Sports Voice for the Hobby
Collectors
Digest
The hobby's oldest and largest publication

22ND EDITION

2008

Baseball Card

PRICE GUIDE

Published by

kp **krause publications**
An Imprint of F+W Publications

700 East State Street • Iola, WI 54990-0001
715-445-2214 • 888-457-2873
www.krausebooks.com

Our toll-free number to place an order or obtain
a free catalog is (800) 258-0929.

ISSN 1549-6309

ISBN-13: 978-0-89689-618-5
ISBN-10: 0-89689-618-8

Designed by Stacy Bloch
Edited by Joe Clemens

Printed in United States of America

TABLE OF CONTENTS

How To Use This Price Guide

This price guide has been uniquely designed to serve the needs of collectors and dealers at all levels from beginning to advanced. It provides a comprehensive guide to more than 26 years of baseball card issues, arranged so that even the most novice hobbyist can consult it with confidence and ease.

The following explanations summarize the general practices used in preparing this price guide's listings. However, because of specialized requirements which may vary from card set to card set, these must not be considered ironclad. Where these standards have been set aside, appropriate notations are usually incorporated.

ARRANGEMENT

The most important feature in identifying and pricing a baseball card is its set of origin. Therefore, the main body of this price guide, covering cards issued from 1981-date, has been alphabetically arranged within specific eras of issue according to the name by which the set is most popularly known to collectors, or by which it can be most easily identified by a person examining a card.

Among those card issuers who produced sets for more than a single year, their sets are then listed chronologically, from earliest to most recent, again within specific eras.

Within each set, the cards are listed by their designated card number, or in the absence of card numbers, alphabetically according to the last name of the player pictured. Listing numbers found in parentheses indicate the number does not appear on the card. Certain cards which fall outside the parameters of the normal card numbering for a specific set may be found at the beginning or end of the listings for that set.

VINTAGE-MODERN ISSUES

The main body of the book details modern major league baseball card issues from 1981-2007, as produced by the major national card companies. In general, prior to about 1990, this will include issues which picture one or more baseball players, usually contemporary with their playing days, printed on paper or cardboard in a variety of shapes and sizes and given away as a premium with the purchase of another product or service. After 1990 or so the definition is broadened to remove the restriction of the card as an ancillary product and to include those printed on plastic, wood, metal, etc.

IDENTIFICATION

While most modern baseball cards are well identified on front, back or both, as to date and is-

sue, such has not always been the case. In general, the back of the card is more useful in identifying the set of origin than the front. The issuer or sponsor's name will usually appear on the back since, after all, baseball cards were first produced as a promotional item to stimulate sales of other products. More often than not, that issuer's name is the name by which the set is known to collectors and under which it will be found listed in this price guide.

In some difficult cases, identifying a baseball card's general age, if not specific year of issue, can usually be accomplished by studying the biological or statistical information on the back of the card. The last year mentioned in either the biography or stats is usually the year which preceded the year of issue.

PHOTOGRAPHS

A photograph of the front of at least one representative card from virtually every set listed in this price guide has been incorporated into the listings to aid in identification.

Photographs have been printed in reduced size. The actual size of cards in each set is given in the introductory text preceding its listing, unless the card is the standard size (2.5" by 3.5").

DATING

The dating of baseball cards by year of issue on the front or back of the card itself is a relatively new phenomenon. In most cases, to accurately determine a date of issue for an unidentified card, it must be studied for clues. As mentioned, the biography, career summary or statistics on the back of the card are the best way to pinpoint a year of issue. In most cases, the year of issue will be the year after the last season mentioned on the card.

NUMBERING

While many baseball card issues as far back as the 1880s have contained card numbers assigned by the issuer to facilitate the collecting of a complete set, the practice has by no means been universal. Even today, not every set bears card numbers.

Logically, those baseball cards which were numbered by their manufacturer are presented in that numerical order within the listings of this catalog whenever possible. In a few cases, complete player checklists were obtained from earlier published sources which did not note card numbers, and so numbers have been arbitrarily assigned. Many other unnumbered issues have been assigned catalog numbers to facilitate their universal identification within the hobby, especially when buying and selling by mail.

In all cases, numbers which have been assigned, or which otherwise do not appear on the card through error or by design, are shown in this catalog within parentheses. In virtually all cases, unless a more natural system suggested itself by the unique matter of a particular set, the assignment of numbers by the cataloging staff has been done by alphabetical arrangement of the players' last names or the card's principal title.

Significant collectible variations for any particular card are noted within the listings by the application of a suffix letter. In instances of variations, the suffix "a" is assigned to the variation which was created first, when it can be so identified.

NAMES

The identification of a player by full name on the front of his baseball card has been a common practice only since the 1920s. Prior to that, the player's last name and team were the usual information found on the card front.

As a general — though not universally applied — practice, the listings in this volume present the player's name exactly as it appears on the front of the card. If the player's full name only appears on the back, rather than on the front of the card, the listing may correspond to that designation.

Cards which contain misspelled first or last names, or even wrong initials, will have included in their listings the incorrect information, with a correction accompanying in parentheses. This extends, also, to cases where the name on the card does not correspond to the player actually pictured.

In some cases, to facilitate efficient presentations, to maintain ease of use for the reader, or to allow for proper computer sorting of data, a player's name or card title may be listed other than as it appears on the card.

GRADING

It is necessary that some sort of card grading standard be used so that buyer and seller (especially when dealing by mail) may reach an informed agreement on the value of a card.

Modern issues, which have been preserved in top condition in considerable number, are listed only in grade of Near Mint-to-Mint (NM/M), reflective of the fact that there exists in the current market little or no demand for cards of the recent past in lower grades.

Values for lower-grade cards from 1981-date may be generally figured by using a figure of 75 percent of the Mint price for Near Mint specimens, and 40 percent of the Mint price for Excellent cards.

For the benefit of the reader, we present herewith the grading guide which was originally formulated in 1981 by Baseball Cards magazine and Sports Collectors Digest, and has been continually refined since that time.

These grading definitions have been used in the pricing of cards in this book, but they are by no means a universally accepted grading standard.

The potential buyer of a baseball card should keep that in mind when encountering cards of nominally the same grade, but at a price which differs widely from that quoted in this book.

Ultimately, the collector himself must formulate his own personal grading standards in deciding whether cards available for purchase meet the needs of his own collection.

Mint (MT): A perfect card. Well-centered, with parallel borders which appear equal to the naked eye. Four sharp, square corners. No creases, edge dents, surface scratches, paper flaws, loss of luster, yellowing or fading, regardless of age. No imperfectly printed card — out of register, badly cut or ink flawed — or card stained by contact with gum, wax or other substances can be considered truly Mint, even if new out of the pack. Generally, to be considered in Mint condition, a card's borders must exist in a ratio of 60/40 side to side and top to bottom.

Near Mint (NR MT): A nearly perfect card. At first glance, a Near Mint card appears perfect; upon closer examination, however, a minor flaw will be discovered. On well-centered cards, three of the four corners must be perfectly sharp; only one corner shows a minor imperfection upon close inspection. A slightly off-center card with one or more borders being noticeably unequal — but no worse than in a ratio of 70/30 S/S or T/B — would also fit this grade.

Excellent (EX): Corners are still fairly sharp with only moderate wear. Card borders may be off center as much as 80/20. No creases. May have very minor gum, wax or product stains, front or back. Surfaces may show slight loss of luster from rubbing across other cards.

Very Good (VG): Shows obvious handling. Corners rounded and/or perhaps showing minor creases. Other minor creases may be visible. Surfaces may exhibit loss of luster, but all printing is intact. May show major gum, wax or other packaging stains. No major creases, tape marks or extraneous markings or writing. All four borders visible, though the ratio may be as poor as 95/5. Exhibits honest wear.

Good (G): A well-worn card, but exhibits no intentional damage or abuse. May have major or multiple creases. Corners rounded well beyond the border. A good card will generally sell for about 50 percent the value of a card in Very Good condition.

Fair (F or Fr.): Shows excessive wear, along with damage or abuse. Will show all the wear characteristics of a Good card, along with such damage as thumb tack holes in or near margins, evidence of having been taped or pasted, perhaps small tears around the edges, or creases so heavy as to break the cardboard. Backs may show minor added pen or pencil writing, or be missing small bits of paper. Still, basically a complete card. A Fair card will generally sell for 50 percent the value of a Good specimen.

Poor (P): A card that has been tortured to death. Corners or other areas may be torn off. Card may have been trimmed, show holes from a paper punch or have been used for BB gun practice. Front may have extraneous pen or pencil writing, or other defacement. Major portions of front or back design may be missing. Not a pretty sight.

In addition to these terms, collectors may encounter intermediate grades, such as NM-MT or EX-MT. These cards usually have characteristics of both the lower and higher grades, and are generally priced midway between those two values.

Grading and pricing reflected in this book are for cards which have not been authenticated, graded and encapsulated by one of the third-party certification services. Cards which have been "slabbed" by these services generally sell for a premium above the price which a "raw" card will bring.

ROOKIE CARDS

While the status (and automatic premium value) which a player's rookie card carries has fallen and risen in recent years, and though the hobby still has not reached a universal definition of a rookie card, many significant rookie cards are noted in this price guide's listings by the use of **RC** or **(RC)**. For purposes of this catalog, a player's rookie card is considered to be any card in a licensed set from a major manufacturer in the first year in which that player appears on a card. Beginning with products issued in 2006, cards with a **(RC)** logo indicate the featured player has a rookie card issued prior to that year.

VALUATIONS

Values quoted in this book represent the current retail market at the time of compilation (January, 2008). The quoted values are the result of a unique system of evaluation and verification created by the price guide's editors. Utilizing specialized computer analysis and drawing upon recommendations provided through their daily involvement in the publication of the hobby's leading sports collectors' periodicals, as well as the input of consultants, dealers and collectors, each listing is, in the final analysis, the interpretation of that data by one or more of the editors.

It should be stressed, however, that this book is intended to serve only as an aid in evaluating cards; actual market conditions are constantly changing. This is especially true of the cards of current players, whose on-field performance during the course of a season can greatly affect the value of their cards — upwards or downwards. Because of the extremely volatile nature of new card prices, especially high-end issues, we have chosen not to include the very latest releases such as premium-

price brands from the major companies, feeling it is better to have no listings at all for those cards than to have inaccurate values in print.

Because this volume is intended to reflect the national market, users will find regional price variances caused by demand differences. Cards of Astros slugger Jeff Bagwell will, for instance, often sell at prices greater than quoted herein at shops and shows in the Houston area. Conversely, his cards may be acquired at a discount from these valuations when purchased on the East or West Coast.

Publication of this book is not intended as a solicitation to buy or sell the listed cards by the editors, publishers or contributors.

Again, the values here are retail prices — what a collector can expect to pay when buying a card from a dealer. The wholesale price, that which a collector can expect to receive from a dealer when selling cards, will be significantly lower.

Most dealers operate on a 100 percent mark-up, generally paying about 50 percent of a card's retail value for cards which they are purchasing for inventory. On some high-demand cards, dealers will pay up to 75 percent or even 100 percent or more of retail value, anticipating continued price increases. Conversely, for many low-demand cards, such as common players' cards, dealers may pay as little as 10 percent or even less of retail with many base-brand cards of recent years having no resale value at all.

SETS

Collectors may note that the complete set prices for newer issues quoted in these listings are usually significantly lower than the total of the value of the individual cards which comprise the set. This reflects two factors in the baseball card market. First, a seller is often willing to take a lower composite price for a complete set as a "volume discount" and to avoid carrying in inventory a large number of common player or other lower-demand cards.

Second, to a degree, the value of common cards can be said to be inflated as a result of having a built-in overhead charge to justify the dealer's time in sorting cards, carrying them in stock and filling orders. This accounts for the fact that even new base-brand baseball cards, which cost the dealer around one cent each when bought in bulk, carry individual price tags of five cents or higher.

Some set prices shown, especially for old cards in top condition, are merely theoretical in that it is unlikely that a complete set exists in that condition. In general among older cards the range of conditions found in even the most painstakingly assembled complete set make the set values quoted useful only as a starting point for price negotiations.

ERRORS/VARIATIONS

It is often hard for the beginning collector to understand that an error on a baseball card, in and of itself, does not usually add premium value to that card. It is usually only when the correcting of an error in the subsequent printing creates a variation that premium value attaches to an error.

Minor errors, such as wrong stats or personal data, misspellings, inconsistencies, etc. — usually affecting the back of the card — are very common, especially in recent years. Unless a corrected variation was also printed, these errors are not noted in the listings of this book because they are not generally perceived by collectors to have premium value.

Many scarce and valuable variations are included in these listings because they are widely collected and often have significant premium value.

Beginning in the early 1990s, some card companies began production of their basic sets at more than one printing facility. This frequently resulted in numerous minor variations. Combined with a general decline in quality control from the mid-1980s through the early 1990s, which allowed unprecedented numbers of uncorrected error cards to be released, this caused a softening of collector interest in errors and variations. Despite the fact most of these modern variations have no premium value, they are listed here as a matter of record.

COUNTERFEITS/REPRINTS

As the value of baseball cards has risen, certain cards and sets have become too expensive for the average collector to obtain. This, along with changes in the technology of color printing, has given rise to increasing numbers of counterfeit and reprint cards.

While both terms describe essentially the same thing — a modern day copy which attempts to duplicate as closely as possible an original baseball card — there are differences which are important to the collector.

Generally, a counterfeit is made with the intention of deceiving somebody into believing it is genuine, thus paying large amounts of money for it. The counterfeiter takes every pain to try to make their fakes look as authentic as possible. In recent years, the 1963 Pete Rose, 1984 Donruss Don Mattingly and more than 100 superstar cards of the late 1960s-early 1990s have been counterfeited — many of which were quickly detected because of the differences in quality of cardboard on which they were printed.

A reprint, on the other hand, while it may have been made to look as close as possible to an original card, is made with the intention of allowing collectors to buy them as substitutes for cards they may never be otherwise able to afford. The big difference is that a reprint is generally marked as such, usually on the back of the card.

In other cases, like the Topps 1952 reprint set and 1953-54 Archives issues, the replicas are printed in a size markedly different from the originals. Collectors should be aware, however, that unscrupulous persons will sometimes cut off or otherwise obliterate the distinguishing word — "Reprint," "Copy," — or modern copyright date on the back of a reprint card in an attempt to pass it as genuine.

A collector's best defense against reprints and counterfeits is to acquire a knowledge of the look and feel of genuine baseball cards of various eras and issues.

Abbreviation Key

OPS: Overprinted "Promotional Sample"

ED: Expansion Draft

AS: All-Star

HL: Hit List

RC: Rookie Class

RC or (RC): Rookie Card

SP: Short Print

DT: Double Team

CC: Curtain Calls

GLR: Gold Leaf Rookies

TP: Top Performers

FF: Future Foundation

DK: Diamond King

RR: Rated Rookie

DP: Double Print

IA: In Action

PC: Promo Card

SR: Star Rookie

MODERN MAJOR LEAGUE CARDS (1981-2007)

The vast majority of cards listed in this section were issued between 1981 and late 2007 and feature major league players only. The term "card" is used rather loosely as in this context it is construed to include virtually any series of cardboard or paper product, of whatever size and/or shape, depicting baseball players. Further, "cards" printed on wood, metal, plastic and other materials are either by their association with other issues or by their compatibility in size with the current 2-1/2" x 3-1/2" card standard also listed here.

Because modern cards are generally not popularly collected in lower grades, cards in this section carry only a Near Mint-to-Mint (NM/M) value quote. In general, post-1980 cards which grade Near Mint (NM) will retail at about 75% of the NM/M price, while Excellent (EX) condition cards bring 40%.

B

1988 Bazooka

	NM/M
Complete Set (22):	3.00
Common Player:	.10
1 George Bell	.10
2 Wade Boggs	.50
3 Jose Canseco	.25
4 Roger Clemens	.60
5 Vince Coleman	.10
6 Eric Davis	.10
7 Tony Fernandez	.10
8 Dwight Gooden	.10
9 Tony Gwynn	.50
10 Wally Joyner	.10
11 Don Mattingly	.60
12 Willie McGee	.10
13 Mark McGwire	.75
14 Kirby Puckett	.50
15 Tim Raines	.10
16 Dave Righetti	.10
17 Cal Ripken, Jr.	1.00
18 Juan Samuel	.10
19 Ryne Sandberg	.50
20 Benny Santiago	.10
21 Darryl Strawberry	.10
22 Todd Worrell	.10

1989 Bazooka

	NM/M
Complete Set (22):	3.00
Common Player:	.10
1 Tim Belcher	.10
2 Damon Berryhill	.10
3 Wade Boggs	.75
4 Jay Buhner	.10
5 Jose Canseco	.25
6 Vince Coleman	.10
7 Cecil Espy	.10
8 Dave Gallagher	.10
9 Ron Gant	.10
10 Kirk Gibson	.10
11 Paul Gibson	.10
12 Mark Grace	.10
13 Tony Gwynn	.75
14 Rickey Henderson	.50
15 Orel Hershiser	.10
16 Gregg Jefferies	.10
17 Ricky Jordan	.10
18 Chris Sabo	.10
19 Gary Sheffield	.40
20 Darryl Strawberry	.10
21 Frank Viola	.10
22 Walt Weiss	.10

1990 Bazooka

	NM/M
Complete Set (22):	3.00
Common Player:	.10
1 Kevin Mitchell	.10
2 Robin Yount	.40
3 Mark Davis	.10
4 Bret Saberhagen	.10
5 Fred McGriff	.10
6 Tony Gwynn	.50
7 Kirby Puckett	.50
8 Vince Coleman	.10
9 Rickey Henderson	.40
10 Ben McDonald	.10
11 Gregg Olson	.10
12 Todd Zeile	.10
13 Carlos Martinez	.10
14 Gregg Jefferies	.10
15 Craig Worthington	.10
16 Gary Sheffield	.25
17 Greg Briley	.10
18 Ken Griffey Jr.	1.50
19 Jerome Walton	.10
20 Bob Geren	.10
21 Tom Gordon	.10
22 Jim Abbott	.10

1991 Bazooka

	NM/M
Complete Set (22):	5.00

Common Player:	.10
1 Barry Bonds	3.50
2 Rickey Henderson	.50
3 Bob Welch	.10
4 Doug Drabek	.10
5 Alex Fernandez	.10
6 Jose Offerman	.10
7 Frank Thomas	.50
8 Cecil Fielder	.10
9 Ryne Sandberg	.75
10 George Brett	1.00
11 Willie McGee	.10
12 Vince Coleman	.10
13 Hal Morris	.10
14 Delino DeShields	.10
15 Robin Ventura	.10
16 Jeff Huson	.10
17 Felix Jose	.10
18 Dave Justice	.10
19 Larry Walker	.10
20 Sandy Alomar, Jr.	.10
21 Kevin Appier	.10
22 Scott Radinsky	.10

1992 Bazooka

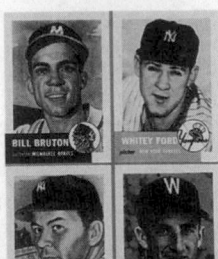

	NM/M
Complete Tin-Box Set (22):	16.00
Complete Set (22):	8.00
Common Player:	.25
1 Joe Adcock, Bob Lemon, Willie Mays, Vic Wertz	1.50
2 Carl Furillo, Don Newcombe, Phil Rizzuto, Hank Sauer	.25
3 Ferris Fain, John Logan, Ed Mathews, Bobby Shantz	.25
4 Yogi Berra, Del Crandall, Howie Pollett, Gene Woodling	.25
5 Richie Ashburn, Leo Durocher, Allie Reynolds, Early Wynn	.25
6 Hank Aaron, Ray Boone, Luke Easter, Dick Williams	1.50
7 Ralph Branca, Bob Feller, Rogers Hornsby, Bobby Thomson	.25
8 Jim Gilliam, Billy Martin, Orestes Minoso, Hal Newhouser	.25
9 Smoky Burgess, John Mize, Preacher Roe, Warren Spahn	.25
10 Monte Irvin, Bobo Newsom, Duke Snider, Wes Westrum	.25
11 Carl Erskine, Jackie Jensen, George Kell, Al Schoendienst	.25
12 Bill Bruton, Whitey Ford, Ed Lopat, Mickey Vernon	.25
13 Joe Black, Lew Burdette, Johnny Pesky, Enos Slaughter	.25
14 Gus Bell, Mike Garcia, Mel Parnell, Jackie Robinson	1.25
15 Alvin Dark, Dick Groat, Pee Wee Reese, John Sain	.25
16 Gil Hodges, Sal Maglie, Wilmer Mizell, Billy Pierce	.45
17 Nellie Fox, Ralph Kiner, Ted Kluszewski, Eddie Stanky	.25
18 Ewell Blackwell, Vern Law, Satchell Paige, Jim Wilson	.45
19 Lou Boudreau, Roy Face, Harvey Haddix, Bill Rigney	.25
20 Roy Campanella, Walt Dropo, Harvey Kuenn, Al Rosen	.45
21 Joe Garagiola, Robin Roberts, Casey Stengel, Hoyt Wilhelm	.25
22 John Antonelli, Bob Friend, Dixie Walker, Ted Williams	1.00

1993 Bazooka Team USA

	NM/M
Complete Set (22):	100.00
Complete Tin Set (22):	150.00
Common Player:	.50
1 Terry Harvey	.50

TODD HELTON
TEAM USA

		NM/M
2	Dante Powell	.50
3	Andy Barkett	.50
4	Steve Reich	.50
5	Charlie Nelson	.50
6	Todd Walker	1.00
7	Dustin Hermanson	1.00
8	Pat Clougherty	.50
9	Danny Graves	.50
10	Paul Wilson	.75
11	Todd Helton	90.00
12	Russ Johnson	.50
13	Darren Grass	.50
14	A.J. Hinch	.50
15	Mark Merila	.50
16	John Powell	.50
17	Bob Scafa	.50
18	Matt Beaumont	.50
19	Todd Dunn	.50
20	Mike Martin	.50
21	Carlton Loewer	.50
22	Bret Wagner	.50

1995 Bazooka

CALIFORNIA ANGELS

		NM/M
Complete Set (132):		3.00
Factory Set (132+5):		5.00
Common Player:		.05
Pack (5):		.30
Wax Box (36):		7.00
1	Greg Maddux	
2	Cal Ripken Jr.	1.00
3	Lee Smith	.05
4	Sammy Sosa	.50
5	Jason Bere	.05
6	Dave Justice	.05
7	Kevin Mitchell	.05
8	Ozzie Guillen	.05
9	Roger Clemens	.60
10	Mike Mussina	.30
11	Sandy Alomar	.05
12	Cecil Fielder	.05
13	Dennis Martinez	.05
14	Randy Myers	.05
15	Jay Buhner	.05
16	Ivan Rodriguez	.35
17	Mo Vaughn	.05
18	Ryan Klesko	.05
19	Chuck Finley	.05
20	Barry Bonds	1.00
21	Dennis Eckersley	.35
22	Kenny Lofton	.05
23	Rafael Palmeiro	.35
24	Mike Stanley	.05
25	Gregg Jefferies	.05
26	Robin Ventura	.05
27	Mark McGwire	.75
28	Ozzie Smith	.50
29	Troy Neel	.05
30	Tony Gwynn	.50
31	Ken Griffey Jr.	.65
32	Will Clark	.05

33	Craig Biggio	.05
34	Shawon Dunston	.05
35	Wilson Alvarez	.05
36	Bobby Bonilla	.05
37	Marquis Grissom	.05
38	Ben McDonald	.05
39	Delino DeShields	.05
40	Barry Larkin	.05
41	John Olerud	.05
42	Jose Canseco	.30
43	Greg Vaughn	.05
44	Gary Sheffield	.20
45	Paul O'Neill	.05
46	Bob Hamelin	.05
47	Don Mattingly	.60
48	John Franco	.05
49	Bret Boone	.05
50	Rick Aguilera	.05
51	Tim Wallach	.05
52	Roberto Kelly	.05
53	Danny Tartabull	.05
54	Randy Johnson	.40
55	Greg McMichael	.05
56	Bip Roberts	.05
57	David Cone	.05
58	Raul Mondesi	.05
59	Travis Fryman	.05
60	Jeff Conine	.05
61	Jeff Bagwell	.40
62	Rickey Henderson	.40
63	Fred McGriff	.05
64	Matt Williams	.05
65	Rick Wilkins	.05
66	Eric Karros	.05
67	Mel Rojas	.05
68	Juan Gonzalez	.20
69	Chuck Carr	.05
70	Moises Alou	.05
71	Mark Grace	.05
72	Alex Fernandez	.05
73	Rod Beck	.05
74	Ray Lankford	.05
75	Dean Palmer	.05
76	Joe Carter	.05
77	Mike Piazza	.65
78	Eddie Murray	.40
79	Dave Nilsson	.05
80	Brett Butler	.05
81	Roberto Alomar	.10
82	Jeff Kent	.05
83	Andres Galarraga	.05
84	Brady Anderson	.05
85	Jimmy Key	.05
86	Bret Saberhagen	.05
87	Chili Davis	.05
88	Jose Rijo	.05
89	Wade Boggs	.50
90	Len Dykstra	.05
91	Steve Howe	.05
92	Hal Morris	.05
93	Larry Walker	.05
94	Jeff Montgomery	.05
95	Wil Cordero	.05
96	Jay Bell	.05
97	Tom Glavine	.15
98	Chris Hoiles	.05
99	Steve Avery	.05
100	Ruben Sierra	.05
101	Mickey Tettleton	.05
102	Paul Molitor	.40
103	Carlos Baerga	.05
104	Walt Weiss	.05
105	Darren Daulton	.05
106	Jack McDowell	.05
107	Doug Drabek	.05
108	Mark Langston	.05
109	Manny Ramirez	.40
110	Kevin Appier	.05
111	Andy Benes	.05
112	Chuck Knoblauch	.05
113	Kirby Puckett	.50
114	Dante Bichette	.05
115	Deion Sanders	.10
116	Albert Belle	.05
117	Todd Zeile	.05
118	Devon White	.05
119	Tim Salmon	.05
120	Frank Thomas	.40
121	John Wetteland	.05
122	James Mouton	.05
123	Javy Lopez	.05
124	Carlos Delgado	.25
125	Cliff Floyd	.05
126	Alex Gonzalez	.05
127	Billy Ashley	.05
128	Rondell White	.05
129	Rico Brogna	.05
130	Melvin Nieves	.05
131	Jose Oliva	.05
132	J.R. Phillips	.05

Red Hot Inserts

	NM/M
Complete Set (22):	7.00

PAUL MOLITOR
TORONTO BLUE JAYS

Common Player:		.15
1	Greg Maddux	1.00
2	Cal Ripken Jr.	2.00
3	Barry Bonds	2.00
4	Kenny Lofton	.15
5	Mike Stanley	.15
6	Tony Gwynn	1.00
7	Ken Griffey Jr.	1.50
8	Barry Larkin	.15
9	Jose Canseco	.35
10	Paul O'Neill	.15
11	Randy Johnson	.75
12	David Cone	.15
13	Jeff Bagwell	.75
14	Matt Williams	.15
15	Mike Piazza	1.50
16	Roberto Alomar	.25
17	Jimmy Key	.15
18	Wade Boggs	1.00
19	Paul Molitor	.75
20	Carlos Baerga	.15
21	Albert Belle	.15
22	Frank Thomas	.75

1996 Bazooka

David Segui

		NM/M
Unopened Fact. Set (133):		9.00
Complete Set (132):		6.00
Common Player:		.05
Pack (5):		.40
Wax Box (36):		9.00
1	Ken Griffey Jr.	.75
2	J.T. Snow	.05
3	Rondell White	.05
4	Reggie Sanders	.05
5	Jeff Montgomery	.05
6	Mike Stanley	.05
7	Bernie Williams	.05
8	Mike Piazza	.75
9	Brian Hunter	.05
10	Len Dykstra	.05
11	Ray Lankford	.05
12	Kenny Lofton	.05
13	Robin Ventura	.05
14	Devon White	.05
15	Cal Ripken Jr.	1.50
16	Heathcliff Slocumb	.05
17	Ryan Klesko	.05
18	Terry Steinbach	.05
19	Travis Fryman	.05
20	Sammy Sosa	.50
21	Jim Thome	.35
22	Kenny Rogers	.05
23	Don Mattingly	.60
24	Kirby Puckett	.50
25	Matt Williams	.05
26	Larry Walker	.05
27	Tim Wakefield	.05
28	Greg Vaughn	.05
29	Denny Neagle	.05
30	Ken Caminiti	.05

31	Garret Anderson	.05
32	Brady Anderson	.05
33	Carlos Baerga	.05
34	Wade Boggs	.50
35	Roberto Alomar	.15
36	Eric Karros	.05
37	Jay Buhner	.05
38	Dante Bichette	.05
39	Darren Daulton	.05
40	Jeff Bagwell	.40
41	Jay Bell	.05
42	Dennis Eckersley	.35
43	Will Clark	.05
44	Tom Glavine	.20
45	Rick Aguilera	.05
46	Kevin Seitzer	.05
47	Bret Boone	.05
48	Mark Grace	.05
49	Ray Durham	.05
50	Rico Brogna	.05
51	Kevin Appier	.05
52	Moises Alou	.05
53	Jeff Conine	.05
54	Marty Cordova	.05
55	Jose Mesa	.05
56	Rod Beck	.05
57	Marquis Grissom	.05
58	David Cone	.05
59	Albert Belle	.05
60	Lee Smith	.05
61	Frank Thomas	.40
62	Roger Clemens	.60
63	Bobby Bonilla	.05
64	Paul Molitor	.40
65	Chuck Knoblauch	.05
66	Steve Finley	.05
67	Craig Biggio	.05
68	Ramon Martinez	.05
69	Jason Isringhausen	.05
70	Mark Wohlers	.05
71	Vinny Castilla	.05
72	Ron Gant	.05
73	Juan Gonzalez	.20
74	Mark McGwire	1.00
75	Jeff King	.05
76	Pedro Martinez	.40
77	Chad Curtis	.05
78	John Olerud	.05
79	Greg Maddux	.50
80	Derek Jeter	1.50
81	Mike Mussina	.25
82	Gregg Jefferies	.05
83	Jim Edmonds	.05
84	Carlos Perez	.05
85	Mo Vaughn	.05
86	Todd Hundley	.05
87	Roberto Hernandez	.05
88	Derek Bell	.05
89	Andres Galarraga	.05
90	Brian McRae	.05
91	Joe Carter	.05
92	Orlando Merced	.05
93	Cecil Fielder	.05
94	Dean Palmer	.05
95	Randy Johnson	.40
96	Chipper Jones	.50
97	Barry Larkin	.05
98	Hideo Nomo	.25
99	Gary Gaetti	.05
100	Edgar Martinez	.05
101	John Wetteland	.05
102	Rafael Palmeiro	.35
103	Chuck Finley	.05
104	Ivan Rodriguez	.35
105	Shawn Green	.10
106	Manny Ramirez	.40
107	Lance Johnson	.05
108	Jose Canseco	.20
109	Fred McGriff	.05
110	David Segui	.05
111	Tim Salmon	.05
112	Hal Morris	.05
113	Tino Martinez	.05
114	Bret Saberhagen	.05
115	Brian Jordan	.05
116	David Justice	.05
117	Jack McDowell	.05
118	Barry Bonds	1.50
119	Mark Langston	.05
120	John Valentin	.05
121	Raul Mondesi	.05
122	Quilvio Veras	.05
123	Randy Myers	.05
124	Tony Gwynn	.50
125	Johnny Damon	.20
126	Doug Drabek	.05
127	Bill Pulsipher	.05
128	Paul O'Neill	.05
129	Rickey Henderson	.40
130	Deion Sanders	.10
131	Orel Hershiser	.05
132	Gary Sheffield	.20

Mickey Mantle
1959 Reprint

MICKEY MANTLE
OUTFIELD   N.Y. YANKEES

	NM/M
Mickey Mantle	7.50

1989 Bowman

	NM/M
Unopened Fact. Set (484):	20.00
Complete Set (484):	15.00
Common Player:	.05
Wax Pack (12+1):	.75
Wax Box (36):	15.00
Rack Pack (40):	1.00
Rack Box (24):	20.00

1	Oswald Peraza	.05
2	Brian Holton	.05
3	Jose Bautista	.05
4	Pete Harnisch RC	.10
5	Dave Schmidt	.05
6	Gregg Olson	.05
7	Jeff Ballard	.05
8	Bob Melvin	.05
9	Cal Ripken, Jr.	.75
10	Randy Milligan	.05
11	Juan Bell RC	.05
12	Billy Ripken	.05
13	Jim Trabor	.05
14	Pete Stanicek	.05
15	Steve Finley RC	.25
16	Larry Sheets	.05
17	Phil Bradley	.05
18	Brady Anderson	.05
19	Lee Smith	.05
20	Tom Fischer	.05
21	Mike Boddicker	.05
22	Rob Murphy	.05
23	Wes Gardner	.05
24	John Dopson	.05
25	Bob Stanley	.05
26	Roger Clemens	.60
27	Rich Gedman	.05
28	Marty Barrett	.05
29	Luis Rivera	.05
30	Jody Reed	.05
31	Nick Esasky	.05
32	Wade Boggs	.50
33	Jim Rice	.20
34	Mike Greenwell	.05
35	Dwight Evans	.05
36	Ellis Burks	.05
37	Chuck Finley	.05
38	Kirk McCaskill	.05
39	Jim Abbott	.05
40	Bryan Harvey RC	.05
41	Bert Blyleven	.05
42	Mike Witt	.05
43	Bob McClure	.05
44	Bill Schroeder	.05
45	Lance Parrish	.05
46	Dick Schofield	.05
47	Wally Joyner	.05
48	Jack Howell	.05
49	Johnny Ray	.05
50	Chili Davis	.05
51	Tony Armas	.05
52	Claudell Washington	.05
53	Brian Downing	.05
54	Devon White	.05
55	Bobby Thigpen	.05
56	Bill Long	.05
57	Jerry Reuss	.05
58	Shawn Hillegas	.05
59	Melido Perez	.05
60	Jeff Bittiger	.05
61	Jack McDowell	.05
62	Carlton Fisk	.40
63	Steve Lyons	.05
64	Ozzie Guillen	.05
65	Robin Ventura	.05
66	Fred Manrique	.05
67	Dan Pasqua	.05
68	Ivan Calderon	.05
69	Ron Kittle	.05
70	Daryl Boston	.05
71	Dave Gallagher	.05
72	Harold Baines	.05
73	Charles Nagy RC	.15
74	John Farrell	.05
75	Kevin Wickander	.05
76	Greg Swindell	.05
77	Mike Walker	.05
78	Doug Jones	.05
79	Rich Yett	.05
80	Tom Candiotti	.05
81	Jesse Orosco	.05
82	Bud Black	.05
83	Andy Allanson	.05
84	Pete O'Brien	.05
85	Jerry Browne	.05
86	Brook Jacoby	.05
87	Mark Lewis RC	.05
88	Luis Aguayo	.05
89	Cory Snyder	.05
90	Oddibe McDowell	.05
91	Joe Carter	.05
92	Frank Tanana	.05
93	Jack Morris	.05
94	Doyle Alexander	.05
95	Steve Searcy	.05
96	Randy Bockus	.05
97	Jeff Robinson	.05
98	Mike Henneman	.05
99	Paul Gibson	.05
100	Frank Williams	.05
101	Matt Nokes	.05
102	Rico Brogna	.05
103	Lou Whitaker	.05
104	Al Pedrique	.05
105	Alan Trammell	.05
106	Chris Brown	.05
107	Pat Sheridan	.05
108	Gary Pettis	.05
109	Keith Moreland	.05
110	Mel Stottlemyre, Jr.	.05
111	Bret Saberhagen	.05
112	Floyd Bannister	.05
113	Jeff Montgomery	.05
114	Steve Farr	.05
115	Tom Gordon	.05
116	Charlie Leibrandt	.05
117	Mark Gubicza	.05
118	Mike MacFarlane	.05
119	Bob Boone	.05
120	Kurt Stillwell	.05
121	George Brett	.60
122	Frank White	.05
123	Kevin Seitzer	.05
124	Willie Wilson	.05
125	Pat Tabler	.05
126	Bo Jackson	.10
127	Hugh Walker	.05
128	Danny Tartabull	.05
129	Teddy Higuera	.05
130	Don August	.05
131	Juan Nieves	.05
132	Mike Birkbeck	.05
133	Dan Plesac	.05
134	Chris Bosio	.05
135	Bill Wegman	.05
136	Chuck Crim	.05
137	B.J. Surhoff	.05
138	Joey Meyer	.05
139	Dale Sveum	.05
140	Paul Molitor	.40
141	Jim Gantner	.05
142	Gary Sheffield RC	.75
143	Greg Brock	.05
144	Robin Yount	.40
145	Glenn Braggs	.05
146	Rob Deer	.05
147	Fred Toliver	.05
148	Jeff Reardon	.05
149	Allan Anderson	.05
150	Frank Viola	.05
151	Shane Rawley	.05
152	Juan Berenguer	.05
153	Johnny Ard	.05
154	Tim Laudner	.05
155	Brian Harper	.05
156	Al Newman	.05
157	Kent Hrbek	.05
158	Gary Gaetti	.05
159	Wally Backman	.05
160	Gene Larkin	.05
161	Greg Gagne	.05
162	Kirby Puckett	.50
163	Danny Gladden	.05
164	Randy Bush	.05
165	Dave LaPoint	.05
166	Andy Hawkins	.05
167	Dave Righetti	.05
168	Lance McCullers	.05
169	Jimmy Jones	.05
170	Al Leiter	.05
171	John Candelaria	.05
172	Don Slaught	.05
173	Jamie Quirk	.05
174	Rafael Santana	.05
175	Mike Pagliarulo	.05
176	Don Mattingly	.60
177	Ken Phelps	.05
178	Steve Sax	.05
179	Dave Winfield	.40
180	Stan Jefferson	.05
181	Rickey Henderson	.40
182	Bob Brower	.05
183	Roberto Kelly	.05
184	Curt Young	.05
185	Gene Nelson	.05
186	Bob Welch	.05
187	Rick Honeycutt	.05
188	Dave Stewart	.05
189	Mike Moore	.05
190	Dennis Eckersley	.35
191	Eric Plunk	.05
192	Storm Davis	.05
193	Terry Steinbach	.05
194	Ron Hassey	.05
195	Stan Royer	.05
196	Walt Weiss	.05
197	Mark McGwire	.65
198	Carney Lansford	.05
199	Glenn Hubbard	.05
200	Dave Henderson	.05
201	Jose Canseco	.30
202	Dave Parker	.05
203	Scott Bankhead	.05
204	Tom Niedenfuer	.05
205	Mark Langston	.05
206	Erik Hanson RC	.05
207	Mike Jackson	.05
208	Dave Valle	.05
209	Scott Bradley	.05
210	Harold Reynolds	.05
211	Tino Martinez	.05
212	Rich Renteria	.05
213	Rey Quinones	.05
214	Jim Presley	.05
215	Alvin Davis	.05
216	Edgar Martinez	.05
217	Darnell Coles	.05
218	Jeffrey Leonard	.05
219	Jay Buhner	.05
220	Ken Griffey Jr. RC	6.00
221	Drew Hall	.05
222	Bobby Witt	.05
223	Jamie Moyer	.05
224	Charlie Hough	.05
225	Nolan Ryan	.75
226	Jeff Russell	.05
227	Jim Sundberg	.05
228	Julio Franco	.05
229	Buddy Bell	.05
230	Scott Fletcher	.05
231	Jeff Kunkel	.05
232	Steve Buechele	.05
233	Monty Fariss	.05
234	Rick Leach	.05
235	Ruben Sierra	.05
236	Cecil Espy	.05
237	Rafael Palmeiro	.35
238	Pete Incaviglia	.05
239	Dave Steib	.05
240	Jeff Musselman	.05
241	Mike Flanagan	.05
242	Todd Stottlemyre	.05
243	Jimmy Key	.05
244	Tony Castillo	.05
245	Alex Sanchez	.05
246	Tom Henke	.05
247	John Cerutti	.05
248	Ernie Whitt	.05
249	Bob Brenly	.05
250	Rance Mulliniks	.05
251	Kelly Gruber	.05
252	Ed Sprague	.05
253	Fred McGriff	.05
254	Tony Fernandez	.05
255	Tom Lawless	.05
256	George Bell	.05
257	Jesse Barfield	.05
258	Sandy Alomar, Sr.	.05
259	Ken Griffey (With Ken Griffey Jr.)	.30
260	Cal Ripken, Sr.	.05
261	Mel Stottlemyre, Sr.	.05
262	Zane Smith	.05
263	Charlie Puleo	.05
264	Derek Lilliquist	.05
265	Paul Assenmacher	.05
266	John Smoltz	.05
267	Tom Glavine	.25
268	Steve Avery RC	.05
269	Pete Smith RC	.05
270	Jody Davis	.05
271	Bruce Benedict	.05
272	Andres Thomas	.05
273	Gerald Perry	.05
274	Ron Gant	.05
275	Darrell Evans	.05
276	Dale Murphy	.25
277	Dion James	.05
278	Lonnie Smith	.05
279	Geronimo Berroa	.05
280	Steve Wilson	.05
281	Rick Suctcliffe	.05
282	Kevin Coffman	.05
283	Mitch Williams	.05
284	Greg Maddux	.50
285	Paul Kilgus	.05
286	Mike Harkey	.05
287	Lloyd McClendon	.05
288	Damon Berryhill	.05
289	Ty Griffin	.05
290	Ryne Sandberg	.50
291	Mark Grace	.05
292	Curt Wilkerson	.05
293	Vance Law	.05
294	Shawon Dunston	.05
295	Jerome Walton	.05
296	Mitch Webster	.05
297	Dwight Smith	.05
298	Andre Dawson	.25
299	Jeff Sellers	.05
300	Jose Rijo	.05
301	John Franco	.05
302	Rick Mahler	.05
303	Ron Robinson	.05
304	Danny Jackson	.05
305	Rob Dibble	.05
306	Tom Browning	.05
307	Bo Diaz	.05
308	Manny Trillo	.05
309	Chris Sabo	.05
310	Ron Oester	.05
311	Barry Larkin	.05
312	Todd Benzinger	.05
313	Paul O'Neill	.05
314	Kal Daniels	.05
315	Joel Youngblood	.05
316	Eric Davis	.05
317	Dave Smith	.05
318	Mark Portugal	.05
319	Brian Meyer	.05
320	Jim Deshaies	.05
321	Juan Agosto	.05
322	Mike Scott	.05
323	Rick Rhoden	.05
324	Jim Clancy	.05
325	Larry Andersen	.05
326	Alex Trevino	.05
327	Alan Ashby	.05
328	Craig Reynolds	.05
329	Bill Doran	.05
330	Rafael Ramirez	.05
331	Glenn Davis	.05
332	Willie Ansley RC	.05
333	Gerald Young	.05
334	Cameron Drew	.05
335	Jay Howell	.05
336	Tim Belcher	.05
337	Fernando Valenzuela	.05
338	Ricky Horton	.05
339	Tim Leary	.05
340	Bill Bene	.05
341	Orel Hershiser	.05
342	Mike Scioscia	.05
343	Rick Dempsey	.05
344	Willie Randolph	.05
345	Alfredo Griffin	.05
346	Eddie Murray	.40
347	Mickey Hatcher	.05
348	Mike Sharperson	.05
349	John Shelby	.05
350	Mike Marshall	.05
351	Kirk Gibson	.05
352	Mike Davis	.05
353	Bryn Smith	.05
354	Pascual Perez	.05
355	Kevin Gross	.05

356	Andy McGaffigan	.05
357	Brian Holman	.05
358	Dave Wainhouse	.05
359	Denny Martinez	.05
360	Tim Burke	.05
361	Nelson Santovenia	.05
362	Tim Wallach	.05
363	Spike Owen	.05
364	Rex Hudler	.05
365	Andres Galarraga	.05
366	Otis Nixon	.05
367	Hubie Brooks	.05
368	Mike Aldrete	.05
369	Rock Raines	.05
370	Dave Martinez	.05
371	Bob Ojeda	.05
372	Ron Darling	.05
373	Wally Whitehurst	.05
374	Randy Myers	.05
375	David Cone	.05
376	Dwight Gooden	.05
377	Sid Fernandez	.05
378	Dave Proctor	.05
379	Gary Carter	.40
380	Keith Miller	.05
381	Gregg Jefferies	.05
382	Tim Teufel	.05
383	Kevin Elster	.05
384	Dave Magadan	.05
385	Keith Hernandez	.05
386	Mookie Wilson	.05
387	Darryl Strawberry	.05
388	Kevin McReynolds	.05
389	Mark Carreon	.05
390	Jeff Parrett	.05
391	Mike Maddux	.05
392	Don Carman	.05
393	Bruce Ruffin	.05
394	Ken Howell	.05
395	Steve Bedrosian	.05
396	Floyd Youmans	.05
397	Larry McWilliams	.05
398	Pat Combs	.05
399	Steve Lake	.05
400	Dickie Thon	.05
401	Ricky Jordan	.05
402	Mike Schmidt	.60
403	Tom Herr	.05
404	Chris James	.05
405	Juan Samuel	.05
406	Von Hayes	.05
407	Ron Jones	.05
408	Curt Ford	.05
409	Bob Walk	.05
410	Jeff Robinson	.05
411	Jim Gott	.05
412	Scott Medvin	.05
413	John Smiley	.05
414	Bob Kipper	.05
415	Brian Fisher	.05
416	Doug Drabek	.05
417	Mike Lavalliere	.05
418	Ken Oberkfell	.05
419	Sid Bream	.05
420	Austin Manahan	.05
421	Jose Lind	.05
422	Bobby Bonilla	.05
423	Glenn Wilson	.05
424	Andy Van Slyke	.05
425	Gary Redus	.05
426	Barry Bonds	.75
427	Don Heinkel	.05
428	Ken Dayley	.05
429	Todd Worrell	.05
430	Brad DuVall	.05
431	Jose DeLeon	.05
432	Joe Magrane	.05
433	John Ericks	.05
434	Frank DiPino	.05
435	Tony Pena	.05
436	Ozzie Smith	.50
437	Terry Pendleton	.05
438	Jose Oquendo	.05
439	Tim Jones	.05
440	Pedro Guerrero	.05
441	Milt Thompson	.05
442	Willie McGee	.05
443	Vince Coleman	.05
444	Tom Brunansky	.05
445	Walt Terrell	.05
446	Eric Show	.05
447	Mark Davis	.05
448	Andy Benes RC	.10
449	Eddie Whitson	.05
450	Dennis Rasmussen	.05
451	Bruce Hurst	.05
452	Pat Clements	.05
453	Benito Santiago	.05
454	Sandy Alomar, Jr.	.05
455	Garry Templeton	.05
456	Jack Clark	.05
457	Tim Flannery	.05
458	Roberto Alomar	.25
459	Camelo Martinez	.05
460	John Kruk	.05
461	Tony Gwynn	.50
462	Jerald Clark	.05
463	Don Robinson	.05
464	Craig Lefferts	.05
465	Kelly Downs	.05
466	Rick Rueschel	.05
467	Scott Garrelts	.05
468	Wil Tejada	.05
469	Kirt Manwaring	.05
470	Terry Kennedy	.05
471	Jose Uribe	.05
472	Royce Clayton RC	.10
473	Robby Thompson	.05
474	Kevin Mitchell	.05
475	Ernie Riles	.05
476	Will Clark	.05
477	Donnell Nixon	.05
478	Candy Maldonado	.05
479	Tracy Jones	.05
480	Brett Butler	.05
481	Checklist 1-121	.05
482	Checklist 122-242	.05
483	Checklist 243-363	.05
484	Checklist 364-484	.05

Inserts

		NM/M
Complete Set (11):		3.50
Common Player:		.10
(1)	Richie Ashburn	.10
(2)	Yogi Berra	.10
(3)	Whitey Ford	.10
(4)	Gil Hodges	.10
(5)	Mickey Mantle/1951	2.00
(6)	Mickey Mantle/1953	1.50
(7)	Willie Mays	.50
(8)	Satchel Paige	.25
(9)	Jackie Robinson	1.00
(10)	Duke Snider	.10
(11)	Ted Williams	1.00

Tiffany

	NM/M
Unopened Set (495):	165.00
Complete Set (495):	100.00
Common Player:	.25
(Star/rookie cards valued at 4-5X regular-issue 1989 Bowman.)	

1990 Bowman

	NM/M
Unopened Factory Set	
(528):	20.00
Complete Set (528):	15.00
Common Player:	.05
Wax Pack (15):	.75
Wax Box (36):	15.00
Jumbo Pack (31):	1.00

Jumbo Box (24):		15.00
Rack Pack (39):		1.50
Rack Box (24):		20.00
1	Tommy Greene RC	.05
2	Tom Glavine	.30
3	Andy Nezelek	.05
4	Mike Stanton	.05
5	Rick Lueken	.05
6	Kent Mercker	.05
7	Derek Lilliquist	.05
8	Charlie Liebrandt	.05
9	Steve Avery	.05
10	John Smoltz	.05
11	Mark Lemke	.05
12	Lonnie Smith	.05
13	Oddibe McDowell	.05
14	Tyler Houston RC	.05
15	Jeff Blauser	.05
16	Ernie Whitt	.05
17	Alexis Infante	.05
18	Jim Presley	.05
19	Dale Murphy	.25
20	Nick Esasky	.05
21	Rick Sutcliffe	.05
22	Mike Bielecki	.05
23	Steve Wilson	.05
24	Kevin Blankenship	.05
25	Mitch Williams	.05
26	Dean Wilkins	.05
27	Greg Maddux	.50
28	Mike Harkey	.05
29	Mark Grace	.05
30	Ryne Sandberg	.50
31	Greg Smith	.05
32	Dwight Smith	.05
33	Damon Berryhill	.05
34	Earl Cunningham	.05
35	Jerome Walton	.05
36	Lloyd McClendon	.05
37	Ty Griffin	.05
38	Shawon Dunston	.05
39	Andre Dawson	.25
40	Luis Salazar	.05
41	Tim Layana	.05
42	Rob Dibble	.05
43	Tom Browning	.05
44	Danny Jackson	.05
45	Jose Rijo	.05
46	Scott Scudder	.05
47	Randy Myers	.05
48	Brian Lane	.05
49	Paul O'Neill	.05
50	Barry Larkin	.05
51	Reggie Jefferson	.05
52	Jeff Branson	.05
53	Chris Sabo	.05
54	Joe Oliver	.05
55	Todd Benzinger	.05
56	Rolando Roomes	.05
57	Hal Morris	.05
58	Eric Davis	.05
59	Scott Bryant	.05
60	Ken Griffey	.05
61	Darryl Kile RC	.05
62	Dave Smith	.05
63	Mark Portugal	.05
64	Jeff Juden RC	.05
65	Bill Gullickson	.05
66	Danny Darwin	.05
67	Larry Andersen	.05
68	Jose Cano	.05
69	Dan Schatzeder	.05
70	Jim Deshaies	.05
71	Mike Scott	.05
72	Gerald Young	.05
73	Ken Caminiti	.05
74	Ken Oberkfell	.05
75	Dave Rohde	.05
76	Bill Doran	.05
77	Andujar Cedeno	.05
78	Craig Biggio	.05
79	Karl Rhodes	.05
80	Glenn Davis	.05
81	Eric Anthony RC	.05
82	John Wetteland	.05
83	Jay Howell	.05
84	Orel Hershiser	.05
85	Tim Belcher	.05
86	Kiki Jones	.05
87	Mike Hartley	.05
88	Ramon Martinez	.05
89	Mike Scioscia	.05
90	Willie Randolph	.05
91	Juan Samuel	.05
92	Jose Offerman RC	.05
93	Dave Hansen	.05
94	Jeff Hamilton	.05
95	Alfredo Griffin	.05
96	Tom Goodwin	.05
97	Kirk Gibson	.05
98	Jose Vizcaino	.05
99	Kal Daniels	.05
100	Hubie Brooks	.05
101	Eddie Murray	.40
102	Dennis Boyd	.05
103	Tim Burke	.05
104	Bill Sampen	.05
105	Brett Gideon	.05
106	Mark Gardner	.05
107	Howard Farmer	.05
108	Mel Rojas	.05
109	Kevin Gross	.05
110	Dave Schmidt	.05
111	Denny Martinez	.05
112	Jerry Goff	.05
113	Andres Galarraga	.05
114	Tim Welch	.05
115	Marquis Grissom RC	.25
116	Spike Owen	.05
117	Larry Walker RC	1.00
118	Rock Raines	.05
119	Delino DeShields RC	.10
120	Tom Foley	.05
121	Dave Martinez	.05
122	Frank Viola	.05
123	Julio Valera	.05
124	Alejandro Pena	.05
125	David Cone	.05
126	Dwight Gooden	.05
127	Kevin Brown	.05
128	John Franco	.05
129	Terry Bross	.05
130	Blaine Beatty	.05
131	Sid Fernandez	.05
132	Mike Marshall	.05
133	Howard Johnson	.05
134	Jaime Roseboro	.05
135	Alan Zinter	.05
136	Keith Miller	.05
137	Kevin Elster	.05
138	Kevin McReynolds	.05
139	Barry Lyons	.05
140	Gregg Jefferies	.05
141	Darryl Strawberry	.05
142	Todd Hundley RC	.10
143	Scott Service	.05
144	Chuck Malone	.05
145	Steve Ontiveros	.05
146	Roger McDowell	.05
147	Ken Howell	.05
148	Pat Combs	.05
149	Jeff Parrett	.05
150	Chuck McElroy	.05
151	Jason Grimsley	.05
152	Len Dykstra	.05
153	Mickey Morandini	.05
154	John Kruk	.05
155	Dickie Thon	.05
156	Ricky Jordan	.05
157	Jeff Jackson	.05
158	Darren Daulton	.05
159	Tom Herr	.05
160	Von Hayes	.05
161	Dave Hollins RC	.05
162	Carmelo Martinez	.05
163	Bob Walk	.05
164	Doug Drabek	.05
165	Walt Terrell	.05
166	Bill Landrum	.05
167	Scott Ruskin	.05
168	Bob Patterson	.05
169	Bobby Bonilla	.05
170	Jose Lind	.05
171	Andy Van Slyke	.05
172	Mike LaValliere	.05
173	Willie Greene RC	.05
174	Jay Bell	.05
175	Sid Bream	.05
176	Tom Prince	.05
177	Wally Backman	.05
178	Moises Alou RC	.25
179	Steve Carter	.05
180	Gary Redus	.05
181	Barry Bonds	1.00
182	Don Slaught	.05
183	Joe Magrane	.05
184	Bryn Smith	.05
185	Todd Worrell	.05
186	Jose Deleon	.05
187	Frank DiPino	.05
188	John Tudor	.05
189	Howard Hilton	.05
190	John Ericks	.05
191	Ken Dayley	.05
192	Ray Lankford RC	.10
193	Todd Zeile	.05
194	Willie McGee	.05
195	Ozzie Smith	.50
196	Milt Thompson	.05
197	Terry Pendleton	.05
198	Vince Coleman	.05
199	Paul Coleman	.05
200	Jose Oquendo	.05
201	Pedro Guerrero	.05
202	Tom Brunansky	.05
203	Roger Smithberg	.05
204	Eddie Whitson	.05
205	Dennis Rasmussen	.05

No.	Player	Price
206	Craig Lefferts	.05
207	Andy Benes	.05
208	Bruce Hurst	.05
209	Eric Show	.05
210	Rafael Valdez	.05
211	Joey Cora	.05
212	Thomas Howard	.05
213	Rob Nelson	.05
214	Jack Clark	.05
215	Garry Templeton	.05
216	Fred Lynn	.05
217	Tony Gwynn	.50
218	Benny Santiago	.05
219	Mike Pagliarulo	.05
220	Joe Carter	.05
221	Roberto Alomar	.25
222	Bip Roberts	.05
223	Rick Reuschel	.05
224	Russ Swan	.05
225	Eric Gunderson	.05
226	Steve Bedrosian	.05
227	Mike Remlinger	.05
228	Scott Garrelts	.05
229	Ernie Camacho	.05
230	Andres Santana	.05
231	Will Clark	.05
232	Kevin Mitchell	.05
233	Robby Thompson	.05
234	Bill Bathe	.05
235	Tony Perezchica	.05
236	Gary Carter	.40
237	Brett Butler	.05
238	Matt Williams	.05
239	Ernie Riles	.05
240	Kevin Bass	.05
241	Terry Kennedy	.05
242	Steve Hosey RC	.05
243	Ben McDonald RC	.15
244	Jeff Ballard	.05
245	Joe Price	.05
246	Curt Schilling	.30
247	Pete Harnisch	.05
248	Mark Williamson	.05
249	Gregg Olson	.05
250	Chris Myers	.05
251a	David Segui (No bio. data on back.)	3.50
251b	David Segui (Bio. data on back.)	.05
252	Joe Orsulak	.05
253	Craig Worthington	.05
254	Mickey Tettleton	.05
255	Cal Ripken, Jr.	1.00
256	Billy Ripken	.05
257	Randy Milligan	.05
258	Brady Anderson	.05
259	Chris Hoiles RC	.05
260	Mike Devereaux	.05
261	Phil Bradley	.05
262	Leo Gomez RC	.05
263	Lee Smith	.05
264	Mike Rochford	.05
265	Jeff Reardon	.05
266	Wes Gardner	.05
267	Mike Boddicker	.05
268	Roger Clemens	.60
269	Rob Murphy	.05
270	Mickey Pina	.05
271	Tony Pena	.05
272	Jody Reed	.05
273	Kevin Romine	.05
274	Mike Greenwell	.05
275	Mo Vaughn RC	.60
276	Danny Heep	.05
277	Scott Cooper	.05
278	Greg Blosser RC	.05
279	Dwight Evans	.05
280	Ellis Burks	.05
281	Wade Boggs	.50
282	Marty Barrett	.05
283	Kirk McCaskill	.05
284	Mark Langston	.05
285	Bert Blyleven	.05
286	Mike Fetters	.05
287	Kyle Abbott	.05
288	Jim Abbott	.05
289	Chuck Finley	.05
290	Gary DiSarcina	.05
291	Dick Schofield	.05
292	Devon White	.05
293	Bobby Rose	.05
294	Brian Downing	.05
295	Lance Parrish	.05
296	Jack Howell	.05
297	Claudell Washington	.05
298	John Orton	.05
299	Wally Joyner	.05
300	Lee Stevens	.05
301	Chili Davis	.05
302	Johnny Ray	.05
303	Greg Hibbard	.05
304	Eric King	.05
305	Jack McDowell	.05
306	Bobby Thigpen	.05
307	Adam Peterson	.05
308	Scott Radinsky RC	.05
309	Wayne Edwards	.05
310	Melido Perez	.05
311	Robin Ventura	.05
312	Sammy Sosa RC	2.00
313	Dan Pasqua	.05
314	Carlton Fisk	.40
315	Ozzie Guillen	.05
316	Ivan Calderon	.05
317	Daryl Boston	.05
318	Craig Grebeck	.05
319	Scott Fletcher	.05
320	Frank Thomas RC	3.00
321	Steve Lyons	.05
322	Carlos Martinez	.05
323	Joe Skalski	.05
324	Tom Candiotti	.05
325	Greg Swindell	.05
326	Steve Olin	.05
327	Kevin Wickander	.05
328	Doug Jones	.05
329	Jeff Shaw	.05
330	Kevin Bearse	.05
331	Dion James	.05
332	Jerry Browne	.05
333	Albert Belle	.05
334	Felix Fermin	.05
335	Candy Maldonado	.05
336	Cory Snyder	.05
337	Sandy Alomar	.05
338	Mark Lewis	.05
339	Carlos Baerga RC	.10
340	Chris James	.05
341	Brook Jacoby	.05
342	Keith Hernandez	.05
343	Frank Tanana	.05
344	Scott Aldred	.05
345	Mike Henneman	.05
346	Steve Wapnick	.05
347	Greg Gohr	.05
348	Eric Stone	.05
349	Brian DuBois	.05
350	Kevin Ritz	.05
351	Rico Brogna	.05
352	Mike Heath	.05
353	Alan Trammell	.05
354	Chet Lemon	.05
355	Dave Bergman	.05
356	Lou Whitaker	.05
357	Cecil Fielder	.05
358	Milt Cuyler	.05
359	Tony Phillips	.05
360	Travis Fryman RC	.10
361	Ed Romero	.05
362	Lloyd Moseby	.05
363	Mark Gubicza	.05
364	Bret Saberhagen	.05
365	Tom Gordon	.05
366	Steve Farr	.05
367	Kevin Appier	.05
368	Storm Davis	.05
369	Mark Davis	.05
370	Jeff Montgomery	.05
371	Frank White	.05
372	Brent Mayne	.05
373	Bob Boone	.05
374	Jim Eisenreich	.05
375	Danny Tartabull	.05
376	Kurt Stillwell	.05
377	Bill Pecota	.05
378	Bo Jackson	.10
379	Bob Hamelin RC	.05
380	Kevin Seitzer	.05
381	Rey Palacios	.05
382	George Brett	.60
383	Gerald Perry	.05
384	Teddy Higuera	.05
385	Tom Filer	.05
386	Dan Plesac	.05
387	Cal Eldred RC	.05
388	Jaime Navarro	.05
389	Chris Bosio	.05
390	Randy Veres	.05
391	Gary Sheffield	.25
392	George Canale	.05
393	B.J. Surhoff	.05
394	Tim McIntosh	.05
395	Greg Brock	.05
396	Greg Vaughn	.05
397	Darryl Hamilton	.05
398	Dave Parker	.05
399	Paul Molitor	.40
400	Jim Gantner	.05
401	Rob Deer	.05
402	Billy Spiers	.05
403	Glenn Braggs	.05
404	Robin Yount	.40
405	Rick Aguilera	.05
406	Johnny Ard	.05
407	Kevin Tapani RC	.10
408	Park Pittman	.05
409	Allan Anderson	.05
410	Juan Berenguer	.05
411	Willie Banks	.05
412	Rich Yett	.05
413	Dave West	.05
414	Greg Gagne	.05
415	Chuck Knoblauch RC	.50
416	Randy Bush	.05
417	Gary Gaetti	.05
418	Kent Hrbek	.05
419	Al Newman	.05
420	Danny Gladden	.05
421	Paul Sorrento	.05
422	Derek Parks	.05
423	Scott Leius	.05
424	Kirby Puckett	.50
425	Willie Smith	.05
426	Dave Righetti	.05
427	Jeff Robinson	.05
428	Alan Mills	.05
429	Tim Leary	.05
430	Pascual Perez	.05
431	Alvaro Espinoza	.05
432	Dave Winfield	.40
433	Jesse Barfield	.05
434	Randy Velarde	.05
435	Rick Cerone	.05
436	Steve Balboni	.05
437	Mel Hall	.05
438	Bob Geren	.05
439	Bernie Williams RC	1.00
440	Kevin Maas RC	.05
441	Mike Blowers	.05
442	Steve Sax	.05
443	Don Mattingly	.60
444	Roberto Kelly	.05
445	Mike Moore	.05
446	Reggie Harris	.05
447	Scott Sanderson	.05
448	Dave Otto	.05
449	Dave Stewart	.05
450	Rick Honeycutt	.05
451	Dennis Eckersley	.35
452	Carney Lansford	.05
453	Scott Hemond	.05
454	Mark McGwire	.75
455	Felix Jose	.05
456	Terry Steinbach	.05
457	Rickey Henderson	.40
458	Dave Henderson	.05
459	Mike Gallego	.05
460	Jose Canseco	.30
461	Walt Weiss	.05
462	Ken Phelps	.05
463	Darren Lewis RC	.05
464	Ron Hassey	.05
465	Roger Salkeld RC	.05
466	Scott Bankhead	.05
467	Keith Comstock	.05
468	Randy Johnson	.40
469	Erik Hanson	.05
470	Mike Schooler	.05
471	Gary Eave	.05
472	Jeffrey Leonard	.05
473	Dave Valle	.05
474	Omar Vizquel	.05
475	Pete O'Brien	.05
476	Henry Cotto	.05
477	Jay Buhner	.05
478	Harold Reynolds	.05
479	Alvin Davis	.05
480	Darnell Coles	.05
481	Ken Griffey Jr.	.65
482	Greg Briley	.05
483	Scott Bradley	.05
484	Tino Martinez	.05
485	Jeff Russell	.05
486	Nolan Ryan	1.00
487	Robb Nen	.05
488	Kevin Brown	.05
489	Brian Bohanon	.05
490	Ruben Sierra	.05
491	Pete Incaviglia	.05
492	Juan Gonzalez RC	1.00
493	Steve Buechele	.05
494	Scott Coolbaugh	.05
495	Geno Petralli	.05
496	Rafael Palmeiro	.35
497	Julio Franco	.05
498	Gary Pettis	.05
499	Donald Harris	.05
500	Monty Fariss	.05
501	Harold Baines	.05
502	Cecil Espy	.05
503	Jack Daugherty	.05
504	Willie Blair	.05
505	Dave Steib	.05
506	Tom Henke	.05
507	John Cerutti	.05
508	Paul Kilgus	.05
509	Jimmy Key	.05
510	John Olerud RC	.75
511	Ed Sprague	.05
512	Manny Lee	.05
513	Fred McGriff	.05
514	Glenallen Hill	.05
515	George Bell	.05
516	Mookie Wilson	.05
517	Luis Sojo	.05
518	Nelson Liriano	.05
519	Kelly Gruber	.05
520	Greg Myers	.05
521	Pat Borders	.05
522	Junior Felix	.05
523	Eddie Zosky	.05
524	Tony Fernandez	.05
525	Checklist	.05
526	Checklist	.05
527	Checklist	.05
528	Checklist	.05

Tiffany

	NM/M
Unopened Set (539):	200.00
Complete Set (539):	60.00
Common Player:	.25

(Star/rookie cards valued about 4-5X regular-issue 1990 Bowman.)

1991 Bowman

REGGIE SANDERS

	NM/M
Unopened Factory Set (704):	30.00
Complete Set (704):	20.00
Common Player:	.05
Wax Pack (14):	.75
Wax Box (36):	17.50
Cello Pack (29):	1.50
Cello Box (24):	25.00

No.	Player	Price
1	Rod Carew-I	.10
2	Rod Carew-II	.10
3	Rod Carew-III	.10
4	Rod Carew-IV	.10
5	Rod Carew-V	.10
6	Willie Fraser	.05
7	John Olerud	.05
8	William Suero	.05
9	Roberto Alomar	.20
10	Todd Stottlemyre	.05
11	Joe Carter	.05
12	Steve Karsay RC	.10
13	Mark Whiten	.05
14	Pat Borders	.05
15	Mike Timlin	.05
16	Tom Henke	.05
17	Eddie Zosky	.05
18	Kelly Gruber	.05
19	Jimmy Key	.05
20	Jerry Schunk	.05
21	Manny Lee	.05
22	Dave Steib	.05
23	Pat Hentgen	.05
24	Glenallen Hill	.05
25	Rene Gonzales	.05
26	Ed Sprague	.05
27	Ken Dayley	.05
28	Pat Tabler	.05
29	Denis Boucher RC	.05
30	Devon White	.05
31	Dante Bichette	.05
32	Paul Molitor	.40
33	Greg Vaughn	.05
34	Dan Plesac	.05
35	Chris George	.05
36	Tim McIntosh	.05
37	Franklin Stubbs	.05
38	Bo Dodson	.05
39	Ron Robinson	.05
40	Ed Nunez	.05
41	Greg Brock	.05
42	Jaime Navarro	.05
43	Chris Bosio	.05
44	B.J. Surhoff	.05
45	Chris Johnson	.05
46	Willie Randolph	.05
47	Narciso Elvira	.05
48	Jim Gantner	.05
49	Kevin Brown	.05

No.	Player	Value
50	Julio Machado	.05
51	Chuck Crim	.05
52	Gary Sheffield	.30
53	Angel Miranda	.05
54	Teddy Higuera	.05
55	Robin Yount	.40
56	Cal Eldred	.05
57	Sandy Alomar	.05
58	Greg Swindell	.05
59	Brook Jacoby	.05
60	Efrain Valdez	.05
61	Ever Magallanes	.05
62	Tom Candiotti	.05
63	Eric King	.05
64	Alex Cole	.05
65	Charles Nagy	.05
66	Mitch Webster	.05
67	Chris James	.05
68	Jim Thome RC	3.00
69	Carlos Baerga	.05
70	Mark Lewis	.05
71	Jerry Browne	.05
72	Jesse Orosco	.05
73	Mike Huff	.05
74	Jose Escobar	.05
75	Jeff Manto	.05
76	Turner Ward RC	.05
77	Doug Jones	.05
78	Bruce Egloff RC	.05
79	Tim Costo	.05
80	Beau Allred	.05
81	Albert Belle	.05
82	John Farrell	.05
83	Glenn Davis	.05
84	Joe Orsulak	.05
85	Mark Williamson	.05
86	Ben McDonald	.05
87	Billy Ripken	.05
88	Leo Gomez	.05
89	Bob Melvin	.05
90	Jeff Robinson	.05
91	Jose Mesa	.05
92	Gregg Olson	.05
93	Mike Devereaux	.05
94	Luis Mercedes	.05
95	Arthur Rhodes RC	.10
96	Juan Bell	.05
97	Mike Mussina RC	3.00
98	Jeff Ballard	.05
99	Chris Hoiles	.05
100	Brady Anderson	.05
101	Bob Milacki	.05
102	David Segui	.05
103	Dwight Evans	.05
104	Cal Ripken, Jr.	1.00
105	Mike Linskey	.05
106	Jeff Tackett RC	.05
107	Jeff Reardon	.05
108	Dana Kiecker	.05
109	Ellis Burks	.05
110	Dave Owen	.05
111	Danny Darwin	.05
112	Mo Vaughn	.05
113	Jeff McNeely	.05
114	Tom Bolton	.05
115	Greg Blosser	.05
116	Mike Greenwell	.05
117	Phil Plantier RC	.05
118	Roger Clemens	.60
119	John Marzano	.05
120	Jody Reed	.05
121	Scott Taylor	.05
122	Jack Clark	.05
123	Derek Livernois	.05
124	Tony Pena	.05
125	Tom Brunansky	.05
126	Carlos Quintana	.05
127	Tim Naehring	.05
128	Matt Young	.05
129	Wade Boggs	.50
130	Kevin Morton	.05
131	Pete Incaviglia	.05
132	Rob Deer	.05
133	Bill Gullickson	.05
134	Rico Brogna	.05
135	Lloyd Moseby	.05
136	Cecil Fielder	.05
137	Tony Phillips	.05
138	Mark Leiter	.05
139	John Cerutti	.05
140	Mickey Tettleton	.05
141	Milt Cuyler	.05
142	Greg Gohr	.05
143	Tony Bernazard	.05
144	Dan Gakeler	.05
145	Travis Fryman	.05
146	Dan Petry	.05
147	Scott Aldred	.05
148	John DeSilva	.05
149	Rusty Meacham	.05
150	Lou Whitaker	.05
151	Dave Haas	.05
152	Luis de los Santos	.05
153	Ivan Cruz	.05
154	Alan Trammell	.05
155	Pat Kelly	.05
156	Carl Everett RC	.25
157	Greg Cadaret	.05
158	Kevin Maas	.05
159	Jeff Johnson	.05
160	Willie Smith	.05
161	Gerald Williams	.05
162	Mike Humphreys	.05
163	Alvaro Espinoza	.05
164	Matt Nokes	.05
165	Wade Taylor	.05
166	Roberto Kelly	.05
167	John Habyan	.05
168	Steve Farr	.05
169	Jesse Barfield	.05
170	Steve Sax	.05
171	Jim Leyritz	.05
172	Robert Eenhoorn	.05
173	Bernie Williams	.05
174	Scott Lusader	.05
175	Torey Lovullo	.05
176	Chuck Cary	.05
177	Scott Sanderson	.05
178	Don Mattingly	.60
179	Mel Hall	.05
180	Juan Gonzalez	.30
181	Hensley Meulens	.05
182	Jose Offerman	.05
183	Jeff Bagwell RC	2.50
184	Jeff Conine RC	.25
185	Henry Rodriguez RC	.05
186	Jimmie Reese	.05
187	Kyle Abbott	.05
188	Lance Parrish	.05
189	Rafael Montalvo	.05
190	Floyd Bannister	.05
191	Dick Schofield	.05
192	Scott Lewis	.05
193	Jeff Robinson	.05
194	Kent Anderson	.05
195	Wally Joyner	.05
196	Chuck Finley	.05
197	Luis Sojo	.05
198	Jeff Richardson	.05
199	Dave Parker	.05
200	Jim Abbott	.05
201	Junior Felix	.05
202	Mark Langston	.05
203	Tim Salmon RC	1.00
204	Cliff Young	.05
205	Scott Bailes	.05
206	Bobby Rose	.05
207	Gary Gaetti	.05
208	Ruben Amaro	.05
209	Luis Polonia	.05
210	Dave Winfield	.40
211	Bryan Harvey	.05
212	Mike Moore	.05
213	Rickey Henderson	.40
214	Steve Chitren	.05
215	Bob Welch	.05
216	Terry Steinbach	.05
217	Ernie Riles	.05
218	Todd Van Poppel RC	.10
219	Mike Gallego	.05
220	Curt Young	.05
221	Todd Burns	.05
222	Vance Law	.05
223	Eric Show	.05
224	Don Peters RC	.05
225	Dave Stewart	.05
226	Dave Henderson	.05
227	Jose Canseco	.30
228	Walt Weiss	.05
229	Dann Howitt	.05
230	Willie Wilson	.05
231	Harold Baines	.05
232	Scott Hemond	.05
233	Joe Slusarski	.05
234	Mark McGwire	.75
235	Kirk Dressendorfer RC	.05
236	Craig Paquette RC	.05
237	Dennis Eckersley	.35
238	Dana Allison	.05
239	Scott Bradley	.05
240	Brian Holman	.05
241	Mike Schooler	.05
242	Rich Delucia	.05
243	Edgar Martinez	.05
244	Henry Cotto	.05
245	Omar Vizquel	.05
246a	Ken Griffey Jr.	.65
246b	Ken Griffey Sr. (Should be #255.)	.10
247	Jay Buhner	.05
248	Bill Krueger	.05
249	Dave Fleming RC	.05
250	Patrick Lennon RC	.05
251	Dave Valle	.05
252	Harold Reynolds	.05
253	Randy Johnson	.40
254	Scott Bankhead	.05
255	(Not issued, see #246b.)	
256	Greg Briley	.05
257	Tino Martinez	.05
258	Alvin Davis	.05
259	Pete O'Brien	.05
260	Erik Hanson	.05
261	Bret Boone RC	.50
262	Roger Salkeld	.05
263	Dave Burba	.05
264	Kerry Woodson RC	.05
265	Julio Franco	.05
266	Dan Peltier	.05
267	Jeff Russell	.05
268	Steve Buechele	.05
269	Donald Harris	.05
270	Robb Nen	.05
271	Rich Gossage	.05
272	Ivan Rodriguez RC	3.00
273	Jeff Huson	.05
274	Kevin Brown	.05
275	Dan Smith RC	.05
276	Gary Pettis	.05
277	Jack Daugherty	.05
278	Mike Jeffcoat	.05
279	Brad Arnsberg	.05
280	Nolan Ryan	1.00
281	Eric McCray	.05
282	Scott Chiamparino	.05
283	Ruben Sierra	.05
284	Geno Petralli	.05
285	Monty Fariss	.05
286	Rafael Palmeiro	.35
287	Bobby Witt	.05
288	Dean Palmer	.05
289	Tony Scruggs	.05
290	Kenny Rogers	.05
291	Bret Saberhagen	.05
292	Brian McRae RC	.05
293	Storm Davis	.05
294	Danny Tartabull	.05
295	David Howard	.05
296	Mike Boddicker	.05
297	Joel Johnston	.05
298	Tim Spehr	.05
299	Hector Wagner	.05
300	George Brett	.60
301	Mike Macfarlane	.05
302	Kirk Gibson	.05
303	Harvey Pulliam	.05
304	Jim Eisenreich	.05
305	Kevin Seitzer	.05
306	Mark Davis	.05
307	Kurt Stillwell	.05
308	Jeff Montgomery	.05
309	Kevin Appier	.05
310	Bob Hamelin	.05
311	Tom Gordon	.05
312	Kerwin Moore RC	.05
313	Hugh Walker	.05
314	Terry Shumpert	.05
315	Warren Cromartie	.05
316	Gary Thurman	.05
317	Steve Bedrosian	.05
318	Danny Gladden	.05
319	Jack Morris	.05
320	Kirby Puckett	.50
321	Kent Hrbek	.05
322	Kevin Tapani	.05
323	Denny Neagle	.05
324	Rich Garces	.05
325	Larry Casian	.05
326	Shane Mack	.05
327	Allan Anderson	.05
328	Junior Ortiz	.05
329	Paul Abbott RC	.05
330	Chuck Knoblauch	.05
331	Chili Davis	.05
332	Todd Ritchie RC	.05
333	Brian Harper	.05
334	Rick Aguilera	.05
335	Scott Erickson	.05
336	Pedro Munoz	.05
337	Scott Leius	.05
338	Greg Gagne	.05
339	Mike Pagliarulo	.05
340	Terry Leach	.05
341	Willie Banks	.05
342	Bobby Thigpen	.05
343	Roberto Hernandez RC	.10
344	Melido Perez	.05
345	Carlton Fisk	.40
346	Norberto Martin RC	.05
347	Johnny Ruffin RC	.05
348	Jeff Carter RC	.05
349	Lance Johnson	.05
350	Sammy Sosa	.50
351	Alex Fernandez	.05
352	Jack McDowell	.05
353	Bob Wickman RC	.05
354	Wilson Alvarez	.05
355	Charlie Hough	.05
356	Ozzie Guillen	.05
357	Cory Snyder	.05
358	Robin Ventura	.05
359	Scott Fletcher	.05
360	Cesar Bernhardt	.05
361	Dan Pasqua	.05
362	Tim Raines	.05
363	Brian Drahman	.05
364	Wayne Edwards	.05
365	Scott Radinsky	.05
366	Frank Thomas	.40
367	Cecil Fielder	.05
368	Julio Franco	.05
369	Kelly Gruber	.05
370	Alan Trammell	.05
371	Rickey Henderson	.30
372	Jose Canseco	.15
373	Ellis Burks	.05
374	Lance Parrish	.05
375	Dave Parker	.05
376	Eddie Murray	.30
377	Ryne Sandberg	.35
378	Matt Williams	.05
379	Barry Larkin	.05
380	Barry Bonds	.75
381	Bobby Bonilla	.05
382	Darryl Strawberry	.05
383	Benny Santiago	.05
384	Don Robinson	.05
385	Paul Coleman	.05
386	Milt Thompson	.05
387	Lee Smith	.05
388	Ray Lankford	.05
389	Tom Pagnozzi	.05
390	Ken Hill	.05
391	Jamie Moyer	.05
392	Greg Carmona RC	.05
393	John Ericks	.05
394	Bob Tewksbury	.05
395	Jose Oquendo	.05
396	Rheal Cormier	.05
397	Mike Milchin RC	.05
398	Ozzie Smith	.50
399	Aaron Holbert RC	.05
400	Jose DeLeon	.05
401	Felix Jose	.05
402	Juan Agosto	.05
403	Pedro Guerrero	.05
404	Todd Zeile	.05
405	Gerald Perry	.05
406	Not Issued	
407	Bryn Smith	.05
408	Bernard Gilkey	.05
409	Rex Hudler	.05
410a	Ralph Branca, Bobby Thomson	.10
410b	Donovan Osborne	.05
411	Lance Dickson	.05
412	Danny Jackson	.05
413	Jerome Walton	.05
414	Sean Cheetham	.05
415	Joe Girardi	.05
416	Ryne Sandberg	.50
417	Mike Harkey	.05
418	George Bell	.05
419	Rick Wilkins RC	.05
420	Earl Cunningham	.05
421	Heathcliff Slocumb	.05
422	Mike Bielecki	.05
423	Jessie Hollins RC	.05
424	Shawon Dunston	.05
425	Dave Smith	.05
426	Greg Maddux	.50
427	Jose Vizcaino	.05
428	Luis Salazar	.05
429	Andre Dawson	.25
430	Rick Sutcliffe	.05
431	Paul Assenmacher	.05
432	Erik Pappas	.05
433	Mark Grace	.05
434	Denny Martinez	.05
435	Marquis Grissom	.05
436	Wil Cordero RC	.05
437	Tim Wallach	.05
438	Brian Barnes RC	.05
439	Barry Jones	.05
440	Ivan Calderon	.05
441	Stan Spencer RC	.05
442	Larry Walker	.05
443	Chris Haney RC	.05
444	Hector Rivera	.05
445	Delino DeShields	.05
446	Andres Galarraga	.05
447	Gilberto Reyes	.05
448	Willie Greene	.05
449	Greg Colbrunn	.05
450	Rondell White RC	.25
451	Steve Frey	.05
452	Shane Andrews RC	.10
453	Mike Fitzgerald	.05
454	Spike Owen	.05
455	Dave Martinez	.05
456	Dennis Boyd	.05
457	Eric Bullock	.05
458	Reid Cornelius RC	.05
459	Chris Nabholz	.05
460	David Cone	.05
461	Hubie Brooks	.05

462	Sid Fernandez	.05
463	Doug Simons RC	.05
464	Howard Johnson	.05
465	Chris Donnels	.05
466	Anthony Young	.05
467	Todd Hundley	.05
468	Rick Cerone	.05
469	Kevin Elster	.05
470	Wally Whitehurst	.05
471	Vince Coleman	.05
472	Dwight Gooden	.05
473	Charlie O'Brien	.05
474	Jeromy Burnitz RC	.50
475	John Franco	.05
476	Daryl Boston	.05
477	Frank Viola	.05
478	D.J. Dozier	.05
479	Kevin McReynolds	.05
480	Tom Herr	.05
481	Gregg Jefferies	.05
482	Pete Schourek	.05
483	Ron Darling	.05
484	Dave Magadan	.05
485	Andy Ashby RC	.05
486	Dale Murphy	.20
487	Von Hayes	.05
488	Kim Batiste RC	.05
489	Tony Longmire RC	.05
490	Wally Backman	.05
491	Jeff Jackson	.05
492	Mickey Morandini	.05
493	Darrel Akerfelds	.05
494	Ricky Jordan	.05
495	Randy Ready	.05
496	Darrin Fletcher	.05
497	Chuck Malone	.05
498	Pat Combs	.05
499	Dickie Thon	.05
500	Roger McDowell	.05
501	Len Dykstra	.05
502	Joe Boever	.05
503	John Kruk	.05
504	Terry Mulholland	.05
505	Wes Chamberlain	.05
506	Mike Lieberthal RC	.75
507	Darren Daulton	.05
508	Charlie Hayes	.05
509	John Smiley	.05
510	Gary Varsho	.05
511	Curt Wilkerson	.05
512	Orlando Merced RC	.05
513	Barry Bonds	1.00
514	Mike Lavalliere	.05
515	Doug Drabek	.05
516	Gary Redus	.05
517	William Pennyfeather RC	.05
518	Randy Tomlin	.05
519	Mike Zimmerman RC	.05
520	Jeff King	.05
521	Kurt Miller RC	.05
522	Jay Bell	.05
523	Bill Landrum	.05
524	Zane Smith	.05
525	Bobby Bonilla	.05
526	Bob Walk	.05
527	Austin Manahan	.05
528	Joe Ausanio RC	.05
529	Andy Van Slyke	.05
530	Jose Lind	.05
531	Carlos Garcia RC	.05
532	Don Slaught	.05
533	Colin Powell	.25
534	Frank Bolick RC	.05
535	Gary Scott RC	.05
536	Nikco Riesgo	.05
537	Reggie Sanders RC	.25
538	Tim Howard RC	.05
539	Ryan Bowen RC	.05
540	Eric Anthony	.05
541	Jim Deshaies	.05
542	Tom Nevers	.05
543	Ken Caminiti	.05
544	Karl Rhodes	.05
545	Xavier Hernandez	.05
546	Mike Scott	.05
547	Jeff Juden	.05
548	Darryl Kile	.05
549	Willie Ansley	.05
550	Luis Gonzalez RC	1.00
551	Mike Simms RC	.05
552	Mark Portugal	.05
553	Jimmy Jones	.05
554	Jim Clancy	.05
555	Pete Harnisch	.05
556	Craig Biggio	.05
557	Eric Yelding	.05
558	Dave Rohde	.05
559	Casey Candaele	.05
560	Curt Schilling	.25
561	Steve Finley	.05
562	Javier Ortiz	.05
563	Andujar Cedeno	.05
564	Rafael Ramirez	.05
565	Kenny Lofton RC	.50
566	Steve Avery	.05
567	Lonnie Smith	.05
568	Kent Mercker	.05
569	Chipper Jones RC	3.00
570	Terry Pendleton	.05
571	Otis Nixon	.05
572	Juan Berenguer	.05
573	Charlie Leibrandt	.05
574	Dave Justice	.05
575	Keith Mitchell	.05
576	Tom Glavine	.25
577	Greg Olson	.05
578	Rafael Belliard	.05
579	Ben Rivera	.05
580	John Smoltz	.05
581	Tyler Houston	.05
582	Mark Wohlers RC	.05
583	Ron Gant	.05
584	Ramon Caraballo	.05
585	Sid Bream	.05
586	Jeff Treadway	.05
587	Javier Lopez RC	.75
588	Deion Sanders	.10
589	Mike Heath	.05
590	Ryan Klesko RC	.20
591	Bob Ojeda	.05
592	Alfredo Griffin	.05
593	Raul Mondesi RC	.25
594	Greg Smith	.05
595	Orel Hershiser	.05
596	Juan Samuel	.05
597	Brett Butler	.05
598	Gary Carter	.40
599	Stan Javier	.05
600	Kal Daniels	.05
601	Jamie McAndrew RC	.05
602	Mike Sharperson	.05
603	Jay Howell	.05
604	Eric Karros RC	.25
605	Tim Belcher	.05
606	Dan Opperman	.05
607	Lenny Harris	.05
608	Tom Goodwin	.05
609	Darryl Strawberry	.05
610	Ramon Martinez	.05
611	Kevin Gross	.05
612	Zakary Shinall	.05
613	Mike Scioscia	.05
614	Eddie Murray	.40
615	Ronnie Walden	.05
616	Will Clark	.05
617	Adam Hyzdu	.05
618	Matt Williams	.05
619	Don Robinson	.05
620	Jeff Brantley	.05
621	Greg Litton	.05
622	Steve Decker	.05
623	Robby Thompson	.05
624	Mark Leonard RC	.05
625	Kevin Bass	.05
626	Scott Garrelts	.05
627	Jose Uribe	.05
628	Eric Gunderson	.05
629	Steve Hosey	.05
630	Trevor Wilson	.05
631	Terry Kennedy	.05
632	Dave Righetti	.05
633	Kelly Downs	.05
634	Johnny Ard	.05
635	Eric Christopherson RC	.05
636	Kevin Mitchell	.05
637	John Burkett	.05
638	Kevin Rogers RC	.05
639	Bud Black	.05
640	Willie McGee	.05
641	Royce Clayton	.05
642	Tony Fernandez	.05
643	Ricky Bones	.05
644	Thomas Howard	.05
645	Dave Staton	.05
646	Jim Presley	.05
647	Tony Gwynn	.50
648	Marty Barrett	.05
649	Scott Coolbaugh	.05
650	Craig Lefferts	.05
651	Eddie Whitson	.05
652	Oscar Azocar	.05
653	Wes Gardner	.05
654	Bip Roberts	.05
655	Robbie Beckett RC	.05
656	Benny Santiago	.05
657	Greg W. Harris	.05
658	Jerald Clark	.05
659	Fred McGriff	.05
660	Larry Andersen	.05
661	Bruce Hurst	.05
662	Steve Martin	.05
663	Rafael Valdez	.05
664	Paul Faries RC	.05
665	Andy Benes	.05
666	Randy Myers	.05
667	Rob Dibble	.05
668	Glenn Sutko	.05
669	Glenn Braggs	.05
670	Billy Hatcher	.05
671	Joe Oliver	.05
672	Freddie Benavides	.05
673	Barry Larkin	.05
674	Chris Sabo	.05
675	Mariano Duncan	.05
676	Chris Jones RC	.05
677	Gino Minutelli RC	.05
678	Reggie Jefferson	.05
679	Jack Armstrong	.05
680	Chris Hammond	.05
681	Jose Rijo	.05
682	Bill Doran	.05
683	Terry Lee	.05
684	Tom Browning	.05
685	Paul O'Neill	.05
686	Eric Davis	.05
687	Dan Wilson RC	.05
688	Ted Power	.05
689	Tim Layana	.05
690	Norm Charlton	.05
691	Hal Morris	.05
692	Rickey Henderson	.35
693	Sam Militello RC	.05
694	Matt Mieske RC	.05
695	Paul Russo RC	.05
696	Domingo Mota RC	.05
697	Todd Guggiana RC	.05
698	Marc Newfield	.05
699	Checklist	.05
700	Checklist	.05
701	Checklist	.05
702	Checklist	.05
703	Checklist	.05
704	Checklist	.05

1992 Bowman

FRED McGRIFF

	NM/M
Complete Set (705):	120.00
Common Player:	.10
Pack (15):	4.00
Wax Box (36):	135.00
Jumbo Pack (25):	8.00
Jumbo Box (36):	200.00

1	Ivan Rodriguez	1.25
2	Kirk McCaskill	.10
3	Scott Livingstone	.10
4	Salomon Torres RC	.10
5	Carlos Hernandez	.10
6	Dave Hollins	.10
7	Scott Fletcher	.10
8	Jorge Fabregas	.10
9	Andujar Cedeno	.10
10	Howard Johnson	.10
11	Trevor Hoffman RC	2.00
12	Roberto Kelly	.10
13	Gregg Jefferies	.10
14	Marquis Grissom	.10
15	Mike Ignasiak	.10
16	Jack Morris	.10
17	William Pennyfeather	.10
18	Todd Stottlemyre	.10
19	Chito Martinez	.10
20	Roberto Alomar	.30
21	Sam Militello	.10
22	Hector Fajardo	.10
23	Paul Quantrill RC	.10
24	Chuck Knoblauch	.10
25	Reggie Jefferson	.10
26	Jeremy McGarity	.10
27	Jerome Walton	.10
28	Chipper Jones	8.00
29	Brian Barber RC	.10
30	Ron Darling	.10
31	Roberto Petagine RC	.10
32	Chuck Finley	.10
33	Edgar Martinez	.10
34	Napoleon Robinson	.10
35	Andy Van Slyke	.10
36	Bobby Thigpen	.10
37	Travis Fryman	.10
38	Eric Christopherson	.10
39	Terry Mulholland	.10
40	Darryl Strawberry	.10
41	Manny Alexander RC	.10
42	Tracey Sanders RC	.10
43	Pete Incaviglia	.10
44	Kim Batiste	.10
45	Frank Rodriguez	.10
46	Greg Swindell	.10
47	Delino DeShields	.10
48	John Ericks	.10
49	Franklin Stubbs	.10
50	Tony Gwynn	2.00
51	Clifton Garrett RC	.10
52	Mike Gardella	.10
53	Scott Erickson	.10
54	Gary Caballo	.10
55	Jose Oliva RC	.10
56	Brook Fordyce	.10
57	Mark Whiten	.10
58	Joe Slusarski	.10
59	J.R. Phillips RC	.10
60	Barry Bonds	4.00
61	Bob Milacki	.10
62	Keith Mitchell	.10
63	Angel Miranda	.10
64	Raul Mondesi	.10
65	Brian Koelling	.10
66	Brian McRae	.10
67	John Patterson	.10
68	John Wetteland	.10
69	Wilson Alvarez	.10
70	Wade Boggs	2.00
71	Darryl Ratliff	.10
72	Jeff Jackson	.10
73	Jeremy Hernandez	.10
74	Darryl Hamilton	.10
75	Rafael Belliard	.10
76	Ricky Trilcek	.10
77	Felipe Crespo RC	.10
78	Carney Lansford	.10
79	Ryan Long	.10
80	Kirby Puckett	2.00
81	Earl Cunningham	.10
82	Pedro Martinez	1.50
83	Scott Hatteberg	.10
84	Juan Gonzalez	.75
85	Robert Nutting	.10
86	Calvin Reese RC	.50
87	Dave Silvestri	.10
88	Scott Ruffcorn RC	.10
89	Rick Aguilera	.10
90	Cecil Fielder	.10
91	Kirk Dressendorfer	.10
92	Jerry DiPoto	.10
93	Mike Felder	.10
94	Craig Paquette	.10
95	Elvin Paulino	.10
96	Donovan Osborne	.10
97	Hubie Brooks	.10
98	Derek Lowe RC	4.00
99	David Zancanaro	.10
100	Ken Griffey Jr.	2.75
101	Todd Hundley	.10
102	Mike Trombley	.10
103	Ricky Gutierrez RC	.10
104	Braulio Castillo	.10
105	Craig Lefferts	.10
106	Rick Sutcliffe	.10
107	Dean Palmer	.10
108	Henry Rodriguez	.10
109	Mark Clark RC	.10
110	Kenny Lofton	.10
111	Mark Carreon	.10
112	J.T. Bruett RC	.10
113	Gerald Williams	.10
114	Frank Thomas	1.50
115	Kevin Reimer	.10
116	Sammy Sosa	2.00
117	Mickey Tettleton	.10
118	Reggie Sanders	.10
119	Trevor Wilson	.10
120	Cliff Brantley	.10
121	Spike Owen	.10
122	Jeff Montgomery	.10
123	Alex Sutherland	.10
124	Brien Taylor RC	.10
125	Brian Williams	.10
126	Kevin Seitzer	.10
127	Carlos Delgado RC	15.00
128	Gary Scott	.10
129	Scott Cooper	.10
130	Domingo Jean RC	.10
131	Pat Mahomes RC	.10
132	Mike Boddicker	.10
133	Roberto Hernandez	.10
134	Dave Valle	.10
135	Kurt Stillwell	.10
136	Brad Pennington RC	.10
137	Jermaine Swifton	.10
138	Ryan Hawblitzel	.10
139	Tito Navarro	.10
140	Sandy Alomar	.10
141	Todd Benzinger	.10
142	Danny Jackson	.10

No.	Player	Value
143	Melvin Nieves RC	.25
144	Jim Campanis	.10
145	Luis Gonzalez	.10
146	Dave Doorneweerd	.10
147	Charlie Hayes	.10
148	Greg Maddux	2.00
149	Brian Harper	.10
150	Brent Miller	.10
151	Shawn Estes RC	.75
152	Mike Williams	.10
153	Charlie Hough	.10
154	Randy Myers	.10
155	Kevin Young RC	.10
156	Rick Wilkins	.10
157	Terry Schumpert	.10
158	Steve Karsay	.10
159	Gary DiSarcina	.10
160	Deion Sanders	.10
161	Tom Browning	.10
162	Dickie Thon	.10
163	Luis Mercedes	.10
164	Ricardo Ingram	.10
165	Tavo Alavarez RC	.10
166	Rickey Henderson	1.50
167	Jaime Navarro	.10
168	Billy Ashley RC	.10
169	Phil Dauphin	.10
170	Ivan Cruz	.10
171	Harold Baines	.10
172	Bryan Harvey	.10
173	Alex Cole	.10
174	Curtis Shaw	.10
175	Matt Williams	.10
176	Felix Jose	.10
177	Sam Horn	.10
178	Randy Johnson	1.50
179	Ivan Calderon	.10
180	Steve Avery	.10
181	William Suero	.10
182	Bill Swift	.10
183	Howard Battle RC	.10
184	Ruben Amaro	.10
185	Jim Abbott	.10
186	Mike Fitzgerald	.10
187	Bruce Hurst	.10
188	Jeff Juden	.10
189	Jeromy Burnitz	.10
190	Dave Burba	.10
191	Kevin Brown	.10
192	Patrick Lennon	.10
193	Jeffrey McNeely	.10
194	Wil Cordero	.10
195	Chili Davis	.10
196	Milt Cuyler	.10
197	Von Hayes	.10
198	Todd Revening RC	.10
199	Joel Johnson	.10
200	Jeff Bagwell	1.50
201	Alex Fernandez	.10
202	Todd Jones	.10
203	Charles Nagy	.10
204	Tim Raines	.10
205	Kevin Maas	.10
206	Julio Franco	.10
207	Randy Velarde	.10
208	Lance Johnson	.10
209	Scott Leius	.10
210	Derek Lee	.10
211	Joe Sondrini	.10
212	Royce Clayton	.10
213	Chris George	.10
214	Gary Sheffield	.60
215	Mark Gubicza	.10
216	Mike Moore	.10
217	Rick Huisman	.10
218	Jeff Russell	.10
219	D.J. Dozier	.10
220	Dave Martinez	.10
221	Al Newman	.10
222	Nolan Ryan	4.00
223	Teddy Higuera	.10
224	Damon Buford RC	.10
225	Ruben Sierra	.10
226	Tom Nevers	.10
227	Tommy Greene	.10
228	Nigel Wilson RC	.10
229	John DeSilva	.10
230	Bobby Witt	.10
231	Greg Cadaret	.10
232	John VanderWal	.10
233	Jack Clark	.10
234	Bill Doran	.10
235	Bobby Bonilla	.10
236	Steve Olin	.10
237	Derek Bell	.10
238	David Cone	.10
239	Victor Cole	.10
240	Rod Bolton	.10
241	Tom Pagnozzi	.10
242	Rob Dibble	.10
243	Michael Carter	.10
244	Don Peters	.10
245	Mike LaValliere	.10
246	Joe Perona	.10
247	Mitch Williams	.10
248	Jay Buhner	.10
249	Andy Benes	.10
250	Alex Ochoa RC	.10
251	Greg Blosser	.10
252	Jack Armstrong	.10
253	Juan Samuel	.10
254	Terry Pendleton	.10
255	Ramon Martinez	.10
256	Rico Brogna	.10
257	John Smiley	.10
258	Carl Everett	.10
259	Tim Salmon	.10
260	Will Clark	.10
261	Ugueth Urbina RC	.40
262	Jason Wood	.10
263	Dave Magadan	.10
264	Dante Bichette	.10
265	Jose DeLeon	.10
266	Mike Neill RC	.10
267	Paul O'Neill	.10
268	Anthony Young	.10
269	Greg Harris	.10
270	Todd Van Poppel	.10
271	Pete Castellano	.10
272	Tony Phillips	.10
273	Mike Gallego	.10
274	Steve Cooke RC	.10
275	Robin Ventura	.10
276	Kevin Mitchell	.10
277	Doug Linton	.10
278	Robert Eenhorn	.10
279	Gabe White RC	.10
280	Dave Stewart	.10
281	Mo Sanford	.10
282	Greg Perschke	.10
283	Kevin Flora	.10
284	Jeff Williams	.10
285	Keith Miller	.10
286	Andy Ashby	.10
287	Doug Dascenzo	.10
288	Eric Karros	.10
289	Glenn Murray RC	.10
290	Troy Percival RC	.75
291	Orlando Merced	.10
292	Peter Hoy	.10
293	Tony Fernandez	.10
294	Juan Guzman	.10
295	Jesse Barfield	.10
296	Sid Fernandez	.10
297	Scott Cepicky	.10
298	Garret Anderson RC	6.00
299	Cal Eldred	.10
300	Ryne Sandberg	2.00
301	Jim Gantner	.10
302	Mariano Rivera RC	25.00
303	Ron Lockett	.10
304	Jose Offerman	.10
305	Denny Martinez	.10
306	Luis Ortiz RC	.10
307	David Howard	.10
308	Russ Springer	.10
309	Chris Howard	.10
310	Kyle Abbott	.10
311	Aaron Sele RC	1.00
312	Dave Justice	.10
313	Pete O'Brien	.10
314	Greg Hansell	.10
315	Dave Winfield	1.50
316	Lance Dickson	.10
317	Eric King	.10
318	Vaughn Eshelman	.10
319	Tim Belcher	.10
320	Andres Galarraga	.10
321	Scott Bullett	.10
322	Doug Strange	.10
323	Jerald Clark	.10
324	Dave Righetti	.10
325	Greg Hibbard	.10
326	Eric Dillman	.10
327	Shane Reynolds RC	.25
328	Chris Hammond	.10
329	Albert Belle	.10
330	Rich Becker RC	.10
331	Eddie Williams	.10
332	Donald Harris	.10
333	Dave Smith	.10
334	Steve Fireovid	.10
335	Steve Buechele	.10
336	Mike Schooler	.10
337	Kevin McReynolds	.10
338	Hensley Meulens	.10
339	Benji Gil RC	.10
340	Don Mattingly	2.50
341	Alvin Davis	.10
342	Alan Mills	.10
343	Kelly Downs	.10
344	Leo Gomez	.10
345	Tarrik Brock RC	.10
346	Ryan Turner	.10
347	John Smoltz	.10
348	Bill Sampen	.10
349	Paul Byrd	.10
350	Mike Bordick	.10
351	Jose Lind	.10
352	David Wells	.10
353	Barry Larkin	.10
354	Bruce Ruffin	.10
355	Luis Rivera	.10
356	Sid Bream	.10
357	Julian Vasquez	.10
358	Jason Bere RC	.10
359	Ben McDonald	.10
360	Scott Stahoviak	.10
361	Kirt Manwaring	.10
362	Jeff Johnson	.10
363	Rob Deer	.10
364	Tony Pena	.10
365	Melido Perez	.10
366	Clay Parker	.10
367	Dale Sveum	.10
368	Mike Scioscia	.10
369	Roger Salkeld	.10
370	Mike Stanley	.10
371	Jack McDowell	.10
372	Tim Wallach	.10
373	Billy Ripken	.10
374	Mike Christopher	.10
375	Paul Molitor	1.50
376	Dave Stieb	.10
377	Pedro Guerrero	.10
378	Russ Swan	.10
379	Bob Ojeda	.10
380	Donn Pall	.10
381	Eddie Zosky	.10
382	Darnell Coles	.10
383	Tom Smith	.10
384	Mark McGwire	3.00
385	Gary Carter	1.50
386	Rich Amaral	.10
387	Alan Embree	.10
388	Jonathan Hurst	.10
389	Bobby Jones RC	.10
390	Rico Rossy	.10
391	Dan Smith	.10
392	Terry Steinbach	.10
393	Jon Farrell	.10
394	Dave Anderson	.10
395	Benito Santiago	.10
396	Mark Wohlers	.10
397	Mo Vaughn	.10
398	Randy Kramer	.10
399	John Jaha RC	.10
400	Cal Ripken, Jr.	4.00
401	Ryan Bowen	.10
402	Tim McIntosh	.10
403	Bernard Gilkey	.10
404	Junior Felix	.10
405	Cris Colon	.10
406	Marc Newfield	.10
407	Bernie Williams	.10
408	Jay Howell	.10
409	Zane Smith	.10
410	Jeff Shaw	.10
411	Kerry Woodson	.10
412	Wes Chamberlain	.10
413	Dave Mlicki	.10
414	Benny Distefano	.10
415	Kevin Rogers	.10
416	Tim Naehring	.10
417	Clemente Nunez	.10
418	Luis Sojo	.10
419	Kevin Ritz	.10
420	Omar Oliveras	.10
421	Manuel Lee	.10
422	Julio Valera	.10
423	Omar Vizquel	.10
424	Darren Burton	.10
425	Mel Hall	.10
426	Dennis Powell	.10
427	Lee Stevens	.10
428	Glenn Davis	.10
429	Willie Greene	.10
430	Kevin Wickander	.10
431	Dennis Eckersley	1.25
432	Joe Orsulak	.10
433	Eddie Murray	1.50
434	Matt Stairs RC	.10
435	Wally Joyner	.10
436	Rondell White	.10
437	Rob Mauer	.10
438	Joe Redfield	.10
439	Mark Lewis	.10
440	Darren Daulton	.10
441	Mike Henneman	.10
442	John Cangelosi	.10
443	Vince Moore RC	.10
444	John Wehner	.10
445	Kent Hrbek	.10
446	Mark McLemore	.10
447	Bill Wegman	.10
448	Robby Thompson	.10
449	Mark Anthony	.10
450	Archi Cianfrocco	.10
451	Johnny Ruffin	.10
452	Javier Lopez	.10
453	Greg Gohr	.10
454	Tim Scott	.10
455	Stan Belinda	.10
456	Darrin Jackson	.10
457	Chris Gardner	.10
458	Esteban Beltre	.10
459	Phil Plantier	.10
460	Jim Thome	1.25
461	Mike Piazza RC	25.00
462	Matt Sinatro	.10
463	Scott Servais	.10
464	Brian Jordan RC	.75
465	Doug Drabek	.10
466	Carl Willis	.10
467	Bret Barbarie	.10
468	Hal Morris	.10
469	Steve Sax	.10
470	Jerry Willard	.10
471	Dan Wilson	.10
472	Chris Hoiles	.10
473	Rheal Cormier	.10
474	John Morris	.10
475	Jeff Reardon	.10
476	Mark Leiter	.10
477	Tom Gordon	.10
478	Kent Bottenfield RC	.10
479	Gene Larkin	.10
480	Dwight Gooden	.10
481	B.J. Surhoff	.10
482	Andy Stankiewicz	.10
483	Tino Martinez	.10
484	Craig Biggio	.10
485	Denny Neagle	.10
486	Rusty Meacham	.10
487	Kal Daniels	.10
488	Dave Henderson	.10
489	Tim Costo	.10
490	Doug Davis	.10
491	Frank Viola	.10
492	Cory Snyder	.10
493	Chris Martin	.10
494	Dion James	.10
495	Randy Tomlin	.10
496	Greg Vaughn	.10
497	Dennis Cook	.10
498	Rosario Rodriguez	.10
499	Dave Staton	.10
500	George Brett	2.50
501	Brian Barnes	.10
502	Butch Henry	.10
503	Harold Reynolds	.10
504	David Nied RC	.10
505	Lee Smith	.10
506	Steve Chitren	.10
507	Ken Hill	.10
508	Robbie Beckett	.10
509	Troy Afenir	.10
510	Kelly Gruber	.10
511	Bret Boone	.10
512	Jeff Branson	.10
513	Mike Jackson	.10
514	Pete Harnisch	.10
515	Chad Kreuter	.10
516	Joe Vitko	.10
517	Orel Hershiser	.10
518	John Doherty RC	.10
519	Jay Bell	.10
520	Mark Langston	.10
521	Dann Howitt	.10
522	Bobby Reed	.10
523	Roberto Munoz	.10
524	Todd Ritchie	.10
525	Bip Roberts	.10
526	Pat Listach RC	.10
527	Scott Brosius RC	.10
528	John Roper RC	.10
529	Phil Hiatt RC	.10
530	Denny Walling	.10
531	Carlos Baerga	.10
532	Manny Ramirez RC	20.00
533	Pat Clements	.10
534	Ron Gant	.10
535	Pat Kelly	.10
536	Billy Spiers	.10
537	Darren Reed	.10
538	Ken Caminiti	.10
539	Butch Huskey RC	.10
540	Matt Nokes	.10
541	John Kruk	.10
542	John Jaha/SP (Foil)	.35
543	Justin Thompson RC	.10
544	Steve Hosey	.10
545	Joe Kmak	.10
546	John Franco	.10
547	Devon White	.10
548	Elston Hansen/SP (Foil)	.35
549	Ryan Klesko	.10
550	Danny Tartabull	.10
551	Frank Thomas/SP (Foil)	1.50

ABBREVIATIONS

SP - Short Print

552 Kevin Tapani	.10
553a Willie Banks	.10
553b Pat Clements	.10
554 B.J. Wallace/SP RC (Foil)	.35
555 Orlando Miller RC	.10
556 Mark Smith RC	.10
557 Tim Wallach (Foil)	.10
558 Bill Gullickson	.10
559 Derek Bell (Foil)	.10
560 Joe Randa (Foil)	.10
561 Frank Seminara	.10
562 Mark Gardner	.10
563 Rick Greene (Foil)	.10
564 Gary Gaetti	.10
565 Ozzie Guillen	.10
566 Charles Nagy (Foil)	.10
567 Mike Milchin	.10
568 Ben Shelton (Foil)	.10
569 Chris Roberts (Foil)	.10
570 Ellis Burks	.10
571 Scott Scudder	.10
572 Jim Abbott (Foil)	.10
573 Joe Carter	.10
574 Steve Finley	.10
575 Jim Olander (Foil)	.10
576 Carlos Garcia	.10
577 Greg Olson	.10
578 Greg Swindell (Foil)	.10
579 Matt Williams (Foil)	.10
580 Mark Grace	.10
581 Howard House (Foil)	.10
582 Luis Polonia	.10
583 Erik Hanson	.10
584 Salomon Torres (Foil)	.10
585 Carlton Fisk	1.50
586 Bret Saberhagen	.10
587 Chad McDonnell RC (Foil)	.10
588 Jimmy Key	.10
589 Mike MacFarlane	.10
590 Barry Bonds (Foil)	3.50
591 Jamie McAndrew	.10
592 Shane Mack	.10
593 Kerwin Moore	.10
594 Joe Oliver	.10
595 Chris Sabo	.10
596 Alex Gonzalez RC	.50
597 Brett Butler	.10
598 Mark Hutton	.10
599 Andy Benes (Foil)	.10
600 Jose Canseco	.60
601 Darryl Kile	.10
602 Matt Stairs/SP (Foil)	.35
603 Rob Butler (Foil)	.10
604 Willie McGee	.10
605 Jack McDowell	.10
606 Tom Candiotti	.10
607 Ed Martel	.10
608 Matt Mieske (Foil)	.10
609 Darrin Fletcher	.10
610 Rafael Palmeiro	1.25
611 Bill Swift	.10
612 Mike Mussina	.65
613 Vince Coleman	.10
614 Scott Cepicky (Foil)	.10
615 Mike Greenwell	.10
616 Kevin McGehee	.10
617 Jeffrey Hammonds (Foil)	.10
618 Scott Taylor	.10
619 Dave Otto	.10
620 Mark McGwire (Foil)	3.00
621 Kevin Tatar	.10
622 Steve Farr	.10
623 Ryan Klesko (Foil)	.10
625 Andre Dawson	.40
626 Tino Martinez/SP (Foil)	.35
627 Chad Curtis/SP	.50
628 Mickey Morandini	.10
629 Gregg Olson/SP (Foil)	.35
630 Lou Whitaker	.10
631 Arthur Rhodes	.10
632 Brandon Wilson	.10
633 Lance Jennings RC	.10
634 Allen Watson RC	.10
635 Len Dykstra	.10
636 Joe Girardi	.10
637 Kiki Hernandez/SP (Foil)	.35
638 Mike Hampton RC	1.00
639 Al Osuna	.10
640 Kevin Appier	.10
641 Rick Helling/SP (Foil)	.35
642 Jody Reed	.10
643 Ray Lankford	.10
644 John Olerud	.10
645 Paul Molitor/SP (Foil)	1.50
646 Pat Borders	.10
647 Mike Morgan	.10
648 Larry Walker	.10
649 Pete Castellano/SP (Foil)	.35
650 Fred McGriff	.10

651 Walt Weiss	.10
652 Calvin Murray/SP RC (Foil)	.35
653 Dave Nilsson	.10
654 Greg Pirkl	.10
655 Robin Ventura/SP (Foil)	.35
656 Mark Portugal	.10
657 Roger McDowell	.10
658 Rick Hirtensteiner/SP (Foil)	.35
659 Glenallen Hill	.10
660 Greg Gagne	.10
661 Charles Johnson/SP (Foil)	.35
662 Brian Hunter	.10
663 Mark Lemke	.10
664 Tim Belcher/SP (Foil)	.35
665 Rich DeLucia	.10
666 Bob Walk	.10
667 Joe Carter/SP (Foil)	.35
668 Jose Guzman	.10
669 Otis Nixon	.10
670 Phil Nevin (Foil)	.10
671 Eric Davis	.10
672 Damion Easley RC	.25
673 Will Clark (Foil)	.10
674 Mark Kiefer	.10
675 Ozzie Smith	2.00
676 Manny Ramirez (Foil)	6.00
677 Gregg Olson	.10
678 Cliff Floyd RC	1.00
679 Duane Singleton	.10
680 Jose Rijo	.10
681 Willie Randolph	.10
682 Michael Tucker RC (Foil)	.25
683 Darren Lewis	.10
684 Dale Murphy	.35
685 Mike Pagliarulo	.10
686 Paul Miller	.10
687 Mike Robertson	.10
688 Mike Devereaux	.10
689 Pedro Astacio	.10
690 Alan Trammell	.10
691 Roger Clemens	2.50
692 Bud Black	.10
693 Turk Wendell	.10
694 Barry Larkin/SP (Foil)	.35
695 Todd Zeile	.10
696 Pat Hentgen	.10
697 Eddie Taubensee RC	.10
698 Guillermo Vasquez	.10
699 Tom Glavine	.30
700 Robin Yount	1.50
701 Checklist	.10
702 Checklist	.10
703 Checklist	.10
704 Checklist	.10
705 Checklist	.10

1993 Bowman

	NM/M
Complete Set (708):	35.00
Common Player:	.10
Pack (15):	1.50
Wax Box (24):	35.00
Jumbo Pack (22):	2.50
Jumbo Box (20):	40.00
1 Glenn Davis	.10
2 Hector Roa RC	.10
3 Ken Ryan RC	.10
4 Derek Wallace RC	.10
5 Jorge Fabregas	.10
6 Joe Oliver	.10
7 Brandon Wilson	.10
8 Mark Thompson RC	.10
9 Tracy Sanders	.10
10 Rich Renteria	.10
11 Lou Whitaker	.10
12 Brian Hunter RC	.10
13 Joe Vitiello	.10
14 Eric Karros	.10
15 Joe Kmak	.10
16 Tavo Alvarez	.10

17 Steve Dunn RC	.10
18 Tony Fernandez	.10
19 Melido Perez	.10
20 Mike Lieberthal	.10
21 Terry Steinbach	.10
22 Stan Belinda	.10
23 Jay Buhner	.10
24 Allen Watson	.10
25 Daryl Henderson RC	.10
26 Ray McDavid RC	.10
27 Shawn Green	.30
28 Bud Black	.10
29 Sherman Obando RC	.10
30 Mike Hostetler RC	.10
31 Nate Hinchey RC	.10
32 Randy Myers	.10
33 Brian Grebeck RC	.10
34 John Roper	.10
35 Larry Thomas	.10
36 Alex Cole	.10
37 Tom Kramer RC	.10
38 Matt Whisenant RC	.10
39 Chris Gomez RC	.10
40 Luis Gonzalez	.10
41 Kevin Appier	.10
42 Omar Daal RC	.10
43 Duane Singleton	.10
44 Bill Risley	.10
45 Pat Meares RC	.10
46 Butch Huskey	.10
47 Bobby Munoz	.10
48 Juan Bell	.10
49 Scott Lydy RC	.10
50 Dennis Moeller	.10
51 Marc Newfield	.10
52 Tripp Cromer RC	.10
53 Kurt Miller	.10
54 Jim Pena	.10
55 Juan Guzman	.10
56 Matt Williams	.10
57 Harold Reynolds	.10
58 Donnie Elliott RC	.10
59 Jon Shave RC	.10
60 Kevin Roberson RC	.10
61 Hilly Hathaway RC	.10
62 Jose Rijo	.10
63 Kerry Taylor RC	.10
64 Ryan Hawblitzel	.10
65 Glenallen Hill	.10
66 Ramon D. Martinez RC	.10
67 Travis Fryman	.10
68 Tom Nevers	.10
69 Phil Hiatt	.10
70 Tim Wallach	.10
71 B.J. Surhoff	.10
72 Rondell White	.10
73 Denny Hocking RC	.10
74 Mike Oquist RC	.10
75 Paul O'Neill	.10
76 Willie Banks	.10
77 Bob Welch	.10
78 Jose Sandoval RC	.10
79 Bill Haselman	.10
80 Rheal Cormier	.10
81 Dean Palmer	.10
82 Pat Gomez RC	.10
83 Steve Karsay	.10
84 Carl Hanselman RC	.10
85 T.R. Lewis RC	.10
86 Chipper Jones	2.00
87 Scott Hatteberg	.10
88 Greg Hibbard	.10
89 Lance Painter RC	.10
90 Chad Mottola RC	.10
91 Jason Bere	.10
92 Dante Bichette	.10
93 Sandy Alomar	.10
94 Carl Everett	.10
95 Danny Bautista RC	.10
96 Steve Finley	.10
97 David Cone	.10
98 Todd Hollandsworth	.10
99 Matt Mieske	.10
100 Larry Walker	.10
101 Shane Mack	.10
102 Aaron Ledesma RC	.10
103 Andy Pettitte RC	4.00
104 Kevin Stocker	.10
105 Mike Mobler	.10
106 Tony Menedez	.10
107 Derek Lowe	.10
108 Basil Shabazz	.10
109 Dan Smith	.10
110 Scott Sanders RC	.10
111 Todd Stottlemyre	.10
112 Benji Sikonton RC	.10
113 Rick Sutcliffe	.10
114 Lee Heath RC	.10
115 Jeff Russell	.10
116 Dave Stevens RC	.10
117 Mark Holzemer RC	.10
118 Tim Belcher	.10
119 Bobby Thigpen	.10
120 Roger Bailey RC	.10

121 Tony Mitchell RC	.10
122 Junior Felix	.10
123 Rich Robertson RC	.10
124 Andy Cook RC	.10
125 Brian Bevil RC	.10
126 Darryl Strawberry	.10
127 Cal Eldred	.10
128 Cliff Floyd	.10
129 Alan Newman	.10
130 Howard Johnson	.10
131 Jim Abbott	.10
132 Chad McConnell RC	.10
133 Miguel Jimenez RC	.10
134 Brett Backlund RC	.10
135 John Cummings RC	.10
136 Brian Barber	.10
137 Rafael Palmeiro	1.25
138 Tim Worrell RC	.10
139 Jose Pett RC	.10
140 Barry Bonds	4.00
141 Damon Buford	.10
142 Jeff Blauser	.10
143 Frankie Rodriguez	.10
144 Mike Morgan	.10
145 Gary DeSarcina	.10
146 Calvin Reese	.10
147 Johnny Ruffin	.10
148 David Nied	.10
149 Charles Nagy	.10
150 Mike Myers RC	.10
151 Kenny Carlyle RC	.10
152 Eric Anthony	.10
153 Jose Lind	.10
154 Pedro Martinez	1.50
155 Mark Kiefer	.10
156 Tim Laker RC	.10
157 Pat Mahomes	.10
158 Bobby Bonilla	.10
159 Domingo Jean	.10
160 Darren Daulton	.10
161 Mark McGwire	3.50
162 Jason Kendall RC	1.00
163 Desi Relaford	.10
164 Ozzie Canseco	.10
165 Rick Helling	.10
166 Steve Pegues RC	.10
167 Paul Molitor	1.50
168 Larry Carter RC	.10
169 Arthur Rhodes	.10
170 Damon Hollins RC	.10
171 Frank Viola	.10
172 Steve Trachsel RC	.25
173 J.T. Snow RC	.50
174 Keith Gordon RC	.10
175 Carlton Fisk	1.50
176 Jason Bates RC	.10
177 Mike Crosby RC	.10
178 Benny Santiago	.10
179 Mike Moore	.10
180 Jeff Juden	.10
181 Darren Burton	.10
182 Todd Williams RC	.10
183 John Jaha	.10
184 Mike Lansing RC	.50
185 Pedro Grifol RC	.10
186 Vince Coleman	.10
187 Pat Kelly	.10
188 Clemente Alvarez RC	.10
189 Ron Darling	.10
190 Orlando Merced	.10
191 Chris Bosio	.10
192 Steve Dixon RC	.10
193 Doug Dascenzo	.10
194 Ray Holbert RC	.10
195 Howard Battle	.10
196 Willie McGee	.10
197 John O'Donoghue RC	.10
198 Steve Avery	.10
199 Greg Blosser	.10
200 Ryne Sandberg	2.00
201 Joe Grahe	.10
202 Dan Wilson	.10
203 Domingo Martinez RC	.10
204 Andres Galarraga	.10
205 Jamie Taylor RC	.10
206 Darrell Whitmore RC	.10
207 Ben Blomdahl RC	.10
208 Doug Drabek	.10
209 Keith Miller	.10
210 Billy Ashley	.10
211 Mike Farrell RC	.10
212 John Wetteland	.10
213 Randy Tomlin	.10
214 Sid Fernandez	.10
215 Quilvio Veras RC	.10
216 Dave Hollins	.10
217 Mike Neill	.10
218 Andy Van Slyke	.10
219 Bret Boone	.10
220 Tom Pagnozzi	.10
221 Mike Welch RC	.10
222 Frank Seminara	.10
223 Ron Villone	.10
224 D.J. Thielen RC	.10

#	Player	Price	#	Player	Price	#	Player	Price	#	Player	Price
225	Cal Ripken, Jr.	4.00	329	Craig Paquette	.10	432	Omar Olivares	.10	536	Mo Vaughn	.10
226	Pedro Borbon RC	.10	330	Jay Bell	.10	433	Charlie Leibrandt	.10	537	Brian Harper	.10
227	Carlos Quintana	.10	331	Jose Martinez RC	.10	434	Kurt Stillwell	.10	538	Juan Castillo	.10
228	Tommy Shields RC	.10	332	Rob Deer	.10	435	Scott Brow RC	.10	539	Steve Farr	.10
229	Tim Salmon	.10	333	Brook Fordyce	.10	436	Robby Thompson	.10	540	John Kruk	.10
230	John Smiley	.10	334	Matt Nokes	.10	437	Ben McDonald	.10	541	Troy Neel	.10
231	Ellis Burks	.10	335	Derek Lee	.10	438	Deion Sanders	.10	542	Danny Clyburn RC	.10
232	Pedro Castellano	.10	336	Paul Ellis RC	.10	439	Tony Pena	.10	543	Jim Converse RC	.10
233	Paul Byrd	.10	337	Desi Wilson RC	.10	440	Mark Grace	.10	544	Gregg Jefferies	.10
234	Bryan Harvey	.10	338	Roberto Alomar	.30	441	Eduardo Perez	.10	545	Jose Canseco	.40
235	Scott Livingstone	.10	339	Jim Tatum (Foil)	.10	442	Tim Pugh RC	.10	546	Julio Bruno RC	.10
236	James Mouton RC	.10	340	J.T. Snow (Foil)	.10	443	Scott Ruffcorn	.10	547	Rob Butler	.10
237	Joe Randa	.10	341	Tim Salmon (Foil)	.10	444	Jay Gainer RC	.10	548	Royce Clayton	.10
238	Pedro Astacio	.10	342	Russ Davis RC (Foil)	.25	445	Albert Belle	.10	549	Chris Hoiles	.10
239	Darryl Hamilton	.10	343	Javier Lopez (Foil)	.10	446	Bret Barberie	.10	550	Greg Maddux	2.00
240	Joey Eischen RC	.10	344	Troy O'Leary RC (Foil)	.10	447	Justin Mashore	.10	551	Joe Ciccarella RC	.10
241	Edgar Herrera RC	.10	345	Marty Cordova RC (Foil)	.60	448	Pete Harnisch	.10	552	Ozzie Timmons	.10
242	Dwight Gooden	.10	346	Bubba Smith RC (Foil)	.10	449	Greg Gagne	.10	553	Chili Davis	.10
243	Sam Militello	.10	347	Chipper Jones (Foil)	1.50	450	Eric Davis	.10	554	Brian Koelling	.10
244	Ron Blazier RC	.10	348	Jessie Hollins (Foil)	.10	451	Dave Mlicki	.10	555	Frank Thomas	1.50
245	Ruben Sierra	.10	349	Willie Greene (Foil)	.10	452	Moises Alou	.10	556	Vinny Castilla	.10
246	Al Martin	.10	350	Mark Thompson (Foil)	.10	453	Rick Aguilera	.10	557	Reggie Jefferson	.10
247	Mike Felder	.10	351	Nigel Wilson (Foil)	.10	454	Eddie Murray	1.50	558	Rob Natal	.10
248	Bob Tewksbury	.10	352	Todd Jones (Foil)	.10	455	Bob Wickman	.10	559	Mike Henneman	.10
249	Craig Lefferts	.10	353	Raul Mondesi (Foil)	.10	456	Wes Chamberlain	.10	560	Craig Biggio	.10
250	Luis Lopez	.10	354	Cliff Floyd (Foil)	.10	457	Brent Gates	.10	561	Billy Brewer RC	.10
251	Devon White	.10	355	Bobby Jones (Foil)	.10	458	Paul Weber	.10	562	Dan Melendez	.10
252	Will Clark	.10	356	Kevin Stocker (Foil)	.10	459	Mike Hampton	.10	563	Kenny Felder RC	.10
253	Mark Smith	.10	357	Midre Cummings (Foil)	.10	460	Ozzie Smith	2.00	564	Miguel Batista RC	.10
254	Terry Pendleton	.10	358	Allen Watson (Foil)	.10	461	Tom Henke	.10	565	Dave Winfield	1.50
255	Aaron Sele	.10	359	Ray McDavid (Foil)	.10	462	Ricky Gutuerrez	.10	566	Al Shirley	.10
256	Jose Viera RC	.10	360	Steve Hosey (Foil)	.10	463	Jack Morris	.10	567	Robert Eenhoorn	.10
257	Damion Easley	.10	361	Brad Pennington (Foil)	.10	464	Joel Chimelis RC	.10	568	Mike Williams	.10
258	Rod Lofton RC	.10	362	Frankie Rodriguez (Foil)	.10	465	Gregg Olson	.10	569	Tanyon Sturtze RC	.10
259	Chris Snopek RC	.10	363	Troy Percival (Foil)	.10	466	Javier Lopez	.10	570	Tim Wakefield	.10
260	Quinton McCracken RC	.10	364	Jason Bere (Foil)	.10	467	Scott Cooper	.10	571	Greg Pirkl	.10
261	Mike Matthews RC	.10	365	Manny Ramirez (Foil)	.75	468	Willie Wilson	.10	572	Sean Lowe RC	.25
262	Hector Carrasco RC	.10	366	Justin Thompson (Foil)	.10	469	Mark Langston	.10	573	Terry Burows RC	.10
263	Rick Greene	.10	367	Joe Vitello (Foil)	.10	470	Barry Larkin	.10	574	Kevin Higgins RC	.10
264	Chris Bolt RC	.10	368	Tyrone Hill (Foil)	.10	471	Rod Bolton	.10	575	Joe Carter	.10
265	George Brett	2.50	369	David McCarty (Foil)	.10	472	Freddie Benavides	.10	576	Kevin Rogers	.10
266	Rick Gorecki RC	.10	370	Brien Taylor (Foil)	.10	473	Ken Ramos RC	.10	577	Manny Alexander	.10
267	Francisco Gamez RC	.10	371	Todd Van Poppel (Foil)	.10	474	Chuck Carr	.10	578	Dave Justice	.10
268	Marquis Grissom	.10	372	Marc Newfield (Foil)	.10	475	Cecil Fielder	.10	579	Brian Conroy RC	.10
269	Kevin Tapani	.10	373	Terrell Lowery RC (Foil)	.10	476	Eddie Taubensee	.10	580	Jessie Hollins RC	.10
270	Ryan Thompson	.10	374	Alex Gonzalez (Foil)	.10	477	Chris Eddy RC	.10	581	Ron Watson RC	.10
271	Gerald Williams	.10	375	Ken Griffey Jr.	3.00	478	Greg Hansell	.10	582	Bip Roberts	.10
272	Paul Fletcher RC	.10	376	Donovan Osborne	.10	479	Kevin Reimer	.10	583	Tom Urbani RC	.10
273	Lance Blankenship	.10	377	Ritchie Moody RC	.10	480	Denny Martinez	.10	584	Jason Hutchins RC	.10
274	Marty Heff RC	.10	378	Shane Andrews	.10	481	Chuck Knoblauch	.10	585	Carlos Baerga	.10
275	Shawn Estes	.10	379	Carlos Delgado	.65	482	Mike Draper	.10	586	Jeff Mutis	.10
276	Rene Arocha RC	.10	380	Bill Swift	.10	483	Spike Owen	.10	587	Justin Thompson	.10
277	Scott Evre RC	.10	381	Leo Gomez	.10	484	Terry Mulholland	.10	588	Orlando Miller	.10
278	Phil Plantier	.10	382	Ron Gant	.10	485	Dennis Eckersley	1.25	589	Brian McRae	.10
279	Paul Spoljaric RC	.10	383	Scott Fletcher	.10	486	Blas Minor	.10	590	Ramon Martinez	.10
280	Chris Gahbs	.10	384	Matt Walbeck RC	.10	487	Dave Fleming	.10	591	Dave Nilsson	.10
281	Harold Baines	.10	385	Chuck Finley	.10	488	Dan Cholonsky	.10	592	Jose Vidro RC	1.50
282	Jose Oliva RC	.10	386	Kevin Mitchell	.10	489	Ivan Rodriguez	1.25	593	Rich Becker	.10
283	Matt Whiteside	.10	387	Wilson Alvarez	.10	490	Gary Sheffield	.45	594	Preston Wilson RC	1.50
284	Brant Brown RC	.10	388	John Burke RC	.10	491	Ed Sprague	.10	595	Don Mattingly	2.50
285	Russ Springer	.10	389	Alan Embree	.10	492	Steve Hosey	.10	596	Tony Longmire	.10
286	Chris Sabo	.10	390	Trevor Hoffman	.10	493	Jimmy Haynes RC	.10	597	Kevin Seitzer	.10
287	Ozzie Guillen	.10	391	Alan Trammell	.10	494	John Smoltz	.10	598	Midre Cummings RC	.10
288	Marcus Moore RC	.10	392	Todd Jones	.10	495	Andre Dawson	.35	599	Omar Vizquel	.10
289	Chad Ogea	.10	393	Felix Jose	.10	496	Rey Sanchez	.10	600	Lee Smith	.10
290	Walt Weiss	.10	394	Orel Hershiser	.10	497	Ty Van Burkleo RC	.10	601	David Hulse RC	.10
291	Brian Edmondson	.10	395	Pat Listach	.10	498	Bobby Ayala RC	.10	602	Darrell Sherman RC	.10
292	Jimmy Gonzalez	.10	396	Gabe White	.10	499	Tim Raines	.10	603	Alex Gonzalez	.10
293	Danny Miceli RC	.10	397	Dan Serafini RC	.10	500	Charlie Hayes	.10	604	Geronimo Pena	.10
294	Jose Offerman	.10	398	Todd Hundley	.10	501	Paul Sorrento	.10	605	Mike Devereaux	.10
295	Greg Vaughn	.10	399	Wade Boggs	2.00	502	Richie Lewis RC	.10	606	Sterling Hitchcock RC	.25
296	Frank Bolick	.10	400	Tyler Green	.10	503	Jason Pfaff RC	.10	607	Mike Greenwell	.10
297	Mike Maksudian RC	.10	401	Mike Bordick	.10	504	Ken Caminiti	.10	608	Steve Buechele	.10
298	John Franco	.10	402	Scott Bullett	.10	505	Mike Macfarlane	.10	609	Troy Percival	.10
299	Danny Tartabull	.10	403	Lagrande Russell RC	.10	506	Jody Reed	.10	610	Bobby Kelly	.10
300	Len Dykstra	.10	404	Ray Lankford	.10	507	Bobby Hughes RC	.10	611	James Baldwin RC	.10
301	Bobby Witt	.10	405	Nolan Ryan	4.00	508	Wil Cordero	.10	612	Jerald Clark	.10
302	Trey Beamon RC	.10	406	Robbie Beckett	.10	509	George Tsanis RC	.10	613	Albie Lopez RC	.10
303	Tino Martinez	.10	407	Brent Bowers RC	.10	510	Bret Saberhagen	.10	614	Dave Magadan	.10
304	Aaron Holbert	.10	408	Adell Davenport RC	.10	511	Derek Jeter RC	20.00	615	Mickey Tettleton	.10
305	Juan Gonzalez	.75	409	Brady Anderson	.10	512	Gene Schall	.10	616	Sean Runyan RC	.10
306	Billy Hall RC	.10	410	Tom Glavine	.35	513	Curtis Shaw	.10	617	Bob Hamelin	.10
307	Duane Ward	.10	411	Doug Hecker RC	.10	514	Steve Cooke	.10	618	Raul Mondesi	.10
308	Rod Beck	.10	412	Jose Guzman	.10	515	Edgar Martinez	.10	619	Tyrone Hill	.10
309	Jose Mercedes RC	.10	413	Luis Polonia	.10	516	Mike Milchin	.10	620	Darrin Fletcher	.10
310	Otis Nixon	.10	414	Brian Williams	.10	517	Billy Ripken	.10	621	Mike Trombley	.10
311	Gettys Glaze RC	.10	415	Bo Jackson	.15	518	Andy Benes	.10	622	Jeromy Burnitz	.10
312	Candy Maldonado	.10	416	Eric Young	.10	519	Juan de la Rosa RC	.10	623	Bernie Williams	.10
313	Chad Curtis	.10	417	Kenny Lofton	.10	520	John Burkett	.10	624	Mike Farmer RC	.10
314	Tim Costo	.10	418	Orestes Destrade	.10	521	Alex Ochoa	.10	625	Rickey Henderson	1.50
315	Mike Robertson	.10	419	Tony Phillips	.10	522	Tony Tarasco RC	.10	626	Carlos Garcia	.10
316	Nigel Wilson	.10	420	Jeff Bagwell	1.50	523	Luis Ortiz	.10	627	Jeff Darwin RC	.10
317	Greg McMichael RC	.10	421	Hark Gardner	.10	524	Rick Williams	.10	628	Todd Zeile	.10
318	Scott Pose RC	.10	422	Brett Butler	.10	525	Chris Turner RC	.10	629	Benji Gil	.10
319	Ivan Cruz	.10	423	Graeme Lloyd RC	.10	526	Rob Dibble	.10	630	Tony Gwynn	2.00
320	Greg Swindell	.10	424	Delino DeShields	.10	527	Jack McDowell	.10	631	Aaron Small RC	.10
321	Kevin McReynolds	.10	425	Scott Erickson	.10	528	Daryl Boston	.10	632	Joe Rosselli RC	.10
322	Tom Candiotti	.10	426	Jeff Kent	.10	529	Bill Wertz RC	.10	633	Mike Mussina	1.00
323	Bob Wishnevski RC	.10	427	Jimmy Key	.10	530	Charlie Hough	.10	634	Ryan Klesko	.10
324	Ken Hill	.10	428	Mickey Morandini	.10	531	Sean Bergman	.10	635	Roger Clemens	2.50
325	Kirby Puckett	2.00	429	Marcos Arkas RC	.10	532	Doug Jones	.10	636	Sammy Sosa	2.00
326	Tim Bogar RC	.10	430	Don Slaught	.10	533	Jeff Montgomery	.10	637	Orlando Palmeiro RC	.10
327	Mariano Rivera	.30	431	Randy Johnson	1.50	534	Roger Cedeno RC	.25	638	Willie Greene	.10
328	Mitch Williams	.10				535	Robin Yount	1.50	639	George Bell	.10

640	Garvin Alston RC	.10
641	Pete Janicki RC	.10
642	Chris Sheff RC	.10
643	Felipe Lira RC	.10
644	Roberto Petagine	.10
645	Wally Joyner	.10
646	Mike Piazza	3.00
647	Jaime Navarro	.10
648	Jeff Hartsock RC	.10
649	David McCarty	.10
650	Bobby Jones	.10
651	Mark Hutton	.10
652	Kyle Abbott	.10
653	Steve Cox RC	.10
654	Jeff King	.10
655	Norm Charlton	.10
656	Mike Gulan RC	.10
657	Julio Franco	.10
658	Cameron Cairncross RC	.10
659	John Olerud	.10
660	Salomon Torres	.10
661	Brad Pennington	.10
662	Melvin Nieves	.10
663	Ivan Calderon	.10
664	Turk Wendell	.10
665	Chris Pritchett	.10
666	Reggie Sanders	.10
667	Robin Ventura	.10
668	Joe Girardi	.10
669	Manny Ramirez	1.50
670	Jeff Conine	.10
671	Greg Gohr	.10
672	Andujar Cedeno	.10
673	Les Norman RC	.10
674	Mike James RC	.10
675	Marshall Boze RC	.10
676	B.J. Wallace	.10
677	Kent Hrbek	.10
678	Jack Voight	.10
679	Brien Taylor	.10
680	Curt Schilling	.35
681	Todd Van Poppel	.10
682	Kevin Young	.10
683	Tommy Adams	.10
684	Bernard Gilkey	.10
685	Kevin Brown	.10
686	Fred McGriff	.10
687	Pat Borders	.10
688	Kirt Manwaring	.10
689	Sid Bream	.10
690	John Valentin	.10
691	Steve Olsen RC	.10
692	Roberto Mejia RC	.10
693	Carlos Delgado (Foil)	.50
694	Steve Gibralter RC (Foil)	.10
695	Gary Mota (Foil)	.10
696	Jose Malave RC (Foil)	.10
697	Larry Sutton RC (Foil)	.10
698	Dan Frye RC (Foil)	.10
699	Tim Clark RC (Foil)	.10
700	Brian Rupp RC (Foil)	.10
701	Felipe Alou, Moises Alou (Foil)	.10
702	Bobby Bonds, Barry Bonds (Foil)	1.00
703	Ken Griffey Sr., Ken Griffey Jr. (Foil)	1.00
704	Hal McRae, Brian McRae (Foil)	.10
705	Checklist 1	.10
706	Checklist 2	.10
707	Checklist 3	.10
708	Checklist 4	.10

1994 Bowman Previews

		NM/M
Complete Set (10):		7.00
Common Player:		.50
1	Frank Thomas	1.50
2	Mike Piazza	3.00
3	Albert Belle	.50
4	Javier Lopez	.50

5	Cliff Floyd	.50
6	Alex Gonzalez	.50
7	Ricky Bottalico	.50
8	Tony Clark	.50
9	Mac Suzuki	.50
10	James Mouton (Foil)	.50

1994 Bowman

		NM/M
Complete Set (682):		40.00
Common Player:		.10
Pack (12):		1.50
Wax Box (24):		30.00
1	Joe Carter	.10
2	Marcus Moore	.10
3	Doug Creek RC	.10
4	Pedro Martinez	1.50
5	Ken Griffey Jr.	3.00
6	Greg Swindell	.10
7	J.J. Johnson	.10
8	Homer Bush RC	.10
9	Arquimedez Pozo RC	.10
10	Bryan Harvey	.10
11	J.T. Snow	.10
12	Alan Benes RC	.10
13	Chad Kreuter	.10
14	Eric Karros	.10
15	Frank Thomas	1.50
16	Bret Saberhagen	.10
17	Terrell Lowery	.10
18	Rod Bolton	.10
19	Harold Baines	.10
20	Matt Walbeck	.10
21	Tom Glavine	.30
22	Todd Jones	.10
23	Alberto Castillo	.10
24	Ruben Sierra	.10
25	Don Mattingly	2.50
26	Mike Morgan	.10
27	Jim Musselwhite RC	.10
28	Matt Brunson RC	.10
29	Adam Meinershagen RC	.10
30	Joe Girardi	.10
31	Shane Halter	.10
32	Jose Paniagua RC	.10
33	Paul Perkins	.10
34	John Hudek RC	.10
35	Frank Viola	.10
36	David Lamb RC	.10
37	Marshall Boze	.10
38	Jorge Posada RC	6.00
39	Brian Anderson RC	.25
40	Mark Whiten	.10
41	Sean Bergman	.10
42	Jose Parra RC	.10
43	Mike Robertson	.10
44	Pete Walker RC	.10
45	Juan Gonzalez	.75
46	Cleveland Ladell RC	.10
47	Mark Smith	.10
48	Kevin Jarvis RC	.10
49	Amaury Telemaco RC	.10
50	Andy Van Slyke	.10
51	Rikkert Faneyte RC	.10
52	Curtis Shaw	.10
53	Matt Drews RC	.10
54	Wilson Alvarez	.10
55	Manny Ramirez	1.50
56	Bobby Munoz	.10
57	Ed Sprague	.10
58	Jamey Wright RC	.10
59	Jeff Montgomery	.10
60	Kirk Rueter	.10
61	Edgar Martinez	.10
62	Luis Gonzalez	.10
63	Tim Vanegmond RC	.10
64	Bip Roberts	.10
65	John Jaha	.10
66	Chuck Carr	.10
67	Chuck Finley	.10
68	Aaron Holbert	.10
69	Cecil Fielder	.10

70	Tom Engle RC	.10
71	Ron Karkovice	.10
72	Joe Orsulak	.10
73	Duff Brumley RC	.10
74	Craig Clayton RC	.10
75	Cal Ripken, Jr.	4.00
76	Brad Fullmer RC	.50
77	Tony Tarasco	.10
78	Terry Farrar RC	.10
79	Matt Williams	.10
80	Rickey Henderson	1.50
81	Terry Mulholland	.10
82	Sammy Sosa	2.00
83	Paul Sorrento	.10
84	Pete Incaviglia	.10
85	Darren Hall RC	.10
86	Scott Klingenbeck	.10
87	Dario Perez RC	.10
88	Ugueth Urbina	.10
89	Dave Vanhof RC	.10
90	Domingo Jean	.10
91	Otis Nixon	.10
92	Andres Berumen	.10
93	Jose Valentin	.10
94	Edgar Renteria RC	5.00
95	Chris Turner	.10
96	Ray Lankford	.10
97	Danny Bautista	.10
98	Chan Ho Park RC	1.00
99	Glenn DiSarcina RC	.10
100	Butch Huskey	.10
101	Ivan Rodriguez	1.00
102	Johnny Ruffin	.10
103	Alex Ochoa	.10
104	Torii Hunter RC	6.00
105	Ryan Klesko	.10
106	Jay Bell	.10
107	Kurt Peltzer RC	.10
108	Miguel Jimenez	.10
109	Russ Davis	.10
110	Derek Wallace	.10
111	Keith Lockhart RC	.10
112	Mike Lieberthal	.10
113	Dave Stewart	.10
114	Tom Schmidt	.10
115	Brian McRae	.10
116	Moises Alou	.10
117	Dave Fleming	.10
118	Jeff Bagwell	1.50
119	Luis Ortiz	.10
120	Tony Gwynn	2.00
121	Jaime Navarro	.10
122	Benny Santiago	.10
123	Darrel Whitmore	.10
124	John Mabry RC	.15
125	Mickey Tettleton	.10
126	Tom Candiotti	.10
127	Tim Raines	.10
128	Bobby Bonilla	.10
129	John Dettmer	.10
130	Hector Carrasco	.10
131	Chris Hoiles	.10
132	Rick Aguilera	.10
133	Dave Justice	.10
134	Esteban Loaiza RC	1.50
135	Barry Bonds	4.00
136	Bob Welch	.10
137	Mike Stanley	.10
138	Roberto Hernandez	.10
139	Sandy Alomar	.10
140	Darren Daulton	.10
141	Angel Martinez RC	.10
142	Howard Johnson	.10
143	Bob Hamelin	.10
144	J.J. Thobe RC	.10
145	Roger Salkeld	.10
146	Orlando Miller	.10
147	Dmitri Young	.10
148	Tim Hyers RC	.10
149	Mark Loretta RC	3.00
150	Chris Hammond	.10
151	Joel Moore RC	.10
152	Todd Zeile	.10
153	Wil Cordero	.10
154	Chris Smith	.10
155	James Baldwin	.10
156	Edgardo Alfonzo RC	1.00
157	Kym Ashworth RC	.10
158	Paul Bako RC	.10
159	Rick Krivda RC	.10
160	Pat Mahomes	.10
161	Damon Hollins	.10
162	Felix Martinez RC	.10
163	Jason Myers RC	.10
164	Izzy Molina RC	.10
165	Brien Taylor	.10
166	Kevin Orie RC	.10
167	Casey Whitten RC	.10
168	Tony Longmire	.10
169	John Olerud	.10
170	Mark Thompson	.10
171	Jorge Fabregas	.10
172	John Wetteland	.10
173	Dan Wilson	.10

174	Doug Drabek	.10
175	Jeffrey McNeely	.10
176	Melvin Nieves	.10
177	Doug Glanville RC	.10
178	Javier De La Hoya RC	.10
179	Chad Curtis	.10
180	Brian Barber	.10
181	Mike Henneman	.10
182	Jose Offerman	.10
183	Robert Ellis RC	.10
184	John Franco	.10
185	Benji Gil	.10
186	Hal Morris	.10
187	Chris Sabo	.10
188	Blaise Ilsley RC	.10
189	Steve Avery	.10
190	Rick White RC	.10
191	Rod Beck	.10
(192)	Mark McGwire (No card number.)	3.00
193	Jim Abbott	.10
194	Randy Myers	.10
195	Kenny Lofton	.10
196	Mariano Duncan	.10
197	Lee Daniels RC	.10
198	Armando Reynoso	.10
199	Joe Randa	.10
200	Cliff Floyd	.10
201	Tim Harkrider RC	.10
202	Kevin Gallaher RC	.10
203	Scott Cooper	.10
204	Phil Stidham RC	.10
205	Jeff D'Amico RC	.25
206	Matt Whisenant	.10
207	De Shawn Warren	.10
208	Rene Arocha	.10
209	Tony Clark RC	.50
210	Jason Jacome RC	.10
211	Scott Christman RC	.10
212	Bill Pulsipher	.10
213	Dean Palmer	.10
214	Chad Mottola	.10
215	Manny Alexander	.10
216	Rich Becker	.10
217	Andre King RC	.10
218	Carlos Garcia	.10
219	Ron Pezzoni RC	.10
220	Steve Karsay	.10
221	Jose Musset RC	.10
222	Karl Rhodes	.10
223	Frank Cimorelli RC	.10
224	Kevin Jordan RC	.10
225	Duane Ward	.10
226	John Burke	.10
227	Mike MacFarlane	.10
228	Mike Lansing	.10
229	Chuck Knoblauch	.10
230	Ken Caminiti	.10
231	Gar Finnvold RC	.10
232	Derrek Lee RC	12.00
233	Brady Anderson	.10
234	Vic Darensbourg RC	.10
235	Mark Langston	.10
236	T.J. Mathews RC	.10
237	Lou Whitaker	.10
238	Roger Cedeno	.10
239	Alex Fernandez	.10
240	Ryan Thompson	.10
241	Kerry Lacy RC	.10
242	Reggie Sanders	.10
243	Brad Pennington	.10
244	Bryan Eversgerd RC	.10
245	Greg Maddux	2.00
246	Jason Kendall	.10
247	J.R. Phillips	.10
248	Bobby Witt	.10
249	Paul O'Neill	.10
250	Ryne Sandberg	2.00
251	Charles Nagy	.10
252	Kevin Stocker	.10
253	Shawn Green	.30
254	Charlie Hayes	.10
255	Donnie Elliott	.10
256	Rob Fitzpatrick RC	.10
257	Tim Davis	.10
258	James Mouton	.10
259	Mike Greenwell	.10
260	Ray McDavid	.10
261	Mike Kelly	.10
262	Andy Larkin RC	.10
(263)	Marquis Riley (No card number.)	.10
264	Bob Tewksbury	.10
265	Brian Edmondson	.10
266	Eduardo Lantigua RC	.10
267	Brandon Wilson	.10
268	Mike Welch	.10
269	Tom Henke	.10
270	Calvin Reese	.10
271	Gregg Zaun RC	.10
272	Todd Ritchie	.10
273	Javier Lopez	.10
274	Kevin Young	.10
275	Kirt Manwaring	.10

#	Player	Price
276	Bill Taylor RC	.10
277	Robert Eenhoorn	.10
278	Jessie Hollins	.10
279	Julian Tavarez RC	.10
280	Gene Schall	.10
281	Paul Molitor	1.50
282	Neifi Perez RC	.10
283	Greg Gagne	.10
284	Marquis Grissom	.10
285	Randy Johnson	1.50
286	Pete Harnisch	.10
287	Joel Bennett RC	.10
288	Derek Bell	.10
289	Darryl Hamilton	.10
290	Gary Sheffield	.40
291	Eduardo Perez	.10
292	Basil Shabazz	.10
293	Eric Davis	.10
294	Pedro Astacio	.10
295	Robin Ventura	.10
296	Jeff Kent	.10
297	Rick Helling	.10
298	Joe Oliver	.10
299	Lee Smith	.10
300	Dave Winfield	1.50
301	Deion Sanders	.10
302	Ravelo Manzanillo RC	.10
303	Mark Portugal	.10
304	Brent Gates	.10
305	Wade Boggs	2.00
306	Rick Wilkins	.10
307	Carlos Baerga	.10
308	Curt Schilling	.35
309	Shannon Stewart	.10
310	Darren Holmes	.10
311	Robert Toth RC	.10
312	Gabe White	.10
313	Mac Suzuki RC	.10
314	Alvin Morman RC	.10
315	Mo Vaughn	.10
316	Bryce Florie RC	.10
317	Gabby Martinez RC	.10
318	Carl Everett	.10
319	Kerwin Moore	.10
320	Tom Pagnozzi	.10
321	Chris Gomez	.10
322	Todd Williams	.10
323	Pat Hentgen	.10
324	Kirk Presley RC	.10
325	Kevin Brown	.10
326	Jason Isringhausen RC	.25
327	Rick Forney RC	.10
328	Carlos Pulido RC	.10
329	Terrell Wade RC	.10
330	Al Martin	.10
331	Dan Carlson RC	.10
332	Mark Acre RC	.10
333	Sterling Hitchcock	.10
334	Jon Ratliff RC	.10
335	Alex Ramirez RC	.10
336	Phil Geisler RC	.10
337	Eddie Zambrano RC (Foil)	.10
338	Jim Thome (Foil)	.60
339	James Mouton (Foil)	.10
340	Cliff Floyd (Foil)	.10
341	Carlos Delgado (Foil)	.40
342	Roberto Petagine (Foil)	.10
343	Tim Clark (Foil)	.10
344	Bubba Smith (Foil)	.10
345	Randy Curtis RC (Foil)	.10
346	Joe Biasucci (Foil)	.10
347	D.J. Boston RC (Foil)	.10
348	Ruben Rivera RC (Foil)	.75
349	Bryan Link RC (Foil)	.10
350	Mike Bell RC (Foil)	.25
351	Marty Watson RC (Foil)	.10
352	Jason Myers (Foil)	.10
353	Chipper Jones (Foil)	1.25
354	Brooks Kieschnick (Foil)	.10
355	Calvin Reese (Foil)	.10
356	John Burke (Foil)	.10
357	Kurt Miller (Foil)	.10
358	Orlando Miller (Foil)	.10
359	Todd Hollandsworth (Foil)	.10
360	Rondell White (Foil)	.10
361	Bill Pulsipher (Foil)	.10
362	Tyler Green (Foil)	.10
363	Midre Cummings (Foil)	.10
364	Brian Barber (Foil)	.10
365	Melvin Nieves (Foil)	.10
366	Salomon Torres (Foil)	.10
367	Alex Ochoa (Foil)	.10
368	Frank Rodriguez (Foil)	.10
369	Brian Anderson (Foil)	.10
370	James Baldwin (Foil)	.10
371	Manny Ramirez (Foil)	.75
372	Justin Thompson (Foil)	.10
373	Johnny Damon (Foil)	.50
374	Jeff D'Amico (Foil)	.10
375	Rich Becker (Foil)	.10
376	Derek Jeter (Foil)	3.00
377	Steve Karsay (Foil)	.10
378	Mac Suzuki (Foil)	.10
379	Benji Gil (Foil)	.10
380	Alex Gonzalez (Foil)	.10
381	Jason Bere (Foil)	.10
382	Brett Butler (Foil)	.10
383	Jeff Conine (Foil)	.10
384	Darren Daulton (Foil)	.10
385	Jeff Kent (Foil)	.10
386	Don Mattingly (Foil)	1.50
387	Mike Piazza (Foil)	2.00
388	Ryne Sandberg (Foil)	1.25
389	Rich Amaral	.10
390	Craig Biggio	.10
391	Jeff Suppan RC	.35
392	Andy Benes	.10
393	Cal Eldred	.10
394	Jeff Conine	.10
395	Tim Salmon	.10
396	Ray Suplee RC	.10
397	Tony Phillips	.10
398	Ramon Martinez	.10
399	Julio Franco	.10
400	Dwight Gooden	.10
401	Kevin Lomon RC	.10
402	Jose Rijo	.10
403	Mike Devereaux	.10
404	Mike Zolecki RC	.10
405	Fred McGriff	.10
406	Danny Clyburn	.10
407	Robby Thompson	.10
408	Terry Steinbach	.10
409	Luis Polonia	.10
410	Mark Grace	.10
411	Albert Belle	.10
412	John Kruk	.10
413	Scott Spiezio RC	.25
414	Ellis Burks	.10
415	Joe Vitiello	.10
416	Tim Costo	.10
417	Marc Newfield	.10
418	Oscar Henriquez RC	.10
419	Matt Perisho RC	.10
420	Julio Bruno	.10
421	Kenny Felder	.10
422	Tyler Green	.10
423	Jim Edmonds	.10
424	Ozzie Smith	2.00
425	Rick Greene	.10
426	Todd Hollandsworth	.10
427	Eddie Pearson RC	.10
428	Quilvio Veras	.10
429	Kenny Rogers	.10
430	Willie Greene	.10
431	Vaughn Eshelman	.10
432	Pat Meares	.10
433	Jermaine Dye RC	8.00
434	Steve Cooke	.10
435	Bill Swift	.10
436	Fausto Cruz RC	.10
437	Mark Hutton	.10
438	Brooks Kieschnick RC	.10
439	Yorkis Perez	.10
440	Len Dykstra	.10
441	Pat Borders	.10
442	Doug Walls RC	.10
443	Wally Joyner	.10
444	Ken Hill	.10
445	Eric Anthony	.10
446	Mitch Williams	.10
447	Cory Bailey RC	.10
448	Dave Staton	.10
449	Greg Vaughn	.10
450	Dave Magadan	.10
451	Chili Davis	.10
452	Gerald Santos RC	.10
453	Joe Perona	.10
454	Delino DeShields	.10
455	Jack McDowell	.10
456	Todd Hundley	.10
457	Ritchie Moody	.10
458	Bret Boone	.10
459	Ben McDonald	.10
460	Kirby Puckett	2.00
461	Gregg Olson	.10
462	Rich Aude RC	.10
463	John Burkett	.10
464	Troy Neel	.10
465	Jimmy Key	.10
466	Ozzie Timmons	.10
467	Eddie Murray	1.50
468	Mark Tranberg RC	.10
469	Alex Gonzalez	.10
470	David Nied	.10
471	Barry Larkin	.10
472	Brian Looney RC	.10
473	Shawn Estes	.10
474	A.J. Sager RC	.10
475	Roger Clemens	2.50
476	Vince Moore	.10
477	Scott Karl RC	.10
478	Kurt Miller	.10
479	Garret Anderson	.10
480	Allen Watson	.10
481	Jose Lima RC	.10
482	Rick Gorecki	.10
483	Jimmy Hurst RC	.10
484	Preston Wilson	.10
485	Will Clark	.10
486	Mike Ferry RC	.10
487	Curtis Goodwin RC	.10
488	Mike Myers	.10
489	Chipper Jones	2.00
490	Jeff King	.10
491	Bill Van Landingham RC	.10
492	Carlos Reyes RC	.10
493	Andy Pettitte	.30
494	Brant Brown	.10
495	Daron Kirkreit	.10
496	Ricky Bottalico RC	.25
497	Devon White	.10
498	Jason Johnson RC	.10
499	Vince Coleman	.10
500	Larry Walker	.10
501	Bobby Ayala	.10
502	Steve Finley	.10
503	Scott Fletcher	.10
504	Brad Ausmus	.10
505	Scott Talanoa RC	.10
506	Orestes Destrade	.10
507	Gary DiSarcina	.10
508	Willie Smith RC	.10
509	Alan Trammell	.10
510	Mike Piazza	3.00
511	Ozzie Guillen	.10
512	Jeromy Burnitz	.10
513	Darren Oliver	.10
514	Kevin Mitchell	.10
515	Rafael Palmeiro	1.00
516	David McCarty	.10
517	Jeff Blauser	.10
518	Trey Beamon	.10
519	Royce Clayton	.10
520	Dennis Eckersley	1.00
521	Bernie Williams	.10
522	Steve Buechele	.10
523	Denny Martinez	.10
524	Dave Hollins	.10
525	Joey Hamilton	.10
526	Andres Galarraga	.10
527	Jeff Granger	.10
528	Joey Eischen	.10
529	Desi Relaford	.10
530	Roberto Petagine	.10
531	Andre Dawson	.30
532	Ray Holbert	.10
533	Duane Singleton	.10
534	Kurt Abbott RC	.20
535	Bo Jackson	.20
536	Gregg Jefferies	.10
537	David Mysel	.10
538	Raul Mondesi	.10
539	Chris Snopek	.10
540	Brook Fordyce	.10
541	Ron Frazier RC	.10
542	Brian Koelling	.10
543	Jimmy Haynes	.10
544	Marty Cordova	.10
545	Jason Green RC	.10
546	Orlando Merced	.10
547	Lou Pote RC	.10
548	Todd Van Poppel	.10
549	Pat Kelly	.10
550	Turk Wendell	.10
551	Herb Perry RC	.10
552	Ryan Karp RC	.10
553	Juan Guzman	.10
554	Bryan Rekar RC	.10
555	Kevin Appier	.10
556	Chris Schwab RC	.10
557	Jay Buhner	.10
558	Andujar Cedeno	.10
559	Ryan McGuire RC	.10
560	Ricky Gutierrez	.10
561	Keith Kimsey RC	.10
562	Tim Clark	.10
563	Damion Easley	.10
564	Clint Davis RC	.10
565	Mike Moore	.10
566	Orel Hershiser	.10
567	Jason Bere	.10
568	Kevin McReynolds	.10
569	Leland Macon RC	.10
570	John Courtright RC	.10
571	Sid Fernandez	.10
572	Chad Roper	.10
573	Terry Pendleton	.10
574	Danny Miceli	.10
575	Joe Rosselli	.10
576	Mike Bordick	.10
577	Danny Tartabull	.10
578	Jose Guzman	.10
579	Omar Vizquel	.10
580	Tommy Greene	.10
581	Paul Spoljaric	.10
582	Walt Weiss	.10
583	Oscar Jimenez RC	.10
584	Rod Henderson	.10
585	Derek Lowe	.10
586	Richard Hidalgo RC	1.00
587	Shayne Bennett RC	.10
588	Tim Belk RC	.10
589	Matt Mieske	.10
590	Nigel Wilson	.10
591	Jeff Knox RC	.10
592	Bernard Gilkey	.10
593	David Cone	.10
594	Paul LoDuca RC	5.00
595	Scott Ruffcorn	.10
596	Chris Roberts	.10
597	Oscar Munoz RC	.10
598	Scott Sullivan RC	.10
599	Matt Jarvis RC	.10
600	Jose Canseco	.35
601	Tony Graffanino RC	.10
602	Don Slaught	.10
603	Brett King RC	.10
604	Jose Herrera RC	.10
605	Melido Perez	.10
606	Mike Hubbard RC	.10
607	Chad Ogea	.10
608	Wayne Gomes RC	.10
609	Roberto Alomar	.25
610	Angel Echevarria RC	.10
611	Jose Lind	.10
612	Darrin Fletcher	.10
613	Chris Bosio	.10
614	Darryl Kile	.10
615	Frank Rodriguez	.10
616	Phil Plantier	.10
617	Pat Listach	.10
618	Charlie Hough	.10
619	Ryan Hancock RC	.10
620	Darrel Deak RC	.10
621	Travis Fryman	.10
622	Brett Butler	.10
623	Lance Johnson	.10
624	Pete Smith	.10
625	James Hurst	.10
626	Roberto Kelly	.10
627	Mike Mussina	.50
628	Kevin Tapani	.10
629	John Smoltz	.10
630	Midre Cummings	.10
631	Salomon Torres	.10
632	Willie Adams	.10
633	Derek Jeter	4.00
634	Steve Trachsel	.10
635	Albie Lopez	.10
636	Jason Moler	.10
637	Carlos Delgado	.50
638	Roberto Mejia	.10
639	Darren Burton	.10
640	B.J. Wallace	.10
641	Brad Clontz RC	.10
642	Billy Wagner RC	1.00
643	Aaron Sele	.10
644	Cameron Cairncross	.10
645	Brian Harper	.10
(646)	Marc Valdes (No card number.)	
647	Mark Ratekin	.10
648	Terry Bradshaw RC	.10
649	Justin Thompson	.10
650	Mike Busch RC	.10
651	Joe Hall RC	.10
652	Bobby Jones	.10
653	Kelly Stinnett RC	.10
654	Rod Steph RC	.10
655	Jay Powell RC	.10
(656)	Keith Garagozzo RC (No card number.)	
657	Todd Dunn	.10
658	Charles Peterson RC	.10
659	Darren Lewis	.10
660	John Wasdin RC	.10
661	Tate Seefried RC	.10
662	Hector Trinidad RC	.10
663	John Carter RC	.10
664	Larry Mitchell	.10
665	David Catlett RC	.10
666	Dante Bichette	.10
667	Felix Jose	.10
668	Rondell White	.10
669	Tino Martinez	.10
670	Brian Hunter	.10
671	Jose Malave	.10
672	Archi Cianfrocco	.10
673	Mike Matheny RC	.15
674	Bret Barberie	.10
675	Andrew Lorraine RC	.10
676	Brian Jordan	.10
677	Tim Belcher	.10
678	Antonio Osuna RC	.10
679	Checklist I	.10
680	Checklist II	.10
681	Checklist III	.10
682	Checklist IV	.10

1994 Bowman's Best

	NM/M
Complete Set (200):	30.00

Roy McDavid

Red Set (90):	10.00
Blue Set (90):	20.00
Common Player:	.15
Pack (8):	1.50
Wax Box (24):	30.00

RED SET

1	Paul Molitor	1.50
2	Eddie Murray	1.50
3	Ozzie Smith	2.00
4	Rickey Henderson	1.50
5	Lee Smith	.15
6	Dave Winfield	1.50
7	Roberto Alomar	.30
8	Matt Williams	.15
9	Mark Grace	.15
10	Lance Johnson	.15
11	Darren Daulton	.15
12	Tom Glavine	.35
13	Gary Sheffield	.40
14	Rod Beck	.15
15	Fred McGriff	.15
16	Joe Carter	.15
17	Dante Bichette	.15
18	Danny Tartabull	.15
19	Juan Gonzalez	.75
20	Steve Avery	.15
21	John Wetteland	.15
22	Ben McDonald	.15
23	Jack McDowell	.15
24	Jose Canseco	.65
25	Tim Salmon	.15
26	Wilson Alvarez	.15
27	Gregg Jefferies	.15
28	John Burkett	.15
29	Greg Vaughn	.15
30	Robin Ventura	.15
31	Paul O'Neill	.15
32	Cecil Fielder	.15
33	Kevin Mitchell	.15
34	Jeff Conine	.15
35	Carlos Baerga	.15
36	Greg Maddux	2.00
37	Roger Clemens	2.25
38	Deion Sanders	.15
39	Delino DeShields	.15
40	Ken Griffey Jr.	2.50
41	Albert Belle	1.50
42	Wade Boggs	2.00
43	Andres Galarraga	.15
44	Aaron Sele	.15
45	Don Mattingly	2.25
46	David Cone	.15
47	Lenny Dykstra	.15
48	Brett Butler	.15
49	Bill Swift	.15
50	Bobby Bonilla	.15
51	Rafael Palmeiro	1.25
52	Moises Alou	.15
53	Jeff Bagwell	1.50
54	Mike Mussina	.50
55	Frank Thomas	1.50
56	Jose Rijo	.15
57	Ruben Sierra	.15
58	Randy Myers	.15
59	Barry Bonds	4.00
60	Jimmy Key	.15
61	Travis Fryman	.15
62	John Olerud	.15
63	David Justice	.15
64	Ray Lankford	.15
65	Bob Tewksbury	.15
66	Chuck Carr	.15
67	Jay Buhner	.15
68	Kenny Lofton	.15
69	Marquis Grissom	.15
70	Sammy Sosa	2.00
71	Cal Ripken Jr.	4.00
72	Ellis Burks	.15
73	Jeff Montgomery	.15
74	Julio Franco	.15
75	Kirby Puckett	2.00
76	Larry Walker	.15
77	Andy Van Slyke	.15
78	Tony Gwynn	2.00
79	Will Clark	.15
80	Mo Vaughn	.15
81	Mike Piazza	2.50
82	James Mouton	.15
83	Carlos Delgado	.60
84	Ryan Klesko	.15
85	Javy Lopez	.15
86	Raul Mondesi	.15
87	Cliff Floyd	.15
88	Manny Ramirez	1.50
89	Hector Carrasco	.15
90	Jeff Granger	.15

BLUE SET

1	Chipper Jones	2.00
2	Derek Jeter	4.00
3	Bill Pulsipher	.15
4	James Baldwin	.15
5	Brooks Kieschnick RC	.50
6	Justin Thompson	.15
7	Midre Cummings	.15
8	Joey Hamilton	.15
9	Calvin Reese	.15
10	Brian Barber	.15
11	John Burke	.15
12	De Shawn Warren	.15
13	Edgardo Alfonzo RC	.75
14	Eddie Pearson RC	.15
15	Jimmy Haynes	.15
16	Danny Bautista	.15
17	Roger Cedeno	.15
18	Jon Lieber	.15
19	Billy Wagner RC	.75
20	Tate Seefried RC	.15
21	Chad Mottola	.15
22	Jose Malave	.15
23	Terrell Wade RC	.15
24	Shane Andrews	.15
25	Chan Ho Park RC	.75
26	Kirk Presley RC	.15
27	Robbie Beckett	.15
28	Orlando Miller	.15
29	Jorge Posada RC	8.00
30	Frank Rodriguez	.15
31	Brian Hunter	.15
32	Billy Ashley	.15
33	Rondell White	.15
34	John Roper	.15
35	Marc Valdes	.15
36	Scott Ruffcorn	.15
37	Rod Henderson	.15
38	Curt Goodwin	.15
39	Russ Davis	.15
40	Rick Gorecki	.15
41	Johnny Damon	.60
42	Roberto Petagine	.15
43	Chris Snopek	.15
44	Mark Acre	.15
45	Todd Hollandsworth	.15
46	Shawn Green	.35
47	John Carter	.15
48	Jim Pittsley	.15
49	John Wasdin RC	.15
50	D.J. Boston	.15
51	Tim Clark	.15
52	Alex Ochoa	.15
53	Chad Roper	.15
54	Mike Kelly	.15
55	Brad Fullmer RC	.50
56	Carl Everett	.15
57	Tim Belk RC	.15
58	Jimmy Hurst RC	.15
59	Mac Suzuki RC	.15
60	Michael Moore	.15
61	Alan Benes RC	.15
62	Tony Clark RC	1.00
63	Edgar Renteria RC	8.00
64	Trey Beamon	.15
65	LaTroy Hawkins RC	.15
66	Wayne Gomes RC	.15
67	Ray McDavid	.15
68	John Dettmer	.15
69	Willie Greene	.15
70	Dave Stevens	.15
71	Kevin Orie RC	.15
72	Chad Ogea	.15
73	Ben Van Ryn	.15
74	Kym Ashworth	.15
75	Dmitri Young	.15
76	Herb Perry	.15
77	Joey Eischen	.15
78	Arquimedez Pozo RC	.15
79	Ugueth Urbina	.15
80	Keith Williams	.15
81	John Frascatore RC	.15
82	Garey Ingram	.15
83	Aaron Small	.15
84	Olmedo Saenz RC	.15
85	Jesus Tavarez	.15
86	Jose Silva RC	.15
87	Gerald Witasick Jr. RC	.15
88	Jay Maldonado	.15
89	Keith Heberling	.15
90	Rusty Greer RC	.50

MIRROR IMAGES

91	Frank Thomas,	
	Kevin Young	.60
92	Fred McGriff,	
	Brooks Kieschnick RC	.15
93	Matt Williams,	
	Shane Andrews	.15
94	Cal Ripken Jr.,	
	Kevin Orie RC	1.50
95	Barry Larkin,	
	Derek Jeter	1.50
96	Ken Griffey Jr.,	
	Johnny Damon	1.50
97	Barry Bonds,	
	Rondell White	1.50
98	Albert Belle,	
	Jimmy Hurst RC	.15
99	Raul Mondesi,	
	Ruben Rivera RC	.15
100	Roger Clemens,	
	Scott Ruffcorn	1.00
101	Greg Maddux,	
	John Wasdin RC	.75
102	Tim Salmon,	
	Chad Mottola	.15
103	Carlos Baerga,	
	Arquimedez Pozo RC	.15
104	Mike Piazza,	
	Bobby Hughes	1.00
105	Carlos Delgado,	
	Melvin Nieves	.50
106	Javy Lopez,	
	Jorge Posada RC	2.00
107	Manny Ramirez,	
	Jose Malave	.65
108	Travis Fryman,	
	Chipper Jones	.75
109	Steve Avery,	
	Bill Pulsipher	.15
110	John Olerud,	
	Shawn Green	.50

Refractors

Superstars:	8-10X
Stars:	4-8X

(See 1994 Bowman's Best for checklist and base card values.)

1995 Bowman

BUHNER

	NM/M
Complete Set (439):	150.00
Common Player:	.10
Pack (10):	6.00
Wax Box (24):	125.00
Rack Pack (15):	5.00
Rack Box (24):	125.00

1	Billy Wagner RC	.10
2	Chris Widger	.10
3	Brent Bowers	.10
4	Bob Abreu RC	10.00
5	Lou Collier RC	.10
6	Juan Acevedo RC	.25
7	Jason Kelley RC	.10
8	Brian Sackinsky RC	.10
9	Scott Christman	.10
10	Damon Hollins	.10
11	Willis Otanez RC	.10
12	Jason Ryan RC	.10
13	Jason Giambi	.75
14	Andy Taulbee RC	.10
15	Mark Thompson	.10
16	Hugo Pivaral RC	.10
17	Brien Taylor	.10
18	Antonio Osuna	.10
19	Edgardo Alfonzo	.10
20	Carl Everett	.10
21	Matt Drews	.10
22	Bartolo Colon RC	4.00
23	Andruw Jones RC	30.00
24	Robert Person RC	.40
25	Derrek Lee	.75
26	John Ambrose RC	.10
27	Eric Knowles RC	.10
28	Chris Roberts	.10
29	Don Wengert	.10
30	Marcus Jensen RC	.10
31	Brian Barber	.10
32	Kevin Brown	.10
33	Benji Gil	.10
34	Mike Hubbard	.10
35	Bart Evans RC	.10
36	Enrique Wilson RC	.50
37	Brian Buchanan RC	.10
38	Ken Ray RC	.10
39	Micah Franklin RC	.10
40	Ricky Otero RC	.10
41	Jason Kendall	.10
42	Jimmy Hurst	.10
43	Jerry Wolak RC	.10
44	Jayson Peterson RC	.10
45	Allen Battle RC	.10
46	Scott Stahoviak	.10
47	Steve Schrenk RC	.10
48	Travis Miller RC	.25
49	Eddie Rios RC	.10
50	Mike Hampton	.10
51	Chad Frontera RC	.10
52	Tom Evans RC	.10
53	C.J. Nitkowski	.10
54	Clay Caruthers RC	.10
55	Shannon Stewart	.10
56	Jorge Posada	.50
57	Aaron Holbert	.10
58	Harry Berrios RC	.10
59	Steve Rodriguez	.10
60	Shane Andrews	.10
61	Will Cunnane RC	.10
62	Richard Hidalgo	.10
63	Bill Selby RC	.10
64	Jay Cranford RC	.10
65	Jeff Suppan	.10
66	Curtis Goodwin	.10
67	John Thomson RC	.10
68	Justin Thompson	.10
69	Troy Percival	.10
70	Matt Wagner RC	.10
71	Terry Bradshaw	.10
72	Greg Hansell	.10
73	John Burke	.10
74	Jeff D'Amico	.10
75	Ernie Young	.10
76	Jason Bates	.10
77	Chris Stynes	.10
78	Cade Gaspar RC	.10
79	Melvin Nieves	.10
80	Rick Gorecki	.10
81	Felix Rodriguez RC	.50
82	Ryan Hancock	.10
83	Chris Carpenter RC	6.00
84	Ray McDavid	.10
85	Chris Wimmer	.10
86	Doug Glanville	.10
87	DeShawn Warren	.10
88	Damian Moss RC	.50
89	Rafael Orellano RC	.10
90	Vladimir Guerrero RC	50.00
91	Raul Casanova RC	.40
92	Karim Garcia RC	.75
93	Bryce Florie	.10
94	Kevin Orie	.10
95	Ryan Nye RC	.10
96	Matt Sachse RC	.10
97	Ivan Arteaga RC	.10
98	Glenn Murray	.10
99	Stacy Hollins RC	.10
100	Jim Pittsley	.10
101	Craig Mattson RC	.40
102	Neifi Perez	.10
103	Keith Williams	.10
104	Roger Cedeno	.10
105	Tony Terry RC	.10
106	Jose Malave	.10
107	Joe Rosselli	.10
108	Kevin Jordan	.10
109	Sid Roberson RC	.10

110	Alan Embree	.10
111	Terrell Wade	.10
112	Bob Wolcott	.10
113	Carlos Perez RC	.10
114	Mike Bovee RC	.10
115	Tommy Davis RC	.10
116	Jeremey Kendall RC	.10
117	Rich Aude	.10
118	Rick Huisman	.10
119	Tim Belk	.10
120	Edgar Renteria	.25
121	Calvin Maduro RC	.10
122	Jerry Martin RC	.10
123	Ramon Fermin RC	.10
124	Kimera Bartee RC	.10
125	Mark Farris	.10
126	Frank Rodriguez	.10
127	Bobby Higginson RC	.50
128	Bret Wagner	.10
129	Edwin Diaz RC	.10
130	Jimmy Haynes	.10
131	Chris Weinke RC	.75
132	Damian Jackson RC	.10
133	Felix Martinez	.10
134	Edwin Hurtado RC	.25
135	Matt Raleigh RC	.10
136	Paul Wilson	.10
137	Ron Villone	.10
138	Eric Stuckenschneider RC	.10
139	Tate Seefried	.10
140	Rey Ordonez RC	.75
141	Eddie Pearson	.10
142	Kevin Gallaher	.10
143	Torii Hunter	.25
144	Daron Kirkreit	.10
145	Craig Wilson	.10
146	Ugueth Urbina	.10
147	Chris Snopek	.10
148	Kym Ashworth	.10
149	Wayne Gomes	.10
150	Mark Loretta	.10
151	Ramon Morel RC	.10
152	Trot Nixon	.20
153	Desi Relaford	.10
154	Scott Sullivan	.10
155	Marc Barcelo	.10
156	Willie Adams	.10
157	Derrick Gibson RC	.10
158	Brian Meadows RC	.10
159	Julian Tavarez	.10
160	Bryan Rekar	.10
161	Steve Gibralter	.10
162	Esteban Loaiza	.10
163	John Wasdin	.10
164	Kirk Presley	.10
165	Mariano Rivera	.50
166	Andy Larkin	.10
167	Sean Whiteside RC	.10
168	Matt Apana RC	.10
169	Shawn Senior RC	.10
170	Scott Gentile	.10
171	Quilvio Veras	.10
172	Elieser Marrero RC	1.00
173	Mendy Lopez RC	.10
174	Homer Bush	.10
175	Brian Stephenson RC	.10
176	Jon Nunnally	.10
177	Jose Herrera	.10
178	Corey Avrard RC	.10
179	David Bell	.10
180	Jason Isringhausen	.10
181	Jamey Wright	.10
182	Lonell Roberts RC	.10
183	Marty Cordova	.10
185	Amaury Telemaco	.10
185	John Mabry	.10
186	Andrew Vessel RC	.10
187	Jim Cole RC	.10
188	Marquis Riley	.10
189	Todd Dunn	.10
190	John Carter	.10
191	Donnie Sadler RC	.25
192	Mike Bell	.10
193	Chris Cumberland RC	.10
194	Jason Schmidt	.25
195	Matt Brunson	.10
196	James Baldwin	.10
197	Bill Simas RC	.10
198	Gus Gandarillas	.10
199	Mac Suzuki	.10
200	Rick Holifield RC	.10
201	Fernando Lunar RC	.10
202	Kevin Jarvis	.10
203	Everett Stull RC	.10
204	Steve Wojciechowski	.10
205	Shawn Estes	.10
206	Jermaine Dye	.10
207	Marc Kroon	.10
208	Peter Munro RC	.10
209	Pat Watkins	.10
210	Matt Smith	.10
211	Joe Vitiello	.10
212	Gerald Witasick Jr.	.10
213	Freddy Garcia RC	.10
214	Glenn Dishman RC	.10
215	Jay Canizaro RC	.10
216	Angel Martinez	.10
217	Yamil Benitez RC	.10
218	Fausto Macey RC	.10
219	Eric Owens	.10
220	Checklist	.10
221	Dwayne Hosey RC	.10
222	Brad Woodall RC	.25
223	Billy Ashley	.10
224	Mark Grudzielanek RC	2.00
225	Mark Johnson RC	.10
226	Tim Unroe RC	.10
227	Todd Greene	.10
228	Larry Sutton	.10
229	Derek Jeter	3.00
230	Sal Fasano RC	.10
231	Ruben Rivera	.10
232	Chris Truby RC	.10
233	John Donati	.10
234	Decomba Conner RC	.10
235	Sergio Nunez RC	.10
236	Ray Brown RC	.10
237	Juan Melo RC	.10
238	Hideo Nomo RC	4.00
239	Jaime Bluma RC	.10
240	Jay Payton RC	1.50
241	Paul Konerko	.75
242	Scott Elarton RC	.50
243	Jeff Abbott RC	.25
244	Jim Brower RC	.10
245	Geoff Blum RC	.40
246	Aaron Boone RC	1.00
247	J.R. Phillips	.10
248	Alex Ochoa	.10
249	Nomar Garciaparra	5.00
250	Garret Anderson	.25
251	Ray Durham	.10
252	Paul Shuey	.10
253	Tony Clark	.10
254	Johnny Damon	1.00
255	Duane Singleton	.10
256	LaTroy Hawkins	.10
257	Andy Pettitte	.40
258	Ben Grieve	.10
259	Marc Newfield	.10
260	Terrell Lowery	.10
261	Shawn Green	.40
262	Chipper Jones	1.50
263	Brooks Kieschnick	.10
264	Calvin Reese	.10
265	Doug Million	.10
266	Marc Valdes	.10
267	Brian Hunter	.10
268	Todd Hollandsworth	.10
269	Rod Henderson	.10
270	Bill Pulsipher	.10
271	Scott Rolen	15.00
272	Trey Beamon	.10
273	Alan Benes	.10
274	Dustin Hermanson	.10
275	Ricky Bottalico	.10
276	Albert Belle	.10
277	Deion Sanders	.25
278	Matt Williams	.10
279	Jeff Bagwell	.75
280	Kirby Puckett	1.50
281	Dave Hollins	.10
282	Don Mattingly	1.50
283	Joey Hamilton	.10
284	Bobby Bonilla	.10
285	Moises Alou	.25
286	Tom Glavine	.25
287	Brett Butler	.10
288	Chris Hoiles	.10
289	Kenny Rogers	.10
290	Larry Walker	.25
291	Tim Raines	.10
292	Kevin Appier	.10
293	Roger Clemens	2.00
294a	Chuck Carr	.10
294b	Cliff Floyd (Should be #394.)	.10
295	Randy Myers	.10
296	Dave Nilsson	.10
297	Joe Carter	.10
298	Chuck Finley	.10
299	Ray Lankford	.10
300	Roberto Kelly	.10
301	Jon Lieber	.10
302	Travis Fryman	.10
303	Mark McGwire	1.50
304	Tony Gwynn	1.00
305	Kenny Lofton	.10
306	Mark Whiten	.10
307	Doug Drabek	.10
308	Terry Steinbach	.10
309	Ryan Klesko	.10
310	Mike Piazza	1.50
311	Ben McDonald	.10
312	Reggie Sanders	.10
313	Alex Fernandez	.10
314	Aaron Sele	.10
315	Gregg Jefferies	.10
316	Rickey Henderson	.75
317	Brian Anderson	.10
318	Jose Valentin	.10
319	Rod Beck	.10
320	Marquis Grissom	.10
321	Ken Griffey Jr.	2.00
322	Bret Saberhagen	.10
323	Juan Gonzalez	.50
324	Paul Molitor	.75
325	Gary Sheffield	.40
326	Darren Daulton	.10
327	Bill Swift	.10
328	Brian McRae	.10
329	Robin Ventura	.10
330	Lee Smith	.10
331	Fred McGriff	.20
332	Delino DeShields	.10
333	Edgar Martinez	.10
334	Mike Mussina	.50
335	Orlando Merced	.10
336	Carlos Baerga	.10
337	Wil Cordero	.10
338	Tom Pagnozzi	.10
339	Pat Hentgen	.10
340	Chad Curtis	.10
341	Darren Lewis	.10
342	Jeff Kent	.20
343	Bip Roberts	.10
344	Ivan Rodriguez	.50
345	Jeff Montgomery	.10
346	Hal Morris	.10
347	Danny Tartabull	.10
348	Raul Mondesi	.10
349	Ken Hill	.10
350	Pedro Martinez	1.00
351	Frank Thomas	.75
352	Manny Ramirez	1.00
353	Tim Salmon	.10
354	William Van Landingham	.10
355	Andres Galarraga	.10
356	Paul O'Neill	.25
357	Brady Anderson	.10
358	Ramon Martinez	.10
359	John Olerud	.10
360	Ruben Sierra	.10
361	Cal Eldred	.10
362	Jay Buhner	.10
363	Jay Bell	.10
364	Wally Joyner	.10
365	Chuck Knoblauch	.10
366	Len Dykstra	.10
367	John Wetteland	.10
368	Roberto Alomar	.25
369	Craig Biggio	.25
370	Ozzie Smith	1.50
371	Terry Pendleton	.10
372	Sammy Sosa	1.00
373	Carlos Garcia	.10
374	Jose Rijo	.10
375	Chris Gomez	.10
376	Barry Bonds	2.00
377	Steve Avery	.10
378	Rick Wilkins	.10
379	Pete Harnisch	.10
380	Dean Palmer	.10
381	Bob Hamelin	.10
382	Jason Bere	.10
383	Jimmy Key	.10
384	Dante Bichette	.10
385	Rafael Palmeiro	.50
386	David Justice	.10
387	Chili Davis	.10
388	Mike Greenwell	.10
389	Todd Zeile	.10
390	Jeff Conine	.10
391	Rick Aguilera	.10
392	Eddie Murray	.50
393	Mike Stanley	.10
394	(Not Issued, See #294.)	
395	Randy Johnson	1.00
396	David Nied	.10
397	Devon White	.10
398	Royce Clayton	.10
399	Andy Benes	.10
400	John Hudek	.10
401	Bobby Jones	.10
402	Eric Karros	.10
403	Will Clark	.25
404	Mark Langston	.10
405	Kevin Brown	.10
406	Greg Maddux	1.50
407	David Cone	.10
408	Wade Boggs	.75
409	Steve Trachsel	.10
410	Greg Vaughn	.10
411	Mo Vaughn	.10
412	Wilson Alvarez	.10
413	Cal Ripken Jr.	3.00
414	Rico Brogna	.10
415	Barry Larkin	.40
416	Cecil Fielder	.10
417	Jose Canseco	.50
418	Jack McDowell	.10
419	Mike Lieberthal	.10
420	Andrew Lorraine	.10
421	Rich Becker	.10
422	Tony Phillips	.10
423	Scott Ruffcorn	.10
424	Jeff Granger	.10
425	Greg Pirkl	.10
426	Dennis Eckersley	.50
427	Jose Lima	.10
428	Russ Davis	.10
429	Armando Benitez	.10
430	Alex Gonzalez	.10
431	Carlos Delgado	.75
432	Chan Ho Park	.10
433	Mickey Tettleton	.10
434	Dave Winfield	.75
435	John Burkett	.10
436	Orlando Miller	.10
437	Rondell White	.10
438	Jose Oliva	.10
439	Checklist	.10

Mirror Image: .50

1	Ben Davis, Ivan Rodriguez	1.00
2	Mark Redman, Manny Ramirez	1.50
3	Reggie Taylor, Deion Sanders	.50
4	Ryan Jaroncyk, Shawn Green	.50
5	Juan LeBron, Juan Gonzalez	1.00
6	Toby McKnight, Craig Biggio	.50
7	Michael Barrett, Travis Fryman	1.00
8	Corey Jenkins, Mo Vaughn	.50
9	Ruben Rivera, Frank Thomas	1.50
10	Curtis Goodwin, Kenny Lofton	.50
11	Brian Hunter, Tony Gwynn	1.75
12	Todd Greene, Ken Griffey Jr.	2.50
13	Karim Garcia, Matt Williams	.75
14	Billy Wagner, Randy Johnson	1.50
15	Pat Watkins, Jeff Bagwell	1.50

1995 Bowman's Best

	NM/M
Complete Set (195):	200.00
Common Player:	.25
Pack (7):	12.00
Wax Box (24):	275.00
Complete Set Red (90):	45.00
1 Randy Johnson	1.50
2 Joe Carter	.25
3 Chili Davis	.25
4 Moises Alou	.25
5 Gary Sheffield	.40
6 Kevin Appier	.25
7 Denny Neagle	.25
8 Ruben Sierra	.25
9 Darren Daulton	.25
10 Cal Ripken Jr.	4.00
11 Bobby Bonilla	.25
12 Manny Ramirez	1.50
13 Barry Bonds	4.00
14 Eric Karros	.25
15 Greg Maddux	2.00
16 Jeff Bagwell	1.50
17 Paul Molitor	1.50
18 Ray Lankford	.25
19 Mark Grace	.25
20 Kenny Lofton	.25
21 Tony Gwynn	2.00
22 Will Clark	.25
23 Roger Clemens	2.25
24 Dante Bichette	.25
25 Barry Larkin	.25
26 Wade Boggs	2.00
27 Kirby Puckett	2.00
28 Cecil Fielder	.25

29	Jose Canseco	.50
30	Juan Gonzalez	.75
31	David Cone	.25
32	Craig Biggio	.25
33	Tim Salmon	.25
34	David Justice	.25
35	Sammy Sosa	2.00
36	Mike Piazza	2.50
37	Carlos Baerga	.25
38	Jeff Conine	.25
39	Rafael Palmeiro	1.25
40	Bret Saberhagen	.25
41	Len Dykstra	.25
42	Mo Vaughn	.25
43	Wally Joyner	.25
44	Chuck Knoblauch	.25
45	Robin Ventura	.25
46	Don Mattingly	2.25
47	Dave Hollins	.25
48	Andy Benes	.25
49	Ken Griffey Jr.	2.50
50	Albert Belle	.25
51	Matt Williams	.25
52	Rondell White	.25
53	Raul Mondesi	.25
54	Brian Jordan	.25
55	Greg Vaughn	.25
56	Fred McGriff	.25
57	Roberto Alomar	.40
58	Dennis Eckersley	1.25
59	Lee Smith	.25
60	Eddie Murray	1.50
61	Kenny Rogers	.25
62	Ron Gant	.25
63	Larry Walker	.25
64	Chad Curtis	.25
65	Frank Thomas	1.50
66	Paul O'Neill	.25
67	Kevin Seitzer	.25
68	Marquis Grissom	.25
69	Mark McGwire	3.00
70	Travis Fryman	.25
71	Andres Galarraga	.25
72	Carlos Perez RC	.25
73	Tyler Green	.25
74	Marty Cordova	.25
75	Shawn Green	.40
76	Vaughn Eshelman	.25
77	John Mabry	.25
78	Jason Bates	.25
79	Jon Nunnally	.25
80	Ray Durham	.25
81	Edgardo Alfonzo	.25
82	Esteban Loaiza	.25
83	Hideo Nomo RC	10.00
84	Orlando Miller	.25
85	Alex Gonzalez	.25
86	Mark Grudzielanek RC	.65
87	Julian Tavarez	.25
88	Benji Gil	.25
89	Quilvio Veras	.25
90	Ricky Bottalico	.25

Complete Set Blue (90): 150.00

1	Derek Jeter	3.00
2	Vladimir Guerrero RC	80.00
3	Bob Abreu RC	25.00
4	Chan Ho Park	.25
5	Paul Wilson	.25
6	Chad Ogea	.25
7	Andruw Jones RC	50.00
8	Brian Barber	.25
9	Andy Larkin	.25
10	Richie Sexson RC	10.00
11	Everett Stull RC	.25
12	Brooks Kieschnick	.25
13	Matt Murray	.25
14	John Wasdin	.25
15	Shannon Stewart	.25
16	Luis Ortiz	.25
17	Marc Kroon	.25
18	Todd Greene	.25
19	Juan Acevedo	.25
20	Tony Clark	.25
21	Jermaine Dye	.25
22	Derrek Lee	1.00
23	Pat Watkins	.25
24	Calvin Reese	.25
25	Ben Grieve	.25
26	Julio Santana RC	.25
27	Felix Rodriguez RC	.50
28	Paul Konerko	.25
29	Nomar Garciaparra	2.00
30	Pat Ahearne	.25
31	Jason Schmidt	.25
32	Billy Wagner	.25
33	Rey Ordonez RC	1.00
34	Curtis Goodwin	.25
35	Sergio Nunez RC	.25
36	Tim Belk	.25
37	Scott Elarton RC	1.00
38	Jason Isringhausen	.25
39	Trot Nixon	.35
40	Sid Roberson	.25
41	Ron Villone	.25
42	Ruben Rivera	.25
43	Rick Huisman	.25
44	Todd Hollandsworth	.25
45	Johnny Damon	1.00
46	Garret Anderson	.25
47	Jeff D'Amico	.25
48	Dustin Hermanson	.25
49	Juan Encarnacion RC	4.00
50	Andy Pettitte	.50
51	Chris Stynes	.25
52	Troy Percival	.25
53	LaTroy Hawkins	.25
54	Roger Cedeno	.25
55	Alan Benes	.25
56	Karim Garcia RC	1.50
57	Andrew Lorraine	.25
58	Gary Rath RC	.25
59	Bret Wagner	.25
60	Jeff Suppan	.25
61	Bill Pulsipher	.25
62	Jay Payton RC	3.00
63	Alex Ochoa	.25
64	Ugueth Urbina	.25
65	Armando Benitez	.25
66	George Arias	.25
67	Raul Casanova RC	.50
68	Matt Drews	.25
69	Jimmy Haynes	.25
70	Jimmy Hurst	.25
71	C.J. Nitkowski	.25
72	Tommy Davis RC	.25
73	Bartolo Colon RC	5.00
74	Chris Carpenter RC	10.00
75	Trey Beamon	.25
76	Bryan Rekar	.25
77	James Baldwin	.25
78	Marc Valdes	.25
79	Tom Fordham RC	.25
80	Marc Newfield	.25
81	Angel Martinez	.25
82	Brian Hunter	.25
83	Jose Herrera	.25
84	Glenn Dishman RC	.25
85	Jacob Cruz RC	.25
86	Paul Shuey	.25
87	Scott Rolen RC	25.00
88	Doug Million	.25
89	Desi Relaford	.25
90	Michael Tucker	.25

Gold

	NM/M
Complete Set (54):	100.00
Common Player:	.50
Stars/RC's:	2.5X

(See 1995 Bowman #221-274 for checklist and base card values.)

Refractors

	NM/M
Common Player:	1.00
Stars:	3-6X
Rookies:	2-3X

(See 1995 Bowman's Best for checklist and base card values.)

1996 Bowman

KATSUHIRO MAEDA

	NM/M
Complete Set (385):	50.00
Common Player:	.10
Foils:	1.5X
Pack (11):	2.00
Wax Box (24):	40.00

1	Cal Ripken Jr.	2.00
2	Ray Durham	.10
3	Ivan Rodriguez	.50
4	Fred McGriff	.20
5	Hideo Nomo	.50
6	Troy Percival	.10
7	Moises Alou	.20
8	Mike Stanley	.10
9	Jay Buhner	.10
10	Shawn Green	.25
11	Ryan Klesko	.10
12	Andres Galarraga	.10
13	Dean Palmer	.10
14	Jeff Conine	.10
15	Brian Hunter	.10
16	J.T. Snow	.10
17	Larry Walker	.25
18	Barry Larkin	.40
19	Alex Gonzalez	.10
20	Edgar Martinez	.10
21	Mo Vaughn	.25
22	Mark McGwire	1.50
23	Jose Canseco	.50
24	Jack McDowell	.10
25	Dante Bichette	.10
26	Wade Boggs	.25
27	Mike Piazza	1.00
28	Ray Lankford	.10
29	Craig Biggio	.25
30	Rafael Palmeiro	.50
31	Ron Gant	.10
32	Javy Lopez	.10
33	Brian Jordan	.10
34	Paul O'Neill	.20
35	Mark Grace	.25
36	Matt Williams	.20
37	Pedro Martinez	.75
38	Rickey Henderson	.50
39	Bobby Bonilla	.10
40	Todd Hollandsworth	.10
41	Jim Thome	.75
42	Gary Sheffield	.40
43	Tim Salmon	.10
44	Gregg Jefferies	.10
45	Roberto Alomar	.25
45p	Roberto Alomar (Unmarked promo card, photo on front.)	3.00
46	Carlos Baerga	.10
47	Mark Grudzielanek	.10
48	Randy Johnson	.75
49	Tino Martinez	.10
50	Robin Ventura	.10
51	Ryne Sandberg	1.50
52	Jay Bell	.10
53	Jason Schmidt	.10
54	Frank Thomas	.75
55	Kenny Lofton	.25
56	Ariel Prieto	.10
57	David Cone	.10
58	Reggie Sanders	.10
59	Michael Tucker	.10
60	Vinny Castilla	.10
61	Lenny Dykstra	.10
62	Todd Hundley	.10
63	Brian McRae	.10
64	Dennis Eckersley	.40
65	Rondell White	.10
66	Eric Karros	.10
67	Greg Maddux	1.50
68	Kevin Appier	.10
69	Eddie Murray	.50
70	John Olerud	.10
71	Tony Gwynn	.75
72	David Justice	.10
73	Ken Caminiti	.10
74	Terry Steinbach	.10
75	Alan Benes	.10
76	Chipper Jones	1.00
77	Jeff Bagwell	.50
77p	Jeff Bagwell (Unmarked promo card, name in gold.)	6.00
78	Barry Bonds	2.00
79	Ken Griffey Jr.	1.50
80	Roger Cedeno	.10
81	Joe Carter	.10
82	Henry Rodriguez	.10
83	Jason Isringhausen	.10
84	Chuck Knoblauch	.10
85	Manny Ramirez	.75
86	Tom Glavine	.30
87	Jeffrey Hammonds	.10
88	Paul Molitor	.75
89	Roger Clemens	2.00
90	Greg Vaughn	.10
91	Marty Cordova	.10
92	Albert Belle	.10
93	Mike Mussina	.40
94	Garret Anderson	.10
95	Juan Gonzalez	.40
96	John Valentin	.10
97	Jason Giambi	.50
98	Kirby Puckett	1.50
99	Jim Edmonds	.25
100	Cecil Fielder	.10
101	Mike Aldrete	.10
102	Marquis Grissom	.10
103	Derek Bell	.10
104	Raul Mondesi	.10
105	Sammy Sosa	1.00
106	Travis Fryman	.10
107	Rico Brogna	.10
108	Will Clark	.25
109	Bernie Williams	.40
110	Brady Anderson	.10
111	Torii Hunter	.10
112	Derek Jeter	2.00
113	Mike Kusiewicz RC	.10
114	Scott Rolen	1.00
115	Ramon Castro	.10
116	Jose Guillen RC	2.50
117	Wade Walker RC	.10
118	Shawn Senior	.10
119	Onan Masaoka RC	.10
120	Marlon Anderson RC	.75
121	Katsuhiro Maeda RC	.25
122	Garrett Stephenson RC	.25
123	Butch Huskey	.10
124	D'Angelo Jimenez RC	.50
125	Tony Mounce RC	.20
126	Jay Canizaro	.10
127	Juan Melo	.10
128	Steve Gibralter	.10
129	Freddy Garcia	.10
130	Julio Santana	.10
131	Richard Hidalgo	.10
132	Jermaine Dye	.10
133	Willie Adams	.10
134	Everett Stull	.10
135	Ramon Morel	.10
136	Chan Ho Park	.10
137	Jamey Wright	.10
138	Luis Garcia RC	.10
139	Dan Serafini	.10
140	Ryan Dempster RC	.50
141	Tate Seefried	.10
142	Jimmy Hurst	.10
143	Travis Miller	.10
144	Curtis Goodwin	.10
145	Rocky Coppinger RC	.10
146	Enrique Wilson	.10
147	Jaime Bluma	.10
148	Andrew Vessel	.10
149	Damian Moss	.10
150	Shawn Gallagher RC	.10
151	Pat Watkins	.10
152	Jose Paniagua	.10
153	Danny Graves	.10
154	Bryon Gainey RC	.10
155	Steve Soderstrom	.10
156	Cliff Brumbaugh RC	.10
157	Eugene Kingsale RC	.10
158	Lou Collier	.10
159	Todd Walker	.10
160	Kris Detmers RC	.10
161	Josh Booty RC	.25
162	Greg Whiteman RC	.10
163	Damian Jackson	.10
164	Tony Clark	.10
165	Jeff D'Amico	.10
166	Johnny Damon	.50

167	Rafael Orellano	.10
168	Ruben Rivera	.10
169	Alex Ochoa	.10
170	Jay Powell	.10
171	Tom Evans	.10
172	Ron Villone	.10
173	Shawn Estes	.10
174	John Wasdin	.10
175	Bill Simas	.10
176	Kevin Brown	.10
177	Shannon Stewart	.10
178	Todd Greene	.10
179	Bob Wolcott	.10
180	Chris Snopek	.10
181	Nomar Garciaparra	1.00
182	Cameron Smith RC	.10
183	Matt Drews	.10
184	Jimmy Haynes	.10
185	Chris Carpenter	.25
186	Desi Relaford	.10
187	Ben Grieve	.10
188	Mike Bell	.10
189	Luis Castillo RC	.75
190	Ugueth Urbina	.10
191	Paul Wilson	.10
191p	Paul Wilson (Unmarked promo card, name in gold.)	1.00
192	Andruw Jones	.75
193	Wayne Gomes	.10
194	Craig Counsell RC	.75
195	Jim Cole	.10
196	Brooks Kieshnick	.10
197	Trey Beamon	.10
198	Marino Santana RC	.10
199	Bob Abreu	.25
200	Calvin Reese	.10
201	Dante Powell	.10
202	George Arias	.10
202p	George Arias (Unmarked promo card, name in gold.)	1.00
203	Jorge Velandia RC	.10
204	George Lombard RC	.10
205	Byron Browne RC	.10
206	John Frascatore	.10
207	Terry Adams	.10
208	Wilson Delgado RC	.10
209	Billy McMillon	.10
210	Jeff Abbott	.10
211	Trot Nixon	.10
212	Amaury Telemaco	.10
213	Scott Sullivan	.10
214	Justin Thompson	.10
215	Decomba Conner	.10
216	Ryan McGuire	.10
217	Matt Luke RC	.10
218	Doug Million	.10
219	Jason Dickson	.25
220	Ramon Hernandez RC	.50
221	Mark Bellhorn RC	.25
222	Eric Ludwick RC	.10
223	Luke Wilcox RC	.10
224	Marty Malloy RC	.10
225	Gary Coffee RC	.10
226	Wendell Magee RC	.10
227	Brett Tomko RC	.25
228	Derek Lowe	.10
229	Jose Rosado RC	.10
230	Steve Bourgeois RC	.10
231	Neil Weber RC	.10
232	Jeff Ware	.10
233	Edwin Diaz	.10
234	Greg Norton	.10
235	Aaron Boone	.10
236	Jeff Suppan	.10
237	Bret Wagner	.10
238	Elieser Marrero	.10
239	Will Cunnane	.10
240	Brian Barkley RC	.10
241	Jay Payton	.10
242	Marcus Jensen	.10
243	Ryan Nye	.10
244	Chad Mottola	.10
245	Scott McClain RC	.10
246	Jesse Ibarra RC	.10
247	Mike Darr RC	.10
248	Bobby Estalella RC	.50
249	Michael Barrett	.10
250	Jamie Lopiccolo RC	.10
251	Shane Spencer RC	.40
252	Ben Petrick RC	.50
253	Jason Bell RC	.10
254	Arnold Gooch RC	.10
255	T.J. Mathews	.10
256	Jason Ryan	.10
257	Pat Cline RC	.10
258	Rafael Carmona RC	.10
259	Carl Pavano RC	1.00
260	Ben Davis	.10
261	Matt Lawton RC	1.00
262	Kevin Sefcik RC	.10
263	Chris Fussell RC	.10
264	Mike Cameron RC	1.50
265	Marty Janzen RC	.10
266	Livan Hernandez RC	1.00
267	Raul Ibanez RC	1.50
268	Juan Encarnacion	.10
269	David Yocum RC	.10
270	Jonathan Johnson RC	.10
271	Reggie Taylor	.10
272	Danny Buxbaum RC	.10
273	Jacob Cruz	.10
274	Bobby Morris RC	.10
275	Andy Fox RC	.10
276	Greg Keagle	.10
277	Charles Peterson	.10
278	Derrek Lee	.50
279	Bryant Nelson RC	.10
280	Antone Williamson	.10
281	Scott Elarton	.10
282	Shad Williams RC	.10
283	Rich Hunter RC	.10
284	Chris Sheff	.10
285	Derrick Gibson	.10
286	Felix Rodriguez	.10
287	Brian Banks RC	.10
288	Jason McDonald RC	.10
289	Glendon Rusch RC	.50
290	Gary Rath	.10
291	Peter Munro	.10
292	Tom Fordham	.10
293	Jason Kendall	.10
294	Russ Johnson	.10
295	Joe Long RC	.10
296	Robert Smith RC	.10
297	Jarrod Washburn RC	.75
298	Dave Coggin RC	.10
299	Jeff Yoder RC	.10
300	Jed Hansen RC	.10
301	Matt Morris RC	1.00
302	Josh Bishop RC	.10
303	Dustin Hermanson	.10
304	Mike Gulan	.10
305	Felipe Crespo	.10
306	Quinton McCracken	.10
307	Jim Bonnici RC	.10
308	Sal Fasano RC	.10
309	Gabe Alvarez RC	.10
310	Heath Murray RC	.10
311	Jose Valentin RC	.10
312	Bartolo Colon	.10
313	Olmedo Saenz RC	.10
314	Norm Hutchins RC	.10
315	Chris Holt RC	.10
316	David Doster RC	.10
317	Robert Person	.10
318	Donne Wall RC	.10
319	Adam Riggs RC	.10
320	Homer Bush	.10
321	Brad Rigby RC	.10
322	Lou Merloni RC	.25
323	Neifi Perez	.10
324	Chris Cumberland RC	.10
325	Alvie Shepherd RC	.10
326	Jarrod Patterson RC	.10
327	Ray Ricken RC	.10
328	Danny Klassen RC	.10
329	David Miller RC	.10
330	Chad Alexander RC	.10
331	Matt Beaumont	.10
332	Damon Hollins	.10
333	Todd Dunn	.10
334	Mike Sweeney RC	1.50
335	Richie Sexson	.40
336	Billy Wagner	.10
337	Ron Wright RC	.10
338	Paul Konerko	.25
339	Tommy Phelps RC	.10
340	Karim Garcia	.10
341	Mike Grace RC	.10
342	Russell Branyan RC	.40
343	Randy Winn RC	.50
344	A.J. Pierzynski RC	1.50
345	Mike Busby RC	.10
346	Matt Beech RC	.10
347	Jose Cepeda RC	.10
348	Brian Stephenson	.10
349	Rey Ordonez	.10
350	Rich Aurilia RC	1.00
351	Edgard Velazquez RC	.25
352	Raul Casanova	.10
353	Carlos Guillen RC	1.00
354	Bruce Aven RC	.10
355	Ryan Jones RC	.10
356	Derek Aucoin RC	.10
357	Brian Rose RC	.10
358	Richard Almanzar RC	.10
359	Fletcher Bates RC	.10
360	Russ Ortiz RC	.75
361	Wilton Guerrero RC	.10
362	Geoff Jenkins RC	1.00
363	Pete Janicki	.10
364	Yamil Benitez	.10
365	Aaron Holbert	.10
366	Tim Belk	.10
367	Terrell Wade	.10
368	Terrence Long	.10
369	Brad Fullmer	.10
370	Matt Wagner	.10
371	Craig Wilson	.10
372	Mark Loretta	.10
373	Eric Owens	.10
374	Vladimir Guerrero	1.00
375	Tommy Davis	.10
376	Donnie Sadler	.10
377	Edgar Renteria	.25
378	Todd Helton	.50
379	Ralph Milliard RC	.10
380	Darin Blood RC	.10
381	Shayne Bennett	.10
382	Mark Redman	.10
383	Felix Martinez	.10
384	Sean Watkins RC	.10
385	Oscar Henriquez	.10

Bowman's Best Preview

NOMAR GARCIAPARRA

		NM/M
Complete Set (30):		18.50
Common Player:		.20
Refractors:		1.5X
Atomic Refractors:		2X
1	Chipper Jones	1.50
2	Alan Benes	.25
3	Brooks Kieshnick	.25
4	Barry Bonds	3.00
5	Rey Ordonez	.25
6	Tim Salmon	.25
7	Mike Piazza	2.00
8	Billy Wagner	.25
9	Andruw Jones	1.00
10	Tony Gwynn	1.50
11	Paul Wilson	.25
12	Calvin Reese	.25
13	Frank Thomas	1.00
14	Greg Maddux	1.50
15	Derek Jeter	3.00
16	Jeff Bagwell	1.00
17	Barry Larkin	.25
18	Todd Greene	.25
19	Ruben Rivera	.25
20	Richard Hidalgo	.25
21	Larry Walker	.25
22	Carlos Baerga	.25
23	Derrick Gibson	.25
24	Richie Sexson	.25
25	Mo Vaughn	.25
26	Hideo Nomo	.25
27	Nomar Garciaparra	1.50
28	Cal Ripken Jr.	3.00
29	Karim Garcia	.25
30	Ken Griffey Jr.	2.00

Minor League Player of the Year

ALEX OCHOA 1996 MINOR LEAGUE PLAYER OF THE YEAR CANDIDATE

	NM/M
Complete Set (15):	12.50

Common Player:		.50
1	Andruw Jones	4.00
2	Derrick Gibson	.50
3	Bob Abreu	.75
4	Todd Walker	.50
5	Jamey Wright	.50
6	Wes Helms	.50
7	Karim Garcia	.75
8	Bartolo Colon	2.00
9	Alex Ochoa	.50
10	Mike Sweeney	2.00
11	Ruben Rivera	.50
12	Gabe Alvarez	.50
13	Billy Wagner	.50
14	Vladimir Guerrero	4.00
15	Edgard Velazquez	.50

1952 Mickey Mantle Reprints

		NM/M
Complete Set (4):		20.00
Common Card:		2.50
20	Mickey Mantle/Reprint	2.50
20	Mickey Mantle/Finest	5.00
20	Mickey Mantle/Refractor	7.50
20	Mickey Mantle/Atomic Refractor	10.00

1996 Bowman's Best

CHUCK KNOBLAUCH

		NM/M
Complete Set (180):		30.00
Common Player:		.25
Refractors:		2X
Atomics:		15X
1952 Mickey Mantle:		2.50
1952 Mantle Finest:		5.00
1952 Mantle Refractor:		7.50
1952 Mantle Atomic:		10.00
Pack (6):		2.50
Wax Box (24):		40.00
1	Hideo Nomo	.75
2	Edgar Martinez	.25
3	Cal Ripken Jr.	4.00
4	Wade Boggs	1.00
5	Cecil Fielder	.25
6	Albert Belle	.25
7	Chipper Jones	1.50
8	Ryne Sandberg	2.00
9	Tim Salmon	.25
10	Barry Bonds	3.00
11	Ken Caminiti	.25
12	Ron Gant	.25
13	Frank Thomas	1.00
14	Dante Bichette	.25
15	Jason Kendall	.25
16	Mo Vaughn	.25
17	Rey Ordonez	.25
18	Henry Rodriguez	.25
19	Ryan Klesko	.25

20	Jeff Bagwell	1.00
21	Randy Johnson	1.50
22	Jim Edmonds	.50
23	Kenny Lofton	.25
24	Andy Pettitte	.50
25	Brady Anderson	.25
26	Mike Piazza	2.50
27	Greg Vaughn	.25
28	Joe Carter	.25
29	Jason Giambi	1.00
30	Ivan Rodriguez	1.00
31	Jeff Conine	.25
32	Rafael Palmeiro	.75
33	Roger Clemens	3.00
34	Chuck Knoblauch	.25
35	Reggie Sanders	.25
36	Andres Galarraga	.25
37	Paul O'Neill	.50
38	Tony Gwynn	2.00
39	Paul Wilson	.25
40	Garret Anderson	.25
41	David Justice	.25
42	Eddie Murray	1.00
43	Mike Grace RC	.25
44	Marty Cordova	.25
45	Kevin Appier	.25
46	Raul Mondesi	.25
47	Jim Thome	1.00
48	Sammy Sosa	2.00
49	Craig Biggio	.50
50	Marquis Grissom	.25
51	Alan Benes	.25
52	Manny Ramirez	1.50
53	Gary Sheffield	.75
54	Mike Mussina	.50
55	Robin Ventura	.25
56	Johnny Damon	1.00
57	Jose Canseco	.75
58	Juan Gonzalez	.75
59	Tino Martinez	.25
60	Brian Hunter	.25
61	Fred McGriff	.25
62	Jay Buhner	.25
63	Carlos Delgado	.75
64	Moises Alou	.50
65	Roberto Alomar	.50
66	Barry Larkin	.25
67	Vinny Castilla	.25
68	Ray Durham	.25
69	Travis Fryman	.25
70	Jason Isringhausen	.25
71	Ken Griffey Jr.	2.50
72	John Smoltz	.50
73	Matt Williams	.25
74	Chan Ho Park	.25
75	Mark McGwire	2.50
76	Jeffrey Hammonds	.25
77	Will Clark	.50
78	Kirby Puckett	2.00
79	Derek Jeter	4.00
80	Derek Bell	.25
81	Eric Karros	.25
82	Lenny Dykstra	.25
83	Larry Walker	.50
84	Mark Grudzielanek	.25
85	Greg Maddux	2.50
86	Carlos Baerga	.25
87	Paul Molitor	1.00
88	John Valentin	.25
89	Mark Grace	.50
90	Ray Lankford	.25
91	Andruw Jones	1.50
92	Nomar Garciaparra	2.00
93	Alex Ochoa	.25
94	Derrick Gibson	.25
95	Jeff D'Amico	.25
96	Ruben Rivera	.25
97	Vladimir Guerrero	1.50
98	Calvin Reese	.25
99	Richard Hidalgo	.25
100	Bartolo Colon	.25
101	Karim Garcia	.25
102	Ben Davis	.25
103	Jay Powell	.25
104	Chris Snopek	.25
105	Glendon Rusch RC	1.00
106	Enrique Wilson	.25
107	Antonio Alfonseca RC	.75
108	Wilton Guerrero RC	.50
109	Jose Guillen RC	3.00
110	Miguel Mejia RC	.25
111	Jay Payton	.25
112	Scott Elarton	.25
113	Brooks Kieschnick	.25
114	Dustin Hermanson	.25
115	Roger Cedeno	.25
116	Matt Wagner	.25
117	Lee Daniels	.25
118	Ben Grieve	.25
119	Ugueth Urbina	.25
120	Danny Graves	.25
121	Dan Donato RC	.25
122	Matt Ruebel RC	.25
123	Mark Sievert RC	.25

124	Chris Stynes	.25
125	Jeff Abbott	.25
126	Rocky Coppinger RC	.25
127	Jermaine Dye	.25
128	Todd Greene	.15
129	Chris Carpenter	1.00
130	Edgar Renteria	.50
131	Matt Drews	.25
132	Edgard Velazquez RC	.50
133	Casey Whitten	.25
134	Ryan Jones RC	.25
135	Todd Walker	.20
136	Geoff Jenkins RC	2.00
137	Matt Morris RC	2.00
138	Richie Sexson	.75
139	Todd Dunwoody RC	.50
140	Gabe Alvarez RC	.50
141	J.J. Johnson	.25
142	Shannon Stewart	.25
143	Brad Fullmer	.25
144	Julio Santana	.25
145	Scott Rolen	1.00
146	Amaury Telemaco	.25
147	Trey Beamon	.25
148	Billy Wagner	.20
149	Todd Hollandsworth	.25
150	Doug Million	.25
151	Jose Valentin RC	.25
152	Wes Helms RC	.50
153	Jeff Suppan	.25
154	Luis Castillo RC	1.50
155	Bob Abreu	.50
156	Paul Konerko	.50
157	Jamey Wright	.25
158	Eddie Pearson	.25
159	Jimmy Haynes	.25
160	Derrek Lee	.75
161	Damian Moss	.15
162	Carlos Guillen RC	2.00
163	Chris Fussell RC	.25
164	Mike Sweeney RC	3.00
165	Donnie Sadler	.15
166	Desi Relaford	.25
167	Steve Gibralter	.25
168	Neifi Perez	.25
169	Antone Williamson	.25
170	Marty Janzen RC	.25
171	Todd Helton	1.00
172	Raul Ibanez RC	2.00
173	Bill Selby	.25
174	Shane Monahan RC	.35
175	Robin Jennings RC	.25
176	Bobby Chouinard RC	.25
177	Einar Diaz	.25
178	Jason Thompson	.15
179	Rafael Medina RC	.25
180	Kevin Orie	.25

Mirror Image

	NM/M
Complete Set (10):	24.00
Common Card:	1.50
Refractors:	1.5X
Atomics:	2X
1	Jeff Bagwell, Todd Helton, Frank Thomas, Richie Sexson	3.00
2	Craig Biggio, Luis Castillo, Roberto Alomar, Desi Relaford	1.50
3	Chipper Jones, Scott Rolen, Wade Boggs, George Arias	3.50
4	Barry Larkin, Neifi Perez, Cal Ripken Jr., Mark Bellhorn	6.00
5	Larry Walker, Karim Garcia, Albert Belle, Ruben Rivera	1.50

6	Barry Bonds, Andruw Jones, Kenny Lofton, Donnie Sadler	6.00
7	Tony Gwynn, Vladimir Guerrero, Ken Griffey Jr., Ben Grieve	4.50
8	Mike Piazza, Ben Davis, Ivan Rodriguez, Jose Valentin	4.50
9	Greg Maddux, Jamey Wright, Mike Mussina, Bartolo Colon	3.50
10	Tom Glavine, Billy Wagner, Randy Johnson, Jarrod Washburn	1.50

Cuts

KEN GRIFFEY JR.

	NM/M
Complete Set (15):	15.00
Common Player:	.25
Refractors:	1.5X
Atomic Refractors:	2X
1	Ken Griffey Jr.	2.50
2	Jason Isringhausen	.25
3	Derek Jeter	4.00
4	Andruw Jones	1.00
5	Chipper Jones	2.00
6	Ryan Klesko	.25
7	Raul Mondesi	.25
8	Hideo Nomo	.50
9	Mike Piazza	2.50
10	Manny Ramirez	1.00
11	Cal Ripken Jr.	4.00
12	Ruben Rivera	.25
13	Tim Salmon	.25
14	Frank Thomas	1.00
15	Jim Thome	.75

1997 Bowman

JOSE GUILLEN

	NM/M
Complete Set (440):	50.00
Complete Series 1 (221):	25.00
Complete Series 2 (219):	25.00
Common Player:	.10
Series 1 Pack (10):	2.00
Series 1 Wax Box (24):	35.00
Series 2 Pack (10):	2.00
Series 2 Wax Box (24):	35.00
1	Derek Jeter	2.00
2	Edgar Renteria	.10
3	Chipper Jones	1.00
4	Hideo Nomo	.40
5	Tim Salmon	.10
6	Jason Giambi	.50
7	Robin Ventura	.10
8	Tony Clark	.25
9	Barry Larkin	.25
10	Paul Molitor	.75

11	Bernard Gilkey	.10
12	Jack McDowell	.10
13	Andy Benes	.10
14	Ryan Klesko	.10
15	Mark McGwire	1.50
16	Ken Griffey Jr.	1.50
17	Robb Nen	.10
18	Cal Ripken Jr.	2.00
19	John Valentin	.10
20	Ricky Bottalico	.10
21	Mike Lansing	.10
22	Ryne Sandberg	1.00
23	Carlos Delgado	.50
24	Craig Biggio	.25
25	Eric Karros	.10
26	Kevin Appier	.10
27	Mariano Rivera	.50
28	Vinny Castilla	.10
29	Juan Gonzalez	.40
30	Al Martin	.10
31	Jeff Cirillo	.10
32	Eddie Murray	.75
33	Ray Lankford	.10
34	Manny Ramirez	.75
35	Roberto Alomar	.25
36	Will Clark	.25
37	Chuck Knoblauch	.10
38	Harold Baines	.10
39	Trevor Hoffman	.10
40	Edgar Martinez	.10
41	Geronimo Berroa	.10
42	Rey Ordonez	.10
43	Mike Stanley	.10
44	Mike Mussina	.40
45	Kevin Brown	.10
46	Dennis Eckersley	.50
47	Henry Rodriguez	.10
48	Tino Martinez	.10
49	Eric Young	.10
50	Bret Boone	.10
51	Raul Mondesi	.10
52	Sammy Sosa	1.00
53	John Smoltz	.25
54	Billy Wagner	.10
55	Jeff D'Amico	.10
56	Ken Caminiti	.10
57	Jason Kendall	.10
58	Wade Boggs	.75
59	Andres Galarraga	.10
60	Jeff Brantley	.10
61	Mel Rojas	.10
62	Brian Hunter	.10
63	Bobby Bonilla	.10
64	Roger Clemens	1.50
65	Jeff Kent	.20
66	Matt Williams	.10
67	Albert Belle	.10
68	Jeff King	.10
69	John Wetteland	.10
70	Deion Sanders	.25
71	Bubba Trammell RC	.25
72	Felix Heredia RC	.25
73	Billy Koch RC	.25
74	Sidney Ponson RC	.25
75	Ricky Ledee RC	.25
76	Brett Tomko	.10
77	Braden Looper RC	.25
78	Damian Jackson	.10
79	Jason Dickson	.10
80	Chad Green RC	.10
81	R.A. Dickey RC	.10
82	Jeff Liefer	.10
83	Matt Wagner	.10
84	Richard Hidalgo	.10
85	Adam Riggs	.10
86	Robert Smith	.10
87	Chad Hermansen RC	.10
88	Felix Martinez	.10
89	J.J. Johnson	.10
90	Todd Dunwoody	.10
91	Katsuhiro Maeda	.10
92	Darin Erstad	.25
93	Elieser Marrero	.10
94	Bartolo Colon	.10
95	Chris Fussell	.10
96	Ugueth Urbina	.10
97	Josh Paul RC	.10
98	Jaime Bluma	.10
99	Seth Greisinger RC	.10
100	Jose Cruz RC	.25
101	Todd Dunn	.10
102	Joe Young RC	.10
103	Jonathan Johnson	.10
104	Justin Towle RC	.10
105	Brian Rose	.10
106	Jose Guillen	.75
107	Andruw Jones	.75
108	Mark Kotsay RC	1.00
109	Wilton Guerrero	.10
110	Jacob Cruz	.10
111	Mike Sweeney	.10
112	Julio Mosquera	.10
113	Matt Morris	.10
114	Wendell Magee	.10

115	John Thomson	.10
116	Javier Valentin RC	.10
117	Tom Fordham	.10
118	Ruben Rivera	.10
119	Mike Drumright RC	.10
120	Chris Holt	.10
121	Sean Maloney RC	.10
122	Michael Barrett	.10
123	Tony Saunders RC	.10
124	Kevin Brown	.10
125	Richard Almanzar	.10
126	Mark Redman	.10
127	Anthony Sanders RC	.10
128	Jeff Abbott	.10
129	Eugene Kingsale	.10
130	Paul Konerko	.40
131	Randall Simon RC	.25
132	Andy Larkin	.10
133	Rafael Medina	.10
134	Mendy Lopez	.10
135	Freddy Garcia	.10
136	Karim Garcia	.15
137	Larry Rodriguez RC	.10
138	Carlos Guillen	.10
139	Aaron Boone	.10
140	Donnie Sadler	.10
141	Brooks Kieschnick	.10
142	Scott Spiezio	.10
143	Everett Stull	.10
144	Enrique Wilson	.10
145	Milton Bradley RC	1.50
146	Kevin Orie	.10
147	Derek Wallace	.10
148	Russ Johnson	.10
149	Joe Lagarde RC	.10
150	Luis Castillo	.10
151	Jay Payton	.10
152	Joe Long	.10
153	Livan Hernandez	.10
154	Vladimir Nunez RC	.15
155	Not Issued	
156a	George Arias	.10
156b	Calvin Reese (Should be #155.)	.10
157	Homer Bush	.10
158	Not Issued	
159a	Eric Milton RC	.50
159b	Chris Carpenter (Should be #158.)	.50
160	Richie Sexson	.40
161	Carl Pavano	.10
162	Chris Gissell RC	.10
163	Mac Suzuki	.10
164	Pat Cline	.10
165	Ron Wright	.10
166	Dante Powell	.10
167	Mark Bellhorn	.10
168	George Lombard	.10
169	Pee Wee Lopez RC	.10
170	Paul Wilder RC	.10
171	Brad Fullmer	.10
172	Willie Martinez RC	.10
173	Dario Veras RC	.10
174	Dave Coggin	.10
175	Kris Benson RC	1.00
176	Torii Hunter	.25
177	D.T. Cromer RC	.10
178	Nelson Figueroa RC	.10
179	Hiram Bocachica RC	.15
180	Shane Monahan	.10
181	Jimmy Anderson RC	.10
182	Juan Melo	.10
183	Pablo Ortega RC	.10
184	Calvin Pickering RC	.50
185	Reggie Taylor	.10
186	Jeff Farnsworth RC	.10
187	Terrence Long	.10
188	Geoff Jenkins	.10
189	Steve Rain RC	.10
190	Nerio Rodriguez RC	.10
191	Derrick Gibson	.10
192	Darin Blood	.10
193	Ben Davis	.10
194	Adrian Beltre RC	2.00
195	Damian Sapp RC	.10
196	Kerry Wood RC	3.00
197	Nate Rolison RC	.10
198	Fernando Tatis RC	.25
199	Brad Penny RC	2.00
200	Jake Westbrook RC	.15
201	Edwin Diaz	.10
202	Joe Fontenot RC	.10
203	Matt Halloran RC	.10
204	Blake Stein RC	.10
205	Onan Masaoka	.10
206	Ben Petrick	.10
207	Matt Clement RC	1.00
208	Todd Greene	.10
209	Ray Ricken	.10
210	Eric Chavez RC	3.00
211	Edgard Velazquez	.10
212	Bruce Chen RC	.10
213	Danny Patterson RC	.10
214	Jeff Yoder	.10

215	Luis Ordaz RC	.10
216	Chris Widger	.10
217	Jason Brester	.10
218	Carlton Loewer	.10
219	Chris Reitsma RC	.10
220	Neifi Perez	.10
221	Hideki Irabu RC	.25
222	Ellis Burks	.10
223	Pedro Martinez	.75
224	Kenny Lofton	.10
225	Randy Johnson	.75
226	Terry Steinbach	.10
227	Bernie Williams	.25
228	Dean Palmer	.10
229	Alan Benes	.10
230	Marquis Grissom	.10
231	Gary Sheffield	.40
232	Curt Schilling	.40
233	Reggie Sanders	.10
234	Bobby Higginson	.10
235	Moises Alou	.20
236	Tom Glavine	.25
237	Mark Grace	.25
238	Ramon Martinez	.10
239	Rafael Palmeiro	.50
240	John Olerud	.10
241	Dante Bichette	.10
242	Greg Vaughn	.10
243	Jeff Bagwell	.50
244	Barry Bonds	2.00
245	Pat Hentgen	.10
246	Jim Thome	.50
247	Jermaine Allensworth	.10
248	Andy Pettitte	.25
249	Jay Bell	.10
250	John Jaha	.10
251	Jim Edmonds	.25
252	Ron Gant	.10
253	David Cone	.10
254	Jose Canseco	.40
255	Jay Buhner	.10
256	Greg Maddux	1.50
257	Brian McRae	.10
258	Lance Johnson	.10
259	Travis Fryman	.10
260	Paul O'Neill	.20
261	Ivan Rodriguez	.50
262	Gregg Jefferies	.10
263	Fred McGriff	.20
264	Derek Bell	.10
265	Jeff Conine	.10
266	Mike Piazza	1.50
267	Mark Grudzielanek	.10
268	Brady Anderson	.10
269	Marty Cordova	.10
270	Ray Durham	.10
271	Joe Carter	.10
272	Brian Jordan	.10
273	David Justice	.10
274	Tony Gwynn	1.00
275	Larry Walker	.20
276	Cecil Fielder	.10
277	Mo Vaughn	.10
278	Alex Fernandez	.10
279	Michael Tucker	.10
280	Jose Valentin	.10
281	Sandy Alomar	.10
282	Todd Hollandsworth	.10
283	Rico Brogna	.10
284	Rusty Greer	.10
285	Roberto Hernandez	.10
286	Hal Morris	.10
287	Johnny Damon	.10
288	Todd Hundley	.10
289	Rondell White	.10
290	Frank Thomas	.75
291	Don Denbow RC	.10
292	Derrek Lee	.50
293	Todd Walker	.10
294	Scott Rolen	.50
295	Wes Helms	.10
296	Bob Abreu	.25
297	John Patterson RC	1.50
298	Alex Gonzalez RC	.25
299	Grant Roberts RC	.25
300	Jeff Suppan	.10
301	Luke Wilcox	.10
302	Marlon Anderson	.10
303	Ray Brown	.10
304	Mike Caruso RC	.10
305	Sam Marsonek RC	.10
306	Brady Raggio RC	.10
307	Kevin McGlinchy RC	.25
308	Roy Halladay RC	3.00
309	Jeremi Gonzalez RC	.25
310	Aramis Ramirez RC	4.00
311	Dermal Brown RC	.10
312	Justin Thompson	.10
313	Jay Tessmer RC	.10
314	Mike Johnson	.10
315	Danny Clyburn	.10
316	Bruce Aven	.10
317	Keith Foulke RC	1.50
318	Jimmy Osting RC	.10

319	Valerio De Los Santos RC	.25
320	Shannon Stewart	.10
321	Willie Adams	.10
322	Larry Barnes	.10
323	Mark Johnson	.10
324	Chris Stowers RC	.10
325	Brandon Reed	.10
326	Randy Winn	.10
327	Steven Chavez	.10
328	Nomar Garciaparra	1.00
329	Jacque Jones	1.00
330	Chris Clemons	.10
331	Todd Helton	.50
332	Ryan Brannan RC	.10
333	Alex Sanchez RC	.25
334	Arnold Gooch	.10
335	Russell Branyan	.10
336	Daryle Ward	.10
337	John LeRoy RC	.10
338	Steve Cox	.10
339	Kevin Witt	.10
340	Norm Hutchins	.10
341	Gabby Martinez	.10
342	Kris Detmers	.10
343	Mike Villano RC	.10
344	Preston Wilson	.10
345	Jim Manias RC	.10
346	Deivi Cruz RC	.25
347	Donzell McDonald RC	.10
348	Rod Myers RC	.10
349	Shawn Chacon RC	.25
350	Elvin Hernandez RC	.10
351	Orlando Cabrera RC	1.00
352	Brian Banks	.10
353	Robbie Bell	.10
354	Brad Rigby	.10
355	Scott Elarton	.10
356	Kevin Sweeney RC	.10
357	Steve Soderstrom	.10
358	Ryan Nye	.10
359	Marlon Allen RC	.10
360	Donny Leon RC	.10
361	Garrett Neubart RC	.10
362	Abraham Nunez RC	.25
363	Adam Eaton RC	.50
364	Octavio Dotel RC	.40
365	Dean Crow RC	.10
366	Jason Baker RC	.10
367	Sean Casey	.10
368	Joe Lawrence RC	.10
369	Adam Johnson RC	.10
370	Scott Schoeneweis RC	.25
371	Gerald Witasick Jr.	.10
372	Ronnie Belliard RC	.25
373	Russ Ortiz	.10
374	Robert Stratton RC	.10
375	Bobby Estalella	.10
376	Corey Lee RC	.10
377	Carlos Beltran	.50
378	Mike Cameron	.10
379	Scott Randall RC	.10
380	Corey Erickson	.10
381	Jay Canizaro	.10
382	Kerry Robinson RC	.10
383	Todd Noel RC	.10
384	A.J. Zapp RC	.10
385	Jarrod Washburn	.10
386	Ben Grieve	.10
387	Javier Vazquez RC	1.50
388	Tony Graffanino	.10
389	Travis Lee RC	.25
390	DaRond Stovall	.10
391	Dennis Reyes RC	.25
392	Danny Buxbaum	.10
393	Marc Lewis RC	.10
394	Kelvim Escobar RC	.25
395	Danny Klassen	.10
396	Ken Cloude RC	.25
397	Gabe Alvarez	.10
398	Jaret Wright RC	.50
399	Raul Casanova	.10
400	Clayton Brunner RC	.10
401	Jason Marquis RC	.50
402	Marc Kroon	.10
403	Jamey Wright	.10
404	Matt Snyder RC	.10
405	Josh Garrett RC	.10
406	Juan Encarnacion	.10
407	Heath Murray	.10
408	Brett Herbison RC	.10
409	Brent Butler RC	.25
410	Danny Peoples RC	.25
411	Miguel Tejada RC	10.00
412	Damian Moss	.10
413	Jim Pittsley	.10
414	Dmitri Young	.10
415	Glendon Rusch	.10
416	Vladimir Guerrero	.75
417	Cole Liniak RC	.10
418	Ramon Hernandez	.10
419	Cliff Politte RC	.25
420	Mel Rosario RC	.10
421	Jorge Carrion RC	.10
422	John Barnes RC	.10

423	Chris Stowe RC	.10
424	Vernon Wells RC	4.00
425	Brett Caradonna RC	.10
426	Scott Hodges RC	.10
427	Jon Garland RC	1.50
428	Nathan Haynes RC	.25
429	Geoff Goetz RC	.25
430	Adam Kennedy RC	.50
431	T.J. Tucker RC	.10
432	Aaron Akin RC	.10
433	Jayson Werth RC	.50
434	Glenn Davis RC	.10
435	Mark Mangum RC	.10
436	Troy Cameron RC	.10
437	J.J. Davis RC	.10
438	Lance Berkman RC	4.00
439	Jason Standridge RC	.25
440	Jason Dellaero RC	.10
441	Hideki Irabu RC	.25

International

	NM/M
Complete Set (440):	75.00
Complete Series 1 (221):	40.00
Complete Series 2 (219):	40.00
Common Player:	.25
Stars and Rookies:	1.5X

(See 1997 Bowman for checklist and base card values.)

Bowman's Best Preview

NOMAR GARCIAPARRA

	NM/M
Complete Set (20):	30.00
Common Player:	.75
Refractors:	1.5X
Atomic Refractors:	2X
1 Frank Thomas	1.50
2 Ken Griffey Jr.	3.00
3 Barry Bonds	5.00
4 Derek Jeter	5.00
5 Chipper Jones	2.00
6 Mark McGwire	4.00
7 Cal Ripken Jr.	5.00
8 Kenny Lofton	.75
9 Gary Sheffield	.75
10 Jeff Bagwell	1.50
11 Wilton Guerrero	.75
12 Scott Rolen	1.00
13 Todd Walker	.75
14 Ruben Rivera	.75
15 Andruw Jones	1.50
16 Nomar Garciaparra	2.00
17 Vladimir Guerrero	1.50
18 Miguel Tejada	1.00
19 Bartolo Colon	.75
20 Katsuhiro Maeda	.75

International Best

	NM/M
Complete Set (20):	20.00

Common Player:	.60
Refractors:	1.5X
Atomic Refractors:	2X
1 Frank Thomas	1.50
2 Ken Griffey Jr.	2.50
3 Juan Gonzalez	1.50
4 Bernie Williams	.60
5 Hideo Nomo	1.50
6 Sammy Sosa	3.50
7 Larry Walker	.60
8 Vinny Castilla	.60
9 Mariano Rivera	.75
10 Rafael Palmeiro	1.00
11 Nomar Garciaparra	3.50
12 Todd Walker	.60
13 Andruw Jones	1.50
14 Vladimir Guerrero	1.50
15 Ruben Rivera	.60
16 Bob Abreu	.75
17 Karim Garcia	.75
18 Katsuhiro Maeda	.60
19 Jose Cruz Jr.	1.00
20 Damian Moss	.60

Scout's Honor Roll

	NM/M
Complete Set (15):	12.50
Common Player:	.50
1 Dmitri Young	.50
2 Bob Abreu	.75
3 Vladimir Guerrero	2.00
4 Paul Konerko	.75
5 Kevin Orie	.50
6 Todd Walker	.50
7 Ben Grieve	.50
8 Darin Erstad	1.00
9 Derrek Lee	1.00
10 Jose Cruz	.50
11 Scott Rolen	1.00
12 Travis Lee	.75
13 Andruw Jones	2.00
14 Wilton Guerrero	.50
15 Nomar Garciaparra	2.50

Rookie of the Year Candidates

	NM/M
Complete Set (15):	9.00
Common Player:	.50
1 Jeff Abbott	.50
2 Karim Garcia	.50
3 Todd Helton	2.50
4 Richard Hidalgo	.50
5 Geoff Jenkins	.50
6 Russ Johnson	.50
7 Paul Konerko	.75
8 Mark Kotsay	.50
9 Ricky Ledee	.50
10 Travis Lee	.75
11 Derrek Lee	1.50
12 Elieser Marrero	.50

13 Juan Melo	.50
14 Brian Rose	.50
15 Fernando Tatis	.50

Certified Autographs

	NM/M
Common Blue:	2.00
Black:	1.5X
Gold:	4X
Derek Jeter Green:	1.5X
1 Jeff Abbott	2.00
2 Bob Abreu	40.00
3 Willie Adams	2.00
4 Brian Banks	2.00
5 Kris Benson	15.00
6 Darin Blood	2.00
7 Jaime Bluma	2.00
8 Kevin Brown	5.00
9 Ray Brown	2.00
10 Homer Bush	4.00
11 Mike Cameron	8.00
12 Jay Canizaro	3.00
13 Luis Castillo	5.00
14 Dave Coggin	2.00
15 Bartolo Colon	15.00
16 Rocky Coppinger	3.00
17 Jacob Cruz	5.00
18 Jose Cruz	8.00
19 Jeff D'Amico	5.00
20 Ben Davis	5.00
21 Mike Drumbright	5.00
22 Scott Elarton	5.00
23 Darin Erstad	10.00
24 Bobby Estalella	5.00
25 Joe Fontenot	4.00
26 Tom Fordham	2.00
27 Brad Fullmer	5.00
28 Chris Fussell	2.00
29 Karim Garcia	5.00
30 Kris Detmers	2.00
31 Todd Greene	4.00
32 Ben Grieve	5.00
33 Vladimir Guerrero	75.00
34 Jose Guillen	15.00
35 Roy Halladay	65.00
36 Wes Helms	5.00
37 Chad Hermansen	3.00
38 Richard Hidalgo	8.00
39 Todd Hollandsworth	3.00
40 Damian Jackson	3.00
41 Derek Jeter	120.00
42 Andruw Jones	40.00
43 Brooks Kieschnick	3.00
44 Eugene Kingsale	5.00
45 Paul Konerko	15.00
46 Marc Kroon	2.00
47 Derrek Lee	40.00
48 Travis Lee	5.00
49 Terrence Long	4.00
50 Curt Lyons	2.00
51 Elieser Marrero	3.00
52 Rafael Medina	2.00
53 Juan Melo	3.00
54 Shane Monahan	2.00
55 Julio Mosquera	2.00
56 Heath Murray	2.00
57 Ryan Nye	2.00
58 Kevin Orie	4.00
59 Russ Ortiz	5.00
60 Carl Pavano	30.00
61 Jay Payton	5.00
62 Neifi Perez	3.00
63 Sidney Ponson	10.00
64 Calvin Reese	8.00
65 Ray Ricken	3.00
66 Brad Rigby	3.00
67 Adam Riggs	3.00
68 Ruben Rivera	4.00
69 J.J. Johnson	2.00
70 Scott Rolen	40.00
71 Tony Saunders	3.00
72 Donnie Sadler	5.00
73 Richie Sexson	15.00

74 Scott Spiezio	6.00
75 Everett Stull	2.00
76 Mike Sweeney	15.00
77 Fernando Tatis	4.00
78 Miguel Tejada	120.00
79 Justin Thompson	5.00
80 Justin Towle	6.00
81 Billy Wagner	20.00
82 Todd Walker	5.00
83 Luke Wilcox	2.00
84 Paul Wilder	4.00
85 Enrique Wilson	5.00
86 Kerry Wood	60.00
87 Jamey Wright	5.00
88 Ron Wright	5.00
89 Dmitri Young	10.00
90 Nelson Figueroa	2.00

1997 Bowman Chrome

	NM/M
Complete Set (300):	150.00
Common Player:	.25
Pack (3):	5.00
Wax Box (24):	100.00
1 Derek Jeter	4.00
2 Chipper Jones	2.00
3 Hideo Nomo	.75
4 Tim Salmon	.25
5 Robin Ventura	.25
6 Tony Clark	.25
7 Barry Larkin	.50
8 Paul Molitor	1.00
9 Andy Benes	.25
10 Ryan Klesko	.25
11 Mark McGwire	3.00
12 Ken Griffey Jr.	2.50
13 Robb Nen	.25
14 Cal Ripken Jr.	4.00
15 John Valentin	.25
16 Ricky Bottalico	.25
17 Mike Lansing	.25
18 Ryne Sandberg	2.00
19 Carlos Delgado	1.00
20 Craig Biggio	.50
21 Eric Karros	.25
22 Kevin Appier	.25
23 Mariano Rivera	.75
24 Vinny Castilla	.25
25 Juan Gonzalez	.50
26 Al Martin	.25
27 Jeff Cirillo	.25
28 Ray Lankford	.25
29 Manny Ramirez	1.50
30 Roberto Alomar	.40
31 Will Clark	.50
32 Chuck Knoblauch	.25
33 Harold Baines	.25
34 Edgar Martinez	.25
35 Mike Mussina	.50
36 Kevin Brown	.25
37 Dennis Eckersley	.75
38 Tino Martinez	.25
39 Raul Mondesi	.25
40 Sammy Sosa	1.50
41 John Smoltz	.75
42 Billy Wagner	.25
43 Ken Caminiti	.25
44 Wade Boggs	1.50
45 Andres Galarraga	.25
46 Roger Clemens	3.00
47 Matt Williams	.25
48 Albert Belle	.25
49 Jeff King	.25
50 John Wetteland	.25
51 Deion Sanders	.50
52 Ellis Burks	.25
53 Pedro Martinez	1.50
54 Kenny Lofton	.25
55 Randy Johnson	1.50
56 Bernie Williams	.50
57 Marquis Grissom	.25
58 Gary Sheffield	.50

59 Curt Schilling	1.00
60 Reggie Sanders	.25
61 Bobby Higginson	.25
62 Moises Alou	.50
63 Tom Glavine	.50
64 Mark Grace	.50
65 Rafael Palmeiro	1.00
66 John Olerud	.25
67 Dante Bichette	.25
68 Jeff Bagwell	1.00
69 Barry Bonds	3.00
70 Pat Hentgen	.25
71 Jim Thome	1.00
72 Andy Pettitte	.50
73 Jay Bell	.25
74 Jim Edmonds	.50
75 Ron Gant	.25
76 David Cone	.25
77 Jose Canseco	.75
78 Jay Buhner	.25
79 Greg Maddux	2.50
80 Lance Johnson	.25
81 Travis Fryman	.25
82 Paul O'Neill	.50
83 Ivan Rodriguez	1.00
84 Fred McGriff	.25
85 Mike Piazza	2.50
86 Brady Anderson	.25
87 Marty Cordova	.25
88 Joe Carter	.25
89 Brian Jordan	.25
90 David Justice	.25
91 Tony Gwynn	2.00
92 Larry Walker	.40
93 Mo Vaughn	.25
94 Sandy Alomar	.25
95 Rusty Greer	.25
96 Roberto Hernandez	.25
97 Hal Morris	.25
98 Todd Hundley	.25
99 Rondell White	.25
100 Frank Thomas	1.50
101 Bubba Trammell RC	.75
102 Sidney Ponson RC	1.50
103 Ricky Ledee RC	.50
104 Brett Tomko	.25
105 Braden Looper RC	.50
106 Jason Dickson	.25
107 Chad Green RC	.25
108 R.A. Dickey RC	.25
109 Jeff Liefer	.25
110 Richard Hidalgo	.25
111 Chad Hermansen RC	.50
112 Felix Martinez	.25
113 J.J. Johnson	.25
114 Todd Dunwoody	.25
115 Katsuhiro Maeda	.25
116 Darin Erstad	.50
117 Elieser Marrero	.25
118 Bartolo Colon	.25
119 Ugueth Urbina	.25
120 Jaime Bluma	.25
121 Seth Greisinger RC	.50
122 Jose Cruz Jr. RC	1.50
123 Todd Dunn	.25
124 Justin Towle RC	.25
125 Brian Rose	.25
126 Jose Guillen	.25
127 Andruw Jones	1.50
128 Mark Kotsay RC	2.50
129 Wilton Guerrero	.25
130 Jacob Cruz	.25
131 Mike Sweeney	.25
132 Matt Morris	.25
133 John Thomson	.25
134 Javier Valentin RC	.25
135 Mike Drumbright RC	.25
136 Michael Barrett	.25
137 Tony Saunders RC	.25
138 Kevin Brown	.25
139 Anthony Sanders RC	.25
140 Jeff Abbott	.25
141 Eugene Kingsale	.25
142 Paul Konerko	.50
143 Randall Simon RC	.50
144 Freddy Garcia	.25
145 Karim Garcia	.25
146 Carlos Guillen	.25
147 Aaron Boone	.25
148 Donnie Sadler	.25
149 Brooks Kieschnick	.25
150 Scott Spiezio	.25
151 Kevin Orie	.25
152 Russ Johnson	.25
153 Livan Hernandez	.25
154 Vladimir Nunez RC	.75
155 Calvin Reese	.25
156 Chris Carpenter	.25
157 Eric Milton RC	1.50
158 Richie Sexson	.50
159 Carl Pavano	.25
160 Pat Cline	.25
161 Ron Wright	.25
162 Dante Powell	.25

163	Mark Bellhorn	.25
164	George Lombard	.25
165	Paul Wilder RC	.25
166	Brad Fullmer	.25
167	Kris Benson RC	2.00
168	Torii Hunter	.50
169	D.T. Cromer	.25
170	Nelson Figueroa RC	.50
171	Hiram Bocachica RC	.50
172	Shane Monahan	.25
173	Juan Melo	.25
174	Calvin Pickering RC	1.50
175	Reggie Taylor	.25
176	Geoff Jenkins	.25
177	Steve Rain RC	.25
178	Nerio Rodriguez	.25
179	Derrick Gibson	.25
180	Darin Blood	.25
181	Ben Davis	.25
182	Adrian Beltre RC	8.00
183	Kerry Wood RC	8.00
184	Nate Rolison	.25
185	Fernando Tatis RC	.50
186	Jake Westbrook RC	2.00
187	Edwin Diaz	.25
188	Joe Fontenot RC	.50
189	Matt Halloran RC	.25
190	Matt Clement RC	3.00
191	Todd Greene	.25
192	Eric Chavez RC	10.00
193	Edgard Velazquez	.25
194	Bruce Chen RC	.25
195	Jason Brester	.25
196	Chris Reitsma RC	.50
197	Neifi Perez	.25
198	Hideki Irabu RC	.50
199	Don Denbow RC	.25
200	Derrek Lee	.75
201	Todd Walker	1.00
202	Scott Rolen	1.00
203	Wes Helms	.25
204	Bob Abreu	.50
205	John Patterson RC	2.00
206	Alex Gonzalez RC	1.00
207	Grant Roberts RC	.50
208	Jeff Suppan	.25
209	Luke Wilcox	.25
210	Marlon Anderson	.25
211	Mike Caruso RC	.75
212	Roy Halladay RC	8.00
213	Jeremi Gonzalez RC	.50
214	Aramis Ramirez RC	10.00
215	Dermal Brown RC	.25
216	Justin Thompson	.25
217	Danny Clyburn	.25
218	Bruce Aven	.25
219	Keith Foulke RC	2.00
220	Shannon Stewart	.25
221	Larry Barnes	.25
222	Mark Johnson RC	.25
223	Randy Winn	.25
224	Nomar Garciaparra	2.00
225	Jacque Jones RC	4.00
226	Chris Clemons	.25
227	Todd Helton	1.00
228	Ryan Brannan RC	.25
229	Alex Sanchez RC	.50
230	Russell Branyan	.25
231	Daryle Ward	.25
232	Kevin Witt	.25
233	Gabby Martinez	.25
234	Preston Wilson	.25
235	Donzell McDonald RC	.25
236	Orlando Cabrera RC	5.00
237	Brian Banks	.25
238	Robbie Bell	.25
239	Brad Rigby	.25
240	Scott Elarton	.25
241	Donny Leon RC	.25
242	Abraham Nunez RC	1.00
243	Adam Eaton RC	2.00
244	Octavio Dotel RC	1.00
245	Sean Casey	.35
246	Joe Lawrence RC	.50
247	Adam Johnson RC	.25
248	Ronnie Belliard RC	1.00
249	Bobby Estalella	.25
250	Corey Lee RC	.25
251	Mike Cameron	.25
252	Kerry Robinson RC	.25
253	A.J. Zapp RC	.25
254	Jarrod Washburn	.25
255	Ben Grieve RC	.25
256	Javier Vazquez RC	3.00
257	Travis Lee RC	1.00
258	Dennis Reyes RC	.50
259	Danny Buxbaum	.25
260	Kelvim Escobar RC	1.00
261	Danny Klassen	.25
262	Ken Cloude RC	.50
263	Gabe Alvarez	.25
264	Clayton Brunner RC	.25
265	Jason Marquis RC	1.50
266	Jamey Wright	.25
267	Matt Snyder RC	.25

268	Josh Garrett RC	.25
269	Juan Encarnacion	.25
270	Heath Murray	.25
271	Brent Butler RC	1.00
272	Danny Peoples RC	.50
273	Miguel Tejada RC	30.00
274	Jim Pittsley	.25
275	Dmitri Young	.25
276	Vladimir Guerrero	1.50
277	Cole Liniak RC	.50
278	Ramon Hernandez	.25
279	Cliff Politte RC	.50
280	Mel Rosario RC	.25
281	Jorge Carrion RC	.25
282	John Barnes RC	.25
283	Chris Stowe RC	.25
284	Vernon Wells RC	15.00
285	Brett Caradonna RC	.25
286	Scott Hodges RC	.25
287	Jon Garland RC	4.00
288	Nathan Haynes RC	.50
289	Geoff Goetz RC	.50
290	Adam Kennedy RC	1.00
291	T.J. Tucker RC	.25
292	Aaron Akin RC	.25
293	Jayson Werth RC	2.50
294	Glenn Davis RC	.25
295	Mark Mangum RC	.25
296	Troy Cameron RC	.25
297	J.J. Davis RC	.25
298	Lance Berkman RC	15.00
299	Jason Standridge RC	.75
300	Jason Dellaero RC	.25

Refractors

NM/M

Common Player: 1.00
Stars: 4X
(See 1997 Bowman Chrome for checklist and base card values.)

International

NM/M

Common Player: 1.00
Stars: 3X
Inserted 1:4
(See 1997 Bowman Chrome for checklist and base card values.)

International Refractors

NM/M

Common Player: 2.00
Stars: 6X
(See 1997 Bowman Chrome for checklist and base card values.)

ROY Candidates

NM/M

Complete Set (15): 9.00
Common Player: .50
Refractors: 1.5X

1	Jeff Abbott	.50
2	Karim Garcia	.75
3	Todd Helton	2.50
4	Richard Hidalgo	.50
5	Geoff Jenkins	.50
6	Russ Johnson	.50
7	Paul Konerko	1.00
8	Mark Kotsay	.50
9	Ricky Ledee	.50
10	Travis Lee	.75
11	Ben Grieve	1.50
12	Elieser Marrero	.50
13	Juan Melo	.50
14	Brian Rose	.50
15	Fernando Tatis	.50

Scout's Honor Roll

NM/M

Complete Set (15): 12.00

Common Player: .50
Refractors: 1.5X

1	Dmitri Young	.75
2	Bob Abreu	.75
3	Vladimir Guerrero	2.00
4	Paul Konerko	.75
5	Kevin Orie	.50
6	Todd Walker	.50
7	Ben Grieve	.50
8	Darin Erstad	1.00
9	Derrek Lee	1.00
10	Jose Cruz, Jr.	.50
11	Scott Rolen	1.00
12	Travis Lee	.50
13	Andruw Jones	2.00
14	Wilton Guerrero	.50
15	Nomar Garciaparra	2.50

1997 Bowman's Best

NM/M

Complete Set (200): 25.00
Common Player: .25
Star Refractors: 4X
Star Atomics: 6X
Pack (6): 2.00
Wax Box (24): 40.00

1	Ken Griffey Jr.	1.50
2	Cecil Fielder	.25
3	Albert Belle	.25
4	Todd Hundley	.25
5	Mike Piazza	1.00
6	Matt Williams	.25
7	Mo Vaughn	.25
8	Ryne Sandberg	1.50
9	Chipper Jones	1.00
10	Edgar Martinez	.25
11	Kenny Lofton	.25
12	Ron Gant	.25
13	Moises Alou	.25
14	Pat Hentgen	.25
15	Steve Finley	.25
16	Mark Grace	.25
17	Jay Buhner	.25
18	Jeff Conine	.25
19	Jim Edmonds	.25
20	Todd Hollandsworth	.25
21	Andy Petitte	.50
22	Jim Thome	.75
23	Eric Young	.25
24	Ray Lankford	.25
25	Marquis Grissom	.25
26	Tony Clark	.25
27	Jermaine Allensworth	.25
28	Ellis Burks	.25
29	Tony Gwynn	1.50
30	Barry Larkin	.25
31	John Olerud	.25
32	Mariano Rivera	.40
33	Paul Molitor	1.00
34	Ken Caminiti	.25

35	Gary Sheffield	.45
36	Al Martin	.25
37	John Valentin	.25
38	Frank Thomas	.75
39	John Jaha	.25
40	Greg Maddux	1.50
41	Alex Fernandez	.25
42	Dean Palmer	.25
43	Bernie Williams	.25
44	Deion Sanders	.25
45	Mark McGwire	2.00
46	Brian Jordan	.25
47	Bernard Gilkey	.25
48	Will Clark	.25
49	Kevin Appier	.25
50	Tom Glavine	.40
51	Chuck Knoblauch	.25
52	Rondell White	.25
53	Greg Vaughn	.25
54	Mike Mussina	.50
55	Brian McRae	.25
56	Chili Davis	.25
57	Wade Boggs	1.50
58	Jeff Bagwell	.75
59	Roberto Alomar	.35
60	Dennis Eckersley	.50
61	Ryan Klesko	.25
62	Manny Ramirez	1.00
63	John Wetteland	.25
64	Cal Ripken Jr.	2.00
65	Edgar Renteria	.25
66	Tino Martinez	.25
67	Larry Walker	.25
68	Gregg Jefferies	.25
69	Lance Johnson	.25
70	Carlos Delgado	.50
71	Craig Biggio	.25
72	Jose Canseco	.50
73	Barry Bonds	2.00
74	Juan Gonzalez	.50
75	Eric Karros	.25
76	Reggie Sanders	.25
77	Robin Ventura	.25
78	Hideo Nomo	.50
79	David Justice	.25
80	Vinny Castilla	.25
81	Travis Fryman	.25
82	Derek Jeter	2.00
83	Sammy Sosa	1.50
84	Ivan Rodriguez	.75
85	Rafael Palmeiro	.75
86	Roger Clemens	2.00
87	Jason Giambi	.50
88	Andres Galarraga	.25
89	Jermaine Dye	.25
90	Joe Carter	.25
91	Brady Anderson	.25
92	Derek Bell	.25
93	Randy Johnson	1.00
94	Fred McGriff	.25
95	John Smoltz	.25
96	Harold Baines	.25
97	Raul Mondesi	.25
98	Tim Salmon	.25
99	Carlos Baerga	.25
100	Dante Bichette	.25
101	Vladimir Guerrero	1.00
102	Richard Hidalgo	.25
103	Paul Konerko	.25
104	Alex Gonzalez RC	.50
105	Jason Dickson	.25
106	Jose Rosado	.25
107	Todd Walker	.25
108	Seth Greisinger RC	.40
109	Todd Helton	.75
110	Ben Davis	.25
111	Bartolo Colon	.25
112	Elieser Marrero	.25
113	Jeff D'Amico	.25
114	Miguel Tejada RC	8.00
115	Darin Erstad	.50
116	Kris Benson RC	1.00
117	Adrian Beltre RC	2.00
118	Neifi Perez	.25
119	Calvin Reese	.25
120	Carl Pavano	.25
121	Juan Melo	.25
122	Kevin McGlinchy RC	.50
123	Pat Cline	.25
124	Felix Heredia RC	.40
125	Aaron Boone	.25
126	Glendon Rusch	.25
127	Mike Cameron	.25
128	Justin Thompson	.25
129	Chad Hermansen RC	.25
130	Sidney Ponson RC	1.00
131	Willie Martinez RC	.25
132	Paul Wilder RC	.25
133	Geoff Jenkins	.25
134	Roy Halladay RC	2.00
135	Carlos Guillen	.25
136	Tony Batista	.25
137	Todd Greene	.25
138	Luis Castillo	.25

139	Jimmy Anderson RC	.25
140	Edgard Velazquez	.25
141	Chris Snopek	.25
142	Ruben Rivera	.25
143	Javier Valentin RC	.25
144	Brian Rose	.25
145	Fernando Tatis RC	.50
146	Dean Crow RC	.25
147	Karim Garcia	.25
148	Dante Powell	.25
149	Hideki Irabu RC	.40
150	Matt Morris	.25
151	Wes Helms	.25
152	Russ Johnson	.25
153	Jarrod Washburn	.25
154	Kerry Wood RC	4.00
155	Joe Fontenot RC	.25
156	Eugene Kingsale	.25
157	Terrence Long	.25
158	Calvin Maduro	.25
159	Jeff Suppan	.25
160	DaRond Stovall	.25
161	Mark Redman	.25
162	Ken Cloude RC	.25
163	Bobby Estalella	.25
164	Abraham Nunez RC	.75
165	Derrick Gibson	.25
166	Mike Drumright RC	.25
167	Katsuhiro Maeda	.25
168	Jeff Liefer	.25
169	Ben Grieve	.25
170	Bob Abreu	.25
171	Shannon Stewart	.25
172	Braden Looper RC	.40
173	Brant Brown	.25
174	Marlon Anderson	.25
175	Brad Fullmer	.25
176	Carlos Beltran	.25
177	Nomar Garciaparra	1.50
178	Derrek Lee	.75
179	Valerio De Los Santos RC	.25
180	Dmitri Young	.25
181	Jamey Wright	.25
182	Hiram Bocachica RC	.25
183	Wilton Guerrero	.25
184	Chris Carpenter	.25
185	Scott Spiezio	.25
186	Andruw Jones	1.00
187	Travis Lee RC	.75
188	Jose Cruz Jr. RC	1.00
189	Jose Guillen	.25
190	Jeff Abbott	.25
191	Ricky Ledee RC	.40
192	Mike Sweeney	.25
193	Donnie Sadler	.25
194	Scott Rolen	.75
195	Kevin Orie	.25
196	Jason Conti RC	.25
197	Mark Kotsay RC	.75
198	Eric Milton RC	1.00
199	Russell Branyan	.25
200	Alex Sanchez RC	.50

Autographs

		NM/M
Complete Set (10):		150.00
Common Player:		5.00
Refractors:		1.5X
Atomics:		2X
29	Tony Gwynn	30.00
33	Paul Molitor	20.00
82	Derek Jeter	100.00
91	Brady Anderson	7.50
98	Tim Salmon	10.00
107	Todd Walker	5.00
183	Wilton Guerrero	5.00
185	Scott Spiezio	5.00
188	Jose Cruz Jr.	6.00
194	Scott Rolen	20.00

Cuts

	NM/M
Complete Set (20):	20.00

Common Player:		.35
Refractors:		1.5X
Atomic Refractors:		2X
1	Derek Jeter	4.00
2	Chipper Jones	1.50
3	Frank Thomas	1.00
4	Cal Ripken Jr.	4.00
5	Mark McGwire	3.00
6	Ken Griffey Jr.	2.00
7	Jeff Bagwell	1.00
8	Mike Piazza	2.00
9	Ken Caminiti	.35
10	Albert Belle	.35
11	Jose Cruz Jr.	.35
12	Wilton Guerrero	.35
13	Darin Erstad	.50
14	Andruw Jones	1.00
15	Scott Rolen	.75
16	Jose Guillen	.35
17	Bob Abreu	.35
18	Vladimir Guerrero	1.00
19	Todd Walker	.35
20	Nomar Garciaparra	1.50

Mirror Image

		NM/M
Complete Set (10):		35.00
Common Card:		2.00
Refractors:		1.5X
Atomic Refractors:		2X
1	Nomar Garciaparra, Derek Jeter, Hiram Bocachica, Barry Larkin	7.50
2	Travis Lee, Frank Thomas, Derrek Lee, Jeff Bagwell	3.50
3	Kerry Wood, Greg Maddux, Kris Benson, John Smoltz	3.50
4	Kevin Brown, Ivan Rodriguez, Elieser Marrero, Mike Piazza	5.00
5	Jose Cruz Jr., Ken Griffey Jr., Andruw Jones, Barry Bonds	7.50
6	Jose Guillen, Juan Gonzalez, Richard Hidalgo, Gary Sheffield	2.00
7	Paul Konerko, Mark McGwire, Todd Helton, Rafael Palmeiro	6.00
8	Wilton Guerrero, Craig Biggio, Donnie Sadler, Chuck Knoblauch	2.00
9	Russell Branyan, Matt Williams, Adrian Beltre, Chipper Jones	3.50
10	Bob Abreu, Kenny Lofton, Vladimir Guerrero, Albert Belle	3.00

1998 Bowman

		NM/M
Complete Set (441):		40.00
Series 1 (221):		20.00
Series 2 (220):		20.00
Common Player:		.10
Series 1 Pack (10):		2.00
Series 1 Wax Box (24):		30.00
Series 2 Pack (10):		1.50
Series 2 Wax Box (24):		25.00
1	Nomar Garciaparra	1.50
2	Scott Rolen	.75
3	Andy Pettitte	.30
4	Ivan Rodriguez	.65
5	Mark McGwire	2.50
6	Jason Dickson	.10
7	Jose Cruz Jr.	.10
8	Jeff Kent	.10
9	Mike Mussina	.30
10	Jason Kendall	.10
11	Brett Tomko	.10
12	Jeff King	.10
13	Brad Radke	.10
14	Robin Ventura	.10
15	Jeff Bagwell	1.00
16	Greg Maddux	1.50
17	John Jaha	.10
18	Mike Piazza	2.00
19	Edgar Martinez	.10
20	David Justice	.10
21	Todd Hundley	.10
22	Tony Gwynn	1.50
23	Larry Walker	.10
24	Bernie Williams	.10
25	Edgar Renteria	.10
26	Rafael Palmeiro	.75
27	Tim Salmon	.10
28	Matt Morris	.10
29	Shawn Estes	.10
30	Vladimir Guerrero	1.00
31	Fernando Tatis	.10
32	Justin Thompson	.10
33	Ken Griffey Jr.	2.00
34	Edgardo Alfonzo	.10
35	Mo Vaughn	.10
36	Marty Cordova	.10
37	Craig Biggio	.10
38	Roger Clemens	1.75
39	Mark Grace	.10
40	Ken Caminiti	.10
41	Tony Womack	.10
42	Albert Belle	.10
43	Tino Martinez	.10
44	Sandy Alomar	.10
45	Jeff Cirillo	.10
46	Jason Giambi	.50
47	Darin Erstad	.25
48	Livan Hernandez	.10
49	Mark Grudzielanek	.10
50	Sammy Sosa	1.50
51	Curt Schilling	.30
52	Brian Hunter	.10
53	Neifi Perez	.10
54	Todd Walker	.10
55	Jose Guillen	.10
56	Jim Thome	.10
57	Tom Glavine	.30
58	Todd Greene	.10
59	Rondell White	.10
60	Roberto Alomar	.25
61	Tony Clark	.10
62	Vinny Castilla	.10
63	Barry Larkin	.10
64	Hideki Irabu	.10
65	Johnny Damon	.35

66	Juan Gonzalez	.50
67	John Olerud	.10
68	Gary Sheffield	.25
69	Raul Mondesi	.10
70	Chipper Jones	1.50
71	David Ortiz	.50
72	Warren Morris RC	.50
73	Alex Gonzalez	.10
74	Nick Bierbrodt	.10
75	Roy Halladay	.10
76	Danny Buxbaum	.10
77	Adam Kennedy	.10
78	Jared Sandberg RC	.75
79	Michael Barrett	.10
80	Gil Meche	.10
81	Jayson Werth	.10
82	Abraham Nunez	.10
83	Ben Petrick	.10
84	Brett Caradonna	.10
85	Mike Lowell RC	3.00
86	Clay Bruner RC	.10
87	John Curtice RC	.10
88	Bobby Estalella	.10
89	Juan Melo	.10
90	Arnold Gooch	.10
91	Kevin Millwood RC	1.00
92	Richie Sexson	.10
93	Orlando Cabrera	.10
94	Pat Cline	.10
95	Anthony Sanders	.10
96	Russ Johnson	.10
97	Ben Grieve	.10
98	Kevin McGlinchy	.10
99	Paul Wilder	.10
100	Russ Ortiz	.10
101	Ryan Jackson RC	.10
102	Heath Murray	.10
103	Brian Rose	.10
104	Ryan Radmanovich RC	.10
105	Ricky Ledee	.10
106	Jeff Wallace RC	.10
107	Ryan Minor RC	.10
108	Dennis Reyes	.10
109	James Manias RC	.10
110	Chris Carpenter	.10
111	Daryle Ward	.10
112	Vernon Wells	.10
113	Chad Green	.10
114	Mike Stoner RC	.10
115	Brad Fullmer	.10
116	Adam Eaton	.10
117	Jeff Liefer	.10
118	Corey Koskie RC	1.00
119	Todd Helton	.75
120	Jaime Jones RC	.10
121	Mel Rosario	.10
122	Geoff Goetz	.10
123	Adrian Beltre	.40
124	Jason Dellaero	.10
125	Gabe Kapler RC	.50
126	Scott Schoeneweis	.10
127	Ryan Brannan	.10
128	Aaron Akin	.10
129	Ryan Anderson RC	.25
130	Brad Penny	.10
131	Bruce Chen	.10
132	Eli Marrero	.10
133	Eric Chavez	.30
134	Troy Glaus RC	3.00
135	Troy Cameron	.10
136	Brian Sikorski RC	.10
137	Mike Kinkade RC	.25
138	Braden Looper	.10
139	Mark Mangum	.10
140	Danny Peoples	.10
141	J.J. Davis	.10
142	Ben Davis	.10
143	Jacque Jones	.10
144	Derrick Gibson	.10
145	Bronson Arroyo	.10
146	Cristian Guzman RC	.50
147	Jeff Abbott	.10
148	Mike Cuddyer RC	1.00
149	Jason Romano	.10
150	Shane Monahan	.10
151	Ntema Ndungidi RC	.10
152	Alex Sanchez	.10
153	Jack Cust RC	1.50
154	Brent Butler	.10
155	Ramon Hernandez	.10
156	Norm Hutchins	.10
157	Jason Marquis	.10
158	Jacob Cruz	.10
159	Rob Burger RC	.10
160	Eric Milton	.10
161	Preston Wilson	.10
162	Jason Fitzgerald RC	.10
163	Dan Serafini	.10
164	Peter Munro	.10
165	Trot Nixon	.10
166	Homer Bush	.10
167	Dermal Brown	.10
168	Chad Hermansen	.10
169	Julio Moreno RC	.10

#	Player	Value
170	John Roskos RC	.10
171	Grant Roberts	.10
172	Ken Cloude	.10
173	Jason Brester	.10
174	Jason Conti	.10
175	Jon Garland	.10
176	Robbie Bell	.10
177	Nathan Haynes	.10
178	Ramon Ortiz RC	.50
179	Shannon Stewart	.10
180	Pablo Ortega	.10
181	Jimmy Rollins RC	4.00
182	Sean Casey	.30
183	Ted Lilly RC	.25
184	Chris Enochs RC	.10
185	Magglio Ordonez RC	3.00
186	Mike Drumright	.10
187	Aaron Boone	.10
188	Matt Clement	.10
189	Todd Dunwoody	.10
190	Larry Rodriguez	.10
191	Todd Noel	.10
192	Geoff Jenkins	.10
193	George Lombard	.10
194	Lance Berkman	.10
195	Marcus McCain RC	.10
196	Ryan McGuire	.10
197	Jhensy Sandoval RC	.10
198	Corey Lee	.10
199	Mario Valdez	.10
200	Robert Fick RC	.20
201	Donnie Sadler	.10
202	Marc Kroon	.10
203	David Miller	.10
204	Jarrod Washburn	.10
205	Miguel Tejada	.30
206	Raul Ibanez	.10
207	John Patterson	.10
208	Calvin Pickering	.10
209	Felix Martinez	.10
210	Mark Redman	.10
211	Scott Elarton	.10
212	Jose Amado RC	.10
213	Kerry Wood	.40
214	Dante Powell	.10
215	Aramis Ramirez	.10
216	A.J. Hinch	.10
217	Dustin Carr RC	.10
218	Mark Kotsay	.10
219	Jason Standridge	.10
220	Luis Ordaz	.10
221	Orlando Hernandez RC	.50
222	Cal Ripken Jr.	3.00
223	Paul Molitor	1.00
224	Derek Jeter	3.00
225	Barry Bonds	3.00
226	Jim Edmonds	.10
227	John Smoltz	.10
228	Eric Karros	.10
229	Ray Lankford	.10
230	Rey Ordonez	.10
231	Kenny Lofton	.10
232	Alex Rodriguez	2.50
233	Dante Bichette	.10
234	Pedro Martinez	1.00
235	Carlos Delgado	.45
236	Rod Beck	.10
237	Matt Williams	.10
238	Charles Johnson	.10
239	Rico Brogna	.10
240	Frank Thomas	1.00
241	Paul O'Neill	.10
242	Jaret Wright	.10
243	Brant Brown	.10
244	Ryan Klesko	.10
245	Chuck Finley	.10
246	Derek Bell	.10
247	Delino DeShields	.10
248	Chan Ho Park	.10
249	Wade Boggs	1.50
250	Jay Buhner	.10
251	Butch Huskey	.10
252	Steve Finley	.10
253	Will Clark	.10
254	John Valentin	.10
255	Bobby Higginson	.10
256	Darryl Strawberry	.10
257	Randy Johnson	1.00
258	Al Martin	.10
259	Travis Fryman	.10
260	Fred McGriff	.10
261	Jose Valentin	.10
262	Andruw Jones	1.00
263	Kenny Rogers	.10
264	Moises Alou	.10
265	Denny Neagle	.10
266	Ugueth Urbina	.10
267	Derrek Lee	.45
268	Ellis Burks	.10
269	Mariano Rivera	.30
270	Dean Palmer	.10
271	Eddie Taubensee	.10
272	Brady Anderson	.10
273	Brian Giles	.10
274	Quinton McCracken	.10
275	Henry Rodriguez	.10
276	Andres Galarraga	.10
277	Jose Canseco	.45
278	David Segui	.10
279	Bret Saberhagen	.10
280	Kevin Brown	.10
281	Chuck Knoblauch	.10
282	Jeromy Burnitz	.10
283	Jay Bell	.10
284	Manny Ramirez	1.00
285	Rick Helling	.10
286	Francisco Cordova	.10
287	Bob Abreu	.20
288	J.T. Snow Jr.	.10
289	Hideo Nomo	.50
290	Brian Jordan	.10
291	Javy Lopez	.10
292	Travis Lee	.10
293	Russell Branyan	.10
294	Paul Konerko	.10
295	Masato Yoshii RC	.50
296	Kris Benson	.10
297	Juan Encarnacion	.10
298	Eric Milton	.10
299	Mike Caruso	.10
300	Ricardo Aramboles RC	.10
301	Bobby Smith	.10
302	Billy Koch	.10
303	Richard Hidalgo	.10
304	Justin Baughman RC	.10
305	Chris Gissell	.10
306	Donnie Bridges RC	.10
307	Nelson Lara RC	.10
308	Randy Wolf RC	1.00
309	Jason LaRue RC	.25
310	Jason Gooding RC	.10
311	Edgar Clemente RC	.10
312	Andrew Vessel	.10
313	Chris Reitsma	.10
314	Jesus Sanchez RC	.10
315	Buddy Carlyle RC	.10
316	Randy Winn	.10
317	Luis Rivera	.10
318	Marcus Thames RC	1.50
319	A.J. Pierzynski	.10
320	Scott Randall	.10
321	Damian Sapp	.10
322	Eddie Yarnell RC	.10
323	Luke Allen RC	.10
324	J.D. Smart	.10
325	Willie Martinez	.10
326	Alex Ramirez	.10
327	Eric DuBose RC	.10
328	Kevin Witt	.10
329	Dan McKinley RC	.10
330	Cliff Politte	.10
331	Vladimir Nunez	.10
332	John Halama RC	.25
333	Nerio Rodriguez	.10
334	Desi Relaford	.10
335	Robinson Checo	.10
336	John Nicholson RC	.10
337	Tom LaRosa RC	.10
338	Kevin Nicholson RC	.10
339	Javier Vazquez	.10
340	A.J. Zapp	.10
341	Tom Evans	.10
342	Kerry Robinson	.10
343	Gabe Gonzalez RC	.10
344	Ralph Milliard	.10
345	Enrique Wilson	.10
346	Elvin Hernandez	.10
347	Mike Lincoln RC	.10
348	Cesar King RC	.10
349	Cristian Guzman RC	1.00
350	Donzell McDonald	.10
351	Jim Parque RC	.25
352	Mike Saipe RC	.10
353	Carlos Febles RC	.40
354	Dernell Stenson RC	.25
355	Mark Osborne RC	.10
356	Odalis Perez RC	.40
357	Jason Dewey RC	.10
358	Joe Fontenot	.10
359	Jason Grilli RC	.40
360	Kevin Haverbusch RC	.25
361	Jay Yennaco RC	.10
362	Brian Buchanan	.10
363	John Barnes	.10
364	Chris Fussell	.10
365	Kevin Gibbs RC	.10
366	Joe Lawrence	.10
367	DaRond Stovall	.10
368	Brian Fuentes RC	.10
369	Jimmy Anderson	.10
370	Laril Gonzalez RC	.10
371	Scott Williamson RC	.40
372	Milton Bradley	.10
373	Jason Halper RC	.10
374	Brent Billingsley RC	.10
375	Joe DePastino RC	.10
376	Jake Westbrook	.10
377	Octavio Dotel	.10
378	Jason Williams RC	.10
379	Julio Ramirez RC	.10
380	Seth Greisinger	.10
381	Mike Judd RC	.10
382	Ben Ford RC	.10
383	Tom Bennett	.10
384	Adam Butler RC	.10
385	Wade Miller RC	.75
386	Kyle Peterson RC	.10
387	Tommy Peterman RC	.10
388	Onan Masaoka	.10
389	Jason Rakers RC	.10
390	Rafael Medina	.10
391	Luis Lopez	.10
392	Jeff Yoder	.10
393	Vance Wilson RC	.25
394	Fernando Seguignol RC	.25
395	Ron Wright	.10
396	Ruben Mateo RC	.40
397	Steve Lomasney RC	.25
398	Damian Jackson	.10
399	Mike Jerzembeck RC	.10
400	Luis Rivas RC	.25
401	Kevin Burford	.10
402	Glenn Davis	.10
403	Robert Luce RC	.10
404	Cole Liniak	.10
405	Matthew LeCroy RC	.20
406	Jeremy Giambi RC	.40
407	Shawn Chacon	.10
408	Dewayne Wise RC	.10
409	Steve Woodard RC	.25
410	Francisco Cordero RC	.25
411	Damon Minor RC	.20
412	Lou Collier	.10
413	Justin Towle	.10
414	Juan LeBron	.10
415	Michael Coleman	.10
416	Felix Rodriguez	.10
417	Paul Ah Yat RC	.10
418	Kevin Barker RC	.25
419	Brian Meadows	.10
420	Darnell McDonald RC	.20
421	Matt Kinney RC	.25
422	Mike Vavrek RC	.10
423	Courtney Duncan RC	.10
424	Kevin Millar RC	.50
425	Ruben Rivera	.10
426	Steve Shoemaker RC	.10
427	Dan Reichert RC	.10
428	Carlos Lee RC	2.00
429	Rod Barajas	.10
430	Pablo Ozuna RC	.20
431	Todd Belitz RC	.10
432	Sidney Ponson	.10
433	Steve Carver RC	.10
434	Esteban Yan	.10
435	Cedrick Bowers RC	.10
436	Marlon Anderson	.10
437	Carl Pavano	.10
438	Jae Weong Seo RC	.50
439	Jose Taveras RC	.10
440	Matt Anderson RC	.25
441	Darron Ingram RC	.10

International

NM/M
Common Player: .25
Stars: 1.5X
Inserted 1:1
(See 1998 Bowman for check-list and base card values.)

Golden Anniversary

NM/M
Common Player: 4.00

Veteran Stars: 15-30X
Young Stars: 5-10X
Rookie Cards: 5-10X
(See 1998 Bowman for check-list and base card values.)

Autographs

Nomar Garciaparra

NM/M
Common Player: 3.00
Inserted 1:149
Silvers (1:992): 1.5-2.5X
Golds (1:2,976): 2-4X

#	Player	Value
1	Adrian Beltre	15.00
2	Brad Fullmer	5.00
3	Ricky Ledee	5.00
4	David Ortiz	35.00
5	Fernando Tatis	3.00
6	Kerry Wood	20.00
7	Mel Rosario	3.00
8	Cole Liniak	5.00
9	A.J. Hinch	5.00
10	Jhensy Sandoval	3.00
11	Jose Cruz Jr.	5.00
12	Richard Hidalgo	6.00
13	Geoff Jenkins	8.00
14	Carl Pavano	10.00
15	Richie Sexson	12.00
16	Tony Womack	5.00
17	Scott Rolen	20.00
18	Ryan Minor	5.00
19	Elieser Marrero	5.00
20	Jason Marquis	5.00
21	Mike Lowell	20.00
22	Todd Helton	20.00
23	Chad Green	3.00
24	Scott Elarton	3.00
25	Russell Branyan	5.00
26	Mike Drumright	3.00
27	Ben Grieve	5.00
28	Jacque Jones	8.00
29	Jared Sandberg	5.00
30	Grant Roberts	5.00
31	Mike Stoner	3.00
32	Brian Rose	3.00
33	Randy Winn	5.00
34	Justin Towle	3.00
35	Anthony Sanders	3.00
36	Rafael Medina	3.00
37	Corey Lee	3.00
38	Mike Kinkade	5.00
39	Norm Hutchins	3.00
40	Jason Brester	3.00
41	Ben Davis	5.00
42	Nomar Garciaparra	75.00
43	Jeff Liefer	3.00
44	Eric Milton	6.00
45	Preston Wilson	8.00
46	Miguel Tejada	30.00
47	Luis Ordaz	3.00
48	Travis Lee	5.00
49	Kris Benson	6.00
50	Jacob Cruz	5.00
51	Dermal Brown	3.00
52	Marc Kroon	3.00
53	Chad Hermansen	5.00
54	Roy Halladay	15.00
55	Eric Chavez	10.00
56	Jason Conti	3.00
57	Juan Encarnacion	5.00
58	Paul Wilder	3.00
59	Aramis Ramirez	15.00
60	Cliff Politte	3.00
61	Todd Dunwoody	5.00
62	Paul Konerko	10.00
63	Shane Monahan	3.00
64	Alex Sanchez	3.00
65	Jeff Abbott	3.00
66	John Patterson	3.00
67	Peter Munro	3.00
68	Jarrod Washburn	5.00
69	Derek Lee	20.00
70	Ramon Hernandez	

Japanese Rookies

Hideo Nomo (P)

		NM/M
Complete Set (3):		15.00
Common Player:		5.00
11	Hideo Nomo	10.00
17	Shigetosi Hasegawa	5.00
	Hideki Irabu	5.00

Minor League MVP

		NM/M
Complete Set (11):		9.00
Common Player:		.50
1	Jeff Bagwell	1.00
2	Andres Galarraga	.50
3	Juan Gonzalez	.60
4	Tony Gwynn	1.50
5	Vladimir Guerrero	1.00
6	Derek Jeter	3.00
7	Andruw Jones	1.00
8	Tino Martinez	.50
9	Manny Ramirez	1.00
10	Gary Sheffield	.60
11	Jim Thome	.65

Rookie of the Year Favorites

		NM/M
Complete Set (10):		6.00
Common Player:		.50
1	Adrian Beltre	.75
2	Troy Glaus	3.00
3	Chad Hermansen	.50
4	Matt Clement	.50
5	Eric Chavez	.75
6	Kris Benson	.50
7	Richie Sexson	.50
8	Randy Wolf	.50

9	Ryan Minor	.50
10	Alex Gonzalez	.50

Scout's Choice

Abraham Nunez

		NM/M
Complete Set (21):		8.00
Common Player:		.25
Inserted 1:12		
1	Paul Konerko	.50
2	Richard Hidalgo	.25
3	Mark Kotsay	.25
4	Ben Grieve	.25
5	Chad Hermansen	.25
6	Matt Clement	.25
7	Brad Fullmer	.25
8	Eli Marrero	.25
9	Kerry Wood	1.50
10	Adrian Beltre	1.50
11	Ricky Ledee	.25
12	Travis Lee	.25
13	Abraham Nunez	.25
14	Ryan Anderson	.25
15	Dermal Brown	.25
16	Juan Encarnacion	.25
17	Aramis Ramirez	.25
18	Todd Helton	2.50
19	Kris Benson	.25
20	Russell Branyan	.25
21	Mike Stoner	.25

1998 Bowman Chrome

NOMAR GARCIAPARRA

		NM/M
Complete Set (441):		100.00
Complete Series 1 (221):		60.00
Complete Series 2 (220):		50.00
Common Player:		.20
Series 1 Pack (4):		2.50
Series 2 Pack (4):		2.00
Series 1 Box (24):		45.00
Series 2 Box (24):		35.00
1	Nomar Garciaparra	1.00
2	Scott Rolen	.75
3	Andy Pettitte	.40
4	Ivan Rodriguez	.75
5	Mark McGwire	2.50
6	Jason Dickson	.20
7	Jose Cruz Jr.	.20
8	Jeff Kent	.20
9	Mike Mussina	.50
10	Jason Kendall	.20
11	Brett Tomko	.20
12	Jeff King	.20
13	Brad Radke	.20
14	Robin Ventura	.20
15	Jeff Bagwell	1.00
16	Greg Maddux	1.50
17	John Jaha	.20
18	Mike Piazza	2.00
19	Edgar Martinez	.20
20	David Justice	.20
21	Todd Hundley	.20

22	Tony Gwynn	1.50
23	Larry Walker	.20
24	Bernie Williams	.20
25	Edgar Renteria	.20
26	Rafael Palmeiro	.75
27	Tim Salmon	.20
28	Matt Morris	.20
29	Shawn Estes	.20
30	Vladimir Guerrero	1.00
31	Fernando Tatis	.20
32	Justin Thompson	.20
33	Ken Griffey Jr.	2.00
34	Edgardo Alfonzo	.20
35	Mo Vaughn	.20
36	Marty Cordova	.20
37	Craig Biggio	.20
38	Roger Clemens	2.00
39	Mark Grace	.20
40	Ken Caminiti	.20
41	Tony Womack	.20
42	Albert Belle	.20
43	Tino Martinez	.20
44	Sandy Alomar	.20
45	Jeff Cirillo	.20
46	Jason Giambi	.50
47	Darin Erstad	.45
48	Livan Hernandez	.20
49	Mark Grudzielanek	.20
50	Sammy Sosa	1.50
51	Curt Schilling	.50
52	Brian Hunter	.20
53	Neifi Perez	.20
54	Todd Walker	.20
55	Jose Guillen	.20
56	Jim Thome	.20
57	Tom Glavine	.40
58	Todd Greene	.20
59	Rondell White	.20
60	Roberto Alomar	.35
61	Tony Clark	.20
62	Vinny Castilla	.20
63	Barry Larkin	.20
64	Hideki Irabu	.20
65	Johnny Damon	.60
66	Juan Gonzalez	.50
67	John Olerud	.20
68	Gary Sheffield	.45
69	Raul Mondesi	.20
70	Chipper Jones	1.50
71	David Ortiz	.75
72	Warren Morris RC	.50
73	Alex Gonzalez	.20
74	Nick Bierbrodt	.20
75	Roy Halladay	.20
76	Danny Buxbaum	.20
77	Adam Kennedy	.20
78	Jared Sandberg RC	.50
79	Michael Barrett	.20
80	Gil Meche	.20
81	Jayson Werth	.20
82	Abraham Nunez	.20
83	Ben Petrick	.20
84	Brett Caradonna	.20
85	Mike Lowell RC	5.00
86	Clay Bruner RC	.20
87	John Curtice RC	.20
88	Bobby Estalella	.20
89	Juan Melo	.20
90	Arnold Gooch	.20
91	Kevin Millwood RC	4.00
92	Richie Sexson	.20
93	Orlando Cabrera	.20
94	Pat Cline	.20
95	Anthony Sanders	.20
96	Russ Johnson	.20
97	Ben Grieve	.20
98	Kevin McGlinchy	.20
99	Paul Wilder	.20
100	Russ Ortiz	.20
101	Ryan Jackson RC	.50
102	Heath Murray	.20
103	Brian Rose	.20
104	Ryan Radmanovich RC	.20
105	Ricky Ledee	.20
106	Jeff Wallace RC	.20
107	Ryan Minor RC	.45
108	Dennis Reyes	.20
109	James Manias RC	.20
110	Chris Carpenter	.20
111	Daryle Ward	.20
112	Vernon Wells	.20
113	Chad Green	.20
114	Mike Stoner RC	.20
115	Brad Fullmer	.20
116	Adam Eaton	.20
117	Jeff Liefer	.20
118	Corey Koskie RC	1.50
119	Todd Helton	.75
120	Jaime Jones RC	.20
121	Mel Rosario	.20
122	Geoff Goetz	.20
123	Adrian Beltre	.40
124	Jason Dellaero	.20

125	Gabe Kapler RC	1.00
126	Scott Schoeneweis	.20
127	Ryan Brannan	.20
128	Aaron Akin	.20
129	Ryan Anderson RC	.50
130	Brad Penny	.20
131	Bruce Chen	.20
132	Eli Marrero	.20
133	Eric Chavez	.35
134	Troy Glaus RC	10.00
135	Troy Cameron	.20
136	Brian Sikorski RC	.20
137	Mike Kinkade	.50
138	Braden Looper	.20
139	Mark Mangum	.20
140	Danny Peoples	.20
141	J.J. Davis	.20
142	Ben Davis	.20
143	Jacque Jones	.20
144	Derrick Gibson	.20
145	Bronson Arroyo	.20
146	Luis De Los Santos RC	.20
147	Jeff Abbott	.20
148	Mike Cuddyer RC	1.50
149	Jason Romano	.20
150	Shane Monahan	.20
151	Ntema Ndungidi RC	.20
152	Alex Sanchez	.20
153	Jack Cust RC	5.00
154	Brent Butler	.20
155	Ramon Hernandez	.20
156	Norm Hutchins	.20
157	Jason Marquis	.20
158	Jacob Cruz	.20
159	Rob Burger RC	.20
160	Eric Milton	.20
161	Preston Wilson	.20
162	Jason Fitzgerald RC	.20
163	Dan Serafini	.20
164	Peter Munro	.20
165	Trot Nixon	.40
166	Homer Bush	.20
167	Dermal Brown	.20
168	Chad Hermansen	.20
169	Julio Moreno RC	.20
170	John Roskos RC	.20
171	Grant Roberts	.20
172	Ken Cloude	.20
173	Jason Brester	.20
174	Jason Conti	.20
175	Jon Garland	.20
176	Robbie Bell	.20
177	Nathan Haynes	.20
178	Ramon Ortiz RC	.50
179	Shannon Stewart	.20
180	Pablo Ortega	.20
181	Jimmy Rollins RC	10.00
182	Sean Casey	.45
183	Ted Lilly RC	.20
184	Chris Enochs RC	.20
185	Magglio Ordonez RC	3.00
186	Mike Drumright	.20
187	Aaron Boone	.20
188	Matt Clement	.20
189	Todd Dunwoody	.20
190	Larry Rodriguez	.20
191	Todd Noel	.20
192	Geoff Jenkins	.20
193	George Lombard	.20
194	Lance Berkman	.20
195	Marcus McCain RC	.20
196	Ryan McGuire	.20
197	Jhensy Sandoval RC	.20
198	Corey Lee	.20
199	Mario Valdez	.20
200	Robert Fick RC	.20
201	Donnie Sadler	.20
202	Marc Kroon	.20
203	David Miller	.20
204	Jarrod Washburn	.20
205	Miguel Tejada	.40
206	Raul Ibanez	.20
207	John Patterson	.20
208	Calvin Pickering	.20
209	Felix Martinez	.20
210	Mark Redman	.20
211	Scott Elarton	.20
212	Jose Amado RC	.20
213	Kerry Wood	.50
214	Dante Powell	.20
215	Aramis Ramirez	.20
216	A.J. Hinch	.20
217	Dustin Carr RC	.20
218	Mark Kotsay	.20
219	Jason Standridge	.20
220	Luis Ordaz	.20
221	Orlando Hernandez RC	3.00
222	Cal Ripken Jr.	3.00
223	Paul Molitor	1.00
224	Derek Jeter	3.00
225	Barry Bonds	3.00
226	Jim Edmonds	.20

227	John Smoltz	.20
228	Eric Karros	.20
229	Ray Lankford	.20
230	Rey Ordonez	.20
231	Kenny Lofton	.20
232	Alex Rodriguez	2.50
233	Dante Bichette	.20
234	Pedro Martinez	1.00
235	Carlos Delgado	.50
236	Rod Beck	.20
237	Matt Williams	.20
238	Charles Johnson	.20
239	Rico Brogna	.20
240	Frank Thomas	1.00
241	Paul O'Neill	.20
242	Jaret Wright	.20
243	Brant Brown	.20
244	Ryan Klesko	.20
245	Chuck Finley	.20
246	Derek Bell	.20
247	Delino DeShields	.20
248	Chan Ho Park	.20
249	Wade Boggs	1.50
250	Jay Buhner	.20
251	Butch Huskey	.20
252	Steve Finley	.20
253	Will Clark	.20
254	John Valentin	.20
255	Bobby Higginson	.20
256	Darryl Strawberry	.20
257	Randy Johnson	1.00
258	Al Martin	.20
259	Travis Fryman	.20
260	Fred McGriff	.20
261	Jose Valentin	.20
262	Andruw Jones	1.00
263	Kenny Rogers	.20
264	Moises Alou	.20
265	Denny Neagle	.20
266	Ugueth Urbina	.20
267	Derrek Lee	.50
268	Ellis Burks	.20
269	Mariano Rivera	.40
270	Dean Palmer	.20
271	Eddie Taubensee	.20
272	Brady Anderson	.20
273	Brian Giles	.20
274	Quinton McCracken	.20
275	Henry Rodriguez	.20
276	Andres Galarraga	.20
277	Jose Canseco	.40
278	David Segui	.20
279	Bret Saberhagen	.20
280	Kevin Brown	.20
281	Chuck Knoblauch	.20
282	Jeromy Burnitz	.20
283	Jay Bell	.20
284	Manny Ramirez	1.00
285	Rick Helling	.20
286	Francisco Cordova	.20
287	Bob Abreu	.30
288	J.T. Snow Jr.	.20
289	Hideo Nomo	.50
290	Brian Jordan	.20
291	Javy Lopez	.20
292	Aaron Akin RC	.20
293	Russell Branyan	.20
294	Paul Konerko	.20
295	Masato Yoshii RC	1.00
296	Kris Benson	.20
297	Juan Encarnacion	.20
298	Eric Milton	.20
299	Mike Caruso	.20
300	Ricardo Aramboles RC	.20
301	Bobby Smith	.20
302	Billy Koch	.20
303	Richard Hidalgo	.20
304	Justin Baughman RC	.20
305	Chris Gissell	.20
306	Donnie Bridges RC	.20
307	Nelson Lara RC	.20
308	Randy Wolf RC	1.00
309	Jason LaRue RC	.50
310	Jason Gooding RC	.20
311	Edgar Clemente RC	.20
312	Andrew Vessel	.20
313	Chris Reitsma	.20
314	Jesus Sanchez RC	.20
315	Buddy Carlyle RC	.20
316	Randy Winn	.20
317	Luis Rivera	.20
318	Marcus Thames RC	5.00
319	A.J. Pierzynski	.20
320	Scott Randall	.20
321	Damian Sapp	.20
322	Eddie Yarnell RC	.20
323	Luke Allen RC	.20
324	J.D. Smart	.20
325	Willie Martinez	.20
326	Alex Ramirez	.20
327	Eric DuBose RC	.20
328	Kevin Witt	.20
329	Dan McKinley RC	.20
330	Cliff Politte	.20
331	Vladimir Nunez	.20
332	John Halama RC	.50
333	Nerio Rodriguez	.20
334	Desi Relaford	.20
335	Robinson Checo	.20
336	John Nicholson RC	.20
337	Tom LaRosa RC	.20
338	Kevin Nicholson RC	.20
339	Javier Vazquez	.20
340	A.J. Zapp	.20
341	Tom Evans	.20
342	Kerry Robinson	.20
343	Gabe Gonzalez RC	.20
344	Ralph Milliard	.20
345	Enrique Wilson	.20
346	Elvin Hernandez	.20
347	Mike Lincoln RC	.35
348	Cesar King RC	.20
349	Cristian Guzman RC	.50
350	Donzell McDonald	.20
351	Jim Parque RC	.20
352	Mike Saipe RC	.20
353	Carlos Febles RC	.50
354	Dernell Stenson RC	.20
355	Mark Osborne RC	.20
356	Odalis Perez RC	2.00
357	Jason Dewey RC	.20
358	Joe Fontenot	.20
359	Jason Grilli RC	.40
360	Kevin Haverbusch RC	.20
361	Jay Yennaco RC	.20
362	Brian Buchanan	.20
363	John Barnes	.20
364	Chris Fussell	.20
365	Kevin Gibbs RC	.20
366	Joe Lawrence	.20
367	DaRond Stovall	.20
368	Brian Fuentes RC	.20
369	Jimmy Anderson	.20
370	Laril Gonzalez RC	.20
371	Scott Williamson RC	1.00
372	Milton Bradley	.20
373	Jason Halper RC	.20
374	Brent Billingsley RC	.20
375	Joe DePastino RC	.20
376	Jake Westbrook	.20
377	Octavio Dotel	.20
378	Jason Williams RC	.20
379	Julio Ramirez RC	.20
380	Seth Greisinger	.20
381	Mike Judd RC	.20
382	Ben Ford RC	.20
383	Tom Bennett RC	.20
384	Adam Butler RC	.20
385	Wade Miller RC	1.50
386	Kyle Peterson RC	.20
387	Tommy Peterman RC	.20
388	Onan Masaoka	.20
389	Jason Rakers RC	.20
390	Rafael Medina	.20
391	Luis Lopez	.20
392	Jeff Yoder	.20
393	Vance Wilson RC	.20
394	Fernando Seguignol RC	.35
395	Ron Wright	.20
396	Ruben Mateo RC	1.00
397	Steve Lomasney RC	.50
398	Damian Jackson	.20
399	Mike Jerzembeck RC	.20
400	Luis Rivas RC	.50
401	Kevin Burford RC	.20
402	Glenn Davis	.20
403	Robert Luce RC	.20
404	Cole Liniak	.20
405	Matthew LeCroy RC	.50
406	Jeremy Giambi RC	.50
407	Shawn Chacon	.20
408	Dewayne Wise RC	.20
409	Steve Woodard RC	.50
410	Francisco Cordero RC	.20
411	Damon Minor RC	.20
412	Lou Collier	.20
413	Justin Towle	.20
414	Juan LeBron	.20
415	Michael Coleman	.20
416	Felix Rodriguez	.20
417	Paul Ah Yat RC	.20
418	Kevin Barker RC	.20
419	Brian Meadows	.20
420	Darnell McDonald RC	.40
421	Matt Kinney RC	.40
422	Mike Vavrek RC	.20
423	Courtney Duncan RC	.20
424	Kevin Millar RC	1.50
425	Ruben Rivera	.20
426	Steve Shoemaker RC	.20
427	Dan Reichert RC	.20
428	Carlos Lee RC	6.00
429	Rod Barajas RC	.20
430	Pablo Ozuna RC	.50
431	Todd Belitz RC	.20
432	Sidney Ponson	.20
433	Steve Carver RC	.20
434	Esteban Yan RC	.20
435	Cedrick Bowers RC	.20
436	Marlon Anderson	.20
437	Carl Pavano	.20
438	Jae Weong Seo RC	1.00
439	Jose Taveras RC	.20
440	Matt Anderson RC	.50
441	Darron Ingram RC	.20

International

	NM/M
Common Player:	.50
Stars and Rookies:	1.5X
Inserted 1:4	

(See 1998 Bowman Chrome for checklist and base card values.)

Refractors

	NM/M
Common Player:	2.00
Stars:	3X
Inserted 1:12	
Int'l Refractors:	6X
Inserted 1:24	

(See 1998 Bowman Chrome for checklist and base card values.)

Golden Anniversary

	NM/M
Common Player:	5.00
Stars:	20X
Common Refractor:	20.00

(See 1998 Bowman Chrome for checklist and base card values.)

Reprints

		NM/M
Complete Set (50):		20.00
Common Player:		.25
Inserted 1:12		
Refractors:		1.5X
Inserted 1:36		
1	Yogi Berra	.50
2	Jackie Robinson	2.00
3	Don Newcombe	.25
4	Satchel Paige	.50
5	Willie Mays	2.00
6	Gil McDougald	.25
7	Don Larsen	.25
8	Elston Howard	.25
9	Robin Ventura	.25
10	Brady Anderson	.25
11	Gary Sheffield	.35
12	Tino Martinez	.25
13	Ken Griffey Jr.	1.25
14	John Smoltz	.25
15	Sandy Alomar Jr.	.25
16	Larry Walker	.25
17	Todd Hundley	.25
18	Mo Vaughn	.25
19	Sammy Sosa	1.00
20	Frank Thomas	.50
21	Chuck Knoblauch	.25
22	Bernie Williams	.25
23	Juan Gonzalez	.40
24	Mike Mussina	.35
25	Jeff Bagwell	.50
26	Tim Salmon	.25
27	Ivan Rodriguez	.35
28	Kenny Lofton	.25
29	Chipper Jones	1.00
30	Javier Lopez	.25
31	Ryan Klesko	.25
32	Raul Mondesi	.25
33	Jim Thome	.35
34	Carlos Delgado	.25
35	Mike Piazza	1.25
36	Manny Ramirez	.50
37	Andy Pettitte	.35
38	Derek Jeter	2.00
39	Brad Fullmer	.25
40	Richard Hidalgo	.25
41	Tony Clark	.25
42	Andruw Jones	.50
43	Vladimir Guerrero	.50
44	Nomar Garciaparra	1.00
45	Paul Konerko	.35
46	Ben Grieve	.25
47	Hideo Nomo	.40
48	Scott Rolen	.40
49	Jose Guillen	.25
50	Livan Hernandez	.25

1998 Bowman's Best

		NM/M
Complete Set (200):		30.00
Common Player:		.25
Pack (6):		2.50
Wax Box (24):		35.00
1	Mark McGwire	2.00
2	Hideo Nomo	.50
3	Barry Bonds	3.00
4	Dante Bichette	.25
5	Chipper Jones	1.50
6	Frank Thomas	1.00
7	Kevin Brown	.25
8	Juan Gonzalez	.50
9	Jay Buhner	.25
10	Chuck Knoblauch	.25
11	Cal Ripken Jr.	3.00
12	Matt Williams	.25
13	Jim Edmonds	.25
14	Manny Ramirez	1.00
15	Tony Clark	.25
16	Mo Vaughn	.25
17	Bernie Williams	.25
18	Scott Rolen	.75
19	Gary Sheffield	.40
20	Albert Belle	.25
21	Mike Piazza	2.00
22	John Olerud	.25
23	Tony Gwynn	1.50
24	Jay Bell	.25
25	Jose Cruz Jr.	.25
26	Justin Thompson	.25
27	Ken Griffey Jr.	2.00
28	Sandy Alomar	.25
29	Mark Grudzielanek	.25
30	Mark Grace	.25
31	Ron Gant	.25
32	Javy Lopez	.25
33	Jeff Bagwell	1.00
34	Fred McGriff	.25
35	Rafael Palmeiro	.75
36	Vinny Castilla	.25
37	Andy Benes	.25
38	Pedro Martinez	1.00
39	Andy Pettitte	.40
40	Marty Cordova	.25
41	Rusty Greer	.25
42	Kevin Orie	.25

43	Chan Ho Park	.25
44	Ryan Klesko	.25
45	Alex Rodriguez	2.50
46	Travis Fryman	.25
47	Jeff King	.25
48	Roger Clemens	2.00
49	Darin Erstad	.50
50	Brady Anderson	.25
51	Jason Kendall	.25
52	John Valentin	.25
53	Ellis Burks	.25
54	Brian Hunter	.25
55	Paul O'Neill	.25
56	Ken Caminiti	.25
57	David Justice	.25
58	Eric Karros	.25
59	Pat Hentgen	.25
60	Greg Maddux	1.50
61	Craig Biggio	.25
62	Edgar Martinez	.25
63	Mike Mussina	.50
64	Larry Walker	.25
65	Tino Martinez	.25
66	Jim Thome	.60
67	Tom Glavine	.40
68	Raul Mondesi	.25
69	Marquis Grissom	.25
70	Randy Johnson	1.00
71	Steve Finley	.25
72	Jose Guillen	.25
73	Nomar Garciaparra	1.50
74	Wade Boggs	1.50
75	Bobby Higginson	.25
76	Robin Ventura	.25
77	Derek Jeter	3.00
78	Andruw Jones	1.00
79	Ray Lankford	.25
80	Vladimir Guerrero	1.00
81	Kenny Lofton	.25
82	Ivan Rodriguez	.75
83	Neifi Perez	.25
84	John Smoltz	.25
85	Tim Salmon	.25
86	Carlos Delgado	.50
87	Sammy Sosa	1.50
88	Jaret Wright	.25
89	Roberto Alomar	.40
90	Paul Molitor	1.00
91	Dean Palmer	.25
92	Barry Larkin	.25
93	Jason Giambi	.50
94	Curt Schilling	.40
95	Eric Young	.25
96	Denny Neagle	.25
97	Moises Alou	.25
98	Livan Hernandez	.25
99	Todd Hundley	.25
100	Andres Galarraga	.25
101	Travis Lee	.25
102	Lance Berkman	.25
103	Orlando Cabrera	.25
104	Mike Lowell RC	2.00
105	Ben Grieve	.25
106	Jae Weong Seo RC	.50
107	Richie Sexson	.25
108	Eli Marrero	.25
109	Aramis Ramirez	.25
110	Paul Konerko	.25
111	Carl Pavano	.25
112	Brad Fullmer	.25
113	Matt Clement	.25
114	Donzell McDonald	.25
115	Todd Helton	.75
116	Mike Caruso	.25
117	Donnie Sadler	.25
118	Bruce Chen	.25
119	Jarrod Washburn	.25
120	Adrian Beltre	.40
121	Ryan Jackson RC	.50
122	Kevin Millar RC	1.50
123	Corey Koskie RC	1.00
124	Dermal Brown	.25
125	Kerry Wood	.50
126	Juan Melo	.25
127	Ramon Hernandez	.25
128	Roy Halladay	.25
129	Ron Wright	.25
130	Darnell McDonald RC	.50
131	Odalis Perez RC	.75
132	Alex Cora RC	.25
133	Justin Towle	.25
134	Juan Encarnacion	.25
135	Brian Rose	.25
136	Russell Branyan	.25
137	Cesar King RC	.25
138	Ruben Rivera	.25
139	Ricky Ledee	.25
140	Vernon Wells	.25
141	Luis Rivas RC	.50
142	Brent Butler	.25
143	Karim Garcia	.25
144	George Lombard	.25
145	Masato Yoshii RC	.25
146	Braden Looper	.25
147	Alex Sanchez	.25
148	Kris Benson	.25
149	Mark Kotsay	.25
150	Richard Hidalgo	.25
151	Scott Elarton	.25
152	Ryan Minor RC	.25
153	Troy Glaus RC	5.00
154	Carlos Lee RC	2.00
155	Michael Coleman	.25
156	Jason Grilli RC	.50
157	Julio Ramirez RC	.50
158	Randy Wolf RC	.75
159	Ryan Brannan	.25
160	Edgar Clemente RC	.50
161	Miguel Tejada	.40
162	Chad Hermansen	.25
163	Ryan Anderson RC	.50
164	Ben Petrick	.25
165	Alex Gonzalez	.25
166	Ben Davis	.25
167	John Patterson	.25
168	Cliff Politte	.25
169	Randall Simon	.25
170	Javier Vazquez	.25
171	Kevin Witt	.25
172	Geoff Jenkins	.25
173	David Ortiz	.60
174	Derrick Gibson	.25
175	Abraham Nunez	.25
176	A.J. Hinch	.25
177	Ruben Mateo RC	.75
178	Magglio Ordonez RC	2.50
179	Todd Dunwoody	.25
180	Daryle Ward	.25
181	Mike Kinkade RC	.50
182	Willie Martinez	.25
183	Orlando Hernandez RC	1.50
184	Eric Milton	.25
185	Eric Chavez	.50
186	Damian Jackson	.25
187	Jim Parque RC	.50
188	Dan Reichert RC	.25
189	Mike Drumright	.25
190	Todd Walker	.25
191	Shane Monahan	.25
192	Derrek Lee	.65
193	Jeremy Giambi RC	.50
194	Dan McKinley RC	.25
195	Tony Armas RC	.75
196	Matt Anderson RC	.50
197	Jim Chamblee RC	.25
198	Francisco Cordero RC	.25
199	Calvin Pickering	.25
200	Reggie Taylor	.25

Refractors

	NM/M
Common Player:	4.00
Stars:	8X

Production 400 Sets
(See 1998 Bowman's Best for checklist and base card values.)

Atomic Refractors

	NM/M
Common Player:	6.00
Stars:	12X

Production 100 Sets
(See 1998 Bowman's Best for checklist and base card values.)

Autographs

	NM/M
Complete Set (10):	65.00
Common Player:	5.00
Inserted 1:180	
Refractors:	1.5X
Inserted 1:2,158	
Atomics:	2X
Inserted 1:6,437	
5 Chipper Jones	30.00
10 Chuck Knoblauch	5.00
15 Tony Clark	5.00
20 Albert Belle	8.00
25 Jose Cruz Jr.	5.00
105 Ben Grieve	5.00
110 Paul Konerko	15.00
115 Todd Helton	15.00
120 Adrian Beltre	15.00
125 Kerry Wood	20.00

Mirror Image Fusion

	NM/M
Complete Set (20):	35.00
Common Player (1:12):	.50
Refractor (1:809):	6X
Atomic (1:3,237):	12X
1 Frank Thomas, David Ortiz	2.00
2 Chuck Knoblauch, Enrique Wilson	.50
3 Nomar Garciaparra, Miguel Tejada	2.50
4 Alex Rodriguez, Mike Caruso	3.50
5 Cal Ripken Jr., Ryan Minor	4.50
6 Ken Griffey Jr., Ben Grieve	3.00
7 Juan Gonzalez, Juan Encarnacion	.75
8 Jose Cruz Jr., Ruben Mateo	.50
9 Randy Johnson, Ryan Anderson	1.50
10 Ivan Rodriguez, A.J. Hinch	1.25
11 Jeff Bagwell, Paul Konerko	1.50
12 Mark McGwire, Travis Lee	3.50
13 Craig Biggio, Chad Hermanson	.50
14 Mark Grudzielanek, Alex Gonzalez	.50
15 Chipper Jones, Adrian Beltre	2.50
16 Larry Walker, Mark Kotsay	.50
17 Tony Gwynn, Preston Wilson	2.50
18 Barry Bonds, Richard Hidalgo	4.50
19 Greg Maddux, Kerry Wood	2.50
20 Mike Piazza, Ben Petrick	3.00

Performers

	NM/M
Complete Set (10):	4.00
Common Player:	.35
Refractor (1:309):	3X
Atomic Refractor (1:3,237):	5X
1 Ben Grieve	.35
2 Travis Lee	.35
3 Ryan Minor	.35
4 Todd Helton	2.00
5 Brad Fullmer	.35
6 Paul Konerko	.50
7 Adrian Beltre	.75
8 Richie Sexson	.35
9 Aramis Ramirez	.35
10 Russell Branyan	.35

1999 Bowman

	NM/M
Complete Set (440):	60.00
Complete Series 1 (220):	30.00
Complete Series 2 (220):	35.00
Common Player:	.10
Series 1 Pack (10):	2.00
Series 1 Box (24):	35.00

Series 2 Pack (10):		3.00
Series 2 Box (24):		50.00
1	Ben Grieve	.10
2	Kerry Wood	.40
3	Ruben Rivera	.10
4	Sandy Alomar	.10
5	Cal Ripken Jr.	2.00
6	Mark McGwire	1.75
7	Vladimir Guerrero	.75
8	Moises Alou	.10
9	Jim Edmonds	.10
10	Greg Maddux	1.00
11	Gary Sheffield	.40
12	John Valentin	.10
13	Chuck Knoblauch	.10
14	Tony Clark	.10
15	Rusty Greer	.10
16	Al Leiter	.10
17	Travis Lee	.10
18	Jose Cruz Jr.	.10
19	Pedro Martinez	.75
20	Paul O'Neill	.10
21	Todd Walker	.10
22	Vinny Castilla	.10
23	Barry Larkin	.10
24	Curt Schilling	.40
25	Jason Kendall	.10
26	Scott Erickson	.10
27	Andres Galarraga	.10
28	Jeff Shaw	.10
29	John Olerud	.10
30	Orlando Hernandez	.10
31	Larry Walker	.10
32	Andruw Jones	.75
33	Jeff Cirillo	.10
34	Barry Bonds	2.00
35	Manny Ramirez	.75
36	Mark Kotsay	.10
37	Ivan Rodriguez	.60
38	Jeff King	.10
39	Brian Hunter	.10
40	Ray Durham	.10
41	Bernie Williams	.10
42	Darin Erstad	.30
43	Chipper Jones	1.00
44	Pat Hentgen	.10
45	Eric Young	.10
46	Jaret Wright	.10
47	Juan Guzman	.10
48	Jorge Posada	.10
49	Bobby Higginson	.10
50	Jose Guillen	.10
51	Trevor Hoffman	.10
52	Ken Griffey Jr.	1.50
53	David Justice	.10
54	Matt Williams	.10
55	Eric Karros	.10
56	Derek Bell	.10
57	Ray Lankford	.10
58	Mariano Rivera	.25
59	Brett Tomko	.10
60	Mike Mussina	.40
61	Kenny Lofton	.10
62	Chuck Finley	.10
63	Alex Gonzalez	.10
64	Mark Grace	.10
65	Raul Mondesi	.10
66	David Cone	.10
67	Brad Fullmer	.10
68	Andy Benes	.10
69	John Smoltz	.10
70	Shane Reynolds	.10
71	Bruce Chen	.10
72	Adam Kennedy	.10
73	Jack Cust	.10
74	Matt Clement	.10
75	Derrick Gibson	.10
76	Darnell McDonald	.10
77	Adam Everett RC	.50
78	Ricardo Aramboles	.10
79	Mark Quinn RC	.25
80	Jason Rakers	.10
81	Seth Etherton RC	.35

82	Jeff Urban RC	.25
83	Manny Aybar	.10
84	Mike Nannini RC	.25
85	Onan Masaoka	.10
86	Rod Barajas	.10
87	Mike Frank	.10
88	Scott Randall	.10
89	Justin Bowles RC	.25
90	Chris Haas	.10
91	Arturo McDowell RC	.10
92	Matt Belisle RC	.35
93	Scott Elarton	.10
94	Vernon Wells	.10
95	Pat Cline	.10
96	Ryan Anderson	.10
97	Kevin Barker	.10
98	Ruben Mateo	.10
99	Robert Fick	.10
100	Corey Koskie	.10
101	Ricky Ledee	.10
102	Rick Elder RC	.25
103	Jack Cressend RC	.10
104	Joe Lawrence	.10
105	Mike Lincoln	.10
106	Kit Pellow RC	.35
107	Matt Burch RC	.10
108	Brent Butler	.10
109	Jason Dewey	.10
110	Cesar King	.10
111	Julio Ramirez	.10
112	Jake Westbrook	.10
113	Eric Valent RC	.35
114	Roosevelt Brown RC	.10
115	Choo Freeman RC	.50
116	Juan Melo	.10
117	Jason Grilli	.10
118	Jared Sandberg	.10
119	Glenn Davis	.10
120	David Riske RC	.25
121	Jacque Jones	.10
122	Corey Lee	.10
123	Michael Barrett	.10
124	Lariel Gonzalez	.10
125	Mitch Meluskey	.10
126	Freddy Garcia	.10
127	Tony Torcato RC	.25
128	Jeff Liefer	.10
129	Ntema Ndungidi	.10
130	Andy Brown RC	.35
131	Ryan Mills RC	.25
132	Andy Abad RC	.25
133	Carlos Febles	.10
134	Jason Tyner RC	.25
135	Mark Osborne	.10
136	Phil Norton RC	.10
137	Nathan Haynes	.10
138	Roy Halladay	.10
139	Juan Encarnacion	.10
140	Brad Penny	.10
141	Grant Roberts	.10
142	Aramis Ramirez	.10
143	Cristian Guzman	.10
144	Mamon Tucker RC	.25
145	Ryan Bradley	.10
146	Brian Simmons	.10
147	Dan Reichert	.10
148	Russ Branyon	.10
149	Victor Valencia RC	.25
150	Scott Schoeneweis	.10
151	Sean Spencer RC	.10
152	Odalis Perez	.10
153	Joe Fontenot	.10
154	Milton Bradley	.10
155	Josh McKinley RC	.25
156	Terrence Long	.10
157	Danny Klassen	.10
158	Paul Hoover RC	.25
159	Ron Belliard	.10
160	Armando Rios	.10
161	Ramon Hernandez	.10
162	Jason Conti	.10
163	Chad Hermansen	.10
164	Jason Standridge	.10
165	Jason Dellaero	.10
166	John Curtice	.10
167	Clayton Andrews RC	.25
168	Jeremy Giambi	.10
169	Alex Ramirez	.10
170	Gabe Molina RC	.25
171	Mario Encarnacion RC	.25
172	Mike Zywica RC	.25
173	Chip Ambres RC	.25
174	Trot Nixon	.10
175	Pat Burrell RC	2.00
176	Jeff Yoder	.10
177	Chris Jones RC	.25
178	Kevin Witt	.10
179	Keith Luuloa RC	.25
180	Billy Koch	.10
181	Damaso Marte RC	.25
182	Ryan Glynn RC	.25
183	Calvin Pickering	.10
184	Michael Cuddyer	.10
185	Nick Johnson RC	.75

186	Doug Mientkiewicz RC	1.00
187	Nate Cornejo RC	.35
188	Octavio Dotel	.10
189	Wes Helms	.10
190	Nelson Lara	.10
191	Chuck Abbott RC	.25
192	Tony Armas Jr.	.10
193	Gil Meche	.10
194	Ben Petrick	.10
195	Chris George RC	.25
196	Scott Hunter RC	.25
197	Ryan Brannan	.10
198	Amaury Garcia RC	.25
199	Chris Gissell	.10
200	Austin Kearns RC	1.50
201	Alex Gonzalez	.10
202	Wade Miller	.10
203	Scott Williamson	.10
204	Chris Enochs	.10
205	Fernando Seguignol	.10
206	Marlon Anderson	.10
207	Todd Sears RC	.25
208	Nate Bump RC	.25
209	J.M. Gold RC	.25
210	Matt LeCroy	.10
211	Alex Hernandez	.10
212	Luis Rivera	.10
213	Troy Cameron	.10
214	Alex Escobar RC	.50
215	Jason LaRue	.10
216	Kyle Peterson	.10
217	Brent Butler	.10
218	Dernell Stenson	.10
219	Adrian Beltre	.40
220	Daryle Ward	.10
----	Series 1 Checklist Folder	.10
221	Jim Thome	.60
222	Cliff Floyd	.10
223	Rickey Henderson	.75
224	Garret Anderson	.10
225	Ken Caminiti	.10
226	Bret Boone	.10
227	Jeromy Burnitz	.10
228	Steve Finley	.10
229	Miguel Tejada	.40
230	Greg Vaughn	.10
231	Jose Offerman	.10
232	Andy Ashby	.10
233	Albert Belle	.10
234	Fernando Tatis	.10
235	Todd Helton	.65
236	Sean Casey	.25
237	Brian Giles	.10
238	Andy Pettitte	.25
239	Fred McGriff	.10
240	Roberto Alomar	.30
241	Edgar Martinez	.10
242	Lee Stevens	.10
243	Shawn Green	.25
244	Ryan Klesko	.10
245	Sammy Sosa	1.00
246	Todd Hundley	.10
247	Shannon Stewart	.10
248	Randy Johnson	.75
249	Rondell White	.10
250	Mike Piazza	1.50
251	Craig Biggio	.10
252	David Wells	.10
253	Brian Jordan	.10
254	Edgar Renteria	.10
255	Bartolo Colon	.10
256	Frank Thomas	.75
257	Will Clark	.10
258	Dean Palmer	.10
259	Dmitri Young	.10
260	Scott Rolen	.60
261	Jeff Kent	.10
262	Dante Bichette	.10
263	Nomar Garciaparra	1.00
264	Tony Gwynn	1.00
265	Alex Rodriguez	1.75
266	Jose Canseco	.45
267	Jason Giambi	.40
268	Jeff Bagwell	.75
269	Carlos Delgado	.40
270	Tom Glavine	.40
271	Eric Davis	.10
272	Edgardo Alfonzo	.10
273	Tim Salmon	.10
274	Johnny Damon	.35
275	Rafael Palmeiro	.65
276	Denny Neagle	.10
277	Neifi Perez	.10
278	Roger Clemens	1.25
279	Brant Brown	.10
280	Kevin Brown	.10
281	Jay Bell	.10
282	Jay Buhner	.10
283	Matt Lawton	.10
284	Robin Ventura	.10
285	Juan Gonzalez	.35
286	Mo Vaughn	.10
287	Kevin Millwood	.10

288	Tino Martinez	.10
289	Justin Thompson	.10
290	Derek Jeter	2.00
291	Ben Davis	.10
292	Mike Lowell	.10
293	Joe Crede RC	.75
294	Micah Bowie RC	.25
295	Lance Berkman	.10
296	Jason Marquis	.10
297	Chad Green	.10
298	Dee Brown	.10
299	Jerry Hairston Jr.	.10
300	Gabe Kapler	.10
301	Brent Stentz RC	.25
302	Scott Mullen RC	.25
303	Brandon Reed	.10
304	Shea Hillenbrand RC	.50
305	J.D. Closser RC	.25
306	Gary Matthews Jr.	.10
307	Toby Hall RC	.25
308	Jason Phillips RC	.25
309	Jose Macias RC	.25
310	Jung Bong RC	.25
311	Ramon Soler RC	.25
312	Kelly Dransfeldt RC	.25
313	Carlos Hernandez RC	.25
314	Kevin Haverbusch RC	.10
315	Aaron Myette RC	.25
316	Chad Harville RC	.35
317	Kyle Farnsworth RC	.50
318	Travis Dawkins RC	.50
319	Willie Martinez	.10
320	Carlos Lee	.10
321	Carlos Pena RC	1.00
322	Peter Bergeron RC	.25
323	A.J. Burnett RC	.50
324	Bucky Jacobsen RC	.25
325	Mo Bruce RC	.25
326	Reggie Taylor	.10
327	Jackie Rexrode	.10
328	Alvin Morrow RC	.25
329	Carlos Beltran	.40
330	Eric Chavez	.25
331	John Patterson	.10
332	Jayson Werth	.10
333	Richie Sexson	.10
334	Randy Wolf	.10
335	Eli Marrero	.10
336	Paul LoDuca	.10
337	J.D. Smart	.10
338	Ryan Minor	.10
339	Kris Benson	.10
340	George Lombard	.10
341	Troy Glaus	.75
342	Eddie Yarnell	.10
343	Kip Wells RC	.50
344	C.C. Sabathia RC	1.00
345	Sean Burroughs RC	.50
346	Felipe Lopez RC	1.50
347	Ryan Rupe RC	.25
348	Orber Moreno RC	.25
349	Rafael Roque RC	.10
350	Alfonso Soriano RC	5.00
351	Pablo Ozuna	.10
352	Corey Patterson RC	1.00
353	Braden Looper	.10
354	Robbie Bell	.10
355	Mark Mulder RC	2.00
356	Angel Pena	.10
357	Kevin McGlinchy	.10
358	Michael Restovich RC	.35
359	Eric DuBose	.10
360	Geoff Jenkins	.10
361	Mark Harriger RC	.25
362	Junior Herndon RC	.25
363	Tim Raines Jr. RC	.25
364	Rafael Furcal RC	.75
365	Marcus Giles RC	1.00
366	Ted Lilly	.10
367	Jorge Toca RC	.25
368	David Kelton RC	.35
369	Adam Dunn RC	5.00
370	Guillermo Mota RC	.35
371	Brett Laxton RC	.25
372	Travis Harper RC	.25
373	Tom Davey RC	.25
374	Darren Blakely RC	.25
375	Tim Hudson RC	3.00
376	Jason Romano	.10
377	Dan Reichert	.10
378	Julio Lugo RC	.75
379	Jose Garcia RC	.25
380	Erubiel Durazo RC	.25
381	Jose Jimenez	.10
382	Chris Fussell	.10
383	Steve Lomasney	.10
384	Juan Pena RC	.25
385	Allen Levrault RC	.25
386	Juan Rivera RC	.25
387	Steve Colyer RC	.25
388	Joe Nathan RC	.25
389	Ron Walker RC	.10
390	Nick Bierbrodt	.10
391	Luke Prokopec RC	.25

392	Dave Roberts RC	.40
393	Mike Darr	.10
394	Abraham Nunez RC	.35
395	Giuseppe Chiaramonte RC	.25
396	Jermaine Van Buren RC	.25
397	Mike Kusiewicz	.10
398	Matt Wise RC	.25
399	Joe McEwing RC	.40
400	Matt Holliday RC	5.00
401	Willi Mo Pena RC	1.50
402	Ruben Quevedo RC	.25
403	Rob Ryan RC	.25
404	Freddy Garcia RC	1.00
405	Kevin Eberwein RC	.25
406	Jesus Colome RC	.25
407	Chris Singleton RC	.25
408	Bubba Crosby RC	.50
409	Jesus Cordero RC	.25
410	Donny Leon	.10
411	Goefrey Tomlinson RC	.25
412	Jeff Winchester RC	.25
413	Adam Piatt RC	.50
414	Robert Stratton	.10
415	T.J. Tucker	.10
416	Ryan Langerhans RC	.25
417	Anthony Shumaker RC	.25
418	Matt Miller RC	.25
419	Doug Clark RC	.25
420	Kory DeHaan RC	.25
421	David Eckstein RC	.75
422	Brian Cooper RC	.25
423	Brady Clark RC	.25
424	Chris Magruder RC	.25
425	Bobby Seay RC	.25
426	Aubrey Huff RC	1.00
427	Mike Jerzembeck	.10
428	Matt Blank RC	.25
429	Benny Agbayani RC	.25
430	Kevin Beirne RC	.25
431	Josh Hamilton RC	4.00
432	Josh Girdley RC	.25
433	Kyle Snyder RC	.25
434	Mike Paradis RC	.25
435	Jason Jennings RC	.25
436	David Walling RC	.25
437	Omar Ortiz RC	.25
438	Jay Gehrke RC	.25
439	Casey Burns RC	.25
440	Carl Crawford RC	2.50

Gold

	NM/M
Common Player:	3.00
Gold Stars:	10X

(See 1999 Bowman for checklist and base card values.)

International

	NM/M
Common Player:	.25

Int'l Stars: 1.5X
(See 1999 Bowman for
checklist and base card values.)

1999 Bowman Pre-Production

		NM/M
Complete Set (6):		4.00
Common Player:		.60
1	Andres Galarraga	.60
2	Raul Mondesi	.60
3	Vinny Castilla	.60
4	Corey Koskie	2.00
5	Octavio Dotel	.60
6	Dernell Stenson	.60

Autographs

		NM/M
Common Player:		3.00
Blues inserted 1:162 or 1:85		
Silvers inserted 1:485 or 1:256		
Golds inserted 1:1,954 or 1:1,024		
1	Ruben Mateo/S	5.00
2	Troy Glaus/G	40.00
3	Ben Davis/G	8.00
4	Jayson Werth/B	5.00
5	Jerry Hairston Jr./S	6.00
6	Darnell McDonald/B	4.00
7	Calvin Pickering/S	8.00
8	Ryan Minor/S	4.00
9	Alex Escobar/B	6.00
10	Grant Roberts/B	5.00
11	Carlos Guillen/B	10.00
12	Ryan Anderson/S	6.00
13	Gil Meche/S	5.00
14	Russell Branyan/S	5.00
15	Alex Ramirez/S	5.00
16	Jason Rakers/S	5.00
17	Eddie Yarnall/B	5.00
18	Freddy Garcia/B	20.00
19	Jason Conti/B	3.00
20	Corey Koskie/B	5.00
21	Roosevelt Brown/B	5.00
22	Willie Martinez/B	3.00
23	Mike Jerzembeck/B	3.00
24	Lariel Gonzalez/B	3.00
25	Fernando Seguignol/B	3.00
26	Robert Fick/S	5.00
27	J.D. Smart/B	3.00
28	Ryan Mills/B	3.00
29	Chad Hermansen/G	6.00
30	Jason Grilli/B	5.00
31	Michael Cuddyer/B	5.00
32	Jacque Jones/S	10.00
33	Reggie Taylor/B	3.00
34	Richie Sexson/G	15.00
35	Michael Barrett/B	8.00
36	Paul LoDuca/B	8.00
37	Adrian Beltre/G	30.00
38	Peter Bergeron/B	4.00
39	Joe Fontenot/B	3.00
40	Randy Wolf/B	6.00
41	Nick Johnson/B	12.00
42	Ryan Bradley/B	4.00
43	Mike Lowell/S	10.00
44	Ricky Ledee/B	5.00
45	Mike Lincoln/S	4.00
46	Jeremy Giambi/B	5.00
47	Dermal Brown/B	3.00
48	Derrick Gibson/B	3.00
49	Scott Randall/B	3.00
50	Ben Petrick/S	3.00
51	Jason LaRue/B	3.00
52	Cole Liniak/B	3.00
53	John Curtice/B	3.00
54	Jackie Rexrode/B	3.00
55	John Patterson/B	4.00
56	Brad Penny/S	6.00
57	Jared Sandberg/B	6.00
58	Kerry Wood/G	20.00
59	Eli Marrero/B	5.00
60	Jason Marquis/B	8.00
61	George Lombard/S	5.00
62	Bruce Chen/S	3.00
63	Kevin Witt/S	4.00
64	Vernon Wells/B	15.00
65	Billy Koch/B	3.00
66	Roy Halladay/B	20.00
67	Nathan Haynes/B	3.00
68	Ben Grieve/G	8.00
69	Eric Chavez/G	10.00
70	Lance Berkman/S	15.00

Early Risers

		NM/M
Complete Set (11):		8.00
Common Player:		.25
Inserted 1:12		
1	Mike Piazza	1.00
2	Cal Ripken Jr.	2.00
3	Jeff Bagwell	.50
4	Ben Grieve	.25
5	Kerry Wood	.40
6	Mark McGwire	1.50
7	Nomar Garciaparra	.75
8	Derek Jeter	2.00
9	Scott Rolen	.50
10	Jose Canseco	.45
11	Raul Mondesi	.25

Late Bloomers

		NM/M
Complete Set (10):		4.00
Common Player:		.25
Inserted 1:12		
LB1	Mike Piazza	2.00
LB2	Jim Thome	.75
LB3	Larry Walker	.25
LB4	Vinny Castilla	.25
LB5	Andy Pettitte	.50
LB6	Jim Edmonds	.25
LB7	Kenny Lofton	.25
LB8	John Smoltz	.25
LB9	Mark Grace	.25
LB10	Trevor Hoffman	.25

Scout's Choice

		NM/M
Complete Set (21):		12.00
Common Player:		.40
Inserted 1:12		
SC1	Ruben Mateo	.40
SC2	Ryan Anderson	.40
SC3	Pat Burrell	3.00
SC4	Troy Glaus	4.00
SC5	Eric Chavez	1.00
SC6	Adrian Beltre	1.00
SC7	Bruce Chen	.40
SC8	Carlos Beltran	1.00
SC9	Alex Gonzalez	.40
SC10	Carlos Lee	.50
SC11	George Lombard	.40
SC12	Matt Clement	.40
SC13	Calvin Pickering	.40
SC14	Marlon Anderson	.40
SC15	Chad Hermansen	.40
SC16	Russell Branyan	.40
SC17	Jeremy Giambi	.40
SC18	Ricky Ledee	.40
SC19	John Patterson	.40
SC20	Roy Halladay	.75
SC21	Michael Barrett	.40

2000 Rookie of the Year

		NM/M
Complete Set (10):		7.00
Common Player:		.50
Inserted 1:12		
1	Ryan Anderson	.50
2	Pat Burrell	2.50
3	A.J. Burnett	.50
4	Ruben Mateo	.50
5	Alex Escobar	.50
6	Pablo Ozuna	.50
7	Mark Mulder	1.00
8	Corey Patterson	1.00
9	George Lombard	.50
10	Nick Johnson	.50

1999 Bowman Chrome

JUAN GONZALEZ

		NM/M
Complete Set (440):		175.00
Complete Series 1 (220):		65.00
Complete Series 2 (220):		125.00
Common Player:		.25
Series 1 Pack (4):		3.00
Series 1 Wax Box (24):		50.00
Series 2 Pack (4):		5.00
Series 2 Wax Box (24):		100.00
1	Ben Grieve	.25
2	Kerry Wood	.45
3	Ruben Rivera	.25
4	Sandy Alomar	.25
5	Cal Ripken Jr.	3.00
6	Mark McGwire	2.50
7	Vladimir Guerrero	1.00
8	Moises Alou	.25
9	Jim Edmonds	.25
10	Greg Maddux	1.50
11	Gary Sheffield	.50
12	John Valentin	.25
13	Chuck Knoblauch	.25
14	Tony Clark	.25
15	Rusty Greer	.25
16	Al Leiter	.25
17	Travis Lee	.25
18	Jose Cruz Jr.	.25
19	Pedro Martinez	1.00
20	Paul O'Neill	.25
21	Todd Walker	.25
22	Vinny Castilla	.25
23	Barry Larkin	.25
24	Curt Schilling	.40
25	Jason Kendall	.25
26	Scott Erickson	.25
27	Andres Galarraga	.25
28	Jeff Shaw	.25
29	John Olerud	.25
30	Orlando Hernandez	.40
31	Larry Walker	.25
32	Andruw Jones	↑.00
33	Jeff Cirillo	.25
34	Barry Bonds	3.00
35	Manny Ramirez	1.00
36	Mark Kotsay	.25
37	Ivan Rodriguez	.75
38	Jeff King	.25
39	Brian Hunter	.25
40	Ray Durham	.25
41	Bernie Williams	.25
42	Darin Erstad	.50
43	Chipper Jones	1.50
44	Pat Hentgen	.25
45	Eric Young	.25
46	Jaret Wright	.25
47	Juan Guzman	.25
48	Jorge Posada	.25
49	Bobby Higginson	.25
50	Jose Guillen	.25
51	Trevor Hoffman	.25
52	Ken Griffey Jr.	2.00
53	David Justice	.25
54	Matt Williams	.25
55	Eric Karros	.25
56	Derek Bell	.25
57	Ray Lankford	.25
58	Mariano Rivera	.40
59	Brett Tomko	.25
60	Mike Mussina	.50
61	Kenny Lofton	.25
62	Chuck Finley	.25
63	Alex Gonzalez	.25
64	Mark Grace	.25
65	Raul Mondesi	.25
66	David Cone	.25
67	Brad Fullmer	.25
68	Andy Benes	.25
69	John Smoltz	.25
70	Shane Reynolds	.25
71	Bruce Chen	.25
72	Adam Kennedy	.25
73	Jack Cust	.25
74	Matt Clement	.25
75	Derrick Gibson	.25
76	Darnell McDonald	.25
77	Adam Everett RC	.75
78	Ricardo Aramboles	.25
79	Mark Quinn RC	.50
80	Jason Rakers	.25
81	Seth Etherton RC	.50
82	Jeff Urban RC	.35
83	Manny Aybar	.25
84	Mike Nannini RC	.35
85	Onan Masaoka	.25

86	Rod Barajas	.25
87	Mike Frank	.25
88	Scott Randall	.25
89	Justin Bowles RC	.35
90	Chris Haas	.25
91	Arturo McDowell RC	.35
92	Matt Belisle RC	.50
93	Scott Elarton	.25
94	Vernon Wells	.25
95	Pat Cline	.25
96	Ryan Anderson	.25
97	Kevin Barker	.25
98	Ruben Mateo	.25
99	Robert Fick	.25
100	Corey Koskie	.25
101	Ricky Ledee	.25
102	Rick Elder RC	.25
103	Jack Cressend RC	.35
104	Joe Lawrence	.25
105	Mike Lincoln	.25
106	Kit Pellow RC	.50
107	Matt Burch RC	.35
108	Brent Butler	.25
109	Jason Dewey	.25
110	Cesar King	.25
111	Julio Ramirez	.25
112	Jake Westbrook	.25
113	Eric Valent RC	1.00
114	Roosevelt Brown RC	.50
115	Choo Freeman RC	1.50
116	Juan Melo	.25
117	Jason Grilli	.25
118	Jared Sandberg	.25
119	Glenn Davis	.25
120	David Riske RC	.35
121	Jacque Jones	.25
122	Corey Lee	.25
123	Michael Barrett	.25
124	Lariel Gonzalez	.25
125	Mitch Meluskey	.25
126	Freddy Garcia	.25
127	Tony Torcato RC	.35
128	Jeff Liefer	.25
129	Ntema Ndungidi	.25
130	Andy Brown RC	.50
131	Ryan Mills RC	.35
132	Andy Abad RC	.50
133	Carlos Febles	.25
134	Jason Tyner RC	.50
135	Mark Osborne	.25
136	Phil Norton RC	.35
137	Nathan Haynes	.25
138	Roy Halladay	.25
139	Juan Encarnacion	.25
140	Brad Penny	.25
141	Grant Roberts	.25
142	Aramis Ramirez	.25
143	Cristian Guzman	.25
144	Mamon Tucker RC	.35
145	Ryan Bradley	.25
146	Brian Simmons	.25
147	Dan Reichert	.25
148	Russ Branyon	.25
149	Victor Valencia RC	.25
150	Scott Schoeneweis	.25
151	Sean Spencer RC	.25
152	Odalis Perez	.25
153	Joe Fontenot	.25
154	Milton Bradley	.25
155	Josh McKinley RC	.35
156	Terrence Long	.25
157	Danny Klassen	.25
158	Paul Hoover RC	.35
159	Ron Belliard	.25
160	Armando Rios	.25
161	Ramon Hernandez	.25
162	Jason Conti	.25
163	Chad Hermansen	.25
164	Jason Standridge	.25
165	Jason Dellaero	.25
166	John Curtice	.25
167	Clayton Andrews RC	.35
168	Jeremy Giambi	.25
169	Alex Ramirez	.25
170	Gabe Molina RC	.35
171	Mario Encarnacion RC	.35
172	Mike Zywica RC	.35
173	Chip Ambres RC	.35
174	Trot Nixon	.25
175	Pat Burrell RC	10.00
176	Jeff Yoder	.25
177	Chris Jones RC	.35
178	Kevin Witt	.25
179	Keith Luuloa RC	.35
180	Billy Koch	.25
181	Damaso Marte RC	.35
182	Ryan Glynn RC	.35
183	Calvin Pickering	.25
184	Michael Cuddyer	.25
185	Nick Johnson RC	4.00
186	Doug Mientkiewicz RC	2.00
187	Nate Cornejo RC	1.00
188	Octavio Dotel	.25
189	Wes Helms	.25
190	Nelson Lara	.25
191	Chuck Abbott RC	.35
192	Tony Armas Jr.	.25
193	Gil Meche	.25
194	Ben Petrick	.25
195	Chris George RC	.35
196	Scott Hunter RC	.35
197	Ryan Brannan	.25
198	Amaury Garcia RC	.35
199	Chris Gissell	.25
200	Austin Kearns RC	5.00
201	Alex Gonzalez	.25
202	Wade Miller	.25
203	Scott Williamson	.25
204	Chris Enochs	.25
205	Fernando Seguignol	.25
206	Marlon Anderson	.25
207	Todd Sears RC	.35
208	Nate Bump RC	.35
209	J.M. Gold RC	.50
210	Matt LeCroy RC	.35
211	Alex Hernandez	.25
212	Luis Rivera	.25
213	Troy Cameron	.25
214	Alex Escobar RC	1.00
215	Jason LaRue	.25
216	Kyle Peterson	.25
217	Brent Butler	.25
218	Dernell Stenson	.25
219	Adrian Beltre	.40
220	Daryle Ward	.25
221	Jim Thome	.65
222	Cliff Floyd	.25
223	Rickey Henderson	1.00
224	Garret Anderson	.25
225	Ken Caminiti	.25
226	Bret Boone	.25
227	Jeromy Burnitz	.25
228	Steve Finley	.25
229	Miguel Tejada	.40
230	Greg Vaughn	.25
231	Jose Offerman	.25
232	Andy Ashby	.25
233	Albert Belle	.25
234	Fernando Tatis	.25
235	Todd Helton	.75
236	Sean Casey	.40
237	Brian Giles	.25
238	Andy Pettitte	.40
239	Fred McGriff	.25
240	Roberto Alomar	.40
241	Edgar Martinez	.25
242	Lee Stevens	.25
243	Shawn Green	.40
244	Ryan Klesko	.25
245	Sammy Sosa	1.50
246	Todd Hundley	.25
247	Shannon Stewart	.25
248	Randy Johnson	1.00
249	Rondell White	.25
250	Mike Piazza	2.00
251	Craig Biggio	.25
252	David Wells	.25
253	Brian Jordan	.25
254	Edgar Renteria	.25
255	Bartolo Colon	.25
256	Frank Thomas	1.00
257	Will Clark	.25
258	Dean Palmer	.25
259	Dmitri Young	.25
260	Scott Rolen	.65
261	Jeff Kent	.25
262	Dante Bichette	.25
263	Nomar Garciaparra	1.50
264	Tony Gwynn	1.50
265	Alex Rodriguez	2.00
266	Jose Canseco	.50
267	Jason Giambi	.50
268	Jeff Bagwell	1.00
269	Carlos Delgado	.65
270	Tom Glavine	.50
271	Eric Davis	.25
272	Edgardo Alfonzo	.25
273	Tim Salmon	.25
274	Johnny Damon	.50
275	Rafael Palmeiro	.75
276	Denny Neagle	.25
277	Neifi Perez	.25
278	Roger Clemens	1.75
279	Brant Brown	.25
280	Kevin Brown	.25
281	Jay Bell	.25
282	Jay Buhner	.25
283	Matt Lawton	.25
284	Robin Ventura	.25
285	Juan Gonzalez	.50
286	Mo Vaughn	.25
287	Kevin Millwood	.25
288	Tino Martinez	.25
289	Justin Thompson	.25
290	Derek Jeter	3.00
291	Ben Davis	.25
292	Mike Lowell	.25
293	Joe Crede RC	3.00
294	Micah Bowie RC	.50
295	Lance Berkman	.25
296	Jason Marquis	.25
297	Chad Green	.25
298	Dee Brown	.25
299	Jerry Hairston Jr.	.25
300	Gabe Kapler	.25
301	Brent Stentz RC	.35
302	Scott Mullen RC	.25
303	Brandon Reed	.25
304	Shea Hillenbrand RC	2.50
305	J.D. Closser RC	1.00
306	Gary Matthews Jr.	.25
307	Toby Hall RC	1.00
308	Jason Phillips RC	.35
309	Jose Macias RC	.50
310	Jung Bong RC	.35
311	Ramon Soler RC	.35
312	Kelly Dransfeldt RC	.75
313	Carlos Hernandez RC	.50
314	Kevin Haverbusch	.25
315	Aaron Myette RC	.75
316	Chad Harville RC	.75
317	Kyle Farnsworth RC	1.00
318	Travis Dawkins RC	.75
319	Willie Martinez	.25
320	Carlos Lee	.35
321	Carlos Pena RC	4.00
322	Peter Bergeron RC	.50
323	A.J. Burnett RC	4.00
324	Bucky Jacobsen RC	1.00
325	Mo Bruce RC	.35
326	Reggie Taylor	.25
327	Jackie Rexrode	.25
328	Alvin Morrow RC	.35
329	Carlos Beltran	.50
330	Eric Chavez	.50
331	John Patterson	.25
332	Jayson Werth	.25
333	Richie Sexson	.25
334	Randy Wolf	.25
335	Eli Marrero	.25
336	Paul LoDuca	.25
337	J.D. Smart	.25
338	Ryan Minor	.25
339	Kris Benson	.25
340	George Lombard	.25
341	Troy Glaus	.75
342	Eddie Yarnell	.25
343	Kip Wells RC	1.00
344	C.C. Sabathia RC	4.00
345	Sean Burroughs RC	1.00
346	Felipe Lopez RC	5.00
347	Ryan Rupe RC	.75
348	Orber Moreno RC	.50
349	Rafael Roque RC	.35
350	Alfonso Soriano RC	25.00
351	Pablo Ozuna	.25
352	Corey Patterson RC	3.00
353	Braden Looper	.25
354	Robbie Bell	.25
355	Mark Mulder RC	4.00
356	Angel Pena	.25
357	Kevin McGlinchy	.25
358	Michael Restovich RC	1.00
359	Eric DuBose	.25
360	Geoff Jenkins	.25
361	Mark Harriger RC	.35
362	Junior Herndon RC	.35
363	Tim Raines Jr. RC	.35
364	Rafael Furcal RC	3.00
365	Marcus Giles RC	2.00
366	Ted Lilly	.25
367	Jorge Toca RC	.35
368	David Kelton RC	1.50
369	Adam Dunn RC	25.00
370	Guillermo Mota RC	.35
371	Brett Laxton RC	.35
372	Travis Harper RC	.35
373	Tom Davey RC	.35
374	Darren Blakely RC	.35
375	Tim Hudson RC	10.00
376	Jason Romano RC	.25
377	Dan Reichert RC	.25
378	Julio Lugo RC	.35
379	Jose Garcia RC	.35
380	Erubiel Durazo RC	1.50
381	Jose Jimenez	.25
382	Chris Fussell	.25
383	Steve Lomasney	.25
384	Juan Pena RC	.75
385	Allen Levrault RC	.35
386	Juan Rivera RC	.35
387	Steve Colyer RC	.35
388	Joe Nathan RC	1.50
389	Ron Walker RC	.35
390	Nick Bierbrodt	.25
391	Luke Prokopec RC	.35
392	Dave Roberts RC	.50
393	Mike Darr	.25
394	Abraham Nunez RC	1.00
395	Giuseppe Chiaramonte RC	.35
396	Jermaine Van Buren RC	.35
397	Mike Kusiewicz	.25
398	Matt Wise RC	.35
399	Joe McEwing RC	.50
400	Matt Holliday RC	20.00
401	Willi Mo Pena RC	4.00
402	Ruben Quevedo RC	.35
403	Rob Ryan RC	.35
404	Freddy Garcia RC	3.00
405	Kevin Eberwein RC	.35
406	Jesus Colome RC	.35
407	Chris Singleton RC	.35
408	Bubba Crosby RC	1.50
409	Jesus Cordero RC	.35
410	Donny Leon	.25
411	Goefrey Tomlinson RC	.35
412	Jeff Winchester RC	.35
413	Adam Piatt RC	.50
414	Robert Stratton	.25
415	T.J. Tucker RC	.25
416	Ryan Langerhans RC	1.50
417	Chris Wakeland RC	.35
418	Matt Miller RC	.35
419	Doug Clark RC	.35
420	Kory DeHaan RC	.35
421	David Eckstein RC	2.00
422	Brian Cooper RC	.35
423	Brady Clark RC	1.50
424	Chris Magruder RC	.35
425	Bobby Seay RC	.50
426	Aubrey Huff RC	5.00
427	Mike Jerzembeck	.25
428	Matt Blank RC	.35
429	Benny Agbayani RC	.35
430	Kevin Beirne RC	.35
431	Josh Hamilton RC	15.00
432	Josh Girdley RC	.35
433	Kyle Snyder RC	.35
434	Mike Paradis RC	.35
435	Jason Jennings RC	.75
436	David Walling RC	.35
437	Omar Ortiz RC	.35
438	Jay Gehrke RC	.35
439	Casey Burns RC	.35
440	Carl Crawford RC	12.00

Refractors

PAT HENTGEN

NM/M

Common Player:	1.00
Refractor Stars:	5X

(See 1999 Bowman Chrome for checklist and base card values.)

International

BRUCE CHEN

NM/M

Common Player, Series 1:	.25
Common Player, Series 2:	.50
Stars:	1.5X
Common Refractor:	5.00
Refractors:	12X

(See 1999 Bowman Chrome for checklist and base card values.)

Gold

NM/M

Common Player, Series 1:	1.50
Common Player, Series 2:	2.00
Stars:	3X
Gold Refractors:	30X

(See 1999 Bowman Chrome for checklist and base card values.)

Diamond Aces

NM/M

Complete Set (18): 24.00
Common Player: .50
Inserted 1:21
Refractors: 1.5X
Inserted 1:84

DA1	Troy Glaus	1.50
DA2	Eric Chavez	.75
DA3	Fernando Seguignol	.50
DA4	Ryan Anderson	.50
DA5	Ruben Mateo	.50
DA6	Carlos Beltran	1.00
DA7	Adrian Beltre	.75
DA8	Bruce Chen	.50
DA9	Pat Burrell	2.00
DA10	Mike Piazza	3.00
DA11	Ken Griffey Jr.	3.00
DA12	Chipper Jones	2.00
DA13	Derek Jeter	4.00
DA14	Mark McGwire	3.50
DA15	Nomar Garciaparra	2.00
DA16	Sammy Sosa	2.00
DA17	Juan Gonzalez	.75
DA18	Alex Rodriguez	3.50

Early Impact

NM/M

Complete Set (20): 35.00

Common Player: .75
Inserted 1:15
Refractor: 1.5X
Inserted 1:75

1	Alfonso Soriano	2.00
2	Pat Burrell	2.00
3	Ruben Mateo	.75
4	A.J. Burnett	.75
5	Corey Patterson	1.00
6	Daryle Ward	.75
7	Eric Chavez	1.00
8	Troy Glaus	2.00
9	Sean Casey	1.00
10	Joe McEwing	.75
11	Gabe Kapler	.75
12	Michael Barrett	.75
13	Sammy Sosa	2.50
14	Alex Rodriguez	4.00
15	Mark McGwire	4.00
16	Derek Jeter	5.00
17	Nomar Garciaparra	2.50
18	Mike Piazza	3.00
19	Chipper Jones	2.50
20	Ken Griffey Jr.	3.00

Scout's Choice

NM/M

Complete Set (21): 20.00
Common Player: .75
Inserted 1:12
Refractors: 1.5X
Inserted 1:48

SC1	Ruben Mateo	.75
SC2	Ryan Anderson	.75
SC3	Pat Burrell	3.00
SC4	Troy Glaus	4.00
SC5	Eric Chavez	2.00
SC6	Adrian Beltre	1.50
SC7	Bruce Chen	.75
SC8	Carlos Beltran	2.50
SC9	Alex Gonzalez	.75
SC10	Carlos Lee	1.00
SC11	George Lombard	.75
SC12	Matt Clement	.75
SC13	Calvin Pickering	.75
SC14	Marlon Anderson	.75
SC15	Chad Hermansen	.75
SC16	Russell Branyan	.75
SC17	Jeremy Giambi	.75
SC18	Ricky Ledee	.75
SC19	John Patterson	.75
SC20	Roy Halladay	1.00
SC21	Michael Barrett	.75

2000 Rookie of the Year

NM/M

Complete Set (10): 12.00
Common Player: 1.00
Inserted 1:20
Refractors: 1.5-3X
Inserted 1:100

1	Ryan Anderson	1.00
2	Pat Burrell	4.00
3	A.J. Burnett	1.00
4	Ruben Mateo	1.00
5	Alex Escobar	1.00
6	Pablo Ozuna	1.00
7	Mark Mulder	1.50
8	Corey Patterson	2.00
9	George Lombard	1.00
10	Nick Johnson	2.00

1999 Bowman's Best

NM/M

Complete Set (200): 30.00
Common Player: 2.00
Pack (6): 2.00
Wax Box (24): 40.00

1	Chipper Jones	1.50
2	Brian Jordan	.25
3	David Justice	.25
4	Jason Kendall	.25
5	Mo Vaughn	.25
6	Jim Edmonds	.25
7	Wade Boggs	1.50
8	Jeromy Burnitz	.25
9	Todd Hundley	.25
10	Rondell White	.25
11	Cliff Floyd	.25
12	Sean Casey	.40
13	Bernie Williams	.25
14	Dante Bichette	.25
15	Greg Vaughn	.25
16	Andres Galarraga	.25
17	Ray Durham	.25
18	Jim Thome	.60
19	Gary Sheffield	.45
20	Frank Thomas	1.00
21	Orlando Hernandez	.35
22	Ivan Rodriguez	.75
23	Jose Cruz Jr.	.25
24	Jason Giambi	.50
25	Craig Biggio	.25
26	Kerry Wood	.45
27	Manny Ramirez	1.00
28	Curt Schilling	.45
29	Mike Mussina	.45
30	Tim Salmon	.25
31	Mike Piazza	2.00
32	Roberto Alomar	.40
33	Larry Walker	.25
34	Barry Larkin	.25
35	Nomar Garciaparra	1.50
36	Paul O'Neill	.25
37	Todd Walker	.25
38	Eric Karros	.25
39	Brad Fullmer	.25
40	John Olerud	.25
41	Todd Helton	.75
42	Raul Mondesi	.25
43	Jose Canseco	.50
44	Matt Williams	.25
45	Ray Lankford	.25
46	Carlos Delgado	.50
47	Darin Erstad	.50
48	Vladimir Guerrero	1.00
49	Robin Ventura	.25
50	Alex Rodriguez	2.50
51	Vinny Castilla	.25
52	Tony Clark	.25
53	Pedro Martinez	1.00
54	Rafael Palmeiro	.65
55	Scott Rolen	.65
56	Tino Martinez	.25
57	Tony Gwynn	1.50
58	Barry Bonds	3.00
59	Kenny Lofton	.25
60	Javy Lopez	.25
61	Mark Grace	.25
62	Travis Lee	.25
63	Kevin Brown	.25
64	Al Leiter	.25
65	Albert Belle	.25
66	Sammy Sosa	1.50
67	Greg Maddux	1.50
68	Mark Kotsay	.25
69	Dmitri Young	.25
70	Mark McGwire	2.50
71	Juan Gonzalez	.50
72	Andruw Jones	1.00
73	Derek Jeter	3.00
74	Randy Johnson	1.00
75	Cal Ripken Jr.	3.00
76	Shawn Green	.35
77	Moises Alou	.25
78	Tom Glavine	.45
79	Sandy Alomar	.25
80	Ken Griffey Jr.	2.00
81	Ryan Klesko	.25
82	Jeff Bagwell	1.00
83	Ben Grieve	.25
84	John Smoltz	.25
85	Roger Clemens	1.75
86	Ken Griffey Jr.	1.00
87	Roger Clemens	.85
88	Derek Jeter	1.50
89	Nomar Garciaparra	.75
90	Mark McGwire	1.25
91	Sammy Sosa	.75
92	Alex Rodriguez	1.25
93	Greg Maddux	.75
94	Vladimir Guerrero	1.00
95	Chipper Jones	.75
96	Kerry Wood	.30
97	Ben Grieve	.25
98	Tony Gwynn	.75
99	Juan Gonzalez	.30
100	Mike Piazza	1.00
101	Eric Chavez	.40
102	Billy Koch	.25
103	Dernell Stenson	.25
104	Marlon Anderson	.25
105	Ron Belliard	.25
106	Bruce Chen	.25
107	Carlos Beltran	.40
108	Chad Hermansen	.25
109	Ryan Anderson	.25
110	Michael Barrett	.25
111	Matt Clement	.25
112	Ben Davis	.25
113	Calvin Pickering	.25
114	Brad Penny	.25
115	Paul Konerko	.35
116	Alex Gonzalez	.25
117	George Lombard	.25
118	John Patterson	.25
119	Rob Bell	.25
120	Ruben Mateo	.25
121	Troy Glaus	.75
122	Ryan Bradley	.25
123	Carlos Lee	.35
124	Gabe Kapler	.25
125	Ramon Hernandez	.25
126	Carlos Febles	.25
127	Mitch Meluskey	.25
128	Michael Cuddyer	.25
129	Pablo Ozuna	.25
130	Jayson Werth	.25
131	Ricky Ledee	.25
132	Jeremy Giambi	.25
133	Danny Klassen	.25
134	Mark DeRosa	.25
135	Randy Wolf	.25
136	Roy Halladay	.35
137	Derrick Gibson	.25
138	Ben Petrick	.25
139	Warren Morris	.25
140	Lance Berkman	.25
141	Russell Branyan	.25
142	Adrian Beltre	.40
143	Juan Encarnacion	.25
144	Fernando Seguignol	.25
145	Corey Koskie	.25
146	Preston Wilson	.25
147	Homer Bush	.25
148	Daryle Ward	.25
149	Joe McEwing RC	.50
150	Peter Bergeron RC	.50
151	Pat Burrell RC	3.00
152	Choo Freeman RC	.50
153	Matt Belisle RC	.50
154	Carlos Pena RC	1.00
155	A.J. Burnett RC	.75
156	Doug Mientkiewicz RC	.75
157	Sean Burroughs RC	.50
158	Mike Zywica RC	.35
159	Corey Patterson RC	1.50
160	Austin Kearns RC	2.00
161	Chip Ambres RC	.35
162	Kelly Dransfeldt RC	.35
163	Mike Nannini RC	.35
164	Mark Mulder RC	2.00
165	Jason Tyner RC	.35
166	Bobby Seay RC	.50
167	Alex Escobar RC	.75
168	Nick Johnson RC	1.00
169	Alfonso Soriano RC	4.00
170	Clayton Andrews RC	.35
171	C.C. Sabathia RC	1.00
172	Matt Holliday RC	5.00
173	Brad Lidge RC	1.00
174	Kit Pellow RC	.50
175	J.M. Gold RC	.50
176	Roosevelt Brown RC	.50
177	Eric Valent RC	.50
178	Adam Everett RC	.75
179	Jorge Toca RC	.35
180	Matt Roney RC	.35
181	Andy Brown RC	.35
182	Phil Norton RC	.35
183	Mickey Lopez RC	.35
184	Chris George RC	.35
185	Arturo McDowell RC	.35
186	Jose Fernandez RC	.35
187	Seth Etherton RC	.50
188	Josh McKinley RC	.50
189	Nate Cornejo RC	.50
190	Giuseppe Chiaramonte RC	.35
191	Mamon Tucker RC	.35
192	Ryan Mills RC	.50
193	Chad Moeller RC	.50
194	Tony Torcato RC	.35
195	Jeff Winchester RC	.35
196	Rick Elder RC	.35
197	Matt Burch RC	.35
198	Jeff Urban RC	.35
199	Chris Jones RC	.35
200	Masao Kida RC	.50

Refractors

NM/M

Complete Set (200):	250.00
Common Player:	1.00
Stars:	6X

Production 400 Sets
(See 1999 Bowman's Best for
checklist and base card values.)

Atomic Refractors

	NM/M
Common Player:	3.00
Stars:	12X

Production 100 Sets
(See 1999 Bowman's Best for
checklist and base card values.)

Franchise Best

		NM/M
Complete Set (10):		15.00
Common Player:		.75
Production 3,000 Sets		
Mach II (1,000):		1.5X
Mach III (500):		2.5X
1	Mark McGwire	2.50
2	Ken Griffey Jr.	1.50
3	Sammy Sosa	1.25
4	Nomar Garciaparra	1.25
5	Alex Rodriguez	2.50
6	Derek Jeter	3.50
7	Mike Piazza	1.50
8	Frank Thomas	1.00
9	Chipper Jones	1.25
10	Juan Gonzalez	.75

Franchise Favorites

		NM/M
Complete Set (6):		12.00
Common Player:		.50
Inserted 1:75		
1A	Derek Jeter	5.00
1B	Don Mattingly	2.00
1C	Derek Jeter, Don Mattingly	5.00

2A	Scott Rolen	.50
2B	Mike Schmidt	1.50
2C	Scott Rolen, Mike Schmidt	1.00

Franchise Favorites Autographs

		NM/M
Common Player:		15.00
Version A & B 1:1,548		
Version C 1:6,191		
1A	Derek Jeter	100.00
1B	Don Mattingly	60.00
1C	Derek Jeter, Don Mattingly	300.00
2A	Scott Rolen	20.00
2B	Mike Schmidt	50.00
2C	Scott Rolen, Mike Schmidt	100.00

Future Foundations

		NM/M
Complete Set (10):		16.00
Common Player:		.75
Production 3,000 Sets		
Mach II (1,000):		1.5X
Mach III (500):		2.5X
1	Ruben Mateo	.75
2	Troy Glaus	4.00
3	Eric Chavez	1.50
4	Pat Burrell	4.00
5	Adrian Beltre	1.50
6	Ryan Anderson	.75
7	Alfonso Soriano	3.00
8	Brad Penny	.75
9	Derrick Gibson	.75
10	Bruce Chen	.75

Mirror Image

		NM/M
Complete Set (10):		20.00
Common Player:		1.50
Inserted 1:24		
Refractors (1:96):		1.5X
Atomic Refractors (1:192):		2X
1	Alex Rodriguez, Alex Rodriguez	2.50
2	Ken Griffey Jr., Ruben Mateo	2.00
3	Derek Jeter, Alfonso Soriano	4.00
4	Sammy Sosa, Corey Patterson	1.50
5	Greg Maddux, Bruce Chen	1.50
6	Chipper Jones, Eric Chavez	1.50
7	Vladimir Guerrero, Carlos Beltran	1.50

8	Frank Thomas, Nick Johnson	1.50
9	Nomar Garciaparra, Pablo Ozuna	1.50
10	Mark McGwire, Pat Burrell	3.00

Rookie of the Year

		NM/M
Complete Set (2):		4.00
1	Ben Grieve	2.00
2	Kerry Wood	2.00
A1	Ben Grieve/Auto.	6.00

Rookie Locker Room Autographs

		NM/M
Common Player:		4.00
Inserted 1:248		
1	Pat Burrell	10.00
2	Michael Barrett	4.00
3	Troy Glaus	10.00
4	Gabe Kapler	4.00
5	Eric Chavez	7.50

Rookie Locker Room Game-Used Lumber

		NM/M
Complete Set (6):		35.00
Common Player:		4.00
Inserted 1:258		
1	Pat Burrell	10.00
2	Michael Barrett	4.00
3	Troy Glaus	10.00
4	Gabe Kapler	4.00
5	Eric Chavez	7.50
6	Richie Sexson	5.00

Rookie Locker Room Game-Worn Jerseys

		NM/M
Complete Set (4):		12.00
Common Player:		3.00
Inserted 1:270		
1	Richie Sexson	3.00

2	Michael Barrett	3.00
3	Troy Glaus	7.50
4	Eric Chavez	4.50

2000 Bowman

		NM/M
Complete Set (440):		65.00
Common Player:		.15
Common Rookie:		.25
Pack (10):		2.50
Box (24):		40.00
1	Vladimir Guerrero	.75
2	Chipper Jones	.75
3	Todd Walker	.15
4	Barry Larkin	.25
5	Bernie Williams	.40
6	Todd Helton	.75
7	Jermaine Dye	.15
8	Brian Giles	.15
9	Freddy Garcia	.15
10	Greg Vaughn	.15
11	Alex Gonzalez	.15
12	Luis Gonzalez	.25
13	Ron Belliard	.15
14	Ben Grieve	.15
15	Carlos Delgado	.50
16	Brian Jordan	.15
17	Fernando Tatis	.15
18	Ryan Rupe	.15
19	Miguel Tejada	.50
20	Mark Grace	.30
21	Kenny Lofton	.15
22	Eric Karros	.15
23	Cliff Floyd	.15
24	John Halama	.15
25	Cristian Guzman	.15
26	Scott Williamson	.15
27	Mike Lieberthal	.15
28	Tim Hudson	.40
29	Warren Morris	.15
30	Pedro Martinez	1.00
31	John Smoltz	.15
32	Ray Durham	.15
33	Chad Allen	.15
34	Tony Clark	.15
35	Tino Martinez	.15
36	J.T. Snow Jr.	.15
37	Kevin Brown	.25
38	Bartolo Colon	.15
39	Rey Ordonez	.15
40	Jeff Bagwell	.50
41	Ivan Rodriguez	.50
42	Eric Chavez	.25
43	Eric Milton	.15
44	Jose Canseco	.50
45	Shawn Green	.25
46	Rich Aurilia	.15
47	Roberto Alomar	.40
48	Brian Daubach	.15
49	Magglio Ordonez	.25
50	Derek Jeter	2.00
51	Kris Benson	.15
52	Albert Belle	.15
53	Rondell White	.15
54	Justin Thompson	.15
55	Nomar Garciaparra	.75
56	Chuck Finley	.15
57	Omar Vizquel	.15
58	Luis Castillo	.15
59	Richard Hidalgo	.15
60	Barry Bonds	2.00

#	Player	Price
61	Craig Biggio	.15
62	Doug Glanville	.15
63	Gabe Kapler	.15
64	Johnny Damon	.15
65	Pokey Reese	.15
66	Andy Pettitte	.25
67	B.J. Surhoff	.15
68	Richie Sexson	.40
69	Javy Lopez	.15
70	Raul Mondesi	.15
71	Darin Erstad	.25
72	Kevin Millwood	.15
73	Ricky Ledee	.15
74	John Olerud	.15
75	Sean Casey	.25
76	Carlos Febles	.15
77	Paul O'Neill	.15
78	Bob Abreu	.15
79	Neifi Perez	.15
80	Tony Gwynn	.75
81	Russ Ortiz	.15
82	Matt Williams	.15
83	Chris Carpenter	.15
84	Roger Cedeno	.15
85	Tim Salmon	.30
86	Billy Koch	.15
87	Jeromy Burnitz	.15
88	Edgardo Alfonzo	.15
89	Jay Bell	.15
90	Manny Ramirez	.75
91	Frank Thomas	.75
92	Mike Mussina	.50
93	J.D. Drew	.25
94	Adrian Beltre	.25
95	Alex Rodriguez	2.00
96	Larry Walker	.15
97	Juan Encarnacion	.15
98	Mike Sweeney	.15
99	Rusty Greer	.15
100	Randy Johnson	.75
101	Jose Vidro	.15
102	Preston Wilson	.15
103	Greg Maddux	1.50
104	Jason Giambi	.50
105	Cal Ripken Jr.	2.00
106	Carlos Beltran	.50
107	Vinny Castilla	.15
108	Mariano Rivera	.25
109	Mo Vaughn	.50
110	Rafael Palmeiro	.50
111	Shannon Stewart	.15
112	Mike Hampton	.15
113	Joe Nathan	.15
114	Ben Davis	.15
115	Andruw Jones	.50
116	Robin Ventura	.15
117	Damion Easley	.15
118	Jeff Cirillo	.15
119	Kerry Wood	.25
120	Scott Rolen	.75
121	Sammy Sosa	.75
122	Ken Griffey Jr.	1.50
123	Shane Reynolds	.15
124	Troy Glaus	.40
125	Tom Glavine	.35
126	Michael Barrett	.15
127	Al Leiter	.15
128	Jason Kendall	.15
129	Roger Clemens	2.00
130	Juan Gonzalez	.40
131	Corey Koskie	.15
132	Curt Schilling	.50
133	Mike Piazza	1.00
134	Gary Sheffield	.40
135	Jim Thome	.40
136	Orlando Hernandez	.25
137	Ray Lankford	.15
138	Geoff Jenkins	.15
139	Jose Lima	.15
140	Mark McGwire	1.50
141	Adam Piatt	.15
142	Pat Manning **RC**	.25
143	Marcos Castillo **RC**	.25
144	Lesli Brea **RC**	.25
145	Humberto Cota **RC**	.25
146	Ben Petrick	.15
147	Kip Wells	.15
148	Willi Mo Pena	.15
149	Chris Wakeland	.15
150	Brad Baker **RC**	.25
151	Robbie Morrison **RC**	.25
152	Reggie Taylor	.15
153	Brian Cole **RC**	.25
154	Peter Bergeron	.15
155	Roosevelt Brown	.15
156	Matt Cepicky **RC**	.15
157	Ramon Castro	.15
158	Brad Baisley **RC**	.25
159	Jeff Goldbach **RC**	.15
160	Mitch Meluskey	.15
161	Chad Harville	.15
162	Brian Cooper	.15
163	Marcus Giles	.15
164	Jim Morris	.50
165	Geoff Goetz	.15
166	Bobby Bradley **RC**	.25
167	Rob Bell	.15
168	Joe Crede **RC**	.15
169	Michael Restovich	.15
170	Quincy Foster **RC**	.25
171	Enrique Cruz **RC**	.25
172	Mark Quinn	.15
173	Nick Johnson	.15
174	Jeff Liefer	.15
175	Kevin Mench **RC**	.75
176	Steve Lomasney	.15
177	Jayson Werth	.15
178	Tim Drew	.15
179	Chip Ambres	.15
180	Ryan Anderson	.15
181	Matt Blank	.15
182	Giuseppe Chiaramonte	.15
183	Corey Myers **RC**	.25
184	Jeff Yoder	.15
185	Craig Dingman	.25
186	Jon Hamilton **RC**	.25
187	Toby Hall	.15
188	Russell Branyan	.15
189	Brian Falkenborg **RC**	.25
190	Aaron Harang **RC**	.75
191	Juan Pena	.15
192	Travis Thompson **RC**	.25
193	Alfonso Soriano	.50
194	Alejandro Diaz **RC**	.25
195	Carlos Pena	.15
196	Kevin Nicholson	.15
197	Mo Bruce	.15
198	C.C. Sabathia	.15
199	Carl Crawford	.15
200	Rafael Furcal	.15
201	Andrew Beinbrink **RC**	.25
202	Jimmy Osting	.15
203	Aaron McNeal **RC**	.25
204	Brett Laxton	.15
205	Chris George	.15
206	Felipe Lopez	.15
207	Ben Sheets **RC**	2.00
208	Mike Meyers **RC**	.40
209	Jason Conti	.15
210	Milton Bradley	.15
211	Chris Mears **RC**	.25
212	Carlos Hernandez **RC**	.50
213	Jason Romano	.15
214	Goefrey Tomlinson	.15
215	Jimmy Rollins	.40
216	Pablo Ozuna	.15
217	Steve Cox	.15
218	Terrence Long	.15
219	Jeff DaVanon **RC**	.40
220	Rick Ankiel	.25
221	Jason Standridge	.15
222	Tony Armas	.15
223	Jason Tyner	.15
224	Ramon Ortiz	.15
225	Daryle Ward	.15
226	Enger Veras **RC**	.25
227	Chris Jones **RC**	.25
228	Eric Cammack **RC**	.25
229	Ruben Mateo	.15
230	Ken Harvey **RC**	.50
231	Jake Westbrook	.15
232	Rob Purvis **RC**	.25
233	Choo Freeman	.15
234	Aramis Ramirez	.15
235	A.J. Burnett	.15
236	Kevin Barker	.15
237	Chance Caple **RC**	.25
238	Jarrod Washburn	.15
239	Lance Berkman	.15
240	Michael Wenner **RC**	.25
241	Alex Sanchez	.15
242	Jake Esteves **RC**	.25
243	Grant Roberts	.15
244	Mark Ellis **RC**	.50
245	Donny Leon	.15
246	David Eckstein	.15
247	Dicky Gonzalez **RC**	.25
248	John Patterson	.15
249	Chad Green	.15
250	Scot Shields **RC**	.25
251	Troy Cameron	.15
252	Jose Molina	.15
253	Rob Pugmire **RC**	.25
254	Rick Elder	.15
255	Sean Burroughs	.25
256	Josh Kalinowski **RC**	.25
257	Matt LeCroy	.15
258	Alex Graman **RC**	.50
259	Tomokazu Ohka **RC**	.50
260	Brady Clark	.15
261	Rico Washington **RC**	.25
262	Gary Matthews Jr.	.15
263	Matt Wise	.15
264	Keith Reed **RC**	.25
265	Santiago Ramirez **RC**	.25
266	Ben Broussard **RC**	.50
267	Ryan Langerhans	.15
268	Juan Rivera	.15
269	Shawn Gallagher	.15
270	Jorge Toca	.15
271	Brad Lidge	.15
272	Leo Estrella **RC**	.25
273	Ruben Quevedo	.15
274	Jack Cust	.15
275	T.J. Tucker	.15
276	Mike Colangelo	.15
277	Brian Schneider	.15
278	Calvin Murray	.15
279	Josh Girdley	.15
280	Mike Paradis	.15
281	Chad Hermansen	.15
282	Ty Howington **RC**	.50
283	Aaron Myette	.15
284	D'Angelo Jimenez	.15
285	Dernell Stenson	.15
286	Jerry Hairston Jr.	.15
287	Gary Majewski **RC**	.25
288	Derrin Ebert **RC**	.25
289	Steve Fish **RC**	.25
290	Carlos Hernandez	.15
291	Allen Levrault	.15
292	Sean McNally **RC**	.25
293	Randey Dorame **RC**	.25
294	Wes Anderson **RC**	.50
295	B.J. Ryan	.15
296	Alan Webb **RC**	.25
297	Brandon Inge **RC**	.75
298	David Walling	.15
299	Sun-Woo Kim **RC**	.40
300	Pat Burrell	.25
301	Rick Guttormson **RC**	.25
302	Gil Meche	.15
303	Carlos Zambrano **RC**	3.00
304	Eric Byrnes **RC** (Photo actually Bo Porter.)	1.00
305	Robb Quinlan **RC**	.25
306	Jackie Rexrode	.15
307	Nate Bump	.15
308	Sean DePaula **RC**	.25
309	Matt Riley	.15
310	Ryan Minor	.15
311	J.J. Davis	.15
312	Randy Wolf	.15
313	Jason Jennings	.15
314	Scott Seabol **RC**	.25
315	Doug Davis	.15
316	Todd Moser **RC**	.25
317	Rob Ryan	.15
318	Bubba Crosby	.15
319	Lyle Overbay **RC**	1.00
320	Mario Encarnacion	.15
321	Francisco Rodriguez **RC**	2.00
322	Michael Cuddyer	.15
323	Eddie Yarnall	.15
324	Cesar Saba **RC**	.25
325	Travis Dawkins	.15
326	Alex Escobar	.15
327	Julio Zuleta **RC**	.40
328	Josh Hamilton	.25
329	Nick Neugebauer **RC**	.25
330	Matt Belisle	.15
331	Kurt Ainsworth **RC**	.50
332	Tim Raines Jr.	.15
333	Eric Munson	.15
334	Donzell McDonald	.15
335	Larry Bigbie **RC**	.25
336	Matt Watson	.15
337	Aubrey Huff	.15
338	Julio Ramirez	.15
339	Jason Grabowski **RC**	.25
340	Jon Garland	.15
341	Austin Kearns	.25
342	Josh Pressley	.15
343	Miguel Olivo **RC**	.25
344	Julio Lugo	.15
345	Roberto Vaz	.15
346	Ramon Soler	.15
347	Brandon Phillips **RC**	2.00
348	Vince Faison **RC**	.25
349	Mike Venafro	.15
350	Rick Asadoorian **RC**	.25
351	B.J. Garbe **RC**	.25
352	Dan Reichert	.15
353	Jason Stumm **RC**	.25
354	Ruben Salazar **RC**	.25
355	Francisco Cordero	.15
356	Juan Guzman **RC**	.25
357	Mike Bacsik **RC**	.25
358	Jared Sandberg	.15
359	Rod Barajas	.15
360	Junior Brignac **RC**	.25
361	J.M. Gold	.15
362	Octavio Dotel	.15
363	David Kelton	.15
364	Scott Morgan **RC**	.25
365	Wascar Serrano **RC**	.25
366	Wilton Veras	.15
367	Eugene Kingsale	.15
368	Ted Lilly	.15
369	George Lombard	.15
370	Chris Haas	.15
371	Wilton Pena **RC**	.50
372	Vernon Wells	.15
373	Jason Royer **RC**	.25
374	Jeff Heaverlo **RC**	.25
375	Calvin Pickering	.15
376	Mike Lamb **RC**	.40
377	Kyle Snyder	.15
378	Javier Cardona **RC**	.25
379	Aaron Rowand **RC**	1.00
380	Dee Brown	.15
381	Brett Myers **RC**	1.00
382	Abraham Nunez	.20
383	Eric Valent	.15
384	Jody Gerut **RC**	.25
385	Adam Dunn	.50
386	Jay Gehrke	.15
387	Omar Ortiz	.15
388	Darnell McDonald	.15
389	Chad Alexander	.15
390	J.D. Closser	.15
391	Ben Christensen **RC**	.25
392	Adam Kennedy	.15
393	Nick Green **RC**	.25
394	Ramon Hernandez	.15
395	Roy Oswalt **RC**	4.00
396	Andy Tracy **RC**	.50
397	Eric Gagne	.15
398	Michael Tejera **RC**	.25
399	Adam Everett	.15
400	Corey Patterson	.25
401	Gary Knotts **RC**	.15
402	Ryan Christianson **RC**	.50
403	Eric Ireland **RC**	.25
404	Andrew Good **RC**	.25
405	Brad Penny	.15
406	Jason LaRue	.15
407	Kit Pellow	.15
408	Kevin Beirne	.15
409	Kelly Dransfeldt	.15
410	Jason Grilli	.15
411	Scott Downs **RC**	.25
412	Jesus Colome	.15
413	John Sneed **RC**	.25
414	Tony McKnight **RC**	.25
415	Luis Rivera	.15
416	Adam Eaton	.15
417	Mike MacDougal **RC**	.50
418	Mike Nannini	.15
419	Barry Zito **RC**	2.00
420	Dewayne Wise	.15
421	Jason Dellaero	.15
422	Chad Moeller	.15
423	Jason Marquis	.15
424	Tim Redding **RC**	.50
425	Mark Mulder	.15
426	Josh Paul	.15
427	Chris Enochs	.15
428	Wilfredo Rodriguez **RC**	.50
429	Kevin Witt	.15
430	Scott Sobkowiak **RC**	.25
431	McKay Christensen	.15
432	Jung Bong	.15
433	Keith Evans **RC**	.25
434	Garry Maddox Jr.	.15
435	Ramon Santiago **RC**	.50
436	Alex Cora	.15
437	Carlos Lee	.15
438	Jason Repko **RC**	.25
439	Matt Burch	.15
440	Shawn Sonnier **RC**	.25

Gold

Stars:	10-20X
Rookies:	4-8X

Production 99 Sets
(See 2000 Bowman for checklist and base card values.)

Retro/Future

	NM/M
Common Player:	.25
Stars:	2-3X
Rookies:	.75-2X

Inserted 1:1
(See 2000 Bowman for checklist and base card values.)

Autographs

	NM/M
Common Autograph:	5.00

Blue Inserted 1:144
Silver 1:312

Jose Vidro

Gold 1:1,604		
CA	Chip Ambres/B	5.00
RA	Rick Ankiel/G	15.00
CB	Carlos Beltran/G	40.00
LB	Lance Berkman/S	20.00
DB	Dee Brown/S	8.00
SB	Sean Burroughs/S	8.00
JDC	J.D. Closser/B	5.00
SC	Steve Cox/B	5.00
MC	Michael Cuddyer/S	10.00
JC	Jack Cust/B	15.00
SD	Scott Downs/S	10.00
JDD	J.D. Drew/G	25.00
AD	Adam Dunn/B	25.00
CF	Choo Freeman/B	5.00
RF	Rafael Furcal/S	15.00
AH	Aubrey Huff/B	8.00
JJ	Jason Jennings/B	8.00
NJ	Nick Johnson/S	10.00
AK	Austin Kearns/B	15.00
DK	David Kelton/B	5.00
RM	Ruben Mateo/G	15.00
MM	Mike Meyers/B	5.00
CP	Corey Patterson/S	20.00
BWP	Brad Penny/G	5.00
BP	Ben Petrick/B	10.00
AP	Adam Piatt/S	8.00
MQ	Mark Quinn/S	8.00
MR	Mike Restovich/B	5.00
MR	Matt Riley/S	8.00
JR	Jason Romano/B	5.00
BS	Ben Sheets/B	30.00
AS	Alfonso Soriano/S	40.00
EV	Eric Valent/B	5.00
JV	Jose Vidro/B	10.00
VW	Vernon Wells/G	20.00
SW	Scott Williamson/G	10.00
KJW	Kevin Witt/S	10.00
KLW	Kerry Wood/S	25.00
EY	Eddie Yarnall/B	10.00
JZ	Julio Zuleta/B	5.00

Bowman's Best Previews

DEREK JETER

		NM/M
Complete Set (10):		15.00
Common Player:		.50
Inserted 1:18		
1	Derek Jeter	4.00
2	Ken Griffey Jr.	3.00
3	Nomar Garciaparra	2.00
4	Mike Piazza	2.00
5	Alex Rodriguez	4.00
6	Sammy Sosa	2.00
7	Mark McGwire	3.00
8	Pat Burrell	1.00
9	Josh Hamilton	.50
10	Adam Piatt	.50

Early Indications

	NM/M
Complete Set (10):	18.00

EARLY INDICATIONS
ALEX RODRIGUEZ
SS Seattle Mariners

Common Player:		1.00
Inserted 1:24		
1	Nomar Garciaparra	1.50
2	Cal Ripken Jr.	4.00
3	Derek Jeter	4.00
4	Mark McGwire	3.00
5	Alex Rodriguez	3.00
6	Chipper Jones	1.50
7	Todd Helton	1.00
8	Vladimir Guerrero	1.50
9	Mike Piazza	1.50
10	Jose Canseco	1.00

Major Power

MAJOR POWER
ALEX RODRIGUEZ

		NM/M
Complete Set (10):		20.00
Common Player:		1.00
Inserted 1:24		
1	Mark McGwire	4.00
2	Chipper Jones	2.50
3	Alex Rodriguez	4.00
4	Sammy Sosa	3.00
5	Rafael Palmeiro	1.00
6	Ken Griffey Jr.	3.00
7	Nomar Garciaparra	3.00
8	Barry Bonds	5.00
9	Derek Jeter	5.00
10	Jeff Bagwell	1.50

Tool Time

RUBEN MATEO

		NM/M
Complete Set (20):		8.00
Common Player:		.40
Inserted 1:8		
1	Pat Burrell	1.00
2	Aaron Rowand	.40
3	Chris Wakeland	.40
4	Ruben Mateo	.40
5	Pat Burrell	1.00

6	Adam Piatt	.50
7	Nick Johnson	1.00
8	Jack Cust	.40
9	Rafael Furcal	.40
10	Julio Ramirez	.40
11	Travis Dawkins	.40
12	Corey Patterson	1.00
13	Ruben Mateo	.40
14	Jason Dellaero	.40
15	Sean Burroughs	.40
16	Ryan Langerhans	.40
17	D'Angelo Jimenez	.40
18	Corey Patterson	1.00
19	Troy Cameron	.40
20	Michael Cuddyer	.50

2000 Bowman Chrome

Mike Mussina

		NM/M
Complete Set (440):		120.00
Common Player:		.25
Common Rookie:		.50
Pack (4):		2.50
Box (24):		50.00
1	Vladimir Guerrero	1.00
2	Chipper Jones	1.00
3	Todd Walker	.25
4	Barry Larkin	.25
5	Bernie Williams	.50
6	Todd Helton	.75
7	Jermaine Dye	.25
8	Brian Giles	.25
9	Freddy Garcia	.25
10	Greg Vaughn	.25
11	Alex Gonzalez	.25
12	Luis Gonzalez	.25
13	Ron Belliard	.25
14	Ben Grieve	.25
15	Carlos Delgado	.75
16	Brian Jordan	.25
17	Fernando Tatis	.25
18	Ryan Rupe	.25
19	Miguel Tejada	.40
20	Mark Grace	.35
21	Kenny Lofton	.25
22	Eric Karros	.25
23	Cliff Floyd	.25
24	John Halama	.25
25	Cristian Guzman	.25
26	Scott Williamson	.25
27	Mike Lieberthal	.25
28	Tim Hudson	.40
29	Warren Morris	.25
30	Pedro Martinez	1.00
31	John Smoltz	.25
32	Ray Durham	.25
33	Chad Allen	.25
34	Tony Clark	.25
35	Tino Martinez	.25
36	J.T. Snow Jr.	.25
37	Kevin Brown	.40
38	Bartolo Colon	.25
39	Rey Ordonez	.25
40	Jeff Bagwell	.50
41	Ivan Rodriguez	.75
42	Eric Chavez	.50
43	Eric Milton	.25
44	Jose Canseco	.50
45	Shawn Green	.50
46	Rich Aurilia	.25
47	Roberto Alomar	.50
48	Brian Daubach	.25
49	Magglio Ordonez	.50
50	Derek Jeter	2.00
51	Kris Benson	.25
52	Albert Belle	.25
53	Rondell White	.25
54	Justin Thompson	.25
55	Nomar Garciaparra	1.00
56	Chuck Finley	.25
57	Omar Vizquel	.25
58	Luis Castillo	.25
59	Richard Hidalgo	.25
60	Barry Bonds	2.00

61	Craig Biggio	.25
62	Doug Glanville	.25
63	Gabe Kapler	.25
64	Johnny Damon	.40
65	Pokey Reese	.25
66	Andy Pettitte	.50
67	B.J. Surhoff	.25
68	Richie Sexson	.50
69	Javy Lopez	.25
70	Raul Mondesi	.25
71	Darin Erstad	.40
72	Kevin Millwood	.40
73	Ricky Ledee	.25
74	John Olerud	.25
75	Sean Casey	.25
76	Carlos Febles	.25
77	Paul O'Neill	.25
78	Bob Abreu	.25
79	Neifi Perez	.25
80	Tony Gwynn	1.00
81	Russ Ortiz	.25
82	Matt Williams	.25
83	Chris Carpenter	.25
84	Roger Cedeno	.25
85	Tim Salmon	.35
86	Billy Koch	.25
87	Jeromy Burnitz	.25
88	Edgardo Alfonzo	.25
89	Jay Bell	.15
90	Manny Ramirez	.75
91	Frank Thomas	.75
92	Mike Mussina	.50
93	J.D. Drew	.40
94	Adrian Beltre	.40
95	Alex Rodriguez	2.00
96	Larry Walker	.25
97	Juan Encarnacion	.25
98	Mike Sweeney	.25
99	Rusty Greer	.25
100	Randy Johnson	.75
101	Jose Vidro	.25
102	Preston Wilson	.25
103	Greg Maddux	1.50
104	Jason Giambi	.75
105	Cal Ripken Jr.	3.00
106	Carlos Beltran	.25
107	Vinny Castilla	.25
108	Mariano Rivera	.35
109	Mo Vaughn	.25
110	Rafael Palmeiro	.50
111	Shannon Stewart	.25
112	Mike Hampton	.25
113	Joe Nathan	.25
114	Ben Davis	.25
115	Andruw Jones	.75
116	Robin Ventura	.25
117	Damion Easley	.25
118	Jeff Cirillo	.25
119	Kerry Wood	.40
120	Scott Rolen	.75
121	Sammy Sosa	1.00
122	Ken Griffey Jr.	2.00
123	Shane Reynolds	.25
124	Troy Glaus	.50
125	Tom Glavine	.40
126	Michael Barrett	.25
127	Al Leiter	.25
128	Jason Kendall	.25
129	Roger Clemens	2.00
130	Juan Gonzalez	.50
131	Corey Koskie	.25
132	Curt Schilling	.75
133	Mike Piazza	1.00
134	Gary Sheffield	.50
135	Jim Thome	.50
136	Orlando Hernandez	.40
137	Ray Lankford	.25
138	Geoff Jenkins	.25
139	Jose Lima	.25
140	Mark McGwire	1.50
141	Adam Piatt	.25
142	Pat Manning **RC**	.50
143	Marcos Castillo **RC**	.50
144	Lesli Brea **RC**	.50
145	Humberto Cota **RC**	.50
146	Ben Petrick	.25
147	Kip Wells	.25
148	Willi Mo Pena	.40
149	Chris Wakeland	.25
150	Brad Baker **RC**	.50
151	Robbie Morrison **RC**	.50
152	Reggie Taylor	.25
153	Matt Ginter **RC**	.50
154	Peter Bergeron	.25
155	Roosevelt Brown	.25
156	Matt Cepicky **RC**	.50
157	Ramon Castro	.25
158	Brad Baisley **RC**	.50
159	Jason Hart **RC**	1.00
160	Mitch Meluskey	.25
161	Chad Harville	.25
162	Brian Cooper	.25
163	Marcus Giles	.25
164	Jim Morris	.50

165	Geoff Goetz	.25
166	Bobby Bradley RC	.50
167	Rob Bell	.25
168	Joe Crede	.25
169	Michael Restovich	.25
170	Quincy Foster RC	.50
171	Enrique Cruz RC	.50
172	Mark Quinn	.25
173	Nick Johnson	.40
174	Jeff Liefer	.25
175	Kevin Mench RC	3.00
176	Steve Lomasney	.25
177	Jayson Werth	.25
178	Tim Drew	.25
179	Chip Ambres	.25
180	Ryan Anderson	.25
181	Matt Blank	.25
182	Giuseppe Chiaramonte	.25
183	Corey Myers RC	.25
184	Jeff Yoder	.25
185	Craig Dingman RC	.25
186	Jon Hamilton RC	.50
187	Toby Hall	.25
188	Russell Branyan	.25
189	Brian Falkenborg RC	.50
190	Aaron Harang RC	3.00
191	Juan Pena	.25
192	Chin-Hui Tsao RC	3.00
193	Alfonso Soriano	.75
194	Alejandro Diaz RC	.25
195	Carlos Pena	.25
196	Kevin Nicholson	.25
197	Mo Bruce	.25
198	C.C. Sabathia	.25
199	Carl Crawford	.25
200	Rafael Furcal	.25
201	Andrew Beinbrink RC	.50
202	Jimmy Osting	.25
203	Aaron McNeal RC	.50
204	Brett Laxton	.25
205	Chris George	.25
206	Felipe Lopez	.25
207	Ben Sheets RC	6.00
208	Mike Meyers RC	.50
209	Jason Conti	.25
210	Milton Bradley	.25
211	Chris Mears RC	.25
212	Carlos Hernandez RC	.50
213	Jason Romano	.25
214	Goefrey Tomlinson	.25
215	Jimmy Rollins	.75
216	Pablo Ozuna	.25
217	Steve Cox	.25
218	Terrence Long	.25
219	Jeff DaVanon RC	.50
220	Rick Ankiel	.25
221	Jason Standridge	.25
222	Tony Armas	.25
223	Jason Tyner	.25
224	Ramon Ortiz	.25
225	Daryle Ward	.25
226	Enger Veras RC	.50
227	Chris Jones RC	.50
228	Eric Cammack RC	.50
229	Ruben Mateo	.25
230	Ken Harvey RC	1.00
231	Jake Westbrook	.25
232	Rob Purvis RC	.25
233	Choo Freeman	.25
234	Aramis Ramirez	.25
235	A.J. Burnett	.25
236	Kevin Barker	.25
237	Chance Caple RC	.25
238	Jarrod Washburn	.25
239	Lance Berkman	.25
240	Michael Wenner RC	.50
241	Alex Sanchez	.25
242	Jake Esteves RC	.50
243	Grant Roberts	.25
244	Mark Ellis RC	.50
245	Donny Leon	.25
246	David Eckstein	.25
247	Dicky Gonzalez RC	.50
248	John Patterson	.25
249	Chad Green	.25
250	Scot Shields RC	.50
251	Troy Cameron	.25
252	Jose Molina	.25
253	Rob Pugmire RC	.50
254	Rick Elder	.25
255	Sean Burroughs	.50
256	Josh Kalinowski RC	.50
257	Matt LeCroy	.25
258	Alex Graman RC	.50
259	Juan Silvestre RC	.50
260	Brady Clark	.25
261	Rico Washington RC	.50
262	Gary Matthews Jr.	.25
263	Matt Wise	.25
264	Keith Reed RC	.50
265	Santiago Ramirez RC	.50
266	Ben Broussard RC	.50
267	Ryan Langerhans	.25
268	Juan Rivera	.25

269	Shawn Gallagher	.25
270	Jorge Toca	.25
271	Brad Lidge	.25
272	Leo Estrella RC	.50
273	Ruben Quevedo	.25
274	Jack Cust	.25
275	T.J. Tucker	.25
276	Mike Colangelo	.25
277	Brian Schneider	.25
278	Calvin Murray	.25
279	Josh Girdley	.25
280	Mike Paradis	.25
281	Chad Hermansen	.25
282	Ty Howington RC	.50
283	Aaron Myette	.25
284	D'Angelo Jimenez	.25
285	Dernell Stenson	.25
286	Jerry Hairston Jr.	.25
287	Gary Majewski RC	.50
288	Derrin Ebert RC	.50
289	Steve Fish RC	.50
290	Carlos Hernandez	.25
291	Allen Levrault	.25
292	Sean McNally RC	.50
293	Randey Dorame RC	.50
294	Wes Anderson RC	.50
295	B.J. Ryan	.25
296	Alan Webb RC	.50
297	Brandon Inge RC	2.00
298	David Walling	.25
299	Sun-Woo Kim RC	1.00
300	Pat Burrell	.50
301	Rick Guttormson RC	.50
302	Gil Meche	.25
303	Carlos Zambrano RC	10.00
304	Eric Byrnes RC (Photo actually Bo Porter.)	5.00
305	Robb Quinlan RC	.50
306	Jackie Rexrode	.25
307	Nate Bump	.25
308	Sean DePaula RC	.50
309	Matt Riley	.25
310	Ryan Minor	.25
311	J.J. Davis	.25
312	Randy Wolf	.25
313	Jason Jennings	.25
314	Scott Seabol RC	.50
315	Doug Davis	.25
316	Todd Moser RC	.50
317	Rob Ryan	.25
318	Bubba Crosby	.25
319	Lyle Overbay RC	2.50
320	Mario Encarnacion	.25
321	Francisco Rodriguez RC	6.00
322	Michael Cuddyer	.25
323	Eddie Yarnall	.25
324	Cesar Saba RC	.50
325	Travis Dawkins	.25
326	Alex Escobar	.25
327	Julio Zuleta RC	.50
328	Josh Hamilton	.25
329	Carlos Urquiola RC	.50
330	Matt Belisle	.25
331	Kurt Ainsworth RC	1.00
332	Tim Raines Jr.	.25
333	Eric Munson	.25
334	Donzell McDonald	.25
335	Larry Bigbie RC	.50
336	Matt Watson	.25
337	Aubrey Huff	.25
338	Julio Ramirez	.25
339	Jason Grabowski RC	.25
340	Jon Garland	.25
341	Austin Kearns	.50
342	Josh Pressley	.25
343	Miguel Olivo RC	.50
344	Julio Lugo	.25
345	Roberto Vaz	.25
346	Ramon Soler	.25
347	Brandon Phillips RC	5.00
348	Vince Faison RC	.50
349	Mike Venafro	.25
350	Rick Asadoorian RC	.50
351	B.J. Garbe RC	.50
352	Dan Reichert	.25
353	Jason Sturm RC	.50
354	Ruben Salazar RC	.50
355	Francisco Cordero	.25
356	Juan Guzman RC	.50
357	Mike Bacsik RC	.50
358	Jared Sandberg	.25
359	Rod Barajas	.25
360	Junior Brignac RC	.50
361	J.M. Gold	.25
362	Octavio Dotel	.25
363	David Kelton	.25
364	Scott Morgan RC	.50
365	Wascar Serrano RC	.50
366	Wilton Veras	.25
367	Eugene Kingsale	.25
368	Ted Lilly	.25
369	George Lombard	.25
370	Chris Haas	.25

371	Wilton Pena RC	.50
372	Vernon Wells	.50
373	Keith Ginter RC	.50
374	Jeff Heaverlo RC	.50
375	Calvin Pickering	.25
376	Mike Lamb RC	.50
377	Kyle Snyder	.25
378	Javier Cardona RC	.50
379	Aaron Rowand RC	3.00
380	Dee Brown	.25
381	Brett Myers RC	4.00
382	Abraham Nunez	.25
383	Eric Valent	.25
384	Jody Gerut RC	.50
385	Adam Dunn	.50
386	Jay Gehrke	.25
387	Omar Ortiz	.25
388	Darnell McDonald	.25
389	Chad Alexander	.25
390	J.D. Closser	.25
391	Ben Christianson RC	.50
392	Adam Kennedy	.50
393	Nick Green RC	.50
394	Ramon Hernandez	.25
395	Roy Oswalt RC	20.00
396	Andy Tracy RC	1.00
397	Eric Gagne	.25
398	Michael Tejera RC	.50
399	Adam Everett	.25
400	Corey Patterson	.50
401	Gary Knotts RC	.50
402	Ryan Christianson RC	.50
403	Eric Ireland RC	.50
404	Andrew Good RC	.50
405	Brad Penny	.25
406	Jason LaRue	.25
407	Kit Pellow	.25
408	Kevin Beirne	.25
409	Kelly Dransfeldt	.25
410	Jason Grilli	.25
411	Scott Downs RC	.50
412	Jesus Colome	.25
413	John Sneed RC	.50
414	Tony McKnight RC	.50
415	Luis Rivera	.25
416	Adam Eaton	.25
417	Mike MacDougal RC	1.00
418	Mike Nannini	.25
419	Barry Zito RC	6.00
420	Dewayne Wise	.25
421	Jason Dellaero	.25
422	Chad Moeller	.25
423	Jason Marquis	.25
424	Tim Redding RC	.50
425	Mark Mulder	.25
426	Josh Paul	.25
427	Chris Enochs	.25
428	Wilfredo Rodriguez RC	.50
429	Kevin Witt	.25
430	Scott Sobkowiak RC	.50
431	McKay Christensen	.25
432	Jung Bong	.25
433	Keith Evans RC	.50
434	Garry Maddox Jr.	.25
435	Ramon Santiago RC	.50
436	Alex Cora	.25
437	Carlos Lee	.25
438	Jason Repko RC	.50
439	Matt Burch	.25
440	Shawn Sonnier RC	1.00

Rookies: 1-3X
Inserted 1:60
(See 2000 Bowman Chrome for checklist and base values.)

Bidding for the Call

		NM/M
Complete Set (15):		10.00
Common Player:		.50
Inserted 1:16		
Refractors:		2-4X
Inserted 1:160		
1	Adam Piatt	.50
2	Pat Burrell	1.00
3	Mark Mulder	1.00
4	Nick Johnson	1.00
5	Alfonso Soriano	2.00
6	Chin-Feng Chen	2.50
7	Scott Sobkowiak	.50
8	Corey Patterson	1.00
9	Jack Cust	.50
10	Sean Burroughs	.50
11	Josh Hamilton	1.00
12	Corey Myers	.50
13	Eric Munson	.50
14	Wes Anderson	.50
15	Lyle Overbay	1.00

Meteoric Rise

		NM/M
Complete Set (10):		20.00
Common Player:		1.50
Inserted 1:24		
Refractors:		2-4X
Inserted 1:240		
1	Nomar Garciaparra	3.00
2	Mark McGwire	4.00
3	Ken Griffey Jr.	3.00
4	Chipper Jones	2.50
5	Manny Ramirez	2.00
6	Mike Piazza	3.00
7	Cal Ripken Jr.	5.00
8	Ivan Rodriguez	1.00
9	Greg Maddux	3.00
10	Randy Johnson	2.00

Refractors

Mariano Rivera

Stars:	4-8X
Rookies:	2-4X
Inserted 1:12	

(See 2000 Bowman Chrome for checklist and base card values.)

Retro/Future

Stars:	1.5-3X
Rookies:	.75X
Inserted 1:6	
Refractors:	6-8X

Oversize

	NM/M
Complete Set (8):	8.00

Common Player: .75
Inserted 1:Box
1	Pat Burrell	2.00
2	Josh Hamilton	1.00
3	Rafael Furcal	1.00
4	Corey Patterson	1.50
5	A.J. Burnett	.75
6	Eric Munson	.75
7	Nick Johnson	1.00
8	Alfonso Soriano	2.00

Rookie Class 2000

NM/M
Complete Set (10): 8.00
Common Player: 1.50
Inserted 1:24
Refractors: 2-4X
Inserted 1:240
1	Pat Burrell	2.00
2	Rick Ankiel	.75
3	Ruben Mateo	.75
4	Vernon Wells	1.50
5	Mark Mulder	1.50
6	A.J. Burnett	.75
7	Chad Hermansen	.75
8	Corey Patterson	1.50
9	Rafael Furcal	1.00
10	Mike Lamb	.75

Teen Idols

NM/M
Complete Set (15): 15.00
Common Player: 1.50
Inserted 1:16
Refractors: 2-4X
Inserted 1:160
1	Alex Rodriguez	5.00
2	Andruw Jones	1.50
3	Juan Gonzalez	1.00
4	Ivan Rodriguez	1.50
5	Ken Griffey Jr.	3.00
6	Bobby Bradley	.75
7	Brett Myers	.75
8	C.C. Sabathia	.75
9	Ty Howington	.75
10	Brandon Phillips	1.00
11	Rick Asadoorian	.75
12	Wily Pena	1.00
13	Sean Burroughs	.75
14	Josh Hamilton	1.00
15	Rafael Furcal	1.00

2000 Bowman Chrome Draft Picks and Prospects

NM/M
Complete Set (110): 50.00
Common Player: .25
1	Pat Burrell	.50

Jon Rauch

2	Rafael Furcal	.50
3	Grant Roberts	.25
4	Barry Zito	2.00
5	Julio Zuleta	.50
6	Mark Mulder	.25
7	Rob Bell	.25
8	Adam Piatt	.50
9	Mike Lamb	.25
10	Pablo Ozuna	.25
11	Jason Tyner	.25
12	Jason Marquis	.25
13	Eric Munson	.25
14	Seth Etherton	.25
15	Milton Bradley	.25
16	Nick Green	.25
17	Chin-Feng Chen RC	2.00
18	Matt Boone RC	.50
19	Kevin Gregg RC	.50
20	Eddy Garabito RC	.50
21	Aaron Capista RC	.50
22	Esteban German RC	.50
23	Derek Thompson RC	.50
24	Phil Merrell RC	.50
25	Brian O'Connor RC	.50
26	Yamid Haad	.25
27	Hector Mercado RC	.50
28	Jason Woolf RC	.50
29	Eddie Furniss RC	.50
30	Cha Sueng Baek RC	.50
31	Colby Lewis RC	.50
32	Pasqual Coco RC	.50
33	Jorge Cantu RC	2.00
34	Erasmo Ramirez RC	.50
35	Bobby Kielty RC	1.00
36	Joaquin Benoit RC	.50
37	Brian Esposito RC	.50
38	Michael Wenner	.25
39	Juan Rincon RC	.50
40	Yorvit Torrealba RC	.50
41	Chad Durham RC	.50
42	Jim Mann RC	.50
43	Shane Loux RC	.50
44	Luis Rivas	.25
45	Ken Chenard RC	.50
46	Mike Lockwood RC	.50
47	Giovanni Lara RC	.50
48	Bubba Carpenter RC	.50
49	Ryan Dittfurth RC	.50
50	John Stephens RC	.50
51	Pedro Feliz RC	2.00
52	Kenny Kelly RC	.50
53	Neil Jenkins RC	.50
54	Mike Glendenning RC	.50
55	Bo Porter	.25
56	Eric Byrnes	.25
57	Tony Alvarez RC	.50
58	Kazuhiro Sasaki RC	1.00
59	Chad Durbin RC	.50
60	Mike Bynum RC	.50
61	Travis Wilson RC	.50
62	Jose Leon RC	.50
63	Ryan Vogelsong RC	.50
64	Geraldo Guzman RC	.50
65	Craig Anderson RC	.50
66	Carlos Silva RC	1.00
67	Brad Thomas RC	.50
68	Chin-Hui Tsao RC	1.50
69	Mark Buehrle RC	6.00
70	Juan Salas RC	.50
71	Denny Abreu RC	.50
72	Keith McDonald RC	.50
73	Chris Richard RC	.50
74	Tomas de la Rosa RC	.50
75	Vicente Padilla RC	1.00
76	Justin Brunette RC	.50
77	Scott Linebrink RC	.50
78	Jeff Sparks RC	.50
79	Tike Redman RC	.50
80	John Lackey RC	3.00
81	Joe Strong RC	.50
82	Brian Tollberg RC	.50
83	Steve Sisco RC	.50
84	Chris Clapinski	.25
85	Augie Ojeda RC	.50
86	Adrian Gonzalez RC	6.00
87	Mike Stodolka RC	.50
88	Adam Johnson RC	.50
89	Matt Wheatland RC	.50
90	Corey Smith RC	.50
91	Rocco Baldelli RC	4.00
92	Keith Bucktrot RC	.50
93	Adam Wainwright RC	4.00
94	Blaine Boyer RC	.50
95	Aaron Herr RC	.50
96	Scott Thorman RC	2.00
97	Brian Digby RC	.50
98	Josh Shortslef RC	.50
99	Sean Smith RC	.50
100	Alex Cruz RC	.50
101	Marc Love RC	.50
102	Kevin Lee RC	.50
103	Timoniel Perez RC	.50
104	Alex Cabrera RC	1.00
105	Shane Heams RC	.50
106	Tripper Johnson RC	.50
107	Brent Abernathy RC	.50
108	John Cotton RC	.50
109	Brad Wilkerson RC	3.00
110	Jon Rauch RC	.50

2000 Bowman Draft Picks and Prospects

Pedro Feliz

NM/M
Complete Set (110): 40.00
Common Player: .15
1	Pat Burrell	.25
2	Rafael Furcal	.15
3	Grant Roberts	.15
4	Barry Zito	.50
5	Julio Zuleta	.25
6	Mark Mulder	.25
7	Rob Bell	.15
8	Adam Piatt	.15
9	Mike Lamb	.15
10	Pablo Ozuna	.15
11	Jason Tyner	.15
12	Jason Marquis	.15
13	Eric Munson	.15
14	Seth Etherton	.15
15	Milton Bradley	.15
16	Nick Green	.15
17	Chin-Feng Chen RC	1.00
18	Matt Boone RC	.25
19	Kevin Gregg RC	.25
20	Eddy Garabito RC	.25
21	Aaron Capista RC	.25
22	Esteban German RC	.25
23	Derek Thompson RC	.25
24	Phil Merrell RC	.25
25	Brian O'Connor RC	.25
26	Yamid Haad	.15
27	Hector Mercado RC	.25
28	Jason Woolf RC	.25
29	Eddie Furniss RC	.25
30	Cha Sueng Baek RC	.25
31	Colby Lewis RC	.25
32	Pasqual Coco RC	.25
33	Jorge Cantu RC	.50
34	Erasmo Ramirez RC	.25
35	Bobby Kielty RC	.50
36	Joaquin Benoit RC	.25
37	Brian Esposito RC	.25
38	Michael Wenner	.15
39	Juan Rincon RC	.25
40	Yorvit Torrealba RC	.25
41	Chad Durham RC	.25
42	Jim Mann RC	.25
43	Shane Loux RC	.25
44	Luis Rivas	.15
45	Ken Chenard RC	.25
46	Mike Lockwood RC	.25
47	Yovanny Lara RC	.25
48	Bubba Carpenter RC	.25
49	Jeremy Griffiths RC	.25
50	John Stephens RC	.25
51	Pedro Feliz RC	.75
52	Kenny Kelly RC	.25
53	Neil Jenkins RC	.25
54	Mike Glendenning RC	.25
55	Bo Porter	.15
56	Eric Byrnes	.15
57	Tony Alvarez RC	.25
58	Kazuhiro Sasaki RC	.50
59	Chad Durbin RC	.25
60	Mike Bynum RC	.25
61	Travis Wilson RC	.25
62	Jose Leon RC	.25
63	Bill Ortega RC	.25
64	Geraldo Guzman RC	.25
65	Craig Anderson RC	.25
66	Carlos Silva RC	.50
67	Brad Thomas RC	.25
68	Chin-Hui Tsao RC	.75
69	Mark Buehrle RC	2.00
70	Juan Salas RC	.25
71	Denny Abreu RC	.25
72	Keith McDonald RC	.25
73	Chris Richard RC	.25
74	Tomas de la Rosa RC	.25
75	Vicente Padilla RC	.50
76	Justin Brunette RC	.25
77	Scott Linebrink RC	.25
78	Jeff Sparks RC	.25
79	Tike Redman RC	.25
80	John Lackey RC	1.50
81	Joe Strong RC	.25
82	Brian Tollberg RC	.25
83	Steve Sisco RC	.25
84	Chris Clapinski	.15
85	Augie Ojeda RC	.25
86	Adrian Gonzalez RC	2.50
87	Mike Stodolka RC	.25
88	Adam Johnson RC	.25
89	Matt Wheatland RC	.25
90	Corey Smith RC	.25
91	Rocco Baldelli RC	3.00
92	Keith Bucktrot RC	.25
93	Adam Wainwright RC	2.00
94	Blaine Boyer RC	.25
95	Aaron Herr RC	.25
96	Scott Thorman RC	1.50
97	Brian Digby RC	.25
98	Josh Shortslef RC	.25
99	Sean Smith RC	.25
100	Alex Cruz RC	.25
101	Marc Love RC	.25
102	Kevin Lee RC	.25
103	Victor Ramos RC	.25
104	Jason Kanoi RC	.25
105	Luis Escobar RC	.25
106	Tripper Johnson RC	.25
107	Phil Dumatrait RC	.25
108	Bryan Edwards RC	.25
109	Grady Sizemore RC	20.00
110	Thomas Mitchell RC	.25

Autograph

Pat Burrell

NM/M
Common Autograph: 5.00
Inserted 1:Set
1	Pat Burrell	20.00
2	Rafael Furcal	15.00
3	Grant Roberts	5.00
4	Barry Zito	40.00
5	Julio Zuleta	5.00
6	Mark Mulder	15.00
7	Bob Bell	5.00
8	Adam Piatt	5.00
9	Mike Lamb	15.00
10	Pablo Ozuna	5.00
11	Jason Tyner	5.00
12	Jason Marquis	10.00
13	Eric Munson	6.00
14	Seth Etherton	5.00
15	Milton Bradley	15.00
16	Not Issued	
17	Michael Wenner	5.00

18	Mike Glendenning	5.00
19	Tony Alvarez	5.00
20	Adrian Gonzalez	80.00
21	Corey Smith	10.00
22	Matt Wheatland	5.00
23	Adam Johnson	8.00
24	Mike Stodolka	5.00
25	Rocco Baldelli	40.00
26	Juan Rincon	5.00
27	Chad Durbin	5.00
28	Yorvit Torrealba	5.00
29	Nick Green	10.00
30	Derek Thompson	5.00
31	John Lackey	40.00
32	Not Issued	
33	Kevin Gregg	5.00
34	Not Issued	
35	Denny Abreu	5.00
36	Brian Tollberg	5.00
37	Yamid Haad	5.00
38	Grady Sizemore	300.00
39	Carlos Silva	10.00
40	Jorge Cantu	20.00
41	Bobby Kielty	8.00
42	Scott Thorman	30.00
43	Juan Salas	10.00
44	Phil Dumatrait	5.00
45	Not Issued	
46	Mike Lockwood	5.00
47	Yovanny Lara	5.00
48	Tripper Johnson	10.00
49	Colby Lewis	5.00
50	Neil Jenkins	5.00
51	Keith Bucktrot	5.00
52	Eric Byrnes	30.00
53	Aaron Herr	5.00
54	Erasmo Ramirez	5.00
55	Chris Richard	5.00
56	Not Issued	
57	Mike Bynum	5.00
58	Brian Esposito	5.00
59	Chris Clapinski	5.00
60	Augie Ojeda	5.00

2000 Bowman's Best

JUAN GONZALEZ

		NM/M
Complete Set (200):		275.00
Common Player:		.20
Common Rookie (151-200):		5.00
Production 2,999 Sets		
Pack (4):		4.00
Box (24):		75.00
1	Nomar Garciaparra	2.00
2	Chipper Jones	1.50
3	Damion Easley	.20
4	Bernie Williams	.40
5	Barry Bonds	3.00
6	Jermaine Dye	.20
7	John Olerud	.20
8	Mike Hampton	.20
9	Cal Ripken Jr.	3.00
10	Jeff Bagwell	1.00
11	Troy Glaus	1.00
12	J.D. Drew	.40
13	Jeromy Burnitz	.20
14	Carlos Delgado	.75
15	Shawn Green	.40
16	Kevin Millwood	.40
17	Rondell White	.20
18	Scott Rolen	.75
19	Jeff Cirillo	.20
20	Barry Larkin	.20
21	Brian Giles	.20
22	Roger Clemens	1.75
23	Manny Ramirez	1.00
24	Alex Gonzalez	.20
25	Mark Grace	.35
26	Fernando Tatis	.20
27	Randy Johnson	1.00
28	Roger Cedeno	.20
29	Brian Jordan	.20
30	Kevin Brown	.40
31	Greg Vaughn	.20

32	Roberto Alomar	.50
33	Larry Walker	.20
34	Rafael Palmeiro	.75
35	Curt Schilling	.50
36	Orlando Hernandez	.20
37	Todd Walker	.20
38	Juan Gonzalez	1.00
39	Sean Casey	.35
40	Tony Gwynn	1.50
41	Albert Belle	.20
42	Gary Sheffield	.40
43	Michael Barrett	.20
44	Preston Wilson	.20
45	Jim Thome	.40
46	Shannon Stewart	.20
47	Mo Vaughn	.20
48	Ben Grieve	.20
49	Adrian Beltre	.35
50	Sammy Sosa	2.00
51	Bob Abreu	.20
52	Edgardo Alfonzo	.20
53	Carlos Febles	.20
54	Frank Thomas	1.00
55	Alex Rodriguez	2.50
56	Cliff Floyd	.20
57	Jose Canseco	.40
58	Erubiel Durazo	.20
59	Tim Hudson	.50
60	Craig Biggio	.20
61	Eric Karros	.20
62	Mike Mussina	.50
63	Robin Ventura	.20
64	Carlos Beltran	.50
65	Pedro Martinez	1.00
66	Gabe Kapler	.20
67	Jason Kendall	.20
68	Derek Jeter	3.00
69	Magglio Ordonez	.50
70	Mike Piazza	2.00
71	Mike Lieberthal	.20
72	Andres Galarraga	.20
73	Raul Mondesi	.20
74	Eric Chavez	.40
75	Greg Maddux	1.50
76	Matt Williams	.30
77	Kris Benson	.20
78	Ivan Rodriguez	.50
79	Pokey Reese	.20
80	Vladimir Guerrero	1.00
81	Mark McGwire	2.50
82	Vinny Castilla	.20
83	Todd Helton	1.00
84	Andruw Jones	.75
85	Ken Griffey Jr.	2.00
86	Mark McGwire	1.25
87	Derek Jeter	1.50
88	Chipper Jones	.75
89	Nomar Garciaparra	1.00
90	Sammy Sosa	.75
91	Cal Ripken Jr.	1.50
92	Juan Gonzalez	.50
93	Alex Rodriguez	1.25
94	Barry Bonds	1.50
95	Sean Casey	.25
96	Vladimir Guerrero	.50
97	Mike Piazza	1.00
98	Shawn Green	.25
99	Jeff Bagwell	.50
100	Ken Griffey Jr.	1.00
101	Rick Ankiel	.35
102	John Patterson	.20
103	David Walling	.20
104	Michael Restovich	.20
105	A.J. Burnett	.20
106	Matt Riley	.20
107	Chad Hermansen	.20
108	Choo Freeman	.20
109	Mark Quinn	.20
110	Corey Patterson	.40
111	Ramon Ortiz	.20
112	Vernon Wells	.40
113	Milton Bradley	.20
114	Travis Dawkins	.20
115	Sean Burroughs	.35
116	Willi Mo Pena	.40
117	Dee Brown	.20
118	C.C. Sabathia	.20
119	Larry Bigbie RC	.20
120	Octavio Dotel	.20
121	Kip Wells	.20
122	Ben Petrick	.20
123	Mark Mulder	.40
124	Jason Standridge	.20
125	Adam Piatt	.20
126	Steve Lomasney	.20
127	Jayson Werth	.20
128	Alex Escobar	.20
129	Ryan Anderson	.20
130	Adam Dunn	.50
131	Omar Ortiz	.20
132	Brad Penny	.20
133	Daryle Ward	.20
134	Eric Munson	.20
135	Nick Johnson	.50

136	Jason Jennings	.20
137	Tim Raines Jr.	.20
138	Ruben Mateo	.20
139	Jack Cust	.20
140	Rafael Furcal	.20
141	Eric Gagne	.35
142	Tony Armas	.20
143	Mike Paradis	.20
144	Chris George	.20
145	Alfonso Soriano	.75
146	Josh Hamilton	.50
147	Michael Cuddyer	.35
148	Jay Gehrke	.20
149	Josh Girdley	.20
150	Pat Burrell	.75
151	Brett Myers RC	10.00
152	Scott Seabol RC	5.00
153	Keith Reed RC	5.00
154	Francisco Rodriguez RC	20.00
155	Barry Zito RC	20.00
156	Pat Manning RC	5.00
157	Ben Christensen RC	5.00
158	Corey Myers RC	5.00
159	Wascar Serrano RC	5.00
160	Wes Anderson RC	5.00
161	Andy Tracy RC	5.00
162	Cesar Saba RC	5.00
163	Mike Lamb RC	5.00
164	Bobby Bradley RC	5.00
165	Vince Faison RC	5.00
166	Ty Howington RC	8.00
167	Ken Harvey RC	8.00
168	Josh Kalinowski RC	5.00
169	Ruben Salazar RC	5.00
170	Aaron Rowand RC	10.00
171	Ramon Santiago RC	5.00
172	Scott Sobkowiak RC	5.00
173	Lyle Overbay RC	10.00
174	Rico Washington RC	5.00
175	Rick Asadoorian RC	5.00
176	Matt Ginter RC	5.00
177	Jason Stumm RC	5.00
178	B.J. Garbe RC	5.00
179	Mike MacDougal RC	5.00
180	Ryan Christianson RC	5.00
181	Kurt Ainsworth RC	5.00
182	Brad Baisley RC	5.00
183	Ben Broussard RC	5.00
184	Aaron McNeal RC	5.00
185	John Sneed RC	5.00
186	Junior Brignac RC	5.00
187	Chance Caple RC	5.00
188	Scott Downs RC	5.00
189	Matt Cepicky RC	5.00
190	Chin-Feng Chen RC	20.00
191	Johan Santana RC	75.00
192	Brad Baker RC	5.00
193	Jason Repko RC	5.00
194	Craig Dingman RC	5.00
195	Chris Wakeland RC	5.00
196	Rogelio Arias RC	5.00
197	Luis Matos RC	8.00
198	Robert Ramsay RC	5.00
199	Willie Bloomquist RC	20.00
200	Tony Pena Jr. RC	5.00

Bets

RUBEN MATEO

		NM/M
Complete Set (10):		10.00
Common Player:		.75
Inserted 1:15		
1	Pat Burrell	2.00
2	Alfonso Soriano	2.00
3	Corey Patterson	1.50
4	Eric Munson	.75
5	Sean Burroughs	1.00
6	Rafael Furcal	.75
7	Rick Ankiel	1.00
8	Nick Johnson	1.50
9	Ruben Mateo	.75
10	Josh Hamilton	1.00

Franchise 2000

		NM/M
Complete Set (25):		60.00
Common Player:		1.00
Inserted 1:18		
1	Cal Ripken Jr.	8.00
2	Nomar Garciaparra	6.00
3	Frank Thomas	2.00
4	Manny Ramirez	2.00
5	Juan Gonzalez	1.50
6	Carlos Beltran	2.00
7	Derek Jeter	8.00
8	Alex Rodriguez	6.00
9	Ben Grieve	1.00
10	Jose Canseco	1.50
11	Ivan Rodriguez	1.50
12	Mo Vaughn	1.00
13	Randy Johnson	3.00
14	Chipper Jones	4.00
15	Sammy Sosa	5.00
16	Ken Griffey Jr.	5.00
17	Larry Walker	1.00
18	Preston Wilson	1.00
19	Jeff Bagwell	2.00
20	Shawn Green	1.00
21	Vladimir Guerrero	2.00
22	Mike Piazza	5.00
23	Scott Rolen	2.00
24	Tony Gwynn	3.50
25	Barry Bonds	8.00

Franchise Favorites Autograph

		NM/M
Common Player:		20.00
Version A & B 1:1,291		
Version C 1:5,153		
1A	Sean Casey	20.00
1B	Johnny Bench	50.00
1C	Sean Casey, Johnny Bench	100.00
2A	Cal Ripken Jr.	125.00
2B	Brooks Robinson	50.00
2C	Cal Ripken Jr., Brooks Robinson	250.00

Franchise Favorites

	NM/M
Complete Set (6):	15.00

Common Player:		1.00
Inserted 1:17		
1A	Sean Casey	1.00
1B	Johnny Bench	3.00
1C	Sean Casey, Johnny Bench	3.00
2A	Cal Ripken Jr.	5.00
2B	Brooks Robinson	2.00
2C	Cal Ripken Jr., Brooks Robinson	5.00

Locker Room Collection Autographs

	NM/M
Common Player:	8.00
Inserted 1:57	

1	Carlos Beltran	25.00
2	Rick Ankiel	8.00
3	Vernon Wells	12.00
4	Ruben Mateo	8.00
5	Ben Petrick	8.00
6	Adam Piatt	8.00
7	Eric Munson	8.00
8	Alfonso Soriano	40.00
9	Kerry Wood	25.00
10	Jack Cust	8.00
11	Rafael Furcal	15.00
12	Josh Hamilton	10.00
13	Brad Penny	8.00
14	Dee Brown	8.00
15	Milton Bradley	12.00
16	Ryan Anderson	8.00
17	John Patterson	8.00
18	Nick Johnson	10.00
19	Peter Bergeron	8.00

Locker Room Collection Lumber

	NM/M
Common Player:	5.00
Inserted 1:376	

1	Carlos Beltran	15.00
2	Rick Ankiel	5.00
3	Vernon Wells	10.00
4	Adam Kennedy	5.00
5	Ben Petrick	5.00
6	Adam Piatt	5.00
7	Eric Munson	5.00
8	Rafael Furcal	8.00
9	J.D. Drew	8.00
10	Pat Burrell	10.00

Locker Room Collection Jerseys

	NM/M
Common Player:	4.00
Inserted 1:206	

1	Carlos Beltran	12.00
2	Rick Ankiel	5.00
3	Adam Kennedy	4.00
4	Ben Petrick	4.00
5	Adam Piatt	4.00

Rookie Signed Baseballs

	NM/M
Complete Set (5):	75.00
Common Player:	10.00
Inserted 1:688	

1	Josh Hamilton	30.00
2	Rick Ankiel	15.00
3	Alfonso Soriano	50.00
4	Nick Johnson	30.00
5	Corey Patterson	20.00

Selections

	NM/M
Complete Set (15):	50.00

Common Player:		1.00
Inserted 1:30		
1	Alex Rodriguez	7.50
2	Ken Griffey Jr.	6.00
3	Pat Burrell	2.00
4	Mark McGwire	7.50
5	Derek Jeter	10.00
6	Nomar Garciaparra	6.00
7	Mike Piazza	6.00
8	Josh Hamilton	1.00
9	Cal Ripken Jr.	10.00
10	Jeff Bagwell	2.50
11	Chipper Jones	4.50
12	Jose Canseco	1.50
13	Carlos Beltran	2.00
14	Kerry Wood	2.00
15	Ben Grieve	1.00

Year By Year

	NM/M
Complete Set (10):	25.00
Common Card:	1.50
Inserted 1:23	

1	Sammy Sosa, Ken Griffey Jr.	4.00
2	Nomar Garciaparra, Vladimir Guerrero	4.00
3	Alex Rodriguez, Jeff Cirillo	5.00
4	Mike Piazza, Pedro Martinez	4.00
5	Derek Jeter, Edgardo Alfonzo	6.00
6	Alfonso Soriano, Rick Ankiel	2.00
7	Mark McGwire, Barry Bonds	6.00
8	Juan Gonzalez, Larry Walker	1.50
9	Ivan Rodriguez, Jeff Bagwell	1.50
10	Shawn Green, Manny Ramirez	1.50

2001 Bowman

Complete Set (440): 140.00
Common Player: .15
Common Rookie: .25

Golds:		1-2X
Inserted 1:1		
Pack (10):		8.00
Box (24):		160.00
1	Jason Giambi	.40
2	Rafael Furcal	.15
3	Rick Ankiel	.15
4	Freddy Garcia	.15
5	Magglio Ordonez	.25
6	Bernie Williams	.40
7	Kenny Lofton	.15
8	Al Leiter	.15
9	Albert Belle	.15
10	Craig Biggio	.15
11	Mark Mulder	.15
12	Carlos Delgado	.40
13	Darin Erstad	.25
14	Richie Sexson	.15
15	Randy Johnson	.75
16	Greg Maddux	1.50
17	Cliff Floyd	.15
18	Mark Buehrle	.15
19	Chris Singleton	.15
20	Orlando Hernandez	.20
21	Javier Vazquez	.15
22	Jeff Kent	.15
23	Jim Thome	.50
24	John Olerud	.15
25	Jason Kendall	.15
26	Scott Rolen	.50
27	Tony Gwynn	.75
28	Edgardo Alfonzo	.15
29	Pokey Reese	.15
30	Todd Helton	.50
31	Mark Quinn	.15
32	Dan Tosca RC	.25
33	Dean Palmer	.15
34	Jacque Jones	.15
35	Ray Durham	.15
36	Rafael Palmeiro	.50
37	Carl Everett	.15
38	Ryan Dempster	.15
39	Randy Wolf	.15
40	Vladimir Guerrero	.75
41	Livan Hernandez	.15
42	Mo Vaughn	.15
43	Shannon Stewart	.15
44	Preston Wilson	.15
45	Jose Vidro	.15
46	Fred McGriff	.15
47	Kevin Brown	.25
48	Peter Bergeron	.15
49	Miguel Tejada	.50
50	Chipper Jones	.75
51	Edgar Martinez	.15
52	Tony Batista	.15
53	Jorge Posada	.40
54	Ricky Ledee	.15
55	Sammy Sosa	1.00
56	Steve Cox	.15
57	Tony Armas Jr.	.15
58	Gary Sheffield	.40
59	Bartolo Colon	.15
60	Pat Burrell	.40
61	Jay Payton	.15
62	Sean Casey	.25
63	Larry Walker	.15
64	Mike Mussina	.40
65	Nomar Garciaparra	1.00
66	Darren Dreifort	.15
67	Richard Hidalgo	.15
68	Troy Glaus	.40
69	Ben Grieve	.15
70	Jim Edmonds	.40
71	Raul Mondesi	.15
72	Andruw Jones	.50
73	Luis Castillo	.15
74	Mike Sweeney	.15
75	Derek Jeter	2.00
76	Ruben Mateo	.15
77	Carlos Lee	.15
78	Cristian Guzman	.15
79	Mike Hampton	.25
80	J.D. Drew	.25
81	Matt Lawton	.15
82	Moises Alou	.15
83	Terrence Long	.15
84	Geoff Jenkins	.15
85	Manny Ramirez	.75
86	Johnny Damon	.15
87	Barry Larkin	.15
88	Pedro Martinez	.75
89	Juan Gonzalez	.40
90	Roger Clemens	2.00
91	Carlos Beltran	.50
92	Brad Radke	.15
93	Orlando Cabrera	.15
94	Roberto Alomar	.50
95	Barry Bonds	2.00
96	Tim Hudson	.25
97	Tom Glavine	.25
98	Jeromy Burnitz	.15
99	Adrian Beltre	.15
100	Mike Piazza	1.00

101	Kerry Wood	.40
102	Steve Finley	.15
103	Alex Cora	.15
104	Bob Abreu	.15
105	Neifi Perez	.15
106	Mark Redman	.15
107	Paul Konerko	.15
108	Jermaine Dye	.15
109	Brian Giles	.15
110	Ivan Rodriguez	.50
111	Vinny Castilla	.15
112	Adam Kennedy	.15
113	Eric Chavez	.25
114	Billy Koch	.15
115	Shawn Green	.25
116	Matt Williams	.15
117	Greg Vaughn	.15
118	Gabe Kapler	.15
119	Jeff Cirillo	.15
120	Frank Thomas	.50
121	David Justice	.15
122	Cal Ripken Jr.	3.00
123	Rich Aurilia	.15
124	Curt Schilling	.40
125	Barry Zito	.25
126	Brian Jordan	.15
127	Chan Ho Park	.15
128	J.T. Snow Jr.	.15
129	Kazuhiro Sasaki	.15
130	Alex Rodriguez	2.00
131	Mariano Rivera	.25
132	Eric Milton	.15
133	Andy Pettitte	.25
134	Scott Elarton	.15
135	Ken Griffey Jr.	1.50
136	Bengie Molina	.15
137	Jeff Bagwell	.50
138	Kevin Millwood	.15
139	Tino Martinez	.25
140	Mark McGwire	1.50
141	Larry Barnes	.15
142	John Buck RC	.25
143	Freddie Bynum RC	.25
144	Abraham Nunez	.15
145	Felix Diaz RC	.25
146	Horatio Estrada RC	.25
147	Ben Diggins	.15
148	Tsuyoshi Shinjo RC	.50
149	Rocco Baldelli	.25
150	Rod Barajas	.15
151	Luis Terrero	.15
152	Milton Bradley	.15
153	Kurt Ainsworth	.15
154	Russell Branyan	.15
155	Ryan Anderson	.15
156	Mitch Jones RC	.25
157	Chip Ambres	.15
158	Steve Bennett RC	.25
159	Ivanon Coffie	.15
160	Sean Burroughs	.15
161	Keith Bucktrot	.15
162	Tony Alvarez	.15
163	Joaquin Benoit	.15
164	Rick Asadoorian	.15
165	Ben Broussard	.25
166	Ryan Madson RC	1.50
167	Dee Brown	.15
168	Sergio Contreras RC	.25
169	John Barnes	.15
170	Ben Washburn RC	.50
171	Erick Almonte RC	.25
172	Shawn Fagan RC	.25
173	Gary Johnson RC	.25
174	Brady Clark	.15
175	Grant Roberts	.15
176	Tony Torcato	.15
177	Ramon Castro	.15
178	Esteban German	.15
179	Joe Hamer RC	.25
180	Nick Neugebauer	.25
181	Dernell Stenson	.15
182	Yhency Brazoban RC	.40
183	Aaron Myette	.15
184	Juan Sosa	.15
185	Brandon Inge	.15
186	Domingo Guante RC	.25
187	Adrian Brown	.15
188	Deivi Mendez RC	.25
189	Luis Matos	.15
190	Pedro Liriano RC	.50
191	Donnie Bridges	.15
192	Alex Cintron	.15
193	Jace Brewer	.15
194	Ron Davenport RC	.50
195	Jason Belcher RC	.25
196	Adrian Hernandez RC	.25
197	Bobby Kielty	.15
198	Reggie Griggs RC	.25
199	Reggie Abercrombie RC	1.00
200	Troy Farnsworth RC	.50
201	Matt Belisle	.15
202	Miguel Villilo RC	.50
203	Adam Everett	.15

#	Player	Price
204	John Lackey	.15
205	Pasqual Coco	.15
206	Adam Wainwright	.25
207	Matt White RC	.25
208	Chin-Feng Chen RC	.25
209	Jeff Andra RC	.25
210	Willie Bloomquist	.15
211	Wes Anderson	.15
212	Enrique Cruz	.15
213	Jerry Hairston Jr.	.15
214	Mike Bynum	.15
215	Brian Hitchcox RC	.25
216	Ryan Christianson	.15
217	J.J. Davis	.15
218	Jovanny Cedeno	.15
219	Elvin Nina	.15
220	Alex Graman	.15
221	Arturo McDowell	.15
222	Deivi Santos RC	.25
223	Jody Gerut	.15
224	Sun-Woo Kim	.15
225	Jimmy Rollins	.25
226	Pappy Ndungidi	.15
227	Ruben Salazar	.15
228	Josh Girdley	.15
229	Carl Crawford	.15
230	Luis Montanez RC	.50
231	Ramon Carvajal RC	.25
232	Matt Riley	.15
233	Ben Davis	.15
234	Jason Grabowski	.15
235	Chris George	.15
236	Hank Blalock RC	5.00
237	Roy Oswalt	.25
238	Eric Reynolds RC	.25
239	Brian Cole	.15
240	Denny Bautista RC	.75
241	Hector Garcia RC	.25
242	Joe Thurston RC	.25
243	Brad Cresse	.25
244	Corey Patterson	.25
245	Brett Evert RC	.25
246	Elpidio Guzman RC	.25
247	Vernon Wells	.15
248	Roberto Miniel RC	.25
249	Brian Bass RC	.50
250	Mark Burnett RC	.25
251	Juan Silvestre	.15
252	Pablo Ozuna	.15
253	Jayson Werth	.15
254	Russ Jacobsen RC	.25
255	Chad Hermansen	.15
256	Travis Hafner RC	8.00
257	Bradley Baker	.15
258	Gookie Dawkins	.15
259	Michael Cuddyer	.15
260	Mark Buehrle	.15
261	Ricardo Aramboles	.15
262	Esix Snead RC	.25
263	Wilson Betemit RC	.50
264	Albert Pujols	85.00
265	Joe Lawrence	.15
266	Ramon Ortiz	.15
267	Ben Sheets	.50
268	Luke Lockwood RC	.25
269	Toby Hall	.15
270	Jack Cust	.15
271	Pedro Feliz	.15
272	Noel Devarez RC	.15
273	Josh Beckett	.15
274	Alex Escobar	.15
275	Doug Gredvig RC	.25
276	Marcus Giles	.15
277	Jon Rauch	.15
278	Brian Schmitt RC	.25
279	Seung Song RC	.50
280	Kevin Mench	.15
281	Adam Eaton	.15
282	Shawn Sonnier	.15
283	Andy Van Hekken RC	.25
284	Aaron Rowand	.15
285	Tony Blanco RC	.25
286	Ryan Kohlmeier	.15
287	C.C. Sabathia	.25
288	Bubba Crosby	.15
289	Josh Hamilton	.25
290	Dee Haynes RC	.15
291	Jason Marquis	.15
292	Julio Zuleta	.15
293	Carlos Hernandez	.15
294	Matt LeCroy	.15
295	Andy Beal RC	.25
296	Carlos Pena	.25
297	Reggie Taylor	.15
298	Bob Keppel RC	.25
299	Miguel Cabrera (Photo actually Manuel Esquivia.)	.75
300	Ryan Franklin	.15
301	Brandon Phillips	.15
302	Victor Hall RC	.25
303	Tony Pena Jr.	.15
304	Jim Journell RC	.25
305	Cristian Guerrero	.25
306	Miguel Olivo	.15
307	Jin Ho Cho	.15
308	Choo Freeman	.15
309	Danny Borrell RC	.25
310	Doug Mientkiewicz	.15
311	Aaron Herr	.15
312	Keith Ginter	.15
313	Felipe Lopez	.15
314	Jeff Goldbach RC	.25
315	Travis Harper	.15
316	Paul LoDuca	.15
317	Joe Torres	.15
318	Eric Byrnes	.15
319	George Lombard	.15
320	David Krynzel	.15
321	Ben Christensen	.15
322	Aubrey Huff	.15
323	Lyle Overbay	.15
324	Sean McGowan	.15
325	Jeff Heaverlo	.15
326	Timo Perez	.15
327	Octavio Martinez RC	.25
328	Vince Faison	.15
329	David Parrish RC	.25
330	Bobby Bradley	.15
331	Jason Miller RC	.25
332	Corey Spencer RC	.25
333	Craig House	.15
334	Maxim St. Pierre RC	.25
335	Adam Johnson	.15
336	Joe Crede	.15
337	Greg Nash RC	.25
338	Chad Durbin	.15
339	Pat Magness RC	.25
340	Matt Wheatland	.15
341	Julio Lugo	.15
342	Grady Sizemore	.50
343	Adrian Gonzalez	.25
344	Tim Raines Jr.	.15
345	Rainier Olmedo RC	.15
346	Phil Dumatrait	.15
347	Brandon Mims RC	.25
348	Jason Jennings	.15
349	Phil Wilson RC	.25
350	Jason Hart	.15
351	Cesar Izturis	.15
352	Matt Butler RC	.25
353	David Kelton	.15
354	Luke Prokopec	.15
355	Corey Smith	.15
356	Joel Pineiro	.75
357	Ken Chenard	.15
358	Keith Reed	.15
359	David Walling	.15
360	Alexis Gomez RC	.50
361	Justin Morneau RC	10.00
362	Josh Fogg RC	.50
363	J.R. House	.15
364	Andy Tracy	.15
365	Kenny Kelly	.15
366	Aaron McNeal	.15
367	Nick Johnson	.15
368	Brian Esposito	.15
369	Charles Frazier RC	.25
370	Scott Heard	.15
371	Patrick Strange	.15
372	Mike Meyers	.15
373	Ryan Ludwick RC	.50
374	Brad Wilkerson	.15
375	Allen Levrault	.15
376	Seth McClung RC	.40
377	Joe Nathan	.15
378	Rafael Soriano RC	.75
379	Chris Richard	.15
380	Xavier Nady	.15
381	Tike Redman	.15
382	Adam Dunn	.15
383	Jared Abruzzo RC	.25
384	Jason Richardson RC	.25
385	Matt Holliday	.50
386	Darwin Cubillian RC	.25
387	Mike Nannini	.15
388	Blake Williams RC	.25
389	Valentino Pascucci RC	.25
390	Jon Garland	.15
391	Josh Pressley	.15
392	Jose Ortiz	.15
393	Ryan Hannaman RC	.25
394	Steve Smyth RC	.25
395	John Patterson	.15
396	Chad Petty RC	.25
397	Jake Peavy RC	10.00
398	Onix Mercado RC	.25
399	Jason Romano	.15
400	Luis Torres RC	.25
401	Casey Fossum RC	.25
402	Eduardo Figueroa RC	.25
403	Bryan Barnowski RC	.25
404	Tim Redding	.15
405	Jason Standridge	.15
406	Marvin Seale RC	.25
407	Todd Moser	.15
408	Alex Gordon	.15
409	Steve Smitherman RC	.75
410	Ben Petrick	.15
411	Eric Munson	.15
412	Luis Rivas	.15
413	Matt Ginter	.15
414	Alfonso Soriano	.50
415	Rafael Boitel RC	.25
416	Dany Morban RC	.25
417	Justin Woodrowc RC	.25
418	Wilfredo Rodriguez	.15
419	Derrick Van Dusen RC	.25
420	Josh Spoerl RC	.25
421	Juan Pierre	.15
422	J.C. Romero	.15
423	Ed Rogers RC	.25
424	Tomokazu Ohka	.25
425	Ben Hendrickson RC	.25
426	Carlos Zambrano	.15
427	Brett Myers	.15
428	Scott Seabol	.15
429	Thomas Mitchell	.15
430	Jose Reyes	35.00
431	Kip Wells	.15
432	Willi Mo Pena	.15
433	Adam Pettyjohn RC	.25
434	Austin Kearns	.15
435	Rico Washington	.15
436	Doug Nickle RC	.25
437	Steve Lomasney	.15
438	Jason Jones RC	.25
439	Bobby Seay	.15
440	Justin Wayne RC	.50

Autographs

JOSH PRESSLEY

		NM/M
Common Autograph:		5.00
Inserted 1:74		
BB	Brian Barnowski	5.00
WB	Wilson Betemit	15.00
JB	Jason Botts	15.00
SB	Sean Burroughs	5.00
FB	Freddie Bynum	5.00
ND	Noel Devarez	5.00
JD	Jose Diaz	5.00
BD	Ben Diggins	5.00
AE	Alex Escobar	8.00
RF	Rafael Furcal	10.00
AG	Adrian Gonzalez	15.00
AKG	Alex Gordon	5.00
AJG	Alex Graman	5.00
CG	Cristian Guerrero	5.00
TH	Travis Hafner	100.00
JH	Josh Hamilton	30.00
JWH	Jason Hart	5.00
JRH	J.R. House	5.00
RJ	Russ Jacobson	5.00
AJ	Adam Johnson	5.00
TJ	Tripper Johnson	5.00
DWK	David Kelton	5.00
DK	David Krynzel	5.00
PR	Pedro Liriano	5.00
SM	Sean McGowan	5.00
KM	Kevin Mench	8.00
LM	Luis Montanez	8.00
JM	Justin Morneau	140.00
LO	Lyle Overbay	12.00
ADP	Adam Piatt	8.00
JP	Josh Pressley	6.00
AP	Albert Pujols	650.00
KS	Kazuhiro Sasaki	
BS	Ben Sheets	20.00
SDS	Steve Smyth	5.00
SS	Shawn Sonnier	5.00
SU	Sixto Urena	5.00
MV	Miguel Villilo	5.00
BW	Brad Wilkerson	10.00
BZ	Barry Zito	25.00

Autoproofs

Common Player:
Inserted 1:18,259H
Inserted 1:8,306HTA
Redemption Expired 4/30/03
Values Undetermined

Autographed Rookie Reprints

WILLIE MAYS

		NM/M
Common Autograph:		20.00
Inserted 1:2,467		
1	Yogi Berra	70.00
2	Willie Mays	200.00
3	Stan Musial	100.00
4	Duke Snider	35.00
5	Warren Spahn	50.00
6	Ralph Kiner	25.00
7	Don Larsen	30.00
9	Don Zimmer	20.00
10	Minnie Minoso	20.00

Autographed Game-Used Bat Rookie Reprints

Inserted 1:18,259
No pricing due to scarcity.

Autographed Three-Piece Game-Used

No pricing due to scarcity.
AE Alex Escobar
JH Josh Hamilton
EM Eric Munson
CP Corey Patterson
BW Brad Wilkerson

Futures Game-Worn Jersey

2000 All-Star Futures Game

		NM/M
Common Player:		5.00
Inserted 1:82		
KA	Kurt Ainsworth	6.00
CA	Craig Anderson	5.00
RA	Ryan Anderson	5.00
BB	Bobby Bradley	5.00
MB	Mike Bynum	5.00
RC	Ramon Castro	25.00
CC	Chin-Feng Chen	5.00
JC	Jack Cust	5.00
TD	Travis Dawkins	5.00
RD	Randey Dorame	5.00
AE	Alex Escobar	5.00
CG	Chris George	5.00
MG	Marcus Giles	6.00
JH	Josh Hamilton	8.00
CH	Carlos Hernandez	5.00
SK	Sun-Woo Kim	5.00
FL	Felipe Lopez	5.00
EM	Eric Munson	5.00
AM	Aaron Myette	5.00
NN	Ntema Ndungidi	5.00
TO	Tomokazu Ohka	6.00
RO	Ramon Ortiz	5.00
DCP	Corey Patterson	8.00
CP	Carlos Pena	5.00
BP	Ben Petrick	5.00
GR	Grant Roberts	5.00
JR	Jason Romano	5.00
BS	Ben Sheets	6.00
CT	Chin-Hui Tsao	15.00
VW	Vernon Wells	8.00
BW	Brad Wilkerson	5.00
TW	Travis Wilson	5.00
BZ	Barry Zito	15.00
JZ	Julio Zuleta	5.00

Futures Game Three-Piece Game-Used

		NM/M
Common Player:		20.00
RC	Ramon Castro	20.00
CC	Chin-Feng Chen	80.00

JC	Jack Cust	20.00
TD	Travis Dawkins	20.00
AE	Alex Escobar	20.00
MG	Marcus Giles	20.00
JH	Josh Hamilton	20.00
FL	Felipe Lopez	20.00
EM	Eric Munson	25.00
NN	Ntema Ndungidi	20.00
DCP	Corey Patterson	25.00
CP	Carlos Pena	20.00
BP	Ben Petrick	20.00
JR	Jason Romano	20.00
VW	Vernon Wells	30.00
BW	Brad Wilkerson	20.00
TW	Travis Wilson	20.00
JZ	Julio Zuleta	20.00

Game-Used Bat Rookie Reprints

		NM/M
Common Player:		10.00
Inserted 1:1,954		
1	Willie Mays	60.00
2	Duke Snider	25.00
3	Minnie Minoso	10.00
4	Hank Bauer	10.00
5	Al Rosen	10.00

Rookie Reprints

		NM/M
Complete Set (25):		50.00
Common Player:		1.50
Inserted 1:12		
1	Yogi Berra	5.00
2	Ralph Kiner	2.50
3	Stan Musial	6.00
4	Warren Spahn	4.00
5	Roy Campanella	4.00
6	Bob Lemon	1.50
7	Robin Roberts	2.00
8	Duke Snider	4.00
9	Early Wynn	1.50
10	Richie Ashburn	1.50
11	Gil Hodges	2.00
12	Hank Bauer	2.00
13	Don Newcombe	1.50
14	Al Rosen	1.50
15	Willie Mays	8.00
16	Joe Garagiola	2.00
17	Whitey Ford	4.00
18	Lew Burdette	1.50
19	Gil McDougald	1.50
20	Minnie Minoso	1.50
21	Eddie Mathews	4.00
22	Harvey Kuenn	2.00
23	Don Larsen	3.00
24	Elston Howard	2.00
25	Don Zimmer	1.50

Rookie of the Year Dual Jersey

	NM/M
Inserted 1:2,202	
ROYR Kazuhiro Sasaki, Rafael Furcal	30.00

2001 Bowman Chrome

	NM/M
Complete Set (351):	

RAFAEL PALMEIRO • 1B
TEXAS RANGERS

Common (1-110, 201-310):		.20
Common Ref. (111-200, 311-330):		4.00
Inserted 1:4		
Common Ref. Auto. (331-350):		25.00
Production 500		
Pack (4):		20.00
Box (24):		450.00
1	Jason Giambi	.60
2	Rafael Furcal	.40
3	Bernie Williams	.50
4	Kenny Lofton	.20
5	Al Leiter	.20
6	Albert Belle	.20
7	Craig Biggio	.40
8	Mark Mulder	.40
9	Carlos Delgado	.75
10	Darin Erstad	.75
11	Richie Sexson	.40
12	Randy Johnson	1.00
13	Greg Maddux	1.50
14	Orlando Hernandez	.20
15	Javier Vazquez	.20
16	Jeff Kent	.40
17	Jim Thome	.50
18	John Olerud	.20
19	Jason Kendall	.20
20	Scott Rolen	.75
21	Tony Gwynn	1.00
22	Edgardo Alfonzo	.20
23	Pokey Reese	.20
24	Todd Helton	.75
25	Mark Quinn	.20
26	Dean Palmer	.20
27	Ray Durham	.20
28	Rafael Palmeiro	.75
29	Carl Everett	.20
30	Vladimir Guerrero	1.00
31	Livan Hernandez	.20
32	Preston Wilson	.20
33	Jose Vidro	.20
34	Fred McGriff	.20
35	Kevin Brown	.20
36	Miguel Tejada	.50
37	Chipper Jones	1.00
38	Edgar Martinez	.20
39	Tony Batista	.20
40	Jorge Posada	.50
41	Sammy Sosa	1.00
42	Gary Sheffield	.50
43	Bartolo Colon	.20
44	Pat Burrell	.50
45	Jay Payton	.20
46	Mike Mussina	.60
47	Nomar Garciaparra	1.00
48	Darren Dreifort	.20
49	Richard Hidalgo	.20
50	Troy Glaus	.50
51	Ben Grieve	.20
52	Jim Edmonds	.40
53	Raul Mondesi	.20
54	Andruw Jones	.75
55	Mike Sweeney	.20
56	Derek Jeter	3.00
57	Ruben Mateo	.20
58	Cristian Guzman	.20
59	Mike Hampton	.20
60	J.D. Drew	.40
61	Matt Lawton	.20
62	Moises Alou	.40
63	Terrence Long	.20
64	Geoff Jenkins	.20
65	Manny Ramirez	1.00
66	Johnny Damon	1.00
67	Pedro Martinez	1.00
68	Juan Gonzalez	.50
69	Roger Clemens	2.00
70	Carlos Beltran	.75
71	Roberto Alomar	.50
72	Barry Bonds	3.00
73	Tim Hudson	.50
74	Tom Glavine	.50
75	Jeromy Burnitz	.20

76	Adrian Beltre	.40
77	Mike Piazza	1.00
78	Kerry Wood	.40
79	Steve Finley	.20
80	Bobby Abreu	.40
81	Neifi Perez	.20
82	Mark Redman	.20
83	Paul Konerko	.40
84	Jermaine Dye	.20
85	Brian Giles	.20
86	Ivan Rodriguez	.75
87	Adam Kennedy	.20
88	Eric Chavez	.40
89	Billy Koch	.20
90	Shawn Green	.40
91	Matt Williams	.20
92	Greg Vaughn	.20
93	Jeff Cirillo	.20
94	Frank Thomas	.75
95	David Justice	.20
96	Cal Ripken Jr.	3.00
97	Curt Schilling	.75
98	Barry Zito	.40
99	Brian Jordan	.20
100	Chan Ho Park	.20
101	J.T. Snow Jr.	.20
102	Kazuhiro Sasaki	.20
103	Alex Rodriguez	2.50
104	Mariano Rivera	.50
105	Eric Milton	.20
106	Andy Pettitte	.50
107	Ken Griffey Jr.	2.00
108	Bengie Molina	.20
109	Jeff Bagwell	.75
110	Mark McGwire	2.00
111	Dan Tosca RC	4.00
112	Sergio Contreras RC	4.00
113	Mitch Jones RC	4.00
114	Ramon Carvajal RC	4.00
115	Ryan Madson RC	12.00
116	Hank Blalock RC	30.00
117	Ben Washburn RC	4.00
118	Erick Almonte RC	4.00
119	Shawn Fagan RC	4.00
120	Gary Johnson RC	4.00
121	Brett Evert RC	4.00
122	Joe Hamer RC	4.00
123	Yhency Brazoban RC	6.00
124	Domingo Guante RC	4.00
125	Deivi Mendez RC	4.00
126	Adrian Hernandez RC	4.00
127	Reggie Abercrombie RC	8.00
128	Steve Bennett RC	4.00
129	Matt White RC	4.00
130	Brian Hitchcox RC	4.00
131	Deivis Santos RC	4.00
132	Luis Montanez RC	4.00
133	Eric Reynolds RC	4.00
134	Denny Bautista RC	8.00
135	Hector Garcia RC	4.00
136	Joe Thurston RC	8.00
137	Tsuyoshi Shinjo RC	8.00
138	Elpidio Guzman RC	4.00
139	Brian Bass RC	4.00
140	Mark Burnett RC	4.00
141	Russ Jacobsen RC	4.00
142	Travis Hafner RC	50.00
143	Wilson Betemit RC	12.00
144	Luke Lockwood RC	4.00
145	Noel Devarez RC	4.00
146	Doug Gredvig RC	4.00
147	Seung Jun Song RC	6.00
148	Andy Van Hekken RC	4.00
149	Ryan Kohlmeier RC	4.00
150	Dee Haynes RC	4.00
151	Jim Journell RC	6.00
152	Chad Petty RC	4.00
153	Danny Borrell RC	4.00
154	David Krynzel RC	4.00
155	Octavio Martinez RC	4.00
156	David Parrish RC	4.00
157	Jason Miller RC	4.00
158	Corey Spencer RC	4.00
159	Maxim St. Pierre RC	4.00
160	Pat Magness RC	4.00
161	Rainier Olmedo RC	4.00
162	Brandon Mims RC	4.00
163	Phil Wilson RC	4.00
164	Jose Reyes RC	150.00
165	Matt Butler RC	4.00
166	Joel Pineiro RC	4.00
167	Ken Chenard RC	4.00
168	Alexis Gomez RC	6.00
169	Justin Morneau RC	75.00
170	Josh Fogg RC	5.00
171	Charles Frazier RC	4.00
172	Ryan Ludwick RC	15.00
173	Seth McClung RC	6.00
174	Justin Wayne RC	6.00
175	Rafael Soriano RC	6.00
176	Jared Abruzzo RC	4.00
177	Jason Richardson RC	4.00
178	Darwin Cubillan RC	4.00
179	Blake Williams RC	4.00
180	Valentino Pascucci RC	4.00

181	Ryan Hannaman RC	4.00
182	Steve Smyth RC	4.00
183	Jake Peavy RC	65.00
184	Onix Mercado RC	4.00
185	Luis Torres RC	4.00
186	Casey Fossum RC	6.00
187	Eduardo Figueroa RC	4.00
188	Bryan Barnowski RC	4.00
189	Jason Standridge RC	4.00
190	Marvin Seale RC	4.00
191	Steve Smitherman RC	8.00
192	Rafael Boitel RC	4.00
193	Dany Morban RC	4.00
194	Justin Woodrowc RC	4.00
195	Ed Rogers RC	4.00
196	Ben Hendrickson RC	4.00
197	Thomas Mitchell RC	4.00
198	Adam Pettyjohn RC	4.00
199	Doug Nickle RC	4.00
200	Jason Jones RC	4.00
201	Larry Barnes	.20
202	Ben Diggins	.20
203	Dee Brown	.20
204	Rocco Baldelli	1.00
205	Luis Terrero	.20
206	Milton Bradley	.20
207	Kurt Ainsworth	.20
208	Sean Burroughs	.20
209	Rick Asadoorian	.20
210	Ramon Castro	.20
211	Nick Neugebauer	.20
212	Aaron Myette	.20
213	Luis Matos	.20
214	Donnie Bridges	.20
215	Alex Cintron	.20
216	Bobby Kielty	.20
217	Matt Belisle	.20
218	Adam Everett	.20
219	John Lackey	.20
220	Adam Wainwright	.50
221	Jerry Hairston Jr.	.20
222	Mike Bynum	.20
223	Ryan Christianson	.20
224	J.J. Davis	.20
225	Alex Graman	.20
226	Abraham Nunez	.20
227	Sun-Woo Kim	.20
228	Jimmy Rollins	.50
229	Ruben Salazar	.20
230	Josh Girdley	.20
231	Carl Crawford	.20
232	Ben Davis	.20
233	Jason Grabowski	.20
234	Chris George	.20
235	Roy Oswalt	.75
236	Brian Cole	.20
237	Corey Patterson	.40
238	Vernon Wells	.20
239	Bradley Baker	.20
240	Gookie Dawkins	.20
241	Michael Cuddyer	.20
242	Ricardo Aramboles	.20
243	Ben Sheets	.50
244	Toby Hall	.20
245	Jack Cust	.20
246	Pedro Feliz	.20
247	Josh Beckett	.50
248	Alex Escobar	.20
249	Marcus Giles	.20
250	Jon Rauch	.20
251	Kevin Mench	.20
252	Shawn Sonnier	.20
253	Aaron Rowand	.20
254	C.C. Sabathia	.20
255	Bubba Crosby	.20
256	Josh Hamilton	.25
257	Carlos Hernandez	.20
258	Carlos Pena	.20
259	Miguel Cabrera (Photo actually Manuel Esquivia.)	2.50
260	Brandon Phillips	.20
261	Tony Pena Jr.	.20
262	Cristian Guerrero	.20
263	Jin Ho Cho	.20
264	Aaron Herr	.20
265	Keith Ginter	.20
266	Felipe Lopez	.20
267	Travis Harper	.20
268	Joe Torres	.20
269	Eric Byrnes	.20
270	Ben Christensen	.20
271	Aubrey Huff	.20
272	Lyle Overbay	.20
273	Vince Faison	.20
274	Bobby Bradley	.20
275	Joe Crede	.20
276	Matt Wheatland	.20
277	Grady Sizemore	1.50
278	Adrian Gonzalez	.50
279	Timothy Raines Jr.	.20
280	Phil Dumatrait	.20
281	Jason Hart	.20
282	David Kelton	.20
283	David Walling	.20

284	J.R. House	.50
285	Kenny Kelly	.20
286	Aaron McNeal	.20
287	Nick Johnson	.20
288	Scott Heard	.20
289	Brad Wilkerson	.20
290	Allen Levrault	.20
291	Chris Richard	.20
292	Jared Sandberg	.20
293	Tike Redman	.20
294	Adam Dunn	.75
295	Josh Pressley	.20
296	Jose Ortiz	.20
297	Jason Romano	.20
298	Tim Redding	.20
299	Alex Gordon	.20
300	Ben Petrick	.20
301	Eric Munson	.20
302	Luis Rivas	.20
303	Matt Ginter	.20
304	Alfonso Soriano	.75
305	Wilfredo Rodriguez	.20
306	Brett Myers	.20
307	Scott Seabol	.20
308	Tony Alvarez	.20
309	Donzell McDonald	.20
310	Austin Kearns	.20
311	Will Ohman RC	4.00
312	Ryan Soules RC	4.00
313	Cody Ross RC	4.00
314	Bill Whitecotton RC	4.00
315	Mike Burns RC	4.00
316	Manuel Acosta RC	4.00
317	Lance Niekro RC	10.00
318	Travis Thompson RC	4.00
319	Zach Sorensen RC	4.00
320	Austin Evans RC	4.00
321	Brad Stiles RC	4.00
322	Joe Kennedy RC	4.00
323	Luke Martin RC	4.00
324	Juan Diaz RC	4.00
325	Pat Hallmark RC	4.00
326	Christian Parker RC	4.00
327	Ronny Corona RC	4.00
328	Jermaine Clark RC	4.00
329	Scott Dunn RC	4.00
330	Scott Chiasson RC	4.00
331	Greg Nash/Auto. RC	25.00
332	Brad Cresse/Auto.	25.00
333	John Buck/Auto.	50.00
334	Freddie Bynum/ Auto. RC	25.00
335	Felix Diaz/Auto. RC	25.00
336	Jason Belcher/ Auto. RC	25.00
337	Troy Farnsworth RC	25.00
338	Roberto Miniel RC	25.00
339	Esix Snead RC	25.00
340	Albert Pujols RC	2,800
341	Jeff Andra RC	25.00
342	Victor Hall RC	25.00
343	Pedro Liriano RC	25.00
344	Andy Beal RC	25.00
345	Bob Keppel RC	40.00
346	Brian Schmitt RC	25.00
347	Ron Davenport RC	150.00
348	Tony Blanco RC	50.00
349	Reggie Griggs RC	25.00
350	Derrick Van Dusen RC	25.00
351a	Ichiro Suzuki Eng. RC	100.00
351b	Ichiro Suzuki Japanese RC	100.00

Gold Refractors

Stars:	8-15X
Rookies:	1.5-3X

Production 99 Sets
(See 2001 Bowman Chrome for checklist and base card values.)

X-Fractors

Stars:	4-8X

Rookies:		.75-1.5X

Inserted 1:23
(See 2001 Bowman Chrome for checklist and base card values.)

Futures Game Memorabilia

		NM/M
Common Player:		6.00
Inserted 1:460		
KA	Kurt Ainsworth	8.00
CA	Craig Anderson	6.00
RA	Ryan Anderson	6.00
BB	Bobby Bradley	6.00
MB	Mike Bynum	6.00
RC	Ramon Castro	6.00
CC	Chin-Feng Chen	30.00
JC	Jack Cust	6.00
RD	Randey Dorame	6.00
AE	Alex Escobar	6.00
CG	Chris George	6.00
MG	Marcus Giles	6.00
JH	Josh Hamilton	8.00
CH	Carlos Hernandez	6.00
SK	Sun-Woo Kim	6.00
FL	Felipe Lopez	8.00
EM	Eric Munson	6.00
AM	Aaron Myette	6.00
NN	Ntema Ndungidi	6.00
TO	Tomokazu Ohka	6.00
DCP	Corey Patterson	10.00
CP	Carlos Pena	6.00
BP	Ben Petrick	6.00
JR	Jason Romano	6.00
BS	Ben Sheets	8.00
CT	Chin-Hui Tsao	40.00
BW	Brad Wilkerson	6.00
TW	Travis Wilson	6.00
BZ	Barry Zito	15.00
JZ	Julio Zuleta	6.00

Rookie Reprints

Don James Larsen

		NM/M
Complete Set (25):		50.00
Common Player:		2.00
Inserted 1:12		
Refractors:		2-3X
Production 299 Sets		
1	Yogi Berra	5.00
2	Ralph Kiner	3.00
3	Stan Musial	6.00
4	Warren Spahn	4.00
5	Roy Campanella	4.00
6	Bob Lemon	2.00
7	Robin Roberts	2.00
8	Duke Snider	4.00
9	Early Wynn	2.00
10	Richie Ashburn	3.00
11	Gil Hodges	3.00
12	Hank Bauer	2.00
13	Don Newcombe	2.00
14	Al Rosen	2.00
15	Willie Mays	8.00
16	Joe Garagiola	3.00
17	Whitey Ford	4.00
18	Lew Burdette	2.00
19	Gil McDougald	2.00
20	Minnie Minoso	2.00
21	Eddie Mathews	4.00
22	Harvey Kuenn	2.00
23	Don Larsen	3.00
24	Elston Howard	2.00
25	Don Zimmer	2.00

Rookie Reprint Relics

		NM/M
Common Player:		8.00
Inserted 1:244		
1	David Justice	8.00
2	Richie Sexson	12.00

3	Sean Casey	8.00
4	Mike Piazza	50.00
5	Carlos Delgado	8.00
6	Chipper Jones	25.00

2001 Bowman Draft Picks & Prospects

ICHIRO • OF
SEATTLE MARINERS

		NM/M
Complete Set (110):		35.00
Complete Factory Set (112):		40.00
Common Player:		.10
1	Alfredo Amezaga RC	.25
2	Andrew Good	.10
3	Kelly Johnson RC	3.00
4	Larry Bigbie	.10
5	Matt Thompson RC	.40
6	Wilton Chavez RC	.40
7	Joe Borchard RC	.50
8	David Espinosa	.10
9	Zach Day RC	.50
10	Brad Hawpe RC	3.00
11	Nate Cornejo	.10
12	Jim Kavourias RC	.25
13	Brad Lidge RC	.10
14	Angel Berroa RC	.75
15	Lamont Matthews RC	.25
16	Jose Garcia	.10
17	Grant Balfour RC	.25
18	Ron Chiavacci RC	.25
19	Jae Seo	.10
20	Juan Rivera	.10
21	D'Angelo Jimenez	.10
22	Aaron Harang	.10
23	Marlon Byrd RC	.50
24	Sean Burnett	.10
25	Josh Pearce RC	.25
26	Brandon Duckworth RC	.25
27	Jack Taschner RC	.25
28	Bo Robinson RC	.25
29	Brent Abernathy	.10
30	David Elder RC	.25
31	Scott Cassidy RC	.25
32	Dennis Tankersley RC	.40
33	Denny Stark	.10
34	Dave Williams RC	.25
35	Boof Bonser RC	1.00
36	Kris Foster RC	.25
37	Neal Musser RC	.25
38	Shawn Chacon	.10
39	Mike Rivera RC	.25
40	Will Smith RC	.25
41	Morgan Ensberg RC	1.50
42	Ken Harvey RC	.10
43	Ricardo Rodriguez RC	.25
44	Jose Mieses RC	.25
45	Luis Maza RC	.25
46	Julio Perez RC	.25
47	Billy Traber RC	.25
48	David Martinez RC	.25

49	Covelli Crisp RC	2.00
50	Mario Ramos RC	.25
51	Matt Thornton RC	.25
52	Xavier Nady RC	.10
53	Ryan Vogelsong	.10
54	Jim Magrane RC	.25
55	Domingo Valdez RC	.25
56	Brent Butler	.10
57	Brian Tallet RC	.25
58	Brian Reith RC	.25
59	Mario Valenzuela RC	.25
60	Bobby Hill RC	.50
61	Rich Rundles RC	.25
62	Rick Elder	.10
63	J.D. Closser	.10
64	Scot Shields	.10
65	Miguel Olivo	.10
66	Stubby Clapp RC	.25
67	Jerome Williams RC	.40
68	Jason Lane RC	.75
69	Chase Utley RC	20.00
70	Erik Bedard RC	5.00
71	Alex Herrera RC	.20
72	Juan Cruz RC	.40
73	Billy Martin RC	.20
74	Ronnie Merrill RC	.20
75	Jason Kinchen RC	.20
76	Wilken Ruan RC	.20
77	Cody Ransom RC	.20
78	Bud Smith RC	.25
79	Wily Mo Pena	.20
80	Jeff Nettles RC	.20
81	Jamal Strong RC	.25
82	Bill Ortega	.10
83	Junior Zamora	.10
84	Ichiro Suzuki RC	10.00
85	Fernando Rodney RC	.20
86	Chris Smith RC	.40
87	John Van Benschoten RC	.50
88	Bobby Crosby RC	3.00
89	Kenny Baugh RC	.25
90	Jake Gautreau RC	.40
91	Gabe Gross RC	.75
92	Kris Honel RC	.40
93	Daniel Denham RC	.25
94	Aaron Heilman RC	1.00
95	Irvin Guzman RC	5.00
96	Mike Jones RC	.50
97	John-Ford Griffin RC	.25
98	Macay McBride RC	.50
99	John Rheineckar RC	.50
100	Bronson Sardinha RC	.25
101	Jason Weintraub RC	.25
102	J.D. Martin RC	.25
103	Jayson Nix RC	.40
104	Noah Lowry RC	3.00
105	Richard Lewis RC	.25
106	Brad Hennessey RC	.40
107	Jeff Mathis RC	.75
108	Jon Skaggs RC	.40
109	Justin Pope RC	.25
110	Josh Burrus RC	.25

Autographs

KEARNS 75

		NM/M
Common Autograph:		5.00
Inserted 1:Set		
JA	Jared Abruzzo	5.00
AA	Alfredo Amezaga	10.00
GA	Garrett Atkins	50.00
BB	Bobby Bradley	5.00
ANC	Antoine Cameron	5.00
ROC	Ramon Carvajal	5.00
RC	Ryan Church	15.00
AC	Alex Cintron	5.00
RD	Ryan Dittfurth	5.00
AE	Alex Everett	5.00
AF	Alex Fernandez	5.00
AG	Alexis Gomez	10.00
CG	Cristian Guerrero	5.00
BH	Beau Hale	5.00
SH	Scott Heard	5.00

AH	Aaron Herr	5.00
CI	Cesar Izturis	5.00
GJ	Gary Johnson	5.00
NJ	Nick Johnson	10.00
AK	Austin Kearns	15.00
JK	Joe Kennedy	5.00
JL	John Lackey	12.00
FL	Felipe Lopez	8.00
RI	Ryan Ludwick	10.00
RMM	Ryan Madson	15.00
TO	Tomo Ohka	8.00
RO	Roy Oswalt	35.00
CP	Christian Parra	5.00
BP	Brandon Phillips	15.00
JP	Joel Pineiro	15.00
NR	Nick Regilio	5.00
ER	Ed Rogers	5.00
SS	Scott Seabol	5.00
BS	Bud Smith	5.00
BJS	Brian Specht	5.00
JT	Joe Torres	5.00
JMW	Justin Wayne	8.00

Futures Game Relics

2000 All-Star Futures Game

		NM/M
Common Player:		4.00
One per factory set.		
AA	Alfredo Amezaga	4.00
AD	Adam Dunn	10.00
AG	Adrian Gonzalez	8.00
AH	Alex Herrera	4.00
BM	Brett Myers	8.00
CD	Cody Ransom	4.00
CG	Chris George	4.00
CH	Carlos Hernandez	5.00
CU	Chase Utley	25.00
EB	Eric Bedard	15.00
GB	Grant Balfour	4.00
HB	Hank Blalock	18.00
JB	Joe Borchard	10.00
JC	Juan Cruz	5.00
JP	Josh Pearce	4.00
JR	Juan Rivera	4.00
LG	Luis Garcia	4.00
MC	Miguel Cabrera	10.00
MR	Mike Rivera	4.00
RR	Ricardo Rodriguez	4.00
SC	Scott Chiasson	4.00
SS	Seung Jun Song	6.00
TB	Toby Hall	4.00
WB	Wilson Betemit	4.00
WP	Wily Mo Pena	5.00
JAP	Juan Pena	4.00

Draft Pick Relics

		NM/M
Common Player:		4.00
One per factory set.		
CI	Cesar Izturis	4.00
GJ	Gary Johnson	4.00
NR	Nick Regilio	4.00
RC	Ryan Church	4.00
BJS	Brian Specht	4.00
JRH	J.R. House	4.00

2001 Bowman Heritage

		NM/M
Complete Set (440):		200.00
Common Player:		.15
Common (331-440):		1.00
Inserted 1:2		
Pack (10):		5.00
Box (24):		100.00
1	Chipper Jones	1.25
2	Pete Harnisch	.15
3	Brian Giles	.15
4	J.T. Snow	.15
5	Bartolo Colon	.15
6	Jorge Posada	.25
7	Shawn Green	.25
8	Derek Jeter	2.50
9	Benito Santiago	.15
10	Ramon Hernandez	.15
11	Bernie Williams	.40
12	Greg Maddux	1.50
13	Barry Bonds	2.50
14	Roger Clemens	2.00
15	Miguel Tejada	.50
16	Pedro Feliz	.15
17	Jim Edmonds	.40
18	Tom Glavine	.40
19	David Justice	.25
20	Rich Aurilia	.15
21	Jason Giambi	.75
22	Orlando Hernandez	.15
23	Shawn Estes	.15
24	Nelson Figueroa	.15
25	Terrence Long	.15
26	Mike Mussina	.15
27	Eric Davis	.15
28	Jimmy Rollins	.50
29	Andy Pettitte	.50
30	Shawon Dunston	.15
31	Tim Hudson	.40
32	Jeff Kent	.25
33	Scott Brosius	.15
34	Livan Hernandez	.15
35	Alfonso Soriano	1.00
36	Mark McGwire	1.50
37	Russ Ortiz	.15
38	Fernando Vina	.15
39	Ken Griffey Jr.	1.50
40	Edgar Renteria	.15
41	Kevin Brown	.15
42	Robb Nen	.15
43	Paul LoDuca	.15
44	Bobby Abreu	.25
45	Adam Dunn	.50
46	Osvaldo Fernandez	.15
47	Marvin Benard	.15
48	Mark Gardner	.15
49	Alex Rodriguez	2.00
50	Preston Wilson	.15
51	Roberto Alomar	.40
52	Ben Davis	.15
53	Derek Bell	.15
54	Ken Caminiti	.15
55	Barry Zito	.40
56	Scott Rolen	.75
57	Geoff Jenkins	.15
58	Mike Cameron	.15
59	Ben Grieve	.15
60	Chuck Knoblauch	.15
61	Matt Lawton	.15
62	Chan Ho Park	.15
63	Lance Berkman	.40
64	Carlos Beltran	.50
65	Dean Palmer	.15
66	Alex Gonzalez	.15
67	Larry Walker	.25
68	Magglio Ordonez	.25
69	Ellis Burks	.15
70	Mark Mulder	.25
71	Randy Johnson	.75
72	John Smoltz	.40
73	Jerry Hairston Jr.	.15
74	Pedro Martinez	.75
75	Fred McGriff	.15
76	Sean Casey	.25
77	C.C. Sabathia	.15
78	Todd Helton	.75
79	Brad Penny	.15
80	Mike Sweeney	.15
81	Billy Wagner	.15
82	Mark Buehrle	.25
83	Cristian Guzman	.15
84	Jose Vidro	.15
85	Pat Burrell	.40
86	Jermaine Dye	.15
87	Brandon Inge	.15
88	David Wells	.15
89	Mike Piazza	1.00
90	Jose Cabrera	.15
91	Cliff Floyd	.15
92	Matt Morris	.15
93	Raul Mondesi	.15
94	Joe Kennedy RC	.50
95	Jack Wilson RC	1.00
96	Andruw Jones	.75
97	Mariano Rivera	.50
98	Mike Hampton	.15
99	Roger Cedeno	.15
100	Jose Cruz	.15
101	Mike Lowell	.15
102	Pedro Astacio	.15
103	Joe Mays	.15
104	John Franco	.15
105	Tim Redding	.15
106	Sandy Alomar	.15
107	Bret Boone	.15
108	Josh Towers RC	.50
109	Matt Stairs	.15
110	Chris Truby	.15
111	Jeff Suppan	.15
112	J.C. Romero	.15
113	Felipe Lopez	.15
114	Ben Sheets	.40
115	Frank Thomas	.75
116	A.J. Burnett	.15
117	Tony Clark	.15
118	Mac Suzuki	.15
119	Brad Radke	.15
120	Jeff Shaw	.15
121	Nick Neugebauer	.15
122	Kenny Lofton	.15
123	Jacque Jones	.15
124	Brent Mayne	.15
125	Carlos Hernandez	.15
126	Shane Spencer	.15
127	John Lackey	.15
128	Sterling Hitchcock	.15
129	Darren Dreifort	.15
130	Rusty Greer	.15
131	Michael Cuddyer	.15
132	Tyler Houston	.15
133	Chin-Feng Chen	.15
134	Ken Harvey	.15
135	Marquis Grissom	.15
136	Russell Branyan	.15
137	Eric Karros	.15
138	Josh Beckett	.25
139	Todd Zeile	.15
140	Corey Koskie	.15
141	Steve Sparks	.15
142	Bobby Seay	.15
143	Tim Raines	.15
144	Julio Zuleta	.15
145	Jose Lima	.15
146	Dante Bichette	.15
147	Randy Keisler	.15
148	Brent Butler	.15
149	Antonio Alfonseca	.15
150	Bryan Rekar	.15
151	Jeffrey Hammonds	.15
152	Larry Bigbie	.15
153	Blake Stein	.15
154	Robin Ventura	.15
155	Rondell White	.15
156	Juan Silvestre	.15
157	Marcus Thames	.15
158	Sidney Ponson	.15
159	Juan Pena	.15
160	Charles Johnson	.15
161	Adam Everett	.15
162	Eric Munson	.15
163	Jason Isringhausen	.15
164	Brad Fullmer	.15
165	Miguel Olivo	.15
166	Fernando Tatis	.15
167	Freddy Garcia	.15
168	Tom Goodwin	.15
169	Armando Benitez	.15
170	Paul Konerko	.40
171	Jeff Cirillo	.15
172	Shane Reynolds	.15
173	Kevin Tapani	.15
174	Joe Crede	.25
175	Omar Infante RC	.50
176	Jake Peavy RC	5.00
177	Corey Patterson	.25
178	Alfredo Amezaga RC	.25
179	Jeromy Burnitz	.15
180	David Segui	.15
181	Marcus Giles	.15
182	Paul O'Neill	.25
183	John Olerud	.15
184	Andy Benes	.15
185	Brad Cresse RC	.25
186	Ricky Ledee	.15
187	Allen Levrault	.15
188	Royce Clayton	.15
189	Kelly Johnson RC	4.00
190	Quilvio Veras	.15
191	Mike Williams	.15
192	Jason Lane RC	1.00
193	Rick Helling	.15
194	Tim Wakefield	.15
195	James Baldwin	.15
196	Cody Ransom RC	.25
197	Bobby Kielty	.15
198	Bobby Jones	.15
199	Steve Cox	.15
200	Jamal Strong RC	.25
201	Steve Lomasney	.15
202	Bill Ortega	.15
203	Mike Matheny	.15
204	Jeff Randazzo RC	.25
205	Aubrey Huff	.15
206	Chuck Finley	.15
207	Denny Bautista RC	1.50
208	Terry Mulholland	.15
209	Rey Ordonez	.15
210	Jason Belcher RC	.25
211	Orlando Cabrera	.15
212	Juan Encarnacion	.15
213	Dustin Hermanson	.15
214	Luis Rivas	.15
215	Mark Quinn	.15
216	Randy Velarde	.15
217	Billy Koch	.15
218	Ryan Rupe	.15
219	Keith Ginter	.15
220	Woody Williams	.15
221	Blake Williams RC	.25
222	Aaron Myette	.15
223	Joe Borchard RC	.75
224	Nate Cornejo	.15
225	Julian Tavarez	.15
226	Kevin Millwood	.15
227	Travis Hafner RC	5.00
228	Charles Nagy	.15
229	Mike Lieberthal	.15
230	Jeff Nelson	.15
231	Ryan Dempster	.15
232	Andres Galarraga	.15
233	Chad Durbin	.15
234	Timoniel Perez	.15
235	Troy O'Leary	.15
236	Kevin Young	.15
237	Gabe Kapler	.15
238	Juan Cruz RC	.50
239	Masato Yoshii	.15
240	Aramis Ramirez	.40
241	Matt Cooper RC	.25
242	Randy Flores RC	.25
243	Rafael Furcal	.25
244	David Eckstein	.15
245	Matt Clement	.15
246	Craig Biggio	.40
247	Rick Reed	.15
248	Jose Macias	.15
249	Alex Escobar	.15
250	Roberto Hernandez	.15
251	Andy Ashby	.15
252	Tony Armas	.15
253	Jamie Moyer	.15
254	Jason Tyner	.15
255	Ryan Ludwick RC	.50
256	Jeff Conine	.15
257	Francisco Cordova	.15
258	Ted Lilly	.15
259	Joe Randa	.15
260	Jeff D'Amico	.15
261	Albie Lopez	.15
262	Kevin Appier	.15
263	Richard Hidalgo	.15
264	Omar Daal	.15
265	Ricky Gutierrez	.15
266	John Rocker	.15
267	Ray Lankford	.15
268	Beau Hale RC	.25
269	Tony Blanco RC	.25
270	Derrek Lee	.75
271	Jamey Wright	.15
272	Alex Gordon	.15
273	Jeff Weaver	.15
274	Jaret Wright	.15
275	Jose Hernandez	.15
276	Bruce Chen	.15
277	Todd Hollandsworth	.15
278	Wade Miller	.15
279	Luke Prokopec	.15
280	Rafael Soriano RC	.75
281	Damion Easley	.15
282	Darren Oliver	.15
283	Brandon Duckworth RC	.50
284	Aaron Herr	.15
285	Ray Durham	.15
286	Adrian Hernandez RC	.40
287	Ugueth Urbina	.15
288	Scott Seabol	.15
289	Lance Niekro RC	1.00
290	Trot Nixon	.15
291	Adam Kennedy	.15
292	Brian Schmitt RC	.25
293	Grant Roberts	.15
294	Benny Agbayani	.15
295	Travis Lee	.15
296	Erick Almonte RC	.40
297	Jim Thome	.50
298	Eric Young	.15
299	Daniel Denham RC	.25

300	Boof Bonser RC	2.00
301	Denny Neagle	.15
302	Kenny Rogers	.15
303	J.D. Closser	.15
304	Chase Utley RC	15.00
305	Rey Sanchez	.15
306	Sean McGowan	.15
307	Justin Pope RC	.25
308	Torii Hunter	.40
309	B.J. Surhoff	.15
310	Aaron Heilman RC	.50
311	Gabe Gross RC	.75
312	Lee Stevens	.15
313	Todd Hundley	.15
314	Macay McBride RC	.50
315	Edgar Martinez	.15
316	Omar Vizquel	.15
317	Reggie Sanders	.15
318	John-Ford Griffin RC	.50
319	Tim Salmon (Photo actually Troy Glaus.)	.50
320	Pokey Reese	.15
321	Jay Payton	.15
322	Doug Glanville	.15
323	Greg Vaughn	.15
324	Ruben Sierra	.15
325	Kip Wells	.15
326	Carl Everett	.15
327	Garret Anderson	.15
328	Jay Bell	.15
329	Barry Larkin	.15
330	Jeff Mathis RC	.75
331	Adrian Gonzalez	2.00
332	Juan Rivera	1.00
333	Tony Alvarez	1.00
334	Xavier Nady	1.00
335	Josh Hamilton	1.00
336	Will Smith RC	1.50
337	Israel Alcantara	1.00
338	Chris George	1.00
339	Sean Burroughs	1.00
340	Jack Cust	1.00
341	Eric Byrnes	1.00
342	Carlos Pena	1.00
343	J.R. House	1.00
344	Carlos Silva	1.00
345	Mike Rivera RC	1.00
346	Adam Johnson	1.00
347	Scott Heard	1.00
348	Alex Cintron	1.00
349	Miguel Cabrera	3.00
350	Nick Johnson	1.00
351	Albert Pujols RC	60.00
352	Ichiro Suzuki RC	30.00
353	Carlos Delgado	1.50
354	Troy Glaus	2.00
355	Sammy Sosa	3.00
356	Ivan Rodriguez	2.00
357	Vladimir Guerrero	2.00
358	Manny Ramirez	2.00
359	Luis Gonzalez	1.00
360	Roy Oswalt	1.50
361	Moises Alou	1.00
362	Juan Gonzalez	1.50
363	Tony Gwynn	2.00
364	Hideo Nomo	2.00
365	Tsuyoshi Shinjo RC	1.00
366	Kazuhiro Sasaki	1.00
367	Cal Ripken Jr.	8.00
368	Rafael Palmeiro	2.00
369	J.D. Drew	1.50
370	Doug Mientkiewicz	1.00
371	Jeff Bagwell	2.00
372	Darin Erstad	2.00
373	Tom Gordon	1.00
374	Ben Petrick	1.00
375	Eric Milton	1.00
376	Nomar Garciaparra	3.00
377	Julio Lugo	1.00
378	Tino Martinez	1.50
379	Javier Vazquez	1.00
380	Jeremy Giambi	1.00
381	Marty Cordova	1.00
382	Adrian Beltre	1.50
383	John Burkett	1.00
384	Aaron Boone	1.00
385	Eric Chavez	1.00
386	Curt Schilling	1.50
387	Cory Lidle	1.00
388	Jason Schmidt	1.00
389	Johnny Damon	3.00
390	Steve Finley	1.00
391	Edgardo Alfonzo	1.00
392	Jose Valentin	1.00
393	Jose Canseco	1.50
394	Ryan Klesko	1.00
395	David Cone	1.00
396	Jason Kendall	1.00
397	Placido Polanco	1.00
398	Glendon Rusch	1.00
399	Aaron Sele	1.00
400	D'Angelo Jimenez	1.00
401	Mark Grace	1.50
402	Al Leiter	1.00

403	Brian Jordan	1.00
404	Phil Nevin	1.00
405	Brent Abernathy	1.00
406	Kerry Wood	1.00
407	Alex Gonzalez	1.00
408	Robert Fick	1.00
409	Dmitri Young	1.00
410	Wes Helms	1.00
411	Trevor Hoffman	1.00
412	Rickey Henderson	2.00
413	Bobby Higginson	1.00
414	Gary Sheffield	1.50
415	Darryl Kile	1.00
416	Richie Sexson	1.50
417	Frank Menechino	1.00
418	Javy Lopez	1.00
419	Carlos Lee	1.00
420	Jon Lieber	1.00
421	Hank Blalock RC	6.00
422	Marlon Byrd RC	1.50
423	Jason Kinchen RC	1.00
424	Morgan Ensberg RC	5.00
425	Greg "Toe" Nash RC	1.00
426	Dennis Tankersley RC	1.00
427	Joel Pineiro	1.00
428	Chris Smith RC	1.00
429	Jake Gautreau RC	1.00
430	John Van Benschoten RC	1.50
431	Travis Thompson	1.00
432	Orlando Hudson RC	3.00
433	Jerome Williams RC	2.00
434	Kevin Reese	1.00
435	Ed Rogers RC	1.00
436	Grant Balfour RC	1.00
437	Adam Pettyjohn RC	1.00
438	Hee Seop Choi RC	2.00
439	Justin Morneau RC	15.00
440	Mitch Jones RC	1.00

Chrome

Stars:	4-8X
SP's:	2-4X

Inserted 1:12
(See 2001 Bowman Heritage for checklist and base card values.)

Autographs

		NM/M
	Common Player:	90.00
BB	Barry Bonds	180.00
RC	Roger Clemens	120.00
AR	Alex Rodriguez	90.00

2001 Bowman Heritage Promos

		NM/M
	Complete Set (5):	60.00
	Common Player:	6.00
1	Roberto Alomar	6.00

2	Albert Pujols	50.00
3	C.C. Sabathia	6.00
4	Mark McGwire	12.50
5	Juan Gonzalez	6.00

Team Topps Legends Autographs

		NM/M
	Common Autograph:	30.00
	Inserted 1:332	
TT13F	Warren Spahn/ 1965	40.00
TT21R	Bob Feller/1952	30.00

1948 Bowman Reprints

		NM/M
	Complete Set (13):	10.00
	Common Player:	.75
	Inserted 1:2	
1	Ralph Kiner	.75
2	Johnny Mize	.75
3	Bobby Thomson	.75
4	Yogi Berra	1.50
5	Phil Rizzuto	1.00
6	Bob Feller	1.00
7	Enos Slaughter	.75
8	Stan Musial	2.00
9	Hank Sauer	.75
10	Ferris Fain	.75
11	Red Schoendienst	.75
12	Allie Reynolds	.75
13	Johnny Sain	.75

1948 Reprint Relics

		NM/M
	Common Player:	8.00
	Inserted 1:44	
YB1	Yogi Berra	20.00
YB2	Yogi Berra	35.00
FF	Ferris Fain	8.00
BF	Bob Feller	12.00

RK	Ralph Kiner	15.00
JM	Johnny Mize	15.00
SM1	Stan Musial	30.00
PR	Phil Rizzuto	15.00
HS	Hank Sauer	8.00
RS	Red Schoendienst	10.00
ES	Enos Slaughter	10.00
BT	Bobby Thomson	8.00

1948 Bowman Reprint Autographs

		NM/M
1	Warren Spahn	40.00
2	Bob Feller	40.00

2001 Bowman's Best

		NM/M
	Complete Set (200):	
	Common Player:	.20
	Common SP (151-200):	5.00
	Production 2,999	
	Pack (5):	10.00
	Box (24):	200.00
1	Vladimir Guerrero	1.00
2	Miguel Tejada	.50
3	Geoff Jenkins	.20
4	Jeff Bagwell	.75
5	Todd Helton	.75
6	Ken Griffey Jr.	2.00
7	Nomar Garciaparra	1.00
8	Chipper Jones	1.00
9	Darin Erstad	.40
10	Frank Thomas	1.00
11	Jim Thome	.50
12	Preston Wison	.20
13	Kevin Brown	.20
14	Derek Jeter	3.00
15	Scott Rolen	1.00
16	Ryan Klesko	.20
17	Jeff Kent	.40
18	Raul Mondesi	.20
19	Greg Vaughn	.20
20	Bernie Williams	.40
21	Mike Piazza	1.00
22	Richard Hidalgo	.20
23	Dean Palmer	.20
24	Roberto Alomar	.40
25	Sammy Sosa	1.00
26	Randy Johnson	1.00
27	Manny Ramirez	1.00
28	Roger Clemens	2.00
29	Terrence Long	.20
30	Jason Kendall	.20
31	Richie Sexson	.40
32	David Wells	.20
33	Andruw Jones	1.00
34	Pokey Reese	.20
35	Juan Gonzalez	.50
36	Carlos Beltran	.75
37	Shawn Green	.40

38	Mariano Rivera	.50
39	John Olerud	.20
40	Jim Edmonds	.40
41	Andres Galarraga	.20
42	Carlos Delgado	.75
43	Kris Benson	.20
44	Andy Pettitte	.40
45	Jeff Cirillo	.20
46	Magglio Ordonez	.40
47	Tom Glavine	.40
48	Garret Anderson	.20
49	Cal Ripken Jr.	3.00
50	Pedro Martinez	1.00
51	Barry Bonds	3.00
52	Alex Rodriguez	2.50
53	Ben Grieve	.20
54	Edgar Martinez	.20
55	Jason Giambi	.75
56	Jeromy Burnitz	.20
57	Mike Mussina	.75
58	Moises Alou	.40
59	Sean Casey	.20
60	Greg Maddux	1.50
61	Tim Hudson	.50
62	Mark McGwire	2.00
63	Rafael Palmeiro	.75
64	Tony Batista	.20
65	Kazuhiro Sasaki	.20
66	Jorge Posada	.50
67	Johnny Damon	1.00
68	Brian Giles	.20
69	Jose Vidro	.20
70	Jermaine Dye	.20
71	Craig Biggio	.40
72	Larry Walker	.40
73	Eric Chavez	.40
74	David Segui	.20
75	Tim Salmon	.40
76	Javy Lopez	.20
77	Paul Konerko	.40
78	Barry Larkin	.40
79	Mike Hampton	.20
80	Bobby Higginson	.20
81	Mark Mulder	.40
82	Pat Burrell	.50
83	Kerry Wood	.50
84	J.T. Snow	.20
85	Ivan Rodriguez	.75
86	Edgardo Alfonzo	.20
87	Orlando Hernandez	.20
88	Gary Sheffield	.50
89	Mike Sweeney	.20
90	Carlos Lee	.20
91	Rafael Furcal	.40
92	Troy Glaus	.50
93	Bartolo Colon	.20
94	Cliff Floyd	.20
95	Barry Zito	.50
96	J.D. Drew	.40
97	Eric Karros	.20
98	Jose Valentin	.20
99	Ellis Burks	.20
100	David Justice	.20
101	Larry Barnes	.20
102	Rod Barajas	.20
103	Tony Pena	.20
104	Jerry Hairston Jr.	.20
105	Keith Ginter	.20
106	Corey Patterson	.40
107	Aaron Rowand	.20
108	Miguel Olivo	.20
109	Gookie Dawkins	.20
110	C.C. Sabathia	.20
111	Ben Petrick	.20
112	Eric Munson	.20
113	Ramon Castro	.20
114	Alex Escobar	.20
115	Josh Hamilton	.40
116	Jason Marquis	.20
117	Ben Davis	.20
118	Alex Cintron	.20
119	Julio Zuleta	.20
120	Ben Broussard	.20
121	Adam Everett	.20
122	Ramon Carvajal RC	.75
123	Felipe Lopez	.20
124	Alfonso Soriano	1.00
125	Jayson Werth	.20
126	Donzell McDonald	.20
127	Jason Hart	.25
128	Joe Crede	.50
129	Sean Burroughs	.20
130	Jack Cust	.20
131	Corey Smith	.20
132	Adrian Gonzalez	.40
133	J.R. House	.20
134	Steve Lomasney	.20
135	Tim Raines Jr.	.20
136	Tony Alvarez	.20
137	Doug Mientkiewicz	.20
138	Rocco Baldelli	.75
139	Jason Romano	.20
140	Vernon Wells	.40
141	Mike Bynum	.20
142	Xavier Nady	.20
143	Brad Wilkerson	.20
144	Ben Diggins	.20
145	Aubrey Huff	.20
146	Eric Byrnes	.20
147	Alex Gordon	.20
148	Roy Oswalt	.50
149	Brian Esposito	.20
150	Scott Seabol	.20
151	Erick Almonte RC	5.00
152	Gary Johnson RC	5.00
153	Pedro Liriano RC	5.00
154	Matt White RC	5.00
155	Luis Montanez RC	5.00
156	Brad Cresse	5.00
157	Wilson Betemit	6.00
158	Octavio Martinez RC	5.00
159	Adam Pettyjohn RC	5.00
160	Corey Spencer RC	5.00
161	Mark Burnett RC	5.00
162	Ichiro Suzuki RC	60.00
163	Alexis Gomez RC	5.00
164	Greg "Toe" Nash RC	5.00
165	Roberto Miniel RC	5.00
166	Justin Morneau RC	50.00
167	Ben Washburn RC	5.00
168	Bob Keppel RC	5.00
169	Deivi Mendez RC	5.00
170	Tsuyoshi Shinjo RC	5.00
171	Jared Abruzzo RC	5.00
172	Derrick Van Dusen RC	5.00
173	Hee Seop Choi RC	8.00
174	Albert Pujols RC	300.00
175	Travis Hafner RC	25.00
176	Ron Davenport RC	6.00
177	Luis Torres RC	5.00
178	Jake Peavy RC	30.00
179	Elvis Corporan RC	5.00
180	David Krynzel RC	5.00
181	Tony Blanco RC	5.00
182	Elpidio Guzman RC	5.00
183	Matt Butler RC	5.00
184	Joe Thurston RC	5.00
185	Andy Beal RC	5.00
186	Kevin Nulton RC	5.00
187	Sneideer Santos RC	5.00
188	Joe Dillon RC	5.00
189	Jeremy Blevins RC	5.00
190	Chris Amador RC	5.00
191	Mark Hendrickson RC	5.00
192	Willy Aybar RC	10.00
193	Antoine Cameron RC	5.00
194	Jonathan Johnson RC	5.00
195	Ryan Ketchner RC	5.00
196	Bjorn Ivy RC	5.00
197	Josh Kroeger RC	5.00
198	Ty Wigginton RC	5.00
199	Stubby Clapp RC	5.00
200	Jerrod Riggan RC	5.00

Autographs

ADRIAN GONZALEZ
FLORIDA MARLINS

		NM/M
Common Player:		8.00
Inserted 1:95		
SB	Sean Burroughs	8.00
BC	Brad Cresse	8.00
AG	Adrian Gonzalez	15.00
JH	Josh Hamilton	30.00
JRH	J.R. House	8.00
TL	Terrence Long	8.00
JR	Jon Rauch	8.00

Exclusive Rookie Autographs

		NM/M
Common Player:		6.00
Inserted 1:50		
WA	Willy Aybar	25.00
SC	Stubby Clapp	6.00
BI	Bjorn Ivy	6.00
JJ	Jonathan Johnson	6.00
TW	Ty Wigginton	6.00

JONATHAN JOHNSON
CHICAGO CUBS

JR	Jerrod Riggan	6.00
SS	Sneideer Santos	6.00
JB	Jeremy Blevins	6.00
MH	Mark Hendrickson	6.00

Franchise Favorites

		NM/M
Complete Set (8):		30.00
Common Player:		1.50
Inserted 1:16		
DM	Don Mattingly	6.00
AR	Alex Rodriguez	6.00
DE	Darin Erstad	1.50
DW	Dave Winfield	1.50
NR	Nolan Ryan	8.00
RJ	Reggie Jackson	2.00
MW	Don Mattingly, Dave Winfield	4.00
RR	Nolan Ryan, Alex Rodriguez	8.00
EJ	Darin Erstad, Reggie Jackson	2.00

Franchise Favorites Autographs

		NM/M
Common Player:		25.00
Inserted 1:556		
Combo 1:4,436		
DE	Darin Erstad	20.00
RJ	Reggie Jackson	40.00
EJ	Darin Erstad, Reggie Jackson	65.00
DM	Don Mattingly	60.00
MW	Don Mattingly, Dave Winfield	150.00
AR	Alex Rodriguez	80.00
NR	Nolan Ryan	80.00
RR	Nolan Ryan, Alex Rodriguez	300.00
DW	Dave Winfield	25.00

Franchise Favorites Relics

FRANCHISE FAVORITES

	NM/M
Common Player:	6.00
Jersey 1:139	

Pants 1:307
Combo Relic 1:1,114

JB	Jeff Bagwell	10.00
CB	Craig Biggio	6.00
BB	Craig Biggio, Jeff Bagwell	25.00
DE	Darin Erstad	6.00
RJ	Reggie Jackson	10.00
EJ	Reggie Jackson, Darin Erstad	25.00
DM	Don Mattingly	30.00
MW	Don Mattingly, Dave Winfield	65.00
AR	Alex Rodriguez	20.00
NR	Nolan Ryan	40.00
RR	Nolan Ryan, Alex Rodriguez	60.00
DW	Dave Winfield	8.00

Franchise Futures

NICK JOHNSON

		NM/M
Complete Set (12):		15.00
Common Player:		1.00
Inserted 1:24		
FF1	Josh Hamilton	1.00
FF2	Wes Helms	1.00
FF3	Alfonso Soriano	4.00
FF4	Nick Johnson	1.50
FF5	Jose Ortiz	1.00
FF6	Ben Sheets	1.50
FF7	Sean Burroughs	1.50
FF8	Ben Petrick	1.00
FF9	Corey Patterson	1.50
FF10	J.R. House	1.00
FF11	Alex Escobar	1.00
FF12	Travis Hafner	1.50

Game-Used Bats

PAT BURRELL

		NM/M
Common Player:		5.00
Inserted 1:267		
PB	Pat Burrell	10.00
SB	Sean Burroughs	5.00
AG	Adrian Gonzalez	10.00
EM	Eric Munson	5.00
CP	Corey Patterson	8.00

Game-Worn Jerseys

ERIC CHAVEZ

		NM/M
Common Player:		5.00
Inserted 1:133		
EC	Eric Chavez	8.00
MM	Mark Mulder	8.00
JP	Jay Payton	5.00
PR	Pokey Reese	5.00
PW	Preston Wilson	5.00

Impact Players

	NM/M
Complete Set (20):	15.00
Common Player:	.50

IMPACT PLAYERS

KEITH GINTER

Inserted 1:7

IP1	Mark McGwire	3.00
IP2	Sammy Sosa	2.00
IP3	Manny Ramirez	1.00
IP4	Troy Glaus	1.00
IP5	Ken Griffey Jr.	2.00
IP6	Gary Sheffield	.75
IP7	Vladimir Guerrero	1.00
IP8	Carlos Delgado	.75
IP9	Jason Giambi	.75
IP10	Frank Thomas	1.50
IP11	Vernon Wells	.60
IP12	Carlos Pena	.50
IP13	Joe Crede	.50
IP14	Keith Ginter	.50
IP15	Aubrey Huff	.50
IP16	Brad Cresse	.50
IP17	Austin Kearns	.75
IP18	Nick Johnson	.50
IP19	Josh Hamilton	.50
IP20	Corey Patterson	.60

Rookie Fever

ROOKIE FEVER

TEXAS

IVAN RODRIGUEZ

		NM/M
Complete Set (10):		10.00
Common Player:		.50
Inserted 1:10		
RF1	Chipper Jones	2.00
RF2	Preston Wilson	.50
RF3	Todd Helton	1.00
RF4	Jay Payton	.50
RF5	Ivan Rodriguez	.75
RF6	Manny Ramirez	1.00
RF7	Derek Jeter	4.00
RF8	Orlando Hernandez	.50
RF9	Marcus Quinn	.50
RF10	Terrence Long	.50

Team Topps

INDIANS

PITCHER

LUIS TIANT

	NM/M
Common Player:	10.00
Overall odds 1:71.	
13R Warren Spahn/1952	40.00
37R Tug McGraw/1965	10.00
48R Bobby Richardson/1957	15.00
25R Luis Tiant/1965 + Exchange	10.00
31R Clete Boyer/1957	15.00
23R Gil McDougald/1952	15.00
27R Andy Pafko/1952	15.00
28R Herb Score/1956	15.00
18R Bob Gibson/1959	40.00
29R Moose Skowron/1954	15.00
37F Tug McGraw/1985	10.00
28F Herb Score/1962	15.00

2002 Bowman

CHRIS SNELLING

MARINERS

OF SEATTLE MARINERS

	NM/M
Complete Set (440):	70.00
Common Player:	.15
Common Rookie:	.40
Pack (10):	4.50
Box (24):	90.00
1 Adam Dunn	.50
2 Derek Jeter	2.00
3 Alex Rodriguez	1.50
4 Miguel Tejada	.50
5 Nomar Garciaparra	1.00
6 Toby Hall	.15
7 Brandon Duckworth	.15
8 Paul LoDuca	.15
9 Brian Giles	.15
10 C.C. Sabathia	.15
11 Curt Schilling	.75
12 Tsuyoshi Shinjo	.15
13 Ramon Hernandez	.15
14 Jose Cruz Jr.	.15
15 Albert Pujols	2.00
16 Joe Mays	.15
17 Javy Lopez	.15
18 J.T. Snow	.15
19 David Segui	.15
20 Jorge Posada	.40
21 Doug Mientkiewicz	.15
22 Jerry Hairston Jr.	.15
23 Bernie Williams	.40
24 Mike Sweeney	.15
25 Jason Giambi	.50
26 Ryan Dempster	.15
27 Ryan Klesko	.15
28 Mark Quinn	.15
29 Jeff Kent	.25
30 Eric Chavez	.30
31 Adrian Beltre	.25
32 Andruw Jones	.50
33 Alfonso Soriano	1.00
34 Aramis Ramirez	.40
35 Greg Maddux	1.00
36 Andy Pettitte	.50
37 Bartolo Colon	.15
38 Ben Sheets	.40
39 Bobby Higginson	.15
40 Ivan Rodriguez	.50
41 Brad Penny	.15
42 Carlos Lee	.25
43 Damion Easley	.15
44 Preston Wilson	.15
45 Jeff Bagwell	.50
46 Eric Milton	.15
47 Rafael Palmeiro	.50
48 Gary Sheffield	.40
49 J.D. Drew	.25
50 Jim Thome	.50
51 Ichiro Suzuki	1.50
52 Bud Smith	.15
53 Chan Ho Park	.15
54 D'Angelo Jimenez	.15
55 Ken Griffey Jr.	1.50
56 Wade Miller	.15
57 Vladimir Guerrero	.50
58 Troy Glaus	.40
59 Shawn Green	.40
60 Kerry Wood	.40
61 Jack Wilson	.15
62 Kevin Brown	.25
63 Marcus Giles	.15
64 Pat Burrell	.40
65 Larry Walker	.25
66 Sammy Sosa	.75
67 Raul Mondesi	.15
68 Tim Hudson	.25
69 Lance Berkman	.40
70 Mike Mussina	.40
71 Barry Zito	.40
72 Jimmy Rollins	.15
73 Barry Bonds	2.00
74 Craig Biggio	.40
75 Todd Helton	.50
76 Roger Clemens	1.50
77 Frank Catalanotto	.15
78 Josh Towers	.15
79 Roy Oswalt	.40
80 Chipper Jones	1.00
81 Cristian Guzman	.15
82 Darin Erstad	.40
83 Freddy Garcia	.15
84 Jason Tyner	.15
85 Carlos Delgado	.40
86 Jon Lieber	.15
87 Juan Pierre	.15
88 Matt Morris	.15
89 Phil Nevin	.15
90 Jim Edmonds	.40
91 Magglio Ordonez	.25
92 Mike Hampton	.15
93 Rafael Furcal	.25
94 Richie Sexson	.40
95 Luis Gonzalez	.25
96 Scott Rolen	.50
97 Tim Redding	.15
98 Moises Alou	.25
99 Jose Vidro	.15
100 Mike Piazza	1.00
101 Pedro Martinez	.75
102 Geoff Jenkins	.15
103 Johnny Damon	.75
104 Mike Cameron	.15
105 Randy Johnson	.75
106 David Eckstein	.15
107 Javier Vazquez	.15
108 Mark Mulder	.25
109 Robert Fick	.15
110 Roberto Alomar	.40
111 Wilson Betemit	.15
112 Chris Tritle RC	.50
113 Ed Rogers	.15
114 Juan Pena	.15
115 Josh Beckett	.50
116 Juan Cruz	.15
117 Noochie Varner RC	.50
118 Taylor Buchholz RC	.50
119 Mike Rivera	.15
120 Hank Blalock	.40
121 Hansel Izquierdo RC	.50
122 Orlando Hudson	.15
123 Bill Hall	.15
124 Jose Reyes	.50
125 Juan Rivera	.15
126 Eric Valent	.15
127 Scotty Layfield RC	.40
128 Austin Kearns	.50
129 Nic Jackson RC	.50
130 Chris Baker RC	.50
131 Chad Qualls RC	.40
132 Marcus Thames	.15
133 Nathan Haynes	.15
134 Brett Evert	.15
135 Joe Borchard	.15
136 Ryan Christianson	.15
137 Josh Hamilton	.15
138 Corey Patterson	.15
139 Travis Wilson	.15
140 Alex Escobar	.15
141 Alexis Gomez	.15
142 Nick Johnson	.15
143 Kenny Kelly	.15
144 Marlon Byrd	.15
145 Kory DeHaan	.15
146 Matt Belisle	.15
147 Carlos Hernandez	.15
148 Sean Burroughs	.15
149 Angel Berroa	.15
150 Aubrey Huff	.15
151 Travis Hafner	.40
152 Brandon Berger	.15
153 David Krynzel	.15
154 Ruben Salazar	.15
155 J.R. House	.15
156 Juan Silvestre	.15
157 Dewon Brazelton	.15
158 Jayson Werth	.15
159 Larry Barnes	.15
160 Elvis Pena	.15
161 Ruben Gotay RC	.40
162 Tommy Marx RC	.50
163 John Suomi RC	.40
164 Javier Colina	.15
165 Greg Sain RC	.40
166 Robert Cosby RC	.40
167 Angel Pagan RC	2.00
168 Ralph Santana RC	.40
169 Joe Orloski RC	.40
170 Shayne Wright RC	.40
171 Jay Caligiuri RC	.25
172 Greg Montalbano RC	.50
173 Rich Harden RC	3.00
174 Rich Thompson RC	.40
175 Fred Bastardo RC	.40
176 Alejandro Giron RC	.40
177 Jesus Medrano RC	.40
178 Kevin Deaton RC	.40
179 Mike Rosamond RC	.50
180 Jon Guzman RC	.40
181 Gerard Oakes RC	.40
182 Francisco Liriano RC	8.00
183 Matt Allegra RC	.50
184 Mike Snyder RC	.40
185 James Shanks RC	.40
186 Anderson Hernandez RC	.40
187 Dan Trumble RC	.40
188 Luis DePaula RC	.40
189 Randall Shelley RC	.40
190 Richard Lane RC	.40
191 Antwon Rollins RC	.50
192 Ryan Bukvich RC	.40
193 Derrick Lewis	.15
194 Eric Miller RC	.40
195 Justin Schuda RC	.40
196 Brian West RC	.40
197 Adam Roller RC	.40
198 Neal Frendling RC	.40
199 Jeremy Hill RC	.40
200 James Barrett RC	.50
201 Brett Kay RC	.50
202 Ryan Mottl RC	.50
203 Brad Nelson RC	.50
204 Juan Gonzalez	.15
205 Curtis Legendre RC	.40
206 Ronald Acuna RC	.40
207 Chris Flinn RC	.40
208 Nick Alvarez RC	.40
209 Jason Ellison RC	.40
210 Blake McGinley RC	.40
211 Dan Phillips RC	.50
212 Demetrius Heath RC	.40
213 Eric Bruntlett RC	.40
214 Joe Jiannetti RC	.40
215 Mike Hill RC	.40
216 Ricardo Cordova RC	.40
217 Mark Hamilton RC	.50
218 David Mattox RC	.40
219 Jose Morban RC	.50
220 Scott Wiggins RC	.50
221 Steve Green	.15
222 Brian Rogers	.15
223 Chin-Hui Tsao	.40
224 Kenny Baugh	.15
225 Nate Teut	.15
226 Josh Wilson RC	.40
227 Christian Parker	.15
228 Tim Raines Jr.	.15
229 Anastacio Martinez RC	.40
230 Richard Lewis	.15
231 Tim Kalita RC	.40
232 Edwin Almonte RC	.40
233 Hee Seop Choi	.25
234 Ty Howington	.15
235 Victor Alvarez RC	.40
236 Morgan Ensberg	.15
237 Jeff Austin RC	.40
238 Luis Terrero	.15
239 Adam Wainwright	.15
240 Clint Weibl RC	.40
241 Eric Cyr RC	.40
242 Marlyn Tisdale RC	.40
243 John VanBenschoten	.15
244 Ryan Raburn RC	.40
245 Miguel Cabrera	.75
246 Jung Bong	.15
247 Raul Chavez RC	.50
248 Erik Bedard	.15
249 Chris Snelling	.50
250 Joe Rogers RC	.40
251 Nate Field RC	.40
252 Matt Herges	.15
253 Matt Childers RC	.50
254 Erick Almonte	.15
255 Nick Neugebauer	.15
256 Ron Calloway RC	.40
257 Seung Jun Song	.15
258 Brandon Phillips	.15
259 Cole Barthel	.25
260 Jason Lane	.15
261 Jae Weong Seo	.15
262 Randy Flores	.15
263 Scott Chiasson	.15

264	Chase Utley	1.00
265	Tony Alvarez	.15
266	Ben Howard RC	.40
267	Nelson Castro RC	.40
268	Mark Lukasiewicz	.15
269	Eric Glaser RC	.40
270	Rob Henkel RC	.40
271	Jose Valverde RC	.40
272	Ricardo Rodriguez	.15
273	Chris Smith	.15
274	Mark Prior	.75
275	Miguel Olivo RC	.15
276	Ben Broussard	.15
277	Zach Sorensen	.15
278	Brian Mallette RC	.40
279	Brad Wilkerson	.15
280	Carl Crawford RC	.40
281	Chone Figgins RC	.40
282	Jimmy Alvarez RC	.40
283	Gavin Floyd	1.50
284	Josh Bonifay RC	.50
285	Garrett Guzman RC	.50
286	Blake Williams	.15
287	Matt Holliday	.50
288	Ryan Madson	.15
289	Luis Torres	.15
290	Jeff Verplancke RC	.40
291	Nate Espy RC	.50
292	Jeff Lincoln RC	.40
293	Ryan Snare RC	.40
294	Jose Ortiz	.15
295	Eric Munson	.15
296	Denny Bautista	.15
297	Willy Aybar	.15
298	Kelly Johnson	.15
299	Justin Morneau	.50
300	Derrick Van Dusen	.15
301	Chad Petty	.15
302	Mike Restovich	.15
303	Shawn Fagan	.15
304	Yurendell DeCaster RC	.40
305	Justin Wayne	.15
306	Mike Peeples RC	.40
307	Joel Guzman RC	.75
308	Ryan Vogelsong	.15
309	Jorge Padilla RC	.50
310	Grady Sizemore	.50
311	Joe Jester RC	.40
312	Jim Journell	.15
313	Bobby Seay	.15
314	Ryan Church RC	1.00
315	Grant Balfour	.15
316	Mitch Jones	.15
317	Travis Foley	.50
318	Bobby Crosby	.15
319	Adrian Gonzalez	.15
320	Ronnie Merrill	.15
321	Joel Pineiro	.15
322	John-Ford Griffin	.15
323	Brian Forystek RC	.40
324	Sean Douglass	.15
325	Manny Delcarmen RC	.40
326	Donnie Bridges	.15
327	Jim Kavourias	.15
328	Gabe Gross	.15
329	Greg "Toe" Nash	.15
330	Bill Ortega	.15
331	Joey Hammond RC	.40
332	Ramon Moreta RC	.40
333	Ron Davenport	.15
334	Brett Myers	.15
335	Carlos Pena	.15
336	Ezequiel Astacio RC	.40
337	Edwin Yan RC	.50
338	Josh Girdley	.15
339	Shaun Boyd	.15
340	Juan Rincon	.15
341	Chris Duffy RC	.50
342	Jason Kinchen	.15
343	Brad Thomas	.15
344	David Kelton	.15
345	Rafael Soriano	.15
346	Colin Young RC	.50
347	Eric Byrnes	.15
348	Chris Narveson RC	.50
349	John Rheinecker RC	.40
350	Mike Wilson RC	.40
351	Justin Sherrod RC	.50
352	Deivi Mendez	.15
353	Wily Mo Pena	.15
354	Brett Roneberg RC	.50
355	Trey Lunsford RC	.40
356	Jimmy Gobble RC	.50
357	Brent Butler	.15
358	Aaron Heilman	.15
359	Wilkin Ruan	.15
360	Brian Wolfe RC	.40
361	Cody Ransom	.15
362	Koyie Hill	.40
363	Brett Cassidy	.15
364	Tony Fontana RC	.50
365	Mark Teixeira	.75
366	Doug Sessions RC	.40
367	Victor Hall	.15

368	Josh Cisneros RC	.40
369	Kevin Mench	.15
370	Tike Redman	.15
371	Jeff Heaverlo	.15
372	Carlos Brackley RC	.40
373	Brad Hawpe	.50
374	Jesus Colome	.15
375	David Espinosa	.15
376	Jesse Foppert	.75
377	Ross Peeples RC	.40
378	Alexander Requena RC	.40
379	Joe Mauer RC	10.00
380	Carlos Silva	.15
381	David Wright	40.00
382	Craig Kuzmic RC	.50
383	Peter Zamora RC	.40
384	Matt Harper RC	.40
385	Ricardo Rodriguez	.15
386	Gary Cates Jr. RC	.40
387	Justin Reid RC	.40
388	Jake Mauer RC	.50
389	John-Ford Griffin	.15
390	Josh Barfield	2.00
391	Luis Maza	.15
392	Henry Pichardo RC	.40
393	Michael Floyd RC	.40
394	Clint Nageotte RC	.75
395	Jim Warden	.15
396	Mauricio Lara RC	.50
397	Alejandro Cadena RC	.40
398	Jonny Gomes RC	3.00
399	Jason Bulger RC	.50
400	Bobby Jenks RC	1.00
401	David Gil RC	.40
402	Joel Crump RC	.40
403	Kazuhisa Ishii RC	.75
404	So Taguchi RC	.75
405	Ryan Doumit RC	1.00
406	Macay McBride	.15
407	Brandon Claussen	.15
408	Chin-Feng Chen	.15
409	Josh Phelps	.25
410	Freddie Money RC	.40
411	Clifford Bartosh RC	.40
412	Josh Pearce	.15
413	Lyle Overbay	.15
414	Ryan Anderson	.15
415	Terrance Hill RC	.40
416	John Rodriguez RC	.40
417	Richard Stahl RC	.40
418	Brian Specht	.15
419	Chris Latham RC	.50
420	Carlos Cabrera RC	.40
421	Jose Bautista RC	.50
422	Kevin Frederick RC	.40
423	Jerome Williams	.15
424	Napoleon Calzado RC	.50
425	Benito Baez	.15
426	Xavier Nady	.15
427	Jason Botts RC	.40
428	Steve Bechler RC	.50
429	Reed Johnson RC	.40
430	Mark Outlaw RC	.40
431	Billy Sylvester	.15
432	Luke Lockwood	.15
433	Jake Peavy	.25
434	Alfredo Amezaga	.15
435	Aaron Cook RC	.50
436	Josh Shaffer RC	.40
437	Dan Wright	.15
438	Ryan Gripp RC	.50
439	Alex Herrera	.15
440	Jason Bay RC	4.00

Gold

Stars:	1-2.5X
Rookies:	1-2X
Inserted 1:1	

Uncirculated

	NM/M
Common Player:	4.00
Production 1,000 Sets	
112 Chris Trittle	6.00
113 Ed Rogers	4.00
114 Juan Pena	4.00
115 Josh Beckett	8.00
116 Juan Cruz	4.00
117 Noochie Varner	6.00
118 Taylor Buchholz	4.00
119 Mike Rivera	4.00
120 Hank Blalock	8.00
121 Hansel Izquierdo	4.00
122 Orlando Hudson	4.00
123 Bill Hall	4.00
124 Jose Reyes	8.00
125 Juan Rivera	4.00
126 Eric Valent	4.00
127 Scotty Layfield	4.00
128 Austin Kearns	8.00
129 Nic Jackson	4.00
130 Chris Baker	4.00
131 Chad Qualls	4.00

Autographs

		NM/M
Common Autograph:		5.00
Inserted 1:37		
AA	Alfredo Amezaga	5.00
GA	Garrett Atkins	20.00
JB	Josh Beckett	35.00
WB	Wilson Betemit	5.00
LB	Larry Bigbie	5.00
HB	Hank Blalock	20.00
TB	Tony Blanco	5.00
JAB	Jason Botts	5.00
MB	Marlon Byrd	10.00
BDC	Brian Cardwell	5.00
BC	Ben Christensen	5.00
BAC	Brandon Claussen	8.00
JD	Jeff Davanon	5.00
MD	Manny Delcarmen	8.00
RF	Randy Flores	5.00
RF	Ryan Franklin	5.00
KG	Keith Ginter	5.00
TH	Toby Hall	5.00
AH	Aubrey Huff	10.00
GJ	Gary Johnson	5.00
NJ	Nick Johnson	10.00
CK	Charles Kegley	5.00
JL	Jason Lane	10.00
NN	Nick Neugebauer	5.00
RO	Roy Oswalt	15.00
JP	Juan Pena	5.00
MP	Mark Prior	20.00
CR	Cody Ransom	5.00
JS	Juan Silvestre	5.00
TS	Terrmel Sledge	8.00
BS	Bud Smith	5.00
CS	Chris Smith	5.00
WS	Will Smith	5.00
BJS	Brian Specht	5.00
CT	Chris Trittle	8.00
CU	Chase Utley	75.00
DV	Domingo Valdez	5.00
NV	Noochie Varner	5.00
RV	Ryan Vogelsong	5.00
JLW	Jerome Williams	8.00
DW	Dan Wright	5.00

Autographed Futures Game Game-Worn Jersey

		NM/M
Common Player:		15.00
Inserted 1:193		
WB	Wilson Betemit	15.00
CH	Carlos Hernandez	15.00
JRH	J.R. House	15.00
NJ	Nick Johnson	20.00
RL	Ryan Ludwick	15.00
CP	Carlos Pena	15.00
DT	Dennis Tankersley	15.00
JW	Jerome Williams	20.00

Autographed Futures Game Game-Used Base

		NM/M
Randomly Inserted		
TB	Toby Hall	15.00

Game-Used Relics

		NM/M
Common Player:		4.00
Inserted 1:165		
JA1	Jared Abruzzo	4.00
JA2	Jared Abruzzo	4.00
GA	Garrett Atkins	8.00
AB	Angel Berroa	6.00
AC	Antoine Cameron	4.00
RC	Ryan Church	6.00

ALC	Alex Cintron	4.00
NC	Nate Cornejo	4.00
RD	Ryan Dittfurth	4.00
AE	Adam Everett	4.00
AF1	Alex Fernandez	4.00
AF2	Alex Fernandez	4.00
AG	Alexis Gomez	4.00
CG	Cristian Guerrero	4.00
CI	Cesar Izturis	4.00
DJ	D'Angelo Jimenez	4.00
FJ	Forrest Johnson	4.00
AK	Austin Kearns	6.00
JL	Jason Lane	4.00
RM	Ryan Madson	4.00
NN	Nick Neugebauer	4.00
CP	Corey Patterson	6.00
RS	Ruben Salazar	4.00
RST	Richard Stahl	4.00
JS	Jamal Strong	4.00
CY	Colin Young	4.00

2002 Bowman Chrome

	NM/M
Complete Set (405):	
Common Player:	.25
Common SP:	3.00
Inserted 1:3	
Common Auto.	
(384-402,405):	10.00
Inserted 1:18	
Pack (4):	12.00
Box (18):	200.00
1 Adam Dunn	.50
2 Derek Jeter	3.00
3 Alex Rodriguez	2.50
4 Miguel Tejada	.50
5 Nomar Garciaparra	1.00
6 Toby Hall	.25
7 Brandon Duckworth	.25
8 Paul LoDuca	.25
9 Brian Giles	.25
10 C.C. Sabathia	.25
11 Curt Schilling	.75
12 Tsuyoshi Shinjo	.25
13 Ramon Hernandez	.25
14 Jose Cruz Jr.	.25
15 Albert Pujols	3.00
16 Joe Mays	.25
17 Javy Lopez	.25
18 J.T. Snow	.25
19 David Segui	.25
20 Jorge Posada	.50
21 Doug Mientkiewicz	.25
22 Jerry Hairston Jr.	.25
23 Bernie Williams	.50
24 Mike Sweeney	.25
25 Jason Giambi	.75
26 Ryan Dempster	.25
27 Ryan Klesko	.25
28 Mark Quinn	.25
29 Jeff Kent	.25

#	Player	Price
30	Eric Chavez	.40
31	Adrian Beltre	.40
32	Andruw Jones	1.00
33	Alfonso Soriano	1.00
34	Aramis Ramirez	.50
35	Greg Maddux	1.50
36	Andy Pettitte	.50
37	Bartolo Colon	.25
38	Ben Sheets	.40
39	Bobby Higginson	.25
40	Ivan Rodriguez	.60
41	Brad Penny	.25
42	Carlos Lee	.40
43	Damion Easley	.25
44	Preston Wilson	.25
45	Jeff Bagwell	1.00
46	Eric Milton	.25
47	Rafael Palmeiro	.75
48	Gary Sheffield	.50
49	J.D. Drew	.40
50	Jim Thome	.75
51	Ichiro Suzuki	2.00
52	Bud Smith	.25
53	Chan Ho Park	.25
54	D'Angelo Jimenez	.25
55	Ken Griffey Jr.	2.00
56	Wade Miller	.25
57	Vladimir Guerrero	1.00
58	Troy Glaus	.50
59	Shawn Green	.40
60	Kerry Wood	.50
61	Jack Wilson	.25
62	Kevin Brown	.25
63	Marcus Giles	.25
64	Pat Burrell	.50
65	Larry Walker	.40
66	Sammy Sosa	1.00
67	Raul Mondesi	.25
68	Tim Hudson	.40
69	Lance Berkman	.50
70	Mike Mussina	.50
71	Barry Zito	.50
72	Jimmy Rollins	.75
73	Barry Bonds	3.00
74	Craig Biggio	.40
75	Todd Helton	.75
76	Roger Clemens	2.00
77	Frank Catalanotto	.25
78	Josh Towers	.25
79	Roy Oswalt	.40
80	Chipper Jones	1.00
81	Cristian Guzman	.25
82	Darin Erstad	.60
83	Freddy Garcia	.25
84	Jason Tyner	.25
85	Carlos Delgado	.50
86	Jon Lieber	.25
87	Juan Pierre	.25
88	Matt Morris	.25
89	Phil Nevin	.25
90	Jim Edmonds	.40
91	Magglio Ordonez	.40
92	Mike Hampton	.25
93	Rafael Furcal	.40
94	Richie Sexson	.40
95	Luis Gonzalez	.40
96	Scott Rolen	.75
97	Tim Redding	.25
98	Moises Alou	.25
99	Jose Vidro	.25
100	Mike Piazza	1.50
101	Pedro Martinez	1.00
102	Geoff Jenkins	.25
103	Johnny Damon	1.00
104	Mike Cameron	.25
105	Randy Johnson	1.00
106	David Eckstein	.25
107	Javier Vazquez	.25
108	Mark Mulder	.40
109	Robert Fick	.25
110	Roberto Alomar	.40
111	Wilson Betemit	.25
112	Chris Tritle/SP RC	4.00
113	Ed Rogers	.25
114	Juan Pena	.25
115	Josh Beckett	.50
116	Juan Cruz	.25
117	Noochie Varner/SP RC	5.00
118	Blake Williams	.25
119	Mike Rivera	.25
120	Hank Blalock	.50
121	Hansel Izquierdo/ SP RC	4.00
122	Orlando Hudson	.25
123	Bill Hall	.25
124	Jose Reyes	1.00
125	Juan Rivera	.25
126	Eric Valent	.25
127	Scotty Layfield/SP RC	.25
128	Austin Kearns	.50
129	Nic Jackson/SP RC	5.00
130	Scott Chiasson	.25
131	Chad Qualls/SP RC	4.00
132	Marcus Thames	.25
133	Nathan Haynes	.25
134	Joe Borchard	.25
135	Josh Hamilton	.25
136	Corey Patterson	.25
137	Travis Wilson	.25
138	Alex Escobar	.25
139	Alexis Gomez	.25
140	Nick Johnson	.25
141	Marlon Byrd	.25
142	Kory DeHaan	.25
143	Carlos Hernandez	.25
144	Sean Burroughs	.25
145	Angel Berroa	.25
146	Aubrey Huff	.25
147	Travis Hafner	.75
148	Brandon Berger	.25
149	J.R. House	.25
150	Dewon Brazelton	.25
151	Jayson Werth	.25
152	Larry Barnes	.25
153	Ruben Gotay/SP	6.00
154	Tommy Marx/SP RC	3.00
155	John Suomi/SP RC	4.00
156	Javier Colina/SP	3.00
157	Greg Sain/SP RC	3.00
158	Robert Cosby/SP RC	4.00
159	Angel Pagan/SP RC	8.00
160	Ralph Santana RC	1.50
161	Joe Orloski/SP	1.50
162	Shayne Wright/SP RC	3.00
163	Jay Caligiuri/SP RC	4.00
164	Greg Montalbano/ SP RC	5.00
165	Rich Harden/SP RC	25.00
166	Rich Thompson/ SP RC	3.00
167	Fred Bastardo/SP RC	3.00
168	Alejandro Giron/SP RC	3.00
169	Jesus Medrano/SP RC	3.00
170	Kevin Deaton/SP RC	4.00
171	Mike Rosamond RC	1.50
172	Jon Guzman/SP RC	3.00
173	Gerard Oakes/SP RC	4.00
174	Francisco Liriano/ SP	40.00
175	Matt Allegra/SP RC	4.00
176	Mike Snyder/SP RC	4.00
177	James Shanks/SP RC	3.00
178	Anderson Hernandez/ SP RC	4.00
179	Dan Trumble/SP RC	3.00
180	Luis DePaula/SP RC	4.00
181	Randall Shelley/SP RC	4.00
182	Richard Lane/SP RC	3.00
183	Antwon Rollins/SP RC	4.00
184	Ryan Bukvich/SP RC	4.00
185	Derrick Lewis/SP	3.00
186	Eric Miller/SP RC	3.00
187	Justin Schuda/SP RC	3.00
188	Brian West/SP RC	4.00
189	Brad Wilkerson	.25
190	Neal Frendling/SP RC	3.00
191	Jeremy Hill/SP RC	3.00
192	James Barrett/SP RC	4.00
193	Brett Kay/SP RC	3.00
194	Ryan Mottl/SP RC	4.00
195	Brad Nelson/SP RC	5.00
196	Juan Gonzalez/SP	3.00
197	Curtis Legendre/SP RC	3.00
198	Ronald Acuna/SP RC	3.00
199	Chris Flinn/SP RC	3.00
200	Nick Alvarez/SP RC	3.00
201	Jason Ellison/SP RC	4.00
202	Blake McGinley/SP RC	3.00
203	Dan Phillips/SP RC	3.00
204	Demetrius Heath/ SP RC	3.00
205	Eric Bruntlett/SP RC	3.00
206	Joe Jiannetti/SP RC	3.00
207	Mike Hill/SP RC	3.00
208	Ricardo Cordova/ SP RC	3.00
209	Mark Hamilton/SP RC	3.00
210	David Mattox/SP RC	3.00
211	Jose Morban/SP RC	5.00
212	Scott Wiggins/SP RC	3.00
213	Steve Green	.25
214	Brian Rogers/SP	3.00
215	Kenny Baugh	.25
216	Anastacio Martinez/ SP RC	3.00
217	Richard Lewis	.25
218	Tim Kalita/SP RC	3.00
219	Edwin Almonte/SP RC	3.00
220	Hee Seop Choi	.25
221	Ty Howington	.25
222	Victor Alvarez/SP RC	3.00
223	Morgan Ensberg	.25
224	Jeff Austin/SP RC	3.00
225	Clint Weibl/SP RC	4.00
226	Eric Cyr RC	1.00
227	Marlyn Tisdale/SP RC	3.00
228	John VanBenschoten	.25
229	Ruben Salazar	.25
230	Raul Chavez/SP RC	4.00
231	Brett Evert	.25
232	Joe Rogers/SP RC	4.00
233	Adam Wainwright	.50
234	Matt Herges	.50
235	Matt Childers/SP RC	4.00
236	Nick Neugebauer	.25
237	Carl Crawford	1.00
238	Seung Jun Song	.25
239	Randy Flores	.25
240	Jason Lane	.25
241	Chase Utley	4.00
242	Ben Howard/SP RC	3.00
243	Eric Glaser/SP RC	3.00
244	Josh Wilson RC	1.00
245	Jose Valverde/SP RC	4.00
246	Chris Smith	.25
247	Mark Prior	1.00
248	Brian Mallette/SP RC	3.00
249	Chone Figgins/SP RC	8.00
250	Jimmy Alvarez/SP RC	3.00
251	Luis Terrero	.25
252	Josh Bonifay/SP RC	4.00
253	Garrett Guzman/ SP RC	3.00
254	Jeff Verplancke/SP RC	4.00
255	Nate Espy/SP RC	4.00
256	Jeff Lincoln/SP RC	3.00
257	Ryan Snare/SP RC	4.00
258	Jose Ortiz	.25
259	Denny Bautista	.25
260	Willy Aybar	.25
261	Kelly Johnson	1.00
262	Shawn Fagan	.25
263	Yurendell DeCaster/ SP RC	3.00
264	Mike Peeples/SP RC	3.00
265	Joel Guzman RC	3.00
266	Ryan Vogelsong	.25
267	Jorge Padilla/SP RC	3.00
268	Joe Jester/SP RC	3.00
269	Ryan Church/SP RC	10.00
270	Mitch Jones	.25
271	Travis Foley/SP	3.00
272	Bobby Crosby	2.00
273	Adrian Gonzalez	.75
274	Ronnie Merrill	.25
275	Joel Pineiro	.25
276	John-Ford Griffin	.25
277	Brian Forystek/SP RC	3.00
278	Sean Douglass	.25
279	Manny Delcarmen/ SP RC	5.00
280	Jim Kavourias/SP	3.00
281	Gabe Gross	.25
282	Bill Ortega	.25
283	Joey Hammond/SP RC	3.00
284	Brett Myers	.50
285	Carlos Pena	.50
286	Ezequiel Astacio/ SP RC	3.00
287	Edwin Yan/SP RC	3.00
288	Chris Duffy/SP RC	6.00
289	Jason Kinchen	.25
290	Rafael Soriano	.25
291	Colin Young RC	.50
292	Eric Byrnes	.25
293	Chris Narveson/SP RC	5.00
294	John Rheinecker RC	.50
295	Mike Wilson/SP RC	4.00
296	Justin Sherrod/SP RC	5.00
297	Deivi Mendez	.25
298	Wily Mo Pena	.25
299	Brett Roneberg/SP RC	4.00
300	Trey Lunsford/SP RC	3.00
301	Christian Parker	.25
302	Brent Butler	.25
303	Aaron Heilman	.25
304	Wilkin Ruan	.25
305	Kenny Kelly	.25
306	Cody Ransom	.25
307	Koyie Hill/SP	3.00
308	Tony Fontana/SP RC	3.00
309	Mark Teixeira	2.00
310	Doug Sessions/SP RC	3.00
311	Josh Cisneros/SP RC	3.00
312	Carlos Brackley/SP RC	3.00
313	Tim Raines Jr.	.25
314	Ross Peeples/SP RC	5.00
315	Alexander Requena/ SP RC	5.00
316	Chin-Hui Tsao	.25
317	Tony Alvarez	.25
318	Craig Kuzmic/SP RC	3.00
319	Peter Zamora/SP RC	3.00
320	Matt Parker/SP RC	3.00
321	Keith Ginter	.25
322	Gary Cates Jr./SP RC	3.00
323	Matt Belisle	.25
324	Ben Broussard	.25
324	Jake Mauer/auto RC	10.00
325	Dennis Tankersley	.25
326	Juan Silvestre	.25
327	Henry Pichardo/SP RC	3.00
328	Michael Floyd/SP RC	3.00
329	Clint Nageotte/SP RC	6.00
330	Raymond Cabrera/ SP RC	3.00
331	Mauricio Lara/SP RC	4.00
332	Alejandro Cadena/ SP RC	3.00
333	Jonny Gomes/SP RC	15.00
334	Jason Bulger/SP RC	4.00
335	Nate Teut	.25
336	David Gil/SP RC	3.00
337	Joel Crump/SP RC	3.00
338	Brandon Phillips	.25
339	Macay McBride	.50
340	Brandon Claussen	1.00
341	Josh Phelps	.25
342	Freddie Money/SP RC	4.00
343	Clifford Bartosh/SP RC	3.00
344	Terrance Hill/SP RC	3.00
345	John Rodriguez/SP RC	4.00
346	Chris Latham/SP RC	3.00
347	Carlos Cabrera/SP RC	3.00
348	Jose Bautista/SP RC	5.00
349	Kevin Frederick/SP RC	3.00
350	Jerome Williams	.75
351	Napoleon Calzado/ SP RC	3.00
352	Benito Baez/SP	3.00
353	Xavier Nady	.25
354	Jason Botts/SP RC	8.00
355	Steve Bechler/SP RC	4.00
356	Reed Johnson/SP RC	8.00
357	Mark Outlaw/SP RC	3.00
358	Jake Peavy	1.00
359	Josh Shaffer/SP RC	3.00
360	Dan Wright/SP	3.00
361	Ryan Gripp/SP RC	3.00
362	Nelson Castro/SP RC	3.00
363	Jason Bay/SP RC	30.00
364	Franklin German/ SP RC	3.00
365	Corwin Malone/SP	3.00
366	Kelly Ramos/SP RC	3.00
367	John Ennis/SP RC	3.00
368	George Perez/SP	3.00
369	Rene Reyes/SP RC	3.00
370	Rolando Viera/SP RC	3.00
371	Earl Snyder/SP RC	4.00
372	Kyle Kane/SP RC	3.00
373	Mario Ramos/SP	3.00
374	Tyler Yates/SP RC	3.00
375	Jason Young/SP RC	5.00
376	Chris Bootcheck/ SP RC	5.00
377	Jesus Cota/SP RC	5.00
378	Corky Miller/SP	3.00
379	Matt Erickson/SP RC	3.00
380	Justin Huber/SP RC	5.00
381	Felix Escalona/SP RC	3.00
382	Kevin Cash/SP RC	3.00
383	J.J. Putz/SP RC	3.00
384	Chris Snelling RC	20.00
385	David Wright	450.00
386	Brian Wolfe RC	10.00
387	Justin Reid RC	10.00
389	Ryan Raburn RC	10.00
390	Josh Barfield	30.00
391	Joe Mauer RC	150.00
392	Bobby Jenks RC	25.00
393	Rob Henkel RC	10.00
394	Jimmy Gobble RC	10.00
395	Jesse Foppert	15.00
396	Gavin Floyd	25.00
397	Nate Field RC	10.00
398	Ryan Doumit RC	25.00
399	Ron Calloway RC	10.00
400	Taylor Buchholz RC	15.00
401	Adam Roller RC	10.00
402	Cole Barthel	10.00
403	Kazuhisa Ishii/SP RC	6.00
404	So Taguchi/SP RC	4.00
405	Chris Baker RC	10.00

Refractors

Star Refractors (1-220):	2-3X
SP Refractors:	.5-1.5X
Production 500	
X-Fractors (1-220):	3-5X
SP X-Fractors:	.75-2X
Production 250:	
Gold Refractors (1-220):	8-15X
SP Gold Refractors:	2-4X
Production 50	
Refractor Autos.	
(384-402,405):	.75-1.5X
Production 500	
X-Fractor Autos.:	.75-2X
Production 250	

ABBREVIATIONS

SP - Short Print

Gold Autographs: 2-4X
Production 50

Uncirculated

Cards: 1-3X
Production 350
Autos. 10 cards of each player.
No Pricing

Rookie Reprints

		NM/M
Complete Set (20):		25.00
Common Player:		1.00
Inserted 1:6		
Refractors:		1.5-2X
Inserted 1:18		
JB	Jeff Bagwell	1.50
BC	Bartolo Colon	1.00
CD	Carlos Delgado	1.00
JG	Juan Gonzalez	1.50
LG	Luis Gonzalez	1.00
KG	Ken Griffey Jr.	3.00
VG	Vladimir Guerrero	2.00
DJ	Derek Jeter	5.00
AJ	Andruw Jones	1.50
CJ	Chipper Jones	2.50
JK	Jason Kendall	1.00
MP	Mike Piazza	3.00
JP	Jorge Posada	1.00
IR	Ivan Rodriguez	1.00
SR	Scott Rolen	1.00
GS	Gary Sheffield	1.00
MS	Mike Sweeney	1.00
FT	Frank Thomas	1.50
LW	Larry Walker	1.00
BW	Bernie Williams	1.00

Ishii & Taguchi Autographs

	NM/M
Refractors:	.75-1.5X
Production 100	
X-Fractors:	2-4X
Production 50	
Golds:	Production 10
403 Kazuhisa Ishii	50.00
404 So Taguchi	25.00

2002 Bowman Chrome Draft Picks & Prospects

	NM/M
Complete Set (175):	275.00
Common Player:	.25
Common RC:	.75
1-165 Two Per Pack	
Common Auto. (166-175):	10.00
Auto's Inserted 1:45	
BDP1 Clint Everts RC	2.00
BDP2 Fred Lewis RC	4.00
BDP3	Jonathan
	Broxton RC	2.00
BDP4	Jason Anderson RC	.75
BDP5	Mike Eusebio RC	.75
BDP6	Zack Greinke RC	5.00
BDP7	Joe Blanton RC	5.00
BDP8	Sergio Santos RC	1.50
BDP9	Jason Cooper RC	1.50
BDP10	Delwyn Young RC	3.00
BDP11	Jeremy
	Hermida RC	15.00
BDP12	Dan Ortmeyer RC	1.50
BDP13	Kevin Jepsen RC	2.00
BDP14	Russ Adams RC	2.00
BDP15	Mike Nixon RC	.75
BDP16	Nick Swisher RC	15.00
BDP17	Cole Hamels RC	35.00
BDP18	Brian Dopirak RC	3.00
BDP19	James Loney RC	15.00
BDP20	Denard Span RC	2.00
BDP21	Billy Petrick RC	.75
BDP22	Jared Doyle RC	.75
BDP23	Jeff Francoeur RC	50.00
BDP24	Nick Bourgeois RC	.75
BDP25	Matt Cain RC	30.00
BDP26	John McCurdy RC	.75
BDP27	Mark Kiger RC	.75
BDP28	Bill Murphy RC	1.00
BDP29	Matt Craig RC	1.00
BDP30	Mike Megrew RC	1.00
BDP31	Ben Crockett RC	.75
BDP32	Luke Hagerty RC	1.50
BDP33	Matt Whitney RC	1.00
BDP34	Dan Meyer RC	1.50
BDP35	Jeremy Brown RC	1.00
BDP36	Doug Johnson RC	.75
BDP37	Steve Obenchain RC	.75
BDP38	Matt Clanton RC	1.00
BDP39	Mark Teahen RC	4.00
BDP40	Thomas Carrow RC	.75
BDP41	Micah Schilling RC	1.00
BDP42	Blair Johnson RC	1.00
BDP43	Jason Pridie RC	1.00
BDP44	Joey Votto RC	15.00
BDP45	Taber Lee RC	.75
BDP46	Adam Peterson RC	.75
BDP47	Adam Donachie RC	1.00
BDP48	Josh Murray RC	1.00
BDP49	Brent Clevlen RC	4.00
BDP50	Chad Pleiness RC	1.00
BDP51	Zach Hammes RC	1.50
BDP52	Chris Snyder RC	1.50
BDP53	Chris Smith	.50
BDP54	Justin Maureau RC	.75
BDP55	David Bush RC	3.00
BDP56	Tim Gilhooly RC	.75
BDP57	Blair Barbier RC	.75
BDP58	Zach Segovia RC	1.00
BDP59	Jeremy Reed RC	4.00
BDP60	Matt Pender RC	.75
BDP61	Eric Thomas RC	.75
BDP62	Justin Jones RC	1.50
BDP63	Brian Slocum RC	1.00
BDP64	Larry Broadway RC	1.50
BDP65	Bo Flowers RC	.75
BDP66	Scott White RC	1.00
BDP67	Steve Stanley RC	.75
BDP68	Alex Merricks RC	.75
BDP69	Josh Womack RC	.75
BDP70	Dave Jensen RC	.75
BDP71	Curtis
	Granderson RC	15.00
BDP72	Pat Osborn RC	1.50
BDP73	Nic Carter RC	.75
BDP74	Mitch Talbot RC	.75
BDP75	Don Murphy RC	.75
BDP76	Val Majewski RC	1.50
BDP77	Javy Rodriguez RC	.75
BDP78	Fernando
	Pacheco RC	1.00
BDP79	Steve Russell RC	.75
BDP80	Jon Slack RC	.75
BDP81	John Baker RC	.75

BDP82	Aaron Coonrod RC	.75
BDP83	Josh Johnson RC	6.00
BDP84	Jake Blalock RC	1.50
BDP85	Alex Hart RC	1.50
BDP86	Wes Bankston RC	5.00
BDP87	Josh Rupe RC	1.00
BDP88	Dan Cevette RC	1.00
BDP89	Kiel Fisher RC	1.00
BDP90	Alan Rick RC	.75
BDP91	Charlie Morton RC	1.00
BDP92	Chad Spann RC	1.00
BDP93	Kyle Boyer RC	1.00
BDP94	Bob Malek RC	.75
BDP95	Ryan Rodriguez RC	.75
BDP96	Jordan Renz RC	.75
BDP97	Randy Frye RC	.75
BDP98	Rich Hill RC	10.00
BDP99	B.J. Upton RC	15.00
BDP100	Dan
	Christensen RC	1.00
BDP101	Casey Kotchman	4.00
BDP102	Eric Good RC	.75
BDP103	Mike Fontenot RC	2.00
BDP104	John Webb RC	.75
BDP105	Jason Dubois RC	1.50
BDP106	Ryan Kibler RC	.75
BDP107	Jhonny Peralta RC	8.00
BDP108	Kirk Saarloos RC	1.50
BDP109	Rhett Parrott RC	.75
BDP110	Jason Grove RC	.75
BDP111	Colt Griffin	1.00
BDP112	Dallas McPherson	2.50
BDP113	Oliver Perez RC	4.00
BDP114	Marshall
	McDougall RC	.75
BDP115	Mike Wood RC	1.00
BDP116	Scott Hairston RC	1.50
BDP117	Jason
	Simontacchi RC	1.00
BDP118	Taggert Bozied RC	1.50
BDP119	Shelley Duncan RC	4.00
BDP120	Dontrelle Willis RC	15.00
BDP121	Sean Burnett RC	.25
BDP122	Aaron Cook RC	.75
BPD123	Brett Evert	.25
BDP124	Jimmy Journell	.25
BDP125	Brett Myers	.25
BDP126	Brad Baker	.25
BDP127	Billy Traber	1.50
BDP128	Adam Wainwright	.50
BDP129	Jason Young	1.00
BDP130	John Buck	.25
BDP131	Kevin Cash	.25
BDP132	Jason Stokes RC	1.50
BDP133	Drew Henson	.50
BDP134	Chad Tracy RC	4.00
BDP135	Orlando Hudson	.50
BDP136	Brandon Phillips	.25
BDP137	Joe Borchard	.25
BDP138	Marlon Byrd	.25
BDP139	Carl Crawford	.25
BDP140	Michael Restovich	.25
BDP141	Corey Hart RC	6.00
BDP142	Edwin Almonte	.25
BDP143	Francis Beltran RC	1.00
BDP144	Jorge De La
	Rosa RC	.75
BDP145	Gerardo Garcia RC	.75
BDP146	Franklyn
	German RC	.75
BDP147	Francisco Liriano	10.00
BDP148	Francisco
	Rodriguez	.50
BDP149	Ricardo Rodriguez	.25
BDP150	Seung Jun Song	.25
BDP151	John Stephens	.25
BDP152	Justin Huber	2.00
BDP153	Victor Martinez	.50
BDP154	Hee Seop Choi	.25
BDP155	Justin Morneau	.75
BDP156	Miguel Cabrera	2.00
BDP157	Victor Diaz RC	2.00
BDP158	Jose Reyes	.75
BDP159	Omar Infante RC	.75
BDP160	Angel Berroa	.25
BDP161	Tony Alvarez	.25
BDP162	Shin-Soo Choo RC	4.00
BDP163	Wily Mo Pena	.25
BDP164	Andres Torres	.25
BDP165	Jose Lopez RC	4.00
BDP166	Scott Moore/
	Auto. RC	15.00
BDP167	Chris Gruler/
	Auto. RC	15.00
BDP168	Joe Saunders/
	Auto. RC	20.00
BDP169	Jeff Francis/
	Auto. RC	30.00
BDP170	Royce Ring/
	Auto. RC	10.00
BDP171	Greg Miller/Auto.	20.00
BDP172	Brandon Weeden/
	Auto. RC	10.00

BDP173	Drew Meyer/
	Auto. RC	10.00
BDP174	Khalil Greene/
	Auto. RC	50.00
BDP175	Mark Schramek/
	Auto. RC	10.00

Refractor

Cards 1-165:	2-4X
Rookies 1-175:	2-3X
1-165 Production 300 Sets	
166-175 Inserted 1:154	

Gold Refractor

Cards 1-165:	8-15X
Rookies 1-165:	5-10X
1-165 Production 50 Sets	
166-175 No Pricing	

X-Fractor

Cards 1-165:	2-5X
Rookies 1-165:	3-4X
Rookies 166-175:	.75-1.5X
1-165 Production 150 Sets	
166-175 Inserted 1:309	

2002 Bowman Draft Picks & Prospects

		NM/M
Complete Set (165):		35.00
Common Player:		.15
Common RC:		.25
Pack: (4 + 2 Chrome):		10.00
Box (24):		200.00
BDP1	Clint Everts RC	.75
BDP2	Fred Lewis RC	1.00
BDP3	Jonathan
	Broxton RC	.75
BDP4	Jason Anderson RC	.25
BDP5	Mike Eusebio RC	.25
BDP6	Zack Greinke RC	2.00
BDP7	Joe Blanton RC	2.00
BDP8	Sergio Santos RC	.50
BDP9	Jason Cooper RC	.50
BDP10	Delwyn Young RC	1.00
BDP11	Jeremy
	Hermida RC	3.00
BDP12	Dan Ortmeyer RC	.40
BDP13	Kevin Jepsen RC	.50
BDP14	Russ Adams RC	1.00
BDP15	Mike Nixon RC	.40
BDP16	Nick Swisher RC	4.00
BDP17	Cole Hamels RC	10.00
BDP18	Brian Dopirak RC	1.00
BDP19	James Loney RC	4.00
BDP20	Denard Span RC	.50
BDP21	Billy Petrick RC	.25
BDP22	Jared Doyle RC	.25
BDP23	Jeff Francoeur RC	15.00
BDP24	Nick Bourgeois RC	.25
BDP25	Matt Cain RC	8.00

BDP26	John McCurdy RC	.40
BDP27	Mark Kiger RC	.15
BDP28	Bill Murphy RC	.40
BDP29	Matt Craig RC	.25
BDP30	Mike Megrew RC	.50
BDP31	Ben Crockett RC	.25
BDP32	Luke Hagerty RC	.50
BDP33	Matt Whitney RC	1.00
BDP34	Dan Meyer RC	.50
BDP35	Jeremy Brown RC	.50
BDP36	Doug Johnson RC	.25
BDP37	Steve Obenchain RC	.25
BDP38	Matt Clanton RC	.40
BDP39	Mark Teahen RC	1.50
BDP40	Thomas Carrow RC	.25
BDP41	Micah Schilling RC	.50
BDP42	Blair Johnson RC	.25
BDP43	Jason Pridie RC	.75
BDP44	Joey Votto RC	4.00
BDP45	Taber Lee RC	.25
BDP46	Adam Peterson RC	.25
BDP47	Adam Donachie RC	.40
BDP48	Josh Murray RC	.40
BDP49	Brent Clevlen RC	1.50
BDP50	Chad Pleiness RC	.40
BDP51	Zach Hammes RC	.50
BDP52	Chris Snyder RC	.50
BDP53	Chris Smith	.25
BDP54	Justin Maureau RC	.25
BDP55	David Bush RC	1.00
BDP56	Tim Gilhooly RC	.25
BDP57	Blair Barbier RC	.25
BDP58	Zach Segovia RC	.50
BDP59	Jeremy Reed RC	2.00
BDP60	Matt Pender RC	.25
BDP61	Eric Thomas RC	.25
BDP62	Justin Jones RC	1.00
BDP63	Brian Slocum RC	.40
BDP64	Larry Broadway RC	1.00
BDP65	Bo Flowers RC	.25
BDP66	Scott White RC	.75
BDP67	Steve Stanley RC	.25
BDP68	Alex Merricks RC	.25
BDP69	Josh Womack RC	.40
BDP70	Dave Jensen RC	.25
BDP71	Curtis Granderson RC	4.00
BDP72	Pat Osborn RC	.40
BDP73	Nic Carter RC	.25
BDP74	Mitch Talbot RC	.25
BDP75	Don Murphy RC	.25
BDP76	Val Majewski RC	.50
BDP77	Javy Rodriguez RC	.25
BDP78	Fernando Pacheco RC	.40
BDP79	Steve Russell RC	.25
BDP80	Jon Slack RC	.25
BDP81	John Baker RC	.25
BDP82	Aaron Coonrod RC	.25
BDP83	Josh Johnson RC	2.00
BDP84	Jake Blalock RC	.75
BDP85	Alex Hart RC	.50
BDP86	Wes Bankston RC	1.50
BDP87	Josh Rupe RC	.40
BDP88	Dan Cevette RC	.75
BDP89	Kiel Fisher RC	.50
BDP90	Alan Rick RC	.25
BDP91	Charlie Morton RC	.50
BDP92	Chad Spann RC	.50
BDP93	Kyle Boyer RC	.25
BDP94	Bob Malek RC	.25
BDP95	Ryan Rodriguez RC	.25
BDP96	Jordan Renz RC	.25
BDP97	Randy Frye RC	.25
BDP98	Rich Hill RC	3.00
BDP99	B.J. Upton RC	5.00
BDP100	Dan Christensen RC	.50
BDP101	Casey Kotchman RC	1.00
BDP102	Eric Good RC	.25
BDP103	Mike Fontenot RC	.75
BDP104	John Webb RC	.25
BDP105	Jason Dubois RC	.75
BDP106	Ryan Kibler RC	.25
BDP107	Jhonny Peralta RC	2.50
BDP108	Kirk Saarloos RC	.75
BDP109	Rhett Parrott RC	.25
BDP110	Jason Grove RC	.25
BDP111	Colt Griffin RC	.25
BDP112	Dallas McPherson RC	1.00
BDP113	Oliver Perez RC	1.50
BDP114	Marshall McDougall RC	.25
BDP115	Mike Wood RC	.40
BDP116	Scott Hairston RC	1.00
BDP117	Jason Simontacchi RC	.50
BDP118	Taggert Bozied RC	1.00
BDP119	Shelley Duncan RC	.25
BDP120	Dontrelle Willis RC	6.00
BDP121	Sean Burnett	.15
BDP122	Aaron Cook RC	.25
BPD123	Brett Evert	.15
BDP124	Jimmy Journell	.15
BDP125	Brett Myers	.15
BDP126	Brad Baker	.15
BDP127	Billy Traber	.50
BDP128	Adam Wainwright	.15
BDP129	Jason Young RC	.40
BDP130	John Buck	.15
BDP131	Kevin Cash RC	.25
BDP132	Jason Stokes RC	.50
BDP133	Drew Henson	.25
BDP134	Chad Tracy RC	1.50
BDP135	Orlando Hudson	.15
BDP136	Brandon Phillips	.25
BDP137	Joe Borchard	.15
BDP138	Marlon Byrd	.15
BDP139	Carl Crawford	.25
BDP140	Michael Restovich	.15
BDP141	Corey Hart RC	1.50
BDP142	Edwin Almonte	.15
BDP143	Francis Beltran RC	.25
BDP144	Jorge De La Rosa RC	.50
BDP145	Gerardo Garcia RC	.25
BDP146	Franklyn German RC	.25
BDP147	Francisco Liriano	4.00
BDP148	Francisco Rodriguez	.50
BDP149	Ricardo Rodriguez	.15
BDP150	Seung Jun Song	.15
BDP151	John Stephens	.15
BDP152	Justin Huber RC	1.00
BDP153	Victor Martinez	.50
BDP154	Hee Seop Choi	.15
BDP155	Justin Morneau	.50
BDP156	Miguel Cabrera	.75
BDP157	Victor Diaz RC	1.00
BDP158	Jose Reyes	.50
BDP159	Omar Infante RC	.25
BDP160	Angel Berroa	.15
BDP161	Tony Alvarez	.15
BDP162	Shin-Soo Choo RC	1.00
BDP163	Wily Mo Pena	.15
BDP164	Andres Torres	.15
BDP165	Jose Lopez RC	2.00

Gold

Rookies: .75-1.5X
Inserted 1:1

Fabric of Future

		NM/M
Common Player:		4.00
Inserted 1:55		
EA	Edwin Almonte	4.00
TA	Tony Alvarez	4.00
FB	Francis Beltran	4.00
AB	Angel Berroa	5.00
SB	Sean Burnett	4.00
KC	Kevin Cash	4.00
HC	Hee Seop Choi	5.00
SC	Shin-Soo Choo	10.00
CC	Carl Crawford	6.00
JR	Jorge de la Rosa	4.00
VD	Victor Diaz	6.00
GG	Gerardo Garcia	4.00
FG	Franklyn German	4.00
CH	Corey Hart	10.00
DH	Drew Henson	6.00
JH	Justin Huber	6.00
JK	Josh Karp	4.00
FL	Francisco Liriano	15.00
JL	Jose Lopez	8.00
BM	Brett Myers	6.00
WP	Wily Mo Pena	6.00
MR	Michael Restovich	4.00
JS	John Stephens	4.00
JS	Jason Stokes	5.00
AT	Andres Torres	4.00
BT	Billy Traber	4.00
CT	Chad Tracy	8.00
AW	Adam Wainwright	10.00

Freshman Fiber

		NM/M
Common Player:		4.00
Bat inserted 1:605		
Jersey 1:45		
BA	Brent Abernathy	4.00
DB	Dewon Brazelton	4.00
MB	Marlon Byrd/Bat	4.00
TH	Toby Hall	4.00
JH	Josh Hamilton	8.00
AH	Aubrey Huff	6.00
AK	Austin Kearns/Bat	4.00
JK	Joe Kennedy	4.00
JS	Jared Sandberg	4.00
JWS	Jason Standridge	4.00
MT	Mark Teixeira/Bat	10.00
JV	John Van Benschoten	4.00

Signs of the Future

	NM/M
Common Autograph:	5.00

EB	Erik Bedard	40.00
LB	Larry Bigbie	5.00
TB	Taylor Buchholz	5.00
DD	Daniel Denham	5.00
ME	Morgan Ensberg	10.00
MF	Mike Fontenot	8.00
KH	Kris Honel	5.00
BI	Brandon Inge	10.00
NJ	Nic Jackson	5.00
MJ	Mitch Jones	5.00
BK	Bob Keppel	5.00
TL	Todd Linden	8.00
JM	Jake Mauer	8.00
JEM	Justin Morneau	25.00
LN	Lance Niekro	8.00
CP	Christian Parra	5.00
BP	Brandon Phillips	15.00
JR	Juan Rivera	5.00
BS	Bud Smith	5.00
AT	Chad Tracy	15.00
JW	Jerome Williams	8.00

2002 Bowman Heritage

		NM/M
Complete Set (439):		190.00
Common Player:		.25
Common SP:		1.00
Inserted 1:2		
Black Box Variations:		2-3X
Inserted 1:2		
Pack (10):		3.00
Box (24):		60.00
1	Brent Abernathy	.25
2	Jermaine Dye	.25
3	James Shanks RC	.40
4	Chris Flinn RC	.40
5	Mike Peeples/SP RC	1.50
6	Gary Sheffield	.50
7	Livan Hernandez/SP	1.00
8	Jeff Austin RC	.40
9	Jeremy Giambi	.25
10	Adam Roller RC	.50
11	Sandy Alomar Jr./SP	1.00
12	Matt Williams/SP	1.00
13	Hee Seop Choi	.25
14	Jose Offerman	.25
15	Robin Ventura	.25
16	Craig Biggio	.50
17	David Wells	.40
18	Rob Henkel RC	.40
19	Edgar Martinez	.25
20	Matt Morris/SP	2.00
21	Jose Valentin	.25
22	Barry Bonds	2.50
23	Justin Schuda RC	.50
24	Josh Phelps	.25
25	John Rodriguez RC	.50
26	Angel Pagan RC	1.50
27	Aramis Ramirez	.50
28	Jack Wilson	.25
29	Roger Clemens	2.00
30	Kazuhisa Ishii RC	.50
31	Carlos Beltran	.75
32	Drew Henson/SP	1.50
33	Kevin Young/SP	1.00
34	Juan Cruz	.25
35	Curtis Legendre RC	.40
36	Jose Morban RC	.50
37	Ricardo Cordova/SP RC	1.50
38	Adam Everett	.25
39	Mark Prior	.75
40	Jose Bautista RC	.75
41	Travis Foley	.25
42	Kerry Wood	.50
43	B.J. Surhoff	.25
44	Moises Alou	.40
45	Joey Hammond RC	.50
46	Eric Bruntlett RC	.50
47	Carlos Guillen	.25
48	Joe Crede	.40
49	Dan Phillips RC	.50
50	Jason LaRue	.25
51	Javy Lopez	.25
52	Larry Bigbie/SP	1.00
53	Chris Baker RC	.75
54	Marty Cordova	.25
55	C.C. Sabathia	.25
56	Mike Piazza	.25
57	Brian Giles	.25
58	Mike Bordick/SP	1.00
59	Tyler Houston/SP	1.00
60	Gabe Kapler	.25
61	Ben Broussard	.25
62	Steve Finley/SP	1.50
63	Koyie Hill	.25
64	Jeff D'Amico	.25
65	Edwin Almonte RC	.50
66	Pedro J. Martinez	1.00
67	Travis Fryman/SP	1.50
68	Brady Clark	.25
69	Reed Johnson/SP RC	2.00
70	Mark Grace/SP	4.00
71	Tony Batista/SP	1.00
72	Roy Oswalt	.50
73	Pat Burrell	.50
74	Dennis Tankersley	.25
75	Ramon Ortiz	.25
76	Neal Frendling/SP RC	1.50
77	Omar Vizquel/SP	2.00
78	Hideo Nomo	.50
79	Orlando Hernandez/SP	1.50
80	Andy Pettitte	.50
81	Cole Barthel	.25
82	Bret Boone	.25
83	Alfonso Soriano	1.00
84	Brandon Duckworth	.25
85	Ben Grieve	.25
86	Mike Rosamond/SP RC	1.50
87	Luke Prokopec	.25
88	Chone Figgins RC	1.50
89	Rick Ankiel/SP	1.50
90	David Eckstein	.25
91	Corey Koskie	.25
92	David Justice	.25
93	Jimmy Alvarez RC	.40
94	Jason Schmidt	.40
95	Reggie Sanders	.25
96	Victor Alvarez RC	.40
97	Brett Roneberg RC	.40
98	D'Angelo Jimenez	.25
99	Hank Blalock	.50
100	Juan Rivera	.25
101	Mark Buehrle/SP	1.50
102	Juan Uribe	.25
103	Royce Clayton/SP	1.00
104	Brett Kay RC	.50
105	John Olerud	.25
106	Richie Sexson	.40
107	Chipper Jones	1.00
108	Adam Dunn	.75
109	Tim Salmon/SP	1.50
110	Eric Karros	.25
111	Jose Vidro	.25
112	Jerry Hairston Jr.	.25
113	Anastacio Martinez RC	.40
114	Robert Fick/SP	1.50
115	Randy Johnson	1.00
116	Trot Nixon/SP	2.00
117	Nick Bierbrodt/SP	1.00
118	Jim Edmonds	.40
119	Rafael Palmeiro	.75
120	Jose Macias	.25
121	Josh Beckett	.50
122	Sean Douglass	.25
123	Jeff Kent	.40
124	Tim Redding	.25
125	Xavier Nady	.25
126	Carl Everett	.25
127	Joe Randa	.25
128	Luke Hudson/SP	1.00
129	Eric Miller RC	.40
130	Melvin Mora	.25
131	Adrian Gonzalez	.25
132	Larry Walker/SP	1.50
133	Nic Jackson/SP RC	2.00
134	Mike Lowell/SP	1.00
135	Jim Thome	.75
136	Eric Milton	.25
137	Rich Thompson/SP RC	1.50
138	Placido Polanco/SP	1.00
139	Juan Pierre	.25
140	David Segui	.25
141	Chuck Finley	.25
142	Felipe Lopez	.25
143	Toby Hall	.25
144	Fred Bastardo/SP	.50
145	Troy Glaus	.75
146	Todd Helton	.75
147	Ruben Gotay/SP RC	1.50
148	Darin Erstad	.40
149	Ryan Gripp/SP RC	1.50
150	Orlando Cabrera	.25
151	Jason Young RC	.50
152	Sterling Hitchcock/SP	1.00
153	Miguel Tejada	.75
154	Al Leiter	.25
155	Taylor Buchholz RC	.40
156	Juan Gonzalez	.50

157	Damion Easley	.25
158	Jimmy Gobble RC	1.00
159	Dennis Ulacia/SP	1.00
160	Shane Reynolds/SP	1.00
161	Javier Colina	.25
162	Frank Thomas	1.00
163	Chuck Knoblauch	.25
164	Sean Burroughs	.25
165	Greg Maddux	1.50
166	Jason Ellison RC	.50
167	Tony Womack	.25
168	Randall Shelley/SP RC	1.50
169	Jason Marquis	.25
170	Brian Jordan	.25
171	Darryl Kile	.25
172	Barry Zito	.50
173	Matt Allegra/SP RC	1.50
174	Ralph Santana/SP RC	1.50
175	Carlos Lee	.40
176	Richard Hidalgo/SP	1.00
177	Kevin Deaton RC	.50
178	Juan Encarnacion	.25
179	Mark Quinn	.25
180	Rafael Furcal	.40
181	Garret Anderson	.50
182	David Wright	15.00
183	Jose Reyes	.50
184	Mario Ramos/SP	1.00
185	J.D. Drew	.25
186	Juan Gonzalez	.50
187	Nick Neugebauer	.25
188	Alejandro Giron RC	.50
189	John Burkett	.25
190	Ben Sheets	.50
191	Vinny Castilla/SP	1.00
192	Cory Lidle	.25
193	Fernando Vina	.25
194	Russell Branyan/SP	1.00
195	Ben Davis	.25
196	Angel Berroa	.25
197	Alex Gonzalez	.25
198	Jared Sandberg	.25
199	Travis Lee/SP	1.00
200	Luis DePaula/SP RC	1.50
201	Ramon Hernandez/SP	1.00
202	Brandon Inge	.25
203	Aubrey Huff	.25
204	Mike Rivera	.25
205	Brad Nelson RC	.50
206	Colt Griffin/SP	2.00
207	Joel Pineiro	.25
208	Adam Pettyjohn	.25
209	Mark Redman	.25
210	Roberto Alomar/SP	3.00
211	Denny Neagle	.25
212	Adam Kennedy	.25
213	Jason Arnold/SP	2.00
214	Jamie Moyer	.25
215	Aaron Boone	.25
216	Doug Glanville	.25
217	Nick Johnson/SP	1.00
218	Mike Cameron/SP	1.50
219	Tim Wakefield/SP	1.50
220	Todd Stottlemyre/SP	1.00
221	Mo Vaughn	.25
222	Vladimir Guerrero	1.00
223	Bill Ortega	.25
224	Kevin Brown	.25
225	Peter Bergeron/SP	1.00
226	Shannon Stewart/SP	1.50
227	Eric Chavez	.25
228	Clint Weibl RC	.40
229	Todd Hollandsworth/SP	1.00
230	Jeff Bagwell	.75
231	Chad Qualls RC	.40
232	Ben Howard RC	1.00
233	Rondell White/SP	1.50
234	Fred McGriff	.20
235	Steve Cox/SP	1.00
236	Chris Tritle RC	1.50
237	Eric Valent	.25
238	Joe Mauer RC	5.00
239	Shawn Green	.40
240	Jimmy Rollins	.75
241	Edgar Renteria	.25
242	Edwin Yan RC	.40
243	Noochie Varner RC	.40
244	Kris Benson/SP	1.50
245	Mike Hampton	.25
246	So Taguchi RC	1.00
247	Sammy Sosa	1.00
248	Terrence Long	.25
249	Jason Bay RC	4.00
250	Kevin Mitchell/SP	1.00
251	Albert Pujols	2.50
252	Chris Latham RC	.40
253	Eric Byrnes	.25
254	Napoleon Calzado/SP RC	1.50

ABBREVIATIONS

SP - Short Print

255	Bobby Higginson	.25
256	Ben Molina	.25
257	Torii Hunter/SP	3.00
258	Jason Giambi	.75
259	Bartolo Colon	.25
260	Benito Baez	.25
261	Ichiro Suzuki	2.00
262	Mike Sweeney	.25
263	Brian West RC	.40
264	Brad Penny	.25
265	Kevin Millwood/SP	2.00
266	Orlando Hudson	.25
267	Doug Mientkiewicz	.25
268	Luis Gonzalez/SP	1.50
269	Jay Caligiuri/SP	.40
270	Nate Cornejo/SP	1.00
271	Lee Stevens	.25
272	Eric Hinske	.25
273	Antwon Rollins RC	.50
274	Bobby Jenks RC	1.00
275	Joe Mays	.25
276	Josh Shaffer RC	.40
277	Jonny Gomes RC	3.00
278	Bernie Williams	.50
279	Ed Rogers	.25
280	Carlos Delgado	.50
281	Raul Mondesi/SP	1.50
282	Jose Ortiz	.25
283	Cesar Izturis	.25
284	Ryan Dempster/SP	1.00
285	Brian Daubach	.25
286	Hansel Izquierdo RC	.40
287	Mike Lieberthal/SP	1.00
288	Marcus Thames	.25
289	Nomar Garciaparra	1.00
290	Brad Fullmer	.25
291	Tino Martinez	.25
292	James Barrett RC	.40
293	Jacque Jones	.25
294	Nick Alvarez/SP RC	1.50
295	Jason Grove/SP RC	1.50
296	Mike Wilson/SP RC	1.50
297	J.T. Snow	.25
298	Cliff Floyd	.25
299	Todd Hundley/SP	1.00
300	Tony Clark/SP	1.00
301	Demetrius Heath RC	.40
302	Morgan Ensberg	.25
303	Cristian Guzman	.25
304	Frank Catalanotto	.25
305	Jeff Weaver	.25
306	Tim Hudson	.25
307	Scott Wiggins/SP RC	1.50
308	Shea Hillenbrand/SP	2.00
309	Todd Walker/SP	1.00
310	Tsuyoshi Shinjo	.25
311	Adrian Beltre	.40
312	Craig Kuzmic RC	.40
313	Paul Konerko	.40
314	Scott Hairston	1.50
315	Chan Ho Park	.25
316	Jorge Posada	.40
317	Chris Snelling RC	.75
318	Keith Foulke	.25
319	John Smoltz	.25
320	Ryan Church/SP RC	3.00
321	Mike Mussina	.75
322	Tony Armas Jr./SP	1.00
323	Craig Counsell	.25
324	Marcus Giles	.25
325	Greg Vaughn	.25
326	Curt Schilling	.75
327	Jeromy Burnitz	.25
328	Eric Byrnes	.25
329	Johnny Damon	.75
330	Michael Floyd/SP RC	1.50
331	Edgardo Alfonzo	.25
332	Jeremy Hill RC	.40
333	Josh Bonifay RC	.40
334	Byung-Hyun Kim	.25
335	Keith Ginter	.25
336	Ronald Acuna/SP RC	1.50
337	Mike Hill/SP RC	1.50
338	Sean Casey	.25
339	Matt Anderson/SP	1.00
340	Dan Wright	.25
341	Ben Petrick	.25
342	Mike Sirotka/SP	1.00
343	Alex Rodriguez	2.50
344	Einar Diaz	.25
345	Derek Jeter	2.50
346	Jeff Conine	.25
347	Ray Durham/SP	1.00
348	Wilson Betemit/SP	1.00
349	Jeffrey Hammonds	.25
350	Dan Trumble RC	.40
351	Phil Nevin/SP	1.50
352	A.J. Burnett	.25
353	Bill Mueller	.25
354	Charles Nagy	.25
355	Rusty Greer/SP	1.00
356	Jason Botts RC	.50
357	Magglio Ordonez	.50
358	Kevin Appier	.25
359	Brad Radke	.25
360	Chris George	.25

Chrome Refractor

Stars: 3-6X

361	Chris Piersoll RC	.25
362	Ivan Rodriguez	.75
363	Jim Kavourias	.25
364	Rick Helling/SP	1.00
365	Dean Palmer	.25
366	Rich Aurilia/SP	1.00
367	Ryan Vogelsong	.25
368	Matt Lawton	.25
369	Wade Miller	.25
370	Dustin Hermanson	.25
371	Craig Wilson	.25
372	Todd Zeile/SP	1.00
373	Jon Guzman RC	.40
374	Ellis Burks	.25
375	Robert Cosby/SP RC	1.50
376	Jason Kendall	.25
377	Scott Rolen/SP	4.00
378	Andruw Jones	1.00
379	Greg Sain RC	.40
380	Paul LoDuca	.25
381	Scotty Layfield RC	.40
382	Drew Henson	.50
383	Garrett Guzman RC	.40
384	Jack Cust	.25
385	Shayne Wright RC	.40
386	Derrek Lee	.75
387	Jesus Medrano RC	.25
388	Javier Vazquez	.25
389	Preston Wilson/SP	1.50
390	Gavin Floyd	1.50
391	Sidney Ponson/SP	1.00
392	Jose Hernandez	.25
393	Scott Erickson/SP	1.00
394	Jose Valverde RC	.40
395	Mark Hamilton/SP RC	1.50
396	Brad Cresse	.25
397	Danny Bautista	.25
398	Ray Lankford/SP	1.00
399	Miguel Batista/SP	1.00
400	Brent Butler	.25
401	Manny Delcarmen/SP RC	1.50
402	Kyle Farnsworth/SP	1.00
403	Freddy Garcia	.25
404	Joe Jiannetti RC	.40
405	Josh Barfield	2.00
406	Corey Patterson	.25
407	Josh Towers	.25
408	Carlos Pena	.25
409	Jeff Cirillo	.25
410	Jon Lieber	.25
411	Woody Williams/SP	1.00
412	Richard Lane/SP RC	1.50
413	Alex Gonzalez	.25
414	Wilkin Ruan	.25
415	Geoff Jenkins	.25
416	Carlos Hernandez	.25
417	Matt Clement/SP	1.50
418	Jose Cruz Jr.	.25
419	Jake Mauer RC	.50
420	Matt Childers RC	.50
421	Tom Glavine/SP	2.50
422	Ken Griffey Jr.	2.00
423	Anderson Hernandez RC	.40
424	John Suomi RC	.40
425	Doug Sessions RC	.40
426	Jaret Wright	.25
427	Rolando Viera/SP RC	1.50
428	Aaron Sele	.25
429	Dmitri Young	.25
430	Ryan Klesko	.25
431	Kevin Tapani/SP	1.00
432	Joe Kennedy	.25
433	Austin Kearns	.40
434	Roger Cedeno	.25
435	Lance Berkman	.50
436	Frank Menechino	.25
437	Brett Myers	.25
438	Bobby Abreu	.50
439	Shawn Estes	.25

SP's: 1-2X
Inserted 1:16
Gold Refractors: 4-8X
SP's: 2-3X
Inserted 1:32

Autographs

		NM/M
Common Player:		8.00
Inserted 1:45		
LB	Lance Berkman	20.00
HB	Hank Blalock	15.00
KG	Keith Ginter	8.00
TH	Toby Hall	8.00
DH	Drew Henson	15.00
KI	Kazuhisa Ishii	25.00
CI	Cesar Izturis	10.00
PL	Paul LoDuca	15.00
JM	Joe Mauer	75.00
RO	Roy Oswalt	15.00
MP	Mark Prior	20.00
AP	Albert Pujols	250.00
JR	Juan Rivera	8.00

Relics

DARIN ERSTAD

		NM/M
Common Player:		4.00
Inserted 1:47		
EA	Edgardo Alfonzo	4.00
JB	Josh Beckett	8.00
BB	Barry Bonds	20.00
EC	Eric Chavez	6.00
CD	Carlos Delgado	6.00
JE	Jim Edmonds	4.00
DE	Darin Erstad	4.00
NG	Nomar Garciaparra	15.00
TG	Tony Gwynn	10.00
TH	Todd Helton	8.00
CJ	Chipper Jones	10.00
PK	Paul Konerko	8.00
GM	Greg Maddux	15.00
EM	Edgar Martinez	8.00
MP	Mike Piazza	10.00
AP	Albert Pujols	20.00
MR	Mariano Rivera	8.00
IR	Ivan Rodriguez	8.00
SR	Scott Rolen	10.00
TS	Tim Salmon	5.00
KS	Kazuhiro Sasaki	4.00
JS	John Smoltz	8.00
FT	Frank Thomas	8.00
JT	Jim Thome	8.00
LW	Larry Walker	4.00
PW	Preston Wilson	4.00

Team Topps Legends Autographs

		NM/M
Common Player:		8.00
	Gil McDougald	8.00

Joe Pepitone	8.00
Bobby Richardson	8.00
Robin Roberts	12.00
Warren Spahn	30.00
Luis Tiant	8.00
Carl Yastrzemski	40.00

1954 Bowman Reprints

	NM/M
Complete Set (20):	40.00
Common Player:	2.00
Inserted 1:12	
RA Richie Ashburn	2.00
YB Yogi Berra	4.00
DC Del Crandell	2.00
BF Bob Feller	2.50
WF Whitey Ford	4.00
NF Nellie Fox	2.00
CL Clem Labine	2.00
DL Don Larsen	3.00
JL Johnny Logan	2.00
WM Willie Mays	6.00
GM Gil McDougald	2.00
DM Don Mueller	2.00
JP Jimmy Piersall	2.00
AR Allie Reynolds	2.00
PR Phil Rizzuto	3.00
ES Enos Slaughter	2.00
DS Duke Snider	4.00
WW Wes Westrum	2.00
HW Hoyt Wilhelm	2.00
DW Davey Williams	2.00

1954 Bowman Reprint Autographs

	NM/M
Common Player:	10.00
Inserted 1:118	
YB Yogi Berra	50.00
DC Del Crandell	15.00
CL Clem Labine	15.00
JL Johnny Logan	15.00
DM Don Mueller	10.00
DW Davey Williams	10.00

2002 Bowman's Best

	NM/M
Complete Set (181):	
Common Player:	.40
Common (91-181):	4.00
Inserted 1:Pack	
Blue (1-90):	1-2X
Production 300	
Red (1-90):	1-2X
Production 200	
Gold (1-90):	3-6X
Production 50	
Blue (91-181):	.75-1X
Production 500	
Red (91-181):	1-1.5X
Production 150	
Gold (91-181):	1-2X
Production 50	
Pack (5):	20.00
Box (10):	180.00
1 Josh Beckett	.75
2 Derek Jeter	4.00
3 Alex Rodriguez	3.00
4 Miguel Tejada	1.00
5 Nomar Garciaparra	1.50
6 Aramis Ramirez	.75
7 Jeremy Giambi	.40
8 Bernie Williams	.50
9 Juan Pierre	.40
10 Chipper Jones	1.50
11 Jimmy Rollins	.75
12 Alfonso Soriano	1.00
13 Daryle Ward	.40
14 Paul Konerko	.75
15 Tim Hudson	.75
16 Doug Mientkiewicz	.40

17	Todd Helton	1.00
18	Moises Alou	.75
19	Juan Gonzalez	.75
20	Jorge Posada	.75
21	Jeff Kent	.50
22	Roger Clemens	3.00
23	Phil Nevin	.40
24	Brian Giles	.40
25	Carlos Delgado	1.00
26	Jason Giambi	.75
27	Vladimir Guerrero	1.50
28	Cliff Floyd	.40
29	Shea Hillenbrand	.40
30	Ken Griffey Jr.	2.50
31	Mike Piazza	1.50
32	Carlos Pena	.40
33	Larry Walker	.50
34	Magglio Ordonez	.50
35	Mike Mussina	.75
36	Andruw Jones	1.00
37	Mark Teixeira	.75
38	Curt Schilling	1.00
39	Eric Chavez	.60
40	Bartolo Colon	.40
41	Eric Hinske	.40
42	Sean Burroughs	.40
43	Randy Johnson	1.00
44	Adam Dunn	.75
45	Pedro Martinez	1.50
46	Garret Anderson	.40
47	Jim Thome	1.00
48	Gary Sheffield	1.00
49	Tsuyoshi Shinjo	.40
50	Albert Pujols	4.00
51	Ichiro Suzuki	3.00
52	C.C. Sabathia	.40
53	Bobby Abreu	.75
54	Ivan Rodriguez	.75
55	J.D. Drew	.50
56	Jacque Jones	.40
57	Jason Kendall	.40
58	Javier Vazquez	.40
59	Jeff Bagwell	.75
60	Greg Maddux	2.50
61	Jim Edmonds	.50
62	Austin Kearns	.50
63	Jose Vidro	.40
64	Kevin Brown	.40
65	Preston Wilson	.40
66	Sammy Sosa	1.50
67	Lance Berkman	.75
68	Mark Mulder	.60
69	Marty Cordova	.40
70	Frank Thomas	1.00
71	Mike Cameron	.40
72	Mike Sweeney	.40
73	Barry Bonds	4.00
74	Troy Glaus	.75
75	Barry Zito	.75
76	Pat Burrell	.50
77	Paul LoDuca	.40
78	Rafael Palmeiro	.75
79	Mark Prior	1.00
80	Darin Erstad	.50
81	Richie Sexson	.75
82	Roberto Alomar	.75
83	Roy Oswalt	.75
84	Ryan Klesko	.40
85	Luis Gonzalez	.50
86	Scott Rolen	1.00
87	Shannon Stewart	.40
88	Shawn Green	.60
89	Toby Hall	.40
90	Bret Boone	.40
91	Casey Kotchman/Bat	10.00
92	Jose Valverde/	
	Auto. RC	8.00
93	Cole Barthel/Bat	4.00
94	Blake Nelson/Auto. RC	8.00
95	Mauricio Lara/	
	Auto. RC	8.00
96	Ryan Gripp/Bat RC	4.00
97	Brian West/Auto. RC	8.00
98	Chris Piersoll/Auto. RC	8.00
99	Ryan Church/	
	Auto. RC	15.00
100	Javier Colina/Auto.	8.00
101	Juan Gonzalez/Auto.	8.00
102	Benito Baez/Auto.	8.00
103	Mike Hill/Bat RC	4.00
104	Jason Grove/Auto. RC	8.00
105	Koyie Hill/Auto.	8.00
106	Mark Outlaw/Auto. RC	8.00
107	Jason Bay/Bat RC	15.00
108	Jorge Padilla/Auto. RC	8.00
109	Peter Zamora/	
	Auto. RC	8.00
110	Joe Mauer/Auto. RC	80.00
111	Franklyn German/	
	Auto.	8.00
112	Chris Flinn/Auto. RC	8.00
113	David Wright/Bat	80.00
114	Anastacio Martinez/	
	Auto. RC	8.00

115	Nic Jackson/Bat RC	8.00
116	Rene Reyes/Auto. RC	8.00
117	Colin Young/Auto. RC	8.00
118	Joe Orloski/Auto. RC	8.00
119	Mike Wilson/Auto. RC	8.00
120	Rich Thompson/	
	Auto. RC	8.00
121	Jake Mauer/Auto. RC	8.00
122	Mario Ramos/Auto. RC	8.00
123	Doug Sessions/	
	Auto. RC	8.00
124	Doug DeVore/Bat RC	4.00
125	Travis Foley/Auto.	10.00
126	Chris Baker/Auto. RC	8.00
127	Michael Floyd/	
	Auto. RC	8.00
128	Josh Barfield/Bat	15.00
129	Jose Bautista/Bat RC	6.00
130	Gavin Floyd/Auto.	15.00
131	Jason Botts/Bat RC	4.00
132	Clint Nageotte/	
	Auto. RC	10.00
133	Jesus Cota/Auto. RC	10.00
134	Ron Calloway/Bat RC	4.00
135	Kevin Cash/Bat RC	4.00
136	Jonny Gomes/	
	Auto. RC	15.00
137	Dennis Ulacia/Auto.	8.00
138	Ryan Snare/Auto. RC	8.00
139	Kevin Deaton/Auto. RC	8.00
140	Bobby Jenks/	
	Auto. RC	15.00
141	Casey Kotchman/	
	Auto.	25.00
142	Adam Walker/	
	Auto. RC	8.00
143	Mike Gonzalez/	
	Auto. RC	8.00
144	Ruben Gotay/Bat RC	8.00
145	Jason Grove/Bat RC	4.00
146	Freddy Sanchez/	
	Auto. RC	20.00
147	Jason Arnold/Auto.	10.00
148	Scott Hairston/Auto.	10.00
149	Jason St. Clair/	
	Auto. RC	8.00
150	Chris Tritle/Bat RC	8.00
151	Edwin Yan/Bat RC	4.00
152	Freddy Sanchez/	
	Bat RC	10.00
153	Greg Sain/Bat RC	4.00
154	Yurendell DeCaster/	
	Bat RC	6.00
155	Noochie Varner/	
	Bat RC	6.00
156	Nelson Castro/	
	Auto. RC	8.00
157	Randall Shelley/	
	Bat RC	6.00
158	Reed Johnson/	
	Bat RC	10.00
159	Ryan Raburn/Auto. RC	8.00
160	Jose Morban/Bat RC	5.00
161	Justin Schuda/	
	Auto. RC	8.00
162	Henry Pichardo/	
	Auto. RC	8.00
163	Josh Bard/Auto. RC	10.00
164	Josh Bonifay/Auto. RC	8.00
165	Brandon League/	
	Auto.	8.00
166	Julio DePaula/	
	Auto. RC	10.00
167	Todd Linden/Auto. RC	10.00
168	Francisco Liriano/	
	Auto. RC	100.00
169	Chris Snelling/	
	Auto. RC	15.00
170	Cody McKay/Auto. RC	8.00
171	Cody McKay/Auto. RC	8.00
172	Jason Stanford/	
	Auto. RC	8.00
173	Lenny Dinardo/	
	Auto. RC	8.00
174	Greg Montalbano/	
	Auto. RC	8.00
175	Earl Snyder/Auto. RC	8.00
176	Justin Huber/Auto. RC	10.00
177	Chris Narveson/	
	Auto. RC	8.00
178	Jon Switzer/Auto.	8.00
179	Ronald Acuna/	
	Auto. RC	8.00
180	Chris Duffy/Bat RC	8.00
181	Kazuhisa Ishii/Bat RC	8.00

2003 Bowman

	NM/M
Complete Set (330):	75.00
Common Player:	.15
Common Rookie:	.40
Pack (10):	3.00
Box (24):	60.00

1	Garret Anderson	.15
2	Derek Jeter	2.00
3	Gary Sheffield	.40
4	Matt Morris	.25
5	Derek Lowe	.15
6	Andy Van Hekken	.15
7	Sammy Sosa	1.00
8	Ken Griffey Jr.	1.50
9	Omar Vizquel	.15
10	Jorge Posada	.40
11	Lance Berkman	.40
12	Mike Sweeney	.15
13	Adrian Beltre	.25
14	Richie Sexson	.25
15	A.J. Pierzynski	.15
16	Bartolo Colon	.15
17	Mike Mussina	.40
18	Paul Byrd	.15
19	Bobby Abreu	.40
20	Miguel Tejada	.50
21	Aramis Ramirez	.40
22	Edgardo Alfonzo	.15
23	Edgar Martinez	.25
24	Albert Pujols	2.00
25	Carl Crawford	.25
26	Eric Hinske	.15
27	Tim Salmon	.25
28	Luis Gonzalez	.25
29	Jay Gibbons	.15
30	John Smoltz	.40
31	Tim Wakefield	.15
32	Mark Prior	.75
33	Magglio Ordonez	.25
34	Adam Dunn	.50
35	Larry Walker	.25
36	Luis Castillo	.15
37	Wade Miller	.15
38	Carlos Beltran	.50
39	Odalis Perez	.15
40	Alex Sanchez	.15
41	Torii Hunter	.25
42	Cliff Floyd	.15
43	Andy Pettitte	.25
44	Francisco Rodriguez	.15
45	Eric Chavez	.40
46	Kevin Millwood	.25
47	Dennis Tankersley	.15
48	Hideo Nomo	.25
49	Freddy Garcia	.15
50	Randy Johnson	.75
51	Aubrey Huff	.15
52	Carlos Delgado	.40
53	Troy Glaus	.50
54	Junior Spivey	.15
55	Mike Hampton	.15
56	Sidney Ponson	.15
57	Aaron Boone	.15
58	Kerry Wood	.40
59	Willie Harris	.15
60	Nomar Garciaparra	1.00
61	Todd Helton	.50
62	Mike Lowell	.15
63	Roy Oswalt	.40
64	Raul Ibanez	.15
65	Brian Jordan	.15
66	Geoff Jenkins	.15
67	Jermaine Dye	.15
68	Tom Glavine	.25
69	Bernie Williams	.40
70	Vladimir Guerrero	.75
71	Mark Mulder	.25
72	Jimmy Rollins	.40
73	Oliver Perez	.15
74	Rich Aurilia	.15
75	Joel Pineiro	.15
76	J.D. Drew	.25
77	Ivan Rodriguez	.50
78	Josh Phelps	.15
79	Darin Erstad	.40
80	Curt Schilling	.75
81	Paul LoDuca	.15
82	Marty Cordova	.15
83	Manny Ramirez	.75

84	Bobby Hill	.15
85	Paul Konerko	.40
86	Austin Kearns	.25
87	Jason Jennings	.15
88	Brad Penny	.15
89	Jeff Bagwell	.75
90	Shawn Green	.40
91	Jason Schmidt	.40
92	Doug Mientkiewicz	.15
93	Jose Vidro	.15
94	Bret Boone	.15
95	Jason Giambi	.50
96	Barry Zito	.40
97	Roy Halliday	.40
98	Pat Burrell	.40
99	Sean Burroughs	.15
100	Barry Bonds	2.00
101	Kazuhiro Sasaki	.15
102	Fernando Vina	.15
103	Chan Ho Park	.15
104	Andruw Jones	.75
105	Adam Kennedy	.15
106	Shea Hillenbrand	.15
107	Greg Maddux	1.50
108	Jim Edmonds	.40
109	Pedro J. Martinez	1.00
110	Moises Alou	.25
111	Jeff Weaver	.15
112	C.C. Sabathia	.15
113	Robert Fick	.15
114	A.J. Burnett	.25
115	Jeff Kent	.25
116	Kevin Brown	.15
117	Rafael Furcal	.25
118	Cristian Guzman	.15
119	Brad Wilkerson	.15
120	Mike Piazza	1.00
121	Alfonso Soriano	.75
122	Mark Ellis	.15
123	Vicente Padilla	.15
124	Eric Gagne	.15
125	Ryan Klesko	.15
126	Ichiro Suzuki	1.50
127	Tony Batista	.15
128	Roberto Alomar	.40
129	Alex Rodriguez	2.00
130	Jim Thome	.75
131	Jarrod Washburn	.15
132	Orlando Hudson	.15
133	Chipper Jones	1.00
134	Rodrigo Lopez	.15
135	Johnny Damon	.75
136	Matt Clement	.15
137	Frank Thomas	.75
138	Ellis Burks	.15
139	Carlos Pena	.15
140	Josh Beckett	.25
141	Joe Randa	.15
142	Brian Giles	.25
143	Kazuhisa Ishii	.15
144	Corey Koskie	.15
145	Orlando Cabrera	.15
146	Mark Buehrle	.25
147	Roger Clemens	2.00
148	Tim Hudson	.40
149	Randy Wolf	.15
150	Josh Fogg	.15
151	Phil Nevin	.15
152	John Olerud	.15
153	Scott Rolen	.15
154	Joe Kennedy	.15
155	Rafael Palmeiro	.75
156	Chad Hutchinson	.40
157	Quincy Carter	.15
158	Hee Seop Choi	.15
159	Joe Borchard	.15
160	Brandon Phillips	.15
161	Wily Mo Pena	.15
162	Victor Martinez	.25
163	Jason Stokes	.15
164	Ken Harvey	.15
165	Juan Rivera	.15
166	Jose Contreras RC	1.00
167	Dan Haren RC	1.00
168	Michel Hernandez RC	.40
169	Eider Torres RC	.40
170	Chris De La Cruz RC	.50
171	Ramon A. Martinez RC	.50
172	Mike Adams RC	.40
173	Justin Arneson RC	.50
174	Jamie Athas RC	.50
175	Dwaine Bacon RC	.40
176	Clint Barmes RC	.50
177	B.J. Barns RC	.40
178	Tyler Johnson RC	.40
179	Bobby Basham RC	.50
180	T.J. Bohn RC	.50
181	J.D. Durbin RC	.50
182	Brandon Bowe RC	.40
183	Craig Brazell RC	.50
184	Dusty Brown RC	.50
185	Brian Bruney RC	.50
186	Greg Bruso RC	.40
187	Jaime Bubela RC	.50

188	Bryan Bullington RC	.50
189	Brian Burgamy RC	.40
190	Eny Cabreja RC	.50
191	Daniel Cabrera RC	1.00
192	Ryan Cameron RC	.40
193	Lance Caraccioli RC	.40
194	David Cash RC	.40
195	Bernie Castro RC	.40
196	Ismael Castro RC	.40
197	Daryl Clark RC	.50
198	Jeff Clark RC	.50
199	Chris Colton RC	.40
200	Dexter Cooper RC	.40
201	Callix Crabbe RC	.40
202	Chien-Ming Wang RC	5.00
203	Eric Crozier RC	.40
204	Nook Logan RC	.40
205	David DeJesus RC	.75
206	Matt DeMarco RC	.40
207	Chris Duncan RC	3.00
208	Eric Eckenstahler RC	.40
209	Willie Eyre RC	.40
210	Evel Bastida-Martinez RC	.40
211	Chris Fallon RC	.75
212	Mike Flannery RC	.40
213	Mike O'Keefe RC	.40
214	Ben Francisco RC	.50
215	Kason Gabbard RC	1.00
216	Mike Gallo RC	.40
217	Jairo Garcia RC	.40
218	Angel Garcia RC	.40
219	Michael Garciaparra RC	.50
220	Joey Gomes RC	.40
221	Dusty Gomon RC	.40
222	Bryan Grace RC	.40
223	Tyson Graham RC	.40
224	Henry Guerrero RC	.40
225	Franklin Gutierrez RC	.50
226	Carlos Guzman RC	.50
227	Matthew Hagen RC	.40
228	Josh Hall RC	.50
229	Rob Hammock RC	.50
230	Brendan Harris RC	.75
231	Gary Harris RC	.40
232	Clay Hensley RC	.75
233	Michael Hinckley RC	.40
234	Luis Hodge RC	.40
235	Donnie Hood RC	.50
236	Travis Ishikawa RC	.50
237	Edwin Jackson RC	.50
238	Ardley Jansen RC	.50
239	Ferenc Jongejan RC	.40
240	Matt Kata RC	.50
241	Kazuhiro Takeoka RC	.40
242	Beau Kemp RC	.40
243	Il Kim RC	.50
244	Brennan King RC	.40
245	Cris Kroski RC	.40
246	Jason Kubel RC	2.00
247	Pete LaForest RC	.40
248	Wilfredo Ledezma RC	.40
249	Jeremy Bonderman RC	3.00
250	Gonzalo Lopez RC	.40
251	Brian Luderer RC	.50
252	Ruddy Lugo RC	.40
253	Wayne Lydon RC	.40
254	Mark Malaska RC	.40
255	Andy Marte RC	1.50
256	Tyler Martin RC	.40
257	Branden Florence RC	.40
258	Aneudis Mateo RC	.40
259	Derell McCall RC	.40
260	Brian McCann RC	5.00
261	Mike McNutt RC	.40
262	Jacabo Meque RC	.50
263	Derek Michaelis RC	.40
264	Aaron Miles RC	1.00
265	Jose Morales RC	.40
266	Dustin Moseley RC	.40
267	Adrian Myers RC	.40
268	Dan Neil RC	.40
269	Jon Nelson RC	.50
270	Mike Neu RC	.40
271	Leigh Neuage RC	.40
272	Weston O'Brien RC	.40
273	Trent Oeltjen RC	.50
274	Tim Olson RC	.50
275	David Pahucki RC	.40
276	Nathan Panther RC	.50
277	Arnie Munoz RC	.40
278	David Pember RC	.40
279	Jason Perry RC	.50
280	Matthew Peterson RC	.40
281	Ryan Shealy RC	1.50
282	Jorge Piedra RC	.40
283	Simon Pond RC	.40
284	Aaron Rakers RC	.40
285	Hanley Ramirez RC	5.00
286	Manuel Ramirez RC	.40
287	Kevin Randel RC	.50
288	Darrell Rasner RC	.40
289	Prentice Redman RC	.50
290	Eric Reed RC	.50

291	Wilton Reynolds RC	.40
292	Eric Riggs RC	.40
293	Carlos Rijo RC	.40
294	Rajai Davis RC	.50
295	Aron Weston RC	.40
296	Arturo Rivas RC	.50
297	Kyle Roat RC	.40
298	Bubba Nelson RC	.50
299	Levi Robinson RC	.40
300	Ray Sadler RC	.40
301	Gary Schneidmiller RC	.50
302	Jon Schuerholz RC	.75
303	Corey Shafer RC	.40
304	Brian Shackelford RC	.40
305	Bill Simon RC	.40
306	Haj Turay RC	.40
307	Sean Smith RC	.40
308	Ryan Spataro RC	.40
309	Jemel Spearman RC	.50
310	Keith Stamler RC	.40
311	Luke Steidlmayer RC	.50
312	Adam Stern RC	.50
313	Jay Sitzman RC	.40
314	Thomari Story-Harden RC	.50
315	Terry Tiffee RC	.40
316	Nick Trzesniak RC	.40
317	Denny Tussen RC	.40
318	Scott Tyler RC	.40
319	Shane Victorino RC	.40
320	Doug Waechter RC	.50
321	Brandon Watson RC	.50
322	Todd Wellemeyer RC	.50
323	Eli Whiteside RC	.50
324	Josh Willingham RC	1.00
325	Travis Wong RC	.50
326	Brian Wright RC	.40
327	Kevin Youkilis RC	3.00
328	Andy Sisco RC	.50
329	Dustin Yount RC	.50
330	Andrew Dominique RC	.40

Gold

Stars (1-165):	1-2X
Rookies (166-330):	1-2X
Inserted 1:1	

Uncirculated

Stars (1-165):	3-5X
Rookies (166-330):	2-4X
Production 250 Sets	

Future Fiber Relics

		NM/M
Common Player:		4.00
RB	Rocco Baldelli	10.00
WB	Wilson Betemit	6.00
HB	Hank Blalock	10.00
JB	Jason Botts	5.00
SB	Sean Burroughs	8.00
KC	Kevin Cash	4.00
KD	Kory DeHaan	5.00
CD	Chris Duffy	4.00
PF	Pedro Feliz	5.00
AG	Adrian Gonzalez	5.00
JG	Jason Grove	5.00
JH	Josh Hamilton	8.00
NH	Nathan Haynes	4.00
DH	Drew Henson	8.00
AH	Aubrey Huff	5.00
RJ	Reed Johnson	6.00
AK	Austin Kearns	5.00
CK	Casey Kotchman	6.00
RK	Ryan Langerhans	5.00
JDM	Jake Mauer	6.00
JM	Joe Mauer	15.00
XN	Xavier Nady	6.00
MR	Michael Restovich	6.00
WR	Wilkin Ruan	6.00
FS	Freddy Sanchez	8.00
RS	Randall Shelley	6.00
BS	Bud Smith	4.00
ES	Esix Snead	6.00
ST	So Taguchi	8.00
JW	Justin Wayne	5.00
TW	Travis Wilson	6.00
DW	David Wright	15.00
EY	Edwin Yan	4.00

Futures Game Gear Relics

	NM/M
Common Player:	4.00

Inserted 1:26		
EA	Edwin Almonte	4.00
TA	Tony Alvarez	4.00
BB	Brad Baker	4.00
FB	Francis Beltran	4.00
JEB	Joe Borchard	4.00
JB	John Buck	4.00
SB	Sean Burnett	6.00
MB	Marlon Byrd	4.00
MC	Miguel Cabrera	10.00
KC	Kevin Cash	4.00
HC	Hee Seop Choi	5.00
SC	Shin-Soo Choo	6.00
AC	Aaron Cook	5.00
CC	Carl Crawford	5.00
JDR	Jorge De La Rosa	4.00
VD	Victor Diaz	4.00
RD	Ryan Dittfurth	4.00
BE	Brett Evert	4.00
GG	Gerardo Garcia	4.00
BH	Bill Hall	4.00
CH	Corey Hart	4.00
DH	Drew Henson	8.00
JH	Justin Huber	6.00
OH	Orlando Hudson	4.00
OI	Omar Infante	4.00
JJ	Jimmy Journell	4.00
JK	Josh Karp	4.00
FL	Francisco Liriano	4.00
JL	Jose Lopez	4.00
VM	Victor Martinez	8.00
JM	Justin Morneau	10.00
BM	Brett Myers	6.00
LO	Lyle Overbay	6.00
WP	Wily Mo Pena	6.00
BP	Brandon Phillips	6.00
MR	Mike Restovich	8.00
JR	Jose Reyes	10.00
FR	Francisco Rodriguez	5.00
RR	Ricardo Rodriguez	4.00
SS	Seung Jun Song	6.00
JMS	John Stephens	4.00
JS	Jason Stokes	8.00
BT	Billy Traber	5.00
CT	Chad Tracey	4.00
AW	Adam Wainwright	10.00
JY	Jason Young	4.00

Futures Game MVP Autograph

		NM/M
Complete Set (1):		
JR	Jose Reyes	40.00

ROY Dual Relic

		NM/M
Inserted 1:765		
JH	Eric Hinske, Jason Jennings	10.00

Signs of the Future

		NM/M
Common Autograph:		5.00
Red Autographs:		1-2.5X
Production 50 Sets		
JA	Jason Arnold	8.00
JB	John Buck	10.00
BB	Bryan Bullington	10.00
QC	Quincy Carter	10.00
NC	Nelson Castro	8.00
RC	Ryan Church	10.00
JC	Jesus Cota	5.00
JOG	Jonny Gomes	20.00
DG	Doug Gredvig	5.00
KG	Khalil Greene	25.00
ZG	Zack Greinke	10.00
JG	Jason Grove	5.00
JGU	Jeremy Guthrie	10.00
CH	Cole Hamels	80.00
JRH	Joel Hanrahan	8.00
CJH	Corey Hart	30.00

KH	Koyie Hill	8.00
CMH	Chad Hutchinson	10.00
BJ	Bobby Jenks	15.00
BK	Ben Kozlowski	5.00
BL	Brandon League	5.00
DL	Donald Levinski	5.00
FL	Fred Lewis	25.00
TL	Todd Linden	5.00
JL	James Loney	35.00
VM	Val Majewski	8.00
DHM	Dustin McGowan	15.00
CP	Chris Piersoll	8.00
HR	Hanley Ramirez	40.00
PR	Prentice Redman	8.00
JR	Jose Reyes	40.00
JSC	Jason St. Clair	6.00
FS	Freddy Sanchez	15.00
ZS	Zach Segovia	8.00
DS	Doug Sessions	5.00
BS	Brian Slocum	6.00
RS	Ryan Snare	8.00
MT	Mitch Talbot	5.00
AT	Andres Torres	5.00
AV	Andy Van Hekken	5.00
OV	Oscar Villarreal	8.00

Dual Signs of the Future Autograph

NM/M

Inserted 1:9,220
CH Quincy Carter, Chad Hutchinson 85.00

2003 Bowman Chrome

CRAIG BRAZELL

	NM/M
Complete Set (351):	400.00
Common Player:	.25
Common Rookie:	1.00
Common RC Auto. (331-350):	10.00
Pack (4):	7.00
Box (18):	100.00
1 Garret Anderson	.25
2 Derek Jeter	3.00
3 Gary Sheffield	.50
4 Matt Morris	.35
5 Derek Lowe	.25
6 Andy Van Hekken	.25
7 Sammy Sosa	1.00
8 Ken Griffey Jr.	2.00
9 Omar Vizquel	.40
10 Jorge Posada	.50
11 Lance Berkman	.50
12 Mike Sweeney	.25
13 Adrian Beltre	.50
14 Richie Sexson	.50
15 A.J. Pierzynski	.25
16 Bartolo Colon	.25
17 Mike Mussina	.75
18 Paul Byrd	.25
19 Bobby Abreu	.50
20 Miguel Tejada	.75
21 Aramis Ramirez	.50
22 Edgardo Alfonzo	.25
23 Edgar Martinez	.40
24 Albert Pujols	3.00
25 Carl Crawford	.40
26 Eric Hinske	.25
27 Tim Salmon	.40
28 Luis Gonzalez	.40
29 Jay Gibbons	.25
30 John Smoltz	.50
31 Tim Wakefield	.25
32 Mark Prior	1.00
33 Magglio Ordonez	.40
34 Adam Dunn	.75
35 Larry Walker	.40
36 Luis Castillo	.25
37 Wade Miller	.25
38 Carlos Beltran	.75
39 Odalis Perez	.25
40 Alex Sanchez	.25

41	Torii Hunter	.50
42	Cliff Floyd	.25
43	Andy Pettitte	.50
44	Francisco Rodriguez	.25
45	Eric Chavez	.50
46	Kevin Millwood	.40
47	Dennis Tankersley	.25
48	Hideo Nomo	.50
49	Freddy Garcia	.25
50	Randy Johnson	1.00
51	Aubrey Huff	.25
52	Carlos Delgado	.50
53	Troy Glaus	.50
54	Junior Spivey	.25
55	Mike Hampton	.25
56	Sidney Ponson	.25
57	Aaron Boone	.25
58	Kerry Wood	.50
59	Willie Harris	.25
60	Nomar Garciaparra	1.00
61	Todd Helton	.75
62	Mike Lowell	.25
63	Roy Oswalt	.50
64	Raul Ibanez	.25
65	Brian Jordan	.25
66	Geoff Jenkins	.25
67	Jermaine Dye	.25
68	Tom Glavine	.50
69	Bernie Williams	.50
70	Vladimir Guerrero	1.00
71	Mark Mulder	.40
72	Jimmy Rollins	.50
73	Oliver Perez	.25
74	Rich Aurilia	.25
75	Joel Pineiro	.25
76	J.D. Drew	.40
77	Ivan Rodriguez	.75
78	Josh Phelps	.25
79	Darin Erstad	.40
80	Curt Schilling	1.00
81	Paul LoDuca	.25
82	Marty Cordova	.25
83	Manny Ramirez	1.00
84	Bobby Hill	.25
85	Paul Konerko	.50
86	Austin Kearns	.40
87	Jason Jennings	.25
88	Brad Penny	.25
89	Jeff Bagwell	.75
90	Shawn Green	.40
91	Jason Schmidt	.40
92	Doug Mientkiewicz	.25
93	Jose Vidro	.25
94	Bret Boone	.25
95	Jason Giambi	.75
96	Barry Zito	.50
97	Roy Halliday	.50
98	Pat Burrell	.50
99	Sean Burroughs	.25
100	Barry Bonds	3.00
101	Kazuhiro Sasaki	.25
102	Fernando Vina	.25
103	Chan Ho Park	.25
104	Andruw Jones	1.00
105	Adam Kennedy	.25
106	Shea Hillenbrand	.25
107	Greg Maddux	2.00
108	Jim Edmonds	.40
109	Pedro J. Martinez	1.00
110	Moises Alou	.40
111	Jeff Weaver	.25
112	C.C. Sabathia	.25
113	Robert Fick	.25
114	A.J. Burnett	.40
115	Jeff Kent	.40
116	Kevin Brown	.25
117	Rafael Furcal	.40
118	Cristian Guzman	.25
119	Brad Wilkerson	.25
120	Mike Piazza	1.00
121	Alfonso Soriano	1.00
122	Mark Ellis	.25
123	Vicente Padilla	.25
124	Eric Gagne	.50
125	Ryan Klesko	.25
126	Ichiro Suzuki	2.00
127	Tony Batista	.25
128	Roberto Alomar	.50
129	Alex Rodriguez	2.50
130	Jim Thome	.75
131	Jarrod Washburn	.25
132	Orlando Hudson	.25
133	Chipper Jones	1.00
134	Rodrigo Lopez	.25
135	Johnny Damon	1.00
136	Matt Clement	.25
137	Frank Thomas	1.00
138	Ellis Burks	.25
139	Carlos Pena	.25
140	Josh Beckett	.50
141	Joe Randa	.25
142	Brian Giles	.25
143	Kazuhisa Ishii	.25
144	Corey Koskie	.25

145	Orlando Cabrera	.25
146	Mark Buehrle	.40
147	Roger Clemens	2.00
148	Tim Hudson	.50
149	Randy Wolf	.25
150	Josh Fogg	.25
151	Phil Nevin	.25
152	John Olerud	.25
153	Scott Rolen	1.00
154	Joe Kennedy	.25
155	Rafael Palmeiro	.75
156	Chad Hutchinson	.50
157	Quincy Carter	.50
158	Hee Seop Choi	.40
159	Joe Borchard	.25
160	Brandon Phillips	.25
161	Wily Mo Pena	.25
162	Victor Martinez	.50
163	Jason Stokes	.25
164	Ken Harvey	.25
165	Juan Rivera	.25
166	Joe Valentine RC	1.50
167	Dan Haren	4.00
168	Michel Hernandez RC	1.00
169	Eider Torres RC	1.00
170	Chris De La Cruz RC	1.00
171	Ramon A. Martinez RC	1.50
172	Mike Adams RC	1.00
173	Justin Arneson RC	1.00
174	Jamie Athas RC	1.00
175	Dwaine Bacon RC	1.00
176	Clint Barmes RC	1.50
177	B.J. Barns RC	1.00
178	Tyler Johnson RC	1.00
179	Brandon Webb RC	8.00
180	T.J. Bohn RC	1.00
181	Ozzie Chavez RC	1.50
182	Brandon Bowe RC	1.00
183	Craig Brazell RC	1.00
184	Dusty Brown RC	1.50
185	Brian Bruney RC	1.00
186	Greg Bruso RC	1.00
187	Jaime Bubela RC	1.00
188	Matt Diaz RC	2.00
189	Brian Burgamy RC	1.00
190	Eny Cabreja RC	2.00
191	Daniel Cabrera RC	3.00
192	Ryan Cameron RC	1.00
193	Lance Caraccioli RC	1.50
194	David Cash RC	1.00
195	Bernie Castro RC	1.00
196	Ismael Castro RC	1.00
197	Cory Doyne RC	1.00
198	Jeff Clark RC	1.00
199	Chris Colton RC	1.00
200	Dexter Cooper RC	1.00
201	Callix Crabbe RC	1.00
202	Chien-Ming Wang RC	15.00
203	Eric Crozier RC	1.00
204	Noah Logan RC	1.50
205	David DeJesus RC	4.00
206	Matt DeMarco RC	1.00
207	Chris Duncan RC	12.00
208	Eric Eckenstahler RC	1.00
209	Willie Eyre RC	1.00
210	Evel Bastida-Martinez RC	1.00
211	Chris Fallon RC	1.50
212	Mike Flannery RC	1.00
213	Mike O'Keefe RC	1.00
214	Lew Ford RC	1.50
215	Kason Gabbard RC	3.00
216	Mike Gallo RC	1.00
217	Jairo Garcia RC	1.00
218	Angel Garcia RC	1.00
219	Michael Garciaparra RC	1.00
220	Jeremy Griffiths RC	1.50
221	Dusty Gomon RC	1.50
222	Bryan Grace RC	1.00
223	Tyson Graham RC	1.50
224	Henry Guerrero RC	1.00
225	Franklin Gutierrez RC	4.00
226	Carlos Guzman RC	2.00
227	Matthew Hagen RC	2.00
228	Josh Hall RC	1.50
229	Rob Hammock RC	1.50
230	Brendan Harris RC	2.00
231	Gary Harris RC	1.00
232	Clay Hensley RC	1.50
233	Michael Hinckley RC	2.00
234	Luis Hodge RC	1.00
235	Donnie Hood RC	2.00
236	Matt Hensley RC	1.00
237	Edwin Jackson RC	1.50
238	Ardley Jansen RC	2.00
239	Ferenc Jongejan RC	1.00
240	Matt Kata RC	1.50
241	Kazuhiro Takeoka RC	1.00
242	Charlie Manning RC	1.00
243	Il Kim RC	1.00
244	Brennan King RC	1.00
245	Cris Kroski RC	1.00
246	David Martinez RC	1.50
247	Pete LaForest RC	1.00

248	Wilfredo Ledezma RC	1.00
249	Jeremy Bonderman RC	12.00
250	Gonzalo Lopez RC	1.00
251	Brian Luderer RC	1.50
252	Ruddy Lugo RC	1.50
253	Wayne Lydon RC	1.00
254	Mark Malaska RC	1.00
255	Andy Marte RC	8.00
256	Tyler Martin RC	1.00
257	Branden Florence RC	1.00
258	Aneudis Mateo RC	1.00
259	Derell McCall RC	1.00
260	Elizardo Ramirez RC	2.00
261	Mike McNutt RC	1.00
262	Jacabo Meque RC	1.00
263	Derek Michaelis RC	1.50
264	Aaron Miles RC	2.00
265	Jose Morales RC	1.00
266	Dustin Moseley RC	1.00
267	Adrian Myers RC	1.00
268	Dan Neil RC	1.00
269	Jon Nelson RC	2.00
270	Mike Neu RC	1.00
271	Leigh Neuage RC	1.00
272	Weston O'Brien RC	1.00
273	Trent Oeltjen RC	2.00
274	Tim Olson RC	2.00
275	David Pahucki RC	1.00
276	Nathan Panther RC	1.50
277	Arnie Munoz RC	1.00
278	David Pember RC	1.00
279	Jason Perry RC	2.00
280	Matthew Peterson RC	1.00
281	Greg Aquino RC	1.50
282	Jorge Piedra RC	1.00
283	Simon Pond RC	1.50
284	Aaron Rakers RC	1.00
285	Felix Sanchez RC	1.50
286	Manuel Ramirez RC	1.00
287	Kevin Randel RC	1.00
288	Kelly Shoppach RC	3.00
289	Prentice Redman RC	2.00
290	Eric Reed RC	1.00
291	Wilton Reynolds RC	1.00
292	Eric Riggs RC	1.00
293	Carlos Rijo RC	1.00
294	Tyler Adamczyk RC	2.00
295	Jon-Mark Sprowl RC	2.00
296	Arturo Rivas RC	2.00
297	Kyle Roat RC	1.00
298	Bubba Nelson RC	2.00
299	Levi Robinson RC	1.00
300	Ray Sadler RC	1.00
301	Rylan Reed RC	1.00
302	Jon Schuerholz RC	1.00
303	Nobuaki Yoshida RC	1.50
304	Brian Shackelford RC	1.00
305	Bill Simon RC	1.00
306	Haj Turay RC	1.00
307	Sean Smith RC	1.00
308	Ryan Spataro RC	1.00
309	Jemel Spearman RC	1.50
310	Keith Stamler RC	1.00
311	Luke Steidlmayer RC	1.00
312	Adam Stern RC	1.00
313	Jay Sitzman RC	1.00
314	Mike Wodnicki RC	1.50
315	Terry Tiffee RC	1.00
316	Nick Trzesniak RC	1.00
317	Denny Tussen RC	1.00
318	Scott Tyler RC	1.00
319	Shane Victorino RC	3.00
320	Doug Waechter RC	1.50
321	Brandon Watson RC	1.50
322	Todd Wellemeyer RC	1.50
323	Eli Whiteside RC	1.50
324	Josh Willingham RC	4.00
325	Travis Wong RC	1.50
326	Brian Wright RC	1.00
327	Felix Pie RC	12.00
328	Andy Sisco RC	1.00
329	Dustin Yount RC	1.00
330	Andrew Dominique RC	1.50
331	Brian McCann RC	80.00
332	Jose Contreras RC	100.00
333	Corey Shafer RC	10.00
334	Hanley Ramirez RC	180.00
335	Ryan Shealy RC	30.00
336	Kevin Youkilis RC	50.00
337	Jason Kubel RC	25.00
338	Aron Weston RC	10.00
339	J.D. Durbin RC	10.00
340	Gary Schneidmiller RC	10.00
341	Travis Ishikawa RC	15.00
342	Ben Francisco RC	10.00
343	Bobby Basham RC	10.00
344	Joey Gomes RC	10.00
345	Beau Kemp RC	10.00
346	Thomari Story-Harden RC	10.00
347	Daryl Clark RC	10.00
348	Bryan Bullington RC	25.00
349	Rajai Davis RC	10.00

350	Darrell Rasner	10.00
351	Willie Mays	3.00

Refractors

TOM GLAVINE

Stars (1-165, 351):	2-4X
Rookies (166-350):	.5-1.5X
X-Fractors (1-165, 351):	3-6X
X-Fractors (166-350):	1-2X
Uncirc.Gold Refractors (1-165):	5-10X
Gold Refractors (166-350):	2-3X
Production 170 Sets	
Gold Refractors (331-350):	1-3X

Willie Mays Autograph

	NM/M
Production 150	
351AU Willie Mays	225.00

2003 Bowman Chrome Draft Picks & Prospects

BO HART

		NM/M
Complete Set (176):		500.00
Common Player:		.25
Common Rookie:		1.00
Common Rk Autograph (166-176):		10.00
BDP1	Dontrelle Willis	.75
BDP2	Freddy Sanchez	.25
BDP3	Miguel Cabrera	.75
BDP4	Ryan Ludwick	.25
BDP5	Ty Wigginton	.25
BDP6	Mark Teixeira	.75
BDP7	Trey Hodges	.25
BDP8	Laynce Nix	.25
BDP9	Antonio Perez	.25
BDP10	Jody Gerut	.25
BDP11	Jae Weong Seo	.25
BDP12	Erick Almonte	.25
BDP13	Lyle Overbay	.25
BDP14	Billy Traber	.25
BDP15	Andres Torres	.25
BDP16	Jose Valverde	.25
BDP17	Aaron Heilman	.25
BDP18	Brandon Larson	.25
BDP19	Jung Bong	.25
BDP20	Jesse Foppert	.25
BDP21	Angel Berroa	.25
BDP22	Jeff DaVanon	.25
BDP23	Kurt Ainsworth	.25
BDP24	Brandon Claussen	.25
BDP25	Xavier Nady	.25
BDP26	Travis Hafner	.75
BDP27	Jerome Williams	.25
BDP28	Jose Reyes	.50
BDP29	Sergio Mitre RC	1.00
BDP30	Bo Hart RC	1.00
BDP31	Adam Miller RC	12.00
BDP32	Brian Finch RC	1.00
BDP33	Taylor Mattingly RC	2.00

BDP34	Daric Barton RC	6.00
BDP35	Chris Ray RC	2.00
BDP36	Jarrod Saltalamacchia RC	15.00
BDP37	Dennis Dove RC	1.00
BDP38	James Houser RC	1.50
BDP39	Clinton King RC	2.00
BDP40	Lou Palmisano RC	2.00
BDP41	Dan Moore RC	1.00
BDP42	Craig Stansberry RC	1.50
BDP43	Jo Jo Reyes RC	2.00
BDP44	Jake Stevens RC	1.00
BDP45	Tom Gorzelanny RC	3.00
BDP46	Brian Marshall RC	1.50
BDP47	Scott Beerer RC	1.00
BDP48	Javi Herrera RC	1.50
BDP49	Steve Lerud RC	2.00
BDP50	Josh Banks RC	2.00
BDP51	Jonathan Papelbon RC	30.00
BDP52	Juan Valdes RC	1.50
BDP53	Beau Vaghan RC	1.50
BDP54	Matt Chico RC	2.00
BDP55	Todd Jennings RC	1.50
BDP56	Tony Gwynn Jr. RC	5.00
BDP57	Matt Harrison RC	2.00
BDP58	Aaron Mardsen RC	1.00
BDP59	Casey Abrams RC	1.00
BDP60	Cory Stuart RC	1.00
BDP61	Mike Wagner RC	1.00
BDP62	Jordan Pratt RC	1.50
BDP63	Andre Randolph RC	1.00
BDP64	Blake Balkcom RC	1.00
BDP65	Josh Muecke RC	1.00
BDP66	Jamie D'Antona RC	3.00
BDP67	Cole Seifrig RC	2.00
BDP68	Josh Anderson RC	1.00
BDP69	Matt Lorenzo RC	1.00
BDP70	Nate Spears RC	1.00
BDP71	Chris Goodman RC	1.50
BDP72	Brian McFall RC	1.50
BDP73	Billy Hogan RC	1.50
BDP74	Jamie Romak RC	1.50
BDP75	Jeff Cook RC	1.50
BDP76	Brooks McNiven RC	1.00
BDP77	Xavier Paul RC	1.50
BDP78	Bob Zimmerman RC	1.00
BDP79	Mickey Hall RC	1.00
BDP80	Shaun Marcum RC	1.00
BDP81	Matt Nachreiner RC	1.00
BDP82	Chris Kinsey RC	1.00
BDP83	Jonathan Fulton RC	1.50
BDP84	Edgardo Baez RC	1.50
BDP85	Robert Valido RC	1.00
BDP86	Kenny Lewis RC	1.50
BDP87	Trent Peterson RC	1.00
BDP88	Johnny Woodard RC	1.00
BDP89	Wes Littleton RC	1.50
BDP90	Sean Rodriguez RC	4.00
BDP91	Kyle Pearson RC	1.00
BDP92	Josh Rainwater RC	2.00
BDP93	Travis Schlichting RC	1.50
BDP94	Tim Battle RC	2.00
BDP95	Aaron Hill RC	3.00
BDP96	Bob McCrory RC	1.00
BDP97	Rick Guarno RC	1.00
BDP98	Brandon Yarbrough RC	1.00
BDP99	Peter Stonard RC	1.50
BDP100	Darin Downs RC	1.50
BDP101	Matt Bruback RC	1.00
BDP102	Danny Garcia RC	1.00
BDP103	Cory Stewart RC	1.00
BDP104	Ferdin Tejeda RC	1.50
BDP105	Kade Johnson RC	1.00
BDP106	Andrew Brown RC	2.00
BDP107	Aquilino Lopez RC	1.00
BDP108	Stephen Randolph RC	1.00
BDP109	Dave Matranga RC	1.00
BDP110	Dustin McGowan RC	3.00
BDP111	Juan Camacho RC	1.50
BDP112	Cliff Lee	.15
BDP113	Jeff Duncan RC	1.00
BDP114	C.J. Wilson	.50
BDP115	Brandon Roberson RC	1.00
BDP116	David Corrente RC	1.00
BDP117	Kevin Beavers RC	1.00
BDP118	Anthony Webster RC	1.50
BDP119	Oscar Villarreal RC	1.00
BDP120	Hong-Chih Kuo RC	6.00
BDP121	Josh Barfield	.15
BDP122	Denny Bautista	.15
BDP123	Chris Burke	2.50

BDP124	Robinson Cano RC	20.00
BDP125	Jose Castillo	.15
BDP126	Neal Cotts	.15
BDP127	Jorge De La Rosa	.15
BDP128	J.D. Durbin	.15
BDP129	Edwin Encarnacion	2.00
BDP130	Gavin Floyd	.15
BDP131	Alexis Gomez	.15
BDP132	Edgar Gonzalez RC	1.00
BDP133	Khalil Greene	.50
BDP134	Zack Greinke	.15
BDP135	Franklin Gutierrez	1.50
BDP136	Rich Harden	.15
BDP137	J.J. Hardy	8.00
BDP138	Ryan Howard	50.00
BDP139	Justin Huber	.15
BDP140	David Kelton	.15
BDP141	David Krynzel	.15
BDP142	Pete LaForest	.15
BDP143	Adam LaRoche	.15
BDP144	Preston Larrison	1.00
BDP145	John Maine RC	15.00
BDP146	Andy Marte	4.00
BDP147	Jeff Mathis	.15
BDP148	Joe Mauer	1.00
BDP149	Clint Nageotte	.15
BDP150	Chris Narveson	.15
BDP151	Ramon Nivar RC	1.00
BDP152	Felix Pie	6.00
BDP153	Guillermo Quiroz RC	1.00
BDP154	Rene Reyes	.15
BDP155	Royce Ring	.15
BDP156	Alexis Rios	2.50
BDP157	Grady Sizemore	1.00
BDP158	Stephen Smitherman	.15
BDP159	Seung Jun Song	.15
BDP160	Scott Thorman	.15
BDP161	Chad Tracy	.15
BDP162	Chin-Hui Tsao	.15
BDP163	John Van Benschoten RC	1.00
BDP164	Kevin Youkilis	5.00
BDP165	Chien-Ming Wang	6.00
BDP166	Chris Lubanski/ Auto. RC	40.00
BDP167	Ryan Harvey/ Auto. RC	20.00
BDP168	Matt Murton/ Auto. RC	20.00
BDP169	Jay Sborz/ Auto. RC	10.00
BDP170	Brandon Wood/ Auto. RC	65.00
BDP171	Nicholas Markakis/ Auto. RC	75.00
BDP172	Rickie Weeks/ Auto. RC	40.00
BDP173	Eric Duncan/ Auto. RC	20.00
BDP174	Chad Billingsley/ Auto. RC	50.00
BDP175	Ryan Wagner/ Auto. RC	10.00
BDP176	Delmon Young/ Auto. RC	125.00

Refractor

JOHN MAINE

Rookies (29-165):	2-4X
Inserted 1:11	
Autos. (166-176):	.75-1.5X
Inserted 1:196	

X-Fractor

BROOKS McNIVEN

Rookies (29-165):	2-4X
Production 130 Sets	
Autos. (166-176):	.75-2X
Inserted 1:393	

Gold Refractor

Rookies (29-165):	3-5X
Production 50 Sets	
Autos. (166-176):	No Pricing
Inserted 1:1,479	

2003 Bowman Draft Picks & Prospects

GRADY SIZEMORE

		NM/M
Complete Set (165):		35.00
Common Player:		.15
Common Rookie:		.25
Pack (5 + 2 Chrome):		10.00
Box (24):		220.00
BDP1	Dontrelle Willis	.40
BDP2	Freddy Sanchez	.15
BDP3	Miguel Cabrera	.50
BDP4	Ryan Ludwick	.15
BDP5	Ty Wigginton	.15
BDP6	Mark Teixeira	.50
BDP7	Trey Hodges	.15
BDP8	Laynce Nix	.15
BDP9	Antonio Perez	.15
BDP10	Jody Gerut	.15
BDP11	Jae Weong Seo	.15
BDP12	Erick Almonte	.15
BDP13	Lyle Overbay	.15
BDP14	Billy Traber	.15
BDP15	Andres Torres	.15
BDP16	Jose Valverde	.15
BDP17	Aaron Heilman	.15
BDP18	Brandon Larson	.15
BDP19	Jung Bong	.15
BDP20	Jesse Foppert	.15
BDP21	Angel Berroa	.15
BDP22	Jeff DaVanon	.15
BDP23	Kurt Ainsworth	.15
BDP24	Brandon Claussen	.15
BDP25	Xavier Nady	.15
BDP26	Travis Hafner	.40
BDP27	Jerome Williams	.15
BDP28	Jose Reyes	.40
BDP29	Sergio Mitre RC	.25
BDP30	Bo Hart RC	.50
BDP31	Adam Miller RC	4.00
BDP32	Brian Finch RC	.25
BDP33	Taylor Mattingly RC	.75
BDP34	Daric Barton RC	3.00
BDP35	Chris Ray RC	.25
BDP36	Jarrod Saltalamacchia RC	4.00
BDP37	Dennis Dove RC	.25
BDP38	James Houser RC	.50

BDP39	Clinton King RC	.50
BDP40	Lou Palmisano RC	.50
BDP41	Dan Moore RC	.25
BDP42	Craig Stansberry RC	.50
BDP43	Jo Jo Reyes RC	.75
BDP44	Jake Stevens RC	.50
BDP45	Tom Gorzelanny RC	1.00
BDP46	Brian Marshall RC	.50
BDP47	Scott Beerer RC	.25
BDP48	Javi Herrera RC	.50
BDP49	Steve Lerud RC	.75
BDP50	Josh Banks RC	.75
BDP51	Jonathan Papelbon RC	10.00
BDP52	Juan Valdes RC	.50
BDP53	Beau Vaghan	.50
BDP54	Matt Chico RC	.25
BDP55	Todd Jennings RC	.50
BDP56	Tony Gwynn Jr. RC	1.00
BDP57	Matt Harrison RC	.25
BDP58	Aaron Mardsen	.25
BDP59	Casey Abrams RC	.25
BDP60	Cory Stuart RC	.25
BDP61	Mike Wagner RC	.25
BDP62	Jordan Pratt RC	.50
BDP63	Andre Randolph RC	.25
BDP64	Blake Nachbcom RC	.25
BDP65	Josh Muecke RC	.25
BDP66	Jamie D'Antona RC	1.00
BDP67	Cole Seifrig RC	.50
BDP68	Josh Anderson RC	.25
BDP69	Matt Lorenzo RC	.25
BDP70	Nate Spears RC	.50
BDP71	Chris Goodman RC	.50
BDP72	Brian McFall RC	.50
BDP73	Billy Hogan RC	.50
BDP74	Jamie Romak RC	.50
BDP75	Jeff Cook RC	.50
BDP76	Brooks McNiven RC	.25
BDP77	Xavier Paul RC	1.00
BDP78	Bob Zimmerman RC	.25
BDP79	Mickey Hall RC	.50
BDP80	Shaun Marcum RC	.25
BDP81	Matt Nachreiner RC	.25
BDP82	Chris Kinsey RC	.25
BDP83	Jonathan Fulton RC	.50
BDP84	Edgardo Baez RC	.50
BDP85	Robert Valido RC	.75
BDP86	Kenny Lewis RC	.50
BDP87	Trent Peterson RC	.25
BDP88	Johnny Woodard RC	.25
BDP89	Wes Littleton RC	.50
BDP90	Sean Rodriguez RC	1.00
BDP91	Kyle Pearson RC	.25
BDP92	Josh Rainwater RC	.75
BDP93	Travis Schlichting RC	.50
BDP94	Tim Battle RC	.75
BDP95	Aaron Hill RC	.75
BDP96	Bob McCrory RC	.25
BDP97	Rick Guarno RC	.25
BDP98	Brandon Yarbrough RC	.25
BDP99	Peter Stonard RC	.50
BDP100	Darin Downs RC	.50
BDP101	Matt Bruback RC	.25
BDP102	Danny Garcia RC	.25
BDP103	Cory Stewart RC	.25
BDP104	Ferdin Tejeda RC	.50
BDP105	Kade Johnson RC	.25
BDP106	Andrew Brown RC	.25
BDP107	Aquilino Lopez RC	.25
BDP108	Stephen Randolph RC	.25
BDP109	Dave Matranga RC	.25
BDP110	Dustin McGowan RC	1.00
BDP111	Juan Camacho RC	1.00
BDP112	Cliff Lee	.15
BDP113	Jeff Duncan RC	.50
BDP114	C.J. Wilson	.25
BDP115	Brandon Roberson RC	.25
BDP116	David Corrente RC	.25
BDP117	Kevin Beavers RC	.25
BDP118	Anthony Webster RC	.50
BDP119	Oscar Villarreal RC	.25
BDP120	Hong-Chih Kuo RC	2.00
BDP121	Josh Barfield	.15
BDP122	Denny Bautista	.15
BDP123	Chris Burke	.75
BDP124	Robinson Cano RC	10.00
BDP125	Jose Castillo	.15
BDP126	Neal Cotts	.15
BDP127	Jorge De La Rosa	.15
BDP128	J.D. Durbin	.15
BDP129	Edwin Encarnacion	.50
BDP130	Gavin Floyd	.15
BDP131	Alexis Gomez	.15
BDP132	Edgar Gonzalez RC	.25
BDP133	Khalil Greene	.15
BDP134	Zack Greinke	.15

BDP135	Franklin Gutierrez	.15
BDP136	Rich Harden	.15
BDP137	J.J. Hardy	3.00
BDP138	Ryan Howard	20.00
BDP139	Justin Huber	.15
BDP140	David Kelton	.15
BDP141	David Krynzel	.15
BDP142	Pete LaForest	.15
BDP143	Adam LaRoche	.15
BDP144	Preston Larrison	.15
BDP145	John Maine RC	4.00
BDP146	Andy Marte	1.00
BDP147	Jeff Mathis	.15
BDP148	Joe Mauer	.50
BDP149	Clint Nageotte	.15
BDP150	Chris Narveson	.15
BDP151	Ramon Nivar RC	.25
BDP152	Felix Pie RC	4.00
BDP153	Guillermo Quiroz RC	.50
BDP154	Rene Reyes	.15
BDP155	Royce Ring	.15
BDP156	Alexis Rios	.75
BDP157	Grady Sizemore	.75
BDP158	Stephen Smitherman	.15
BDP159	Seung Jun Song	.15
BDP160	Scott Thorman	.15
BDP161	Chad Tracy	.15
BDP162	Chin-Hui Tsao	.15
BDP163	John Van Benschoten RC	.25
BDP164	Kevin Youkilis	1.00
BDP165	Chien-Ming Wang	3.00

Gold

Cards (1-165): 1-2X
Inserted 1:1

Fabric of Future

		NM/M
	Common Player:	4.00
JB	Josh Barfield	6.00
RC	Robinson Cano	25.00
JD	J.D. Durbin	4.00
GF	Gavin Floyd	4.00
EG	Edgar Gonzalez	4.00
KG	Khalil Greene	8.00
ZG	Zack Greinke	4.00
FG	Franklin Gutierrez	4.00
RH	Rich Harden	6.00
RJH	Ryan Howard	50.00
JH	Justin Huber	5.00
AL	Adam LaRoche	8.00
AM	Andy Marte	8.00
JSM	Jeff Mathis	6.00
JM	Joe Mauer	10.00
CN	Chris Narveson	6.00
FP	Felix Pie	15.00
RR	Rene Reyes	4.00
RRR	Royce Ring	4.00
GS	Grady Sizemore	10.00

Prospect Premiums

		NM/M
	Common Player:	4.00
RB	Rocco Baldelli	6.00
HB	Hank Blalock	6.00
CC	Carl Crawford	5.00
TH	Travis Hafner	8.00
BH	Brendan Harris	4.00
NH	Nathan Haynes	4.00

JM	Justin Morneau	8.00
CS	Chris Snelling	4.00
JT	Joe Thurston	4.00
CU	Chase Utley	10.00

Signs of the Future

		NM/M
	Common Player:	5.00
JA	Jason Arnold	5.00
ZG	Zack Greinke	15.00
CS	Cory Stewart	5.00
DT	Dennis Tankersley	5.00
AT	Andres Torres	8.00

2003 Bowman Heritage

MIGUEL CABRERA • Third Base • MARLINS

	NM/M
Complete Set (280):	60.00
Common Player:	.25

Cards 171-180 have 3 versions.

Pack (8):		3.00
Box (24):		65.00
1	Jorge Posada	.50
2	Todd Helton	.75
3	Marcus Giles	.25
4	Eric Chavez	.40
5	Edgar Martinez	.25
6	Luis Gonzalez	.40
7	Corey Patterson	.25
8	Preston Wilson	.25
9	Ryan Klesko	.25
10	Randy Johnson	1.00
11	Eric Byrnes	.25
12	Carlos Lee	.40
13	Steve Finley	.25
14	A.J. Pierzynski	.25
15	Troy Glaus	.50
16	Darin Erstad	.40
17	Moises Alou	.40
18	Torii Hunter	.50
19	Marlon Byrd	.25
20	Mark Prior	.75
21	Shannon Stewart	.25
22	Craig Biggio	.40
23	Johnny Damon	.75
24	Robert Fick	.25
25	Jason Giambi	.75
26	Fernando Vina	.25
27	Aubrey Huff	.25
28	Benito Santiago	.25
29	Jay Gibbons	.25
30	Ken Griffey Jr.	2.00
31	Rocco Baldelli	.50
32	Pat Burrell	.50
33	A.J. Burnett	.25
34	Omar Vizquel	.25
35	Greg Maddux	1.50
36	Jae Weong Seo	.25
37	C.C. Sabathia	.25
38	Geoff Jenkins	.25
39	Ty Wigginton	.25
40	Jeff Kent	.40
41	Orlando Hudson	.25
42	Edgardo Alfonzo	.25
43	Greg Myers	.25
44	Melvin Mora	.25
45	Sammy Sosa	1.00
46	Russ Ortiz	.25
47	Josh Beckett	.50
48	David Wells	.25
49	Woody Williams	.25
50	Alex Rodriguez	2.00
51	Randy Wolf	.25
52	Carlos Beltran	.75
53	Austin Kearns	.40
54	Trot Nixon	.25
55	Ivan Rodriguez	.75
56	Shea Hillenbrand	.25
57	Roberto Alomar	.40
58	John Olerud	.25
59	Michael Young	.25
60	Garret Anderson	.25
61	Mike Lieberthal	.25
62	Adam Dunn	.50
63	Raul Ibanez	.25
64	Kenny Lofton	.25
65	Ichiro Suzuki	1.50
66	Jarrod Washburn	.25
67	Shawn Chacon	.25
68	Alex Gonzalez	.25
69	Roy Halladay	.40
70	Vladimir Guerrero	1.00
71	Hee Seop Choi	.25

72	Brandon Phillips	.25
73	Ray Durham	.25
74	Mark Teixeira	.75
75	Hank Blalock	.40
76	Jerry Hairston Jr.	.25
77	Erubiel Durazo	.25
78	Frank Catalanotto	.25
79	Jacque Jones	.25
80	Bobby Abreu	.50
81	Mike Hampton	.25
82	Zach Day	.25
83	Jimmy Rollins	.50
84	Joel Pineiro	.25
85	Brett Myers	.25
86	Frank Thomas	.75
87	Aramis Ramirez	.40
88	Paul LoDuca	.25
89	Bobby Higginson	.25
90	Brian Giles	.25
91	Jose Cruz Jr.	.25
92	Derek Lowe	.25
93	Mark Buehrle	.25
94	Wade Miller	.25
95	Derek Jeter	2.00
96	Bret Boone	.25
97	Tony Batista	.25
98	Sean Casey	.25
99	Eric Hinske	.25
100	Albert Pujols	2.00
101	Runelvys Hernandez	.25
102	Vernon Wells	.40
103	Kerry Wood	.40
104	Lance Berkman	.50
105	Alfonso Soriano	1.00
106	Ken Harvey	.25
107	Bartolo Colon	.25
108	Andy Pettitte	.40
109	Rafael Furcal	.40
110	Dontrelle Willis	.40
111	Carl Crawford	.40
112	Scott Rolen	.75
113	Chipper Jones	1.00
114	Magglio Ordonez	.50
115	Bernie Williams	.50
116	Roy Oswalt	.50
117	Kevin Brown	.35
118	Cristian Guzman	.25
119	Kazuhisa Ishii	.25
120	Larry Walker	.40
121	Miguel Tejada	.50
122	Manny Ramirez	1.00
123	Mike Mussina	.50
124	Mike Lowell	.25
125	Barry Bonds	2.00
126	Aaron Boone	.25
127	Carlos Delgado	.60
128	Jose Vidro	.25
129	Brad Radke	.25
130	Rafael Palmeiro	.75
131	Mark Mulder	.40
132	Jason Schmidt	.40
133	Gary Sheffield	.50
134	Richie Sexson	.50
135	Barry Zito	.50
136	Tom Glavine	.50
137	Jim Edmonds	.40
138	Andruw Jones	.75
139	Pedro J. Martinez	1.00
140	Curt Schilling	.75
141	Joe Kennedy	.25
142	Nomar Garciaparra	1.00
143	Vicente Padilla	.25
144	Kevin Millwood	.40
145	Shawn Green	.40
146	Jeff Bagwell	.75
147	Hideo Nomo	.50
148	Fred McGriff	.25
149	Matt Morris	.25
150	Roger Clemens	2.00
151	Damian Moss	.25
152	Orlando Cabrera	.25
153	Tim Hudson	.40
154	Mike Sweeney	.25
155	Jim Thome	.75
156	Rich Aurilia	.25
157	Mike Piazza	1.00
158	Edgar Renteria	.25
159	Javy Lopez	.25
160	Jamie Moyer	.25
161	Miguel Cabrera	.75
162	Adam Loewen RC	1.00
163	Jose Reyes	.50
164	Zack Greinke	.50
165	Cole Hamels	.25
166	Jeremy Guthrie	.25
167	Victor Martinez	.40
168	Rich Harden	.25
169	Joe Mauer	.50
170	Khalil Greene	.25
171	Willie Mays	2.00
172	Phil Rizzuto	.50
173	Al Kaline	1.00
174	Warren Spahn	1.00
175	Jimmy Piersall	.50

176	Luis Aparicio	.50
177	Whitey Ford	1.00
178	Harmon Killebrew	1.00
179	Duke Snider	1.00
180	Bobby Richardson	.50
181	David Martinez	.25
182	Felix Pie RC	3.00
183	Kevin Correia RC	.50
184	Brandon Webb RC	2.50
185	Matt Diaz RC	.50
186	Lew Ford RC	.50
187	Jeremy Griffiths	.25
188	Matt Hensley RC	.75
189	Danny Garcia RC	.50
190	Elizardo Ramirez RC	.50
191	Greg Aquino RC	.50
192	Felix Sanchez RC	.50
193	Kelly Shoppach RC	.75
194	Bubba Nelson RC	.50
195	Mike O'Keefe RC	.50
196	Hanley Ramirez RC	5.00
197	Todd Wellemeyer RC	.50
198	Dustin Moseley RC	.75
199	Eric Crozier RC	.50
200	Ryan Shealy RC	1.50
201	Jeremy Bonderman	2.00
202	Bo Hart RC	.50
203	Dusty Brown RC	.50
204	Rob Hammock RC	.50
205	Jorge Piedra RC	.50
206	Jason Kubel RC	1.00
207	Stephen Randolph RC	.50
208	Andy Sisco RC	.50
209	Matt Kata RC	.50
210	Robinson Cano RC	10.00
211	Ben Francisco RC	.50
212	Arnie Munoz RC	.50
213	Ozzie Chavez RC	.50
214	Beau Kemp RC	.50
215	Travis Wong RC	.50
216	Brian McCann RC	5.00
217	Aquilino Lopez RC	.50
218	Bobby Basham RC	.50
219	Tim Olson RC	.50
220	Nathan Panther RC	.50
221	Wilfredo Ledezma RC	.50
222	Josh Willingham RC	1.00
223	David Cash RC	.50
224	Oscar Villarreal RC	.50
225	Jeff Duncan RC	.75
226	Dan Haren	2.00
227	Michel Hernandez RC	.50
228	Matt Murton RC	1.50
229	Clay Hensley RC	.75
230	Tyler Johnson RC	.50
231	Tyler Martin RC	.50
232	J.D. Durbin RC	.75
233	Shane Victorino RC	.50
234	Rajai Davis RC	.50
235	Chien-Ming Wang RC	6.00
236	Travis Ishikawa RC	.50
237	Eric Eckenstahler	.25
238	Dustin McGowan RC	1.00
239	Prentice Redman RC	.50
240	Haj Turay RC	.50
241	Matt DeMarco RC	.50
242	Lou Palmisano RC	.50
243	Eric Reed RC	.50
244	Willie Eyre RC	.50
245	Ferdin Tejeda RC	.50
246	Michael Garciaparra RC	.25
247	Michael Hinckley RC	.50
248	Branden Florence RC	.50
249	Trent Oeltjen RC	.50
250	Mike Neu RC	.75
251	Chris Lubanski RC	1.50
252	Brandon Wood RC	5.00
253	Delmon Young RC	5.00
253	Delmon Young/ Auto. RC	75.00
254	Matt Harrison RC	.50
255	Chad Billingsley RC	2.50
256	Josh Anderson RC	.50
257	Brian McFall	.75
258	Ryan Wagner RC	.50
259	Billy Hogan RC	.50
260	Nate Spears RC	.50
261	Ryan Harvey RC	2.00
262	Wes Littleton RC	.50
263	Xavier Paul RC	.75
264	Sean Rodriguez RC	1.50
265	Brian Finch RC	.50
266	Josh Rainwater RC	.50
267	Brian Snyder RC	.75
268	Eric Duncan RC	1.50
269	Rickie Weeks RC	3.00
270	Tim Battle RC	.50
271	Scott Beerer RC	.50
272	Aaron Hill RC	.75
273	Casey Abrams RC	.50
274	Jonathan Fulton RC	.50
275	Todd Jennings RC	.50
276	Jordan Pratt RC	.50
277	Tom Gorzelanny RC	1.00

278	Matt Lorenzo RC	.75
279	Jarrod Saltalamacchia RC	3.00
280	Mike Wagner RC	.50

Diamond Cuts

	NM/M
Common Player:	4.00
Red:	1-2X
Production 56 Sets	
JA	Jeremy Affeldt	4.00
MA	Moises Alou	5.00
TA	Tony Armas Jr.	4.00
JB	Jeff Bagwell	6.00
CB	Craig Biggio	6.00
HB	Hank Blalock	6.00
BB	Bret Boone	4.00
EC	Eric Chavez	4.00
JE	Jim Edmonds	6.00
JG	Jason Giambi	8.00
TG	Troy Glaus	6.00
MG	Mark Grace	6.00
VG	Vladimir Guerrero	8.00
CG	Cristian Guzman	4.00
TH	Todd Helton	6.00
RH	Rickey Henderson	12.00
JJ	Jason Jennings	4.00
AJ	Andruw Jones	6.00
CJ1	Chipper Jones/Jsy	8.00
CJ2	Chipper Jones/Bat	8.00
AK	Austin Kearns	6.00
PL	Paul LoDuca	4.00
JL	Javy Lopez	4.00
PM	Pedro J. Martinez	8.00
KM	Kevin Millwood	4.00
MM	Mark Mulder	4.00
BM	Brett Myers	4.00
HN	Hideo Nomo	8.00
RP1	Rafael Palmeiro/Jsy	8.00
RP2	Rafael Palmeiro/Bat	8.00
JLP	Josh Phelps	4.00
AP	Albert Pujols	15.00
JR	Jose Reyes	6.00
AR1	Alex Rodriguez/Jsy	10.00
AR2	Alex Rodriguez/Bat	10.00
SR1	Scott Rolen/Jsy	8.00
SR2	Scott Rolen/Bat	10.00
KI	Kazuhiro Sasaki	4.00
GS	Gary Sheffield	6.00
AS	Alfonso Soriano	8.00
SS1	Sammy Sosa/Jsy	10.00
SS2	Sammy Sosa/Bat	10.00
MS	Mike Sweeney	4.00
MT	Miguel Tejada	6.00
JV	Javier Vazquez	4.00
JW	Jarrod Washburn	4.00
VW	Vernon Wells	4.00
BW	Bernie Williams	6.00
KW	Kerry Wood	5.00
BZ	Barry Zito	6.00

Keith Olbermann Autograph

	NM/M
Inserted 1:1,421	
KO	Keith Olbermann	50.00

Signs of Greatness

	NM/M
Common Player:	6.00

2003 Bowman's Best

	NM/M
Complete Set:	
Common Player:	.50
Pack (5):	50.00
Box (10):	450.00
First-Year Players	
JB	Jeremy Bonderman	4.00
TJB	T.J. Bohn	1.00
MB	Matt Bruback RC	1.00
BC	Bernie Castro RC	1.00
JC	Jose Contreras RC	2.00
MD	Matt Diaz RC	2.00
BJH	Bo Hart RC	1.00
RM	Ramon Martinez	1.00
MO	Mike O'Keefe RC	1.00
JMS	Jon-Mark Sprowl RC	1.00
TT	Terry Tiffee	1.00
HT	Haj Turay RC	2.00
SV	Shane Victorino RC	3.00
CW	Chien-Ming Wang RC	15.00
DY	Dustin Yount RC	1.00
First-Year Player Autographs	
Common Auto.:	8.00
Inserted 1:1	
TA	Tyler Adamczyk RC	8.00
GA	Greg Aquino RC	8.00
BWB	Bobby Basham RC	10.00
GB	Gregor Blanco RC	8.00
AB	Andrew Brown RC	8.00
BB	Bryan Bullington RC	20.00
RC	Ryan Cameron RC	8.00
DC	David Cash RC	8.00
OC	Ozzie Chavez RC	8.00
RD	Rajai Davis RC	10.00
CDC	Chris De La Cruz RC	10.00
MD	Matt Diaz RC	10.00
CAD	Carlos Duran RC	10.00
JDD	J.D. Durbin RC	10.00
WE	Willie Eyre RC	8.00
BF	Branden Florence RC	10.00
LF	Lew Ford RC	10.00
BLF	Ben Francisco RC	10.00
JG	Joey Gomes RC	10.00
JRG	Jeremy Griffiths	10.00

MNH	Matt Hagen RC	10.00
RWH	Robby Hammock RC	10.00
DH	Dan Haren	30.00
BH	Brendan Harris RC	15.00
MDH	Matt Hensley RC	8.00
MH	Michel Hernandez RC	10.00
MHI	Michael Hinckley RC	10.00
RH	Ryan Howard	400.00
TI	Travis Ishikawa RC	10.00
KJ	Kade Johnson RC	8.00
TJ	Tyler Johnson RC	8.00
MK	Matt Kata RC	10.00
BK	Beau Kemp RC	8.00
JK	Jason Kubel RC	15.00
PL	Pete LaForest RC	10.00
WL	Wilfredo Ledezma RC	10.00
NL	Nook Logan RC	10.00
MDM	Mark Malaska RC	8.00
CM	Charlie Manning RC	8.00
DM	David Martinez	10.00
AM	Aneudis Mateo RC	8.00
BM	Brian McCann	60.00
DMM	Dustin McGowan RC	30.00
JM	Jose Morales	10.00
DAM	Dustin Moseley RC	10.00
TO	Tim Olson RC	10.00
FP	Felix Pie RC	60.00
ER	Elizardo Ramirez RC	10.00
HR	Hanley Ramirez RC	100.00
DR	Darrell Rasner RC	8.00
PR	Prentice Redman RC	8.00
FS	Felix Sanchez RC	10.00
GS	Gary Schneidmiller RC	8.00
CSS	Corey Shafer RC	10.00
RS	Ryan Shealy RC	15.00
KS	Kelly Shoppach RC	15.00
CS	Cory Stewart RC	10.00
TSH	Thomari Story-Harden RC	8.00
FT	Ferdin Tejeda RC	10.00
ET	Eider Torres RC	10.00
ST	Scott Tyler	10.00
JV	Joe Valentine RC	8.00
OV	Oscar Villarreal RC	
DW	Doug Waechter RC	10.00
AW	Aron Weston RC	8.00
JW	Josh Willingham RC	20.00
CJW	C.J. Wilson	8.00
KY	Kevin Youkilis RC	40.00
CW	Chien-Ming Wang	250.00
Veterans		
GJA	Garret Anderson	.50
LB	Lance Berkman	.75
BLB	Barry Bonds	4.00
PB	Pat Burrell	.50
WRC	Roger Clemens	3.00
NG	Nomar Garciaparra	1.50
JGG	Jason Giambi	1.00
BSG	Brian Giles	.50
SG	Shawn Green	.50
KG	Ken Griffey Jr.	2.50
VG	Vladimir Guerrero	1.50
TH	Todd Helton	1.00
TKH	Torii Hunter	.75
DJ	Derek Jeter	4.00
RJ	Randy Johnson	1.50
CJ	Chipper Jones	1.50
AK	Austin Kearns	.50
JFK	Jeff Kent	.50
GM	Greg Maddux	2.50
PM	Pedro J. Martinez	1.50
MOR	Magglio Ordonez	.50
MJP	Mike Piazza	1.50
MP	Mark Prior	1.00
AP	Albert Pujols	4.00
MR	Manny Ramirez	1.50
AR	Alex Rodriguez	3.00
CMS	Curt Schilling	1.50
AS	Alfonso Soriano	1.50
SS	Sammy Sosa	1.50
IS	Ichiro Suzuki	2.50
MS	Mike Sweeney	.50
MT	Miguel Tejada	1.00
JT	Jim Thome	1.00
LW	Larry Walker	.50
BZ	Barry Zito	.75

Red

Red Autographs:	2-4X
Inserted 1:63	
Red Base Card:	4-8X
Red Rookies:	2-3X
Production 50	

Blue

Blue Autographs:	1-1.5X
Inserted 1:32	
Blue Base Card:	3-5X
Blue Rookies:	1-2X
Production 100	

Double Play

	NM/M
Common Card:	20.00

Inserted 1:55
EB	Elizardo Ramirez, Bryan Bullington	25.00
GK	Joey Gomes, Jason Kubel	50.00
SR	Felix Sanchez, Darrell Rasner	15.00
YS	Kevin Youkilis, Kelly Shoppach	40.00
HV	Dan Haren, Joe Valentine	25.00
GM	Jeremy Griffiths, David Martinez	15.00
HM	Michael Hinckley, Brian McCann	15.00
RS	Prentice Redman, Gary Schneidmiller	15.00
LL	Nook Logan, Wilfredo Ledezma	25.00
SB	Corey Shafer, Gregor Blanco	25.00

First-Year Player Relics

		NM/M
	Common Player:	5.00
RLD	Rajai Davis	5.00
JLF	Lew Ford	8.00
JGG	Joey Gomes	5.00
RJH	Ryan Howard	60.00
JJK	Jason Kubel	8.00
HRB	Hanley Ramirez	20.00
RNS	Ryan Shealy	8.00
KBS	Kelly Shoppach	8.00
KEY	Kevin Youkilis	10.00

Triple Play

		NM/M
	Inserted 1:219	
DRS	Rajai Davis, Hanley Ramirez, Ryan Shealy	85.00
BCS	Andrew Brown, David Cash, Cory Stewart	30.00

2004 Bowman

ROGER CLEMENS

		NM/M
	Complete Set (330):	70.00
	Common Player:	.15
	Common Rookie:	.50
	Pack (10):	3.00
	Box (24):	60.00
1	Garret Anderson	.15
2	Larry Walker	.25
3	Derek Jeter	2.00
4	Curt Schilling	.75
5	Carlos Zambrano	.40
6	Shawn Green	.25
7	Manny Ramirez	.75
8	Randy Johnson	.75
9	Jeremy Bonderman	.25
10	Alfonso Soriano	.75
11	Scott Rolen	.75
12	Kerry Wood	.25
13	Eric Gagne	.25
14	Ryan Klesko	.15
15	Kevin Millar	.15
16	Ty Wigginton	.15
17	David Ortiz	.75
18	Luis Castillo	.15
19	Bernie Williams	.40
20	Edgar Renteria	.25
21	Matt Kata	.15
22	Bartolo Colon	.25
23	Derrek Lee	.50
24	Gary Sheffield	.40
25	Nomar Garciaparra	.75
26	Kevin Millwood	.25
27	Corey Patterson	.25
28	Carlos Beltran	.50
29	Mike Lieberthal	.15
30	Troy Glaus	.40
31	Preston Wilson	.15
32	Jorge Posada	.50
33	Bo Hart	.15
34	Mark Prior	.40
35	Hideo Nomo	.25
36	Jason Kendall	.15
37	Shea Hillenbrand	.15
38	Dmitri Young	.15
39	Aaron Boone	.15
40	Jim Edmonds	.40
41	Ryan Ludwick	.15
42	Brandon Webb	.25
43	Todd Helton	.50
44	Jacque Jones	.15
45	Xavier Nady	.15
46	Tim Salmon	.25
47	Kelvim Escobar	.15
48	Tony Batista	.15
49	Nick Johnson	.15
50	Jim Thome	.50
51	Casey Blake	.15
52	Trot Nixon	.25
53	Luis Gonzalez	.25
54	Dontrelle Willis	.25
55	Mike Mussina	.40
56	Carl Crawford	.25
57	Mark Buehrle	.15
58	Scott Podsednik	.25
59	Brian Giles	.15
60	Rafael Furcal	.25
61	Miguel Cabrera	.75
62	Rich Harden	.15
63	Mark Teixeira	.50
64	Frank Thomas	.75
65	Johan Santana	.50
66	Jason Schmidt	.25
67	Aramis Ramirez	.40
68	Jose Reyes	.75
69	Magglio Ordonez	.25
70	Mike Sweeney	.15
71	Eric Chavez	.25
72	Rocco Baldelli	.25
73	Jerry Hairston	.15
74	Javy Lopez	.15
75	Roy Oswalt	.25
76	Raul Ibanez	.15
77	Ivan Rodriguez	.50
78	Jerome Williams	.15
79	Carlos Lee	.25
80	Geoff Jenkins	.15
81	Sean Burroughs	.15
82	Marcus Giles	.15
83	Mike Lowell	.25
84	Barry Zito	.40
85	Aubrey Huff	.15
86	Esteban Loaiza	.15
87	Torii Hunter	.25
88	Phil Nevin	.15
89	Andruw Jones	.50
90	Josh Beckett	.40
91	Mark Mulder	.25
92	Hank Blalock	.25
93	Jason Phillips	.15
94	Russ Ortiz	.15
95	Juan Pierre	.15
96	Tom Glavine	.25
97	Gil Meche	.15
98	Ramon Ortiz	.15
99	Richie Sexson	.40
100	Albert Pujols	2.00
101	Javier Vazquez	.15
102	Johnny Damon	.75
103	Alex Rodriguez	1.50
104	Omar Vizquel	.25
105	Chipper Jones	.75
106	Lance Berkman	.40
107	Tim Hudson	.40
108	Carlos Delgado	.40
109	Austin Kearns	.25
110	Orlando Cabrera	.25
111	Edgar Martinez	.25
112	Melvin Mora	.15
113	Jeff Bagwell	.50
114	Marlon Byrd	.15
115	Vernon Wells	.25
116	C.C. Sabathia	.25
117	Cliff Floyd	.15
118	Ichiro Suzuki	1.00
119	Miguel Olivo	.15
120	Mike Piazza	.75
121	Adam Dunn	.40
122	Paul Lo Duca	.15
123	Brett Myers	.25
124	Michael Young	.25
125	Larry Bigbie	.15
126	Greg Maddux	1.00
127	Vladimir Guerrero	.75
128	Miguel Tejada	.40
129	Andy Pettitte	.40
130	Jose Cruz	.15
131	Ken Griffey Jr.	1.50
132	Shannon Stewart	.15
133	Joel Pineiro	.15
134	Luis Matos	.15
135	Jeff Kent	.25
136	Randy Wolf	.15
137	Chris Woodward	.15
138	Jody Gerut	.15
139	Jose Vidro	.15
140	Bret Boone	.15
141	Bill Mueller	.15
142	Angel Berroa	.15
143	Bobby Abreu	.25
144	Roy Halladay	.25
145	Delmon Young	.50
146	Jonny Gomes	.15
147	Rickie Weeks	.40
148	Edwin Jackson	.15
149	Neal Cotts	.15
150	Jason Bay	.40
151	Khalil Greene	.25
152	Joe Mauer	.40
153	Bobby Jenks	.15
154	Chin-Feng Chen	.15
154	Chin-Feng Chen/Jsy	10.00
155	Chien-Ming Wang	.75
155	Chien-Ming Wang/Jsy	25.00
156	Mickey Hall	.15
156	Mickey Hall/Jsy	5.00
157	James Houser	.15
157	James Houser/Jsy	5.00
158	Jay Sborz	.15
158	Jay Sborz/Jsy	5.00
159	Jonathan Fulton	.15
159	Jonathan Fulton/Jsy	5.00
160	Steve Lerud	.15
160	Steve Lerud/Jsy	5.00
161	Grady Sizemore	.50
161	Grady Sizemore/Auto.	40.00
162	Felix Pie	.50
162	Felix Pie/Auto.	15.00
163	Dustin McGowan	.15
163	Dustin McGowan/Auto.	10.00
164	Chris Lubanski	.15
164	Chris Lubanski/Auto.	10.00
164	Chris Lubanski/Jsy	5.00
165	Tom Gorzelanny	.15
165	Tom Gorzelanny/Auto.	15.00
166	Rudy Guillen RC	1.00
166	Rudy Guillen/Auto. RC	10.00
167	Bobby Brownlie RC	1.00
167	Bobby Brownlie/Auto. RC	10.00
168	Conor Jackson	1.50
168	Conor Jackson/Auto.	30.00
169	Matt Moses	1.00
169	Matt Moses/Auto.	20.00
170	Ervin Santana RC	1.50
170	Ervin Santana/Auto. RC	15.00
171	Merkin Valdez RC	.50
171	Merkin Valdez/Auto. RC	10.00
172	Erick Aybar RC	1.00
172	Erick Aybar/Auto. RC	15.00
173	Brad Sullivan	.50
173	Brad Sullivan/Auto.	10.00
174	David Aardsma	.50
174	David Aardsma/Auto.	10.00
175	Brad Snyder	.75
175	Brad Snyder/Auto.	10.00
176	Alberto Callaspo RC	.75
177	Brandon Medders RC	.50
178	Zach Miner RC	1.00
179	Charlie Zink RC	.40
180	Adam Greenberg RC	.75
181	Kevin Howard RC	.50
182	Wanell Severino RC	.50
183	Kevin Kouzmanoff RC	2.00
184	Joel Zumaya RC	4.00
185	Skip Schumaker RC	.50
186	Nic Ungs RC	.50
187	Todd Self RC	.50
188	Brian Steffek RC	.50
189	Brock Peterson RC	.50
190	Greg Thissen RC	.50
191	Frank Brooks RC	.50
192	Estee Harris RC	.50
192	Estee Harris/Jsy RC	5.00
193	Chris Mabeus RC	.50
194	Daniel Giese RC	.50
195	Jared Wells RC	.50
196	Carlos Sosa RC	.50
197	Bobby Madritsch RC	.50
198	Calvin Hayes RC	.50
199	Omar Quintanilla RC	.50
200	Chris O'Riordan RC	.50
201	Tim Hutting RC	.50
202	Carlos Quentin RC	3.00
203	Brayan Pena RC	.50
204	Jeff Salazar RC	.50
205	David Murphy RC	1.00
206	Alberto Garcia RC	.50
207	Ramon Ramirez RC	.50
208	Luis Bolivar RC	.50
209	Rodney Choy Foo RC	.50
210	Kyle Sleeth	.50
211	Anthony Acevedo RC	.50
212	Chad Santos RC	.50
213	Jason Frasor RC	.75
214	Jesse Roman RC	.50
215	James Tomlin RC	.50
216	Josh Labandeira RC	.75
217	Joaquin Arias RC	.50
218	Don Sutton RC (Photo actually Nick Swisher.)	1.50
219	Danny Gonzalez RC	.50
220	Javier Guzman RC	.50
221	Anthony Lerew RC	.50
221	Anthony Lerew/Jsy RC	5.00
222	Jon Knott RC	.50
223	Jesse English RC	.50
224	Felix Hernandez RC	5.00
225	Travis Hanson	.50
226	Jesse Floyd RC	.50
227	Nick Gorneault RC	.50
228	Craig Ansman RC	.50
229	Wardell Starling RC	.50
230	Carl Loadenthal RC	.50
231	David Crouthers	.50
232	Harvey Garcia RC	.50
233	Casey Kopitzke RC	.50
234	Ricky Nolasco	1.00
235	Miguel Perez RC	.50
236	Ryan Mulhern RC	.50
237	Chris Aguila RC	.50
238	Brooks Conrad RC	.50
239	Damaso Espino RC	.50
240	Jereme Milons RC	.50
241	Luke Hughes RC	.50
242	Kory Casto	.50
243	Jose Valdez RC	.50
244	J.T. Stotts	.50
245	Lee Gwaltney RC	.50
246	Yoann Torrealba RC	.50
247	Omar Falcon RC	.50
248	Jon Coutlangus RC	.50
249	George Sherrill RC	.50
250	John Santor RC	.50
251	Tony Richie RC	.50
252	Kevin Richardson RC	.50
253	Tim Bittner RC	.50
254	Dustin Nippert RC	1.00
255	Jose Capellan RC	.50
256	Donald Levinski	.50
257	Jerome Gamble RC	.50
258	Jeff Keppinger RC	.50
259	Jason Szuminski RC	.50
260	Akinori Otsuka RC	.75
261	Ryan Budde	.50
262	Shingo Takatsu RC	.75
263	Jeffrey Allison	.40
264	Hector Gimenez RC	.50
265	Tim Frend RC	.50
266	Tom Farmer RC	.50
267	Shawn Hill RC	.50
268	Lastings Milledge	5.00
269	Scott Proctor RC	.75
270	Jorge Mejia RC	.50
271	Terry Jones RC	.50
272	Zachary Duke RC	1.50
273	Tim Stauffer	.75
274	Luke Anderson RC	.50
275	Hunter Brown RC	.50
276	Matt Lemanczyk RC	.50
277	Fernando Cortez RC	.50
278	Vince Perkins RC	.50
279	Tommy Murphy RC	.50
280	Mike Gosling	.50
281	Paul Bacot	.50
282	Matt Capps RC	.75
283	Juan Gutierrez RC	.50
284	Teodoro Encarnacion RC	.50
285	Juan Cedeno RC	.50
286	Matt Creighton RC	.50
287	Ryan Hankins RC	.50
288	Leo Nunez RC	.50
289	Dave Wallace RC	.50
290	Rob Tejeda RC	.75
291	Lincoln Holdzkom RC	.50
292	Jason Hirsh	1.50
293	Tydus Meadows RC	.50
294	Khalid Ballouli RC	.50
295	Benji DeQuin RC	.50
296	Tyler Davidson	1.00
297	Brent Colamarino RC	.50
298	Marcus McBeth RC	.50
299	Brad Eldred RC	.75
300	David Pauley RC	.50
301	Yadier Molina RC	1.00
302	Chris Shelton RC	1.00
303	Travis Blackley RC	.50
304	Jon DeVries	.50
305	Sheldon Fulse RC	.50
306	Vito Chiaravalloti RC	.50
307	Warner Madrigal RC	.75
308	Reid Gorecki RC	.50
309	Sung Jung RC	.50
310	Peter Shier RC	.50
311	Michael Mooney RC	.50
312	Kenny Perez RC	.50
313	Mike Mallory RC	.50
314	Ben Himes RC	.50
315	Ivan Ochoa	.50

316	Donald Kelly RC	.50
317	Logan Kensing RC	.50
318	Kevin Davidson RC	.50
319	Brian Pilkington RC	.50
320	Alex Romero RC	.50
321	Chad Chop RC	.50
322	Dioner Navarro RC	.75
323	Casey Myers RC	.50
324	Mike Rouse	.50
325	Sergio Silva RC	.50
326	J.J. Furmaniak RC	.75
327	Brad Vericker RC	.50
328	Blake Hawksworth RC	1.00
329	Brock Jacobsen RC	.50
330	Alec Zumwalt RC	.50

Gold

Stars: 1-2X
Rookies: 1-2X
Inserted 1:1

1st Edition

NM/M
Stars: 3-5X
Rookies: 1-2X
HTA Exclusive
Pack (10): 4.00
Box (20): 75.00

Uncirculated

BOBBY ABREU OF

Stars: 4-8X
Rookies: 3-5X
Production 245 Sets

Base of the Future Autographed Relic

NM/M
HTA Exclusive
GS Grady Sizemore 40.00

Futures Game Gear

		NM/M
	Common Player:	4.00
DB	Denny Bautista	6.00
CB	Chris Burke	6.00
JC	Jose Castillo	4.00
NC	Neal Cotts	5.00
JD	Jorge De La Rosa	4.00
EE	Edwin Encarnacion	8.00

SH	Shawn Hill	4.00
EJ	Edwin Jackson	4.00
DK	David Kelton	4.00
DBK	David Krynzel	4.00
PL	Pete LaForest	4.00
JM	John Maine	10.00
CN	Clint Nageotte	6.00
RN	Ramon Nivar	4.00
GQ	Guillermo Quiroz	4.00
AR	Alexis Rios	8.00
ES	Ervin Santana	8.00
SS	Stephen Smitherman	4.00
SJS	Seung Jun Song	4.00
CT	Chad Tracy	8.00
ST	Scott Thorman	8.00
MV	Merkin Valdez	4.00
JV	John VanBenschoten	6.00
CW	Chien-Ming Wang	40.00
KY	Kevin Youkilis	10.00

Rookie of the Year Dual Relic

NM/M
Inserted 1:829
BW Angel Berroa, Dontrelle Willis 15.00

Signs of Future

NM/M
Common Autograph: 8.00
Red Ink: No Pricing
Production 25 Sets

JB	Justin Backsmeyer	10.00
IC	Ismael Castro	8.00
BC	Brent Clevelen	15.00
ED	Eric Duncan	15.00
BF	Brian Finch	8.00
RH	Ryan Harvey	15.00
AH	Aaron Hill	15.00
JH	James Houser	8.00
TJ	Tyler Johnson	8.00
TL	Todd Linden	8.00
NM	Nicholas Markakis	25.00
BM	Brandon Medders	8.00
MM	Matt Murton	15.00
CS	Corey Shafer	8.00
GS	Grady Sizemore	40.00
BS	Brian Snyder	8.00
DS	Denard Span	8.00
JV	Joey Votto	30.00
BW	Brandon Wood	20.00

2004 Bowman Chrome

FIRST Chrome YEAR
FELIX HERNANDEZ P

NM/M
Complete Set (350):
Common Player: .25
Common Rookie: 1.00
Common Rookie Auto.
(331-350): 10.00
Inserted 1:18
Pack (4): 7.00
Box (18): 120.00

1	Garret Anderson	.50
2	Larry Walker	.50
3	Derek Jeter	2.50
4	Curt Schilling	.75
5	Carlos Zambrano	.50
6	Shawn Green	.50
7	Manny Ramirez	1.00
8	Randy Johnson	1.00
9	Jeremy Bonderman	.50
10	Alfonso Soriano	1.00
11	Scott Rolen	1.00
12	Kerry Wood	.50
13	Eric Gagne	.50
14	Ryan Klesko	.25
15	Kevin Millar	.25
16	Ty Wigginton	.25
17	David Ortiz	1.50
18	Luis Castillo	.25
19	Bernie Williams	.50
20	Edgar Renteria	.50
21	Matt Kata	.25
22	Bartolo Colon	.50
23	Derrek Lee	.75
24	Gary Sheffield	.75
25	Nomar Garciaparra	1.00
26	Kevin Millwood	.25
27	Corey Patterson	.50
28	Carlos Beltran	.75
29	Mike Lieberthal	.25
30	Troy Glaus	.50
31	Preston Wilson	.25
32	Jorge Posada	.50
33	Bo Hart	.25
34	Mark Prior	.75
35	Hideo Nomo	.50
36	Jason Kendall	.25
37	Roger Clemens	2.50
38	Dmitri Young	.25
39	Jason Giambi	.75
40	Jim Edmonds	.75
41	Ryan Ludwick	.25
42	Brandon Webb	.50
43	Todd Helton	.75
44	Jacque Jones	.25
45	Jamie Moyer	.25
46	Tim Salmon	.50
47	Kelvim Escobar	.25
48	Tony Batista	.25
49	Nick Johnson	.25
50	Jim Thome	1.00
51	Casey Blake	.25
52	Trot Nixon	.50
53	Luis Gonzalez	.50
54	Dontrelle Willis	.50
55	Mike Mussina	.50
56	Carl Crawford	.50
57	Mark Buehrle	.50
58	Scott Podsednik	.50
59	Brian Giles	.50
60	Rafael Furcal	.50
61	Miguel Cabrera	1.00
62	Rich Harden	.50
63	Mark Teixeira	.75
64	Frank Thomas	.75
65	Johan Santana	.75
66	Jason Schmidt	.50
67	Aramis Ramirez	.50
68	Jose Reyes	.75
69	Magglio Ordonez	.50
70	Mike Sweeney	.25
71	Eric Chavez	.50
72	Rocco Baldelli	.50
73	Sammy Sosa	.75
74	Javy Lopez	.25
75	Roy Oswalt	.50
76	Raul Ibanez	.25
77	Ivan Rodriguez	.75
78	Jerome Williams	.25
79	Carlos Lee	.50
80	Geoff Jenkins	.25
81	Sean Burroughs	.25
82	Marcus Giles	.25
83	Mike Lowell	.50
84	Barry Zito	.50
85	Aubrey Huff	.25
86	Esteban Loaiza	.25
87	Torii Hunter	.50
88	Phil Nevin	.25
89	Andruw Jones	.75
90	Josh Beckett	.50
91	Mark Mulder	.50
92	Hank Blalock	.50
93	Jason Phillips	.25
94	Russ Ortiz	.25
95	Juan Pierre	.50
96	Tom Glavine	.50
97	Gil Meche	.25
98	Ramon Ortiz	.25
99	Richie Sexson	.50
100	Albert Pujols	2.50
101	Javier Vazquez	.25
102	Johnny Damon	1.00
103	Alex Rodriguez	2.50
104	Omar Vizquel	.50
105	Chipper Jones	1.00
106	Lance Berkman	.50
107	Tim Hudson	.50
108	Carlos Delgado	.50
109	Austin Kearns	.40
110	Orlando Cabrera	.25
111	Edgar Martinez	.50
112	Melvin Mora	.25
113	Jeff Bagwell	.75
114	Marlon Byrd	.25
115	Vernon Wells	.50
116	C.C. Sabathia	.50
117	Cliff Floyd	.25
118	Ichiro Suzuki	2.00
119	Miguel Olivo	.25
120	Mike Piazza	1.00
121	Adam Dunn	.75
122	Paul Lo Duca	.25
123	Brett Myers	.50
124	Michael Young	.50
125	Sidney Ponson	.25
126	Greg Maddux	2.00
127	Vladimir Guerrero	1.00
128	Miguel Tejada	.50
129	Andy Pettitte	.50
130	Rafael Palmeiro	.75
131	Ken Griffey Jr.	2.00
132	Shannon Stewart	.25
133	Joel Pineiro	.25
134	Luis Matos	.25
135	Jeff Kent	.50
136	Randy Wolf	.25
137	Chris Woodward	.25
138	Jody Gerut	.25
139	Jose Vidro	.25
140	Bret Boone	.25
141	Bill Mueller	.25
142	Angel Berroa	.25
143	Bobby Abreu	.50
144	Roy Halladay	.50
145	Delmon Young	.50
146	Jonny Gomes	.25
147	Rickie Weeks	.50
148	Edwin Jackson	.25
149	Neal Cotts	.25
150	Jason Bay	.50
151	Khalil Greene	.50
152	Joe Mauer	.50
153	Bobby Jenks	.25
154	Chin-Feng Chen	.25
155	Chien-Ming Wang	.75
156	Mickey Hall	.25
157	James Houser	.25
158	Jay Sborz	.25
159	Jonathan Fulton	.25
160	Steve Lerud	.25
161	Grady Sizemore	.75
162	Felix Pie	.50
163	Dustin McGowan	.25
164	Chris Lubanski	.25
165	Tom Gorzelanny	.50
166	Rudy Guillen	.25
167	Aarom Baldiris RC	2.00
168	Conor Jackson	8.00
169	Matt Moses	2.00
170	Ervin Santana RC	2.00
171	Merkin Valdez RC	2.00
172	Erick Aybar RC	3.00
173	Brad Sullivan	1.00
174	Joey Gathright RC	2.00
175	Brad Snyder	2.00
176	Alberto Callaspo RC	3.00
177	Brandon Medders RC	1.00
178	Zach Miner RC	3.00
179	Charlie Zink RC	1.50
180	Adam Greenberg	2.50
181	Kevin Howard RC	1.00
182	Wanell Severino RC	1.00
183	Chin-Lung Hu RC	3.00
184	Joel Zumaya RC	10.00
185	Skip Schumaker RC	1.00
186	Nic Ungs RC	1.00
187	Todd Self RC	2.00
188	Brian Steffek RC	1.00
189	Brock Peterson RC	2.00
190	Greg Thissen RC	1.00
191	Frank Brooks RC	1.00
192	Scott Olsen RC	3.00
193	Chris Mabeus RC	1.00
194	Daniel Giese RC	2.00
195	Jared Wells RC	1.00
196	Carlos Sosa RC	2.00
197	Bobby Madritsch RC	1.00
198	Calvin Hayes RC	1.50
199	Omar Quintanilla RC	2.00
200	Chris O'Riordan RC	1.00
201	Tim Hutting RC	1.00
202	Carlos Quentin	10.00
203	Brayan Pena RC	1.00
204	Jeff Salazar RC	2.00
205	David Murphy	3.00
206	Alberto Garcia RC	2.00
207	Ramon Ramirez RC	2.00
208	Luis Bolivar RC	1.00
209	Rodney Choy Foo RC	1.00
210	Fausto Carmona RC	5.00
211	Anthony Acevedo RC	2.00
212	Chad Santos RC	1.00
213	Jason Frasor RC	1.50
214	Jesse Roman RC	1.00
215	James Tomlin RC	1.00
216	Josh Labandeira RC	1.00
217	Ryan Meaux RC	1.00
218	Don Sutton RC	3.00
219	Danny Gonzalez RC	1.00
220	Javier Guzman RC	2.00
221	Anthony Lerew RC	2.00
222	Jon Connolly RC	3.00
223	Jesse English RC	1.00
224	Hector Made RC	2.50
225	Travis Hanson	1.50
226	Jesse Floyd RC	2.00
227	Nick Gorneault RC	1.00
228	Craig Ansman RC	1.00
229	Paul McAnulty RC	2.50

230	Carl Loadenthal RC	1.50
231	David Crouthers RC	1.00
232	Harvey Garcia RC	1.00
233	Casey Kopitzke RC	1.00
234	Ricky Nolasco RC	3.00
235	Miguel Perez RC	1.00
236	Ryan Mulhern RC	1.00
237	Chris Aguila RC	1.00
238	Brooks Conrad RC	1.00
239	Damaso Espino RC	1.00
240	Jereme Milons RC	1.50
241	Luke Hughes RC	1.00
242	Kory Casto RC	1.50
243	Jose Valdez RC	1.00
244	J.T. Stotts RC	1.00
245	Lee Gwaltney RC	1.50
246	Yoann Torrealba RC	1.00
247	Omar Falcon RC	1.00
248	Jon Coutlangus RC	1.00
249	George Sherrill RC	2.00
250	John Santor RC	1.00
251	Tony Richie RC	1.00
252	Kevin Richardson RC	1.00
253	Tim Bittner RC	1.00
254	Chris Saenz RC	1.50
255	Jose Capellan RC	2.00
256	Donald Levinski RC	1.00
257	Jerome Gamble RC	1.00
258	Jeff Keppinger RC	1.00
259	Jason Szuminski RC	1.00
260	Akinori Otsuka RC	1.50
261	Ryan Budde RC	1.00
262	Marland Williams RC	2.00
263	Jeffrey Allison RC	1.00
264	Hector Gimenez RC	1.00
265	Tim Frend RC	1.00
266	Tom Farmer RC	1.00
267	Shawn Hill RC	1.00
268	Mike Huggins RC	2.00
269	Scott Proctor RC	1.50
270	Jorge Mejia RC	1.00
271	Terry Jones RC	1.50
272	Zachary Duke RC	4.00
273	Jesse Crain RC	3.00
274	Luke Anderson RC	1.00
275	Hunter Brown RC	1.00
276	Matt Lemanczyk RC	1.00
277	Fernando Cortez RC	1.00
278	Vince Perkins RC	1.00
279	Tommy Murphy RC	1.00
280	Mike Gosling RC	1.00
281	Paul Bacot RC	1.50
282	Matt Capps RC	2.00
283	Juan Gutierrez RC	1.00
284	Teodoro Encarnacion RC	2.00
285	Chad Bentz RC	1.50
286	Kazuo Matsui RC	1.50
287	Ryan Hankins RC	1.00
288	Leo Nunez RC	1.00
289	Dave Wallace RC	1.00
290	Rob Tejeda RC	2.50
291	Paul Maholm RC	3.00
292	Casey Daigle RC	1.00
293	Tydus Meadows RC	1.00
294	Khalid Ballouli RC	1.00
295	Benji DeQuin RC	1.00
296	Tyler Davidson RC	2.00
297	Brent Colamarino RC	3.00
298	Marcus McBeth RC	1.00
299	Brad Eldred RC	2.50
300	David Pauley RC	3.00
301	Yadier Molina RC	4.00
302	Chris Shelton RC	2.00
303	Nyjer Morgan RC	1.00
304	Jon DeVries RC	1.00
305	Sheldon Fulse RC	1.00
306	Vito Chiaravalloti RC	1.50
307	Warner Madrigal RC	3.00
308	Reid Gorecki RC	1.00
309	Sung Jung RC	1.00
310	Peter Shier RC	1.00
311	Michael Mooney RC	1.00
312	Kenny Perez RC	1.00
313	Mike Mallory RC	1.00
314	Ben Himes RC	1.00
315	Ivan Ochoa RC	1.00
316	Donald Kelly RC	1.00
317	Tom Mastny RC	1.00
318	Kevin Davidson RC	1.50
319	Brian Pilkington RC	1.00
320	Alex Romero RC	1.00
321	Chad Chop RC	1.00
322	Kody Kirkland RC	2.50
323	Casey Myers RC	1.00
324	Mike Rouse RC	1.00
325	Sergio Silva RC	1.00
326	J.J. Furmaniak RC	3.00
327	Brad Vericker RC	1.00
328	Blake Hawksworth RC	2.00
329	Brock Jacobsen RC	1.00
330	Alec Zumwalt RC	1.00
331	Wardell Starling RC	10.00
332	Estee Harris RC	10.00
333	Kyle Sleeth RC	15.00
334	Dioner Navarro RC	15.00
335	Logan Kensing RC	10.00
336	Travis Blackley RC	10.00
337	Lincoln Holdzkom RC	10.00
338	Jason Hirsh RC	20.00
339	Juan Cedeno RC	10.00
340	Matt Creighton RC	10.00
341	Tim Stauffer RC	10.00
342	Shingo Takatsu RC	10.00
343	Lastings Milledge RC	60.00
344	Dustin Nippert RC	10.00
345	Felix Hernandez RC	100.00
346	Joaquin Arias RC	10.00
347	Kevin Kouzmanoff RC	30.00
348	Bobby Brownlie RC	10.00
349	David Aardsma RC	10.00
350	Jon Knott RC	10.00

Refractor

Stars (1-165):	2-4X
Rookies (166-330):	1-2X
Inserted 1:4	
Autograph (331-350):	1-2X
Inserted 1:100	

Gold Refractor

Stars (1-165):	4-8X
Rookies (166-330):	3-5X
Production 50	
Autograph (331-350):	No Pricing
Inserted 1:1,003	

X-Fractor

Stars (1-165):	3-5X
Rookies (166-330):	2-4X
Production 173	
Autograph (331-350):	No Pricing
Inserted 1:200	

Stars Of The Future

NM/M

Inserted 1:600

YSS	Delmon Young, Kyle Sleeth, Tim Stauffer	70.00
LHC	Chris Lubanski, Ryan Harvey, Chad Cordero	50.00
MHD	Nicholas Markakis, Aaron Hill, Eric Duncan	50.00

2004 Bowman Chrome Draft Picks & Prospects

NM/M

Complete Set (175):	
Common Player:	.25
Common Rookie:	1.00

Common RC Auto. (166-175):		15.00
Inserted 1:60		
BDP1	Lyle Overbay	.50
BDP2	David Newhan	.25
BDP3	J.R. House	.25
BDP4	Chad Tracy	.25
BDP5	Humberto Quintero	.25
BDP6	David Bush	.25
BDP7	Scott Hairston	.25
BDP8	Mike Wood	.25
BDP9	Alexis Rios	.50
BDP10	Sean Burnett	.25
BDP11	Wilson Valdez	.25
BDP12	Lew Ford	.25
BDP13	Freddie Thon RC	1.00
BDP14	Zack Greinke	.25
BDP15	Bucky Jacobsen	.25
BDP16	Kevin Youkilis	.50
BDP17	Grady Sizemore	.75
BDP18	Denny Bautista	.25
BDP19	David DeJesus	.25
BDP20	Casey Kotchman	.25
BDP21	David Kelton	.25
BDP22	Charles Thomas RC	1.00
BDP23	Kazuhito Tadano RC	1.50
BDP24	Justin Leone RC	1.00
BDP25	Eduardo Villacis RC	1.00
BDP26	Brian Dallimore RC	1.00
BDP27	Nick Green RC	1.00
BDP28	Sam McConnell RC	1.00
BDP29	Brad Halsey RC	1.00
BDP30	Roman Colon RC	1.00
BDP31	Josh Fields RC	6.00
BDP32	Cody Bunkelman RC	1.00
BDP33	Jay Rainville RC	4.00
BDP34	Richie Robnett RC	3.00
BDP35	Jon Poterson RC	2.50
BDP36	Huston Street RC	5.00
BDP37	Erick San Pedro RC	1.00
BDP38	Cory Dunlap RC	3.00
BDP39	Kurt Suzuki RC	3.00
BDP40	Anthony Swarzak RC	2.00
BDP41	Ian Desmond RC	3.00
BDP42	Chris Covington RC	1.50
BDP43	Christian Garcia RC	1.50
BDP44	Gaby Hernandez RC	5.00
BDP45	Steven Register RC	1.00
BDP46	Eduardo Morlan RC	2.50
BDP47	Collin Balester RC	1.00
BDP48	Nathan Phillips RC	1.00
BDP49	Dan Schwartzbauer RC	1.00
BDP50	Rafael Gonzalez RC	1.00
BDP51	K.C. Herren RC	2.00
BDP52	William Susdorf RC	1.00
BDP53	Rob Johnson RC	1.00
BDP54	Louis Marson RC	2.00
BDP55	Joe Koshansky RC	5.00
BDP56	Jamar Walton RC	3.00
BDP57	Mark Lowe RC	2.50
BDP58	Matt Macri RC	3.00
BDP59	Donny Lucy RC	1.00
BDP60	Mike Ferris RC	2.00
BDP61	Mike Nickeas RC	1.00
BDP62	Eric Hurley RC	3.00
BDP63	Scott Elbert RC	4.00
BDP64	Blake DeWitt RC	5.00
BDP65	Danny Putnam RC	2.00
BDP66	J.P. Howell RC	3.00
BDP67	John Wiggins RC	1.00
BDP68	Justin Orenduff RC	2.00
BDP69	Ray Liotta RC	2.00
BDP70	Billy Buckner RC	1.00
BDP71	Eric Campbell RC	4.00
BDP72	Olin Wick RC	2.00
BDP73	Sean Gamble RC	1.50
BDP74	Seth Smith RC	3.00
BDP75	Wade Davis RC	4.00
BDP76	Joe Jacobitz RC	1.00
BDP77	J.A. Happ RC	2.00
BDP78	Eric Ridener RC	1.00
BDP79	Matt Tuiasosopo RC	3.00
BDP80	Bradley Bergesen RC	1.00
BDP81	Javy Guerra RC	1.50
BDP82	Buck Shaw RC	2.00
BDP83	Paul Janish RC	2.00
BDP84	Sean Kazmar RC	1.00
BDP85	Josh Johnson RC	1.50
BDP86	Angel Salome RC	1.00
BDP87	Jordan Parraz RC	1.00
BDP88	Kelvin Vazquez RC	1.00
BDP89	Grant Hansen RC	1.00
BDP90	Matt Fox RC	1.00
BDP91	Trevor Plouffe RC	4.00
BDP92	Wes Whisler RC	1.00
BDP93	Curtis Thigpen RC	2.00
BDP94	Donnie Smith RC	1.00
BDP95	Luis Rivera RC	1.50
BDP96	Jesse Hoover RC	1.00
BDP97	Jason Vargas RC	4.00
BDP98	Clary Carlsen RC	1.00
BDP99	Mark Robinson RC	1.00
BDP100	J.C. Holt RC	1.50
BDP101	Chad Blackwell RC	1.00
BDP102	Daryl Jones RC	2.00
BDP103	Jonathan Tierce RC	1.00
BDP104	Patrick Bryant RC	1.00
BDP105	Eddie Prasch RC	1.50
BDP106	Mitch Einertson RC	2.00
BDP107	Kyle Waldrop RC	4.00
BDP108	Jeff Marquez RC	2.00
BDP109	Zach Jackson RC	2.00
BDP110	Josh Wahpepah RC	1.00
BDP111	Adam Lind RC	5.00
BDP112	Kyle Bloom RC	1.00
BDP113	Ben Harrison RC	1.00
BDP114	Taylor Tankersley RC	2.00
BDP115	Steven Jackson RC	1.00
BDP116	David Purcey RC	1.50
BDP117	Jacob McGee RC	4.00
BDP118	Lucas Harrell RC	1.00
BDP119	Brandon Allen RC	2.50
BDP120	Van Pope RC	1.50
BDP121	Jeff Francis	.25
BDP122	Joe Blanton	.25
BDP123	Wilfredo Ledezma	.25
BDP124	Bryan Bullington	.25
BDP125	Jairo Garcia	.25
BDP126	Matt Cain	.75
BDP127	Arnie Munoz	.25
BDP128	Clint Everts	.25
BDP129	Jesus Cota	.25
BDP130	Gavin Floyd	.25
BDP131	Edwin Encarnacion	.25
BDP132	Koyie Hill	.25
BDP133	Ruben Gotay	.25
BDP134	Jeff Mathis	.25
BDP135	Andy Marte	.50
BDP136	Dallas McPherson	.50
BDP137	Justin Morneau	.25
BDP138	Rickie Weeks	.40
BDP139	Joel Guzman	.25
BDP140	Shin-Soo Choo	.25
BDP141	Yusmeiro Petit RC	6.00
BDP142	Jorge Cortes	.25
BDP143	Val Majewski	.25
BDP144	Felix Pie	.25
BDP145	Aaron Hill	.25
BDP146	Jose Capellan	.25
BDP147	Dioner Navarro RC	1.00
BDP148	Fausto Carmona RC	1.00
BDP149	Robinson Diaz RC	1.00
BDP150	Felix Hernandez RC	5.00
BDP151	Andres Blanco RC	1.00
BDP152	Jason Kubel	.25
BDP153	Willy Taveras RC	2.50
BDP154	Merkin Valdez	1.00
BDP155	Robinson Cano	1.00
BDP156	Bill Murphy RC	.50
BDP157	Chris Burke	.25
BDP158	Kyle Sleeth	.75
BDP159	B.J. Upton	.75
BDP160	Tim Stauffer	1.00
BDP161	David Wright	2.50
BDP162	Conor Jackson	3.00
BDP163	Brad Thompson RC	2.00
BDP164	Delmon Young	.50
BDP165	Jeremy Reed	.25
BDP166	Matt Bush RC	20.00
BDP167	Mark Rogers RC	15.00
BDP168	Thomas Diamond RC	15.00
BDP169	Greg Golson RC	20.00
BDP170	Homer Bailey RC	60.00
BDP171	Chris Lambert RC	10.00
BDP172	Neil Walker RC	30.00
BDP173	Bill Bray RC	10.00
BDP174	Phillip Hughes RC	140.00
BDP175	Gio Gonzalez RC	40.00

Refractor

Rookies:	2-4X
Inserted 1:11	
Rookie Autos. (166-175):	.75-1.5X
Inserted 1:204	

Gold Refractor

Rookies:	10-20X
Production 50	
Rookie Autos. (166-175):	3-5X
Inserted 1:2,045	

X-Fractor

KAZUHITO TADANO P

Rookies:	3-6X
Production 125	
Rookie Autos. (166-175):	1-2X
Inserted 1:407	

2004 Bowman Chrome Draft Picks AFLAC

	NM/M
Complete Set (12):	35.00
One redemption per box.	
1	C.J. Henry	4.00
2	John Drennen	2.00
3	Beau Jones	2.00
4	Jeff Lyman	1.00
5	Andrew McCutchen	8.00
6	Chris Volstad	2.00
7	Jonathan Egan	1.00
8	P.J. Phillips	2.00
9	Steve Johnson	1.00
10	Ryan Tucker	1.00
11	Cameron Maybin	25.00
12	Shane Funk	1.00

Gold Refractor

No Pricing
Production 50 Sets

Refractor

Refractors:	4-6X
Production 550 Sets	

X-Fractor

X-Refractors:	10-15X
Production 125 Sets	

Red Refractor

No Pricing
Production One Set

2004 Bowman Draft Picks & Prospects

JOSE CAPELLAN P

	NM/M
Complete Set (1-165):	30.00
Common Player:	.15
Common Rookie:	.25
Pack (5 Bowman +	
2 Chrome):	7.00
Box (24):	140.00
BDP1	Lyle Overbay	.25
BDP2	David Newhan	.15
BDP3	J.R. House	.15
BDP4	Chad Tracy	.25
BDP5	Humberto Quintero	.15
BDP6	David Bush	.15
BDP7	Scott Hairston	.15
BDP8	Mike Wood	.15
BDP9	Alexis Rios	.25

BDP10	Sean Burnett	.15
BDP11	Wilson Valdez	.15
BDP12	Lew Ford	.15
BDP13	Freddy Thon RC	.25
BDP14	Zack Greinke	.15
BDP15	Bucky Jacobsen	.15
BDP16	Kevin Youkilis	.25
BDP17	Grady Sizemore	.25
BDP18	Denny Bautista	.15
BDP19	David DeJesus	.15
BDP20	Casey Kotchman	.15
BDP21	David Kelton	.15
BDP22	Charles Thomas RC	.25
BDP23	Kazuhito Tadano RC	.50
BDP24	Justin Leone RC	.25
BDP25	Eduardo Villacis	.25
BDP26	Brian Dallimore RC	.25
BDP27	Nick Green	.25
BDP28	Sam McConnell	.25
BDP29	Brad Halsey RC	.25
BDP30	Roman Colon RC	.25
BDP31	Josh Fields RC	2.00
BDP32	Cody Bunkelman	.50
BDP33	Jay Rainville RC	1.00
BDP34	Richie Robnett RC	1.00
BDP35	Jon Poterson RC	.75
BDP36	Huston Street RC	1.00
BDP37	Erick San Pedro RC	.25
BDP38	Cory Dunlap	1.00
BDP39	Kurt Suzuki RC	.75
BDP40	Anthony Swarzak	.50
BDP41	Ian Desmond	1.00
BDP42	Chris Covington	.40
BDP43	Christian Garcia	.40
BDP44	Gaby Hernandez RC	1.00
BDP45	Steven Register	.25
BDP46	Eduardo Morlan	.25
BDP47	Collin Balester	.50
48	Nathan Phillips	.25
49	Dan Schwartzbauer	.25
50	Rafael Gonzalez	.25
51	K.C. Herren RC	.50
52	William Susdorf	.25
53	Rob Johnson	.25
54	Louis Marson	.50
55	Joe Koshansky RC	1.50
56	Jamar Walton	1.00
57	Mark Lowe	.75
58	Matt Macri RC	.75
59	Donny Lucy	.25
60	Mike Ferris	.50
61	Mike Nickeas	.50
62	Eric Hurley RC	.75
63	Scott Elbert RC	1.00
64	Blake DeWitt RC	1.50
65	Danny Putnam RC	.50
66	J.P. Howell RC	.75
67	John Wiggins	.25
68	Justin Orenduff RC	.50
69	Ray Liotta RC	.75
70	Billy Buckner RC	.25
71	Eric Campbell RC	1.50
72	Olin Wick	.25
73	Sean Gamble	.40
74	Seth Smith	1.00
75	Wade Davis RC	1.00
76	Joe Jacobitz	.25
77	J.A. Happ	.50
78	Eric Ridener	.25
79	Matt Tuiasosopo RC	1.00
80	Bradley Bergesen	.25
81	Javy Guerra	.40
82	Buck Shaw	.50
83	Paul Janish	.50
84	Sean Kazmar	.25
85	Josh Johnson RC	.50
86	Angel Salome	.75
87	Jordan Parraz RC	.50
88	Kelvin Vazquez	.25
89	Grant Hansen	.50
90	Matt Fox RC	.50
91	Trevor Plouffe RC	1.50
92	Wes Whisler	.50
93	Curtis Thigpen	.50
94	Donnie Smith RC	.25
95	Luis Rivera	.40
96	Jesse Hoover	.25
97	Jason Vargas RC	1.00
98	Clary Carlsen	.25
99	Mark Robinson	.25
100	J.C. Holt RC	.40
101	Chad Blackwell	.25
102	Daryl Jones RC	.75
103	Jonathan Tierce	.25
104	Patrick Bryant	.25
105	Eddie Prasch	.40
106	Mitch Einertson RC	.75
107	Kyle Waldrop RC	.75
108	Jeff Marquez RC	.50
109	Zach Jackson RC	.50
110	Josh Wahpepah	.25
111	Adam Lind RC	2.00
112	Kyle Bloom	.25
113	Ben Harrison	.25

114	Taylor Tankersley RC	.75
115	Steven Jackson	.25
116	David Purcey RC	.50
117	Jacob McGee	1.50
118	Lucas Harrell RC	.25
119	Brandon Allen	.75
120	Van Pope	.50
121	Jeff Francis	.15
122	Joe Blanton	.15
123	Wilfredo Ledezma	.15
124	Bryan Bullington	.15
125	Jairo Garcia	.15
126	Matt Cain	.40
127	Arnie Munoz	.15
128	Clint Everts	.15
129	Jesus Cota	.15
130	Gavin Floyd	.15
131	Edwin Encarnacion	.15
132	Koyie Hill	.15
133	Ruben Gotay	.15
134	Jeff Mathis	.15
135	Andy Marte	.25
136	Dallas McPherson	.15
137	Justin Morneau	.40
138	Rickie Weeks	.25
139	Joel Guzman	.15
140	Shin-Soo Choo	.15
141	Yusmeiro Petit RC	2.00
142	Jorge Cortes	.25
143	Val Majewski	.15
144	Felix Pie	.15
145	Aaron Hill	.15
146	Jose Capellan	.25
147	Dioner Navarro RC	.25
148	Fausto Carmona RC	.50
149	Robinzon Diaz	.25
150	Felix Hernandez	2.00
151	Andres Blanco	.25
152	Jason Kubel	.15
153	Willy Taveras RC	1.00
154	Merkin Valdez	.40
155	Robinson Cano	.50
156	Bill Murphy	.25
157	Chris Burke	.15
158	Kyle Sleeth	.25
159	B.J. Upton	.25
160	Tim Stauffer	.25
161	David Wright	1.00
162	Conor Jackson	.25
163	Brad Thompson RC	.25
164	Delmon Young	.40
165	Jeremy Reed	.15

Gold

COLLIN BALESTER

Rookies:	.75-1.5X
Inserted 1:1	

Red

No Pricing
Production One Set

Printing Plates

No Pricing
Production one for each color.

Prospect Premiums

		NM/M
Common Player:		4.00
AB	Angel Berroa	4.00
KC	Kevin Cash	4.00
RH	Ryan Harvey	6.00
CJ	Conor Jackson	10.00
EJ	Edwin Jackson	4.00
LM	Lastings Milledge	15.00
DN	Dioner Navarro	4.00
CQ	Carlos Quentin	8.00
JR	Jeremy Reed	6.00
NS	Nick Swisher	8.00
BU	B.J. Upton	8.00
DY	Delmon Young	6.00

Signs of the Future

	NM/M
Common Player:	8.00

CC	Chad Cordero	10.00
JH	James Houser	8.00
AL	Adam Loewen	15.00
PM	Paul Maholm	8.00
TP	Tyler Pelland	8.00
TT	Terry Tiffee	8.00

AFLAC

	NM/M
Complete Set (12):	10.00
One redemption per box.	
Red:	No Pricing
Production One Set	
1	C.J. Henry	1.00
2	John Drennen	.75
3	Beau Jones	.75
4	Jeff Lyman	.50
5	Andrew McCutchen	2.50
6	Chris Volstad	1.00
7	Jonathan Egan	.50
8	P.J. Phillips	1.00
9	Steve Johnson	.50
10	Ryan Tucker	.50
11	Cameron Maybin	8.00
12	Shane Funk	.50

2004 Bowman Heritage

		NM/M
Complete Set (347):		
Common Player:		.15
Common SP:		4.00
Common SP Rookie:		4.00
SP's inserted 1:3		
Pack (8):		5.00
Box (24):		100.00
1	Tom Glavine	.40
2	Mike Piazza/SP	8.00
3	Sidney Ponson	.15
4	Jerry Hairston Jr.	.15
5	Jermaine Dye	.25
6	Bobby Crosby	.15
7	Carlos Zambrano	.25
8	Moises Alou	.25
9	Alex Rodriguez/SP	10.00
10	Derek Jeter	2.00
11	Rafael Furcal	.25
12	J.D. Drew	.25
13	Joe Mauer/SP	6.00
14	Brad Radke	.15
15	Johnny Damon	.75
16	Derek Lowe	.15
17	Pat Burrell	.25
18	Mike Lieberthal	.15
19	Cliff Lee	.15
20	Ronnie Belliard	.15
21	Eric Gagne/SP	4.00
22	Brad Penny	.15
23	Al Kaline	.50
24	Mike Maroth	.15
25	Magglio Ordonez/SP	4.00
26	Mark Buehrle	.25
27	Jack Wilson	.15
28	Oliver Perez	.15
29	Al "Red" Schoendienst	.15
30	Yadier Molina RC	1.50
31	Ryan Freel	.15
32	Adam Dunn	.50
33	Paul Konerko	.40
34	Esteban Loaiza	.15
35	Ivan Rodriguez	.50
36	Carlos Guillen	.15
37	Adrian Beltre	.25
38	C.C. Sabathia	.25
39	Hideo Nomo	.40
40	Victor Martinez/SP	4.00
41	Bobby Abreu	.25
42	Randy Wolf	.15
43	Johnny Estrada	.15
44	Russ Ortiz	.15
45	Kenny Rogers	.15
46	Hank Blalock/SP	4.00
47	David Ortiz	1.00
48	Pedro Martinez/SP	6.00
49	Austin Kearns	.15
50	Ken Griffey Jr./SP	6.00
51	Mark Prior	.50
52	Kerry Wood	.40
53	Eric Chavez	.25
54	Tim Hudson	.25
55	Rafael Palmeiro/SP	5.00
56	Javy Lopez	.15
57	Jason Bay	.40

#	Player	Price
58	Craig Wilson	.15
59	Ed "Whitey" Ford	.50
60	Jason Giambi	.50
61	Scott Rolen/SP	6.00
62	Matt Morris	.15
63	Javier Vazquez	.15
64	Jim Thome	.50
65	Don Zimmer	.25
66	Shawn Green	.25
67	Don Larsen	.50
68	Gary Sheffield	.40
69	Jorge Posada	.50
70	Bernie Williams	.40
71	Chipper Jones	.75
72	Andruw Jones	.50
73	John Thomson	.15
74	Jim Edmonds	.50
75	Albert Pujols	2.00
76	Chris Carpenter	.15
77	Aubrey Huff/SP	4.00
78	Carl Crawford	.40
79	Victor Zambrano	.15
80	Alfonso Soriano/SP	5.00
81	Lance Berkman	.40
82	Mike Sweeney	.15
83	Ken Harvey	.15
84	Angel Berroa	.15
85	A.J. Burnett	.15
86	Mike Lowell	.15
87	Miguel Cabrera/SP	5.00
88	Preston Wilson	.15
89	Todd Helton/SP	4.00
90	Larry Walker	.25
91	Vladimir Guerrero	.75
92	Garret Anderson	.15
93	Bartolo Colon	.15
94	Scott Hairston	.15
95	Richie Sexson/SP	4.00
96	Sean Casey	.25
97	Johnny Podres	.40
98	Andy Pettitte	.40
99	Roy Oswalt	.25
100	Roger Clemens/SP	8.00
101	Scott Podsednik	.25
102	Ben Sheets	.25
103	Lyle Overbay	.25
104	Nick Johnson/SP	4.00
105	Zach Day	.15
106	Jose Reyes	.75
107	Khalil Greene	.25
108	Sean Burroughs	.15
109	David Wells/SP	4.00
110	Jason Schmidt	.25
111	Neifi Perez	.15
112	Edgar Renteria	.25
113	Rich Aurilia	.15
114	Edgar Martinez	.15
115	Joel Pineiro	.15
116	Mark Teixeira	.40
117	Michael Young	.25
118	Ricardo Rodriguez	.15
119	Carlos Delgado	.50
120	Roy Halladay	.25
121	Jose Guillen	.15
122	Troy Glaus	.40
123	Shea Hillenbrand	.15
124	Luis Gonzalez	.25
125	Horacio Ramirez	.15
126	Melvin Mora	.15
127	Miguel Tejada/SP	4.00
128	Manny Ramirez	.75
129	Tim Wakefield	.15
130	Curt Schilling/SP	5.00
131	Aramis Ramirez	.40
132	Sammy Sosa/SP	6.00
133	Matt Clement	.15
134	Juan Uribe	.15
135	Dontrelle Willis	.25
136	Paul LoDuca	.15
137	Juan Pierre	.15
138	Kevin Brown	.15
139	Brian Giles, Marcus Giles	.15
140	Brian Giles	.15
141	Nomar Garciaparra/SP	6.00
142	Cesar Izturis	.15
143	Don Newcombe	.15
144	Craig Biggio	.25
145	Carlos Beltran	.50
146	Torii Hunter	.25
147	Livan Hernandez	.15
148	Cliff Floyd	.15
149	Barry Zito	.40
150	Mark Mulder	.25
151	Rocco Baldelli	.25
152	Bret Boone	.15
153	Jamie Moyer	.15
154	Ichiro Suzuki	1.50
155	Brett Myers	.25
156	Carl Pavano	.15
157	Josh Beckett	.25
158	Randy Johnson	.75
159	Trot Nixon	.15
160	Dmitri Young	.15
161	Jacque Jones	.15
162	Lew Ford	.15
163	Jose Vidro	.15
164	Mark Kotsay	.15
165	A.J. Pierzynski	.15
166	Dewon Brazelton	.15
167	Jeromy Burnitz	.15
168	Johan Santana	.50
169	Greg Maddux	1.00
170	Carl Erskine	.15
171	Robin Roberts	.15
172	Freddy Garcia	.15
173	Carlos Lee	.25
174	Jeff Bagwell	.40
175	Jeff Kent	.25
176	Kazuhisa Ishii	.15
177	Orlando Cabrera	.25
178	Shannon Stewart	.15
179	Mike Cameron	.15
180	Mike Mussina	.40
181	Frank Thomas	.75
182	Jaret Wright	.15
183	Alex Gonzalez/SP	4.00
184	Matt Lawton	.15
185	Derrek Lee	.50
186	Omar Vizquel	.25
187	Jeremy Bonderman	.25
188	Jake Westbrook	.15
189	Zack Greinke/SP	4.00
190	Chad Tracy	.15
191	Rondell White	.15
192	Alex Gonzalez	.15
193	Geoff Jenkins	.15
194	Ralph Kiner	.40
195	Al Leiter	.15
196	Kevin Millwood	.25
197	Jason Kendall	.15
198	Kris Benson	.15
199	Ryan Klesko	.15
200	Mark Loretta	.15
201	Richard Hidalgo	.15
202	Reed Johnson	.15
203	Luis Castillo	.15
204	Jon Zeringue/SP RC	6.00
205	Matt Bush RC	2.00
206	Kurt Suzuki/SP RC	5.00
207	Mark Rogers RC	2.00
208	Jason Vargas/SP RC	5.00
209	Homer Bailey RC	5.00
210	Ray Liotta/SP RC	5.00
211	Eric Campbell RC	2.00
212	Thomas Diamond RC	2.00
213	Gaby Hernandez/SP RC	8.00
214	Neil Walker RC	2.00
215	Bill Bray RC	1.00
216	Wade Davis/SP RC	5.00
217	David Purcey RC	2.00
218	Scott Elbert RC	2.00
219	Josh Fields RC	3.00
220	Josh Johnson/SP RC	4.00
221	Chris Lambert RC	2.00
222	Trevor Plouffe RC	3.00
223	Bruce Froemming	.15
224	Matt Macri/SP RC	5.00
225	Greg Golson RC	2.00
226	Phillip Hughes RC	10.00
227	Kyle Waldrop RC	2.00
228	Matt Tuiasosopo/SP RC	5.00
229	Richie Robnett RC	2.00
230	Taylor Tankersley RC	1.50
231	Blake DeWitt RC	2.50
232	Charlie Reliford	.15
233	Eric Hurley RC	1.00
234	Jordan Parraz/SP RC	4.00
235	J.P. Howell RC	2.00
236	Dana DeMuth	.15
237	Zach Jackson RC	1.00
238	Justin Orenduff RC	1.00
239	Brad Thompson RC	1.00
240	J.C. Holt/SP RC	5.00
241	Matt Fox RC	1.00
242	Danny Putnam RC	1.00
243	Daryl Jones/SP RC	5.00
244	Jon Poterson RC	1.00
245	Gio Gonzalez RC	2.00
246	Lucas Harrell/SP RC	4.00
247	Jerry Crawford	.15
248	Jay Rainville RC	2.00
249	Donnie Smith/SP RC	5.00
250	Huston Street RC	2.00
251	Jeff Marquez RC	1.00
252	Reid Brignac RC	3.00
253	Yusmeiro Petit RC	2.00
254	K.C. Herren RC	1.00
255	Dale Scott	.15
256	Erick San Pedro RC	1.00
257	Ed Montague	.15
258	Billy Buckner RC	1.00
259	Mitch Einertson/SP RC	4.00
260	Aarom Baldiris RC	1.00
261	Conor Jackson	2.00
262	Rick Reed	.15
263	Ervin Santana RC	2.00
264	Gerry Davis	.15
265	Merkin Valdez RC	1.00
266	Joey Gathright RC	1.00
267	Alberto Callaspo RC	.75
268	Carlos Quentin/SP	6.00
269	Gary Darling	.15
270	Jeff Salazar/SP RC	4.00
271	Akinori Otsuka/SP RC	4.00
272	Joe Brinkman	.15
273	Omar Quintanilla	.50
274	Brian Runge	.15
275	Tom Mastny RC	.50
276	John Hirschbeck	.15
277	Warner Madrigal RC	.50
278	Joe West	.15
279	Paul Maholm RC	1.00
280	Larry Young	.15
281	Mike Reilly	.15
282	Kazuo Matsui/SP RC	4.00
283	Randy Marsh	.15
284	Frank Francisco RC	.50
285	Zachary Duke RC	2.00
286	Tim McClelland	.15
287	Jesse Crain	.75
288	Hector Gimenez RC	.50
289	Marland Williams RC	.50
290	Brian Gorman	.15
291	Jose Capellan/SP RC	4.00
292	Tim Welke	.15
293	Javier Guzman RC	.50
294	Paul McAnulty RC	.50
295	Hector Made RC	.50
296	Jon Connolly RC	.50
297	Don Sutton RC	1.00
298	Fausto Carmona RC	1.00
299	Ramon Ramirez RC	.50
300	Brad Snyder	1.00
301	Chin-Lung Hu RC	1.00
302	Rudy Guillen RC	.50
303	Matt Moses	1.00
304	Brad Halsey/SP RC	4.00
305	Erick Aybar RC	1.50
306	Brad Sullivan	1.00
307	Nick Gorneault RC	1.00
308	Craig Ansman RC	1.00
309	Rocky Nolasco	1.00
310	Luke Hughes RC	1.00
311	Danny Gonzalez RC	1.00
312	Josh Labandeira RC	.50
313	Donald Levinski	.50
314	Vince Perkins RC	.50
315	Tommy Murphy RC	.50
316	Chad Bentz RC	.50
317	Chris Shelton RC	2.00
318	Nyjer Morgan/SP RC	4.00
319	Kody Kirkland RC	1.00
320	Blake Hawksworth RC	.50
321	Alex Romero RC	.50
322	Mike Gosling	.50
323	Ryan Budde	.50
324	Kevin Howard RC	.50
325	Wanell Macia RC	.50
326	Travis Blackley RC	1.00
327	Kazuhito Tadano/SP RC	4.00
328	Shingo Takatsu RC	1.00
329	Joaquin Arias RC	1.00
330	Juan Cedeno RC	.75
331	Bobby Brownlie RC	1.00
332	Lastings Milledge	5.00
333	Estee Harris RC	.75
334	Tim Stauffer/SP	5.00
335	Jon Knott	.50
336	David Aardsma	.50
337	Wardell Starling RC	1.00
338	Dioner Navarro RC	1.00
339	Logan Kensing RC	.50
340	Jason Hirsh	1.50
341	Matt Creighton RC	.50
342	Felix Hernandez/SP RC	10.00
343	Kyle Sleeth	.50
344	Dustin Nippert RC	.50
345	Anthony Lerew RC	.50
346	Chris Saenz RC	.50
347	Steve Palermo	.15
348	Barry Bonds	20.00

Abbreviations
SP - Short Print

Black & White

Stars:	2X
SP Stars:	.5-1X
Rookies:	1-2X
SP Rookies:	.5-.75X
Inserted 1:1	

Mohagany

Stars:	15-25X

SP Stars:	3-4X
Rookies:	4-8X
SP Rookies:	3-5X
Production 25 Sets	

Printing Plates
No Pricing
Production One Set

Commissioner's Cut
Production One
FF   Ford Frick   .15

Signs of Authority

	NM/M
Common Autograph:	15.00
Inserted 1:49	
Red Ink:	1.5-2X
Production 55 Sets	
JB Joe Brinkman	15.00
JC Jerry Crawford	15.00
GDA Gary Darling	15.00
GD Gerry Davis	15.00
DD Dana DeMuth	15.00
BF Bruce Froemming	20.00
BG Brian Gorman	15.00
JH John Hirschbeck	15.00
RM Randy Marsh	15.00
TM Tim McClelland	15.00
EM Ed Montague	15.00
SP Steve Palermo	15.00
ER Rick Reed	15.00
MR Mike Reilly	15.00
CM Charlie Reliford	15.00
BR Brian Runge	15.00
DS Dale Scott	20.00
TW Tim Welke	15.00
JW Joe West	20.00
LY Larry Young	15.00

Signs of Glory

	NM/M
Common Autograph:	25.00
Inserted 1:246	
Red Ink:	2X
Production 55 Sets	
GK George Kell	25.00
BK Bob Kuzava	25.00
PR Elwin "Preacher" Roe	30.00
BS Bobby Shantz	25.00
MS Bill "Moose" Skowron	30.00

Signs of Greatness

	NM/M
Common Autograph:	10.00
Inserted 1:57	
Red Ink:	2-4X
Production 55 Sets	
MB Matt Bush	15.00
TD Thomas Diamond	15.00
GG Greg Golson	15.00
PH Phillip Hughes	100.00
CL Chris Lambert	10.00
JM Jeff Marquez	10.00
TP Trevor Plouffe	15.00
JR Jay Rainville	15.00
MR Mark Rogers	15.00
NW Neil Walker	20.00

Threads of Greatness

PAT BURRELL

	NM/M
Common Player:	4.00
Inserted 1:12	
Gold:	2-3X
Production 55 Sets	
MA Moises Alou	5.00
JB Jeff Bagwell	8.00
JB2 Jeff Bagwell	8.00
RB Rocco Baldelli	4.00
TB Tony Batista	4.00
JB Josh Beckett	4.00

JB2	Josh Beckett	4.00
AB	Adrian Beltre	6.00
AGB	Armando Benitez	4.00
LB	Lance Berkman	4.00
LB2	Lance Berkman	6.00
AMB	Angel Berroa	4.00
HB	Hank Blalock	6.00
HB2	Hank Blalock	6.00
WB3	Wade Boggs	8.00
BB	Bret Boone	4.00
BB2	Bret Boone	4.00
PB	Pat Burrell	4.00
MC	Miguel Cabrera	8.00
EC	Eric Chavez	4.00
EC2	Eric Chavez	4.00
RC	Roger Clemens	10.00
BC	Bobby Cox	4.00
JD	Johnny Damon	15.00
CE	Carl Everett	4.00
NG	Nomar Garciaparra	6.00
JG	Jason Giambi	6.00
JG2	Jason Giambi	6.00
JAG	Juan Gonzalez	6.00
RH	Roy Halladay	6.00
TH	Todd Helton	6.00
AJ	Andruw Jones	6.00
DJ	David Justice	4.00
PL	Paul LoDuca	4.00
JL	Javy Lopez	4.00
ML	Mike Lowell	4.00
JM	Joe Mauer	10.00
MCD	Mike McDougal	4.00
KM	Kevin Millwood	4.00
MM	Mark Mulder	4.00
MM2	Mark Mulder	4.00
HN	Hideo Nomo	8.00
JO	John Olerud	4.00
JO2	John Olerud	4.00
AEP	Andy Pettitte	4.00
MP	Mike Piazza	10.00
MP2	Mike Piazza	10.00
AP	Albert Pujols	15.00
AP2	Albert Pujols	15.00
MR	Manny Ramirez	8.00
MR2	Manny Ramirez	8.00
JR	Jose Reyes	10.00
AR	Alex Rodriguez	15.00
CS	C.C. Sabathia	6.00
JDS	Jason Schmidt	6.00
GS	Gary Sheffield	6.00
RS	Ruben Sierra	4.00
JS	John Smoltz	6.00
JS2	John Smoltz	6.00
AS	Alfonso Soriano	8.00
SS	Sammy Sosa	8.00
SS2	Sammy Sosa	8.00
SS3	Sammy Sosa	8.00
MS	Mike Sweeney	4.00
MCT	Mark Teixeira	6.00
MT	Miguel Tejada	6.00
MT2	Miguel Tejada	6.00
MT3	Miguel Tejada	6.00
FT	Frank Thomas	8.00
JT	Jim Thome	8.00
JT2	Jim Thome	8.00
OV	Omar Vizquel	4.00
JW	Jarrod Washburn	4.00
VW	Vernon Wells	6.00
BW	Bernie Williams	6.00
DW	Dontrelle Willis	6.00
KW	Kerry Wood	4.00
KW2	Kerry Wood	4.00
MY	Michael Young	4.00
BZ	Barry Zito	4.00

2004 Bowman Sterling

Common Rookie:		5.00
Pack (5):		60.00
Box (6):		325.00

Rookie Relic Autographs

HB	Homer Bailey RC	40.00
BB	Brian Bixler RC	10.00
MB	Matt Bush RC	15.00
BD	Blake DeWitt RC	20.00
CG	Christian Garcia RC	10.00
SK	Scott Kazmir	35.00
JM	Jeff Marquez RC	10.00
SO	Scott Olsen RC	15.00
TP	Trevor Plouffe RC	20.00
DP	Danny Putnam RC	10.00
HS	Huston Street RC	20.00
TT	Taylor Tankersley RC	10.00
MT	Matt Tuiasosopo RC	15.00
KWA	Kyle Waldrop RC	15.00

Prospect Relic Autographs

RC	Robinson Cano	50.00
CC	Chad Cordero	10.00
DD	David DeJesus	15.00
RH	Ryan Harvey	15.00
CL	Chris Lubanski	15.00
FP	Felix Pie	20.00
BU	B.J. Upton	25.00
AW	Adam Wainwright	20.00
DW	David Wright	50.00

DY	Delmon Young	20.00
ABA	Aarom Baldiris RC	5.00
BBR	Bill Bray RC	5.00
RBR	Reid Brignac RC	15.00
BBU	Billy Buckner RC	5.00
JC	Jose Capellan RC	5.00
FC	Fausto Carmona RC	10.00
JCR	Jesse Crain RC	6.00
TD	Thomas Diamond RC	10.00
ZD	Zachary Duke RC	5.00
ME	Mitch Einertson RC	5.00
BE	Brad Eldred RC	5.00
MF	Mike Ferris RC	5.00
JFI	Josh Fields RC	10.00
MFO	Matt Fox RC	5.00
JG	Joey Gathright RC	5.00
GG	Greg Golson RC	8.00
GIG	Gio Gonzalez RC	10.00
FG	Freddy Guzman RC	5.00
GH	Gaby Hernandez RC	8.00
FH	Felix Hernandez RC	20.00
KCH	K.C. Herren RC	5.00
JH	Jesse Hoover RC	5.00
JPH	J.P. Howell RC	5.00
PH	Phillip Hughes RC	30.00
EH	Eric Hurley RC	5.00
CJ	Conor Jackson	15.00
ZJ	Zach Jackson RC	5.00
CLA	Chris Lambert RC	5.00
CH	Chin-Lung Hu RC	8.00
MMC	Matt Macri RC	5.00
HM	Hector Made RC	5.00
PGM	Paul Maholm RC	6.00
NM	Nyjer Morgan RC	5.00
CN	Chris Nelson RC	8.00
JO	Justin Orenduff RC	5.00
YP	Yusmeiro Petit RC	15.00
DPU	David Purcey RC	5.00
OQ	Omar Quintanilla RC	5.00
MRO	Mark Rogers RC	8.00
ESP	Erick San Pedro RC	5.00
NS	Nate Schierholtz RC	8.00
SSM	Seth Smith RC	8.00
KS	Kurt Suzuki RC	8.00
KT	Kazuhito Tadano RC	5.00
CT	Curtis Thigpen RC	5.00
BT	Brad Thompson RC	5.00
NW	Neil Walker RC	10.00
AWH	Anthony Whittington RC	5.00
MW	Marland Williams RC	5.00
JZ	Jon Zeringue RC	5.00

Rookie Autographs

CA	Chris Aguila RC	8.00
AC	Alberto Callaspo RC	15.00
HG	Hector Gimenez RC	10.00
BH	Blake Hawksworth RC	10.00
LH	Lincoln Holdzkom RC	10.00
RM	Ryan Meaux RC	8.00
MM	Matt Moses RC	10.00
VP	Vince Perkins RC	8.00
CQ	Carlos Quentin	25.00
JR	Jay Rainville RC	10.00
AR	Alex Romero RC	8.00
MR	Mike Rouse RC	8.00
JS	Jeremy Sowers RC	15.00
AZ	Alec Zumwalt RC	8.00

Relics

		5.00
MA	Moises Alou	5.00
JB	Jeff Bagwell	8.00
RB	Rocco Baldelli	5.00
CIB	Carlos Beltran	10.00
LB	Lance Berkman	5.00
AB	Angel Berroa	5.00
CB	Craig Biggio	5.00
HJB	Hank Blalock	5.00
MC	Miguel Cabrera	8.00
LC	Luis Castillo	5.00
HC	Hee Seop Choi	5.00
BC2	Bobby Crosby	5.00
JD	Johnny Damon	10.00
AD	Adam Dunn	8.00
JE	Johnny Estrada	5.00
EG	Eric Gagne	5.00
TG	Troy Glaus	5.00
TMG	Tom Glavine	8.00
VG	Vladimir Guerrero	10.00
TLH	Todd Helton	8.00
RJH	Richard Hidalgo	5.00
NJ	Nick Johnson	5.00
AJ	Andruw Jones	8.00
AK	Austin Kearns	5.00
JK	Jason Kendall	5.00
PL	Paul LoDuca	5.00
TM	Tino Martinez	5.00
MAM	Mark Mulder	5.00
LN	Laynce Nix	5.00
RO	Russ Ortiz	5.00
RP	Rafael Palmeiro	6.00
MJP	Mike Piazza	10.00
JP	Juan Pierre	5.00
MP	Mark Prior	8.00
AP	Albert Pujols	20.00
ANR	Aramis Ramirez	8.00

MAR	Manny Ramirez	8.00
PR	Pokey Reese	5.00
AER	Alex Rodriguez	15.00
IR	Ivan Rodriguez	8.00
GS	Gary Sheffield	8.00
SS	Sammy Sosa	10.00
MCT	Mark Teixeira	5.00
MT1	Miguel Tejada/bat	8.00
MT2	Miguel Tejada/jsy	8.00
FT	Frank Thomas	10.00
BW	Bernie Williams	8.00
DWW	Dontrelle Willis	5.00
KW	Kerry Wood	5.00
MY	Michael Young	5.00

Refractors

Regular Rookies:	1.5-2X
Rookie Relic Autos.:	1-2X
Rookie Autos.:	1-2X
Prospect Relic Autos.:	1-2X
Relics:	1-2X
Production 199 Sets	

Black Refractors

No Pricing
Production 25 Sets

Red Refractor

No Pricing
Production One Set

Uncirculated

No Pricing
Production 16 Sets

Autographed Originals

No Pricing

2004 Bowman's Best

		NM/M
Complete Set:		
Common Player:		.25
Pack (5):		15.00
Box (10):		125.00

First-Year Players

Common Rookie		1.00
JJC	Jon Connolly RC	2.00
JRG	Joey Gathright RC	2.00
DG	Danny Gonzalez RC	1.00
NG	Nick Gorneault RC	1.00
MG	Mike Gosling RC	1.00
CH	Chin-Lung Hu RC	2.00
TJ	Terry Jones	1.00
AL	Anthony Lerew RC	1.00
HM	Hector Made RC	2.00
WM	Warner Madrigal RC	2.00
PMM	Paul McAnulty RC	2.00
AO	Akinori Otsuka RC	1.00
TS	Todd Self RC	1.00
KS	Kyle Sleeth RC	1.00
DS	Don Sutton RC	1.00

Veterans		
GA	Garret Anderson	.25
CB	Carlos Beltran	.75
HB	Hank Blalock	.50
MTC	Miguel Cabrera	1.00
EC	Eric Chavez	.50
RC	Roger Clemens	2.50
CD	Carlos Delgado	.50
NAG	Nomar Garciaparra	1.00
JGG	Jason Giambi	.75
BG	Brian Giles	.25
VG	Vladimir Guerrero	1.00
TLH	Todd Helton	.75
RJ	Randy Johnson	1.00
LWJ	Chipper Jones	1.00
JLO	Javy Lopez	.25
MO	Magglio Ordonez	.25
LO	Lyle Overbay	.25
MJP	Mike Piazza	1.50
JP	Jorge Posada	.50
MWP	Mark Prior	.75
AP	Albert Pujols	3.00
MAR	Manny Ramirez	1.00
AER	Alex Rodriguez	2.50
IR	Ivan Rodriguez	.75
SR	Scott Rolen	1.00
CMS	Curt Schilling	1.00
JDS	Jason Schmidt	.50
RS	Richie Sexson	.50
AS	Alfonso Soriano	1.00
SS	Sammy Sosa	1.00
IS	Ichiro Suzuki	2.00
MT	Miguel Tejada	.50
JT	Jim Thome	.75
JAV	Jose Vidro	.25
MY	Michael Young	.25

First-Year Player Autographs

Common Autograph:		8.00
DA	David Aardsma	10.00
CMA	Craig Ansman RC	10.00
JA	Joaquin Arias RC	10.00
EA	Erick Aybar RC	15.00
BB	Bobby Brownlie RC	10.00
RB	Ryan Budde RC	10.00
KC	Kory Casto	10.00
JC	Juan Cedeno RC	10.00
VC	Vito Chiaravalloti RC	10.00
MDC	Matt Creighton RC	8.00
DC	David Crouthers	10.00
TD	Tyler Davidson	10.00
ZD	Zachary Duke RC	15.00
JE	Jesse English RC	10.00
AG	Adam Greenberg	10.00
RG	Rudy Guillen RC	10.00
TOH	Travis Hanson	10.00
EH	Estee Harris RC	10.00
FH	Felix Hernandez RC	75.00
SH	Shawn Hill	10.00
JH	Jason Hirsh	15.00
LTH	Luke Hughes RC	8.00
CJ	Conor Jackson	25.00
LK	Logan Kensing RC	10.00
JK	Jon Knott RC	10.00
KK	Kevin Kouzmanoff	20.00
JL	Josh Labandeira RC	8.00
DL	Donald Levinski	10.00
PM	Paul Maholm RC	15.00
TRM	Tom Mastny RC	10.00
BEM	Brandon Medders RC	8.00
LM	Lastings Milledge	50.00
YM	Yadier Molina RC	20.00
DM	David Murphy	15.00
DN	Dioner Navarro RC	10.00
DDN	Dustin Nippert RC	15.00
RN	Ricky Nolasco	15.00
BP	Brayan Pena RC	8.00
QQ	Omar Quintanilla	10.00
RR	Ramon Ramirez RC	10.00
JS	Jeff Salazar RC	10.00
ES	Ervin Santana RC	15.00
BMS	Brad Snyder	15.00
WS	Wardell Starling RC	8.00
TJS	Tim Stauffer	10.00
BS	Brad Sullivan	10.00
JSZ	Jason Szuminski RC	10.00
RT	Rob Tejeda RC	10.00
NU	Nic Ungs RC	10.00
MV	Merkin Valdez RC	10.00
CZ	Charlie Zink RC	10.00

First-Year Player Relics

TB	Travis Blackley RC	5.00
KRK	Kody Kirkland RC	6.00
KM	Kazuo Matsui RC	6.00
KT	Kazuhito Tadano RC	6.00
ST	Shingo Takatsu RC	8.00

Green

Green Stars:	4-8X
Green Non-Auto. RC's:	1.5-3X
Production 100	
Green RC Autos.:	1-2X

Red

Red Stars:	No Pricing

Production 20
Red Non-Auto. RC's: No Pricing
Red RC Autos.: No Pricing

Double Play Autographs

		NM/M
Common Duo:		20.00
Inserted 1:33		
MH	Lastings Milledge, Estee Harris	40.00
QS	Omar Quintanilla, Brad Snyder	20.00
SC	Tim Stauffer, Vito Chiaravalloti	20.00
HJ	Travis Hanson, Conor Jackson	25.00
MN	Brandon Medders, Dustin Nippert	20.00
UK	Nic Ungs, Kevin Kouzmanoff	25.00
CC	Matt Creighton, David Crouthers	20.00
EN	Jesse English, Ricky Nolasco	20.00
SV	Ervin Santana, Merkin Valdez	30.00
SK	Jeff Salazar, Jon Knott	20.00

Triple Play Autographs

		NM/M
Common Trio:		30.00
Inserted 1:109		
CBA	Juan Cedeno, Bobby Brownlie, Joaquin Arias	30.00
ALS	David Aardsma, Donald Levinski, Brad Sullivan	25.00
SSV	Tim Stauffer, Ervin Santana, Merkin Valdez	50.00

2005 Bowman

		NM/M
Complete Set (330):		60.00
Common Player:		.15
Common Rookie:		.50
Pack (10):		3.00
Box (24):		60.00
1	Gavin Floyd	.15
2	Eric Chavez	.25
3	Miguel Tejada	.50
4	Dmitri Young	.15
5	Hank Blalock	.25
6	Kerry Wood	.25
7	Andy Pettitte	.40
8	Pat Burrell	.25
9	Johnny Estrada	.15
10	Frank Thomas	.50
11	Juan Pierre	.25
12	Tom Glavine	.40
13	Lyle Overbay	.25
14	Jim Edmonds	.40
15	Steve Finley	.15
16	Jermaine Dye	.25
17	Omar Vizquel	.15
18	Nick Johnson	.15
19	Brian Giles	.25
20	Justin Morneau	.50
21	Preston Wilson	.15
22	Wily Mo Pena	.15
23	Rafael Palmeiro	.50
24	Scott Kazmir	.25
25	Derek Jeter	2.00
26	Barry Zito	.25
27	Mike Lowell	.15
28	Jason Bay	.25
29	Ken Harvey	.15
30	Nomar Garciaparra	.75
31	Roy Halladay	.25
32	Todd Helton	.50
33	Mark Kotsay	.15
34	Jake Peavy	.40
35	David Wright	1.00
36	Dontrelle Willis	.40
37	Marcus Giles	.15
38	Chone Figgins	.15
39	Sidney Ponson	.15
40	Randy Johnson	.75
41	John Smoltz	.15
42	Kevin Millar	.15
43	Mark Teixeira	.50
44	Alex Rios	.25
45	Mike Piazza	1.00
46	Victor Martinez	.25
47	Jeff Bagwell	.50
48	Shawn Green	.25
49	Ivan Rodriguez	.50
50	Alex Rodriguez	1.50
51	Kazuo Matsui	.15
52	Mark Mulder	.40
53	Michael Young	.25
54	Javy Lopez	.15
55	Johnny Damon	.75
56	Jeff Francis	.25
57	Rich Harden	.25
58	Bobby Abreu	.40
59	Mark Loretta	.15
60	Gary Sheffield	.40
61	Jamie Moyer	.15
62	Garret Anderson	.25
63	Vernon Wells	.25
64	Orlando Cabrera	.25
65	Magglio Ordonez	.15
66	Ronnie Belliard	.15
67	Carlos Lee	.25
68	Carl Pavano	.15
69	Jon Lieber	.15
70	Aubrey Huff	.15
71	Rocco Baldelli	.25
72	Jason Schmidt	.25
73	Bernie Williams	.40
74	Hideki Matsui	1.50
75	Ken Griffey Jr.	1.50
76	Josh Beckett	.25
77	Mark Buehrle	.15
78	David Ortiz	.75
79	Luis Gonzalez	.25
80	Scott Rolen	.75
81	Joe Mauer	.75
82	Jose Reyes	.75
83	Adam Dunn	.25
84	Greg Maddux	1.00
85	Bartolo Colon	.15
86	Bret Boone	.15
87	Mike Mussina	.50
88	Ben Sheets	.40
89	Lance Berkman	.40
90	Miguel Cabrera	.75
91	C.C. Sabathia	.25
92	Mike Maroth	.15
93	Andruw Jones	.50
94	Jack Wilson	.15
95	Ichiro Suzuki	1.50
96	Geoff Jenkins	.15
97	Zack Greinke	.25
98	Jorge Posada	.40
99	Travis Hafner	.40
100	Barry Bonds	2.00
101	Aaron Rowand	.15
102	Aramis Ramirez	.40
103	Curt Schilling	.75
104	Melvin Mora	.15
105	Albert Pujols	2.00
106	Austin Kearns	.25
107	Shannon Stewart	.15
108	Carl Crawford	.40
109	Carlos Zambrano	.25
110	Roger Clemens	2.00
111	Javier Vazquez	.15
112	Randy Wolf	.15
113	Chipper Jones	.75
114	Larry Walker	.25
115	Alfonso Soriano	.75
116	Brad Wilkerson	.15
117	Bobby Crosby	.25
118	Jim Thome	.75
119	Oliver Perez	.25
120	Vladimir Guerrero	.75
121	Roy Oswalt	.40
122	Torii Hunter	.25
123	Rafael Furcal	.25
124	Luis Castillo	.15
125	Carlos Beltran	.50
126	Mike Sweeney	.15
127	Johan Santana	.50
128	Tim Hudson	.40
129	Troy Glaus	.25
130	Manny Ramirez	.75
131	Jeff Kent	.25
132	Jose Vidro	.15
133	Edgar Renteria	.25
134	Russ Ortiz	.15
135	Sammy Sosa	.75
136	Carlos Delgado	.40
137	Richie Sexson	.25
138	Pedro Martinez	.75
139	Adrian Beltre	.25
140	Mark Prior	.40
141	Omar Quintanilla	.15
142	Carlos Quentin	.25
143	Dan Johnson	.15
144	Jake Stevens	.15
145	Nate Schierholtz	.15
146	Neil Walker	.15
147	Bill Bray	.15
148	Taylor Tankersley	.15
149	Trevor Plouffe	.15
150	Felix Hernandez	.50
151	Phillip Hughes	.50
152	James Houser	.15
153	David Murphy	.15
154	Ervin Santana	.15
155	Anthony Whittington	.15
156	Chris Lambert	.15
157	Jeremy Sowers	.15
158	Gio Gonzalez	.15
159	Blake DeWitt	.15
160	Thomas Diamond	.15
161	Greg Golson	.15
162	David Aardsma	.15
163	Paul Maholm	.15
164	Mark Rogers	.15
165	Homer Bailey	.50
166	Chip Cannon RC	1.00
167	Tony Giarratano RC	.75
168	Darren Fenster RC	.50
169	Elvys Quezada RC	.75
170	Glen Perkins RC	1.00
171	Ian Kinsler RC	3.00
172	Michael Bourn RC	1.00
173	Jeremy West RC	.75
174	Justin Verlander RC	3.00
175	Kevin West RC	.50
176	Luis Hernandez RC	1.00
177	Matt Campbell RC	.75
178	Nate McLouth RC	.50
179	Ryan Goleski RC	.50
180	Matt Lindstrom RC	.50
181	Matt DeSalvo RC	1.00
182	Kole Strayhorn RC	.50
183	Jose Vaquedano RC	.50
184	James Jurries RC	.50
185	Ian Bladergroen RC	.75
186	Eric Nielsen RC	.75
187	Chris Vines RC	1.00
188	Chris Denorfia RC	.50
189	Kevin Melillo RC	.50
190	Melky Cabrera RC	2.00
191	Ryan Sweeney RC	1.50
192	Sean Marshall RC	1.00
193	Andy LaRoche RC	3.00
194	Tyler Pelland RC	1.50
195	Mike Morse RC	.75
196	Wes Swackhamer RC	.50
197	Wade Robinson RC	.50
198	Dan Santin RC	.50
199	Steven Doetsch RC	.50
200	Shane Costa RC	.50
201	Scott Mathieson RC	.50
202	Ben Jones RC	.75
203	Michael Rogers RC	.50
204	Matt Rogelstad RC	.50
205	Luis Ramirez RC	1.00
206	Landon Powell RC	.75
207	Erik Cordier RC	1.00
208	Chris Seddon RC	.50
209	Chris Roberson RC	.75
210	Tom Oldham RC	.50
211	Dana Eveland RC	1.00
212	Cody Haerther RC	.50
213	Danny Core RC	.50
214	Craig Tatum RC	.75
215	Elliot Johnson RC	.75
216	Ender Chavez RC	.75
217	Errol Simonitsch RC	.75
218	Matt Van Der Bosch RC	.75
219	Eulogio de la Cruz RC	.50
220	C.J. Smith RC	.50
221	Adam Boeve RC	.75
222	Adam Harben RC	.75
223	Baltazar Lopez RC	.75
224	Russ Martin RC	2.50
225	Brian Bannister RC	1.00
226	Brian Miller RC	.50
227	Casey McGehee RC	.50
228	Humberto Sanchez RC	1.50
229	Javon Moran RC	.50
230	Brandon McCarthy RC	1.50
231	Danny Zell RC	.50
232	Jake Postlewait RC	.50
233	Juan Tejeda RC	.50
234	Keith Ramsey RC	.50
235	Lorenzo Scott RC	.75
236	Wladimir Balentien RC	1.50
237	Martin Prado RC	.50
238	Matt Albers RC	1.00
239	Brian Schweiger RC	.50
240	Brian Stavisky RC	.50
241	Pat Misch RC	.50
242	Pat Osborn RC	.50
243	Ryan Feierabend RC	1.00
244	Shaun Marcum RC	.50
245	Kevin Collins RC	.50
246	Stuart Pomeranz RC	.50
247	Tetsu Yofu RC	.75
248	Hernan Iribarren RC	1.00
249	Mike Spiegel RC	.50
250	Tony Arnerich RC	.50
251	Manny Parra RC	.75
252	Drew Anderson RC	.75
253	T.J. Beam RC	1.00
254	Pedro Lopez RC	.75
255	Andy Sides RC	.75
256	Bear Bay RC	.50
257	Bill McCarthy RC	1.00
258	Daniel Haigwood RC	1.50
259	Brian Sprout RC	.75
260	Bryan Triplett RC	.75
261	Steve Bondurant RC	.50
262	Darwinson Salazar RC	.75
263	David Shepard RC	.50
264	Johan Silva RC	.75
265	J.B. Thurmond RC	.50
266	Brandon Moorhead RC	.50
267	Kyle Nichols RC	.50
268	Jonathan Sanchez RC	1.00
269	Mike Esposito RC	.50
270	Erik Schindewolf RC	.75
271	Peeter Ramos RC	.75
272	Juan Senreiso RC	.50
273	Matthew Kemp RC	3.00
274	Vinny Rottino RC	.50
275	Micah Furtado RC	.50
276	George Kottaras RC	1.00
277	Billy Butler RC	5.00
278	Buck Coats RC	.50
279	Ken Durost RC	.50
280	Nic Touchstone RC	.50
281	Jerry Owens RC	1.00
282	Stefan Bailie RC	.50
283	Jesse Gutierrez RC	.75
284	Chuck Tiffany RC	1.00
285	Brendan Ryan RC	.50
286	Hayden Penn RC	2.00
287	Shawn Bowman RC	.50
288	Alexander Smit RC	.50
289	Micah Schnurstein RC	.75
290	Jared Gothreaux RC	.50
291	Jair Jurrjens RC	1.50
292	Bobby Livingston RC	.75
293	Ryan Speier RC	.50
294	Zachary Parker RC	.50
295	Christian Colonel RC	.75
296	Scott Mitchinson RC	.50
297	Neil Wilson RC	.50
298	Chuck James RC	2.00
299	Heath Totten RC	.50
300	Sean Tracey RC	.75
301	Ismael Ramirez RC	.50
302	Matt Brown RC	.50
303	Franklin Morales RC	1.00
304	Brandon Sing RC	1.00
305	D.J. Houlton RC	.50
306	Jayce Tingler RC	.50
307	Mitchell Arnold RC	.50
308	Jim Burt RC	.75
309	Jason Motte RC	.50
310	David Gassner RC	.75
311	Andy Santana RC	.50
312	Kelvin Pichardo RC	.50
313	Carlos Carrasco RC	1.50
314	Willy Mota RC	.50
315	Frank Mata RC	.50
316	Carlos Gonzalez RC	2.50
317	Jeff Niemann RC	1.00
318	Chris Young RC	3.00
319	Billy Sadler RC	.50
320	Ricky Barrett RC	.50
321	Benjamin Harrison RC	.50
322	Steve Nelson RC	.50
323	Daryl Thompson RC	.75
324	Philip Humber RC	1.50
325	Jeremy Harts RC	.50
326	Nick Masset RC	.50
327	Mike Rodriguez RC	.50
328	Mike Garber RC	.50
329	Kennard Bibbs RC	.50
330	Ryan Garko RC	1.50

Gold

Stars:	1-2X
Rookies:	1-2X
Inserted 1:1	

White

Stars:	3-6X
Rookies:	3-6X
Production 240 Sets	

Printing Plates

No Pricing
Production One Set

1st Edition

		NM/M
Stars:		3-5X
Rookies:		1-2X
HTA Exclusive		
Pack (10):		3.50
Box (20):		60.00

A-Rod Throwbacks

		NM/M
Complete Set (4):		6.00
Common A-Rod:		2.00
94-AR	Alex Rodriguez	2.00
95-AR	Alex Rodriguez	2.00
96-AR	Alex Rodriguez	2.00
97-AR	Alex Rodriguez	2.00

A-Rod Throwbacks Autographs

		NM/M
Production 1-225		
96A-AR	Alex Rodriguez/99	150.00
97A-AR	Alex Rodriguez/225	150.00

A-Rod Throwbacks Relic

		NM/M
Quantity produced listed		
96R-AR	Alex Rodriguez/99	20.00
97R-AR	Alex Rodriguez/800	15.00

Autographed Base Card Variations

		NM/M
	Inserted 1:1,599	
141	Omar Quintanilla	8.00
142	Carlos Quentin	20.00
143	Dan Johnson	10.00
144	Jake Stevens	10.00
145	Nate Schierholtz	10.00
146	Neil Walker	15.00
147	Bill Bray	8.00
148	Taylor Tankersley	10.00
149	Trevor Plouffe	12.00
150	Felix Hernandez	30.00
151	Phillip Hughes	50.00
152	James Houser	10.00
153	David Murphy	15.00
154	Ervin Santana	15.00
155	Anthony Whittington	8.00
156	Chris Lambert	12.00
157	Jeremy Sowers	15.00
158	Gio Gonzalez	15.00
159	Blake DeWitt	15.00
160	Thomas Diamond	15.00
161	Greg Golson	12.00
162	David Aardsma	10.00
163	Paul Maholm	12.00
164	Mark Rogers	15.00
165	Homer Bailey	25.00

Dual Rookie of the Year Relic

		NM/M
Inserted 1:668		
ROY-BC	Jason Bay, Bobby Crosby	15.00

Futures Game Gear

		NM/M
JB	Joe Blanton	5.00
BB	Bryan Bullington	5.00
MC	Matt Cain	5.00
SC	Shin-Soo Choo	6.00
JCO	Jorge Cortes	5.00
JC	Jesus Cota	5.00
EE	Edwin Encarnacion	5.00
CE	Clint Everts	5.00
GF	Gavin Floyd	5.00
JF	Jeff Francis	5.00
JG	Jairo Garcia	5.00
RG	Ruben Gotay	5.00
JGU	Joel Guzman	5.00
AH	Aaron Hill	5.00
KH	Koyie Hill	5.00
WL	Wilfredo Ledezma	5.00
VM	Val Majewski	5.00
AMA	Andy Marte	8.00
JM	Jeff Mathis	5.00
DM	Dallas McPherson	8.00
JMO	Justin Morneau	8.00
AM	Arnie Munoz	5.00
YP	Yusmeiro Petit	8.00
FP	Felix Pie	8.00
RW	Rickie Weeks	8.00

Relic Base Card Variations

		NM/M
	Inserted 1:50	
2	Eric Chavez	5.00
5	Hank Blalock	8.00
23	Rafael Palmeiro	8.00
43	Mark Teixeira	8.00
49	Ivan Rodriguez	8.00
50	Alex Rodriguez	15.00
60	Gary Sheffield	8.00
65	Magglio Ordonez	5.00
78	David Ortiz	10.00
83	Adam Dunn	8.00
90	Miguel Cabrera	8.00
93	Andruw Jones	5.00
100	Barry Bonds	25.00
104	Melvin Mora	5.00
105	Albert Pujols	20.00
115	Alfonso Soriano	8.00
120	Vladimir Guerrero	8.00
125	Carlos Beltran	10.00
130	Manny Ramirez	8.00
135	Sammy Sosa	12.00

Signs of the Future

		NM/M
BB	Brian Bixler	10.00
MC	Melky Cabrera	25.00
RC	Robinson Cano	45.00
CC	Chad Cordero	10.00
BC	Bobby Crosby	15.00
BD	Blake DeWitt	20.00
CG	Christian Garcia	10.00
TG	Tom Gorzelanny	10.00
PH	Phillip Hughes	40.00
TH	Tim Hutting	10.00
SK	Scott Kazmir	15.00
AL	Adam Loewen	10.00
PM	Paul Maholm	10.00
DM	Dallas McPherson	10.00
SO	Scott Olson	10.00
TP	Trevor Plouffe	15.00
DP	Dan Putnam	10.00
JR	Jay Rainville	15.00
RR	Richie Robnett	8.00
ES	Ervin Santana	15.00
JS	Jay Sborz	10.00
BMS	Brad Snyder	10.00
HS	Huston Street	25.00
BS	Brad Sullivan	10.00
TT	Taylor Tankersley	12.00
RW	Ryan Wagner	10.00
KW	Kyle Waldrop	10.00
AW	Anthony Whittington	10.00
DW	David Wright	70.00

Two of a Kind Autograph

No Pricing
Production 13

2005 Bowman Chrome

		NM/M
Complete Set (352):		
Common Player:		.25
Common Rookie:		1.00
Common RC Auto.		
(331-352):		10.00
Pack (4):		8.00
Box (18):		125.00
1	Gavin Floyd	.25
2	Eric Chavez	.50
3	Miguel Tejada	.75
4	Dmitri Young	.25
5	Hank Blalock	.50
6	Kerry Wood	.50
7	Andy Pettitte	.50
8	Pat Burrell	.50
9	Johnny Estrada	.25
10	Frank Thomas	.75
11	Juan Pierre	.25
12	Tom Glavine	.50
13	Lyle Overbay	.25
14	Jim Edmonds	.50
15	Steve Finley	.25
16	Jermaine Dye	.25
17	Omar Vizquel	.25
18	Nick Johnson	.25
19	Brian Giles	.25
20	Justin Morneau	.50
21	Preston Wilson	.25
22	Wily Mo Pena	.25
23	Rafael Palmeiro	.75
24	Scott Kazmir	.50
25	Derek Jeter	3.00
26	Barry Zito	.50
27	Mike Lowell	.25
28	Jason Bay	.50
29	Ken Harvey	.25
30	Nomar Garciaparra	1.00
31	Roy Halladay	.50
32	Todd Helton	.75
33	Mark Kotsay	.25
34	Jake Peavy	.50
35	David Wright	1.00
36	Dontrelle Willis	.50
37	Marcus Giles	.25
38	Chone Figgins	.25
39	Sidney Ponson	.25
40	Randy Johnson	1.00
41	John Smoltz	.50
42	Kevin Millar	.25
43	Mark Teixeira	.75
44	Alex Rios	.25
45	Mike Piazza	1.00
46	Victor Martinez	.50
47	Jeff Bagwell	.75
48	Shawn Green	.50
49	Ivan Rodriguez	.75
50	Alex Rodriguez	2.50
51	Kazuo Matsui	.25
52	Mark Mulder	.50
53	Michael Young	.50
54	Javy Lopez	.25
55	Johnny Damon	1.00
56	Jeff Francis	.25
57	Rich Harden	.50
58	Bobby Abreu	.50
59	Mark Loretta	.25
60	Gary Sheffield	.50
61	Jamie Moyer	.25
62	Garret Anderson	.50
63	Vernon Wells	.50
64	Orlando Cabrera	.25
65	Magglio Ordonez	.25
66	Ronnie Belliard	.25
67	Carlos Lee	.50
68	Carl Pavano	.25
69	Jon Lieber	.25
70	Aubrey Huff	.25
71	Rocco Baldelli	.25
72	Jason Schmidt	.50
73	Bernie Williams	.50
74	Hideki Matsui	2.00
75	Ken Griffey Jr.	2.00
76	Josh Beckett	.50
77	Mark Buehrle	.40
78	David Ortiz	1.00
79	Luis Gonzalez	.25
80	Scott Rolen	1.00
81	Joe Mauer	.75
82	Jose Reyes	.75
83	Adam Dunn	.75
84	Greg Maddux	2.00
85	Bartolo Colon	.40
86	Bret Boone	.25
87	Mike Mussina	.50
88	Ben Sheets	.50
89	Lance Berkman	.50
90	Miguel Cabrera	1.00
91	C.C. Sabathia	.25
92	Mark Maroth	.25
93	Andruw Jones	.50
94	Jack Wilson	.25
95	Ichiro Suzuki	2.00
96	Geoff Jenkins	.25
97	Zack Greinke	.25
98	Jorge Posada	.50
99	Travis Hafner	.50
100	Barry Bonds	3.00
101	Aaron Rowand	.25
102	Aramis Ramirez	.50
103	Curt Schilling	1.00
104	Melvin Mora	.25
105	Albert Pujols	3.00
106	Austin Kearns	.40
107	Shannon Stewart	.25
108	Carl Crawford	.50
109	Carlos Zambrano	.50
110	Roger Clemens	3.00
111	Javier Vazquez	.25
112	Randy Wolf	.25
113	Chipper Jones	1.00
114	Larry Walker	.50
115	Alfonso Soriano	1.00
116	Brad Wilkerson	.25
117	Bobby Crosby	.25
118	Jim Thome	.75
119	Oliver Perez	.25
120	Vladimir Guerrero	1.00
121	Roy Oswalt	.50
122	Torii Hunter	.40
123	Rafael Furcal	.25
124	Luis Castillo	.25
125	Carlos Beltran	.75
126	Mike Sweeney	.25
127	Johan Santana	.75
128	Tim Hudson	.50
129	Troy Glaus	.50
130	Manny Ramirez	1.00
131	Jeff Kent	.40
132	Jose Vidro	.25

#	Player	Price
133	Edgar Renteria	.40
134	Russ Ortiz	.25
135	Sammy Sosa	1.00
136	Carlos Delgado	.50
137	Richie Sexson	.50
138	Pedro Martinez	1.00
139	Adrian Beltre	.50
140	Mark Prior	.75
141	Omar Quintanilla	.25
142	Carlos Quentin	.25
143	Dan Johnson	.25
144	Jake Stevens	.25
145	Nate Schierholtz	.25
146	Neil Walker	.25
147	Bill Bray	.25
148	Taylor Tankersley	.25
149	Trevor Plouffe	.25
150	Felix Hernandez	1.00
151	Phillip Hughes	.50
152	James Houser	.25
153	David Murphy	.25
154	Ervin Santana	.25
155	Anthony Whittington	.25
156	Chris Lambert	.25
157	Jeremy Sowers	.25
158	Gio Gonzalez	.25
159	Blake DeWitt	.25
160	Thomas Diamond	.25
161	Greg Golson	.25
162	David Aardsma	.25
163	Paul Maholm	.25
164	Mark Rogers	.25
165	Homer Bailey	.50
166	Elvin Puello RC	1.00
167	Tony Giarratano RC	1.50
168	Darren Fenster RC	1.00
169	Elvys Quezada RC	1.00
170	Glen Perkins RC	2.50
171	Ian Kinsler RC	10.00
172	Adam Bostick RC	1.00
173	Jeremy West RC	2.00
174	Brett Harper RC	2.00
175	Kevin West RC	1.00
176	Luis Hernandez RC	1.00
177	Matt Campbell RC	1.00
178	Nate McLouth RC	1.50
179	Ryan Goleski RC	2.00
180	Matt Lindstrom RC	1.00
181	Matt DeSalvo RC	3.00
182	Kole Strayhorn RC	1.00
183	Jose Vaquedano RC	1.00
184	James Jurries RC	2.00
185	Ian Bladergroen RC	2.50
186	Kila Kaaihue RC	4.00
187	Luke Scott RC	4.00
188	Chris Denorfia RC	3.00
189	Jai Miller RC	1.50
190	Melky Cabrera RC	6.00
191	Ryan Sweeney RC	4.00
192	Sean Marshall RC	2.00
193	Eric Abreu RC	2.00
194	Tyler Pelland RC	1.50
195	Cole Armstrong RC	1.50
196	John Hudgins RC	1.00
197	Wade Robinson RC	1.00
198	Dan Santin RC	1.50
199	Steven Doetsch RC	1.50
200	Shane Costa RC	1.00
201	Scott Mathieson RC	2.00
202	Ben Jones RC	2.00
203	Michael Rogers RC	1.00
204	Matt Rogelstad RC	1.50
205	Luis Ramirez RC	1.00
206	Landon Powell RC	2.00
207	Erik Cordier RC	1.50
208	Chris Seddon RC	1.00
209	Chris Roberson RC	1.50
210	Tom Oldham RC	1.00
211	Dana Eveland RC	2.50
212	Cody Haerther RC	1.00
213	Danny Core RC	1.00
214	Craig Tatum RC	1.00
215	Elliot Johnson RC	2.50
216	Ender Chavez RC	1.00
217	Errol Simonitsch RC	1.50
218	Matt Van Der Bosch RC	1.00
219	Eulogio de la Cruz RC	1.00
220	Drew Toussaint RC	1.50
221	Adam Boeve RC	2.00
222	Adam Harben RC	1.50
223	Baltazar Lopez RC	2.00
224	Russell Martin RC	8.00
225	Brian Bannister RC	2.00
226	Chris Walker RC	1.00
227	Casey McGehee RC	1.50
228	Humberto Sanchez RC	6.00
229	Javon Moran RC	1.00
230	Brandon McCarthy RC	2.00
231	Danny Zell RC	1.00
232	Kevin Barry RC	1.00
233	Juan Tejeda RC	1.50
234	Keith Ramsey RC	1.00
235	Lorenzo Scott RC	1.00
236	Jonathan Barratt RC	1.00
237	Martin Prado RC	2.00
238	Matt Albers RC	3.00
239	Brian Schweiger RC	1.00
240	Raul Tablado RC	1.00
241	Pat Misch RC	1.00
242	Pat Osborn RC	1.00
243	Ryan Feierabend RC	1.00
244	Shaun Marcum RC	1.00
245	Kevin Collins RC	1.00
246	Stuart Pomeranz RC	1.00
247	Tetsu Yofu RC	1.00
248	Hernan Iribarren RC	3.00
249	Michael Spidale RC	1.00
250	Tony Americh RC	1.00
251	Manny Parra RC	1.00
252	Drew Anderson RC	1.00
253	T.J. Beam RC	3.00
254	Claudio Arias RC	2.00
255	Andy Sides RC	1.00
256	Bear Bay RC	2.00
257	Bill McCarthy RC	1.00
258	Daniel Haigwood RC	2.00
259	Brian Sprout RC	1.00
260	Bryan Triplett RC	1.00
261	Steve Bondurant RC	1.00
262	Darwinson Salazar RC	1.00
263	David Shepard RC	1.00
264	Johan Silva RC	1.50
265	J.B. Thurmond RC	1.00
266	Brandon Moorhead RC	1.00
267	Kyle Nichols RC	2.00
268	Jonathan Sanchez RC	3.00
269	Mike Esposito RC	1.00
270	Erik Schindewolf RC	1.00
271	Peeter Ramos RC	1.00
272	Juan Senreiso RC	1.00
273	Travis Chick RC	2.00
274	Vinny Rottino RC	1.00
275	Micah Furtado RC	1.00
276	George Kottaras RC	2.00
277	Abel Gomez RC	1.50
278	Buck Coats RC	1.00
279	Ken Durost RC	1.00
280	Nick Touchstone RC	1.00
281	Jerry Owens RC	1.00
282	Stefan Bailie RC	1.00
283	Jesse Gutierrez RC	1.00
284	Chuck Tiffany RC	3.00
285	Brendan Ryan RC	1.50
286	Julio Pimentel RC	1.50
287	Shawn Bowman RC	1.50
288	Alexander Smit RC	1.50
289	Micah Schnurstein RC	1.50
290	Jared Gothreaux RC	1.00
291	Jair Jurrjens RC	4.00
292	Bobby Livingston RC	1.00
293	Ryan Speier RC	1.00
294	Zachary Parker RC	1.00
295	Christian Colonel RC	1.00
296	Scott Mitchinson RC	1.00
297	Neil Wilson RC	1.00
298	Chuck James RC	5.00
299	Heath Totten RC	1.00
300	Sean Tracey RC	1.00
301	Tadahito Iguchi RC	2.50
302	Matt Brown RC	1.00
303	Franklin Morales RC	3.00
304	Brandon Sing RC	3.00
305	D.J. Houlton RC	1.50
306	Jayce Tingler RC	1.00
307	Mitchell Arnold RC	1.00
308	Jim Burt RC	1.00
309	Jason Motte RC	1.00
310	David Gassner RC	1.00
311	Andy Santana RC	1.00
312	Kelvin Pichardo RC	1.00
313	Carlos Carrasco RC	5.00
314	Willy Mota RC	2.00
315	Frank Mata RC	1.00
316	Carlos Gonzalez RC	10.00
317	Jesse Floyd RC	1.00
318	Chris Young RC	6.00
319	Billy Sadler RC	1.00
320	Ricky Barrett RC	1.00
321	Benjamin Harrison RC	1.00
322	Steve Nelson RC	1.00
323	Daryl Thompson RC	1.00
324	Davis Romero RC	1.00
325	Jeremy Harts RC	1.00
326	Nick Masset RC	1.00
327	Thomas Pauly RC	1.00
328	Mike Garber RC	1.00
329	Kennard Bibbs RC	1.00
330	Colter Bean RC	1.00
331	Justin Verlander RC	80.00
332	Chip Cannon RC	25.00
333	Kevin Melillo RC	20.00
334	Jake Postlewait RC	10.00
335	Wes Swackhamer RC	15.00
336	Mike Rodriguez RC	15.00
337	Philip Humber RC	30.00
338	Jeff Niemann RC	30.00
339	Brian Miller RC	10.00
340	Chris Vines RC	10.00
341	Andy LaRoche RC	50.00
342	Michael Bourn	20.00
343	Eric Nielsen RC	15.00
344	Wladimir Balentien RC	40.00
345	Ismael Ramirez RC	15.00
346	Pedro Lopez RC	10.00
347	Shawn Bowman RC	15.00
348	Hayden Penn RC	20.00
349	Matthew Kemp RC	70.00
350	Brian Stavisky RC	10.00
351	C.J. Smith RC	10.00
352	Mike Morse RC	15.00
353	Billy Butler RC	90.00

Refractor

Stars (1-165):	2-4X
Rookies (166-330):	1-2X
Inserted 1:4	
Autograph (331-353):	1-2X
Production 500	

X-Fractor

Stars (1-165):	3-5X
Rookies (166-330):	2-5X
Autograph (331-353):	1-2.5X
Production 225 Sets	

Blue Refractor

Stars (1-165):	3-5X
Rookies (166-330):	2-5X
Autograph (331-353):	1-2.5X
Production 150 Sets	

Gold Refractor

Stars (1-165):	8-15X
Rookies (166-330):	15-25X
Autograph (331-353):	3-6X
Production 50 Sets	

Red Refractor

No Pricing
Production 5 Sets

Superfractor

No Pricing
Production One Set

Printing Plates

No Pricing
Production one set per color.

A-Rod Throwback

	NM/M
Complete Set (4):	6.00
Common A-Rod	2.00
Inserted 1:9	
Refractor:	2-3X
Production 499 Sets	
X-Fractor:	3-5X
Production 99 Sets	
Superfractor:	No Pricing
Production One Set	

A-Rod Throwback Autograph

	NM/M
Quantity produced listed	
96AR Alex Rodriguez/50	160.00
97AR Alex Rodriguez/99	150.00

One Of A Kind Autograph

No Pricing
Production 13

2005 Bowman Chrome Draft Picks & Prospects

	NM/M
Complete Set (180):	
Common Player:	.25
Common Rookie:	1.00
Common Rk Auto. (166-180):	15.00

#	Player	Price
BDP1	Rickie Weeks	.40
BDP2	Kyle Davies	.25
BDP3	Garrett Atkins	.25
BDP4	Chien-Ming Wang	.75
BDP5	Dallas McPherson	.25
BDP6	Dan Johnson	.25
BDP7	Andy Sisco	.25
BDP8	Ryan Doumit	.25
BDP9	J.P. Howell	.25
BDP10	Tim Stauffer	.25
BDP11	Willy Taveras	.25
BDP12	Aaron Hill	.25
BDP13	Victor Diaz	.25
BDP14	Wilson Betemit	.25
BDP15	Ervin Santana	.25
BDP16	Mike Morse	.25
BDP17	Yadier Molina	.25
BDP18	Kelly Johnson	.25
BDP19	Clint Barmes	.25
BDP20	Robinson Cano	.75
BDP21	Brad Thompson	.25
BDP22	Jorge Cantu	.25
BDP23	Brad Halsey	.25
BDP24	Lance Niekro	.25
BDP25	D.J. Houlton	.25
BDP26	Ryan Church	.25
BDP27	Hayden Penn	.25
BDP28	Chris Young	1.00
BDP29	Chad Orvella	.50
BDP30	Mark Teahen	.25
BDP31	Mark McCormick RC	1.00
BDP32	Jay Bruce RC	15.00
BDP33	Beau Jones RC	2.50
BDP34	Tyler Greene RC	1.50
BDP35	Zach Ward RC	2.50
BDP36	Josh Bell RC	4.00
BDP37	Josh Wall RC	2.00
BDP38	Nick Webber RC	1.00
BDP39	Travis Buck RC	3.00
BDP40	Kyle Winters RC	1.00
BDP41	Mitch Boggs RC	1.00
BDP42	Tommy Mendoza RC	2.00
BDP43	Brad Corley RC	1.50
BDP44	Drew Butera RC	1.50
BDP45	Ryan Mount RC	1.50
BDP46	Tyler Herron RC	1.50
BDP47	Nick Weglarz RC	3.00
BDP48	Brandon Erbe RC	4.00
BDP49	Cody Allen RC	1.00
BDP50	Eric Fowler RC	1.00
BDP51	James Boone RC	1.50
BDP52	Josh Flores RC	3.00
BDP53	Brandon Monk RC	2.00
BDP54	Kieron Pope RC	2.50
BDP55	Kyle Cofield RC	1.50
BDP56	Brent Lillibridge RC	2.50
BDP57	Daryl Jones RC	1.50
BDP58	Eli Iorg RC	2.00
BDP59	Brett Hayes RC	1.00
BDP60	Mike Durant RC	3.00
BDP61	Michael Bowden RC	5.00
BDP62	Paul Kelly RC	2.00
BDP63	Andrew McCutchen RC	8.00
BDP64	Travis Wood RC	3.00
BDP65	Cesar Ramos RC	1.00
BDP66	Chaz Roe RC	1.50
BDP67	Matt Torra RC	2.00
BDP68	Kevin Slowey RC	6.00
BDP69	Trayvon Robinson RC	1.50
BDP70	Reid Engel RC	1.50
BDP71	Kris Harvey RC	2.00
BDP72	Craig Italiano RC	2.50
BDP73	Matt Maloney RC	3.00
BDP74	Sean West RC	1.50
BDP75	Henry Sanchez RC	2.50

BDP76	Scott Blue RC	1.00
BDP77	Jordan Schafer RC	4.00
BDP78	Chris Robinson RC	1.00
BDP79	Chris Hobdy RC	1.00
BDP80	Brandon Durden RC	1.00
BDP81	Clay Buchholz RC	20.00
BDP82	Josh Geer RC	1.00
BDP83	Sam LeCure RC	1.00
BDP84	Justin Thomas RC	1.00
BDP85	Brett Gardner RC	1.50
BDP86	Tommy Manzella RC	1.00
BDP87	Matt Green RC	1.00
BDP88	Yunel Escobar RC	3.00
BDP89	Mike Costanzo RC	3.00
BDP90	Nick Hundley RC	1.00
BDP91	Zach Simons RC	1.00
BDP92	Jacob Marceaux RC	1.00
BDP93	Jed Lowrie RC	3.00
BDP94	Brandon Snyder RC	4.00
BDP95	Matt Goyen RC	1.00
BDP96	Jon Egan RC	1.50
BDP97	Drew Thompson RC	1.50
BDP98	Bryan Anderson RC	4.00
BDP99	Clayton Richard RC	1.00
BDP100	Jimmy Shull RC	1.00
BDP101	Mark Pawelek RC	5.00
BDP102	P.J. Phillips RC	1.50
BDP103	John Drennen RC	3.00
BDP104	Nolan Reimold RC	4.00
BDP105	Troy Tulowitzki RC	15.00
BDP106	Kevin Whelan RC	1.00
BDP107	Wade Townsend RC	2.00
BDP108	Micah Owings RC	4.00
BDP109	Ryan Tucker RC	1.50
BDP110	Jeff Clement RC	4.00
BDP111	Josh Sullivan RC	1.00
BDP112	Jeff Lyman RC	1.00
BDP113	Brian Bogusevic RC	1.50
BDP114	Trevor Bell RC	2.00
BDP115	Brent Cox RC	1.50
BDP116	Michael Billek RC	1.00
BDP117	Garrett Olson RC	4.00
BDP118	Steven Johnson RC	1.00
BDP119	Chase Headley RC	4.00
BDP120	Daniel Carte RC	2.00
BDP121	Francisco Liriano	1.50
BDP122	Fausto Carmona	.25
BDP123	Zach Jackson	.25
BDP124	Adam Loewen	.25
BDP125	Chris Lambert	.25
BDP126	Scott Mathieson RC	1.00
BDP127	Paul Maholm	.25
BDP128	Fernando Nieve	.25
BDP129	Justin Verlander	3.00
BDP130	Yusmeiro Petit	.25
BDP131	Joel Zumaya	1.00
BDP132	Merkin Valdez	.25
BDP133	Ryan Garko RC	4.00
BDP134	Edinson Volquez RC	4.00
BDP135	Russell Martin	3.00
BDP136	Conor Jackson	.25
BDP137	Miguel Montero RC	3.00
BDP138	Josh Barfield	.15
BDP139	Delmon Young	.50
BDP140	Andy LaRoche	2.00
BDP141	William Bergolla	.25
BDP142	B.J. Upton	.25
BDP143	Hernan Iribarren	1.00
BDP144	Brandon Wood	1.00
BDP145	Jose Bautista	.25
BDP146	Edwin Encarnacion	.25
BDP147	Javier Herrera RC	.25
BDP148	Jeremy Hermida	.25
BDP149	Frank Diaz RC	1.00
BDP150	Chris Young	2.00
BDP151	Shin-Soo Choo	.25
BDP152	Kevin Thompson	.25
BDP153	Hanley Ramirez	.25
BDP154	Lastings Milledge	.50
BDP155	Luis Montanez	.25
BDP156	Justin Huber	.25
BDP157	Zachary Duke	.25
BDP158	Jeff Francoeur	.50
BDP159	Melky Cabrera	3.00
BDP160	Bobby Jenks	.25
BDP161	Ian Snell	.25
BDP162	Fernando Cabrera	.25
BDP163	Troy Patton	2.00
BDP164	Anthony Lerew	.25
BDP165	Nelson Cruz RC	3.00
BDP166	Stephen Drew RC	75.00
BDP167	Jered Weaver RC	60.00
BDP168	Ryan Braun RC	180.00
BDP169	John Mayberry Jr. RC	30.00

BDP170	Aaron Thompson RC	20.00
BDP171	Cesar Carrillo RC	25.00
BDP172	Jacoby Ellsbury RC	125.00
BDP173	Matt Garza RC	50.00
BDP174	Cliff Pennington RC	10.00
BDP175	Colby Rasmus RC	80.00
BDP176	Chris Volstad RC	30.00
BDP177	Ricky Romero RC	15.00
BDP178	Ryan Zimmerman RC	100.00
BDP179	C.J. Henry RC	30.00
BDP180	Eddy Martinez RC	25.00

Refractor

Rookies:		2-4X
Inserted 1:11		
Rk Autos: (166-180):		1-1.5X
Production 500		

Blue Refract

Rookies:		4-6X
Rk Autos. (166-180):		1.5-3X
Production 150 Sets		

Gold Refract

Rookies:		8-15X
Rk Autos. (166-180):		4-6X
Production 50 Sets		

Red Refract

No Pricing
Production One Set

X-Fractor

Rookies:		4-6X
Rk Autos. (166-180):		1-2X
Production 250 Sets		

SuperFractor

No Pricing
Production One Set

2005 Bowman Draft Picks & Prospects

		NM/M
Complete Set (165):		30.00
Commmon Player:		.15
Common Rookie		.25
Pack (5 + 2 Chrome):		7.00
Box (24):		140.00
BDP1	Rickie Weeks	.15
BDP2	Kyle Davies	.15
BDP3	Garrett Atkins	.15
BDP4	Chien-Ming Wang	.50
BDP5	Dallas McPherson	.15
BDP6	Dan Johnson	.15
BDP7	Andy Sisco	.15
BDP8	Ryan Doumit	.15
BDP9	J.P. Howell	.15
BDP10	Tim Stauffer	.15
BDP11	Willy Taveras	.15
BDP12	Aaron Hill	.15
BDP13	Victor Diaz	.15
BDP14	Wilson Betemit	.15
BDP15	Erwin Santana	.15
BDP16	Mike Morse	.15
BDP17	Yadier Molina	.15
BDP18	Kelly Johnson	.15
BDP19	Clint Barmes	.15
BDP20	Robinson Cano	.40
BDP21	Brad Thompson	.15
BDP22	Jorge Cantu	.15
BDP23	Brad Halsey	.15
BDP24	Lance Niekro	.15
BDP25	D.J. Houlton	.15
BDP26	Ryan Church	.15
BDP27	Hayden Penn	.15
BDP28	Chris Young	.50
BDP29	Chad Orvella	.15

BDP30	Mark Teahen	.15
BDP31	Mark McCormick RC	.25
BDP32	Jay Bruce RC	6.00
BDP33	Beau Jones RC	.75
BDP34	Tyler Greene RC	.40
BDP35	Zach Ward RC	.75
BDP36	Josh Bell RC	1.00
BDP37	Josh Wall RC	.50
BDP38	Nick Webber RC	.25
BDP39	Travis Buck RC	1.00
BDP40	Kyle Winters RC	.25
BDP41	Mitch Boggs RC	.25
BDP42	Tommy Mendoza RC	.50
BDP43	Brad Corley RC	.40
BDP44	Drew Butera RC	.25
BDP45	Ryan Mount RC	.40
BDP46	Tyler Herron RC	.25
BDP47	Nick Weglarz RC	1.00
BDP48	Brandon Erbe RC	1.00
BDP49	Cody Allen RC	.25
BDP50	Eric Fowler RC	.25
BDP51	James Boone RC	.50
BDP52	Josh Flores RC	.75
BDP53	Brandon Monk RC	.25
BDP54	Kieron Pope RC	.75
BDP55	Kyle Cofield RC	.40
BDP56	Brent Lillibridge RC	.75
BDP57	Daryl Jones RC	.40
BDP58	Eli Iorg RC	.50
BDP59	Brett Hayes RC	.25
BDP60	Mike Durant RC	.75
BDP61	Michael Bowden RC	1.50
BDP62	Paul Kelly RC	.50
BDP63	Andrew McCutchen RC	1.50
BDP64	Travis Wood RC	.75
BDP65	Cesar Ramos RC	.25
BDP66	Chaz Roe RC	.40
BDP67	Matt Torra RC	.50
BDP68	Kevin Slowey RC	2.00
BDP69	Trayvon Robinson RC	.40
BDP70	Reid Engel RC	.40
BDP71	Kris Harvey RC	.50
BDP72	Craig Italiano RC	.50
BDP73	Matt Maloney RC	1.00
BDP74	Sean West RC	1.00
BDP75	Henry Sanchez RC	.50
BDP76	Scott Blue RC	.25
BDP77	Jordan Schafer RC	1.00
BDP78	Chris Robinson RC	.25
BDP79	Chris Hobdy RC	.25
BDP80	Brandon Durden RC	.25
BDP81	Clay Buchholz RC	5.00
BDP82	Josh Geer RC	.25
BDP83	Sam LeCure RC	.25
BDP84	Justin Thomas RC	.25
BDP85	Brett Gardner RC	.50
BDP86	Tommy Manzella RC	.25
BDP87	Matt Green RC	.25
BDP88	Yunel Escobar RC	.75
BDP89	Mike Costanzo RC	.75
BDP90	Nick Hundley RC	.25
BDP91	Zach Simons RC	.25
BDP92	Jacob Marceaux RC	.25
BDP93	Jed Lowrie RC	.75
BDP94	Brandon Snyder RC	1.00
BDP95	Matt Goyen RC	.25
BDP96	Jon Egan RC	.40
BDP97	Drew Thompson RC	.40
BDP98	Bryan Anderson RC	1.00
BDP99	Clayton Richard RC	.25
BDP100	Jimmy Shull RC	.25
BDP101	Mark Pawelek RC	1.00
BDP102	P.J. Phillips RC	.40
BDP103	John Drennen RC	.75
BDP104	Nolan Reimold RC	1.50
BDP105	Troy Tulowitzki RC	4.00
BDP106	Kevin Whelan RC	.25
BDP107	Wade Townsend RC	.15
BDP108	Micah Owings RC	1.50
BDP109	Ryan Tucker RC	.40
BDP110	Jeff Clement RC	1.50
BDP111	Josh Sullivan RC	.25
BDP112	Jeff Lyman RC	.25
BDP113	Brian Bogusevic RC	.40
BDP114	Trevor Bell RC	.50
BDP115	Brent Cox RC	.75
BDP116	Michael Billek RC	.25
BDP117	Garrett Olson RC	1.00
BDP118	Steven Johnson RC	.25
BDP119	Chase Headley RC	.75
BDP120	Daniel Carte RC	.50
BDP121	Francisco Liriano	.75
BDP122	Fausto Carmona	.15
BDP123	Zach Jackson	.15
BDP124	Adam Loewen	.15
BDP125	Chris Lambert	.15
BDP126	Scott Mathieson RC	.25
BDP127	Paul Maholm	.15
BDP128	Fernando Nieve	.15
BDP129	Justin Verlander	.75
BDP130	Yusmeiro Petit	.40

BDP131	Joel Zumaya	.25
BDP132	Merkin Valdez	.15
BDP133	Ryan Garko RC	.75
BDP134	Edinson Volquez RC	1.00
BDP135	Russell Martin	.50
BDP136	Conor Jackson	.25
BDP137	Miguel Montero RC	.50
BDP138	Josh Barfield	.15
BDP139	Delmon Young	.25
BDP140	Andy LaRoche	.75
BDP141	William Bergolla	.15
BDP142	B.J. Upton	.15
BDP143	Hernan Iribarren RC	.25
BDP144	Brandon Wood	.40
BDP145	Jose Bautista	.15
BDP146	Edwin Encarnacion	.15
BDP147	Javier Herrera RC	1.00
BDP148	Jeremy Hermida	.25
BDP149	Frank Diaz RC	.25
BDP150	Chris Young	.50
BDP151	Shin-Soo Choo	.15
BDP152	Kevin Thompson	.15
BDP153	Hanley Ramirez	.50
BDP154	Lastings Milledge	.25
BDP155	Luis Montanez	.15
BDP156	Justin Huber	.15
BDP157	Zachary Duke	.15
BDP158	Jeff Francoeur	.25
BDP159	Melky Cabrera	1.00
BDP160	Bobby Jenks	.15
BDP161	Ian Snell	.15
BDP162	Fernando Cabrera	.15
BDP163	Troy Patton	.50
BDP164	Anthony Lerew	.15
BDP165	Nelson Cruz RC	.75

White

Rookies:		3-5X
Production 225 Sets		

Red

No Pricing
Production One Set

Base Relic Variations

		NM/M
Common Player:		4.00
BDP121	Francisco Liriano	8.00
BDP122	Fausto Carmona	4.00
BDP123	Zach Jackson	4.00
BDP124	Adam Loewen	4.00
BDP125	Chris Lambert	4.00
BDP126	Scott Mathieson	4.00
BDP127	Paul Maholm	4.00
BDP128	Fernando Nieve	4.00
BDP129	Justin Verlander	8.00
BDP130	Yusmeiro Petit	6.00
BDP131	Joel Zumaya	10.00
BDP132	Merkin Valdez	4.00
BDP133	Ryan Garko	6.00
BDP134	Edinson Volquez	5.00
BDP135	Russell Martin	6.00
BDP136	Conor Jackson	6.00
BDP137	Miguel Montero	6.00
BDP138	Josh Barfield	4.00
BDP139	Delmon Young	6.00
BDP140	Andy LaRoche	6.00
BDP141	William Bergolla	4.00
BDP142	B.J. Upton	4.00
BDP143	Hernan Iribarren	4.00
BDP144	Brandon Wood	10.00
BDP145	Jose Bautista	4.00
BDP146	Edwin Encarnacion	4.00
BDP147	Javier Herrera	6.00
BDP148	Jeremy Hermida	6.00
BDP149	Frank Diaz	6.00
BDP150	Chris Young	6.00

Signs of the Future

		NM/M
Common Player:		8.00
HB	Homer Bailey	25.00
BB	Bill Bray	8.00
JF	Jeff Frazier	8.00
GG	Greg Golson	8.00
AG	Angel Guzman	10.00
JH	Justin Hoyman	8.00
JJ	Justin Jones	8.00
DL	Donald Lucey	8.00
TL	Tyler Lumsden	8.00
DM	David Murphy	10.00
JP	Jonathan Poterson	8.00
DP	David Purcey	8.00
RR	Richie Robnett	8.00
JS	Jeremy Sowers	10.00

2005 Bowman Heritage

	NM/M
Complete Set (349):	
Common Player (1-300):	.15
Common SP (301-349):	3.00
Inserted 1:3	

RYAN BRAUN

Draft Pick Variations
(325-349):		1-1.5X

One DPV pack per hobby box.
Pack (8):	4.00
Box (24):	85.00

#	Player	Price
1	Steven White RC	.75
2	Jorge Posada	.25
3	Brett Myers	.15
4	Pat Burrell	.25
5	Grady Sizemore	.50
6	Jeff Weaver	.15
7	Jeff Kent	.25
8	Mark Kotsay	.15
9	Nick Swisher	.15
10	Scott Rolen	.50
11	Matt Morris	.25
12	Luis Castillo	.15
13	Pedro Feliz	.15
14	Omar Vizquel	.15
15	Edgar Renteria	.25
16	David Wells	.15
17	Chad Cordero	.15
18	Brad Wilkerson	.15
19	Kelly Johnson	.15
20	Johnny Estrada	.15
21	Brian Roberts	.25
22	Jeromy Burnitz	.15
23	Magglio Ordonez	.15
24	Adam Dunn	.50
25	Randy Johnson	.75
26	Derek Jeter	2.00
27	Jon Lieber	.15
28	Jim Thome	.50
29	Ronnie Belliard	.15
30	Jake Westbrook	.15
31	Bengie Molina	.15
32	J.D. Drew	.25
33	Rich Harden	.25
34	David Eckstein	.15
35	Scott Podsednik	.25
36	Mark Buehrle	.25
37	Barry Bonds	2.00
38	Brian Schneider	.15
39	Tim Wakefield	.15
40	Craig Wilson	.15
41	Jose Vidro	.15
42	Jacque Jones	.15
43	Felix Hernandez	.50
44	Nomar Garciaparra	.75
45	Neifi Perez	.15
46	Brandon Inge	.15
47	Felipe Lopez	.15
48	Ken Griffey Jr.	1.50
49	Robinson Cano	.40
50	Jason Giambi	.50
51	Mike Lieberthal	.15
52	Bobby Abreu	.25
53	C.C. Sabathia	.15
54	Aaron Boone	.15
55	Milton Bradley	.15
56	Derek Lowe	.15
57	Barry Zito	.25
58	Jim Edmonds	.40
59	Jon Garland	.15
60	Tadahito Iguchi RC	1.50
61	Jason Schmidt	.25
62	David Ortiz	.75
63	Matt Lawton	.15
64	Zachary Duke	.25
65	Gary Sheffield	.40
66	Chipper Jones	.75
67	Sammy Sosa	.75
68	Rafael Palmeiro	.50
69	Carlos Zambrano	.25
70	Aramis Ramirez	.25
71	Chris Shelton	.15
72	Wily Mo Pena	.15
73	Mike Mussina	.25
74	Chien-Ming Wang	.50
75	Randy Wolf	.15
76	Jimmy Rollins	.25
77	Chase Utley	.25
78	Kevin Millwood	.15
79	Victor Martinez	.25
80	Morgan Ensberg	.25
81	Bartolo Colon	.25
82	Bobby Crosby	.15
83	Dan Johnson	.15
84	Danny Haren	.15
85	Yadier Molina	.15
86	Mark Mulder	.25
87	Russell Branyan	.15
88	Lyle Overbay	.15
89	Edgardo Alfonzo	.15
90	Mike Matheny	.15
91	J.T. Snow	.15
92	Curt Schilling	.75
93	Oliver Perez	.15
94	Mark Redman	.15
95	Esteban Loaiza	.15
96	Livan Hernandez	.15
97	Ryan Church	.15
98	Kyle Davies	.15
99	Mike Hampton	.15
100	Jeff Francoeur	.15
101	Javy Lopez	.15
102	Mark Prior	.75
103	Kerry Wood	.25
104	Carlos Guillen	.15
105	Dmitri Young	.15
106	David Wright	1.00
107	Cliff Floyd	.15
108	Carlos Beltran	.50
109	Melky Cabrera RC	2.00
110	Carl Pavano	.15
111	Jamie Moyer	.15
112	Joel Pineiro	.15
113	Adrian Beltre	.25
114	Jhonny Peralta	.15
115	Travis Hafner	.40
116	Cesar Izturis	.15
117	Brad Penny	.15
118	Garret Anderson	.25
119	Scott Kazmir	.15
120	Aubrey Huff	.15
121	Larry Walker	.25
122	Albert Pujols	2.00
123	Paul Konerko	.25
124	Frank Thomas	.50
125	Phil Nevin	.15
126	Brian Giles	.15
127	Ramon Hernandez	.15
128	Johnny Damon	.75
129	Trot Nixon	.15
130	Rocco Baldelli	.15
131	Carl Crawford	.25
132	Alfonso Soriano	.50
133	Mark Teixeira	.50
134	Gustavo Chacin	.15
135	Vernon Wells	.25
136	Erik Bedard	.15
137	Daniel Cabrera	.15
138	Michael Barrett	.15
139	Greg Maddux	1.00
140	Javier Vazquez	.15
141	Chad Tracy	.15
142	Michael Young	.15
143	Kenny Rogers	.15
144	Mike Piazza	.75
145	Jose Reyes	.40
146	Geoff Jenkins	.15
147	Carlos Lee	.25
148	Brady Clark	.15
149	Torii Hunter	.25
150	Johan Santana	.75
151	Steve Finley	.15
152	Darin Erstad	.25
153	Jake Peavy	.25
154	Xavier Nady	.15
155	Ryan Klesko	.15
156	Ichiro Suzuki	1.50
157	Richie Sexson	.40
158	Raul Ibanez	.15
159	Freddy Garcia	.15
160	Brad Hawpe	.15
161	Jeff Francis	.15
162	Todd Helton	.40
163	Clint Barmes	.15
164	Rodrigo Lopez	.15
165	Melvin Mora	.15
166	Brandon Webb	.15
167	Shawn Green	.25
168	Moises Alou	.15
169	Matt Clement	.15
170	John Smoltz	.40
171	Rafael Furcal	.25
172	Jeff Bagwell	.25
173	Roger Clemens	2.00
174	Dontrelle Willis	.40
175	Paul LoDuca	.15
176	Zack Greinke	.25
177	David DeJesus	.15
178	Mike Sweeney	.15
179	Ben Sheets	.25
180	Doug Davis	.15
181	Mike Cameron	.15
182	Lance Berkman	.40
183	Craig Biggio	.25
184	Shannon Stewart	.15
185	Joe Mauer	.50
186	Justin Morneau	.25
187	Mike Maroth	.15
188	Ivan Rodriguez	.50
189	Luis Gonzalez	.15
190	Troy Glaus	.25
191	Adam Eaton	.15
192	Khalil Greene	.25
193	Mike Lowell	.15
194	Miguel Cabrera	.75
195	Roy Halladay	.25
196	Ted Lilly	.15
197	Alex Rios	.15
198	Josh Beckett	.25
199	A.J. Burnett	.15
200	Juan Pierre	.15
201	Marcus Giles	.15
202	Craig Tatum RC	.50
203	Hayden Penn RC	.50
204	C.J. Smith RC	.25
205	Matt Albers RC	1.00
206	Jared Gothreaux RC	.25
207	Mike Rodriguez RC	.25
208	Hernan Iribarren RC	.25
209	Manny Parra RC	.25
210	Kevin Collins RC	.25
211	Buck Coats RC	.50
212	Jeremy West RC	.50
213	Ian Bladergroen RC	.25
214	Chuck Tiffany RC	1.50
215	Andy LaRoche RC	2.00
216	Frank Diaz RC	.25
217	Jai Miller RC	.25
218	Tony Giarratano RC	.50
219	Danny Zell RC	.25
220	Justin Verlander RC	5.00
221	Ryan Sweeney RC	1.00
222	Brandon McCarthy RC	1.00
223	Jerry Owens RC	.25
224	Glen Perkins RC	.50
225	Kevin West RC	.25
226	Billy Butler RC	4.00
227	Shane Costa RC	.50
228	Erik Schindewolf RC	.25
229	Miguel Montero RC	.75
230	Stephen Drew RC	4.00
231	Matt DeSalvo RC	1.00
232	Ben Jones RC	.75
233	Bill McCarthy RC	.25
234	Chuck James RC	2.00
235	Brandon Sing RC	.75
236	Andy Santana RC	.25
237	Brendan Ryan RC	.50
238	Wes Swackhamer RC	.25
239	Jeff Niemann RC	1.00
240	Ian Kinsler RC	3.00
241	Micah Furtado RC	.50
242	Ryan Mount RC	.50
243	P.J. Phillips RC	.50
244	Trevor Bell RC	1.00
245	Jered Weaver RC	4.00
246	Eddy Martinez-Esteve RC	.75
247	Brian Bannister RC	1.00
248	Philip Humber RC	1.00
249	Michael Rogers RC	.50
250	Landon Powell RC	.50
251	Kennard Bibbs RC	.50
252	Nelson Cruz RC	1.00
253	Paul Kelly RC	.75
254	Kevin Slowey RC	2.00
255	Brandon Snyder RC	1.00
256	Nolan Reimold RC	1.50
257	Brian Stavisky RC	.25
258	Javier Herrera RC	1.50
259	Russell Martin RC	3.00
260	Matthew Kemp RC	3.00
261	Wade Townsend RC	.75
262	Nick Touchstone RC	.50
263	Ryan Feierabend RC	.50
264	Bobby Livingston RC	.50
265	Wladimir Balentien RC	.75
266	Keiichi Yabu RC	1.00
267	Craig Italiano RC	.50
268	Ryan Goleski RC	.50
269	Ryan Garko RC	1.50
270	Michael Bourn RC	.50
271	Scott Mathieson RC	.75
272	Scott Mitchinson RC	.75
273	Tyler Greene RC	1.00
274	Mark McCormick RC	.50
275	Daryl James RC	.50
276	Travis Chick RC	.50
277	Luis Hernandez RC	.25
278	Steven Doetsch RC	.25
279	Chris Vines RC	.50
280	Mike Costanzo RC	1.00
281	Matt Maloney RC	1.00
282	Matt Goyen RC	.25
283	Jacob Marceaux RC	.25
284	David Gassner RC	.25
285	Ricky Barrett RC	.50
286	Jon Egan RC	.50
287	Scott Blue RC	.50
288	Steve Bondurant RC	.50
289	Kevin Melillo RC	.50
290	Brad Corley RC	.50
291	Brent Lillibridge RC	1.00
292	Mike Morse RC	.25
293	Justin Thomas RC	.50
294	Nick Webber RC	.25
295	Mitch Boggs RC	.25
296	Jeff Lyman RC	.50
297	Jordan Schafer RC	1.50
298	Ismael Ramirez RC	.25
299	Chris Young RC	2.50
300	Brian Miller RC	.50
301	Jason Bay	4.00
302	Tim Hudson	3.00
303	Miguel Tejada	4.00
304	Jeremy Bonderman	3.00
305	Alex Rodriguez	8.00
306	Rickie Weeks	3.00
307	Manny Ramirez	6.00
308	Nick Johnson	3.00
309	Andruw Jones	4.00
310	Hideki Matsui	6.00
311	Jeremy Reed	5.00
312	Dallas McPherson	3.00
313	Vladimir Guerrero	5.00
314	Eric Chavez	3.00
315	Chris Carpenter	4.00
316	Aaron Hill	3.00
317	Derrek Lee	5.00
318	Mark Loretta	3.00
319	Garrett Atkins	3.00
320	Hank Blalock	3.00
321	Chris Young	5.00
322	Roy Oswalt	3.00
323	Carlos Delgado	4.00
324	Pedro Martinez	5.00
325	Jeff Clement RC	4.00
326	Jimmy Shull RC	4.00
327	Daniel Carte RC	4.00
328	Travis Buck RC	4.00
329	Chris Volstad RC	3.00
330	Andrew McCutchen RC	8.00
331	Cliff Pennington RC	4.00
332	John Mayberry Jr. RC	4.00
333	C.J. Henry RC	4.00
334	Ricky Romero RC	5.00
335	Aaron Thompson RC	5.00
336	Cesar Carrillo RC	4.00
337	Jacoby Ellsbury RC	12.00
338	Matt Garza RC	8.00
339	Colby Rasmus RC	6.00
340	Ryan Zimmerman RC	12.00
341	Ryan Braun RC	20.00
342	Brent Lillibridge RC	3.00
343	Jay Bruce RC	12.00
344	Matt Green RC	6.00
345	Brent Cox RC	6.00
346	Jed Lowrie RC	4.00
347	Beau Jones RC	3.00
348	Eli Iorg RC	4.00
349	Chaz Roe RC	4.00

Mahogany

Stars (1-300):	1-2X
SP's (301-349):	.5-1X
Inserted 1:1	

Red

No Pricing
Production One Set

Printing Plates

No Pricing
Production one set per color.

Mini

Stars (1-300):	1-2X
SP's (301-349):	.5-1X
Inserted 1:1	

Draft Pick Variation

	NM/M

Variations (325-349): 1-1.5X Base
One DPV pack per hobby box.
325	Jeff Clement	10.00
326	Jimmy Shull	6.00
327	Daniel Carte	6.00
328	Travis Buck	5.00
329	Chris Volstad	5.00
330	Andrew McCutchen	12.00
331	Cliff Pennington	6.00
332	John Mayberry Jr.	6.00
333	C.J. Henry	8.00
334	Ricky Romero	6.00
335	Aaron Thompson	6.00
336	Cesar Carrillo	6.00
337	Jacoby Ellsbury	20.00
338	Matt Garza	10.00
339	Colby Rasmus	10.00
340	Ryan Zimmerman	15.00

#	Player	Price
341	Ryan Braun	30.00
342	Brent Lillibridge	6.00
343	Jay Bruce	15.00
344	Matt Green	6.00
345	Brent Cox	6.00
346	Jed Lowrie	6.00
347	Beau Jones	5.00
348	Eli Iorg	6.00
349	Chaz Roe	6.00

Future Greatness

NM/M

	Player	Price
	Common Player:	4.00
TB	Tony Blanco	4.00
JB	Joe Blanton	4.00
BB	Bryan Bullington	4.00
MC	Matt Cain	8.00
FC	Fausto Carmona	4.00
SC	Shin-Soo Choo	4.00
JC	Jorge Cortes	4.00
JCO	Jesus Cota	4.00
EE	Edwin Encarnacion	4.00
CE	Clint Everts	4.00
GF	Gavin Floyd	4.00
JF	Jeff Francis	4.00
JGA	Jairo Garcia	4.00
RG	Ruben Gotay	6.00
JG	Joel Guzman	4.00
AH	Aaron Hill	4.00
KH	Koyie Hill	4.00
JK	Jason Kubel	4.00
WL	Wilfredo Ledezma	4.00
VM	Val Majewski	4.00
AMA	Andy Marte	8.00
JMA	Jeff Mathis	8.00
DM	Dallas McPherson	4.00
JM	Justin Morneau	8.00
AM	Arnie Munoz	4.00
JP	Juan Perez	4.00
YP	Yusmeiro Petit	4.00
FP	Felix Pie	4.00
BT	Brad Thompson	15.00
RW	Rickie Weeks	6.00
DY	Delmon Young	8.00

Pieces of Greatness

NM/M

	Player	Price
	Common Player:	4.00
JB	Josh Beckett	4.00
CB	Carlos Beltran	6.00
BB	Barry Bonds	20.00
MC	Miguel Cabrera	8.00
EC	Eric Chavez	4.00
RC	Roger Clemens	10.00
BC	Bobby Crosby	4.00
JD	Johnny Damon	8.00
CD	Carlos Delgado	6.00
AD	Adam Dunn	8.00
JG	Josh Gibson	15.00
TG	Troy Glaus	4.00
RH	Rich Harden	4.00
TH	Todd Helton	6.00
JK	Jeff Kent	4.00
PK	Paul Konerko	6.00
PM	Pedro Martinez	8.00
MMO	Melvin Mora	4.00
MM	Mark Mulder	4.00
BM	Brett Myers	4.00
AP	Albert Pujols	20.00
MR	Manny Ramirez	8.00
BR	Brian Roberts	4.00
AR	Alex Rodriguez	15.00
JS	John Smoltz	8.00
IS	Ichiro Suzuki	15.00
MT	Miguel Tejada	6.00
JT	Jim Thome	6.00
DW	Dontrelle Willis	6.00
DWR	David Wright	15.00
BZ	Barry Zito	4.00

Signs of Greatness

NM/M

	Player	Price
	Common Player:	6.00
RB	Ryan Braun	100.00
JB	Jay Bruce	50.00
PB	Patrick Bryant	10.00
MB	Matt Bush	15.00
TC	Travis Chick	6.00
TD	Thomas Diamond	6.00
SE	Scott Elbert	15.00
MG	Matt Green	8.00
AG	Angel Guzman	8.00
JH	J.P. Howell	8.00
PH	Philip Humber	20.00
ZJ	Zach Jackson	8.00
JJ	Jason Jaramillo	10.00
DJ	Dan Johnson	8.00
BL	Brent Lillibridge	10.00
DL	Donald Lucey	8.00
EM	Eddy Martinez-Esteve	8.00
JM	John Mayberry	20.00
AM	Andrew McCutchen	35.00
JP	Jonathan Papelbon	40.00

	Player	Price
DP	David Purcey	8.00
RR	Ricky Romero	10.00
HS	Huston Street	20.00
CT	Curtis Thigpen	10.00
WW	Wes Whisler	10.00
JZ	Jon Zeringue	8.00
RZ	Ryan Zimmerman	40.00

51 Topps Heritage Blue Back

NM/M

#	Player	Price
	Common Player:	1.00
1	Adam Dunn	3.00
2	Zachary Duke	1.50
3	Alex Rodriguez	8.00
4	Vladimir Guerrero	3.00
5	Andruw Jones	2.00
6	Travis Chick	2.00
7	Alfonso Soriano	2.00
8	Scott Rolen	3.00
9	Brian Bannister	2.00
10	Randy Johnson	3.00
11	Barry Bonds	8.00
12	Pat Burrell	1.50
13	Barry Zito	1.50
14	Nomar Garciaparra	3.00
15	C.C. Sabathia	1.00
16	Miguel Tejada	2.00
17	Hideki Matsui	6.00
18	John Smoltz	2.00
19	Ken Griffey Jr.	5.00
20	Chris Carpenter	1.50
21	Ian Kinsler	2.00
22	Chuck Tiffany	1.50
23	Gary Sheffield	2.00
24	Mark Mulder	1.50
25	Ichiro Suzuki	5.00
26	Kerry Wood	1.50
27	Jose Reyes	1.00
28	Derrek Lee	2.00
29	Justin Verlander	2.00
30	Johnny Damon	3.00
31	Chris Volstad	1.00
32	Jeremy Bonderman	1.00
33	David Ortiz	3.00
34	Morgan Ensberg	1.00
35	Mark Buehrle	1.00
36	Chuck James	2.00
37	Miguel Cabrera	3.00
38	Magglio Ordonez	1.00
39	Michael Young	1.00
40	Carlos Beltran	2.00
41	Nick Johnson	1.00
42	Billy Butler	2.00
43	Brian Giles	1.00
44	Paul Konerko	1.50
45	Roy Oswalt	1.50
46	Bobby Abreu	1.50
47	Sammy Sosa	3.00
48	Aramis Ramirez	1.50
49	Torii Hunter	1.00
50	Aubrey Huff	1.00
51	Vernon Wells	1.00
52	Joe Mauer	1.50

51 Topps Heritage Red Back

NM/M

#	Player	Price
	Common Player:	1.00
1	Andy LaRoche	3.00
2	Mike Piazza	4.00
3	Pedro Martinez	3.00
4	Wladimir Balentien	1.00
5	Tim Hudson	1.50
6	Richie Sexson	1.50
7	Carlos Delgado	1.00
8	Derek Jeter	8.00
9	Ryan Zimmerman	6.00
10	Mark Teixeira	2.00
11	David Wright	3.00
12	Jake Peavy	1.50
13	Jose Vidro	1.00
14	Jim Thome	2.00
15	Carlos Zambrano	1.50
16	Hank Blalock	1.50
17	Johan Santana	2.00
18	Cliff Pennington	1.00
19	Rafael Palmeiro	1.50
20	Curt Schilling	2.00
21	Brandon McCarthy	2.00
22	Stephen Drew	8.00
23	Jeff Niemann	2.00
24	Eric Chavez	1.00
25	Hernan Iribarren	1.00
26	Jered Weaver	2.00
27	Edgar Renteria	1.00
28	Travis Hafner	1.00
29	Frank Thomas	1.50
30	Brian Roberts	1.00
31	Anthony Reyes	1.00
32	Scott Kazmir	1.00
33	Carlos Lee	1.00
34	Jimmy Rollins	1.00
35	Garret Anderson	1.00
36	Jason Schmidt	1.00
37	Jon Garland	1.00
38	Dontrelle Willis	1.50
39	C.J. Henry	3.00
40	Greg Maddux	4.00
41	Todd Helton	2.00
42	Ivan Rodriguez	2.00
43	Chipper Jones	3.00
44	Rich Harden	1.50
45	Mark Prior	3.00
46	Roy Halladay	1.50
47	Albert Pujols	8.00
48	Roger Clemens	8.00
49	Andrew McCutchen	4.00
50	Scott Podsednik	1.50
51	Manny Ramirez	3.00
52	Carl Crawford	1.00
53	Jim Edmonds	1.50
54	Wily Mo Pena	1.00

2005 Bowman Sterling

TYLER HERRON

NM/M

		Price
Pack (5):		45.00
Box (6):		250.00

First Year Autographs

	Player	Price
MA	Matt Albers RC	20.00
RB	Ryan Braun RC	125.00
TC	Travis Chick RC	10.00
MG	Matt Green RC	10.00
CH	C.J. Henry RC	15.00
GK	George Kottaras RC	20.00
EM	Eddy Martinez-Esteve RC	15.00
JM	John Mayberry Jr. RC	20.00
GO	Garrett Olson RC	20.00
CP	Cliff Pennington RC	10.00
HS	Humberto Sanchez RC	25.00
BS	Brandon Sing RC	15.00
AT	Aaron Thompson RC	15.00
CV	Chris Volstad RC	10.00
SW	Steven White RC	10.00

Autographed Prospect Base Relics

	Player	Price
BB	Billy Buckner	15.00
SE	Scott Elbert	15.00
BE	Brad Eldred	15.00
JF	Josh Fields	20.00
AL	Adam Lind	15.00
CN	Chris Nelson	15.00
DP	Dustin Pedroia	60.00
CT	Curtis Thigpen	10.00

Autographed First Year Relics

	Player	Price
TB	Trevor Bell RC	15.00
MB	Michael Bowden RC	30.00
JB	Jay Bruce RC	80.00
MC	Mike Conroy RC	15.00
BC	J. Brent Cox RC	15.00
JE	Jacoby Ellsbury RC	100.00
JG	Josh Geer RC	15.00
PH	Philip Humber RC	25.00
EI	Eli Iorg RC	15.00
BJ	Beau Jones RC	15.00
BL	Bobby Livingston RC	15.00
JL	Jed Lowrie RC	25.00
SM	Steve Marek RC	15.00
RM	Russell Martin RC	40.00
BM	Brandon McCarthy RC	15.00
AM	Andrew McCutchen RC	40.00
TM	Tyler Minges RC	15.00
JCN	John Nelson RC	15.00
JN	Jeff Niemann RC	20.00
JO	Justin Olson RC	10.00
CPP	Carmen Pignatiello RC	15.00
CR	Colby Rasmus RC	60.00
CRO	Chaz Roe RC	15.00
CS	C.J. Smith RC	10.00
RT	Raul Tablado RC	15.00
JV	Justin Verlander RC	60.00

First Year Base Cards

	Player	Price
BA	Brian Anderson	4.00
BRB	Brian Bogusevic RC	4.00
CBU	Clay Buchholz RC	35.00
TBU	Travis Buck RC	6.00
BBU	Billy Butler RC	20.00
CC	Cesar Carrillo RC	6.00
DC	Daniel Carte RC	4.00
JC	Jeff Clement RC	15.00
MCO	Mike Constanzo RC	6.00
BCR	Brad Corley RC	4.00
JDR	John Drennen RC	8.00
SD	Stephen Drew RC	10.00
JEG	Jon Egan RC	4.00
YE	Yunel Escobar RC	6.00
MGA	Matt Garza RC	10.00
TG	Tyler Greene RC	6.00
BH	Brett Hayes RC	4.00
CHE	Chase Headley RC	6.00
THE	Tyler Herron RC	5.00
NH	Nick Hundley RC	4.00
TI	Tadahito Iguchi RC	6.00
HI	Hernan Iribarren RC	4.00
CI	Craig Italiano RC	6.00
CJ	Chuck James RC	8.00
PK	Paul Kelly RC	8.00
ACL	Andy LaRoche RC	10.00
JLY	Jeff Lyman RC	4.00
MAM	Matt Maloney RC	8.00
JMA	Jacob Marceaux RC	4.00
MMC	Mark McCormick RC	4.00
RMO	Ryan Mount RC	6.00
PP	P.J. Phillips RC	6.00
CRA	Cesar Ramos RC	4.00
NR	Nolan Reimold RC	8.00
RR	Ricky Romero RC	6.00
HAS	Henry Sanchez RC	6.00
ZS	Zach Simons RC	4.00
KS	Kevin Slowey RC	15.00
BSN	Brandon Snyder RC	8.00
DT	Drew Thompson RC	4.00
CLT	Chuck Tiffany RC	6.00
MTO	Matt Torra RC	6.00
WT	Wade Townsend RC	4.00
TT	Troy Tulowitzki RC	20.00
JW	Josh Wall RC	6.00
JWE	Jered Weaver RC	15.00
NW	Nick Webber RC	4.00
KW	Kevin Whelan RC	4.00
TW	Travis Wood RC	4.00
RZ	Ryan Zimmerman RC	25.00

Refractors

Rookies:	1.5-2X
Rookie Auto.:	1-2X
Rookie Relic Auto.:	1-2X
Production 199 Sets	

Black Refractors

No Pricing
Production 25 Sets

Red Refractors

No Pricing
Production One Set

MLB Logo Patch

No Pricing
Production One Set

Original Autographs

NM/M

Production 1-160

	Player		Price
AJ4	Andruw Jones	02 B/122	25.00
AJ6	Andruw Jones	03 B/112	25.00
AJ8	Andruw Jones	04 B/71	25.00
DL1	Derrek Lee	95 B/27	25.00
DL2	Derrek Lee	96 B/29	25.00
DL5	Derrek Lee	98 B/22	25.00
DL6	Derrek Lee	04 B/92	20.00
DL7	Derrek Lee	04 BC/26	25.00
DW1	David Wright	04 BD/98	85.00
DW3	David Wright	05 B/139	85.00
GA1	Garret Anderson	04 BC/36	20.00
GA2	Garret Anderson	05 B/48	20.00
JR1	Jeremy Reed	04 BD/82	15.00
JR2	Jeremy Reed	04 BCD/48	20.00
MC2	Miguel Cabrera	02 BD/26	50.00

MC4	Miguel Cabrera 03 BD/27	50.00
MC5	Miguel Cabrera 03 BCD/25	50.00
MC6	Miguel Cabrera 04 B/127	25.00
MC7	Miguel Cabrera 04 BC/25	50.00
MC8	Miguel Cabrera 05 B/154	25.00
MC9	Miguel Cabrera 05 BC/25	50.00
MK3	Mark Kotsay 98 B/56	15.00
MK5	Mark Kotsay 99 B/75	15.00
MK7	Mark Kotsay 05 B/160	10.00
MK8	Mark Kotsay 05 BC/46	15.00
MY1	Michael Young 04 B/148	15.00
MY2	Michael Young 04 BC/64	15.00
MY3	Michael Young 05 B/92	15.00

Relics

NM/M
Common Player:		4.00
Refractor:		1-1.5X
Production 199 Sets		
Black Refractor:		2-4X
Production 25 Sets		
JBE	Josh Beckett	4.00
RBE	Ronnie Belliard	4.00
CB	Carlos Beltran	6.00
HB	Hank Blalock	4.00
BLB	Barry Bonds	20.00
MCA	Miguel Cabrera	8.00
EC	Eric Chavez	4.00
JD	Johnny Damon	8.00
CD	Carlos Delgado	4.00
JPE	Jim Edmonds	6.00
RF	Rafael Furcal	4.00
JGI	Josh Gibson	15.00
MGI	Marcus Giles	4.00
KG	Khalil Greene	6.00
VG	Vladimir Guerrero	8.00
TLH	Todd Helton	6.00
THU	Tim Hudson	4.00
TH	Torii Hunter	4.00
LWJ	Chipper Jones	8.00
DL	Derrek Lee	6.00
PL	Paul LoDuca	4.00
GM	Greg Maddux	10.00
PM	Pedro Martinez	8.00
TM	Tino Martinez	4.00
VM	Victor Martinez	4.00
HM	Hideki Matsui	15.00
KM	Kevin Millar	4.00
BMU	Bill Mueller	4.00
MM	Mark Mulder	4.00
TN	Trot Nixon	4.00
DO	David Ortiz	10.00
MP	Mike Piazza	8.00
JP	Jorge Posada	6.00
MPR	Mark Prior	6.00
AP	Albert Pujols	20.00
ARA	Aramis Ramirez	4.00
MR	Manny Ramirez	8.00
AR	Alex Rodriguez	20.00
IR	Ivan Rodriguez	6.00
SR	Scott Rolen	8.00
CSU	Curt Schilling	6.00
GS	Gary Sheffield	6.00
JS	John Smoltz	6.00
AS	Alfonso Soriano	8.00
SS	Sammy Sosa	8.00
MTE	Mark Teixeira	8.00
MT	Miguel Tejada	6.00
DW	Dontrelle Willis	6.00

MY	Michael Young	4.00
BZ	Barry Zito	4.00

2005 Bowman's Best

NM/M
Common Player:		.25
Common Rookie:		1.00
Common Rookie Auto. (101-143):		10.00
Production 974		
Pack (5):		14.00
Box (10):		120.00
1	Jose Vidro	.25
2	Adam Dunn	.50
3	Manny Ramirez	.75
4	Miguel Tejada	.50
5	Ken Griffey Jr.	1.00
6	Pedro Martinez	1.00
7	Alex Rodriguez	1.50
8	Ichiro Suzuki	1.50
9	Alfonso Soriano	.75
10	Brian Giles	.25
11	Roger Clemens	2.00
12	Todd Helton	.50
13	Ivan Rodriguez	.50
14	David Ortiz	.75
15	Sammy Sosa	1.00
16	Chipper Jones	.75
17	Mark Buehrle	.50
18	Miguel Cabrera	.75
19	Johan Santana	.75
20	Randy Johnson	.75
21	Jim Thome	.50
22	Vladimir Guerrero	.75
23	Dontrelle Willis	.50
24	Nomar Garciaparra	.75
25	Barry Bonds	2.00
26	Curt Schilling	.75
27	Carlos Beltran	.50
28	Albert Pujols	2.00
29	Mark Prior	.75
30	Derek Jeter	2.00
31	Ryan Garko RC	4.00
32	Eulogio de la Cruz RC	1.00
33	Luke Scott RC	3.00
34	Shane Costa RC	1.00
35	Casey McGehee RC	1.00
36	Jered Weaver RC	8.00
37	Kevin Melillo RC	2.00
38	D.J. Houlton RC	2.00
39	Brandon Moorhead RC	1.00
40	Jerry Owens RC	1.00
41	Elliot Johnson RC	1.50
42	Kevin West RC	2.00
43	Hernan Iribarren RC	1.00
44	Miguel Montero RC	6.00
45	Craig Tatum RC	1.00
46	Ryan Sweeney RC	2.00
47	Micah Furtado RC	1.00
48	Cody Haerther RC	1.00
49	Erik Abreu RC	1.00
50	Chuck Tiffany RC	2.00
51	Tadahito Iguchi RC	4.00
52	Frank Diaz RC	3.00
53	Errol Simonitsch RC	1.00
54	Wade Robinson RC	2.00
55	Adam Boeve RC	1.00
56	Steve Bondurant RC	1.00
57	Jason Motte RC	1.00
58	Juan Senreiso RC	1.00
59	Vinny Rottino RC	1.00
60	Jai Miller RC	1.00
61	Thomas Pauly RC	1.00
62	Tony Giarratano RC	1.00
63	Alexander Smit RC	1.00
64	Keiichi Yabu RC	1.00
65	Brian Bannister RC	2.50
66	Kennard Bibbs RC	1.00
67	Anthony Reyes RC	4.00
68	Tom Oldham RC	1.00
69	Benjamin Harrison RC	1.00
70	Daryl Thompson RC	1.00

71	Kevin Collins RC	1.00
72	Wes Swackhamer RC	1.50
73	Landon Powell RC	1.50
74	Matt Brown RC	1.00
75	Russell Martin RC	6.00
76	Nick Touchstone RC	1.00
77	Steven White RC	1.00
78	Ian Bladergroen RC	1.00
79	Sean Marshall RC	2.00
80	Nick Masset RC	1.00
81	Ryan Goleski RC	1.50
82	Matt Campbell RC	1.00
83	Manny Parra RC	1.00
84	Melky Cabrera RC	5.00
85	Ryan Feierabend RC	1.50
86	Nate McLouth RC	1.50
87	Glen Perkins RC	2.50
88	Kila Kaaihue RC	1.50
89	Dana Eveland RC	1.50
90	Tyler Pelland RC	1.00
91	Matt Van Der Bosch RC	1.00
92	Andy Santana RC	1.00
93	Eric Nielsen RC	1.00
94	Brendan Ryan RC	1.00
95	Ian Kinsler RC	4.00
96	Matthew Kemp RC	8.00
97	Stephen Drew RC	10.00
98	Peeter Ramos RC	2.00
99	Chris Seddon RC	2.00
100	Chuck James RC	6.00
101	Travis Chick RC	10.00
102	Justin Verlander RC	60.00
103	Billy Butler RC	50.00
104	Chris Young RC	80.00
105	Jake Postlewait RC	10.00
106	C.J. Smith RC	10.00
107	Mike Rodriguez RC	12.00
108	Philip Humber RC	25.00
109	Jeff Niemann RC	20.00
110	Brian Miller RC	10.00
111	Chris Vines RC	12.00
112	Andy LaRoche RC	30.00
113	Mike Bourn RC	12.00
114	Wladimir Balentien RC	30.00
115	Ismael Ramirez RC	10.00
116	Hayden Penn RC	15.00
117	Pedro Lopez RC	10.00
118	Shawn Bowman RC	15.00
119	Chad Orvella RC	10.00
120	Sean Tracey RC	10.00
121	Bobby Livingston RC	10.00
122	Michael Rogers RC	10.00
123	Willy Mota RC	15.00
124	Brandon McCarthy RC	15.00
125	Mike Morse RC	15.00
126	Matt Lindstrom RC	10.00
127	Brian Stavisky RC	10.00
128	Rich Gardner RC	10.00
129	Scott Mitchinson RC	10.00
130	Billy McCarthy RC	10.00
131	Brandon Sing RC	15.00
132	Matt Albers RC	12.00
133	George Kottaras RC	15.00
134	Luis Hernandez RC	10.00
135	Humberto Sanchez RC	20.00
136	Buck Coats RC	12.00
137	Jonathan Barratt RC	10.00
138	Raul Tablado RC	12.00
139	Jake Mullinax RC	15.00
140	Edgar Varela RC	12.00
141	Ryan Garko RC	25.00
142	Nate McLouth RC	10.00
143	Shane Costa RC	10.00

Blue Refractor

Stars:	2-4X
Rookies:	1-2X
Production 499	
Rookie Autos.:	1-1.5X
Production 299	

Gold Refractor

No Pricing
Production 25 Sets

Green Refractor

Stars:	2-3X
Rookies:	1-2X
Production 899	
Rookie Autos.:	1-1.5X
Production 399	

Red Refractor

Stars:	3-5X
Rookies:	2-3X
Rookie Autos.:	1.5-2X
Production 199 Sets	

Silver Refractor

Stars:	4-6X

Rookies:	2-3X
Rookie Autos.:	1.5-3X
Production 99 Sets	

Printing Plates

No Pricing
Production one set for each color.

Printing Plates Autograph

No Pricing
Production one set for each color.

A-Rod Throwback Autograph

NM/M
Production 100
AR	Alex Rodriguez	150.00

Bowman's Best Shortstops

Production 25
No Pricing

Mirror Image Spokesmen

Production 10
No Pricing

Mirror Image Throwback

NM/M
Production 50
RR	Cal Ripken Jr., Alex Rodriguez	450.00

2006 Bowman

NM/M
Complete Set (231):		
Common Player (1-200):		.15
Common RC (201-220):		.25
Common Auto (219-231):		10.00
Pack (10):		4.00
Box (24):		85.00
1	Nick Swisher	.15
2	Ted Lilly	.15
3	John Smoltz	.25
4	Lyle Overbay	.15
5	Alfonso Soriano	.50
6	Javier Vazquez	.15
7	Ronnie Belliard	.15
8	Jose Reyes	.50
9	Brian Roberts	.25
10	Curt Schilling	.75
11	Adam Dunn	.50
12	Zack Greinke	.15
13	Carlos Guillen	.15
14	Jon Garland	.15
15	Robinson Cano	.25
16	Chris Burke	.15
17	Barry Zito	.25
18	Russ Adams	.15
19	Chris Capuano	.15
20	Scott Rolen	.50
21	Kerry Wood	.25
22	Scott Kazmir	.25
23	Brandon Webb	.25

#	Player		#	Player	
24	Jeff Kent	.25	127	Cliff Floyd	.15
25	Albert Pujols	2.00	128	Jeremy Reed	.15
26	C.C. Sabathia	.15	129	Jake Westbrook	.15
27	Adrian Beltre	.15	130	Wily Mo Pena	.15
28	Brad Wilkerson	.15	131	Toby Hall	.15
29	Randy Wolf	.15	132	David Ortiz	.75
30	Jason Bay	.15	133	David Eckstein	.15
31	Austin Kearns	.25	134	Brady Clark	.15
32	Clint Barmes	.15	135	Marcus Giles	.15
33	Mike Sweeney	.15	136	Aaron Hill	.15
34	Justin Verlander	.25	137	Mark Kotsay	.15
35	Justin Morneau	.15	138	Carlos Lee	.40
36	Scott Podsednik	.25	139	Roy Oswalt	.40
37	Jason Giambi	.50	140	Chone Figgins	.15
38	Steve Finley	.15	141	Mike Mussina	.50
39	Morgan Ensberg	.25	142	Orlando Hernandez	.15
40	Eric Chavez	.25	143	Magglio Ordonez	.15
41	Roy Halladay	.25	144	Jim Edmonds	.40
42	Horacio Ramirez	.15	145	Bobby Abreu	.40
43	Ben Sheets	.25	146	Nick Johnson	.15
44	Chris Carpenter	.40	147	Carlos Beltran	.50
45	Andruw Jones	.50	148	Jhonny Peralta	.15
46	Carlos Zambrano	.25	149	Pedro Feliz	.15
47	Jonny Gomes	.25	150	Miguel Tejada	.50
48	Shawn Green	.15	151	Luis Gonzalez	.15
49	Moises Alou	.25	152	Carl Crawford	.25
50	Ichiro Suzuki	1.50	153	Yadier Molina	.15
51	Juan Pierre	.15	154	Rich Harden	.25
52	Grady Sizemore	.40	155	Tim Wakefield	.15
53	Kazuo Matsui	.15	156	Rickie Weeks	.25
54	Jose Vidro	.15	157	Johnny Estrada	.15
55	Jake Peavy	.25	158	Gustavo Chacin	.15
56	Dallas McPherson	.15	159	Dan Johnson	.15
57	Ryan Howard	1.00	160	Willy Taveras	.15
58	Zachary Duke	.15	161	Garret Anderson	.25
59	Michael Young	.15	162	Randy Johnson	.75
60	Todd Helton	.50	163	Jermaine Dye	.15
61	David DeJesus	.15	164	Joe Mauer	.50
62	Ivan Rodriguez	.50	165	Ervin Santana	.15
63	Johan Santana	.50	166	Jeremy Bonderman	.15
64	Danny Haren	.15	167	Garrett Atkins	.15
65	Derek Jeter	2.00	168	Manny Ramirez	.75
66	Greg Maddux	1.00	169	Brad Eldred	.15
67	Jorge Cantu	.15	170	Chase Utley	.25
68	Conor Jackson (RC)	.15	171	Mark Loretta	.15
69	Victor Martinez	.25	172	John Patterson	.15
70	David Wright	1.00	173	Tom Glavine	.40
71	Ryan Church	.15	174	Dontrelle Willis	.25
72	Khalil Greene	.15	175	Mark Teixeira	.50
73	Jimmy Rollins	.25	176	Felix Hernandez	.40
74	Hank Blalock	.25	177	Cliff Lee	.15
75	Pedro Martinez	.75	178	Jason Schmidt	.25
76	Jonathan Papelbon (RC)	3.00	179	Chad Tracy	.15
77	Felipe Lopez	.15	180	Rocco Baldelli	.15
78	Jeff Francis	.15	181	Aramis Ramirez	.25
79	Andrew Sisco	.15	182	Andy Pettitte	.25
80	Hideki Matsui	1.50	183	Mark Mulder	.25
81	Ken Griffey Jr.	1.50	184	Geoff Jenkins	.15
82	Nomar Garciaparra	.75	185	Chipper Jones	.75
83	Kevin Millwood	.25	186	Vernon Wells	.25
84	Paul Konerko	.25	187	Bobby Crosby	.15
85	A.J. Burnett	.15	188	Lance Berkman	.40
86	Mike Piazza	.75	189	Vladimir Guerrero	.75
87	Brian Giles	.25	190	Jose Capellan (RC)	.15
88	Johnny Damon	.75	191	Brad Penny	.15
89	Jim Thome	.50	192	Jose Guillen	.15
90	Roger Clemens	2.00	193	Brett Myers	.15
91	Aaron Rowand	.15	194	Miguel Cabrera	.75
92	Rafael Furcal	.25	195	Bartolo Colon	.15
93	Gary Sheffield	.50	196	Craig Biggio	.25
94	Mike Cameron	.15	197	Tim Hudson	.25
95	Carlos Delgado	.50	198	Mark Prior	.50
96	Jorge Posada	.40	199	Mark Buehrle	.15
97	Denny Bautista	.15	200	Barry Bonds	2.00
98	Mike Maroth	.15	201	Anderson Hernandez (RC)	.25
99	Brad Radke	.15	202	Charlton Jimerson (RC)	.25
100	Alex Rodriguez	2.00	203	Jeremy Accardo RC	.50
101	Freddy Garcia	.15	204	Hanley Ramirez (RC)	.50
102	Oliver Perez	.15	205	Matt Capps (RC)	.25
103	Jon Lieber	.15	206	John-Ford Griffin (RC)	.25
104	Melvin Mora	.25	207	Chuck James (RC)	.25
105	Travis Hafner	.40	208	Jaime Bubela (RC)	.25
106	Matt Cain (RC)	.25	209	Mark Woodyard (RC)	.25
107	Derek Lowe	.15	210	Jason Botts (RC)	.25
108	Luis Castillo	.15	211	Chris Demaria RC	.75
109	Livan Hernandez	.15	212	Miguel Perez (RC)	.25
110	Tadahito Iguchi	.15	213	Tom Gorzelanny (RC)	.25
111	Shawn Chacon	.15	214	Adam Wainwright (RC)	.25
112	Frank Thomas	.40	215	Ryan Garko (RC)	.25
113	Josh Beckett	.25	216	Jason Bergmann RC	1.00
114	Aubrey Huff	.15	217	J.J. Furmaniak (RC)	.25
115	Derrek Lee	.50	218	Francisco Liriano (RC)	.50
116	Chien-Ming Wang	.25	219	Kenji Johjima RC	2.50
117	Joe Crede	.15	219	Kenji Johjima/ Auto. RC	75.00
118	Torii Hunter	.25	220	Craig Hansen RC	1.50
119	J.D. Drew	.25	220	Craig Hansen/ Auto. RC	20.00
120	Troy Glaus	.40	221	Ryan Zimmerman/ Auto. (RC)	40.00
121	Sean Casey	.15	222	Joey Devine/Auto. RC	10.00
122	Edgar Renteria	.25	223	Scott Olsen/ Auto. (RC)	10.00
123	Craig Wilson	.15			
124	Adam Eaton	.15			
125	Jeff Francoeur	.15			
126	Bruce Chen	.15			

#	Player	
224	Darrell Rasner/ Auto. (RC)	10.00
225	Craig Breslow/ Auto. RC	10.00
226	Reggie Abercrombie/ Auto. (RC)	10.00
227	Dan Uggla/Auto. (RC)	20.00
228	Willie Eyre/Auto. (RC)	10.00
229	Joel Zumaya/ Auto. (RC)	20.00
230	Ricky Nolasco/ Auto. (RC)	10.00
231	Ian Kinsler/Auto. (RC)	20.00

Blue

Stars:	2-4X
Rookies (201-220):	2-4X
RC Auto. (219-231):	1-1.5X
Production 500 Sets	

Red

No Pricing
Production One Set

White

Stars:	3-6X
Rookies (201-220):	3-6X
RC Auto. (219-231):	1-2X
Production 120 Sets	

Base of the Future

		NM/M
JH	Justin Huber	20.00

Chrome Prospects

		NM/M
Common Prospect:		.50
BC1	Alex Gordon	25.00
BC2	Jonathan George	.50
BC3	Scott Walter	.50
BC4	Brian Holliday	.50
BC5	Ben Copeland	1.00
BC6	Bobby Wilson	1.50
BC7	Mayker Sandoval	1.50
BC8	Alejandro de Aza	2.00
BC9	David Munoz	.75
BC10	Josh LeBlanc	1.00
BC11	Philippe Valiquette	1.00
BC12	Edwin Bellorin	1.00
BC13	Jason Quarles	1.00
BC14	Mark Trumbo	2.00
BC15	Steve Kelly	.75
BC16	Jamie Hoffman	.75
BC17	Joseph Bauserman	1.00
BC18	Nick Adenhart	8.00
BC19	Mike Butia	.75
BC20	Jon Weber	.75
BC21	Luis Valdez	1.00
BC22	Rafael Rodriguez	1.50
BC23	Wyatt Toregas	1.50
BC24	John Vanden Berg	.75
BC25	Mike Connolly	.75
BC26	Mike O'Connor	3.00
BC27	Garrett Mock	.75
BC28	Bill Layman	.75
BC29	Luis Pena	.75
BC30	Billy Killian	1.00
BC31	Ross Ohlendorf	.50
BC32	Mark Kaiser	.75
BC33	Ryan Costello	.75
BC34	Dale Thayer	.50
BC35	Steve Garrabrants	.75
BC36	Samuel Deduno	.75
BC37	Juan Portes	3.00
BC38	Javier Martinez	.75
BC39	Clint Sammons	1.00
BC40	Andrew Kown	1.50
BC41	Matt Tolbert	.75
BC42	Michael Ekstrom	.75
BC43	Shawn Norris	.75
BC44	Diory Hernandez	.75
BC45	Chris Maples	.75
BC46	Aaron Hathaway	1.00
BC47	Steven Baker	.75
BC48	Greg Creek	1.00
BC49	Collin Mahoney	.75
BC50	Corey Ragsdale	1.50
BC51	Ariel Nunez	.50
BC52	Max Ramirez	4.00
BC53	Eric Rodland	1.00
BC54	Dante Brinkley	1.00
BC55	Casey Craig	1.00
BC56	Ryan Spilborghs	2.50
BC57	Fredy Deza	.75
BC58	Jeff Frazier	.50
BC59	Vince Cordova	.50
BC60	Oswaldo Navarro	1.50
BC61	Jarod Rine	.75
BC62	Jordan Tata	1.50
BC63	Ben Julianel	1.00
BC64	Yung-Chi Chen	5.00
BC65	Carlos Torres	1.50
BC66	Juan Francia	1.50
BC67	Brett Smith	1.00
BC68	Francisco Leandro	1.00
BC69	Chris Turner	3.00
BC70	Matt Joyce	2.00
BC71	Jason Jones	1.00
BC72	Jose Diaz	.50
BC73	Kevin Ool	.75
BC74	Nate Bumstead	1.00
BC75	Omir Santos	1.00
BC76	Shawn Riggans	1.00
BC77	Ofilio Castro	.50
BC78	Mike Rozier	1.50
BC79	Wilkin Ramirez	2.00
BC80	Yobal Duenas	1.00
BC81	Adam Bourassa	1.00
BC82	Tony Granadillo	1.00
BC83	Brad McCann	4.00
BC84	Dustin Majewski	1.00
BC85	Kelvin Jimenez	.50
BC86	Mark Reed	4.00
BC87	Asdrubal Cabrera	3.00
BC88	James Barthmaier	1.00
BC89	Brandon Boggs	.75
BC90	Raul Valdez	.50
BC91	Jose Campusano	1.50
BC92	Henry Owens	1.00
BC93	Tug Hulett	1.00
BC94	Nate Gold	1.00
BC95	Lee Mitchell	1.00
BC96	John Hardy	.75
BC97	Aaron Wideman	.75
BC98	Brandon Roberts	1.50
BC99	Lou Santangelo	.75
BC100	Kyle Kendrick	2.50
BC101	Michael Collins	2.00
BC102	Camilo Vazquez	.75
BC103	Mark McLemore	.50
BC104	Alexander Peralta	.75
BC105	Josh Whitesell	1.00
BC106	Carlos Guevara	.50
BC107	Michael Aubrey	1.50
BC108	Brandon Chaves	1.00
BC109	Leonard Davis	1.00
BC110	Kendry Morales	2.00

Chrome Prospects Refractor

Refractor (1-110):	2-4X
Production 500 Sets	

Chrome Prospects Blue Refractor

Blue Refractor (1-110):	4-6X
Production 150 Sets	

Chrome Prospects Gold Refractor

Gold Refractor (1-110):	8-15X
Production 50 Sets	

Chrome Prospects Orange Refractor

No Pricing
Production 25 Sets

Chrome Prospects Red Refractor

No Pricing
Production Five Sets

Chrome Prospects X-Fractor

X-Fractor (1-110):	3-6X
Production 250 Sets	

Prospects

		NM/M
Common Player:		.25
B1	Alex Gordon	10.00

B2	Jonathan George	.25
B3	Scott Walter	.25
B4	Brian Holliday	.25
B5	Ben Copeland	.50
B6	Bobby Wilson	.50
B7	Mayker Sandoval	.50
B8	Alejandro de Aza	.25
B9	David Munoz	.25
B10	Josh LeBlanc	.50
B11	Philippe Valiquette	.50
B12	Edwin Bellorin	.50
B13	Jason Quarles	.50
B14	Mark Trumbo	.75
B15	Steve Kelly	.25
B16	Jamie Hoffman	.25
B17	Joseph Bauserman	.50
B18	Nick Adenhart	2.50
B19	Mike Butia	.25
B20	Jon Weber	.25
B21	Luis Valdez	.50
B22	Rafael Rodriguez	.75
B23	Wyatt Toregas	.75
B24	John Vanden Berg	.25
B25	Mike Connolly	.25
B26	Mike O'Connor	1.00
B27	Garrett Mock	.25
B28	Bill Layman	.25
B29	Luis Pena	.25
B30	Billy Killian	.50
B31	Ross Ohlendorf	.25
B32	Mark Kaiser	.25
B33	Ryan Costello	.25
B34	Dale Thayer	.25
B35	Steve Garrabrants	.25
B36	Samuel Deduno	.25
B37	Juan Portes	1.00
B38	Javier Martinez	.25
B39	Clint Sammons	.25
B40	Andrew Kown	.75
B41	Matt Tolbert	.25
B42	Michael Ekstrom	.25
B43	Shawn Norris	.25
B44	Diory Hernandez	.25
B45	Chris Maples	.25
B46	Aaron Hathaway	.50
B47	Steven Baker	.50
B48	Greg Creek	.50
B49	Collin Mahoney	.25
B50	Corey Ragsdale	.50
B51	Ariel Nunez	.25
B52	Max Ramirez	1.50
B53	Eric Rodland	.50
B54	Dante Brinkley	.50
B55	Casey Craig	.50
B56	Ryan Spilborghs	1.00
B57	Fredy Deza	.25
B58	Jeff Frazier	.25
B59	Vince Cordova	.25
B60	Oswaldo Navarro	.75
B61	Jarod Rine	.25
B62	Jordan Tata	.75
B63	Ben Julianel	.50
B64	Yung-Chi Chen	1.50
B65	Carlos Torres	.50
B66	Juan Francia	.50
B67	Brett Smith	.50
B68	Francisco Leandro	.25
B69	Chris Turner	1.00
B70	Matt Joyce	.75
B71	Jason Jones	.25
B72	Jose Diaz	.25
B73	Kevin Ool	.25
B74	Nate Bumstead	.25
B75	Omir Santos	.25
B76	Shawn Riggans	.25
B77	Ofilio Castro	.25
B78	Mike Rozier	.75
B79	Wilkin Ramirez	.75
B80	Yobal Duenas	.25
B81	Adam Bourassa	.50
B82	Tony Granadillo	.25
B83	Brad McCann	1.50
B84	Dustin Majewski	.50

B85	Kelvin Jimenez	.25
B86	Mark Reed	1.50
B87	Asdrubal Cabrera	1.00
B88	James Barthmaier	.25
B89	Brandon Boggs	.25
B90	Raul Valdez	.25
B91	Jose Campusano	.50
B92	Henry Owens	.25
B93	Tug Hulett	.50
B94	Nate Gold	.25
B95	Lee Mitchell	.25
B96	John Hardy	.25
B97	Aaron Wideman	.25
B98	Brandon Roberts	.50
B99	Lou Santangelo	.25
B100	Kyle Kendrick	.75
B101	Michael Collins	.75
B102	Camilo Vazquez	.25
B103	Mark McLemore	.25
B104	Alexander Peralta	.25
B105	Josh Whitesell	.50
B106	Carlos Guevara	.25
B107	Michael Aubrey	.50
B108	Brandon Chaves	.25
B109	Leonard Davis	.25
B110	Kendry Morales	1.50
B111	Koby Clemens	25.00
B112	Lance Broadway	15.00
B113	Cameron Maybin	100.00
B114	Mike Aviles	10.00
B115	Kyle Blanks	40.00
B116	Chris Dickerson	15.00
B117	Sean Gallagher	20.00
B118	Jamar Hill	15.00
B119	Garrett Mock	15.00
B120	Kendry Morales	15.00
B121	Russel Rohlicek	15.00
B122	Clete Thomas	15.00
B123	Josh Kinney	15.00
B124	Justin Huber	10.00

Prospects Blue

Blue:	2-3X
Blue Autos.:	1.5X
Production 500 Sets	

Prospects Gold

Gold:	1-1.5X
Inserted 1:1	

Prospects White

White:	4-6X
White Autos.:	1.5-2X
Production 120 Sets	

Signs of the Future

		NM/M
Common Auto.:		10.00
BB	Brian Bogusevic	10.00
MB	Mark Bowden	20.00
RB	Ryan Braun	60.00
TB	Travis Buck	15.00
JC	Jeff Clement	15.00
BC	Ben Copeland	15.00
MC	Mike Costanzo	10.00
TC	Trevor Crowe	15.00
JD	John Drennen	10.00
JE	Jacoby Ellsbury	30.00
YE	Yunel Escobar	15.00
JM	John Mayberry Jr.	15.00
GO	Garrett Olson	10.00
CR	Cesar Ramos	10.00
RR	Ricky Romero	10.00
HS	Henry Sanchez	10.00
DS	Denard Span	10.00
AT	Aaron Thompson	15.00
RT	Ryan Tucker	10.00
TT	Troy Tulowitzki	30.00
SW	Sean West	10.00

2006 Bowman Chrome

RYAN HOWARD
PHILADELPHIA PHILLIES

	NM/M
Complete Set (224):	

Common Player:		.25
Common Rookie (201-220):		.50
Pack (4):		8.00
Box (18):		125.00
1	Nick Swisher	.25
2	Ted Lilly	.25
3	John Smoltz	.50
4	Lyle Overbay	.25
5	Alfonso Soriano	.75
6	Javier Vazquez	.25
7	Ronnie Belliard	.25
8	Jose Reyes	.75
9	Brian Roberts	.25
10	Curt Schilling	.25
11	Adam Dunn	.75
12	Zack Greinke	.25
13	Carlos Guillen	.25
14	Jon Garland	.25
15	Robinson Cano	.50
16	Chris Burke	.25
17	Barry Zito	.50
18	Russ Adams	.25
19	Chris Capuano	.25
20	Scott Rolen	.75
21	Kerry Wood	.25
22	Scott Kazmir	.50
23	Brandon Webb	.50
24	Jeff Kent	.40
25	Albert Pujols	2.50
26	C.C. Sabathia	.25
27	Adrian Beltre	.25
28	Brad Wilkerson	.25
29	Randy Wolf	.25
30	Jason Bay	.50
31	Austin Kearns	.25
32	Clint Barmes	.25
33	Mike Sweeney	.25
34	Kevin Youkilis	.25
35	Justin Morneau	.50
36	Scott Podsednik	.40
37	Jason Giambi	.75
38	Steve Finley	.25
39	Morgan Ensberg	.25
40	Eric Chavez	.40
41	Roy Halladay	.50
42	Horacio Ramirez	.25
43	Ben Sheets	.40
44	Chris Carpenter	.50
45	Andruw Jones	.75
46	Carlos Zambrano	.40
47	Jonny Gomes	.40
48	Shawn Green	.40
49	Moises Alou	.40
50	Ichiro Suzuki	1.50
51	Juan Pierre	.25
52	Grady Sizemore	.75
53	Kazuo Matsui	.25
54	Jose Vidro	.25
55	Jake Peavy	.50
56	Dallas McPherson	.25
57	Ryan Howard	2.00
58	Zachary Duke	.25
59	Michael Young	.50
60	Todd Helton	.75
61	David DeJesus	.25
62	Ivan Rodriguez	.75
63	Johan Santana	.75
64	Danny Haren	.25
65	Derek Jeter	2.50
66	Greg Maddux	1.50
67	Jorge Cantu	.25
68	J.J. Hardy	.25
69	Victor Martinez	.50
70	David Wright	1.50
71	Ryan Church	.25
72	Khalil Greene	.25
73	Jimmy Rollins	.40
74	Hank Blalock	.40
75	Pedro Martinez	1.00
76	Chris Shelton	.25
77	Felipe Lopez	.25
78	Jeff Francis	.25
79	Andrew Sisco	.25
80	Hideki Matsui	1.50
81	Ken Griffey Jr.	1.50
82	Nomar Garciaparra	.75
83	Kevin Millwood	.25
84	Paul Konerko	.50
85	A.J. Burnett	.25
86	Mike Piazza	1.00
87	Brian Giles	.40
88	Johnny Damon	1.00
89	Jim Thome	.75
90	Roger Clemens	2.50
91	Aaron Rowand	.25
92	Rafael Furcal	.40
93	Gary Sheffield	.50
94	Mike Cameron	.25
95	Carlos Delgado	.50
96	Jorge Posada	.50
97	Denny Bautista	.25
98	Mike Maroth	.25
99	Brad Radke	.25
100	Alex Rodriguez	2.50

101	Freddy Garcia	.25
102	Oliver Perez	.25
103	Jon Lieber	.25
104	Melvin Mora	.25
105	Travis Hafner	.50
106	Alex Rios	.25
107	Derek Lowe	.25
108	Luis Castillo	.25
109	Livan Hernandez	.25
110	Tadahito Iguchi	.25
111	Shawn Chacon	.25
112	Frank Thomas	.75
113	Josh Beckett	.50
114	Aubrey Huff	.25
115	Derrek Lee	.75
116	Chien-Ming Wang	.75
117	Joe Crede	.50
118	Torii Hunter	.50
119	J.D. Drew	.40
120	Troy Glaus	.50
121	Sean Casey	.40
122	Edgar Renteria	.40
123	Craig Wilson	.25
124	Adam Eaton	.25
125	Jeff Francoeur	.40
126	Bruce Chen	.25
127	Cliff Floyd	.25
128	Jeremy Reed	.25
129	Jake Westbrook	.25
130	Wily Mo Pena	.25
131	Toby Hall	.25
132	David Ortiz	1.00
133	David Eckstein	.25
134	Brady Clark	.25
135	Marcus Giles	.25
136	Aaron Hill	.25
137	Mark Kotsay	.25
138	Carlos Lee	.50
139	Roy Oswalt	.50
140	Chone Figgins	.25
141	Mike Mussina	.75
142	Orlando Hernandez	.25
143	Magglio Ordonez	.40
144	Jim Edmonds	.50
145	Bobby Abreu	.50
146	Nick Johnson	.25
147	Carlos Beltran	.75
148	Jhonny Peralta	.25
149	Pedro Feliz	.25
150	Miguel Tejada	.75
151	Luis Gonzalez	.40
152	Carl Crawford	.50
153	Yadier Molina	.25
154	Rich Harden	.40
155	Tim Wakefield	.25
156	Rickie Weeks	.50
157	Johnny Estrada	.25
158	Gustavo Chacin	.25
159	Dan Johnson	.25
160	Willy Taveras	.25
161	Garret Anderson	.40
162	Randy Johnson	1.00
163	Jermaine Dye	.25
164	Joe Mauer	.75
165	Ervin Santana	.25
166	Jeremy Bonderman	.50
167	Garrett Atkins	.25
168	Manny Ramirez	1.00
169	Brad Eldred	.25
170	Chase Utley	.75
171	Mark Loretta	.25
172	John Patterson	.25
173	Tom Glavine	.50
174	Dontrelle Willis	.50
175	Mark Teixeira	.50
176	Felix Hernandez	.50
177	Cliff Lee	.25
178	Jason Schmidt	.40
179	Chad Tracy	.25
180	Rocco Baldelli	.25
181	Aramis Ramirez	.40
182	Andy Pettitte	.50
183	Mark Mulder	.40
184	Geoff Jenkins	.25
185	Chipper Jones	.75
186	Vernon Wells	.50
187	Bobby Crosby	.25
188	Lance Berkman	.50
189	Vladimir Guerrero	.75
190	Coco Crisp	.25
191	Brad Penny	.25
192	Jose Guillen	.25
193	Brett Myers	.25
194	Miguel Cabrera	.75
195	Bartolo Colon	.25
196	Craig Biggio	.40
197	Tim Hudson	.50
198	Mark Prior	.50
199	Mark Buehrle	.40
200	Barry Bonds	2.50
201	Anderson Hernandez (RC)	.50
202	Jose Capellan (RC)	.50
203	Jeremy Accardo RC	1.00

204	Hanley Ramirez (RC)	1.00
205	Matt Capps (RC)	.50
206	Jonathan Papelbon (RC)	4.00
207	Chuck James (RC)	.50
208	Matt Cain (RC)	1.00
209	Cole Hamels (RC)	1.00
210	Jason Botts (RC)	.50
211	Lastings Milledge (RC)	.50
212	Conor Jackson (RC)	.50
213	Yusmeiro Petit (RC)	.50
214	Alay Soler RC	2.00
215	Willy Aybar (RC)	.50
216	Adam Loewen (RC)	.50
217	Justin Verlander (RC)	4.00
218	Francisco Liriano (RC)	4.00
219	Kenji Johjima RC	4.00
219	Kenji Johjima/ Auto. RC	75.00
220	Craig Hansen RC	2.00
221	Prince Fielder/ Auto. (RC)	120.00
222	Josh Barfield/ Auto. (RC)	15.00
223	Fausto Carmona/ Auto. (RC)	25.00
224	James Loney/ Auto. (RC)	30.00

Refractor
Refractor (1-200): 2-4X
Refractor (201-220): 2-3X
Inserted 1:4
Autograph (219, 221-224):1-1.5X
Production 500

Blue Refractor
Blue Refractor (1-200): 3-6X
Blue Refractor (201-220): 4-6X
Production 150
Blue Ref. Auto.
 (219, 221-224): 1-2.5X
Production 150

Gold Refractor
Gold Refractor (1-200): 8-15X
Gold Refractor (201-220): 8-15X
Production 50
Gold Ref. Auto.
 (219, 221-224): 3-5X
Production 50

Orange Refractor
Orange Refractor (1-200):15-25X
Orange Refractor
 (201-220): 15-25X
Production 25
Orange Ref. Auto.
 (221-224): No Pricing
Production 25

Red Refractor
No Pricing
Production Five Sets

Super Fractor
No Pricing
Production One Set

X-Fractor
X-Refractor (1-200): 3-5X
X-Refractor (201-220): 3-5X
Production 250
X-Fractor Auto.
 (219, 221-224): 1-2X
Production 225

Printing Plates
No Pricing
Production One Set

Bowman Chrome Prospects

DEXTER FOWLER
COLORADO ROCKIES™

		NM/M
	Common Prospect:	.50
BC111	Koby Clemens	2.00
BC112	Lance Broadway	1.50
BC113	Cameron Maybin	15.00
BC114	Mike Aviles	.50
BC115	Kyle Blanks	2.00
BC116	Chris Dickerson	1.00
BC117	Sean Gallagher	3.00
BC118	Jamar Hill	.50
BC119	Garrett Mock	.75
BC120	Russel Rohlicek	.50
BC121	Clete Thomas	1.00
BC122	Elvis Andrus	5.00
BC123	Brandon Moss	.75
BC124	Mark Holliman	3.00
BC125	Jose Tabata	15.00
BC126	Corey Wimberly	2.00
BC127	Bobby Wilson	1.00
BC128	Edward Mujica	1.50
BC129	Hunter Pence	6.00
BC130	Adam Heether	.50
BC131	Andy Wilson	.50
BC132	Radhames Liz	3.00
BC133	Garrett Patterson	.50
BC134	Carlos Gomez	15.00
BC135	Jared Lansford	1.00
BC136	Jose Arredondo	2.00
BC137	Renee Cortez	1.00
BC138	Francisco Rosario	.50
BC139	Brian Stokes	.50
BC140	Will Thompson	.50
BC141	Ernesto Frieri	1.00
BC142	Jose Mijares	1.00
BC143	Jeremy Slayden	2.00
BC144	Brandon Fahey	1.00
BC145	Jason Windsor	1.50
BC146	Shawn Nottingham	1.00
BC147	Dallas Trahern	1.00
BC148	Jon Niese	3.00
BC149	A.J. Shappi	.50
BC150	Jordan Pals	.50
BC151	Tim Moss	.50
BC152	Stephen Marek	1.00
BC153	Mat Gamel	3.00
BC154	Sean Henn	.50
BC155	Matt Guillory	.50
BC156	Brandon Jones	4.00
BC157	Gary Galvez	1.00
BC158	Shane Lindsay	1.50
BC159	Jesus Reina	4.00
BC160	Lorenzo Cain	4.00
BC161	Chris Britton	1.00
BC162	Yovani Gallardo	4.00
BC163	Matt Walker	1.00
BC164	Shaun Cumberland	1.00
BC165	Ryan Patterson	2.00
BC166	Michael Hollimon	1.00
BC167	Eude Brito	.50
BC168	John Bowker	.50
BC169	James Avery	.50
BC170	John Bannister	.50
BC171	Juan Ciriaco	.50
BC172	Manuel Corpas	1.00
BC173	Leo Rosales	.50
BC174	Tim Kennelly	.50
BC175	Adam Russell	.50
BC176	Jeremy Hellickson	4.00
BC177	Ryan Klosterman	.50
BC178	Evan Meek	1.00
BC179	Steve Murphy	2.00
BC180	Scott Feldman	.50
BC181	Pablo Sandoval	1.50
BC182	Dexter Fowler	2.00
BC183	Jairo Cuevas	1.50
BC184	Andrew Pinckney	1.00
BC185	Marino Salas	.50
BC186	Justin Christian	.50
BC187	Ching-Lung Lo	3.00
BC188	Randy Roth	2.00
BC189	Andrew Sonnanstine	3.00
BC190	Josh Outman	3.00
BC191	Yuber A. Rodriguez	1.00
BC192	Hainley Statia	2.00
BC193	Kevin Estrada	1.50
BC194	Jeff Karstens	1.50
BC195	Corey Coles	.50
BC196	Gustavo Espinoza	1.00
BC197	Brian Horwitz	.50
BC198	Landon Jacobsen	.50
BC199	Ben Krosschell	1.00
BC200	Jason Jaramillo	1.00
BC201	Josh Wilson	.50
BC202	Jason Ray	.50
BC203	Brent Dlugach	1.00
BC204	Cesar Jimenez	1.00
BC205	Eric Haberer	.50
BC206	Felipe Paulino	.50
BC207	Alcides Escobar	2.00
BC208	Jose Ascanio	1.00
BC209	Yoel Hernandez	1.00
BC210	Geoff Vandel	1.00
BC211	Travis Denker	1.50
BC212	Ramon Alvarado	1.00
BC213	Welinson Baez	1.50
BC214	Chris Kolkhorst	.50
BC215	Emiliano Fruto	1.00
BC216	Luis Cota	1.00
BC217	Mark Worrell	.50
BC218	Cla Meredith	1.50
BC219	Emmanuel Garcia	1.50
BC220	B.J. Szymanski	1.00
BC221	Alex Gordon	125.00
BC222	Mark Pawelek	25.00
BC223	Justin Upton	150.00
BC224	Sean West	15.00
BC225	Tyler Greene	15.00
BC226	Josh Kinney	15.00
BC227	Pedro Lopez	10.00
BC228	Troy Patton	25.00
BC229	Chris Iannetta	20.00
BC230	Jared Wells	10.00
BC231	Brandon Wood	20.00
BC232	Josh Geer	15.00
BC233	Cesar Carrillo	10.00
BC234	Franklin Gutierrez	15.00
BC235	Matt Garza	25.00
BC236	Eli Iorg	15.00
BC237	Trevor Bell	15.00
BC238	Jeff Lyman	15.00
BC239	Jon Lester	40.00
BC240	Kendry Morales	15.00
BC241	J. Brent Cox	15.00
BC242	Jose Bautista	15.00
BC243	Josh Sullivan	15.00
BC244	Brandon Snyder	15.00
BC245	Elvin Puello	10.00
BC246	Henry Sanchez	15.00
BC247	Jacob Marceaux	15.00

Prospects Refractors
Refractor (111-220): 2-4X
Refractor Auto. (221-247):1-1.5X
Production 500 Sets

Prospects Blue Refractors
Blue Refractor (111-220): 4-6X
Blue Refractor Auto.
 (221-247): 1-2.5X
Production 150 Sets

Prospects Gold Refractors
Gold Refractor (111-220): 8-15X
Gold Refractor Auto.
 (221-247): 3-5X
Production 50 Sets

Prospects Orange Refractors
Orange Refractor
 (111-220): 15-25X
Orange Refractor Auto.
 (221-247): 4-6X
Production 25 Sets

Prospects Red Refractors
No Pricing
Production Five Sets

Prospects Super Fractors
No Pricing
Production One Set

Prospects X-Fractors
X-Refractor (111-220): 3-5X
X-Refractor Auto. (221-247):1-2X
Production 225

2006 Bowman Chrome Draft

		NM/M
	Complete Set (55):	25.00
	Common Player:	.50
1	Matthew Kemp (RC)	1.50
2	Taylor Tankersley (RC)	.50
3	Michael Napoli RC	1.50
4	Brian Bannister (RC)	.50
5	Melky Cabrera (RC)	.50
6	Bill Bray (RC)	.50
7	Brian Anderson (RC)	.50
8	Jered Weaver (RC)	2.00
9	Chris Duncan (RC)	.50
10	Boof Bonser (RC)	1.00
11	Mike Rouse (RC)	.50
12	David Pauley (RC)	.50
13	Russell Martin (RC)	1.00
14	Jeremy Sowers (RC)	.50
15	Kevin Reese (RC)	.50
16	John Rheinecker (RC)	.50
17	Tommy Murphy (RC)	.50
18	Sean Marshall (RC)	.50
19	Jason Kubel (RC)	.50
20	Chad Billingsley (RC)	1.50
21	Kendry Morales (RC)	1.00
22	Jon Lester (RC)	2.00
23	Brandon Fahey RC	.50
24	Josh Johnson (RC)	.50
25	Kevin Frandsen (RC)	.50
26	Casey Janssen RC	.50
27	Scott Thorman (RC)	1.00
28	Scott Mathieson (RC)	.50
29	Jeremy Hermida (RC)	.50
30	Dustin Nippert (RC)	.50
31	Kevin Thompson (RC)	.50
32	Bobby Livingston (RC)	.50
33	Travis Ishikawa (RC)	.50
34	Jeff Mathis (RC)	.50
35	Charlie Haeger RC	1.00
36	Josh Willingham (RC)	.50
37	Taylor Buchholz (RC)	.50
38	Joel Guzman (RC)	.50
39	Zach Jackson (RC)	.50
40	Howie Kendrick (RC)	1.00
41	T.J. Beam RC	1.00
42	Ty Taubenheim RC	1.00
43	Erick Aybar (RC)	.50
44	Anibal Sanchez (RC)	1.00
45	Mike Pelfrey RC	6.00
46	Shawn Hill (RC)	.50
47	Chris Roberson (RC)	.50
48	Carlos Villanueva RC	.50
49	Andre Ethier (RC)	1.50
50	Anthony Reyes (RC)	1.00
51	Franklin Gutierrez (RC)	.50
52	Angel Guzman (RC)	.50
53	Michael O'Connor RC	.50
54	James Shields RC	2.50
55	Nate McLouth (RC)	.50

Refractor
Refractor (1-55): 2-4X

Gold Refractor
Gold Refractor (1-55): 8-15X
Production 50 Sets

Orange Refractor
Orange Refractor (1-55): 15-25X
Production 25 Sets

Red Refractor
No Pricing
Production Five Sets

X-Fractor
X-Fractor (1-55): 3-6X
Production 299 Sets

SuperFractor
No Pricing
Production One Set

Draft Picks

		NM/M
	Complete Set (90):	
	Common Draft Pick (1-65):	1.00
	Common Auto. (66-90):	20.00
1	Tyler Colvin	3.00
2	Chris Marrero	4.00
3	Hank Conger	4.00
4	Chris Parmelee	5.00
5	Jason Place	5.00
6	Billy Rowell	6.00
7	Travis Snider	8.00
8	Colton Willems	3.00
9	Chase Fontaine	2.00
10	Jon Jay	2.00
11	Wade Leblanc	3.00
12	Justin Masterson	5.00
13	Gary Daley	1.50
14	Justin Edwards	1.50
15	Charlie Yarbrough	1.50
16	Cyle Hankerd	4.00
17	Zach McAllister	1.50
18	Tyler Robertson	1.00
19	Joe Smith	1.00
20	Nate Culp	1.00
21	John Holdzkom	1.00
22	Patrick Bresnehan	1.00
23	Chad Lee	1.00
24	Ryan Morris	1.00
25	D'Arby Myers	2.50
26	Garrett Olson	2.00
27	Jon Still	1.50
28	Brandon Rice	1.00
29	Chris Davis	4.00
30	Zack Daeges	1.50
31	Bobby Henson	2.00
32	George Kontos	2.00
33	Jermaine Mitchell	2.50
34	Adam Coe	2.00
35	Dustin Richardson	1.50
36	Allen Craig	1.00
37	Austin McClune	1.50
38	Doug Fister	1.00
39	Corey Madden	1.00
40	Justin Jacobs	1.50

41	Jim Negrych	1.00
42	Tyler Norrick	1.50
43	Adam Davis	1.00
44	Brett Logan	1.00
45	Brian Omogrosso	1.00
46	Kyle Drabek	4.00
47	Jamie Ortiz	2.00
48	Alex Presley	2.00
49	Terrance Warren	1.50
50	David Christensen	2.00
51	Helder Velazquez	2.00
52	Matt McBride	1.50
53	Quintin Berry	2.00
54	Michael Eisenberg	1.00
55	Dan Garcia	1.00
56	Scott Cousins	1.00
57	Sean Land	1.00
58	Kristopher Medlen	1.00
59	Tyler Reves	1.00
60	John Shelby	1.50
61	Jordan Newton	1.50
62	Ricky Orta	1.00
63	Jason Donald	1.00
64	David Huff	1.50
65	Brett Sinkbeil	2.00
66	Evan Longoria/Auto.	125.00
67	Cody Johnson/Auto.	40.00
68	Kris Johnson/Auto.	25.00
69	Kasey Kiker/Auto.	20.00
70	Ronny Bourquin/Auto.	20.00
71	Adrian Cardenas/Auto.	40.00
72	Matt Antonelli/Auto.	50.00
73	Brooks Brown/Auto.	20.00
74	Steven Evarts/Auto.	25.00
75	Joshua Butler/Auto.	20.00
76	Chad Huffman/Auto.	20.00
77	Steven Wright/Auto.	15.00
78	Cory Rasmus/Auto.	20.00
79	Brad Furnish/Auto.	15.00
80	Andrew Carpenter/Auto.	20.00
81	Dustin Evans/Auto.	15.00
82	Tommy Hickman/Auto.	25.00
83	Matt Long/Auto.	15.00
84	Clayton Kershaw/Auto.	80.00
85	Kyle McCulloch/Auto.	20.00
86	Pedro Beato/Auto.	30.00
87	Kyler Burke/Auto.	25.00
88	Stephen Englund/Auto.	20.00
89	Michael Felix/Auto.	15.00
90	Sean Watson/Auto.	20.00

Draft Picks Refractor

EVAN LONGORIA
TAMPA BAY DEVIL RAYS

Refractor (1-65): 2-4X
Refractor Auto. (66-90): 1-1.5X
Production 500 for #'s 66-90

Draft Picks Blue Refractor

Blue Refractor (1-65): 4-8X
Production 199 Sets
Blue Auto. (66-90): 1-2.5X
Production 150 Sets

Draft Picks Gold Refractor

Gold Refractor (1-65): 8-15X
Production 50 Sets
Gold Auto. (66-90): 3-5X
Production 50 Sets

Draft Picks Orange Refractor

Orange Refractor (1-65): 15-25X
Production 25 Sets
Orange Auto. (66-90): No Pricing
Production 25 Sets

Draft Picks Red Refractor

No Pricing
Production Five Sets

Draft Picks SuperFractor

No Pricing
Production One Set

Draft Picks X-Fractor

X-Fractor (1-65): 3-6X
Production 299 Sets
X-Fractor Auto. (66-90): 1-2X
Production 225 Sets

Future's Game Prospects

		NM/M
Complete Set (45):		20.00
Common Player:		.50
1	Nick Adenhart	1.00
2	Joel Guzman	.50
3	Ryan Braun	.50
4	Carlos Carrasco	.50
5	Neil Walker	.50
6	Pablo Sandoval	.50
7	Gio Gonzalez	.50
8	Joey Votto	.50
9	Luis Cruz	.50
10	Nolan Reimold	.50
11	Juan Salas	.50
12	Josh Fields	1.00
13	Yovani Gallardo	1.00
14	Radhames Liz	.50
15	Eric Patterson	.50
16	Cameron Maybin	2.50
17	Edgar Martinez	.50
18	Hunter Pence	1.50
19	Phillip Hughes	2.00
20	Trent Oeltjen	.50
21	Nick Pereira	.50
22	Wladimir Balentien	.50
23	Stephen Drew	1.50
24	Davis Romero	.50
25	Joe Koshansky	.50
26	Chin-Lung Hu	2.00
27	Jason Hirsh	.50
28	Jose Tabata	2.00
29	Eric Hurley	.50
30	Yung-Chi Chen	2.50
31	Howie Kendrick	1.00
32	Humberto Sanchez	1.00
33	Alex Gordon	4.00
34	Yunel Escobar	.50
35	Travis Buck	.75
36	Billy Butler	1.00
37	Homer Bailey	1.00
38	George Kottaras	.50
39	Kurt Suzuki	.50
40	Joaquin Arias	.50
41	Matt Lindstrom	.50
42	Sean Smith	.50
43	Carlos Gonzalez	.50
44	Jaime Garcia	1.00
45	Jose Garcia	1.00

Future's Game Refractor

Refractor (1-45): 2-4X

Future's Game Blue Refractor

Blue (1-45): 4-8X
Production 199 Sets

Future's Game Gold Refractor

Gold (1-45): 8-15X
Production 50 Sets

Future's Game Orange Refractor

Orange (1-45): 15-30X
Production 25 Sets

Future's Game Red Refractor

No Pricing
Production Five Sets

Future's Game X-Fractor

X-Fractor (1-45): 3-6X
Production 299 Sets

Head of the Class Dual Autograph

	NM/M
Production 174	
Refractor:	1-1.5X
Production 50	
Gold Refractor:	No Pricing
Production 25	
RU Alex Rodriguez, Justin Upton	150.00

2006 Bowman Draft

		NM/M
Complete Set (55):		10.00
Common Player:		.25
Pack (5 + 2 Chrome):		3.50
Box (24):		75.00
1	Matthew Kemp (RC)	.50
2	Taylor Tankersley (RC)	.25
3	Michael Napoli RC	.50
4	Brian Bannister (RC)	.25
5	Melky Cabrera (RC)	.25
6	Bill Bray (RC)	.25
7	Brian Anderson (RC)	.25
8	Jered Weaver (RC)	.75
9	Chris Duncan (RC)	.25
10	Boof Bonser (RC)	.50
11	Mike Rouse (RC)	.25
12	David Pauley (RC)	.25
13	Russell Martin (RC)	.25
14	Jeremy Sowers (RC)	.25
15	Kevin Reese (RC)	.25
16	John Rheinecker (RC)	.25
17	Tommy Murphy (RC)	.25
18	Sean Marshall (RC)	.25
19	Jason Kubel (RC)	.25
20	Chad Billingsley (RC)	.75
21	Kendry Morales (RC)	.50
22	Jon Lester (RC)	.75
23	Brandon Fahey RC	.25
24	Josh Johnson (RC)	.25
25	Kevin Frandsen (RC)	.25
26	Casey Janssen RC	.25
27	Scott Thorman (RC)	.25
28	Scott Mathieson (RC)	.25
29	Jeremy Hermida (RC)	.25
30	Dustin Nippert (RC)	.25
31	Kevin Thompson (RC)	.25
32	Bobby Livingston (RC)	.25
33	Travis Ishikawa (RC)	.25
34	Jeff Mathis (RC)	.25
35	Charlie Haeger RC	.50
36	Josh Willingham (RC)	.50
37	Taylor Buchholz (RC)	.25
38	Joel Guzman (RC)	.25
39	Zach Jackson (RC)	.25
40	Howie Kendrick (RC)	.50
41	T.J. Beam (RC)	.25
42	Ty Taubenheim RC	.50
43	Erick Aybar (RC)	.25
44	Anibal Sanchez (RC)	.25
45	Mike Pelfrey RC	2.00
46	Shawn Hill (RC)	.25
47	Chris Roberson (RC)	.25
48	Carlos Villanueva RC	.25
49	Andre Ethier (RC)	.50
50	Anthony Reyes (RC)	.25
51	Franklin Gutierrez (RC)	.25
52	Angel Guzman (RC)	.25
53	Michael O'Connor RC	.25
54	James Shields RC	.50
55	Nate McLouth (RC)	.25

Gold

Gold (1-55): 1-2X
Inserted 1:1

Red

No Pricing
Production One Set

White

White (1-55): 2-5X
Production 225 Sets

Printing Plates

No Pricing
Production one set per color.

Draft Picks

		NM/M
Complete Set (65):		20.00
Common Draft Pick (1-65):		.50
1	Tyler Colvin	1.00
2	Chris Marrero	1.00
3	Hank Conger	1.00
4	Chris Parmelee	1.00
5	Jason Place	1.00
6	Billy Rowell	1.00
7	Travis Snider	2.00
8	Colton Willems	.75
9	Chase Fontaine	.50
10	Jon Jay	.50
11	Wade Leblanc	1.00
12	Justin Masterson	1.50
13	Gary Daley	.50
14	Justin Edwards	.50
15	Charlie Yarbrough	.50
16	Cyle Hankerd	1.00
17	Zach McAllister	.50
18	Tyler Robertson	.50
19	Joe Smith	.50
20	Nate Culp	.50
21	John Holdzkom	.50
22	Patrick Bresnehan	.50
23	Chad Lee	.50
24	Ryan Morris	.50
25	D'Arby Myers	.75
26	Garrett Olson	.75
27	Jon Still	.50
28	Brandon Rice	.50
29	Chris Davis	1.00
30	Zack Daeges	.50
31	Bobby Henson	.50
32	George Kontos	.50
33	Jermaine Mitchell	.75
34	Adam Coe	.50
35	Dustin Richardson	.50
36	Allen Craig	.50
37	Austin McClune	.50
38	Doug Fister	.50
39	Corey Madden	.50
40	Justin Jacobs	.50
41	Jim Negrych	.50
42	Tyler Norrick	.50
43	Adam Davis	.50
44	Brett Logan	.50
45	Brian Omogrosso	1.00
46	Kyle Drabek	1.00
47	Jamie Ortiz	.50
48	Alex Presley	.50
49	Terrance Warren	.50
50	David Christensen	.50
51	Helder Velazquez	.50
52	Matt McBride	.50
53	Quintin Berry	.50
54	Michael Eisenberg	.50
55	Dan Garcia	.50
56	Scott Cousins	.50
57	Sean Land	.50
58	Kristopher Medlen	.50
59	Tyler Reves	.50
60	John Shelby	.50
61	Jordan Newton	.50
62	Ricky Orta	.50
63	Jason Donald	.50
64	David Huff	.50
65	Brett Sinkbeil	.50

Future's Game Prospects

		NM/M
Complete Set (45):		10.00
Common Player:		.25
1	Nick Adenhart	.50
2	Joel Guzman	.25
3	Ryan Braun	.50
4	Carlos Carrasco	.25
5	Neil Walker	.25
6	Pablo Sandoval	.25
7	Gio Gonzalez	.25
8	Joey Votto	.25
9	Luis Cruz	.25
10	Nolan Reimold	.25
11	Juan Salas	.25
12	Josh Fields	.50
13	Yovani Gallardo	.50
14	Radhames Liz	.25
15	Eric Patterson	.25
16	Cameron Maybin	1.00
17	Edgar Martinez	.25
18	Hunter Pence	.75
19	Phillip Hughes	.75
20	Trent Oeltjen	.25
21	Nick Pereira	.25
22	Wladimir Balentien	.25
23	Stephen Drew	.50
24	Davis Romero	.25
25	Joe Koshansky	.25
26	Chin-Lung Hu	.25
27	Jason Hirsh	.25
28	Jose Tabata	.75
29	Eric Hurley	.25
30	Yung-Chi Chen	.75
31	Howie Kendrick	.50
32	Humberto Sanchez	.50
33	Alex Gordon	1.50
34	Yunel Escobar	.25
35	Travis Buck	.25
36	Billy Butler	.50
37	Homer Bailey	.50
38	George Kottaras	.25
39	Kurt Suzuki	.25
40	Joaquin Arias	.25
41	Matt Lindstrom	.25

42 Sean Smith .25
43 Carlos Gonzalez .25
44 Jaime Garcia .25
45 Jose Garcia .50

Future's Game Prospects Relics

NM/M
Common Player: 4.00
1 Nick Adenhart 8.00
2 Joel Guzman 4.00
3 Ryan Braun 8.00
4 Carlos Carrasco 4.00
5 Neil Walker 4.00
6 Pablo Sandoval 4.00
7 Gio Gonzalez 4.00
8 Joey Votto 6.00
9 Luis Cruz 4.00
10 Nolan Reimold 4.00
11 Juan Salas 4.00
12 Josh Fields 6.00
13 Yovani Gallardo 6.00
14 Radhames Liz 4.00
15 Eric Patterson 6.00
16 Cameron Maybin 10.00
17 Edgar Martinez 4.00
18 Hunter Pence 8.00
19 Phillip Hughes 20.00
20 Trent Oeltjen 4.00
21 Nick Pereira 4.00
22 Wladimir Balentien 4.00
23 Stephen Drew 8.00
24 Davis Romero 4.00
25 Joe Koshansky 4.00
26 Chin-Lung Hu 25.00
27 Jason Hirsh 4.00
28 Jose Tabata 15.00
29 Eric Hurley 4.00
30 Yung-Chi Chen 35.00
31 Howie Kendrick 8.00
32 Humberto Sanchez 6.00
33 Alex Gordon 20.00
34 Yunel Escobar 4.00
35 Travis Buck 4.00
36 Billy Butler 8.00
37 Homer Bailey 10.00
38 George Kottaras 4.00
39 Kurt Suzuki 4.00
40 Joaquin Arias 4.00
41 Matt Lindstrom 4.00
42 Sean Smith 4.00
43 Carlos Gonzalez 4.00
44 Jaime Garcia 4.00
45 Jose Garcia 4.00

Signs of the Future

NM/M
Common Autograph: 6.00
BS Brandon Snyder 8.00
KC Koby Clemens 15.00
AG Alex Gordon 80.00
CI Chris Iannetta 15.00
MO Micah Owings 15.00
JC Jeff Clement 15.00
CR Clayton Richard 15.00
TB Travis Buck 15.00
BJ Beau Jones 15.00
DJ Daryl Jones 8.00
CDR Chaz Roe 8.00
JM Jacob Marceaux 6.00
CTI Craig Italiano 8.00
JB Jay Bruce 25.00
WT Wade Townsend 8.00
MM Mark McCormick 8.00
HS Henry Sanchez 6.00
MC Mike Costanzo 8.00
CRA Cesar Ramos 8.00

2006 Bowman Heritage

NM/M
Complete Set (300): .15

Common Player (1-200): .15
Common SP
(even #'s 202-300): 3.00
Inserted 1:3
Pack (8): 3.00
Box (24): 60.00
1 David Wright 1.00
2 Andruw Jones .50
3 Ryan Howard 1.50
4 Jason Bay .25
5 Paul Konerko .25
6 Jake Peavy .25
7 Todd Jones .15
8 Troy Glaus .25
9 Rocco Baldelli .15
10 Rafael Furcal .25
11 Freddy Sanchez .15
12 Jermaine Dye .15
13 A.J. Burnett .15
14 Michael Cuddyer .15
15 Barry Zito .25
16 Chipper Jones .75
17 Paul LoDuca .15
18 Mark Mulder .15
19 Raul Ibanez .15
20 Carlos Delgado .40
21 Marcus Giles .15
22 Danny Haren .15
23 Justin Morneau .40
24 Livan Hernandez .15
25 Ken Griffey Jr. 1.50
26 Aaron Hill .15
27 Tadahito Iguchi .15
28 Nate Robertson .15
29 Kevin Millwood .15
30 Jim Thome .50
31 Aubrey Huff .15
32 Dontrelle Willis .25
33 Khalil Greene .25
34 Doug Davis .15
35 Ivan Rodriguez .50
36 Rickie Weeks .25
37 Jhonny Peralta .15
38 Yadier Molina .15
39 Eric Chavez .25
40 Alfonso Soriano .75
41 Pat Burrell .25
42 B.J. Ryan .15
43 Carl Crawford .25
44 Preston Wilson .15
45 Jorge Posada .40
46 Carlos Zambrano .25
47 Mark Teahen .15
48 Nick Johnson .15
49 Mark Kotsay .15
50 Derek Jeter 2.00
51 Moises Alou .25
52 Ryan Freel .15
53 Shannon Stewart .15
54 Casey Blake .15
55 Edgar Renteria .15
56 Frank Thomas .50
57 Ty Wigginton .15
58 Jeff Kent .25
59 Chien-Ming Wang .50
60 Josh Beckett .25
61 Chase Utley .40
62 Gary Matthews .15
63 Torii Hunter .25
64 Bobby Jenks .15
65 Wilson Betemit .15
66 Jeremy Bonderman .25
67 Scott Rolen .25
68 Brad Penny .15
69 Jacque Jones .15
70 Jose Reyes .50
71 Brian Roberts .15
72 John Smoltz .25
73 Johnny Estrada .15
74 Ronnie Belliard .15
75 Vladimir Guerrero .75
76 A.J. Pierzynski .15
77 Garrett Atkins .15
78 Adam LaRoche .15
79 Mark Loretta .15
80 Todd Helton .50
81 Jose Vidro .15
82 Carlos Guillen .15
83 Michael Barrett .15
84 Lyle Overbay .15
85 Travis Hafner .25
86 Shea Hillenbrand .15
87 Julio Lugo .15
88 Tim Hudson .25
89 Scott Podsednik .15
90 Roy Halladay .25
91 Bartolo Colon .15
92 Ryan Langerhans .15
93 Tom Glavine .40
94 Ken Rogers .15
95 Robinson Cano .50
96 Mark Prior .50
97 Jason Schmidt .25
98 Bengie Molina .15

99 Jon Lieber .15
100 Alex Rodriguez 2.00
101 Scott Kazmir .25
102 Jeff Francoeur .25
103 Chris Carpenter .40
104 Juan Uribe .15
105 Mariano Rivera .40
106 Rich Harden .15
107 Jack Wilson .15
108 Austin Kearns .15
109 Marcus Thames .15
110 Miguel Tejada .25
111 Chone Figgins .15
112 Bronson Arroyo .15
113 Chad Cordero .15
114 Bill Hall .15
115 Curt Schilling .50
116 David Eckstein .15
117 Ramon Hernandez .15
118 Eric Byrnes .15
119 Clint Barmes .15
120 Bobby Abreu .25
121 Joe Crede .15
122 Derek Lowe .15
123 Jason Marquis .15
124 Erik Bedard .15
125 Derrek Lee .50
126 Brian McCann .25
127 Magglio Ordonez .25
128 Ben Sheets .25
129 Brandon Inge .15
130 Miguel Cabrera .75
131 Jim Edmonds .25
132 John Lackey .15
133 Kevin Mench .15
134 Adrian Beltre .25
135 Curtis Granderson .15
136 Shawn Green .15
137 Jose Contreras .15
138 Joe Nathan .15
139 Bobby Crosby .15
140 Johnny Damon .50
141 Brad Hawpe .15
142 Brandon Phillips .15
143 Victor Martinez .15
144 Jimmy Rollins .50
145 Corey Patterson .15
146 Grady Sizemore .40
147 Placido Polanco .15
148 Mike Lowell .15
149 Francisco Rodriguez .15
150 Ichiro Suzuki 1.50
151 Kris Benson .15
152 Scott Hatteberg .15
153 Akinori Otsuka .15
154 Cesar Izturis .15
155 Roger Clemens 2.00
156 Kerry Wood .25
157 Tom Gordon .15
158 Sean Casey .15
159 Jose Lopez .15
160 Orlando Hernandez .15
161 Aramis Ramirez .25
162 J.D. Drew .25
163 David DeJesus .15
164 Craig Biggio .25
165 Brad Myers .15
166 C.C. Sabathia .15
167 Zachary Duke .15
168 Luis Castillo .15
169 Hideki Matsui 1.00
170 Brian Giles .15
171 Coco Crisp .15
172 Richie Sexson .25
173 Nomar Garciaparra .75
174 Roy Oswalt .25
175 David Ortiz .75
176 Matt Morris .15
177 Felipe Lopez .15
178 Garret Anderson .15
179 Kevin Youkilis .25
180 Alex Rios .15
181 John Garland .15
182 Luis Gonzalez .15
183 Cliff Floyd .15
184 Juan Encarnacion .15
185 Nick Swisher .25
186 Mike Cameron .15
187 Jose Castillo .15
188 Ray Durham .15
189 Jorge Cantu .15
190 Andy Pettitte .25
191 Chad Tracy .15
192 Adrian Gonzalez .15
193 Jose Valentin .15
194 Mark Buehrle .15
195 Huston Street .15
196 Chris Capuano .15
197 Aaron Rowand .15
198 Billy Wagner .15
199 Orlando Cabrera .15
200 Albert Pujols 2.00
201 Dan Uggla (RC) .50
202 Alay Soler RC 3.00

203 Matthew Kemp (RC) 1.00
204 Michael Napoli RC 3.00
205 Joel Zumaya (RC) 3.00
206 Mike Pelfrey RC 4.00
207 Ian Kinsler (RC) .50
208 Josh Willingham (RC) 3.00
209 Erick Aybar (RC) .50
210 Willie Eyre (RC) 3.00
211 Kendry Morales (RC) .50
212 Scott Thorman (RC) 3.00
213 Hanley Ramirez (RC) 1.00
214 Boof Bonser (RC) 4.00
215 Anthony Reyes (RC) .50
216 Justin Huber (RC) 3.00
217 Yusmeiro Petit (RC) .50
218 Jason Bartlett (RC) 3.00
219 Shin-Soo Choo (RC) 1.00
220 Francisco Liriano (RC) 5.00
221 Craig Hansen RC 2.00
222 Ricky Nolasco (RC) 3.00
223 Adam Loewen (RC) .50
224 Scott Olsen (RC) 3.00
225 Cole Hamels (RC) 1.50
226 Martin Prado (RC) 3.00
227 James Loney (RC) 1.00
228 Kevin Thompson (RC) 3.00
229 Adam Jones (RC) 1.00
230 Josh Johnson (RC) 3.00
231 Anderson Hernandez (RC) .40
232 Tony Gwynn Jr. (RC) 3.00
233 Casey Janssen RC .50
234 Taylor Tankersley (RC) 3.00
235 Mike Thompson (RC) .50
236 Jeremy Sowers (RC) 3.00
237 Anibal Sanchez (RC) .50
238 Adam Wainwright (RC) 4.00
239 Rich Hill (RC) .50
240 Russell Martin (RC) 4.00
241 Joe Inglett RC .50
242 Tony Pena (RC) 3.00
243 Joshua Sharpless RC .50
244 Darrell Rasner (RC) 3.00
245 Joe Saunders (RC) .50
246 Jon Lester (RC) 6.00
247 Jeremy Hermida (RC) .50
248 Chad Billingsley (RC) 4.00
249 Bobby Livingston (RC) .50
250 Justin Verlander (RC) 5.00
251 Mickey Mantle 10.00
252 Hank Blalock 3.00
253 Manny Ramirez 1.00
254 Mike Mussina 5.00
255 Greg Maddux 2.00
256 Jason Giambi 4.00
257 Mark Teixeira .75
258 Carlos Beltran 4.00
259 Matt Holliday 1.00
260 Pedro Martinez 5.00
261 Joe Mauer 1.00
262 Melvin Mora 3.00
263 Mike Piazza 1.50
264 B.J. Upton 4.00
265 Vernon Wells .75
266 Gary Sheffield 4.00
267 Randy Johnson 1.00
268 Ryan Zimmerman 4.00
269 Lance Berkman .75
270 Johan Santana 5.00
271 Carlos Lee .50
272 Brandon Webb 3.00
273 Adam Dunn .75
274 Michael Young 3.00
275 Barry Bonds 2.00
276 Jonathan Papelbon (RC) 6.00
277 Howie Kendrick (RC) 1.00
278 Melky Cabrera (RC) 3.00
279 Jered Weaver (RC) 2.00
280 Josh Barfield (RC) 3.00
281 Chuck James (RC) 1.00
282 Lastings Milledge (RC) 5.00
283 Nicholas Markakis (RC) 1.00
284 Jose Capellan (RC) 3.00
285 Prince Fielder (RC) 3.00
286 Jason Botts (RC) 3.00
287 Eliezer Alfonzo RC .50
288 Sean Marshall (RC) 3.00
289 Ryan Garko (RC) .75
290 Stephen Drew (RC) 5.00
291 Joel Guzman (RC) .50
292 Hong-Chih Kuo (RC) 3.00
293 Zach Miner (RC) .50
294 Angel Guzman (RC) 3.00
295 Andre Ethier (RC) 1.00
296 Fausto Carmona (RC) 3.00
297 Ronny Paulino (RC) .75
298 Matt Cain (RC) 5.00
299 Carlos Quentin (RC) .75
300 Kenji Johjima RC 5.00

Foil

Foil (1-300): 1-2X
Foil (301-350): .5-1X
Inserted 1:1

Black

No Pricing
Production One Set

Printing Plates

No Pricing
Production One Set

Mini

Mini (1-300): 1-2X
Inserted 1:1

Draft Pick Variations

		NM/M
	One five card pack per box.	
BHP76	Evan Longoria	6.00
BHP77	Adrian Cardenas	1.00
BHP78	Steven Wright	1.00
BHP79	Andrew Carpenter	2.00
BHP80	Dustin Evans	2.00
BHP81	Chad Tracy	1.00
BHP82	Matthew Sulentic	4.00
BHP83	Adam Ottavino	2.00
BHP84	Matt Long	1.00
BHP85	Clayton Kershaw	3.00
BHP86	Matt Antonelli	3.00
BHP87	Chris Parmelee	2.00
BHP88	Billy Rowell	3.00
BHP89	Chase Fontaine	1.00
BHP90	Chris Murrero	2.00
BHP91	Jamie Ortiz	2.00
BHP92	Sean Watson	1.00
BHP93	Brooks Brown	1.00
BHP94	Brad Furnish	3.00
BHP95	Chad Huffman	2.00
BHP96	Pedro Beato	3.00
BHP97	Kyler Burke	1.00
BHP98	Stephen Englund	1.00
BHP99	Tyler Norrick	1.00
BHP100	Brent Sinkbeil	1.00

Pieces of Greatness

		NM/M
	Common Player:	5.00
	Inserted 1:12	
	White:	1.5-3X
	Production 49 Sets	
	Black:	No Pricing
	Production One Set	
LB	Lance Berkman	5.00
CB	Craig Biggio	8.00
HB	Hank Blalock	5.00
BB	Barry Bonds	25.00
MB	Milton Bradley	5.00
RC	Robinson Cano	20.00
AD	Adam Dunn	5.00
JD	Jermaine Dye	5.00
DE	David Eckstein	15.00
EE	Edwin Encarnacion	5.00

ME	Morgan Ensberg	5.00
CF	Cliff Floyd	5.00
JF	Jeff Francoeur	10.00
RF	Rafael Furcal	5.00
VG	Vladimir Guerrero	10.00
THE	Todd Helton	8.00
RH	Ryan Howard	25.00
TH	Torii Hunter	5.00
AJ	Andruw Jones	8.00
AJ2	Andruw Jones	8.00
CJ	Chipper Jones	8.00
CJ2	Chipper Jones	8.00
NJ	Nick Johnson	5.00
JK	Jeff Kent	5.00
AL	Adam LaRoche	5.00
DL	Derrek Lee	8.00
JL	Javy Lopez	5.00
ML	Mike Lowell	5.00
GM	Greg Maddux	10.00
VM	Victor Martinez	5.00
XN	Xavier Nady	5.00
MO	Magglio Ordonez	5.00
DO	David Ortiz	15.00
AJP	A.J. Pierzynski	5.00
SP	Scott Podsednik	10.00
AP	Albert Pujols	25.00
AP2	Albert Pujols	25.00
ARA	Aramis Ramirez	5.00
MR	Manny Ramirez	8.00
BR	Brian Roberts	5.00
AR	Alex Rodriguez	20.00
CS	Curt Schilling	8.00
GS	Gary Sheffield	5.00
NS	Nick Swisher	8.00
JT	Jim Thome	8.00
CU	Chase Utley	8.00
BW	Brad Wilkerson	5.00
DW	Dontrelle Willis	5.00
MY	Michael Young	5.00
BZ	Barry Zito	5.00

Prospects

		NM/M
	Common Prospect:	.50
	Inserted 2:Pack	
	Black:	No Pricing
	Production One Set	
BHP1	Justin Upton	5.00
BHP2	Koby Clemens	6.00
BHP3	Lance Broadway	1.00
BHP4	Cameron Maybin	8.00
BHP5	Garrett Mock	1.00
BHP6	Alex Gordon	6.00
BHP7	Ben Copeland	1.00
BHP8	Nick Adenhart	2.00
BHP9	Yung-Chi Chen	3.00
BHP10	Tim Moss	1.00
BHP11	Francisco Leandro	.50
BHP12	Brad McCann	1.00
BHP13	Dallas Trahern	1.00
BHP14	Dustin Majewski	2.00
BHP15	James Barthmaier	1.00
BHP16	Nate Gold	1.00
BHP17	John Hardy	.50
BHP18	Mark McLemore	.50
BHP19	Michael Aubrey	1.00
BHP20	Mark Holliman	2.00
BHP21	Bobby Wilson	.50
BHP22	Radhames Liz	1.00
BHP23	Jose Tabata	8.00
BHP24	Jared Lansford	.50
BHP25	Brent Dlugach	1.00
BHP26	Steve Garrabrants	.50
BHP27	Eric Haberer	1.00
BHP28	Chris Dickerson	.50
BHP29	Welinson Baez	1.00
BHP30	Chris Kolkhorst	.50
BHP31	Brandon Moss	2.00
BHP32	Corey Wimberly	.50
BHP33	Ryan Patterson	2.00
BHP34	Michael Hollimon	1.00
BHP35	John Bannister	.50
BHP36	Pablo Sandoval	.50
BHP37	Dexter Fowler	.50

BHP38	Elvis Andrus	2.00
BHP39	Jason Windsor	1.00
BHP40	B.J. Szymanski	1.00
BHP41	Yovani Gallardo	4.00
BHP42	John Bowker	.50
BHP43	Justin Christian	2.00
BHP44	Andrew Sonnanstine	2.00
BHP45	Jeremy Slayden	.50
BHP46	Brandon Jones	.50
BHP47	Travis Denker	.50
BHP48	Emmanuel Garcia	3.00
BHP49	Landon Jacobsen	6.00
BHP50	Kevin Estrada	1.00
BHP51	Ross Ohlendorf	.50
BHP52	Wyatt Toregas	.50
BHP53	Andrew Kown	1.00
BHP54	Steve Kelly	.50
BHP55	Mike Butia	.50
BHP56	Mike Connolly	.50
BHP57	Brian Horwitz	.50
BHP58	Dale Thayer	.50
BHP59	Diory Hernandez	1.00
BHP60	Samuel Deduno	.50
BHP61	Jamie Hoffman	1.00
BHP62	Matt Tolbert	3.00
BHP63	Michael Ekstrom	.50
BHP64	Chris Maples	1.00
BHP65	Adam Coe	1.00
BHP66	Max Ramirez	1.00
BHP67	Evan MacLane	.50
BHP68	Jose Campusano	.50
BHP69	Lou Santangelo	1.00
BHP70	Shawn Riggans	1.00
BHP71	Kyle Kendrick	.75
BHP72	Oswaldo Navarro	.50
BHP73	Eric Rodland	1.00
BHP74	Omir Santos	2.00
BHP75	Kyle McCulloch	.50
BHP76	Evan Longoria	5.00
BHP77	Adrian Cardenas	2.00
BHP78	Steven Wright	.50
BHP79	Andrew Carpenter	2.00
BHP80	Dustin Evans	1.50
BHP81	Chad Tracy	.50
BHP82	Matthew Sulentic	4.00
BHP83	Adam Ottavino	2.00
BHP84	Matt Long	.50
BHP85	Clayton Kershaw	3.00
BHP86	Matt Antonelli	2.00
BHP87	Chris Parmelee	2.00
BHP88	Billy Rowell	3.00
BHP89	Chase Fontaine	1.00
BHP90	Chris Murrero	2.00
BHP91	Jamie Ortiz	2.00
BHP92	Sean Watson	1.00
BHP93	Brooks Brown	1.00
BHP94	Brad Furnish	2.00
BHP95	Chad Huffman	2.00
BHP96	Pedro Beato	3.00
BHP97	Kyler Burke	1.00
BHP98	Stephen Englund	1.00
BHP99	Tyler Norrick	.50
BHP100	Brent Sinkbeil	.50

Signs of Greatness

		NM/M
	Common Autograph:	10.00
	White:	No Pricing
	Production 5 Sets	
	Black:	No Pricing
	Production One Set	
BB	Brian Bogusevic	10.00
LB	Lance Broadway	15.00
KC	Koby Clemens	20.00
JCL	Jeff Clement	15.00
JC	Jesus Cota	10.00
TC	Trevor Crowe	15.00
JD	John Drennen	15.00
SG	Sean Gallagher	15.00
AG	Alex Gordon	60.00
JH	Justin Huber	15.00
CI	Craig Italiano	15.00
SL	Sam LeCure	10.00
MM	Matt Maloney	15.00
CM	Cameron Maybin	50.00
JS	Jarrod Saltalamacchia	25.00
BS	Brandon Snyder	10.00
ST	Steve Tolleson	15.00
WT	Wade Townsend	15.00
RT	Ryan Tucker	15.00
JU	Justin Upton	75.00
KW	Kevin Whelan	10.00
BW	Brandon Wood	25.00

2006 Bowman Originals

		NM/M
	Complete Set (55):	50.00
	Common Player (1-35):	1.00
	Common Player (36-55):	2.00
	Pack (7):	60.00
	Box (6):	350.00
1	David Wright	3.00
2	Derek Jeter	5.00

35

3	Eric Chavez	1.00
4	Ken Griffey Jr.	4.00
5	Albert Pujols	5.00
6	Ryan Howard	5.00
7	Joe Mauer	1.50
8	Andruw Jones	1.50
9	Nomar Garciaparra	2.00
10	Michael Young	1.00
11	Miguel Tejada	1.50
12	Alfonso Soriano	2.00
13	Alex Rodriguez	5.00
14	Paul Konerko	1.50
15	Carl Crawford	1.00
16	Nick Johnson	1.00
17	Jim Thome	1.50
18	Ivan Rodriguez	1.50
19	Chipper Jones	2.00
20	Pedro Martinez	2.00
21	Carlos Delgado	1.50
22	Roger Clemens	5.00
23	Mark Teixeira	1.50
24	Manny Ramirez	2.00
25	Barry Bonds	2.00
26	Vernon Wells	1.00
27	Vladimir Guerrero	2.00
28	Miguel Cabrera	2.00
29	Victor Martinez	1.00
30	Derrek Lee	1.50
31	Carlos Lee	1.00
32	Ichiro Suzuki	3.00
33	Johan Santana	1.50
34	David Ortiz	2.00
35	Jason Bay	1.50
36	Kendry Morales (RC)	3.00
37	Nicholas Markakis (RC)	5.00
38	Conor Jackson (RC)	2.00
39	Justin Verlander (RC)	5.00
40	Ryan Zimmerman (RC)	5.00
41	Jeremy Hermida (RC)	2.00
42	Dan Uggla (RC)	3.00
43	Matthew Kemp (RC)	5.00
44	Lastings Milledge (RC)	5.00
45	Kenji Johjima RC	5.00
46	Ian Kinsler (RC)	3.00
47	Hanley Ramirez (RC)	3.00
48	Melky Cabrera (RC)	5.00
49	Willy Aybar (RC)	2.00
50	Jonathan Papelbon (RC)	6.00
51	Prince Fielder (RC)	5.00
52	Cole Hamels (RC)	5.00
53	Josh Barfield (RC)	2.00
54	Alay Soler RC	3.00
55	Russell Martin (RC)	3.00

Blue

Blue (1-55): 2-3X
Production 249 Sets

Black

Black (1-55): 3-5X
Production 99 Sets

Red

No Pricing
Production One Set

Printing Plates

No Pricing
Production one set per color.

Buyback Autographs

	NM/M
Adam Loewen/68	15.00
Adam Loewen/719	10.00
Adam Loewen/198	15.00
Adrian Gonzalez/976	20.00
Albert Pujols/44	250.00
Albert Pujols/50	250.00
Alex Gordon/49	250.00
Alex Gordon/32	280.00
Andrew McCutchen/391	40.00
Andrew McCutchen/33	60.00
Andrew McCutchen/561	35.00
Andruw Jones/34	50.00
Andruw Jones/22	60.00
Andruw Jones/24	60.00
Andruw Jones/28	60.00
Andruw Jones/48	50.00
Andy LaRoche/109	40.00
Andy LaRoche/60	40.00
Andy LaRoche/66	40.00
Andy LaRoche/734	25.00
Alex Rodriguez/21	150.00
Alex Rodriguez/22	150.00
B.J. Upton/58	30.00
B.J. Upton/136	25.00
B.J. Upton/667	20.00
B.J. Upton/251	25.00
Beau Jones/576	15.00
Beau Jones/63	30.00
Beau Jones/329	20.00
Beau Jones/33	30.00
Billy Buckner/99	25.00
Billy Buckner/432	20.00
Billy Buckner/182	20.00
Billy Buckner/33	30.00
Billy Wagner/56	30.00
Billy Wagner/47	30.00
Billy Wagner/64	25.00
Billy Wagner/90	20.00
Billy Wagner/99	20.00
Billy Wagner/37	30.00
Billy Wagner/38	30.00
Brandon Phillips/46	15.00
Brandon Phillips/26	20.00
Brandon Phillips/67	10.00
Brandon Phillips/28	20.00
Brandon Phillips/32	15.00
Brandon Phillips/140	10.00
Brandon Phillips/35	15.00
Brandon Phillips/335	10.00
Brandon Phillips/257	10.00
Brandon Snyder/461	15.00
Brandon Wood/70	30.00
Brandon Wood/100	30.00
Brandon Wood/627	20.00
Brandon Wood/239	30.00
Brent Cox/240	15.00
Brent Cox/66	20.00
Brent Cox/688	15.00
Carl Crawford/37	25.00
Carl Crawford/40	25.00
Carl Crawford/20	30.00
Carl Crawford/30	25.00
Carl Crawford/71	20.00
Carl Crawford/71	20.00
Carl Crawford/334	15.00
Carl Crawford/279	15.00
Carlos Silva/996	10.00
Cesar Ramos/25	25.00

Cesar Ramos/76	25.00
Cesar Ramos/161	15.00
Cesar Ramos/732	10.00
Chase Utley/23	75.00
Chase Utley/150	40.00
Chase Utley/303	40.00
Chase Utley/23	75.00
Chaz Roe/73	15.00
Chaz Roe/774	10.00
Chaz Roe/132	10.00
Chien-Ming Wang/25	500.00
Chien-Ming Wang/25	600.00
Chien-Ming Wang/25	500.00
Chien-Ming Wang/25	600.00
Chipper Jones/20	80.00
Chipper Jones/20	80.00
Chipper Jones/20	80.00
Chipper Jones/20	80.00
Chipper Jones/20	80.00
Chris Young/70	20.00
Chris Young/772	20.00
Chris Young/146	20.00
Chris Young/211	20.00
Chris Young/44	75.00
Chris Young/88	40.00
Chris Young/81	40.00
Chris Young/558	25.00
Clint Barmes/61	20.00
Clint Barmes/113	15.00
Clint Barmes/375	10.00
Clint Barmes/430	10.00
Conor Jackson/70	30.00
Conor Jackson/78	50.00
Conor Jackson/457	20.00
Conor Jackson/360	20.00
Craig Italiano/160	15.00
Craig Italiano/658	10.00
Craig Italiano/163	15.00
Dan Johnson/276	15.00
Dan Johnson/575	15.00
Dan Johnson/101	15.00
Dan Johnson/29	20.00
David Wright/543	60.00
David Wright/264	150.00
David Wright/45	80.00
David Wright/64	80.00
Derrek Lee/61	20.00
Dontrelle Willis/147	20.00
Dontrelle Willis/55	25.00
Dontrelle Willis/525	25.00
Dontrelle Willis/79	25.00
Dontrelle Willis/78	25.00
Dontrelle Willis/24	25.00
Dontrelle Willis/36	25.00
Eli Iorg/167	15.00
Eli Iorg/151	15.00
Eli Iorg/672	15.00
Eric Chavez/34	20.00
Eric Chavez/301	15.00
Eric Chavez/25	20.00
Eric Chavez/70	20.00
Eric Chavez/62	20.00
Ervin Santana/369	15.00
Ervin Santana/544	15.00
Ervin Santana/51	20.00
Ervin Santana/109	20.00
Ervin Santana/76	20.00
Ervin Santana/67	20.00
Ervin Santana/62	50.00
Fausto Carmona/131	10.00
Fausto Carmona/56	15.00
Fausto Carmona/263	10.00
Francisco Cordero/64	10.00
Francisco Cordero/87	10.00
Francisco Cordero/49	10.00
Francisco Cordero/138	10.00
Francisco Cordero/140	10.00
Francisco Liriano/142	35.00
Francisco Liriano/63	40.00
Francisco Liriano/47	35.00
Francisco Liriano/222	30.00
Francisco Liriano/350	25.00
Francisco Liriano/212	65.00
Garrett Atkins/121	15.00
Garrett Atkins/27	20.00
Garrett Atkins/209	15.00
Garrett Atkins/581	15.00
Garrett Atkins/35	15.00
Hanley Ramirez/435	20.00
Hanley Ramirez/98	25.00
Hanley Ramirez/466	20.00
Jason Bay/24	30.00
Jason Bay/298	25.00
Jason Bay/50	25.00
Jason Bay/58	25.00
Jason Bay/70	25.00
Jason Botts/29	15.00
Jason Botts/31	15.00

Jason Botts/269	10.00
Jason Botts/46	15.00
Jason Botts/59	15.00
Jason Botts/577	10.00
Jason Kubel/232	15.00
Jason Kubel/127	15.00
Jason Kubel/25	25.00
Jason Kubel/77	20.00
Jason Marquis/944	8.00
Jason Marquis/26	20.00
Jay Bruce/66	80.00
Jay Bruce/434	50.00
Jed Lowrie/123	15.00
Jed Lowrie/141	15.00
Jed Lowrie/716	15.00
Jeff Mathis/127	15.00
Jeff Mathis/185	15.00
Jeff Mathis/97	15.00
Jerome Williams/292	8.00
Jerome Williams/48	10.00
Jerome Williams/45	10.00
Jerome Williams/97	8.00
Joel Guzman/274	15.00
Joel Guzman/54	20.00
Joel Guzman/53	20.00
Joel Zumaya/233	50.00
Joel Zumaya/57	50.00
Joel Zumaya/96	80.00
Joel Zumaya/582	40.00
Joel Zumaya/163	50.00
John Drennen/78	30.00
John Drennen/387	15.00
John Van Benschoten/51	15.00
John Van Benschoten/24	20.00
John Van Benschoten/130	15.00
John Van Benschoten/272	10.00
Jonny Gomes/341	15.00
Jonny Gomes/27	50.00
Jonny Gomes/175	15.00
Jonny Gomes/363	10.00
Josh Barfield/158	20.00
Josh Barfield/557	15.00
Josh Barfield/178	30.00
Josh Geer/343	10.00
Josh Geer/138	10.00
Justin Huber/32	15.00
Justin Huber/99	15.00
Justin Huber/572	10.00
Justin Huber/212	10.00
Justin Huber/26	20.00
Justin Huber/37	15.00
Justin Upton/1000	100.00
Kevin Gregg/988	10.00
Lastings Milledge/166	35.00
Lastings Milledge/166	35.00
Lastings Milledge/632	25.00
Mark Mulder/20	25.00
Mark Mulder/20	25.00
Mark Mulder/20	25.00
Mark Mulder/20	25.00
Matt Cain/36	30.00
Matt Cain/389	25.00
Matt Maloney/350	25.00
Matt Maloney/50	60.00
Matt Maloney/20	75.00
Matt Maloney/60	60.00
Matt Torra/456	15.00
Matt Torra/37	30.00
Melky Cabrera/606	30.00
Melky Cabrera/191	35.00
Melky Cabrera/60	50.00
Melky Cabrera/24	70.00
Melky Cabrera/95	40.00
Melky Cabrera/12	12.00
Merkin Valdez/41	15.00
Merkin Valdez/325	8.00
Merkin Valdez/70	15.00
Merkin Valdez/66	15.00
Micah Owings/138	30.00
Micah Owings/648	20.00
Michael Bowden/27	40.00
Michael Bowden/24	40.00
Michael Bowden/449	20.00
Miguel Cabrera/70	30.00
Miguel Cabrera/70	30.00
Miguel Cabrera/69	30.00
Miguel Cabrera/98	30.00
Miguel Cabrera/63	30.00
Miguel Cabrera/130	40.00
Mike Costanzo/466	15.00
Mike Lamb/993	10.00
Morgan Ensberg/74	15.00
Morgan Ensberg/334	10.00
Morgan Ensberg/64	15.00
Nick Swisher/342	20.00
Nick Swisher/73	25.00
Nick Swisher/31	30.00
Nolan Reimold/41	60.00
Nolan Reimold/419	20.00

Nolan Reimold/30	60.00
Rich Harden/87	20.00
Rich Harden/82	20.00
Rich Harden/70	20.00
Rich Harden/68	20.00
Rich Harden/68	30.00
Ricky Nolasco/52	15.00
Ricky Nolasco/256	10.00
Ricky Nolasco/148	15.00
Robinson Cano/90	50.00
Robinson Cano/72	50.00
Robinson Cano/101	50.00
Robinson Cano/222	40.00
Roy Oswalt/96	25.00
Roy Oswalt/42	30.00
Roy Oswalt/61	30.00
Roy Oswalt/63	40.00
Roy Oswalt/25	50.00
Roy Oswalt/199	25.00
Russell Martin/33	40.00
Russell Martin/96	30.00
Russell Martin/577	25.00
Russell Martin/252	25.00
Ryan Howard/50	350.00
Scott Elbert/79	50.00
Scott Elbert/330	35.00
Scott Elbert/60	50.00
Scott Kazmir/99	25.00
Scott Kazmir/36	30.00
Scott Kazmir/153	20.00
Scott Kazmir/26	30.00
Scott Kazmir/661	20.00
Scott Mathieson/472	8.00
Scott Mathieson/108	20.00
Scott Mathieson/72	25.00
Scott Thorman/980	10.00
Sean West/394	20.00
Sean West/70	30.00
Shaun Marcum/133	15.00
Shaun Marcum/26	20.00
Shaun Marcum/138	20.00
Shaun Marcum/153	20.00
Shaun Marcum/33	25.00
Travis Buck/60	40.00
Travis Buck/44	60.00
Travis Buck/747	20.00
Travis Hafner/114	20.00
Travis Hafner/96	20.00
Travis Hafner/386	20.00
Travis Hafner/45	25.00
Travis Hafner/280	20.00
Trevor Bell/146	15.00
Trevor Bell/28	15.00
Trevor Bell/689	15.00
Troy Patton/211	15.00
Troy Patton/50	30.00
Troy Patton/736	15.00
Vernon Wells/52	25.00
Vernon Wells/100	25.00
Vernon Wells/25	40.00
Vernon Wells/96	25.00
Vernon Wells/68	25.00
Vernon Wells/56	25.00
Vernon Wells/40	40.00
Vernon Wells/29	40.00
Vernon Wells/426	20.00
Vladimir Guerrero/21	80.00
Vladimir Guerrero/45	60.00
Vladimir Guerrero/20	80.00
Wade Townsend/423	15.00
Wade Townsend/53	20.00
Wily Mo Pena/79	20.00
Wily Mo Pena/70	20.00
Wily Mo Pena/69	20.00
Wily Mo Pena/134	20.00
Wily Mo Pena/62	20.00
Xavier Nady/20	20.00
Xavier Nady/72	20.00
Xavier Nady/192	15.00
Xavier Nady/213	15.00
Xavier Nady/294	15.00
Xavier Nady/41	20.00
Yunel Escobar/69	30.00
Yunel Escobar/395	25.00
Yusmeiro Petit/68	20.00
Yusmeiro Petit/102	20.00
Yusmeiro Petit/160	15.00
Yusmeiro Petit/630	15.00

Prospects

	NM/M
Common Player:	2.00
Blue:	1.5-2X
Production 249 Sets	
Black:	2-4X
Production 99 Sets	
Red:	No Pricing
Production One Set	
1 Cameron Maybin	15.00
2 Koby Clemens	5.00
3 Lance Broadway	2.00
4 Chris Dickerson	2.00
5 Garrett Mock	2.00
6 Ben Copeland	2.00

DEXTER FOWLER

7	Nick Adenhart	2.00
8	Brad McCann	3.00
9	Dustin Majewski	2.00
10	Jimmy Barthmaier	2.00
11	Michael Aubrey	2.00
12	Evan Longoria	20.00
13	Clayton Kershaw	8.00
14	Juan Francia	2.00
15	Elvis Andrus	6.00
16	Mark Trumbo	2.00
17	Shawn Riggans	2.00
18	Asdrubal Cabrera	2.00
19	Mark McLemore	2.00
20	Radhames Liz	2.00
21	Mat Gamel	2.00
22	Wilkin Ramirez	2.00
23	Jared Lansford	2.00
24	Hunter Pence	4.00
25	Justin Upton	15.00
26	Brent Dlugach	2.00
27	B.J. Szymanski	4.00
28	Stephen Marek	4.00
29	Shaun Cumberland	2.00
30	Yovani Gallardo	4.00
31	Will Venable	2.00
32	A.J. Shappi	2.00
33	Dallas Trahern	2.00
34	Jason Jaramillo	2.00
35	Jose Tabata	5.00
36	Jose Campusano	2.00
37	Ryan Patterson	3.00
38	Andrew Pinckney	2.00
39	Dexter Fowler	2.00
40	Cody Johnson	3.00
41	Steve Murphy	2.00
42	Mark Reed	2.00
43	Chris Iannetta	4.00
44	Michael Hollimon	4.00
45	Omir Santos	2.00
46	Diory Hernandez	2.00
47	Matt Tolbert	4.00
48	Jeff Frazier	2.00
49	Max Ramirez	3.00
50	Alex Gordon	20.00
51	Steve Garrabrants	2.00
52	Steven Baker	2.00
53	Ryan Klosterman	3.00
54	Michael Collins	2.00
55	Corey Wimberly	2.00

2006 Bowman Sterling

JONES

		NM/M
	Common Relic:	5.00
	Pack (5):	50.00
	Box (6):	260.00
CB	Carlos Beltran	8.00
CB2	Carlos Beltran	8.00
LB	Lance Berkman	5.00
HB	Hank Blalock	5.00
BLB	Barry Bonds	20.00
MC	Miguel Cabrera	10.00

MC2	Miguel Cabrera	10.00
RC	Robinson Cano	15.00
CC	Chris Carpenter	8.00
EC	Eric Chavez	5.00
JDD	Johnny Damon	8.00
AD	Adam Dunn	5.00
ME	Morgan Ensberg	5.00
VG	Vladimir Guerrero	10.00
JRH	Rich Harden	5.00
TH	Todd Helton	8.00
RH	Ryan Howard	25.00
AJ	Andruw Jones	8.00
LWJ	Chipper Jones	8.00
PK	Paul Konerko	8.00
MCM	Mickey Mantle	120.00
PM	Pedro Martinez	8.00
HM	Hideki Matsui	20.00
MM	Mark Mulder	5.00
DO	David Ortiz	10.00
MJP	Mike Piazza	10.00
AP	Albert Pujols	25.00
AP2	Albert Pujols	25.00
AR	Aramis Ramirez	8.00
MR	Manny Ramirez	10.00
MR2	Manny Ramirez	10.00
BR	Brian Roberts	5.00
AER	Alex Rodriguez	20.00
IR	Ivan Rodriguez	8.00
SR	Scott Rolen	8.00
JAS	Johan Santana	8.00
CS	Curt Schilling	8.00
GS	Grady Sizemore	8.00
APS	Alfonso Soriano	10.00
IS	Ichiro Suzuki	25.00
MCT	Mark Teixeira	8.00
MT	Miguel Tejada	8.00
JHT	Jim Thome	8.00
DWW	Dontrelle Willis	5.00
DW	David Wright	20.00
Common Rookie:		4.00
BA	Brian Anderson (RC)	4.00
WA	Willy Aybar (RC)	4.00
BB	Brian Bannister (RC)	4.00
CRB	Chad Billingsley (RC)	10.00
BON	Boof Bonser (RC)	6.00
MCC	Melky Cabrera (RC)	6.00
JD	Joey Devine RC	4.00
SD	Stephen Drew (RC)	10.00
KF	Kevin Frandsen (RC)	4.00
RK	Ryan Garko (RC)	6.00
DG	David Gassner (RC)	4.00
EG	Enrique Gonzalez (RC)	4.00
FG	Franklin Gutierrez (RC)	4.00
TGJ	Tony Gwynn Jr. (RC)	6.00
CRH	Craig Hansen RC	8.00
CJ	Conor Jackson (RC)	4.00
CHJ	Chuck James (RC)	6.00
CJJ	Casey Janssen RC	4.00
KJ	Kenji Johjima RC	10.00
JJ	Josh Johnson (RC)	6.00
JK	Jeff Karstens RC	6.00
MK	Matthew Kemp (RC)	6.00
HK	Howie Kendrick (RC)	6.00
FL	Francisco Liriano (RC)	10.00
JL	James Loney (RC)	6.00
NM	Nicholas Markakis (RC)	8.00
RM	Russell Martin (RC)	6.00
SM	Scott Mathieson (RC)	6.00
JM	Jeff Mathis (RC)	6.00
KM	Kendry Morales (RC)	4.00
SO	Scott Olsen (RC)	4.00
JP	Jonathan Papelbon (RC)	10.00
DP	David Pauley (RC)	6.00
MPP	Mike Pelfrey RC	15.00
HP	Hayden Penn (RC)	4.00
CQ	Carlos Quentin (RC)	6.00
HR	Hanley Ramirez (RC)	6.00
AS	Anibal Sanchez (RC)	4.00
JS	James Shields RC	8.00
MS	Matt Smith (RC)	4.00
ALS	Alay Soler (RC)	6.00
JBS	Jeremy Sowers (RC)	4.00
TT	Taylor Tankersley (RC)	4.00
JTA	Jordan Tata RC	6.00
DU	Dan Uggla (RC)	6.00
JV	Justin Verlander (RC)	10.00
JW	Jered Weaver (RC)	8.00
RZ	Ryan Zimmerman (RC)	15.00
BZ	Benjamin Zobrist (RC)	6.00
JZ	Joel Zumaya (RC)	10.00
Common Rookie Autograph:		
JLB	Josh Barfield (RC)	15.00
JCB	Jason Botts (RC)	10.00
AE	Andre Ethier (RC)	20.00
JI	Joe Inglett RC	15.00
IK	Ian Kinsler (RC)	20.00
LM	Lastings Milledge (RC)	20.00

ZM	Zach Miner (RC)	15.00
RN	Ricky Nolasco (RC)	15.00
Common Rookie Relic Auto.:		
JB	Jason Bulger (RC)	15.00
PF	Prince Fielder (RC)	80.00
CI	Chris Iannetta RC	20.00
CH	Cole Hamels (RC)	50.00
HK	Howie Kendrick (RC)	20.00
JTL	Jon Lester (RC)	30.00
BL	Bobby Livingston (RC)	15.00
MN	Erik Naposki RC	20.00
RP	Ronny Paulino (RC)	15.00
YP	Yusmeiro Petit (RC)	20.00
MP	Martin Prado (RC)	20.00
ALR	Anthony Reyes (RC)	20.00
JT	Jack Taschner (RC)	15.00
ST	Scott Thorman (RC)	15.00

Refractors

Rookies:	1.5-2X
Rookie Auto.:	1-2X
Rookie Relic Auto.:	1-2X
Relics:	1-2X
Prospects:	1.5-2X
Prospect Auto.:	1-2X
Production 199 Sets	

Black Refractors

No Pricing
Production 25 Sets

Gold Refractors

No Pricing
Production 10 Sets

Red Refractors

No Pricing
Production One Set

Printing Plates

No Pricing
Production One Set

Prospect

		NM/M
NA	Nick Adenhart	5.00
EA	Elvis Andrus	15.00
MRA	Michael Aubrey	5.00
JRB	Jimmy Barthmaier	5.00
AJC	Asdrubal Cabrera	6.00
JAC	Jose Campusano	5.00
YC	Yung-Chi Chen	20.00
ADC	Adam Coe	8.00
MC	Michael Collins	8.00
BC	Ben Copeland	5.00
SC	Shaun Cumberland	5.00
CD	Chris Dickerson	5.00
BD	Brent Dlugach	5.00
DF	Dexter Fowler	5.00
JF	Juan Francia	5.00
JKF	Jeff Frazier	5.00
YG	Yovani Gallardo	8.00
MG	Mat Gamel	5.00
SGG	Steve Garrabrants	8.00
DIH	Diory Hernandez	5.00
MH	Michael Hollimon	5.00
JJ	Jason Jaramillo	5.00
BJ	Brandon Jones	8.00
RK	Ryan Klosterman	8.00
JTL	Jared Lansford	8.00
RL	Radhames Liz	8.00
EM	Evan MacLane	5.00
DM	Dustin Majewski	6.00
SM	Stephen Marek	5.00
BWM	Brad McCann	5.00
MSM	Mark McLemore	5.00
GLM	Garrett Mock	5.00
SMM	Steve Murphy	5.00
ON	Oswaldo Navarro	5.00
RP	Ryan Patterson	6.00
HP	Hunter Pence	5.00

AP	Andrew Pinckney	8.00
MRR	Max Ramirez	6.00
WR	Wilkin Ramirez	5.00
MR	Mark Reed	5.00
SR	Shawn Riggans	5.00
OS	Omir Santos	5.00
AS	A.J. Shappi	5.00
BJS	B.J. Szymanski	5.00
JT	Jose Tabata	25.00
CMT	Matt Tolbert	8.00
DT	Dallas Trahern	5.00
MT	Mark Trumbo	6.00
WV	Will Venable	5.00
CW	Corey Wimberly	5.00

Prospect Autographs

		NM/M
BA	Brandon Allen	8.00
MAA	Matt Antonelli	25.00
MA	Mike Aviles	10.00
PB	Pedro Beato	20.00
RB	Ronny Bourquin	15.00
BB	Brooks Brown	15.00
TB	Travis Buck	15.00
KB	Kyler Burke	15.00
JBU	Joshua Butler	15.00
AC	Adrian Cardenas	25.00
KC	Koby Clemens	20.00
JC	Jeff Clement	15.00
TC	Tyler Colvin	35.00
HC	Hank Conger	25.00
TC	Trevor Crowe	20.00
CD	Chris Dickerson	10.00
KD	Kyle Drabek	25.00
DE	Dustin Evans	15.00
SE	Steven Evarts	15.00
MF	Michael Felix	15.00
BF	Brad Furnish	15.00
AG	Alex Gordon	80.00
DH	Daniel Haigwood	15.00
BH	Brett Hayes	15.00
CH	Chase Headley	20.00
LH	Luke Hochevar	40.00
DHU	David Huff	15.00
CHH	Chad Huffman	15.00
JJ	Jeremy Jeffress	20.00
CJ	Cody Johnson	20.00
KJ	Kris Johnson	15.00
CK	Clayton Kershaw	40.00
KK	Kasey Kiker	15.00
EL	Evan Longoria	60.00
PL	Pedro Lopez	8.00
CM	Cameron Maybin	80.00
MM	Mark McCormick	15.00
KM	Kyle McCulloch	15.00
GM	Garrett Mock	15.00
BM	Brandon Moss	20.00
JN	Jason Neighborgall	10.00
AO	Adam Ottavino	15.00
MO	Micah Owings	20.00
CP	Chris Parmelee	35.00
TP	Troy Patton	25.00
EP	Elvin Puello	10.00
CR	Cory Rasmus	15.00
JR	Joshua Rodriguez	15.00
BR	Billy Rowell	60.00
JS	Jarrod Saltalamacchia	20.00
BSI	Brett Sinkbeil	20.00
BS	Brandon Snyder	15.00
WT	Wade Townsend	15.00
CT	Chad Tracy	15.00
JU	Justin Upton	80.00
SWA	Sean Watson	15.00
JW	Johnny Whittleman	15.00
CW	Colten Willems	15.00
BW	Brandon Wood	25.00
SW	Steven Wright	15.00

2007 Bowman

MILLER

		NM/M
Complete Set (237):		
Common Player:		.15
Common RC (201-220):		.25

#	Player	Price
	Common RC Auto.:	10.00
	Pack (10):	3.50
	Box (24):	75.00
1	Hanley Ramirez	.50
2	Justin Verlander	.50
3	Ryan Zimmerman	.40
4	Jered Weaver	.50
5	Stephen Drew	.50
6	Jonathan Papelbon	.50
7	Melky Cabrera	.25
8	Francisco Liriano	.25
9	Prince Fielder	.75
10	Dan Uggla	.15
11	Jeremy Sowers	.15
12	Carlos Quentin	.15
13	Chuck James	.15
14	Andre Ethier	.15
15	Cole Hamels	.50
16	Kenji Johjima	.25
17	Chad Bilingsley	.15
18	Ian Kinsler	.25
19	Jason Hirsh	.15
20	Nicholas Markakis	.25
21	Jeremy Hermida	.15
22	Ryan Shealy	.15
23	Scott Olsen	.15
24	Russell Martin	.25
25	Conor Jackson	.15
26	Erik Bedard	.25
27	Brian McCann	.15
28	Michael Barrett	.25
29	Brandon Phillips	.15
30	Garrett Atkins	.25
31	Freddy Garcia	.15
32	Mark Loretta	.15
33	Craig Biggio	.25
34	Jeremy Bonderman	.25
35	Johan Santana	.75
36	Jorge Posada	.40
37	Brian Bannister	.15
38	Carlos Delgado	.50
39	Gary Mathews Jr.	.15
40	Mike Cameron	.15
41	Adrian Beltre	.25
42	Freddy Sanchez	.15
43	Austin Kearns	.15
44	Mark Buehrle	.15
45	Miguel Cabrera	.75
46	Josh Beckett	.25
47	Chone Figgins	.15
48	Edgar Renteria	.25
49	Derek Lowe	.15
50	Ryan Howard	1.50
51	Shawn Green	.15
52	Jason Giambi	.50
53	Ervin Santana	.15
54	Jack Wilson	.15
55	Roy Oswalt	.50
56	Danny Haren	.25
57	Jose Vidro	.15
58	Kevin Millwood	.15
59	Jim Edmonds	.25
60	Carl Crawford	.50
61	Randy Wolf	.15
62	Paul LoDuca	.15
63	Johnny Estrada	.15
64	Brian Roberts	.25
65	Manny Ramirez	.75
66	Jose Contreras	.15
67	Josh Barfield	.15
68	Juan Pierre	.15
69	David DeJesus	.15
70	Gary Sheffield	.40
71	Jon Lieber	.15
72	Randy Johnson	.75
73	Rickie Weeks	.25
74	Brian Giles	.15
75	Ichiro Suzuki	1.00
76	Nick Swisher	.25
77	Justin Morneau	.50
78	Scott Kazmir	.25
79	Lyle Overbay	.15
80	Alfonso Soriano	.75
81	Brandon Webb	.25
82	Joe Crede	.15
83	Corey Patterson	.15
84	Kenny Rogers	.15
85	Ken Griffey Jr.	1.50
86	Cliff Lee	.15
87	Mike Lowell	.15
88	Marcus Giles	.15
89	Orlando Cabrera	.15
90	Derek Jeter	2.00
91	Josh Johnson	.15
92	Carlos Guillen	.15
93	Bill Hall	.25
94	Michael Cuddyer	.15
95	Miguel Tejada	.50
96	Todd Helton	.50
97	C.C. Sabathia	.25
98	Tadahito Iguchi	.15
99	Jose Reyes	.75
100	David Wright	1.00
101	Barry Zito	.25
102	Jake Peavy	.25
103	Richie Sexson	.40
104	A.J. Burnett	.15
105	Eric Chavez	.25
106	Jorge Cantu	.15
107	Grady Sizemore	.50
108	Bronson Arroyo	.15
109	Mike Mussina	.40
110	Magglio Ordonez	.25
111	Anibal Sanchez	.15
112	Jeff Francoeur	.25
113	Kevin Youkilis	.25
114	Aubrey Huff	.15
115	Carlos Zambrano	.25
116	Mark Teahen	.15
117	Carlos Silva	.15
118	Pedro Martinez	.50
119	Hideki Matsui	.75
120	Mike Piazza	.75
121	Jason Schmidt	.25
122	Greg Maddux	1.50
123	Joe Blanton	.15
124	Chris Carpenter	.75
125	David Ortiz	.75
126	Alex Rios	.15
127	Nick Johnson	.15
128	Carlos Lee	.25
129	Pat Burrell	.25
130	Ben Sheets	.25
131	Kazuo Matsui	.15
132	Adam Dunn	.50
133	Jermaine Dye	.25
134	Curt Schilling	.75
135	Chad Tracy	.15
136	Vladimir Guerrero	.75
137	Melvin Mora	.15
138	John Smoltz	.25
139	Craig Monroe	.15
140	Dontrelle Willis	.25
141	Jeff Francis	.15
142	Chipper Jones	.75
143	Frank Thomas	.50
144	Brett Myers	.15
145	Xavier Nady	.15
146	Robinson Cano	.40
147	Jeff Kent	.15
148	Scott Rolen	.50
149	Roy Halladay	.25
150	Joe Mauer	.25
151	Bobby Abreu	.25
152	Matt Cain	.25
153	Hank Blalock	.15
154	Chris Capuano	.15
155	Jake Westbrook	.15
156	Javier Vazquez	.15
157	Garret Anderson	.15
158	Aramis Ramirez	.40
159	Mark Kotsay	.15
160	Matthew Kemp	.15
161	Adrian Gonzalez	.25
162	Felix Hernandez	.25
163	David Eckstein	.15
164	Curtis Granderson	.15
165	Paul Konerko	.25
166	Orlando Hudson	.15
167	Tim Hudson	.25
168	J.D. Drew	.25
169	Chien-Ming Wang	.50
170	Jimmy Rollins	.50
171	Matt Morris	.15
172	Raul Ibanez	.15
173	Mark Teixeira	.40
174	Ted Lilly	.15
175	Albert Pujols	2.00
176	Carlos Beltran	.50
177	Lance Berkman	.40
178	Ivan Rodriguez	.50
179	Torii Hunter	.25
180	Johnny Damon	.50
181	Chase Utley	.75
182	Jason Bay	.40
183	Jeff Weaver	.15
184	Troy Glaus	.25
185	Rocco Baldelli	.15
186	Rafael Furcal	.25
187	Jim Thome	.50
188	Travis Hafner	.40
189	Matt Holliday	.50
190	Andruw Jones	.50
191	Ramon Hernandez	.15
192	Victor Martinez	.25
193	Aaron Hill	.15
194	Michael Young	.25
195	Vernon Wells	.25
196	Mark Mulder	.15
197	Derrek Lee	.50
198	Tom Glavine	.40
199	Chris Young	.25
200	Alex Rodriguez	2.00
201	Delmon Young (RC)	.50
202	Alexi Casilla RC	.25
203	Shawn Riggans (RC)	.25
204	Jeff Baker (RC)	.25
205	Hector Gimenez (RC)	.25
206	Ubaldo Jimenez (RC)	.25
207	Adam Lind (RC)	.25
208	Joaquin Arias (RC)	.25
209	David Murphy (RC)	.25
210	Daisuke Matsuzaka RC	10.00
211	Jerry Owens (RC)	.25
212	Ryan Sweeney (RC)	.25
213	Kei Igawa RC	1.00
214	Fred Lewis (RC)	.25
215	Philip Humber (RC)	.25
216	Kevin Hooper (RC)	.25
217	Jeff Fiorentino (RC)	.25
218	Michael Bourn (RC)	.25
219	Hideki Okajima RC	3.00
219	Hideki Okajima/ Auto.	50.00
220	Josh Fields (RC)	.25
221	Andrew Miller/ Auto. (RC)	40.00
222	Troy Tulowitzki/ Auto. (RC)	20.00
223	Ryan Braun/ Auto. RC	15.00
224	Oswaldo Navarro/ Auto. RC	10.00
225	Philip Humber/ Auto. (RC)	15.00
226	Mitch Maier/ Auto. (RC)	15.00
227	Jerry Owens/ Auto. (RC)	15.00
228	Mike Rabelo/ Auto. RC	20.00
229	Delwyn Young/ Auto. (RC)	10.00
230	Miguel Montero/ Auto. (RC)	15.00
231	Akinori Iwamura/ Auto. RC	30.00
232	Matt Lindstrom/ Auto. (RC)	10.00
233	Josh Hamilton/ Auto. (RC)	20.00
235	Elijah Dukes/ Auto. RC	20.00
236	Sean Henn/Auto. (RC)	15.00
237	Barry Bonds	2.00

Blue

Blue:	2-4X
Blue RC Auto.:	1X
Production 500 Sets	

Gold

Gold (1-220):	1-2X
Inserted 1:1	

Orange

Orange:	3-6X
Orange RC Auto.:	1-1.5X
Production 250 Sets	

Red

No Pricing
Production One Set

Printing Plates

No Pricing
Production one set per color.

Alex Rodriguez Road to 500

Common Rodriguez:	2.00
Inserted 2:Box	
Autograph:	No Pricing
Production One Set	

Chrome Prospects

NM/M

Complete Set (110):	50.00
Common Player:	.50
Inserted 2:Hobby Pack	

#	Player	Price
1	Cooper Brannon	1.00
2	Jason Taylor	2.50
3	Shawn O'Malley	1.00
4	Robert Alcombrack	1.00
5	Dellin Betances	4.00
6	Jeremy Papelbon	2.00
7	Adam Carr	1.00
8	Matthew Clarkson	.50
9	Darin McDonald	1.00
10	Brandon Rice	1.00
11	Matthew Sweeney	2.50
12	Scott Deal	.50
13	Brennan Boesch	1.00
14	Scott Taylor	1.00
15	Michael Brantley	2.00
16	Yahmed Yema	1.00
17	Brandon Morrow	5.00
18	Cole Garner	1.00
19	Erik Lis	1.50
20	Lucas French	1.00
21	Aaron Cunningham	3.00
22	Ryan Schreppel	.50
23	Kevin Russo	1.00
24	Yohan Pino	1.00
25	Michael Sullivan	.50
26	Trey Shields	.50
27	Danny Matienzo	.50
28	Chuck Lofgren	2.00
29	Gerrit Simpson	.50
30	David Haehnel	.50
31	Marvin Lowrance	1.00
32	Kevin Ardoin	.50
33	Edwin Maysonet	.50
34	Derek Griffith	.50
35	Sam Fuld	1.00
36	Chase Wright	1.50
37	Brandon Roberts	.50
38	Kyle Aselton	.50
39	Steven Sollmann	1.00
40	Michael Devaney	1.00
41	Charlie Fermaint	.50
42	Jesse Litsch	1.50
43	Bryan Hansen	1.00
44	Ramon Garcia	.50
45	John Otness	1.50
46	Trey Hearne	.50
47	Habelito Hernandez	1.00
48	Edgar Garcia	1.50
49	Seth Fortenberry	1.00
50	Reid Brignac	2.00
51	Derek Rodriguez	.50
52	Ervin Alcantara	1.00
53	Tom Hottovy	1.00
54	Jesus Flores	1.00
55	Matt Palmer	.50
56	Brian Henderson	.50
57	John Gragg	.50
58	Jay Garthwaite	1.00
59	Esmerling Vasquez	1.00
60	Gilberto Mejia	1.00
61	Aaron Jensen	.50
62	Cedric Brooks	.50
63	Brandon Mann	.50
64	Myron Leslie	1.00
65	Ray Aguilar	.50
66	Jesus Guzman	.50
67	Sean Thompson	.50
68	Jarrett Hoffpauir	1.00
69	Matt Goodson	.50
70	Neal Musser	.50
71	Tony Abreu	4.00
72	Tony Peguero	.50
73	Michael Bertram	1.00
74	Randy Wells	1.00
75	Bradley Davis	.50
76	Jay Sawatski	1.00
77	Vic Buttler	.50
78	Jose Oyervidez	.50
79	Doug Deeds	1.00
80	Daniel Dement	1.00
81	Spike Lundberg	.50
82	Ricardo Nanita	.50
83	Brad Knox	1.00
84	Will Venable	1.00
85	Greg Smith	1.50
86	Pedro Powell	1.00
87	Gabriel Medina	1.00
88	Duke Sardinha	.50
89	Mike Madsen	1.50
90	Rayner Bautista	.50
91	T.J. Nall	.50
92	Neil Sellers	1.00
93	Andrew Dobies	.50
94	Leo Daigle	.50
95	Brian Duensing	1.50
96	Vincent Blue	1.00
97	Fernando Rodriguez	1.00
98	Derin McMains	.50
99	Adam Bass	1.00
100	Justin Ruggiano	1.50
101	Jared Burton	1.00
102	Mike Parisi	1.00
103	Aaron Peel	1.00
104	Evan Englebrook	1.00

105	Sendy Vasquez	.50
106	Desmond Jennings	3.00
107	Clay Harris	1.00
108	Cody Strait	1.00
109	Ryan Mullins	1.00
110	Ryan Webb	1.00

Chrome Prospects Refractor
Refractor (1-110): 2-4X
Production 500 Sets

Chrome Prospects Blue Refractor
Blue Refractor (1-110): 4-6X
Production 150 Sets

Chrome Prospects Gold Refractor
Gold Refractor (1-110): 10-20X
Production 50 Sets

Chrome Prospects Orange Refractor
Orange Refractor (1-110): No Pricing
Production 25 Sets

Chrome Prospects Red Refractor
Red Refractor (1-110):No Pricing
Production 5 Sets

Chrome Prospects SuperFractor
Superfractor (1-110): No Pricing
Production One Set

Chrome Prospects X-Fractor
X-Fractor (1-110): 3-6X
Production 275 Sets

Prospects

REID BRIGNAC SS

		NM/M
Complete Set (135):		
Common Player (1-110):		.25
Common Auto. (111-135):		10.00
1	Cooper Brannon	.25
2	Jason Taylor	.75
3	Shawn O'Malley	.25
4	Robert Alcombrack	.25
5	Dellin Betances	1.00
6	Jeremy Papelbon	.50
7	Adam Carr	.25
8	Matthew Clarkson	.25
9	Darin McDonald	.25
10	Brandon Rice	.25
11	Matthew Sweeney	.50
12	Scott Deal	.25
13	Brennan Boesch	.25
14	Scott Taylor	.25
15	Michael Brantley	.50
16	Yahmed Yema	.25
17	Brandon Morrow	1.50
18	Cole Garner	.50
19	Erik Lis	.25
20	Lucas French	.25
21	Aaron Cunningham	1.00
22	Ryan Schreppel	.25
23	Kevin Russo	.25
24	Yohan Pino	.25
25	Michael Sullivan	.25
26	Trey Shields	.25
27	Danny Matienzo	.25
28	Chuck Lofgren	.50
29	Gerrit Simpson	.25
30	David Haehnel	.25
31	Marvin Lowrance	.25
32	Kevin Ardoin	.25
33	Edwin Maysonet	.25
34	Derek Griffith	.25
35	Sam Fuld	.25
36	Chase Wright	.50
37	Brandon Roberts	.25
38	Kyle Aselton	.25
39	Steven Sollmann	.25
40	Michael Devaney	.25
41	Charlie Fermaint	.25
42	Jesse Litsch	.50
43	Bryan Hansen	.25
44	Ramon Garcia	.25
45	John Otness	.50
46	Trey Hearne	.25
47	Habelito Hernandez	.25
48	Edgar Garcia	.50
49	Seth Fortenberry	.25
50	Reid Brignac	.50
51	Derek Rodriguez	.25
52	Ervin Alcantara	.25
53	Tom Hottovy	.25
54	Jesus Flores	.25
55	Matt Palmer	.25
56	Brian Henderson	.25
57	John Gragg	.25
58	Jay Garthwaite	.25
59	Esmerling Vasquez	.25
60	Gilberto Mejia	.25
61	Aaron Jensen	.25
62	Cedric Brooks	.25
63	Brandon Mann	.25
64	Myron Leslie	.25
65	Ray Aguilar	.25
66	Jesus Guzman	.25
67	Sean Thompson	.25
68	Jarrett Hoffpauir	.25
69	Matt Goodson	.25
70	Neal Musser	.25
71	Tony Abreu	1.50
72	Tony Peguero	.25
73	Michael Bertram	.25
74	Randy Wells	.25
75	Bradley Davis	.25
76	Jay Sawatski	.25
77	Vic Buttler	.25
78	Jose Oyervidez	.25
79	Doug Deeds	.25
80	Daniel Dement	.25
81	Spike Lundberg	.25
82	Ricardo Nanita	.25
83	Brad Knox	.25
84	Will Venable	.25
85	Greg Smith	.50
86	Pedro Powell	.25
87	Gabriel Medina	.25
88	Duke Sardinha	.25
89	Mike Madsen	.50
90	Rayner Bautista	.25
91	T.J. Nall	.25
92	Neil Sellers	.25
93	Andrew Dobies	.25
94	Leo Daigle	.25
95	Brian Duensing	.50
96	Vincent Blue	.25
97	Fernando Rodriguez	.25
98	Derin McMains	.25
99	Adam Bass	.25
100	Justin Ruggiano	.50
101	Jared Burton	.25
102	Mike Parisi	.25
103	Aaron Peel	.25
104	Evan Englebrook	.25
105	Sendy Vasquez	.25
106	Desmond Jennings	.75
107	Clay Harris	.25
108	Cody Strait	.25
109	Ryan Mullins	.25
110	Ryan Webb	.25
111	Kyle Drabek	20.00
112	Evan Longoria	30.00
113	Tyler Colvin	20.00
114	Matt Long	10.00
115	Jeremy Jeffress	15.00
116	Kasey Kiker	15.00
117	Hank Conger	15.00
118	Cody Johnson	15.00
119	David Huff	15.00
120	Tommy Hickman	10.00
121	Chris Parmelee	20.00
122	Dustin Evans	10.00
123	Brett Sinkbeil	15.00
124	Andrew Carpenter	15.00
125	Colton Willems	10.00
126	Matt Antonelli	15.00
127	Marcus Sanders	15.00
128	Joshua Rodriguez	15.00
129	Keith Weiser	20.00
130	Chad Tracy	15.00
131	Matthew Sulentic	20.00
132	Adam Ottavino	15.00
133	Jarrod Saltalamacchia	25.00
134	Kyle Blanks	15.00
135	Brad Emaus	10.00

Prospects Blue
Blue (1-110): 2-4X
Blue RC Auto.(111-135): 1X
Production 500 Sets

Prospects Gold
Gold (1-110): 1-2X
Inserted 1:1

Prospects Orange
Orange (1-110): 3-6X
Orange RC Auto.
(111-135): 1-1.5X
Production 250 Sets

Prospects Red
No Pricing
Production One Set

Signs of the Future

		NM/M
KD	Kyle Drabek	20.00
DB	Dellin Betances	60.00
JBC	J. Brent Cox	15.00
JD	John Drennen	10.00
DS	Denard Span	15.00
KC	Koby Clemens	25.00
EH	Estee Harris	20.00
MN	Mike Neu	15.00
RO	Ross Ohlendorf	15.00
CG	Chris Getz	10.00
AR	Adam Russell	15.00
JC	Jesus Cota	10.00
JB	John Baker	10.00
BM	Brandon Moss	10.00
CS	Chad Santos	10.00
KS	Kurt Suzuki	10.00
JJ	Jair Jurrjens	20.00
MA	Mike Aviles	10.00
TT	Taylor Teagarden	15.00
SK	Shane Komine	15.00
ME	Mike Edwards	10.00
MM	Matthew Merricks	10.00
JDA	Jamie D'Antona	10.00
JBB	John Bowker	10.00
CR	Chris Robinson	10.00
JW	Jared Wells	10.00
BF	Ben Fritz	10.00
BB	Brian Bixler	10.00
CM	Christopher McConnell	10.00
JCB	Jordan Brown	15.00
FP	Felix Pie	20.00
ER	Eric Reed	10.00
AM	Andrew McCutchen	20.00
MR	Michael Rogers	10.00
RB	Reid Brignac	20.00
RG	Rich Gardner	10.00
SG	Sean Gallagher	10.00
CJS	Chris Seddon	10.00

2007 Bowman Chrome

		NM/M
Common Player:		.25
Common RC:		.50
Pack (4):		5.00
Box (18):		85.00
1	Hanley Ramirez	.75
2	Justin Verlander	.75
3	Ryan Zimmerman	.50
4	Jered Weaver	.50
5	Stephen Drew	.40
6	Jonathan Papelbon	.50
7	Melky Cabrera	.50
8	Francisco Liriano	.25
9	Prince Fielder	1.00
10	Dan Uggla	.25
11	Jeremy Sowers	.25
12	Carlos Quentin	.25
13	Chuck James	.25
14	Andre Ethier	.25
15	Cole Hamels	.50
16	Kenji Johjima	.25
17	Chad Billingsley	.50
18	Ian Kinsler	.25
19	Jason Hirsh	.25
20	Nicholas Markakis	.50
21	Jeremy Hermida	.25
22	Ryan Shealy	.25
23	Scott Olsen	.25
24	Russell Martin	.50
25	Conor Jackson	.25
26	Erik Bedard	.50
27	Brian McCann	.50
28	Michael Barrett	.25
29	Brandon Phillips	.25
30	Garrett Atkins	.25
31	Freddy Garcia	.25
32	Mark Loretta	.25
33	Craig Biggio	.50
34	Jeremy Bonderman	.50
35	Johan Santana	.75
36	Jorge Posada	.75
37	Victor Martinez	.50
38	Carlos Delgado	.75
39	Gary Matthews	.50
40	Mike Cameron	.25
41	Adrian Beltre	.25
42	Freddy Sanchez	.25
43	Austin Kearns	.25
44	Mark Buehrle	.25
45	Miguel Cabrera	1.00
46	Josh Beckett	.75
47	Chone Figgins	.50
48	Edgar Renteria	.50
49	Derek Lowe	.25
50	Ryan Howard	2.00
51	Shawn Green	.25
52	Jason Giambi	.50
53	Ervin Santana	.25
54	Aaron Hill	.25
55	Roy Oswalt	.50
56	Danny Haren	.25
57	Jose Vidro	.25
58	Kevin Millwood	.25
59	Jim Edmonds	.50
60	Carl Crawford	.50
61	Randy Wolf	.25
62	Paul LoDuca	.25
63	Johnny Estrada	.25
64	Brian Roberts	.50
65	Manny Ramirez	1.00
66	Jose Contreras	.25
67	Josh Barfield	.25
68	Juan Pierre	.25
69	David DeJesus	.25
70	Gary Sheffield	.75
71	Michael Young	.50
72	Randy Johnson	.75
73	Rickie Weeks	.25
74	Brian Giles	.25
75	Ichiro Suzuki	1.50
76	Nick Swisher	.50
77	Justin Morneau	.75
78	Scott Kazmir	.50
79	Lyle Overbay	.25
80	Alfonso Soriano	1.00
81	Brandon Webb	.50
82	Joe Crede	.25
83	Corey Patterson	.25
84	Kenny Rogers	.25
85	Ken Griffey Jr.	2.00
86	Cliff Lee	.25
87	Mike Lowell	.50
88	Marcus Giles	.25
89	Orlando Cabrera	.25
90	Derek Jeter	2.50
91	Ramon Hernandez	.25
92	Carlos Guillen	.25
93	Bill Hall	.25
94	Michael Cuddyer	.25
95	Miguel Tejada	.75
96	Todd Helton	.75
97	C.C. Sabathia	.50
98	Tadahito Iguchi	.25
99	Jose Reyes	1.00
100	David Wright	1.00
101	Barry Zito	.50
102	Jake Peavy	.50
103	Richie Sexson	.50
104	A.J. Burnett	.25
105	Eric Chavez	.25
106	Vernon Wells	.50
107	Grady Sizemore	.75
108	Bronson Arroyo	.50
109	Mike Mussina	.50
110	Magglio Ordonez	.50
111	Anibal Sanchez	.25
112	Jeff Francoeur	.50
113	Kevin Youkilis	.50
114	Aubrey Huff	.25
115	Carlos Zambrano	.50
116	Mark Teahen	.25
117	Mark Mulder	.50
118	Pedro Martinez	1.00
119	Hideki Matsui	1.50
120	Mike Piazza	1.00
121	Jason Schmidt	.25
122	Greg Maddux	2.00
123	Joe Blanton	.25
124	Chris Carpenter	.75
125	David Ortiz	1.00
126	Alex Rios	.25
127	Nick Johnson	.25
128	Carlos Lee	.50
129	Pat Burrell	.50
130	Ben Sheets	.50
131	Derrek Lee	.50
132	Adam Dunn	.50
133	Jermaine Dye	.25
134	Curt Schilling	.75
135	Chad Tracy	.25
136	Vladimir Guerrero	1.00
137	Melvin Mora	.25
138	John Smoltz	.50
139	Craig Monroe	.25
140	Dontrelle Willis	.25

141	Jeff Francis	.25
142	Chipper Jones	1.00
143	Frank Thomas	1.00
144	Brett Myers	.25
145	Tom Glavine	.75
146	Robinson Cano	.75
147	Jeff Kent	.50
148	Scott Rolen	.75
149	Roy Halladay	.50
150	Joe Mauer	.50
151	Bobby Abreu	.50
152	Matt Cain	.50
153	Hank Blalock	.50
154	Chris Young	.50
155	Jake Westbrook	.25
156	Javier Vazquez	.25
157	Garret Anderson	.25
158	Aramis Ramirez	.50
159	Mark Kotsay	.25
160	Matthew Kemp	.50
161	Adrian Gonzalez	.50
162	Felix Hernandez	.50
163	David Eckstein	.25
164	Curtis Granderson	.50
165	Paul Konerko	.50
166	Alex Rodriguez	2.50
167	Tim Hudson	.50
168	J.D. Drew	.25
169	Chien-Ming Wang	1.00
170	Jimmy Rollins	.75
171	Matt Morris	.25
172	Raul Ibanez	.25
173	Mark Teixeira	.75
174	Ted Lilly	.25
175	Albert Pujols	2.50
176	Carlos Beltran	1.00
177	Lance Berkman	.50
178	Ivan Rodriguez	.75
179	Torii Hunter	.50
180	Johnny Damon	.75
181	Chase Utley	1.00
182	Jason Bay	.50
183	Jeff Weaver	.25
184	Troy Glaus	.50
185	Rocco Baldelli	.25
186	Rafael Furcal	.50
187	Jim Thome	.75
188	Travis Hafner	.50
189	Matt Holliday	.50
190	Andruw Jones	.50
191	Andrew Miller **RC**	5.00
192	Ryan Braun **RC**	.50
193	Oswaldo Navarro **RC**	.50
194	Mike Rabelo **RC**	.50
195	Delwyn Young **(RC)**	.50
196	Miguel Montero **(RC)**	.50
197	Matt Lindstrom **(RC)**	.50
198	Josh Hamilton **(RC)**	2.00
199	Elijah Dukes **RC**	1.00
200	Sean Henn **(RC)**	.50
201	Delmon Young **(RC)**	1.00
202	Alexi Casilla **RC**	1.00
203	Hunter Pence **(RC)**	10.00
204	Jeff Baker **(RC)**	.50
205	Hector Gimenez **(RC)**	.50
206	Ubaldo Jimenez **(RC)**	.50
207	Adam Lind **(RC)**	1.00
208	Joaquin Arias **(RC)**	1.00
209	David Murphy **(RC)**	.50
210	Daisuke Matsuzaka **RC**	8.00
211	Jerry Owens **(RC)**	.50
212	Ryan Sweeney **(RC)**	.50
213	Kei Igawa **RC**	1.00
214	Mitch Maier **RC**	.50
215	Philip Humber **(RC)**	1.00
216	Troy Tulowitzki **(RC)**	2.00
217	Tim Lincecum **RC**	10.00
218	Michael Bourn **(RC)**	.50
219	Hideki Okajima **RC**	2.00
220	Josh Fields **(RC)**	1.00

Refractors

Refractor RC (1-190): 2-4X
Refractor RC (191-220): 1.5-2X
Inserted 4:Box

Blue Refractor

Blue Refractor (1-190): 4-6X
Blue Refractor RC
  (191-220): 3-5X
Production 150 Sets

Gold Refractor

Gold Refractor (1-190): 10-15X
Gold Refractor RC
  (191-220): 8-15X
Production 50 Sets

Orange Refractor

Orange Refractor (1-190):10-20X
Orange Refractor RC
  (191-220): 10-20X
Production 25 Sets

Red Refractor

Production 5 Sets

Super-Fractor

Production One Set

X-Fractor

X-Fractor (1-190): 3-5X
X-Fractor RC (191-220): 2-4X
Production 250 Sets

Printing Plates

Production One Set

Chrome Prospects

		NM/M
	Common Player:	.50
	Common Auto. (221-256):	10.00
BC1	Cooper Brannon	1.00
BC2	Jason Taylor	1.00
BC3	Shawn O'Malley	.50
BC4	Robert Alcombrack	.50
BC5	Dellin Betances	4.00
BC6	Jeremy Papelbon	1.00
BC7	Adam Carr	.50
BC8	Matthew Clarkson	.50
BC9	Darin McDonald	.50
BC10	Brandon Rice	.50
BC11	Matthew Sweeney	3.00
BC12	Scott Deal	.50
BC13	Brennan Boesch	.50
BC14	Scott Taylor	.50
BC15	Michael Brantley	1.00
BC16	Yahmed Yema	.50
BC17	Brandon Morrow	.50
BC18	Cole Garner	.50
BC19	Erik Lis	1.00
BC20	Lucas French	.50
BC21	Aaron Cunningham	2.00
BC22	Ryan Schreppel	.50
BC23	Kevin Russo	.50
BC24	Yohan Pino	1.00
BC25	Michael Sullivan	.50
BC26	Trey Shields	1.00
BC27	Danny Matienzo	.50
BC28	Chuck Lofgren	.50
BC29	Gerrit Simpson	.50
BC30	David Haehnel	.50
BC31	Marvin Lowrance	.50
BC32	Kevin Ardoin	.50
BC33	Edwin Maysonet	.50
BC34	Derek Griffith	.50
BC35	Sam Fuld	1.00
BC36	Chase Wright	2.00
BC37	Brandon Roberts	.50
BC38	Kyle Aselton	.50
BC39	Steven Sollmann	.50
BC40	Michael Devaney	.50
BC41	Charlie Fermaint	.50
BC42	Jesse Litsch	1.00
BC43	Bryan Hansen	.50
BC44	Ramon Garcia	1.00
BC45	John Otness	.50
BC46	Trey Hearne	.50
BC47	Habelito Hernandez	.50
BC48	Edgar Garcia	.50
BC49	Seth Fortenberry	.50
BC50	Reid Brignac	1.00
BC51	Derek Rodriguez	.50
BC52	Ervin Alcantara	.50
BC53	Tom Hottovy	.50
BC54	Jesus Flores	1.00
BC55	Matt Palmer	.50
BC56	Brian Henderson	.50
BC57	John Gragg	.50
BC58	Jay Garthwaite	.50
BC59	Esmerling Vasquez	.50
BC60	Gilberto Mejia	1.00
BC61	Aaron Jensen	.50
BC62	Cedric Brooks	1.00
BC63	Brandon Mann	.50
BC64	Myron Leslie	1.00
BC65	Ray Aguilar	.50

BC66	Jesus Guzman	2.00
BC67	Sean Thompson	.50
BC68	Jarrett Hoffpauir	1.00
BC69	Matt Goodson	.50
BC70	Neal Musser	.50
BC71	Tony Abreu	1.50
BC72	Tony Peguero	1.00
BC73	Michael Bertram	.50
BC74	Randy Wells	.50
BC75	Bradley Davis	.50
BC76	Jay Sawatski	.50
BC77	Vic Buttler	1.00
BC78	Jose Oyervidez	1.00
BC79	Doug Deeds	1.00
BC80	Daniel Dement	.50
BC81	Spike Lundberg	.50
BC82	Ricardo Nanita	1.00
BC83	Brad Knox	.50
BC84	Will Venable	1.00
BC85	Greg Smith	.50
BC86	Pedro Powell	.50
BC87	Gabriel Medina	.50
BC88	Duke Sardinha	.50
BC89	Mike Madsen	.50
BC90	Rayner Bautista	.50
BC91	T.J. Nall	.50
BC92	Neil Sellers	.50
BC93	Andrew Dobies	.50
BC94	Leo Daigle	.50
BC95	Brian Duensing	2.00
BC96	Vincent Blue	.50
BC97	Fernando Rodriguez	.50
BC98	Derin McMains	.50
BC99	Adam Bass	.50
BC100	Justin Ruggiano	1.00
BC101	Jared Burton	1.00
BC102	Mike Parisi	.50
BC103	Aaron Peel	1.00
BC104	Evan Englebrook	.50
BC105	Sendy Vasquez	.50
BC106	Desmond Jennings	1.50
BC107	Clay Harris	.50
BC108	Cody Strait	.50
BC109	Ryan Mullins	.50
BC110	Ryan Webb	.50
BC111	Mike Carp	1.00
BC112	Greg Porter	.50
BC113	Joe Ness	.50
BC114	Matt Camp	.50
BC115	Carlos Fisher	.50
BC116	Bryan Bass	.50
BC117	Jeff Baisley	.50
BC118	Burke Badenhop	1.00
BC119	Grant Psomas	.50
BC120	Eric Young Jr.	1.00
BC121	Henry Rodriguez	1.00
BC122	Carlos Fernandez	1.00
BC123	Chris Errecart	.50
BC124	Brandon Hynick	1.50
BC125	Jose Constanza	.50
BC126	Steve Delabar	.50
BC127	Raul Barron	.50
BC128	Nick DeBarr	.50
BC129	Reegie Corona	1.00
BC130	Thomas Fairchild	.50
BC131	Bryan Byrne	.50
BC132	Kurt Mertins	.50
BC133	Erik Averill	.50
BC134	Matt Young	.50
BC135	Ryan Rogowski	.50
BC136	Andrew Bailey	2.00
BC137	Jonathan Van Every	.50
BC138	Scott Shoemaker	.50
BC139	Steve Singleton	.50
BC140	Mitch Atkins	.50
BC141	Robert Rohrbaugh	1.00
BC142	Ole Sheldon	.50
BC143	Adam Ricks	.50
BC144	Daniel Mayora	1.50
BC145	Johnny Cueto	4.00
BC146	Jim Fasano	.50
BC147	Jared Goedert	1.50
BC148	Jonathan Ash	.50
BC149	Derek Miller	.50
BC150	Juan Miranda	1.50
BC151	J.R. Mathes	.50
BC152	Craig Cooper	.50
BC153	Drew Locke	.50
BC154	Michael MacDonald	.50
BC155	Ryan Norwood	.50
BC156	Tony Butler	1.50
BC157	Pat Dobson	.50
BC158	Cody Ehlers	.50
BC159	Dan Fournier	.50
BC160	Joe Gaetti	.50
BC161	Mark Wagner	1.50
BC162	Tommy Hanson	1.00
BC163	Sharlon Schoop	.50
BC164	Woods Fines	.50
BC165	Chad Boyd	.50
BC166	Kala Kaaihu	2.00
BC167	Chris Salamida	1.00
BC168	Brendan Katin	1.00
BC169	Terrance Blunt	.50

BC170	Tobi Stoner	1.00
BC171	Phil Coke	.50
BC172	O.D. Gonzalez	.50
BC173	Christopher Cody	.50
BC174	Cedric Hunter	2.00
BC175	Whit Robbins	.50
BC176	Chris Begg	.50
BC177	Nathan Southard	.50
BC178	Dan Brauer	.50
BC179	Jared Keel	.50
BC180	Chance Douglass	1.00
BC181	Daniel Murphy	2.00
BC182	Anthony Hatch	.50
BC183	Justin Byler	1.00
BC184	Scott Lewis	.50
BC185	Andrew Fie	1.00
BC186	Chorye Spoone	1.00
BC187	Cole Bruce	.50
BC188	Adam Cowart	1.00
BC189	Chris Nowak	.50
BC190	Gorkys Hernandez	5.00
BC191	Devin Ivany	.50
BC192	Jordan Smith	.50
BC193	Philip Britton	.50
BC194	Cole Gillespie	1.00
BC195	Brett Anderson	2.00
BC196	Joe Mather	.50
BC197	Eddie Degerman	.50
BC198	Ronald Prettyman	.50
BC199	Patrick Reilly	.50
BC200	Tyler Clippard	1.00
BC201	Nick Van Stratten	.50
BC202	Todd Redmond	.50
BC203	Michael Martinez	.50
BC204	Alberto Bastardo	.50
BC205	Vasili Spanos	.50
BC206	Shane Benson	.50
BC207	Brent Johnson	.50
BC208	Brett Campbell	.50
BC209	Dustin Martin	.50
BC210	Chris Carter	4.00
BC211	Alfred Joseph	.50
BC212	Carlos Leon	.50
BC213	Gabriel Sanchez	1.00
BC214	Carlos Corporan	.50
BC215	Emerson Frostad	.50
BC216	Karl Gelinas	.50
BC217	Ryan Finan	.50
BC218	Noe Rodriguez	.50
BC219	Archie Gilbert	.50
BC220	Jeff Locke	3.00
BC221	Fernando Martinez	100.00
BC222	Jeremy Papelbon	20.00
BC223	Ryan Adams	10.00
BC224	Chris Perez	10.00
BC225	J.R. Towles	20.00
BC226	Tommy Mendoza	15.00
BC227	Jeff Samardzija	40.00
BC228	Sergio Perez	20.00
BC229	Justin Reed	20.00
BC230	Luke Hochevar	30.00
BC231	Ivan DeJesus	20.00
BC232	Kevin Mulvey	30.00
BC233	Chris Coghlan	20.00
BC234	Trevor Cahill	40.00
BC235	Peter Bourjos	20.00
BC236	Joba Chamberlain	180.00
BC237	Josh Rodriguez	15.00
BC238	Tim Lincecum	100.00
BC239	Josh Papelbon	20.00
BC240	Greg Reynolds	25.00
BC241	Wes Hodges	25.00
BC242	Chad Reineke	20.00
BC243	Emmanuel Burriss	20.00
BC244	Henry Sosa	25.00
BC245	Cesar Nicolas	15.00
BC246	Young Il Jung	20.00
BC247	Eric Patterson	15.00
BC248	Hunter Pence	40.00
BC249	Dellin Betances	60.00
BC250	Will Venable	20.00
BC251	Zach McAllister	25.00
BC252	Mark Hamilton	20.00
BC253	Paul Estrada	15.00
BC254	Brad Lincoln	20.00
BC255	Cedric Hunter	50.00
BC256	Chad Rodgers	20.00

Chrome Prospects
Refractor

Refractor (1-200): 3-5X
Refractor Auto. (201-256):1-1.5X
Production 500 Sets

Chrome Prospects
Blue Refractor

Blue Refractor (1-200): 5-10X
Blue Refractor Auto.
  (201-256): 1.5-2.5X
Production 150 Sets

Chrome Prospects
Gold Refractor

Gold Refractor (1-200):	15-25X
Gold Refractor Auto.	
(201-256):	3-5X
Production 50 Sets	

Chrome Prospects
Orange Refractor

Orange Refractor	
(1-200):	No Pricing
Orange Refract Auto.	
(201-256):	No Pricing
Production 25 Sets	

Chrome Prospects
Red Refractor

No Pricing
Production 5 Sets

Chrome Prospects
X-Fractor

X-Fractor (1-200):	4-8X
Production 250 Sets	
X-Fractor Auto. (201-256):	1-2X
Production 225 Sets	

2007 Bowman
Heritage

	NM/M
Complete Set (251):	
Common Player (1-200):	.25
Common RC (201-251):	.50
Common SP:	3.00
Inserted 1:3	
SP's don't have auto. on front.	
Pack (8):	
Box (24):	
1	Jeff Francoeur	.50
2	Jered Weaver	.40
3	Derrek Lee	.50
4	Todd Helton	.50
5	Shawn Hill	.25
6	Ivan Rodriguez	.50
7	Mickey Mantle	5.00
8	Ramon Hernandez	.25
9	Randy Johnson	.75
10	Jermaine Dye	.25
11	Brian Roberts	.40
12	Hank Blalock	.40
13	Chien-Ming Wang	.75
14	Mike Lowell	.50
15	Brandon Webb	.50
16	Kelly Johnson	.25
17	Nick Johnson	.25
18	Zach Duke	.25
19	Aaron Hill	.25
20	Miguel Tejada	.40
21	Mark Buehrle	.40
22	Michael Young	.40
23	Carlos Delgado	.50
24	Anibal Sanchez	.25
25	Vladimir Guerrero	.75
26	Russell Martin	.40
27	Lance Berkman	.25
28	Bobby Crosby	.25
29	Javier Vazquez	.25
30	Manny Ramirez	.75
31	Rich Hill	.25
32	Mike Sweeney	.25
33	Jeff Kent	.40
34	Noah Lowry	.25
35	Alfonso Soriano	.75
36	Paul LoDuca	.25
37	J.D. Drew	.25
38	C.C. Sabathia	.50
39	Craig Biggio	.40
40	Adam Dunn	.50
41	Josh Beckett	.50
42	Carlos Guillen	.25
43	Jeff Francis	.25
44	Orlando Hudson	.25
45	Grady Sizemore	.75
46	Jason Jennings	.25
47	Mark Teixeira	.50
48	Freddy Garcia	.25
49	Adrian Gonzalez	.40
50	Albert Pujols	2.00
51	Tom Glavine	.40
52	J.J. Hardy	.40
53	Bobby Abreu	.40
54	Bartolo Colon	.25
55	Garrett Atkins	.40
56	Moises Alou	.40
57	Cliff Lee	.25
58	Mike Cuddyer	.25
59	Brandon Phillips	.40
60	Jeremy Bonderman	.40
61	Rickie Weeks	.40
62	Chris Carpenter	.50

63	Frank Thomas	.75
64	Victor Martinez	.50
65	Dontrelle Willis	.40
66	Jim Thome	.50
67	Aaron Rowand	.40
68	Andy Pettitte	.50
69	Brian McCann	.40
70	Roger Clemens	2.00
71	Gary Matthews	.25
72	Bronson Arroyo	.25
73	Jeremy Hermida	.25
74	Eric Chavez	.40
75	David Ortiz	.75
76	Stephen Drew	.50
77	Ronnie Belliard	.25
78	James Shields	.25
79	Richie Sexson	.40
80	Johan Santana	.75
81	Orlando Cabrera	.25
82	Aramis Ramirez	.50
83	Greg Maddux	1.00
84	Reggie Sanders	.25
85	Carlos Zambrano	.50
86	Bengie Molina	.25
87	David DeJesus	.25
88	Adam Wainwright	.40
89	Conor Jackson	.25
90	David Wright	1.00
91	Ryan Garko	.25
92	Bill Hall	.25
93	Marcus Giles	.25
94	Kenny Rogers	.25
95	Joe Mauer	.40
96	Hanley Ramirez	.75
97	Brian Giles	.25
98	Danny Haren	.25
99	Robinson Cano	.50
100	Ryan Howard	1.00
101	Andruw Jones	.40
102	Aaron Harang	.25
103	Hideki Matsui	1.50
104	Nick Swisher	.40
105	Pedro Martinez	.75
106	Felipe Lopez	.25
107	Erik Bedard	.50
108	Rafael Furcal	.40
109	Curt Schilling	.50
110	Jose Reyes	.75
111	Adam LaRoche	.40
112	Mike Mussina	.50
113	Melvin Mora	.25
114	Zack Greinke	.25
115	Justin Morneau	.75
116	Ervin Santana	.25
117	Ken Griffey Jr.	1.50
118	David Eckstein	.25
119	Jamie Moyer	.25
120	Jorge Posada	.50
121	Justin Verlander	.50
122	Sammy Sosa	.75
123	Jason Schmidt	.25
124	Josh Willingham	.25
125	Roy Oswalt	.50
126	Travis Hafner	.40
127	John Maine	.40
128	Willy Taveras	.25
129	Magglio Ordonez	.50
130	Barry Zito	.40
131	Prince Fielder	1.00
132	Michael Barrett	.25
133	Livan Hernandez	.25
134	Troy Glaus	.40
135	Rocco Baldelli	.40
136	Jason Giambi	.50
137	Austin Kearns	.25
138	Dan Uggla	.25
139	Pat Burrell	.40
140	Carlos Beltran	.50
141	Carlos Quentin	.25
142	Johnny Estrada	.25
143	Torii Hunter	.40
144	Carlos Lee	.50
145	Mike Piazza	.75
146	Mark Teahen	.25
147	Juan Pierre	.40
148	Paul Konerko	.50
149	Freddy Sanchez	.25
150	Derek Jeter	2.00
151	Orlando Hernandez	.25
152	Raul Ibanez	.25
153	John Smoltz	.50
154	Scott Rolen	.50
155	Jimmy Rollins	.50
156	A.J. Burnett	.25
157	Jason Varitek	.50
158	Ben Sheets	.40
159	Matt Cain	.40
160	Carl Crawford	.50
161	Jeff Suppan	.25
162	Tadahito Iguchi	.25
163	Kevin Millwood	.25
164	Chris Duncan	.25
165	Rich Harden	.25
166	Joe Crede	.25

167	Chipper Jones	.75
168	Gary Sheffield	.50
169	Cole Hamels	.50
170	Jason Bay	.40
171	Jhonny Peralta	.40
172	Aubrey Huff	.25
173	Xavier Nady	.25
174	Kazuo Matsui	.25
175	Vernon Wells	.40
176	Johnny Damon	.50
177	Jim Edmonds	.40
178	Jose Vidro	.25
179	Garret Anderson	.25
180	Alex Rios	.40
181	Ichiro Suzuki	1.50
181	Ichiro Suzuki/SP	6.00
182	Jake Peavy	.50
182	Jake Peavy/SP	4.00
183	Ian Kinsler	.50
183	Ian Kinsler/SP	3.00
184	Tom Gorzelanny	.25
184	Tom Gorzelanny/SP	3.00
185	Miguel Cabrera	.75
185	Miguel Cabrera/SP	5.00
186	Scott Kazmir	.40
186	Scott Kazmir/SP	3.00
187	Matt Holliday	.50
187	Matt Holliday/SP	5.00
188	Roy Halladay	.50
188	Roy Halladay/SP	4.00
189	Ryan Zimmerman	.50
189	Ryan Zimmerman/SP	4.00
190	Alex Rodriguez	2.00
190	Alex Rodriguez/SP	8.00
191	Kenji Johjima	.25
191	Kenji Johjima/SP	3.00
192	Gil Meche	.25
192	Gil Meche/SP	3.00
193	Chase Utley	.75
193	Chase Utley/SP	5.00
194	Jeremy Sowers	.25
194	Jeremy Sowers/SP	3.00
195	John Lackey	.25
195	John Lackey/SP	3.00
196	Nick Markakis	.50
196	Nick Markakis/SP	4.00
197	Tim Hudson	.40
197	Tim Hudson/SP	3.00
198	B.J. Upton	.50
198	B.J. Upton/SP	4.00
199	Felix Hernandez	.50
199	Felix Hernandez/SP	4.00
200	Barry Bonds	2.00
200	Barry Bonds/SP	8.00
201	Jarrod Saltalamacchia (RC)	.50
202	Tim Lincecum RC	5.00
203	Kory Casto (RC)	.50
204	Sean Henn (RC)	.50
205	Hector Gimenez (RC)	.50
206	Homer Bailey (RC)	1.00
207	Yunel Escobar (RC)	.50
208	Matt Lindstrom (RC)	.50
209	Tyler Clippard (RC)	.50
210	Joe Smith RC	.50
211	Tony Abreu RC	.50
212	Billy Butler (RC)	1.00
213	Gustavo Molina RC	.50
214	Brian Stokes (RC)	.50
215	Kevin Slowey (RC)	.50
216	Curtis Thigpen (RC)	.50
217	Carlos Gomez RC	2.00
218	Rick Vanden Hurk RC	.50
219	Michael Bourn (RC)	.50
220	Jeff Baker (RC)	.50
221	Andy LaRoche (RC)	1.00
222	Andrew Sonnanstine RC	.50
223	Chase Wright RC	.50
224	Mark Reynolds RC	2.00
225	Matt Chico (RC)	.50
226	Hunter Pence (RC)	2.00
226	Hunter Pence SP	6.00
227	John Danks (RC)	.50
227	John Danks/SP	3.00
228	Elijah Dukes RC	.50
228	Elijah Dukes/SP	3.00
229	Kei Igawa RC	1.00
229	Kei Igawa/SP	4.00
230	Felix Pie (RC)	.75
230	Felix Pie/SP	3.00
231	Jesus Flores RC	.50
231	Jesus Flores/SP	3.00
232	Dallas Braden RC	.50
232	Dallas Braden/SP	3.00
233	Akinori Iwamura RC	1.00
233	Akinori Iwamura/SP	4.00
234	Ryan Braun (RC)	2.50
234	Ryan Braun/SP	8.00
235	Alex Gordon RC	2.00
235	Alex Gordon/SP	6.00
236	Micah Owings (RC)	.50
236	Micah Owings/SP	3.00
237	Kevin Kouzmanoff (RC)	.75
237	Kevin Kouzmanoff/SP	3.00

238	Glen Perkins (RC)	.50
238	Glen Perkins/SP	3.00
239	Danny Putnam (RC)	.50
239	Danny Putnam/SP	3.00
240	Phil Hughes (RC)	2.00
240	Phil Hughes/SP	6.00
241	Ryan Sweeney (RC)	.50
241	Ryan Sweeney/SP	3.00
242	Josh Hamilton (RC)	1.00
242	Josh Hamilton/SP	6.00
243	Hideki Okajima (RC)	1.00
243	Hideki Okajima/SP	4.00
244	Adam Lind (RC)	.50
244	Adam Lind/SP	3.00
245	Travis Buck (RC)	.50
245	Travis Buck/SP	3.00
246	Miguel Montero (RC)	.50
246	Miguel Montero/SP	3.00
247	Brandon Morrow RC	1.00
247	Brandon Morrow/SP	4.00
248	Troy Tulowitzki (RC)	2.00
248	Troy Tulowitzki/SP	6.00
249	Delmon Young (RC)	1.00
249	Delmon Young/SP	4.00
250	Daisuke Matsuzaka RC	5.00
250	Daisuke Matsuzaka/SP	15.00
251	Joba Chamberlain RC	10.00

Red

Production One Set

Black

Black:	10-15X
Black SP's:	3-5X
Production 52 Sets	

Printing Plates

Production one set per color.

Rainbow

Rainbow:	1-2X
Rainbow SP's:	.5-1X
Inserted 1:1	

A-Rod Road to 500

	NM/M
Common A-Rod (351-375):	2.00
Inserted 2:Box	
Autograph:	No Pricing
Production One Set	

Box Topper

	NM/M
Common Player:	3.00
Inserted 1:Box	
1	Alex Rodriguez	10.00
2	Barry Bonds	10.00
3	Ryan Howard	6.00
4	David Wright	6.00
5	Ichiro Suzuki	6.00
6	Hideki Matsui	6.00
7	Mickey Mantle	15.00
8	Manny Ramirez	3.00
9	David Ortiz	4.00
10	Vladimir Guerrero	3.00
11	Jose Reyes	5.00
12	Albert Pujols	10.00
13	Alfonso Soriano	3.00
14	Matt Holliday	3.00
15	Miguel Cabrera	3.00
16	Phil Hughes	8.00
17	Daisuke Matsuzaka	10.00
18	Delmon Young	3.00
19	Troy Tulowitzki	5.00
20	Felix Pie	3.00
21	Alex Gordon	8.00
22	Hunter Pence	5.00
23	Akinori Iwamura	3.00
24	Josh Hamilton	3.00
25	Kei Igawa	3.00

Mickey Mantle
Shortprints

	NM/M
Complete Set (5):	40.00
Common Mantle:	10.00
Black:	4-8X
Production 52 Sets	
Red:	No Pricing
Production One Set	

Pieces of Greatness

	NM/M
Common Player:	4.00
Black:	2-3X
Production 52 Sets	
Red:	No Pricing
RB	Rocco Baldelli	4.00
LB	Lance Berkman	6.00
CB	Craig Biggio	6.00
JB	Jeremy Bonderman	4.00

Code	Player	Price
BB	Barry Bonds	20.00
MC	Miguel Cabrera	8.00
RC	Robinson Cano	8.00
RC2	Robinson Cano	8.00
EC	Eric Chavez	4.00
BC	Bobby Crosby	4.00
JD	Johnny Damon	8.00
JDD	J.D. Drew	4.00
AD	Adam Dunn	6.00
JE	Juan Encarnacion	4.00
DE	Darin Erstad	4.00
AE	Andre Ethier	4.00
JF	Jeff Francoeur	10.00
JFR	Jeff Francis	4.00
RF	Rafael Furcal	4.00
BG	Brian Giles	4.00
AG	Alex Gonzalez	4.00
LG	Luis Gonzalez	4.00
SG	Shawn Green	4.00
VG	Vladimir Guerrero	8.00
CH	Cole Hamels	10.00
RH	Rich Harden	4.00
TH	Todd Helton	8.00
TH2	Todd Helton	8.00
THU	Tim Hudson	6.00
TI	Tadahito Iguchi	4.00
AJ	Andruw Jones	6.00
JK	Jeff Kent	4.00
PK	Paul Konerko	6.00
PK2	Paul Konerko	6.00
CK	Corey Koskie	4.00
AL	Adam LaRoche	4.00
BL	Brad Lidge	4.00
ML	Mike Lowell	6.00
GM	Greg Maddux	10.00
HM	Hideki Matsui	15.00
JM	Joe Mauer	6.00
YM	Yadier Molina	4.00
MM	Mark Mulder	4.00
TN	Trot Nixon	4.00
MO	Magglio Ordonez	4.00
DO	David Ortiz	8.00
DO2	David Ortiz	8.00
CP	Corey Patterson	4.00
MP	Mike Piazza	8.00
AR	Aramis Ramirez	8.00
MR	Manny Ramirez	8.00
MR2	Manny Ramirez	8.00
JR	Jose Reyes	10.00
ARO	Alex Rodriguez	15.00
IR	Ivan Rodriguez	6.00
CS	Curt Schilling	6.00
GS	Gary Sheffield	6.00
GSI	Grady Sizemore	10.00
NS	Nick Swisher	4.00
MT	Mark Teixeira	8.00
MTE	Miguel Tejada	6.00
FT	Frank Thomas	8.00
CU	Chase Utley	8.00
TW	Tim Wakefield	4.00
DW	Dontrelle Willis	4.00
DWR	David Wright	10.00
BZ	Barry Zito	4.00
CBE	Carlos Beltran	8.00
CT	Chad Tracy	4.00

Prospects

NM/M

Common Prospect: .50
Inserted 2:Pack
Black: 10-15X
Production 52 Sets
Red: No Pricing
Production One Set

#	Player	Price
1	Thomas Fairchild	.50
2	Peter Bourjos	.50
3	Brett Campbell	.50
4	Cesar Nicolas	.50
5	Kala Kaaihu	1.00
6	Zach McAllister	1.00
7	Chad Reineke	.50
8	Anthony Hatch	.50
9	Cedric Hunter	1.00
10	Chris Carter	1.50
11	Tommy Hanson	1.50
12	Dellin Betances	2.00
13	John Otness	.50
14	Derin McMains	.50
15	Greg Reynolds	.50
16	Jonathan Van Every	.50
17	Eddie Degerman	.50
18	Cody Strait	.50
19	Noe Rodriguez	.50
20	Young-Il Jung	.50
21	Reegie Corona	1.00
22	Carlos Corporan	.50
23	Chance Douglass	.50
24	Leo Daigle	.50
25	Jeff Samardzija	2.00
26	Mark Wagner	.50
27	Chuck Lofgren	1.00
28	Bryan Byrne	1.00
29	Daniel Mayora	1.00
30	Gorkys Hernandez	2.00
31	Joshua Rodriguez	.50
32	Brad Knox	.50
33	Scott Lewis	.50
34	Joe Gaetti	.50
35	Mike Saunders	.50
36	Brendan Katin	.50
37	Brennan Boesch	.50
38	Jay Garthwaite	.50
39	Michael Devaney	.50
40	J.R. Towles	1.50
41	Joe Ness	1.00
42	Michael Martinez	1.00
43	Justin Byler	1.00
44	Chris Coghlan	1.00
45	Eric Young Jr.	1.00
46	J.R. Mathes	1.00
47	Ivan DeJesus Jr.	.50
48	Woods Fines	.50
49	Andrew Fie	.50
50	Luke Hochevar	2.00
51	Will Venable	.50
52	Todd Redmond	.50
53	Matthew Sweeney	.50
54	Trevor Cahill	2.00
55	Mike Carp	.50
56	Henry Sosa	.50
57	Emerson Frostad	.50
58	Jeremy Jeffress	1.00
59	Whit Robbins	.50
60	Joba Chamberlain	10.00
61	Raul Barron	.50
62	Aaron Cunningham	1.00
63	Greg Smith	1.00
64	Jeff Baisley	.50
65	Vic Buttler	.50
66	Steve Singleton	.50
67	Josh Papelbon	1.00
68	Ryan Finan	.50
69	Deolis Guerra	1.50
70	Vasili Spanos	1.00
71	Patrick Reilly	.50
72	Tom Hottovy	1.00
73	Daniel Murphy	.50
74	Matt Young	1.00
75	Brian Bocock	1.00
76	Chris Salamida	.50
77	Nathan Southard	.50
78	Brandon Hynick	1.50
79	Chris Nowak	.50
80	Reid Brignac	1.00
81	Cole Garner	.50
82	Nick Van Stratten	1.00
83	Jeremy Papelbon	.50
84	Jarrett Hoffpauir	.50
85	Kevin Mulvey	1.00
86	Matt Miller	.50
87	Devin Ivany	1.00
88	Marcus Sanders	.50
89	Michael MacDonald	.50
90	Gabriel Sanchez	.50
91	Ryan Norwood	.50
92	Jim Fasano	.50
93	Ryan Adams	.50
94	Evan Englebrook	.50
95	Juan Miranda	2.00
96	Greg Porter	.50
97	Shane Benson	.50
98	Sam Fuld	1.00
99	Cooper Brannon	.50
100	Fernando Martinez	4.00

Signs of Greatness

NM/M

Common Autograph: 8.00
Black: 1.5-2X
Production 52 Sets
Red: No Pricing
Production One Set

Code	Player	Price
DW	David Wright	75.00
CJ	Chipper Jones	50.00
CC	Carl Crawford	15.00
CH	Cole Hamels	30.00
JH	J.P. Howell	8.00
BJ	Blake Johnson	15.00
JP	Jorge Posada	35.00
NR	Nolan Reimold	15.00
CA	Carlos Arroyo	15.00
JB	John Buck	15.00
JC	Jorge Cantu	8.00
GM	Garrett Mock	10.00
AO	Adam Ottavino	20.00
RD	Rajai Davis	8.00
MM	Matt Maloney	10.00
WJB	Joe Benson	15.00
JCB	Jordan Brown	20.00
TG	Tony Giarratano	8.00
GG	Glenn Gibson	15.00
EJ	Elliot Johnson	10.00
JM	Jeff Manship	20.00
SS	Scott Sizemore	15.00
MT	Mike Thompson	8.00
SE	Stephen Englund	10.00
AF	Andrew Fie	15.00
SJ	Seth Johnston	10.00
SK	Sean Kazmar	10.00
JL	Jeff Locke	20.00
SP	Steve Pearce	30.00
CS	Chorye Spoone	15.00
WCS	Cody Strait	10.00
JT	J.R. Towles	15.00
JW	Johnny Whittleman	10.00

C

1996 Circa

NM/M

Complete Set (200): 15.00
Common Player: .10
Raves: 30X
Pack (8): 1.50
Wax Box (24): 25.00

#	Player	Price
1	Roberto Alomar	.25
2	Brady Anderson	.10
3	Rocky Coppinger RC	.10
4	Eddie Murray	.75
5	Mike Mussina	.35
6	Randy Myers	.10
7	Rafael Palmeiro	.65
8	Cal Ripken Jr.	2.00
9	Jose Canseco	.50
10	Roger Clemens	1.00
11	Mike Greenwell	.10
12	Tim Naehring	.10
13	John Valentin	.10
14	Mo Vaughn	.10
15	Tim Wakefield	.10
16	Jim Abbott	.10
17	Garret Anderson	.10
18	Jim Edmonds	.10
19	Darin Erstad RC	2.00
20	Chuck Finley	.10
21	Troy Percival	.10
22	Tim Salmon	.10
23	J.T. Snow	.10
24	Wilson Alvarez	.10
25	Harold Baines	.10
26	Ray Durham	.10
27	Alex Fernandez	.10
28	Tony Phillips	.10
29	Frank Thomas	.75
30	Robin Ventura	.10
31	Sandy Alomar Jr.	.10
32	Albert Belle	.10
33	Kenny Lofton	.10
34	Dennis Martinez	.10
35	Jose Mesa	.10
36	Charles Nagy	.10
37	Manny Ramirez	.75
37p	Manny Ramirez/OPS	2.00
38	Jim Thome	.60
39	Travis Fryman	.10
40	Bob Higginson	.10
41	Melvin Nieves	.10
42	Alan Trammell	.10
43	Kevin Appier	.10
44	Johnny Damon	.30
45	Keith Lockhart	.10
46	Jeff Montgomery	.10
47	Joe Randa	.10
48	Bip Roberts	.10
49	Ricky Bones	.10
50	Marc Newfield	.10
51	Dave Nilsson	.10
52	Kevin Seitzer	.10
53	Ron Coomer	.10
54	Marty Cordova	.10
55	Paul Molitor	.75
56	Roberto Kelly	.10
57	Chuck Knoblauch	.10
58	Paul Molitor	.75
59	Kirby Puckett	1.00
60	Scott Stahoviak	.10
61	Wade Boggs	1.00
62	David Cone	.10
63	Cecil Fielder	.10
64	Dwight Gooden	.10
65	Derek Jeter	2.00
66	Tino Martinez	.10
67	Paul O'Neill	.10
68	Andy Pettitte	.35
69	Ruben Rivera	.10
70	Bernie Williams	.10
71	Geronimo Berroa	.10
72	Jason Giambi	.45
73	Mark McGwire	1.50
74	Terry Steinbach	.10
75	Todd Van Poppel	.10
76	Jay Buhner	.10
77	Norm Charlton	.10
78	Ken Griffey Jr.	1.25
79	Randy Johnson	.75
80	Edgar Martinez	.10
81	Alex Rodriguez	1.50
82	Paul Sorrento	.10
83	Dan Wilson	.10
84	Will Clark	.10
85	Kevin Elster	.10
86	Juan Gonzalez	.40
87	Rusty Greer	.10
88	Ken Hill	.10
89	Mark McLemore	.10
90	Dean Palmer	.10
91	Roger Pavlik	.10
92	Ivan Rodriguez	.65
93	Joe Carter	.10
94	Carlos Delgado	.35
95	Juan Guzman	.10
96	John Olerud	.10
97	Ed Sprague	.10
98	Jermaine Dye	.10
99	Tom Glavine	.30
100	Marquis Grissom	.10
101	Andruw Jones	.75
102	Chipper Jones	1.00
103	David Justice	.10
104	Ryan Klesko	.10
105	Greg Maddux	1.00
106	Fred McGriff	.10
107	John Smoltz	.10
108	Brant Brown	.10
109	Mark Grace	.10
110	Brian McRae	.10
111	Ryne Sandberg	1.00
112	Sammy Sosa	1.00
113	Steve Trachsel	.10
114	Bret Boone	.10
115	Eric Davis	.10
116	Steve Gibralter	.10
117	Barry Larkin	.10
118	Reggie Sanders	.10
119	John Smiley	.10
120	Dante Bichette	.10
121	Ellis Burks	.10
122	Vinny Castilla	.10
123	Andres Galarraga	.10
124	Larry Walker	.10
125	Eric Young	.10
126	Kevin Brown	.10
127	Greg Colbrunn	.10
128	Jeff Conine	.10
129	Charles Johnson	.10
130	Al Leiter	.10
131	Gary Sheffield	.50
132	Devon White	.10
133	Jeff Bagwell	.75
134	Derek Bell	.10
135	Craig Biggio	.10
136	Doug Drabek	.10
137	Brian Hunter	.10
138	Darryl Kile	.10
139	Shane Reynolds	.10
140	Brett Butler	.10
141	Eric Karros	.10
142	Ramon Martinez	.10
143	Raul Mondesi	.10
144	Hideo Nomo	.40
145	Chan Ho Park	.10
146	Mike Piazza	1.25
147	Moises Alou	.10
148	Yamil Benitez	.10
149	Mark Grudzielanek	.10
150	Pedro Martinez	.75
151	Henry Rodriguez	.10
152	David Segui	.10
153	Rondell White	.10
154	Carlos Baerga	.10
155	John Franco	.10
156	Bernard Gilkey	.10
157	Todd Hundley	.10
158	Jason Isringhausen	.10
159	Lance Johnson	.10
160	Alex Ochoa	.10
161	Rey Ordonez	.10
162	Paul Wilson	.10
163	Ron Blazier	.10
164	Ricky Bottalico	.10
165	Jim Eisenreich	.10
166	Pete Incaviglia	.10
167	Mickey Morandini	.10

168	Ricky Otero	.10
169	Curt Schilling	.25
170	Jay Bell	.10
171	Charlie Hayes	.10
172	Jason Kendall	.10
173	Jeff King	.10
174	Al Martin	.10
175	Alan Benes	.10
176	Royce Clayton	.10
177	Brian Jordan	.10
178	Ray Lankford	.10
179	John Mabry	.10
180	Willie McGee	.10
181	Ozzie Smith	1.00
182	Todd Stottlemyre	.10
183	Andy Ashby	.10
184	Ken Caminiti	.10
185	Steve Finley	.10
186	Tony Gwynn	1.00
187	Rickey Henderson	.75
188	Wally Joyner	.10
189	Fernando Valenzuela	.10
190	Greg Vaughn	.10
191	Rod Beck	.10
192	Barry Bonds	2.00
193	Shawon Dunston	.10
194	Chris Singleton	.10
195	Robby Thompson	.10
196	Matt Williams	.10
197	Barry Bonds Checklist	.75
198	Ken Griffey Jr. Checklist	.65
199	Cal Ripken Jr. Checklist	.75
200	Frank Thomas Checklist	.40

Rave

	NM/M
Common Player:	2.00
Stars:	30X

(See 1996 Circa for checklist and base card values.)

Access

		NM/M
Complete Set (30):		50.00
Common Player:		.60
1	Cal Ripken Jr.	6.00
2	Mo Vaughn	.60
3	Tim Salmon	.75
4	Frank Thomas	2.00
5	Albert Belle	.75
6	Kenny Lofton	.60
7	Manny Ramirez	2.00
8	Paul Molitor	2.00
9	Kirby Puckett	3.00
10	Paul O'Neill	.60
11	Mark McGwire	5.00
12	Ken Griffey Jr.	4.00
13	Randy Johnson	2.00
14	Greg Maddux	3.00
15	John Smoltz	.60
16	Sammy Sosa	4.00
17	Barry Larkin	.60
18	Gary Sheffield	1.00
19	Jeff Bagwell	2.00
20	Hideo Nomo	2.00
21	Mike Piazza	4.00
22	Moises Alou	.60
23	Henry Rodriguez	.60
24	Rey Ordonez	.60
25	Jay Bell	.60
26	Ozzie Smith	3.00
27	Tony Gwynn	3.00
28	Rickey Henderson	2.00
29	Barry Bonds	6.00
30	Matt Williams	.60
30p	Matt Williams/OPS	1.00

Boss

		NM/M
Complete Set (50):		50.00
Common Player:		.45
1	Roberto Alomar	1.00
2	Cal Ripken Jr.	5.00
2p	Cal Ripken Jr./OPS	3.00
3	Jose Canseco	1.50
4	Mo Vaughn	.45
5	Tim Salmon	.60
6	Frank Thomas	2.00
7	Robin Ventura	.45
8	Albert Belle	.60
9	Kenny Lofton	.45
10	Manny Ramirez	2.00
11	Dave Nilsson	.45
12	Chuck Knoblauch	.45
13	Paul Molitor	2.00
14	Kirby Puckett	3.00
15	Wade Boggs	3.00
16	Dwight Gooden	.45
17	Paul O'Neill	.45
18	Mark McGwire	4.00
19	Jay Buhner	.45
20	Ken Griffey Jr.	3.50
21	Randy Johnson	2.00
22	Will Clark	.60
23	Juan Gonzalez	2.00
24	Joe Carter	.45
25	Tom Glavine	.45
26	Ryan Klesko	.45
27	Greg Maddux	3.00
28	John Smoltz	.45
29	Ryne Sandberg	3.00
30	Sammy Sosa	3.50
31	Barry Larkin	.45
32	Reggie Sanders	.45
33	Dante Bichette	.45
34	Andres Galarraga	.45
35	Charles Johnson	.45
36	Gary Sheffield	1.50
37	Jeff Bagwell	2.00
38	Hideo Nomo	2.00
39	Mike Piazza	3.50
40	Moises Alou	.45
41	Henry Rodriguez	.45
42	Rey Ordonez	.45
43	Ricky Otero	.45
44	Jay Bell	.45
45	Royce Clayton	.45
46	Ozzie Smith	3.00
47	Tony Gwynn	3.00
48	Rickey Henderson	2.00
49	Barry Bonds	5.00
50	Matt Williams	.45

1997 Circa

	NM/M
Complete Set (400):	15.00
Common Player:	.10
Pack (8):	1.00
Retail Wax Box (18):	15.00
Hobby Wax Box (36):	30.00

1	Kenny Lofton	.10
2	Ray Durham	.10
3	Mariano Rivera	.20
4	Jon Lieber	.10
5	Tim Salmon	.10
6	Mark Grudzielanek	.10
7	Neifi Perez	.10
8	Cal Ripken Jr.	3.00
9	John Olerud	.10
10	Edgar Renteria	.10
11	Jose Rosado	.10
12	Mickey Morandini	.10
13	Orlando Miller	.10
14	Ben McDonald	.10
15	Hideo Nomo	.40
16	Fred McGriff	.10
17	Sean Berry	.10
18	Roger Pavlik	.10
19	Aaron Sele	.10
20	Joey Hamilton	.10
21	Roger Clemens	1.25
22	Jose Herrera	.10
23	Ryne Sandberg	1.00
24	Ken Griffey Jr.	1.50
25	Barry Bonds	3.00
26	Dan Naulty	.10
27	Wade Boggs	1.00
28	Ray Lankford	.10
29	Rico Brogna	.10
30	Wally Joyner	.10
31	F.P. Santangelo	.10
32	Vinny Castilla	.10
33	Eddie Murray	.75
34	Kevin Elster	.10
35	Mike Macfarlane	.10
36	Jeff Kent	.10
37	Orlando Merced	.10
38	Jason Isringhausen	.10
39	Chad Ogea	.10
40	Greg Gagne	.10
41	Curt Lyons	.10
42	Mo Vaughn	.10
43	Rusty Greer	.10
44	Shane Reynolds	.10
45	Frank Thomas	.75
46	Chris Hoiles	.10
47	Scott Sanders	.10
48	Mark Lemke	.10
49	Fernando Vina	.10
50	Mark McGwire	2.00
51	Bernie Williams	.10
52	Bobby Higginson	.10
53	Kevin Tapani	.10
54	Rich Becker	.10
55	Felix Heredia RC	.30
56	Delino DeShields	.10
57	Rick Wilkins	.10
58	Edgardo Alfonzo	.10
59	Brett Butler	.10
60	Ed Sprague	.10
61	Joe Randa	.10
62	Ugueth Urbina	.10
63	Todd Greene	.10
64	Devon White	.10
65	Bruce Ruffin	.10
66	Mark Gardner	.10
67	Omar Vizquel	.10
68	Luis Gonzalez	.10
69	Tom Glavine	.25
70	Cal Eldred	.10
71	William Van Landingham	.10
72	Jay Buhner	.10
73	James Baldwin	.10

ABBREVIATIONS

OPS - Overprinted "Promotional Sample"

74	Robin Jennings	.10
75	Terry Steinbach	.10
76	Billy Taylor	.10
77	Armando Benitez	.10
78	Joe Girardi	.10
79	Jay Bell	.10
80	Damon Buford	.10
81	Deion Sanders	.15
82	Bill Haselman	.10
83	John Flaherty	.10
84	Todd Stottlemyre	.10
85	J.T. Snow	.10
86	Felipe Lira	.10
87	Steve Avery	.10
88	Trey Beamon	.10
89	Alex Gonzalez	.10
90	Mark Clark	.10
91	Shane Andrews	.10
92	Randy Myers	.10
93	Gary Gaetti	.10
94	Jeff Blauser	.10
95	Tony Batista	.10
96	Todd Worrell	.10
97	Jim Edmonds	.10
98	Eric Young	.10
99	Roberto Kelly	.10
100	Alex Rodriguez	2.00
100p	Alex Rodriguez/OPS	2.00
101	Julio Franco	.10
102	Jeff Bagwell	.75
103	Bobby Witt	.10
104	Tino Martinez	.10
105	Shannon Stewart	.10
106	Brian Banks	.10
107	Eddie Taubensee	.10
108	Terry Mulholland	.10
109	Lyle Mouton	.10
110	Jeff Conine	.10
111	Johnny Damon	.30
112	Quilvio Veras	.10
113	Wilton Guerrero	.10
114	Dmitri Young	.10
115	Garret Anderson	.10
116	Bill Pulsipher	.10
117	Jacob Brumfield	.10
118	Mike Lansing	.10
119	Jose Canseco	.50
120	Mike Bordick	.10
121	Kevin Stocker	.10
122	Frank Rodriguez	.10
123	Mike Cameron	.10
124	Tony Womack RC	.25
125	Bret Boone	.10
126	Moises Alou	.10
127	Tim Naehring	.10
128	Brant Brown	.10
129	Todd Zeile	.10
130	Dave Nilsson	.10
131	Donne Wall	.10
132	Jose Mesa	.10
133	Mark McLemore	.10
134	Mike Stanton	.10
135	Dan Wilson	.10
136	Jose Offerman	.10
137	David Justice	.10
138	Kirt Manwaring	.10
139	Raul Casanova	.10
140	Ron Coomer	.10
141	Dave Hollins	.10
142	Shawn Estes	.10
143	Darren Daulton	.10
144	Turk Wendell	.10
145	Darrin Fletcher	.10
146	Marquis Grissom	.10
147	Andy Benes	.10
148	Nomar Garciaparra	1.00
149	Andy Pettitte	.30
150	Tony Gwynn	1.00
151	Robb Nen	.10
152	Kevin Seitzer	.10
153	Ariel Prieto	.10
154	Scott Karl	.10
155	Carlos Baerga	.10
156	Wilson Alvarez	.10
157	Thomas Howard	.10
158	Kevin Appier	.10
159	Russ Davis	.10
160	Justin Thompson	.10
161	Pete Schourek	.10
162	John Burkett	.10
163	Roberto Alomar	.25
164	Darren Holmes	.10
165	Travis Miller	.10
166	Mark Langston	.10
167	Juan Guzman	.10
168	Pedro Astacio	.10
169	Mark Johnson	.10
170	Mark Leiter	.10
171	Heathcliff Slocumb	.10
172	Dante Bichette	.10
173	Brian Giles RC	1.00
174	Paul Wilson	.10
175	Eric Davis	.10
176	Charles Johnson	.10

177	Willie Greene	.10
178	Geronimo Berroa	.10
179	Mariano Duncan	.10
180	Robert Person	.10
181	David Segui	.10
182	Ozzie Guillen	.10
183	Osvaldo Fernandez	.10
184	Dean Palmer	.10
185	Bob Wickman	.10
186	Eric Karros	.10
187	Travis Fryman	.10
188	Andy Ashby	.10
189	Scott Stahoviak	.10
190	Norm Charlton	.10
191	Craig Paquette	.10
192	John Smoltz	.10
193	Orel Hershiser	.10
194	Glenallen Hill	.10
195	George Arias	.10
196	Brian Jordan	.10
197	Greg Vaughn	.10
198	Rafael Palmeiro	.60
199	Darryl Kile	.10
200	Derek Jeter	3.00
201	Jose Vizcaino	.10
202	Rick Aguilera	.10
203	Jason Schmidt	.10
204	Trot Nixon	.10
205	Tom Pagnozzi	.10
206	Mark Wohlers	.10
207	Lance Johnson	.10
208	Carlos Delgado	.40
209	Cliff Floyd	.10
210	Kent Mercker	.10
211	Matt Mieske	.10
212	Ismael Valdes	.10
213	Shawon Dunston	.10
214	Melvin Nieves	.10
215	Tony Phillips	.10
216	Scott Spiezio	.10
217	Michael Tucker	.10
218	Matt Williams	.10
219	Ricky Otero	.10
220	Kevin Ritz	.10
221	Darryl Strawberry	.10
222	Troy Percival	.10
223	Eugene Kingsale	.10
224	Julian Tavarez	.10
225	Jermaine Dye	.10
226	Jason Kendall	.10
227	Sterling Hitchcock	.10
228	Jeff Cirillo	.10
229	Roberto Hernandez	.10
230	Ricky Bottalico	.10
231	Bobby Bonilla	.10
232	Edgar Martinez	.10
233	John Valentin	.10
234	Ellis Burks	.10
235	Benito Santiago	.10
236	Terrell Wade	.10
237	Armando Reynoso	.10
238	Danny Graves	.10
239	Ken Hill	.10
240	Dennis Eckersley	.65
241	Darin Erstad	.25
242	Lee Smith	.10
243	Cecil Fielder	.10
244	Tony Clark	.10
245	Scott Erickson	.10
246	Bob Abreu	.10
247	Ruben Sierra	.10
248	Chili Davis	.10
249	Darryl Hamilton	.10
250	Albert Belle	.10
251	Todd Hollandsworth	.10
252	Terry Adams	.10
253	Rey Ordonez	.10
254	Steve Finley	.10
255	Jose Valentin	.10
256	Royce Clayton	.10
257	Sandy Alomar	.10
258	Mike Lieberthal	.10
259	Ivan Rodriguez	.65
260	Rod Beck	.10
261	Ron Karkovice	.10
262	Mark Gubicza	.10
263	Chris Holt	.10
264	Jaime Bluma	.10
265	Francisco Cordova	.10
266	Javy Lopez	.10
267	Reggie Jefferson	.10
268	Kevin Brown	.10
269	Scott Brosius	.10
270	Dwight Gooden	.10
271	Marty Cordova	.10
272	Jeff Brantley	.10
273	Joe Carter	.10
274	Todd Jones	.10
275	Sammy Sosa	1.00
276	Randy Johnson	.75
277	B.J. Surhoff	.10
278	Chan Ho Park	.10
279	Jamey Wright	.10
280	Manny Ramirez	.75

281	John Franco	.10
282	Tim Worrell	.10
283	Scott Rolen	.60
284	Reggie Sanders	.10
285	Mike Fetters	.10
286	Tim Wakefield	.10
287	Trevor Hoffman	.10
288	Donovan Osborne	.10
289	Phil Nevin	.10
290	Jermaine Allensworth	.10
291	Rocky Coppinger	.10
292	Tim Raines	.10
293	Henry Rodriguez	.10
294	Paul Sorrento	.10
295	Tom Goodwin	.10
296	Raul Mondesi	.10
297	Allen Watson	.10
298	Derek Bell	.10
299	Gary Sheffield	.45
300	Paul Molitor	.75
301	Shawn Green	.15
302	Darren Oliver	.10
303	Jack McDowell	.10
304	Denny Neagle	.10
305	Doug Drabek	.10
306	Mel Rojas	.10
307	Andres Galarraga	.10
308	Alex Ochoa	.10
309	Gary DiSarcina	.10
310	Ron Gant	.10
311	Gregg Jefferies	.10
312	Ruben Rivera	.10
313	Vladimir Guerrero	.75
314	Willie Adams	.10
315	Bip Roberts	.10
326	Mark Grace	.10
317	Bernard Gilkey	.10
318	Marc Newfield	.10
319	Al Leiter	.10
320	Otis Nixon	.10
321	Tom Candiotti	.10
322	Mike Stanley	.10
323	Jeff Fassero	.10
324	Billy Wagner	.10
325	Todd Walker	.10
326	Chad Curtis	.10
327	Quinton McCracken	.10
328	Will Clark	.10
329	Andruw Jones	.75
330	Robin Ventura	.10
331	Curtis Pride	.10
332	Barry Larkin	.10
333	Jimmy Key	.10
334	David Wells	.10
335	Mike Holtz	.10
336	Paul Wagner	.10
337	Greg Maddux	1.00
338	Curt Schilling	.35
339	Steve Trachsel	.10
340	John Wetteland	.10
341	Rickey Henderson	.75
342	Ernie Young	.10
343	Harold Baines	.10
344	Bobby Jones	.10
345	Jeff D'Amico	.10
346	John Mabry	.10
347	Pedro Martinez	.75
348	Mark Lewis	.10
349	Dan Miceli	.10
350	Chuck Knoblauch	.10
351	John Smiley	.10
352	Brady Anderson	.10
353	Jim Leyritz	.10
354	Al Martin	.10
355	Pat Hentgen	.10
356	Mike Piazza	1.50
357	Charles Nagy	.10
358	Luis Castillo	.10
359	Paul O'Neill	.10
360	Steve Reed	.10
361	Tom Gordon	.10
362	Craig Biggio	.40
363	Jeff Montgomery	.10
364	Jamie Moyer	.10
365	Ryan Klesko	.10
366	Todd Hundley	.10
367	Bobby Estalella	.10
368	Jason Giambi	.50
369	Brian Hunter	.10
370	Ramon Martinez	.10
371	Carlos Garcia	.10
372	Hal Morris	.10
373	Juan Gonzalez	.40
374	Brian McRae	.10
375	Mike Mussina	.40
376	John Ericks	.10
377	Larry Walker	.10
378	Chris Gomez	.10
379	John Jaha	.10
380	Rondell White	.10
381	Chipper Jones	1.00
382	David Cone	.10
383	Alan Benes	.10
384	Troy O'Leary	.10

385	Ken Caminiti	.10
386	Jeff King	.10
387	Mike Hampton	.10
388	Jaime Navarro	.10
389	Brad Radke	.10
390	Joey Cora	.10
391	Jim Thome	.60
392	Alex Fernandez	.10
393	Chuck Finley	.10
394	Andruw Jones Checklist	.35
395	Ken Griffey Jr. Checklist	.60
396	Frank Thomas Checklist	.35
397	Alex Rodriguez Checklist	.75
398	Cal Ripken Jr. Checklist	1.00
399	Mike Piazza Checklist	.60
400	Greg Maddux Checklist	.45

Rave

Common Player:	3.00
Stars/Rookies:	10-15X

(See 1997 Circa for checklist and base card values.)

Boss

	NM/M
Complete Set (20):	10.00
Common Player:	.15
Super Boss:	2X
1	Jeff Bagwell	.60
2	Albert Belle	.15
3	Barry Bonds	2.00
4	Ken Caminiti	.15
5	Juan Gonzalez	.30
6	Ken Griffey Jr.	1.00
7	Tony Gwynn	.75
8	Derek Jeter	2.00
9	Andruw Jones	.60
10	Chipper Jones	.75
11	Greg Maddux	.75
12	Mark McGwire	1.50
13	Mike Piazza	1.00
14	Manny Ramirez	.60
15	Cal Ripken Jr.	2.00
16	Alex Rodriguez	1.50
17	John Smoltz	.15
18	Frank Thomas	.60
19	Mo Vaughn	.15
20	Bernie Williams	.15

Emerald Autographs

	NM/M
Complete Set (6):	100.00
Common Player:	7.50
100	Alex Rodriguez	75.00

241	Darin Erstad	9.00
251	Todd Hollandsworth	6.00
283	Scott Rolen	12.00
308	Alex Ochoa	6.00
325	Todd Walker	6.00

Fast Track

		NM/M
Complete Set (10):		12.00
Common Player:		.50
1	Vladimir Guerrero	1.50
2	Todd Hollandsworth	.50
3	Derek Jeter	4.00
4	Andruw Jones	1.50
5	Chipper Jones	2.50
6	Andy Pettitte	1.00
7	Mariano Rivera	.75
8	Alex Rodriguez	3.00
9	Scott Rolen	1.25
10	Todd Walker	.50

Icons

		NM/M
Complete Set (12):		25.00
Common Player:		.50
1	Juan Gonzalez	.75
2	Ken Griffey Jr.	3.00
3	Tony Gwynn	2.00
4	Derek Jeter	5.00
5	Chipper Jones	2.00
6	Greg Maddux	2.00
7	Mark McGwire	4.00
8	Mike Piazza	3.00
9	Cal Ripken Jr.	5.00
10	Alex Rodriguez	4.00
11	Frank Thomas	1.50
12	Matt Williams	.50

Limited Access

		NM/M
Complete Set (300):		10.00
Common Player:		.10
Pack (8):		1.00
Wax Box (36):		20.00
1	Ben Grieve	.10
2	Derek Jeter	2.50
3	Alex Rodriguez	2.00
4	Paul Molitor	.75
5	Nomar Garciaparra	1.00
6	Fred McGriff	.10
7	Kenny Lofton	.10
8a	Cal Ripken Jr.	2.50
8b	Marquis Grissom (Should be #280.)	.10
8s	Cal Ripken Jr./OPS	2.50
9	Matt Williams	.10
10	Chipper Jones	1.00
11	Barry Larkin	.10
12	Steve Finley	.10
13	Billy Wagner	.10
14	Rico Brogna	.10
15	Tim Salmon	.10
16	Hideo Nomo	.40
17	Tony Clark	.10
18	Jason Kendall	.10
19	Juan Gonzalez	.40
20	Jeromy Burnitz	.10
21	Roger Clemens	1.25
22	Mark Grace	.10
23	Robin Ventura	.10
24	Manny Ramirez	.75
25	Mark McGwire	2.00
26	Gary Sheffield	.50
27	Vladimir Guerrero	.75
28	Butch Huskey	.10
29	Cecil Fielder	.10
30	Roderick Myers	.10
31	Greg Maddux	1.00
32	Bill Mueller	.10
33	Larry Walker	.10
34	Henry Rodriguez	.10
35	Mike Mussina	.35
36	Ricky Ledee	.10
37	Bobby Bonilla	.10
38	Curt Schilling	.35
39	Luis Gonzalez	.10
40	Troy Percival	.10
41	Eric Milton	.10
42	Mo Vaughn	.10
43	Raul Mondesi	.10
44	Kenny Rogers	.10
45	Frank Thomas	.75
46	Jose Canseco	.50
47	Tom Glavine	.35
48	Rich Butler RC	.10
49	Jay Buhner	.10
50	Jose Cruz Jr.	.10
51	Bernie Williams	.10
52	Doug Glanville	.10
53	Travis Fryman	.10
54	Rey Ordonez	.10
55	Jeff Conine	.10
56	Trevor Hoffman	.10
57	Kirk Rueter	.10
58	Ron Gant	.10
59	Carl Everett	.10
60	Joe Carter	.10
61	Livan Hernandez	.10
62	John Jaha	.10
63	Ivan Rodriguez	.65
64	Willie Blair	.10
65	Todd Helton	.65
66	Kevin Young	.10
67	Mike Caruso	.10
68	Steve Trachsel	.10
69	Marty Cordova	.10
70	Alex Fernandez	.10
71	Eric Karros	.10
72	Reggie Sanders	.10
73	Russ Davis	.10
74	Roberto Hernandez	.10
75	Barry Bonds	2.50
76	Alex Gonzalez	.10
77	Roberto Alomar	.25
78	Troy O'Leary	.10
79	Bernard Gilkey	.10
80	Ismael Valdes	.10
81	Travis Lee	.10
82	Brant Brown	.10
83	Gary DiSarcina	.10
84	Joe Randa	.10
85	Jaret Wright	.10
86	Quilvio Veras	.10
87	Rickey Henderson	.75
88	Randall Simon	.10
89	Mariano Rivera	.25
90	Ugueth Urbina	.10
91	Fernando Vina	.10
92	Alan Benes	.10
93	Dante Bichette	.10
94	Karim Garcia	.10
95	A.J. Hinch	.10
96	Shane Reynolds	.10

		NM/M
Complete Set (15):		30.00
Common Player:		1.25
1	Jeff Bagwell	2.00
2	Albert Belle	1.25
3	Barry Bonds	5.00
4	Juan Gonzalez	1.50
5	Ken Griffey Jr.	3.25
6	Tony Gwynn	2.50
7	Derek Jeter	5.00
8	Chipper Jones	2.50
9	Greg Maddux	2.50
10	Mark McGwire	4.00
11	Mike Piazza	3.50
12	Cal Ripken Jr.	5.00
13	Alex Rodriguez	4.00
14	Frank Thomas	2.00
15	Mo Vaughn	1.25

Rave Reviews

		NM/M
Complete Set (12):		75.00
Common Player:		3.00
1	Albert Belle	3.00
2	Barry Bonds	12.00
3	Juan Gonzalez	3.00
4	Ken Griffey Jr.	7.50
5	Tony Gwynn	6.00
6	Greg Maddux	6.00
7	Mark McGwire	9.00
8	Eddie Murray	4.00
9	Mike Piazza	7.50
10	Cal Ripken Jr.	12.00
11	Alex Rodriguez	9.00
12	Frank Thomas	4.50

1998 Circa Thunder

97	Kevin Stocker	.10
98	John Wetteland	.10
99	Terry Steinbach	.10
100	Ken Griffey Jr.	1.50
101	Mike Cameron	.10
102	Damion Easley	.10
103	Randy Myers	.10
104	Jason Schmidt	.10
105	Jeff King	.10
106	Gregg Jefferies	.10
107	Sean Casey	.15
108	Mark Kotsay	.10
109	Brad Fullmer	.10
110	Wilson Alvarez	.10
111	Sandy Alomar Jr.	.10
112	Walt Weiss	.10
113	Doug Jones	.10
114	Andy Benes	.10
115	Paul O'Neill	.10
116	Dennis Eckersley	.65
117	Todd Greene	.10
118	Bobby Jones	.10
119	Darrin Fletcher	.10
120	Eric Young	.10
121	Jeffrey Hammonds	.10
122	Mickey Morandini	.10
123	Chuck Knoblauch	.10
124	Moises Alou	.10
125	Miguel Tejada	.15
126	Brian Anderson	.10
127	Edgar Renteria	.10
128	Mike Lansing	.10
129	Quinton McCracken	.10
130	Ray Lankford	.10
131	Andy Ashby	.10
132	Kelvim Escobar	.10
133	Mike Lowell RC	.40
134	Randy Johnson	.75
135	Andres Galarraga	.10
136	Armando Benitez	.10
137	Rusty Greer	.10
138	Jose Guillen	.10
139	Paul Konerko	.15
140	Edgardo Alfonzo	.10
141	Jim Leyritz	.10
142	Mark Clark	.10
143	Brian Johnson	.10
144	Scott Rolen	.60
145	David Cone	.10
146	Jeff Shaw	.10
147	Shannon Stewart	.10
148	Brian Hunter	.10
149	Garret Anderson	.10
150	Jeff Bagwell	.75
151	James Baldwin	.10
152	Devon White	.10
153	Jim Thome	.60
154	Wally Joyner	.10
155	Mark Wohlers	.10
156	Jeff Cirillo	.10
157	Jason Giambi	.60
158	Royce Clayton	.10
159	Dennis Reyes	.10
160	Raul Casanova	.10
161	Pedro Astacio	.10
162	Todd Dunwoody	.10
163	Sammy Sosa	1.00
164	Todd Hundley	.10
165	Wade Boggs	1.00
166	Robb Nen	.10
167	Dan Wilson	.10
168	Hideki Irabu	.10
169	B.J. Surhoff	.10
170	Carlos Delgado	.40
171	Fernando Tatis	.10
172	Bob Abreu	.15
173	David Ortiz	.50
174	Tony Womack	.10
175	Magglio Ordonez RC	1.00
176	Aaron Boone	.10
177	Brian Giles	.10
178	Kevin Appier	.10
179	Chuck Finley	.10
180	Brian Rose	.10
181	Ryan Klesko	.10
182	Mike Stanley	.10
183	Dave Nilsson	.10
184	Carlos Perez	.10
185	Jeff Blauser	.10
186	Richard Hidalgo	.10
187	Charles Johnson	.10
188	Vinny Castilla	.10
189	Joey Hamilton	.10
190	Bubba Trammell	.10
191	Eli Marrero	.10
192	Scott Erickson	.10
193	Pat Hentgen	.10
194	Jorge Fabregas	.10
195	Tino Martinez	.10
196	Bobby Higginson	.10
197	Dave Hollins	.10
198	Rolando Arrojo RC	.25
199	Joey Cora	.10
200	Mike Piazza	1.50

201	Reggie Jefferson	.10
202	John Smoltz	.10
203	Bobby Smith	.10
204	Tom Goodwin	.10
205	Omar Vizquel	.10
206	John Olerud	.10
207	Matt Stairs	.10
208	Bobby Estalella	.10
209	Miguel Cairo	.10
210	Shawn Green	.20
211	Jon Nunnally	.10
212	Al Leiter	.10
213	Matt Lawton	.10
214	Brady Anderson	.10
215	Jeff Kent	.10
216	Ray Durham	.10
217	Al Martin	.10
218	Jeff D'Amico	.10
219	Kevin Tapani	.10
220	Jim Edmonds	.10
221	Jose Vizcaino	.10
222	Jay Bell	.10
223	Ken Caminiti	.10
224	Craig Biggio	.10
225	Bartolo Colon	.10
226	Neifi Perez	.10
227	Delino DeShields	.10
228	Javier Lopez	.10
229	David Wells	.10
230	Brad Rigby	.10
231	John Franco	.10
232	Michael Coleman	.10
233	Edgar Martinez	.10
234	Francisco Cordova	.10
235	Johnny Damon	.30
236	Deivi Cruz	.10
237	J.T. Snow	.10
238	Enrique Wilson	.10
239	Rondell White	.10
240	Aaron Sele	.10
241	Tony Saunders	.10
242	Ricky Bottalico	.10
243	Cliff Floyd	.10
244	Chili Davis	.10
245	Brian McRae	.10
246	Brad Radke	.10
247	Chan Ho Park	.10
248	Lance Johnson	.10
249	Rafael Palmeiro	.65
250	Tony Gwynn	1.00
251	Denny Neagle	.10
252	Dean Palmer	.10
253	Jose Valentin	.10
254	Matt Morris	.10
255	Ellis Burks	.10
256	Jeff Suppan	.10
257	Jimmy Key	.10
258	Justin Thompson	.10
259	Brett Tomko	.10
260	Mark Grudzielanek	.10
261	Mike Hampton	.10
262	Jeff Fassero	.10
263	Charles Nagy	.10
264	Pedro Martinez	.75
265	Todd Zeile	.10
266	Will Clark	.10
267	Abraham Nunez	.10
268	Dave Martinez	.10
269	Jason Dickson	.10
270	Eric Davis	.10
271	Kevin Orie	.10
272	Derrek Lee	.50
273	Andruw Jones	.75
274	Juan Encarnacion	.10
275	Carlos Baerga	.10
276	Andy Pettitte	.35
277	Brent Brede	.10
278	Paul Sorrento	.10
279	Mike Lieberthal	.10
280	(Not issued, see #8)	.10
281	Darin Erstad	.25
282	Willie Greene	.10
283	Derek Bell	.10
284	Scott Spiezio	.10
285	David Segui	.10
286	Albert Belle	.10
287	Ramon Martinez	.10
288	Jeremi Gonzalez	.10
289	Shawn Estes	.10
290	Ron Coomer	.10
291	John Valentin	.10
292	Kevin Brown	.10
293	Michael Tucker	.10
294	Brian Jordan	.10
295	Darryl Kile	.10
296	David Justice	.10
297	Jose Cruz Jr. Checklist	.10
298	Alex Rodriguez Checklist	1.00
299	Ken Griffey Jr. Checklist	.75
300	Frank Thomas Checklist	.65

Rave

Javier Lopez
Atlanta Braves™ - C

	NM/M
Common Player:	2.00
Stars:	15X

(See 1998 Circa Thunder for
checklist andbase card values.)

Super Rave

	NM/M
Common Player:	6.00
Stars:	40X

(See 1998 Circa Thunder for
checklist andbase card values.)

Boss

	NM/M
Complete Set (20):	10.00
Common Player:	.25
Inserted 1:6	
1B	Jeff Bagwell	.75
2B	Barry Bonds	2.00
3B	Roger Clemens	1.00
4B	Jose Cruz Jr.	.25
5B	Nomar Garciaparra	1.00
6B	Juan Gonzalez	.40
7B	Ken Griffey Jr.	1.25
8B	Tony Gwynn	1.00
9B	Derek Jeter	2.00
10B	Chipper Jones	1.00
11B	Travis Lee	.25
12B	Greg Maddux	1.00
13B	Pedro Martinez	.75
14B	Mark McGwire	1.50
15B	Mike Piazza	1.25
16B	Cal Ripken Jr.	2.00
17B	Alex Rodriguez	1.50
18B	Scott Rolen	.65
19B	Frank Thomas	.75
20B	Larry Walker	.25

Fast Track

	NM/M
Complete Set (10):	8.00
Common Player:	.25
Inserted 1:24	
1FT	Jose Cruz Jr.	.25
2FT	Juan Encarnacion	.25
3FT	Brad Fullmer	.25
4FT	Nomar Garciaparra	4.00
5FT	Todd Helton	2.50
6FT	Livan Hernandez	.25
7FT	Travis Lee	.25
8FT	Neifi Perez	.25
9FT	Scott Rolen	1.50
10FT	Jaret Wright	.25

Limited Access

	NM/M
Complete Set (15):	17.50
Common Player:	.50
Inserted 1:18	
1LA	Jeff Bagwell	1.25
2LA	Roger Clemens	1.75
3LA	Jose Cruz Jr.	.50
4LA	Nomar Garciaparra	1.50
5LA	Juan Gonzalez	1.00
6LA	Ken Griffey Jr.	2.00
7LA	Tony Gwynn	1.50
8LA	Derek Jeter	3.00
9LA	Greg Maddux	1.50
10LA	Pedro Martinez	1.25
11LA	Mark McGwire	2.50
12LA	Mike Piazza	2.00
13LA	Alex Rodriguez	2.50
14LA	Frank Thomas	1.25
15LA	Larry Walker	.50

Quick Strike

	NM/M
Complete Set (12):	20.00
Common Player:	.50
Inserted 1:36	
1QS	Jeff Bagwell	2.00
2QS	Roger Clemens	2.75
3QS	Jose Cruz Jr.	.50
4QS	Nomar Garciaparra	2.50
5QS	Ken Griffey Jr.	3.00
6QS	Greg Maddux	2.50
7QS	Pedro Martinez	2.00
8QS	Mark McGwire	4.00
9QS	Mike Piazza	3.00
10QS	Alex Rodriguez	4.00
11QS	Frank Thomas	2.00
12QS	Larry Walker	.50

Rave Reviews

	NM/M
Complete Set (15):	100.00
Common Player:	2.00
Inserted 1:288	
1RR	Jeff Bagwell	5.00

		NM/M
2RR	Barry Bonds	15.00
3RR	Roger Clemens	7.50
4RR	Jose Cruz Jr.	2.00
5RR	Nomar Garciaparra	6.00
6RR	Juan Gonzalez	3.50
7RR	Ken Griffey Jr.	10.00
8RR	Tony Gwynn	6.00
9RR	Derek Jeter	15.00
10RR	Greg Maddux	6.00
11RR	Mark McGwire	12.50
12RR	Mike Piazza	10.00
13RR	Alex Rodriguez	12.50
14RR	Frank Thomas	5.00
15RR	Larry Walker	2.00

Thunder Boomers

		NM/M
Complete Set (12):		50.00
Common Player:		1.50
Inserted 1:96		
1TB	Jeff Bagwell	6.00
2TB	Barry Bonds	10.00
3TB	Jay Buhner	1.50
4TB	Andres Galarraga	1.50
5TB	Juan Gonzalez	3.00
6TB	Ken Griffey Jr.	7.50
7TB	Tino Martinez	1.50
8TB	Mark McGwire	9.00
9TB	Mike Piazza	7.50
10TB	Frank Thomas	6.00
11TB	Jim Thome	4.50
12TB	Larry Walker	1.50

1994 Collector's Choice

		NM/M
Unopened Fact. Set (675):		25.00
Complete Set (670):		20.00
Common Player:		.05
Silver Signature:		2.5X
Gold Signature:		15X
Series 1 Pack (12):		.35
Series 1 Box (36):		8.00
Series 2 Pack (12):		.75
Series 2 Box (36):		17.50
1	Rich Becker RC	.05
2	Greg Blosser	.05
3	Midre Cummings	.05
4	Carlos Delgado	.30
5	Steve Dreyer RC	.05
6	Carl Everett RC	.50
7	Cliff Floyd	.05
8	Alex Gonzalez	.05
9	Shawn Green	.10
10	Butch Huskey	.05
11	Mark Hutton	.05
12	Miguel Jimenez	.05
13	Steve Karsay	.05
14	Marc Newfield	.05
15	Luis Ortiz	.05
16	Manny Ramirez	.60
17	Johnny Ruffin	.05
18	Scott Stahoviak RC	.05
19	Salomon Torres	.05
20	Gabe White RC	.10
21	Brian Anderson RC	.05
22	Wayne Gomes RC	.05
23	Jeff Granger	.05
24	Steve Soderstrom RC	.05
25	Trot Nixon RC	.50
26	Kirk Presley RC	.05
27	Matt Brunson RC	.05
28	Brooks Kieschnick RC	.05
29	Billy Wagner RC	.50
30	Matt Drews RC	.05
31	Kurt Abbott RC	.05
32	Luis Alicea	.05
33	Roberto Alomar	.20
34	Sandy Alomar Jr.	.05
35	Moises Alou	.05
36	Wilson Alvarez	.05
37	Rich Amaral	.05
38	Eric Anthony	.05
39	Luis Aquino	.05
40	Jack Armstrong	.05
41	Rene Arocha	.05
42	Rich Aude RC	.05
43	Brad Ausmus	.05
44	Steve Avery	.05
45	Bob Ayrault	.05
46	Willie Banks	.05
47	Bret Barberie	.05
48	Kim Batiste	.05
49	Rod Beck	.05
50	Jason Bere	.05
51	Sean Berry	.05
52	Dante Bichette	.05
53	Jeff Blauser	.05
54	Mike Blowers	.05
55	Tim Bogar	.05
56	Tom Bolton	.05
57	Ricky Bones	.05
58	Bobby Bonilla	.05
59	Bret Boone	.05
60	Pat Borders	.05
61	Mike Bordick	.05
62	Daryl Boston	.05
63	Ryan Bowen	.05
64	Jeff Branson	.05
65	George Brett	.85
66	Steve Buechele	.05
67	Dave Burba	.05
68	John Burkett	.05
69	Jeromy Burnitz	.05
70	Brett Butler	.05
71	Rob Butler	.05
72	Ken Caminiti	.05
73	Cris Carpenter	.05
74	Vinny Castilla	.05
75	Andujar Cedeno	.05
76	Wes Chamberlain	.05
77	Archi Cianfrocco	.05
78	Dave Clark	.05
79	Jerald Clark	.05
80	Royce Clayton	.05
81	David Cone	.05
82	Jeff Conine	.05
83	Steve Cooke	.05
84	Scott Cooper	.05
85	Joey Cora	.05
86	Tim Costa	.05
87	Chad Curtis	.05
88	Ron Darling	.05
89	Danny Darwin	.05
90	Rob Deer	.05
91	Jim Deshaies	.05
92	Delino DeShields	.05
93	Rob Dibble	.05
94	Gary DiSarcina	.05
95	Doug Drabek	.05
96	Scott Erickson	.05
97	Rikkert Faneyte RC	.05
98	Jeff Fassero	.05
99	Alex Fernandez	.05
100	Cecil Fielder	.05
101	Dave Fleming	.05
102	Darrin Fletcher	.05
103	Scott Fletcher	.05
104	Mike Gallego	.05
105	Carlos Garcia	.05
106	Jeff Gardner	.05
107	Brent Gates	.05
108	Benji Gil	.05
109	Bernard Gilkey	.05

#	Player	Price	#	Player	Price	#	Player	Price	#	Player	Price
110	Chris Gomez	.05	214	Bobby Munoz	.05	315	Kenny Lofton/TP	.05	379	Kevin Seitzer	.05
111	Luis Gonzalez	.05	215	Troy Neel	.05	316	Barry Bonds Checklist 1-64	.50	380	Wade Boggs	.75
112	Tom Gordon	.05	216	Dave Nilsson	.05	317	Ken Griffey Jr. Checklist 65-128	.35	381	Wally Whitehurst	.05
113	Jim Gott	.05	217	John O'Donoghue	.05	318	Mike Piazza Checklist 129-192	.35	382	Scott Leius	.05
114	Mark Grace	.05	218	Paul O'Neill	.05	319	Kirby Puckett Checklist 193-256	.25	383	Danny Tartabull	.05
115	Tommy Greene	.05	219	Jose Offerman	.05	320	Nolan Ryan Checklist 257-320	.50	384	Harold Reynolds	.05
116	Willie Greene	.05	220	Joe Oliver	.05	321	Roberto Alomar Checklist 321-370	.10	385	Tim Raines	.05
117	Ken Griffey Jr.	1.00	221	Greg Olson	.05	322	Roger Clemens Checklist 371-420	.30	386	Darryl Hamilton	.05
118	Bill Gullickson	.05	222	Donovan Osborne	.05	323	Juan Gonzalez Checklist 421-470	.10	387	Felix Fermin	.05
119	Ricky Gutierrez	.05	223	Jayhawk Owens	.05	324	Ken Griffey Jr. Checklist 471-520	.35	388	Jim Eisenreich	.05
120	Juan Guzman	.05	224	Mike Pagliarulo	.05	325	David Justice Checklist 521-570	.05	389	Kurt Abbott	.05
121	Chris Gwynn	.05	225	Craig Paquette	.05	326	John Kruk Checklist 571-620	.05	390	Kevin Appier	.05
122	Tony Gwynn	.75	226	Roger Pavlik	.05	327	Frank Thomas Checklist 621-670	.20	391	Chris Bosio	.05
123	Jeffrey Hammonds	.05	227	Brad Pennington	.05	328	Tim Salmon/ Angels Checklist	.05	392	Randy Tomlin	.05
124	Erik Hanson	.05	228	Eduardo Perez	.05	329	Jeff Bagwell/ Astros Checklist	.20	393	Bob Hamelin	.05
125	Gene Harris	.05	229	Mike Perez	.05	330	Mark McGwire/ Athletics Checklist	.45	394	Kevin Gross	.05
126	Greg Harris	.05	230	Tony Phillips	.05	331	Roberto Alomar/ Blue Jays Checklist	.10	395	Wil Cordero	.05
127	Bryan Harvey	.05	231	Hipolito Pichardo	.05	332	David Justice/ Braves Checklist	.05	396	Joe Girardi	.05
128	Billy Hatcher	.05	232	Phil Plantier	.05	333	Pat Listach/ Brewers Checklist	.05	397	Orestes Destrade	.05
129	Hilly Hathaway	.05	233	Curtis Pride RC	.05	334	Ozzie Smith/ Cardinals Checklist	.25	398	Chris Haney	.05
130	Charlie Hayes	.05	234	Tim Pugh	.05	335	Ryne Sandberg/ Cubs Checklist	.25	399	Xavier Hernandez	.05
131	Rickey Henderson	.60	235	Scott Radinsky	.05	336	Mike Piazza/ Dodgers Checklist	.35	400	Mike Piazza	1.00
132	Mike Henneman	.05	236	Pat Rapp	.05	337	Cliff Floyd/ Expos Checklist	.05	401	Alex Arias	.05
133	Pat Hentgen	.05	237	Kevin Reimer	.05	338	Barry Bonds/ Giants Checklist	.50	402	Tom Candiotti	.05
134	Roberto Hernandez	.05	238	Armando Reynoso	.05	339	Albert Belle/ Indians Checklist	.05	403	Kirk Gibson	.05
135	Orel Hershiser	.05	239	Jose Rijo	.05	340	Ken Griffey Jr./ Mariners Checklist	.35	404	Chuck Carr	.05
136	Phil Hiatt	.05	240	Cal Ripken, Jr.	2.00	341	Gary Sheffield/ Marlins Checklist	.10	405	Brady Anderson	.05
137	Glenallen Hill	.05	241	Kevin Roberson	.05	342	Dwight Gooden/ Mets Checklist	.05	406	Greg Gagne	.05
138	Ken Hill	.05	242	Kenny Rogers	.05	343	Cal Ripken, Jr./ Orioles Checklist	.50	407	Bruce Ruffin	.05
139	Eric Hillman	.05	243	Kevin Rogers	.05	344	Tony Gwynn/ Padres Checklist	.25	408	Scott Hemond	.05
140	Chris Hoiles	.05	244	Mel Rojas	.05	345	Lenny Dykstra/ Phillies Checklist	.05	409	Keith Miller	.05
141	Dave Hollins	.05	245	John Roper	.05	346	Andy Van Slyke/ Pirates Checklists	.05	410	John Wetteland	.05
142	David Hulse	.05	246	Kirk Rueter	.05	347	Juan Gonzalez/ Rangers Checklist	.10	411	Eric Anthony	.05
143	Todd Hundley	.05	247	Scott Ruffcorn	.05	348	Roger Clemens/ Red Sox Checklist	.30	412	Andre Dawson	.25
144	Pete Incaviglia	.05	248	Ken Ryan	.05	349	Barry Larkin/ Reds Checklist	.05	413	Doug Henry	.05
145	Danny Jackson	.05	249	Nolan Ryan	2.00	350	Andres Galarraga/ Rockies Checklist	.05	414	John Franco	.05
146	John Jaha	.05	250	Bret Saberhagen	.05	351	Kevin Appier/ Royals Checklist	.05	415	Julio Franco	.05
147	Domingo Jean	.05	251	Tim Salmon	.05	352	Cecil Fielder/ Tigers Checklist	.05	416	Dave Hansen	.05
148	Gregg Jefferies	.05	252	Reggie Sanders	.05	353	Kirby Puckett/ Twins Checklist	.25	417	Mike Harkey	.05
149	Reggie Jefferson	.05	253	Curt Schilling	.20	354	Frank Thomas/ White Sox Checklist	.20	418	Jack Armstrong	.05
150	Lance Johnson	.05	254	David Segui	.05	355	Don Mattingly/ Yankees Checklist	.30	419	Joe Orsulak	.05
151	Bobby Jones	.05	255	Aaron Sele	.05	356	Bo Jackson	.10	420	John Smoltz	.05
152	Chipper Jones	.75	256	Scott Servais	.05	357	Randy Johnson	.60	421	Scott Livingstone	.05
153	Todd Jones	.05	257	Gary Sheffield	.30	358	Darren Daulton	.05	422	Darren Holmes	.05
154	Brian Jordan	.05	258	Ruben Sierra	.05	359	Charlie Hough	.05	423	Ed Sprague	.05
155	Wally Joyner	.05	259	Don Slaught	.05	360	Andres Galarraga	.05	424	Jay Buhner	.05
156	Dave Justice	.05	260	Lee Smith	.05	361	Mike Felder	.05	425	Kirby Puckett	.75
157	Ron Karkovice	.05	261	Cory Snyder	.05	362	Chris Hammond	.05	426	Phil Clark	.05
158	Eric Karros	.05	262	Paul Sorrento	.05	363	Shawon Dunston	.05	427	Anthony Young	.05
159	Jeff Kent	.05	263	Sammy Sosa	.75	364	Junior Felix	.05	428	Reggie Jefferson	.05
160	Jimmy Key	.05	264	Bill Spiers	.05	365	Ray Lankford	.05	429	Mariano Duncan	.05
161	Mike Kiefer	.05	265	Mike Stanley	.05	366	Darryl Strawberry	.05	430	Tom Glavine	.20
162	Darryl Kile	.05	266	Dave Staton	.05	367	Dave Magadan	.05	431	Dave Henderson	.05
163	Jeff King	.05	267	Terry Steinbach	.05	368	Gregg Olson	.05	432	Melido Perez	.05
164	Wayne Kirby	.05	268	Kevin Stocker	.05	369	Len Dykstra	.05	433	Paul Wagner	.05
165	Ryan Klesko	.05	269	Todd Stottlemyre	.05	370	Darrin Jackson	.05	434	Tim Worrell	.05
166	Chuck Knoblauch	.05	270	Doug Strange	.05	371	Dave Stewart	.05	435	Ozzie Guillen	.05
167	Chad Kreuter	.05	271	Bill Swift	.05	372	Terry Pendleton	.05	436	Mike Butcher	.05
168	John Kruk	.05	272	Kevin Tapani	.05	373	Arthur Rhodes	.05	437	Jim Deshaies	.05
169	Mark Langston	.05	273	Tony Tarasco	.05	374	Benito Santiago	.05	438	Kevin Young	.05
170	Mike Lansing	.05	274	Julian Tavarez RC	.05	375	Travis Fryman	.05	439	Tom Browning	.05
171	Barry Larkin	.05	275	Mickey Tettleton	.05	376	Scott Brosius	.05	440	Mike Greenwell	.05
172	Manuel Lee	.05	276	Ryan Thompson	.05	377	Stan Belinda	.05	441	Mike Stanton	.05
173	Phil Leftwich RC	.05	277	Chris Turner	.05	378	Derek Parks	.05	442	John Doherty	.05
174	Darren Lewis	.05	278	John Valentin	.05				443	John Dopson	.05
175	Derek Lilliquist	.05	279	Todd Van Poppel	.05				444	Carlos Baerga	.05
176	Jose Lind	.05	280	Andy Van Slyke	.05				445	Jack McDowell	.05
177	Albie Lopez	.05	281	Mo Vaughn	.05				446	Kent Mercker	.05
178	Javier Lopez	.05	282	Robin Ventura	.05				447	Ricky Jordan	.05
179	Torey Lovullo	.05	283	Frank Viola	.05				448	Jerry Browne	.05
180	Scott Lydy	.05	284	Jose Vizcaino	.05				449	Fernando Vina	.05
181	Mike Macfarlane	.05	285	Omar Vizquel	.05				450	Jim Abbott	.05
182	Shane Mack	.05	286	Larry Walker	.05				451	Teddy Higuera	.05
183	Greg Maddux	.75	287	Duane Ware	.05				452	Tim Naehring	.05
184	Dave Magadan	.05	288	Allen Watson	.05				453	Jim Leyritz	.05
185	Joe Magrane	.05	289	Bill Wegman	.05				454	Frank Castillo	.05
186	Kirt Manwaring	.05	290	Turk Wendell	.05				455	Joe Carter	.05
187	Al Martin	.05	291	Lou Whitaker	.05				456	Craig Biggio	.05
188	Pedro A. Martinez RC	.05	292	Devon White	.05				457	Geronimo Pena	.05
189	Pedro Martinez	.60	293	Rondell White	.05				458	Alejandro Pena	.05
190	Ramon Martinez	.05	294	Mark Whiten	.05				459	Mike Moore	.05
191	Tino Martinez	.05	295	Darrell Whitmore	.05				460	Randy Myers	.05
192	Don Mattingly	.85	296	Bob Wickman	.05				461	Greg Myers	.05
193	Derrick May	.05	297	Rick Wilkins	.05				462	Greg Hibbard	.05
194	David McCarty	.05	298	Bernie Williams	.05				463	Jose Guzman	.05
195	Ben McDonald	.05	299	Matt Williams	.05				464	Tom Pagnozzi	.05
196	Roger McDowell	.05	300	Woody Williams	.05				465	Marquis Grissom	.05
197	Fred McGriff	.05	301	Nigel Wilson	.05				466	Tim Wallach	.05
198	Mark McLemore	.05	302	Dave Winfield	.60				467	Joe Grahe	.05
199	Greg McMichael	.05	303	Anthony Young	.05				468	Bob Tewksbury	.05
200	Jeff McNeely	.05	304	Eric Young	.05				469	B.J. Surhoff	.05
201	Brian McRae	.05	305	Todd Zeile	.05				470	Kevin Mitchell	.05
202	Pat Meares	.05	306	Jack McDowell, John Burkett, Tom Glavine/TP	.05				471	Bobby Witt	.05
203	Roberto Mejia	.05	307	Randy Johnson/TP	.25				472	Milt Thompson	.05
204	Orlando Merced	.05	308	Randy Myers/TP	.05				473	John Smiley	.05
205	Jose Mesa	.05	309	Jack McDowell/TP	.05				474	Alan Trammell	.05
206	Blas Minor	.05	310	Mike Piazza/TP	.40				475	Mike Mussina	.30
207	Angel Miranda	.05	311	Barry Bonds/TP	.60				476	Rick Aguilera	.05
208	Paul Molitor	.60	312	Andres Galarraga/TP	.05				477	Jose Valentin	.05
209	Raul Mondesi	.05	313	Juan Gonzalez, Barry Bonds/TP	.45				478	Harold Baines	.05
210	Jeff Montgomery	.05	314	Albert Belle/TP	.05				479	Bip Roberts	.05
211	Mickey Morandini	.05							480	Edgar Martinez	.05
212	Mike Morgan	.05							481	Rheal Cormier	.05
213	Jamie Moyer	.05							482	Hal Morris	.05

483	Pat Kelly	.05
484	Roberto Kelly	.05
485	Chris Sabo	.05
486	Kent Hrbek	.05
487	Scott Kamieniecki	.05
488	Walt Weiss	.05
489	Karl Rhodes	.05
490	Derek Bell	.05
491	Chili Davis	.05
492	Brian Harper	.05
493	Felix Jose	.05
494	Trevor Hoffman	.05
495	Dennis Eckersley	.50
496	Pedro Astacio	.05
497	Jay Bell	.05
498	Randy Velarde	.05
499	David Wells	.05
500	Frank Thomas	.60
501	Mark Lemke	.05
502	Mike Devereaux	.05
503	Chuck McElroy	.05
504	Luis Polonia	.05
505	Damion Easley	.05
506	Greg A. Harris	.05
507	Chris James	.05
508	Terry Mulholland	.05
509	Pete Smith	.05
510	Rickey Henderson	.60
511	Sid Fernandez	.05
512	Al Leiter	.05
513	Doug Jones	.05
514	Steve Farr	.05
515	Chuck Finley	.05
516	Bobby Thigpen	.05
517	Jim Edmonds	.05
518	Graeme Lloyd	.05
519	Dwight Gooden	.05
520	Pat Listach	.05
521	Kevin Bass	.05
522	Willie Banks	.05
523	Steve Finley	.05
524	Delino DeShields	.05
525	Mark McGwire	1.50
526	Greg Swindell	.05
527	Chris Nabholz	.05
528	Scott Sanders	.05
529	David Segui	.05
530	Howard Johnson	.05
531	Jaime Navarro	.05
532	Jose Vizcaino	.05
533	Mark Lewis	.05
534	Pete Harnisch	.05
535	Robby Thompson	.05
536	Marcus Moore	.05
537	Kevin Brown	.05
538	Mark Clark	.05
539	Sterling Hitchcock	.05
540	Will Clark	.05
541	Denis Boucher	.05
542	Jack Morris	.05
543	Pedro Munoz	.05
544	Bret Boone	.05
545	Ozzie Smith	.75
546	Dennis Martinez	.05
547	Dan Wilson	.05
548	Rick Sutcliffe	.05
549	Kevin McReynolds	.05
550	Roger Clemens	.85
551	Todd Benzinger	.05
552	Bill Haselman	.05
553	Bobby Munoz	.05
554	Ellis Burks	.05
555	Ryne Sandberg	.75
556	Lee Smith	.05
557	Danny Bautista	.05
558	Rey Sanchez	.05
559	Norm Charlton	.05
560	Jose Canseco	.35
561	Tim Belcher	.05
562	Denny Neagle	.05
563	Eric Davis	.05
564	Jody Reed	.05
565	Kenny Lofton	.05
566	Gary Gaetti	.05
567	Todd Worrell	.05
568	Mark Portugal	.05
569	Dick Schofield	.05
570	Andy Benes	.05
571	Zane Smith	.05
572	Bobby Ayala	.05
573	Chip Hale	.05
574	Bob Welch	.05
575	Deion Sanders	.10
576	Dave Nied	.05
577	Pat Mahomes	.05
578	Charles Nagy	.05
579	Otis Nixon	.05
580	Dean Palmer	.05

581	Roberto Petagine	.05
582	Dwight Smith	.05
583	Jeff Russell	.05
584	Mark Dewey	.05
585	Greg Vaughn	.05
586	Brian Hunter	.05
587	Willie McGee	.05
588	Pedro J. Martinez	.60
589	Roger Salkeld	.05
590	Jeff Bagwell	.60
591	Spike Owen	.05
592	Jeff Reardon	.05
593	Erik Pappas	.05
594	Brian Williams	.05
595	Eddie Murray	.60
596	Henry Rodriguez	.05
597	Erik Hanson	.05
598	Stan Javier	.05
599	Mitch Williams	.05
600	John Olerud	.05
601	Vince Coleman	.05
602	Damon Berryhill	.05
603	Tom Brunansky	.05
604	Robb Nen	.05
605	Rafael Palmeiro	.50
606	Cal Eldred	.05
607	Jeff Brantley	.05
608	Alan Mills	.05
609	Jeff Nelson	.05
610	Barry Bonds	2.00
611	Carlos Pulido RC	.05
612	Tim Hyers RC	.05
613	Steve Howe	.05
614	Brian Turang RC	.05
615	Leo Gomez	.05
616	Jesse Orosco	.05
617	Dan Pasqua	.05
618	Marvin Freeman	.05
619	Tony Fernandez	.05
620	Albert Belle	.05
621	Eddie Taubensee	.05
622	Mike Jackson	.05
623	Jose Bautista	.05
624	Jim Thome	.40
625	Ivan Rodriguez	.50
626	Ben Rivera	.05
627	Dave Valle	.05
628	Tom Henke	.05
629	Omar Vizquel	.05
630	Juan Gonzalez	.30
631	Roberto Alomar	.10
632	Barry Bonds	.60
633	Juan Gonzalez	.15
634	Ken Griffey Jr.	.50
635	Michael Jordan	1.50
636	Dave Justice	.05
637	Mike Piazza	.50
638	Kirby Puckett	.25
639	Tim Salmon	.05
640	Frank Thomas	.35
641	Alan Benes/FF RC	.05
642	Johnny Damon/FF	.35
643	Brad Fullmer/FF RC	.25
644	Derek Jeter/FF	2.00
645	Derrek Lee/FF RC	.75
646	Alex Ochoa/FF	.05
647	Alex Rodriguez/FF RC	6.00
648	Jose Silva/FF RC	.05
649	Terrell Wade/FF RC	.05
650	Preston Wilson/FF	.05
651	Shane Andrews	.05
652	James Baldwin	.05
653	Ricky Bottalico RC	.10
654	Tavo Alvarez	.05
655	Donnie Elliott	.05
656	Joey Eischen	.05
657	Jason Giambi	.50
658	Todd Hollandsworth/RC	.05
659	Brian Hunter/RC	.05
660	Charles Johnson/RC	.05
661	Michael Jordan/RC RC	3.00
662	Jeff Juden/RC	.05
663	Mike Kelly/RC	.05
664	James Mouton/RC	.05
665	Ray Holbert/RC	.05
666	Pokey Reese/RC	.05
667	Ruben Santana/RC RC	.05
668	Paul Spoljaric/RC	.05
669	Luis Lopez/RC	.05
670	Matt Walbeck/RC	.05

1994 Collector's Choice Gold Signature

NM/M

Common Player:	2.00
Stars:	15X

(See 1994 Collector's Choice for checklist and base card values.)

1994 Collector's Choice Silver Signature

NM/M

Common Player:	.15
Stars:	2.5X

(See 1994 Collector's Choice for checklist and base card values.)

647 Alex Rodriguez (White Letters. Some A-Rod Silver Signature parallels were mistakenly printed on base cards with his name and other details on front and back printed in white, rather than gray.) 100.00

Home Run All-Stars

NM/M

Complete Set (8):		4.00
Common Player:		.25
1HA	Juan Gonzalez	.50
2HA	Ken Griffey Jr.	1.50
3HA	Barry Bonds	2.50
4HAa	Bobby Bonilla	.25
4HAb	Cecil Fielder	.25
6HA	Albert Belle	.25
7HA	David Justice	.25
8HA	Mike Piazza	1.50

1995 Collector's Choice

NM/M

Unopened Fact. Set (545):	17.50
Complete Set (530):	12.50

Common Player:		.05
Silver Stars:		2X
Gold Stars:		6X
Pack (12):		1.00
Wax Box (36):		20.00
1	Charles Johnson	.05
2	Scott Ruffcorn	.05
3	Ray Durham	.05
4	Armando Benitez	.05
5	Alex Rodriguez	1.25
6	Julian Tavarez	.05
7	Chad Ogea	.05
8	Quilvio Veras	.05
9	Phil Nevin	.05
10	Michael Tucker	.05
11	Mark Thompson	.05
12	Rod Henderson	.05
13	Andrew Lorraine	.05
14	Joe Randa	.05
15	Derek Jeter	1.50
16	Tony Clark	.05
17	Juan Castillo	.05
18	Mark Acre	.05
19	Orlando Miller	.05
20	Paul Wilson	.05
21	John Mabry	.05
22	Garey Ingram	.05
23	Garret Anderson	.05
24	Dave Stevens	.05
25	Dustin Hermanson	.05
26	Paul Shuey	.05
27	J.R. Phillips	.05
28	Ruben Rivera/FF	.05
29	Nomar Garciaparra/FF	.75
30	John Wasdin/FF	.05
31	Jim Pittsley/FF	.05
32	Scott Elarton/FF RC	.15
33	Raul Casanova/FF RC	.05
34	Todd Greene/FF	.05
35	Bill Pulsipher/FF	.05
36	Trey Beamon/FF	.05
37	Curtis Goodwin/FF	.05
38	Doug Million/FF	.05
39	Karim Garcia/FF RC	1.00
40	Ben Grieve/FF	.05
41	Mark Farris/FF	.05
42	Juan Acevedo/FF RC	.05
43	C.J. Nitkowski/FF	.05
44	Travis Miller/FF RC	.10
45	Reid Ryan/FF	.10
46	Nolan Ryan	1.50
47	Robin Yount	.50
48	Ryne Sandberg	.75
49	George Brett	.85
50	Mike Schmidt	.85
51	Cecil Fielder	.05
52	Nolan Ryan	.75
53	Rickey Henderson	.20
54	George Brett, Robin Yount, Dave Winfield	.25
55	Sid Bream	.05
56	Carlos Baerga	.05
57	Lee Smith	.05
58	Mark Whiten	.05
59	Joe Carter	.05
60	Barry Bonds	.75
61	Tony Gwynn	.40
62	Ken Griffey Jr.	.50
63	Greg Maddux	.40
64	Frank Thomas	.35
65	Dennis Martinez, Kenny Rogers	.05
66	David Cone (Cy Young)	.05
67	Greg Maddux (Cy Young)	.75
68	Jimmy Key (Most Victories)	.05
69	Fred McGriff (All-Star MVP)	.05
70	Ken Griffey Jr. (HR Champ)	1.00
71	Matt Williams (HR Champ)	.05
72	Paul O'Neill (Batting Title)	.05
73	Tony Gwynn (Batting Title)	.40
74	Randy Johnson (K's Leader)	.60
75	Frank Thomas (MVP)	.60
76	Jeff Bagwell (MVP)	.60
77	Kirby Puckett (RBI Leader)	.75
78	Bob Hamelin (ROY)	.05
79	Raul Mondesi (ROY)	.05
80	Mike Piazza/AS	1.00
81	Kenny Lofton (SB Leader)	.05
82	Barry Bonds (Gold Glove)	1.50
83	Albert Belle/AS	.05
84	Juan Gonzalez (HR Champ)	.30

ABBREVIATIONS

TP - Top Performers

#	Player	Value
85	Cal Ripken Jr. (2,000 Straight Games)	1.50
86	Barry Bonds	.75
87	Mike Piazza	.60
88	Ken Griffey Jr.	.50
89	Frank Thomas	.35
90	Juan Gonzalez	.10
91	Jorge Fabregas	.05
92	J.T. Snow	.05
93	Spike Owen	.05
94	Eduardo Perez	.05
95	Bo Jackson	.10
96	Damion Easley	.05
97	Gary DiSarcina	.05
98	Jim Edmonds	.05
99	Chad Curtis	.05
100	Tim Salmon	.05
101	Chili Davis	.05
102	Chuck Finley	.05
103	Mark Langston	.05
104	Brian Anderson	.05
105	Lee Smith	.05
106	Phil Leftwich	.05
107	Chris Donnels	.05
108	John Hudek	.05
109	Craig Biggio	.05
110	Luis Gonzalez	.05
111	Brian L. Hunter	.05
112	James Mouton	.05
113	Scott Servais	.05
114	Tony Eusebio	.05
115	Derek Bell	.05
116	Doug Drabek	.05
117	Shane Reynolds	.05
118	Darryl Kile	.05
119	Greg Swindell	.05
120	Phil Plantier	.05
121	Todd Jones	.05
122	Steve Ontiveros	.05
123	Bobby Witt	.05
124	Brent Gates	.05
125	Rickey Henderson	.60
126	Scott Brosius	.05
127	Mike Bordick	.05
128	Fausto Cruz	.05
129	Stan Javier	.05
130	Mark McGwire	1.25
131	Geronimo Berroa	.05
132	Terry Steinbach	.05
133	Steve Karsay	.05
134	Dennis Eckersley	.50
135	Ruben Sierra	.05
136	Ron Darling	.05
137	Todd Van Poppel	.05
138	Alex Gonzalez	.05
139	John Olerud	.05
140	Roberto Alomar	.20
141	Darren Hall	.05
142	Ed Sprague	.05
143	Devon White	.05
144	Shawn Green	.20
145	Paul Molitor	.60
146	Pat Borders	.05
147	Carlos Delgado	.35
148	Juan Guzman	.05
149	Pat Hentgen	.05
150	Joe Carter	.05
151	Dave Stewart	.05
152	Todd Stottlemyre	.05
153	Dick Schofield	.05
154	Chipper Jones	.75
155	Ryan Klesko	.05
156	Dave Justice	.05
157	Mike Kelly	.05
158	Roberto Kelly	.05
159	Tony Tarasco	.05
160	Javier Lopez	.05
161	Steve Avery	.05
162	Greg McMichael	.05
163	Kent Mercker	.05
164	Mark Lemke	.05
165	Tom Glavine	.20
166	Jose Oliva	.05
167	John Smoltz	.05
168	Jeff Blauser	.05
169	Troy O'Leary	.05
170	Greg Vaughn	.05
171	Jody Reed	.05
172	Kevin Seitzer	.05
173	Jeff Cirillo	.05
174	B.J. Surhoff	.05
175	Cal Eldred	.05
176	Jose Valentin	.05
177	Turner Ward	.05
178	Darryl Hamilton	.05
179	Pat Listach	.05
180	Matt Mieske	.05
181	Brian Harper	.05
182	Dave Nilsson	.05
183	Mike Fetters	.05
184	John Jaha	.05
185	Ricky Bones	.05
186	Geronimo Pena	.05
187	Bob Tewksbury	.05
188	Todd Zeile	.05
189	Danny Jackson	.05
190	Ray Lankford	.05
191	Bernard Gilkey	.05
192	Brian Jordan	.05
193	Tom Pagnozzi	.05
194	Rick Sutcliffe	.05
195	Mark Whiten	.05
196	Tom Henke	.05
197	Rene Arocha	.05
198	Allen Watson	.05
199	Mike Perez	.05
200	Ozzie Smith	.75
201	Anthony Young	.05
202	Rey Sanchez	.05
203	Steve Buechele	.05
204	Shawon Dunston	.05
205	Mark Grace	.05
206	Glenallen Hill	.05
207	Eddie Zambrano	.05
208	Rick Wilkins	.05
209	Derrick May	.05
210	Sammy Sosa	.75
211	Kevin Roberson	.05
212	Steve Trachsel	.05
213	Willie Banks	.05
214	Kevin Foster	.05
215	Randy Myers	.05
216	Mike Morgan	.05
217	Rafael Bournigal	.05
218	Delino DeShields	.05
219	Tim Wallach	.05
220	Eric Karros	.05
221	Jose Offerman	.05
222	Tom Candiotti	.05
223	Ismael Valdes	.05
224	Henry Rodriguez	.05
225	Billy Ashley	.05
226	Darren Dreifort	.05
227	Ramon Martinez	.05
228	Pedro Astacio	.05
229	Orel Hershiser	.05
230	Brett Butler	.05
231	Todd Hollandsworth	.05
232	Chan Ho Park	.05
233	Mike Lansing	.05
234	Sean Berry	.05
235	Rondell White	.05
236	Ken Hill	.05
237	Marquis Grissom	.05
238	Larry Walker	.05
239	John Wetteland	.05
240	Cliff Floyd	.05
241	Joey Eischen	.05
242	Lou Frazier	.05
243	Darrin Fletcher	.05
244	Pedro J. Martinez	.60
245	Wil Cordero	.05
246	Jeff Fassero	.05
247	Butch Henry	.05
248	Mel Rojas	.05
249	Kirk Rueter	.05
250	Moises Alou	.05
251	Rod Beck	.05
252	John Patterson	.05
253	Robby Thompson	.05
254	Royce Clayton	.05
255	William Van Landingham	.05
256	Darren Lewis	.05
257	Kirt Manwaring	.05
258	Mark Portugal	.05
259	Bill Swift	.05
260	Rikkert Faneyte	.05
261	Mike Jackson	.05
262	Todd Benzinger	.05
263	Bud Black	.05
264	Salomon Torres	.05
265	Eddie Murray	.60
266	Mark Clark	.05
267	Paul Sorrento	.05
268	Jim Thome	.45
269	Omar Vizquel	.05
270	Carlos Baerga	.05
271	Jeff Russell	.05
272	Herbert Perry	.05
273	Sandy Alomar Jr.	.05
274	Dennis Martinez	.05
275	Manny Ramirez	.60
276	Wayne Kirby	.05
277	Charles Nagy	.05
278	Albie Lopez	.05
279	Jeromy Burnitz	.05
280	Dave Winfield	.60
281	Tim Davis	.05
282	Marc Newfield	.05
283	Tino Martinez	.05
284	Mike Blowers	.05
285	Goose Gossage	.05
286	Luis Sojo	.05
287	Edgar Martinez	.05
288	Rich Amaral	.05
289	Felix Fermin	.05
290	Jay Buhner	.05
291	Dan Wilson	.05
292	Bobby Ayala	.05
293	Dave Fleming	.05
294	Greg Pirkl	.05
295	Reggie Jefferson	.05
296	Greg Hibbard	.05
297	Yorkis Perez	.05
298	Kurt Miller	.05
299	Chuck Carr	.05
300	Gary Sheffield	.30
301	Jerry Browne	.05
302	Dave Magadan	.05
303	Kurt Abbott	.05
304	Pat Rapp	.05
305	Jeff Conine	.05
306	Benito Santiago	.05
307	Dave Weathers	.05
308	Robb Nen	.05
309	Chris Hammond	.05
310	Bryan Harvey	.05
311	Charlie Hough	.05
312	Greg Colbrunn	.05
313	David Segui	.05
314	Rico Brogna	.05
315	Jeff Kent	.05
316	Jose Vizcaino	.05
317	Jim Lindeman	.05
318	Carl Everett	.05
319	Ryan Thompson	.05
320	Bobby Bonilla	.05
321	Joe Orsulak	.05
322	Pete Harnisch	.05
323	Doug Linton	.05
324	Todd Hundley	.05
325	Bret Saberhagen	.05
326	Kelly Stinnett	.05
327	Jason Jacome	.05
328	Bobby Jones	.05
329	John Franco	.05
330	Rafael Palmeiro	.50
331	Chris Hoiles	.05
332	Leo Gomez	.05
333	Chris Sabo	.05
334	Brady Anderson	.05
335	Jeffrey Hammonds	.05
336	Dwight Smith	.05
337	Jack Voigt	.05
338	Harold Baines	.05
339	Ben McDonald	.05
340	Mike Mussina	.30
341	Bret Barberie	.05
342	Jamie Moyer	.05
343	Mike Oquist	.05
344	Sid Fernandez	.05
345	Eddie Williams	.05
346	Joey Hamilton	.05
347	Brian Williams	.05
348	Luis Lopez	.05
349	Steve Finley	.05
350	Andy Benes	.05
351	Andujar Cedeno	.05
352	Bip Roberts	.05
353	Ray McDavid	.05
354	Ken Caminiti	.05
355	Trevor Hoffman	.05
356	Mel Nieves	.05
357	Brad Ausmus	.05
358	Andy Ashby	.05
359	Scott Sanders	.05
360	Gregg Jefferies	.05
361	Mariano Duncan	.05
362	Dave Hollins	.05
363	Kevin Stocker	.05
364	Fernando Valenzuela	.05
365	Lenny Dykstra	.05
366	Jim Eisenreich	.05
367	Ricky Bottalico	.05
368	Doug Jones	.05
369	Ricky Jordan	.05
370	Darren Daulton	.05
371	Mike Lieberthal	.05
372	Bobby Munoz	.05
373	John Kruk	.05
374	Curt Schilling	.20
375	Orlando Merced	.05
376	Carlos Garcia	.05
377	Lance Parrish	.05
378	Steve Cooke	.05
379	Jeff King	.05
380	Jay Bell	.05
381	Al Martin	.05
382	Paul Wagner	.05
383	Rick White	.05
384	Midre Cummings	.05
385	Jon Lieber	.05
386	Dave Clark	.05
387	Don Slaught	.05
388	Denny Neagle	.05
389	Zane Smith	.05
390	Andy Van Slyke	.05
391	Ivan Rodriguez	.50
392	David Hulse	.05
393	John Burkett	.05
394	Kevin Brown	.05
395	Dean Palmer	.05
396	Otis Nixon	.05
397	Rick Helling	.05
398	Kenny Rogers	.05
399	Darren Oliver	.05
400	Will Clark	.05
401	Jeff Frye	.05
402	Kevin Gross	.05
403	John Dettmer	.05
404	Manny Lee	.05
405	Rusty Greer	.05
406	Aaron Sele	.05
407	Carlos Rodriguez	.05
408	Scott Cooper	.05
409	John Valentin	.05
410	Roger Clemens	.85
411	Mike Greenwell	.05
412	Tim Vanegmond	.05
413	Tom Brunansky	.05
414	Steve Farr	.05
415	Jose Canseco	.35
416	Joe Hesketh	.05
417	Ken Ryan	.05
418	Tim Naehring	.05
419	Frank Viola	.05
420	Andre Dawson	.25
421	Mo Vaughn	.05
422	Jeff Brantley	.05
423	Pete Schourek	.05
424	Hal Morris	.05
425	Deion Sanders	.10
426	Brian L. Hunter	.05
427	Bret Boone	.05
428	Willie Greene	.05
429	Ron Gant	.05
430	Barry Larkin	.05
431	Reggie Sanders	.05
432	Eddie Taubensee	.05
433	Jack Morris	.05
434	Jose Rijo	.05
435	Johnny Ruffin	.05
436	John Smiley	.05
437	John Roper	.05
438	David Nied	.05
439	Roberto Mejia	.05
440	Andres Galarraga	.05
441	Mike Kingery	.05
442	Curt Leskanic	.05
443	Walt Weiss	.05
444	Marvin Freeman	.05
445	Charlie Hayes	.05
446	Eric Young	.05
447	Ellis Burks	.05
448	Joe Girardi	.05
449	Lance Painter	.05
450	Dante Bichette	.05
451	Bruce Ruffin	.05
452	Jeff Granger	.05
453	Wally Joyner	.05
454	Jose Lind	.05
455	Jeff Montgomery	.05
456	Gary Gaetti	.05
457	Greg Gagne	.05
458	Vince Coleman	.05
459	Mike Macfarlane	.05
460	Brian McRae	.05
461	Tom Gordon	.05
462	Kevin Appier	.05
463	Billy Brewer	.05
464	Mark Gubicza	.05
465	Travis Fryman	.05
466	Danny Bautista	.05
467	Sean Bergman	.05
468	Mike Henneman	.05
469	Mike Moore	.05
470	Cecil Fielder	.05
471	Alan Trammell	.05
472	Kirk Gibson	.05
473	Tony Phillips	.05
474	Mickey Tettleton	.05
475	Lou Whitaker	.05
476	Chris Gomez	.05
477	John Doherty	.05
478	Greg Gohr	.05
479	Bill Gullickson	.05
480	Rick Aguilera	.05
481	Matt Walbeck	.05
482	Kevin Tapani	.05
483	Scott Erickson	.05
484	Steve Dunn	.05
485	David McCarty	.05
486	Scott Leius	.05
487	Pat Meares	.05
488	Jeff Reboulet	.05
489	Pedro Munoz	.05
490	Chuck Knoblauch	.05

ABBREVIATIONS

AS - All-Star
FF - Future Foundation

491	Rich Becker	.05
492	Alex Cole	.05
493	Pat Mahomes	.05
494	Ozzie Guillen	.05
495	Tim Raines	.05
496	Kirk McCaskill	.05
497	Olmedo Saenz	.05
498	Scott Sanderson	.05
499	Lance Johnson	.05
500	Michael Jordan	1.50
501	Warren Newson	.05
502	Ron Karkovice	.05
503	Wilson Alvarez	.05
504	Jason Bere	.05
505	Robin Ventura	.05
506	Alex Fernandez	.05
507	Roberto Hernandez	.05
508	Norberto Martin	.05
509	Bob Wickman	.05
510	Don Mattingly	.85
511	Melido Perez	.05
512	Pat Kelly	.05
513	Randy Velarde	.05
514	Tony Fernandez	.05
515	Jack McDowell	.05
516	Luis Polonia	.05
517	Bernie Williams	.05
518	Danny Tartabull	.05
519	Mike Stanley	.05
520	Wade Boggs	.75
521	Jim Leyritz	.05
522	Steve Howe	.05
523	Scott Kamieniecki	.05
524	Russ Davis	.05
525	Jim Abbott	.05
526	Eddie Murray Checklist 1-106	.20
527	Alex Rodriguez Checklist 107-212	.40
528	Jeff Bagwell Checklist 213-318	.20
529	Joe Carter Checklist 319-424	.05
530	Fred McGriff Checklist 425-530	.05
---	National Packtime Offer Card	.05

Gold Signature

NM/M
Common Player: .50
Stars: 6X
(See 1995 Collector's Choice for checklist and base card values.)

Silver Signature

NM/M
Common Player: .10
Stars: 2X
(See 1995 Collector's Choice for checklist and base card values.)

Michael Jordan Jumbo

NM/M
661 Michael Jordan 15.00

1995 Collector's Choice/SE

		NM/M
	Complete Set (265):	17.50
	Common Player:	.05
	Pack (12):	1.25
	Wax Box (36):	25.00
1	Alex Rodriguez	1.50
2	Derek Jeter	2.00
3	Dustin Hermanson	.05
4	Bill Pulsipher	.05
5	Terrell Wade	.05
6	Darren Dreifort	.05
7	LaTroy Hawkins	.05
8	Alex Ochoa	.05
9	Paul Wilson	.05
10	Ernie Young	.05
11	Alan Benes	.05
12	Garret Anderson	.05
13	Armando Benitez	.05
14	Robert Perez	.05
15	Herbert Perry	.05
16	Jose Silva	.05
17	Orlando Miller	.05
18	Russ Davis	.05
19	Jason Isringhausen	.05
20	Ray McDavid	.05
21	Duane Singleton	.05
22	Paul Shuey	.05
23	Steve Dunn	.05
24	Mike Lieberthal	.05
25	Chan Ho Park	.05
26	Ken Griffey Jr. (Record Pace)	.65
27	Tony Gwynn (Record Pace)	.40
28	Chuck Knoblauch (Record Pace)	.05
29	Frank Thomas (Record Pace)	.35
30	Matt Williams (Record Pace)	.05
31	Chili Davis	.05
32	Chad Curtis	.05
33	Brian Anderson	.05
34	Chuck Finley	.05
35	Tim Salmon	.05
36	Bo Jackson	.10
37	Doug Drabek	.05
38	Craig Biggio	.05
39	Ken Caminiti	.05
40	Jeff Bagwell	.65
41	Darryl Kile	.05
42	John Hudek	.05
43	Brian L. Hunter	.05

44	Dennis Eckersley	.60
45	Mark McGwire	1.50
46	Brent Gates	.05
47	Steve Karsay	.05
48	Rickey Henderson	.65
49	Terry Steinbach	.05
50	Ruben Sierra	.05
51	Roberto Alomar	.25
52	Carlos Delgado	.25
53	Alex Gonzalez	.05
54	Joe Carter	.05
55	Paul Molitor	.65
56	Juan Guzman	.05
57	John Olerud	.05
58	Shawn Green	.25
59	Tom Glavine	.25
60	Greg Maddux	.75
61	Roberto Kelly	.05
62	Ryan Klesko	.05
63	Javier Lopez	.05
64	Jose Oliva	.05
65	Fred McGriff	.05
66	Steve Avery	.05
67	Dave Justice	.05
68	Ricky Bones	.05
69	Cal Eldred	.05
70	Greg Vaughn	.05
71	Dave Nilsson	.05
72	Jose Valentin	.05
73	Matt Mieske	.05
74	Todd Zeile	.05
75	Ozzie Smith	.75
76	Bernard Gilkey	.05
77	Ray Lankford	.05
78	Bob Tewksbury	.05
79	Mark Whiten	.05
80	Gregg Jefferies	.05
81	Randy Myers	.05
82	Shawon Dunston	.05
83	Mark Grace	.05
84	Derrick May	.05
85	Sammy Sosa	.75
86	Steve Trachsel	.05
87	Brett Butler	.05
88	Delino DeShields	.05
89	Orel Hershiser	.05
90	Mike Piazza	1.00
91	Todd Hollandsworth	.05
92	Eric Karros	.05
93	Ramon Martinez	.05
94	Tim Wallach	.05
95	Raul Mondesi	.05
96	Larry Walker	.05
97	Wil Cordero	.05
98	Marquis Grissom	.05
99	Ken Hill	.05
100	Cliff Floyd	.05
101	Pedro J. Martinez	.65
102	John Wetteland	.05
103	Rondell White	.05
104	Moises Alou	.05
105	Barry Bonds	2.00
106	Darren Lewis	.05
107	Mark Portugal	.05
108	Matt Williams	.05
109	William Van Landingham	.05
110	Bill Swift	.05
111	Robby Thompson	.05
112	Rod Beck	.05
113	Darryl Strawberry	.05
114	Jim Thome	.50
115	Dave Winfield	.65
116	Eddie Murray	.65
117	Manny Ramirez	.75
118	Carlos Baerga	.05
119	Kenny Lofton	.05
120	Albert Belle	.05
121	Mark Clark	.05
122	Dennis Martinez	.05
123	Randy Johnson	.65
124	Jay Buhner	.05
125	Ken Griffey Jr.	1.00
125a	Ken Griffey Jr./OPS	1.50
126	Rich Gossage	.05
127	Tino Martinez	.05
128	Reggie Jefferson	.05
129	Edgar Martinez	.05
130	Gary Sheffield	.30
131	Pat Rapp	.05
132	Bret Barberie	.05
133	Chuck Carr	.05
134	Jeff Conine	.05
135	Charles Johnson	.05
136	Benito Santiago	.05
137	Matt Williams	.05
138	Jeff Bagwell	.35
139	Kenny Lofton	.05
140	Tony Gwynn	.40
141	Jimmy Key	.05
142	Greg Maddux	.40
143	Randy Johnson	.25
144	Lee Smith	.05
145	Bobby Bonilla	.05
146	Jason Jacome	.05
147	Jeff Kent	.05

148	Ryan Thompson	.05
149	Bobby Jones	.05
150	Bret Saberhagen	.05
151	John Franco	.05
152	Lee Smith	.05
153	Rafael Palmeiro	.60
154	Brady Anderson	.05
155	Cal Ripken Jr.	2.00
156	Jeffrey Hammonds	.05
157	Mike Mussina	.35
158	Chris Hoiles	.05
159	Ben McDonald	.05
160	Tony Gwynn	.75
161	Joey Hamilton	.05
162	Andy Benes	.05
163	Trevor Hoffman	.05
164	Phil Plantier	.05
165	Derek Bell	.05
166	Bip Roberts	.05
167	Eddie Williams	.05
168	Fernando Valenzuela	.05
169	Mariano Duncan	.05
170	Lenny Dykstra	.05
171	Darren Daulton	.05
172	Danny Jackson	.05
173	Bobby Munoz	.05
174	Doug Jones	.05
175	Jay Bell	.05
176	Zane Smith	.05
177	Jon Lieber	.05
178	Carlos Garcia	.05
179	Orlando Merced	.05
180	Andy Van Slyke	.05
181	Rick Helling	.05
182	Rusty Greer	.05
183	Kenny Rogers	.05
184	Will Clark	.05
185	Jose Canseco	.40
186	Juan Gonzalez	.35
187	Dean Palmer	.05
188	Ivan Rodriguez	.60
189	John Valentin	.05
190	Roger Clemens	.85
191	Aaron Sele	.05
192	Scott Cooper	.05
193	Mike Greenwell	.05
194	Mo Vaughn	.05
195	Andre Dawson	.25
196	Ron Gant	.05
197	Jose Rijo	.05
198	Bret Boone	.05
199	Deion Sanders	.10
200	Barry Larkin	.05
201	Hal Morris	.05
202	Reggie Sanders	.05
203	Kevin Mitchell	.05
204	Marvin Freeman	.05
205	Andres Galarraga	.05
206	Walt Weiss	.05
207	Charlie Hayes	.05
208	David Nied	.05
209	Dante Bichette	.05
210	David Cone	.05
211	Jeff Montgomery	.05
212	Felix Jose	.05
213	Mike Macfarlane	.05
214	Wally Joyner	.05
215	Bob Hamelin	.05
216	Brian McRae	.05
217	Kirk Gibson	.05
218	Lou Whitaker	.05
219	Chris Gomez	.05
220	Cecil Fielder	.05
221	Mickey Tettleton	.05
222	Travis Fryman	.05
223	Tony Phillips	.05
224	Rick Aguilera	.05
225	Scott Erickson	.05
226	Chuck Knoblauch	.05
227	Kent Hrbek	.05
228	Shane Mack	.05
229	Kevin Tapani	.05
230	Kirby Puckett	.75
231	Julio Franco	.05
232	Jack McDowell	.05
233	Jason Bere	.05
234	Alex Fernandez	.05
235	Frank Thomas	.65
236	Ozzie Guillen	.05
237	Robin Ventura	.05
238	Michael Jordan	2.00
239	Wilson Alvarez	.05
240	Don Mattingly	.85
241	Jim Abbott	.05
242	Jim Leyritz	.05
243	Paul O'Neill	.05
244	Melido Perez	.05
245	Wade Boggs	.75
246	Mike Stanley	.05
247	Danny Tartabull	.05
248	Jimmy Key	.05
249	Greg Maddux	.40
250	Randy Johnson	.20
251	Bret Saberhagen	.05
252	John Wetteland	.05
253	Mike Piazza	.50

254	Jeff Bagwell	.35
255	Craig Biggio	.05
256	Matt Williams	.05
257	Wil Cordero	.05
258	Kenny Lofton	.05
259	Barry Bonds	.75
260	Dante Bichette	.05
261	Ken Griffey Jr. Checklist 1-53	.35
262	Goose Gossage Checklist 54-106	.05
263	Cal Ripken Jr. Checklist 107-159	.45
264	Kenny Rogers Checklist 160-212	.05
265	John Valentin Checklist 213-265	.05

Gold

NM/M

Common Player: 1.00
Stars: 8X
(For checklist and base card values, see 1995 Collector's Choice SE.)

Silver

NM/M

Common Player: .15
Stars: 1.5X
(For checklist and base card values, see 1995 Collector's Choice SE.)

1995 Collector's Choice Ichiro Suzuki

NM/M

59	Ichiro Suzuki	1,000

1996 Collector's Choice

NM/M

Unopened Fact. Set (790):		17.50
Complete Set: (760):		12.50
Traded Set: (366T-395T):		3.00
Common Player:		.05
Series 1 Pack (12):		.75
Series 1 Wax Box (36):		22.50
Series 2 Pack (14):		1.00
Series 2 Wax Box (40):		25.00
1	Cal Ripken Jr.	2.00
2	Edgar Martinez, Tony Gwynn	.05
3	Albert Belle, Dante Bichette	.05
4	Albert Belle, Mo Vaughn, Dante Bichette	.05
5	Kenny Lofton, Quilvio Veras	.05
6	Mike Mussina, Greg Maddux	.40
7	Randy Johnson, Hideo Nomo	.25
8	Randy Johnson, Greg Maddux	.40
9	Jose Mesa, Randy Myers	.05
10	Johnny Damon	.35
11	Rick Krivda	.05
12	Roger Cedeno	.05
13	Angel Martinez	.05
14	Ariel Prieto	.05
15	John Wasdin	.05
16	Edwin Hurtado	.05
17	Lyle Mouton	.05
18	Chris Snopek	.05
19	Mariano Rivera	.15
20	Ruben Rivera	.05
21	Juan Castro RC	.05
22	Jimmy Haynes	.05
23	Bob Wolcott	.05
24	Brian Barber	.05
25	Frank Rodriguez	.05
26	Jesus Tavarez	.05
27	Glenn Dishman	.05
28	Jose Herrera	.05
29	Chan Ho Park	.05
30	Jason Isringhausen	.05
31	Doug Johns	.05
32	Gene Schall	.05
33	Kevin Jordan	.05
34	Matt Lawton RC	.10
35	Karim Garcia	.05
36	George Williams	.05
37	Orlando Palmeiro	.05
38	Jamie Brewington	.05
39	Robert Person	.05
40	Greg Maddux	.75
41	Marquis Grissom	.05
42	Chipper Jones	.75
43	David Justice	.05
44	Mark Lemke	.05
45	Fred McGriff	.05
46	Javy Lopez	.05
47	Mark Wohlers	.05
48	Jason Schmidt	.05
49	John Smoltz	.05
50	Curtis Goodwin	.05
51	Gregg Zaun	.05
52	Armando Benitez	.05
53	Manny Alexander	.05
54	Chris Hoiles	.05
55	Harold Baines	.05
56	Ben McDonald	.05
57	Scott Erickson	.05
58	Jeff Manto	.05
59	Luis Alicea	.05
60	Roger Clemens	.85
61	Rheal Cormier	.05
62	Vaughn Eshelman	.05
63	Zane Smith	.05
64	Mike Macfarlane	.05
65	Erik Hanson	.05
66	Tim Naehring	.05
67	Lee Tinsley	.05
68	Troy O'Leary	.05
69	Garret Anderson	.05
70	Chili Davis	.05
71	Jim Edmonds	.05
72	Troy Percival	.05
73	Mark Langston	.05
74	Spike Owen	.05
75	Tim Salmon	.05
76	Brian Anderson	.05
77	Lee Smith	.05
78	Jim Abbott	.05
79	Jim Bullinger	.05
80	Mark Grace	.05
81	Todd Zeile	.05
82	Kevin Foster	.05
83	Howard Johnson	.05
84	Brian McRae	.05
85	Randy Myers	.05
86	Jaime Navarro	.05
87	Luis Gonzalez	.05
88	Ozzie Timmons	.05
89	Wilson Alvarez	.05
90	Frank Thomas	.60
91	James Baldwin	.05
92	Ray Durham	.05
93	Alex Fernandez	.05
94	Ozzie Guillen	.05
95	Tim Raines	.05
96	Roberto Hernandez	.05
97	Lance Johnson	.05
98	John Kruk	.05
99	Mark Portugal	.05
100	Don Mattingly	.65
101	Jose Canseco	.15
102	Raul Mondesi	.05
103	Cecil Fielder	.05
104	Ozzie Smith	.40
105	Frank Thomas	.45
106	Sammy Sosa	.50
107	Fred McGriff	.05
108	Barry Bonds	1.00
109	Thomas Howard	.05
110	Ron Gant	.05
111	Eddie Taubensee	.05
112	Hal Morris	.05
113	Jose Rijo	.05
114	Pete Schourek	.05
115	Reggie Sanders	.05
116	Benito Santiago	.05
117	Jeff Brantley	.05
118	Julian Tavarez	.05
119	Carlos Baerga	.05
120	Jim Thome	.40
121	Jose Mesa	.05
122	Dennis Martinez	.05
123	Dave Winfield	.60
124	Eddie Murray	.60
125	Manny Ramirez	.60
126	Paul Sorrento	.05
127	Kenny Lofton	.05
128	Eric Young	.05
129	Jason Bates	.05
130	Bret Saberhagen	.05
131	Andres Galarraga	.05
132	Joe Girardi	.05
133	John Vander Wal	.05
134	David Nied	.05
135	Dante Bichette	.05
136	Vinny Castilla	.05
137	Kevin Ritz	.05
138	Felipe Lira	.05
139	Joe Boever	.05
140	Cecil Fielder	.05
141	John Flaherty	.05
142	Kirk Gibson	.05
143	Brian Maxcy	.05
144	Lou Whitaker	.05
145	Alan Trammell	.05
146	Bobby Higginson	.05
147	Chad Curtis	.05
148	Quilvio Veras	.05
149	Jerry Browne	.05
150	Andre Dawson	.25
151	Robb Nen	.05
152	Greg Colbrunn	.05
153	Chris Hammond	.05
154	Kurt Abbott	.05
155	Charles Johnson	.05
156	Terry Pendleton	.05
157	Dave Weathers	.05
158	Mike Hampton	.05
159	Craig Biggio	.05
160	Jeff Bagwell	.60
161	Brian L. Hunter	.05
162	Mike Henneman	.05
163	Dave Magadan	.05
164	Shane Reynolds	.05
165	Derek Bell	.05
166	Orlando Miller	.05
167	James Mouton	.05
168	Melvin Bunch	.05
169	Tom Gordon	.05
170	Kevin Appier	.05
171	Tom Goodwin	.05
172	Greg Gagne	.05
173	Gary Gaetti	.05
174	Jeff Montgomery	.05
175	Jon Nunnally	.05
176	Michael Tucker	.05
177	Joe Vitiello	.05
178	Billy Ashley	.05
179	Tom Candiotti	.05
180	Hideo Nomo	.30
181	Chad Fonville	.05
182	Todd Hollandsworth	.05
183	Eric Karros	.05
184	Roberto Kelly	.05
185	Mike Piazza	1.00
186	Ramon Martinez	.05
187	Tim Wallach	.05
188	Jeff Cirillo	.05
189	Sid Roberson	.05
190	Kevin Seitzer	.05
191	Mike Fetters	.05
192	Steve Sparks	.05
193	Matt Mieske	.05
194	Joe Oliver	.05
195	B.J. Surhoff	.05
196	Alberto Reyes	.05
197	Fernando Vina	.05
198	LaTroy Hawkins	.05
199	Marty Cordova	.05
200	Kirby Puckett	.75
201	Brad Radke	.05
202	Pedro Munoz	.05
203	Scott Klingenbeck	.05
204	Pat Meares	.05
205	Chuck Knoblauch	.05
206	Scott Stahoviak	.05
207	Dave Stevens	.05
208	Shane Andrews	.05
209	Moises Alou	.05
210	David Segui	.05
211	Cliff Floyd	.05
212	Carlos Perez	.05
213	Mark Grudzielanek	.05
214	Butch Henry	.05
215	Rondell White	.05
216	Mel Rojas	.05
217	Ugueth Urbina	.05
218	Edgardo Alfonzo	.05
219	Carl Everett	.05
220	John Franco	.05
221	Todd Hundley	.05
222	Bobby Jones	.05
223	Bill Pulsipher	.05
224	Rico Brogna	.05
225	Jeff Kent	.05
226	Chris Jones	.05
227	Butch Huskey	.05
228	Robert Eenhoorn	.05
229	Sterling Hitchcock	.05
230	Wade Boggs	.75
231	Derek Jeter	2.00
232	Tony Fernandez	.05
233	Jack McDowell	.05
234	Andy Pettitte	.35
235	David Cone	.05
236	Mike Stanley	.05
237	Don Mattingly	.85
238	Geronimo Berroa	.05
239	Scott Brosius	.05
240	Rickey Henderson	.60
241	Terry Steinbach	.05
242	Mike Gallego	.05
243	Jason Giambi	.40
244	Steve Ontiveros	.05
245	Dennis Eckersley	.50
246	Dave Stewart	.05
247	Don Wengert	.05
248	Paul Quantrill	.05
249	Ricky Bottalico	.05
250	Kevin Stocker	.05
251	Lenny Dykstra	.05
252	Tony Longmire	.05
253	Tyler Green	.05
254	Mike Mimbs	.05
255	Charlie Hayes	.05
256	Mickey Morandini	.05
257	Heathcliff Slocumb	.05
258	Jeff King	.05
259	Midre Cummings	.05
260	Mark Johnson	.05
261	Freddy Garcia	.05
262	Jon Lieber	.05
263	Esteban Loaiza	.05
264	Danny Miceli	.05
265	Orlando Merced	.05
266	Denny Neagle	.05
267	Steve Parris	.05
268	Greg Maddux Fantasy Team '95	.35
269	Randy Johnson Fantasy Team '95	.20

No.	Player	Price
270	Hideo Nomo Fantasy Team '95	.15
271	Jose Mesa Fantasy Team '95	.05
272	Mike Piazza Fantasy Team '95	.60
273	Mo Vaughn Fantasy Team '95	.05
274	Craig Biggio Fantasy Team '95	.05
275	Edgar Martinez Fantasy Team '95	.05
276	Barry Larkin Fantasy Team '95	.05
277	Sammy Sosa Fantasy Team '95	.50
278	Dante Bichette Fantasy Team '95	.05
279	Albert Belle Fantasy Team '95	.05
280	Ozzie Smith	.75
281	Mark Sweeney	.05
282	Terry Bradshaw	.05
283	Allen Battle	.05
284	Danny Jackson	.05
285	Tom Henke	.05
286	Scott Cooper	.05
287	Tripp Cromer	.05
288	Bernard Gilkey	.05
289	Brian Jordan	.05
290	Tony Gwynn	.75
291	Brad Ausmus	.05
292	Bryce Florie	.05
293	Andres Berumen	.05
294	Ken Caminiti	.05
295	Bip Roberts	.05
296	Trevor Hoffman	.05
297	Roberto Petagine	.05
298	Jody Reed	.05
299	Fernando Valenzuela	.05
300	Barry Bonds	2.00
301	Mark Leiter	.05
302	Mark Carreon	.05
303	Royce Clayton	.05
304	Kirt Manwaring	.05
305	Glenallen Hill	.05
306	Deion Sanders	.10
307	Joe Rosselli	.05
308	Robby Thompson	.05
309	William Van Landingham	.05
310	Ken Griffey Jr.	1.00
311	Bobby Ayala	.05
312	Joey Cora	.05
313	Mike Blowers	.05
314	Darren Bragg	.05
315	Randy Johnson	.60
316	Alex Rodriguez	1.50
317	Andy Benes	.05
318	Tino Martinez	.05
319	Dan Wilson	.05
320	Will Clark	.05
321	Jeff Frye	.05
322	Benji Gil	.05
323	Rick Helling	.05
324	Mark McLemore	.05
325	Dave Nilsson	.05
326	Larry Walker	.05
327	Jose Canseco	.15
328	Raul Mondesi	.05
329	Manny Ramirez	.30
330	Robert Eenhoorn	.05
331	Chili Davis	.05
332	Hideo Nomo	.15
333	Benji Gil	.05
334	Fernando Valenzuela	.05
335	Dennis Martinez	.05
336	Roberto Kelly	.05
337	Carlos Baerga	.05
338	Juan Gonzalez	.15
339	Roberto Alomar	.10
340	Chan Ho Park	.05
341	Andres Galarraga	.05
342	Midre Cummings	.05
343	Otis Nixon	.05
344	Jeff Russell	.05
345	Ivan Rodriguez	.50
346	Mickey Tettleton	.05
347	Bob Tewksbury	.05
348	Domingo Cedeno	.05
349	Lance Parrish	.05
350	Joe Carter	.05
351	Devon White	.05
352	Carlos Delgado	.35
353	Alex Gonzalez	.05
354	Darren Hall	.05
355	Paul Molitor	.60
356	Al Leiter	.05
357	Randy Knorr	.05
358	Checklist 1-46 (12-player Astros-Padres trade.)	.05
359	Hideo Nomo Checklist 47-92	.15
360	Ramon Martinez Checklist 93-138	.05
361	Robin Ventura Checklist 139-184	.05
362	Cal Ripken Jr. Checklist 185-230	.30
363	Ken Caminiti Checklist 231-275	.05
364	Eddie Murray Checklist 276-320	.20
365	Randy Johnson Checklist 321-365	.15
366	Tony Pena A.L. Divisional Series	.10
367	Jim Thome A.L. Divisional Series	.25
368	Don Mattingly A.L. Divisional Series	.60
369	Jim Leyritz A.L. Divisional Series	.10
370	Ken Griffey Jr. A.L. Divisional Series	.60
371	Edgar Martinez A.L. Divisional Series	.10
372	Pete Schourek N.L. Divisional Series	.10
373	Mark Lewis N.L. Divisional Series	.10
374	Chipper Jones N.L. Divisonal Series	.50
375	Fred McGriff N.L. Divisonal Series	.10
376	Javy Lopez N.L. Championship Series	.10
377	Fred McGriff N.L. Championship Series	.10
378	Charlie O'Brien N.L. Championship Series	.10
379	Mike Devereaux N.L. Championship Series	.10
380	Mark Wohlers N.L. Championship Series	.10
381	Bob Wolcott A.L. Championship Series	.10
382	Manny Ramirez A.L. Championship Series	.25
383	Jay Buhner A.L. Championship Series	.10
384	Orel Hershiser A.L. Championship Series	.10
385	Kenny Lofton A.L. Championship Series	.10
386	Greg Maddux World Series	.50
387	Javy Lopez World Series	.10
388	Kenny Lofton World Series	.10
389	Eddie Murray World Series	.10
390	Luis Polonia World Series	.10
391	Pedro Borbon World Series	.10
392	Jim Thome World Series	.25
393	Orel Hershiser World Series	.10
394	David Justice World Series	.10
395	Tom Glavine World Series	.10
396	Greg Maddux/Braves Team Checklist	.25
397	Brett Butler/Mets Team Checklist	.05
398	Darren Daulton/Phillies Team Checklist	.05
399	Gary Sheffield/Marlins Team Checklist	.05
400	Moises Alou/Expos Team Checklist	.05
401	Barry Larkin/Reds Team Checklist	.05
402	Jeff Bagwell/Astros Team Checklist	.20
403	Sammy Sosa/Cubs Team Checklist	.35
404	Ozzie Smith/Cardinals Team Checklist	.25
405	Jeff King Pirates Team Checklist	.05
406	Mike Piazza/Dodgers Team Checklist	.50
407	Dante Bichette/Rockies Team Checklist	.05
408	Tony Gwynn/Padres Team Checklist	.25
409	Barry Bonds/Giants Team Checklist	.45
410	Kenny Lofton/Indians Team Checklist	.05
411	Jon Nunnally/Royals Team Checklist	.05
412	Frank Thomas/White Sox Team Checklist	.20
413	Greg Vaughn/Brewers Team Checklist	.05
414	Paul Molitor/Twins Team Checklist	.20
415	Ken Griffey Jr./Mariners Team Checklist	.35
416	Jim Edmonds/Angels Team Checklist	.05
417	Juan Gonzalez/Rangers Team Checklist	.15
418	Mark McGwire/Athletics Team Checklist	.75
419	Roger Clemens/Red Sox Team Checklist	.30
420	Wade Boggs/Yankees Team Checklist	.35
421	Cal Ripken Jr./Orioles Team Checklist	.40
422	Cecil Fielder/Tigers Team Checklist	.05
423	Joe Carter/Blue Jays Team Checklist	.05
424	Osvaldo Fernandez RC	.15
425	Billy Wagner	.05
426	George Arias	.05
427	Mendy Lopez	.05
428	Jeff Suppan	.05
429	Rey Ordonez	.05
430	Brooks Kieschnick	.05
431	Raul Ibanez RC	.05
432	Livan Hernandez RC	.20
433	Shannon Stewart	.05
434	Steve Cox	.05
435	Trey Beamon	.05
436	Sergio Nunez	.05
437	Jermaine Dye	.05
438	Mike Sweeney RC	.45
439	Richard Hidalgo	.05
440	Todd Greene	.05
441	Robert Smith RC	.05
442	Rafael Orellano	.05
443	Wilton Guerrero RC	.05
444	David Doster RC	.05
445	Jason Kendall	.05
446	Edgar Renteria	.05
447	Scott Spiezio	.05
448	Jay Canizaro	.05
449	Enrique Wilson	.05
450	Bob Abreu	.10
451	Dwight Smith	.05
452	Jeff Blauser	.05
453	Steve Avery	.05
454	Brad Clontz	.05
455	Tom Glavine	.20
456	Mike Mordecai	.05
457	Rafael Belliard	.05
458	Greg McMichael	.05
459	Pedro Borbon	.05
460	Ryan Klesko	.05
461	Terrell Wade	.05
462	Brady Anderson	.05
463	Roberto Alomar	.20
464	Bobby Bonilla	.05
465	Mike Mussina	.40
466	Cesar Devarez RC	.05
467	Jeffrey Hammonds	.05
468	Mike Devereaux	.05
469	B.J. Surhoff	.05
470	Rafael Palmeiro	.50
471	John Valentin	.05
472	Mike Greenwell	.05
473	Dwayne Hosey	.05
474	Tim Wakefield	.05
475	Jose Canseco	.35
476	Aaron Sele	.05
477	Stan Belinda	.05
478	Mike Stanley	.05
479	Jamie Moyer	.05
480	Mo Vaughn	.05
481	Randy Velarde	.05
482	Gary DiSarcina	.05
483	Jorge Fabregas	.05
484	Rex Hudler	.05
485	Chuck Finley	.05
486	Tim Wallach	.05
487	Eduardo Perez	.05
488	Scott Sanderson	.05
489	J.T. Snow	.05
490	Sammy Sosa	.75
491	Terry Adams	.05
492	Matt Franco	.05
493	Scott Servais	.05
494	Frank Castillo	.05
495	Ryne Sandberg	.75
496	Rey Sanchez	.05
497	Steve Trachsel	.05
498	Jose Hernandez	.05
499	Dave Martinez	.05
500	Babe Ruth	1.00
501	Ty Cobb	.50
502	Walter Johnson	.10
503	Christy Mathewson	.10
504	Honus Wagner	.25
505	Robin Ventura	.05
506	Jason Bere	.05
507	Mike Cameron RC	.25
508	Ron Karkovice	.05
509	Matt Karchner	.05
510	Harold Baines	.05
511	Kirk McCaskill	.05
512	Larry Thomas	.05
513	Danny Tartabull	.05
514	Steve Gibralter	.05
515	Bret Boone	.05
516	Jeff Branson	.05
517	Kevin Jarvis	.05
518	Xavier Hernandez	.05
519	Eric Owens	.05
520	Barry Larkin	.05
521	Dave Burba	.05
522	John Smiley	.05
523	Paul Assenmacher	.05
524	Chad Ogea	.05
525	Orel Hershiser	.05
526	Alan Embree	.05
527	Tony Pena	.05
528	Omar Vizquel	.05
529	Mark Clark	.05
530	Albert Belle	.05
531	Charles Nagy	.05
532	Herbert Perry	.05
533	Darren Holmes	.05
534	Ellis Burks	.05
535	Bill Swift	.05
536	Armando Reynoso	.05
537	Curtis Leskanic	.05
538	Quinton McCracken	.05
539	Steve Reed	.05
540	Larry Walker	.05
541	Walt Weiss	.05
542	Bryan Rekar	.05
543	Tony Clark	.05
544	Steve Rodriguez	.05
545	C.J. Nitkowski	.05
546	Todd Steverson	.05
547	Jose Lima	.05
548	Phil Nevin	.05
549	Chris Gomez	.05
550	Travis Fryman	.05
551	Mark Lewis	.05
552	Alex Arias	.05
553	Marc Valdes	.05
554	Kevin Brown	.05
555	Jeff Conine	.05
556	John Burkett	.05
557	Devon White	.05
558	Pat Rapp	.05
559	Jay Powell	.05
560	Gary Sheffield	.30
561	Jim Dougherty	.05
562	Todd Jones	.05
563	Tony Eusebio	.05
564	Darryl Kile	.05
565	Doug Drabek	.05
566	Mike Simms	.05
567	Derrick May	.05
568	Donne Wall RC	.05
569	Greg Swindell	.05
570	Jim Pittsley	.05
571	Bob Hamelin	.05
572	Mark Gubicza	.05
573	Chris Haney	.05
574	Keith Lockhart	.05
575	Mike Macfarlane	.05
576	Les Norman	.05
577	Joe Randa	.05
578	Chris Stynes	.05
579	Greg Gagne	.05
580	Raul Mondesi	.05
581	Delino DeShields	.05
582	Pedro Astacio	.05
583	Antonio Osuna	.05
584	Brett Butler	.05
585	Todd Worrell	.05
586	Mike Blowers	.05
587	Felix Rodriguez	.05
588	Ismael Valdes	.05
589	Ricky Bones	.05
590	Greg Vaughn	.05
591	Mark Loretta	.05
592	Cal Eldred	.05
593	Chuck Carr	.05
594	Dave Nilsson	.05
595	John Jaha	.05
596	Scott Karl	.05
597	Pat Listach	.05
598	Jose Valentin RC	.05
599	Mike Trombley	.05
600	Paul Molitor	.60
601	Dave Hollins	.05
602	Ron Coomer	.05
603	Matt Walbeck	.05
604	Roberto Kelly	.05
605	Rick Aguilera	.05
606	Pat Mahomes	.05
607	Jeff Reboulet	.05
608	Rich Becker	.05
609	Tim Scott	.05
610	Pedro J. Martinez	.60
611	Kirk Rueter	.05
612	Tavo Alvarez	.05
613	Yamil Benitez	.05
614	Darrin Fletcher	.05

615	Mike Lansing	.05
616	Henry Rodriguez	.05
617	Tony Tarasco	.05
618	Alex Ochoa	.05
619	Tim Bogar	.05
620	Bernard Gilkey	.05
621	Dave Mlicki	.05
622	Brent Mayne	.05
623	Ryan Thompson	.05
624	Pete Harnisch	.05
625	Lance Johnson	.05
626	Jose Vizcaino	.05
627	Doug Henry	.05
628	Scott Kamieniecki	.05
629	Jim Leyritz	.05
630	Ruben Sierra	.05
631	Pat Kelly	.05
632	Joe Girardi	.05
633	John Wetteland	.05
634	Melido Perez	.05
635	Paul O'Neill	.05
636	Jorge Posada	.05
637	Bernie Williams	.05
638	Mark Acre	.05
639	Mike Bordick	.05
640	Mark McGwire	1.50
641	Fausto Cruz	.05
642	Ernie Young	.05
643	Todd Van Poppel	.05
644	Craig Paquette	.05
645	Brent Gates	.05
646	Pedro Munoz	.05
647	Andrew Lorraine	.05
648	Sid Fernandez	.05
649	Jim Eisenreich	.05
650	Johnny Damon	.30
651	Dustin Hermanson	.05
652	Joe Randa	.05
653	Michael Tucker	.05
654	Alan Benes	.05
655	Chad Fonville	.05
656	David Bell	.05
657	Jon Nunnally	.05
658	Chan Ho Park	.05
659	LaTroy Hawkins	.05
660	Jamie Brewington	.05
661	Quinton McCracken	.05
662	Tim Unroe	.05
663	Jeff Ware	.05
664	Todd Greene	.05
665	Andrew Lorraine	.05
666	Ernie Young	.05
667	Toby Borland	.05
668	Lenny Webster	.05
669	Benito Santiago	.05
670	Gregg Jefferies	.05
671	Darren Daulton	.05
672	Curt Schilling	.25
673	Mark Whiten	.05
674	Todd Zeile	.05
675	Jay Bell	.05
676	Paul Wagner	.05
677	Dave Clark	.05
678	Nelson Liriano	.05
679	Ramon Morel	.05
680	Charlie Hayes	.05
681	Angelo Encaracion	.05
682	Al Martin	.05
683	Jacob Brumfield	.05
684	Mike Kingery	.05
685	Carlos Garcia	.05
686	Tom Pagnozzi	.05
687	David Bell	.05
688	Todd Stottlemyre	.05
689	Jose Oliva	.05
690	Ray Lankford	.05
691	Mike Morgan	.05
692	John Frascatore	.05
693	John Mabry	.05
694	Mark Petkovsek	.05
695	Alan Benes	.05
696	Steve Finley	.05
697	Marc Newfield	.05
698	Andy Ashby	.05
699	Marc Kroon	.05
700	Wally Joyner	.05
701	Joey Hamilton	.05
702	Dustin Hermanson	.05
703	Scott Sanders	.05
704	Marty Cordova	.05
705	Hideo Nomo	.15
706	Mo Vaughn	.05
707	Barry Larkin	.05
708	Randy Johnson	.20
709	Greg Maddux	.35
710	Mark McGwire	.75
711	Ron Gant	.05
712	Andujar Cedeno	.05
713	Brian Johnson	.05
714	J.R. Phillips	.05
715	Rod Beck	.05
716	Sergio Valdez	.05
717	Marvin Benard **RC**	.25
718	Steve Scarsone	.05

719	Rich Aurilia **RC**	.10
720	Matt Williams	.05
721	John Patterson	.05
722	Shawn Estes	.05
723	Russ Davis	.05
724	Rich Amaral	.05
725	Edgar Martinez	.05
726	Norm Charlton	.05
727	Paul Sorrento	.05
728	Luis Sojo	.05
729	Arquimedez Pozo	.05
730	Jay Buhner	.05
731	Chris Bosio	.05
732	Chris Widger	.05
733	Kevin Gross	.05
734	Darren Oliver	.05
735	Dean Palmer	.05
736	Matt Whiteside	.05
737	Luis Ortiz	.05
738	Roger Pavlik	.05
739	Damon Buford	.05
740	Juan Gonzalez	.30
741	Rusty Greer	.05
742	Lou Frazier	.05
743	Pat Hentgen	.05
744	Tomas Perez	.05
745	Juan Guzman	.05
746	Otis Nixon	.05
747	Robert Perez	.05
748	Ed Sprague	.05
749	Tony Castillo	.05
750	John Olerud	.05
751	Shawn Green	.10
752	Jeff Ware	.05
753	Dante Bichette, Larry Walker, Andres Galarraga, Vinny Castilla Checklist 396-441/Blake St. Bombers	.05
754	Greg Maddux Checklist 442-487	.25
755	Marty Cordova Checklist 488-533	.05
756	Ozzie Smith Checklist 534-579	.35
757	John Vander Wal Checklist 580-625	.05
758	Andres Galarraga Checklist 626-670	.05
759	Frank Thomas Checklist 671-715	.20
760	Tony Gwynn Checklist 716-760	.25
761	Randy Myers	.10
762	Kent Mercker	.10
763	David Wells	.05
764	Tom Gordon	.10
765	Wil Cordero	.10
766	Dave Magadan	.10
767	Doug Jones	.10
768	Kevin Tapani	.10
769	Curtis Goodwin	.10
770	Julio Franco	.10
771	Jack McDowell	.10
772	Al Leiter	.10
773	Sean Berry	.10
774	Bip Roberts	.10
775	Jose Offerman	.10
776	Ben McDonald	.10
777	Dan Serafini	.10
778	Ryan McGuire	.10
779	Tim Raines	.10
780	Tino Martinez	.10
781	Kenny Rogers	.10
782	Bob Tewksbury	.10
783	Rickey Henderson	.60
784	Ron Gant	.10
785	Gary Gaetti	.10
786	Andy Benes	.10
787	Royce Clayton	.10
788	Darryl Hamilton	.10
789	Ken Hill	.10
790	Erik Hanson	.10

Gold Signature

	NM/M
Common Player:	1.00
Stars:	10X

(See 1996 Collector's Choice for checklist and base card values.)

Silver Signature

	NM/M
Common Player:	.10
Stars:	1.5X

(See 1996 Collector's Choice for checklist and base card values.)

A Cut Above

		NM/M
Complete Set (10):		8.00
Common Card:		1.00
CA1	Ken Griffey Jr. (Teenage Rookie)	1.00
CA2	Ken Griffey Jr. (Great Defense)	1.00
CA3	Ken Griffey Jr. (Fun-Loving)	1.00
CA4	Ken Griffey Jr. (All-Star Games)	1.00
CA5	Ken Griffey Jr. ('93 Season)	1.00
CA6	Ken Griffey Jr. ('94 HR Records)	1.00
CA7	Ken Griffey Jr. ('94 Season)	1.00
CA8	Ken Griffey Jr. ('95 Season)	1.00
CA9	Ken Griffey Jr. ('95 Postseason)	1.00
CA10	Ken Griffey Jr. ('96: A Look Ahead)	1.00

Cal Ripken Jr. Jumbo

		NM/M
1	Cal Ripken Jr.	5.00

Nomo Scrapbook

	NM/M
Complete Set (5):	10.00
Common Card:	2.00
Japanese:	3X
1-5 Hideo Nomo	2.00

Ripken Collection

	NM/M
Complete Set (1-4, 9-12)	15.00
Common Card:	2.50
Header Card:	2.00

(See also Upper Deck Series 1 and 2, and Upper Deck/SP.)

1997 Collector's Choice

	NM/M
Factory Set (516):	16.00
Complete Set (506):	12.00

Raul **MONDESI** of

Common Player:		.05
Pack (12):		1.00
Wax Box (36):		20.00
1	Andruw Jones	1.00
2	Rocky Coppinger .053	
3	Jeff D'Amico	.05
4	Dmitri Young	.05
5	Darin Erstad	.75
6	Jermaine Allensworth	.05
7	Damian Jackson	.05
8	Bill Mueller	.05
9	Jacob Cruz	.05
10	Vladimir Guerrero	1.00
11	Marty Janzen	.05
12	Kevin L. Brown	.05
13	Willie Adams	.05
14	Wendell Magee	.05
15	Scott Rolen	.65
16	Matt Beech	.05
17	Neifi Perez	.05
18	Jamey Wright	.05
19	Jose Paniagua	.05
20	Todd Walker	.05
21	Justin Thompson	.05
22	Robin Jennings	.05
23	Dario Veras **RC**	.05
24	Brian Lesher	.05
25	Nomar Garciaparra	1.25
26	Luis Castillo	.05
27	Brian Giles **RC**	.75
28	Jermaine Dye	.05
29	Terrell Wade	.05
30	Fred McGriff	.05
31	Marquis Grissom	.05
32	Ryan Klesko	.05
33	Javier Lopez	.05
34	Mark Wohlers	.05
35	Tom Glavine	.25
36	Denny Neagle	.05
37	Scott Erickson	.05
38	Chris Hoiles	.05
39	Roberto Alomar	.25
40	Eddie Murray	.75
41	Cal Ripken Jr.	2.00
42	Randy Myers	.05
43	B.J. Surhoff	.05
44	Rick Krivda	.05
45	Jose Canseco	.50
46	Heathcliff Slocumb	.05
47	Jeff Suppan	.05
48	Tom Gordon	.05
49	Aaron Sele	.05
50	Mo Vaughn	.05
51	Darren Bragg	.05
52	Wil Cordero	.05
53	Scott Bullett	.05
54	Terry Adams	.05
55	Jackie Robinson	.35
56	Tony Gwynn, Alex Rodriguez (Batting Leaders)	.35
57	Andres Galarraga, Mark McGwire (Homer Leaders)	.50
58	Andres Galarraga, Albert Belle (RBI Leaders)	.05
59	Eric Young, Kenny Lofton (SB Leaders)	.05
60	John Smoltz, Andy Pettitte (Victory Leaders)	.05
61	John Smoltz, Roger Clemens (Strikout Leaders)	.20
62	Kevin Brown, Juan Guzman (ERA Leaders)	.05
63	John Wetteland, Todd Worrell, Jeff Brantley (Save Leaders)	.05
64	Scott Servais	.05
65	Sammy Sosa	1.00
66	Ryne Sandberg	1.00

No.	Player	Price	No.	Player	Price	No.	Player	Price	No.	Player	Price
67	Frank Castillo	.05	171	John Franco	.05	273	Jimmy Key	.05	377	Roberto Kelly	.05
68	Rey Sanchez	.05	172	Pete Harnisch	.05	274	Mike Bordick	.05	378	Bob Tewksbury	.05
69	Steve Trachsel	.05	173	Butch Huskey	.05	275	Brady Anderson	.05	379	Ron Coomer	.05
70	Robin Ventura	.05	174	Paul Wilson	.05	276	Eric Davis	.05	380	Brad Radke	.05
71	Wilson Alvarez	.05	175	Bernie Williams	.05	277	Jeffrey Hammonds	.05	381	Matt Lawton	.05
72	Tony Phillips	.05	176	Dwight Gooden	.05	278	Reggie Jefferson	.05	382	Dan Naulty	.05
73	Lyle Mouton	.05	177	Wade Boggs	1.00	279	Tim Naehring	.05	383	Scott Stahoviak	.05
74	Mike Cameron	.05	178	Ruben Rivera	.05	280	John Valentin	.05	384	Matt Wagner	.05
75	Harold Baines	.05	179	Jim Leyritz	.05	281	Troy O'Leary	.05	385	Jim Bullinger	.05
76	Albert Belle	.05	180	Derek Jeter	2.00	282	Shane Mack	.05	386	Carlos Perez	.05
77	Chris Snopek	.05	181	Tino Martinez	.05	283	Mike Stanley	.05	387	Darrin Fletcher	.05
78	Reggie Sanders	.05	182	Tim Raines	.05	284	Tim Wakefield	.05	388	Chris Widger	.05
79	Jeff Brantley	.05	183	Scott Brosius	.05	285	Brian McRae	.05	389	F.P. Santangelo	.05
80	Barry Larkin	.05	184	Jason Giambi	.60	286	Brooks Kieschnick	.05	390	Lee Smith	.05
81	Kevin Jarvis	.05	185	Geronimo Berroa	.05	287	Shawon Dunston	.05	391	Bobby Jones	.05
82	John Smiley	.05	186	Ariel Prieto	.05	288	Kevin Foster	.05	392	John Olerud	.05
83	Pete Schourek	.05	187	Scott Spiezio	.05	289	Mel Rojas	.05	393	Mark Clark	.05
84	Thomas Howard	.05	188	John Wasdin	.05	290	Mark Grace	.05	394	Jason Isringhausen	.05
85	Lee Smith	.05	189	Ernie Young	.05	291	Brant Brown	.05	395	Todd Hundley	.05
86	Omar Vizquel	.05	190	Mark McGwire	1.50	292	Amaury Telemaco	.05	396	Lance Johnson	.05
87	Julio Franco	.05	191	Jim Eisenreich	.05	293	Dave Martinez	.05	397	Edgardo Alfonzo	.05
88	Orel Hershiser	.05	192	Ricky Bottalico	.05	294	Jaime Navarro	.05	398	Alex Ochoa	.05
89	Charles Nagy	.05	193	Darren Daulton	.05	295	Ray Durham	.05	399	Darryl Strawberry	.05
90	Matt Williams	.05	194	David Doster	.05	296	Ozzie Guillen	.05	400	David Cone	.05
91	Dennis Martinez	.05	195	Gregg Jefferies	.05	297	Roberto Hernandez	.05	401	Paul O'Neill	.05
92	Jose Mesa	.05	196	Lenny Dykstra	.05	298	Ron Karkovice	.05	402	Joe Girardi	.05
93	Sandy Alomar Jr.	.05	197	Curt Schilling	.20	299	James Baldwin	.05	403	Charlie Hayes	.05
94	Jim Thome	.50	198	Todd Stottlemyre	.05	300	Frank Thomas	.75	404	Andy Pettitte	.25
95	Vinny Castilla	.05	199	Willie McGee	.05	301	Eddie Taubensee	.05	405	Mariano Rivera	.25
96	Armando Reynoso	.05	200	Ozzie Smith	1.00	302	Bret Boone	.05	406	Mariano Duncan	.05
97	Kevin Ritz	.05	201	Dennis Eckersley	.65	303	Willie Greene	.05	407	Kenny Rogers	.05
98	Larry Walker	.05	202	Ray Lankford	.05	304	Dave Burba	.05	408	Cecil Fielder	.05
99	Eric Young	.05	203	John Mabry	.05	305	Deion Sanders	.10	409	George Williams	.05
100	Dante Bichette	.05	204	Alan Benes	.05	306	Reggie Sanders	.05	410	Jose Canseco	.35
101	Quinton McCracken	.05	205	Ron Gant	.05	307	Hal Morris	.05	411	Tony Batista	.05
102	John Vander Wal	.05	206	Archi Cianfrocco	.05	308	Pokey Reese	.05	412	Steve Karsay	.05
103	Phil Nevin	.05	207	Fernando Valenzuela	.05	309	Tony Fernandez	.05	413	Dave Telgheder	.05
104	Tony Clark	.05	208	Greg Vaughn	.05	310	Manny Ramirez	.75	414	Billy Taylor	.05
105	Alan Trammell	.05	209	Steve Finley	.05	311	Chad Ogea	.05	415	Mickey Morandini	.05
106	Felipe Lira	.05	210	Tony Gwynn	1.00	312	Jack McDowell	.05	416	Calvin Maduro	.05
107	Curtis Pride	.05	211	Rickey Henderson	.75	313	Kevin Mitchell	.05	417	Mark Leiter	.05
108	Bobby Higginson	.05	212	Trevor Hoffman	.05	314	Chad Curtis	.05	418	Kevin Stocker	.05
109	Mark Lewis	.05	213	Jason Thompson	.05	315	Steve Kline	.05	419	Mike Lieberthal	.05
110	Travis Fryman	.05	214	Osvaldo Fernandez	.05	316	Kevin Seitzer	.05	420	Rico Brogna	.05
111	Al Leiter	.05	215	Glenallen Hill	.05	317	Kirt Manwaring	.05	421	Mark Portugal	.05
112	Devon White	.05	216	William Van Landingham	.05	318	Bill Swift	.05	422	Rex Hudler	.05
113	Jeff Conine	.05				319	Ellis Burks	.05	423	Mark Johnson	.05
114	Charles Johnson	.05	217	Marvin Benard	.05	320	Andres Galarraga	.05	424	Esteban Loaiza	.05
115	Andre Dawson	.25	218	Juan Gonzalez	.10	321	Bruce Ruffin	.05	425	Lou Collier	.05
116	Edgar Renteria	.05	219	Roberto Alomar	.05	322	Mark Thompson	.05	426	Kevin Elster	.05
117	Robb Nen	.05	220	Brian Jordan	.05	323	Walt Weiss	.05	427	Francisco Cordova	.05
118	Kevin Brown	.05	221	John Smoltz	.05	324	Todd Jones	.05	428	Marc Wilkins	.05
119	Derek Bell	.05	222	Javy Lopez	.05	325	Andruw Jones	.50	429	Joe Randa	.05
120	Bob Abreu	.10	223	Bernie Williams	.05	326	Chipper Jones	.65	430	Jason Kendall	.05
121	Mike Hampton	.05	224	Jim Leyritz, John Wetteland	.05	327	Mo Vaughn	.05	431	Jon Lieber	.05
122	Todd Jones	.05	225	Barry Bonds	2.00	328	Frank Thomas	.50	432	Steve Cooke	.05
123	Billy Wagner	.05	226	Rich Aurilia	.05	329	Albert Belle	.10	433	Emil Brown RC	.05
124	Shane Reynolds	.05	227	Jay Canizaro	.05	330	Mark McGwire	1.00	434	Tony Womack RC	.25
125	Jeff Bagwell	.75	228	Dan Wilson	.05	331	Derek Jeter	1.50	435	Al Martin	.05
126	Brian L. Hunter	.05	229	Bob Wolcott	.05	332	Alex Rodriguez	1.00	436	Jason Schmidt	.05
127	Jeff Montgomery	.05	230	Ken Griffey Jr.	1.25	333	Jay Buhner	.05	437	Andy Benes	.05
128	Rod Myers RC	.05	231	Sterling Hitchcock	.05	334	Ken Griffey Jr.	.75	438	Delino DeShields	.05
129	Tim Belcher	.05	232	Edgar Martinez	.05	335	Brian L. Hunter	.05	439	Royce Clayton	.05
130	Kevin Appier	.05	233	Joey Cora	.05	336	Brian Johnson	.05	440	Brian Jordan	.05
131	Mike Sweeney	.05	234	Norm Charlton	.05	337	Omar Olivares	.05	441	Donovan Osborne	.05
132	Craig Paquette	.05	235	Alex Rodriguez	1.50	338	Deivi Cruz RC	.05	442	Gary Gaetti	.05
133	Joe Randa	.05	236	Bobby Witt	.05	339	Damion Easley	.05	443	Tom Pagnozzi	.05
134	Michael Tucker	.05	237	Darren Oliver	.05	340	Melvin Nieves	.05	444	Joey Hamilton	.05
135	Raul Mondesi	.05	238	Kevin Elster	.05	341	Moises Alou	.05	445	Wally Joyner	.05
136	Tim Wallach	.05	239	Rusty Greer	.05	342	Jim Eisenreich	.05	446	John Flaherty	.05
137	Brett Butler	.05	240	Juan Gonzalez	.40	343	Mark Hutton	.05	447	Chris Gomez	.05
138	Karim Garcia	.10	241	Will Clark	.05	344	Alex Fernandez	.05	448	Sterling Hitchcock	.05
139	Todd Hollandsworth	.05	242	Dean Palmer	.05	345	Gary Sheffield	.35	449	Andy Ashby	.05
140	Eric Karros	.05	243	Ivan Rodriguez	.65	346	Pat Rapp	.05	450	Ken Caminiti	.05
141	Hideo Nomo	.40	244	Ken Griffey Jr. Checklist	.25	347	Brad Ausmus	.05	451	Tim Worrell	.05
142	Ismael Valdes	.05	245	Ken Griffey Jr. Checklist	.25	348	Sean Berry	.05	452	Jose Vizcaino	.05
143	Cal Eldred	.05	246	Ken Griffey Jr. Checklist	.25	349	Darryl Kile	.05	453	Rod Beck	.05
144	Scott Karl	.05	247	Ken Griffey Jr. Checklist	.25	350	Craig Biggio	.05	454	Wilson Delgado	.05
145	Matt Mieske	.05	248	Ken Griffey Jr. Checklist	.25	351	Chris Holt	.05	455	Darryl Hamilton	.05
146	Mike Fetters	.05	249	Ken Griffey Jr. Checklist	.25	352	Luis Gonzalez	.05	456	Mark Lewis	.05
147	Mark Loretta	.05	250	Eddie Murray	.75	353	Pat Listach	.05	457	Mark Gardner	.05
148	Fernando Vina	.05	251	Troy Percival	.05	354	Jose Rosado	.05	458	Rick Wilkins	.05
149	Jeff Cirillo	.05	252	Garret Anderson	.05	355	Mike Macfarlane	.05	459	Scott Sanders	.05
150	Dave Nilsson	.05	253	Allen Watson	.05	356	Tom Goodwin	.05	460	Kevin Orie	.05
151	Kirby Puckett	1.00	254	Jason Dickson	.05	357	Chris Haney	.05	461	Glendon Rusch	.05
152	Rich Becker	.05	255	Jim Edmonds	.05	358	Chili Davis	.05	462	Juan Melo	.05
153	Chuck Knoblauch	.05	256	Chuck Finley	.05	359	Jose Offerman	.05	463	Richie Sexson	.05
154	Marty Cordova	.05	257	Randy Velarde	.05	360	Johnny Damon	.30	464	Bartolo Colon	.05
155	Paul Molitor	.75	258	Shigetosi Hasegawa	.05	361	Bip Roberts	.05	465	Jose Guillen	.05
156	Rick Aguilera	.05	259	Todd Greene	.05	362	Ramon Martinez	.05	466	Heath Murray	.05
157	Pat Meares	.05	260	Tim Salmon	.05	363	Pedro Astacio	.05	467	Aaron Boone	.05
158	Frank Rodriguez	.05	261	Mark Langston	.05	364	Todd Zeile	.05	468	Bubba Trammell RC	.05
159	David Segui	.05	262	Dave Hollins	.05	365	Mike Piazza	1.25	469	Jeff Abbott	.05
160	Henry Rodriguez	.05	263	Gary DiSarcina	.05	366	Greg Gagne	.05	470	Derrick Gibson	.05
161	Shane Andrews	.05	264	Kenny Lofton	.05	367	Chan Ho Park	.05	471	Matt Morris	.05
162	Pedro J. Martinez	.75	265	John Smoltz	.05	368	Wilton Guerrero	.05	472	Ryan Jones	.05
163	Mark Grudzielanek	.05	266	Greg Maddux	1.00	369	Todd Worrell	.05	473	Pat Cline	.05
164	Mike Lansing	.05	267	Jeff Blauser	.05	370	John Jaha	.05	474	Adam Riggs	.05
165	Rondell White	.05	268	Alan Embree	.05	371	Steve Sparks	.05	475	Jay Payton	.05
166	Ugueth Urbina	.05	269	Mark Lemke	.05	372	Mike Matheny	.05	476	Derrek Lee	.50
167	Rey Ordonez	.05	270	Chipper Jones	1.00	373	Marc Newfield	.05	477	Elieser Marrero	.05
168	Robert Person	.05	271	Mike Mussina	.65	374	Jeromy Burnitz	.05	478	Lee Tinsley	.05
169	Carlos Baerga	.05	272	Rafael Palmeiro	.65	375	Jose Valentin	.05	479	Jamie Moyer	.05
170	Bernard Gilkey	.05				376	Ben McDonald	.05	480	Jay Buhner	.05

481	Bob Wells	.05
482	Jeff Fassero	.05
483	Paul Sorrento	.05
484	Russ Davis	.05
485	Randy Johnson	.75
486	Roger Pavlik	.05
487	Damon Buford	.05
488	Julio Santana	.05
489	Mark McLemore	.05
490	Mickey Tettleton	.05
491	Ken Hill	.05
492	Benji Gil	.05
493	Ed Sprague	.05
494	Mike Timlin	.05
495	Pat Hentgen	.05
496	Orlando Merced	.05
497	Carlos Garcia	.05
498	Carlos Delgado	.35
499	Juan Guzman	.05
500	Roger Clemens	1.00
501	Erik Hanson	.05
502	Otis Nixon	.05
503	Shawn Green	.10
504	Charlie O'Brien	.05
505	Joe Carter	.05
506	Alex Gonzalez	.05

All-Star Connection

		NM/M
Complete Set (45):		10.00
Common Player:		.10
1	Mark McGwire	1.00
2	Chuck Knoblauch	.10
3	Jim Thome	.35
4	Alex Rodriguez	1.00
5	Ken Griffey Jr.	.75
6	Brady Anderson	.10
7	Albert Belle	.10
8	Ivan Rodriguez	.40
9	Pat Hentgen	.10
10	Frank Thomas	.50
11	Roberto Alomar	.25
12	Robin Ventura	.10
13	Cal Ripken Jr.	1.50
14	Juan Gonzalez	.25
15	Manny Ramirez	.50
16	Bernie Williams	.10
17	Terry Steinbach	.10
18	Andy Pettitte	.25
19	Jeff Bagwell	.50
20	Craig Biggio	.10
21	Ken Caminiti	.10
22	Barry Larkin	.10
23	Tony Gwynn	.60
24	Barry Bonds	1.50
25	Kenny Lofton	.10
26	Mike Piazza	.75
27	John Smoltz	.10
28	Andres Galarraga	.10
29	Ryne Sandberg	.60
30	Chipper Jones	.60
31	Mark Grudzielanek	.10
32	Sammy Sosa	.60
33	Steve Finley	.10
34	Gary Sheffield	.25
35	Todd Hundley	.10
36	Greg Maddux	.60
37	Mo Vaughn	.10
38	Eric Young	.10
39	Vinny Castilla	.10
40	Derek Jeter	1.50
41	Lance Johnson	.10
42	Ellis Burks	.10
43	Dante Bichette	.10
44	Javy Lopez	.10
45	Hideo Nomo	.25

Big Shots

	NM/M
Complete Set (19):	15.00
Common Player:	.25
Gold Signature Edition:	2X

1	Ken Griffey Jr.	2.00
2	Nomar Garciaparra	1.50
3	Brian Jordan	.25
4	Scott Rolen	.75
5	Alex Rodriguez	2.50
6	Larry Walker	.25
7	Mariano Rivera	.35
8	Cal Ripken Jr.	3.00
9	Deion Sanders	.25
10	Frank Thomas	1.00
11	Dean Palmer	.25
12	Ken Caminiti	.25
13	Derek Jeter	3.00
14	Barry Bonds	3.00
15	Chipper Jones	1.50
16	Mo Vaughn	.25
17	Jay Buhner	.25
18	Mike Piazza	2.00
19	Tony Gwynn	1.50

Big Show

		NM/M
Complete Set (45):		7.00
Common Player:		.10
World Headquarters:		8X
1	Greg Maddux	.50
2	Chipper Jones	.50
3	Andruw Jones	.40
4	John Smoltz	.10
5	Cal Ripken Jr.	1.00
6	Roberto Alomar	.25
7	Rafael Palmeiro	.35
8	Eddie Murray	.40
9	Jose Canseco	.30
10	Roger Clemens	.55
11	Mo Vaughn	.10
12	Jim Edmonds	.10
13	Tim Salmon	.10
14	Sammy Sosa	.50
15	Albert Belle	.10
16	Frank Thomas	.40
17	Barry Larkin	.10
18	Kenny Lofton	.10
19	Manny Ramirez	.40
20	Matt Williams	.10
21	Dante Bichette	.10
22	Gary Sheffield	.30
23	Craig Biggio	.10
24	Jeff Bagwell	.40
25	Todd Hollandsworth	.10
26	Raul Mondesi	.10
27	Hideo Nomo	.25
28	Mike Piazza	.60
29	Paul Molitor	.40
30	Kirby Puckett	.50
31	Rondell White	.10
32	Rey Ordonez	.10
33	Paul Wilson	.10
34	Derek Jeter	1.00
35	Andy Pettitte	.25
36	Mark McGwire	.75
37	Jason Kendall	.10
38	Ozzie Smith	.50
39	Tony Gwynn	.50
40	Barry Bonds	1.00
41	Alex Rodriguez	.75
42	Jay Buhner	.10
43	Ken Griffey Jr.	.60
44	Randy Johnson	.40
45	Juan Gonzalez	.25

Big Show World Headquarters

	NM/M
Complete Set (45):	50.00
Common Player:	1.50
Stars:	8X

(See 1997 Collector's Choice Big Show for checklist and base card values.)

Clearly Dominant

	NM/M
Complete Set (5):	16.00
Common Griffey Jr.:	4.00

Clearly Dominant Jumbos

	NM/M
Complete Set (5):	10.00
Common Griffey Jr.:	2.00

Hot List Jumbos

		NM/M
Complete Set (10):		15.00
Common Player:		.50
325	Andruw Jones	1.50
326	Chipper Jones	2.00
327	Mo Vaughn	.50
328	Frank Thomas	1.50
329	Albert Belle	.50
330	Mark McGwire	3.00
331	Derek Jeter	4.00

Andruw JONES or

332	Alex Rodriguez	3.00
333	Jay Buhner	.50
334	Ken Griffey Jr.	2.50

New Frontier

		NM/M
Complete Set (40):		75.00
Common Player:		1.00
1	Alex Rodriguez	5.00
2	Tony Gwynn	3.00
3	Jose Canseco	1.25
4	Hideo Nomo	1.25
5	Mark McGwire	5.00
6	Barry Bonds	6.00
7	Juan Gonzalez	1.25
8	Ken Caminiti	1.00
9	Tim Salmon	1.00
10	Mike Piazza	4.00
11	Ken Griffey Jr.	4.00
12	Andres Galarraga	1.00
13	Jay Buhner	1.00
14	Dante Bichette	1.00
15	Frank Thomas	2.00
16	Ryne Sandberg	3.00
17	Roger Clemens	3.50
18	Andruw Jones	2.00
19	Jim Thome	1.50
20	Sammy Sosa	3.00
21	David Justice	1.00
22	Deion Sanders	1.00
23	Todd Walker	1.00
24	Kevin Orie	1.00
25	Albert Belle	1.00
26	Jeff Bagwell	2.00
27	Manny Ramirez	2.00
28	Brian Jordan	1.00
29	Derek Jeter	6.00
30	Chipper Jones	3.00
31	Mo Vaughn	1.00
32	Gary Sheffield	1.50
33	Carlos Delgado	1.50
34	Vladimir Guerrero	2.00
35	Cal Ripken Jr.	6.00
36	Greg Maddux	3.00
37	Cecil Fielder	1.00
38	Todd Hundley	1.00
39	Mike Mussina	1.25
40	Scott Rolen	1.50

Premier Power

		NM/M
Complete Set (20):		20.00
Common Player:		.40
Gold:		2X
1	Mark McGwire	3.00
2	Brady Anderson	.40
3	Ken Griffey Jr.	2.50
4	Albert Belle	.40
5	Juan Gonzalez	.60
6	Andres Galarraga	.40

Alex Rodriguez Seattle Mariners - SS

7	Jay Buhner	.40
8	Mo Vaughn	.40
9	Barry Bonds	3.50
10	Gary Sheffield	.75
11	Todd Hundley	.40
12	Frank Thomas	1.50
13	Sammy Sosa	2.00
14	Ken Caminiti	.40
15	Vinny Castilla	.40
16	Ellis Burks	.40
17	Rafael Palmeiro	1.00
18	Alex Rodriguez	3.00
19	Mike Piazza	2.50
20	Eddie Murray	1.50

Premier Power Jumbo

		NM/M
Complete Set (20):		15.00
Common Player:		.50
1	Mark McGwire	2.50
2	Brady Anderson	.50
3	Ken Griffey Jr.	2.00
4	Albert Belle	.50
5	Juan Gonzalez	.75
6	Andres Galarraga	.50
7	Jay Buhner	.50
8	Mo Vaughn	.50
9	Barry Bonds	3.00
10	Gary Sheffield	.65
11	Todd Hundley	.50
12	Frank Thomas	1.00
13	Sammy Sosa	1.50
14	Ken Caminiti	.50
15	Vinny Castilla	.50
16	Ellis Burks	.50
17	Rafael Palmeiro	.75
18	Alex Rodriguez	2.50
19	Mike Piazza	2.00
20	Eddie Murray	1.00

Stick' Ums

		NM/M
Complete Set (30):		5.00
Common Player:		.05
1	Ozzie Smith	.50
2	Andruw Jones	.40
3	Alex Rodriguez	.75
4	Paul Molitor	.40
5	Jeff Bagwell	.40
6	Manny Ramirez	.40
7	Kenny Lofton	.05
8	Albert Belle	.05
9	Jay Buhner	.05
10	Chipper Jones	.50
11	Barry Larkin	.05
12	Dante Bichette	.05
13	Mike Piazza	.60
14	Andres Galarraga	.05
15	Barry Bonds	1.00
16	Brady Anderson	.05
17	Gary Sheffield	.20
18	Jim Thome	.35
19	Tony Gwynn	.50
20	Cal Ripken Jr.	1.00
21	Sammy Sosa	.50
22	Juan Gonzalez	.20
23	Greg Maddux	.50
24	Ken Griffey Jr.	.60
25	Mark McGwire	.75
26	Kirby Puckett	.50
27	Mo Vaughn	.05
28	Vladimir Guerrero	.40
29	Ken Caminiti	.05
30	Frank Thomas	.40

Toast of the Town

		NM/M
Complete Set (30):		40.00
Common Player:		.30
1	Andruw Jones	2.00
2	Chipper Jones	2.50
3	Greg Maddux	2.50

4 John Smoltz .30
5 Kenny Lofton .30
6 Brady Anderson .30
7 Cal Ripken Jr. 6.00
8 Mo Vaughn .30
9 Sammy Sosa 2.50
10 Albert Belle .30
11 Frank Thomas 2.00
12 Barry Larkin .30
13 Manny Ramirez 2.00
14 Jeff Bagwell 2.00
15 Mike Piazza 4.00
16 Paul Molitor 2.00
17 Vladimir Guerrero 2.00
18 Todd Hundley .30
19 Derek Jeter 6.00
20 Andy Pettitte .45
21 Bernie Williams .30
22 Mark McGwire 5.00
23 Scott Rolen 1.00
24 Ken Caminiti .30
25 Tony Gwynn 2.50
26 Barry Bonds 6.00
27 Ken Griffey Jr. 4.00
28 Alex Rodriguez 5.00
29 Juan Gonzalez .75
30 Roger Clemens 3.00

1997 Collector's Choice Update

NM/M
Complete Set (30): 2.00
Common Player: .10
1 Jim Leyritz .10
2 Matt Perisho .10
3 Michael Tucker .10
4 Mike Johnson .10
5 Jaime Navarro .10
6 Doug Drabek .10
7 Terry Mulholland .10
8 Brett Tomko .10
9 Marquis Grissom .10
10 David Justice .10
11 Brian Moehler .10
12 Bobby Bonilla .10
13 Todd Dunwoody .10
14 Tony Saunders .10
15 Jay Bell .10
16 Jeff King .10
17 Terry Steinbach .10
18 Steve Bieser .10
19 Takashi Kashiwada RC .10
20 Hideki Irabu .10
21 Damon Mashore .10
22 Quilvio Veras .10
23 Will Cunnane .10
24 Jeff Kent .50
25 J.T. Snow .10
26 Dante Powell .10
27 Jose Cruz Jr. .10
28 John Burkett .10

29 John Wetteland .10
30 Benito Santiago .10

1998 Collector's Choice

NM/M
Unopened Fact. Set (540): 15.00
Complete Set (530): 10.00
Common Player: .05
Pack (14): 1.00
Wax Box (36): 15.00
1 Nomar Garciaparra .50
2 Roger Clemens .50
3 Larry Walker .05
4 Mike Piazza .60
5 Mark McGwire .75
6 Tony Gwynn .45
7 Jose Cruz Jr. .05
8 Frank Thomas .40
9 Tino Martinez .05
10 Ken Griffey Jr. .60
11 Barry Bonds .85
12 Scott Rolen .30
13 Randy Johnson .15
14 Ryne Sandberg .35
15 Eddie Murray .15
16 Kevin Brown .05
17 Greg Maddux .35
18 Sandy Alomar Jr. .05
19 Ken Griffey Jr., Adam Riggs Checklist .40
20 Nomar Garciaparra, Charlie O'Brien Checklist .10
21 Ben Grieve, Ken Griffey Jr., Larry Walker, Mark McGwire Checklist .50
22 Mark McGwire, Cal Ripken Jr. Checklist .50
23 Tino Martinez Checklist .05
24 Jason Dickson .05
25 Darin Erstad .25
26 Todd Greene .05
27 Chuck Finley .05
28 Garret Anderson .05
29 Dave Hollins .05
30 Rickey Henderson .60
31 John Smoltz .05
32 Michael Tucker .05
33 Jeff Blauser .05
34 Javier Lopez .05
35 Andruw Jones .60
36 Denny Neagle .05
37 Randall Simon .05
38 Mark Wohlers .05
39 Harold Baines .05
40 Cal Ripken Jr. 1.50
41 Mike Bordick .05
42 Jimmy Key .05
43 Armando Benitez .05
44 Scott Erickson .05
45 Eric Davis .05
46 Bret Saberhagen .05
47 Darren Bragg .05
48 Steve Avery .05
49 Jeff Frye .05
50 Aaron Sele .05
51 Scott Hatteberg .05
52 Tom Gordon .05
53 Kevin Orie .05
54 Kevin Foster .05
55 Ryne Sandberg .75
56 Doug Glanville .05
57 Tyler Houston .05
58 Steve Trachsel .05
59 Mark Grace .05
60 Frank Thomas .60
61 Scott Eyre RC .05
62 Jeff Abbott .05
63 Chris Clemons .05
64 Jorge Fabregas .05
65 Robin Ventura .05
66 Matt Karchner .05

67 Jon Nunnally .05
68 Aaron Boone .05
69 Pokey Reese .05
70 Deion Sanders .10
71 Jeff Shaw .05
72 Eduardo Perez .05
73 Brett Tomko .05
74 Bartolo Colon .05
75 Manny Ramirez .60
76 Jose Mesa .05
77 Brian Giles .05
78 Richie Sexson .05
79 Orel Hershiser .05
80 Matt Williams .05
81 Walt Weiss .05
82 Jerry DiPoto .05
83 Quinton McCracken .05
84 Neifi Perez .05
85 Vinny Castilla .05
86 Ellis Burks .05
87 John Thomson .05
88 Willie Blair .05
89 Bob Hamelin .05
90 Tony Clark .05
91 Todd Jones .05
92 Deivi Cruz .05
93 Frank Catalanotto RC .15
94 Justin Thompson .05
95 Gary Sheffield .25
96 Kevin Brown .05
97 Charles Johnson .05
98 Bobby Bonilla .05
99 Livan Hernandez .05
100 Paul Konerko .10
101 Craig Counsell .05
102 Magglio Ordonez RC 1.00
103 Garrett Stephenson .05
104 Ken Cloude .05
105 Miguel Tejada .25
106 Juan Encarnacion .05
107 Dennis Reyes .05
108 Orlando Cabrera .05
109 Kelvim Escobar .05
110 Ben Grieve .05
111 Brian Rose .05
112 Fernando Tatis .05
113 Tom Evans .05
114 Tom Fordham .05
115 Mark Kotsay .05
116 Mario Valdez .05
117 Jeremi Gonzalez .05
118 Todd Dunwoody .05
119 Javier Valentin .05
120 Todd Helton .50
121 Jason Varitek .10
122 Chris Carpenter .05
123 Kevin Millwood RC .75
124 Brad Fullmer .05
125 Jaret Wright .05
126 Brad Rigby .05
127 Edgar Renteria .05
128 Robb Nen .05
129 Tony Pena .05
130 Craig Biggio .05
131 Brad Ausmus .05
132 Shane Reynolds .05
133 Mike Hampton .05
134 Billy Wagner .05
135 Richard Hidalgo .05
136 Jose Rosado .05
137 Yamil Benitez .05
138 Felix Martinez .05
139 Jeff King .05
140 Jose Offerman .05
141 Joe Vitiello .05
142 Tim Belcher .05
143 Brett Butler .05
144 Greg Gagne .05
145 Mike Piazza 1.00
146 Ramon Martinez .05
147 Raul Mondesi .05
148 Adam Riggs .05
149 Eddie Murray .50
150 Jeff Cirillo .05
151 Scott Karl .05
152 Mike Fetters .05
153 Dave Nilsson .05
154 Antone Williamson .05
155 Jeff D'Amico .05
156 Jose Valentin .05
157 Brad Radke .05
158 Torii Hunter .05
159 Chuck Knoblauch .05
160 Paul Molitor .60
161 Travis Miller .05
162 Rich Robertson .05
163 Ron Coomer .05
164 Mark Grudzielanek .05
165 Lee Smith .05
166 Vladimir Guerrero .60
167 Dustin Hermanson .05
168 Ugueth Urbina .05
169 F.P. Santangelo .05
170 Rondell White .05

171 Bobby Jones .05
172 Edgardo Alfonzo .05
173 John Franco .05
174 Carlos Baerga .05
175 Butch Huskey .05
176 Rey Ordonez .05
177 Matt Franco .05
178 Dwight Gooden .05
179 Chad Curtis .05
180 Tino Martinez .05
181 Charlie O'Brien .05
182 Sandy Alomar Jr. .05
183 Raul Casanova .05
184 Jim Leyritz .05
185 Mike Piazza .60
186 Ivan Rodriguez .25
187 Charles Johnson .05
188 Brad Ausmus .05
189 Brian Johnson .05
190 Wade Boggs .75
191 David Wells .05
192 Tim Raines .05
193 Ramiro Mendoza .05
194 Willie Adams .05
195 Matt Stairs .05
196 Jason McDonald .05
197 Dave Magadan .05
198 Mark Bellhorn .05
199 Ariel Prieto .05
200 Jose Canseco .35
201 Bobby Estalella .05
202 Tony Barron RC .05
203 Midre Cummings .05
204 Ricky Bottalico .05
205 Mike Grace .05
206 Rico Brogna .05
207 Mickey Morandini .05
208 Lou Collier .05
209 Kevin Polcovich RC .05
210 Kevin Young .05
211 Jose Guillen .05
212 Esteban Loaiza .05
213 Marc Wilkins .05
214 Jason Schmidt .05
215 Gary Gaetti .05
216 Fernando Valenzuela .05
217 Willie McGee .05
218 Alan Benes .05
219 Eli Marrero .05
220 Mark McGwire 1.25
221 Matt Morris .05
222 Trevor Hoffman .05
223 Will Cunnane .05
224 Joey Hamilton .05
225 Ken Caminiti .05
226 Derrek Lee .35
227 Mark Sweeney .05
228 Carlos Hernandez .05
229 Brian Johnson .05
230 Jeff Kent .05
231 Kirk Rueter .05
232 Bill Mueller .05
233 Dante Powell .05
234 J.T. Snow .05
235 Shawn Estes .05
236 Dennis Martinez .05
237 Jamie Moyer .05
238 Dan Wilson .05
239 Joey Cora .05
240 Ken Griffey Jr. 1.00
241 Paul Sorrento .05
242 Jay Buhner .05
243 Hanley Frias RC .05
244 John Burkett .05
245 Juan Gonzalez .30
246 Rick Helling .05
247 Darren Oliver .05
248 Mickey Tettleton .05
249 Ivan Rodriguez .45
250 Joe Carter .05
251 Pat Hentgen .05
252 Marty Janzen .05
253 Frank Thomas, Tony Gwynn .25
254 Mark McGwire, Ken Griffey Jr., Larry Walker .50
255 Ken Griffey Jr., Andres Galarraga .40
256 Brian Hunter, Tony Womack .05
257 Roger Clemens, Denny Neagle .10
258 Roger Clemens, Curt Schilling .30
259 Roger Clemens, Pedro J. Martinez .25
260 Randy Myers, Jeff Shaw .05
261 Nomar Garciaparra, Scott Rolen .25
262 Charlie O'Brien .05
263 Shannon Stewart .05
264 Robert Person .05
265 Carlos Delgado .25

266	Matt Williams, Travis Lee Checklist	.05
267	Nomar Garciaparra, Cal Ripken Jr. Checklist	.50
268	Mark McGwire, Mike Piazza Checklist	.50
269	Tony Gwynn, Ken Griffey Jr. Checklist	.40
270	Fred McGriff, Jose Cruz Jr. Checklist	.05
271	Andruw Jones	.25
272	Alex Rodriguez	.65
273	Juan Gonzalez	.15
274	Nomar Garciaparra	.50
275	Ken Griffey Jr.	.60
276	Tino Martinez	.05
277	Roger Clemens	.40
278	Barry Bonds	.85
279	Mike Piazza	.60
280	Tim Salmon	.05
281	Gary DiSarcina	.05
282	Cecil Fielder	.05
283	Ken Hill	.05
284	Troy Percival	.05
285	Jim Edmonds	.05
286	Allen Watson	.05
287	Brian Anderson	.05
288	Jay Bell	.05
289	Jorge Fabregas	.05
290	Devon White	.05
291	Yamil Benitez	.05
292	Jeff Suppan	.05
293	Tony Batista	.05
294	Brent Brede	.05
295	Andy Benes	.05
296	Felix Rodriguez	.05
297	Karim Garcia	.05
298	Omar Daal	.05
299	Andy Stankiewicz	.05
300	Matt Williams	.05
301	Willie Blair	.05
302	Ryan Klesko	.05
303	Tom Glavine	.25
304	Walt Weiss	.05
305	Greg Maddux	.75
306	Chipper Jones	.75
307	Keith Lockhart	.05
308	Andres Galarraga	.05
309	Chris Hoiles	.05
310	Roberto Alomar	.25
311	Joe Carter	.05
312	Doug Drabek	.05
313	Jeffrey Hammonds	.05
314	Rafael Palmeiro	.40
315	Mike Mussina	.40
316	Brady Anderson	.05
317	B.J. Surhoff	.05
318	Dennis Eckersley	.45
319	Jim Leyritz	.05
320	Mo Vaughn	.05
321	Nomar Garciaparra	.75
322	Reggie Jefferson	.05
323	Tim Naehring	.05
324	Troy O'Leary	.05
325	Pedro J. Martinez	.50
326	John Valentin	.05
327	Mark Clark	.05
328	Rod Beck	.05
329	Mickey Morandini	.05
330	Sammy Sosa	.75
331	Jeff Blauser	.05
332	Lance Johnson	.05
333	Scott Servais	.05
334	Kevin Tapani	.05
335	Henry Rodriguez	.05
336	Jaime Navarro	.05
337	Benji Gil	.05
338	James Baldwin	.05
339	Mike Cameron	.05
340	Ray Durham	.05
341	Chris Snopek	.05
342	Eddie Taubensee	.05
343	Bret Boone	.05
344	Willie Greene	.05
345	Barry Larkin	.05
346	Chris Stynes	.05
347	Pete Harnisch	.05
348	Dave Burba	.05
349	Sandy Alomar Jr.	.05
350	Kenny Lofton	.05
351	Geronimo Berroa	.05
352	Omar Vizquel	.05
353	Travis Fryman	.05
354	Dwight Gooden	.05
355	Jim Thome	.40
356	David Justice	.05
357	Charles Nagy	.05
358	Chad Ogea	.05
359	Pedro Astacio	.05
360	Larry Walker	.05
361	Mike Lansing	.05
362	Kirt Manwaring	.05
363	Dante Bichette	.05
364	Jamey Wright	.05

365	Darryl Kile	.05
366	Luis Gonzalez	.05
367	Joe Randa	.05
368	Raul Casanova	.05
369	Damion Easley	.05
370	Brian L. Hunter	.05
371	Bobby Higginson	.05
372	Brian Moehler	.05
373	Scott Sanders	.05
374	Jim Eisenreich	.05
375	Derrek Lee	.35
376	Jay Powell	.05
377	Cliff Floyd	.05
378	Alex Fernandez	.05
379	Felix Heredia	.05
380	Jeff Bagwell	.60
381	Bill Spiers	.05
382	Chris Holt	.05
383	Carl Everett	.05
384	Derek Bell	.05
385	Moises Alou	.05
386	Ramon Garcia	.05
387	Mike Sweeney	.05
388	Glendon Rusch	.05
389	Kevin Appier	.05
390	Dean Palmer	.05
391	Jeff Conine	.05
392	Johnny Damon	.25
393	Jose Vizcaino	.05
394	Todd Hollandsworth	.05
395	Eric Karros	.05
396	Todd Zeile	.05
397	Chan Ho Park	.05
398	Ismael Valdes	.05
399	Eric Young	.05
400	Hideo Nomo	.25
401	Mark Loretta	.05
402	Doug Jones	.05
403	Jeromy Burnitz	.05
404	John Jaha	.05
405	Marquis Grissom	.05
406	Mike Matheny	.05
407	Todd Walker	.05
408	Marty Cordova	.05
409	Matt Lawton	.05
410	Terry Steinbach	.05
411	Pat Meares	.05
412	Rick Aguilera	.05
413	Otis Nixon	.05
414	Derrick May	.05
415	Carl Pavano	.05
416	A.J. Hinch	.05
417	David Dellucci RC	.10
418	Bruce Chen	.05
419	Darron Ingram RC	.05
420	Sean Casey	.20
421	Mark L. Johnson	.05
422	Gabe Alvarez	.05
423	Alex Gonzalez	.05
424	Daryle Ward	.05
425	Russell Branyan	.05
426	Mike Caruso	.05
427	Mike Kinkade RC	.20
428	Ramon Hernandez	.05
429	Matt Clement	.05
430	Travis Lee	.05
431	Shane Monahan	.05
432	Rich Butler RC	.05
433	Chris Widger	.05
434	Jose Vidro	.05
435	Carlos Perez	.05
436	Ryan McGuire	.05
437	Brian McRae	.05
438	Al Leiter	.05
439	Rich Becker	.05
440	Todd Hundley	.05
441	Dave Mlicki	.05
442	Bernard Gilkey	.05
443	John Olerud	.05
444	Paul O'Neill	.05
445	Andy Pettitte	.30
446	David Cone	.05
447	Chili Davis	.05
448	Bernie Williams	.05
449	Joe Girardi	.05
450	Derek Jeter	1.50
451	Mariano Rivera	.20
452	George Williams	.05
453	Kenny Rogers	.05
454	Tom Candiotti	.05
455	Rickey Henderson	.60
456	Jason Giambi	.40
457	Scott Spiezio	.05
458	Doug Glanville	.05
459	Desi Relaford	.05
460	Curt Schilling	.20
461	Bob Abreu	.10
462	Gregg Jefferies	.05
463	Scott Rolen	.40
464	Mike Lieberthal	.05
465	Tony Womack	.05
466	Jermaine Allensworth	.05
467	Francisco Cordova	.05
468	Jon Lieber	.05

469	Al Martin	.05
470	Jason Kendall	.05
471	Todd Stottlemyre	.05
472	Royce Clayton	.05
473	Brian Jordan	.05
474	John Mabry	.05
475	Ray Lankford	.05
476	Delino DeShields	.05
477	Ron Gant	.05
478	Mark Langston	.05
479	Steve Finley	.05
480	Tony Gwynn	.75
481	Andy Ashby	.05
482	Wally Joyner	.05
483	Greg Vaughn	.05
484	Sterling Hitchcock	.05
485	J. Kevin Brown	.05
486	Orel Hershiser	.05
487	Charlie Hayes	.05
488	Darryl Hamilton	.05
489	Mark Gardner	.05
490	Barry Bonds	1.50
491	Robb Nen	.05
492	Kirk Rueter	.05
493	Randy Johnson	.50
494	Jeff Fassero	.05
495	Alex Rodriguez	1.25
496	David Segui	.05
497	Rich Amaral	.05
498	Russ Davis	.05
499	Bubba Trammell	.05
500	Wade Boggs	.75
501	Roberto Hernandez	.05
502	Dave Martinez	.05
503	Dennis Springer	.05
504	Paul Sorrento	.05
505	Wilson Alvarez	.05
506	Mike Kelly	.05
507	Albie Lopez	.05
508	Tony Saunders	.05
509	John Flaherty	.05
510	Fred McGriff	.05
511	Quinton McCracken	.05
512	Terrell Wade	.05
513	Kevin Stocker	.05
514	Kevin Elster	.05
515	Will Clark	.05
516	Bobby Witt	.05
517	Tom Goodwin	.05
518	Aaron Sele	.05
519	Lee Stevens	.05
520	Rusty Greer	.05
521	John Wetteland	.05
522	Darrin Fletcher	.05
523	Jose Canseco	.35
524	Randy Myers	.05
525	Jose Cruz Jr.	.05
526	Shawn Green	.15
527	Tony Fernandez	.05
528	Alex Gonzalez	.05
529	Ed Sprague	.05
530	Roger Clemens	.85

Cover Glory 5x7

		NM/M
Complete Set (10):		10.00
Common Player:		1.00
1	Nomar Garciaparra	1.50
2	Roger Clemens	2.00
3	Larry Walker	1.00
4	Mike Piazza	2.50
5	Mark McGwire	3.00
6	Tony Gwynn	1.50
7	Jose Cruz Jr.	1.00
8	Frank Thomas	1.25
9	Tino Martinez	1.00
10	Ken Griffey Jr.	2.50

Evolution Revolution

	NM/M
Complete Set (28):	36.00
Common Player:	.40

Inserted 1:13

1	Tim Salmon	.40
2	Greg Maddux	2.50
3	Cal Ripken Jr.	6.00
4	Mo Vaughn	.40
5	Sammy Sosa	2.50
6	Frank Thomas	1.50
7	Barry Larkin	.40
8	Jim Thome	.65
9	Larry Walker	.40
10	Travis Fryman	.40
11	Gary Sheffield	.65
12	Jeff Bagwell	1.50
13	Johnny Damon	.65
14	Mike Piazza	4.00
15	Jeff Cirillo	.40
16	Paul Molitor	1.50
17	Vladimir Guerrero	1.50
18	Todd Hundley	.40
19	Tino Martinez	.40
20	Jose Canseco	.65
21	Scott Rolen	.75
22	Al Martin	.40
23	Mark McGwire	5.00
24	Tony Gwynn	2.50
25	Barry Bonds	6.00
26	Ken Griffey Jr.	4.00
27	Juan Gonzalez	.75
28	Roger Clemens	3.00

Mini Bobbing Heads

		NM/M
Complete Set (30):		20.00
Common Player:		.25
Inserted 1:3		
1	Tim Salmon	.25
2	Travis Lee	.25
3	Matt Williams	.25
4	Chipper Jones	1.00
5	Greg Maddux	1.00
6	Cal Ripken Jr.	2.50
7	Nomar Garciaparra	1.00
8	Mo Vaughn	.25
9	Sammy Sosa	1.00
10	Frank Thomas	.75
11	Kenny Lofton	.25
12	Jaret Wright	.25
13	Larry Walker	.25
14	Tony Clark	.25
15	Edgar Renteria	.25
16	Jeff Bagwell	.75
17	Mike Piazza	1.50
18	Vladimir Guerrero	.75
19	Derek Jeter	2.50
20	Ben Grieve	.25
21	Scott Rolen	.50
22	Mark McGwire	2.00
23	Tony Gwynn	1.00
24	Barry Bonds	2.50
25	Ken Griffey Jr.	1.50
26	Alex Rodriguez	2.00
27	Fred McGriff	.25
28	Juan Gonzalez	.40
29	Roger Clemens	1.25
30	Jose Cruz Jr.	.25

Rookie Class: Prime Choice

		NM/M
Complete Set (18):		30.00
Common Player:		2.00
415	Carl Pavano	2.00
416	A.J. Hinch	2.00
417	David Dellucci	2.00
418	Bruce Chen	2.00
419	Darron Ingram	2.00
420	Sean Casey	5.00
421	Mark L. Johnson	2.00
422	Gabe Alvarez	2.00
423	Alex Gonzalez	2.00
424	Daryle Ward	2.00

rookie class

alex gonzalez

425	Russell Branyan	2.00
426	Mike Caruso	2.00
427	Mike Kinkade	2.00
428	Ramon Hernandez	2.00
429	Matt Clement	2.00
430	Travis Lee	2.50
431	Shane Monahan	2.00
432	Rich Butler	2.00

StarQuest - Series 1

		NM/M
Complete Set (90):		185.00
Common Special Delivery (1-45):		.25
Inserted 1:1		
Common Student of the Game (46-65):		.75
Inserted 1:21		
Common Super Power (66-80):		2.00
Inserted 1:71		
Common Superstar Domain (81-90):		3.00
Inserted 1:145		
1	Nomar Garciaparra	1.50
2	Scott Rolen	.75
3	Jason Dickson	.25
4	Jaret Wright	.25
5	Kevin Orie	.25
6	Jose Guillen	.25
7	Matt Morris	.25
8	Mike Cameron	.25
9	Kevin Polcovich	.25
10	Jose Cruz Jr.	.25
11	Miguel Tejada	.40
12	Fernando Tatis	.25
13	Todd Helton	.65
14	Ken Cloude	.25
15	Ben Grieve	.25
16	Dante Powell	.25
17	Bubba Trammell	.25
18	Juan Encarnacion	.25
19	Derrek Lee	.50
20	Paul Konerko	.35
21	Richard Hidalgo	.25
22	Denny Neagle	.25
23	David Justice	.25
24	Pedro J. Martinez	1.00
25	Greg Maddux	1.50
26	Edgar Martinez	.25
27	Cal Ripken Jr.	2.50
28	Tim Salmon	.25
29	Shawn Estes	.25
30	Ken Griffey Jr.	2.00
31	Brad Radke	.25
32	Andy Pettitte	.40
33	Curt Schilling	.50
34	Raul Mondesi	.25
35	Alex Rodriguez	2.25
36	Jeff Kent	.25
37	Jeff Bagwell	1.00
38	Juan Gonzalez	.50
39	Barry Bonds	2.50
40	Mark McGwire	2.00
41	Frank Thomas	1.00
42	Ray Lankford	.25
43	Tony Gwynn	1.50
44	Mike Piazza	1.75
45	Tino Martinez	.25
46	Nomar Garciaparra	3.00
47	Paul Molitor	1.50
48	Chuck Knoblauch	.75
49	Rusty Greer	.75
50	Cal Ripken Jr.	6.00
51	Roberto Alomar	1.00
52	Scott Rolen	1.00
53	Derek Jeter	6.00
54	Mark Grace	.75
55	Randy Johnson	1.50
56	Craig Biggio	.75
57	Kenny Lofton	.75
58	Eddie Murray	1.50

59	Ryne Sandberg	2.00
60	Rickey Henderson	1.50
61	Darin Erstad	1.00
62	Jim Edmonds	.75
63	Ken Caminiti	.75
64	Ivan Rodriguez	1.25
65	Tony Gwynn	2.00
66	Tony Clark	2.00
67	Andres Galarraga	2.00
68	Rafael Palmeiro	3.00
69	Manny Ramirez	6.00
70	Albert Belle	2.00
71	Jay Buhner	2.00
72	Mo Vaughn	2.00
73	Barry Bonds	15.00
74	Chipper Jones	7.50
75	Jeff Bagwell	6.00
76	Jim Thome	3.00
77	Sammy Sosa	7.50
78	Todd Hundley	2.00
79	Matt Williams	2.00
80	Vinny Castilla	2.00
81	Jose Cruz Jr.	3.00
82	Frank Thomas	7.50
83	Juan Gonzalez	4.00
84	Mike Piazza	15.00
85	Alex Rodriguez	20.00
86	Larry Walker	3.00
87	Tino Martinez	3.00
88	Greg Maddux	12.50
89	Mark McGwire	20.00
90	Ken Griffey Jr.	15.00

StarQuest - Series 2

TONY GWYNN

		NM/M
Complete Set (30):		17.50
Common Player:		.25
Singles 1:1		
Doubles 1:21		2X
Triples 1:71		6X
Home Runs:		15X
1	Ken Griffey Jr.	1.25
2	Jose Cruz Jr.	.25
3	Cal Ripken Jr.	2.00
4	Roger Clemens	1.00
5	Frank Thomas	.75
6	Derek Jeter	2.00
7	Alex Rodriguez	1.50
8	Andruw Jones	.75
9	Vladimir Guerrero	.75
10	Mark McGwire	1.50
11	Kenny Lofton	.25
12	Pedro J. Martinez	.75
13	Greg Maddux	1.00
14	Larry Walker	.25
15	Barry Bonds	2.00
16	Chipper Jones	1.00
17	Jeff Bagwell	.75
18	Juan Gonzalez	.50
19	Tony Gwynn	1.00
20	Mike Piazza	1.25
21	Tino Martinez	.25
22	Mo Vaughn	.20
23	Ben Grieve	.25
24	Scott Rolen	.60
25	Nomar Garciaparra	1.00
26	Paul Konerko	.35
27	Jaret Wright	.25
28	Gary Sheffield	.50
29	Travis Lee	.25
30	Todd Helton	.65

Stickums

		NM/M
Complete Set (30):		7.00
Common Player:		.10
Inserted 1:3		
1	Andruw Jones	.35
2	Chipper Jones	.45
3	Cal Ripken Jr.	1.00
4	Nomar Garciaparra	.45
5	Mo Vaughn	.10

ALBERT BELLE

STICK-UMS Baseball

6	Ryne Sandberg	.45
7	Sammy Sosa	.45
8	Frank Thomas	.35
9	Albert Belle	.10
10	Jim Thome	.30
11	Manny Ramirez	.35
12	Larry Walker	.10
13	Gary Sheffield	.20
14	Jeff Bagwell	.35
15	Mike Piazza	.60
16	Paul Molitor	.35
17	Pedro J. Martinez	.35
18	Todd Hundley	.10
19	Derek Jeter	1.00
20	Tino Martinez	.10
21	Curt Schilling	.25
22	Mark McGwire	.75
23	Tony Gwynn	.45
24	Barry Bonds	1.00
25	Ken Griffey Jr.	.60
26	Alex Rodriguez	.75
27	Juan Gonzalez	.20
28	Ivan Rodriguez	.30
29	Roger Clemens	.50
30	Jose Cruz Jr.	.10

D

1981 Donruss

Reds

TOM SEAVER PITCHER

		NM/M
Complete Set (605):		
Uncut Sheet Set (5):		
Common Player:		.06
Wax Pack (18):		
Wax Box (36):		
1	Ozzie Smith	1.50
2	Rollie Fingers	.70
3	Rick Wise	.06
4	Gene Richards	.06
5	Alan Trammell	.08
6	Tom Brookens	.06
7a	Duffy Dyer (1980 Avg. .185)	.20
7b	Duffy Dyer (1980 Avg. 185)	.06
8	Mark Fidrych	.11
9	Dave Rozema	.06
10	Ricky Peters	.06
11	Mike Schmidt	2.25
12	Willie Stargell	.90
13	Tim Foli	.06
14	Manny Sanguillen	.06
15	Grant Jackson	.06
16	Eddie Solomon	.06
17	Omar Moreno	.06
18	Joe Morgan	.90

19	Rafael Landestoy	.06
20	Bruce Bochy	.06
21	Joe Sambito	.06
22	Manny Trillo	.06
23a	Dave Smith **RC** (Incomplete box around stats.)	.08
23b	Dave Smith **RC** (Complete box around stats.)	.11
24	Terry Puhl	.06
25	Bump Wills	.06
26a	John Ellis (Danny Walton photo - with bat.)	.25
26b	John Ellis (John Ellis photo - with glove.)	.06
27	Jim Kern	.06
28	Richie Zisk	.06
29	John Mayberry	.06
30	Bob Davis	.06
31	Jackson Todd	.06
32	Al Woods	.06
33	Steve Carlton	1.25
34	Lee Mazzilli	.06
35	John Stearns	.06
36	Roy Jackson	.06
37	Mike Scott	.06
38	Lamar Johnson	.06
39	Kevin Bell	.06
40	Ed Farmer	.06
41	Ross Baumgarten	.06
42	Leo Sutherland	.06
43	Dan Meyer	.06
44	Ron Reed	.06
45	Mario Mendoza	.06
46	Rick Honeycutt	.06
47	Glenn Abbott	.06
48	Leon Roberts	.06
49	Rod Carew	1.25
50	Bert Campaneris	.06
51a	Tom Donahue (Incorrect spelling.)	.20
51b	Tom Donohue (Donohue on front.)	.06
52	Dave Frost	.06
53	Ed Halicki	.06
54	Dan Ford	.06
55	Garry Maddox	.06
56a	Steve Garvey (Surpassed 25 HR.)	.90
56b	Steve Garvey (Surpassed 21 HR.)	.45
57	Bill Russell	.06
58	Don Sutton	.70
59	Reggie Smith	.06
60	Rick Monday	.06
61	Ray Knight	.08
62	Johnny Bench	1.25
63	Mario Soto	.06
64	Doug Bair	.06
65	George Foster	.08
66	Jeff Burroughs	.06
67	Keith Hernandez	.08
68	Tom Herr	.06
69	Bob Forsch	.06
70	John Fulgham	.06
71a	Bobby Bonds (Lifetime HR 986.)	.25
71b	Bobby Bonds (Lifetime HR 326.)	.11
72a	Rennie Stennett ("...breaking broke leg..." on back)	.20
72b	Rennie Stennett ("...breaking leg..." on back)	.06
73	Joe Strain	.06
74	Ed Whitson	.06
75	Tom Griffin	.06
76	Bill North	.06
77	Gene Garber	.06
78	Mike Hargrove	.06
79	Dave Rosello	.06
80	Ron Hassey	.06
81	Sid Monge	.06
82a	Joe Charboneau **RC** ("For some reason, Phillies..." on back.)	1.50
82b	Joe Charboneau **RC** ("Phillies..." on back.)	.20
83	Cecil Cooper	.06
84	Sal Bando	.06
85	Moose Haas	.06
86	Mike Caldwell	.06
87a	Larry Hisle ("...Twins with 28 RBI." on back.)	.20
87b	Larry Hisle ("...Twins with 28 HR" on back.)	.06
88	Luis Gomez	.06
89	Larry Parrish	.06
90	Gary Carter	.90
91	Bill Gullickson **RC**	.11

#	Player	Price
92	Fred Norman	.06
93	Tommy Hutton	.06
94	Carl Yastrzemski	1.25
95	Glenn Hoffman	.06
96	Dennis Eckersley	.90
97a	Tom Burgmeier (Throws: Right)	.20
97b	Tom Burgmeier (Throws: Left)	.06
98	Win Remmerswaal	.06
99	Bob Horner	.06
100	George Brett	2.25
101	Dave Chalk	.06
102	Dennis Leonard	.06
103	Renie Martin	.06
104	Amos Otis	.06
105	Graig Nettles	.11
106	Eric Soderholm	.06
107	Tommy John	.08
108	Tom Underwood	.06
109	Lou Piniella	.11
110	Mickey Klutts	.06
111	Bobby Murcer	.06
112	Eddie Murray	1.25
113	Rick Dempsey	.06
114	Scott McGregor	.06
115	Ken Singleton	.06
116	Gary Roenicke	.06
117	Dave Revering	.06
118	Mike Norris	.06
119	Rickey Henderson	1.50
120	Mike Heath	.06
121	Dave Cash	.06
122	Randy Jones	.06
123	Eric Rasmussen	.06
124	Jerry Mumphrey	.06
125	Richie Hebner	.06
126	Mark Wagner	.06
127	Jack Morris	.08
128	Dan Petry	.06
129	Bruce Robbins	.06
130	Champ Summers	.06
131a	Pete Rose ("See card 251" on back.)	1.50
131b	Pete Rose ("See card 371" on back.)	1.50
132	Willie Stargell	.90
133	Ed Ott	.06
134	Jim Bibby	.06
135	Bert Blyleven	.08
136	Dave Parker	.08
137	Bill Robinson	.06
138	Enos Cabell	.06
139	Dave Bergman	.06
140	J.R. Richard	.08
141	Ken Forsch	.06
142	Larry Bowa	.08
143	Frank LaCorte (Photo actually Randy Niemann.)	.06
144	Dennis Walling	.06
145	Buddy Bell	.08
146	Fergie Jenkins	.70
147	Danny Darwin	.06
148	John Grubb	.06
149	Alfredo Griffin	.06
150	Jerry Garvin	.06
151	Paul Mirabella RC	.06
152	Rick Bosetti	.06
153	Dick Ruthven	.06
154	Frank Taveras	.06
155	Craig Swan	.06
156	Jeff Reardon RC	.70
157	Steve Henderson	.06
158	Jim Morrison	.06
159	Glenn Borgmann	.06
160	Lamarr Hoyt (LaMarr) RC	.08
161	Rich Wortham	.06
162	Thad Bosley	.06
163	Julio Cruz	.06
164a	Del Unser (No 3B in stat heads.)	.20
164b	Del Unser (3B in stat heads)	.06
165	Jim Anderson	.06
166	Jim Beattie	.06
167	Shane Rawley	.06
168	Joe Simpson	.06
169	Rod Carew	1.25
170	Fred Patek	.06
171	Frank Tanana	.06
172	Alfredo Martinez	.06
173	Chris Knapp	.06
174	Joe Rudi	.06
175	Greg Luzinski	.06
176	Steve Garvey	.45
177	Joe Ferguson	.06
178	Bob Welch	.06
179	Dusty Baker	.08
180	Rudy Law	.06
181	Dave Concepcion	.06
182	Johnny Bench	1.25
183	Mike LaCoss	.06
184	Ken Griffey	.08
185	Dave Collins	.06
186	Brian Asselstine	.06
187	Garry Templeton	.06
188	Mike Phillips	.06
189	Pete Vukovich	.06
190	John Urrea	.06
191	Tony Scott	.06
192	Darrell Evans	.08
193	Milt May	.06
194	Bob Knepper	.06
195	Randy Moffitt	.06
196	Larry Herndon	.06
197	Rick Camp	.06
198	Andre Thornton	.06
199	Tom Veryzer	.06
200	Gary Alexander	.06
201	Rick Waits	.06
202	Rick Manning	.06
203	Paul Molitor	.90
204	Jim Gantner	.06
205	Paul Mitchell	.06
206	Reggie Cleveland	.06
207	Sixto Lezcano	.06
208	Bruce Benedict	.06
209	Rodney Scott	.06
210	John Tamargo	.06
211	Bill Lee	.06
212	Andre Dawson	.60
213	Rowland Office	.06
214	Carl Yastrzemski	1.25
215	Jerry Remy	.06
216	Mike Torrez	.06
217	Skip Lockwood	.06
218	Fred Lynn	.06
219	Chris Chambliss	.06
220	Willie Aikens	.06
221	John Wathan	.06
222	Dan Quisenberry	.06
223	Willie Wilson	.08
224	Clint Hurdle	.06
225	Bob Watson	.06
226	Jim Spencer	.06
227	Ron Guidry	.11
228	Reggie Jackson	1.50
229	Oscar Gamble	.06
230	Jeff Cox	.06
231	Luis Tiant	.06
232	Rich Dauer	.06
233	Dan Graham	.06
234	Mike Flanagan	.06
235	John Lowenstein	.06
236	Benny Ayala	.06
237	Wayne Gross	.06
238	Rick Langford	.06
239	Tony Armas	.06
240a	Bob Lacy (Incorrect spelling.)	.20
240b	Bob Lacey (Correct spelling.)	.06
241	Gene Tenace	.06
242	Bob Shirley	.06
243	Gary Lucas	.06
244	Jerry Turner	.06
245	John Wockenfuss	.06
246	Stan Papi	.06
247	Milt Wilcox	.06
248	Dan Schatzeder	.06
249	Steve Kemp	.06
250	Jim Lentine	.06
251	Pete Rose	1.50
252	Bill Madlock	.08
253	Dale Berra	.06
254	Kent Tekulve	.06
255	Enrique Romo	.06
256	Mike Easler	.06
257	Chuck Tanner	.06
258	Art Howe	.08
259	Alan Ashby	.06
260	Nolan Ryan	3.75
261a	Vern Ruhle (Ken Forsch photo - head shot.)	.20
261b	Vern Ruhle (Vern Ruhle photo - waist to head shot.)	.08
262	Bob Boone	.08
263	Cesar Cedeno	.06
264	Jeff Leonard	.06
265	Pat Putnam	.06
266	Jon Matlack	.06
267	Dave Rajsich	.06
268	Billy Sample	.06
269	Damaso Garcia RC	.08
270	Tom Buskey	.06
271	Joey McLaughlin	.06
272	Barry Bonnell	.06
273	Tug McGraw	.08
274	Mike Jorgensen	.06
275	Pat Zachry	.06
276	Neil Allen	.06
277	Joel Youngblood	.06
278	Greg Pryor	.06
279	Britt Burns RC	.08
280	Rich Dotson RC	.20
281	Chet Lemon	.06
282	Rusty Kuntz	.06
283	Ted Cox	.06
284	Sparky Lyle	.06
285	Larry Cox	.06
286	Floyd Bannister	.06
287	Byron McLaughlin	.06
288	Rodney Craig	.06
289	Bobby Grich	.06
290	Dickie Thon	.06
291	Mark Clear	.06
292	Dave Lemanczyk	.06
293	Jason Thompson	.06
294	Rick Miller	.06
295	Lonnie Smith	.06
296	Ron Cey	.06
297	Steve Yeager	.06
298	Bobby Castillo	.06
299	Manny Mota	.06
300	Jay Johnstone	.06
301	Dan Driessen	.06
302	Joe Nolan	.06
303	Paul Householder	.06
304	Harry Spilman	.06
305	Cesar Geronimo	.06
306a	Gary Mathews (Mathews on front.)	.25
306b	Gary Matthews (Matthews on front.)	.06
307	Ken Reitz	.06
308	Ted Simmons	.06
309	John Littlefield	.06
310	George Frazier	.06
311	Dane Iorg	.06
312	Mike Ivie	.06
313	Dennis Littlejohn	.06
314	Gary LaVelle (Lavelle)	.06
315	Jack Clark	.08
316	Jim Wohlford	.06
317	Rick Matula	.06
318	Toby Harrah	.06
319a	Dwane Kuiper (Dwane on front.)	.20
319b	Duane Kuiper (Duane on front.)	.06
320	Len Barker	.06
321	Victor Cruz	.06
322	Dell Alston	.06
323	Robin Yount	.90
324	Charlie Moore	.06
325	Lary Sorensen	.06
326a	Gorman Thomas ("...30-HR mark 4th..." on back)	.20
326b	Gorman Thomas ("...30-HR mark 3rd..." on back)	.06
327	Bob Rodgers	.06
328	Phil Niekro	.70
329	Chris Speier	.06
330a	Steve Rodgers (Rodgers on front.)	.20
330b	Steve Rogers (Rogers on front.)	.06
331	Woodie Fryman	.06
332	Warren Cromartie	.06
333	Jerry White	.06
334	Tony Perez	.90
335	Carlton Fisk	.90
336	Dick Drago	.06
337	Steve Renko	.06
338	Jim Rice	.60
339	Jerry Royster	.06
340	Frank White	.06
341	Jamie Quirk	.06
342a	Paul Spittorff (Spittorff on front.)	.20
342b	Paul Splittorff (Splittorff on front.)	.06
343	Marty Pattin	.06
344	Pete LaCock	.06
345	Willie Randolph	.06
346	Rick Cerone	.06
347	Rich Gossage	.08
348	Reggie Jackson	1.50
349	Ruppert Jones	.06
350	Dave McKay	.06
351	Yogi Berra	.40
352	Doug Decinces (DeCinces)	.08
353	Jim Palmer	.90
354	Tippy Martinez	.06
355	Al Bumbry	.06
356	Earl Weaver	.40
357a	Bob Picciolo (Bob on front.)	.20
357b	Rob Picciolo (Rob on front.)	.06
358	Matt Keough	.06
359	Dwayne Murphy	.06
360	Brian Kingman	.06
361	Bill Fahey	.06
362	Steve Mura	.06
363	Dennis Kinney	.06
364	Dave Winfield	.90
365	Lou Whitaker	.08
366	Lance Parrish	.08
367	Tim Corcoran	.06
368	Pat Underwood	.06
369	Al Cowens	.06
370	Sparky Anderson	.40
371	Pete Rose	2.25
372	Phil Garner	.06
373	Steve Nicosia	.06
374	John Candelaria	.06
375	Don Robinson	.06
376	Lee Lacy	.06
377	John Milner	.06
378	Craig Reynolds	.06
379a	Luis Pujols (Pujols on front.)	.20
379b	Luis Pujols (Pujols on front.)	.06
380	Joe Niekro	.06
381	Joaquin Andujar	.06
382	Keith Moreland RC	.11
383	Jose Cruz	.06
384	Bill Virdon	.06
385	Jim Sundberg	.06
386	Doc Medich	.06
387	Al Oliver	.08
388	Jim Norris	.06
389	Bob Bailor	.06
390	Ernie Whitt	.06
391	Otto Velez	.06
392	Roy Howell	.06
393	Bob Walk RC	.08
394	Doug Flynn	.06
395	Pete Falcone	.06
396	Tom Hausman	.06
397	Elliott Maddox	.06
398	Mike Squires	.06
399	Marvis Foley	.06
400	Steve Trout	.06
401	Wayne Nordhagen	.06
402	Tony Larussa (LaRussa)	.08
403	Bruce Bochte	.06
404	Bake McBride	.06
405	Jerry Narron	.06
406	Rob Dressler	.06
407	Dave Heaverlo	.06
408	Tom Paciorek	.06
409	Carney Lansford	.06
410	Brian Downing	.06
411	Don Aase	.06
412	Jim Barr	.06
413	Don Baylor	.08
414	Jim Fregosi	.06
415	Dallas Green	.06
416	Dave Lopes	.06
417	Jerry Reuss	.06
418	Rick Sutcliffe	.08
419	Derrel Thomas	.06
420	Tommy LaSorda (Lasorda)	.40
421	Charlie Leibrandt RC	.20
422	Tom Seaver	1.25
423	Ron Oester	.06
424	Junior Kennedy	.06
425	Tom Seaver	1.25
426	Bobby Cox	.08
427	Leon Durham RC	.15
428	Terry Kennedy	.06
429	Silvio Martinez	.06
430	George Hendrick	.06
431	Red Schoendienst	.40
432	John LeMaster	.06
433	Vida Blue	.08
434	John Montefusco	.06
435	Terry Whitfield	.06
436	Dave Bristol	.06
437	Dale Murphy	.60
438	Jerry Dybzinski	.06
439	Jorge Orta	.06
440	Wayne Garland	.06
441	Miguel Dilone	.06
442	Dave Garcia	.06
443	Don Money	.06
444a	Buck Martinez (Photo reversed.)	.25
444b	Buck Martinez (Photo correct.)	.08
445	Jerry Augustine	.06
446	Ben Oglivie	.06
447	Jim Slaton	.06
448	Doyle Alexander	.06
449	Tony Bernazard	.06
450	Scott Sanderson	.06
451	Dave Palmer	.06
452	Stan Bahnsen	.06
453	Dick Williams	.06
454	Rick Burleson	.06
455	Gary Allenson	.06
456	Bob Stanley	.06
457a	John Tudor RC (Lifetime W/L 9.7.)	.30
457b	John Tudor RC (Lifetime W/L 9-7.)	.15
458	Dwight Evans	.08

459	Glenn Hubbard	.06
460	U L Washington	.06
461	Larry Gura	.06
462	Rich Gale	.06
463	Hal McRae	.06
464	Jim Frey	.06
465	Bucky Dent	.06
466	Dennis Werth	.06
467	Ron Davis	.06
468	Reggie Jackson	2.00
469	Bobby Brown	.08
470	Mike Davis **RC**	.08
471	Gaylord Perry	.90
472	Mark Belanger	.06
473	Jim Palmer	.90
474	Sammy Stewart	.06
475	Tim Stoddard	.06
476	Steve Stone	.08
477	Jeff Newman	.06
478	Steve McCatty	.06
479	Billy Martin	.08
480	Mitchell Page	.06
481	Steve Carlton (CY)	.30
482	Bill Buckner	.08
483a	Ivan DeJesus (Lifetime hits 702.)	.20
483b	Ivan DeJesus (Lifetime hits 642.)	.06
484	Cliff Johnson	.06
485	Lenny Randle	.06
486	Larry Milbourne	.06
487	Roy Smalley	.06
488	John Castino	.06
489	Ron Jackson	.06
490a	Dave Roberts (1980 highlights begins "Showed pop...")	.20
490b	Dave Roberts (1980 highlights begins "Declared himself...")	.06
491	George Brett (MVP)	1.25
492	Mike Cubbage	.06
493	Rob Wilfong	.06
494	Danny Goodwin	.06
495	Jose Morales	.06
496	Mickey Rivers	.06
497	Mike Edwards	.06
498	Mike Sadek	.06
499	Lenn Sakata	.06
500	Gene Michael	.06
501	Dave Roberts	.06
502	Steve Dillard	.06
503	Jim Essian	.06
504	Rance Mulliniks	.06
505	Darrell Porter	.06
506	Joe Torre	.40
507	Terry Crowley	.06
508	Bill Travers	.06
509	Nelson Norman	.06
510	Bob McClure	.06
511	Steve Howe **RC**	.11
512	Dave Rader	.06
513	Mick Kelleher	.06
514	Kiko Garcia	.06
515	Larry Biittner	.06
516a	Willie Norwood (1980 highlights begins "Spent most...")	.20
516b	Willie Norwood (1980 highlights begins "Traded to...")	.06
517	Bo Diaz	.06
518	Juan Beniquez	.06
519	Scot Thompson	.06
520	Jim Tracy	.06
521	Carlos Lezcano	.06
522	Joe Amalfitano	.06
523	Preston Hanna	.06
524a	Ray Burris (1980 highlights begins "Went on...")	.20
524b	Ray Burris (1980 highlights begins "Drafted by...")	.06
525	Broderick Perkins	.06
526	Mickey Hatcher	.06
527	John Goryl	.06
528	Dick Davis	.06
529	Butch Wynegar	.06
530	Sal Butera	.06
531	Jerry Koosman	.06
532a	Jeff (Geoff) Zahn (1980 highlights begins "Was 2nd in...")	.20
532b	Jeff (Geoff) Zahn (1980 highlights begins "Signed a 3 year ...")	.06
533	Dennis Martinez	.06
534	Gary Thomasson	.06
535	Steve Macko	.06
536	Jim Kaat	.11
537	George Brett, Rod Carew Best Hitters	1.25
538	Tim Raines **RC**	2.25
539	Keith Smith	.06
540	Ken Macha	.06

541	Burt Hooton	.06
542	Butch Hobson	.06
543	Bill Stein	.06
544	Dave Stapleton	.06
545	Bob Pate	.06
546	Doug Corbett	.06
547	Darrell Jackson	.06
548	Pete Redfern	.06
549	Roger Erickson	.06
550	Al Hrabosky	.06
551	Dick Tidrow	.06
552	Dave Ford	.06
553	Dave Kingman	.08
554a	Mike Vail (1980 highlights begins "After...")	.20
554b	Mike Vail (1980 highlights begins "Traded...")	.06
555a	Jerry Martin (1980 highlights begins "Overcame...")	.20
555b	Jerry Martin (1980 highlights begins "Traded...")	.06
556a	Jesus Figueroa (1980 highlights begins "Had...")	.20
556b	Jesus Figueroa (1980 highlights begins "Traded...")	.06
557	Don Stanhouse	.06
558	Barry Foote	.06
559	Tim Blackwell	.06
560	Bruce Sutter	.90
561	Rick Reuschel	.06
562	Lynn McGlothen	.06
563a	Bob Owchinko (1980 highlights begins "Traded...")	.20
563b	Bob Owchinko (1980 highlights begins "Involved...")	.06
564	John Verhoeven	.06
565	Ken Landreaux	.06
566a	Glen Adams (Glen on front.)	.20
566b	Glenn Adams (Glenn on front.)	.06
567	Hosken Powell	.06
568	Dick Noles	.06
569	Danny Ainge **RC**	1.50
570	Bobby Mattick	.06
571	Joe LeFebvre (Lefebvre)	.06
572	Bobby Clark	.06
573	Dennis Lamp	.06
574	Randy Lerch	.06
575	Mookie Wilson **RC**	.25
576	Ron LeFlore	.06
577	Jim Dwyer	.06
578	Bill Castro	.06
579	Greg Minton	.06
580	Mark Littell	.06
581	Andy Hassler	.06
582	Dave Stieb	.06
583	Ken Oberkfell	.06
584	Larry Bradford	.06
585	Fred Stanley	.06
586	Bill Caudill	.06
587	Doug Capilla	.06
588	George Riley	.06
589	Willie Hernandez	.06
590	Mike Schmidt (MVP)	1.25
591	Steve Stone (Cy Young 1980)	.08
592	Rick Sofield	.06
593	Bombo Rivera	.06
594	Gary Ward	.06
595a	Dave Edwards (1980 highlights begins "Sidelined...")	.20
595b	Dave Edwards (1980 highlights begins "Traded...")	.06
596	Mike Proly	.06
597	Tommy Boggs	.06
598	Greg Gross	.06
599	Elias Sosa	.06
600	Pat Kelly	.06
----	Checklist 1-120 (51 Tom Donohue)	.20
----	Checklist 1-120 (51 Tom Donahue)	.08
----	Checklist 121-240	.08
----	Checklist 241-360 (306 Gary Mathews)	.20
----	Checklist 241-360 (306 Gary Matthews)	.08
----	Checklist 361-480 (379 Luis Pujois)	.20
----	Checklist 361-480 (379 Luis Pujols)	.08
----	Checklist 481-600 (566 Glen Adams)	.20
----	Checklist 481-600 (566 Glenn Adams)	.08

1982 Donruss

Brewers — CECIL COOPER 1b

	NM/M
Unopened Fact. Set (660):	50.00
Complete Set (660):	45.00
Complete Set, Uncut Sheets (5):	175.00
Common Player:	.10
Babe Ruth Puzzle:	1.00
Wax Pack (15):	2.50
Wax Box (36):	80.00

1	Pete Rose/DK	4.00
2	Gary Carter/DK	1.25
3	Steve Garvey/DK	.45
4	Vida Blue/DK	.10
5a	Alan Trammell/DK (Last name incorrect.)	1.00
5b	Alan Trammell/DK (Corrected)	.30
6	Len Barker/DK	.10
7	Dwight Evans/DK	.15
8	Rod Carew/DK	1.25
9	George Hendrick/DK	.10
10	Phil Niekro/DK	1.00
11	Richie Zisk/DK	.10
12	Dave Parker/DK	.10
13	Nolan Ryan/DK	5.00
14	Ivan DeJesus/DK	.10
15	George Brett/DK	2.00
16	Tom Seaver/DK	1.25
17	Dave Kingman/DK	.15
18	Dave Winfield/DK	1.25
19	Mike Norris/DK	.10
20	Carlton Fisk/DK	1.25
21	Ozzie Smith/DK	1.50
22	Roy Smalley/DK	.10
23	Buddy Bell/DK	.10
24	Ken Singleton/DK	.10
25	John Mayberry/DK	.10
26	Gorman Thomas/DK	.10
27	Earl Weaver	.50
28	Rollie Fingers	1.00
29	Sparky Anderson	.50
30	Dennis Eckersley	1.25
31	Dave Winfield	1.25
32	Burt Hooton	.10
33	Rick Waits	.10
34	George Brett	2.00
35	Steve McCatty	.10
36	Steve Rogers	.10
37	Bill Stein	.10
38	Steve Renko	.10
39	Mike Squires	.10
40	George Hendrick	.10
41	Bob Knepper	.10
42	Steve Carlton	1.25
43	Larry Biittner	.10
44	Chris Welsh	.10
45	Steve Nicosia	.10
46	Jack Clark	.10
47	Chris Chambliss	.10
48	Ivan DeJesus	.10
49	Lee Mazzilli	.10
50	Julio Cruz	.10
51	Pete Redfern	.10
52	Dave Stieb	.10
53	Doug Corbett	.10
54	George Bell **RC**	.50
55	Joe Simpson	.10
56	Rusty Staub	.10
57	Hector Cruz	.10
58	Claudell Washington	.10

ABBREVIATIONS

DK - Diamond King
RR - Rated Rookie
SP - Short Print

59	Enrique Romo	.10
60	Gary Lavelle	.10
61	Tim Flannery	.10
62	Joe Nolan	.10
63	Larry Bowa	.10
64	Sixto Lezcano	.10
65	Joe Sambito	.10
66	Bruce Kison	.10
67	Wayne Nordhagen	.10
68	Woodie Fryman	.10
69	Billy Sample	.10
70	Amos Otis	.10
71	Matt Keough	.10
72	Toby Harrah	.10
73	Dave Righetti **RC**	.30
74	Carl Yastrzemski	1.50
75	Bob Welch	.10
76a	Alan Trammel (Last name misspelled.)	1.00
76b	Alan Trammell (Corrected)	.10
77	Rick Dempsey	.10
78	Paul Molitor	1.25
79	Dennis Martinez	.10
80	Jim Slaton	.10
81	Champ Summers	.10
82	Carney Lansford	.10
83	Barry Foote	.10
84	Steve Garvey	.45
85	Rick Manning	.10
86	John Wathan	.10
87	Brian Kingman	.10
88	Andre Dawson	.50
89	Jim Kern	.10
90	Bobby Grich	.10
91	Bob Forsch	.10
92	Art Howe	.10
93	Marty Bystrom	.10
94	Ozzie Smith	1.50
95	Dave Parker	.10
96	Doyle Alexander	.10
97	Al Hrabosky	.10
98	Frank Taveras	.10
99	Tim Blackwell	.10
100	Floyd Bannister	.10
101	Alfredo Griffin	.10
102	Dave Engle	.10
103	Mario Soto	.10
104	Ross Baumgarten	.10
105	Ken Singleton	.10
106	Ted Simmons	.10
107	Jack Morris	.10
108	Bob Watson	.10
109	Dwight Evans	.50
110	Tom Lasorda	.50
111	Bert Blyleven	.10
112	Dan Quisenberry	.10
113	Rickey Henderson	1.25
114	Gary Carter	1.25
115	Brian Downing	.10
116	Al Oliver	.10
117	LaMarr Hoyt	.10
118	Cesar Cedeno	.10
119	Keith Moreland	.10
120	Bob Shirley	.10
121	Terry Kennedy	.10
122	Frank Pastore	.10
123	Gene Garber	.10
124	Tony Pena	.10
125	Allen Ripley	.10
126	Randy Martz	.10
127	Richie Zisk	.10
128	Mike Scott	.10
129	Lloyd Moseby	.10
130	Rob Wilfong	.10
131	Tim Stoddard	.10
132	Gorman Thomas	.10
133	Dan Petry	.10
134	Bob Stanley	.10
135	Lou Piniella	.15
136	Pedro Guerrero	.10
137	Len Barker	.10
138	Richard Gale	.10
139	Wayne Gross	.10
140	Tim Wallach **RC**	.50
141	Gene Mauch	.10
142	Doc Medich	.10
143	Tony Bernazard	.10
144	Bill Virdon	.10
145	John Littlefield	.10
146	Dave Bergman	.10
147	Dick Davis	.10
148	Tom Seaver	1.50
149	Matt Sinatro	.10
150	Chuck Tanner	.10
151	Leon Durham	.10
152	Gene Tenace	.10
153	Al Bumbry	.10
154	Mark Brouhard	.10
155	Rick Peters	.10
156	Jerry Remy	.10
157	Rick Reuschel	.10
158	Steve Howe	.10
159	Alan Bannister	.10

#	Player	Value	#	Player	Value	#	Player	Value	#	Player	Value
160	U L Washington	.10	264	Dennis Leonard	.10	364	Ken Brett	.10	462	Fernando Valenzuela	.10
161	Rick Langford	.10	265	Jim Spencer	.10	365	Tony Armas	.10	463	Ron Hassey	.10
162	Bill Gullickson	.10	266	John Milner	.10	366	Chris Speier	.10	464	Paul Splittorff	.10
163	Mark Wagner	.10	267	Don Aase	.10	367	Fred Lynn	.10	465	Rob Picciolo	.10
164	Geoff Zahn	.10	268	Jim Sundberg	.10	368	Buddy Bell	.10	466	Larry Parrish	.10
165	Ron LeFlore	.10	269	Lamar Johnson	.10	369	Jim Essian	.10	467	Johnny Grubb	.10
166	Dane Iorg	.10	270	Frank LaCorte	.10	370	Terry Puhl	.10	468	Dan Ford	.10
167	Joe Niekro	.10	271	Barry Evans	.10	371	Greg Gross	.10	469	Silvio Martinez	.10
168	Pete Rose	3.00	272	Enos Cabell	.10	372	Bruce Sutter	1.25	470	Kiko Garcia	.10
169	Dave Collins	.10	273	Del Unser	.10	373	Joe Lefebvre	.10	471	Bob Boone	.10
170	Rick Wise	.10	274	George Foster	.10	374	Ray Knight	.10	472	Luis Salazar	.10
171	Jim Bibby	.10	275	Brett Butler RC	.50	375	Bruce Benedict	.10	473	Randy Niemann	.10
172	Larry Herndon	.10	276	Lee Lacy	.10	376	Tim Foli	.10	474	Tom Griffin	.10
173	Bob Horner	.10	277	Ken Reitz	.10	377	Al Holland	.10	475	Phil Niekro	1.00
174	Steve Dillard	.10	278	Keith Hernandez	.10	378	Ken Kravec	.10	476	Hubie Brooks	.10
175	Mookie Wilson	.10	279	Doug DeCinces	.10	379	Jeff Burroughs	.10	477	Dick Tidrow	.10
176	Dan Meyer	.10	280	Charlie Moore	.10	380	Pete Falcone	.10	478	Jim Beattie	.10
177	Fernando Arroyo	.10	281	Lance Parrish	.10	381	Ernie Whitt	.10	479	Damaso Garcia	.10
178	Jackson Todd	.10	282	Ralph Houk	.10	382	Brad Havens	.10	480	Mickey Hatcher	.10
179	Darrell Jackson	.10	283	Rich Gossage	.10	383	Terry Crowley	.10	481	Joe Price	.10
180	Al Woods	.10	284	Jerry Reuss	.10	384	Don Money	.10	482	Ed Farmer	.10
181	Jim Anderson	.10	285	Mike Stanton	.10	385	Dan Schatzeder	.10	483	Eddie Murray	1.25
182	Dave Kingman	.10	286	Frank White	.10	386	Gary Allenson	.10	484	Ben Oglivie	.10
183	Steve Henderson	.10	287	Bob Owchinko	.10	387	Yogi Berra	.50	485	Kevin Saucier	.10
184	Brian Asselstine	.10	288	Scott Sanderson	.10	388	Ken Landreaux	.10	486	Bobby Murcer	.10
185	Rod Scurry	.10	289	Bump Wills	.10	389	Mike Hargrove	.10	487	Bill Campbell	.10
186	Fred Breining	.10	290	Dave Frost	.10	390	Darryl Motley	.10	488	Reggie Smith	.10
187	Danny Boone	.10	291	Chet Lemon	.10	391	Dave McKay	.10	489	Wayne Garland	.10
188	Junior Kennedy	.10	292	Tito Landrum	.10	392	Stan Bahnsen	.10	490	Jim Wright	.10
189	Sparky Lyle	.10	293	Vern Ruhle	.10	393	Ken Forsch	.10	491	Billy Martin	.10
190	Whitey Herzog	.10	294	Mike Schmidt	2.00	394	Mario Mendoza	.10	492	Jim Fanning	.10
191	Dave Smith	.10	295	Sam Mejias	.10	395	Jim Morrison	.10	493	Don Baylor	.10
192	Ed Ott	.10	296	Gary Lucas	.10	396	Mike Ivie	.10	494	Rick Honeycutt	.10
193	Greg Luzinski	.10	297	John Candelaria	.10	397	Broderick Perkins	.10	495	Carlton Fisk	1.25
194	Bill Lee	.10	298	Jerry Martin	.10	398	Darrell Evans	.10	496	Denny Walling	.10
195	Don Zimmer	.10	299	Dale Murphy	.50	399	Ron Reed	.10	497	Bake McBride	.10
196	Hal McRae	.10	300	Mike Lum	.10	400	Johnny Bench	1.50	498	Darrell Porter	.10
197	Mike Norris	.10	301	Tom Hausman	.10	401	Steve Bedrosian RC	.20	499	Gene Richards	.10
198	Duane Kuiper	.10	302	Glenn Abbott	.10	402	Bill Robinson	.10	500	Ron Oester	.10
199	Rick Cerone	.10	303	Roger Erickson	.10	403	Bill Buckner	.10	501	Ken Dayley RC	.10
200	Jim Rice	.45	304	Otto Velez	.10	404	Ken Oberkfell	.10	502	Jason Thompson	.10
201	Steve Yeager	.10	305	Danny Goodwin	.10	405	Cal Ripken, Jr. RC	40.00	503	Milt May	.10
202	Tom Brookens	.10	306	John Mayberry	.10	406	Jim Gantner	.10	504	Doug Bird	.10
203	Jose Morales	.10	307	Lenny Randle	.10	407	Kirk Gibson	.10	505	Bruce Bochte	.10
204	Roy Howell	.10	308	Bob Bailor	.10	408	Tony Perez	1.00	506	Neil Allen	.10
205	Tippy Martinez	.10	309	Jerry Morales	.10	409	Tommy John	.10	507	Joey McLaughlin	.10
206	Moose Haas	.10	310	Rufino Linares	.10	410	Dave Stewart RC	2.50	508	Butch Wynegar	.10
207	Al Cowens	.10	311	Kent Tekulve	.10	411	Dan Spillner	.10	509	Gary Roenicke	.10
208	Dave Stapleton	.10	312	Joe Morgan	1.25	412	Willie Aikens	.10	510	Robin Yount	1.25
209	Bucky Dent	.10	313	John Urrea	.10	413	Mike Heath	.10	511	Dave Tobik	.10
210	Ron Cey	.10	314	Paul Householder	.10	414	Ray Burris	.10	512	Rich Gedman RC	.15
211	Jorge Orta	.10	315	Garry Maddox	.10	415	Leon Roberts	.10	513	Gene Nelson RC	.10
212	Jamie Quirk	.10	316	Mike Ramsey	.10	416	Mike Witt RC	.15	514	Rick Monday	.10
213	Jeff Jones	.10	317	Alan Ashby	.10	417	Bobby Molinaro	.10	515	Miguel Dilone	.10
214	Tim Raines	.25	318	Bob Clark	.10	418	Steve Braun	.10	516	Clint Hurdle	.10
215	Jon Matlack	.10	319	Tony LaRussa	.15	419	Nolan Ryan	4.00	517	Jeff Newman	.10
216	Rod Carew	1.50	320	Charlie Lea	.10	420	Tug McGraw	.10	518	Grant Jackson	.10
217	Jim Kaat	.15	321	Danny Darwin	.10	421	Dave Concepcion	.10	519	Andy Hassler	.10
218	Joe Pittman	.10	322	Cesar Geronimo	.10	422a	Juan Eichelberger (Gary Lucas photo - white player.)	.50	520	Pat Putnam	.10
219	Larry Christenson	.10	323	Tom Underwood	.10	422b	Juan Eichelberger (Correct photo - black player.)	.10	521	Greg Pryor	.10
220	Juan Bonilla	.10	324	Andre Thornton	.10	423	Rick Rhoden	.10	522	Tony Scott	.10
221	Mike Easler	.10	325	Rudy May	.10	424	Frank Robinson	.50	523	Steve Mura	.10
222	Vida Blue	.10	326	Frank Tanana	.10	425	Eddie Miller	.10	524	Johnnie LeMaster	.10
223	Rick Camp	.10	327	Davey Lopes	.10	426	Bill Caudill	.10	525	Dick Ruthven	.10
224	Mike Jorgensen	.10	328	Richie Hebner	.10	427	Doug Flynn	.10	526	John McNamara	.10
225	Jody Davis RC	.15	329	Mike Flanagan	.10	428	Larry Anderson (Andersen)	.10	527	Larry McWilliams	.10
226	Mike Parrott	.10	330	Mike Caldwell	.10	429	Al Williams	.10	528	Johnny Ray RC	.15
227	Jim Clancy	.10	331	Scott McGregor	.10	430	Jerry Garvin	.10	529	Pat Tabler RC	.15
228	Hosken Powell	.10	332	Jerry Augustine	.10	431	Glenn Adams	.10	530	Tom Herr	.10
229	Tom Hume	.10	333	Stan Papi	.10	432	Barry Bonnell	.10	531a	San Diego Chicken (W/trademark symbol.)	.75
230	Britt Burns	.10	334	Rick Miller	.10	433	Jerry Narron	.10	531b	San Diego Chicken (No trademark symbol.)	.50
231	Jim Palmer	1.25	335	Graig Nettles	.15	434	John Stearns	.10	532	Sal Butera	.10
232	Bob Rodgers	.10	336	Dusty Baker	.10	435	Mike Tyson	.10	533	Mike Griffin	.10
233	Milt Wilcox	.10	337	Dave Garcia	.10	436	Glenn Hubbard	.10	534	Kelvin Moore	.10
234	Dave Revering	.10	338	Larry Gura	.10	437	Eddie Solomon	.10	535	Reggie Jackson	2.00
235	Mike Torrez	.10	339	Cliff Johnson	.10	438	Jeff Leonard	.10	536	Ed Romero	.10
236	Robert Castillo	.10	340	Warren Cromartie	.10	439	Randy Bass	.10	537	Derrel Thomas	.10
237	Von Hayes RC	.25	341	Steve Comer	.10	440	Mike LaCoss	.10	538	Mike O'Berry	.10
238	Renie Martin	.10	342	Rick Burleson	.10	441	Gary Matthews	.10	539	Jack O'Connor	.10
239	Dwayne Murphy	.10	343	John Martin	.10	442	Mark Littell	.10	540	Bob Ojeda RC	.25
240	Rodney Scott	.10	344	Craig Reynolds	.10	443	Don Sutton	1.00	541	Roy Lee Jackson	.10
241	Fred Patek	.10	345	Mike Proly	.10	444	John Harris	.10	542	Lynn Jones	.10
242	Mickey Rivers	.10	346	Ruppert Jones	.10	445	Vada Pinson	.10	543	Gaylord Perry	1.00
243	Steve Trout	.10	347	Omar Moreno	.10	446	Elias Sosa	.10	544a	Phil Garner (Photo reversed.)	.50
244	Jose Cruz	.10	348	Greg Minton	.10	447	Charlie Hough	.10	544b	Phil Garner (Photo correct.)	.10
245	Manny Trillo	.10	349	Rick Mahler RC	.10	448	Willie Wilson	.10	545	Garry Templeton	.10
246	Lary Sorensen	.10	350	Alex Trevino	.10	449	Fred Stanley	.10	546	Rafael Ramirez	.10
247	Dave Edwards	.10	351	Mike Krukow	.10	450	Tom Veryzer	.10	547	Jeff Reardon	.10
248	Dan Driessen	.10	352a	Shane Rawley (Jim Anderson photo - shaking hands.)	.50	451	Ron Davis	.10	548	Ron Guidry	.10
249	Tommy Boggs	.10	352b	Shane Rawley (Correct photo - kneeling.)	.15	452	Mark Clear	.10	549	Tim Laudner RC	.15
250	Dale Berra	.10	353	Garth Iorg	.10	453	Bill Russell	.10	550	John Henry Johnson	.10
251	Ed Whitson	.10	354	Pete Mackanin	.10	454	Lou Whitaker	.10	551	Chris Bando	.10
252	Lee Smith RC	4.00	355	Paul Moskau	.10	455	Dan Graham	.10	552	Bobby Brown	.10
253	Tom Paciorek	.10	356	Richard Dotson	.10	456	Reggie Cleveland	.10	553	Larry Bradford	.10
254	Pat Zachry	.10	357	Steve Stone	.10	457	Sammy Stewart	.10	554	Scott Fletcher RC	.20
255	Luis Leal	.10	358	Larry Hisle	.10	458	Pete Vuckovich	.10	555	Jerry Royster	.10
256	John Castino	.10	359	Aurelio Lopez	.10	459	John Wockenfuss	.10	556	Shooty Babbitt	.10
257	Rich Dauer	.10	360	Oscar Gamble	.10	460	Glenn Hoffman	.10	557	Kent Hrbek RC	2.00
258	Cecil Cooper	.10	361	Tom Burgmeier	.10	461	Willie Randolph	.10	558	Ron Guidry, Tommy John Yankee Winners	.15
259	Dave Rozema	.10	362	Terry Forster	.10						
260	John Tudor	.10	363	Joe Charboneau	.25						
261	Jerry Mumphrey	.10									
262	Jay Johnstone	.10									
263	Bo Diaz	.10									

559	Mark Bomback	.10
560	Julio Valdez	.10
561	Buck Martinez	.10
562	Mike Marshall RC	.15
563	Rennie Stennett	.10
564	Steve Crawford	.10
565	Bob Babcock	.10
566	Johnny Podres	.10
567	Paul Serna	.10
568	Harold Baines	1.00
569	Dave LaRoche	.10
570	Lee May	.10
571	Gary Ward	.10
572	John Denny	.10
573	Roy Smalley	.10
574	Bob Brenly RC	.20
575	Reggie Jackson,	
	Dave Winfield/	
	Bronx Bombers	1.50
576	Luis Pujols	.10
577	Butch Hobson	.10
578	Harvey Kuenn	.10
579	Cal Ripken, Sr.	.10
580	Juan Berenguer	.10
581	Benny Ayala	.10
582	Vance Law	.10
583	Rick Leach RC	.15
584	George Frazier	.10
585	Pete Rose, Mike Schmidt	
	Phillies Finest	1.00
586	Joe Rudi	.10
587	Juan Beniquez	.10
588	Luis DeLeon RC	.10
589	Craig Swan	.10
590	Dave Chalk	.10
591	Billy Gardner	.10
592	Sal Bando	.10
593	Bert Campaneris	.10
594	Steve Kemp	.10
595a	Randy Lerch (Braves)	.25
595b	Randy Lerch (Brewers)	.10
596	Bryan Clark	.10
597	Dave Ford	.10
598	Mike Scioscia	.10
599	John Lowenstein	.10
600	Rene Lachmann	
	(Lachemann)	.10
601	Mick Kelleher	.10
602	Ron Jackson	.10
603	Jerry Koosman	.10
604	Dave Goltz	.10
605	Ellis Valentine	.10
606	Lonnie Smith	.10
607	Joaquin Andujar	.10
608	Garry Hancock	.10
609	Jerry Turner	.10
610	Bob Bonner	.10
611	Jim Dwyer	.10
612	Terry Bulling	.10
613	Joel Youngblood	.10
614	Larry Milbourne	.10
615	Phil Roof (Photo actually	
	Gene Roof.)	.10
616	Keith Drumright	.10
617	Dave Rosello	.10
618	Rickey Keeton	.10
619	Dennis Lamp	.10
620	Sid Monge	.10
621	Jerry White	.10
622	Luis Aguayo RC	.10
623	Jamie Easterly	.10
624	Steve Sax RC	.50
625	Dave Roberts	.10
626	Rick Bosetti	.10
627	Terry Francona RC	.15
628	Johnny Bench, Tom Seaver	
	Pride of the Reds	1.00
629	Paul Mirabella	.10
630	Rance Mulliniks	.10
631	Kevin Hickey	.10
632	Reid Nichols	.10
633	Dave Geisel	.10
634	Ken Griffey	.10
635	Bob Lemon	.15
636	Orlando Sanchez	.10
637	Bill Almon	.10
638	Danny Ainge	1.00
639	Willie Stargell	1.25
640	Bob Sykes	.10
641	Ed Lynch	.10
642	John Ellis	.10
643	Fergie Jenkins	1.00
644	Lenn Sakata	.10
645	Julio Gonzales	.10
646	Jesse Orosco	.10
647	Jerry Dybzinski	.10
648	Tommy Davis	.10
649	Ron Gardenhire	.10
650	Felipe Alou	.10
651	Harvey Haddix	.10
652	Willie Upshaw	.10
653	Bill Madlock	.10
----	Checklist 1-26 DK	
	(5 Trammel)	.25

----	Checklist 1-26 DK	
	(5 Trammell)	.10
----	Checklist 27-130	.10
----	Checklist 131-234	.10
----	Checklist 235-338	.10
----	Checklist 339-442	.10
----	Checklist 443-544	.10
----	Checklist 545-653	.10

1983 Donruss

RICK RHODEN

		NM/M
Unopened Fact. Set (660):		50.00
Complete Set (660):		40.00
Common Player:		.10
Ty Cobb Puzzle:		2.50
Wax Pack (15):		2.50
Wax Box (36):		80.00
1	Fernando	
	Valenzuela/DK	.15
2	Rollie Fingers/DK	.75
3	Reggie Jackson/DK	2.50
4	Jim Palmer/DK	1.00
5	Jack Morris/DK	.15
6	George Foster/DK	.15
7	Jim Sundberg/DK	.10
8	Willie Stargell/DK	1.00
9	Dave Stieb/DK	.15
10	Joe Niekro/DK	.15
11	Rickey Henderson/DK	1.25
12	Dale Murphy/DK	.50
13	Toby Harrah/DK	.10
14	Bill Buckner/DK	.15
15	Willie Wilson/DK	.10
16	Steve Carlton/DK	1.25
17	Ron Guidry/DK	.15
18	Steve Rogers/DK	.10
19	Ken Hrbek/DK	.10
20	Keith Hernandez/DK	.10
21	Floyd Bannister/DK	.10
22	Johnny Bench/DK	2.00
23	Britt Burns/DK	.10
24	Joe Morgan/DK	1.25
25	Carl Yastrzemski/DK	2.00
26	Terry Kennedy/DK	.10
27	Gary Roenicke	.10
28	Dwight Bernard	.10
29	Pat Underwood	.10
30	Gary Allenson	.10
31	Ron Guidry	.10
32	Burt Hooton	.10
33	Chris Bando	.10
34	Rudy May	.10
35	Rickey Henderson	1.25
36	Ray Burris	.10
37	John Butcher	.10
38	Don Aase	.10
39	Jerry Koosman	.10
40	Bruce Sutter	1.00
41	Jose Cruz	.10
42	Pete Rose	3.00
43	Cesar Cedeno	.10
44	Floyd Chiffer	.10
45	Larry McWilliams	.10
46	Alan Fowlkes	.10
47	Dale Murphy	.50
48	Doug Bird	.10
49	Hubie Brooks	.10
50	Floyd Bannister	.10
51	Jack O'Connor	.10
52	Steve Senteney	.10
53	Gary Gaetti RC	1.00
54	Damaso Garcia	.10
55	Gene Nelson	.10
56	Mookie Wilson	.10
57	Allen Ripley	.10
58	Bob Horner	.10
59	Tony Pena	.10
60	Gary Lavelle	.10
61	Tim Lollar	.10
62	Frank Pastore	.10
63	Garry Maddox	.10
64	Bob Forsch	.10

65	Harry Spilman	.10
66	Geoff Zahn	.10
67	Salome Barojas	.10
68	David Palmer	.10
69	Charlie Hough	.10
70	Dan Quisenberry	.10
71	Tony Armas	.10
72	Rick Sutcliffe	.10
73	Steve Balboni	.10
74	Jerry Remy	.10
75	Mike Scioscia	.10
76	John Wockenfuss	.10
77	Jim Palmer	1.00
78	Rollie Fingers	.75
79	Joe Nolan	.10
80	Pete Vuckovich	.10
81	Rick Leach	.10
82	Rick Miller	.10
83	Graig Nettles	.15
84	Ron Cey	.10
85	Miguel Dilone	.10
86	John Wathan	.10
87	Kelvin Moore	.10
88a	Byrn Smith	
	(First name incorrect.)	.35
88b	Bryn Smith	
	(First name correct.)	.10
89	Dave Hostetler	.10
90	Rod Carew	1.50
91	Lonnie Smith	.10
92	Bob Knepper	.10
93	Marty Bystrom	.10
94	Chris Welsh	.10
95	Jason Thompson	.10
96	Tom O'Malley	.10
97	Phil Niekro	.75
98	Neil Allen	.10
99	Bill Buckner	.10
100	Ed Vande Berg RC	.10
101	Jim Clancy	.10
102	Robert Castillo	.10
103	Bruce Berenyi	.10
104	Carlton Fisk	1.25
105	Mike Flanagan	.10
106	Cecil Cooper	.10
107	Jack Morris	.10
108	Mike Morgan	.10
109	Luis Aponte	.10
110	Pedro Guerrero	.10
111	Len Barker	.10
112	Willie Wilson	.10
113	Dave Beard	.10
114	Mike Gates	.10
115	Reggie Jackson	2.50
116	George Wright	.10
117	Vance Law	.10
118	Nolan Ryan	4.00
119	Mike Krukow	.10
120	Ozzie Smith	2.00
121	Broderick Perkins	.10
122	Tom Seaver	1.50
123	Chris Chambliss	.10
124	Chuck Tanner	.10
125	Johnnie LeMaster	.10
126	Mel Hall RC	.15
127	Bruce Bochte	.10
128	Charlie Puleo RC	.10
129	Luis Leal	.10
130	John Pacella	.10
131	Glenn Gulliver	.10
132	Don Money	.10
133	Dave Rozema	.10
134	Bruce Hurst	.10
135	Rudy May	.10
136	Tom LaSorda (Lasorda)	.40
137	Dan Spillner (Photo actually	
	Ed Whitson.)	.10
138	Jerry Martin	.10
139	Mike Norris	.10
140	Al Oliver	.10
141	Daryl Sconiers	.10
142	Lamar Johnson	.10
143	Harold Baines	.10
144	Alan Ashby	.10
145	Garry Templeton	.10
146	Al Holland	.10
147	Bo Diaz	.10
148	Dave Concepcion	.10
149	Rick Camp	.10
150	Jim Morrison	.10
151	Randy Martz	.10
152	Keith Hernandez	.10
153	John Lowenstein	.10
154	Mike Caldwell	.10
155	Milt Wilcox	.10
156	Rich Gedman	.10
157	Rich Gossage	.20
158	Jerry Reuss	.10
159	Ron Hassey	.10
160	Larry Gura	.10
161	Dwayne Murphy	.10
162	Woodie Fryman	.10
163	Steve Comer	.10
164	Ken Forsch	.10

165	Dennis Lamp	.10
166	David Green	.10
167	Terry Puhl	.10
168	Mike Schmidt	2.50
169	Eddie Milner RC	.10
170	John Curtis	.10
171	Don Robinson	.10
172	Richard Gale	.10
173	Steve Bedrosian	.10
174	Willie Hernandez	.10
175	Ron Gardenhire	.10
176	Jim Beattie	.10
177	Tim Laudner	.10
178	Buck Martinez	.10
179	Kent Hrbek	.10
180	Alfredo Griffin	.10
181	Larry Andersen	.10
182	Pete Falcone	.10
183	Jody Davis	.10
184	Glenn Hubbard	.10
185	Dale Berra	.10
186	Greg Minton	.10
187	Gary Lucas	.10
188	Dave Van Gorder	.10
189	Bob Dernier	.10
190	Willie McGee RC	1.50
191	Dickie Thon	.10
192	Bob Boone	.10
193	Britt Burns	.10
194	Jeff Reardon	.10
195	Jon Matlack	.10
196	Don Slaught RC	.15
197	Fred Stanley	.10
198	Rick Manning	.10
199	Dave Righetti	.10
200	Dave Stapleton	.10
201	Steve Yeager	.10
202	Enos Cabell	.10
203	Sammy Stewart	.10
204	Moose Haas	.10
205	Lenn Sakata	.10
206	Charlie Moore	.10
207	Alan Trammell	.40
208	Jim Rice	.40
209	Roy Smalley	.10
210	Bill Russell	.10
211	Andre Thornton	.10
212	Willie Aikens	.10
213	Dave McKay	.10
214	Tim Blackwell	.10
215	Buddy Bell	.10
216	Doug DeCinces	.10
217	Tom Herr	.10
218	Frank LaCorte	.10
219	Steve Carlton	1.25
220	Terry Kennedy	.10
221	Mike Easler	.10
222	Jack Clark	.10
223	Gene Garber	.10
224	Scott Holman	.10
225	Mike Proly	.10
226	Terry Bulling	.10
227	Jerry Garvin	.10
228	Ron Davis	.10
229	Tom Hume	.10
230	Marc Hill	.10
231	Dennis Martinez	.10
232	Jim Gantner	.10
233	Larry Pashnick	.10
234	Dave Collins	.10
235	Tom Burgmeier	.10
236	Ken Landreaux	.10
237	John Denny	.10
238	Hal McRae	.10
239	Matt Keough	.10
240	Doug Flynn	.10
241	Fred Lynn	.10
242	Billy Sample	.10
243	Tom Paciorek	.10
244	Joe Sambito	.10
245	Sid Monge	.10
246	Ken Oberkfell	.10
247	Joe Pittman (Photo actually	
	Juan Eichelberger.)	.10
248	Mario Soto	.10
249	Claudell Washington	.10
250	Rick Rhoden	.10
251	Darrell Evans	.10
252	Steve Henderson	.10
253	Manny Castillo	.10
254	Craig Swan	.10
255	Joey McLaughlin	.10
256	Pete Redfern	.10
257	Ken Singleton	.10
258	Robin Yount	1.25
259	Elias Sosa	.10
260	Bob Ojeda	.10
261	Bobby Murcer	.10
262	Candy Maldonado RC	.10
263	Rick Waits	.10
264	Greg Pryor	.10
265	Bob Owchinko	.10
266	Chris Speier	.10
267	Bruce Kison	.10

Num	Name	Price
268	Mark Wagner	.10
269	Steve Kemp	.10
270	Phil Garner	.10
271	Gene Richards	.10
272	Renie Martin	.10
273	Dave Roberts	.10
274	Dan Driessen	.10
275	Rufino Linares	.10
276	Lee Lacy	.10
277	Ryne Sandberg RC	12.00
278	Darrell Porter	.10
279	Cal Ripken, Jr.	4.00
280	Jamie Easterly	.10
281	Bill Fahey	.10
282	Glenn Hoffman	.10
283	Willie Randolph	.10
284	Fernando Valenzuela	.10
285	Alan Bannister	.10
286	Paul Splittorff	.10
287	Joe Rudi	.10
288	Bill Gullickson	.10
289	Danny Darwin	.10
290	Andy Hassler	.10
291	Ernesto Escarrega	.10
292	Steve Mura	.10
293	Tony Scott	.10
294	Manny Trillo	.10
295	Greg Harris	.10
296	Luis DeLeon	.10
297	Kent Tekulve	.10
298	Atlee Hammaker	.10
299	Bruce Benedict	.10
300	Fergie Jenkins	.75
301	Dave Kingman	.10
302	Bill Caudill	.10
303	John Castino	.10
304	Ernie Whitt	.10
305	Randy S. Johnson	.10
306	Garth Iorg	.10
307	Gaylord Perry	.75
308	Ed Lynch	.10
309	Keith Moreland	.10
310	Rafael Ramirez	.10
311	Bill Madlock	.10
312	Milt May	.10
313	John Montefusco	.10
314	Wayne Krenchicki	.10
315	George Vukovich	.10
316	Joaquin Andujar	.10
317	Craig Reynolds	.10
318	Rick Burleson	.10
319	Richard Dotson	.10
320	Steve Rogers	.10
321	Dave Schmidt	.10
322	Bud Black RC	.15
323	Jeff Burroughs	.10
324	Von Hayes	.10
325	Butch Wynegar	.10
326	Carl Yastrzemski	1.50
327	Ron Roenicke	.10
328	Howard Johnson RC	1.00
329	Rick Dempsey	.10
330a	Jim Slaton (One yellow box on back.)	.25
330b	Jim Slaton (Two yellow boxes on back.)	.10
331	Benny Ayala	.10
332	Ted Simmons	.10
333	Lou Whitaker	.10
334	Chuck Rainey	.10
335	Lou Piniella	.15
336	Steve Sax	.10
337	Toby Harrah	.10
338	George Brett	2.50
339	Davey Lopes	.10
340	Gary Carter	1.25
341	John Grubb	.10
342	Tim Foli	.10
343	Jim Kaat	.15
344	Mike LaCoss	.10
345	Larry Christenson	.10
346	Juan Bonilla	.10
347	Omar Moreno	.10
348	Chili Davis	.10
349	Tommy Boggs	.10
350	Rusty Staub	.15
351	Bump Wills	.10
352	Rick Sweet	.10
353	Jim Gott RC	.15
354	Terry Felton	.10
355	Jim Kern	.10
356	Bill Almon	.10
357	Tippy Martinez	.10
358	Roy Howell	.10
359	Dan Petry	.10
360	Jerry Mumphrey	.10
361	Mark Clear	.10
362	Mike Marshall	.10
363	Lary Sorensen	.10
364	Amos Otis	.10
365	Rick Langford	.10
366	Brad Mills	.10
367	Brian Downing	.10
368	Mike Richardt	.10
369	Aurelio Rodriguez	.10
370	Dave Smith	.10
371	Tug McGraw	.10
372	Doug Bair	.10
373	Ruppert Jones	.10
374	Alex Trevino	.10
375	Ken Dayley	.10
376	Rod Scurry	.10
377	Bob Brenly	.10
378	Scot Thompson	.10
379	Julio Cruz	.10
380	John Stearns	.10
381	Dale Murray	.10
382	Frank Viola RC	1.50
383	Al Bumbry	.10
384	Ben Oglivie	.10
385	Dave Tobik	.10
386	Bob Stanley	.10
387	Andre Robertson	.10
388	Jorge Orta	.10
389	Ed Whitson	.10
390	Don Hood	.10
391	Tom Underwood	.10
392	Tim Wallach	.10
393	Steve Renko	.10
394	Mickey Rivers	.10
395	Greg Luzinski	.10
396	Art Howe	.10
397	Alan Wiggins	.10
398	Jim Barr	.10
399	Ivan DeJesus	.10
400	Tom Lawless RC	.10
401	Bob Walk	.10
402	Jimmy Smith	.10
403	Lee Smith	.20
404	George Hendrick	.10
405	Eddie Murray	1.25
406	Marshall Edwards	.10
407	Lance Parrish	.10
408	Carney Lansford	.10
409	Dave Winfield	1.25
410	Bob Welch	.10
411	Larry Milbourne	.10
412	Dennis Leonard	.10
413	Dan Meyer	.10
414	Charlie Lea	.10
415	Rick Honeycutt	.10
416	Mike Witt	.10
417	Steve Trout	.10
418	Glenn Brummer	.10
419	Denny Walling	.10
420	Gary Matthews	.10
421	Charlie Liebrandt (Leibrandt)	.10
422	Juan Eichelberger	.10
423	Matt Guante (Cecilio) RC	.10
424	Bill Laskey	.10
425	Jerry Royster	.10
426	Dickie Noles	.10
427	George Foster	.10
428	Mike Moore RC	.25
429	Gary Ward	.10
430	Barry Bonnell	.10
431	Ron Washington	.10
432	Rance Mulliniks	.10
433	Mike Stanton	.10
434	Jesse Orosco	.10
435	Larry Bowa	.10
436	Biff Pocoroba	.10
437	Johnny Ray	.10
438	Joe Morgan	1.25
439	Eric Show RC	.15
440	Larry Biittner	.10
441	Greg Gross	.10
442	Gene Tenace	.10
443	Danny Heep	.10
444	Bobby Clark	.10
445	Kevin Hickey	.10
446	Scott Sanderson	.10
447	Frank Tanana	.10
448	Cesar Geronimo	.10
449	Jimmy Sexton	.10
450	Mike Hargrove	.10
451	Doyle Alexander	.10
452	Dwight Evans	.10
453	Terry Forster	.10
454	Tom Brookens	.10
455	Rich Dauer	.10
456	Rob Picciolo	.10
457	Terry Crowley	.10
458	Ned Yost	.10
459	Kirk Gibson	.10
460	Reid Nichols	.10
461	Oscar Gamble	.10
462	Dusty Baker	.10
463	Jack Perconte	.10
464	Frank White	.10
465	Mickey Klutts	.10
466	Warren Cromartie	.10
467	Larry Parrish	.10
468	Bobby Grich	.10
469	Dane Iorg	.10
470	Joe Niekro	.10
471	Ed Farmer	.10
472	Tim Flannery	.10
473	Dave Parker	.10
474	Jeff Leonard	.10
475	Al Hrabosky	.10
476	Ron Hodges	.10
477	Leon Durham	.10
478	Jim Essian	.10
479	Roy Lee Jackson	.10
480	Brad Havens	.10
481	Joe Price	.10
482	Tony Bernazard	.10
483	Scott McGregor	.10
484	Paul Molitor	1.25
485	Mike Ivie	.10
486	Ken Griffey	.10
487	Dennis Eckersley	1.00
488	Steve Garvey	.40
489	Mike Fischlin	.10
490	U.L. Washington	.10
491	Steve McCatty	.10
492	Roy Johnson	.10
493	Don Baylor	.10
494	Bobby Johnson	.10
495	Mike Squires	.10
496	Bert Roberge	.10
497	Dick Ruthven	.10
498	Tito Landrum	.10
499	Sixto Lezcano	.10
500	Johnny Bench	1.50
501	Larry Whisenton	.10
502	Manny Sarmiento	.10
503	Fred Breining	.10
504	Bill Campbell	.10
505	Todd Cruz	.10
506	Bob Bailor	.10
507	Dave Stieb	.10
508	Al Williams	.10
509	Dan Ford	.10
510	Gorman Thomas	.10
511	Chet Lemon	.10
512	Mike Torrez	.10
513	Shane Rawley	.10
514	Mark Belanger	.10
515	Rodney Craig	.10
516	Onix Concepcion	.10
517	Mike Heath	.10
518	Andre Dawson	.50
519	Luis Sanchez	.10
520	Terry Bogener	.10
521	Rudy Law	.10
522	Ray Knight	.10
523	Joe Lefebvre	.10
524	Jim Wohlford	.10
525	Julio Franco RC	2.00
526	Ron Oester	.10
527	Rick Mahler	.10
528	Steve Nicosia	.10
529	Junior Kennedy	.10
530a	Whitey Herzog (One yellow box on back.)	.25
530b	Whitey Herzog (Two yellow boxes on back.)	.15
531a	Don Sutton (Blue frame.)	.75
531b	Don Sutton (Green frame.)	.75
532	Mark Brouhard	.10
533a	Sparky Anderson (One yellow box on back.)	.50
533b	Sparky Anderson (Two yellow boxes on back.)	.50
534	Roger LaFrancois	.10
535	George Frazier	.10
536	Tom Niedenfuer	.10
537	Ed Glynn	.10
538	Lee May	.10
539	Bob Kearney	.10
540	Tim Raines	.10
541	Paul Mirabella	.10
542	Luis Tiant	.10
543	Ron LeFlore	.10
544	Dave LaPoint RC	.15
545	Randy Moffitt	.10
546	Luis Aguayo	.10
547	Brad Lesley	.10
548	Luis Salazar	.10
549	John Candelaria	.10
550	Dave Bergman	.10
551	Bob Watson	.10
552	Pat Tabler	.10
553	Brent Gaff	.10
554	Al Cowens	.10
555	Tom Brunansky	.10
556	Lloyd Moseby	.10
557a	Pascual Perez (Twins)	.25
557b	Pascual Perez (Braves)	.10
558	Willie Upshaw	.10
559	Richie Zisk	.10
560	Pat Zachry	.10
561	Jay Johnstone	.10
562	Carlos Diaz	.10
563	John Tudor	.10
564	Frank Robinson	.50
565	Dave Edwards	.10
566	Paul Householder	.10
567	Ron Reed	.10
568	Mike Ramsey	.10
569	Kiko Garcia	.10
570	Tommy John	.10
571	Tony LaRussa	.10
572	Joel Youngblood	.10
573	Wayne Tolleson RC	.10
574	Keith Creel	.10
575	Billy Martin	.10
576	Jerry Dybzinski	.10
577	Rick Cerone	.10
578	Tony Perez	1.00
579	Greg Brock RC	.10
580	Glen Wilson (Glenn)	.10
581	Tim Stoddard	.10
582	Bob McClure	.10
583	Jim Dwyer	.10
584	Ed Romero	.10
585	Larry Herndon	.10
586	Wade Boggs RC	10.00
587	Jay Howell	.10
588	Dave Stewart	.10
589	Bert Blyleven	.10
590	Dick Howser	.10
591	Wayne Gross	.10
592	Terry Francona	.10
593	Don Werner	.10
594	Bill Stein	.10
595	Jesse Barfield	.10
596	Bobby Molinaro	.10
597	Mike Vail	.10
598	Tony Gwynn RC	12.00
599	Gary Rajsich	.10
600	Jerry Ujdur	.10
601	Cliff Johnson	.10
602	Jerry White	.10
603	Bryan Clark	.10
604	Joe Ferguson	.10
605	Guy Sularz	.10
606a	Ozzie Virgil (Green frame around photo.)	.25
606b	Ozzie Virgil (Orange frame around photo.)	.10
607	Terry Harper	.10
608	Harvey Kuenn	.10
609	Jim Sundberg	.10
610	Willie Stargell	1.25
611	Reggie Smith	.10
612	Rob Wilfong	.10
613	Joe Niekro, Phil Niekro Niekro Brothers	.25
614	Lee Elia	.10
615	Mickey Hatcher	.10
616	Jerry Hairston Sr.	.10
617	John Martin	.10
618	Wally Backman	.10
619	Storm Davis RC	.15
620	Alan Knicely	.10
621	John Stuper	.10
622	Matt Sinatro	.10
623	Gene Petralli RC	.10
624	Duane Walker	.10
625	Dick Williams	.10
626	Pat Corrales	.10
627	Vern Ruhle	.10
628	Joe Torre	.10
629	Anthony Johnson	.10
630	Steve Howe	.10
631	Gary Woods	.10
632	Lamarr Hoyt (LaMarr)	.10
633	Steve Swisher	.10
634	Terry Leach	.10
635	Jeff Newman	.10
636	Brett Butler	.10
637	Gary Gray	.10
638	Lee Mazzilli	.10
639a	Ron Jackson/A's	2.50
639b	Ron Jackson/Angels (Green frame around photo.)	.25
639c	Ron Jackson/Angels (Red frame around photo.)	.15
640	Juan Beniquez	.10
641	Dave Rucker	.10
642	Luis Pujols	.10
643	Rick Monday	.10
644	Hosken Powell	.10
645	San Diego Chicken	.20
646	Dave Engle	.10
647	Dick Davis	.10
648	Vida Blue, Joe Morgan, Frank Robinson MVP's	.15
649	Al Chambers	.10
650	Jesus Vega	.10
651	Jeff Jones	.10
652	Marvis Foley	.10
653	Ty Cobb (Puzzle)	.10
----	Dick Perez DK checklist (No word "Checklist" on back.)	.25
----	Dick Perez DK Checklist (Word "Checklist" on back.)	.10

#	Player	Price
----	Checklist 27-130	.10
----	Checklist 131-234	.10
----	Checklist 235-338	.10
----	Checklist 339-442	.10
----	Checklist 443-546	.10
----	Checklist 547-653	.10

1984 Donruss

JOE NIEKRO P

		NM/M
	Unopened Fact. Set (658):	150.00
	Complete Set (660):	75.00
	Common Player:	.15
	Duke Snider Puzzle:	2.00
	Wax Pack (15):	4.50
	Wax Box (36):	150.00
	Rack Pack (45):	15.00
A	Rollie Fingers, Gaylord Perry Living Legends	1.50
B	Johnny Bench, Carl Yastrzemski Living Legends	4.00
1a	Robin Yount/DK (Steel)	2.50
1b	Robin Yount/DK (Steele)	3.00
2a	Dave Concepcion/DK (Steel)	.25
2b	Dave Concepcion/DK (Steele)	.35
3a	Dwayne Murphy/DK (Steel)	.25
3b	Dwayne Murphy/DK (Steele)	.35
4a	John Castino/DK (Steel)	.25
4b	John Castino/DK (Steele)	.35
5a	Leon Durham/DK (Steel)	.25
5b	Leon Durham/DK (Steele)	.35
6a	Rusty Staub/DK (Steel)	.30
6b	Rusty Staub/DK (Steele)	.45
7a	Jack Clark/DK (Steel)	.25
7b	Jack Clark/DK (Steele)	.35
8a	Dave Dravecky/DK (Steel)	.25
8b	Dave Dravecky/DK (Steele)	.35
9a	Al Oliver/DK (Steel)	.35
9b	Al Oliver/DK (Steele)	.50
10a	Dave Righetti/DK (Steel)	.25
10b	Dave Righetti/DK (Steele)	.35
11a	Hal McRae/DK (Steel)	.25
11b	Hal McRae/DK (Steele)	.35
12a	Ray Knight/DK (Steel)	.25
12b	Ray Knight/DK (Steele)	.35
13a	Bruce Sutter/DK (Steel)	2.50
13b	Bruce Sutter/DK (Steele)	3.00
14a	Bob Horner/DK (Steel)	.25
14b	Bob Horner/DK (Steele)	.35
15a	Lance Parrish/DK (Steel)	.25
15b	Lance Parrish/DK (Steele)	.35
16a	Matt Young/DK (Steel)	.25
16b	Matt Young/DK (Steele)	.35
17a	Fred Lynn/DK (Steel)	.35
17b	Fred Lynn/DK (Steele)	.50
18a	Ron Kittle/DK (Steel)	.35
18b	Ron Kittle/DK (Steele)	.35
19a	Jim Clancy/DK (Steel)	.35
19b	Jim Clancy/DK (Steele)	.35
20a	Bill Madlock/DK (Steel)	.25
20b	Bill Madlock/DK (Steele)	.35
21a	Larry Parrish/DK (Steel)	.25
21b	Larry Parrish/DK (Steele)	.35
22a	Eddie Murray/DK (Steel)	2.50
22b	Eddie Murray/DK (Steele)	3.00
23a	Mike Schmidt/DK (Steel)	3.00
23b	Mike Schmidt/DK (Steele)	4.00
24a	Pedro Guerrero/DK (Steel)	.25
24b	Pedro Guerrero/DK (Steele)	.35
25a	Andre Thornton/DK (Steel)	.25
25b	Andre Thornton/DK (Steele)	.35
26a	Wade Boggs/DK (Steel)	3.00
26b	Wade Boggs/DK (Steele)	3.00
27	Joel Skinner/RR RC	.15
28	Tom Dunbar/RR	.15
29a	Mike Stenhouse/RR (no number on back)	.15
29b	Mike Stenhouse/RR (29 on back)	1.00
30a	Ron Darling/RR RC (no number on back)	1.50
30b	Ron Darling/RR RC (30 on back)	2.50
31	Dion James/RR RC	.15
32	Tony Fernandez/RR RC	3.00
33	Angel Salazar/RR	.15
34	Kevin McReynolds/RR RC	1.50
35	Dick Schofield/RR RC	.20
36	Brad Komminsk/RR RC	.15
37	Tim Teufel/RR RC	.25
38	Doug Frobel/RR	.15
39	Greg Gagne/RR RC	1.00
40	Mike Fuentes/RR	.15
41	Joe Carter/RR RC	8.00
42	Mike Brown/RR	.15
43	Mike Jeffcoat/RR	.15
44	Sid Fernandez/RR RC	2.00
45	Brian Dayett/RR	.15
46	Chris Smith/RR	.15
47	Eddie Murray	3.00
48	Robin Yount	3.00
49	Lance Parrish	.15
50	Jim Rice	1.00
51	Dave Winfield	3.00
52	Fernando Valenzuela	.15
53	George Brett	5.00
54	Rickey Henderson	3.00
55	Gary Carter	3.00
56	Buddy Bell	.15
57	Reggie Jackson	5.00
58	Harold Baines	.15
59	Ozzie Smith	4.00
60	Nolan Ryan	8.00
61	Pete Rose	7.50
62	Ron Oester	.15
63	Steve Garvey	.75
64	Jason Thompson	.15
65	Jack Clark	.15
66	Dale Murphy	1.50
67	Leon Durham	.15
68	Darryl Strawberry	2.00
69	Richie Zisk	.15
70	Kent Hrbek	.15
71	Dave Stieb	.15
72	Ken Schrom	.15
73	George Bell	.15
74	John Moses	.15
75	Ed Lynch	.15
76	Chuck Rainey	.15
77	Biff Pocoroba	.15
78	Cecilio Guante	.15
79	Jim Barr	.15
80	Kurt Bevacqua	.15
81	Tom Foley	.15
82	Joe Lefebvre	.15
83	Andy Van Slyke RC	2.00
84	Bob Lillis	.15
85	Rick Adams	.15
86	Jerry Hairston Sr.	.15
87	Bob James	.15
88	Joe Altobelli	.15
89	Ed Romero	.15
90	John Grubb	.15
91	John Henry Johnson	.15
92	Juan Espino	.15
93	Candy Maldonado	.15
94	Andre Thornton	.15
95	Onix Concepcion	.15
96	Don Hill RC	.15
97	Andre Dawson	1.50
98	Frank Tanana	.15
99	Curt Wilkerson RC	.15
100	Larry Gura	.15
101	Dwayne Murphy	.15
102	Tom Brennan	.15
103	Dave Righetti	.15
104	Steve Sax	.15
105	Dan Petry	.15
106	Cal Ripken, Jr.	8.00
107	Paul Molitor	3.00
108	Fred Lynn	.15
109	Neil Allen	.15
110	Joe Niekro	.15
111	Steve Carlton	3.00
112	Terry Kennedy	.15
113	Bill Madlock	.15
114	Chili Davis	.15
115	Jim Gantner	.15
116	Tom Seaver	4.00
117	Bill Buckner	.15
118	Bill Caudill	.15
119	Jim Clancy	.15
120	John Castino	.15
121	Dave Concepcion	.15
122	Greg Luzinski	.15
123	Mike Boddicker	.15
124	Pete Ladd	.15
125	Juan Berenguer	.15
126	John Montefusco	.15
127	Ed Jurak	.15
128	Tom Niedenfuer	.15
129	Bert Blyleven	.25
130	Bud Black	.15
131	Gorman Heimueller	.15
132	Dan Schatzeder	.15
133	Ron Jackson	.15
134	Tom Henke RC	1.00
135	Kevin Hickey	.15
136	Mike Scott	.15
137	Bo Diaz	.15
138	Glenn Brummer	.15
139	Sid Monge	.15
140	Rich Gale	.15
141	Brett Butler	.15
142	Brian Harper	.15
143	John Rabb	.15
144	Gary Woods	.15
145	Pat Putnam	.15
146	Jim Acker RC	.15
147	Mickey Hatcher	.15
148	Todd Cruz	.15
149	Tom Tellmann	.15
150	John Wockenfuss	.15
151	Wade Boggs	5.00
152	Don Baylor	.15
153	Bob Welch	.15
154	Alan Bannister	.15
155	Willie Aikens	.15
156	Jeff Burroughs	.15
157	Bryan Little	.15
158	Bob Boone	.15
159	Dave Hostetler	.15
160	Jerry Dybzinski	.15
161	Mike Madden	.15
162	Luis DeLeon	.15
163	Willie Hernandez	.15
164	Frank Pastore	.15
165	Rick Camp	.15
166	Lee Mazzilli	.15
167	Scot Thompson	.15
168	Bob Forsch	.15
169	Mike Flanagan	.15
170	Rick Manning	.15
171	Chet Lemon	.15
172	Jerry Remy	.15
173	Ron Guidry	.20
174	Pedro Guerrero	.15
175	Willie Wilson	.15
176	Carney Lansford	.15
177	Al Oliver	.15
178	Jim Sundberg	.15
179	Bobby Grich	.15
180	Richard Dotson	.15
181	Joaquin Andujar	.15
182	Jose Cruz	.15
183	Mike Schmidt	5.00
184	Gary Redus RC	.25
185	Garry Templeton	.15
186	Tony Pena	.15
187	Greg Minton	.15
188	Phil Niekro	1.50
189	Fergie Jenkins	1.50
190	Mookie Wilson	.15
191	Jim Beattie	.15
192	Gary Ward	.15
193	Jesse Barfield	.15
194	Pete Filson	.15
195	Roy Lee Jackson	.15
196	Rick Sweet	.15
197	Jesse Orosco	.15
198	Steve Lake RC	.15
199	Ken Dayley	.15
200	Manny Sarmiento	.15
201	Mark Davis	.15
202	Tim Flannery	.15
203	Bill Scherrer	.15
204	Al Holland	.15
205	David Von Ohlen	.15
206	Mike LaCoss	.15
207	Juan Beniquez	.15
208	Juan Agosto RC	.15
209	Bobby Ramos	.15
210	Al Bumbry	.15
211	Mark Brouhard	.15
212	Howard Bailey	.15
213	Bruce Hurst	.15
214	Bob Shirley	.15
215	Pat Zachry	.15
216	Julio Franco	.15
217	Mike Armstrong	.15
218	Dave Beard	.15
219	Steve Rogers	.15
220	John Butcher	.15
221	Mike Smithson RC	.15
222	Frank White	.15
223	Mike Heath	.15
224	Chris Bando	.15
225	Roy Smalley	.15
226	Dusty Baker	.15
227	Lou Whitaker	.15
228	John Lowenstein	.15
229	Ben Oglivie	.15
230	Doug DeCinces	.15
231	Lonnie Smith	.15
232	Ray Knight	.15
233	Gary Matthews	.15
234	Juan Bonilla	.15
235	Rod Scurry	.15
236	Atlee Hammaker	.15
237	Mike Caldwell	.15
238	Keith Hernandez	.15
239	Larry Bowa	.15
240	Tony Bernazard	.15
241	Damaso Garcia	.15
242	Tom Brunansky	.15
243	Dan Driessen	.15
244	Ron Kittle	.15
245	Tim Stoddard	.15
246	Bob L. Gibson	.15
247	Marty Castillo	.15
248	Don Mattingly RC	25.00
249	Jeff Newman	.15
250	Alejandro Pena RC	.15
251	Toby Harrah	.15
252	Cesar Geronimo	.15
253	Tom Underwood	.15
254	Doug Flynn	.15
255	Andy Hassler	.15
256	Odell Jones	.15
257	Rudy Law	.15
258	Harry Spilman	.15
259	Marty Bystrom	.15
260	Dave Rucker	.15
261	Ruppert Jones	.15
262	Jeff Jones	.15
263	Gerald Perry RC	.15
264	Gene Tenace	.15
265	Brad Wellman	.15
266	Dickie Noles	.15
267	Jamie Allen	.15
268	Jim Gott	.15
269	Ron Davis	.15
270	Benny Ayala	.15
271	Ned Yost	.15
272	Dave Rozema	.15
273	Dave Stapleton	.15
274	Lou Piniella	.25
275	Jose Morales	.15
276	Brod Perkins	.15
277	Butch Davis	.15
278	Tony Phillips	.15
279	Jeff Reardon	.15
280	Ken Forsch	.15
281	Pete O'Brien RC	.15
282	Tom Paciorek	.15
283	Frank LaCorte	.15
284	Tim Lollar	.15
285	Greg Gross	.15
286	Alex Trevino	.15
287	Gene Garber	.15
288	Dave Parker	.15
289	Lee Smith	.25
290	Dave LaPoint	.15
291	John Shelby RC	.15
292	Charlie Moore	.15
293	Alan Trammell	.15
294	Tony Armas	.15
295	Shane Rawley	.15
296	Greg Brock	.15
297	Hal McRae	.15
298	Mike Davis	.15
299	Tim Raines	.15
300	Bucky Dent	.15
301	Tommy John	.25
302	Carlton Fisk	3.00
303	Darrell Porter	.15
304	Dickie Thon	.15
305	Garry Maddox	.15
306	Cesar Cedeno	.15
307	Gary Lucas	.15

#	Player	Price
308	Johnny Ray	.15
309	Andy McGaffigan	.15
310	Claudell Washington	.15
311	Ryne Sandberg	5.00
312	George Foster	.15
313	Spike Owen RC	.25
314	Gary Gaetti	.15
315	Willie Upshaw	.15
316	Al Williams	.15
317	Jorge Orta	.15
318	Orlando Mercado	.15
319	Junior Ortiz RC	.15
320	Mike Proly	.15
321	Randy S. Johnson	.15
322	Jim Morrison	.15
323	Max Venable	.15
324	Tony Gwynn	5.00
325	Duane Walker	.15
326	Ozzie Virgil	.15
327	Jeff Lahti	.15
328	Bill Dawley RC	.15
329	Rob Wilfong	.15
330	Marc Hill	.15
331	Ray Burris	.15
332	Allan Ramirez	.15
333	Chuck Porter	.15
334	Wayne Krenchicki	.15
335	Gary Allenson	.15
336	Bob Meacham RC	.15
337	Joe Beckwith	.15
338	Rick Sutcliffe	.15
339	Mark Huismann RC	.15
340	Tim Conroy RC	.15
341	Scott Sanderson	.15
342	Larry Biittner	.15
343	Dave Stewart	.15
344	Darryl Motley	.15
345	Chris Codiroli RC	.15
346	Rick Behenna	.15
347	Andre Robertson	.15
348	Mike Marshall	.15
349	Larry Herndon	.15
350	Rich Dauer	.15
351	Cecil Cooper	.15
352	Rod Carew	3.00
353	Willie McGee	.15
354	Phil Garner	.15
355	Joe Morgan	3.00
356	Luis Salazar	.15
357	John Candelaria	.15
358	Bill Laskey	.15
359	Bob McClure	.15
360	Dave Kingman	.15
361	Ron Cey	.15
362	Matt Young RC	.15
363	Lloyd Moseby	.15
364	Frank Viola	.15
365	Eddie Milner	.15
366	Floyd Bannister	.15
367	Dan Ford	.15
368	Moose Haas	.15
369	Doug Bair	.15
370	Ray Fontenot RC	.15
371	Luis Aponte	.15
372	Jack Fimple	.15
373	Neal Heaton RC	.15
374	Greg Pryor	.15
375	Wayne Gross	.15
376	Charlie Lea	.15
377	Steve Lubratich	.15
378	Jon Matlack	.15
379	Julio Cruz	.15
380	John Mizerock	.15
381	Kevin Gross RC	.15
382	Mike Ramsey	.15
383	Doug Gwosdz	.15
384	Kelly Paris	.15
385	Pete Falcone	.15
386	Milt May	.15
387	Fred Breining	.15
388	Craig Lefferts RC	.25
389	Steve Henderson	.15
390	Randy Moffitt	.15
391	Ron Washington	.15
392	Gary Roenicke	.15
393	Tom Candiotti RC	.75
394	Larry Pashnick	.15
395	Dwight Evans	.15
396	Goose Gossage	.25
397	Derrel Thomas	.15
398	Juan Eichelberger	.15
399	Leon Roberts	.15
400	Davey Lopes	.15
401	Bill Gullickson	.15
402	Geoff Zahn	.15
403	Billy Sample	.15
404	Mike Squires	.15
405	Craig Reynolds	.15
406	Eric Show	.15
407	John Denny	.15
408	Dann Bilardello	.15
409	Bruce Benedict	.15
410	Kent Tekulve	.15
411	Mel Hall	.15

#	Player	Price
412	John Stuper	.15
413	Rick Dempsey	.15
414	Don Sutton	1.50
415	Jack Morris	.15
416	John Tudor	.15
417	Willie Randolph	.15
418	Jerry Reuss	.15
419	Don Slaught	.15
420	Steve McCatty	.15
421	Tim Wallach	.15
422	Larry Parrish	.15
423	Brian Downing	.15
424	Britt Burns	.15
425	David Green	.15
426	Jerry Mumphrey	.15
427	Ivan DeJesus	.15
428	Mario Soto	.15
429	Gene Richards	.15
430	Dale Berra	.15
431	Darrell Evans	.15
432	Glenn Hubbard	.15
433	Jody Davis	.15
434	Danny Heep	.15
435	Ed Nunez RC	.15
436	Bobby Castillo	.15
437	Ernie Whitt	.15
438	Scott Ullger	.15
439	Doyle Alexander	.15
440	Domingo Ramos	.15
441	Craig Swan	.15
442	Warren Brusstar	.15
443	Len Barker	.15
445	Mike Easler	.15
445	Renie Martin	.15
446	Dennis Rasmussen RC	.25
447	Ted Power	.15
448	Charlie Hudson RC	.15
449	Danny Cox RC	.15
450	Kevin Bass	.15
451	Daryl Sconiers	.15
452	Scott Fletcher	.15
453	Bryn Smith	.15
454	Jim Dwyer	.15
455	Rob Picciolo	.15
456	Enos Cabell	.15
457	Dennis Boyd RC	.20
458	Butch Wynegar	.15
459	Burt Hooton	.15
460	Ron Hassey	.15
461	Danny Jackson RC	.15
462	Bob Kearney	.15
463	Terry Francona	.15
464	Wayne Tolleson	.15
465	Mickey Rivers	.15
466	John Wathan	.15
467	Bill Almon	.15
468	George Vukovich	.15
469	Steve Kemp	.15
470	Ken Landreaux	.15
471	Milt Wilcox	.15
472	Tippy Martinez	.15
473	Ted Simmons	.15
474	Tim Foli	.15
475	George Hendrick	.15
476	Terry Puhl	.15
477	Von Hayes	.15
478	Bobby Brown	.15
479	Lee Lacy	.15
480	Joel Youngblood	.15
481	Jim Slaton	.15
482	Mike Fitzgerald RC	.15
483	Keith Moreland	.15
484	Ron Roenicke	.15
485	Luis Leal	.15
486	Bryan Oelkers	.15
487	Bruce Berenyi	.15
488	LaMarr Hoyt	.15
489	Joe Nolan	.15
490	Marshall Edwards	.15
491	Mike Laga RC	.15
492	Rick Cerone	.15
493	Mike Miller (Rick)	.15
494	Rick Honeycutt	.15
495	Mike Hargrove	.15
496	Joe Simpson	.15
497	Keith Atherton RC	.15
498	Chris Welsh	.15
499	Bruce Kison	.15
500	Bob Johnson	.15
501	Jerry Koosman	.15
502	Frank DiPino	.15
503	Tony Perez	2.00
504	Ken Oberkfell	.15
505	Mark Thurmond RC	.15
506	Joe Price	.15
507	Pascual Perez	.15
508	Marvell Wynne RC	.15
509	Mike Krukow	.15
510	Dick Ruthven	.15
511	Al Cowens	.15
512	Cliff Johnson	.15
513	Randy Bush RC	.15
514	Sammy Stewart	.15
515	Bill Schroeder RC	.15

#	Player	Price
516	Aurelio Lopez	.15
517	Mike Brown	.15
518	Graig Nettles	.25
519	Dave Sax	.15
520	Gerry Willard	.15
521	Paul Splittorff	.15
522	Tom Burgmeier	.15
523	Chris Speier	.15
524	Bobby Clark	.15
525	George Wright	.15
526	Dennis Lamp	.15
527	Tony Scott	.15
528	Ed Whitson	.15
529	Ron Reed	.15
530	Charlie Puleo	.15
531	Jerry Royster	.15
532	Don Robinson	.15
533	Steve Trout	.15
534	Bruce Sutter	2.50
535	Bob Horner	.15
536	Pat Tabler	.15
537	Chris Chambliss	.15
538	Bob Ojeda	.15
539	Alan Ashby	.15
540	Jay Johnstone	.15
541	Bob Dernier	.15
542	Brook Jacoby RC	.15
543	U.L. Washington	.15
544	Danny Darwin	.15
545	Kiko Garcia	.15
546	Vance Law	.15
547	Tug McGraw	.15
548	Dave Smith	.15
549	Len Matuszek	.15
550	Tom Hume	.15
551	Dave Dravecky	.15
552	Rick Rhoden	.15
553	Duane Kuiper	.15
554	Rusty Staub	.20
555	Bill Campbell	.15
556	Mike Torrez	.15
557	Dave Henderson	.15
558	Len Whitehouse	.15
559	Barry Bonnell	.15
560	Rick Lysander	.15
561	Garth Iorg	.15
562	Bryan Clark	.15
563	Brian Giles	.15
564	Vern Ruhle	.15
565	Steve Bedrosian	.15
566	Larry McWilliams	.15
567	Jeff Leonard	.15
568	Alan Wiggins	.15
569	Jeff Russell RC	.15
570	Salome Barojas	.15
571	Dane Iorg	.15
572	Bob Knepper	.15
573	Gary Lavelle	.15
574	Gorman Thomas	.15
575	Manny Trillo	.15
576	Jim Palmer	3.00
577	Dale Murray	.15
578	Tom Brookens	.15
579	Rich Gedman	.15
580	Bill Doran RC	.25
581	Steve Yeager	.15
582	Dan Spillner	.15
583	Dan Quisenberry	.15
584	Rance Mulliniks	.15
585	Storm Davis	.15
586	Dave Schmidt	.15
587	Bill Russell	.15
588	Pat Sheridan RC	.15
589	Rafael Ramirez	.15
590	Bud Anderson	.15
591	George Frazier	.15
592	Lee Tunnell RC	.15
593	Kirk Gibson	.15
594	Scott McGregor	.15
595	Bob Bailor	.15
596	Tom Herr	.15
597	Luis Sanchez	.15
598	Dave Engle	.15
599	Craig McMurtry RC	.15
600	Carlos Diaz	.15
601	Tom O'Malley	.15
602	Nick Esasky RC	.15
603	Ron Hodges	.15
604	Ed Vande Berg	.15
605	Alfredo Griffin	.15
606	Glenn Hoffman	.15
607	Hubie Brooks	.15
608	Richard Barnes (Photo actually Neal Heaton.)	
609	Greg Walker RC	.15
610	Ken Singleton	.15
611	Mark Clear	.15
612	Buck Martinez	.15
613	Ken Griffey	.20
614	Reid Nichols	.15
615	Doug Sisk RC	.15
616	Bob Brenly	.15
617	Joey McLaughlin	.15
618	Glenn Wilson	.15

#	Player	Price
619	Bob Stoddard	.15
620	Len Sakata (Lenn)	.15
621	Mike Young RC	.15
622	John Stefero	.15
623	Carmelo Martinez RC	.15
624	Dave Bergman	.15
625	David Green, Willie McGee, Lonnie Smith, Ozzie Smith Runnin' Reds	.75
626	Rudy May	.15
627	Matt Keough	.15
628	Jose DeLeon RC	.15
629	Jim Essian	.15
630	Darnell Coles RC	.15
631	Mike Warren	.15
632	Del Crandall	.15
633	Dennis Martinez	.15
634	Mike Moore	.15
635	Lary Sorensen	.15
636	Ricky Nelson	.15
637	Omar Moreno	.15
638	Charlie Hough	.15
639	Dennis Eckersley	2.50
640	Walt Terrell RC	.15
641	Denny Walling	.15
642	Dave Anderson RC	.15
643	Jose Oquendo RC	.15
644	Bob Stanley	.15
645	Dave Geisel	.15
646	Scott Garrelts RC	.15
647	Gary Pettis RC	.15
648	Duke Snider Puzzle Card	.15
649	Johnnie LeMaster	.15
650	Dave Collins	.15
651	San Diego Chicken	.25
----	Checklist 1-26 DK (Perez-Steel on back.)	.15
----	Checklist 1-26 DK (Perez-Steele on back.)	.15
----	Checklist 27-130	.15
----	Checklist 131-234	.15
----	Checklist 235-338	.15
----	Checklist 339-442	.15
----	Checklist 443-546	.15
----	Checklist 547-651	.15

1985 Donruss

CAL RIPKEN SS

	NM/M
Unopened Fact. Set (660):	75.00
Complete Set (660):	50.00
Common Player:	.10
Lou Gehrig Puzzle:	3.00
Wax Pack (15):	4.00
Wax Box (36):	120.00
Rack Pack (45):	7.00

#	Player	Price
1	Ryne Sandberg/DK	2.50
2	Doug DeCinces/DK	.10
3	Rich Dotson/DK	.10
4	Bert Blyleven/DK	.25
5	Lou Whitaker/DK	.10
6	Dan Quisenberry/DK	.10
7	Don Mattingly/DK	4.00
8	Carney Lansford/DK	.10
9	Frank Tanana/DK	.10
10	Willie Upshaw/DK	.10
11	Claudell Washington/DK	.10
12	Mike Marshall/DK	.10
13	Joaquin Andujar/DK	.10
14	Cal Ripken, Jr./DK	6.00
15	Jim Rice/DK	.75
16	Don Sutton/DK	1.00
17	Frank Viola/DK	.10
18	Alvin Davis/DK	.10
19	Mario Soto/DK	.10
20	Jose Cruz/DK	.10
21	Charlie Lea/DK	.10
22	Jesse Orosco/DK	.10
23	Juan Samuel/DK	.10
24	Tony Pena/DK	.10
25	Tony Gwynn/DK	2.50

No.	Player	Price	No.	Player	Price	No.	Player	Price	No.	Player	Price
26	Bob Brenly/DK	.10	122	Vance Law	.10	226	Jerry Reuss	.10	330	Scott Fletcher	.10
27	Danny Tartabull/RR RC	1.50	123	Gary Roenicke	.10	227	Darrell Evans	.10	331	Jeff Reardon	.10
28	Mike Bielecki/RR RC	.10	124	Bill Schroeder	.10	228	Wayne Gross	.10	332	Rick Dempsey	.10
29	Steve Lyons/RR RC	.25	125	Dave Rozema	.10	229	Jim Gantner	.10	333	Ben Oglivie	.10
30	Jeff Reed/RR RC	.10	126	Bobby Meacham	.10	230	Bob Boone	.10	334	Dan Petry	.10
31	Tony Brewer/RR	.10	127	Marty Barrett	.10	231	Lonnie Smith	.10	335	Jackie Gutierrez	.10
32	John Morris/RR RC	.10	128	R.J. Reynolds RC	.15	232	Frank DiPino	.10	336	Dave Righetti	.10
33	Daryl Boston/RR RC	.15	129	Ernie Camacho	.10	233	Jerry Koosman	.10	337	Alejandro Pena	.10
34	Alfonso Pulido/RR	.10	130	Jorge Orta	.10	234	Graig Nettles	.15	338	Mel Hall	.10
35	Steve Kiefer/RR RC	.10	131	Lary Sorensen	.10	235	John Tudor	.10	339	Pat Sheridan	.10
36	Larry Sheets/RR RC	.10	132	Terry Francona	.10	236	John Rabb	.10	340	Keith Atherton	.10
37	Scott Bradley/RR RC	.10	133	Fred Lynn	.10	237	Rick Manning	.10	341	David Palmer	.10
38	Calvin Schiraldi/RR RC	.10	134	Bobby Jones	.10	238	Mike Fitzgerald	.10	342	Gary Ward	.10
39	Shawon Dunston/RR RC	1.50	135	Jerry Hairston Sr.	.10	239	Gary Matthews	.10	343	Dave Stewart	.10
40	Charlie Mitchell/RR	.10	136	Kevin Bass	.10	240	Jim Presley RC	.10	344	Mark Gubicza RC	.50
41	Billy Hatcher/RR RC	.15	137	Garry Maddox	.10	241	Dave Collins	.10	345	Carney Lansford	.10
42	Russ Stephans/RR	.10	138	Dave LaPoint	.10	242	Gary Gaetti	.10	346	Jerry Willard	.10
43	Alejandro Sanchez/RR	.10	139	Kevin McReynolds	.10	243	Dann Bilardello	.10	347	Ken Griffey	.10
44	Steve Jeltz/RR RC	.10	140	Wayne Krenchicki	.10	244	Rudy Law	.10	348	Franklin Stubbs RC	.10
45	Jim Traber/RR RC	.10	141	Rafael Ramirez	.10	245	John Lowenstein	.10	349	Aurelio Lopez	.10
46	Doug Loman/RR	.10	142	Rod Scurry	.10	246	Tom Tellmann	.10	350	Al Bumbry	.10
47	Eddie Murray	2.00	143	Greg Minton	.10	247	Howard Johnson	.10	351	Charlie Moore	.10
48	Robin Yount	2.00	144	Tim Stoddard	.10	248	Ray Fontenot	.10	352	Luis Sanchez	.10
49	Lance Parrish	.10	145	Steve Henderson	.10	249	Tony Armas	.10	353	Darrell Porter	.10
50	Jim Rice	.75	146	George Bell	.10	250	Candy Maldonado	.10	354	Bill Dawley	.10
51	Dave Winfield	2.00	147	Dave Meier	.10	251	Mike Jeffcoat RC	.10	355	Charlie Hudson	.10
52	Fernando Valenzuela	.10	148	Sammy Stewart	.10	252	Dane Iorg	.10	356	Garry Templeton	.10
53	George Brett	3.00	149	Mark Brouhard	.10	253	Bruce Bochte	.10	357	Cecilio Guante	.10
54	Dave Kingman	.10	150	Larry Herndon	.10	254	Pete Rose	5.00	358	Jeff Leonard	.10
55	Gary Carter	2.00	151	Oil Can Boyd	.10	255	Don Aase	.10	359	Paul Molitor	2.00
56	Buddy Bell	.10	152	Brian Dayett	.10	256	George Wright	.10	360	Ron Gardenhire	.10
57	Reggie Jackson	3.00	153	Tom Niedenfuer	.10	257	Britt Burns	.10	361	Larry Bowa	.10
58	Harold Baines	.10	154	Brook Jacoby	.10	258	Mike Scott	.10	362	Bob Kearney	.10
59	Ozzie Smith	2.00	155	Onix Concepcion	.10	259	Len Matuszek	.10	363	Garth Iorg	.10
60	Nolan Ryan	6.00	156	Tim Conroy	.10	260	Dave Rucker	.10	364	Tom Brunansky	.10
61	Mike Schmidt	3.00	157	Joe Hesketh RC	.15	261	Craig Lefferts	.10	365	Brad Gulden	.10
62	Dave Parker	.10	158	Brian Downing	.10	262	Jay Tibbs RC	.10	366	Greg Walker	.10
63	Tony Gwynn	2.50	159	Tommy Dunbar	.10	263	Bruce Benedict	.10	367	Mike Young	.10
64	Tony Pena	.10	160	Marc Hill	.10	264	Don Robinson	.10	368	Rick Waits	.10
65	Jack Clark	.10	161	Phil Garner	.10	265	Gary Lavelle	.10	369	Doug Bair	.10
66	Dale Murphy	.60	162	Jerry Davis	.10	266	Scott Sanderson	.10	370	Bob Shirley	.10
67	Ryne Sandberg	2.50	163	Bill Campbell	.10	267	Matt Young	.10	371	Bob Ojeda	.10
68	Keith Hernandez	.10	164	John Franco RC	1.50	268	Ernie Whitt	.10	372	Bob Welch	.10
69	Alvin Davis	.10	165	Len Barker	.10	269	Houston Jimenez	.10	373	Neal Heaton	.10
70	Kent Hrbek	.10	166	Benny Distefano RC	.10	270	Ken Dixon RC	.10	374	Danny Jackson (Photo actually Steve Farr.)	.10
71	Willie Upshaw	.10	167	George Frazier	.10	271	Peter Ladd	.10	375	Donnie Hill	.10
72	Dave Engle	.10	168	Tito Landrum	.10	272	Juan Berenguer	.10	376	Mike Stenhouse	.10
73	Alfredo Griffin	.10	169	Cal Ripken, Jr.	6.00	273	Roger Clemens	35.00	377	Bruce Kison	.10
74a	Jack Perconte (Last line of highlights begins "Batted .346...")		170	Cecil Cooper	.10	274	Rick Cerone	.10	378	Wayne Tolleson	.10
			171	Alan Trammell	.10	275	Dave Anderson	.10	379	Floyd Bannister	.10
74b	Jack Perconte (Last line of highlights begins "Led the ...")	.15	172	Wade Boggs	2.50	276	George Vukovich	.10	380	Vern Ruhle	.10
75	Jesse Orosco	.10	173	Don Baylor	.10	277	Greg Pryor	.10	381	Tim Corcoran	.10
76	Jody Davis	.10	174	Pedro Guerrero	.10	278	Mike Warren	.10	382	Kurt Kepshire	.10
77	Bob Horner	.10	175	Frank White	.10	279	Bob James	.10	383	Bobby Brown	.10
78	Larry McWilliams	.10	176	Rickey Henderson	2.00	280	Bobby Grich	.10	384	Dave Van Gorder	.10
79	Joel Youngblood	.10	177	Charlie Lea	.10	281	Mike Mason RC	.10	385	Rick Mahler	.10
80	Alan Wiggins	.10	178	Pete O'Brien	.10	282	Ron Reed	.10	386	Lee Mazzilli	.10
81	Ron Oester	.10	179	Doug DeCinces	.10	283	Alan Ashby	.10	387	Bill Laskey	.10
82	Ozzie Virgil	.10	180	Ron Kittle	.10	284	Mark Thurmond	.10	388	Thad Bosley	.10
83	Ricky Horton RC	.10	181	George Hendrick	.10	285	Joe Lefebvre	.10	389	Al Chambers	.10
84	Bill Doran	.10	182	Joe Niekro	.10	286	Ted Power	.10	390	Tony Fernandez	.10
85	Rod Carew	2.00	183	Juan Samuel	.10	287	Chris Chambliss	.10	391	Ron Washington	.10
86	LaMarr Hoyt	.10	184	Mario Soto	.10	288	Lee Tunnell	.10	392	Bill Swaggerty	.10
87	Tim Wallach	.10	185	Goose Gossage	.15	289	Rich Bordi	.10	393	Bob L. Gibson	.10
88	Mike Flanagan	.10	186	Johnny Ray	.10	290	Glenn Brummer	.10	394	Marty Castillo	.10
89	Jim Sundberg	.10	187	Bob Brenly	.10	291	Mike Boddicker	.10	395	Steve Crawford	.10
90	Chet Lemon	.10	188	Craig McMurtry	.10	292	Rollie Fingers	1.00	396	Clay Christiansen	.10
91	Bob Stanley	.10	189	Leon Durham	.10	293	Lou Whitaker	.10	397	Bob Bailor	.10
92	Willie Randolph	.10	190	Dwight Gooden	.25	294	Dwight Evans	.10	398	Mike Hargrove	.10
93	Bill Russell	.10	191	Barry Bonnell	.10	295	Don Mattingly	5.00	399	Charlie Leibrandt	.10
94	Julio Franco	.10	192	Tim Teufel	.10	296	Mike Marshall	.10	400	Tom Burgmeier	.10
95	Dan Quisenberry	.10	193	Dave Stieb	.10	297	Willie Wilson	.10	401	Razor Shines	.10
96	Bill Caudill	.10	194	Mickey Hatcher	.10	298	Mike Heath	.10	402	Rob Wilfong	.10
97	Bill Gullickson	.10	195	Jesse Barfield	.10	299	Tim Raines	.10	403	Tom Henke	.10
98	Danny Darwin	.10	196	Al Cowens	.10	300	Larry Parrish	.10	404	Al Jones	.10
99	Curtis Wilkerson	.10	197	Hubie Brooks	.10	301	Geoff Zahn	.10	405	Mike LaCoss	.10
100	Bud Black	.10	198	Steve Trout	.10	302	Rich Dotson	.10	406	Luis DeLeon	.10
101	Tony Phillips	.10	199	Glenn Hubbard	.10	303	David Green	.10	407	Greg Gross	.10
102	Tony Bernazard	.10	200	Bill Madlock	.10	304	Jose Cruz	.10	408	Tom Hume	.10
103	Jay Howell	.10	201	Jeff Robinson RC	.10	305	Steve Carlton	2.00	409	Rick Camp	.10
104	Burt Hooton	.10	202	Eric Show	.10	306	Gary Redus	.10	410	Milt May	.10
105	Milt Wilcox	.10	203	Dave Concepcion	.10	307	Steve Garvey	.40	411	Henry Cotto RC	.10
106	Rich Dauer	.10	204	Ivan DeJesus	.10	308	Jose DeLeon	.10	412	Dave Von Ohlen	.10
107	Don Sutton	1.00	205	Neil Allen	.10	309	Randy Lerch	.10	413	Scott McGregor	.10
108	Mike Witt	.10	206	Jerry Mumphrey	.10	310	Claudell Washington	.10	414	Ted Simmons	.10
109	Bruce Sutter	1.50	207	Mike Brown	.10	311	Lee Smith	.25	415	Jack Morris	.10
110	Enos Cabell	.10	208	Carlton Fisk	2.00	312	Darryl Strawberry	.10	416	Bill Buckner	.10
111	John Denny	.10	209	Bryn Smith	.10	313	Jim Beattie	.10	417	Butch Wynegar	.10
112	Dave Dravecky	.10	210	Tippy Martinez	.10	314	John Butcher	.10	418	Steve Sax	.10
113	Marvell Wynne	.10	211	Dion James	.10	315	Damaso Garcia	.10	419	Steve Balboni	.10
114	Johnnie LeMaster	.10	212	Willie Hernandez	.10	316	Mike Smithson	.10	420	Dwayne Murphy	.10
115	Chuck Porter	.10	213	Mike Easler	.10	317	Luis Leal	.10	421	Andre Dawson	.65
116	John Gibbons	.10	214	Ron Guidry	.10	318	Ken Phelps	.10	422	Charlie Hough	.10
117	Keith Moreland	.10	215	Rick Honeycutt	.10	319	Wally Backman	.10	423	Tommy John	.15
118	Darnell Coles	.10	216	Brett Butler	.10	320	Ron Cey	.10	424a	Tom Seaver (Floyd Bannister photo, left-hander.)	2.00
119	Dennis Lamp	.10	217	Larry Gura	.10	321	Brad Komminsk	.10	424b	Tom Seaver (Correct photo.)	7.50
120	Ron Davis	.10	218	Ray Burris	.10	322	Jason Thompson	.10	425	Tom Herr	.10
121	Nick Esasky	.10	219	Steve Rogers	.10	323	Frank Williams RC	.10	426	Terry Puhl	.10
			220	Frank Tanana	.10	324	Tim Lollar	.10	427	Al Holland	.10
			221	Ned Yost	.10	325	Eric Davis RC	1.50	428	Eddie Milner	.10
			222	Bret Saberhagen	.25	326	Von Hayes	.10			
			223	Mike Davis	.10	327	Andy Van Slyke	.50			
			224	Bert Blyleven	.15	328	Craig Reynolds	.10			
			225	Steve Kemp	.10	329	Dick Schofield	.10			

No.	Player	Price
429	Terry Kennedy	.10
430	John Candelaria	.10
431	Manny Trillo	.10
432	Ken Oberkfell	.10
433	Rick Sutcliffe	.10
434	Ron Darling	.10
435	Spike Owen	.10
436	Frank Viola	.10
437	Lloyd Moseby	.10
438	Kirby Puckett	8.00
439	Jim Clancy	.10
440	Mike Moore	.10
441	Doug Sisk	.10
442	Dennis Eckersley	1.50
443	Gerald Perry	.10
444	Dale Berra	.10
445	Dusty Baker	.10
446	Ed Whitson	.10
447	Cesar Cedeno	.10
448	Rick Schu RC	.10
449	Joaquin Andujar	.10
450	Mark Bailey RC	.10
451	Ron Romanick RC	.10
452	Julio Cruz	.10
453	Miguel Dilone	.10
454	Storm Davis	.10
455	Jaime Cocanower	.10
456	Barbaro Garbey	.10
457	Rich Gedman	.10
458	Phil Niekro	1.00
459	Mike Scioscia	.10
460	Pat Tabler	.10
461	Darryl Motley	.10
462	Chris Codoroli (Codiroli)	.10
463	Doug Flynn	.10
464	Billy Sample	.10
465	Mickey Rivers	.10
466	John Wathan	.10
467	Bill Krueger	.10
468	Andre Thornton	.10
469	Rex Hudler	.10
470	Sid Bream RC	.25
471	Kirk Gibson	.10
472	John Shelby	.10
473	Moose Haas	.10
474	Doug Corbett	.10
475	Willie McGee	.10
476	Bob Knepper	.10
477	Kevin Gross	.10
478	Carmelo Martinez	.10
479	Kent Tekulve	.10
480	Chili Davis	.10
481	Bobby Clark	.10
482	Mookie Wilson	.10
483	Dave Owen	.10
484	Ed Nunez	.10
485	Rance Mulliniks	.10
486	Ken Schrom	.10
487	Jeff Russell	.10
488	Tom Paciorek	.10
489	Dan Ford	.10
490	Mike Caldwell	.10
491	Scottie Earl	.10
492	Jose Rijo	.10
493	Bruce Hurst	.10
494	Ken Landreaux	.10
495	Mike Fischlin	.10
496	Don Slaught	.10
497	Steve McCatty	.10
498	Gary Lucas	.10
499	Gary Pettis	.10
500	Marvis Foley	.10
501	Mike Squires	.10
502	Jim Pankovitz RC	.10
503	Luis Aguayo	.10
504	Ralph Citarella	.10
505	Bruce Bochy	.10
506	Bob Owchinko	.10
507	Pascual Perez	.10
508	Lee Lacy	.10
509	Atlee Hammaker	.10
510	Bob Dernier	.10
511	Ed Vande Berg	.10
512	Cliff Johnson	.10
513	Len Whitehouse	.10
514	Dennis Martinez	.10
515	Ed Romero	.10
516	Rusty Kuntz	.10
517	Rick Miller	.10
518	Dennis Rasmussen	.10
519	Steve Yeager	.10
520	Chris Bando	.10
521	U.L. Washington	.10
522	Curt Young RC	.10
523	Angel Salazar	.10
524	Curt Kaufman	.10
525	Odell Jones	.10
526	Juan Agosto	.10
527	Denny Walling	.10
528	Andy Hawkins	.10
529	Sixto Lezcano	.10
530	Skeeter Barnes	.10
531	Randy S. Johnson	.10
532	Jim Morrison	.10
533	Warren Brusstar	.10
534a	Jeff Pendleton RC (Error)	1.00
534b	Terry Pendleton RC (Correct)	4.50
535	Vic Rodriguez	.10
536	Bob McClure	.10
537	Dave Bergman	.10
538	Mark Clear	.10
539	Mike Pagliarulo RC	.25
540	Terry Whitfield	.10
541	Joe Beckwith	.10
542	Jeff Burroughs	.10
543	Dan Schatzeder	.10
544	Donnie Scott	.10
545	Jim Slaton	.10
546	Greg Luzinski	.10
547	Mark Salas RC	.10
548	Dave Smith	.10
549	John Wockenfuss	.10
550	Frank Pastore	.10
551	Tim Flannery	.10
552	Rick Rhoden	.10
553	Mark Davis	.10
554	Jeff Dedmon RC	.15
555	Gary Woods	.10
556	Danny Heep	.10
557	Mark Langston	.10
558	Darrell Brown	.10
559	Jimmy Key	.10
560	Rick Lysander	.10
561	Doyle Alexander	.10
562	Mike Stanton	.10
563	Sid Fernandez	.10
564	Richie Hebner	.10
565	Alex Trevino	.10
566	Brian Harper	.10
567	Dan Gladden RC	.25
568	Luis Salazar	.10
569	Tom Foley	.10
570	Larry Andersen	.10
571	Danny Cox	.10
572	Joe Sambito	.10
573	Juan Beniquez	.10
574	Joel Skinner	.10
575	Randy St. Claire RC	.10
576	Floyd Rayford	.10
577	Roy Howell	.10
578	John Grubb	.10
579	Ed Jurak	.10
580	John Montefusco	.10
581	Orel Hershiser RC	3.00
582	Tom Waddell RC	.10
583	Mark Huismann	.10
584	Joe Morgan	2.00
585	Jim Wohlford	.10
586	Dave Schmidt	.10
587	Jeff Kunkel RC	.10
588	Hal McRae	.10
589	Bill Almon	.10
590	Carmen Castillo	.10
591	Omar Moreno	.10
592	Ken Howell RC	.10
593	Tom Brookens	.10
594	Joe Nolan	.10
595	Willie Lozado	.10
596	Tom Nieto RC	.10
597	Walt Terrell	.10
598	Al Oliver	.10
599	Shane Rawley	.10
600	Denny Gonzalez RC	.10
601	Mark Grant RC	.10
602	Mike Armstrong	.10
603	George Foster	.10
604	Davey Lopes	.10
605	Salome Barojas	.10
606	Roy Lee Jackson	.10
607	Pete Filson	.10
608	Duane Walker	.10
609	Glenn Wilson	.10
610	Rafael Santana RC	.10
611	Roy Smith	.10
612	Ruppert Jones	.10
613	Joe Cowley	.10
614	Al Nipper RC (Photo actually Mike Brown.)	.15
615	Gene Nelson	.10
616	Joe Carter	.10
617	Ray Knight	.10
618	Chuck Rainey	.10
619	Dan Driessen	.10
620	Daryl Sconiers	.10
621	Bill Stein	.10
622	Roy Smalley	.10
623	Ed Lynch	.10
624	Jeff Stone RC	.10
625	Bruce Berenyi	.10
626	Kelvin Chapman	.10
627	Joe Price	.10
628	Steve Bedrosian	.10
629	Vic Mata	.10
630	Mike Krukow	.10
631	Phil Bradley RC	.15
632	Jim Gott	.10
633	Randy Bush	.10
634	Tom Browning RC	.25
635	Lou Gehrig Puzzle Card	.10
636	Reid Nichols	.10
637	Dan Pasqua RC	.25
638	German Rivera	.10
639	Don Schulze RC	.10
640a	Mike Jones (Last line of highlights begins "Was 11- 7...")	.10
640b	Mike Jones (Last line of highlights begins "Spent some ...")	.15
641	Pete Rose	4.00
642	Wade Rowdon RC	.10
643	Jerry Narron	.10
644	Darrell Miller RC	.10
645	Tim Hulett RC	.10
646	Andy McGaffigan	.10
647	Kurt Bevacqua	.10
648	John Russell RC	.10
649	Ron Robinson RC	.10
650	Donnie Moore	.10
651a	Don Mattingly, Dave Winfield Two for the Title (Yellow letters.)	3.00
651b	Don Mattingly, Dave Winfield Two for the Title (White letters.)	4.50
652	Tim Laudner	.10
653	Steve Farr RC	.10
----	Checklist 1-26 DK	.10
----	Checklist 27-130	.10
----	Checklist 131-234	.10
----	Checklist 235-338	.10
----	Checklist 339-442	.10
----	Checklist 443-546	.10
----	Checklist 547-653	.10

1986 Donruss

BILL BUCKNER 1B

	NM/M
Unopened Factory Set (660):	35.00
Complete Set (660):	30.00
Common Player:	.05
Hank Aaron Puzzle:	3.00
Wax Pack (15):	1.25
Wax Box (36):	35.00
Rack Pack (45):	2.50
1	Kirk Gibson/DK	.15
2	Goose Gossage/DK	.15
3	Willie McGee/DK	.10
4	George Bell/DK	.05
5	Tony Armas/DK	.05
6	Chili Davis/DK	.05
7	Cecil Cooper/DK	.05
8	Mike Boddicker/DK	.05
9	Davey Lopes/DK	.05
10	Bill Doran/DK	.05
11	Bret Saberhagen/DK	.10
12	Brett Butler/DK	.10
13	Harold Baines/DK	.15
14	Mike Davis/DK	.05
15	Tony Perez/DK	1.00
16	Willie Randolph/DK	.05
17	Bob Boone/DK	.10
18	Orel Hershiser/DK)	.10
19	Johnny Ray/DK	.05
20	Gary Ward/DK	.05
21	Rick Mahler/DK	.05
22	Phil Bradley/DK	.05
23	Jerry Koosman/DK	.10
24	Tom Brunansky/DK	.05
25	Andre Dawson/DK	.50
26	Dwight Gooden/DK	.10
27	Kal Daniels/RR RC	.15
28	Fred McGriff/RR RC	4.00
29	Cory Snyder/RR RC	.10
30	Jose Guzman/RR RC	.05
31	Ty Gainey/RR RC	.05
32	Johnny Abrego/RR RC	.05
33a	Andres Galarraga/RR RC (Accent mark over e of Andres on back.)	2.00
33b	Andres Galarraga/RR RC (No accent mark.)	2.00
34	Dave Shipanoff/RR RC	.05
35	Mark McLemore/RR RC	.50
36	Marty Clary/RR RC	.05
37	Paul O'Neill/RR RC	2.00
38	Danny Tartabull/RR	.05
39	Jose Canseco/RR RC	6.00
40	Juan Nieves/RR RC	.05
41	Lance McCullers/RR RC	.05
42	Rick Surhoff/RR RC	.05
43	Todd Worrell/RR RC	.25
44	Bob Kipper/RR	.05
45	John Habyan/RR RC	.05
46	Mike Woodard/RR RC	.05
47	Mike Boddicker	.05
48	Robin Yount	1.50
49	Lou Whitaker	.05
50	Dennis Boyd	.05
51	Rickey Henderson	1.50
52	Mike Marshall	.05
53	George Brett	2.50
54	Dave Kingman	.05
55	Hubie Brooks	.05
56	Oddibe McDowell RC	.15
57	Doug DeCinces	.05
58	Britt Burns	.05
59	Ozzie Smith	2.00
60	Jose Cruz	.05
61	Mike Schmidt	2.50
62	Pete Rose	3.00
63	Steve Garvey	.40
64	Tony Pena	.05
65	Chili Davis	.05
66	Dale Murphy	.40
67	Ryne Sandberg	2.00
68	Gary Carter	1.50
69	Alvin Davis	.05
70	Kent Hrbek	.05
71	George Bell	.05
72	Kirby Puckett	2.00
73	Lloyd Moseby	.05
74	Bob Kearney	.05
75	Dwight Gooden	.05
76	Gary Matthews	.05
77	Rick Mahler	.05
78	Benny Distefano	.05
79	Jeff Leonard	.05
80	Kevin McReynolds	.05
81	Ron Oester	.05
82	John Russell	.05
83	Tommy Herr	.05
84	Jerry Mumphrey	.05
85	Ron Romanick	.05
86	Daryl Boston	.05
87	Andre Dawson	.50
88	Eddie Murray	1.50
89	Dion James	.05
90	Chet Lemon	.05
91	Bob Stanley	.05
92	Willie Randolph	.05
93	Mike Scioscia	.05
94	Tom Waddell	.05
95	Danny Jackson	.05
96	Mike Davis	.05
97	Mike Fitzgerald	.05
98	Gary Ward	.05
99	Pete O'Brien	.05
100	Bret Saberhagen	.05
101	Alfredo Griffin	.05
102	Brett Butler	.05
103	Ron Guidry	.15
104	Jerry Reuss	.05
105	Jack Morris	.50
106	Rick Dempsey	.05
107	Ray Burris	.05
108	Brian Downing	.05
109	Willie McGee	.05
110	Bill Doran	.05
111	Kent Tekulve	.05
112	Tony Gwynn	2.00
113	Marvell Wynne	.05
114	David Green	.05
115	Jim Gantner	.05
116	George Foster	.05
117	Steve Trout	.05
118	Mark Langston	.05
119	Tony Fernandez	.05
120	John Butcher	.05
121	Ron Robinson	.05
122	Dan Spillner	.05
123	Mike Young	.05
124	Paul Molitor	1.50
125	Kirk Gibson	.05
126	Ken Griffey	.05
127	Tony Armas	.05
128	Mariano Duncan RC	.15
129	Pat Tabler (Mr. Clutch)	.05
130	Frank White	.05
131	Carney Lansford	.05
132	Vance Law	.05

#	Player	Price
133	Dick Schofield	.05
134	Wayne Tolleson	.05
135	Greg Walker	.05
136	Denny Walling	.05
137	Ozzie Virgil	.05
138	Ricky Horton	.05
139	LaMarr Hoyt	.05
140	Wayne Krenchicki	.05
141	Glenn Hubbard	.05
142	Cecilio Guante	.05
143	Mike Krukow	.05
144	Lee Smith	.15
145	Edwin Nunez	.05
146	Dave Stieb	.05
147	Mike Smithson	.05
148	Ken Dixon	.05
149	Danny Darwin	.05
150	Chris Pittaro	.05
151	Bill Buckner	.05
152	Mike Pagliarulo	.05
153	Bill Russell	.05
154	Brook Jacoby	.05
155	Pat Sheridan	.05
156	Mike Gallego RC	.05
157	Jim Wohlford	.05
158	Gary Pettis	.05
159	Toby Harrah	.05
160	Richard Dotson	.05
161	Bob Knepper	.05
162	Dave Dravecky	.05
163	Greg Gross	.05
164	Eric Davis	.05
165	Gerald Perry	.05
166	Rick Rhoden	.05
167	Keith Moreland	.05
168	Jack Clark	.05
169	Storm Davis	.05
170	Cecil Cooper	.05
171	Alan Trammell	.05
172	Roger Clemens	2.50
173	Don Mattingly	2.50
174	Pedro Guerrero	.05
175	Willie Wilson	.05
176	Dwayne Murphy	.05
177	Tim Raines	.05
178	Larry Parrish	.05
179	Mike Witt	.05
180	Harold Baines	.05
181	Vince Coleman RC	.35
182	Jeff Heathcock RC	.05
183	Steve Carlton	1.50
184	Mario Soto	.05
185	Goose Gossage	.10
186	Johnny Ray	.05
187	Dan Gladden	.05
188	Bob Horner	.05
189	Rick Sutcliffe	.05
190	Keith Hernandez	.05
191	Phil Bradley	.05
192	Tom Brunansky	.05
193	Jesse Barfield	.05
194	Frank Viola	.05
195	Willie Upshaw	.05
196	Jim Beattie	.05
197	Darryl Strawberry	.05
198	Ron Cey	.05
199	Steve Bedrosian	.05
200	Steve Kemp	.05
201	Manny Trillo	.05
202	Garry Templeton	.05
203	Dave Parker	.05
204	John Denny	.05
205	Terry Pendleton	.05
206	Terry Puhl	.05
207	Bobby Grich	.05
208	Ozzie Guillen RC	2.00
209	Jeff Reardon	.05
210	Cal Ripken, Jr.	3.00
211	Bill Schroeder	.05
212	Dan Petry	.05
213	Jim Rice	.50
214	Dave Righetti	.05
215	Fernando Valenzuela	.05
216	Julio Franco	.05
217	Darryl Motley	.05
218	Dave Collins	.05
219	Tim Wallach	.05
220	George Wright	.05
221	Tommy Dunbar	.05
222	Steve Balboni	.05
223	Jay Howell	.05
224	Joe Carter	.05
225	Ed Whitson	.05
226	Orel Hershiser	.05
227	Willie Hernandez	.05
228	Lee Lacy	.05
229	Rollie Fingers	1.00
230	Bob Boone	.05
231	Joaquin Andujar	.05
232	Craig Reynolds	.05
233	Shane Rawley	.05
234	Eric Show	.05
235	Jose DeLeon	.05
236	Jose Uribe RC	.05
237	Moose Haas	.05
238	Wally Backman	.05
239	Dennis Eckersley	1.25
240	Mike Moore	.05
241	Damaso Garcia	.05
242	Tim Teufel	.05
243	Dave Concepcion	.05
244	Floyd Bannister	.05
245	Fred Lynn	.05
246	Charlie Moore	.05
247	Walt Terrell	.05
248	Dave Winfield	1.50
249	Dwight Evans	.05
250	Dennis Powell RC	.05
251	Andre Thornton	.05
252	Onix Concepcion	.05
253	Mike Heath	.05
254a	David Palmer (2B on front.)	.05
254b	David Palmer (P on front.)	.15
255	Donnie Moore	.05
256	Curtis Wilkerson	.05
257	Julio Cruz	.05
258	Nolan Ryan	3.00
259	Jeff Stone	.05
260a	John Tudor (1981 Games is .18)	.05
260b	John Tudor (1981 Games is 18)	.15
261	Mark Thurmond	.05
262	Jay Tibbs	.05
263	Rafael Ramirez	.05
264	Larry McWilliams	.05
265	Mark Davis	.05
266	Bob Dernier	.05
267	Matt Young	.05
268	Jim Clancy	.05
269	Mickey Hatcher	.05
270	Sammy Stewart	.05
271	Bob L. Gibson	.05
272	Nelson Simmons	.05
273	Rich Gedman	.05
274	Butch Wynegar	.05
275	Ken Howell	.05
276	Mel Hall	.05
277	Jim Sundberg	.05
278	Chris Codiroli	.05
279	Herman Winningham RC	.05
280	Rod Carew	1.50
281	Don Slaught	.05
282	Scott Fletcher	.05
283	Bill Dawley	.05
284	Andy Hawkins	.05
285	Glenn Wilson	.05
286	Nick Esasky	.05
287	Claudell Washington	.05
288	Lee Mazzilli	.05
289	Jody Davis	.05
290	Darrell Porter	.05
291	Scott McGregor	.05
292	Ted Simmons	.05
293	Aurelio Lopez	.05
294	Marty Barrett	.05
295	Dale Berra	.05
296	Greg Brock	.05
297	Charlie Leibrandt	.05
298	Bill Krueger	.05
299	Bryn Smith	.05
300	Burt Hooton	.05
301	Stu Cliburn RC	.05
302	Luis Salazar	.05
303	Ken Dayley	.05
304	Frank DiPino	.05
305	Von Hayes	.05
306a	Gary Redus (1983 2B is .20)	.05
306b	Gary Redus (1983 2B is 20)	.15
307	Craig Lefferts	.05
308	Sam Khalifa	.05
309	Scott Garrelts	.05
310	Rick Cerone	.05
311	Shawon Dunston	.05
312	Howard Johnson	.05
313	Jim Presley	.05
314	Gary Gaetti	.05
315	Luis Leal	.05
316	Mark Salas	.05
317	Bill Caudill	.05
318	Dave Henderson	.05
319	Rafael Santana	.05
320	Leon Durham	.05
321	Bruce Sutter	1.25
322	Jason Thompson	.05
323	Bob Brenly	.05
324	Carmelo Martinez	.05
325	Eddie Milner	.05
326	Juan Samuel	.05
327	Tom Nieto	.05
328	Dave Smith	.05
329	Urbano Lugo RC	.05
330	Joel Skinner	.05
331	Bill Gullickson	.05
332	Floyd Rayford	.05
333	Ben Oglivie	.05
334	Lance Parrish	.05
335	Jackie Gutierrez	.05
336	Dennis Rasmussen	.05
337	Terry Whitfield	.05
338	Neal Heaton	.05
339	Jorge Orta	.05
340	Donnie Hill	.05
341	Joe Hesketh	.05
342	Charlie Hough	.05
343	Dave Rozema	.05
344	Greg Pryor	.05
345	Mickey Tettleton	.05
346	George Vukovich	.05
347	Don Baylor	.05
348	Carlos Diaz	.05
349	Barbaro Garbey	.05
350	Larry Sheets	.05
351	Ted Higuera RC	.10
352	Juan Beniquez	.05
353	Bob Forsch	.05
354	Mark Bailey	.05
355	Larry Andersen	.05
356	Terry Kennedy	.05
357	Don Robinson	.05
358	Jim Gott	.05
359	Earnest Riles RC	.05
360	John Christensen RC	.05
361	Ray Fontenot	.05
362	Spike Owen	.05
363	Jim Acker	.05
364a	Ron Davis (Last line in highlights ends with "...in May.")	.05
364b	Ron Davis (Last line in highlights ends with "...relievers (9).")	.15
365	Tom Hume	.05
366	Carlton Fisk	1.50
367	Nate Snell	.05
368	Rick Manning	.05
369	Darrell Evans	.05
370	Ron Hassey	.05
371	Wade Boggs	2.00
372	Rick Honeycutt	.05
373	Chris Bando	.05
374	Bud Black	.05
375	Steve Henderson	.05
376	Charlie Lea	.05
377	Reggie Jackson	2.50
378	Dave Schmidt	.05
379	Bob James	.05
380	Glenn Davis	.05
381	Tim Corcoran	.05
382	Danny Cox	.05
383	Tim Flannery	.05
384	Tom Browning	.05
385	Rick Camp	.05
386	Jim Morrison	.05
387	Dave LaPoint	.05
388	Davey Lopes	.05
389	Al Cowens	.05
390	Doyle Alexander	.05
391	Tim Laudner	.05
392	Don Aase	.05
393	Jaime Cocanower	.05
394	Randy O'Neal	.05
395	Mike Easler	.05
396	Scott Bradley	.05
397	Tom Niedenfuer	.05
398	Jerry Willard	.05
399	Lonnie Smith	.05
400	Bruce Bochte	.05
401	Terry Francona	.05
402	Jim Slaton	.05
403	Bill Stein	.05
404	Tim Hulett	.05
405	Alan Ashby	.05
406	Tim Stoddard	.05
407	Garry Maddox	.05
408	Ted Power	.05
409	Len Barker	.05
410	Denny Gonzalez	.05
411	George Frazier	.05
412	Andy Van Slyke	.05
413	Jim Dwyer	.05
414	Paul Householder	.05
415	Alejandro Sanchez	.05
416	Steve Crawford	.05
417	Dan Pasqua	.05
418	Enos Cabell	.05
419	Mike Jones	.05
420	Steve Kiefer	.05
421	Tim Burke RC	.05
422	Mike Mason	.05
423	Ruppert Jones	.05
424	Jerry Hairston Sr.	.05
425	Tito Landrum	.05
426	Jeff Calhoun	.05
427	Don Carman RC	.05
428	Tony Perez	1.00
429	Jerry Davis	.05
430	Bob Walk	.05
431	Brad Wellman	.05
432	Terry Forster	.05
433	Billy Hatcher	.05
434	Clint Hurdle	.05
435	Ivan Calderon RC	.05
436	Pete Filson	.05
437	Tom Henke	.05
438	Dave Engle	.05
439	Tom Filer	.05
440	Gorman Thomas	.05
441	Rick Aguilera RC	.25
442	Scott Sanderson	.05
443	Jeff Dedmon	.05
444	Joe Orsulak RC	.10
445	Atlee Hammaker	.05
446	Jerry Royster	.05
447	Buddy Bell	.05
448	Dave Rucker	.05
449	Ivan DeJesus	.05
450	Jim Pankovits	.05
451	Jerry Narron	.05
452	Bryan Little	.05
453	Gary Lucas	.05
454	Dennis Martinez	.05
455	Ed Romero	.05
456	Bob Melvin RC	.05
457	Glenn Hoffman	.05
458	Bob Shirley	.05
459	Bob Welch	.05
460	Carmen Castillo	.05
461	Dave Leeper	.05
462	Tim Birtsas RC	.05
463	Randy St. Claire	.05
464	Chris Welsh	.05
465	Greg Harris	.05
466	Lynn Jones	.05
467	Dusty Baker	.05
468	Roy Smith	.05
469	Andre Robertson	.05
470	Ken Landreaux	.05
471	Dave Bergman	.05
472	Gary Roenicke	.05
473	Pete Vuckovich	.05
474	Kirk McCaskill RC	.10
475	Jeff Lahti	.05
476	Mike Scott	.05
477	Darren Daulton RC	1.50
478	Graig Nettles	.15
479	Bill Almon	.05
480	Greg Minton	.05
481	Randy Ready	.05
482	Len Dykstra RC	1.50
483	Thad Bosley	.05
484	Harold Reynolds RC	1.00
485	Al Oliver	.05
486	Roy Smalley	.05
487	John Franco	.05
488	Juan Agosto	.05
489	Al Pardo	.05
490	Bill Wegman RC	.05
491	Frank Tanana	.05
492	Brian Fisher RC	.05
493	Mark Clear	.05
494	Len Matuszek	.05
495	Ramon Romero	.05
496	John Wathan	.05
497	Rob Picciolo	.05
498	U.L. Washington	.05
499	John Candelaria	.05
500	Duane Walker	.05
501	Gene Nelson	.05
502	John Mizerock	.05
503	Luis Aguayo	.05
504	Kurt Kepshire	.05
505	Ed Wojna	.05
506	Joe Price	.05
507	Milt Thompson RC	.05
508	Junior Ortiz	.05
509	Vida Blue	.05
510	Steve Engel	.05
511	Karl Best	.05
512	Cecil Fielder RC	2.00
513	Frank Eufemia	.05
514	Tippy Martinez	.05
515	Billy Robidoux RC	.05
516	Bill Scherrer	.05
517	Bruce Hurst	.05
518	Rich Bordi	.05
519	Steve Yeager	.05
520	Tony Bernazard	.05
521	Hal McRae	.05
522	Jose Rijo	.05
523	Mitch Webster RC	.05
524	Jack Howell RC	.05
525	Alan Bannister	.05
526	Ron Kittle	.05
527	Phil Garner	.05
528	Kurt Bevacqua	.05
529	Kevin Gross	.05
530	Bo Diaz	.05
531	Ken Oberkfell	.05
532	Rick Reuschel	.05
533	Ron Meridith	.05

534	Steve Braun	.05
535	Wayne Gross	.05
536	Ray Searage	.05
537	Tom Brookens	.05
538	Al Nipper	.05
539	Billy Sample	.05
540	Steve Sax	.05
541	Dan Quisenberry	.05
542	Tony Phillips	.05
543	Floyd Youmans RC	.05
544	Steve Buechele RC	.05
545	Craig Gerber	.05
546	Joe DeSa	.05
547	Brian Harper	.05
548	Kevin Bass	.05
549	Tom Foley	.05
550	Dave Van Gorder	.05
551	Bruce Bochy	.05
552	R.J. Reynolds	.05
553	Chris Brown RC	.05
554	Bruce Benedict	.05
555	Warren Brusstar	.05
556	Danny Heep	.05
557	Darnell Coles	.05
558	Greg Gagne	.05
559	Ernie Whitt	.05
560	Ron Washington	.05
561	Jimmy Key	.05
562	Billy Swift	.05
563	Ron Darling	.05
564	Dick Ruthven	.05
565	Zane Smith	.05
566	Sid Bream	.05
567a	Joel Youngblood (P on front)	.05
567b	Joel Youngblood (IF on front)	.15
568	Mario Ramirez	.05
569	Tom Runnells	.05
570	Rick Schu	.05
571	Bill Campbell	.05
572	Dickie Thon	.05
573	Al Holland	.05
574	Reid Nichols	.05
575	Bert Roberge	.05
576	Mike Flanagan	.05
577	Tim Leary	.05
578	Mike Laga	.05
579	Steve Lyons	.05
580	Phil Niekro	1.00
581	Gilberto Reyes	.05
582	Jamie Easterly	.05
583	Mark Gubicza	.05
584	Stan Javier RC	.15
585	Bill Laskey	.05
586	Jeff Russell	.05
587	Dickie Noles	.05
588	Steve Farr	.05
589	Steve Ontiveros RC	.05
590	Mike Hargrove	.05
591	Marty Bystrom	.05
592	Franklin Stubbs	.05
593	Larry Herndon	.05
594	Bill Swaggerty	.05
595	Carlos Ponce	.05
596	Pat Perry RC	.05
597	Ray Knight	.05
598	Steve Lombardozzi RC	.05
599	Brad Havens	.05
600	Pat Clements RC	.05
601	Joe Niekro	.05
602	Hank Aaron Puzzle Card	.05
603	Dwayne Henry RC	.05
604	Mookie Wilson	.05
605	Buddy Biancalana	.05
606	Rance Mulliniks	.05
607	Alan Wiggins	.05
608	Joe Cowley	.05
609a	Tom Seaver (Green stripes around name.)	1.50
609b	Tom Seaver (Yellow stripes around name.)	2.00
610	Neil Allen	.05
611	Don Sutton	1.00
612	Fred Toliver RC	.05
613	Jay Baller	.05
614	Marc Sullivan	.05
615	John Grubb	.05
616	Bruce Kison	.05
617	Bill Madlock	.05
618	Chris Chambliss	.05
619	Dave Stewart	.05
620	Tim Lollar	.05
621	Gary Lavelle	.05
622	Charles Hudson	.05
623	Joel Davis RC	.05
624	Joe Johnson RC	.05
625	Sid Fernandez	.05
626	Dennis Lamp	.05
627	Terry Harper	.05
628	Jack Lazorko	.05
629	Roger McDowell RC	.25
630	Mark Funderburk	.05

631	Ed Lynch	.05
632	Rudy Law	.05
633	Roger Mason m RC	.05
634	Mike Felder RC	.05
635	Ken Schrom	.05
636	Bob Ojeda	.05
637	Ed Vande Berg	.05
638	Bobby Meacham	.05
639	Cliff Johnson	.05
640	Garth Iorg	.05
641	Dan Driessen	.05
642	Mike Brown	.05
643	John Shelby	.05
644	Pete Rose (RB)	.50
645	Joe Niekro, Phil Niekro Knuckle Brothers	.25
646	Jesse Orosco	.05
647	Billy Beane RC	.05
648	Cesar Cedeno	.05
649	Bert Blyleven	.15
650	Max Venable	.05
651	Vince Coleman, Willie McGee Fleet Feet	.25
652	Calvin Schiraldi	.05
653	Pete Rose King of Kings	3.00
----	Checklist 1-26 DK	.05
----	Checklist 27-130 (45 is Beane)	.05
----	Checklist 27-130 (45 is Habyan)	.05
----	Checklist 131-234	.05
----	Checklist 235-338	.05
----	Checklist 339-442	.05
----	Checklist 443-546	.05
----	Checklist 547-653	.05

Rookies

NM/M

Unopened Set (56):		35.00
Opened Set (56):		30.00
Common Player:		.05
1	Wally Joyner RC	.50
2	Tracy Jones	.05
3	Allan Anderson	.05
4	Ed Correa	.05
5	Reggie Williams	.05
6	Charlie Kerfeld	.05
7	Andres Galarraga	.15
8	Bob Tewksbury	.05
9	Al Newman	.05
10	Andres Thomas	.05
11	Barry Bonds RC	25.00
12	Juan Nieves	.05
13	Mark Eichhorn	.05
14	Dan Plesac	.05
15	Cory Snyder	.05
16	Kelly Gruber	.05
17	Kevin Mitchell RC	.25
18	Steve Lombardozzi	.05
19	Mitch Williams	.05
20	John Cerutti	.05
21	Todd Worrell	.05
22	Jose Canseco	2.00
23	Pete Incaviglia RC	.15
24	Jose Guzman	.05
25	Scott Bailes	.05
26	Greg Mathews	.05
27	Eric King	.05
28	Paul Assenmacher	.05
29	Jeff Sellers	.05
30	Bobby Bonilla RC	.25
31	Doug Drabek RC	.25
32	Will Clark RC	1.00
33	Bip Roberts	.05
34	Jim Deshaies	.05
35	Mike LaValliere	.05
36	Scott Bankhead	.05
37	Dale Sveum	.05
38	Bo Jackson RC	2.00
39	Rob Thompson	.05

40	Eric Plunk	.05
41	Bill Bathe	.05
42	John Kruk RC	.25
43	Andy Allanson	.05
44	Mark Portugal	.05
45	Danny Tartabull	.05
46	Bob Kipper	.05
47	Gene Walter	.05
48	Rey Quinonez	.05
49	Bobby Witt	.05
50	Bill Mooneyham	.05
51	John Cangelosi	.05
52	Ruben Sierra RC	.25
53	Rob Woodward	.05
54	Ed Hearn	.05
55	Joel McKeon	.05
56	Checklist 1-56	.05

1987 Donruss

LANCE McCULLERS P

NM/M

Unopened Fact. Set (660):		40.00
Complete Set (660):		30.00
Common Player:		.05
Roberto Clemente Puzzle:		2.50
Wax Pack (15):		1.25
Wax Box (36):		35.00
Rack Pack (45):		3.00
Jumbo Rack (75):		4.00
1	Wally Joyner/DK	.25
2	Roger Clemens/DK	1.00
3	Dale Murphy/DK	.25
4	Darryl Strawberry/DK	.10
5	Ozzie Smith/DK	.75
6	Jose Canseco/DK	.40
7	Charlie Hough/DK	.05
8	Brook Jacoby/DK	.05
9	Fred Lynn/DK	.10
10	Rick Rhoden/DK	.05
11	Chris Brown/DK	.05
12	Von Hayes/DK	.05
13	Jack Morris/DK	.10
14a	Kevin McReynolds/DK (No yellow stripe on back.)	.25
14b	Kevin McReynolds/DK (Yellow stripe on back.)	.25
15	George Brett/DK	1.00
16	Ted Higuera/DK	.05
17	Hubie Brooks/DK	.05
18	Mike Scott/DK	.05
19	Kirby Puckett/DK	.75
20	Dave Winfield/DK	.60
21	Lloyd Moseby/DK	.05
22a	Eric Davis/DK (No yellow stripe on back.)	.25
22b	Eric Davis/DK (Yellow stripe on back.)	.15
23	Jim Presley/DK	.05
24	Keith Moreland/DK	.05
25a	Greg Walker/DK (No yellow stripe on back.)	.25
25b	Greg Walker/DK (Yellow stripe on back.)	.10
26	Steve Sax/DK	.10
27	Checklist 1-27	.05
28	B.J. Surhoff/RR RC	.30
29	Randy Myers/RR RC	.50
30	Ken Gerhart/RR RC	.05
31	Benito Santiago/RR	.05
32	Greg Swindell/RR RC	.15
33	Mike Birkbeck/RR RC	.05
34	Terry Steinbach/RR RC	.25
35	Bo Jackson/RR	1.50
36	Greg Maddux/RR RC	6.00
37	Jim Lindeman/RR RC	.05
38	Devon White/RR RC	.75
39	Eric Bell/RR RC	.05
40	Will Fraser/RR RC	.05
41	Jerry Browne/RR RC	.05
42	Chris James/RR RC	.05
43	Rafael Palmeiro/RR RC	4.00
44	Pat Dodson/RR RC	.05
45	Duane Ward/RR RC	.10
46	Mark McGwire/RR	6.00

47	Bruce Fields/RR RC (Photo actually Darnell Coles.)	.10
48	Eddie Murray	.60
49	Ted Higuera	.05
50	Kirk Gibson	.05
51	Oil Can Boyd	.05
52	Don Mattingly	1.00
53	Pedro Guerrero	.05
54	George Brett	1.00
55	Jose Rijo	.05
56	Tim Raines	.05
57	Ed Correa RC	.05
58	Mike Witt	.05
59	Greg Walker	.05
60	Ozzie Smith	.75
61	Glenn Davis	.05
62	Glenn Wilson	.05
63	Tom Browning	.05
64	Tony Gwynn	.75
65	R.J. Reynolds	.05
66	Will Clark	.25
67	Ozzie Virgil	.05
68	Rick Sutcliffe	.05
69	Gary Carter	.60
70	Mike Moore	.05
71	Bert Blyleven	.10
72	Tony Fernandez	.05
73	Kent Hrbek	.05
74	Lloyd Moseby	.05
75	Alvin Davis	.05
76	Keith Hernandez	.05
77	Ryne Sandberg	.75
78	Dale Murphy	.40
79	Sid Bream	.05
80	Chris Brown	.05
81	Steve Garvey	.25
82	Mario Soto	.05
83	Shane Rawley	.05
84	Willie McGee	.05
85	Jose Cruz	.05
86	Brian Downing	.05
87	Ozzie Guillen	.05
88	Hubie Brooks	.05
89	Cal Ripken, Jr.	2.50
90	Juan Nieves	.05
91	Lance Parrish	.05
92	Jim Rice	.25
93	Ron Guidry	.10
94	Fernando Valenzuela	.05
95	Andy Allanson RC	.05
96	Willie Wilson	.05
97	Jose Canseco	.40
98	Jeff Reardon	.05
99	Bobby Witt RC	.20
100	Checklist 28-133	.05
101	Jose Guzman	.05
102	Steve Balboni	.05
103	Tony Phillips	.05
104	Brook Jacoby	.05
105	Dave Winfield	.60
106	Orel Hershiser	.05
107	Lou Whitaker	.05
108	Fred Lynn	.05
109	Bill Wegman	.05
110	Donnie Moore	.05
111	Jack Clark	.05
112	Bob Knepper	.05
113	Von Hayes	.05
114	Bip Roberts RC	.25
115	Tony Pena	.05
116	Scott Garrelts	.05
117	Paul Molitor	.60
118	Darryl Strawberry	.05
119	Shawon Dunston	.05
120	Jim Presley	.05
121	Jesse Barfield	.05
122	Gary Gaetti	.05
123	Kurt Stillwell RC	.10
124	Joel Davis	.05
125	Mike Boddicker	.05
126	Robin Yount	.60
127	Alan Trammell	.05
128	Dave Righetti	.05
129	Dwight Evans	.05
130	Mike Scioscia	.05
131	Julio Franco	.05
132	Bret Saberhagen	.05
133	Mike Davis	.05
134	Joe Hesketh	.05
135	Wally Joyner	.05
136	Don Slaught	.05
137	Daryl Boston	.05
138	Nolan Ryan	2.50
139	Mike Schmidt	1.00
140	Tommy Herr	.05
141	Garry Templeton	.05
142	Kal Daniels	.05
143	Billy Sample	.05
144	Johnny Ray	.05
145	Rob Thompson RC	.10
146	Bob Dernier	.05
147	Danny Tartabull	.05
148	Ernie Whitt	.05

No.	Player	Price
149	Kirby Puckett	.75
150	Mike Young	.05
151	Ernest Riles	.05
152	Frank Tanana	.05
153	Rich Gedman	.05
154	Willie Randolph	.05
155a	Bill Madlock (Name in brown band.)	.10
155b	Bill Madlock (Name in red band.)	.25
156a	Joe Carter (Name in brown band.)	.10
156b	Joe Carter (Name in red band.)	.25
157	Danny Jackson	.05
158	Carney Lansford	.05
159	Bryn Smith	.05
160	Gary Pettis	.05
161	Oddibe McDowell	.05
162	John Cangelosi RC	.10
163	Mike Scott	.05
164	Eric Show	.05
165	Juan Samuel	.05
166	Nick Esasky	.05
167	Zane Smith	.05
168	Mike Brown	.05
169	Keith Moreland	.05
170	John Tudor	.05
171	Ken Dixon	.05
172	Jim Gantner	.05
173	Jack Morris	.05
174	Bruce Hurst	.05
175	Dennis Rasmussen	.05
176	Mike Marshall	.05
177	Dan Quisenberry	.05
178	Eric Plunk	.05
179	Tim Wallach	.05
180	Steve Buechele	.05
181	Don Sutton	.50
182	Dave Schmidt	.05
183	Terry Pendleton	.05
184	Jim Deshaies RC	.05
185	Steve Bedrosian	.05
186	Pete Rose	2.00
187	Dave Dravecky	.05
188	Rick Reuschel	.05
189	Dan Gladden	.05
190	Rick Mahler	.05
191	Thad Bosley	.05
192	Ron Darling	.05
193	Matt Young	.05
194	Tom Brunansky	.05
195	Dave Stieb	.05
196	Frank Viola	.05
197	Tom Henke	.05
198	Karl Best	.05
199	Dwight Gooden	.05
200	Checklist 134-239	.05
201	Steve Trout	.05
202	Rafael Ramirez	.05
203	Bob Walk	.05
204	Roger Mason	.05
205	Terry Kennedy	.05
206	Ron Oester	.05
207	John Russell	.05
208	Greg Mathews RC	.05
209	Charlie Kerfeld	.05
210	Reggie Jackson	1.00
211	Floyd Bannister	.05
212	Vance Law	.05
213	Rich Bordi	.05
214	Dan Plesac RC	.10
215	Dave Collins	.05
216	Bob Stanley	.05
217	Joe Niekro	.05
218	Tom Niedenfuer	.05
219	Brett Butler	.05
220	Charlie Leibrandt	.05
221	Steve Ontiveros	.05
222	Tim Burke	.05
223	Curtis Wilkerson	.05
224	Pete Incaviglia RC	.10
225	Lonnie Smith	.05
226	Chris Codiroli	.05
227	Scott Bailes RC	.05
228	Rickey Henderson	.60
229	Ken Howell	.05
230	Darnell Coles	.05
231	Don Aase	.05
232	Tim Leary	.05
233	Bob Boone	.05
234	Ricky Horton	.05
235	Mark Bailey	.05
236	Kevin Gross	.05
237	Lance McCullers	.05
238	Cecilio Guante	.05
239	Bob Melvin	.05
240	Billy Jo Robidoux	.05
241	Roger McDowell	.05
242	Leon Durham	.05
243	Ed Nunez	.05
244	Jimmy Key	.05
245	Mike Smithson	.05
246	Bo Diaz	.05
247	Carlton Fisk	.60
248	Larry Sheets	.05
249	Juan Castillo RC	.05
250	Eric King RC	.05
251	Doug Drabek	.05
252	Wade Boggs	.75
253	Mariano Duncan	.05
254	Pat Tabler	.05
255	Frank White	.05
256	Alfredo Griffin	.05
257	Floyd Youmans	.05
258	Rob Wilfong	.05
259	Pete O'Brien	.05
260	Tim Hulett	.05
261	Dickie Thon	.05
262	Darren Daulton	.05
263	Vince Coleman	.05
264	Andy Hawkins	.05
265	Eric Davis	.05
266	Andres Thomas RC	.05
267	Mike Diaz RC	.05
268	Chili Davis	.05
269	Jody Davis	.05
270	Phil Bradley	.05
271	George Bell	.05
272	Keith Atherton	.05
273	Storm Davis	.05
274	Rob Deer	.05
275	Walt Terrell	.05
276	Roger Clemens	1.00
277	Mike Easler	.05
278	Steve Sax	.05
279	Andre Thornton	.05
280	Jim Sundberg	.05
281	Bill Bathe	.05
282	Jay Tibbs	.05
283	Dick Schofield	.05
284	Mike Mason	.05
285	Jerry Hairston Sr.	.05
286	Bill Doran	.05
287	Tim Flannery	.05
288	Gary Redus	.05
289	John Franco	.05
290	Paul Assenmacher RC	.10
291	Joe Orsulak	.05
292	Lee Smith	.10
293	Mike Laga	.05
294	Rick Dempsey	.05
295	Mike Felder	.05
296	Tom Brookens	.05
297	Al Nipper	.05
298	Mike Pagliarulo	.05
299	Franklin Stubbs	.05
300	Checklist 240-345	.05
301	Steve Farr	.05
302	Bill Mooneyham RC	.05
303	Andres Galarraga	.05
304	Scott Fletcher	.05
305	Jack Howell	.05
306	Russ Morman RC	.05
307	Todd Worrell	.05
308	Dave Smith	.05
309	Jeff Stone	.05
310	Ron Robinson	.05
311	Bruce Bochy	.05
312	Jim Winn	.05
313	Mark Davis	.05
314	Jeff Dedmon	.05
315	Jamie Moyer RC	.10
316	Wally Backman	.05
317	Ken Phelps	.05
318	Steve Lombardozzi	.05
319	Rance Mulliniks	.05
320	Tim Laudner	.05
321	Mark Eichhorn RC	.10
322	Lee Guetterman RC	.05
323	Sid Fernandez	.05
324	Jerry Mumphrey	.05
325	David Palmer	.05
326	Bill Almon	.05
327	Candy Maldonado	.05
328	John Kruk	.05
329	John Denny	.05
330	Milt Thompson	.05
331	Mike LaValliere RC	.10
332	Alan Ashby	.05
333	Doug Corbett	.05
334	Ron Karkovice RC	.05
335	Mitch Webster	.05
336	Lee Lacy	.05
337	Glenn Braggs RC	.05
338	Dwight Lowry	.05
339	Don Baylor	.05
340	Brian Fisher	.05
341	Reggie Williams RC	.05
342	Tom Candiotti	.05
343	Rudy Law	.05
344	Curt Young	.05
345	Mike Fitzgerald	.05
346	Ruben Sierra RC	.05
347	Mitch Williams RC	.25
348	Jorge Orta	.05
349	Mickey Tettleton	.05
350	Ernie Camacho	.05
351	Ron Kittle	.05
352	Ken Landreaux	.05
353	Chet Lemon	.05
354	John Shelby	.05
355	Mark Clear	.05
356	Doug DeCinces	.05
357	Ken Dayley	.05
358	Phil Garner	.05
359	Steve Jeltz	.05
360	Ed Whitson	.05
361	Barry Bonds	10.00
362	Vida Blue	.05
363	Cecil Cooper	.05
364	Bob Ojeda	.05
365	Dennis Eckersley	.50
366	Mike Morgan	.05
367	Willie Upshaw	.05
368	Allan Anderson RC	.05
369	Bill Gullickson	.05
370	Bobby Thigpen RC	.10
371	Juan Beniquez	.05
372	Charlie Moore	.05
373	Dan Petry	.05
374	Rod Scurry	.05
375	Tom Seaver	.75
376	Ed Vande Berg	.05
377	Tony Bernazard	.05
378	Greg Pryor	.05
379	Dwayne Murphy	.05
380	Andy McGaffigan	.05
381	Kirk McCaskill	.05
382	Greg Harris	.05
383	Rich Dotson	.05
384	Craig Reynolds	.05
385	Greg Gross	.05
386	Tito Landrum	.05
387	Craig Lefferts	.05
388	Dave Parker	.05
389	Bob Horner	.05
390	Pat Clements	.05
391	Jeff Leonard	.05
392	Chris Speier	.05
393	John Moses	.05
394	Garth Iorg	.05
395	Greg Gagne	.05
396	Nate Snell	.05
397	Bryan Clutterbuck RC	.05
398	Darrell Evans	.05
399	Steve Crawford	.05
400	Checklist 346-451	.05
401	Phil Lombardi RC	.05
402	Rick Honeycutt	.05
403	Ken Schrom	.05
404	Bud Black	.05
405	Donnie Hill	.05
406	Wayne Krenchicki	.05
407	Chuck Finley RC	.35
408	Toby Harrah	.05
409	Steve Lyons	.05
410	Kevin Bass	.05
411	Marvell Wynne	.05
412	Ron Roenicke	.05
413	Tracy Jones RC	.05
414	Gene Garber	.05
415	Mike Bielecki	.05
416	Frank DiPino	.05
417	Andy Van Slyke	.05
418	Jim Dwyer	.05
419	Ben Oglivie	.05
420	Dave Bergman	.05
421	Joe Sambito	.05
422	Bob Tewksbury RC	.30
423	Len Matuszek	.05
424	Mike Kingery RC	.05
425	Dave Kingman	.05
426	Al Newman RC	.05
427	Gary Ward	.05
428	Ruppert Jones	.05
429	Harold Baines	.05
430	Pat Perry	.05
431	Terry Puhl	.05
432	Don Carman	.05
433	Eddie Milner	.05
434	LaMarr Hoyt	.05
435	Rick Rhoden	.05
436	Jose Uribe	.05
437	Ken Oberkfell	.05
438	Ron Davis	.05
439	Jesse Orosco	.05
440	Scott Bradley	.05
441	Randy Bush	.05
442	John Cerutti RC	.05
443	Roy Smalley	.05
444	Kelly Gruber	.05
445	Bob Kearney	.05
446	Ed Hearn RC	.05
447	Scott Sanderson	.05
448	Bruce Benedict	.05
449	Junior Ortiz	.05
450	Mike Aldrete RC	.05
451	Kevin McReynolds	.05
452	Rob Murphy RC	.05
453	Kent Tekulve	.05
454	Curt Ford	.05
455	Davey Lopes	.05
456	Bobby Grich	.05
457	Jose DeLeon	.05
458	Andre Dawson	.35
459	Mike Flanagan	.05
460	Joey Meyer RC	.05
461	Chuck Cary RC	.05
462	Bill Buckner	.05
463	Bob Shirley	.05
464	Jeff Hamilton RC	.05
465	Phil Niekro	.50
466	Mark Gubicza	.05
467	Jerry Willard	.05
468	Bob Sebra RC	.05
469	Larry Parrish	.05
470	Charlie Hough	.05
471	Hal McRae	.05
472	Dave Leiper RC	.05
473	Mel Hall	.05
474	Dan Pasqua	.05
475	Bob Welch	.05
476	Johnny Grubb	.05
477	Jim Traber	.05
478	Chris Bosio RC	.05
479	Mark McLemore	.05
480	John Morris	.05
481	Billy Hatcher	.05
482	Dan Schatzeder	.05
483	Rich Gossage	.10
484	Jim Morrison	.05
485	Bob Brenly	.05
486	Bill Schroeder	.05
487	Mookie Wilson	.05
488	Dave Martinez RC	.10
489	Harold Reynolds	.05
490	Jeff Hearron	.05
491	Mickey Hatcher	.05
492	Barry Larkin RC	2.00
493	Bob James	.05
494	John Habyan	.05
495	Jim Adduci RC	.05
496	Mike Heath	.05
497	Tim Stoddard	.05
498	Tony Armas	.05
499	Dennis Powell	.05
500	Checklist 452-557	.05
501	Chris Bando	.05
502	David Cone RC	2.00
503	Jay Howell	.05
504	Tom Foley	.05
505	Ray Chadwick RC	.05
506	Mike Loynd RC	.05
507	Neil Allen	.05
508	Danny Darwin	.05
509	Rick Schu	.05
510	Jose Oquendo	.05
511	Gene Walter	.05
512	Terry McGriff RC	.05
513	Ken Griffey	.05
514	Benny Distefano	.05
515	Terry Mulholland RC	.25
516	Ed Lynch	.05
517	Bill Swift	.05
518	Manny Lee	.05
519	Andre David	.05
520	Scott McGregor	.05
521	Rick Manning	.05
522	Willie Hernandez	.05
523	Marty Barrett	.05
524	Wayne Tolleson	.05
525	Jose Gonzalez RC	.05
526	Cory Snyder	.05
527	Buddy Biancalana	.05
528	Moose Haas	.05
529	Wilfredo Tejada RC	.05
530	Stu Cliburn	.05
531	Dale Mohorcic RC	.05
532	Ron Hassey	.05
533	Ty Gainey	.05
534	Jerry Royster	.05
535	Mike Maddux RC	.05
536	Ted Power	.05
537	Ted Simmons	.05
538	Rafael Belliard RC	.05
539	Chico Walker	.05
540	Bob Forsch	.05
541	John Stefero	.05
542	Dale Sveum RC	.05
543	Mark Thurmond	.05
544	Jeff Sellers RC	.05
545	Joel Skinner	.05
546	Alex Trevino	.05
547	Randy Kutcher RC	.05
548	Joaquin Andujar	.05
549	Casey Candaele RC	.10
550	Jeff Russell	.05
551	John Candelaria	.05
552	Joe Cowley	.05
553	Danny Cox	.05
554	Denny Walling	.05
555	Bruce Ruffin RC	.10
556	Buddy Bell	.05
557	Jimmy Jones RC	.05
558	Bobby Bonilla	.05

559	Jeff Robinson	.05
560	Ed Olwine	.05
561	Glenallen Hill RC	.25
562	Lee Mazzilli	.05
563	Mike Brown	.05
564	George Frazier	.05
565	Mike Sharperson RC	.10
566	Mark Portugal RC	.05
567	Rick Leach	.05
568	Mark Langston	.05
569	Rafael Santana	.05
570	Manny Trillo	.05
571	Cliff Speck	.05
572	Bob Kipper	.05
573	Kelly Downs RC	.05
574	Randy Asadoor RC	.05
575	Dave Magadan RC	.25
576	Marvin Freeman RC	.05
577	Jeff Lahti	.05
578	Jeff Calhoun	.05
579	Gus Polidor	.05
580	Gene Nelson	.05
581	Tim Teufel	.05
582	Odell Jones	.05
583	Mark Ryal	.05
584	Randy O'Neal	.05
585	Mike Greenwell RC	.50
586	Ray Knight	.05
587	Ralph Bryant RC	.05
588	Carmen Castillo	.05
589	Ed Wojna	.05
590	Stan Javier	.05
591	Jeff Musselman RC	.05
592	Mike Stanley RC	.05
593	Darrell Porter	.05
594	Drew Hall RC	.05
595	Rob Nelson RC	.05
596	Bryan Oelkers	.05
597	Scott Nielsen RC	.05
598	Brian Holton RC	.05
599	Kevin Mitchell	.05
600	Checklist 558-660	.05
601	Jackie Gutierrez	.05
602	Barry Jones RC	.05
603	Jerry Narron	.05
604	Steve Lake	.05
605	Jim Pankovits	.05
606	Ed Romero	.05
607	Dave LaPoint	.05
608	Don Robinson	.05
609	Mike Krukow	.05
610	Dave Valle RC	.05
611	Len Dykstra	.05
612	Roberto Clemente Puzzle Card	.25
613	Mike Trujillo	.05
614	Damaso Garcia	.05
615	Neal Heaton	.05
616	Juan Berenguer	.05
617	Steve Carlton	.75
618	Gary Lucas	.05
619	Geno Petralli	.05
620	Rick Aguilera	.05
621	Fred McGriff	.05
622	Dave Henderson	.05
623	Dave Clark RC	.05
624	Angel Salazar	.05
625	Randy Hunt	.05
626	John Gibbons	.05
627	Kevin Brown RC	2.00
628	Bill Dawley	.05
629	Aurelio Lopez	.05
630	Charlie Hudson	.05
631	Ray Soff	.05
632	Ray Hayward RC	.05
633	Spike Owen	.05
634	Glenn Hubbard	.05
635	Kevin Elster RC	.10
636	Mike LaCoss	.05
637	Dwayne Henry	.05
638	Rey Quinones RC	.05
639	Jim Clancy	.05
640	Larry Andersen	.05
641	Calvin Schiraldi	.05
642	Stan Jefferson RC	.05
643	Marc Sullivan	.05
644	Mark Grant	.05
645	Cliff Johnson	.05
646	Howard Johnson	.05
647	Dave Sax	.05
648	Dave Stewart	.05
649	Danny Heep	.05
650	Joe Johnson	.05
651	Bob Brower RC	.05
652	Rob Woodward	.05
653	John Mizerock	.05
654	Tim Pyznarski RC	.05
655	Luis Aquino RC	.05
656	Mickey Brantley	.05
657	Doyle Alexander	.05
658	Sammy Stewart	.05
659	Jim Acker	.05
660	Pete Ladd	.05

Rookies

KEVIN SEITZER 3B

		NM/M
Unopened Fact. Set (56):		15.00
Complete Set (56):		10.00
Common Player:		.05
1	Mark McGwire	6.00
2	Eric Bell	.05
3	Mark Williamson	.05
4	Mike Greenwell	.05
5	Ellis Burks	.05
6	DeWayne Buice	.05
7	Mark Mclemore (McLemore)	.05
8	Devon White	.05
9	Willie Fraser	.05
10	Lester Lancaster	.05
11	Ken Williams	.05
12	Matt Nokes	.05
13	Jeff Robinson	.05
14	Bo Jackson	.25
15	Kevin Seitzer	.05
16	Billy Ripken	.05
17	B.J. Surhoff	.05
18	Chuck Crim	.05
19	Mike Birbeck	.05
20	Chris Bosio	.05
21	Les Straker	.05
22	Mark Davidson	.05
23	Gene Larkin	.05
24	Ken Gerhart	.05
25	Luis Polonia	.05
26	Terry Steinbach	.05
27	Mickey Brantley	.05
28	Mike Stanley	.05
29	Jerry Browne	.05
30	Todd Benzinger	.05
31	Fred McGriff	.25
32	Mike Henneman	.05
33	Casey Candaele	.05
34	Dave Magadan	.05
35	David Cone	.05
36	Mike Jackson	.05
37	John Mitchell	.05
38	Mike Dunne	.05
39	John Smiley	.05
40	Joe Magrane	.05
41	Jim Lindeman	.05
42	Shane Mack	.05
43	Stan Jefferson	.05
44	Benito Santiago	.05
45	Matt Williams RC	1.50
46	Dave Meads	.05
47	Rafael Palmeiro	4.00
48	Bill Long	.05
49	Bob Brower	.05
50	James Steels	.05
51	Paul Noce	.05
52	Greg Maddux	5.00
53	Jeff Musselman	.05
54	Brian Holton	.05
55	Chuck Jackson	.05
56	Checklist 1-56	.03

1988 Donruss

		NM/M
Unopened Fact. Set (660):		10.00
Complete Set (660):		8.00
Common Player:		.05
Stan Musial Puzzle:		1.00
Wax Pack (15):		.40
Wax Box (36):		10.00
Cello Pack (36):		.75
Cello Box (24):		12.00
Rack Pack (45):		.75
1	Mark McGwire/DK	.75
2	Tim Raines/DK	.05
3	Benito Santiago/DK	.05
4	Alan Trammell/DK	.05
5	Danny Tartabull/DK	.05
6	Ron Darling/DK	.05
7	Paul Molitor/DK	.40
8	Devon White/DK	.05

Darryl Strawberry OF

9	Andre Dawson/DK	.25
10	Julio Franco/DK	.05
11	Scott Fletcher/DK	.05
12	Tony Fernandez/DK	.05
13	Shane Rawley/DK	.05
14	Kal Daniels/DK	.05
15	Jack Clark/DK	.05
16	Dwight Evans/DK	.05
17	Tommy John/DK	.05
18	Andy Van Slyke/DK	.05
19	Gary Gaetti/DK	.05
20	Mark Langston/DK	.05
21	Will Clark/DK	.05
22	Glenn Hubbard/DK	.05
23	Billy Hatcher/DK	.05
24	Bob Welch/DK	.05
25	Ivan Calderon/DK	.05
26	Cal Ripken, Jr./DK	1.00
27	Checklist 1-27	.05
28	Mackey Sasser/RR RC	.05
29	Jeff Treadway/RR RC	.05
30	Mike Campbell /RR RC	.05
31	Lance Johnson/RR RC	.15
32	Nelson Liriano/RR RC	.05
33	Shawn Abner/RR	.05
34	Roberto Alomar/RR RC	1.00
35	Shawn Hillegas/RR RC	.05
36	Joey Meyer/RR	.05
37	Kevin Elster/RR	.05
38	Jose Lind/RR RC	.05
39	Kirt Manwaring/RR RC	.05
40	Mark Grace/RR RC	.50
41	Jody Reed/RR RC	.10
42	John Farrell/RR RC	.05
43	Al Leiter/RR RC	.20
44	Gary Thurman/RR RC	.05
45	Vicente Palacios/RR RC	.05
46	Eddie Williams/RR RC	.05
47	Jack McDowell/RR RC	.20
48	Ken Dixon	.05
49	Mike Birkbeck	.05
50	Eric King	.05
51	Roger Clemens	.60
52	Pat Clements	.05
53	Fernando Valenzuela	.05
54	Mark Gubicza	.05
55	Jay Howell	.05
56	Floyd Youmans	.05
57	Ed Correa	.05
58	DeWayne Buice RC	.05
59	Jose DeLeon	.05
60	Danny Cox	.05
61	Nolan Ryan	1.00
62	Steve Bedrosian	.05
63	Tom Browning	.05
64	Mark Davis	.05
65	R.J. Reynolds	.05
66	Kevin Mitchell	.05
67	Ken Oberkfell	.05
68	Rick Sutcliffe	.05
69	Dwight Gooden	.05
70	Scott Bankhead	.05
71	Bert Blyleven	.10
72	Jimmy Key	.05
73	Les Straker RC	.05
74	Jim Clancy	.05
75	Mike Moore	.05
76	Ron Darling	.05
77	Ed Lynch	.05
78	Dale Murphy	.20
79	Doug Drabek	.05
80	Scott Garrelts	.05
81	Ed Whitson	.05
82	Rob Murphy	.05
83	Shane Rawley	.05
84	Greg Mathews	.05
85	Jim Deshaies	.05
86	Mike Witt	.05
87	Donnie Hill	.05
88	Jeff Reed	.05
89	Mike Boddicker	.05
90	Ted Higuera	.05
91	Walt Terrell	.05

92	Bob Stanley	.05
93	Dave Righetti	.05
94	Orel Hershiser	.05
95	Chris Bando	.05
96	Bret Saberhagen	.05
97	Curt Young	.05
98	Tim Burke	.05
99	Charlie Hough	.05
100a	Checklist 28-137	.05
100b	Checklist 28-133	.05
101	Bobby Witt	.05
102	George Brett	.60
103	Mickey Tettleton	.05
104	Scott Bailes	.05
105	Mike Pagliarulo	.05
106	Mike Scioscia	.05
107	Tom Brookens	.05
108	Ray Knight	.05
109	Dan Plesac	.05
110	Wally Joyner	.05
111	Bob Forsch	.05
112	Mike Scott	.05
113	Kevin Gross	.05
114	Benito Santiago	.05
115	Bob Kipper	.05
116	Mike Krukow	.05
117	Chris Bosio	.05
118	Sid Fernandez	.05
119	Jody Davis	.05
120	Mike Morgan	.05
121	Mark Eichhorn	.05
122	Jeff Reardon	.05
123	John Franco	.05
124	Richard Dotson	.05
125	Eric Bell	.05
126	Juan Nieves	.05
127	Jack Morris	.05
128	Rick Rhoden	.05
129	Rich Gedman	.05
130	Ken Howell	.05
131	Brook Jacoby	.05
132	Danny Jackson	.05
133	Gene Nelson	.05
134	Neal Heaton	.05
135	Willie Fraser	.05
136	Jose Guzman	.05
137	Ozzie Guillen	.05
138	Bob Knepper	.05
139	Mike Jackson RC	.05
140	Joe Magrane RC	.05
141	Jimmy Jones	.05
142	Ted Power	.05
143	Ozzie Virgil	.05
144	Felix Fermin RC	.05
145	Kelly Downs	.05
146	Shawon Dunston	.05
147	Scott Bradley	.05
148	Dave Stieb	.05
149	Frank Viola	.05
150	Terry Kennedy	.05
151	Bill Wegman	.05
152	Matt Nokes RC	.10
153	Wade Boggs	.50
154	Wayne Tolleson	.05
155	Mariano Duncan	.05
156	Julio Franco	.05
157	Charlie Leibrandt	.05
158	Terry Steinbach	.05
159	Mike Fitzgerald	.05
160	Jack Lazorko	.05
161	Mitch Williams	.05
162	Greg Walker	.05
163	Alan Ashby	.05
164	Tony Gwynn	.50
165	Bruce Ruffin	.05
166	Ron Robinson	.05
167	Zane Smith	.05
168	Junior Ortiz	.05
169	Jamie Moyer	.05
170	Tony Pena	.05
171	Cal Ripken, Jr.	1.00
172	B.J. Surhoff	.05
173	Lou Whitaker	.05
174	Ellis Burks RC	.20
175	Ron Guidry	.10
176	Steve Sax	.05
177	Danny Tartabull	.05
178	Carney Lansford	.05
179	Casey Candaele	.05
180	Scott Fletcher	.05
181	Mark McLemore	.05
182	Ivan Calderon	.05
183	Jack Clark	.05
184	Glenn Davis	.05
185	Luis Aguayo	.05
186	Bo Diaz	.05
187	Stan Jefferson	.05
188	Sid Bream	.05
189	Bob Brenly	.05
190	Dion James	.05
191	Leon Durham	.05
192	Jesse Orosco	.05
193	Alvin Davis	.05
194	Gary Gaetti	.05

No.	Player	Value
195	Fred McGriff	.05
196	Steve Lombardozzi	.05
197	Rance Mulliniks	.05
198	Rey Quinones	.05
199	Gary Carter	.40
200a	Checklist 138-247	.05
200b	Checklist 134-239	.05
201	Keith Moreland	.05
202	Ken Griffey	.05
203	Tommy Gregg RC	.05
204	Will Clark	.05
205	John Kruk	.05
206	Buddy Bell	.05
207	Von Hayes	.05
208	Tommy Herr	.05
209	Craig Reynolds	.05
210	Gary Pettis	.05
211	Harold Baines	.05
212	Vance Law	.05
213	Ken Gerhart	.05
214	Jim Gantner	.05
215	Chet Lemon	.05
216	Dwight Evans	.05
217	Don Mattingly	.60
218	Franklin Stubbs	.05
219	Pat Tabler	.05
220	Bo Jackson	.10
221	Tony Phillips	.05
222	Tim Wallach	.05
223	Ruben Sierra	.05
224	Steve Buechele	.05
225	Frank White	.05
226	Alfredo Griffin	.05
227	Greg Swindell	.05
228	Willie Randolph	.05
229	Mike Marshall	.05
230	Alan Trammell	.05
231	Eddie Murray	.40
232	Dale Sveum	.05
233	Dick Schofield	.05
234	Jose Oquendo	.05
235	Bill Doran	.05
236	Milt Thompson	.05
237	Marvell Wynne	.05
238	Bobby Bonilla	.05
239	Chris Speier	.05
240	Glenn Braggs	.05
241	Wally Backman	.05
242	Ryne Sandberg	.50
243	Phil Bradley	.05
244	Kelly Gruber	.05
245	Tom Brunansky	.05
246	Ron Oester	.05
247	Bobby Thigpen	.05
248	Fred Lynn	.05
249	Paul Molitor	.40
250	Darrell Evans	.05
251	Gary Ward	.05
252	Bruce Hurst	.05
253	Bob Welch	.05
254	Joe Carter	.05
255	Willie Wilson	.05
256	Mark McGwire	.75
257	Mitch Webster	.05
258	Brian Downing	.05
259	Mike Stanley	.05
260	Carlton Fisk	.40
261	Billy Hatcher	.05
262	Glenn Wilson	.05
263	Ozzie Smith	.50
264	Randy Ready	.05
265	Kurt Stillwell	.05
266	David Palmer	.05
267	Mike Diaz	.05
268	Rob Thompson	.05
269	Andre Dawson	.25
270	Lee Guetterman	.05
271	Willie Upshaw	.05
272	Randy Bush	.05
273	Larry Sheets	.05
274	Rob Deer	.05
275	Kirk Gibson	.05
276	Marty Barrett	.05
277	Rickey Henderson	.40
278	Pedro Guerrero	.05
279	Brett Butler	.05
280	Kevin Seitzer	.05
281	Mike Davis	.05
282	Andres Galarraga	.05
283	Devon White	.05
284	Pete O'Brien	.05
285	Jerry Hairston Sr.	.05
286	Kevin Bass	.05
287	Carmelo Martinez	.05
288	Juan Samuel	.05
289	Kal Daniels	.05
290	Albert Hall	.05
291	Andy Van Slyke	.05
292	Lee Smith	.10
293	Vince Coleman	.05
294	Tom Niedenfuer	.05
295	Robin Yount	.40
296	Jeff Robinson RC	.05
297	Todd Benzinger RC	.10
298	Dave Winfield	.40
299	Mickey Hatcher	.05
300a	Checklist 248-357	.05
300b	Checklist 240-345	.05
301	Bud Black	.05
302	Jose Canseco	.25
303	Tom Foley	.05
304	Pete Incaviglia	.05
305	Bob Boone	.05
306	Bill Long RC	.05
307	Willie McGee	.05
308	Ken Caminiti RC	.20
309	Darren Daulton	.05
310	Tracy Jones	.05
311	Greg Booker	.05
312	Mike LaValliere	.05
313	Chili Davis	.05
314	Glenn Hubbard	.05
315	Paul Noce RC	.05
316	Keith Hernandez	.05
317	Mark Langston	.05
318	Keith Atherton	.05
319	Tony Fernandez	.05
320	Kent Hrbek	.05
321	John Cerutti	.05
322	Mike Kingery	.05
323	Dave Magadan	.05
324	Rafael Palmeiro	.35
325	Jeff Dedmon	.05
326	Barry Bonds	1.00
327	Jeffrey Leonard	.05
328	Tim Flannery	.05
329	Dave Concepcion	.05
330	Mike Schmidt	.60
331	Bill Dawley	.05
332	Larry Andersen	.05
333	Jack Howell	.05
334	Ken Williams RC	.05
335	Bryn Smith	.05
336	Billy Ripken RC	.10
337	Greg Brock	.05
338	Mike Heath	.05
339	Mike Greenwell	.05
340	Claudell Washington	.05
341	Jose Gonzalez	.05
342	Mel Hall	.05
343	Jim Eisenreich	.05
344	Tony Bernazard	.05
345	Tim Raines	.05
346	Bob Brower	.05
347	Larry Parrish	.05
348	Thad Bosley	.05
349	Dennis Eckersley	.35
350	Cory Snyder	.05
351	Rick Cerone	.05
352	John Shelby	.05
353	Larry Herndon	.05
354	John Habyan	.05
355	Chuck Crim RC	.05
356	Gus Polidor	.05
357	Ken Dayley	.05
358	Danny Darwin	.05
359	Lance Parrish	.05
360	James Steels RC	.05
361	Al Pedrique RC	.05
362	Mike Aldrete	.05
363	Juan Castillo	.05
364	Len Dykstra	.05
365	Luis Quinones	.05
366	Jim Presley	.05
367	Lloyd Moseby	.05
368	Kirby Puckett	.50
369	Eric Davis	.05
370	Gary Redus	.05
371	Dave Schmidt	.05
372	Mark Clear	.05
373	Dave Bergman	.05
374	Charles Hudson	.05
375	Calvin Schiraldi	.05
376	Alex Trevino	.05
377	Tom Candiotti	.05
378	Steve Farr	.05
379	Mike Gallego	.05
380	Andy McGaffigan	.05
381	Kirk McCaskill	.05
382	Oddibe McDowell	.05
383	Floyd Bannister	.05
384	Denny Walling	.05
385	Don Carman	.05
386	Todd Worrell	.05
387	Eric Show	.05
388	Dave Parker	.05
389	Rick Mahler	.05
390	Mike Dunne	.10
391	Candy Maldonado	.05
392	Bob Dernier	.05
393	Dave Valle	.05
394	Ernie Whitt	.05
395	Juan Berenguer	.05
396	Mike Young	.05
397	Mike Felder	.05
398	Willie Hernandez	.05
399	Jim Rice	.25
400a	Checklist 358-467	.05
400b	Checklist 346-451	.05
401	Tommy John	.10
402	Brian Holton	.05
403	Carmen Castillo	.05
404	Jamie Quirk	.05
405	Dwayne Murphy	.05
406	Jeff Parrett RC	.05
407	Don Sutton	.35
408	Jerry Browne	.05
409	Jim Winn	.05
410	Dave Smith	.05
411	Shane Mack RC	.05
412	Greg Gross	.05
413	Nick Esasky	.05
414	Damaso Garcia	.05
415	Brian Fisher	.05
416	Brian Dayett	.05
417	Curt Ford	.05
418	Mark Williamson RC	.05
419	Bill Schroeder	.05
420	Mike Henneman RC	.10
421	John Marzano RC	.05
422	Ron Kittle	.05
423	Matt Young	.05
424	Steve Balboni	.05
425	Luis Polonia RC	.05
426	Randy St. Claire	.05
427	Greg Harris	.05
428	Johnny Ray	.05
429	Ray Searage	.05
430	Ricky Horton	.05
431	Gerald Young RC	.05
432	Rick Schu	.05
433	Paul O'Neill	.05
434	Rich Gossage	.10
435	John Cangelosi	.05
436	Mike LaCoss	.05
437	Gerald Perry	.05
438	Dave Martinez	.05
439	Darryl Strawberry	.05
440	John Moses	.05
441	Greg Gagne	.05
442	Jesse Barfield	.05
443	George Frazier	.05
444	Garth Iorg	.05
445	Ed Nunez	.05
446	Rick Aguilera	.05
447	Jerry Mumphrey	.05
448	Rafael Ramirez	.05
449	John Smiley RC	.10
450	Atlee Hammaker	.05
451	Lance McCullers	.05
452	Guy Hoffman	.05
453	Chris James	.05
454	Terry Pendleton	.05
455	Dave Meads RC	.05
456	Bill Buckner	.05
457	John Pawlowski RC	.05
458	Bob Sebra	.05
459	Jim Dwyer	.05
460	Jay Aldrich RC	.05
461	Frank Tanana	.05
462	Oil Can Boyd	.05
463	Dan Pasqua	.05
464	Tim Crews RC	.10
465	Andy Allanson	.05
466	Bill Pecota RC	.05
467	Steve Ontiveros	.05
468	Hubie Brooks	.05
469	Paul Kilgus RC	.05
470	Dale Mohorcic	.05
471	Dan Quisenberry	.05
472	Dave Stewart	.05
473	Dave Clark	.05
474	Joel Skinner	.05
475	Dave Anderson	.05
476	Dan Petry	.05
477	Carl Nichols RC	.05
478	Ernest Riles	.05
479	George Hendrick	.05
480	John Morris	.05
481	Manny Hernandez RC	.05
482	Jeff Stone	.05
483	Chris Brown	.05
484	Mike Bielecki	.05
485	Dave Dravecky	.05
486	Rick Manning	.05
487	Bill Almon	.05
488	Jim Sundberg	.05
489	Ken Phelps	.05
490	Tom Henke	.05
491	Dan Gladden	.05
492	Barry Larkin	.05
493	Fred Manrique RC	.05
494	Mike Griffin	.05
495	Mark Knudson RC	.05
496	Bill Madlock	.05
497	Tim Stoddard	.05
498	Sam Horn RC	.05
499	Tracy Woodson RC	.05
500a	Checklist 468-577	.05
500b	Checklist 452-557	.05
501	Ken Schrom	.05
502	Angel Salazar	.05
503	Eric Plunk	.05
504	Joe Hesketh	.05
505	Greg Minton	.05
506	Geno Petralli	.05
507	Bob James	.05
508	Robbie Wine RC	.05
509	Jeff Calhoun	.05
510	Steve Lake	.05
511	Mark Grant	.05
512	Frank Williams	.05
513	Jeff Blauser RC	.10
514	Bob Walk	.05
515	Craig Lefferts	.05
516	Manny Trillo	.05
517	Jerry Reed	.05
518	Rick Leach	.05
519	Mark Davidson RC	.05
520	Jeff Ballard RC	.05
521	Dave Stapleton RC	.05
522	Pat Sheridan	.05
523	Al Nipper	.05
524	Steve Trout	.05
525	Jeff Hamilton	.05
526	Tommy Hinzo RC	.05
527	Lonnie Smith	.05
528	Greg Cadaret RC	.05
529	Rob McClure (Bob)	.05
530	Chuck Finley	.05
531	Jeff Russell	.05
532	Steve Lyons	.05
533	Terry Puhl	.05
534	Eric Nolte RC	.05
535	Kent Tekulve	.05
536	Pat Pacillo RC	.05
537	Charlie Puleo	.05
538	Tom Prince RC	.05
539	Greg Maddux	.50
540	Jim Lindeman	.05
541	Pete Stanicek RC	.05
542	Steve Kiefer	.05
543	Jim Morrison	.05
544	Spike Owen	.05
545	Jay Buhner RC	.50
546	Mike Devereaux RC	.10
547	Jerry Don Gleaton	.05
548	Jose Rijo	.05
549	Dennis Martinez	.05
550	Mike Loynd	.05
551	Darrell Miller	.05
552	Dave LaPoint	.05
553	John Tudor	.05
554	Rocky Childress RC	.05
555	Wally Ritchie RC	.05
556	Terry McGriff	.05
557	Dave Leiper	.05
558	Jeff Robinson	.05
559	Jose Uribe	.05
560	Ted Simmons	.05
561	Lester Lancaster RC	.10
562	Keith Miller RC	.05
563	Harold Reynolds	.05
564	Gene Larkin RC	.05
565	Cecil Fielder	.05
566	Roy Smalley	.05
567	Duane Ward	.05
568	Bill Wilkinson RC	.05
569	Howard Johnson	.05
570	Frank DiPino	.05
571	Pete Smith RC	.05
572	Darnell Coles	.05
573	Don Robinson	.05
574	Rob Nelson	.05
575	Dennis Rasmussen	.05
576	Steve Jeltz (Photo actually Juan Samuel.)	.05
577	Tom Pagnozzi RC	.05
578	Ty Gainey	.05
579	Gary Lucas	.05
580	Ron Hassey	.05
581	Herm Winningham	.05
582	Rene Gonzales RC	.05
583	Brad Komminsk	.05
584	Doyle Alexander	.05
585	Jeff Sellers	.05
586	Bill Gullickson	.05
587	Tim Belcher	.05
588	Doug Jones RC	.05
589	Melido Perez RC	.05
590	Rick Honeycutt	.05
591	Pascual Perez	.05
592	Curt Wilkerson	.05
593	Steve Howe	.05
594	John Davis RC	.05
595	Storm Davis	.05
596	Sammy Stewart	.05
597	Neil Allen	.05
598	Alejandro Pena	.05
599	Mark Thurmond	.05
600a	Checklist 578-BC26	.05
600b	Checklist 558-660	.05
601	Jose Mesa RC	.10
602	Don August RC	.05
603	Terry Leach/SP	.10
604	Tom Newell RC	.05

605	Randall Byers/SP RC	.10
606	Jim Gott	.05
607	Harry Spilman	.05
608	John Candelaria	.05
609	Mike Brumley RC	.05
610	Mickey Brantley	.05
611	Jose Nunez/SP RC	.10
612	Tom Nieto	.05
613	Rick Reuschel	.05
614	Lee Mazzilli/SP	.10
615	Scott Lusader RC	.05
616	Bobby Meacham	.05
617	Kevin McReynolds/SP	.10
618	Gene Garber	.05
619	Barry Lyons/SP RC	.10
620	Randy Myers	.05
621	Donnie Moore	.05
622	Domingo Ramos	.05
623	Ed Romero	.05
624	Greg Myers RC	.10
625	Billy Ripken,	
	Cal Ripken, Jr.,	
	Cal Ripken, Sr. Ripken	
	Baseball Family	.40
626	Pat Perry	.05
627	Andres Thomas/SP	.10
628	Matt Williams/SP	.15
629	Dave Hengel RC	.05
630	Jeff Musselman/SP	.10
631	Tim Laudner	.05
632	Bob Ojeda/SP	.10
633	Rafael Santana	.05
634	Wes Gardner RC	.05
635	Roberto Kelly/SP	.15
636	Mike Flanagan/SP	.10
637	Jay Bell RC	.35
638	Bob Melvin	.05
639	Damon Berryhill RC	.05
640	David Wells/SP RC	.40
641	Stan Musial	
	Puzzle Card	.05
642	Doug Sisk	.05
643	Keith Hughes RC	.05
644	Tom Glavine RC	1.00
645	Al Newman	.05
646	Scott Sanderson	.05
647	Scott Terry	.05
648	Tim Teufel/SP	.10
649	Garry Templeton/SP	.10
650	Manny Lee/SP	.10
651	Roger McDowell/SP	.10
652	Mookie Wilson/SP	.10
653	David Cone/SP	.10
654	Ron Gant/SP RC	.20
655	Joe Price/SP	.10
656	George Bell/SP	.10
657	Gregg Jefferies/SP RC	.25
658	Todd Stottlemyre/SP RC	.25
659	Geronimo Berroa/SP RC	.20
660	Jerry Royster/SP	.10

Rookies

		NM/M
	Complete Set (56):	4.00
	Common Player:	.05
1	Mark Grace	.25
2	Mike Campbell	.05
3	Todd Frowirth	.05
4	Dave Stapleton	.05
5	Shawn Abner	.05
6	Jose Cecena	.05
7	Dave Gallagher	.05
8	Mark Parent	.05
9	Cecil Espy	.05
10	Pete Smith	.05
11	Jay Buhner	.25
12	Pat Borders	.05
13	Doug Jennings	.05
14	Brady Anderson RC	1.00
15	Pete Stanicek	.05
16	Roberto Kelly	.05
17	Jeff Treadway	.05

18	Walt Weiss	.05
19	Paul Gibson	.05
20	Tim Crews	.05
21	Melido Perez	.05
22	Steve Peters	.05
23	Craig Worthington	.05
24	John Trautwein	.05
25	DeWayne Vaughn	.05
26	David Wells	.15
27	Al Leiter	.15
28	Tim Belcher	.05
29	Johnny Paredes	.05
30	Chris Sabo	.05
31	Damon Berryhill	.05
32	Randy Milligan	.05
33	Gary Thurman	.05
34	Kevin Elster	.05
35	Roberto Alomar	1.50
36	Edgar Martinez RC (Photo	
	actually Edwin Nunez.)	1.50
37	Todd Stottlemyre	.15
38	Joey Meyer	.05
39	Carl Nichols	.05
40	Jack McDowell	.05
41	Jose Bautista	.05
42	Sil Campusano	.05
43	John Dopson	.05
44	Jody Reed	.05
45	Darrin Jackson	.05
46	Mike Capel	.05
47	Ron Gant	.05
48	John Davis	.05
49	Kevin Coffman	.05
50	Cris Carpenter	.05
51	Mackey Sasser	.05
52	Luis Alicea	.05
53	Bryan Harvey	.05
54	Steve Ellsworth	.05
55	Mike Macfarlane	.05
56	Checklist 1-56	.05

1989 Donruss

Fred McGriff 1B

		NM/M
	Unopened Fact. Set (660):	17.50
	Complete Set (660):	15.00
	Common Player:	.05
	Warren Spahn Puzzle:	.50
	Wax Pack (15):	.75
	Wax Box (36):	15.00
	Cello Pack (32):	1.00
	Cello Box (24):	15.00
	Rack Pack (45):	.75
1	Mike Greenwell/DK	.05
2	Bobby Bonilla/DK	.05
3	Pete Incaviglia/DK	.05
4	Chris Sabo/DK	.05
5	Robin Yount/DK	.40
6	Tony Gwynn/DK	.50
7	Carlton Fisk/DK	.40
8	Cory Snyder/DK	.05
9	David Cone/DK	.05
10	Kelly Seitzer/DK	.05
11	Rick Reuschel/DK	.05
12	Johnny Ray/DK	.05
13	Dave Schmidt/DK	.05
14	Andres Galarraga/DK	.05
15	Kirk Gibson/DK	.05
16	Fred McGriff/DK	.15
17	Mark Grace/DK	.15
18	Jeff Robinson/DK	.05
19	Vince Coleman/DK	.05
20	Dave Henderson/DK	.05
21	Harold Reynolds/DK	.05
22	Gerald Perry/DK	.05
23	Frank Viola/DK	.05
24	Steve Bedrosian/DK	.05
25	Glenn Davis/DK	.05
26	Don Mattingly/DK	.60
27	Checklist 1-27	.05
28	Sandy Alomar, Jr./RR RC	.35
29	Steve Searcy/RR RC	.05
30	Cameron Drew/RR RC	.05

31	Gary Sheffield/RR RC	1.00
32	Erik Hanson/RR RC	.05
33	Ken Griffey Jr./RR RC	6.00
34	Greg Harris/RR RC	.05
35	Gregg Jefferies/RR	.05
36	Luis Medina/RR RC	.05
37	Carlos Quintana/RR RC	.05
38	Felix Jose/RR RC	.05
39	Cris Carpenter/RR RC	.05
40	Ron Jones/RR RC	.05
41	Dave West/RR RC	.05
42	Randy Johnson/RR RC	3.00
43	Mike Harkey/RR RC	.05
44	Pete Harnisch/RR RC	.10
45	Tom Gordon/RR RC	.25
46	Gregg Olson/RR RC	.10
47	Alex Sanchez/RR RC	.05
48	Ruben Sierra	.35
49	Rafael Palmeiro	.35
50	Ron Gant	.05
51	Cal Ripken, Jr.	1.00
52	Wally Joyner	.05
53	Gary Carter	.40
54	Andy Van Slyke	.05
55	Robin Yount	.40
56	Pete Incaviglia	.05
57	Greg Brock	.05
58	Melido Perez	.05
59	Craig Lefferts	.05
60	Gary Pettis	.05
61	Danny Tartabull	.05
62	Guillermo Hernandez	.05
63	Ozzie Smith	.50
64	Gary Gaetti	.05
65	Mark Davis	.05
66	Lee Smith	.05
67	Dennis Eckersley	.35
68	Wade Boggs	.50
69	Mike Scott	.05
70	Fred McGriff	.05
71	Tom Browning	.05
72	Claudell Washington	.05
73	Mel Hall	.05
74	Don Mattingly	.60
75	Steve Bedrosian	.05
76	Juan Samuel	.05
77	Mike Scioscia	.05
78	Dave Righetti	.05
79	Alfredo Griffin	.05
80	Eric Davis	.05
81	Juan Berenguer	.05
82	Todd Worrell	.05
83	Joe Carter	.05
84	Steve Sax	.05
85	Frank White	.05
86	John Kruk	.05
87	Rance Mulliniks	.05
88	Alan Ashby	.05
89	Charlie Leibrandt	.05
90	Frank Tanana	.05
91	Jose Canseco	.25
92	Barry Bonds	1.00
93	Harold Reynolds	.05
94	Mark McLemore	.05
95	Mark McGwire	.75
96	Eddie Murray	.40
97	Tim Raines	.05
98	Rob Thompson	.05
99	Kevin McReynolds	.05
100	Checklist 28-137	.05
101	Carlton Fisk	.40
102	Dave Martinez	.05
103	Glenn Braggs	.05
104	Dale Murphy	.15
105	Ryne Sandberg	.50
106	Dennis Martinez	.05
107	Pete O'Brien	.05
108	Dick Schofield	.05
109	Henry Cotto	.05
110	Mike Marshall	.05
111	Keith Moreland	.05
112	Tom Brunansky	.05
113	Kelly Gruber	.05
114	Brook Jacoby	.05
115	Keith Brown RC	.05
116	Matt Nokes	.05
117	Keith Hernandez	.05
118	Bob Forsch	.05
119	Bert Blyleven	.10
120	Willie Wilson	.05
121	Tommy Gregg	.05
122	Jim Rice	.25
123	Bob Knepper	.05
124	Danny Jackson	.05
125	Eric Plunk	.05
126	Brian Fisher	.05
127	Mike Pagliarulo	.05
128	Tony Gwynn	.50
129	Lance McCullers	.05
130	Andres Galarraga	.05
131	Jose Uribe	.05
132	Kirk Gibson	.05
133	David Palmer	.05
134	R.J. Reynolds	.05

135	Greg Walker	.05
136	Kirk McCaskill	.05
137	Shawon Dunston	.05
138	Andy Allanson	.05
139	Rob Murphy	.05
140	Mike Aldrete	.05
141	Terry Kennedy	.05
142	Scott Fletcher	.05
143	Steve Balboni	.05
144	Bret Saberhagen	.05
145	Ozzie Virgil	.05
146	Dale Sveum	.05
147	Darryl Strawberry	.05
148	Harold Baines	.10
149	George Bell	.05
150	Dave Parker	.05
151	Bobby Bonilla	.05
152	Mookie Wilson	.05
153	Ted Power	.05
154	Nolan Ryan	1.00
155	Jeff Reardon	.05
156	Tim Wallach	.05
157	Jamie Moyer	.05
158	Rich Gossage	.10
159	Dave Winfield	.40
160	Von Hayes	.05
161	Willie McGee	.05
162	Rich Gedman	.05
163	Tony Pena	.05
164	Mike Morgan	.05
165	Charlie Hough	.05
166	Mike Stanley	.05
167	Andre Dawson	.20
168	Joe Boever	.05
169	Pete Stanicek	.05
170	Bob Boone	.05
171	Ron Darling	.05
172	Bob Walk	.05
173	Rob Deer	.05
174	Steve Buechele	.05
175	Ted Higuera	.05
176	Ozzie Guillen	.05
177	Candy Maldonado	.05
178	Doyle Alexander	.05
179	Mark Gubicza	.05
180	Alan Trammell	.05
181	Vince Coleman	.05
182	Kirby Puckett	.50
183	Chris Brown	.05
184	Marty Barrett	.05
185	Stan Javier	.05
186	Mike Greenwell	.05
187	Billy Hatcher	.05
188	Jimmy Key	.05
189	Nick Esasky	.05
190	Don Slaught	.05
191	Cory Snyder	.05
192	John Candelaria	.05
193	Mike Schmidt	.60
194	Kevin Gross	.05
195	John Tudor	.05
196	Neil Allen	.05
197	Orel Hershiser	.05
198	Kal Daniels	.05
199	Kent Hrbek	.05
200	Checklist 138-247	.05
201	Joe Magrane	.05
202	Scott Bailes	.05
203	Tim Belcher	.05
204	George Brett	.60
205	Benito Santiago	.05
206	Tony Fernandez	.05
207	Gerald Young	.05
208	Bo Jackson	.10
209	Chet Lemon	.05
210	Storm Davis	.05
211	Doug Drabek	.05
212	Mickey Brantley	
	(Photo actually	
	Nelson Simmons.)	.05
213	Devon White	.05
214	Dave Stewart	.05
215	Dave Schmidt	.05
216	Bryn Smith	.05
217	Brett Butler	.05
218	Bob Ojeda	.05
219	Steve Rosenberg RC	.05
220	Hubie Brooks	.05
221	B.J. Surhoff	.05
222	Rick Mahler	.05
223	Rick Sutcliffe	.05
224	Neal Heaton	.05
225	Mitch Williams	.05
226	Chuck Finley	.05
227	Mark Langston	.05
228	Jesse Orosco	.05
229	Ed Whitson	.05
230	Terry Pendleton	.05
231	Lloyd Moseby	.05
232	Greg Swindell	.05
233	John Franco	.05
234	Jack Morris	.05
235	Howard Johnson	.05
236	Glenn Davis	.05

No.	Player	Price
237	Frank Viola	.05
238	Kevin Seitzer	.05
239	Gerald Perry	.05
240	Dwight Evans	.05
241	Jim Deshaies	.05
242	Bo Diaz	.05
243	Carney Lansford	.05
244	Mike LaValliere	.05
245	Rickey Henderson	.40
246	Roberto Alomar	.20
247	Jimmy Jones	.05
248	Pascual Perez	.05
249	Will Clark	.05
250	Fernando Valenzuela	.05
251	Shane Rawley	.05
252	Sid Bream	.05
253	Steve Lyons	.05
254	Brian Downing	.05
255	Mark Grace	.05
256	Tom Candiotti	.05
257	Barry Larkin	.05
258	Mike Krukow	.05
259	Billy Ripken	.05
260	Cecilio Guante	.05
261	Scott Bradley	.05
262	Floyd Bannister	.05
263	Pete Smith	.05
264	Jim Gantner	.05
265	Roger McDowell	.05
266	Bobby Thigpen	.05
267	Jim Clancy	.05
268	Terry Steinbach	.05
269	Mike Dunne	.05
270	Dwight Gooden	.05
271	Mike Heath	.05
272	Dave Smith	.05
273	Keith Atherton	.05
274	Tim Burke	.05
275	Damon Berryhill	.05
276	Vance Law	.05
277	Rich Dotson	.05
278	Lance Parrish	.05
279	Geronimo Berroa	.05
280	Roger Clemens	.60
281	Greg Mathews	.05
282	Tom Niedenfuer	.05
283	Paul Kilgus	.05
284	Jose Guzman	.05
285	Calvin Schiraldi	.05
286	Charlie Puleo	.05
287	Joe Orsulak	.05
288	Jack Howell	.05
289	Kevin Elster	.05
290	Jose Lind	.05
291	Paul Molitor	.40
292	Cecil Espy	.05
293	Bill Wegman	.05
294	Dan Pasqua	.05
295	Scott Garrelts	.05
296	Walt Terrell	.05
297	Ed Hearn	.05
298	Lou Whitaker	.05
299	Ken Dayley	.05
300	Checklist 248-357	.05
301	Tommy Herr	.05
302	Mike Brumley	.05
303	Ellis Burks	.05
304	Curt Young	.05
305	Jody Reed	.05
306	Bill Doran	.05
307	David Wells	.05
308	Ron Robinson	.05
309	Rafael Santana	.05
310	Julio Franco	.05
311	Jack Clark	.05
312	Chris James	.05
313	Milt Thompson	.05
314	John Shelby	.05
315	Al Leiter	.05
316	Mike Davis	.05
317	Chris Sabo RC	.15
318	Greg Gagne	.05
319	Jose Oquendo	.05
320	John Farrell	.05
321	Franklin Stubbs	.05
322	Kurt Stillwell	.05
323	Shawn Abner	.05
324	Mike Flanagan	.05
325	Kevin Bass	.05
326	Pat Tabler	.05
327	Mike Henneman	.05
328	Rick Honeycutt	.05
329	John Smiley	.05
330	Rey Quinones	.05
331	Johnny Ray	.05
332	Bob Welch	.05
333	Larry Sheets	.05
334	Jeff Parrett	.05
335	Rick Reuschel	.05
336	Randy Myers	.05
337	Ken Williams	.05
338	Andy McGaffigan	.05
339	Joey Meyer	.05
340	Dion James	.05
341	Les Lancaster	.05
342	Tom Foley	.05
343	Geno Petralli	.05
344	Dan Petry	.05
345	Alvin Davis	.05
346	Mickey Hatcher	.05
347	Marvell Wynne	.05
348	Danny Cox	.05
349	Dave Stieb	.05
350	Jay Bell	.05
351	Jeff Treadway	.05
352	Luis Salazar	.05
353	Len Dykstra	.05
354	Juan Agosto	.05
355	Gene Larkin	.05
356	Steve Farr	.05
357	Paul Assenmacher	.05
358	Todd Benzinger	.05
359	Larry Andersen	.05
360	Paul O'Neill	.05
361	Ron Hassey	.05
362	Jim Gott	.05
363	Ken Phelps	.05
364	Tim Flannery	.05
365	Randy Ready	.05
366	Nelson Santovenia RC	.05
367	Kelly Downs	.05
368	Danny Heep	.05
369	Phil Bradley	.05
370	Jeff Robinson	.05
371	Ivan Calderon	.05
372	Mike Witt	.05
373	Greg Maddux	.50
374	Carmen Castillo	.05
375	Jose Rijo	.05
376	Joe Price	.05
377	R.C. Gonzalez	.05
378	Oddibe McDowell	.05
379	Jim Presley	.05
380	Brad Wellman	.05
381	Tom Glavine	.20
382	Dan Plesac	.05
383	Wally Backman	.05
384	Dave Gallagher RC	.05
385	Tom Henke	.05
386	Luis Polonia	.05
387	Junior Ortiz	.05
388	David Cone	.05
389	Dave Bergman	.05
390	Danny Darwin	.05
391	Dan Gladden	.05
392	John Dopson RC	.05
393	Frank DiPino	.05
394	Al Nipper	.05
395	Willie Randolph	.05
396	Don Carman	.05
397	Scott Terry	.05
398	Rick Cerone	.05
399	Tom Pagnozzi	.05
400	Checklist 358-467	.05
401	Mickey Tettleton	.05
402	Curtis Wilkerson	.05
403	Jeff Russell	.05
404	Pat Perry	.05
405	Jose Alvarez RC	.05
406	Rick Schu	.05
407	Sherman Corbett RC	.05
408	Dave Magadan	.05
409	Bob Kipper	.05
410	Don August	.05
411	Bob Brower	.05
412	Chris Bosio	.05
413	Jerry Reuss	.05
414	Atlee Hammaker	.05
415	Jim Walewander	.05
416	Mike Macfarlane RC	.10
417	Pat Sheridan	.05
418	Pedro Guerrero	.05
419	Allan Anderson	.05
420	Mark Parent RC	.05
421	Bob Stanley	.05
422	Mike Gallego	.05
423	Bruce Hurst	.05
424	Dave Meads	.05
425	Jesse Barfield	.05
426	Rob Dibble RC	.15
427	Joel Skinner	.05
428	Ron Kittle	.05
429	Rick Rhoden	.05
430	Bob Dernier	.05
431	Steve Jeltz	.05
432	Rick Dempsey	.05
433	Roberto Kelly	.05
434	Dave Anderson	.05
435	Herm Winningham	.05
436	Al Newman	.05
437	Jose DeLeon	.05
438	Doug Jones	.05
439	Brian Holton	.05
440	Jeff Montgomery	.05
441	Dickie Thon	.05
442	Cecil Fielder	.05
443	John Fishel RC	.05
444	Jerry Don Gleaton	.05
445	Paul Gibson RC	.05
446	Walt Weiss	.05
447	Glenn Wilson	.05
448	Mike Moore	.05
449	Chili Davis	.05
450	Dave Henderson	.05
451	Jose Bautista RC	.05
452	Rex Hudler	.05
453	Bob Brenly	.05
454	Mackey Sasser	.05
455	Daryl Boston	.05
456	Mike Fitzgerald	.05
457	Jeffery Leonard	.05
458	Bruce Sutter	.35
459	Mitch Webster	.05
460	Joe Hesketh	.05
461	Bobby Witt	.05
462	Stew Cliburn	.05
463	Scott Bankhead	.05
464	Ramon Martinez RC	.25
465	Dave Leiper	.05
466	Luis Alicea RC	.05
467	John Cerutti	.05
468	Ron Washington	.05
469	Jeff Reed	.05
470	Jeff Robinson	.05
471	Sid Fernandez	.05
472	Terry Puhl	.05
473	Charlie Lea	.05
474	Israel Sanchez RC	.05
475	Bruce Benedict	.05
476	Oil Can Boyd	.05
477	Craig Reynolds	.05
478	Frank Williams	.05
479	Greg Cadaret	.05
480	Randy Kramer RC	.05
481	Dave Eiland RC	.05
482	Eric Show	.05
483	Garry Templeton	.05
484	Wallace Johnson	.05
485	Kevin Mitchell	.05
486	Tim Crews	.05
487	Mike Maddux	.05
488	Dave LaPoint	.05
489	Fred Manrique	.05
490	Greg Minton	.05
491	Doug Dascenzo RC	.05
492	Willie Upshaw	.05
493	Jack Armstrong RC	.05
494	Kirt Manwaring	.05
495	Jeff Ballard	.05
496	Jeff Kunkel	.05
497	Mike Campbell	.05
498	Gary Thurman	.05
499	Zane Smith	.05
500	Checklist 468-577	.05
501	Mike Birkbeck	.05
502	Terry Leach	.05
503	Shawn Hillegas	.05
504	Manny Lee	.05
505	Doug Jennings RC	.05
506	Ken Oberkfell	.05
507	Tim Teufel	.05
508	Tom Brookens	.05
509	Rafael Ramirez	.05
510	Fred Toliver	.05
511	Brian Holman RC	.05
512	Mike Bielecki	.05
513	Jeff Pico RC	.05
514	Charles Hudson	.05
515	Bruce Ruffin	.05
516	Larry McWilliams	.05
517	Jeff Sellers	.05
518	John Costello RC	.05
519	Brady Anderson	.05
520	Craig McMurtry	.05
521	Ray Hayward	.05
522	Drew Hall	.05
523	Mark Lemke RC	.05
524	Oswald Peraza RC	.05
525	Bryan Harvey RC	.05
526	Rick Aguilera	.05
527	Tom Prince	.05
528	Mark Clear	.05
529	Jerry Browne	.05
530	Juan Castillo	.05
531	Jack McDowell	.05
532	Chris Speier	.05
533	Darrell Evans	.05
534	Luis Aquino	.05
535	Eric King	.05
536	Ken Hill RC	.05
537	Randy Bush	.05
538	Shane Mack	.05
539	Tom Bolton	.05
540	Gene Nelson	.05
541	Wes Gardner	.05
542	Ken Caminiti	.05
543	Duane Ward	.05
544	Norm Charlton RC	.10
545	Hal Morris RC	.25
546	Rich Yett	.05
547	Hensley Meulens RC	.10
548	Greg Harris	.05
549	Darren Daulton	.05
550	Jeff Hamilton	.05
551	Luis Aguayo	.05
552	Tim Leary	.05
553	Ron Oester	.05
554	Steve Lombardozzi	.05
555	Tim Jones RC	.05
556	Bud Black	.05
557	Alejandro Pena	.05
558	Jose DeJesus RC	.05
559	Dennis Rasmussen	.05
560	Pat Borders RC	.25
561	Craig Biggio	.05
562	Luis de los Santos RC	.05
563	Fred Lynn	.05
564	Todd Burns RC	.05
565	Felix Fermin	.05
566	Darnell Coles	.05
567	Willie Fraser	.05
568	Glenn Hubbard	.05
569	Craig Worthington RC	.05
570	Johnny Paredes RC	.05
571	Don Robinson	.05
572	Barry Lyons	.05
573	Bill Long	.05
574	Tracy Jones	.05
575	Juan Nieves	.05
576	Andres Thomas	.05
577	Rolando Roomes RC	.05
578	Luis Rivera	.05
579	Chad Kreuter RC	.10
580	Tony Armas	.05
581	Jay Buhner	.05
582	Ricky Horton	.05
583	Andy Hawkins	.05
584	Sil Campusano RC	.05
585	Dave Clark	.05
586	Van Snider RC	.05
587	Todd Frohwirth	.05
588	Warren Spahn Puzzle Card	.05
589	William Brennan RC	.05
590	German Gonzalez RC	.05
591	Ernie Whitt	.05
592	Jeff Blauser	.05
593	Spike Owen	.05
594	Matt Williams	.05
595	Lloyd McClendon	.05
596	Steve Ontiveros	.05
597	Scott Medvin RC	.05
598	Hipolito Pena RC	.05
599	Jerald Clark RC	.05
600a	Checklist 578-BC26 (#635 is Kurt Schilling)	.10
600b	Checklist 578-BC26 (#635 is Kurt Schilling)	.05
601	Carmelo Martinez	.05
602	Mike LaCoss	.05
603	Mike Devereaux	.05
604	Alex Madrid RC	.05
605	Gary Redus	.05
606	Lance Johnson	.05
607	Terry Clark RC	.05
608	Manny Trillo	.05
609	Scott Jordan RC	.05
610	Jay Howell	.05
611	Francisco Melendez RC	.05
612	Mike Boddicker	.05
613	Kevin Brown	.05
614	Dave Valle	.05
615	Tim Laudner	.05
616	Andy Nezelek RC	.05
617	Chuck Crim	.05
618	Jack Savage	.05
619	Adam Peterson	.05
620	Todd Stottlemyre	.05
621	Lance Blankenship RC	.05
622	Miguel Garcia RC	.05
623	Keith Miller	.05
624	Ricky Jordan RC	.05
625	Ernest Riles	.05
626	John Moses	.05
627	Nelson Liriano	.05
628	Mike Smithson	.05
629	Scott Sanderson	.05
630	Dale Mohorcic	.05
631	Marvin Freeman	.05
632	Mike Young	.05
633	Dennis Lamp	.05
634	Dante Bichette RC	.25
635	Curt Schilling RC	3.00
636	Scott May RC	.05
637	Mike Schooler RC	.05
638	Rick Leach	.05
639	Tom Lampkin RC	.05
640	Brian Meyer RC	.05
641	Brian Harper	.05
642	John Smoltz	.05
643	Jose Canseco (40/40)	.15
644	Bill Schroeder	.05
645	Edgar Martinez	.10
646	Dennis Cook RC	.05
647	Barry Jones	.05

648 Orel Hershiser (59 and Counting) .05
649 Rod Nichols RC .05
650 Jody Davis .05
651 Bob Milacki RC .05
652 Mike Jackson .05
653 Derek Lilliquist RC .05
654 Paul Mirabella .05
655 Mike Diaz .05
656 Jeff Musselman .05
657 Jerry Reed .05
658 Kevin Blankenship RC .05
659 Wayne Tolleson .05
660 Eric Hetzel RC .05

Rookies

		NM/M
Complete Set (56):		8.00
Common Player:		.05
1	Gary Sheffield	.75
2	Gregg Jefferies	.05
3	Ken Griffey Jr.	5.00
4	Tom Gordon	.05
5	Billy Spiers	.05
6	Deion Sanders RC	.50
7	Donn Pall	.05
8	Steve Carter	.05
9	Francisco Oliveras	.05
10	Steve Wilson	.05
11	Bob Geren	.05
12	Tony Castillo	.05
13	Kenny Rogers	.05
14	Carlos Martinez	.05
15	Edgar Martinez	.05
16	Jim Abbott	.05
17	Torey Lovullo	.05
18	Mark Carreon	.05
19	Geronimo Berroa	.05
20	Luis Medina	.05
21	Sandy Alomar, Jr.	.05
22	Bob Milacki	.05
23	Joe Girardi RC	.10
24	German Gonzalez	.05
25	Craig Worthington	.05
26	Jerome Walton	.05
27	Gary Wayne	.05
28	Tim Jones	.05
29	Dante Bichette	.05
30	Alexis Infante	.05
31	Ken Hill	.05
32	Dwight Smith	.05
33	Luis de los Santos	.05
34	Eric Yelding	.05
35	Gregg Olson	.05
36	Phil Stephenson	.05
37	Ken Patterson	.05
38	Rick Wrona	.05
39	Mike Brumley	.05
40	Cris Carpenter	.05
41	Jeff Brantley	.05
42	Ron Jones	.05
43	Randy Johnson	2.00
44	Kevin Brown	.05
45	Ramon Martinez	.05
46	Greg Harris	.05
47	Steve Finley	.05
48	Randy Kramer	.05
49	Erik Hanson	.05
50	Matt Merullo	.05
51	Mike Devereaux	.05
52	Clay Parker	.05
53	Omar Vizquel	.05
54	Derek Lilliquist	.05
55	Junior Felix	.05
56	Checklist	.05

1989 Donruss Traded

Rafael Palmeiro OF

		NM/M
Complete Set (56):		2.00
Common Player:		.05
1	Jeffrey Leonard	.05
2	Jack Clark	.05
3	Kevin Gross	.05
4	Tommy Herr	.05
5	Bob Boone	.05
6	Rafael Palmeiro	.30
7	John Dopson	.05
8	Willie Randolph	.05
9	Chris Brown	.05
10	Wally Backman	.05
11	Steve Ontiveros	.05
12	Eddie Murray	.45
13	Lance McCullers	.05
14	Spike Owen	.05
15	Rob Murphy	.05
16	Pete O'Brien	.05
17	Ken Williams	.05
18	Nick Esasky	.05
19	Nolan Ryan	1.50
20	Brian Holton	.05
21	Mike Moore	.05
22	Joel Skinner	.05
23	Steve Sax	.05
24	Rick Mahler	.05
25	Mike Aldrete	.05
26	Jesse Orosco	.05
27	Dave LaPoint	.05
28	Walt Terrell	.05
29	Eddie Williams	.05
30	Mike Devereaux	.05
31	Julio Franco	.05
32	Jim Clancy	.05
33	Felix Fermin	.05
34	Curtis Wilkerson	.05
35	Bert Blyleven	.05
36	Mel Hall	.05
37	Eric King	.05
38	Mitch Williams	.05
39	Jamie Moyer	.05
40	Rick Rhoden	.05
41	Phil Bradley	.05
42	Paul Kilgus	.05
43	Milt Thompson	.05
44	Jerry Browne	.05
45	Bruce Hurst	.05
46	Claudell Washington	.05
47	Todd Benzinger	.05
48	Steve Balboni	.05
49	Oddibe McDowell	.05
50	Charles Hudson	.05
51	Ron Kittle	.05
52	Andy Hawkins	.05
53	Tom Brookens	.05
54	Tom Niedenfuer	.05
55	Jeff Parrett	.05
56	Checklist	.05

1990 Donruss Previews

1990 PREVIEW CARDS
No. 10 of 12
JEROME WALTON
OUTFIELDER
CAREER HIGHLIGHTS

		NM/M
Complete Set (12):		85.00
Common Player:		3.00
1	Todd Zeile	3.00
2	Ben McDonald	3.00
3	Bo Jackson	7.50
4	Will Clark	3.00
5	Dave Stewart	3.00
6	Kevin Mitchell	3.00
7	Nolan Ryan	50.00
8	Howard Johnson	3.00
9	Tony Gwynn	25.00
10	Jerome Walton	3.00
11	Wade Boggs	25.00
12	Kirby Puckett	25.00

1990 Donruss

	NM/M
Unopened Factory Set (716):	10.00
Complete Set (716):	7.50
Common Player:	.05
Carl Yastrzemski Puzzle:	1.00
Wax Pack (16):	.50
Wax Box (36):	10.00
Rack Pack (48):	1.00
Blister Rack (78):	1.50
1 Bo Jackson/DK	.15
2 Steve Sax/DK	.05
3a Ruben Sierra/DK (No vertical black line at top-right on back.)	.25
3b Ruben Sierra/DK (Vertical line at top-right on back.)	.10
4 Ken Griffey Jr./DK	.65
5 Mickey Tettleton/DK	.05
6 Dave Stewart/DK	.05
7 Jim Deshaies/DK	.05
8 John Smoltz/DK	.05
9 Mike Bielecki/DK	.05
10a Brian Downing /DK (Reversed negative.)	.25
10b Brian Downing/DK (Corrected)	.05
11 Kevin Mitchell/DK	.05
12 Kelly Gruber/DK	.05
13 Joe Magrane/DK	.05
14 John Franco/DK	.05
15 Ozzie Guillen/DK	.05
16 Lou Whitaker/DK	.05
17 John Smiley/DK	.05
18 Howard Johnson/DK	.05
19 Willie Randolph/DK	.05
20 Chris Bosio/DK	.05
21 Tommy Herr/DK	.05
22 Dan Gladden/DK	.05
23 Ellis Burks/DK	.05
24 Pete O'Brien/DK	.05
25 Bryn Smith/DK	.05
26 Ed Whitson/DK	.05
27 Checklist 1-27	.05
28 Robin Ventura/RR	.05
29 Todd Zeile/RR RC	.15
30 Sandy Alomar, Jr./RR	.05
31 Kent Mercker/RR RC	.10
32 Ben McDonald/RR RC	.25
33a Juan Gonzalez/RR (Reversed negative.) RC	2.00
33b Juan Gonzalez/RR (Corrected)	1.50
34 Eric Anthony/RR RC	.05
35 Mike Fetters/RR RC	.05
36 Marquis Grissom/RR RC	.50
37 Greg Vaughn/RR RC	.25
38 Brian DuBois/RR RC	.05
39 Steve Avery/RR RC	.10
40 Mark Gardner/RR RC	.05
41 Andy Benes/RR	.05
42 Delino DeShields/RR RC	.15
43 Scott Coolbaugh/RR RC	.05
44 Pat Combs/RR RC	.10
45 Alex Sanchez/RR RC	.05
46 Kelly Mann/RR RC	.05
47 Julio Machado/RR RC	.05
48 Pete Incaviglia	.05
49 Shawon Dunston	.05
50 Jeff Treadway	.05
51 Jeff Ballard	.05

52	Claudell Washington	.05
53	Juan Samuel	.05
54	John Smiley	.05
55	Rob Deer	.05
56	Geno Petralli	.05
57	Chris Bosio	.05
58	Carlton Fisk	.40
59	Kirt Manwaring	.05
60	Chet Lemon	.05
61	Bo Jackson	.10
62	Doyle Alexander	.05
63	Pedro Guerrero	.05
64	Allan Anderson	.05
65	Greg Harris	.05
66	Mike Greenwell	.05
67	Walt Weiss	.05
68	Wade Boggs	.50
69	Jim Clancy	.05
70	Junior Felix RC	.05
71	Barry Larkin	.05
72	Dave LaPoint	.05
73	Joel Skinner	.05
74	Jesse Barfield	.05
75	Tommy Herr	.05
76	Ricky Jordan	.05
77	Eddie Murray	.40
78	Steve Sax	.05
79	Tim Belcher	.05
80	Danny Jackson	.05
81	Kent Hrbek	.05
82	Milt Thompson	.05
83	Brook Jacoby	.05
84	Mike Marshall	.05
85	Kevin Seitzer	.05
86	Tony Gwynn	.50
87	Dave Steib	.05
88	Dave Smith	.05
89	Bret Saberhagen	.05
90	Alan Trammell	.05
91	Tony Phillips	.05
92	Doug Drabek	.05
93	Jeffrey Leonard	.05
94	Wally Joyner	.05
95	Carney Lansford	.05
96	Cal Ripken, Jr.	1.00
97	Andres Galarraga	.05
98	Kevin Mitchell	.05
99	Howard Johnson	.05
100a	Checklist 28-129	.05
100b	Checklist 28-125	.05
101	Melido Perez	.05
102	Spike Owen	.05
103	Paul Molitor	.40
104	Geronimo Berroa	.05
105	Ryne Sandberg	.50
106	Bryn Smith	.05
107	Steve Buechele	.05
108	Jim Abbott	.05
109	Alvin Davis	.05
110	Lee Smith	.05
111	Roberto Alomar	.20
112	Rick Reuschel	.05
113a	Kelly Gruber (Born 2/22)	.05
113b	Kelly Gruber (Born 2/26)	.20
114	Joe Carter	.05
115	Jose Rijo	.05
116	Greg Minton	.05
117	Bob Ojeda	.05
118	Glenn Davis	.05
119	Jeff Reardon	.05
120	Kurt Stillwell	.05
121	John Smoltz	.05
122	Dwight Evans	.05
123	Eric Yelding	.05
124	John Franco	.05
125	Jose Canseco	.20
126	Barry Bonds	1.00
127	Lee Guetterman	.05
128	Jack Clark	.05
129	Dave Valle	.05
130	Hubie Brooks	.05
131	Ernest Riles	.05
132	Mike Morgan	.05
133	Steve Jeltz	.05
134	Jeff Robinson	.05
135	Ozzie Guillen	.05
136	Chili Davis	.05
137	Mitch Webster	.05
138	Jerry Browne	.05
139	Bo Diaz	.05
140	Robby Thompson	.05
141	Craig Worthington	.05
142	Julio Franco	.05
143	Brian Holman	.05
144	George Brett	.60
145	Tom Glavine	.20
146	Robin Yount	.40
147	Gary Carter	.40
148	Ron Kittle	.05
149	Tony Fernandez	.05
150	Dave Stewart	.05
151	Gary Gaetti	.05

No.	Player	Price	No.	Player	Price	No.	Player	Price	No.	Player	Price
152	Kevin Elster	.05	249	Brett Butler	.05	352	Brian Downing	.05	448	Jay Buhner	.05
153	Gerald Perry	.05	250	Willie Randolph	.05	353	Frank Viola	.05	449	Lee Stevens RC	.05
154	Jesse Orosco	.05	251	Roger McDowell	.05	354	Terry Puhl	.05	450	Ron Hassey	.05
155	Wally Backman	.05	252	Rafael Belliard	.05	355	Brian Harper	.05	451	Bob Melvin	.05
156	Dennis Martinez	.05	253	Steve Rosenberg	.05	356	Steve Farr	.05	452	Dave Martinez	.05
157	Rick Sutcliffe	.05	254	Jack Howell	.05	357	Joe Boever	.05	453	Greg Litton RC	.05
158	Greg Maddux	.50	255	Marvell Wynne	.05	358	Danny Heep	.05	454	Mark Carreon	.05
159	Andy Hawkins	.05	256	Tom Candiotti	.05	359	Larry Andersen	.05	455	Scott Fletcher	.05
160	John Kruk	.05	257	Todd Benzinger	.05	360	Rolando Roomes	.05	456	Otis Nixon	.05
161	Jose Oquendo	.05	258	Don Robinson	.05	361	Mike Gallego	.05	457	Tony Fossas RC	.05
162	John Dopson	.05	259	Phil Bradley	.05	362	Bob Kipper	.05	458	John Russell	.05
163	Joe Magrane	.05	260	Cecil Espy	.05	363	Clay Parker	.05	459	Paul Assenmacher	.05
164	Billy Ripken	.05	261	Scott Bankhead	.05	364	Mike Pagliarulo	.05	460	Zane Smith	.05
165	Fred Manrique	.05	262	Frank White	.05	365	Ken Griffey Jr.	.65	461	Jack Daugherty RC	.05
166	Nolan Ryan	1.00	263	Andres Thomas	.05	366	Rex Hudler	.05	462	Rich Monteleone RC	.05
167	Damon Berryhill	.05	264	Glenn Braggs	.05	367	Pat Sheridan	.05	463	Greg Briley	.05
168	Dale Murphy	.20	265	David Cone	.05	368a	Kirk Gibson (May 25 birthdate.)	.05	464	Mike Smithson	.05
169	Mickey Tettleton	.05	266	Bobby Thigpen	.05	368b	Kirk Gibson (May 28 birthdate.)	.05	465	Benito Santiago	.05
170a	Kirk McCaskill (Born 4/19.)	.05	267	Nelson Liriano	.05	369	Jeff Parrett	.05	466	Jeff Brantley RC	.05
170b	Kirk McCaskill (Born 4/9.)	.10	268	Terry Steinbach	.05	370	Bob Walk	.05	467	Jose Nunez	.05
171	Dwight Gooden	.05	269	Kirby Puckett	.50	371	Ken Patterson	.05	468	Scott Bailes	.05
172	Jose Lind	.05	270	Gregg Jefferies	.05	372	Bryan Harvey	.05	469	Ken Griffey	.05
173	B.J. Surhoff	.05	271	Jeff Blauser	.05	373	Mike Bielecki	.05	470	Bob McClure	.05
174	Ruben Sierra	.05	272	Cory Snyder	.05	374	Tom Magrann RC	.05	471	Mackey Sasser	.05
175	Dan Plesac	.05	273	Roy Smith	.05	375	Rick Mahler	.05	472	Glenn Wilson	.05
176	Dan Pasqua	.05	274	Tom Foley	.05	376	Craig Lefferts	.05	473	Kevin Tapani RC	.10
177	Kelly Downs	.05	275	Mitch Williams	.05	377	Gregg Olson	.05	474	Bill Buckner	.05
178	Matt Nokes	.05	276	Paul Kilgus	.05	378	Jamie Moyer	.05	475	Ron Gant	.05
179	Luis Aquino	.05	277	Don Slaught	.05	379	Randy Johnson	.40	476	Kevin Romine	.05
180	Frank Tanana	.05	278	Von Hayes	.05	380	Jeff Montgomery	.05	477	Juan Agosto	.05
181	Tony Pena	.05	279	Vince Coleman	.05	381	Marty Clary	.05	478	Herm Winningham	.05
182	Dan Gladden	.05	280	Mike Boddicker	.05	382	Bill Spiers RC	.05	479	Storm Davis	.05
183	Bruce Hurst	.05	281	Ken Dayley	.05	383	Dave Magadan	.05	480	Jeff King	.05
184	Roger Clemens	.60	282	Mike Devereaux	.05	384	Greg Hibbard RC	.05	481	Kevin Mmahat RC	.05
185	Mark McGwire	.75	283	Kenny Rogers RC	.05	385	Ernie Whitt	.05	482	Carmelo Martinez	.05
186	Rob Murphy	.05	284	Jeff Russell	.05	386	Rick Honeycutt	.05	483	Omar Vizquel	.05
187	Jim Deshaies	.05	285	Jerome Walton RC	.10	387	Dave West	.05	484	Jim Dwyer	.05
188	Fred McGriff	.05	286	Derek Lilliquist	.05	388	Keith Hernandez	.05	485	Bob Knepper	.05
189	Rob Dibble	.05	287	Joe Orsulak	.05	389	Jose Alvarez	.05	486	Dave Anderson	.05
190	Don Mattingly	.60	288	Dick Schofield	.05	390	Albert Belle	.05	487	Ron Jones	.05
191	Felix Fermin	.05	289	Ron Darling	.05	391	Rick Aguilera	.05	488	Jay Bell	.05
192	Roberto Kelly	.05	290	Bobby Bonilla	.05	392	Mike Fitzgerald	.05	489	Sammy Sosa RC	3.00
193	Dennis Cook	.05	291	Jim Gantner	.05	393	Dwight Smith RC	.05	490	Kent Anderson RC	.05
194	Darren Daulton	.05	292	Bobby Witt	.05	394	Steve Wilson RC	.05	491	Domingo Ramos	.05
195	Alfredo Griffin	.05	293	Greg Brock	.05	395	Bob Geren RC	.05	492	Dave Clark	.05
196	Eric Plunk	.05	294	Ivan Calderon	.05	396	Randy Ready	.05	493	Tim Birtsas	.05
197	Orel Hershiser	.05	295	Steve Bedrosian	.05	397	Ken Hill	.05	494	Ken Oberkfell	.05
198	Paul O'Neill	.05	296	Mike Henneman	.05	398	Jody Reed	.05	495	Larry Sheets	.05
199	Randy Bush	.05	297	Tom Gordon	.05	399	Tom Brunansky	.05	496	Jeff Kunkel	.05
200a	Checklist 130-231	.05	298	Lou Whitaker	.05	400a	Checklist 334-435	.05	497	Jim Presley	.05
200b	Checklist 126-223	.05	299	Terry Pendleton	.05	400b	Checklist 322-419	.05	498	Mike Macfarlane	.05
201	Ozzie Smith	.50	300a	Checklist 232-333	.05	401	Rene Gonzales	.05	499	Pete Smith	.05
202	Pete O'Brien	.05	300b	Checklist 224-321	.05	402	Harold Baines	.05	500a	Checklist 436-537	.05
203	Jay Howell	.05	301	Juan Berenguer	.05	403	Cecilio Guante	.05	500b	Checklist 420-517	.05
204	Mark Gubicza	.05	302	Mark Davis	.05	404	Joe Girardi	.05	501	Gary Sheffield	.20
205	Ed Whitson	.05	303	Nick Esasky	.05	405a	Sergio Valdez RC (Black line crosses S in Sergio.)	.10	502	Terry Bross RC	.05
206	George Bell	.05	304	Rickey Henderson	.40	405b	Sergio Valdez (Corrected)	.05	503	Jerry Kutzler RC	.05
207	Mike Scott	.05	305	Rick Cerone	.05	406	Mark Williamson	.05	504	Lloyd Moseby	.05
208	Charlie Leibrandt	.05	306	Craig Biggio	.05	407	Glenn Hoffman	.05	505	Curt Young	.05
209	Mike Heath	.05	307	Duane Ward	.05	408	Jeff Innis RC	.05	506	Al Newman	.05
210	Dennis Eckersley	.35	308	Tom Browning	.05	409	Randy Kramer	.05	507	Keith Miller	.05
211	Mike LaValliere	.05	309	Walt Terrell	.05	410	Charlie O'Brien	.05	508	Mike Stanton RC	.20
212	Darnell Coles	.05	310	Greg Swindell	.05	411	Charlie Hough	.05	509	Rich Yett	.05
213	Lance Parrish	.05	311	Dave Righetti	.05	412	Gus Polidor	.05	510	Tim Drummond RC	.05
214	Mike Moore	.05	312	Mike Maddux	.05	413	Ron Karkovice	.05	511	Joe Hesketh	.05
215	Steve Finley RC	.20	313	Len Dykstra	.05	414	Trevor Wilson	.05	512	Rick Wrona RC	.05
216	Tim Raines	.05	314	Jose Gonzalez	.05	415	Kevin Ritz RC	.05	513	Luis Salazar	.05
217a	Scott Garrelts (Born 10/20.)	.05	315	Steve Balboni	.05	416	Gary Thurman	.05	514	Hal Morris	.05
217b	Scott Garrelts (Born 10/30.)	.10	316	Mike Scioscia	.05	417	Jeff Robinson	.05	515	Terry Mullholland	.05
218	Kevin McReynolds	.05	317	Ron Oester	.05	418	Scott Terry	.05	516	John Morris	.05
219	Dave Gallagher	.05	318	Gary Wayne RC	.05	419	Tim Laudner	.05	517	Carlos Quintana	.05
220	Tim Wallach	.05	319	Todd Worrell	.05	420	Dennis Rasmussen	.05	518	Frank DiPino	.05
221	Chuck Crim	.05	320	Doug Jones	.05	421	Luis Rivera	.05	519	Randy Milligan	.05
222	Lonnie Smith	.05	321	Jeff Hamilton	.05	422	Jim Corsi	.05	520	Chad Kreuter	.05
223	Andre Dawson	.20	322	Danny Tartabull	.05	423	Dennis Lamp	.05	521	Mike Jeffcoat	.05
224	Nelson Santovenia	.05	323	Chris James	.05	424	Ken Caminiti	.05	522	Mike Harkey	.05
225	Rafael Palmeiro	.35	324	Mike Flanagan	.05	425	David Wells	.05	523a	Andy Nezelek (Born 1985.)	.05
226	Devon White	.05	325	Gerald Young	.05	426	Norm Charlton	.05	523b	Andy Nezelek (Born 1965.)	.05
227	Harold Reynolds	.05	326	Bob Boone	.05	427	Deion Sanders	.05	524	Dave Schmidt	.05
228	Ellis Burks	.05	327	Frank Williams	.05	428	Dion James	.05	525	Tony Armas	.05
229	Mark Parent	.05	328	Dave Parker	.05	429	Chuck Cary	.05	526	Barry Lyons	.05
230	Will Clark	.05	329	Sid Bream	.05	430	Ken Howell	.05	527	Rick Reed RC	.05
231	Jimmy Key	.05	330	Mike Schooler	.05	431	Steve Lake	.05	528	Jerry Reuss	.05
232	John Farrell	.05	331	Bert Blyleven	.10	432	Kal Daniels	.05	529	Dean Palmer RC	.10
233	Eric Davis	.05	332	Bob Welch	.05	433	Lance McCullers	.05	530	Jeff Peterek RC	.05
234	Johnny Ray	.05	333	Bob Milacki	.05	434	Lenny Harris	.05	531	Carlos Martinez RC	.05
235	Darryl Strawberry	.05	334	Tim Burke	.05	435	Scott Scudder RC	.05	532	Atlee Hammaker	.05
236	Bill Doran	.05	335	Jose Uribe	.05	436	Gene Larkin	.05	533	Mike Brumley	.05
237	Greg Gagne	.05	336	Randy Myers	.05	437	Dan Quisenberry	.05	534	Terry Leach	.05
238	Jim Eisenreich	.05	337	Eric King	.05	438	Steve Olin RC	.05	535	Doug Strange RC	.05
239	Tommy Gregg	.05	338	Mark Langston	.05	439	Mickey Hatcher	.05	536	Jose DeLeon	.05
240	Marty Barrett	.05	339	Ted Higuera	.05	440	Willie Wilson	.05	537	Shane Rawley	.05
241	Rafael Ramirez	.05	340	Oddibe McDowell	.05	441	Mark Grant	.05	538	Joey Cora	.05
242	Chris Sabo	.05	341	Lloyd McClendon	.05	442	Mookie Wilson	.05	539	Eric Hetzel	.05
243	Dave Henderson	.05	342	Pascual Perez	.05	443	Alex Trevino	.05	540	Gene Nelson	.05
244	Andy Van Slyke	.05	343	Kevin Brown	.05	444	Pat Tabler	.05	541	Wes Gardner	.05
245	Alvaro Espinoza	.05	344	Chuck Finley	.05	445	Dave Bergman	.05	542	Mark Portugal	.05
246	Garry Templeton	.05	345	Erik Hanson	.05	446	Todd Burns	.05	543	Al Leiter	.05
247	Gene Harris	.05	346	Rich Gedman	.05	447	R.J. Reynolds	.05	544	Jack Armstrong	.05
248	Kevin Gross	.05	347	Bip Roberts	.05				545	Greg Cadaret	.05
			348	Matt Williams	.05				546	Rod Nichols	.05
			349	Tom Henke	.05				547	Luis Polonia	.05
			350	Brad Komminsk	.05						
			351	Jeff Reed	.05						

548	Charlie Hayes	.05
549	Dickie Thon	.05
550	Tim Crews	.05
551	Dave Winfield	.40
552	Mike Davis	.05
553	Ron Robinson	.05
554	Carmen Castillo	.05
555	John Costello	.05
556	Bud Black	.05
557	Rick Dempsey	.05
558	Jim Acker	.05
559	Eric Show	.05
560	Pat Borders	.05
561	Danny Darwin	.05
562	Rick Luecken RC	.05
563	Edwin Nunez	.05
564	Felix Jose	.05
565	John Cangelosi	.05
566	Billy Swift	.05
567	Bill Schroeder	.05
568	Stan Javier	.05
569	Jim Traber	.05
570	Wallace Johnson	.05
571	Donell Nixon	.05
572	Sid Fernandez	.05
573	Lance Johnson	.05
574	Andy McGaffigan	.05
575	Mark Knudson	.05
576	Tommy Greene RC	.05
577	Mark Grace	.05
578	Larry Walker RC	1.00
579	Mike Stanley	.05
580	Mike Witt	.05
581	Scott Bradley	.05
582	Greg Harris	.05
583a	Kevin Hickey (Black stripe over top of "K" vertical stroke.)	.05
583b	Kevin Hickey (Black stripe under "K.")	.05
584	Lee Mazzilli	.05
585	Jeff Pico	.05
586	Joe Oliver RC	.05
587	Willie Fraser	.05
588	Carl Yastrzemski Puzzle Card	.05
589	Kevin Bass	.05
590	John Moses	.05
591	Tom Pagnozzi	.05
592	Tony Castillo RC	.05
593	Jerald Clark	.05
594	Dan Schatzeder	.05
595	Luis Quinones	.05
596	Pete Harnisch	.05
597	Gary Redus	.05
598	Mel Hall	.05
599	Rick Schu	.05
600a	Checklist 538-639	.05
600b	Checklist 518-617	.05
601	Mike Kingery	.05
602	Terry Kennedy	.05
603	Mike Sharperson	.05
604	Don Carman	.05
605	Jim Gott	.05
606	Donn Pall	.05
607	Rance Mulliniks	.05
608	Curt Wilkerson	.05
609	Mike Felder	.05
610	Guillermo Hernandez	.05
611	Candy Maldonado	.05
612	Mark Thurmond	.05
613	Rick Leach	.05
614	Jerry Reed	.05
615	Franklin Stubbs	.05
616	Billy Hatcher	.05
617	Don August	.05
618	Tim Teufel	.05
619	Shawn Hillegas	.05
620	Manny Lee	.05
621	Gary Ward	.05
622	Mark Guthrie RC	.05
623	Jeff Musselman	.05
624	Mark Lemke	.05
625	Fernando Valenzuela	.05
626	Paul Sorrento RC	.05
627	Glenallen Hill	.05
628	Les Lancaster	.05
629	Vance Law	.05
630	Randy Velarde	.05
631	Todd Frohwirth	.05
632	Willie McGee	.05
633	Oil Can Boyd	.05
634	Cris Carpenter	.05
635	Brian Holton	.05
636	Tracy Jones	.05
637	Terry Steinbach/AS	.05
638	Brady Anderson	.05
639a	Jack Morris (Black line crosses J of Jack.)	.10
639b	Jack Morris (Corrected)	.05
640	Jaime Navarro RC	.05
641	Darrin Jackson	.05
642	Mike Dyer RC	.05
643	Mike Schmidt	.60

644	Henry Cotto	.05
645	John Cerutti	.05
646	Francisco Cabrera RC	.05
647	Scott Sanderson	.05
648	Brian Meyer	.05
649	Ray Searage	.05
650	Bo Jackson/AS	.25
651	Steve Lyons	.05
652	Mike LaCoss	.05
653	Ted Power	.05
654	Howard Johnson/AS	.05
655	Mauro Gozzo RC	.05
656	Mike Blowers RC	.05
657	Paul Gibson	.05
658	Neal Heaton	.05
659a	Nolan Ryan 5,000 K's (King of Kings (#665) back.)	1.50
659b	Nolan Ryan 5,000 K's (Correct back.)	.60
660a	Harold Baines/AS (Black line through star on front, Recent Major League Performance on back.)	.25
660b	Harold Baines/AS (Black line through star on front, All-Star Game Performance on back.)	.25
660c	Harold Baines/AS (Black line behind star on front, Recent Major League Performance on back.)	.25
660d	Harold Baines/AS (Black line behind star on front, All-Star Game Performance on back.)	.10
661	Gary Pettis	.05
662	Clint Zavaras RC	.05
663	Rick Reuschel	.05
664	Alejandro Pena	.05
665a	Nolan Ryan (King of Kings) (5,000 K's (#659) back.)	1.50
665b	Nolan Ryan (King of Kings) (Correct back.)	1.00
665c	Nolan Ryan (King of Kings) (No number on back.)	1.00
666	Ricky Horton	.05
667	Curt Schilling	.05
668	Bill Landrum	.05
669	Todd Stottlemyre	.05
670	Tim Leary	.05
671	John Wetteland RC	.25
672	Calvin Schiraldi	.05
673	Ruben Sierra/AS	.05
674	Pedro Guerrero/AS	.05
675	Ken Phelps	.05
676	Cal Ripken/AS	.50
677	Denny Walling	.05
678	Goose Gossage	.05
679	Gary Mielke RC	.05
680	Bill Bathe	.05
681	Tom Lawless	.05
682	Xavier Hernandez RC	.05
683	Kirby Puckett/AS	.25
684	Mariano Duncan	.05
685	Ramon Martinez	.05
686	Tim Jones	.05
687	Tom Filer	.05
688	Steve Lombardozzi	.05
689	Bernie Williams RC	1.00
690	Chip Hale RC	.05
691	Beau Allred RC	.05
692	Ryne Sandberg/AS	.25
693	Jeff Huson RC	.05
694	Curt Ford	.05
695	Eric Davis/AS	.05
696	Scott Lusader	.05
697	Mark McGwire/AS	.40
698	Steve Cummings RC	.05
699	George Canale RC	.05
700a	Checklist 640-715/ BC1-BC26	.05
700b	Checklist 640-716/ BC1-BC26	.05
700c	Checklist 618-716	.05
701	Julio Franco/AS	.05
702	Dave Johnson RC	.05
703	Dave Stewart/AS	.05
704	Dave Justice RC	.50
705	Tony Gwynn/AS	.25
706	Greg Myers	.05
707	Will Clark/AS	.05
708	Benito Santiago/AS	.05

ABBREVIATIONS

AS - All-Star

DK - Diamond King

RR - Rated Rookie

SP - Short Print

709	Larry McWilliams	.05
710	Ozzie Smith/AS	.25
711	John Olerud RC	.50
712	Wade Boggs/AS	.25
713	Gary Eave RC	.05
714	Bob Tewksbury	.05
715	Kevin Mitchell/AS	.25
716	A. Bartlett Giamatti	.25

Rookies

		NM/M
Complete Set (56):		1.00
Common Player:		.05
1	Sandy Alomar	.05
2	John Olerud	.40
3	Pat Combs	.05
4	Brian Dubois	.05
5	Felix Jose	.05
6	Delino DeShields	.05
7	Mike Stanton	.05
8	Mike Munoz	.05
9	Craig Grebeck	.05
10	Joe Kraemer	.05
11	Jeff Huson	.05
12	Bill Sampen	.05
13	Brian Bohanon	.05
14	Dave Justice	.40
15	Robin Ventura	.05
16	Greg Vaughn	.05
17	Wayne Edwards	.05
18	Shawn Boskie	.05
19	Carlos Baerga RC	.20
20	Mark Gardner	.05
21	Kevin Appier	.05
22	Mike Harkey	.05
23	Tim Layana	.05
24	Glenallen Hill	.05
25	Jerry Kutzler	.05
26	Mike Blowers	.05
27	Scott Ruskin	.05
28	Dana Kiecker	.05
29	Willie Blair	.05
30	Ben McDonald	.05
31	Todd Zeile	.05
32	Scott Coolbaugh	.05
33	Xavier Hernandez	.05
34	Mike Hartley	.05
35	Kevin Tapani	.05
36	Kevin Wickander	.05
37	Carlos Hernandez	.05
38	Brian Traxler	.05
39	Marty Brown	.05
40	Scott Radinsky	.05
41	Julio Machado	.05
42	Steve Avery	.05
43	Mark Lemke	.05
44	Alan Mills	.05
45	Marquis Grissom	.05
46	Greg Olson	.05
47	Dave Hollins	.05
48	Jerald Clark	.05
49	Eric Anthony	.05
50	Tim Drummond	.05
51	John Burkett	.05
52	Brent Knackert	.05
53	Jeff Shaw	.05
54	John Orton	.05
55	Terry Shumpert	.05
56	Checklist	.05

1991 Donruss

	NM/M
Factory Set w/Previews (788):	12.00
Factory Collector's Set (792):	12.00
Complete Set (770):	8.00
Common Player:	.05
Willie Stargell Puzzle	.50
Series 1 or 2 Pack (15):	.50
Series 1 or 2 Wax Box (36):	12.50

1	Dave Steib/DK	.05
2	Craig Biggio/DK	.05
3	Cecil Fielder/DK	.05
4	Barry Bonds/DK	1.00
5	Barry Larkin/DK	.05
6	Dave Parker/DK	.05
7	Len Dykstra/DK	.05
8	Bobby Thigpen/DK	.05
9	Roger Clemens/DK	.60
10	Ron Gant/DK	.05
11	Delino DeShields/DK	.05
12	Roberto Alomar/DK	.20
13	Sandy Alomar/DK	.05
14	Ryne Sandberg/DK	.50
15	Ramon Martinez/DK	.05
16	Edgar Martinez/DK	.05
17	Dave Magadan/DK	.05
18	Matt Williams/DK	.05
19	Rafael Palmeiro/DK	.40
20	Bob Welch/DK	.05
21	Dave Righetti/DK	.05
22	Brian Harper/DK	.05
23	Gregg Olson/DK	.05
24	Kurt Stillwell/DK	.05
25	Pedro Guerrero/DK	.05
26	Chuck Finley/DK	.05
27	Diamond King Checklist	.05
28	Tino Martinez/RR	.05
29	Mark Lewis/RR	.05
30	Bernard Gilkey/RR RC	.10
31	Hensley Meulens/RR	.05
32	Derek Bell/RR RC	.30
33	Jose Offerman/RR	.05
34	Terry Bross/RR	.05
35	Leo Gomez/RR RC	.05
36	Derrick May/RR	.05
37	Kevin Morton/RR RC	.05
38	Moises Alou/RR	.05
39	Julio Valera/RR RC	.05
40	Milt Cuyler/RR	.05
41	Phil Plantier/RR RC	.10
42	Scott Chiamparino/RR RC	.05
43	Ray Lankford/RR RC	.20
44	Mickey Morandini/RR RC	.10
45	Dave Hansen/RR	.05
46	Kevin Belcher/RR RC	.05
47	Darrin Fletcher/RR	.05
48	Steve Sax/AS	.05
49	Ken Griffey Jr./AS	.30
50a	Jose Canseco/AS (A's in stat line on back.)	.10
50b	Jose Canseco/AS (AL in stat line on back.)	.25
51	Sandy Alomar, Jr./AS	.05
52	Cal Ripken, Jr./AS	.50
53	Rickey Henderson/AS	.20
54	Bob Welch/AS	.05
55	Wade Boggs/AS	.25
56	Mark McGwire/AS	.50
57a	Jack McDowell (Career Games 30)	.05
57b	Jack McDowell (Career Games 63)	.25
58	Jose Lind	.05
59	Alex Fernandez	.05
60	Pat Combs	.05
61	Mike Walker RC	.05
62	Juan Samuel	.05
63	Mike Blowers	.05
64	Mark Guthrie	.05
65	Mark Salas	.05
66	Tim Jones	.05
67	Tim Leary	.05
68	Andres Galarraga	.05
69	Bob Milacki	.05
70	Tim Belcher	.05
71	Todd Zeile	.05
72	Jerome Walton	.05
73	Kevin Seitzer	.05
74	Jerald Clark	.05
75	John Smoltz	.05

#	Player	Val	#	Player	Val	#	Player	Val	#	Player	Val
76	Mike Henneman	.05	180	Tom Foley	.05	280	Orel Hershiser	.05	384	Norm Charlton	.05
77	Ken Griffey Jr.	.65	181	Pete Harnisch	.05	281	Jose Oquendo	.05	385	Gene Nelson	.05
78	Jim Abbott	.05	182	Mike Morgan	.05	282	Mike Witt	.05	386a	Checklist 256-331 (Blue Borders)	.05
79	Gregg Jefferies	.05	183	Bob Tewksbury	.05	283	Mitch Webster	.05	386b	Checklist 256-331 (Green Borders)	.05
80	Kevin Reimer	.05	184	Joe Girardi	.05	284	Greg Gagne	.05	387	Rickey Henderson/ MVP	.20
81	Roger Clemens	.60	185	Storm Davis	.05	285	Greg Olson RC	.05	388	Lance Parrish/MVP	.05
82	Mike Fitzgerald	.05	186	Ed Whitson	.05	286	Tony Phillips	.05	389	Fred McGriff/MVP	.05
83	Bruce Hurst	.05	187	Steve Avery	.05	287	Scott Bradley	.05	390	Dave Parker/MVP	.05
84	Eric Davis	.05	188	Lloyd Moseby	.05	288	Cory Snyder	.05	391	Candy Maldonado/MVP	.05
85	Paul Molitor	.40	189	Scott Bankhead	.05	289	Jay Bell	.05	392	Ken Griffey Jr./MVP	.50
86	Will Clark	.05	190	Mark Langston	.05	290	Kevin Romine	.05	393	Gregg Olson/MVP	.05
87	Mike Bielecki	.05	191	Kevin McReynolds	.05	291	Jeff Robinson	.05	394	Rafael Palmeiro/MVP	.20
88	Bret Saberhagen	.05	192	Julio Franco	.05	292	Steve Frey	.05	395	Roger Clemens/MVP	.30
89	Nolan Ryan	1.00	193	John Dopson	.05	293	Craig Worthington	.05	396	George Brett/MVP	.30
90	Bobby Thigpen	.05	194	Oil Can Boyd	.05	294	Tim Crews	.05	397	Cecil Fielder/MVP	.05
91	Dickie Thon	.05	195	Bip Roberts	.05	295	Joe Magrane	.05	398	Brian Harper/MVP	.05
92	Duane Ward	.05	196	Billy Hatcher	.05	296	Hector Villanueva RC	.05	399	Bobby Thigpen/MVP	.05
93	Luis Polonia	.05	197	Edgar Diaz	.05	297	Terry Shumpert RC	.05	400	Roberto Kelly/MVP	.05
94	Terry Kennedy	.05	198	Greg Litton	.05	298	Joe Carter	.05	401	Danny Darwin/MVP	.05
95	Kent Hrbek	.05	199	Mark Grace	.05	299	Kent Mercker	.05	402	Dave Justice/MVP	.05
96	Danny Jackson	.05	200	Checklist 104-179	.05	300	Checklist 180-255	.05	403	Lee Smith/MVP	.05
97	Sid Fernandez	.05	201	George Brett	.60	301	Chet Lemon	.05	404	Ryne Sandberg/MVP	.25
98	Jimmy Key	.05	202	Jeff Russell	.05	302	Mike Schooler	.05	405	Eddie Murray/MVP	.20
99	Franklin Stubbs	.05	203	Ivan Calderon	.05	303	Dante Bichette	.05	406	Tim Wallach/MVP	.05
100	Checklist 28-103	.05	204	Ken Howell	.05	304	Kevin Elster	.05	407	Kevin Mitchell/MVP	.05
101	R.J. Reynolds	.05	205	Tom Henke	.05	305	Jeff Huson	.05	408	Darryl Strawberry/MVP	.05
102	Dave Stewart	.05	206	Bryan Harvey	.05	306	Greg Harris	.05	409	Joe Carter/MVP	.05
103	Dan Pasqua	.05	207	Steve Bedrosian	.05	307	Marquis Grissom	.05	410	Len Dykstra/MVP	.05
104	Dan Plesac	.05	208	Al Newman	.05	308	Calvin Schiraldi	.05	411	Doug Drabek/MVP	.05
105	Mark McGwire	.75	209	Randy Myers	.05	309	Mariano Duncan	.05	412	Chris Sabo/MVP	.05
106	John Farrell	.05	210	Daryl Boston	.05	310	Bill Spiers	.05	413	Paul Marak/RR RC	.05
107	Don Mattingly	.60	211	Manny Lee	.05	311	Scott Garrelts	.05	414	Tim McIntosh/RR	.05
108	Carlton Fisk	.40	212	Dave Smith	.05	312	Mitch Williams	.05	415	Brian Barnes/RR RC	.05
109	Ken Oberkfell	.05	213	Don Slaught	.05	313	Mike Macfarlane	.05	416	Eric Gunderson/RR RC	.05
110	Darrel Akerfelds	.05	214	Walt Weiss	.05	314	Kevin Brown	.05	417	Mike Gardiner/RR RC	.05
111	Gregg Olson	.05	215	Donn Pall	.05	315	Robin Ventura	.05	418	Steve Carter/RR	.05
112	Mike Scioscia	.05	216	Jamie Navarro	.05	316	Darren Daulton	.05	419	Gerald Alexander/RR RC	.05
113	Bryn Smith	.05	217	Willie Randolph	.05	317	Pat Borders	.05	420	Rich Garces/RR RC	.05
114	Bob Geren	.05	218	Rudy Seanez	.05	318	Mark Eichhorn	.05	421	Chuck Knoblauch/RR RC	.50
115	Tom Candiotti	.05	219	Jim Leyritz RC	.15	319	Jeff Brantley	.05	422	Scott Aldred/RR RC	.05
116	Kevin Tapani	.05	220	Ron Karkovice	.05	320	Shane Mack	.05	423	Wes Chamberlain/RR RC	.05
117	Jeff Treadway	.05	221	Ken Caminiti	.05	321	Rob Dibble	.05	424	Lance Dickson/RR RC	.05
118	Alan Trammell	.05	222a	Von Hayes (Traded players' first names included in How Acquired on back.)	.05	322	John Franco	.05	425	Greg Colbrunn/RR RC	.10
119	Pete O'Brien	.05				323	Junior Felix	.05	426	Rich Delucia/RR RC	.05
120	Joel Skinner	.05	222b	Von Hayes (No first names.)	.05	324	Casey Candaele	.05	427	Jeff Conine/RR RC	.50
121	Mike LaValliere	.05	223	Cal Ripken, Jr.	1.00	325	Bobby Bonilla	.05	428	Steve Decker/RR RC	.05
122	Dwight Evans	.05	224	Lenny Harris	.05	326	Dave Henderson	.05	429	Turner Ward/RR RC	.05
123	Jody Reed	.05	225	Milt Thompson	.05	327	Wayne Edwards	.05	430	Mo Vaughn/RR	.05
124	Lee Guetterman	.05	226	Alvaro Espinoza	.05	328	Mark Knudson	.05	431	Steve Chitren/RR RC	.05
125	Tim Burke	.05	227	Chris James	.05	329	Terry Steinbach	.05	432	Mike Benjamin/RR	.05
126	Dave Johnson	.05	228	Dan Gladden	.05	330	Colby Ward RC	.05	433	Ryne Sandberg/AS	.25
127	Fernando Valenzuela	.05	229	Jeff Blauser	.05	331	Oscar Azocar RC	.05	434	Len Dykstra/AS	.05
128	Jose DeLeon	.05	230	Mike Heath	.05	332	Scott Radinsky RC	.10	435	Andre Dawson/AS	.15
129	Andre Dawson	.20	231	Omar Vizquel	.05	333	Eric Anthony	.05	436	Mike Scioscia/AS	.05
130	Gerald Perry	.05	232	Doug Jones	.05	334	Steve Lake	.05	437	Ozzie Smith/AS	.25
131	Greg Harris	.05	233	Jeff King	.05	335	Bob Melvin	.05	438	Kevin Mitchell/AS	.05
132	Tom Glavine	.25	234	Luis Rivera	.05	336	Kal Daniels	.05	439	Jack Armstrong/AS	.05
133	Lance McCullers	.05	235	Ellis Burks	.05	337	Tom Pagnozzi	.05	440	Chris Sabo/AS	.05
134	Randy Johnson	.40	236	Greg Cadaret	.05	338	Alan Mills RC	.05	441	Will Clark/AS	.05
135	Lance Parrish	.05	237	Dave Martinez	.05	339	Steve Olin	.05	442	Mel Hall	.05
136	Mackey Sasser	.05	238	Mark Williamson	.05	340	Juan Berenguer	.05	443	Mark Gardner	.05
137	Geno Petralli	.05	239	Stan Javier	.05	341	Francisco Cabrera	.05	444	Mike Devereaux	.05
138	Dennis Lamp	.05	240	Ozzie Smith	.50	342	Dave Bergman	.05	445	Kirk Gibson	.05
139	Dennis Martinez	.05	241	Shawn Boskie RC	.05	343	Henry Cotto	.05	446	Terry Pendleton	.05
140	Mike Pagliarulo	.05	242	Tom Gordon	.05	344	Sergio Valdez	.05	447	Mike Harkey	.05
141	Hal Morris	.05	243	Tony Gwynn	.50	345	Bob Patterson	.05	448	Jim Eisenreich	.05
142	Dave Parker	.05	244	Tommy Gregg	.05	346	John Marzano	.05	449	Benito Santiago	.05
143	Brett Butler	.05	245	Jeff Robinson	.05	347	Dana Kiecker RC	.05	450	Oddibe McDowell	.05
144	Paul Assenmacher	.05	246	Keith Comstock	.05	348	Dion James	.05	451	Cecil Fielder	.05
145	Mark Gubicza	.05	247	Jack Howell	.05	349	Hubie Brooks	.05	452	Ken Griffey Sr.	.05
146	Charlie Hough	.05	248	Keith Miller	.05	350	Bill Landrum	.05	453	Bert Blyleven	.10
147	Sammy Sosa	.50	249	Bobby Witt	.05	351	Bill Sampen RC	.05	454	Howard Johnson	.05
148	Randy Ready	.05	250	Rob Murphy	.05	352	Greg Briley	.05	455	Monty Farris	.05
149	Kelly Gruber	.05	251	Spike Owen	.05	353	Paul Gibson	.05	456	Tony Pena	.05
150	Devon White	.05	252	Garry Templeton	.05	354	Dave Eiland	.05	457	Tim Raines	.05
151	Gary Carter	.40	253	Glenn Braggs	.05	355	Steve Finley	.05	458	Dennis Rasmussen	.05
152	Gene Larkin	.05	254	Ron Robinson	.05	356	Bob Boone	.05	459	Luis Quinones	.05
153	Chris Sabo	.05	255	Kevin Mitchell	.05	357	Steve Buechele	.05	460	B.J. Surhoff	.05
154	David Cone	.05	256	Les Lancaster	.05	358	Chris Hoiles	.05	461	Ernest Riles	.05
155	Todd Stottlemyre	.05	257	Mel Stottlemyre RC	.10	359	Larry Walker	.05	462	Rick Sutcliffe	.05
156	Glenn Wilson	.05	258	Kenny Rogers	.05	360	Frank DiPino	.05	463	Danny Tartabull	.05
157	Bob Walk	.05	259	Lance Johnson	.05	361	Mark Grant	.05	464	Pete Incaviglia	.05
158	Mike Gallego	.05	260	John Kruk	.05	362	Dave Magadan	.05	465	Carlos Martinez	.05
159	Greg Hibbard	.05	261	Fred McGriff	.05	363	Robby Thompson	.05	466	Ricky Jordan	.05
160	Chris Bosio	.05	262	Dick Schofield	.05	364	Lonnie Smith	.05	467	John Cerutti	.05
161	Mike Moore	.05	263	Trevor Wilson	.05	365	Steve Farr	.05	468	Dave Winfield	.40
162	Jerry Browne	.05	264	David West	.05	366	Dave Valle	.05	469	Francisco Oliveras	.05
163	Steve Sax	.05	265	Scott Scudder	.05	367	Tim Naehring RC	.05	470	Roy Smith	.05
164	Melido Perez	.05	266	Dwight Gooden	.05	368	Jim Acker	.05	471	Barry Larkin	.05
165	Danny Darwin	.05	267	Willie Blair RC	.05	369	Jeff Reardon	.05	472	Ron Darling	.05
166	Roger McDowell	.05	268	Mark Portugal	.05	370	Tim Teufel	.05	473	David Wells	.05
167	Bill Ripken	.05	269	Doug Drabek	.05	371	Juan Gonzalez	.20	474	Glenn Davis	.05
168	Mike Sharperson	.05	270	Dennis Eckersley	.35	372	Luis Salazar	.05	475	Neal Heaton	.05
169	Lee Smith	.05	271	Eric King	.05	373	Rick Honeycutt	.05	476	Ron Hassey	.05
170	Matt Nokes	.05	272	Robin Yount	.40	374	Greg Maddux	.50	477	Frank Thomas	.40
171	Jesse Orosco	.05	273	Carney Lansford	.05	375	Jose Uribe	.05	478	Greg Vaughn	.05
172	Rick Aguilera	.05	274	Carlos Baerga	.05	376	Donnie Hill	.05	479	Todd Burns	.05
173	Jim Presley	.05	275	Dave Righetti	.05	377	Don Carman	.05	480	Candy Maldonado	.05
174	Lou Whitaker	.05	276	Scott Fletcher	.05	378	Craig Grebeck RC	.05			
175	Harold Reynolds	.05	277	Eric Yelding	.05	379	Willie Fraser	.05			
176	Brook Jacoby	.05	278	Charlie Hayes	.05	380	Glenallen Hill	.05			
177	Wally Backman	.05	279	Jeff Ballard	.05	381	Joe Oliver	.05			
178	Wade Boggs	.50				382	Randy Bush	.05			
179	Chuck Cary	.05				383	Alex Cole	.05			

481	Dave LaPoint	.05
482	Alvin Davis	.05
483	Mike Scott	.05
484	Dale Murphy	.20
485	Ben McDonald	.05
486	Jay Howell	.05
487	Vince Coleman	.05
488	Alfredo Griffin	.05
489	Sandy Alomar	.05
490	Kirby Puckett	.50
491	Andres Thomas	.05
492	Jack Morris	.05
493	Matt Young	.05
494	Greg Myers	.05
495	Barry Bonds	1.00
496	Scott Cooper	.05
497	Dan Schatzeder	.05
498	Jesse Barfield	.05
499	Jerry Goff	.05
500	Checklist 332-408	.05
501	Anthony Telford RC	.05
502	Eddie Murray	.40
503	Omar Olivares RC	.05
504	Ryne Sandberg	.50
505	Jeff Montgomery	.05
506	Mark Parent	.05
507	Ron Gant	.05
508	Frank Tanana	.05
509	Jay Buhner	.05
510	Max Venable	.05
511	Wally Whitehurst	.05
512	Gary Pettis	.05
513	Tom Brunansky	.05
514	Tim Wallach	.05
515	Craig Lefferts	.05
516	Tim Layana RC	.05
517	Darryl Hamilton	.05
518	Rick Reuschel	.05
519	Steve Wilson	.05
520	Kurt Stillwell	.05
521	Rafael Palmeiro	.30
522	Ken Patterson	.05
523	Len Dykstra	.05
524	Tony Fernandez	.05
525	Kent Anderson	.05
526	Mark Leonard RC	.05
527	Allan Anderson	.05
528	Tom Browning	.05
529	Frank Viola	.05
530	John Olerud	.05
531	Juan Agosto	.05
532	Zane Smith	.05
533	Scott Sanderson	.05
534	Barry Jones	.05
535	Mike Felder	.05
536	Jose Canseco	.20
537	Felix Fermin	.05
538	Roberto Kelly	.05
539	Brian Holman	.05
540	Mark Davidson	.05
541	Terry Mulholland	.05
542	Randy Milligan	.05
543	Jose Gonzalez	.05
544	Craig Wilson RC	.05
545	Mike Hartley	.05
546	Greg Swindell	.05
547	Gary Gaetti	.05
548	Dave Justice	.05
549	Steve Searcy	.05
550	Erik Hanson	.05
551	Dave Stieb	.05
552	Andy Van Slyke	.05
553	Mike Greenwell	.05
554	Kevin Maas	.05
555	Delino Deshields	.05
556	Curt Schilling	.20
557	Ramon Martinez	.05
558	Pedro Guerrero	.05
559	Dwight Smith	.05
560	Mark Davis	.05
561	Shawn Abner	.05
562	Charlie Leibrandt	.05
563	John Shelby	.05
564	Bill Swift	.05
565	Mike Fetters	.05
566	Alejandro Pena	.05
567	Ruben Sierra	.05
568	Carlos Quintana	.05
569	Kevin Gross	.05
570	Derek Lilliquist	.05
571	Jack Armstrong	.05
572	Greg Brock	.05
573	Mike Kingery	.05
574	Greg Smith	.05
575	Brian McRae RC	.10
576	Jack Daugherty	.05
577	Ozzie Guillen	.05
578	Joe Boever	.05
579	Luis Sojo	.05
580	Chili Davis	.05
581	Don Robinson	.05
582	Brian Harper	.05
583	Paul O'Neill	.05
584	Bob Ojeda	.05
585	Mookie Wilson	.05
586	Rafael Ramirez	.05
587	Gary Redus	.05
588	Jamie Quirk	.05
589	Shawn Hilligas	.05
590	Tom Edens RC	.05
591	Joe Klink	.05
592	Charles Nagy	.05
593	Eric Plunk	.05
594	Tracy Jones	.05
595	Craig Biggio	.05
596	Jose DeJesus	.05
597	Mickey Tettleton	.05
598	Chris Gwynn	.05
599	Rex Hudler	.05
600	Checklist 409-506	.05
601	Jim Gott	.05
602	Jeff Manto	.05
603	Nelson Liriano	.05
604	Mark Lemke	.05
605	Clay Parker	.05
606	Edgar Martinez	.05
607	Mark Whiten RC	.10
608	Ted Power	.05
609	Tom Bolton	.05
610	Tom Herr	.05
611	Andy Hawkins	.05
612	Scott Ruskin	.05
613	Ron Kittle	.05
614	John Wetteland	.05
615	Mike Perez RC	.05
616	Dave Clark	.05
617	Brent Mayne	.05
618	Jack Clark	.05
619	Marvin Freeman	.05
620	Edwin Nunez	.05
621	Russ Swan	.05
622	Johnny Ray	.05
623	Charlie O'Brien	.05
624	Joe Bitker RC	.05
625	Mike Marshall	.05
626	Otis Nixon	.05
627	Andy Benes	.05
628	Ron Oester	.05
629	Ted Higuera	.05
630	Kevin Bass	.05
631	Damon Berryhill	.05
632	Bo Jackson	.10
633	Brad Arnsberg	.05
634	Jerry Willard	.05
635	Tommy Greene	.05
636	Bob MacDonald RC	.05
637	Kirk McCaskill	.05
638	John Burkett	.05
639	Paul Abbott RC	.05
640	Todd Benzinger	.05
641	Todd Hundley	.05
642	George Bell	.05
643	Javier Ortiz RC	.05
644	Sid Bream	.05
645	Bob Welch	.05
646	Phil Bradley	.05
647	Bill Krueger	.05
648	Rickey Henderson	.40
649	Kevin Wickander	.05
650	Steve Balboni	.05
651	Gene Harris	.05
652	Jim Deshaies	.05
653	Jason Grimsley	.05
654	Joe Orsulak	.05
655	Jimmy Poole RC	.05
656	Felix Jose	.05
657	Dennis Cook	.05
658	Tom Brookens	.05
659	Junior Ortiz	.05
660	Jeff Parrett	.05
661	Jerry Don Gleaton	.05
662	Brent Knackert	.05
663	Rance Mulliniks	.05
664	John Smiley	.05
665	Larry Andersen	.05
666	Willie McGee	.05
667	Chris Nabholz RC	.05
668	Brady Anderson	.05
669	Darren Holmes RC	.10
670	Ken Hill	.05
671	Gary Varsho	.05
672	Bill Pecota	.05
673	Fred Lynn	.05
674	Kevin D. Brown	.05
675	Dan Petry	.05
676	Mike Jackson	.05
677	Wally Joyner	.05
678	Danny Jackson	.05
679	Bill Haselman RC	.05
680	Mike Boddicker	.05
681	Mel Rojas RC	.05
682	Roberto Alomar	.20
683	Dave Justice (R.O.Y.)	.05
684	Chuck Crim	.05
685a	Matt Williams (Last line of Career Highlights ends, "most DP's in.")	.10
685b	Matt Williams (Last line ends "8/24-27/87.")	.25
686	Shawon Dunston	.05
687	Jeff Schulz RC	.05
688	John Barfield RC	.05
689	Gerald Young	.05
690	Luis Gonzalez RC	.75
691	Frank Wills	.05
692	Chuck Finley	.05
693	Sandy Alomar (R.O.Y.)	.05
694	Tim Drummond	.05
695	Herm Winningham	.05
696	Darryl Strawberry	.05
697	Al Leiter	.05
698	Karl Rhodes RC	.05
699	Stan Belinda	.05
700	Checklist 507-604	.05
701	Lance Blankenship	.05
702	Willie Stargell (Puzzle Card)	.05
703	Jim Gantner	.05
704	Reggie Harris RC	.05
705	Rob Ducey	.05
706	Tim Hulett	.05
707	Atlee Hammaker	.05
708	Xavier Hernandez	.05
709	Chuck McElroy	.05
710	John Mitchell	.05
711	Carlos Hernandez	.05
712	Geronimo Pena	.05
713	Jim Neidlinger RC	.05
714	John Orton	.05
715	Terry Leach	.05
716	Mike Stanton	.05
717	Walt Terrell	.05
718	Luis Aquino	.05
719	Bud Black	.05
720	Bob Kipper	.05
721	Jeff Gray RC	.05
722	Jose Rijo	.05
723	Curt Young	.05
724	Jose Vizcaino	.05
725	Randy Tomlin RC	.05
726	Junior Noboa	.05
727	Bob Welch (Award Winner)	.05
728	Gary Ward	.05
729	Rob Deer	.05
730	David Segui RC	.05
731	Mark Carreon	.05
732	Vicente Palacios	.05
733	Sam Horn	.05
734	Howard Farmer RC	.05
735	Ken Dayley	.05
736	Kelly Mann	.05
737	Joe Grahe RC	.05
738	Kelly Downs	.05
739	Jimmy Kremers RC	.05
740	Kevin Appier	.05
741	Jeff Reed	.05
742	Jose Rijo (World Series)	.05
743	Dave Rohde RC	.05
744	Len Dykstra, Dale Murphy Dr. Dirt/Mr. Clean	.10
745	Paul Sorrento	.05
746	Thomas Howard	.05
747	Matt Stark RC	.05
748	Harold Baines	.05
749	Doug Dascenzo	.05
750	Doug Drabek (Award Winner)	.05
751	Gary Sheffield	.20
752	Terry Lee RC	.05
753	Jim Vatcher RC	.05
754	Lee Stevens	.05
755	Randy Veres	.05
756	Bill Doran	.05
757	Gary Wayne	.05
758	Pedro Munoz RC	.05
759	Chris Hammond	.05
760	Checklist 605-702	.05
761	Rickey Henderson/MVP	.20
762	Barry Bonds/MVP	.50
763	Billy Hatcher (World Series)	.05
764	Julio Machado	.05
765	Jose Mesa	.05
766	Willie Randolph (World Series)	.05
767	Scott Erickson RC	.10
768	Travis Fryman	.05
769	Rich Rodriguez RC	.05
770	Checklist 703-770; BC1-BC22	.05

THE ELITE SERIES

GEORGE BRETT

6	Cecil Fielder	7.50
7	Rickey Henderson	25.00
8	Matt Williams	7.50
---	Nolan Ryan (Legend)	65.00
---	Ryne Sandberg (Signature)	100.00

Rookies

Brian Hunter FIRST BASE

		NM/M
Complete Set (56):		4.00
Common Player:		.05
1	Pat Kelly	.05
2	Rich DeLucia	.05
3	Wes Chamberlain	.05
4	Scott Leius	.05
5	Darryl Kile	.05
6	Milt Cuyler	.05
7	Todd Van Poppel	.05
8	Ray Lankford	.05
9	Brian Hunter	.05
10	Tony Perezchica	.05
11	Ced Landrum	.05
12	Dave Burba	.05
13	Ramon Garcia	.05
14	Ed Sprague	.05
15	Warren Newson	.05
16	Paul Faries	.05
17	Luis Gonzalez	.15
18	Charles Nagy	.05
19	Chris Hammond	.05
20	Frank Castillo	.05
21	Pedro Munoz	.05
22	Orlando Merced	.05
23	Jose Melendez	.05
24	Kirk Dressendorfer	.05
25	Heathcliff Slocumb	.05
26	Doug Simons	.05
27	Mike Timlin	.05
28	Jeff Fassero	.05
29	Mark Leiter	.05
30	Jeff Bagwell RC	2.50
31	Brian McRae	.05
32	Mark Whiten	.05
33	Ivan Rodriguez RC	1.50
34	Wade Taylor	.05
35	Darren Lewis	.05
36	Mo Vaughn	.25
37	Mike Remlinger	.05
38	Rick Wilkins	.05
39	Chuck Knoblauch	.05
40	Kevin Morton	.05
41	Carlos Rodriguez	.05
42	Mark Lewis	.05
43	Brent Mayne	.05
44	Chris Haney	.05
45	Denis Boucher	.05
46	Mike Gardiner	.05
47	Jeff Johnson	.05
48	Dean Palmer	.05
49	Chuck McElroy	.05
50	Chris Jones	.05

Elite

		NM/M
Complete Set (10):		250.00
Common Player:		15.00
1	Barry Bonds	60.00
2	George Brett	40.00
3	Jose Canseco	25.00
4	Andre Dawson	15.00
5	Doug Drabek	7.50

51	Scott Kamieniecki	.05
52	Al Osuna	.05
53	Rusty Meacham	.05
54	Chito Martinez	.05
55	Reggie Jefferson	.05
56	Checklist	.05

1992 Donruss

JOHN KRUK
PHILLIES • FIRST BASE

	NM/M
Unopened Retail Set (788):	15.00
Unopened Hobby Set (784):	12.50
Unopened "Coca-Cola" Set (784):	25.00
Complete Set (784):	12.00
Common Player:	.05
Rod Carew Puzzle:	.50
Series 1 or 2 Pack (15):	.50
Series 1 or 2 Wax Box (36):	15.00
Blister Rack (92):	1.50

1	Mark Wohlers/RR RC	.05
2	Wil Cordero/RR	.05
3	Kyle Abbott/RR	.05
4	Dave Nilsson/RR RC	.05
5	Kenny Lofton/RR	.15
6	Luis Mercedes/RR RC	.05
7	Roger Salkeld/RR RC	.05
8	Eddie Zosky/RR	.05
9	Todd Van Poppel/RR RC	.10
10	Frank Seminara/RR RC	.05
11	Andy Ashby/RR RC	.10
12	Reggie Jefferson/RR	.05
13	Ryan Klesko/RR	.05
14	Carlos Garcia/RR RC	.10
15	John Ramos/RR RC	.05
16	Eric Karros/RR	.05
17	Pat Lennon/RR RC	.05
18	Eddie Taubensee/RR RC	.05
19	Roberto Hernandez/RR RC	.05
20	D.J. Dozier/RR	.05
21	Dave Henderson/AS	.05
22	Cal Ripken, Jr./AS	.50
23	Wade Boggs/AS	.25
24	Ken Griffey Jr./AS	.35
25	Jack Morris/AS	.05
26	Danny Tartabull/AS	.05
27	Cecil Fielder/AS	.05
28	Roberto Alomar/AS	.10
29	Sandy Alomar/AS	.05
30	Rickey Henderson/AS	.25
31	Ken Hill	.05
32	John Habyan	.05
33	Otis Nixon (Highlight)	.05
34	Tim Wallach	.05
35	Cal Ripken, Jr.	1.00
36	Gary Carter	.35
37	Juan Agosto	.05
38	Doug Dascenzo	.05
39	Kirk Gibson	.05
40	Benito Santiago	.05
41	Otis Nixon	.05
42	Andy Allanson	.05
43	Brian Holman	.05
44	Dick Schofield	.05
45	Dave Magadan	.05
46	Rafael Palmeiro	.35
47	Jody Reed	.05
48	Ivan Calderon	.05
49	Greg Harris	.05
50	Chris Sabo	.05
51	Paul Molitor	.35
52	Robby Thompson	.05
53	Dave Smith	.05
54	Mark Davis	.05
55	Kevin Brown	.05
56	Donn Pall	.05
57	Len Dykstra	.05
58	Roberto Alomar	.15
59	Jeff Robinson	.05

60	Willie McGee	.05
61	Jay Buhner	.05
62	Mike Pagliarulo	.05
63	Paul O'Neill	.05
64	Hubie Brooks	.05
65	Kelly Gruber	.05
66	Ken Caminiti	.05
67	Gary Redus	.05
68	Harold Baines	.05
69	Charlie Hough	.05
70	B.J. Surhoff	.05
71	Walt Weiss	.05
72	Shawn Hillegas	.05
73	Roberto Kelly	.05
74	Jeff Ballard	.05
75	Craig Biggio	.05
76	Pat Combs	.05
77	Jeff Robinson	.05
78	Tim Belcher	.05
79	Cris Carpenter	.05
80	Checklist 1-79	.05
81	Steve Avery	.05
82	Chris James	.05
83	Brian Harper	.05
84	Charlie Leibrandt	.05
85	Mickey Tettleton	.05
86	Pete O'Brien	.05
87	Danny Darwin	.05
88	Bob Walk	.05
89	Jeff Reardon	.05
90	Bobby Rose	.05
91	Danny Jackson	.05
92	John Morris	.05
93	Bud Black	.05
94	Tommy Greene (Highlight)	.05
95	Rick Aguilera	.05
96	Gary Gaetti	.05
97	David Cone	.05
98	John Olerud	.05
99	Joel Skinner	.05
100	Jay Bell	.05
101	Bob Milacki	.05
102	Norm Charlton	.05
103	Chuck Crim	.05
104	Terry Steinbach	.05
105	Juan Samuel	.05
106	Steve Howe	.05
107	Rafael Belliard	.05
108	Joey Cora	.05
109	Tommy Greene	.05
110	Gregg Olson	.05
111	Frank Tanana	.05
112	Lee Smith	.05
113	Greg Harris	.05
114	Dwayne Henry	.05
115	Chili Davis	.05
116	Kent Mercker	.05
117	Brian Barnes	.05
118	Rich DeLucia	.05
119	Andre Dawson	.20
120	Carlos Baerga	.05
121	Mike LaValliere	.05
122	Jeff Gray	.05
123	Bruce Hurst	.05
124	Alvin Davis	.05
125	John Candelaria	.05
126	Matt Nokes	.05
127	George Bell	.05
128	Bret Saberhagen	.05
129	Jeff Russell	.05
130	Jim Abbott	.05
131	Bill Gullickson	.05
132	Todd Zeile	.05
133	Dave Winfield	.35
134	Wally Whitehurst	.05
135	Matt Williams	.05
136	Tom Browning	.05
137	Marquis Grissom	.05
138	Erik Hanson	.05
139	Rob Dibble	.05
140	Don August	.05
141	Tom Henke	.05
142	Dan Pasqua	.05
143	George Brett	.60
144	Jerald Clark	.05
145	Robin Ventura	.05
146	Dale Murphy	.20
147	Dennis Eckersley	.30
148	Eric Yelding	.05
149	Mario Diaz	.05
150	Casey Candaele	.05
151	Steve Olin	.05
152	Luis Salazar	.05
153	Kevin Maas	.05
154	Nolan Ryan (Highlight)	.50
155	Barry Jones	.05
156	Chris Hoiles	.05
157	Bobby Ojeda	.05
158	Pedro Guerrero	.05
159	Paul Assenmacher	.05
160	Checklist 80-157	.05
161	Mike Macfarlane	.05
162	Craig Lefferts	.05

163	Brian Hunter RC	.05
164	Alan Trammell	.05
165	Ken Griffey Jr.	.65
166	Lance Parrish	.05
167	Brian Downing	.05
168	John Barfield	.05
169	Jack Clark	.05
170	Chris Nabholz	.05
171	Tim Teufel	.05
172	Chris Hammond	.05
173	Robin Yount	.35
174	Dave Righetti	.05
175	Joe Girardi	.05
176	Mike Boddicker	.05
177	Dean Palmer	.05
178	Greg Hibbard	.05
179	Randy Ready	.05
180	Devon White	.05
181	Mark Eichhorn	.05
182	Mike Felder	.05
183	Joe Klink	.05
184	Steve Bedrosian	.05
185	Barry Larkin	.05
186	John Franco	.05
187	Ed Sprague RC	.05
188	Mark Portugal	.05
189	Jose Lind	.05
190	Bob Welch	.05
191	Alex Fernandez	.05
192	Gary Sheffield	.20
193	Rickey Henderson	.35
194	Rod Nichols	.05
195	Scott Kamieniecki RC	.05
196	Mike Flanagan	.05
197	Steve Finley	.05
198	Darren Daulton	.05
199	Leo Gomez	.05
200	Mike Morgan	.05
201	Bob Tewksbury	.05
202	Sid Bream	.05
203	Sandy Alomar	.05
204	Greg Gagne	.05
205	Juan Berenguer	.05
206	Cecil Fielder	.05
207	Randy Johnson	.35
208	Tony Pena	.05
209	Doug Drabek	.05
210	Wade Boggs	.45
211	Bryan Harvey	.05
212	Jose Vizcaino	.05
213	Alonzo Powell RC	.05
214	Will Clark	.05
215	Rickey Henderson (Highlight)	.20
216	Jack Morris	.05
217	Junior Felix	.05
218	Vince Coleman	.05
219	Jimmy Key	.05
220	Alex Cole	.05
221	Bill Landrum	.05
222	Randy Milligan	.05
223	Jose Rijo	.05
224	Greg Vaughn	.05
225	Dave Stewart	.05
226	Lenny Harris	.05
227	Scott Sanderson	.05
228	Jeff Blauser	.05
229	Ozzie Guillen	.05
230	John Kruk	.05
231	Bob Melvin	.05
232	Milt Cuyler	.05
233	Felix Jose	.05
234	Ellis Burks	.05
235	Pete Harnisch	.05
236	Kevin Tapani	.05
237	Terry Pendleton	.05
238	Mark Gardner	.05
239	Harold Reynolds	.05
240	Checklist 158-237	.05
241	Mike Harkey	.05
242	Felix Fermin	.05
243	Barry Bonds	1.00
244	Roger Clemens	.60
245	Dennis Rasmussen	.05
246	Jose DeLeon	.05
247	Orel Hershiser	.05
248	Mel Hall	.05
249	Rick Wilkins RC	.05
250	Tom Gordon	.05
251	Kevin Reimer	.05
252	Luis Polonia	.05
253	Mike Henneman	.05
254	Tom Pagnozzi	.05
255	Chuck Finley	.05
256	Mackey Sasser	.05
257	John Burkett	.05
258	Hal Morris	.05
259	Larry Walker	.05
260	Billy Swift	.05
261	Joe Oliver	.05
262	Julio Machado	.05
263	Todd Stottlemyre	.05
264	Matt Merullo	.05
265	Brent Mayne	.05

266	Thomas Howard	.05
267	Lance Johnson	.05
268	Terry Mulholland	.05
269	Rick Honeycutt	.05
270	Luis Gonzalez	.05
271	Jose Guzman	.05
272	Jimmy Jones	.05
273	Mark Lewis	.05
274	Rene Gonzales	.05
275	Jeff Johnson RC	.05
276	Dennis Martinez (Highlight)	.05
277	Delino DeShields	.05
278	Sam Horn	.05
279	Kevin Gross	.05
280	Jose Oquendo	.05
281	Mark Grace	.05
282	Mark Gubicza	.05
283	Fred McGriff	.05
284	Ron Gant	.05
285	Lou Whitaker	.05
286	Edgar Martinez	.05
287	Ron Tingley	.05
288	Kevin McReynolds	.05
289	Ivan Rodriguez	.30
290	Mike Gardiner	.05
291	Chris Haney RC	.05
292	Darrin Jackson	.05
293	Bill Doran	.05
294	Ted Higuera	.05
295	Jeff Brantley	.05
296	Les Lancaster	.05
297	Jim Eisenreich	.05
298	Ruben Sierra	.05
299	Scott Radinsky	.05
300	Jose DeJesus	.05
301	Mike Timlin RC	.05
302	Luis Sojo	.05
303	Kelly Downs	.05
304	Scott Bankhead	.05
305	Pedro Munoz	.05
306	Scott Scudder	.05
307	Kevin Elster	.05
308	Duane Ward	.05
309	Darryl Kile RC	.10
310	Orlando Merced	.05
311	Dave Henderson	.05
312	Tim Raines	.05
313	Mark Lee	.05
314	Mike Gallego	.05
315	Charles Nagy	.05
316	Jesse Barfield	.05
317	Todd Frohwirth	.05
318	Al Osuna	.05
319	Darrin Fletcher	.05
320	Checklist 238-316	.05
321	David Segui	.05
322	Stan Javier	.05
323	Bryn Smith	.05
324	Jeff Treadway	.05
325	Mark Whiten	.05
326	Kent Hrbek	.05
327	Dave Justice	.05
328	Tony Phillips	.05
329	Rob Murphy	.05
330	Kevin Morton	.05
331	John Smiley	.05
332	Luis Rivera	.05
333	Wally Joyner	.05
334	Heathcliff Slocumb RC	.05
335	Rick Cerone	.05
336	Mike Remlinger RC	.05
337	Mike Moore	.05
338	Lloyd McClendon	.05
339	Al Newman	.05
340	Kirk McCaskill	.05
341	Howard Johnson	.05
342	Greg Myers	.05
343	Kal Daniels	.05
344	Bernie Williams	.05
345	Shane Mack	.05
346	Gary Thurman	.05
347	Dante Bichette	.05
348	Mark McGwire	.75
349	Travis Fryman	.05
350	Ray Lankford	.05
351	Mike Jeffcoat	.05
352	Jack McDowell	.05
353	Mitch Williams	.05
354	Mike Devereaux	.05
355	Andres Galarraga	.05
356	Henry Cotto	.05
357	Scott Bailes	.05
358	Jeff Bagwell	.35
359	Scott Leius	.05
360	Zane Smith	.05
361	Bill Pecota	.05
362	Tony Fernandez	.05
363	Glenn Braggs	.05
364	Bill Spiers	.05
365	Vicente Palacios	.05
366	Tim Burke	.05
367	Randy Tomlin	.05
368	Kenny Rogers	.05

#	Player	Value
369	Brett Butler	.05
370	Pat Kelly	.05
371	Bip Roberts	.05
372	Gregg Jefferies	.05
373	Kevin Bass	.05
374	Ron Karkovice	.05
375	Paul Gibson	.05
376	Bernard Gilkey	.05
377	Dave Gallagher	.05
378	Bill Wegman	.05
379	Pat Borders	.05
380	Ed Whitson	.05
381	Gilberto Reyes	.05
382	Russ Swan	.05
383	Andy Van Slyke	.05
384	Wes Chamberlain	.05
385	Steve Chitren	.05
386	Greg Olson	.05
387	Brian McRae	.05
388	Rich Rodriguez	.05
389	Steve Decker	.05
390	Chuck Knoblauch	.05
391	Bobby Witt	.05
392	Eddie Murray	.35
393	Juan Gonzalez	.20
394	Scott Ruskin	.05
395	Jay Howell	.05
396	Checklist 317-396	.05
397	Royce Clayton/RR	.05
398	John Jaha/RR RC	.05
399	Dan Wilson/RR	.05
400	Archie Corbin/RR RC	.05
401	Barry Manuel/RR RC	.05
402	Kim Batiste/RR	.05
403	Pat Mahomes/RR RC	.05
404	Dave Fleming/RR	.05
405	Jeff Juden/RR)	.05
406	Jim Thome/RR	.40
407	Sam Militello/RR	.05
408	Jeff Nelson/RR RC	.05
409	Anthony Young/RR	.05
410	Tino Martinez/RR	.05
411	Jeff Mutis/RR RC	.05
412	Rey Sanchez/RR RC	.05
413	Chris Gardner/RR RC	.05
414	John Vander Wal/RR RC	.10
415	Reggie Sanders/RR	.05
416	Brian Williams/RR RC	.05
417	Mo Sanford/RR	.05
418	David Weathers/RR RC	.05
419	Hector Fajardo/RR RC	.05
420	Steve Foster/RR RC	.05
421	Lance Dickson	.05
422	Andre Dawson/AS	.15
423	Ozzie Smith/AS	.25
424	Chris Sabo/AS	.05
425	Tony Gwynn/AS	.25
426	Tom Glavine/AS	.05
427	Bobby Bonilla/AS	.05
428	Will Clark/AS	.25
429	Ryne Sandberg/AS	.25
430	Benito Santiago/AS	.05
431	Ivan Calderon/AS	.05
432	Ozzie Smith	.45
433	Tim Leary	.05
434	Bret Saberhagen (Highlight)	.05
435	Mel Rojas	.05
436	Ben McDonald	.05
437	Tim Crews	.05
438	Rex Hudler	.05
439	Chico Walker	.05
440	Kurt Stillwell	.05
441	Tony Gwynn	.45
442	John Smoltz	.05
443	Lloyd Moseby	.05
444	Mike Schooler	.05
445	Joe Grahe	.05
446	Dwight Gooden	.05
447	Oil Can Boyd	.05
448	John Marzano	.05
449	Bret Barberie	.05
450	Mike Maddux	.05
451	Jeff Reed	.05
452	Dale Sveum	.05
453	Jose Uribe	.05
454	Bob Scanlan	.05
455	Kevin Appier	.05
456	Jeff Huson	.05
457	Ken Patterson	.05
458	Ricky Jordan	.05
459	Tom Candiotti	.05
460	Lee Stevens	.05
461	Rod Beck RC	.10
462	Dave Valle	.05
463	Scott Erickson	.05
464	Chris Jones	.05
465	Mark Carreon	.05
466	Rob Ducey	.05
467	Jim Corsi	.05
468	Jeff King	.05
469	Curt Young	.05
470	Bo Jackson	.15
471	Chris Bosio	.05
472	Jamie Quirk	.05
473	Jesse Orosco	.05
474	Alvaro Espinoza	.05
475	Joe Orsulak	.05
476	Checklist 397-477	.05
477	Gerald Young	.05
478	Wally Backman	.05
479	Juan Bell	.05
480	Mike Scioscia	.05
481	Omar Olivares	.05
482	Francisco Cabrera	.05
483	Greg Swindell	.05
484	Terry Leach	.05
485	Tommy Gregg	.05
486	Scott Aldred	.05
487	Greg Briley	.05
488	Phil Plantier	.05
489	Curtis Wilkerson	.05
490	Tom Brunansky	.05
491	Mike Fetters	.05
492	Frank Castillo	.05
493	Joe Boever	.05
494	Kirt Manwaring	.05
495	Wilson Alvarez (Highlight)	.05
496	Gene Larkin	.05
497	Gary DiSarcina	.05
498	Frank Viola	.05
499	Manuel Lee	.05
500	Albert Belle	.05
501	Stan Belinda	.05
502	Dwight Evans	.05
503	Eric Davis	.05
504	Darren Holmes	.05
505	Mike Bordick	.05
506	Dave Hansen	.05
507	Lee Guetterman	.05
508	Keith Mitchell RC	.05
509	Melido Perez	.05
510	Dickie Thon	.05
511	Mark Williamson	.05
512	Mark Salas	.05
513	Milt Thompson	.05
514	Mo Vaughn	.05
515	Jim Deshaies	.05
516	Rich Garces	.05
517	Lonnie Smith	.05
518	Spike Owen	.05
519	Tracy Jones	.05
520	Greg Maddux	.45
521	Carlos Martinez	.05
522	Neal Heaton	.05
523	Mike Greenwell	.05
524	Andy Benes	.05
525	Jeff Schaefer	.05
526	Mike Sharperson	.05
527	Wade Taylor	.05
528	Jerome Walton	.05
529	Storm Davis	.05
530	Jose Hernandez RC	.05
531	Mark Langston	.05
532	Rob Deer	.05
533	Geronimo Pena	.05
534	Juan Guzman RC	.10
535	Pete Schourek	.05
536	Todd Benzinger	.05
537	Billy Hatcher	.05
538	Tom Foley	.05
539	Dave Cochrane	.05
540	Mariano Duncan	.05
541	Edwin Nunez	.05
542	Rance Mulliniks	.05
543	Carlton Fisk	.35
544	Luis Aquino	.05
545	Ricky Bones	.05
546	Craig Grebeck	.05
547	Charlie Hayes	.05
548	Jose Canseco	.25
549	Andujar Cedeno	.05
550	Geno Petralli	.05
551	Javier Ortiz	.05
552	Rudy Seanez	.05
553	Rich Gedman	.05
554	Eric Plunk	.05
555	Nolan Ryan, Rich Gossage (Highlight)	.25
556	Checklist 478-555	.05
557	Greg Colbrunn	.05
558	Chito Martinez RC	.05
559	Darryl Strawberry	.05
560	Luis Alicea	.05
561	Dwight Smith	.05
562	Terry Shumpert	.05
563	Jim Vatcher	.05
564	Deion Sanders	.10
565	Walt Terrell	.05
566	Dave Burba	.05
567	Dave Howard	.05
568	Todd Hundley	.05
569	Jack Daugherty	.05
570	Scott Cooper	.05
571	Bill Sampen	.05
572	Jose Melendez	.05
573	Freddie Benavides	.05
574	Jim Gantner	.05
575	Trevor Wilson	.05
576	Ryne Sandberg	.45
577	Kevin Seitzer	.05
578	Gerald Alexander	.05
579	Mike Huff	.05
580	Von Hayes	.05
581	Derek Bell	.05
582	Mike Stanley	.05
583	Kevin Mitchell	.05
584	Mike Jackson	.05
585	Dan Gladden	.05
586	Ted Power	.05
587	Jeff Innis	.05
588	Bob MacDonald	.05
589	Jose Tolentino RC	.05
590	Bob Patterson	.05
591	Scott Brosius RC	.10
592	Frank Thomas	.35
593	Darryl Hamilton	.05
594	Kirk Dressendorfer	.05
595	Jeff Shaw	.05
596	Don Mattingly	.60
597	Glenn Davis	.05
598	Andy Mota	.05
599	Jason Grimsley	.05
600	Jimmy Poole	.05
601	Jim Gott	.05
602	Stan Royer	.05
603	Marvin Freeman	.05
604	Denis Boucher	.05
605	Denny Neagle	.05
606	Mark Lemke	.05
607	Jerry Don Gleaton	.05
608	Brent Knackert	.05
609	Carlos Quintana	.05
610	Bobby Bonilla	.05
611	Joe Hesketh	.05
612	Daryl Boston	.05
613	Shawon Dunston	.05
614	Danny Cox	.05
615	Darren Lewis	.05
616	Alejandro Pena, Kent Mercker, Mark Wohlers (Highlight)	.05
617	Kirby Puckett	.45
618	Franklin Stubbs	.05
619	Chris Donnels	.05
620	David Wells	.05
621	Mike Aldrete	.05
622	Bob Kipper	.05
623	Anthony Telford	.05
624	Randy Myers	.05
625	Willie Randolph	.05
626	Joe Slusarski	.05
627	John Wetteland	.05
628	Greg Cadaret	.05
629	Tom Glavine	.20
630	Wilson Alvarez	.05
631	Wally Ritchie	.05
632	Mike Mussina	.25
633	Mark Leiter	.05
634	Gerald Perry	.05
635	Matt Young	.05
636	Checklist 556-635	.05
637	Scott Hemond	.05
638	David West	.05
639	Jim Clancy	.05
640	Doug Piatt	.05
641	Omar Vizquel	.05
642	Rick Sutcliffe	.05
643	Glenallen Hill	.05
644	Gary Varsho	.05
645	Tony Fossas	.05
646	Jack Howell	.05
647	Jim Campanis RC	.05
648	Chris Gwynn	.05
649	Jim Leyritz	.05
650	Chuck McElroy	.05
651	Sean Berry	.05
652	Donald Harris	.05
653	Don Slaught	.05
654	Rusty Meacham RC	.05
655	Scott Terry	.05
656	Ramon Martinez	.05
657	Keith Miller	.05
658	Ramon Garcia	.05
659	Milt Hill RC	.05
660	Steve Frey	.05
661	Bob McClure	.05
662	Ced Landrum RC	.05
663	Doug Henry RC	.05
664	Candy Maldonado	.05
665	Carl Willis	.05
666	Jeff Montgomery	.05
667	Craig Shipley RC	.05
668	Warren Newson RC	.05
669	Mickey Morandini	.05
670	Brook Jacoby	.05
671	Ryan Bowen RC	.05
672	Bill Krueger	.05
673	Rob Mallicoat	.05
674	Doug Jones	.05
675	Scott Livingstone	.05
676	Danny Tartabull	.05
677	Joe Carter (Highlight)	.05
678	Cecil Espy	.05
679	Randy Velarde	.05
680	Bruce Ruffin	.05
681	Ted Wood RC	.05
682	Dan Plesac	.05
683	Eric Bullock	.05
684	Junior Ortiz	.05
685	Dave Hollins	.05
686	Dennis Martinez	.05
687	Larry Andersen	.05
688	Doug Simons	.05
689	Tim Spehr RC	.05
690	Calvin Jones RC	.05
691	Mark Guthrie	.05
692	Alfredo Griffin	.05
693	Joe Carter	.05
694	Terry Mathews RC	.05
695	Pascual Perez	.05
696	Gene Nelson	.05
697	Gerald Williams	.05
698	Chris Cron RC	.05
699	Steve Buechele	.05
700	Paul McClellan	.05
701	Jim Lindeman	.05
702	Francisco Oliveras	.05
703	Rob Maurer RC	.05
704	Pat Hentgen RC	.15
705	Jaime Navarro	.05
706	Mike Magnante RC	.05
707	Nolan Ryan	1.00
708	Bobby Thigpen	.05
709	John Cerutti	.05
710	Steve Wilson	.05
711	Hensley Meulens	.05
712	Rheal Cormier RC	.05
713	Scott Bradley	.05
714	Mitch Webster	.05
715	Roger Mason	.05
716	Checklist 636-716	.05
717	Jeff Fassero RC	.05
718	Cal Eldred	.05
719	Sid Fernandez	.05
720	Bob Zupcic RC	.05
721	Jose Offerman	.05
722	Cliff Brantley RC	.05
723	Ron Darling	.05
724	Dave Stieb	.05
725	Hector Villanueva	.05
726	Mike Hartley	.05
727	Arthur Rhodes RC	.05
728	Randy Bush	.05
729	Steve Sax	.05
730	Dave Otto	.05
731	John Wehner RC	.05
732	Dave Martinez	.05
733	Ruben Amaro RC	.05
734	Billy Ripken	.05
735	Steve Farr	.05
736	Shawn Abner	.05
737	Gil Heredia RC	.05
738	Ron Jones	.05
739	Tony Castillo	.05
740	Sammy Sosa	.45
741	Julio Franco	.05
742	Tim Naehring	.05
743	Steve Wapnick RC	.05
744	Craig Wilson	.05
745	Darrin Chapin RC	.05
746	Chris George RC	.05
747	Mike Simms	.05
748	Rosario Rodriguez	.05
749	Skeeter Barnes	.05
750	Roger McDowell	.05
751	Dann Howitt	.05
752	Paul Sorrento	.05
753	Braulio Castillo RC	.05
754	Yorkis Perez RC	.05
755	Willie Fraser	.05
756	Jeremy Hernandez RC	.05
757	Curt Schilling	.20
758	Steve Lyons	.05
759	Dave Anderson	.05
760	Willie Banks	.05
761	Mark Leonard	.05
762	Jack Armstrong	.05
763	Scott Servais	.05
764	Ray Stephens	.05
765	Junior Noboa	.05
766	Jim Olander RC	.05
767	Joe Magrane	.05
768	Lance Blankenship	.05
769	Mike Humphreys RC	.05
770	Jarvis Brown RC	.05
771	Damon Berryhill	.05
772	Alejandro Pena	.05
773	Jose Mesa	.05
774	Gary Cooper RC	.05
775	Carney Lansford	.05
776	Mike Bielecki	.05
777	Charlie O'Brien	.05
778	Carlos Hernandez	.05

779	Howard Farmer	.05
780	Mike Stanton	.05
781	Reggie Harris	.05
782	Xavier Hernandez	.05
783	Bryan Hickerson **RC**	.05
784	Checklist 717-BC8	.05

Diamond Kings

FRED McGRIFF

		NM/M
Complete Set (27):		17.50
Common Player:		.40
1	Paul Molitor	2.00
2	Will Clark	.50
3	Joe Carter	.50
4	Julio Franco	.50
5	Cal Ripken, Jr.	6.00
6	Dave Justice	.50
7	George Bell	.50
8	Frank Thomas	2.00
9	Wade Boggs	4.00
10	Scott Sanderson	.50
11	Jeff Bagwell	2.00
12	John Kruk	.50
13	Felix Jose	.50
14	Harold Baines	.50
15	Dwight Gooden	.50
16	Brian McRae	.50
17	Jay Bell	.50
18	Brett Butler	.50
19	Hal Morris	.50
20	Mark Langston	.50
21	Scott Erickson	.50
22	Randy Johnson	2.00
23	Greg Swindell	.50
24	Dennis Martinez	.50
25	Tony Phillips	.50
26	Fred McGriff	.50
27	Checklist	.10

Elite

KEN GRIFFEY, JR.

		NM/M
Complete Set (12):		300.00
Common Player:		7.50
9	Wade Boggs	15.00
10	Joe Carter	7.50
11	Will Clark	7.50
12	Dwight Gooden	7.50
13	Ken Griffey Jr.	30.00
14	Tony Gwynn	15.00
15	Howard Johnson	7.50
16	Terry Pendleton	7.50
17	Kirby Puckett	15.00
18	Frank Thomas	15.00
---	Rickey Henderson (Legend)	20.00
---	Cal Ripken, Jr. (Signature)	250.00

1992 Donruss Previews

RYAN KLESKO
BRAVES • FIRST BASE

		NM/M
Complete Set (12):		25.00
Common Player:		.50
1	Wade Boggs	2.50
2	Barry Bonds	7.50
3	Will Clark	.50
4	Andre Dawson	.75
5	Dennis Eckersley	1.50
6	Robin Ventura	.50
7	Ken Griffey Jr.	4.00
8	Kelly Gruber	.50
9	Ryan Klesko/RR	.50
10	Cal Ripken, Jr.	7.50
11	Nolan Ryan (Highlight)	7.50
12	Todd Van Poppel	.50

Rookies

HARVEY PULLIAM
ROYALS • OUTFIELD

		NM/M
Complete Set (132):		6.00
Common Player:		.05
Pack (12):		.50
Wax Box (36):		10.00
1	Kyle Abbott	.05
2	Troy Afenir	.05
3	Rich Amaral	.05
4	Ruben Amaro	.05
5	Billy Ashley	.05
6	Pedro Astacio	.05
7	Jim Austin	.05
8	Robert Ayrault	.05
9	Kevin Baez	.05
10	Estaban Beltre	.05
11	Brian Bohanon	.05
12	Kent Bottenfield	.05
13	Jeff Branson	.05
14	Brad Brink	.05
15	John Briscoe	.05
16	Doug Brocail	.05
17	Rico Brogna	.05
18	J.T. Bruett	.05
19	Jacob Brumfield	.05
20	Jim Bullinger	.05
21	Kevin Campbell	.05
22	Pedro Castellano	.05
23	Mike Christopher	.05
24	Archi Cianfrocco	.05
25	Mark Clark	.05
26	Craig Colbert	.05
27	Victor Cole	.05
28	Steve Cooke	.05
29	Tim Costo	.05
30	Chad Curtis	.05
31	Doug Davis	.05
32	Gary DiSarcina	.05
33	John Doherty	.05
34	Mike Draper	.05
35	Monty Fariss	.05
36	Bien Figueroa	.05
37	John Flaherty	.05

38	Tim Fortugno	.05
39	Eric Fox	.05
40	Jeff Frye **RC**	.05
41	Ramon Garcia	.05
42	Brent Gates	.05
43	Tom Goodwin	.05
44	Buddy Groom	.05
45	Jeff Grotewold	.05
46	Juan Guerrero	.05
47	Johnny Guzman	.05
48	Shawn Hare	.05
49	Ryan Hawblitzel	.05
50	Bert Heffernan	.05
51	Butch Henry	.05
52	Cesar Hernandez	.05
53	Vince Horsman	.05
54	Steve Hosey	.05
55	Pat Howell	.05
56	Peter Hoy	.05
57	Jon Hurst	.05
58	Mark Hutton	.05
59	Shawn Jeter	.05
60	Joel Johnston	.05
61	Jeff Kent	1.00
62	Kurt Knudsen	.05
63	Kevin Koslofski	.05
64	Danny Leon	.05
65	Jesse Levis	.05
66	Tom Marsh	.05
67	Ed Martel	.05
68	Al Martin	.05
69	Pedro Martinez	2.00
70	Derrick May	.05
71	Matt Maysey	.05
72	Russ McGinnis	.05
73	Tim McIntosh	.05
74	Jim McNamara	.05
75	Jeff McNeely	.05
76	Rusty Meacham	.05
77	Tony Melendez	.05
78	Henry Mercedes	.05
79	Paul Miller	.05
80	Joe Millette	.05
81	Blas Minor	.05
82	Dennis Moeller	.05
83	Raul Mondesi	.25
84	Rob Natal	.05
85	Troy Neel	.05
86	David Nied	.05
87	Jerry Nielsen	.05
88	Donovan Osborne	.05
89	John Patterson	.05
90	Roger Pavlik	.05
91	Dan Peltier	.05
92	Jim Pena	.05
93	William Pennyfeather	.05
94	Mike Perez	.05
95	Hipolito Pichardo	.05
96	Greg Pirkl	.05
97	Harvey Pulliam	.05
98	Manny Ramirez **RC**	3.00
99	Pat Rapp	.05
100	Jeff Reboulet	.05
101	Darren Reed	.05
102	Shane Reynolds	.05
103	Bill Risley	.05
104	Ben Rivera	.05
105	Henry Rodriguez	.05
106	Rico Rossy	.05
107	Johnny Ruffin	.05
108	Steve Scarsone	.05
109	Tim Scott	.05
110	Steve Shifflett	.05
111	Dave Silvestri	.05
112	Matt Stairs	.05
113	William Suero	.05
114	Jeff Tackett	.05
115	Eddie Taubensee	.05
116	Rick Trlicek	.05
117	Scooter Tucker	.05
118	Shane Turner	.05
119	Julio Valera	.05
120	Paul Wagner	.05
121	Tim Wakefield	.05
122	Mike Walker	.05
123	Bruce Walton	.05
124	Lenny Webster	.05
125	Bob Wickman	.05
126	Mike Williams	.05
127	Kerry Woodson	.05
128	Eric Young	.05
129	Kevin Young	.05
130	Pete Young	.05
131	Checklist	.05
132	Checklist	.05

Rookie Phenoms

		NM/M
Complete Set (20):		12.50
Common Player:		.25
1	Moises Alou	.25
2	Bret Boone	.50
3	Jeff Conine	.25
4	Dave Fleming	.25

PHENOMS

BRET BOONE
SEATTLE MARINERS • 43/2B

5	Tyler Green	.25
6	Eric Karros	.25
7	Pat Listach	.25
8	Kenny Lofton	.25
9	Mike Piazza	10.00
10	Tim Salmon	.50
11	Andy Stankiewicz	.25
12	Dan Walters	.25
13	Ramon Caraballo	.25
14	Brian Jordan	.25
15	Ryan Klesko	.25
16	Sam Militello	.25
17	Frank Seminara	.25
18	Salomon Torres	.25
19	John Valentin	.25
20	Wil Cordero	.25

Update

		NM/M
Complete Set (22):		15.00
Common Player:		.50
1	Pat Listach/RR	.50
2	Andy Stankiewicz/RR	.50
3	Brian Jordan/RR	.50
4	Dan Walters/RR	.50
5	Chad Curtis/RR	.50
6	Kenny Lofton/RR	1.50
7	Mark McGwire (Highlight)	8.00
8	Eddie Murray (Highlight)	1.00
9	Jeff Reardon (Highlight)	.50
10	Frank Viola	.50
11	Gary Sheffield	.75
12	George Bell	.50
13	Rick Sutcliffe	.50
14	Wally Joyner	.50
15	Kevin Seitzer	.50
16	Bill Krueger	.50
17	Danny Tartabull	.50
18	Dave Winfield	2.00
19	Gary Carter	1.50
20	Bobby Bonilla	.50
21	Cory Snyder	.50
22	Bill Swift	.50

1993 Donruss

		NM/M
Complete Set (792):		10.00
Common Player:		.05
Series 1 or 2 Pack (14):		.50
Series 1 or 2 Box (36):		10.00
1	Craig Lefferts	.05
2	Kent Mercker	.05
3	Phil Plantier	.05
4	Alex Arias **RC**	.05
5	Julio Valera	.05
6	Dan Wilson	.05
7	Frank Thomas	.50

ROBERTO ALOMAR 2B

No.	Name	Price
8	Eric Anthony	.05
9	Derek Lilliquist	.05
10	Rafael Bournigal RC	.05
11	Manny Alexander/RR RC	.05
12	Bret Barberie	.05
13	Mickey Tettleton	.05
14	Anthony Young	.05
15	Tim Spehr	.05
16	Bob Ayrault RC	.05
17	Bill Wegman	.05
18	Jay Bell	.05
19	Rick Aguilera	.05
20	Todd Zeile	.05
21	Steve Farr	.05
22	Andy Benes	.05
23	Lance Blankenship	.05
24	Ted Wood	.05
25	Omar Vizquel	.05
26	Steve Avery	.05
27	Brian Bohanon	.05
28	Rick Wilkins	.05
29	Devon White	.05
30	Bobby Ayala RC	.05
31	Leo Gomez	.05
32	Mike Simms	.05
33	Ellis Burks	.05
34	Steve Wilson	.05
35	Jim Abbott	.05
36	Tim Wallach	.05
37	Wilson Alvarez	.05
38	Daryl Boston	.05
39	Sandy Alomar, Jr.	.05
40	Mitch Williams	.05
41	Rico Brogna	.05
42	Gary Varsho	.05
43	Kevin Appier	.05
44	Eric Wedge/RR	.05
45	Dante Bichette	.05
46	Jose Oquendo	.05
47	Mike Trombley RC	.05
48	Dan Walters	.05
49	Gerald Williams	.05
50	Bud Black	.05
51	Bobby Witt	.05
52	Mark Davis	.05
53	Shawn Barton RC	.05
54	Paul Assenmacher	.05
55	Kevin Reimer	.05
56	Billy Ashley/RR RC	.05
57	Eddie Zosky	.05
58	Chris Sabo	.05
59	Billy Ripken	.05
60	Scooter Tucker RC	.05
61	Tim Wakefield/RR RC	.10
62	Mitch Webster	.05
63	Jack Clark	.05
64	Mark Gardner	.05
65	Lee Stevens	.05
66	Todd Hundley	.05
67	Bobby Thigpen	.05
68	Dave Hollins	.05
69	Jack Armstrong	.05
70	Alex Cole	.05
71	Mark Carreon	.05
72	Todd Worrell	.05
73	Steve Shifflett RC	.05
74	Jerald Clark	.05
75	Paul Molitor	.50
76	Larry Carter RC	.05
77	Rich Rowland	.05
78	Damon Berryhill	.05
79	Willie Banks	.05
80	Hector Villanueva	.05
81	Mike Gallego	.05
82	Tim Belcher	.05
83	Mike Bordick	.05
84	Craig Biggio	.05
85	Lance Parrish	.05
86	Brett Butler	.05
87	Mike Timlin	.05
88	Brian Barnes	.05
89	Brady Anderson	.05
90	D.J. Dozier	.05
91	Frank Viola	.05
92	Darren Daulton	.05
93	Chad Curtis	.05
94	Zane Smith	.05
95	George Bell	.05
96	Rex Hudler	.05
97	Mark Whiten	.05
98	Tim Teufel	.05
99	Kevin Ritz	.05
100	Jeff Brantley	.05
101	Jeff Conine	.05
102	Vinny Castilla	.05
103	Greg Vaughn	.05
104	Steve Buechele	.05
105	Darren Reed	.05
106	Bip Roberts	.05
107	John Habyan	.05
108	Scott Servais	.05
109	Walt Weiss	.05
110	J.T. Snow/RR RC	.50
111	Jay Buhner	.05
112	Darryl Strawberry	.05
113	Roger Pavlik RC	.05
114	Chris Nabholz	.05
115	Pat Borders	.05
116	Pat Howell RC	.05
117	Gregg Olson	.05
118	Curt Schilling	.25
119	Roger Clemens	.65
120	Victor Cole RC	.05
121	Gary DiSarcina	.05
122	Checklist 1-80	.05
123	Steve Sax	.05
124	Chuck Carr	.05
125	Mark Lewis	.05
126	Tony Gwynn	.60
127	Travis Fryman	.05
128	Dave Burba	.05
129	Wally Joyner	.05
130	John Smoltz	.05
131	Cal Eldred	.05
132	Checklist 81-159	.05
133	Arthur Rhodes	.05
134	Jeff Blauser	.05
135	Scott Cooper	.05
136	Doug Strange	.05
137	Luis Sojo	.05
138	Jeff Branson RC	.05
139	Alex Fernandez	.05
140	Ken Caminiti	.05
141	Charles Nagy	.05
142	Tom Candiotti	.05
143	Willie Green/RR	.05
144	John Vander Wal	.05
145	Kurt Knudsen RC	.05
146	John Franco	.05
147	Eddie Pierce RC	.05
148	Kim Batiste	.05
149	Darren Holmes	.05
150	Steve Cooke RC	.05
151	Terry Jorgensen	.05
152	Mark Clark RC	.05
153	Randy Velarde	.05
154	Greg Harris	.05
155	Kevin Campbell RC	.05
156	John Burkett	.05
157	Kevin Mitchell	.05
158	Deion Sanders	.25
159	Jose Canseco	.25
160	Jeff Hartsock RC	.05
161	Tom Quinlan RC	.05
162	Tim Pugh RC	.05
163	Glenn Davis	.05
164	Shane Reynolds RC	.10
165	Jody Reed	.05
166	Mike Sharperson	.05
167	Scott Lewis	.05
168	Dennis Martinez	.05
169	Scott Radinsky	.05
170	Dave Gallagher	.05
171	Jim Thome	.45
172	Terry Mulholland	.05
173	Milt Cuyler	.05
174	Bob Patterson	.05
175	Jeff Montgomery	.05
176	Tim Salmon/RR	.25
177	Franklin Stubbs	.05
178	Donovan Osborne	.05
179	Jeff Reboulet RC	.05
180	Jeremy Hernandez	.05
181	Charlie Hayes	.05
182	Matt Williams	.05
183	Mike Raczka	.05
184	Francisco Cabrera	.05
185	Rich DeLucia	.05
186	Sammy Sosa	.60
187	Ivan Rodriguez	.45
188	Bret Boone/RR	.15
189	Juan Guzman	.05
190	Tom Browning	.05
191	Randy Milligan	.05
192	Steve Finley	.05
193	John Patterson/RR	.05
194	Kip Gross	.05
195	Tony Fossas	.05
196	Ivan Calderon	.05
197	Junior Felix	.05
198	Pete Schourek	.05
199	Craig Grebeck	.05
200	Juan Bell	.05
201	Glenallen Hill	.05
202	Danny Jackson	.05
203	John Kiely	.05
204	Bob Tewksbury	.05
205	Kevin Koslofski RC	.05
206	Craig Shipley	.05
207	John Jaha	.05
208	Royce Clayton	.05
209	Mike Piazza/RR	2.00
210	Ron Gant	.05
211	Scott Erickson	.05
212	Doug Dascenzo	.05
213	Andy Stankiewicz	.05
214	Geronimo Berroa	.05
215	Dennis Eckersley	.45
216	Al Osuna	.05
217	Tino Martinez	.05
218	Henry Rodriguez RC	.05
219	Ed Sprague	.05
220	Ken Hill	.05
221	Chito Martinez	.05
222	Bret Saberhagen	.05
223	Mike Greenwell	.05
224	Mickey Morandini	.05
225	Chuck Finley	.05
226	Denny Neagle	.05
227	Kirk McCaskill	.05
228	Rheal Cormier	.05
229	Paul Sorrento	.05
230	Darrin Jackson	.05
231	Rob Deer	.05
232	Bill Swift	.05
233	Kevin McReynolds	.05
234	Terry Pendleton	.05
235	Dave Nilsson	.05
236	Chuck McElroy	.05
237	Derek Parks	.05
238	Norm Charlton	.05
239	Matt Nokes	.05
240	Juan Guerrero RC	.05
241	Jeff Parrett	.05
242	Ryan Thompson/RR	.05
243	Dave Fleming	.05
244	Dave Hansen	.05
245	Monty Fariss	.05
246	Archi Cianfrocco RC	.05
247	Pat Hentgen	.05
248	Bill Pecota	.05
249	Ben McDonald	.05
250	Cliff Brantley	.05
251	John Valentin RC	.05
252	Jeff King	.05
253	Reggie Williams RC	.05
254	Checklist 160-238	.05
255	Ozzie Guillen	.05
256	Mike Perez	.05
257	Thomas Howard	.05
258	Kurt Stillwell	.05
259	Mike Henneman	.05
260	Steve Decker	.05
261	Brent Mayne	.05
262	Otis Nixon	.05
263	Mark Keifer RC	.05
264	Checklist 239-317	.05
265	Richie Lewis RC	.05
266	Pat Gomez RC	.05
267	Scott Taylor RC	.05
268	Shawon Dunston	.05
269	Greg Myers	.05
270	Tim Costo	.05
271	Greg Hibbard	.05
272	Pete Harnisch	.05
273	Dave Mlicki RC	.05
274	Orel Hershiser	.05
275	Sean Berry/RR	.05
276	Doug Simons	.05
277	John Doherty RC	.05
278	Eddie Murray	.50
279	Chris Haney	.05
280	Stan Javier	.05
281	Jaime Navarro	.05
282	Orlando Merced	.05
283	Kent Hrbek	.05
284	Bernard Gilkey	.05
285	Russ Springer	.05
286	Mike Maddux	.05
287	Eric Fox RC	.05
288	Mark Leonard	.05
289	Tim Leary	.05
290	Brian Hunter	.05
291	Donald Harris	.05
292	Bob Scanlan	.05
293	Turner Ward	.05
294	Hal Morris	.05
295	Jimmy Poole	.05
296	Doug Jones	.05
297	Tony Pena	.05
298	Ramon Martinez	.05
299	Tim Fortugno RC	.05
300	Marquis Grissom	.05
301	Lance Johnson	.05
302	Jeff Kent RC	1.00
303	Reggie Jefferson	.05
304	Wes Chamberlain	.05
305	Shawn Hare RC	.05
306	Mike LaValliere	.05
307	Gregg Jefferies	.05
308	Troy Neel/RR RC	.05
309	Pat Listach	.05
310	Geronimo Pena	.05
311	Pedro Munoz	.05
312	Guillermo Velasquez RC	.05
313	Roberto Kelly	.05
314	Mike Jackson	.05
315	Rickey Henderson	.50
316	Mark Lemke	.05
317	Erik Hanson	.05
318	Derrick May	.05
319	Geno Petralli	.05
320	Melvin Nieves/RR	.05
321	Doug Linton RC	.05
322	Rob Dibble	.05
323	Chris Hoiles	.05
324	Jimmy Jones	.05
325	Dave Staton/RR	.05
326	Pedro Martinez	.05
327	Paul Quantrill RC	.05
328	Greg Colbrunn	.05
329	Hilly Hathaway RC	.05
330	Jeff Innis	.05
331	Ron Karkovice	.05
332	Keith Shepherd RC	.05
333	Alan Embree RC	.05
334	Paul Wagner RC	.05
335	Dave Haas RC	.05
336	Ozzie Canseco	.05
337	Bill Sampen	.05
338	Rich Rodriguez	.05
339	Dean Palmer	.05
340	Greg Litton	.05
341	Jim Tatum/RR	.05
342	Todd Haney RC	.05
343	Larry Casian	.05
344	Ryne Sandberg	.60
345	Sterling Hitchcock RC	.10
346	Chris Hammond	.05
347	Vince Horsman RC	.05
348	Butch Henry RC	.05
349	Dann Howitt	.05
350	Roger McDowell	.05
351	Jack Morris	.05
352	Bill Krueger	.05
353	Cris Colon RC	.05
354	Joe Vitko RC	.05
355	Willie McGee	.05
356	Jay Baller	.05
357	Pat Mahomes	.05
358	Roger Mason	.05
359	Jerry Nielsen RC	.05
360	Tom Pagnozzi	.05
361	Kevin Baez RC	.05
362	Tim Scott RC	.05
363	Domingo Martinez RC	.05
364	Kirt Manwaring	.05
365	Rafael Palmeiro	.45
366	Ray Lankford	.05
367	Tim McIntosh	.05
368	Jessie Hollins RC	.05
369	Scott Leius	.05
370	Bill Doran	.05
371	Sam Militello RC	.05
372	Ryan Bowen	.05
373	Dave Henderson	.05
374	Dan Smith/RR	.05
375	Steve Reed RC	.05
376	Jose Offerman	.05
377	Kevin Brown	.05
378	Darrin Fletcher	.05
379	Duane Ward	.05
380	Wayne Kirby/RR	.05
381	Steve Scarsone RC	.05
382	Mariano Duncan	.05
383	Ken Ryan RC	.05
384	Lloyd McClendon	.05
385	Brian Holman	.05
386	Braulio Castillo	.05
387	Danny Leon RC	.05
388	Omar Olivares	.05
389	Kevin Wickander	.05
390	Fred McGriff	.05
391	Phil Clark	.05
392	Darren Lewis	.05
393	Phil Hiatt RC	.10
394	Mike Morgan	.05
395	Shane Mack	.05
396	Checklist 318-396	.05
397	David Segui	.05
398	Rafael Belliard	.05
399	Tim Naehring	.05
400	Frank Castillo	.05
401	Joe Grahe	.05

#	Player	Value
402	Reggie Sanders	.05
403	Roberto Hernandez	.05
404	Luis Gonzalez	.05
405	Carlos Baerga	.05
406	Carlos Hernandez	.05
407	Pedro Astacio/RR	.05
408	Mel Rojas	.05
409	Scott Livingstone	.05
410	Chico Walker	.05
411	Brian McRae	.05
412	Ben Rivera	.05
413	Ricky Bones	.05
414	Andy Van Slyke	.05
415	Chuck Knoblauch	.05
416	Luis Alicea	.05
417	Bob Wickman	.05
418	Doug Brocail	.05
419	Scott Brosius	.05
420	Rod Beck	.05
421	Edgar Martinez	.05
422	Ryan Klesko	.05
423	Nolan Ryan	1.50
424	Rey Sanchez	.05
425	Roberto Alomar	.20
426	Barry Larkin	.05
427	Mike Mussina	.30
428	Jeff Bagwell	.50
429	Mo Vaughn	.05
430	Eric Karros	.05
431	John Orton	.05
432	Wil Cordero	.05
433	Jack McDowell	.05
434	Howard Johnson	.05
435	Albert Belle	.05
436	John Kruk	.05
437	Skeeter Barnes	.05
438	Don Slaught	.05
439	Rusty Meacham	.05
440	Tim Laker/RR	.05
441	Robin Yount	.50
442	Brian Jordan	.05
443	Kevin Tapani	.05
444	Gary Sheffield	.25
445	Rich Monteleone	.05
446	Will Clark	.05
447	Jerry Browne	.05
448	Jeff Treadway	.05
449	Mike Schooler	.05
450	Mike Harkey	.05
451	Julio Franco	.05
452	Kevin Young/RR	.05
453	Kelly Gruber	.05
454	Jose Rijo	.05
455	Mike Devereaux	.05
456	Andujar Cedeno	.05
457	Damion Easley/RR	.05
458	Kevin Gross	.05
459	Matt Young	.05
460	Matt Stairs	.05
461	Luis Polonia	.05
462	Dwight Gooden	.05
463	Warren Newson	.05
464	Jose DeLeon	.05
465	Jose Mesa	.05
466	Danny Cox	.05
467	Dan Gladden	.05
468	Gerald Perry	.05
469	Mike Boddicker	.05
470	Jeff Gardner	.05
471	Doug Henry	.05
472	Mike Benajmin	.05
473	Dan Peltier/RR	.05
474	Mike Stanton	.05
475	John Smiley	.05
476	Dwight Smith	.05
477	Jim Leyritz	.05
478	Dwayne Henry	.05
479	Mark McGwire	1.00
480	Pete Incaviglia	.05
481	Dave Cochrane	.05
482	Eric Davis	.05
483	John Olerud	.05
484	Ken Bottenfield	.05
485	Mark McLemore	.05
486	Dave Magadan	.05
487	John Marzano	.05
488	Ruben Amaro	.05
489	Rob Ducey	.05
490	Stan Belinda	.05
491	Dan Pasqua	.05
492	Joe Magrane	.05
493	Brook Jacoby	.05
494	Gene Harris	.05
495	Mark Leiter	.05
496	Bryan Hickerson	.05
497	Tom Gordon	.05
498	Pete Smith	.05
499	Chris Bosio	.05
500	Shawn Boskie	.05
501	Dave West	.05
502	Milt Hill	.05
503	Pat Kelly	.05
504	Joe Boever	.05
505	Terry Steinbach	.05

#	Player	Value
506	Butch Huskey/RR	.05
507	David Valle	.05
508	Mike Scioscia	.05
509	Kenny Rogers	.05
510	Moises Alou	.05
511	David Wells	.05
512	Mackey Sasser	.05
513	Todd Frohwirth	.05
514	Ricky Jordan	.05
515	Mike Gardiner	.05
516	Gary Redus	.05
517	Gary Gaetti	.05
518	Checklist 397-476	.05
519	Carlton Fisk	.50
520	Ozzie Smith	.60
521	Rod Nichols	.05
522	Benito Santiago	.05
523	Bill Gullickson	.05
524	Robby Thompson	.05
525	Mike Macfarlane	.05
526	Sid Bream	.05
527	Darryl Hamilton	.05
528	Checklist 477-555	.05
529	Jeff Tackett	.05
530	Greg Olson	.05
531	Bob Zupcic	.05
532	Mark Grace	.05
533	Steve Frey	.05
534	Dave Martinez	.05
535	Robin Ventura	.05
536	Casey Candaele	.05
537	Kenny Lofton	.05
538	Jay Howell	.05
539	Fernando Ramsey/RR	.05
540	Larry Walker	.05
541	Cecil Fielder	.05
542	Lee Guetterman	.05
543	Keith Miller	.05
544	Len Dykstra	.05
545	B.J. Surhoff	.05
546	Bob Walk	.05
547	Brian Harper	.05
548	Lee Smith	.05
549	Danny Tartabull	.05
550	Frank Seminara	.05
551	Henry Mercedes	.05
552	Dave Righetti	.05
553	Ken Griffey Jr.	.75
554	Tom Glavine	.25
555	Juan Gonzalez	.25
556	Jim Bullinger	.05
557	Derek Bell	.05
558	Cesar Hernandez	.05
559	Cal Ripken, Jr.	1.50
560	Eddie Taubensee	.05
561	John Flaherty	.05
562	Todd Benzinger	.05
563	Hubie Brooks	.05
564	Delino DeShields	.05
565	Tim Raines	.05
566	Sid Fernandez	.05
567	Steve Olin	.05
568	Tommy Greene	.05
569	Buddy Groom	.05
570	Randy Tomlin	.05
571	Hipolito Pichardo	.05
572	Rene Arocha/RR	.05
573	Mike Fetters	.05
574	Felix Jose	.05
575	Gene Larkin	.05
576	Bruce Hurst	.05
577	Bernie Williams	.05
578	Trevor Wilson	.05
579	Bob Welch	.05
580	Dave Justice	.05
581	Randy Johnson	.50
582	Jose Vizcaino	.05
583	Jeff Huson	.05
584	Rob Maurer/RR	.05
585	Todd Stottlemyre	.05
586	Joe Oliver	.05
587	Bob Milacki	.05
588	Rob Murphy	.05
589	Greg Pirkl/RR	.05
590	Lenny Harris	.05
591	Luis Rivera	.05
592	John Wetteland	.05
593	Mark Langston	.05
594	Bobby Bonilla	.05
595	Esteban Beltre	.05
596	Mike Hartley	.05
597	Felix Fermin	.05
598	Carlos Garcia	.05
599	Frank Tanana	.05
600	Gordon Guerrero	.05
601	Terry Shumpert	.05

ABBREVIATIONS

ED - Expansion Draft
RR - Rated Rookie

#	Player	Value
602	Wally Whitehurst	.05
603	Kevin Seitzer	.05
604	Chris James	.05
605	Greg Gohr/RR	.05
606	Mark Wohlers	.05
607	Kirby Puckett	.60
608	Greg Maddux	.60
609	Don Mattingly	.65
610	Greg Cadaret	.05
611	Dave Stewart	.05
612	Mark Portugal	.05
613	Pete O'Brien	.05
614	Bobby Ojeda	.05
615	Joe Carter	.05
616	Pete Young	.05
617	Sam Horn	.05
618	Vince Coleman	.05
619	Wade Boggs	.60
620	Todd Pratt RC	.05
621	Ron Tingley	.05
622	Doug Drabek	.05
623	Scott Hemond	.05
624	Tim Jones	.05
625	Dennis Cook	.05
626	Jose Melendez	.05
627	Mike Munoz	.05
628	Jim Pena	.05
629	Gary Thurman	.05
630	Charlie Leibrandt	.05
631	Scott Fletcher	.05
632	Andre Dawson	.25
633	Greg Gagne	.05
634	Greg Swindell	.05
635	Kevin Maas	.05
636	Xavier Hernandez	.05
637	Ruben Sierra	.05
638	Dimitri Young/RR	.05
639	Harold Reynolds	.05
640	Tom Goodwin	.05
641	Todd Burns	.05
642	Jeff Fassero	.05
643	Dave Winfield	.50
644	Willie Randolph	.05
645	Luis Mercedes	.05
646	Dale Murphy	.20
647	Danny Darwin	.05
648	Dennis Moeller	.05
649	Chuck Crim	.05
650	Checklist 556-634	.05
651	Shawn Abner	.05
652	Tracy Woodson	.05
653	Scott Scudder	.05
654	Tom Lampkin	.05
655	Alan Trammell	.05
656	Cory Snyder	.05
657	Chris Gwynn	.05
658	Lonnie Smith	.05
659	Jim Austin	.05
660	Checklist 635-713	.05
661	Tim Hulett	.05
662	Marvin Freeman	.05
663	Greg Harris	.05
664	Heathcliff Slocumb	.05
665	Mike Butcher	.05
666	Steve Foster	.05
667	Donn Pall	.05
668	Darryl Kile	.05
669	Jesse Levis	.05
670	Jim Gott	.05
671	Mark Hutton RC	.05
672	Brian Drahman	.05
673	Chad Kreuter	.05
674	Tony Fernandez	.05
675	Jose Lind	.05
676	Kyle Abbott	.05
677	Dan Plesac	.05
678	Barry Bonds	1.50
679	Chili Davis	.05
680	Stan Royer	.05
681	Scott Kamieniecki	.05
682	Carlos Martinez	.05
683	Mike Moore	.05
684	Candy Maldanado	.05
685	Jeff Nelson	.05
686	Lou Whitaker	.05
687	Jose Guzman	.05
688	Manuel Lee	.05
689	Bob MacDonald	.05
690	Scott Bankhead	.05
691	Alan Mills	.05
692	Brian Williams	.05
693	Tom Brunansky	.05
694	Lenny Webster	.05
695	Greg Briley	.05
696	Paul O'Neill	.05
697	Joey Cora	.05
698	Charlie O'Brien	.05
699	Junior Ortiz	.05
700	Ron Darling	.05
701	Tony Phillips	.05
702	William Pennyfeather	.05
703	Mark Gubicza	.05
704	Steve Hosey/RR	.05
705	Henry Cotto	.05

#	Player	Value
706	David Hulse RC	.05
707	Mike Pagliarulo	.05
708	Dave Stieb	.05
709	Melido Perez	.05
710	Jimmy Key	.05
711	Jeff Russell	.05
712	David Cone	.05
713	Russ Swan	.05
714	Mark Guthrie	.05
715	Checklist 714-792	.05
716	Al Martin/RR	.05
717	Randy Knorr	.05
718	Mike Stanley	.05
719	Rick Sutcliffe	.05
720	Terry Leach	.05
721	Chipper Jones/RR	1.00
722	Jim Eisenreich	.05
723	Tom Henke	.05
724	Jeff Frye	.05
725	Harold Baines	.05
726	Scott Sanderson	.05
727	Tom Foley	.05
728	Bryan Harvey/ED	.05
729	Tom Edens	.05
730	Eric Young/ED	.05
731	Dave Weathers/ED	.05
732	Spike Owen	.05
733	Scott Aldred/ED	.05
734	Cris Carpenter/ED	.05
735	Dion James	.05
736	Joe Girardi/ED	.05
737	Nigel Wilson/ED	.05
738	Scott Chiamparino/ED	.05
739	Jeff Reardon	.05
740	Willie Blair/ED	.05
741	Jim Corsi/ED	.05
742	Ken Patterson	.05
743	Andy Ashby/ED	.05
744	Rob Natal/ED	.05
745	Kevin Bass	.05
746	Freddie Benavides/ED	.05
747	Chris Donnels/ED	.05
748	Kerry Woodson RC	.05
749	Calvin Jones/ED	.05
750	Gary Scott	.05
751	Joe Orsulak	.05
752	Armando Reynoso/ED	.05
753	Monty Farriss/ED	.05
754	Billy Hatcher	.05
755	Denis Boucher/ED	.05
756	Walt Weiss	.05
757	Mike Fitzgerald	.05
758	Rudy Seanez	.05
759	Bret Barberie/ED	.05
760	Mo Sanford/ED	.05
761	Pedro Castellano/ED RC	.05
762	Chuck Carr/ED	.05
763	Steve Howe	.05
764	Andres Galarraga	.05
765	Jeff Conine/ED	.05
766	Ted Power	.05
767	Butch Henry/ED	.05
768	Steve Decker/ED	.05
769	Storm Davis	.05
770	Vinny Castilla/ED	.05
771	Junior Felix/ED	.05
772	Walt Terrell	.05
773	Brad Ausmus/ED	.05
774	Jamie McAndrew/ED	.05
775	Milt Thompson	.05
776	Charlie Hayes/ED	.05
777	Jack Armstrong/ED	.05
778	Dennis Rasmussen	.05
779	Darren Holmes/ED	.05
780	Alex Arias RC	.05
781	Randy Bush	.05
782	Javier Lopez/RR	.05
783	Dante Bichette	.05
784	John Johnstone/ED	.05
785	Rene Gonzales	.05
786	Alex Cole/ED	.05
787	Jeromy Burnitz/ED	.05
788	Michael Huff	.05
789	Anthony Telford	.05
790	Jerald Clark/ED	.05
791	Joel Johnston	.05
792	David Nied/RR	.05

Diamond Kings

		NM/M
	Complete Set (31):	17.50
	Common Player:	.25
1	Ken Griffey Jr.	4.00
2	Ryne Sandberg	3.00
3	Roger Clemens	3.50
4	Kirby Puckett	3.00
5	Bill Swift	.25
6	Larry Walker	.25
7	Juan Gonzalez	.75
8	Wally Joyner	.25
9	Andy Van Slyke	.25
10	Robin Ventura	.25
11	Bip Roberts	.25

ROGER CLEMENS

12	Roberto Kelly	.25
13	Carlos Baerga	.25
14	Orel Hershiser	.25
15	Cecil Fielder	.25
16	Robin Yount	1.50
17	Darren Daulton	.25
18	Mark McGwire	4.00
19	Tom Glavine	.75
20	Roberto Alomar	.50
21	Gary Sheffield	.75
22	Bob Tewksbury	.25
23	Brady Anderson	.25
24	Craig Biggio	.25
25	Eddie Murray	1.50
26	Luis Polonia	.25
27	Nigel Wilson	.25
28	David Nied	.25
29	Pat Listach	.25
30	Eric Karros	.25
31	Checklist	.05

Elite

PAUL MOLITOR

		NM/M
Complete Set (20):		150.00
Common Player:		10.00
19	Fred McGriff	10.00
20	Ryne Sandberg	20.00
21	Eddie Murray	15.00
22	Paul Molitor	15.00
23	Barry Larkin	10.00
24	Don Mattingly	25.00
25	Dennis Eckersley	15.00
26	Roberto Alomar	12.50
27	Edgar Martinez	10.00
28	Gary Sheffield	12.50
29	Darren Daulton	10.00
30	Larry Walker	10.00
31	Barry Bonds	30.00
32	Andy Van Slyke	10.00
33	Mark McGwire	25.00
34	Cecil Fielder	10.00
35	Dave Winfield	15.00
36	Juan Gonzalez	12.50
---	Robin Yount (Legend)	17.50
---	Will Clark (Signature)	40.00

1993 Donruss Elite
Dominators

		NM/M
Complete Set (20):		135.00
Common Player:		3.00
1	Ryne Sandberg	10.00
2	Fred McGriff	3.00
3	Greg Maddux	10.00
4	Ron Gant	3.00
5	Dave Justice	3.00
6	Don Mattingly	12.00
7	Tim Salmon	3.00
8	Mike Piazza	12.00
9	John Olerud	3.00

Nolan Ryan

10	Nolan Ryan	20.00
11	Juan Gonzalez	5.00
12	Ken Griffey Jr.	12.00
13	Frank Thomas	7.50
14	Tom Glavine	4.50
15	George Brett	12.00
16	Barry Bonds	20.00
17	Albert Belle	3.00
18	Paul Molitor	7.50
19	Cal Ripken, Jr.	20.00
20	Roberto Alomar	5.00
Autographed Cards:		
6	Don Mattingly	35.00
10	Nolan Ryan	65.00
11	Juan Gonzalez	20.00
18	Paul Molitor	20.00

Long Ball Leaders

460 FEET

ALBERT BELLE • INDIANS

		NM/M
Complete Set (18):		5.00
Common Player:		.10
1	Rob Deer	.10
2	Fred McGriff	.10
3	Albert Belle	.10
4	Mark McGwire	2.00
5	Dave Justice	.10
6	Jose Canseco	.25
7	Kent Hrbek	.10
8	Roberto Alomar	.20
9	Ken Griffey Jr.	1.50
10	Frank Thomas	.50
11	Darryl Strawberry	.10
12	Felix Jose	.10
13	Cecil Fielder	.10
14	Juan Gonzalez	.20
15	Ryne Sandberg	.75
16	Gary Sheffield	.20
17	Jeff Bagwell	.50
18	Larry Walker	.10

Masters of the Game

		NM/M
Complete Set (16):		15.00
Common Player:		1.00
1	Frank Thomas	1.50
2	Nolan Ryan	3.00
3	Gary Sheffield	1.25
4	Fred McGriff	1.00
5	Ryne Sandberg	1.75
6	Cal Ripken, Jr.	3.00
7	Jose Canseco	1.25
8	Ken Griffey Jr.	2.50
9	Will Clark	1.00
10	Roberto Alomar	1.00
11	Juan Gonzalez	1.25
12	David Justice	1.00
13	Kirby Puckett	1.75
14	Barry Bonds	3.00
15	Robin Yount	1.50
16	Deion Sanders	1.00

MVPs

Paul Molitor — MVP — Brewers

		NM/M
Complete Set (26):		10.00
Common Player:		.10
1	Luis Polonia	.10
2	Frank Thomas	.60
3	George Brett	.75
4	Paul Molitor	.60
5	Don Mattingly	.75
6	Roberto Alomar	.25
7	Terry Pendleton	.10
8	Eric Karros	.10
9	Larry Walker	.10
10	Eddie Murray	.60
11	Darren Daulton	.10
12	Ray Lankford	.10
13	Will Clark	.10
14	Cal Ripken, Jr.	2.00
15	Roger Clemens	.75
16	Carlos Baerga	.10
17	Cecil Fielder	.10
18	Kirby Puckett	.65
19	Mark McGwire	1.50
20	Ken Griffey Jr.	1.25
21	Juan Gonzalez	.30
22	Ryne Sandberg	.65
23	Bip Roberts	.10
24	Jeff Bagwell	.60
25	Barry Bonds	2.00
26	Gary Sheffield	.25

Spirit of the Game

		NM/M
Complete Set (20):		5.00
Common Player:		.25
1	Dave Winfield, Mike Bordick Turning Two	.35
2	David Justice Play at the Plate	.25
3	Roberto Alomar In There	.30
4	Dennis Eckersley Pumped	.60
5	Juan Gonzalez, Jose Canseco Dynamic Duo	.50
6	Frank Thomas, George Bell Gone	.60
7	Wade Boggs Safe or Out?	.75
8	Will Clark The Thrill	.30
9	Damon Berryhill, Bip Roberts, Glenn Braggs Safe at Home	.25
10	Cecil Fielder, Mickey Tettleton, Rob Deer Thirty X 31	.25
11	Kenny Lofton Bag Bandit	.25

12	Fred McGriff, Gary Sheffield Back to Back	.30
13	Greg Gagne, Barry Larkin Range Rovers	.25
14	Ryne Sandberg The Ball Stops Here	.75
15	Carlos Baerga, Gary Gaetti Over the Top	.25
16	Danny Tartabull At the Wall	.25
17	Brady Anderson Head First	.25
18	Frank Thomas Big Hurt	.65
19	Kevin Gross No-Hitter	.25
20	Robin Yount 3,000	.65

1993 Donruss Previews

ROGER CLEMENS — RHP

		NM/M
Complete Set (22):		60.00
Common Player:		1.50
1	Tom Glavine	2.00
2	Ryne Sandberg	5.00
3	Barry Larkin	1.50
4	Jeff Bagwell	4.00
5	Eric Karros	1.50
6	Larry Walker	1.50
7	Eddie Murray	4.00
8	Darren Daulton	1.50
9	Andy Van Slyke	1.50
10	Gary Sheffield	2.00
11	Will Clark	1.50
12	Cal Ripken Jr.	9.00
13	Roger Clemens	6.00
14	Frank Thomas	4.00
15	Cecil Fielder	1.50
16	George Brett	6.00
17	Robin Yount	4.00
18	Don Mattingly	6.00
19	Dennis Eckersley	3.50
20	Ken Griffey Jr.	7.50
21	Jose Canseco	2.50
22	Roberto Alomar	2.00

1994 Donruss

JOHN KRUK

		NM/M
Complete Set (660):		15.00
Common Player:		.05
Series 1 or 2 Pack (13):		.50
Series 1 or 2 Box (36):		12.50
1	Nolan Ryan (Career Salute 27 Years.)	2.00
2	Mike Piazza	1.00
3	Moises Alou	.05
4	Ken Griffey Jr.	1.00
5	Gary Sheffield	.25
6	Roberto Alomar	.20
7	John Kruk	.05
8	Gregg Olson	.05
9	Gregg Jefferies	.05

No.	Player	Value	No.	Player	Value	No.	Player	Value	No.	Player	Value
10	Tony Gwynn	.65	112	Damion Easley	.05	216	Ben Rivera	.05	320	Rondell White/RR	.05
11	Chad Curtis	.05	113	Pete Harnisch	.05	217	Don Slaught	.05	321	Frank Viola	.05
12	Craig Biggio	.05	114	Danny Cox	.05	218	Bob Patterson	.05	322	Manny Ramirez/RR	.75
13	John Burkett	.05	115	Kevin Tapani	.05	219	Carlos Quintana	.05	323	Gary Wayne	.05
14	Carlos Baerga	.05	116	Roberto Hernandez	.05	220	Tim Raines 2,000 Hits Checklist	.05	324	Mike Macfarlane	.05
15	Robin Yount	.60	117	Domingo Jean	.05	221	Hal Morris	.05	325	Russ Springer	.05
16	Dennis Eckersley	.50	118	Sid Bream	.05	222	Darren Holmes	.05	326	Tim Wallach	.05
17	Dwight Gooden	.05	119	Doug Henry	.05	223	Chris Gwynn	.05	327	Salomon Torres/RR	.05
18	Ryne Sandberg	.65	120	Omar Olivares	.05	224	Chad Kreuter	.05	328	Omar Vizquel	.05
19	Rickey Henderson	.60	121	Mike Harkey	.05	225	Mike Hartley	.05	329	Andy Tomberlin RC	.05
20	Jack McDowell	.05	122	Carlos Hernandez	.05	226	Scott Lydy	.05	330	Chris Sabo	.05
21	Jay Bell	.05	123	Jeff Fassero	.05	227	Eduardo Perez	.05	331	Mike Mussina	.30
22	Kevin Brown	.05	124	Dave Burba	.05	228	Greg Swindell	.05	332	Andy Benes	.05
23	Robin Ventura	.05	125	Wayne Kirby	.05	229	Al Leiter	.05	333	Darren Daulton	.05
24	Paul Molitor	.60	126	John Cummings	.05	230	Scott Radinsky	.05	334	Orlando Merced	.05
25	Dave Justice	.05	127	Bret Barberie	.05	231	Bob Wickman	.05	335	Mark McGwire	1.50
26	Rafael Palmeiro	.50	128	Todd Hundley	.05	232	Otis Nixon	.05	336	Dave Winfield	.60
27	Cecil Fielder	.05	129	Tim Hulett	.05	233	Kevin Reimer	.05	337	Sammy Sosa	.65
28	Chuck Knoblauch	.05	130	Phil Clark	.05	234	Geronimo Pena	.05	338	Eric Karros	.05
29	Dave Hollins	.05	131	Danny Jackson	.05	235	Kevin Roberson/RR	.05	339	Greg Vaughn	.05
30	Jimmy Key	.05	132	Tom Foley	.05	236	Jody Reed	.05	340	Don Mattingly	.75
31	Mark Langston	.05	133	Donald Harris	.05	237	Kirk Rueter/RR	.05	341	Frank Thomas	.60
32	Darryl Kile	.05	134	Scott Fletcher	.05	238	Willie McGee	.05	342	Fred McGriff	.05
33	Ruben Sierra	.05	135	Johnny Ruffin/RR	.05	239	Charles Nagy	.05	343	Kirby Puckett	.65
34	Ron Gant	.05	136	Jerald Clark	.05	240	Tim Leary	.05	344	Roberto Kelly	.05
35	Ozzie Smith	.65	137	Billy Brewer	.05	241	Carl Everett	.05	345	Wally Joyner	.05
36	Wade Boggs	.65	138	Dan Gladden	.05	242	Charlie O'Brien	.05	346	Andres Galarraga	.05
37	Marquis Grissom	.05	139	Eddie Guardado	.05	243	Mike Pagliarulo	.05	347	Bobby Bonilla	.05
38	Will Clark	.05	140	Cal Ripken, Jr. 2,000 Hits Checklist	.35	244	Kerry Taylor	.05	348	Benito Santiago	.05
39	Kenny Lofton	.05	141	Scott Hemond	.05	245	Kevin Stocker	.05	349	Barry Bonds	2.00
40	Cal Ripken, Jr.	2.00	142	Steve Frey	.05	246	Joel Johnston	.05	350	Delino DeShields	.05
41	Steve Avery	.05	143	Xavier Hernandez	.05	247	Geno Petralli	.05	351	Albert Belle	.05
42	Mo Vaughn	.05	144	Mark Eichhorn	.05	248	Jeff Russell	.05	352	Randy Johnson	.60
43	Brian McRae	.05	145	Ellis Burks	.05	249	Joe Oliver	.05	353	Tim Salmon	.05
44	Mickey Tettleton	.05	146	Jim Leyritz	.05	250	Robert Mejia	.05	354	John Olerud	.05
45	Barry Larkin	.05	147	Mark Lemke	.05	251	Chris Haney	.05	355	Dean Palmer	.05
46	Charlie Hayes	.05	148	Pat Listach	.05	252	Bill Krueger	.05	356	Roger Clemens	.75
47	Kevin Appier	.05	149	Donovan Osborne	.05	253	Shane Mack	.05	357	Jim Abbott	.05
48	Robby Thompson	.05	150	Glenallen Hill	.05	254	Terry Steinbach	.05	358	Mark Grace	.05
49	Juan Gonzalez	.30	151	Orel Hershiser	.05	255	Luis Polonia	.05	359	Ozzie Guillen	.05
50	Paul O'Neill	.05	152	Darrin Fletcher	.05	256	Eddie Taubensee	.05	360	Lou Whitaker	.05
51	Marcos Armas	.05	153	Royce Clayton	.05	257	Dave Stewart	.05	361	Jose Rijo	.05
52	Mike Butcher	.05	154	Derek Lilliquist	.05	258	Tim Raines	.05	362	Jeff Montgomery	.05
53	Ken Caminiti	.05	155	Mike Felder	.05	259	Bernie Williams	.05	363	Chuck Finley	.05
54	Pat Borders	.05	156	Jeff Conine	.05	260	John Smoltz	.05	364	Tom Glavine	.25
55	Pedro Munoz	.05	157	Ryan Thompson	.05	261	Kevin Seitzer	.05	365	Jeff Bagwell	.60
56	Tim Belcher	.05	158	Ben McDonald	.05	262	Bob Tewksbury	.05	366	Joe Carter	.05
57	Paul Assenmacher	.05	159	Ricky Gutierrez	.05	263	Bob Scanlan	.05	367	Ray Lankford	.05
58	Damon Berryhill	.05	160	Terry Mulholland	.05	264	Henry Rodriguez	.05	368	Ramon Martinez	.05
59	Ricky Bones	.05	161	Carlos Garcia	.05	265	Tim Scott	.05	369	Jay Buhner	.05
60	Rene Arocha	.05	162	Tom Henke	.05	266	Scott Sanderson	.05	370	Matt Williams	.05
61	Shawn Boskie	.05	163	Mike Greenwell	.05	267	Eric Plunk	.05	371	Larry Walker	.05
62	Pedro Astacio	.05	164	Thomas Howard	.05	268	Edgar Martinez	.05	372	Jose Canseco	.30
63	Frank Bolick	.05	165	Joe Girardi	.05	269	Charlie Hough	.05	373	Len Dykstra	.05
64	Bud Black	.05	166	Hubie Brooks	.05	270	Joe Orsulak	.05	374	Bryan Harvey	.05
65	Sandy Alomar, Jr.	.05	167	Greg Gohr	.05	271	Harold Reynolds	.05	375	Andy Van Slyke	.05
66	Rich Amaral	.05	168	Chip Hale	.05	272	Tim Teufel	.05	376	Ivan Rodriguez	.50
67	Luis Aquino	.05	169	Rick Honeycutt	.05	273	Bobby Thigpen	.05	377	Kevin Mitchell	.05
68	Kevin Baez	.05	170	Hilly Hathaway	.05	274	Randy Tomlin	.05	378	Travis Fryman	.05
69	Mike Devereaux	.05	171	Todd Jones	.05	275	Gary Redus	.05	379	Duane Ward	.05
70	Andy Ashby	.05	172	Tony Fernandez	.05	276	Ken Ryan	.05	380	Greg Maddux	.65
71	Larry Andersen	.05	173	Bo Jackson	.10	277	Tim Pugh	.05	381	Scott Servais	.05
72	Steve Cooke	.05	174	Bobby Munoz	.05	278	Jayhawk Owens	.05	382	Greg Olson	.05
73	Mario Diaz	.05	175	Greg McMichael	.05	279	Phil Hiatt/RR	.05	383	Rey Sanchez	.05
74	Rob Deer	.05	176	Graeme Lloyd	.05	280	Alan Trammell	.05	384	Tom Kramer	.05
75	Bobby Ayala	.05	177	Tom Pagnozzi	.05	281	Dave McCarty/RR	.05	385	David Valle	.05
76	Freddie Benavides	.05	178	Derrick May	.05	282	Bob Welch	.05	386	Eddie Murray	.60
77	Stan Belinda	.05	179	Pedro Martinez	.60	283	J.T. Snow	.05	387	Kevin Higgins	.05
78	John Doherty	.05	180	Ken Hill	.05	284	Brian Williams	.05	388	Dan Wilson	.05
79	Willie Banks	.05	181	Bryan Hickerson	.05	285	Devon White	.05	389	Todd Frohwirth	.05
80	Spike Owen	.05	182	Jose Mesa	.05	286	Steve Sax	.05	390	Gerald Williams	.05
81	Mike Bordick	.05	183	Dave Fleming	.05	287	Tony Tarasco	.05	391	Hipolito Pichardo	.05
82	Chili Davis	.05	184	Henry Cotto	.05	288	Bill Spiers	.05	392	Pat Meares	.05
83	Luis Gonzalez	.05	185	Jeff Kent	.05	289	Allen Watson	.05	393	Luis Lopez	.05
84	Ed Sprague	.05	186	Mark McLemore	.05	290	Rickey Henderson 2,000 Hits Checklist	.05	394	Ricky Jordan	.05
85	Jeff Reboulet	.05	187	Trevor Hoffman	.05	291	Joe Vizcaino	.05	395	Bob Walk	.05
86	Jason Bere	.05	188	Todd Pratt	.05	292	Darryl Strawberry	.05	396	Sid Fernandez	.05
87	Mark Hutton	.05	189	Blas Minor	.05	293	John Wetteland	.05	397	Todd Worrell	.05
88	Jeff Blauser	.05	190	Charlie Leibrandt	.05	294	Bill Swift	.05	398	Darryl Hamilton	.05
89	Cal Eldred	.05	191	Tony Pena	.05	295	Jeff Treadway	.05	399	Randy Myers	.05
90	Bernard Gilkey	.05	192	Larry Luebbers RC	.05	296	Tino Martinez	.05	400	Rod Brewer	.05
91	Frank Castillo	.05	193	Greg Harris	.05	297	Richie Lewis	.05	401	Lance Blankenship	.05
92	Jim Gott	.05	194	David Cone	.05	298	Bret Saberhagen	.05	402	Steve Finley	.05
93	Greg Colbrunn	.05	195	Bill Gullickson	.05	299	Arthur Rhodes	.05	403	Phil Leftwich RC	.05
94	Jeff Brantley	.05	196	Brian Harper	.05	300	Guillermo Velasquez	.05	404	Juan Guzman	.05
95	Jeremy Hernandez	.05	197	Steve Karsay/RR	.05	301	Milt Thompson	.05	405	Anthony Young	.05
96	Norm Charlton	.05	198	Greg Myers	.05	302	Doug Strange	.05	406	Jeff Gardner	.05
97	Alex Arias	.05	199	Mark Portugal	.05	303	Aaron Sele	.05	407	Ryan Bowen	.05
98	John Franco	.05	200	Pat Hentgen	.05	304	Bip Roberts	.05	408	Fernando Valenzuela	.05
99	Chris Hoiles	.05	201	Mike La Valliere	.05	305	Bruce Ruffin	.05	409	David West	.05
100	Brad Ausmus	.05	202	Mike Stanley	.05	306	Jose Lind	.05	410	Kenny Rogers	.05
101	Wes Chamberlain	.05	203	Kent Mercker	.05	307	David Wells	.05	411	Bob Zupcic	.05
102	Mark Dewey	.05	204	Dave Nilsson	.05	308	Bobby Witt	.05	412	Eric Young	.05
103	Benji Gil/RR	.05	205	Erik Pappas	.05	309	Mark Wohlers	.05	413	Bret Boone	.05
104	John Dopson	.05	206	Mike Morgan	.05	310	B.J. Surhoff	.05	414	Danny Tartabull	.05
105	John Smiley	.05	207	Roger McDowell	.05	311	Mark Whiten	.05	415	Bob MacDonald	.05
106	David Nied	.05	208	Mike Lansing	.05	312	Turk Wendell	.05	416	Ron Karkovice	.05
107	George Brett (Career Salute 21 Years.)	.75	209	Kirt Manwaring	.05	313	Raul Mondesi	.05	417	Scott Cooper	.05
108	Kirk Gibson	.05	210	Randy Milligan	.05	314	Brian Turang RC	.05	418	Dante Bichette	.05
109	Larry Casian	.05	211	Erik Hanson	.05	315	Chris Hammond	.05	419	Tripp Cromer	.05
110	Ryne Sandberg 2,000 Hits Checklist	.25	212	Orestes Destrade	.05	316	Tim Bogar	.05	420	Billy Ashley	.05
111	Brent Gates	.05	213	Mike Maddux	.05	317	Brad Pennington	.05	421	Roger Smithberg	.05
			214	Alan Mills	.05	318	Tim Worrell	.05	422	Dennis Martinez	.05
			215	Tim Mauser	.05	319	Mitch Williams	.05	423	Mike Blowers	.05
									424	Darren Lewis	.05
									425	Junior Ortiz	.05

426 Butch Huskey .05
427 Jimmy Poole .05
428 Walt Weiss .05
429 Scott Bankhead .05
430 Deion Sanders .05
431 Scott Bullett .05
432 Jeff Huson .05
433 Tyler Green .05
434 Billy Hatcher .05
435 Bob Hamelin .05
436 Reggie Sanders .05
437 Scott Erickson .05
438 Steve Reed .05
439 Randy Velarde .05
440 Checklist (Tony Gwynn 2,000 Hits) .15
441 Terry Leach .05
442 Danny Bautista .05
443 Kent Hrbek .05
444 Rick Wilkins .05
445 Tony Phillips .05
446 Dion James .05
447 Joey Cora .05
448 Andre Dawson .15
449 Pedro Castellano .05
450 Tom Gordon .05
451 Rob Dibble .05
452 Ron Darling .05
453 Chipper Jones .65
454 Joe Grahe .05
455 Domingo Cedeno .05
456 Tom Edens .05
457 Mitch Webster .05
458 Jose Bautista .05
459 Troy O'Leary .05
460 Todd Zeile .05
461 Sean Berry .05
462 Brad Holman RC .05
463 Dave Martinez .05
464 Mark Lewis .05
465 Paul Carey .05
466 Jack Armstrong .05
467 David Telgheder .05
468 Gene Harris .05
469 Danny Darwin .05
470 Kim Batiste .05
471 Tim Wakefield .05
472 Craig Lefferts .05
473 Jacob Brumfield .05
474 Lance Painter .05
475 Milt Cuyler .05
476 Melido Perez .05
477 Derek Parks .05
478 Gary DiSarcina .05
479 Steve Bedrosian .05
480 Eric Anthony .05
481 Julio Franco .05
482 Tommy Greene .05
483 Pat Kelly .05
484 Nate Minchey/RR .05
485 William Pennyfeather .05
486 Harold Baines .05
487 Howard Johnson .05
488 Angel Miranda .05
489 Scott Sanders .05
490 Shawon Dunston .05
491 Mel Rojas .05
492 Jeff Nelson .05
493 Archi Cianfrocco .05
494 Al Martin .05
495 Mike Gallego .05
496 Mike Henneman .05
497 Armando Reynoso .05
498 Mickey Morandini .05
499 Rick Renteria .05
500 Rick Sutcliffe .05
501 Bobby Jones/RR .05
502 Gary Gaetti .05
503 Rick Aguilera .05
504 Todd Stottlemyre .05
505 Mike Mohler .05
506 Mike Stanton .05
507 Jose Guzman .05
508 Kevin Rogers .05
509 Chuck Carr .05
510 Chris Jones .05
511 Brent Mayne .05
512 Greg Harris .05
513 Dave Henderson .05
514 Eric Hillman .05
515 Dan Peltier .05
516 Craig Shipley .05
517 John Valentin .05
518 Wilson Alvarez .05
519 Andujar Cedeno .05
520 Troy Neel .05
521 Tom Candiotti .05
522 Matt Mieske .05
523 Jim Thome .50
524 Lou Frazier .05
525 Mike Jackson .05
526 Pedro Martinez .05
527 Roger Pavlik .05
528 Kent Bottenfield .05
529 Felix Jose .05
530 Mark Guthrie .05

531 Steve Farr .05
532 Craig Paquette .05
533 Doug Jones .05
534 Luis Alicea .05
535 Cory Snyder .05
536 Paul Sorrento .05
537 Nigel Wilson .05
538 Jeff King .05
539 Willie Green .05
540 Kirk McCaskill .05
541 Al Osuna .05
542 Greg Hibbard .05
543 Brett Butler .05
544 Jose Valentin .05
545 Wil Cordero .05
546 Chris Bosio .05
547 Jamie Moyer .05
548 Jim Eisenreich .05
549 Vinny Castilla .05
550 Checklist (Dave Winfield 3,000 Hits) .05
551 John Roper .05
552 Lance Johnson .05
553 Scott Kamieniecki .05
554 Mike Moore .05
555 Steve Buechele .05
556 Terry Pendleton .05
557 Todd Van Poppel .05
558 Rob Butler .05
559 Zane Smith .05
560 David Hulse .05
561 Tim Costo .05
562 John Habyan .05
563 Terry Jorgensen .05
564 Matt Nokes .05
565 Kevin McReynolds .05
566 Phil Plantier .05
567 Chris Turner .05
568 Carlos Delgado .40
569 John Jaha .05
570 Dwight Smith .05
571 John Vander Wal .05
572 Trevor Wilson .05
573 Felix Fermin .05
574 Marc Newfield/RR .05
575 Jeromy Burnitz .05
576 Leo Gomez .05
577 Curt Schilling .25
578 Kevin Young .05
579 Jerry Spradlin RC .05
580 Curt Leskanic .05
581 Carl Willis .05
582 Alex Fernandez .05
583 Mark Holzemer .05
584 Domingo Martinez .05
585 Pete Smith .05
586 Brian Jordan .05
587 Kevin Gross .05
588 J.R. Phillips/RR .05
589 Chris Nabholz .05
590 Bill Wertz .05
591 Derek Bell .05
592 Brady Anderson .05
593 Matt Turner .05
594 Pete Incaviglia .05
595 Greg Gagne .05
596 John Flaherty .05
597 Scott Livingstone .05
598 Rod Bolton .05
599 Mike Perez .05
600 Checklist (Roger Clemens 2,000 Strikeouts) .25
601 Tony Castillo .05
602 Henry Mercedes .05
603 Mike Fetters .05
604 Rod Beck .05
605 Damon Buford .05
606 Matt Whiteside .05
607 Shawn Green .25
608 Midre Cummings/RR .05
609 Jeff McNeeley .05
610 Danny Sheaffer .05
611 Paul Wagner .05
612 Torey Lovullo .05
613 Javier Lopez .05
614 Mariano Duncan .05
615 Doug Brocail .05
616 Dave Hansen .05
617 Ryan Klesko .05
618 Eric Davis .05
619 Scott Ruffcorn/RR .05
620 Mike Trombley .05
621 Jaime Navarro .05
622 Rheal Cormier .05
623 Jose Offerman .05
624 David Segui .05
625 Robb Nenv .05
626 Dave Gallagher .05
627 Julian Tavarez RC .05
628 Chris Gomez .05
629 Jeffrey Hammonds/RR .05
630 Scott Brosius .05
631 Willie Blair .05
632 Doug Drabek .05
633 Bill Wegman .05
634 Jeff McKnight .05

635 Rich Rodriguez .05
636 Steve Trachsel .05
637 Buddy Groom .05
638 Sterling Hitchcock .05
639 Chuck McElroy .05
640 Rene Gonzales .05
641 Dan Plesac .05
642 Jeff Branson .05
643 Darrell Whitmore .05
644 Paul Quantrill .05
645 Rich Rowland .05
646 Curtis Pride RC .05
647 Erik Plantenberg .05
648 Albie Lopez .05
649 Rich Batchelor RC .05
650 Lee Smith .05
651 Cliff Floyd .05
652 Pete Schourek .05
653 Reggie Jefferson .05
654 Bill Haselman .05
655 Steve Hosey .05
656 Mark Clark .05
657 Mark Davis .05
658 Dave Magadan .05
659 Candy Maldonado .05
660 Checklist (Mark Langston 2,000 Strikeouts) .05

Special Edition - Gold

	NM/M
Complete Set (100):	7.50
Common Player:	.10
1 Nolan Ryan	1.50
2 Mike Piazza	1.00
3 Moises Alou	.10
4 Ken Griffey Jr.	1.00
5 Gary Sheffield	.25
6 Roberto Alomar	.20
7 John Kruk	.10
8 Gregg Olson	.10
9 Gregg Jefferies	.10
10 Tony Gwynn	.65
11 Chad Curtis	.10
12 Craig Biggio	.10
13 John Burkett	.10
14 Carlos Baerga	.10
15 Robin Yount	.60
16 Dennis Eckersley	.50
17 Dwight Gooden	.10
18 Ryne Sandberg	.65
19 Rickey Henderson	.60
20 Jack McDowell	.10
21 Jay Bell	.10
22 Kevin Brown	.10
23 Robin Ventura	.10
24 Paul Molitor	.60
25 David Justice	.10
26 Rafael Palmeiro	.10
27 Cecil Fielder	.10
28 Chuck Knoblauch	.10
29 Dave Hollins	.10
30 Jimmy Key	.10
31 Mark Langston	.10
32 Darryl Kile	.10
33 Ruben Sierra	.10
34 Ron Gant	.10
35 Ozzie Smith	.65
36 Wade Boggs	.35
37 Marquis Grissom	.10
38 Will Clark	.25
39 Kenny Lofton	.10
40 Cal Ripken, Jr.	1.50
41 Steve Avery	.10
42 Mo Vaughn	.10
43 Brian McRae	.10
44 Mickey Tettleton	.10
45 Barry Larkin	.10
46 Charlie Hayes	.10
47 Kevin Appier	.10
48 Robby Thompson	.10
49 Juan Gonzalez	.30
50 Paul O'Neill	.10
51 Mike Mussina	.40
52 Andy Benes	.10
53 Darren Daulton	.10
54 Orlando Merced	.10
55 Mark McGwire	1.25
56 Dave Winfield	.60
57 Sammy Sosa	.65
58 Eric Karros	.10
59 Greg Vaughn	.10
60 Don Mattingly	.75
61 Frank Thomas	.60
62 Fred McGriff	.10
63 Kirby Puckett	.65
64 Roberto Kelly	.10
65 Wally Joyner	.10
66 Andres Galarraga	.10
67 Bobby Bonilla	.10
68 Benito Santiago	.10
69 Barry Bonds	1.50
70 Delino DeShields	.10
71 Albert Belle	.10
72 Randy Johnson	.60
73 Tim Salmon	.10
74 John Olerud	.10
75 Dean Palmer	.10
76 Roger Clemens	.75
77 Jim Abbott	.10
78 Mark Grace	.10
79 Ozzie Guillen	.10
80 Lou Whitaker	.10
81 Jose Rijo	.10
82 Jeff Montgomery	.10
83 Chuck Finley	.10
84 Tom Glavine	.25
85 Jeff Bagwell	.60
86 Joe Carter	.10
87 Ray Lankford	.10
88 Ramon Martinez	.10
89 Jay Buhner	.10
90 Matt Williams	.10
91 Larry Walker	.10
92 Jose Canseco	.25
93 Len Dykstra	.10
94 Bryan Harvey	.10
95 Andy Van Slyke	.10
96 Ivan Rodriguez	.50
97 Kevin Mitchell	.10
98 Travis Fryman	.10
99 Duane Ward	.10
100 Greg Maddux	.65

Anniversary-1984

RICKEY HENDERSON of

	NM/M
Complete Set (10):	20.00
Common Player:	1.00
1 Joe Carter	1.00
2 Robin Yount	1.50
3 George Brett	2.50
4 Rickey Henderson	1.50
5 Nolan Ryan	6.00
6 Cal Ripken, Jr.	6.00
7 Wade Boggs	2.00
8 Don Mattingly	2.50
9 Ryne Sandberg	2.00
10 Tony Gwynn	2.00

Decade Dominators

	NM/M
Complete Set (20):	15.00
Common Player:	.35
Series 1	
1 Cecil Fielder	.35
2 Barry Bonds	2.50
3 Fred McGriff	.35
4 Matt Williams	.35
5 Joe Carter	.35
6 Juan Gonzalez	.40
7 Jose Canseco	.50
8 Ron Gant	.35
9 Ken Griffey Jr.	1.50
10 Mark McGwire	2.00
Series 2	
1 Tony Gwynn	1.00

DOMINATORS
CECIL FIELDER
HOMERUNS

2	Frank Thomas	.75
3	Paul Molitor	.75
4	Edgar Martinez	.35
5	Kirby Puckett	1.00
6	Ken Griffey, Jr.	1.50
7	Barry Bonds	2.50
8	Willie McGee	.35
9	Len Dykstra	1.50
10	John Kruk	.35

Diamond Kings

DIAMOND KINGS
Bobby Bonilla

		NM/M
Complete Set (30):		12.00
Common Player:		.25
1	Barry Bonds	2.50
2	Mo Vaughn	.25
3	Steve Avery	.25
4	Tim Salmon	.25
5	Rick Wilkins	.25
6	Brian Harper	.25
7	Andres Galarraga	.25
8	Albert Belle	.25
9	John Kruk	.25
10	Ivan Rodriguez	.75
11	Tony Gwynn	1.25
12	Brian McRae	.25
13	Bobby Bonilla	.25
14	Ken Griffey Jr.	2.00
15	Mike Piazza	2.00
16	Don Mattingly	1.50
17	Barry Larkin	.25
18	Ruben Sierra	.25
19	Orlando Merced	.25
20	Greg Vaughn	.25
21	Gregg Jefferies	.25
22	Cecil Fielder	.25
23	Moises Alou	.25
24	John Olerud	.25
25	Gary Sheffield	.25
26	Mike Mussina	.60
27	Jeff Bagwell	1.00
28	Frank Thomas	1.00
29	Dave Winfield (King of Kings)	1.00
30	Dick Perez (Checklist)	.25

Elite

		NM/M
Complete Set (12):		50.00
Common Player:		4.00
37	Frank Thomas	6.00
38	Tony Gwynn	7.50
39	Tim Salmon	4.00
40	Albert Belle	4.00
41	John Kruk	4.00
42	Juan Gonzalez	5.00
43	John Olerud	4.00
44	Barry Bonds	12.00
45	Ken Griffey Jr.	9.00

ANGELS
TIM SALMON
ELITE SERIES

46	Mike Piazza	9.00
47	Jack McDowell	4.00
48	Andres Galarraga	4.00

Long Ball Leaders

		NM/M
Complete Set (10):		6.00
Common Player:		.30
1	Cecil Fielder	.30
2	Dean Palmer	.30
3	Andres Galarraga	.30
4	Bo Jackson	.40
5	Ken Griffey Jr.	1.50
6	Dave Justice	.30
7	Mike Piazza	1.50
8	Frank Thomas	1.00
9	Barry Bonds	3.00
10	Juan Gonzalez	.50

MVPs

MVP
ANDRES GALARRAGA-1B

		NM/M
Complete Set (28):		20.00
Common Player:		.25
1	Dave Justice	.25
2	Mark Grace	.25
3	Jose Rijo	.25
4	Andres Galarraga	.25
5	Bryan Harvey	.25
6	Jeff Bagwell	1.00
7	Bret Boone	2.50
8	Moises Alou	.25
9	Bobby Bonilla	.25
10	Len Dykstra	.25
11	Jeff King	.25
12	Gregg Jefferies	.25
13	Tony Gwynn	1.50
14	Barry Bonds	4.00
15	Cal Ripken, Jr.	4.00
16	Mo Vaughn	.25
17	Tim Salmon	.25
18	Frank Thomas	1.00
19	Albert Belle	.25
20	Cecil Fielder	.25
21	Wally Joyner	.25
22	Greg Vaughn	.25
23	Kirby Puckett	1.50
24	Don Mattingly	2.00
25	Ruben Sierra	.25
26	Ken Griffey Jr.	2.50
27	Juan Gonzalez	.50
28	John Olerud	.25

Spirit of the Game

		NM/M
Complete Set (10):		10.00
Common Player:		.70
1	John Olerud	.50
2	Barry Bonds	2.50
3	Ken Griffey Jr.	2.00
4	Mike Piazza	2.00

★ Spirit of the Game ★

5	Juan Gonzalez	.60
6	Frank Thomas	1.00
7	Tim Salmon	.50
8	Dave Justice	.50
9	Don Mattingly	1.50
10	Len Dykstra	.50

1995 Donruss

		NM/M
Complete Set (550):		20.00
Common Player:		.05
Series 1 or 2 Pack (12):		.75
Series 1 or 2 Wax Box (36):		20.00
1	Dave Justice	.05
2	Rene Arocha	.05
3	Sandy Alomar Jr.	.05
4	Luis Lopez	.05
5	Mike Piazza	1.50
6	Bobby Jones	.05
7	Damion Easley	.05
8	Barry Bonds	2.50
9	Mike Mussina	.40
10	Kevin Seitzer	.05
11	John Smiley	.05
12	W. Van Landingham	.05
13	Ron Darling	.05
14	Walt Weiss	.05
15	Mike Lansing	.05
16	Allen Watson	.05
17	Aaron Sele	.05
18	Randy Johnson	.65
19	Dean Palmer	.05
20	Jeff Bagwell	.65
21	Curt Schilling	.25
22	Darrell Whitmore	.05
23	Steve Trachsel	.05
24	Dan Wilson	.05
25	Steve Finley	.05
26	Bret Boone	.05
27	Charles Johnson	.05
28	Mike Stanton	.05
29	Ismael Valdes	.05
30	Salomon Torres	.05
31	Eric Anthony	.05
32	Spike Owen	.05
33	Joey Cora	.05
34	Robert Eenhoorn	.05
35	Rick White	.05
36	Omar Vizquel	.05
37	Carlos Delgado	.45
38	Eddie Williams	.05
39	Shawon Dunston	.05
40	Darrin Fletcher	.05
41	Leo Gomez	.05
42	Juan Gonzalez	.40
43	Luis Alicea	.05
44	Ken Ryan	.05
45	Lou Whitaker	.05
46	Mike Blowers	.05
47	Willie Blair	.05
48	Todd Van Poppel	.05
49	Roberto Alomar	.25
50	Ozzie Smith	.75
51	Sterling Hitchcock	.05
52	Mo Vaughn	.05
53	Rick Aguilera	.05
54	Kent Mercker	.05
55	Don Mattingly	1.00
56	Bob Scanlan	.05
57	Wilson Alvarez	.05
58	Jose Mesa	.05
59	Scott Kamieniecki	.05
60	Todd Jones	.05
61	John Kruk	.05
62	Mike Stanley	.05
63	Tino Martinez	.05
64	Eddie Zambrano	.05
65	Todd Hundley	.05
66	Jamie Moyer	.05
67	Rich Amaral	.05
68	Jose Valentin	.05
69	Alex Gonzalez	.05
70	Kurt Abbott	.05
71	Delino DeShields	.05
72	Brian Anderson	.05
73	John Vander Wal	.05
74	Turner Ward	.05
75	Tim Raines	.05
76	Mark Acre	.05
77	Jose Offerman	.05
78	Jimmy Key	.05
79	Mark Whiten	.05
80	Mark Gubicza	.05
81	Darren Hall	.05
82	Travis Fryman	.05
83	Cal Ripken, Jr.	2.50
84	Geronimo Berroa	.05
85	Bret Barberie	.05
86	Andy Ashby	.05
87	Steve Avery	.05
88	Rich Becker	.05
89	John Valentin	.05
90	Glenallen Hill	.05
91	Carlos Garcia	.05
92	Dennis Martinez	.05
93	Pat Kelly	.05
q4	Orlando Miller	.05
95	Felix Jose	.05
96	Mike Kingery	.05
97	Jeff Kent	.05
98	Pete Incaviglia	.05
99	Chad Curtis	.05
100	Thomas Howard	.05
101	Hector Carrasco	.05
102	Tom Pagnozzi	.05
103	Danny Tartabull	.05
104	Donnie Elliott	.05
105	Danny Jackson	.05
106	Steve Dunn	.05
107	Roger Salkeld	.05
108	Jeff King	.05
109	Cecil Fielder	.05
110	Checklist	.05
111	Denny Neagle	.05
112	Troy Neel	.05
113	Rod Beck	.05
114	Alex Rodriguez	2.00
115	Joey Eischen	.05
116	Tom Candiotti	.05
117	Ray McDavid	.05
118	Vince Coleman	.05
119	Pete Harnisch	.05
120	David Nied	.05
121	Pat Rapp	.05
122	Sammy Sosa	.75
123	Steve Reed	.05
124	Jose Oliva	.05
125	Rick Bottalico	.05
126	Jose DeLeon	.05
127	Pat Hentgen	.05
128	Will Clark	.05
129	Mark Dewey	.05
130	Greg Vaughn	.05
131	Darren Dreifort	.05
132	Ed Sprague	.05
133	Lee Smith	.05
134	Charles Nagy	.05
135	Phil Plantier	.05
136	Jason Jacome	.05
137	Jose Lima	.05
138	J.R. Phillips	.05
139	J.T. Snow	.05
140	Mike Huff	.05
141	Billy Brewer	.05
142	Jeromy Burnitz	.05
143	Ricky Bones	.05
144	Carlos Rodriguez	.05
145	Luis Gonzalez	.05
146	Mark Lemke	.05
147	Al Martin	.05
148	Mike Bordick	.05
149	Robb Nen	.05
150	Wil Cordero	.05
151	Edgar Martinez	.05
152	Gerald Williams	.05
153	Esteban Beltre	.05
154	Mike Moore	.05
155	Mark Langston	.05
156	Mark Clark	.05
157	Bobby Ayala	.05
158	Rick Wilkins	.05
159	Bobby Munoz	.05
160	Checklist	.05
161	Scott Erickson	.05

#	Player	Price	#	Player	Price	#	Player	Price	#	Player	Price
162	Paul Molitor	.65	266	Joe Orsulak	.05	370	Manny Ramirez	.65	474	Todd Worrell	.05
163	Jon Lieber	.05	267	Joey Hamilton	.05	371	Kenny Lofton	.05	475	Mark Eichhorn	.05
164	Jason Grimsley	.05	268	Mark Portugal	.05	372	Mark Smith	.05	476	Bruce Ruffin	.05
165	Norberto Martin	.05	269	Kevin Tapani	.05	373	Dave Fleming	.05	477	Chuck Finley	.05
166	Javier Lopez	.05	270	Sid Fernandez	.05	374	Dave Stewart	.05	478	Marc Newfield	.05
167	Brian McRae	.05	271	Steve Dreyer	.05	375	Roger Pavlik	.05	479	Paul Shuey	.05
168	Gary Sheffield	.40	272	Denny Hocking	.05	376	Hipolito Pichardo	.05	480	Bob Tewksbury	.05
169	Marcus Moore	.05	273	Troy O'Leary	.05	377	Bill Taylor	.05	481	Ramon Martinez	.05
170	John Hudek	.05	274	Milt Cuyler	.05	378	Robin Ventura	.05	482	Melvin Nieves	.05
171	Kelly Stinett	.05	275	Frank Thomas	.65	379	Bernard Gilkey	.05	483	Todd Zeile	.05
172	Chris Gomez	.05	276	Jorge Fabregas	.05	380	Kirby Puckett	.75	484	Benito Santiago	.05
173	Rey Sanchez	.05	277	Mike Gallego	.05	381	Steve Howe	.05	485	Stan Javier	.05
174	Juan Guzman	.05	278	Mickey Morandini	.05	382	Devon White	.05	486	Kirk Rueter	.05
175	Chan Ho Park	.05	279	Roberto Hernandez	.05	383	Roberto Mejia	.05	487	Andre Dawson	.25
176	Terry Shumpert	.05	280	Henry Rodriguez	.05	384	Darrin Jackson	.05	488	Eric Karros	.05
177	Steve Ontiveros	.05	281	Garret Anderson	.05	385	Mike Morgan	.05	489	Dave Magadan	.05
178	Brad Ausmus	.05	282	Bob Wickman	.05	386	Rusty Meacham	.05	490	Checklist	.05
179	Tim Davis	.05	283	Gar Finnvold	.05	387	Bill Swift	.05	491	Randy Velarde	.05
180	Billy Ashley	.05	284	Paul O'Neill	.05	388	Lou Frazier	.05	492	Larry Walker	.05
181	Vinny Castilla	.05	285	Royce Clayton	.05	389	Andy Van Slyke	.05	493	Cris Carpenter	.05
182	Bill Spiers	.05	286	Chuck Knoblauch	.05	390	Brett Butler	.05	494	Tom Gordon	.05
183	Randy Knorr	.05	287	Johnny Ruffin	.05	391	Bobby Witt	.05	495	Dave Burba	.05
184	Brian Hunter	.05	288	Dave Nilsson	.05	392	Jeff Conine	.05	496	Darren Bragg	.05
185	Pat Meares	.05	289	David Cone	.05	393	Tim Hyers	.05	497	Darren Daulton	.05
186	Steve Buechele	.05	290	Chuck McElroy	.05	394	Terry Pendleton	.05	498	Don Slaught	.05
187	Kirt Manwaring	.05	291	Kevin Stocker	.05	395	Ricky Jordan	.05	499	Pat Borders	.05
188	Tim Naehring	.05	292	Jose Rijo	.05	396	Eric Plunk	.05	500	Lenny Harris	.05
189	Matt Mieske	.05	293	Sean Berry	.05	397	Melido Perez	.05	501	Joe Ausanio	.05
190	Josias Manzanillo	.05	294	Ozzie Guillen	.05	398	Darryl Kile	.05	502	Alan Trammell	.05
191	Greg McMichael	.05	295	Chris Hoiles	.05	399	Mark McLemore	.05	503	Mike Fetters	.05
192	Chuck Carr	.05	296	Kevin Foster	.05	400	Greg Harris	.05	504	Scott Ruffcorn	.05
193	Midre Cummings	.05	297	Jeff Frye	.05	401	Jim Leyritz	.05	505	Rich Rowland	.05
194	Darryl Strawberry	.05	298	Lance Johnson	.05	402	Doug Strange	.05	506	Juan Samuel	.05
195	Greg Gagne	.05	299	Mike Kelly	.05	403	Tim Salmon	.05	507	Bo Jackson	.10
196	Steve Cooke	.05	300	Ellis Burks	.05	404	Terry Mulholland	.05	508	Jeff Branson	.05
197	Woody Williams	.05	301	Roberto Kelly	.05	405	Robby Thompson	.05	509	Bernie Williams	.05
198	Ron Karkovice	.05	302	Dante Bichette	.05	406	Ruben Sierra	.05	510	Paul Sorrento	.05
199	Phil Leftwich	.05	303	Alvaro Espinoza	.05	407	Tony Phillips	.05	511	Dennis Eckersley	.60
200	Jim Thome	.50	304	Alex Cole	.05	408	Moises Alou	.05	512	Pat Mahomes	.05
201	Brady Anderson	.05	305	Rickey Henderson	.65	409	Felix Fermin	.05	513	Rusty Greer	.05
202	Pedro Martinez	.65	306	Dave Weathers	.05	410	Pat Listach	.05	514	Luis Polonia	.05
203	Steve Karsay	.05	307	Shane Reynolds	.05	411	Kevin Bass	.05	515	Willie Banks	.05
204	Reggie Sanders	.05	308	Bobby Bonilla	.05	412	Ben McDonald	.05	516	John Wetteland	.05
205	Bill Risley	.05	309	Junior Felix	.05	413	Scott Cooper	.05	517	Mike LaVaillere	.05
206	Jay Bell	.05	310	Jeff Fassero	.05	414	Jody Reed	.05	518	Tommy Greene	.05
207	Kevin Brown	.05	311	Darren Lewis	.05	415	Deion Sanders	.05	519	Mark Grace	.05
208	Tim Scott	.05	312	John Doherty	.05	416	Ricky Gutierrez	.05	520	Bob Hamelin	.05
209	Len Dykstra	.05	313	Scott Servais	.05	417	Gregg Jefferies	.05	521	Scott Sanderson	.05
210	Willie Greene	.05	314	Rick Helling	.05	418	Jack McDowell	.05	522	Joe Carter	.05
211	Jim Eisenreich	.05	315	Pedro Martinez	.65	419	Al Leiter	.05	523	Jeff Brantley	.05
212	Cliff Floyd	.05	316	Wes Chamberlain	.05	420	Tony Longmire	.05	524	Andrew Lorraine	.05
213	Otis Nixon	.05	317	Bryan Eversgerd	.05	421	Paul Wagner	.05	525	Rico Brogna	.05
214	Eduardo Perez	.05	318	Trevor Hoffman	.05	422	Geronimo Pena	.05	526	Shane Mack	.05
215	Manuel Lee	.05	319	John Patterson	.05	423	Ivan Rodriguez	.60	527	Mark Wohlers	.05
216	Armando Benitez RC	.10	320	Matt Walbeck	.05	424	Kevin Gross	.05	528	Scott Sanders	.05
217	Dave McCarty	.05	321	Jeff Montgomery	.05	425	Kirk McCaskill	.05	529	Chris Bosio	.05
218	Scott Livingstone	.05	322	Mel Rojas	.05	426	Greg Myers	.05	530	Andujar Cedeno	.05
219	Chad Kreuter	.05	323	Eddie Taubensee	.05	427	Roger Clemens	1.00	531	Kenny Rogers	.05
220	Checklist	.05	324	Ray Lankford	.05	428	Chris Hammond	.05	532	Doug Drabek	.05
221	Brian Jordan	.05	325	Jose Vizcaino	.05	429	Randy Myers	.05	533	Curt Leskanic	.05
222	Matt Whiteside	.05	326	Carlos Baerga	.05	430	Roger Mason	.05	534	Craig Shipley	.05
223	Jim Edmonds	.05	327	Jack Voigt	.05	431	Bret Saberhagen	.05	535	Craig Grebeck	.05
224	Tony Gwynn	.75	328	Julio Franco	.05	432	Jeff Reboulet	.05	536	Cal Eldred	.05
225	Jose Lind	.05	329	Brent Gates	.05	433	John Olerud	.05	537	Mickey Tettleton	.05
226	Marvin Freeman	.05	330	Checklist	.05	434	Bill Gullickson	.05	538	Harold Baines	.05
227	Ken Hill	.05	331	Greg Maddux	.75	435	Eddie Murray	.65	539	Tim Wallach	.05
228	David Hulse	.05	332	Jason Bere	.05	436	Pedro Munoz	.05	540	Damon Buford	.05
229	Joe Hesketh	.05	333	Bill Wegman	.05	437	Charlie O'Brien	.05	541	Lenny Webster	.05
230	Roberto Petagine	.05	334	Tuffy Rhodes	.05	438	Jeff Nelson	.05	542	Kevin Appier	.05
231	Jeffrey Hammonds	.05	335	Kevin Young	.05	439	Mike Macfarlane	.05	543	Raul Mondesi	.05
232	John Jaha	.05	336	Andy Benes	.05	440	Checklist	.05	544	Eric Young	.05
233	John Burkett	.05	337	Pedro Astacio	.05	441	Derrick May	.05	545	Russ Davis	.05
234	Hal Morris	.05	338	Reggie Jefferson	.05	442	John Roper	.05	546	Mike Benjamin	.05
235	Tony Castillo	.05	339	Tim Belcher	.05	443	Darryl Hamilton	.05	547	Mike Greenwell	.05
236	Ryan Bowen	.05	340	Ken Griffey Jr.	1.50	444	Dan Miceli	.05	548	Scott Brosius	.05
237	Wayne Kirby	.05	341	Mariano Duncan	.05	445	Tony Eusebio	.05	549	Brian Dorsett	.05
238	Brent Mayne	.05	342	Andres Galarraga	.05	446	Jerry Browne	.05	550	Checklist	.05
239	Jim Bullinger	.05	343	Rondell White	.05	447	Wally Joyner	.05			
240	Mike Lieberthal	.05	344	Cory Bailey	.05	448	Brian Harper	.05			
241	Barry Larkin	.05	345	Bryan Harvey	.05	449	Scott Fletcher	.05			
242	David Segui	.05	346	John Franco	.05	450	Bip Roberts	.05			
243	Jose Bautista	.05	347	Greg Swindell	.05	451	Pete Smith	.05			
244	Hector Fajardo	.05	348	David West	.05	452	Chili Davis	.05			
245	Orel Hershiser	.05	349	Fred McGriff	.05	453	Dave Hollins	.05			
246	James Mouton	.05	350	Jose Canseco	.35	454	Tony Pena	.05			
247	Scott Leius	.05	351	Orlando Merced	.05	455	Butch Henry	.05			
248	Tom Glavine	.25	352	Rheal Cormier	.05	456	Craig Biggio	.05			
249	Danny Bautista	.05	353	Carlos Pulido	.05	457	Zane Smith	.05			
250	Jose Mercedes	.05	354	Terry Steinbach	.05	458	Ryan Thompson	.05			
251	Marquis Grissom	.05	355	Wade Boggs	.75	459	Mike Jackson	.05			
252	Charlie Hayes	.05	356	B.J. Surhoff	.05	460	Mark McGwire	2.00			
253	Ryan Klesko	.05	357	Rafael Palmeiro	.60	461	John Smoltz	.05			
254	Vicente Palacios	.05	358	Anthony Young	.05	462	Steve Scarsone	.05			
255	Matias Carrillo	.05	359	Tom Brunansky	.05	463	Greg Colbrunn	.05			
256	Gary DiSarcina	.05	360	Todd Stottlemyre	.05	464	Shawn Green	.25			
257	Kirk Gibson	.05	361	Chris Turner	.05	465	David Wells	.05			
258	Garey Ingram	.05	362	Joe Boever	.05	466	Jose Hernandez	.05			
259	Alex Fernandez	.05	363	Jeff Blauser	.05	467	Chip Hale	.05			
260	John Mabry	.05	364	Derek Bell	.05	468	Tony Tarasco	.05			
261	Chris Howard	.05	365	Matt Williams	.05	469	Kevin Mitchell	.05			
262	Miguel Jimenez	.05	366	Jeremy Hernandez	.05	470	Billy Hatcher	.05			
263	Heath Slocumb	.05	367	Joe Girardi	.05	471	Jay Buhner	.05			
264	Albert Belle	.05	368	Mike Devereaux	.05	472	Ken Caminiti	.05			
265	Dave Clark	.05	369	Jim Abbott	.05	473	Tom Henke	.05			

Press Proofs

NM/M

Complete Set (550):	150.00
Common Player:	1.00

Stars: 15X
(See 1995 Donruss for checklist and base card values.)

All-Stars

		NM/M
Complete Set (18):		26.00
Common Player:		.40
AL1	Jimmy Key	.40
AL2	Ivan Rodriguez	1.25
AL3	Frank Thomas	1.50
AL4	Roberto Alomar	.60
AL5	Wade Boggs	2.00
AL6	Cal Ripken, Jr.	4.50
AL7	Joe Carter	.40
AL8	Ken Griffey Jr.	3.00
AL9	Kirby Puckett	2.00
NL1	Greg Maddux	2.00
NL2	Mike Piazza	3.00
NL3	Gregg Jefferies	.40
NL4	Mariano Duncan	.40
NL5	Matt Williams	.40
NL6	Ozzie Smith	2.00
NL7	Barry Bonds	4.50
NL8	Tony Gwynn	2.00
NL9	Dave Justice	.40

Bomb Squad

		NM/M
Complete Set (6):		3.00
Common Player:		.50
1	Ken Griffey Jr., Matt Williams	1.00
2	Frank Thomas, Jeff Bagwell	.75
3	Albert Belle, Barry Bonds	1.50
4	Jose Canseco, Fred McGriff	.60
5	Cecil Fielder, Andres Galarraga	.50
6	Joe Carter, Kevin Mitchell	.50

Diamond Kings

		NM/M
Complete Set (29):		35.00
Common Player:		.75
1	Frank Thomas	3.00
2	Jeff Bagwell	3.00
3	Chili Davis	.75
4	Dante Bichette	.75
5	Ruben Sierra	.75
6	Jeff Conine	.75
7	Paul O'Neill	.75
8	Bobby Bonilla	.75
9	Joe Carter	.75
10	Moises Alou	.75
11	Kenny Lofton	.75
12	Matt Williams	.75
13	Kevin Seitzer	.75
14	Sammy Sosa	3.50
15	Scott Cooper	.75
16	Raul Mondesi	.75
17	Will Clark	.75
18	Lenny Dykstra	.75
19	Kirby Puckett	3.50
20	Hal Morris	.75
21	Travis Fryman	.75
22	Greg Maddux	3.50
23	Rafael Palmeiro	2.50
24	Tony Gwynn	3.50
25	David Cone	.75
26	Al Martin	.75
27	Ken Griffey Jr.	5.00
28	Gregg Jefferies	.75
29	Checklist	.10

Dominators

		NM/M
Complete Set (9):		7.50
Common Player:		.50
1	David Cone, Mike Mussina, Greg Maddux	1.00
2	Ivan Rodriguez, Mike Piazza, Darren Daulton	2.00
3	Fred McGriff, Frank Thomas, Jeff Bagwell	1.50
4	Roberto Alomar, Carlos Baerga, Craig Biggio	.75
5	Robin Ventura, Travis Fryman, Matt Williams	.50
6	Cal Ripken Jr., Barry Larkin, Wil Cordero	2.50
7	Albert Belle, Barry Bonds, Moises Alou	2.50
8	Ken Griffey Jr., Kenny Lofton, Marquis Grissom	2.00
9	Kirby Puckett, Paul O'Neill, Tony Gwynn	2.00

Elite

JEFF BAGWELL

		NM/M
Complete Set (12):		100.00
Common Player:		6.00
49	Jeff Bagwell	12.00
50	Paul O'Neill	6.00
51	Greg Maddux	15.00
52	Mike Piazza	17.50
53	Matt Williams	6.00
54	Ken Griffey Jr.	17.50
55	Frank Thomas	12.00
56	Barry Bonds	20.00
57	Kirby Puckett	15.00
58	Fred McGriff	6.00
59	Jose Canseco	9.00
60	Albert Belle	6.00

Long Ball Leaders

		NM/M
Complete Set (8):		7.50
Common Player:		.50
1	Frank Thomas	1.50
2	Fred McGriff	.50
3	Ken Griffey Jr.	2.00
4	Matt Williams	.50
5	Mike Piazza	2.00
6	Jose Canseco	.75
7	Barry Bonds	2.50
8	Jeff Bagwell	1.50

Mound Marvels

MIKE MUSSINA

		NM/M
Complete Set (8):		7.50
Common Player:		1.00
1	Greg Maddux	4.00
2	David Cone	1.00
3	Mike Mussina	2.00
4	Bret Saberhagen	1.00
5	Jimmy Key	1.00
6	Doug Drabek	1.00
7	Randy Johnson	3.00
8	Jason Bere	1.00

1996 Donruss

DANTE BICHETTE

		NM/M
Complete Set (550):		20.00
Complete Series 1 (330):		12.00
Complete Series 2 (220):		10.00
Common Player:		.05
Series 1 Pack (12):		1.00
Series 1 Wax Box (36):		20.00
Series 2 Pack (12):		1.00
Series 2 Wax Box (18):		12.50
1	Frank Thomas	1.00
2	Jason Bates	.05
3	Steve Sparks	.05
4	Scott Servais	.05
5	Angelo Encarnacion	.05
6	Scott Sanders	.05
7	Billy Ashley	.05
8	Alex Rodriguez	2.00
9	Sean Bergman	.05
10	Brad Radke	.05
11	Andy Van Slyke	.05
12	Joe Girardi	.05
13	Mark Grudzielanek	.05
14	Rick Aguilera	.05
15	Randy Veres	.05
16	Tim Bogar	.05
17	Dave Veres	.05
18	Kevin Stocker	.05
19	Marquis Grissom	.05
20	Will Clark	.05
21	Jay Bell	.05
22	Allen Battle	.05
23	Frank Rodriguez	.05
24	Terry Steinbach	.05
25	Gerald Williams	.05
26	Sid Roberson	.05
27	Gregg Zaun	.05
28	Ozzie Timmons	.05
29	Vaughn Eshelman	.05
30	Ed Sprague	.05
31	Gary DiSarcina	.05
32	Joe Boever	.05
33	Steve Avery	.05
34	Brad Ausmus	.05
35	Kirt Manwaring	.05
36	Gary Sheffield	.25
37	Jason Bere	.05
38	Jeff Manto	.05
39	David Cone	.05
40	Manny Ramirez	1.00
41	Sandy Alomar	.05
42	Curtis Goodwin/RR	.05
43	Tino Martinez	.05
44	Woody Williams	.05
45	Dean Palmer	.05
46	Hipolito Pichardo	.05
47	Jason Giambi	.60
48	Lance Johnson	.05
49	Bernard Gilkey	.05
50	Kirby Puckett	1.25
51	Tony Fernandez	.05
52	Alex Gonzalez	.05
53	Bret Saberhagen	.05
54	Lyle Mouton/RR	.05
55	Brian McRae	.05
56	Mark Gubicza	.05
57	Sergio Valdez	.05
58	Darrin Fletcher	.05
59	Steve Parris	.05
60	Johnny Damon/RR	.35
61	Rickey Henderson	1.00
62	Darrell Whitmore	.05
63	Roberto Petagine	.05
64	Trenidad Hubbard	.05
65	Heathcliff Slocumb	.05
66	Steve Finley	.05
67	Mariano Rivera	.25
68	Brian Hunter	.05
69	Jamie Moyer	.05
70	Ellis Burks	.05
71	Pat Kelly	.05
72	Mickey Tettleton	.05
73	Garret Anderson	.05
74	Andy Pettitte/RR	.75
75	Glenallen Hill	.05
76	Brent Gates	.05
77	Lou Whitaker	.05
78	David Segui	.05
79	Dan Wilson	.05
80	Pat Listach	.05
81	Jeff Bagwell	1.00
82	Ben McDonald	.05
83	John Valentin	.05
84	John Jaha	.05
85	Pete Schourek	.05
86	Bryce Florie	.05
87	Brian Jordan	.05
88	Ron Karkovice	.05
89	Al Leiter	.05
90	Tony Longmire	.05
91	Nelson Liriano	.05
92	David Bell	.05
93	Kevin Gross	.05
94	Tom Candiotti	.05
95	Dave Martinez	.05
96	Greg Myers	.05
97	Rheal Cormier	.05
98	Chris Hammond	.05
99	Randy Myers	.05
100	Bill Pulsipher/RR	.05
101	Jason Isringhausen/RR	.05
102	Dave Stevens	.05
103	Roberto Alomar	.20
104	Bob Higginson/RR	.05
105	Eddie Murray	1.00
106	Matt Walbeck	.05
107	Mark Wohlers	.05
108	Jeff Nelson	.05
109	Tom Goodwin	.05
110	Cal Ripken Jr. Checklist 1-83 (2,131 Consecutive Games)	1.25
111	Rey Sanchez	.05
112	Hector Carrasco	.05
113	B.J. Surhoff	.05
114	Dan Miceli	.05
115	Dean Hartgraves	.05
116	John Burkett	.05
117	Gary Gaetti	.05
118	Ricky Bones	.05
119	Mike Macfarlane	.05
120	Bip Roberts	.05
121	Dave Milcki	.05
122	Chili Davis	.05
123	Mark Whiten	.05
124	Herbert Perry	.05
125	Butch Henry	.05
126	Derek Bell	.05
127	Al Martin	.05
128	John Franco	.05
129	William Van Landingham	.05
130	Mike Bordick	.05
131	Mike Mordecai	.05
132	Robby Thompson	.05
133	Greg Colbrunn	.05
134	Domingo Cedeno	.05
135	Chad Curtis	.05
136	Jose Hernandez	.05
137	Scott Klingenbeck	.05

No.	Player	Val	No.	Player	Val	No.	Player	Val	No.	Player	Val
138	Ryan Klesko	.05	240	Scott Leius	.05	341	Gregg Jefferies	.05	445	Rick Wilkins	.05
139	John Smiley	.05	241	Russ Davis	.05	342	Larry Walker	.05	446	Quilvio Veras	.05
140	Charlie Hayes	.05	242	Ray Durham/RR	.05	343	Pedro Martinez	.05	447	Greg Gagne	.05
141	Jay Buhner	.05	243	Matt Mieske	.05	344	Dwayne Hosey	.05	448	Mark Kiefer	.05
142	Doug Drabek	.05	244	Brent Mayne	.05	345	Terry Pendleton	.05	449	Bobby Witt	.05
143	Roger Pavlik	.05	245	Thomas Howard	.05	346	Pete Harnisch	.05	450	Andy Ashby	.05
144	Todd Worrell	.05	246	Troy O'Leary	.05	347	Tony Castillo	.05	451	Alex Ochoa	.05
145	Cal Ripken Jr.	2.50	247	Jacob Brumfield	.05	348	Paul Quantrill	.05	452	Jorge Fabregas	.05
146	Steve Reed	.05	248	Mickey Morandini	.05	349	Fred McGriff	.05	453	Gene Schall	.05
147	Chuck Finley	.05	249	Todd Hundley	.05	350	Ivan Rodriguez	.65	454	Ken Hill	.05
148	Mike Blowers	.05	250	Chris Bosio	.05	351	Butch Huskey	.05	455	Tony Tarasco	.05
149	Orel Hershiser	.05	251	Omar Vizquel	.05	352	Ozzie Smith	1.25	456	Donnie Wall	.05
150	Allen Watson	.05	252	Mike Lansing	.05	353	Marty Cordova	.05	457	Carlos Garcia	.05
151	Ramon Martinez	.05	253	John Mabry	.05	354	John Wasdin	.05	458	Ryan Thompson	.05
152	Melvin Nieves	.05	254	Mike Perez	.05	355	Wade Boggs	1.25	459	Marvin Benard RC	.05
153	Tripp Cromer	.05	255	Delino DeShields	.05	356	Dave Nilsson	.05	460	Jose Herrera	.05
154	Yorkis Perez	.05	256	Wil Cordero	.05	357	Rafael Palmeiro	.65	461	Jeff Blauser	.05
155	Stan Javier	.05	257	Mike James	.05	358	Luis Gonzalez	.05	462	Chris Hook	.05
156	Mel Rojas	.05	258	Todd Van Poppel	.05	359	Reggie Jefferson	.05	463	Jeff Conine	.05
157	Aaron Sele	.05	259	Joey Cora	.05	360	Carlos Delgado	.60	464	Devon White	.05
158	Eric Karros	.05	260	Andre Dawson	.25	361	Orlando Palmeiro	.05	465	Danny Bautista	.05
159	Robb Nen	.05	261	Jerry DiPoto	.05	362	Chris Gomez	.05	466	Steve Trachsel	.05
160	Raul Mondesi	.05	262	Rick Krivda	.05	363	John Smoltz	.05	467	C.J. Nitkowski	.05
161	John Wetteland	.05	263	Glenn Dishman	.05	364	Marc Newfield	.05	468	Mike Devereaux	.05
162	Tim Scott	.05	264	Mike Mimbs	.05	365	Matt Williams	.05	469	David Wells	.05
163	Kenny Rogers	.05	265	John Ericks	.05	366	Jesus Tavarez	.05	470	Jim Eisenreich	.05
164	Melvin Bunch	.05	266	Jose Canseco	.35	367	Bruce Ruffin	.05	471	Edgar Martinez	.05
165	Rod Beck	.05	267	Jeff Branson	.05	368	Sean Berry	.05	472	Craig Biggio	.05
166	Andy Benes	.05	268	Curt Leskanic	.05	369	Randy Velarde	.05	473	Jeff Frye	.05
167	Lenny Dykstra	.05	269	Jon Nunnally	.05	370	Tony Pena	.05	474	Karim Garcia	.05
168	Orlando Merced	.05	270	Scott Stahoviak	.05	371	Jim Thome	.60	475	Jimmy Haynes	.05
169	Tomas Perez	.05	271	Jeff Montgomery	.05	372	Jeffrey Hammonds	.05	476	Darren Holmes	.05
170	Xavier Hernandez	.05	272	Hal Morris	.05	373	Bob Wolcott	.05	477	Tim Salmon	.05
171	Ruben Sierra	.05	273	Esteban Loaiza	.05	374	Juan Guzman	.05	478	Randy Johnson	1.00
172	Alan Trammell	.05	274	Rico Brogna	.05	375	Juan Gonzalez	.50	479	Eric Plunk	.05
173	Mike Fetters	.05	275	Dave Winfield	1.00	376	Michael Tucker	.05	480	Scott Cooper	.05
174	Wilson Alvarez	.05	276	J.R. Phillips	.05	377	Doug Johns	.05	481	Chan Ho Park	.05
175	Erik Hanson	.05	277	Todd Zeile	.05	378	Mike Cameron RC	.75	482	Ray McDavid	.05
176	Travis Fryman	.05	278	Tom Pagnozzi	.05	379	Ray Lankford	.05	483	Mark Petkovsek	.05
177	Jim Abbott	.05	279	Mark Lemke	.05	380	Jose Parra	.05	484	Greg Swindell	.05
178	Bret Boone	.05	280	Dave Magadan	.05	381	Jimmy Key	.05	485	George Williams	.05
179	Sterling Hitchcock	.05	281	Greg McMichael	.05	382	John Olerud	.05	486	Yamil Benitez	.05
180	Pat Mahomes	.05	282	Mike Morgan	.05	383	Kevin Ritz	.05	487	Tim Wakefield	.05
181	Mark Acre	.05	283	Moises Alou	.05	384	Tim Raines	.05	488	Kevin Tapani	.05
182	Charles Nagy	.05	284	Dennis Martinez	.05	385	Rich Amaral	.05	489	Derrick May	.05
183	Rusty Greer	.05	285	Jeff Kent	.05	386	Keith Lockhart	.05	490	Ken Griffey Jr. Checklist	1.00
184	Mike Stanley	.05	286	Mark Johnson	.05	387	Steve Scarsone	.05	491	Derek Jeter	2.50
185	Jim Bullinger	.05	287	Darren Lewis	.05	388	Cliff Floyd	.05	492	Jeff Fassero	.05
186	Shane Andrews	.05	288	Brad Clontz	.05	389	Rich Aude	.05	493	Benito Santiago	.05
187	Brian Keyser	.05	289	Chad Fonville/RR	.05	390	Hideo Nomo	.50	494	Tom Gordon	.05
188	Tyler Green	.05	290	Paul Sorrento	.05	391	Geronimo Berroa	.05	495	Jamie Brewington	.05
189	Mark Grace	.05	291	Lee Smith	.05	392	Pat Rapp	.05	496	Vince Coleman	.05
190	Bob Hamelin	.05	292	Tom Glavine	.25	393	Dustin Hermanson	.05	497	Kevin Jordan	.05
191	Luis Ortiz	.05	293	Antonio Osuna	.05	394	Greg Maddux	1.25	498	Jeff King	.05
192	Joe Carter	.05	294	Kevin Foster	.05	395	Darren Daulton	.05	499	Mike Simms	.05
193	Eddie Taubensee	.05	295	Sandy Martinez RC	.05	396	Kenny Lofton	.05	500	Jose Rijo	.05
194	Brian Anderson	.05	296	Mark Leiter	.05	397	Ruben Rivera	.05	501	Denny Neagle	.05
195	Edgardo Alfonzo	.05	297	Julian Tavarez	.05	398	Billy Wagner	.05	502	Jose Lima	.05
196	Pedro Munoz	.05	298	Mike Kelly	.05	399	Kevin Brown	.05	503	Kevin Seitzer	.05
197	David Justice	.05	299	Joe Oliver	.05	400	Mike Kingery	.05	504	Alex Fernandez	.05
198	Trevor Hoffman	.05	300	John Flaherty	.05	401	Bernie Williams	.05	505	Mo Vaughn	.05
199	Bobby Ayala	.05	301	Don Mattingly	1.50	402	Otis Nixon	.05	506	Phil Nevin	.05
200	Tony Eusebio	.05	302	Pat Meares	.05	403	Damion Easley	.05	507	J.T. Snow	.05
201	Jeff Russell	.05	303	John Doherty	.05	404	Paul O'Neill	.05	508	Andujar Cedeno	.05
202	Mike Hampton	.05	304	Joe Vitiello	.05	405	Deion Sanders	.05	509	Ozzie Guillen	.05
203	Walt Weiss	.05	305	Vinny Castilla	.05	406	Dennis Eckersley	1.00	510	Mark Clark	.05
204	Joey Hamilton	.05	306	Jeff Brantley	.05	407	Tony Clark	.05	511	Mark McGwire	2.00
205	Roberto Hernandez	.05	307	Mike Greenwell	.05	408	Rondell White	.05	512	Jeff Reboulet	.05
206	Greg Vaughn	.05	308	Midre Cummings	.05	409	Luis Sojo	.05	513	Armando Benitez	.05
207	Felipe Lira	.05	309	Curt Schilling	.25	410	David Hulse	.05	514	LaTroy Hawkins	.05
208	Harold Baines	.05	310	Ken Caminiti	.05	411	Shane Reynolds	.05	515	Brett Butler	.05
209	Tim Wallach	.05	311	Scott Erickson	.05	412	Chris Hoiles	.05	516	Tavo Alvarez	.05
210	Manny Alexander	.05	312	Carl Everett	.05	413	Lee Tinsley	.05	517	Chris Snopek	.05
211	Tim Laker	.05	313	Charles Johnson	.05	414	Scott Karl	.05	518	Mike Mussina	.50
212	Chris Haney	.05	314	Alex Diaz	.05	415	Ron Gant	.05	519	Darryl Kile	.05
213	Brian Maxcy	.05	315	Jose Mesa	.05	416	Brian Johnson	.05	520	Wally Joyner	.05
214	Eric Young	.05	316	Mark Carreon	.05	417	Jose Oliva	.05	521	Willie McGee	.05
215	Darryl Strawberry	.05	317	Carlos Perez/RR	.05	418	Jack McDowell	.05	522	Kent Mercker	.05
216	Barry Bonds	2.50	318	Ismael Valdes	.05	419	Paul Molitor	1.00	523	Mike Jackson	.05
217	Tim Naehring	.05	319	Frank Castillo	.05	420	Ricky Bottalico	.05	524	Troy Percival	.05
218	Scott Brosius	.05	320	Tom Henke	.05	421	Paul Wagner	.05	525	Tony Gwynn	1.25
219	Reggie Sanders	.05	321	Spike Owen	.05	422	Terry Bradshaw	.05	526	Ron Coomer	.05
220	Eddie Murray Checklist 84-166 (3,000 Career Hits)	.35	322	Joe Orsulak	.05	423	Bob Tewksbury	.05	527	Darryl Hamilton	.05
221	Luis Alicea	.05	323	Paul Menhart	.05	424	Mike Piazza	1.75	528	Phil Plantier	.05
222	Albert Belle	.05	324	Pedro Borbon	.05	425	Luis Andujar RC	.05	529	Norm Charlton	.05
223	Benji Gil	.05	325	Paul Molitor Checklist 167-249 (1,000 Career RBI)	.35	426	Mark Langston	.05	530	Craig Paquette	.05
224	Dante Bichette	.05	326	Jeff Cirillo	.05	427	Stan Belinda	.05	531	Dave Burba	.05
225	Bobby Bonilla	.05	327	Edwin Hurtado	.05	428	Kurt Abbott	.05	532	Mike Henneman	.05
226	Todd Stottlemyre	.05	328	Orlando Miller	.05	429	Shawon Dunston	.05	533	Terrell Wade	.05
227	Jim Edmonds	.05	329	Steve Ontiveros	.05	430	Bobby Jones	.05	534	Eddie Williams	.05
228	Todd Jones	.05	330	Kirby Puckett Checklist 250-330 (1,000 Career RBI)	.75	431	Jose Vizcaino	.05	535	Robin Ventura	.05
229	Shawn Green	.25	331	Scott Bullett	.05	432	Matt Lawton RC	.05	536	Chuck Knoblauch	.05
230	Javy Lopez	.05	332	Andres Galarraga	.05	433	Pat Hentgen	.05	537	Les Norman	.05
231	Ariel Prieto	.05	333	Cal Eldred	.05	434	Cecil Fielder	.05	538	Brady Anderson	.05
232	Tony Phillips	.05	334	Sammy Sosa	1.25	435	Carlos Baerga	.05	539	Roger Clemens	1.50
233	James Mouton	.05	335	Don Slaught	.05	436	Rich Becker	.05	540	Mark Portugal	.05
234	Jose Oquendo	.05	336	Jody Reed	.05	437	Chipper Jones	1.25	541	Mike Matheny	.05
235	Royce Clayton	.05	337	Roger Cedeno	.05	438	Bill Risley	.05	542	Jeff Parrett	.05
236	Chuck Carr	.05	338	Ken Griffey Jr.	1.75	439	Kevin Appier	.05	543	Roberto Kelly	.05
237	Doug Jones	.05	339	Todd Hollandsworth	.05	440	Checklist	.05	544	Damon Buford	.05
238	Mark Mclemore (McLemore)	.05	340	Mike Trombley	.05	441	Jaime Navarro	.05	545	Chad Ogea	.05
239	Bill Swift	.05				442	Barry Larkin	.05	546	Jose Offerman	.05
						443	Jose Valentin RC	.05	547	Brian Barber	.05
						444	Bryan Rekar	.05			

548	Danny Tartabull	.05
549	Duane Singleton	.05
550	Tony Gwynn Checklist	.75

Press Proofs

	NM/M
Complete Set (550):	150.00
Common Player:	.50

(Star cards valued 7X corresponding regular-issue cards.)

Diamond Kings

Frank Thomas

		NM/M
Complete Set (31):		160.00
Common Player:		2.25
1	Frank Thomas	7.50
2	Mo Vaughn	2.50
3	Manny Ramirez	7.50
4	Mark McGwire	13.50
5	Juan Gonzalez	4.00
6	Roberto Alomar	3.00
7	Tim Salmon	2.50
8	Barry Bonds	15.00
9	Tony Gwynn	10.00
10	Reggie Sanders	2.50
11	Larry Walker	2.50
12	Pedro Martinez	7.50
13	Jeff King	2.50
14	Mark Grace	2.50
15	Greg Maddux	10.00
16	Don Mattingly	12.50
17	Gregg Jefferies	2.50
18	Chad Curtis	2.50
19	Jason Isringhausen	2.50
20	B.J. Surhoff	2.50
21	Jeff Conine	2.50
22	Kirby Puckett	10.00
23	Derek Bell	2.50
24	Wally Joyner	2.50
25	Brian Jordan	2.50
26	Edgar Martinez	2.50
27	Hideo Nomo	4.00
28	Mike Mussina	5.00
29	Eddie Murray	7.50
30	Cal Ripken Jr.	15.00
31	Checklist	.25

Elite

		NM/M
Complete Set (12):		55.00
Complete Series 1 (61-66):		27.50
Complete Series 2 (67-72):		32.50
Common Player Series 1:		2.50
Common Player Series 2:		1.75
61	Cal Ripken Jr.	12.00
62	Hideo Nomo	3.00
63	Reggie Sanders	2.50
64	Mo Vaughn	2.50
65	Tim Salmon	2.50
66	Chipper Jones	9.00

67	Manny Ramirez	6.00
68	Greg Maddux	7.50
69	Frank Thomas	6.00
70	Ken Griffey Jr.	10.00
71	Dante Bichette	1.75
72	Tony Gwynn	7.50

Freeze Frame

		NM/M
Complete Set (8):		16.00
Common Player:		1.00
1	Frank Thomas	2.00
2	Ken Griffey Jr.	3.00
3	Cal Ripken Jr.	4.00
4	Hideo Nomo	1.50
5	Greg Maddux	2.50
6	Albert Belle	1.00
7	Chipper Jones	2.50
8	Mike Piazza	3.00

Hit List

		NM/M
Complete Set (16):		30.00
Common Player:		.60
1	Tony Gwynn	3.00
2	Ken Griffey Jr.	5.00
3	Will Clark	.60
4	Mike Piazza	5.00
5	Carlos Baerga	.60
6	Mo Vaughn	.60
7	Mark Grace	.60
8	Kirby Puckett	3.00
9	Frank Thomas	2.00
10	Barry Bonds	6.00
11	Jeff Bagwell	2.00
12	Edgar Martinez	.60
13	Tim Salmon	.60
14	Wade Boggs	3.00
15	Don Mattingly	4.00
16	Eddie Murray	2.00

Long Ball Leaders

		NM/M
Complete Set (8):		45.00
Common Player:		1.50
1	Barry Bonds	15.00
2	Ryan Klesko	1.50
3	Mark McGwire	15.00
4	Raul Mondesi	1.50
5	Cecil Fielder	1.50
6	Ken Griffey Jr.	12.00

7	Larry Walker	1.50
8	Frank Thomas	6.00

Power Alley

		NM/M
Complete Set (10):		30.00
Common Player		2.00
Die-Cuts:		2X
1	Frank Thomas	4.00
2	Barry Bonds	7.50
3	Reggie Sanders	2.00
4	Albert Belle	2.00
5	Tim Salmon	2.00
6	Dante Bichette	2.00
7	Mo Vaughn	2.00
8	Jim Edmonds	2.00
9	Manny Ramirez	4.00
10	Ken Griffey Jr.	6.00

Pure Power

		NM/M
Complete Set (8):		25.00
Common Player:		2.25
1	Raul Mondesi	2.25
2	Barry Bonds	10.00
3	Albert Belle	2.25
4	Frank Thomas	4.50
5	Mike Piazza	7.50
6	Dante Bichette	2.25
7	Manny Ramirez	4.50
8	Mo Vaughn	2.25

Round Trippers

		NM/M
Complete Set (10):		35.00
Common Player:		2.50
1	Albert Belle	2.50
2	Barry Bonds	7.50
3	Jeff Bagwell	4.00
4	Tim Salmon	2.50
5	Mo Vaughn	2.50
6	Ken Griffey Jr.	5.00
7	Mike Piazza	5.00
8	Cal Ripken Jr.	7.50
9	Frank Thomas	4.00
9p	Frank Thomas/Promo	2.50
10	Dante Bichette	2.50

Showdown

		NM/M
Complete Set (8):		22.50
Common Player:		.75
1	Frank Thomas, Hideo Nomo	3.00
2	Barry Bonds, Randy Johnson	6.00
3	Greg Maddux, Ken Griffey Jr.	5.00
4	Roger Clemens, Tony Gwynn	4.50
5	Mike Piazza, Mike Mussina	5.00
6	Cal Ripken Jr., Pedro Martinez	6.00
7	Tim Wakefield, Matt Williams	.75
8	Manny Ramirez, Carlos Perez	2.50

1997 Donruss

Derek Jeter

		NM/M
Complete Set (450):		20.00
Series 1 Set (270):		10.00
Update Set (180):		10.00
Common Player:		.05
Press Proof Set (450):		250.00
Common Press Proof:		.50
Common Press Proof Gold:		2.00
Press Proof Gold Stars:		10X
Wax Pack (10):		1.50
Hobby Wax Box (18):		25.00
Retail Wax Box (36):		40.00
Magazine Pack (13):		1.50
Magazine Box (24):		20.00
Update Pack (10):		1.50
Update Wax Box (24):		30.00
1	Juan Gonzalez	.40
2	Jim Edmonds	.05
3	Tony Gwynn	1.00
4	Andres Galarraga	.05
5	Joe Carter	.05
6	Raul Mondesi	.05
7	Greg Maddux	1.00
8	Travis Fryman	.05
9	Brian Jordan	.05
10	Henry Rodriguez	.05
11	Manny Ramirez	.75
12	Mark McGwire	1.75
13	Marc Newfield	.05
14	Craig Biggio	.05
15	Sammy Sosa	1.00
16	Brady Anderson	.05
17	Wade Boggs	1.00
18	Charles Johnson	.05
19	Matt Williams	.05
20	Denny Neagle	.05
21	Ken Griffey Jr.	1.50
22	Robin Ventura	.05
23	Barry Larkin	.05
24	Todd Zeile	.05
25	Chuck Knoblauch	.05
26	Todd Hundley	.05
27	Roger Clemens	1.25
28	Michael Tucker	.05
29	Rondell White	.05
30	Osvaldo Fernandez	.05
31	Ivan Rodriguez	.65
32	Alex Fernandez	.05
33	Jason Isringhausen	.05
34	Chipper Jones	1.00
35	Paul O'Neill	.05
36	Hideo Nomo	.40
37	Roberto Alomar	.20
38	Derek Bell	.05
39	Paul Molitor	.75
40	Andy Benes	.05
41	Steve Trachsel	.05
42	J.T. Snow	.05
43	Jason Kendall	.05
44	Alex Rodriguez	1.75
45	Joey Hamilton	.05

No	Name	Price	No	Name	Price	No	Name	Price	No	Name	Price
46	Carlos Delgado	.50	150	Kevin Elster	.05	254	Jaime Navarro	.05	355	Vladimir Guerrero	.75
47	Jason Giambi	.50	151	Bob Wells	.05	255	Shawon Dunston	.05	356	Darin Erstad	.30
48	Larry Walker	.05	152	Wally Joyner	.05	256	Ron Wright	.05	357	Scott Rolen	.60
49	Derek Jeter	2.00	153	Rico Brogna	.05	257	Tim Belk	.05	358	Andruw Jones	.75
50	Kenny Lofton	.05	154	Dwight Gooden	.05	258	Jeff Darwin	.05	359	Scott Spiezio	.05
51	Devon White	.05	155	Jermaine Allensworth	.05	259	Ruben Sierra	.05	360	Karim Garcia	.05
52	Matt Mieske	.05	156	Ray Durham	.05	260	Chuck Finley	.05	361	Hideki Irabu RC	.25
53	Melvin Nieves	.05	157	Cecil Fielder	.05	261	Darryl Strawberry	.05	362	Nomar Garciaparra	1.00
54	Jose Canseco	.40	158	Ryan Hancock	.05	262	Shannon Stewart	.05	363	Dmitri Young	.05
55	Tino Martinez	.05	159	Gary Sheffield	.30	263	Pedro Martinez	.05	364	Bubba Trammell RC	.25
56	Rafael Palmeiro	.65	160	Albert Belle	.05	264	Neifi Perez	.05	365	Kevin Orie	.05
57	Edgardo Alfonzo	.05	161	Tomas Perez	.05	265	Jeff Conine	.05	366	Jose Rosado	.05
58	Jay Buhner	.05	162	David Doster	.05	266	Orel Hershiser	.05	367	Jose Guillen	.05
59	Shane Reynolds	.05	163	John Valentin	.05	267	Eddie Murray Checklist 1-90 (500 Career HR)	.05	368	Brooks Kieschnick	.05
60	Steve Finley	.05	164	Danny Graves	.05	268	Paul Molitor Checklist 91-180 (3,000 Career Hits)	.05	369	Pokey Reese	.05
61	Bobby Higginson	.05	165	Jose Paniagua	.05	269	Barry Bonds Checklist 181-270 (300 Career HR)	.90	370	Glendon Rusch	.05
62	Dean Palmer	.05	166	Brian Giles RC	.50	270	Mark McGwire Checklist - inserts (300 Career HR)	.75	371	Jason Dickson	.05
63	Terry Pendleton	.05	167	Barry Bonds	2.00	271	Matt Williams	.05	372	Todd Walker	.05
64	Marquis Grissom	.05	168	Sterling Hitchcock	.05	272	Todd Zeile	.05	373	Justin Thompson	.05
65	Mike Stanley	.05	169	Bernie Williams	.05	273	Roger Clemens	1.25	374	Todd Greene	.05
66	Moises Alou	.05	170	Fred McGriff	.05	274	Michael Tucker	.05	375	Jeff Suppan	.05
67	Ray Lankford	.05	171	George Williams	.05	275	J.T. Snow	.05	376	Trey Beamon	.05
68	Marty Cordova	.05	172	Amaury Telemaco	.05	276	Kenny Lofton	.05	377	Damon Mashore	.05
69	John Olerud	.05	173	Ken Caminiti	.05	277	Jose Canseco	.40	378	Wendell Magee	.05
70	David Cone	.05	174	Ron Gant	.05	278	Marquis Grissom	.05	379	Shigetosi Hasegawa	.05
71	Benito Santiago	.05	175	David Justice	.05	279	Moises Alou	.05	380	Bill Mueller	.05
72	Ryne Sandberg	1.00	176	James Baldwin	.05	280	Benito Santiago	.05	381	Chris Widger	.05
73	Rickey Henderson	.75	177	Pat Hentgen	.05	281	Willie McGee	.05	382	Tony Grafannino	.05
74	Roger Cedeno	.05	178	Ben McDonald	.05	282	Chili Davis	.05	383	Derrek Lee	.50
75	Wilson Alvarez	.05	179	Tim Naehring	.05	283	Ron Coomer	.05	384	Brian Moehler	.05
76	Tim Salmon	.05	180	Jim Eisenreich	.05	284	Orlando Merced	.05	385	Quinton McCracken	.05
77	Orlando Merced	.05	181	Ken Hill	.05	285	Delino DeShields	.05	386	Matt Morris	.05
78	Vinny Castilla	.05	182	Paul Wilson	.05	286	John Wetteland	.05	387	Marvin Benard	.05
79	Ismael Valdes	.05	183	Marvin Benard	.05	287	Darren Daulton	.05	388	Deivi Cruz RC	.25
80	Dante Bichette	.05	184	Alan Benes	.05	288	Lee Stevens	.05	389	Javier Valentin RC	.05
81	Kevin Brown	.05	185	Ellis Burks	.05	289	Albert Belle	.05	390	Todd Dunwoody	.05
82	Andy Pettitte	.40	186	Scott Servais	.05	290	Sterling Hitchcock	.05	391	Derrick Gibson	.05
83	Scott Stahoviak	.05	187	David Segui	.05	291	David Justice	.05	392	Raul Casanova	.05
84	Mickey Tettleton	.05	188	Scott Brosius	.05	292	Eric Davis	.05	393	George Arias	.05
85	Jack McDowell	.05	189	Jose Offerman	.05	293	Brian Hunter	.05	394	Tony Womack RC	.25
86	Tom Glavine	.30	190	Eric Davis	.05	294	Darryl Hamilton	.05	395	Antone Williamson	.05
87	Gregg Jefferies	.05	191	Brett Butler	.05	295	Steve Avery	.05	396	Jose Cruz Jr. RC	.50
88	Chili Davis	.05	192	Curtis Pride	.05	296	Joe Vitiello	.05	397	Desi Relaford	.05
89	Randy Johnson	.75	193	Yamil Benitez	.05	297	Jaime Navarro	.05	398	Frank Thomas/HL	.40
90	John Mabry	.05	194	Chan Ho Park	.05	298	Eddie Murray	.75	399	Ken Griffey Jr./HL	.65
91	Billy Wagner	.05	195	Bret Boone	.05	299	Randy Myers	.05	400	Cal Ripken Jr./HL	1.00
92	Jeff Cirillo	.05	196	Omar Vizquel	.05	300	Francisco Cordova	.05	401	Chipper Jones/HL	.50
93	Trevor Hoffman	.05	197	Orlando Miller	.05	301	Javier Lopez	.05	402	Mike Piazza/HL	.65
94	Juan Guzman	.05	198	Ramon Martinez	.05	302	Geronimo Berroa	.05	403	Gary Sheffield/HL	.15
95	Geronimo Berroa	.05	199	Harold Baines	.05	303	Jeffrey Hammonds	.05	404	Alex Rodriguez/HL	.75
96	Bernard Gilkey	.05	200	Eric Young	.05	304	Deion Sanders	.05	405	Wade Boggs/HL	.50
97	Danny Tartabull	.05	201	Fernando Vina	.05	305	Jeff Fassero	.05	406	Juan Gonzalez/HL	.20
98	Johnny Damon	.35	202	Alex Gonzalez	.05	306	Curt Schilling	.25	407	Tony Gwynn/HL	.50
99	Charlie Hayes	.05	203	Fernando Valenzuela	.05	307	Robb Nen	.05	408	Edgar Martinez/HL	.05
100	Reggie Sanders	.05	204	Steve Avery	.05	308	Mark McLemore	.05	409	Jeff Bagwell/HL	.40
101	Robby Thompson	.05	205	Ernie Young	.05	309	Jimmy Key	.05	410	Larry Walker/HL	.05
102	Bobby Bonilla	.05	206	Kevin Appier	.05	310	Quilvio Veras	.05	411	Kenny Lofton/HL	.05
103	Reggie Jefferson	.05	207	Randy Myers	.05	311	Bip Roberts	.05	412	Manny Ramirez/HL	.05
104	John Smoltz	.05	208	Jeff Suppan	.05	312	Esteban Loaiza	.05	413	Mark McGwire/HL	.75
105	Jim Thome	.60	209	James Mouton	.05	313	Andy Ashby	.05	414	Roberto Alomar/HL	.10
106	Ruben Rivera	.05	210	Russ Davis	.05	314	Sandy Alomar Jr.	.05	415	Derek Jeter/HL	1.00
107	Darren Oliver	.05	211	Al Martin	.05	315	Shawn Green	.20	416	Brady Anderson/HL	.05
108	Mo Vaughn	.05	212	Troy Percival	.05	316	Luis Castillo	.05	417	Paul Molitor/HL	.35
109	Roger Pavlik	.05	213	Al Leiter	.05	317	Benji Gil	.05	418	Dante Bichette/HL	.05
110	Terry Steinbach	.05	214	Dennis Eckersley	.65	318	Otis Nixon	.05	419	Jim Edmonds/HL	.05
111	Jermaine Dye	.05	215	Mark Johnson	.05	319	Aaron Sele	.05	420	Mo Vaughn/HL	.05
112	Mark Grudzielanek	.05	216	Eric Karros	.05	320	Brad Ausmus	.05	421	Barry Bonds/HL	.90
113	Rick Aguilera	.05	217	Royce Clayton	.05	321	Troy O'Leary	.05	422	Rusty Greer/HL	.05
114	Jamey Wright	.05	218	Tony Phillips	.05	322	Terrell Wade	.05	423	Greg Maddux	.50
115	Eddie Murray	.75	219	Tim Wakefield	.05	323	Jeff King	.05	424	Andy Pettitte	.15
116	Brian Hunter	.05	220	Alan Trammell	.05	324	Kevin Seitzer	.05	425	John Smoltz	.05
117	Hal Morris	.05	221	Eduardo Perez	.05	325	Mark Wohlers	.05	426	Randy Johnson	.40
118	Tom Pagnozzi	.05	222	Butch Huskey	.05	326	Edgar Renteria	.05	427	Hideo Nomo	.20
119	Mike Mussina	.40	223	Tim Belcher	.05	327	Dan Wilson	.05	428	Roger Clemens	.60
120	Mark Grace	.05	224	Jamie Moyer	.05	328	Brian McRae	.05	429	Tom Glavine	.15
121	Cal Ripken Jr.	2.00	225	F.P. Santangelo	.05	329	Rod Beck	.05	430	Pat Hentgen	.05
122	Tom Goodwin	.05	226	Rusty Greer	.05	330	Julio Franco	.05	431	Kevin Brown	.05
123	Paul Sorrento	.05	227	Jeff Brantley	.05	331	Dave Nilsson	.05	432	Mike Mussina	.20
124	Jay Bell	.05	228	Mark Langston	.05	332	Glenallen Hill	.05	433	Alex Fernandez	.05
125	Todd Hollandsworth	.05	229	Ray Montgomery	.05	333	Kevin Elster	.05	434	Kevin Appier	.05
126	Edgar Martinez	.05	230	Rich Becker	.05	334	Joe Girardi	.05	435	David Cone	.05
127	George Arias	.05	231	Ozzie Smith	1.00	335	David Wells	.05	436	Jeff Fassero	.05
128	Greg Vaughn	.05	232	Rey Ordonez	.05	336	Jeff Blauser	.05	437	John Wetteland	.05
129	Roberto Hernandez	.05	233	Ricky Otero	.05	337	Darryl Kile	.05	438	Barry Bonds, Ivan Rodriguez/IS	.90
130	Delino DeShields	.05	234	Mike Cameron	.05	338	Jeff Kent	.05	439	Ken Griffey Jr., Andres Galarraga/IS	.65
131	Bill Pulsipher	.05	235	Mike Sweeney	.05	339	Jim Leyritz	.05	440	Fred McGriff, Rafael Palmeiro/IS	.05
132	Joey Cora	.05	236	Mark Lewis	.05	340	Todd Stottlemyre	.05	441	Barry Larkin, Jim Thome/IS	.05
133	Mariano Rivera	.15	237	Luis Gonzalez	.05	341	Tony Clark	.05	442	Sammy Sosa, Albert Belle/IS	.50
134	Mike Piazza	1.50	238	Marcus Jensen	.05	342	Chris Hoiles	.05	443	Bernie Williams, Todd Hundley/IS	.05
135	Carlos Baerga	.05	239	Ed Sprague	.05	343	Mike Lieberthal	.05	444	Chuck Knoblauch, Brian Jordan/IS	.05
136	Jose Mesa	.05	240	Jose Valentin	.05	344	Matt Lawton	.05	445	Mo Vaughn, Jeff Conine/IS	.05
137	Will Clark	.05	241	Jeff Frye	.05	345	Alex Ochoa	.05	446	Ken Caminiti, Jason Giambi/IS	.25
138	Frank Thomas	.75	242	Charles Nagy	.05	346	Chris Snopek	.05	447	Raul Mondesi, Tim Salmon/IS	.05
139	John Wetteland	.05	243	Carlos Garcia	.05	347	Rudy Pemberton	.05	448	Cal Ripken Jr. Checklist	.75
140	Shawn Estes	.05	244	Mike Hampton	.05	348	Eric Owens	.05	449	Greg Maddux Checklist	.60
141	Garret Anderson	.05	245	B.J. Surhoff	.05	349	Joe Randa	.05	450	Ken Griffey Jr. Checklist	.50
142	Andre Dawson	.25	246	Wilton Guerrero	.05	350	John Olerud	.05			
143	Eddie Taubensee	.05	247	Frank Rodriguez	.05	351	Steve Karsay	.05			
144	Ryan Klesko	.05	248	Gary Gaetti	.05	352	Mark Whiten	.05			
145	Rocky Coppinger	.05	249	Lance Johnson	.05	353	Bob Abreu	.10			
146	Jeff Bagwell	.75	250	Darren Bragg	.05	354	Bartolo Colon	.05			
147	Donovan Osborne	.05	251	Darryl Hamilton	.05						
148	Greg Myers	.05	252	John Jaha	.05						
149	Brant Brown	.05	253	Craig Paquette	.05						

Press Proofs

	NM/M
Complete Set (270):	150.00
Common Player:	.50
Stars/Rookies:	5X
Complete Gold Set (270):	350.00
Common Gold Player:	2.00
Gold Stars/Rookies:	10X

(See 1997 Donruss for checklist and base card values.)

Armed and Dangerous

		NM/M
	Complete Set (15):	35.00
	Common Player:	1.00
1	Ken Griffey Jr.	4.00
2	Raul Mondesi	1.00
3	Chipper Jones	3.00
4	Ivan Rodriguez	1.50
5	Randy Johnson	2.00
6	Alex Rodriguez	5.00
7	Larry Walker	1.00
8	Cal Ripken Jr.	6.00
9	Kenny Lofton	1.00
10	Barry Bonds	6.00
11	Derek Jeter	6.00
12	Charles Johnson	1.00
13	Greg Maddux	3.00
14	Roberto Alomar	1.00
15	Barry Larkin	1.00

Diamond Kings

		NM/M
	Complete Set (10):	35.00
	Common Player:	.70
	Canvas (1st 500):	2X
1	Ken Griffey Jr.	6.00
2	Cal Ripken Jr.	9.00
3	Mo Vaughn	.75
4	Chuck Knoblauch	.75
5	Jeff Bagwell	3.00
6	Henry Rodriguez	.75
7	Mike Piazza	6.00
8	Ivan Rodriguez	2.50
9	Frank Thomas	3.00
10	Chipper Jones	4.50

Elite Inserts

		NM/M
	Complete Set (12):	100.00
	Common Player:	3.00
	Promos:	50%
1	Frank Thomas	7.50
2	Paul Molitor	7.50
3	Sammy Sosa	10.00
4	Barry Bonds	20.00
5	Chipper Jones	10.00
6	Alex Rodriguez	15.00
7	Ken Griffey Jr.	12.50

8	Jeff Bagwell	7.50
9	Cal Ripken Jr.	20.00
10	Mo Vaughn	3.00
11	Mike Piazza	12.50
12	Juan Gonzalez	4.50

Frank Thomas The Big Heart

		NM/M
	Complete Set (4):	20.00
	Common Card:	5.00
1	Frank Thomas, Rod Carew	5.00
2	Frank Thomas	5.00
3	Frank Thomas	5.00
4	Frank Thomas	5.00

Jackie Robinson Rookie Reprint

		NM/M
79	Jackie Robinson	10.00

Longball Leaders

		NM/M
	Complete Set (15):	20.00
	Common Player:	.50
1	Frank Thomas	2.00
2	Albert Belle	.50
3	Mo Vaughn	.50
4	Brady Anderson	.50
5	Greg Vaughn	.50

ABBREVIATIONS

RC (RC) - Rookie Card
SP - Short Print

6	Ken Griffey Jr.	3.00
7	Jay Buhner	.50
8	Juan Gonzalez	.75
9	Mike Piazza	3.00
10	Jeff Bagwell	2.00
11	Sammy Sosa	2.50
12	Mark McGwire	4.00
13	Cecil Fielder	.50
14	Ryan Klesko	.50
15	Jose Canseco	.85

Rated Rookies

		NM/M
	Complete Set (30):	10.00
	Common Player:	.50
1	Jason Thompson	.50
2	LaTroy Hawkins	.50
3	Scott Rolen	1.50
4	Trey Beamon	.50
5	Kimera Bartee	.50
6	Nerio Rodriguez	.50
7	Jeff D'Amico	.50
8	Quinton McCracken	.50
9	John Wasdin	.50
10	Robin Jennings	.50
11	Steve Gibralter	.50
12	Tyler Houston	.50
13	Tony Clark	.50
14	Ugueth Urbina	.50
15	Billy McMillon	.50
16	Raul Casanova	.50
17	Brooks Kieschnick	.50
18	Luis Castillo	.50
19	Edgar Renteria	.50
20	Andruw Jones	2.00
21	Chad Mottola	.50
22	Makoto Suzuki	.50
23	Justin Thompson	.50
24	Darin Erstad	1.00
25	Todd Walker	.50
26	Todd Greene	.50
27	Vladimir Guerrero	2.00
28	Darren Dreifort	.50
29	John Burke	.50
30	Damon Mashore	.50

Rocket Launchers

		NM/M
	Complete Set (15):	25.00
	Common Player:	.75
1	Frank Thomas	2.50
2	Albert Belle	.75
3	Chipper Jones	3.00
4	Mike Piazza	4.00
5	Mo Vaughn	.75
6	Juan Gonzalez	1.00
7	Fred McGriff	.75
8	Jeff Bagwell	2.50
9	Matt Williams	.75
10	Gary Sheffield	1.00
11	Barry Bonds	5.00

12	Manny Ramirez	2.00
13	Henry Rodriguez	.75
14	Jason Giambi	1.50
15	Cal Ripken Jr.	5.00

Update Press Proofs

	NM/M
Complete Set (180):	200.00
Common Player:	.50
Stars:	7X
Complete Set, Gold (180):	400.00
Common Player, Gold:	2.00
Gold Stars:	15X

(See 1997 Donruss (#271-450) for checklist, base card values.)

Update Cal Ripken

		NM/M
	Complete Set (10):	75.00
	Common Card:	10.00
1-9	Cal Ripken Jr.	10.00
10	Cal Ripken Jr. (Book insert.)	10.00

Update Dominators

	NM/M
Complete Set (20):	22.50

Common Player: .50
1	Frank Thomas	1.25
2	Ken Griffey Jr.	2.25
3	Greg Maddux	1.50
4	Cal Ripken Jr.	3.00
5	Alex Rodriguez	2.50
6	Albert Belle	.50
7	Mark McGwire	2.50
8	Juan Gonzalez	.65
9	Chipper Jones	1.50
10	Hideo Nomo	.65
11	Roger Clemens	2.00
12	John Smoltz	.50
13	Mike Piazza	2.25
14	Sammy Sosa	1.50
15	Matt Williams	.50
16	Kenny Lofton	.50
17	Barry Larkin	.50
18	Rafael Palmeiro	1.00
19	Ken Caminiti	.50
20	Gary Sheffield	.75

Update Franchise Features

		NM/M
Complete Set (15):		45.00
Common Player:		2.00
1	Ken Griffey Jr., Andruw Jones	4.00
2	Frank Thomas, Darin Erstad	2.50
3	Alex Rodriguez, Nomar Garciaparra	5.00
4	Chuck Knoblauch, Wilton Guerrero	2.00
5	Juan Gonzalez, Bubba Trammell	2.00
6	Chipper Jones, Todd Walker	3.00
7	Barry Bonds, Vladimir Guerrero	6.00
8	Mark McGwire, Dmitri Young	5.00
9	Mike Piazza, Mike Sweeney	4.00
10	Mo Vaughn, Tony Clark	2.00
11	Gary Sheffield, Jose Guillen	2.00
12	Kenny Lofton, Shannon Stewart	2.00
13	Cal Ripken Jr., Scott Rolen	6.00
14	Derek Jeter, Pokey Reese	6.00
15	Tony Gwynn, Bob Abreu	3.00

Update Power Alley

		NM/M
Complete Set (24):		100.00
Common Gold:		7.50
Common Blue:		3.00
Common Green:		1.50
Die-Cuts:		3X
1	Frank Thomas/G	7.50
2	Ken Griffey Jr./G	10.00
3	Cal Ripken Jr./G	15.00
4	Jeff Bagwell/B	5.00
5	Mike Piazza/B	7.50
6	Andruw Jones/GR	3.50
7	Alex Rodriguez/G	12.50
8	Albert Belle/GR	1.50
9	Mo Vaughn/GR	1.50
10	Chipper Jones/B	6.00
11	Juan Gonzalez/B	3.00
12	Ken Caminiti/GR	1.50
13	Manny Ramirez/GR	3.50
14	Mark McGwire/GR	6.00
15	Kenny Lofton/B	3.00
16	Barry Bonds/GR	7.50
17	Gary Sheffield/GR	1.50
18	Tony Gwynn/GR	4.50
19	Vladimir Guerrero/B	5.00
20	Ivan Rodriguez/B	3.50
21	Paul Molitor/B	5.00
22	Sammy Sosa/GR	4.50
23	Matt Williams/GR	1.50
24	Derek Jeter/GR	7.50

Update Rookie Diamond Kings

		NM/M
Complete Set (10):		20.00
Common Player:		1.50
Canvas:		1.5X
1	Andruw Jones	4.00
2	Vladimir Guerrero	10.00
3	Scott Rolen	2.00
4	Todd Walker	1.50
5	Bartolo Colon	2.00
6	Jose Guillen	1.50
7	Nomar Garciaparra	6.00
8	Darin Erstad	2.00
9	Dmitri Young	1.50
10	Wilton Guerrero	1.50

1997 Donruss Elite

		NM/M
Complete Set (150):		10.00
Common Player:		.10
Common Elite Star:		.50
Elite Stars Stars/RC's:		4X
Pack (6):		2.50
Wax Box (18):		35.00
1	Juan Gonzalez	.40
2	Alex Rodriguez	2.00
3	Frank Thomas	.75
4	Greg Maddux	1.00
5	Ken Griffey Jr.	1.50
6	Cal Ripken Jr.	2.50
7	Mike Piazza	1.50
8	Chipper Jones	1.00
9	Albert Belle	.10
10	Andruw Jones	.75
11	Vladimir Guerrero	.75
12	Mo Vaughn	.10
13	Ivan Rodriguez	.65
14	Andy Pettitte	.40
15	Tony Gwynn	1.00
16	Barry Bonds	2.50
17	Jeff Bagwell	.75
18	Manny Ramirez	.75
19	Kenny Lofton	.10
20	Roberto Alomar	.20
21	Mark McGwire	2.00
22	Ryan Klesko	.10
23	Tim Salmon	.10
24	Derek Jeter	2.50
25	Eddie Murray	.75
26	Jermaine Dye	.10
27	Ruben Rivera	.10
28	Jim Edmonds	.10
29	Mike Mussina	.40
30	Randy Johnson	.75
31	Sammy Sosa	1.00
32	Hideo Nomo	.40
33	Chuck Knoblauch	.10
34	Paul Molitor	.75
35	Rafael Palmeiro	.75
36	Brady Anderson	.10
37	Will Clark	.10
38	Craig Biggio	.10
39	Jason Giambi	.50
40	Roger Clemens	1.25
41	Jay Buhner	.10
42	Edgar Martinez	.10
43	Gary Sheffield	.35
44	Fred McGriff	.10
45	Bobby Bonilla	.10
46	Tom Glavine	.25
47	Wade Boggs	1.00
48	Jeff Conine	.10
49	John Smoltz	.10
50	Jim Thome	.60
51	Billy Wagner	.10
52	Jose Canseco	.40
53	Javy Lopez	.10
54	Cecil Fielder	.10
55	Garret Anderson	.10
56	Alex Ochoa	.10
57	Scott Rolen	.60
58	Darin Erstad	.30
59	Rey Ordonez	.10
60	Dante Bichette	.10
61	Joe Carter	.10
62	Moises Alou	.10
63	Jason Isringhausen	.10
64	Karim Garcia	.10
65	Brian Jordan	.10
66	Ruben Sierra	.10
67	Todd Hollandsworth	.10
68	Paul Wilson	.10
69	Ernie Young	.10
70	Ryne Sandberg	1.00
71	Raul Mondesi	.10
72	George Arias	.10
73	Ray Durham	.10
74	Dean Palmer	.10
75	Shawn Green	.30
76	Eric Young	.10
77	Jason Kendall	.10
78	Greg Vaughn	.10
79	Terrell Wade	.10
80	Bill Pulsipher	.10
81	Bobby Higginson	.10
82	Mark Grudzielanek	.10
83	Ken Caminiti	.10
84	Todd Greene	.10
85	Carlos Delgado	.50
86	Mark Grace	.10
87	Rondell White	.10
88	Barry Larkin	.10
89	J.T. Snow	.10
90	Alex Gonzalez	.10
91	Raul Casanova	.10
92	Marc Newfield	.10
93	Jermaine Allensworth	.10
94	John Mabry	.10
95	Kirby Puckett	1.00
96	Travis Fryman	.10
97	Kevin Brown	.15
98	Andres Galarraga	.10
99	Marty Cordova	.10
100	Henry Rodriguez	.10
101	Sterling Hitchcock	.10
102	Trey Beamon	.10
103	Brett Butler	.10
104	Rickey Henderson	.75
105	Tino Martinez	.10
106	Kevin Appier	.10
107	Brian Hunter	.10
108	Eric Karros	.10
109	Andre Dawson	.10
110	Darryl Strawberry	.10
111	James Baldwin	.10
112	Chad Mottola	.10
113	Dave Nilsson	.10
114	Carlos Baerga	.10
115	Chan Ho Park	.10
116	John Jaha	.10
117	Alan Benes	.10
118	Mariano Rivera	.20
119	Ellis Burks	.10
120	Tony Clark	.10
121	Todd Walker	.10
122	Dwight Gooden	.10
123	Ugueth Urbina	.10
124	David Cone	.10
125	Ozzie Smith	1.00
126	Kimera Bartee	.10
127	Rusty Greer	.10
128	Pat Hentgen	.10
129	Charles Johnson	.10
130	Quinton McCracken	.10
131	Troy Percival	.10
132	Shane Reynolds	.10
133	Charles Nagy	.10
134	Tom Goodwin	.10
135	Ron Gant	.10
136	Dan Wilson	.10
137	Matt Williams	.10
138	LaTroy Hawkins	.10
139	Kevin Seitzer	.10
140	Michael Tucker	.10
141	Todd Hundley	.10
142	Alex Fernandez	.10
143	Marquis Grissom	.10
144	Steve Finley	.10
145	Curtis Pride	.10
146	Derek Bell	.10
147	Butch Huskey	.10
148	Dwight Gooden	.10
149	Al Leiter	.10
150	Hideo Nomo	.40

Elite Stars

	NM/M
Complete Set (150):	60.00
Common Player:	1.00

(Star players in the Elite Star parallel issue valued at 4X regular Elites.)

Leather & Lumber

		NM/M
Complete Set (10):		140.00
Common Player:		4.00
1	Ken Griffey Jr.	20.00
2	Alex Rodriguez	25.00
3	Frank Thomas	9.00
4	Chipper Jones	12.50
5	Ivan Rodriguez	7.50
6	Cal Ripken Jr.	35.00
7	Barry Bonds	35.00
8	Chuck Knoblauch	4.00
9	Manny Ramirez	9.00
10	Mark McGwire	25.00

Passing the Torch

		NM/M
Complete Set (12):		110.00
Common Player:		4.50
1	Cal Ripken Jr.	20.00
2	Alex Rodriguez	15.00
3	Cal Ripken Jr., Alex Rodriguez	17.50
4	Kirby Puckett	10.00
5	Andruw Jones	7.50
6	Kirby Puckett, Andruw Jones	7.50
7	Cecil Fielder	4.50
8	Frank Thomas	7.50
9	Cecil Fielder, Frank Thomas	6.00
10	Ozzie Smith	10.00
11	Derek Jeter	20.00
12	Ozzie Smith, Derek Jeter	12.00

Passing the Torch Autographs

		NM/M
	Common Card:	15.00
1	Cal Ripken Jr.	200.00
2	Alex Rodriguez	275.00
3	Cal Ripken Jr., Alex Rodriguez	750.00
4	Kirby Puckett	80.00
5	Andruw Jones	40.00
6	Kirby Puckett, Andruw Jones	140.00
7	Cecil Fielder	45.00
8	Frank Thomas	75.00
9	Cecil Fielder, Frank Thomas	125.00
10	Ozzie Smith	120.00
11	Derek Jeter	160.00
12	Ozzie Smith, Derek Jeter	325.00

Turn of the Century

Scott Rolen

		NM/M
	Complete Set (20):	55.00
	Common Player:	1.00
	Die-Cuts:	3X
	Samples:	1X
1	Alex Rodriguez	10.00
2	Andruw Jones	6.00
3	Chipper Jones	7.50
4	Todd Walker	1.00
5	Scott Rolen	4.00
6	Trey Beamon	1.00
7	Derek Jeter	12.50
8	Darin Erstad	3.00
9	Tony Clark	1.00
10	Todd Walker	1.00
11	Jason Giambi	3.00
12	Justin Thompson	1.00
13	Ernie Young	1.00
14	Jason Kendall	1.00
15	Alex Ochoa	1.00
16	Brooks Kieschnick	1.00
17	Bobby Higginson	1.00
18	Ruben Rivera	1.00
19	Chan Ho Park	1.00
20	Chad Mottola	1.00

1997 Donruss Limited

	NM/M
Complete Set (200):	450.00
Common Counterpart:	.20
Common Double Team:	.75
Common Star Factor:	1.50
Common Unlimited Potential:	1.25
Pack (5):	2.00
Wax Box (24):	45.00

1	Ken Griffey Jr., Rondell White	1.00
2	Greg Maddux, David Cone	.75
3	Gary Sheffield, Moises Alou/DT	1.25
4	Frank Thomas/SF	10.00
5	Cal Ripken Jr., Kevin Orie	2.00
6	Vladimir Guerrero, Barry Bonds/UPT	20.00
7	Eddie Murray, Reggie Jefferson	.60
8	Manny Ramirez, Marquis Grissom/DT	2.50
9	Mike Piazza/SF	15.00
10	Barry Larkin, Rey Ordonez	.20
11	Jeff Bagwell, Eric Karros	.60
12	Chuck Knoblauch, Ray Durham	.20
13	Alex Rodriguez, Edgar Renteria	1.50
14	Matt Williams, Vinny Castilla	.20
15	Todd Hollandsworth, Bob Abreu	.20
16	John Smoltz, Pedro Martinez	.60
17	Jose Canseco, Chili Davis	.40
18	Jose Cruz, Jr., Ken Griffey Jr./UPT	15.00
19	Ken Griffey Jr./SF	15.00
20	Paul Molitor, John Olerud	.60
21	Roberto Alomar, Luis Castillo	.35
22	Derek Jeter, Lou Collier	2.00
23	Chipper Jones, Robin Ventura	.75
24	Gary Sheffield, Ron Gant	.25
25	Ramon Martinez, Bobby Jones	.20
26	Mike Piazza, Raul Mondesi/DT	7.50
27	Darin Erstad, Jeff Bagwell/UPT	7.50
28	Ivan Rodriguez/SF	7.50
29	J.T. Snow, Kevin Young	.20
30	Ryne Sandberg, Julio Franco	.75
31	Travis Fryman, Chris Snopek (Counterparts)	.20
32	Wade Boggs, Russ Davis	.75
33	Brooks Kieschnick, Marty Cordova	.20
34	Andy Pettitte, Denny Neagle	.35
35	Paul Molitor, Matt Lawton/DT	2.50
36	Scott Rolen, Cal Ripken Jr./UPT	20.00
37	Cal Ripken Jr./SF	20.00
38	Jim Thome, Dave Nilsson	.50
39	Tony Womack, Carlos Baerga	.20
40	Nomar Garciaparra, Mark Grudzielanek	.75
41	Todd Greene, Chris Widger	.20
42	Deion Sanders, Bernard Gilkey	.20
43	Hideo Nomo, Charles Nagy	.50
44	Ivan Rodriguez, Rusty Greer/DT	2.00
45	Todd Walker, Chipper Jones/UPT	10.00
46	Greg Maddux/SF	12.00
47	Mo Vaughn, Cecil Fielder	.20
48	Craig Biggio, Scott Spiezio	.20
49	Pokey Reese, Jeff Blauser	.20
50	Ken Caminiti, Joe Randa	.20
51	Albert Belle, Shawn Green (Counterparts)	.20
52	Randy Johnson, Jason Dickson (Counterparts)	.60
53	Hideo Nomo, Chan Ho Park/DT	2.00
54	Scott Spiezio, Chuck Knoblauch/UPT	1.25
55	Chipper Jones/SF	12.00
56	Tino Martinez, Ryan McGuire	.20
57	Eric Young, Wilton Guerrero	.20
58	Ron Coomer, Dave Hollins	.20
59	Sammy Sosa, Angel Echevarria (Counterparts)	.75
60	Dennis Reyes, Jimmy Key (Counterparts)	.20
61	Barry Larkin, Deion Sanders/DT	.75
62	Wilton Guerrero, Roberto Alomar/UPT	2.00
63	Albert Belle/SF	1.50
64	Mark McGwire, Andres Galarraga	1.50
65	Edgar Martinez, Todd Walker	.20
66	Steve Finley, Rich Becker	.20
67	Tom Glavine, Andy Ashby	.30
68	Sammy Sosa, Ryne Sandberg/DT	5.00
69	Nomar Garciaparra, Alex Rodriguez/UPT	15.00
70	Jeff Bagwell/SF	10.00
71	Darin Erstad, Mark Grace	.40
72	Scott Rolen, Edgardo Alfonzo	.50
73	Kenny Lofton, Lance Johnson	.20
74	Joey Hamilton, Brett Tomko	.20
75	Eddie Murray, Tim Salmon/DT	2.50
76	Dmitri Young, Mo Vaughn/UPT	1.25
77	Juan Gonzalez/SF	3.00
78	Frank Thomas, Tony Clark	.60
79	Shannon Stewart, Bip Roberts (Counterparts)	.20
80	Shawn Estes, Alex Fernandez	.20
81	John Smoltz, Javier Lopez/DT	.75
82	Todd Greene, Mike Piazza/UPT	15.00
83	Derek Jeter/SF	20.00
84	Dmitri Young, Antone Williamson	.20
85	Rickey Henderson, Darryl Hamilton	.60
86	Billy Wagner, Dennis Eckersley	.60
87	Larry Walker, Eric Young/DT	.75
88	Mark Kotsay, Juan Gonzalez/UPT	3.00
89	Barry Bonds/SF	20.00
90	Will Clark, Jeff Conine	.20
91	Tony Gwynn, Brett Butler	.75
92	John Wetteland, Rod Beck	.20
93	Bernie Williams, Tino Martinez/DT	1.25
94	Andruw Jones, Kenny Lofton/UPT	7.50
95	Mo Vaughn/SF	1.50
96	Joe Carter, Derrek Lee	.50
97	John Mabry, F.P. Santangelo	.20
98	Esteban Loaiza, Wilson Alvarez	.20
99	Matt Williams, David Justice/DT	.75
100	Derek Lee, Frank Thomas/UPT	7.50
101	Mark McGwire/SF	17.50
102	Fred McGriff, Paul Sorrento	.20
103	Jermaine Allensworth, Bernie Williams	.20
104	Ismael Valdes, Chris Holt	.20
105	Fred McGriff, Ryan Klesko/DT	.75
106	Tony Clark, Mark McGwire/UPT	17.50
107	Tony Gwynn/SF	12.00
108	Jeffrey Hammonds, Ellis Burks	.20
109	Shane Reynolds, Andy Benes	.20
110	Roger Clemens, Carlos Delgado/DT	10.00
111	Karim Garcia, Albert Belle/UPT	1.25
112	Paul Molitor/SF	10.00
113	Trey Beamon, Eric Owens	.20
114	Curt Schilling, Darryl Kile	.30
115	Tom Glavine, Michael Tucker/DT	.75
116	Pokey Reese, Derek Jeter/UPT	20.00
117	Manny Ramirez/SF	10.00
118	Juan Gonzalez, Brant Brown	.40
119	Juan Guzman, Francisco Cordova	.20
120	Randy Johnson, Edgar Martinez/DT	2.50
121	Hideki Irabu, Greg Maddux/UPT	10.00
122	Alex Rodriguez/SF	17.50
123	Barry Bonds, Quinton McCracken	2.00
124	Roger Clemens, Alan Benes	.85
125	Wade Boggs, Paul O'Neill/DT	1.75
126	Mike Cameron, Larry Walker/UPT	1.25
127	Gary Sheffield/SF	2.50
128	Andruw Jones, Raul Mondesi	.60
129	Brian Anderson, Terrell Wade	.20
130	Brady Anderson, Rafael Palmeiro/DT	2.00
131	Neifi Perez, Barry Larkin/UPT	1.25
132	Ken Caminiti/SF	1.50
133	Larry Walker, Rusty Greer	.20
134	Mariano Rivera, Mark Wohlers	.30
135	Hideki Irabu, Andy Pettitte/DT	1.50
136	Jose Guillen, Tony Gwynn/UPT	10.00
137	Hideo Nomo/SF	3.00
138	Vladimir Guerrero, Jim Edmonds	.60
139	Justin Thompson, Dwight Gooden	.20
140	Andres Galarraga, Dante Bichette/DT	.75
141	Kenny Lofton/SF	1.50
142	Tim Salmon, Manny Ramirez	.60
143	Kevin Brown, Matt Morris	.20
144	Craig Biggio, Bob Abreu/DT	.75
145	Roberto Alomar/SF	2.00
146	Jose Guillen, Brian Jordan	.20
147	Bartolo Colon, Kevin Appier	.20
148	Ray Lankford, Brian Jordan/DT	.75
149	Chuck Knoblauch/SF	1.50
150	Henry Rodriguez, Ray Lankford	.20

ABBREVIATIONS

DT - Double Team
SF - Star Factor
UPT - Unlimited Potential/Talent

151 Jaret Wright, Ben McDonald .20
152 Bobby Bonilla, Kevin Brown/DT .75
153 Barry Larkin/SF 1.50
154 David Justice, Reggie Sanders .20
155 Mike Mussina, Ken Hill .40
156 Mark Grace, Brooks Kieschnick/DT .75
157 Jim Thome/SF 2.50
158 Michael Tucker, Curtis Goodwin .20
159 Jeff Suppan, Jeff Fassero .20
160 Mike Mussina, Jeffrey Hammonds/DT 1.00
161 John Smoltz/SF 1.50
162 Moises Alou, Eric Davis .20
163 Sandy Alomar Jr., Dan Wilson .20
164 Rondell White, Henry Rodriguez/DT .75
165 Roger Clemens/SF 12.50
166 Brady Anderson, Al Martin .20
167 Jason Kendall, Charles Johnson .20
168 Jason Giambi, Jose Canseco/DT 2.00
169 Larry Walker/SF 1.50
170 Jay Buhner, Geronimo Berroa .20
171 Ivan Rodriguez, Mike Sweeney .50
172 Kevin Appier, Jose Rosado/DT .75
173 Bernie Williams/SF 1.50
174 Todd Dunwoody, Brian Giles RC .40
175 Javier Lopez, Scott Hatteberg .20
176 John Jaha, Jeff Cirillo/DT .75
177 Andy Pettitte/SF 2.00
178 Dante Bichette, Butch Huskey .20
179 Raul Casanova, Todd Hundley .20
180 Jim Edmonds, Garret Anderson/DT .75
181 Deion Sanders SF 1.50
182 Ryan Klesko, Paul O'Neill .20
183 Joe Carter, Pat Hentgen/DT .75
184 Brady Anderson/SF 1.50
185 Carlos Delgado, Wally Joyner .50
186 Jermaine Dye, Johnny Damon/DT 1.00
187 Randy Johnson/SF 7.50
188 Todd Hundley, Carlos Baerga/DT .75
189 Tom Glavine/SF 2.50
190 Damon Mashore, Jason McDonald/DT .75
191 Wade Boggs/SF 12.00
192 Al Martin, Jason Kendall/DT .75
193 Matt Williams/SF 1.50
194 Will Clark, Dean Palmer/DT .75
195 Sammy Sosa/SF 12.00
196 Jose Cruz, Jr., Jay Buhner/DT .75
197 Eddie Murray/SF 10.00
198 Darin Erstad, Jason Dickson/DT 1.00
199 Fred McGriff/SF 1.50
200 Bubba Trammell, Bobby Higginson/DT .75

Exposure

	NM/M
Common Counterparts:	.75
Common Double Team:	3.00
Common Star Factor:	6.50
Common Unlimited:	4.50
Stars:	4X

(See 1997 Donruss Limited for checklist and base card values.)

Exposure Non-Glossy

	NM/M
Common Non-Glossy:	.50
Stars:	25%

(See 1997 Donruss Limited and Limited Exposure to calculate base card values.)

Fabric of the Game

	NM/M
Complete Set: (69):	275.00
Common Player:	1.50
Complete Canvas Set (23):	80.00
Rickey Henderson/100	12.00
Barry Bonds/250	15.00
Kenny Lofton/250	2.50
Roberto Alomar/250	4.50
Ryne Sandberg/250	12.00
Tony Gwynn/500	7.50
Barry Larkin/500	2.00
Brady Anderson/500	2.00
Chuck Knoblauch /500	2.00
Craig Biggio/500	2.00
Sammy Sosa/750	7.50
Gary Sheffield/750	2.00
Eric Young/750	1.50
Larry Walker/750	1.50
Ken Griffey Jr. /750	10.00
Deion Sanders/750	1.50
Raul Mondesi/1,000	1.50
Rondell White/1,000	1.50
Derek Jeter/1,000	10.00
Nomar Garciaparra/1,000	6.00
Wilton Guerrero/1,000	1.50
Pokey Reese/1,000	1.50
Darin Erstad/1,000	2.00
Complete Leather Set (23):	90.00
Paul Molitor/100	15.00
Wade Boggs/250	12.00
Cal Ripken Jr./250	20.00
Tony Gwynn/250	12.00
Joe Carter/250	2.50
Rafael Palmeiro/500	5.00
Mark Grace/500	1.50
Bobby Bonilla/500	1.50
Andres Galarraga/500	1.50
Edgar Martinez/500	1.50
Ken Caminiti/750	1.50
Ivan Rodriguez/750	4.50
Frank Thomas/750	6.00
Jeff Bagwell/750	6.00
Albert Belle/750	1.50
Bernie Williams/750	1.50
Chipper Jones/1,000	7.50
Rusty Greer/1,000	1.50
Todd Walker/1,000	1.50
Scott Rolen/1,000	3.00
Bob Abreu/1,000	1.50
Jose Guillen/1,000	1.50
Jose Cruz, Jr./1,000	1.50
Complete Wood Set (23):	110.00
Eddie Murray/100	12.00
Cal Ripken Jr./250	20.00
Barry Bonds/250	20.00
Mark McGwire/250	17.50
Fred McGriff/250	3.50
Ken Griffey Jr./500	7.50
Albert Belle/500	2.00
Frank Thomas/500	6.50
Juan Gonzalez/500	5.00
Matt Williams/500	2.00
Mike Piazza/750	7.50
Jeff Bagwell/750	6.00
Mo Vaughn/750	1.50
Gary Sheffield/750	2.00
Tim Salmon/750	1.50
David Justice/750	1.50
Manny Ramirez/1,000	1.50
Jim Thome/1,000	2.50
Tino Martinez/1,000	1.50
Andruw Jones/1,000	3.50
Vladimir Guerrero/1,000	5.00
Tony Clark/1,000	1.50
Dmitri Young/1,000	1.50

1997 Donruss Preferred

	NM/M
Complete Set (200):	225.00
Common Bronze:	.10
Common Silver:	.60
Common Gold:	1.25
Common Platinum:	6.00
Cut to the Chase:	1.5X
Tin Pack (5):	2.50
Tin Box (24):	40.00

1 Frank Thomas/P 7.50
2 Ken Griffey Jr./P 12.50
3 Cecil Fielder/P .10
4 Chuck Knoblauch/B 1.25
5 Garret Anderson/B .10
6 Greg Maddux/P 10.00
7 Matt Williams/S .60
8 Marquis Grissom/S .60
9 Jason Isringhausen/B .10
10 Larry Walker/S .60
11 Charles Nagy/B .10
12 Dan Wilson/B .10
13 Albert Belle/G 1.25
14 Javier Lopez/B .10
15 David Cone/B .10
16 Bernard Gilkey/B .10
17 Andres Galarraga/B .60
18 Bill Pulsipher/B .10
19 Alex Fernandez/B .10
20 Andy Pettitte/B 1.25
21 Mark Grudzielanek/B .10
22 Juan Gonzalez/P 6.00
23 Reggie Sanders/B .10
24 Kenny Lofton/B 1.25
25 Andy Ashby/B .10
26 John Wetteland/B .10
27 Bobby Bonilla/B .10
28 Hideo Nomo/G 2.50
29 Joe Carter/B .10
30 Jose Canseco/B .40
31 Ellis Burks/B .10
32 Edgar Martinez/B .60
33 Chan Ho Park/B .10
34 David Justice/B .10
35 Carlos Delgado/B .50
36 Jeff Cirillo/S .60
37 Charles Johnson/B .10
38 Manny Ramirez/G 4.50
39 Greg Vaughn/B .10
40 Henry Rodriguez/B .10
41 Darryl Strawberry/B .10
42 Jim Thome/B 2.50
43 Ryan Klesko/B .10
44 Jermaine Allensworth/B .10
45 Brian Jordan/B 1.25
46 Tony Gwynn/G 10.00
47 Rafael Palmeiro/S 3.50
48 Dante Bichette/S .60
49 Ivan Rodriguez/S 3.50
50 Mark McGwire/G 8.00
51 Tim Salmon/B .60
52 Roger Clemens/S 1.50
53 Matt Lawton/B .10
54 Wade Boggs/S 3.50
55 Travis Fryman/B .10
56 Bobby Higginson/B .60
57 John Jaha/B .60
58 Rondell White/B .60
59 Tom Glavine/B 1.25
60 Eddie Murray/S 2.50
61 Vinny Castilla/B .10
62 Todd Hundley/B .60
63 Jay Buhner/B .60
64 Paul O'Neill/B .10
65 Steve Finley/B .10
66 Kevin Appier/B .10
67 Ray Durham/B .10
68 Dave Nilsson/B .10
69 Jeff Bagwell/G 4.50
70 Al Martin/S .60
71 Paul Molitor/G 4.50
72 Kevin Brown/S .60
73 Ron Gant/B .10
74 Dwight Gooden/B .10
75 Quinton McCracken/B .10
76 Rusty Greer/S .60
77 Juan Guzman/B .10
78 Fred McGriff/S .60
79 Tino Martinez/B .10
80 Ray Lankford/B .10
81 Ken Caminiti/G 1.25
82 James Baldwin/B .10
83 Jermaine Dye/G 1.25
84 Mark Grace/S .60
85 Pat Hentgen/S .60
86 Jason Giambi/S 1.50
87 Brian Hunter/B .10
88 Andy Benes/B .10
89 Jose Rosado/B .10
90 Shawn Green/B .25
91 Jason Kendall/B .10
92 Alex Rodriguez/P 15.00
93 Chipper Jones/P 10.00
94 Barry Bonds/G 10.00
95 Brady Anderson/G 1.25
96 Ryne Sandberg/S 3.50
97 Lance Johnson/B .10
98 Cal Ripken Jr./P 17.50
99 Craig Biggio/S .60
100 Dean Palmer/B .10
101 Gary Sheffield/G 1.50
102 Johnny Damon/B .35
103 Mo Vaughn/B 1.25
104 Randy Johnson/S 2.50
105 Raul Mondesi/S .60
106 Roberto Alomar/S 2.00
107 Mike Piazza/S 12.50
108 Rey Ordonez/B .10
109 Barry Larkin/G 1.25
110 Tony Clark/S .60
111 Bernie Williams/S .60
112 John Smoltz/G 1.25
113 Moises Alou/B .10
114 Will Clark/B .10
115 Sammy Sosa/G 6.00
116 Jim Edmonds/S .60
117 Jeff Conine/B .10
118 Joey Hamilton/B .10
119 Todd Hollandsworth/B .10
120 Troy Percival/B .10
121 Paul Wilson/B .10
122 Ken Hill/B .10
123 Mariano Rivera/S .75
124 Eric Karros/B .10
125 Derek Jeter/G 10.00
126 Eric Young/B .60
127 John Mabry/B .10
128 Gregg Jefferies/B .10
129 Ismael Valdes/S .60
130 Marty Cordova/B .10
131 Omar Vizquel/B .10
132 Mike Mussina/B 1.25
133 Darin Erstad/B .30
134 Edgar Renteria/B .60
135 Billy Wagner/B .10
136 Alex Ochoa/B .10
137 Luis Castillo/B .10
138 Rocky Coppinger/B .10
139 Mike Sweeney/B .10
140 Michael Tucker/B .10
141 Chris Snopek/B .10
142 Dmitri Young/B .10
143 Andruw Jones/P 7.50
144 Mike Cameron/S .60
145 Brant Brown/B .10
146 Todd Walker/B 1.25
147 Nomar Garciaparra/P 6.00
148 Glendon Rusch/B .10
149 Karim Garcia/S .60
150 Bubba Trammell/S RC .60
151 Todd Greene/B .10
152 Wilton Guerrero/G 1.25
153 Scott Spiezio/B .10
154 Brooks Kieschnick/B .10
155 Vladimir Guerrero/G 4.50
156 Brian Giles/S RC 1.50
157 Pokey Reese/B .10
158 Jason Dickson/G 1.25
159 Kevin Orie/S .60
160 Scott Rolen/B 3.00
161 Bartolo Colon/S .60
162 Shannon Stewart/B 1.25
163 Wendell Magee/B .10
164 Jose Guillen/B .60
165 Bob Abreu/B .60
166 Deivi Cruz/B RC .60
167 Alex Rodriguez/B 3.00
168 Frank Thomas/B .75
169 Cal Ripken Jr./B 4.00
170 Chipper Jones/B 1.25
171 Mike Piazza/B 2.50

172	Tony Gwynn/S	3.50
173	Juan Gonzalez/B	.40
174	Kenny Lofton/S	.60
175	Ken Griffey Jr./B	2.50
176	Mark McGwire/B	3.00
177	Jeff Bagwell/B	.75
178	Paul Molitor/S	2.50
179	Andruw Jones/B	.75
180	Manny Ramirez/S	2.50
181	Ken Caminiti/B	.60
182	Barry Bonds/B	4.00
183	Mo Vaughn/B	.10
184	Derek Jeter/B	4.00
185	Barry Larkin/S	.60
186	Ivan Rodriguez/B	.65
187	Albert Belle/S	.60
188	John Smoltz/S	.60
189	Chuck Knoblauch/S	.60
190	Brian Jordan/S	.60
191	Gary Sheffield/S	1.00
192	Jim Thome/S	2.00
193	Brady Anderson/S	.60
194	Hideo Nomo/S	1.50
195	Sammy Sosa/S	3.50
196	Greg Maddux/B	1.25
197	Vladimir Guerrero/B Checklist	.40
198	Scott Rolen/B Checklist	.15
199	Todd Walker/B Checklist	.10
200	Nomar Garciaparra/B Checklist	.60

Cut To The Chase

Typical Value: 1.5X
(See 1997 Donruss Preferred for checklist and base card values.)

Precious Metals

		NM/M
	Common Player:	7.50
1	Frank Thomas/P	45.00
2	Ken Griffey Jr./P	75.00
3	Greg Maddux/P	60.00
4	Albert Belle/G	7.50
5	Juan Gonzalez/P	25.00
6	Kenny Lofton/G	7.50
7	Tony Gwynn/P	60.00
8	Ivan Rodriguez/P	30.00
9	Mark McGwire/G	90.00
10	Matt Williams/G	7.50
11	Wade Boggs/S	60.00
12	Eddie Murray/G	45.00
13	Jeff Bagwell/G	45.00
14	Ken Caminiti/G	7.50
15	Alex Rodriguez/P	90.00
16	Chipper Jones/G	60.00
17	Barry Bonds/G	125.00
18	Cal Ripken Jr./P	125.00
19	Mo Vaughn/G	7.50
20	Mike Piazza/P	75.00
21	Derek Jeter/G	125.00

22	Bernie Williams/S	7.50
23	Andruw Jones/P	45.00
24	Vladimir Guerrero/G	45.00
25	Jose Guillen/S	7.50

Staremasters

		NM/M
	Complete Set (20):	55.00
	Common Player:	1.00
	Samples:	50%
1	Alex Rodriguez	6.00
2	Frank Thomas	3.00
3	Chipper Jones	4.00
4	Cal Ripken Jr.	7.50
5	Mike Piazza	4.50
6	Juan Gonzalez	2.25
7	Derek Jeter	7.50
8	Jeff Bagwell	3.00
9	Ken Griffey Jr.	4.50
10	Tony Gwynn	4.00
11	Barry Bonds	7.50
12	Albert Belle	1.00
13	Greg Maddux	4.00
14	Mark McGwire	6.00
15	Ken Caminiti	1.00
16	Hideo Nomo	2.25
17	Gary Sheffield	1.50
18	Andruw Jones	3.00
19	Mo Vaughn	1.00
20	Ivan Rodriguez	2.25

X-Ponential Power

		NM/M
	Complete Set (20):	50.00
	Common Player:	1.00
1A	Manny Ramirez	3.50
1B	Jim Thome	2.00
2A	Paul Molitor	3.50
2B	Chuck Knoblauch	1.00
3A	Ivan Rodriguez	2.50
3B	Juan Gonzalez	2.00
4A	Albert Belle	1.00
4B	Frank Thomas	3.50
5A	Roberto Alomar	1.25
5B	Cal Ripken Jr.	9.00
6A	Tim Salmon	1.00
6B	Jim Edmonds	1.00
7A	Ken Griffey Jr.	6.00
7B	Alex Rodriguez	7.50
8A	Chipper Jones	4.50
8B	Andruw Jones	3.50
9A	Mike Piazza	6.00
9B	Raul Mondesi	1.00
10A	Tony Gwynn	4.50
10B	Ken Caminiti	1.00

1997 Donruss Signature

	NM/M
Complete Set (100):	15.00
Common Player:	.10

Michael Tucker - Braves

Platinum Stars/RC's:		12X
Pack (5):		7.50
Wax Box (12):		80.00
1	Mark McGwire	1.25
2	Kenny Lofton	.10
3	Tony Gwynn	.75
4	Tony Clark	.10
5	Tim Salmon	.10
6	Ken Griffey Jr.	1.00
7	Mike Piazza	1.00
8	Greg Maddux	.75
9	Roberto Alomar	.20
10	Andres Galarraga	.10
11	Roger Clemens	.90
12	Bernie Williams	.10
13	Rondell White	.10
14	Kevin Appier	.10
15	Ray Lankford	.10
16	Frank Thomas	.65
17	Will Clark	.10
18	Chipper Jones	.75
19	Jeff Bagwell	.65
20	Manny Ramirez	.65
21	Ryne Sandberg	.75
22	Paul Molitor	.65
23	Gary Sheffield	.10
24	Jim Edmonds	.10
25	Barry Larkin	.10
26	Rafael Palmeiro	.60
27	Alan Benes	.10
28	David Justice	.10
29	Randy Johnson	.65
30	Barry Bonds	1.50
31	Mo Vaughn	.10
32	Michael Tucker	.10
33	Larry Walker	.10
34	Tino Martinez	.10
35	Jose Guillen	.10
36	Carlos Delgado	.40
37	Jason Dickson	.10
38	Tom Glavine	.25
39	Raul Mondesi	.10
40	Jose Cruz Jr. RC	.50
41	Johnny Damon	.20
42	Mark Grace	.10
43	Juan Gonzalez	.35
44	Vladimir Guerrero	.65
45	Kevin Brown	.10
46	Justin Thompson	.10
47	Eric Young	.10
48	Ron Coomer	.10
49	Mark Kotsay	.10
50	Scott Rolen	.60
51	Derek Jeter	1.50
52	Jim Thome	.50
53	Fred McGriff	.10
54	Albert Belle	.10
55	Garret Anderson	.10
56	Wilton Guerrero	.10
57	Jose Canseco	.40
58	Cal Ripken Jr.	1.50
59	Sammy Sosa	.75
60	Dmitri Young	.10
61	Alex Rodriguez	1.25
62	Javier Lopez	.10
63	Sandy Alomar Jr.	.10
64	Joe Carter	.10
65	Dante Bichette	.10
66	Al Martin	.10
67	Darin Erstad	.30
68	Pokey Reese	.10
69	Brady Anderson	.10
70	Andruw Jones	.65
71	Ivan Rodriguez	.50
72	Nomar Garciaparra	.75
73	Moises Alou	.10
74	Andy Pettitte	.35
75	Jay Buhner	.10
76	Craig Biggio	.10
77	Wade Boggs	.75
78	Shawn Estes	.10
79	Neifi Perez	.10
80	Rusty Greer	.10
81	Pedro Martinez	.60
82	Mike Mussina	.40

83	Jason Giambi	.40
84	Hideo Nomo	.35
85	Todd Hundley	.10
86	Deion Sanders	.10
87	Mike Cameron	.10
88	Bobby Bonilla	.10
89	Todd Greene	.10
90	Kevin Orie	.10
91	Ken Caminiti	.10
92	Chuck Knoblauch	.10
93	Matt Morris	.10
94	Matt Williams	.10
95	Pat Hentgen	.10
96	John Smoltz	.10
97	Edgar Martinez	.10
98	Jason Kendall	.10
99	Ken Griffey Jr. Checklist	.50
100	Frank Thomas Checklist	.30

Platinum Press Proofs

	NM/M
Common Player:	2.00
Stars:	12X

(See 1997 Donruss Signature for checklist and base card prices.)

Autographs (Red)

		NM/M
	Complete Set (116):	700.00
	Common Player:	2.00
(1)	Jeff Abbott/3,900	2.00
(2)	Bob Abreu/3,900	8.00
(3)	Edgardo Alfonzo/3,900	3.00
(4)	Roberto Alomar/150	50.00
(5)	Sandy Alomar Jr./1,400	6.00
(6)	Moises Alou/3,900	10.00
(7)	Garret Anderson/3,900	7.00
(8)	Andy Ashby/3,900	3.00
(10)	Trey Beamon/3,900	2.00
(12)	Alan Benes/3,900	2.00
(13)	Geronimo Berroa/3,900	2.00
(14)	Wade Boggs/150	175.00
(18)	Kevin L. Brown/3,900	2.00
(20)	Brett Butler/1,400	3.50
(21)	Mike Cameron/3,900	7.00
(22)	Giovanni Carrara/2,900	2.00
(23)	Luis Castillo/3,900	4.00
(24)	Tony Clark/3,900	3.00
(25)	Will Clark/1,400	12.00
(27)	Lou Collier/3,900	2.00
(28)	Bartolo Colon/3,900	12.50
(29)	Ron Coomer/3,900	2.00
(30)	Marty Cordova/3,900	3.00
(31)	Jacob Cruz/3,900	2.00
(32)	Jose Cruz Jr./900	8.00

(33) Russ Davis/3,900 3.00
(34) Jason Dickson/3,900 2.00
(35) Todd Dunwoody/3,900 2.00
(36) Jermaine Dye/3,900 3.00
(37) Jim Edmonds/3,900 12.00
(38) Darin Erstad/900 8.00
(39) Bobby Estalella/3,900 3.00
(40) Shawn Estes/3,900 3.00
(41) Jeff Fassero/3,900 2.00
(42) Andres Galarraga/900 6.00
(43) Karim Garcia/3,900 3.00
(45) Derrick Gibson/3,900 2.00
(46) Brian Giles/3,900 8.00
(47) Tom Glavine/150 50.00
(49) Rick Gorecki/900 4.50
(50) Shawn Green/1,900 15.00
(51) Todd Greene/3,900 3.00
(52) Rusty Greer/3,900 3.00
(53) Ben Grieve/3,900 3.00
(54) Mark Grudzielanek/3,900 3.00
(55) Vladimir Guerrero/1,900 20.00
(56) Wilton Guerrero/2,150 3.00
(57) Jose Guillen/2,900 8.00
(59) Jeffrey Hammonds/2,150 3.50
(60) Todd Helton/1,400 16.00
(61) Todd Hollandsworth/2,900 9.00
(62) Trenidad Hubbard/900 4.00
(63) Todd Hundley/1,400 3.00
(66) Bobby Jones/3,900 2.00
(68) Brian Jordan/1,400 4.00
(69) David Justice/900 10.00
(70) Eric Karros/650 4.50
(71) Jason Kendall/3,900 6.00
(72) Jimmy Key/3,900 5.00
(73) Brooks Kieschnick/3,900 2.00
(74) Ryan Klesko/225 10.00
(76) Paul Konerko/3,900 10.00
(77) Mark Kotsay/2,400 3.00
(78) Ray Lankford/3,900 4.00
(79) Barry Larkin/150 35.00
(80) Derrek Lee/3,900 10.00
(81) Esteban Loaiza/3,900 3.00
(82) Javier Lopez/1,400 10.00
(84) Edgar Martinez/150 50.00
(85) Pedro Martinez/900 35.00
(87) Rafael Medina/3,900 2.00
(88) Raul Mondesi (Exchange Card) 3.00
(89) Matt Morris/3,900 10.00
(92) Paul O'Neill/900 15.00
(93) Kevin Orie/3,900 2.00
(94) David Ortiz/3,900 50.00
(95) Rafael Palmeiro/900 30.00
(96) Jay Payton/3,900 2.50
(97) Neifi Perez/3,900 9.00
(99) Manny Ramirez/900 40.00
(100) Joe Randa/3,900 2.00
(101) Calvin Reese/3,900 3.00
(102) Edgar Renteria (?) 20.00
(102) Edgar Renteria (Exchange card) 20.00
(103) Dennis Reyes/3,900 2.00
(106) Henry Rodriguez/3,900 2.00
(108) Scott Rolen/1,900 25.00
(109) Kirk Rueter/2,900 3.00
(110) Ryne Sandberg/400 60.00
(112) Dwight Smith/2,900 3.00
(113) J.T. Snow/900 4.00
(114) Scott Spiezio/2,900 2.00
(115) Shannon Stewart/2,900 3.00
(116) Jeff Suppan/1,900 3.00
(117) Mike Sweeney/3,900 6.00
(118) Miguel Tejada/3,900 25.00
(121) Justin Thompson/2,400 3.00
(122) Brett Tomko/3,900 3.00
(123) Bubba Trammell/3,900 2.50
(124) Michael Tucker/3,900 2.00
(125) Javier Valentin/3,900 2.00
(126) Mo Vaughn/150 12.00
(127) Robin Ventura/1,400 8.00
(128) Terrell Wade/3,900 2.00
(129) Billy Wagner/3,900 12.00
(130) Larry Walker/3,900 25.00
(131) Todd Walker/2,400 3.00
(132) Rondell White/3,900 6.00
(133) Kevin Wickander/900 4.00
(134) Chris Widger/3,900 2.00
(136) Matt Williams/150 25.00
(137) Antone Williamson/3,900 2.00

(138) Dan Wilson/3,900 2.00
(139) Tony Womack/3,900 5.00
(140) Jaret Wright/3,900 12.00
(141) Dmitri Young/3,900 8.00
(142) Eric Young/3,900 2.50
(143) Kevin Young/3,900 2.50

Autographs Promo

NM/M
Frank Thomas 6.00

Century Marks (Blue)

NM/M
Common Player: 20.00
(1) Jeff Abbott 20.00
(2) Bob Abreu 30.00
(3) Edgardo Alfonzo 20.00
(4) Roberto Alomar 75.00
(5) Sandy Alomar Jr. 25.00
(6) Moises Alou 35.00
(7) Garret Anderson 60.00
(8) Andy Ashby 20.00
(9) Jeff Bagwell 80.00
(10) Trey Beamon 20.00
(11) Albert Belle 30.00
(12) Alan Benes 20.00
(13) Geronimo Berroa 20.00
(14) Wade Boggs 100.00
(15) Barry Bonds 300.00
(16) Bobby Bonilla 20.00
(17) Kevin Brown 75.00
(18) Kevin L. Brown 20.00
(19) Jay Buhner 30.00
(20) Brett Butler 30.00
(21) Mike Cameron 25.00
(22) Giovanni Carrara 20.00
(23) Luis Castillo 20.00
(24) Tony Clark 20.00
(25) Will Clark 100.00
(26) Roger Clemens 200.00
(27) Lou Collier 20.00
(28) Bartolo Colon 30.00
(29) Ron Coomer 20.00
(30) Marty Cordova 20.00
(31) Jacob Cruz 20.00
(32) Jose Cruz Jr. 30.00
(33) Russ Davis 20.00
(34) Jason Dickson 25.00
(35) Todd Dunwoody 25.00
(36) Jermaine Dye 20.00
(37) Jim Edmonds 60.00
(38) Darin Erstad 40.00
(39) Bobby Estalella 20.00
(40) Shawn Estes 20.00
(41) Jeff Fassero 20.00
(42) Andres Galarraga 30.00
(43) Karim Garcia 20.00
(44) Nomar Garciaparra SP/62 225.00
(45) Derrick Gibson 20.00
(46) Brian Giles 30.00

(47) Tom Glavine 100.00
(48) Juan Gonzalez 55.00
(49) Rick Gorecki 20.00
(50) Shawn Green 90.00
(51) Todd Greene 20.00
(52) Rusty Greer 20.00
(53) Ben Grieve 20.00
(54) Mark Grudzielanek 20.00
(55) Vladimir Guerrero 100.00
(56) Wilton Guerrero 20.00
(57) Jose Guillen 30.00
(58) Tony Gwynn 95.00
(59) Jeffrey Hammonds 20.00
(60) Todd Helton 60.00
(61) Todd Hollandsworth 20.00
(62) Trenidad Hubbard 20.00
(63) Todd Hundley 25.00
(64) Derek Jeter 200.00
(65) Andruw Jones 50.00
(66) Bobby Jones 20.00
(67) Chipper Jones 100.00
(68) Brian Jordan 35.00
(69) David Justice 30.00
(70) Eric Karros 25.00
(71) Jason Kendall 30.00
(72) Jimmy Key 50.00
(73) Brooks Kieschnick 25.00
(74) Ryan Klesko 25.00
(75) Chuck Knoblauch 20.00
(76) Paul Konerko 25.00
(77) Mark Kotsay 25.00
(78) Ray Lankford 20.00
(79) Barry Larkin 60.00
(80) Derrek Lee 40.00
(81) Esteban Loaiza 20.00
(82) Javy Lopez 45.00
(83) Greg Maddux 175.00
(84) Edgar Martinez 50.00
(85) Pedro Martinez 100.00
(86) Tino Martinez 50.00
(87) Rafael Medina 20.00
(88) Raul Mondesi 35.00
(88) Raul Mondesi (Exchange card.) 5.00
(89) Matt Morris 40.00
(90) Eddie Murray 75.00
(91) Mike Mussina 80.00
(92) Paul O'Neill 40.00
(93) Kevin Orie 20.00
(94) David Ortiz 100.00
(95) Rafael Palmeiro 80.00
(96) Jay Payton 20.00
(97) Neifi Perez 20.00
(98) Andy Petitte 50.00
(99) Manny Ramirez 100.00
(100) Joe Randa 20.00
(101) Calvin Reese 20.00
(102) Edgar Renteria 50.00
(102) Edgar Renteria (Exchange card.) 5.00
(103) Dennis Reyes 20.00
(104) Cal Ripken Jr. 225.00
(105) Alex Rodriguez 180.00
(106) Henry Rodriguez 20.00
(107) Ivan Rodriguez 75.00
(108) Scott Rolen 75.00
(109) Kirk Rueter 20.00
(110) Ryne Sandberg 125.00
(111) Gary Sheffield 50.00
(112) Dwight Smith 20.00
(113) J.T. Snow 25.00
(114) Scott Spiezio 20.00
(115) Shannon Stewart 25.00
(116) Jeff Suppan 20.00
(117) Mike Sweeney 25.00
(118) Miguel Tejada 120.00
(119) Frank Thomas 80.00
(120) Jim Thome 75.00
(120) Jim Thome (Exchange card.) 5.00
(121) Justin Thompson 20.00
(122) Brett Tomko 20.00
(123) Bubba Trammell 20.00
(124) Michael Tucker 20.00
(125) Javier Valentin 20.00
(126) Mo Vaughn 25.00
(127) Robin Ventura 30.00
(128) Terrell Wade 20.00
(129) Billy Wagner 40.00
(130) Larry Walker 80.00
(131) Todd Walker 25.00
(132) Rondell White 25.00
(133) Kevin Wickander 20.00
(134) Chris Widger 20.00
(135) Bernie Williams 75.00
(136) Matt Williams 30.00
(137) Antone Williamson 20.00
(138) Dan Wilson 20.00
(139) Tony Womack 25.00
(140) Jaret Wright 35.00
(141) Dmitri Young 30.00
(142) Eric Young 30.00
(143) Kevin Young 20.00

Millennium Marks (Green)

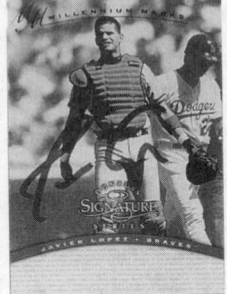

NM/M
Complete Set (143): 1,450
Common Player: 2.00
(1) Jeff Abbott 2.00
(2) Bob Abreu 8.00
(3) Edgardo Alfonzo 5.00
(4) Roberto Alomar 20.00
(5) Sandy Alomar Jr. 8.00
(6) Moises Alou 15.00
(7) Garret Anderson 10.00
(8) Andy Ashby 5.00
(9) Jeff Bagwell/400 75.00
(10) Trey Beamon 2.00
(11) Albert Belle/400 12.50
(12) Alan Benes 2.00
(13) Geronimo Berroa 2.00
(14) Wade Boggs 30.00
(15) Barry Bonds/400 200.00
(16) Bobby Bonilla/900 7.50
(17) Kevin Brown/900 20.00
(18) Kevin L. Brown 10.00
(19) Jay Buhner/900 10.00
(20) Brett Butler 6.00
(21) Mike Cameron 4.00
(22) Giovanni Carrara 2.00
(23) Luis Castillo 5.00
(24) Tony Clark 5.00
(25) Will Clark 12.00
(26) Roger Clemens/400 120.00
(27) Lou Collier 2.00
(28) Bartolo Colon 8.00
(29) Ron Coomer 2.00
(30) Marty Cordova 2.00
(31) Jacob Cruz 2.00
(32) Jose Cruz Jr. 6.00
(33) Russ Davis 2.00
(34) Jason Dickson 5.00
(35) Todd Dunwoody 5.00
(36) Jermaine Dye 5.00
(37) Jim Edmonds 30.00
(38) Darin Erstad 10.00
(39) Bobby Estalella 3.00
(40) Shawn Estes 2.00
(41) Jeff Fassero 4.00
(42) Andres Galarraga 10.00
(43) Karim Garcia 3.50
(44) Nomar Garciaparra/650 75.00
(45) Derrick Gibson 4.00
(46) Brian Giles 8.00
(47) Tom Glavine 25.00
(48) Juan Gonzalez/900 25.00
(49) Rick Gorecki 2.00
(50) Shawn Green 20.00
(51) Todd Greene 7.50
(52) Rusty Greer 7.50
(53) Ben Grieve 5.00
(54) Mark Grudzielanek 2.00
(55) Vladimir Guerrero 25.00
(56) Wilton Guerrero 2.00
(57) Jose Guillen 6.00
(58) Tony Gwynn/900 30.00
(59) Jeffrey Hammonds 2.00
(60) Todd Helton 30.00
(61) Todd Hollandsworth 2.00
(62) Trenidad Hubbard 2.00
(63) Todd Hundley 6.00
(64) Derek Jeter/400 100.00
(65) Andruw Jones/900 15.00
(66) Bobby Jones 2.00
(67) Chipper Jones 30.00
(68) Brian Jordan 7.50
(69) David Justice 10.00
(70) Eric Karros 6.00
(71) Jason Kendall 8.00
(72) Jimmy Key 2.00
(73) Brooks Kieschnick 4.00
(74) Ryan Klesko 5.00
(75) Chuck Knoblauch/900 5.00

		NM/M
(76)	Paul Konerko	5.00
(77)	Mark Kotsay	6.00
(78)	Ray Lankford	2.00
(79)	Barry Larkin	30.00
(80)	Derrek Lee	20.00
(81)	Esteban Loaiza	2.00
(82)	Javy Lopez	8.00
(83)	Greg Maddux/400	80.00
(84)	Edgar Martinez	25.00
(85)	Pedro Martinez	40.00
(86)	Tino Martinez/900	15.00
(87)	Rafael Medina	2.00
(88)	Raul Mondesi	10.00
(88)	Raul Mondesi (Exchange card.)	2.00
(89)	Matt Morris	15.00
(90)	Eddie Murray/900	27.50
(91)	Mike Mussina/900	20.00
(92)	Paul O'Neill	12.50
(93)	Kevin Orie	2.00
(94)	David Ortiz	40.00
(95)	Rafael Palmeiro	30.00
(96)	Jay Payton	5.00
(97)	Neifi Perez	2.00
(98)	Andy Petitte/900	25.00
(99)	Manny Ramirez	30.00
(100)	Joe Randa	2.00
(101)	Calvin Reese	2.00
(102)	Edgar Renteria	30.00
(102)	Edgar Renteria (Exchange card.)	2.00
(103)	Dennis Reyes	3.00
(104)	Cal Ripken Jr./400	135.00
(105)	Alex Rodriguez/400	100.00
(106)	Henry Rodriguez	3.00
(107)	Ivan Rodriguez/200	20.00
(108)	Scott Rolen	25.00
(109)	Kirk Rueter	2.00
(110)	Ryne Sandberg	40.00
(111)	Gary Sheffield/400	25.00
(112)	Dwight Smith	2.00
(113)	J.T. Snow	7.50
(114)	Scott Spiezio	5.00
(115)	Shannon Stewart	2.00
(116)	Jeff Suppan	2.00
(117)	Mike Sweeney	5.00
(118)	Miguel Tejada	40.00
(119)	Frank Thomas/400	50.00
(120)	Jim Thome/900	30.00
(120)	Jim Thome (Exchange card.)	2.00
(121)	Justin Thompson	2.00
(122)	Brett Tomko	2.00
(123)	Bubba Trammell	4.00
(124)	Michael Tucker	2.00
(125)	Javier Valentin	2.00
(126)	Mo Vaughn	8.00
(127)	Robin Ventura	8.00
(128)	Terrell Wade	2.00
(129)	Billy Wagner	10.00
(130)	Larry Walker	20.00
(131)	Todd Walker	6.00
(132)	Rondell White	6.00
(133)	Kevin Wickander	2.00
(134)	Chris Widger	2.00
(135)	Bernie Williams/400	60.00
(136)	Matt Williams	10.00
(137)	Antone Williamson	2.00
(138)	Dan Wilson	2.00
(139)	Tony Womack	2.00
(140)	Jaret Wright	15.00
(141)	Dmitri Young	5.00
(142)	Eric Young	5.00
(143)	Kevin Young	2.00

Notable Nicknames

		NM/M
Common Player:		20.00
(1)	Ernie Banks (Mr. Cub)	150.00
(2)	Tony Clark (The Tiger)	20.00

(3)	Roger Clemens (The Rocket)	300.00
(4)	Reggie Jackson (Mr. October)	125.00
(5)	Randy Johnson (Big Unit)	300.00
(6)	Stan Musial (The Man)	180.00
(7)	Ivan Rodriguez (Pudge)	100.00
(8)	Frank Thomas (The Big Hurt)	125.00
(9)	Mo Vaughn (Hit Dog)	20.00
(10)	Billy Wagner (The Kid)	40.00

Significant Signatures

		NM/M
Common Player:		15.00
(1)	Ernie Banks	25.00
(2)	Johnny Bench	30.00
(3)	Yogi Berra	30.00
(4)	George Brett	40.00
(5)	Lou Brock	25.00
(6)	Rod Carew	25.00
(7)	Steve Carlton	20.00
(8)	Larry Doby	35.00
(9)	Carlton Fisk	30.00
(10)	Bob Gibson	25.00
(11)	Reggie Jackson	25.00
(12)	Al Kaline	25.00
(13)	Harmon Killebrew	30.00
(14)	Don Mattingly	40.00
(15)	Stan Musial	45.00
(16)	Jim Palmer	15.00
(17)	Brooks Robinson	30.00
(18)	Frank Robinson	15.00
(19)	Mike Schmidt	35.00
(20)	Tom Seaver	30.00
(21)	Duke Snider	20.00
(22)	Carl Yastrzemski	40.00

1997 Donruss Team Sets

		NM/M
Comp. Angels Set (1-15):		1.25
Comp. Braves Set (16-30):		3.00
Comp. Orioles Set (31-45):		2.50
Comp. Red Sox Set (46-60):		1.50
Comp. White Sox Set (61-75):		2.00
Comp. Indians Set (76-90):		1.50
Comp. Rockies Set (91-105):		1.50
Comp. Dodgers Set (106-120):		2.25
Comp. Yankees Set (121-135):		4.50
Comp. Mariners Set (136-150):		4.50
Comp. Cardinals Set (151-165):		2.00
Common Player:		.05
Pennant Edition Stars:		3X
1	Jim Edmonds	.05
2	Tim Salmon	.05
3	Tony Phillips	.05
4	Garret Anderson	.05
5	Troy Percival	.05
6	Mark Langston	.05
7	Chuck Finley	.05
8	Eddie Murray	.75
9	Jim Leyritz	.05
10	Darin Erstad	.30
11	Jason Dickson	.05
12	Allen Watson	.05
13	Shigetosi Hasegawa	.05
14	Dave Hollins	.05
15	Gary DiSarcina	.05
16	Greg Maddux	1.00
17	Denny Neagle	.05
18	Chipper Jones	1.00
19	Tom Glavine	.25
20	John Smoltz	.05
21	Ryan Klesko	.05
22	Fred McGriff	.05
23	Michael Tucker	.05
24	Kenny Lofton	.05
25	Javier Lopez	.05
26	Mark Wohlers	.05
27	Jeff Blauser	.05
28	Andruw Jones	.75
29	Tony Graffanino	.05
30	Terrell Wade	.05
31	Brady Anderson	.05
32	Roberto Alomar	.15
33	Rafael Palmeiro	.65
34	Mike Mussina	.35
35	Cal Ripken Jr.	2.00
36	Rocky Coppinger	.05
37	Randy Myers	.05
38	B.J. Surhoff	.05
39	Eric Davis	.05
40	Armando Benitez	.05
41	Jeffrey Hammonds	.05
42	Jimmy Key	.05
43	Chris Hoiles	.05
44	Mike Bordick	.05
45	Pete Incaviglia	.05
46	Mike Stanley	.05
47	Reggie Jefferson	.05
48	Mo Vaughn	.05
49	John Valentin	.05
50	Tim Naehring	.05
51	Jeff Suppan	.05
52	Tim Wakefield	.05
53	Jeff Frye	.05
54	Darren Bragg	.05
55	Steve Avery	.05
56	Shane Mack	.05
57	Aaron Sele	.05
58	Troy O'Leary	.05
59	Rudy Pemberton	.05
60	Nomar Garciaparra	1.00
61	Robin Ventura	.05
62	Wilson Alvarez	.05
63	Roberto Hernandez	.05
64	Frank Thomas	.75
65	Ray Durham	.05
66	James Baldwin	.05
67	Harold Baines	.05
68	Doug Drabek	.05
69	Mike Cameron	.05
70	Albert Belle	.05
71	Jaime Navarro	.05
72	Chris Snopek	.05
73	Lyle Mouton	.05
74	Dave Martinez	.05
75	Ozzie Guillen	.05
76	Manny Ramirez	.75
77	Jack McDowell	.05
78	Jim Thome	.50
79	Jose Mesa	.05
80	Brian Giles	.05
81	Omar Vizquel	.05
82	Charles Nagy	.05
83	Orel Hershiser	.05
84	Matt Williams	.05
85	Marquis Grissom	.05
86	David Justice	.05
87	Sandy Alomar	.05
88	Kevin Seitzer	.05
89	Julio Franco	.05
90	Bartolo Colon	.05
91	Andres Galarraga	.05
92	Larry Walker	.05
93	Vinny Castilla	.05
94	Dante Bichette	.05
95	Jamey Wright	.05
96	Ellis Burks	.05
97	Eric Young	.05
98	Neifi Perez	.05
99	Quinton McCracken	.05
100	Bruce Ruffin	.05
101	Walt Weiss	.05
102	Roger Bailey	.05
103	Jeff Reed	.05
104	Bill Swift	.05
105	Kirt Manwaring	.05
106	Raul Mondesi	.05
107	Hideo Nomo	.35
108	Roger Cedeno	.05
109	Ismael Valdes	.05
110	Todd Hollandsworth	.05
111	Mike Piazza	1.50
112	Brett Butler	.05
113	Chan Ho Park	.05
114	Ramon Martinez	.05
115	Eric Karros	.05
116	Wilton Guerrero	.05
117	Todd Zeile	.05
118	Karim Garcia	.05
119	Greg Gagne	.05
120	Darren Dreifort	.05
121	Wade Boggs	1.00
122	Paul O'Neill	.05
123	Derek Jeter	2.00
124	Tino Martinez	.05
125	David Cone	.05
126	Andy Pettitte	.25
127	Charlie Hayes	.05
128	Mariano Rivera	.15
129	Dwight Gooden	.05
130	Cecil Fielder	.05
131	Not Issued	
132	Darryl Strawberry	.05
133	Joe Girardi	.05
134	David Wells	.05
135	Hideki Irabu	.05
136	Ken Griffey Jr.	1.25
137	Alex Rodriguez	1.50
138	Jay Buhner	.05
139	Randy Johnson	.75
140	Paul Sorrento	.05
141	Edgar Martinez	.05
142	Joey Cora	.05
143	Bob Wells	.05
144	Not Issued	
145	Jamie Moyer	.05
146	Jeff Fassero	.05
147	Dan Wilson	.05
148	Jose Cruz, Jr.	.05
149	Scott Sanders	.05
150	Rich Amaral	.05
151	Brian Jordan	.05
152	Andy Benes	.05
153	Ray Lankford	.05
154	John Mabry	.05
155	Tom Pagnozzi	.05
156	Ron Gant	.05
157	Alan Benes	.05
158	Dennis Eckersley	.65
159	Royce Clayton	.05
160	Todd Stottlemyre	.05
161	Gary Gaetti	.05
162	Willie McGee	.05
163	Delino DeShields	.05
164	Dmitri Young	.05
165	Matt Morris	.05

1997 Donruss Team Sets MVP

		NM/M
Complete Set (18):		45.00
Common Player:		.50
1	Ivan Rodriguez	1.50
2	Mike Piazza	5.50
3	Frank Thomas	2.50
4	Jeff Bagwell	2.50
5	Chuck Knoblauch	.50
6	Eric Young	.50
7	Alex Rodriguez	6.00
8	Barry Larkin	.50
9	Cal Ripken Jr.	7.50
10	Chipper Jones	4.00
11	Albert Belle	.50
12	Barry Bonds	7.50
13	Ken Griffey Jr.	5.50
14	Kenny Lofton	.50
15	Juan Gonzalez	1.00
16	Larry Walker	.50
17	Roger Clemens	5.00
18	Greg Maddux	4.00

1997 Donruss VXP 1.0

		NM/M
Complete Set (50):		17.50
Common Player:		.25
1	Darin Erstad	.40

2	Jim Thome	.50
3	Alex Rodriguez	1.50
4	Greg Maddux	1.00
5	Scott Rolen	.65
6	Roberto Alomar	.30
7	Tony Gwynn	.25
8	Randy Johnson	.75
9	Sammy Sosa	1.00
10	Jose Guillen	.25
11	Cal Ripken Jr.	2.00
12	Paul Molitor	.75
13	Jose Cruz Jr.	.20
14	Barry Larkin	.25
15	Ken Caminiti	.25
16	Rafael Palmeiro	.65
17	Chuck Knoblauch	.25
18	Juan Gonzalez	.40
19	Larry Walker	.25
20	Tony Gwynn	1.00
21	Brady Anderson	.25
22	Derek Jeter	2.00
23	Rusty Greer	.25
24	Gary Sheffield	.35
25	Barry Bonds	2.00
26	Mo Vaughn	.20
27	Tino Martinez	.25
28	Ivan Rodriguez	.65
29	Jeff Bagwell	.75
30	Tim Salmon	.25
31	Nomar Garciaparra	1.00
32	Bernie Williams	.25
33	Kenny Lofton	.25
34	Mike Piazza	1.25
35	Jim Edmonds	.25
36	Frank Thomas	.75
37	Andy Pettitte	.35
38	Andruw Jones	.75
39	Raul Mondesi	.25
40	John Smoltz	.25
41	Albert Belle	.25
42	Mark McGwire	1.50
43	Chipper Jones	1.00
44	Hideo Nomo	.40
45	David Justice	.25
46	Manny Ramirez	.75
47	Ken Griffey Jr.	1.25
48	Roger Clemens	1.00
49	Vladimir Guerrero	.75
50	Ryne Sandberg	1.00

1997 Donruss VXP 1.0 CDs

		NM/M
Complete Set (6):		12.00
Common Player:		2.00
(1)	Ken Griffey Jr.	2.25
(2)	Greg Maddux	2.00
(3)	Mike Piazza	2.25
(4)	Cal Ripken Jr.	3.00
(5)	Alex Rodriguez	2.50
(6)	Frank Thomas	2.00

1998 Donruss

	NM/M
Complete Set (420):	30.00
Complete Series 1 (170):	10.00
Complete Update 2 (250):	15.00
Common Player:	.05
Pack (10):	1.00
Wax Box (24):	16.00

1	Paul Molitor	.75
2	Juan Gonzalez	.40
3	Darryl Kile	.05
4	Randy Johnson	.75
5	Tom Glavine	.25
6	Pat Hentgen	.05
7	David Justice	.05
8	Kevin Brown	.05
9	Mike Mussina	.45
10	Ken Caminiti	.05
11	Todd Hundley	.05
12	Frank Thomas	.75
13	Ray Lankford	.05
14	Justin Thompson	.05
15	Jason Dickson	.05
16	Kenny Lofton	.05
17	Ivan Rodriguez	.65
18	Pedro Martinez	.75
19	Brady Anderson	.05
20	Barry Larkin	.05
21	Chipper Jones	1.50
22	Tony Gwynn	1.50
23	Roger Clemens	1.50
24	Sandy Alomar Jr.	.05
25	Tino Martinez	.05
26	Jeff Bagwell	.75
27	Shawn Estes	.05
28	Ken Griffey Jr.	1.75
29	Javier Lopez	.05
30	Denny Neagle	.05
31	Mike Piazza	1.75
32	Andres Galarraga	.05
33	Larry Walker	.05
34	Alex Rodriguez	2.00
35	Greg Maddux	1.50
36	Albert Belle	.05
37	Barry Bonds	2.50
38	Mo Vaughn	.05
39	Kevin Appier	.05
40	Wade Boggs	1.50
41	Garret Anderson	.05
42	Jeffrey Hammonds	.05
43	Marquis Grissom	.05
44	Jim Edmonds	.05
45	Brian Jordan	.05
46	Raul Mondesi	.05
47	John Valentin	.05
48	Brad Radke	.05
49	Ismael Valdes	.05
50	Matt Stairs	.05
51	Matt Williams	.05
52	Reggie Jefferson	.05
53	Alan Benes	.05
54	Charles Johnson	.05
55	Chuck Knoblauch	.05
56	Edgar Martinez	.05
57	Nomar Garciaparra	1.50
58	Craig Biggio	.05
59	Bernie Williams	.05
60	David Cone	.05
61	Cal Ripken Jr.	2.50
62	Mark McGwire	2.00
63	Roberto Alomar	.20
64	Fred McGriff	.05
65	Eric Karros	.05
66	Robin Ventura	.05
67	Darin Erstad	.30
68	Michael Tucker	.05
69	Jim Thome	.60
70	Mark Grace	.05
71	Lou Collier	.05
72	Karim Garcia	.05
73	Alex Fernandez	.05
74	J.T. Snow	.05
75	Reggie Sanders	.05
76	John Smoltz	.05
77	Tim Salmon	.05
78	Paul O'Neill	.05
79	Vinny Castilla	.05
80	Rafael Palmeiro	.65
81	Jaret Wright	.05
82	Jay Buhner	.05
83	Brett Butler	.05
84	Todd Greene	.05
85	Scott Rolen	.65
86	Sammy Sosa	1.50
87	Jason Giambi	.50
88	Carlos Delgado	.50
89	Deion Sanders	.05
90	Wilton Guerrero	.05
91	Andy Pettitte	.30
92	Brian Giles	.05
93	Dmitri Young	.05
94	Ron Coomer	.05
95	Mike Cameron	.05
96	Edgardo Alfonzo	.05
97	Jimmy Key	.05
98	Ryan Klesko	.05
99	Andy Benes	.05
100	Derek Jeter	2.50
101	Jeff Fassero	.05
102	Neifi Perez	.05
103	Hideo Nomo	.40
104	Andruw Jones	.75
105	Todd Helton	.50
106	Livan Hernandez	.05
107	Brett Tomko	.05
108	Shannon Stewart	.05
109	Bartolo Colon	.05
110	Matt Morris	.05
111	Miguel Tejada	.20
112	Pokey Reese	.05
113	Fernando Tatis	.05
114	Todd Dunwoody	.05
115	Jose Cruz Jr.	.05
116	Chan Ho Park	.05
117	Kevin Young	.05
118	Rickey Henderson	.75
119	Hideki Irabu	.05
120	Francisco Cordova	.05
121	Al Martin	.05
122	Tony Clark	.05
123	Curt Schilling	.25
124	Rusty Greer	.05
125	Jose Canseco	.40
126	Edgar Renteria	.05
127	Todd Walker	.05
128	Wally Joyner	.05
129	Bill Mueller	.05
130	Jose Guillen	.05
131	Manny Ramirez	.75
132	Bobby Higginson	.05
133	Kevin Orie	.05
134	Will Clark	.05
135	Jon Nilsson	.05
136	Jason Kendall	.05
137	Ivan Cruz	.05
138	Gary Sheffield	.25
139	Bubba Trammell	.05
140	Vladimir Guerrero	.75
141	Dennis Reyes	.05
142	Bobby Bonilla	.05
143	Ruben Rivera	.05
144	Ben Grieve	.05
145	Moises Alou	.05
146	Tony Womack	.05
147	Eric Young	.05
148	Paul Konerko	.10
149	Dante Bichette	.05
150	Joe Carter	.05
151	Rondell White	.05
152	Chris Holt	.05
153	Shawn Green	.20
154	Mark Grudzielanek	.05
155	Jermaine Dye	.05
156	Ken Griffey Jr.	.90
157	Frank Thomas	.50
158	Chipper Jones	.75
159	Mike Piazza	.90
160	Cal Ripken Jr.	1.25
161	Greg Maddux	.75
162	Juan Gonzalez	.20
163	Alex Rodriguez	1.00
164	Mark McGwire	1.00
165	Derek Jeter	1.25
166	Larry Walker Checklist	.05
167	Tony Gwynn Checklist	.60
168	Tino Martinez Checklist	.05
169	Scott Rolen Checklist	.15
170	Nomar Garciaparra Checklist	.60
171	Mike Sweeney	.05
172	Dustin Hermanson	.05
173	Darren Dreifort	.05
174	Ron Gant	.05
175	Todd Hollandsworth	.05
176	John Jaha	.05
177	Kerry Wood	.30
178	Chris Stynes	.05
179	Kevin Elster	.05
180	Derek Bell	.05
181	Darryl Strawberry	.05
182	Damion Easley	.05
183	Jeff Cirillo	.05
184	John Thomson	.05
185	Dan Wilson	.05
186	Jay Bell	.05
187	Bernard Gilkey	.05
188	Marc Valdes	.05
189	Ramon Martinez	.05
190	Charles Nagy	.05
191	Derek Lowe	.05
192	Andy Benes	.05
193	Delino DeShields	.05
194	Ryan Jackson RC	.05
195	Kenny Lofton	.05
196	Chuck Knoblauch	.05
197	Andres Galarraga	.05
198	Jose Canseco	.50
199	John Olerud	.05
200	Lance Johnson	.05
201	Darryl Kile	.05
202	Luis Castillo	.05
203	Joe Carter	.05
204	Dennis Eckersley	.65
205	Steve Finley	.05
206	Esteban Loaiza	.05
207	Ryan Christenson RC	.05
208	Deivi Cruz	.05
209	Mariano Rivera	.15
210	Mike Judd RC	.05
211	Billy Wagner	.05
212	Scott Spiezio	.05
213	Russ Davis	.05
214	Jeff Suppan	.05
215	Doug Glanville	.05
216	Dmitri Young	.05
217	Rey Ordonez	.05
218	Cecil Fielder	.05
219	Masato Yoshii RC	.10
220	Raul Casanova	.05
221	Rolando Arrojo RC	.20
222	Ellis Burks	.05
223	Butch Huskey	.05
224	Brian Hunter	.05
225	Marquis Grissom	.05
226	Kevin Brown	.05
227	Joe Randa	.05
228	Henry Rodriguez	.05
229	Omar Vizquel	.05
230	Fred McGriff	.05
231	Matt Williams	.05
232	Moises Alou	.05
233	Travis Fryman	.05
234	Wade Boggs	1.50
235	Pedro Martinez	.75
236	Rickey Henderson	.75
237	Bubba Trammell	.05
238	Mike Caruso	.05
239	Wilson Alvarez	.05
240	Geronimo Berroa	.05
241	Eric Milton	.05
242	Scott Erickson	.05
243	Todd Erdos RC	.05
244	Bobby Hughes	.05
245	Dave Hollins	.05
246	Dean Palmer	.05
247	Carlos Baerga	.05
248	Jose Silva	.05
249	Jose Cabrera RC	.05
250	Tom Evans	.05
251	Marty Cordova	.05
252	Hanley Frias RC	.05
253	Javier Valentin	.05
254	Mario Valdez	.05
255	Joey Cora	.05
256	Mike Lansing	.05
257	Jeff Kent	.05
258	David Dellucci RC	.10
259	Curtis King RC	.05
260	David Segui	.05
261	Royce Clayton	.05
262	Jeff Blauser	.05
263	Manny Aybar RC	.05
264	Mike Cather RC	.05
265	Todd Zeile	.05
266	Richard Hidalgo	.05
267	Dante Powell	.05
268	Mike DeJean RC	.05
269	Ken Cloude	.05
270	Danny Klassen	.05
271	Sean Casey	.15
272	A.J. Hinch	.05
273	Rich Butler RC	.05
274	Ben Ford RC	.05
275	Billy McMillon	.05
276	Wilson Delgado	.05
277	Orlando Cabrera	.05
278	Geoff Jenkins	.05
279	Enrique Wilson	.05
280	Derrek Lee	.60
281	Marc Pisciotta RC	.05
282	Abraham Nunez	.05
283	Aaron Boone	.05
284	Brad Fullmer	.05
285	Rob Stanifer RC	.05
286	Preston Wilson	.05
287	Greg Norton	.05
288	Bobby Smith	.05
289	Josh Booty	.05
290	Russell Branyan	.05
291	Jeremi Gonzalez	.05
292	Michael Coleman	.05
293	Cliff Politte	.05
294	Eric Ludwick	.05
295	Rafael Medina	.05
296	Jason Varitek	.05
297	Ron Wright	.05

298	Mark Kotsay	.05
299	David Ortiz	.50
300	Frank Catalanotto RC	.20
301	Robinson Checo	.05
302	Kevin Millwood RC	.75
303	Jacob Cruz	.05
304	Javier Vazquez	.05
305	Magglio Ordonez RC	1.50
306	Kevin Witt	.05
307	Derrick Gibson	.05
308	Shane Monahan	.05
309	Brian Rose	.05
310	Bobby Estalella	.05
311	Felix Heredia	.05
312	Desi Relaford	.05
313	Esteban Yan RC	.05
314	Ricky Ledee	.05
315	Steve Woodard RC	.05
316	Pat Watkins	.05
317	Damian Moss	.05
318	Bob Abreu	.05
319	Jeff Abbott	.05
320	Miguel Cairo	.05
321	Rigo Beltran RC	.05
322	Tony Saunders	.05
323	Randall Simon	.05
324	Hiram Bocachica	.05
325	Richie Sexson	.05
326	Karim Garcia	.05
327	Mike Lowell RC	.50
328	Pat Cline	.05
329	Matt Clement	.05
330	Scott Elarton	.05
331	Manuel Barrios	.05
332	Bruce Chen	.05
333	Juan Encarnacion	.05
334	Travis Lee	.05
335	Wes Helms	.05
336	Chad Fox RC	.05
337	Donnie Sadler	.05
338	Carlos Mendoza RC	.05
339	Damian Jackson	.05
340	Julio Ramirez RC	.05
341	John Halama RC	.05
342	Edwin Diaz	.05
343	Felix Martinez	.05
344	Eli Marrero	.05
345	Carl Pavano	.05
346	Vladimir Guerrero/HL	.40
347	Barry Bonds/HL	1.25
348	Darin Erstad/HL	.10
349	Albert Belle/HL	.05
350	Kenny Lofton/HL	.05
351	Mo Vaughn/HL	.05
352	Jose Cruz Jr./HL	.05
353	Tony Clark/HL	.05
354	Roberto Alomar/HL	.10
355	Manny Ramirez/HL	.40
356	Paul Molitor/HL	.40
357	Jim Thome/HL	.05
358	Tino Martinez/HL	.05
359	Tim Salmon/HL	.05
360	David Justice/HL	.05
361	Raul Mondesi/HL	.05
362	Mark Grace/HL	.05
363	Craig Biggio/HL	.05
364	Larry Walker/HL	.05
365	Mark McGwire/HL	1.00
366	Juan Gonzalez/HL	.20
367	Derek Jeter/HL	1.25
368	Chipper Jones/HL	.75
369	Frank Thomas/HL	.50
370	Alex Rodriguez/HL	1.00
371	Mike Piazza/HL	.90
372	Tony Gwynn/HL	.75
373	Jeff Bagwell/HL	.40
374	Nomar Garciaparra/HL	.75
375	Ken Griffey Jr./HL	.90
376	Livan Hernandez	.05
377	Chan Ho Park	.05
378	Mike Mussina	.20
379	Andy Pettitte	.05
380	Greg Maddux	.75
381	Hideo Nomo	.20
382	Roger Clemens	.80
383	Randy Johnson	.40
384	Pedro Martinez	.40
385	Jaret Wright	.05
386	Ken Griffey Jr.	.90
387	Todd Helton	.05
388	Paul Konerko	.05
389	Cal Ripken Jr.	1.25
390	Larry Walker	.05
391	Ken Caminiti	.05
392	Jose Guillen	.05
393	Jim Edmonds	.05
394	Barry Larkin	.05
395	Bernie Williams	.05
396	Tony Clark	.05
397	Jose Cruz Jr.	.05
398	Ivan Rodriguez	.30
399	Darin Erstad	.10
400	Scott Rolen	.15
401	Mark McGwire	1.00
402	Andruw Jones	.40
403	Juan Gonzalez	.20

404	Derek Jeter	1.25
405	Chipper Jones	.75
406	Greg Maddux	.75
407	Frank Thomas	.50
408	Alex Rodriguez	1.00
409	Mike Piazza	.90
410	Tony Gwynn	.75
411	Jeff Bagwell	.40
412	Nomar Garciaparra	.75
413	Hideo Nomo	.20
414	Barry Bonds	1.25
415	Ben Grieve	.05
416	Barry Bonds Checklist	1.25
417	Mark McGwire Checklist	1.00
418	Roger Clemens Checklist	.65
419	Livan Hernandez Checklist	.05
420	Ken Griffey Jr. Checklist	.75

Gold Press Proofs

	NM/M
Complete Set (420):	300.00
Common Player:	1.00
Stars/RC's:	6X

Production 500 Sets
(See 1998 Donruss for checklist and base card values.)

Silver Press Proofs

	NM/M
Complete Set (420):	150.00
Common Player:	.50
Stars/RC's:	2X

Production 1,500 Sets
(See 1998 Donruss for checklist and base card values.)

Crusade

		NM/M
	Common Player:	6.00
	Production 250 Sets	
	Purples (100 Sets):	2X
	Reds (25 Sets):	5X
5	Jason Dickson	6.00
6	Todd Greene	6.00
7	Roberto Alomar	7.50
8	Cal Ripken Jr.	60.00
12	Mo Vaughn	6.00
13	Nomar Garciaparra	30.00
16	Mike Cameron	6.00
20	Sandy Alomar Jr.	6.00
21	David Justice	6.00
25	Justin Thompson	6.00
27	Kevin Appier	6.00
33	Tino Martinez	6.00
36	Hideki Irabu	6.00
37	Jose Canseco	10.00
39	Ken Griffey Jr.	40.00
42	Edgar Martinez	6.00
45	Will Clark	6.00
47	Rusty Greer	6.00
50	Shawn Green	9.00
51	Jose Cruz Jr.	6.00
52	Kenny Lofton	6.00
53	Chipper Jones	30.00
62	Kevin Orie	6.00
65	Deion Sanders	6.00
67	Larry Walker	6.00
68	Dante Bichette	6.00
71	Todd Helton	15.00
74	Bobby Bonilla	6.00
75	Kevin Brown	6.00
78	Craig Biggio	6.00
82	Wilton Guerrero	6.00
85	Pedro Martinez	20.00
86	Edgardo Alfonzo	6.00
88	Scott Rolen	15.00
89	Francisco Cordova	6.00
90	Jose Guillen	6.00
92	Ray Lankford	6.00
93	Mark McGwire	45.00
94	Matt Morris	6.00
100	Shawn Estes	6.00

Days

		NM/M
	Complete Set (14):	16.00
	Common Player:	.50
1	Frank Thomas	1.00
2	Tony Clark	.50
3	Ivan Rodriguez	.65
4	David Justice	.50
5	Nomar Garciaparra	1.50
6	Mark McGwire	2.50
7	Travis Lee	.50
8	Cal Ripken Jr.	3.00
9	Jeff Bagwell	1.00
10	Barry Bonds	3.00
11	Ken Griffey Jr.	2.00
12	Derek Jeter	3.00
13	Raul Mondesi	.50
14	Greg Maddux	1.50

Diamond Kings

		NM/M
	Complete Set (20):	65.00
	Common Player:	2.00
	Production 9,500 Sets	
	Canvas (1st 500 Sets):	2X
1	Cal Ripken Jr.	9.00
2	Greg Maddux	4.50
3	Ivan Rodriguez	2.50
4	Tony Gwynn	4.50
5	Paul Molitor	3.00
6	Kenny Lofton	2.00
7	Andy Pettitte	2.00
8	Darin Erstad	2.00
9	Randy Johnson	3.00
10	Derek Jeter	9.00
11	Hideo Nomo	2.50

12	David Justice	2.00
13	Bernie Williams	2.00
14	Roger Clemens	5.00
15	Barry Larkin	2.00
16	Andruw Jones	3.00
17	Mike Piazza	6.50
18	Frank Thomas	3.00
18s	Frank Thomas (Sample)	3.00
19	Alex Rodriguez	7.50
20	Ken Griffey Jr.	6.50

Longball Leaders

		NM/M
	Complete Set (24):	50.00
	Common Player:	1.00
	Production 5,000 Sets	
1	Ken Griffey Jr.	5.00
2	Mark McGwire	6.00
3	Tino Martinez	1.00
4	Barry Bonds	7.50
5	Frank Thomas	3.00
6	Albert Belle	1.00
7	Mike Piazza	5.00
8	Chipper Jones	4.00
9	Vladimir Guerrero	3.00
10	Matt Williams	1.00
11	Sammy Sosa	4.00
12	Tim Salmon	1.00
13	Raul Mondesi	1.00
14	Jeff Bagwell	3.00
15	Mo Vaughn	1.00
16	Manny Ramirez	3.00
17	Jim Thome	2.00
18	Jim Edmonds	1.00
19	Tony Clark	1.00
20	Nomar Garciaparra	4.00
21	Juan Gonzalez	1.50
22	Scott Rolen	2.00
23	Larry Walker	1.00
24	Andres Galarraga	1.00

Production Line-Ob

		NM/M
	Complete Set (20):	85.00
	Common Player:	1.50
1	Frank Thomas/456	6.00
2	Edgar Martinez/456	1.50
3	Roberto Alomar/390	2.00
4	Chuck Knoblauch/390	1.50
5	Mike Piazza/431	10.00
6	Barry Larkin/440	1.50
7	Kenny Lofton/390	1.50
8	Jeff Bagwell/425	6.00
9	Barry Bonds/446	15.00
10	Rusty Greer/405	1.50
11	Gary Sheffield/424	2.00
12	Mark McGwire/393	12.00
13	Chipper Jones/371	8.00
14	Tony Gwynn/409	8.00
15	Craig Biggio/415	1.50
16	Mo Vaughn/420	1.50
17	Bernie Williams/408	1.50
18	Ken Griffey Jr./382	10.00
19	Brady Anderson/393	1.50
20	Derek Jeter/370	6.00

Production Line-Pi

		NM/M
	Complete Set (20):	85.00
	Common Player:	1.50
1	Frank Thomas/1,067	5.00
2	Mark McGwire/1,039	12.00
3	Barry Bonds/1,031	12.50
4	Jeff Bagwell/1,017	5.00
5	Ken Griffey Jr./1,028	10.00
6	Alex Rodriguez/390	12.00
7	Chipper Jones/850	7.00
8	Mike Piazza/1,070	10.00
9	Mo Vaughn/980	1.50
10	Brady Anderson/863	1.50
11	Manny Ramirez/953	5.00

12	Albert Belle/823	1.50
13	Jim Thome/1,001	2.50
14	Bernie Williams/952	1.50
15	Scott Rolen/846	2.00
16	Vladimir Guerrero/833	5.00
17	Larry Walker/1,172	1.50
18	David Justice/1,013	1.50
19	Tino Martinez/948	1.50
20	Tony Gwynn/957	7.00

Production Line-Sg

		NM/M
Complete Set (20):		135.00
Common Player:		3.00
1	Mark McGwire/646	20.00
2	Ken Griffey Jr./646	12.50
3	Andres Galarraga/585	3.00
4	Barry Bonds/585	22.50
5	Juan Gonzalez/589	4.50
6	Mike Piazza/638	12.50
7	Jeff Bagwell/592	7.50
8	Manny Ramirez/538	7.50
9	Jim Thome/579	4.50
10	Mo Vaughn/560	3.00
11	Larry Walker/720	3.00
12	Tino Martinez/577	3.00
13	Frank Thomas/611	7.50
14	Tim Salmon/517	3.00
15	Raul Mondesi/541	3.00
16	Alex Rodriguez/496	15.00
17	Nomar Garciaparra/534	10.00
18	Jose Cruz Jr./499	3.00
19	Tony Clark/500	3.00
20	Cal Ripken Jr./402	25.00

Rated Rookies

	NM/M
Complete Set (30):	32.50
Common Player:	1.00

Medalists (250 Sets):		6X
1	Mark Kotsay	1.00
2	Neifi Perez	1.00
3	Paul Konerko	1.50
4	Jose Cruz Jr.	1.00
5	Hideki Irabu	1.00
6	Mike Cameron	1.00
7	Jeff Suppan	1.00
8	Kevin Orie	1.00
9	Pokey Reese	1.00
10	Todd Dunwoody	1.00
11	Miguel Tejada	1.50
12	Jose Guillen	1.00
13	Bartolo Colon	1.50
14	Derek Lee	2.50
15	Antone Williamson	1.00
16	Wilton Guerrero	1.00
17	Jaret Wright	1.00
18	Todd Helton	4.00
19	Shannon Stewart	1.00
20	Nomar Garciaparra	6.00
21	Brett Tomko	1.00
22	Fernando Tatis	1.00
23	Raul Ibanez	1.00
24	Dennis Reyes	1.00
25	Bobby Estalella	1.00
26	Lou Collier	1.00
27	Bubba Trammell	1.00
28	Ben Grieve	1.00
29	Ivan Cruz	1.00
30	Karim Garcia	1.00

Update Crusade

	NM/M
Complete Set, Green (30):	325.00
Common Player:	6.00
Production 250 Sets	
Purples (100 Sets):	3X
Reds (25 Sets):	10X

1	Tim Salmon	6.00
2	Garret Anderson	6.00
9	Rafael Palmeiro	15.00
10	Brady Anderson	6.00
14	Frank Thomas	15.00
17	Robin Ventura	6.00
22	Matt Williams	6.00
23	Tony Clark	6.00
29	Chuck Knoblauch	6.00
31	Bernie Williams	6.00
32	Derek Jeter	50.00
38	Jason Giambi	10.00
43	Jay Buhner	6.00
44	Juan Gonzalez	7.50
49	Carlos Delgado	9.00
55	Greg Maddux	20.00
57	Tom Glavine	9.00
60	Mark Grace	6.00
61	Sammy Sosa	20.00
63	Barry Larkin	6.00
69	Neifi Perez	6.00
72	Gary Sheffield	7.50
77	Jeff Bagwell	15.00
80	Raul Mondesi	6.00
81	Hideo Nomo	7.50
83	Rondell White	6.00
84	Vladimir Guerrero	15.00
87	Todd Hundley	6.00
96	Brian Jordan	6.00
99	Barry Bonds	50.00

Update Dominators

	NM/M
Complete Set (30):	25.00
Common Player:	.25
Approx:	1:12

1	Roger Clemens	1.50
2	Tony Clark	.25
3	Darin Erstad	.50
4	Jeff Bagwell	1.00
5	Ken Griffey Jr.	1.75
6	Andruw Jones	1.00

7	Juan Gonzalez	.50
8	Ivan Rodriguez	.75
9	Randy Johnson	1.00
10	Tino Martinez	.25
11	Mark McGwire	2.00
12	Chuck Knoblauch	.25
13	Jim Thome	.65
14	Alex Rodriguez	2.00
15	Hideo Nomo	.50
16	Jose Cruz Jr.	.25
17	Chipper Jones	1.50
18	Tony Gwynn	1.50
19	Barry Bonds	2.50
20	Mo Vaughn	.25
21	Cal Ripken Jr.	2.50
22	Greg Maddux	1.50
23	Manny Ramirez	1.00
24	Andres Galarraga	.25
25	Vladimir Guerrero	1.00
26	Albert Belle	.25
27	Nomar Garciaparra	1.50
28	Kenny Lofton	.25
29	Mike Piazza	1.75
30	Frank Thomas	1.00

Update Elite

		NM/M
Complete Set (20):		115.00
Common Player:		3.00
Production 2,500 Sets		
1	Jeff Bagwell	4.50
2	Andruw Jones	4.50
3	Ken Griffey Jr.	7.50
4	Derek Jeter	15.00
5	Juan Gonzalez	3.50
6	Mark McGwire	10.00
7	Ivan Rodriguez	3.50
8	Paul Molitor	4.50
9	Hideo Nomo	3.50
10	Mo Vaughn	3.00
11	Chipper Jones	6.00
12	Nomar Garciaparra	6.00
13	Mike Piazza	7.50
14	Frank Thomas	4.50
15	Greg Maddux	6.00
16	Cal Ripken Jr.	15.00
17	Alex Rodriguez	10.00
18	Scott Rolen	3.50
19	Barry Bonds	15.00
20	Tony Gwynn	6.00

Update FANtasy Team

	NM/M
Complete Set (20):	35.00
Common Player (1-10) (1,750 Sets):	1.50
Common Player (11-20) (3,750 Sets):	1.00
Die-Cuts (250 Each):	2X

1	Frank Thomas	2.00
2	Ken Griffey Jr.	3.50
3	Cal Ripken Jr.	5.00
4	Jose Cruz Jr.	1.00
5	Travis Lee	1.00
6	Greg Maddux	2.50
7	Alex Rodriguez	4.00
8	Mark McGwire	4.00
9	Chipper Jones	2.50
10	Andruw Jones	2.00
11	Mike Piazza	3.50
12	Tony Gwynn	2.50
13	Larry Walker	1.00
14	Nomar Garciaparra	3.00
15	Jaret Wright	1.00
16	Livan Hernandez	1.00
17	Roger Clemens	2.75
18	Derek Jeter	5.00
19	Scott Rolen	1.25
20	Jeff Bagwell	1.50

Update Rookie Diamond Kings

		NM/M
Complete Set (12):		20.00
Common Player:		2.00
Production 9,500 Sets		
Canvas (500 Sets):		2X
1	Travis Lee	2.00
2	Fernando Tatis	2.00
3	Livan Hernandez	2.00
4	Todd Helton	5.00
5	Derek Lee	3.50
6	Jaret Wright	2.00
7	Ben Grieve	2.00
8	Paul Konerko	2.50
9	Jose Cruz Jr.	2.00
10	Mark Kotsay	2.00
11	Todd Greene	2.00
12	Brad Fullmer	2.00

Update Sony MLB 99

		NM/M
Complete Set (20):		3.00
Common Player:		.05
1	Cal Ripken Jr.	.75
2	Nomar Garciaparra	.40
3	Barry Bonds	.75
4	Mike Mussina	.20
5	Pedro Martinez	.25
6	Derek Jeter	.75
7	Andruw Jones	.25
8	Kenny Lofton	.05
9	Gary Sheffield	.15
10	Raul Mondesi	.05
11	Jeff Bagwell	.25
12	Tim Salmon	.05
13	Tom Glavine	.15
14	Ben Grieve	.05
15	Matt Williams	.05
16	Juan Gonzalez	.15
17	Mark McGwire	.50
18	Bernie Williams	.05
19	Andres Galarraga	.05
20	Jose Cruz Jr.	.05

1998 Donruss Collections

	NM/M
Complete Donruss Set (200):	100.00
Complete Leaf Set (200):	125.00
Complete Elite Set (150):	125.00
Complete Preferred Set (200):	300.00
Prized Collections Parallel:	2X
Pack (5):	4.00
Wax Box (20):	75.00
Samples:	6X
DONRUSS	

#	Player	Price
1	Paul Molitor	2.00
2	Juan Gonzalez	1.00
3	Darryl Kile	.25
4	Randy Johnson	2.00
5	Tom Glavine	.50
6	Pat Hentgen	.25
7	David Justice	.25
8	Kevin Brown	.25
9	Mike Mussina	.50
10	Ken Caminiti	.25
11	Todd Hundley	.25
12	Frank Thomas	2.00
13	Ray Lankford	.25
14	Justin Thompson	.25
15	Jason Dickson	.25
16	Kenny Lofton	.25
17	Ivan Rodriguez	1.50
18	Pedro Martinez	2.00
19	Brady Anderson	.25
20	Barry Larkin	.25
21	Chipper Jones	3.00
22	Tony Gwynn	3.00
23	Roger Clemens	3.25
24	Sandy Alomar Jr.	.25
25	Tino Martinez	.25
26	Jeff Bagwell	2.00
27	Shawn Estes	.25
28	Ken Griffey Jr.	3.50
29	Javier Lopez	.25
30	Denny Neagle	.25
31	Mike Piazza	3.50
32	Andres Galarraga	.25
33	Larry Walker	.25
34	Alex Rodriguez	4.50
35	Greg Maddux	3.00
36	Albert Belle	.25
37	Barry Bonds	6.00
38	Mo Vaughn	.25
39	Kevin Appier	.25
40	Wade Boggs	3.00
41	Garret Anderson	.25
42	Jeffrey Hammonds	.25
43	Marquis Grissom	.25
44	Jim Edmonds	.25
45	Brian Jordan	.25
46	Raul Mondesi	.25
47	John Valentin	.25
48	Brad Radke	.25
49	Ismael Valdes	.25
50	Matt Stairs	.25
51	Matt Williams	.25
52	Reggie Jefferson	.25
53	Alan Benes	.25
54	Charles Johnson	.25
55	Chuck Knoblauch	.25
56	Edgar Martinez	.25
57	Nomar Garciaparra	3.00
58	Craig Biggio	.25
59	Bernie Williams	.50
60	David Cone	.25
61	Cal Ripken Jr.	6.00
62	Mark McGwire	4.50
63	Roberto Alomar	.50
64	Fred McGriff	.25
65	Eric Karros	.25
66	Robin Ventura	.25
67	Darin Erstad	.50
68	Michael Tucker	.25
69	Jim Thome	1.00
70	Mark Grace	.25
71	Lou Collier	.25
72	Karim Garcia	.25
73	Alex Fernandez	.25
74	J.T. Snow	.25
75	Reggie Sanders	.25
76	John Smoltz	.25
77	Tim Salmon	.25
78	Paul O'Neill	.25
79	Vinny Castilla	.25
80	Rafael Palmeiro	1.50
81	Jaret Wright	.25
82	Jay Buhner	.25
83	Brett Butler	.25
84	Todd Greene	.25
85	Scott Rolen	1.50
86	Sammy Sosa	3.00
87	Jason Giambi	1.00
88	Carlos Delgado	.75
89	Deion Sanders	.25
90	Wilton Guerrero	.25
91	Andy Pettitte	.45
92	Brian Giles	.25
93	Dmitri Young	.25
94	Ron Coomer	.25
95	Mike Cameron	.25
96	Edgardo Alfonzo	.25
97	Jimmy Key	.25
98	Ryan Klesko	.25
99	Andy Benes	.25
100	Derek Jeter	6.00
101	Jeff Fassero	.25
102	Neifi Perez	.25
103	Hideo Nomo	1.00
104	Andruw Jones	2.00
105	Todd Helton	1.50
106	Livan Hernandez	.25
107	Brett Tomko	.25
108	Shannon Stewart	.25
109	Bartolo Colon	.25
110	Matt Morris	.25
111	Miguel Tejada	.40
112	Pokey Reese	.25
113	Fernando Tatis	.25
114	Todd Dunwoody	.25
115	Jose Cruz Jr.	.25
116	Chan Ho Park	.25
117	Kevin Young	.25
118	Rickey Henderson	2.00
119	Hideki Irabu	.25
120	Francisco Cordova	.25
121	Al Martin	.25
122	Tony Clark	.25
123	Curt Schilling	.40
124	Rusty Greer	.25
125	Jose Canseco	.60
126	Edgar Renteria	.25
127	Todd Walker	.25
128	Wally Joyner	.25
129	Bill Mueller	.25
130	Jose Guillen	.25
131	Manny Ramirez	2.00
132	Bobby Higginson	.25
133	Kevin Orie	.25
134	Will Clark	.25
135	Dave Nilsson	.25
136	Jason Kendall	.25
137	Ivan Cruz	.25
138	Gary Sheffield	.40
139	Bubba Trammell	.25
140	Vladimir Guerrero	2.00
141	Dennis Reyes	.25
142	Bobby Bonilla	.25
143	Ruben Rivera	.25
144	Ben Grieve	.25
145	Moises Alou	.25
146	Tony Womack	.25
147	Eric Young	.25
148	Paul Konerko	.35
149	Dante Bichette	.25
150	Joe Carter	.25
151	Rondell White	.25
152	Chris Holt	.25
153	Shawn Green	.40
154	Mark Grudzielanek	.25
155	Jermaine Dye	.25
156	Ken Griffey Jr.	1.75
157	Frank Thomas	1.00
158	Chipper Jones	1.50
159	Mike Piazza	1.75
160	Cal Ripken Jr.	3.00
161	Greg Maddux	1.50
162	Juan Gonzalez	.50
163	Alex Rodriguez	2.25
164	Mark McGwire	2.25
165	Derek Jeter	3.00
166	Larry Walker (Checklist)	.25
167	Tony Gwynn (Checklist)	.75
168	Tino Martinez (Checklist)	.25
169	Scott Rolen (Checklist)	.40
170	Nomar Garciaparra (Checklist)	.75

DONRUSS RATED ROOKIES

#	Player	Price
1	Mark Kotsay	.50
2	Neifi Perez	.50
3	Paul Konerko	1.00
4	Jose Cruz Jr.	.50
5	Hideki Irabu	.50
6	Mike Cameron	.50
7	Jeff Suppan	.50
8	Kevin Orie	.50
9	Pokey Reese	.50
10	Todd Dunwoody	.50
11	Miguel Tejada	1.00
12	Jose Guillen	.50
13	Bartolo Colon	.50
14	Derrek Lee	.75
15	Antone Williamson	.50
16	Wilton Guerrero	.50
17	Jaret Wright	.50
18	Todd Helton	2.00
19	Shannon Stewart	.50
20	Nomar Garciaparra	3.00
21	Brett Tomko	.50
22	Fernando Tatis	.50
23	Raul Ibanez	.50
24	Dennis Reyes	.50
25	Bobby Estalella	.50
26	Lou Collier	.50
27	Bubba Trammell	.50
28	Ben Grieve	.50
29	Ivan Cruz	.50
30	Karim Garcia	.50

LEAF

#	Player	Price
1	Rusty Greer	.25
2	Tino Martinez	.25
3	Bobby Bonilla	.25
4	Jason Giambi	.65
5	Matt Morris	.25
6	Craig Counsell	.25
7	Reggie Jefferson	.25
8	Brian Rose	.25
9	Ruben Rivera	.25
10	Shawn Estes	.25
11	Tony Gwynn	3.00
12	Jeff Abbott	.25
13	Jose Cruz Jr.	.25
14	Francisco Cordova	.25
15	Ryan Klesko	.25
16	Tim Salmon	.25
17	Brett Tomko	.25
18	Matt Williams	.25
19	Joe Carter	.25
20	Harold Baines	.25
21	Gary Sheffield	.40
22	Charles Johnson	.25
23	Aaron Boone	.35
24	Eddie Murray	2.00
25	Matt Stairs	.25
26	David Cone	.25
27	Jon Nunnally	.25
28	Chris Stynes	.25
29	Enrique Wilson	.25
30	Randy Johnson	2.00
31	Garret Anderson	.25
32	Manny Ramirez	2.00
33	Jeff Suppan	.25
34	Rickey Henderson	2.00
35	Scott Spiezio	.25
36	Rondell White	.25
37	Todd Greene	.25
38	Delino DeShields	.25
39	Kevin Brown	.25
40	Chili Davis	.25
41	Jimmy Key	.25
42	Not Issued	
43	Mike Mussina	1.00
44	Joe Randa	.25
45	Chan Ho Park	.25
46	Brad Radke	.25
47	Geronimo Berroa	.25
48	Wade Boggs	3.00
49	Kevin Appier	.25
50	Moises Alou	.25
51	David Justice	.25
52	Ivan Rodriguez	1.50
53	J.T. Snow	.25
54	Brian Giles	.25
55	Will Clark	.25
56	Justin Thompson	.25
57	Javier Lopez	.25
58	Hideki Irabu	.25
59	Mark Grudzielanek	.25
60	Abraham Nunez	.25
61	Todd Hollandsworth	.25
62	Jay Bell	.25
63	Nomar Garciaparra	3.00
64	Vinny Castilla	.25
65	Lou Collier	.25
66	Kevin Orie	.25
67	John Valentin	.25
68	Robin Ventura	.25
69	Denny Neagle	.25
70	Tony Womack	.25
71	Dennis Reyes	.25
72	Wally Joyner	.25
73	Kevin Brown	.35
74	Ray Durham	.25
75	Mike Cameron	.25
76	Dante Bichette	.25
77	Jose Guillen	.25
78	Carlos Delgado	.60
79	Paul Molitor	2.00
80	Jason Kendall	.25
81	Mark Belhorn	.25
82	Damian Jackson	.25
83	Bill Mueller	.25
84	Kevin Young	.25
85	Curt Schilling	.50
86	Jeffrey Hammonds	.25
87	Sandy Alomar Jr.	.25
88	Bartolo Colon	.25
89	Wilton Guerrero	.25
90	Bernie Williams	.25
91	Deion Sanders	.25
92	Mike Piazza	3.50
93	Butch Huskey	.25
94	Edgardo Alfonzo	.25
95	Alan Benes	.25
96	Craig Biggio	.25
97	Mark Grace	.25
98	Shawn Green	.40
99	Derek Lee	1.00
100	Ken Griffey Jr.	3.50
101	Tim Raines	.25
102	Pokey Reese	.25
103	Lee Stevens	.25
104	Shannon Stewart	.25
105	John Smoltz	.25
106	Frank Thomas	2.00
107	Jeff Fassero	.25
108	Jay Buhner	.25
109	Jose Canseco	.45
110	Omar Vizquel	.25
111	Travis Fryman	.25
112	Dave Nilsson	.25
113	John Olerud	.25
114	Larry Walker	.25
115	Jim Edmonds	.25
116	Bobby Higginson	.25
117	Todd Hundley	.25
118	Paul O'Neill	.25
119	Bip Roberts	.25
120	Ismael Valdes	.25
121	Pedro Martinez	2.00
122	Jeff Cirillo	.25
123	Andy Benes	.25
124	Bobby Jones	.25
125	Brian Hunter	.25
126	Darryl Kile	.25
127	Pat Hentgen	.25
128	Marquis Grissom	.25
129	Eric Davis	.25
130	Chipper Jones	3.00
131	Edgar Martinez	.25
132	Andy Pettitte	.50
133	Cal Ripken Jr.	6.00
134	Scott Rolen	1.50
135	Ron Coomer	.25
136	Luis Castillo	.25
137	Fred McGriff	.25
138	Neifi Perez	.25
139	Eric Karros	.25
140	Alex Fernandez	.25
141	Jason Dickson	.25
142	Lance Johnson	.25
143	Ray Lankford	.25
144	Sammy Sosa	3.00
145	Eric Young	.25
146	Bubba Trammell	.25
147	Todd Walker	.25
148	Mo Vaughn/CC	.25
149	Jeff Bagwell/CC	2.00
150	Kenny Lofton/CC	.25
151	Raul Mondesi/CC	.25
152	Mike Piazza/CC	3.50
153	Chipper Jones/CC	3.00
154	Larry Walker/CC	.25
155	Greg Maddux/CC	3.00
156	Ken Griffey Jr./CC	3.50
157	Frank Thomas/CC	2.00
158	Darin Erstad/GLS	2.00
159	Roberto Alomar/GLS	1.50
160	Albert Belle/GLS	1.00
161	Jim Thome/GLS	2.00
162	Tony Clark/GLS	1.00
163	Chuck Knoblauch/GLS	1.00
164	Derek Jeter/GLS	12.00
165	Alex Rodriguez/GLS	8.00
166	Tony Gwynn/GLS	6.00
167	Roger Clemens/GLS	7.00
168	Barry Larkin/GLS	1.00
169	Andres Galarraga/GLS	1.00
170	Vladimir Guerrero/GLS	4.50
171	Mark McGwire/GLS	8.00
172	Barry Bonds/GLS	12.00
173	Juan Gonzalez/GLS	2.50
174	Andruw Jones/GLS	4.50
175	Paul Molitor/GLS	4.50
176	Hideo Nomo/GLS	2.50
177	Cal Ripken Jr./GLS	12.50
178	Brad Fullmer/GLR	1.00
179	Jaret Wright/GLR	1.00
180	Bobby Estalella/GLR	1.00
181	Ben Grieve/GLR	1.00
182	Paul Konerko/GLR	1.50
183	David Ortiz/GLR	3.00
184	Todd Helton/GLR	3.00
185	Juan Encarnacion/GLR	1.00
186	Miguel Tejada/GLR	1.50
187	Jacob Cruz/GLR	1.00
188	Mark Kotsay/GLR	1.00
189	Fernando Tatis/GLR	1.00

190	Ricky Ledee/GLR	1.00
191	Richard Hidalgo/GLR	1.00
192	Richie Sexson/GLR	1.00
193	Luis Ordaz/GLR	1.00
194	Eli Marrero/GLR	1.00
195	Livan Hernandez/GLR	1.00
196	Homer Bush/GLR	1.00
197	Raul Ibanez/GLR	1.00
198	Nomar Garciaparra Checklist	1.00
199	Scott Rolen Checklist	.75
200	Jose Cruz Jr. Checklist	.25
201	Al Martin	.25

ELITE

1	Ken Griffey Jr.	4.00
2	Frank Thomas	2.50
3	Alex Rodriguez	6.00
4	Mike Piazza	4.00
5	Greg Maddux	3.00
6	Cal Ripken Jr.	7.00
7	Chipper Jones	3.00
8	Derek Jeter	7.00
9	Tony Gwynn	3.00
10	Andruw Jones	2.50
11	Juan Gonzalez	1.25
12	Jeff Bagwell	2.50
13	Mark McGwire	6.00
14	Roger Clemens	3.00
15	Albert Belle	.50
16	Barry Bonds	7.00
17	Kenny Lofton	.50
18	Ivan Rodriguez	2.00
19	Manny Ramirez	2.50
20	Jim Thome	1.50
21	Chuck Knoblauch	.50
22	Paul Molitor	2.50
23	Barry Larkin	.50
24	Andy Pettitte	1.00
25	John Smoltz	.50
26	Randy Johnson	2.50
27	Bernie Williams	.50
28	Larry Walker	.50
29	Mo Vaughn	.50
30	Bobby Higginson	.50
31	Edgardo Alfonzo	.50
32	Justin Thompson	.50
33	Jeff Suppan	.50
34	Roberto Alomar	1.00
35	Hideo Nomo	1.25
36	Rusty Greer	.50
37	Tim Salmon	.50
38	Jim Edmonds	.50
39	Gary Sheffield	.75
40	Ken Caminiti	.50
41	Sammy Sosa	3.00
42	Tony Womack	.50
43	Matt Williams	.50
44	Andres Galarraga	.50
45	Garret Anderson	.50
46	Rafael Palmeiro	2.00
47	Mike Mussina	1.00
48	Craig Biggio	.50
49	Wade Boggs	3.00
50	Tom Glavine	.75
51	Jason Giambi	1.00
52	Will Clark	.50
53	David Justice	.50
54	Sandy Alomar Jr.	.50
55	Edgar Martinez	.50
56	Brady Anderson	.50
57	Eric Young	.50
58	Ray Lankford	.50
59	Kevin Brown	.60
60	Raul Mondesi	.50
61	Bobby Bonilla	.50
62	Javier Lopez	.50
63	Fred McGriff	.50
64	Rondell White	.50
65	Todd Hundley	.50
66	Mark Grace	.50
67	Alan Benes	.50
68	Jeff Abbott	.50
69	Bob Abreu	.50
70	Deion Sanders	.50
71	Tino Martinez	.50
72	Shannon Stewart	.50
73	Homer Bush	.50
74	Carlos Delgado	1.50
75	Raul Ibanez	.50
76	Hideki Irabu	.50
77	Jose Cruz Jr.	.50
78	Tony Clark	.50
79	Wilton Guerrero	.50
80	Vladimir Guerrero	2.50
81	Scott Rolen	2.25
82	Nomar Garciaparra	3.00
83	Darin Erstad	1.00
84	Chan Ho Park	.50
85	Mike Cameron	.50
86	Todd Walker	.50
87	Todd Dunwoody	.50
88	Neifi Perez	.50
89	Brett Tomko	.50
90	Jose Guillen	.50
91	Matt Morris	.50
92	Bartolo Colon	.50
93	Jaret Wright	.50
94	Shawn Estes	.50
95	Livan Hernandez	.50
96	Bobby Estalella	.50
97	Ben Grieve	.50
98	Paul Konerko	.75
99	David Ortiz	1.00
100	Todd Helton	2.00
101	Juan Encarnacion	.50
102	Bubba Trammell	.50
103	Miguel Tejada	1.00
104	Jacob Cruz	.50
105	Todd Greene	.50
106	Kevin Orie	.50
107	Mark Kotsay	.50
108	Fernando Tatis	.50
109	Jay Payton	.50
110	Pokey Reese	.50
111	Derek Lee	1.50
112	Richard Hidalgo	.50
113	Ricky Ledee	.50
114	Lou Collier	.50
115	Ruben Rivera	.50
116	Shawn Green	1.00
117	Moises Alou	.50
118	Ken Griffey Jr.	2.00
119	Frank Thomas	1.25
120	Alex Rodriguez	3.00
121	Mike Piazza	2.00
122	Greg Maddux	1.75
123	Cal Ripken Jr.	3.50
124	Chipper Jones	1.75
125	Derek Jeter	3.50
126	Tony Gwynn	1.75
127	Andruw Jones	1.25
128	Juan Gonzalez	.75
129	Jeff Bagwell	1.25
130	Mark McGwire	3.00
131	Roger Clemens	1.75
132	Albert Belle	.50
133	Barry Bonds	3.50
134	Kenny Lofton	.50
135	Ivan Rodriguez	1.00
136	Manny Ramirez	1.25
137	Jim Thome	1.00
138	Chuck Knoblauch	.50
139	Paul Molitor	1.25
140	Barry Larkin	.50
141	Mo Vaughn	.50
142	Hideki Irabu	.50
143	Jose Cruz Jr.	.50
144	Tony Clark	.50
145	Vladimir Guerrero	1.25
146	Scott Rolen	1.00
147	Nomar Garciaparra	2.00
148	Nomar Garciaparra Checklist	1.00
149	Larry Walker Checklist	.50
150	Tino Martinez Checklist	.50

PREFERRED

1	Ken Griffey Jr./EX	12.00
2	Frank Thomas/EX	7.50
3	Cal Ripken Jr./EX	17.50
4	Alex Rodriguez/EX	15.00
5	Greg Maddux/EX	10.00
6	Mike Piazza/EX	12.00
7	Chipper Jones/EX	10.00
8	Tony Gwynn/FB	10.00
9	Derek Jeter/FB	17.50
10	Jeff Bagwell/EX	7.50
11	Juan Gonzalez/EX	4.00
12	Nomar Garciaparra/EX	10.00
13	Andruw Jones/FB	7.50
14	Hideo Nomo/FB	4.00
15	Roger Clemens/FB	13.50
16	Mark McGwire/FB	15.00
17	Scott Rolen/FB	6.00
18	Vladimir Guerrero/FB	7.50
19	Barry Bonds/FB	17.50
20	Darin Erstad/FB	4.00
21	Albert Belle/FB	2.00
22	Kenny Lofton/FB	2.00
23	Mo Vaughn/FB	2.00
24	Tony Clark/FB	2.00
25	Ivan Rodriguez/FB	6.00
26	Larry Walker/CL	2.00
27	Eddie Murray/CL	7.50
28	Andy Pettitte/CL	4.00
29	Roberto Alomar/CL	2.00
30	Randy Johnson/CL	7.50
31	Manny Ramirez/CL	7.50
32	Paul Molitor/FB	7.50
33	Mike Mussina/CL	4.00
34	Jim Thome/FB	2.00
35	Tino Martinez/CL	2.00
36	Gary Sheffield/CL	3.00
37	Chuck Knoblauch/CL	2.00
38	Bernie Williams/CL	2.00
39	Tim Salmon/CL	2.00
40	Sammy Sosa/CL	10.00
41	Wade Boggs/MZ	10.00
42	Will Clark/GS	2.00
43	Andres Galarraga/CL	2.00
44	Raul Mondesi/CL	2.00
45	Rickey Henderson/GS	6.50
46	Jose Canseco/GS	4.00
47	Pedro Martinez/GS	6.50
48	Jay Buhner/GS	2.00
49	Ryan Klesko/GS	2.00
50	Barry Larkin/CL	2.00
51	Charles Johnson/GS	2.00
52	Tom Glavine/GS	3.00
53	Edgar Martinez/CL	2.00
54	Fred McGriff/GS	2.00
55	Moises Alou/MZ	2.00
56	Dante Bichette/GS	2.00
57	Jim Edmonds/CL	2.00
58	Mark Grace/MZ	2.00
59	Chan Ho Park/MZ	2.00
60	Justin Thompson/MZ	2.00
61	John Smoltz/MZ	2.00
62	Craig Biggio/CL	2.00
63	Ken Caminiti/MZ	2.00
64	Deion Sanders/MZ	2.00
65	Carlos Delgado/MZ	2.00
66	David Justice/CL	2.00
67	J.T. Snow/GS	2.00
68	Jason Giambi/CL	4.00
69	Garret Anderson/MZ	2.00
70	Rondell White/MZ	2.00
71	Matt Williams/MZ	2.00
72	Brady Anderson/MZ	2.00
73	Eric Karros/GS	2.00
74	Javier Lopez/GS	2.00
75	Pat Hentgen/GS	2.00
76	Todd Hundley/GS	2.00
77	Ray Lankford/GS	2.00
78	Denny Neagle/GS	2.00
79	Henry Rodriguez/GS	2.00
80	Sandy Alomar Jr./MZ	2.00
81	Rafael Palmeiro/MZ	5.00
82	Robin Ventura/GS	2.00
83	John Olerud/GS	2.00
84	Omar Vizquel/GS	2.00
85	Joe Randa/GS	2.00
86	Lance Johnson/GS	2.00
87	Kevin Brown/GS	2.00
88	Curt Schilling/GS	4.00
89	Ismael Valdes/GS	2.00
90	Francisco Cordova/GS	2.00
91	David Cone/GS	2.00
92	Paul O'Neill/GS	2.00
93	Jimmy Key/GS	2.00
94	Brad Radke/GS	2.00
95	Kevin Appier/GS	2.00
96	Al Martin/GS	2.00
97	Rusty Greer/MZ	2.00
98	Reggie Jefferson/GS	2.00
99	Ron Coomer/GS	2.00
100	Vinny Castilla/GS	2.00
101	Bobby Bonilla/MZ	2.00
102	Eric Young/GS	2.00
103	Tony Womack/GS	2.00
104	Jason Kendall/GS	2.00
105	Jeff Suppan/GS	2.00
106	Shawn Estes/MZ	2.00
107	Shawn Green/GS	2.00
108	Edgardo Alfonzo/MZ	2.00
109	Alan Benes/MZ	2.00
110	Bobby Higginson/GS	2.00
111	Mark Grudzielanek/GS	2.00
112	Wilton Guerrero/GS	2.00
113	Todd Greene/GS	2.00
114	Pokey Reese/GS	2.00
115	Jose Guillen/GS	2.00
116	Neifi Perez/MZ	2.00
117	Luis Castillo/GS	2.00
118	Edgar Renteria/GS	2.00
119	Karim Garcia/GS	2.00
120	Butch Huskey/GS	2.00
121	Michael Tucker/GS	2.00
122	Jason Dickson/GS	2.00
123	Todd Walker/MZ	2.00
124	Brian Jordan/GS	2.00
125	Joe Carter/GS	2.00
126	Matt Morris/MZ	2.00
127	Brett Tomko/MZ	2.00
128	Mike Cameron/CL	2.00
129	Russ Davis/GS	2.00
130	Shannon Stewart/MZ	2.00
131	Kevin Orie/GS	2.00
132	Scott Spiezio/GS	2.00
133	Brian Giles/GS	2.00
134	Raul Casanova/GS	2.00
135	Jose Cruz Jr./CL	2.00
136	Hideki Irabu/GS	2.00
137	Bubba Trammell/GS	2.00
138	Richard Hidalgo/CL	2.00
139	Paul Konerko/CL	2.50
140	Todd Helton/FB	5.00
141	Miguel Tejada/GS	3.00
142	Fernando Tatis/GS	2.00
143	Ben Grieve/FB	2.00
144	Travis Lee/FB	2.00
145	Mark Kotsay/CL	2.00
146	Eli Marrero/MZ	2.00
147	David Ortiz/CL	4.00
148	Juan Encarnacion/MZ	2.00
149	Jaret Wright/MZ	2.00
150	Livan Hernandez/CL	2.00
151	Ruben Rivera/GS	2.00
152	Brad Fullmer/MZ	2.00
153	Dennis Reyes/MZ	2.00
154	Enrique Wilson/MZ	2.00
155	Todd Dunwoody/MZ	2.00
156	Derrick Gibson/MZ	2.00
157	Aaron Boone/MZ	2.00
158	Ron Wright/MZ	2.00
159	Preston Wilson/MZ	2.00
160	Abraham Nunez/GS	2.00
161	Shane Monahan/GS	2.00
162	Carl Pavano/GS	2.00
163	Derrek Lee/GS	4.00
164	Jeff Abbott/GS	2.00
165	Wes Helms/MZ	2.00
166	Brian Rose/GS	2.00
167	Bobby Estalella/GS	2.00
168	Ken Griffey Jr./GS	9.00
169	Frank Thomas/GS	6.00
170	Cal Ripken Jr./GS	15.00
171	Alex Rodriguez/GS	12.00
172	Greg Maddux/GS	7.50
173	Mike Piazza/GS	9.00
174	Chipper Jones/GS	7.50
175	Tony Gwynn/GS	7.50
176	Derek Jeter/GS	15.00
177	Jeff Bagwell/GS	6.00
178	Juan Gonzalez/GS	3.00
179	Nomar Garciaparra/GS	7.50
180	Andruw Jones/GS	6.00
181	Hideo Nomo/GS	3.00
182	Roger Clemens/GS	8.00
183	Mark McGwire/GS	12.00
184	Scott Rolen/GS	3.00
185	Barry Bonds/GS	15.00
186	Darin Erstad/GS	3.00
187	Mo Vaughn/GS	2.00
188	Ivan Rodriguez/GS	5.00
189	Larry Walker/MZ	2.00
190	Andy Pettitte/GS	3.00
191	Randy Johnson/MZ	2.00
192	Paul Molitor/GS	6.00
193	Jim Thome/GS	4.00
194	Tino Martinez/MZ	2.00
195	Gary Sheffield/GS	3.00
196	Albert Belle/GS	2.00
197	Jose Cruz Jr./GS	2.00
198	Todd Helton/GS	5.00
199	Ben Grieve/GS	2.00
200	Paul Konerko/GS	2.50

1998 Donruss Elite

	NM/M
Complete Set (150):	15.00
Common Player:	.10
Aspirations (750 Sets):	2.5X
Status (100 Sets):	15X
Pack (5):	2.50
Wax Box (18):	40.00
1 Ken Griffey Jr.	1.50
2 Frank Thomas	.75
3 Alex Rodriguez	2.00
4 Mike Piazza	1.50
5 Greg Maddux	1.00
6 Cal Ripken Jr.	2.50
7 Chipper Jones	1.00
8 Derek Jeter	2.50
9 Tony Gwynn	1.00
10 Andruw Jones	.75
11 Juan Gonzalez	.40
12 Jeff Bagwell	.75
13 Mark McGwire	2.00
14 Roger Clemens	1.25
15 Albert Belle	.10

16	Barry Bonds	2.50	
17	Kenny Lofton	.10	
18	Ivan Rodriguez	.65	
19	Manny Ramirez	.75	
20	Jim Thome	.50	
21	Chuck Knoblauch	.10	
22	Paul Molitor	.75	
23	Barry Larkin	.10	
24	Andy Pettitte	.40	
25	John Smoltz	.10	
26	Randy Johnson	.75	
27	Bernie Williams	.10	
28	Larry Walker	.10	
29	Mo Vaughn	.10	
30	Bobby Higginson	.10	
31	Edgardo Alfonzo	.10	
32	Justin Thompson	.10	
33	Jeff Suppan	.10	
34	Roberto Alomar	.30	
35	Hideo Nomo	.40	
36	Rusty Greer	.10	
37	Tim Salmon	.10	
38	Jim Edmonds	.10	
39	Gary Sheffield	.25	
40	Ken Caminiti	.10	
41	Sammy Sosa	1.00	
42	Tony Womack	.10	
43	Matt Williams	.10	
44	Andres Galarraga	.10	
45	Garret Anderson	.10	
46	Rafael Palmeiro	.65	
47	Mike Mussina	.40	
48	Craig Biggio	.10	
49	Wade Boggs	1.00	
50	Tom Glavine	.25	
51	Jason Giambi	.50	
52	Will Clark	.10	
53	David Justice	.10	
54	Sandy Alomar Jr.	.10	
55	Edgar Martinez	.10	
56	Brady Anderson	.10	
57	Eric Young	.10	
58	Ray Lankford	.10	
59	Kevin Brown	.10	
60	Raul Mondesi	.10	
61	Bobby Bonilla	.10	
62	Javier Lopez	.10	
63	Fred McGriff	.10	
64	Rondell White	.10	
65	Todd Hundley	.10	
66	Mark Grace	.10	
67	Alan Benes	.10	
68	Jeff Abbott	.10	
69	Bob Abreu	.10	
70	Deion Sanders	.10	
71	Tino Martinez	.10	
72	Shannon Stewart	.10	
73	Homer Bush	.10	
74	Carlos Delgado	.50	
75	Raul Ibanez	.10	
76	Hideki Irabu	.10	
77	Jose Cruz Jr.	.10	
78	Tony Clark	.10	
79	Wilton Guerrero	.10	
80	Vladimir Guerrero	.75	
81	Scott Rolen	.60	
82	Nomar Garciaparra	1.00	
83	Darin Erstad	.30	
84	Chan Ho Park	.10	
85	Mike Cameron	.10	
86	Todd Walker	.10	
87	Todd Dunwoody	.10	
88	Neifi Perez	.10	
89	Brett Tomko	.10	
90	Jose Guillen	.10	
91	Matt Morris	.10	
92	Bartolo Colon	.10	
93	Jaret Wright	.10	
94	Shawn Estes	.10	
95	Livan Hernandez	.10	
96	Bobby Estalella	.10	
97	Ben Grieve	.10	
98	Paul Konerko	.15	
99	David Ortiz	.40	
100	Todd Helton	.65	
101	Juan Encarnacion	.10	
102	Bubba Trammell	.10	
103	Miguel Tejada	.25	
104	Jacob Cruz	.10	
105	Todd Greene	.10	
106	Kevin Orie	.10	
107	Mark Kotsay	.10	
108	Fernando Tatis	.10	
109	Jay Payton	.10	
110	Pokey Reese	.10	
111	Derrek Lee	.10	
112	Richard Hidalgo	.10	
113	Ricky Ledee	.10	
114	Lou Collier	.10	
115	Ruben Rivera	.10	
116	Shawn Green	.20	
117	Moises Alou	.10	
118	Ken Griffey Jr.	.65	
119	Frank Thomas	.40	
120	Alex Rodriguez	.75	
121	Mike Piazza	.65	
122	Greg Maddux	.50	
123	Cal Ripken Jr.	1.00	
124	Chipper Jones	.50	
125	Derek Jeter	1.00	
126	Tony Gwynn	.50	
127	Andruw Jones	.40	
128	Juan Gonzalez	.20	
129	Jeff Bagwell	.40	
130	Mark McGwire	.75	
131	Roger Clemens	.65	
132	Albert Belle	.10	
133	Barry Bonds	1.00	
134	Kenny Lofton	.10	
135	Ivan Rodriguez	.25	
136	Manny Ramirez	.40	
137	Jim Thome	.25	
138	Chuck Knoblauch	.10	
139	Paul Molitor	.40	
140	Barry Larkin	.10	
141	Mo Vaughn	.10	
142	Hideki Irabu	.10	
143	Jose Cruz Jr.	.10	
144	Tony Clark	.10	
145	Vladimir Guerrero	.10	
146	Scott Rolen	.20	
147	Nomar Garciaparra	.50	
148	Nomar Garciaparra Checklist (Hit Streaks)	.40	
149	Larry Walker Checklist (Long HR-Coors)	.10	
150	Tino Martinez Checklist (3 HR in game)	.10	

Aspirations

	NM/M
Complete Set (150):	60.00
Common Player:	.50
Stars/Rookies:	2.5X

(See 1998 Donruss Elite for checklist and base card values.)

Status

	NM/M
Complete Set (150):	350.00
Common Player:	1.50
Stars/Rookies:	15X

(See 1998 Donruss Elite for checklist and base card values.)

Back to the Future

		NM/M
Complete Set (8):		40.00
Common Player:		2.50

Production 1,400 Sets

1	Cal Ripken Jr., Paul Konerko	9.00
2	Jeff Bagwell, Todd Helton	4.50
3	Eddie Mathews, Chipper Jones	5.00
4	Juan Gonzalez, Ben Grieve	2.50
5	Hank Aaron, Jose Cruz Jr.	7.50
6	Frank Thomas, David Ortiz	4.50
7	Nolan Ryan, Greg Maddux	9.00
8	Alex Rodriguez, Nomar Garciaparra	9.00

Back to the Future Autographs

		NM/M

Production 100 Sets

1a	Paul Konerko	30.00
1b	Cal Ripken Jr.	150.00
2	Jeff Bagwell, Todd Helton	120.00
3	Eddie Mathews, Chipper Jones	200.00
4	Juan Gonzalez, Ben Grieve	30.00
5	Hank Aaron, Jose Cruz Jr.	180.00
6	Not Issued In Autographed Form	
7	Nolan Ryan, Greg Maddux	850.00
8	Alex Rodriguez, Nomar Garciaparra	450.00
2	Frank Thomas (Specially autographed Elite)	45.00

Craftsmen

	NM/M
Complete Set (30):	40.00
Common Player:	.50

Production 3,500 Sets
Master Craftsman (100 Sets): 10X

1	Ken Griffey Jr.	3.00
2	Frank Thomas	1.50
3	Alex Rodriguez	4.00
4	Cal Ripken Jr.	5.00
5	Greg Maddux	2.00
6	Mike Piazza	3.00
7	Chipper Jones	2.00
8	Derek Jeter	5.00
9	Tony Gwynn	2.00
10	Nomar Garciaparra	2.00
11	Scott Rolen	1.25
12	Jose Cruz Jr.	.50
13	Tony Clark	.50
14	Vladimir Guerrero	1.50
15	Todd Helton	1.25
16	Ben Grieve	.50
17	Andruw Jones	1.50
18	Jeff Bagwell	1.50
19	Mark McGwire	4.00
20	Juan Gonzalez	.75
21	Roger Clemens	2.50
22	Albert Belle	.50
23	Barry Bonds	5.00
24	Kenny Lofton	.50
25	Ivan Rodriguez	1.25
26	Paul Molitor	1.50

Abbreviations

CC - Curtain Calls
GLR - Gold Leaf Rookies
GLS - Gold Leaf Stars
HL - Hit List
RR - Rated Rookie

27	Barry Larkin (Incorrect "CARDINALS" on front.)	.50
28	Mo Vaughn	.50
29	Larry Walker	.50
30	Tino Martinez	.50

Prime Numbers

	NM/M
Common Card:	5.00
Samples: 50% Player's Common	

1A	Ken Griffey Jr. 2/94	25.00
1B	Ken Griffey Jr. 9/204	20.00
1C	Ken Griffey Jr. 4/290	17.50
2A	Frank Thomas 4/56	25.00
2B	Frank Thomas 5/406	7.50
2C	Frank Thomas 6/450	7.50
3A	Mark McGwire 3/87	30.00
3B	Mark McGwire 8/307	20.00
3C	Mark McGwire 7/380	20.00
4A	Cal Ripken Jr. 5/17	135.00
4B	Cal Ripken Jr. 1/507	13.50
4C	Cal Ripken Jr. 7/510	13.50
5A	Mike Piazza 5/76	30.00
5B	Mike Piazza 7/506	12.00
5C	Mike Piazza 6/570	12.00
6A	Chipper Jones 4/89	25.00
6B	Chipper Jones 8/409	9.00
6C	Chipper Jones 9/480	9.00
7A	Tony Gwynn 3/72	25.00
7B	Tony Gwynn 7/302	9.00
7C	Tony Gwynn 2/370	9.00
8A	Barry Bonds 3/74	45.00
8B	Barry Bonds 7/304	12.00
8C	Barry Bonds 4/370	12.00
9A	Jeff Bagwell 4/25	25.00
9B	Jeff Bagwell 2/405	7.50
9C	Jeff Bagwell 5/420	7.50
10A	Juan Gonzalez 5/89	9.00
10B	Juan Gonzalez 8/509	6.00
10C	Juan Gonzalez 9/580	6.00
11A	Alex Rodriguez 5/34	55.00
11B	Alex Rodriguez 3/504	12.00
11C	Alex Rodriguez 4/530	12.00
12A	Kenny Lofton 3/54	15.00
12B	Kenny Lofton 5/304	5.00
12C	Kenny Lofton 4/350	5.00

1998 Donruss Preferred

	NM/M
Complete Set (200):	90.00
Common Grand Stand (5:1):	.10
Common Mezzanine (1:6):	.20
Common Club Level (1:12):	.30
Common Field Box: (1:23):	.40
Common Executive Suite (1:65):	1.50
Tin Pack (5):	3.00
Tin Box (24):	40.00

1	Ken Griffey Jr./EX	4.00
2	Frank Thomas/EX	2.50

3	Cal Ripken Jr./EX	7.50
4	Alex Rodriguez/EX	5.00
5	Greg Maddux/EX	3.00
6	Mike Piazza/EX	4.00
7	Chipper Jones/EX	3.00
8	Tony Gwynn/EX	2.50
9	Derek Jeter/FB	6.00
10	Jeff Bagwell/EX	2.50
11	Juan Gonzalez/EX	1.50
12	Nomar Garciaparra/EX	3.00
13	Andruw Jones/FB	2.00
14	Hideo Nomo/FB	.65
15	Roger Clemens/FB	3.00
16	Mark McGwire/FB	5.00
17	Scott Rolen/FB	.75
18	Vladimir Guerrero/FB	2.00
19	Barry Bonds/FB	6.00
20	Darin Erstad/FB	.60
21	Albert Belle/FB	.40
22	Kenny Lofton/FB	.40
23	Mo Vaughn/FB	.40
24	Tony Clark/FB	.40
25	Ivan Rodriguez/FB	1.50
26	Larry Walker/CL	.30
27	Eddie Murray/CL	1.00
28	Andy Pettitte/CL	.45
29	Roberto Alomar/CL	.40
30	Randy Johnson/CL	1.00
31	Manny Ramirez/CL	1.00
32	Paul Molitor/FB	2.00
33	Mike Mussina/CL	.50
34	Jim Thome/FB	.75
35	Tino Martinez/CL	.30
36	Gary Sheffield/CL	.45
37	Chuck Knoblauch/CL	.30
38	Bernie Williams/CL	.30
39	Tim Salmon/CL	.30
40	Sammy Sosa/CL	1.50
41	Wade Boggs/MZ	.75
42	Will Clark/MZ	.10
43	Andres Galarraga/CL	.30
44	Raul Mondesi/CL	.30
45	Rickey Henderson/CL	.50
46	Jose Canseco/GS	.35
47	Pedro Martinez/GS	.50
48	Jay Buhner/GS	.10
49	Ryan Klesko/GS	.10
50	Barry Larkin/CL	.30
51	Charles Johnson/GS	.10
52	Tom Glavine/GS	.25
53	Edgar Martinez/GS	.30
54	Fred McGriff/GS	.10
55	Moises Alou/MZ	.20
56	Dante Bichette/MZ	.10
57	Jim Edmonds/CL	.30
58	Mark Grace/MZ	.20
59	Chan Ho Park/MZ	.20
60	Justin Thompson/MZ	.20
61	John Smoltz/MZ	.20
62	Craig Biggio/CL	.30
63	Ken Caminiti/MZ	.20
64	Deion Sanders/MZ	.20
65	Carlos Delgado/GS	.30
66	David Justice/CL	.30
67	J.T. Snow/GS	.10
68	Jason Giambi/CL	.50
69	Garret Anderson/MZ	.20
70	Rondell White/MZ	.20
71	Matt Williams/MZ	.20
72	Brady Anderson/MZ	.20
73	Eric Karros/GS	.10
74	Javier Lopez/GS	.10
75	Pat Hentgen/GS	.10
76	Todd Hundley/GS	.10
77	Ray Lankford/GS	.10
78	Denny Neagle/GS	.10
79	Henry Rodriguez/GS	.10
80	Sandy Alomar Jr./MZ	.20
81	Rafael Palmeiro/MZ	.50
82	Robin Ventura/GS	.10
83	John Olerud/GS	.10
84	Omar Vizquel/GS	.10
85	Joe Randa/GS	.10
86	Lance Johnson/GS	.10
87	Kevin Brown/GS	.10
88	Curt Schilling/GS	.25
89	Ismael Valdes/GS	.10
90	Francisco Cordova/GS	.10
91	David Cone/GS	.10
92	Paul O'Neill/GS	.10
93	Jimmy Key/GS	.10
94	Brad Radke/GS	.10
95	Kevin Appier/GS	.10
96	Al Martin/GS	.10
97	Rusty Greer/MZ	.20
98	Reggie Jefferson/GS	.10
99	Ron Coomer/GS	.10
100	Vinny Castilla/GS	.10
101	Bobby Bonilla/MZ	.20
102	Eric Young/GS	.10
103	Tony Womack/GS	.10
104	Jason Kendall/GS	.10
105	Jeff Suppan/GS	.10
106	Shawn Estes/MZ	.20
107	Shawn Green/GS	.25
108	Edgardo Alfonzo/MZ	.20
109	Alan Benes/MZ	.20
110	Bobby Higginson/GS	.10
111	Mark Grudzielanek/GS	.10
112	Wilton Guerrero/GS	.10
113	Todd Greene/MZ	.20
114	Pokey Reese/GS	.10
115	Jose Guillen/CL	.30
116	Neifi Perez/MZ	.20
117	Luis Castillo/GS	.10
118	Edgar Renteria/GS	.10
119	Karim Garcia/GS	.10
120	Butch Huskey/GS	.10
121	Michael Tucker/GS	.10
122	Jason Dickson/GS	.10
123	Todd Walker/MZ	.20
124	Brian Jordan/GS	.10
125	Joe Carter/GS	.10
126	Matt Morris/MZ	.20
127	Brett Tomko/MZ	.20
128	Mike Cameron/CL	.30
129	Russ Davis/GS	.10
130	Shannon Stewart/MZ	.20
131	Kevin Orie/GS	.10
132	Scott Spiezio/GS	.10
133	Brian Giles/GS	.10
134	Raul Casanova/GS	.10
135	Jose Cruz Jr./CL	.30
136	Hideki Irabu/GS	.10
137	Bubba Trammell/GS	.10
138	Richard Hidalgo/CL	.30
139	Paul Konerko/CL	.35
140	Todd Helton/FB	1.00
141	Miguel Tejada/MZ	.40
142	Fernando Tatis/MZ	.20
143	Ben Grieve/FB	.40
144	Travis Lee/FB	.65
145	Mark Kotsay/CL	.30
146	Eli Marrero/MZ	.20
147	David Ortiz/CL	.50
148	Juan Encarnacion/MZ	.20
149	Jaret Wright/MZ	.20
150	Livan Hernandez/CL	.30
151	Ruben Rivera/GS	.10
152	Brad Fullmer/MZ	.20
153	Dennis Reyes/GS	.10
154	Enrique Wilson/MZ	.20
155	Todd Dunwoody/MZ	.20
156	Derrick Gibson/MZ	.20
157	Aaron Boone/MZ	.20
158	Ron Wright/MZ	.20
159	Preston Wilson/MZ	.20
160	Abraham Nunez/GS	.10
161	Shane Monahan/GS	.10
162	Carl Pavano/GS	.10
163	Derrek Lee/GS	.35
164	Jeff Abbott/GS	.10
165	Wes Helms/MZ	.20
166	Brian Rose/GS	.10
167	Bobby Estalella/GS	.10
168	Ken Griffey Jr./GS	.75
169	Frank Thomas/GS	.75
170	Cal Ripken Jr./GS	1.50
171	Alex Rodriguez/GS	1.00
172	Greg Maddux/GS	.60
173	Mike Piazza/GS	.75
174	Chipper Jones/GS	.60
175	Tony Gwynn/GS	.60
176	Derek Jeter/GS	1.50
177	Jeff Bagwell/GS	.50
178	Juan Gonzalez/GS	.30
179	Nomar Garciaparra/GS	.60
180	Andruw Jones/GS	.50
181	Hideo Nomo/GS	.30
182	Roger Clemens/GS	.65
183	Mark McGwire/GS	1.00
184	Scott Rolen/GS	.35
185	Barry Bonds/GS	1.50
186	Darin Erstad/GS	.25
187	Mo Vaughn/GS	.10
188	Ivan Rodriguez/GS	.40
189	Larry Walker/MZ	.20
190	Andy Pettitte/GS	.30
191	Randy Johnson/MZ	.60
192	Paul Molitor/GS	.50
193	Jim Thome/GS	.35
194	Tino Martinez/MZ	.20
195	Gary Sheffield/GS	.30
196	Albert Belle/GS	.10
197	Jose Cruz Jr./GS	.10
198	Todd Helton/GS	.40
199	Ben Grieve/GS	.10
200	Paul Konerko/GS	.20

Seating

	NM/M
Common Grand Stand:	.50
Stars and Rookies:	4X
Common Mezzanine:	.50
Stars and Rookies:	2X
Common Club Level:	.50
Stars and Rookies:	2X
Common Field Box:	1.00
Stars and Rookies:	1.5X
Common Executive Suite:	2.50
Stars and Rookies:	1X

(See 1998 Donruss Preferred for checklistand base card values.)

Great X-pectations

		NM/M
Complete Set (26):		35.00
Common Player:		.75
Die-Cuts:		3X
Samples:		1X
1	Jeff Bagwell, Travis Lee	1.25
2	Jose Cruz Jr., Ken Griffey Jr.	2.00
3	Larry Walker, Ben Grieve	.75
4	Frank Thomas, Todd Helton	1.25
5	Jim Thome, Paul Konerko	1.00
6	Alex Rodriguez, Miguel Tejada	2.50
7	Greg Maddux, Livan Hernandez	1.75
8	Roger Clemens, Jaret Wright	1.75
9	Albert Belle, Juan Encarnacion	.75
10	Mo Vaughn, David Ortiz	1.00
11	Manny Ramirez, Mark Kotsay	1.25
12	Tim Salmon, Brad Fullmer	.75
13	Cal Ripken Jr., Fernando Tatis	3.50
14	Hideo Nomo, Hideki Irabu	1.50
15	Mike Piazza, Todd Greene	2.00
16	Gary Sheffield, Richard Hidalgo	.75
17	Paul Molitor, Darin Erstad	1.25
18	Ivan Rodriguez, Eli Marrero	1.00
19	Ken Caminiti, Todd Walker	.75
20	Tony Gwynn, Jose Guillen	1.75
21	Derek Jeter, Nomar Garciaparra	3.50
22	Chipper Jones, Scott Rolen	1.75
23	Juan Encarnacion, Andruw Jones	1.25
24	Barry Bonds, Vladimir Guerrero	3.50
25	Mark McGwire, Tony Clark	2.50
26	Bernie Williams, Mike Cameron	.75

Precious Metals

		NM/M
Complete Set (30):		850.00
Common Player:		7.50
1	Ken Griffey Jr.	50.00
2	Frank Thomas	35.00
3	Cal Ripken Jr.	75.00
4	Alex Rodriguez	60.00
5	Greg Maddux	45.00
6	Mike Piazza	50.00
7	Chipper Jones	45.00
8	Tony Gwynn	45.00
9	Derek Jeter	75.00
10	Jeff Bagwell	35.00
11	Juan Gonzalez	15.00
12	Nomar Garciaparra	45.00
13	Andruw Jones	35.00
14	Hideo Nomo	15.00
15	Roger Clemens	45.00
16	Mark McGwire	60.00
17	Scott Rolen	25.00
18	Barry Bonds	75.00
19	Darin Erstad	15.00
20	Kenny Lofton	7.50
21	Mo Vaughn	7.50
22	Ivan Rodriguez	25.00
23	Randy Johnson	35.00
24	Paul Molitor	35.00
25	Jose Cruz Jr.	7.50
26	Paul Konerko	7.50
27	Todd Helton	25.00
28	Ben Grieve	7.50
29	Travis Lee	7.50
30	Mark Kotsay	7.50

Title Waves

		NM/M
Complete Set (30):		100.00
Common Player:		
1	Nomar Garciaparra	5.00
2	Scott Rolen	2.50
3	Roger Clemens	5.50
4	Gary Sheffield	1.50
5	Jeff Bagwell	3.50
6	Cal Ripken Jr.	10.00
7	Frank Thomas	3.50
8	Ken Griffey Jr.	6.00
9	Larry Walker	1.00
10	Derek Jeter	10.00
11	Juan Gonzalez	2.00
12	Bernie Williams	1.00
13	Andruw Jones	3.50
14	Andy Pettitte	1.50
15	Ivan Rodriguez	2.50
16	Alex Rodriguez	8.00
17	Mark McGwire	8.00
18	Andres Galarraga	1.00
19	Hideo Nomo	2.00
20	Mo Vaughn	1.00
21	Randy Johnson	3.50
22	Chipper Jones	5.00
23	Greg Maddux	5.00
24	Manny Ramirez	3.50
25	Tony Gwynn	5.00
26	Albert Belle	1.00
27	Kenny Lofton	1.00
28	Mike Piazza	6.00
29	Paul Molitor	3.50
30	Barry Bonds	10.00

1998 Donruss Signature Series

	NM/M
Complete Set (140):	30.00
Common Player:	.10
Signature Proofs:	12X
Pack (5):	12.50

Wax Box (12): 150.00
1 David Justice .10
2 Derek Jeter 2.50
3 Nomar Garciaparra 1.00
4 Ryan Klesko .10
5 Jeff Bagwell .75
6 Dante Bichette .10
7 Ivan Rodriguez .65
8 Albert Belle .10
9 Cal Ripken Jr. 2.50
10 Craig Biggio .10
11 Barry Larkin .10
12 Jose Guillen .10
13 Will Clark .10
14 J.T. Snow .10
15 Chuck Knoblauch .10
16 Todd Walker .10
17 Scott Rolen .60
18 Rickey Henderson .75
19 Juan Gonzalez .40
20 Justin Thompson .10
21 Roger Clemens 1.25
22 Ray Lankford .10
23 Jose Cruz Jr. .10
24 Ken Griffey Jr. 1.50
25 Andruw Jones .75
26 Darin Erstad .30
27 Jim Thome .50
28 Wade Boggs 1.00
29 Ken Caminiti .10
30 Todd Hundley .10
31 Mike Piazza 1.50
32 Sammy Sosa 1.00
33 Larry Walker .10
34 Matt Williams .10
35 Frank Thomas .75
36 Gary Sheffield .30
37 Alex Rodriguez 2.00
38 Hideo Nomo .40
39 Kenny Lofton .10
40 John Smoltz .10
41 Mo Vaughn .10
42 Edgar Martinez .10
43 Paul Molitor .75
44 Rafael Palmeiro .65
45 Barry Bonds 2.50
46 Vladimir Guerrero .75
47 Carlos Delgado .50
48 Bobby Higginson .10
49 Greg Maddux 1.00
50 Jim Edmonds .10
51 Randy Johnson .75
52 Mark McGwire 2.00
53 Rondell White .10
54 Raul Mondesi .10
55 Manny Ramirez .75
56 Pedro Martinez .75
57 Tim Salmon .10
58 Moises Alou .10
59 Fred McGriff .10
60 Garret Anderson .10
61 Sandy Alomar Jr. .10
62 Chan Ho Park .10
63 Mark Kotsay .10
64 Mike Mussina .50
65 Tom Glavine .25
66 Tony Clark .10
67 Mark Grace .10
68 Tony Gwynn 1.00
69 Tino Martinez .10
70 Kevin Brown .10
71 Todd Greene .10
72 Andy Pettitte .30
73 Livan Hernandez .10
74 Curt Schilling .25
75 Andres Galarraga .10
76 Rusty Greer .10
77 Jay Buhner .10
78 Bobby Bonilla .10
79 Chipper Jones 1.00
80 Eric Young .10
81 Jason Giambi .50
82 Javy Lopez .10

83 Roberto Alomar .25
84 Bernie Williams .10
85 A.J. Hinch .10
86 Kerry Wood .40
87 Juan Encarnacion .10
88 Brad Fullmer .10
89 Ben Grieve .10
90 Magglio Ordonez RC 2.00
91 Todd Helton .65
92 Richard Hidalgo .10
93 Paul Konerko .15
94 Aramis Ramirez .10
95 Ricky Ledee .10
96 Derrek Lee .50
97 Travis Lee .15
98 Matt Anderson RC .25
99 Jaret Wright .10
100 David Ortiz .35
101 Carl Pavano .10
102 Orlando
  Hernandez RC .50
103 Fernando Tatis .10
104 Miguel Tejada .30
105 Rolando Arrojo RC .50
106 Kevin Millwood RC 1.00
107 Ken Griffey Jr. .50
108 Frank Thomas .30
109 Cal Ripken Jr. .75
110 Greg Maddux .40
111 John Olerud .10
112 David Cone .10
113 Vinny Castilla .10
114 Jason Kendall .10
115 Brian Jordan .10
116 Hideki Irabu .10
117 Bartolo Colon .10
118 Greg Vaughn .10
119 David Segui .10
120 Bruce Chen .10
121 Julio Ramirez RC .10
122 Troy Glaus RC 4.00
123 Jeremy Giambi RC .50
124 Ryan Minor RC .15
125 Richie Sexson .10
126 Dermal Brown .10
127 Adrian Beltre .15
128 Eric Chavez .30
129 J.D. Drew RC 4.00
130 Gabe Kapler RC .30
131 Masato Yoshii RC .25
132 Mike Lowell RC 1.00
133 Jim Parque RC .25
134 Roy Halladay .10
135 Carlos Lee RC 1.00
136 Jin Ho Cho RC .25
137 Michael Barrett .10
138 Fernando
  Seguignol RC .40
139 Odalis Perez RC .50
140 Mark McGwire .65

Proofs

	NM/M
Complete Set (140):	450.00
Common Player:	1.00
Stars/Rookies:	12X

(See 1998 Donruss Signature
Series for checklist and base card
values.)

Autographs (Red)

	NM/M
Common Player:	2.50

(1) Roberto Alomar/150 35.00
(2) Sandy Alomar Jr./
  700 10.00
(3) Moises Alou/900 15.00
(4) Gabe Alvarez/2,900 2.50
(5) Wilson Alvarez/1,600 4.00
(6) Jay Bell/1,500 4.00
(7) Adrian Beltre/1,900 25.00
(8) Andy Benes/2,600 4.00

(9) Aaron Boone/3,400 8.00
(10) Russell Branyan/
  1,650 4.00
(11) Orlando Cabrera/
  3,100 8.00
(12) Mike Cameron/1,150 8.00
(13) Joe Carter/400 10.00
(14) Sean Casey/2,275 8.00
(15) Bruce Chen/150 5.00
(16) Tony Clark/2,275 5.00
(17) Will Clark/1,400 15.00
(18) Matt Clement/1,400 4.00
(19) Pat Cline/400 5.00
(20) Ken Cloude/3,400 2.50
(21) Michael Coleman/
  2,800 2.50
(22) David Cone/25 50.00
(23) Jeff Conine/1,400 5.00
(24) Jacob Cruz/3,200 2.50
(25) Russ Davis/3,500 2.50
(26) Jason Dickson/1,400 4.00
(27) Todd Dunwoody/3,500 2.50
(28) Juan Encarnacion/
  3,400 5.00
(29) Darin Erstad/700) 10.00
(30) Bobby Estalella/3,400 4.00
(31) Jeff Fassero/3,400 2.50
(32) John Franco/1,800 2.50
(33) Brad Fullmer/3,100 5.00
(34) Jason Giambi/3,100 15.00
(35) Derrick Gibson/1,200 5.00
(36) Todd Greene/1,400 5.00
(37) Ben Grieve/1,400 5.00
(38) Mark Grudzielanek/
  3,200 4.00
(39) Vladimir Guerrero/
  2,100 25.00
(40) Wilton Guerrero/
  1,900 4.00
(41) Jose Guillen/2,400 5.00
(42) Todd Helton/1,300 20.00
(43) Richard Hidalgo/
  3,400 4.00
(44) A.J. Hinch/2,900 4.00
(45) Butch Huskey/1,900 4.00
(46) Raul Ibanez/3,300 2.50
(47) Damian Jackson/900 2.50
(48) Geoff Jenkins/3,100 6.00
(49) Eric Karros/650 8.00
(50) Ryan Klesko/400 8.00
(51) Mark Kotsay/3,600 5.00
(52) Ricky Ledee/2,200 5.00
(53) Derrek Lee/3,400 15.00
(54) Travis Lee/150 10.00
(54s) Travis Lee
  (Facsimile autograph,
  "SAMPLE" on back.) 3.00
(55) Javier Lopez/650 8.00
(56) Mike Lowell/3,500 10.00
(57) Greg Maddux/12 625.00
(58) Eli Marrero/3,400 5.00
(59) Al Martin/1,300 4.00
(60) Rafael Medina/1,400 2.50
(61) Scott Morgan/900 4.50
(62) Abraham Nunez/3,500 2.50
(63) Paul O'Neill/1,000 20.00
(64) Luis Ordaz/2,700 2.50
(65) Magglio Ordonez/
  3,200 15.00
(66) Kevin Orie/1,350 5.00
(67) David Ortiz/3,400 25.00
(68) Rafael Palmeiro/
  1,000 20.00
(69) Carl Pavano/2,600 5.00
(70) Neifi Perez/3,300 2.50
(71) Dante Powell/3,050 2.50
(72) Aramis Ramirez/
  2,800 10.00
(73) Mariano Rivera/900 35.00
(74) Felix Rodriguez/1,400 3.00
(75) Henry Rodriguez/
  3,400 3.00
(76) Scott Rolen/1,900 30.00

(77) Brian Rose/1,400 3.00
(78) Curt Schilling/900 30.00
(79) Richie Sexson/3,500 8.00
(80) Randall Simon/3,500 3.00
(81) J.T. Snow/400 10.00
(82) Jeff Suppan/1,400 5.00
(83) Fernando Tatis/3,900 3.00
(84) Miguel Tejada/3,800 15.00
(85) Brett Tomko/3,400 2.50
(86) Bubba Trammell/3,900 2.50
(87) Ismael Valdez/1,900 5.00
(88) Robin Ventura/1,400 5.00
(89) Billy Wagner/3,900 10.00
(90) Todd Walker/1,900 5.00
(91) Daryle Ward/400 4.00
(92) Rondell White/3,400 5.00
(93) Antone Williamson/
  3,350 2.50
(94) Dan Wilson/2,400 4.00
(95) Enrique Wilson/3,400 2.50
(96) Preston Wilson/2,100 5.00
(97) Tony Womack/3,500 2.50
(98) Kerry Wood/3,400 10.00

Century Marks (Blue)

	NM/M
Common Player:	10.00

(1) Roberto Alomar 60.00
(2) Sandy Alomar Jr. 15.00
(3) Moises Alou 40.00
(4) Gabe Alvarez 10.00
(5) Wilson Alvarez 10.00
(6) Brady Anderson 15.00
(7) Jay Bell 15.00
(8) Albert Belle 20.00
(9) Adrian Beltre 25.00
(10) Andy Benes 10.00
(11) Wade Boggs 60.00
(12) Barry Bonds 250.00
(13) Aaron Boone 25.00
(14) Russell Branyan 10.00
(15) Jay Buhner 10.00
(16) Ellis Burks 10.00
(17) Orlando Cabrera 25.00
(18) Mike Cameron 10.00
(19) Ken Caminiti 25.00
(20) Joe Carter 20.00
(21) Sean Casey 15.00
(22) Bruce Chen 10.00
(23) Tony Clark 10.00
(24) Will Clark 40.00
(25) Roger Clemens 200.00
(26) Matt Clement 20.00
(27) Pat Cline 10.00
(28) Ken Cloude 10.00
(29) Michael Coleman 10.00
(30) David Cone 25.00
(31) Jeff Conine 10.00
(32) Jacob Cruz 10.00
(33) Jose Cruz Jr. 15.00
(34) Russ Davis 10.00
(35) Jason Dickson 10.00
(36) Todd Dunwoody 10.00
(37) Scott Elarton 10.00
(38) Darin Erstad 25.00
(39) Bobby Estalella 10.00
(40) Jeff Fassero 10.00
(41) John Franco 10.00
(42) Brad Fullmer 10.00
(43) Andres Galarraga 15.00
(44) Nomar Garciaparra 80.00
(45) Jason Giambi 40.00
(46) Derrick Gibson 10.00
(47) Tom Glavine 75.00
(48) Juan Gonzalez 50.00
(49) Todd Greene 10.00
(50) Ben Grieve 10.00
(51) Mark Grudzielanek 10.00
(52) Vladimir Guerrero 75.00
(53) Wilton Guerrero 10.00
(54) Jose Guillen 10.00
(55) Tony Gwynn 80.00
(56) Todd Helton 60.00

(57)	Richard Hidalgo	10.00
(58)	A.J. Hinch	10.00
(59)	Butch Huskey	10.00
(60)	Raul Ibanez	10.00
(61)	Damian Jackson	10.00
(62)	Geoff Jenkins	10.00
(63)	Derek Jeter	200.00
(64)	Randy Johnson	150.00
(65)	Chipper Jones	100.00
(66)	Eric Karros/50	15.00
(67)	Jason Kendall (Unsigned)	20.00
(68)	Ryan Klesko	10.00
(69)	Chuck Knoblauch	10.00
(70)	Mark Kotsay	10.00
(71)	Ricky Ledee	10.00
(72)	Derrek Lee	25.00
(73)	Travis Lee	15.00
(74)	Javier Lopez	25.00
(75)	Mike Lowell	30.00
(76)	Greg Maddux	150.00
(77)	Eli Marrero	10.00
(78)	Al Martin	10.00
(79)	Rafael Medina	10.00
(80)	Paul Molitor	50.00
(81)	Scott Morgan	10.00
(82)	Mike Mussina	75.00
(83)	Abraham Nunez	15.00
(84)	Paul O'Neill	40.00
(85)	Luis Ordaz	10.00
(86)	Magglio Ordonez	30.00
(87)	Kevin Orie	10.00
(88)	David Ortiz	75.00
(89)	Rafael Palmeiro	75.00
(90)	Carl Pavano	25.00
(91)	Neifi Perez	10.00
(92)	Andy Pettitte	50.00
(93)	Aramis Ramirez	25.00
(94)	Cal Ripken Jr.	200.00
(95)	Mariano Rivera	75.00
(96)	Alex Rodriguez	200.00
(97)	Felix Rodriguez	10.00
(98)	Henry Rodriguez	10.00
(99)	Scott Rolen	70.00
(100)	Brian Rose	10.00
(101)	Curt Schilling	50.00
(102)	Richie Sexson	20.00
(103)	Randall Simon	10.00
(104)	J.T. Snow	10.00
(105)	Darryl Strawberry	40.00
(106)	Jeff Suppan	10.00
(107)	Fernando Tatis	10.00
(108)	Brett Tomko	10.00
(109)	Bubba Trammell	10.00
(110)	Ismael Valdez	10.00
(111)	Robin Ventura	20.00
(112)	Billy Wagner	40.00
(113)	Todd Walker	15.00
(114)	Daryle Ward	10.00
(115)	Rondell White	20.00
(116)	Matt Williams/80	35.00
(117)	Antone Williamson	10.00
(118)	Dan Wilson	15.00
(119)	Enrique Wilson	10.00
(120)	Preston Wilson	15.00
(121)	Tony Womack	10.00
(122)	Kerry Wood	40.00

Millennium Marks (Green)

		NM/M
Common Player:		3.00
(1)	Roberto Alomar	25.00
(2)	Sandy Alomar Jr.	5.00
(3)	Moises Alou	10.00
(4)	Gabe Alvarez	3.00
(5)	Wilson Alvarez	3.00
(6)	Brady Anderson/800	8.00
(7)	Jay Bell	3.00
(8)	Albert Belle/400	10.00
(9)	Adrian Beltre	15.00
(10)	Andy Benes	3.00

(11)	Wade Boggs/900	20.00
(12)	Barry Bonds/400	150.00
(13)	Aaron Boone	4.00
(14)	Russell Branyan	3.00
(15)	Jay Buhner/400	10.00
(16)	Ellis Burks/900	5.00
(17)	Orlando Cabrera	6.00
(18)	Mike Cameron	5.00
(19)	Ken Caminiti/900	20.00
(20)	Joe Carter	8.00
(21)	Sean Casey	8.00
(22)	Bruce Chen	3.00
(23)	Tony Clark	5.00
(24)	Will Clark	25.00
(25)	Roger Clemens/400	75.00
(26)	Matt Clement/900	8.00
(27)	Pat Cline	3.00
(28)	Ken Cloude	3.00
(29)	Michael Coleman	3.00
(30)	David Cone	10.00
(31)	Jeff Conine	3.00
(32)	Jacob Cruz	3.00
(33)	Jose Cruz Jr./850	5.00
(34)	Russ Davis/950	3.00
(35)	Jason Dickson/950	3.00
(36)	Todd Dunwoody	3.00
(37)	Scott Elarton/900	3.00
(38)	Juan Encarnacion	5.00
(39)	Darin Erstad	5.00
(40)	Bobby Estalella	3.00
(41)	Jeff Fassero	3.00
(42)	John Franco/950	5.00
(43)	Brad Fullmer	3.00
(44)	Andres Galarraga/900	10.00
(45)	Nomar Garciaparra/400	60.00
(46)	Jason Giambi	20.00
(47)	Derrick Gibson	3.00
(48)	Tom Glavine/700	25.00
(49)	Juan Gonzalez	20.00
(50)	Todd Greene	3.00
(51)	Ben Grieve	4.00
(52)	Mark Grudzielanek	3.00
(53)	Vladimir Guerrero	30.00
(54)	Wilton Guerrero	3.00
(55)	Jose Guillen	3.00
(56)	Tony Gwynn/900	30.00
(57)	Todd Helton	20.00
(58)	Richard Hidalgo	3.00
(59)	A.J. Hinch	3.00
(60)	Butch Huskey	3.00
(61)	Raul Ibanez	3.00
(62)	Damian Jackson	3.00
(63)	Geoff Jenkins	3.00
(64)	Derek Jeter/400	100.00
(65)	Randy Johnson/900	50.00
(66)	Chipper Jones/900	30.00
(67)	Eric Karros	5.00
(68)	Ryan Klesko	5.00
(69)	Chuck Knoblauch/900	10.00
(70)	Mark Kotsay	5.00
(71)	Ricky Ledee	3.00
(72)	Derrek Lee	20.00
(73)	Travis Lee	5.00
(74)	Javier Lopez/800	10.00
(75)	Mike Lowell	10.00
(76)	Greg Maddux/400	85.00
(77)	Eli Marrero	3.00
(78)	Al Martin/950	3.00
(79)	Rafael Medina/850	3.00
(80)	Paul Molitor/900	20.00
(81)	Scott Morgan	3.00
(82)	Mike Mussina/900	15.00
(83)	Abraham Nunez	3.00
(84)	Paul O'Neill/900	20.00
(85)	Luis Ordaz	3.00
(86)	Magglio Ordonez	15.00
(87)	Kevin Orie	3.00
(88)	David Ortiz	40.00
(89)	Rafael Palmeiro/900	30.00
(90)	Carl Pavano	10.00
(91)	Neifi Perez	3.00
(92)	Andy Pettitte/900	20.00
(93)	Dante Powell/950	3.00
(94)	Aramis Ramirez	10.00
(95)	Cal Ripken Jr./375	100.00
(96)	Mariano Rivera	30.00
(97)	Alex Rodriguez/350	75.00
(98)	Felix Rodriguez	5.00
(99)	Henry Rodriguez	3.00
(100)	Scott Rolen	20.00
(101)	Brian Rose	3.00
(102)	Curt Schilling	20.00
(103)	Richie Sexson	8.00
(104)	Randall Simon	3.00
(105)	J.T. Snow	4.00
(106)	Darryl Strawberry/900	40.00
(107)	Jeff Suppan	3.00
(108)	Fernando Tatis	5.00
(109)	Miguel Tejada	40.00
(110)	Brett Tomko	3.00
(111)	Bubba Trammell	3.00
(112)	Ismael Valdes	3.00
(113)	Robin Ventura	5.00

(114)	Billy Wagner/900	10.00
(115)	Todd Walker	4.00
(116)	Daryle Ward	5.00
(117)	Rondell White	5.00
(118)	Matt Williams/820	8.00
(119)	Antone Williamson	3.00
(120)	Dan Wilson	3.00
(121)	Enrique Wilson	3.00
(122)	Preston Wilson/400	10.00
(123)	Tony Womack	3.00
(124)	Kerry Wood	20.00

Preview Autographs

		NM/M
Common Player:		10.00
(1)	Sandy Alomar Jr./96	30.00
(2)	Moises Alou	50.00
(3)	Andy Benes/135	15.00
(4)	Russell Branyan/188	15.00
(5)	Sean Casey	85.00
(6)	Tony Clark/188	20.00
(7)	Juan Encarnacion/193	15.00
(8)	Brad Fullmer/396	10.00
(9)	Juan Gonzalez/108	115.00
(10)	Ben Grieve/100	35.00
(11)	Todd Helton/101	50.00
(12)	Richard Hidalgo/380	10.00
(13)	A.J. Hinch/400	10.00
(14)	Damian Jackson/15	65.00
(15)	Geoff Jenkins	185.00
(16)	Derek Jeter	1,225
(17)	Chipper Jones/112	125.00
(18)	Chuck Knoblauch/98	50.00
(19)	Travis Lee/101	20.00
(20)	Mike Lowell/450	15.00
(21)	Greg Maddux/92	165.00
(22)	Kevin Millwood/395	30.00
(23)	Magglio Ordonez/420	50.00
(24)	David Ortiz/393	75.00
(25)	Rafael Palmeiro/107	50.00
(26)	Cal Ripken Jr./22	850.00
(27)	Alex Rodriguez/23	1,150
(28)	Curt Schilling/100	100.00
(29)	Randall Simon/380	10.00
(30)	Fernando Tatis/100	10.00
(31)	Miguel Tejada/375	40.00
(32)	Robin Ventura/95	30.00
(33)	Dan Wilson	85.00
(34)	Kerry Wood/373	40.00

Redemption Baseballs

		NM/M
Common Autographed Ball:		15.00
Redemption Card:		10%
(1)	Roberto Alomar/60	35.00
(2)	Sandy Alomar Jr./60	20.00
(3)	Ernie Banks/12	85.00
(4)	Ken Caminiti/60	20.00
(5)	Tony Clark/60	20.00
(6)	Jacob Cruz/12	20.00
(7)	Russ Davis/60	15.00
(8)	Juan Encarnacion/60	20.00
(9)	Bobby Estalella/60	15.00
(10)	Jeff Fassero/60	15.00
(11)	Mark Grudzielanek/60	15.00
(12)	Ben Grieve/30	20.00
(13)	Jose Guillen/120	20.00
(14)	Tony Gwynn/60	100.00
(15)	Al Kaline/12	75.00
(16)	Paul Konerko/100	15.00
(17)	Travis Lee/100	20.00
(18)	Mike Lowell/60	15.00
(19)	Eli Marrero/60	15.00
(20)	Eddie Mathews/12	80.00
(21)	Paul Molitor/60	65.00
(22)	Stan Musial/12	125.00
(23)	Abraham Nunez/12	20.00
(24)	Luis Ordaz/12	20.00
(25)	Magglio Ordonez/12	50.00

(26)	Scott Rolen/60	45.00
(27)	Bubba Trammell/24	25.00
(28)	Robin Ventura/60	20.00
(29)	Billy Wagner/60	20.00
(30)	Rondell White/60	20.00
(31)	Antone Williamson/12	15.00
(32)	Tony Womack/60	15.00

Significant Signatures

	NM/M
Complete Set (18):	425.00
Common Player:	10.00
Ernie Banks	25.00
Yogi Berra	25.00
George Brett	40.00
Catfish Hunter	35.00
Al Kaline	25.00
Harmon Killebrew	25.00
Ralph Kiner	10.00
Sandy Koufax	100.00
Eddie Mathews	25.00
Don Mattingly	50.00
Willie McCovey	25.00
Stan Musial	40.00
Phil Rizzuto (Edition of 1,000.)	20.00
Nolan Ryan	60.00
Nolan Ryan (Exchange card.)	5.00
Ozzie Smith	20.00
Ozzie Smith (Exchange card.)	5.00
Duke Snider	25.00
Don Sutton	12.00
Billy Williams	12.00

2001 Donruss

	NM/M
Complete Set (220):	
Common Player:	.15
Common Rated Rookie (151-200):	4.00
Production 2001	
Hobby Pack (5):	6.00
Hobby Box (24):	120.00
The Rookies Coupon:	1.00
Inserted 1:72	
Baseball's Best Coupon:	1.00
Inserted 1:720	
Exchange Deadline 11/01/01	

1	Alex Rodriguez	2.00
2	Barry Bonds	2.50
3	Cal Ripken Jr.	2.50
4	Chipper Jones	1.00
5	Derek Jeter	2.50
6	Troy Glaus	.50
7	Frank Thomas	.75
8	Greg Maddux	1.00
9	Ivan Rodriguez	.50
10	Jeff Bagwell	.50
11	Jose Canseco	.40

12	Todd Helton	.50
13	Ken Griffey Jr.	1.50
14	Manny Ramirez	.75
15	Mark McGwire	2.00
16	Mike Piazza	1.50
17	Nomar Garciaparra	1.00
18	Pedro Martinez	1.00
19	Randy Johnson	.75
20	Rick Ankiel	.15
21	Ricky Henderson	.75
22	Roger Clemens	2.00
23	Sammy Sosa	1.00
24	Tony Gwynn	1.00
25	Vladimir Guerrero	.75
26	Eric Davis	.15
27	Roberto Alomar	.25
28	Mark Mulder	.25
29	Pat Burrell	.40
30	Harold Baines	.15
31	Carlos Delgado	.40
32	J.D. Drew	.25
33	Jim Edmonds	.40
34	Darin Erstad	.25
35	Jason Giambi	.50
36	Tom Glavine	.30
37	Juan Gonzalez	.35
38	Mark Grace	.25
39	Shawn Green	.25
40	Tim Hudson	.25
41	Andruw Jones	.75
42	David Justice	.15
43	Jeff Kent	.25
44	Barry Larkin	.25
45	Pokey Reese	.15
46	Mike Mussina	.40
47	Hideo Nomo	.35
48	Rafael Palmeiro	.50
49	Adam Piatt	.15
50	Scott Rolen	.75
51	Gary Sheffield	.40
52	Bernie Williams	.25
53	Bob Abreu	.25
54	Edgardo Alfonzo	.15
55	Jermaine Clark RC	.15
56	Albert Belle	.15
57	Craig Biggio	.25
58	Andres Galarraga	.15
59	Edgar Martinez	.15
60	Fred McGriff	.15
61	Magglio Ordonez	.15
62	Jim Thome	.50
63	Matt Williams	.15
64	Kerry Wood	.25
65	Moises Alou	.15
66	Brady Anderson	.15
67	Garret Anderson	.15
68	Tony Armas Jr.	.15
69	Tony Batista	.15
70	Jose Cruz Jr.	.15
71	Carlos Beltran	.50
72	Adrian Beltre	.25
73	Kris Benson	.15
74	Lance Berkman	.40
75	Kevin Brown	.15
76	Jay Buhner	.15
77	Jeromy Burnitz	.15
78	Ken Caminiti	.15
79	Sean Casey	.25
80	Luis Castillo	.15
81	Eric Chavez	.25
82	Jeff Cirillo	.15
83	Bartolo Colon	.15
84	David Cone	.15
85	Freddy Garcia	.15
86	Johnny Damon	.50
87	Ray Durham	.15
88	Jermaine Dye	.15
89	Juan Encarnacion	.15
90	Terrence Long	.15
91	Carl Everett	.15
92	Steve Finley	.15
93	Cliff Floyd	.15
94	Brad Fullmer	.15
95	Brian Giles	.15
96	Luis Gonzalez	.15
97	Rusty Greer	.15
98	Jeffrey Hammonds	.15
99	Mike Hampton	.15
100	Orlando Hernandez	.15
101	Richard Hidalgo	.15
102	Geoff Jenkins	.15
103	Jacque Jones	.15
104	Brian Jordan	.15
105	Gabe Kapler	.15
106	Eric Karros	.15
107	Jason Kendall	.15
108	Adam Kennedy	.15
109	Byung-Hyun Kim	.15
110	Ryan Klesko	.15
111	Chuck Knoblauch	.15
112	Paul Konerko	.40
113	Carlos Lee	.25
114	Kenny Lofton	.15
115	Javy Lopez	.15

116	Tino Martinez	.15
117	Ruben Mateo	.15
118	Kevin Millwood	.15
119	Ben Molina	.15
120	Raul Mondesi	.15
121	Trot Nixon	.15
122	John Olerud	.15
123	Paul O'Neill	.15
124	Chan Ho Park	.15
125	Andy Pettitte	.25
126	Jorge Posada	.25
127	Mark Quinn	.15
128	Aramis Ramirez	.40
129	Mariano Rivera	.25
130	Tim Salmon	.15
131	Curt Schilling	.75
132	Richie Sexson	.40
133	John Smoltz	.25
134	J.T. Snow	.15
135	Jay Payton	.15
136	Shannon Stewart	.15
137	B.J. Surhoff	.15
138	Mike Sweeney	.15
139	Fernando Tatis	.15
140	Miguel Tejada	.40
141	Jason Varitek	.40
142	Greg Vaughn	.15
143	Mo Vaughn	.15
144	Robin Ventura	.15
145	Jose Vidro	.15
146	Omar Vizquel	.15
147	Larry Walker	.15
148	David Wells	.15
149	Rondell White	.15
150	Preston Wilson	.15
151	Brent Abernathy	4.00
152	Cory Aldridge RC	4.00
153	Gene Altman RC	4.00
154	Josh Beckett	4.00
155	Wilson Betemit RC	8.00
156	Albert Pujols/500 RC	275.00
157	Joe Crede	8.00
158	Jack Cust	4.00
159	Ben Sheets/500	40.00
160	Alex Escobar	4.00
161	Adrian Hernandez RC	4.00
162	Pedro Feliz	4.00
163	Nate Frese RC	4.00
164	Carlos Garcia RC	4.00
165	Marcus Giles	4.00
166	Alexis Gomez RC	4.00
167	Jason Hart	4.00
168	Eric Hinske RC	8.00
169	Cesar Izturis	4.00
170	Nick Johnson	4.00
171	Mike Young	4.00
172	Brian Lawrence RC	6.00
173	Steve Lomasney	4.00
174	Nick Maness RC	4.00
175	Jose Mieses RC	4.00
176	Greg Miller RC	4.00
177	Eric Munson	4.00
178	Xavier Nady	4.00
179	Blaine Neal RC	4.00
180	Abraham Nunez	4.00
181	Jose Ortiz	4.00
182	Jeremy Owens RC	4.00
183	Pablo Ozuna	4.00
184	Corey Patterson	4.00
185	Carlos Pena	4.00
186	Wily Mo Pena	4.00
187	Timo Perez	4.00
188	Adam Pettyjohn RC	4.00
189	Luis Rivas	4.00
190	Jackson Melian RC	4.00
191	Wilken Ruan RC	4.00
192	Duaner Sanchez RC	4.00
193	Alfonso Soriano	5.00
194	Rafael Soriano RC	6.00
195	Ichiro Suzuki RC	60.00
196	Billy Sylvester RC	4.00
197	Juan Uribe RC	4.00
198	Eric Valent	4.00
199	Carlos Valderrama RC	4.00
200	Matt White RC	4.00
201	Alex Rodriguez	2.50
202	Barry Bonds	3.00
203	Cal Ripken Jr.	3.00
204	Chipper Jones	1.00
205	Derek Jeter	2.50
206	Troy Glaus	.50
207	Frank Thomas	.75
208	Greg Maddux	1.50
209	Ivan Rodriguez	.50
210	Jeff Bagwell	.50
211	Todd Helton	.50
212	Ken Griffey Jr.	1.50
213	Manny Ramirez	.75
214	Mark McGwire	1.50
215	Mike Piazza	1.50
216	Pedro Martinez	.75
217	Sammy Sosa	1.50
218	Tony Gwynn	1.00
219	Vladimir Guerrero	.75
220	Nomar Garciaparra	1.00

Stat Line Career

		NM/M
Cards #1-150 print run		
251-400:		3-6X
1-150 p/r 201-250:		4-8X
1-150 p/r 151-200:		4-8X
1-150 p/r 101-150:		5-10X
1-150 p/r 61-100:		10-20X
1-150 p/r 41-60:		20-30X
1-150 p/r 21-40:		25-40X
1-150 p/r 15-20:		30-60X
Common (151-200)		
p/r 251-400:		1.00
Common (151-200)		
p/r 151-250:		1.00
Common (151-200)		
p/r 101-150:		2.00
Common (151-200)		
p/r 76-100:		2.00
Common (151-200)		
p/r 31-75:		4.00
Common (151-200)		
p/r 20-30:		6.00
cards 201-220 p/r 201-400:		1-2X
201-220 p/r 101-200:		2-4X
201-220 p/r 75-100:		3-5X
201-220 p/r 40-74:		4-8X
156	Albert Pujols/154	150.00
190	Jackson Melian/26	50.00
195	Ichiro Suzuki/106	200.00

Stat Line Season

		NM/M
Cards #1-150 print run		
151-200:		4-8X
1-150 p/r 101-150:		4-8X
1-150 p/r 76-100:		10-20X
1-150 p/r 51-75:		10-20X
1-150 p/r 36-50:		15-25X
1-150 p/r 21-35:		20-40X
Common (151-200)		
p/r 151-200:		1.00
Common (151-200)		
p/r 101-150:		1.00
Common (151-200)		
p/r 101-150:		1.00
Common (151-200)		
p/r 76-100:		2.00
Common (151-200)		
p/r 31-75:		3.00
Common (151-200)		
p/r 20-30:		6.00
cards 201-220 p/r 151-200:		1-3X
201-220 p/r 101-150:		2-4X
201-220 p/r 75-100:		3-5X
201-220 p/r 40-74:		4-8X
156	Albert Pujols/17	400.00
190	Jackson Melian/73	40.00
195	Ichiro Suzuki/153	150.00

All-Time Diamond Kings

		NM/M
Complete Set (10):		150.00
Common Player:		8.00
Production 2,500 Sets		
Studio Series:		2-3X
Production 250		
#9 Undetermined Redemp.		
1a	Frank Robinson	8.00
1b	Willie Mays (Should have been ATDK-9.)	25.00
2	Harmon Killebrew	8.00
3	Mike Schmidt	20.00
4	Reggie Jackson	8.00
5	Nolan Ryan	35.00
6	George Brett	25.00
7	Tom Seaver	10.00
8	Hank Aaron	25.00

| 9 | Redemption, Willie Mays (See #1b.) | |
| 10 | Stan Musial | 20.00 |

All-Time Diamond Kings Autograph

		NM/M
Production 50 Sets		
1	Frank Robinson	100.00
1	Willie Mays	200.00
2	Harmon Killebrew	80.00
3	Mike Schmidt	200.00
4	Reggie Jackson	80.00
5	Nolan Ryan	250.00
6	George Brett	225.00
7	Tom Seaver	85.00
8	Hank Aaron	200.00
10	Stan Musial	120.00

Bat Kings

		NM/M
Common Card:		20.00
Production 250 Sets		
1	Ivan Rodriguez	20.00
2	Tony Gwynn	35.00
3	Barry Bonds	75.00
4	Todd Helton	20.00
5	Troy Glaus	20.00
6	Mike Schmidt	50.00
7	Reggie Jackson	20.00
8	Harmon Killebrew	20.00
9	Frank Robinson	20.00
10	Hank Aaron	75.00

Bat Kings Autograph

		NM/M
Production 50 Sets		
1	Ivan Rodriguez	75.00
2	Tony Gwynn	120.00
3	Barry Bonds/No Auto.	50.00
4	Todd Helton	65.00
5	Troy Glaus	65.00
6	Mike Schmidt	150.00
7	Reggie Jackson	100.00
8	Harmon Killebrew	100.00
9	Frank Robinson	85.00
10	Hank Aaron	200.00

2001 Donruss Baseball's Best

		NM/M
Complete Set, Bronze (330):		100.00
999 Produced		
Stars:		2-3X
Complete Set, Silver (330):		300.00

499 Produced
Stars: 2-4X
Complete Set, Gold (330):550.00
99 Produced
Stars: 4-8X
(See 2001 Donruss, The Rookies, Rookies DK for checklists and base values.)

Diamond Kings Reprints

		NM/M
Complete Set (20):		160.00
Common Player:		5.00
#'d to yr. produced		
1	Rod Carew	5.00
2	Nolan Ryan	25.00
3	Tom Seaver	10.00
4	Carlton Fisk	10.00
5	Reggie Jackson	12.00
6	Steve Carlton	5.00
7	Johnny Bench	10.00
8	Joe Morgan	5.00
9	Mike Schmidt	20.00
10	Wade Boggs	15.00
11	Cal Ripken Jr.	25.00
12	Tony Gwynn	15.00
13	Andre Dawson	5.00
14	Ozzie Smith	15.00
15	George Brett	20.00
16	Dave Winfield	5.00
17	Paul Molitor	10.00
18	Will Clark	5.00
19	Robin Yount	10.00
20	Ken Griffey Jr.	17.50

Diamond Kings Reprints Autograph

PAUL MOLITOR

		NM/M
Common Player:		
DKR1	Rod Carew/82	40.00
DKR2	Nolan Ryan/82	150.00
DKR3	Tom Seaver/82	75.00
DKR4	Carlton Fisk/82	65.00
DKR5	Reggie Jackson/ 83	60.00
DKR6	Steve Carlton/83	40.00
DKR7	Johnny Bench/83	80.00
DKR8	Joe Morgan/83	30.00
DKR9	Mike Schmidt/84	120.00
DKR10	Wade Boggs/84	60.00
DKR11	Cal Ripken Jr./85	180.00
DKR12	Tony Gwynn/86	80.00
DKR13	Andre Dawson/ 86	35.00
DKR14	Ozzie Smith/87	80.00
DKR15	George Brett/87	120.00
DKR16	Dave Winfield/87	40.00
DKR17	Paul Molitor/88	60.00
DKR18	Will Clark/88	75.00

DKR19	Robin Yount/89	80.00
DKR20	Ken Griffey Jr./ 89/No Auto.	25.00

Elite Series

		NM/M
Complete Set (20):		75.00
Common Player:		2.00
Production 2,500 Sets		
Dominators:		5-8X
Production 25 Sets		
1	Vladimir Guerrero	4.00
2	Cal Ripken Jr.	10.00
3	Greg Maddux	5.00
4	Alex Rodriguez	8.00
5	Barry Bonds	10.00
6	Chipper Jones	5.00
7	Derek Jeter	10.00
8	Ivan Rodriguez	2.50
9	Ken Griffey Jr.	7.00
10	Mark McGwire	8.00
11	Mike Piazza	7.00
12	Nomar Garciaparra	7.00
13	Pedro Martinez	4.00
14	Randy Johnson	4.00
15	Roger Clemens	6.00
16	Sammy Sosa	7.00
17	Tony Gwynn	5.00
18	Darin Erstad	3.00
19	Andruw Jones	4.00
20	Bernie Williams	2.00

Jersey Kings

		NM/M
Common Card:		25.00
Production 250 Sets		
1	Vladimir Guerrero	20.00
2	Cal Ripken Jr.	80.00
3	Greg Maddux	40.00
4	Chipper Jones	25.00
5	Roger Clemens	40.00
6	George Brett	50.00
7	Tom Seaver	20.00
8	Nolan Ryan	85.00
9	Stan Musial	45.00
10	Willie Mays	

Jersey Kings Autographs

		NM/M
Production 50 Sets		
1	Vladimir Guerrero	90.00
2	Cal Ripken Jr.	225.00
3	Greg Maddux	150.00
4	Chipper Jones	85.00
5	Roger Clemens	175.00
6	George Brett	200.00
7	Tom Seaver	75.00
8	Nolan Ryan	200.00

9	Stan Musial	120.00
10	Ozzie Smith	100.00

Longball Leaders

		NM/M
Complete Set (20):		50.00
Common Player:		1.00
Production 1,000 Sets		
Die-Cut Parallel:		3-5X
#'d to '00 HR Total		
1	Vladimir Guerrero	4.00
2	Alex Rodriguez	8.00
3	Barry Bonds	10.00
4	Troy Glaus	4.00
5	Frank Thomas	4.00
6	Jeff Bagwell	4.00
7	Todd Helton	4.00
8	Ken Griffey Jr.	6.00
9	Manny Ramirez	4.00
10	Mike Piazza	6.00
11	Sammy Sosa	6.00
12	Carlos Delgado	2.00
13	Jim Edmonds	1.00
14	Jason Giambi	3.00
15	David Justice	1.00
16	Rafael Palmeiro	3.00
17	Gary Sheffield	2.00
18	Jim Thome	1.00
19	Tony Batista	1.00
20	Richard Hidalgo	1.00

Production Line

		NM/M
Complete Set (60):		150.00
Common Player:		.50
Die-Cut OBP (1-20):		1-2X
Die-Cut SLG (21-40):		1-2.5X
Die-Cut PI (41-60):		1.5-3X
Production 100 Sets		
1	Jason Giambi/476	3.00
2	Carlos Delgado/470	2.00
3	Todd Helton/463	3.00
4	Manny Ramirez/457	3.00
5	Barry Bonds/440	15.00
6	Gary Sheffield/438	2.00
7	Frank Thomas/436	3.00
8	Nomar Garciaparra/ 434	10.00
9	Brian Giles/432	1.00
10	Edgardo Alfonzo/425	.50
11	Jeff Kent/424	.75
12	Jeff Bagwell/424	3.00
13	Edgar Martinez/423	.75
14	Alex Rodriguez/420	10.00
15	Will Clark/418	.50
16	Will Clark/418	2.50
17	Jorge Posada/417	2.00
18	Derek Jeter/416	12.00
19	Bob Abreu/416	1.00
20	Moises Alou/416	.75
21	Todd Helton/698	3.00
22	Manny Ramirez/697	3.00
23	Barry Bonds/688	15.00
24	Carlos Delgado/664	2.00
25	Vladimir Guerrero/664	3.00
26	Jason Giambi/647	3.00
27	Gary Sheffield/643	2.00
28	Richard Hidalgo/636	.50
29	Sammy Sosa/634	8.00
30	Frank Thomas/625	3.00
31	Moises Alou/623	.75
32	Jeff Bagwell/615	3.00
33	Mike Piazza/614	8.00
34	Alex Rodriguez/606	10.00
35	Troy Glaus/604	3.00
36	Nomar Garciaparra/ 599	10.00
37	Jeff Kent/596	.75
38	Brian Giles/594	.75
39	Geoff Jenkins/588	.50
40	Carl Everett/587	.50
41	Todd Helton/1,161	3.00

42	Manny Ramirez/1,154	3.00
43	Carlos Delgado/1,134	2.00
44	Barry Bonds/1,128	12.00
45	Jason Giambi/1,123	3.00
46	Gary Sheffield/1,081	2.00
47	Vladimir Guerrero/ 1,074	3.00
48	Frank Thomas/1,061	3.00
49	Sammy Sosa/1,040	8.00
50	Moises Alou/1,039	1.00
51	Jeff Bagwell/1,039	3.00
52	Nomar Garciaparra/ 1,033	10.00
53	Richard Hidalgo/1,027	.50
54	Alex Rodriguez/ 1,026.	10.00
55	Brian Giles/1,026	1.00
56	Jeff Kent/1,020	1.00
57	Mike Piazza/1,012	8.00
58	Troy Glaus/1,008	3.00
59	Edgar Martinez/1,002	1.00
60	Jim Edmonds/994	1.00

Rookie Reprints

		NM/M
Complete Set (40):		200.00
Common Player:		3.00
#'d to Original Yr. issued.		
1	Cal Ripken Jr.	20.00
2	Wade Boggs	10.00
3	Tony Gwynn	10.00
4	Ryne Sandberg	10.00
5	Don Mattingly	12.00
6	Joe Carter	3.00
7	Roger Clemens	15.00
8	Kirby Puckett	10.00
9	Orel Hershiser	3.00
10	Andres Galarraga	3.00
11	Jose Canseco	5.00
12	Fred McGriff	3.00
13	Paul O'Neill	3.00
14	Mark McGwire	15.00
15	Barry Bonds	20.00
16	Kevin Brown	3.00
17	David Cone	3.00
18	Rafael Palmeiro	8.00
19	Barry Larkin	3.00
20	Bo Jackson	5.00
21	Greg Maddux	10.00
22	Roberto Alomar	4.00
23	Mark Grace	3.00
24	David Wells	3.00
25	Tom Glavine	4.00
26	Matt Williams	3.00
27	Ken Griffey Jr.	12.00
28	Randy Johnson	8.00
29	Gary Sheffield	5.00
30	Craig Biggio	3.00
31	Curt Schilling	5.00
32	Larry Walker	3.00
33	Bernie Williams	4.00
34	Sammy Sosa	12.00
35	Juan Gonzalez	8.00
36	David Justice	3.00
37	Ivan Rodriguez	6.00
38	Jeff Bagwell	8.00
39	Jeff Kent	3.00
40	Manny Ramirez	8.00

Rookie Reprints Autographs

		NM/M
Common Player:		
#'d to last 2 digits of yr. issued		
1	Cal Ripken/82	150.00
2	Wade Boggs/83	40.00
3	Tony Gwynn/83	75.00
4	Ryne Sandberg/83	100.00
5	Don Mattingly/84	100.00
6	Joe Carter/84	20.00
7	Roger Clemens/85	200.00
8	Kirby Puckett/85	60.00

9	Orel Hershiser/85	25.00
10	Andres Galarraga/86	30.00
15	Barry Bonds/87	200.00
16	Kevin Brown/87	30.00
17	David Cone/87	30.00
18	Rafael Palmeiro/87	50.00
20	Bo Jackson/87	85.00
21	Greg Maddux/87	150.00
22	Roberto Alomar/88	40.00
24	David Wells/88	25.00
25	Tom Glavine/88	40.00
28	Randy Johnson/89	100.00
29	Gary Sheffield/89	50.00
31	Curt Schilling/89	75.00
35	Juan Gonzalez/90	40.00
36	David Justice/90	25.00
37	Ivan Rodriguez/91	40.00
39	Manny Ramirez/92	100.00

1999 Diamond Kings

NM/M
Complete Set (5): 40.00
Common Player: 8.00
Production 2,500 Sets

1	Scott Rolen	8.00
2	Sammy Sosa	10.00
3	Juan Gonzalez	8.00
4	Ken Griffey Jr.	10.00
5	Derek Jeter	20.00

1999 Retro

NM/M
Complete Set (100): 200.00
Common Player: .25
Inserted 1:Hobby Pack
Common (81-100): 3.00
Production 1,999

1	Ken Griffey Jr.	2.00
2	Nomar Garciaparra	3.00
3	Alex Rodriguez	3.00
4	Mark McGwire	2.50
5	Sammy Sosa	2.00
6	Chipper Jones	1.50
7	Mike Piazza	2.00
8	Barry Larkin	.50
9	Andruw Jones	1.00
10	Albert Belle	.25
11	Jeff Bagwell	1.00
12	Tony Gwynn	1.50
13	Manny Ramirez	1.00
14	Mo Vaughn	.25
15	Barry Bonds	4.00
16	Frank Thomas	1.00
17	Vladimir Guerrero	1.00
18	Derek Jeter	3.00
19	Randy Johnson	1.00
20	Greg Maddux	1.50
21	Pedro Martinez	1.00
22	Cal Ripken Jr.	3.00
23	Ivan Rodriguez	.75
24	Matt Williams	.25
25	Javy Lopez	.25
26	Tim Salmon	.25
27	Raul Mondesi	.25
28	Todd Helton	1.00
29	Magglio Ordonez	.75
30	Sean Casey	.25
31	Jeromy Burnitz	.25
32	Jeff Kent	.25
33	Jim Edmonds	.25
34	Jim Thome	.75
35	Dante Bichette	.25
36	Larry Walker	.25
37	Will Clark	.50
38	Omar Vizquel	.25
39	Mike Mussina	.50
40	Eric Karros	.25
41	Kenny Lofton	.25
42	David Justice	.50
43	Craig Biggio	.50
44	J.D. Drew	.25
45	Rickey Henderson	1.00
46	Bernie Williams	.50
47	Brian Giles	.25
48	Paul O'Neill	.50
49	Orlando Hernandez	.25
50	Jason Giambi	.50
51	Curt Schilling	1.00
52	Scott Rolen	1.00
53	Mark Grace	.50
54	Moises Alou	.50
55	Jason Kendall	.25
56	Ray Lankford	.25
57	Kerry Wood	.50
58	Gary Sheffield	.75
59	Ruben Mateo	.25
60	Darin Erstad	.25
61	Troy Glaus	1.00
62	Jose Canseco	.50
63	Wade Boggs	1.50
64	Tom Glavine	.50
65	Gabe Kapler	.25
66	Juan Gonzalez	1.00
67	Rafael Palmeiro	.75
68	Richie Sexson	.25
69	Carl Everett	.25
70	David Wells	.75
71	Carlos Delgado	.75
72	Eric Davis	.25
73	Shawn Green	.50
74	Andres Galarraga	.25
75	Edgar Martinez	.25
76	Roberto Alomar	.50
77	John Olerud	.25
78	Luis Gonzalez	.25
79	Kevin Brown	.25
80	Roger Clemens	2.00
81	Josh Beckett	5.00
82	Alfonso Soriano	8.00
83	Alex Escobar	.50
84	Pat Burrell	.50
85	Eric Chavez	.50
86	Erubiel Durazo	.50
87	Abraham Nunez	.50
88	Carlos Pena	2.00
89	Nick Johnson	.50
90	Eric Munson	.50
91	Corey Patterson	.50
92	Wily Mo Pena	.50
93	Rafael Furcal	1.00
94	Eric Valent	.50
95	Mark Mulder	.50
96	Chad Hutchinson	1.00
97	Freddy Garcia	.50
98	Tim Hudson	1.00
99	Rick Ankiel	1.00
100	Kip Wells	.50

1999 Retro Stat Line Career

NM/M
Cards #1-80 print run

251-400:	2-3X
(1-80) p/r 151-250:	2-4X
(1-80) p/r 101-150:	3-6X
(1-80) p/r 76-100:	4-8X
(1-80) p/r 51-75:	5-10X
(1-80) p/r 30-50:	8-15X

1	Ken Griffey Jr./350	20.00
2	Nomar Garciaparra/309	20.00
3	Alex Rodriguez/313	20.00
4	Mark McGwire/219	25.00
5	Sammy Sosa/273	12.00
6	Chipper Jones/297	15.00
7	Mike Piazza/333	20.00
8	Barry Larkin/305	5.00
9	Andruw Jones/273	6.00
10	Albert Belle/321	2.50
11	Jeff Bagwell/304	8.00
12	Tony Gwynn/339	12.00
13	Manny Ramirez/154	15.00
14	Mo Vaughn/304	2.50
15	Barry Bonds/290	12.00
16	Frank Thomas/286	10.00
17	Vladimir Guerrero/305	10.00
18	Derek Jeter/308	25.00
19	Randy Johnson/336	8.00
20	Greg Maddux/202	20.00
21	Pedro Martinez/298	10.00
22	Cal Ripken Jr./276	25.00
23	Ivan Rodriguez/232	8.00
24	Matt Williams/299	4.00
25	Javy Lopez/333	2.50
26	Tim Salmon/179	4.00
27	Raul Mondesi/295	2.50
28	Todd Helton/310	8.00
29	Magglio Ordonez/173	4.00
30	Sean Casey/269	2.50
31	Jeromy Burnitz/294	2.50
32	Jeff Kent/193	5.00
33	Jim Edmonds/294	5.00
34	Jim Thome/163	4.00
35	Dante Bichette/300	2.50
36	Larry Walker/225	8.00
37	Will Clark/302	6.00
38	Omar Vizquel/196	4.00
39	Mike Mussina/118	10.00
40	Eric Karros/177	4.00
41	Kenny Lofton/311	2.50
42	David Justice/214	5.00
43	Craig Biggio/318	2.50
44	J.D. Drew/35	25.00
45	Rickey Henderson/283	6.00
46	Bernie Williams/213	6.00
47	Brian Giles/157	4.00
48	Paul O'Neill/223	5.00
49	Orlando Hernandez/313	2.50
50	Jason Giambi/73	15.00
51	Curt Schilling/336	2.50
52	Scott Rolen/220	5.00
53	Mark Grace/310	6.00
54	Moises Alou/201	3.00
55	Jason Kendall/308	2.50
56	Ray Lankford/225	3.00
57	Kerry Wood/233	3.00
58	Gary Sheffield/202	5.00
59	Ruben Mateo/384	2.50
60	Darin Erstad/179	8.00
61	Troy Glaus/218	10.00
62	Jose Canseco/296	6.00
63	Wade Boggs/329	8.00
64	Tom Glavine/331	5.00
66	Juan Gonzalez/301	8.00
67	Rafael Palmeiro/314	5.00
68	Richie Sexson/308	2.50
69	Carl Everett/209	3.00
70	David Wells/124	6.00
71	Carlos Delgado/333	6.00
72	Eric Davis/342	7.50
73	Shawn Green/77	15.00
74	Andres Galarraga/364	4.00
75	Edgar Martinez/318	4.00
76	Roberto Alomar/302	6.00
77	John Olerud/301	2.50
78	Luis Gonzalez/237	3.00
79	Kevin Brown/330	2.50
80	Roger Clemens/295	12.00
82	Alfonso Soriano/113	15.00
83	Alex Escobar/181	10.00
84	Pat Burrell/303	12.00
85	Eric Chavez/314	2.50
86	Erubiel Durazo/147	5.00
87	Abraham Nunez/106	15.00
88	Carlos Pena/46	25.00
89	Nick Johnson/259	6.00
90	Eric Munson/7	6.00
91	Corey Patterson/117	15.00
92	Wily Mo Pena/247	8.00
93	Rafael Furcal/137	20.00
94	Eric Valent/53	10.00
95	Mark Mulder/340	4.00
97	Freddy Garcia/397	6.00
98	Tim Hudson/17	50.00
99	Rick Ankiel/222	10.00
100	Kip Wells/371	2.50

1999 Retro Stat Line Season

NM/M
Cards #1-80 print run

251-400:	2-3X
(1-80) p/r 151-250:	2-4X
(1-80) p/r 101-150:	3-6X
(1-80) p/r 76-100:	4-8X
(1-80) p/r 51-75:	5-10X
(1-80) p/r 30-50:	8-15X

1	Ken Griffey Jr./56	70.00
2	Nomar Garciaparra/35	100.00
3	Alex Rodriguez/42	100.00
4	Mark McGwire/70	80.00
5	Sammy Sosa/66	40.00
6	Chipper Jones/123	30.00
7	Mike Piazza/111	50.00
8	Barry Larkin/166	8.00
9	Andruw Jones/31	30.00
10	Albert Belle/49	8.00
11	Jeff Bagwell/164	12.00
12	Tony Gwynn/148	25.00
13	Manny Ramirez/145	20.00
14	Mo Vaughn/40	10.00
15	Barry Bonds/120	25.00
16	Frank Thomas/155	15.00
17	Vladimir Guerrero/38	40.00
18	Derek Jeter/127	60.00
19	Randy Johnson/70	75.00
21	Pedro Martinez/19	80.00
22	Cal Ripken Jr./163	40.00
23	Ivan Rodriguez/186	12.00
24	Matt Williams/136	8.00
25	Javy Lopez/106	6.00
26	Tim Salmon/139	5.00
27	Raul Mondesi/66	4.00
28	Todd Helton/25	60.00
29	Magglio Ordonez/151	4.00
30	Sean Casey/82	8.00
31	Jeromy Burnitz/125	5.00
32	Jeff Kent/128	8.00
33	Jim Edmonds/115	12.00
34	Jim Thome/129	6.00
35	Dante Bichette/122	5.00
36	Larry Walker/113	15.00
37	Will Clark/169	10.00
38	Omar Vizquel/166	4.00
39	Mike Mussina/175	10.00
40	Eric Karros/150	5.00
41	Kenny Lofton/54	10.00
42	David Justice/151	6.00
43	Craig Biggio/51	10.00
45	Rickey Henderson/66	25.00
46	Bernie Williams/26	30.00
47	Brian Giles/94	6.00
48	Paul O'Neill/116	10.00
49	Orlando Hernandez/12	35.00
50	Jason Giambi/166	10.00
51	Curt Schilling/15	40.00
52	Scott Rolen/31	60.00
53	Mark Grace/92	15.00
54	Moises Alou/124	5.00
55	Jason Kendall/175	4.00
56	Ray Lankford/156	4.00
57	Kerry Wood/13	50.00
58	Gary Sheffield/132	10.00
59	Ruben Mateo/134	5.00
60	Darin Erstad/159	10.00
62	Jose Canseco/46	30.00
63	Wade Boggs/122	15.00
64	Tom Glavine/50	50.00
65	Gabe Kapler/25	20.00
66	Juan Gonzalez/30	30.00
67	Rafael Palmeiro/121	10.00
69	Carl Everett/138	5.00
70	David Wells/163	4.00

71	Carlos Delgado/155	10.00
72	Eric Davis/148	5.00
73	Shawn Green/100	12.00
74	Andres Galarraga/44	20.00
75	Edgar Martinez/102	10.00
76	Roberto Alomar/166	15.00
77	John Olerud/22	20.00
78	Luis Gonzalez/146	5.00
79	Kevin Brown/18	25.00
80	Roger Clemens/20	120.00
81	Josh Beckett/178	10.00
83	Alex Escobar/27	40.00
85	Eric Chavez/33	15.00
86	Erubiel Durazo/19	20.00
87	Abraham Nunez/95	10.00
88	Carlos Pena/319	6.00
89	Nick Johnson/17	50.00
90	Eric Munson/16	40.00
91	Corey Patterson/22	40.00
93	Rafael Furcal/88	20.00
95	Mark Mulder/113	6.00
96	Chad Hutchinson/51	6.00
98	Tim Hudson/152	15.00
99	Rick Ankiel/12	40.00
100	Kip Wells/135	2.50

2000 Diamond Kings

		NM/M
Complete Set (5):		35.00
Common Player:		8.00
Production 2,500 Sets		
Studio:		1-2X
Production 250 Sets		
1	Frank Thomas	8.00
2	Greg Maddux	9.00
3	Alex Rodriguez	10.00
4	Jeff Bagwell	8.00
5	Manny Ramirez	8.00

2000 Retro

		NM/M
Complete Set (100):		90.00
Common Player:		.25
Common (81-100):		3.00
Production 2,000		
1	Vladimir Guerrero	1.00
2	Alex Rodriguez	4.00
3	Ken Griffey Jr.	2.50
4	Nomar Garciaparra	1.00
5	Mike Piazza	1.50
6	Mark McGwire	2.00
7	Sammy Sosa	1.50
8	Chipper Jones	1.00
9	Jim Edmonds	.50
10	Tony Gwynn	1.00
11	Andruw Jones	.75
12	Albert Belle	.25
13	Jeff Bagwell	.75
14	Manny Ramirez	1.00
15	Mo Vaughn	.25
16	Barry Bonds	4.00
17	Frank Thomas	1.00
18	Ivan Rodriguez	.75
19	Derek Jeter	4.00
20	Randy Johnson	1.00
21	Greg Maddux	1.00
22	Pedro Martinez	1.00
23	Cal Ripken Jr.	4.00
24	Mark Grace	.50
25	Javy Lopez	.25
26	Ray Durham	.25
27	Todd Helton	1.00
28	Magglio Ordonez	.75
29	Sean Casey	.25
30	Darin Erstad	.50
31	Barry Larkin	.50
32	Will Clark	.50
33	Jim Thome	.75
34	Dante Bichette	.25
35	Larry Walker	.50
36	Ken Caminiti	.25
37	Omar Vizquel	.25

38	Miguel Tejada	.50
39	Eric Karros	.25
40	Gary Sheffield	.75
41	Jeff Cirillo	.25
42	Rondell White	.25
43	Rickey Henderson	.75
44	Bernie Williams	.50
45	Brian Giles	.25
46	Paul O'Neill	.50
47	Orlando Hernandez	.25
48	Ben Grieve	.25
49	Jason Giambi	.50
50	Curt Schilling	1.00
51	Scott Rolen	.50
52	Bobby Abreu	.50
53	Jason Kendall	.25
54	Fernando Tatis	.25
55	Jeff Kent	.25
56	Mike Mussina	.50
57	Troy Glaus	.75
58	Jose Canseco	.50
59	Wade Boggs	1.00
60	Fred McGriff	.25
61	Juan Gonzalez	.75
62	Rafael Palmeiro	.75
63	Rusty Greer	.25
64	Carl Everett	.25
65	David Wells	.25
66	Carlos Delgado	.50
67	Shawn Green	.40
68	David Justice	.25
69	Edgar Martinez	.25
70	Andres Galarraga	.25
71	Roberto Alomar	.50
72	Jermaine Dye	.25
73	John Olerud	.25
74	Luis Gonzalez	.25
75	Craig Biggio	.50
76	Kevin Millwood	.25
77	Kevin Brown	.25
78	John Smoltz	.50
79	Roger Clemens	3.00
80	Mike Hampton	.25
81	Tomas De La Rosa	.25
82	C.C. Sabathia	1.00
83	Ryan Christenson	.25
84	Pedro Feliz	.50
85	Jose Ortiz	.25
86	Xavier Nady	.50
87	Julio Zuleta	.25
88	Jason Hart	.25
89	Keith Ginter	.25
90	Brent Abernathy	.25
91	Timo Perez	.50
92	Juan Pierre	.50
93	Tike Redman	.25
94	Mike Lamb	.50
95	Ben Sheets	1.00
96	Kazuhiro Sasaki	.50
97	Barry Zito	1.00
98	Adam Bernero	.25
99	Chad Durbin	.25
100	Matt Ginter	.25

2000 Retro Stat Line Career

	NM/M
Cards #1-80 print run	
251-400:	2-3X
1-80 p/r 151-250:	2-4X
1-80 p/r 101-150:	3-6X
1-80 p/r 76-100:	4-8X
1-80 p/r 51-75:	5-10X
1-80 p/r 31-50:	8-15X
1-80 p/r 21-30:	15-25X
Common (81-100)	
p/r 251-400:	1.00
Common (81-100)	
p/r 151-250:	1.00
Common (81-100)	
p/r 101-150:	2.00
Common (81-100)	
p/r 76-100:	2.00
Common (81-100) p/r 31-75	3.00

2000 Retro Stat Line Season

	NM/M
Cards #1-80 print run	
251-400:	2-3X
1-80 p/r 151-250:	2-4X
1-80 p/r 101-150:	3-6X
1-80 p/r 76-100:	4-8X
1-80 p/r 51-75:	5-10X
1-80 p/r 31-50:	8-15X
1-80 p/r 21-30:	15-25X
Common (81-100)	
p/r 151-200:	1.00
Common (81-100)	
p/r 81-150:	2.00
Common (81-100)	
p/r 51-80:	2.00

2001 Diamond Kings

		NM/M
Complete Set (20):		150.00
Common Player:		5.00
Production 2,500 Sets		
Studio Canvas Parallel:		1-2X
Production 250		
1	Alex Rodriguez	12.50
2	Cal Ripken Jr.	15.00
3	Mark McGwire	12.50
4	Ken Griffey Jr.	10.00
5	Derek Jeter	15.00
6	Nomar Garciaparra	10.00
7	Mike Piazza	10.00
8	Roger Clemens	9.00
9	Greg Maddux	8.00
10	Chipper Jones	8.00
11	Tony Gwynn	8.00
12	Barry Bonds	15.00
13	Sammy Sosa	10.00
14	Vladimir Guerrero	6.00
15	Frank Thomas	6.00
16	Troy Glaus	6.00
17	Todd Helton	6.00
18	Ivan Rodriguez	5.00
19	Pedro Martinez	6.00
20	Carlos Delgado	5.00

2001 Diamond Kings Studio Series Auto.

		NM/M
Common Autograph:		50.00
Production 50 Sets		
1	Alex Rodriguez	180.00
2	Cal Ripken Jr.	250.00
8	Roger Clemens	150.00
9	Greg Maddux	150.00
10	Chipper Jones	85.00
11	Tony Gwynn	80.00
14	Vladimir Guerrero	100.00
16	Troy Glaus	50.00
17	Todd Helton	60.00
18	Ivan Rodriguez	60.00

2001 Donruss Class of 2001

		NM/M
Complete Set (300):		.20
Common Player:		.20
Common (101-200):		3.00
Production 1,875		
Common (201-300):		3.00
Production 625		
Pack (3):		6.00
Box (24 + Bobble Head):		125.00
1	Alex Rodriguez	2.00
2	Barry Bonds	2.50
3	Vladimir Guerrero	.75
4	Jim Edmonds	.20
5	Derek Jeter	2.50

6	Jose Canseco	.40
7	Rafael Furcal	.20
8	Cal Ripken Jr.	2.50
9	Brad Radke	.20
10	Miguel Tejada	.40
11	Pat Burrell	.50
12	Ken Griffey Jr.	1.50
13	Cliff Floyd	.20
14	Luis Gonzalez	.20
15	Frank Thomas	.75
16	Mike Sweeney	.20
17	Paul LoDuca	.20
18	Lance Berkman	.20
19	Tony Gwynn	1.00
20	Chipper Jones	1.00
21	Eric Chavez	.40
22	Kerry Wood	.35
23	Jorge Posada	.40
24	J.D. Drew	.50
25	Garret Anderson	.20
26	Mike Piazza	1.50
27	Kenny Lofton	.20
28	Mike Mussina	.40
29	Paul Konerko	.20
30	Bernie Williams	.20
31	Eric Milton	.20
32	Shawn Green	.40
33	Paul O'Neill	.40
34	Juan Gonzalez	.35
35	Andres Galarraga	.20
36	Gary Sheffield	.40
37	Ben Grieve	.20
38	Scott Rolen	.60
39	Mark Grace	.20
40	Hideo Nomo	.35
41	Barry Zito	.50
42	Edgar Martinez	.20
43	Jarrod Washburn	.20
44	Greg Maddux	1.00
45	Mark Buehrle	.20
46	Larry Walker	.20
47	Trot Nixon	.20
48	Nomar Garciaparra	1.50
49	Robert Fick	.20
50	Sean Casey	.40
51	Joe Mays	.20
52	Roger Clemens	1.50
53	Chan Ho Park	.20
54	Carlos Delgado	.50
55	Phil Nevin	.20
56	Jason Giambi	.50
57	Raul Mondesi	.20
58	Roberto Alomar	.35
59	Ryan Klesko	.20
60	Andruw Jones	.75
61	Gabe Kapler	.20
62	Darin Erstad	.35
63	Cristian Guzman	.20
64	Kazuhiro Sasaki	.20
65	Doug Mientkiewicz	.20
66	Sammy Sosa	1.50
67	Mike Hampton	.20
68	Rickey Henderson	.75
69	Mark Mulder	.30
70	Mark McGwire	2.00
71	Freddy Garcia	.20
72	Ivan Rodriguez	.60
73	Terrence Long	.20
74	Jeff Bagwell	.75
75	Moises Alou	.20
76	Todd Helton	.65
77	Preston Wilson	.20
78	Pedro Martinez	.75
79	Bobby Abreu	.20
80	Manny Ramirez	.75
81	Jose Vidro	.20
82	Randy Johnson	.75
83	Richie Sexson	.20
84	Troy Glaus	.65
85	Kevin Brown	.20
86	Carlos Lee	.20
87	Adrian Beltre	.30
88	Brian Giles	.20
89	Jermaine Dye	.20
90	Craig Biggio	.20
91	Richard Hidalgo	.20
92	Magglio Ordonez	.20
93	Aramis Ramirez	.20
94	Jeff Kent	.20
95	Curt Schilling	.50
96	Tim Hudson	.40
97	Fred McGriff	.20
98	Barry Larkin	.20
99	Jim Thome	.60
100	Tom Glavine	.40
101	Sean Douglass RC	3.00
102	Rob Mackowiak RC	3.00
103	Jeremy Fikac RC	3.00
104	Henry Mateo RC	3.00
105	Geronimo Gil RC	3.00
106	Ramon Vazquez RC	5.00
107	Pedro Santana RC	3.00
108	Ryan Jensen RC	3.00
109	Paul Phillips RC	3.00
110	Saul Rivera RC	3.00
111	Larry Bigbie	3.00

112	Josh Phelps	3.00
113	Justin Kaye RC	3.00
114	Kris Keller RC	3.00
115	Adam Bernero	3.00
116	Victor Zambrano RC	3.00
117	Felipe Lopez	3.00
118	Brian Roberts RC	10.00
119	Kurt Ainsworth RC	3.00
120	George Perez RC	3.00
121	Wilson Guzman RC	3.00
122	Derrick Lewis RC	3.00
123	Nate Teut RC	3.00
124	Martin Vargas RC	3.00
125	Brandon Inge	3.00
126	Travis Phelps RC	3.00
127	Les Walrond RC	3.00
128	Justin Atchley RC	3.00
129	Stubby Clapp RC	3.00
130	Bret Prinz RC	3.00
131	Bert Snow RC	3.00
132	Joe Crede RC	3.00
133	Nick Punto RC	3.00
134	Carlos Hernandez RC	3.00
135	Ken Vining RC	3.00
136	Luis Pineda RC	3.00
137	Winston Abreu RC	3.00
138	Matt Ginter	3.00
139	Jason Smith RC	3.00
140	Gene Altman RC	3.00
141	Brian Rogers RC	3.00
142	Michael Cuddyer	3.00
143	Mike Penney RC	3.00
144	Scott Podsednik RC	10.00
145	Esix Snead RC	3.00
146	Steve Watkins RC	3.00
147	Orlando Woodards RC	3.00
148	Mike Young	3.00
149	Chris George	3.00
150	Blaine Neal RC	3.00
151	Ben Sheets	3.00
152	Scott Stewart RC	3.00
153	Mike Koplove RC	3.00
154	Kyle Lohse RC	8.00
155	Dee Brown	3.00
156	Aubrey Huff	3.00
157	Pablo Ozuna	3.00
158	Bill Ortega	3.00
159	Toby Hall	3.00
160	Kevin Olsen RC	3.00
161	Will Ohman RC	3.00
162	Nate Cornejo	3.00
163	Jack Cust	3.00
164	Juan Rivera	3.00
165	Jerrod Riggan RC	3.00
166	Dustan Mohr RC	3.00
167	Doug Nickle RC	3.00
168	Craig Monroe RC	3.00
169	Jason Jennings	3.00
170	Bart Miadich RC	3.00
171	Luis Rivas	3.00
172	Tim Christman RC	3.00
173	Luke Hudson RC	3.00
174	Brett Jodie RC	3.00
175	Jorge Julio RC	4.00
176	David Espinosa	3.00
177	Mike Maroth RC	3.00
178	Keith Ginter	3.00
179	Juan Moreno RC	3.00
180	Brandon Knight RC	3.00
181	Steve Lomasney	3.00
182	John Grabow RC	3.00
183	Steve Green RC	3.00
184	Jason Karnuth RC	3.00
185	Bob File RC	3.00
186	Brent Abernathy	3.00
187	Morgan Ensberg RC	10.00
188	Wily Mo Pena	3.00
189	Ken Harvey	3.00
190	Josh Pearce RC	3.00
191	Cesar Izturis	3.00
192	Eric Hinske RC	5.00
193	Joe Beimel RC	3.00
194	Timo Perez	3.00
195	Troy Mattes RC	3.00
196	Eric Valent	3.00
197	Ed Rogers RC	3.00
198	Grant Balfour RC	3.00
199	Benito Baez RC	3.00
200	Vernon Wells	3.00
201	Joe Kennedy RC	4.00
202	Wilson Betemit RC	8.00
203	Christian Parker RC	3.00
204	Jay Gibbons RC	10.00
205	Carlos Garcia RC	4.00
206	Jack Wilson RC	4.00
207	Johnny Estrada RC	10.00
208	Wilkin Ruan RC	3.00
209	Brandon Duckworth RC	5.00
210	Willie Harris RC	3.00
211	Marlon Byrd RC	10.00
212	C.C. Sabathia	3.00
213	Dennis Tankersley RC	5.00
214	Brandon Larson RC	5.00
215	Alexis Gomez RC	4.00
216	Bill Hall RC	10.00
217	Antonio Perez RC	3.00

218	Jeremy Affeldt RC	4.00
219	Junior Spivey RC	8.00
220	Casey Fossum RC	8.00
221	Brandon Lyon RC	4.00
222	Angel Santos RC	4.00
223	Lance Davis RC	3.00
224	Zach Day RC	4.00
225	David Williams RC	3.00
226	Cesar Crespo RC	3.00
227	Jose Acevedo RC	3.00
228	Travis Hafner RC	20.00
229	Orlando Hudson RC	10.00
230	Jose Mieses RC	3.00
231	Ricardo Rodriguez RC	3.00
232	Alfonso Soriano	3.00
233	Jason Hart	3.00
234	Endy Chavez RC	3.00
235	Delvin James RC	3.00
236	Ryan Drese RC	3.00
237	Jeremy Owens RC	3.00
238	Brad Voyles RC	3.00
239	Nate Frese	3.00
240	Josh Beckett	3.00
241	Roy Oswalt	3.00
242	Juan Uribe RC	5.00
243	Cory Aldridge RC	3.00
244	Adam Dunn	3.00
245	Bud Smith RC	3.00
246	Adrian Hernandez RC	3.00
247	Matt Guerrier RC	3.00
248	Jimmy Rollins	3.00
249	Wilmy Caceres RC	3.00
250	Jason Michaels RC	3.00
251	Ichiro Suzuki RC	60.00
252	John Buck RC	3.00
253	Andres Torres RC	3.00
254	Alfredo Amezaga RC	3.00
255	Corky Miller RC	3.00
256	Rafael Soriano RC	10.00
257	Donaldo Mendez RC	3.00
258	Victor Martinez RC	50.00
259	Corey Patterson	3.00
260	Horacio Ramirez RC	8.00
261	Elpidio Guzman RC	3.00
262	Juan Diaz RC	3.00
263	Mike Rivera RC	3.00
264	Brian Lawrence RC	3.00
265	Josue Perez RC	3.00
266	Jose Nunez	3.00
267	Erik Bedard RC	20.00
268	Albert Pujols RC	200.00
269	Duaner Sanchez RC	3.00
270	Cody Ransom RC	3.00
271	Greg Miller RC	3.00
272	Adam Pettyjohn RC	3.00
273	Tsuyoshi Shinjo RC	3.00
274	Claudio Vargas RC	3.00
275	Justin Duchscherer RC	5.00
276	Tim Spooneybarger RC	3.00
277	Rick Bauer RC	3.00
278	Josh Fogg RC	5.00
279	Brian Reith RC	3.00
280	Scott MacRae RC	3.00
281	Ryan Ludwick RC	5.00
282	Erick Almonte RC	3.00
283	Josh Towers RC	8.00
284	Juan Pena	3.00
285	David Brous RC	3.00
286	Erik Hiljus RC	3.00
287	Nick Neugebauer RC	3.00
288	Jackson Melian RC	3.00
289	Billy Sylvester RC	3.00
290	Carlos Valderrama RC	3.00
291	Jose Cueto RC	3.00
292	Matt White RC	3.00
293	Nick Maness RC	3.00
294	Jason Lane RC	10.00
295	Brandon Berger RC	3.00
296	Angel Berroa RC	6.00
297	Juan Cruz RC	4.00
298	Dewon Brazelton RC	3.00
299	Mark Prior RC	15.00
300	Mark Teixeira RC	40.00

First Class

Stars (1-100):		5-10X
Production 100		
SP's (101-300):		1-3X
Production 50		

Aces

		NM/M
Complete Set (20):		70.00
Common Player:		3.00
Inserted 1:30		
1	Roger Clemens	12.00
2	Randy Johnson	7.50
3	Freddy Garcia	3.00
4	Greg Maddux	10.00
5	Tim Hudson	5.00
6	Curt Schilling	5.00
7	Mark Buehrle	3.00
8	Matt Morris	3.00
9	Joe Mays	3.00
10	Javier Vazquez	3.00

11	Mark Mulder	4.00
12	Wade Miller	3.00
13	Barry Zito	5.00
14	Pedro Martinez	7.50
15	Al Leiter	3.00
16	Chan Ho Park	3.00
17	John Burkett	3.00
18	C.C. Sabathia	3.00
19	Jamie Moyer	3.00
20	Mike Mussina	5.00

Bobblehead

		NM/M
Common Bobblehead:		10.00
One per box.		
1	Ichiro Suzuki	40.00
2	Cal Ripken Jr.	40.00
3	Derek Jeter	35.00
4	Mark McGwire	35.00
5	Albert Pujols	40.00
6	Ken Griffey Jr.	20.00
7	Nomar Garciaparra	20.00
8	Mike Piazza	20.00
9	Alex Rodriguez	20.00
10	Manny Ramirez	10.00
11	Tsuyoshi Shinjo	10.00
12	Hideo Nomo	10.00
13	Chipper Jones	15.00
14	Sammy Sosa	20.00
15	Roger Clemens	17.50
16	Tony Gwynn	15.00
17	Barry Bonds	35.00
18	Kazuhiro Sasaki	10.00
19	Pedro Martinez	10.00
20	Jeff Bagwell	10.00
21	Ichiro Suzuki ROY	40.00
22	Albert Pujols ROY	40.00

Bobblehead Cards

		NM/M
Common Player:		4.00
1-20 2,000 Produced		
21-22 1,000 Produced		
1	Ichiro Suzuki	15.00
2	Cal Ripken Jr.	12.00
3	Derek Jeter	12.00
4	Mark McGwire	10.00
5	Albert Pujols	10.00
6	Ken Griffey Jr.	8.00
7	Nomar Garciaparra	8.00
8	Mike Piazza	8.00
9	Alex Rodriguez	8.00
10	Manny Ramirez	5.00
11	Tsuyoshi Shinjo	4.00
12	Hideo Nomo	4.00
13	Chipper Jones	6.00
14	Sammy Sosa	8.00
15	Roger Clemens	7.00
16	Tony Gwynn	6.00
17	Barry Bonds	15.00
18	Kazuhiro Sasaki	4.00

19	Pedro Martinez	5.00
20	Jeff Bagwell	5.00
21	Ichiro Suzuki	15.00
22	Albert Pujols	15.00

Crusade

		NM/M
Complete Set (25):		125.00
Common Player:		3.00
1	Roger Clemens/275	15.00
2	Luis Gonzalez/275	3.00
3	Troy Glaus/275	6.00
4	Freddy Garcia/300	3.00
5	Sean Casey/285	5.00
6	Bobby Abreu/300	3.00
7	Matt Morris/300	3.00
8	Cal Ripken Jr./275	25.00
9	Miguel Tejada/285	5.00
10	Vladimir Guerrero/275	8.00
11	Mark Buehrle/100	5.00
12	Mike Sweeney/300	3.00
13	Ivan Rodriguez/275	8.00
14	Jeff Bagwell/275	8.00
15	Joe Mays/250	3.00
16	Cliff Floyd/300	3.00
17	Lance Berkman/300	3.00
18	Aramis Ramirez/100	5.00
19	Tony Gwynn/300	10.00
20	Shannon Stewart/100	5.00
21	Todd Helton/300	5.00
22	Chipper Jones/275	12.00
23	Javier Vazquez/100	5.00
24	Shawn Green/275	5.00
25	Barry Bonds/300	25.00

Crusade Autographs

		NM/M
Common Player:		
11	Mark Buehrle/200	10.00
15	Joe Mays/50	10.00
18	Aramis Ramirez/200	8.00
20	Shannon Stewart/200	8.00
23	Javier Vazquez/200	8.00
26	Albert Pujols/50	750.00
27	Wilson Betemit/200	10.00
29	Roy Oswalt/200	12.00
30	Johnny Estrada/200	8.00
31	Nick Johnson/200	12.00
32	Aubrey Huff/200	8.00
33	Corey Patterson/200	10.00
34	Jay Gibbons/200	20.00
35	Marcus Giles/200	8.00
36	Juan Cruz/200	8.00
39	Bud Smith/200	8.00
40	Alex Escobar/200	8.00
41	Joe Kennedy/200	8.00
42	Alexis Gomez/200	10.00
44	Josh Towers/200	8.00
45	Joe Crede/200	10.00
46	Brandon Duckworth/200	12.00

Stars / SP designations

19	Pedro Martinez	5.00
20	Jeff Bagwell	5.00
21	Ichiro Suzuki	15.00
22	Albert Pujols	15.00

48	Jose Ortiz/200	8.00
49	Casey Fossum/200	12.00
50	Adam Dunn/100	30.00

Diamond Aces

Common Player: **NM/M** 5.00
Varying quantities produced

1	Roger Clemens/200	30.00
2	Randy Johnson/750	10.00
3	Freddy Garcia/350	5.00
4	Greg Maddux/750	20.00
5	Tim Hudson/550	8.00
6	Curt Schilling/525	8.00
7	Mark Buehrle/750	5.00
9	Joe Mays/750	5.00
10	Javier Vazquez/500	5.00
11	Mark Mulder/300	6.00
12	Wade Miller/525	5.00
13	Barry Zito/550	8.00
14	Pedro Martinez/550	15.00
15	Al Leiter/525	5.00
16	Chan Ho Park/400	5.00
17	John Burkett/700	5.00
18	C.C. Sabathia/550	5.00
19	Jamie Moyer/700	5.00

Diamond Dominators

Common Player: **NM/M** 4.00
Varying quantities produced

1	Manny Ramirez/725	8.00
2	Lance Berkman/725	4.00
3	Juan Gonzalez/500	6.00
4	Albert Pujols/125	65.00
5	Jason Giambi/250	8.00
6	Mike Sweeney/325	4.00
7	Rafael Palmeiro/550	8.00
8	Luis Gonzalez/725	4.00
10	Cliff Floyd/725	4.00
11	Roberto Alomar/200	8.00
12	Paul LoDuca/600	4.00
13	Shannon Stewart/725	6.00
14	Barry Bonds/250	30.00
15	Larry Walker/250	6.00
16	Shawn Green/500	6.00
17	Moises Alou/550	4.00
18	Cal Ripken/250	50.00
19	Brian Giles/725	5.00
20	Magglio Ordonez/725	5.00
21	Jose Vidro/725	4.00
22	Edgar Martinez/200	6.00
23	Aramis Ramirez/200	5.00
24	Tony Gwynn/500	10.00
25	Richie Sexson/725	6.00
26	Todd Helton/725	8.00
27	Garret Anderson/725	6.00
28	Chipper Jones/725	12.00
29	Troy Glaus/200	8.00
30	Jeff Bagwell/325	8.00

Dominators

NM/M
Complete Set (30): 90.00
Common Player: 2.00
Inserted 1:20

1	Manny Ramirez	4.00
2	Lance Berkman	2.00
3	Juan Gonzalez	4.00
4	Albert Pujols	10.00
5	Jason Giambi	3.00
6	Mike Sweeney	2.00
7	Rafael Palmeiro	4.00
8	Luis Gonzalez	2.00
9	Ichiro Suzuki	10.00
10	Cliff Floyd	2.00
11	Roberto Alomar	4.00
12	Paul LoDuca	2.00
13	Shannon Stewart	2.00
14	Barry Bonds	10.00

15	Larry Walker	2.00
16	Shawn Green	3.00
17	Moises Alou	2.00
18	Cal Ripken Jr.	10.00
19	Brian Giles	2.00
20	Magglio Ordonez	3.00
21	Jose Vidro	2.00
22	Edgar Martinez	2.00
23	Aramis Ramirez	2.00
24	Tony Gwynn	5.00
25	Richie Sexson	2.00
26	Todd Helton	4.00
27	Garret Anderson	2.00
28	Chipper Jones	5.00
29	Troy Glaus	4.00
30	Jeff Bagwell	4.00

Final Rewards

NM/M
Common Player: 5.00
Varying quantities produced

1	Jason Giambi/250	10.00
2	Ichiro Suzuki/50	120.00
3	Roger Clemens/200	30.00
4	Freddy Garcia/250	5.00
5	Ichiro Suzuki/50	120.00
6	Albert Pujols/125	60.00
7	Barry Bonds/200	40.00
8	Albert Pujols/125	60.00
9	Randy Johnson/150	15.00

First Class Autographs

NM/M
Common Player:

10	Miguel Tejada/75	50.00
17	Paul LoDuca/100	20.00
21	Eric Chavez/100	20.00
41	Barry Zito/100	30.00

45	Mark Buehrle/100	25.00
49	Robert Fick/100	15.00
50	Sean Casey/100	25.00
51	Joe Mays/100	15.00
59	Ryan Kiesko/50	20.00
69	Mark Mulder/100	25.00
73	Terrence Long/100	15.00
81	Jose Vidro/100	15.00
83	Richie Sexson/100	25.00
84	Troy Glaus/100	25.00
89	Jermaine Dye/100	20.00
91	Richard Hidalgo/100	15.00
93	Aramis Ramirez/100	20.00
96	Tim Hudson/100	25.00

Rewards

NM/M
Common Player: 5.00
Inserted 1:212

1	Jason Giambi	7.50
2	Ichiro Suzuki	40.00
3	Roger Clemens	20.00
4	Freddy Garcia	5.00
5	Ichiro Suzuki	40.00
6	Albert Pujols	30.00
7	Barry Bonds	30.00
8	Albert Pujols	30.00
9	Randy Johnson	10.00
10	Matt Morris	5.00

Rookie Autographs

NM/M
Common Autograph: 8.00

109	Paul Phillips/250	8.00
114	Kris Keller/250	8.00
115	Adam Bernero/250	8.00
120	George Perez/250	8.00
123	Nate Teut/250	8.00
124	Martin Vargas/250	8.00
127	Les Walrond/250	8.00
132	Joe Crede/250	10.00
137	Winston Abreu/250	8.00
138	Matt Ginter/250	8.00
140	Gene Altman/250	8.00
142	Michael Cuddyer/250	8.00
143	Mike Penney/250	8.00
145	Esix Snead/250	8.00
147	Orlando Woodards/250	8.00
148	Jeff Deardorff/100	8.00
150	Blaine Neal/250	8.00
156	Aubrey Huff/250	10.00
157	Pablo Ozuna/250	8.00
158	Bill Ortega/250	8.00
160	Kevin Olsen/250	8.00
161	Will Ohman/250	8.00
163	Jack Cust/250	10.00
168	Craig Monroe/250	8.00
169	Jason Jennings/250	8.00
171	Luis Rivas/250	8.00
173	Luke Hudson/250	12.00
176	David Espinosa/250	8.00
177	Mike Maroth/250	8.00
178	Keith Ginter/250	8.00
181	Steve Lomasney/250	8.00
182	John Grabow/250	8.00
184	Jason Karnuth/250	8.00
186	Brent Abernathy/250	8.00
188	Wily Mo Pena/250	15.00
191	Cesar Izturis/250	8.00
192	Eric Hinske/250	10.00
194	Timo Perez/100	8.00
196	Eric Valent/250	8.00
201	Joe Kennedy/100	8.00
202	Wilson Betemit/100	15.00
203	Christian Parker/100	8.00
204	Jay Gibbons/100	20.00
205	Carlos Garcia/200	8.00
206	Jack Wilson/100	15.00
207	Johnny Estrada/200	20.00
208	Wilkin Ruan/200	8.00
209	Brandon Duckworth/100	8.00

211	Marlon Byrd/100	20.00
213	Dennis Tankersley/100	10.00
214	Brandon Larson/200	8.00
215	Alexis Gomez/200	10.00
216	Bill Hall/100	50.00
217	Antonio Perez/100	8.00
218	Jeremy Affeldt/200	10.00
220	Casey Fossum/200	10.00
224	Zach Day/200	8.00
225	David Williams/200	8.00
227	Jose Acevedo/200	8.00
229	Orlando Hudson/100	25.00
230	Jose Mieses/200	8.00
231	Ric Rodriguez/200	8.00
232	Alfonso Soriano/100	40.00
233	Jason Hart/100	8.00
234	Endy Chavez/200	8.00
235	Delvin James/100	8.00
237	Jeremy Owens/200	8.00
238	Brad Voyles/200	8.00
239	Nate Frese/200	8.00
240	Josh Beckett/25	80.00
241	Roy Oswalt/100	25.00
242	Juan Uribe/150	10.00
243	Cory Aldridge/200	8.00
244	Adam Dunn/100	30.00
245	Bud Smith/100	8.00
246	Adrian Hernandez/100	8.00
249	Wilmy Caceres/200	8.00
250	Jason Michaels/200	8.00
252	John Buck/100	15.00
253	Andres Torres/100	8.00
255	Corky Miller/100	8.00
256	Rafael Soriano/200	10.00
257	Donaldo Mendez/200	8.00
259	Corey Patterson/100	15.00
260	Horacio Ramirez/200	8.00
261	Elpidio Guzman/200	8.00
262	Juan Diaz/200	8.00
264	Brian Lawrence/200	10.00
265	Josue Perez/200	8.00
266	Jose Nunez/200	8.00
268	Albert Pujols/100	500.00
269	Duaner Sanchez/200	8.00
271	Greg Miller/200	8.00
272	Adam Pettyjohn/200	8.00
274	Claudio Vargas/200	8.00
279	Brian Reith/200	8.00
283	Josh Towers/100	8.00
285	David Brous/200	8.00
287	Nick Neugebauer/100	8.00
289	Billy Sylvester/200	8.00
290	Carlos Valderrama/200	8.00
292	Matt White/200	8.00
293	Nick Maness/200	8.00
296	Angel Berroa/100	15.00
297	Juan Cruz/100	8.00
298	Dewon Brazelton/100	8.00
299	Mark Prior/100	100.00
300	Mark Teixeira/100	250.00

Rookie Crusade

NM/M
Complete Set (25): 110.00
Common Player: 3.00

26	Albert Pujols/250	30.00
27	Wilson Betemit/100	3.00
28	C.C. Sabathia/290	3.00
29	Roy Oswalt/100	4.00
30	Johnny Estrada/100	3.00
31	Nick Johnson/100	4.00
32	Aubrey Huff/100	3.00
33	Corey Patterson/200	4.00
34	Jay Gibbons/100	4.00
35	Marcus Giles/100	3.00
36	Juan Cruz/100	3.00
37	Tsuyoshi Shinjo/300	3.00
38	Ben Sheets/285	3.00
39	Bud Smith/100	3.00
40	Alex Escobar/100	3.00

41	Joe Kennedy/100	3.00
42	Alexis Gomez/100	3.00
43	Jimmy Rollins/300	3.00
44	Josh Towers/100	3.00
45	Joe Crede/100	3.00
46	Brandon Duckworth/100	3.00
47	Ichiro Suzuki/300	40.00
48	Jose Ortiz/100	3.00
49	Casey Fossum/100	3.00
50	Adam Dunn/100	5.00

Rookie Team

		NM/M
Complete Set (15):		65.00
Common Player:		3.00
Inserted 1:83		
1	Jay Gibbons	5.00
2	Alfonso Soriano	6.00
3	Jimmy Rollins	3.00
4	Wilson Betemit	3.00
5	Albert Pujols	20.00
6	Johnny Estrada	3.00
7	Ichiro Suzuki	15.00
8	Tsuyoshi Shinjo	4.00
9	Adam Dunn	5.00
10	C.C. Sabathia	3.00
11	Ben Sheets	3.00
12	Roy Oswalt	4.00
13	Bud Smith	3.00
14	Josh Towers	3.00
15	Juan Cruz	3.00

Rookie Team Materials

		NM/M
Common Player:		5.00
Varying quantities produced		
1	Jay Gibbons/100	8.00
2	Alfonso Soriano/100	15.00
3	Jimmy Rollins/200	5.00
5	Albert Pujols/100	65.00
6	Johnny Estrada/100	5.00
7	Ichiro Suzuki/50	120.00
8	Tsuyoshi Shinjo/200	10.00
9	Adam Dunn/200	8.00
10	C.C. Sabathia/200	5.00
11	Ben Sheets/200	5.00
13	Bud Smith/250	5.00
14	Josh Towers/200	5.00
15	Juan Cruz/200	5.00

Yearbook

		NM/M
Complete Set (25):		85.00
Common Player:		2.00
Inserted 1:24		
1	Barry Bonds	12.00
2	Mark Mulder	3.00
3	Luis Gonzalez	2.00
4	Lance Berkman	2.00

5	Matt Morris	2.00
6	Roy Oswalt	2.50
7	Todd Helton	3.00
8	Tsuyoshi Shinjo	2.00
9	C.C. Sabathia	2.00
10	Curt Schilling	3.00
11	Rickey Henderson	4.00
12	Jamie Moyer	2.00
13	Shawn Green	3.00
14	Randy Johnson	4.00
15	Jim Thome	2.00
16	Larry Walker	2.00
17	Jimmy Rollins	2.00
18	Kazuhiro Sasaki	2.00
19	Hideo Nomo	3.00
20	Roger Clemens	7.50
21	Bud Smith	2.00
22	Ichiro Suzuki	10.00
23	Albert Pujols	15.00
24	Cal Ripken Jr.	15.00
25	Tony Gwynn	5.00

Yearbook Scrapbook

		NM/M
Common Player:		4.00
Varying quantities produced		
1	Barry Bonds/525	30.00
2	Mark Mulder/500	6.00
3	Luis Gonzalez/500	4.00
4	Lance Berkman/525	4.00
6	Roy Oswalt/150	6.00
7	Todd Helton/525	6.00
8	Tsuyoshi Shinjo/75	15.00
9	C.C. Sabathia/500	4.00
10	Curt Schilling/525	6.00
11	Rickey Henderson/200	15.00
12	Jamie Moyer/500	4.00
13	Shawn Green/525	5.00
14	Randy Johnson/500	8.00
15	Jim Thome/400	4.00
16	Larry Walker/500	4.00
18	Kazuhiro Sasaki/500	4.00
19	Hideo Nomo/150	5.00
20	Roger Clemens/475	20.00
21	Bud Smith/525	4.00
22	Ichiro Suzuki/75	80.00
23	Albert Pujols/150	50.00
24	Cal Ripken/525	30.00
25	Tony Gwynn/500	10.00

2001 Donruss Classics

		NM/M
Common Player:		.50
Common SP (101-150):		5.00
Production 585		
Common SP (151-200):		3.00
Production 1,755		
Pack (6):		12.00
Box (18):		180.00
1	Alex Rodriguez	3.00

2	Barry Bonds	3.00
3	Cal Ripken Jr.	4.00
4	Chipper Jones	2.00
5	Derek Jeter	3.00
6	Troy Glaus	.75
7	Frank Thomas	1.00
8	Greg Maddux	2.00
9	Ivan Rodriguez	1.00
10	Jeff Bagwell	1.00
11	Cliff Floyd	.50
12	Todd Helton	1.00
13	Ken Griffey Jr.	2.00
14	Manny Ramirez	1.00
15	Mark McGwire	3.00
16	Mike Piazza	2.00
17	Nomar Garciaparra	3.00
18	Pedro Martinez	1.50
19	Randy Johnson	1.50
20	Rick Ankiel	.50
21	Rickey Henderson	.75
22	Roger Clemens	3.00
23	Sammy Sosa	2.50
24	Tony Gwynn	1.50
25	Vladimir Guerrero	1.50
26	Kazuhiro Sasaki	.50
27	Roberto Alomar	.75
28	Barry Zito	.75
29	Pat Burrell	.75
30	Harold Baines	.50
31	Carlos Delgado	.75
32	J.D. Drew	.50
33	Jim Edmonds	.75
34	Darin Erstad	.75
35	Jason Giambi	1.00
36	Tom Glavine	.75
37	Juan Gonzalez	1.00
38	Mark Grace	.75
39	Shawn Green	.75
40	Tim Hudson	.75
41	Andruw Jones	.75
42	Jeff Kent	.50
43	Barry Larkin	.75
44	Rafael Furcal	.50
45	Mike Mussina	.75
46	Hideo Nomo	.75
47	Rafael Palmeiro	1.00
48	Scott Rolen	1.00
49	Gary Sheffield	.75
50	Bernie Williams	.75
51	Bob Abreu	.50
52	Edgardo Alfonzo	.50
53	Edgar Martinez	.50
54	Magglio Ordonez	.75
55	Kerry Wood	.75
56	Adrian Beltre	.50
57	Lance Berkman	.75
58	Kevin Brown	.75
59	Sean Casey	.50
60	Eric Chavez	.75
61	Bartolo Colon	.50
62	Johnny Damon	.50
63	Jermaine Dye	.50
64	Juan Encarnacion	.50
65	Carl Everett	.50
66	Brian Giles	.75
67	Mike Hampton	.50
68	Richard Hidalgo	.50
69	Geoff Jenkins	.75
70	Jacque Jones	.50
71	Jason Kendall	.75
72	Ryan Klesko	.50
73	Chan Ho Park	.50
74	Richie Sexson	.50
75	Mike Sweeney	.50
76	Fernando Tatis	.50
77	Miguel Tejada	.75
78	Jose Vidro	.50
79	Larry Walker	.75
80	Preston Wilson	.50
81	Craig Biggio	.75
82	Fred McGriff	.50
83	Jim Thome	1.00
84	Garret Anderson	.75
85	Russell Branyan	.50

86	Tony Batista	.50
87	Terrence Long	.50
88	Brad Fullmer	.50
89	Rusty Greer	.50
90	Orlando Hernandez	.50
91	Gabe Kapler	.50
92	Paul Konerko	.50
93	Carlos Lee	.50
94	Kenny Lofton	.75
95	Raul Mondesi	.50
96	Jorge Posada	.75
97	Tim Salmon	.75
98	Greg Vaughn	.50
99	Mo Vaughn	.50
100	Omar Vizquel	.50
101	Aubrey Huff	5.00
102	Jimmy Rollins	5.00
103	Cory Aldridge RC	5.00
104	Wilmy Caceres RC	5.00
105	Josh Beckett RC	6.00
106	Wilson Betemit RC	5.00
107	Timo Perez	5.00
108	Albert Pujols RC	240.00
109	Bud Smith RC	5.00
110	Jack Wilson RC	10.00
111	Alex Escobar	5.00
112	Johnny Estrada RC	10.00
113	Pedro Feliz	5.00
114	Nate Frese RC	5.00
115	Carlos Garcia RC	5.00
116	Brandon Larson RC	5.00
117	Alexis Gomez RC	5.00
118	Jason Hart	5.00
119	Adam Dunn	5.00
120	Marcus Giles	5.00
121	Christian Parker RC	5.00
122	Jackson Melian RC	5.00
123	Eric Chavez	5.00
124	Adrian Hernandez RC	5.00
125	Joe Kennedy RC	5.00
126	Jose Mieses RC	5.00
127	C.C. Sabathia	5.00
128	Eric Munson	5.00
129	Xavier Nady	5.00
130	Horacio Ramirez RC	10.00
131	Abraham Nunez	5.00
132	Jose Ortiz	5.00
133	Jeremy Owens RC	5.00
134	Claudio Vargas RC	5.00
135	Corey Patterson	5.00
136	Audres Torres	5.00
137	Ben Sheets	5.00
138	Joe Crede	5.00
139	Adam Pettyjohn RC	5.00
140	Elpidio Guzman RC	5.00
141	Jay Gibbons RC	10.00
142	Wilkin Ruan RC	5.00
143	Tsuyoshi Shinjo RC	10.00
144	Alfonso Soriano	5.00
145	Nick Johnson	5.00
146	Ichiro Suzuki RC	80.00
147	Juan Uribe RC	8.00
148	Jack Cust	5.00
149	Carlos Valderrama RC	5.00
150	Matt White RC	5.00
151	Hank Aaron	10.00
152	Ernie Banks	4.00
153	Johnny Bench	6.00
154	George Brett	10.00
155	Lou Brock	3.00
156	Rod Carew	3.00
157	Steve Carlton	3.00
158	Bob Feller	3.00
159	Bob Gibson	5.00
160	Reggie Jackson	5.00
161	Al Kaline	6.00
162	Sandy Koufax	600.00
163	Don Mattingly	10.00
164	Willie Mays	10.00
165	Willie McCovey	5.00
166	Joe Morgan	3.00
167	Stan Musial	8.00
168	Jim Palmer	3.00
169	Brooks Robinson	5.00
170	Frank Robinson	3.00
171	Nolan Ryan	15.00
172	Mike Schmidt	10.00
173	Tom Seaver	5.00
174	Warren Spahn	4.00
175	Robin Yount	5.00
176	Wade Boggs	4.00
177	Ty Cobb	10.00
178	Lou Gehrig	10.00
179	Luis Aparicio	5.00
180	Babe Ruth	15.00
181	Ryne Sandberg	10.00
182	Yogi Berra	5.00
183	Roberto Clemente	10.00
184	Eddie Murray	5.00
185	Robin Roberts	5.00
186	Duke Snider	5.00
187	Orlando Cepeda	5.00
188	Billy Williams	3.00
189	Juan Marichal	5.00
190	Harmon Killebrew	5.00
191	Kirby Puckett	8.00

192	Carlton Fisk	4.00
193	Dave Winfield	3.00
194	Whitey Ford	4.00
195	Paul Molitor	4.00
196	Tony Perez	3.00
197	Ozzie Smith	6.00
198	Ralph Kiner	3.00
199	Fergie Jenkins	3.00
200	Phil Rizzuto	4.00

Benchmarks

		NM/M
Common Player:		5.00
Inserted 1:18		
1	Todd Helton	5.00
2	Roberto Clemente	40.00
3	Mark McGwire	30.00
4	Barry Bonds	40.00
5	Bob Gibson	10.00
6	Ken Griffey Jr.	20.00
7	Frank Robinson	8.00
8	Greg Maddux	15.00
9	Reggie Jackson	10.00
10	Sammy Sosa	20.00
11	Willie Stargell	8.00
12	Vladimir Guerrero	8.00
13	Johnny Bench	15.00
14	Tony Gwynn	10.00
15	Mike Schmidt	17.50
16	Ivan Rodriguez	6.00
17	Jeff Bagwell	10.00
18	Cal Ripken Jr.	40.00
20	Kirby Puckett	15.00
21	Frank Thomas	8.00
22	Joe Morgan	5.00
23	Mike Piazza	20.00
24	Hank Aaron	
25	Andruw Jones	5.00

Benchmarks Autographs

		NM/M
5	Bob Gibson	60.00
7	Frank Robinson	50.00
9	Reggie Jackson	100.00
15	Mike Schmidt	100.00
22	Joe Morgan	50.00
25	Andruw Jones	60.00

Classic Combos

		NM/M
Common Card:		20.00
1	Roberto Clemente	125.00
2	Willie Stargell	25.00
3	Babe Ruth	450.00
4	Lou Gehrig	300.00
5	Hank Aaron	100.00
6	Eddie Mathews	30.00
7	Johnny Bench	40.00
8	Joe Morgan	20.00
9	Robin Yount	40.00
10	Paul Molitor	35.00
11	Steve Carlton	25.00
12	Mike Schmidt	75.00
13	Stan Musial	75.00
14	Lou Brock	20.00
15	Yogi Berra	25.00
16	Phil Rizzuto	25.00
17	Ernie Banks	40.00
18	Billy Williams	20.00
19	Don Mattingly	70.00
21	Jackie Robinson	100.00
22	Duke Snider	30.00
23	Frank Robinson	25.00
24	Brooks Robinson	40.00
26	Willie McCovey	30.00
27	Ryne Sandberg	60.00
29	Harmon Killebrew	40.00
30	Rod Carew	40.00
31	Roberto Clemente, Willie Stargell	200.00
32	Babe Ruth, Lou Gehrig	1,000
33	Hank Aaron, Eddie Mathews	200.00
34	Johnny Bench, Joe Morgan	80.00
35	Robin Yount, Paul Molitor	100.00
36	Steve Carlton, Mike Schmidt	200.00
37	Stan Musial, Lou Brock	150.00
38	Phil Rizzuto, Yogi Berra	100.00
41	Jackie Robinson, Duke Snider	150.00
42	Brooks Robinson, Frank Robinson	75.00
43	Willie McCovey, Orlando Cepeda	60.00
45	Harmon Killebrew, Rod Carew	100.00

Classic Combos Autographs

No pricing due to scarcity.

Legendary Lumberjacks

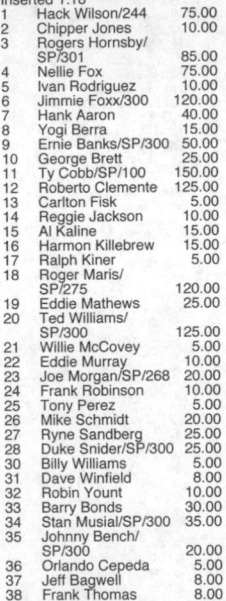

		NM/M
Common Player:		5.00
Inserted 1:18		
1	Hack Wilson/244	75.00
2	Chipper Jones	10.00
3	Rogers Hornsby/SP/301	85.00
4	Nellie Fox	75.00
5	Ivan Rodriguez	10.00
6	Jimmie Foxx/300	120.00
7	Hank Aaron	40.00
8	Yogi Berra	15.00
9	Ernie Banks/SP/300	50.00
10	George Brett	25.00
11	Ty Cobb/SP/100	150.00
12	Roberto Clemente	125.00
13	Carlton Fisk	5.00
14	Reggie Jackson	10.00
15	Al Kaline	15.00
16	Harmon Killebrew	15.00
17	Ralph Kiner	5.00
18	Roger Maris/SP/275	120.00
19	Eddie Mathews	25.00
20	Ted Williams/SP/300	125.00
21	Willie McCovey	5.00
22	Eddie Murray	10.00
23	Joe Morgan/SP/268	20.00
24	Frank Robinson	10.00
25	Tony Perez	5.00
26	Mike Schmidt	20.00
27	Ryne Sandberg	25.00
28	Duke Snider/SP/300	25.00
30	Billy Williams	5.00
31	Dave Winfield	8.00
32	Robin Yount	10.00
33	Barry Bonds	30.00
34	Stan Musial/SP/300	35.00
35	Johnny Bench/SP/300	20.00
36	Orlando Cepeda	5.00
37	Jeff Bagwell	8.00
38	Frank Thomas	8.00
39	Juan Gonzalez	8.00
40	Cal Ripken Jr.	40.00
41	Rafael Palmeiro	8.00
42	Troy Glaus/SP/100	15.00
43	Manny Ramirez	8.00
44	Paul Molitor	15.00
45	Tony Gwynn	8.00
46	Rod Carew	8.00
47	Lou Brock	8.00
48	Wade Boggs	5.00
49	Babe Ruth/SP	225.00
50	Lou Gehrig/SP	150.00

Legendary Lumberjacks Autographs

		NM/M
No pricing due to scarcity.		
LL24	Frank Robinson	200.00

Significant Signatures

		NM/M
Common Autograph:		5.00
Inserted 1:18		
101	Aubrey Huff	6.00
103	Cory Aldridge	5.00
105	Josh Beckett/SP	30.00
106	Wilson Betemit	5.00
107	Timo Perez	5.00
108	Albert Pujols	600.00
110	Jack Wilson	10.00
111	Alex Escobar	5.00
112	Johnny Estrada	20.00
113	Pedro Feliz	5.00
114	Nate Frese	5.00
115	Carlos Garcia	5.00
116	Brandon Larson	8.00
118	Jason Hart	5.00
119	Adam Dunn/SP	25.00
120	Marcus Giles	8.00
121	Christian Parker	5.00
126	Jose Mieses	5.00
127	C.C. Sabathia	10.00
129	Xavier Nady	8.00
130	Horacio Ramirez	10.00
131	Abraham Nunez	5.00
132	Jose Ortiz	5.00
133	Jeremy Owens	5.00
134	Claudio Vargas	5.00
135	Corey Patterson/SP	20.00
136	Andres Torres	5.00
137	Ben Sheets/SP	25.00
138	Joe Crede	8.00
139	Adam Pettyjohn	5.00
140	Elpidio Guzman	5.00
141	Jay Gibbons	15.00
142	Wilkin Ruan	5.00
144	Alfonso Soriano/SP	40.00
145	Nick Johnson	10.00
147	Juan Uribe	10.00
149	Carlos Valderrama	5.00
151	Hank Aaron/SP	200.00
152	Ernie Banks	35.00
153	Johnny Bench/SP	100.00
154	George Brett/SP	150.00
155	Lou Brock	15.00
156	Rod Carew	25.00
157	Steve Carlton	25.00
158	Bob Feller	15.00
159	Bob Gibson	25.00
160	Reggie Jackson/SP	65.00
161	Al Kaline	40.00
162	Nolan Ryan/SP	150.00
163	Don Mattingly	80.00
164	Willie Mays/SP	160.00
165	Willie McCovey	20.00
166	Joe Morgan	10.00
167	Stan Musial/SP	85.00
168	Jim Palmer	15.00
169	Brooks Robinson	40.00
170	Frank Robinson	20.00
171	Nolan Ryan/SP	150.00
172	Mike Schmidt	75.00
173	Tom Seaver	30.00
174	Warren Spahn	40.00
175	Robin Yount/SP	100.00
176	Wade Boggs/SP	50.00
179	Luis Aparicio	10.00
181	Ryne Sandberg	75.00
182	Yogi Berra	30.00
184	Eddie Murray	50.00
185	Ron Santo	25.00
186	Duke Snider	25.00
187	Orlando Cepeda	10.00
188	Billy Williams	10.00
189	Juan Marichal	15.00
190	Harmon Killebrew	20.00
191	Kirby Puckett/SP	60.00
192	Carlton Fisk	20.00
193	Dave Winfield/SP	50.00
194	Whitey Ford	25.00
195	Paul Molitor/SP	50.00
196	Tony Perez	15.00
197	Ozzie Smith/SP	80.00
198	Ralph Kiner	25.00
199	Fergie Jenkins	10.00
200	Phil Rizzuto	40.00

Stadium Stars

		NM/M
Common Player:		4.00
Inserted 1:18		
1	Babe Ruth	40.00
2	Cal Ripken Jr.	20.00
3	Brooks Robinson	8.00
4	Tony Gwynn	10.00
5	Ty Cobb	25.00
6	Vladimir Guerrero	8.00
7	Lou Gehrig	35.00
8	Nomar Garciaparra	12.00
9	Sammy Sosa	12.00
10	Reggie Jackson	8.00
11	Alex Rodriguez	12.00
12	Derek Jeter	20.00
13	Willie McCovey	4.00
14	Mark McGwire	15.00
15	Chipper Jones	10.00
16	Honus Wagner	10.00
17	Ken Griffey Jr.	12.00
18	Frank Robinson	8.00
19	Barry Bonds	20.00
20	Yogi Berra	8.00
21	Mike Piazza	12.00
22	Roger Clemens	10.00
23	Duke Snider	8.00
24	Frank Thomas	8.00
25	Andruw Jones	8.00

Stadium Stars Autographs

No pricing

Timeless Treasures

		NM/M
Inserted 1:420		
1	Mark McGwire/Ball	200.00
2	Babe Ruth/Seat	60.00
3	Harmon Killebrew/Bat	30.00
4	Derek Jeter/Base	25.00
5	Barry Bonds/Ball	85.00

Timeless Tributes

Stars (1-100)	4-8X
SP's (101-150)	1-1.5X
SP's (151-200)	1-2.5X
Production 100 Sets	

(See 2001 Donruss Classics for checklist and base cards values.)

2001 Donruss Elite

Geoff Jenkins

	NM/M
Complete Set (200):	
Common Player:	.25
Common (151-200):	5.00
Production 900	
Common 201-250:	4.00
(#201-250 available by redemption)	
Pack (5):	12.00
Box (18):	200.00
1 Alex Rodriguez	2.00
2 Barry Bonds	2.50
3 Cal Ripken Jr.	2.50
4 Chipper Jones	1.50
5 Derek Jeter	2.50
6 Troy Glaus	.75
7 Frank Thomas	1.00
8 Greg Maddux	1.50
9 Ivan Rodriguez	.75
10 Jeff Bagwell	1.00
11 Jose Canseco	.50
12 Todd Helton	.75
13 Ken Griffey Jr.	1.75
14 Manny Ramirez	1.00
15 Mark McGwire	2.00
16 Mike Piazza	1.75
17 Nomar Garciaparra	1.50
18 Pedro Martinez	1.00
19 Randy Johnson	1.00
20 Rick Ankiel	.25
21 Ricky Henderson	1.00
22 Roger Clemens	1.75
23 Sammy Sosa	1.50
24 Tony Gwynn	1.50
25 Vladimir Guerrero	1.00
26 Eric Davis	.25
27 Roberto Alomar	.35
28 Mark Mulder	.35
29 Pat Burrell	.50
30 Harold Baines	.25
31 Carlos Delgado	.60
32 J.D. Drew	.40
33 Jim Edmonds	.25
34 Darin Erstad	.35
35 Jason Giambi	.50
36 Tom Glavine	.50
37 Juan Gonzalez	.50
38 Mark Grace	.25
39 Shawn Green	.40
40 Tim Hudson	.40
41 Andruw Jones	1.00
42 David Justice	.25
43 Jeff Kent	.25
44 Barry Larkin	.25
45 Pokey Reese	.25
46 Mike Mussina	.40
47 Hideo Nomo	.50
48 Rafael Palmeiro	.65
49 Adam Piatt	.25
50 Scott Rolen	.65
51 Gary Sheffield	.40
52 Bernie Williams	.25
53 Bob Abreu	.25
54 Edgardo Alfonzo	.25
55 Jermaine Clark RC	.25
56 Albert Belle	.25
57 Craig Biggio	.25
58 Andres Galarraga	.25
59 Edgar Martinez	.25
60 Fred McGriff	.25
61 Magglio Ordonez	.25
62 Jim Thome	.65
63 Matt Williams	.25
64 Kerry Wood	.25
65 Moises Alou	.25
66 Brady Anderson	.25
67 Garret Anderson	.25
68 Tony Armas Jr.	.25
69 Tony Batista	.25
70 Jose Cruz Jr.	.25
71 Carlos Beltran	.50
72 Adrian Beltre	.40

73 Kris Benson	.25
74 Lance Berkman	.25
75 Kevin Brown	.25
76 Jay Buhner	.25
77 Jeromy Burnitz	.25
78 Ken Caminiti	.25
79 Sean Casey	.40
80 Luis Castillo	.25
81 Eric Chavez	.40
82 Jeff Cirillo	.25
83 Bartolo Colon	.25
84 David Cone	.25
85 Freddy Garcia	.25
86 Johnny Damon	.50
87 Ray Durham	.25
88 Jermaine Dye	.25
89 Juan Encarnacion	.25
90 Terrence Long	.25
91 Carl Everett	.25
92 Steve Finley	.25
93 Cliff Floyd	.25
94 Brad Fulmer	.25
95 Brian Giles	.25
96 Luis Gonzalez	.25
97 Rusty Greer	.25
98 Jeffrey Hammonds	.25
99 Mike Hampton	.25
100 Orlando Hernandez	.35
101 Richard Hidalgo	.25
102 Geoff Jenkins	.25
103 Jacque Jones	.25
104 Brian Jordan	.25
105 Gabe Kapler	.25
106 Eric Karros	.25
107 Jason Kendall	.25
108 Adam Kennedy	.25
109 Byung-Hyun Kim	.25
110 Ryan Klesko	.25
111 Chuck Knoblauch	.25
112 Paul Konerko	.25
113 Carlos Lee	.25
114 Kenny Lofton	.25
115 Javy Lopez	.25
116 Tino Martinez	.25
117 Ruben Mateo	.25
118 Kevin Millwood	.25
119 Ben Molina	.25
120 Raul Mondesi	.25
121 Trot Nixon	.25
122 John Olerud	.25
123 Paul O'Neill	.25
124 Chan Ho Park	.25
125 Andy Pettitte	.40
126 Jorge Posada	.35
127 Mark Quinn	.25
128 Aramis Ramirez	.25
129 Mariano Rivera	.35
130 Tim Salmon	.25
131 Curt Schilling	.40
132 Richie Sexson	.25
133 John Smoltz	.25
134 J.T. Snow	.25
135 Jay Payton	.25
136 Shannon Stewart	.25
137 B.J. Surhoff	.25
138 Mike Sweeney	.25
139 Fernando Tatis	.25
140 Miguel Tejada	.40
141 Jason Varitek	.25
142 Greg Vaughn	.25
143 Mo Vaughn	.25
144 Robin Ventura	.25
145 Jose Vidro	.25
146 Omar Vizquel	.25
147 Larry Walker	.25
148 David Wells	.25
149 Rondell White	.25
150 Preston Wilson	.25
151 Brent Abernathy	5.00
152 Cory Aldridge RC	5.00
153 Gene Altman RC	5.00
154 Josh Beckett	6.00
155 Wilson Betemit RC	5.00
156 Albert Pujols RC	400.00
157 Joe Crede	5.00
158 Jack Cust	5.00
159 Ben Sheets	5.00
160 Alex Escobar	5.00
161 Adrian Hernandez RC	5.00
162 Pedro Feliz	5.00
163 Nate Frese RC	5.00
164 Carlos Garcia RC	5.00
165 Marcus Giles	5.00
166 Alexis Gomez RC	5.00
167 Jason Hart	5.00
168 Aubrey Huff	5.00
169 Cesar Izturis	5.00
170 Nick Johnson	5.00
171 Jack Wilson RC	10.00
172 Brian Lawrence RC	5.00
173 Christian Parker RC	5.00
174 Nick Maness RC	5.00
175 Jose Mieses RC	5.00
176 Greg Miller RC	5.00

177 Eric Munson	5.00
178 Xavier Nady	5.00
179 Blaine Neal RC	5.00
180 Abraham Nunez	5.00
181 Jose Ortiz	5.00
182 Jeremy Owens RC	5.00
183 Jay Gibbons RC	10.00
184 Corey Patterson	5.00
185 Carlos Pena	5.00
186 C.C. Sabathia	5.00
187 Timo Perez	5.00
188 Adam Pettyjohn RC	5.00
189 Donaldo Mendez RC	5.00
190 Jackson Melian RC	5.00
191 Wilken Ruan RC	5.00
192 Duaner Sanchez RC	5.00
193 Alfonso Soriano	5.00
194 Rafael Soriano RC	10.00
195 Ichiro Suzuki RC	150.00
196 Billy Sylvester RC	5.00
197 Juan Uribe RC	5.00
198 Tsuyoshi Shinjo RC	10.00
199 Carlos Valderrama RC	5.00
200 Matt White RC	5.00
201 Adam Dunn	6.00
202 Joe Kennedy	4.00
203 Mike Rivera	4.00
204 Erick Almonte	4.00
205 Brandon Duckworth	4.00
206 Victor Martinez RC	100.00
207 Rick Bauer	4.00
208 Jeff Deardorff	4.00
209 Antonio Perez	4.00
210 Bill Hall	30.00
211 Dennis Tankersley	6.00
212 Jeremy Affeldt	8.00
213 Junior Spivey	8.00
214 Casey Fossum	6.00
215 Brandon Lyon	4.00
216 Angel Santos	4.00
217 Cody Ransom	4.00
218 Jason Lane	35.00
219 David Williams	4.00
220 Alex Herrera	4.00
221 Ryan Drese	4.00
222 Travis Hafner	40.00
223 Bud Smith	4.00
224 Johnny Estrada	25.00
225 Ricardo Rodriguez	4.00
226 Brandon Berger	4.00
227 Claudio Vargas	4.00
228 Luis Garcia	4.00
229 Marlon Byrd	20.00
230 Hee Seop Choi	20.00
231 Corky Miller	4.00
232 Justin Duchscherer	6.00
233 Tim Spooneybarger	4.00
234 Roy Oswalt	4.00
235 Willie Harris	4.00
236 Josh Towers	4.00
237 Juan Pena	4.00
238 Alfredo Amezaga	4.00
239 Geronimo Gil	4.00
240 Juan Cruz	4.00
241 Ed Rogers	4.00
242 Joe Thurston	4.00
243 Orlando Hudson RC	10.00
244 John Buck RC	8.00
245 Martin Vargas	4.00
246 David Brous	4.00
247 Dewon Brazelton	4.00
248 Mark Prior	50.00
249 Angel Berroa	10.00
250 Mark Teixeira	100.00

Aspirations

Cards 1-150 print run	
76-100:	5-10X
1-150 p/r 51-75:	8-15X
1-150 p/r 26-50:	10-25X
Cards 151-200 print run	
76-100:	1X
151-200 p/r 51-75:	1.5X
151-200 p/r 26-50:	1.5-2X
Varying quantities produced	

Status

Cards 1-150 print run	
76-100:	5-10X
1-150 p/r 51-75:	8-15X
1-150 p/r 26-50:	10-25X
Cards 151-200 print run	
76-100:	1X
151-200 p/r 51-75:	1.5X
151-200 p/r 26-50:	1.5-2X
Varying quantities produced	

Back 2 Back Jacks

	NM/M
Common Player:	15.00
Singles production 100.	
Doubles production 50.	
SP print runs listed.	
1 Ernie Banks/75	20.00
2 Ryne Sandberg/75	40.00

3	Babe Ruth	200.00
4	Lou Gehrig	150.00
5	Eddie Matthews	25.00
6	Troy Glaus	15.00
7	Don Mattingly/50	50.00
8	Todd Helton	20.00
9	Wade Boggs	15.00
10	Tony Gwynn	25.00
11	Robin Yount	25.00
12	Paul Molitor/50	25.00
13	Mike Schmidt/50	40.00
14	Scott Rolen/75	20.00
15	Reggie Jackson	20.00
16	Dave Winfield	15.00
17	Johnny Bench/50	40.00
18	Joe Morgan	15.00
19	Brooks Robinson/50	40.00
20	Cal Ripken Jr.	50.00
21	Ty Cobb	100.00
22	Al Kaline/50	40.00
23	Frank Robinson/50	25.00
24	Frank Thomas	20.00
25	Roberto Clemente	80.00
26	Vladimir Guerrero/50	25.00
27	Harmon Killebrew/50	25.00
28	Kirby Puckett	20.00
29	Yogi Berra/75	35.00
30	Phil Rizzuto/75	30.00
31	Ernie Banks, Ryne Sandberg	80.00
32	Babe Ruth, Lou Gehrig	350.00
33	Troy Glaus, Eddie Matthews	40.00
34	Don Mattingly, Todd Helton	100.00
35	Tony Gwynn, Wade Boggs	75.00
36	Paul Molitor, Robin Yount	50.00
37	Mike Schmidt, Scott Rolen	80.00
38	Dave Winfield, Reggie Jackson	40.00
39	Joe Morgan, Johnny Bench	50.00
40	Brooks Robinson, Cal Ripken Jr.	100.00
41	Al Kaline, Ty Cobb	175.00
42	Frank Robinson, Frank Thomas	40.00
43	Roberto Clemente, Vladimir Guerrero	100.00
44	Harmon Killebrew, Kirby Puckett	50.00
45	Phil Rizzuto, Yogi Berra/25	100.00

Back 2 Back Jacks Autograph

	NM/M
Common Autograph:	60.00
Print runs listed.	
1 Ernie Banks/25	200.00
2 Ryne Sandberg/25	250.00
6 Troy Glaus/50	50.00
7 Don Mattingly/50	200.00
12 Paul Molitor/50	75.00
13 Mike Schmidt/50	150.00
14 Scott Rolen/25	60.00
17 Johnny Bench/50	100.00
19 Brooks Robinson/50	75.00
22 Al Kaline/50	100.00
23 Frank Robinson/50	50.00
26 Vladimir Guerrero/50	100.00
27 Harmon Killebrew/50	100.00
29 Yogi Berra/25	125.00
30 Phil Rizzuto/25	125.00
45 Phil Rizzuto, Yogi Berra/25	200.00

Passing the Torch

		NM/M
Common Player:		3.00

Singles production 1,000.
Doubles production 500.

1	Stan Musial	8.00
2	Tony Gwynn	6.00
3	Willie Mays	10.00
4	Barry Bonds	15.00
5	Mike Schmidt	10.00
6	Scott Rolen	4.00
7	Cal Ripken Jr.	15.00
8	Alex Rodriguez	10.00
9	Hank Aaron	10.00
10	Andruw Jones	4.00
11	Nolan Ryan	15.00
12	Pedro Martinez	5.00
13	Wade Boggs	6.00
14	Nomar Garciaparra	8.00
15	Don Mattingly	10.00
16	Todd Helton	5.00
17	Stan Musial, Tony Gwynn	10.00
18	Barry Bonds, Willie Mays	20.00
19	Mike Schmidt, Scott Rolen	15.00
20	Alex Rodriguez, Cal Ripken Jr.	25.00
21	Andruw Jones, Hank Aaron	15.00
22	Nolan Ryan, Pedro Martinez	25.00
23	Nomar Garciaparra, Wade Boggs	15.00
24	Don Mattingly, Todd Helton	15.00

Passing the Torch Autographs

		NM/M
Common Player:		30.00

Singles production 100.
Doubles production 50.

1	Stan Musial	100.00
2	Tony Gwynn	75.00
3	Willie Mays	200.00
4	Barry Bonds	275.00
5	Mike Schmidt	100.00
6	Scott Rolen	50.00
7	Cal Ripken Jr.	150.00
8	Alex Rodriguez	120.00
9	Hank Aaron	200.00
10	Andruw Jones	30.00
11	Nolan Ryan	125.00
12	Pedro Martinez	75.00
13	Wade Boggs	30.00
14	Nomar Garciaparra	125.00
15	Don Mattingly	100.00
16	Todd Helton	40.00
17	Stan Musial, Tony Gwynn	175.00
18	Barry Bonds, Willie Mays	900.00
19	Mike Schmidt, Scott Rolen	150.00
20	Alex Rodriguez, Cal Ripken Jr.	400.00
21	Andruw Jones, Hank Aaron	250.00
22	Nolan Ryan, Pedro Martinez	300.00
22	Nolan Ryan, Roger Clemens FB redemp.	375.00
23	Wade Boggs, FB Redemp.	25.00
24	Don Mattingly, Todd Helton	200.00

Prime Numbers

		NM/M

Print runs listed.

1a	Alex Rodriguez/300	8.00
1b	Alex Rodriguez/308	8.00
1c	Alex Rodriguez/350	8.00
2a	Ken Griffey Jr./400	6.00
2b	Ken Griffey Jr./408	6.00
2c	Ken Griffey Jr./430	6.00
3a	Mark McGwire/500	8.00
3b	Mark McGwire/504	8.00
3c	Mark McGwire/550	8.00
4a	Cal Ripken Jr./400	10.00
4b	Cal Ripken Jr./407	10.00
4c	Cal Ripken Jr./410	10.00
5a	Derek Jeter/300	10.00
5b	Derek Jeter/302	10.00
5c	Derek Jeter/320	10.00
6a	Mike Piazza/300	6.00
6b	Mike Piazza/302	6.00
6c	Mike Piazza/360	6.00
7a	Nomar Garciaparra/300	6.00
7b	Nomar Garciaparra/302	6.00
7c	Nomar Garciaparra/370	6.00
8a	Sammy Sosa/300	6.00
8b	Sammy Sosa/306	6.00
8c	Sammy Sosa/380	6.00
9a	Vladimir Guerrero/300	4.00
9b	Vladimir Guerrero/305	4.00
9c	Vladimir Guerrero/340	4.00
10a	Tony Gwynn/300	4.00
10b	Tony Gwynn/304	4.00
10c	Tony Gwynn/390	4.00

Primary Colors

		NM/M
Complete Set (40):		100.00
Common Player:		1.00

Production 975 Sets

Red Die-Cut:	3-5X

Production 25

Blues:	1-1.5X

Production 200

Blue Die-Cut:	1.5-3X

Production 50

Yellows:	3-5X

Production 25

Yellow Die-Cut:	1.5-2X

Production 75

1	Alex Rodriguez	8.00
2	Barry Bonds	10.00
3	Cal Ripken Jr.	10.00
4	Chipper Jones	5.00
5	Derek Jeter	10.00
6	Troy Glaus	4.00
7	Frank Thomas	4.00
8	Greg Maddux	5.00
9	Ivan Rodriguez	2.50
10	Jeff Bagwell	4.00
11	Todd Helton	4.00
12	Ken Griffey Jr.	6.00
13	Manny Ramirez	4.00
14	Mark McGwire	8.00
15	Mike Piazza	6.00
16	Nomar Garciaparra	6.00
17	Pedro Martinez	4.00
18	Randy Johnson	4.00
19	Rick Ankiel	1.25
20	Roger Clemens	5.50
21	Sammy Sosa	6.00
22	Tony Gwynn	5.00
23	Vladimir Guerrero	4.00
24	Carlos Delgado	2.00
25	Jason Giambi	2.50
26	Andruw Jones	4.00
27	Bernie Williams	1.50
28	Roberto Alomar	1.50
29	Shawn Green	1.50
30	Barry Larkin	1.00
31	Scott Rolen	3.00
32	Gary Sheffield	2.00
33	Rafael Palmeiro	3.00
34	Albert Belle	1.00
35	Magglio Ordonez	1.50
36	Jim Thome	1.00
37	Jim Edmonds	1.00
38	Darin Erstad	2.00
39	Kris Benson	1.00
40	Sean Casey	1.50

Throwback Threads

		NM/M
Common Player:		15.00

Singles production 100.
Doubles production 50.
SP production listed.

1	Stan Musial/75	50.00
2	Tony Gwynn/75	25.00
3	Willie McCovey	15.00
4	Barry Bonds	50.00
5	Babe Ruth	250.00
6	Lou Gehrig	200.00
7	Mike Schmidt/75	40.00
8	Scott Rolen	20.00
9	Harmon Killebrew/75	30.00
10	Kirby Puckett	20.00
11	Al Kaline/75	40.00
12	Eddie Matthews	25.00
13	Hank Aaron/75	60.00
14	Andruw Jones/50	20.00
15	Lou Brock	15.00
16	Ozzie Smith	25.00
17	Ernie Banks/75	35.00
18	Ryne Sandberg	50.00
19	Roberto Clemente	100.00
20	Vladimir Guerrero/50	30.00
21	Frank Robinson/50	25.00
22	Frank Thomas	15.00
23	Brooks Robinson/50	25.00
24	Cal Ripken Jr.	50.00
25	Roger Clemens	30.00
26	Pedro Martinez	20.00
27	Reggie Jackson	15.00
28	Dave Winfield	15.00
29	Don Mattingly/50	60.00
30	Todd Helton	15.00
31	Stan Musial, Tony Gwynn/25	120.00
32	Barry Bonds, Willie McCovey	85.00
33	Babe Ruth, Lou Gehrig	500.00
34	Mike Schmidt, Scott Rolen/25	150.00
35	Harmon Killebrew, Kirby Puckett	50.00
36	Al Kaline, Eddie Matthews	50.00
37	Andruw Jones, Hank Aaron	85.00
38	Lou Brock, Ozzie Smith	50.00
39	Ernie Banks, Ryne Sandberg/25	125.00
40	Roberto Clemente, Vladimir Guerrero	90.00
41	Frank Robinson, Frank Thomas	40.00
42	Brooks Robinson, Cal Ripken Jr.	85.00
43	Pedro Martinez, Roger Clemens	60.00
44	Dave Winfield, Reggie Jackson	30.00
45	Don Mattingly, Todd Helton	75.00

Throwback Threads Autograph

		NM/M

Production listed
Football Exchange for 21 & 22 will be redeemed for #'s listed for 21 & 22.

1	Stan Musial/25	150.00
2	Tony Gwynn/25	100.00
7	Mike Schmidt/25	200.00
9	Harmon Killebrew/25	125.00
11	Al Kaline/25	120.00
13	Hank Aaron/25	150.00
14	Andruw Jones/50	50.00
17	Ernie Banks/25	150.00
20	Vladimir Guerrero/50	75.00
21	Frank Robinson/50 FB Redemp	40.00
22	Frank Thomas/50 FB redemp	50.00
23	Brooks Robinson/50	100.00
29	Don Mattingly/50	150.00
31	Stan Musial, Tony Gwynn/25	225.00
34	Mike Schmidt, Scott Rolen/25	225.00
39	Ernie Banks, Ryne Sandberg/25	250.00

Title Waves

		NM/M
Common Player:		1.00

Numbered to title year.

Holofoil:	2-3X

Production 100 Sets

1	Tony Gwynn/1994	5.00
2	Todd Helton/2000	4.00
3	Nomar Garciaparra/2000	6.00
4	Frank Thomas/1997	4.00
5	Alex Rodriguez/1996	8.00
6	Jeff Bagwell/1994	4.00
7	Mark McGwire/1998	8.00
8	Sammy Sosa/2000	6.00
9	Ken Griffey Jr./1997	6.00
10	Albert Belle/1995	1.00
11	Barry Bonds/1993	10.00
12	Jose Canseco/1991	2.00
13	Manny Ramirez/1999	4.00
14	Sammy Sosa/1998	6.00
15	Andres Galarraga/1996	1.00
16	Todd Helton/2000	4.00
17	Ken Griffey Jr./1997	6.00
18	Jeff Bagwell/1994	4.00
19	Mike Piazza/1995	6.00
20	Alex Rodriguez/1995	8.00
21	Jason Giambi/2000	2.00
22	Ivan Rodriguez/1999	2.50
23	Greg Maddux/1997	5.00
24	Pedro Martinez/1994	4.00
25	Derek Jeter/2000	10.00
26	Bernie Williams/1998	1.50
27	Roger Clemens/1999	8.00
28	Chipper Jones/1995	4.00
29	Mark McGwire/1998	8.00
30	Cal Ripken Jr./1983	10.00

Turn of the Century Autographs

		NM/M
Common Autograph:		8.00

Production 100 Sets
Redemp. deadline 5/01/03.

151	Brent Abernathy	8.00
152	Cory Aldridge	8.00
153	Gene Altman	8.00
154	Josh Beckett	80.00
155	Wilson Betemit	25.00
156	Albert Pujols	900.00
157	Joe Crede	30.00
158	Jack Cust	10.00
159	Ben Sheets	30.00
160	Alex Escobar	8.00
161	Adrian Hernandez	8.00
162	Pedro Feliz	8.00
163	Nate Frese	8.00
164	Carlos Garcia	8.00
165	Marcus Giles	20.00
166	Alexis Gomez	10.00
167	Jason Hart	8.00
168	Aubrey Huff	20.00
169	Cesar Izturis	10.00
170	Nick Johnson	20.00
171	Jack Wilson	15.00
172	Brian Lawrence	10.00
173	Christian Parker	8.00
174	Nick Maness	8.00
175	Jose Mieses	10.00
176	Greg Miller	8.00
177	Eric Munson	10.00
178	Xavier Nady	15.00
179	Blaine Neal	8.00
180	Abraham Nunez	10.00
181	Jose Ortiz	10.00
182	Jeremy Owens	10.00
183	Jay Gibbons	25.00
184	Corey Patterson	20.00
185	Carlos Pena	25.00
186	C.C. Sabathia	30.00
187	Timoniel Perez	8.00
188	Adam Pettyjohn	8.00
189	Donaldo Mendez	8.00
190	Jackson Melian	8.00
191	Wilken Ruan	8.00
192	Duaner Sanchez	8.00
193	Alfonso Soriano	60.00
194	Rafael Soriano	10.00
196	Billy Sylvester	8.00
197	Juan Uribe	20.00
199	Carlos Valderrama	10.00
200	Matt White	10.00

2001 Donruss Signature Series

		NM/M
Complete Set (311):		
Common Player:		.50
Common (111-165):		8.00
Auto. Print Run 330		
Common (166-311):		4.00
Production 800		
Box:		100.00
1	Alex Rodriguez	3.00
2	Barry Bonds	4.00
3	Cal Ripken Jr.	4.00
4	Chipper Jones	2.00
5	Derek Jeter	4.00
6	Troy Glaus	1.50
7	Frank Thomas	1.50
8	Greg Maddux	2.00
9	Ivan Rodriguez	1.00
10	Jeff Bagwell	1.50
11	John Olerud	.50
12	Todd Helton	1.50
13	Ken Griffey Jr.	2.50
14	Manny Ramirez	1.50
15	Mark McGwire	3.00
16	Mike Piazza	2.50
17	Nomar Garciaparra	2.50
18	Moises Alou	.50
19	Aramis Ramirez	.50
20	Curt Schilling	.75
21	Pat Burrell	.75

22	Doug Mientkiewicz	.50
23	Carlos Delgado	.75
24	J.D. Drew	.50
25	Cliff Floyd	.50
26	Freddy Garcia	.50
27	Roberto Alomar	.75
28	Barry Zito	.75
29	Juan Encarnacion	.50
30	Paul Konerko	.50
31	Mark Mulder	.75
32	Andy Pettitte	.75
33	Jim Edmonds	.50
34	Darin Erstad	1.00
35	Jason Giambi	1.00
36	Tom Glavine	.75
37	Juan Gonzalez	1.50
38	Fred McGriff	.50
39	Shawn Green	.75
40	Tim Hudson	.75
41	Andruw Jones	1.50
42	Jeff Kent	.50
43	Barry Larkin	.50
44	Brad Radke	.50
45	Mike Mussina	.75
46	Hideo Nomo	.75
47	Rafael Palmeiro	1.50
48	Scott Rolen	1.50
49	Gary Sheffield	.75
50	Bernie Williams	.75
51	Bobby Abreu	.50
52	Edgardo Alfonzo	.50
53	Edgar Martinez	.50
54	Magglio Ordonez	.75
55	Kerry Wood	.75
56	Adrian Beltre	.75
57	Lance Berkman	.50
58	Kevin Brown	.65
59	Sean Casey	.65
60	Eric Chavez	.75
61	Bartolo Colon	.50
62	Sammy Sosa	2.50
63	Jermaine Dye	.50
64	Tony Gwynn	2.00
65	Carl Everett	.50
66	Brian Giles	.50
67	Mike Hampton	.50
68	Richard Hidalgo	.50
69	Geoff Jenkins	.50
70	Tony Clark	.50
71	Roger Clemens	2.25
72	Ryan Klesko	.50
73	Chan Ho Park	.50
74	Richie Sexson	.50
75	Mike Sweeney	.50
76	Kazuhiro Sasaki	.75
77	Miguel Tejada	.75
78	Jose Vidro	.50
79	Larry Walker	.50
80	Preston Wilson	.50
81	Craig Biggio	.50
82	Andres Galarraga	.50
83	Jim Thome	.50
84	Vladimir Guerrero	1.50
85	Rafael Furcal	.50
86	Cristian Guzman	.50
87	Terrence Long	.50
88	Bret Boone	.50
89	Wade Miller	.50
90	Eric Milton	.50
91	Gabe Kapler	.50
92	Johnny Damon	.75
93	Carlos Lee	.50
94	Kenny Lofton	.50
95	Raul Mondesi	.50
96	Jorge Posada	.65
97	Mark Grace	.65
98	Robert Fick	.50
99	Joe Mays	.50
100	Aaron Sele	.50
101	Ben Grieve	.50
102	Luis Gonzalez	.65
103	Ray Durham	.50
104	Mark Quinn	.50
105	Jose Canseco	1.00
106	David Justice	.50
107	Pedro Martinez	1.50
108	Randy Johnson	1.50
109	Phil Nevin	.50
110	Ricky Henderson	1.50
111	Alex Escobar/Auto.	8.00
112	Johnny Estrada/ Auto.	15.00
113	Pedro Feliz/Auto.	8.00
114	Nate Frese/Auto.	8.00
115	Ricardo Rodriguez/ Auto.	8.00
116	Brandon Larson/ Auto. RC	8.00
117	Alexis Gomez/ Auto. RC	8.00
118	Jason Hart/Auto.	8.00
119	C.C. Sabathia/Auto.	15.00
120	Endy Chavez/Auto. RC	8.00
121	Christian Parker/ Auto. RC	8.00
122	Jackson Melian RC	8.00

123	Joe Kennedy/ Auto. RC	10.00
124	Adrian Hernandez/ Auto. RC	8.00
125	Cesar Izturis/Auto.	10.00
126	Jose Mieses/Auto. RC	8.00
127	Roy Oswalt/Auto.	30.00
128	Eric Munson/Auto.	8.00
129	Xavier Nady/Auto.	8.00
130	Horacio Ramirez/ Auto. RC	15.00
131	Abraham Nunez/ Auto.	8.00
132	Jose Ortiz/Auto.	8.00
133	Jeremy Owens/ Auto. RC	8.00
134	Claudio Vargas/ Auto. RC	8.00
135	Corey Patterson/ Auto.	15.00
136	Carlos Pena	15.00
137	Bud Smith/Auto.	8.00
138	Adam Dunn/Auto.	25.00
139	Adam Pettyjohn/Auto.	8.00
140	Elpidio Guzman/ Auto. RC	8.00
141	Jay Gibbons/Auto. RC	15.00
142	Wilken Ruan/Auto. RC	8.00
143	Tsuyoshi Shinjo RC	8.00
144	Alfonso Soriano/Auto.	30.00
145	Marcus Giles/Auto.	10.00
146	Ichiro Suzuki RC	75.00
147	Juan Uribe/Auto.	10.00
148	David Williams/ Auto. RC	8.00
149	Carlos Valderrama/ Auto. RC	8.00
150	Matt White/Auto. RC	8.00
151	Albert Pujols/ Auto. RC	800.00
152	Donaldo Mendez/ Auto. RC	8.00
153	Cory Aldridge/ Auto. RC	8.00
154	Brandon Duckworth/ Auto. RC	8.00
155	Josh Beckett/Auto.	30.00
156	Wilson Betemit/ Auto. RC	15.00
157	Ben Sheets/Auto.	25.00
158	Andres Torres/ Auto. RC	8.00
159	Aubrey Huff/Auto.	15.00
160	Jack Wilson/Auto. RC	15.00
161	Rafael Soriano/ Auto. RC	8.00
162	Nick Johnson/Auto.	12.00
163	Carlos Garcia/ Auto. RC	8.00
164	Josh Towers/ Auto. RC	10.00
165	Jason Michaels/ Auto. RC	8.00
166	Ryan Drese RC	4.00
167	Dewon Brazelton RC	4.00
168	Kevin Olsen RC	4.00
169	Benito Baez RC	4.00
170	Mark Prior RC	20.00
171	Wilmy Caceres RC	4.00
172	Mark Teixeira RC	35.00
173	Willie Harris RC	4.00
174	Mike Koplove RC	4.00
175	Brandon Knight RC	4.00
176	John Grabow RC	4.00
177	Jeremy Affeldt RC	4.00
178	Brandon Inge RC	4.00
179	Casey Fossum RC	6.00
180	Scott Stewart RC	4.00
181	Luke Hudson RC	4.00
182	Ken Vining RC	4.00
183	Toby Hall RC	4.00
184	Eric Knott RC	4.00
185	Kris Foster RC	4.00
186	David Brous RC	4.00
187	Roy Smith RC	4.00
188	Grant Balfour RC	4.00
189	Jeremy Fikac RC	4.00
190	Morgan Ensberg RC	10.00
191	Ryan Freel RC	6.00
192	Ryan Jensen RC	4.00
193	Lance Davis RC	4.00
194	Delvin James RC	4.00
195	Timo Perez RC	4.00
196	Michael Cuddyer RC	4.00
197	Bob File RC	4.00
198	Martin Vargas RC	4.00
199	Kris Keller RC	4.00
200	Tim Spooneybarger RC	4.00
201	Adam Everett RC	4.00
202	Josh Fogg RC	6.00
203	Kip Wells RC	4.00
204	Rick Bauer RC	4.00
205	Brent Abernathy RC	4.00
206	Erick Almonte RC	4.00
207	Pedro Santana RC	4.00
208	Ken Harvey RC	4.00

209	Jerrod Riggan RC	4.00
210	Nick Punto RC	4.00
211	Steve Green RC	4.00
212	Nick Neugebauer RC	4.00
213	Chris George	4.00
214	Mike Penny	4.00
215	Bret Prinz RC	4.00
216	Tim Christman RC	4.00
217	Sean Douglass RC	4.00
218	Brett Jodie RC	4.00
219	Juan Diaz RC	4.00
220	Carlos Hernandez RC	4.00
221	Alex Cintron	4.00
222	Juan Cruz RC	4.00
223	Larry Bigbie	4.00
224	Junior Spivey RC	8.00
225	Luis Rivas	4.00
226	Brandon Lyon RC	4.00
227	Tony Cogan RC	4.00
228	Justin Duchscherer RC	6.00
229	Tike Redman RC	4.00
230	Jimmy Rollins	5.00
231	Scott Podsednik RC	15.00
232	Jose Acevedo RC	4.00
233	Luis Pineda RC	4.00
234	Josh Phelps RC	4.00
235	Paul Phillips RC	4.00
236	Brian Roberts RC	10.00
237	Orlando Woodwards	4.00
238	Bart Miadich RC	4.00
239	Les Walrond RC	4.00
240	Brad Voyles RC	4.00
241	Joe Crede	8.00
242	Juan Moreno RC	4.00
243	Matt Ginter	4.00
244	Brian Rogers RC	4.00
245	Pablo Ozuna	4.00
246	Geronimo Gil RC	4.00
247	Mike Maroth RC	4.00
248	Josue Perez RC	4.00
249	Dee Brown	4.00
250	Victor Zambrano RC	4.00
251	Nick Maness RC	4.00
252	Kyle Lohse RC	6.00
253	Greg Miller RC	4.00
254	Henry Mateo RC	4.00
255	Duaner Sanchez RC	4.00
256	Rob Mackowiak RC	6.00
257	Steve Lomasney	4.00
258	Angel Santos RC	4.00
259	Winston Abreu RC	4.00
260	Brandon Berger RC	4.00
261	Tomas De La Rosa	4.00
262	Ramon Vazquez RC	4.00
263	Mickey Callaway	4.00
264	Corky Miller RC	4.00
265	Keith Ginter	4.00
266	Cody Ransom RC	4.00
267	Doug Nickle RC	4.00
268	Derrick Lewis RC	4.00
269	Eric Hinske RC	6.00
270	Travis Phelps RC	4.00
271	Eric Valent	4.00
272	Michael Rivera RC	4.00
273	Esix Snead RC	4.00
274	Troy Mattes RC	4.00
275	Jermaine Clark	4.00
276	Nate Cornejo	4.00
277	George Perez RC	4.00
278	Juan Rivera RC	4.00
279	Justin Atchley RC	4.00
280	Adam Johnson	4.00
281	Gene Altman RC	4.00
282	Jason Jennings	4.00
283	Scott MacRae RC	4.00
284	Craig Monroe RC	6.00
285	Bert Snow RC	4.00
286	Stubby Clapp RC	4.00
287	Jack Cust	4.00
288	Will Ohman RC	4.00
289	Wily Mo Pena	4.00
290	Joe Beimel RC	4.00
291	Jason Karnuth RC	4.00
292	Bill Ortega	4.00
293	Nate Teut RC	4.00
294	Erik Hiljus RC	4.00
295	Jason Smith RC	4.00
296	Juan Pena	4.00
297	David Espinosa	4.00
298	Tim Redding	4.00
299	Brian Lawrence RC	4.00
300	Brian Reith RC	4.00
301	Chad Durbin	4.00
302	Kurt Ainsworth	4.00
303	Blaine Neal RC	4.00
304	Jorge Julio RC	4.00
305	Adam Bernero	4.00
306	Travis Hafner RC	20.00
307	Dustan Mohr RC	4.00
308	Cesar Crespo RC	4.00
309	Billy Sylvester RC	4.00
310	Zach Day RC	6.00
311	Angel Berroa RC	8.00

Signature Stats

NM/M

Quantity produced listed

Roberto Alomar/120	40.00
Moises Alou/124	6.00
Luis Aparicio/313	10.00
Lance Berkman/297	15.00
Wade Boggs/51	75.00
Lou Brock/118	15.00
Gary Carter/32	50.00
Joe Carter/121	10.00
Sean Casey/103	10.00
Darin Erstad/100	15.00
Bob Feller/26	50.00
Cliff Floyd/45	15.00
Whitey Ford/72	40.00
Andres Galarraga/150	8.00
Bob Gibson/112	25.00
Brian Giles/123	10.00
Troy Glaus/102	20.00
Luis Gonzalez/114	10.00
Vladimir Guerrero/131	30.00
Richard Hidalgo/314	6.00
Bo Jackson/32	85.00
Al Kaline/128	45.00
Gabe Kapler/302	6.00
Ralph Kiner/54	30.00
Carlos Lee/261	10.00
Kenny Lofton/210	6.00
Edgar Martinez/145	20.00
Joe Mays/115	6.00
Paul Molitor/41	50.00
Mark Mulder/88	25.00
Magglio Ordonez/126	10.00
Rafael Palmeiro/47	40.00
Kirby Puckett/31	100.00
Manny Ramirez/45	60.00
Alex Rodriguez/132	85.00
Ivan Rodriguez/113	30.00
Shannon Stewart/319	6.00
Mike Sweeney/144	6.00
Miguel Tejada/115	35.00
Joe Torre/230	25.00
Javier Vazquez/405	6.00
Jose Vidro/330	6.00
Hoyt Wilhelm/243	6.00

Signature Proofs

Stars (1-110): 2-3X
Production 175
Cards (111-311) Production 25

Award Winning Signatures

NM/M

Common Player:	20.00
Jeff Bagwell/94	65.00
Carlos Beltran/99	40.00

Johnny Bench/68	75.00
Yogi Berra/55	50.00
Craig Biggio/97	25.00
Barry Bonds/93	200.00
Rod Carew/77	50.00
Orlando Cepeda/67	20.00
Andre Dawson/77	20.00
Dennis Eckersley/92	25.00
Dennis Eckersley/92	25.00
Whitey Ford/61	50.00
Jason Giambi/100	20.00
Bob Gibson/68	40.00
Juan Gonzalez/96	35.00
Orel Hershiser/88	25.00
Al Kaline/67	75.00
Fred Lynn/75	15.00
Fred Lynn/75	15.00
Jim Palmer/76	25.00
Cal Ripken/83	150.00
Phil Rizzuto/50	40.00
Brooks Robinson/64	40.00
Scott Rolen/97	30.00
Ryne Sandberg/84	90.00
Warren Spahn/57	50.00
Frank Thomas/94	35.00
Billy Williams/61	20.00
Kerry Wood/98	40.00
Robin Yount/89	60.00

Century Marks

NM/M

Common Autograph:	5.00
Brent Abernathy/184	5.00
Roberto Alomar/102	40.00
Rick Ankiel/119	8.00
Lance Berkman/121	15.00
Mark Buehrle/224	10.00
Wilmy Caceres/194	5.00
Eric Chavez/170	10.00
Joe Crede/154	5.00
Jack Cust/178	10.00
Brandon Duckworth/183	5.00
David Espinosa/199	5.00
Johnny Estrada/198	5.00
Pedro Feliz/180	5.00
Robert Fick/232	5.00
Cliff Floyd/146	8.00
Casey Fossum/100	10.00
Jay Gibbons/175	15.00
Keith Ginter/163	5.00
Troy Glaus/144	20.00
Luis Gonzalez/101	10.00
Vladimir Guerrero/187	30.00
Richard Hidalgo/173	5.00
Tim Hudson/145	25.00
Adam Johnson/130	5.00
Gabe Kapler/150	8.00
Joe Kennedy/219	5.00
Ryan Klesko/176	10.00
Carlos Lee/179	8.00
Terrence Long/180	5.00
Edgar Martinez/110	20.00
Joe Mays/209	5.00
Greg Miller/194	5.00
Wade Miller/180	5.00
Mark Mulder/203	20.00
Xavier Nady/180	5.00
Magglio Ordonez/104	10.00
Jose Ortiz/187	5.00
Roy Oswalt/192	20.00
Wily Mo Pena/203	10.00
Brad Penny/198	5.00
Aramis Ramirez/241	20.00
Luis Rivas/163	5.00
Alex Rodriguez/110	120.00
Scott Rolen/106	30.00
Mike Sweeney/99	10.00
Eric Valent/163	5.00
Kip Wells/223	5.00
Kerry Wood/109	25.00

Milestone Marks

NM/M

Common Player:	10.00
Ernie Banks/285	35.00
Yogi Berra/120	50.00
Wade Boggs/98	60.00
Barry Bonds/55	200.00
George Brett/27	150.00
George Brett/23	150.00
Lou Brock/83	25.00
Rod Carew/110	30.00
Steve Carlton/75	35.00
Gary Carter/213	20.00
Bobby Doerr/192	15.00
Bob Feller/202	15.00
Whitey Ford/186	25.00
Steve Garvey/175	10.00
Tony Gwynn/99	50.00
Fergie Jenkins/149	15.00
Al Kaline/149	40.00
Harmon Killebrew/127	40.00
Ralph Kiner/105	20.00
Willie McCovey/20	75.00
Paul Molitor/41	40.00
Eddie Murray/46	70.00
Eddie Murray/17	
Stan Musial/109	75.00
Phil Niekro/300	10.00
Tony Perez/146	15.00
Cal Ripken/25	200.00
Frank Robinson/136	20.00
Mike Schmidt/40	125.00
Mike Schmidt/23	150.00
Enos Slaughter/117	20.00
Warren Spahn/300	40.00
Alan Trammell/154	25.00
Hoyt Wilhelm/227	10.00
Dave Winfield/31	50.00
Dave Winfield/15	80.00

Notable Nicknames

NM/M

Common Player:	30.00
Production 100	
Ernie Banks	75.00
Orlando Cepeda	40.00
Will Clark	80.00
Roger Clemens/50	250.00
Andre Dawson	30.00
Bob Feller	50.00
Carlton Fisk	70.00
Andres Galarraga	40.00
Luis Gonzalez	30.00
Reggie Jackson	75.00
Harmon Killebrew	80.00
Stan Musial	120.00
Brooks Robinson	80.00
Nolan Ryan	250.00

Ryne Sandberg	150.00
Enos Slaughter	60.00
Duke Snider	75.00
Frank Thomas	100.00

Team Trademarks

NM/M

Rick Ankiel/179	10.00
Ernie Banks/180	50.00
Johnny Bench/20	75.00
Yogi Berra/124	40.00
Wade Boggs/89	75.00
Barry Bonds/77	200.00
Lou Brock/29	35.00
Steve Carlton/174	25.00
Sean Casey/123	15.00
Orlando Cepeda/100	20.00
Roger Clemens/30 (Red Sox)	125.00
Roger Clemens/21 (Yankees)	150.00
Andre Dawson/176	15.00
Bobby Doerr/193	20.00
Whitey Ford/94	40.00
Steve Garvey/182	20.00
Bob Gibson/98	30.00
Juan Gonzalez/70	40.00
Shawn Green/109	20.00
Orel Hershiser/210	25.00
Reggie Jackson/53	50.00
Fergie Jenkins/213	15.00
Chipper Jones/74	50.00
Pedro Martinez/27	85.00
Don Mattingly/72	125.00
Willie Mays/197	125.00
Willie McCovey/26	70.00
Joe Morgan/33	80.00
Eddie Murray/45	75.00
Stan Musial/65	90.00
Mike Mussina/85 (Orioles)	40.00
Mike Mussina/95 (Yankees)	50.00
Phil Niekro/187	10.00
Rafael Palmeiro/99	30.00
Jim Palmer/142	15.00
Tony Perez/73	15.00
Manny Ramirez/57	50.00
Cal Ripken Jr./47	200.00
Phil Rizzuto/98	40.00
Brooks Robinson/146	25.00
Frank Robinson/118 (Orioles)	25.00
Frank Robinson/116 (Reds)	25.00
Alex Rodriguez/100	100.00
Ivan Rodriguez/62	50.00
Scott Rolen/39	40.00
Nolan Ryan/153	100.00
Ryne Sandberg/52	100.00
Curt Schilling/163	40.00
Mike Schmidt/107	75.00
Tom Seaver/25	125.00
Gary Sheffield/194	20.00
Enos Slaughter/215	20.00
Duke Snider/47	50.00
Warren Spahn/140	40.00
Joe Torre/90	40.00
Billy Williams/194	10.00
Kerry Wood/52	40.00

2001 Donruss Studio

NM/M

Complete Set (200):	
Common Player:	.25
Common SP (151-200):	4.00
Production 700	
Pack (6):	8.00
Box (18) + 5x7 Auto.	140.00
1 Alex Rodriguez	2.00
2 Barry Bonds	2.50
3 Cal Ripken Jr.	2.50
4 Chipper Jones	1.00

Jason Giambi · 1B
OAKLAND ATHLETICS

5	Derek Jeter	2.50
6	Troy Glaus	.65
7	Frank Thomas	.75
8	Greg Maddux	1.00
9	Ivan Rodriguez	.65
10	Jeff Bagwell	.75
11	Mark Quinn	.25
12	Todd Helton	.65
13	Ken Griffey Jr.	1.50
14	Manny Ramirez	.75
15	Mark McGwire	2.00
16	Mike Piazza	1.50
17	Nomar Garciaparra	1.00
18	Robin Ventura	.25
19	Aramis Ramirez	.25
20	J.T. Snow	.25
21	Pat Burrell	.60
22	Curt Schilling	.50
23	Carlos Delgado	.50
24	J.D. Drew	.40
25	Cliff Floyd	.25
26	Brian Jordan	.25
27	Roberto Alomar	.35
28	Barry Zito	.40
29	Harold Baines	.25
30	Brad Penny	.25
31	Jose Cruz	.25
32	Andy Pettitte	.40
33	Jim Edmonds	.25
34	Darin Erstad	.35
35	Jason Giambi	.60
36	Tom Glavine	.50
37	Juan Gonzalez	.35
38	Mark Grace	.25
39	Shawn Green	.50
40	Tim Hudson	.50
41	Andruw Jones	.75
42	Jeff Kent	.25
43	Barry Larkin	.25
44	Rafael Furcal	.25
45	Mike Mussina	.50
46	Hideo Nomo	.50
47	Rafael Palmeiro	.65
48	Scott Rolen	.60
49	Gary Sheffield	.50
50	Bernie Williams	.25
51	Bobby Abreu	.25
52	Edgardo Alfonzo	.25
53	Edgar Martinez	.25
54	Magglio Ordonez	.25
55	Kerry Wood	.50
56	Matt Morris	.25
57	Lance Berkman	.25
58	Kevin Brown	.25
59	Sean Casey	.40
60	Eric Chavez	.40
61	Bartolo Colon	.25
62	Johnny Damon	.50
63	Jermaine Dye	.25
64	Juan Encarnacion	.25
65	Carl Everett	.25
66	Brian Giles	.25
67	Mike Hampton	.25
68	Richard Hidalgo	.25
69	Geoff Jenkins	.25
70	Jacque Jones	.25
71	Jason Kendall	.25
72	Ryan Klesko	.25
73	Chan Ho Park	.25
74	Richie Sexson	.25
75	Mike Sweeney	.25
76	Fernando Tatis	.25
77	Miguel Tejada	.50
78	Jose Vidro	.25
79	Larry Walker	.25
80	Preston Wilson	.25
81	Craig Biggio	.25
82	Fred McGriff	.25
83	Jim Thome	.65
84	Garret Anderson	.25
85	Mark Mulder	.40
86	Tony Batista	.25
87	Terrence Long	.25
88	Brad Fullmer	.25

89	Rusty Greer	.25
90	Orlando Hernandez	.25
91	Gabe Kapler	.25
92	Paul Konerko	.25
93	Carlos Lee	.25
94	Kenny Lofton	.25
95	Raul Mondesi	.25
96	Jorge Posada	.40
97	Tim Salmon	.25
98	Greg Vaughn	.25
99	Mo Vaughn	.25
100	Omar Vizquel	.25
101	Ben Grieve	.25
102	Luis Gonzalez	.25
103	Ray Durham	.25
104	Ryan Dempster	.25
105	Eric Karros	.25
106	David Justice	.25
107	Pedro Martinez	.75
108	Randy Johnson	.75
109	Rick Ankiel	.25
110	Rickey Henderson	.75
111	Roger Clemens	1.25
112	Sammy Sosa	1.00
113	Tony Gwynn	1.00
114	Vladimir Guerrero	.75
115	Kazuhiro Sasaki	.25
116	Phil Nevin	.25
117	Ruben Mateo	.25
118	Shannon Stewart	.25
119	Matt Williams	.25
120	Tino Martinez	.25
121	Ken Caminiti	.25
122	Edgar Renteria	.25
123	Charles Johnson	.25
124	Aaron Sele	.25
125	Javy Lopez	.25
126	Mariano Rivera	.35
127	Shea Hillenbrand	.25
128	Jeff D'Amico	.25
129	Brady Anderson	.25
130	Kevin Millwood	.25
131	Trot Nixon	.25
132	Mike Lieberthal	.25
133	Juan Pierre	.25
134	Russ Ortiz	.25
135	Jose Macias	.25
136	John Smoltz	.25
137	Jason Varitek	.25
138	Dean Palmer	.25
139	Jeff Cirillo	.25
140	Paul O'Neill	.25
141	Andres Galarraga	.25
142	David Wells	.25
143	Brad Radke	.25
144	Wade Miller	.25
145	John Olerud	.25
146	Moises Alou	.25
147	Carlos Beltran	.50
148	Jeromy Burnitz	.25
149	Steve Finley	.25
150	Joe Mays	.25
151	Alex Escobar	4.00
152	Johnny Estrada RC	8.00
153	Pedro Feliz	4.00
154	Nate Frese RC	4.00
155	Dee Brown	4.00
156	Brandon Larson RC	5.00
157	Alexis Gomez RC	4.00
158	Jason Hart	4.00
159	C.C. Sabathia	4.00
160	Josh Towers RC	6.00
161	Christian Parker RC	4.00
162	Jackson Melian RC	4.00
163	Joe Kennedy RC	4.00
164	Adrian Hernandez RC	4.00
165	Jimmy Rollins	4.00
166	Jose Mieses RC	4.00
167	Roy Oswalt	5.00
168	Eric Munson	4.00
169	Xavier Nady	4.00
170	Horacio Ramirez RC	8.00
171	Abraham Nunez	4.00
172	Jose Ortiz	4.00
173	Jeremy Owens RC	4.00
174	Claudio Vargas RC	4.00
175	Corey Patterson	4.00
176	Carlos Pena	4.00
177	Bud Smith RC	4.00
178	Adam Dunn	4.00
179	Adam Pettyjohn RC	4.00
180	Elpidio Guzman RC	4.00
181	Jay Gibbons RC	10.00
182	Wilkin Ruan RC	4.00
183	Tsuyoshi Shinjo RC	4.00
184	Alfonso Soriano	6.00
185	Marcus Giles	4.00
186	Ichiro Suzuki RC	85.00
187	Juan Uribe RC	6.00
188	David Williams RC	4.00
189	Carlos Valderrama RC	4.00
190	Matt White RC	4.00
191	Albert Pujols RC	240.00
192	Donaldo Mendez RC	4.00
193	Cory Aldridge RC	4.00
194	Endy Chavez RC	4.00

195	Josh Beckett	4.00
196	Wilson Betemit RC	4.00
197	Ben Sheets	4.00
198	Andres Torres RC	4.00
199	Aubrey Huff	4.00
200	Jack Wilson RC	8.00

Proofs

Chipper Jones · 3B
ATLANTA BRAVES

Values Undetermined
Production 25 Sets
(See 2001 Studio for checklist.)

Diamond Collection

		NM/M
Common Player:		5.00
1	Vladimir Guerrero	10.00
2	Barry Bonds	30.00
3	Cal Ripken Jr.	30.00
4	Nomar Garciaparra	20.00
5	Greg Maddux	15.00
6	Frank Thomas	10.00
7	Roger Clemens	20.00
8	Luis Gonzalez/SP	6.00
9	Tony Gwynn	15.00
10	Carlos Lee/SP	6.00
11	Troy Glaus	8.00
12	Randy Johnson	10.00
13	Manny Ramirez/SP	15.00
14	Pedro Martinez	10.00
15	Todd Helton	10.00
16	Jeff Bagwell	10.00
17	Rickey Henderson	10.00
18	Kazuhiro Sasaki	5.00
19	Albert Pujols/SP	50.00
20	Ivan Rodriguez	8.00
21	Darin Erstad	6.00
22	Andruw Jones	8.00
23	Roberto Alomar	6.00
25	Juan Gonzalez	10.00
26	Shawn Green	7.50
27	Lance Berkman	5.00
28	Scott Rolen	9.00
29	Rafael Palmeiro	8.00
31	J.D. Drew	5.00
32	Kerry Wood	8.00
32	Jim Edmonds	8.00
33	Tom Glavine/SP	8.00
34	Hideo Nomo/SP	50.00
36	Tim Hudson	5.00
37	Miguel Tejada	5.00
38	Chipper Jones	15.00
39	Edgar Martinez/SP	8.00
40	Chan Ho Park	5.00
41	Magglio Ordonez	5.00
42	Sean Casey	5.00
43	Larry Walker	5.00
45	Cliff Floyd	5.00
46	Mike Sweeney	5.00
47	Kevin Brown	5.00
48	Richie Sexson	5.00
49	Jermaine Dye	5.00
50	Craig Biggio	5.00

Leather & Lumber

		NM/M
Common Player:		5.00
Combos:		No Pricing
Production 25 Sets		
1	Barry Bonds	25.00
2	Cal Ripken Jr.	25.00
3	Miguel Tejada	5.00
5	Frank Thomas	8.00

Bobby Abreu · OF
PHILLIES

6	Greg Maddux	10.00
7	Ivan Rodriguez	8.00
8	Jeff Bagwell/SP	10.00
9	Sean Casey/SP	6.00
10	Todd Helton	8.00
11	Cliff Floyd	5.00
12	Hideo Nomo	40.00
13	Chipper Jones	10.00
14	Rickey Henderson	8.00
15	Richard Hidalgo	5.00
16	Mike Piazza	15.00
17	Larry Walker	8.00
18	Tony Gwynn	10.00
19	Vladimir Guerrero	8.00
20	Rafael Furcal	5.00
21	Roberto Alomar/SP	8.00
23	Albert Pujols	60.00
24	Raul Mondesi	5.00
25	J.D. Drew	5.00
26	Jim Edmonds	5.00
27	Darin Erstad/SP	6.00
28	Craig Biggio	5.00
29	Kenny Lofton	5.00
30	Juan Gonzalez	8.00
31	John Olerud	5.00
32	Shawn Green	5.00
33	Andruw Jones/SP	8.00
34	Moises Alou	5.00
35	Jeff Kent	5.00
36	Ryan Klesko	5.00
37	Luis Gonzalez	5.00
38	Rafael Palmeiro	8.00
40	Scott Rolen	8.00
41	Carlos Lee	5.00
42	Bobby Abreu	5.00
43	Edgardo Alfonzo	5.00
44	Bernie Williams	5.00
45	Brian Giles	5.00
46	Jermaine Dye	5.00
47	Lance Berkman	5.00
48	Edgar Martinez	5.00
49	Richie Sexson	5.00
50	Magglio Ordonez	5.00

Masterstokes

		NM/M
Common Player:		8.00
Production 200 Sets		
1	Tony Gwynn	25.00
2	Ivan Rodriguez	10.00
3	J.D. Drew	8.00
4	Cal Ripken Jr.	60.00
5	Hideo Nomo	50.00
6	Darin Erstad	8.00
7	Frank Thomas	12.00
8	Andruw Jones	12.00
9	Roberto Alomar	8.00
10	Larry Walker	8.00
11	Vladimir Guerrero	12.00
12	Barry Bonds	65.00
14	Luis Gonzalez	8.00
16	Juan Gonzalez	12.00
17	Todd Helton	12.00
18	Jeff Bagwell	12.00
19	Albert Pujols	75.00
20	Shawn Green	8.00
21	Magglio Ordonez	8.00
22	Scott Rolen	12.00
23	Rafael Palmeiro	10.00
24	Sean Casey	8.00
25	Jim Edmonds	8.00

26	Chipper Jones	20.00
27	Cliff Floyd	8.00
28	Carlos Lee	8.00
29	Edgar Martinez	8.00
30	Lance Berkman	8.00

Private Signings

Rick Ankiel • P
ST. LOUIS CARDINALS

		NM/M
Common Player:		8.00
Inserted 1:Hobby Box		
1	Alex Rodriguez	80.00
2	Miguel Tejada	25.00
3	Ben Sheets	15.00
4	Tony Gwynn SP/190	60.00
5	Wilson Betemit	8.00
6	Rick Ankiel	20.00
7	Ivan Rodriguez/ SP/150	30.00
8	Ryan Klesko	8.00
9	Jason Giambi/SP/250	15.00
10	Brad Penny	8.00
11	Gabe Kapler	8.00
12	Vladimir Guerrero	30.00
13	Alex Escobar	8.00
14	Edgar Martinez	15.00
15	Cal Ripken/SP/50	200.00
16	Brian Giles	8.00
17	Todd Helton/SP/125	25.00
18	Mike Sweeney	8.00
19	Cliff Floyd	8.00
20	Corey Patterson	12.00
21	Alfonso Soriano	40.00
22	Bobby Abreu	8.00
23	Shawn Green/SP/190	20.00
24	C.C. Sabathia	8.00
25	Luis Gonzalez	8.00
26	Barry Bonds/SP/95	200.00
27	Rafael Palmeiro/ SP/250	30.00
28	Mike Mussina/ SP/144	40.00
29	Roger Clemens/ SP/200	100.00
30	Greg Maddux/ SP/200	80.00
31	Troy Glaus	20.00
32	Kerry Wood	15.00
33	Roberto Alomar/ SP/200	30.00
34	Tom Glavine	40.00
35	Frank Thomas	20.00
36	Carlos Lee	8.00
37	Scott Rolen	20.00
38	Andruw Jones/ SP/250	20.00
39	Manny Ramirez/ SP/115	40.00
40	Magglio Ordonez	12.00
41	Lance Berkman	8.00
42	Josh Beckett	30.00
43	Adam Dunn	15.00
44	Albert Pujols/SP/50	600.00
45	Darin Erstad	12.00
46	Curt Schilling	40.00
47	Barry Zito	12.00
48	Sean Casey	8.00

Round Trip Tickets

No Pricing
Production 25 Sets

Warning Track

		NM/M
Common Player:		4.00
1	Andruw Jones	8.00
2	Rafael Palmeiro	7.00
3	Gary Sheffield	5.00
4	Larry Walker	4.00
5	Shawn Green	4.00
6	Mike Piazza	12.00
7	Barry Bonds	20.00
8	J.D. Drew	4.00
9	Magglio Ordonez	4.00
10	Todd Helton	8.00
11	Juan Gonzalez	8.00
12	Pat Burrell	5.00
13	Mark McGwire	15.00
14	Frank Robinson	4.00
15	Manny Ramirez	8.00
16	Lance Berkman	4.00
17	Johnny Bench	10.00
18	Chipper Jones	10.00
19	Mike Schmidt	15.00
21	Vladimir Guerrero	8.00
22	Sammy Sosa	12.00
23	Cal Ripken Jr.	20.00
24	Roberto Alomar	4.00
25	Willie Stargell	4.00
27	Scott Rolen	7.00
28	Roberto Clemente/SP	50.00
29	Tony Gwynn	10.00
30	Ivan Rodriguez	5.00
31	Sean Casey	4.00
32	Frank Thomas	8.00
33	Jeff Bagwell	8.00
34	Jeff Kent	4.00
35	Reggie Jackson	8.00

2001 Donruss The Rookies

MARK TEIXEIRA • TEXAS RANGERS

		NM/M
Complete Set (105):		80.00
Complete Factory Set (106):		100.00
Common Player:		.25
1	Adam Dunn	.50
2	Ryan Drese RC	.40
3	Bud Smith RC	.25
4	Tsuyoshi Shinjo RC	.50
5	Roy Oswalt	.50
6	Wilmy Caceres RC	.25
7	Willie Harris RC	.25
8	Andres Torres RC	.25
9	Brandon Knight RC	.25
10	Horacio Ramirez RC	.75
11	Benito Baez RC	.25
12	Jeremy Affeldt RC	.25
13	Ryan Jensen RC	.25
14	Casey Fossum RC	.50
15	Ramon Vazquez RC	.50
16	Dustan Mohr RC	.25
17	Saul Rivera RC	.25
18	Zach Day RC	.50
19	Erik Hiljus RC	.25
20	Cesar Crespo RC	.25
21	Wilson Guzman RC	.25
22	Travis Hafner RC	6.00
23	Grant Balfour RC	.25
24	Johnny Estrada RC	1.50
25	Morgan Ensberg RC	1.00

26	Jack Wilson RC	1.50
27	Aubrey Huff RC	.25
28	Endy Chavez RC	.50
29	Delvin James RC	.25
30	Michael Cuddyer RC	.25
31	Jason Michaels RC	.25
32	Martin Vargas RC	.25
33	Donaldo Mendez RC	.25
34	Jorge Julio RC	.25
35	Tim Spooneybarger RC	.25
36	Kurt Ainsworth RC	.25
37	Josh Fogg RC	.50
38	Brian Reith RC	.25
39	Rick Baurer RC	.25
40	Tim Redding	.25
41	Erick Almonte RC	.50
42	Juan Pena	.25
43	Ken Harvey RC	.25
44	David Brous RC	.25
45	Kevin Olsen RC	.25
46	Henry Mateo RC	.25
47	Nick Neugebauer RC	.25
48	Mike Penney RC	.25
49	Jay Gibbons RC	1.00
50	Tim Christman RC	.25
51	Brandon Duckworth RC	.50
52	Brett Jodie RC	.25
53	Christian Parker RC	.25
54	Carlos Hernandez RC	.25
55	Brandon Larson RC	.50
56	Nick Punto RC	.25
57	Elpidio Guzman RC	.25
58	Joe Beimel RC	.25
59	Junior Spivey RC	.50
60	Will Ohman RC	.25
61	Brandon Lyon RC	.25
62	Stubby Clapp RC	.25
63	Justin Duchscherer RC	.50
64	Jimmy Rollins	.40
65	David Williams RC	.40
66	Craig Monroe RC	.40
67	Jose Acevedo RC	.25
68	Jason Jennings RC	.25
69	Josh Phelps	.25
70	Brian Roberts RC	2.00
71	Claudio Vargas RC	.25
72	Adam Johnson RC	.25
73	Bart Miadich RC	.25
74	Juan Rivera RC	.25
75	Brad Voyles RC	.25
76	Nate Cornejo RC	.25
77	Juan Moreno RC	.25
78	Brian Rogers RC	.25
79	Ricardo Rodriguez RC	.40
80	Geronimo Gil RC	.25
81	Joe Kennedy RC	.40
82	Kevin Joseph RC	.25
83	Josue Perez RC	.25
84	Victor Zambrano RC	.25
85	Josh Towers RC	.40
86	Mike Rivera RC	.25
87	Mark Prior RC	6.00
88	Juan Cruz RC	.40
89	Dewon Brazelton RC	.40
90	Angel Berroa RC	1.00
91	Mark Teixeira RC	15.00
92	Cody Ransom RC	.25
93	Angel Santos RC	.25
94	Corky Miller RC	.40
95	Brandon Berger RC	.40
96	Corey Patterson	.25
97	Albert Pujols RC	60.00
98	Josh Beckett	.50
99	C.C. Sabathia	.25
100	Alfonso Soriano	.75
101	Ben Sheets	.25
102	Rafael Soriano RC	.50
103	Wilson Betemit RC	.50
104	Ichiro Suzuki RC	10.00
105	Jose Ortiz	.25

Rookie Diamond Kings

	NM/M
Complete Set (5):	40.00

Inserted 1:Rookies Set		
106	C.C. Sabathia	5.00
107	Tsuyoshi Shinjo	8.00
108	Albert Pujols	25.00
109	Roy Oswalt	8.00
110	Ichiro Suzuki	12.00

2002 Donruss

		NM/M
Complete Set (220):		100.00
Common Player:		.15
Common (151-200):		1.00
Inserted 1:4		
Common (201-220):		1.00
Inserted 1:8		
Pack (5):		2.00
Box (24):		40.00
1	Alex Rodriguez	1.50
2	Barry Bonds	2.00
3	Derek Jeter	2.00
4	Robert Fick	.15
5	Juan Pierre	.20
6	Torii Hunter	.25
7	Todd Helton	.75
8	Cal Ripken Jr.	2.00
9	Manny Ramirez	.75
10	Johnny Damon	.25
11	Mike Piazza	1.25
12	Nomar Garciaparra	1.25
13	Pedro Martinez	.75
14	Brian Giles	.15
15	Albert Pujols	1.50
16	Roger Clemens	1.00
17	Sammy Sosa	1.25
18	Vladimir Guerrero	.75
19	Tony Gwynn	1.00
20	Pat Burrell	.35
21	Carlos Delgado	.50
22	Tino Martinez	.15
23	Jim Edmonds	.15
24	Jason Giambi	.50
25	Tom Glavine	.30
26	Mark Grace	.20
27	Tony Armas Jr.	.15
28	Andruw Jones	.75
29	Ben Sheets	.15
30	Jeff Kent	.15
31	Barry Larkin	.15
32	Joe Mays	.15
33	Mike Mussina	.40
34	Hideo Nomo	.60
35	Rafael Palmeiro	.65
36	Scott Brosius	.15
37	Scott Rolen	.65
38	Gary Sheffield	.35
39	Bernie Williams	.35
40	Bobby Abreu	.15
41	Edgardo Alfonzo	.15
42	C.C. Sabathia	.15
43	Jeremy Giambi	.15
44	Craig Biggio	.15
45	Andres Galarraga	.15
46	Edgar Martinez	.15
47	Fred McGriff	.25
48	Magglio Ordonez	.25
49	Jim Thome	.15
50	Matt Williams	.15
51	Kerry Wood	.50
52	Moises Alou	.15
53	Brady Anderson	.15
54	Garret Anderson	.15
55	Juan Gonzalez	.75
56	Bret Boone	.15
57	Jose Cruz Jr.	.15
58	Carlos Beltran	.50
59	Adrian Beltre	.25
60	Joe Kennedy	.25
61	Lance Berkman	.15
62	Kevin Brown	.25
63	Tim Hudson	.35
64	Jeromy Burnitz	.15
65	Jarrod Washburn	.15
66	Sean Casey	.20
67	Eric Chavez	.25

68	Bartolo Colon	.15
69	Freddy Garcia	.15
70	Jermaine Dye	.15
71	Terrence Long	.15
72	Cliff Floyd	.15
73	Luis Gonzalez	.25
74	Ichiro Suzuki	1.50
75	Mike Hampton	.15
76	Richard Hidalgo	.15
77	Geoff Jenkins	.15
78	Gabe Kapler	.15
79	Ken Griffey Jr.	1.25
80	Jason Kendall	.15
81	Josh Towers	.15
82	Ryan Klesko	.15
83	Paul Konerko	.15
84	Carlos Lee	.15
85	Kenny Lofton	.15
86	Josh Beckett	.15
87	Raul Mondesi	.15
88	Trot Nixon	.15
89	John Olerud	.15
90	Paul O'Neill	.15
91	Chan Ho Park	.15
92	Andy Pettitte	.35
93	Jorge Posada	.30
94	Mark Quinn	.15
95	Aramis Ramirez	.15
96	Curt Schilling	.40
97	Richie Sexson	.15
98	John Smoltz	.15
99	Wilson Betemit	.15
100	Shannon Stewart	.15
101	Alfonso Soriano	.75
102	Mike Sweeney	.15
103	Miguel Tejada	.40
104	Greg Vaughn	.15
105	Robin Ventura	.15
106	Jose Vidro	.15
107	Larry Walker	.15
108	Preston Wilson	.15
109	Corey Patterson	.20
110	Mark Mulder	.25
111	Tony Clark	.15
112	Roy Oswalt	.25
113	Jimmy Rollins	.40
114	Kazuhiro Sasaki	.15
115	Barry Zito	.40
116	Javier Vazquez	.15
117	Mike Cameron	.15
118	Phil Nevin	.15
119	Bud Smith	.15
120	Cristian Guzman	.15
121	Al Leiter	.15
122	Brad Radke	.15
123	Bobby Higginson	.15
124	Robert Person	.15
125	Adam Dunn	.50
126	Ben Grieve	.15
127	Rafael Furcal	.15
128	Jay Gibbons	.15
129	Paul LoDuca	.15
130	Wade Miller	.15
131	Tsuyoshi Shinjo	.15
132	Eric Milton	.15
133	Rickey Henderson	.75
134	Roberto Alomar	.40
135	Darin Erstad	.50
136	J.D. Drew	.35
137	Shawn Green	.25
138	Randy Johnson	.75
139	Mark McGwire	1.50
140	Jose Canseco	.40
141	Jeff Bagwell	.75
142	Greg Maddux	1.00
143	Mark Buehrle	.15
144	Ivan Rodriguez	.65
145	Frank Thomas	.75
146	Rich Aurilia	.15
147	Troy Glaus	.75
148	Ryan Dempster	.15
149	Chipper Jones	1.00
150	Matt Morris	.15
151	Marlon Byrd	2.00
152	Ben Howard RC	4.00
153	Brandon Backe RC	2.00
154	Jorge De La Rosa RC	2.00
155	Corky Miller	1.00
156	Dennis Tankersley	1.00
157	Kyle Kane RC	3.00
158	Justin Duchscherer	1.00
159	Brian Mallette RC	3.00
160	Chris Baker RC	3.00
161	Jason Lane	1.00
162	Hee Seop Choi	1.50
163	Juan Cruz	1.00
164	Rodrigo Rosario RC	2.00
165	Matt Guerrier	1.00
166	Anderson Machado RC	3.00
167	Geronimo Gil	1.00
168	Dewon Brazelton	1.00
169	Mark Prior	5.00
170	Bill Hall	1.00
171	Jorge Padilla RC	4.00
172	Jose Cueto	1.00
173	Allan Simpson RC	3.00
174	Doug DeVore RC	3.00
175	Josh Pearce	1.00
176	Angel Berroa	1.00
177	Steve Bechler RC	3.00
178	Antonio Perez	1.00
179	Mark Teixeira	3.00
180	Erick Almonte	1.00
181	Orlando Hudson	1.00
182	Mike Rivera	1.00
183	Raul Chavez RC	2.00
184	Juan Pena	1.00
185	Travis Hughes RC	2.00
186	Ryan Ludwick	1.00
187	Ed Rogers	1.00
188	Andy Pratt RC	2.00
189	Nick Neugebauer	1.00
190	Tom Shearn RC	3.00
191	Eric Cyr RC	3.00
192	Victor Martinez	1.00
193	Brandon Berger	1.00
194	Erik Bedard	1.00
195	Fernando Rodney	1.00
196	Joe Thurston	1.00
197	John Buck	1.00
198	Jeff Deardorff RC	2.00
199	Ryan Jamison RC	2.00
200	Alfredo Amezaga	1.00
201	Luis Gonzalez	1.00
202	Roger Clemens	4.00
203	Barry Zito	1.25
204	Bud Smith	1.00
205	Magglio Ordonez	1.25
206	Kerry Wood	1.50
207	Freddy Garcia	1.00
208	Adam Dunn	1.50
209	Curt Schilling	2.00
210	Lance Berkman	1.50
211	Rafael Palmeiro	2.00
212	Ichiro Suzuki	4.00
213	Bobby Abreu	1.00
214	Mark Mulder	1.00
215	Roy Oswalt	1.50
216	Mike Sweeney	1.00
217	Paul LoDuca	1.00
218	Aramis Ramirez	1.00
219	Randy Johnson	2.00
220	Albert Pujols	5.00

Stat Line Career

	NM/M
Cards 1-150 print run	
251-400:	2-4X
1-150 p/r 151-250:	3-6X
1-150 p/r 101-150:	4-8X
1-150 p/r 61-100:	5-10X
1-150 p/r 31-60:	8-20X
1-150 p/r 15-30:	15-30X
Common 151-200 p/r 251-400:	1.00
Common 151-200 p/r 151-250:	1.00
Common 151-200 p/r 76-150:	2.00
Common 151-200 p/r 30-75:	4.00

Stat Line Season

	NM/M
cards 1-150 print run	
151-200:	3-6X
1-150 p/r 101-150:	4-8X
1-150 p/r 76-100:	5-10X
1-150 p/r 51-75:	6-12X
1-150 p/r 31-50:	8-20X
1-150 p/r 15-30:	15-30X
Comm. 151-200 p/r 151-200:	1.00
Comm. 151-200 p/r 101-150:	1.50

ABBREVIATIONS

SP - Short Print

	NM/M
Comm. 151-200 p/r 76-100:	2.00
Comm. 151-200 p/r 30-75:	4.00

All-Time Diamond Kings

		NM/M
Complete Set (10):		80.00
Common Player:		5.00
Production 2,500 Sets		
Studio Series:		2-3X
Production 250 Sets		
1	Ted Williams	15.00
2	Cal Ripken Jr.	15.00
3	Lou Gehrig	10.00
4	Babe Ruth	15.00
5	Roberto Clemente	10.00
6	Don Mattingly	8.00
7	Kirby Puckett	8.00
8	Stan Musial	8.00
9	Yogi Berra	5.00
10	Ernie Banks	5.00

Autographs

		NM/M
Common Autograph:		15.00
Varying quantities produced		
203	Barry Zito/200	25.00
204	Bud Smith/200	15.00
205	Magglio Ordonez/200	20.00
206	Kerry Wood/200	30.00
207	Freddy Garcia/200	15.00
208	Adam Dunn/200	25.00
210	Lance Berkman/175	15.00
211	Rafael Palmeiro/25	20.00
213	Bobby Abreu/200	15.00
214	Mark Mulder/200	15.00
215	Roy Oswalt/200	15.00
216	Mike Sweeney/200	15.00
217	Paul LoDuca/200	15.00
218	Aramis Ramirez/200	15.00
220	Albert Pujols/200	75.00

Bat Kings

		NM/M
Quantities produced listed		
Studio Series:		1.5-3X
Production 25 or 50		
1	Jason Giambi	15.00
2	Alex Rodriguez/250	25.00
3	Mike Piazza/250	20.00
4	Roberto Clemente/125	100.00
5	Babe Ruth/125	220.00

Diamond Kings

		NM/M
Complete Set (20):		80.00
Common Player:		2.00
Production 2,500 Sets		
Studio Series:		2-3X
Production 250 Sets		
1	Nomar Garciaparra	6.00
2	Shawn Green	2.00
3	Randy Johnson	4.00
4	Derek Jeter	7.50
5	Carlos Delgado	3.00
6	Roger Clemens	5.00
7	Jeff Bagwell	4.00
8	Vladimir Guerrero	4.00
9	Luis Gonzalez	2.00
10	Mike Piazza	6.00
11	Ichiro Suzuki	6.00
12	Pedro Martinez	4.00
13	Todd Helton	4.00
14	Sammy Sosa	6.00
15	Ivan Rodriguez	3.50
16	Barry Bonds	7.50
17	Albert Pujols	6.00
18	Jim Thome	2.00
19	Alex Rodriguez	6.00
20	Jason Giambi	3.00

Elite Series

		NM/M
Complete Set (15):		30.00
Common Player:		2.00
Production 2,500 Sets		
Autographs:		No Pricing
Production 25		
1	Barry Bonds	8.00
2	Lance Berkman	2.00
3	Jason Giambi	2.50
4	Nomar Garciaparra	6.00
5	Curt Schilling	2.50
6	Vladimir Guerrero	3.00
7	Shawn Green	2.00
8	Troy Glaus	2.00
9	Jeff Bagwell	3.00
10	Manny Ramirez	2.00
11	Eric Chavez	2.00
12	Carlos Delgado	2.50
13	Mike Sweeney	2.00
14	Todd Helton	3.00
15	Luis Gonzalez	2.00

Elite Series Legends

		NM/M
Complete Set (5):		15.00
Common Player:		3.00
Production 2,500		
16	Enos Slaughter	3.00
17	Frank Robinson	4.00
18	Bob Gibson	4.00
19	Warren Spahn	4.00
20	Whitey Ford	4.00

Elite Series Legends Autographs

		NM/M
Production 250 Sets		
16	Enos Slaughter	30.00
17	Frank Robinson	30.00
18	Bob Gibson	35.00
19	Warren Spahn	40.00
20	Whitey Ford	40.00

Jersey Kings

		NM/M
Quantity produced listed		
Studio Series:		1.5-3X
Production 25 or 50		
1	Alex Rodriguez/250	15.00
2	Jason Giambi/250	10.00
3	Carlos Delgado/250	8.00
4	Barry Bonds/250	25.00
5	Randy Johnson/250	10.00
6	Jim Thome/250	8.00
7	Shawn Green/250	8.00
8	Pedro Martinez/250	10.00
9	Jeff Bagwell/250	10.00
10	Vladimir Guerrero/250	10.00
11	Ivan Rodriguez/250	10.00
12	Nomar Garciaparra/250	15.00
13	Don Mattingly/125	80.00
14	Ted Williams/125	125.00
15	Lou Gehrig/125	200.00

Longball Leaders

		NM/M
Complete Set (20):		40.00
Common Player:		1.00
Production 1,000 Sets		
Seasonal Sum Parallel:		2-4X
Parallel #'d to 2001 HR Total		
1	Barry Bonds	8.00
2	Sammy Sosa	6.00
3	Luis Gonzalez	1.00
4	Alex Rodriguez	6.00
5	Shawn Green	1.50
6	Todd Helton	3.00
7	Jim Thome	1.00
8	Rafael Palmeiro	2.50
9	Richie Sexson	1.00
10	Troy Glaus	3.00
11	Manny Ramirez	3.00
12	Phil Nevin	1.00
13	Jeff Bagwell	3.00
14	Carlos Delgado	2.00
15	Jason Giambi	2.00
16	Chipper Jones	4.00
17	Larry Walker	1.00
18	Albert Pujols	6.00
19	Brian Giles	1.00
20	Bret Boone	1.00

Production Line

		NM/M
Common Card:		2.00
Numbered to category stat.		
1	Barry Bonds/515	8.00
2	Jason Giambi/477	4.00
3	Larry Walker/449	2.50
4	Sammy Sosa/437	6.00
5	Todd Helton/432	3.00
6	Lance Berkman/430	2.00
7	Luis Gonzalez/429	2.00
8	Chipper Jones/427	6.00
9	Edgar Martinez/423	2.00
10	Gary Sheffield/417	3.00
11	Jim Thome/416	3.00
12	Roberto Alomar/415	3.00
13	J.D. Drew/414	2.00

14	Jim Edmonds/410	2.00
15	Carlos Delgado/408	3.00
16	Manny Ramirez/405	4.00
17	Brian Giles/404	2.00
18	Albert Pujols/403	8.00
19	John Olerud/401	2.00
20	Alex Rodriguez/399	8.00
21	Barry Bonds/863	6.00
22	Sammy Sosa/737	5.00
23	Luis Gonzalez/688	1.50
24	Todd Helton/685	2.00
25	Larry Walker/662	1.50
26	Jason Giambi/660	2.00
27	Jim Thome/624	2.00
28	Alex Rodriguez/620	5.00
29	Lance Berkman/620	1.50
30	J.D. Drew/613	1.50
31	Albert Pujols/610	5.00
32	Manny Ramirez/609	2.00
33	Chipper Jones/605	3.00
34	Shawn Green/598	1.50
35	Brian Giles/590	1.50
36	Juan Gonzalez/590	2.00
37	Phil Nevin/588	1.50
38	Gary Sheffield/583	1.50
39	Bret Boone/578	1.50
40	Cliff Floyd/578	1.50
41	Barry Bonds/1,378	5.00
42	Sammy Sosa/1,174	4.00
43	Jason Giambi/1,137	1.50
44	Todd Helton/1,117	1.50
45	Luis Gonzalez/1,117	1.00
46	Larry Walker/1,111	1.00
47	Lance Berkman/1,050	1.00
48	Jim Thome/1,040	1.00
49	Chipper Jones/1,032	2.50
50	J.D. Drew/1,027	1.00
51	Alex Rodriguez/1,021	4.00
52	Manny Ramirez/1,014	1.50
53	Albert Pujols/1,013	4.00
54	Gary Sheffield/1,000	1.50
55	Brian Giles/994	1.00
56	Phil Nevin/976	1.00
57	Jim Edmonds/974	1.50
58	Shawn Green/970	1.00
59	Cliff Floyd/968	1.00
60	Edgar Martinez/966	1.00

Recollection Collection

NM/M
Some not priced due to scarcity.

6	Steve Carlton 83/30	40.00
7	Steve Carlton 87/30	40.00
8	Gary Carter 87/100	25.00
9	Gary Carter 89/100	25.00
11	Joe Carter 87/45	25.00
13	Andre Dawson 81/50	20.00
14	Andre Dawson 83/50	20.00
16	Andre Dawson 87/45	20.00
17	Dennis Eckersley 81/45	20.00
24	Steve Garvey 87/75	20.00
26	Fergie Jenkins 81/40	25.00
46	Tom Seaver 87/60	60.00
47	Don Sutton 87/200	15.00

Rookie Year Materials - Bats

NM/M
Production 250 Sets

1	Barry Bonds	40.00
2	Cal Ripken Jr.	40.00
3	Kirby Puckett	15.00
4	Johnny Bench	15.00

Rookie Year Materials - Jerseys

NM/M
Quantity produced listed
Parallel #'d to 25 or 50.

1	Nomar Garciaparra/250	20.00
2	Randy Johnson/250	10.00
3	Ivan Rodriguez/250	10.00
4	Vladimir Guerrero/250	15.00
5	Stan Musial/50	80.00
6	Yogi Berra/50	50.00

Rookie Year Materials - Bats Autograph

NM/M
Numbered to debut year.

1	Barry Bonds/86	125.00
2	Cal Ripken Jr/81	140.00
3	Kirby Puckett/84	120.00
4	Johnny Bench/68	75.00

2002 Donruss Classics

NM/M

Complete Set (200):
Common Player:
Common (101-150): .50
Common (101-150): 3.00
Common (151-200): 2.00
Production 1,500
Pack (6): 5.00
Box (18): 70.00

1	Alex Rodriguez	3.00
2	Barry Bonds	4.00
3	C.C. Sabathia	.50
4	Chipper Jones	2.00
5	Derek Jeter	4.00
6	Troy Glaus	1.50
7	Frank Thomas	1.50
8	Greg Maddux	2.00
9	Ivan Rodriguez	1.25
10	Jeff Bagwell	1.50
11	Mark Buehrle	.50
12	Todd Helton	1.50
13	Ken Griffey Jr.	2.50
14	Manny Ramirez	1.50
15	Brad Penny	.50
16	Mike Piazza	2.50
17	Morgan Garciaparra	2.50
18	Pedro J. Martinez	1.50
19	Randy Johnson	1.50
20	Bud Smith	.50
21	Rickey Henderson	1.50
22	Roger Clemens	2.25
23	Sammy Sosa	2.50
24	Brandon Duckworth	.50
25	Vladimir Guerrero	1.50
26	Kazuhiro Sasaki	.50
27	Roberto Alomar	.65
28	Barry Zito	.75
29	Rich Aurilia	.50
30	Ben Sheets	.50
31	Carlos Delgado	1.00
32	J.D. Drew	.75
33	Jermaine Dye	.50
34	Darin Erstad	.75
35	Jason Giambi	1.00
36	Tom Glavine	.60
37	Juan Gonzalez	1.50
38	Luis Gonzalez	.35
39	Shawn Green	.75
40	Tim Hudson	.65
41	Andruw Jones	1.50
42	Shannon Stewart	.50
43	Barry Larkin	.50
44	Wade Miller	.50
45	Mike Mussina	.65
46	Hideo Nomo	1.00
47	Rafael Palmeiro	1.25
48	Scott Rolen	1.00
49	Gary Sheffield	.75
50	Bernie Williams	.65
51	Bobby Abreu	.50
52	Javier Vazquez	.50
53	Edgar Martinez	.50
54	Magglio Ordonez	.75
55	Kerry Wood	1.00
56	Adrian Beltre	.65
57	Lance Berkman	.50
58	Kevin Brown	.50
59	Sean Casey	.50
60	Eric Chavez	.75
61	Robert Person	.50
62	Jeremy Giambi	.50
63	Freddy Garcia	.50
64	Alfonso Soriano	1.50
65	Doug Davis	.50
66	Brian Giles	.50
67	Moises Alou	.50
68	Richard Hidalgo	.50
69	Paul LoDuca	.50
70	Aramis Ramirez	.50
71	Andres Galarraga	.50
72	Ryan Klesko	.50
73	Chan Ho Park	.50
74	Richie Sexson	.50
75	Mike Sweeney	.50
76	Aubrey Huff	.50
77	Miguel Tejada	.75
78	Jose Vidro	.50
79	Larry Walker	.50
80	Roy Oswalt	.75
81	Craig Biggio	.50
82	Juan Pierre	.50
83	Jim Thome	.50
84	Josh Towers	.50
85	Alex Escobar	.50
86	Cliff Floyd	.50
87	Terrence Long	.50
88	Curt Schilling	.75
89	Carlos Beltran	1.00
90	Albert Pujols	2.50
91	Gabe Kapler	.50
92	Mark Mulder	.50
93	Carlos Lee	.50
94	Robert Fick	.50
95	Raul Mondesi	.50
96	Ichiro Suzuki	2.50
97	Adam Dunn	.75
98	Corey Patterson	.75
99	Tsuyoshi Shinjo	.50
100	Joe Mays	.50
101	Juan Cruz	3.00
102	Marlon Byrd	5.00
103	Luis Garcia	3.00
104	Jorge Padilla RC	6.00
105	Dennis Tankersley	3.00
106	Josh Pearce	3.00
107	Ramon Vazquez	3.00
108	Chris Baker RC	5.00
109	Eric Cyr RC	5.00
110	Reed Johnson RC	5.00
111	Ryan Jamison RC	5.00
112	Antonio Perez	3.00
113	Satoru Komiyama RC	3.00
114	Austin Kearns	4.00
115	Juan Pena	3.00
116	Orlando Hudson	3.00
117	Kazuhisa Ishii RC	6.00
118	Eric Bedard	3.00
119	Luis Ugueto RC	3.00
120	Ben Howard RC	3.00
121	Doug Ensberg	3.00
122	Doug DeVore RC	4.00
123	Josh Phelps	3.00
124	Angel Berroa	3.00
125	Ed Rogers	3.00
126	Takahito Nomura RC	3.00
127	John Ennis RC	3.00
128	Bill Hall	3.00
129	Dewon Brazelton	3.00
130	Hank Blalock	5.00
131	So Taguchi RC	3.00
132	Jorge De La Rosa RC	3.00
133	Matt Thornton	3.00
134	Brandon Backe RC	3.00
135	Jeff Deardorff RC	3.00
136	Steve Smyth	3.00
137	Anderson Machado RC	5.00
138	John Buck	3.00
139	Mark Prior	15.00
140	Sean Burroughs	3.00
141	Alex Herrera	3.00
142	Francis Beltran RC	3.00
143	Jason Romano	3.00
144	Michael Cuddyer	3.00
145	Steve Bechler RC	3.00
146	Alfredo Amezaga	3.00
147	Ryan Ludwick	3.00
148	Martin Vargas	3.00
149	Allan Simpson RC	3.00
150	Mark Teixeira	4.00
151	Hank Aaron	8.00
152	Ernie Banks	6.00
153	Johnny Bench	6.00
154	George Brett	10.00
155	Lou Brock	3.00
156	Rod Carew	3.00
157	Steve Carlton	4.00
158	Joe Torre	3.00
159	Dennis Eckersley	2.50
160	Reggie Jackson	5.00
161	Al Kaline	6.00
162	Dave Parker	2.00
163	Don Mattingly	10.00
164	Tony Gwynn	6.00
165	Willie McCovey	3.00
166	Joe Morgan	3.00
167	Stan Musial	8.00
168	Jim Palmer	3.00
169	Brooks Robinson	5.00
170	Bo Jackson	6.00
171	Nolan Ryan	15.00
172	Mike Schmidt	8.00
173	Tom Seaver	6.00
174	Cal Ripken Jr.	15.00
175	Robin Yount	6.00
176	Wade Boggs	5.00
177	Gary Carter	3.00
178	Ron Santo	2.00
179	Luis Aparicio	2.00
180	Bobby Doerr	3.00
181	Ryne Sandberg	6.00
182	Yogi Berra	5.00
183	Will Clark	5.00
184	Eddie Murray	4.00
185	Andre Dawson	3.00
186	Duke Snider	5.00
187	Orlando Cepeda	3.00
188	Billy Williams	2.00
189	Juan Marichal	4.00
190	Harmon Killebrew	5.00
191	Kirby Puckett	6.00
192	Carlton Fisk	4.00
193	Dave Winfield	3.00
194	Alan Trammell	3.00
195	Paul Molitor	6.00
196	Tony Perez	3.00
197	Ozzie Smith	6.00
198	Ralph Kiner	3.00
199	Fergie Jenkins	2.00
200	Phil Rizzuto	3.00

Timeless Tributes

Stars (1-100): 2-4X
SP's (101-150): 1-2X
SP's (151-200): 2-3X
Production 100 Sets

Classic Combos

Too scarce to price.

Classic Singles

NM/M
Common Player: 10.00
Some too scarce to price.

1	Cal Ripken Jr/Jsy/50	40.00
2	Eddie Murray/Jsy/100	15.00
3	George Brett/Jsy/100	35.00
4	Bo Jackson/Jsy/100	20.00
5	Ted Williams/Bat/50	200.00
6	Jimmie Foxx/Bat/50	60.00
7	Reggie Jackson/Jsy/100	15.00
8	Steve Carlton/Jsy/50	30.00
9	Mel Ott/Jsy/50	70.00
10	"Catfish" Hunter/Jsy/100	10.00
11	Nolan Ryan/Jsy/100	40.00
12	Rickey Henderson/Jsy/100	25.00
13	Robin Yount/Jsy/100	25.00
14	Orlando Cepeda/Jsy/100	10.00
15	Ty Cobb/Bat/50	150.00
16	Babe Ruth/Bat/50	275.00
17	Dave Parker/Jsy/100	10.00
18	Willie Stargell/Jsy/100	10.00
19	Ernie Banks/Bat/100	25.00
20	Mike Schmidt/Jsy/100	35.00
21	Duke Snider/Jsy/50	25.00

22	Jackie Robinson/Jsy/50	75.00
23	Rickey Henderson/Bat/100	25.00
24	TBD	
25	Lou Gehrig/Bat/50	175.00
26	Jimmie Foxx/Bat/50	65.00
28	Tony Gwynn/Bat/100	20.00
29	Bobby Doerr/Jsy/100	15.00
30	Joe Torre/Jsy/100	10.00

Legendary Hats

NM/M

50 sets produced

1	Don Mattingly/50	150.00
2	George Brett	150.00
3	Wade Boggs	30.00
5	Ryne Sandberg	120.00

Legendary Spikes

NM/M

50 sets produced

1	Don Mattingly	125.00
2	Eddie Murray	30.00
3	Paul Molitor	50.00
4	Harmon Killebrew	40.00
5	Mike Schmidt	100.00

Legendary Leather

NM/M

50 sets produced

1	Don Mattingly	125.00
2	Wade Boggs	30.00
4	Kirby Puckett	50.00
5	Mike Schmidt	80.00

Legendary Lumberjacks

NM/M

Varying quantities produced

1	Don Mattingly/50	20.00
2	George Brett/400	20.00
3	Stan Musial/100	35.00
4	Lou Gehrig/50	175.00
5	Mike Piazza/500	10.00
6	Mel Ott/50	75.00
7	Ted Williams/50	150.00
8	Bo Jackson/500	8.00
9	Kirby Puckett/500	15.00
10	Rafael Palmeiro/500	10.00
11	Andre Dawson/500	5.00
12	Ozzie Smith/500	15.00
13	Paul Molitor/500	15.00
14	Babe Ruth/500	220.00
15	Carlton Fisk/500	8.00
16	Rickey Henderson/500	10.00
17	Gary Carter/500	5.00
18	Cal Ripken Jr/100	40.00
19	Eddie Matthews/100	20.00
20	Luis Aparicio/500	5.00
21	Al Kaline/100	25.00
22	Eddie Murray/500	8.00
23	Yogi Berra/100	25.00
24	Alex Rodriguez/500	10.00
25	Tony Gwynn/500	10.00
26	Roberto Clemente/100	80.00
27	Mike Schmidt/400	20.00
28	Reggie Jackson/500	10.00
29	Ryne Sandberg/500	20.00
30	Joe Morgan/400	5.00
31	Joe Torre/500	5.00
32	Gary Sheffield/500	5.00
33	Nomar Garciaparra/500	10.00
34	Jeff Bagwell/500	8.00
35	Manny Ramirez/500	8.00

New Millennium Classics

NM/M

Common Player: 4.00

Varying quantities produced

All jerseys unless noted.

1	Curt Schilling/500	6.00
2	Vladimir Guerrero/100	15.00
3	Jim Thome/500	8.00
4	Troy Glaus/400	6.00
5	Ivan Rodriguez/200	6.00
6	Todd Helton/400	8.00
7	Sean Casey/500	4.00
8	Scott Rolen/475	8.00
9	Ken Griffey Jr./150/Base	10.00
10	Hideo Nomo/100	25.00
11	Tom Glavine/350	5.00
12	Pedro Martinez/100	15.00
13	Cliff Floyd/500	4.00
14	Shawn Green/125	8.00
15	Rafael Palmeiro/250	8.00
16	Luis Gonzalez/100	5.00
17	Lance Berkman/100	6.00
18	Frank Thomas/500	8.00
19	Randy Johnson/400	8.00
20	Moises Alou/500	4.00
21	Chipper Jones/500	8.00
22	Larry Walker/300	4.00
23	Mike Sweeney/500	4.00
24	Juan Gonzalez/300	6.00
25	Roger Clemens/100	20.00
26	Albert Pujols/300/Base	15.00
27	Magglio Ordonez/500	5.00
28	Alex Rodriguez/400	10.00
29	Jeff Bagwell/125	10.00
30	Kazuhiro Sasaki/500	4.00
31	Barry Larkin/300	6.00
32	Andruw Jones/350	8.00
33	Kerry Wood/200	8.00
34	Rickey Henderson/100	10.00
35	Greg Maddux/100	15.00
36	Brian Giles/400	4.00
37	Craig Biggio/100	5.00
38	Roberto Alomar/400	6.00
39	Mike Piazza/400	10.00
40	Bernie Williams/100	10.00
41	Ichiro Suzuki/150/Ball	30.00
42	Kenny Lofton/450	4.00
43	Mark Mulder/500	4.00
44	Kazuhisa Ishii/100	15.00
45	Darin Erstad/500	4.00
46	Jose Vidro/500	4.00
47	Miguel Tejada/475	6.00
48	Roy Oswalt/500	5.00
50	Barry Zito/500	6.00
51	Manny Ramirez/500	8.00
52	Nomar Garciaparra/400	10.00
53	C.C. Sabathia/500	4.00
54	Carlos Delgado/500	8.00
55	Gary Sheffield/500	6.00
56	J.D. Drew/500	5.00
57	Barry Bonds/150/Ball	25.00
58	Derek Jeter/150/Ball	25.00
59	Edgar Martinez/400	5.00
60	Sammy Sosa/150/Ball	15.00

Significant Signatures

NM/M

Common Prospect Autograph: 5.00

Varying quantities produced, many not priced due to scarcity

101	Juan Cruz/400	6.00
102	Marlon Byrd/500	10.00
103	Luis Garcia/500	6.00
104	Jorge Padilla/500	10.00
105	Dennis Tankersley/250	10.00
106	Josh Pearce/500	8.00
107	Ramon Vazquez/500	8.00
108	Chris Baker/500 RC	8.00
109	Eric Cyr/500	6.00
110	Reed Johnson/500	10.00
111	Ryan Jamison/500	5.00
112	Antonio Perez/500	5.00
113	Satoru Komiyama/50	40.00
114	Austin Kearns/500	15.00
115	Juan Pena/500	5.00
116	Orlando Hudson/400	10.00
117	Kazuhisa Ishii/50	40.00
118	Eric Bedard/500	15.00
119	Luis Ugueto/250	10.00
120	Ben Howard/500	8.00
121	Morgan Ensberg/500	10.00
122	Doug DeVore/500	8.00
123	Josh Phelps/500	8.00
124	Angel Berroa/500	10.00
125	Ed Rogers/500	5.00
127	John Ennis/500	5.00
128	Bill Hall/400	10.00
129	Dewon Brazelton/400	8.00
130	Hank Blalock/100	20.00
131	So Taguchi/150	30.00
132	Jorge De La Rosa/500	5.00
133	Matt Thornton/500	5.00
134	Brandon Backe/500	5.00
135	Jeff Deardorff/500	5.00
136	Steve Smyth/400	5.00
137	Anderson Machado/500	10.00
138	John Buck/500	5.00
139	Mark Prior/250	25.00
140	Sean Burroughs/50	10.00
141	Alex Herrera/500	5.00
142	Francis Beltran/500	5.00
143	Jason Romano/500	5.00
144	Michael Cuddyer/400	8.00
145	Steve Bechler/500	8.00
146	Alfredo Amezaga/500	5.00
147	Ryan Ludwick/500	8.00
148	Martin Vargas/500	5.00
149	Allan Simpson/500	5.00
150	Mark Teixeira/200	30.00
152	Ernie Banks/25	100.00
153	Johnny Bench/25	125.00
154	George Brett/25	260.00
155	Lou Brock/100	30.00
157	Steve Carlton/125	35.00
159	Dennis Eckersley/500	15.00
161	Al Kaline/125	35.00
162	Dave Parker/500	10.00
163	Don Mattingly/50	75.00
168	Jim Palmer/125	25.00
169	Brooks Robinson/125	40.00
177	Gary Carter/150	25.00
178	Ron Santo/500	20.00
179	Luis Aparicio/400	10.00
180	Bobby Doerr/500	15.00
182	Yogi Berra/25	80.00
184	Eddie Murray/25	60.00
185	Andre Dawson/200	20.00
186	Duke Snider/25	70.00
187	Orlando Cepeda/125	25.00
188	Billy Williams/200	15.00
189	Juan Marichal/500	15.00
190	Harmon Killebrew/100	50.00
194	Alan Trammell/200	25.00
195	Paul Molitor/25	60.00
196	Tony Perez/150	15.00
198	Ralph Kiner/125	20.00
199	Fergie Jenkins/200	15.00
200	Phil Rizzuto/125	40.00

Timeless Treasures

NM/M

Some not priced.

5	Ted Williams/Bat/42	140.00
6	Ted Williams/Bat/47	140.00
7	Ted Williams/Bat/46	140.00
8	Ted Williams/Bat/49	140.00
10	Cal Ripken Jr./Jsy/98	50.00
11	Cal Ripken Jr./Jsy/82	50.00
12	Cal Ripken Jr./Jsy/83	50.00
13	Cal Ripken Jr./Jsy/91	50.00

2002 Donruss Diamond Kings

NM/M

Complete Set (150):	150.00
Common Player:	.40
Common SP (101-150):	2.00
Inserted 1:3	
Pack (4):	4.50
Box (24):	80.00

1	Vladimir Guerrero	1.00
2	Adam Dunn	.75
3	Tsuyoshi Shinjo	.40
4	Adrian Beltre	.60
5	Troy Glaus	1.00
6	Albert Pujols	2.00
7	Trot Nixon	.40
8	Alex Rodriguez	2.50
9	Tom Glavine	.50
10	Alfonso Soriano	1.00
11	Todd Helton	1.00
12	Joe Torre	.40
13	Tim Hudson	.50
14	Andruw Jones	1.00
15	Shawn Green	.50
16	Aramis Ramirez	.40
17	Shannon Stewart	.40
18	Barry Bonds	3.00
19	Sean Casey	.40
20	Barry Larkin	.40
21	Scott Rolen	.75
22	Barry Zito	.50
23	Sammy Sosa	2.00
24	Bartolo Colon	.40
25	Ryan Klesko	.40
26	Ben Grieve	.40
27	Roy Oswalt	.50
28	Kazuhiro Sasaki	.40
29	Roger Clemens	1.75
30	Bernie Williams	.50
31	Roberto Alomar	.50
32	Bobby Abreu	.40
33	Robert Fick	.40
34	Bret Boone	.40
35	Rickey Henderson	1.00
36	Brian Giles	.40
37	Richie Sexson	.40
38	Bud Smith	.40
39	Richard Hidalgo	.40
40	C.C. Sabathia	.40
41	Rich Aurilia	.40
42	Carlos Beltran	.75
43	Raul Mondesi	.40
44	Carlos Delgado	.50
45	Randy Johnson	1.00
46	Chan Ho Park	.40
47	Rafael Palmeiro	.75
48	Chipper Jones	1.50
49	Phil Nevin	.40
50	Cliff Floyd	.40
51	Pedro Martinez	1.00
52	Craig Biggio	.40
53	Paul LoDuca	.40
54	Cristian Guzman	.40
55	Pat Burrell	.50
56	Curt Schilling	.50
57	Orlando Cabrera	.40
58	Darin Erstad	.65
59	Omar Vizquel	.40
60	Derek Jeter	3.00
61	Nomar Garciaparra	2.00
62	Edgar Martinez	.40
63	Moises Alou	.40
64	Eric Chavez	.50
65	Mike Sweeney	.40
66	Frank Thomas	1.00
67	Mike Piazza	2.00
68	Gary Sheffield	.50
69	Mike Mussina	.50
70	Greg Maddux	1.50
71	Juan Gonzalez	1.00
72	Hideo Nomo	.65
73	Miguel Tejada	.50
74	Ichiro Suzuki	2.00
75	Matt Morris	.40
76	Ivan Rodriguez	.75
77	Mark Mulder	.40
78	J.D. Drew	.40
79	Mark Grace	.50
80	Jason Giambi	.50
81	Mark Buehrle	.40
82	Jose Vidro	.40
83	Manny Ramirez	1.00

84	Jeff Bagwell	1.00
85	Magglio Ordonez	.50
86	Ken Griffey Jr.	2.00
87	Luis Gonzalez	.40
88	Jim Edmonds	.40
89	Larry Walker	.40
90	Jim Thome	.40
91	Lance Berkman	.40
92	Jorge Posada	.50
93	Kevin Brown	.40
94	Joe Mays	.40
95	Kerry Wood	.75
96	Mark Ellis	.40
97	Austin Kearns	.75
98	Jorge De La Rosa RC	.50
99	Brandon Berger	.40
100	Ryan Ludwick	.40
101	Marlon Byrd	2.00
102	Brandon Backe RC	2.00
103	Juan Cruz	2.00
104	Anderson Machado RC	3.00
105	So Taguchi RC	4.00
106	Dewon Brazelton	2.00
107	Josh Beckett	3.00
108	John Buck	2.00
109	Jorge Padilla RC	3.00
110	Hee Seop Choi	3.00
111	Angel Berroa	2.00
112	Mark Teixeira	3.00
113	Victor Martinez	2.00
114	Kazuhisa Ishii RC	6.00
115	Dennis Tankersley	2.00
116	Wilson Valdez RC	2.00
117	Antonio Perez	2.00
118	Ed Rogers	2.00
119	Wilson Betemit	2.00
120	Mike Rivera	2.00
121	Mark Prior	6.00
122	Roberto Clemente	6.00
123	Roberto Clemente	6.00
124	Roberto Clemente	6.00
125	Roberto Clemente	6.00
126	Roberto Clemente	6.00
127	Babe Ruth	10.00
128	Ted Williams	8.00
129	Andre Dawson	2.00
130	Eddie Murray	3.00
131	Juan Marichal	3.00
132	Kirby Puckett	5.00
133	Alan Trammell	2.00
134	Bobby Doerr	2.00
135	Carlton Fisk	3.00
136	Eddie Mathews	4.00
137	Mike Schmidt	6.00
138	Jim "Catfish" Hunter	2.00
139	Nolan Ryan	10.00
140	George Brett	6.00
141	Gary Carter	2.00
142	Paul Molitor	4.00
143	Lou Brock	8.00
144	Ryne Sandberg	5.00
145	Tony Gwynn	5.00
146	Ron Santo	2.00
147	Cal Ripken Jr.	10.00
148	Al Kaline	4.00
149	Bo Jackson	3.00
150	Don Mattingly	8.00

Bronze Foil

Cards 1-100:	1-2X
Cards 101-150:	.5X
Inserted 1:6	
Gold Foil (1-100):	4-8X
Gold Foil (101-150):	2-3X
Production 100 Sets	
Silver Foil (1-100):	3-4X
Silver Foil (101-150):	1-2X
Production 400 Sets	

Diamond Cut

		NM/M
Common Signature (1-30):		5.00
1	Vladimir Guerrero/400	30.00
2	Mark Prior/400	50.00
3	Victor Martinez/500	10.00
4	Marlon Byrd/500	15.00
5	Bud Smith/400	10.00
6	Joe Mays/500	10.00
7	Troy Glaus/500	20.00
8	Ron Santo/500	15.00
9	Roy Oswalt/500	20.00

10	Angel Berroa/500	10.00
11	Mark Buehrle/500	15.00
12	John Buck/500	10.00
13	Barry Larkin/250	40.00
14	Gary Carter/300	30.00
15	Mark Teixeira/300	25.00
16	Alan Trammell/500	20.00
17	Kazuhisa Ishii/100	65.00
18	Rafael Palmeiro/125	50.00
19	Austin Kearns/500	25.00
20	Joe Torre/125	40.00
21	J.D. Drew/400	20.00
22	So Taguchi/400	20.00
23	Juan Marichal/500	15.00
24	Bobby Doerr/500	15.00
25	Carlos Beltran/500	10.00
26	Robert Fick/500	10.00
27	Albert Pujols/200	70.00
28	Shannon Stewart/500	10.00
29	Antonio Perez/500	10.00
30	Wilson Betemit/500	10.00

Jerseys (31-80):

31	Alex Rodriguez/500	15.00
32	Curt Schilling/500	8.00
33	George Brett/300	30.00
34	Hideo Nomo/100	40.00
35	Ivan Rodriguez/500	8.00
36	Don Mattingly/200	40.00
37	Joe Mays/500	5.00
38	Lance Berkman/400	5.00
39	Tony Gwynn/500	10.00
40	Darin Erstad/400	5.00
41	Adrian Beltre/400	5.00
42	Frank Thomas/500	8.00
43	Cal Ripken Jr./300	30.00
44	Jose Vidro/500	5.00
45	Randy Johnson/300	8.00
46	Carlos Delgado/500	6.00
47	Roger Clemens/400	20.00
48	Luis Gonzalez/500	5.00
49	Marlon Byrd/500	5.00
50	Carlton Fisk/500	8.00
51	Manny Ramirez/500	8.00
52	Vladimir Guerrero/500	8.00
53	Barry Larkin/500	8.00
54	Aramis Ramirez/500	5.00
55	Todd Helton/300	8.00
56	Carlos Beltran/250	5.00
57	Jeff Bagwell/250	8.00
58	Larry Walker/500	5.00
59	Al Kaline/200	25.00
60	Chipper Jones/500	8.00
61	Bernie Williams/500	6.00
62	Bud Smith/500	5.00
63	Edgar Martinez/500	5.00
64	Pedro Martinez/500	5.00
65	Andre Dawson/200	6.00
66	Mike Piazza/100	40.00
67	Barry Zito/500	6.00
68	Bo Jackson/300	8.00
69	Nolan Ryan/400	50.00
70	Troy Glaus/500	6.00
71	Jorge Posada/500	6.00
72	Ted Williams/100	200.00
73	Nomar Garciaparra/500	15.00
74	"Catfish" Hunter/100	25.00
75	Gary Carter/500	8.00
76	Craig Biggio/500	5.00
77	Andruw Jones/500	8.00
78	Rickey Henderson/250	30.00
79	Greg Maddux/400	15.00
80	Kerry Wood/500	10.00

Bats (81-100):

81	Alex Rodriguez/500	20.00
82	Don Mattingly/425	30.00
83	Craig Biggio/500	5.00
84	Kazuhisa Ishii/375	8.00
85	Eddie Murray/500	8.00
86	Carlton Fisk/500	8.00
87	Tsuyoshi Shinjo/500	5.00
88	Bo Jackson/500	10.00
89	Eddie Mathews/100	30.00
90	Chipper Jones/500	8.00
91	Adam Dunn/375	6.00
92	Tony Gwynn/200	10.00
93	Kirby Puckett/500	15.00
94	Andre Dawson/500	5.00
95	Bernie Williams/500	6.00
96	Roberto Clemente/300	70.00
97	Babe Ruth/100	250.00
98	Roberto Alomar/500	8.00
99	Frank Thomas/500	8.00
100	So Taguchi/500	6.00

DK Originals

	NM/M
Complete Set (15):	50.00
Common Player:	2.00
Production 1,000 Sets	
1 Alex Rodriguez	7.00
2 Kazuhisa Ishii	2.00
3 Pedro Martinez	3.00

4	Nomar Garciaparra	6.00
5	Albert Pujols	6.00
6	Chipper Jones	5.00
7	So Taguchi	2.00
8	Jeff Bagwell	3.00
9	Vladimir Guerrero	3.00
10	Derek Jeter	8.00
11	Sammy Sosa	6.00
12	Ichiro Suzuki	6.00
13	Barry Bonds	8.00
14	Jason Giambi	3.00
15	Mike Piazza	6.00

Heritage Collection

	NM/M
Complete Set (25):	100.00
Common Player:	2.00
Inserted 1:23	
1 Lou Gehrig	8.00
2 Nolan Ryan	10.00
3 Ryne Sandberg	4.00
4 Ted Williams	8.00
5 Roberto Clemente	8.00
6 Mike Schmidt	6.00
7 Roger Clemens	5.00
8 Kirby Puckett	4.00
9 Andre Dawson	2.00
10 Carlton Fisk	2.00
11 Don Mattingly	8.00
12 Juan Marichal	2.00
13 George Brett	8.00
14 Bo Jackson	3.00
15 Eddie Mathews	3.00
16 Randy Johnson	3.00
17 Alan Trammell	2.00
18 Tony Gwynn	4.00
19 Paul Molitor	3.00
20 Barry Bonds	10.00
21 Eddie Murray	3.00
22 Jim "Catfish" Hunter	2.00
23 Rickey Henderson	3.00
24 Cal Ripken Jr.	10.00
25 Babe Ruth	10.00

2002 Donruss Diamond Kings Original Paintings

(See 2002 Donruss Diamond
Kings for checklist.)

Recollection Collection

		NM/M
Most not priced.		
Common Player:		
22	Fred Lynn 87 DK/28	15.00
30	Roy Oswalt 01 RDK Black/48	20.00
47	Alan Trammell 88 DK/110	30.00

Ramly T204

		NM/M
Complete Set (25):		120.00
Common Player:		3.00
Production 1,000 Sets		
1	Vladimir Guerrero	4.00
2	Jeff Bagwell	4.00
3	Barry Bonds	15.00
4	Rickey Henderson	4.00
5	Mike Piazza	8.00
6	Derek Jeter	15.00
7	Kazuhisa Ishii	3.00
8	Ichiro Suzuki	10.00
9	Chipper Jones	5.00
10	Sammy Sosa	8.00
11	Don Mattingly	10.00
12	Shawn Green	3.00
13	Nomar Garciaparra	10.00
14	Luis Gonzalez	3.00
15	Albert Pujols	8.00
16	Cal Ripken Jr.	15.00
17	Todd Helton	4.00
18	Hideo Nomo	3.00
19	Alex Rodriguez	10.00
20	So Taguchi	3.00
21	Lance Berkman	3.00
22	Tony Gwynn	5.00
23	Roger Clemens	6.00
24	Jason Giambi	4.00
25	Ken Griffey Jr.	8.00

Timeline

		NM/M
Complete Set (10):		60.00
Common Card:		3.00
Inserted 1:60		
1	Lou Gehrig, Don Mattingly	10.00
2	Hideo Nomo, Ichiro Suzuki	6.00
3	Cal Ripken Jr., Alex Rodriguez	10.00
4	Mike Schmidt, Scott Rolen	8.00
5	Ichiro Suzuki, Albert Pujols	8.00
6	Curt Schilling, Randy Johnson	5.00
7	Chipper Jones, Eddie Mathews	5.00
8	Lou Gehrig, Cal Ripken Jr.	10.00
9	Derek Jeter, Roger Clemens	10.00
10	Kazuhiko Ishimine, So Taguchi	3.00

2002 Donruss Diamond Kings Samples

	NM/M
Common Player:	.25

Stars: 1.5-2X
Gold: 10X
(See 2002 Donruss Diamond Kings for checklist and base card values.)

2002 Donruss Elite

		NM/M
Complete Set (200):		
Common Player:		.25
Common (101-150):		2.00
Inserted 1:10		
Common (151-200):		3.00
Production 1,500		
Pack (5):		3.00
Box (20):		50.00
1	Vladimir Guerrero	.75
2	Bernie Williams	.35
3	Ichiro Suzuki	1.50
4	Roger Clemens	1.25
5	Greg Maddux	1.00
6	Fred McGriff	.25
7	Jermaine Dye	.25
8	Ken Griffey Jr.	1.50
9	Todd Helton	.75
10	Torii Hunter	.40
11	Pat Burrell	.40
12	Chipper Jones	1.00
13	Ivan Rodriguez	.50
14	Roy Oswalt	.40
15	Shannon Stewart	.25
16	Magglio Ordonez	.40
17	Lance Berkman	.25
18	Mark Mulder	.25
19	Al Leiter	.25
20	Sammy Sosa	1.50
21	Scott Rolen	.75
22	Aramis Ramirez	.25
23	Alfonso Soriano	.75
24	Phil Nevin	.25
25	Barry Bonds	2.50
26	Joe Mays	.25
27	Jeff Kent	.25
28	Mark Quinn	.25
29	Adrian Beltre	.35
30	Freddy Garcia	.25
31	Pedro J. Martinez	.75
32	Darryl Kile	.25
33	Mike Cameron	.25
34	Frank Catalanotto	.25
35	Jose Vidro	.25
36	Jim Thome	.25
37	Javy Lopez	.25
38	Paul Konerko	.25
39	Jeff Bagwell	.75
40	Curt Schilling	.40
41	Miguel Tejada	.40
42	Jim Edmonds	.25
43	Ellis Burks	.25
44	Mark Grace	.35
45	Robb Nen	.25
46	Jeff Conine	.25
47	Derek Jeter	2.50
48	Mike Lowell	.25
49	Javier Vazquez	.25
50	Manny Ramirez	.75
51	Bartolo Colon	.25
52	Carlos Beltran	.50
53	Tim Hudson	.40
54	Rafael Palmeiro	.65
55	Jimmy Rollins	.50
56	Andruw Jones	.75
57	Orlando Cabrera	.25
58	Dean Palmer	.25
59	Bret Boone	.25
60	Carlos Febles	.25
61	Ben Grieve	.25
62	Richie Sexson	.25
63	Alex Rodriguez	2.00
64	Juan Pierre	.25
65	Bobby Higginson	.25
66	Barry Zito	.40

67	Raul Mondesi	.25
68	Albert Pujols	2.00
69	Omar Vizquel	.25
70	Bobby Abreu	.25
71	Corey Koskie	.25
72	Tom Glavine	.40
73	Paul LoDuca	.25
74	Terrence Long	.25
75	Matt Morris	.25
76	Andy Pettitte	.40
77	Rich Aurilia	.25
78	Todd Walker	.25
79	John Olerud	.25
80	Mike Sweeney	.25
81	Ray Durham	.25
82	Fernando Vina	.25
83	Nomar Garciaparra	1.50
84	Mariano Rivera	.35
85	Mike Piazza	1.50
86	Mark Buehrle	.25
87	Adam Dunn	.50
88	Luis Gonzalez	.35
89	Richard Hidalgo	.25
90	Brad Radke	.25
91	Russ Ortiz	.25
92	Brian Giles	.25
93	Billy Wagner	.25
94	Cliff Floyd	.25
95	Eric Milton	.25
96	Bud Smith	.25
97	Wade Miller	.25
98	Jon Lieber	.25
99	Derrek Lee	.25
100	Jose Cruz Jr.	.25
101	Dmitri Young	2.00
102	Mo Vaughn	2.00
103	Tino Martinez	2.00
104	Larry Walker	2.50
105	Chuck Knoblauch	2.00
106	Troy Glaus	3.00
107	Jason Giambi	4.00
108	Travis Fryman	2.00
109	Josh Beckett	4.00
110	Edgar Martinez	2.00
111	Tim Salmon	2.00
112	C.C. Sabathia	2.00
113	Randy Johnson	5.00
114	Juan Gonzalez	4.00
115	Carlos Delgado	4.00
116	Hideo Nomo	4.00
117	Kerry Wood	4.00
118	Brian Jordan	2.00
119	Carlos Pena	2.00
120	Roger Cedeno	2.00
121	Chan Ho Park	2.00
122	Rafael Furcal	2.00
123	Frank Thomas	4.00
124	Mike Mussina	4.00
125	Rickey Henderson	5.00
126	Sean Casey	2.00
127	Barry Larkin	2.00
128	Kazuhiro Sasaki	2.00
129	Moises Alou	2.00
130	Jeff Cirillo	2.00
131	Jason Kendall	2.00
132	Gary Sheffield	3.00
133	Ryan Klesko	2.00
134	Kevin Brown	2.00
135	Darin Erstad	2.00
136	Roberto Alomar	3.00
137	Brad Fullmer	2.00
138	Eric Chavez	2.00
139	Ben Sheets	2.00
140	Trot Nixon	2.00
141	Garret Anderson	2.00
142	Shawn Green	2.50
143	Troy Percival	2.00
144	Craig Biggio	2.50
145	Jorge Posada	2.50
146	J.D. Drew	3.00
147	Johnny Damon	2.00
148	Jeromy Burnitz	2.00
149	Robin Ventura	2.00
150	Aaron Sele	2.00
151	Cam Esslinger RC	3.00
152	Ben Howard RC	4.00
153	Brandon Backe RC	3.00
154	Jorge De La Rosa RC	3.00
155	Austin Kearns	5.00
156	Carlos Zambrano	3.00
157	Kyle Kane RC	3.00
158	So Taguchi RC	5.00
159	Brian Mallette RC	3.00
160	Brett Jodie	3.00
161	Elio Serrano RC	3.00
162	Joe Thurston	3.00
163	Kevin Olsen	3.00
164	Rodrigo Rosario RC	4.00
165	Matt Guerrier	3.00
166	Anderson Machado RC	5.00
167	Bert Snow	3.00
168	Franklyn German RC	3.00
169	Brandon Claussen	3.00
170	Jason Romano	3.00

171	Jorge Padilla RC	5.00
172	Jose Cueto	3.00
173	Allan Simpson RC	3.00
174	Doug DeVore RC	3.00
175	Justin Duchscherer	3.00
176	Josh Pearce	3.00
177	Steve Bechler RC	3.00
178	Josh Phelps	3.00
179	Juan Diaz	3.00
180	Victor Alvarez RC	3.00
181	Ramon Vazquez	3.00
182	Mike Rivera	3.00
183	Kazuhisa Ishii RC	6.00
184	Henry Mateo	3.00
185	Travis Hughes RC	5.00
186	Zach Day	3.00
187	Brad Voyles	3.00
188	Sean Douglass	3.00
189	Nick Neugebauer	3.00
190	Tom Shearn RC	3.00
191	Eric Cyr RC	3.00
192	Adam Johnson	3.00
193	Michael Cuddyer	3.00
194	Erik Bedard	3.00
195	Mark Ellis	3.00
196	Carlos Hernandez	3.00
197	Deivi Santos	3.00
198	Morgan Ensberg	3.00
199	Ryan Jamison RC	3.00
200	Cody Ransom	3.00

Aspirations

1-100 print run 26-50:	15-30X
1-100 p/r 51-80:	8-15X
101-150 p/r 26-50:	1.5-3X
101-150 p/r 51-99:	1-2X

Status

1-100 print run 36-70:	10-20X
1-100 p/r 71-100:	5-10X
101-150 p/r 36-70:	1-2X
101-150 p/r 71-100:	1X

All-Star Salutes

		NM/M
Common Player:		1.00
Century:		1-2X
Production 100		
1	Ichiro Suzuki	5.00
2	Tony Gwynn	4.00
3	Magglio Ordonez	1.50
4	Cal Ripken Jr.	8.00
5	Tony Gwynn	4.00
6	Kazuhiro Sasaki	1.00
7	Freddy Garcia	1.00
8	Luis Gonzalez	1.00
9	Lance Berkman	1.00
10	Derek Jeter	8.00
11	Chipper Jones	4.00
12	Randy Johnson	3.00
13	Andruw Jones	3.00
14	Pedro J. Martinez	3.00
15	Jim Thome	1.00
16	Rafael Palmeiro	2.50
17	Barry Larkin	1.00
18	Ivan Rodriguez	2.50
19	Omar Vizquel	1.00
20	Edgar Martinez	1.00
21	Larry Walker	1.00
22	Javy Lopez	1.00
23	Mariano Rivera	1.25
24	Frank Thomas	3.00
25	Greg Maddux	3.00

Back to the Future

		NM/M
Complete Set (24):		75.00
Common Player:		2.00
Duals 500 produced, singles 1,000		
1	Scott Rolen, Marlon Byrd	5.00

2	Joe Crede, Frank Thomas	6.00
3	Lance Berkman, Jeff Bagwell	6.00
4	Marcus Giles, Chipper Jones	10.00
5	Shawn Green, Paul LoDuca	4.00
7	Kerry Wood, Juan Cruz	4.00
8	Vladimir Guerrero, Orlando Cabrera	6.00
9	Scott Rolen	3.00
10	Marlon Byrd	2.00
11	Frank Thomas	4.00
12	Joe Crede	2.00
13	Jeff Bagwell	4.00
14	Lance Berkman	2.00
15	Chipper Jones	6.00
16	Marcus Giles	2.00
17	Shawn Green	2.50
18	Paul LoDuca	2.00
19	Jim Edmonds	2.00
20	Kerry Wood	3.00
21	Juan Cruz	2.00
22	Vladimir Guerrero	4.00
23	Orlando Cabrera	2.00

Back to the Future Threads

		NM/M
Common Card:		10.00
Duals 50 produced, singles 100		
1	Scott Rolen, Marlon Byrd	30.00
2	Joe Crede, Frank Thomas	40.00
3	Lance Berkman, Jeff Bagwell	40.00
4	Marcus Giles, Chipper Jones	50.00
5	Shawn Green, Paul LoDuca	30.00
7	Kerry Wood, Juan Cruz	35.00
8	Vladimir Guerrero, Orlando Cabrera	40.00
9	Scott Rolen	15.00
10	Marlon Byrd	20.00
11	Frank Thomas	25.00
12	Joe Crede	10.00
13	Jeff Bagwell	25.00
14	Lance Berkman	15.00
15	Chipper Jones	25.00
16	Marcus Giles	10.00
17	Shawn Green	15.00
18	Paul LoDuca	10.00
19	Jim Edmonds	10.00
20	So Taguchi	50.00
21	Kerry Wood	15.00
22	Juan Cruz	10.00
23	Vladimir Guerrero	25.00
24	Orlando Cabrera	10.00

Back 2 Back Jacks

	NM/M
Common Card:	10.00
Dual Production 75	
Single Production 150	

1	Ivan Rodriguez,	
	Alex Rodriguez	40.00
2	Kirby Puckett,	
	Dave Winfield	50.00
3	Ted Williams,	
	Nomar Garciaparra	150.00
4	Jeff Bagwell,	
	Craig Biggio	25.00
5	Eddie Murray,	
	Cal Ripken Jr.	125.00
6	Andruw Jones,	
	Chipper Jones	25.00
7	Roberto Clemente,	
	Willie Stargell	120.00
8	Lou Gehrig,	
	Don Mattingly	180.00
9	Larry Walker,	
	Todd Helton	20.00
10	Manny Ramirez,	
	Trot Nixon	25.00
11	Alex Rodriguez	30.00
12	Ivan Rodriguez	15.00
13	Kirby Puckett	40.00
14	Dave Winfield	15.00
15	Ted Williams	100.00
16	Nomar Garciaparra	40.00
17	Jeff Bagwell	15.00
18	Craig Biggio	10.00
19	Eddie Murray	20.00
20	Cal Ripken Jr.	60.00
21	Andruw Jones	10.00
22	Chipper Jones	20.00
23	Roberto Clemente	80.00
25	Lou Gehrig	160.00
26	Don Mattingly	65.00
27	Larry Walker	10.00
28	Todd Helton	15.00
29	Manny Ramirez	20.00
30	Trot Nixon	10.00

Career Bests

		NM/M
Common Player:		2.00
1	Albert Pujols/1,013	8.00
2	Alex Rodriguez/52	20.00
3	Alex Rodriguez/135	15.00
4	Andruw Jones/104	6.00
5	Barry Bonds/73	25.00
6	Barry Bonds/1,379	10.00
7	Barry Bonds/177	20.00
8	C.C. Sabathia/171	4.00
9	Carlos Beltran/876	2.00
10	Chipper Jones/330	6.00
11	Derek Jeter/900	15.00
12	Eric Chavez/114	4.00
13	Frank Catalanotto/330	2.00
14	Ichiro Suzuki/838	10.00
15	Ichiro Suzuki/127	15.00
16	Ichiro Suzuki/8	
17	J.D. Drew/27	20.00
18	J.D. Drew/1,027	2.00
19	Jason Giambi/660	5.00
20	Jim Thome/49	25.00
21	Jim Thome/624	4.00
22	Jorge Posada/95	8.00
23	Jose Cruz Jr/856	2.00
24	Kazuhiro Sasaki/45	15.00
25	Kerry Wood/336	5.00
26	Lance Berkman/1,050	3.00
27	Magglio Ordonez/382	3.00
28	Mark Mulder/345	2.00
29	Pat Burrell/27	20.00
30	Pat Burrell/469	3.00
31	Randy Johnson/372	6.00
32	Randy Johnson/21	
33	Richie Sexson/547	3.00
34	Roberto Alomar/956	3.00
35	Sammy Sosa/160	12.00
36	Sammy Sosa/1,174	6.00
37	Shawn Green/547	4.00
38	Tsuyoshi Shinjo/10	
39	Trot Nixon/150	3.00
40	Troy Glaus/108	5.00

Passing the Torch

		NM/M
Common Card:		4.00
Dual 500, single 1,000 produced.		
1	Fergie Jenkins,	
	Mark Prior	10.00
2	Nolan Ryan,	
	Roy Oswalt	25.00
3	Ozzie Smith,	
	J.D. Drew	8.00
4	George Brett,	
	Carlos Beltran	15.00
5	Kirby Puckett,	
	Michael Cuddyer	10.00
6	Johnny Bench,	
	Adam Dunn	8.00
7	Duke Snider,	
	Paul LoDuca	6.00
8	Tony Gwynn,	
	Xavier Nady	10.00
9	Fergie Jenkins	4.00
10	Mark Prior	8.00
11	Nolan Ryan	15.00
12	Roy Oswalt	5.00
13	Ozzie Smith	6.00
14	J.D. Drew	4.00
15	George Brett	10.00
16	Carlos Beltran	6.00
17	Kirby Puckett	6.00
18	Michael Cuddyer	4.00
19	Johnny Bench	6.00
20	Adam Dunn	6.00
21	Duke Snider	6.00
22	Paul LoDuca	4.00
23	Tony Gwynn	6.00
24	Xavier Nady	4.00

Passing the Torch Autographs

		NM/M
Common Autograph:		15.00
1	Ferguson Jenkins,	
	Mark Prior/50	100.00
2	Nolan Ryan,	
	Roy Oswalt/50	180.00
3	Ozzie Smith,	
	J.D. Drew/50	125.00
4	George Brett,	
	Carlos Beltran/25	300.00
5	Kirby Puckett,	
	Michael Cuddyer/50	100.00
6	Johnny Bench,	
	Adam Dunn/50	100.00
7	Duke Snider,	
	Paul LoDuca/50	80.00
8	Tony Gwynn,	
	Xavier Nady/50	120.00
9	Fergie Jenkins/50	40.00
10	Mark Prior/100	80.00
11	Nolan Ryan/100	125.00
12	Roy Oswalt/100	25.00
13	Ozzie Smith/25	160.00
14	J.D. Drew/100	30.00
15	George Brett/25	300.00
16	Carlos Beltran/100	40.00
17	Kirby Puckett/25	150.00
18	Michael Cuddyer/100	15.00
19	Johnny Bench/100	50.00
20	Adam Dunn/100	40.00
21	Duke Snider/100	30.00
22	Paul LoDuca/100	15.00
23	Tony Gwynn/100	50.00
24	Xavier Nady/100	15.00

Recollection Collection

		NM/M
Common Player:		
2	Alfredo Amezaga	
	01/50	15.00
13	Orlando Hudson	
	01/50	20.00
18	Antonio Perez 01/50	15.00
20	Mike Rivera 01/50	15.00
22	Claudio Vargas 01/50	15.00
23	Martin Vargas 01/50	15.00

Throwback Threads

		NM/M
Common Card:		15.00

Dual 50, single 100 produced.

1	Manny Ramirez,	
	Ted Williams	125.00
2	Mike Piazza,	
	Carlton Fisk	50.00
3	George Brett,	
	Bo Jackson	125.00
4	Randy Johnson,	
	Curt Schilling	40.00
5	Don Mattingly,	
	Lou Gehrig	250.00
6	Bernie Williams,	
	Dave Winfield	25.00
7	Rickey Henderson	75.00
8	Paul Molitor,	
	Robin Yount	75.00
9	J.D. Drew,	
	Stan Musial	100.00
10	Andre Dawson,	
	Ryne Sandberg	100.00
11	Babe Ruth,	
	Reggie Jackson	325.00
12	Brooks Robinson,	
	Cal Ripken Jr.	120.00
13	Ted Williams,	
	Nomar Garciaparra	125.00
14	Shawn Green,	
	Jackie Robinson	80.00
15	Tony Gwynn,	
	Cal Ripken Jr.	120.00
16	Ted Williams	75.00
17	Manny Ramirez	20.00
18	Carlton Fisk	25.00
19	Mike Piazza	20.00
20	Bo Jackson	20.00
21	George Brett	50.00
22	Curt Schilling	20.00
23	Randy Johnson	20.00
24	Don Mattingly	50.00
25	Lou Gehrig	200.00
26	Bernie Williams	15.00
27	Dave Winfield	15.00
29	Rickey Henderson	40.00
30	Robin Yount	30.00
31	Paul Molitor	25.00
32	Stan Musial	65.00
33	J.D. Drew	15.00
34	Andre Dawson	15.00
35	Ryne Sandberg	50.00
36	Babe Ruth	250.00
37	Reggie Jackson	25.00
38	Brooks Robinson	25.00
39	Cal Ripken Jr.	75.00
40	Nomar Garciaparra	40.00
41	Jackie Robinson	80.00
42	Shawn Green	15.00
43	Pedro J. Martinez	20.00
44	Nolan Ryan	80.00
45	Kazuhiro Sasaki	15.00
46	Tony Gwynn	25.00
47	Carlton Fisk	20.00
48	Cal Ripken Jr.	75.00
49	Rod Carew	20.00
50	Nolan Ryan	80.00
51	Alex Rodriguez	25.00
52	Greg Maddux	25.00
53	Pedro J. Martinez	20.00
54	Rickey Henderson	30.00
55	Rod Carew	20.00
56	Roberto Clemente	100.00
57	Hideo Nomo	40.00
58	Rickey Williams	40.00
59	Dave Parker	15.00
60	Eddie Mathews	25.00
61	Eddie Murray	20.00
62	Nolan Ryan	80.00
63	Tom Seaver	25.00
64	Roger Clemens	40.00
65	Rickey Henderson	40.00

Throwback Threads Autographs

Production 5-25

Turn of the Century

		NM/M
Common Player:		8.00
154	Jorge De La Rosa/50	8.00
156	Carlos Zambrano/50	8.00
157	Kyle Kane/50	8.00
158	So Taguchi/25	15.00
159	Brian Mallette/50	8.00
160	Brett Jodie/50	8.00
165	Matt Guerrier/50	8.00
168	Franklin German/50	8.00
169	Brandon Claussen/50	15.00
171	Jorge Padilla/50	10.00
172	Jose Cueto/50	8.00
176	Josh Pearce/50	8.00
177	Steve Bechler/50	8.00
178	Josh Phelps/50	8.00
180	Victor Alvarez/50	8.00
182	Michael Rivera/50	8.00
183	Kazuhisa Ishii/125	20.00
184	Henry Mateo/50	8.00
186	Zach Day/50	8.00
189	Nick Neugebauer/100	8.00
192	Adam Johnson/125	8.00
193	Michael Cuddyer/50	8.00
195	Mark Ellis/25	10.00
196	Carlos Hernandez/150	8.00
198	Morgan Ensberg/50	8.00
200	Cody Ransom/150	8.00

Turn of the Century Autographs

		NM/M
Common Autograph:		10.00
151	Cam Esslinger/150	10.00
152	Ben Howard/150	10.00
153	Brandon Backe/150	15.00
154	Jorge De La Rosa/	
	100	10.00
155	Austin Kearns/150	15.00
156	Carlos Zambrano/100	20.00
157	Kyle Kane/100	10.00
158	So Taguchi/125	20.00
159	Brian Mallette/100	10.00
160	Brett Jodie/100	10.00
161	Elio Serrano/150	10.00
162	Joe Thurston/150	10.00
163	Kevin Olsen/150	10.00
164	Rodrigo Rosario/150	10.00
165	Matt Guerrier/150	10.00
166	Anderson Machado/	
	150	10.00
167	Bert Snow/150	10.00
168	Franklin German/100	10.00
169	Brandon Claussen/	
	100	15.00
170	Jason Romano/150	10.00
171	Jorge Padilla/100	15.00
172	Jose Cueto/100	10.00
173	Allan Simpson/150	10.00
174	Doug DeVore/150	15.00
175	Justin Duchscherer/	
	150	10.00
176	Josh Pearce/100	10.00
177	Steve Bechler/100	10.00
178	Josh Phelps/100	15.00
179	Juan Diaz/150	10.00
180	Victor Alvarez/100	10.00
181	Ramon Vazquez/150	10.00
182	Michael Rivera/100	10.00
183	Kazuhisa Ishii/25	150.00
184	Henry Mateo/100	10.00
185	Travis Hughes/150	10.00
186	Zach Day/100	10.00
187	Brad Voyles/150	10.00
188	Sean Douglass/150	10.00
189	Nick Neugebauer/50	10.00
190	Tom Shearn/150	10.00
191	Eric Cyr/150	10.00
192	Adam Johnson/25	10.00
193	Michael Cuddyer/100	10.00
194	Erik Bedard/150	20.00
195	Mark Ellis/125	10.00
197	Deivis Santos/150	10.00
198	Morgan Ensberg/100	10.00
199	Ryan Jamison/150	10.00

2002 Donruss Fan Club

		NM/M
Complete Set (300):		
Common Player:		.25
Common (201-260):		3.00
Production 1,350		
Common (261-300):		2.00
Production 2,025		
Pack (5):		3.50
Box (20):		60.00
1	Alex Rodriguez	2.00
2	Pedro Martinez	.75
3	Vladimir Guerrero	.75
4	Jim Edmonds	.25

#	Player	Price
5	Derek Jeter	2.50
6	Johnny Damon	.40
7	Rafael Furcal	.25
8	Cal Ripken Jr.	2.50
9	Brad Radke	.25
10	Bret Boone	.25
11	Pat Burrell	.50
12	Roy Oswalt	.50
13	Cliff Floyd	.25
14	Robin Ventura	.25
15	Frank Thomas	.75
16	Mariano Rivera	.35
17	Paul LoDuca	.25
18	Geoff Jenkins	.25
19	Tony Gwynn	1.00
20	Chipper Jones	1.00
21	Eric Chavez	.40
22	Kerry Wood	.60
23	Jorge Posada	.35
24	J.D. Drew	.40
25	Garret Anderson	.25
26	Javier Vazquez	.25
27	Kenny Lofton	.25
28	Mike Mussina	.45
29	Paul Konerko	.25
30	Bernie Williams	.45
31	Eric Milton	.25
32	Craig Wilson	.25
33	Paul O'Neill	.25
34	Dmitri Young	.25
35	Andres Galarraga	.25
36	Gary Sheffield	.40
37	Ben Grieve	.25
38	Scott Rolen	.75
39	Mark Grace	.35
40	Albert Pujols	2.00
41	Barry Zito	.40
42	Edgar Martinez	.25
43	Jarrod Washburn	.25
44	Juan Pierre	.25
45	Mark Buehrle	.25
46	Larry Walker	.25
47	Trot Nixon	.25
48	Wade Miller	.25
49	Robert Fick	.25
50	Sean Casey	.40
51	Joe Mays	.25
52	Brad Fullmer	.25
53	Chan Ho Park	.25
54	Carlos Delgado	.50
55	Phil Nevin	.25
56	Mike Cameron	.25
57	Raul Mondesi	.25
58	Roberto Alomar	.40
59	Ryan Klesko	.25
60	Andruw Jones	.75
61	Gabe Kapler	.25
62	Darin Erstad	.65
63	Cristian Guzman	.25
64	Kazuhiro Sasaki	.25
65	Doug Mientkiewicz	.25
66	Sammy Sosa	1.50
67	Mike Hampton	.25
68	Rickey Henderson	.75
69	Mark Mulder	.35
70	Jeff Conine	.25
71	Freddy Garcia	.25
72	Ivan Rodriguez	.65
73	Terrence Long	.25
74	Adam Dunn	.50
75	Moises Alou	.25
76	Todd Helton	.75
77	Preston Wilson	.25
78	Roger Cedeno	.25
79	Tony Armas Jr.	.25
80	Manny Ramirez	.75
81	Jose Vidro	.25
82	Randy Johnson	.75
83	Richie Sexson	.25
84	Troy Glaus	.75
85	Kevin Brown	.35
86	Woody Williams	.25
87	Adrian Beltre	.40
88	Brian Giles	.25
89	Jermaine Dye	.25
90	Craig Biggio	.25
91	Richard Hidalgo	.25
92	Magglio Ordonez	.40
93	Al Leiter	.25
94	Jeff Kent	.25
95	Curt Schilling	.50
96	Tim Hudson	.50
97	Fred McGriff	.25
98	Barry Larkin	.25
99	Jim Thome	.25
100	Tom Glavine	.40
101	Alfonso Soriano	.75
102	Jamie Moyer	.25
103	Vinny Castilla	.25
104	Rich Aurilia	.25
105	Matt Morris	.25
106	Rafael Palmeiro	.65
107	Joe Crede	.25
108	Barry Bonds	2.50
109	Robert Person	.25
110	Nomar Garciaparra	1.50
111	Brandon Duckworth	.25
112	Russ Ortiz	.25
113	Jeff Weaver	.25
114	Carlos Beltran	.50
115	Ellis Burks	.25
116	Jeremy Giambi	.25
117	Carlos Lee	.25
118	Ken Griffey Jr.	1.50
119	Torii Hunter	.40
120	Andy Petitte	.40
121	Jose Canseco	.40
122	Charles Johnson	.25
123	Nick Johnson	.25
124	Luis Gonzalez	.35
125	Rondell White	.25
126	Miguel Tejada	.50
127	Jose Cruz Jr.	.25
128	Brent Abernathy	.25
129	Scott Brosius	.25
130	Jon Lieber	.25
131	John Smoltz	.25
132	Mike Sweeney	.25
133	Shannon Stewart	.25
134	Derrek Lee	.25
135	Brian Jordan	.25
136	Rusty Greer	.25
137	Mike Piazza	1.50
138	Billy Wagner	.25
139	Shawn Green	.35
140	Orlando Cabrera	.25
141	Jeff Bagwell	.75
142	Aaron Sele	.25
143	Hideo Nomo	.75
144	Marlon Anderson	.25
145	Todd Walker	.25
146	Bobby Higginson	.25
147	Ichiro Suzuki	2.00
148	Juan Uribe	.25
149	Jason Kendall	.25
150	Mark Quinn	.25
151	Ben Sheets	.25
152	Paul Abbott	.25
153	Aubrey Huff	.25
154	Greg Maddux	1.00
155	Darryl Kile	.25
156	John Burkett	.25
157	Juan Gonzalez	.75
158	Javy Lopez	.25
159	Aramis Ramirez	.25
160	Lance Berkman	.25
161	David Cone	.25
162	Edgar Renteria	.25
163	Roger Clemens	1.25
164	Frank Catalanotto	.25
165	Bartolo Colon	.25
166	Mark McGwire	2.00
167	Jay Gibbons	.25
168	Tony Clark	.25
169	Tsuyoshi Shinjo	.25
170	Brad Penny	.25
171	Marcus Giles	.25
172	Matt Williams	.25
173	Bud Smith	.25
174	Tino Martinez	.25
175	Ryan Dempster	.25
176	Jimmy Rollins	.40
177	Edgardo Alfonzo	.25
178	Jason Giambi	.50
179	Aaron Boone	.25
180	Matt Dunigan	.25
181	Mike Lowell	.25
182	Jose Ortiz	.25
183	Johnny Estrada	.25
184	Shane Reynolds	.25
185	Joe Kennedy	.25
186	Corey Patterson	.25
187	Jeromy Burnitz	.25
188	C.C. Sabathia	.25
189	Doug Davis	.25
190	Omar Vizquel	.25
191	John Olerud	.25
192	Dee Brown	.25
193	Kip Wells	.25
194	A.J. Burnett	.25
195	Josh Towers	.25
196	Jason Varitek	.25
197	Jason Isringhausen	.25
198	Fernando Vina	.25
199	Ramon Ortiz	.25
200	Bobby Abreu	.25
201	Willie Harris	3.00
202	Angel Santos	3.00
203	Corky Miller	3.00
204	Mike Rivera	3.00
205	Justin Duchscherer	3.00
206	Rick Bauer	3.00
207	Angel Berroa	3.00
208	Juan Cruz	3.00
209	Dewon Brazelton	3.00
210	Mark Prior	10.00
211	Mark Teixeira	8.00
212	Geronimo Gil	3.00
213	Casey Fossum	3.00
214	Ken Harvey	3.00
215	Michael Cuddyer	3.00
216	Wilson Betemit	3.00
217	David Brous	3.00
218	Juan Pena	3.00
219	Travis Hafner	4.00
220	Erick Almonte	3.00
221	Morgan Ensberg	3.00
222	Martin Vargas	3.00
223	Brandon Berger	3.00
224	Zach Day	3.00
225	Brad Voyles	3.00
226	Jeremy Affeldt	3.00
227	Nick Neugebauer	3.00
228	Tim Redding	3.00
229	Adam Johnson	3.00
230	Doug DeVore RC	4.00
231	Cody Ransom	3.00
232	Marlon Byrd	3.00
233	Delvin James	3.00
234	Eric Munson	3.00
235	Dennis Tankersley	3.00
236	Josh Beckett	8.00
237	Bill Hall	3.00
238	Kevin Olsen	3.00
239	Francis Beltran RC	5.00
240	Antonio Perez	3.00
241	Orlando Hudson	3.00
242	Anderson Machado RC	6.00
243	Tom Shearn RC	4.00
244	Brian Mallette RC	4.00
245	Raul Chavez RC	4.00
246	Andy Pratt RC	4.00
247	Jorge De La Rosa RC	4.00
248	Jeff Deardorff RC	4.00
249	Ben Howard RC	4.00
250	Brandon Backe RC	4.00
251	Ed Rogers	3.00
252	Travis Hughes RC	5.00
253	Rodrigo Rosario RC	5.00
254	Alfredo Amezaga	3.00
255	Jorge Padilla RC	5.00
256	Victor Martinez	4.00
257	Steve Bechler RC	4.00
258	Chris Baker	4.00
259	Ryan Freel	3.00
260	Allan Simpson RC	3.00
261	Alex Rodriguez	6.00
262	Vladimir Guerrero	3.00
263	Bud Smith	2.00
264	Miguel Tejada	2.00
265	Craig Biggio	2.00
266	Luis Gonzalez	2.00
267	Ivan Rodriguez	3.00
268	C.C. Sabathia	2.00
269	Jeff Bagwell	3.00
270	Aramis Ramirez	2.00
271	Bobby Abreu	2.00
272	Rich Aurilia	2.00
273	Jason Giambi	3.00
274	Rickey Henderson	3.00
275	Wade Miller	2.00
276	Andruw Jones	3.00
277	Troy Glaus	2.00
278	Roy Oswalt	2.00
279	Tony Gwynn	3.00
280	Adam Dunn	3.00
281	Larry Walker	2.00
282	Jose Canseco	3.00
283	Todd Helton	2.00
284	Lance Berkman	2.00
285	Cal Ripken Jr.	10.00
286	Albert Pujols	8.00
287	Alfonso Soriano	3.00
288	Mark Mulder	2.00
289	Mike Hampton	2.00
290	Andres Galarraga	2.00
291	Barry Bonds	8.00
292	Ben Sheets	2.00
293	Ichiro Suzuki	6.00
294	J.D. Drew	2.00
295	Jose Ortiz	2.00
296	Kerry Wood	3.00
297	Mark McGwire	8.00
298	Mike Sweeney	2.00
299	Pat Burrell	3.00
300	Tim Hudson	3.00

Artist

		NM/M
Complete Set (14):		60.00
Common Player:		3.00
Production 300 Sets		
1	Pedro Martinez	8.00
2	Curt Schilling	6.00
3	Kevin Brown	3.00
4	Tim Hudson	5.00
5	Kerry Wood	7.50
6	Barry Zito	4.00
7	Hideo Nomo	6.00
8	Randy Johnson	8.00
9	Greg Maddux	10.00
10	Roger Clemens	15.00
11	Kazuhiro Sasaki	3.00
12	Joe Mays	3.00
13	Mark Mulder	3.00
14	Javier Vazquez	3.00

Artist Autographs

	NM/M
Production 15-100	
6 Barry Zito/100	35.00

Autographs

		NM/M
Common Player:		5.00
Varying quantities produced		
201	Willie Harris/500	5.00
203	Corky Miller/500	5.00
205	Justin Duchscherer/500	8.00
207	Angel Berroa/100	15.00
208	Juan Cruz/175	8.00
209	Dewon Brazelton/52	15.00
210	Mark Prior/425	40.00
211	Mark Teixeira/425	25.00
213	Casey Fossum/100	10.00
215	Michael Cuddyer/52	15.00
216	Wilson Betemit/500	8.00
217	David Brous/500	5.00
218	Juan A. Pena/188	8.00
219	Travis Hafner/375	5.00
221	Morgan Ensberg/52	15.00
222	Martin Vargas/500	5.00
223	Brandon Berger/500	5.00
224	Zach Day/500	5.00
225	Brad Voyles/500	5.00
226	Jeremy Affeldt/250	5.00
227	Nick Neugebauer/225	8.00
228	Tim Redding/500	5.00
229	Adam Johnson/425	5.00
230	Doug DeVore/300	8.00
231	Cody Ransom/500	5.00
232	Marlon Byrd/475	15.00
233	Delvin James/375	5.00
234	Eric Munson/325	8.00
235	Dennis Tankersley/500	5.00
238	Kevin Olsen/325	5.00
240	Antonio Perez/525	5.00
241	Orlando Hudson/525	10.00
248	Jeff Deardorff/475	5.00
251	Ed Rogers/400	5.00
255	Jorge Padilla/450	15.00
260	Allan Simpson/475	8.00
278	Roy Oswalt/75	35.00

Craftsmen

		NM/M
Complete Set (18):		80.00
Common Player:		3.00
Production 300 Sets		
1	Ichiro Suzuki	10.00
2	Todd Helton	5.00
3	Manny Ramirez	5.00
4	Luis Gonzalez	3.00
5	Roberto Alomar	3.50
6	Moises Alou	3.00
7	Darin Erstad	5.00
8	Mike Piazza	10.00
9	Edgar Martinez	3.00
10	Vladimir Guerrero	6.00
11	Juan Gonzalez	3.00
12	Nomar Garciaparra	10.00
13	Tony Gwynn	6.00
14	Jeff Bagwell	3.00
15	Albert Pujols	15.00
16	Larry Walker	3.00
17	Paul LoDuca	3.00
18	Lance Berkman	3.00

Craftsmen Autographs

		NM/M
Common Player:		
17	Paul LoDuca/100	20.00

Master Craftsmen

		NM/M
Common Player:		5.00
Production 150 Sets/H		
1	Ichiro Suzuki/Ball/51	75.00
2	Todd Helton	10.00
3	Manny Ramirez	10.00
4	Luis Gonzalez	8.00
5	Roberto Alomar	8.00
6	Moises Alou	8.00
7	Darin Erstad	8.00
8	Mike Piazza	15.00
9	Edgar Martinez	8.00
10	Vladimir Guerrero	15.00
11	Juan Gonzalez	8.00
12	Nomar Garciaparra	20.00
13	Tony Gwynn/175	20.00
14	Jeff Bagwell	10.00
15	Albert Pujols/175	25.00
16	Larry Walker/175	5.00
17	Paul LoDuca/175	5.00
18	Lance Berkman	8.00

Double Features

		NM/M
Complete Set (10):		80.00
Common Card:		8.00
Production 125 Sets		
1	Larry Walker, Todd Helton	10.00
2	Jose Vidro, Vladimir Guerrero	10.00
3	Jason Giambi, Jeremy Giambi	8.00
4	Nomar Garciaparra, Manny Ramirez	15.00
5	Troy Glaus, Darin Erstad	8.00
6	Shawn Green, Paul LoDuca	8.00
7	Jeff Bagwell, Craig Biggio	10.00
8	Pedro Martinez, Hideo Nomo	12.00
9	Curt Schilling, Randy Johnson	10.00
10	Andruw Jones, Chipper Jones	12.50

Double Features Game-Used

		NM/M
Common Card:		10.00
Production 50 Sets		
1	Larry Walker, Todd Helton	15.00
2	Jose Vidro, Vladimir Guerrero	20.00
3	Jason Giambi, Jeremy Giambi	15.00
4	Nomar Garciaparra, Manny Ramirez	30.00
5	Troy Glaus, Darin Erstad	15.00
6	Shawn Green, Paul LoDuca	10.00
7	Jeff Bagwell, Craig Biggio	15.00
8	Pedro Martinez, Hideo Nomo	30.00
9	Curt Schilling, Randy Johnson	20.00
10	Andruw Jones, Chipper Jones	20.00

Franchise Features

		NM/M
Complete Set (40):		180.00
Common Player:		3.00
Production 300 Sets		

1	Cliff Floyd	3.00
2	Mike Piazza	12.00
3	Cal Ripken Jr.	25.00
4	Mike Sweeney	3.00
5	Curt Schilling	5.00
6	Aramis Ramirez	3.00
7	Vladimir Guerrero	8.00
8	Andruw Jones	8.00
9	Tim Hudson	3.00
10	Bernie Williams	3.00
11	Pedro Martinez	8.00
12	Roberto Alomar	3.00
13	Joe Mays	3.00
14	Jason Giambi	5.00
15	Kazuhiro Sasaki	3.00
16	Magglio Ordonez	3.00
17	Nomar Garciaparra	12.00
18	Juan Gonzalez	8.00
19	Carlos Beltran	5.00
20	Javier Vazquez	3.00
21	Miguel Tejada	3.00
22	Luis Gonzalez	3.00
23	Greg Maddux	10.00
24	Rafael Palmeiro	6.00
25	Freddy Garcia	3.00
26	Barry Zito	4.00
27	Paul LoDuca	3.00
28	Robert Fick	3.00
29	Roger Clemens	10.00
30	Eric Chavez	3.00
31	Ivan Rodriguez	6.00
32	Chipper Jones	10.00
33	Kerry Wood	6.00
34	Randy Johnson	8.00
35	Alex Rodriguez	12.00
36	Manny Ramirez	8.00
37	Mark Buehrle	3.00
38	Mark Mulder	3.00
39	Ichiro Suzuki	15.00
40	Troy Glaus	4.00

Franchise Features Game-Used

		NM/M
Common Player:		4.00
Production 150 Sets		
All jerseys unless noted.		
1	Cliff Floyd	4.00
2	Mike Piazza	15.00
3	Cal Ripken Jr.	30.00
4	Mike Sweeney	4.00
5	Curt Schilling	8.00
6	Aramis Ramirez	6.00
7	Vladimir Guerrero	8.00
8	Andruw Jones	8.00
9	Tim Hudson	6.00
10	Bernie Williams	6.00
11	Pedro Martinez	10.00
12	Roberto Alomar	6.00
13	Joe Mays	4.00
14	Jason Giambi	8.00
15	Kazuhiro Sasaki	5.00
16	Magglio Ordonez	6.00
17	Nomar Garciaparra	20.00
18	Juan Gonzalez	8.00
19	Carlos Beltran	8.00
20	Javier Vazquez	4.00
21	Miguel Tejada	8.00
22	Luis Gonzalez	5.00
23	Greg Maddux	15.00
24	Rafael Palmeiro	10.00
25	Freddy Garcia	4.00
26	Barry Zito	8.00
27	Paul LoDuca	4.00
28	Robert Fick	4.00
29	Roger Clemens	20.00
30	Eric Chavez/bat	4.00
31	Ivan Rodriguez	8.00
32	Chipper Jones	8.00
33	Kerry Wood	10.00
34	Randy Johnson	10.00
35	Alex Rodriguez	15.00
36	Manny Ramirez	8.00
37	Mark Buehrle	4.00
38	Mark Mulder	6.00
39	Ichiro Suzuki/Ball	80.00
40	Troy Glaus	6.00

Franchise Features Autographs

		NM/M
Production 15-100		
6	Aramis Ramirez/100	20.00
9	Tim Hudson/50	25.00
13	Joe Mays/75	10.00
19	Carlos Beltran/100	20.00
25	Freddy Garcia/100	20.00
26	Barry Zito/100	30.00
27	Paul LoDuca/100	15.00
28	Robert Fick/100	15.00
30	Eric Chavez/50	20.00
37	Mark Buehrle/100	15.00

League Leaders

		NM/M
Common Player:		3.00
Production 300 Sets		
1	Roger Clemens	12.00
2	Curt Schilling	5.00
3	Matt Morris	3.00
4	Randy Johnson	6.00
5	Mark Mulder	4.00
6	Curt Schilling	5.00
7	Mike Mussina	4.00
8	Joe Mays	3.00
9	Matt Morris	3.00
10	Tim Hudson	4.00
11	Mark Buehrle	3.00
12	Greg Maddux	10.00
13	Freddy Garcia	3.00
14	Randy Johnson	6.00
15	Curt Schilling	5.00
16	Chan Ho Park	3.00
17	Roger Clemens	12.00
18	Mike Mussina	4.00
19	Javier Vazquez	3.00
20	Kerry Wood	6.00
21	Randy Johnson	6.00
22	Barry Zito	4.00
23	Hideo Nomo	8.00
24	Ichiro Suzuki	10.00
25	Todd Helton	6.00
26	Albert Pujols	20.00
27	Alex Rodriguez	12.00
28	Shannon Stewart	3.00
29	Luis Gonzalez	3.00
30	Alex Rodriguez	12.00
31	Barry Bonds	20.00
32	Sammy Sosa	15.00
33	Luis Gonzalez	3.00
34	Todd Helton	6.00
35	Jim Thome	3.00
36	Shawn Green	4.00
37	Jeff Bagwell	7.50
38	Todd Helton	5.00
39	Luis Gonzalez	3.00
40	Lance Berkman	3.00
41	Juan Gonzalez	3.00
42	Larry Walker	3.00
43	Ichiro Suzuki	10.00
44	Lance Berkman	3.00
45	Todd Helton	5.00

League Leaders Autographs

		NM/M
Production 15-100		
5	Mark Mulder/100	20.00
11	Mark Buehrle/100	15.00
13	Freddy Garcia/100	15.00
19	Javier Vazquez/100	15.00
26	Albert Pujols/100	150.00
28	Shannon Stewart/100	15.00

League Leaders Game-Used

		NM/M
Common Player:		4.00
Production 150 or 175		
1	Roger Clemens	20.00
2	Curt Schilling	10.00
3	Randy Johnson	8.00
5	Mark Mulder	6.00
6	Curt Schilling	10.00
7	Mike Mussina/Shoe/50	25.00
8	Joe Mays	6.00
10	Tim Hudson	6.00
11	Mark Buehrle	6.00
12	Greg Maddux	15.00
13	Freddy Garcia	4.00
14	Randy Johnson	8.00
15	Curt Schilling	10.00
16	Chan Ho Park	4.00
17	Roger Clemens	20.00
18	Mike Mussina/Shoe/50	25.00
19	Javier Vazquez	4.00
20	Kerry Wood	10.00
21	Randy Johnson	8.00
22	Barry Zito	6.00
23	Hideo Nomo	10.00
24	Ichiro Suzuki/Ball/51	75.00
25	Todd Helton	8.00
26	Albert Pujols	20.00
27	Alex Rodriguez	15.00
28	Shannon Stewart	4.00
29	Luis Gonzalez	5.00
30	Alex Rodriguez	15.00
31	Barry Bonds	25.00
32	Sammy Sosa	15.00
33	Luis Gonzalez	4.00
34	Todd Helton	8.00
35	Jim Thome	10.00
36	Shawn Green	5.00
37	Jeff Bagwell	8.00
38	Todd Helton	8.00
39	Luis Gonzalez	4.00
40	Lance Berkman	5.00
41	Juan Gonzalez	6.00
42	Larry Walker	4.00
43	Ichiro Suzuki/Ball/51	75.00
44	Lance Berkman	4.00
45	Todd Helton	8.00

Master Artists

		NM/M
Common Player:		5.00
Production 150 Sets		
1	Pedro Martinez	15.00
2	Curt Schilling	10.00
3	Kevin Brown	5.00
4	Tim Hudson	6.00
5	Kerry Wood	5.00
6	Barry Zito	8.00
7	Hideo Nomo	15.00
8	Randy Johnson	15.00
9	Greg Maddux	15.00
10	Roger Clemens	20.00
11	Kazuhiro Sasaki	5.00
12	Joe Mays	5.00
13	Mark Mulder	5.00
14	Javier Vazquez	5.00

Pure Power

		NM/M
Complete Set (18):		65.00
Common Player:		2.00
Production 300 Sets		
1	Sammy Sosa	8.00
2	Lance Berkman	2.00
3	Chipper Jones	6.00
4	Troy Glaus	4.00
5	Barry Bonds	12.00
6	Todd Helton	4.00
7	Manny Ramirez	4.00
8	Jason Giambi	3.00
9	Juan Gonzalez	4.00
10	Albert Pujols	10.00
11	Jim Thome	2.00
12	Mike Piazza	8.00
13	Frank Thomas	4.00
14	Richie Sexson	2.00
15	Jeff Bagwell	4.00
16	Rafael Palmeiro	3.00
17	Luis Gonzalez	2.00
18	Shawn Green	2.50

Pure Power Autographs

		NM/M
Varying quantities produced		
14	Richie Sexson/100	20.00

Pure Power Masters

		NM/M
Complete Set (18)		125.00
Common Player:		5.00
Production 150		
1	Sammy Sosa	15.00
2	Lance Berkman	5.00
3	Chipper Jones	10.00
4	Troy Glaus	8.00
5	Barry Bonds	25.00
6	Todd Helton	8.00
7	Manny Ramirez	8.00

#	Player	NM/M
8	Jason Giambi	6.00
9	Juan Gonzalez	8.00
10	Albert Pujols	20.00
11	Jim Thome	5.00
12	Mike Piazza	15.00
13	Frank Thomas	8.00
14	Richie Sexson	5.00
15	Jeff Bagwell	8.00
16	Rafael Palmeiro	6.00
17	Luis Gonzalez	5.00
18	Shawn Green	6.00

Records

		NM/M
Complete Set (5):		50.00
Common Player:		8.00
Production 300		
1	Barry Bonds	15.00
2	Barry Bonds	15.00
3	Barry Bonds	15.00
4	Rickey Henderson	8.00
5	Rickey Henderson	8.00

Records Game-Used

		NM/M
Production 150		
1	Barry Bonds	40.00
2	Barry Bonds	40.00
3	Barry Bonds	40.00
4	Rickey Henderson	20.00
5	Rickey Henderson	20.00

2002 Donruss Originals

Mike Piazza c

		NM/M
Complete Set (400):		75.00
Common Player:		.10
Common Rated Rookie:		.50
Pack (5):		2.00
Hobby Box (24):		40.00
1	So Taguchi/RR RC	.75
2	Allan Simpson/RR RC	.50
3	Brian Mallette/RR RC	.50
4	Ben Howard/RR RC	.50
5	Kazuhisa Ishii/RR RC	2.00
6	Francis Beltran/RR RC	.50
7	Jorge Padilla/RR RC	.50
8	Brandon Puffer/RR RC	.50
9	Oliver Perez/RR RC	1.50
10	Kirk Saarloos/RR	.50
11	Travis Driskill/RR RC	.50
12	Jeremy Lambert/RR RC	.50
13	John Foster/RR RC	.50
14	Steve Kent/RR RC	.50
15	Shawn Sedlacek/RR RC	.50
16	Alex Rodriguez	1.25
17	Lance Berkman	.10
18	Kevin Brown	.10
19	Garret Anderson	.10
20	Bobby Abreu	.10
21	Richard Hidalgo	.10
22	Matt Morris	.10
23	Manny Ramirez	.60
24	Derek Jeter	1.50
25	Kerry Wood	.50
26	Mark Grace	.15
27	Edgar Martinez	.10
28	Nomar Garciaparra	1.00
29	Roberto Alomar	.25
30	Jason Giambi	.50
31	Juan Gonzalez	.60
32	Albert Pujols	1.00
33	Juan Cruz	.10
34	Troy Glaus	.60
35	Greg Maddux	.75
36	Adam Dunn	.40
37	J.D. Drew	.25
38	Tsuyoshi Shinjo	.10
39	Vladimir Guerrero	.60
40	Barry Bonds	1.50
41	Carlos Delgado	.40
42	Ken Griffey Jr.	1.00
43	Carlos Pena	.10
44	Jeff Kent	.10
45	Roger Clemens	.75
46	Frank Thomas	.60
47	Larry Walker	.10
48	Pedro J. Martinez	.60
49	Moises Alou	.10
50	Andruw Jones	.60
51	Luis Gonzalez	.25
52	Adrian Beltre	.10
53	Bobby Hill	.10
54	Roy Oswalt	.20
55	Tim Hudson	.20
56	Trot Nixon	.10
57	Jeff Bagwell	.60
58	Bernie Williams	.30
59	Magglio Ordonez	.25
60	Bartolo Colon	.10
61	Shawn Green	.20
62	Mark Buehrle	.10
63	Sean Casey	.10
64	Rickey Henderson	.60
65	Aramis Ramirez	.10
66	Ichiro Suzuki	1.00
67	Cliff Floyd	.10
68	Darin Erstad	.40
69	Paul LoDuca	.10
70	Ivan Rodriguez	.50
71	Mo Vaughn	.10
72	Todd Helton	.60
73	Raul Mondesi	.10
74	Sammy Sosa	1.00
75	Cristian Guzman	.10
76	Jimmy Rollins	.25
77	Hideo Nomo	.50
78	C.C. Sabathia	.10
79	Wade Miller	.10
80	Drew Henson	.20
81	Chipper Jones	.75
82	Miguel Tejada	.25
83	Freddy Garcia	.10
84	Richie Sexson	.10
85	Robin Ventura	.10
86	Jose Vidro	.10
87	Rich Aurilia	.10
88	Scott Rolen	.60
89	Carlos Beltran	.40
90	Austin Kearns	.25
91	Kazuhiro Sasaki	.10
92	Carlos Hernandez	.10
93	Randy Johnson	.60
94	Jim Thome	.10
95	Curt Schilling	.40
96	Alfonso Soriano	.50
97	Barry Larkin	.10
98	Rafael Palmeiro	.50
99	Tom Glavine	.25
100	Barry Zito	.20
101	Craig Biggio	.20
102	Mike Piazza	1.00
103	Ben Sheets	.20
104	Mark Mulder	.20
105	Mike Mussina	.25
106	Jim Edmonds	.10
107	Paul Konerko	.10
108	Pat Burrell	.25
109	Chan Ho Park	.10
110	Mike Sweeney	.10
111	Phil Nevin	.10
112	Brian Giles	.10
113	Eric Chavez	.20
114	Corey Patterson	.20
115	Gary Sheffield	.25
116	Kazuhisa Ishii/RR	2.00
117	Kyle Kane/RR RC	.50
118	Eric Junge/RR RC	.50
119	Luis Ugueto/RR RC	.50
120	Cam Esslinger/RR RC	.50
121	Earl Snyder/RR RC	.50
122	Oliver Perez/RR RC	1.50
123	Victor Alvarez/RR RC	.50
124	Tom Shearn/RR RC	.50
125	Corey Thurman/RR RC	.50
126	Satoru Komiyama/RR RC	.50
127	Hansel Izquierdo/RR RC	.50
128	Elio Serrano/RR RC	.50
129	Michael Crudale/RR RC	.50
130	Chris Snelling/RR RC	1.50
131	Nomar Garciaparra	1.00
132	Roger Clemens	.75
133	Hank Blalock	.25
134	Eric Chavez	.20
135	Corey Patterson	.20
136	Richie Sexson	.10
137	Freddy Garcia	.10
138	Miguel Tejada	.25
139	Alex Rodriguez/SP	1.50
140	Adrian Beltre	.10
141	Bobby Abreu	.10
142	Bret Boone	.10
143	Tim Hudson	.20
144	Roy Oswalt	.20
145	Derek Jeter	1.50
146	Rich Aurilia	.10
147	Mark Grace	.15
148	Kerry Wood/SP	1.00
149	Geronimo Gil	.10
150	Mark Buehrle	.10
151	Jim Edmonds	.10
152	Ichiro Suzuki	1.00
153	Juan Gonzalez	.60
154	Darin Erstad	.40
155	Barry Bonds/SP	2.50
156	Greg Maddux	.75
157	Adam Dunn	.40
158	Todd Helton	.60
159	Roberto Alomar	.25
160	Sammy Sosa	1.00
161	Sean Burroughs	.10
162	Albert Pujols	1.00
163	Carlos Delgado	.25
164	Frank Thomas	.60
165	Ken Griffey Jr.	1.00
166	Jason Giambi/SP	1.00
167	Chipper Jones	.75
168	Ivan Rodriguez	.50
169	Pedro Martinez/SP	1.00
170	Gary Sheffield	.25
171	Andruw Jones	.60
172	Luis Gonzalez	.25
173	Raul Mondesi	.10
174	Jose Vidro	.10
175	Garret Anderson/SP	.50
176	Scott Rolen	.60
177	Kazuhiro Sasaki	.10
178	Jeff Bagwell	.60
179	Manny Ramirez	.60
180	Jim Thome	.10
181	Ben Sheets	.20
182	Randy Johnson	.60
183	Lance Berkman	.10
184	Shawn Green	.20
185	Rickey Henderson	.60
186	Edgar Martinez	.10
187	Barry Larkin	.10
188	Bernie Williams	.30
189	Luis Aparicio	.10
190	Troy Glaus/SP	.50
191	Mike Mussina	.30
192	Pee Wee Reese	.20
193	Craig Biggio	.10
194	Vladimir Guerrero	.60
195	J.D. Drew	.20
196	Jeff Kent	.10
197	Dewon Brazelton	.10
198	Tsuyoshi Shinjo/SP	.40
199	Sean Casey	.10
200	Hideo Nomo	.50
201	C.C. Sabathia	.10
202	Larry Walker	.10
203	Mark Teixeira	.20
204	Mike Sweeney	.10
205	Moises Alou	.10
206	Mark Prior	.75
207	Javier Vazquez	.10
208	Phil Nevin	.10
209	Harmon Killebrew	.50
210	Brian Giles	.10
211	Carlos Beltran	.40
212	Don Drysdale	.40
213	Matt Morris	.10
214	Trot Nixon	.10
215	Magglio Ordonez	.25
216	Curt Schilling/SP	.75
217	Mark Mulder	.20
218	Alfonso Soriano	1.00
219	Rafael Palmeiro/SP	.75
220	Tom Glavine	.25
221	Barry Zito	.25
222	Mike Piazza	1.00
223	Bartolo Colon	.10
224	Cliff Floyd	.10
225	Paul LoDuca	.10
226	Cristian Guzman	.10
227	Mo Vaughn	.10
228	Aramis Ramirez	.10
229	Pat Burrell	.25
230	Chan Ho Park	.10
231	Satoru Komiyama/RR	.50
232	Brandon Backe/RR RC	.50
233	Anderson Machado/RR RC	.50
234	Doug DeVore/RR RC	.50
235	Steve Bechler/RR RC	.50
236	John Ennis/RR RC	.50
237	Rodrigo Rosario/RR RC	.50
238	Jorge Sosa/RR RC	.50
239	Ken Huckaby/RR RC	.50
240	Mike Moriarty/RR RC	.50
241	Kirk Saarloos/RR	1.00
242	Kevin Frederick/RR RC	.50
243	Aaron Guiel/RR RC	.50
244	Jose Rodriguez/RR RC	.50
245	So Taguchi/RR	1.00
246	Albert Pujols	1.00
247	Derek Jeter	1.50
248	Brian Giles	.10
249	Mike Cameron	.10
250	Josh Beckett	.25
251	Ken Griffey Jr./SP	1.50
252	Aramis Ramirez	.10
253	Miguel Tejada	.25
254	Carlos Delgado	.25
255	Pedro J. Martinez	.60
256	Raul Mondesi	.10
257	Roger Clemens	.75
258	Gary Sheffield	.25
259	Jose Vidro	.10
260	Alex Rodriguez	1.25
261	Larry Walker	.10
262	Mark Mulder	.20
263	Scott Rolen	.60
264	Tim Hudson	.20
265	Manny Ramirez	.60
266	Rich Aurilia	.10
267	Roy Oswalt	.20
268	Mark Grace	.15
269	Lance Berkman	.10
270	Nomar Garciaparra	1.00
271	Barry Bonds	1.50
272	Ryan Klesko	.10
273	Ichiro Suzuki	1.00
274	Shawn Green	.20
275	Darin Erstad	.40
276	Bernie Williams	.30
277	Greg Maddux/SP	1.00
278	Eric Hinske	.10
279	Randy Johnson	.60
280	Todd Helton	.60
281	Sammy Sosa	1.50
282	Nick Johnson	.10
283	Jose Cruz Jr.	.10
284	Frank Thomas	.60
285	Tsuyoshi Shinjo	.10
286	Troy Glaus	.60
287	Jason Giambi	.60
288	Chipper Jones/SP	1.00
289	Roberto Alomar	.30
290	Bobby Hill	.10
291	Garret Anderson	.10
292	Andruw Jones	.60
293	Luis Gonzalez	.15
294	Mike Mussina	.30
295	Ivan Rodriguez/SP	.75
296	Barry Larkin	.10
297	Kazuhiro Sasaki	.10
298	Alfonso Soriano	.50
299	Jeff Bagwell/SP	.75
300	Bobby Abreu	.10
301	Ben Sheets	.20
302	Curt Schilling	.40
303	Jim Thome	.10
304	Kerry Wood	.50
305	Mark Buehrle	.10
306	Rickey Henderson	.60
307	Rafael Palmeiro	.50
308	Jim Edmonds	.10
309	Mike Piazza	1.00
310	Edgar Martinez	.10
311	Tom Glavine	.25
312	Adrian Beltre	.10
313	Adam Dunn	.40
314	Craig Biggio	.10
315	Vladimir Guerrero/SP	1.00
316	Bret Boone	.10
317	Hideo Nomo/SP	.75
318	Jeff Kent	.10
319	Juan Gonzalez	.60
320	Sean Casey	.10
321	C.C. Sabathia	.10
322	J.D. Drew	.20
323	Torii Hunter/SP	.40
324	Chan Ho Park	.10
325	Mike Sweeney	.10
326	Javier Vazquez	.10
327	Jorge Posada	.25
328	Barry Zito	.25
329	Willie McCovey	.50
330	Kevin Brown	.20
331	Mo Vaughn	.10
332	Carlos Beltran	.40
333	Bobby Doerr	.10
334	Matt Morris	.10
335	Trot Nixon	.10
336	Magglio Ordonez	.25
337	Paul LoDuca	.10
338	Phil Nevin	.10
339	Eric Chavez	.20
340	Corey Patterson	.10
341	Richie Sexson	.10
342	Pat Burrell	.25
343	Freddy Garcia	.10
344	Bartolo Colon	.10
345	Cliff Floyd	.10
346	Deivis Santos/RR	.50
347	Felix Escalona/RR RC	.50
348	Miguel Asencio/RR RC	.50
349	Takahito Nomura/RR RC	.50
350	Jorge Padilla/RR	.50
351	Vladimir Guerrero	.50
352	Ichiro Suzuki	1.00

353	Jay Gibbons	.10
354	Alfonso Soriano	.50
355	Mark Buehrle	.10
356	Shawn Green	.20
357	Barry Larkin	.10
358	Josh Fogg	.10
359	Shannon Stewart	.10
360	Andruw Jones	.60
361	Juan Gonzalez	.60
362	Ken Griffey Jr.	1.00
363	Tim Hudson	.20
364	Roy Oswalt/SP	.50
365	Carlos Delgado	.40
366	Albert Pujols/SP	2.00
367	Willie Stargell	.25
368	Roger Clemens	.75
369	Luis Gonzalez	.25
370	Barry Zito	.25
371	Alex Rodriguez	1.25
372	Troy Glaus	.60
373	Vladimir Guerrero	.60
374	Jeff Bagwell	.60
375	Randy Johnson	.60
376	Manny Ramirez	.60
377	Derek Jeter/SP	2.00
378	C.C. Sabathia	.10
379	Rickey Henderson	.60
380	J.D. Drew	.20
381	Nomar Garciaparra	1.00
382	Darin Erstad	.40
383	Ben Sheets	.20
384	Frank Thomas	.60
385	Barry Bonds	1.50
386	Pedro J. Martinez	.60
387	Mark Mulder	.20
388	Greg Maddux	.75
389	Todd Helton	.60
390	Lance Berkman	.10
391	Sammy Sosa	1.00
392	Mike Piazza	1.00
393	Chipper Jones	.75
394	Adam Dunn	.40
395	Jason Giambi	.50
396	Eric Chavez	.20
397	Bobby Abreu	.10
398	Aramis Ramirez	.10
399	Paul LoDuca	.10
400	Miguel Tejada	.25

Aqueous Glossy

Stars (1-400): 3-5X
Average of 1:Box

All-Stars

		NM/M
Complete Set (25):		90.00
Common Player:		2.00
Inserted 1:30		
1	George Brett	8.00
2	Rickey Henderson	4.00
3	Mike Schmidt	6.00
4	Vladimir Guerrero	3.00
5	Tony Gwynn	3.00
6	Curt Schilling	2.00
7	Don Mattingly	8.00
8	Roberto Alomar	2.00
9	Cal Ripken Jr.	8.00
10	Carlton Fisk	2.00
11	Roger Clemens	5.00
12	Jeff Bagwell	3.00
13	Kirby Puckett	8.00
14	Nolan Ryan	10.00
15	Ryne Sandberg	5.00
16	Ivan Rodriguez	2.00
17	Sammy Sosa	5.00
18	Greg Maddux	5.00
19	Alex Rodriguez	8.00
20	Todd Helton	2.00
21	Randy Johnson	3.00
22	Troy Glaus	2.00
23	Ichiro Suzuki	6.00
24	Barry Bonds	8.00
25	Derek Jeter	10.00

Champions

		NM/M
Complete Set (25):		75.00
Common Player:		2.00
Production 800 Sets		
1	Nolan Ryan	10.00
2	George Brett	6.00
3	Edgar Martinez	2.00
4	Mike Schmidt	6.00
5	Randy Johnson	3.00
6	Tony Gwynn	4.00
7	John Smoltz	2.00
8	Roger Clemens	4.00
9	Mel Ott	2.00
10	Todd Helton	3.00
11	Bernie Williams	2.00
12	Troy Glaus	3.00
13	Steve Carlton	2.00
14	Ryne Sandberg	4.00
15	Ted Williams	8.00
16	Alex Rodriguez	8.00
17	Lou Boudreau	2.00
18	Luis Gonzalez	2.00
19	Rickey Henderson	3.00
20	Jose Canseco	2.00
21	Stan Musial	5.00
22	Randy Johnson	3.00
23	Don Mattingly	6.00
24	Nomar Garciaparra	5.00
25	Wade Boggs	4.00

Champions Materials

		NM/M
Common Player:		8.00
Varying quantities produced		
1	Nolan Ryan/78	65.00
2	George Brett/80	30.00
3	Edgar Martinez/92	10.00
4	Mike Schmidt/80	40.00
5	Randy Johnson/94	15.00
6	Tony Gwynn/84	20.00
7	John Smoltz/96	8.00
8	Roger Clemens/88	20.00
10	Todd Helton/100	10.00
11	Bernie Williams/98	10.00
12	Troy Glaus/100	10.00
13	Steve Carlton/80	15.00
14	Ryne Sandberg/90	40.00
15	Ted Williams/42	200.00
16	Alex Rodriguez/96	20.00
17	Lou Boudreau/44	15.00
18	Luis Gonzalez/99	8.00
19	Rickey Henderson/82	20.00
21	Stan Musial/50	60.00
22	Randy Johnson/88	15.00
23	Don Mattingly/84	60.00
24	Nomar Garciaparra/100	30.00
25	Wade Boggs/88	15.00

Gamers

		NM/M
Common Player:		3.00
Varying quantities produced		
1	Alfonso Soriano/400	8.00
2	Shawn Green/500	5.00
3	Curt Schilling/250	8.00
4	Hideo Nomo/100	20.00
5	Toby Hall/500	4.00
6	Andruw Jones/500	8.00
7	Cliff Floyd/500	3.00
8	Mark Ellis/500	4.00
9	Gabe Kapler/500	3.00
10	Andres Galarraga/500	3.00
11	Freddy Garcia/500	3.00
12	Tsuyoshi Shinjo/200	4.00
13	Robin Ventura/500	3.00
14	Paul LoDuca/500	3.00
15	Manny Ramirez/500	8.00
16	Garret Anderson/250	5.00
17	Joe Kennedy/500	3.00
18	Roger Clemens/500	15.00
19	Gary Sheffield/500	6.00
20	Vernon Wells/500	4.00
22	Hideo Nomo/100	40.00
23	Tim Hudson/500	6.00
24	Larry Bigbie/500	4.00
25	Larry Walker/500	4.00
27	John Olerud/500	3.00
28	Chipper Jones/500	8.00
29	Tony Gwynn/500	10.00
30	Juan Gonzalez/500	8.00
31	Jacque Jones/500	5.00
32	Frank Thomas/500	8.00
33	Luis Gonzalez/500	4.00
34	Geoff Jenkins/500	6.00
35	J.D. Drew/500	5.00
36	Edgardo Alfonzo/500	3.00
37	Todd Helton/500	8.00
38	Brad Penny/500	3.00
39	Robert Fick/500	3.00
40	Will Clark/500	15.00
41	Tony Armas Jr./500	4.00
42	Nick Johnson/400	3.00
43	Ben Grieve/500	3.00
44	Vladimir Guerrero/500	8.00
45	Jason Jennings/500	3.00
46	Carlos Lee/500	3.00
47	Carlos Delgado/500	6.00
48	Chan Ho Park/500	3.00
49	Juan Diaz/500	3.00
50	Alex Rodriguez/400	15.00

Hit List

		NM/M
Complete Set (20):		40.00
Common Player:		1.00
Production 1,500 Sets		
1	Ichiro Suzuki	4.00
2	Shawn Green	1.00
3	Alex Rodriguez	5.00
4	Nomar Garciaparra	4.00
5	Derek Jeter	6.00
6	Barry Bonds	6.00
7	Mike Piazza	4.00
8	Albert Pujols	4.00
9	Chipper Jones	3.00
10	Sammy Sosa	4.00
11	Rickey Henderson	2.00
12	Frank Thomas	2.00
13	Jeff Bagwell	2.00
14	Vladimir Guerrero	2.00
15	Todd Helton	2.00
16	Adam Dunn	1.00
17	Rafael Palmeiro	1.00
18	Manny Ramirez	2.00
19	Lance Berkman	1.00
20	Jason Giambi	1.00

Hit List Total Bases

		NM/M
Common Player:		4.00
Numbered to career high total bases.		
1	Ichiro Suzuki/Base/316	15.00
2	Shawn Green/Bat/370	5.00
3	Alex Rodriguez/Bat/393	15.00
4	Nomar Garciaparra/Bat/365	10.00
5	Derek Jeter/346/Base	20.00
6	Barry Bonds/Base/411	20.00
7	Mike Piazza/Bat/355	10.00
8	Albert Pujols/Base/360	10.00
9	Chipper Jones/Bat/359	8.00
10	Sammy Sosa/Base/425	10.00
11	Rickey Henderson/Bat/285	10.00
12	Frank Thomas/Bat/364	8.00
13	Jeff Bagwell/Bat/363	8.00
14	Vladimir Guerrero/Bat/379	8.00
15	Todd Helton/Bat/405	8.00
16	Adam Dunn/Bat/141	8.00
17	Rafael Palmeiro/Bat/356	8.00
18	Manny Ramirez/Bat/346	8.00
19	Lance Berkman/Bat/358	5.00
20	Jason Giambi/Base/343	6.00

Making History

		NM/M
Complete Set (10):		30.00
Common Player:		2.00
Production 800 Sets		
1	Rafael Palmeiro	2.00
2	Roger Clemens	5.00
3	Greg Maddux	4.00
4	Randy Johnson	3.00
5	Barry Bonds	8.00
6	Mike Piazza	6.00
7	Roberto Alomar	2.00
8	Rickey Henderson	2.00
9	Sammy Sosa	6.00
10	Tom Glavine	2.00

Making History Materials

		NM/M
Production 100 Sets		
1	Rafael Palmeiro	15.00
2	Roger Clemens	20.00
3	Greg Maddux	15.00
4	Randy Johnson	10.00
5	Barry Bonds/Base	20.00
6	Mike Piazza	15.00
7	Roberto Alomar	8.00
8	Rickey Henderson	25.00
9	Sammy Sosa/base	15.00
10	Tom Glavine	10.00

Mound Marvels

		NM/M
Complete Set (15):		30.00
Common Player:		1.00
Inserted 1:40		
1	Roger Clemens	6.00
2	Matt Morris	1.00
3	Pedro J. Martinez	5.00
4	Randy Johnson	5.00
5	Wade Miller	1.00
6	Tim Hudson	1.50
7	Mike Mussina	3.00
8	C.C. Sabathia	1.00
9	Kazuhiro Sasaki	1.00
10	Curt Schilling	4.00
11	Hideo Nomo	2.50
12	Roger Clemens	6.00
13	Mark Buehrle	1.00
14	Barry Zito	1.50
15	Roy Oswalt	1.50

Mound Marvels High Heat

		NM/M
Production 100 Sets		
1	Roger Clemens	25.00
2	Matt Morris	10.00
3	Pedro J. Martinez	20.00
4	Randy Johnson	15.00
5	Wade Miller	8.00
6	Tim Hudson	10.00
7	Mike Mussina	15.00
8	C.C. Sabathia	10.00
9	Kazuhiro Sasaki	10.00
10	Curt Schilling	15.00
11	Hideo Nomo	40.00
12	Roger Clemens	25.00
13	Mark Buehrle	8.00
14	Barry Zito	15.00
15	Roy Oswalt	8.00

Nifty Fifty Bats

	NM/M
Common Player:	5.00

Production 50 Sets

1	Alex Rodriguez	20.00
2	Kerry Wood	15.00
3	Ivan Rodriguez	15.00
4	Geronimo Gil	5.00
5	Vladimir Guerrero	15.00
6	Corky Miller	5.00
7	Todd Helton	12.00
8	Rickey Henderson	15.00
9	Andruw Jones	10.00
10	Barry Bonds/Ball	30.00
11	Tom Glavine	10.00
12	Mark Teixeira	10.00
13	Mike Piazza	15.00
14	Austin Kearns	8.00
15	Rickey Henderson	15.00
16	Derek Jeter/Ball	20.00
17	Barry Larkin	8.00
18	Jeff Bagwell	10.00
19	Bernie Williams	10.00
20	Frank Thomas	10.00
21	Lance Berkman	8.00
22	Marlon Byrd	6.00
23	Randy Johnson	15.00
24	Ichiro Suzuki/Ball	40.00
25	Darin Erstad	8.00
26	Jason Lane	5.00
27	Roberto Alomar	10.00
28	Ken Griffey Jr./Ball	20.00
29	Tsuyoshi Shinjo	8.00
30	Pedro Martinez	15.00
31	Rickey Henderson	15.00
32	Albert Pujols/Ball	20.00
33	Nomar Garciaparra	15.00
34	Troy Glaus	10.00
35	Chipper Jones	15.00
36	Adam Dunn	8.00
37	Jason Giambi/Ball	10.00
38	Greg Maddux	20.00
39	Mike Piazza	15.00
40	So Taguchi	8.00
41	Manny Ramirez	10.00
42	Scott Rolen	15.00
43	Sammy Sosa/Ball	15.00
44	Shawn Green	8.00
45	Rickey Henderson	15.00
46	Alex Rodriguez	20.00
47	Hideo Nomo	30.00
48	Kazuhisa Ishii	8.00
49	Luis Gonzalez	8.00
50	Jim Thome	15.00

Nifty Fifty Combos

		NM/M
	Production 50 Sets	
	All bat & jerseys unless noted.	
1	Alex Rodriguez	30.00
2	Kerry Wood	20.00
3	Ivan Rodriguez	20.00
4	Geronimo Gil	10.00
5	Vladimir Guerrero	20.00
6	Corky Miller	10.00
7	Todd Helton	20.00
8	Rickey Henderson	25.00
9	Andruw Jones	15.00
10	Barry Bonds/Base/Ball	40.00
11	Tom Glavine	20.00
12	Mark Teixeira	20.00
13	Mike Piazza	25.00
14	Austin Kearns	15.00
15	Rickey Henderson	25.00
16	Derek Jeter/Base/Ball	30.00
17	Barry Larkin	15.00
18	Jeff Bagwell	20.00
19	Bernie Williams	20.00
20	Frank Thomas	20.00
21	Lance Berkman	15.00
22	Marlon Byrd	15.00
23	Randy Johnson	20.00

24	Ichiro Suzuki/Base/Ball	60.00
25	Darin Erstad	15.00
26	Jason Lane	10.00
27	Roberto Alomar	15.00
28	Ken Griffey Jr./Base/Ball	25.00
29	Tsuyoshi Shinjo	10.00
30	Pedro Martinez	20.00
31	Rickey Henderson	25.00
32	Albert Pujols/Base/Ball	50.00
33	Nomar Garciaparra	30.00
34	Troy Glaus	15.00
35	Chipper Jones	20.00
36	Adam Dunn	15.00
37	Jason Giambi	20.00
38	Greg Maddux	25.00
39	Mike Piazza	25.00
40	So Taguchi	15.00
41	Manny Ramirez	20.00
42	Scott Rolen	20.00
43	Sammy Sosa/Base/Ball	25.00
44	Shawn Green	10.00
45	Rickey Henderson	25.00
46	Alex Rodriguez	30.00
47	Hideo Nomo	30.00
48	Kazuhisa Ishii	15.00
49	Luis Gonzalez	10.00
50	Jim Thome	20.00

Nifty Fifty Jersey

		NM/M
	Common Player:	5.00
	Production 50 Sets	
1	Alex Rodriguez	
2	Kerry Wood	15.00
3	Ivan Rodriguez	15.00
4	Geronimo Gil	5.00
5	Vladimir Guerrero	15.00
6	Corky Miller	5.00
7	Todd Helton	12.00
8	Rickey Henderson	15.00
9	Andruw Jones	10.00
10	Barry Bonds/Base	
11	Tom Glavine	10.00
12	Mark Teixeira	10.00
13	Mike Piazza	15.00
14	Austin Kearns	8.00
15	Rickey Henderson	15.00
16	Derek Jeter/Base	20.00
17	Barry Larkin	8.00
18	Jeff Bagwell	10.00
19	Bernie Williams	10.00
20	Frank Thomas	10.00
21	Lance Berkman	8.00
22	Marlon Byrd	8.00
23	Randy Johnson	15.00
24	Ichiro Suzuki/Base	40.00
25	Darin Erstad	8.00
26	Jason Lane	5.00
27	Roberto Alomar	10.00
28	Ken Griffey Jr./Base	20.00
29	Tsuyoshi Shinjo	8.00
30	Pedro Martinez	15.00
31	Rickey Henderson	15.00
32	Albert Pujols/Base	20.00
33	Nomar Garciaparra	20.00
34	Troy Glaus	10.00
35	Chipper Jones	15.00
36	Adam Dunn	8.00
37	Jason Giambi/Base	10.00
38	Greg Maddux	20.00
39	Mike Piazza	15.00
40	So Taguchi	8.00
41	Manny Ramirez	10.00
42	Scott Rolen	15.00
43	Sammy Sosa/Base	15.00
44	Shawn Green	8.00
45	Rickey Henderson	15.00
46	Alex Rodriguez	20.00
47	Hideo Nomo	30.00
48	Kazuhisa Ishii	8.00
49	Luis Gonzalez	10.00
50	Jim Thome	15.00

On The Record

		NM/M
	Complete Set (15):	60.00
	Common Player:	3.00
	Production 800 Sets	
1	Ty Cobb	6.00
2	Jimmie Foxx	4.00

3	Lou Gehrig	10.00
4	Dale Murphy	5.00
5	Steve Carlton	3.00
6	Randy Johnson	4.00
7	Greg Maddux	6.00
8	Roger Clemens	8.00
9	Yogi Berra	5.00
10	Don Mattingly	8.00
11	Rickey Henderson	4.00
12	Stan Musial	6.00
13	Jackie Robinson	8.00
14	Roberto Clemente	10.00
15	Mike Schmidt	6.00

On the Record Materials

		NM/M
	Varying quantities produced	
1	Ty Cobb/9	
3	Lou Gehrig/34	220.00
4	Dale Murphy/83	10.00
5	Steve Carlton/72	10.00
6	Randy Johnson/100	10.00
7	Greg Maddux/93	15.00
8	Roger Clemens/87	20.00
9	Yogi Berra/51	12.00
10	Don Mattingly/85	25.00
11	Rickey Henderson/90	15.00
13	Jackie Robinson/49	50.00
14	Roberto Clemente/66	75.00
15	Mike Schmidt/80	25.00

Power Alley

		NM/M
	Complete Set (15):	30.00
	Common Player:	1.00
	Production 1,500 Sets	
	Die-Cut Parallel:	1.5-2X
	Production 100 Sets	
1	Barry Bonds	6.00
2	Sammy Sosa	3.00
3	Lance Berkman	1.00
4	Luis Gonzalez	1.00
5	Alex Rodriguez	5.00
6	Troy Glaus	2.00
7	Vladimir Guerrero	2.00
8	Jason Giambi	1.50
9	Mike Piazza	3.00
10	Todd Helton	2.00
11	Mike Schmidt	4.00
12	Don Mattingly	4.00
13	Andre Dawson	1.50
14	Reggie Jackson	2.00
15	Dale Murphy	1.50

Signature Marks

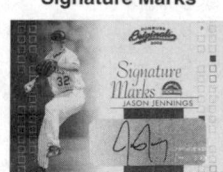

		NM/M
	Common Autograph:	5.00
	Varying quantities produced	
	Many not priced, lack of market info.	
1	Kazuhisa Ishii/50	
2	Eric Hinske/200	8.00
3	Cesar Izturis/200	5.00
4	Roy Oswalt/100	20.00
5	Jack Cust/200	8.00
6	Nick Johnson/200	8.00
7	Jason Hart/200	6.00
8	Mark Prior/100	30.00
9	Luis Garcia/200	5.00
10	Jay Gibbons/200	10.00
11	Corky Miller/200	8.00
12	Antonio Perez/100	8.00
13	Andres Torres/200	5.00
14	Brandon Claussen/200	8.00
15	Ed Rogers/200	5.00
16	Jorge Padilla/200	10.00
17	Francis Beltran/200	6.00
18	Kip Wells/200	6.00
19	Ryan Ludwick/200	8.00
20	Juan Cruz/100	8.00
21	Juan Diaz/200	5.00
22	Marcus Giles/200	10.00
23	Joe Kennedy/200	10.00
24	Wade Miller/100	10.00
25	Corey Patterson/100	10.00
26	Angel Berroa/200	10.00
27	Ricardo Rodriguez/200	5.00
28	Toby Hall/200	8.00
29	Carlos Pena/50	10.00
30	Jason Jennings/200	8.00

31	Rafael Soriano/200	10.00
32	Marlon Byrd/100	10.00
33	Rodrigo Rosario/200	5.00
35	Brent Abernathy/200	5.00
36	Bill Hall/200	15.00
37	Fernando Rodney/200	10.00
38	Josh Pearce/200	8.00
39	Brian Lawrence/200	8.00
40	Tim Redding/200	5.00
42	Jeremy Giambi/200	5.00
43	Victor Martinez/200	25.00
44	Hank Blalock/50	25.00
46	Geronimo Gil/200	5.00
47	So Taguchi/50	25.00
48	Austin Kearns/200	25.00
49	Alfonso Soriano/50	40.00

What If - Rookies

		NM/M
	Complete Set (23):	75.00
	Common Player:	1.50
	Inserted 1:12	
1	Wade Boggs	6.00
2	Ryne Sandberg	6.00
3	Cal Ripken Jr.	12.50
4	Tony Gwynn	6.00
5	Don Mattingly	10.00
6	Wade Boggs	6.00
7	Roger Clemens	7.50
8	Kirby Puckett	6.00
9	Eric Davis	1.50
10	Dwight Gooden	1.50
11	Eric Davis	1.50
12	Roger Clemens	7.50
13	Kirby Puckett	6.00
14	Dwight Gooden	1.50
15	Barry Bonds	12.50
16	Will Clark	1.50
17	Barry Larkin	1.50
18	Greg Maddux	6.00
19	Rafael Palmeiro	4.00
20	Craig Biggio	1.50
21	Gary Sheffield	1.50
22	Randy Johnson	5.00
23	Curt Schilling	3.00

What If - '78

		NM/M
	Complete Set (27):	75.00
	Common Player:	1.50
	Inserted 1:12	
1	Paul Molitor	4.00
2	Alan Trammell	1.50
3	Ozzie Smith	6.00
4	George Brett	10.00
5	Johnny Bench	6.00
6	Rod Carew	2.00
7	Carlton Fisk	1.50
8	Reggie Jackson	5.00
9	Dale Murphy	2.00
10	Joe Morgan	1.50
11	Eddie Murray	4.00
12	Jim Palmer	2.00
13	Tom Seaver	4.00
14	Willie Stargell	2.00
15	Dave Winfield	2.00
16	Dave Parker	1.50
17	Mike Schmidt	8.00
18	Eddie Mathews	4.00
19	Lou Brock	1.50
20	Willie McCovey	1.50
21	Andre Dawson	1.50
22	Dennis Eckersley	4.00
23	Robin Yount	4.00
24	Nolan Ryan	15.00
25	Steve Carlton	1.50
26	Paul Molitor	4.00
27	Ozzie Smith	6.00

What If - '80

		NM/M
	Complete Set (25):	75.00
	Common Player:	1.50
	Inserted 1:12	
1	Rickey Henderson	3.00
2	Johnny Bench	6.00
3	George Brett	10.00
4	Steve Carlton	2.50
5	Rod Carew	2.00
6	Gary Carter	1.50
7	Carlton Fisk	1.50
8	Reggie Jackson	5.00
9	Dave Parker	1.50
10	Dale Murphy	3.00
11	Paul Molitor	4.00
12	Mike Schmidt	8.00
13	Alan Trammell	1.50
14	Dave Winfield	4.00
15	Robin Yount	4.00
16	Joe Morgan	1.50
17	Jim Palmer	1.50
18	Nolan Ryan	15.00

19	Tom Seaver	4.00
20	Ozzie Smith	6.00
21	Willie McCovey	1.50
22	Andre Dawson	1.50
23	Eddie Murray	2.00
24	Al Kaline	5.00
25	Duke Snider	4.00

2002 Donruss Studio

BRIAN GILES / OF

		NM/M
Complete Set (250):		150.00
Common Player:		.25
Common (201-250):		3.00
Production 1,500		
Pack (5):		3.00
Box (18):		45.00
1	Vladimir Guerrero	.75
2	Chipper Jones	1.00
3	Bobby Abreu	.25
4	Barry Zito	.40
5	Larry Walker	.40
6	Miguel Tejada	.40
7	Mike Sweeney	.25
8	Shannon Stewart	.25
9	Sammy Sosa	1.50
10	Bud Smith	.25
11	Wilson Betemit	.25
12	Kevin Brown	.35
13	Ellis Burks	.25
14	Pat Burrell	.40
15	Cliff Floyd	.25
16	Marcus Giles	.25
17	Troy Glaus	.75
18	Barry Larkin	.25
19	Carlos Lee	.25
20	Brian Lawrence	.25
21	Paul LoDuca	.25
22	Ben Grieve	.25
23	Shawn Green	.40
24	Mike Cameron	.25
25	Roger Clemens	1.25
26	Joe Crede	.25
27	Jose Cruz	.25
28	Jeremy Affeldt	.25
29	Adrian Beltre	.25
30	Josh Beckett	.50
31	Roberto Alomar	.40
32	Toby Hall	.25
33	Mike Hampton	.25
34	Eric Milton	.25
35	Eric Munson	.25
36	Trot Nixon	.25
37	Roy Oswalt	.40
38	Chan Ho Park	.25
39	Charles Johnson	.25
40	Nick Johnson	.25
41	Tim Hudson	.40
42	Cristian Guzman	.25
43	Drew Henson	.25
44	Mark Grace	.35
45	Luis Gonzalez	.35
46	Pedro J. Martinez	.75
47	Joe Mays	.25
48	Jorge Posada	.40
49	Aramis Ramirez	.25
50	Kip Wells	.25
51	Moises Alou	.25
52	Omar Vizquel	.25
53	Ichiro Suzuki	1.50
54	Jimmy Rollins	.40
55	Freddy Garcia	.25
56	Steve Green	.25
57	Brian Jordan	.25
58	Paul Konerko	.35
59	Jack Cust	.25
60	Sean Casey	.25
61	Bret Boone	.25
62	Hideo Nomo	.60
63	Magglio Ordonez	.40
64	Frank Thomas	.75
65	Josh Towers	.25
66	Javier Vazquez	.25

67	Robin Ventura	.25
68	Aubrey Huff	.25
69	Richard Hidalgo	.25
70	Brandon Claussen	.25
71	Bartolo Colon	.25
72	John Buck	.25
73	Dee Brown	.25
74	Barry Bonds	2.00
75	Jason Giambi	.50
76	Erick Almonte	.25
77	Ryan Dempster	.25
78	Jim Edmonds	.25
79	Jay Gibbons	.25
80	Shigetoshi Hasegawa	.25
81	Todd Helton	.75
82	Erik Bedard	.25
83	Carlos Beltran	.50
84	Rafael Soriano	.25
85	Gary Sheffield	.40
86	Richie Sexson	.25
87	Mike Rivera	.25
88	Jose Ortiz	.25
89	Abraham Nunez	.25
90	Dave Williams	.25
91	Preston Wilson	.25
92	Jason Jennings	.25
93	Juan Diaz	.25
94	Steve Smyth	.25
95	Phil Nevin	.25
96	John Olerud	.25
97	Brad Penny	.25
98	Andy Pettitte	.40
99	Juan Pierre	.25
100	Manny Ramirez	.75
101	Edgardo Alfonzo	.25
102	Michael Cuddyer	.25
103	Johnny Damon	.40
104	Carlos Zambrano	.35
105	Jose Vidro	.25
106	Tsuyoshi Shinjo	.25
107	Ed Rogers	.25
108	Scott Rolen	.75
109	Mariano Rivera	.35
110	Tim Redding	.25
111	Josh Phelps	.25
112	Gabe Kapler	.25
113	Edgar Martinez	.25
114	Fred McGriff	.25
115	Raul Mondesi	.25
116	Wade Miller	.25
117	Mike Mussina	.40
118	Rafael Palmeiro	.65
119	Adam Johnson	.25
120	Rickey Henderson	.75
121	Bill Hall	.25
122	Ken Griffey Jr.	1.50
123	Geronimo Gil	.25
124	Robert Fick	.25
125	Darin Erstad	.50
126	Brandon Duckworth	.25
127	Garret Anderson	.25
128	Pedro Feliz	.25
129	Jeff Cirillo	.25
130	Brian Giles	.25
131	Craig Biggio	.25
132	Willie Harris	.25
133	Doug Davis	.25
134	Jeff Kent	.25
135	Terrence Long	.25
136	Carlos Delgado	.50
137	Tino Martinez	.25
138	Donaldo Mendez	.25
139	Sean Douglass	.25
140	Eric Chavez	.40
141	Rick Ankiel	.25
142	Jeremy Giambi	.25
143	Juan Pena	.25
144	Bernie Williams	.40
145	Craig Wilson	.25
146	Ricardo Rodriguez	.25
147	Albert Pujols	1.50
148	Antonio Perez	.25
149	Russ Ortiz	.25
150	Corky Miller	.25
151	Rich Aurilia	.25
152	Kerry Wood	.50
153	Joe Thurston	.25
154	Jeff Deardorff RC	.25
155	Jermaine Dye	.25
156	Andruw Jones	.75
157	Victor Martinez	.25
158	Nick Neugebauer	.25
159	Matt Morris	.25
160	Casey Fossum	.25
161	J.D. Drew	.40
162	Matt Childers RC	.50

163	Mark Buehrle	.25
164	Jeff Bagwell	.75
165	Kazuhiro Sasaki	.25
166	Ben Sheets	.40
167	Alex Rodriguez	1.50
168	Adam Pettyjohn	.25
169	Chris Snelling RC	.50
170	Robert Person	.25
171	Juan Uribe	.25
172	Mo Vaughn	.25
173	Alfredo Amezaga	.25
174	Ryan Drese	.25
175	Corey Thurman RC	.25
176	Jim Thome	.25
177	Orlando Cabrera	.25
178	Eric Cyr RC	.50
179	Greg Maddux	1.00
180	Earl Snyder RC	.25
181	C.C. Sabathia	.40
182	Mark Mulder	.40
183	Jose Mieses	.25
184	Joe Kennedy	.25
185	Randy Johnson	.75
186	Tom Glavine	.40
187	Eric Junge RC	.25
188	Mike Piazza	1.50
189	Corey Patterson	.40
190	Carlos Pena	.25
191	Curt Schilling	.40
192	Nomar Garciaparra	1.50
193	Lance Berkman	.25
194	Ryan Klesko	.25
195	Ivan Rodriguez	.65
196	Alfonso Soriano	.75
197	Derek Jeter	2.00
198	David Justice	.25
199	Juan Gonzalez	.75
200	Adam Dunn	.50
201	Victor Alvarez RC	3.00
202	Miguel Asencio RC	3.00
203	Brandon Backe RC	3.00
204	Chris Baker RC	4.00
205	Steve Bechler RC	4.00
206	Francis Beltran RC	4.00
207	Angel Berroa	3.00
208	Hank Blalock	4.00
209	Dewon Brazelton	3.00
210	Sean Burroughs	3.00
211	Marlon Byrd	3.00
212	Raul Chavez RC	4.00
213	Juan Cruz	3.00
214	Jorge De La Rosa RC	3.00
215	Doug DeVore RC	3.00
216	John Ennis RC	3.00
217	Felix Escalona RC	3.00
218	Morgan Ensberg	3.00
219	Cam Esslinger RC	3.00
220	Kevin Frederick RC	3.00
221	Franklyn German RC	3.00
222	Eric Hinske	4.00
223	Ben Howard RC	3.00
224	Orlando Hudson	3.00
225	Travis Hughes RC	5.00
226	Kazuhisa Ishii RC	6.00
227	Ryan Jamison RC	3.00
228	Reed Johnson RC	4.00
229	Kyle Kane RC	3.00
230	Austin Kearns	3.00
231	Satoru Komiyama RC	4.00
232	Jason Lane	3.00
233	Jeremy Lambert RC	3.00
234	Anderson Machado RC	4.00
235	Brian Mallette RC	3.00
236	Takahito Nomura RC	3.00
237	Jorge Padilla RC	4.00
238	Luis Ugueto RC	3.00
239	Mark Prior	10.00
240	Rene Reyes RC	3.00
241	Deivis Santos	3.00
242	Elio Serrano RC	3.00
243	Tom Shearn RC	3.00
244	Allan Simpson RC	3.00
245	So Taguchi RC	5.00
246	Dennis Tankersley	3.00
247	Mark Teixeira	6.00
248	Matt Thornton	3.00
249	Bobby Hill	3.00
250	Ramon Vazquez	3.00

Proof

Proofs (1-200):	4-8X
Proofs (201-250):	1-2X
Production 100 Sets	

Classic Studio

	NM/M
Complete Set (25):	90.00
Common Player:	3.00
Production 1,000 Sets	
First Ballot:	3-4X
Print Run based on HOF Year	
1 Kirby Puckett	5.00
2 George Brett	8.00
3 Nolan Ryan	10.00

WILLIE McCOVEY · 1B · SAN FRANCISCO GIANTS

4	Mike Schmidt	8.00
5	Steve Carlton	3.00
6	Reggie Jackson	5.00
7	Tom Seaver	3.00
8	Joe Morgan	3.00
9	Jim Palmer	3.00
10	Johnny Bench	5.00
11	Willie McCovey	3.00
12	Brooks Robinson	4.00
13	Al Kaline	5.00
14	Stan Musial	6.00
15	Ozzie Smith	6.00
16	Dave Winfield	3.00
17	Robin Yount	5.00
18	Rod Carew	3.00
19	Willie Stargell	3.00
20	Lou Brock	3.00
21	Ernie Banks	5.00
22	Ted Williams	10.00
23	Jackie Robinson	8.00
24	Roberto Clemente	10.00
25	Lou Gehrig	10.00

Classic Studio Autograph

Production 15-20
No Pricing

Diamond Collection

JASON GIAMBI · 1B

		NM/M
Complete Set (25):		65.00
Common Player:		1.50
Inserted 1:17		
1	Todd Helton	3.00
2	Chipper Jones	4.00
3	Lance Berkman	1.50
4	Derek Jeter	8.00
5	Hideo Nomo	3.00
6	Kazuhisa Ishii	1.50
7	Barry Bonds	8.00
8	Alex Rodriguez	6.00
9	Ichiro Suzuki	5.00
10	Mike Piazza	5.00
11	Jim Thome	1.50
12	Greg Maddux	4.00
13	Jeff Bagwell	3.00
14	Vladimir Guerrero	3.00
15	Ken Griffey Jr.	5.00
16	Jason Giambi	2.50
17	Nomar Garciaparra	5.00
18	Albert Pujols	6.00
19	Manny Ramirez	3.00
20	Pedro J. Martinez	3.00
21	Roger Clemens	4.50
22	Randy Johnson	3.00
23	Mark Prior	2.00
24	So Taguchi	1.50
25	Sammy Sosa	5.00

Diamond Collection Artist's Proof

	NM/M
Common Jersey card:	4.00
Varying quantities produced	
1 Todd Helton/200	8.00
2 Chipper Jones/150	10.00
3 Lance Berkman/200	6.00
4 Derek Jeter/200/Base	20.00
5 Hideo Nomo/150	25.00

6	Kazuhisa Ishii/150	8.00
7	Barry Bonds/200/Base	25.00
8	Alex Rodriguez/150	15.00
9	Ichiro Suzuki/200/Base	25.00
10	Mike Piazza/150	15.00
11	Jim Thome/150	10.00
12	Greg Maddux/150	15.00
13	Jeff Bagwell/150	8.00
14	Vladimir Guerrero/200	8.00
15	Ken Griffey Jr./200/Base	10.00
16	Jason Giambi/200/Base	6.00
17	Nomar Garciaparra/150	15.00
18	Albert Pujols/Base/200	10.00
19	Manny Ramirez/150	8.00
20	Pedro Martinez/150	8.00
21	Roger Clemens/150	15.00
22	Randy Johnson/150	8.00
24	So Taguchi/200	5.00
25	Sammy Sosa/200/Base	15.00

Hats Off

		NM/M
Common Player:		8.00
Production 100		
MLB Logo:		No Pricing
Production One Set		
10	Carlos Lee	10.00
14	Mark Buehrle	10.00
16	Paul LoDuca	10.00
22	Brandon Duckworth	10.00
26	J.D. Drew	12.00
28	Wade Miller	10.00
30	Brian Giles	10.00
31	Lance Berkman	10.00
32	Shannon Stewart	10.00
33	Kazuhisa Ishii/50	20.00
35	Rafael Palmeiro	20.00
36	Roy Oswalt	15.00
37	Jason Lane	10.00
38	Andruw Jones	15.00
39	Brad Penny	10.00
40	Bud Smith	8.00
41	Carlos Beltran	15.00
42	Magglio Ordonez	20.00
43	Craig Biggio	15.00
45	Jeff Bagwell	25.00
47	Juan Cruz	8.00
48	Kerry Wood	25.00
49	Brandon Berger	8.00
50	Juan Pierre	8.00

Leather & Lumber

		NM/M
Common Player:		5.00
Production 200 unless noted.		
Artist's Proofs:		1.5-2X
Production 50		
1	Nomar Garciaparra	15.00
2	Jeff Bagwell/150	8.00
3	Alex Rodriguez	15.00
4	Vladimir Guerrero/100	10.00
5	Luis Gonzalez	5.00
6	Chipper Jones	10.00
7	Shawn Green	5.00
8	Kirby Puckett/100	15.00
9	Juan Gonzalez	8.00
10	Troy Glaus	8.00
11	Don Mattingly/100	30.00
12	Todd Helton	8.00
13	Jim Thome	10.00
14	Rickey Henderson	15.00
15	Mike Schmidt/100	35.00
16	Adam Dunn/100	10.00
17	Ivan Rodriguez	10.00
18	Manny Ramirez/150	10.00
19	Tsuyoshi Shinjo	8.00
20	Andruw Jones/150	10.00
21	Roberto Alomar	8.00
22	Lance Berkman	5.00
23	Derek Jeter/50/Ball	30.00
24	Ichiro Suzuki/50/Ball	60.00
25	Mike Piazza	15.00

Masterstrokes

		NM/M
Complete Set (25):		50.00
Common Player:		1.50
Inserted 1:17		
1	Vladimir Guerrero	3.00
2	Frank Thomas	3.00
3	Alex Rodriguez	6.00
4	Manny Ramirez	3.00
5	Jeff Bagwell	3.00
6	Jim Thome	1.50
7	Ichiro Suzuki	5.00
8	Andruw Jones	3.00
9	Troy Glaus	3.00
10	Chipper Jones	4.00
11	Juan Gonzalez	3.00
12	Lance Berkman	1.50
13	Mike Piazza	5.00
14	Darin Erstad	2.00
15	Albert Pujols	6.00
16	Kazuhisa Ishii	1.50
17	Shawn Green	1.50
18	Rafael Palmeiro	2.00
19	Todd Helton	3.00
20	Carlos Delgado	1.50
21	Ivan Rodriguez	2.00
22	Luis Gonzalez	1.50
23	Derek Jeter	8.00
24	Nomar Garciaparra	5.00
25	J.D. Drew	1.50

Masterstrokes Artist's Proof

		NM/M
All Jersey/bat unless noted.		
Varying quantities produced.		
1	Vladimir Guerrero/200	15.00
2	Frank Thomas/200	15.00
3	Alex Rodriguez/100	25.00
4	Manny Ramirez/200	10.00
5	Jeff Bagwell/150	10.00
6	Jim Thome/200	15.00
7	Ichiro Suzuki/100/Ball/Base	50.00
8	Andruw Jones/200	10.00
9	Troy Glaus/200	10.00
10	Chipper Jones/200	15.00
11	Juan Gonzalez/200	10.00
12	Lance Berkman/200	8.00
13	Mike Piazza/200	25.00
14	Darin Erstad/200	10.00
15	Albert Pujols/100/Ball/Base	30.00
16	Kazuhisa Ishii/150	15.00
17	Shawn Green/200	10.00
18	Rafael Palmeiro/200	20.00
19	Todd Helton/200	15.00
20	Carlos Delgado/200	10.00
21	Ivan Rodriguez/200	15.00
22	Luis Gonzalez/200	10.00
23	Derek Jeter/100/Ball/Base	35.00
24	Nomar Garciaparra/150	25.00
25	J.D. Drew/150	8.00

Private Signings

		NM/M
Common Autograph:		5.00
Varying quantities produced		
1	Vladimir Guerrero/25	75.00
2	Chipper Jones/15	150.00
3	Bobby Abreu/50	20.00
4	Barry Zito/25	25.00
6	Miguel Tejada/50	25.00
7	Mike Sweeney/50	15.00
8	Shannon Stewart/100	10.00
10	Bud Smith/100	5.00
11	Wilson Betemit/250	8.00
12	Kevin Brown/25	25.00
15	Cliff Floyd/50	15.00
16	Marcus Giles/50	10.00
17	Troy Glaus/50	25.00
18	Barry Larkin/25	50.00
19	Carlos Lee/25	20.00
20	Brian Lawrence/250	8.00
21	Paul LoDuca/25	15.00
25	Roger Clemens/15	175.00
26	Joe Crede/250	8.00
28	Jeremy Affeldt/250	8.00
29	Adrian Beltre/25	20.00
30	Josh Beckett/25	40.00
31	Roberto Alomar/25	50.00
32	Toby Hall/250	8.00
37	Roy Oswalt/50	20.00
40	Nick Johnson/250	8.00
43	Drew Henson/150	15.00
45	Luis Gonzalez/15	25.00
47	Joe Mays/100	8.00
49	Aramis Ramirez/50	20.00
50	Kip Wells/250	8.00
51	Moises Alou/15	25.00
55	Freddy Garcia/50	10.00
56	Steve Green/250	5.00
59	Jack Cust/250	10.00
60	Sean Casey/50	10.00
63	Magglio Ordonez/15	40.00
65	Josh Towers/250	8.00
66	Javier Vazquez/100	15.00
68	Aubrey Huff/250	10.00
69	Richard Hidalgo/25	15.00
70	Brandon Claussen/250	10.00
72	John Buck/250	5.00
73	Dee Brown/250	5.00
75	Jason Giambi/25	
76	Erick Almonte/250	8.00
79	Jay Gibbons/250	15.00
81	Todd Helton/15	85.00
82	Erik Bedard/250	15.00
83	Carlos Beltran/15	
84	Rafael Soriano/250	10.00
85	Gary Sheffield/15	40.00
86	Richie Sexson/50	20.00
87	Mike Rivera/250	8.00
88	Jose Ortiz/250	8.00
89	Abraham Nunez/250	5.00
90	Dave Williams/250	5.00
92	Jason Jennings/250	8.00
93	Juan Diaz/250	5.00
94	Steve Smyth/250	5.00
97	Brad Penny/80	10.00
99	Juan Pierre/100	5.00
100	Manny Ramirez/15	75.00
102	Michael Cuddyer/250	10.00
104	Carlos Zambrano/250	15.00
105	Jose Vidro/100	10.00
107	Ed Rogers/250	5.00
110	Tim Redding/250	5.00
111	Josh Phelps/250	5.00
112	Gabe Kapler/100	10.00
113	Edgar Martinez/50	40.00
116	Wade Miller/250	10.00
118	Rafael Palmeiro/25	40.00
121	Bill Hall/250	10.00
123	Geronimo Gil/250	10.00
124	Robert Fick/150	10.00
126	Brandon Duckworth/250	8.00
128	Pedro Feliz/250	8.00
130	Brian Giles/15	25.00
131	Craig Biggio/15	40.00
132	Willie Harris/250	8.00
133	Doug Davis/250	8.00
135	Terrence Long/150	10.00
138	Donaldo Mendez/250	5.00
139	Sean Douglass/250	8.00
140	Eric Chavez/15	25.00
141	Rick Ankiel/250	15.00
142	Jeremy Giambi/100	6.00
143	Juan Pena/250	8.00
144	Bernie Williams/15	75.00
145	Craig Wilson/250	10.00
146	Ricardo Rodriguez/250	10.00
147	Albert Pujols/25	200.00
148	Antonio Perez/250	5.00
150	Corky Miller/250	5.00
151	Ron Aurilia/250	15.00
152	Kerry Wood/25	30.00
153	Joe Thurston/250	5.00
154	Jeff Deardorff/250	8.00
155	Jermaine Dye/15	25.00
157	Victor Martinez/250	15.00
158	Nick Neugebauer/150	5.00
160	Casey Fossum/250	8.00
161	J.D. Drew/25	25.00
162	Matt Childers/250	5.00
163	Mark Buehrle/150	10.00
166	Ben Sheets/100	15.00
167	Alex Rodriguez/15	165.00
168	Adam Pettyjohn/250	5.00
169	Chris Snelling/250	10.00
170	Robert Person/250	5.00
171	Juan Uribe/250	5.00
173	Alfredo Amezaga/250	5.00
175	Corey Thurman/250	5.00
178	Eric Cyr/250	5.00
179	Greg Maddux/15	200.00
180	Earl Snyder/250	5.00
181	C.C. Sabathia/50	20.00
182	Mark Mulder/50	15.00
183	Jose Mieses/250	5.00
184	Joe Kennedy/250	5.00
187	Eric Junge/250	5.00
189	Corey Patterson/205	20.00
190	Carlos Pena/250	10.00
191	Curt Schilling/15	80.00
195	Ivan Rodriguez/15	50.00
196	Alfonso Soriano/50	40.00
201	Victor Alvarez/250	5.00
203	Brandon Backe/250	5.00
204	Chris Baker/250	5.00
205	Steve Bechler/250	8.00
206	Francis Beltran/250	5.00
207	Angel Berroa/250	10.00
208	Hank Blalock/100	20.00
209	Dewon Brazelton/200	5.00
210	Sean Burroughs/50	20.00
211	Marlon Byrd/200	5.00
212	Raul Chavez/250	5.00
213	Juan Cruz/50	15.00
214	Jorge De La Rosa/250	5.00
215	Doug DeVore/250	5.00
216	John Ennis/250	5.00
217	Felix Escalona/250	5.00
218	Morgan Ensberg/250	10.00
219	Cam Esslinger/250	5.00
220	Kevin Frederick/250	5.00
221	Franklyn German/250	5.00
222	Eric Hinske/250	8.00
223	Ben Howard/250	5.00
224	Orlando Hudson/250	10.00
225	Travis Hughes/250	5.00
226	Kazuhisa Ishii/50	25.00
227	Ryan Jamison/250	5.00
228	Reed Johnson/250	5.00
229	Kyle Kane/250	5.00
230	Austin Kearns/250	20.00
231	Satoru Komiyama/50	10.00
232	Jason Lane/200	5.00
233	Jeremy Lambert/250	5.00
234	Anderson Machado/200	10.00
235	Brian Mallette/250	5.00
236	Takahito Nomura/100	20.00
237	Jorge Padilla/200	10.00
238	Luis Ugueto/250	5.00
239	Mark Prior/100	30.00
240	Rene Reyes/250	5.00
241	Deivis Santos/250	5.00
242	Elio Serrano/250	5.00
243	Tom Shearn/250	5.00
244	Allan Simpson/250	5.00
245	So Taguchi/150	15.00
246	Dennis Tankersley/100	10.00
247	Mark Teixeira/50	40.00
248	Matt Thornton/250	5.00
249	Bobby Hill/100	10.00
250	Ramon Vazquez/250	5.00

Spirit of the Game

		NM/M
Complete Set (50):		60.00
Common Player:		1.00
Inserted 1:9		
1	Alex Rodriguez	5.00
2	Curt Schilling	1.50
3	Hideo Nomo	2.00
4	Derek Jeter	6.00
5	Mike Sweeney	1.00
6	Mike Piazza	4.00
7	Roger Clemens	3.00
8	Shawn Green	1.50
9	Vladimir Guerrero	2.00
10	Carlos Lee	1.00
11	Edgar Martinez	1.00
12	Albert Pujols	5.00
13	Mark Prior	2.00
14	Mark Buehrle	1.00
15	Chipper Jones	3.00
16	Paul LoDuca	1.00
17	Frank Thomas	3.00
18	Randy Johnson	2.00
19	Cliff Floyd	1.00
20	Todd Helton	2.00
21	Luis Gonzalez	1.00

22	Brandon Duckworth	1.00
23	Jason Giambi	1.50
24	Juan Uribe	1.00
25	Dewon Brazelton	1.00
26	J.D. Drew	1.00
27	Troy Glaus	2.00
28	Wade Miller	1.00
29	Darin Erstad	1.50
30	Brian Giles	1.00
31	Lance Berkman	1.00
32	Shannon Stewart	1.00
33	Kazuhisa Ishii	1.00
34	Corey Patterson	1.00
35	Rafael Palmeiro	1.50
36	Roy Oswalt	1.00
37	Jason Lane	1.00
38	Andruw Jones	2.00
39	Brad Penny	1.00
40	Bud Smith	1.00
41	Carlos Beltran	1.50
42	Magglio Ordonez	1.50
43	Craig Biggio	1.00
44	Hank Blalock	1.50
45	Jeff Bagwell	2.00
46	Josh Beckett	1.50
47	Juan Cruz	1.00
48	Kerry Wood	1.50
49	Brandon Berger	1.00
50	Juan Pierre	1.00

Studio Stars

		NM/M
Complete Set (50):		60.00
Common Player:		1.00
Production 700 Sets		
Golds:		1.5-2X
Production 250 Sets		
Platinums:		3-5X
Production 50 Sets		
1	Mike Piazza	3.00
2	Ivan Rodriguez	1.50
3	Albert Pujols	4.00
4	Scott Rolen	2.00
5	Alex Rodriguez	4.00
6	Curt Schilling	1.50
7	Vladimir Guerrero	2.00
8	Jim Thome	1.00
9	Derek Jeter	5.00
10	C.C. Sabathia	1.00
11	Sammy Sosa	3.00
12	Adam Dunn	1.50
13	Bernie Williams	1.00
14	Ichiro Suzuki	4.00
15	Barry Bonds	5.00
16	Rickey Henderson	2.00
17	Ken Griffey Jr.	3.00
18	Kazuhisa Ishii	1.00
19	Kerry Wood	1.50
20	Todd Helton	1.50
21	Hideo Nomo	2.00
22	Frank Thomas	2.00
23	Manny Ramirez	2.00
24	Luis Gonzalez	1.00
25	Rafael Palmeiro	1.50
26	Mike Mussina	1.50
27	Roy Oswalt	1.00
28	Darin Erstad	1.00
29	Barry Larkin	1.00
30	Randy Johnson	2.00
31	Tom Glavine	1.00
32	Lance Berkman	1.00
33	Juan Gonzalez	2.00
34	Shawn Green	1.00
35	Nomar Garciaparra	3.00
36	Troy Glaus	2.00
37	Tim Hudson	1.00
38	Carlos Delgado	1.50
39	Jason Giambi	1.50
40	Andruw Jones	2.00
41	Roberto Alomar	1.00
42	Greg Maddux	2.50
43	Pedro J. Martinez	2.00
44	Tony Gwynn	3.00
45	Alfonso Soriano	1.50
46	Chipper Jones	2.50
47	J.D. Drew	1.00
48	Roger Clemens	2.75
49	Barry Zito	1.00
50	Jeff Bagwell	1.50

2002 Donruss
The Rookies

		NM/M
Complete Set (110):		20.00
Common Player:		.15
Common Rookie:		
Pack (5):		2.00
Box (24):		40.00
1	Kazuhisa Ishii RC	1.00
2	P.J. Bevis RC	.25
3	Jason Simontacchi RC	.50
4	John Lackey RC	.15
5	Travis Driskill RC	.25
6	Carl Sadler RC	.25
7	Tim Kalita RC	.25
8	Nelson Castro RC	.25
9	Francis Beltran RC	.25
10	So Taguchi RC	.50
11	Ryan Bukvich RC	.25
12	Brian Fitzgerald	.15
13	Kevin Frederick RC	.25
14	Chone Figgins RC	.75
15	Marlon Byrd	.15
16	Ron Calloway RC	.25
17	Jason Lane	.15
18	Satoru Komiyama RC	.25
19	John Ennis RC	.25
20	Juan Brito RC	.25
21	Gustavo Chacin RC	.50
22	Josh Bard RC	.50
23	Brett Myers	.15
24	Mike Smith RC	.25
25	Eric Hinske RC	.15
26	Jake Peavy	.15
27	Todd Donovan RC	.25
28	Luis Ugueto RC	.25
29	Corey Thurman RC	.25
30	Takahito Nomura RC	.25
31	Andy Shibilo RC	.25
32	Mike Crudale RC	.25
33	Earl Snyder RC	.25
34	Brian Tallet	.50
35	Miguel Asencio RC	.25
36	Felix Escalona RC	.25
37	Drew Henson	.40
38	Steve Kent RC	.25
39	Rene Reyes RC	.25
40	Edwin Almonte RC	.25
41	Chris Snelling RC	.75
42	Franklyn German RC	.25
43	Jeriome Robertson RC	.25
44	Colin Young RC	.25
45	Jeremy Lambert RC	.25
46	Kirk Saarloos RC	.75
47	Matt Childers RC	.25
48	Justin Wayne	.15
49	Jose Valverde RC	.25
50	Wily Mo Pena	.15
51	Victor Alvarez RC	.25
52	Julius Matos RC	.25
53	Aaron Cook RC	.40
54	Jeff Austin RC	.25
55	Adrian Burnside RC	.25
56	Brandon Puffer RC	.25
57	Jeremy Hill RC	.25
58	Jaime Cerda RC	.25
59	Aaron Guiel RC	.25
60	Ron Chiavacci	.15
61	Kevin Cash RC	.25
62	Elio Serrano	.15
63	Julio Mateo RC	.25
64	Cam Esslinger RC	.25
65	Ken Huckaby RC	.25
66	Wiki Nieves RC	.25
67	Luis Martinez RC	.25
68	Scotty Layfield RC	.25
69	Jeremy Guthrie RC	.75
70	Hansel Izquierdo RC	.25
71	Shane Nance RC	.25
72	Jeff Baker RC	.50
73	Clifford Bartosh RC	.25
74	Mitch Wylie RC	.25

75	Oliver Perez RC	.75
76	Matt Thornton	.15
77	John Foster RC	.25
78	Joe Borchard	.15
79	Eric Junge RC	.25
80	Jorge Sosa RC	.25
81	Runelvys Hernandez RC	.25
82	Kevin Mench	.15
83	Ben Kozlowski RC	.50
84	Trey Hodges RC	.40
85	Reed Johnson RC	.25
86	Eric Eckenstahler RC	.25
87	Franklin Nunez RC	.25
88	Victor Martinez	.50
89	Kevin Gryboski RC	.25
90	Jason Jennings	.15
91	Jim Rushford RC	.25
92	Jeremy Ward RC	.25
93	Adam Walker RC	.25
94	Freddy Sanchez RC	.50
95	Wilson Valdez RC	.25
96	Lee Gardner	.15
97	Eric Good RC	.25
98	Hank Blalock	.50
99	Mark Corey	.15
100	Jason Davis RC	.40
101	Mike Gonzalez RC	.25
102	David Ross RC	.25
103	Tyler Yates RC	.25
104	Cliff Lee RC	.50
105	Mike Moriarty RC	.25
106	Josh Hancock RC	.25
107	Jason Beverlin RC	.25
108	Clay Condrey RC	.25
109	Shawn Sedlacek RC	.25
110	Sean Burroughs	.15

Donruss Originals

401	Runelvys Hernandez RC	.50
402	Wilson Valdez RC	.25
403	Brian Tallet	1.00
404	Chone Figgins RC	.25
405	Jeriome Robertson RC	.50
406	Shane Nance RC	.25
407	Aaron Cook RC	.75
408	Trey Hodges RC	.75
409	Matt Childers RC	.40
410	Mitch Wylie RC	.25
411	Rene Reyes RC	.25
412	Mike Smith	.25
413	Jason Simontacchi RC	.75
414	Luis Martinez	.40
415	Kevin Cash RC	.40
416	Todd Donovan	.25
417	Scotty Layfield	.25
418	Joe Borchard	.25
419	Adrian Burnside	.25
420	Ben Kozlowski	.25
421	Clay Condrey	.25
422	Cliff Lee	1.00
423	Josh Bard	.25
424	Freddy Sanchez	1.00
425	Ron Calloway	.25

Donruss Studio

Common Studio RC:		3.00
Production 1,500		
251	Freddy Sanchez RC	5.00
252	Josh Bard RC	3.00
253	Trey Hodges RC	3.00
254	Jorge Sosa RC	3.00
255	Ben Kozlowski RC	3.00
256	Eric Good RC	3.00
257	Brian Tallet	3.00
258	P.J. Bevis RC	3.00
259	Rodrigo Rosario RC	3.00
260	Kirk Saarloos	5.00
261	Runelvys Hernandez RC	4.00
262	Josh Hancock RC	3.00
263	Tim Kalita RC	3.00
264	Jason Simontacchi RC	5.00
265	Clay Condrey RC	3.00
266	Cliff Lee RC	8.00
267	Aaron Guiel RC	4.00
268	Andy Pratt RC	4.00
269	Wilson Valdez RC	3.00
270	Oliver Perez RC	6.00
271	Joe Borchard	3.00
272	Jeriome Robertson RC	4.00
273	Aaron Cook RC	5.00
274	Kevin Cash RC	3.00
275	Chone Figgins RC	3.00

Best of Fan Club

Common Best of Fan Club RC:		3.00
Production 1,350		
Best of Fan Club Spotlights:		1.5-3X
Production 100 Sets		
201	Kirk Saarloos RC	4.00
202	Oliver Perez RC	5.00
203	So Taguchi RC	6.00

204	Runelvys Hernandez RC	5.00
205	Freddy Sanchez RC	5.00
206	Cliff Lee RC	8.00
207	Kazuhisa Ishii RC	8.00
208	Kevin Cash RC	5.00
209	Trey Hodges RC	6.00
210	Wilson Valdez RC	3.00
211	Satoru Komiyama RC	3.00
212	Luis Ugueto RC	3.00
213	Joe Borchard	3.00
214	Brian Tallet	4.00
215	Jeriome Robertson RC	5.00
216	Eric Junge RC	4.00
217	Aaron Cook RC	5.00
218	Jason Simontacchi RC	3.00
219	Miguel Asencio RC	3.00
220	Josh Bard RC	3.00
221	Earl Snyder RC	3.00
222	Felix Escalona RC	3.00
223	Rene Reyes RC	3.00
224	Chone Figgins RC	3.00
225	Chris Snelling RC	5.00

Fan Club

Inserted 1:4 Retail		
201	Kirk Saarloos RC	1.50
202	Oliver Perez RC	3.00
203	So Taguchi RC	2.00
204	Runelvys Hernandez RC	1.50
205	Freddy Sanchez RC	3.00
206	Cliff Lee	3.00
207	Kazuhisa Ishii RC	3.00
208	Kevin Cash	1.00
209	Trey Hodges	1.50
210	Wilson Valdez	1.00
211	Satoru Komiyama RC	1.00
212	Luis Ugueto RC	1.50
213	Joe Borchard	2.00
214	Brian Tallet	3.00
215	Jeriome Robertson RC	1.50
216	Eric Junge	1.50
217	Aaron Cook	1.50
218	Jason Simontacchi	1.50
219	Miguel Asencio	1.50
220	Josh Bard	1.50
221	Earl Snyder RC	1.00
222	Felix Escalona	1.00
223	Rene Reyes	1.00
224	Chone Figgins	1.50
225	Chris Snelling RC	4.00

Elite

Common Elite RC:		4.00
Production 1,000		
Elite Turn of the Century:		1-2.5X
Production 100 Sets		
201	Chris Snelling RC	5.00
202	Satoru Komiyama RC	5.00
203	Jason Simontacchi RC	8.00
204	Tim Kalita RC	4.00
205	Runelvys Hernandez RC	5.00
206	Kirk Saarloos RC	4.00
207	Aaron Cook RC	6.00
208	Luis Ugueto RC	5.00
209	Gustavo Chacin RC	5.00
210	Francis Beltran RC	5.00
211	Takahito Nomura RC	5.00
212	Oliver Perez RC	8.00
213	Miguel Asencio RC	4.00
214	Rene Reyes RC	5.00
215	Jeff Baker RC	15.00
216	Jon Adkins RC	5.00
217	Carlos Rivera RC	5.00
218	Corey Thurman RC	5.00
219	Earl Snyder RC	5.00
220	Felix Escalona RC	5.00
221	Jeremy Guthrie RC	15.00
222	Josh Hancock RC	5.00
223	Ben Kozlowski RC	5.00
224	Eric Good RC	5.00
225	Eric Junge RC	5.00
226	Andy Pratt RC	5.00
227	Matt Thornton RC	5.00
228	Jorge Sosa RC	5.00
229	Mike Smith RC	5.00
230	Mitch Wylie RC	5.00
231	John Ennis RC	5.00
232	Reed Johnson RC	5.00
233	Joe Borchard	8.00
234	Ron Calloway RC	5.00
235	Brian Tallet	5.00
236	Chris Baker RC	5.00
237	Cliff Lee RC	15.00
238	Matt Childers RC	5.00
239	Freddy Sanchez RC	5.00
240	Chone Figgins RC	8.00
241	Kevin Cash RC	5.00
242	Josh Bard RC	5.00
243	Jeriome Robertson RC	5.00
244	Jeremy Hill RC	5.00
245	Shane Nance RC	5.00
246	Wes Obermueller RC	5.00
247	Trey Hodges RC	5.00

248	Eric Eckenstahler RC	5.00
249	Jim Rushford RC	5.00
250	Jose Castillo RC	10.00
251	Garrett Atkins RC	20.00
252	Alexis Rios RC	100.00
253	Ryan Church RC	10.00
254	Jimmy Gobble RC	8.00
255	Corwin Malone	6.00
257	Nic Jackson RC	6.00
258	Tommy Whiteman RC	8.00
259	Mario Ramos	5.00
260	Rob Bowen RC	8.00
261	Josh Wilson RC	5.00
262	Tim Hummel RC	5.00
264	Gerald Laird RC	15.00
265	Vinnie Chulk RC	5.00
266	Jesus Medrano RC	5.00
272	Adam LaRoche RC	20.00
273	Adam Morrissey RC	5.00
274	Henri Stanley RC	5.00
275	Walter Young RC	10.00

Donruss Classics
Common Classics RC: 3.00
Production 1,500
Classics Timeless
Tributes: 1.5-3X
Production 100 Sets

201	Oliver Perez RC	5.00
202	Aaron Cook RC	5.00
203	Eric Junge RC	3.00
204	Freddy Sanchez RC	5.00
205	Cliff Lee RC	5.00
206	Runelvys Hernandez RC	5.00
207	Chone Figgins RC	3.00
208	Rodrigo Rosario RC	3.00
209	Kevin Cash RC	3.00
210	Josh Bard RC	3.00
211	Felix Escalona RC	3.00
212	Jeriome Robertson RC	5.00
213	Jason Simontacchi RC	5.00
214	Shane Nance RC	3.00
215	Ben Kozlowski RC	3.00
216	Brian Tallet RC	5.00
217	Earl Snyder RC	3.00
218	Andy Pratt RC	3.00
219	Trey Hodges RC	5.00
220	Kirk Saarloos RC	3.00
221	Rene Reyes RC	3.00
222	Joe Borchard RC	3.00
223	Wilson Valdez RC	3.00
224	Miguel Asencio RC	3.00
225	Chris Snelling RC	5.00

Diamond Kings
Common DK RC: 3.00
Inserted 1:10

151	Chris Snelling RC	4.00
152	Satoru Komiyama RC	3.00
153	Oliver Perez RC	4.00
154	Kirk Saarloos RC	3.00
155	Rene Reyes RC	5.00
156	Runelvys Hernandez RC	3.00
157	Rodrigo Rosario RC	3.00
158	Jason Simontacchi RC	3.00
159	Miguel Asencio RC	3.00
160	Aaron Cook RC	3.00

Autographs

NM/M
Production 15-100   5.00
Print runs listed.

2	P.J. Bevis/50	20.00
9	Francis Beltran/100	5.00
13	Kevin Frederick/100	5.00
14	Chone Figgins/100	20.00
15	Marlon Byrd/100	10.00
17	Jason Lane/100	8.00
19	John Ennis/100	10.00
22	Josh Bard/100	10.00
25	Eric Hinske/100	10.00
28	Luis Ugueto/100	5.00
29	Corey Thurman/100	5.00
30	Takahito Nomura/100	20.00
33	Earl Snyder/100	10.00
34	Brian Tallet/100	15.00
37	Drew Henson/50	20.00
39	Rene Reyes/50	15.00
40	Edwin Almonte/50	15.00
41	Chris Snelling/50	20.00
42	Franklyn German/100	5.00
45	Jeremy Lambert/100	5.00
46	Kirk Saarloos/50	10.00
47	Matt Childers/100	5.00
50	Wily Mo Pena/100	15.00
51	Victor Alvarez/100	10.00
61	Kevin Cash/100	8.00
62	Elio Serrano/100	5.00
64	Cam Esslinger/100	5.00
69	Jeremy Guthrie/100	15.00
71	Shane Nance/100	8.00
72	Jeff Baker/100	20.00
76	Matt Thornton/100	5.00
78	Joe Borchard/100	10.00
82	Kevin Mench/100	10.00
83	Ben Kozlowski/100	8.00
84	Trey Hodges/100	5.00
85	Reed Johnson/100	15.00
88	Victor Martinez/100	25.00
90	Jason Jennings/100	8.00
95	Wilson Valdez/100	10.00
97	Eric Good/100	10.00
98	Hank Blalock/100	20.00
104	Cliff Lee/100	25.00
110	Sean Burroughs/100	10.00

Best of Fan Club Autograph

NM/M
Production 10-100
Print runs listed.

201	Kirk Saarloos/100	10.00
208	Kevin Cash/100	10.00
209	Trey Hodges/100	10.00
210	Wilson Valdez/50	10.00
212	Luis Ugueto/75	10.00
213	Joe Borchard/50	15.00
214	Brian Tallet/50	15.00
220	Josh Bard/50	8.00
221	Earl Snyder/100	8.00
223	Rene Reyes/50	8.00
224	Chone Figgins/100	8.00
225	Chris Snelling/50	15.00

Donruss Classics Signatures

NM/M
Print runs listed.

203	Eric Junge/50	10.00
205	Cliff Lee/100	30.00
207	Chone Figgins/100	10.00
208	Rodrigo Rosario/250	10.00
209	Kevin Cash/100	10.00
210	Josh Bard/100	10.00
214	Shane Nance/200	10.00
215	Ben Kozlowski/200	10.00
216	Brian Tallet/100	15.00
217	Earl Snyder/100	10.00
218	Andy Pratt/250	10.00
219	Trey Hodges/250	15.00
220	Kirk Saarloos/50	20.00
221	Rene Reyes/50	10.00
222	Joe Borchard/100	10.00
223	Wilson Valdez/100	10.00
225	Chris Snelling/100	25.00

Donruss Studio Private Signing

NM/M
Print runs listed.

252	Josh Bard/100	10.00
253	Trey Hodges/250	10.00
255	Ben Kozlowski/200	5.00
257	Brian Tallet/50	15.00
258	P.J. Bevis/50	15.00
259	Rodrigo Rosario/250	5.00
260	Kirk Saarloos/100	10.00
263	Tim Kalita/50	8.00
266	Cliff Lee/100	25.00
268	Andy Pratt/250	8.00
269	Wilson Valdez/200	5.00
271	Joe Borchard/100	15.00
274	Kevin Cash/100	8.00
275	Chone Figgins/100	8.00

Elite Turn of the Century Autograph

NM/M
Common Autograph:
Print runs listed.

201	Chris Snelling/50	30.00
206	Kirk Saarloos/50	20.00
215	Jeff Baker/100	40.00
216	Jon Adkins/100	10.00
217	Carlos Rivera/100	15.00
221	Jeremy Guthrie/100	25.00
223	Ben Kozlowski/100	10.00
240	Chone Figgins/100	30.00
241	Kevin Cash/100	10.00
247	Trey Hodges/100	15.00
251	Garrett Atkins/100	50.00
253	Ryan Church/100	35.00
254	Jimmy Gobble/100	10.00
255	Corwin Malone/100	15.00
258	Tom Whiteman/100	15.00
259	Mario Ramos/100	15.00
260	Rob Bowen/100	15.00
262	Tim Hummel/100	10.00
264	Gerald Laird/100	25.00
266	Jesus Medrano/100	10.00
272	Adam LaRoche/100	60.00
273	Adam Morrissey/100	15.00
274	Henri Stanley/100	15.00

Fan Club Autograph

NM/M
Common Autograph:
Print runs listed.

201	Kirk Saarloos/100	10.00
208	Kevin Cash/50	8.00
209	Trey Hodges/50	10.00
210	Wilson Valdez/50	10.00
212	Luis Ugueto/75	10.00
213	Joe Borchard/50	15.00
214	Brian Tallet/50	15.00
220	Josh Bard/50	8.00
221	Earl Snyder/100	8.00
223	Rene Reyes/50	8.00
224	Chone Figgins/100	8.00

Phenoms

NM/M
Common Player: 3.00
Production 1,000 Sets

1	Kazuhisa Ishii	5.00
2	Eric Hinske	3.00
3	Jason Lane	5.00
4	Victor Martinez	5.00
5	Mark Prior	6.00
6	Antonio Perez	3.00
7	John Buck	3.00
8	Joe Borchard	3.00
9	Alexis Gomez	3.00
10	Sean Burroughs	3.00
11	Carlos Pena	3.00
12	Bill Hall	3.00
13	Alfredo Amezaga	3.00
14	Ed Rogers	3.00
15	Mark Teixeira	5.00
16	Chris Snelling	4.00
17	Nick Johnson	3.00
18	Angel Berroa	3.00
19	Orlando Hudson	3.00
20	Drew Henson	3.00
21	Austin Kearns	3.00
22	Dewon Brazelton	3.00
23	Dennis Tankersley	3.00
24	Josh Beckett	4.00
25	Marlon Byrd	4.00

Phenoms Autographs

NM/M
Common Autograph: 5.00
Print runs listed.

1	Kazuhisa Ishii/25	
2	Eric Hinske/500	10.00
3	Jason Lane/500	5.00
4	Victor Martinez/225	10.00
5	Mark Prior/100	50.00
6	Antonio Perez/500	5.00
7	John Buck/500	8.00
8	Joe Borchard/100	10.00
9	Alexis Gomez/400	5.00
10	Sean Burroughs/150	10.00
11	Carlos Pena/150	8.00
12	Bill Hall/200	8.00
13	Alfredo Amezaga/500	5.00
14	Ed Rogers/500	5.00
15	Mark Teixeira/100	20.00
16	Chris Snelling/100	15.00
17	Nick Johnson/250	8.00
18	Angel Berroa/500	8.00
19	Orlando Hudson/400	15.00
20	Drew Henson/500	25.00
21	Austin Kearns/75	20.00
22	Dewon Brazelton/350	5.00
23	Dennis Tankersley/100	8.00
24	Josh Beckett/125	30.00
25	Marlon Byrd/500	10.00

Rookie Crusade

NM/M
Common Player: 3.00
Production 1,500 Sets

1	Corky Miller	3.00
2	Jack Cust	3.00
3	Erik Bedard	3.00
4	Andres Torres	3.00
5	Geronimo Gil	3.00
6	Rafael Soriano	3.00
7	Johnny Estrada	3.00
8	Steve Bechler	3.00
9	Adam Johnson	3.00
10	So Taguchi	3.00
11	Dee Brown	3.00
12	Kevin Frederick	3.00
13	Allan Simpson	3.00
14	Ricardo Rodriguez	3.00
15	Jason Hart	3.00
16	Matt Childers	3.00
17	Jason Jennings	3.00
18	Anderson Machado	3.00
19	Fernando Rodney	3.00
20	Brandon Larson	3.00
21	Satoru Komiyama	3.00
22	Francis Beltran	3.00
23	Joe Thurston	3.00
24	Josh Pearce	3.00
25	Carlos Hernandez	3.00
26	Ben Howard	3.00
27	Wilson Valdez	3.00
28	Victor Alvarez	3.00
29	Cesar Izturis	3.00
30	Endy Chavez	3.00
31	Michael Cuddyer	4.00
32	Bobby Hill	3.00
33	Willie Harris	3.00
34	Joe Crede	3.00
35	Jorge Padilla	3.00
36	Brandon Backe	3.00
37	Franklyn German	3.00
38	Xavier Nady	3.00
39	Raul Chavez	3.00
40	Shane Nance	3.00
41	Brandon Claussen	4.00
42	Tom Shearn	3.00
43	Freddy Sanchez	3.00
44	Chone Figgins	3.00
45	Cliff Lee	4.00

46	Brian Mallette	3.00
47	Mike Rivera	3.00
48	Elio Serrano	3.00
49	Rodrigo Rosario	3.00
50	Earl Snyder	3.00

Rookie Crusade Autograph

NM/M

Common Autograph: 5.00
Print runs listed.

1	Corky Miller/500	5.00
2	Jack Cust/500	6.00
3	Erik Bedard/100	10.00
4	Andres Torres/500	5.00
5	Geronimo Gil/500	5.00
6	Rafael Soriano/500	8.00
7	Johnny Estrada/400	5.00
8	Steve Bechler/500	6.00
9	Adam Johnson/500	5.00
11	Dee Brown/500	5.00
12	Kevin Frederick/150	5.00
13	Allan Simpson/150	5.00
14	Ricardo Rodriguez/500	5.00
15	Jason Hart/500	5.00
16	Matt Childers/150	5.00
17	Jason Jennings/500	5.00
18	Anderson Machado/500	8.00
19	Fernando Rodney/500	5.00
20	Brandon Larson/400	5.00
22	Francis Beltran/500	5.00
23	Joe Thurston/500	5.00
24	Josh Pearce/500	5.00
25	Carlos Hernandez/500	5.00
26	Ben Howard/500	6.00
27	Wilson Valdez/500	5.00
28	Victor Alvarez/500	5.00
29	Cesar Izturis/500	8.00
30	Endy Chavez/500	5.00
31	Michael Cuddyer/375	10.00
32	Bobby Hill/250	5.00
33	Willie Harris/300	5.00
34	Joe Crede/100	8.00
35	Jorge Padilla/475	10.00
36	Brandon Backe/350	5.00
37	Franklyn German/500	5.00
38	Xavier Nady/500	8.00
39	Raul Chavez/500	5.00
40	Shane Nance/500	5.00
41	Brandon Claussen/150	10.00
42	Tom Shearn/500	5.00
44	Chone Figgins/500	5.00
45	Cliff Lee/500	10.00
46	Brian Mallette/150	5.00
47	Mike Rivera/400	5.00
48	Elio Serrano/500	5.00
49	Rodrigo Rosario/100	10.00
50	Earl Snyder/100	10.00

2003 Donruss

GARRET ANDERSON OF

NM/M

Complete Set (400): 40.00
Common Player: .15
Pack (13): 1.50
Box (24): 30.00

1	Vladimir Guerrero	.75
2	Derek Jeter	2.00
3	Adam Dunn	.50
4	Greg Maddux	1.00
5	Lance Berkman	.40
6	Ichiro Suzuki	2.00
7	Mike Piazza	1.00
8	Alex Rodriguez	2.00
9	Tom Glavine	.25
10	Randy Johnson	.75
11	Nomar Garciaparra	1.00
12	Jason Giambi	.50
13	Sammy Sosa	1.00
14	Barry Zito	.25
15	Chipper Jones	1.00
16	Magglio Ordonez	.25
17	Larry Walker	.25
18	Alfonso Soriano	.75
19	Curt Schilling	.50
20	Barry Bonds	2.00
21	Joe Borchard	.15
22	Chris Snelling	.15
23	Brian Tallet	.15
24	Cliff Lee	.15
25	Freddy Sanchez	.15
26	Chone Figgins	.15
27	Kevin Cash	.15
28	Josh Bard	.15
29	Jeriome Robertson	.15
30	Jeremy Hill	.15
31	Shane Nance	.15
32	Jake Peavy Padres	.15
33	Trey Hodges	.15
34	Eric Eckenstahler	.15
35	Jim Rushford	.15
36	Oliver Perez	.15
37	Kirk Saarloos	.15
38	Hank Blalock	.50
39	Francisco Rodriguez	.25
40	Runelvys Hernandez	.15
41	Aaron Cook	.15
42	Josh Hancock	.15
43	P.J. Bevis	.15
44	Jon Adkins	.15
45	Tim Kalita	.15
46	Nelson Castro	.15
47	Colin Young	.15
48	Adrian Burnside	.15
49	Luis Martinez	.15
50	Peter Zamora	.15
51	Todd Donovan	.15
52	Jeremy Ward	.15
53	Wilson Valdez	.15
54	Eric Good	.15
55	Jeff Baker	.15
56	Mitch Wylie	.15
57	Ron Calloway	.15
58	Jose Valverde	.15
59	Jason Davis	.15
60	Scotty Layfield	.15
61	Matt Thornton	.15
62	Adam Walker	.15
63	Gustavo Chacin	.15
64	Ron Chiavacci	.15
65	Wiki Nieves	.15
66	Clifford Bartosh	.15
67	Mike Gonzalez	.15
68	Justin Wayne	.15
69	Eric Junge	.15
70	Ben Kozlowski	.15
71	Darin Erstad	.25
72	Garret Anderson	.40
73	Troy Glaus	.40
74	David Eckstein	.15
75	Adam Kennedy	.15
76	Kevin Appier	.15
77	Jarrod Washburn	.15
78	Scott Spiezio	.15
79	Tim Salmon	.25
80	Ramon Ortiz	.15
81	Bengie Molina	.15
82	Brad Fullmer	.15
83	Troy Percival	.15
84	David Segui	.15
85	Jay Gibbons	.15
86	Tony Batista	.15
87	Scott Erickson	.15
88	Jeff Conine	.15
89	Melvin Mora	.15
90	Buddy Groom	.15
91	Rodrigo Lopez	.15
92	Marty Cordova	.15
93	Geronimo Gil	.15
94	Kenny Lofton	.15
95	Shea Hillenbrand	.15
96	Manny Ramirez	.50
97	Pedro Martinez	.75
98	Nomar Garciaparra	1.00
99	Rickey Henderson	.40
100	Johnny Damon	.25
101	Trot Nixon	.15
102	Derek Lowe	.15
103	Hee Seop Choi	.15
104	Mark Teixeira	.40
105	Tim Wakefield	.15
106	Jason Varitek	.25
107	Frank Thomas	.50
108	Joe Crede	.15
109	Magglio Ordonez	.25
110	Ray Durham	.15
111	Mark Buehrle	.15
112	Paul Konerko	.25
113	Jose Valentin	.15
114	Carlos Lee	.15
115	Royce Clayton	.15
116	C.C. Sabathia	.15
117	Ellis Burks	.15
118	Omar Vizquel	.25
119	Jim Thome	.75
120	Matt Lawton	.15
121	Travis Fryman	.15
122	Earl Snyder	.15
123	Ricky Gutierrez	.15
124	Einar Diaz	.15
125	Danys Baez	.15
126	Robert Fick	.15
127	Bobby Higginson	.15
128	Steve Sparks	.15
129	Mike Rivera	.15
130	Wendell Magee	.15
131	Randall Simon	.15
132	Carlos Pena	.15
133	Mark Redman	.15
134	Juan Acevedo	.15
135	Mike Sweeney	.15
136	Aaron Guiel	.15
137	Carlos Beltran	.40
138	Joe Randa	.15
139	Paul Byrd	.15
140	Shawn Sedlacek	.15
141	Raul Ibanez	.15
142	Michael Tucker	.15
143	Torii Hunter	.40
144	Jacque Jones	.15
145	David Ortiz	.40
146	Corey Koskie	.15
147	Brad Radke	.15
148	Doug Mientkiewicz	.15
149	A.J. Pierzynski	.15
150	Dustan Mohr	.15
151	Michael Cuddyer	.15
152	Eddie Guardado	.15
153	Cristian Guzman	.15
154	Derek Jeter	2.00
155	Bernie Williams	.50
156	Roger Clemens	1.50
157	Mike Mussina	.50
158	Jorge Posada	.40
159	Alfonso Soriano	.75
160	Jason Giambi	.50
161	Robin Ventura	.25
162	Andy Pettitte	.25
163	David Wells	.15
164	Nick Johnson	.15
165	Jeff Weaver	.15
166	Raul Mondesi	.15
167	Rondell White	.15
168	Tim Hudson	.25
169	Barry Zito	.40
170	Mark Mulder	.25
171	Miguel Tejada	.40
172	Eric Chavez	.25
173	Billy Koch	.15
174	Jermaine Dye	.15
175	Scott Hatteberg	.15
176	Terrence Long	.15
177	David Justice	.25
178	Ramon Hernandez	.15
179	Ted Lilly	.15
180	Ichiro Suzuki	1.50
181	Edgar Martinez	.25
182	Mike Cameron	.15
183	John Olerud	.15
184	Bret Boone	.25
185	Dan Wilson	.15
186	Freddy Garcia	.15
187	Jamie Moyer	.15
188	Carlos Guillen	.15
189	Ruben Sierra	.15
190	Kazuhiro Sasaki	.15
191	Mark McLemore	.15
192	Chris Snelling	.15
193	Joel Pineiro	.15
194	Jeff Cirillo	.15
195	Rafael Soriano	.15
196	Ben Grieve	.15
197	Aubrey Huff	.15
198	Steve Cox	.15
199	Toby Hall	.15
200	Randy Winn	.15
201	Brent Abernathy	.15
202	Chris Gomez	.15
203	John Flaherty	.15
204	Paul Wilson	.15
205	Chan Ho Park	.15
206	Alex Rodriguez	2.00
207	Juan Gonzalez	.50
208	Rafael Palmeiro	.50
209	Ivan Rodriguez	.50
210	Rusty Greer	.15
211	Kenny Rogers	.15
212	Ismael Valdes	.15
213	Frank Catalanotto	.15
214	Hank Blalock	.50
215	Michael Young	.15
216	Kevin Mench	.15
217	Herbert Perry	.15
218	Gabe Kapler	.25
219	Carlos Delgado	.25
220	Shannon Stewart	.15
221	Eric Hinske	.15
222	Roy Halladay	.25
223	Felipe Lopez	.15
224	Vernon Wells	.15
225	Josh Phelps	.15
226	Jose Cruz	.15
227	Curt Schilling	.50
228	Randy Johnson	.75
229	Luis Gonzalez	.25
230	Mark Grace	.40
231	Junior Spivey	.15
232	Tony Womack	.15
233	Matt Williams	.25
234	Steve Finley	.15
235	Byung-Hyun Kim	.15
236	Craig Counsell	.15
237	Greg Maddux	1.00
238	Tom Glavine	.40
239	John Smoltz	.25
240	Chipper Jones	1.00
241	Gary Sheffield	.25
242	Andruw Jones	.40
243	Vinny Castilla	.15
244	Damian Moss	.15
245	Rafael Furcal	.15
246	Javy Lopez	.25
247	Kevin Millwood	.15
248	Kerry Wood	.75
249	Fred McGriff	.25
250	Sammy Sosa	1.00
251	Alex Gonzalez	.15
252	Corey Patterson	.25
253	Moises Alou	.25
254	Juan Cruz	.15
255	Jon Lieber	.15
256	Matt Clement	.15
257	Mark Prior	.75
258	Ken Griffey Jr.	1.00
259	Barry Larkin	.25
260	Adam Dunn	.50
261	Sean Casey	.15
262	Jose Rijo	.15
263	Elmer Dessens	.15
264	Austin Kearns	.25
265	Corky Miller	.15
266	Todd Walker	.15
267	Chris Reitsma	.15
268	Ryan Dempster	.15
269	Aaron Boone	.15
270	Danny Graves	.15
271	Brandon Larson	.15
272	Larry Walker	.25
273	Todd Helton	.50
274	Juan Uribe	.15
275	Juan Pierre	.15
276	Mike Hampton	.15
277	Todd Zeile	.15
278	Todd Hollandsworth	.15
279	Jason Jennings	.15
280	Josh Beckett	.40
281	Mike Lowell	.25
282	Derrek Lee	.25
283	A.J. Burnett	.25
284	Luis Castillo	.15
285	Tim Raines	.15
286	Preston Wilson	.15
287	Juan Encarnacion	.15
288	Charles Johnson	.15
289	Jeff Bagwell	.50
290	Craig Biggio	.25
291	Lance Berkman	.40
292	Daryle Ward	.15
293	Roy Oswalt	.40
294	Richard Hidalgo	.15
295	Octavio Dotel	.15
296	Wade Miller	.15
297	Julio Lugo	.15
298	Billy Wagner	.15
299	Shawn Green	.40
300	Adrian Beltre	.25
301	Paul LoDuca	.15
302	Eric Karros	.15
303	Kevin Brown	.15
304	Hideo Nomo	.40
305	Odalis Perez	.15
306	Eric Gagne	.40
307	Brian Jordan	.15
308	Cesar Izturis	.15
309	Mark Grudzielanek	.15
310	Kazuhisa Ishii	.15
311	Geoff Jenkins	.15
312	Richie Sexson	.40
313	Jose Hernandez	.15
314	Ben Sheets	.25
315	Ruben Quevedo	.15
316	Jeffrey Hammonds	.15
317	Alex Sanchez	.15
318	Eric Young	.15
319	Takahito Nomura	.15
320	Vladimir Guerrero	.75
321	Jose Vidro	.15
322	Orlando Cabrera	.15
323	Michael Barrett	.15
324	Javier Vazquez	.15
325	Tony Armas Jr.	.15
326	Andres Galarraga	.15
327	Tomokazu Ohka	.15
328	Bartolo Colon	.15
329	Fernando Tatis	.15
330	Brad Wilkerson	.15
331	Masato Yoshii	.15
332	Mike Piazza	1.00
333	Jeromy Burnitz	.15
334	Roberto Alomar	.50

335	Mo Vaughn	.15
336	Al Leiter	.25
337	Pedro Astacio	.15
338	Edgardo Alfonzo	.15
339	Armando Benitez	.15
340	Timoniel Perez	.15
341	Jay Payton	.15
342	Roger Cedeno	.15
343	Rey Ordonez	.15
344	Steve Trachsel	.15
345	Satoru Komiyama	.15
346	Scott Rolen	.75
347	Pat Burrell	.40
348	Bobby Abreu	.25
349	Mike Lieberthal	.15
350	Brandon Duckworth	.15
351	Jimmy Rollins	.25
352	Marlon Anderson	.15
353	Travis Lee	.15
354	Vicente Padilla	.15
355	Randy Wolf	.15
356	Jason Kendall	.15
357	Brian Giles	.25
358	Aramis Ramirez	.40
359	Pokey Reese	.15
360	Kip Wells	.15
361	Josh Fogg	.15
362	Mike Williams	.15
363	Jack Wilson	.15
364	Craig Wilson	.15
365	Kevin Young	.15
366	Ryan Klesko	.15
367	Phil Nevin	.15
368	Brian Lawrence	.15
369	Mark Kotsay	.15
370	Brett Tomko	.15
371	Trevor Hoffman	.15
372	Deivi Cruz	.15
373	Bubba Trammell	.15
374	Sean Burroughs	.15
375	Barry Bonds	2.00
376	Jeff Kent	.25
377	Rich Aurilia	.15
378	Tsuyoshi Shinjo	.15
379	Benito Santiago	.15
380	Kirk Rueter	.15
381	Livan Hernandez	.15
382	Russ Ortiz	.15
383	David Bell	.15
384	Jason Schmidt	.40
385	Reggie Sanders	.15
386	J.T. Snow	.15
387	Robb Nen	.15
388	Ryan Jensen	.15
389	Jim Edmonds	.40
390	J.D. Drew	.25
391	Albert Pujols	1.50
392	Fernando Vina	.15
393	Tino Martinez	.15
394	Edgar Renteria	.40
395	Matt Morris	.15
396	Woody Williams	.15
397	Jason Isringhausen	.15
398	Placido Polanco	.15
399	Eli Marrero	.15
400	Jason Simontacchi	.15

Stat Line Career

Cards serial numbered		
251-400:		3-6X
Print run 151-250:		4-8X
Print run 101-150:		5-10X
Print run 61-100:		8-15X
Print run 31-60:		10-20X
Numbered to career stat.		

Stat Line Season

Cards serial numbered		
151-200:		4-8X
Print run 151-150:		5-10X
Print run 61-100:		8-15X
Print run 31-60:		10-20X
Numbered to 2002 stat.		

All-Stars

		NM/M
Complete Set (10):		25.00
Common Player:		1.50
Retail only		
1	Ichiro Suzuki	5.00
2	Alex Rodriguez	6.00
3	Nomar Garciaparra	3.00
4	Derek Jeter	6.00
5	Manny Ramirez	2.00
6	Barry Bonds	6.00
7	Adam Dunn	1.50
8	Mike Piazza	3.00
9	Sammy Sosa	4.00
10	Todd Helton	1.50

Anniversary 1983

		NM/M
Complete Set (20):		50.00
Common Player:		1.50
Inserted 1:12		
1	Dale Murphy	2.00
2	Jim Palmer	2.00
3	Nolan Ryan	6.00
4	Ozzie Smith	4.00
5	Tom Seaver	4.00
6	Mike Schmidt	5.00
7	Steve Carlton	2.00
8	Robin Yount	3.00
9	Ryne Sandberg	4.00
10	Cal Ripken Jr.	8.00
11	Fernando Valenzuela	1.50
12	Andre Dawson	2.00
13	George Brett	6.00
14	Eddie Murray	3.00
15	Dave Winfield	2.00
16	Johnny Bench	4.00
17	Wade Boggs	2.00
18	Tony Gwynn	4.00
19	San Diego Chicken	1.50
20	Ty Cobb	5.00

Bat Kings

		NM/M
Common Player:		10.00
Studio Series:		1.5-3X
Production 25 or 50		
1	Scott Rolen/250	20.00
2	Frank Thomas/250	15.00
3	Chipper Jones/250	20.00
4	Ivan Rodriguez/250	15.00
5	Stan Musial/100	40.00
6	Nomar Garciaparra/ 250	25.00
7	Vladimir Guerrero/ 250	15.00
8	Adam Dunn/250	15.00
9	Lance Berkman/250	15.00
10	Magglio Ordonez/250	10.00
11	Ernie Banks/50	40.00

12	Manny Ramirez/100	25.00
13	Mike Piazza/100	40.00
14	Alex Rodriguez/100	25.00
15	Todd Helton/100	20.00
16	Andre Dawson/100	20.00
17	Cal Ripken Jr/100	60.00
18	Tony Gwynn/100	25.00
19	Don Mattingly/100	60.00
20	Ryne Sandberg/100	45.00

Diamond Kings

		NM/M
Complete Set (20):		120.00
Common Player:		2.00
Production 2,500 Sets		
Studio Series:		1.5-3X
Production 250 Sets		
1	Vladimir Guerrero	5.00
2	Derek Jeter	15.00
3	Adam Dunn	5.00
4	Greg Maddux	8.00
5	Lance Berkman	3.00
6	Ichiro Suzuki	10.00
7	Mike Piazza	10.00
8	Alex Rodriguez	10.00
9	Tom Glavine	3.00
10	Randy Johnson	8.00
11	Nomar Garciaparra	10.00
12	Jason Giambi	5.00
13	Sammy Sosa	8.00
14	Barry Zito	3.00
15	Chipper Jones	8.00
16	Magglio Ordonez	5.00
17	Larry Walker	2.00
18	Alfonso Soriano	8.00
19	Curt Schilling	4.00
20	Barry Bonds	15.00

Elite Series

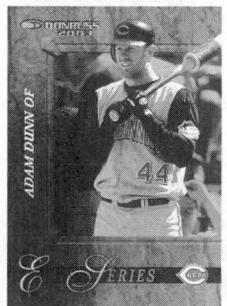

		NM/M
Complete Set (15):		50.00
Common Player:		2.00
Production 2,500 Sets		
Dominators:		No Pricing
Production 25 Sets		
1	Alex Rodriguez	8.00
2	Barry Bonds	10.00
3	Ichiro Suzuki	8.00
4	Vladimir Guerrero	5.00
5	Randy Johnson	4.00
6	Pedro Martinez	4.00
7	Adam Dunn	3.00
8	Sammy Sosa	6.00
9	Jim Edmonds	2.00
10	Greg Maddux	6.00
11	Kazuhisa Ishii	2.00
12	Jason Giambi	6.00
13	Nomar Garciaparra	6.00
14	Tom Glavine	2.00
15	Todd Helton	3.00

Jersey Kings

		NM/M
Common Player:		10.00
Studio Series:		1.5-3X
Production 25 or 50		
1	Juan Gonzalez/250	15.00
2	Greg Maddux/250	20.00
3	Nomar Garciaparra/ 250	20.00
4	Troy Glaus/250	10.00
5	Reggie Jackson/100	20.00
6	Alex Rodriguez/250	25.00
7	Alfonso Soriano/250	15.00
8	Curt Schilling/250	12.00
9	Vladimir Guerrero/ 250	15.00
10	Adam Dunn/250	15.00
11	Mark Grace/100	25.00
12	Roger Clemens/100	30.00
13	Jeff Bagwell/100	25.00
14	Tom Glavine/100	20.00
15	Mike Piazza/100	25.00
16	Rod Carew/100	20.00
17	Rickey Henderson/ 100	25.00
18	Mike Schmidt/100	40.00
19	Cal Ripken Jr/100	60.00
20	Dale Murphy/100	15.00

Longball Leaders

		NM/M
Complete Set (10):		30.00
Common Player:		1.50
Production 1,000 Sets		
Seasonal Sum:		4-6X
Numbered to 2002 HR total.		
1	Alex Rodriguez	6.00
2	Alfonso Soriano	4.00
3	Rafael Palmeiro	2.00
4	Jim Thome	3.00
5	Jason Giambi	3.00
6	Sammy Sosa	5.00
7	Barry Bonds	8.00
8	Lance Berkman	2.00
9	Shawn Green	1.50
10	Vladimir Guerrero	4.00

Production Line

		NM/M
Complete Set (30):		120.00
Common Player:		2.00
Numbered to selected stat.		
Die-Cuts:		1-3X
Production 100 Sets		
1	Alex Rodriguez/1,015	6.00
2	Jim Thome/1,122	3.00
3	Lance Berkman/357	8.00
4	Barry Bonds/1,381	8.00
5	Sammy Sosa/993	5.00
6	Vladimir Guerrero/ 1,010	3.00
7	Barry Bonds/582	10.00
8	Jason Giambi/435	6.00
9	Vladimir Guerrero/417	4.00
10	Adam Dunn/400	3.00
11	Chipper Jones/435	6.00
12	Todd Helton/429	3.00
13	Rafael Palmeiro/571	2.00
14	Sammy Sosa/594	6.00
15	Alex Rodriguez/623	8.00
16	Larry Walker/602	2.00
17	Lance Berkman/578	2.00
18	Alfonso Soriano/547	5.00
19	Ichiro Suzuki/321	8.00
20	Mike Sweeney/340	6.00
21	Manny Ramirez/349	4.00
22	Larry Walker/338	2.00
23	Barry Bonds/370	12.00
24	Jim Edmonds/311	2.00
25	Alfonso Soriano/300	6.00
26	Jason Giambi/335	6.00
27	Miguel Tejada/336	4.00
28	Brian Giles/309	3.00
29	Vladimir Guerrero/364	5.00
30	Pat Burrell/319	6.00

Timber and Threads

		NM/M
Common Player:		6.00
1	Al Kaline/Bat/125	25.00
2	Alex Rodriguez/ Bat/350	20.00
3	Carlos Delgado/ Bat/250	8.00
4	Cliff Floyd/Bat/250	8.00
5	Eddie Mathews/ Bat/125	25.00
6	Edgar Martinez/ Bat/125	10.00
7	Ernie Banks/Bat/50	40.00
8	Ivan Rodriguez/ Bat/125	15.00
9	J.D. Drew/Bat/125	8.00

10	Jorge Posada/Bat/300	10.00
11	Lou Brock/Bat/125	20.00
12	Mike Piazza/Bat/125	25.00
13	Mike Schmidt/Bat/125	50.00
14	Reggie Jackson/Bat/125	20.00
15	Rickey Henderson/Bat/125	25.00
16	Robin Yount/Bat/125	35.00
17	Rod Carew/Bat/125	20.00
18	Scott Rolen/Bat/125	20.00
19	Shawn Green/Bat/200	8.00
20	Willie Stargell/Bat/125	
21	Alex Rodriguez/Jsy/175	20.00
22	Andruw Jones/Jsy/275	8.00
23	Brooks Robinson/Jsy/150	25.00
24	Chipper Jones/Jsy/150	20.00
25	Greg Maddux/Jsy/175	20.00
26	Hideo Nomo/Jsy/300	40.00
27	Ivan Rodriguez/Jsy/225	10.00
28	Jack Morris/Jsy/150	8.00
29	J.D. Drew/Jsy/150	8.00
30	Jeff Bagwell/Jsy/500	15.00
31	Jim Thome/Jsy/200	15.00
32	John Smoltz/Jsy/175	8.00
33	John Olerud/Jsy/450	8.00
34	Kerry Wood/Jsy/200	15.00
35	Harmon Killebrew/Jsy/50	60.00
36	Larry Walker/Jsy/500	6.00
37	Magglio Ordonez/Jsy/150	10.00
38	Manny Ramirez/Jsy/500	15.00
39	Mike Piazza/Jsy/300	15.00
40	Mike Sweeney/Jsy/200	8.00
41	Nomar Garciaparra/Jsy/200	25.00
42	Paul Konerko/Jsy/500	10.00
43	Pedro Martinez/Jsy/175	15.00
44	Randy Johnson/Jsy/175	15.00
45	Roger Clemens/Jsy/350	20.00
46	Shawn Green/Jsy/250	8.00
47	Todd Helton/Jsy/175	8.00
48	Tom Glavine/Jsy/525	12.00
49	Tony Gwynn/Jsy/150	25.00
50	Vladimir Guerrero/Jsy/450	15.00

2003 Donruss Champions

RUNELVYS HERNANDEZ

		NM/M
	Complete Set (300):	40.00
	Common Player:	.15
	Pack (8):	2.00
	Box (24):	40.00
1	Adam Kennedy	.15
2	Alfredo Amezaga	.15
3	Chone Figgins	.15
4	Darin Erstad	.25
5	David Eckstein	.15
6	Garret Anderson	.40
7	Jarrod Washburn	.15
8	Nolan Ryan	2.00
9	Tim Salmon	.25
10	Troy Glaus	.40
11	Troy Percival	.15
12	Curt Schilling	.50
13	Junior Spivey	.15
14	Luis Gonzalez	.25
15	Mark Grace	.50
16	Randy Johnson	1.00
17	Steve Finley	.15
18	Andruw Jones	.40
19	Chipper Jones	.75
20	Dale Murphy	.50
21	Gary Sheffield	.40
22	Greg Maddux	1.00
23	John Smoltz	.25
24	Andy Pratt	.15
25	Adam LaRoche	.15
26	Trey Hodges	.15
27	Warren Spahn	.75
28	Cal Ripken Jr.	3.00
29	Ed Rogers	.15
30	Brian Roberts	.15
31	Geronimo Gil	.15
32	Jay Gibbons	.15
33	Josh Towers	.15
34	Casey Fossum	.15
35	Cliff Floyd	.15
36	Derek Lowe	.15
37	Fred Lynn	.15
38	Freddy Sanchez	.15
39	Manny Ramirez	.50
40	Nomar Garciaparra	1.00
41	Pedro J. Martinez	.75
42	Rickey Henderson	.50
43	Shea Hillenbrand	.15
44	Trot Nixon	.15
45	Bobby Hill	.15
46	Corey Patterson	.25
47	Fred McGriff	.25
48	Hee Seop Choi	.15
49	Juan Cruz	.15
50	Kerry Wood	.75
51	Mark Prior	1.00
52	Moises Alou	.25
53	Nic Jackson	.15
54	Ryne Sandberg	1.00
55	Sammy Sosa	1.50
56	Carlos Lee	.15
57	Corwin Malone	.15
58	Frank Thomas	.50
59	Joe Borchard	.15
60	Joe Crede	.15
61	Magglio Ordonez	.25
62	Mark Buehrle	.15
63	Paul Konerko	.15
64	Tim Hummel	.15
65	Jon Adkins	.15
66	Adam Dunn	.50
67	Austin Kearns	.25
68	Barry Larkin	.40
69	Jose Acevedo	.15
70	Corky Miller	.15
71	Eric Davis	.15
72	Ken Griffey Jr.	1.00
73	Sean Casey	.25
74	Wily Mo Pena	.25
75	Bob Feller	.50
76	Brian Tallet	.15
77	C.C. Sabathia	.15
78	Cliff Lee	.15
79	Earl Snyder	.15
80	Ellis Burks	.15
81	Jeremy Guthrie	.15
82	Travis Hafner	.25
83	Luis Garcia	.15
84	Omar Vizquel	.25
85	Ricardo Rodriguez	.15
86	Ryan Church	.15
87	Victor Martinez	.15
88	Brandon Phillips	.15
89	Jack Cust	.15
90	Jason Jennings	.15
91	Jeff Baker	.15
92	Garrett Atkins	.15
93	Juan Uribe	.15
94	Larry Walker	.25
95	Rene Reyes	.15
96	Todd Helton	.50
97	Alan Trammell	.15
98	Fernando Rodney	.15
99	Carlos Pena	.15
100	Jack Morris	.15
101	Bobby Higginson	.15
102	Mike Maroth	.15
103	Robert Fick	.15
104	Jesus Medrano	.15
105	Josh Beckett	.40
106	Luis Castillo	.15
107	Mike Lowell	.25
108	Juan Pierre	.15
109	Josh Wilson	.15
110	Tim Redding	.15
111	Carlos Hernandez	.15
112	Craig Biggio	.25
113	Henri Stanley	.15
114	Jason Lane	.15
115	Jeff Bagwell	.50
116	John Buck	.15
117	Kirk Saarloos	.15
118	Lance Berkman	.75
119	Nolan Ryan	2.00
120	Richard Hidalgo	.15
121	Rodrigo Rosario	.15
122	Roy Oswalt	.25
123	Tommy Whiteman RC	.15
124	Wade Miller	.15
125	Alexis Gomez	.15
126	Angel Berroa	.15
127	Brandon Berger	.15
128	Carlos Beltran	.40
129	George Brett	2.00
130	Jimmy Gobble	.15
131	Dee Brown	.15
132	Mike Sweeney	.15
133	Raul Ibanez	.15
134	Runelvys Hernandez	.15
135	Adrian Beltre	.40
136	Brian Jordan	.15
137	Cesar Izturis	.15
138	Victor Alvarez	.15
139	Hideo Nomo	.50
140	Joe Thurston	.15
141	Kazuhisa Ishii	.15
142	Kevin Brown	.25
143	Odalis Perez	.15
144	Paul LoDuca	.15
145	Shawn Green	.25
146	Ben Sheets	.25
147	Bill Hall	.15
148	Nick Neugebauer	.15
149	Richie Sexson	.40
150	Robin Yount	1.00
151	Shane Nance	.15
152	Takahito Nomura	.15
153	A.J. Pierzynski	.15
154	Joe Mays	.15
155	Kirby Puckett	1.00
156	Adam Johnson	.15
157	Rob Bowen	.15
158	Torii Hunter	.40
159	Andres Galarraga	.15
160	Endy Chavez	.15
161	Javier Vazquez	.15
162	Jose Vidro	.15
163	Vladimir Guerrero	.75
164	Dwight Gooden	.15
165	Mike Piazza	1.00
166	Roberto Alomar	.40
167	Tom Glavine	.40
168	Alfonso Soriano	.75
169	Bernie Williams	.40
170	Brandon Claussen	.15
171	Derek Jeter	2.00
172	Don Mattingly	1.50
173	Drew Henson	.15
174	Jason Giambi	.50
175	Joe Torre	.25
176	Jorge Posada	.40
177	Mike Mussina	.50
178	Nick Johnson	.15
179	Roger Clemens	1.50
180	Whitey Ford	.75
181	Adam Morrissey	.15
182	Barry Zito	.15
183	David Justice	.15
184	Eric Chavez	.40
185	Jermaine Dye	.15
186	Mark Mulder	.25
187	Miguel Tejada	.40
188	Reggie Jackson	.75
189	Terrence Long	.15
190	Tim Hudson	.25
191	Anderson Machado	.15
192	Bobby Abreu	.40
193	Brandon Duckworth	.15
194	Jim Thome	.75
195	Eric Junge	.15
196	Jeremy Giambi	.15
197	Johnny Estrada	.15
198	Jorge Padilla	.15
199	Marlon Byrd	.15
200	Mike Schmidt	1.50
201	Pat Burrell	.50
202	Steve Carlton	.25
203	Aramis Ramirez	.25
204	Brian Giles	.25
205	Carlos Rivera	.15
206	Craig Wilson	.15
207	Dave Williams	.15
208	Jack Wilson	.15
209	Jose Castillo	.15
210	Kip Wells	.15
211	Roberto Clemente	1.50
212	Walter Young	.15
213	Ben Howard	.15
214	Brian Lawrence	.15
215	Clifford Bartosh	.15
216	Dennis Tankersley	.15
217	Oliver Perez	.15
218	Phil Nevin	.25
219	Ryan Klesko	.25
220	Sean Burroughs	.15
221	Tony Gwynn	.75
222	Xavier Nady	.15
223	Mike Rivera	.15
224	Barry Bonds	2.00
225	Benito Santiago	.15
226	Jason Schmidt	.40
227	Jeff Kent	.25
228	Kenny Lofton	.15
229	Rich Aurilia	.15
230	Robb Nen	.15
231	Tsuyoshi Shinjo	.15
232	Bret Boone	.15
233	Chris Snelling	.15
234	Edgar Martinez	.25
235	Freddy Garcia	.15
236	Ichiro Suzuki	1.50
237	John Olerud	.25
238	Kazuhiro Sasaki	.15
239	Mike Cameron	.15
240	Rafael Soriano	.15
241	Albert Pujols	1.50
242	J.D. Drew	.40
243	Jim Edmonds	.40
244	Ozzie Smith	1.00
245	Scott Rolen	.75
246	So Taguchi	.15
247	Stan Musial	1.00
248	Antonio Perez	.15
249	Aubrey Huff	.15
250	Dewon Brazelton	.15
251	Delvin James	.15
252	Joe Kennedy	.15
253	Toby Hall	.15
254	Alex Rodriguez	2.00
255	Ben Kozlowski	.15
256	Gerald Laird	.15
257	Hank Blalock	.50
258	Ivan Rodriguez	.50
259	Juan Gonzalez	.50
260	Kevin Mench	.15
261	Mario Ramos	.15
262	Mark Teixeira	.25
263	Nolan Ryan	2.00
264	Rafael Palmeiro	.50
265	Alexis Rios	.15
266	Carlos Delgado	.40
267	Eric Hinske	.15
268	Josh Phelps	.15
269	Kevin Cash	.15
270	Orlando Hudson	.15
271	Roy Halladay	.15
272	Shannon Stewart	.15
273	Vernon Wells	.15
274	Vinnie Chulk	.15
275	Jason Anderson	.15
276	Craig Brazell RC	.50
277	Terrmel Sledge RC	.50
278	Ryan Cameron RC	.50
279	Clint Barmes RC	.50
280	Jhonny Peralta	.50
281	Todd Wellemeyer RC	.50
282	Jon Leicester RC	.40
283	Brandon Webb RC	1.00
284	Tim Olson RC	.50
285	Matt Kata RC	.75
286	Rob Hammock RC	.50
287	Pete LaForest RC	.50
288	Nook Logan RC	.50
289	Prentice Redman RC	.40
290	Joe Valentine RC	.40
291	Jose Contreras RC	1.00
292	Josh Stewart RC	.40
293	Mike Nicolas RC	.40
294	Marshall McDougall	.15
295	Travis Chapman	.15
296	Jose Morban	.15
297	Michael Hessman RC	.40
298	Buddy Hernandez RC	.40
299	Shane Victorino RC	.40
300	Jason Dubois	.15
301	Hideki Matsui RC	3.00

Metalized

ROOKIE

Stars: 4-8X
RC's: 1-3X

Production 100 Sets
Holofoils: No Pricing
Production 25 Sets

Autographs

		NM/M
Common Autograph:		5.00
2	Alfredo Amezaga/325	8.00
3	Chone Figgins/375	10.00
13	Junior Spivey/45	10.00
24	Andy Pratt/475	8.00
25	Adam LaRoche/400	10.00
26	Trey Hodges/305	5.00
29	Ed Rogers/305	5.00
30	Brian Roberts/305	35.00
31	Geronimo Gil/150	8.00
32	Jay Gibbons/475	8.00
33	Josh Towers/500	10.00
34	Casey Fossum/160	5.00
35	Cliff Floyd/70	20.00
37	Fred Lynn/80	20.00
38	Freddy Sanchez/400	15.00
46	Corey Patterson/100	15.00
49	Juan Cruz/250	8.00
51	Mark Prior/50	30.00
53	Nic Jackson/100	10.00
57	Corwin Malone/400	8.00
59	Joe Borchard/215	8.00
64	Tim Hummel/250	5.00
65	Jon Adkins/400	5.00
66	Adam Dunn/100	30.00
67	Austin Kearns/50	20.00
69	Jose Acevedo/315	5.00
70	Corky Miller/295	5.00
71	Eric Davis/45	25.00
74	Wily Mo Pena/450	15.00
76	Brian Tallet/250	8.00
78	Cliff Lee/330	10.00
79	Earl Snyder/225	8.00
81	Jeremy Guthrie/400	8.00
83	Luis Garcia/395	5.00
86	Ryan Church/395	10.00
87	Victor Martinez/250	25.00
88	Brandon Phillips/375	10.00
89	Jack Cust/498	10.00
90	Jason Jennings/375	8.00
91	Jeff Baker/400	8.00
92	Garrett Atkins/400	8.00
95	Rene Reyes/350	8.00
98	Fernando Rodney/500	8.00
100	Jack Morris/50	20.00
102	Mike Maroth/400	8.00
104	Jesus Medrano/500	8.00
109	Josh Wilson/400	8.00
110	Tim Redding/375	8.00
111	Carlos Hernandez/250	8.00
113	Henri Stanley/390	5.00
114	Jason Lane/250	10.00
117	Kirk Saarloos/149	8.00
120	Richard Hidalgo/120	10.00
121	Rodrigo Rosario/500	10.00
122	Roy Oswalt/100	20.00
124	Wade Miller/125	10.00
126	Angel Berroa/400	8.00
127	Brandon Berger/325	8.00
130	Jimmy Gobble/400	8.00
131	Dee Brown/500	8.00
132	Mike Sweeney/45	20.00
134	Runelvys Hernandez/400	5.00
138	Victor Alvarez/308	8.00
144	Paul LoDuca/50	20.00
146	Ben Sheets/50	20.00
147	Bill Hall/450	10.00
148	Nick Neugebauer/375	5.00
151	Shane Nance/150	8.00
152	Takahito Nomura/50	20.00
153	A.J. Pierzynski/50	10.00
156	Adam Johnson/500	8.00
157	Rob Bowen/375	8.00
158	Torii Hunter/45	20.00
160	Endy Chavez/280	10.00
161	Javier Vazquez/50	15.00
162	Jose Vidro/45	15.00

164	Dwight Gooden/45	30.00
170	Brandon Claussen/475	10.00
178	Nick Johnson/500	8.00
181	Adam Morrissey/395	8.00
185	Jermaine Dye/125	15.00
189	Terrence Long/250	10.00
191	Anderson Machado/500	8.00
193	Brandon Duckworth/100	10.00
195	Eric Junge/279	8.00
196	Jeremy Giambi/195	8.00
205	Carlos Rivera/400	10.00
206	Craig Wilson/245	8.00
207	Dave Williams/265	8.00
208	Jack Wilson/500	15.00
212	Walter Young/400	8.00
213	Ben Howard/500	8.00
214	Brian Lawrence/500	8.00
215	Clifford Bartosh/400	8.00
222	Xavier Nady/250	8.00
223	Mike Rivera/90	8.00
233	Chris Snelling/200	8.00
240	Rafael Soriano/500	8.00
248	Antonio Perez/500	8.00
249	Aubrey Huff/475	15.00
250	Dewon Brazelton/50	15.00
251	Delvin James/400	8.00
252	Joe Kennedy/250	8.00
253	Toby Hall/500	8.00
255	Ben Kozlowski/400	8.00
256	Gerald Laird/483	8.00
257	Hank Blalock/50	25.00
260	Kevin Mench/475	10.00
261	Mario Ramos/475	5.00
262	Mark Teixeira/40	40.00
265	Alexis Rios/400	20.00
267	Eric Hinske/390	10.00
269	Kevin Cash/375	8.00
274	Vinnie Chulk/100	10.00
275	Jason Anderson/493	15.00
276	Craig Brazell/15	15.00
277	Terrmel Sledge/500	10.00
278	Ryan Cameron/475	8.00
279	Clint Barmes/475	15.00
280	Jhonny Peralta/500	8.00
281	Todd Wellemeyer/477	10.00
282	Jon Leicester/480	8.00
283	Brandon Webb/500	30.00
284	Tim Olson/500	8.00
285	Matt Kata/487	10.00
286	Rob Hammock/486	10.00
287	Pete LaForest/500	10.00
288	Nook Logan/500	8.00
289	Prentice Redman/488	10.00
290	Joe Valentine/475	8.00
291	Jose Contreras/100	25.00
292	Josh Stewart/485	10.00
293	Mike Nicolas/500	10.00
295	Travis Chapman/100	15.00
296	Jose Morban/475	8.00
297	Michael Hessman/500	8.00
298	Buddy Hernandez/500	8.00
299	Shane Victorino/480	8.00
300	Jason Dubois/480	10.00
302	Ryan Wagner/100	15.00
303	Adam Loewen/100	10.00
304	Chien-Ming Wang/100	200.00
305	Hong-Chih Kuo/100	80.00
307	Dan Haren/100	25.00
309	Ramon Nivar/100	15.00

Call to the Hall

to the Hall
hoyt wilhelm
rp

		NM/M
Complete Set (10):		30.00
Common Player:		2.00
Metalized:		2-4X
Production 100 Sets		
Holofoils:		No Pricing
Production 25 Sets		
1	Nolan Ryan/2,490	10.00
2	Tom Seaver/2,490	4.00

3	Phil Rizzuto/2,500	4.00
4	Orlando Cepeda/2,500	2.00
5	Al Kaline/2,500	5.00
6	Hoyt Wilhelm/2,500	2.00
7	Luis Aparicio/2,500	2.00
8	Billy Williams/2,500	2.00
9	Jim Palmer/2,500	2.00
10	Mike Schmidt/2,500	6.00

Call to the Hall
Autographs

No Pricing
Quantity produced listed

Grand Champions

GRAND CHAMPIONS
Phillies
MIKE SCHMIDT
• 1986 •

		NM/M
Complete Set (25):		80.00
Common Player:		2.00
Inserted 1:18		
Metalized:		2-4X
Production 100 Sets		
Holo Foils:		No Pricing
Production 25 Sets		
1	Stan Musial	6.00
2	Bob Feller	2.00
3	Reggie Jackson	3.00
4	George Brett	8.00
5	Jim Palmer	2.00
6	Harmon Killebrew	4.00
7	Ernie Banks	4.00
8	Frank Robinson	2.00
9	Greg Maddux	4.00
10	Whitey Ford	4.00
11	Bob Gibson	4.00
12	Mike Schmidt	6.00
13	Nolan Ryan	10.00
14	Warren Spahn	4.00
15	Rod Carew	3.00
16	Hoyt Wilhelm	2.00
17	Duke Snider	4.00
18	Tom Seaver	4.00
19	Steve Carlton	3.00
20	Yogi Berra	4.00
21	Cal Ripken Jr.	10.00
22	Tony Gwynn	4.00
23	Wade Boggs	2.00
24	Rickey Henderson	3.00
25	Roger Clemens	8.00

Grand Champions
Autographs

No Pricing

Numbers Game

		NM/M
Quantity produced listed		
1	Vladimir Guerrero/Jsy/200	10.00
2	Nomar Garciaparra/Jsy/200	20.00
3	Magglio Ordonez/Jsy/100	8.00
4	Garret Anderson/Jsy/50	15.00
5	Derek Jeter/Base/200	20.00
6	Jim Thome/Jsy/200	8.00
7	Torii Hunter/Jsy/200	10.00
8	Todd Helton/Jsy/200	10.00
9	Andruw Jones/Jsy/200	6.00
10	Alfonso Soriano/Jsy/25	
11	Luis Gonzalez/Jsy/200	5.00
12	Manny Ramirez/Jsy/200	12.00
13	Paul Konerko/Jsy/200	6.00
14	Alex Rodriguez/Jsy/200	10.00
15	Carlos Beltran/Jsy/200	4.00
16	Bernie Williams/Jsy/200	8.00
17	Barry Bonds/Base/200	20.00
18	Miguel Tejada/Jsy/50	15.00
19	Jason Giambi/Base/200	8.00
20	Ichiro Suzuki/Base/200	25.00
21	Ivan Rodriguez/Jsy/100	15.00
22	Rafael Palmeiro/Jsy/200	10.00

23	Carlos Delgado/Jsy/200	5.00
24	Vernon Wells/Jsy/200	4.00
25	Sammy Sosa/Jsy/200	20.00
26	Chipper Jones/Jsy/200	12.00
27	Adam Dunn/Jsy/44	25.00
28	Larry Walker/Jsy/200	8.00
29	Shawn Green/Jsy/100	10.00
30	Richie Sexson/Jsy/200	6.00
31	Jose Vidro/Jsy/200	4.00
32	Mike Piazza/Jsy/50	40.00
33	Roberto Alomar/Jsy/100	15.00
34	Bobby Abreu/Jsy/200	5.00
35	Pat Burrell/Jsy/200	8.00
36	Brian Giles/Jsy/200	6.00
37	Albert Pujols/Base/200	15.00
38	Lance Berkman/Jsy/50	15.00
39	Ryan Klesko/Jsy/200	6.00
40	Jeff Kent/Jsy/200	4.00

Team Colors

		NM/M
Complete Set (30):		60.00
Common Player:		1.00
Inserted 1:10		
1	Miguel Tejada	1.50
2	Mike Schmidt	5.00
3	George Brett	6.00
4	Magglio Ordonez	1.00
5	Ryne Sandberg	4.00
6	Adam Dunn	1.50
7	Mark Prior	2.00
8	Tony Gwynn	2.00
9	Troy Glaus	1.50
10	Stan Musial	4.00
11	Kirby Puckett	3.00
12	Don Mattingly	5.00
13	Bobby Abreu	1.00
14	Ichiro Suzuki	4.00
15	Cal Ripken Jr.	8.00
16	Chipper Jones	3.00
17	Carlos Beltran	1.50
18	Alfonso Soriano	2.00
19	Albert Pujols	5.00
20	Andruw Jones	1.50
21	Bernie Williams	1.50
22	Todd Helton	1.50
23	Roberto Clemente	6.00
24	Jim Thome	1.50
25	Carlos Delgado	1.00
26	Derek Jeter	6.00
27	Garret Anderson	1.00
28	Nomar Garciaparra	4.00
29	Torii Hunter	1.00
30	Vladimir Guerrero	2.00

Team Colors Materials

		NM/M
Quantity produced listed		
1	Miguel Tejada/Jsy/50	15.00
2	Mike Schmidt/Jsy/200	35.00
3	George Brett/Jsy/100	35.00
4	Magglio Ordonez/Jsy/100	8.00
5	Ryne Sandberg/Jsy/200	30.00
6	Adam Dunn/Jsy/44	20.00
7	Mark Prior/Jsy/200	8.00
8	Tony Gwynn/Jsy/200	15.00
9	Troy Glaus/Jsy/200	8.00
10	Stan Musial/Jsy/200	35.00
11	Kirby Puckett/Jsy/200	15.00
12	Don Mattingly/Jsy/200	40.00

13	Bobby Abreu/Jsy/200	5.00
14	Ichiro Suzuki/Base/200	25.00
15	Cal Ripken Jr./Jsy/200	40.00
16	Chipper Jones/Jsy/200	12.00
17	Carlos Beltran/Jsy/200	8.00
18	Alfonso Soriano/Jsy/25	
19	Albert Pujols/Base/200	15.00
20	Andruw Jones/Jsy/200	6.00
21	Bernie Williams/Jsy/200	8.00
22	Todd Helton/Jsy/200	10.00
23	Roberto Clemente/Jsy/200	80.00
24	Jim Thome/Jsy/200	8.00
25	Carlos Delgado/Jsy/200	5.00
26	Derek Jeter/Base/200	20.00
27	Garret Anderson/Jsy/50	12.00
28	Nomar Garciaparra/Jsy/200	20.00
29	Torii Hunter/Jsy/200	10.00
30	Vladimir Guerrero/Jsy/200	10.00

Total Game

NM/M

Complete Set (40):		60.00
Common Player:		1.00
Inserted 1:9		
1	Vladimir Guerrero	2.00
2	Nomar Garciaparra	4.00
3	Magglio Ordonez	1.00
4	Garret Anderson	1.00
5	Derek Jeter	6.00
6	Jim Thome	1.50
7	Torii Hunter	1.50
8	Todd Helton	1.50
9	Andruw Jones	1.50
10	Alfonso Soriano	2.00
11	Luis Gonzalez	1.00
12	Manny Ramirez	1.50
13	Paul Konerko	1.00
14	Alex Rodriguez	5.00
15	Carlos Beltran	1.00
16	Bernie Williams	1.50
17	Barry Bonds	6.00
18	Miguel Tejada	1.00
19	Jason Giambi	1.00
20	Ichiro Suzuki	4.00
21	Ivan Rodriguez	1.50
22	Rafael Palmeiro	1.50
23	Carlos Delgado	1.00
24	Vernon Wells	1.00
25	Sammy Sosa	4.00
26	Chipper Jones	2.00
27	Adam Dunn	1.50
28	Larry Walker	1.00
29	Shawn Green	1.00
30	Richie Sexson	1.00
31	Jose Vidro	1.00
32	Mike Piazza	3.00
33	Roberto Alomar	1.50
34	Bobby Abreu	1.00
35	Pat Burrell	1.00
36	Brian Giles	1.00
37	Albert Pujols	5.00
38	Lance Berkman	1.00
39	Ryan Klesko	1.00
40	Jeff Kent	1.00

Statistical Champs

NM/M

Complete Set (30):		40.00
Common Player:		1.00
Inserted 1:10		

1	Alex Rodriguez	5.00
2	Alfonso Soriano	2.00
3	Curt Schilling	1.50
4	Eddie Mathews	2.00
5	Fred Lynn	1.00
6	Harmon Killebrew	2.00
7	Hideo Nomo	1.00
8	Jim Thome	1.50
9	Kirby Puckett	3.00
10	Luis Gonzalez	1.00
11	Manny Ramirez	1.50
12	Jason Giambi	1.00
13	Mike Schmidt	4.00
14	Nomar Garciaparra	4.00
15	Lou Brock	1.50
16	Randy Johnson	2.00
17	Reggie Jackson	2.00
18	Rickey Henderson	1.50
19	Roberto Clemente	5.00
20	Barry Zito	1.50
21	Todd Helton	1.50
22	Tom Seaver	3.00
23	Tony Gwynn	2.00
24	Torii Hunter	1.00
25	Troy Glaus	1.00
26	Wade Boggs	1.50
27	Rod Carew	1.50
28	Juan Gonzalez	1.50
29	Sammy Sosa	3.00
30	Warren Spahn	2.00

Statistical Champs Materials

NM/M

Quantity produced listed		
1	Alex Rodriguez/Jsy/250	20.00
3	Curt Schilling/Jsy/225	8.00
4	Eddie Mathews/Jsy/200	20.00
6	Harmon Killebrew/Jsy/200	20.00
7	Hideo Nomo/Jsy/110	50.00
8	Jim Thome/Jsy/250	8.00
9	Kirby Puckett/Jsy/200	20.00
10	Luis Gonzalez/Jsy/250	5.00
11	Manny Ramirez/Jsy/155	10.00
12	Jason Giambi/Jsy/250	10.00
13	Mike Schmidt/Jsy/250	35.00
14	Nomar Garciaparra/Jsy/99	30.00
15	Lou Brock/Jsy/250	15.00
16	Randy Johnson/Jsy/100	15.00
17	Reggie Jackson/Jsy/200	15.00
18	Rickey Henderson/Jsy/184	15.00
20	Barry Zito/Jsy/100	10.00
21	Todd Helton/Jsy/250	10.00
22	Tom Seaver/Jsy/100	30.00
23	Tony Gwynn/Jsy/200	15.00
24	Torii Hunter/Jsy/250	10.00
25	Troy Glaus/Jsy/125	10.00
26	Wade Boggs/Jsy/250	15.00
27	Rod Carew/Hat/150	15.00
28	Juan Gonzalez/Jsy/250	8.00
29	Sammy Sosa/Jsy/250	20.00
30	Warren Spahn/Jsy/150	30.00

World Series Champions

NM/M

Complete Set (15):		20.00
Common Player:		1.50
Production 2,002 Sets		
Metalized:		2-3X
Production 100 Sets		
Holo Foil:		No Pricing
Production 25 Sets		
1	Troy Glaus	3.00
2	Jarrod Washburn	1.50
3	Darin Erstad	2.50
4	Troy Percival	1.50

5	David Eckstein	1.50
6	Francisco Rodriguez	2.00
7	Garret Anderson	2.50
8	John Lackey	1.50
9	Tim Salmon	2.00
10	Chone Figgins	1.50
11	Adam Kennedy	1.50
12	Scott Spiezio	1.50
13	Ben Molina	1.50
14	Brad Fullmer	1.50
15	Troy Glaus MVP	3.00

World Series Champions Autograph

No Pricing

2003 Donruss Classics

NM/M

Complete Set (200):		
Common Player:		.40
Common Legends (101-150):		3.00
Production 1,500		
Common Prospect (151-200):		3.00
Production 1,500		
Pack (7):		4.50
Box (18):		70.00
1	Troy Glaus	.50
2	Barry Bonds	3.00
3	Miguel Tejada	.50
4	Randy Johnson	1.00
5	Eric Hinske	.40
6	Barry Zito	.50
7	Jason Jennings	.40
8	Derek Jeter	3.00
9	Vladimir Guerrero	1.00
10	Corey Patterson	.50
11	Manny Ramirez	.75
12	Edgar Martinez	.50
13	Roy Oswalt	.50
14	Andruw Jones	.75
15	Alex Rodriguez	3.00
16	Mark Mulder	.50
17	Kazuhisa Ishii	.40
18	Gary Sheffield	.50
19	Jay Gibbons	.40
20	Roberto Alomar	.50
21	A.J. Pierzynski	.40
22	Eric Chavez	.50
23	Roger Clemens	2.00
24	C.C. Sabathia	.40
25	Jose Vidro	.40
26	Shannon Stewart	.40
27	Mark Teixeira	.50
28	Joe Thurston	.40
29	Josh Beckett	.75
30	Jeff Bagwell	.75
31	Geronimo Gil	.40
32	Curt Schilling	.75
33	Frank Thomas	.75
34	Lance Berkman	.50
35	Adam Dunn	.75
36	Christian Parker	.40
37	Jim Thome	1.00
38	Shawn Green	.50
39	Drew Henson	.40
40	Chipper Jones	1.00
41	Kevin Mench	.40
42	Hideo Nomo	.50
43	Andres Galarraga	.40
44	Doug Davis	.40
45	Mark Prior	1.00
46	Sean Casey	.40
47	Magglio Ordonez	.50
48	Tom Glavine	.50
49	Marlon Byrd	.40
50	Albert Pujols	2.00
51	Mark Buehrle	.40
52	Aramis Ramirez	.50
53	Pat Burrell	.50

54	Craig Biggio	.50
55	Alfonso Soriano	1.00
56	Kerry Wood	1.00
57	Wade Miller	.40
58	Hank Blalock	.75
59	Cliff Floyd	.40
60	Jason Giambi	.50
61	Carlos Beltran	.50
62	Brian Roberts	.40
63	Paul LoDuca	.40
64	Tim Redding	.40
65	Sammy Sosa	2.00
66	Joe Borchard	.40
67	Ryan Klesko	.40
68	Richie Sexson	.50
69	Carlos Lee	.40
70	Rickey Henderson	.75
71	Brian Tallet	.40
72	Luis Gonzalez	.50
73	Satoru Komiyama	.40
74	Tim Hudson	.50
75	Ken Griffey Jr.	1.50
76	Adam Johnson	.40
77	Bobby Abreu	.60
78	Adrian Beltre	.40
79	Rafael Palmeiro	.75
80	Ichiro Suzuki	2.00
81	Kenny Lofton	.40
82	Brian Giles	.50
83	Barry Larkin	.50
84	Robert Fick	.40
85	Ben Sheets	.50
86	Scott Rolen	1.00
87	Nomar Garciaparra	1.50
88	Brandon Phillips	.40
89	Ben Kozlowski	.40
90	Bernie Williams	.75
91	Pedro J. Martinez	1.00
92	Todd Helton	.75
93	Jermaine Dye	.40
94	Carlos Delgado	.50
95	Mike Piazza	1.50
96	Junior Spivey	.40
97	Torii Hunter	.50
98	Mike Sweeney	.40
99	Ivan Rodriguez	.75
100	Greg Maddux	1.50
101	Ernie Banks	5.00
102	Steve Garvey	3.00
103	George Brett	8.00
104	Lou Brock	3.00
105	Hoyt Wilhelm	3.00
106	Steve Carlton	4.00
107	Joe Torre	3.00
108	Dennis Eckersley	4.00
109	Reggie Jackson	5.00
110	Al Kaline	8.00
111	Harold Reynolds	3.00
112	Don Mattingly	8.00
113	Tony Gwynn	5.00
114	Willie McCovey	4.00
115	Joe Morgan	3.00
116	Stan Musial	8.00
117	Jim Palmer	3.00
118	Brooks Robinson	5.00
119	Don Sutton	3.00
120	Nolan Ryan	10.00
121	Mike Schmidt	6.00
122	Tom Seaver	5.00
123	Cal Ripken Jr.	8.00
124	Robin Yount	5.00
125	Bob Feller	3.00
126	Joe Carter	3.00
127	Jack Morris	3.00
128	Luis Aparicio	3.00
129	Bobby Doerr	3.00
130	Dave Parker	3.00
131	Yogi Berra	5.00
132	Will Clark	3.00
133	Fred Lynn	3.00
134	Andre Dawson	3.00
135	Duke Snider	4.00
136	Orlando Cepeda	3.00
137	Billy Williams	3.00
138	Dale Murphy	4.00
139	Harmon Killebrew	5.00
140	Kirby Puckett	6.00
141	Carlton Fisk	3.00
142	Eric Davis	3.00
143	Alan Trammell	3.00
144	Paul Molitor	5.00
145	Jose Canseco	3.00
146	Ozzie Smith	5.00
147	Ralph Kiner	3.00
148	Dwight Gooden	5.00
149	Phil Rizzuto	5.00
150	Lenny Dykstra	3.00
151	Adam LaRoche	4.00
152	Tim Hummel	3.00
153	Matt Kata RC	4.00
154	Jeff Baker	3.00
155	Josh Stewart RC	3.00
156	Marshall McDougall	4.00
157	Jhonny Peralta	4.00

158	Mike Nicolas RC	3.00
159	Jeremy Guthrie	3.00
160	Craig Brazell RC	4.00
161	Joe Valentine RC	4.00
162	Buddy Hernandez	3.00
163	Freddy Sanchez	4.00
164	Shane Victorino RC	4.00
165	Corwin Malone	3.00
166	Jason Dubois	3.00
167	Josh Wilson	3.00
168	Tim Olson RC	3.00
169	Clifford Bartosh	3.00
170	Michael Hessman RC	4.00
171	Ryan Church	5.00
172	Garrett Atkins	4.00
173	Jose Morban	3.00
174	Ryan Cameron RC	4.00
175	Todd Wellemeyer RC	4.00
176	Travis Chapman	3.00
177	Jason Anderson	4.00
178	Adam Morrissey	3.00
179	Jose Contreras RC	5.00
180	Nic Jackson	3.00
181	Rob Hammock RC	4.00
182	Carlos Rivera	3.00
183	Vinnie Chulk	3.00
184	Pete LaForest RC	4.00
185	Jon Leicester RC	4.00
186	Terrmel Sledge RC	3.00
187	Jose Castillo	3.00
188	Gerald Laird	3.00
189	Nook Logan RC	4.00
190	Clint Barmes RC	5.00
191	Jesus Medrano	3.00
192	Henri Stanley	4.00
193	Hideki Matsui RC	10.00
194	Walter Young	3.00
195	Jon Adkins	3.00
196	Tommy Whiteman RC	4.00
197	Rob Bowen	3.00
198	Brandon Webb RC	4.00
199	Prentice Redman RC	4.00
200	Jimmy Gobble	3.00

Combos

NM/M

Varying quantities produced

CC1	Babe Ruth, Lou Gehrig/50	475.00
CC2	Jackie Robinson, Pee Wee Reese/50	80.00
CC3	Bobby Doerr, Fred Lynn/25	65.00
CC4	Honus Wagner, Roberto Clemente/50	150.00
CC5	Kirby Puckett, Torii Hunter/25	75.00
CC6	Sammy Sosa, Ryne Sandberg/25	100.00
CC7	Hideo Nomo, Kazuhisa Ishii/25	75.00
CC8	Mike Schmidt, Steve Carlton/25	150.00
CC9	Robin Yount, Paul Molitor/25	100.00
CC12	Don Mattingly, Jason Giambi/25	150.00
CC13	Stan Musial, Ozzie Smith/25	100.00

Dress Code

NM/M

Common Player: 4.00

Quantity produced listed

1	Roger Clemens/Jsy/500	15.00
2	M. Tejada/Jsy/Hat/Bat/250	20.00
3	V. Guerrero/Jsy/425	8.00
4	Kazuhisa Ishii/Jsy/250	10.00
5	Chipper Jones/Jsy/425	10.00
6	Troy Glaus/Jsy/425	8.00
7	Rafael Palmeiro/Jsy/425	8.00
8	Rickey Henderson/Jsy/250	10.00
9	Pedro Martinez/Jsy/425	8.00
10	Andruw Jones/Jsy/500	6.00
11	Nomar Garciaparra/Jsy/500	12.00
12	Carlos Delgado/Jsy/500	5.00
13	R.Henderson/Jsy/Hat/250	20.00
14	K. Wood/Jsy/Hat/250	20.00
15	L. Berkman/Jsy/Hat/50	20.00
16	Tony Gwynn/Jsy/Quad/100	65.00
17	Mark Mulder/Jsy/425	8.00
18	Jim Thome/Jsy/500	8.00
19	Mike Piazza/Jsy/500	15.00
20	Mike Mussina/Jsy/500	10.00
21	Luis Gonzalez/Jsy/500	5.00
22	Ryan Klesko/Jsy/500	5.00
23	Richie Sexson/Jsy/500	6.00
24	Curt Schilling/Jsy/200	10.00
25	A. Rodriguez/Jsy/500	12.00
26	B. Williams/Jsy/425	8.00
27	Cal Ripken Jr./Jsy/500	35.00
28	C.C. Sabathia/Jsy/500	4.00
29	M. Piazza/Bat/Jsy/200	30.00
30	Rickey Henderson/Hat/Jsy/500	15.00
31	Torii Hunter/Jsy/425	8.00
32	Mark Teixeira/Jsy/425	8.00
33	D. Murphy/Jsy/Bat/300	15.00
34	Todd Helton/Jsy/425	8.00
35	Eric Chavez/Jsy/425	8.00
36	Vernon Wells/Jsy/425	5.00
37	J. Bagwell/Jsy/Hat/100	25.00
38	Nick Johnson/Jsy/425	5.00
39	Tim Hudson/Jsy/Hat/250	10.00
40	Shawn Green/Jsy/425	5.00
41	Mark Buehrle/Jsy/500	5.00
42	Garret Anderson/Jsy/100	5.00
43	Alex Rodriguez/Jsy/500	12.00
44	Jason Giambi/Jsy/500	8.00
45	Carlos Beltran/Jsy/500	5.00
46	Adam Dunn/Jsy/Hat/100	30.00
47	Jorge Posada/Jsy/425	8.00
48	Roy Oswalt/Jsy/Hat/200	15.00
49	Rich Aurilia/Jsy/500	5.00
50	Jason Jennings/Quad/100	15.00
51	Mark Prior/Quad/250	40.00
52	Jim Edmonds/Jsy/500	8.00
53	Fred McGriff/Jsy/500	8.00
54	A. Soriano/Jsy/Shoe/100	15.00
55	Jeff Kent/Jsy/425	5.00
56	Hideo Nomo/Jsy/200	30.00
57	Manny Ramirez/Jsy/425	8.00
58	J. Canseco/Jsy/Bat/300	15.00
59	M. Ordonez/Jsy/500	6.00
60	A. Trammell/Jsy/Bat/250	10.00
61	Bobby Abreu/Jsy/500	6.00
62	R.Henderson/Dual Jsy/200	20.00
63	Josh Beckett/Jsy/500	6.00
64	Barry Larkin/Jsy/500	8.00
65	Randy Johnson/Jsy/200	10.00
66	Juan Gonzalez/Jsy/500	8.00
67	Barry Zito/Jsy/Hat/125	15.00
68	Roger Clemens/Jsy/500	15.00
69	Rickey Henderson/Hat/Jsy/100	25.00
70	Hideo Nomo/Jsy/100	50.00
71	Paul Konerko/Jsy/400	6.00
72	Pat Burrell/Jsy/400	8.00
73	F.Thomas/Jsy/Pants/250	15.00
74	Sammy Sosa/Jsy/500	15.00
75	G. Maddux/Glove/Jsy/50	60.00

Legendary Hats

NM/M

Varying quantities produced

1	Roberto Clemente/80	100.00
2	Kirby Puckett/50	50.00
3	Mike Schmidt/50	75.00
4	Tony Gwynn/50	50.00
5	Rickey Henderson/50	60.00

Legendary Spikes

NM/M

Production 50 Sets

1	Kirby Puckett	60.00
2	Tony Gwynn	50.00
3	Don Mattingly	125.00
4	Frank Robinson	35.00
5	Gary Carter	30.00

Legendary Leather

NM/M

Varying quantities produced

1	Nolan Ryan/80	110.00

Legendary Lumberjacks

NM/M

Common Player: 10.00

Varying quantities produced

1	Babe Ruth/100	180.00
2	Lou Gehrig/80	125.00
3	George Brett/250	25.00
4	Duke Snider/250	20.00
5	Roberto Clemente/25	165.00
6	Ryne Sandberg/400	35.00
7	Robin Yount/300	25.00
8	Harmon Killebrew/250	25.00
9	Al Kaline/250	25.00
10	Eddie Mathews/225	20.00
11	Brooks Robinson/400	15.00
12	Kirby Puckett/375	25.00
13	Jose Canseco/400	15.00
14	Nellie Fox/325	15.00
15	Don Mattingly/400	35.00
16	Joe Torre/250	10.00
17	Cal Ripken Jr/250	40.00
18	Richie Ashburn/250	20.00
19	Mike Schmidt/250	30.00
20	Dale Murphy/250	25.00
21	Thurman Munson/400	15.00
22	Tony Gwynn/400	10.00
23	Orlando Cepeda/225	10.00
24	Ty Cobb/25	225.00
25	Paul Molitor/325	10.00
26	Ralph Kiner/200	10.00
27	Frank Robinson/225	20.00
28	Yogi Berra/50	50.00
29	Reggie Jackson/375	20.00
30	Rod Carew/325	15.00
31	Carlton Fisk/325	15.00
32	Rogers Hornsby/50	60.00
33	Mel Ott/50	30.00
34	Jimmie Foxx/50	60.00

Legends of the Fall

NM/M

Complete Set (10): 40.00

Common Player: 3.00

Production 2,500 Sets

1	Reggie Jackson	4.00
2	Duke Snider	4.00
3	Roberto Clemente	8.00
4	Mel Ott	5.00
5	Yogi Berra	5.00
6	Jackie Robinson	6.00
7	Enos Slaughter	3.00
8	Willie Stargell	4.00
9	Bobby Doerr	3.00
10	Thurman Munson	5.00

Legends of the Fall Fabrics

NM/M

Quantity produced listed 3.00

1	Reggie Jackson/100	20.00
3	Roberto Clemente/50	120.00
6	Jackie Robinson/50	80.00
8	Willie Stargell/100	20.00
9	Bobby Doerr/100	20.00

Membership

NM/M

Complete Set (15): 65.00

Common Player: 3.00

Production 2,500 Sets

1	Babe Ruth	10.00
2	Steve Carlton	3.00
3	Honus Wagner	6.00
4	Warren Spahn	5.00
5	Eddie Mathews	5.00
6	Nolan Ryan	10.00
7	Rogers Hornsby	5.00
8	Ernie Banks	5.00
9	Harmon Killebrew	5.00
10	Tom Seaver	5.00
11	Jimmie Foxx	6.00
12	Ty Cobb	6.00
13	Frank Robinson	4.00
14	Mel Ott	5.00
15	Lou Gehrig	8.00

Membership VIP Memorabilia

NM/M

Varying quantities produced

1	Babe Ruth/Bat/29	325.00
2	Steve Carlton/Jsy/81	25.00
4	Warren Spahn/Jsy/61	50.00
5	Eddie Mathews/Bat/67	60.00
6	Nolan Ryan/Jsy/80	75.00
7	R. Hornsby/Bat/31	75.00
8	Ernie Banks/Jsy/70	35.00
9	H. Killebrew/Jsy/71	60.00
10	Tom Seaver/Jsy/81	30.00
11	Jimmie Foxx/Bat/40	60.00
13	F. Robinson/Jsy/71	25.00
14	Mel Ott/Jsy/45	50.00
15	Lou Gehrig/Bat/31	

Significant Signatures

NM/M

Common Autograph: 8.00

#'s 201-211 exclusive to Donruss Rookies

5	Eric Hinske/250	15.00
6	Barry Zito/25	40.00

7	Jason Jennings/250	10.00
10	Corey Patterson/100	15.00
13	Roy Oswalt/100	20.00
16	Mark Mulder/100	25.00
19	Jay Gibbons/250	10.00
21	A.J. Pierzynski/75	20.00
22	Eric Chavez/20	40.00
25	Jose Vidro/75	15.00
27	Mark Teixeira/50	40.00
31	Geronimo Gil/50	10.00
35	Adam Dunn/100	40.00
36	Christian Parker/250	10.00
39	Drew Henson/100	20.00
41	Kevin Mench/250	10.00
45	Mark Prior/50	30.00
56	Kerry Wood/15	60.00
57	Wade Miller/200	10.00
58	Hank Blalock/50	25.00
62	Brian Roberts/250	25.00
63	Paul LoDuca/100	15.00
64	Tim Redding/50	8.00
66	Joe Borchard/100	15.00
68	Richie Sexson/20	40.00
69	Carlos Lee/25	20.00
73	Satoru Komiyama/124	20.00
76	Adam Johnson/200	8.00
84	Robert Fick/50	10.00
88	Brandon Phillips/250	10.00
89	Ben Kozlowski/150	8.00
93	Jermaine Dye/100	20.00
96	Junior Spivey/100	15.00
97	Torii Hunter/50	25.00
102	Steve Garvey/100	20.00
108	Dennis Eckersley/50	30.00
111	Harold Reynolds/50	25.00
119	Don Sutton/100	20.00
120	Nolan Ryan/50	200.00
123	Cal Ripken Jr./50	220.00
126	Joe Carter/100	25.00
127	Jack Morris/100	20.00
128	Luis Aparicio/50	20.00
132	Will Clark/20	125.00
133	Fred Lynn/50	15.00
134	Andre Dawson/50	30.00
136	Orlando Cepeda/100	20.00
137	Billy Williams/100	15.00
142	Eric Davis/50	25.00
143	Alan Trammell/50	35.00
148	Dwight Gooden/50	40.00
149	Phil Rizzuto/20	75.00
150	Lenny Dykstra/50	25.00
151	Adam LaRoche/250	15.00
152	Tim Hummel/500	8.00
153	Matt Kata/500	15.00
154	Jeff Baker/500	10.00
155	Josh Stewart/177	10.00
156	Marshall McDougall/500	10.00
157	Jhonny Peralta/500	20.00
158	Mike Nicolas/500	8.00
159	Jeremy Guthrie/500	10.00
160	Craig Brazell/500	15.00
161	Joe Valentine/172	10.00
162	Buddy Hernandez/500	8.00
163	Freddy Sanchez/500	10.00
164	Shane Victorino/351	8.00
165	Corwin Malone/500	8.00
166	Jason Dubois/500	12.00
167	Josh Wilson/500	8.00
168	Tim Olson/500	8.00
169	Clifford Bartosh/500	8.00
170	Michael Hessman/427	8.00
171	Ryan Church/500	10.00
172	Garrett Atkins/500	8.00
173	Jose Morban/500	8.00
174	Ryan Cameron/500	10.00
175	Todd Wellemeyer/500	10.00
176	Travis Chapman/477	10.00
177	Jason Anderson/500	15.00
178	Adam Morrissey/500	8.00
179	Jose Contreras/100	20.00
180	Nic Jackson/500	8.00
181	Rob Hammock/500	10.00
182	Carlos Rivera/500	8.00
183	Vinnie Chulk/500	8.00
184	Pete LaForest/177	10.00
185	Jon Leicester/500	8.00
186	Terrmel Sledge/500	8.00
187	Jose Castillo/500	10.00
188	Gerald Laird/500	8.00
189	Nook Logan/427	8.00
190	Clint Barmes/100	20.00
191	Jesus Medrano/500	8.00
192	Henri Stanley/500	8.00
194	Walter Young/500	10.00
195	Jon Adkins/500	8.00
196	Tommy Whiteman/500	8.00
197	Rob Bowen/500	8.00
198	Brandon Webb/500	30.00
199	Prentice Redman/127	10.00
200	Jimmy Gobble/500	10.00
201	Jeremy Bonderman/100	50.00

202	Adam Loewen/100	10.00
203	Chien-Ming Wang/50	220.00
205	Ryan Wagner/100	10.00
206	Dan Haren/100	40.00
209	Ramon Nivar/100	15.00

Singles

		NM/M
Common Player:		10.00
Varying quantities produced		
1	Babe Ruth/Jsy/100	275.00
2	Lou Gehrig/Jsy/80	200.00
3	Jackie Robinson/Jsy/80	75.00
5	Bobby Doerr/Jsy/100	15.00
6	Fred Lynn/Jsy/100	12.00
7	Honus Wagner/Seat/100	35.00
8	Roberto Clemente/Jsy/80	100.00
9	Kirby Puckett/Jsy/100	40.00
10	Torii Hunter/Jsy/100	10.00
11	Sammy Sosa/Jsy/100	25.00
12	Ryne Sandberg/Jsy/100	10.00
13	Hideo Nomo/Jsy/50	90.00
14	Kazuhisa Ishii/Jsy/50	15.00
15	Mike Schmidt/Jsy/100	45.00
16	Steve Carlton/Jsy/100	15.00
17	Robin Yount/Jsy/100	30.00
18	Paul Molitor/Jsy/100	20.00
19	Mike Piazza/Jsy/100	20.00
20	Duke Snider/Jsy/50	35.00
21	Al Kaline/Jsy/50	50.00
23	Don Mattingly/Jsy/100	60.00
24	Jason Giambi/Jsy/100	10.00
26	Ozzie Smith/Jsy/100	40.00
27	Roger Clemens/Jsy/100	25.00
28	Pedro Martinez/Jsy/100	20.00
29	Thurman Munson/Jsy/50	50.00
30	Yogi Berra/Jsy/25	70.00

Timeless Treasures

		NM/M
Varying quantities produced		
1	Tony Gwynn, Stan Musial/50	100.00
3	Vladimir Guerrero, Roberto Clemente/50	125.00
5	Jason Giambi, Don Mattingly/50	100.00

2003 Donruss Diamond Kings

		NM/M
Complete Set (176):		90.00
Common Player:		.40
Common (151-176):		1.00
Pack (5):		4.00
Box (24):		75.00
1	Darin Erstad	.50
2	Garret Anderson	.50
3	Troy Glaus	.50
4	David Eckstein	.40
5	Jarrod Washburn	.40
6	Adam Kennedy	.40
7	Jay Gibbons	.40
8	Tony Batista	.40
9	Melvin Mora	.40
10	Rodrigo Lopez	.40
11	Manny Ramirez	.75
12	Pedro J. Martinez	1.00

13	Nomar Garciaparra	1.50
14	Rickey Henderson	.60
15	Johnny Damon	.50
16	Derek Lowe	.40
17	Cliff Floyd	.40
18	Frank Thomas	.75
19	Magglio Ordonez	.40
20	Paul Konerko	.40
21	Mark Buehrle	.40
22	C.C. Sabathia	.40
23	Omar Vizquel	.40
24	Jim Thome	.75
25	Ellis Burks	.40
26	Robert Fick	.40
27	Bobby Higginson	.40
28	Randall Simon	.40
29	Carlos Pena	.40
30	Carlos Beltran	.75
31	Paul Byrd	.40
32	Raul Ibanez	.40
33	Mike Sweeney	.40
34	Torii Hunter	.50
35	Corey Koskie	.40
36	A.J. Pierzynski	.40
37	Cristian Guzman	.40
38	Jacque Jones	.40
39	Derek Jeter	3.00
40	Bernie Williams	.60
41	Roger Clemens	2.00
42	Mike Mussina	.60
43	Jorge Posada	.40
44	Alfonso Soriano	1.00
45	Jason Giambi	.50
46	Robin Ventura	.40
47	David Wells	.40
48	Tim Hudson	.50
49	Barry Zito	.40
50	Mark Mulder	.50
51	Miguel Tejada	.50
52	Eric Chavez	.50
53	Jermaine Dye	.40
54	Ichiro Suzuki	2.00
55	Edgar Martinez	.50
56	John Olerud	.40
57	Dan Wilson	.40
58	Joel Pineiro	.40
59	Kazuhiro Sasaki	.40
60	Freddy Garcia	.40
61	Aubrey Huff	.40
62	Steve Cox	.40
63	Randy Winn	.40
64	Alex Rodriguez	2.50
65	Juan Gonzalez	.50
66	Rafael Palmeiro	.75
67	Ivan Rodriguez	.75
68	Kenny Rogers	.40
69	Carlos Delgado	.40
70	Eric Hinske	.40
71	Roy Halladay	.40
72	Vernon Wells	.40
73	Shannon Stewart	.40
74	Curt Schilling	.75
75	Randy Johnson	1.00
76	Luis Gonzalez	.40
77	Mark Grace	.50
78	Junior Spivey	.40
79	Greg Maddux	1.50
80	Tom Glavine	.50
81	John Smoltz	.40
82	Chipper Jones	1.00
83	Gary Sheffield	.40
84	Andruw Jones	.50
85	Kerry Wood	1.00
86	Fred McGriff	.40
87	Sammy Sosa	1.50
88	Mark Prior	1.00
89	Ken Griffey Jr.	1.50
90	Barry Larkin	.50
91	Adam Dunn	.75
92	Sean Casey	.40
93	Austin Kearns	.50
94	Aaron Boone	.40
95	Larry Walker	.40
96	Todd Helton	.75
97	Jason Jennings	.40
98	Jay Payton	.40
99	Josh Beckett	.50
100	Mike Lowell	.40
101	A.J. Burnett	.40
102	Jeff Bagwell	.75
103	Craig da Luz	.40
104	Lance Berkman	.50
105	Roy Oswalt	.40
106	Wade Miller	.40
107	Shawn Green	.50
108	Adrian Beltre	.50
109	Hideo Nomo	.50
110	Kazuhisa Ishii	.40
111	Odalis Perez	.40
112	Paul LoDuca	.40
113	Ben Sheets	.40
114	Richie Sexson	.40
115	Jose Hernandez	.40
116	Vladimir Guerrero	1.00

117	Jose Vidro	.40
118	Tomokazu Ohka	.40
119	Andres Galarraga	.40
120	Bartolo Colon	.40
121	Mike Piazza	1.50
122	Roberto Alomar	.50
123	Mo Vaughn	.40
124	Al Leiter	.40
125	Edgardo Alfonzo	.40
126	Pat Burrell	.75
127	Bobby Abreu	.50
128	Mike Lieberthal	.40
129	Vicente Padilla	.40
130	Marlon Byrd	.40
131	Jason Kendall	.40
132	Brian Giles	.40
133	Aramis Ramirez	.50
134	Kip Wells	.40
135	Ryan Klesko	.40
136	Phil Nevin	.40
137	Brian Lawrence	.40
138	Sean Burroughs	.40
139	Mark Kotsay	.40
140	Barry Bonds	3.00
141	Jeff Kent	.40
142	Benito Santiago	.40
143	Kirk Reuter	.40
144	Jason Schmidt	.50
145	Jim Edmonds	.50
146	J.D. Drew	.50
147	Albert Pujols	2.00
148	Tino Martinez	.40
149	Matt Morris	.40
150	Scott Rolen	1.00
151	Joe Borchard	2.00
152	Cliff Lee	1.00
153	Brian Tallet	1.00
154	Freddy Sanchez	1.00
155	Chone Figgins	1.00
156	Kevin Cash	1.00
157	Justin Wayne	1.00
158	Ben Kozlowski	1.00
159	Babe Ruth	6.00
160	Jackie Robinson	4.00
161	Ozzie Smith	4.00
162	Lou Gehrig	5.00
163	Stan Musial	4.00
164	Mike Schmidt	5.00
165	Carlton Fisk	2.00
166	George Brett	6.00
167	Dale Murphy	4.00
168	Cal Ripken Jr.	8.00
169	Tony Gwynn	3.00
170	Don Mattingly	6.00
171	Jack Morris	2.00
172	Ty Cobb	5.00
173	Nolan Ryan	6.00
174	Ryne Sandberg	5.00
175	Thurman Munson	4.00
176	Jose Contreras RC	8.00

Diamond Cut

Common Signature (1-25):		10.00
Quantity produced listed		
1	Barry Zito/75	50.00
2	Edgar Martinez/125	50.00
3	Jay Gibbons/150	25.00
4	Joe Borchard/150	20.00
5	Marlon Byrd/150	20.00
6	Adam Dunn/150	40.00
7	Torii Hunter/150	40.00
8	Vladimir Guerrero/25	150.00
9	Wade Miller/150	25.00
10	Alfonso Soriano/100	60.00
11	Brian Lawrence/150	10.00
12	Cliff Floyd/100	25.00
13	Dale Murphy/75	75.00
14	Jack Morris/150	25.00
15	Eric Hinske/150	25.00
16	Jason Jennings/150	20.00
17	Mark Buehrle/150	30.00
18	Mark Prior/150	40.00
19	Mark Mulder/150	30.00
20	Mike Sweeney/150	25.00
21	Nolan Ryan/50	200.00
22	Don Mattingly/75	100.00
23	Andruw Jones/75	40.00
24	Aubrey Huff/75	20.00
Common Jerseys (26-75):		5.00
26	Nolan Ryan/250	50.00
27	Ozzie Smith/450	15.00
28	Rickey Henderson/300	10.00
29	Jack Morris/500	5.00
30	George Brett/350	25.00
31	Cal Ripken Jr./300	40.00
32	Ryne Sandberg/450	20.00
33	Don Mattingly/400	25.00
34	Tony Gwynn/400	15.00
35	Dale Murphy/350	10.00
36	Carlton Fisk/400	10.00
38	Lou Gehrig/50	240.00
39	Garret Anderson/450	8.00

40	Pedro J. Martinez/400	10.00
41	Nomar Garciaparra/350	15.00
42	Magglio Ordonez/450	8.00
43	C.C. Sabathia/500	5.00
44	Omar Vizquel/250	8.00
45	Jim Thome/350	10.00
46	Torii Hunter/500	8.00
47	Roger Clemens/500	15.00
48	Alfonso Soriano/400	10.00
49	Tim Hudson/500	8.00
50	Barry Zito/350	6.00
51	Mark Mulder/500	6.00
52	Miguel Tejada/400	8.00
53	John Olerud/350	5.00
54	Alex Rodriguez/500	15.00
55	Rafael Palmeiro/500	8.00
56	Curt Schilling/500	8.00
57	Randy Johnson/400	10.00
58	Greg Maddux/350	12.00
59	John Smoltz/400	6.00
60	Chipper Jones/450	10.00
61	Andruw Jones/500	8.00
62	Kerry Wood/500	10.00
63	Mark Prior/500	10.00
64	Adam Dunn/350	10.00
65	Larry Walker/500	5.00
66	Todd Helton/500	8.00
67	Jeff Bagwell/500	10.00
68	Roy Oswalt/500	8.00
69	Hideo Nomo/150	15.00
70	Kazuhisa Ishii/250	5.00
71	Vladimir Guerrero/500	10.00
72	Mike Piazza/500	15.00
73	Joe Borchard/500	5.00
74	Ryan Klesko/500	5.00
75	Shawn Green/500	6.00
Common Bat (76-105):		
76	George Brett/350	25.00
77	Ozzie Smith/450	15.00
78	Cal Ripken Jr./150	50.00
79	Don Mattingly/400	25.00
80	Babe Ruth/50	200.00
81	Dale Murphy/50	10.00
82	Rickey Henderson/500	10.00
83	Ivan Rodriguez/500	8.00
84	Marlon Byrd/500	5.00
85	Eric Chavez/500	8.00
86	Nomar Garciaparra/500	15.00
87	Alex Rodriguez/500	15.00
88	Vladimir Guerrero/500	10.00
89	Paul LoDuca/500	5.00
90	Richie Sexson/500	6.00
91	Mike Piazza/350	15.00
92	J.D. Drew/500	8.00
93	Juan Gonzalez/500	8.00
94	Pat Burrell/500	8.00
95	Adam Dunn/250	15.00
96	Mike Schmidt/500	20.00
97	Ryne Sandberg/500	20.00
98	Edgardo Alfonzo/500	5.00
99	Andruw Jones/500	8.00
100	Carlos Beltran/500	6.00
101	Jeff Bagwell/500	10.00
102	Lance Berkman/500	8.00
103	Luis Gonzalez/500	5.00
104	Carlos Delgado/500	6.00
105	Jim Edmonds/250	8.00
Combos (106-110):		
Some Combos & Autos. not priced.		
106	Alfonso Soriano/75	40.00
107	Greg Maddux/Jsy/Auto./50	140.00
109	Adam Dunn/Bat/Auto./50	60.00
110	Rickey Henderson/Jsy/Bat/50	20.00

DK Evolution

TODD HELTON FIRST BASE

		NM/M
Complete Set (25):		85.00
Common Player:		2.00
Inserted 1:18		
1	Cal Ripken Jr.	10.00
2	Ichiro Suzuki	6.00
3	Randy Johnson	4.00
4	Pedro J. Martinez	4.00
5	Nolan Ryan	10.00
6	Derek Jeter	10.00
7	Kerry Wood	4.00
8	Alex Rodriguez	8.00
9	Magglio Ordonez	2.00
10	Greg Maddux	5.00
11	Todd Helton	3.00
12	Sammy Sosa	5.00
13	Lou Gehrig	8.00
14	Lance Berkman	2.00
15	Barry Zito	2.00
16	Barry Bonds	10.00
17	Tom Glavine	2.00
18	Shawn Green	2.00
19	Roger Clemens	8.00
20	Nomar Garciaparra	6.00
21	Tony Gwynn	4.00
22	Vladimir Guerrero	3.00
23	Albert Pujols	8.00
24	Chipper Jones	8.00
25	Alfonso Soriano	4.00

Framed Portraits Bronze

Cards (1-150):	1-2.5X
Cards (151-176):	.75-1.5X
Silvers (1-150):	3-5X
Silvers (151-176):	2-3X
Production 400 Sets	
Golds (1-150):	5-10X
Golds (151-176):	3-6X
Production 100 Sets	

Hall of Fame Heroes

		NM/M
Complete Set (10):		40.00
Common Card:		3.00
Inserted 1:43		
1	Bob Feller	3.00
2	Al Kaline	6.00
3	Lou Boudreau	3.00
4	Duke Snider	4.00
5	Jackie Robinson	6.00
6	Early Wynn	3.00
7	Yogi Berra	4.00
8	Stan Musial	6.00
9	Ty Cobb	6.00
10	Ted Williams	6.00

HOF Heroes Materials

		NM/M
Common Player:		30.00
Production 50 Sets		
1	Bob Feller/Jsy	70.00
2	Al Kaline/Bat	45.00
3	Lou Boudreau/Jsy	40.00
4	Duke Snider/Bat	30.00
7	Yogi Berra/Bat	40.00
8	Stan Musial/Bat	100.00
9	Ty Cobb/Bat	110.00
10	Ted Williams/Jsy	175.00

Heritage Collection

		NM/M
Complete Set (25):		100.00
Common Player:		2.00
Inserted 1:23		
1	Ozzie Smith	5.00
2	Lou Gehrig	8.00
3	Stan Musial	6.00
4	Mike Schmidt	6.00
5	Carlton Fisk	2.00
6	George Brett	10.00
7	Dale Murphy	4.00

8	Cal Ripken Jr.	10.00
9	Tony Gwynn	4.00
10	Don Mattingly	8.00
11	Jack Morris	2.00
12	Ty Cobb	8.00
13	Nolan Ryan	12.00
14	Ryne Sandberg	6.00
15	Thurman Munson	4.00
16	Ichiro Suzuki	6.00
17	Derek Jeter	10.00
18	Greg Maddux	5.00
19	Sammy Sosa	5.00
20	Pedro J. Martinez	4.00
21	Alex Rodriguez	8.00
22	Roger Clemens	5.00
23	Barry Bonds	10.00
24	Lance Berkman	2.00
25	Vladimir Guerrero	3.00

Team Timelines

		NM/M
Complete Set (10):		85.00
Common Card:		4.00
Production 1,000 Sets		
1	Nolan Ryan, Roy Oswalt	15.00
2	Dale Murphy, Chipper Jones	8.00
3	Stan Musial, Jim Edmonds	10.00
4	George Brett, Mike Sweeney	12.00
5	Tony Gwynn, Ryan Klesko	6.00
6	Carlton Fisk, Magglio Ordonez	4.00
7	Mike Schmidt, Pat Burrell	12.00
8	Don Mattingly, Bernie Williams	12.00
9	Ryne Sandberg, Kerry Wood	10.00
10	Lou Gehrig, Alfonso Soriano	10.00

Team Timelines Materials

		NM/M
Common Card:		30.00
Production 100 unless noted.		
1	Nolan Ryan, Roy Oswalt	120.00
2	Dale Murphy, Chipper Jones	40.00
3	Stan Musial, Jim Edmonds	45.00
4	George Brett, Mike Sweeney	65.00
5	Tony Gwynn, Ryan Klesko	40.00
6	Carlton Fisk, Magglio Ordonez	30.00
7	Mike Schmidt, Pat Burrell	90.00
8	Don Mattingly, Bernie Williams	70.00
9	Ryne Sandberg, Kerry Wood	60.00
10	Lou Gehrig, Alfonso Soriano/50	200.00

Recollection

Production 2-15
No Pricing

Recollection Autographs

		NM/M
Common Player:		
1	Adrian Beltre/40	15.00
2	Brandon Berger/99	10.00

9	Mark Buehrle/73	10.00
15	Andre Dawson/24	25.00
16	Andre Dawson/50	20.00
17	Andre Dawson/28	25.00
19	Jorge De La Rosa/148	5.00
24	Rob Fick/150	8.00
37	Tim Hudson/50	15.00
42	Ryan Ludwick/130	8.00
55	Roy Oswalt/65	15.00
56	Roy Oswalt/100	15.00
70	Bud Smith/114	5.00
72	Shannon Stewart/50	8.00

2003 Donruss Elite

Scott Rolen THIRD BASE

		NM/M
Complete Set (200):		
Common Player:		.25
Common Rookie (181-200):		3.00
Production 1,750		
Pack (5):		3.50
Box (20):		60.00
1	Darin Erstad	.40
2	David Eckstein	.25
3	Garret Anderson	.40
4	Jarrod Washburn	.25
5	Tim Salmon	.40
6	Troy Glaus	.50
7	Marty Cordova	.25
8	Melvin Mora	.25
9	Rodrigo Lopez	.25
10	Tony Batista	.25
11	Derek Lowe	.25
12	Johnny Damon	.40
13	Manny Ramirez	.50
14	Nomar Garciaparra	1.50
15	Pedro J. Martinez	.75
16	Shea Hillenbrand	.25
17	Carlos Lee	.25
18	Joe Crede	.25
19	Frank Thomas	.50
20	Magglio Ordonez	.40
21	Mark Buehrle	.25
22	Paul Konerko	.25
23	C.C. Sabathia	.25
24	Ellis Burks	.25
25	Omar Vizquel	.40
26	Brian Tallet	.25
27	Bobby Higginson	.25
28	Carlos Pena	.25
29	Mark Redman	.25
30	Steve Sparks	.25
31	Carlos Beltran	.50
32	Joe Randa	.25
33	Mike Sweeney	.25
34	Raul Ibanez	.25
35	Runelvys Hernandez	.25
36	Brad Radke	.25
37	Corey Koskie	.25
38	Cristian Guzman	.25
39	David Ortiz	.50
40	Doug Mientkiewicz	.25
41	Jacque Jones	.25
42	Torii Hunter	.40
43	Alfonso Soriano	.75
44	Andy Pettitte	.40
45	Bernie Williams	.50
46	David Wells	.25
47	Derek Jeter	2.00
48	Jason Giambi	.40
49	Jeff Weaver	.25
50	Jorge Posada	.40
51	Mike Mussina	.50
52	Roger Clemens	1.50
53	Barry Zito	.40
54	Eric Chavez	.40
55	Jermaine Dye	.25
56	Mark Mulder	.40
57	Miguel Tejada	.40
58	Tim Hudson	.40
59	Bret Boone	.25
60	Chris Snelling	.25
61	Edgar Martinez	.40

62	Freddy Garcia	.25
63	Ichiro Suzuki	1.50
64	Jamie Moyer	.25
65	John Olerud	.25
66	Kazuhiro Sasaki	.25
67	Aubrey Huff	.25
68	Joe Kennedy	.25
69	Paul Wilson	.25
70	Alex Rodriguez	1.50
71	Chan Ho Park	.25
72	Hank Blalock	.50
73	Juan Gonzalez	.50
74	Kevin Mench	.25
75	Rafael Palmeiro	.50
76	Carlos Delgado	.40
77	Eric Hinske	.25
78	Josh Phelps	.25
79	Roy Halladay	.40
80	Shannon Stewart	.25
81	Vernon Wells	.25
82	Curt Schilling	.50
83	Junior Spivey	.25
84	Luis Gonzalez	.40
85	Mark Grace	.50
86	Randy Johnson	.75
87	Steve Finley	.25
88	Andruw Jones	.50
89	Chipper Jones	.75
90	Gary Sheffield	.50
91	Greg Maddux	1.00
92	John Smoltz	.40
93	Corey Patterson	.40
94	Kerry Wood	.75
95	Mark Prior	1.00
96	Moises Alou	.40
97	Sammy Sosa	1.50
98	Adam Dunn	.50
99	Austin Kearns	.40
100	Barry Larkin	.40
101	Ken Griffey Jr.	1.00
102	Sean Casey	.25
103	Jason Jennings	.25
104	Jay Payton	.25
105	Larry Walker	.40
106	Todd Helton	.50
107	A.J. Burnett	.25
108	Josh Beckett	.50
109	Juan Encarnacion	.25
110	Mike Lowell	.25
111	Craig Biggio	.40
112	Daryle Ward	.25
113	Jeff Bagwell	.50
114	Lance Berkman	.40
115	Roy Oswalt	.40
116	Jason Lane	.25
117	Adrian Beltre	.50
118	Hideo Nomo	.50
119	Kazuhisa Ishii	.25
120	Kevin Brown	.40
121	Odalis Perez	.25
122	Paul LoDuca	.25
123	Shawn Green	.40
124	Ben Sheets	.40
125	Jeffrey Hammonds	.25
126	Jose Hernandez	.25
127	Richie Sexson	.50
128	Bartolo Colon	.25
129	Brad Wilkerson	.25
130	Javier Vazquez	.25
131	Jose Vidro	.25
132	Michael Barrett	.25
133	Vladimir Guerrero	.75
134	Al Leiter	.25
135	Mike Piazza	1.00
136	Mo Vaughn	.25
137	Pedro Astacio	.25
138	Roberto Alomar	.40
139	Pat Burrell	.40
140	Vicente Padilla	.25
141	Jimmy Rollins	.40
142	Bobby Abreu	.40
143	Marlon Byrd	.25
144	Brian Giles	.40
145	Jason Kendall	.40
146	Aramis Ramirez	.40
147	Josh Fogg	.25
148	Ryan Klesko	.40
149	Phil Nevin	.25
150	Sean Burroughs	.25
151	Mark Kotsay	.25
152	Barry Bonds	2.00
153	Damian Moss	.25
154	Jason Schmidt	.50
155	Benito Santiago	.25
156	Rich Aurilia	.25
157	Scott Rolen	.75
158	J.D. Drew	.40
159	Jim Edmonds	.40
160	Matt Morris	.40
161	Tino Martinez	.25
162	Albert Pujols	1.50
163	Russ Ortiz	.25
164	Rey Ordonez	.25
165	Paul Byrd	.25
166	Kenny Lofton	.25
167	Kenny Rogers	.25
168	Rickey Henderson	.50
169	Fred McGriff	.40
170	Charles Johnson	.25
171	Mike Hampton	.25
172	Jim Thome	.75
173	Travis Hafner	.25
174	Ivan Rodriguez	.50
175	Ray Durham	.25
176	Jeremy Giambi	.25
177	Jeff Kent	.40
178	Cliff Floyd	.25
179	Kevin Millwood	.25
180	Tom Glavine	.50
181	Hideki Matsui RC	10.00
182	Jose Contreras RC	5.00
183	Terrmel Sledge RC	3.00
184	Lew Ford RC	6.00
185	Jhonny Peralta	4.00
186	Alexis Rios	4.00
187	Jeff Baker	3.00
188	Jeremy Guthrie	3.00
189	Jose Castillo	3.00
190	Garrett Atkins	3.00
191	Jeremy Bonderman	8.00
192	Adam LaRoche	3.00
193	Vinnie Chulk	3.00
194	Walter Young	3.00
195	Jimmy Gobble	3.00
196	Prentice Redman RC	4.00
197	Jason Anderson	3.00
198	Nic Jackson	3.00
199	Travis Chapman	3.00
200	Shane Victorino RC	3.00

Aspirations

		NM/M
Stars print run 25-50:		10-15X
Rookies (181-200)		
p/r 25-50:		1-3X
Stars p/r 51-99:		5-10X

Serial numbered to jersey number.
Gold One-of-One's exist.

181	Hideki Matsui/45	125.00

Status

		NM/M
Stars print run 25-50:		10-15X
Rookies (181-200)		
p/r 25-50:		1-3X
Stars p/r 51-99:		5-10X
Gold Status:		No Pricing

Production 24 Sets

181	Hideki Matsui/55	120.00

All-Time Career Best

		NM/M
Complete Set (45):		120.00
Common Player:		2.00

Inserted 1:9

Gold print run 25-50:		4-8X
Gold print run 51-100:		3-5X
Gold p/r 101-239:		1.5-3X

Numbered to career stat.

1	Babe Ruth	6.00
2	Ty Cobb	4.00
3	Jackie Robinson	4.00
4	Lou Gehrig	5.00
5	Thurman Munson	2.00
6	Nolan Ryan	8.00
7	Mike Schmidt	4.00
8	Don Mattingly	5.00
9	Yogi Berra	3.00
10	Rod Carew	2.00
11	Reggie Jackson	3.00
12	Al Kaline	4.00
13	Harmon Killebrew	4.00
14	Eddie Mathews	3.00
15	Stan Musial	4.00
16	Jim Palmer	2.00
17	Phil Rizzuto	2.00
18	Brooks Robinson	3.00
19	Tom Seaver	3.00
20	Robin Yount	4.00
21	Carlton Fisk	3.00
22	Dale Murphy	4.00
23	Cal Ripken Jr.	8.00
24	Tony Gwynn	4.00
25	Andre Dawson	2.00
26	Derek Jeter	6.00
27	Ken Griffey Jr.	4.00
28	Albert Pujols	4.00
29	Sammy Sosa	4.00
30	Jason Giambi	3.00
31	Randy Johnson	3.00
32	Greg Maddux	4.00
33	Rickey Henderson	3.00
34	Pedro Martinez	3.00
35	Jeff Bagwell	3.00
36	Alex Rodriguez	5.00
37	Vladimir Guerrero	3.00
38	Chipper Jones	3.00
39	Shawn Green	2.00
40	Tom Glavine	2.00
41	Curt Schilling	2.00
42	Todd Helton	2.00
43	Roger Clemens	4.00
44	Lance Berkman	2.00
45	Nomar Garciaparra	5.00

All-Time Career Best Materials

		NM/M
Common Player:		5.00

Varying quantities produced

1	Babe Ruth/Bat/25	250.00
2	Ty Cobb/Bat/25	150.00
3	Jackie Robinson/Jsy/50	50.00
4	Lou Gehrig/Bat/100	100.00
5	Thurman Munson/Bat/200	15.00
6	Nolan Ryan/Jsy/400	40.00
7	Mike Schmidt/Jsy/400	30.00
8	Don Mattingly/Jsy/250	40.00
9	Yogi Berra/Bat/100	25.00
10	Rod Carew/Bat/400	10.00
11	Reggie Jackson/Bat/400	10.00
12	Al Kaline/Bat/400	20.00
13	Harmon Killebrew/Jsy/400	15.00
14	Eddie Mathews/Bat/200	25.00
15	Stan Musial/Bat/100	40.00
16	Jim Palmer/Jsy/200	10.00
17	Phil Rizzuto/Bat/400	10.00
18	Brooks Robinson/Bat/400	15.00
19	Tom Seaver/Jsy/400	15.00
20	Robin Yount/Bat/400	15.00
21	Carlton Fisk/Bat/400	10.00
22	Dale Murphy/Bat/400	10.00
23	Cal Ripken Jr./Bat/400	35.00
24	Tony Gwynn/Jsy/400	12.00
25	Andre Dawson/Bat/400	5.00
26	Derek Jeter/Base/400	15.00
27	Ken Griffey Jr./Base/400	10.00
28	Albert Pujols/Base/400	15.00
29	Sammy Sosa/Bat/400	12.00
30	Jason Giambi/Bat/400	8.00
31	Randy Johnson/Jsy/400	8.00
32	Greg Maddux/Jsy/400	10.00
33	Rickey Henderson/Bat/400	10.00
34	Pedro Martinez/Jsy/400	10.00
35	Jeff Bagwell/Jsy/400	8.00
36	Alex Rodriguez/Bat/400	12.00
37	Vladimir Guerrero/Bat/400	8.00
38	Chipper Jones/Bat/400	10.00
39	Shawn Green/Bat/400	5.00
40	Tom Glavine/Jsy/400	5.00
41	Curt Schilling/Jsy/400	8.00
42	Todd Helton/Bat/400	8.00
43	Roger Clemens/Jsy/400	20.00
44	Lance Berkman/Bat/400	5.00
45	Nomar Garciaparra/Bat/400	15.00

All-Time Career Best Materials Gold

		NM/M

Numbered to career stat.
Some not priced yet.

1	Babe Ruth/60	125.00
4	Lou Gehrig/49	125.00
5	Thurman Munson/105	25.00
7	Mike Schmidt/48	50.00
8	Don Mattingly/53	60.00
9	Yogi Berra/30	50.00
10	Rod Carew/239	10.00
11	Reggie Jackson/39	25.00
12	Al Kaline/29	50.00
13	Harmon Killebrew/140	20.00
14	Eddie Mathews/31	50.00
15	Stan Musial/39	60.00
18	Brooks Robinson/118	20.00
20	Robin Yount/49	40.00
21	Carlton Fisk/107	15.00
22	Dale Murphy/44	40.00
23	Cal Ripken Jr./211	40.00
24	Tony Gwynn/220	10.00
25	Andre Dawson/49	15.00
27	Ken Griffey Jr./56	25.00
28	Albert Pujols/37	30.00
29	Sammy Sosa/66	35.00
30	Jason Giambi/137	10.00
33	Rickey Henderson/130	20.00
35	Jeff Bagwell/47	15.00
36	Alex Rodriguez/393	10.00
37	Vladimir Guerrero/44	25.00
38	Chipper Jones/45	15.00
39	Shawn Green/49	15.00
41	Curt Schilling/35	20.00
42	Todd Helton/59	15.00
44	Lance Berkman/15	15.00
45	Nomar Garciaparra/35	50.00

Back to the Future

		NM/M
Complete Set (15):		35.00
Common Card:		2.00

#'s 1-10 production 1,000:
#'s 11-15 production 500

1	Kerry Wood	4.00
2	Mark Prior	4.00
3	Magglio Ordonez	2.50
4	Joe Borchard	2.00
5	Lance Berkman	3.00
6	Jason Lane	2.00
7	Rafael Palmeiro	3.00
8	Mark Teixeira	3.00
9	Carlos Delgado	3.00
10	Josh Phelps.	2.00
11	Kerry Wood, Mark Prior.	4.00
12	Joe Borchard, Magglio Ordonez.	2.50
13	Jason Lane, Lance Berkman.	3.00
14	Mark Teixeira, Rafael Palmeiro.	3.00
15	Carlos Delgado, Josh Phelps.	3.00

Back to the Future Threads

		NM/M
Common Card:		4.00

Singles production 250:
Doubles production 125:

1	Kerry Wood	10.00
2	Mark Prior	12.00
3	Magglio Ordonez	5.00
4	Joe Borchard	5.00
5	Lance Berkman	6.00
6	Jason Lane	4.00
7	Rafael Palmeiro	8.00
8	Mark Teixeira	10.00
9	Carlos Delgado	8.00
11	Josh Phelps	6.00
11	Kerry Wood, Mark Prior	20.00
12	Joe Borchard, Magglio Ordonez	8.00
13	Jason Lane, Lance Berkman	8.00
14	Mark Teixeira, Rafael Palmeiro	15.00
15	Carlos Delgado, Josh Phelps	8.00

Back 2 Back Jacks

		NM/M
Common Player:		
1	Adam Dunn/250	10.00
2	Alex Rodriguez/250	15.00
3	Alfonso Soriano/250	10.00
4	Andruw Jones/250	8.00
5	Chipper Jones/250	10.00
6	Jason Giambi/250	8.00
7	Jeff Bagwell/250	8.00
8	Jim Thome/250	8.00
9	Juan Gonzalez/250	8.00
10	Lance Berkman/250	6.00
11	Magglio Ordonez/250	4.00
12	Manny Ramirez/250	8.00
13	Miguel Tejada/250	6.00
14	Mike Piazza/250	15.00

15	Nomar Garciaparra/250	15.00
16	Rafael Palmeiro/250	8.00
17	Rickey Henderson/250	10.00
18	Sammy Sosa/250	15.00
19	Scott Rolen/250	8.00
20	Shawn Green/250	6.00
21	Todd Helton/250	8.00
22	Vladimir Guerrero/250	8.00
23	Ivan Rodriguez/250	8.00
24	Eric Chavez/250	6.00
25	Larry Walker/250	6.00
26	Troy Glaus/250, Garret Anderson	8.00
27	Adam Dunn, Austin Kearns/125	20.00
28	Alex Rodriguez, Rafael Palmeiro/125	20.00
29	Eric Chavez, Miguel Tejada/125	10.00
30	Frank Thomas, Magglio Ordonez/125	15.00
31	Jeff Bagwell, Lance Berkman/125	15.00
32	Manny Ramirez, Nomar Garciaparra/125	30.00
33	Jose Vidro, Vladimir Guerrero/125	15.00
34	Mike Piazza, Roberto Alomar/125	20.00
35	Larry Walker, Todd Helton/125	15.00
36	Babe Ruth/100	150.00
37	Cal Ripken Jr./100	65.00
38	Don Mattingly/100	50.00
39	Kirby Puckett/100	20.00
40	Roberto Clemente/100	75.00
41	Alfonso Soriano, Phil Rizzuto/75	25.00
42	Andre Dawson, Sammy Sosa/75	40.00
43	Ozzie Smith, Scott Rolen/75	60.00
44	Don Mattingly, Jason Giambi/75	75.00
45	Rickey Henderson, Ty Cobb/75	125.00
46	Joe Morgan, Johnny Bench/50	35.00
47	Brooks Robinson, Cal Ripken Jr./50	100.00
48	Bo Jackson, George Brett/50	100.00
49	Babe Ruth, Lou Gehrig/50	375.00
50	Thurman Munson, Yogi Berra/50	60.00

Career Best

NM/M

Common Player:		3.00

Numbered to statistic.

3	Garret Anderson/56	6.00
4	Andruw Jones/83	6.00
6	Magglio Ordonez/38	6.00
7	Magglio Ordonez/135	4.00
8	Adam Dunn/26	15.00
10	Lance Berkman/42	6.00
11	Lance Berkman/128	3.00
12	Shawn Green/385	3.00
13	Alfonso Soriano/39	12.00
14	Alfonso Soriano/300	5.00
15	Jason Giambi/120	5.00
16	Derek Jeter/32	30.00
17	Vladimir Guerrero/40	12.00
18	Vladimir Guerrero/417	5.00
19	Barry Zito/23	8.00
20	Miguel Tejada/34	8.00
21	Barry Bonds/198	15.00
22	Barry Bonds/370	15.00
23	Ichiro Suzuki/388	8.00
24	Alex Rodriguez/57	15.00
25	Alex Rodriguez/142	10.00

Career Best Materials

NM/M

Common Player:		4.00

Production 500 Sets

1	Randy Johnson/Jsy	8.00
2	Curt Schilling/Jsy	8.00
3	Garret Anderson/Bat	4.00
4	Andruw Jones/Bat	6.00
5	Kerry Wood/Shoe	10.00
6	Magglio Ordonez/Bat	4.00
7	Magglio Ordonez/Bat	4.00
8	Adam Dunn/Bat	6.00
9	Roy Oswalt/Jsy	5.00
10	Lance Berkman/Bat	5.00
11	Lance Berkman/Bat	5.00
12	Shawn Green/Bat	4.00
13	Alfonso Soriano/Bat	10.00
14	Alfonso Soriano/Bat	10.00
15	Jason Giambi/Bat	8.00
16	Derek Jeter/Base	15.00
17	Vladimir Guerrero/Bat	8.00
18	Vladimir Guerrero/Bat	8.00
19	Barry Zito/Jsy	6.00
20	Miguel Tejada/Bat	6.00
21	Barry Bonds/Base	15.00
22	Barry Bonds/Base	15.00
23	Ichiro Suzuki/Base	15.00
24	Alex Rodriguez/Jsy	10.00
25	Alex Rodriguez/Jsy	10.00

Career Best Materials Autograph

NM/M

Quantity produced listed

3	Garret Anderson/Bat/75	35.00
8	Adam Dunn/Bat/100	50.00
9	Roy Oswalt/Jsy/250	30.00
17	Vladimir Guerrero/Bat/50	75.00
18	Vladimir Guerrero/Bat/50	75.00
19	Barry Zito/Jsy/75	40.00

Elite Dominators

No pricing, 25 sets produced.

Highlights

NM/M

Production 500 Sets

1	Sammy Sosa	10.00
2	Rafael Palmeiro	8.00
3	Hideki Matsui	10.00
4	Jose Contreras	4.00
5	Kevin Millwood	4.00

Highlights Autographs

NM/M

Production 50 Sets

2	Rafael Palmeiro	75.00
4	Jose Contreras	25.00

Passing the Torch

NM/M

Complete Set (15):		50.00

Common Player:

1	Stan Musial	6.00
2	Jim Edmonds	2.00
3	Dale Murphy	3.00
4	Andruw Jones	3.00
5	Roger Clemens	8.00
6	Mark Prior	3.00
7	Tom Seaver	3.00
8	Tom Glavine	1.50
9	Mike Schmidt	8.00
10	Pat Burrell	2.00
11	Jim Edmonds,	8.00
12	Andruw Jones, Dale Murphy	5.00
13	Mark Prior, Roger Clemens	8.00
14	Tom Glavine, Tom Seaver	5.00
15	Mike Schmidt, Pat Burrell	10.00

Passing the Torch Autograph

NM/M

Common Auto (1-10): 30.00
#'s 1-10 Production 50
#'s 11-15 Production 25
No pricing for #'s 11-15.

1	Stan Musial	80.00
2	Jim Edmonds	40.00
3	Dale Murphy	50.00
4	Andruw Jones	30.00
5	Roger Clemens	125.00
6	Mark Prior	40.00
7	Tom Seaver	60.00
8	Tom Glavine	50.00
9	Mike Schmidt	100.00
10	Pat Burrell	30.00

Recollection Autographs

NM/M

Some not priced due to scarcity.

1	Jeremy Affeldt/75	15.00
2	Erick Almonte/75	8.00
4	Adrian Beltre/36	30.00
7	Brandon Berger/83	8.00
8	Angel Berroa/28	25.00
13	Jeff Deardorff/53	8.00
14	Ryan Drese/100	25.00
21	Luis Garcia/28	15.00
22	Geronimo Gil/75	8.00
28	Travis Hafner Black/52	30.00
30	Bill Hall/27	15.00
35	Gerald Laird/46	30.00
36	Jason Lane/27	15.00
44	Victor Martinez/52	100.00
46	Roy Oswalt/Black/61	20.00
51	Ricardo Rodriguez/75	8.00
55	Bud Smith/50	10.00
56	Bud Smith/28	10.00
58	Junior Spivey/45	20.00
59	Tim Spooneybarger/100	15.00
61	Shannon Stewart/35	20.00
64	Claudio Vargas/51	8.00

Throwback Threads

NM/M

Common Player:		4.00
1	Randy Johnson/Jsy	8.00
2	Randy Johnson/Hat	10.00
3	Roger Clemens/Jsy	20.00
4	Roger Clemens/Jsy	20.00
5	Manny Ramirez/Jsy	8.00
6	Greg Maddux/Jsy	15.00
7	Jason Giambi/Jsy	6.00
8	Jason Giambi/Jsy	6.00
9	Alex Rodriguez/Jsy	10.00
10	Alex Rodriguez/Jsy	10.00
11	Miguel Tejada/Jsy	6.00
12	Alfonso Soriano/Jsy	8.00
13	Nomar Garciaparra/Jsy	15.00
14	Pedro J. Martinez/Jsy	8.00
15	Pedro J. Martinez/Jsy	8.00
16	Andruw Jones/Jsy	6.00
17	Chipper Jones/Jsy	8.00
18	Barry Zito/Jsy	8.00
19	Mark Mulder/Jsy	4.00
20	Lance Berkman/Jsy	6.00
21	Magglio Ordonez/Jsy	4.00
22	Mike Piazza/Jsy	15.00
23	Mike Piazza/Jsy	15.00
24	Rickey Henderson/Jsy	8.00
25	Rickey Henderson/Jsy	8.00
26	Rickey Henderson/Jsy	8.00
27	Sammy Sosa/Jsy	15.00
28	Shawn Green/Jsy	5.00
29	Troy Glaus/Jsy	6.00
30	Vladimir Guerrero/Jsy	8.00
31	Adam Dunn/Jsy	8.00
32	Jeff Bagwell/Jsy	8.00
33	Curt Schilling/Jsy	8.00
34	Hideo Nomo/Jsy	20.00
35	Hideo Nomo/Jsy	20.00
36	Hideo Nomo/Jsy	20.00
37	Kerry Wood/Jsy	10.00
38	Mark Prior/Jsy	8.00
39	Roberto Alomar/Jsy	6.00
40	Todd Helton/Jsy	8.00
41	Jim Thome/Jsy	8.00
42	Rafael Palmeiro/Jsy	8.00
43	Juan Gonzalez/Jsy	8.00
44	Vernon Wells/Jsy	4.00
45	Torii Hunter/Jsy	6.00
46	Randi Johnson/Jsy	15.00
47	Roger Clemens/Jsy	30.00
48	Jason Giambi/Jsy	10.00
49	Alex Rodriguez/Jsy	25.00
50	Pedro J. Martinez/Jsy	20.00
51	Mike Piazza/Jsy	25.00
52	Rickey Henderson	20.00
53	Rickey Henderson	20.00
54	Rickey Henderson/Hat, Rickey Henderson/Jsy	20.00
55	Hideo Nomo/Jsy	40.00
56	Randy Johnson/Jsy	15.00
57	Curt Schilling, Randy Johnson/Jsy	15.00
58	Alfonso Soriano, Jason Giambi	20.00
59	Barry Zito, Mark Mulder	15.00
60	Andruw Jones, Chipper Jones/Jsy	20.00
61	Greg Maddux, Tom Glavine	40.00
62	Jeff Bagwell, Lance Berkman/Jsy	15.00
63	Mark Prior, Roger Clemens/Jsy	20.00
64	Alex Rodriguez, Rafael Palmeiro/Jsy	20.00
65	Jim Thome, Roberto Alomar/Jsy	20.00
66	Mike Piazza, Roberto Alomar/Jsy	20.00
67	Mark Grace, Sammy Sosa/Jsy	25.00
68	Larry Walker, Todd Helton/Jsy	20.00
69	Adam Dunn, Austin Kearns/Jsy	20.00
70	Alex Rodriguez, Ivan Rodriguez/Jsy	20.00
71	Bobby Abreu, Marlon Byrd/Jsy	15.00
72	Eric Chavez, Miguel Tejada/Jsy	15.00
73	Greg Maddux, John Smoltz/Jsy	30.00
74	Kerry Wood, Mark Prior/Jsy	10.00
75	Barry Zito, Tim Hudson/Jsy	10.00
76	Babe Ruth	250.00
77	Ty Cobb	100.00
78	Jackie Robinson	75.00
79	Lou Gehrig	125.00
80	Thurman Munson	30.00
81	Nolan Ryan	40.00
82	Don Mattingly	50.00
83	Mike Schmidt	40.00
84	Reggie Jackson	20.00
85	George Brett	40.00
86	Cal Ripken Jr.	50.00
87	Tony Gwynn	15.00
88	Yogi Berra	25.00
89	Stan Musial	40.00
90	Jim Palmer	10.00
91	Thurman Munson	50.00
92	Chipper Jones, Dale Murphy	50.00
93	Don Mattingly, Jason Giambi	80.00
94	Andre Dawson, Sammy Sosa	40.00
95	Mark Prior, Nolan Ryan	50.00
96	Babe Ruth, Lou Gehrig	475.00
97	Joe Morgan, Tom Seaver	40.00
98	Harmon Killebrew, Rod Carew	40.00
99	Nolan Ryan	90.00
100	Reggie Jackson	35.00

Throwback Threads Autograph

NM/M

Production 5-75		4.00
30	Vladimir Guerrero/50	75.00
31	Adam Dunn/50	75.00
37	Kerry Wood/50	75.00
38	Mark Prior/75	50.00
39	Roberto Alomar/50	75.00

Turn of the Century Autographs

NM/M

Common Autograph:		10.00

Production 50 Sets

182	Jose Contreras	40.00
183	Terrmel Sledge	15.00
184	Lew Ford	20.00
185	Jhonny Peralta	35.00
186	Alexis Rios	40.00
187	Jeff Baker	15.00

188	Jeremy Guthrie	15.00
189	Jose Castillo	15.00
190	Garrett Atkins	20.00
191	Jeremy Bonderman	75.00
192	Adam LaRoche	15.00
193	Vinnie Chulk	15.00
194	Walter Young	15.00
195	Jimmy Gobble	10.00
196	Prentice Redman	15.00
197	Jason Anderson	15.00
198	Nic Jackson	15.00
199	Travis Chapman	10.00
200	Shane Victorino	10.00

2003 Donruss Rookie & Traded

		NM/M
Complete Set (65):		8.00
Common Player:		.25
Pack (8):		8.00
Box (24):		150.00
1	Jeremy Bonderman	1.00
2	Adam Loewen	.50
3	Dan Haren	.50
4	Jose Contreras RC	.50
5	Hideki Matsui RC	2.00
6	Arnie Munoz	.25
7	Miguel Cabrera	.25
8	Andrew Brown RC	.25
9	Josh Hall RC	.25
10	Josh Stewart RC	.25
11	Clint Barmes RC	.25
12	Luis Ayala RC	.25
13	Brandon Webb RC	.75
14	Greg Aquino	.25
15	Chien-Ming Wang RC	2.00
16	Rickie Weeks RC	1.50
17	Edgar Gonzalez RC	.25
18	Dontrelle Willis	.25
19	Bo Hart RC	.25
20	Rosman Garcia RC	.25
21	Jeremy Griffiths	.25
22	Craig Brazell RC	.50
23	Daniel Cabrera RC	.50
24	Fernando Cabrera RC	.25
25	Terrmel Sledge RC	.25
26	Ramon Nivar	.25
27	Rob Hammock RC	.25
28	Francisco Rosario RC	.25
29	Cory Stewart	.25
30	Felix Sanchez	.25
31	Jorge Cordova	.25
32	Rocco Baldelli	.25
33	Beau Kemp RC	.25
34	Micheal Nakamura RC	.25
35	Rett Johnson RC	.25
36	Guillermo Quiroz RC	.25
37	Hong-Chih Kuo RC	1.00
38	Ian Ferguson RC	.25
39	Franklin Perez	.25
40	Tim Olson RC	.25

41	Jerome Williams	.25
42	Rich Fischer	.25
43	Phil Seibel RC	.25
44	Aaron Looper RC	.25
45	Jae Weong Seo	.25
46	Chad Gaudin RC	.25
47	Matt Kata RC	.25
48	Ryan Wagner RC	.25
49	Michel Hernandez RC	.25
50	Diegomar Markwell	.25
51	Doug Waechter	.25
52	Mike Nicolas	.25
53	Prentice Redman RC	.25
54	Shane Bazzell	.25
55	Delmon Young RC	2.00
56	Brian Stokes	.25
57	Matt Bruback	.25
58	Nook Logan RC	.25
59	Oscar Villarreal RC	.25
60	Pete LaForest RC	.25
61	Shea Hillenbrand	.25
62	Aramis Ramirez	.40
63	Aaron Boone	.25
64	Roberto Alomar	.50
65	Rickey Henderson	.50

Team Heroes
Common Player (541-548):		.25
Team Heroes Glossy:		1-2X
541	Rickie Weeks RC	1.00
542	Hideki Matsui RC	1.50
543	Ramon Nivar	.25
544	Adam Loewen RC	.25
545	Brandon Webb RC	.75
546	Dan Haren	.50
547	Delmon Young RC	2.00
548	Ryan Wagner RC	.25

Champions
Common Player (302-309):		.25
Metalized:		4-8X
Production 100		
302	Ryan Wagner RC	.25
303	Adam Loewen RC	.25
304	Chien-Ming Wang RC	2.50
305	Hong-Chih Kuo RC	1.00
306	Delmon Young RC	2.00
307	Dan Haren	.50
308	Rickie Weeks RC	1.50
309	Ramon Nivar	.25

Leaf
Common Player (321-329):		.25
Leaf Red Press Proofs:		4-8X
Production 100		
Leaf Blue Press Proofs:		5-10X
Production 50		
321	Hideki Matsui RC	1.50
322	Ramon Nivar	.25
323	Adam Loewen RC	.25
324	Brandon Webb RC	.75
325	Chien-Ming Wang RC	2.50
326	Delmon Young RC	2.00
327	Ryan Wagner RC	.25
328	Dan Haren	.50
329	Rickie Weeks RC	1.50

Playoff Prestige
Common Player (201-210):		.25
Prestige X-Tra Points:		5-10X
Production 50		
201	Jeremy Bonderman	1.00
202	Brandon Webb RC	.75
203	Adam Loewen RC	.25
204	Chien-Ming Wang RC	2.50
205	Hong-Chih Kuo RC	1.00
206	Delmon Young RC	2.00
207	Ryan Wagner RC	.25
208	Dan Haren	.50
209	Rickie Weeks RC	1.50
210	Ramon Nivar	.25

Classics
Common Player (201-211):		4.00
Production 1,000		
Classics Timeless		
Tributes:		.75-1.5X
Production 100		
201	Jeremy Bonderman	8.00
202	Adam Loewen RC	6.00
203	Chien-Ming Wang RC	25.00
204	Hong-Chih Kuo RC	8.00
205	Ryan Wagner RC	4.00
206	Dan Haren	6.00
207	Dontrelle Willis	4.00
208	Rickie Weeks RC	8.00
209	Ramon Nivar	4.00
210	Chad Gaudin RC	4.00
211	Delmon Young RC	10.00

Studio
Common Player (201-211):		3.00
Production 1,500		
Studio Proof:		1-1.5X
Production 100		
201	Adam Loewen RC	3.00
202	Jeremy Bonderman	6.00
203	Brandon Webb RC	8.00
204	Chien-Ming Wang RC	25.00
205	Chad Gaudin RC	3.00

206	Ryan Wagner RC	3.00
207	Hong-Chih Kuo RC	8.00
208	Dan Haren	6.00
209	Rickie Weeks RC	8.00
210	Ramon Nivar	3.00
211	Delmon Young RC	10.00

Diamond Kings
Common Player (177-201):		3.00
Inserted 1:30		
DK Portraits Bronze:		.5-1X
DK Portraits Silver:		1-1.5X
Production 100		
DK Portraits Gold:		1-2X
Production 50		
177	Hideki Matsui RC	10.00
178	Jeremy Bonderman	8.00
179	Brandon Webb RC	8.00
180	Adam Loewen RC	4.00
181	Chien-Ming Wang RC	15.00
182	Hong-Chih Kuo RC	8.00
183	Clint Barmes RC	3.00
184	Guillermo Quiroz RC	4.00
185	Edgar Gonzalez RC	3.00
186	Todd Wellemeyer RC	3.00
187	Dan Haren	4.00
188	Dustin McGowan	5.00
189	Preston Larrison	3.00
191	Kevin Youkilis	8.00
192	Bubba Nelson	3.00
193	Chris Burke	3.00
194	J.D. Durbin	4.00
195	Ryan Howard	30.00
196	Jason Kubel RC	6.00
197	Brendan Harris	6.00
198	Brian Bruney	3.00
199	Ramon Nivar	3.00
200	Rickie Weeks RC	8.00
201	Delmon Young RC	10.00

Leaf Certified Materials
Mirror Red Signature:		.75-1.5X
Production 100 or 50		
Mirror Blue Signature:		1-1.5X
Mirror Gold Signature:		No Pricing
Mirror Emerald		
Signature:		No Pricing
Mirror Reds:		.2-.4X
Production 100		
Mirror Blues:		.4-.6X
Production 50		
Mirror Golds:		No Pricing
Production 25		
251	Adam Loewen/ Auto./250 RC	15.00
252	Dan Haren/Auto./250	30.00
253	Dontrelle Willis/ Auto./250	25.00
254	Ramon Nivar/ Auto./250	10.00
255	Chad Gaudin/ Auto./250	20.00
256	Kevin Correia/ Auto./250	10.00
257	Rickie Weeks/ Auto./100 RC	80.00
258	Ryan Wagner/ Auto./250 RC	15.00
259	Delmon Young/ Auto./100 RC	150.00

Playoff Absolute
Common Player (201-208):		4.00
Production 1,000		
Spectrum:		1-2X
Production 100		
201	Adam Loewen RC	4.00
202	Ramon Nivar	4.00
203	Dan Haren	5.00
204	Dontrelle Willis	4.00
205	Chad Gaudin	4.00
206	Rickie Weeks RC	8.00
207	Ryan Wagner RC	4.00
208	Delmon Young RC	12.00

Elite Extra Edition
Common Player (1-58):		4.00
Production 900		
Elite Status:		1-3X
Numbered to Jersey Number		
Elite Aspirations:		1-2X
Varying quantities produced		
Turn of Century non-Auto:		1-2X
Production 100		
Elite Gold Status:		No Pricing
Production 24		
1	Adam Loewen RC	4.00
2	Brandon Webb RC	10.00
3	Chien-Ming Wang RC	30.00
4	Hong-Chih Kuo RC	20.00
5	Clint Barmes RC	4.00
6	Guillermo Quiroz RC	3.00
7	Edgar Gonzalez RC	3.00
8	Todd Wellemeyer RC	4.00
9	Alfredo Gonzalez RC	3.00
10	Craig Brazell RC	3.00
11	Tim Olson RC	3.00
12	Rich Fischer	3.00
13	Daniel Cabrera RC	5.00

14	Francisco Rosario RC	4.00
15	Francisco Cruceta RC	4.00
16	Alejandro Machado	4.00
17	Andrew Brown RC	4.00
18	Rob Hammock RC	4.00
19	Arnie Munoz	4.00
20	Felix Sanchez	4.00
21	Nook Logan RC	4.00
22	Cory Stewart	4.00
23	Michel Hernandez RC	4.00
24	Rett Johnson RC	4.00
25	Josh Hall RC	4.00
26	Doug Waechter	4.00
27	Matt Kata RC	4.00
28	Dan Haren	8.00
29	Dontrelle Willis	4.00
30	Ramon Nivar	4.00
31	Chad Gaudin RC	5.00
32	Rickie Weeks RC	10.00
33	Ryan Wagner RC	4.00
34	Kevin Correia RC	4.00
35	Bo Hart RC	4.00
36	Oscar Villarreal RC	4.00
37	Josh Willingham RC	5.00
38	Jeff Duncan RC	6.00
39	David DeJesus RC	6.00
40	Dustin McGowan RC	6.00
41	Preston Larrison	4.00
43	Kevin Youkilis	8.00
44	Bubba Nelson	4.00
45	Chris Burke	6.00
46	J.D. Durbin	4.00
47	Ryan Howard	80.00
48	Jason Kubel RC	8.00
49	Brendan Harris	6.00
50	Brian Bruney	4.00
52	Byron Gettis	4.00
53	Edwin Jackson RC	4.00
55	Daniel Garcia	4.00
57	Chad Cordero RC	4.00
58	Delmon Young RC	20.00

Common Leaf Limited Phenom:
Silver Spotlights:		1X
Production 50		
Gold Spotlights:		No Pricing
Production 10 or 25		
201	Delmon Young/ Auto./99 RC	180.00
202	Rickie Weeks/ Auto./99 RC	80.00
203	Edwin Jackson/ Auto./99 RC	20.00
204	Dan Haren/Auto./99	40.00

Signature Series:
151	Delmon Young/ Auto./200 RC	100.00
152	Rickie Weeks/ Auto./200 RC	50.00
153	Edwin Jackson/ Auto./200	15.00

Stat Line Season/Career

Cards serial #'d from 101-150:		1-2X
Cards serial #'d from 50-100:		2-3X
Cards serial #'d from 26-49:		3-4X
Cards numbered under 25 not priced.		

Autographs

		NM/M
Common Autograph:		5.00
1	Jeremy Bonderman/ 50	50.00
2	Adam Loewen/500	10.00
3	Dan Haren/100	30.00
4	Jose Contreras/100	25.00
6	Arnie Munoz/584	5.00
7	Miguel Cabrera/50	50.00
8	Andrew Brown/584	5.00

9	Josh Hall/1,000	10.00
10	Josh Stewart/300	5.00
11	Clint Barmes/129	15.00
12	Luis Ayala/1,000	5.00
13	Brandon Webb/100	35.00
14	Greg Aquino/1,000	5.00
15	Chien-Ming Wang/100	200.00
17	Edgar Gonzalez/400	5.00
19	Bo Hart/150	5.00
20	Rosman Garcia/250	5.00
21	Jeremy Griffiths/812	5.00
22	Craig Brazell/205	5.00
23	Daniel Cabrera/383	15.00
24	Fernando Cabrera/1,000	5.00
25	Terrmel Sledge/250	5.00
26	Ramon Nivar/100	5.00
27	Rob Hammock/201	10.00
29	Cory Stewart/1,000	5.00
30	Felix Sanchez/1,000	5.00
31	Jorge Cordova/1,000	5.00
33	Beau Kemp/1,000	5.00
34	Micheal Nakamura/1,000	5.00
35	Rett Johnson/1,000	8.00
36	Guillermo Quiroz/90	15.00
37	Hong-Chih Kuo/50	150.00
38	Ian Ferguson/1,000	5.00
39	Franklin Perez/1,000	5.00
40	Tim Olson/150	5.00
41	Jerome Williams/50	10.00
42	Rich Fischer/734	5.00
43	Phil Seibel/1,000	5.00
44	Aaron Looper/513	5.00
45	Jae Weong Seo/50	30.00
47	Matt Kata/203	10.00
48	Ryan Wagner/100	10.00
50	Diegomar Markwell/1,000	5.00
51	Doug Waechter/583	5.00
52	Mike Nicolas/1,000	5.00
53	Prentice Redman/425	5.00
54	Shane Bazell/1,000	5.00
55	Delmon Young/75	125.00
56	Brian Stokes/1,000	5.00
57	Matt Bruback/513	5.00
58	Nook Logan/150	5.00
59	Oscar Villarreal/150	5.00
60	Pete LaForest/250	5.00

Gamers

		NM/M
Common Player:		4.00
Production 500		
Position:		1-2X
Production 100		
Number:		1-2X
Production 100		
Patch:		No Pricing
Production 25		
Rewards:		No Pricing
Production 10		
1	Nomar Garciaparra	8.00
2	Alex Rodriguez	8.00
3	Mike Piazza	8.00
4	Greg Maddux	8.00
5	Roger Clemens	10.00
6	Sammy Sosa	8.00
7	Randy Johnson	8.00
8	Albert Pujols	15.00
9	Alfonso Soriano	8.00
10	Chipper Jones	8.00
11	Mark Prior	6.00
12	Hideo Nomo	6.00
13	Adam Dunn	6.00
14	Juan Gonzalez	5.00
15	Vladimir Guerrero	8.00
16	Pedro J. Martinez	8.00
17	Jim Thome	6.00
18	Brandon Webb/200	6.00
19	Mike Mussina	6.00
20	Mark Teixeira	5.00
21	Barry Larkin	5.00
22	Ivan Rodriguez	6.00
23	Hank Blalock	6.00
24	Rafael Palmeiro	6.00
25	Curt Schilling	6.00
26	Troy Glaus	5.00
27	Bernie Williams	6.00
28	Scott Rolen	6.00
29	Torii Hunter	5.00
30	Nick Johnson	4.00

31	Kazuhisa Ishii	4.00
32	Shawn Green	5.00
33	Jeff Bagwell	6.00
34	Lance Berkman	4.00
35	Roy Oswalt	4.00
36	Kerry Wood	4.00
37	Todd Helton	6.00
38	Manny Ramirez	8.00
39	Andruw Jones	5.00
40	Frank Thomas	8.00
41	Gary Sheffield	5.00
42	Magglio Ordonez	5.00
43	Mike Sweeney	4.00
44	Carlos Beltran	6.00
45	Richie Sexson	5.00
46	Jeff Kent	5.00
47	Carlos Delgado	5.00
48	Vernon Wells	4.00
49	Dontrelle Willis	8.00
50	Jae Weong Seo	4.00

Gamers Autograph

		NM/M
Production 5-50		4.00
Many not priced due to scarcity.		
20	Mark Teixeira/50	30.00
23	Hank Blalock/50	30.00
29	Torii Hunter/50	20.00
35	Roy Oswalt/50	20.00
43	Mike Sweeney/50	15.00
48	Vernon Wells/30	20.00
49	Dontrelle Willis/50	25.00

Leaf Autographs

		NM/M
Common Autograph:		
304	Jose Contreras/100	25.00
322	Ramon Nivar/100	10.00
323	Adam Loewen/100	10.00
324	Brandon Webb/100	30.00
325	Chien-Ming Wang/50	250.00
327	Ryan Wagner/100	10.00
328	Dan Haren/100	25.00

Playoff Prestige Autograph

		NM/M
Quantity produced listed		
201	Jeremy Bonderman/100	50.00
202	Brandon Webb/100	30.00
203	Adam Loewen/100	10.00
204	Chien-Ming Wang/50	300.00
205	Hong-Chih Kuo/100	150.00
207	Ryan Wagner/100	10.00
208	Dan Haren/100	25.00
210	Ramon Nivar/100	15.00

Recollection Autographs

		NM/M
Common Player:		
7	Jack McDowell 88/75	20.00

Turn of the Century Autograph

		NM/M
Common Player:		10.00
Production 100		
Aspirations:		.75-1.5X
Varying quantities produced		
1	Adam Loewen	15.00
2	Brandon Webb	80.00
3	Chien-Ming Wang	300.00
4	Hong-Chih Kuo	150.00
5	Clint Barmes	25.00
6	Guillermo Quiroz	20.00
7	Edgar Gonzalez	10.00

8	Todd Wellemeyer	10.00
9	Alfredo Gonzalez	10.00
10	Craig Brazell	10.00
11	Tim Olson	10.00
12	Rich Fischer	10.00
13	Daniel Cabrera	30.00
14	Francisco Rosario	10.00
15	Francisco Cruceta	10.00
16	Alejandro Machado	10.00
17	Andrew Brown	10.00
18	Rob Hammock	10.00
19	Arnie Munoz	10.00
20	Felix Sanchez	10.00
21	Nook Logan	10.00
22	Cory Stewart	10.00
23	Michel Hernandez	10.00
24	Rett Johnson	10.00
25	Josh Hall	15.00
26	Doug Waechter	10.00
27	Matt Kata	10.00
28	Dan Haren	60.00
29	Dontrelle Willis/25	60.00
30	Ramon Nivar	10.00
31	Chad Gaudin	20.00
32	Rickie Weeks/25	120.00
33	Ryan Wagner	10.00
35	Bo Hart	10.00
36	Oscar Villarreal	10.00
37	Josh Willingham	30.00
38	Jeff Duncan	15.00
40	Dustin McGowan	25.00
41	Preston Larrison	10.00
43	Kevin Youkilis	50.00
44	Bubba Nelson	15.00
45	Chris Burke	40.00
46	J.D. Durbin	15.00
47	Ryan Howard	1,100
48	Jason Kubel	40.00
49	Brendan Harris	20.00
50	Brian Bruney	10.00
52	Byron Gettis	10.00
53	Edwin Jackson	10.00
55	Daniel Garcia	10.00
58	Delmon Young	250.00

2003 Donruss Signature Series

		NM/M
Complete Set (150):		150.00
Common Player:		.50
Common Rk (101-150):		1.00
Inserted 1:Tin		
Tin:		35.00
1	Garret Anderson	.75
2	Tim Salmon	.75
3	Troy Glaus	.75
4	Curt Schilling	1.00
5	Luis Gonzalez	.75
6	Mark Grace	.75
7	Matt Williams	.50
8	Randy Johnson	1.50
9	Andruw Jones	1.00
10	Chipper Jones	1.50
11	Gary Sheffield	.75
12	Greg Maddux	2.00
13	Johnny Damon	.75
14	Manny Ramirez	1.00
15	Nomar Garciaparra	1.50
16	Pedro J. Martinez	1.50
17	Corey Patterson	.75
18	Kerry Wood	1.50
19	Mark Prior	2.00
20	Sammy Sosa	2.50
21	Bartolo Colon	.50
22	Frank Thomas	1.00
23	Magglio Ordonez	1.00
24	Paul Konerko	.50
25	Adam Dunn	1.00
26	Austin Kearns	.75
27	Barry Larkin	.75
28	Ken Griffey Jr.	2.00
29	C.C. Sabathia	.50
30	Omar Vizquel	.50
31	Larry Walker	.50
32	Todd Helton	1.00
33	Ivan Rodriguez	1.00
34	Josh Beckett	.75
35	Craig Biggio	.75
36	Jeff Bagwell	1.00
37	Jeff Kent	.50
38	Lance Berkman	.75
39	Richard Hidalgo	.50
40	Roy Oswalt	.75
41	Carlos Beltran	1.00
42	Mike Sweeney	.50
43	Runelvys Hernandez	.50
44	Hideo Nomo	.75
45	Kazuhisa Ishii	.50
46	Paul LoDuca	.50
47	Shawn Green	.75
48	Ben Sheets	.75
49	Richie Sexson	.50
50	A.J. Pierzynski	.50

51	Torii Hunter	.75
52	Javier Vazquez	.50
53	Jose Vidro	.50
54	Vladimir Guerrero	1.50
55	Cliff Floyd	.50
56	David Cone	.50
57	Mike Piazza	2.00
58	Roberto Alomar	.75
59	Tom Glavine	.75
60	Alfonso Soriano	1.50
61	Derek Jeter	4.00
62	Drew Henson	.50
63	Jason Giambi	.75
64	Mike Mussina	1.00
65	Nick Johnson	.50
66	Roger Clemens	3.00
67	Barry Zito	.75
68	Eric Chavez	.75
69	Mark Mulder	.75
70	Miguel Tejada	.75
71	Tim Hudson	.75
72	Bobby Abreu	.75
73	Jim Thome	1.00
74	Kevin Millwood	.50
75	Pat Burrell	.50
76	Brian Giles	.50
77	Jason Kendall	.50
78	Kenny Lofton	.50
79	Phil Nevin	.50
80	Ryan Klesko	.50
81	Andres Galarraga	.50
82	Barry Bonds	4.00
83	Rich Aurilia	.50
84	Edgar Martinez	.50
85	Freddy Garcia	.50
86	Ichiro Suzuki	2.50
87	Albert Pujols	3.00
88	Jim Edmonds	.75
89	Scott Rolen	1.50
90	So Taguchi	.50
91	Rocco Baldelli	.50
92	Alex Rodriguez	3.00
93	Hank Blalock	1.00
94	Juan Gonzalez	1.00
95	Mark Teixeira	.75
96	Rafael Palmeiro	1.00
97	Carlos Delgado	1.00
98	Eric Hinske	.50
99	Roy Halladay	.75
100	Vernon Wells	.50
101	Hideki Matsui RC	10.00
102	Jose Contreras RC	3.00
103	Jeremy Bonderman RC	4.00
104	Bernie Castro RC	1.00
105	Alfredo Gonzalez RC	1.00
106	Arnie Munoz RC	1.00
107	Andrew Brown RC	1.50
108	Josh Hall RC	1.50
109	Josh Stewart RC	1.50
110	Clint Barmes RC	1.50
111	Brandon Webb RC	2.50
112	Chien-Ming Wang RC	15.00
113	Edgar Gonzalez RC	1.00
114	Alejandro Machado RC	1.00
115	Jeremy Griffiths	1.00
116	Craig Brazell RC	1.00
117	Shane Bazell RC	1.50
118	Fernando Cabrera RC	1.50
119	Terrmel Sledge RC	1.50
120	Rob Hammock RC	1.50
121	Francisco Rosario RC	1.50
122	Francisco Cruceta RC	1.50
123	Rett Johnson RC	1.50
124	Guillermo Quiroz RC	2.00
125	Hong-Chih Kuo RC	2.00
126	Ian Ferguson RC	1.50
127	Tim Olson RC	1.00
128	Todd Wellemeyer RC	1.50
129	Richard Fischer RC	1.50
130	Phil Seibel RC	1.00
131	Joe Valentine RC	1.00
132	Matt Kata RC	1.00
133	Michael Hessman RC	1.00
134	Michel Hernandez RC	1.00
135	Doug Waechter RC	1.50
136	Prentice Redman RC	1.50
137	Nook Logan RC	1.00
138	Oscar Villarreal RC	1.00
139	Pete LaForest RC	1.00
140	Matt Bruback RC	1.00
141	Dontrelle Willis	1.50
142	Greg Aquino RC	1.00
143	Lew Ford RC	4.00
144	Jeff Duncan RC	2.00
145	Dan Haren RC	2.00
146	Miguel Ojeda RC	1.00
147	Rosman Garcia RC	1.00
148	Felix Sanchez RC	1.00
149	Jon Leicester RC	1.00
150	Roger Deago RC	1.00

Authentic Cuts

Quantity produced listed

Autographs

		NM/M
Common Auto:		8.00
Some not priced due to scarcity.		
1	Garret Anderson	15.00
6	Mark Grace/141	50.00
7	Matt Williams	10.00
8	Randy Johnson/50	60.00
10	Chipper Jones/50	45.00
14	Manny Ramirez/50	40.00
17	Barry Larkin/159	25.00
33	Ivan Rodriguez/50	35.00
38	Lance Berkman/75	15.00
39	Richard Hidalgo	8.00
40	Roy Oswalt/150	15.00
42	Mike Sweeney	8.00
50	A.J. Pierzynski	8.00
51	Torii Hunter	10.00
53	Jose Vidro	6.00
54	Vladimir Guerrero	20.00
55	Cliff Floyd	8.00
56	David Cone/35	20.00
58	Roberto Alomar/50	40.00
65	Nick Johnson	10.00
67	Barry Zito/150	15.00
68	Eric Chavez	10.00
69	Mark Mulder/50	20.00
72	Bobby Abreu	10.00
78	Kenny Lofton/229	10.00
80	Ryan Klesko/150	10.00
81	Andres Galarraga	8.00
83	Rich Aurilia/122	8.00
84	Edgar Martinez	15.00
88	Jim Edmonds/25	
89	Scott Rolen/200	25.00
90	So Taguchi/220	10.00
92	Alex Rodriguez/25	
95	Mark Teixeira/50	20.00
96	Rafael Palmeiro/25	
100	Vernon Wells	10.00
102	Jose Contreras	20.00
141	Dontrelle Willis/150	25.00

Century

		NM/M
Common Auto.:		15.00
Production 100 Sets		
Decades:		No Pricing
Production 10 Sets		
1	Garret Anderson	15.00
7	Matt Williams	15.00
27	Barry Larkin	30.00
39	Richard Hidalgo	15.00
42	Mike Sweeney	15.00
50	A.J. Pierzynski	15.00
51	Torii Hunter	20.00
53	Jose Vidro	15.00
54	Vladimir Guerrero	30.00
55	Cliff Floyd	15.00
62	Drew Henson	15.00
65	Nick Johnson	15.00
69	Mark Mulder	25.00
72	Bobby Abreu	20.00
78	Kenny Lofton	15.00
81	Andres Galarraga	15.00
84	Edgar Martinez	25.00
89	Scott Rolen	30.00
90	So Taguchi	15.00
100	Vernon Wells	15.00
102	Jose Contreras	25.00

Century Notations

		NM/M
Production 100 Sets		
Decade Notations:		No Pricing
Production 10 Sets		
1	Garret Anderson	20.00
7	Matt Williams	15.00
50	A.J. Pierzynski	15.00
68	Eric Chavez	15.00
78	Kenny Lofton	15.00
84	Edgar Martinez	25.00

Century Proofs

Stars (1-100):	2-4X
Century (101-150):	1-2X
Production 100 Sets	

Decade Proofs

Production 10 Sets
No pricing due to scarcity.

INKredible - Three

		NM/M
Production 50 Sets		
1	Barry Zito, Mark Mulder, Tim Hudson	300.00
2	Andruw Jones, Chipper Jones, Greg Maddux	325.00
3	Ernie Banks, Kerry Wood, Mark Prior	300.00

4	Harmon Killebrew, Kirby Puckett, Torii Hunter	175.00
5	Javier Vazquez, Jose Vidro, Vladimir Guerrero	90.00

INKredible - Four

		NM/M
Production 25 Sets		
Limited pricing due to scarcity.		
4	Brooks Robinson, Cal Ripken Jr., Frank Robinson, Jim Palmer	500.00
6	Bo Jackson, Carlos Beltran, George Brett, Mike Sweeney	225.00
7	Curt Schilling, Junior Spivey, Mark Grace, Randy Johnson	475.00
10	Joe Carter, Roberto Alomar, Ryan Klesko, Tony Gwynn	200.00

INKredible - Six

		NM/M
Production 10 Sets		
Limited pricing due to scarcity.		
3	Andre Dawson, Ernie Banks, Kerry Wood, Mark Grace, Mark Prior, Ryne Sandberg	1,500
5	Alex Rodriguez, Don Mattingly, George Brett, Hideo Nomo, Nolan Ryan, Roger Clemens	3,100

Legends of Summer

		NM/M
Complete Set (40):		125.00
Common Player:		3.00
Production 250 Sets		
Century:		1X
Production 100 Sets		
Decades:		No Pricing
Production 10 Sets		
1	Al Kaline	5.00
2	Alan Trammell	3.00
3	Andre Dawson	3.00
4	Babe Ruth	10.00
5	Billy Williams	3.00
6	Bo Jackson	4.00
7	Bob Feller	3.00
8	Bobby Doerr	3.00
9	Brooks Robinson	5.00
10	Dale Murphy	5.00
11	Dennis Eckersley	3.00
12	Don Mattingly	8.00
13	Duke Snider	5.00
14	Eric Davis	3.00
15	Frank Robinson	5.00
16	Fred Lynn	3.00
17	Gary Carter	3.00
18	Harmon Killebrew	5.00
19	Jack Morris	3.00
20	Jim Palmer	3.00
21	Jim Abbott	3.00
22	Joe Morgan	3.00
23	Joe Torre	3.00
24	Johnny Bench	5.00
25	Jose Canseco	3.00
26	Kirby Puckett	5.00
27	Lenny Dykstra	3.00
28	Lou Brock	3.00
29	Ralph Kiner	3.00
30	Mike Schmidt	6.00
31	Nolan Ryan	10.00
32	Nolan Ryan	10.00
33	Orel Hershiser	3.00
34	Phil Rizzuto	3.00
35	Orlando Cepeda	4.00
36	Ryne Sandberg	8.00
37	Stan Musial	6.00
38	Steve Garvey	3.00
39	Tony Perez	3.00
40	Ty Cobb	6.00

Legends of Summer Autograph

		NM/M
Common Autograph:		8.00
1	Al Kaline	20.00
2	Alan Trammell	10.00
3	Andre Dawson	10.00
5	Billy Williams	8.00
6	Bo Jackson/100	50.00
7	Bob Feller	15.00
8	Bobby Doerr	15.00
9	Brooks Robinson	25.00
10	Dale Murphy/75	40.00
11	Dennis Eckersley	10.00
12	Don Mattingly/50	75.00
13	Duke Snider/225	20.00
14	Eric Davis	8.00
15	Frank Robinson	10.00
16	Fred Lynn	8.00
17	Gary Carter	10.00
18	Harmon Killebrew/171	20.00
19	Jack Morris	8.00
20	Jim Palmer	10.00
21	Jim Abbott	8.00
22	Joe Morgan/125	15.00
23	Joe Torre	10.00
24	Johnny Bench/75	30.00
25	Jose Canseco/75	30.00
26	Kirby Puckett/75	35.00
27	Lenny Dykstra	10.00
28	Lou Brock	15.00
29	Ralph Kiner	10.00
30	Mike Schmidt/75	60.00
31	Nolan Ryan/75	110.00
33	Orel Hershiser	20.00
34	Phil Rizzuto	15.00
35	Orlando Cepeda	15.00
36	Ryne Sandberg/75	60.00
37	Stan Musial/200	40.00
38	Steve Garvey	10.00
39	Tony Perez	10.00

Legends of Summer Century

		NM/M
Production 100 Sets		
Decades:		No Pricing
Production 10 Sets		
1	Al Kaline	25.00
2	Alan Trammell	20.00
3	Andre Dawson	15.00
5	Billy Williams	15.00
6	Bo Jackson	50.00
7	Bob Feller	25.00
8	Bobby Doerr	20.00
9	Brooks Robinson	30.00
11	Dennis Eckersley	15.00
12	Don Mattingly	65.00
14	Eric Davis	15.00
15	Frank Robinson	15.00
16	Fred Lynn	15.00
17	Gary Carter	20.00
19	Jack Morris	15.00
20	Jim Palmer	20.00
21	Jim Abbott	15.00
23	Joe Torre	15.00
27	Lenny Dykstra	15.00
28	Lou Brock	25.00
29	Ralph Kiner	15.00
33	Orel Hershiser	60.00
34	Phil Rizzuto	30.00
35	Orlando Cepeda	20.00
36	Ryne Sandberg	65.00
37	Stan Musial	60.00
38	Steve Garvey	15.00
39	Tony Perez	15.00

Notations

		NM/M
Varying quantities produced		
Many not priced due to scarcity.		
1	Garret Anderson/75	20.00
7	Matt Williams/250	20.00
7	Matt Williams/50	20.00
45	Kazuhisa Ishii/35	35.00
50	A.J. Pierzynski/200	10.00
53	Jose Vidro/40	15.00
62	Drew Henson/73	20.00
68	Eric Chavez/50	20.00
78	Kenny Lofton/150	15.00
80	Ryan Klesko/75	15.00
83	Rich Aurilia/61	15.00
84	Edgar Martinez/250	10.00
84	Edgar Martinez/60	20.00
100	Vernon Wells/75	15.00

Notable Nicknames

		NM/M
Complete Set (20):		75.00
Common Player:		3.00
Production 750 Sets		

Century:	1-1.5X
Production 100 Sets	
Decade:	No Pricing
Production 10 Sets	
1	Andre Dawson	3.00
2	Torii Hunter	3.00
3	Brooks Robinson	5.00
4	Carlton Fisk	3.00
5	Mike Mussina	4.00
6	Don Mattingly	8.00
7	Duke Snider	4.00
8	Eric Davis	3.00
9	Frank Thomas	4.00
10	Randy Johnson	5.00
11	Lenny Dykstra	3.00
12	Ivan Rodriguez	3.00
13	Nolan Ryan	10.00
14	Phil Rizzuto	3.00
15	Reggie Jackson	4.00
16	Roger Clemens	8.00
17	Ryne Sandberg	8.00
18	Stan Musial	6.00
19	Luis Gonzalez	3.00
20	Will Clark	4.00

Notable Nicknames Autograph

		NM/M
Quantity produced listed		
Decades:		No Pricing
Production 10 Sets		
1	Andre "The Hawk" Dawson/100	30.00
2	Torii "Spiderman" Hunter/100	30.00
3	Brooks "Hoover" Robinson	60.00
4	Carlton "Pudge" Fisk/100	50.00
5	Mike "Moose" Mussina/100	80.00
6	Don "Donnie Baseball" Mattingly/100	100.00
7	Duke "Duke of Flatbush" Snider/100	60.00
8	Eric "The Red" Davis/40	50.00
9	Frank "The Big Hurt" Thomas/100	60.00
10	Randy "Big Unit" Johnson/100	100.00
11	Lenny "Nails" Dykstra/100	20.00
12	Ivan "Pudge" Rodriguez/75	50.00
14	Phil "Scooter" Rizzuto/100	50.00
15	Reggie "Mr. October" Jackson/100	60.00
16	Roger "The Rocket" Clemens/100	150.00
17	Ryne "Ryno" Sandberg/100	75.00
18	Stan "The Man" Musial/100	85.00
19	Luis "Gonzo" Gonzalez/100	25.00
20	Will "The Thrill" Clark/100	60.00

Players Collection Autograph

		NM/M
Quantity produced listed		
	Roberto Alomar/75	30.00
	Adrian Beltre/104	30.00
	Lance Berkman/50	20.00
	Craig Biggio/26	35.00
	Joe Borchard/53	10.00
	J.D. Drew/52	20.00
	Jim Edmonds/50	25.00
	Todd Helton/50	40.00
	Jason Jennings/49	10.00
	Chipper Jones/51	50.00
	Paul LoDuca/227	8.00
	Magglio Ordonez/102	20.00
	Mark Prior/27	100.00
	Ivan Rodriguez/52	35.00
	Richie Sexson/50	20.00
	Matt Williams/482	8.00

Signature Cuts

		NM/M
Some not priced due to scarcity.		
Decades:		No Pricing
Production 10 Sets		
8	Randy Johnson/40	60.00
33	Ivan Rodriguez/122	30.00
54	Vladimir Guerrero/34	35.00
58	Roberto Alomar/100	30.00
64	Mike Mussina/82	40.00
73	Jim Thome/127	30.00

80	Ryan Klesko/35	20.00
81	Andres Galarraga/51	20.00
89	Scott Rolen/36	40.00

Team Trademarks

		NM/M
Complete Set (40):		150.00
Common Player:		3.00
Production 100 Sets		
Century:		1X
Production 100 Sets		
Decade:		No Pricing
Production 10 Sets		
1	Adam Dunn	3.00
2	Andre Dawson	3.00
3	Babe Ruth	10.00
4	Barry Bonds	10.00
5	Brooks Robinson	4.00
6	Cal Ripken Jr.	10.00
7	Derek Jeter	8.00
8	Don Mattingly	8.00
9	Frank Robinson	3.00
10	Fred Lynn	3.00
11	Gary Carter	3.00
12	George Brett	6.00
13	Greg Maddux	5.00
14	Ichiro Suzuki	6.00
15	Jim Palmer	3.00
16	Jose Contreras	3.00
17	Kerry Wood	4.00
18	Lou Gehrig	8.00
19	Magglio Ordonez	3.00
20	Mark Grace	3.00
21	Mike Schmidt	8.00
22	Nolan Ryan	10.00
23	Nolan Ryan	10.00
24	Reggie Jackson	4.00
25	Rickey Henderson	3.00
26	Roberto Clemente	6.00
27	Roger Clemens	6.00
28	Roger Clemens	6.00
29	Ryne Sandberg	6.00
30	Sammy Sosa	6.00
31	Stan Musial	6.00
32	Steve Carlton	3.00
33	Tim Hudson	3.00
34	Tom Glavine	3.00
35	Tom Seaver	4.00
36	Tony Gwynn	4.00
37	Torii Hunter	3.00
38	Ty Cobb	6.00
39	Vladimir Guerrero	4.00
40	Will Clark	4.00

Team Trademarks Autograph

		NM/M
Quantity produced listed		
1	Adam Dunn/50	35.00
2	Andre Dawson/250	10.00
5	Brooks Robinson/250	20.00
6	Cal Ripken Jr./50	200.00
8	Don Mattingly/75	85.00
10	Fred Lynn/250	8.00
11	Gary Carter/250	10.00
12	George Brett/50	100.00
13	Greg Maddux/50	85.00
16	Jose Contreras/250	15.00
17	Kerry Wood/50	40.00
19	Magglio Ordonez/75	15.00
20	Mark Grace/25	90.00
23	Nolan Ryan/50	110.00
24	Reggie Jackson/75	25.00
25	Rickey Henderson/50	100.00
27	Roger Clemens/50	110.00
28	Roger Clemens/50	110.00
29	Ryne Sandberg/100	60.00
31	Stan Musial/200	50.00
32	Steve Carlton/150	20.00
33	Tim Hudson/100	35.00
34	Tom Glavine/50	35.00
35	Tom Seaver/50	35.00
36	Tony Gwynn/50	60.00
37	Torii Hunter/250	10.00
39	Vladimir Guerrero/250	20.00
40	Will Clark/125	30.00

Team Trademarks Century

		NM/M
Production 100 Sets		
Decade:		No Pricing
Production 10 Sets		
2	Andre Dawson	15.00
5	Brooks Robinson	30.00
9	Frank Robinson	15.00
10	Fred Lynn	15.00
11	Gary Carter	20.00
15	Jim Palmer	15.00
16	Jose Contreras	25.00
20	Mark Grace	60.00
29	Ryne Sandberg	65.00
31	Stan Musial	65.00
32	Steve Carlton	25.00
34	Tom Glavine	25.00
37	Steve Hunter	15.00
39	Vladimir Guerrero	25.00

Team Trademarks Notations

		NM/M
Quantity produced listed		
2	Andre Dawson/250	10.00
2	Andre Dawson/150	10.00
5	Brooks Robinson/75	35.00
5	Brooks Robinson/125	30.00
10	Fred Lynn/50	20.00
15	Jim Palmer/32	25.00
15	Jim Palmer/128	15.00
15	Jim Palmer/150	15.00
29	Ryne Sandberg/40	80.00
29	Ryne Sandberg/55	75.00
32	Steve Carlton/50	35.00
33	Tim Hudson/50	45.00
40	Will Clark/52	60.00

2003 Donruss Studio

		NM/M
Complete Set (200):		35.00
Common Player:		.25
Pack (6):		4.00
Box (20):		60.00
1	Darin Erstad	.40
2	David Eckstein	.25
3	Garret Anderson	.50
4	Jarrod Washburn	.25
5	Tim Salmon	.50
6	Troy Glaus	.50
7	Jay Gibbons	.25
8	Melvin Mora	.25
9	Rodrigo Lopez	.25
10	Tony Batista	.25
11	Freddy Sanchez	.25
12	Derek Lowe	.25
13	Johnny Damon	.40
14	Manny Ramirez	.75
15	Nomar Garciaparra	1.50
16	Pedro J. Martinez	1.00
17	Rickey Henderson	.50
18	Shea Hillenbrand	.25
19	Carlos Lee	.25
20	Frank Thomas	.75
21	Magglio Ordonez	.40
22	Bartolo Colon	.25
23	Paul Konerko	.25
24	Josh Stewart RC	.50
25	C.C. Sabathia	.25
26	Jeremy Guthrie	.25
27	Ellis Burks	.25
28	Omar Vizquel	.40
29	Victor Martinez	.25
30	Cliff Lee	.25
31	Jhonny Peralta	.50
32	Brian Tallet	.25
33	Bobby Higginson	.25
34	Carlos Pena	.25
35	Nook Logan RC	.25

36	Steve Sparks	.25
37	Travis Chapman	.25
38	Carlos Beltran	.75
39	Joe Randa	.25
40	Mike Sweeney	.25
41	Jimmy Gobble	.25
42	Michael Tucker	.25
43	Runelvys Hernandez	.25
44	Brad Radke	.25
45	Corey Koskie	.25
46	Cristian Guzman	.25
47	J.C. Romero	.25
48	Doug Mientkiewicz	.25
49	Lew Ford RC	1.50
50	Jacque Jones	.40
51	Torii Hunter	.50
52	Alfonso Soriano	.75
53	Nick Johnson	.25
54	Bernie Williams	.50
55	Jose Contreras RC	1.50
56	Derek Jeter	3.00
57	Jason Giambi	.50
58	Brandon Claussen	.25
59	Jorge Posada	.50
60	Mike Mussina	.50
61	Roger Clemens	2.00
62	Hideki Matsui RC	5.00
63	Barry Zito	.50
64	Adam Morrissey	.25
65	Eric Chavez	.40
66	Jermaine Dye	.25
67	Mark Mulder	.40
68	Miguel Tejada	.50
69	Joe Valentine RC	.25
70	Tim Hudson	.50
71	Bret Boone	.40
72	Chris Snelling	.25
73	Edgar Martinez	.25
74	Freddy Garcia	.25
75	Ichiro Suzuki	2.00
76	Jamie Moyer	.25
77	John Olerud	.40
78	Kazuhiro Sasaki	.25
79	Aubrey Huff	.25
80	Joe Kennedy	.25
81	Dewon Brazelton	.25
82	Pete LaForest RC	.25
83	Alex Rodriguez	2.50
84	Chan Ho Park	.25
85	Hank Blalock	.75
86	Juan Gonzalez	.75
87	Kevin Mench	.25
88	Rafael Palmeiro	.75
89	Carlos Delgado	.50
90	Eric Hinske	.25
91	Josh Phelps	.25
92	Roy Halladay	.40
93	Shannon Stewart	.25
94	Vernon Wells	.40
95	Vinnie Chulk	.25
96	Curt Schilling	.75
97	Junior Spivey	.25
98	Luis Gonzalez	.50
99	Mark Grace	.25
100	Randy Johnson	1.00
101	Andruw Jones	.75
102	Chipper Jones	1.00
103	Gary Sheffield	.50
104	Greg Maddux	1.50
105	John Smoltz	.50
106	Mike Hampton	.25
107	Adam LaRoche	.25
108	Michael Hessman RC	.50
109	Corey Patterson	.40
110	Kerry Wood	1.00
111	Mark Prior	1.00
112	Moises Alou	.50
113	Sammy Sosa	1.50
114	Adam Dunn	.75
115	Austin Kearns	.40
116	Barry Larkin	.40
117	Ken Griffey Jr.	1.50
118	Sean Casey	.25
119	Jason Jennings	.25
120	Jay Payton	.25
121	Larry Walker	.40
122	Todd Helton	.75
123	Jeff Baker	.25
124	Clint Barmes RC	1.00
125	Ivan Rodriguez	.75
126	Josh Beckett	.50
127	Juan Encarnacion	.25
128	Mike Lowell	.25
129	Craig Biggio	.40
130	Jason Lane	.25
131	Jeff Bagwell	.75
132	Lance Berkman	.50
133	Roy Oswalt	.40
134	Jeff Kent	.40
135	Hideo Nomo	.50
136	Kazuhisa Ishii	.25
137	Kevin Brown	.40
138	Odalis Perez	.25
139	Paul LoDuca	.25

140	Shawn Green	.50
141	Adrian Beltre	.50
142	Ben Sheets	.40
143	Bill Hall	.25
144	Jeffrey Hammonds	.25
145	Richie Sexson	.50
146	Terrmel Sledge RC	.75
147	Brad Wilkerson	.25
148	Javier Vazquez	.25
149	Jose Vidro	.25
150	Michael Barrett	.25
151	Vladimir Guerrero	.75
152	Al Leiter	.25
153	Mike Piazza	2.00
154	Mo Vaughn	.25
155	Cliff Floyd	.25
156	Roberto Alomar	.50
157	Roger Cedeno	.25
158	Tom Glavine	.50
159	Prentice Redman RC	.50
160	Bobby Abreu	.50
161	Jimmy Rollins	.40
162	Mike Lieberthal	.25
163	Pat Burrell	.50
164	Vicente Padilla	.25
165	Jim Thome	.75
166	Kevin Millwood	.40
167	Aramis Ramirez	.50
168	Brian Giles	.40
169	Jason Kendall	.40
170	Josh Fogg	.25
171	Kip Wells	.25
172	Jose Castillo	.25
173	Mark Kotsay	.25
174	Oliver Perez	.25
175	Phil Nevin	.25
176	Ryan Klesko	.40
177	Sean Burroughs	.25
178	Brian Lawrence	.25
179	Shane Victorino RC	.25
180	Barry Bonds	3.00
181	Benito Santiago	.25
182	Ray Durham	.25
183	Rich Aurilia	.25
184	Damian Moss	.25
185	Albert Pujols	2.00
186	J.D. Drew	.25
187	Jim Edmonds	.50
188	Matt Morris	.40
189	Tino Martinez	.25
190	Scott Rolen	.75
191	Troy Glaus, Tim Salmon	.50
192	Sean Casey, Corky Miller	.25
193	Carlos Lee, Frank Thomas	.50
194	Lance Berkman, Jeff Kent	.25
195	Jose Contreras, Mariano Rivera	1.00
196	Alex Rodriguez, Juan Gonzalez	1.00
197	Andy Pettitte, David Wells	.25
198	Shawn Green, Dave Roberts	.25
199	Mike Lieberthal, Jimmy Rollins	.40
200	Mike Mussina, Hideki Matsui	2.00

Proofs

Stars (1-200):	4-8X
Rookies (1-200):	2-3X
Production 100 Sets	

Big League Challenge

		NM/M
Complete Set (50):		125.00
Common Player:		1.50
Production 400 Sets		
Proofs:		4-8X
Production 25 Sets		
1	Jose Canseco	2.00
2	Magglio Ordonez	1.50
3	Alex Rodriguez	5.00
4	Lance Berkman	1.50
5	Rafael Palmeiro	3.00
6	Nomar Garciaparra	5.00
7	Nomar Garciaparra	5.00
9	Troy Glaus	2.00
10	Mark McGwire	6.00
11	Mark McGwire	6.00
12	Mark McGwire	6.00
13	Jim Thome	3.00
14	Chipper Jones	3.00
15	Shawn Green	1.50
16	Alex Rodriguez	5.00
17	Alex Rodriguez	5.00
18	Alex Rodriguez	5.00
19	Alex Rodriguez	5.00
20	Jason Giambi	2.00

21	Pat Burrell	1.50
22	Mike Piazza	4.00
23	Mike Piazza	4.00
24	Mike Piazza	4.00
25	Frank Thomas	2.00
26	Rafael Palmeiro	2.00
27	Todd Helton	2.00
28	Jose Canseco	2.00
29	Albert Pujols	5.00
30	Troy Glaus	2.00
31	Barry Bonds	6.00
32	Barry Bonds	6.00
33	Barry Bonds	6.00
34	Todd Helton	3.00
35	Rafael Palmeiro	3.00
36	Jim Thome	3.00
37	Ozzie Smith	3.00
38	Troy Glaus	2.00
39	Shawn Green	1.50
40	Barry Bonds	6.00
41	Barry Bonds	6.00
42	Barry Bonds	6.00
43	Magglio Ordonez	1.50
44	Alex Rodriguez	5.00
45	Alex Rodriguez	5.00
46	Alex Rodriguez	5.00
47	Lance Berkman	1.50
48	Rafael Palmeiro	3.00
49	Pat Burrell	1.50
50	Albert Pujols	5.00

Big League Challenge Materials

		NM/M
Common Player:		4.00
Inserted 1:20		
2	Magglio Ordonez/Jsy	4.00
3	Alex Rodriguez/Jsy	10.00
4	Lance Berkman/Jsy	4.00
15	Shawn Green/Jsy	4.00
29	Albert Pujols/Jsy	15.00
36	Jim Thome/Jsy	6.00
39	Shawn Green/Pants	4.00
40	Barry Bonds/Base	10.00
41	Barry Bonds/Base	10.00
42	Barry Bonds/Base	10.00
43	Magglio Ordonez/Jsy	4.00
45	Alex Rodriguez/Jsy	10.00
46	Alex Rodriguez/Pants	10.00
47	Lance Berkman/Jsy	4.00
48	Rafael Palmeiro/Jsy	6.00
50	Albert Pujols/Pants	10.00

Big League Challenge Prime Material

		NM/M
Common Player:		10.00
2	Magglio Ordonez/100	10.00
3	Alex Rodriguez/100	25.00
15	Shawn Green/50	15.00
29	Albert Pujols/100	25.00
36	Jim Thome/50	20.00
45	Alex Rodriguez/100	25.00
48	Rafael Palmeiro/100	15.00

Enshrinement

		NM/M
Complete Set (50):		180.00
Common Player:		3.00
Production 750 Sets		
Proofs:		5-10X
Production 20 or 21		
1	Gary Carter	4.00
2	Ozzie Smith	10.00
3	Kirby Puckett	6.00
4	Carlton Fisk	4.00
5	Tony Perez	3.00
6	Nolan Ryan	15.00
7	George Brett	12.00

8	Robin Yount	10.00
9	Orlando Cepeda	3.00
10	Phil Niekro	3.00
11	Mike Schmidt	10.00
12	Richie Ashburn	6.00
13	Steve Carlton	4.00
14	Phil Rizzuto	4.00
15	Reggie Jackson	6.00
16	Tom Seaver	5.00
17	Rollie Fingers	3.00
18	Rod Carew	5.00
19	Gaylord Perry	3.00
20	Fergie Jenkins	3.00
21	Jim Palmer	3.00
22	Joe Morgan	3.00
23	Johnny Bench	6.00
24	Willie Stargell	4.00
25	Billy Williams	3.00
26	Jim "Catfish" Hunter	3.00
27	Willie McCovey	3.00
28	Bobby Doerr	3.00
29	Lou Brock	4.00
30	Enos Slaughter	3.00
31	Hoyt Wilhelm	3.00
32	Harmon Killebrew	6.00
33	Pee Wee Reese	3.00
34	Luis Aparicio	3.00
35	Brooks Robinson	6.00
36	Juan Marichal	4.00
37	Frank Robinson	5.00
38	Bob Gibson	4.00
39	Al Kaline	6.00
40	Duke Snider	6.00
41	Eddie Mathews	5.00
42	Robin Roberts	3.00
43	Ralph Kiner	3.00
44	Whitey Ford	5.00
45	Roberto Clemente	10.00
46	Warren Spahn	4.00
47	Yogi Berra	5.00
48	Early Wynn	3.00
49	Stan Musial	6.00
50	Bob Feller	4.00

Enshrinement Autographs

		NM/M
Varying quantities produced		
1	Gary Carter/50	30.00
5	Tony Perez/50	50.00
9	Orlando Cepeda/50	25.00
10	Phil Niekro/50	20.00
13	Steve Carlton/50	40.00
14	Phil Rizzuto/15	50.00
20	Fergie Jenkins/50	20.00
21	Jim Palmer/25	35.00
22	Joe Morgan/10	50.00
28	Bobby Doerr/100	20.00
31	Hoyt Wilhelm/50	25.00
34	Luis Aparicio/100	15.00
35	Brooks Robinson/25	65.00
37	Frank Robinson/25	50.00
43	Ralph Kiner/25	40.00
50	Bob Feller/100	25.00

Leather & Lumber

		NM/M
Common Player:		5.00
1	Adam Dunn/400	10.00
2	Alex Rodriguez/250	12.00
3	Alfonso Soriano/250	10.00
4	Andruw Jones/400	8.00
5	Austin Kearns/400	8.00
6	Chipper Jones/400	10.00
7	Derek Jeter/100	35.00
8	Don Mattingly/100	40.00
9	Edgar Martinez	5.00
10	Frank Thomas/400	8.00
11	Fred McGriff/400	8.00
13	Greg Maddux/150	15.00
14	Hideki Matsui/Ball/100	40.00
15	Hideo Nomo/150	15.00
16	Ichiro Suzuki/Ball/100	40.00
17	Ivan Rodriguez/250	8.00
18	Jason Giambi/400	8.00
19	Jeff Bagwell/400	8.00
20	Jim Edmonds/150	8.00
21	Jim Thome/400	10.00
22	Juan Gonzalez/400	8.00
23	Kerry Wood/250	10.00
24	Kirby Puckett/100	25.00
25	Lance Berkman/400	5.00
26	Magglio Ordonez/400	5.00
27	Manny Ramirez/250	10.00
28	Mark Prior/400	8.00
29	Miguel Tejada/200	5.00
30	Mike Piazza/400	10.00
31	Mike Schmidt/200	25.00
32	Nomar Garciaparra/400	15.00
33	Pat Burrell/400	8.00
34	Pedro Martinez/150	10.00

35	Rafael Palmeiro/400	8.00
36	Randy Johnson/250	10.00
37	Rickey Henderson/175	10.00
38	Sammy Sosa/300	10.00
39	Shawn Green/400	5.00
40	Vladimir Guerrero/400	8.00

Leather & Lumber Dual

		NM/M
Common Player:		
Those without bat & ball are noted.		
1	Adam Dunn/50	25.00
2	Alex Rodriguez/50	30.00
4	Andruw Jones/50	25.00
5	Austin Kearns/Shoe/50	25.00
6	Chipper Jones/25	45.00
8	Don Mattingly/50	80.00
10	Frank Thomas/50	30.00
13	Greg Maddux/Shoe/50	35.00
17	Ivan Rodriguez/50	25.00
19	Jeff Bagwell/25	35.00
23	Kerry Wood/50	35.00
24	Kirby Puckett/25	50.00
25	Lance Berkman/50	12.00
28	Mark Prior/Shoe/50	50.00
29	Miguel Tejada/25	15.00
32	Nomar Garciaparra/Base/25	
33	Pat Burrell/25	20.00
36	Randy Johnson/25	40.00
38	Sammy Sosa/Shoe/25	60.00

Masterstrokes

ALBERT PUJOLS - OUTFIELD

		NM/M
Complete Set (25):		50.00
Common Player:		1.00
Production 1,000 Sets		
1	Adam Dunn	2.00
2	Albert Pujols	3.00
3	Alex Rodriguez	5.00
4	Alfonso Soriano	3.00
5	Andruw Jones	1.50
6	Chipper Jones	3.00
7	Derek Jeter	6.00
8	Greg Maddux	3.00
9	Hideki Matsui	8.00
10	Hideo Nomo	1.50
11	Ivan Rodriguez	2.00
12	Jason Giambi	1.50
13	Jeff Bagwell	2.00
14	Juan Gonzalez	1.50
15	Ken Griffey Jr.	3.00
16	Lance Berkman	1.00
17	Magglio Ordonez	1.00
18	Manny Ramirez	2.00
19	Mark Prior	2.00
20	Miguel Tejada	1.00
21	Mike Piazza	4.00
22	Nomar Garciaparra	4.00
23	Pat Burrell	1.50
24	Sammy Sosa	4.00
25	Vladimir Guerrero	1.50

Masterstrokes Artist's Proof

		NM/M
Common Player:		15.00
Production 50 Sets		
1	Adam Dunn	25.00
2	Albert Pujols	50.00
3	Alex Rodriguez	50.00
4	Alfonso Soriano	25.00
5	Andruw Jones	20.00
6	Chipper Jones	30.00
7	Derek Jeter	50.00
8	Greg Maddux	25.00

9	Hideki Matsui	75.00
10	Hideo Nomo	100.00
11	Ivan Rodriguez	20.00
12	Jason Giambi	15.00
13	Jeff Bagwell	25.00
14	Juan Gonzalez	25.00
15	Ken Griffey Jr.	30.00
16	Lance Berkman	15.00
17	Magglio Ordonez	15.00
18	Manny Ramirez	20.00
19	Mark Prior	20.00
20	Miguel Tejada	15.00
21	Mike Piazza	35.00
22	Nomar Garciaparra	40.00
23	Pat Burrell	15.00
24	Sammy Sosa	40.00
25	Vladimir Guerrero	25.00

Players Collection

		NM/M
Common Player:		4.00
Production 300 Sets		
1	Adam Dunn	8.00
2	Adrian Beltre	6.00
3	Alex Rodriguez	10.00
4	Alfonso Soriano	8.00
5	Andruw Jones	6.00
6	Andy Pettitte	4.00
7	Barry Larkin	6.00
8	Barry Zito	4.00
9	Ben Grieve	4.00
10	Bernie Williams	8.00
11	Cal Ripken Jr.	30.00
12	Carlos Delgado	5.00
13	C.C. Sabathia	4.00
14	Chipper Jones	10.00
15	Craig Biggio	4.00
16	Curt Schilling	6.00
17	Alex Rodriguez	10.00
18	Frank Thomas	8.00
19	Freddy Garcia	4.00
20	Jay Bell	4.00
21	Roger Clemens	12.00
22	Tony Gwynn	10.00
23	Ivan Rodriguez	6.00
24	Jason Giambi	6.00
25	Jason Jennings	4.00
26	Jay Payton	4.00
27	J.D. Drew	4.00
28	Jeff Bagwell	8.00
29	Jeromy Burnitz	4.00
30	Jim Edmonds	6.00
31	Jim Thome	8.00
32	Joe Borchard	4.00
33	Joe Mays	4.00
34	John Olerud	4.00
35	David Wells	4.00
36	Juan Gonzalez	6.00
37	Kazuhiro Sasaki	4.00
38	Chan Ho Park	4.00
39	Kerry Wood	8.00
40	Kevin Brown	5.00
41	Lance Berkman	4.00
42	Larry Walker	4.00
43	Bret Boone	4.00
44	Magglio Ordonez	4.00
45	Manny Ramirez	6.00
46	Mark Mulder	4.00
47	Mark Prior	8.00
48	Matt Williams	4.00
49	Miguel Tejada	6.00
50	Mike Piazza	10.00
51	Nomar Garciaparra	10.00
52	Doug Davis	4.00
53	Paul Konerko	4.00
54	Paul LoDuca	4.00
55	Pedro J. Martinez	8.00
56	Preston Wilson	4.00
57	Rafael Palmeiro	8.00
58	Marlon Byrd	4.00
59	Reggie Sanders	4.00
60	Richie Sexson	5.00

61	Rickey Henderson	10.00
62	Rickey Henderson	10.00
63	Robert Person	4.00
64	Jeff Bagwell	8.00
65	Roger Clemens	12.00
66	Roy Oswalt	4.00
67	Ryan Klesko	4.00
68	Sammy Sosa	12.00
69	Shawn Green	5.00
70	Steve Finley	4.00
71	Terrence Long	4.00
72	Tim Hudson	5.00
73	Toby Hall	4.00
74	Todd Helton	8.00
75	Travis Lee	4.00
76	Troy Glaus	6.00
77	Tsuyoshi Shinjo	4.00
78	Vernon Wells	4.00
79	Vladimir Guerrero	8.00
80	Wes Helms	4.00
81	Alex Rodriguez	10.00
82	Alfonso Soriano	8.00
83	Barry Larkin	6.00
84	Roberto Alomar	6.00
85	Ivan Rodriguez	6.00
86	Jason Giambi	6.00
87	Jeff Bagwell	8.00
88	Juan Gonzalez	6.00
89	Larry Walker	4.00
90	Luis Gonzalez	4.00
91	Magglio Ordonez	4.00
92	Manny Ramirez	8.00
93	Marlon Byrd	4.00
94	Mike Piazza	10.00
95	Pat Burrell	8.00
96	Todd Helton	8.00
97	Rickey Henderson	10.00
98	Andruw Jones	6.00
99	Craig Biggio	4.00
100	Mark Prior	8.00

Private Signings

NM/M

7	Jay Gibbons/100	10.00
11	Freddy Sanchez/150	25.00
24	Josh Stewart/200	8.00
26	Jeremy Guthrie/125	8.00
29	Victor Martinez/200	20.00
30	Cliff Lee/150	10.00
31	Jhonny Peralta/200	20.00
35	Nook Logan/100	8.00
37	Travis Chapman/150	8.00
41	Jimmy Gobble/200	8.00
47	J.C. Romero/200	8.00
49	Lew Ford/200	15.00
51	Torii Hunter/50	20.00
53	Nick Johnson/100	10.00
55	Jose Contreras/100	25.00
58	Brandon Claussen/200	10.00
69	Joe Valentine/200	8.00
79	Aubrey Huff/50	20.00
81	Dewon Brazelton/75	10.00
82	Pete LaForest/200	10.00
85	Hank Blalock/50	20.00
87	Kevin Mench/200	8.00
90	Eric Hinske/125	8.00
95	Vinnie Chulk/100	8.00
97	Junior Spivey/50	10.00
107	Adam LaRoche/200	15.00
108	Michael Hessman/200	8.00
111	Mark Prior/50	30.00
119	Jason Jennings/50	10.00
123	Jeff Baker/75	10.00
124	Clint Barmes/200	10.00
130	Jason Lane/100	10.00
139	Paul LoDuca/75	15.00
143	Bill Hall/50	20.00
146	Terrmel Sledge/125	10.00
149	Jose Vidro/50	15.00
159	Prentice Redman/200	10.00
160	Bobby/Abreu/50	20.00
171	Kip Wells/100	10.00
172	Jose Castillo/175	8.00
178	Brian Lawrence/100	10.00
179	Shane Victorino/200	10.00
201	Adam Loewen/100	20.00
202	Jeremy Bonderman/50	40.00
203	Brandon Webb/100	35.00
204	Chien-Ming Wang/50	250.00
206	Ryan Wagner/100	10.00
207	Hong-Chih Kuo/25	175.00
208	Dan Haren/100	25.00
210	Ramon Nivar/100	15.00

Recollection
Autographs 5x7

NM/M

1	Josh Beckett/3	
3	Sean Casey/125	15.00
5	Troy Glaus/82	20.00

8	Vladimir Guerrero/125	35.00
10	Todd Helton/55	35.00
12	Ryan Klesko/75	15.00
18	Ivan Rodriguez/50	40.00
19	C.C. Sabathia/50	20.00
20	Curt Schilling/75	30.00
23	Mike Sweeney/42	15.00
24	Miguel Tejada/44	30.00
26	Kerry Wood/200	25.00
27	Barry Zito/200	15.00

Spirit of the Game

NM/M

Complete Set (35):		60.00
Common Player:		1.00
Production 1,250 Sets		
1	Garret Anderson	1.00
2	Nomar Garciaparra	3.00
3	Pedro J. Martinez	2.00
4	Rickey Henderson	1.50
5	Magglio Ordonez	1.00
6	Torii Hunter	1.50
7	Alfonso Soriano	2.00
8	Jose Contreras	1.00
9	Derek Jeter	5.00
10	Jason Giambi	1.50
11	Roger Clemens	4.00
12	Hideki Matsui	6.00
13	Barry Zito	1.50
14	Ichiro Suzuki	3.00
15	Alex Rodriguez	4.00
16	Curt Schilling	2.00
17	Randy Johnson	2.00
18	Andruw Jones	1.50
19	Chipper Jones	2.00
20	Greg Maddux	3.00
21	Sammy Sosa	3.00
22	Adam Dunn	2.00
23	Ken Griffey Jr.	3.00
24	Todd Helton	2.00
25	Ivan Rodriguez	2.00
26	Lance Berkman	1.00
27	Hideo Nomo	1.50
28	Shawn Green	1.00
29	Vladimir Guerrero	2.00
30	Mike Piazza	3.00
31	Roberto Alomar	1.50
32	Jim Thome	2.00
33	Barry Bonds	5.00
34	Albert Pujols	3.00
35	Scott Rolen	2.00

Stars

NM/M

Complete Set (50):		65.00
Common Player:		1.00
Inserted 1:5		
Golds:		3-5X
Production 100 Sets		
1	Troy Glaus	1.50
2	Manny Ramirez	2.00
3	Nomar Garciaparra	3.00
4	Pedro J. Martinez	2.00
5	Rickey Henderson	1.50
6	Torii Hunter	1.50
7	Frank Thomas	1.50
8	Magglio Ordonez	1.00
9	Alfonso Soriano	2.00
10	Jose Contreras	1.00
11	Derek Jeter	5.00
12	Jason Giambi	1.50
13	Roger Clemens	4.00
14	Mike Mussina	1.50
15	Barry Zito	1.50
16	Miguel Tejada	1.00
17	Ichiro Suzuki	4.00
18	Alex Rodriguez	1.00
19	Juan Gonzalez	1.00
20	Rafael Palmeiro	2.00
21	Hank Blalock	2.00

22	Curt Schilling	2.00
23	Randy Johnson	2.00
24	Junior Spivey	1.00
25	Andruw Jones	1.50
26	Chipper Jones	2.00
27	Greg Maddux	3.00
28	Kerry Wood	2.00
29	Mark Prior	1.50
30	Sammy Sosa	3.00
31	Adam Dunn	2.00
32	Ken Griffey Jr.	3.00
33	Austin Kearns	1.50
34	Larry Walker	1.00
35	Todd Helton	2.00
36	Ivan Rodriguez	2.00
37	Jeff Bagwell	2.00
38	Lance Berkman	1.00
39	Craig Biggio	1.00
40	Hideo Nomo	1.50
41	Shawn Green	1.00
42	Vladimir Guerrero	2.00
43	Mike Piazza	3.00
44	Tom Glavine	1.50
45	Roberto Alomar	1.50
46	Pat Burrell	1.50
47	Jim Thome	2.00
48	Barry Bonds	5.00
49	Albert Pujols	4.00
50	Scott Rolen	2.00

2003 Donruss Team Heroes

NM/M

Complete Set (540):		55.00
Common Player:		.15
Pack (13):		1.50
Box (24):		25.00
1	Adam Kennedy	.15
2	Steve Green	.15
3	Rod Carew	.40
4	Alfredo Amezaga	.15
5	Reggie Jackson	.50
6	Jarrod Washburn	.15
7	Nolan Ryan	3.00
8	Tim Salmon	.25
9	Garret Anderson	.25
10	Darin Erstad	.25
11	Elpidio Guzman	.15
12	David Eckstein	.15
13	Troy Percival	.15
14	Troy Glaus	.75
15	Doug DeVore	.15
16	Tony Womack	.15
17	Matt Williams	.25
18	Junior Spivey	.15
19	Mark Grace	.50
20	Curt Schilling	.75
21	Erubiel Durazo	.15
22	Craig Counsell	.15
23	Byung-Hyun Kim	.15
24	Randy Johnson	1.00
25	Luis Gonzalez	.40
26	John Smoltz	.15
27	Tim Spooneybarger	.15
28	Dale Murphy	.50
29	Warren Spahn	.50
30	Jason Marquis	.15
31	Kevin Millwood	.15
32	Javy Lopez	.15
33	Vinny Castilla	.15
34	Julio Franco	.15
35	Trey Hodges	.15
36	Chipper Jones	1.50
37	Gary Sheffield	.25
38	Billy Sylvester	.15
39	Tom Glavine	.40
40	Rafael Furcal	.15
41	Cory Aldridge	.15
42	Greg Maddux	1.50
43	John Ennis	.15
44	Wes Helms	.15
45	Horacio Ramirez	.15

46	Derrick Lewis	.15
47	Marcus Giles	.15
48	Eddie Mathews	.75
49	Wilson Betemit	.15
50	Andruw Jones	.50
51	Josh Towers	.15
52	Ed Rogers	.15
53	Kris Foster	.15
54	Brooks Robinson	.75
55	Cal Ripken Jr.	3.00
56	Brian Roberts	.15
57	Luis Rivera	.15
58	Rodrigo Lopez	.15
59	Geronimo Gil	.15
60	Erik Bedard	.15
61	Jim Palmer	.40
62	Jay Gibbons	.15
63	Travis Driskill	.15
64	Larry Bigbie	.15
65	Eddie Murray	.40
66	Hoyt Wilhelm	.15
67	Bobby Doerr	.15
68	Pedro J. Martinez	1.00
69	Roger Clemens	1.50
70	Nomar Garciaparra	2.00
71	Trot Nixon	.15
72	Dennis Eckersley	.40
73	John Burkett	.15
74	Tim Wakefield	.15
75	Wade Boggs	.40
76	Cliff Floyd	.15
77	Casey Fossum	.15
78	Johnny Damon	.15
79	Fred Lynn	.15
80	Rickey Henderson	.40
81	Juan Diaz	.15
82	Manny Ramirez	.75
83	Carlton Fisk	.50
84	Jorge De La Rosa	.15
85	Shea Hillenbrand	.15
86	Derek Lowe	.15
87	Jason Varitek	.15
88	Carlos Baerga	.15
89	Freddy Sanchez	.15
90	Ugueth Urbina	.15
91	Rey Sanchez	.15
92	Josh Hancock	.15
93	Tony Clark	.15
94	Dustin Hermanson	.15
95	Ryne Sandberg	1.50
96	Fred McGriff	.25
97	Alex Gonzalez	.15
98	Mark Belhorn	.15
99	Fergie Jenkins	.25
100	Jon Lieber	.15
101	Francis Beltran	.15
102	Greg Maddux	1.50
103	Nate Frese	.15
104	Andre Dawson	.25
105	Carlos Zambrano	.15
106	Steve Smyth	.15
107	Ernie Banks	1.00
108	Will Ohman	.15
109	Kerry Wood	.50
110	Bobby Hill	.15
111	Moises Alou	.15
112	Hee Seop Choi	.15
113	Corey Patterson	.15
114	Sammy Sosa	1.50
115	Mark Prior	.50
116	Juan Cruz	.15
117	Ron Santo	.15
118	Billy Williams	.15
119	Antonio Alfonseca	.15
120	Matt Clement	.15
121	Carlton Fisk	.50
122	Joe Crede	.15
123	Magglio Ordonez	.40
124	Frank Thomas	.75
125	Joe Borchard	.15
126	Royce Clayton	.15
127	Luis Aparicio	.15
128	Willie Harris	.15
129	Kyle Kane	.15
130	Paul Konerko	.25
131	Matt Ginter	.15
132	Carlos Lee	.15
133	Mark Buehrle	.15
134	Adam Dunn	.75
135	Eric Davis	.15
136	Johnny Bench	1.00
137	Joe Morgan	.25
138	Austin Kearns	.40
139	Barry Larkin	.40
140	Ken Griffey Jr.	2.00
141	Luis Pineda	.15
142	Corky Miller	.15
143	Brandon Larson	.15
144	Wily Mo Pena	.15
145	Lance Davis	.15
146	Tom Seaver	1.00
147	Luke Hudson	.15
148	Sean Casey	.15
149	Tony Perez	.15

#	Player	Price		#	Player	Price		#	Player	Price		#	Player	Price
150	Todd Walker	.15		254	Odalis Perez	.15		360	David Wells	.15		466	Ruben Sierra	.15
151	Aaron Boone	.15		255	Hideo Nomo	.50		361	Enos Slaughter	.15		467	Mark McLemore	.15
152	Jose Rijo	.15		256	Kevin Brown	.15		362	Whitey Ford	.50		468	Carlos Guillen	.15
153	Ryan Dempster	.15		257	Eric Karros	.15		363	Eric Chavez	.25		469	Dan Wilson	.15
154	Danny Graves	.15		258	Joe Thurston	.15		364	Miguel Tejada	.40		470	Shigetoshi Hasegawa	.15
155	Matt Lawton	.15		259	Carlos Garcia	.15		365	Barry Zito	.25		471	Ben Davis	.15
156	Cliff Lee	.15		260	Shawn Green	.40		366	Bert Snow	.15		472	Ozzie Smith	1.00
157	Ryan Drese	.15		261	Paul LoDuca	.15		367	Rickey Henderson	.50		473	Matt Morris	.15
158	Danys Baez	.15		262	Kazuhisa Ishii	.15		368	Juan A. Pena	.15		474	Edgar Renteria	.15
159	Einar Diaz	.15		263	Victor Alvarez	.15		369	Terrence Long	.15		475	Les Walrond	.15
160	Milton Bradley	.15		264	Eric Gagne	.15		370	Dennis Eckersley	.40		476	Albert Pujols	1.00
161	Earl Snyder	.15		265	Don Sutton	.15		371	Mark Ellis	.15		477	Stan Musial	1.50
162	Ellis Burks	.15		266	Orel Hershiser	.15		372	Tim Hudson	.25		478	J.D. Drew	.15
163	Lou Boudreau	.15		267	Dave Roberts	.15		373	Jose Canseco	.50		479	Josh Pearce	.15
164	Bob Feller	.15		268	Adrian Beltre	.15		374	Reggie Jackson	.50		480	Enos Slaughter	.15
165	Ricardo Rodriguez	.15		269	Don Drysdale	.50		375	Mark Mulder	.25		481	Jason Simontacchi	.15
166	Victor Martinez	.15		270	Jackie Robinson	1.50		376	David Justice	.15		482	Jeremy Lambert	.15
167	Alex Herrera	.15		271	Tyler Houston	.15		377	Jermaine Dye	.15		483	Tino Martinez	.15
168	Omar Vizquel	.15		272	Omar Daal	.15		378	Brett Myers	.15		484	Rogers Hornsby	.50
169	David Elder	.15		273	Marquis Grissom	.15		379	Lenny Dykstra	.15		485	Rick Ankiel	.15
170	C.C. Sabathia	.15		274	Paul Quantrill	.15		380	Vicente Padilla	.15		486	Jim Edmonds	.25
171	Alex Escobar	.15		275	Paul Molitor	.50		381	Bobby Abreu	.15		487	Scott Rolen	.50
172	Brian Tallet	.15		276	Jose Hernandez	.15		382	Pat Burrell	.50		488	Kevin Joseph	.15
173	Jim Thome	.75		277	Takahito Nomura	.15		383	Jorge Padilla	.15		489	Fernando Vina	.15
174	Rene Reyes	.15		278	Nick Neugebauer	.15		384	Jeremy Giambi	.15		490	Jason Isringhausen	.15
175	Juan Uribe	.15		279	Jose Mieses	.15		385	Mike Lieberthal	.15		491	Lou Brock	.40
176	Jason Romano	.15		280	Richie Sexson	.40		386	Anderson Machado	.15		492	Joe Torre	.25
177	Juan Pierre	.15		281	Matt Childers	.15		387	Marlon Byrd	.15		493	Bob Gibson	.50
178	Jason Jennings	.15		282	Bill Hall	.15		388	Bud Smith	.15		494	Chuck Finley	.15
179	Jose Ortiz	.15		283	Ben Sheets	.15		389	Eric Valent	.15		495	So Taguchi	.15
180	Larry Walker	.25		284	Brian Mallette	.15		390	Elio Serrano	.15		496	Ben Grieve	.15
181	Cam Esslinger	.15		285	Geoff Jenkins	.15		391	Jimmy Rollins	.25		497	Toby Hall	.15
182	Todd Helton	.50		286	Robin Yount	.75		392	Brandon Duckworth	.15		498	Brent Abernathy	.15
183	Aaron Cook	.15		287	Jeff Deardorff	.15		393	Robin Roberts	.15		499	Brandon Backe	.15
184	Jack Cust	.15		288	Luis Rivas	.15		394	Marlon Anderson	.15		500	Felix Escalona	.15
185	Jack Morris	.15		289	Harmon Killebrew	.50		395	Robert Person	.15		501	Matt White	.15
186	Mike Rivera	.15		290	Michael Cuddyer	.15		396	Johnny Estrada	.15		502	Randy Winn	.15
187	Bobby Higginson	.15		291	Torii Hunter	.15		397	Mike Schmidt	1.00		503	Carl Crawford	.15
188	Fernando Rodney	.15		292	Kevin Frederick	.15		398	Eric Junge	.15		504	Dewon Brazelton	.15
189	Al Kaline	1.00		293	Adam Johnson	.15		399	Jason Michaels	.15		505	Joe Kennedy	.15
190	Carlos Pena	.15		294	Jack Morris	.15		400	Steve Carlton	.40		506	Wade Boggs	.50
191	Alan Trammell	.15		295	Rod Carew	.40		401	Placido Polanco	.15		507	Aubrey Huff	.15
192	Mike Maroth	.15		296	Kirby Puckett	1.50		402	John Grabow	.15		508	Alex Rodriguez	2.50
193	Adam Pettyjohn	.15		297	Joe Mays	.15		403	Tomas De La Rosa	.15		509	Ivan Rodriguez	.50
194	David Espinosa	.15		298	Jacque Jones	.15		404	Tike Redman	.15		510	Will Clark	.75
195	Adam Bernero	.15		299	Cristian Guzman	.15		405	Willie Stargell	.40		511	Hank Blalock	.15
196	Franklyn German	.15		300	Kyle Lohse	.15		406	Dave Williams	.15		512	Travis Hughes	.15
197	Robert Fick	.15		301	Eric Milton	.15		407	John Candelaria	.15		513	Travis Hafner	.15
198	Andres Torres	.15		302	Brad Radke	.15		408	Jack Wilson	.15		514	Ryan Ludwick	.15
199	Luis Castillo	.15		303	Doug Mientkiewicz	.15		409	Matt Guerrier	.15		515	Doug Davis	.15
200	Preston Wilson	.15		304	Corey Koskie	.15		410	Jason Kendall	.15		516	Juan Gonzalez	.50
201	Pablo Ozuna	.15		305	Jose Vidro	.15		411	Josh Fogg	.15		517	Jason Hart	.15
202	Brad Penny	.15		306	Claudio Vargas	.15		412	Aramis Ramirez	.15		518	Mark Teixeira	.40
203	Josh Beckett	.15		307	Gary Carter	.15		413	Dave Parker	.15		519	Nolan Ryan	3.00
204	Charles Johnson	.15		308	Andre Dawson	.25		414	Roberto Clemente	2.00		520	Rafael Palmeiro	.50
205	Wilson Valdez	.15		309	Henry Mateo	.15		415	Kip Wells	.15		521	Kevin Mench	.15
206	A.J. Burnett	.15		310	Andres Galarraga	.15		416	Brian Giles	.25		522	Chan Ho Park	.15
207	Abraham Nunez	.15		311	Zach Day	.15		417	Honus Wagner	1.50		523	Kenny Rogers	.15
208	Mike Lowell	.15		312	Bartolo Colon	.15		418	Ramon Vazquez	.15		524	Rusty Greer	.15
209	Jose Cueto	.15		313	Endy Chavez	.15		419	Oliver Perez	.15		525	Michael Young	.15
210	Jeriome Robertson	.15		314	Javier Vazquez	.15		420	Ryan Klesko	.15		526	Carlos Delgado	.40
211	Jeff Bagwell	.75		315	Michael Barrett	.15		421	Brian Lawrence	.15		527	Vernon Wells	.15
212	Kirk Saarloos	.15		316	Vladimir Guerrero	1.00		422	Ben Howard	.15		528	Orlando Hudson	.15
213	Craig Biggio	.25		317	Orlando Cabrera	.15		423	Ozzie Smith	1.00		529	Shannon Stewart	.15
214	Rodrigo Rosario	.15		318	Al Leiter	.15		424	Dennis Tankersley	.15		530	Joe Carter	.15
215	Roy Oswalt	.25		319	Timoniel Perez	.15		425	Tony Gwynn	1.00		531	Chris Baker	.15
216	John Buck	.15		320	Rey Ordonez	.15		426	Sean Burroughs	.15		532	Eric Hinske	.15
217	Tim Redding	.15		321	Gary Carter	.15		427	Xavier Nady	.15		533	Corey Thurman	.15
218	Morgan Ensberg	.15		322	Armando Benitez	.15		428	Phil Nevin	.15		534	Josh Phelps	.15
219	Richard Hidalgo	.15		323	Dwight Gooden	.15		429	Trevor Hoffman	.15		535	Reed Johnson	.15
220	Wade Miller	.15		324	Pedro Astacio	.15		430	Jake Peavy	.15		536	Brian Bowles	.15
221	Lance Berkman	.50		325	Roberto Alomar	.50		431	Cody Ransom	.15		537	Roy Halladay	.15
222	Raul Chavez	.15		326	Edgardo Alfonzo	.15		432	Kenny Lofton	.15		538	Jose Cruz Jr.	.15
223	Carlos Hernandez	.15		327	Nolan Ryan	3.00		433	Mel Ott	.50		539	Kelvim Escobar	.15
224	Greg Miller	.15		328	Mo Vaughn	.25		434	Tsuyoshi Shinjo	.15		540	Chris Carpenter	.15
225	Tom Shearn	.15		329	Ryan Jamison	.15		435	Deivis Santos	.15				
226	Jason Lane	.15		330	Satoru Komiyama	.15		436	Rich Aurilia	.15				
227	Nolan Ryan	3.00		331	Mike Piazza	2.50		437	Will Clark	.50				
228	Billy Wagner	.15		332	Tom Seaver	1.00		438	Pedro Feliz	.15				
229	Octavio Dotel	.15		333	Jorge Posada	.40		439	J.T. Snow	.15				
230	Shane Reynolds	.15		334	Derek Jeter	2.50		440	Robb Nen	.15				
231	Julio Lugo	.15		335	Babe Ruth	3.00		441	Carlos Valderrama	.15				
232	Daryle Ward	.15		336	Lou Gehrig	2.50		442	Willie McCovey	.15				
233	Mike Sweeney	.15		337	Andy Pettitte	.40		443	Jeff Kent	.25				
234	Angel Berroa	.15		338	Mariano Rivera	.25		444	Orlando Cepeda	.15				
235	George Brett	1.50		339	Robin Ventura	.15		445	Barry Bonds	2.50				
236	Brad Voyles	.15		340	Yogi Berra	1.00		446	Alex Rodriguez	2.50				
237	Brandon Berger	.15		341	Phil Rizzuto	.50		447	Allan Simpson	.15				
238	Chad Durbin	.15		342	Bernie Williams	.50		448	Antonio Perez	.15				
239	Alexis Gomez	.15		343	Alfonso Soriano	1.50		449	Edgar Martinez	.15				
240	Jeremy Affeldt	.15		344	Drew Henson	.15		450	Freddy Garcia	.15				
241	Bo Jackson	.75		345	Erick Almonte	.15		451	Chris Snelling	.15				
242	Dee Brown	.15		346	Rondell White	.15		452	Matt Thornton	.15				
243	Tony Cogan	.15		347	Christian Parker	.15		453	Kazuhiro Sasaki	.15				
244	Carlos Beltran	.15		348	Joe Torre	.25		454	Harold Reynolds	.15				
245	Joe Randa	.15		349	Nick Johnson	.15		455	Randy Johnson	1.00				
246	Pee Wee Reese	.25		350	Raul Mondesi	.15		456	Bret Boone	.15				
247	Andy Ashby	.15		351	Brandon Claussen	.15		457	Rafael Soriano	.15				
248	Cesar Izturis	.15		352	Reggie Jackson	.50		458	Luis Ugueto	.15				
249	Duke Snider	.50		353	Roger Clemens	1.50		459	Ken Griffey Jr.	2.00				
250	Mark Grudzielanek	.15		354	Don Mattingly	2.00		460	Ichiro Suzuki	2.00				
251	Chin-Feng Chen	.15		355	Jason Giambi	1.50		461	Jamie Moyer	.15				
252	Brian Jordan	.15		356	Adrian Hernandez	.15		462	Joel Pineiro	.15				
253	Steve Garvey	.15		357	Jeff Weaver	.15		463	Jeff Cirillo	.15				
				358	Mike Mussina	.50		464	John Olerud	.15				
				359	Brett Jodie	.15		465	Mike Cameron	.15				

Glossy

Stars: 1-2.5X
Inserted 1:1

Stat Line

Cards serial numbered
151-250: 4-8X
Print run 101-150: 5-10X

Print run 51-100:	8-15X
Print run 26-50:	10-20X

Autographs

		NM/M
Common Player:		6.00

Some not priced due to scarcity.

4	Alfredo Amezaga/250	6.00
11	Elpidio Guzman/100	10.00
15	Doug DeVore/122	10.00
35	Trey Hodges/250	8.00
38	Billy Sylvester/250	6.00
41	Cory Aldridge/250	8.00
45	Horacio Ramirez/200	8.00
46	Derrick Lewis/250	6.00
47	Marcus Giles/200	8.00
49	Wilson Betemit/75	8.00
51	Josh Towers/110	10.00
52	Ed Rogers/250	6.00
53	Kris Foster/250	6.00
56	Brian Roberts/250	35.00
59	Geronimo Gil/60	10.00
60	Erik Bedard/250	8.00
62	Jay Gibbons/181	10.00
64	Larry Bigbie/100	10.00
77	Casey Fossum/250	6.00
79	Fred Lynn/50	20.00
81	Juan Diaz/250	6.00
84	Jorge De La Rosa/250	6.00
99	Fergie Jenkins/50	25.00
101	Francis Beltran/250	8.00
103	Nate Frese/250	6.00
105	Carlos Zambrano/150	20.00
108	Will Ohman/50	10.00
110	Bobby Hill/150	8.00
115	Mark Prior/250	40.00
116	Juan Cruz/50	10.00
122	Joe Crede/250	10.00
125	Joe Borchard/250	10.00
127	Luis Aparicio/250	20.00
128	Willie Harris/129	8.00
129	Kyle Kane/100	10.00
131	Matt Ginter/250	6.00
132	Carlos Lee/50	15.00
133	Mark Buehrle/50	20.00
135	Eric Davis/75	20.00
138	Austin Kearns/71	20.00
142	Corky Miller/250	6.00
143	Brandon Larson/143	10.00
144	Wily Mo Pena/250	15.00
147	Luke Hudson/50	12.00
149	Tony Perez/250	20.00
156	Cliff Lee/250	10.00
161	Earl Snyder/250	8.00
165	Ricardo Rodriguez/250	8.00
166	Victor Martinez/250	25.00
167	Alex Herrera/250	6.00
171	Alex Escobar/125	10.00
172	Brian Tallet/250	10.00
174	Rene Reyes/50	6.00
176	Jason Romano/50	15.00
177	Juan Pierre/66	15.00
178	Jason Jennings/250	10.00
179	Jose Ortiz/250	8.00
181	Cam Esslinger/250	6.00
184	Jack Cust/250	10.00
185	Jack Morris/250	20.00
186	Mike Rivera/250	6.00
188	Fernando Rodney/250	6.00
190	Carlos Pena/96	12.00
192	Mike Maroth/250	6.00
193	Adam Pettyjohn/250	6.00
194	David Espinosa/250	6.00
195	Adam Bernero/250	6.00
196	Franklyn German/250	8.00
197	Robert Fick/50	10.00
198	Andres Torres/250	6.00
201	Pablo Ozuna/250	6.00
205	Wilson Valdez/250	6.00
207	Abraham Nunez/250	8.00
212	Kirk Saarloos/250	8.00
214	Rodrigo Rosario/250	6.00
215	Roy Oswalt/50	20.00
217	Tim Redding/250	6.00
218	Morgan Ensberg/250	6.00
219	Richard Hidalgo/100	10.00
220	Wade Miller/200	10.00
222	Raul Chavez/125	15.00
223	Carlos Hernandez/250	10.00
224	Greg Miller/90	10.00
226	Jason Lane/250	10.00
234	Angel Berroa/200	10.00
236	Brad Voyles/200	10.00
237	Brandon Berger/250	8.00
238	Chad Durbin/250	8.00
239	Alexis Gomez/165	10.00
240	Jeremy Affeldt/250	6.00
242	Dee Brown/50	12.00
243	Tony Cogan/250	6.00
248	Cesar Izturis/250	10.00
253	Steve Garvey/75	30.00
258	Joe Thurston/108	10.00

259	Carlos Garcia/100	8.00
261	Paul LoDuca/50	20.00
263	Victor Alvarez/250	6.00
265	Don Sutton/50	20.00
277	Takahito Nomura/100	20.00
279	Jose Mieses/50	15.00
281	Matt Childers/50	12.00
283	Ben Sheets/100	20.00
284	Brian Mallette/250	6.00
287	Jeff Deardorff/100	6.00
288	Luis Rivas/200	8.00
290	Michael Cuddyer/250	10.00
291	Torii Hunter/100	25.00
294	Jack Morris/50	20.00
305	Jose Vidro/50	15.00
306	Claudio Vargas/150	6.00
309	Henry Mateo/250	6.00
311	Zach Day/250	6.00
313	Endy Chavez/250	6.00
314	Javier Vazquez/50	15.00
321	Gary Carter/20	
323	Dwight Gooden/75	25.00
344	Drew Henson/250	25.00
345	Erick Almonte/250	6.00
347	Christian Parker/200	6.00
351	Brandon Claussen/250	6.00
356	Adrian Hernandez/200	6.00
359	Brett Jodie/250	8.00
366	Bert Snow/250	6.00
368	Juan Pena/250	8.00
371	Mark Ellis/150	6.00
379	Lenny Dykstra/75	25.00
383	Jorge Padilla/250	8.00
384	Jeremy Giambi/100	10.00
386	Anderson Machado/250	6.00
387	Marlon Byrd/200	10.00
388	Bud Smith/125	8.00
389	Eric Valent/100	8.00
390	Elio Serrano/250	8.00
392	Brandon Duckworth/100	10.00
395	Robert Person/100	10.00
396	Johnny Estrada/209	15.00
398	Eric Junge/250	6.00
399	Jason Michaels/221	6.00
402	John Grabow/250	6.00
406	Dave Williams/250	6.00
407	John Candelaria/100	10.00
408	Jack Wilson/250	6.00
409	Matt Guerrier/200	6.00
412	Aramis Ramirez/50	30.00
413	Dave Parker/250	20.00
415	Kip Wells/250	8.00
418	Ramon Vazquez/200	6.00
419	Oliver Perez/150	15.00
421	Brian Lawrence/250	8.00
422	Ben Howard/250	6.00
427	Xavier Nady/50	15.00
431	Cody Ransom/100	10.00
435	Deivis Santos/100	6.00
438	Pedro Feliz/50	15.00
441	Carlos Valderrama/250	6.00
447	Allan Simpson/250	6.00
448	Antonio Perez/250	6.00
451	Chris Snelling/100	10.00
452	Matt Thornton/200	6.00
454	Harold Reynolds/100	15.00
457	Rafael Soriano/250	6.00
458	Luis Ugueto/50	10.00
475	Les Walrond/50	12.00
479	Josh Pearce/200	6.00
497	Toby Hall/200	8.00
498	Brent Abernathy/250	6.00
499	Brandon Backe/250	8.00
500	Felix Escalona/50	10.00
504	Dewon Brazelton/100	10.00
505	Joe Kennedy/250	6.00
507	Aubrey Huff/100	15.00
512	Travis Hughes/200	6.00
514	Ryan Ludwick/250	6.00
515	Doug Davis/250	6.00
517	Jason Hart/123	6.00
518	Mark Teixeira/50	40.00
521	Kevin Mench/250	10.00
528	Orlando Hudson/120	10.00
531	Chris Baker/250	6.00
532	Eric Hinske/250	10.00
533	Corey Thurman/250	8.00
534	Josh Phelps/150	10.00
535	Reed Johnson/250	6.00
536	Brian Bowles/250	6.00
543	Ramon Nivar/100	15.00
544	Adam Loewen/100	10.00
545	Brandon Webb/100	30.00
546	Dan Haren/100	25.00
548	Ryan Wagner/100	15.00

Timeline Threads

		NM/M

Common Player:
Quantity produced listed

1	Bobby Doerr/39	20.00
2	Phil Rizzuto/47	30.00
3	Yogi Berra/47	35.00
4	Pee Wee Reese/48	15.00
5	Stan Musial/42	
6	Al Kaline/64	40.00
7	Orlando Cepeda/65	15.00
8	Eddie Mathews/66	40.00
9	Lou Brock/66	15.00
10	Juan Marichal/67	15.00
11	Ernie Banks/68	40.00
12	Willie Stargell/68	15.00
13	Jim Palmer/69	15.00
14	Luis Aparicio/69	15.00
15	Tom Seaver/69	30.00
16	Harmon Killebrew/71	50.00
17	Joe Morgan/74	15.00
18	Brooks Robinson/76	30.00
19	Mike Schmidt/81	65.00
20	Willie McCovey/77	15.00
21	Robin Yount/78	40.00
22	Reggie Jackson/79	20.00
23	Rod Carew/85	25.00
24	Nolan Ryan/91	80.00
25	Tony Gwynn/98	15.00
26	Alex Rodriguez/100	25.00
27	Carlos Delgado/101	10.00
28	Lance Berkman/102	10.00
29	Randy Johnson/100	20.00
30	Josh Beckett/101	15.00
31	Eric Davis/89	15.00
32	Todd Helton/100	15.00
33	Jose Canseco/89	15.00
34	Mike Piazza/101	25.00
35	Fred Lynn/75	15.00
36	Mike Sweeney/101	10.00
37	Miguel Tejada/101	15.00
38	Curt Schilling/101	15.00
39	Dale Murphy/87	40.00
40	Jim Thome/101	20.00
41	Adam Dunn/102	15.00
42	Nomar Garciaparra/100	
43	Vladimir Guerrero/100	25.00
44	Alfonso Soriano/102	15.00
45	Wade Boggs/90	15.00
46	Randy Johnson/89	15.00
47	Hal Newhouser/55	15.00
48	Chipper Jones/93	20.00
49	Andruw Jones/96	15.00
50	Frank Thomas/94	15.00

2003 Donruss Timeless Treasures

		NM/M
Complete Set (100):		
Common Player:		2.00
Production 900 Sets		
Tin (4):		100.00
1	Adam Dunn	3.00
2	Al Kaline	5.00
3	Alan Trammell	2.00
4	Albert Pujols	8.00
5	Alex Rodriguez	8.00
6	Alfonso Soriano	4.00
7	Andre Dawson	2.00
8	Andruw Jones	3.00
9	Austin Kearns	2.00
10	Babe Ruth	10.00

11	Barry Bonds	10.00
12	Barry Larkin	2.00
13	Barry Zito	3.00
14	Bernie Williams	4.00
15	Bo Jackson	4.00
16	Brooks Robinson	4.00
17	Cal Ripken Jr.	10.00
18	Carlton Fisk	2.00
19	Chipper Jones	4.00
20	Curt Schilling	3.00
21	Dale Murphy	2.00
22	Derek Jeter	10.00
23	Don Mattingly	10.00
24	Duke Snider	3.00
25	Eddie Mathews	4.00
26	Frank Robinson	2.00
27	Frank Thomas	4.00
28	Garret Anderson	2.00
29	Gary Carter	2.00
30	George Brett	8.00
31	Greg Maddux	6.00
32	Harmon Killebrew	4.00
33	Hideki Matsui **RC**	10.00
34	Hideo Nomo	3.00
35	Ichiro Suzuki	6.00
36	Juan Rodriguez	4.00
37	Jackie Robinson	6.00
38	Jason Giambi	3.00
39	Jeff Bagwell	4.00
40	Jim Edmonds	3.00
41	Jim Palmer	3.00
42	Jim Thome	4.00
43	Joe Morgan	2.00
44	Jorge Posada	3.00
45	Jose Contreras **RC**	5.00
46	Juan Gonzalez	3.00
47	Kazuhisa Ishii	2.00
48	Ken Griffey Jr.	5.00
49	Kerry Wood	4.00
50	Kirby Puckett	5.00
51	Lance Berkman	2.00
52	Larry Walker	2.00
53	Lou Brock	3.00
54	Lou Gehrig	8.00
55	Magglio Ordonez	2.00
56	Mark Prior	4.00
57	Miguel Tejada	3.00
58	Mike Mussina	3.00
59	Mike Piazza	6.00
60	Mike Schmidt	8.00
61	Nolan Ryan	10.00
62	Nomar Garciaparra	6.00
63	Ozzie Smith	5.00
64	Pat Burrell	2.00
65	Pedro J. Martinez	4.00
66	Pee Wee Reese	4.00
67	Phil Rizzuto	2.00
68	Rafael Palmeiro	3.00
69	Randy Johnson	5.00
70	Reggie Jackson	4.00
71	Richie Ashburn	2.00
72	Rickey Henderson	3.00
73	Roberto Alomar	3.00
74	Roberto Clemente	8.00
75	Robin Yount	4.00
76	Rod Carew	4.00
77	Roger Clemens	8.00
78	Rogers Hornsby	4.00
79	Roy Oswalt	2.00
80	Ryan Klesko	2.00
81	Ryne Sandberg	6.00
82	Sammy Sosa	6.00
83	Scott Rolen	4.00
84	Shawn Green	3.00
85	Stan Musial	6.00
86	Steve Carlton	3.00
87	Thurman Munson	5.00
88	Todd Helton	4.00
89	Tom Glavine	2.00
90	Tom Seaver	4.00
91	Tony Gwynn	4.00
92	Tony Perez	2.00
93	Torii Hunter	2.00
94	Troy Glaus	3.00
95	Ty Cobb	6.00
96	Vernon Wells	2.00
97	Vladimir Guerrero	4.00
98	Warren Spahn	4.00
99	Willie McCovey	3.00
100	Yogi Berra	5.00

Silver

Stars (1-100):	3-5X
Production 50 Sets	
Golds:	No Pricing
Production 10 Sets	
Platinum 1-of-1's exist.	

Award Materials

		NM/M

Quantity produced listed

1	Ivan Rodriguez/100	10.00
2	Mike Schmidt/50	60.00
3	Roberto Clemente/50	80.00
4	Roger Clemens/50	25.00

5	Randy Johnson/100	15.00
6	Pedro J. Martinez/100	15.00
7	Ivan Rodriguez/100	10.00
8	Jeff Bagwell/100	15.00
9	Frank Thomas/100	15.00
10	Cal Ripken Jr./75	50.00
11	Tom Seaver/50	25.00

Award Materials Autographs

Complete Set (1):

6	Pedro J. Martinez/5	

Award Prime Materials

NM/M

Quantity produced listed

6	Pedro J. Martinez/50	30.00
9	Frank Thomas/50	25.00

Award Winning MLB Logos

No Pricing

Classic Combos

NM/M

Quantity produced listed

1	Jason Giambi/100	15.00
2	Adrian Beltre/100	10.00
3	Alex Rodriguez/100	25.00
4	Alfonso Soriano/100	30.00
5	Andruw Jones/100	15.00
6	Andre Dawson/100	15.00
7	Barry Larkin/100	10.00
8	Barry Zito/100	15.00
9	Cal Ripken Jr./100	60.00
10	Chipper Jones/100	20.00
11	Don Mattingly/10	50.00
12	Eric Chavez/100	10.00
13	Frank Thomas/100	15.00
14	Greg Maddux/100	25.00
15	Ivan Rodriguez/100	15.00
16	Jeff Bagwell/100	15.00
17	Jim Thome/100	15.00
18	Juan Gonzalez/100	15.00
19	Kazuhisa Ishii/100	10.00
20	Kerry Wood/100	15.00
21	Lance Berkman/100	15.00
22	Magglio Ordonez/100	10.00
23	Manny Ramirez/100	15.00
24	Miguel Tejada/100	10.00
25	Mike Piazza/100	20.00
26	Nomar Garciaparra/100	20.00
27	Pedro J. Martinez/100	20.00
28	Randy Johnson/100	15.00
29	Rickey Henderson/100	20.00
30	Ryne Sandberg/100	30.00
31	Sammy Sosa	
32	Shawn Green/100	10.00
33	Todd Helton/100	10.00
34	Tony Gwynn/100	20.00
35	Vladimir Guerrero/100	15.00

Classic Combos Autographs

NM/M

Quantity produced listed

8	Barry Zito/25	100.00
22	Magglio Ordonez/25	65.00
34	Tony Gwynn/25	100.00

Classic Prime Combos

NM/M

Quantity produced listed

6	Andre Dawson/25	40.00
11	Don Mattingly/25	75.00
16	Jeff Bagwell/25	50.00

Game Day Materials

NM/M

Quantity produced listed

1	Tony Gwynn/100	15.00
2	Magglio Ordonez/100	8.00
3	George Brett/100	40.00
4	Rickey Henderson/100	15.00
5	Billy Williams/100	10.00
6	Frank Thomas/100	10.00
7	Tony Gwynn/75	20.00
10	Ryne Sandberg/100	30.00
11	Miguel Tejada/100	10.00

Game Day Materials Autograph

Quantity produced listed
No Pricing

HOF Materials

NM/M

Quantity produced listed

1	Al Kaline	25.00
2	Babe Ruth/75	140.00
3	Carlton Fisk/100	15.00
4	Eddie Mathews/100	20.00
5	Gary Carter/100	15.00
6	George Brett/100	35.00
7	Harmon Killebrew/100	25.00
8	Joe Morgan/100	10.00
9	Kirby Puckett/100	20.00
10	Lou Gehrig/100	110.00
11	Luis Aparicio/100	10.00
12	Mike Schmidt/100	25.00
13	Ozzie Smith/100	25.00
14	Phil Rizzuto/100	10.00
15	Reggie Jackson/100	15.00
16	Richie Ashburn/100	15.00
17	Roberto Clemente/100	60.00
18	Robin Yount/100	20.00
19	Rod Carew/100	15.00
20	Rogers Hornsby/100	45.00
21	Stan Musial/100	35.00
22	Ty Cobb/100	120.00
23	Willie McCovey/100	10.00
24	Yogi Berra/100	30.00
25	Al Kaline/100	25.00
26	Babe Ruth/50	300.00
27	Bobby Doerr/100	15.00
28	Brooks Robinson/100	15.00
29	Eddie Mathews/100	20.00
30	Harmon Killebrew/100	25.00
31	Ty Cobb/50	150.00
32	Joe Morgan/100	10.00
33	Lou Brock/100	10.00
34	Lou Gehrig/50	225.00
35	Mike Schmidt/100	25.00
36	Nolan Ryan/100	40.00
37	Nolan Ryan/100	40.00
38	Nolan Ryan/100	40.00
39	Phil Rizzuto/100	10.00
40	Reggie Jackson/25	25.00
41	Reggie Jackson/100	15.00
42	Roberto Clemente/50	90.00
43	Robin Yount/100	20.00
44	Rod Carew/100	15.00
45	Stan Musial/100	35.00
46	Tom Seaver/100	20.00
47	Steve Carlton/100	15.00
48	Carlton Fisk/100	15.00
49	Pee Wee Reese/100	15.00
50	Jackie Robinson/50	85.00

HOF Materials Autographs

NM/M

Quantity produced listed

7	Harmon Killebrew/25	80.00
12	Mike Schmidt/15	180.00
24	Yogi Berra/15	150.00
28	Brooks Robinson/25	75.00
30	Harmon Killebrew/50	75.00
39	Phil Rizzuto/25	65.00
43	Robin Yount/25	175.00

HOF Cuts

NM/M

Production One Set
Ty Cobb
(8/03 Auction) 6,500

HOF Combos

NM/M

Quantity produced listed

1	Al Kaline/50	50.00
4	Kirby Puckett/75	40.00

6	Mike Schmidt/100	50.00
7	Nolan Ryan/50	100.00
8	Phil Rizzuto/50	30.00
9	Reggie Jackson/50	40.00
11	Rod Carew/100	25.00
14	George Brett/25	85.00
15	Carlton Fisk/100	20.00

HOF Combos Autographs

Quantity produced listed
No Pricing

HOF Letters

Quantity produced listed
No Pricing

Induction Year Combos

NM/M

Production 25 Sets

6	Enos Slaughter, Lou Brock/25	60.00
8	Phil Rizzuto, Steve Carlton/25	45.00
10	George Brett, Robin Yount/25	185.00

HOF Logos

NM/M

Quantity produced listed

29	Eddie Mathews/35	65.00
36	Nolan Ryan/35	100.00
37	Nolan Ryan/35	100.00
38	Nolan Ryan/35	100.00
43	Robin Yount/35	50.00

HOF Numbers

NM/M

Quantity produced listed

35	Mike Schmidt/50	40.00
36	Nolan Ryan/35	100.00
43	Robin Yount/35	50.00
47	Steve Carlton/40	20.00
48	Carlton Fisk/35	45.00

HOF Prime Combos

Quantity produced listed
No Pricing

Home Run Materials

NM/M

Quantity produced listed

1	Harmon Killebrew/100	20.00
2	Harmon Killebrew/100	20.00
3	Jose Canseco/100	15.00
4	Magglio Ordonez/100	8.00
5	Rafael Palmeiro/100	15.00
6	Rafael Palmeiro/100	15.00
7	Rafael Palmeiro/100	15.00
8	Alex Rodriguez/100	15.00
9	Alex Rodriguez/100	15.00
10	Alex Rodriguez/100	15.00
11	Alex Rodriguez/20	75.00
12	Adam Dunn/100	15.00

Home Run Materials Autograph

NM/M

Quantity produced listed

1	Harmon Killebrew/25	80.00
3	Jose Canseco/25	100.00

Material Ink

NM/M

Quantity produced listed

1	Adam Dunn/50	45.00
2	Alan Trammell/100	30.00
3	Alex Rodriguez/25	150.00
5	Andre Dawson/100	30.00
6	Barry Zito/100	45.00
7	Bo Jackson/100	60.00
8	Bob Feller/25	70.00
9	Bobby Doerr/50	45.00
11	Cal Ripken Jr./50	200.00
12	Cal Ripken Jr./50	200.00
13	Cal Ripken Jr./25	225.00
14	Dale Murphy/50	45.00
15	Dave Parker/75	35.00
16	David Cone/100	30.00
17	Don Mattingly/100	85.00
18	Duke Snider/25	75.00
19	Edgar Martinez/50	50.00
20	Gary Carter/100	30.00
21	Harmon Killebrew/75	70.00
22	Jim Edmonds/25	55.00
23	Jim Thome/50	50.00
24	Joe Carter/100	30.00
25	Jose Canseco/50	50.00
26	Jose Vidro/100	20.00
27	Kazuhisa Ishii/100	40.00
28	Kerry Wood/50	60.00
29	Lance Berkman/50	40.00
30	Mark Mulder/25	65.00
32	Mike Schmidt/50	90.00
33	Nick Johnson/100	25.00
34	Nolan Ryan/25	225.00
35	Nolan Ryan/25	225.00
36	Nolan Ryan/25	225.00
37	Paul LoDuca/25	25.00
38	Paul Molitor/50	45.00
40	Reggie Jackson/40	85.00
41	Roberto Alomar/50	50.00
42	Roberto Alomar/100	40.00
43	Robin Yount/50	75.00
47	Ryan Klesko/75	25.00
48	Ryne Sandberg/25	140.00
50	Stan Musial/25	150.00
51	Steve Carlton/25	35.00
52	Steve Carlton/100	35.00
53	Todd Helton/50	60.00
54	Tom Seaver/50	50.00
55	Tony Gwynn/25	100.00
56	Torii Hunter/100	40.00
57	Vladimir Guerrero/100	40.00
58	Will Clark/50	85.00

Material MLB Logo Ink

No Pricing

Milestone Materials

NM/M

Quantity produced listed

3	Rickey Henderson/100	15.00

Past and Present

NM/M

Production 100 Sets

1	Alex Rodriguez/100	20.00
2	Hideo Nomo/100	25.00
3	Jason Giambi/100	20.00
4	Juan Gonzalez/100	15.00
5	Mike Piazza/100	20.00
6	Pedro J. Martinez/100	15.00
7	Randy Johnson/100	15.00
8	Rickey Henderson/100	20.00
9	Roberto Alomar/100	15.00
10	Roger Clemens/100	20.00
11	Sammy Sosa/100	35.00

Past & Present Letters

NM/M

Quantity produced listed

1	Alex Rodriguez/75	30.00
2	Hideo Nomo/25	90.00
4	Juan Gonzalez/50	25.00
6	Pedro J. Martinez/75	35.00
7	Randy Johnson/75	40.00

Past and Present Logos

NM/M

Quantity produced listed

2	Hideo Nomo/25	90.00
3	Jason Giambi/75	40.00
5	Mike Piazza/50	40.00

Past & Present Numbers

Quantity produced listed

		NM/M
2	Hideo Nomo/75	75.00
3	Jason Giambi/75	40.00
6	Pedro J. Martinez/50	40.00
7	Randy Johnson/50	40.00

Past & Present Patches

Quantity produced listed
No Pricing

Post Season Materials

Quantity produced listed
No Pricing

Post Season Materials Autograph

Quantity produced listed

		NM/M
1	Ozzie Smith/15	125.00
8	Alfonso Soriano/25	

Post Season Prime Material

No Pricing

		NM/M
1	Ozzie Smith/75	50.00

Prime Materials

Quantity produced listed

		NM/M
1	Tony Gwynn/100	15.00
2	Magglio Ordonez/100	8.00
4	Rickey Henderson/100	15.00
6	Frank Thomas/100	10.00
7	Tony Gwynn/100	20.00
10	Ryne Sandberg/100	30.00
11	Miguel Tejada/100	10.00

Prime Material Ink

Quantity produced listed

		NM/M
2	Alan Trammell/50	50.00
5	Andre Dawson/25	60.00
7	Bo Jackson/50	100.00
20	Gary Carter/50	50.00
24	Joe Carter/50	50.00
26	Jose Vidro/50	40.00
27	Kazuhisa Ishii/50	50.00
33	Nick Johnson/50	45.00
53	Steve Carlton/50	50.00
58	Torii Hunter/50	50.00
59	Vladimir Guerrero/50	70.00
60	Will Clark/25	180.00

Rookie Year Materials

		NM/M
Common Player:		8.00
1	Cal Ripken Jr./100	50.00
2	Mike Schmidt/50	40.00
3	Rafael Palmeiro/100	15.00
4	Nomar Garciaparra/100	20.00
5	Sean Casey	
6	Stan Musial/42	70.00
7	Yogi Berra/100	30.00
8	Bernie Williams	
9	Ivan Rodriguez/102	10.00
10	J.D. Drew	
11	Scott Rolen	
12	Vladimir Guerrero/100	15.00
13	Johnny Bench	
14	Ivan Rodriguez/91	10.00
15	Andruw Jones/96	15.00
16	Andruw Jones/100	15.00
17	Fred Lynn/100	10.00
18	Jeff Kent/100	8.00
19	Gary Sheffield/100	10.00
20	Ron Santo/100	15.00
21	Juan Gonzalez/100	15.00
22	Alfonso Soriano/100	25.00
23	Ryan Klesko/92	10.00
24	Adam Dunn/100	12.00

25	Hideo Nomo/100	25.00
26	Mark Prior/100	15.00
27	Pat Burrell/99	10.00
28	Magglio Ordonez/100	8.00
29	Kirby Puckett/84	25.00
30	Albert Pujols/100	30.00
31	Albert Pujols/100	30.00

Rookie Year Materials Autograph

Quantity produced listed

		NM/M
7	Yogi Berra/15	150.00
26	Mark Prior/25	150.00
28	Magglio Ordonez/25	50.00

Rookie Year Combos

Quantity produced listed

		NM/M
6	Mark Prior/50	40.00
7	Albert Pujols/50	80.00

Rookie Year Materials Letter

Quantity produced listed

		NM/M
4	Nomar Garciaparra/35	40.00
9	Ivan Rodriguez/35	20.00
12	Vladimir Guerrero/35	25.00
15	Andruw Jones/25	35.00
30	Albert Pujols/25	90.00

Rookie Year Materials Logos

Quantity produced listed

		NM/M
12	Vladimir Guerrero/50	25.00
15	Andruw Jones/50	25.00
17	Fred Lynn/25	25.00
18	Jeff Kent/50	20.00
19	Gary Sheffield/50	25.00
22	Alfonso Soriano/20	60.00
23	Ryan Klesko/50	15.00
30	Albert Pujols/50	75.00

Rookie Year Materials Numbers

Quantity produced listed

		NM/M
12	Vladimir Guerrero/50	25.00
15	Andruw Jones/15	25.00
17	Fred Lynn/30	25.00
18	Jeff Kent/25	20.00
19	Gary Sheffield/25	30.00
21	Juan Gonzalez/30	30.00
22	Alfonso Soriano/35	50.00
23	Ryan Klesko/35	20.00
26	Mark Prior/35	40.00
30	Albert Pujols/25	90.00

Rookie Year Materials Patches

Quantity produced listed
No Pricing

2004 Donruss

Jeff Bagwell

		NM/M
Complete Set (400):		75.00
Common Player:		.10
Pack (10):		3.50
Box (24):		65.00
1	Derek Jeter	2.00
2	Greg Maddux	1.00
3	Albert Pujols	1.50
4	Ichiro Suzuki	1.00
5	Alex Rodriguez	1.50
6	Roger Clemens	1.50
7	Andruw Jones	.50
8	Barry Bonds	2.00
9	Jeff Bagwell	.50
10	Randy Johnson	.75
12	Scott Rolen	.50
13	Lance Berkman	.40
14	Barry Zito	.25
15	Manny Ramirez	.50
16	Carlos Delgado	.50
17	Alfonso Soriano	.75
18	Todd Helton	.50
19	Mike Mussina	.50
20	Nomar Garciaparra	1.50
21	Chipper Jones	1.00
22	Mark Prior	2.00
23	Jim Thome	.50
24	Vladimir Guerrero	.75
25	Pedro Martinez	.75
26	Sergio Mitre	.10
27	Adam Loewen	.10
28	Alfredo Gonzalez	.10
29	Miguel Ojeda	.10
30	Rosman Garcia	.10
31	Arnie Munoz	.10
32	Andrew Brown	.10
33	Josh Hall	.10
34	Josh Stewart	.10
35	Clint Barmes	.10
36	Brandon Webb	.10
37	Chien-Ming Wang	.40
38	Edgar Gonzalez	.10
39	Alejandro Machado	.10
40	Jeremy Griffiths	.10
41	Craig Brazell	.10
42	Daniel Cabrera	.10
43	Fernando Cabrera	.10
44	Terrmel Sledge	.10
45	Rob Hammock	.10
46	Francisco Rosario	.10
47	Francisco Cruceta	.10
48	Rett Johnson	.10
49	Guillermo Quiroz	.10
50	Hong-Chih Kuo	.10
51	Ian Ferguson	.10
52	Tim Olson	.10
53	Todd Wellemeyer	.10
54	Rich Fischer	.10
55	Phil Seibel	.10
56	Joe Valentine	.10
57	Matt Kata	.10
58	Michael Hessman	.10
59	Michel Hernandez	.10
60	Doug Waechter	.10
61	Prentice Redman	.10
62	Nook Logan	.10
63	Oscar Villarreal	.10
64	Pete LaForest	.10
65	Matt Bruback	.10
66	Dan Haren	.10
67	Greg Aquino	.10
68	Lew Ford	.10
69	Jeff Duncan	.10
70	Ryan Wagner	.10
71	Bengie Molina	.10
72	Brad Fullmer	.10
73	Darin Erstad	.25
74	David Eckstein	.10
75	Garret Anderson	.25
76	Jarrod Washburn	.10
77	Kevin Appier	.10
78	Scott Spiezio	.10
79	Tim Salmon	.25
80	Troy Glaus	.40
81	Troy Percival	.10
82	Jason Johnson	.10
83	Jay Gibbons	.25
84	Melvin Mora	.10
85	Sidney Ponson	.10
86	Tony Batista	.10
87	Bill Mueller	.10
88	Byung-Hyun Kim	.10
89	David Ortiz	.25
90	Derek Lowe	.25
91	Johnny Damon	.25
92	Casey Fossum	.10
93	Manny Ramirez	.50
94	Nomar Garciaparra	1.50
95	Pedro J. Martinez	.75
96	Todd Walker	.10
97	Trot Nixon	.10
98	Bartolo Colon	.25
99	Carlos Lee	.10
100	D'Angelo Jimenez	.10
101	Esteban Loaiza	.10
102	Frank Thomas	.50
103	Joe Crede	.10
104	Jose Valentin	.10
105	Magglio Ordonez	.25
106	Mark Buehrle	.10
107	Paul Konerko	.10
108	Brandon Phillips	.10
109	C.C. Sabathia	.10
110	Ellis Burks	.10
111	Jeremy Guthrie	.10
112	Josh Bard	.10
113	Matt Lawton	.10
114	Milton Bradley	.10
115	Omar Vizquel	.20
116	Travis Hafner	.10
117	Bobby Higginson	.10
118	Carlos Pena	.10
119	Dmitri Young	.20
120	Eric Munson	.10
121	Jeremy Bonderman	.10
122	Nate Cornejo	.10
123	Omar Infante	.10
124	Ramon Santiago	.10
125	Angel Berroa	.10
126	Carlos Beltran	.25
127	Desi Relaford	.10
128	Jeremy Affeldt	.10
129	Joe Randa	.10
130	Ken Harvey	.10
131	Mike MacDougal	.10
132	Michael Tucker	.10
133	Mike Sweeney	.20
134	Raul Ibanez	.20
135	Runelvys Hernandez	.10
136	A.J. Pierzynski	.10
137	Brad Radke	.10
138	Corey Koskie	.10
139	Cristian Guzman	.10
140	Doug Mientkiewicz	.10
141	Dustan Mohr	.10
142	Jacque Jones	.10
143	Kenny Rogers	.10
144	Bobby Kielty	.10
145	Kyle Lohse	.10
146	Luis Rivas	.10
147	Torii Hunter	.25
148	Alfonso Soriano	.75
149	Andy Pettitte	.40
150	Bernie Williams	.40
151	David Wells	.10
152	Derek Jeter	2.00
153	Hideki Matsui	2.00
154	Jason Giambi	.75
155	Jorge Posada	.50
156	Jose Contreras	.40
157	Mike Mussina	.50
158	Nick Johnson	.10
159	Robin Ventura	.20
160	Roger Clemens	1.50
161	Barry Zito	.25
162	Chris Singleton	.10
163	Eric Byrnes	.10
164	Eric Chavez	.25
165	Erubiel Durazo	.10
166	Keith Foulke	.10
167	Mark Ellis	.10
168	Miguel Tejada	.40
169	Mark Mulder	.25
170	Ramon Hernandez	.10
171	Ted Lilly	.10
172	Terrence Long	.10
173	Tim Hudson	.25
174	Bret Boone	.25
175	Carlos Guillen	.10
176	Dan Wilson	.10
177	Edgar Martinez	.25
178	Freddy Garcia	.10
179	Gil Meche	.10
180	Ichiro Suzuki	1.00
181	Jamie Moyer	.10
182	Joel Pineiro	.10
183	John Olerud	.20
184	Mike Cameron	.10
185	Randy Winn	.10
186	Ryan Franklin	.10
187	Kazuhiro Sasaki	.10
188	Aubrey Huff	.10
189	Carl Crawford	.10
190	Joe Kennedy	.10
191	Marlon Anderson	.10
192	Rey Ordonez	.10
193	Rocco Baldelli	.25
194	Toby Hall	.10
195	Travis Lee	.10
196	Alex Rodriguez	1.50
197	Carl Everett	.10
198	Chan Ho Park	.10
199	Einar Diaz	.10
200	Hank Blalock	.50
201	Ismael Valdes	.10
202	Juan Gonzalez	.50
203	Mark Teixeira	.40
204	Mike Young	.10
205	Rafael Palmeiro	.50
206	Carlos Delgado	.50
207	Kelvim Escobar	.10
208	Eric Hinske	.10
209	Frank Catalanotto	.10
210	Josh Phelps	.10
211	Orlando Hudson	.10
212	Roy Halladay	.25
213	Shannon Stewart	.10
214	Vernon Wells	.25
215	Carlos Baerga	.10
216	Curt Schilling	.40
217	Junior Spivey	.10
218	Luis Gonzalez	.25
219	Lyle Overbay	.10
220	Mark Grace	.25

221	Matt Williams	.20
222	Randy Johnson	.75
223	Shea Hillenbrand	.10
224	Steve Finley	.10
225	Andruw Jones	.50
226	Chipper Jones	1.00
227	Gary Sheffield	.40
228	Greg Maddux	1.00
229	Javy Lopez	.25
230	John Smoltz	.25
231	Marcus Giles	.20
232	Mike Hampton	.10
233	Rafael Furcal	.25
234	Robert Fick	.10
235	Russ Ortiz	.10
236	Alex Gonzalez	.10
237	Carlos Zambrano	.10
238	Corey Patterson	.10
239	Hee Seop Choi	.10
240	Kerry Wood	.50
241	Mark Belhorn	.10
242	Mark Prior	1.50
243	Moises Alou	.25
244	Sammy Sosa	1.50
245	Aaron Boone	.10
246	Adam Dunn	.40
247	Austin Kearns	.25
248	Barry Larkin	.10
249	Felipe Lopez	.10
250	Jose Guillen	.10
251	Ken Griffey Jr.	1.00
252	Jason LaRue	.10
253	Scott Williamson	.10
254	Sean Casey	.20
255	Shawn Chacon	.10
256	Chris Stynes	.10
257	Jason Jennings	.10
258	Jay Payton	.20
259	Jose Hernandez	.10
260	Larry Walker	.25
261	Preston Wilson	.20
262	Ronnie Belliard	.10
263	Todd Helton	.50
264	A.J. Burnett	.10
265	Alex Gonzalez	.10
266	Brad Penny	.10
267	Derek Lee	.10
268	Ivan Rodriguez	.50
269	Josh Beckett	.50
270	Juan Encarnacion	.10
271	Juan Pierre	.10
272	Luis Castillo	.10
273	Mike Lowell	.10
274	Todd Hollandsworth	.10
275	Billy Wagner	.25
276	Brad Ausmus	.10
277	Craig Biggio	.25
278	Jeff Bagwell	.50
279	Jeff Kent	.25
280	Lance Berkman	.25
281	Richard Hidalgo	.10
282	Roy Oswalt	.25
283	Wade Miller	.10
284	Adrian Beltre	.10
285	Brian Jordan	.10
286	Cesar Izturis	.10
287	Dave Roberts	.10
288	Eric Gagne	.25
289	Fred McGriff	.25
290	Hideo Nomo	.40
291	Kazuhisa Ishii	.10
292	Kevin Brown	.25
293	Paul LoDuca	.10
294	Shawn Green	.40
295	Ben Sheets	.25
296	Geoff Jenkins	.25
297	Rey Sanchez	.10
298	Richie Sexson	.40
299	Wes Helms	.10
300	Brad Wilkerson	.10
301	Claudio Vargas	.10
302	Endy Chavez	.10
303	Fernando Tatis	.10
304	Javier Vazquez	.25
305	Jose Vidro	.10
306	Michael Barrett	.10
307	Orlando Cabrera	.20
308	Tony Armas Jr.	.10
309	Vladimir Guerrero	.75
310	Zach Day	.10
311	Al Leiter	.10
312	Cliff Floyd	.10
313	Jae Weong Seo	.10
314	Jeromy Burnitz	.10
315	Mike Piazza	1.00
316	Mo Vaughn	.10
317	Roberto Alomar	.40
318	Roger Cedeno	.10
319	Tom Glavine	.25
320	Jose Reyes	.40
321	Bobby Abreu	.20
322	Brett Myers	.10
323	David Bell	.10
324	Jim Thome	.50
325	Jimmy Rollins	.25
326	Kevin Millwood	.25

327	Marlon Byrd	.10
328	Mike Lieberthal	.10
329	Pat Burrell	.40
330	Randy Wolf	.10
331	Aramis Ramirez	.10
332	Brian Giles	.25
333	Jason Kendall	.20
334	Kenny Lofton	.20
335	Kip Wells	.10
336	Kris Benson	.10
337	Randall Simon	.10
338	Reggie Sanders	.10
339	Albert Pujols	2.00
340	Edgar Renteria	.10
341	Fernando Vina	.10
342	J.D. Drew	.10
343	Jim Edmonds	.25
344	Matt Morris	.10
345	Mike Matheny	.10
346	Scott Rolen	.50
347	Tino Martinez	.10
348	Woody Williams	.10
349	Brian Lawrence	.10
350	Mark Kotsay	.10
351	Mark Loretta	.10
352	Ramon Vazquez	.10
353	Rondell White	.10
354	Ryan Klesko	.25
355	Sean Burroughs	.10
356	Trevor Hoffman	.10
357	Xavier Nady	.10
358	Andres Galarraga	.10
359	Barry Bonds	2.00
360	Benito Santiago	.10
361	Deivi Cruz	.10
362	Edgardo Alfonzo	.10
363	J.T. Snow	.10
364	Jason Schmidt	.10
365	Kirk Rueter	.10
366	Kurt Ainsworth	.10
367	Marquis Grissom	.10
368	Ray Durham	.10
369	Rich Aurilia	.10
370	Tim Worrell	.10
371	Troy Glaus	.20
372	Melvin Mora	.10
373	Nomar Garciaparra	.75
374	Magglio Ordonez	.20
375	Omar Vizquel	.10
376	Dmitri Young	.10
377	Mike Sweeney	.10
378	Torii Hunter	.20
379	Derek Jeter	1.00
380	Barry Zito	.20
381	Ichiro Suzuki	.20
382	Rocco Baldelli	.20
383	Alex Rodriguez	.75
384	Carlos Delgado	.25
385	Randy Johnson	.40
386	Greg Maddux	.50
387	Sammy Sosa	.75
388	Ken Griffey Jr.	.50
389	Todd Helton	.25
390	Ivan Rodriguez	.25
391	Jeff Bagwell	.25
392	Hideo Nomo	.20
393	Richie Sexson	.20
394	Vladimir Guerrero	.40
395	Mike Piazza	.50
396	Jim Thome	.25
397	Jason Kendall	.10
398	Albert Pujols	1.00
399	Ryan Klesko	.10
400	Barry Bonds	1.00

Black Press Proofs

No pricing due to scarcity.
Production 10 Sets
Hot Pack exclusive.

Career Stat Line

Cards Serial #'d from

251-500:	3-5X
Print run 101-250:	4-6X

Print run 61-100: 4-8X
Print run 26-60: 8-15X
No pricing for P/R 25 or less.
Numbered to career statistic.

Season Stat Line

Print run 101-261:	4-6X
Print run 61-100:	4-8X
Print run 26-60:	8-15X

No pricing for P/R 25 or less.
Numbered to 2003 statistic.

All-Stars

AUSTIN KEARNS

	NM/M
Complete Set (20):	40.00
Common Player:	1.50
Production 1,000 Sets	
Black:	1-2X
Production 250 Sets	
1	Alex Rodriguez	5.00
2	Roger Clemens	5.00
3	Ichiro Suzuki	3.00
4	Barry Zito	1.50
5	Garret Anderson	1.50
6	Derek Jeter	5.00
7	Manny Ramirez	2.00
8	Pedro J. Martinez	2.00
9	Alfonso Soriano	2.50
10	Carlos Delgado	1.50
11	Barry Bonds	5.00
12	Andruw Jones	2.00
13	Scott Rolen	2.00
14	Austin Kearns	1.50
15	Mark Prior	4.00
16	Vladimir Guerrero	2.00
17	Jeff Bagwell	2.00
18	Mike Piazza	3.00
19	Albert Pujols	5.00
20	Randy Johnson	2.50

Bat Kings

	NM/M
Common Player:	5.00
Studio Current Player:	1.5X
Production 50	
Studio Retired:	No Pricing
Production 25	
1	Alex Rodriguez/250	10.00
2	Albert Pujols/250	15.00
3	Chipper Jones/250	12.00
4	Lance Berkman/250	5.00
5	Cal Ripken Jr./100	50.00
6	George Brett/100	30.00
7	Don Mattingly/100	40.00
8	Roberto Clemente/ 100	75.00

Craftsmen

	NM/M
Complete Set (15):	40.00

Common Player:		2.00
Production 2,000 Sets		
Black:		1-2X
Production 275 Sets		
Master Craftsmen:		1-2X
Production 150 Sets		
1	Alex Rodriguez	5.00
2	Mark Prior	4.00
3	Ichiro Suzuki	3.00
4	Barry Bonds	5.00
5	Ken Griffey Jr.	3.00
6	Alfonso Soriano	3.00
7	Mike Piazza	3.00
8	Chipper Jones	3.00
9	Derek Jeter	5.00
10	Randy Johnson	2.50
11	Sammy Sosa	4.00
12	Roger Clemens	4.00
13	Nomar Garciaparra	4.00
14	Greg Maddux	3.00
15	Albert Pujols	5.00

Diamond Kings Insert

	NM/M
Complete Set (25):	80.00
Common Player:	2.00
Production 2,500 Sets	
Studio Series:	1-2X
Production 250 Sets	
Black:	1.5-2X
Production 100 Sets	
1	Derek Jeter	8.00
2	Greg Maddux	6.00
3	Albert Pujols	8.00
4	Ichiro Suzuki	6.00
5	Alex Rodriguez	6.00
6	Roger Clemens	6.00
7	Andruw Jones	3.00
8	Barry Bonds	8.00
9	Jeff Bagwell	3.00
10	Randy Johnson	3.00
11	Scott Rolen	3.00
12	Lance Berkman	2.00
13	Barry Zito	2.00
14	Manny Ramirez	3.00
15	Carlos Delgado	2.50
16	Alfonso Soriano	4.00
17	Todd Helton	3.00
18	Mike Mussina	2.00
19	Austin Kearns	2.00
20	Nomar Garciaparra	6.00
21	Chipper Jones	4.00
22	Mark Prior	4.00
23	Jim Thome	3.00
24	Vladimir Guerrero	3.00
25	Pedro J. Martinez	3.00

Elite Series

	NM/M
Complete Set (15):	60.00
Common Player:	2.00

Production 1,500 Sets
Black: 1-2X
Production 150 Sets
Dominators: No Pricing
Production 25 Sets

1	Albert Pujols	8.00
2	Barry Zito	3.00
3	Gary Sheffield	3.00
4	Mike Mussina	3.00
5	Lance Berkman	2.00
6	Alfonso Soriano	4.00
7	Randy Johnson	4.00
8	Nomar Garciaparra	8.00
9	Austin Kearns	3.00
10	Manny Ramirez	3.00
11	Mark Prior	6.00
12	Alex Rodriguez	6.00
13	Derek Jeter	8.00
14	Barry Bonds	8.00
15	Roger Clemens	6.00

Inside View

NM/M
Complete Set (25): 50.00
Common Player: 1.00
Production 1,250 Sets

1	Derek Jeter	5.00
2	Greg Maddux	3.00
3	Albert Pujols	5.00
4	Ichiro Suzuki	3.00
5	Alex Rodriguez	4.00
6	Roger Clemens	5.00
7	Andruw Jones	1.50
8	Barry Bonds	5.00
9	Jeff Bagwell	2.00
10	Randy Johnson	2.00
11	Scott Rolen	2.00
12	Lance Berkman	1.00
13	Barry Zito	1.50
14	Manny Ramirez	2.00
15	Carlos Delgado	1.50
16	Alfonso Soriano	2.00
17	Todd Helton	2.00
18	Mike Mussina	1.50
19	Austin Kearns	1.50
20	Nomar Garciaparra	4.00
21	Chipper Jones	3.00
22	Mark Prior	4.00
23	Jim Thome	2.00
24	Vladimir Guerrero	2.00
25	Pedro J. Martinez	2.50

Jersey Kings

NM/M
Quantity produced listed
Studio Current Player: 1.5X
Production 50
Studio Retired: No Pricing
Production 25

1	Alfonso Soriano/250	10.00
2	Sammy Sosa/250	15.00
3	Roger Clemens/250	15.00
4	Nomar Garciaparra/250	12.00
5	Mark Prior/250	10.00
6	Vladimir Guerrero/250	8.00
7	Don Mattingly/100	40.00
8	Roberto Clemente/100	80.00
9	George Brett/100	35.00
10	Nolan Ryan/100	40.00
11	Cal Ripken Jr./100	55.00
12	Mike Schmidt/100	40.00

Longball Leaders

NM/M
Complete Set (10): 20.00
Common Player: 1.50
Production 1,500 Sets
Black: 1-2X
Production 250 Sets
Die-Cuts: 1.5-3X

Production 50 Sets

1	Barry Bonds	5.00
2	Alfonso Soriano	3.00
3	Adam Dunn	1.50
4	Alex Rodriguez	5.00
5	Jim Thome	2.00
6	Garret Anderson	1.50
7	Juan Gonzalez	2.00
8	Jeff Bagwell	2.00
9	Gary Sheffield	1.50
10	Sammy Sosa	4.00

Mound Marvels

NM/M
Complete Set (15): 20.00
Common Player: 1.00
Production 750 Sets
Black: 1-2X
Production 175 Sets

1	Mark Prior	4.00
2	Curt Schilling	1.50
3	Mike Mussina	1.50
4	Kevin Brown	1.50
5	Pedro J. Martinez	2.50
6	Mark Mulder	1.00
7	Kerry Wood	1.50
8	Greg Maddux	3.00
9	Kevin Millwood	1.00
10	Barry Zito	1.50
11	Roger Clemens	5.00
12	Randy Johnson	2.50
13	Hideo Nomo	1.50
14	Tim Hudson	1.50
15	Tom Glavine	1.50

Power Alley Red

NM/M
Complete Set (20): 50.00
Common Player: 2.00
Production 2,500 Sets
Red Die-Cut: 1-2X
Production 250 Sets
Blues: 1X
Production 1,000 Sets
Blue Die-Cuts: 1.5-2X
Production 100 Sets
Purples: 1-2X
Production 250 Sets
Purple Die-Cuts: No Pricing
Production 25 Sets
Yellows: 1.5-2X
Production 100 Sets
Yellow Die-Cuts: No Pricing
Greens: No Pricing
Production 25 Sets
Green Die-Cuts: No Pricing
Production 5 Sets

1	Albert Pujols	8.00
2	Mike Piazza	5.00
3	Carlos Delgado	2.00
4	Barry Bonds	8.00
5	Jim Edmonds	2.00
6	Nomar Garciaparra	6.00
7	Alfonso Soriano	4.00
8	Alex Rodriguez	6.00
9	Lance Berkman	2.00
10	Scott Rolen	3.00
11	Manny Ramirez	3.00
12	Rafael Palmeiro	4.00
13	Sammy Sosa	6.00
14	Adam Dunn	2.00
15	Andruw Jones	2.00
16	Jim Thome	3.00
17	Jason Giambi	3.00
18	Jeff Bagwell	3.00
19	Juan Gonzalez	3.00
20	Austin Kearns	3.00

Production Line OPS

NM/M
Complete Set (10): 25.00
Varying quanties produced
Black: 1-2X
Production 125 Sets
Die-Cuts: 1-2X
Production 100 Sets

1	Albert Pujols/1,106	5.00
2	Barry Bonds/1,278	5.00
3	Gary Sheffield/1,023	1.50
4	Todd Helton/1,088	2.00
5	Scott Rolen/910	3.00
6	Manny Ramirez/1,014	3.00
7	Alex Rodriguez/995	5.00
8	Jim Thome/958	3.00
9	Jason Giambi/939	3.00
10	Frank Thomas/952	3.00

Production Line Slugging

NM/M
Complete Set (10): 25.00
Varying quantities produced
Black: 1-2X
Production 75 Sets
Die-Cuts: 1-2X
Production 100 Sets

1	Alex Rodriguez/604	6.00
2	Frank Thomas/562	3.00
3	Garret Anderson/541	2.00
4	Albert Pujols/667	6.00
5	Sammy Sosa/553	5.00
6	Gary Sheffield/604	2.00
7	Manny Ramirez/587	3.00
8	Jim Edmonds/617	2.00
9	Barry Bonds/688	6.00
10	Todd Helton/630	3.00

Production Line OBP

NM/M
Complete Set (10): 25.00
Common Player: 2.00
Die-Cuts: 1-2X
Production 100 Sets
Black: 2-3X
Production 40 Sets

1	Todd Helton/458	3.00
2	Albert Pujols/439	6.00
3	Larry Walker/422	2.00
4	Barry Bonds/529	6.00
5	Chipper Jones/402	4.00
6	Manny Ramirez/427	3.00
7	Gary Sheffield/419	2.00
8	Lance Berkman/412	2.00
9	Alex Rodriguez/396	6.00
10	Jason Giambi/412	3.00

Production Line Average

NM/M
Complete Set (10): 35.00
Common Player: 2.00
Die-Cuts: 1-2X
Production 100 Sets
Black: 2-3X
Production 35 Sets

1	Gary Sheffield/330	2.00
2	Ichiro Suzuki/312	5.00
3	Todd Helton/358	3.00
4	Manny Ramirez/325	3.00
5	Garret Anderson/315	2.00
6	Barry Bonds/341	8.00
7	Albert Pujols/359	8.00
8	Derek Jeter/324	8.00
9	Nomar Garciaparra/301	6.00
10	Hank Blalock/300	3.00

Timber & Threads

NM/M
Common Player: 4.00
Inserted 1:40
Studio Series: 1.5X
Production 50 Sets

1	Adam Dunn	6.00
2	Alex Rodriguez - Blue	10.00
3	Alex Rodriguez - White	10.00
4	Andruw Jones	6.00
5	Austin Kearns	6.00
6	Carlos Beltran	4.00
7	Carlos Lee	4.00
8	Frank Thomas	8.00
9	Greg Maddux	10.00
10	Hideo Nomo	10.00

11	Jeff Bagwell	8.00
12	Lance Berkman	4.00
13	Magglio Ordonez	4.00
14	Mike Sweeney	4.00
15	Randy Johnson	8.00
16	Rocco Baldelli	10.00
17	Roger Clemens	12.00
18	Sammy Sosa	12.00
19	Shawn Green	4.00
20	Tom Glavine	6.00
21	Adam Dunn	6.00
22	Andruw Jones	6.00
23	Bobby Abreu	4.00
24	Hank Blalock	6.00
25	Ivan Rodriguez	6.00
26	Jim Edmonds	6.00
27	Josh Phelps	4.00
28	Juan Gonzalez	6.00
29	Lance Berkman	4.00
30	Larry Walker	4.00
31	Magglio Ordonez	4.00
32	Manny Ramirez	8.00
33	Mike Piazza	10.00
34	Nomar Garciaparra	10.00
35	Paul LoDuca	4.00
36	Roberto Alomar	6.00
37	Rocco Baldelli	10.00
38	Sammy Sosa	12.00
39	Vernon Wells	4.00
40	Vladimir Guerrero	8.00

2004 Donruss Classics

NM/M
Complete Set (213):
Common Player: .40
Common (151-210): 3.00
Production 1,999
Pack (6): 6.00
Box (18): 90.00

1	Albert Pujols	2.50
2	Derek Jeter	3.00
3	Hank Blalock	.50
4	Shannon Stewart	.40
5	Jason Giambi	1.00
6	Carlos Lee	.40
7	Trot Nixon	.40
8	Bret Boone	.50
9	Mark Mulder	.40
10	Mariano Rivera	.50
11	Scott Podsednik	.75
12	Jim Edmonds	.50
13	Mike Lowell	.50
14	Robin Ventura	.40
15	Brian Giles	.50
16	Jose Vidro	.40
17	Manny Ramirez	.75
18	Alex Rodriquez	2.50
19	Carlos Beltran	.50
20	Hideki Matsui	2.50
21	Johan Santana	.40
22	Richie Sexson	.50
23	Chipper Jones	1.00
24	Steve Finley	.40
25	Mark Prior	1.50
26	Alexis Rios	.40
27	Rafael Palmeiro	.75
28	Jorge Posada	.50
29	Barry Zito	.50
30	Jamie Moyer	.40
31	Preston Wilson	.40
32	Miguel Cabrera	.75
33	Pedro Martinez	1.00
34	Curt Schilling	.75
35	Hee Seop Choi	.40
36	Dontrelle Willis	.50
37	Rafael Soriano	.40
38	Richard Fischer	.40
39	Brian Tallet	.40
40	Jose Castillo	.40
41	Wade Miller	.40
42	Jose Contreras	.40
43	Runelvys Hernandez	.40
44	Joe Borchard	.40
45	Kazuhisa Ishii	.40

46	Jose Reyes	.50
47	Adam Dunn	.50
48	Randy Johnson	1.00
49	Brandon Phillips	.40
50	Scott Rolen	1.00
51	Ken Griffey Jr.	1.50
52	Tom Glavine	.50
53	Cliff Lee	.40
54	Chien-Ming Wang	.50
55	Roy Oswalt	.40
56	Austin Kearns	.50
57	Jhonny Peralta	.50
58	Greg Maddux	1.50
59	Mark Grace	.50
60	Jae Weong Seo	.40
61	Nic Jackson	.40
62	Roger Clemens	2.50
63	Jimmy Gobble	.40
64	Travis Hafner	.40
65	Paul Konerko	.40
66	Jerome Williams	.40
67	Ryan Klesko	.50
68	Alexis Gomez	.40
69	Omar Vizquel	.40
70	Zach Day	.40
71	Rickey Henderson	.50
72	Morgan Ensberg	.40
73	Josh Beckett	.75
74	Garrett Atkins	.40
75	Sean Casey	.40
76	Julio Franco	.40
77	Lyle Overbay	.40
78	Josh Phelps	.40
79	Juan Gonzalez	.75
80	Rich Harden	.40
81	Bernie Williams	.50
82	Torii Hunter	.40
83	Angel Berroa	.40
84	Jody Gerut	.40
85	Roberto Alomar	.50
86	Byung-Hyun Kim	.40
87	Jay Gibbons	.40
88	Chone Figgins	.40
89	Fred McGriff	.50
90	Rich Aurilia	.40
91	Xavier Nady	.40
92	Marlon Byrd	.40
93	Mike Piazza	1.50
94	Vladimir Guerrero	1.00
95	Shawn Green	.50
96	Jeff Kent	.50
97	Ivan Rodriguez	.75
98	Jay Payton	.40
99	Barry Larkin	.50
100	Mike Sweeney	.40
101	Adrian Beltre	.40
102	Robby Hammock	.40
103	Orlando Hudson	.40
104	Mark Teixeira	.50
105	Hong-Chih Kuo	.40
106	Eric Chavez	.50
107	Nick Johnson	.40
108	Jacque Jones	.40
109	Ken Harvey	.40
110	Aramis Ramirez	.40
111	Victor Martinez	.40
112	Joe Crede	.40
113	Jason Varitek	.40
114	Troy Glaus	.50
115	Billy Wagner	.40
116	Kerry Wood	1.00
117	Hideo Nomo	.50
118	Brandon Webb	.40
119	Craig Biggio	.40
120	Orlando Cabrera	.40
121	Sammy Sosa	2.00
122	Bobby Abreu	.50
123	Andruw Jones	.75
124	Jeff Bagwell	.75
125	Jim Thome	1.00
126	Javy Lopez	.50
127	Luis Castillo	.40
128	Todd Helton	.75
129	Roy Halladay	.50
130	Mike Mussina	.50
131	Eric Byrnes	.40
132	Eric Hinske	.40
133	Nomar Garciaparra	2.00
134	Edgar Martinez	.50
135	Rocco Baldelli	.50
136	Miguel Tejada	.50
137	Alfonso Soriano	1.00
138	Carlos Delgado	.75
139	Rafael Furcal	.50
140	Ichiro Suzuki	2.00
141	Aubrey Huff	.40
142	Garret Anderson	.50
143	Vernon Wells	.40
144	Magglio Ordonez	.50
145	Brett Myers	.40
146	Luis Gonzalez	.40
147	Lance Berkman	.50
148	Frank Thomas	.75
149	Gary Sheffield	.50
150	Tim Hudson	.50
151	Duke Snider	3.00

152	Carl Yastrzemski	4.00
153	Whitey Ford	3.00
154	Cal Ripken Jr.	8.00
155	Dwight Gooden	2.00
156	Warren Spahn	4.00
157	Bob Gibson	3.00
158	Don Mattingly	6.00
159	Jack Morris	2.00
160	Jim Bunning	2.00
161	Fergie Jenkins	2.00
162	Brooks Robinson	3.00
163	George Kell	2.00
164	Darryl Strawberry	2.00
165	Robin Roberts	2.00
166	Monte Irvin	2.00
167	Ernie Banks	4.00
168	Wade Boggs	3.00
169	Gaylord Perry	2.00
170	Keith Hernandez	2.00
171	Lou Brock	3.00
172	Frank Robinson	3.00
173	Nolan Ryan	8.00
174	Stan Musial	5.00
175	Eddie Murray	3.00
176	Byron Gettis	3.00
177	Merkin Valdez RC	3.00
178	Rickie Weeks	4.00
179	Akinori Otsuka RC	3.00
180	Brian Bruney	3.00
181	Freddy Guzman RC	3.00
182	Brendan Harris	3.00
183	John Gall RC	3.00
184	Jason Kubel	3.00
185	Delmon Young	4.00
186	Ryan Howard	3.00
187	Adam Loewen	3.00
188	J.D. Durbin	3.00
189	Dan Haren	3.00
190	Dustin McGowan	3.00
191	Chad Gaudin	3.00
192	Preston Larrison	3.00
193	Ramon Nivar	3.00
194	Ronald Belisario RC	3.00
195	Mike Gosling	3.00
196	Kevin Youkilis	3.00
197	Ryan Wagner	3.00
198	Bubba Nelson	3.00
199	Edwin Jackson	3.00
200	Chris Burke	3.00
201	Carlos Hines RC	3.00
202	Greg Dobbs RC	3.00
203	Jamie Brown RC	3.00
204	David Crouthers	3.00
205	Ian Snell RC	5.00
206	Gary Carter	3.00
207	Dale Murphy	3.00
208	Ryne Sandberg	5.00
209	Phil Niekro	2.00
210	Don Sutton	5.00
211	Alex Rodriguez/ Yankees/SP	5.00
212	Alfonso Soriano/ Rangers/SP	1.00
213	Greg Maddux/ Cubs/SP	3.00

Timeless Tributes Green

Cards (1-150):	4-6X
Cards (151-210):	1-2X
Production 50 Sets	

Timeless Tributes Platinum

No Pricing
Production One Set

Timeless Tributes Red

Red (1-150):	2-4X
Red (151-210):	1-1.5X
Production 100 Sets	

Classic Singles Jersey

NM/M

Quantity produced listed
Prime: No Pricing
Production One Set

2	Nolan Ryan/50	35.00
3	Stan Musial/15	50.00
6	Eddie Murray/100	10.00
7	Roy Campanella/Pants/50	20.00
8	Robin Yount/100	15.00
9	Roberto Clemente/25	75.00
10	Don Mattingly/100	20.00
11	Bob Gibson/15	25.00
12	Carl Yastrzemski/50	20.00
13	Mark Grace/25	20.00
14	Jack Morris/100	6.00
15	Rickey Henderson/25	20.00
16	Reggie Jackson/50	15.00
17	Pee Wee Reese/25	25.00
18	Marty Marion/100	6.00
19	Tommy John/100	6.00
20	Roger Maris/25	50.00
21	Cal Ripken Jr./25	75.00
22	Red Schoendienst/25	10.00
23	Willie Stargell/100	15.00
24	Paul Molitor/100	10.00
25	Whitey Ford/50	15.00
26	Alan Trammell/100	10.00
27	Sammy Sosa/50	20.00
28	Bobby Doerr/50	8.00
29	Rod Carew/100	10.00
30	Yogi Berra/15	35.00
31	Phil Rizzuto/25	20.00
32	George Brett/50	40.00

Classic Singles Bat

NM/M

Quantity produced listed

1	Babe Ruth/15	250.00
3	Stan Musial/25	30.00
4	Ted Williams/25	100.00
5	Lou Gehrig/50	125.00
6	Eddie Murray/50	15.00
7	Roy Campanella/50	20.00
8	Robin Yount/50	20.00
9	Roberto Clemente/25	70.00
10	Don Mattingly/50	25.00
12	Carl Yastrzemski/50	20.00
13	Mark Grace/50	15.00
15	Rickey Henderson/50	15.00
16	Reggie Jackson/50	15.00
17	Pee Wee Reese/50	15.00
20	Roger Maris/25	40.00
21	Cal Ripken Jr./50	60.00
23	Willie Stargell/50	15.00
24	Paul Molitor/50	20.00
26	Alan Trammell/50	12.00
27	Sammy Sosa/50	20.00
28	Bobby Doerr/50	8.00
29	Rod Carew/50	15.00
30	Yogi Berra/25	20.00
32	George Brett/50	30.00

Classic Singles Jersey-Bat

NM/M

Quantity produced listed
Prime: No Pricing
Production One Set

2	Nolan Ryan/25	50.00
3	Stan Musial/15	45.00
6	Eddie Murray/25	25.00
7	Roy Campanella/Pants/25	35.00
8	Robin Yount/25	40.00
9	Roberto Clemente/25	125.00
10	Don Mattingly/25	40.00
12	Carl Yastrzemski/25	50.00
13	Mark Grace/25	20.00
15	Rickey Henderson/25	25.00
16	Reggie Jackson/25	25.00
17	Pee Wee Reese/25	25.00
20	Roger Maris/25	75.00
21	Cal Ripken Jr./25	75.00
23	Willie Stargell/25	20.00
24	Paul Molitor/25	25.00
26	Alan Trammell/25	20.00
27	Sammy Sosa/25	25.00
28	Bobby Doerr/25	25.00
29	Rod Carew/25	30.00
30	Yogi Berra/15	40.00
32	George Brett/25	40.00

Classic Combos Jersey

NM/M

Quantity produced listed
Prime: No Pricing
Production One Set

1	Babe Ruth/Pants, Lou Gehrig/Pants/15	500.00
2	Roy Campanella/Pants, Pee Wee Reese/25	30.00
3	Ted Williams, Carl Yastrzemski/15	200.00
4	Roberto Clemente, Willie Stargell/25	85.00
5	Eddie Murray, Cal Ripken Jr./25	75.00
6	Roger Maris, Yogi Berra/25	65.00
8	Whitey Ford, Yogi Berra/25	30.00
9	Marty Marion, Stan Musial/25	40.00
10	Nolan Ryan, Rod Carew/25	40.00
11	Don Mattingly, Rickey Henderson/50	40.00
12	Jack Morris, Alan Trammell/50	15.00
13	Whitey Ford, Phil Rizzuto/50	30.00
14	Marty Marion, Red Schoendienst/25	15.00
15	Robin Yount, Paul Molitor/50	40.00
16	Mark Grace, Sammy Sosa/50	30.00
17	Ted Williams, Bobby Doerr/15	150.00
18	Reggie Jackson, Rod Carew/50	25.00

Classic Combos Bat

NM/M

Quantity produced listed

1	Babe Ruth, Lou Gehrig/25	375.00
2	Roy Campanella, Pee Wee Reese/50	25.00
3	Ted Williams, Carl Yastrzemski/25	125.00
4	Roberto Clemente, Willie Stargell/25	100.00
5	Eddie Murray, Cal Ripken Jr./50	50.00
6	Roger Maris, Yogi Berra/25	65.00
10	Nolan Ryan, Rod Carew/50	35.00
11	Don Mattingly, Rickey Henderson/50	40.00
15	Robin Yount, Paul Molitor/50	40.00
16	Mark Grace, Sammy Sosa/50	30.00
17	Ted Williams, Bobby Doerr/25	80.00
18	Reggie Jackson, Rod Carew/50	25.00

Classic Combos Quad

NM/M

Quantity produced listed
Prime: No Pricing
Production One Set

2	Roy Campanella/Pants, Pee Wee Reese/25	50.00
3	Ted Williams, Carl Yastrzemski/15	250.00
4	Roberto Clemente, Willie Stargell/25	200.00
5	Eddie Murray, Cal Ripken Jr./25	125.00
6	Roger Maris, Yogi Berra/15	150.00
10	Nolan Ryan, Rod Carew/25	70.00
11	Don Mattingly, Rickey Henderson/25	80.00
15	Robin Yount, Paul Molitor/25	75.00
16	Mark Grace, Sammy Sosa/25	60.00
17	Ted Williams, Bobby Doerr/15	200.00
18	Reggie Jackson, Rod Carew/25	40.00

Dress Code Jersey

		NM/M
Common Player:		4.00
Production 100 Sets		
Number:		1X
Production 100 Sets		
Prime:		2X
Production 25 Sets		
1	Derek Jeter	25.00
2	Kerry Wood	15.00
3	Nomar Garciaparra	10.00
4	Jacque Jones	4.00
5	Mark Teixeira	5.00
6	Troy Glaus	6.00
7	Todd Helton	6.00
8	Miguel Tejada	6.00
9	Mike Piazza	10.00
11	Mike Sweeney	4.00
12	Albert Pujols	15.00
13	Rickey Henderson	8.00
14	Chipper Jones	8.00
15	Don Mattingly	25.00
16	Shawn Green	5.00
17	Mark Grace	10.00
18	Jason Giambi	8.00
19	Barry Zito	8.00
20	Sammy Sosa	12.00
21	Jay Gibbons	4.00
22	Rafael Palmeiro	8.00
23	Frank Thomas	8.00
24	Manny Ramirez	6.00
25	Mike Mussina	8.00
26	Magglio Ordonez	6.00
27	Rocco Baldelli	6.00
28	Andruw Jones	8.00
29	Torii Hunter	6.00
30	Ivan Rodriguez	8.00
31	Jeff Bagwell	8.00
32	Mark Mulder	6.00
33	Trot Nixon	5.00
34	Cal Ripken Jr./25	80.00
35	Dontrelle Willis	6.00
36	Hank Blalock	5.00
37	Brandon Webb	4.00
38	Miguel Cabrera	12.00
39	Hideo Nomo	8.00
40	Shannon Stewart	4.00
41	Tim Hudson	6.00
42	Pedro Martinez	8.00
43	Hee Seop Choi	4.00
44	Randy Johnson	8.00
45	Tony Gwynn	10.00
46	Mark Prior	10.00
47	Eric Chavez	6.00
48	Alex Rodriguez	10.00
49	Johan Santana	4.00
50	Alfonso Soriano	8.00

Dress Code Bat

		NM/M
Common Player:		5.00
Production 50 Sets		
Combo Material:		1-1.5X
Production 50 Sets		
1	Derek Jeter	25.00
2	Kerry Wood	15.00
3	Nomar Garciaparra	15.00
4	Jacque Jones	5.00
5	Mark Teixeira	6.00
6	Troy Glaus	8.00
7	Todd Helton	10.00
8	Miguel Tejada	6.00
9	Mike Piazza	12.00
11	Mike Sweeney	5.00
12	Albert Pujols	20.00
13	Rickey Henderson	10.00
14	Chipper Jones	10.00
15	Don Mattingly	25.00
16	Shawn Green	5.00
17	Mark Grace	10.00
18	Jason Giambi	8.00
19	Barry Zito	8.00
20	Sammy Sosa	15.00
22	Rafael Palmeiro	10.00
23	Frank Thomas	10.00
24	Manny Ramirez	8.00
25	Mike Mussina	10.00
26	Magglio Ordonez	6.00
27	Rocco Baldelli	12.00
28	Andruw Jones	8.00
29	Torii Hunter	6.00
30	Ivan Rodriguez	10.00

31	Jeff Bagwell	10.00
32	Mark Mulder	6.00
33	Trot Nixon	10.00
34	Cal Ripken Jr.	60.00
35	Dontrelle Willis	8.00
36	Hank Blalock	8.00
37	Brandon Webb	8.00
38	Miguel Cabrera	10.00
39	Hideo Nomo	10.00
40	Shannon Stewart	
41	Tim Hudson	8.00
42	Pedro Martinez	12.00
43	Hee Seop Choi	6.00
44	Randy Johnson	10.00
45	Tony Gwynn	15.00
46	Mark Prior	10.00
47	Eric Chavez	8.00
48	Alex Rodriguez	15.00
50	Alfonso Soriano	12.00

Dress Code Combos Signature

		NM/M
Quantity produced listed		
Prime:		No Pricing
Production One Set		
4	Jacque Jones/Jsy/25	15.00
21	Jay Gibbons/Jsy/25	25.00
32	Mark Mulder/Jsy/25	35.00
33	Trot Nixon/Jsy/25	50.00
35	Dontrelle Willis/Jsy/25	40.00
38	Miguel Cabrera/Jsy/25	70.00
40	Shannon Stewart/Jsy/25	20.00
49	Johan Santana/Jsy/25	40.00

Famous Foursomes

		NM/M
Production 99 Sets		
1	Roy Campanella, Pee Wee Reese, Jackie Robinson, Duke Snider	15.00
2	Stan Musial, Bob Gibson, Red Schoendienst, Clete Boyer	15.00

Famous Foursomes Jersey

No Pricing
Production 10 Sets
Prime: No Pricing
Production One Set

Legendary Lumberjacks

		NM/M
Common Player:		2.00
Production 1,000 Sets		
Spikes:		1-2X
Production 100 Sets		
Hats:		2-3X
Production 50 Sets		
Jackets:		2-3X
Production 50 Sets		
Jerseys:		1X
Production 500 Sets		
Leather:		1-2X
Production 100 Sets		
Pants:		2-3X
Production 50 Sets		
1	Tony Gwynn	3.00
2	Mike Schmidt	5.00
3	Johnny Bench	4.00
4	Roger Maris	5.00
5	Ted Williams	8.00
6	George Brett	6.00
7	Carlton Fisk	2.00
8	Reggie Jackson	3.00
9	Joe Morgan	2.00
10	Bo Jackson	3.00
11	Stan Musial	4.00
12	Andre Dawson	2.00
13	Rickey Henderson	2.00
14	Cal Ripken Jr.	8.00
15	Dale Murphy	2.00
16	Kirby Puckett	4.00
17	Don Mattingly	5.00
18	Brooks Robinson	3.00
19	Orlando Cepeda	2.00
20	Reggie Jackson	3.00
21	Roberto Clemente	6.00
22	Ernie Banks	4.00
23	Frank Robinson	3.00
24	Harmon Killebrew	3.00
25	Willie Stargell	3.00
26	Al Kaline	4.00
27	Carl Yastrzemski	4.00
28	Duke Snider	3.00
29	Dave Winfield	2.00
30	Eddie Murray	3.00
31	Eddie Matthews	3.00
32	Gary Carter	2.00
33	Rod Carew	3.00
34	Jimmie Foxx	4.00
35	Mel Ott	3.00
36	Paul Molitor	3.00
37	Thurman Munson	4.00
38	Rogers Hornsby	3.00
39	Robin Yount	4.00
40	Wade Boggs	3.00
41	Jackie Robinson	5.00
42	Rickey Henderson	2.00
43	Ty Cobb	5.00
44	Yogi Berra	3.00
45	Roy Campanella	3.00
46	Luis Aparicio	2.00
47	Phil Rizzuto	3.00
48	Roger Maris	5.00
49	Reggie Jackson	3.00
50	Lou Gehrig	6.00
51	Rafael Palmeiro	3.00
52	Sammy Sosa	5.00
53	Roger Clemens	6.00
54	Nolan Ryan	8.00
55	Steve Carlton	3.00
56	Rod Carew	3.00
57	Whitey Ford	3.00
58	Fergie Jenkins	2.00
59	Babe Ruth	8.00
60	R Henderson	2.00

Legendary Lumberjacks Material

		NM/M
Quantity produced listed		
1	Tony Gwynn/100	15.00

		NM/M
2	Mike Schmidt/100	15.00
3	Johnny Bench/100	12.00
4	Roger Maris /25	40.00
5	Ted Williams/25	100.00
6	George Brett/100	25.00
7	Carlton Fisk/100	10.00
8	Reggie Jackson/100	12.00
9	Joe Morgan/100	5.00
10	Bo Jackson/100	15.00
11	Stan Musial/25	35.00
12	Andre Dawson/100	5.00
13	R Henderson/100	5.00
14	Cal Ripken Jr./100	40.00
15	Dale Murphy/100	12.00
16	Kirby Puckett/100	15.00
17	Don Mattingly/100	20.00
18	Brooks Robinson/100	15.00
19	Orlando Cepeda/100	5.00
20	Reggie Jackson/100	12.00
21	Roberto Clemente/25	65.00
22	Ernie Banks/100	15.00
23	Frank Robinson/100	15.00
24	Harmon Killebrew/100	20.00
25	Willie Stargell/100	15.00
26	Al Kaline/100	15.00
27	Carl Yastrzemski/100	15.00
29	Dave Winfield/100	5.00
30	Eddie Murray/100	15.00
31	Eddie Mathews/50	20.00
32	Gary Carter/100	8.00
33	Rod Carew/100	10.00
35	Mel Ott/25	35.00
36	Paul Molitor/100	10.00
37	Thurman Munson/50	20.00
38	Rogers Hornsby/25	50.00
39	Robin Yount/100	5.00
40	Wade Boggs/100	10.00
42	Rickey Henderson/50	10.00
44	Yogi Berra/25	20.00
45	Roy Campanella/25	30.00
46	Luis Aparicio/100	8.00
48	Roger Maris/25	40.00
49	Reggie Jackson/100	15.00
50	Lou Gehrig/25	125.00
51	Rafael Palmeiro/100	8.00
52	Sammy Sosa/100	15.00
56	Rod Carew/100	8.00
60	R Henderson/100	10.00

Legendary Leather Material

		NM/M
Quantity produced listed		
16	Kirby Puckett/ Fld Glv/25	40.00
32	Gary Carter/ Fld Glv/25	35.00
51	Rafael Palmeiro/ Fld Glv/25	25.00
52	Sammy Sosa/ Btg Glv/25	50.00
55	Steve Carlton/ Fld Glv/25	15.00
58	Fergie Jenkins/ Fld Glv/25	15.00

Legendary Jerseys Material

		NM/M
Quantity produced listed		
Number:		1X
Production 3-50		
No pricing for production 15 or less.		
Prime:		No Pricing
Production One Set		
1	Tony Gwynn/50	20.00
2	Mike Schmidt/25	35.00
3	Johnny Bench/50	15.00
6	George Brett/25	50.00

7	Carlton Fisk/50	10.00
8	Reggie Jackson/25	30.00
9	Joe Morgan/25	15.00
10	Bo Jackson/25	50.00
12	Andre Dawson/50	10.00
13	R Henderson/25	20.00
14	Cal Ripken Jr./25	85.00
15	Dale Murphy/25	30.00
16	Kirby Puckett/50	15.00
17	Don Mattingly/50	25.00
18	Brooks Robinson/50	20.00
19	Orlando Cepeda/50	8.00
20	Reggie Jackson/25	25.00
21	Roberto Clemente/25	75.00
23	Frank Robinson/50	10.00
24	Harmon Killebrew/50	15.00
25	Willie Stargell/50	20.00
27	Carl Yastrzemski/50	25.00
29	Dave Winfield/50	10.00
30	Eddie Murray/50	20.00
31	Eddie Mathews/25	25.00
32	Gary Carter/50	8.00
33	Rod Carew/25	20.00
36	Paul Molitor/50	15.00
39	Robin Yount/50	25.00
40	Wade Boggs/50	15.00
42	Rickey Henderson/25	25.00
44	Yogi Berra/15	35.00
46	Luis Aparicio/50	8.00
47	Phil Rizzuto/25	20.00
48	Roger Maris/25	40.00
49	Reggie Jackson/25	15.00
51	Rafael Palmeiro/50	10.00
52	Sammy Sosa/50	20.00
53	Roger Clemens/25	25.00
p4	Nolan Ryan/50	30.00
55	Steve Carlton/50	8.00
56	Rod Carew/50	15.00
57	Whitey Ford/25	35.00
59	Babe Ruth/5	

Legendary Spikes Material

NM/M

Quantity produced listed

13	R Henderson/Yanks/25	30.00
17	Don Mattingly/50	40.00
29	Dave Winfield/50	15.00
42	Rickey Henderson/A's/25	30.00
51	Rafael Palmeiro/25	25.00
52	Sammy Sosa/50	30.00
60	R Henderson/Angels/25	30.00

Legendary Pants Material

NM/M

Quantity produced listed

1	Tony Gwynn/25	25.00
12	Andre Dawson/25	10.00
24	Harmon Killebrew/50	20.00
26	Al Kaline/50	20.00
45	Roy Campanella/25	25.00
46	Luis Aparicio/50	10.00
47	Phil Rizzuto/50	15.00
48	Roger Maris/A's/25	30.00
51	Rafael Palmeiro/25	20.00
56	Rod Carew/Angels/50	15.00
57	Whitey Ford/25	25.00
58	Fergie Jenkins/25	20.00
59	Babe Ruth/3	

Legendary Jackets Material

NM/M

Production 100 Sets

2	Mike Schmidt	15.00
8	Reggie Jackson/A's	15.00
17	Don Mattingly	20.00
32	Gary Carter	5.00
54	Nolan Ryan	30.00
56	Rod Carew/Angels	10.00

Legendary Hats Material

NM/M

Quantity produced listed

1	Tony Gwynn/10	
2	Mike Schmidt/25	50.00
6	George Brett/25	60.00
14	Cal Ripken Jr./25	100.00
16	Kirby Puckett/25	30.00
20	Reggie Jackson/Yanks/25	25.00
22	Ernie Banks/25	35.00
29	Dave Winfield/25	15.00
40	Wade Boggs/25	25.00
42	Rickey Henderson/A'S/25	20.00

49	Reggie Jackson/Angels/25	25.00
51	Rafael Palmeiro/25	20.00
52	Sammy Sosa/25	30.00
55	Steve Carlton/25	15.00
56	Rod Carew/Angels/25	20.00
60	R Henderson/Angels/25	20.00

Membership

NM/M

Complete Set (25):		70.00
Common Player:		2.00

Production 2,499 Sets

1	Stan Musial	4.00
2	Ted Williams	5.00
3	Early Wynn	2.00
4	Roberto Clemente	5.00
5	Al Kaline	4.00
6	Bob Gibson	3.00
7	Lou Brock	2.00
8	Carl Yastrzemski	4.00
9	Gaylord Perry	2.00
10	Fergie Jenkins	2.00
11	Steve Carlton	2.00
12	Reggie Jackson	3.00
13	Rod Carew	3.00
14	Bert Blyleven	2.00
15	Mike Schmidt	4.00
16	Nolan Ryan	6.00
17	Robin Yount	4.00
18	George Brett	6.00
19	Eddie Murray	3.00
20	Tony Gwynn	3.00
21	Cal Ripken Jr.	8.00
22	Randy Johnson	4.00
23	Sammy Sosa	5.00
24	Rafael Palmeiro	3.00
25	Roger Clemens	5.00

Membership VIP Bat

NM/M

Quantity produced listed

1	Stan Musial/25	40.00
2	Ted Williams/25	100.00
4	Roberto Clemente/25	65.00
5	Al Kaline/25	20.00
7	Lou Brock/25	20.00
8	Carl Yastrzemski/25	25.00
11	Steve Carlton/25	15.00
12	Reggie Jackson/25	20.00
13	Rod Carew/25	20.00
15	Mike Schmidt/25	30.00
17	Robin Yount/25	25.00
19	Eddie Murray/25	25.00
20	Tony Gwynn/25	25.00
22	Randy Johnson/25	20.00
23	Sammy Sosa/25	30.00
24	Rafael Palmeiro/25	20.00
25	Roger Clemens/25	25.00

Membership VIP Combos Material

NM/M

Quantity produced listed

Prime: No Pricing

Production One Set

1	Stan Musial/Bat-Jsy/15	40.00
4	Roberto Clemente/Bat-Jsy/25	100.00
5	Al Kaline/Bat-Pants/25	30.00
8	Carl Yastrzemski/Bat-Jsy/25	50.00
10	Fergie Jenkins/Fld Glv-Pants/25	15.00

11	Steve Carlton/Bat-Jsy/25	15.00
12	Reggie Jackson/Bat-Jsy/25	30.00
13	Rod Carew/Bat-Pants/25	25.00
15	Mike Schmidt/Bat-Jsy/25	40.00
16	Nolan Ryan/Bat-Jsy/25	50.00
17	Robin Yount/Bat-Jsy/25	40.00
18	George Brett/Bat-Jsy/25	50.00
19	Eddie Murray/Bat-Jsy/25	30.00
20	Tony Gwynn/Bat-Jsy/25	40.00
21	Cal Ripken Jr./Bat-Jsy/25	80.00
22	Randy Johnson/Bat-Jsy/25	25.00
23	Sammy Sosa/Bat-Jsy/25	35.00
24	Rafael Palmeiro/Bat-Jsy/25	25.00
25	Roger Clemens/Bat-Jsy/25	30.00

Membership VIP Combos Signature

NM/M

Quantity produced listed

Prime: No Pricing

Production One Set

5	Al Kaline/Pants/25	50.00
9	Gaylord Perry/Jsy/50	15.00
10	Fergie Jenkins/Pants/50	20.00
11	Steve Carlton/Jsy/50	40.00
14	Bert Blyleven/Jsy/50	15.00

Membership VIP Signatures

NM/M

Quantity produced listed

5	Al Kaline/20	50.00
9	Gaylord Perry/50	15.00
10	Fergie Jenkins/50	20.00
11	Steve Carlton/20	30.00
14	Bert Blyleven/50	10.00

Membership VIP Jersey

NM/M

Quantity produced listed

Prime: No Pricing

Production One Set

1	Stan Musial/15	40.00
4	Roberto Clemente/25	75.00
5	Al Kaline Pants/25	20.00
8	Carl Yastrzemski/25	30.00
9	Gaylord Perry/25	10.00
10	Fergie Jenkins/Pants/25	15.00
11	Steve Carlton/25	15.00
12	Reggie Jackson/25	25.00
13	Rod Carew/25	20.00
14	Bert Blyleven/25	10.00
15	Mike Schmidt/25	30.00
16	Nolan Ryan/25	35.00
17	Robin Yount/25	25.00
18	George Brett/25	40.00
19	Eddie Murray/25	25.00
20	Tony Gwynn/25	25.00
21	Cal Ripken Jr./25	85.00
22	Randy Johnson/25	20.00
23	Sammy Sosa/25	30.00
24	Rafael Palmeiro/25	20.00
25	Roger Clemens/25	25.00

October Heroes

NM/M

Production 2,499 Sets

1	Reggie Jackson	3.00
2	Bob Gibson	3.00
3	Carlton Fisk	2.00
4	Whitey Ford	2.00
5	George Brett	5.00

6	Roberto Clemente	5.00
7	Roy Campanella	3.00
8	Babe Ruth	6.00

October Heroes Bat

NM/M

Quantity produced listed

1	Reggie Jackson/25	25.00
3	Carlton Fisk/25	25.00
6	Roberto Clemente/25	65.00
7	Roy Campanella/25	25.00

October Heroes Combos Material

NM/M

Quantity produced listed

1	Reggie Jackson/Bat-Hat/25	40.00
3	Carlton Fisk/Bat-Jsy/25	30.00
5	George Brett/Bat-Jsy/25	50.00
7	Roy Campanella/Bat-Pants/25	35.00

October Heroes Combos Signature

NM/M

Quantity produced listed

4	Whitey Ford/Jsy/50	45.00

October Heroes Fabric

NM/M

Quantity produced listed

2	Bob Gibson/Jsy/15	30.00
3	Carlton Fisk/Jsy/25	20.00
4	Whitey Ford/Jsy/50	20.00
5	George Brett/Jsy/25	40.00
7	Roy Campanella/Pants/25	20.00

October Heroes Signature

NM/M

Quantity produced listed

4	Whitey Ford/50	40.00

Significant Signatures Green

NM/M

Quantity produced listed

3	Hank Blalock/25	40.00
4	Shannon Stewart/50	10.00
7	Trot Nixon/25	30.00
13	Mike Lowell/25	25.00
14	Robin Ventura/25	15.00
19	Carlos Beltran/25	50.00
21	Johan Santana/25	35.00
24	Steve Finley/25	25.00
26	Alexis Rios/100	25.00
32	Miguel Cabrera/50	50.00
36	Dontrelle Willis/25	25.00
37	Rafael Soriano/100	6.00
38	Richard Fischer/100	6.00
39	Brian Tallet/100	6.00
40	Jose Castillo/100	6.00
41	Wade Miller/25	20.00
43	Runelvys Hernandez/20	10.00
44	Joe Borchard/50	8.00
47	Adam Dunn/25	30.00
49	Brandon Phillips/50	6.00
53	Cliff Lee/50	10.00
54	Chien-Ming Wang/50	150.00
57	Jhonny Peralta/100	6.00
60	Jae Weong Seo/50	15.00
61	Nic Jackson/100	8.00
63	Jimmy Gobble/45	10.00
64	Travis Hafner/50	12.00
66	Jerome Williams/50	20.00
68	Alexis Gomez/50	6.00
70	Zach Day/50	6.00
72	Morgan Ensberg/50	8.00
74	Garrett Atkins/99	6.00
77	Lyle Overbay/100	15.00
78	Josh Phelps/25	10.00
79	Juan Gonzalez/25	45.00
80	Rich Harden/50	15.00

#	Player	Price
84	Jody Gerut/50	15.00
87	Jay Gibbons/50	15.00
88	Chone Figgins/50	10.00
98	Jay Payton/50	10.00
99	Barry Larkin/25	40.00
102	Robby Hammock/50	6.00
103	Orlando Hudson/50	8.00
105	Hong-Chih Kuo/50	30.00
106	Eric Chavez/25	35.00
108	Jacque Jones/50	10.00
109	Ken Harvey/100	8.00
110	Aramis Ramirez/50	20.00
111	Victor Martinez/50	15.00
112	Joe Crede/50	10.00
113	Jason Varitek/25	40.00
118	Brandon Webb/25	15.00
121	Sammy Sosa/25	150.00
127	Luis Castillo/25	10.00
134	Edgar Martinez/25	40.00
145	Brett Myers/50	8.00
149	Gary Sheffield/25	25.00
151	Duke Snider/25	35.00
153	Whitey Ford/25	40.00
155	Dwight Gooden/50	20.00
158	Don Mattingly/25	100.00
159	Jack Morris/50	10.00
160	Jim Bunning/25	25.00
161	Fergie Jenkins/50	15.00
163	George Kell/50	15.00
164	Darryl Strawberry/50	20.00
165	Robin Roberts/25	30.00
166	Monte Irvin/25	20.00
167	Ernie Banks/25	60.00
168	Wade Boggs/25	40.00
169	Gaylord Perry/50	10.00
170	Keith Hernandez/50	20.00
172	Frank Robinson/25	30.00
173	Nolan Ryan/25	120.00
174	Stan Musial/25	70.00
175	Eddie Murray/25	50.00
176	Byron Gettis/100	6.00
177	Merkin Valdez/100	20.00
178	Rickie Weeks/25	50.00
180	Brian Bruney/100	6.00
181	Freddy Guzman/100	6.00
182	Brendan Harris/100	6.00
183	John Gall/100	8.00
184	Jason Kubel/100	12.00
185	Delmon Young/100	30.00
186	Ryan Howard/100	80.00
187	Adam Loewen/100	15.00
188	J.D. Durbin/100	8.00
189	Dan Haren/100	10.00
190	Dustin McGowan/100	10.00
191	Chad Gaudin/100	6.00
192	Preston Larrison/100	6.00
193	Ramon Nivar/100	6.00
195	Mike Gosling/100	6.00
196	Kevin Youkilis/100	15.00
197	Ryan Wagner/100	10.00
198	Bubba Nelson/100	8.00
199	Edwin Jackson/100	10.00
200	Chris Burke/100	6.00
201	Carlos Hines/100	10.00
202	Greg Dobbs/50	6.00
203	Jamie Brown/100	8.00
204	David Crouthers/100	6.00
205	Ian Snell/100	30.00
206	Gary Carter/50	25.00
207	Dale Murphy/50	40.00
208	Ryne Sandberg/50	75.00
209	Phil Niekro/50	20.00
210	Don Sutton/50	15.00

Significant Signatures Red

DARRYL STRAWBERRY • OF

NM/M
Quantity produced listed

#	Player	Price
3	Hank Blalock/50	30.00
4	Shannon Stewart/100	8.00
6	Carlos Lee/25	20.00
7	Trot Nixon/50	20.00
9	Mark Mulder/25	30.00
12	Jim Edmonds/25	30.00
13	Mike Lowell/50	20.00
14	Robin Ventura/50	10.00
16	Jose Vidro/25	8.00
19	Carlos Beltran/25	50.00
21	Johan Santana/100	30.00
24	Steve Finley/100	8.00
26	Alexis Rios/250	6.00
27	Rafael Palmeiro/25	65.00
28	Jorge Posada/25	45.00
32	Miguel Cabrera/100	40.00
36	Dontrelle Willis/100	25.00
37	Rafael Soriano/250	6.00
38	Richard Fischer/250	6.00
39	Brian Tallet/250	6.00
40	Jose Castillo/250	6.00
41	Wade Miller/92	15.00
42	Jose Contreras/25	25.00
43	Runelvys Hernandez/50	8.00
44	Joe Borchard/250	6.00
47	Adam Dunn/25	30.00
49	Brandon Phillips/70	6.00
50	Scott Rolen/25	35.00
53	Cliff Lee/100	8.00
54	Chien-Ming Wang/250	100.00
55	Roy Oswalt/25	30.00
56	Austin Kearns/25	20.00
57	Jhonny Peralta/250	6.00
60	Jae Weong Seo/100	10.00
61	Nic Jackson/250	8.00
63	Jimmy Gobble/200	10.00
64	Travis Hafner/100	12.00
65	Paul Konerko/25	15.00
66	Jerome Williams/250	20.00
68	Alexis Gomez/100	6.00
70	Zach Day/100	8.00
72	Morgan Ensberg/100	8.00
74	Garrett Atkins/245	6.00
76	Julio Franco/25	20.00
77	Lyle Overbay/250	15.00
78	Josh Phelps/50	8.00
79	Juan Gonzalez/25	45.00
80	Rich Harden/150	10.00
82	Torii Hunter/50	30.00
84	Jody Gerut/50	15.00
87	Jay Gibbons/100	15.00
88	Chone Figgins/100	10.00
90	Rich Aurilia/25	15.00
92	Marlon Byrd/25	15.00
98	Jay Payton/100	8.00
99	Barry Larkin/25	40.00
102	Robby Hammock/150	6.00
103	Orlando Hudson/100	8.00
105	Hong-Chih Kuo/100	30.00
106	Eric Chavez/25	35.00
107	Nick Johnson/25	15.00
108	Jacque Jones/100	8.00
109	Ken Harvey/250	8.00
110	Aramis Ramirez/100	20.00
111	Victor Martinez/99	20.00
112	Joe Crede/250	10.00
113	Jason Varitek/50	35.00
114	Troy Glaus/25	30.00
118	Brandon Webb/50	15.00
119	Craig Biggio/25	30.00
120	Orlando Cabrera/25	10.00
121	Sammy Sosa/25	150.00
122	Bobby Abreu/25	15.00
123	Andruw Jones/25	30.00
124	Jeff Bagwell/25	65.00
127	Luis Castillo/50	10.00
131	Eric Byrnes/25	10.00
132	Eric Hinske/25	15.00
134	Edgar Martinez/25	30.00
135	Rocco Baldelli/25	40.00
143	Vernon Wells/25	15.00
144	Magglio Ordonez/25	30.00
145	Brett Myers/100	8.00
149	Gary Sheffield/50	20.00
150	Tim Hudson/50	40.00
151	Duke Snider/50	30.00
153	Whitey Ford/50	40.00
155	Dwight Gooden/100	20.00
156	Warren Spahn/25	45.00
158	Don Mattingly/100	100.00
159	Jack Morris/100	10.00
160	Jim Bunning/100	20.00
161	Fergie Jenkins/100	15.00
163	George Kell/100	15.00
164	Darryl Strawberry/100	20.00
165	Robin Roberts/100	15.00
166	Monte Irvin/100	15.00
167	Ernie Banks/50	50.00
168	Wade Boggs/50	30.00
169	Gaylord Perry/100	10.00
170	Keith Hernandez/100	20.00
171	Lou Brock/50	30.00
172	Frank Robinson/25	25.00
173	Nolan Ryan/50	85.00
174	Stan Musial/50	60.00
175	Eddie Murray/50	50.00
176	Byron Gettis/250	6.00
177	Merkin Valdez/250	15.00
178	Rickie Weeks/250	40.00
180	Brian Bruney/250	6.00
181	Freddy Guzman/250	6.00
182	Brendan Harris/250	6.00
183	John Gall/250	6.00
184	Jason Kubel/250	10.00
185	Delmon Young/100	30.00
186	Ryan Howard/250	70.00
187	Adam Loewen/250	15.00
188	J.D. Durbin/250	8.00
189	Dan Haren/250	10.00
190	Dustin McGowan/250	10.00
191	Chad Gaudin/250	6.00
192	Preston Larrison/250	6.00
193	Ramon Nivar/250	6.00
195	Mike Gosling/250	6.00
196	Kevin Youkilis/250	15.00
197	Ryan Wagner/250	10.00
198	Bubba Nelson/250	8.00
200	Chris Burke/250	6.00
201	Carlos Hines/250	10.00
202	Greg Dobbs/100	6.00
203	Jamie Brown/250	6.00
204	David Crouthers/250	6.00
205	Ian Snell/250	25.00
206	Gary Carter/100	20.00
207	Dale Murphy/50	40.00
208	Ryne Sandberg/50	85.00
209	Phil Niekro/100	15.00
210	Don Sutton/100	15.00

Team Colors Jersey

NM/M
Quantity produced listed
Prime: No Pricing
Production One Set

#	Player	Price
1	Lenny Dykstra/Mets/Fld Glv/25	15.00
2	Steve Garvey/100	6.00
3	Eric Davis/25	15.00
5	Nolan Ryan/50	30.00
6	Bobby Doerr/25	20.00
7	Paul Molitor/50	10.00
8	Dale Murphy/50	20.00
9	Harold Baines/50	8.00
10	Dwight Gooden/50	10.00
11	Jose Canseco/25	15.00
12	Jim Rice/100	8.00
13	Will Clark/50	25.00
14	Alan Trammell/100	8.00
15	Lee Smith/100	5.00
16	Dwight Evans/50	15.00
17	Tony Oliva/100	8.00
18	Dave Parker/Pirates/25	10.00
19	Jack Morris/100	5.00
20	Luis Tiant/100	6.00
21	Andre Dawson/Expos/100	6.00
22	Darryl Strawberry/Dgr/100	8.00
23	George Foster/100	5.00
24	Marty Marion/50	6.00
25	Dennis Eckersley/100	6.00
26	Bo Jackson/50	30.00
27	Cal Ripken Jr./100	35.00
28	Deion Sanders/50	8.00
29	Don Mattingly/Jkt/100	20.00
30	Mark Grace/50	15.00
31	Fred Lynn/50	8.00
33	Ernie Banks/25	30.00
37	Keith Hernandez/25	15.00
38	Tony Gwynn/50	15.00
39	Jim Palmer/25	15.00
40	Red Schoendienst/50	15.00
41	Steve Carlton/50	15.00
42	Wade Boggs/25	25.00
43	Tommy John/100	5.00
44	Luis Aparicio/25	10.00
46	Andre Dawson/Cubs/25	15.00
47	Bert Blyleven/100	5.00
48	Darryl Strawberry/Mets/100	15.00
49	Dave Parker Reds/100	5.00

Team Colors Bat

NM/M
Quantity produced listed

#	Player	Price
2	Steve Garvey/50	10.00
3	Eric Davis/25	15.00
4	Al Oliver/25	8.00
6	Bobby Doerr/25	20.00
7	Paul Molitor/50	15.00
8	Dale Murphy/50	20.00
11	Jose Canseco/50	20.00
12	Jim Rice/50	12.00
13	Will Clark/50	25.00
14	Alan Trammell/50	12.00
16	Dwight Evans/50	15.00
18	Dave Parker/Pirates/25	10.00
21	Andre Dawson/Expos/50	10.00
22	Darryl Strawberry/Dgr/50	10.00
23	George Foster/50	8.00
26	Bo Jackson/50	30.00
27	Cal Ripken Jr./50	50.00
28	Deion Sanders/25	15.00
29	Don Mattingly/Jkt/50	25.00
30	Mark Grace/50	15.00
31	Fred Lynn/50	8.00
33	Ernie Banks/25	30.00
34	Gary Carter/25	12.00
35	Roger Maris/25	40.00
36	Ron Santo/50	12.00
38	Tony Gwynn/50	15.00
40	Red Schoendienst/25	15.00
41	Steve Carlton/25	15.00
42	Wade Boggs/25	25.00
44	Luis Aparicio/25	10.00
46	Andre Dawson/Cubs/25	12.00
48	Darryl Strawberry/Mets/50	10.00
49	Dave Parker Reds/50	8.00

Team Colors Combos Material

NM/M
Production 25 Sets
Prime: No Pricing
Production One Set

#	Player	Price
2	Steve Garvey/Bat-Jsy	15.00
3	Eric Davis/Bat-Jsy	20.00
5	Nolan Ryan/Bat-Jsy	50.00
6	Bobby Doerr/Bat-Jsy	25.00
7	Paul Molitor/Bat-Jsy	25.00
8	Dale Murphy/Bat-Jsy	25.00
11	Jose Canseco/Bat-Jsy	30.00
12	Jim Rice/Bat-Jsy	25.00
13	Will Clark/Bat-Jsy	40.00
14	Alan Trammell/Bat-Jsy	30.00
16	Dwight Evans/Bat-Jsy	25.00
18	Dave Parker/Pirates/Bat-Jsy	20.00
21	Andre Dawson/Expos/Bat-Jsy	15.00
22	Darryl Strawberry/Dgr/Bat-Jsy	20.00
23	George Foster/Bat-Jsy	10.00
26	Bo Jackson/Bat-Jsy	40.00
27	Cal Ripken Jr./Bat-Jsy	65.00
28	Deion Sanders/Bat-Jsy	25.00
29	Don Mattingly/Bat-Jsy	45.00
30	Mark Grace/Bat-Jsy	25.00
33	Ernie Banks/Bat-Jsy	45.00
34	Gary Carter/Bat-Jkt	25.00
38	Tony Gwynn/Bat-Jsy	40.00
40	Red Schoendienst/Bat-Jsy	15.00
41	Steve Carlton/Bat-Jsy	20.00
42	Wade Boggs/Bat-Jsy	25.00
44	Luis Aparicio/Bat-Jsy	15.00
46	Andre Dawson/Cubs/Bat-Jsy	15.00
48	Darryl Strawberry/Mets/Bat-Jsy	20.00
49	Dave Parker/Reds/Bat-Jsy	20.00

Team Colors Combos Signature

NM/M
Quantity produced listed
Prime: No Pricing
Production One Set

#	Player	Price
1	Lenny Dykstra/Mets/Fld Glv/100	15.00
2	Steve Garvey/Jsy/100	15.00
3	Eric Davis/Jsy/100	25.00
4	Al Oliver/Bat/100	20.00
6	Bobby Doerr/Jsy/100	20.00
9	Harold Baines/Jsy/100	20.00
10	Dwight Gooden/Jsy/100	25.00
12	Jim Rice/Jsy/100	25.00

14	Alan Trammell/Jsy/100	25.00
15	Lee Smith/Jsy/100	20.00
16	Dwight Evans/Jsy/100	25.00
17	Tony Oliva/Jsy/100	20.00
18	Dave Parker/Pirates/Jsy/100	15.00
19	Jack Morris/Jsy/100	20.00
20	Luis Tiant/Jsy/100	20.00
21	Andre Dawson/Expos/Jsy/50	25.00
22	Darryl Strawberry/Dgr/Jsy/100	25.00
23	George Foster/Jsy/100	20.00
24	Marty Marion/Jsy/100	20.00
25	Dennis Eckersley/Jsy/100	25.00
31	Fred Lynn/Jsy/100	20.00
33	Ernie Banks/Jsy/25	90.00
34	Gary Carter/Jkt/50	40.00
36	Ron Santo/Bat/25	50.00
37	Keith Hernandez/Jsy/25	45.00
39	Jim Palmer/Jsy/50	35.00
40	Red Schoendienst/Jsy/100	15.00
43	Tommy John/Jsy/100	20.00
44	Luis Aparicio/Jsy/100	15.00
46	Andre Dawson/Cubs/Jsy/50	25.00
47	Bert Blyleven/Jsy/100	25.00
48	Darryl Strawberry/Mets/Jsy/100	25.00
49	Dave Parker/Reds/Jsy/100	15.00
50	Lenny Dykstra/Phils/Btg Glv/30	25.00

Team Colors Signatures
NM/M

Quantity produced listed

1	Lenny Dykstra/Mets/50	15.00
2	Steve Garvey/50	25.00
3	Eric Davis/50	20.00
4	Al Oliver/50	15.00
6	Bobby Doerr/50	20.00
9	Harold Baines/50	25.00
10	Dwight Gooden/50	20.00
12	Jim Rice/50	20.00
14	Alan Trammell/50	20.00
15	Lee Smith/50	15.00
16	Dwight Evans/50	15.00
17	Tony Oliva/50	20.00
18	Dave Parker/Pirates/50	15.00
19	Jack Morris/50	10.00
20	Luis Tiant/50	15.00
21	Andre Dawson/Expos/25	25.00
22	Darryl Strawberry/Dgr/50	20.00
23	George Foster/50	15.00
24	Marty Marion/50	15.00
25	Dennis Eckersley/50	25.00
31	Fred Lynn/50	15.00
34	Gary Carter/20	35.00
37	Keith Hernandez/25	35.00
39	Jim Palmer/20	20.00
40	Red Schoendienst/50	15.00
41	Steve Carlton/20	35.00
43	Tommy John/50	15.00
44	Luis Aparicio/50	20.00
45	Bob Feller/50	20.00
46	Andre Dawson/Cubs/25	25.00
47	Bert Blyleven/50	12.00
48	Darryl Strawberry/Mets/50	20.00
49	Dave Parker/Reds/50	15.00
50	Lenny Dykstra/Phils/50	15.00

Timeless Triples
NM/M

Complete Set (6):		40.00
Common Player:		
Production 500 Sets		
1	Ted Williams, Carl Yastrzemski, Carlton Fisk	10.00
2	Lou Gehrig, Roger Maris, Thurman Munson	8.00
3	Brooks Robinson, Frank Robinson, Cal Ripken Jr.	10.00

4	Roger Clemens, Andy Pettitte, Roy Oswalt	6.00
5	Greg Maddux, Mark Prior, Kerry Wood	8.00
6	Alex Rodriguez, Derek Jeter, Gary Sheffield	10.00

Timeless Triples Bat
NM/M

Production 25 Sets

1	Ted Williams, Carl Yastrzemski, Carlton Fisk	185.00
2	Lou Gehrig, Roger Maris, Thurman Munson	200.00
3	Brooks Robinson, Frank Robinson, Cal Ripken Jr.	140.00

Timeless Triples Jersey

NM/M

Quantity produced listed
Prime: No Pricing
Production One Set

3	Brooks Robinson, Frank Robinson, Cal Ripken Jr./25	140.00

2004 Donruss Diamond Kings

NM/M

Complete Set (175):		75.00
Common Player:		.25
Common (151-175):		1.50
Pack (5):		7.50
Box (12):		80.00
1	Alex Rodriguez	2.50
2	Andruw Jones	.75
3	Nomar Garciaparra	2.00
4	Kerry Wood	.75
5	Magglio Ordonez	.50
6	Victor Martinez	.25
7	Jeremy Bonderman	.25
8	Josh Beckett	.75
9	Jeff Kent	.40
10	Carlos Beltran	.50
11	Hideo Nomo	.50
12	Richie Sexson	.25
13	Jose Vidro	.25
14	Jae Weong Seo	.25
15	Alfonso Soriano	1.00
16	Barry Zito	.50
17	Brett Myers	.25
18	Brian Giles	.40
19	Edgar Martinez	.40
20	Jim Edmonds	.50
21	Rocco Baldelli	.75
22	Mark Teixeira	.50
23	Carlos Delgado	.75
24	Julius Matos	.25
25	Jose Reyes	.50
26	Marlon Byrd	.25
27	Albert Pujols	2.50
28	Vernon Wells	.40
29	Garret Anderson	.50
30	Jerome Williams	.25

31	Chipper Jones	1.00
32	Rich Harden	.25
33	Manny Ramirez	.75
34	Derek Jeter	3.00
35	Brandon Webb	.25
36	Mark Prior	1.50
37	Roy Halladay	.50
38	Frank Thomas	.75
39	Rafael Palmeiro	.75
40	Adam Dunn	.50
41	Aubrey Huff	.25
42	Todd Helton	.75
43	Matt Morris	.40
44	Dontrelle Willis	.40
45	Lance Berkman	.50
46	Mike Sweeney	.25
47	Kazuhisa Ishii	.25
48	Torii Hunter	.50
49	Vladimir Guerrero	1.00
50	Mike Piazza	1.50
51	Alexis Rios	.25
52	Shannon Stewart	.25
53	Eric Hinske	.25
54	Jason Jennings	.25
55	Jason Giambi	1.00
56	Brandon Claussen	.25
57	Joe Thurston	.25
58	Ramon Nivar	.25
59	Jay Gibbons	.25
60	Eric Chavez	.50
61	Jimmy Gobble	.25
62	Walter Young	.25
63	Mark Grace	.50
64	Austin Kearns	.50
65	Bobby Abreu	.25
66	Hee Seop Choi	.25
67	Brandon Phillips	.25
68	Rickie Weeks	.50
69	Luis Gonzalez	.50
70	Mariano Rivera	.50
71	Jason Lane	.25
72	Xavier Nady	.25
73	Runelvys Hernandez	.25
74	Aramis Ramirez	.25
75	Ichiro Suzuki	2.00
76	Cliff Lee	.25
77	Chris Snelling	.25
78	Ryan Wagner	.25
79	Miguel Tejada	.50
80	Juan Gonzalez	.75
81	Joe Borchard	.25
82	Gary Sheffield	.50
83	Wade Miller	.25
84	Jeff Bagwell	.75
85	Ryan Church	.25
86	Adrian Beltre	.25
87	Jeff Baker	.25
88	Adam Loewen	.25
89	Bernie Williams	.50
90	Pedro J. Martinez	1.00
91	Carlos Rivera	.25
92	Junior Spivey	.25
93	Tim Hudson	.50
94	Troy Glaus	.50
95	Ken Griffey Jr.	1.50
96	Alexis Gomez	.25
97	Antonio Perez	.25
98	Dan Haren	.25
99	Ivan Rodriguez	.75
100	Randy Johnson	1.00
101	Lyle Overbay	.25
102	Oliver Perez	.25
103	Miguel Cabrera	.75
104	Scott Rolen	1.00
105	Roger Clemens	2.00
106	Brian Tallet	.25
107	Nic Jackson	.25
108	Angel Berroa	.25
109	Hank Blalock	.50
110	Ryan Klesko	.40
111	Jose Castillo	.25
112	Paul Konerko	.25
113	Greg Maddux	1.50
114	Mark Mulder	.50
115	Pat Burrell	.50
116	Garrett Atkins	.25
117	Jeremy Guthrie	.25
118	Orlando Cabrera	.25
119	Nick Johnson	.25
120	Tom Glavine	.50
121	Morgan Ensberg	.25
122	Sean Casey	.25
123	Orlando Hudson	.25
124	Hideki Matsui	2.50
125	Craig Biggio	.25
126	Adam LaRoche	.25
127	Hong-Chih Kuo	.25
128	Paul LoDuca	.25
129	Shawn Green	.50
130	Luis Castillo	.25
131	Joe Crede	.25
132	Ken Harvey	.25
133	Freddy Sanchez	.25
134	Roy Oswalt	.50

135	Curt Schilling	.75
136	Alfredo Amezaga	.25
137	Chien-Ming Wang	.50
138	Barry Larkin	.50
139	Trot Nixon	.25
140	Jim Thome	1.00
141	Bret Boone	.40
142	Jacque Jones	.25
143	Travis Hafner	.25
144	Sammy Sosa	2.00
145	Mike Mussina	.50
146	Vinnie Chulk	.25
147	Chad Gaudin	.25
148	Delmon Young	.50
149	Mike Lowell	.40
150	Rickey Henderson	.50
151	Roger Clemens	4.00
152	Mark Grace	2.00
153	Rickey Henderson	2.00
154	Alex Rodriguez	5.00
155	Rafael Palmeiro	2.00
156	Greg Maddux	3.00
157	Mike Piazza	3.00
158	Mike Mussina	1.50
159	Dale Murphy	1.50
160	Cal Ripken Jr.	6.00
161	Carl Yastrzemski	2.00
162	Marty Marion	1.50
163	Don Mattingly	4.00
164	Robin Yount	2.00
165	Andre Dawson	1.50
166	Jim Palmer	1.50
167	George Brett	5.00
168	Whitey Ford	2.00
169	Roy Campanella	2.00
170	Roger Maris	4.00
171	Duke Snider	2.00
172	Steve Carlton	2.00
173	Stan Musial	3.00
174	Nolan Ryan	6.00
175	Deion Sanders	1.50

Bronze

Bronze (1-150):	4-6X
Bronze (151-175):	2-3X
Production 100 Sets	
Bronze Sepia:	2-3X
Production 100	

Platinum

Platinum:	No Pricing
Production One Set	
Platinum Sepia:	No Pricing
Production One Set	

Silver

Silver (1-150):	5-10X
Silver (151-175):	2-4X
Production 50 Sets	
Silver Sepia:	2-4X
Production 50	

Framed Bronze

Framed Bronze (1-150):	2-3X
Framed Bronze (151-175):	1-2X
Framed Bronze Sepia:	1-2X
Inserted 1:6	

Framed Silver

Framed Silver (1-150):	4-8X
Framed Silver (151-175):	2-3X
Production 100 Sets	
Framed Silver Sepia:	2-3X
Production 100	

Framed Platinum

Framed Platinum:	No Pricing
Production One Set	

Diamond Cut Bat
NM/M

Common Player:		6.00
Production 100 unless noted.		
1	Alex Rodriguez	15.00
2	Nomar Garciaparra	12.00
3	Hideo Nomo	8.00
4	Alfonso Soriano	10.00
6	Edgar Martinez	8.00
7	Rocco Baldelli	10.00
8	Mark Teixeira	10.00
9	Albert Pujols	20.00
10	Vernon Wells	8.00
11	Garret Anderson	8.00
14	Brandon Webb	6.00
15	Mark Prior	15.00
16	Rafael Palmeiro	10.00
17	Adam Dunn	10.00
18	Dontrelle Willis	8.00
19	Kazuhisa Ishii	6.00
20	Torii Hunter	8.00
21	Vladimir Guerrero	10.00
22	Mike Piazza	15.00
23	Jason Giambi	10.00
26	Bobby Abreu	6.00

27	Hee Seop Choi	6.00
28	Rickie Weeks	12.00
30	Troy Glaus	8.00
31	Ivan Rodriguez	10.00
32	Hank Blalock	10.00
33	Greg Maddux	15.00
34	Nick Johnson	6.00
35	Shawn Green	8.00
36	Sammy Sosa	15.00
37	Dale Murphy/50	15.00
38	Cal Ripken Jr./50	50.00
39	Carl Yastrzemski	15.00
41	Don Mattingly	25.00
43	George Brett/50	40.00
45	Duke Snider/1	
46	Steve Carlton/50	15.00
47	Stan Musial/25	40.00
48	Nolan Ryan/50	35.00
49	Deion Sanders/50	15.00
50	Roberto Clemente/25	120.00

Diamond Cut Jersey

NM/M

Common Player: 6.00
Production 100 unless noted.

1	Alex Rodriguez	15.00
2	Nomar Garciaparra	15.00
3	Hideo Nomo/50	15.00
4	Alfonso Soriano	10.00
5	Brett Myers/50	10.00
6	Edgar Martinez	8.00
7	Rocco Baldelli	12.00
8	Mark Teixeira	10.00
9	Albert Pujols	20.00
10	Vernon Wells	8.00
11	Garret Anderson/50	8.00
12	Jerome Williams	8.00
13	Rich Harden	8.00
14	Brandon Webb	6.00
15	Mark Prior	15.00
16	Rafael Palmeiro	10.00
17	Adam Dunn	10.00
18	Dontrelle Willis	8.00
19	Kazuhisa Ishii	6.00
20	Torii Hunter	8.00
21	Vladimir Guerrero/50	15.00
22	Mike Piazza	15.00
23	Jason Giambi	10.00
25	Ramon Nivar	6.00
26	Bobby Abreu	6.00
27	Hee Seop Choi	6.00
30	Troy Glaus	8.00
31	Ivan Rodriguez	10.00
32	Hank Blalock	10.00
33	Greg Maddux	15.00
34	Nick Johnson	6.00
35	Shawn Green	8.00
36	Sammy Sosa	15.00
37	Dale Murphy/50	20.00
38	Cal Ripken Jr./50	50.00
39	Carl Yastrzemski	20.00
40	Marty Marion/50	15.00
41	Don Mattingly	25.00
42	Jim Palmer/25	20.00
43	George Brett/50	35.00
44	Whitey Ford/25	25.00
45	Duke Snider/10	
46	Steve Carlton/50	15.00
47	Stan Musial/50	
48	Nolan Ryan/50	40.00
49	Deion Sanders/50	15.00
50	Roberto Clemente/10	

Diamond Cut Signature

NM/M

Many not priced due to scarcity.

7	Rocco Baldelli/25	45.00
8	Mark Teixeira/25	30.00
13	Rich Harden/50	25.00
14	Brandon Webb/50	25.00
20	Torii Hunter/25	30.00
24	Ryan Wagner/50	20.00
25	Ramon Nivar/50	10.00
28	Rickie Weeks/50	40.00
29	Adam Loewen/50	20.00
32	Hank Blalock/50	30.00
40	Marty Marion/25	25.00
41	Don Mattingly/23	110.00
42	Jim Palmer/22	45.00
46	Steve Carlton/25	35.00
48	Nolan Ryan/34	125.00

Diamond Cut Combo

NM/M

Common Player: 10.00
Production 50 unless noted.

1	Alex Rodriguez	30.00
2	Nomar Garciaparra	25.00
3	Hideo Nomo/50	30.00
4	Alfonso Soriano	15.00
6	Edgar Martinez/25	15.00

7	Rocco Baldelli/25	25.00
8	Mark Teixeira/25	20.00
9	Albert Pujols	40.00
10	Vernon Wells/25	15.00
11	Garret Anderson/25	15.00
14	Brandon Webb/25	15.00
15	Mark Prior/25	20.00
16	Rafael Palmeiro/25	20.00
17	Adam Dunn/25	15.00
18	Dontrelle Willis/25	15.00
19	Kazuhisa Ishii/25	15.00
20	Torii Hunter/25	15.00
21	Vladimir Guerrero/25	25.00
22	Mike Piazza	20.00
23	Jason Giambi/25	25.00
26	Bobby Abreu	10.00
27	Hee Seop Choi	10.00
30	Troy Glaus/25	20.00
31	Ivan Rodriguez/25	20.00
32	Hank Blalock/25	20.00
33	Greg Maddux	25.00
34	Nick Johnson/25	12.00
35	Shawn Green/25	15.00
36	Sammy Sosa	25.00
41	Don Mattingly/23	50.00
42	Jim Palmer/22	20.00
46	Steve Carlton/32	20.00
48	Nolan Ryan/34	50.00
49	Deion Sanders/24	25.00
50	Roberto Clemente/21	150.00

Diamond Cut Signature Combo

NM/M

Varying quantities produced

40	Marty Marion/25	30.00
46	Steve Carlton/32	45.00

DK Combos Bronze

NM/M

Varying quantities produced

26	Marlon Byrd/Bat-Jsy/30	20.00
32	Rich Harden/Jsy-Jsy/15	50.00
53	Eric Hinske/Bat-Jsy/30	20.00
57	Joe Thurston/Bat-Jsy/25	15.00
59	Jay Gibbons/Jsy-Jsy/15	35.00
74	Aramis Ramirez/Bat-Bat/15	25.00
92	Junior Spivey/Bat-Jsy/15	30.00
101	Lyle Overbay/Bat-Jsy/30	15.00
103	Miguel Cabrera/Bat-Jsy/15	35.00
108	Angel Berroa/Bat-Pants/30	15.00
109	Hank Blalock/Bat-Jsy/30	35.00
111	Jose Castillo/Bat-Bat/15	15.00
121	Morgan Ensberg/Bat-Jsy/30	15.00
123	Orlando Hudson/Bat-Jsy/30	15.00
126	Adam LaRoche/Bat-Bat/30	15.00
130	Luis Castillo/Bat-Jsy/30	15.00
143	Travis Hafner/Bat-Jsy/30	12.00
147	Chad Gaudin/Jsy-Jsy/25	12.00

DK Combos Gold

Gold Combos: No Pricing
Production 1-5
Gold Combos Sepia: No Pricing
Production One Set

DK Combos Silver

NM/M

Varying quantities produced

26	Marlon Byrd/Bat-Jsy/15	15.00

101	Lyle Overbay/Bat-Jsy/15	15.00
102	Miguel Cabrera/Bat-Jsy/5	50.00
108	Angel Berroa/Bat-Pants/15	20.00
109	Hank Blalock/Bat-Jsy/5	50.00
121	Morgan Ensberg/Bat-Jsy/15	20.00
123	Orlando Hudson/Bat-Jsy/15	15.00
126	Adam LaRoche/Bat-Bat/15	20.00

DK Combos Platinum

Platinum Combos: No Pricing
Production One Set
Platinum Combos Sepia: No Pricing
Production One Set

DK Combos Framed Bronze

NM/M

Varying quantities produced

26	Marlon Byrd/Bat-Jsy/25	12.00
35	Brandon Webb/Bat-Jsy/25	25.00
53	Eric Hinske/Bat-Jsy/25	15.00
57	Joe Thurston/Bat-Jsy/25	12.00
59	Jay Gibbons/Jsy-Jsy/15	15.00
62	Walter Young/Bat-Bat/25	12.00
65	Bobby Abreu/Bat-Jsy/25	15.00
71	Jason Lane/Bat-Hat/25	15.00
74	Aramis Ramirez/Bat-Bat/25	20.00
77	Chris Snelling/Bat-Jsy/25	12.00
81	Joe Borchard/Bat-Jsy/25	10.00
92	Junior Spivey/Bat-Jsy/25	12.00
97	Antonio Perez/Bat-Pants/25	12.00
98	Dan Haren/Bat-Jsy/25	15.00
101	Lyle Overbay/Bat-Jsy/25	10.00
103	Miguel Cabrera/Bat-Jsy/25	40.00
107	Nic Jackson/Bat-Bat/25	10.00
108	Angel Berroa/Bat-Pants/25	12.00
109	Hank Blalock/Bat-Jsy/25	30.00
110	Ryan Klesko/Bat-Jsy/15	20.00
111	Jose Castillo/Bat-Bat/25	10.00
121	Morgan Ensberg/Bat-Jsy/15	15.00
123	Orlando Hudson/Bat-Jsy/25	12.00
126	Adam LaRoche/Bat-Jsy/15	15.00
127	Hong-Chih Kuo/Bat-Bat/25	10.00
130	Luis Castillo/Bat-Jsy/25	12.00
136	Alfredo Amezaga/Bat-Jsy/15	15.00
143	Travis Hafner/Bat-Jsy/15	15.00
147	Chad Gaudin/Jsy-Jsy/25	10.00

DK Combos Framed Gold

Framed Gold Combos: No Pricing
Production 1-5
Framed Gold Sepia: No Pricing
Production 1-5

DK Combos Framed Platinum

Framed Platinum: No Pricing
Production One Set

DK Combos Framed Silver

Framed Silver: No Pricing
Production 1-15

Framed Silver Sepia: No Pricing
Production 1-5

DK Materials Bronze

NM/M

Common Player:
No pricing for production 15 or less.
Framed Bronze: 1-1.5X
Production 5-100
Framed Bronze Sepia: 1.5-2X
Production 5-50
Silver: 1-2X
Production 5-50
Silver Sepia: 1.5-2X
Production 1-30
Framed Silver: 1-2X
Production 5-75
Framed Silver Sepia: 1.5-2X
Production 1-30
Gold: 1.5-2X
Production 1-50
Gold Sepia: No Pricing
Production 1-15
Framed Gold: 1.5-2X
Production 5-50
Framed Gold Sepia: No Pricing
Production 1-15
Platinums: No Pricing
All Platinums limited to one set.

1	Alex Rodriguez/Bat-Jsy/150	20.00
2	Andruw Jones/Bat-Jsy/150	8.00
3	Nomar Garciaparra/Bat-Jsy/150	15.00
4	Kerry Wood/Bat-Jsy/150	15.00
5	Magglio Ordonez/Bat-Jsy/150	8.00
6	Victor Martinez/Bat-Bat/100	6.00
7	Jeremy Bonderman/Jsy-Jsy/30	10.00
8	Josh Beckett/Bat-Jsy/150	10.00
9	Jeff Kent/Bat-Jsy/150	8.00
10	Carlos Beltran/Bat-Jsy/150	8.00
11	Hideo Nomo/Bat-Jsy/150	10.00
12	Richie Sexson/Bat-Jsy/150	8.00
13	Jose Vidro/Bat-Jsy/50	8.00
14	Jae Weong Seo/Jsy-Jsy/100	8.00
15	Alfonso Soriano/Bat-Jsy/150	10.00
16	Barry Zito/Bat-Jsy/100	10.00
17	Brett Myers/Jsy-Jsy/30	10.00
18	Brian Giles/Bat-Bat/100	8.00
19	Edgar Martinez/Bat-Jsy/150	8.00
20	Jim Edmonds/Bat-Jsy/150	8.00
21	Rocco Baldelli/Bat-Jsy/100	12.00
22	Mark Teixeira/Bat-Jsy/100	8.00
23	Carlos Delgado/Bat-Jsy/150	8.00
25	Jose Reyes/Bat-Jsy/100	8.00
26	Marlon Byrd/Bat-Jsy/100	8.00
27	Albert Pujols/Bat-Jsy/150	25.00
28	Vernon Wells/Bat-Jsy/150	8.00
29	Garret Anderson/Bat-Jsy/15	20.00
30	Jerome Williams/Jsy-Jsy/100	8.00
31	Chipper Jones/Bat-Jsy/150	12.00
32	Rich Harden/Jsy-Jsy/100	8.00
33	Manny Ramirez/Bat-Jsy/150	10.00
34	Derek Jeter/Base-Base/100	20.00
35	Brandon Webb/Bat-Jsy/100	8.00
36	Mark Prior/Bat-Jsy/100	8.00
37	Roy Halladay/Jsy-Jsy/100	8.00
38	Frank Thomas/Bat-Jsy/150	12.00
39	Rafael Palmeiro/Bat-Jsy/150	10.00

#	Player / Description	Price
40	Adam Dunn/ Bat-Jsy/150	8.00
41	Aubrey Huff/ Bat-Jsy/30	10.00
42	Todd Helton/ Bat-Jsy/150	10.00
43	Matt Morris/ Jsy-Jsy/100	8.00
44	Dontrelle Willis/ Bat-Jsy/100	10.00
45	Lance Berkman/ Bat-Jsy/150	6.00
46	Mike Sweeney/ Bat-Jsy/100	8.00
47	Kazuhisa Ishii/ Bat-Jsy/100	8.00
48	Torii Hunter/ Bat-Jsy/100	8.00
49	Vladimir Guerrero/ Bat-Jsy/100	15.00
50	Mike Piazza/ Bat-Jsy/150	15.00
51	Alexis Rios/ Bat-Bat/150	12.00
52	Shannon Stewart/ Bat-Bat/100	6.00
53	Eric Hinske/ Bat-Jsy/100	6.00
54	Jason Jennings/ Bat-Jsy/150	6.00
55	Jason Giambi/ Bat-Jsy/150	10.00
57	Joe Thurston/ Bat-Jsy/150	6.00
58	Ramon Nivar/ Bat-Jsy/100	6.00
59	Jay Gibbons/ Jsy-Jsy/100	8.00
60	Eric Chavez/ Bat-Jsy/150	8.00
62	Walter Young/ Bat-Bat/100	6.00
63	Mark Grace/ Bat-Jsy/150	10.00
64	Austin Kearns/ Bat-Jsy/150	8.00
65	Bob Abreu/ Bat-Jsy/150	6.00
66	Hee Seop Choi/ Bat-Jsy/100	6.00
67	Brandon Phillips/ Bat-Bat/100	6.00
68	Rickie Weeks/ Bat-Bat/100	15.00
69	Luis Gonzalez/ Bat-Jsy/150	6.00
70	Mariano Rivera/ Jsy-Jsy/100	10.00
71	Jason Lane/	15.00
73	Runelvys Hernandez/ Jsy-Jsy/30	8.00
75	Ichiro Suzuki/ Ball-Base/15	50.00
77	Chris Snelling/ Bat-Bat/30	8.00
79	Miguel Tejada/ Bat-Jsy/150	8.00
80	Juan Gonzalez/ Bat-Jsy/150	8.00
82	Gary Sheffield/ Bat-Jsy/150	8.00
83	Wade Miller/ Bat-Jsy/50	6.00
84	Jeff Bagwell/ Bat-Jsy/150	15.00
86	Adrian Beltre/ Bat-Jsy/100	6.00
87	Jeff Baker/Bat-Bat/100	6.00
89	Bernie Williams/ Bat-Jsy/150	10.00
90	Pedro J. Martinez/ Bat-Jsy/100	15.00
92	Junior Spivey/ Bat-Jsy/100	8.00
93	Tim Hudson/ Bat-Jsy/150	8.00
94	Troy Glaus/ Bat-Jsy/100	8.00
95	Ken Griffey Jr./ Base-Base/100	15.00
96	Alexis Gomez/ Bat-Jsy/30	10.00
97	Antonio Perez/ Bat-Pants/100	6.00
98	Dan Haren/ Bat-Jsy/100	6.00
99	Ivan Rodriguez/ Bat-Jsy/100	10.00
100	Randy Johnson/ Bat-Jsy/100	12.00
101	Lyle Overbay/ Bat-Jsy/100	6.00
103	Miguel Cabrera/ Bat-Jsy/100	15.00
104	Scott Rolen/ Bat-Jsy/100	10.00
105	Roger Clemens/ Bat-Jsy/100	20.00
107	Nic Jackson/ Bat-Bat/100	6.00
108	Angel Berroa/ Bat-Pants/30	10.00
109	Hank Blalock/ Bat-Jsy/100	10.00
110	Ryan Klesko/ Bat-Jsy/100	8.00
111	Jose Castillo/ Bat-Bat/100	6.00
112	Paul Konerko/ Bat-Jsy/100	6.00
113	Greg Maddux/ Bat-Jsy/100	15.00
114	Mark Mulder/ Bat-Jsy/100	8.00
115	Pat Burrell/ Bat-Jsy/100	8.00
116	Garrett Atkins/ Jsy-Jsy/100	6.00
118	Orlando Cabrera/ Bat-Jsy/100	8.00
119	Nick Johnson/ Bat-Jsy/100	6.00
120	Tom Glavine/ Bat-Jsy/100	10.00
121	Morgan Ensberg/ Bat-Jsy/100	6.00
123	Orlando Hudson/ Bat-Jsy/100	6.00
124	Hideki Matsui/ Ball-Base/15	70.00
125	Craig Biggio/ Bat-Jsy/100	8.00
126	Adam LaRoche/ Bat-Bat/100	8.00
127	Hong-Chih Kuo/ Bat-Bat/100	6.00
128	Paul LoDuca/ Bat-Jsy/100	6.00
129	Shawn Green/ Bat-Jsy/100	8.00
130	Luis Castillo/ Bat-Jsy/100	6.00
132	Ken Harvey/ Bat-Bat/100	6.00
133	Freddy Sanchez/ Bat-Bat/100	6.00
134	Roy Oswalt/ Bat-Jsy/100	8.00
135	Curt Schilling/ Bat-Jsy/100	8.00
136	Alfredo Amezaga/ Bat-Jsy/15	15.00
139	Trot Nixon/ Bat-Jsy/100	10.00
140	Jim Thome/ Bat-Jsy/100	15.00
141	Bret Boone/ Bat-Jsy/100	8.00
142	Jacque Jones/ Bat-Jsy/100	8.00
143	Todd Hafner/ Bat-Jsy/100	8.00
144	Sammy Sosa/ Bat-Jsy/100	20.00
145	Mike Mussina/ Bat-Jsy/100	12.00
147	Chad Gaudin/ Jsy-Jsy/100	6.00
149	Mike Lowell/ Bat-Jsy/100	8.00
150	Rickey Henderson/ Bat-Jsy/100	15.00
151	Roger Clemens/ FB Bat-Jsy/100	20.00
153	Rickey Henderson/ FB Bat-Jsy/30	30.00
154	Alex Rodriguez/ FB Bat-Jsy/100	20.00
155	Rafael Palmeiro/ FB Bat-Jsy/100	10.00
156	Greg Maddux/ FB Bat-Jsy/100	15.00
157	Mike Piazza/ FB Bat-Jsy/100	15.00
158	Mike Mussina/ FB Bat-Jsy/100	12.00
159	Dale Murphy/ LGD Bat-Jsy/30	20.00
160	Cal Ripken Jr./ LGD Bat-Jsy/100	50.00
161	Carl Yastrzemski/ LGD Bat-Jsy/100	25.00
162	Marty Marion/ LGD Jsy-Jsy/30	10.00
163	Don Mattingly/ LGD Bat-Jsy/100	25.00
164	Robin Yount/ LGD Bat-Jsy/100	25.00
165	Andre Dawson/ LGD Bat-Jsy/30	15.00
167	George Brett/ LGD Bat-Jsy/30	50.00
168	Whitey Ford/ LGD Jsy-Pants/30	20.00
172	Steve Carlton/ LGD Bat-Jsy/100	15.00
173	Stan Musial/ LGD Bat-Jsy/30	25.00
174	Nolan Ryan/ LGD Bat-Jsy/30	50.00
175	Deion Sanders/ LGD Bat-Jsy/100	12.00

DK Signatures Bronze

NM/M

No Pricing For Prod. less than 15.
Framed Bronze: 1X
Production 1-50
Bronze Sepia: No Pricing
Production 1-15

#	Player	Price
6	Victor Martinez/200	10.00
13	Jose Vidro/200	10.00
14	Jae Weong Seo/200	15.00
17	Brett Myers/200	10.00
19	Edgar Martinez/25	40.00
26	Marlon Byrd/200	8.00
32	Rich Harden/200	15.00
35	Brandon Webb/25	30.00
41	Aubrey Huff/100	12.00
48	Torii Hunter/200	20.00
51	Alexis Rios/200	20.00
52	Shannon Stewart/100	10.00
53	Eric Hinske/25	20.00
56	Brandon Claussen/ 200	10.00
57	Joe Thurston/200	8.00
58	Ramon Nivar/100	8.00
59	Jay Gibbons/200	25.00
61	Jimmy Gobble/100	15.00
62	Walter Young/200	8.00
67	Brandon Phillips/100	6.00
68	Rickie Weeks/30	40.00
71	Jason Lane/200	8.00
73	Runelvys Hernandez/ 50	10.00
74	Aramis Ramirez/100	15.00
76	Cliff Lee/200	10.00
77	Chris Snelling/200	8.00
78	Ryan Wagner/100	15.00
81	Joe Borchard/200	8.00
85	Ryan Church/200	8.00
87	Jeff Baker/100	10.00
88	Adam Loewen/100	20.00
91	Carlos Rivera/100	8.00
92	Junior Spivey/25	20.00
96	Alexis Gomez/200	8.00
97	Antonio Perez/46	10.00
98	Dan Haren/100	12.00
101	Lyle Overbay/200	8.00
102	Oliver Perez/200	8.00
103	Miguel Cabrera/100	35.00
106	Brian Tallet/200	8.00
107	Nic Jackson/200	8.00
108	Angel Berroa/25	15.00
109	Hank Blalock/25	35.00
111	Jose Castillo/200	8.00
114	Mark Mulder/25	30.00
116	Garrett Atkins/100	8.00
117	Jeremy Guthrie/200	8.00
118	Orlando Cabrera/75	12.00
121	Morgan Ensberg/200	10.00
123	Orlando Hudson/100	10.00
126	Adam LaRoche/100	15.00
127	Hong-Chih Kuo/75	20.00
130	Luis Castillo/25	20.00
131	Joe Crede/100	8.00
132	Ken Harvey/200	8.00
133	Freddy Sanchez/50	10.00
136	Alfredo Amezaga/90	8.00
137	Chien-Ming Wang/ 25	125.00
139	Trot Nixon/15	
142	Jacque Jones/25	20.00
143	Travis Hafner/200	10.00
146	Vinnie Chulk/200	8.00
147	Chad Gaudin/100	8.00
149	Mike Lowell/25	20.00

DK Signatures Gold

NM/M

Many not priced due to scarcity.
Framed Gold: No Pricing
Production 1-5
Gold Sepia: No Pricing
Production 1-5

#	Player	Price
32	Rich Harden/50	20.00
51	Alexis Rios/50	25.00
56	Brandon Claussen/50	15.00
62	Joe Thurston/50	10.00
62	Walter Young/50	10.00
71	Jason Lane/40	15.00
77	Chris Snelling/50	10.00
81	Joe Borchard/50	15.00
85	Ryan Church/50	10.00
96	Alexis Gomez/50	10.00
101	Lyle Overbay/50	10.00
102	Oliver Perez/50	10.00
106	Brian Tallet/50	10.00
107	Nic Jackson/50	10.00
121	Morgan Ensberg/48	15.00
146	Vinnie Chulk/50	10.00

DK Signatures Silver

NM/M

No pricing for prod. less than 15.
Framed Silver: 1.5-2X
Production 1-25
Silver Sepia: No Pricing
Production 1-10

#	Player	Price
6	Victor Martinez/49	15.00
13	Jose Vidro/20	20.00
14	Jae Weong Seo/80	20.00
17	Brett Myers/90	15.00
26	Marlon Byrd/100	10.00
32	Rich Harden/100	15.00
35	Brandon Webb/15	35.00
41	Aubrey Huff/40	15.00
51	Alexis Rios/100	20.00
52	Shannon Stewart/30	15.00
56	Brandon Claussen/ 100	10.00
57	Joe Thurston/100	8.00
58	Ramon Nivar/30	15.00
61	Jimmy Gobble/30	20.00
62	Walter Young/100	8.00
67	Brandon Phillips/30	10.00
68	Rickie Weeks/50	50.00
71	Jason Lane/100	8.00
73	Runelvys Hernandez/ 30	10.00
74	Aramis Ramirez/30	25.00
76	Cliff Lee/100	10.00
77	Chris Snelling/100	8.00
78	Ryan Wagner/30	20.00
81	Joe Borchard/100	8.00
85	Ryan Church/100	8.00
87	Jeff Baker/30	15.00
88	Adam Loewen/30	25.00
96	Alexis Gomez/100	8.00
98	Dan Haren/30	15.00
101	Lyle Overbay/100	8.00
102	Oliver Perez/100	8.00
103	Miguel Cabrera/30	40.00
106	Brian Tallet/100	8.00
107	Nic Jackson/100	8.00
109	Hank Blalock/25	35.00
111	Jose Castillo/100	8.00
116	Garrett Atkins/30	10.00
117	Jeremy Guthrie/30	15.00
121	Morgan Ensberg/50	15.00
123	Orlando Hudson/30	15.00
126	Adam LaRoche/30	20.00
131	Joe Crede/35	12.00
132	Ken Harvey/30	15.00
136	Alfredo Amezaga/30	10.00
143	Travis Hafner/30	15.00
146	Vinnie Chulk/100	8.00
147	Chad Gaudin/30	10.00

DK Signatures Platinum

No Pricing
Production One Set
Framed Platinum: No Pricing
Platinum Sepia: No Pricing
Production One Set

Gallery of Stars

NM/M

Complete Set (15): 50.00
Common Player: 2.00
Inserted 1:37

#	Player	Price
1	Nolan Ryan	8.00
2	Cal Ripken Jr.	8.00
3	George Brett	6.00
4	Don Mattingly	6.00
5	Deion Sanders	2.00
6	Mike Piazza	4.00
7	Hideo Nomo	2.00
8	Rickey Henderson	2.00
9	Roger Clemens	6.00
10	Greg Maddux	4.00
11	Albert Pujols	6.00
12	Alex Rodriguez	6.00
13	Dale Murphy	3.00
14	Mark Prior	4.00
15	Dontrelle Willis	2.00

Gallery of Stars Autograph

No Pricing

Heritage Collection

		NM/M
Complete Set (25):		75.00
Common Player:		2.00
Inserted 1:22		
1	Dale Murphy	3.00
2	Cal Ripken Jr.	8.00
3	Carl Yastrzemski	4.00
4	Don Mattingly	6.00
5	Jim Palmer	2.00
6	Andre Dawson	2.00
7	Roy Campanella	3.00
8	George Brett	6.00
9	Duke Snider	3.00
10	Marty Marion	2.00
11	Deion Sanders	2.00
12	Whitey Ford	3.00
13	Stan Musial	5.00
14	Nolan Ryan	8.00
15	Steve Carlton	2.00
16	Robin Yount	3.00
17	Albert Pujols	6.00
18	Alex Rodriguez	6.00
19	Mike Piazza	4.00
20	Roger Clemens	6.00
21	Hideo Nomo	2.00
22	Mark Prior	4.00
23	Roger Maris	5.00
24	Greg Maddux	4.00
25	Mark Grace	2.00

Heritage Collection Autograph

No Pricing

Heritage Collection Bat

		NM/M
Production 50 unless noted.		
1	Dale Murphy	20.00
2	Cal Ripken Jr.	40.00
3	Carl Yastrzemski	20.00
4	Don Mattingly	20.00
6	Andre Dawson/25	20.00
7	Roy Campanella/25	30.00
8	George Brett/25	40.00
11	Deion Sanders	10.00
13	Stan Musial/25	35.00
14	Nolan Ryan/25	40.00
15	Steve Carlton/25	20.00
16	Robin Yount	20.00
17	Albert Pujols	25.00
18	Alex Rodriguez	25.00
19	Mike Piazza	15.00
20	Roger Clemens	25.00
21	Hideo Nomo	15.00
22	Mark Prior	15.00
23	Roger Maris/25	50.00
24	Greg Maddux	15.00
25	Mark Grace	10.00

Heritage Collection Jersey

		NM/M
Production 50 unless noted.		
1	Dale Murphy	15.00
2	Cal Ripken Jr.	40.00
3	Carl Yastrzemski	20.00
4	Don Mattingly	30.00
6	Andre Dawson/25	20.00
7	Roy Campanella/25	30.00
8	George Brett/25	40.00
10	Marty Marion	10.00
11	Deion Sanders	10.00
12	Whitey Ford/25	25.00
14	Nolan Ryan/25	40.00
15	Steve Carlton/25	20.00
16	Robin Yount	20.00
17	Albert Pujols	25.00
18	Alex Rodriguez	25.00
19	Mike Piazza	15.00
20	Roger Clemens	25.00
21	Hideo Nomo	15.00
22	Mark Prior	15.00
23	Roger Maris/25	50.00
24	Greg Maddux	15.00
25	Mark Grace	10.00

HOF Heroes

George Brett

		NM/M
Common Player:		2.50
1	George Brett/1,000	6.00
2	George Brett/500	8.00
3	George Brett/250	12.00
4	Mike Schmidt/1,000	5.00
5	Mike Schmidt/250	8.00
6	Nolan Ryan/1,000	8.00
7	Nolan Ryan/500	10.00
8	Nolan Ryan/250	15.00
9	Roberto Clemente/1,000	6.00
10	Roberto Clemente/500	10.00
11	Roberto Clemente/250	15.00
12	Roberto Clemente/100	20.00
13	Carl Yastrzemski/1,000	4.00
14	Robin Yount/1,000	4.00
15	Whitey Ford/1,000	4.00
16	Duke Snider/1,000	4.00
17	Duke Snider/1,000	8.00
18	Carlton Fisk/1,000	3.00
19	Ozzie Smith/1,000	5.00
20	Kirby Puckett/1,000	4.00
21	Bobby Doerr/1,000	2.50
22	Frank Robinson/1,000	3.00
23	Ralph Kiner/1,000	2.50
24	Al Kaline/1,000	4.00
25	Bob Feller/1,000	3.00
26	Yogi Berra/1,000	4.00
27	Stan Musial/1,000	5.00
28	Stan Musial/500	8.00
29	Stan Musial/250	10.00
30	Jim Palmer/1,000	2.50
31	Johnny Bench/1,000	4.00
32	Steve Carlton/1,000	3.00
33	Gary Carter/1,000	3.00
34	Roy Campanella/1,000	3.00
35	Roy Campanella/250	8.00

HOF Heroes Bat

		NM/M
Production 25 unless noted.		
1	George Brett	35.00
2	George Brett	35.00
3	George Brett	35.00
4	Mike Schmidt	35.00
5	Mike Schmidt	35.00
6	Nolan Ryan	40.00
7	Nolan Ryan	40.00
8	Nolan Ryan	40.00
14	Carl Yastrzemski	30.00
14	Robin Yount	35.00
18	Carlton Fisk	25.00
19	Ozzie Smith	30.00
20	Kirby Puckett	30.00
21	Bobby Doerr	20.00
22	Frank Robinson	15.00
23	Ralph Kiner	15.00
24	Al Kaline	25.00
31	Johnny Bench	25.00
32	Steve Carlton	20.00
33	Gary Carter	20.00
34	Roy Campanella	30.00
35	Roy Campanella	30.00

HOF Heroes Combo

		NM/M
Production 25 unless noted.		
1	George Brett	50.00
2	George Brett	50.00
3	George Brett	50.00
4	Mike Schmidt	40.00
5	Mike Schmidt	40.00
6	Nolan Ryan	50.00
7	Nolan Ryan	50.00

Stan Musial

8	Nolan Ryan	50.00
13	Carl Yastrzemski	40.00
14	Robin Yount	40.00
15	Whitey Ford	30.00
18	Carlton Fisk	30.00
19	Ozzie Smith	40.00
20	Kirby Puckett	40.00
21	Bobby Doerr	25.00
23	Ralph Kiner	20.00
24	Al Kaline	35.00
32	Steve Carlton	30.00
33	Gary Carter	25.00
34	Roy Campanella	40.00
35	Roy Campanella	40.00

HOF Heroes Jersey

		NM/M
Production 25 unless noted.		
1	George Brett	35.00
2	George Brett	35.00
3	George Brett	35.00
4	Mike Schmidt	35.00
5	Mike Schmidt	35.00
6	Nolan Ryan	40.00
7	Nolan Ryan	40.00
8	Nolan Ryan	40.00
13	Carl Yastrzemski	30.00
14	Robin Yount	35.00
15	Whitey Ford	30.00
18	Carlton Fisk	25.00
19	Ozzie Smith	30.00
20	Kirby Puckett	30.00
21	Bobby Doerr	20.00
24	Al Kaline	25.00
32	Steve Carlton	20.00
33	Gary Carter	20.00
34	Roy Campanella	30.00
35	Roy Campanella	30.00

HOF Heroes Signature

		NM/M
Many not priced.		
14	Robin Yount/19	70.00
15	Whitey Ford/16	50.00
22	Frank Robinson/20	50.00
25	Bob Feller/19	40.00
30	Jim Palmer/22	40.00
32	Steve Carlton/32	35.00

Recollection Autographs

		NM/M
Varying quantities produced		
6	Clint Barnes 03 DK Black/82	10.00
7	Clint Barnes 03 DK Blue/72	10.00
8	Carlos Beltran 02 DK/23	20.00
9	Carlos Beltran 03 DK/99	15.00
10	Adrian Beltre 02 DK/40	10.00
19	Chris Burke 03 DK/150	10.00
20	Marlon Byrd 02 DK/23	15.00
21	Marlon Byrd 03 DK/100	10.00
24	Kevin Cash 03 DK/103	10.00
25	Jose Cruz 85 DK/59	10.00
26	J.D. Durbin 03 DK/151	10.00
27	Jim Edmonds 03 DK/24	25.00
32	Julio Franco 87 DK/25	20.00
33	Freddy Garcia 03 DK/50	20.00
34	Jay Gibbons 03 DK/100	12.00

39	Brendan Harris 03 DK/150	8.00
42	Runelvys Hernandez 02 DK/100	8.00
43	Eric Hinske 03 DK/20	20.00
44	Tim Hudson 02 DK/25	30.00
45	Tim Hudson 03 DK/25	30.00
46	Aubrey Huff 03 DK/99	15.00
49	Jason Jennings 03 DK/50	10.00
50	Tommy John 88 DK Black/62	15.00
52	Howard Johnson 90 DK/52	10.00
54	Austin Kearns 02 DK/25	30.00
55	Austin Kearns 03 DK/25	30.00
59	Preston Larrison 03 DK Black/74	10.00
60	Preston Larrison 03 DK Blue/77	10.00
67	Dustin McGowan 03 DK/159	8.00
69	Melvin Mora 03 DK/101	8.00
71	Jack Morris 03 DK/60	10.00
72	Jack Morris 03 DK Her/19	20.00
74	Dale Murphy 03 DK Blue/47	30.00
82	Magglio Ordonez 03 DK/25	30.00
85	Dave Parker 82 DK/20	30.00
86	Dave Parker 90 DK/18	30.00
88	Jorge Posada 02 DK/25	50.00
89	Mark Prior 03 DK/25	100.00
92	Mike Rivera 02 DK/24	15.00
97	Ivan Rodriguez 03 DK/22	40.00
100	Rodrigo Rosario 02 DK/50	8.00
105	Ron Santo 02 DK/29	35.00
106	Richie Sexson 02 DK/25	25.00
107	Richie Sexson 03 DK/25	25.00
109	Chris Snelling 02 DK/46	12.00
119	Shannon Stewart 03 DK/50	15.00
120	Shannon Stewart 03 DK Black/92	12.00
126	Gorman Thomas 82 DK Black/22	20.00
127	Gorman Thomas 82 DK Blue/20	20.00
128	Alan Trammell 02 DK/29	30.00
129	Alan Trammell 02 DK Her/25	30.00
130	Robin Ventura 03 DK/25	20.00
131	Jose Vidro 03 DK/25	20.00
132	Rickie Weeks 03 DK/52	50.00
133	Kevin Youkilis 03 DK/153	15.00

Team Timeline

		NM/M
Complete Set (19):		65.00
Common Duo:		2.00
Inserted 1:29		
1	Deion Sanders, Andruw Jones	2.00
2	Rickie Weeks, Robin Yount	3.00
3	Don Mattingly, Whitey Ford	8.00
4	Chipper Jones, Dale Murphy	4.00
5	Nomar Garciaparra, Bobby Doerr	5.00
6	Mark Prior, Sammy Sosa	5.00
7	Hideo Nomo, Kazuhisa Ishii	2.00
8	Andre Dawson, Mark Grace	3.00
9	Roger Clemens, Carl Yastrzemski	6.00
10	Mike Mussina, Cal Ripken Jr.	8.00
11	Stan Musial, Albert Pujols	6.00
12	Jim Palmer, Mike Mussina	2.00
13	Marty Marion, Stan Musial	4.00

14	George Brett, Mike Sweeney	6.00
15	Roger Clemens, Roger Maris	6.00
16	Duke Snider, Shawn Green	3.00
17	Jim Thome, Mike Schmidt	4.00
18	Nolan Ryan, Alex Rodriguez	8.00
19	Roy Campanella, Mike Piazza	4.00

Team Timeline Bat
NM/M
Production 25 unless noted.

1	Deion Sanders, Andruw Jones	15.00
2	Rickie Weeks, Robin Yount	40.00
3	Don Mattingly, Whitey Ford	60.00
4	Chipper Jones, Dale Murphy	35.00
5	Nomar Garciaparra, Bobby Doerr	30.00
6	Mark Prior, Sammy Sosa	40.00
7	Hideo Nomo, Kazuhisa Ishii	40.00
8	Andre Dawson, Mark Grace	20.00
9	Roger Clemens, Carl Yastrzemski	50.00
10	Mike Mussina, Cal Ripken Jr.	75.00
11	Stan Musial, Albert Pujols	65.00
12	Jim Palmer, Mike Mussina	25.00
14	George Brett, Mike Sweeney	30.00
15	Roger Clemens, Roger Maris	60.00
17	Jim Thome, Mike Schmidt	40.00
18	Nolan Ryan, Alex Rodriguez	60.00
19	Roy Campanella, Mike Piazza	40.00

Team Timeline Jersey

NM/M
Production 25 Sets
Prime: No Pricing
Production One Set

1	Deion Sanders, Andruw Jones	15.00
2	Rickie Weeks, Robin Yount	40.00
3	Don Mattingly, Whitey Ford	60.00
4	Chipper Jones, Dale Murphy	35.00
5	Nomar Garciaparra, Bobby Doerr	30.00
6	Mark Prior, Sammy Sosa	40.00
7	Hideo Nomo, Kazuhisa Ishii	40.00
8	Andre Dawson, Mark Grace	20.00
9	Roger Clemens, Carl Yastrzemski	50.00
10	Mike Mussina, Cal Ripken Jr.	75.00
14	George Brett, Mike Sweeney	30.00
15	Roger Clemens, Roger Maris	60.00
17	Jim Thome, Mike Schmidt	40.00
18	Nolan Ryan, Alex Rodriguez	60.00
19	Roy Campanella, Mike Piazza	40.00

Timeline
NM/M
Common Player: 3.00
Inserted 1:92

1	Roger Clemens	6.00
2	Mark Grace	3.00
3	Mike Mussina	3.00
4	Mike Piazza	4.00
5	Nolan Ryan	8.00
6	Rickey Henderson	3.00

Timeline Bat
NM/M
Production 25 Sets

1	Roger Clemens	35.00
2	Mark Grace	25.00
3	Mike Mussina	20.00
4	Mike Piazza	35.00
5	Nolan Ryan	50.00
6	Rickey Henderson	20.00

Timeline Jersey

NM/M
Production 25 Sets
Prime: No Pricing
Production One Set

1	Roger Clemens	35.00
2	Mark Grace	25.00
3	Mike Mussina	20.00
4	Mike Piazza	35.00
5	Nolan Ryan	50.00
6	Rickey Henderson	20.00

2004 Donruss Elite

JASON BARTLETT

NM/M
Complete Set (205): .25
Common Player: .25
Common Auto. (151-180): 5.00
Production 250-1,000
Common (181-200): 2.00
Production 1,000
Pack (5): 5.00
Box (24): 100.00

1	Troy Glaus	.40
2	Darin Erstad	.25
3	Garret Anderson	.40
4	Tim Salmon	.25
5	Bartolo Colon	.25
6	Jose Guillen	.40
7	Miguel Tejada	.40
8	Adam Loewen	.25
9	Jay Gibbons	.25
10	Melvin Mora	.25
11	Javy Lopez	.40
12	Pedro J. Martinez	.75
13	Curt Schilling	.50
14	David Ortiz	.50
15	Keith Foulke	.25
16	Nomar Garciaparra	1.00
17	Magglio Ordonez	.40
18	Frank Thomas	.50
19	Carlos Lee	.40
20	Paul Konerko	.40
21	Mark Buehrle	.25
22	Jody Gerut	.25
23	Victor Martinez	.25
24	C.C. Sabathia	.25
25	Ellis Burks	.25
26	Bobby Higginson	.25
27	Jeremy Bonderman	.25
28	Fernando Vina	.25
29	Carlos Pena	.25
30	Dmitri Young	.25
31	Carlos Beltran	.50
32	Benito Santiago	.25
33	Mike Sweeney	.25
34	Angel Berroa	.25
35	Runelvys Hernandez	.25
36	Johan Santana	.25
37	Doug Mientkiewicz	.25
38	Shannon Stewart	.25
39	Torii Hunter	.40
40	Derek Jeter	2.00
41	Jason Giambi	.50
42	Bernie Williams	.40
43	Alfonso Soriano	.50
44	Gary Sheffield	.40
45	Mike Mussina	.50
46	Jorge Posada	.40
47	Hideki Matsui	1.00
48	Kevin Brown	.40
49	Javier Vazquez	.40
50	Mariano Rivera	.40
51	Eric Chavez	.40
52	Tim Hudson	.40
53	Mark Mulder	.40
54	Barry Zito	.40
55	Ichiro Suzuki	1.00
56	Edgar Martinez	.40
57	Bret Boone	.40
58	John Olerud	.40
59	Scott Spiezio	.25
60	Aubrey Huff	.40
61	Rocco Baldelli	.40
62	Jose Cruz Jr.	.25
63	Delmon Young	.40
64	Mark Teixeira	.40
65	Hank Blalock	.50
66	Michael Young	.40
67	Alex Rodriguez	2.00
68	Carlos Delgado	.50
69	Eric Hinske	.25
70	Roy Halladay	.40
71	Vernon Wells	.25
72	Randy Johnson	.75
73	Richie Sexson	.50
74	Brandon Webb	.25
75	Luis Gonzalez	.40
76	Steve Finley	.25
77	Chipper Jones	.75
78	Andruw Jones	.50
79	Marcus Giles	.25
80	Rafael Furcal	.25
81	J.D. Drew	.40
82	Sammy Sosa	1.50
83	Kerry Wood	.75
84	Mark Prior	1.00
85	Derrek Lee	.40
86	Moises Alou	.40
87	Corey Patterson	.25
88	Ken Griffey Jr.	1.00
89	Austin Kearns	.40
90	Adam Dunn	.50
91	Barry Larkin	.40
92	Todd Helton	.50
93	Larry Walker	.40
94	Preston Wilson	.25
95	Charles Johnson	.25
96	Luis Castillo	.25
97	Josh Beckett	.40
98	Mike Lowell	.40
99	Miguel Cabrera	.75
100	Juan Pierre	.25
101	Dontrelle Willis	.40
102	Andy Pettitte	.40
103	Wade Miller	.25
104	Jeff Bagwell	.50
105	Craig Biggio	.40
106	Lance Berkman	.40
107	Jeff Kent	.40
108	Roy Oswalt	.40
109	Hideo Nomo	.40
110	Adrian Beltre	.25
111	Paul LoDuca	.25
112	Shawn Green	.40
113	Fred McGriff	.40
114	Eric Gagne	.40
115	Geoff Jenkins	.40
116	Rickie Weeks	.40
117	Scott Podsednik	.40
118	Nick Johnson	.25
119	Orlando Cabrera	.25
120	Jose Vidro	.25
121	Kazuo Matsui RC	5.00
122	Tom Glavine	.40
123	Al Leiter	.25
124	Mike Piazza	1.00
125	Jose Reyes	.50
126	Mike Cameron	.25
127	Pat Burrell	.40
128	Jim Thome	.75
129	Mike Lieberthal	.25
130	Bobby Abreu	.40
131	Kip Wells	.25
132	Jack Wilson	.40
133	Pokey Reese	.25
134	Brian Giles	.40
135	Sean Burroughs	.25
136	Ryan Klesko	.40
137	Trevor Hoffman	.25
138	Jason Schmidt	.40
139	J.T. Snow	.25
140	A.J. Pierzynski	.25
141	Ray Durham	.25
142	Jim Edmonds	.40
143	Albert Pujols	1.50
144	Edgar Renteria	.40
145	Scott Rolen	.75
146	Matt Morris	.25
147	Ivan Rodriguez	.50
148	Vladimir Guerrero	.75
149	Greg Maddux	1.00
150	Kevin Millwood	.40
151	Hector Gimenez/ AU/750 RC	5.00
152	Willy Taveras/ AU/750 RC	15.00
153	Ruddy Yan/AU/750	5.00
154	Graham Koonce/ AU/750	8.00
155	Jose Capellan/ AU/750 RC	15.00
156	Onil Joseph/ AU/750 RC	5.00
157	John Gall/ AU/1000 RC	10.00
158	Carlos Hines/ AU/750 RC	5.00
159	Jerry Gil/AU/750 RC	5.00
160	Mike Gosling/ AU/750	5.00
161	Jason Frasor/ AU/750 RC	5.00
162	Justin Knoedler/ AU/750 RC	5.00
163	Merkin Valdez/ AU/500 RC	10.00
164	Angel Chavez/ AU/1000 RC	5.00
165	Ivan Ochoa/ AU/750 RC	10.00
166	Greg Dobbs/ AU/750 RC.	5.00
167	Ronald Belisario/ AU/750 RC	5.00
168	Aarom Baldiris/ AU/750 RC	10.00
169	Kazuo Matsui RC.	
170	David Crouthers/ AU/750	5.00
171	Freddy Guzman/ AU/750 RC	10.00
172	Akinori Otsuka/ AU/250 RC	25.00
173	Ian Snell/ AU/750 RC	30.00
174	Nick Regilio/ AU/1000 RC	5.00
175	Jamie Brown/ AU/750 RC	5.00
176	Jerome Gamble/ AU/750 RC	5.00
177	Roberto Novoa/ AU/1000 RC.	5.00
178	Sean Henn/ AU/1000.	10.00
179	Ramon Ramirez/ AU/1000 RC	10.00
180	Jason Bartlett/ AU/1000 RC	10.00
181	Bob Gibson/RET	4.00
182	Cal Ripken Jr./RET	8.00
183	Carl Yastrzemski/ RET	4.00
184	Dale Murphy/RET	3.00
185	Don Mattingly/RET	6.00
186	Eddie Murray/RET	2.00
187	George Brett/RET	6.00
188	Jackie Robinson/ RET	4.00
189	Jim Palmer/RET	2.00
190	Lou Gehrig/RET	5.00
191	Mike Schmidt/RET	5.00
192	Ozzie Smith/RET	5.00
193	Nolan Ryan/RET	8.00
194	Reggie Jackson/ RET	3.00
195	Roberto Clemente/ RET	6.00
196	Robin Yount/RET	4.00

197	Stan Musial/RET	5.00
198	Ted Williams/RET	8.00
199	Tony Gwynn/RET	3.00
200	Ty Cobb/RET	5.00
201	James Gandolfini/FG	3.00
202	Freddy Adu/FG	3.00
203	Summer Sanders/FG	1.50
204	Janet Evans/FG	1.50
205	Brandi Chastain/FG	1.50

Aspirations

Cards (1-150) print run
61-99:	4-8X
(1-150) p/r 41-60:	6-10X
(1-150) p/r 21-40:	8-15X
Autos (151-180):	.75-1.5X
(181-200):	2-3X
Production 19-99	

Status

Cards (1-150) print run
61-81:	4-8X
(1-150) p/r 41-60:	6-10X
(1-150) p/r 21-40:	8-15X
Autos. (151-180):	.75-1X
(181-200):	3-4X
Production 1-81	

Status Gold
Gold (1-150):	10-20X
Gold (151-180):	No Pricing
Gold (181-200):	3-6X
Production 24 Sets	

Back 2 Back Jacks
NM/M

Singles Production 25-125
Duals Production 25-50
1	Albert Pujols/125	15.00
2	Alex Rodriguez/125	10.00
3	Alfonso Soriano/125	8.00
4	Andruw Jones/125	5.00
5	Chipper Jones/125	8.00
6	Derek Jeter/125	20.00
7	Frank Thomas/125	8.00
8	Miguel Cabrera/125	8.00
9	Jason Giambi/125	8.00
10	Jim Thome/125	8.00
11	Mike Piazza/125	10.00
12	Nomar Garciaparra/25	35.00
13	Sammy Sosa/125	10.00
14	Shawn Green/125	4.00
15	Vladimir Guerrero/125	8.00
16	Andruw Jones, Chipper Jones/50	20.00
17	Alfonso Soriano, Derek Jeter/50	30.00
18	Jeff Bagwell, Lance Berkman/50	15.00
19	Alex Rodriguez, Rafael Palmeiro/50	20.00
20	Adam Dunn, Austin Kearns/25	20.00
21	Al Kaline/100	15.00
22	Babe Ruth/50	140.00
23	Cal Ripken Jr./100	40.00
24	Dale Murphy/100	10.00
25	Don Mattingly/100	15.00
26	George Brett/100	20.00
27	Lou Gehrig/100	85.00
28	Mike Schmidt/100	15.00
29	Roberto Clemente/100	50.00
30	Roy Campanella/100	15.00
31	Babe Ruth, Roger Maris/25	200.00
32	Harmon Killebrew, Kirby Puckett/50	35.00
33	Paul Molitor, Robin Yount/50	40.00
34	Reggie Jackson/50	15.00
35	Lou Gehrig, Ty Cobb/50	200.00
36	Don Mattingly, Jason Giambi/50	25.00
37	Ted Williams, Nomar Garciaparra/50	75.00
38	Andre Dawson, Sammy Sosa/50	25.00
39	Dale Murphy, Chipper Jones/50	15.00
40	Stan Musial, Jim Edmonds/50	25.00

Back 2 Back Jacks Combos

NM/M

Singles Production 25-50
Duals Production 10-25
1	Albert Pujols/Bat-Jsy/50	30.00
2	Alex Rodriguez/Bat-Jsy/50	20.00
3	Alfonso Soriano/Bat-Jsy/50	15.00
4	Andruw Jones/Bat-Jsy/50	8.00
5	Chipper Jones/Bat-Jsy/50	12.00
6	Derek Jeter/Bat-Jsy/50	35.00
7	Frank Thomas/Bat-Jsy/50	15.00
8	Miguel Cabrera/Bat-Jsy/50	15.00
9	Jason Giambi/Bat-Jsy/50	15.00
10	Jim Thome/Bat-Jsy/50	15.00
11	Mike Piazza/Bat-Jsy/50	20.00
12	Nomar Garciaparra/Bat-Jsy/50	20.00
13	Sammy Sosa/Bat-Jsy/50	20.00
14	Shawn Green/Bat-Jsy/50	6.00
15	Vladimir Guerrero/Bat-Jsy/50	15.00
16	Andruw Jones, Chipper Jones/50	30.00
17	Alfonso Soriano, Lance Berkman/25	50.00
18	Jeff Bagwell, Lance Berkman/25	20.00
19	Alex Rodriguez, Rafael Palmeiro/25	30.00
20	Adam Dunn, Austin Kearns/25	20.00
21	Al Kaline/Bat-Jsy/25	25.00
22	Babe Ruth/Bat-Jsy/25	350.00
23	Cal Ripken Jr./Bat-Jsy/25	60.00
24	Dale Murphy/Bat-Jsy/50	15.00
25	Don Mattingly/Bat-Jsy/50	25.00
26	George Brett/Bat-Jsy/50	30.00
27	Lou Gehrig/Bat-Jsy/25	150.00
28	Mike Schmidt/Bat-Jsy/25	30.00
29	Roberto Clemente/BatJsy/50	80.00
30	Roy Campanella/Bat-Jsy/50	25.00
31	Babe Ruth, Roger Maris/10	185.00
32	Harmon Killebrew, Kirby Puckett/25	50.00
33	Paul Molitor, Robin Yount/25	50.00
34	Reggie Jackson/25	25.00
35	Lou Gehrig, Ty Cobb/25	350.00
36	Don Mattingly, Jason Giambi/25	35.00
37	Ted Williams, Nomar Garciaparra	140.00
38	Andre Dawson, Sammy Sosa/25	40.00
39	Dale Murphy, Chipper Jones	20.00
40	Stan Musial, Jim Edmonds	35.00

Back to the Future
NM/M

#1-6
Production 500
#6-9
Production 250
Black:		1-2X
Production 25 or 50		
Gold:		.75-1.5X
Production 50 or 100		
Red:		1X
Production 125 or 250		
1	Tim Hudson	2.00
2	Rich Harden	1.50
3	Alex Rodriguez/Rgr	5.00
4	Hank Blalock	3.00
5	Sammy Sosa	5.00
6	Hee Seop Choi	1.50
7	Tim Hudson, Rich Harden	3.00
8	Alex Rodriguez, Hank Blalock	6.00
9	Sammy Sosa, Hee Seop Choi	6.00

Back to the Future Bats
NM/M

#1-6
Production 200
#8-9
Production 100
1	Tim Hudson	4.00
3	Alex Rodriguez	10.00
4	Hank Blalock	6.00
5	Sammy Sosa	10.00
6	Hee Seop Choi	4.00
8	Alex Rodriguez, Hank Blalock	12.00
9	Sammy Sosa, Hee Seop Choi	12.00

Back to the Future Jerseys
NM/M

#1-6
Production 200
#7-9
Production 100
Prime:		1.5-2X
Production 25 or 50		
1	Tim Hudson	4.00
2	Rich Harden	4.00
3	Alex Rodriguez/Rgr	10.00
4	Hank Blalock	6.00
5	Sammy Sosa	10.00
6	Hee Seop Choi	4.00
7	Tim Hudson, Rich Harden	8.00
8	Alex Rodriguez, Hank Blalock	12.00
9	Sammy Sosa, Hee Seop Choi	12.00

Career Best
NM/M

Common Player:	1.00
Production 1,000 Sets	
Black:	2X
Production 100 Sets	
Gold Print Run 200-390:	1.5X
Gold P/R 101-200:	2X
Gold P/R 50-100:	3X
Gold P/R 26-50:	3-5X
Gold P/R 15-25:	5-8X

1	Albert Pujols	3.00
2	Alex Rodriguez	3.00
3	Alfonso Soriano	1.50
4	Andruw Jones	1.00
5	Barry Zito	1.00
6	Cal Ripken Jr.	5.00
7	Chipper Jones	1.50
8	Curt Schilling	1.00
9	Derek Jeter	4.00
10	Don Mattingly	4.00
11	Dontrelle Willis	1.00
12	Doc Gooden	1.00
13	Eddie Murray	1.50
14	Frank Thomas	1.50
15	Gary Sheffield	1.00
16	George Brett	4.00
17	Greg Maddux	2.00
18	Hideo Nomo	1.00
19	Ichiro Suzuki	2.00
20	Ivan Rodriguez	1.50
21	Jason Giambi	1.50
22	Jeff Bagwell	1.50
23	Jim Thome	1.50
24	Kerry Wood	1.50
25	Lance Berkman	1.00
26	Magglio Ordonez	1.00
27	Mark Prior	2.00
28	Mike Piazza	2.00
29	Mike Schmidt	3.00
30	Nomar Garciaparra	2.50
31	Pedro J. Martinez	2.00
32	Randy Johnson	2.00
33	Roger Clemens	3.00
34	Sammy Sosa	2.50
35	Tony Gwynn	1.50

Career Best Bats

NM/M

Production 100 Or 200	
Combo Print Run 50:	1-2X
Combo P/R 25:	2X
Production 25 or 50	

1	Albert Pujols/200	15.00
2	Alex Rodriguez/200	10.00
3	Alfonso Soriano/200	8.00
4	Andruw Jones/200	5.00
5	Barry Zito/200	4.00
6	Cal Ripken Jr./200	25.00
7	Chipper Jones/200	8.00
8	Curt Schilling/200	5.00
9	Derek Jeter/200	15.00
10	Don Mattingly/200	15.00
11	Dontrelle Willis/100	6.00
12	Doc Gooden/200	6.00
13	Eddie Murray/200	4.00
14	Frank Thomas/200	15.00
15	Gary Sheffield/200	5.00
16	George Brett/200	15.00
17	Greg Maddux/100	10.00
18	Hideo Nomo/100	8.00
20	Ivan Rodriguez/200	8.00
21	Jason Giambi/200	8.00
22	Jeff Bagwell/200	6.00
23	Jim Thome/200	8.00
24	Kerry Wood/100	10.00
25	Lance Berkman/200	4.00
26	Magglio Ordonez/200	4.00
27	Mark Prior/100	8.00
28	Mike Piazza/200	10.00
29	Mike Schmidt/200	10.00
30	Nomar Garciaparra/200	10.00
31	Pedro J. Martinez/200	8.00
32	Randy Johnson/200	8.00
33	Roger Clemens/200	15.00
34	Sammy Sosa/200	10.00
35	Tony Gwynn/200	8.00

Career Best Jerseys
NM/M

Quantity produced listed
Prime:	1.5-2X

Production 25-50

1	Albert Pujols/200	15.00
2	Alex Rodriguez/200	10.00
3	Alfonso Soriano/200	8.00
4	Andruw Jones/200	5.00
5	Barry Zito/200	4.00
6	Cal Ripken Jr./50	40.00
7	Chipper Jones/200	8.00
8	Curt Schilling/200	5.00
9	Derek Jeter/200	15.00
10	Don Mattingly/50	20.00
11	Dontrelle Willis/200	6.00
12	Doc Gooden/200	6.00
13	Eddie Murray/200	6.00
14	Frank Thomas/200	8.00
15	Gary Sheffield/200	5.00
16	George Brett/50	25.00
17	Greg Maddux/200	10.00
18	Hideo Nomo/200	8.00
20	Ivan Rodriguez/200	8.00
21	Jason Giambi/200	8.00
22	Jeff Bagwell/200	6.00
23	Jim Thome/200	8.00
24	Kerry Wood/200	10.00
25	Lance Berkman/200	4.00
26	Magglio Ordonez/200	4.00
27	Mark Prior/200	8.00
28	Mike Piazza/200	10.00
29	Mike Schmidt/100	10.00
30	Nomar Garciaparra/200	10.00
31	Pedro J. Martinez/200	8.00
32	Randy Johnson/200	8.00
33	Roger Clemens/200	15.00
34	Sammy Sosa/200	10.00
35	Tony Gwynn/200	15.00

Fans of the Game Autographs

		NM/M
201	James Gandolfini	120.00
202	Freddy Adu	80.00
203	Summer Sanders	25.00
204	Janet Evans	25.00
205	Brandi Chastain	35.00

Passing the Torch

		NM/M

#1-30
Production 1,000
#31-45
Production 500

Black: Production 50 or 100	1-2X
Blue: Production 125 or 250	1X
Gold: Production 25 or 50	1.5-3X
Green: Production 250 or 500	.75-1X

1	Whitey Ford	3.00
2	Andy Pettitte	1.50
3	Willie McCovey	2.00
4	Will Clark	3.00
5	Stan Musial	4.00
6	Albert Pujols	5.00
7	Andre Dawson	2.00
8	Vladimir Guerrero	2.00
9	Dale Murphy	2.00
10	Chipper Jones	2.00
11	Joe Morgan	1.50
12	Barry Larkin	1.50
13	Jim "Catfish" Hunter	1.50
14	Tim Hudson	1.50
15	Jim Rice	1.50
16	Manny Ramirez	2.00
17	Greg Maddux	2.50
18	Mark Prior	2.00
19	Don Mattingly	4.00
20	Jason Giambi	2.00
21	Roy Campanella	2.00
22	Mike Piazza	3.00
23	Ozzie Smith	2.00
24	Scott Rolen	2.00
25	Roger Clemens	4.00
26	Mike Mussina	2.00
27	Babe Ruth	6.00
28	Roger Maris	4.00
29	Nolan Ryan	6.00
30	Roy Oswalt	1.50
31	Whitey Ford, Andy Pettitte	3.00
32	Willie McCovey, Will Clark	3.00
33	Stan Musial, Albert Pujols	6.00
34	Andre Dawson, Vladimir Guerrero	3.00
35	Dale Murphy, Chipper Jones	3.00
36	Joe Morgan, Barry Larkin	3.00
37	Jim "Catfish" Hunter, Tim Hudson	2.00
38	Jim Rice, Manny Ramirez	3.00
39	Greg Maddux, Mark Prior	4.00
40	Don Mattingly, Jason Giambi	8.00
41	Roy Campanella, Mike Piazza	5.00
42	Ozzie Smith, Scott Rolen	5.00
43	Roger Clemens, Mike Mussina	5.00
44	Babe Ruth, Roger Maris	10.00
45	Nolan Ryan, Roy Oswalt	8.00

Passing the Torch Autographs

		NM/M

Quantity produced listed
Many not priced due to scarcity.

4	Will Clark/15	100.00
7	Andre Dawson/50	15.00
9	Dale Murphy/50	30.00
14	Joe Morgan/15	25.00
14	Tim Hudson/15	45.00
15	Jim Rice/50	15.00
18	Mark Prior/15	80.00
24	Scott Rolen/15	50.00
30	Roy Oswalt/50	15.00

Passing the Torch Bats

		NM/M

Quantity produced listed

2	Andy Pettitte/200	4.00
3	Willie McCovey/100	6.00
4	Will Clark/100	10.00
5	Stan Musial/100	25.00
6	Albert Pujols/200	15.00
7	Andre Dawson/100	8.00
8	Vladimir Guerrero/200	8.00
9	Dale Murphy/100	10.00
10	Chipper Jones/200	8.00
11	Joe Morgan/200	4.00
12	Barry Larkin/200	5.00
14	Tim Hudson/200	5.00
15	Jim Rice/200	5.00
16	Manny Ramirez/200	8.00
18	Mark Prior/200	8.00
19	Don Mattingly/100	15.00
20	Jason Giambi/200	8.00
21	Roy Campanella/50	30.00
22	Mike Piazza/200	10.00
23	Ozzie Smith/200	15.00
24	Scott Rolen/200	8.00
25	Roger Clemens/200	15.00
26	Mike Mussina/200	8.00
27	Babe Ruth/25	150.00
28	Roger Maris/50	50.00
29	Nolan Ryan/100	25.00
30	Roy Oswalt/200	4.00
32	Willie McCovey, Will Clark/50	20.00
33	Stan Musial, Albert Pujols/50	50.00
34	Andre Dawson, Vladimir Guerrero/50	20.00
35	Dale Murphy, Chipper Jones/50	20.00
36	Joe Morgan, Barry Larkin/50	15.00
38	Jim Rice, Manny Ramirez/50	20.00
39	Greg Maddux, Mark Prior/50	25.00
40	Don Mattingly, Jason Giambi/50	35.00
41	Roy Campanella, Mike Piazza/25	35.00
42	Ozzie Smith, Scott Rolen/50	30.00
43	Roger Clemens, Mike Mussina/50	30.00
44	Babe Ruth, Roger Maris/25	200.00
45	Nolan Ryan, Roy Oswalt/50	35.00

Passing the Torch Jerseys

		NM/M

Quantity produced listed

1	Whitey Ford/100	15.00
2	Andy Pettitte/200	4.00
3	Willie McCovey/100	6.00
4	Will Clark/100	10.00
5	Stan Musial/100	25.00
6	Albert Pujols/200	15.00
7	Andre Dawson/200	8.00
8	Vladimir Guerrero/200	8.00
9	Dale Murphy/100	10.00
10	Chipper Jones/200	8.00
11	Joe Morgan/100	4.00
12	Barry Larkin/200	5.00
13	Jim "Catfish" Hunter/100	5.00
14	Tim Hudson/200	5.00
15	Jim Rice/200	5.00
16	Manny Ramirez/200	8.00
18	Mark Prior/200	8.00
19	Don Mattingly/100	15.00
20	Jason Giambi/200	8.00
21	Roy Campanella/50	30.00
22	Mike Piazza/200	10.00
23	Ozzie Smith/100	12.00
24	Scott Rolen/200	8.00
25	Roger Clemens/200	15.00
26	Mike Mussina/200	8.00
27	Babe Ruth/25	300.00
28	Roger Maris/50	50.00
29	Nolan Ryan/100	25.00
30	Roy Oswalt/200	4.00
31	Whitey Ford, Andy Pettitte/200	20.00
32	Willie McCovey, Will Clark/50	20.00
33	Stan Musial, Albert Pujols/50	50.00
34	Andre Dawson, Vladimir Guerrero/50	20.00
35	Dale Murphy, Chipper Jones/50	20.00
36	Joe Morgan, Barry Larkin/50	15.00
37	Jim "Catfish" Hunter, Tim Hudson/50	15.00
38	Jim Rice, Manny Ramirez/50	20.00
40	Don Mattingly, Jason Giambi/50	35.00
41	Roy Campanella, Mike Piazza/50	35.00
42	Ozzie Smith, Scott Rolen/50	30.00
43	Roger Clemens, Mike Mussina/50	30.00
45	Nolan Ryan, Roy Oswalt/50	35.00

Recollection Autographs

		NM/M
	Common Autograph:	8.00
1	Jeremy Affeldt 01/25	15.00
2	Erick Almonte 01/26	10.00
4	Jeff Baker 02/25	30.00
5	Brandon Berger 01/25	8.00
6	Marlon Byrd 01/24	25.00
8	Ryan Drese 02/45	8.00
9	Brandon Duckworth 01/16	15.00
10	Casey Fossum 01/23	15.00
11	Geronimo Gil 01/25	8.00
13	Jeremy Guthrie 02/25	20.00
14	Nic Jackson 02/95	8.00
21	Ricardo Rodriguez 01/25	8.00
23	Bud Smith 01/25	8.00
24	Sammy Sosa 01/1	
25	Junior Spivey 01/20	20.00
26	Tim Spooneybarger 01/25	10.00
27	Mark Teixeira 01/6	
28	Martin Vargas 01/37	8.00

Team

		NM/M

Production 1,500 Sets

Black: Production 150 Sets	1-2X
Gold: Production 250 Sets	1-1.5X

1	Cal Ripken Jr., Eddie Murray, Jim Palmer	8.00
2	Derek Jeter, Roger Clemens, Bernie Williams, Andy Pettitte	4.00
3	Johnny Bench, Tony Perez, George Foster, Dave Concepcion	4.00
4	Josh Beckett, Dontrelle Willis, Ivan Rodriguez	2.00
5	Randy Johnson, Curt Schilling, Luis Gonzalez, Mark Grace	2.00
6	Derek Jeter, Wade Boggs, Darryl Strawberry	5.00
7	Chipper Jones, Tom Glavine, Greg Maddux, Ryan Klesko	4.00

8	Dwight Gooden, Gary Carter, Darryl Strawberry	2.00
9	Jackie Robinson, Roy Campanella, Duke Snider	3.00
10	Phil Rizzuto, Yogi Berra, Whitey Ford	2.00
11	Stan Musial, Curt Schilling, Marty Marion, Enos Slaughter	4.00

Team Bats

NM/M

Production 100 Sets

2	Derek Jeter, Roger Clemens, Bernie Williams, Andy Pettitte	30.00
3	Johnny Bench, Tony Perez, George Foster, Dave Concepcion	50.00
4	Josh Beckett, Dontrelle Willis, Ivan Rodriguez	15.00
5	Randy Johnson, Curt Schilling, Luis Gonzalez, Mark Grace	25.00
6	Derek Jeter, Wade Boggs, Darryl Strawberry	30.00
7	Chipper Jones, Tom Glavine, Greg Maddux, Ryan Klesko	25.00
8	Dwight Gooden, Gary Carter, Darryl Strawberry	20.00

Team Jerseys

NM/M

Production 100 unless noted.

1	Cal Ripken Jr., Eddie Murray, Jim Palmer	50.00
2	Derek Jeter, Roger Clemens, Bernie Williams, Andy Pettitte	40.00
4	Josh Beckett, Dontrelle Willis, Ivan Rodriguez	15.00
5	Randy Johnson, Curt Schilling, Luis Gonzalez, Mark Grace	25.00
6	Derek Jeter, Wade Boggs, Darryl Strawberry	30.00
7	Chipper Jones, Tom Glavine, Greg Maddux, Ryan Klesko	25.00
9	Jackie Robinson, Roy Campanella, Duke Snider	75.00
10	Phil Rizzuto, Yogi Berra, Whitey Ford	35.00
11	Stan Musial, Curt Schilling, Marty Marion, Enos Slaughter	50.00

Throwback Threads

NM/M

Quantity produced listed
Prime: 1.5-3X
Prime Singles Production 10-25
Prime Duals Production 5-15

1	Albert Pujols/150	60.00
2	Alex Rodriguez/Rgr/150	125.00
3	Alfonso Soriano/150	175.00
4	Chipper Jones/150	120.00
5	Derek Jeter/150	15.00
6	Greg Maddux/150	10.00
7	Hideo Nomo/150	8.00
8	Miguel Cabrera/150	8.00
9	Ivan Rodriguez/150	8.00

10	Jason Giambi/150	8.00
11	Jeff Bagwell/150	8.00
12	Lance Berkman/150	4.00
13	Mark Prior/150	8.00
14	Mike Piazza/150	10.00
15	Nomar Garciaparra/150	10.00
16	Pedro J. Martinez/150	8.00
17	Randy Johnson/150	8.00
18	Sammy Sosa/150	10.00
19	Shawn Green/150	4.00
20	Vladimir Guerrero/150	8.00
21	Adam Dunn, Austin Kearns/75	20.00
22	Barry Zito, Mark Mulder/75	10.00
23	Curt Schilling/75	10.00
24	Derek Jeter, Jason Giambi/75	25.00
25	Dontrelle Willis, Josh Beckett/75	15.00
26	Frank Thomas, Magglio Ordonez/75	15.00
27	Jim Thome/75	15.00
28	Kerry Wood, Mark Prior/75	25.00
29	Hank Blalock, Mark Teixeira/75	15.00
30	Albert Pujols, Scott Rolen/75	40.00
31	Babe Ruth/50	280.00
32	Cal Ripken Jr./100	40.00
33	Carl Yastrzemski/100	20.00
34	Deion Sanders/100	10.00
35	Don Mattingly/100	20.00
36	George Brett/100	20.00
37	Jim Palmer/100	8.00
38	Kirby Puckett/100	15.00
39	Lou Gehrig/100	125.00
40	Mark Grace/100	10.00
41	Mike Schmidt/100	20.00
42	Nolan Ryan/100	25.00
43	Ozzie Smith/100	20.00
44	Reggie Jackson/100	10.00
45	Rickey Henderson/100	10.00
46	Roberto Clemente/100	75.00
47	Roger Clemens/100	15.00
48	Roger Maris/100	40.00
49	Roy Campanella/Pants/100	20.00
50	Tony Gwynn/100	15.00
51	Babe Ruth, Lou Gehrig/25	400.00
52	Cal Ripken Jr., Eddie Murray/50	50.00
53	Ted Williams, Carl Yastrzemski/50	85.00
54	Andre Dawson, Gary Carter/50	20.00
55	Reggie Jackson, Rod Carew/50	20.00
56	Derek Jeter, Phil Rizzuto/50	40.00
57	Nolan Ryan, Roy Oswalt/50	40.00
58	Roger Clemens, Mike Mussina/50	25.00
59	Albert Pujols, Stan Musial/50	40.00
60	Nomar Garciaparra, Stan Musial/50	85.00

Throwback Threads Autographs

NM/M

Production 25 Sets
Prime: No Pricing
Production 5-10

9	Ivan Rodriguez/25	60.00
13	Mark Prior/25	80.00
18	Sammy Sosa/25	175.00
35	Don Mattingly/25	120.00
37	Jim Palmer/25	40.00

Turn of the Century

Stars (1-150): 2-3X
Production 750

Stars (181-200): 1X
Production 250

2004 Donruss Elite Extra Edition

NM/M

Complete Set (288):
Common (1-150): .25
Common (206-215): 2.00
Production 1,000
Common Auto.(216-355): 6.00
Common No Auto.
(234-254): 3.00
No Auto. Production 1,000
Pack (5): 14.00
Box (12): 150.00
Note: Cards 151-205 do not exist.

1	Troy Glaus	.40
2	John Lackey	.25
3	Garret Anderson	.40
4	Francisco Rodriguez	.25
5	Casey Kotchman	.25
6	Jose Guillen	.25
7	Miguel Tejada	.50
8	Rafael Palmeiro	.50
9	Jay Gibbons	.25
10	Melvin Mora	.25
11	Javy Lopez	.25
12	Pedro Martinez	.75
13	Curt Schilling	.75
14	David Ortiz	.75
15	Manny Ramirez	.75
16	Nomar Garciaparra	1.00
17	Magglio Ordonez	.25
18	Frank Thomas	.75
19	Esteban Loaiza	.25
20	Paul Konerko	.50
21	Mark Buehrle	.25
22	Jody Gerut	.25
23	Victor Martinez	.40
24	C.C. Sabathia	.25
25	Travis Hafner	.50
26	Cliff Lee	.25
27	Jeremy Bonderman	.40
28	Dallas McPherson	.25
29	Jermaine Dye	.25
30	Carlos Guillen	.25
31	Carlos Beltran	.50
32	Ken Harvey	.25
33	Mike Sweeney	.25
34	Angel Berroa	.25
35	Joe Nathan	.25
36	Johan Santana	.50
37	Jacque Jones	.25
38	Shannon Stewart	.25
39	Torii Hunter	.40
40	Derek Jeter	2.00
41	Jason Giambi	.50
42	Danny Graves	.25
43	Alfonso Soriano	.75

44	Gary Sheffield	.50
45	Mike Mussina	.50
46	Jorge Posada	.50
47	Hideki Matsui	1.00
48	Francisco Cordero	.25
49	Javier Vazquez	.25
50	Mariano Rivera	.40
51	Eric Chavez	.40
52	Tim Hudson	.40
53	Mark Mulder	.40
54	Barry Zito	.40
55	Ichiro Suzuki	1.50
56	Edgar Martinez	.25
57	Bret Boone	.25
58	Lew Ford	.25
59	B.J. Upton	.40
60	Aubrey Huff	.25
61	Rocco Baldelli	.25
62	Carl Crawford	.40
63	Delmon Young	.40
64	Mark Teixeira	.40
65	Hank Blalock	.50
66	Michael Young	.25
67	Alex Rodriguez	1.50
68	Carlos Delgado	.40
69	Milton Bradley	.25
70	Roy Halladay	.40
71	Vernon Wells	.25
72	Randy Johnson	.75
73	Bobby Crosby	.25
74	Lyle Overbay	.25
75	Luis Gonzalez	.25
76	Steve Finley	.25
77	Chipper Jones	.75
78	Andruw Jones	.40
79	Marcus Giles	.25
80	Rafael Furcal	.25
81	J.D. Drew	.40
82	Sammy Sosa	1.00
83	Kerry Wood	.40
84	Mark Prior	.75
85	Derek Lee	.50
86	Moises Alou	.40
87	Carlos Zambrano	.40
88	Ken Griffey Jr.	1.00
89	Austin Kearns	.40
90	Adam Dunn	.50
91	Barry Larkin	.40
92	Todd Helton	.50
93	Larry Walker	.40
94	Preston Wilson	.25
95	Sean Casey	.25
96	Luis Castillo	.25
97	Josh Beckett	.25
98	Mike Lowell	.40
99	Miguel Cabrera	.75
100	Brad Penny	.25
101	Dontrelle Willis	.25
102	Andy Pettitte	.40
103	Wade Miller	.25
104	Jeff Bagwell	.50
105	Craig Biggio	.25
106	Lance Berkman	.40
107	Jeff Kent	.25
108	Roy Oswalt	.40
109	Hideo Nomo	.40
110	Adrian Beltre	.40
111	Paul LoDuca	.25
112	Shawn Green	.40
113	Roger Clemens	2.00
114	Eric Gagne	.40
115	Danny Kolb	.25
116	Rickie Weeks	.25
117	Scott Podsednik	.25
118	Livan Hernandez	.25
119	Orlando Cabrera	.25
120	Jose Vidro	.25
121	David Wright	1.50
122	Tom Glavine	.40
123	Al Leiter	.25
124	Mike Piazza	1.00
125	Jose Reyes	.50
126	Richard Hidalgo	.25
127	Eric Milton	.25
128	Jim Thome	.75
129	Mike Lieberthal	.25
130	Bobby Abreu	.40
131	Kip Wells	.25
132	Jack Wilson	.25
133	Jason Bay	.40
134	Brian Giles	.25
135	Sean Burroughs	.25
136	Khalil Greene	.25
137	Jake Peavy	.40
138	Jason Schmidt	.40
139	J.T. Snow	.25
140	Craig Wilson	.25
141	Chase Utley	.50
142	Jim Edmonds	.40
143	Albert Pujols	2.00
144	Edgar Renteria	.40
145	Scott Rolen	.75
146	Matt Morris	.25
147	Ivan Rodriguez	.50

#	Player	Price
148	Vladimir Guerrero	.75
149	Greg Maddux	1.00
150	Ben Sheets	.40
206	Will Clark	2.00
207	Nolan Ryan	8.00
208	Bob Feller	2.00
209	Red Schoendienst	2.00
210	Brooks Robinson	3.00
211	Al Kaline	3.00
212	Ozzie Smith	4.00
213	Maury Wills	2.00
214	Steve Carlton	2.00
215	Duke Snider	3.00
216	Scott Lewis/ Auto./603 RC	15.00
217	Josh Johnson/ Auto./597 RC	10.00
218	Jeff Fiorentino/ Auto./597 RC	15.00
219	Grant Hansen/ Auto./599 RC	6.00
220	Yovani Gallardo/ Auto./803 RC	75.00
221	Eddie Prasch/ Auto./603 RC	10.00
222	Danny Hill/ Auto./603 RC	6.00
223	Chuck Lofgren/ Auto./803 RC	25.00
224	Blake Johnson/ Auto./811 RC	10.00
225	Cory Dunlap/ Auto./599 RC	15.00
226	Carlos Vasquez/ Auto./869 RC	8.00
227	Jesse Crain/ Auto./1,000 RC	10.00
228	Yhency Brazoban/ Auto./1,000 RC	6.00
229	Abe Alvarez/ Auto./1,000 RC	8.00
230	Scott Kazmir/ Auto./350	50.00
231	J.A. Happ/ Auto./1195 RC	8.00
232	Mark Jecmen/ Auto./1,047 RC	6.00
234	Kameron Loe/ 1,000 RC	3.00
235	Ervin Santana/ 1,000 RC	5.00
239	Josh Karp/1,000 RC	3.00
242	Alberto Callaspo/ 1,000 RC	3.00
243	Jesse Hoover/ Auto./1,191 RC	8.00
246	Justin Hoyman/ Auto./1,124 RC	8.00
247	Juan Cedeno/ 1,000 RC	3.00
250	Jake Dittler/1,000	4.00
252	Benjamin Zobrist/ Auto./1,178 RC	10.00
253	Jeff Salazar/1,000 RC	3.00
254	Fausto Carmona/ 1,000 RC	4.00
256	Jorge Vasquez/ Auto./1,000 RC	6.00
257	Rafael Gonzalez/ Auto./603 RC	6.00
258	Andrew Dobies/ Auto./601 RC	10.00
259	Colby Miller/ Auto./997 RC	6.00
260	K.C. Herren/ Auto./735 RC	10.00
261	Ryan Meaux/ Auto./546 RC	6.00
262	Dustin Pedroia/ Auto./1,114 RC	75.00
263	Fernando Nieve/ Auto./1,000 RC	10.00
264	Mariano Gomez/ Auto./1,000 RC	6.00
265	Eric Campbell/ Auto./260 RC	60.00
266	Billy Killian/ Auto./703 RC	6.00
267	Mike Rouse/Auto./999	6.00
268	Kyle Bono/ Auto./1203 RC	8.00
269	Mitch Einertson/ Auto./1047 RC	10.00
270	Scott Proctor/ Auto./1000 RC	8.00
271	Tim Bittner/ Auto./1000 RC	6.00
272	Christian Garcia/ Auto./799 RC	10.00
273	Yadier Molina/ Auto./1,000 RC	20.00
275	Charles Thomas/ Auto./907 RC	8.00
276	Travis Blackley/ Auto./1000 RC	8.00
277	Frankie Francisco/ Auto./1000 RC	6.00
278	Dioner Navarro/ Auto./1000 RC	10.00
279	Joey Gathright/ Auto./1000 RC	8.00
280	Kazuhito Tadano/ Auto./1000 RC	15.00
281	Matt Bush/ Auto./1100 RC	20.00
282	David Haehnel/ Auto./865 RC	8.00
283	Tommy Hottovy/ Auto./825 RC	8.00
284	Chris Carter/ Auto./973 RC	25.00
285	Mark Rogers/ Auto./578 RC	20.00
286	Jeremy Sowers/ Auto./537 RC	25.00
287	Homer Bailey/ Auto./1571 RC	50.00
288	Mike Butia/ Auto./825 RC	8.00
289	Chris Nelson/ Auto./465 RC	30.00
290	Thomas Diamond/ Auto./1055 RC	15.00
291	Neil Walker/ Auto./1343 RC	25.00
292	Sean Gamble/ Auto./1229 RC	8.00
293	Bill Bray/ Auto./1073 RC	6.00
294	Reid Brignac/ Auto./522 RC	60.00
295	Ryan Klosterman/ Auto./865 RC	6.00
296	David Purcey/ Auto./1485 RC	8.00
297	Scott Elbert/ Auto./1617 RC	30.00
298	Josh Fields/ Auto./961 RC	30.00
299	Chris Lambert/ Auto./954 RC	8.00
300	Trevor Plouffe/ Auto./1329 RC	15.00
301	Greg Golson/ Auto./1334 RC	15.00
302	Josh Baker/ Auto./525 RC	8.00
303	Phillip Hughes/ Auto./1485 RC	80.00
304	Matt Macri/ Auto./979 RC	10.00
305	Kyle Waldrop/ Auto./823 RC	10.00
306	Richie Robnett/ Auto./1575 RC	15.00
307	Taylor Tankersley/ Auto./1073 RC	8.00
308	Blake DeWitt/ Auto./1562 RC	25.00
309	Daryl Jones/ Auto./575 RC	15.00
310	Eric Hurley/ Auto./1021 RC	30.00
311	J.P. Howell/ Auto./1453 RC	10.00
312	Zach Jackson/ Auto./1069 RC	8.00
313	Justin Orenduff/ Auto./473 RC	10.00
314	Tyler Lumsden/ Auto./473 RC	10.00
315	Matt Fox/ Auto./473 RC	12.00
316	Danny Putnam/ Auto./473 RC	10.00
317	Jon Poterson/ Auto./464 RC	15.00
318	Gio Gonzalez/ Auto./473 RC	30.00
319	Jay Rainville/ Auto./823 RC	12.00
320	Huston Street/ Auto./709 RC	30.00
321	Jeff Marquez/ Auto./493 RC	20.00
322	Eric Beattie/ Auto./930 RC	8.00
323	B.J. Szymanski/ Auto./1,327 RC	8.00
324	Seth Smith/ Auto./1065 RC	20.00
325	Robert Zastryny/ Auto./790 RC	8.00
326	Wes Whisler/ Auto./473 RC	8.00
327	Billy Buckner/ Auto./673 RC	8.00
328	Jon Zeringue/ Auto./473 RC	15.00
329	Curtis Thigpen/ Auto./673 RC	10.00
330	Donny Lucy/ Auto./573 RC	6.00
331	Mike Ferris/ Auto./558 RC	10.00
332	Anthony Swarzak/ Auto./370 RC	25.00
333	Jason Jaramillo/ Auto./573 RC	8.00
334	Hunter Pence/ Auto./672 RC	150.00
335	Mike Rozier/ Auto./628 RC	8.00
336	Kurt Suzuki/ Auto./473 RC	20.00
337	Jason Vargas/ Auto./621 RC	20.00
338	Brian Bixler/ Auto./665 RC	10.00
340	Dexter Fowler/ Auto./623 RC	50.00
341	Mark Trumbo/ Auto./1321 RC	15.00
342	Jeff Frazier/ Auto./423 RC	15.00
343	Steven Register/ Auto./673 RC	8.00
344	Michael Schlact/ Auto./477 RC	8.00
345	Garrett Mock/ Auto./471 RC	12.00
346	Eric Haberer/ Auto./473 RC	8.00
347	Matt Tuiasosopo/ Auto./473 RC	25.00
348	Jason Windsor/ Auto./473 RC	15.00
349	Grant Johnson/ Auto./815 RC	10.00
350	J.C. Holt/ Auto./673 RC	10.00
351	Joseph Bauserman/ Auto./472 RC	8.00
352	Jamar Walton/ Auto./481 RC	15.00
353	Eric Patterson/ Auto./1,571 RC	20.00
354	Tyler Johnson/ Auto./775 RC	15.00
355	Nick Adenhart/ Auto./653 RC	80.00

Aspirations

1-150 print run 61-99:	4-8X
1-150 p/r 41-60:	6-12X
1-150 p/r 26-40:	8-15X
1-150 p/r 25 or less:	No Pricing
206-355 p/r 51-99:1-2X No Auto.	
216-355 p/r 61-99:	.4-1X Auto.
216-355 p/r 41-60:	.75-1X Auto.
216-355 p/r 26-40:	.75-1X Auto.
No Pricing print run 25 or less.	

Aspirations Gold

Gold (1-150):	10-20X
Gold (206-215):	3-6X
Gold (216-355):	No Pricing
Production 25 Sets	

Status

1-150 print run 61-99:	4-8X
1-150 p/r 41-60:	6-12X
1-150 p/r 26-40:	8-15X
1-150 p/r 25 or less:	No Pricing
206-355 p/r 51-99:1-2X No Auto.	
216-355 p/r 61-99:	.4-1X Auto.
216-355 p/r 41-60:	.5-1X Auto.
216-355 p/r 26-40:	.75-1X Auto.
No pricing print run 25 or less.	

Status Gold

No Pricing
Production 10 Sets

Turn of the Century

(1-150):	3-5X
Production 250 Sets	
(206-215):	2-3X
(216-355 No Auto.):	.5-1X
(216-355 Auto.):	.2-.5X
206-355 Production 100	

Back to Back Picks Signatures

NM/M

Quantity produced listed

#	Players	Price
1	Delmon Young, Rickie Weeks/25	50.00
3	Adam Dunn, Austin Kearns/25	50.00
5	Michael Young, Vernon Wells/25	35.00
6	Brian Roberts, Larry Bigbie/50	30.00
7	Ron Cey, Steve Garvey/50	35.00
8	Bill Madlock, Dave Parker/50	40.00
9	Derrek Lee, Torii Hunter, Trot Nixon/50	50.00
11	Chris Nelson, Matt Bush, Reid Brignac/250	65.00
12	B.J. Szymanski, Greg Golson, Jeff Frazier/250	40.00
13	Mark Trumbo, Nick Adenhart, Tyler Johnson/100	50.00
14	Chris Carter, Danny Putnam, Mark Jecmen/100	40.00
15	Billy Killian, Daryl Jones, Matt Bush/100	40.00
16	Blake DeWitt, Justin Orenduff, Scott Elbert/250	40.00
17	Jay Rainville, Kyle Waldrop, Trevor Plouffe/250	40.00
18	Jeff Marquez, Jon Poterson, Phillip Hughes/100	80.00
19	Wes Whisler, Tyler Lumsden, Wes Whisler/100	40.00
20	Curtis Thigpen, David Purcey, Zach Jackson/100	40.00

Career Best All-Stars

NM/M

Common Player:
Production 500 Sets

#	Player	Price
1	Randy Johnson	3.00
2	David Ortiz	3.00
3	Edgar Renteria	2.00
4	Victor Martinez	2.00
5	Albert Pujols	6.00
6	Hideki Matsui	5.00
7	Mariano Rivera	2.00
8	Carlos Zambrano	2.00
9	Hank Blalock	2.00
10	Michael Young	2.00
11	Mike Piazza	4.00
12	Alfonso Soriano	3.00
13	Carl Crawford	2.00
14	Scott Rolen	3.00
15	Vladimir Guerrero	3.00
16	Lance Berkman	2.00
17	Todd Helton	3.00
18	Curt Schilling	3.00
19	Francisco Cordero	3.00
20	Mark Mulder	2.00
21	Sammy Sosa	4.00
22	Roger Clemens	6.00
23	Miguel Cabrera	3.00
24	Manny Ramirez	3.00
25	Jim Thome	3.00

Career Best A-S Jersey

NM/M

Production 50 Sets
Prime: 1-2X
Production 5-25
No pricing 15 or less.

#	Player	Price
1	Randy Johnson	15.00
2	David Ortiz	15.00
3	Edgar Renteria	8.00
4	Victor Martinez	8.00
5	Albert Pujols	25.00
6	Hideki Matsui	40.00
7	Mariano Rivera	10.00
8	Carlos Zambrano	8.00
9	Hank Blalock	10.00
10	Michael Young	8.00
11	Mike Piazza	20.00
12	Alfonso Soriano	15.00
13	Carl Crawford	8.00
14	Scott Rolen	15.00
15	Vladimir Guerrero	15.00
16	Lance Berkman	8.00

17	Todd Helton	10.00
18	Curt Schilling	15.00
19	Francisco Cordero	8.00
20	Mark Mulder	8.00
21	Sammy Sosa	20.00
22	Roger Clemens	20.00
23	Miguel Cabrera	12.00
24	Manny Ramirez	15.00
25	Jim Thome	15.00

Career Best A-S Jersey Prime

NM/M

2	David Ortiz/25	25.00
4	Victor Martinez/25	15.00
5	Albert Pujols/25	40.00
6	Hideki Matsui/25	75.00
8	Carlos Zambrano/25	15.00
9	Hank Blalock/25	20.00
10	Michael Young/25	15.00
11	Mike Piazza/25	30.00
12	Alfonso Soriano/25	25.00
13	Carl Crawford/25	15.00
14	Scott Rolen/25	25.00
15	Vladimir Guerrero/25	25.00
16	Lance Berkman/25	15.00
17	Todd Helton/25	20.00
18	Curt Schilling/25	25.00
20	Mark Mulder/25	15.00
21	Sammy Sosa/25	30.00
22	Roger Clemens/25	40.00
23	Miguel Cabrera/25	20.00
24	Manny Ramirez/25	25.00
25	Jim Thome/25	25.00

Career Best A-S Signature Black

No Pricing
Production 1-5

Career Best A-S Signature Gold

No Pricing
Production 1-10

Career Best A-S Signature Jersey Gold

NM/M
Production 1-25

2	David Ortiz/25	75.00
3	Edgar Renteria/25	40.00
4	Victor Martinez/25	40.00
8	Carlos Zambrano/25	40.00
10	Michael Young/25	35.00
13	Carl Crawford/25	30.00
19	Francisco Cordero/25	20.00

Career Best A-S Signature Jersey Prime

No Pricing
Production 1-10

Draft Class

NM/M
Common Duo: 2.00
Production 500 Sets

1	Johnny Bench, Nolan Ryan	10.00
2	Bert Blyleven, Dwight Evans	2.00
3	Jim Rice, Keith Hernandez	2.00
4	Dennis Eckersley, Gary Carter	3.00
5	Fred Lynn, Robin Yount	5.00
6	Andre Dawson, Lee Smith	2.00
7	Alan Trammell, Jack Morris	2.00
8	Harold Baines, Paul Molitor	3.00
9	Cal Ripken Jr., Kirk Gibson	10.00
10	Don Mattingly, Orel Hershiser	6.00
11	Darryl Strawberry, Eric Davis	2.00
12	Dwight Gooden, Jose Canseco	3.00
13	Rafael Palmeiro, Randy Johnson	4.00
14	Curt Schilling, Gary Sheffield	3.00
15	Mike Piazza, Robin Ventura	4.00
16	Frank Thomas, Jeff Bagwell	3.00
17	Chipper Jones, Mike Mussina	

18	Garret Anderson, Jorge Posada	2.00
19	Scott Rolen, Torii Hunter	3.00
20	Kerry Wood, Todd Helton	3.00
21	Eric Chavez, Roy Oswalt	2.00
22	Johnny Estrada, Vernon Wells	2.00
23	Lance Berkman, Tim Hudson	2.00
24	Mark Buehrle, Mark Mulder	2.00
25	C.C. Sabathia, Sean Burroughs	2.00
26	Albert Pujols, Barry Zito	6.00
27	Rich Harden, Rocco Baldelli	2.00
28	Bobby Crosby, Mark Teixeira	2.00
29	Casey Kotchman, Mark Prior	3.00
30	Dewon Brazelton, Jeremy Bonderman	2.00
31	J.C. Holt, Jon Zeringue	3.00
32	Kyle Bono, Matt Fox	3.00
33	Dexter Fowler, Mike Rozier	3.00
34	Huston Street, J.P. Howell	3.00
35	Grant Johnson, Matt Macri	3.00
36	Eric Beattie, Jeff Frazier	3.00
37	Jason Windsor, Kurt Suzuki	5.00
38	Josh Fields, Matt Tuiasosopo	6.00
39	Joseph Bauserman, K.C. Herren	3.00
40	Chris Lambert, Eric Haberer, Matt Tuiasosopo	3.00

Passing the Torch

NM/M
Common Duo: 3.00
Production 500 Sets

1	Dennis Eckersley, Huston Street	4.00
2	Matt Bush, Tony Gwynn	6.00
3	Homer Bailey, Tom Seaver	4.00
4	Bob Feller, Jeremy Sowers	3.00
5	Josh Fields, Robin Ventura	3.00
6	Nolan Ryan, Thomas Diamond	8.00
7	Eric Patterson, Ryne Sandberg	6.00
8	Richie Robnett, Rickey Henderson	4.00
9	Mike Ferris, Stan Musial	5.00
10	Bobby Doerr, Dustin Pedroia	3.00

Passing the Torch Autograph Black

No Pricing
Production 5-10 Sets

Passing the Torch Autograph Gold

NM/M
Production 5-25

2	Matt Bush, Tony Gwynn/25	90.00
4	Bob Feller, Jeremy Sowers/25	60.00
10	Bobby Doerr, Dustin Pedroia/25	75.00

Round Numbers

NM/M
Common Player: 2.00
Production 500 Sets

1	Ozzie Smith	4.00
2	Derek Jeter	6.00
3	Alex Rodriguez	5.00
4	Paul Molitor	3.00
5	George Brett	6.00
6	Delmon Young	2.00
7	Dontrelle Willis	2.00
8	Gary Carter	2.00
9	Reggie Jackson	3.00
10	Andre Dawson	2.00
11	Neil Walker	2.00
12	Laynce Nix	2.00
13	Matt Bush	6.00
14	Lyle Overbay	2.00
15	Carlos Beltran	3.00
16	Todd Helton	3.00
17	Mark Grace	2.00
18	Fred Lynn	2.00
19	Robin Yount	4.00
20	Mike Schmidt	6.00
21	Roger Clemens	6.00
22	Will Clark	3.00
23	Don Mattingly	5.00
24	Blake DeWitt	2.00
25	Rafael Palmeiro	3.00
26	Wade Boggs	3.00
27	Mark Rogers	5.00
28	Billy Buckner	3.00
29	Jeff Baker	2.00
30	Nolan Ryan	8.00
31	Mike Piazza	4.00
32	Alexis Rios	2.00
33	Eddie Murray	3.00
34	Jose Canseco	3.00
35	Mike Mussina	3.00
36	Eric Beattie	3.00
37	Keith Hernandez	2.00
38	Michael Young	2.00
39	Dwight Evans	2.00
40	Scott Elbert	3.00
41	Adrian Gonzalez	2.00
42	Johnny Bench	3.00
43	Dennis Eckersley	2.00
44	Dale Murphy	3.00
45	Ryne Sandberg	4.00
46	David Wright	3.00
47	Hank Blalock	3.00
48	Orel Hershiser	2.00
49	Sean Casey	2.00
50	Albert Pujols	6.00

Round Numbers Signature

NM/M
Production 5-250

1	Ozzie Smith/25	65.00
4	Paul Molitor/25	35.00
6	Delmon Young/50	25.00
7	Dontrelle Willis/25	20.00
8	Gary Carter/50	20.00
10	Andre Dawson/50	20.00
11	Neil Walker/250	20.00
12	Laynce Nix/50	20.00
13	Matt Bush/100	45.00
14	Lyle Overbay/50	15.00
15	Carlos Beltran/25	35.00
17	Mark Grace/25	35.00
18	Fred Lynn/50	15.00
20	Mike Schmidt/25	85.00
22	Will Clark/20	60.00
23	Don Mattingly/25	80.00
24	Blake DeWitt/50	30.00
27	Mark Rogers/100	40.00
28	Billy Buckner/100	15.00
32	Alexis Rios/50	15.00
34	Jose Canseco/25	50.00
36	Eric Beattie/100	10.00
37	Keith Hernandez/50	20.00
38	Michael Young/50	25.00
39	Dwight Evans/50	15.00
40	Scott Elbert/50	15.00
41	Adrian Gonzalez/50	10.00
43	Dennis Eckersley/50	30.00
44	Dale Murphy/50	15.00
46	David Wright/25	75.00
47	Hank Blalock/25	20.00
49	Sean Casey/25	15.00

Signature

NM/M
Production 1-50

132	Jack Wilson/50	25.00
133	Jason Bay/25	25.00
231	J.A. Happ/50	10.00
233	Mark Jecmen/50	8.00
234	Kameron Loe/50	20.00
235	Ervin Santana/50	40.00
239	Josh Karp/50	15.00
243	Jesse Hoover/50	10.00
246	Justin Hoyman/50	15.00
247	Juan Cedeno/50	15.00
252	Benjamin Zobrist/50	10.00
253	Jeff Salazar/50	30.00
254	Fausto Carmona/50	20.00

Signature Aspirations

NM/M
Production 1-100
Golds: No Pricing
Production 1-25

216	Scott Lewis/50	15.00
217	Josh Johnson/50	15.00
218	Jeff Fiorentino/50	25.00
219	Grant Hansen/50	8.00
220	Yovani Gallardo/50	150.00
221	Eddie Prasch/50	10.00
222	Danny Hill/50	8.00
223	Chuck Lofgren/50	40.00
224	Blake Johnson/50	15.00
225	Cory Dunlap/50	20.00
226	Carlos Vasquez/50	10.00
227	Jesse Crain/50	15.00
228	Yhency Brazoban/50	10.00
229	Abe Alvarez/50	10.00
256	Jorge Vasquez/50	8.00
257	Rafael Gonzalez/50	8.00
258	Andrew Dobies/50	15.00
259	Colby Miller/49	10.00
260	K.C. Herren/50	15.00
261	Ryan Meaux/50	10.00
262	Dustin Pedroia/50	100.00
263	Fernando Nieve/50	8.00
264	Mariano Gomez/50	8.00
266	Billy Killian/50	8.00
267	Mike Rouse/50	10.00
268	Kyle Bono/50	10.00
269	Mitch Einertson/50	25.00
270	Scott Proctor/50	15.00
271	Tim Bittner/50	8.00
272	Christian Garcia/50	10.00
273	Yadier Molina/50	30.00
274	Justin Leone/50	15.00
275	Charles Thomas/50	15.00
276	Travis Blackley/50	10.00
277	Frankie Francisco/50	10.00
278	Dioner Navarro/50	15.00
279	Joey Gathright/50	10.00
280	Kazuhito Tadano/50	20.00
281	Matt Bush/50	30.00
282	David Haehnel/100	15.00
283	Tommy Hottovy/100	10.00
284	Chris Carter/100	30.00
286	Jeremy Sowers/100	40.00
287	Homer Bailey/100	75.00
288	Mike Butia/100	10.00
289	Chris Nelson/100	40.00
290	Thomas Diamond/100	30.00
291	Neil Walker/100	30.00
292	Sean Gamble/100	10.00
293	Bill Bray/100	8.00
294	Reid Brignac/50	80.00
295	Ryan Klosterman/100	8.00
296	David Purcey/100	10.00
297	Scott Elbert/100	50.00
298	Josh Fields/100	40.00
299	Chris Lambert/100	10.00
300	Trevor Plouffe/100	25.00
301	Greg Golson/100	20.00
302	Josh Baker/100	10.00
303	Phillip Hughes/100	125.00
304	Matt Macri/100	12.00
305	Kyle Waldrop/100	10.00
306	Richie Robnett/100	25.00
307	Taylor Tankersley/100	10.00
308	Blake DeWitt/100	50.00
309	Daryl Jones/50	25.00
310	Eric Hurley/100	40.00
311	J.P. Howell/100	10.00
312	Zach Jackson/100	20.00
313	Justin Orenduff/100	15.00
314	Tyler Lumsden/100	15.00
315	Matt Fox/100	15.00
316	Danny Putnam/100	15.00
317	Jon Poterson/100	20.00
318	Gio Gonzalez/100	40.00
319	Jay Rainville/100	25.00
320	Huston Street/100	50.00
321	Jeff Marquez/100	15.00
322	Eric Beattie/100	10.00
323	B.J. Szymanski/100	10.00
324	Seth Smith/100	30.00
325	Robert Johnson/100	10.00
326	Wes Whisler/100	10.00
327	Billy Buckner/100	10.00
328	Jon Zeringue/100	30.00
329	Curtis Thigpen/50	12.00
330	Donny Lucy/50	10.00
331	Mike Ferris/100	12.00
333	Jason Jaramillo/100	10.00
334	Hunter Pence/50	160.00
335	Mike Rozier/100	10.00
336	Kurt Suzuki/100	25.00
337	Jason Vargas/50	50.00
338	Brian Bixler/50	10.00
340	Dexter Fowler/50	80.00
341	Mark Trumbo/50	15.00
342	Jeff Frazier/100	20.00
343	Steven Register/50	15.00
344	Michael Schlact/50	10.00
345	Garrett Mock/50	15.00
346	Eric Haberer/50	10.00
347	Matt Tuiasosopo/100	30.00
348	Jason Windsor/50	20.00
349	Grant Johnson/50	10.00
350	J.C. Holt/50	10.00

351 Joseph Bauserman/50 10.00
352 Jamar Walton/50 10.00
353 Eric Patterson/100 35.00
354 Tyler Johnson/100 25.00
355 Nick Adenhart/100 125.00

Signature Status

NM/M

Production 1-50
Golds: No Pricing
Production 1-10

221 Eddie Prasch/25 15.00
224 Blake Johnson/25 20.00
229 Abe Alvarez/25 15.00
257 Rafael Gonzalez/25 10.00
268 Kyle Bono/25 15.00
272 Christian Garcia/25 15.00
276 Travis Blackley/25 15.00
281 Matt Bush/50 40.00
282 David Haehnel/50 15.00
283 Tommy Hottovy/50 15.00
284 Chris Carter/50 40.00
286 Jeremy Sowers/50 40.00
287 Homer Bailey/50 125.00
288 Mike Butia/50 15.00
289 Chris Nelson/50 40.00
290 Thomas Diamond/50 40.00
291 Neil Walker/50 40.00
292 Sean Gamble/50 15.00
293 Bill Bray/50 10.00
294 Reid Brignac/50 80.00
295 Ryan Klosterman/50 10.00
296 David Purcey/50 15.00
297 Scott Elbert/50 75.00
298 Josh Fields/50 15.00
299 Chris Lambert/50 15.00
300 Trevor Plouffe/50 25.00
301 Greg Golson/50 35.00
302 Josh Baker/50 15.00
303 Phillip Hughes/50 160.00
304 Matt Macri/50 15.00
305 Kyle Waldrop/50 25.00
306 Richie Robnett/50 25.00
307 Taylor Tankersley/50 15.00
308 Blake DeWitt/50 40.00
309 Daryl Jones/50 30.00
310 Eric Hurley/50 50.00
311 J.P. Howell/50 20.00
312 Zach Jackson/50 15.00
313 Justin Orenduff/50 20.00
314 Tyler Lumsden/50 20.00
315 Matt Fox/50 20.00
316 Danny Putnam/50 20.00
317 Jon Poterson/50 20.00
318 Gio Gonzalez/50 50.00
319 Jay Rainville/50 35.00
320 Huston Street/50 60.00
321 Jeff Marquez/50 20.00
322 Eric Beattie/50 15.00
323 B.J. Szymanski/50 15.00
324 Seth Smith/50 40.00
325 Robert Johnson/50 15.00
326 Wes Whisler/50 15.00
327 Billy Buckner/50 15.00
328 Jon Zeringue/50 35.00
329 Curtis Thigpen/50 12.00
330 Donny Lucy/50 15.00
331 Mike Ferris/50 15.00
333 Jason Jaramillo/50 15.00
334 Hunter Pence/50 160.00
335 Mike Rozier/50 15.00
336 Kurt Suzuki/50 25.00
337 Jason Vargas/50 50.00
338 Brian Bixler/50 15.00
340 Dexter Fowler/50 80.00
341 Mark Trumbo/50 25.00
342 Jeff Frazier/50 20.00
343 Steven Register/50 10.00
344 Michael Schlact/50 15.00
345 Garrett Mock/50 15.00
346 Eric Haberer/50 10.00
347 Matt Tuiasosopo/50 40.00
348 Jason Windsor/50 20.00
349 Grant Johnson/50 10.00
350 J.C. Holt/50 10.00
351 Joseph Bauserman/50 10.00
352 Jamar Walton/50 25.00
353 Eric Patterson/50 35.00
354 Tyler Johnson/50 15.00
355 Nick Adenhart/50 125.00

Signature Turn of Century

NM/M

216 Scott Lewis/100 12.00
217 Josh Johnson/100 12.00
218 Jeff Fiorentino/100 10.00
219 Grant Hansen/100 8.00
220 Yovani Gallardo/100 125.00
221 Eddie Prasch/100 10.00

222 Danny Hill/100 8.00
223 Chuck Lofgren/100 35.00
224 Blake Johnson/100 20.00
225 Cory Dunlap/100 20.00
226 Carlos Vasquez/100 10.00
227 Jesse Crain/100 15.00
228 Yhency Brazoban/100 10.00
229 Abe Alvarez/100 10.00
246 Justin Hoyman/250 10.00
252 Benjamin Zobrist/150 10.00
256 Jorge Vasquez/100 8.00
257 Rafael Gonzalez/100 8.00
258 Andrew Dobies/100 15.00
259 Colby Miller/100 10.00
260 K.C. Herren/100 15.00
261 Ryan Meaux/100 10.00
262 Dustin Pedroia/100 75.00
263 Fernando Nieve/100 10.00
264 Mariano Gomez/100 10.00
266 Billy Killian/100 15.00
267 Mike Rouse/100 10.00
268 Kyle Bono/100 10.00
269 Mitch Einertson/100 15.00
270 Scott Proctor/100 10.00
271 Tim Bittner/100 8.00
272 Christian Garcia/100 10.00
273 Yadier Molina/100 30.00
274 Justin Leone/100 15.00
275 Charles Thomas/100 15.00
276 Travis Blackley/100 10.00
277 Frankie Francisco/100 10.00
278 Dioner Navarro/100 15.00
279 Joey Gathright/100 15.00
280 Kazuhito Tadano/100 15.00
281 Matt Bush/250 20.00
282 David Haehnel/250 8.00
283 Tommy Hottovy/250 8.00
284 Chris Carter/250 30.00
285 Mark Rogers/100 30.00
286 Jeremy Sowers/250 30.00
287 Homer Bailey/250 75.00
288 Mike Butia/250 8.00
289 Chris Nelson/250 30.00
290 Thomas Diamond/250 25.00
291 Neil Walker/242 25.00
292 Sean Gamble/250 8.00
293 Bill Bray/250 8.00
294 Reid Brignac/100 60.00
295 Ryan Klosterman/250 8.00
296 David Purcey/250 8.00
297 Scott Elbert/250 50.00
298 Josh Fields/250 40.00
299 Chris Lambert/250 15.00
300 Trevor Plouffe/250 15.00
301 Greg Golson/250 20.00
302 Josh Baker/100 10.00
303 Phillip Hughes/250 100.00
304 Matt Macri/250 15.00
305 Kyle Waldrop/250 15.00
306 Richie Robnett/250 15.00
307 Taylor Tankersley/250 10.00
308 Blake DeWitt/250 25.00
309 Daryl Jones/250 15.00
310 Eric Hurley/250 30.00
311 J.P. Howell/250 10.00
312 Zach Jackson/250 15.00
313 Justin Orenduff/100 15.00
314 Tyler Lumsden/250 15.00
315 Matt Fox/250 12.00
316 Danny Putnam/250 12.00
317 Jon Poterson/238 12.00
318 Gio Gonzalez/250 35.00
319 Jay Rainville/250 20.00
320 Huston Street/250 30.00
321 Jeff Marquez/250 10.00
322 Eric Beattie/250 8.00
323 B.J. Szymanski/250 8.00
324 Seth Smith/250 20.00
325 Robert Johnson/100 10.00
326 Wes Whisler/100 8.00
327 Billy Buckner/100 10.00
328 Jon Zeringue/250 20.00
329 Curtis Thigpen/100 10.00
330 Donny Lucy/100 8.00
331 Mike Ferris/250 10.00
332 Anthony Swarzak/100 25.00
333 Jason Jaramillo/250 8.00
334 Hunter Pence/200 180.00
335 Mike Rozier/250 8.00
336 Kurt Suzuki/250 20.00
337 Jason Vargas/250 8.00
338 Brian Bixler/200 8.00
340 Dexter Fowler/250 40.00
341 Mark Trumbo/250 20.00
342 Jeff Frazier/250 20.00
343 Steven Register/200 8.00
344 Michael Schlact/200 8.00
345 Garrett Mock/200 15.00
346 Eric Haberer/100 8.00

347 Matt Tuiasosopo/250 25.00
348 Jason Windsor/100 15.00
349 Grant Johnson/250 8.00
350 J.C. Holt/100 8.00
351 Joseph Bauserman/100 8.00
352 Jamar Walton/200 12.00
353 Eric Patterson/250 25.00
354 Tyler Johnson/250 15.00
355 Nick Adenhart/100 125.00

Throwback Threads

NM/M

Production 50 Sets
1 Roger Maris 60.00
2 Ted Williams 80.00
3 Cal Ripken Jr. 75.00
4 Duke Snider 20.00
5 George Brett 40.00

Throwback Threads Autograph

No Pricing

2004 Donruss Leather & Lumber

NM/M

Complete Set (175):
Common Player (1-150): .25
Common Auto. (151-173): 6.00
Production 500
Pack (5): 5.00
Box (24): 100.00

1 Bartolo Colon .25
2 Garret Anderson .50
3 Tim Salmon .40
4 Troy Glaus .50
5 Vladimir Guerrero 1.00
6 Brandon Webb .25
7 Luis Gonzalez .40
8 Randy Johnson 1.00
9 Richie Sexson .50
10 Shea Hillenbrand .25
11 Adam LaRoche .25
12 Andruw Jones .50
13 Chipper Jones 1.00
14 Dale Murphy .75
15 J.D. Drew .50
16 Marcus Giles .25
17 Rafael Furcal .25
18 Cal Ripken Jr. 3.00
19 Javy Lopez .50
20 Jay Gibbons .25
21 Luis Matos .25
22 Miguel Tejada .50
23 Rafael Palmeiro .75
24 Curt Schilling .75
25 Jason Varitek .40
26 Manny Ramirez .75
27 Nomar Garciaparra 1.50
28 Pedro J. Martinez 1.00
29 Trot Nixon .25
30 Greg Maddux 1.50
31 Kerry Wood 1.00
32 Mark Prior 1.00
33 Ryne Sandberg 1.50
34 Sammy Sosa 2.00
35 Carlos Lee .25
36 Frank Thomas .75
37 Magglio Ordonez .40
38 Paul Konerko .25
39 Adam Dunn .75
40 Austin Kearns .25
41 Barry Larkin .50
42 Ken Griffey Jr. 1.50
43 Ryan Wagner .25
44 C.C. Sabathia .25
45 Jody Gerut .25
46 Omar Vizquel .25
47 Larry Walker .40
48 Preston Wilson .25
49 Todd Helton .75

50 Alan Trammell .25
51 Ivan Rodriguez .75
52 Jeremy Bonderman .25
53 Dontrelle Willis .25
54 Josh Beckett .50
55 Luis Castillo .25
56 Miguel Cabrera 1.00
57 Mike Lowell .25
58 Andy Pettitte .40
59 Craig Biggio .40
60 Jeff Bagwell .75
61 Jeff Kent .40
62 Lance Berkman .40
63 Roger Clemens 2.50
64 Roy Oswalt .40
65 Angel Berroa .25
66 Carlos Beltran .75
67 George Brett 2.00
68 Juan Gonzalez .50
69 Mike Sweeney .25
70 Eric Gagne .50
71 Hideo Nomo .50
72 Kazuhisa Ishii .25
73 Paul LoDuca .25
74 Shawn Green .50
75 Geoff Jenkins .25
76 Junior Spivey .25
77 Rickie Weeks .25
78 Robin Yount .75
79 Scott Podsednik .25
80 Jacque Jones .25
81 Johan Santana .50
82 Shannon Stewart .25
83 Torii Hunter .40
84 Andre Dawson .50
85 Chad Cordero .25
86 Jose Vidro .25
87 Nick Johnson .25
88 Orlando Cabrera .40
89 Gary Carter .50
90 Jae Weong Seo .25
91 Jose Reyes .50
92 Mike Piazza 1.50
93 Tom Glavine .50
94 Alex Rodriguez 2.50
95 Bernie Williams .50
96 Derek Jeter 2.50
97 Don Mattingly 2.00
98 Gary Sheffield .50
99 Hideki Matsui 1.50
100 Jason Giambi .50
101 Jorge Posada .50
102 Mike Mussina .50
103 Barry Zito .50
104 Bobby Crosby .25
105 Eric Chavez .40
106 Jermaine Dye .25
107 Mark Mulder .40
108 Rich Harden .25
109 Rickey Henderson .25
110 Tim Hudson .40
111 Bobby Abreu .40
112 Brett Myers .25
113 Jim Thome 1.00
114 Kevin Millwood .25
115 Marlon Byrd .25
116 Mike Schmidt 2.00
117 Pat Burrell .25
118 Dave Parker .25
119 Jason Bay .25
120 Jason Kendall .25
121 Brian Giles .25
122 Jay Payton .25
123 Ryan Klesko .25
124 Tony Gwynn 1.00
125 Edgardo Alfonzo .25
126 Jason Schmidt .50
127 Jerome Williams .25
128 Bret Boone .25
129 Edgar Martinez .25
130 Ichiro Suzuki 2.00
131 Jamie Moyer .25
132 John Olerud .25
133 Albert Pujols 2.00
134 Edgar Renteria .40
135 Jim Edmonds .50
136 Matt Morris .25
137 Scott Rolen 1.00
138 Aubrey Huff .25
139 Carl Crawford .25
140 Delmon Young .25
141 Rocco Baldelli .25
142 Alfonso Soriano 1.00
143 Hank Blalock .75
144 Mark Teixeira .50
145 Michael Young .50
146 Nolan Ryan 2.50
147 Carlos Delgado .25
148 Eric Hinske .25
149 Roy Halladay .25
150 Vernon Wells .25
151 Andres Blanco RC 8.00
152 Kevin Cave RC 6.00
153 Ryan Meaux RC 6.00

154	Tim Bausher RC	6.00
155	Jesse Harper RC	6.00
156	Mike Wuertz RC	8.00
157	Colby Miller RC	8.00
158	Donald Kelly RC	6.00
159	Edwin Moreno RC	8.00
160	Mike Johnston RC	6.00
161	Orlando Rodriguez RC RC	6.00
162	Phil Stockman RC	8.00
163	Yadier Molina RC	8.00
164	Jorge Vasquez RC	6.00
165	Scott Proctor RC	8.00
166	Jake Woods RC	6.00
167	Aarom Baldiris RC	8.00
168	Jason Bartlett RC	6.00
169	Casey Daigle RC	6.00
170	Dennis Sarfate RC	6.00
171	Edwardo Sierra RC	8.00
172	Merkin Valdez RC	8.00
173	Eddy Rodriguez RC	8.00
174	Kazuo Matsui RC	8.00
175	David Aardsma RC	4.00

Gold

Stars (1-150):	10-15X
SP's (151-175):	No Pricing
Production 25 Sets	

Platinum

No Pricing	
Production One Set	

Silver

Stars (1-150):	4-8X
SP's (151-175):	.5X
Production 100 Sets	

B/W

	NM/M
Common Player:	1.50
Production 1,000 Sets	
Gold B/W:	4-6X
Production 25 Sets	
Silver B/W:	2-3X
Production 100 Sets	
Platinum B/W:	No Pricing
Production One Set	
13 Chipper Jones	2.00
14 Dale Murphy	1.50
18 Cal Ripken Jr.	8.00
27 Nomar Garciaparra	3.00
30 Greg Maddux	2.50
32 Mark Prior	1.50
33 Ryne Sandberg	3.00
34 Sammy Sosa	3.00
63 Roger Clemens	4.00
67 George Brett	4.00
78 Robin Yount	3.00
89 Gary Carter	1.50
92 Mike Piazza	3.00
94 Alex Rodriguez	5.00
96 Derek Jeter	5.00
97 Don Mattingly	4.00
99 Hideki Matsui	3.00
109 Rickey Henderson	1.50
116 Mike Schmidt	3.00
124 Tony Gwynn	2.00
130 Ichiro Suzuki	4.00
133 Albert Pujols	4.00
142 Alfonso Soriano	2.00
146 Nolan Ryan	5.00
174 Kazuo Matsui	6.00

Bat-Spikes

	NM/M
Bat/Glove:	.75-1.5X
Production 1-50	
Bat/Ball:	.75-1.5X
Production 5-25	
No pricing 15 or less.	
Barrel/Jersey:	No Pricing
Production 1-5	
1 Andruw Jones/25	15.00
3 Angel Berroa/25	10.00
7 Barry Zito/25	15.00
7 Ben Sheets/50	10.00
8 Brad Penny/50	8.00
9 Brian Giles/50	8.00
10 Carlos Lee/50	8.00
11 Corey Patterson/50	15.00
13 Don Mattingly/25	40.00
15 Gary Carter/50	12.00
17 Ivan Rodriguez/50	15.00
18 Jack Cust/50	8.00
19 Jason Jennings/50	8.00
21 Jim Edmonds/50	10.00
22 Joe Borchard/50	8.00
23 Joe Crede/50	8.00
24 Josh Beckett/25	15.00
25 Josh Phelps/50	8.00
26 Juan Pierre/50	8.00
27 Kenny Lofton/50	8.00
29 Lance Berkman/25	15.00
30 Magglio Ordonez/25	10.00
31 Marcus Giles/50	10.00

32	Mark Buehrle/50	8.00
33	Mark Prior/25	20.00
34	Mark Teixeira/25	15.00
35	Marlon Byrd/50	8.00
38	Nick Johnson/25	10.00
39	Orlando Hudson/50	8.00
40	Paul LoDuca/25	10.00
41	Rafael Palmeiro/25	20.00
43	Roy Oswalt/25	15.00
44	Ryan Klesko/50	10.00
46	Sean Casey/50	10.00
48	Travis Hafner/50	15.00
49	Victor Martinez/50	10.00
50	Wade Miller/50	10.00

Cuts

		NM/M
Common Player:		
1	Adam Dunn/192	20.00
2	Al Kaline/192	35.00
3	Alfonso Soriano/160	40.00
4	Andre Dawson/224	15.00
5	Angel Berroa/224	10.00
6	Harmon Killebrew/192	35.00
7	Bob Gibson/96	30.00
8	Brooks Robinson/192	30.00
9	Cal Ripken Jr./32	200.00
10	Dale Murphy/224	25.00
11	Darryl Strawberry/224	15.00
12	Delmon Young/192	20.00
13	Don Mattingly/96	65.00
14	Duke Snider/96	30.00
15	Dwight Gooden/224	15.00
16	Ozzie Smith/96	60.00
18	Garret Anderson/224	15.00
19	Gary Carter/160	20.00
20	George Kell/224	15.00
21	Hank Blalock/224	20.00
22	Jim Palmer/192	20.00
23	Kirk Gibson/160	15.00
24	Lou Brock/192	25.00
25	Ryne Sandberg/160	50.00
26	Mark Prior/160	40.00
27	Miguel Cabrera/224	25.00
28	Mike Lowell/160	15.00
29	Nolan Ryan/96	100.00
30	Luis Aparicio/224	15.00
31	Paul Molitor/160	30.00
32	Red Schoendienst/224	25.00
33	Rickie Weeks/224	15.00
34	Ron Santo/224	25.00
35	Roy Oswalt/224	20.00
36	Stan Musial/96	60.00
37	Steve Carlton/192	20.00
38	Tony Gwynn/192	35.00
39	Vernon Wells/160	10.00
40	Will Clark/192	35.00
41	Bob Feller/224	25.00
42	Bobby Doerr/224	20.00
44	Ralph Kiner/224	30.00
45	Torii Hunter/224	15.00
46	Rollie Fingers/224	15.00
47	Steve Garvey/224	15.00
48	Alan Trammell/224	15.00
49	Maury Wills/224	15.00
50	Gaylord Perry/224	15.00

Fans of the Game

		NM/M
Inserted 1:24		
1	John Travolta	4.00
2	Dennis Haysbert	2.00
3	Chris O'Donnell	2.00
4	Abby Wambach	3.00
5	Jules Asner	3.00

Fans of the Game Signature

		NM/M
Common Auto.:		20.00
1	John Travolta/SP EXCH	220.00
2	Dennis Haysbert/	25.00
3	Chris O'Donnell	20.00
4	Abby Wambach	50.00
5	Jules Asner	50.00

Hall of Fame

		NM/M
Common Player:		2.00
Quantity produced listed		
Silver:		1-2X
Production 100 Sets		
1	Carl Yastrzemski/1989	4.00
2	Carlton Fisk/2000	2.00
3	George Brett/1999	5.00
4	Johnny Bench/1995	4.00
5	Mike Schmidt/1995	5.00
6	Nolan Ryan/1999	6.00
7	Ozzie Smith/2002	4.00
8	Robin Yount/1999	4.00
9	Rod Carew/1991	3.00
10	Tom Seaver/1992	3.00

Hall of Fame Materials

		NM/M
Quantity produced listed		
1	Carl Yastrzemski/Jsy/250	15.00
2	Carlton Fisk/Jsy/250	10.00
3	George Brett/Jsy/250	15.00
4	Johnny Bench/Jsy/100	15.00
5	Mike Schmidt/Jkt/250	15.00
6	Nolan Ryan/Pants/100	25.00
7	Ozzie Smith/Jsy/100	20.00
8	Robin Yount/Jsy/250	12.00
9	Rod Carew/Jkt/250	15.00
10	Tom Seaver/Jsy/200	15.00

Leather Materials

		NM/M
Quantity produced listed		
1	Garret Anderson/Ball/50	8.00
2	Albert Pujols/Ball/50	25.00
3	John Smoltz/Ball/50	20.00
4	Cal Ripken Jr./Ball/50	75.00
5	Ichiro Suzuki/Ball/50	60.00
6	Pedro J. Martinez/Ball/50	15.00
7	Shawn Green/Ball/50	8.00
8	Juan Gonzalez/Ball/50	10.00
9	Mariano Rivera/Ball/50	10.00
10	Jason Giambi/Ball/50	10.00
11	Dave Parker/Btg Glv/25	20.00
12	Dwight Gooden/Btg Glv/25	20.00
13	Eric Munson/Btg Glv/50	8.00
14	Frank Thomas/Btg Glv/50	20.00
15	Joe Carter/Btg Glv/50	10.00
16	Jose Canseco/Btg Glv/50	20.00
17	Paul O'Neill/Btg Glv/50	20.00
18	Tony Gwynn/Btg Glv/50	30.00
19	Wade Boggs/Btg Glv/25	20.00
20	Xavier Nady/Btg Glv/50	8.00
22	Alex Rodriguez/Fld Glv/25	35.00
23	Chipper Jones/Fld Glv/25	30.00
24	Derek Jeter/Fld Glv/25	50.00
25	Jack Wilson/Fld Glv/50	8.00
26	Lenny Dykstra/Fld Glv/50	10.00
27	Mark Grace/Fld Glv/50	15.00
28	Steve Carlton/Fld Glv/50	12.00
29	Tony Perez/Fld Glv/25	15.00
31	Bernie Williams/Spikes/50	10.00
32	Eddie Murray/Spikes/50	30.00
33	Frank Robinson/Spikes/50	10.00
34	Greg Maddux/Spikes/25	30.00
35	Harmon Killebrew/Spikes/25	35.00

Leather Cuts Ball

No Pricing

Leather in Leather

	NM/M
Common Player:	
Production 2,499 Sets	

Cuts Glove

		NM/M
Quantity produced listed		
1	Adam Dunn/192	20.00
2	Al Kaline/192	35.00
3	Alfonso Soriano/160	40.00
4	Andre Dawson/224	15.00
5	Angel Berroa/224	10.00
6	Harmon Killebrew/192	35.00
7	Bob Gibson/96	30.00
8	Brooks Robinson/192	30.00
9	Cal Ripken Jr./32	200.00
10	Dale Murphy/224	25.00
11	Darryl Strawberry/224	15.00
12	Delmon Young/192	20.00
13	Don Mattingly/96	65.00
14	Duke Snider/96	30.00
15	Dwight Gooden/224	15.00

Silver: 1-2X
Production 100 Sets
1	Garret Anderson/BB	1.50
2	Albert Pujols/BB	5.00
3	John Smoltz/BB	1.50
4	Cal Ripken Jr./BB	8.00
5	Ichiro Suzuki/BB	5.00
6	Pedro J. Martinez/BB	2.00
7	Shawn Green/BB	1.50
8	Juan Gonzalez/BB	1.50
9	Mariano Rivera/BB	1.50
10	Jason Giambi/BB	1.50
11	Dave Parker/BG	1.50
12	Dwight Gooden/BG	1.50
13	Eric Munson/BG	1.50
14	Frank Thomas/BG	2.00
15	Joe Carter/BG	1.50
16	Jose Canseco/BG	2.00
17	Paul O'Neill/BG	1.50
18	Tony Gwynn/BG	3.00
19	Wade Boggs/BG	2.00
20	Xavier Nady/BG	1.50
21	Albert Pujols/FG	5.00
22	Alex Rodriguez/FG	6.00
23	Chipper Jones/FG	3.00
24	Derek Jeter/FG	6.00
25	Jack Wilson/FG	1.50
26	Lenny Dykstra/FG	1.50
27	Mark Grace/FG	2.00
28	Steve Carlton/FG	2.00
29	Tony Perez/FG	2.00
30	Vladimir Guerrero/FG	3.00
31	Bernie Williams/SH	2.00
32	Eddie Murray/SH	3.00
33	Frank Robinson/SH	3.00
34	Greg Maddux/SH	4.00
35	Harmon Killebrew/SH	3.00
36	Manny Ramirez/SH	2.00
37	Mike Piazza/SH	4.00
38	Paul Molitor/SH	3.00
39	Sammy Sosa/SH	4.00
40	Tim Hudson/SH	2.00

Materials Jersey

	NM/M
Common Jersey:	4.00

Quantity produced listed
MLB Logo: No Pricing
Production One Set
Prime: 1-1.25X
Production 1-25
No pricing 15 or less.
Barrel: No Pricing
Production 1-5
2	Garret Anderson/50	8.00
3	Tim Salmon/250	4.00
4	Troy Glaus/200	4.00
6	Brandon Webb/100	4.00
7	Luis Gonzalez/250	4.00
8	Randy Johnson/100	10.00
12	Andruw Jones/250	4.00
13	Chipper Jones/250	8.00
14	Dale Murphy/250	10.00
16	Marcus Giles/250	4.00
17	Rafael Furcal/250	4.00
18	Cal Ripken Jr./100	30.00
19	Javy Lopez/150	4.00
20	Jay Gibbons/250	4.00
21	Luis Matos/250	4.00
22	Miguel Tejada/250	6.00
23	Rafael Palmeiro/250	8.00
25	Jason Varitek/250	4.00
26	Manny Ramirez/250	8.00
28	Pedro J. Martinez/250	8.00
29	Trot Nixon/25	10.00
30	Greg Maddux/250	10.00
31	Kerry Wood/250	10.00
32	Mark Prior/250	8.00
33	Ryne Sandberg/50	30.00
34	Sammy Sosa/250	10.00
35	Carlos Lee/250	4.00
36	Frank Thomas/250	8.00

37	Magglio Ordonez/250	4.00
38	Paul Konerko/250	4.00
39	Adam Dunn/250	8.00
40	Austin Kearns/250	4.00
41	Barry Larkin/250	6.00
44	C.C. Sabathia/250	4.00
45	Jody Gerut/250	4.00
46	Omar Vizquel/250	4.00
47	Larry Walker/250	4.00
48	Preston Wilson/250	4.00
49	Todd Helton	8.00
50	Alan Trammell/50	10.00
51	Ivan Rodriguez/100	10.00
52	Jeremy Bonderman/150	4.00
53	Dontrelle Willis/100	4.00
54	Josh Beckett/250	4.00
55	Luis Castillo/250	4.00
56	Miguel Cabrera/50	15.00
57	Mike Lowell/25	10.00
58	Andy Pettitte/25	15.00
59	Craig Biggio/250	4.00
60	Jeff Bagwell/250	8.00
61	Jeff Kent/250	4.00
62	Lance Berkman/250	4.00
64	Roy Oswalt/250	4.00
65	Angel Berroa/50	6.00
66	Carlos Beltran/250	4.00
67	George Brett/250	15.00
69	Mike Sweeney/100	4.00
71	Hideo Nomo/250	6.00
72	Kazuhisa Ishii/250	4.00
73	Paul LoDuca/250	4.00
74	Shawn Green/250	4.00
75	Geoff Jenkins/250	4.00
78	Robin Yount/250	10.00
80	Jacque Jones/250	4.00
81	Johan Santana/250	8.00
82	Shannon Stewart/250	4.00
83	Torii Hunter/250	4.00
84	Andre Dawson/50	10.00
86	Jose Vidro/100	4.00
88	Orlando Cabrera/100	4.00
89	Gary Carter/250	8.00
90	Jae Weong Seo/100	4.00
91	Jose Reyes/250	6.00
92	Mike Piazza/250	10.00
93	Tom Glavine/250	6.00
95	Bernie Williams/250	6.00
96	Derek Jeter/150	20.00
97	Don Mattingly/250	15.00
99	Hideki Matsui/250	20.00
100	Jason Giambi/250	4.00
101	Jorge Posada/50	10.00
102	Mike Mussina/100	8.00
103	Barry Zito/250	4.00
105	Eric Chavez/100	4.00
107	Mark Mulder/250	4.00
108	Rich Harden/50	8.00
109	Rickey Henderson/100	10.00
110	Tim Hudson/250	4.00
111	Bobby Abreu/250	4.00
112	Brett Myers/250	4.00
113	Jim Thome/250	8.00
114	Kevin Millwood/250	4.00
115	Marlon Byrd/250	4.00
116	Mike Schmidt/50	25.00
117	Pat Burrell/250	4.00
118	Dave Parker/250	8.00
120	Jason Kendall/50	6.00
123	Ryan Klesko/250	4.00
124	Tony Gwynn/100	12.00
127	Jerome Williams/200	4.00
129	Edgar Martinez/250	6.00
131	Jamie Moyer/250	4.00
132	John Olerud/150	4.00
133	Albert Pujols/250	15.00
134	Edgar Renteria/100	6.00
135	Jim Edmonds/250	4.00
136	Matt Morris/250	4.00
137	Scott Rolen/250	8.00
138	Aubrey Huff/100	4.00
139	Carl Crawford/250	4.00
141	Rocco Baldelli/250	4.00
143	Hank Blalock/250	6.00
146	Nolan Ryan/250	30.00
147	Carlos Delgado/250	4.00
148	Eric Hinske/100	4.00
149	Roy Halladay/100	4.00
150	Vernon Wells/250	4.00

Materials Jersey B/W

	NM/M
Common Player:	5.00
Jersey Prime B/W:	No Pricing

Production 1-25
13	Chipper Jones/250	8.00
14	Dale Murphy/250	8.00
18	Cal Ripken Jr./10	35.00
30	Greg Maddux/100	10.00
32	Mark Prior/250	8.00
33	Ryne Sandberg/50	30.00
34	Sammy Sosa/250	12.00

67	George Brett/250	15.00
78	Robin Yount/150	10.00
89	Gary Carter/250	5.00
92	Mike Piazza/250	10.00
96	Derek Jeter/100	20.00
97	Don Mattingly/250	15.00
99	Hideki Matsui/250	20.00
109	Rickey Henderson/250	8.00
116	Mike Schmidt/50	25.00
124	Tony Gwynn/100	10.00
133	Albert Pujols/250	15.00
146	Nolan Ryan/100	25.00
174	Kazuo Matsui/50	25.00

Materials Bat B/W

	NM/M

Production 100 unless noted.
13	Chipper Jones	8.00
14	Dale Murphy	10.00
18	Cal Ripken Jr.	30.00
27	Nomar Garciaparra	10.00
30	Greg Maddux	10.00
32	Mark Prior	8.00
33	Ryne Sandberg/30	30.00
34	Sammy Sosa	12.00
63	Roger Clemens/20	20.00
67	George Brett	15.00
78	Robin Yount	12.00
89	Gary Carter	8.00
92	Mike Piazza	10.00
94	Alex Rodriguez	10.00
96	Derek Jeter	20.00
97	Don Mattingly	20.00
109	Rickey Henderson	10.00
116	Mike Schmidt	15.00
124	Tony Gwynn	10.00
133	Albert Pujols	20.00
142	Alfonso Soriano	8.00
146	Nolan Ryan/25	65.00
174	Kazuo Matsui	20.00

Naturals

	NM/M
Common Player:	1.50

Production 1,499 Sets
Silver: 1-2X
Production 100 Sets
1	Eric Chavez	1.50
2	Garret Anderson	1.50
3	Lance Berkman	1.50
4	Paul Molitor	3.00
5	Rafael Palmeiro	2.00
6	Ralph Kiner	3.00
7	Todd Helton	2.00
8	Tony Gwynn	4.00
9	Wade Boggs	2.00
10	Will Clark	2.00

Naturals Materials Bat

	NM/M
Barrel:	No Pricing

Production 1-5
1	Eric Chavez/20	12.00
2	Garret Anderson/250	5.00
3	Lance Berkman/250	5.00
4	Paul Molitor/250	8.00
5	Rafael Palmeiro/250	8.00
6	Ralph Kiner/250	10.00
7	Todd Helton/250	8.00
8	Tony Gwynn/250	12.00
9	Wade Boggs/250	8.00
10	Will Clark/250	10.00

Pennants/Pinstripes

	NM/M
Common Player:	1.50

Production 1,499 Sets
Gold: 1-2X
Production 100 Sets
1	Reggie Jackson	2.50
2	Mike Schmidt	5.00

3	Steve Carlton	2.00
4	Dwight Gooden	1.50
5	Darryl Strawberry	1.50
6	Roger Clemens	5.00
7	Curt Schilling	2.00
8	Mark Grace	2.00
9	Ivan Rodriguez	2.00
10	Josh Beckett	1.50

Pennants/Pinstripes Materials

	NM/M

Quantity produced listed
1	Reggie Jackson/Pants/100	10.00
2	Mike Schmidt/Jsy/25	35.00
3	Steve Carlton/Jsy/100	8.00
4	Dwight Gooden/Jsy/250	8.00
5	Darryl Strawberry/Pants/250	5.00
6	Roger Clemens/Jsy/250	10.00
7	Curt Schilling/Jsy/250	6.00
8	Mark Grace/Jsy/250	8.00
9	Ivan Rodriguez/Jsy/250	8.00
10	Josh Beckett/Jsy/100	5.00

Rivals

	NM/M

Common Duo:
Production 1,499 Sets
Silver: 1-2X
Production 100 Sets
1	Derek Jeter, Nomar Garciaparra	6.00
2	Mark Prior, Albert Pujols	4.00
3	Warren Spahn, Stan Musial	4.00
4	Don Sutton, Reggie Jackson	2.00
5	Roger Clemens, Mike Piazza	4.00
6	Dennis Eckersley, M. Williams	1.50
7	Kerry Wood, Frank Thomas	3.00
8	Jim Palmer, Willie Stargell	2.00
9	Tom Seaver, Mike Schmidt	5.00
10	Jack Morris, George Brett	5.00
11	Randy Johnson, Todd Helton	2.00
12	Tommy John, Rod Carew	2.00
13	Pedro J. Martinez, Jason Giambi	2.00
14	Dwight Gooden, Wade Boggs	1.50
15	Bob Gibson, Ernie Banks	3.00
16	Hideo Nomo, Barry Larkin	1.50
17	Roy Halladay, Vladimir Guerrero	2.00
18	Greg Maddux, Jeff Bagwell	3.00
19	Barry Zito, Alex Rodriguez	5.00
20	Steve Carlton, Andre Dawson	1.50
21	Mariano Rivera, Chipper Jones	2.00
22	Tom Glavine, Manny Ramirez	2.00
23	Whitey Ford, Harmon Killebrew	2.00

#	Player	NM/M
24	Carl Yastrzemski, Jim "Catfish" Hunter	2.00
25	Nolan Ryan, Robin Ventura	5.00
26	Carlton Fisk, Joe Morgan	1.50
27	Phil Rizzuto, Duke Snider	2.00
28	Fergie Jenkins, Lou Brock	1.50
29	Jose Canseco, Will Clark	1.50
30	Mike Mussina, Josh Beckett	1.50
31	Rickey Henderson, Ivan Rodriguez	2.00
32	Don Mattingly, Eddie Murray	5.00
33	Troy Glaus, Eric Chavez	1.50
34	Ryne Sandberg, Steve Garvey	3.00
35	Bob Gibson, Roger Maris	4.00
36	Roger Clemens, Cal Ripken Jr.	8.00
37	Orel Hershiser, Darryl Strawberry	1.50
38	Curt Schilling, Paul Molitor	2.00
39	Ichiro Suzuki, Hideki Matsui	5.00
40	Sammy Sosa, Jim Thome	4.00

Rivals Materials

NM/M

Quantity produced listed

#	Player	NM/M
1	Derek Jeter/Jsy, Nomar Garciaparra/Bat/250	25.00
2	Mark Prior/Jsy, Albert Pujols/Jsy/250	20.00
3	Warren Spahn/Pants, Stan Musial/Jsy/100	30.00
4	Don Sutton/Jsy, Reggie Jackson/Jsy/10	
5	Roger Clemens/Jsy, Mike Piazza/Jsy/250	20.00
7	Kerry Wood/Jsy, Frank Thomas/Jsy/250	10.00
8	Jim Palmer/Jsy, Willie Stargell/Jsy/250	12.00
9	Tom Seaver/Jsy, Mike Schmidt/Jsy/250	20.00
10	Jack Morris/Jsy, George Brett/Jsy/250	15.00
11	Randy Johnson/Jsy, Todd Helton/Jsy/250	12.00
12	Tommy John/Pants, Rod Carew/Jkt/250	12.00
13	Pedro J. Martinez/Jsy, Jason Giambi/Jsy/250	12.00
14	Dwight Gooden/Jsy, Wade Boggs/Jsy/250	10.00
15	Bob Gibson/Jsy, Ernie Banks/Pants/250	20.00
16	Hideo Nomo/Jsy, Barry Larkin/Jsy/250	10.00
17	Roy Halladay/Jsy, Vladimir Guerrero/Jsy/250	10.00
18	Greg Maddux/Jsy/250, Jeff Bagwell/Jsy/250	15.00
19	Barry Zito/Jsy, Alex Rodriguez/Jsy/250	15.00
20	Steve Carlton/Jsy, Andre Dawson/Jsy/250	10.00
21	Mariano Rivera/Jsy, Chipper Jones/Jsy/10	
22	Tom Glavine/Jsy, Manny Ramirez/Jsy/250	10.00
23	Whitey Ford/Pants, Harmon Killebrew/Jsy/100	35.00
24	Carl Yastrzemski/Jsy, Jim "Catfish" Hunter/Jsy/250	20.00
25	Nolan Ryan/Pants, Robin Ventura/Jsy/250	25.00
26	Carlton Fisk/Jsy, Joe Morgan/Jsy/250	10.00
27	Phil Rizzuto/Jsy, Duke Snider/Jsy/5	
28	Fergie Jenkins/Pants, Lou Brock/Jsy/100	20.00
29	Jose Canseco/Bat, Will Clark/Bat/250	15.00
30	Mike Mussina/Jsy, Josh Beckett/Jsy/250	10.00
31	Rickey Henderson/Jsy, Ivan Rodriguez/Jsy/250	10.00
32	Don Mattingly/Pants, Eddie Murray/Jsy/250	20.00
33	Troy Glaus/Jsy, Eric Chavez/Jsy/250	8.00
34	Ryne Sandberg/Jsy, Steve Garvey/Jsy/250	20.00
35	Bob Gibson/Jsy, Roger Maris/Jsy/100	40.00
36	Roger Clemens/Jsy, Cal Ripken Jr./Pants/250	30.00
38	Curt Schilling/Jsy, Paul Molitor/Bat/250	12.00
39	Ichiro Suzuki/Base, Hideki Matsui/Base/250	40.00
40	Sammy Sosa/Jsy, Jim Thome/Jsy/250	12.00

Signatures Bronze

NM/M

Quantity produced listed

#	Player	NM/M
2	Garret Anderson/25	25.00
10	Shea Hillenbrand/100	10.00
11	Adam LaRoche/100	10.00
14	Dale Murphy/25	35.00
16	Marcus Giles/50	15.00
17	Rafael Furcal/25	20.00
20	Jay Gibbons/100	10.00
21	Luis Matos/100	10.00
35	Carlos Lee/100	10.00
39	Adam Dunn/25	30.00
44	C.C. Sabathia/100	15.00
48	Preston Wilson/50	15.00
50	Alan Trammell/50	20.00
52	Jeremy Bonderman/100	10.00
56	Miguel Cabrera/50	30.00
65	Angel Berroa/100	10.00
66	Carlos Beltran/100	25.00
79	Scott Podsednik/100	10.00
80	Jacque Jones/100	10.00
81	Johan Santana/100	40.00
82	Shannon Stewart/100	10.00
83	Torii Hunter/50	10.00
84	Andre Dawson/100	15.00
85	Chad Cordero/100	8.00
86	Jose Vidro/100	10.00
88	Orlando Cabrera/100	10.00
104	Bobby Crosby/100	10.00
106	Jermaine Dye/100	15.00
108	Rich Harden/50	20.00
115	Marlon Byrd/25	15.00
119	Jason Bay/50	15.00
122	Jay Payton/50	10.00
138	Aubrey Huff/50	15.00
139	Carl Crawford/50	20.00
145	Michael Young/100	15.00
151	Andres Blanco/50	10.00
152	Kevin Cave/50	10.00
153	Ryan Meaux/50	10.00
154	Tim Bausher/50	10.00
155	Jesse Harper/50	10.00
156	Mike Wuertz/50	10.00
158	Donald Kelly/50	8.00
159	Edwin Moreno/50	8.00
160	Mike Johnston/50	8.00
161	Orlando Rodriguez/50	8.00
164	Jorge Vasquez/50	10.00
166	Jake Woods/50	10.00
167	Aarom Baldiris/50	10.00
170	Dennis Sarfate/50	8.00
173	Eddy Rodriguez/50	10.00

Signatures Bronze B/W

No Pricing

Signatures Gold

NM/M

Quantity produced listed

#	Player	NM/M
2	Garret Anderson/25	25.00
10	Shea Hillenbrand/25	20.00
11	Adam LaRoche/25	15.00
14	Dale Murphy/25	35.00
16	Marcus Giles/25	20.00
17	Rafael Furcal/25	20.00
20	Jay Gibbons/25	15.00
21	Luis Matos/25	15.00
35	Carlos Lee/25	15.00
39	Adam Dunn/25	30.00
44	C.C. Sabathia/25	15.00
45	Jody Gerut/25	20.00
48	Preston Wilson/25	20.00
50	Alan Trammell/25	25.00
52	Jeremy Bonderman/25	20.00
56	Miguel Cabrera/25	35.00
65	Angel Berroa/25	10.00
66	Carlos Beltran/25	40.00
79	Scott Podsednik/25	20.00
80	Jacque Jones/25	20.00
81	Johan Santana/25	50.00
82	Shannon Stewart/25	20.00
83	Torii Hunter/25	20.00
84	Andre Dawson/25	15.00
85	Chad Cordero/25	10.00
86	Jose Vidro/25	15.00
88	Orlando Cabrera/25	15.00
104	Bobby Crosby/25	30.00
106	Jermaine Dye/25	15.00
115	Marlon Byrd/25	15.00
119	Jason Bay/25	25.00
122	Jay Payton/25	15.00
138	Aubrey Huff/25	20.00
139	Carl Crawford/25	25.00
145	Michael Young/25	30.00
151	Andres Blanco/50	10.00
152	Kevin Cave/50	10.00
153	Ryan Meaux/50	10.00
154	Tim Bausher/50	10.00
155	Jesse Harper/50	10.00
156	Mike Wuertz/50	10.00
158	Donald Kelly/50	8.00
159	Edwin Moreno/50	8.00
160	Mike Johnston/50	8.00
161	Orlando Rodriguez/50	8.00
164	Jorge Vasquez/50	10.00
166	Jake Woods/50	10.00
167	Aarom Baldiris/50	10.00
168	Jason Bartlett/50	12.00
170	Dennis Sarfate/50	10.00
173	Eddy Rodriguez/50	10.00

Signatures Gold B/W

No Pricing

Signatures Silver

NM/M

Quantity produced listed

#	Player	NM/M
2	Garret Anderson/50	20.00
10	Shea Hillenbrand/50	15.00
11	Adam LaRoche/50	15.00
14	Dale Murphy/50	25.00
16	Marcus Giles/50	15.00
17	Rafael Furcal/50	15.00
20	Jay Gibbons/50	10.00
21	Luis Matos/50	10.00
29	Trot Nixon/25	35.00
32	Mark Prior/25	40.00
35	Carlos Lee/50	10.00
39	Adam Dunn/25	30.00
42	Austin Kearns/25	20.00
43	Ryan Wagner/50	10.00
44	C.C. Sabathia/50	15.00
45	Jody Gerut/50	15.00
48	Preston Wilson/50	15.00
50	Alan Trammell/50	20.00
52	Jeremy Bonderman/50	10.00
56	Miguel Cabrera/50	30.00
65	Angel Berroa/50	10.00
66	Carlos Beltran/50	30.00
73	Paul LoDuca/50	20.00
79	Scott Podsednik/50	15.00
80	Jacque Jones/50	15.00
81	Johan Santana/50	40.00
82	Shannon Stewart/50	15.00
83	Torii Hunter/50	15.00
84	Andre Dawson/50	15.00
85	Chad Cordero/50	8.00
86	Jose Vidro/50	10.00
88	Orlando Cabrera/50	12.00
104	Bobby Crosby/50	25.00
106	Jermaine Dye/50	15.00
107	Mark Mulder/25	20.00
108	Rich Harden/50	20.00
115	Marlon Byrd/50	10.00
119	Jason Bay/50	20.00
122	Jay Payton/50	10.00
138	Aubrey Huff/50	15.00
139	Carl Crawford/50	20.00
143	Hank Blalock/50	25.00
145	Michael Young/50	20.00
150	Vernon Wells/50	15.00
151	Andres Blanco/100	10.00
152	Kevin Cave/100	10.00
153	Ryan Meaux/100	8.00
154	Tim Bausher/100	8.00
155	Jesse Harper/100	8.00
156	Mike Wuertz/100	10.00
158	Donald Kelly/100	6.00
159	Edwin Moreno/100	6.00
160	Mike Johnston/100	6.00
161	Orlando Rodriguez/100	6.00
164	Jorge Vasquez/100	8.00
166	Jake Woods/100	8.00
167	Aarom Baldiris/100	8.00
170	Dennis Sarfate/100	6.00
173	Eddy Rodriguez/100	8.00

Signatures Silver B/W

No Pricing

Signatures Platinum

No Pricing
Production One Set

Signatures Platinum B/W

No Pricing

2004 Donruss Studio

CHIPPER JONES

NM/M

	NM/M
Complete Set (220):	
Common Player:	.15
Common SP (201-221):	6.00
Production 400-800:	
Pack (6):	4.00
Box (24):	75.00

#	Player	NM/M
1	Bartolo Colon	.15
2	Garret Anderson	.40
3	Tim Salmon	.25
4	Troy Glaus	.40
5	Vladimir Guerrero	.75
6	Brandon Webb	.15
7	Brian Bruney	.15
8	Casey Fossum	.15
9	Luis Gonzales	.25
10	Randy Johnson	1.00
11	Richie Sexson	.40
12	Robby Hammock	.15
13	Roberto Alomar	.40
14	Shea Hillenbrand	.15
15	Steve Finley	.15
16	Adam LaRoche	.15
17	Andruw Jones	.50
18	Bubba Nelson	.15
19	Chipper Jones	.75
20	Dale Murphy	.50
21	J.D. Drew	.25
22	Marcus Giles	.15
23	Michael Hessman	.15
24	Rafael Furcal	.25
25	Warren Spahn	.50
26	Adam Loewen	.15
27	Cal Ripken Jr.	3.00
28	Javy Lopez	.40
29	Jay Gibbons	.15
30	Luis Matos	.15
31	Miguel Tejada	.40
32	Rafael Palmeiro	.50
33	Curt Schilling	.50
34	Jason Varitek	.25
35	Kevin Youkilis	.15
36	Manny Ramirez	.50
37	Nomar Garciaparra	1.50
38	Pedro Martinez	.75
39	Trot Nixon	.25
40	Aramis Ramirez	.40
41	Brendan Harris	.15
42	Derrek Lee	.25
43	Ernie Banks	1.00
44	Greg Maddux	1.00
45	Kerry Wood	.75
46	Mark Prior	1.00
47	Ryne Sandberg	1.00

48	Sammy Sosa	1.50
49	Todd Wellemeyer	.15
50	Carlos Lee	.15
51	Edwin Almonte	.15
52	Frank Thomas	.50
53	Joe Borchard	.15
54	Joe Crede	.15
55	Magglio Ordonez	.25
56	Adam Dunn	.50
57	Austin Kearns	.25
58	Barry Larkin	.40
59	Brandon Larson	.15
60	Ken Griffey Jr.	1.00
61	Ryan Wagner	.15
62	Sean Casey	.25
63	Brian Tallet	.15
64	C.C. Sabathia	.15
65	Jeremy Guthrie	.15
66	Jody Gerut	.15
67	Travis Hafner	.25
68	Clint Barmes	.15
69	Jeff Baker	.15
70	Joe Kennedy	.15
71	Larry Walker	.25
72	Preston Wilson	.15
73	Todd Helton	.50
74	Dmitri Young	.15
75	Ivan Rodriguez	.50
76	Jeremy Bonderman	.15
77	Preston Larrison	.15
78	Dontrelle Willis	.15
79	Josh Beckett	.50
80	Juan Pierre	.15
81	Luis Castillo	.15
82	Miguel Cabrera	.75
83	Mike Lowell	.25
84	Andy Pettitte	.25
85	Chris Burke	.15
86	Craig Biggio	.25
87	Jeff Bagwell	.50
88	Jeff Kent	.25
89	Lance Berkman	.25
90	Morgan Ensberg	.15
91	Richard Hidalgo	.15
92	Roger Clemens	1.50
93	Roy Oswalt	.25
94	Wade Miller	.15
95	Angel Berroa	.15
96	Byron Gettis	.15
97	Carlos Beltran	.25
98	Juan Gonzalez	.50
99	Mike Sweeney	.15
100	Duke Snider	.15
101	Edwin Jackson	.15
102	Eric Gagne	.50
103	Hideo Nomo	.40
104	Hong-Chih Kuo	.15
105	Kazuhisa Ishii	.15
106	Paul Lo Duca	.15
107	Robin Ventura	.15
108	Shawn Green	.25
109	Junior Spivey	.15
110	Lyle Overbay	.25
111	Rickie Weeks	.25
112	Scott Podsednik	.25
113	J.D. Durbin	.15
114	Jacque Jones	.15
115	Jason Kubel	.15
116	Johan Santana	.15
117	Shannon Stewart	.15
118	Torii Hunter	.25
119	Brad Wilkerson	.15
120	Jose Vidro	.15
121	Nick Johnson	.15
122	Orlando Cabrera	.15
123	Zach Day	.15
124	Gary Carter	.40
125	Jae Weong Seo	.15
126	Kazuo Matsui RC	5.00
127	Mike Piazza	1.00
128	Tom Glavine	.40
129	Alex Rodriguez	2.00
130	Bernie Williams	.40
131	Chien-Ming Wang	.50
132	Derek Jeter	2.00
133	Don Mattingly	2.00
134	Gary Sheffield	.40
135	Hideki Matsui	1.00
136	Jason Giambi	.50
137	Javier Vazquez	.25
138	Jorge Posada	.40
139	Jose Contreras	.15
140	Kevin Brown	.25
141	Mariano Rivera	.40
142	Mike Mussina	.40
143	Whitey Ford	.50
144	Barry Zito	.25
145	Eric Chavez	.25
146	Mark Mulder	.25
147	Rich Harden	.15
148	Tim Hudson	.25
149	Bobby Abreu	.25
150	Jim Thome	.75
151	Kevin Millwood	.15
152	Marlon Byrd	.15
153	Mike Schmidt	1.00
154	Ryan Howard	.75
155	Jack Wilson	.15
156	Jason Kendall	.15
157	Akinori Otsuka RC	1.00
158	Brian Giles	.25
159	David Wells	.15
160	Jay Payton	.15
161	Phil Nevin	.15
162	Ryan Klesko	.15
163	Sean Burroughs	.15
164	A.J. Pierzynski	.15
165	J.T. Snow	.15
166	Jason Schmidt	.25
167	Jerome Williams	.15
168	Merkin Valdez RC	1.00
169	Will Clark	.50
170	Bret Boone	.25
171	Chris Snelling	.15
172	Edgar Martinez	.25
173	Ichiro Suzuki	1.00
174	Jamie Moyer	.15
175	Randy Winn	.15
176	Rich Aurilia	.15
177	Shigetoshi Hasegawa	.15
178	Albert Pujols	1.50
179	Dan Haren	.15
180	Edgar Renteria	.25
181	Jim Edmonds	.25
182	Matt Morris	.25
183	Scott Rolen	.75
184	Stan Musial	1.00
185	Aubrey Huff	.15
186	Chad Gaudin	.15
187	Delmon Young	.15
188	Fred McGriff	.25
189	Rocco Baldelli	.25
190	Alfonso Soriano	.75
191	Hank Blalock	.50
192	Mark Teixeira	.50
193	Nolan Ryan	2.50
194	Alexis Rios	.15
195	Carlos Delgado	.50
196	Dustin McGowan	.15
197	Guillermo Quiroz	.15
198	Josh Phelps	.15
199	Roy Halladay	.25
200	Vernon Wells	.25
201	Mike Gosling/AU/400 AU/76 RC	8.00
202	Ronny Cedeno/ AU/400 RC	8.00
203	Ronald Belisario/ AU/800 RC	8.00
204	Justin Hampson/ AU/800 RC	6.00
205	Carlos Vasquez/ AU/800 RC	6.00
206	Lincoln Holdzkom/ AU/800 RC	6.00
207	Casey Daigle/ AU/550 RC	6.00
208	Jason Bartlett/ AU/700 RC	6.00
209	Mariano Gomez/ AU/800 RC	8.00
210	Mike House/ AU/800 RC	6.00
211	Chris Shelton/ AU/800 RC	25.00
212	Dennis Sarfate/ AU/800 RC	8.00
213	Shingo Takatsu/ AU/400 RC	35.00
214	Justin Leone/ AU/800 RC	15.00
215	Cory Sullivan/ AU/800 RC	8.00
216	Mike Wuertz/ AU/800 RC	8.00
217	Tim Bausher/ AU/800 RC	8.00
218	Jesse Harper/ AU/800 RC	8.00
219	Ryan Meaux/ AU/800 RC	8.00
221	Kevin Cave/ AU/800 RC	8.00

Proofs Gold

Gold (1-200):	5-10X
Gold (201-225):	.5X

#220, 222-225 exist only in parallel set.
Production 50 Sets

Proofs Platinum

No Pricing
Production 10 Sets

Proofs Silver

Silver (1-200):	3-6X
Silver (201-225):	.25X

#220, 222-225 exist only in parallel set.
Production 100 Sets

Big League Challenge

	NM/M
Production 999 Sets	6.00
Die-Cut:	1X
Production 500 Sets	
1 Albert Pujols/Left	6.00
2 Albert Pujols/Right	6.00
3 Alex Rodriguez/Rgr Left	5.00
4 Alex Rodriguez/Rgr Right	5.00
5 Magglio Ordonez	2.00
6 Rafael Palmeiro	3.00
7 Troy Glaus/Follow	2.00
8 Troy Glaus/Start	2.00
9 Albert Pujols/Bat Up	6.00
10 Alex Rodriguez/Rgr Bat Up	5.00

Big League Challenge Material

	NM/M
Production 100 Sets Combo:	15.00 1-2X
Production 50 Sets	
1 Albert Pujols/Jsy	15.00
2 Albert Pujols/Pants	15.00
3 Alex Rodriguez/Rgr Jsy	10.00
4 Alex Rodriguez/Rgr Pants	10.00
5 Magglio Ordonez/Jsy	5.00
6 Rafael Palmeiro/Jsy	8.00
7 Troy Glaus/Jsy	6.00
8 Troy Glaus/Pants	6.00
9 Albert Pujols/Hat	20.00
10 Alex Rodriguez/Rgr Hat	15.00

Diamond Cuts Combo Material

	NM/M
Quantity produced listed	15.00
1 Derek Jeter/Bat-Jsy/50	40.00
2 Greg Maddux/Bat-Jsy/50	25.00
3 Nomar Garciaparra/Bat-Jsy/25	
4 Miguel Cabrera/Bat-Jsy/50	20.00
5 Mark Mulder/Bat-Jsy/50	15.00
6 Rafael Furcal/Bat-Jsy/50	10.00
7 Mark Prior/Bat-Jsy/50	20.00
8 Roy Oswalt/Bat-Jsy/50	10.00
9 Dontrelle Willis/Bat-Jsy/25	15.00
10 Jay Gibbons/Bat-Jsy/50	10.00
11 Josh Beckett/Bat-Jsy/50	15.00
12 Angel Berroa/Bat-Jsy/50	10.00
13 Adam Dunn/Bat-Jsy/50	15.00
14 Hank Blalock/Bat-Jsy/50	15.00
15 Carlos Beltran/Bat-Jsy/50	15.00
16 Shannon Stewart/Bat-Jsy/50	10.00
17 Aubrey Huff/Bat-Jsy/50	10.00
18 Jeff Bagwell/Bat-Jsy/50	20.00
19 Trot Nixon/Bat-Jsy/50	15.00
20 Nolan Ryan/Jacket-Jsy/50	40.00
21 Tony Gwynn/Bat-Jsy/50	30.00
22 Andre Dawson/Bat-Jsy/50	15.00
23 Don Mattingly/Bat-Jacket/50	40.00
24 Dale Murphy/Bat-Jsy/50	20.00
25 Gary Carter/Bat-Jsy/50	15.00

Diamond Cuts Combo Material Signature

Production 1-5 Sets

Diamond Cuts Material Bat

	NM/M
Quantity produced listed	8.00
1 Derek Jeter/100	25.00
2 Greg Maddux/100	10.00
3 Nomar Garciaparra/200	10.00
4 Miguel Cabrera/200	8.00
5 Mark Mulder/200	6.00
6 Rafael Furcal/200	4.00
7 Mark Prior/200	8.00
8 Roy Oswalt/200	4.00
9 Dontrelle Willis/100	6.00
10 Jay Gibbons/200	4.00
11 Josh Beckett/200	4.00
12 Angel Berroa/200	4.00
13 Adam Dunn/200	8.00
14 Hank Blalock/200	4.00
15 Carlos Beltran/200	6.00
16 Shannon Stewart/200	4.00
17 Aubrey Huff/200	4.00
18 Jeff Bagwell/200	8.00
19 Trot Nixon/200	6.00
20 Tony Gwynn/200	10.00
21 Andre Dawson/200	6.00
22 Don Mattingly/200	15.00
23 Dale Murphy/200	10.00
24 Gary Carter/200	6.00

Diamond Cuts Material Jersey

	NM/M
Production 250 Sets	8.00
1 Derek Jeter	20.00
2 Greg Maddux	10.00
3 Nomar Garciaparra	10.00
4 Miguel Cabrera	8.00
5 Mark Mulder	6.00
6 Rafael Furcal	4.00
7 Mark Prior	8.00
8 Roy Oswalt	6.00
9 Dontrelle Willis	6.00
10 Jay Gibbons	6.00
11 Josh Beckett	6.00
12 Angel Berroa	4.00
13 Adam Dunn	8.00
14 Hank Blalock	6.00
15 Carlos Beltran	6.00
16 Shannon Stewart	4.00
17 Aubrey Huff	4.00
18 Jeff Bagwell	8.00
19 Trot Nixon	6.00
20 Nolan Ryan/Jkt	25.00
21 Tony Gwynn	10.00
22 Andre Dawson	6.00
23 Don Mattingly/Jkt	15.00
24 Dale Murphy	10.00
25 Gary Carter	6.00

Fans of the Game

	NM/M
216 Regis Philbin	3.00
217 Denis Leary	3.00
218 Bode Miller	3.00

219	Steve Schirripa	2.00
220	Adam Mesh	2.00

Fans of the Game Autographs

		NM/M
216	Regis Philbin	40.00
217	Denis Leary	30.00
218	Bode Miller	20.00
219	Steve Schirripa	25.00
220	Adam Mesh	25.00

Game Day Souvenirs Number

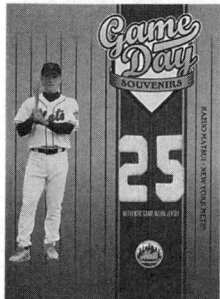

		NM/M
Quantity produced listed		4.00
Position:		.5-1X
Production 25-300		
1	Garret Anderson/Jsy/300	4.00
2	Troy Glaus/Jsy/300	6.00
3	Vladimir Guerrero/Jsy/300	8.00
4	Steve Finley/Jsy/250	4.00
5	Luis Gonzalez/Jsy/25	4.00
6	Richie Sexson/Jsy/250	6.00
7	Andruw Jones/Jsy/300	6.00
8	Chipper Jones/Jsy/250	8.00
9	Rafael Furcal/Jsy/250	4.00
13	Curt Schilling/Jsy/300	6.00
14	Pedro Martinez/Jsy/300	8.00
15	David Ortiz/Jsy/300	8.00
16	Sammy Sosa/Jsy/250	10.00
17	Corey Patterson/Jsy/250	6.00
18	Moises Alou/Jsy/300	6.00
19	Magglio Ordonez/Jsy/250	4.00
20	Paul Konerko/Jsy/300	4.00
21	Frank Thomas/Jsy/300	8.00
22	Austin Kearns/Jsy/50	8.00
23	Sean Casey/Jsy/300	6.00
24	Adam Dunn/Jsy/200	10.00
25	Omar Vizquel/Jsy/250	4.00
26	C.C. Sabathia/Jsy/300	4.00
27	Jody Gerut/Jsy/250	4.00
28	Todd Helton/Jsy/300	8.00
29	Vinny Castilla/Jsy/300	4.00
30	Jeromy Burnitz/Jsy/300	4.00
31	Fernando Vina/Jsy/150	4.00
32	Ivan Rodriguez/Jsy/300	8.00
33	Jeremy Bonderman/Jsy/300	4.00
34	Mike Lowell/Jsy/225	4.00
35	Luis Castillo/Jsy/250	4.00
36	Miguel Cabrera/Jsy/250	8.00
37	Roger Clemens/Jsy/300	10.00
38	Andy Pettitte/Jsy/300	6.00
39	Jeff Bagwell/Jsy/300	6.00
40	Mike Sweeney/Jsy/150	4.00
41	Carlos Beltran/Jsy/200	6.00
42	Angel Berroa/Jsy/100	6.00
43	Paul Lo Duca/Jsy/75	6.00
44	Shawn Green/Jsy/300	4.00
45	Adrian Beltre/Jsy/150	4.00
46	Ben Sheets/Jsy/300	6.00
47	Geoff Jenkins/Jsy/250	4.00
48	Junior Spivey/Jsy/300	4.00
49	Doug Mientkiewicz/Jsy/100	4.00
50	Shannon Stewart/Jsy/100	4.00
51	Torii Hunter/Jsy/300	6.00
52	Livan Hernandez/Jsy/300	4.00
53	Jose Vidro/Jsy/200	4.00
54	Orlando Cabrera/Jsy/300	4.00
55	Mike Piazza/Jsy/250	8.00
56	Mike Cameron/Jsy/250	4.00
57	Kazuo Matsui/Jsy/200	30.00
58	Derek Jeter/Jsy/50	30.00
59	Jason Giambi/Jsy/50	10.00
61	Barry Zito/Jsy/200	6.00
62	Eric Chavez/Jsy/150	4.00
63	Eric Byrnes/Jsy/150	4.00
65	Jim Thome/Jsy/300	8.00
66	Jimmy Rollins/Jsy/250	4.00
67	Jason Kendall/Jsy/250	4.00
68	Craig Wilson/Jsy/250	4.00
69	Jack Wilson/Jsy/250	4.00
70	Ryan Klesko/Jsy/300	4.00
71	Brian Giles/Jsy/300	4.00
72	Sean Burroughs/Jsy/300	4.00
73	A.J. Pierzynski/Jsy/300	4.00
74	J.T. Snow/Jsy/300	4.00
75	Michael Tucker/Jsy/300	4.00
77	Edgar Martinez/Jsy/50	10.00
79	Scott Rolen/Jsy/300	8.00
80	Albert Pujols/Jsy/300	15.00
81	Jim Edmonds/Jsy/300	6.00
82	Aubrey Huff/Jsy/100	4.00
83	Tino Martinez/Jsy/100	4.00
84	Rocco Baldelli/Jsy/100	6.00
85	Alfonso Soriano/Jsy/200	8.00
86	Michael Young/Jsy/250	6.00
87	Hank Blalock/Jsy/200	6.00
88	Eric Hinske/Jsy/200	4.00
89	Carlos Delgado/Jsy/300	4.00
90	Vernon Wells/Jsy/250	4.00

Game Day Souvenirs Signature Number

Production 5 Sets

Heritage

		NM/M
Production 999 Sets		4.00
Die-Cut:		2-3X
Production 100 Sets		
1	George Brett	6.00
2	Nolan Ryan	8.00
3	Cal Ripken Jr.	8.00
4	Mike Schmidt	5.00
5	Roberto Clemente	6.00
6	Don Mattingly	5.00
7	Dale Murphy	4.00
8	Ryne Sandberg	5.00
9	Harmon Killebrew	4.00
10	Stan Musial	5.00

Heritage Material Bat

		NM/M
Production 50 Sets		15.00
1	George Brett	30.00
3	Cal Ripken Jr.	40.00
4	Mike Schmidt	20.00
5	Roberto Clemente	60.00
6	Don Mattingly	30.00
7	Dale Murphy	15.00
8	Ryne Sandberg	20.00
9	Harmon Killebrew	15.00
10	Stan Musial	35.00

Heritage Material Jersey

		NM/M
Quantity produced listed		15.00
1	George Brett/200	15.00
2	Nolan Ryan/Jkt/200	20.00
3	Cal Ripken Jr./200	30.00
4	Mike Schmidt/Pants/200	15.00
5	Roberto Clemente/50	60.00
6	Don Mattingly/Jkt/200	15.00
7	Dale Murphy/200	8.00
8	Ryne Sandberg/200	20.00
9	Harmon Killebrew/Pants/200	15.00
10	Stan Musial/100	20.00

Heritage Signature Material Jersey

Production 5 Sets

Heroes of the Hall

		NM/M
Production 999 Sets		4.00
Die-Cut:		1X
Production 500 Sets		
1	Fergie Jenkins	3.00
2	Gary Carter	3.00
3	Gaylord Perry	3.00
4	George Brett	6.00
5	Jim Palmer	3.00
6	Nolan Ryan	8.00
7	Paul Molitor	4.00
8	Rod Carew	4.00
9	Steve Carlton	3.00
10	Robin Yount	5.00

Heroes of the Hall Material Bat

		NM/M
Production 100 Sets		8.00
2	Gary Carter	8.00
4	George Brett	20.00
7	Paul Molitor	10.00
8	Rod Carew	8.00
9	Steve Carlton	8.00
10	Robin Yount	15.00

Heroes of the Hall Material Jersey

		NM/M
Production 200 unless noted.		
Prime:		No Pricing
Production 10 Sets		
1	Fergie Jenkins/Pants	8.00
2	Gary Carter	8.00
3	Gaylord Perry/100	8.00
4	George Brett	15.00
5	Jim Palmer	8.00
6	Nolan Ryan	25.00
7	Paul Molitor	10.00
8	Rod Carew	10.00
9	Steve Carlton	8.00
10	Robin Yount	15.00

Heroes of the Hall Material Signature

No Pricing

Masterstrokes Combo Material

		NM/M
Production 50 Sets		10.00
1	Todd Helton/Bat-Jsy/50	15.00
2	Jose Vidro/Bat-Jsy/50	8.00
3	Edgar Renteria/Bat-Jsy/50	10.00
4	Mike Lowell/Bat-Jsy/50	10.00
5	Gary Sheffield/Bat-Jsy/50	10.00
6	Albert Pujols/Bat-Jsy/50	30.00
7	Javy Lopez/Bat-Jsy/50	10.00
8	Carlos Delgado/Bat-Jsy/50	10.00
9	Bret Boone/Bat-Jsy/50	8.00
10	Alex Rodriguez/Rgr/Bat-Jsy/50	20.00
11	Vernon Wells/Bat-Jsy/50	8.00
12	Manny Ramirez/Bat-Jsy/50	10.00
13	Jorge Posada/Bat-Jsy/50	10.00
14	Edgar Martinez/Bat-Jsy/50	10.00
15	Bernie Williams/Bat-Jsy/50	10.00
16	Magglio Ordonez/Bat-Jsy/50	8.00
17	Garret Anderson/Bat-Jsy/50	8.00
18	Eric Chavez/Bat-Jsy/50	8.00
19	Alfonso Soriano/Bat-Jsy/50	15.00
20	Jason Giambi/Bat-Jsy/50	10.00
21	Jeff Kent/Bat-Jsy/50	8.00
22	Scott Rolen/Bat-Jsy/50	20.00
23	Vladimir Guerrero/Bat-Jsy/50	20.00
24	Sammy Sosa/Bat-Jsy/50	25.00
25	Mike Piazza/Bat-Jsy/50	20.00

Masterstrokes Combo Material Signature

No Pricing

Masterstrokes Material Bat

		NM/M
Production 200 Sets		6.00
1	Todd Helton	8.00
2	Jose Vidro	4.00
3	Edgar Renteria	6.00

4	Mike Lowell	4.00
5	Gary Sheffield	6.00
6	Albert Pujols	15.00
7	Javy Lopez	6.00
8	Carlos Delgado	6.00
9	Bret Boone	4.00
10	Alex Rodriquez	10.00
11	Vernon Wells	4.00
12	Manny Ramirez	6.00
13	Jorge Posada	6.00
14	Edgar Martinez	4.00
15	Bernie Williams	6.00
16	Magglio Ordonez	4.00
17	Garret Anderson	4.00
18	Eric Chavez	4.00
19	Alfonso Soriano	8.00
20	Jason Giambi	6.00
21	Jeff Kent	4.00
22	Scott Rolen	8.00
23	Vladimir Guerrero	8.00
24	Sammy Sosa	10.00
25	Mike Piazza	8.00

Masterstrokes Material Jersey

		NM/M
Prime:		No Pricing
Production 5 Sets		
1	Todd Helton/250	8.00
2	Jose Vidro/250	4.00
3	Edgar Renteria/250	6.00
4	Mike Lowell/250	4.00
5	Gary Sheffield/250	6.00
6	Albert Pujols/250	15.00
7	Javy Lopez/250	6.00
8	Carlos Delgado/250	6.00
9	Bret Boone/250	4.00
10	Alex Rodriguez/250	10.00
11	Vernon Wells/250	4.00
12	Manny Ramirez/250	6.00
13	Jorge Posada/250	6.00
14	Edgar Martinez/250	4.00
15	Bernie Williams/250	6.00
16	Magglio Ordonez/250	4.00
17	Garret Anderson/250	4.00
18	Eric Chavez/250	4.00
19	Alfonso Soriano/150	8.00
20	Jason Giambi/250	6.00
21	Jeff Kent/250	4.00
22	Scott Rolen/250	8.00
23	Vladimir Guerrero/250	8.00
24	Sammy Sosa/250	10.00
25	Mike Piazza/250	8.00

Players Collection Jersey

		NM/M
Common Jersey:		
Production 150 Sets		
Platinum:		1-2X
Production 50 Sets		
1	Adam Dunn/AS	6.00
2	Adam Dunn/Gray	6.00
3	Adam Dunn/White	6.00
4	Alex Rodriguez	10.00
5	Alex Rodriguez/AS	10.00
6	Alex Rodriguez/Blue	10.00
7	Alex Rodriguez/White	10.00
8	Andruw Jones/Home	6.00
9	Andruw Jones/Road	6.00
10	Austin Kearns	6.00
11	Brandon Webb	4.00
12	C.C. Sabathia	4.00
13	Cal Ripken Jr.	25.00
14	Carlos Beltran	6.00
15	Carlos Delgado	6.00
16	Carlos Lee	4.00
17	Chipper Jones Home	8.00
18	Chipper Jones Road	8.00

19	Craig Biggio	6.00
20	Curt Schilling	6.00
21	David Wells	4.00
22	Don Mattingly	20.00
23	Dontrelle Willis	6.00
24	Frank Thomas/Black	8.00
25	Frank Thomas/White	8.00
26	Fred McGriff	4.00
27	Garret Anderson/AS	6.00
28	Gary Sheffield	6.00
29	Gary Sheffield	6.00
30	Greg Maddux/Gray	8.00
31	Hank Blalock/Home	6.00
32	Hank Blalock/Road	6.00
33	Hee Seop Choi	6.00
34	Hideo Nomo	6.00
35	Hideo Nomo/Gray	6.00
36	Hideo Nomo/White	6.00
37	Ivan Rodriguez	6.00
38	Ivan Rodriguez	6.00
39	Jason Giambi/Home	6.00
40	Jim Edmonds	6.00
41	Jim Thorne	8.00
42	John Olerud	6.00
43	John Smoltz	6.00
44	Josh Beckett	6.00
45	Josh Phelps	4.00
46	Juan Gonzalez	6.00
47	Juan Gonzalez	6.00
48	Kazuhisa Ishii	6.00
49	Lance Berkman	6.00
50	Larry Walker/Home	4.00
51	Larry Walker/Road	4.00
52	Luis Gonzalez/AS	4.00
53	Magglio Ordonez/Home	4.00
54	Magglio Ordonez/Road	4.00
55	Manny Ramirez	8.00
56	Manny Ramirez/AS	8.00
57	Mark Prior/Home	8.00
58	Mark Prior/Road	8.00
59	Mark Teixeira	6.00
60	Mike Mussina	6.00
61	Mike Piazza/AS	8.00
62	Mike Piazza/Black	8.00
63	Mike Piazza/White	8.00
64	Nomar Garciaparra/Gray	8.00
65	Nomar Garciaparra/White	8.00
66	Pat Burrell	4.00
67	Paul Konerko	4.00
68	Paul Lo Duca	4.00
69	Pedro Martinez	8.00
70	Rafael Furcal	4.00
71	Rafael Palmeiro/Blue	6.00
72	Rafael Palmeiro/Gray	6.00
73	Ramon Hernandez	4.00
74	Rickey Henderson	6.00
75	Rickey Henderson/Black	6.00
76	Rickey Henderson/White	6.00
77	Roberto Alomar	6.00
78	Roberto Alomar	6.00
79	Robin Ventura/AS	4.00
80	Roger Clemens Away	10.00
81	Roger Clemens Home	10.00
82	Roy Halladay	6.00
83	Sammy Sosa/AS	12.00
84	Sammy Sosa/Gray	12.00
85	Sammy Sosa/White	12.00
86	Scott Rolen	8.00
87	Shannon Stewart	4.00
88	Shawn Green/Blue	4.00
89	Shawn Green/Gray	4.00
90	Shawn Green/White	4.00
91	Terrence Long	4.00
92	Tim Hudson	6.00
93	Todd Helton/Away	8.00
94	Todd Helton/Home	8.00
95	Tom Glavine	6.00
96	Tom Glavine	6.00
97	Torii Hunter	6.00
98	Vernon Wells	4.00
99	Vladimir Guerrero	8.00
100	Vladimir Guerrero/AS	8.00

Private Signings Silver

		NM/M
2	Garret Anderson/25	25.00
6	Brandon Webb/25	15.00
7	Brian Bruney/200	5.00
8	Casey Fossum/63	8.00
14	Shea Hillenbrand/25	20.00
16	Adam LaRoche/26	15.00
18	Bubba Nelson/25	25.00
22	Marcus Giles/25	30.00
24	Rafael Furcal/25	25.00
26	Adam Loewen/25	20.00
29	Jay Gibbons/50	15.00

MIKE PIAZZA

GARY CARTER

30	Luis Matos/250	10.00
35	Kevin Youkilis/250	20.00
39	Trot Nixon/25	50.00
40	Aramis Ramirez/25	25.00
41	Brendan Harris/100	8.00
43	Ernie Banks/25	75.00
48	Sammy Sosa/21	150.00
50	Carlos Lee/25	20.00
51	Edwin Almonte/227	5.00
53	Joe Borchard/100	5.00
59	Brandon Larson/100	5.00
61	Ryan Wagner/50	10.00
63	Brian Tallet/250	5.00
65	Jeremy Guthrie/89	8.00
66	Jody Gerut/100	5.00
67	Travis Hafner/100	15.00
68	Clint Barmes/100	8.00
70	Joe Kennedy/100	5.00
72	Preston Wilson/25	25.00
77	Preston Larrison/100	8.00
81	Luis Castillo/25	15.00
82	Miguel Cabrera/25	60.00
85	Chris Burke/100	5.00
90	Morgan Ensberg/50	15.00
96	Byron Gettis/250	10.00
97	Carlos Beltran/50	35.00
100	Duke Snider/50	40.00
101	Edwin Jackson/100	15.00
104	Hong-Chih Kuo/250	10.00
105	Kazuhisa Ishii/5	10.00
106	Paul Lo Duca/25	15.00
107	Robin Ventura/25	30.00
109	Junior Spivey/50	15.00
112	Scott Podsednik/100	20.00
113	J.D. Durbin/250	5.00
114	Jacque Jones/25	20.00
115	Jason Kubel/100	15.00
116	Johan Santana/25	25.00
117	Shannon Stewart/25	15.00
120	Jose Vidro/15	30.00
122	Orlando Cabrera/15	25.00
124	Gary Carter/50	25.00
131	Chien-Ming Wang/243	100.00
133	Don Mattingly/25	75.00
134	Gary Sheffield/25	25.00
147	Rich Harden/200	15.00
154	Ryan Howard/65	65.00
160	Jay Payton/50	10.00
167	Jerome Williams/57	25.00
168	Merkin Valdez/250	10.00
169	Will Clark/25	75.00
171	Chris Snelling/200	5.00
177	Shigetoshi Hasegawa/25	75.00
178	Albert Pujols/5	
179	Dan Haren/250	8.00
184	Stan Musial/25	80.00
185	Aubrey Huff/50	10.00
186	Chad Gaudin/100	5.00
187	Delmon Young/25	40.00
192	Mark Teixeira/23	25.00
193	Nolan Ryan/34	100.00
194	Alexis Rios/250	15.00
196	Dustin McGowan/115	10.00
197	Guillermo Quiroz/120	8.00

Private Signings Gold

		NM/M
2	Garret Anderson/16	35.00
6	Brandon Webb/55	15.00
7	Brian Bruney/100	5.00
14	Shea Hillenbrand/28	25.00
16	Adam LaRoche/25	15.00
18	Bubba Nelson/100	5.00
22	Marcus Giles/25	30.00
23	Michael Hessman/25	10.00
29	Jay Gibbons/25	20.00
30	Luis Matos/100	5.00
35	Kevin Youkilis/100	25.00
40	Aramis Ramirez/16	35.00
41	Brendan Harris/75	10.00

49	Todd Wellemeyer/50	10.00
50	Carlos Lee/45	15.00
51	Edwin Almonte/56	10.00
53	Joe Borchard/25	10.00
54	Joe Crede/24	15.00
57	Austin Kearns/28	25.00
59	Brandon Larson/16	15.00
61	Ryan Wagner/38	10.00
63	Brian Tallet/50	10.00
65	Jeremy Guthrie/67	8.00
66	Jody Gerut/25	20.00
67	Travis Hafner/34	25.00
68	Clint Barmes/36	10.00
69	Jeff Baker/62	10.00
70	Joe Kennedy/37	15.00
73	Todd Helton/17	50.00
77	Preston Larrison/56	10.00
78	Dontrelle Willis/35	40.00
82	Miguel Cabrera/24	60.00
85	Chris Burke/46	8.00
89	Lance Berkman/17	50.00
90	Morgan Ensberg/25	15.00
96	Byron Gettis/100	8.00
97	Carlos Beltran/25	50.00
98	Juan Gonzalez/22	35.00
100	Duke Snider/25	50.00
101	Edwin Jackson/50	20.00
104	Hong-Chih Kuo/100	40.00
105	Kazuhisa Ishii/17	50.00
106	Paul Lo Duca/16	30.00
107	Robin Ventura/25	30.00
108	Shawn Green/15	30.00
109	Junior Spivey/17	30.00
112	Scott Podsednik/20	25.00
113	J.D. Durbin/31	15.00
114	Jacque Jones/25	25.00
116	Johan Santana/57	25.00
117	Shannon Stewart/23	15.00
121	Nick Johnson/21	15.00
122	Orlando Cabrera/18	25.00
124	Gary Carter/25	30.00
125	Jae Weong Seo/25	25.00
131	Chien-Ming Wang/100	125.00
147	Rich Harden/53	20.00
152	Marlon Byrd/29	15.00
154	Ryan Howard/100	75.00
160	Jay Payton/17	20.00
167	Jerome Williams/50	20.00
168	Merkin Valdez/100	15.00
171	Chris Snelling/32	10.00
177	Shigetoshi Hasegawa/17	75.00
179	Dan Haren/100	10.00
184	Stan Musial/25	80.00
185	Aubrey Huff/19	25.00
186	Chad Gaudin/100	5.00
187	Delmon Young/73	20.00
192	Mark Teixeira/25	25.00
194	Alexis Rios/50	20.00
196	Dustin McGowan/50	10.00
198	Josh Phelps/15	15.00

Private Signings Platinum

No Pricing
Production 1-10

Rally Caps

NM/M
Production 999 Sets

Die-cut:		1X
Production 500 Sets		
1	Adam Dunn	2.00
2	Adrian Beltre	1.50
3	Albert Pujols	5.00
4	Alex Rodriguez	5.00
5	Andruw Jones	2.00
6	Angel Berroa	1.50
7	Aubrey Huff	1.50
8	Austin Kearns	1.50
9	Ben Sheets	2.00
10	Brad Penny	1.50
11	Carlos Beltran	2.00
12	Carlos Lee	1.50
13	Casey Fossum	1.50
14	Eric Hinske	1.50
15	Geoff Jenkins	1.50
16	Jack Wilson	1.50
17	Jason Jennings	1.50
18	Joe Kennedy	1.50
19	Lance Berkman	1.50
20	Magglio Ordonez	1.50
21	Kerry Wood	3.00
22	Mark Buehrle	1.50
23	Mark Prior	3.00
24	Mark Teixeira	2.00
25	Michael Cuddyer	1.50
26	Jeff Conine	1.50
27	Mike Mussina	2.50
28	Mike Piazza	4.00
29	Jose Reyes	2.00
30	Paul Lo Duca	1.50
31	Pedro Martinez	2.00
32	Roy Oswalt	2.00
33	Ryan Klesko	1.50
34	Sammy Sosa	4.00
35	Tim Hudson	1.50
36	Todd Helton	2.00
37	Torii Hunter	2.00
38	Vernon Wells	1.50
39	Craig Wilson	1.50
40	Edgar Renteria	1.50

Spirit of the Game

		NM/M
Production 999 Sets		
Die-Cut:		1X
Production 500 Sets		
1	Sammy Sosa	4.00
2	Alex Rodriguez/Rgr	4.00
3	Nomar Garciaparra	4.00
4	Derek Jeter	6.00
5	Albert Pujols	5.00
6	Roger Clemens	5.00
7	Mark Prior	3.00
8	Randy Johnson	2.00
9	Pedro Martinez	2.00
10	Vladimir Guerrero	2.00
11	Todd Helton	2.00
12	Jeff Bagwell	2.00
13	Mike Mussina	1.50
14	Josh Beckett	1.50
15	Hideo Nomo	1.50
16	Mike Piazza	4.00
17	Don Mattingly	5.00
18	George Brett	5.00
19	Nolan Ryan	8.00
20	Cal Ripken Jr.	8.00

Spirit of the Game Material Bat

		NM/M
1	Sammy Sosa/100	15.00
2	Alex Rodriguez/Rgr/100	10.00
3	Nomar Garciaparra/100	10.00
4	Derek Jeter/100	20.00
5	Albert Pujols/100	15.00
6	Roger Clemens/50	20.00
7	Mark Prior/100	8.00
8	Randy Johnson/100	10.00
10	Vladimir Guerrero/100	10.00
11	Todd Helton/100	10.00
12	Jeff Bagwell/100	8.00
13	Mike Mussina/100	10.00
14	Josh Beckett/100	8.00
15	Hideo Nomo/100	10.00
16	Mike Piazza/100	10.00
17	Don Mattingly/100	20.00
18	George Brett/100	20.00
20	Cal Ripken Jr./50	50.00

Spirit of the Game Material Jersey

		NM/M
Prime:		No Pricing
Production 1-5		
1	Sammy Sosa/200	10.00
2	Alex Rodriguez/200	10.00
3	Nomar Garciaparra/100	10.00
4	Derek Jeter/200	20.00
5	Albert Pujols/100	20.00
7	Mark Prior/200	8.00
8	Randy Johnson/100	10.00
9	Pedro Martinez/200	10.00
11	Todd Helton/100	10.00
12	Jeff Bagwell/200	8.00
13	Mike Mussina/200	8.00
14	Josh Beckett/200	8.00
15	Hideo Nomo/200	8.00
16	Mike Piazza/200	12.00
17	Don Mattingly/Jkt/200	15.00
18	George Brett/200	15.00
19	Nolan Ryan/100	40.00
20	Cal Ripken Jr./100	40.00

Spirit of the Game Material Signature Jersey

No Pricing

Stars

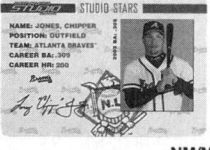

		NM/M
Inserted 1:5		
Gold:		1.5-3X
Production 100 Sets		
Platinum:		3-5X
Production 25 Sets		
1	Albert Pujols	3.00
2	Alex Rodriguez	4.00
3	Alfonso Soriano	1.50
4	Andy Pettitte	.50
5	Angel Berroa	.50
6	Aubrey Huff	.50
7	Austin Kearns	.75
8	Barry Zito	.75
9	Brian Giles	.75
10	Carlos Delgado	.75
11	Chipper Jones	1.50
12	Craig Biggio	.75
13	Curt Schilling	1.00
14	Derek Jeter	4.00
15	Edgar Martinez	.50
16	Eric Gagne	1.00
17	Frank Thomas	1.00
18	Hank Blalock	1.00
19	Hideki Matsui	3.00
20	Hideo Nomo	.75
21	Ichiro Suzuki	2.00
22	Ivan Rodriguez	1.00
23	Jason Kendall	.50
24	Jason Schmidt	.75
25	Jeff Bagwell	1.00
26	Jim Edmonds	1.00
27	Jim Thome	1.50
28	Josh Beckett	.75
29	Kazuo Matsui	4.00
30	Ken Griffey Jr.	2.50
31	Larry Walker	.50
32	Magglio Ordonez	.50
33	Manny Ramirez	1.00
34	Mark Mulder	.75
35	Mark Prior	2.00
36	Mark Teixeira	1.00
37	Miguel Tejada	1.00
38	Mike Mussina	1.00
39	Mike Piazza	2.50
40	Pedro Martinez	1.50
41	Randy Johnson	1.50
42	Roger Clemens	3.00

2004 Donruss Team Heroes

PEDRO MARTINEZ

		NM/M
Complete Set (465):		75.00
Common Player:		.25
Common SP (441-465):		.50
Pack (8):		2.00
Box (24):		40.00
1	Troy Glaus	.40
2	Garret Anderson	.40
3	John Lackey	.25
4	Jarrod Washburn	.25
5	Bengie Molina	.25
6	Adam Kennedy	.25
7	Francisco Rodriguez	.25
8	Darin Erstad	.25
9	Ramon Ortiz	.25
10	Chone Figgins	.25
11	Rich Fischer	.25
12	David Eckstein	.25
13	Troy Percival	.25
14	Tim Salmon	.40
15	Nolan Ryan/Angels	2.00
16	Luis Gonzalez	.40
17	Matt Kata	.25
18	Randy Johnson	.75
19	Oscar Villarreal	.25
20	Tim Olson	.25
21	Rob Hammock	.25
22	Alex Cintron	.25
23	Brian Bruney	.25
24	Brandon Webb	.25
25	Greg Aquino	.25
26	Shea Hillenbrand	.25
27	Steve Finley	.25
28	Rod Barajas	.25
29	Mike Hampton	.25
30	Adam LaRoche	.25
31	Russ Ortiz	.25
32	Chipper Jones	.75
33	John Smoltz	.40
34	Andruw Jones	.50
35	Bubba Nelson	.25
36	Johnny Estrada	.25
37	Marcus Giles	.25
38	Rafael Furcal	.25
39	Horacio Ramirez	.25
40	Dale Murphy	.40
41	Gaylord Perry/Braves	.25
42	Mark DeRosa	.25
43	Adam Loewen	.25
44	Jerry Hairston Jr.	.25
45	Jose Morban	.25
46	Daniel Cabrera	.25
47	Jay Gibbons	.25
48	Larry Bigbie	.25
49	Luis Matos	.25
50	Rodrigo Lopez	.25
51	Melvin Mora	.25
52	Cal Ripken Jr.	2.50
53	Geronimo Gil	.25
54	Tony Batista	.25
55	Jason Johnson	.25
56	Jason Varitek	.25
57	Bill Mueller	.25
58	Todd Walker	.25
59	Trot Nixon	.40
60	Tim Wakefield	.25
61	Kevin Youkilis	.25
62	David Ortiz	.50
63	Johnny Damon	.40
64	Derek Lowe	.25
65	Pedro J. Martinez	.75

43	Roy Halladay	.50
44	Russ Ortiz	.50
45	Sammy Sosa	3.00
46	Scott Podsednik	.50
47	Tim Hudson	.75
48	Todd Helton	1.50
49	Vernon Wells	.50
50	Vladimir Guerrero	2.00

2004 Donruss Team Heroes

66	Carl Yastrzemski	.75
67	Bobby Doerr	.25
68	Matt Clement	.25
69	Sammy Sosa	1.50
70	Randall Simon	.25
71	Nate Frese	.25
72	Carlos Zambrano	.40
73	Moises Alou	.40
74	Mark Prior	1.00
75	Jason Dubois	.25
76	Nic Jackson	.25
77	Corey Patterson	.40
78	John Webb	.25
79	Kerry Wood	.75
80	Aramis Ramirez	.40
81	Brendan Harris	.25
82	Kenny Lofton	.40
83	Alex Gonzalez	.25
84	Gary Matthews Sr.	.25
85	Mark Grace	.40
86	Mark Grudzielanek	.25
87	Joe Borowski	.25
88	Joe Crede	.25
89	Mark Buehrle	.25
90	Paul Konerko	.40
91	Magglio Ordonez	.40
92	Corwin Malone	.25
93	Frank Thomas	.50
94	Jose Valentin	.25
95	Miguel Olivo	.25
96	Esteban Loaiza	.25
97	Carlos Lee	.40
98	Harold Baines	.25
99	Jason LaRue	.25
100	Sean Casey	.40
101	Adam Dunn	.50
102	Josh Hall	.25
103	Danny Graves	.25
104	Barry Larkin	.40
105	Ken Griffey Jr.	1.00
106	Brandon Claussen	.25
107	Austin Kearns	.40
108	D'Angelo Jimenez	.25
109	Ryan Wagner	.25
110	Tim Hummel	.25
111	Johnny Bench	1.00
112	Eric Davis	.25
113	Jose Rijo	.25
114	Travis Hafner	.40
115	Jody Gerut	.25
116	Fernando Cabrera	.25
117	Jhonny Peralta	.25
118	Ryan Church	.25
119	Francisco Cruceta	.25
120	Omar Vizquel	.40
121	Jason Davis	.25
122	Jeremy Guthrie	.25
123	C.C. Sabathia	.40
124	Milton Bradley	.25
125	Cliff Lee	.25
126	Victor Martinez	.25
127	Bob Feller	.50
128	Casey Blake	.25
129	Josh Bard	.25
130	Billy Traber	.25
131	Coco Crisp	.25
132	Larry Walker	.40
133	Jason Jennings	.25
134	Garrett Atkins	.25
135	Rene Reyes	.25
136	Chin-Hui Tsao	.25
137	Preston Wilson	.25
138	Jeff Baker	.25
139	Charles Johnson	.25
140	Shawn Chacon	.25
141	Todd Helton	.50
142	Jay Payton	.25
143	Omar Infante	.25
144	Bobby Higginson	.25
145	Dmitri Young	.25
146	Jorge Cordova	.25
147	Jeremy Bonderman	.25
148	Brandon Inge	.25
149	Franklyn German	.25
150	Nook Logan	.25
151	Alex Sanchez	.25
152	Craig Monroe	.25
153	Preston Larrison	.25
154	Carlos Pena	.40
155	Alan Trammell	.50
156	Jack Morris	.50
157	Eric Munson	.25
158	Mike Maroth	.25
159	Josh Beckett	.40
160	Josh Willingham	.25
161	Mike Lowell	.40
162	Luis Castillo	.25
163	Wilson Valdez	.25
164	Miguel Cabrera	.75
165	Alex Gonzalez	.25
166	Carl Pavano	.25
167	Dontrelle Willis	.40
168	Juan Pierre	.25
169	Juan Encarnacion	.25

170 Brad Penny	.25	
171 Ivan Rodriguez/Marlins	.50	
172 Josh Wilson	.25	
173 Jeff Conine	.25	
174 Mark Redman	.25	
175 A.J. Burnett	.25	
176 Jeff Bagwell	.50	
177 Octavio Dotel	.25	
178 Craig Biggio	.40	
179 John Buck	.25	
180 Rodrigo Rosario	.25	
181 Tommy Whiteman	.25	
182 Kirk Saarloos	.25	
183 Jason Lane	.25	
184 Wade Miller	.25	
185 Lance Berkman	.40	
186 Roy Oswalt	.40	
187 Tim Redding	.25	
188 Jeff Kent	.40	
189 Chris Burke	.25	
190 Morgan Ensberg	.25	
191 Nolan Ryan/Astros	2.00	
192 Geoff Blum	.25	
193 Jeremy Affeldt	.25	
194 Mike Sweeney	.25	
195 Angel Berroa	.25	
196 Jimmy Gobble	.25	
197 Ken Harvey	.25	
198 Carlos Beltran	.50	
199 Alexis Gomez	.25	
200 Byron Gettis	.25	
201 Mike MacDougal	.25	
202 David DeJesus	.25	
203 Runelvys Hernandez	.25	
204 George Brett	1.50	
205 Amos Otis	.25	
206 Joe Randa	.25	
207 Aaron Guiel	.25	
208 Eric Gagne	.40	
209 Shawn Green	.40	
210 Kevin Brown	.40	
211 Cesar Izturis	.25	
212 Kazuhisa Ishii	.25	
213 Joe Thurston	.25	
214 Odalis Perez	.25	
215 Rickey Henderson	.50	
216 Hideo Nomo	.40	
217 Hong-Chih Kuo	.25	
218 Edwin Jackson	.25	
219 Paul LoDuca	.25	
220 Adrian Beltre	.25	
221 Duke Snider	.75	
222 Steve Garvey	.25	
223 Rickie Weeks	.40	
224 Bill Hall	.25	
225 Doug Davis	.25	
226 Geoff Jenkins	.40	
227 Matt Childers	.25	
228 Dan Kolb	.25	
229 Scott Podsednik	.25	
230 Pedro Liriano	.25	
231 Ben Sheets	.40	
232 Robin Yount	.75	
233 Gorman Thomas	.25	
234 Ben Oglivie	.25	
235 Matt LeCroy	.25	
236 Cristian Guzman	.25	
237 Lew Ford	.25	
238 J.C. Romero	.25	
239 Rob Bowen	.25	
240 Corey Koskie	.25	
241 Jacque Jones	.25	
242 Brad Radke	.25	
243 Shannon Stewart	.25	
244 J.D. Durbin	.25	
245 Doug Mientkiewicz	.25	
246 Jason Kubel	.25	
247 Torii Hunter	.40	
248 Johan Santana	.25	
249 Kirby Puckett	.75	
250 Luis Rivas	.25	
251 Orlando Cabrera	.25	
252 Tony Armas Jr.	.25	
253 Brad Wilkerson	.25	
254 Endy Chavez	.25	
255 Jose Vidro	.25	
256 Zach Day	.25	
257 Livan Hernandez	.25	
258 Terrmel Sledge	.25	
259 Michael Barrett	.25	
260 Gary Carter	.50	
261 Andre Dawson	.50	
262 Craig Brazell	.25	
263 Mike Piazza	1.00	
264 Jeff Duncan	.25	
265 Jason Anderson	.25	
266 Tom Glavine	.40	
267 Danny Garcia	.25	
268 Ty Wigginton	.25	
269 Al Leiter	.25	
270 Jeremy Griffiths	.25	
271 Jose Reyes	.40	
272 Prentice Redman	.25	
273 Cliff Floyd	.25	
274 Jae Weong Seo	.25	
275 Nolan Ryan Mets	2.00	
276 Keith Hernandez	.25	
277 Jason Phillips	.25	
278 Kazuo Matsui RC	3.00	
279 Jose Contreras	.25	
280 Aaron Boone	.25	
281 Mike Mussina	.40	
282 Jason Giambi	.50	
283 Hideki Matsui	1.00	
284 Derek Jeter	2.00	
285 Mariano Rivera	.40	
286 Chien-Ming Wang	.40	
287 Bernie Williams	.40	
288 Alfonso Soriano/Yanks	.50	
289 Jorge Posada	.40	
290 Michel Hernandez	.25	
291 Erick Almonte	.25	
292 Don Mattingly	1.50	
293 Roger Clemens/Yanks	1.50	
294 Gaylord Perry/Rgr	.25	
295 Tommy John	.25	
296 Tim Hudson	.40	
297 Rich Harden	.25	
298 Eric Chavez	.40	
299 Antonio Morrissey	.25	
300 Mark Mulder	.40	
301 Eric Byrnes	.25	
302 Jermaine Dye	.25	
303 Barry Zito	.40	
304 Erubiel Durazo	.25	
305 Mark Ellis	.25	
306 Bobby Crosby	.25	
307 Shane Bazzell	.25	
308 Mario Ramos	.25	
309 Jose Canseco	.50	
310 Placido Polanco	.25	
311 Jimmy Rollins	.25	
312 Jim Thome	.75	
313 Brett Myers	.25	
314 Jason Michaels	.25	
315 Vicente Padilla	.25	
316 Bobby Abreu	.40	
317 Ryan Howard	.50	
318 Chase Utley	.50	
319 Pat Burrell	.40	
320 Randy Wolf	.25	
321 Franklin Perez	.25	
322 Marlon Byrd	.25	
323 Kevin Millwood	.40	
324 Mike Lieberthal	.25	
325 Anderson Machado	.25	
326 Travis Chapman	.25	
327 Steve Carlton	.50	
328 Greg Luzinski	.25	
329 David Bell	.25	
330 Craig Wilson	.40	
331 Kris Benson	.25	
332 Jose Castillo	.25	
333 Josh Fogg	.25	
334 Jason Kendall	.25	
335 Walter Young	.25	
336 Oliver Perez	.25	
337 Jason Bay	.25	
338 Duaner Sanchez	.25	
339 Jack Wilson	.25	
340 Carlos Rivera	.25	
341 Kip Wells	.25	
342 Freddy Sanchez	.25	
343 Roberto Clemente	2.00	
344 Al Oliver	.25	
345 Phil Nevin	.25	
346 Trevor Hoffman	.25	
347 Ryan Klesko	.40	
348 Khalil Greene	.25	
349 Freddy Guzman RC	.25	
350 Brian Giles	.40	
351 Brian Lawrence	.25	
352 Sean Burroughs	.25	
353 Ben Howard	.25	
354 Xavier Nady	.25	
355 Mark Loretta	.25	
356 Ramon Vazquez	.25	
357 Tony Gwynn	.75	
358 Adam Eaton	.25	
359 Merkin Valdez RC	.75	
360 Kevin Correia	.25	
361 Edgardo Alfonzo	.25	
362 Mike Cameron	.25	
363 Ray Durham	.25	
364 Jesse Foppert	.25	
365 Robb Nen	.25	
366 Marquis Grissom	.25	
367 Jerome Williams	.25	
368 Jason Schmidt	.40	
369 Will Clark	.50	
370 Bret Boone	.40	
371 Freddy Garcia	.25	
372 Dan Wilson	.25	
373 Rett Johnson	.25	
374 Kazuhiro Sasaki	.25	
375 Ichiro Suzuki	1.00	
376 Edgar Martinez	.40	
377 Jamie Moyer	.25	
378 Joel Pineiro	.25	
379 Carlos Guillen	.25	
380 Randy Winn	.25	
381 J.J. Putz	.25	
382 John Olerud	.40	
383 Matt Thornton	.25	
384 Rafael Soriano	.25	
385 Gil Meche	.25	
386 Albert Pujols	1.50	
387 Woody Williams	.25	
388 Dan Haren	.25	
389 Matt Morris	.40	
390 Jim Edmonds	.40	
391 Edgar Renteria	.40	
392 Scott Rolen	.75	
393 J.D. Drew	.40	
394 Bo Hart	.25	
395 Stan Musial	1.00	
396 Red Schoendienst	.25	
397 Terry Pendleton	.25	
398 Mike Matheny	.25	
399 Dewon Brazelton	.25	
400 Chad Gaudin	.25	
401 Aubrey Huff	.25	
402 Victor Zambrano	.25	
403 Antonio Perez	.25	
404 Carl Crawford	.40	
405 Joe Kennedy	.25	
406 Pete LaForest	.25	
407 Delmon Young	.40	
408 Rocco Baldelli	.40	
409 Doug Waechter	.25	
410 Brian Stokes	.25	
411 Edwin Almonte	.25	
412 Toby Hall	.25	
413 Lance Carter	.25	
414 Greg Maddux/Braves	1.00	
415 Hank Blalock	.50	
416 Colby Lewis	.25	
417 Mark Teixeira	.40	
418 Gerald Laird	.25	
419 Ricardo Rodriguez	.25	
420 Ben Kozlowski	.25	
421 Kevin Mench	.25	
422 Michael Young	.25	
423 Ramon Nivar	.25	
424 Laynce Nix	.25	
425 Nolan Ryan Rgr	2.00	
426 Einar Diaz	.25	
427 Carlos Delgado	.40	
428 Eric Hinske	.25	
429 Dustin McGowan	.25	
430 Frank Catalanotto	.25	
431 Kevin Cash	.25	
432 Roy Halladay	.40	
433 Orlando Hudson	.25	
434 Francisco Rosario	.25	
435 Guillermo Quiroz	.25	
436 Vernon Wells	.25	
437 Josh Phelps	.25	
438 Alexis Rios	.25	
439 Reed Johnson	.25	
440 Chris Woodward	.25	
441 Bartolo Colon/SP	.50	
442 Richie Sexson/SP	.75	
443 Greg Maddux/Cubs/SP	2.00	
444 Javy Lopez/SP	.75	
445 Gary Sheffield/SP	.75	
446 Curt Schilling/SP	1.00	
447 Nomar Garciaparra/SP	2.50	
448 Manny Ramirez/SP	1.50	
449 Derrek Lee/SP	.75	
450 Roberto Alomar/SP	.75	
451 Ivan Rodriguez/Tigers/SP	1.50	
452 Junior Spivey/SP	.50	
453 Alfonso Soriano/Rgr/SP	1.00	
454 Vladimir Guerrero/SP	1.50	
455 Nick Johnson/SP	.50	
456 Javier Vazquez/SP	.50	
457 Andy Pettitte/SP	.75	
458 Miguel Tejada/SP	.75	
459 Rich Aurilia/SP	.50	
460 A.J. Pierzynski/SP	.50	
461 Raul Ibanez/SP	.50	
462 Roger Clemens/Astros/SP	3.00	
463 Juan Gonzalez/SP	1.00	
464 Rafael Palmeiro/SP	1.00	
465 Alex Rodriguez/Yanks/SP	4.00	

Showdown Bronze

Bronze (1-440): 3-5X
Bronze (441-465): 2-3X
Production 150 Sets

Showdown Gold

No Pricing
Production 10 Sets

Showdown Silver

Silver (1-440): 5-10X
Silver (441-465): 3-5X
Production 50 Sets

Autographs

NM/M
Inserted 1:24

10	Chone Figgins	10.00
11	Rich Fischer	5.00
17	Matt Kata	5.00
19	Oscar Villarreal	5.00
20	Tim Olson	5.00
21	Rob Hammock/57	10.00
23	Brian Bruney	5.00
25	Greg Aquino	5.00
35	Bubba Nelson	5.00
45	Jose Morban	5.00
46	Daniel Cabrera	5.00
61	Kevin Youkilis/50	15.00
71	Nate Frese	5.00
75	Jason Dubois	5.00
76	Nic Jackson	5.00
78	John Webb	5.00
81	Brendan Harris	5.00
84	Gary Matthews Sr.	10.00
92	Corwin Malone	5.00
102	Josh Hall/25	15.00
106	Brandon Claussen	10.00
110	Tim Hummel	5.00
116	Francisco Cabrera	5.00
117	Jhonny Peralta	8.00
118	Ryan Church	5.00
119	Francisco Cruceta/75	8.00
146	Jorge Cordova	5.00
149	Franklyn German	5.00
150	Nook Logan	5.00
153	Preston Larrison	8.00
160	Josh Willingham	5.00
163	Wilson Valdez	5.00
172	Josh Wilson	5.00
180	Rodrigo Rosario	8.00
181	Tommy Whiteman	5.00
187	Tim Redding/22	10.00
189	Chris Burke	5.00
197	Ken Harvey	15.00
200	Byron Gettis	8.00
205	Amos Otis	10.00
211	Cesar Izturis	5.00
225	Doug Davis	8.00
227	Matt Childers	5.00
230	Pedro Liriano	5.00
233	Gorman Thomas	15.00
234	Ben Oglivie/86	15.00
237	Lew Ford	10.00
238	J.C. Romero	5.00
239	Rob Bowen	5.00
246	Jason Kubel/50	15.00
258	Terrmel Sledge	5.00
262	Craig Brazell	5.00
264	Jeff Duncan	8.00
265	Jason Anderson	5.00
267	Danny Garcia	5.00
270	Jeremy Griffiths	5.00
272	Prentice Redman	8.00
291	Erick Almonte/66	8.00
307	Shane Bazzell	5.00
308	Mario Ramos	5.00
314	Jason Michaels/42	8.00
321	Franklin Perez	5.00
325	Anderson Machado/50	10.00
326	Travis Chapman	5.00
328	Greg Luzinski	15.00
331	Kris Benson	5.00
335	Walter Young/67	10.00
338	Duaner Sanchez	5.00
353	Ben Howard	5.00
359	Merkin Valdez/50	20.00
360	Kevin Correia	5.00
373	Rett Johnson/76	8.00
381	J.J. Putz	5.00

383	Matt Thornton/50	8.00
384	Rafael Soriano	8.00
406	Pete LaForest	5.00
410	Brian Stokes	5.00
411	Edwin Almonte	5.00
419	Ricardo Rodriguez	5.00
420	Ben Kozlowski	5.00
431	Kevin Cash	5.00
434	Francisco Rosario/48	8.00

2004 Donruss Throwback Threads

NM/M

Complete Set (250):		
Common Player:		.15
Common (201-225):		1.50
Common (226-250):		3.00
Production 1,000		
Hobby Pack (5):		5.00
Hobby Box (24):		90.00
1	Bartolo Colon	.15
2	Darin Erstad	.25
3	David Eckstein	.15
4	Garret Anderson	.25
5	Tim Salmon	.25
6	Troy Glaus	.25
7	Vladimir Guerrero	.75
8	Brandon Webb	.15
9	Luis Gonzalez	.25
10	Randy Johnson	.75
11	Richie Sexson	.40
12	Roberto Alomar	.50
13	Shea Hillenbrand	.15
14	Steve Finley	.15
15	Adam LaRoche	.15
16	Andruw Jones	.50
17	Chipper Jones	.75
18	J.D. Drew	.25
19	John Smoltz	.25
20	Rafael Furcal	.15
21	Russ Ortiz	.15
22	Javy Lopez	.25
23	Jay Gibbons	.15
24	Larry Bigbie	.15
25	Luis Matos	.15
26	Melvin Mora	.15
27	Miguel Tejada	.40
28	Rafael Palmeiro	.50
29	Curt Schilling	.50
30	David Ortiz	.75
31	Derek Lowe	.15
32	Jason Varitek	.15
33	Johnny Damon	.25
34	Manny Ramirez	.50
35	Nomar Garciaparra	1.00
36	Pedro J. Martinez	.75
37	Trot Nixon	.15
38	Aramis Ramirez	.40
39	Corey Patterson	.25
40	Derrek Lee	.25
41	Greg Maddux	1.00
42	Kerry Wood	.75
43	Mark Prior	.75
44	Sammy Sosa	1.50
45	Carlos Lee	.15
46	Esteban Loaiza	.15
47	Frank Thomas	.50
48	Joe Borchard	.15
49	Magglio Ordonez	.25
50	Mark Buehrle	.15
51	Paul Konerko	.15
52	Adam Dunn	.50
53	Austin Kearns	.25
54	Barry Larkin	.40
55	Brandon Larson	.15
56	Ken Griffey Jr.	1.00
57	Ryan Wagner	.15
58	Sean Casey	.15
59	C.C. Sabathia	.15
60	Jody Gerut	.15
61	Omar Vizquel	.15
62	Travis Hafner	.25
63	Victor Martinez	.25
64	Charles Johnson	.15
65	Garrett Atkins	.15
66	Jason Jennings	.15
67	Joe Kennedy	.15
68	Larry Walker	.25
69	Preston Wilson	.15
70	Todd Helton	.50
71	Ivan Rodriguez	.50
72	Jeremy Bonderman	.15
73	A.J. Burnett	.15
74	Brad Penny	.15
75	Dontrelle Willis	.25
76	Josh Beckett	.50
77	Juan Pierre	.15
78	Luis Castillo	.15
79	Miguel Cabrera	.75
80	Mike Lowell	.25
81	Andy Pettitte	.25
82	Craig Biggio	.25
83	Jeff Bagwell	.50
84	Jeff Kent	.25
85	Lance Berkman	.25
86	Morgan Ensberg	.15
87	Richard Hidalgo	.15
88	Roger Clemens	1.50
89	Roy Oswalt	.25
90	Wade Miller	.15
91	Angel Berroa	.15
92	Carlos Beltran	.50
93	Juan Gonzalez	.40
94	Ken Harvey	.15
95	Mike Sweeney	.15
96	Runelvys Hernandez	.15
97	Adrian Beltre	.40
98	Edwin Jackson	.15
99	Eric Gagne	.40
100	Hideo Nomo	.25
101	Hong-Chih Kuo	.15
102	Kazuhisa Ishii	.15
103	Paul LoDuca	.15
104	Shawn Green	.25
105	Ben Sheets	.25
106	Geoff Jenkins	.15
107	Junior Spivey	.15
108	Rickie Weeks	.25
109	Scott Podsednik	.25
110	Corey Koskie	.15
111	Doug Mientkiewicz	.15
112	Jacque Jones	.15
113	Joe Mays	.15
114	Johan Santana	.25
115	Shannon Stewart	.15
116	Torii Hunter	.25
117	Brad Wilkerson	.15
118	Carl Everett	.15
119	Chad Cordero	.15
120	Jose Vidro	.15
121	Nick Johnson	.15
122	Orlando Cabrera	.25
123	Al Leiter	.15
124	Cliff Floyd	.15
125	Jae Weong Seo	.15
126	Jose Reyes	.25
127	Mike Cameron	.15
128	Mike Piazza	1.00
129	Tom Glavine	.25
130	Alex Rodriguez	2.00
131	Bernie Williams	.40
132	Chien-Ming Wang	.40
133	Derek Jeter	2.00
134	Gary Sheffield	.50
135	Hideki Matsui	1.00
136	Jason Giambi	.25
137	Javier Vazquez	.15
138	Jorge Posada	.25
139	Jose Contreras	.15
140	Kevin Brown	.15
141	Mariano Rivera	.25
142	Mike Mussina	.40
143	Barry Zito	.25
144	Bobby Crosby	.15
145	Eric Chavez	.25
146	Erubiel Durazo	.15
147	Jermaine Dye	.15
148	Mark Kotsay	.15
149	Mark Mulder	.25
150	Rich Harden	.15
151	Tim Hudson	.25
152	Billy Wagner	.15
153	Bobby Abreu	.25
154	Brett Myers	.15
155	Jim Thome	.75
156	Jimmy Rollins	.25
157	Kevin Millwood	.25
158	Marlon Byrd	.15
159	Pat Burrell	.25
160	Jason Bay	.15
161	Jason Kendall	.15
162	Brian Giles	.25
163	Jay Payton	.15
164	Ryan Klesko	.15
165	Edgardo Alfonzo	.15
166	Jason Schmidt	.40
167	Jerome Williams	.15
168	Todd Linden	.15
169	Bret Boone	.15
170	Edgar Martinez	.25
171	Freddy Garcia	.15
172	Ichiro Suzuki	1.50
173	Jamie Moyer	.15
174	John Olerud	.15
175	Shigetoshi Hasegawa	.15
176	Albert Pujols	1.50
177	Dan Haren	.15
178	Edgar Renteria	.25
179	Jim Edmonds	.25
180	Matt Morris	.15
181	Scott Rolen	.75
182	Aubrey Huff	.15
183	Carl Crawford	.15
184	Chad Gaudin	.15
185	Dewon Young	.25
186	Dewon Brazelton	.15
187	Fred McGriff	.25
188	Rocco Baldelli	.15
189	Alfonso Soriano	.75
190	Hank Blalock	.50
191	Laynce Nix	.15
192	Mark Teixeira	.25
193	Michael Young	.15
194	Carlos Delgado	.40
195	Eric Hinske	.15
196	Frank Catalanotto	.15
197	Josh Phelps	.15
198	Orlando Hudson	.15
199	Roy Halladay	.15
200	Vernon Wells	.15
201	Dale Murphy	2.00
202	Cal Ripken Jr.	10.00
203	Fred Lynn	1.50
204	Wade Boggs	2.00
205	Nolan Ryan	6.00
206	Rod Carew	2.00
207	Andre Dawson	1.50
208	Ernie Banks	3.00
209	Ryne Sandberg	5.00
210	Bo Jackson	3.00
211	Carlton Fisk	3.00
212	Dave Concepcion	1.50
213	Alan Trammell	1.50
214	George Brett	5.00
215	Robin Yount	4.00
216	Gary Carter	1.50
217	Darryl Strawberry	1.50
218	Dwight Gooden	1.50
219	Babe Ruth	6.00
220	Don Mattingly	5.00
221	Reggie Jackson	5.00
222	Mike Schmidt	5.00
223	Tony Gwynn	4.00
224	Keith Hernandez	2.00
225	Hector Gimenez RC	3.00
226	Graham Koonce	3.00
227	John Gall RC	5.00
228	Jerry Gil RC	3.00
229	Jason Frasor RC	3.00
230	Justin Knoedler RC	3.00
231	Ivan Ochoa RC	3.00
232	Greg Dobbs RC	3.00
233	Ronald Belisario RC	3.00
234	Jerome Gamble RC	3.00
235	Roberto Novoa RC	3.00
236	Sean Henn	4.00
237	Willy Taveras RC	3.00
238	Ramon Ramirez RC	3.00
239	Kazuo Matsui RC	8.00
240	Akinori Otsuka RC	3.00
241	Jason Bartlett RC	5.00
242	Fernando Nieve RC	3.00
243	Freddy Guzman RC	3.00
244	Aarom Baldiris RC	5.00
245	Merkin Valdez RC	3.00
246	Mike Gosling	3.00
247	Shingo Takatsu RC	4.00
248	William Bergolla RC	3.00
249	Shawn Hill RC	3.00
250	Justin Germano RC	3.00

Blast From the Past

Mike Piazza • New York Mets

NM/M

Common Player:		1.50
Production 1,500 Sets		
Spectrum:		2-3X
Production 100 Sets		
1	Albert Pujols	5.00
2	Alex Rodriguez	4.00
3	Babe Ruth	6.00
4	Cal Ripken Jr.	8.00
5	Carlton Fisk	2.00
6	Eddie Mathews	3.00
7	Eddie Murray	2.00
8	Ernie Banks	3.00
9	Frank Robinson	2.00
10	George Foster	1.50
11	Harmon Killebrew	3.00
12	Jim Rice	1.50
13	Jim Thome	2.00
14	Johnny Bench	3.00
15	Jose Canseco	2.00
16	Juan Gonzalez	2.00
17	Ken Griffey Jr.	3.00
18	Mike Piazza	4.00
19	Mike Schmidt	5.00
20	Reggie Jackson	2.00
21	Roger Maris	3.00
22	Sammy Sosa	4.00
23	Stan Musial	4.00
24	Willie McCovey	2.00
25	Willie Stargell	2.00

Blast From the Past Bat

Mike Schmidt • 3B • Philadelphia Phillies

NM/M

Production 250 unless noted.		
1	Albert Pujols	15.00
2	Alex Rodriguez	10.00
3	Babe Ruth/50	150.00
4	Cal Ripken Jr.	25.00
5	Carlton Fisk	8.00
6	Eddie Mathews	10.00
7	Eddie Murray	8.00
8	Ernie Banks	10.00
9	Frank Robinson	8.00
10	George Foster	6.00
11	Harmon Killebrew	10.00
12	Jim Rice	8.00
13	Jim Thome	8.00
14	Johnny Bench	10.00
15	Jose Canseco/100	10.00
16	Juan Gonzalez	8.00
18	Mike Piazza	10.00
19	Mike Schmidt	15.00
20	Reggie Jackson	8.00
21	Roger Maris	30.00
22	Sammy Sosa	10.00
23	Stan Musial	15.00
24	Willie McCovey	8.00
25	Willie Stargell	8.00

Century Collection Material

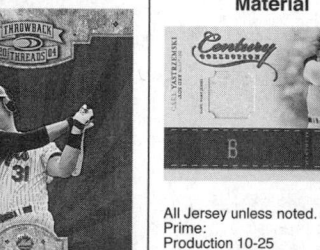

NM/M

All Jersey unless noted.		
Prime:		1.5-3X
Production 10-25		
Combo:		.75-2X
Production 5-50		
Combo Prime:		2-3X
Production 5-25		
No pricing 15 or less.		
1	Alan Trammell/250	8.00
2	Alex Rodriguez/250	10.00
3	Alfonso Soriano/250	8.00
4	Andre Dawson/250	6.00
5	Andy Pettitte/250	6.00
6	Bert Blyleven/250	6.00
7	Bo Jackson/250	12.00
8	Bobby Doerr/250	8.00
9	Brooks Robinson/25	30.00
10	Carl Yastrzemski/250	15.00
11	Carlos Delgado/250	4.00
12	Carlton Fisk/Jkt/250	6.00
13	Curt Schilling/250	6.00
14	Darryl Strawberry/250	6.00
15	Dave Concepcion/250	6.00
16	Dave Parker/100	8.00
17	Dennis Eckersley/250	8.00

#	Player	Price
18	Don Sutton/250	6.00
19	Duke Snider/250	10.00
20	Dwight Gooden/250	6.00
21	Eddie Mathews/25	25.00
22	Enos Slaughter/100	8.00
23	Ernie Banks/Pants/250	15.00
24	Frankie Frisch/Jkt/250	12.00
25	Frank Robinson/50	10.00
26	Frank Thomas/250	10.00
27	Garret Anderson/250	6.00
28	Gary Carter/250	6.00
29	Gary Sheffield/250	6.00
30	Harmon Killebrew/25	25.00
31	Harold Baines/250	6.00
32	Hideo Nomo/250	8.00
33	Jack Morris/250	6.00
34	Jason Giambi/250	6.00
35	Jeff Kent/250	4.00
36	Jim "Catfish" Hunter/250	6.00
37	Jim Palmer/50	10.00
38	Jim Rice/250	8.00
39	Jim Thome/250	10.00
40	John Smoltz/250	8.00
41	Johnny Mize/Pants/250	8.00
42	Jose Canseco/250	8.00
43	Juan Gonzalez/250	6.00
44	Juan Marichal/250	8.00
45	Keith Hernandez/250	6.00
46	Kerry Wood/250	10.00
47	Kevin Brown/250	4.00
48	Lance Berkman/250	6.00
49	Larry Walker/250	6.00
50	Lee Smith/250	6.00
51	Lenny Dykstra/Bat/250	6.00
52	Luis Tiant/250	6.00
53	Magglio Ordonez/250	4.00
54	Manny Ramirez/250	8.00
55	Mariano Rivera/100	8.00
56	Mark Grace/250	8.00
57	Mark Mulder/250	6.00
58	Mark Teixeira/150	6.00
59	Marty Marion/25	15.00
60	Mike Mussina/Pants/250	8.00
61	Mike Piazza/250	10.00
62	Nellie Fox/Bat/250	15.00
63	Nolan Ryan/Jkt/250	20.00
65	Ozzie Smith/250	12.00
66	Pedro J. Martinez/250	8.00
67	Pee Wee Reese/Bat/250	8.00
68	Phil Niekro/250	8.00
69	Phil Rizzuto/Pants/250	10.00
70	Rafael Palmeiro/250	8.00
71	Ralph Kiner/Bat/250	8.00
72	Randy Johnson/250	10.00
73	Reggie Jackson/Jkt/250	8.00
74	Rickey Henderson/250	10.00
75	Roberto Alomar/250	8.00
76	Robin Ventura/250	4.00
77	Rod Carew/250	10.00
78	Roger Clemens/250	15.00
79	Ron Santo Bat/250	10.00
80	Scott Rolen/250	10.00
81	Shawn Green/250	6.00
82	Steve Garvey/250	6.00
83	Tim Hudson/250	4.00
84	Tom Glavine/250	6.00
85	Tom Seaver/25	30.00
86	Adam Dunn/250	8.00
87	Tommy John/250	6.00
88	Tommy Lasorda/250	6.00
89	Tony Oliva/250	8.00
90	Tony Perez/Bat/250	8.00
91	Torii Hunter/250	4.00
92	Troy Glaus/250	4.00
93	Vernon Wells/250	4.00
94	Vladimir Guerrero/250	8.00
95	Wade Boggs/250	8.00
96	Warren Spahn/100	20.00
97	Will Clark/Bat/250	10.00
98	Willie McCovey/250	8.00
99	Willie Stargell/250	8.00
100	George Foster/250	8.00

Century Collection Signature Material

NM/M

All Jersey unless noted.
Prime: No Pricing
Production 5-10
Combo: .75-1.5X
Production 5-25
No pricing 15 or less.
Combo Prime: No Pricing

Production 5-10

#	Player	Price
1	Alan Trammell/50	25.00
3	Alfonso Soriano/50	40.00
4	Andre Dawson/50	25.00
6	Bert Blyleven/50	20.00
8	Bobby Doerr/50	25.00
12	Carlton Fisk/Jkt/10	
14	Darryl Strawberry/50	25.00
15	Dave Concepcion/50	25.00
16	Dave Parker/50	20.00
17	Dennis Eckersley/50	40.00
18	Don Sutton/50	20.00
19	Duke Snider/50	40.00
20	Dwight Gooden/50	25.00
27	Garret Anderson/50	25.00
28	Gary Carter/50	25.00
29	Gary Sheffield/25	30.00
31	Harold Baines/50	20.00
33	Jack Morris/50	15.00
37	Jim Palmer/25	25.00
38	Jim Rice/50	20.00
42	Jose Canseco/25	50.00
44	Juan Marichal/50	25.00
45	Keith Hernandez/50	25.00
50	Lee Smith/50	15.00
51	Lenny Dykstra/Bat/50	20.00
52	Luis Tiant/50	15.00
53	Magglio Ordonez/50	25.00
56	Mark Grace/50	40.00
57	Mark Mulder/25	25.00
58	Mark Teixeira/25	40.00
59	Marty Marion/50	25.00
68	Phil Niekro/50	25.00
71	Ralph Kiner/Bat/50	40.00
75	Roberto Alomar/50	50.00
76	Robin Ventura/50	20.00
82	Steve Garvey/50	25.00
87	Tommy John/50	15.00
90	Tony Perez/Bat/25	40.00
91	Torii Hunter/25	30.00
93	Vernon Wells/25	25.00
94	Vladimir Guerrero/50	40.00
100	George Foster/50	20.00

Century Stars

NM/M

Common Player: 1.50
Production 1,500 Sets
Spectrum: 1.5-3X
Production 100 Sets

#	Player	Price
1	Al Kaline	2.00
2	Albert Pujols	5.00
3	Alex Rodriguez	4.00
4	Barry Larkin	2.00
5	Barry Zito	1.50
6	Billy Williams	1.50
7	Bob Feller	1.50
8	Bob Gibson	3.00
9	Cal Ripken Jr.	8.00
10	Chipper Jones	3.00
11	Curt Schilling	2.00
12	Dale Murphy	2.00
13	Dave Parker	1.50
14	Derek Jeter	6.00
15	Don Drysdale	1.50
16	Don Mattingly	5.00
17	Eddie Murray	2.00
18	Fergie Jenkins	2.00
19	Gary Carter	2.00
20	George Brett	5.00
21	Greg Maddux	3.00
22	Ivan Rodriguez	2.00
23	Jeff Bagwell	2.00
24	Joe Morgan	2.00
25	Johnny Bench	3.00
26	Kirby Puckett	3.00
27	Lou Boudreau	1.50
28	Lou Brock	1.50
29	Luis Aparicio	1.50
30	Manny Ramirez	2.00
31	Mark Prior	2.00
32	Miguel Tejada	2.00
33	Mike Mussina	2.00
34	Mike Piazza	4.00
35	Mike Schmidt	5.00
36	Nolan Ryan	6.00
37	Nomar Garciaparra	4.00
38	Ozzie Smith	4.00
39	Paul Molitor	3.00
40	Pedro J. Martinez	3.00
41	Rafael Palmeiro	2.00
42	Randy Johnson	3.00
43	Red Schoendienst	1.50
44	Reggie Jackson	3.00
45	Rickey Henderson	2.00
46	Roberto Alomar	2.00
47	Roberto Clemente	5.00
48	Robin Yount	3.00
49	Rod Carew	2.00
50	Roger Clemens	5.00
51	Ryne Sandberg	4.00
52	Sammy Sosa	4.00
53	Stan Musial	4.00
54	Steve Carlton	2.00
55	Todd Helton	2.00
56	Tom Glavine	2.00
57	Tom Seaver	3.00
58	Tony Gwynn	3.00
59	Wade Boggs	2.00
60	Whitey Ford	3.00

Century Stars Material

NM/M

All Jersey unless noted.
Prime: No Pricing
Production 5 Sets

#	Player	Price
1	Al Kaline/Pants/25	30.00
2	Albert Pujols/50	25.00
4	Barry Larkin/50	10.00
5	Barry Zito/50	6.00
6	Billy Williams/50	8.00
7	Bob Feller/10	
8	Bob Gibson/25	20.00
9	Cal Ripken Jr./50	60.00
10	Chipper Jones/50	10.00
11	Curt Schilling/50	8.00
12	Dale Murphy/50	12.00
13	Dave Parker/50	8.00
14	Derek Jeter/50	35.00
15	Don Drysdale/50	12.00
16	Don Mattingly/Jkt/50	20.00
17	Eddie Murray/50	15.00
18	Fergie Jenkins/Pants/25	12.00
19	Gary Carter/Pants/50	8.00
20	George Brett/50	25.00
21	Greg Maddux/50	15.00
22	Ivan Rodriguez/50	12.00
23	Jeff Bagwell/50	10.00
24	Joe Morgan/50	10.00
25	Johnny Bench/50	20.00
26	Kirby Puckett/50	15.00
27	Lou Boudreau/50	8.00
28	Lou Brock/25	20.00
29	Luis Aparicio/Pants/50	8.00
30	Manny Ramirez/50	10.00
31	Mark Prior/50	8.00
32	Miguel Tejada/50	8.00
33	Mike Mussina/50	10.00
34	Mike Piazza/50	20.00
35	Mike Schmidt/50	20.00
36	Nolan Ryan/50	35.00
37	Nomar Garciaparra/50	15.00
38	Ozzie Smith/50	25.00
40	Pedro J. Martinez/50	10.00
41	Rafael Palmeiro/25	15.00
42	Randy Johnson/50	12.00
43	Red Schoendienst/50	8.00
44	Reggie Jackson/Pants/50	15.00
45	Rickey Henderson/50	15.00
46	Roberto Alomar/50	12.00
48	Robin Yount/50	20.00
49	Rod Carew Jkt/50	10.00
50	Roger Clemens/50	15.00
51	Ryne Sandberg/50	20.00
52	Sammy Sosa/50	15.00
53	Stan Musial/10	
54	Steve Carlton/25	15.00
55	Todd Helton/50	12.00
56	Tom Glavine/50	10.00
57	Tom Seaver/50	15.00
58	Tony Gwynn/50	15.00
59	Wade Boggs/50	10.00
60	Whitey Ford/Pants/10	

Century Stars Signature

NM/M

Signature Material: No Pricing
Production 5 Sets
Sig. Material Prime: No Pricing
Production 5 Sets

#	Player	Price
1	Al Kaline/25	50.00
6	Billy Williams/25	35.00
7	Bob Feller/25	30.00
8	Bob Gibson/25	35.00
12	Dale Murphy/25	40.00
13	Dave Parker/25	20.00
18	Fergie Jenkins/25	25.00
19	Gary Carter/25	25.00
24	Joe Morgan/25	30.00
28	Lou Brock/25	35.00
29	Luis Aparicio/25	20.00
35	Mike Schmidt/25	60.00
38	Ozzie Smith/25	75.00
53	Stan Musial/25	75.00

Dynasty

NM/M

Common Player: 3.00
Production 1,500 Sets
Spectrum: 2-3X
Production 100 Sets

#	Players	Price
1	Phil Rizzuto, Whitey Ford	3.00
2	Pee Wee Reese, Duke Snider, Tom Lasorda	3.00
3	Jim "Catfish" Hunter, Reggie Jackson	3.00
4	Roger Maris, Whitey Ford	5.00
5	Enos Slaughter, Shawn Marion, Stan Musial	5.00
6	Dwight Gooden, Gary Carter, Darryl Strawberry, Keith Hernandez	3.00
7	Johnny Bench, Tony Perez, Joe Morgan, George Foster	3.00
8	Derek Jeter, Jorge Posada, Bernie Williams, Andy Pettitte	6.00
9	Frank Robinson, Brooks Robinson, Jim Palmer	3.00
10	Willie Stargell, Dave Parker, Bill Madlock	3.00
11	Bob Gibson, Lou Brock, Ken Boyer	3.00
12	Rickey Henderson, Paul Molitor, Joe Carter, Roberto Alomar	3.00

Dynasty Material

NM/M

Quantity produced listed
Prime: No Pricing
Production 5 Sets

3	Jim "Catfish" Hunter, Reggie Jackson/25	25.00
6	Dwight Gooden, Gary Carter, Darryl Strawberry, Keith Hernandez/50	35.00
7	Johnny Bench, Tony Perez, Joe Morgan, George Foster/25	80.00
8	Derek Jeter, Jorge Posada, Bernie Williams, Andy Pettitte/50	50.00
10	Willie Stargell, Dave Parker, Bill Madlock/25	30.00
11	Bob Gibson, Lou Brock, Ken Boyer/25	35.00
12	Rickey Henderson, Paul Molitor, Joe Carter, Roberto Alomar/25	60.00

Fans of the Game

Inserted 1:24
1	Emilio Estevez	3.00
2	Shannon Elizabeth	3.00
3	Joe Montegna/UER	2.00
4	Jamie-Lynn DiScala	2.00
5	Jonathan Silverman	2.00

Fans of the Game Signature

NM/M
1	Emilio Estevez	40.00
2	Shannon Elizabeth	60.00
3	Joe Montegna/UER	20.00
4	Jamie-Lynn DiScala	60.00
5	Jonathan Silverman	20.00

Generations

NM/M
Common Duo:		1.50
Production 1,500 Sets		
Spectrum:		2-3X
Production 100 Sets		
1	George Brett, Albert Pujols	5.00
2	Wade Boggs, Aubrey Huff	2.00
3	Jim "Catfish" Hunter, Tim Hudson	2.00
4	Steve Garvey, Shawn Green	1.50
5	Tony Gwynn, Garret Anderson	4.00
6	Fergie Jenkins, Mark Prior	2.00
7	Robin Yount, Rickie Weeks	4.00
8	Warren Spahn, Greg Maddux	4.00
9	Brooks Robinson, Cal Ripken Jr., Miguel Tejada	8.00
10	Bobby Doerr, Carl Yastrzemski, Manny Ramirez	5.00
11	Al Kaline, Alan Trammell, Ivan Rodriguez	2.50

12	Tom Seaver, Dwight Gooden, Tom Glavine	3.00
13	Stan Musial, Lou Brock, Jim Edmonds	4.00
14	George Foster, Dave Parker, Austin Kearns	1.50
15	Ed Mathews, Dale Murphy, Chipper Jones	3.00
16	Don Sutton, Nolan Ryan, Roger Clemens	8.00
17	Bernie Williams, Andre Dawson, Sammy Sosa	4.00
18	Whitey Ford, Tommy John, Andy Pettitte	2.00
19	Carlton Fisk, Roger Clemens, Nomar Garciaparra	5.00
20	Shawn Marion, Ozzie Smith, Edgar Renteria	4.00
21	Reggie Jackson, Rickey Henderson, Eric Chavez	2.00
22	Babe Ruth, Don Mattingly, Derek Jeter	8.00
23	Roberto Clemente Jr., Reggie Jackson, Sammy Sosa	6.00
24	Bob Feller, Tom Seaver, Roger Clemens	5.00

NM/M
25	Ernie Banks, Cal Ripken Jr., Alex Rodriguez	8.00
26	Pee Wee Reese, Ozzie Smith, Derek Jeter	6.00
27	Harmon Killebrew, Mike Schmidt, Alex Rodriguez	5.00
28	Bob Gibson, Dwight Gooden, Josh Beckett	2.00

Generations Material

NM/M
Quantity produced listed
Prime: No Pricing
Production 5 Sets
1	George Brett, Albert Pujols/50	40.00
2	Wade Boggs, Aubrey Huff/50	10.00
3	Jim "Catfish" Hunter, Tim Hudson/25	20.00
5	Tony Gwynn, Garret Anderson/50	20.00
7	Fergie Jenkins, Mark Prior/25	15.00
7	Robin Yount, Rickie Weeks/Bat/50	20.00
8	Warren Spahn, Greg Maddux/25	40.00
11	Al Kaline, Alan Trammell, Ivan Rodriguez/Bat/25	40.00
14	George Foster, Dave Parker, Austin Kearns/25	20.00
16	Don Sutton, Nolan Ryan, Roger Clemens/Bat/50	50.00
17	Billy Williams, Andre Dawson, Sammy Sosa/50	30.00
18	Whitey Ford, Tommy John, Andy Pettitte/25	40.00
19	Carlton Fisk, Roger Clemens, Nomar Garciaparra	40.00
20	Marty Marion, Ozzie Smith, Edgar Renteria/25	40.00
21	Reggie Jackson, Rickey Henderson, Eric Chavez/25	30.00
24	Bob Feller, Tom Seaver, Roger Clemens/25	40.00
25	Ernie Banks, Cal Ripken Jr., Alex Rodriguez	65.00
26	Pee Wee Reese, Ozzie Smith, Derek Jeter/25	50.00
27	Harmon Killebrew, Mike Schmidt, Alex Rodriguez/Bat/25	50.00
28	Bob Gibson, Dwight Gooden, Josh Beckett/25	30.00

Material

NM/M
Common Player:		4.00
2	Darin Erstad/Jsy/100	6.00
4	Garret Anderson/Jsy/100	6.00
5	Tim Salmon/Jsy/100	6.00
6	Troy Glaus/Jsy/100	6.00
7	Vladimir Guerrero/Bat/100	10.00
8	Brandon Webb/Pants/100	4.00
9	Luis Gonzalez/Jsy/100	4.00
10	Randy Johnson/Jsy/100	10.00
11	Richie Sexson/Bat/50	8.00
12	Roberto Alomar/Bat/100	8.00
14	Steve Finley/Jsy/100	4.00
15	Adam LaRoche/Bat/100	4.00
16	Andruw Jones/Jsy/100	6.00
17	Chipper Jones/Jsy/100	8.00
18	J.D. Drew/Bat/100	6.00
19	John Smoltz/Jsy/100	8.00
20	Rafael Furcal/Jsy/100	4.00
22	Javy Lopez/Bat/100	6.00
23	Jay Gibbons/Jsy/100	4.00
24	Larry Bigbie/Jsy/100	4.00
25	Luis Matos/Jsy/100	4.00
26	Melvin Mora/Jsy/100	4.00
27	Miguel Tejada/Bat/100	6.00
28	Rafael Palmeiro/Jsy/100	8.00
29	Curt Schilling/Jsy/100	6.00
30	David Ortiz/Bat/100	10.00
32	Jason Varitek/Jsy/100	8.00
33	Johnny Damon/Bat/100	6.00
34	Manny Ramirez/Jsy/100	8.00
35	Nomar Garciaparra/Jsy/100	8.00
36	Pedro J. Martinez/Jsy/100	8.00
37	Trot Nixon/Bat/100	4.00
38	Aramis Ramirez/Jsy/100	6.00
39	Corey Patterson/Pants/100	6.00
41	Greg Maddux/Bat/100	10.00
42	Kerry Wood/Pants/100	10.00
43	Mark Prior/Jsy/100	6.00
44	Sammy Sosa/Jsy/100	12.00
47	Carlos Lee/Jsy/100	4.00
47	Frank Thomas/Pants/100	8.00
48	Joe Borchard/Jsy/100	4.00
49	Magglio Ordonez/Jsy/100	4.00
50	Mark Buehrle/Jsy/100	4.00
51	Paul Konerko/Jsy/100	4.00
52	Adam Dunn/Jsy/100	8.00
53	Austin Kearns/Jsy/100	6.00
54	Barry Larkin/Jsy/100	6.00
55	Brandon Larson/Fld Glv/100	4.00
58	Sean Casey/Jsy/100	4.00
59	C.C. Sabathia/Jsy/100	4.00
60	Jody Gerut/Jsy/100	4.00
61	Omar Vizquel/Jsy/100	4.00
62	Travis Hafner/Jsy/100	4.00
63	Victor Martinez/Bat/100	6.00
64	Charles Johnson/Bat/100	4.00
65	Garrett Atkins/Jsy/100	4.00
66	Jason Jennings/Jsy/100	4.00

67	Joe Kennedy/Bat/100	4.00
68	Larry Walker/Jsy/100	6.00
69	Preston Wilson/Jsy/100	4.00
70	Todd Helton/Jsy/100	8.00
71	Ivan Rodriguez/Bat/100	8.00
72	Jeremy Bonderman/Jsy/100	4.00
73	A.J. Burnett/Jsy/100	4.00
74	Brad Penny/Jsy/100	4.00
75	Dontrelle Willis/Jsy/100	4.00
76	Josh Beckett/Jsy/100	6.00
77	Juan Pierre/Bat/100	4.00
78	Luis Castillo/Jsy/100	4.00
79	Miguel Cabrera/Jsy/100	8.00
80	Mike Lowell/Jsy/50	8.00
81	Andy Pettitte/Bat/100	6.00
82	Craig Biggio/Jsy/100	6.00
83	Jeff Bagwell/Jsy/100	8.00
84	Jeff Kent/Jsy/100	4.00
85	Lance Berkman/Jsy/100	4.00
86	Morgan Ensberg/Jsy/100	4.00
87	Richard Hidalgo/Pants/100	4.00
88	Roger Clemens/Bat/50	15.00
89	Roy Oswalt/Jsy/100	4.00
90	Wade Miller Jsy/100	4.00
91	Angel Berroa/Pants/100	4.00
92	Carlos Beltran/Jsy/100	8.00
93	Juan Gonzalez/Bat/100	8.00
94	Ken Harvey/Bat/100	4.00
95	Mike Sweeney/Jsy/100	4.00
96	Runelvys Hernandez/Jsy/100	4.00
97	Adrian Beltre/Jsy/100	6.00
98	Edwin Jackson/Jsy/100	4.00
100	Hideo Nomo/Jsy/100	8.00
101	Hong-Chih Kuo/Bat/100	8.00
102	Kazuhisa Ishii/Jsy/100	4.00
103	Paul LoDuca/Jsy/100	4.00
104	Shawn Green/Jsy/100	6.00
105	Ben Sheets/Jsy/100	4.00
106	Geoff Jenkins/Jsy/100	4.00
107	Junior Spivey/Bat/50	4.00
108	Rickie Weeks/Bat/50	8.00
111	Doug Mientkiewicz/Bat/100	4.00
112	Jacque Jones/Jsy/100	4.00
113	Joe Mays/Jsy/100	4.00
114	Johan Santana/Jsy/100	8.00
115	Shannon Stewart/Jsy/100	4.00
116	Torii Hunter/Jsy/100	6.00
117	Brad Wilkerson/Bat/100	4.00
118	Carl Everett/Bat/100	4.00
120	Jose Vidro/Jsy/100	4.00
121	Nick Johnson/Bat/100	4.00
122	Orlando Cabrera/Jsy/100	4.00
123	Al Leiter/Jsy/100	4.00
124	Cliff Floyd/Bat/100	4.00
125	Jae Weong Seo/Jsy/100	4.00
126	Jose Reyes/Jsy/100	8.00
128	Mike Piazza/Jsy/100	10.00
129	Tom Glavine/Jsy/100	6.00
130	Alex Rodriguez/Bat/100	10.00
131	Bernie Williams/Jsy/100	6.00
133	Derek Jeter/Jsy/100	20.00
134	Gary Sheffield/Bat/100	6.00
135	Hideki Matsui/Jsy/100	20.00
136	Jason Giambi/Jsy/100	6.00
138	Jorge Posada/Jsy/100	6.00
141	Mariano Rivera/Jsy/50	15.00
142	Mike Mussina/Jsy/100	4.00
143	Barry Zito/Jsy/100	4.00
145	Eric Chavez/Jsy/100	4.00
146	Erubiel Durazo/Bat/100	4.00
147	Jermaine Dye/Bat/100	6.00
149	Mark Mulder/Jsy/100	6.00
150	Rich Harden/Jsy/100	4.00
151	Tim Hudson/Jsy/100	4.00
153	Bobby Abreu/Jsy/100	6.00

154 Brett Myers/Jsy/100 4.00
155 Jim Thome/Jsy/100 8.00
157 Kevin Millwood/Jsy/100 4.00
158 Marlon Byrd/Jsy/100 4.00
159 Pat Burrell/Jsy/100 6.00
161 Jason Kendall/Jsy/100 4.00
162 Brian Giles/Bat/100 4.00
164 Ryan Klesko/Jsy/100 4.00
165 Edgardo Alfonzo/Bat/100 4.00
167 Jerome Williams/Jsy/100 4.00
169 Bret Boone/Jsy/29
170 Edgar Martinez/Jsy/100 8.00
171 Freddy Garcia/Jsy/100 4.00
173 Jamie Moyer/Jsy/100 4.00
174 John Olerud/Jsy/100 4.00
176 Albert Pujols/Jsy/100 20.00
177 Dan Haren/Jsy/100 4.00
178 Edgar Renteria/Jsy/100 6.00
179 Jim Edmonds/Jsy/100 6.00
180 Matt Morris/Jsy/100 4.00
181 Scott Rolen/Jsy/100 8.00
182 Aubrey Huff/Jsy/100 4.00
183 Carl Crawford/Jsy/100 4.00
184 Chad Gaudin/Jsy/100 4.00
185 Delmon Young/Bat/100 6.00
186 Dewon Brazelton/Jsy/100 4.00
187 Fred McGriff/Jsy/100 6.00
188 Rocco Baldelli/Jsy/100 4.00
189 Alfonso Soriano/Bat/100 8.00
190 Hank Blalock/Jsy/100 6.00
191 Laynce Nix/Bat/100 4.00
192 Mark Teixeira/Jsy/23 15.00
193 Michael Young/Bat/100 6.00
194 Carlos Delgado/Jsy/100 6.00
195 Eric Hinske/Jsy/100 4.00
196 Frank Catalanotto/Jsy/100 4.00
197 Josh Phelps/Jsy/100 4.00
198 Orlando Hudson/Jsy/100 4.00
199 Roy Halladay/Jsy/100 4.00
200 Vernon Wells/Jsy/100 4.00
201 Dale Murphy/Jsy/100 12.00
202 Cal Ripken Jr./Jsy/100 30.00
203 Fred Lynn/Jsy/100 8.00
204 Wade Boggs/Jsy/100 8.00
205 Nolan Ryan/Jkt/100 25.00
206 Rod Carew/Jkt/100 8.00
207 Andre Dawson/Pants/100 6.00
208 Ernie Banks/Pants/50 20.00
209 Ryne Sandberg/Jsy/50 25.00
210 Bo Jackson/Jsy/100 12.00
211 Carlton Fisk/Jkt/100 10.00
212 Dave Concepcion/Jsy/100 8.00
213 Alan Trammell/Bat/100 8.00
214 George Brett/Jsy/100 15.00
215 Robin Yount/Jsy/100 15.00
216 Gary Carter/Jsy/100 8.00
217 Darryl Strawberry/Pants/100 8.00
218 Dwight Gooden/Jsy/50 8.00
219 Babe Ruth/Jsy/25 400.00
220 Don Mattingly/Jkt/100 15.00
221 Reggie Jackson/Jkt/100 10.00
222 Mike Schmidt/Jkt/100 15.00
223 Tony Gwynn/Jsy/100 10.00
224 Keith Hernandez/Jsy/100 8.00

Player Threads

NM/M
Common Player: 4.00

Production 250 Sets Prime: 2-3X
Production 10-25 No pricing 15 or less.
1 Aaron Boone 4.00
2 Alex Rodriguez/M's-Rgr 15.00
3 Andres Galarraga/Braves-Giants-Rgr 10.00
4 Aramis Ramirez 4.00
5 Bartolo Colon 4.00
6 Ben Grieve/A's-D'Rays
7 Brad Fullmer
8 Bret Boone/Braves-M's 4.00
9 Brian Giles 4.00
10 Brian Jordan 4.00
11 Byung-Hyun Kim 4.00
12 Casey Fossum 4.00
13 Cesar Izturis 4.00
14 Chan Ho Park 4.00
15 Charles Johnson 4.00
16 Cliff Floyd 4.00
17 Darryl Strawberry/Dgr-Met-Ynk 10.00
18 David Ortiz 10.00
19 David Wells/Jays-Yanks 4.00
20 Derrek Lee 6.00
21 Dmitri Young 4.00
22 Edgardo Alfonzo 4.00
23 Ellis Burks 4.00
24 Gary Sheffield/Braves-Brew-Dgr 8.00
25 Hee Seop Choi 4.00
26 Ivan Rodriguez/Marlins-Rgr 10.00
27 J.D. Drew 6.00
28 Javier Vazquez 4.00
29 Jay Payton 4.00
30 Jeff Kent/Astros-Giants-Jays 4.00
31 Jeromy Burnitz 4.00
32 Jim Thome/Indians-Phils 10.00
33 Joe Kennedy 4.00
34 Joe Torre 8.00
35 Jose Cruz Jr. 4.00
36 Juan Encarnacion 4.00
37 Juan Gonzalez/Indians-Rgr 8.00
38 Juan Pierre 4.00
39 Junior Spivey 4.00
40 Kenny Lofton/Brave-Tribe 8.00
41 Kevin Millwood 6.00
42 Manny Ramirez/Indians-Sox 12.00
43 Mark Grace/Cubs-D'backs 10.00
44 Mike Hampton 4.00
45 Mike Piazza/Dgr-Marlins-Mets 20.00
46 Milton Bradley 4.00
47 Moises Alou 6.00
48 Nick Johnson 4.00
49 Nolan Ryan/Ang Jkt-Ast Jkt-Rgr 50.00
50 Preston Wilson/Marlins-Rockies 6.00
51 Rafael Palmeiro/O's-Rgr 10.00
52 Ray Durham 4.00
53 Reggie Jackson/A's-Ang-Yank 15.00
54 Reggie Sanders 4.00
55 Rich Aurilia 4.00
56 Richie Sexson 6.00
57 Rickey Henderson/A's-M's-Yanks/25 50.00
58 Rickey Henderson/Dgr-Mets-Padres 20.00
59 Robert Fick 4.00
60 Roberto Alomar/Mets-Sox 8.00
61 Roberto Alomar/Indians-O's 8.00
62 Robin Ventura/Mets-Sox-Yanks 10.00
63 Rondell/White Cubs-Expos
64 Ryan Klesko/Braves-Padres 6.00
65 Sean Casey 6.00
66 Shannon Stewart/Jays-Twins 6.00
67 Shawn Green/Jays-Dgr 8.00
68 Shea Hillenbrand 4.00
69 Steve Carlton/Giants-Sox 8.00
70 Terrence Long 4.00
71 Tony Batista 4.00

72 Travis Hafner/Indians-Rgr 6.00
73 Travis Lee 4.00
74 Vladimir Guerrero 8.00
75 Wes Helms 4.00

Player Threads Signature

NM/M
Quantity produced listed
4 Aramis Ramirez/25 30.00
17 Darryl Strawberry/Dgr-Met-Ynk/25 40.00
24 Gary Sheffield/Brave-Brw-Dgr/25 40.00
28 Javier Vazquez/25 20.00
29 Jay Payton/25 15.00
37 Juan Gonzalez/Indians-Rgr/25 40.00
39 Junior Spivey/25 15.00
50 Preston Wilson/Marlins-Rockies/25 25.00
55 Rich Aurilia/25 15.00
62 Robin Ventura/Mets-Sox-Yanks/25 40.00
68 Shea Hillenbrand/25 20.00
74 Vladimir Guerrero/25 60.00

Signature Marks

NM/M
Common Autograph: 8.00
4 Garret Anderson/25 25.00
8 Brandon Webb/50 10.00
13 Shea Hillenbrand/50 15.00
15 Adam LaRoche/50 10.00
20 Rafael Furcal/25 25.00
23 Jay Gibbons/50 20.00
24 Larry Bigbie/50 20.00
25 Luis Matos/50 15.00
26 Melvin Mora/50 15.00
30 David Ortiz/25 40.00
37 Trot Nixon/25 30.00
40 Derrek Lee/25 40.00
43 Mark Prior/25 40.00
45 Carlos Lee/50 20.00
46 Esteban Loaiza/50 12.00
48 Joe Borchard/25 10.00
50 Mark Buehrle/25 15.00
53 Austin Kearns/25 15.00
55 Brandon Larson/25 15.00
60 Jody Gerut/50 20.00
62 Travis Hafner/50 20.00
63 Victor Martinez/50 25.00
69 Preston Wilson/50 15.00
74 Brad Penny/50 10.00
79 Miguel Cabrera/25 40.00
80 Mike Lowell/25 20.00
86 Morgan Ensberg/50 12.00
89 Roy Oswalt/25 20.00
91 Angel Berroa/25 12.00
92 Carlos Beltran/25 35.00
98 Edwin Jackson/50 15.00
101 Hong-Chih Kuo/50 30.00
109 Scott Podsednik/50 15.00
112 Jacque Jones/50 15.00
114 Johan Santana/50 50.00
115 Shannon Stewart/50 20.00
116 Torii Hunter/25 25.00
119 Chad Cordero/50 8.00
120 Jose Vidro/25 15.00

122 Orlando Cabrera/50 15.00
132 Chien-Ming Wang/25 100.00
147 Jermaine Dye/50 12.00
160 Jason Bay/50 20.00
163 Jay Payton/50 15.00
168 Todd Linden/50 15.00
175 Shigetoshi Hasegawa/25 50.00
177 Dan Haren/50 15.00
181 Scott Rolen/25 50.00
182 Aubrey Huff/50 15.00
184 Chad Gaudin/50 10.00
186 Dewon Brazelton/50 10.00
187 Fred McGriff/25 40.00
189 Alfonso Soriano/25 50.00
193 Michael Young/50 20.00
203 Fred Lynn/50 15.00
207 Andre Dawson/50 25.00
216 Gary Carter/25 25.00
217 Darryl Strawberry/50 20.00
218 Dwight Gooden/50 15.00
224 Keith Hernandez/50 20.00
225 Hector Gimenez/100 8.00
226 Graham Koonce/100 8.00
228 Jerry Gil/100 8.00
229 Jason Frasor/100 8.00
230 Justin Knoedler/50 10.00
233 Ronald Belisario/200 8.00
234 Jerome Gamble/200 8.00
235 Roberto Novoa/200 8.00
236 Sean Henn/200 10.00
237 Willy Taveras/200 8.00
238 Ramon Ramirez/200 10.00
241 Jason Bartlett/25 20.00
242 Fernando Nieve/25 12.00
243 Freddy Guzman/25 20.00
248 William Bergolla/100 10.00
249 Shawn Hill/100 8.00
250 Justin Germano/100 8.00

2004 Donruss Timeless Treasures

NM/M
Complete Set (100): 200.00
Common Player: 1.50
Production 999 Sets
Tin (4): 125.00
1 Albert Pujols 6.00
2 Garret Anderson 2.00
3 Randy Johnson 3.00
4 Alex Rodriguez/Yanks 8.00
5 Manny Ramirez 3.00
6 Mark Prior 4.00
7 Roberto Alomar 2.00
8 Barry Larkin 2.00
9 Todd Helton 2.50
10 Ivan Rodriguez 3.00
11 Jacque Jones 1.50
12 Jeff Kent 2.00
13 Mike Sweeney 1.50
14 Shawn Green 2.00
15 Richie Sexson 2.00
16 Mike Piazza 5.00
17 Vladimir Guerrero 4.00
18 Mike Mussina 2.00
19 Barry Zito 2.00
20 Don Mattingly 6.00
21 Ichiro Suzuki 5.00
22 Rocco Baldelli 2.00
23 Rafael Palmeiro 3.00
24 Carlos Delgado 2.00
25 Roger Clemens 6.00
26 Luis Gonzalez 2.00
27 Gary Sheffield 2.00
28 Jay Gibbons 1.50
29 Nomar Garciaparra 5.00
30 Aramis Ramirez 2.00
31 Frank Thomas 3.00
32 Ryan Wagner 1.50
33 Preston Wilson 1.50
34 Hideki Matsui 4.00
35 Roy Oswalt 2.00
36 Angel Berroa 1.50
37 Kazuhisa Ishii 1.50
38 Scott Podsednik 2.00
39 Torii Hunter 2.00
40 Tom Glavine 2.00
41 Jason Giambi 3.00
42 Eric Chavez 2.00
43 Jim Thome 3.00
44 Tony Gwynn 3.00
45 Edgar Martinez 2.00
46 Jim Edmonds 2.00
47 Delmon Young 2.00
48 Hank Blalock 2.00
49 Vernon Wells 1.50
50 Curt Schilling 2.50
51 Chipper Jones 3.00
52 Cal Ripken Jr. 8.00
53 Jason Varitek 1.50
54 Kerry Wood 3.00
55 Magglio Ordonez 2.00

56	Adam Dunn	2.00
57	Jay Payton	1.50
58	Josh Beckett	2.00
59	Jeff Bagwell	3.00
60	Carlos Beltran	2.00
61	Hideo Nomo	2.00
62	Rickie Weeks	2.00
63	Alfonso Soriano	2.50
64	Miguel Tejada	2.00
65	Bret Boone	2.00
66	Scott Rolen	3.00
67	Aubrey Huff	1.50
68	Juan Gonzalez	2.50
69	Roy Halladay	2.50
70	Brandon Webb	1.50
71	Andruw Jones	2.50
72	Pedro J. Martinez	3.00
73	Carlos Lee	1.50
74	Lance Berkman	2.00
75	Paul LoDuca	1.50
76	Jorge Posada	2.00
77	Tim Hudson	2.00
78	Stan Musial	4.00
79	Mark Teixeira	2.00
80	Trot Nixon	1.50
81	Fred McGriff	1.50
82	Nick Johnson	1.50
83	Nolan Ryan	8.00
84	Ken Griffey Jr.	4.00
85	Mariano Rivera	2.00
86	Mark Mulder	2.00
87	Bob Gibson	2.50
88	Dale Murphy UER	2.50
89	Bernie Williams	2.00
90	Carl Yastrzemski	3.00
91	Sammy Sosa	5.00
92	Miguel Cabrera	4.00
93	Craig Biggio	2.00
94	George Brett	6.00
95	Rickey Henderson	3.00
96	Derek Jeter	8.00
97	Greg Maddux	4.00
98	Bob Abreu	2.00
99	Troy Glaus	2.00
100	Dontrelle Willis	2.00

Bronze
Bronze: 1-2X
Production 100 Sets

Gold
Gold: No Pricing
Production 10 Sets

Platinum
Platinum: No Pricing
Production One Set

Silver
Silver: 2-4X
Production 25 Sets

Award Materials
NM/M
Common Player: 10.00
Quantity Produced Listed
Prime: 1-2X
Production 1-25
No pricing 10 or less.
Number: .75-1.5X
Production 3-51
No pricing 10 or less.

1	Jimmie Foxx/Bat/9	
2	Stan Musial/Jsy/43	25.00
3	Lou Boudreau/Jsy/19	15.00
4	Roger Maris/Pants/61	40.00
5	Roger Maris/Bat/61	40.00
6	Roberto Clemente/Bat/66	60.00
7	Bob Gibson/68 CY Jsy/68	20.00
8	Bob Gibson/68 MVP Jsy/68	20.00
9	Tom Seaver/Jsy/19	20.00
10	Fred Lynn Jsy/75	8.00
11	Jim Rice/Jsy/78	10.00
12	Mike Schmidt/80 MVP Jsy/80	15.00
13	Mike Schmidt/80 MVP Pants/80	15.00
14	Mike Schmidt/80 MVP Stir/80	15.00
15	Mike Schmidt/81 MVP Jsy/81	15.00
16	Mike Schmidt/81 MVP Bat/81	15.00
17	Dale Murphy/Jsy/82	10.00
18	Mike Schmidt/86 MVP Hat/19	35.00
19	Mike Schmidt/86 MVP Shoe/19	35.00
20	Mike Schmidt/86 MVP Bat/86	15.00
21	Mike Schmidt/86 MVP Stir/19	35.00
22	Jose Canseco/Jsy/88	10.00
23	Frank Thomas/93 MVP Bat/93	10.00
24	Frank Thomas/93 MVP Jsy/93	10.00
25	Jeff Bagwell/Pants/94	10.00
26	Frank Thomas/94 MVP Jsy/94	10.00
27	Frank Thomas/94 MVP Pants/94	10.00
28	Jeff Bagwell/Bat/94	10.00
29	Pedro J. Martinez/97 CY Jsy/97	10.00
30	Ivan Rodriguez/Bat/99	10.00
31	Randy Johnson/00 CY Jsy/25	20.00
32	Pedro J. Martinez/00 CY Jsy/25	20.00
33	Roger Clemens/Jsy/25	20.00
34	Randy Johnson/02 CY Jsy/25	20.00
35	Miguel Tejada/Jsy/25	15.00

Award Material Combo Prime
Production 19 Sets

Award Materials Combos
NM/M
Prime: .75-1.5X
Production 19 Sets

4	Roger Maris/Bat-Pants/25	70.00
12	Mike Schmidt/80M Jsy-Pants/25	40.00
13	Mike Schmidt/80M Pant-Stir/50	30.00
14	Mike Schmidt/80M Jsy-Stir/50	30.00
15	Mike Schmidt/81 Bat-Jsy/25	40.00
16	Mike Schmidt/81M Bat-Stir/50	30.00
18	Mike Schmidt/86M Hat-Shoe/50	30.00
19	Mike Schmidt/86M Hat-Bat/50	30.00
20	Mike Schmidt/86M Hat-Stir/50	30.00
21	Mike Schmidt/86M Bat-Shoe/50	30.00
23	Frank Thomas/93M Bat-Jsy/25	25.00
25	Jeff Bagwell/Bat-Jsy/25	25.00
26	Frank Thomas/94M Bat-Jsy/25	25.00
35	Miguel Tejada/Bat-Jsy/25	15.00

Award Material Combo Signature
No Pricing
Production 5 Sets
Prime: No Pricing
Production One Set

Award Materials Number
Production 3-45

Award Materials Prime
Production 1-25

Award Materials Signature
NM/M
Common Autograph:
Quantity produced listed
Number: 1-2X
Production 1-19
No pricing 10 or less.
Prime: No Pricing

7	Bob Gibson/68 CY Jsy/19	50.00
8	Bob Gibson/68 MVP Jsy/19	50.00
10	Fred Lynn/Jsy/75	15.00
11	Jim Rice/Jsy/78	30.00

Award Material Signature Number
No Pricing

Award Material Signature Prime
No Pricing

Game Day Materials
NM/M
Quantity produced listed

1	Nellie Fox/Bat/58	40.00
2	Frank Robinson/Bat/61	10.00
3	George Brett/Bat/77	20.00
4	George Brett/Hat/82	30.00
5	Nolan Ryan/Hat/19	80.00
6	Cal Ripken Jr./Hat/85	50.00
7	Rod Carew/Hat/19	25.00
8	Ryne Sandberg/Bat/91	20.00
9	Kirby Puckett/Bat/92	15.00
10	Frank Thomas/Bat/93	10.00
11	Tony Gwynn/Pants/99	20.00
12	Vladimir Guerrero/Bat/99	15.00
14	Tony Gwynn/Hat/99	15.00
15	Magglio Ordonez/Hat/15	15.00
16	Rickey Henderson/Bat/50	10.00

Game Day Material Signature
NM/M
Many not priced due to scarcity.

2	Frank Robinson/Bat/25	40.00
15	Magglio Ordonez/Hat/25	30.00

HOF Materials Barrel
Production One Set

HOF Materials Bat
NM/M

1	Al Kaline/25	25.00
2	Babe Ruth/50	200.00
4	Bobby Doerr/25	10.00
5	Brooks Robinson/25	30.00
6	Carl Yastrzemski/25	30.00
7	Carlton Fisk/25	20.00
8	Dave Winfield/25	15.00
10	Eddie Murray/25	25.00
11	Ernie Banks/25	30.00
13	Frank Robinson/25	15.00
18	Joe Morgan/25	15.00
19	Johnny Bench/25	30.00
21	Kirby Puckett/25	30.00
22	Lou Brock/25	20.00
23	Lou Gehrig/50	125.00
24	Luis Aparicio/25	10.00
25	Mel Ott/25	40.00
26	Orlando Cepeda/25	15.00
27	Pee Wee Reese/25	15.00
28	Phil Rizzuto/25	15.00
29	Red Schoendienst/25	10.00
30	Roberto Clemente/25	65.00
31	Roy Campanella/25	25.00
32	Paul Molitor/25	20.00
33	Ty Cobb/25	100.00
35	Willie McCovey/25	15.00
36	Willie Stargell/25	15.00

HOF Materials Bat Signature
NM/M

1	Al Kaline/50	40.00
4	Bobby Doerr/50	40.00
5	Brooks Robinson/50	40.00
11	Ernie Banks/25	75.00
13	Frank Robinson/50	35.00
18	Joe Morgan/25	40.00
19	Johnny Bench/25	60.00
22	Lou Brock/50	30.00
24	Luis Aparicio/50	20.00
26	Orlando Cepeda/50	25.00
28	Phil Rizzuto/50	35.00
29	Red Schoendienst/50	25.00
32	Paul Molitor/25	50.00

HOF Material Combo Bat-Jersey
NM/M
Quantity produced listed
Prime: No Pricing
Production 1-5

1	Al Kaline/25	40.00
2	Babe Ruth/25	500.00
4	Bobby Doerr/25	15.00
5	Brooks Robinson/50	30.00
6	Carl Yastrzemski/50	40.00
7	Carlton Fisk/50	20.00
8	Dave Winfield/50	15.00
10	Eddie Murray/50	35.00
13	Frank Robinson/50	20.00
18	Joe Morgan/50	15.00
21	Kirby Puckett/50	30.00
22	Lou Brock/50	15.00
23	Lou Gehrig/50	220.00
24	Luis Aparicio/25	20.00
25	Mel Ott/25	60.00
27	Pee Wee Reese/50	20.00
28	Phil Rizzuto/50	20.00
29	Red Schoendienst/50	15.00
30	Roberto Clemente/50	80.00
32	Paul Molitor/50	20.00
35	Willie McCovey/50	15.00
36	Willie Stargell/50	20.00

HOF Material Combo Bat-Jersey Signature
NM/M
Quantity produced listed
Prime: No Pricing
Production 1-5

4	Bobby Doerr/25	30.00
5	Brooks Robinson/25	80.00
11	Ernie Banks/25	80.00
13	Frank Robinson/25	65.00
18	Joe Morgan/25	40.00
22	Lou Brock/25	40.00
24	Luis Aparicio/25	30.00
29	Red Schoendienst/25	40.00
32	Paul Molitor/25	60.00

HOF Material Bat-Jersey Signature Prime
No Pricing

HOF Material Combo Bat-Pant
NM/M
Production 25 Sets

1	Al Kaline/25	35.00
2	Babe Ruth/25	350.00
12	Fergie Jenkins/Fld Glv-Pants/25	15.00
23	Lou Gehrig/25	200.00
24	Luis Aparicio/25	15.00
25	Mel Ott/25	60.00
31	Roy Campanella/25	40.00
33	Ty Cobb/25	200.00

HOF Mat Combo Bat-Pant Signature
NM/M

1	Al Kaline/25	75.00
12	Fergie Jenkins/Fld Glv-Pants/25	35.00
24	Luis Aparicio/25	25.00

HOF Material Combo Jersey-Pant
NM/M

1	Al Kaline/10	
2	Babe Ruth/25	500.00
16	Jackie Robinson/Jkt-Jsy/10	
23	Lou Gehrig/25	220.00
24	Luis Aparicio/25	15.00
25	Mel Ott/10	

HOF Material Combo Jersey-Pant Prime
No Pricing

HOF Material Combo Jersy-Pant Signature
NM/M
Prime: No Pricing
Production 1-5

1	Al Kaline/5	
24	Luis Aparicio/25	25.00

HOF Materials Jersey
NM/M
Quantity produced listed
Prime: No Pricing
Production 1-10
Jersey Number: .75-1.5X
Production 1-44
No pricing 15 or less.

2	Babe Ruth/25	500.00
3	Bob Feller/10	10.00
4	Bobby Doerr/25	15.00
5	Brooks Robinson/50	15.00

6	Carl Yastrzemski/50	25.00
7	Carlton Fisk/50	15.00
8	Dave Winfield/50	10.00
10	Eddie Murray/25	5.00
13	Frank Robinson/25	20.00
14	Hal Newhouser/50	10.00
15	Hoyt Wilhelm/50	10.00
17	Jim Palmer/50	10.00
18	Joe Morgan/50	10.00
20	Juan Marichal/50	10.00
21	Kirby Puckett/50	20.00
22	Lou Brock/25	15.00
23	Lou Gehrig/25	140.00
24	Luis Aparicio/25	10.00
25	Mel Ott/25	6.00
27	Pee Wee Reese/50	15.00
28	Phil Rizzuto/50	15.00
29	Red Schoendienst/25	15.00
30	Roberto Clemente/50	60.00
32	Paul Molitor/50	15.00
34	Warren Spahn/50	20.00
35	Willie McCovey/50	10.00
36	Willie Stargell/50	15.00

HOF Material Jersey Number

NM/M

16	Jackie Robinson/42	50.00

HOF Materials Jersey Prime

No Pricing

HOF Materials Jersey Signature

NM/M

Quantity produced listed
Prime: No Pricing
Production 1-10
Number: 1X
Production 10-25

1	Al Kaline/25	50.00
4	Bobby Doerr/50	30.00
5	Brooks Robinson/25	60.00
13	Frank Robinson/50	35.00
15	Hoyt Wilhelm/25	25.00
17	Jim Palmer/50	30.00
18	Joe Morgan/25	30.00
20	Juan Marichal/50	35.00
22	Lou Brock/50	30.00
24	Luis Aparicio/50	25.00
26	Orlando Cepeda/25	25.00
28	Phil Rizzuto/50	40.00
29	Red Schoendienst/50	20.00
32	Paul Molitor/50	30.00
34	Warren Spahn/25	65.00

HOF Material Jersey Signature Number

No Pricing

HOF Material Jersey Signature Prime

NM/M

23	Lou Gehrig/1 (7/04 Auction)	4,950

HOF Materials Pants

NM/M

1	Al Kaline/25	30.00
2	Babe Ruth/50	200.00
12	Fergie Jenkins/25	15.00
23	Lou Gehrig/25	125.00
24	Luis Aparicio/25	15.00
25	Mel Ott/25	40.00
31	Roy Campanella/25	30.00
33	Ty Cobb/25	125.00

HOF Material Pants Signature

NM/M

Production 25 Sets

1	Al Kaline	50.00
12	Fergie Jenkins	30.00
24	Luis Aparicio	25.00
28	Phil Rizzuto	40.00

HOF Materials Signature

NM/M

Quantity produced listed
Prime: No Pricing
Production 1-10

1	Al Kaline/25	50.00
3	Bob Feller/25	25.00
5	Brooks Robinson/50	50.00
7	Carlton Fisk/27	50.00
9	Duke Snider/25	40.00

11	Ernie Banks/25	60.00
12	Fergie Jenkins/31	30.00
13	Frank Robinson/20	40.00
15	Hoyt Wilhelm/25	25.00
17	Jim Palmer/22	30.00
20	Juan Marichal/27	30.00
21	Kirby Puckett/34	60.00
22	Lou Brock/20	40.00
26	Orlando Cepeda/30	30.00
28	Phil Rizzuto/25	40.00
29	Red Schoendienst/25	30.00
32	Paul Molitor/25	50.00
34	Warren Spahn/21	50.00
35	Willie McCovey/25	40.00

Home Away Gamers

NM/M

Quantity produced listed
Prime: No Pricing
Production 3-5

1	Babe Ruth/Jsy-Jsy/25	600.00
3	Wade Boggs/Jsy-Jsy/50	15.00
4	Tony Gwynn/Jsy-Jsy/50	30.00
5	Steve Carlton/Jsy-Jsy/25	15.00
7	Ryne Sandberg/Jsy-Jsy/50	35.00
8	Rod Carew/Jsy-Jsy/50	15.00
9	Rickey Henderson/Jsy-Jsy/50	25.00
11	Ted Williams/Jsy-Jsy/100	85.00
12	Ozzie Smith/Jsy-Jsy/50	25.00
13	Mike Schmidt/Jsy-Jsy/50	30.00
14	Harmon Killebrew/Jsy-Jsy/50	30.00
15	George Brett/Jsy-Jsy/100	30.00
16	Don Mattingly/Jsy-Jsy/50	35.00
17	Dale Murphy/Jsy-Jsy/50	15.00
18	Cal Ripken Jr./Jsy-Jsy/100	50.00
19	Lou Gehrig/Jsy-Jsy/25	200.00
20	Nolan Ryan/Jsy-Jsy/100	40.00

Home Away Gamers Combos

NM/M

Quantity produced listed
Prime: No Pricing
Production 3-10

1	Babe Ruth/25	800.00
2	Yogi Berra/8	
3	Wade Boggs/50	25.00
4	Tony Gwynn/50	40.00
5	Steve Carlton/50	25.00
6	Stan Musial/25	85.00
7	Ryne Sandberg/50	40.00
8	Rod Carew/50	25.00
9	Rickey Henderson/50	35.00
10	Brooks Robinson/5	
11	Ted Williams/100	150.00
12	Ozzie Smith/50	40.00
13	Mike Schmidt/50	50.00
14	Harmon Killebrew/50	40.00
15	George Brett/100	50.00
16	Don Mattingly/50	60.00
17	Dale Murphy/50	25.00
18	Cal Ripken Jr./100	65.00
19	Lou Gehrig/25	400.00
20	Nolan Ryan/100	65.00

Home Away Gamer Combo Prime

No Pricing

Home Away Gamer Combo Signature

No Pricing
Production 1-5
Prime: No Pricing
Production One Set

Home Away Gamers Prime

No Pricing

Home Away Gamers Signature

NM/M

5	Steve Carlton/Jsy-Jsy/25	40.00
13	Mike Schmidt/Jsy-Jsy/20	100.00
14	Harmon Killebrew/Jsy-Jsy/25	90.00
16	Don Mattingly/Jsy-Jsy/25	120.00
17	Dale Murphy/Jsy-Jsy/25	70.00
19	Lou Gehrig/Jsy-Jsy/1 (5/04 auction)	7,100

Home Run Materials

NM/M

1	Roger Maris/Bat/61	40.00
2	Ron Santo/Ball/12	
3	Harmon Killebrew/HR 570 Bat/75	20.00
4	Harmon Killebrew/HR 565 Bat/75	20.00
5	Jose Canseco/Bat/96	10.00
6	Alex Rodriguez/Bat/100	15.00
7	Sammy Sosa/Jsy/100	15.00
8	Rafael Palmeiro/Jsy/25	20.00
9	Ivan Rodriguez/Jsy/25	20.00

Home Run Material Signature

No Pricing

Material Ink Bat

NM/M

1	Adam Dunn/25	40.00
2	Alan Trammell/25	35:00
4	Andre Dawson/25	35.00
5	Bo Jackson/25	60.00
7	Dale Murphy/25	65.00
12	Don Mattingly/50	65.00
20	Mark Prior/25	80.00
25	Paul O'Neill/25	40.00
29	Ron Santo/50	35.00
30	Ryne Sandberg/25	85.00
32	Tony Gwynn/25	80.00
34	Will Clark/25	45.00

Material Ink Combos

NM/M

Quantity produced listed
Prime: No Pricing
Production 1-10

1	Adam Dunn/Bat-Jsy/25	40.00
2	Alan Trammell/Bat-Jsy/25	35.00
4	Andre Dawson/Bat-Jsy/25	35.00
5	Bo Jackson/Bat-Jsy/25	60.00
7	Dale Murphy/Bat-Jsy/25	40.00
12	Don Mattingly/Bat-Jsy/25	100.00
17	Jose Canseco/Bat-Jsy/25	50.00
30	Ryne Sandberg/Bat-Jsy/25	85.00
32	Tony Gwynn/Bat-Jsy/25	80.00
33	Vladimir Guerrero/Bat-Jsy/25	
34	Will Clark/Bat-Jsy/50	40.00

Material Ink Combo Prime

Quantity produced listed
No Pricing

Material Ink Jersey

NM/M

Quantity produced listed
Number: .75-1X
Production 1-100

No pricing 15 or less.
Prime: .75-1.5X
Production 1-25
No pricing 15 or less.

1	Adam Dunn/25	40.00
2	Alan Trammell/100	20.00
4	Andre Dawson/100	25.00
5	Bo Jackson/25	60.00
7	Dale Murphy/50	35.00
8	Darryl Strawberry/100	
9	Dave Parker/25	20.00
11	Doc Gooden/100	20.00
12	Don Mattingly/50	65.00
13	Dontrelle Willis/25	40.00
15	Ivan Rodriguez/25	50.00
16	Joe Carter/25	50.00
17	Jose Canseco/25	50.00
20	Mark Prior/50	60.00
21	Mark Teixeira/25	30.00
22	Marty Marion/25	25.00
26	Rocco Baldelli/25	40.00
30	Ryne Sandberg/50	75.00
31	Ernie Banks/50	75.00
33	Vladimir Guerrero/25	60.00
34	Will Clark/50	75.00

Material Ink Jersey Number

NM/M

Quantity produced listed

1	Adam Dunn/25	40.00
2	Alan Trammell/100	20.00
4	Andre Dawson/100	20.00
5	Bo Jackson/25	75.00
7	Dale Murphy/50	30.00
8	Darryl Strawberry/100	20.00
9	Dave Parker/25	30.00
11	Doc Gooden/100	15.00
12	Don Mattingly/50	75.00
13	Dontrelle Willis/25	40.00
16	Joe Carter/25	30.00
19	Mark Grace/25	40.00
21	Mark Teixeira/25	40.00
22	Marty Marion/25	20.00
26	Rocco Baldelli/25	25.00
31	Ernie Banks/25	65.00
33	Vladimir Guerrero/25	50.00
34	Will Clark/25	25.00

Milestone Materials

Quantity produced listed
Number: .75-1.5X
Production 9-36
Prime: 1-2X
Production 25 Sets

Milestone Material Number

No Pricing

Milestone Material Prime

No Pricing

Milestone Material Signature

NM/M

4	Gaylord Perry/Jsy/82	20.00

Milestone Material Signature Number

4	Gaylord Perry/Jsy/82	20.00

Milestone Material Signature Prime

NM/M

Quantity produced listed

4	Gaylord Perry/Jsy/19	30.00

No-Hitters Quad Signature

No Pricing
Production One Set

Rookie Year Materials

NM/M

Quantity produced listed
Prime: No Pricing
Production 5-10
Number: .75-1.5X
Production 3-51
No pricing 15 or less.

1	Stan Musial Jsy/19	60.00
2	Yogi Berra/Stripe Jsy/19	40.00

3	Yogi Berra/Grey Jsy/47	25.00
4	Whitey Ford/Jsy/50	20.00
5	Jim "Catfish" Hunter/Jsy/65	10.00
6	Johnny Bench/Bat/68	15.00
7	Mike Schmidt/Bat/72	15.00
8	Gary Carter/Jsy/74	8.00
9	Robin Yount/Jsy/74	20.00
11	Cal Ripken Jr./Bat/81	40.00
12	Kirby Puckett/Bat/84	10.00
13	Roger Clemens/Jsy/84	20.00
15	Gary Sheffield/Jsy/89	8.00
16	Juan Gonzalez/Jsy/89	10.00
17	Randy Johnson/Jsy/89	10.00
18	Ivan Rodriguez/Jsy/91	10.00
20	Pedro J. Martinez/Jsy/92	10.00
21	Mike Piazza/Jsy/93	10.00
22	Hideo Nomo/Jsy/95	10.00
23	Hideo Nomo/Pants/95	10.00
24	Alex Rodriguez/Jsy/95	15.00
26	Scott Rolen/Jsy/96	10.00
27	Andruw Jones/Jsy/96	8.00
28	Nomar Garciaparra/Jsy/97	10.00
29	Vladimir Guerrero/Jsy/97	10.00
31	Alfonso Soriano/Jsy/100	10.00
32	Albert Pujols/White Jsy/100	20.00
33	Albert Pujols/Grey Jsy/100	20.00
34	Albert Pujols/Bat/100	20.00
36	Mark Prior/Blue Jsy/100	10.00
37	Mark Prior/Grey Jsy/100	10.00
38	Dontrelle Willis/Jsy/35	15.00

Rookie Year Material Combo

NM/M
Quantity produced listed

2	Yogi Berra/Jsy-Jsy/8	60.00
22	Hideo Nomo/Jsy-Pants/16	30.00
36	Mark Prior/Jsy-Jsy/22	30.00
38	Dontrelle Willis/Jsy-Jsy/35	10.00

Rookie Year Material Combos Prime

NM/M
Quantity produced listed

36	Mark Prior/Jsy-Jsy/22	30.00
38	Dontrelle Willis/Jsy-Jsy/35	10.00

Rookie Year Material Combos Signature

NM/M
Quantity produced listed

36	Mark Prior/Jsy-Jsy/22	100.00
38	Dontrelle Willis/Jsy-Jsy/35	40.00

Rookie Year Material Combo Signature Prime

NM/M
Quantity produced listed

36	Mark Prior/Jsy-Jsy/22	100.00
38	Dontrelle Willis/Jsy-Jsy/35	40.00

Rookie Year Material Dual

NM/M
Production 25 Sets
Prime: No Pricing
Production 10 Sets

40	Roger Clemens/Jsy, Nomar Garciaparra/Jsy	40.00
41	Pedro J. Martinez/Jsy, Mike Piazza/Jsy	35.00
42	Mike Piazza/Jsy, Hideo Nomo/Jsy	35.00
43	Pedro J. Martinez/Jsy, Hideo Nomo/Jsy	20.00
44	Yogi Berra/Jsy, Whitey Ford/Jsy	50.00
45	Mike Schmidt/Bat, Scott Rolen/Jsy	40.00
46	Stan Musial/Jsy, Albert Pujols/Jsy	75.00
47	Juan Gonzalez/Jsy, Ivan Rodriguez/Jsy	15.00

Rookie Year Material Dual Prime

No Pricing
Production 10 Sets

Rookie Year Material Dual Signature

No Pricing
Production 5 Sets

Rookie Year Material Number

Quantity produced listed

Rookie Year Material Prime

Quantity produced listed

Rookie Year Material Signature

NM/M
Quantity produced listed
Prime: 1X
Production 1-35
Number: 1X
No pricing 15 or less.

1	Stan Musial/Jsy/9	125.00
3	Yogi Berra/Grey Jsy/19	100.00
4	Whitey Ford/Jsy/19	85.00
8	Gary Carter/Jsy/19	35.00
10	Fred Lynn/Jsy/75	15.00
14	Lenny Dykstra/Fld Glv/85	20.00
16	Juan Gonzalez/Jsy/19	40.00
25	Garret Anderson/Jsy/95	20.00
30	Shannon Stewart/Jsy/97	15.00
36	Mark Prior/Blue Jsy/22	80.00
37	Mark Prior/Grey Jsy/22	80.00
38	Dontrelle Willis/Jsy/35	40.00
39	Rocco Baldelli/Jsy/19	40.00

Rookie Year Material Signature Number

Quantity produced listed

Rookie Year Material Signature Prime

Quantity produced listed

Signature Bronze

NM/M

1	Albert Pujols/25	125.00
2	Garret Anderson/16	30.00
5	Alex Rodriguez/25	100.00
6	Manny Ramirez/24	40.00
8	Mark Prior/50	50.00
9	Todd Helton/17	40.00
14	Shawn Green/15	30.00
17	Vladimir Guerrero	50.00
20	Don Mattingly/50	60.00
23	Rafael Palmeiro/25	45.00
27	Gary Sheffield/50	25.00
37	Kazuhisa Ishii/17	40.00
40	Tom Glavine/25	30.00
42	Eric Chavez/25	25.00
44	Tony Gwynn/50	40.00
46	Jim Edmonds/15	35.00
47	Delmon Young/73	20.00
49	Vernon Wells/25	20.00
50	Curt Schilling/38	40.00
53	Jason Varitek/33	30.00
56	Adam Dunn/25	30.00
58	Josh Beckett/21	30.00
59	Jeff Bagwell/25	50.00
60	Carlos Beltran/15	40.00
68	Juan Gonzalez/25	40.00
71	Andruw Jones/25	30.00
76	Jorge Posada/25	40.00
78	Stan Musial/50	75.00
79	Mark Teixeira/23	35.00
83	Nolan Ryan/50	90.00
87	Bob Gibson/25	40.00
88	Dale Murphy/25	35.00
90	Carl Yastrzemski/25	60.00
91	Sammy Sosa/50	125.00
92	Miguel Cabrera/24	50.00
94	George Brett/25	100.00
95	Rickey Henderson/25	25.00
97	Greg Maddux/31	75.00
100	Dontrelle Willis/35	30.00

Signature Gold

No Pricing
Production 1-11

Signature Silver

NM/M
Quantity produced listed

2	Garret Anderson/10	10.00
6	Mark Prior/22	50.00
17	Vladimir Guerrero/27	50.00
20	Don Mattingly/23	90.00
27	Gary Sheffield/25	35.00
44	Tony Gwynn/19	75.00
47	Delmon Young/25	30.00
68	Juan Gonzalez/22	35.00
76	Jorge Posada/20	40.00
78	Stan Musial/25	75.00
83	Nolan Ryan/34	120.00
88	Dale Murphy/25	40.00
91	Sammy Sosa/21	125.00

Statistical Champions

NM/M
Number: .75-1.5X
Production 1-51
No pricing 15 or less.
Prime: No Pricing
Production 5-10

2	Stan Musial/43 BA Jsy/19	40.00
3	Ralph Kiner/Bat/49	10.00
4	Stan Musial/57 BA Jsy/57	30.00
5	Ted Williams/Jsy/25	90.00
6	Warren Spahn/Jsy/25	30.00
7	Eddie Mathews/Jsy/19	40.00
8	Roger Maris/61 HR Bat/61	40.00
9	Roger Maris/61 HR Pants/61	40.00
10	Roger Maris/61 RBI Bat/61	40.00
11	Roger Maris/61 RBI Pants/61	40.00
12	Roberto Clemente/Jsy/19	100.00
13	Frank Robinson/Bat/66	10.00
14	Bob Gibson/68 ERA Jsy/68	15.00
15	Bob Gibson/68 K Jsy/68	15.00
16	Tom Seaver/Jsy/19	25.00
18	Harmon Killebrew/Pants/71	15.00
19	Mike Schmidt/Jsy/74	15.00
20	Reggie Jackson/Jsy/19	20.00
21	Phil Niekro/Jsy/5	15.00
22	Rod Carew/Hat/78	15.00
23	Jim Rice/78 HR Jsy/78	10.00
24	Jim Rice/78 RBI Jsy/78	10.00
25	Reggie Jackson/Hat/80	15.00
26	Dale Murphy/82 HR Jsy/82	15.00
27	Steve Carlton/Jsy/83	10.00
28	Dale Murphy/85 HR Jsy/85	15.00
29	Wade Boggs/86 BA Jsy/86	15.00
30	Wade Boggs/87 BA Jsy/87	15.00
31	Will Clark/Jsy/88	15.00
32	Dale Murphy/89 K Jsy/89	20.00
33	Nolan Ryan/90 K Jsy/90	20.00
34	Nolan Ryan/90 K Pants/90	20.00
35	Ryne Sandberg/Jsy/90	20.00
36	Roger Clemens/90 K Jsy/90	20.00
37	George Brett/Jsy/90	20.00
38	Roger Clemens/92 ERA Jsy/100	20.00
39	Roger Clemens/96 K Jsy/100	20.00
40	Tony Gwynn/Jsy/25	35.00
41	Pedro Martinez/Expos Jsy/25	20.00
42	Greg Maddux/Jsy/100	10.00
43	Juan Gonzalez/Pants/25	20.00
44	Manny Ramirez/Bat/25	15.00
45	Nomar Garciaparra/99 BA Jsy/100	10.00
47	Nomar Garciaparra/00 BA Jsy/100	10.00
48	Todd Helton/00 BA Jsy/25	15.00
49	Todd Helton/00 RBI Jsy/25	15.00
50	Troy Glaus/Jsy/25	15.00
51	Randy Johnson/00 K Jsy/25	15.00
52	Tom Glavine/Jsy/25	10.00
53	Sammy Sosa/00 HR Jsy/100	15.00
54	Alex Rodriguez/01 HR Bat/100	15.00
55	Curt Schilling/Jsy/25	10.00
56	Pedro J. Martinez/99 K Jsy/25	20.00
57	Alex Rodriguez/01 HR Jsy/100	15.00
58	Mark Mulder/Jsy/25	10.00
59	Sammy Sosa/01 RBI Jsy/100	15.00
60	Manny Ramirez/Jsy/25	15.00
61	Lance Berkman/Jsy/25	10.00
62	Randy Johnson/02 W Jsy/25	15.00
63	Alex Rodriguez/02 HR Jsy/100	15.00
64	Alex Rodriguez/02 RBI Jsy/100	15.00
65	Alex Rodriguez/02 HR Bat/100	15.00
66	Alex Rodriguez/02 RBI Bat/100	15.00
67	Pedro J. Martinez/02 K Jsy/25	20.00
68	Pedro J. Martinez/02 ERA Jsy/25	20.00
69	Sammy Sosa/02 HR Jsy/25	15.00
70	Jim Thome/Jsy/25	15.00
71	Alex Rodriguez/03 HR Bat/100	15.00
72	Albert Pujols/Bat/100	20.00
73	Alex Rodriguez/03 HR Jsy/100	15.00
74	Albert Pujols/Jsy/100	20.00

Statistical Champions Number

No Pricing

Statistical Champions Signature

NM/M
Quantity produced listed
Number: .5-1.5X
Production 1-47
Prime: No Pricing
Production 1-10

3	Ralph Kiner/Bat/49	35.00
6	Warren Spahn/Jsy/25	75.00
13	Frank Robinson/Bat/66	40.00
14	Bob Gibson/68 ERA Jsy/25	50.00
15	Bob Gibson/68 K Jsy/25	50.00
17	Harmon Killebrew/Jsy/71	50.00
18	Harmon Killebrew/Pants/71	50.00
19	Mike Schmidt/Jsy/25	75.00
20	Reggie Jackson/Jsy/25	65.00
21	Phil Niekro/Jsy/50	30.00
22	Rod Carew/Hat/25	40.00

23	Jim Rice/78 HR Jsy/78	30.00
24	Jim Rice/78 RBI Jsy/78	30.00
25	Reggie Jackson/Hat/25	65.00
26	Dale Murphy/82 RBI Jsy/25	50.00
27	Steve Carlton/Jsy/25	50.00
28	Dale Murphy/85 HR Jsy/25	50.00
29	Wade Boggs/86 BA Jsy/25	40.00
30	Wade Boggs/87 BA Jsy/25	40.00
31	Will Clark Jsy/88	30.00
32	Nolan Ryan/89 K Jsy/25	120.00
33	Nolan Ryan/90 K Jsy/25	120.00
34	Nolan Ryan/90 K Pants/25	120.00
35	Ryne Sandberg/Jsy/25	80.00
40	Tony Gwynn/Jsy/25	70.00
43	Juan Gonzalez/Pants/19	40.00
50	Troy Glaus/Jsy/25	35.00
52	Tom Glavine/Jsy/20	40.00
53	Sammy Sosa/00 HR Jsy/25	150.00
55	Curt Schilling/Jsy/25	40.00
58	Mark Mulder/Jsy/25	30.00
59	Sammy Sosa/01 RBI Jsy/25	150.00
61	Lance Berkman/Jsy/20	40.00
69	Sammy Sosa/02 HR Jsy/25	150.00

Statistical Champions Signature Number

No Pricing

Statistical Champions Signature Prime

No Pricing

World Series Materials

		NM/M
Quantity produced listed		
1	Frank Robinson/Bat/61.	15.00
2	Ozzie Smith/Jsy/87.	15.00
3	Rickey Henderson/Bat/93.	15.00
4	Tom Glavine/Jsy/96.	10.00
5	Roger Clemens/Jsy/100.	15.00

World Series Material Prime

		NM/M
Quantity produced listed		
2	Ozzie Smith/Jsy/19	25.00
4	Tom Glavine/Jsy/19	20.00
5	Roger Clemens/Jsy/20	30.00

World Series Material Signature

		NM/M
Quantity produced listed		
Prime:		No Pricing
Production 9-10		
1	Frank Robinson/Bat/19	50.00
4	Tom Glavine/Jsy/19	40.00

2004 Donruss Timelines

		NM/M
Complete Set (50):		40.00
Common Player:		.75
Pack (5):		40.00
Box (4):		120.00
1	Adam Dunn	.75
2	Albert Pujols	3.00
3	Alex Rodriguez	3.00
4	Alfonso Soriano	1.50
5	Andruw Jones	1.00
6	Austin Kearns	.75
7	Miguel Cabrera	1.00
8	Barry Zito	.75
9	Carlos Beltran	.75
10	Carlos Delgado	1.00
11	Chipper Jones	2.00
12	Curt Schilling	1.00
13	Derek Jeter	4.00
14	Frank Thomas	1.00
15	Garret Anderson	.75
16	Gary Sheffield	.75
17	Greg Maddux	2.00
18	Hank Blalock	.75
19	Hideki Matsui	3.00
20	Hideo Nomo	.75
21	Ichiro Suzuki	2.00
22	Ivan Rodriguez	1.00
23	Jason Giambi	1.50
24	Jeff Bagwell	1.00
25	Jim Thome	1.50
26	Juan Gonzalez	.75
27	Ken Griffey Jr.	2.00
28	Kevin Brown	.75
29	Kerry Wood	1.00
30	Lance Berkman	.75
31	Magglio Ordonez	.75
32	Manny Ramirez	1.00
33	Mark Prior	3.00
34	Mike Mussina	1.00
35	Mike Piazza	2.00
36	Nomar Garciaparra	3.00
37	Pedro J. Martinez	1.50
38	Rafael Palmeiro	1.00
39	Randy Johnson	1.50
40	Richie Sexson	.75
41	Roger Clemens	3.00
42	Roy Halladay	.75
43	Sammy Sosa	2.50
44	Scott Rolen	1.50
45	Shawn Green	.75
46	Tim Hudson	.75
47	Todd Helton	1.00
48	Torii Hunter	.75
49	Vernon Wells	.75
50	Vladimir Guerrero	1.50

Gold

Cards (1-50):	4-6X
Production 25 Sets	

Silver

Cards (1-50):	2X
Production 100 Sets	

Platinum

No Pricing
Production One Set

Gold Autographs

		NM/M
Production 25 Sets		30.00
1	Adam Dunn	40.00
7	Miguel Cabrera	80.00
9	Carlos Beltran	40.00
15	Garret Anderson	30.00
18	Hank Blalock	35.00
22	Ivan Rodriguez	60.00
26	Juan Gonzalez	50.00
31	Magglio Ordonez	40.00
33	Mark Prior	50.00
44	Scott Rolen	45.00
48	Torii Hunter	35.00
49	Vernon Wells	30.00
50	Vladimir Guerrero	70.00

Boys of Summer

		NM/M
Complete Set (25):		75.00
Common Player:		3.00
Production 250 Sets		
Silver:		1-1.5x
Production 100 Sets		
Gold:		3-4X
Production 25 Sets		
Platinum:		No Pricing
Production One Set		
1	Alan Trammell	5.00
2	Marty Marion	3.00
3	Andre Dawson	3.00
4	Bo Jackson	5.00
5	Cal Ripken Jr.	10.00
6	Steve Garvey	3.00
7	Dale Murphy	3.00
8	Darren Daulton	3.00
9	Darryl Strawberry	3.00
10	Dave Parker	3.00
11	Doc Gooden	3.00
12	Don Mattingly	6.00
13	Eric Davis	3.00
14	Dwight Evans	3.00
15	Fred Lynn	3.00
16	Graig Nettles	3.00
17	Jay Buhner	3.00
18	Jim Rice	3.00
19	Jose Canseco	3.00
20	Keith Hernandez	3.00
21	Rickey Henderson	3.00
22	Jack Morris	3.00
23	Tony Gwynn	4.00
24	Vida Blue	3.00
25	Will Clark	3.00

Boys of Summer Autographs

		NM/M
Common Autograph:		10.00
2	Marty Marion	10.00
3	Andre Dawson	15.00
6	Steve Garvey	12.00
8	Darren Daulton	10.00
9	Darryl Strawberry	15.00
10	Dave Parker	15.00
11	Doc Gooden	15.00
13	Eric Davis	10.00
15	Fred Lynn	12.00
16	Graig Nettles	15.00
17	Jay Buhner	15.00
20	Keith Hernandez	12.00
22	Jack Morris	12.00
24	Vida Blue	12.00

Boys of Summer Silver Autographs

		NM/M
Common Autograph:		12.00
Production 100		
2	Marty Marion	12.00
3	Andre Dawson	15.00
6	Steve Garvey	20.00
8	Darren Daulton	12.00
9	Darryl Strawberry	18.00
10	Dave Parker	12.00
11	Doc Gooden	20.00
12	Don Mattingly	65.00
13	Eric Davis	12.00
15	Fred Lynn	15.00
16	Graig Nettles	15.00
18	Jim Rice	20.00
20	Keith Hernandez	15.00
22	Jack Morris	15.00
24	Vida Blue	15.00

Boys of Summer Gold Autographs

		NM/M
Common Autograph:		20.00
Production 25		
1	Alan Trammell	35.00
2	Marty Marion	20.00
3	Andre Dawson	20.00
6	Steve Garvey	20.00
8	Darren Daulton	20.00
9	Darryl Strawberry	20.00
10	Dave Parker	20.00
11	Doc Gooden	20.00
12	Don Mattingly	75.00
13	Eric Davis	20.00
14	Dwight Evans	25.00
15	Fred Lynn	25.00
16	Graig Nettles	20.00
17	Jay Buhner	25.00
18	Jim Rice	25.00
20	Keith Hernandez	20.00
22	Jack Morris	20.00
24	Vida Blue	20.00
25	Will Clark	100.00

ABBREVIATIONS

AS - All-Star
SP - Short Print

Boys of Summer Materials

		NM/M
Common Player:		5.00
Combos:		1-2X
Production 100 Sets		
Prime:		1-2X
Production 100 Sets		
3	Andre Dawson	5.00
4	Bo Jackson	10.00
5	Cal Ripken Jr.	20.00
7	Dale Murphy	6.00
9	Darryl Strawberry	5.00
11	Doc Gooden	5.00
12	Don Mattingly	15.00
19	Jose Canseco	6.00
21	Rickey Henderson	8.00
22	Jack Morris	5.00
23	Tony Gwynn	8.00
25	Will Clark	8.00

Boys of Summer Combo Materials

		NM/M
Production 100 Sets		
3	Andre Dawson	10.00
4	Bo Jackson	15.00
5	Cal Ripken Jr.	30.00
7	Dale Murphy	10.00
12	Don Mattingly	25.00
19	Jose Canseco	10.00
21	Rickey Henderson	15.00
23	Tony Gwynn	10.00
25	Will Clark	10.00

Boys of Summer Material Autographs

		NM/M
Varying quantities produced		
3	Andre Dawson/50	25.00
9	Darryl Strawberry/150	25.00
11	Doc Gooden/100	25.00
12	Don Mattingly/25	80.00
22	Jack Morris/150	12.00

Boys of Summer Prime Materials

		NM/M
Common Player:		8.00
Production 100 Sets		
3	Andre Dawson	8.00
4	Bo Jackson	15.00
5	Cal Ripken Jr.	30.00
9	Darryl Strawberry	8.00
11	Doc Gooden	8.00
12	Don Mattingly	25.00
21	Rickey Henderson	15.00
23	Tony Gwynn	12.00
25	Will Clark	12.00

Call to the Hall

		NM/M
Complete Set (25):		80.00
Common Player:		3.00
Production 250 Sets		
Silver:		1X
Production 100 Sets		
Gold:		3-4X
Production 25 Sets		
Platinum:		No Pricing
Production One Set		
1	Babe Ruth	10.00
2	Billy Williams	3.00
3	Bob Feller	3.00
4	Bobby Doerr	3.00
5	Carlton Fisk	3.00

6	Gary Carter	3.00
7	George Brett	8.00
8	Carl Yastrzemski	5.00
9	Harmon Killebrew	5.00
10	Jim Palmer	3.00
11	Joe Morgan	3.00
12	Johnny Bench	5.00
13	Kirby Puckett	5.00
14	Gaylord Perry	3.00
15	Mike Schmidt	6.00
16	Nolan Ryan	10.00
17	Ozzie Smith	5.00
18	Phil Rizzuto	3.00
19	Reggie Jackson	4.00
20	Roberto Clemente	6.00
21	Robin Yount	4.00
22	Rod Carew	3.00
23	Rollie Fingers	3.00
24	Steve Carlton	3.00
25	Tom Seaver	4.00

Call to the Hall Autographs

		NM/M
Common Autograph:		15.00
Silver Autos.:		1X
Production 100		
3	Bob Feller	15.00
4	Bobby Doerr	15.00
14	Gaylord Perry	15.00
23	Rollie Fingers	15.00

Call to the Hall Gold Autographs

		NM/M
Production 25 Sets		
2	Billy Williams	25.00
3	Bob Feller	40.00
6	Gary Carter	40.00
10	Jim Palmer	30.00
18	Phil Rizzuto	40.00
24	Steve Carlton	40.00

Call to the Hall Materials

		NM/M
Common Player:		6.00
1	Babe Ruth/50	575.00
4	Bobby Doerr	6.00
6	Gary Carter	8.00
7	George Brett	12.00
8	Carl Yastrzemski	12.00
13	Kirby Puckett	10.00
15	Mike Schmidt	12.00
16	Nolan Ryan	20.00
19	Ozzie Smith	8.00
19	Reggie Jackson	8.00
20	Roberto Clemente/100	50.00

Call to the Hall Combo Materials

		NM/M
Production 125 Sets		
6	Gary Carter	12.00
7	George Brett	25.00
13	Kirby Puckett	20.00
15	Mike Schmidt	25.00
16	Nolan Ryan	35.00
19	Reggie Jackson	20.00

Call to the Hall Material Autographs

		NM/M
Varying quantities produced		
4	Bobby Doerr/100	25.00
6	Gary Carter/25	45.00
19	Reggie Jackson/25	50.00

Materials

		NM/M
Common Player:		5.00
Combos:		1-2X
Production 125		
Primes:		1-2X
Production 125		
1	Adam Dunn	5.00
2	Albert Pujols	12.00
3	Alex Rodriguez	10.00
4	Alfonso Soriano	8.00
5	Andruw Jones	5.00
7	Miguel Cabrera/SP	10.00
10	Carlos Delgado	5.00
11	Chipper Jones	8.00
14	Frank Thomas	8.00
17	Greg Maddux	8.00
20	Hideo Nomo	6.00
22	Ivan Rodriguez	6.00
23	Jason Giambi	6.00
24	Jeff Bagwell	6.00
25	Jim Thome	8.00
26	Juan Gonzalez	6.00
30	Lance Berkman	5.00
33	Mark Prior	10.00
35	Mike Piazza	8.00
36	Nomar Garciaparra	10.00
37	Pedro J. Martinez	8.00
39	Randy Johnson	6.00
41	Roger Clemens	10.00
43	Sammy Sosa	10.00
45	Shawn Green	5.00
47	Todd Helton	6.00
49	Vernon Wells	5.00

Materials Combo

		NM/M
Common Player:		8.00
Production 125 Sets		
1	Adam Dunn	8.00
2	Albert Pujols	20.00
3	Alex Rodriguez	15.00
4	Alfonso Soriano	10.00
5	Andruw Jones	8.00
7	Miguel Cabrera	20.00
11	Chipper Jones	15.00
14	Frank Thomas	12.00
17	Greg Maddux	15.00
20	Hideo Nomo	10.00
30	Lance Berkman	8.00
33	Mark Prior	20.00
35	Mike Piazza	15.00
36	Nomar Garciaparra	15.00
37	Pedro J. Martinez	12.00
39	Randy Johnson	10.00
41	Roger Clemens	15.00
43	Sammy Sosa	15.00
45	Shawn Green	10.00
47	Todd Helton	10.00

Materials Autographs

		NM/M
Varying quantities produced		
7	Miguel Cabrera/25	85.00
22	Ivan Rodriguez/25	65.00
33	Mark Prior/50	75.00
49	Vernon Wells/25	25.00

Materials Prime

		NM/M
Common Player:		8.00
Production 125 Sets		
1	Adam Dunn	8.00
2	Albert Pujols	20.00
3	Alex Rodriguez	20.00
4	Alfonso Soriano	10.00
5	Andruw Jones	8.00
7	Miguel Cabrera	20.00
10	Carlos Delgado	8.00
11	Chipper Jones	15.00
14	Frank Thomas	12.00
17	Greg Maddux	15.00
20	Hideo Nomo	10.00
25	Jim Thome	12.00
30	Lance Berkman	8.00
33	Mark Prior	20.00
35	Mike Piazza	15.00
36	Nomar Garciaparra	15.00
37	Pedro J. Martinez	12.00
39	Randy Johnson	10.00
41	Roger Clemens	15.00
43	Sammy Sosa	15.00
45	Shawn Green	10.00
47	Todd Helton	10.00
49	Vernon Wells	8.00

2004 Donruss World Series

		NM/M
Complete Set (200):		
Common Player:		.15
Common SP (176-200):		.25
Pack (6):		6.00
Box (24):		120.00
1	Bartolo Colon	.15
2	Darin Erstad	.25
3	Garret Anderson	.25
4	Tim Salmon	.25
5	Troy Glaus	.25
6	Vladimir Guerrero	.75
7	Brandon Webb	.15
8	Luis Gonzalez	.15
9	Randy Johnson	.75
10	Roberto Alomar	.40
11	Shea Hillenbrand	.15
12	Steve Finley	.15
13	Andruw Jones	.40
14	Chipper Jones	.75
15	J.D. Drew	.25
16	Marcus Giles	.15
17	Rafael Furcal	.25
18	Javy Lopez	.25
19	Jay Gibbons	.15
20	Luis Matos	.15
21	Melvin Mora	.15
22	Miguel Tejada	.40
23	Rafael Palmeiro	.50
24	Curt Schilling	.75
25	Dwight Evans	.15
26	Fred Lynn	.15
27	Jason Varitek	.25
28	Jim Rice	.25
29	Johnny Damon	.40
30	Luis Tiant	.15
31	Manny Ramirez	.50
32	Nomar Garciaparra	1.00
33	Pedro Martinez	.75
34	Trot Nixon	.15
35	Aramis Ramirez	.25
36	Corey Patterson	.25
37	Derek Lee	.25
38	Greg Maddux	1.00
39	Kerry Wood	.75
40	Mark Prior	.75
41	Moises Alou	.25
42	Sammy Sosa	1.50
43	Carlos Lee	.15
44	Frank Thomas	.50
45	Luis Aparicio	.15
46	Magglio Ordonez	.25
47	Mark Buehrle	.15
48	Paul Konerko	.25
49	Adam Dunn	.50
50	Austin Kearns	.15
51	Barry Larkin	.25
52	Dave Concepcion	.15
53	George Foster	.15
54	Joe Morgan	.25
55	Sean Casey	.25
56	Tony Perez	.15
57	C.C. Sabathia	.15
58	Jody Gerut	.15
59	Omar Vizquel	.15
60	Victor Martinez	.15
61	Charles Johnson	.15
62	Jeromy Burnitz	.15
63	Larry Walker	.25
64	Preston Wilson	.15
65	Todd Helton	.50
66	Alan Trammell	.15
67	Dmitri Young	.15
68	Ivan Rodriguez	.50
69	Jeremy Bonderman	.15
70	A.J. Burnett	.15
71	Brad Penny	.15
72	Dontrelle Willis	.15
73	Josh Beckett	.40
74	Juan Pierre	.15
75	Luis Castillo	.15
76	Miguel Cabrera	.75
77	Mike Lowell	.25
78	Andy Pettitte	.25
79	Craig Biggio	.25
80	Jeff Bagwell	.50
81	Jeff Kent	.25
82	Lance Berkman	.25
83	Roger Clemens	2.00
84	Roy Oswalt	.25
85	Wade Miller	.15
86	Angel Berroa	.15
87	Carlos Beltran	.50
88	Juan Gonzalez	.40
89	Ken Harvey	.15
90	Mike Sweeney	.15
91	Adrian Beltre	.40
92	Hideo Nomo	.40
93	Kazuhisa Ishii	.15
94	Milton Bradley	.15
95	Orel Hershiser	.15
96	Paul LoDuca	.15
97	Shawn Green	.25
98	Ben Sheets	.15
99	Geoff Jenkins	.15
100	Junior Spivey	.15
101	Rickie Weeks	.15
102	Scott Podsednik	.15
103	Jack Morris	.15
104	Jacque Jones	.15
105	Johan Santana	.50
106	Shannon Stewart	.15
107	Torii Hunter	.25
108	Jose Vidro	.15
109	Orlando Cabrera	.25
110	Al Leiter	.15
111	Darryl Strawberry	.25
112	Dwight Gooden	.15
113	Jose Reyes	.25
114	Kazuo Matsui RC	2.00
115	Keith Hernandez	.15
116	Lenny Dykstra	.15
117	Mike Piazza	1.00
118	Tom Glavine	.40
119	Alex Rodriguez	2.00
120	Bernie Williams	.40
121	Derek Jeter	2.00
122	Gary Sheffield	.50
123	Jason Giambi	.25
124	Javier Vazquez	.25
125	Jorge Posada	.25
126	Kenny Lofton	.15
127	Kevin Brown	.15
128	Mariano Rivera	.25
129	Mike Mussina	.40
130	Barry Zito	.25
131	Eric Chavez	.25
132	Jermaine Dye	.15
133	Mark Mulder	.25
134	Rich Harden	.25
135	Tim Hudson	.25
136	Brett Myers	.15
137	Jim Thome	.75
138	Kevin Millwood	.15
139	Marlon Byrd	.15
140	Mike Lieberthal	.15
141	Pat Burrell	.15

#	Player	Price
142	Steve Carlton	.25
143	Dave Parker	.15
144	Jason Kendall	.15
145	Brian Giles	.15
146	Jay Payton	.15
147	Ryan Klesko	.15
148	J.T. Snow	.15
149	Jason Schmidt	.25
150	Bret Boone	.15
151	Edgar Martinez	.25
152	Jamie Moyer	.15
153	Rich Aurilia	.15
154	Shigetoshi Hasegawa	.15
155	Albert Pujols	2.00
156	Dan Haren	.15
157	Edgar Renteria	.25
158	Fernando Vina	.15
159	Jim Edmonds	.40
160	Matt Morris	.15
161	Scott Rolen	.75
162	Aubrey Huff	.15
163	Carl Crawford	.15
164	Dewon Brazelton	.15
165	Fred McGriff	.25
166	Rocco Baldelli	.15
167	Alfonso Soriano	.75
168	Hank Blalock	.50
169	Kenny Rogers	.15
170	Mark Teixeira	.25
171	Michael Young	.15
172	Carlos Delgado	.40
173	Eric Hinske	.15
174	Roy Halladay	.15
175	Vernon Wells	.15
176	Ivan Ochoa/ Auto./487 RC	8.00
177	Jason Bartlett/ Auto./1000 RC	8.00
178	Josh Labandeira/ Auto./703 RC	8.00
179	Phil Stockman/ Auto./715 RC	8.00
180	Ronny Cedeno/ Auto./1000 RC	8.00
181	Shawn Camp/ Auto./1000 RC	8.00
182	Ruddy Yan/ Auto./1000	8.00
183	Roberto Novoa/ Auto./568 RC	10.00
184	Justin Knoedler/ Auto./1000 RC	8.00
185	Jesse Harper/ Auto./1000 RC	8.00
186	Jason Szuminski/ Auto./1000 RC	8.00
187	Jamie Brown/ Auto./800 RC	8.00
188	Eddy Rodriguez/ Auto./1000 RC	8.00
189	Dennis Sarfate/ Auto./1000 RC	8.00
190	Ryan Meaux/ Auto./1000 RC	8.00
191	Charles Thomas/ Auto./1000 RC	10.00
192	Frank Francisco/ Auto./1000 RC	8.00
193	Orlando Rodriguez/ Auto./500 RC	8.00
194	Joey Gathright/ Auto./1000 RC	10.00
195	Renyel Pinto/ Auto./1000 RC	10.00
196	Justin Leone/ Auto./1000 RC	10.00
197	Tim Bausher/ Auto./834 RC	8.00
198	Travis Blackley/ Auto./1000 RC	10.00
199	Yadier Molina/ Auto./500 RC	15.00
200	Brad Halsey/ Auto./500 RC	10.00

HoloFoil 100

HoloFoil (1-175):	4-8X
HoloFoil (176-200):	.5X
Production 100 Sets	

HoloFoil 50

HoloFoil (1-175):	6-12X
HoloFoil (176-200):	.75X
Production 50 Sets	

HoloFoil 25

HoloFoil (1-175):	10-20X
HoloFoil (176-200):	No Pricing
Production 25 Sets	

HoloFoil 10

No Pricing
Production 10 Sets

Blue

	NM/M
Complete Set (100):	50.00
Common Player:	.50
Inserted 1:1	
HoloFoil 100:	2-4X
Production 100 Sets	
HoloFoil 50:	4-6X
Production 50 Sets	
HoloFoil 25:	6-10X
Production 25 Sets	
HoloFoil 10:	No Pricing
Production 10 Sets	

#	Player	Price
1	Josh Beckett	.50
2	Miguel Cabrera	1.00
3	Derrek Lee	.50
4	Mike Lowell	.50
5	Brad Penny	.50
6	Ivan Rodriguez	1.00
7	Dontrelle Willis	.50
8	Luis Castillo	.50
9	Garret Anderson	.75
10	Troy Glaus	.75
11	John Lackey	.50
12	Chone Figgins	.50
13	Tim Salmon	.50
14	Darin Erstad	.50
15	Troy Percival	.50
16	Steve Finley	.50
17	Mark Grace	.75
18	Randy Johnson	1.00
19	Curt Schilling	1.00
20	Luis Gonzalez	.50
21	Andy Pettitte	.75
22	Bernie Williams	.75
23	Jorge Posada	.75
24	Mariano Rivera	.75
25	Roger Clemens	3.00
26	Jose Canseco	1.00
27	David Justice	.50
28	Paul O'Neill	.75
29	Darryl Strawberry	.50
30	David Wells	.50
31	Wade Boggs	.75
32	Charles Johnson	.50
33	Cliff Floyd	.50
34	Moises Alou	.50
35	Edgar Renteria	.75
36	Chipper Jones	1.50
37	Tom Glavine	.75
38	John Smoltz	.75
39	Greg Maddux	1.50
40	Ryan Klesko	.50
41	Javy Lopez	.50
42	Fred McGriff	.50
43	Roberto Alomar	.75
44	Joe Carter	.50
45	Rickey Henderson	.50
46	Paul Molitor	1.00
47	Jack Morris	.50
48	Jack Morris	.50
49	Kirby Puckett	1.50
50	Eric Davis	.50
51	Barry Larkin	.75
52	Paul O'Neill	.75
53	Dennis Eckersley	.75
54	Jose Canseco	1.00
55	Rickey Henderson	.75
56	Dave Parker	.50
57	Orel Hershiser	.50
58	Kirk Gibson	.50
59	Bert Blyleven	.50
60	Dwight Gooden	.50
61	Gary Carter	.50
62	Lenny Dykstra	.50
63	Keith Hernandez	.50
64	Darryl Strawberry	.50
65	George Brett	3.00
66	Kirk Gibson	.50
67	Alan Trammell	.50
68	Jim Palmer	.75
69	Eddie Murray	.75
70	Cal Ripken Jr.	5.00
71	Keith Hernandez	.50
72	Ozzie Smith	1.50
73	Steve Garvey	.50
74	Steve Carlton	1.00
75	Mike Schmidt	4.00
76	John Candelaria	.50
77	Bert Blyleven	.50
78	Dave Parker	.50
79	Willie Stargell	1.00
80	Reggie Jackson	1.00
81	Johnny Bench	2.00
82	Dave Concepcion	.50
83	George Foster	.50
84	Joe Morgan	.50
85	Tony Perez	.50
86	Rollie Fingers	.50
87	Jim "Catfish" Hunter	.50
88	Reggie Jackson	1.00
89	Al Oliver	.50
90	Roberto Clemente	3.00
91	Willie Stargell	.75
92	Brooks Robinson	1.00
93	Frank Robinson	.75
94	Nolan Ryan	4.00
95	Tom Seaver	1.50
96	Al Kaline	1.00
97	Bob Gibson	1.00
98	Lou Brock	.75
99	Orlando Cepeda	.50
100	Duke Snider	1.00

Blue Signature

	NM/M

Quantity produced listed

#	Player	Price
2	Miguel Cabrera/25	40.00
3	Derrek Lee/25	30.00
5	Brad Penny/25	15.00
9	Garret Anderson/25	20.00
11	John Lackey/50	10.00
12	Chone Figgins/25	15.00
16	Steve Finley/25	20.00
29	Darryl Strawberry/25	20.00
42	Fred McGriff/25	40.00
47	Jack Morris/25	20.00
48	Jack Morris/25	20.00
50	Eric Davis/25	25.00
53	Dennis Eckersley/25	40.00
56	Dave Parker/25	25.00
59	Bert Blyleven/25	20.00
60	Dwight Gooden/25	25.00
62	Lenny Dykstra/25	25.00
63	Keith Hernandez/25	25.00
64	Darryl Strawberry/25	25.00
67	Alan Trammell/25	25.00
71	Jim Palmer/25	25.00
71	Keith Hernandez/25	25.00
76	John Candelaria/25	25.00
77	Bert Blyleven/25	25.00
78	Dave Parker/25	20.00
82	Dave Concepcion/25	20.00
83	George Foster/25	25.00
85	Tony Perez/25	35.00
86	Rollie Fingers/25	25.00
89	Al Oliver/25	25.00

Blue Material Fabric

	NM/M
Common Player:	4.00

Quantity produced listed

#	Player	Price
1	Josh Beckett/Jsy/103	4.00
2	Miguel Cabrera/ Jsy/103	8.00
3	Derrek Lee/Jsy/103	6.00
4	Mike Lowell/Jsy/103	4.00
5	Brad Penny/Jsy/103	4.00
6	Ivan Rodriguez/ Jsy/103	8.00
7	Dontrelle Willis/ Jsy/103	4.00
9	Garret Anderson/ Jsy/102	4.00
10	Troy Glaus/Jsy/102	4.00
13	Tim Salmon/Jsy/102	4.00
14	Darin Erstad/Jsy/102	4.00
15	Tony Percival/Jsy/102	4.00
16	Steve Finley/Jsy/101	4.00
18	Randy Johnson/ Pants/101	8.00
19	Curt Schilling/Jsy/101	8.00
20	Luis Gonzalez/ Jsy/101	4.00
21	Andy Pettitte/Jsy/100	6.00
22	Bernie Williams/ Jsy/100	6.00
24	Mariano Rivera/ Jsy/100	6.00
25	Roger Clemens/ Jsy/100	12.00
29	Darryl Strawberry/ Jsy/99	6.00
30	David Wells/Jsy/99	6.00
31	Wade Boggs/Jsy/96	8.00
32	Charles Johnson/ Jsy/97	4.00
33	Cliff Floyd/Jsy/97	4.00
36	Chipper Jones/Jsy/95	8.00
37	Tom Glavine/Jsy/95	6.00
39	Greg Maddux/Jsy/95	10.00
40	Ryan Klesko/Jsy/95	4.00
41	Javy Lopez/Jsy/95	4.00
51	Barry Larkin/Jsy/90	8.00
54	Jose Canseco/Jsy/89	10.00
55	Rickey Henderson/ Jsy/89	12.00
57	Orel Hershiser/Jsy/88	8.00
59	Bert Blyleven/Jsy/87	6.00
60	Dwight Gooden/ Jsy/86	8.00
61	Gary Carter/Jkt/86	6.00
64	Darryl Strawberry/ Jsy/86	6.00
65	George Brett/Jsy/85	20.00
68	Jim Palmer/Pants/83	8.00
69	Eddie Murray/Jsy/83	15.00
70	Cal Ripken Jr./ Jsy/83	40.00
71	Keith Hernandez/ Jsy/82	6.00
74	Steve Carlton/Jsy/80	6.00
75	Mike Schmidt/Jkt/80	15.00
78	Dave Parker/Jsy/79	6.00
79	Willie Stargell/Jsy/79	8.00
80	Reggie Jackson/ Jsy/78	8.00
81	Johnny Bench/Jsy/75	12.00
82	Dave Concepcion/ Jsy/75	4.00
83	George Foster/Jsy/75	4.00
86	Rollie Fingers/Jsy/74	4.00
87	Jim "Catfish" Hunter/ Jsy/74	8.00
88	Reggie Jackson/ Jkt/73	8.00
91	Willie Stargell/Jsy/71	8.00
98	Lou Brock/Jkt/67	8.00
100	Duke Snider/ Pants/55	10.00

Blue Material Fabric AL/NL

	NM/M
Common Player:	4.00

Quantity produced listed

#	Player	Price
1	Josh Beckett/Jsy/100	4.00
2	Miguel Cabrera/ Jsy/100	8.00
3	Derrek Lee/Jsy/100	4.00
4	Mike Lowell/Jsy/100	4.00
5	Brad Penny/Jsy/103	4.00
6	Ivan Rodriguez/ Jsy/100	8.00
7	Dontrelle Willis/ Jsy/100	4.00
9	Garret Anderson/ Jsy/100	4.00
10	Troy Glaus/Jsy/100	4.00
13	Tim Salmon/Jsy/100	4.00
14	Darin Erstad/Jsy/100	4.00
15	Tony Percival/Jsy/100	4.00
16	Steve Finley/Jsy/100	4.00
18	Randy Johnson/ Pants/100	8.00
19	Curt Schilling/Jsy/100	8.00
20	Luis Gonzalez/Jsy/100	4.00
21	Andy Pettitte/Jsy/100	6.00
22	Bernie Williams/ Jsy/100	6.00
24	Mariano Rivera/ Jsy/100	6.00
25	Roger Clemens/ Jsy/100	15.00
29	Darryl Strawberry/ Jsy/100	4.00
30	David Wells/Jsy/10	4.00
31	Wade Boggs/Jsy/100	8.00
32	Charles Johnson/ Jsy/100	4.00
33	Cliff Floyd/Jsy/100	4.00
37	Tom Glavine/Jsy/100	6.00
39	Greg Maddux/ Jsy/100	10.00
40	Ryan Klesko/Jsy/100	4.00
41	Javy Lopez/Jsy/10	4.00
51	Barry Larkin/Jsy/100	8.00
54	Jose Canseco/ Jsy/100	10.00
55	Rickey Henderson/ Jsy/100	10.00
57	Orel Hershiser/ Jsy/100	8.00
59	Bert Blyleven/Jsy/50	8.00
60	Dwight Gooden/ Jsy/100	6.00
61	Gary Carter/Jkt/100	6.00
64	Darryl Strawberry/ Jsy/100	6.00
65	George Brett/Jsy/50	25.00
68	Jim Palmer/Pants/50	8.00
69	Eddie Murray/Jsy/50	15.00
70	Cal Ripken Jr./ Jsy/50	65.00
71	Keith Hernandez/ Jsy/50	8.00
74	Steve Carlton/Jsy/50	8.00
75	Mike Schmidt/Jkt/50	25.00
78	Dave Parker/Jsy/50	8.00
79	Willie Stargell/Jsy/50	15.00
80	Reggie Jackson/ Jsy/50	15.00
82	Dave Concepcion/ Jsy/50	8.00
83	George Foster/Jsy/50	8.00
86	Rollie Fingers/Jsy/50	8.00
87	Jim "Catfish" Hunter/ Jsy/50	15.00

88	Reggie Jackson/Jkt/50	15.00
91	Willie Stargell/Jsy/50	15.00
98	Lou Brock/Jkt/50	15.00
100	Duke Snider/Pants/50	15.00

Blue Material Bat

		NM/M
Common Player:		5.00
Production 50 Sets		
1	Josh Beckett	8.00
2	Miguel Cabrera	12.00
3	Derrek Lee	8.00
4	Mike Lowell	5.00
5	Brad Penny	5.00
6	Ivan Rodriguez	12.00
8	Luis Castillo	5.00
9	Garret Anderson	5.00
10	Troy Glaus	8.00
13	Tim Salmon	5.00
14	Darin Erstad	5.00
17	Mark Grace	12.00
19	Curt Schilling	12.00
20	Luis Gonzalez	5.00
21	Andy Pettitte	5.00
22	Bernie Williams	8.00
23	Jorge Posada	10.00
25	Roger Clemens	20.00
27	David Justice	5.00
28	Paul O'Neill	10.00
29	Darryl Strawberry	10.00
31	Wade Boggs	15.00
32	Charles Johnson	5.00
33	Cliff Floyd	5.00
34	Moises Alou	8.00
35	Edgar Renteria	8.00
36	Chipper Jones	15.00
37	Tom Glavine	10.00
39	Greg Maddux	20.00
40	Ryan Klesko	5.00
41	Javy Lopez	5.00
42	Fred McGriff	8.00
43	Roberto Alomar	8.00
44	Joe Carter	5.00
45	Rickey Henderson	15.00
46	Paul Molitor	15.00
49	Kirby Puckett	15.00
50	Eric Davis	5.00
51	Barry Larkin	8.00
52	Paul O'Neill	8.00
55	Rickey Henderson	15.00
56	Dave Parker	8.00
58	Kirk Gibson	10.00
60	Dwight Gooden	8.00
61	Gary Carter	8.00
62	Lenny Dykstra	5.00
63	Keith Hernandez	5.00
64	Darryl Strawberry	5.00
65	George Brett	25.00
66	Kirk Gibson	8.00
67	Alan Trammell	8.00
69	Eddie Murray	20.00
70	Cal Ripken Jr.	70.00
71	Keith Hernandez	8.00
72	Ozzie Smith	20.00
73	Steve Garvey	5.00
74	Steve Carlton	10.00
75	Mike Schmidt	25.00
78	Dave Parker	8.00
79	Willie Stargell	15.00
80	Reggie Jackson	15.00
81	Johnny Bench	20.00
82	Dave Concepcion	5.00
83	George Foster	5.00
84	Joe Morgan	8.00
85	Tony Perez	8.00
88	Reggie Jackson	15.00
89	Al Oliver	5.00
90	Roberto Clemente	60.00
91	Willie Stargell	15.00
92	Brooks Robinson	15.00
93	Frank Robinson	10.00
96	Al Kaline	15.00
98	Lou Brock	15.00
99	Orlando Cepeda	10.00

Face Off

		NM/M
Complete Set (20):		75.00
Common Duo:		2.00
Production 500 Sets		
HoloFoil:		2-4X
Production 25 Sets		
1	Roger Clemens, Mike Piazza	6.00
2	Mike Mussina, Ivan Rodriguez	3.00
3	Mark Grace, Jorge Posada	4.00
4	Greg Maddux, Jim Thome	5.00
5	Rickey Henderson, Curt Schilling	4.00

6	Kirby Puckett, Tom Glavine	4.00
7	Dennis Eckersley, Will Clark	3.00
8	Bernie Williams, Randy Johnson	4.00
9	Cal Ripken Jr., Steve Carlton	12.00
10	Tom Seaver, Reggie Jackson	4.00
11	Mike Schmidt, George Brett	8.00
12	Wade Boggs, Keith Hernandez	3.00
13	Dwight Gooden, Dwight Evans	2.00
14	Johnny Bench, Jim "Catfish" Hunter	4.00
15	Jim Palmer, Dave Parker	4.00
16	Bob Gibson, Al Kaline	4.00
17	Carl Yastrzemski, Lou Brock	6.00
18	Duke Snider, Whitey Ford	4.00
19	Carlton Fisk, Tony Perez	4.00
20	Roberto Clemente, Frank Robinson	

Face Off Material

		NM/M
Common Duo:		10.00
Quantity produced listed		
1	Roger Clemens/Jsy, Mike Piazza/Jsy/100	25.00
2	Mike Mussina/Jsy, Ivan Rodriguez/Jsy/100	20.00
4	Greg Maddux/Jsy, Jim Thome/Jsy/25	35.00
5	Rickey Henderson/Jsy, Curt Schilling/Jsy/100	15.00
6	Kirby Puckett/Jsy, Tom Glavine/Jsy/100	25.00
8	Bernie Williams/Jsy, Randy Johnson/Pants/100	20.00
9	Cal Ripken Jr./Jsy, Steve Carlton/Jsy/50	75.00
11	Mike Schmidt/Jkt, George Brett/Jsy/50	40.00
13	Dwight Gooden/Jsy, Dwight Evans/Jsy/50	25.00
15	Jim Palmer/Jsy, Dave Parker/Jsy/50	10.00
17	Carl Yastrzemski/Jsy, Lou Brock/Jkt/50	40.00
18	Duke Snider/Pants, Whitey Ford/Jsy/50	25.00
19	Carlton Fisk/Jsy, Tony Perez/Fld Glv/50	20.00

Fans of the Game

		NM/M
Complete Set (5):		8.00
Common Player:		1.50
Inserted 1:24		
1	Val Kilmer	2.00
2	Stan Lee	2.00
3	Apolo Anton Ohno	1.50
4	Gene Shalit	1.50
5	Leeann Tweeden	1.50

Fans of the Game Signatures

		NM/M
Common Autograph:		20.00
1	Val Kilmer	50.00
2	Stan Lee	50.00
3	Apolo Anton Ohno	30.00
4	Gene Shalit	20.00
5	Leeann Tweeden	35.00

Legends of the Fall

		NM/M
Complete Set (20):		75.00
Common Player:		3.00
Production 500 Sets		
HoloFoil:		2-4X
Production 25 Sets		
1	Bob Gibson	4.00
2	Brooks Robinson	4.00
3	Cal Ripken Jr.	12.00
4	Carl Yastrzemski	6.00
5	Carlton Fisk	4.00
6	Derek Jeter	8.00
7	Duke Snider	4.00
8	Eddie Murray	4.00
9	Frank Robinson	3.00
10	Gary Carter	3.00
11	George Brett	8.00
12	Jim Palmer	3.00
13	Johnny Bench	4.00
14	Marco Rivera	3.00
15	Mike Schmidt	8.00
16	Phil Rizzuto	3.00
17	Red Schoendienst	4.00
18	Reggie Jackson	4.00
19	Rickey Henderson	3.00
20	Whitey Ford	4.00

Legends of the Fall Material

		NM/M
Common Player:		5.00
Quantity produced listed		
1	Bob Gibson/Jsy/50	12.00
2	Brooks Robinson/Bat/100	10.00
3	Cal Ripken Jr./Jkt/100	40.00
4	Carl Yastrzemski/Bat/50	10.00
5	Carlton Fisk/Bat/50	10.00
7	Duke Snider/Pants/50	15.00
8	Eddie Murray/Jsy/50	15.00
9	Frank Robinson/Bat/100	5.00
10	Gary Carter/Jkt/100	5.00
11	George Brett/Bat/50	25.00
12	Jim Palmer/Pants/25	12.00
13	Johnny Bench/Bat/100	12.00
14	Marco Rivera/Jsy/100	8.00
15	Mike Schmidt/Jkt/50	25.00
16	Phil Rizzuto/Pants/50	10.00
17	Red Schoendienst/Bat/100	5.00
18	Reggie Jackson/Bat/100	10.00
19	Rickey Henderson/Bat/100	10.00

Legends of the Fall Signature

		NM/M
Common Player:		
2	Brooks Robinson/25	30.00
9	Frank Robinson/25	35.00
10	Gary Carter/25	25.00
12	Jim Palmer/25	25.00
16	Phil Rizzuto/25	30.00
17	Red Schoendienst/50	20.00

Legends of the Fall Signature Material

		NM/M
Quantity produced listed		
1	Bob Gibson/Jsy/25	40.00
2	Brooks Robinson/Bat/50	35.00
7	Duke Snide/Pants/50	35.00
9	Frank Robinson/Bat/50	30.00
10	Gary Carter/Jkt/50	25.00
12	Jim Palmer/Pants/25	25.00
13	Johnny Bench/Bat/25	70.00
16	Phil Rizzuto/Pants/50	35.00
17	Red Schoendienst/Bat/100	20.00

Material Bat

		NM/M
Common Player:		4.00
Production 100 Sets		
2	Darin Erstad	4.00
3	Garret Anderson	4.00
4	Tim Salmon	4.00
5	Troy Glaus	4.00
6	Vladimir Guerrero	8.00
8	Luis Gonzalez	4.00
13	Andruw Jones	6.00
14	Chipper Jones	8.00
15	J.D. Drew	4.00
16	Marcus Giles	4.00
17	Rafael Furcal	4.00
18	Javy Lopez	4.00
19	Jay Gibbons	4.00
22	Miguel Tejada	6.00
23	Rafael Palmeiro	8.00
25	Dwight Evans	4.00
26	Fred Lynn	4.00
27	Jason Varitek	8.00
28	Jim Rice	6.00
29	Johnny Damon	10.00
31	Manny Ramirez	8.00
32	Nomar Garciaparra	10.00
33	Pedro Martinez	8.00
34	Trot Nixon	4.00
35	Aramis Ramirez	6.00
37	Derrek Lee	6.00
40	Mark Prior	6.00
41	Moises Alou	4.00
42	Sammy Sosa	12.00
43	Carlos Lee	4.00
44	Frank Thomas	8.00
45	Luis Aparicio	4.00
46	Magglio Ordonez	4.00
47	Mark Buehrle	4.00
48	Paul Konerko	8.00
49	Adam Dunn Jsy	8.00
50	Austin Kearns	4.00
51	Barry Larkin	8.00
52	Dave Concepcion	4.00
53	George Foster	4.00
54	Joe Morgan	6.00
55	Sean Casey	4.00
56	Tony Perez	4.00
59	Omar Vizquel	4.00
60	Victor Martinez	4.00
61	Charles Johnson	4.00
63	Larry Walker	8.00
64	Preston Wilson	4.00
65	Todd Helton	8.00
66	Alan Trammell	4.00
68	Ivan Rodriguez	8.00
71	Brad Penny	4.00
73	Josh Beckett	6.00
74	Juan Pierre	4.00
75	Luis Castillo	4.00
76	Miguel Cabrera	8.00
77	Mike Lowell	4.00
78	Andy Pettitte	6.00
79	Craig Biggio	6.00
80	Jeff Bagwell	8.00

81	Jeff Kent	4.00
82	Lance Berkman	4.00
83	Roger Clemens	15.00
84	Roy Oswalt	4.00
86	Angel Berroa	4.00
87	Carlos Beltran	8.00
88	Juan Gonzalez	6.00
89	Ken Harvey	4.00
90	Mike Sweeney	4.00
91	Adrian Beltre	6.00
93	Kazuhisa Ishii	4.00
96	Paul LoDuca	4.00
97	Shawn Green	4.00
98	Ben Sheets	4.00
99	Geoff Jenkins	4.00
104	Jacque Jones	4.00
106	Shannon Stewart	4.00
107	Torii Hunter	6.00
108	Jose Vidro	4.00
109	Orlando Cabrera	6.00
111	Darryl Strawberry	6.00
112	Dwight Gooden	6.00
113	Jose Reyes	6.00
114	Kazuo Matsui	10.00
115	Keith Hernandez	6.00
116	Lenny Dykstra	4.00
118	Tom Glavine	8.00
122	Gary Sheffield	8.00
123	Jason Giambi	4.00
125	Jorge Posada	8.00
126	Kenny Lofton	4.00
127	Kevin Brown	4.00
129	Mike Mussina	8.00
131	Eric Chavez	4.00
132	Jermaine Dye	4.00
133	Mark Mulder	4.00
135	Tim Hudson	6.00
137	Jim Thome	8.00
139	Marlon Byrd	4.00
141	Pat Burrell	4.00
142	Steve Carlton	6.00
143	Dave Parker	4.00
145	Brian Giles	4.00
147	Ryan Klesko	4.00
151	Edgar Martinez	4.00
153	Rich Aurilia	4.00
155	Albert Pujols	15.00
156	Dan Haren	4.00
157	Edgar Renteria	6.00
159	Jim Edmonds	6.00
161	Scott Rolen	8.00
162	Aubrey Huff	4.00
165	Fred McGriff	4.00
166	Rocco Baldelli	4.00
167	Alfonso Soriano	8.00
168	Hank Blalock	8.00
170	Mark Teixeira	6.00
171	Michael Young	4.00
172	Carlos Delgado	4.00
175	Vernon Wells	4.00

Material Fabric AL/NL

NM/M

Common Player:		4.00

Production 250 unless noted.

2	Darin Erstad/Jsy	4.00
3	Garret Anderson/Jsy	4.00
4	Tim Salmon/Jsy	4.00
5	Troy Glaus/Jsy	4.00
6	Vladimir Guerrero/Jsy	8.00
7	Brandon Webb/Pants	4.00
8	Luis Gonzalez/Jsy	4.00
9	Randy Johnson/ Pants/100	10.00
12	Steve Finley/Jsy	4.00
13	Andruw Jones/Jsy	6.00
14	Chipper Jones/Jsy	8.00
16	Marcus Giles/Jsy	4.00
17	Rafael Furcal/Jsy	4.00
19	Jay Gibbons/Jsy	4.00
20	Luis Matos/Jsy	4.00
21	Melvin Mora/Jsy	4.00

22	Miguel Tejada/Jsy	6.00
23	Rafael Palmeiro/ Jsy/100	8.00
25	Dwight Evans/Jsy	4.00
26	Fred Lynn/Jsy	4.00
28	Jim Rice/Jsy	6.00
31	Manny Ramirez/Jsy	8.00
33	Pedro Martinez/Jsy	8.00
35	Aramis Ramirez/Jsy	6.00
38	Greg Maddux/ Jsy/100	12.00
39	Kerry Wood/Pants	8.00
40	Mark Prior/Jsy	6.00
42	Sammy Sosa/Jsy	10.00
43	Carlos Lee/Jsy	4.00
44	Frank Thomas/Jsy	8.00
47	Mark Buehrle/Jsy	4.00
48	Paul Konerko/Jsy	4.00
49	Adam Dunn/Jsy	8.00
50	Austin Kearns/Jsy	4.00
52	Dave Concepcion/Jsy	4.00
57	C.C. Sabathia/Jsy	4.00
58	Jody Gerut/Jsy	4.00
59	Omar Vizquel/Jsy	4.00
60	Victor Martinez/Jsy	4.00
63	Larry Walker/Jsy	8.00
64	Preston Wilson/Jsy	4.00
65	Todd Helton/Jsy	8.00
70	A.J. Burnett/Jsy	4.00
71	Brad Penny/Jsy	4.00
72	Dontrelle Willis/Jsy	6.00
73	Josh Beckett/Jsy	6.00
76	Miguel Cabrera/Jsy	8.00
77	Mike Lowell/Jsy	4.00
79	Craig Biggio/Jsy	6.00
80	Jeff Bagwell/Pants	8.00
81	Jeff Kent/Jsy	4.00
82	Lance Berkman/Jsy	4.00
86	Angel Berroa/Pants	4.00
90	Mike Sweeney/Jsy	6.00
91	Adrian Beltre/Jsy	6.00
92	Hideo Nomo/Jsy	8.00
93	Kazuhisa Ishii/Jsy	4.00
95	Orel Hershiser/ Jsy/100	6.00
96	Paul LoDuca/Jsy	4.00
97	Shawn Green/Jsy	6.00
98	Ben Sheets/Pants	4.00
99	Geoff Jenkins/Jsy	4.00
104	Jacque Jones/Jsy	4.00
105	Johan Santana/Jsy	8.00
106	Shannon Stewart/Jsy	4.00
110	Al Leiter/Jsy	4.00
111	Darryl Strawberry/ Jsy	4.00
117	Mike Piazza/Jsy	10.00
118	Tom Glavine/Jsy	8.00
120	Bernie Williams/Jsy	6.00
123	Jason Giambi/Jsy	4.00
128	Mariano Rivera/Jsy	6.00
129	Mike Mussina/Jsy	8.00
130	Barry Zito/Jsy	4.00
132	Eric Chavez/Jsy	4.00
133	Mark Mulder/Jsy	4.00
135	Tim Hudson/Jsy	4.00
136	Brett Myers/Jsy	4.00
137	Jim Thome/Jsy	8.00
138	Kevin Millwood/Jsy	4.00
139	Marlon Byrd/Jsy	4.00
141	Pat Burrell/Jsy	4.00
142	Steve Carlton/Jsy/100	6.00
143	Dave Parker/Jsy/100	4.00
147	Ryan Klesko/Jsy	4.00
152	Jamie Moyer/Jsy	4.00
155	Albert Pujols/Jsy/100	15.00
156	Dan Haren/Jsy	4.00
159	Jim Edmonds/Jsy	6.00
161	Scott Rolen/Jsy	8.00
162	Aubrey Huff/Jsy	4.00
163	Carl Crawford/Jsy	4.00
164	Dewon Brazelton/Jsy	4.00
165	Fred McGriff/Jsy	4.00
166	Rocco Baldelli/Jsy	4.00
168	Hank Blalock/Jsy	8.00
174	Roy Halladay/Jsy	4.00
175	Vernon Wells/Jsy	4.00

Material Fabric Number

NM/M

Common Player:

5	Troy Glaus/Jsy/25	10.00
6	Vladimir Guerrero/ Jsy/27	20.00
7	Brandon Webb/ Pants/55	6.00
8	Luis Gonzalez/Jsy/20	8.00
9	Randy Johnson/ Pants/51	15.00
13	Andruw Jones/Jsy/25	10.00
16	Marcus Giles/Jsy/22	8.00
19	Jay Gibbons/Jsy/31	8.00
23	Rafael Palmeiro/ Jsy/25	15.00

25	Dwight Evans/Jsy/24	15.00
26	Fred Lynn/Jsy/19	10.00
30	Luis Tiant/Jsy/23	8.00
31	Manny Ramirez/ Jsy/24	20.00
33	Pedro Martinez/ Jsy/45	15.00
38	Greg Maddux/ Jsy/31	20.00
39	Kerry Wood Pants/34	20.00
40	Mark Prior/Jsy/22	15.00
43	Sammy Sosa/Jsy/21	25.00
44	Carlos Lee/Jsy/45	6.00
46	Frank Thomas/Jsy/35	15.00
46	Magglio Ordonez/ Jsy/30	8.00
47	Mark Buehrle/Jsy/56	6.00
49	Adam Dunn/Jsy/44	12.00
50	Austin Kearns/Jsy/28	10.00
57	C.C. Sabathia/Jsy/52	6.00
60	Victor Martinez/Jsy/41	8.00
63	Larry Walker/Jsy/33	10.00
64	Preston Wilson/ Jsy/44	6.00
65	Todd Helton/Jsy/17	25.00
70	A.J. Burnett/Jsy/34	6.00
71	Brad Penny/Jsy/31	6.00
72	Dontrelle Willis/Jsy/35	6.00
73	Josh Beckett/Jsy/21	15.00
76	Miguel Cabrera/ Jsy/24	20.00
90	Mike Sweeney/Jsy/29	10.00
91	Adrian Beltre/Jsy/29	15.00
95	Orel Hershiser/Jsy/55	8.00
105	Johan Santana/ Jsy/57	15.00
106	Shannon Stewart/ Jsy/23	8.00
107	Torii Hunter/Jsy/48	10.00
110	Al Leiter/Jsy/22	10.00
117	Mike Piazza/Jsy/31	20.00
118	Tom Glavine/Jsy/47	12.00
120	Bernie Williams/ Jsy/51	12.00
123	Jason Giambi/Jsy/25	10.00
125	Jorge Posada/Jsy/20	15.00
128	Mariano Rivera/ Jsy/42	10.00
129	Mike Mussina/Jsy/35	15.00
130	Barry Zito/Jsy/75	8.00
133	Mark Mulder/Jsy/20	15.00
136	Brett Myers/Jsy/39	6.00
137	Jim Thome/Jsy/25	20.00
138	Kevin Millwood/Jsy/34	8.00
139	Marlon Byrd/Jsy/29	8.00
142	Steve Carlton/Jsy/32	12.00
143	Dave Parker/Jsy/39	8.00
147	Ryan Klesko/Jsy/30	10.00
152	Jamie Moyer/Jsy/50	6.00
156	Dan Haren/Jsy/55	6.00
159	Jim Edmonds/Jsy/15	15.00
161	Scott Rolen/Jsy/27	25.00
164	Dewon Brazelton/ Jsy/45	6.00
165	Fred McGriff/Jsy/29	15.00
174	Roy Halladay/Jsy/32	8.00

MVP

NM/M

Complete Set (15):		35.00
Common Player:		2.00

Production 1,000 Sets
HoloFoil: 2-4X
Production 50 Sets

1	Whitey Ford	3.00
2	Bob Gibson	3.00
3	Frank Robinson	2.00
4	Brooks Robinson	3.00
5	Roberto Clemente	6.00
6	Reggie Jackson	3.00
7	Rollie Fingers	2.00
8	Johnny Bench	4.00
9	Reggie Jackson	3.00
10	Mike Schmidt	6.00
11	Alan Trammell	2.00
12	Orel Hershiser	2.00
13	Jack Morris	2.00
14	Paul Molitor	4.00
15	Tom Glavine	3.00

MVP Material

NM/M

Quantity produced listed

1	Whitey Ford/Jsy/50	10.00
2	Bob Gibson/Jsy/50	10.00
3	Frank Robinson/ Jsy/25	12.00
6	Reggie Jackson/ Jkt/100	10.00
7	Rollie Fingers/Jsy/100	5.00
9	Reggie Jackson/ Jsy/25	20.00
10	Mike Schmidt/Jsy/50	25.00
12	Orel Hershiser/ Jsy/100	5.00
15	Tom Glavine/Jsy/100	8.00

MVP Signature

NM/M

Quantity produced listed

11	Alan Trammell/25	20.00
13	Jack Morris/25	20.00

MVP Signature Material

NM/M

Quantity produced listed

2	Bob Gibson/Jsy/50	35.00
3	Frank Robinson/ Shoe/50	40.00
7	Rollie Fingers/ Jsy/100	15.00
12	Orel Hershiser/ Jsy/25	25.00

October Heroes

NM/M

Complete Set (20):		40.00
Common Player:		2.00

Production 500 Sets
HoloFoil: 2-4X
Production 25 Sets

1	Alan Trammell	2.00
2	Andy Pettitte	3.00
3	Jim "Catfish" Hunter	2.00
4	Chipper Jones	4.00
5	Dave Concepcion	2.00
6	David Wells	2.00
7	Jack Morris	2.00
8	Joe Morgan	3.00
9	Josh Beckett	2.00
10	Kirby Puckett	4.00
11	Kirk Gibson	2.00
12	Marty Marion	2.00
13	Miguel Cabrera	4.00
14	Paul Molitor	4.00
15	Paul O'Neill	2.00
16	Randy Johnson	4.00
17	Roger Clemens	6.00
18	Steve Carlton	3.00
19	Steve Garvey	2.00
20	Wade Boggs	3.00

October Heroes Material

NM/M

Common Player:		4.00
1	Alan Trammell/ Jsy/25	10.00
2	Andy Pettitte/Jsy/100	4.00
3	Jim "Catfish" Hunter/ Jsy/25	15.00
4	Chipper Jones/ Jsy/100	8.00
5	Dave Concepcion/ Jsy/100	4.00
6	David Wells/Jsy/25	8.00
8	Josh Beckett/Jsy/25	8.00
10	Kirby Puckett/Jsy/25	25.00
12	Marty Marion/Jsy/100	10.00
13	Miguel Cabrera/ Jsy/100	8.00

16	Randy Johnson/Pants/50	12.00
17	Roger Clemens/Jsy/100	12.00
18	Steve Carlton/Jsy/100	6.00
19	Steve Garvey/Jsy/100	4.00
20	Wade Boggs/Jsy/100	8.00

October Heroes Signatures

NM/M

Quantity produced listed

1	Alan Trammell/25	25.00
5	Dave Concepcion/25	20.00
7	Jack Morris/25	20.00
12	Marty Marion/25	20.00
13	Miguel Cabrera/25	40.00
18	Steve Carlton/25	35.00
19	Steve Garvey/25	20.00

October Heroes Signature Material

NM/M

Quantity produced listed

1	Alan Trammell/Jsy/100	20.00
5	Dave Concepcion/Jsy/100	15.00
12	Marty Marion/Jsy/100	15.00
13	Miguel Cabrera/Jsy/100	30.00
18	Steve Carlton/Jsy/50	35.00
19	Steve Garvey/Jsy/100	15.00

October Legends

NM/M

Complete Set (20):	60.00
Common Player:	2.00
Production 500 Sets	
HoloFoil:	2-4X
Production 25 Sets	

1	Bob Gibson	4.00
2	Cal Ripken Jr.	10.00
3	Carl Yastrzemski	6.00
4	Carlton Fisk	3.00
5	Duke Snider	4.00
6	Eddie Murray	4.00
7	Frank Robinson	3.00
8	George Brett	8.00
9	Joe Morgan	2.00
10	Johnny Bench	4.00
11	Lou Brock	3.00
12	Mike Schmidt	8.00
13	Paul Molitor	4.00
14	Phil Rizzuto	3.00
15	Reggie Jackson	4.00
16	Robin Yount	4.00
17	Stan Musial	6.00
18	Steve Carlton	2.00
19	Whitey Ford	3.00
20	Willie McCovey	2.00

October Legends Materials

NM/M

Common Player:	5.00

Quantity produced listed

1	Bob Gibson/Jsy/50	10.00
2	Cal Ripken Jr./Jsy/100	50.00
3	Carl Yastrzemski/Jsy/100	20.00
4	Carlton Fisk/Jsy/100	8.00
5	Duke Snider/Jsy/25	20.00
6	Eddie Murray/Jsy/100	10.00
7	Frank Robinson/Jsy/50	8.00
8	George Brett/Jsy/50	25.00
10	Johnny Bench/Jsy/50	15.00
11	Lou Brock/Jkt/100	8.00
12	Mike Schmidt/Jkt/100	15.00
14	Phil Rizzuto/Pants/25	15.00
15	Reggie Jackson/Jkt/100	8.00
16	Robin Yount/Jsy/100	10.00
18	Steve Carlton/Jsy/100	5.00
19	Whitey Ford/Pants/50	15.00
20	Willie McCovey/Jsy/25	15.00

October Legends Signature

NM/M

Quantity produced listed

11	Lou Brock/25	35.00
14	Phil Rizzuto/25	35.00
18	Steve Carlton/25	30.00

October Legends Signature Material

NM/M

Quantity produced listed

1	Bob Gibson/Jsy/50	40.00
5	Duke Snider/Jsy/50	40.00
7	Frank Robinson/Jsy/50	30.00
11	Lou Brock/Jsy/50	25.00
13	Paul Molitor/Jsy/25	40.00
14	Phil Rizzuto/Pants/50	30.00
16	Robin Yount/Jsy/25	65.00
17	Stan Musial/Jsy/25	90.00
18	Steve Carlton/Jsy/100	25.00
19	Whitey Ford/Pants/50	40.00
20	Willie McCovey/Jsy/25	40.00

Playoff All-Stars

NM/M

Complete Set (20):	50.00
Common Player:	2.00
Production 500 Sets	
HoloFoil:	2-4X
Production 25 Sets	

1	Mark Prior	3.00
2	Sammy Sosa	6.00
3	Steve Finley	2.00
4	David Ortiz	4.00
5	Mike Piazza	5.00
6	Edgar Martinez	2.00
7	Roy Oswalt	2.00
8	Johan Santana	3.00
9	Jacque Jones	2.00
10	Will Clark	4.00
11	Albert Pujols	8.00
12	Andre Dawson	3.00
13	Nolan Ryan	10.00
14	Fred Lynn	2.00
15	Jim Rice	2.00
16	Dwight Evans	2.00
17	Harmon Killebrew	4.00
18	Maury Wills	2.00
19	Mark Mulder	2.00
20	Frank Thomas	4.00

Playoff All-Stars Material 1

NM/M

Quantity produced listed

1	Mark Prior/Jsy/100	6.00
2	Sammy Sosa/Jsy/100	10.00
3	Steve Finley/Jsy/100	4.00
4	David Ortiz/Jsy/100	10.00
5	Mike Piazza/Jsy/100	10.00
6	Edgar Martinez/Jsy/50	6.00
7	Roy Oswalt/Jsy/100	4.00
8	Johan Santana/Jsy/100	8.00
9	Jacque Jones/Jsy/100	4.00
10	Will Clark/Bat/100	10.00
11	Albert Pujols/Jsy/100	20.00
12	Andre Dawson/Jsy/100	6.00
13	Nolan Ryan/Jsy/100	25.00
14	Fred Lynn/Jsy/50	6.00
15	Jim Rice/Jsy/50	6.00
16	Dwight Evans/Jsy/50	6.00
17	Harmon Killebrew/Jsy/50	20.00
19	Mark Mulder/Jsy/50	6.00
20	Frank Thomas/Jsy/100	8.00

Playoff All-Stars Material 2

NM/M

Common Dual:	6.00

1	Mark Prior/Jsy-Jsy/100	8.00
2	Sammy Sosa/Jsy-Jsy/100	15.00
3	Steve Finley/Jsy-Jsy/100	6.00
4	David Ortiz/Bat-Jsy/100	20.00
5	Mike Piazza/Bat-Jsy/100	15.00
6	Edgar Martinez/Bat-Jsy/50	10.00
7	Roy Oswalt/Bat-Jsy/100	6.00
8	Johan Santana/Jsy-Jsy/100	10.00
9	Jacque Jones/Bat-Jsy/100	6.00
11	Albert Pujols/Jsy-Jsy/100	25.00
12	Andre Dawson/Bat-Jsy/100	8.00
13	Nolan Ryan/Jkt-Jsy/50	40.00
14	Fred Lynn/Bat-Jsy/50	8.00
15	Jim Rice/Bat-Jsy/50	10.00
16	Dwight Evans/Bat-Jsy/50	6.00
17	Harmon Killebrew/Bat-Jsy/50	25.00
19	Mark Mulder/Bat-Jsy/100	6.00
20	Frank Thomas/Bat-Jsy/100	12.00

Playoff All-Stars Material 3

NM/M

Common Triple:	10.00

1	Mark Prior/Bat-Hat-Jsy/100	15.00
2	Sammy Sosa/Bat-Jsy-Jsy/100	20.00
3	Steve Finley/Jsy-Jsy-Jsy/100	10.00
4	David Ortiz/Bat-Jsy-Jsy/100	25.00
5	Mike Piazza/Bat-Jsy-Jsy/100	20.00
6	Edgar Martinez/Bat-Jsy-Jsy/50	10.00
7	Roy Oswalt/Bat-Fld Glv-Jsy/50	10.00
9	Jacque Jones/Bat-Jsy-Jsy/50	10.00
11	Albert Pujols/Bat-Jsy-Jsy/100	40.00
12	Andre Dawson/Bat-Hat-Jsy/100	10.00
13	Nolan Ryan/Bat-Jkt-Jsy/50	65.00
15	Jim Rice/Bat-Jsy-Jsy/100	10.00
16	Dwight Evans/Bat-Hat-Jsy/100	10.00
17	Harmon Killebrew/Bat-Jsy-Shoe/25	50.00
20	Frank Thomas/Jsy-Jsy-Pants/100	20.00

Playoff All-Stars Signature

NM/M

Quantity produced listed

1	Mark Prior/25	40.00
3	Steve Finley/25	20.00
4	David Ortiz/25	60.00
7	Roy Oswalt/25	20.00
8	Johan Santana/25	40.00
9	Jacque Jones/25	20.00
10	Will Clark/25	50.00

12	Andre Dawson/25	20.00
13	Nolan Ryan/25	125.00
14	Fred Lynn/25	20.00
15	Jim Rice/25	25.00
16	Dwight Evans/25	30.00
18	Maury Wills/25	20.00

Playoff All-Stars Signature Material 1

NM/M

Quantity produced listed

Material 2:		.75-1.5X
Production 5-100		
Material 3:		.75-1.5X
Production 5-100		
3	Steve Finley/Jsy/100	15.00
4	David Ortiz/Jsy/100	50.00
6	Edgar Martinez/Jsy/50	30.00
7	Roy Oswalt/Jsy/100	15.00
8	Johan Santana/Jsy/100	35.00
9	Jacque Jones/Jsy/100	15.00
10	Will Clark Bat/25	65.00
12	Andre Dawson/Jsy/100	20.00
14	Fred Lynn/Jsy/25	20.00
15	Jim Rice/Jsy/25	25.00
16	Dwight Evans/Jsy/50	30.00
19	Mark Mulder/Jsy/25	30.00
20	Frank Thomas/Jsy/25	50.00

Records

NM/M

Complete Set (5):	10.00
Common Player:	3.00
Production 1,000 Sets	
HoloFoil:	2-4X
Production 50 Sets	

1	Lou Brock	3.00
2	Yogi Berra	4.00
3	Reggie Jackson	3.00
4	Bob Gibson	3.00
5	Whitey Ford	3.00

Records Material

NM/M

Quantity produced listed

1	Lou Brock/Bat/100	10.00
2	Yogi Berra/Bat/50	20.00
3	Reggie Jackson/Bat/100	10.00
5	Whitey Ford/Pants/25	20.00

Records Signature

NM/M

Common Player:	

1	Lou Brock/25	30.00

Records Signature Material

NM/M

Quantity produced listed

1	Lou Brock/Bat/100	25.00
3	Reggie Jackson/Bat/20	40.00

Signature

NM/M

Common Autograph:	10.00
201-222 Exclusive to Red Sox Champs Sets	

3	Garret Anderson/25	10.00
7	Brandon Webb/25	10.00
11	Shea Hillenbrand/25	10.00
12	Steve Finley/25	15.00
16	Marcus Giles/25	15.00
17	Rafael Furcal/25	20.00
20	Jay Gibbons/25	10.00
21	Luis Matos/25	10.00
21	Melvin Mora/25	20.00
25	Dwight Evans/25	30.00
26	Fred Lynn/25	20.00
28	Jim Rice/25	25.00
30	Luis Tiant/25	20.00
34	Trot Nixon/25	25.00
35	Aramis Ramirez/25	35.00
37	Derrek Lee/25	30.00
40	Mark Prior/25	40.00
43	Carlos Lee/25	10.00
45	Luis Aparicio/25	20.00
47	Magglio Ordonez/25	20.00
48	Mark Buehrle/25	20.00
49	Adam Dunn/25	40.00
50	Austin Kearns/25	20.00
52	Dave Concepcion/25	15.00
53	George Foster/25	15.00
56	Tony Perez/25	35.00

57	C.C. Sabathia/25	20.00
58	Jody Gerut/25	10.00
60	Victor Martinez/25	25.00
64	Preston Wilson/25	15.00
66	Alan Trammell/25	25.00
69	Jeremy Bonderman/25	10.00
71	Brad Penny/25	10.00
76	Miguel Cabrera/25	40.00
84	Roy Oswalt/25	20.00
85	Wade Miller/25	10.00
86	Angel Berroa/25	10.00
87	Carlos Beltran/25	50.00
89	Ken Harvey/25	10.00
94	Milton Bradley/25	20.00
96	Paul LoDuca/25	25.00
101	Rickie Weeks/25	25.00
102	Scott Podsednik/25	20.00
103	Jack Morris/25	20.00
104	Jacque Jones/25	15.00
105	Johan Santana/25	50.00
106	Shannon Stewart/25	15.00
107	Torii Hunter/25	25.00
108	Jose Vidro/25	15.00
109	Orlando Cabrera/25	40.00
111	Darryl Strawberry/25	25.00
112	Dwight Gooden/25	25.00
115	Keith Hernandez/25	25.00
116	Lenny Dykstra/25	20.00
132	Jermaine Dye/25	20.00
133	Mark Mulder/25	25.00
134	Rich Harden/25	25.00
139	Marlon Byrd/25	10.00
142	Steve Carlton/25	35.00
143	Dave Parker/25	25.00
146	Jay Payton/25	10.00
148	J.T. Snow/25	15.00
154	Shigetoshi Hasegawa/25	40.00
156	Dan Haren/25	15.00
162	Aubrey Huff/25	20.00
163	Carl Crawford/25	20.00
164	Dewon Brazelton/25	10.00
168	Hank Blalock/25	25.00
170	Mark Teixeira/25	35.00
171	Michael Young/25	20.00

Signature Trio

		NM/M
Quantity produced listed
2	Derek Lee, Brad Penny, Mike Lowell/25	40.00
3	Garret Anderson, John Lackey, Chone Figgins/25	75.00
8	Roberto Alomar, Paul Molitor, Jack Morris/25	125.00
9	Eric Davis, Barry Larkin, Paul O'Neill/25	100.00
10	Dennis Eckersley, Jose Canseco, Dave Parker/25	125.00
11	Keith Hernandez, Dwight Gooden, Gary Carter/25	75.00
12	Lenny Dykstra, George Foster, Darryl Strawberry/25	65.00
13	Alan Trammell, Kirk Gibson, Jack Morris/25	100.00
15	Bert Blyleven, John Candelaria, Dave Parker/25	75.00

Souvenirs Playoff

		NM/M
Common Player: 5.00
Production 100 Sets
1	Chipper Jones/Ball	10.00
2	Randy Johnson/Ball	10.00
3	Albert Pujols/Ball	20.00
4	Jason Schmidt/Ball	8.00
5	Gary Sheffield/Ball	8.00
6	Miguel Tejada/Ball	8.00
7	J.D. Drew/Ball	5.00
8	John Smoltz/Ball	10.00
9	Eric Milton/Ball	5.00
10	Mark Grace/Ball	10.00
11	Tim Hudson/Ball	5.00
12	Jeff Bagwell/Ball	10.00
13	Jim Edmonds/Ball	8.00
14	Sammy Sosa/Ball	15.00
15	Albert Pujols/Ball	20.00

Souvenirs World Series

		NM/M
Common Player: 5.00
Production 100 Sets
1	Jason Schmidt/Ball	8.00
2	Troy Glaus/Base	5.00

3	Reggie Sanders/Base	5.00
4	Tim Salmon/Base	5.00
5	Garret Anderson/Base	5.00
6	Francisco Rodriguez/Base	5.00
7	Rich Aurilia/Ball	5.00
8	Jeff Kent/Ball	5.00
9	Darin Erstad/Base	5.00
10	Troy Glaus/Base	5.00
11	Jeff Kent/Ball	5.00
12	Scott Spiezio/Base	5.00
13	Tony Percival/Base	5.00
14	Garret Anderson/Base	5.00
15	Darin Erstad/Base	5.00

Triple Threads

		NM/M
Common Player: 10.00
1	Josh Beckett, Miguel Cabrera, Mike Lowell/100	15.00
2	Luis Castillo, Ivan Rodriguez, Dontrelle Willis/100	20.00
3	Garret Anderson, Troy Glaus, Tim Salmon/100	20.00
4	Curt Schilling, Mark Grace, Randy Johnson/50	25.00
5	Jorge Posada, Bernie Williams, Roger Clemens/50	25.00
6	Andy Pettitte, Wade Boggs, Mariano Rivera/50	20.00
7	Charles Johnson, Cliff Floyd, Moises Alou/100	10.00
8	Chipper Jones, Tom Glavine, Greg Maddux/100	30.00
9	Joe Carter, Rickey Henderson, David Wells/100	25.00
10	Eric Davis, Barry Larkin, Paul O'Neill/100	20.00
11	Dwight Gooden, Gary Carter, Darryl Strawberry/100	20.00
12	Frank White, Willie Wilson, George Brett/100	30.00
13	Jim Palmer, Eddie Murray, Cal Ripken Jr./50	125.00
14	Willie Stargell, Dave Parker, Bill Madlock/100	20.00
15	Johnny Bench, Joe Morgan, Tony Perez/100	35.00
16	Dave Concepcion, George Foster, Johnny Bench/50	40.00
17	Al Oliver, Roberto Clemente, Willie Stargell/50	80.00
18	Jim Palmer, Frank Robinson, Brooks Robinson/50	25.00
19	Bob Gibson, Lou Brock, Orlando Cepeda/50	25.00
20	Stan Musial, Red Schoendienst, Marty Marion/50	40.00

2004 Donruss World Series Champions

		NM/M
Complete Boxed Set (25): 25.00
Common Player: .50
201	Curt Schilling	3.00
202	Pedro Martinez	3.00

203	Derek Lowe	.50
204	Tim Wakefield	.50
205	Bronson Arroyo	.50
206	Mike Timlin	.50
207	Curt Leskanic	.50
208	Mike Myers	.50
209	Alan Embree	.50
210	Keith Foulke	.50
211	Jason Varitek	2.00
212	Doug Mirabelli	.50
213	Doug Mientkiewicz	.50
214	Mark Bellhorn	.50
215	Pokey Reese	.50
216	Orlando Cabrera	1.00
217	Bill Mueller	.50
218	Kevin Youkilis	.50
219	Manny Ramirez	3.00
220	Johnny Damon	3.00
221	Dave Roberts	.50
222	Trot Nixon	.50
223	Gabe Kapler	.50
224	David Ortiz	3.00

Box Topper

		NM/M
Inserted 1:Set
WS1	World Series Champions	2.00

2005 Donruss

		NM/M
Complete Set (400): 120.00
Common Player: .15
Common SP (1-70, 371-400): 1.00
Inserted 1:6
Pack (10): 2.50
Box (24): 50.00
1	Garret Anderson	1.00
2	Vladimir Guerrero	2.00
3	Manny Ramirez	2.00
4	Kerry Wood	2.00
5	Sammy Sosa	3.00
6	Magglio Ordonez	1.00
7	Adam Dunn	1.50
8	Todd Helton	1.50
9	Josh Beckett	1.00
10	Miguel Cabrera	2.00
11	Lance Berkman	1.00
12	Carlos Beltran	1.50
13	Shawn Green	1.00
14	Roger Clemens	4.00
15	Mike Piazza	2.50
16	Alex Rodriguez	3.00
17	Derek Jeter	4.00
18	Mark Mulder	1.00
19	Jim Thome	2.00
20	Albert Pujols	3.00
21	Scott Rolen	2.00
22	Aubrey Huff	1.00
23	Alfonso Soriano	2.00
24	Hank Blalock	1.50
25	Vernon Wells	1.00
26	Kazuo Matsui	1.50
27	B.J. Upton	1.50
28	Charles Thomas	1.00
29	Akinori Otsuka	1.00
30	David Aardsma	1.00
31	Travis Blackley	1.00
32	Brad Halsey	1.00
33	David Wright	5.00

34	Kazuhito Tadano	1.00
35	Casey Kotchman	1.50
36	Khalil Greene	2.00
37	Adrian Gonzalez	1.00
38	Zack Greinke	1.00
39	Chad Cordero	1.00
40	Scott Kazmir	4.00
41	Jeremy Guthrie	1.00
42	Noah Lowry	1.00
43	Chase Utley	1.00
44	Billy Traber	1.00
45	Aarom Baldiris	1.00
46	Abe Alvarez	1.00
47	Angel Chavez	1.00
48	Joe Mauer	1.00
49	Joey Gathright	1.00
50	John Gall	1.00
51	Ronald Belisario	1.00
52	Ryan Wing	1.00
53	Scott Proctor	1.00
54	Yadier Molina	1.00
55	Carlos Hines	1.00
56	Frankie Francisco	1.00
57	Graham Koonce	1.00
58	Jake Woods	1.00
59	Jason Bartlett	1.00
60	Mike Rouse	1.00
61	Phil Stockman	1.00
62	Renyel Pinto	1.00
63	Roberto Novoa	1.00
64	Ryan Meaux	1.00
65	David Crouthers	1.00
66	Justin Knoedler	1.00
67	Justin Leone	1.00
68	Nick Regilio	1.00
69	Mike Gosling	1.00
70	Onil Joseph	1.00
71	Bartolo Colon	.15
72	Brad Fullmer	.15
73	Chone Figgins	.15
74	Darin Erstad	.25
75	Francisco Rodriguez	.15
76	Garret Anderson	.25
77	Jarrod Washburn	.15
78	John Lackey	.15
79	Jose Guillen	.15
80	Robb Quinlan	.15
81	Tim Salmon	.25
82	Troy Glaus	.25
83	Troy Percival	.15
84	Vladimir Guerrero	.50
85	Brandon Webb	.15
86	Casey Fossum	.15
87	Luis Gonzalez	.15
88	Randy Johnson	.50
89	Richie Sexson	.25
90	Robby Hammock	.15
91	Roberto Alomar	.25
92	Adam LaRoche	.15
93	Andruw Jones	.25
94	Bubba Nelson	.15
95	Chipper Jones	.50
96	J.D. Drew	.25
97	John Smoltz	.25
98	Johnny Estrada	.15
99	Marcus Giles	.15
100	Mike Hampton	.15
101	Nick Green	.15
102	Rafael Furcal	.15
103	Russ Ortiz	.15
104	Adam Loewen	.15
105	Brian Roberts	.15
106	Javy Lopez	.25
107	Jay Gibbons	.15
108	Larry Bigbie	.15
109	Luis Matos	.15
110	Melvin Mora	.15
111	Miguel Tejada	.40
112	Rafael Palmeiro	.40
113	Rodrigo Lopez	.15
114	Sidney Ponson	.15
115	Bill Mueller	.15
116	Byung-Hyun Kim	.15
117	Curt Schilling	.40
118	David Ortiz	.40
119	Derek Lowe	.15
120	Doug Mientkiewicz	.15
121	Jason Varitek	.25
122	Johnny Damon	.25
123	Keith Foulke	.15
124	Kevin Youkilis	.15
125	Manny Ramirez	.50
126	Orlando Cabrera	.25
127	Pedro J. Martinez	.50
128	Trot Nixon	.15
129	Aramis Ramirez	.25
130	Carlos Zambrano	.25
131	Corey Patterson	.25
132	Derrek Lee	.25
133	Greg Maddux	.75
134	Kerry Wood	.50
135	Mark Prior	.50
136	Matt Clement	.15
137	Moises Alou	.25

138	Nomar Garciaparra	1.00
139	Sammy Sosa	1.00
140	Todd Walker	.15
141	Angel Guzman	.15
142	Billy Koch	.15
143	Carlos Lee	.15
144	Frank Thomas	.40
145	Magglio Ordonez	.25
146	Mark Buehrle	.15
147	Paul Konerko	.25
148	Wilson Valdez	.15
149	Adam Dunn	.40
150	Austin Kearns	.15
151	Barry Larkin	.25
152	Benito Santiago	.15
153	Jason LaRue	.15
154	Ken Griffey Jr.	.75
155	Ryan Wagner	.15
156	Sean Casey	.15
157	Brandon Phillips	.15
158	Brian Tallet	.15
159	C.C. Sabathia	.15
160	Cliff Lee	.15
161	Jeremy Guthrie	.15
162	Jody Gerut	.15
163	Matt Lawton	.15
164	Omar Vizquel	.15
165	Travis Hafner	.15
166	Victor Martinez	.25
167	Charles Johnson	.15
168	Garrett Atkins	.15
169	Jason Jennings	.15
170	Jay Payton	.15
171	Jeromy Burnitz	.15
172	Joe Kennedy	.15
173	Larry Walker	.25
174	Preston Wilson	.15
175	Todd Helton	.40
176	Vinny Castilla	.15
177	Bobby Higginson	.15
178	Brandon Inge	.15
179	Carlos Guillen	.15
180	Carlos Pena	.15
181	Craig Monroe	.15
182	Dmitri Young	.15
183	Eric Munson	.15
184	Fernando Vina	.15
185	Ivan Rodriguez	.40
186	Jeremy Bonderman	.15
187	Rondell White	.15
188	A.J. Burnett	.15
189	Dontrelle Willis	.25
190	Guillermo Mota	.15
191	Hee Seop Choi	.15
192	Jeff Conine	.15
193	Josh Beckett	.25
194	Juan Encarnacion	.15
195	Juan Pierre	.15
196	Luis Castillo	.15
197	Miguel Cabrera	.50
198	Mike Lowell	.15
199	Paul LoDuca	.15
200	Andy Pettitte	.25
201	Brad Ausmus	.15
202	Carlos Beltran	.40
203	Chris Burke	.15
204	Craig Biggio	.25
205	Jeff Bagwell	.40
206	Jeff Kent	.25
207	Lance Berkman	.25
208	Morgan Ensberg	.15
209	Octavio Dotel	.15
210	Roger Clemens	1.50
211	Roy Oswalt	.25
212	Tim Redding	.15
213	Angel Berroa	.15
214	Juan Gonzalez	.25
215	Ken Harvey	.15
216	Mike Sweeney	.15
217	Adrian Beltre	.25
218	Brad Penny	.15
219	Eric Gagne	.25
220	Hideo Nomo	.25
221	Hong-Chih Kuo	.15
222	Jeff Weaver	.15
223	Kazuhisa Ishii	.15
224	Milton Bradley	.15
225	Shawn Green	.25
226	Steve Finley	.15
227	Danny Kolb	.15
228	Geoff Jenkins	.15
229	Junior Spivey	.15
230	Lyle Overbay	.15
231	Rickie Weeks	.15
232	Scott Podsednik	.15
233	Brad Radke	.15
234	Corey Koskie	.15
235	Cristian Guzman	.15
236	Dustan Mohr	.15
237	Eddie Guardado	.15
238	J.D. Durbin	.15
239	Jacque Jones	.15
240	Joe Nathan	.15
241	Johan Santana	.40

242	Lew Ford	.15
243	Michael Cuddyer	.15
244	Shannon Stewart	.15
245	Torii Hunter	.15
246	Brad Wilkerson	.15
247	Carl Everett	.15
248	Jeff Fassero	.15
249	Jose Vidro	.15
250	Livan Hernandez	.15
251	Michael Barrett	.15
252	Tony Batista	.15
253	Zach Day	.15
254	Al Leiter	.15
255	Cliff Floyd	.15
256	Jae Weong Seo	.15
257	John Olerud	.15
258	Jose Reyes	.40
259	Mike Cameron	.15
260	Mike Piazza	1.00
261	Richard Hidalgo	.15
262	Tom Glavine	.25
263	Vance Wilson	.15
264	Alex Rodriguez	1.50
265	Armando Benitez	.15
266	Bernie Williams	.25
267	Bubba Crosby	.15
268	Chien-Ming Wang	.40
269	Derek Jeter	1.50
270	Esteban Loaiza	.15
271	Gary Sheffield	.25
272	Hideki Matsui	1.00
273	Jason Giambi	.25
274	Javier Vazquez	.15
275	Jorge Posada	.25
276	Jose Contreras	.25
277	Kenny Lofton	.15
278	Kevin Brown	.15
279	Mariano Rivera	.25
280	Mike Mussina	.25
281	Barry Zito	.25
282	Bobby Crosby	.15
283	Eric Byrnes	.15
284	Eric Chavez	.25
285	Erubiel Durazo	.15
286	Jermaine Dye	.15
287	Mark Kotsay	.15
288	Mark Mulder	.25
289	Rich Harden	.15
290	Tim Hudson	.15
291	Billy Wagner	.15
292	Bobby Abreu	.25
293	Brett Myers	.15
294	Eric Milton	.15
295	Jim Thome	.50
296	Jimmy Rollins	.25
297	Kevin Millwood	.15
298	Marlon Byrd	.15
299	Mike Lieberthal	.15
300	Pat Burrell	.15
301	Randy Wolf	.15
302	Craig Wilson	.15
303	Jack Wilson	.15
304	Jacob Cruz	.15
305	Jason Bay	.15
306	Jason Kendall	.15
307	Jose Castillo	.15
308	Kip Wells	.15
309	Brian Giles	.15
310	Brian Lawrence	.15
311	Chris Oxspring	.15
312	David Wells	.15
313	Freddy Guzman	.15
314	Jake Peavy	.15
315	Mark Loretta	.15
316	Ryan Klesko	.15
317	Sean Burroughs	.15
318	Trevor Hoffman	.15
319	Xavier Nady	.15
320	A.J. Pierzynski	.15
321	Edgardo Alfonzo	.15
322	J.T. Snow	.15
323	Jason Schmidt	.25
324	Jerome Williams	.15
325	Kirk Rueter	.15
326	Bret Boone	.15
327	Bucky Jacobsen	.15
328	Edgar Martinez	.15
329	Freddy Garcia	.15
330	Ichiro Suzuki	1.00
331	Jamie Moyer	.15
332	Joel Pineiro	.15
333	Scott Spiezio	.15
334	Shigetoshi Hasegawa	.15
335	Albert Pujols	1.50
336	Edgar Renteria	.25
337	Jason Isringhausen	.15
338	Jim Edmonds	.25
339	Matt Morris	.15
340	Mike Matheny	.15
341	Reggie Sanders	.15
342	Scott Rolen	.50
343	Woody Williams	.15
344	Jeff Suppan	.15
345	Aubrey Huff	.15

346	Carl Crawford	.15
347	Chad Gaudin	.15
348	Delmon Young	.15
349	Devon Brazelton	.15
350	Jose Cruz Jr.	.15
351	Rocco Baldelli	.25
352	Tino Martinez	.15
353	Toby Hall	.15
354	Alfonso Soriano	.40
355	Brian Jordan	.15
356	Francisco Cordero	.15
357	Hank Blalock	.40
358	Kenny Rogers	.15
359	Kevin Mench	.15
360	Laynce Nix	.15
361	Mark Teixeira	.25
362	Michael Young	.15
363	Alex Gonzalez	.15
364	Alexis Rios	.15
365	Carlos Delgado	.25
366	Eric Hinske	.15
367	Frank Catalanotto	.15
368	Josh Phelps	.15
369	Roy Halladay	.15
370	Vernon Wells	.15
371	Vladimir Guerrero	2.00
372	Randy Johnson	2.00
373	Chipper Jones	2.00
374	Miguel Tejada	1.50
375	Pedro Martinez	2.00
376	Sammy Sosa	3.00
377	Frank Thomas	1.50
378	Ken Griffey Jr.	3.00
379	Victor Martinez	1.00
380	Todd Helton	1.50
381	Ivan Rodriguez	1.50
382	Miguel Cabrera	2.00
383	Roger Clemens	4.00
384	Ken Harvey	1.00
385	Eric Gagne	1.50
386	Lyle Overbay	1.00
387	Shannon Stewart	1.00
388	Brad Wilkerson	1.00
389	Mike Piazza	2.50
390	Alex Rodriguez	3.00
391	Mark Mulder	1.00
392	Jim Thome	2.00
393	Jack Wilson	1.00
394	Khalil Greene	1.50
395	Jason Schmidt	1.00
396	Ichiro Suzuki	3.00
397	Albert Pujols	4.00
398	Rocco Baldelli	1.00
399	Alfonso Soriano	1.50
400	Vernon Wells	1.00

25th Anniversary

Stars:	10-20X
SP's (1-70, 371-400):	3-6X
Production 25 Sets	

Press Proofs Black

No Pricing
Production 10 Sets

Press Proofs Blue

Blue (71-370):	4-8X
Blue SP's:	2-3X
Production 100 Sets	

Press Proofs Gold

Gold (71-370):	10-20X
Gold SP's:	3-6X
Production 25 Sets	

Press Proofs Red

Red (71-370):	2-4X
Red SP's:	.75-1.5X
Production 200 Sets	

Stat Line Career

	NM/M
#71-370 print run 201-400:	2-4X
71-370 p/r 101-200:	3-6X
71-370 p/r 51-100:	4-8X
71-370 p/r 25 or less:	6-12X
SP's print run 200 or more:	No Pricing
	1-2X
SP's p/r 101-200:	1.5-2X
SP's p/r 51-100:	2-4X
SP's p/r 26-50:	3-5X
SP's p/r 25 or less:	No Pricing
Cards are numbered to career statistic.	

Stat Line Season

#71-370 print run 101-200:	3-6X
71-370 p/r 51-100:	4-8X
71-370 p/r 26-50:	6-12X
71-370 p/r 25 or less:	No Pricing
SP's p/r 101 or more:	1.5-2X
SP's p/r 51-100:	2-4X
SP's p/r 26-50:	3-5X
SP's p/r 25 or less:	No Pricing
Cards are numbered to season statistic.	

'85 Reprints

		NM/M
Complete Set (12):		40.00
Common Player:		2.00
Production 1,985 Sets		
1	Eddie Murray	3.00
2	George Brett	6.00
3	Nolan Ryan	8.00
4	Mike Schmidt	6.00
5	Tony Gwynn	3.00
7	Cal Ripken Jr.	10.00
8	Dwight Gooden	2.00
9	Roger Clemens	8.00
10	Don Mattingly	6.00
11	Kirby Puckett	4.00
12	Orel Hershiser	2.00

'85 Reprints Material

		NM/M
Production 85 Sets		
1	Eddie Murray/Jsy	20.00
2	George Brett/Jsy	35.00
3	Nolan Ryan/Jkt	40.00
4	Mike Schmidt/Jkt	35.00
5	Tony Gwynn/Jsy	20.00
7	Cal Ripken Jr./Jsy	50.00

10	Don Mattingly/Jsy	40.00
9	Roger Clemens/Jsy	40.00
10	Don Mattingly/Jsy	35.00
11	Kirby Puckett/Jsy	20.00
12	Orel Hershiser/Jsy	10.00

All-Stars AL

		NM/M
Common Player:		2.00
Production 1,000 Sets		
Gold:		1-2X
Production 100 Sets		
1	Alex Rodriguez	6.00
2	Alfonso Soriano	3.00
3	Curt Schilling	2.00
4	Derek Jeter	8.00
5	Hank Blalock	2.00
6	Hideki Matsui	6.00
7	Ichiro Suzuki	6.00
8	Ivan Rodriguez	3.00
9	Jason Giambi	2.00
10	Manny Ramirez	3.00
11	Mark Mulder	2.00
12	Michael Young	2.00
13	Tim Hudson	2.00
14	Victor Martinez	2.00
15	Vladimir Guerrero	3.00

All-Stars NL

		NM/M
Common Player:		2.00
Production 1,000 Sets		
Gold:		1-2X
Production 100 Sets		
1	Albert Pujols	8.00
2	Ben Sheets	2.00
3	Edgar Renteria	2.00
4	Eric Gagne	2.00
5	Jack Wilson	2.00
6	Jason Schmidt	2.00
7	Jeff Kent	2.00
8	Jim Thome	3.00
9	Ken Griffey Jr.	4.00
10	Mike Piazza	4.00
11	Roger Clemens	8.00
12	Sammy Sosa	5.00
13	Scott Rolen	3.00
14	Sean Casey	2.00
15	Todd Helton	2.00

Autographs

No Pricing

Bat Kings

	NM/M
Common Player:	5.00
Quantity produced listed	
1 Garret Anderson/250	5.00

2	Vladimir Guerrero/250	8.00
3	Cal Ripken Jr./100	50.00
4	Manny Ramirez/250	8.00
5	Kerry Wood/250	8.00
6	Sammy Sosa/250	12.00
7	Magglio Ordonez/250	5.00
8	Adam Dunn/250	8.00
9	Todd Helton/250	8.00
10	Josh Beckett/250	5.00
11	Miguel Cabrera/250	8.00
12	Carlos Beltran/250	5.00
13	Carlos Beltran/250	8.00
14	Shawn Green/250	5.00
15	Roger Clemens/100	15.00
16	Mike Piazza/250	12.00
17	Nolan Ryan/100	50.00
18	Mark Mulder/250	5.00
19	Jim Thome/250	10.00
20	Albert Pujols/250	20.00
21	Scott Rolen/250	10.00
22	Aubrey Huff/250	5.00
23	Alfonso Soriano/250	8.00

Bat Kings Signatures

No Pricing
Production 5 or 10

2005 Donruss Cal Ripken 10th Anniversary

	NM/M
Cal Ripken Jr.	4.00

Craftsmen

		NM/M
Complete Set (30):		40.00
Common Player:		1.00
Production 1,000 Sets		
Black:		1.5-2X
Production 100 Sets		
Master:		1-2X
Production 250 Sets		
Master Black:		No Pricing
Production 10 Sets		
1	Albert Pujols	5.00
2	Alex Rodriguez	4.00
3	Alfonso Soriano	2.00
4	Andruw Jones	1.00
5	Carlos Beltran	1.50
6	Derek Jeter	5.00
7	Greg Maddux	2.50
8	Hank Blalock	1.50
9	Ichiro Suzuki	4.00
10	Jeff Bagwell	1.50
11	Jim Thome	2.00
12	Josh Beckett	1.00
13	Ken Griffey Jr.	2.50
14	Manny Ramirez	2.00
15	Mark Mulder	1.00
16	Mark Prior	2.00
17	Mark Teixeira	1.00
18	Miguel Tejada	1.50
19	Mike Mussina	1.50
20	Mike Piazza	2.50
21	Nomar Garciaparra	3.00
22	Pedro Martinez	2.00
23	Rafael Palmeiro	1.50
24	Randy Johnson	2.00
25	Roger Clemens	5.00
26	Sammy Sosa	3.00
27	Scott Rolen	2.00
28	Tim Hudson	1.00
29	Vernon Wells	1.00
30	Vladimir Guerrero	2.00

Diamond Kings Inserts

	NM/M
Complete Set (25):	40.00
Common Player:	1.50

Production 2,005 Sets		
Studio:		1.5-2X
Production 250 Sets		
Studio Black:		1.5-3X
Production 100 Sets		
1	Garret Anderson	1.50
2	Vladimir Guerrero	2.00
3	Manny Ramirez	2.00
4	Kerry Wood	1.50
5	Sammy Sosa	4.00
6	Magglio Ordonez	1.50
7	Adam Dunn	1.50
8	Todd Helton	1.50
9	Josh Beckett	1.50
10	Miguel Cabrera	2.00
11	Lance Berkman	1.50
12	Carlos Beltran	2.00
13	Shawn Green	1.50
14	Roger Clemens	6.00
15	Mike Piazza	3.00
16	Alex Rodriguez	5.00
17	Derek Jeter	6.00
18	Mark Mulder	1.50
19	Jim Thome	2.00
20	Albert Pujols	6.00
21	Scott Rolen	2.00
22	Aubrey Huff	1.50
23	Alfonso Soriano	2.00
24	Hank Blalock	1.50
25	Vernon Wells	1.50

Elite Series

		NM/M
Complete Set (25):		50.00
Common Player:		2.00
Production 1,500 Sets		
Black:		1-2X
Production 100 Sets		
Dominator:		1-1.5X
Production 250 Sets		
Dominator Black:		3-5X
Production 25 Sets		
1	Albert Pujols	6.00
2	Alex Rodriguez	5.00
3	Alfonso Soriano	2.00
4	Derek Jeter	6.00
5	Hank Blalock	1.50
6	Ichiro Suzuki	5.00
7	Ivan Rodriguez	2.00
8	Jim Thome	2.00
9	Ken Griffey Jr.	3.00
10	Manny Ramirez	2.00
11	Mark Mulder	1.50
12	Mark Prior	2.00
13	Michael Young	1.50
14	Miguel Cabrera	2.00
15	Miguel Tejada	2.00
16	Mike Piazza	3.00
17	Nomar Garciaparra	4.00
18	Rafael Palmeiro	2.00
19	Randy Johnson	2.00
20	Roger Clemens	6.00
21	Sammy Sosa	4.00
22	Scott Rolen	2.00
23	Tim Hudson	1.50
24	Todd Helton	1.50
25	Vladimir Guerrero	2.00

Fans of the Game

	NM/M
Complete Set (5):	10.00

1	Jesse Ventura	3.00
2	John C. McGinley	2.00
3	Susie Essman	2.00
4	Dean Cain	2.00
5	Meat Loaf	3.00

Fans of the Game Signatures

		NM/M
1	Jesse Ventura	50.00
2	John C. McGinley/SP/300	50.00
3	Susie Essman	60.00
4	Dean Cain/SP/250	90.00
5	Meat Loaf	60.00

Jersey Kings

		NM/M
Common Player:		5.00
1	Garret Anderson/250	5.00
2	Vladimir Guerrero/250	8.00
3	Cal Ripken Jr./100	50.00
4	Manny Ramirez/250	8.00
5	Kerry Wood/250	10.00
6	Sammy Sosa/250	12.00
7	Magglio Ordonez/250	5.00
8	Adam Dunn/250	8.00
9	Todd Helton/250	8.00
10	Josh Beckett/250	5.00
11	Miguel Cabrera/250	8.00
12	Lance Berkman/250	8.00
13	Carlos Beltran/250	8.00
14	Shawn Green/250	8.00
15	Roger Clemens/250	15.00
16	Mike Piazza/250	10.00
17	Nolan Ryan/250	50.00
18	Mark Mulder/250	5.00
19	Jim Thome/250	8.00
20	Albert Pujols/250	20.00
21	Scott Rolen/250	10.00
22	Aubrey Huff/250	5.00
23	Alfonso Soriano/250	8.00
24	Hank Blalock/250	8.00
25	Vernon Wells/250	5.00

Jersey Kings Signatures

No Pricing
Production 5 or 10

Longball Leaders

		NM/M
Complete Set (15):		30.00
Common Player:		2.00
Black:		1-2X
Production 250 Sets		
Die-Cut:		2-3X
Production 50 Sets		
Black Die-Cut:		No Pricing
Production 10 Sets		
1	Adam Dunn	3.00
2	Adrian Beltre	3.00
3	Albert Pujols	6.00
4	Alex Rodriguez	5.00
5	David Ortiz	3.00
6	Hank Blalock	3.00
7	J.D. Drew	2.00
8	Jeromy Burnitz	2.00
9	Jim Edmonds	2.50
10	Jim Thome	3.00
11	Manny Ramirez	3.00
12	Mark Teixeira	2.00
13	Moises Alou	2.00
14	Paul Konerko	2.00
15	Steve Finley	2.00

Mound Marvels

		NM/M
Complete Set (15):		40.00
Common Player:		2.00
Production 1,000 Sets		
Black:		No Pricing
Production 10 Sets		
1	Curt Schilling	4.00
2	Dontrelle Willis	2.00
3	Eric Gagne	4.00
4	Greg Maddux	6.00
5	John Smoltz	3.00
6	Kenny Rogers	2.00
7	Kerry Wood	4.00
8	Mariano Rivera	3.00
9	Mark Mulder	2.00

10	Mark Prior	4.00
11	Mike Mussina	3.00
12	Pedro Martinez	4.00
13	Randy Johnson	4.00
14	Roger Clemens	8.00
15	Tim Hudson	2.00

Power Alley Red

MIKE PIAZZA

NM/M

Common Player:		1.50
Production 2,500 Sets		
Black:		No Pricing
Production 10 Sets		
Black Die-Cut:		No Pricing
Production 5 Sets		
Blue:		1X
Production 1,000 Sets		
Blue Die-Cut:		2-3X
Production 100 Sets		
Green:		3-5X
Production 25 Sets		
Green Die-Cut:		No Pricing
Production 10 Sets		
Purple:		1-2X
Production 250 Sets		
Purple Die-Cut:		2-3X
Production 50 Sets		
Red Die-Cut:		1-2X
Production 250 Sets		
Yellow:		2-3X
Production 100 Sets		
Yellow Die-Cut:		3-5X
Production 25 Sets		
1	Adam Dunn	2.00
2	Adrian Beltre	2.00
3	Albert Pujols	6.00
4	Alex Rodriguez	5.00
5	Alfonso Soriano	3.00
6	Gary Sheffield	2.00
7	Hank Blalock	2.00
8	Hideki Matsui	4.00
9	J.D. Drew	1.50
10	Jeromy Burnitz	1.50
11	Jim Edmonds	2.00
12	Jim Thome	3.00
13	Ken Griffey Jr.	3.00
14	Manny Ramirez	2.00
15	Mark Teixeira	1.50
16	Miguel Cabrera	2.00
17	Miguel Tejada	2.00
18	Mike Lowell	1.50
19	Mike Piazza	3.00
20	Moises Alou	1.50
21	Paul Konerko	1.50
22	Sammy Sosa	4.00
23	Scott Rolen	3.00
24	Todd Helton	2.00
25	Vladimir Guerrero	3.00

Production Line BA

NM/M

Common Player:		3.00
Black:		2-3X
Production 25 Sets		
Die-Cut:		1X
Production 100 Sets		
Black Die-Cut:		No Pricing
Production 10 Sets		
1	Ichiro Suzuki/372	8.00
2	Ivan Rodriguez/334	5.00
3	Juan Pierre/326	3.00
4	Adrian Beltre/334	5.00
5	Albert Pujols/331	10.00
6	Mark Loretta/335	3.00
7	Melvin Mora/340	3.00
8	Sean Casey/324	3.00
9	Todd Helton/347	5.00
10	Vladimir Guerrero/337	5.00

Production Line OBP

NM/M

Common Player:		3.00
Black:		2-3X
Production 25 Sets		

Die-Cut:		1X
Production 100 Sets		
Black Die-Cut:		No Pricing
Production 10 Sets		
1	Albert Pujols/415	8.00
2	Bobby Abreu/428	3.00
3	Lance Berkman/450	3.00
4	J.D. Drew/436	3.00
5	Jorge Posada/400	4.00
6	Ichiro Suzuki/414	8.00
7	Manny Ramirez/397	4.00
8	Melvin Mora/419	3.00
9	Todd Helton/469	4.00
10	Travis Hafner/410	3.00

Production Line OPS

NM/M

Common Player:		3.00
Black:		1.5-2X
Production 50 Sets		
Die-Cut:		1X
Production 100 Sets		
Black Die-Cut:		2-3X
Production 25 Sets		
1	Albert Pujols/1072	8.00
2	Bobby Abreu/983	4.00
3	Lance Berkman/1017	4.00
4	J.D. Drew/1006	3.00
5	Jorge Posada/977	4.00
6	Ichiro Suzuki/1016	3.00
7	Manny Ramirez/1009	4.00
8	Melvin Mora/1007	4.00
9	Todd Helton/1088	4.00
10	Travis Hafner/993	3.00

Production Line Slugging

ADRIAN BELTRE

.629

NM/M

Common Player:		3.00
Black:		1.5-2X
Production 50 Sets		
Die-Cut:		1X
Production 100 Sets		
Black Die-Cut:		2-3X
Production 25 Sets		
1	Adrian Beltre/629	4.00
2	Albert Pujols/657	8.00
3	Todd Helton/620	4.00
4	J.D. Drew/569	3.00
5	Jim Edmonds/643	3.00
6	Jim Thome/581	4.00
7	Vladimir Guerrero/598	4.00
8	Manny Ramirez/613	4.00
9	Scott Rolen/598	4.00
10	Travis Hafner/583	3.00

Rookies

NM/M

Common Player:		2.00
Inserted 1:23		
Black:		No Pricing
Production 10 Sets		
Blue:		1X
Production 100 Sets		
Gold:		2-3X
Production 25 Sets		
Red:		.75-1X
Production 200 Sets		
1	Fernando Nieve	2.00
2	Frankie Francisco	2.00
3	Jorge Vasquez	2.00
4	Travis Blackley	2.00
5	Joey Gathright	4.00
6	Kazuhito Tadano	2.00
7	Edwin Moreno	2.00
8	Lance Cormier	2.00
9	Justin Knoedler	2.00
10	Orlando Rodriguez	2.00
11	Renyel Pinto	2.00
12	Justin Leone	2.00
13	Dennis Sarfate	2.00
14	Sam Narron	2.00
15	Yadier Molina	4.00
16	Carlos Vasquez	2.00

17	Ryan Wing	2.00
18	Brad Halsey	2.00
19	Ryan Meaux	2.00
20	Mike Wuertz	2.00
21	Shawn Camp	2.00
22	Ruddy Yan	2.00
23	Donald Kelly	2.00
24	Jake Woods	2.00
25	Colby Miller	2.00
26	Abe Alvarez	2.00
27	Mike Rouse	2.00
28	Phil Stockman	2.00
29	Kevin Cave	2.00
30	Chris Shelton	4.00
31	Tim Bittner	2.00
32	Mariano Gomez	2.00
33	Angel Chavez	2.00
34	Carlos Hines	2.00
35	Aarom Baldiris	2.00
36	Kazuo Matsui	5.00
37	Nick Regilio	2.00
38	Ivan Ochoa	2.00
39	Graham Koonce	2.00
40	Merkin Valdez	3.00
41	Greg Dobbs	2.00
42	Chris Oxspring	2.00
43	David Crouthers	2.00
44	Freddy Guzman	2.00
45	Akinori Otsuka	3.00
46	Jesse Crain	2.00
47	Casey Daigle	2.00
48	Roberto Novoa	2.00
49	Eddy Rodriguez	2.00
50	Jason Bartlett	2.00

Rookies Autographs

NM/M

Common Autographs:		5.00
1	Fernando Nieve	5.00
2	Frankie Francisco	5.00
3	Jorge Vasquez	5.00
4	Travis Blackley	5.00
5	Joey Gathright	8.00
6	Edwin Moreno	5.00
7	Lance Cormier	5.00
9	Justin Knoedler	5.00
10	Orlando Rodriguez	5.00
11	Renyel Pinto	5.00
13	Dennis Sarfate	5.00
15	Yadier Molina	10.00
16	Carlos Vasquez	8.00
17	Ryan Wing/SP	10.00
18	Brad Halsey	8.00
19	Ryan Meaux	5.00
20	Mike Wuertz	5.00
22	Ruddy Yan	5.00
23	Donald Kelly	5.00
24	Jake Woods	5.00
25	Colby Miller	5.00
26	Abe Alvarez	5.00
27	Mike Rouse/SP	8.00
28	Phil Stockman	5.00
29	Kevin Cave	5.00
30	Chris Shelton/SP	10.00
31	Tim Bittner	5.00
32	Mariano Gomez	5.00
33	Angel Chavez	5.00
34	Carlos Hines	5.00
35	Aarom Baldiris	5.00
37	Nick Regilio	5.00
38	Ivan Ochoa	5.00
39	Graham Koonce	5.00
42	Chris Oxspring	5.00
43	David Crouthers	5.00
48	Roberto Novoa	5.00
49	Eddy Rodriguez	5.00
50	Jason Bartlett	5.00

Rookies Stat Line Career

Print run 201-316:	1X
Print run 101-200:	1X
Print run 51-100:	1-1.5X
Print run 26-50:	1-2X
Print run 25 or less:	No Pricing

Cards are numbered to career statistic.

Rookies Stat Line Season

Print run 101-200:	1X
Print run 51-100:	1-1.5X
Print run 26-50:	1-2X
Print run 25 or less:	No Pricing

Cards are numbered to season statistic.

Timber and Threads Bat

NM/M

Common Player:		5.00
1	Albert Pujols	15.00
2	Alfonso Soriano	8.00
3	Andre Dawson	8.00

4	Austin Kearns	5.00
5	Brad Penny	5.00
6	Carlos Beltran	8.00
7	Carlos Lee	5.00
8	Chipper Jones	8.00
9	Dale Murphy	8.00
10	Don Mattingly	20.00
11	Frank Thomas	8.00
12	Garret Anderson	5.00
13	Gary Carter	8.00
14	Hank Blalock	5.00
15	Jacque Jones	5.00
17	Jay Gibbons	5.00
18	Jeff Bagwell	8.00
20	Jermaine Dye	5.00
21	Jim Thome	8.00
22	Jose Vidro	5.00
23	Lance Berkman	5.00
24	Laynce Nix	5.00
25	Magglio Ordonez	5.00
26	Marcus Giles	5.00
27	Mark Prior	10.00
28	Mark Teixeira	5.00
29	Melvin Mora	5.00
30	Michael Young	5.00
31	Miguel Cabrera	8.00
32	Mike Lowell	5.00
33	Roy Oswalt	5.00
34	Sammy Sosa	10.00
35	Scott Rolen	10.00
36	Sean Burroughs	5.00
37	Sean Casey	5.00
38	Shannon Stewart	5.00
39	Torii Hunter	5.00
40	Travis Hafner	5.00

Timber and Threads Bat Signature

No Pricing
Production 5 or 10

Timber and Threads Combo

NM/M

1	Albert Pujols/Bat-Jsy	25.00
2	Alfonso Soriano/Bat-Jsy	10.00
3	Andre Dawson/Bat-Jsy	8.00
4	Austin Kearns/Bat-Jsy	8.00
5	Brad Penny/Bat-Jsy	6.00
6	Carlos Beltran/Bat-Jsy	12.00
7	Carlos Lee/Bat-Jsy	6.00
8	Chipper Jones/Bat-Jsy	12.00
9	Dale Murphy/Bat-Jsy	10.00
10	Don Mattingly/Bat-Jsy	25.00
11	Frank Thomas/Bat-Jsy	12.00
12	Garret Anderson/Bat-Jsy	8.00
13	Gary Carter/Bat-Jsy	10.00
14	Hank Blalock/Bat-Jsy	10.00
15	Jacque Jones/Bat-Jsy	6.00
17	Jay Gibbons/Bat-Jsy	6.00
18	Jeff Bagwell/Bat-Jsy	12.00
20	Jermaine Dye/Bat-Jsy	6.00
21	Jim Thome/Bat-Jsy	12.00
22	Jose Vidro/Bat-Jsy	6.00
23	Lance Berkman/Bat-Jsy	6.00
24	Laynce Nix/Bat-Jsy	6.00
25	Magglio Ordonez/Bat-Jsy	8.00
26	Marcus Giles/Bat-Jsy	6.00
27	Mark Prior/Bat-Jsy	15.00
28	Mark Teixeira/Bat-Jsy	8.00
29	Melvin Mora/Bat-Jsy	

		NM/M
30	Michael Young/Bat-Jsy	8.00
31	Miguel Cabrera/Bat-Jsy	12.00
32	Mike Lowell/Bat-Jsy	8.00
33	Roy Oswalt/Bat-Jsy	8.00
34	Sammy Sosa/Bat-Jsy	15.00
35	Scott Rolen/Bat-Jsy	15.00
36	Sean Burroughs/Bat-Jsy	6.00
37	Sean Casey/Bat-Jsy	6.00
38	Shannon Stewart/Bat-Jsy	6.00
39	Torii Hunter/Bat-Jsy	8.00
40	Travis Hafner/Bat-Jsy	8.00

Timber and Threads Combo Signture

No Pricing
Production 5 or 10

Timber and Threads Jersey

		NM/M
	Common Player:	5.00
1	Albert Pujols	15.00
2	Alfonso Soriano	8.00
4	Austin Kearns	5.00
5	Brad Penny	5.00
6	Carlos Beltran	8.00
7	Carlos Lee	5.00
8	Dale Murphy	8.00
10	Don Mattingly	25.00
11	Frank Thomas	8.00
12	Garret Anderson	5.00
13	Gary Carter	8.00
14	Hank Blalock	8.00
15	Jacque Jones	5.00
17	Jay Gibbons	5.00
18	Jeff Bagwell	8.00
19	Jeremy Bonderman	5.00
20	Jermaine Dye	5.00
21	Jim Thome	8.00
22	Jose Vidro	5.00
23	Lance Berkman	5.00
24	Laynce Nix	5.00
25	Magglio Ordonez	5.00
26	Marcus Giles	5.00
27	Mark Prior	10.00
28	Mark Teixeira	5.00
29	Melvin Mora	5.00
30	Michael Young	5.00
31	Miguel Cabrera	8.00
32	Mike Lowell	5.00
33	Roy Oswalt	5.00
34	Sammy Sosa	10.00
35	Scott Rolen	10.00
36	Sean Burroughs	5.00
37	Sean Casey	5.00
38	Shannon Stewart	5.00
39	Torii Hunter	5.00
40	Travis Hafner	5.00

Timber and Threads Jersey Signature

No Pricing
Production 5 or 10

2005 Donruss Champions

		NM/M
	Complete Set (450):	
	Common Player:	.25
	Pack (8):	3.75
	Box (24):	75.00
1	Adam Dunn	.50
2	Albert Pujols	2.00
3	Albert Pujols	2.00
4	Ichiro Suzuki	1.50
5	Alex Rodriguez	2.00
6	Andruw Jones	.50
7	Carlos Beltran	.50
8	Derek Lee	.50
9	Hideki Matsui	1.50
10	Ichiro Suzuki	1.50
11	Ichiro Suzuki	1.50
12	Jeff Kent	.25
13	Ken Griffey Jr.	1.50
14	Ken Griffey Jr.	1.50
15	Sammy Sosa	1.00
16	Sean Casey	.25
17	Troy Glaus	.40
18	Derek Jeter	2.00
19	Cal Ripken Jr.	2.00
20	Roberto Alomar	.40
21	B.J. Surhoff	.25
22	Brian Jordan	.25
23	Corey Koskie	.25
24	Doug Davis	.25
25	Jason Varitek	.50
26	Jim Edmonds	.25
27	Kevin Mench	.25
28	Roberto Alomar	.40
29	Tony Armas Jr.	.25
30	Ramon Ortiz	.25
31	Rodrigo Lopez	.25
32	Andres Galarraga	.25
33	Brian Lawrence	.25
34	Jay Payton	.25
35	Ryan Ludwick	.25
36	Hee Seop Choi	.25
37	J.D. Drew	.25
38	Raul Mondesi	.25
39	Brian Jordan	.25
40	Luis Matos	.25
41	Russell Branyan	.25
42	Tony Gwynn	.75
43	Francisco Rodriguez	.25
44	Frank Robinson	.75
45	Jeff Bagwell	.50
46	Tony Gwynn	.75
47	Tony Gwynn	.75
48	Will Clark	.50
49	Antonio Perez	.25
50	Rickey Henderson	.50
51	Brian Lawrence	.25
52	Carlos Beltran	.50
53	Chris Snelling	.25
54	Darryl Strawberry	.25
55	Doug Mientkiewicz	.25
56	Edgardo Alfonzo	.25
57	Eric Chavez	.25
58	Eric Davis	.25
59	Guillermo Quiroz	.25
60	J.D. Drew	.25
61	J.D. Drew	.25
62	Walter Young	.25
63	John Kruk	.25
64	Jose Reyes	.50
65	Jose Vidro	.25
66	Josh Phelps	.25
67	Larry Walker	.25
68	Lyle Overbay	.25
69	Manny Ramirez	.75
70	Marlon Byrd	.25
71	Matt Williams	.25
72	Melvin Mora	.25
73	Nook Logan	.25
74	Orlando Hudson	.25
75	Orlando Hudson	.25
76	Orlando Hudson	.25
77	Paul Konerko	.50
78	Raul Mondesi	.25
79	Reed Johnson	.25
80	Ryan Ludwick	.25
81	So Taguchi	.25
82	Toby Hall	.25
83	Todd Helton	.50
84	Tommy John	.25
85	Tony Clark	.25
86	Victor Martinez	.40
87	Vladimir Guerrero	.75
88	Wade Boggs	.40
89	Roberto Clemente	1.50
90	Angel Berroa	.25
91	Terrmel Sledge	.25
92	Andres Galarraga	.25
93	Brooks Robinson	.50
94	Brooks Robinson	.50
95	Dennis Tankersley	.25
96	Don Mattingly	1.00
97	Ricardo Rodriguez	.25
98	Deivi Cruz	.25
99	Deivi Cruz	.25
100	Pete LaForest	.25
101	Roger Clemens	2.00
102	Frankie Francisco	.25
103	Kevin Millwood	.25
104	Tony Womack	.25
105	Jeff Bagwell	.50
106	Billy Martin	.25
107	J.T. Snow	.25
108	Juan Uribe	.25
109	Ryan Dempster	.25
110	Toby Hall	.25
111	Dennis Tankersley	.25
112	Freddy Garcia	.25
113	Garrett Atkins	.25
114	Troy Glaus	.40
115	Gabe Kapler	.25
116	Jeff Kent	.25
117	Rondell White	.25
118	C.C. Sabathia	.25
119	Javier Vazquez	.25
120	Mike Cameron	.25
121	Pat Burrell	.25
122	Lew Ford	.25
123	Brad Radke	.25
124	Preston Wilson	.25
125	Ray Durham	.25
126	Vernon Wells	.25
127	Bo Jackson	.50
128	Dmitri Young	.25
129	Doug Davis	.25
130	Brandon Duckworth	.25
131	Brandon Backe	.25
132	Juan Encarnacion	.25
133	Mike Maroth	.25
134	Sean Casey	.25
135	Travis Hafner	.40
136	Wes Helms	.25
137	Randy Johnson	.75
138	Larry Walker	.25
139	Luis Gonzalez	.25
140	John Olerud	.25
141	Kazuhisa Ishii	.25
142	Mike Lowell	.25
143	Kevin Millwood	.25
144	Chad Gaudin	.25
145	Bret Boone	.25
146	Cliff Floyd	.25
147	Dale Murphy	.25
148	Rickey Henderson	.50
149	Ricardo Rodriguez	.25
150	Richard Hidalgo	.25
151	Joe Kennedy	.25
152	Juan Pierre	.25
153	Juan Pierre RC	.25
154	Lance Berkman	.50
155	Joe Borchard	.25
156	Craig Monroe	.25
157	Abraham Nunez	.25
158	Willie Wilson	.25
159	Carlos Lee	.25
160	Carl Everett	.25
161	Frank White	.25
162	Craig Biggio	.40
163	Jason Varitek	.50
164	Magglio Ordonez	.25
165	Carlos Delgado	.50
166	Casey Kotchman	.25
167	Kenny Lofton	.25
168	Gil Hodges	.25
169	Rafael Furcal	.25
170	Ramon Vazquez	.25
171	Jeff Bagwell	.50
172	Jason Lane	.25
173	Nomar Garciaparra	.75
174	Willie Harris	.25
175	Adam Dunn	.50
176	Jose Cruz Jr.	.25
177	Robin Ventura	.25
178	Al Oliver	.25
179	Wily Mo Pena	.25
180	Erubiel Durazo	.25
181	Joey Gathright	.25
182	Luis Castillo	.25
183	Mark Teixeira	.50
184	Delmon Young	.25
185	Esteban Loaiza	.25
186	Bo Jackson	.50
187	Freddy Sanchez	.25
188	Jason Bay	.50
189	Rickey Henderson	.50
190	Shawn Green	.25
191	Roger Cedeno	.25
192	Hideki Matsui	1.50
193	Andruw Jones	.50
194	David Wright	1.00
195	Cesar Izturis	.25
196	Chipper Jones	.75
197	Troy Glaus	.40
198	Cliff Floyd	.25
199	Jason Jennings	.25
200	Mike Lowell	.25
201	Johnny Damon	.75
202	Aramis Ramirez	.40
203	John Smoltz	.40
204	Alan Trammell	.25
205	Moises Alou	.25
206	Randy Johnson	.75
207	Reggie Sanders	.25
208	Rickey Henderson	.50
209	Runelvys Hernandez	.25
210	Ryan Klesko	.25
211	Casey Fossum	.25
212	Robert Fick	.25
213	Al Oliver	.25
214	Kazuo Matsui	.25
215	Pedro Martinez	.75
216	Roberto Alomar	.50
217	Greg Maddux	1.50
218	Mark Ellis	.25
219	Shawn Green	.25
220	Shawn Green	.25
221	Willie McCovey	.50
222	Rafael Furcal	.25
223	Richie Ashburn	.25
224	Edgar Martinez	.25
225	Carlos Delgado	.25
226	David Justice	.25
227	Jose Cruz	.25
228	Larry Walker	.25
229	Miguel Tejada	.50
230	Andres Galarraga	.25
231	Trot Nixon	.25
232	Willie Mays	1.50
233	Dennis Eckersley	.25
234	Michael Barrett	.25
235	Jose Cruz Jr.	.25
236	Nolan Ryan	2.00
237	Hal Newhouser	.25
238	Roger Clemens	2.00
239	Victor Martinez	.40
240	Sean Burroughs	.25
241	Andres Galarraga	.25
242	Cal Ripken Jr.	2.00
243	Doug Mientkiewicz	.25
244	Hank Aaron	2.00
245	Vladimir Guerrero	.75
246	Reggie Jackson	.75
247	Terrence Long	.25
248	Tommy Lasorda	.25
249	Bert Blyleven	.25
250	Ken Boyer	.25
251	Maury Wills	.25
252	Lou Brock	.25
253	Don Sutton	.25
254	Enos Slaughter	.25
255	Ernie Banks	.75
256	Gaylord Perry	.25
257	Joe Carter	.25
258	Keith Hernandez	.25
259	Orlando Cabrera	.25
260	Phil Niekro	.25
261	Robin Ventura	.25
262	Rod Carew	.50
263	Rollie Fingers	.25
264	Sammy Sosa	1.00
265	Byung-Hyun Kim	.25
266	Zach Day	.25
267	Richie Ashburn	.25
268	Mike Piazza	1.00
269	Tommy John	.25
270	Craig Biggio	.50
271	Hideki Matsui	1.50
272	Cesar Izturis	.25
273	Paul Molitor	.50
274	Steve Carlton	.50
275	Justin Morneau	.50
276	Albert Pujols	2.00
277	John Olerud	.25
278	Austin Kearns	.25
279	Travis Hafner	.40
280	Charles Johnson	.25
281	Craig Wilson	.25
282	Joe Carter	.25
283	Josh Beckett	.40
284	Dale Murphy	.25
285	Robert Fick	.25
286	David Justice	.25
287	Kirby Puckett	.75
288	Juan Encarnacion	.25
289	Moises Alou	.25
290	Shannon Stewart	.25
291	Alfonso Soriano	.75
292	Jacque Jones	.25
293	Pee Wee Reese	.50
294	Deion Sanders	.50
295	Richard Hidalgo	.25
296	Rocco Baldelli	.25
297	Bill Hall	.25
298	Mike Sweeney	.25
299	Paul Molitor	.50
300	Will Clark	.50
301	Torii Hunter	.40
302	Jim Thome	.75
303	Kevin Mench	.25
304	John Buck	.25
305	Joe Morgan	.25
306	Wilson Betemit	.25
307	Ivan Rodriguez	.50
308	Michael Young	.25
309	Moises Alou	.25
310	So Taguchi	.25
311	Rickey Henderson	.50
312	Kenny Lofton	.25
313	Rickey Henderson	.50
314	Shannon Stewart	.25
315	Fred Lynn	.25
316	Mark Prior	.50
317	Tony Perez	.25
318	Dontrelle Willis	.25
319	Xavier Nady	.25
320	Juan Uribe	.25
321	Chipper Jones	.75
322	Joe Crede	.25
323	Kerry Wood	.40
324	Eric Hinske	.25
325	Carlos Lee	.25
326	Joe Borchard	.25
327	Sean Casey	.25

328	Joe Kennedy	.25
329	Brandon Duckworth	.25
330	Willie Mays	1.50
331	Andruw Jones	.50
332	Brandon Claussen	.25
333	Brandon Claussen	.25
334	Brian Giles	.25
335	Gary Sheffield	.40
336	Mark Grace	.40
337	Ryne Sandberg	.75
338	Sammy Sosa	1.00
339	Steve Carlton	.25
340	Vernon Wells	.40
341	Wade Miller	.25
342	Andre Dawson	.25
343	Darryl Strawberry	.25
344	Nolan Ryan	2.00
345	Curt Schilling	.75
346	Bo Jackson	.50
347	Darin Erstad	.50
348	Alfonso Soriano	.75
349	A.J. Burnett	.25
350	David Ortiz	.75
351	George Foster	.25
352	Rafael Palmeiro	.50
353	Alan Trammell	.25
354	Willie Mays	1.50
355	Bernie Williams	.50
356	Phil Niekro	.25
357	Hank Blalock	.40
358	Miguel Cabrera	.75
359	Carl Yastrzemski	.75
360	Aramis Ramirez	.40
361	Frank Thomas	.75
362	Tony Oliva	.25
363	Roger Clemens	2.00
364	Adam Loewen	.25
365	Alex Cintron	.25
366	Alfredo Simon	.25
367	Angel Guzman	.25
368	Anthony Lerew	.25
369	Ben Hendrickson	.25
370	Brandon McCarthy RC	1.50
371	Bubba Nelson	.25
372	Clint Nageotte	.25
373	Eddy Rodriguez	.25
374	Edwin Moreno	.25
375	J.J. Putz	.25
376	Jake Woods	.25
377	Jeff Suppan	.25
378	Jeremy Affeldt	.25
379	Jose Castillo	.25
380	Justin Leone	.25
381	Justin Verlander RC	4.00
382	Marlon Byrd	.25
383	Mike Gosling	.25
384	Prince Fielder	5.00
385	Randy Wolf	.25
386	Raul Ibanez	.25
387	Raul Tablado RC	.50
388	Rick Dempsey	.25
389	Roberto Novoa	.25
390	Russ Ortiz	.25
391	Ryan Wing	.25
392	Scot Shields	.25
393	Steve Stone	.25
394	Tadahito Iguchi RC	1.50
395	Todd Wellemeyer	.25
396	Travis Blackley	.25
397	Troy Percival	.25
398	Wilson Valdez	.25
399	Kevin Youkilis	.25
400	Jose Guillen	.25
401	Duke Snider	.25
402	Jeff Niemann RC	1.00
403	Johan Santana	.50
404	Nellie Fox	.25
405	Nellie Fox	.25
406	Marlon Byrd	.25
407	Mike Piazza	1.00
408	Bobby Higginson	.25
409	Don Mattingly	1.00
410	Jayson Werth	.25
411	Al Kaline	.50
412	Bobby Higginson	.25
413	Roger Cedeno	.25
414	Roger Cedeno	.25
415	Roger Cedeno	.25
416	Roger Cedeno	.25
417	Roger Cedeno	.25
418	Magglio Ordonez	.25
419	Don Mattingly	1.00
420	Morgan Ensberg	.25
421	Charles Johnson	.25
422	Albert Pujols	2.00
423	Dave Righetti	.25
424	Roy Halladay	.50
425	Tom Seaver	.75
426	Early Wynn	.25
427	Bob Gibson	.50
428	Doug Mientkiewicz	.25
429	Jason Varitek	.50
430	Tom Glavine	.25
431	Erik Bedard	.25
432	Pedro Martinez	.75
433	David Ortiz	.75
434	Kazuhisa Ishii	.25
435	Trevor Hoffman	.25
436	Paul Molitor	.50
437	Derrek Lee	.50
438	Fergie Jenkins	.25
439	Tony Gwynn	.75
440	Jeff Bagwell	.50
441	Steve Carlton	.25
442	Adam Dunn	.25
443	Sean Casey	.25
444	Geoff Jenkins	.25
445	Derek Jeter	2.00
446	J.T. Snow	.25
447	Kenny Lofton	.25
448	Benito Santiago	.25
449	Tim Salmon	.25
450	Ichiro Suzuki	1.50

Press Plates
No Pricing
Production one set per color.

Impressions
Stars: 1.5-3X
Inserted 1:3

Impressions Black
No Pricing
Production 5 Sets

Impressions Blue
Stars: 2-4X
Production 100 Sets

Impressions Gold
Stars: 3-5X
Production 50 Sets

Impressions Green
No Pricing
Production 25 Sets

Impressions Orange
Stars: 2-4X
Production 75 Sets

Impressions Red
Stars: 1.5-2X
Production 250 Sets

Impressions Autograph
NM/M

Tier 1 Production 101-250
Tier 2 Production 251-500
Tier 3 Production 501-800
Tier 4 Production 801-1,200
Tier 5 Production 1,201-1,500
Cards are not serial numbered.

19	Cal Ripken Jr./65	140.00
42	Tony Gwynn/65	35.00
44	Frank Robinson/59	25.00
46	Tony Gwynn/65	35.00
47	Tony Gwynn/65	35.00
206	Randy Johnson/62	65.00
242	Cal Ripken Jr./25	160.00
262	Rod Carew/37	25.00
279	Travis Hafner/49	20.00
297	Bill Hall/52	10.00
322	Joe Crede/34	20.00
364	Adam Loewen T1	10.00
365	Alex Cintron T1	10.00
366	Alfredo Simon T2	8.00
367	Angel Guzman T2	8.00
369	Ben Hendrickson T3	8.00
371	Bubba Nelson T2	8.00
372	Clint Nageotte T2	8.00
373	Eddy Rodriguez/89	8.00
374	Edwin Moreno/55	10.00
375	J.J. Putz T3	8.00
376	Jake Woods T1	8.00
377	Jeff Suppan T4	12.00
378	Jeremy Affeldt T1	8.00
379	Jose Castillo T1	8.00
380	Justin Leone T2	8.00
382	Marlon Byrd T1	10.00
383	Mike Gosling/93	8.00
385	Randy Wolf T1	10.00
386	Raul Ibanez T1	10.00
387	Raul Tablado/74	10.00
388	Rick Dempsey T4	10.00
389	Roberto Novoa T2	8.00
390	Russ Ortiz/49	15.00
391	Ryan Wing T1	8.00
392	Scot Shields T5	8.00
393	Steve Stone/65	15.00
395	Todd Wellemeyer/92	10.00
396	Travis Blackley/87	8.00
397	Troy Percival T1	10.00
398	Wilson Valdez T5	8.00
399	Kevin Youkilis T2	20.00
401	Duke Snider/30	35.00
402	Jeff Niemann/77	15.00
403	Johan Santana/29	40.00
423	Dave Righetti T1	15.00
425	Tom Seaver/28	40.00

Impressions Ball
NM/M

Production 1-100

55	Doug Mientkiewicz/25	8.00
57	Eric Chavez/45	5.00
175	Adam Dunn/25	10.00
192	Hideki Matsui/40	40.00
193	Andruw Jones/30	10.00
197	Troy Glaus/78	8.00
276	Albert Pujols/76	20.00
277	John Olerud/53	5.00
286	David Justice/30	8.00
292	Jacque Jones/37	5.00
301	Torii Hunter/55	8.00
316	Mark Prior/31	8.00
348	Alfonso Soriano/75	8.00
350	David Ortiz/100	10.00
352	Rafael Palmeiro/65	8.00
390	Russ Ortiz/50	5.00

Impressions Batting Glove
NM/M

Production 44-145

306	Wilson Betemit/145	5.00
320	Juan Uribe/125	5.00
322	Joe Crede/89	8.00
325	Carlos Lee/71	8.00
334	Brian Giles/44	8.00
419	Don Mattingly/125	15.00

Impressions Button
No Pricing
Production 1-16

Impressions Combos
NM/M

Production 1-210
Prime: .75-2X
Production 1-50

302A	Jim Thome/105	8.00
302B	Jim Thome/45	10.00
303	Kevin Mench/175	5.00
304	John Buck/150	5.00
305	Joe Morgan/80	8.00
306A	Wilson Betemit/210	5.00
306B	Wilson Betemit/65	8.00
307A	Ivan Rodriguez/175	8.00
307B	Ivan Rodriguez/35	10.00
308A	Michael Young/180	8.00
308B	Michael Young/50	8.00
310	So Taguchi/150	5.00
311	Rickey Henderson/40	15.00
312	Kenny Lofton/1	
313	Rickey Henderson/85	15.00
315A	Fred Lynn/60	5.00
316A	Mark Prior/53	8.00
317	Tony Perez/62	5.00
319A	Xavier Nady/50	5.00
320	Juan Uribe/59	8.00
322A	Joe Crede/190	8.00
322B	Joe Crede/40	10.00
323A	Kerry Wood/33	8.00
324A	Eric Hinske/132	5.00
325A	Carlos Lee/52	8.00
326A	Joe Borchard/57	5.00
332A	Brandon Claussen/165	8.00
334A	Brian Giles/90	8.00
342A	Andre Dawson/165	8.00
342B	Andre Dawson/50	10.00
343	Darryl Strawberry/73	8.00
345	Curt Schilling/89	10.00
350A	David Ortiz/53	15.00
352	Rafael Palmeiro/201	8.00
355	Bernie Williams/43	8.00
357	Hank Blalock/47	5.00
359	Carl Yastrzemski/73	15.00
362	Tony Oliva/93	8.00

Impressions Fielding Glove
NM/M

Production 26-250

317	Tony Perez/49	10.00
319	Xavier Nady/97	5.00
321	Chipper Jones/26	30.00
328	Joe Kennedy/130	5.00
331	Andruw Jones/82	10.00
332	Brandon Claussen/250	5.00
336	Mark Grace/186	10.00
337	Ryne Sandberg/64	20.00
339	Steve Carlton/86	8.00
341	Wade Miller/117	5.00
420	Morgan Ensberg/87	5.00

Impressions Hat
NM/M

Production 1-250

313	Rickey Henderson/219	10.00
314	Shannon Stewart/250	5.00
316	Mark Prior/250	8.00
329	Brandon Duckworth/157	5.00
332	Brandon Claussen/250	5.00
340	Vernon Wells/26	5.00

Impressions Material
NM/M

Tier 1 Production 101-250
Tier 2 Production 251-500
Tier 3 Production 501-800
Tier 4 Production 801-1,200
Tier 5 Production 1,201-1,500
Cards are not serial numbered.
Prime: 1-2.5X
No pricing production 25 or less.

21	B.J. Surhoff T5	4.00
22	Brian Jordan T5	4.00
23	Corey Koskie T5	4.00
24	Doug Davis T5	4.00
25	Jason Varitek T5	8.00
26	Jim Edmonds/65	6.00
27	Kevin Mench T5	4.00
28	Roberto Alomar T5	4.00
29	Tony Armas Jr. T5	4.00
30	Ramon Ortiz T5	4.00
31	Rodrigo Lopez T5	4.00
32	Andres Galarraga T4	4.00
33	Brian Lawrence T5	4.00
34	Jay Payton T5	4.00
36	Hee Seop Choi T5	4.00
37	J.D. Drew T4	4.00
38	Raul Mondesi T4	4.00
39	Brian Jordan T4	4.00
40	Luis Matos T5	4.00
41	Russell Branyan T4	4.00
42	Tony Gwynn T4	8.00
43	Francisco Rodriguez T4	4.00
44	Frank Robinson T5	10.00
45	Jeff Bagwell T5	6.00
46	Tony Gwynn T5	8.00
47	Tony Gwynn T5	8.00
48	Will Clark T5	4.00
50	Rickey Henderson T3	10.00
51	Brian Lawrence T4	4.00
52	Carlos Beltran T5	8.00
53	Chris Snelling T5	4.00
54	Darryl Strawberry/50	6.00
55	Doug Mientkiewicz T5	4.00
56	Edgardo Alfonzo T5	4.00
57	Eric Chavez T5	6.00
58	Eric Davis T5	4.00
59	Guillermo Quiroz T5	4.00
60	J.D. Drew T5	4.00
61	J.D. Drew T5	4.00
62	Walter Young T4	4.00
63	John Kruk T5	6.00
64	Jose Reyes T5	4.00
65	Jose Vidro T5	4.00
66	Josh Phelps T5	4.00
67	Larry Walker T5	6.00
68	Lyle Overbay T5	4.00
69	Manny Ramirez T1	10.00
70	Marlon Byrd T5	4.00
71	Matt Williams T5	6.00
72	Melvin Mora T5	4.00
73	Nook Logan T5	4.00
74	Orlando Hudson T5	4.00
75	Orlando Hudson T5	4.00
76	Orlando Hudson T5	4.00
77	Paul Konerko T5	6.00
78	Raul Mondesi T4	4.00
79	Reed Johnson T5	4.00
81	So Taguchi T4	4.00
82	Toby Hall T5	4.00
83	Todd Helton T5	8.00
84	Tommy John T5	4.00
85	Tony Clark T4	4.00
86	Victor Martinez T5	6.00
87	Vladimir Guerrero/51	10.00
88	Wade Boggs T5	6.00
89	Roberto Clemente T5	35.00
90	Angel Berroa T5	4.00
91	Terrmel Sledge T5	4.00
92	Andres Galarraga T4	4.00
93	Brooks Robinson T5	10.00
94	Brooks Robinson T4	10.00
95	Dennis Tankersley T4	4.00
96	Don Mattingly T5	15.00
97	Ricardo Rodriguez T4	4.00
98	Deivi Cruz T5	4.00
99	Deivi Cruz T3	4.00
100	Pete LaForest T4	4.00
101	Rickey Henderson T3	15.00

102	Frankie Francisco T4	4.00
103	Kevin Millwood T4	4.00
104	Tony Womack T4	4.00
105	Jeff Bagwell T4	6.00
106	Billy Martin T3	8.00
107	J.T. Snow T3	4.00
108	Juan Uribe T4	4.00
109	Ryan Dempster T3	4.00
110	Toby Hall T4	4.00
111	Dennis Tankersley T3	4.00
112	Freddy Garcia T4	4.00
113	Garrett Atkins T4	4.00
114	Troy Glaus T3	4.00
115	Gabe Kapler T4	4.00
116	Jeff Kent T4	4.00
117	Rondell White T3	4.00
118	C.C. Sabathia T3	4.00
119	Javier Vazquez T4	4.00
120	Mike Cameron T3	4.00
121	Pat Burrell T3	6.00
122	Lew Ford T3	4.00
123	Brad Radke T3	4.00
124	Preston Wilson T3	4.00
125	Ray Durham T3	4.00
126	Vernon Wells T3	6.00
127	Bo Jackson T3	8.00
128	Dmitri Young T3	4.00
129	Doug Davis T3	4.00
130	Brandon Duckworth T3	4.00
131	Brandon Backe T3	4.00
132	Juan Encarnacion T3	4.00
133	Mike Maroth T3	4.00
134	Sean Casey T4	4.00
135	Travis Hafner T3	6.00
136	Wes Helms T3	4.00
137	Randy Johnson T3	8.00
138	Larry Walker T2	4.00
139	Luis Gonzalez T2	4.00
140	John Olerud T3	4.00
141	Kazuhisa Ishii T4	4.00
142	Mike Lowell T2	4.00
143	Kevin Millwood T2	4.00
144	Chad Gaudin T2	4.00
145	Bret Boone T2	4.00
146	Cliff Floyd T2	4.00
147A	Dale Murphy T3	6.00
148	Rickey Henderson T4	10.00
149	Ricardo Rodriguez T2	10.00
150	Richard Hidalgo T3	4.00
151	Joe Kennedy T4	4.00
152	Juan Pierre T4	4.00
153	Juan Pierre T4	4.00
154	Lance Berkman T4	6.00
155	Joe Borchard T4	4.00
156	Craig Monroe T4	4.00
157	Abraham Nunez T1	4.00
158	Willie Wilson T4	4.00
159	Carlos Lee T3	6.00
160	Carl Everett T4	4.00
161	Frank White T4	4.00
162	Craig Biggio T4	6.00
163	Jason Varitek T4	8.00
164	Magglio Ordonez T4	4.00
165	Carlos Delgado T4	6.00
166	Casey Kotchman T4	4.00
167	Kenny Lofton T4	4.00
168	Gil Hodges T4	15.00
169	Rafael Furcal T4	4.00
170	Ramon Vazquez T4	4.00
171	Jeff Bagwell T3	6.00
172	Jason Lane T3	4.00
173	Nomar Garciaparra T3	8.00
174	Willie Harris T3	4.00
175	Adam Dunn T3	6.00
176	Jose Cruz Jr. T3	4.00
177	Robin Ventura T3	4.00
178	Al Oliver T3	4.00
179	Wily Mo Pena T3	4.00
180	Erubiel Durazo T3	4.00
181	Joey Gathright T3	4.00
182	Luis Castillo T3	4.00
183	Mark Teixeira T3	8.00
184	Delmon Young T3	8.00
185	Esteban Loaiza T3	4.00
186	Bo Jackson T3	8.00
187	Freddy Sanchez T3	4.00
188	Jason Bay T3	6.00
189	Rickey Henderson T3	10.00
190	Shawn Green T2	4.00
191	Roger Cedeno T4	4.00
192	Hideki Matsui T3	15.00
193	Andruw Jones T3	8.00
194	David Wright T3	10.00
195	Cesar Izturis T3	4.00
196	Chipper Jones T3	8.00
197	Troy Glaus T3	6.00
198	Cliff Floyd T3	4.00
199	Jason Jennings T2	4.00
200	Mike Lowell T3	4.00
201	Johnny Damon T2	10.00
202	Aramis Ramirez T1	6.00
203	John Smoltz T2	6.00
204	Alan Trammell T2	6.00
205	Moises Alou T2	4.00
206	Randy Johnson T2	8.00
207	Reggie Sanders T2	4.00
208	Rickey Henderson T2	10.00
209	Runelvys Hernandez T2	4.00
210	Ryan Klesko T2	4.00
211	Casey Fossum T2	4.00
212	Robert Fick T2	4.00
213	Al Oliver T2	4.00
214	Kazuo Matsui T2	4.00
215	Pedro Martinez T2	8.00
216	Roberto Alomar T1	6.00
217	Greg Maddux T1	10.00
218	Mark Ellis T2	4.00
219	Shawn Green T1	4.00
220	Shawn Green T1	4.00
221	Willie McCovey T2	6.00
222	Rafael Furcal T1	4.00
223	Richie Ashburn T1	6.00
225	Carlos Delgado T2	6.00
226	David Justice T2	4.00
227	Jose Cruz T2	4.00
228	Larry Walker T1	4.00
229	Miguel Tejada T1	6.00
230	Andres Galarraga T1	4.00
231	Trot Nixon T1	6.00
232	Willie Mays T2	30.00
233	Dennis Eckersley T1	4.00
234	Michael Barrett T1	4.00
235	Jose Cruz Jr. T1	4.00
236	Nolan Ryan T1	20.00
237	Hal Newhouser T1	6.00
238	Roger Clemens T1	15.00
239	Victor Martinez/50	8.00
240	Sean Burroughs/90	4.00
241	Andres Galarraga/84	4.00
242	Cal Ripken Jr. T1	40.00
243	Doug Mientkiewicz/68	4.00
244	Hank Aaron/60	40.00
246	Reggie Jackson/35	8.00
247	Terrence Long/73	4.00
265	Byung-Hyun Kim T2	4.00
266	Zach Day T2	4.00
267	Richie Ashburn T2	6.00
268	Mike Piazza T2	10.00
269	Tommy John T1	4.00
270	Craig Biggio T1	6.00
271	Hideki Matsui T1	15.00
272	Cesar Izturis T1	4.00
273	Paul Molitor T1	8.00
274	Steve Carlton/40	4.00
275	Justin Morneau T2	6.00
276	Albert Pujols T2	15.00
277	John Olerud T2	4.00
278	Austin Kearns T2	4.00
279	Travis Hafner T2	6.00
280	Charles Johnson T2	4.00
281	Craig Wilson T2	4.00
282	Joe Carter T2	4.00
283	Josh Beckett T2	6.00
284	Dale Murphy/42	8.00
285	Robert Fick T2	4.00
286	David Justice T2	4.00
287	Kirby Puckett T2	8.00
288	Juan Encarnacion T2	4.00
289	Moises Alou T2	4.00
290	Shannon Stewart T2	4.00
291	Alfonso Soriano T2	8.00
292	Jacque Jones T2	4.00
293	Pee Wee Reese T2	8.00
294	Deion Sanders/81	8.00
295	Richard Hidalgo T2	4.00
296	Rocco Baldelli T2	4.00
297	Bill Hall T2	4.00
298	Mike Sweeney T1	4.00
299	Paul Molitor T2	8.00
300	Will Clark T1	8.00
301	Torii Hunter T1	6.00
305	Joe Morgan/95	8.00
311	Rickey Henderson T1	10.00
315	Fred Lynn/40	4.00
318	Dontrelle Willis/51	8.00
342	Andre Dawson/25	8.00
350	David Ortiz T1	8.00
351	George Foster T1	4.00
353	Alan Trammell T1	6.00
354	Willie Mays T1	30.00
355	Bernie Williams T1	6.00
356	Phil Niekro T1	6.00
357	Hank Blalock T1	4.00
358	Miguel Cabrera T1	8.00
359	Carl Yastrzemski/47	8.00
360	Aramis Ramirez/57	6.00
361	Frank Thomas T1	8.00
363	Roger Clemens/10	
404	Nellie Fox T5	6.00
405	Nellie Fox T5	6.00
406	Marlon Byrd T5	4.00
407	Mike Piazza T2	10.00
408	Bobby Higginson T4	4.00
410	Jayson Werth T5	4.00
411	Al Kaline T5	8.00
412	Bobby Higginson T3	4.00
413	Roger Cedeno T4	4.00
414	Roger Cedeno T4	4.00
415	Roger Cedeno T4	4.00
416	Roger Cedeno T4	4.00
417	Roger Cedeno T4	4.00
418	Magglio Ordonez T5	4.00
424	Roy Halladay/89	6.00
426	Early Wynn T1	6.00
427	Bob Gibson/36	6.00
428	Doug Mientkiewicz T5	4.00
429	Jason Varitek T2	8.00
430	Tom Glavine T1	6.00
431	Erik Bedard T2	4.00
432	Pedro Martinez T2	8.00
433	David Ortiz T3	8.00
434	Kazuhisa Ishii T2	4.00
435	Trevor Hoffman T2	4.00
436	Paul Molitor T1	6.00
437	Derrek Lee T1	8.00
439	Tony Gwynn T5	8.00
440	Jeff Bagwell T4	6.00

Impressions Shoe

NM/M

Production 2-226

310	So Taguchi/226	5.00
312	Kenny Lofton/103	5.00
323	Kerry Wood/89	6.00
324	Eric Hinske/133	5.00
326	Joe Borchard/200	5.00
327	Sean Casey/51	5.00
338	Sammy Sosa/75	10.00
421	Charles Johnson/196	5.00

MLB Logo Patch

No Pricing
Production 1-7

Recollection Autographs

NM/M

Production 1-319

BBR1	Brian Bruney/151	8.00
SB1	Sean Burroughs/72	8.00
MB1	Marlon Byrd/319	8.00
MB2	Marlon Byrd/25	12.00
MB3	Marlon Byrd/25	12.00
MB4	Marlon Byrd/23	12.00
MB5	Marlon Byrd/35	12.00
EC2	Eric Chavez/33	15.00
RD1	Rob Dibble/33	10.00
JD4	Jermaine Dye/33	15.00
CF2	Chone Figgins/68	15.00
JG1	Jason Giambi/25	30.00
JG2	Jason Giambi/25	30.00
JG3	Jason Giambi/25	30.00
JGI1	Jay Gibbons/27	10.00
GG1	Geronimo Gil/40	10.00
BG3	Bobby Grich/68	10.00
JGU1	Jose Guillen/35	10.00
RHA1	Rich Harden/33	10.00
DH1	Danny Haren/146	10.00
RHO1	Ryan Howard/150	200.00
THU2	Torii Hunter/72	15.00
RI1	Raul Ibanez/72	8.00
JJ2	Jacque Jones/33	15.00
PK1	Paul Konerko/33	20.00
JK1	Jason Kubel/110	10.00
BL1	Barry Larkin/33	25.00
CLE2	Cliff Lee/73	8.00
ML2	Mike Lieberthal/27	10.00
MLO1	Mike Lowell/33	10.00
BM4	Bill Madlock/35	10.00
EM3	Edgar Martinez/35	20.00
EM9	Edgar Martinez/33	20.00
WM2	Wade Miller/89	10.00
JM6	Jack Morris/74	10.00
BN1	Bubba Nelson/147	8.00
TN1	Trot Nixon/33	15.00
BO1	Ben Oglivie/44	15.00
BO2	Ben Oglivie/81	10.00
BO3	Ben Oglivie/28	15.00
BO6	Ben Oglivie/62	10.00
BO7	Ben Oglivie/132	10.00
MO4	Magglio Ordonez/33	15.00
MO5	Magglio Ordonez/33	15.00
RO1	Roy Oswalt/73	15.00
GQ1	Guillermo Quiroz/149	8.00
AR2	Aramis Ramirez/34	25.00
AR3	Aramis Ramirez/35	25.00
RR1	Ricardo Rodriguez/63	8.00
JS1	Jae Weong Seo/33	15.00
CS1	Chris Snelling/47	8.00
SS1	Shannon Stewart	10.00
JV2	Jose Vidro/71	8.00
BW2	Brandon Webb/51	15.00
TW1	Todd Wellemeyer/146	8.00
VW1	Vernon Wells/33	15.00
VW2	Vernon Wells/49	15.00

2005 Donruss Classics

NM/M

Complete Set (250):	
Common Player (1-200):	.25
Common Auto. (201-225):	6.00
Common SP (226-250):	3.00
Production 1,000	
Pack (5):	8.00
Box (18):	120.00
1 Scott Rolen	1.00
2 Derek Jeter	3.00
3 Jose Vidro	.25
4 Johnny Damon	1.00
5 Nomar Garciaparra	2.00
6 Jose Guillen	.25
7 Trot Nixon	.25
8 Mark Loretta	.25
9 Jody Gerut	.25
10 Miguel Tejada	.75
11 Barry Larkin	.50
12 Jeff Kent	.40
13 Carl Crawford	.40
14 Paul Konerko	.40
15 Jim Edmonds	.50
16 Garret Anderson	.40
17 Jay Gibbons	.25
18 Moises Alou	.40
19 Mike Lowell	.25
20 Mark Mulder	.40
21 Josh Beckett	.50
22 Tim Salmon	.25
23 Shannon Stewart	.25
24 Miguel Cabrera	1.00
25 Jim Thome	1.00
26 Kevin Youkilis	.25
27 Justin Morneau	.75
28 Austin Kearns	.25
29 Cliff Lee	.25
30 Ken Griffey Jr.	1.50
31 Mike Piazza	1.50
32 Roy Halladay	.40
33 Larry Walker	.50
34 David Ortiz	1.00
35 Dontrelle Willis	.50
36 Craig Wilson	.25
37 Jeff Suppan	.25
38 Curt Schilling	1.00
39 Larry Bigbie	.25
40 Rich Harden	.40
41 Victor Martinez	.40
42 Jorge Posada	.50
43 Joey Gathright	.25
44 Adam Dunn	.75
45 Pedro Martinez	1.00
46 Dallas McPherson	.50
47 Tom Glavine	.40
48 Torii Hunter	.40
49 Angel Berroa	.25
50 Mark Prior	1.00
51 Ichiro Suzuki	2.00
52 C.C. Sabathia	.25
53 Bobby Abreu	.50
54 Shigetoshi Hasegawa	.25
55 Brandon Webb	.50
56 Mark Buehrle	.50
57 Johan Santana	.75
58 Francisco Rodriguez	.25
59 Roy Oswalt	.50
60 Mike Sweeney	.50
61 Jake Peavy	.50
62 Akinori Otsuka	.25
63 Dioner Navarro	.25
64 Kazuhito Tadano	.25
65 Ryan Wagner	.25
66 Abe Alvarez	.25
67 Mark Teixeira	.75
68 Jermaine Dye	.50
69 Todd Walker	.25
70 Octavio Dotel	.25
71 Frank Thomas	.75
72 Javy Lopez	.50
73 Scott Podsednik	.25

#	Player	Price
74	B.J. Upton	.25
75	Barry Zito	.40
76	Raul Ibanez	.25
77	Orlando Cabrera	.25
78	Sean Burroughs	.25
79	Esteban Loaiza	.25
80	Jason Schmidt	.50
81	Vinny Castilla	.25
82	Shingo Takatsu	.25
83	Juan Pierre	.25
84	David Dellucci	.25
85	Travis Blackley	.25
86	Brad Penny	.25
87	Nick Johnson	.25
88	Brian Roberts	.50
89	Kazuo Matsui	.25
90	Mike Lieberthal	.25
91	Craig Biggio	.40
92	Sean Casey	.25
93	Andy Pettitte	.50
94	Milton Bradley	.40
95	Rocco Baldelli	.25
96	Adrian Gonzalez	.25
97	Chad Tracy	.25
98	Chad Cordero	.25
99	Albert Pujols	3.00
100	Jason Kubel	.25
101	Rafael Furcal	.25
102	Jack Wilson	.25
103	Eric Chavez	.40
104	Casey Kotchman	.25
105	Jeff Bagwell	.75
106	Melvin Mora	.25
107	Bobby Crosby	.25
108	Preston Wilson	.25
109	Hank Blalock	.75
110	Vernon Wells	.40
111	Francisco Cordero	.25
112	Steve Finley	.25
113	Omar Vizquel	.25
114	Eric Byrnes	.25
115	Tim Hudson	.50
116	Aramis Ramirez	.50
117	Lance Berkman	.40
118	Shea Hillenbrand	.25
119	Aubrey Huff	.25
120	Lew Ford	.25
121	Sammy Sosa	2.00
122	Marcus Giles	.25
123	Rickie Weeks	.25
124	Manny Ramirez	1.00
125	Jason Giambi	.40
126	Adam LaRoche	.25
127	Vladimir Guerrero	1.00
128	Ken Harvey	.25
129	Adrian Beltre	.50
130	Magglio Ordonez	.25
131	Greg Maddux	1.50
132	Russ Ortiz	.25
133	Jason Varitek	.75
134	Kerry Wood	1.00
135	Mike Mussina	.75
136	Joe Nathan	.25
137	Troy Glaus	.50
138	Carlos Zambrano	.50
139	Ben Sheets	.50
140	Jae Weong Seo	.25
141	Derrek Lee	.50
142	Carlos Beltran	.50
143	John Lackey	.25
144	Aaron Rowand	.25
145	Dewon Brazelton	.25
146	Jason Bay	.25
147	Alfonso Soriano	1.00
148	Travis Hafner	.25
149	Ryan Church	.25
150	Bret Boone	.25
151	Bernie Williams	.50
152	Wade Miller	.25
153	Zack Greinke	.25
154	Scott Kazmir	.25
155	Hideki Matsui	2.00
156	Livan Hernandez	.25
157	Jose Capellan	.25
158	David Wright	1.00
159	Chone Figgins	.25
160	Jeremy Reed	.25
161	J.D. Drew	.40
162	Hideo Nomo	.50
163	Merkin Valdez	.25
164	Shawn Green	.40
165	Alexis Rios	.25
166	Johnny Estrada	.25
167	Danny Graves	.25
168	Carlos Lee	.25
169	John Van Benschoten	.25
170	Randy Johnson	1.00
171	Randy Wolf	.25
172	Luis Gonzalez	.40
173	Chipper Jones	1.00
174	Delmon Young	.50
175	Edwin Jackson	.25
176	Carlos Delgado	.50
177	Matt Clement	.25
178	Jacque Jones	.25
179	Gary Sheffield	.50

Timeless Tributes Gold

Gold (1-200): 4-8X

#	Player	Price
180	Laynce Nix	.25
181	Tom Gordon	.25
182	Jose Castillo	.25
183	Andruw Jones	.50
184	Brian Giles	.40
185	Paul LoDuca	.25
186	Roger Clemens	3.00
187	Todd Helton	.75
188	Keith Foulke	.25
189	Jeremy Bonderman	.25
190	Troy Percival	.25
191	Michael Young	.25
192	Carlos Guillen	.25
193	Rafael Palmeiro	.75
194	Brett Myers	.25
195	Carl Pavano	.40
196	Alex Rodriguez	2.50
197	Lyle Overbay	.25
198	Ivan Rodriguez	.75
199	Khalil Greene	.40
200	Edgar Renteria	.40
201	Justin Verlander/ AU/400 RC	40.00
202	Miguel Negron/ AU/1300 RC	6.00
204	Paul Reynoso/ AU/1200 RC	8.00
205	Colter Bean/ AU/1200 RC	8.00
206	Raul Tablado/ AU/1200 RC	8.00
207	Mark McLemore/ AU/1200 RC	8.00
208	Russel Rohlicek/ AU/1200 RC	8.00
210	Chris Seddon/ AU/785 RC	8.00
213	Mike Morse/ AU/1200 RC	6.00
215	Randy Messenger/ AU/1200 RC	8.00
217	Carlos Ruiz/ AU/1200 RC	8.00
218	Chris Roberson/ AU/1200 RC	8.00
219	Ryan Speier/ AU/1200 RC	8.00
221	Ambiorix Burgos/ AU/750 RC	8.00
223	David Gassner/ AU/1200 RC	6.00
224	Sean Tracey/ AU/1200 RC	8.00
225	Casey Rogowski/ AU/1500 RC	8.00
226	Billy Williams	3.00
227	Ralph Kiner	3.00
228	Ozzie Smith	5.00
229	Rod Carew	3.00
230	Nolan Ryan	8.00
231	Fergie Jenkins	3.00
232	Paul Molitor	4.00
233	Carlton Fisk	4.00
234	Rollie Fingers	3.00
235	Lou Brock	3.00
236	Gaylord Perry	3.00
237	Don Mattingly	6.00
238	Maury Wills	3.00
239	Luis Aparicio	3.00
240	George Brett	8.00
241	Mike Schmidt	6.00
242	Joe Morgan	3.00
243	Dennis Eckersley	3.00
244	Reggie Jackson	8.00
245	Bobby Doerr	3.00
246	Bob Feller	3.00
247	Cal Ripken Jr.	10.00
248	Harmon Killebrew	4.00
249	Frank Robinson	4.00
250	Stan Musial	5.00

Gold (201-225): .4-.75X
Gold (226-250): 2-4X
Production 50 Sets

Timeless Tributes Silver

Gold (1-200): 2-4X
Gold (201-225): .25X
Gold (226-250): 1-2X
Production 100 Sets

Timeless Tributes Platinum

No Pricing
Production One Set

Classic Combos

	NM/M
Common Combo:	4.00

Production 400 Sets
Gold: 2-4X
Production 25 Sets
Platinum: No Pricing
Production One Set

33	Babe Ruth, Ted Williams	10.00
34	Roberto Clemente, Vladimir Guerrero	8.00
35	Willie Mays, Willie McCovey	8.00
36	Yogi Berra, Mike Piazza	6.00
37	Sandy Koufax, Nolan Ryan	30.00
38	Harmon Killebrew, Mike Schmidt	8.00
39	Whitey Ford, Randy Johnson	4.00
40	Cal Ripken Jr., George Brett	15.00
41	Hank Aaron, Stan Musial	8.00
42	Carl Yastrzemski, Frank Robinson	6.00
43	Bob Feller, Roger Clemens	6.00
44	Bob Gibson, Tom Seaver	4.00
45	Roger Maris, Jim Thome	4.00
46	Albert Pujols, Don Mattingly	8.00
47	Duke Snider, Sammy Sosa	4.00
48	Rickey Henderson, Bo Jackson	4.00
49	Ernie Banks, Reggie Jackson	4.00
50	Burleigh Grimes, Greg Maddux	6.00

Classic Combos Bat

No Pricing
Production 5 Sets

Classic Combos Jersey

	NM/M

Production 5-50

Prime: No Pricing
Production 1-5

38	Harmon Killebrew, Mike Schmidt/50	30.00
39	Whitey Ford, Randy Johnson/25	25.00
40	Cal Ripken Jr., George Brett/50	50.00
45	Roger Maris, Jim Thome/25	50.00
46	Albert Pujols, Don Mattingly/50	40.00
47	Duke Snider, Sammy Sosa/25	30.00
48	Rickey Henderson, Bo Jackson/50	25.00

Classic Combos Materials

	NM/M

Production 1-25
Prime: No Pricing
Production 5 Sets

| 46 | Albert Pujols, Don Mattingly/25 | 50.00 |
| 48 | Rickey Henderson, Bo Jackson/25 | 30.00 |

Classic Combos Materials HR

	NM/M

Production 1-25

| 46 | Albert Pujols, Don Mattingly/25 | 50.00 |
| 48 | Rickey Henderson, Bo Jackson/25 | 30.00 |

Classic Combos Signature

No Pricing
Production One Set

Classic Combos Signature Bat

No Pricing
Production One Set

Classic Combos Signature Jersey

No Pricing
Production 1-5

Classic Combos Signature Material

No Pricing
Production One Set

Classic Combos Signature Materials HR

No Pricing
Production One Set

Classic Singles

	NM/M
Complete Set (32):	120.00
Common Player:	3.00

Production 400 Sets
Gold: 2-4X
Production 25 Sets
Platinum: No Pricing
Production One Set

1	Hank Aaron	8.00
2	Tom Seaver	4.00
3	Harmon Killebrew	4.00
4	Paul Molitor	4.00
5	Brooks Robinson	4.00
6	Stan Musial	5.00
7	Bobby Doerr	4.00
8	Cal Ripken Jr.	12.00
9	Phil Niekro	3.00
10	Eddie Murray	4.00
11	Randy Johnson	4.00
12	Steve Carlton	3.00
13	Rickey Henderson	3.00
14	Ernie Banks	4.00
15	Curt Schilling	4.00
16	Whitey Ford	4.00
17	Al Kaline	4.00
18	Gary Carter	3.00
19	Robin Yount	4.00
20	Johnny Bench	4.00
21	Bob Feller	3.00
22	Jim Palmer	3.00
23	Don Mattingly	6.00
24	Willie Mays	6.00
25	Dave Righetti	3.00
26	Roger Clemens	6.00
27	Juan Marichal	3.00
28	Tony Gwynn	4.00
29	Nolan Ryan	8.00

30	Carlton Fisk	3.00
31	Greg Maddux	5.00
32	Sandy Koufax	25.00

Classic Singles Bat

NM/M

Production 25-50

1	Hank Aaron/25	50.00
2	Tom Seaver/50	15.00
4	Paul Molitor/50	15.00
5	Brooks Robinson/50	15.00
6	Stan Musial/25	30.00
7	Bobby Doerr/25	10.00
8	Cal Ripken Jr./25	70.00
9	Phil Niekro/50	8.00
10	Eddie Murray/50	15.00
11	Randy Johnson/25	20.00
12	Steve Carlton/50	10.00
13	Rickey Henderson/50	15.00
14	Ernie Banks/50	20.00
17	Al Kaline/25	25.00
18	Gary Carter/25	8.00
19	Robin Yount/50	15.00
20	Johnny Bench/25	20.00
23	Don Mattingly/25	30.00
24	Willie Mays/25	50.00
28	Tony Gwynn/50	15.00
29	Nolan Ryan/25	40.00
30	Carlton Fisk/50	15.00

Classic Singles Jersey

NM/M

Production 10-100
Prime: No Pricing
Production 1-5

2	Tom Seaver/25	20.00
3	Harmon Killebrew/25	20.00
4	Paul Molitor/25	15.00
5	Brooks Robinson/25	15.00
7	Bobby Doerr/Pants/100	10.00
8	Cal Ripken Jr./25	70.00
9	Phil Niekro/50	8.00
10	Eddie Murray/50	15.00
11	Randy Johnson/100	12.00
12	Steve Carlton/25	12.00
13	Rickey Henderson/100	12.00
14	Ernie Banks/25	25.00
15	Curt Schilling/100	15.00
16	Whitey Ford/25	20.00
18	Gary Carter/100	8.00
19	Robin Yount/25	15.00
20	Johnny Bench/50	15.00
21	Bob Feller Pants/25	20.00
22	Jim Palmer/100	8.00
23	Don Mattingly/100	25.00
24	Willie Mays/50	50.00
25	Dave Righetti/50	8.00
26	Roger Clemens/50	25.00
27	Juan Marichal/50	10.00
28	Tony Gwynn/100	15.00
29	Nolan Ryan/50	30.00
30	Carlton Fisk/25	15.00
31	Greg Maddux/100	15.00
32	Sandy Koufax/25	375.00

Classic Singles Materials

NM/M

Production 10-25
Prime: No Pricing
Production 10-25

2	Tom Seaver/Bat-Jsy/25	20.00
3	Harmon Killebrew/Bat-Jys/25	25.00
4	Paul Molitor/Bat-Jsy/25	20.00
5	Brooks Robinson/Bat-Jsy/25	20.00
7	Bobby Doerr/Bat-Pants/25	10.00
11	Randy Johnson/Bat-Jsy/25	20.00
12	Steve Carlton/Bat-Jsy/25	15.00
13	Rickey Henderson/Bat-Jsy/25	30.00
18	Gary Carter/Bat-Jsy/25	15.00
19	Robin Yount/Bat-Jsy/25	25.00
20	Johnny Bench/Bat-Jsy/25	25.00
23	Don Mattingly/Bat-Jsy/25	35.00
28	Tony Gwynn/Bat-Jsy/25	25.00
29	Nolan Ryan/Bat-Jsy/25	40.00
30	Carlton Fisk/Bat-Jsy/25	15.00

Classic Singles Materials HR

NM/M

Production 10-25

2	Tom Seaver/Bat-Jsy/25	20.00
3	Harmon Killebrew/Bat-Jsy/25	25.00
4	Paul Molitor/Bat-Jsy/25	20.00
5	Brooks Robinson/Bat-Jsy/25	20.00
7	Bobby Doerr/Bat-Pants/25	10.00
11	Randy Johnson/Bat-Jsy/25	20.00
12	Steve Carlton/Bat-Pants/25	15.00
13	Rickey Henderson/Bat-Jsy/25	30.00
18	Gary Carter/Bat-Jsy/25	15.00
19	Robin Yount/Bat-Jsy/25	25.00
20	Johnny Bench/Bat-Jsy/25	25.00
23	Don Mattingly/Bat-Jsy/25	35.00
28	Tony Gwynn/Bat-Jsy/25	25.00

Classic Singles Signature

No Pricing
Production 1-5

Classic Singles Signature Bat

No Pricing
Production 1-10

Classic Singles Signature Jersey

No Pricing
Production 1-5

Classic Singles Signature Materials

No Pricing
Production 1-10

Classic Singles Signature Materials HR

No Pricing
Production 1-10

Dress Code Bat

NM/M

Production 50-100

1	Albert Pujols/100	25.00
2	Bernie Williams/50	10.00
4	Carlos Beltran/100	10.00
5	Chipper Jones/100	10.00
7	David Ortiz/100	12.00
8	Hank Blalock/100	6.00
9	Hideki Matsui/100	30.00
10	Jim Edmonds/100	8.00
11	Jim Thome/100	10.00
14	Mark Prior/50	8.00
15	Mark Teixeira/100	6.00
16	Miguel Cabrera/100	8.00
17	Miguel Tejada/100	6.00
18	Mike Piazza/100	12.00
22	Sammy Sosa/100	12.00
23	Scott Rolen/100	10.00
26	Torii Hunter/100	6.00
30	Vladimir Guerrero/100	10.00

Dress Code Jersey Number

NM/M

Production 5-57

2	Bernie Williams/51	10.00
4	Carlos Beltran/15	20.00
6	Curt Schilling/38	15.00
7	David Ortiz/34	20.00
9	Hideki Matsui/55	30.00
11	Jim Thome/25	15.00
12	Johan Santana/57	12.00
13	Mark Mulder/20	10.00
14	Mark Prior/22	15.00
15	Mark Teixeira/23	10.00
16	Miguel Cabrera/24	15.00
18	Mike Piazza/31	20.00
19	Pedro J. Martinez/45	10.00

20	Randy Johnson/Pants/51	12.00
21	Roger Clemens/23	25.00
22	Sammy Sosa/21	20.00
23	Scott Rolen/27	15.00
26	Torii Hunter/48	6.00
27	Travis Hafner/48	6.00
29	Victor Martinez/51	8.00
30	Vladimir Guerrero/27	20.00

Dress Code Jersey Prime

NM/M

Production 25 Sets

1	Albert Pujols	75.00
2	Bernie Williams	20.00
3	Carl Crawford	12.00
4	Carlos Beltran	25.00
5	Chipper Jones	30.00
6	Curt Schilling	30.00
7	David Ortiz	30.00
8	Hank Blalock	20.00
10	Jim Edmonds	20.00
11	Jim Thome	25.00
12	Johan Santana	30.00
13	Mark Mulder	20.00
14	Mark Prior	20.00
15	Mark Teixeira	15.00
16	Miguel Cabrera	25.00
17	Miguel Tejada	25.00
18	Mike Piazza	30.00
19	Pedro J. Martinez	25.00
20	Randy Johnson	30.00
21	Roger Clemens	50.00
22	Sammy Sosa	30.00
23	Scott Rolen	30.00
24	Tim Hudson	20.00
25	Todd Helton	20.00
26	Torii Hunter	15.00
27	Travis Hafner	10.00
28	Vernon Wells	10.00
29	Victor Martinez	15.00
30	Vladimir Guerrero	30.00

Dress Code Materials

NM/M

Production 5-100
Prime: No Pricing
Production 5 Sets

1	Albert Pujols/Bat-Jsy/100	25.00
2	Bernie Williams/Bat-Jsy/100	10.00
4	Carlos Beltran/Bat-Bat/Jsy/100	10.00
5	Chipper Jones/Bat-Jsy/100	12.00
6	Curt Schilling/Bat-Jsy/100	15.00
7	David Ortiz/Bat-Hat/100	15.00
8	Hank Blalock/Bat-Jsy/100	8.00
9	Hideki Matsui/Bat-Jsy/100	30.00
10	Jim Edmonds	10.00
11	Jim Thome/Jsy-Jsy/100	12.00
15	Mark Teixeira/Bat-Jsy/100	8.00
16	Miguel Cabrera/Jsy-Jsy/100	10.00
17	Miguel Tejada/Bat-Jsy/100	8.00
18	Mike Piazza/Bat-Jsy/100	12.00
19	Pedro J. Martinez/Bat-Jsy/100	12.00
22	Sammy Sosa/Bat-Jsy/100	12.00
23	Scott Rolen/Bat-Jsy/100	12.00
25	Todd Helton/Jsy-Jsy/50	12.00
26	Torii Hunter/Bat-Jsy/100	8.00
27	Travis Hafner/Jsy-Shoes/50	8.00
28	Vernon Wells/Jsy-Jsy/50	8.00
29	Victor Martinez/Jsy-Jsy/50	8.00
30	Vladimir Guerrero/Bat-Jsy/100	12.00

Dress Code Signature Bat

NM/M

Production 1-25

7	David Ortiz/25	50.00
8	Hank Blalock/25	30.00
16	Miguel Cabrera/25	50.00

26	Torii Hunter/25	30.00
27	Travis Hafner/25	25.00
28	Vernon Wells/25	25.00

Dress Code Signature Jersey

NM/M

Production 5-25

7	David Ortiz/25	50.00
8	Hank Blalock/25	30.00
12	Johan Santana/25	50.00
16	Miguel Cabrera/25	50.00
26	Torii Hunter/25	30.00
27	Travis Hafner/25	25.00
28	Vernon Wells/25	25.00
29	Victor Martinez/25	25.00

Dress Code Signature Jersey Number

NM/M

Production 1-25
Prime: No Pricing
Production 1-5

7	David Ortiz/25	50.00
8	Hank Blalock/25	30.00
12	Johan Santana/25	50.00
26	Torii Hunter/25	30.00
27	Travis Hafner/25	25.00
29	Victor Martinez/25	25.00

Dress Code Signature Materials

No Pricing
Production 1-5

Home Run Heroes

NM/M

Complete Set (50):	90.00
Common Player:	1.50

Production 1,000 Sets
Gold: 2-4X
Production 50 Sets
Platinum: No Pricing
Production One Set

1	Mike Schmidt	4.00
2	Ken Griffey Jr.	4.00
3	Babe Ruth	6.00
4	Duke Snider	2.00
5	Johnny Bench	3.00
6	Stan Musial	3.00
7	Willie McCovey	2.00
8	Willie Stargell	2.00
9	Ted Williams	5.00
10	Frank Thomas	2.00
11	Gary Sheffield	2.00
12	Jim Thome	2.00
13	Harmon Killebrew	2.00
14	Ernie Banks	3.00
15	George Foster	1.50
16	Albert Pujols	5.00
17	Tony Perez	1.50
18	Richie Sexson	1.50
19	Juan Gonzalez	1.50
20	Frank Robinson	2.00
21	Sammy Sosa	3.00
22	Jeff Bagwell	1.50
23	Mark Teixeira	1.50
24	Willie Mays	5.00
25	Rafael Palmeiro	2.00
26	Billy Williams	1.50
27	Vladimir Guerrero	2.00
28	Gary Carter	2.00
29	Fred McGriff	1.50
30	Orlando Cepeda	1.50
31	Dave Winfield	2.00
32	Shawn Green	1.50
33	Jose Canseco	1.50
34	Hideki Matsui	4.00
35	Roger Maris	4.00
36	Andre Dawson	2.00
37	Paul Konerko	1.50
38	Darryl Strawberry	1.50
39	Dave Parker	1.50
40	Adam Dunn	2.00
41	Ralph Kiner	2.00
42	Miguel Tejada	2.00
43	Dale Murphy	2.00
44	Hank Aaron	6.00
45	Mike Piazza	3.00
46	Reggie Jackson	2.00

47	Adrian Beltre	2.00
48	Cal Ripken Jr.	8.00
49	Manny Ramirez	3.00
50	Alex Rodriguez	5.00

Home Run Heroes Jersey HR

NM/M

Production 1-66
Prime: No Pricing
Production One Set

1	Mike Schmidt/48	25.00
3	Babe Ruth/25	165.00
5	Johnny Bench/45	15.00
7	Willie McCovey/23	15.00
8	Willie Stargell/48	15.00
9	Ted Williams/43	60.00
10	Frank Thomas/43	12.00
11	Gary Sheffield/36	8.00
12	Jim Thome/47	15.00
13	Harmon Killebrew/49	20.00
14	Ernie Banks/ Pants/47	20.00
15	Gene Foster/25	10.00
16	Albert Pujols/46	35.00
18	Richie Sexson/45	8.00
19	Juan Gonzalez/47	8.00
21	Sammy Sosa/66	12.00
22	Jeff Bagwell/47	10.00
23	Mark Teixeira/38	8.00
24	Willie Mays/51	50.00
25	Rafael Palmeiro/47	10.00
26	Billy Williams/26	10.00
27	Vladimir Guerrero/44	12.00
28	Gary Carter/31	10.00
29	Fred McGriff/32	12.00
30	Orlando Cepeda/ Pants/46	8.00
31	Dave Winfield/34	10.00
32	Shawn Green/49	8.00
33	Jose Canseco/44	10.00
34	Hideki Matsui/ Pants/31	40.00
35	Roger Maris/ Pants/19	50.00
36	Andre Dawson/49	8.00
38	Darryl Strawberry/24	10.00
39	Dave Parker/34	8.00
40	Adam Dunn/46	10.00
42	Miguel Tejada/44	10.00
43	Dale Murphy/44	12.00
44	Hank Aaron/47	50.00
45	Mike Piazza/40	15.00
46	Reggie Jackson/39	12.00
47	Adrian Beltre/48	8.00
48	Cal Ripken Jr./34	12.00
49	Manny Ramirez/43	12.00

Home Run Heroes Materials

NM/M

Production 1-66
Prime: No Pricing
Production One Set

1	Mike Schmidt/ Bat-Jsy/48	30.00
3	Babe Ruth/ Bat-Jsy/43	300.00
5	Johnny Bench/ Bat-Jsy/45	20.00
7	Willie McCovey/ Bat-Jsy/23	20.00
8	Willie Stargell/ Bat-Jsy/48	20.00
9	Ted Williams/ Bat-Jsy/43	85.00
10	Frank Thomas/ Jsy-Jsy/43	15.00
11	Gary Sheffield/ Bat-Jsy/36	10.00
12	Jim Thome/ Bat-Jsy/47	15.00
13	Harmon Killebrew/ Bat-Jsy/49	25.00
14	Ernie Banks/ Bat-Pants/47	25.00
15	George Foster/ Bat-Jsy/52	10.00
16	Albert Pujols/ Jsy-Jsy/43	40.00
17	Tony Perez/ Bat-Fld Glv/24	15.00
18	Richie Sexson/ Bat-Jsy/45	10.00
19	Juan Gonzalez/ Bat-Jsy/47	10.00
21	Sammy Sosa/ Bat-Jsy/66	15.00
22	Jeff Bagwell/ Bat-Jsy/47	12.00
23	Mark Teixeira/ Bat-Jsy/38	10.00
24	Willie Mays/ Bat-Jsy/51	50.00
25	Rafael Palmeiro/ Bat-Jsy/47	12.00
26	Billy Williams/ Bat-Jsy/26	10.00
27	Vladimir Guerrero/ Bat-Jsy/44	15.00
28	Gary Carter/ Bat-Jsy/31	12.00
29	Fred McGriff/ Bat-Jsy/32	15.00
30	Orlando Cepeda/ Bat-Pants/34	12.00
31	Dave Winfield/ Bat-Jsy/34	15.00
32	Shawn Green/ Bat-Jsy/49	10.00
33	Jose Canseco/ Hat-Jsy/44	12.00
34	Hideki Matsui/ Bat-Pants/31	60.00
35	Roger Maris/ Bat-Pants/19	50.00
36	Andre Dawson/ Bat-Jsy/49	10.00
38	Darryl Strawberry/ Jsy-Pants/24	12.00
39	Dave Parker/ Bat-Jsy/34	12.00
40	Adam Dunn/ Bat-Jsy/46	15.00
42	Miguel Tejada/ Bat-Jsy/34	15.00
43	Dale Murphy/ Jsy-Jsy/44	15.00
44	Hank Aaron/ Bat-Jsy/47	50.00
45	Mike Piazza/ Jsy-Jsy/40	15.00
46	Reggie Jackson/ Bat-Jsy/39	15.00
47	Adrian Beltre/ Bat-Jsy/48	12.00
48	Cal Ripken Jr./ Bat-Jsy/34	60.00
49	Manny Ramirez/ Jsy-Jsy/43	15.00

Home Run Heroes Signature

No Pricing
Production 1-10

Home Run Heroes Signature Materials

No Pricing
Production 1-10

Legendary Lumberjacks

NM/M

Common Player: 2.00
Production 400 Sets
Gold: 2-4X
Production 50 Sets
Platinum: No Pricing
Production One Set

1	Al Kaline	4.00
2	Babe Ruth	8.00
3	Billy Williams	2.00
4	Bob Feller	3.00
5	Bob Gibson	3.00
6	Brooks Robinson	4.00
7	Cal Ripken Jr.	10.00
8	Carlton Fisk	3.00
9	Dennis Eckersley	2.00
10	Don Mattingly	6.00
11	Duke Snider	3.00
12	Eddie Murray	3.00
13	Ernie Banks	4.00
14	Fergie Jenkins	2.00
15	Frank Robinson	4.00
16	Gaylord Perry	2.00
17	George Brett	6.00
18	George Kell	2.00
19	Harmon Killebrew	4.00
20	Jim Palmer	2.00
21	Joe Morgan	2.00
22	Johnny Bench	5.00
23	Juan Marichal	2.00
24	Lou Brock	3.00
25	Maury Wills	2.00
26	Mike Schmidt	6.00
27	Nolan Ryan	8.00
28	Ozzie Smith	4.00
29	Paul Molitor	3.00
30	Pee Wee Reese	2.00
31	Phil Niekro	2.00
32	Phil Rizzuto	3.00
33	Ralph Kiner	2.00
34	Reggie Jackson	3.00
35	Rickey Henderson	3.00
36	Roberto Clemente	8.00
37	Robin Yount	4.00
38	Rod Carew	2.00
39	Roger Maris	5.00
40	Stan Musial	5.00
41	Steve Carlton	2.00
42	Ted Williams	8.00
43	Tom Seaver	3.00
44	Tony Gwynn	3.00
45	Tony Perez	2.00
46	Wade Boggs	3.00
47	Warren Spahn	4.00
48	Whitey Ford	4.00
49	Willie McCovey	3.00
50	Yogi Berra	4.00

Legendary Lumberjacks Bat

NM/M

Production 1-50

1	Al Kaline/6	
2	Babe Ruth/25	200.00
6	Brooks Robinson/50	15.00
7	Cal Ripken Jr./50	50.00
8	Carlton Fisk/50	10.00
10	Don Mattingly/50	25.00
12	Eddie Murray/50	15.00
13	Ernie Banks/50	15.00
15	Frank Robinson/50	15.00
17	George Brett/50	20.00
19	Harmon Killebrew/50	15.00
21	Joe Morgan/50	10.00
22	Johnny Bench/50	15.00
24	Lou Brock/50	10.00
26	Mike Schmidt/50	20.00
28	Ozzie Smith/50	15.00
29	Paul Molitor/50	12.00
30	Pee Wee Reese/50	10.00
34	Reggie Jackson/50	12.00
35	Rickey Henderson/50	12.00
36	Roberto Clemente/50	50.00
37	Robin Yount/50	15.00
38	Rod Carew/50	10.00
39	Roger Maris/25	40.00
40	Stan Musial/25	25.00
42	Ted Williams/25	60.00
44	Tony Gwynn/50	15.00
45	Tony Perez/1	
46	Wade Boggs/50	12.00
49	Willie McCovey/50	12.00
50	Yogi Berra/25	25.00

Legendary Lumberjacks Jersey

NM/M

Production 1-50

3	Billy Williams/25	12.00
6	Brooks Robinson/25	20.00
7	Cal Ripken Jr./50	50.00
8	Carlton Fisk/25	15.00
10	Don Mattingly/50	25.00
12	Eddie Murray/50	15.00
13	Ernie Banks/25	20.00
22	Johnny Bench/25	20.00
24	Lou Brock/25	12.00
25	Maury Wills/25	12.00
26	Mike Schmidt/25	25.00
28	Ozzie Smith/25	20.00
29	Paul Molitor/50	12.00
34	Reggie Jackson/25	15.00
35	Rickey Henderson/ 50	12.00
37	Robin Yount/50	15.00
38	Rod Carew/50	10.00

Legendary Lumberjacks Jersey HR

NM/M

Production 1-25

6	Brooks Robinson/25	20.00
7	Cal Ripken Jr./25	60.00
10	Don Mattingly/25	30.00
12	Eddie Murray/25	20.00
29	Paul Molitor/25	20.00
35	Rickey Henderson/25	20.00
37	Robin Yount/25	20.00
45	Tony Gwynn/25	20.00
46	Wade Boggs/25	15.00
49	Willie McCovey/25	15.00

Legendary Lumberjacks Materials

NM/M

Production 1-50

2	Babe Ruth/ Bat-Jsy/25	300.00
6	Brooks Robinson/ Bat-Jsy/50	20.00
7	Cal Ripken Jr./ Bat-Jsy/50	60.00
8	Carlton Fisk/50	15.00
10	Don Mattingly/ Bat-Jsy/50	30.00
12	Eddie Murray/ Bat-Jsy/50	20.00
13	Ernie Banks/ Bat-Jsy/25	25.00
19	Harmon Killebrew/ Bat-Jsy/50	20.00
22	Johnny Bench/ Bat-Jsy/50	20.00
24	Lou Brock/Bat-Jsy/50	12.00
26	Mike Schmidt/ Bat-Jsy/50	25.00
29	Paul Molitor/ Bat-Jsy/50	15.00
34	Reggie Jackson/ Bat-Jsy/50	20.00
35	Rickey Henderson/ Bat-Jsy/50	15.00
37	Robin Yount/ Bat-Jsy/50	20.00
38	Rod Carew/ Bat-Jsy/50	15.00
44	Tony Gwynn/ Bat-Jsy/50	20.00
46	Wade Boggs/ Bat-Jsy/50	15.00
49	Willie McCovey/ Bat-Jsy/44	15.00

Legendary Players

NM/M

Common Player: 1.50
Production 800 Sets
Gold: 2-3X
Production 75 Sets
Platinum: No Pricing
Production One Set

1	Al Kaline	3.00
2	Babe Ruth	6.00
3	Billy Williams	1.50
4	Bob Feller	2.00
5	Bob Gibson	2.00
6	Brooks Robinson	3.00
7	Cal Ripken Jr.	8.00
8	Carlton Fisk	2.00
9	Dennis Eckersley	2.00
10	Don Mattingly	5.00
11	Duke Snider	2.00
12	Eddie Murray	2.00
13	Ernie Banks	3.00
14	Fergie Jenkins	1.50
15	Frank Robinson	3.00
16	Gaylord Perry	1.50
17	George Brett	5.00
18	George Kell	1.50
19	Harmon Killebrew	3.00
20	Jim Palmer	1.50
21	Joe Morgan	1.50
22	Johnny Bench	4.00
23	Juan Marichal	1.50
24	Lou Brock	2.00
25	Maury Wills	1.50
26	Mike Schmidt	5.00
27	Nolan Ryan	6.00
28	Ozzie Smith	3.00
29	Paul Molitor	2.00
30	Pee Wee Reese	1.50
31	Phil Niekro	1.50
32	Phil Rizzuto	2.00
33	Ralph Kiner	1.50
34	Reggie Jackson	2.00
35	Rickey Henderson	2.00
36	Roberto Clemente	6.00
37	Robin Yount	3.00
38	Rod Carew	2.00
39	Roger Maris	4.00
40	Stan Musial	4.00
41	Steve Carlton	1.50
42	Ted Williams	6.00
43	Tom Seaver	2.00
44	Tony Gwynn	2.00
45	Tony Perez	1.50
46	Wade Boggs	3.00
47	Warren Spahn	3.00
48	Whitey Ford	3.00
49	Willie McCovey	2.00
50	Yogi Berra	3.00

Legendary Players Hat

NM/M

Production 1-25

10	Don Mattingly/25	30.00
13	Ernie Banks/25	20.00
17	George Brett/25	30.00
20	Jim Palmer/25	10.00
26	Mike Schmidt/25	30.00
28	Ozzie Smith/25	25.00
37	Robin Yount/25	25.00
44	Tony Gwynn/25	20.00

Legendary Players Jacket

		NM/M
Production 25 Sets		
7	Cal Ripken Jr.	60.00
8	Carlton Fisk	12.00
10	Don Mattingly	40.00
24	Lou Brock	15.00
26	Mike Schmidt	35.00
27	Nolan Ryan	50.00
34	Reggie Jackson	15.00
35	Rickey Henderson	20.00
38	Rod Carew	20.00
42	Ted Williams	85.00

Legendary Players Jersey Number

		NM/M
Production 1-44		
Prime:		No Pricing
Production One Set		
3	Billy Williams/26	10.00
8	Carlton Fisk/72	10.00
9	Dennis Eckersley/43	10.00
10	Don Mattingly/23	30.00
12	Eddie Murray/33	15.00
16	Gaylord Perry/36	8.00
20	Jim Palmer/22	10.00
23	Juan Marichal/27	10.00
24	Lou Brock/20	15.00
25	Maury Wills/30	8.00
26	Mike Schmidt/20	30.00
27	Nolan Ryan/34	40.00
31	Phil Niekro/35	8.00
35	Rickey Henderson/24	15.00
37	Robin Yount/19	25.00
38	Rod Carew/29	15.00
41	Steve Carlton/32	10.00
43	Tom Seaver/41	15.00
44	Tony Gwynn/19	20.00
45	Tony Perez/24	10.00
46	Wade Boggs/26	15.00
47	Warren Spahn/24	20.00
49	Willie McCovey/44	12.00

Legendary Players Leather

		NM/M
Production 10-25		
10	Don Mattingly/ Btg Glv/25	40.00
14	Fergie Jenkins/ Fld Glv/25	15.00
26	Mike Schmidt/ Fld Glv/25	40.00
35	Rickey Henderson/ Btg Glv/25	25.00
41	Steve Carlton/ Fld Glv/25	15.00
44	Tony Gwynn/ Btg Glv/25	30.00
45	Tony Perez/ Fld Glv/25	15.00

Legendary Players Pants

		NM/M
Production 1-25		
4	Bob Feller/19	20.00
7	Cal Ripken Jr./25	60.00
11	Duke Snider/25	20.00
12	Eddie Murray/25	20.00
14	Fergie Jenkins/25	10.00
20	Jim Palmer/25	10.00
23	Juan Marichal/25	10.00
28	Ozzie Smith/25	25.00
29	Paul Molitor/25	15.00
35	Rickey Henderson/25	20.00
38	Rod Carew/25	15.00
39	Roger Maris/25	50.00
43	Tom Seaver/25	15.00
44	Tony Gwynn/25	20.00
47	Warren Spahn/24	20.00
49	Willie McCovey/25	15.00

Legendary Players Signature

No Pricing
Production 1-10

Legendary Players Spikes

		NM/M
Production 1-25		
15	Frank Robinson/25	20.00
44	Tony Gwynn/25	30.00

Membership

		NM/M
Common Player:		1.50
Production 1,000 Sets		
Gold:		2-4X
Production 50 Sets		
Platinum:		No Pricing
Production One Set		
1	Bobby Doerr	1.50
2	Tom Seaver	2.00
3	Cal Ripken Jr.	8.00
4	Paul Molitor	2.00
5	Brooks Robinson	2.00
6	Al Kaline	4.00
7	Steve Carlton	2.00
8	Carl Yastrzemski	4.00
9	Bob Feller	2.00
10	Fred Lynn	1.50
11	Luis Aparicio	1.50
12	Hank Aaron	6.00
13	Willie Mays	6.00
14	Bob Gibson	3.00
15	Joe Morgan	2.00
16	Whitey Ford	3.00
17	Don Sutton	1.50
18	Harmon Killebrew	3.00
19	Tony Gwynn	3.00
20	Lou Brock	1.50
21	Dennis Eckersley	1.50
22	Jim Palmer	1.50
23	Don Mattingly	5.00
24	Carlton Fisk	2.00
25	Gaylord Perry	1.50
26	Mike Schmidt	5.00
27	Nolan Ryan	6.00
28	Sandy Koufax	10.00
29	Rod Carew	2.00
30	Maury Wills	1.50

Membership VIP Bat

		NM/M
Production 25 Sets		
1	Bobby Doerr	10.00
2	Tom Seaver	20.00
3	Cal Ripken Jr.	60.00
4	Paul Molitor	15.00
5	Brooks Robinson	15.00
6	Al Kaline	20.00
7	Steve Carlton	10.00
8	Carl Yastrzemski	20.00
10	Fred Lynn	8.00
11	Luis Aparicio	8.00
12	Hank Aaron	40.00
13	Willie Mays	50.00
15	Joe Morgan	10.00
18	Harmon Killebrew	20.00
19	Tony Gwynn	20.00
20	Lou Brock	15.00
23	Don Mattingly	30.00
24	Carlton Fisk	15.00
29	Rod Carew	12.00

Membership VIP Jersey

		NM/M
Production 5-50		
Prime:		No Pricing
Production One Set		
7	Steve Carlton/25	10.00
10	Fred Lynn/25	10.00
11	Luis Aparicio/25	10.00
15	Joe Morgan/25	10.00
17	Don Sutton/50	8.00
19	Tony Gwynn/50	15.00
20	Lou Brock/25	15.00
21	Dennis Eckersley/50	8.00
22	Jim Palmer/25	10.00
23	Don Mattingly/25	30.00
24	Carlton Fisk/25	15.00
25	Gaylord Perry/50	8.00
26	Mike Schmidt/50	20.00
27	Nolan Ryan/25	40.00
29	Rod Carew/50	10.00

Membership VIP Materials

		NM/M
Production 5-25		
Prime:		No Pricing
Production One Set		

1	Bobby Doerr/ Bat-Pants/25	10.00
2	Tom Seaver/ Bat-Jsy/25	20.00
3	Cal Ripken Jr./ Bat-Jsy/25	75.00
4	Paul Molitor/ Bat-Jsy/25	20.00
5	Brooks Robinson/ Bat-Jsy/25	25.00
7	Steve Carlton/ Bat-Jsy/25	15.00
10	Fred Lynn/Bat-Jsy/25	10.00
11	Luis Aparicio/ Bat-Jsy/25	10.00
15	Joe Morgan/ Bat-Jsy/25	12.00
18	Harmon Killebrew/ Bat-Jsy/25	25.00
19	Tony Gwynn/ Bat-Jsy/25	25.00
20	Lou Brock/Bat-Jsy/25	25.00
23	Don Mattingly/ Bat-Jsy/25	35.00
27	Nolan Ryan/ Bat-Jsy/25	50.00
29	Rod Carew/ Bat-Jsy/25	20.00

Membership VIP Materials Awards

No Pricing
Production 5-10

Membership VIP Materials HOF

No Pricing
Production 10 Sets

Membership VIP Materials HR

		NM/M
Production 6-49		
1	Bobby Doerr/ Jsy-Pants/27	15.00
3	Cal Ripken Jr./ Jsy-Pants/34	60.00
4	Paul Molitor/ Bat-Jsy/22	15.00
8	Carl Yastrzemski/ Bat-Jsy/44	25.00
10	Fred Lynn/Bat-Jsy/39	8.00
12	Hank Aaron/ Bat-Jsy/47	50.00
15	Joe Morgan/ Bat-Jsy/27	12.00
18	Harmon Killebrew/ Bat-Jsy/49	20.00
20	Lou Brock/Bat-Jsy/21	15.00
23	Don Mattingly/ Bat-Jsy/35	40.00
24	Carlton Fisk/ Bat-Jsy/37	15.00
26	Mike Schmidt/ Bat-Jsy/48	25.00

Membership VIP Materials Stats

No Pricing
Production 10 Sets

Membership VIP Signature

No Pricing
Production 1-5

Membership VIP Signature Bat

No Pricing
Production 1-10

Membership VIP Signature Jersey

No Pricing
Production 1-10

Membership VIP Signature Material

		NM/M
Production 1-25		
Prime:		No Pricing
Production One Set		
1	Bobby Doerr/ Bat-Pants/25	35.00
10	Fred Lynn/Bat-Jsy/25	30.00
11	Luis Aparicio/ Bat-Jsy/25	30.00
20	Lou Brock/ Bat-Jsy/25	50.00

Membership VIP Signature Materials Awards

No Pricing
Production 1-10

Membership VIP Signature Materials HOF

No Pricing
Production 1-10

Membership VIP Signature Materials HR

No Pricing
Production 1-10

Membership VIP Signature Material Stats

No Pricing
Production 5-10

Significant Signatures Silver

		NM/M
Production 1-200		
Gold:		.75-1.5X
Production 1-100		
No pricing 20 or less.		
Platinum:		No Pricing
Production One Set		
17	Jay Gibbons/25	15.00
22	Tim Salmon/100	15.00
26	Kevin Youkilis/25	12.00
29	Cliff Lee/200	8.00
37	Jeff Suppan/200	10.00
39	Larry Bigbie/100	15.00
40	Rich Harden/100	15.00
41	Victor Martinez/25	20.00
43	Joey Gathright/100	8.00
61	Jake Peavy/25	40.00
63	Dioner Navarro/100	15.00
64	Kazuhito Tadano/100	15.00
65	Ryan Wagner/50	10.00
66	Abe Alvarez/100	15.00
68	Jermaine Dye/25	15.00
69	Todd Walker/25	15.00
70	Octavio Dotel/25	15.00
73	Scott Podsednik/25	20.00
76	Raul Ibanez/50	10.00
77	Orlando Cabrera/25	20.00
79	Esteban Loaiza/50	15.00
84	David Dellucci/50	20.00
85	Travis Blackley/100	8.00
86	Brad Penny/25	15.00
88	Brian Roberts/100	35.00
90	Mike Lieberthal/25	15.00
94	Milton Bradley/100	15.00
96	Adrian Gonzalez/200	12.00
97	Chad Tracy/100	10.00
98	Chad Cordero/100	8.00
100	Jason Kubel/200	12.00
102	Jack Wilson/100	10.00
104	Casey Kotchman/100	12.00
106	Melvin Mora/100	15.00
107	Bobby Crosby/100	15.00
111	Francisco Cordero/50	15.00
114	Eric Byrnes/50	10.00
118	Shea Hillenbrand/25	15.00
119	Aubrey Huff/25	20.00
120	Lew Ford/25	20.00
126	Adam LaRoche/25	15.00
128	Ken Harvey/50	10.00
132	Russ Ortiz/25	15.00
133	Jason Varitek/25	10.00
136	Joe Nathan/100	20.00
138	Carlos Zambrano/25	35.00
143	John Lackey/100	15.00
145	Dewon Brazelton/200	10.00
146	Jason Bay/25	25.00
148	Travis Hafner/100	12.00
152	Wade Miller/50	12.00
154	Scott Kazmir/25	35.00
156	Livan Hernandez/25	15.00
158	David Wright/25	85.00
159	Chone Figgins/50	12.00
163	Merkin Valdez/200	10.00
165	Alexis Rios/50	15.00
166	Johnny Estrada/200	10.00
167	Danny Graves/50	15.00
168	Carlos Lee/25	25.00
171	Randy Wolf/25	15.00
175	Edwin Jackson/25	15.00
178	Jacque Jones/25	15.00
180	Laynce Nix/200	10.00
181	Tom Gordon/25	15.00
182	Jose Castillo/100	12.00

188	Keith Foulke/25	60.00
189	Jeremy Bonderman/50	20.00
190	Troy Percival/25	15.00
194	Brett Myers/50	15.00
197	Lyle Overbay/25	20.00
202	Miguel Negron/100	8.00
204	Paulino Reynoso/100	8.00
205	Colter Bean/100	10.00
206	Raul Tablado/100	8.00
207	Mark McLemore/100	8.00
208	Russel Rohlicek/100	8.00
210	Chris Seddon/100	8.00
213	Mike Morse/100	20.00
217	Carlos Ruiz/100	15.00
218	Chris Roberson/100	8.00
219	Ryan Speier/100	8.00
221	Ambiorix Burgos/100	8.00
223	David Gassner/100	10.00
224	Sean Tracey/100	8.00
225	Casey Rogowski/100	8.00
236	Gaylord Perry/LGD/25	25.00
245	Bobby Doerr/LGD/25	25.00
246	Bob Feller/LGD/25	30.00

Stars of Summer

		NM/M
Common Player:		1.50
Production 1,000 Sets		
Gold:		2-4X
Production 50 Sets		
Platinum:		No Pricing
Production One Set		
1	Andre Dawson	2.00
2	Bert Blyleven	2.00
3	Bill Madlock	1.50
4	Dale Murphy	3.00
5	Darryl Strawberry	2.00
6	Dave Parker	2.00
7	Dave Righetti	2.00
8	Dwight Evans	2.00
9	Dwight Gooden	2.00
10	Fred Lynn	1.50
11	George Foster	2.00
12	Harold Baines	2.00
13	Jack Morris	1.50
14	Jim Rice	3.00
15	Keith Hernandez	2.00
16	Kirk Gibson	2.00
17	Luis Aparicio	2.00
18	Mark Grace	2.00
19	Marty Marion	1.50
20	Orel Hershiser	2.00
21	Ron Guidry	3.00
22	Ron Santo	2.00
23	Steve Garvey	2.00
24	Tony Oliva	2.00
25	Will Clark	3.00

Stars of Summer Material

		NM/M
Production 100-250		
1	Andre Dawson/Jsy/250	8.00
2	Bert Blyleven/Jsy/150	8.00
3	Bill Madlock/Bat/250	5.00
4	Dale Murphy/Jsy/100	12.00
5	Darryl Strawberry/Jsy/100	10.00
6	Dave Parker/Jsy/100	10.00
7	Dave Righetti/Jsy/150	8.00
8	Dwight Evans/Bat/250	8.00
9	Dwight Gooden/Bat/100	8.00
10	Fred Lynn/Jsy/100	5.00
11	George Foster/Bat/250	5.00
12	Harold Baines/Jsy/250	5.00
13	Jack Morris/Jsy/100	5.00
14	Jim Rice/Pants/250	8.00
15	Keith Hernandez/Bat/100	5.00
16	Kirk Gibson/Jsy/250	8.00
17	Luis Aparicio/Bat/250	8.00
18	Mark Grace/Bat/250	10.00
22	Ron Santo/Bat/150	10.00
23	Steve Garvey/Jsy/250	8.00
24	Tony Oliva/Jsy/250	8.00
25	Will Clark/Bat/250	10.00

Stars of Summer Signature Material

		NM/M
Production 25-100		
1	Andre Dawson/Jsy/100	20.00
2	Bert Blyleven/Jsy/50	20.00
3	Bill Madlock/Bat/100	20.00
4	Dale Murphy/Jsy/25	40.00
6	Dave Parker/Jsy/50	20.00
7	Dave Righetti/Jsy/50	20.00
8	Dwight Evans/Jsy/50	20.00
9	Dwight Gooden/Bat/25	25.00
10	Fred Lynn/Jsy/100	15.00
11	George Foster/Bat/50	20.00
12	Harold Baines/Jsy/100	25.00
13	Jack Morris/Jsy/100	15.00
14	Jim Rice/Pants/50	25.00
15	Keith Hernandez/Jsy/50	20.00
16	Kirk Gibson/Jsy/50	40.00
17	Luis Aparicio/Bat/50	20.00
18	Mark Grace/Bat/25	40.00
22	Ron Santo/Bat/50	35.00
23	Steve Garvey/Jsy/50	20.00
24	Tony Oliva/Jsy/50	20.00
25	Will Clark/Bat/25	40.00

Team Colors

		NM/M
Common Player:		1.50
Production 800 Sets		
Gold:		2-4X
Production 50 Sets		
Platinum:		No Pricing
Production One Set		
1	Adam Dunn	2.00
2	Albert Pujols	6.00
3	Andruw Jones	2.00
4	Aramis Ramirez	2.00
5	Aubrey Huff	1.50
6	Bobby Abreu	2.00
7	Cal Ripken Jr.	8.00
8	Carlos Lee	1.50
9	Craig Biggio	2.00
10	Derrek Lee	2.00
11	Garret Anderson	2.00
12	Gary Carter	2.00
13	Geoff Jenkins	1.50
14	Greg Maddux	4.00
15	Hank Blalock	2.00
16	Hideki Matsui	5.00
17	Jake Peavy	2.00
18	Jim Edmonds	2.00
19	Jim Palmer	2.00
20	Jose Guillen	1.50
21	Jose Vidro	1.50
22	Juan Pierre	1.50
23	Lew Ford	1.50
24	Lyle Overbay	1.50
25	Manny Ramirez	3.00
26	Mark Loretta	1.50
27	Mark Teixeira	3.00
28	Melvin Mora	1.50
29	Michael Young	2.00
30	Miguel Cabrera	4.00
31	Mike Lowell	1.50
32	Mike Mussina	2.00
33	Milton Bradley	2.00
34	Randy Johnson	4.00
35	Roger Clemens	6.00
36	Sean Casey	2.00
37	Shawn Green	2.00
38	Steve Carlton	2.00
39	Todd Helton	2.00
40	Travis Hafner	1.50

Team Colors Bat

		NM/M
Production 100 Sets		
1	Adam Dunn	8.00
2	Albert Pujols	20.00
3	Andruw Jones	5.00
4	Aramis Ramirez	8.00
7	Cal Ripken Jr.	30.00
9	Craig Biggio	8.00
10	Derrek Lee	8.00
11	Garret Anderson	5.00
12	Gary Carter	5.00
15	Hank Blalock	8.00
16	Hideki Matsui	30.00
18	Jim Edmonds	10.00
21	Jose Vidro	5.00
22	Juan Pierre	5.00
23	Lew Ford	5.00
27	Mark Teixeira	8.00
28	Melvin Mora	5.00
29	Michael Young	5.00
30	Miguel Cabrera	10.00
31	Mike Lowell	5.00
36	Sean Casey	5.00
37	Shawn Green	5.00

Team Colors Materials

		NM/M
Production 25-100		
Prime:		No Pricing
Production 5 Sets		
1	Adam Dunn/Bat-Jsy/100	10.00
2	Albert Pujols/Bat-Jsy/100	25.00
3	Andruw Jones/Bat-Jsy/100	8.00
4	Aramis Ramirez/Bat-Jsy/100	10.00
6	Bobby Abreu/Jsy-Jsy/100	10.00
7	Cal Ripken Jr./Bat-Jsy/100	40.00
8	Carlos Lee/Bat-Jsy/100	8.00
9	Craig Biggio/Bat-Jsy/100	10.00
11	Garret Anderson/Bat-Jsy/50	8.00
12	Gary Carter/Bat-Jsy/50	8.00
13	Geoff Jenkins/Jsy-Pants/100	8.00
15	Hank Blalock/Bat-Jsy/100	10.00
16	Hideki Matsui/Bat-Jsy/50	45.00
18	Jim Edmonds/Bat-Jkt/100	12.00
19	Jim Palmer/Jsy-Pants/25	12.00
21	Jose Vidro/Bat-Jsy/100	8.00
23	Lew Ford/Bat-Jsy/100	8.00
25	Manny Ramirez/Jsy-Jsy/100	15.00
27	Mark Teixeira/Bat-Jsy/100	10.00
28	Melvin Mora/Bat-Jsy/100	8.00
29	Michael Young/Bat-Jsy/100	8.00
30	Miguel Cabrera/Bat-Jsy/100	15.00
31	Mike Lowell/Bat-Jsy/100	8.00
36	Sean Casey/Bat-Jsy/100	8.00
37	Shawn Green/Bat-Jsy/100	8.00
39	Todd Helton/Jsy-Jsy/50	10.00

Team Colors Signature

		NM/M
Production 1-25		
4	Aramis Ramirez/25	40.00
5	Aubrey Huff/25	20.00
8	Carlos Lee/25	25.00
17	Jake Peavy/25	40.00
20	Jose Guillen/25	25.00
21	Jose Vidro/25	20.00
23	Lew Ford/25	20.00
24	Lyle Overbay/25	25.00
26	Mark Loretta/25	25.00
28	Melvin Mora/25	25.00
33	Milton Bradley/25	25.00
40	Travis Hafner/25	20.00

Team Colors Signature Bat

		NM/M
Production 5-25		
1	Adam Dunn/25	40.00
4	Aramis Ramirez/25	40.00
5	Aubrey Huff/25	20.00
10	Derrek Lee/25	35.00
11	Garret Anderson/25	25.00
15	Hank Blalock/25	30.00
21	Jose Vidro/25	20.00
23	Lew Ford/25	20.00
29	Michael Young/25	20.00

Team Colors Signature Jersey

		NM/M
Production 1-25		
Prime:		No Pricing
Production One Set		
1	Adam Dunn/25	40.00
4	Aramis Ramirez/25	40.00
5	Aubrey Huff/25	20.00
8	Carlos Lee/25	25.00
11	Garret Anderson/25	25.00
12	Gary Carter/25	25.00
15	Hank Blalock/25	30.00
21	Jose Vidro/25	20.00
23	Lew Ford/25	20.00
24	Lyle Overbay/25	25.00
28	Melvin Mora/25	25.00
29	Michael Young/25	20.00
40	Travis Hafner/25	20.00

Team Colors Signature Materials

		NM/M
Production 5-25		
Prime:		No Pricing
Production One Set		
4	Aramis Ramirez/Bat-Jsy/25	50.00
5	Aubrey Huff/Jsy-Jsy/25	25.00
8	Carlos Lee/Jsy-Jsy/25	30.00
11	Garret Anderson/Bat-Jsy/25	30.00
15	Hank Blalock/Bat-Jsy/25	40.00
21	Jose Vidro/Bat-Jsy/25	25.00
23	Lew Ford/Bat-Jsy/25	25.00
28	Melvin Mora/Bat-Jsy/25	30.00
29	Michael Young/Bat-Jsy/25	30.00
40	Travis Hafner/Jsy-Jsy/25	25.00

Texas Rangers Hall of Fame

		NM/M
Complete Set (9):		7.00
Common Player:		.25
(1)	Buddy Bell	.50
(2)	Mark Holtz (Broadcaster)	.25
(3)	Charlie Hough	.50

(4)	Ferguson Jenkins	.50
(5)	Johnny Oates	.50
(6)	Nolan Ryan	5.00
(7)	Jim Sundberg	.50
(8)	Tom Vandergriff (Broadcaster)	.25
(9)	John Wetteland	.50

2005 Donruss Diamond Kings

		NM/M
	Complete Set (300):	85.00
	Complete Update Set (150):	40.00
	Common Player:	.25
	Pack (5):	8.00
	Box (12):	75.00
	Update Pack (5):	5.00
	Update Box (16):	75.00
1	Garret Anderson	.40
2	Vladimir Guerrero	.75
3	Jose Guillen	.40
4	Troy Glaus	.40
5	Tim Salmon	.25
6	Casey Kotchman	.25
7	Chone Figgins	.25
8	Robb Quinlan	.25
9	Francisco Rodriguez	.25
10	Troy Percival	.25
11	Randy Johnson	.75
12	Brandon Webb	.25
13	Richie Sexson	.40
14	Shea Hillenbrand	.25
15	Chad Tracy	.25
16	Alex Cintron	.25
17	Luis Gonzalez	.25
18	Rafael Furcal	.25
19	Andruw Jones	.50
20	Marcus Giles	.25
21	John Smoltz	.50
22	Adam LaRoche	.25
23	Russ Ortiz	.25
24	J.D. Drew	.25
25	Chipper Jones	.75
26	Nick Green	.25
27	Rafael Palmeiro	.50
28	Miguel Tejada	.50
29	Javy Lopez	.25
30	Luis Matos	.25
31	Larry Bigbie	.25
32	Rodrigo Lopez	.25
33	Brian Roberts	.25
34	Melvin Mora	.25
35	Adam Loewen	.25
36	Manny Ramirez	.75
37	Jason Varitek	.50
38	Trot Nixon	.25
39	Curt Schilling	.75
40	Keith Foulke	.25
41	Pedro Martinez	.75
42	Johnny Damon	.75
43	Kevin Youkilis	.25
44	Orlando Cabrera	.25
45	Abe Alvarez	.25
46	David Ortiz	.75
47	Kerry Wood	.75
48	Mark Prior	.75
49	Aramis Ramirez	.50
50	Greg Maddux	1.00
51	Carlos Zambrano	.40
52	Derrek Lee	.50
53	Corey Patterson	.40
54	Moises Alou	.40
55	Matt Clement	.25
56	Sammy Sosa	1.50
57	Nomar Garciaparra	1.00
58	Todd Walker	.25
59	Angel Guzman	.25
60	Magglio Ordonez	.25
61	Carlos Lee	.25
62	Joe Crede	.25
63	Paul Konerko	.25
64	Shingo Takatsu	.25
65	Frank Thomas	.50
66	Freddy Garcia	.25
67	Aaron Rowand	.25
68	Jose Contreras	.25
69	Adam Dunn	.50
70	Austin Kearns	.25
71	Barry Larkin	.40
72	Ken Griffey Jr.	1.00
73	Ryan Wagner	.25
74	Sean Casey	.25
75	Danny Graves	.25
76	C.C. Sabathia	.25
77	Jody Gerut	.25
78	Omar Vizquel	.25
79	Victor Martinez	.40
80	Matt Lawton	.25
81	Jake Westbrook	.25
82	Kazuhito Tadano	.25
83	Travis Hafner	.25
84	Todd Helton	.50
85	Preston Wilson	.25
86	Matt Holliday	.25
87	Jeromy Burnitz	.25
88	Vinny Castilla	.25
89	Jeremy Bonderman	.25
90	Ivan Rodriguez	.50
91	Carlos Guillen	.25
92	Brandon Inge	.25
93	Rondell White	.25
94	Dontrelle Willis	.25
95	Miguel Cabrera	.75
96	Josh Beckett	.40
97	Mike Lowell	.25
98	Luis Castillo	.25
99	Juan Pierre	.25
100	Paul LoDuca	.25
101	Guillermo Mota	.25
102	Craig Biggio	.25
103	Lance Berkman	.25
104	Roy Oswalt	.25
105	Roger Clemens	2.00
106	Jeff Kent	.25
107	Morgan Ensberg	.25
108	Jeff Bagwell	.50
109	Carlos Beltran	.50
110	Angel Berroa	.25
111	Mike Sweeney	.25
112	Jeremy Affeldt	.25
113	Zack Greinke	.25
114	Juan Gonzalez	.25
115	Andres Blanco	.25
116	Shawn Green	.25
117	Milton Bradley	.25
118	Adrian Beltre	.50
119	Hideo Nomo	.50
120	Steve Finley	.25
121	Eric Gagne	.25
122	Brad Penny	.25
123	Scott Podsednik	.25
124	Ben Sheets	.40
125	Lyle Overbay	.25
126	Junior Spivey	.25
127	Bill Hall	.25
128	Rickie Weeks	.25
129	Jacque Jones	.25
130	Torii Hunter	.40
131	Johan Santana	.50
132	Lew Ford	.25
133	Joe Mauer	.75
134	Justin Morneau	.50
135	Jason Kubel	.25
136	Jose Vidro	.25
137	Chad Cordero	.25
138	Brad Wilkerson	.25
139	Nick Johnson	.25
140	Livan Hernandez	.25
141	Tom Glavine	.40
142	Jae Weong Seo	.25
143	Jose Reyes	.50
144	Al Leiter	.25
145	Mike Piazza	1.00
146	Kazuo Matsui	.25
147	Richard Hidalgo	.25
148	David Wright	.75
149	Mariano Rivera	.50
150	Mike Mussina	.50
151	Alex Rodriguez	1.50
152	Derek Jeter	2.00
153	Jorge Posada	.25
154	Jason Giambi	.25
155	Gary Sheffield	.50
156	Bubba Crosby	.25
157	Javier Vazquez	.25
158	Kevin Brown	.25
159	Tom Gordon	.25
160	Esteban Loaiza	.25
161	Hideki Matsui	1.50
162	Eric Chavez	.40
163	Mark Mulder	.40
164	Barry Zito	.40
165	Tim Hudson	.40
166	Jermaine Dye	.25
167	Octavio Dotel	.25
168	Bobby Crosby	.25
169	Mark Kotsay	.25
170	Scott Hatteberg	.25
171	Jim Thome	.75
172	Bobby Abreu	.40
173	Kevin Millwood	.25
174	Mike Lieberthal	.25
175	Jimmy Rollins	.50
176	Chase Utley	.50
177	Randy Wolf	.25
178	Craig Wilson	.25
179	Jason Kendall	.25
180	Jack Wilson	.25
181	Jose Castillo	.25
182	Robert Mackowiak	.25
183	Oliver Perez	.25
184	Oliver Perez	.25
185	Sean Burroughs	.25
186	Jay Payton	.25
187	Brian Giles	.25
188	Akinori Otsuka	.25
189	Jake Peavy	.25
190	Phil Nevin	.25
191	Mark Loretta	.25
192	Khalil Greene	.40
193	Trevor Hoffman	.25
194	Freddy Guzman	.25
195	Jerome Williams	.25
196	Jason Schmidt	.40
197	Todd Linden	.25
198	Merkin Valdez	.25
199	J.T. Snow	.25
200	A.J. Pierzynski	.25
201	Edgar Martinez	.40
202	Ichiro Suzuki	1.50
203	Raul Ibanez	.25
204	Bret Boone	.25
205	Shigetoshi Hasegawa	.25
206	Miguel Olivo	.25
207	Bucky Jacobsen	.25
208	Jamie Moyer	.25
209	Jim Edmonds	.50
210	Scott Rolen	.75
211	Edgar Renteria	.50
212	Dan Haren	.25
213	Matt Morris	.25
214	Albert Pujols	2.00
215	Larry Walker	.40
216	Jason Isringhausen	.25
217	Chris Carpenter	.25
218	Jason Marquis	.25
219	Jeff Suppan	.25
220	Aubrey Huff	.25
221	Carl Crawford	.25
222	Rocco Baldelli	.25
223	Fred McGriff	.25
224	Dewon Brazelton	.25
225	B.J. Upton	.40
226	Joey Gathright	.25
227	Scott Kazmir	.40
228	Hank Blalock	.50
229	Mark Teixeira	.50
230	Michael Young	.25
231	Adrian Gonzalez	.25
232	Laynce Nix	.25
233	Alfonso Soriano	.75
234	Rafael Palmeiro	.50
235	Kevin Mench	.25
236	David Dellucci	.25
237	Francisco Cordero	.25
238	Kenny Rogers	.25
239	Roy Halladay	.25
240	Carlos Delgado	.40
241	Alexis Rios	.25
242	Vernon Wells	.25
243	Yadier Molina	.25
244	Rene Rivera	.25
245	Logan Kensing	.25
246	Gavin Floyd	.25
247	Russ Adams	.25
248	Dioner Navarro	.25
249	Ryan Howard	1.00
250	Ryan Church	.25
251	Jeff Francis	.25
252	John Van Benschoten	.25
253	Yhency Brazoban	.25
254	David Krynzel	.25
255	Victor Diaz	.25
256	Jairo Garcia	.25
257	Scott Proctor	.25
258	Shawn Hill	.25
259	Jeff Baker	.25
260	Matt Peterson	.25
261	Josh Kroeger	.25
262	Grady Sizemore	.40
263	Clint Nageotte	.25
264	Andy Green	.25
265	Justin Verlander RC	2.00
266	Jim Thome	.75
267	Larry Walker	.40
268	Ivan Rodriguez	.50
269	Brad Penny	.25
270	Carlos Beltran	.50
271	Paul LoDuca	.25
272	Orlando Cabrera	.25
273	Nomar Garciaparra	1.00
274	Esteban Loaiza	.25
275	Richard Hidalgo	.25
276	John Olerud	.25
277	Greg Maddux	1.00
278	Roger Clemens	2.00
279	Alfonso Soriano	.75
280	Dale Murphy	.50
281	Cal Ripken Jr.	4.00
282	Dwight Evans	.25
283	Ron Santo	.25
284	Andre Dawson	.50
285	Harold Baines	.25
286	Jack Morris	.25
287	Kirk Gibson	.25
288	Bo Jackson	.75
289	Orel Hershiser	.25
290	Maury Wills	.25
291	Tony Oliva	.25
292	Darryl Strawberry	.25
293	Roger Maris	1.00
294	Don Mattingly	2.00
295	Rickey Henderson	.50
296	Dave Stewart	.25
297	Dave Parker	.25
298	Steve Garvey	.25
299	Matt Williams	.25
300	Keith Hernandez	.25
301	John Lackey	.25
302	Vladimir Guerrero	.75
303	Garret Anderson	.25
304	Dallas McPherson	.25
305	Orlando Cabrera	.25
306	Steve Finley	.25
307	Luis Gonzalez	.25
308	Randy Johnson	.75
309	Scott Hairston	.25
310	Shawn Green	.25
311	Troy Glaus	.40
312	Javier Vazquez	.25
313	Russ Ortiz	.25
314	Chipper Jones	.75
315	Johnny Estrada	.25
316	Andruw Jones	.50
317	Tim Hudson	.50
318	Danny Kolb	.25
319	Jay Gibbons	.25
320	Melvin Mora	.25
321	Rafael Palmeiro	.50
322	Val Majewski	.25
323	David Ortiz	.75
324	Manny Ramirez	.75
325	Edgar Renteria	.25
326	Matt Clement	.25
327	Curt Schilling	.75
328	Sammy Sosa	1.00
329	Mark Prior	.75
330	Greg Maddux	1.00
331	Nomar Garciaparra	1.00
332	Frank Thomas	.50
333	Mark Buehrle	.25
334	Jermaine Dye	.25
335	Scott Podsednik	.25
336	Sean Casey	.25
337	Adam Dunn	.50
338	Ken Griffey Jr.	1.00
339	Travis Hafner	.25
340	Victor Martinez	.25
341	Cliff Lee	.25
342	Todd Helton	.50
343	Preston Wilson	.25
344	Ivan Rodriguez	.50
345	Dmitri Young	.25
346	Nate Robertson	.25
347	Miguel Cabrera	.75
348	Jeff Bagwell	.40
349	Andy Pettitte	.40
350	Roger Clemens	2.00
351	Ken Harvey	.25
352	Danny Bautista	.25
353	Hideo Nomo	.50

354	Kazuhisa Ishii	.25
355	Edwin Jackson	.25
356	J.D. Drew	.25
357	Jeff Kent	.25
358	Geoff Jenkins	.25
359	Carlos Lee	.25
360	Shannon Stewart	.25
361	Joe Nathan	.25
362	Johan Santana	.50
363	Mike Piazza	1.00
364	Hideki Matsui	.25
365	Carlos Beltran	.50
366	Pedro Martinez	.75
367	Ambiorix Concepcion RC	.40
368	Hideki Matsui	1.50
369	Bernie Williams	.40
370	Gary Sheffield	.50
371	Randy Johnson	.75
372	Jaret Wright	.25
373	Carl Pavano	.25
374	Derek Jeter	2.00
375	Alex Rodriguez	1.50
376	Eric Byrnes	.25
377	Rich Harden	.25
378	Mark Mulder	.40
379	Nick Swisher	.25
380	Eric Chavez	.25
381	Jason Kendall	.25
382	Marlon Byrd	.25
383	Pat Burrell	.25
384	Brett Myers	.25
385	Jim Thome	.50
386	Jason Bay	.25
387	Jake Peavy	.25
388	Moises Alou	.25
389	Omar Vizquel	.25
390	Travis Blackley	.25
391	Jose Lopez	.25
392	Jeremy Reed	.25
393	Adrian Beltre	.25
394	Richie Sexson	.25
395	Wladimir Balentien RC	1.50
396	Ichiro Suzuki	1.50
397	Albert Pujols	2.00
398	Scott Rolen	.75
399	Mark Mulder	.40
400	David Eckstein	.25
401	Delmon Young	.25
402	Aubrey Huff	.25
403	Alfonso Soriano	.50
404	Hank Blalock	.25
405	Richard Hidalgo	.25
406	Vernon Wells	.25
407	Orlando Hudson	.25
408	Alexis Rios	.25
409	Shea Hillenbrand	.25
410	Jose Guillen	.25
411	Vinny Castilla	.25
412	Jose Vidro	.25
413	Nick Johnson	.25
414	Livan Hernandez	.25
415	Miguel Tejada	.50
416	Gary Sheffield	.50
417	Curt Schilling	.75
418	Rafael Palmeiro	.50
419	Scott Rolen	.75
420	Aramis Ramirez	.40
421	Vladimir Guerrero	.75
422	Steve Finley	.25
423	Roger Clemens	2.00
424	Mike Piazza	1.00
425	Ivan Rodriguez	.50
426	David Justice	.25
427	Mark Grace	.40
428	Alan Trammell	.25
429	Bert Blyleven	.25
430	Dwight Gooden	.25
431	Deion Sanders	.25
432	Joe Torre	.25
433	Jose Canseco	.40
434	Tony Gwynn	.75
435	Will Clark	.40
436	Marty Marion	.25
437	Nolan Ryan	3.00
438	Billy Martin	.25
439	Carlos Delgado	.25
440	Magglio Ordonez	.25
441	Sammy Sosa	1.00
442	Keiichi Yabu RC	.50
443	Yuniesky Betancourt RC	1.00
444	Jeff Niemann RC	1.50
445	Brandon McCarthy RC	1.50
446	Philip Humber RC	1.50
447	Tadahito Iguchi RC	2.00
448	Cal Ripken Jr.	4.00
449	Ryne Sandberg	2.00
450	Willie Mays	2.00

Non-Canvas

No Pricing
Production 20 Sets

Bronze

Stars:	3-5X
Production 100 Sets	
Update Bronze (301-450):	3-5X
Production 50	

Gold

Golds:	5-10X
Production 25 Sets	
Gold Update (301-450):	No Pricing
Production 10 Sets	

Platinum

No Pricing
Production One Set
Framed Platinums: No Pricing
Production One Set

Silver

Silvers:	4-8X
Production 50 Sets	
Update (301-450):	No Pricing
Production 25 Sets	

Framed Black

Stars:	5-10X
Production 25 Sets	

Framed Blue

Stars:	5-10X
Production 25 Sets	

Framed Green

Stars:	4-8X
Production 50 Sets	

Framed Red

Stars:	1-3X
Inserted 1:3	

Diamond Cuts Bat

NM/M

	Common Player:	4.00
1	Adam Dunn/200	8.00
2	Adrian Beltre/200	6.00
3	Alfonso Soriano/50	8.00
4	Andruw Jones/200	4.00
5	Andy Pettitte/50	6.00
6	Aramis Ramirez/100	6.00
7	Brian Giles/200	4.00
12	Carlos Beltran/200	4.00
12	Craig Wilson/200	4.00
13	Curt Schilling/50	10.00
14	Darin Erstad/200	4.00
16	Derrek Lee/200	6.00
17	Fred McGriff/100	4.00
19	Ivan Rodriguez/200	8.00
20	Jason Bay/200	4.00
21	Jason Giambi/100	4.00
22	Jay Gibbons/200	4.00
23	Jeff Kent/200	4.00
24	John Olerud/200	4.00
25	Juan Gonzalez/200	4.00
27	Kazuhisa Ishii/50	6.00
28	Kevin Brown/100	4.00
29	Larry Walker/200	6.00
31	Mark Teixeira/200	6.00
32	Melvin Mora/50	6.00
33	Michael Young/200	4.00
34	Miguel Tejada/100	8.00
35	Mike Mussina/50	8.00
36	Paul LoDuca/200	4.00
37	Preston Wilson/200	4.00
38	Randy Johnson/50	10.00
39	Richie Sexson/200	6.00
40	Roger Clemens/50	15.00
41	Scott Rolen/100	8.00
42	Sean Burroughs/200	4.00
43	Sean Casey/200	4.00
44	Shannon Stewart/200	4.00

45	Shawn Green/200	4.00
47	Tim Salmon/200	4.00
48	Tom Glavine/200	6.00
49	Torii Hunter/200	6.00

Diamond Cuts Combos

NM/M

	Common Player:	6.00
	Prime:	No Pricing
	Production One Set	
1	Adam Dunn/ Bat-Jsy/100	10.00
2	Adrian Beltre/ Bat-Jsy/100	8.00
3	Alfonso Soriano/ Bat-Jsy/100	10.00
4	Andruw Jones/ Bat-Jsy/100	8.00
5	Andy Pettitte/ Jsy-Jsy/100	10.00
6	Aramis Ramirez/ Bat-Jsy/100	8.00
7	Brian Giles/ Bat-Jsy/100	6.00
10	Carlos Beltran/ Bat-Jsy/50	15.00
11	Carlos Lee/ Jsy-Jsy/100	6.00
12	Craig Wilson/ Bat-Jsy/100	6.00
13	Curt Schilling/ Bat-Jsy/100	12.00
14	Darin Erstad/ Bat-Jsy/100	6.00
17	Fred McGriff/ Bat-Jsy/100	6.00
19	Ivan Rodriguez/ Bat-Jsy/100	10.00
21	Jason Giambi/ Bat-Jsy/50	8.00
22	Jay Gibbons/ Bat-Jsy/50	8.00
23	Jeff Kent/Bat-Jsy/100	6.00
24	John Olerud/ Bat-Jsy/200	6.00
25	Juan Gonzalez/ Bat-Pants/100	8.00
27	Kazuhisa Ishii/ Bat-Jsy/100	8.00
28	Kevin Brown/ Bat-Jsy/100	6.00
29	Larry Walker/ Bat-Jsy/100	8.00
31	Mark Teixeira/ Bat-Jsy/100	10.00
34	Miguel Tejada/ Jsy-Jsy/100	10.00
35	Mike Mussina/ Bat-Pants/100	12.00
36	Paul LoDuca/ Bat-Jsy/100	8.00
37	Preston Wilson/ Bat-Jsy/100	6.00
38	Randy Johnson/ Bat-Jsy/50	15.00
40	Roger Clemens/ Bat-Jsy/50	20.00
44	Shannon Stewart/ Bat-Jsy/100	6.00
45	Shawn Green/ Bat-Jsy/100	6.00
48	Tom Glavine/ Bat-Jsy/100	8.00
49	Torii Hunter/ Bat-Jsy/25	8.00

Diamond Cuts Jersey

NM/M

	Common Player:	4.00
	Prime:	No Pricing
	Production One Set	
1	Adam Dunn/50	10.00
2	Adrian Beltre/200	6.00
3	Alfonso Soriano/200	8.00
4	Andruw Jones/200	4.00
5	Andy Pettitte/100	6.00
6	Aramis Ramirez/200	4.00
7	Brian Giles/200	4.00
8	C.C. Sabathia/200	4.00
9	Carl Crawford/200	4.00
10	Carlos Beltran/200	8.00
11	Carlos Lee/200	4.00
12	Craig Wilson/200	4.00
13	Curt Schilling/200	10.00
14	Darin Erstad/200	4.00
17	Fred McGriff/200	4.00
18	Greg Maddux/50	12.00
19	Ivan Rodriguez/200	8.00
20	Jason Bay/200	4.00
21	Jason Giambi/200	4.00
22	Jay Gibbons/100	4.00
23	Jeff Kent/200	4.00

24	John Olerud/200	4.00
25	Juan Gonzalez/ Pants/200	4.00
26	Junior Spivey/200	4.00
27	Kazuhisa Ishii/200	6.00
28	Kevin Brown/200	4.00
29	Larry Walker/ Rockies/200	6.00
30	Lyle Overbay/200	4.00
31	Mark Teixeira/100	6.00
32	Melvin Mora/200	4.00
33	Michael Young/200	4.00
34	Miguel Tejada/200	8.00
35	Mike Mussina/100	8.00
36	Paul LoDuca/50	6.00
37	Preston Wilson/200	4.00
38	Randy Johnson/200	8.00
39	Richie Sexson/200	6.00
40	Roger Clemens/50	15.00
41	Scott Rolen/50	10.00
42	Sean Burroughs/200	4.00
43	Sean Casey/200	4.00
44	Shannon Stewart/100	4.00
45	Shawn Green/200	4.00
46	Steve Finley/200	4.00
48	Tom Glavine/200	6.00
50	Travis Hafner/100	4.00

Diamond Cuts Signature

NM/M

	Production 1-100	
8	C.C. Sabathia/25	20.00
9	Carl Crawford/50	20.00
11	Carlos Lee/100	15.00
12	Craig Wilson/100	15.00
20	Jason Bay/100	15.00
22	Jay Gibbons/100	10.00
30	Lyle Overbay/100	15.00
32	Melvin Mora/50	15.00
44	Shannon Stewart/25	20.00
47	Tim Salmon/100	20.00
50	Travis Hafner/100	15.00

Diamond Cuts Signature Bat

NM/M

	Production 5-100	
2	Adrian Beltre/50	35.00
6	Aramis Ramirez/100	30.00
10	Carlos Beltran/50	40.00
12	Craig Wilson/100	15.00
16	Derrek Lee/100	20.00
17	Fred McGriff/25	50.00
22	Jay Gibbons/100	10.00
31	Mark Teixeira/25	40.00
33	Michael Young/100	20.00
36	Paul LoDuca/25	25.00
43	Sean Casey/25	25.00
44	Shannon Stewart/25	20.00
49	Torii Hunter/25	25.00

Diamond Cuts Signature Combos

NM/M

	Production 1-100	
	Prime:	No Pricing
	Production One Set	
1	Adam Dunn/ Bat-Jsy/25	40.00
2	Adrian Beltre/ Bat-Bat/25	40.00
6	Aramis Ramirez/ Bat-Jsy/50	30.00
8	C.C. Sabathia/ Jsy-Jsy/50	25.00
11	Carlos Lee/ Jsy-Jsy/50	20.00
12	Craig Wilson/ Bat-Bat/50	15.00
17	Fred McGriff/ Bat-Bat/50	50.00
22	Jay Gibbons/ Bat-Bat/50	10.00
25	Juan Gonzalez/ Bat-Jsy/25	25.00
27	Kazuhisa Ishii/ Bat-Jsy/25	50.00
31	Mark Teixeira/ Bat-Bat/25	40.00

33	Michael Young/Bat-Jsy/50	25.00
36	Paul LoDuca/Bat-Bat/25	25.00
43	Sean Casey/Bat-Jsy/25	25.00
44	Shannon Stewart/Bat-Jsy/25	20.00
49	Torii Hunter/Bat-Jsy/25	25.00
50	Travis Hafner/Bat-Jsy/25	25.00
51	Aramis Ramirez/Jsy/24	25.00
60	Victor Martinez/25	20.00

Diamond Cuts Signature Jersey
NM/M

Production 5-100
Prime: No Pricing
Production One Set

2	Adrian Beltre/100	25.00
6	Aramis Ramirez/100	30.00
8	C.C. Sabathia/100	15.00
9	Carl Crawford/50	20.00
11	Carlos Lee/100	15.00
12	Craig Wilson/100	15.00
30	Lyle Overbay/100	15.00
31	Mark Teixeira/25	40.00
32	Melvin Mora/50	15.00
33	Michael Young/100	20.00
36	Paul LoDuca/25	25.00
42	Sean Burroughs/50	10.00
43	Sean Casey/25	25.00
44	Shannon Stewart/25	20.00
46	Steve Finley/25	25.00
50	Travis Hafner/50	20.00
57	Mark Mulder/25	25.00
60	Victor Martinez/25	20.00

Heritage Collection

NM/M

Common Player: 1.50
Inserted 1:21
#26-35 inserted 1:76
#26-35 are DK Update exclusive

1	Andre Dawson	1.50
2	Bob Gibson	2.50
3	Cal Ripken Jr.	8.00
4	Dale Murphy	2.00
5	Darryl Strawberry	1.50
6	Dennis Eckersley	1.50
7	Don Mattingly	6.00
8	Duke Snider	3.00
9	Dwight Gooden	1.50
10	Eddie Murray	3.00
11	Frank Robinson	3.00
12	Gary Carter	2.00
13	George Brett	6.00
14	Harmon Killebrew	3.00
15	Jack Morris	1.50
16	Jim Palmer	1.50
17	Lou Brock	2.00
18	Mike Schmidt	6.00
19	Nolan Ryan	8.00
20	Ozzie Smith	4.00
21	Phil Niekro	1.50
22	Rod Carew	2.00
23	Rollie Fingers	1.50
24	Steve Carlton	1.50
25	Tony Gwynn	3.00
26	Curt Schilling	3.00
27	Bobby Doerr	1.50
28	Edgar Martinez	1.50
29	Jim Thorpe	4.00
30	Mark Grace	1.50
31	Matt Williams	1.50
32	Paul Molitor	2.50
33	Robin Yount	4.00
34	Ryne Sandberg	5.00
35	Will Clark	2.00

Heritage Collection Bat
NM/M

Production 50-100

1	Andre Dawson/50	8.00
3	Cal Ripken Jr./100	40.00
4	Dale Murphy/100	10.00
5	Darryl Strawberry/50	8.00
7	Don Mattingly/100	20.00
9	Dwight Gooden/100	5.00
10	Eddie Murray/100	15.00
11	Frank Robinson/50	8.00
12	Gary Carter/100	5.00
13	George Brett/100	15.00
14	Harmon Killebrew/100	10.00
17	Lou Brock/100	8.00
18	Mike Schmidt/100	20.00
19	Nolan Ryan/50	30.00
20	Ozzie Smith/100	15.00
21	Phil Niekro/50	8.00
22	Rod Carew/100	8.00
24	Steve Carlton/100	5.00
25	Tony Gwynn/100	10.00

Heritage Collection Combos
NM/M

Production 25-100
Prime: No Pricing
Production One Set

1	Andre Dawson/Bat-Jsy/25	8.00
3	Cal Ripken Jr./Bat-Jsy/50	60.00
4	Dale Murphy/Bat-Jsy/25	20.00
7	Don Mattingly/Bat-Jkt/100	25.00
8	Duke Snider/Jsy-Pants/25	20.00
9	Dwight Gooden/Bat-Jsy/50	10.00
10	Eddie Murray/Bat-Jsy/100	20.00
14	Harmon Killebrew/Bat-Jsy/100	15.00
16	Jim Palmer/Jsy-Pants/100	10.00
17	Lou Brock/Bat/Bat-Jkt/100	10.00
18	Mike Schmidt/Bat-Jsy/100	25.00
19	Nolan Ryan/Jsy-Pants/50	40.00
20	Ozzie Smith/Bat-Pants/100	20.00
21	Phil Niekro/Bat-Jsy/100	10.00
22	Rod Carew/Bat-Jsy/100	10.00
24	Steve Carlton/Bat-Jsy/100	8.00
25	Tony Gwynn/Bat-Jsy/100	15.00

Heritage Collection Jersey
NM/M

Production 25-100
Prime: No Pricing
Production One Set

1	Andre Dawson/100	8.00
2	Bob Gibson/100	10.00
3	Cal Ripken Jr./100	40.00
4	Dale Murphy/100	10.00
5	Darryl Strawberry/25	10.00
6	Dennis Eckersley/100	5.00
7	Don Mattingly/100	20.00
8	Duke Snider/50	15.00
9	Dwight Gooden/100	5.00
10	Eddie Murray/100	15.00
12	Gary Carter/100	5.00
13	George Brett/50	20.00
14	Harmon Killebrew/100	10.00
15	Jack Morris/100	5.00
16	Jim Palmer/100	5.00
17	Lou Brock/100	8.00
18	Mike Schmidt/Jkt/100	20.00
19	Nolan Ryan/100	25.00
20	Ozzie Smith/Pants/100	15.00
21	Phil Niekro/50	8.00
22	Rod Carew/100	8.00
23	Rollie Fingers/50	8.00
24	Steve Carlton/50	8.00
25	Tony Gwynn/100	10.00

Heritage Collection Signature
NM/M

Production 1-50

1	Andre Dawson/50	25.00
5	Darryl Strawberry/50	25.00
9	Dwight Gooden/50	25.00
15	Jack Morris/50	20.00
23	Rollie Fingers/25	40.00

Heritage Collection Signature Bat
NM/M

Production 5-100
#26-35 are DK Update exclusive.

1	Andre Dawson/50	25.00
4	Dale Murphy/25	40.00
7	Don Mattingly/25	75.00
9	Dwight Gooden/100	25.00
11	Frank Robinson/25	40.00
14	Harmon Killebrew/50	50.00
17	Lou Brock/50	35.00
20	Ozzie Smith/25	65.00
21	Phil Niekro/25	30.00
22	Rod Carew/25	40.00
24	Steve Carlton/25	40.00
25	Tony Gwynn/25	50.00
28	Edgar Martinez/25	40.00
31	Matt Williams/25	35.00
35	Will Clark/25	40.00

Heritage Collection Signature Combos
NM/M

Production 5-100
#26-35 are DK Update exclusive.
Prime: No Pricing
Production One Set

1	Andre Dawson/Bat-Jsy/50	25.00
4	Dale Murphy/Bat-Jsy/25	40.00
6	Dennis Eckersley/Jsy-Jsy/25	25.00
7	Don Mattingly/Bat-Jkt/25	80.00
9	Dwight Gooden/Bat-Jsy/100	25.00
12	Gary Carter/Jkt-Jsy/25	25.00
14	Harmon Killebrew/Bat-Bat/25	50.00
15	Jack Morris/Jsy-Jsy/25	30.00
16	Jim Palmer/Jsy-Pants/25	30.00
17	Lou Brock/Bat-Jsy/50	40.00
21	Phil Niekro/Bat-Jsy/50	25.00
22	Rod Carew/Bat-Jkt/25	40.00
24	Steve Carlton/Bat-Jsy/50	40.00
25	Tony Gwynn/Bat-Jsy/25	50.00
27	Bobby Doerr/Jsy/Pants/25	25.00
28	Edgar Martinez/Bat/Jsy/25	40.00
31	Matt Williams/Bat/Jsy/25	35.00
35	Will Clark/Bat/Jsy/25	40.00

Heritage Collection Signature Jersey
NM/M

Production 5-100
#26-35 are DK Update exclusive
Prime: No Pricing
Production One Set

1	Andre Dawson/100	25.00
2	Bob Gibson/25	40.00
4	Dale Murphy/50	40.00
5	Darryl Strawberry/Pants/100	20.00
6	Dennis Eckersley/50	25.00
7	Don Mattingly/25	85.00
8	Duke Snider/25	35.00
9	Dwight Gooden/100	20.00
11	Frank Robinson/25	40.00
12	Gary Carter/50	25.00
14	Harmon Killebrew/50	50.00
15	Jack Morris/100	15.00
16	Jim Palmer/25	35.00
17	Lou Brock/50	35.00
20	Ozzie Smith/25	60.00
21	Phil Niekro/30	30.00
22	Rod Carew/25	40.00
23	Rollie Fingers/25	30.00
24	Steve Carlton/25	40.00
27	Bobby Doerr/25	25.00
28	Edgar Martinez/25	35.00
31	Matt Williams/25	35.00
35	Will Clark/25	40.00

HOF Heroes
NM/M

#51-100 are DK Update exclusive
Common Player: 1.50
Inserted 1:5

Non Canvas:		No Pricing
Production 20 Sets		
Bronze:		1-2X
Production 100 Sets		
Gold:		3-5X
Production 25 Sets		
Platinum:		No Pricing
Production One Set		
Silver:		2-4X
Production 50 Sets		
Frame Black:		3-5X
Production 25 Sets		
Frame Blue:		1-2X
Production 100 Sets		
Frame Green:		2-4X
Production 50 Sets		
Frame Red:		1X

Inserted 1:18

1	Phil Niekro	1.50
2	Brooks Robinson	2.00
3	Jim Palmer	2.00
4	Carl Yastrzemski	3.00
5	Ted Williams	5.00
6	Duke Snider	3.00
7	Burleigh Grimes	1.50
8	Don Sutton	1.50
9	Nolan Ryan	6.00
10	Fergie Jenkins	1.50
11	Carlton Fisk	2.00
12	Tom Seaver	2.00
13	Bob Feller	2.00
14	Nolan Ryan	6.00
15	George Brett	5.00
16	Warren Spahn	3.00
17	Paul Molitor	3.00
18	Rod Carew	3.00
19	Harmon Killebrew	3.00
20	Monte Irvin	2.00
21	Gary Carter	1.50
22	Phil Rizzuto	2.00
23	Babe Ruth	6.00
24	Reggie Jackson	2.00
25	Mike Schmidt	5.00
26	Roberto Clemente	5.00
27	Juan Marichal	1.50
28	Willie McCovey	2.00
29	Stan Musial	4.00
30	Ozzie Smith	3.00
31	Dennis Eckersley	1.50
32	Phil Niekro	1.50
33	Jim Palmer	2.00
34	Carl Yastrzemski	3.00
35	Duke Snider	3.00
36	Don Sutton	1.50
37	Nolan Ryan	6.00
38	Carlton Fisk	2.00
39	Tom Seaver	2.00
40	Bob Feller	2.00
41	Nolan Ryan	6.00
42	George Brett	5.00
43	Harmon Killebrew	3.00
44	Gary Carter	1.50
45	Mike Schmidt	5.00
46	Stan Musial	4.00
47	Ozzie Smith	3.00
48	Dennis Eckersley	1.50
49	Fergie Jenkins	1.50
50	Brooks Robinson	2.00
51	Eddie Murray	2.00
52	Frank Robinson	2.00
53	Carlton Fisk	1.50
54	Ted Williams	5.00
55	Rod Carew	2.00
56	Ernie Banks	3.00
57	Luis Aparicio	1.50
58	Johnny Bench	3.00
59	Al Kaline	2.00
60	George Kell	1.50
61	Robin Yount	3.00
62	Nolan Ryan	6.00
63	Whitey Ford	1.50
64	Reggie Jackson	2.00
65	Babe Ruth	6.00

#	Player	Price
66	Rollie Fingers	1.50
67	Steve Carlton	1.50
68	Robin Roberts	1.50
69	Ralph Kiner	1.50
70	Willie Stargell	2.00
71	Roberto Clemente	5.00
72	Gaylord Perry	1.50
73	Bob Gibson	2.00
74	Lou Brock	1.50
75	Frankie Frisch	1.50
76	Eddie Murray	2.00
77	Frank Robinson	2.00
78	Carlton Fisk	1.50
79	Ted Williams	5.00
80	Rod Carew	2.00
81	Ernie Banks	3.00
82	Luis Aparicio	1.50
83	Johnny Bench	3.00
84	Al Kaline	2.00
85	Willie Mays	5.00
86	Robin Yount	3.00
87	Nolan Ryan	5.00
88	Whitey Ford	2.00
89	Reggie Jackson	2.00
90	Babe Ruth	6.00
91	Rollie Fingers	1.50
92	Steve Carlton	1.50
93	Wade Boggs	2.00
94	Wade Boggs	2.00
95	Willie Stargell	2.00
96	Roberto Clemente	5.00
97	Gaylord Perry	1.50
98	Bob Gibson	2.00
99	Lou Brock	1.50
100	Frankie Frisch	1.50

HOF Heroes Materials Bronze

NM/M

Production 1-100
No pricing 20 or less.
Gold: .75-1.5X
Production 1-25
Silver: .75-1.5X
Production 10-50
Framed Black: No Pricing
Production 1-10
Framed Blue: .75-1.5X
Production 1-25
Framed Red: .75-1.5X
Production 10-50

#	Player	Price
1	Phil Niekro/Bat-Jsy/100	8.00
2	Brooks Robinson/Bat-Jsy/100	12.00
3	Jim Palmer/Jsy-Pants/100	8.00
4	Carl Yastrzemski/Bat-Pants/50	20.00
6	Duke Snider/Jsy-Pants/50	15.00
7	Burleigh Grimes/Pants-Pants/25	75.00
8	Don Sutton/Jsy-Jsy/100	8.00
9	Nolan Ryan/Bat-Jkt/50	40.00
10	Fergie Jenkins/Pants-Pants/100	8.00
11	Carlton Fisk/Bat-Jkt/100	12.00
12	Tom Seaver/Jsy-Pants/50	15.00
13	Bob Feller/Pants-Pants/25	20.00
14	Nolan Ryan/Bat-Jsy/50	40.00
15	George Brett/Bat-Bat/25	40.00
16	Warren Spahn/Jsy-Pants/25	30.00
17	Paul Molitor/Bat-Jsy/100	15.00
18	Rod Carew/Bat-Jsy/50	15.00
19	Harmon Killebrew/Bat-Jsy/25	20.00
21	Gary Carter/Bat-Jsy/100	8.00
23	Babe Ruth/Bat-Pants/25	300.00
24	Reggie Jackson/Bat-Jkt/100	15.00
25	Mike Schmidt/Bat-Jkt/50	30.00
26	Roberto Clemente/Bat-Bat/25	60.00
27	Juan Marichal/Pants-Pants/25	12.00
28	Willie McCovey/Jsy-Pants/100	10.00
29	Stan Musial/Bat-Bat/25	30.00
30	Ozzie Smith/Bat-Pants/100	20.00
31	Dennis Eckersley/Jsy-Jsy/100	8.00
32	Phil Niekro/Bat-Jsy/100	8.00
33	Jim Palmer/Jsy-Pants/25	12.00
34	Carl Yastrzemski/Bat-Pants/25	30.00
35	Duke Snider/Jsy-Pants	20.00
36	Don Sutton/Jsy-Jsy/100	8.00
37	Nolan Ryan/Bat-Jkt/25	50.00
38	Carlton Fisk/Bat-Jkt/100	12.00
39	Tom Seaver/Bat-Jsy/25	20.00
40	Bob Feller/Pants-Pants/25	20.00
41	Nolan Ryan/Bat-Jkt/25	50.00
42	George Brett/Bat-Bat/25	40.00
43	Harmon Killebrew/Bat-Jsy/25	25.00
44	Gary Carter/Bat-Jsy/100	8.00
45	Mike Schmidt/Bat-Jsy/25	40.00
46	Stan Musial/Bat-Bat/25	30.00
47	Ozzie Smith/Bat-Pants/100	20.00
48	Dennis Eckersley/Jsy-Jsy/100	8.00
49	Fergie Jenkins/Pants-Pants/25	12.00
50	Brooks Robinson/Bat-Jsy/25	20.00
51	Eddie Murray/Bat/Pants/50	12.00
52	Frank Robinson/Bat/Bat/50	12.00
53	Carlton Fisk/Bat/Bat/50	10.00
55	Rod Carew/Bat/Jsy/50	12.00
56	Ernie Banks/Bat/Pants/50	15.00
57	Luis Aparicio/Bat/Bat/50	8.00
58	Johnny Bench/Bat/Jsy/50	15.00
59	Al Kaline/Bat/Bat/25	20.00
61	Robin Yount/Bat/Jsy/50	15.00
62	Nolan Ryan/Bat/Jsy/25	50.00
63	Whitey Ford/Jsy/Jsy/25	25.00
64	Reggie Jackson/Jsy/Jsy/50	15.00
66	Rollie Fingers/Jsy/50	8.00
67	Steve Carlton/Bat/Jsy/50	10.00
70	Willie Stargell/Bat/Jsy/50	15.00
72	Gaylord Perry/Jsy/Jsy/50	8.00
73	Bob Gibson/Jsy/Jsy/25	15.00
74	Lou Brock/Bat/Jsy/50	12.00
76	Eddie Murray/Bat/Bat/50	12.00
77	Frank Robinson/Bat/Bat/50	12.00
78	Carlton Fisk/Bat/Bat/50	12.00
80	Rod Carew/Bat/Jkt/50	12.00
81	Ernie Banks/Bat/Jsy/25	15.00
82	Luis Aparicio/Bat/Bat/50	8.00
83	Johnny Bench/Bat/Jsy/50	15.00
86	Robin Yount/Bat/Jsy/50	15.00
87	Nolan Ryan/Bat/Jsy/25	40.00
88	Whitey Ford/Jsy/25	25.00
89	Reggie Jackson/Jsy/Jsy/50	15.00
91	Rollie Fingers/Jsy/Jsy/50	8.00
92	Steve Carlton/Bat/Jsy/50	10.00
95	Willie Stargell/Jsy/Jsy/50	15.00
97	Gaylord Perry/Jsy/Jsy/50	8.00
99	Lou Brock/Bat/Jsy/50	10.00

HOF Heroes Signatures Bronze

NM/M

Production 1-25
No pricing 20 or less.
Gold: No Pricing
Production 1-10
Platinum: No Pricing
Production One Set
Silver: 1X
Production 1-25
Framed Blue: No Pricing
Production One Set
Framed Black: No Pricing
Production One Set
Framed Green: No Pricing
Production 1-10
Framed Red: No Pricing
Production 1-25
Cards #52-99 are seeded in DK Update.

#	Player	Price
13	Bob Feller/25	35.00
40	Bob Feller/25	35.00
52	Frank Robinson/25	35.00
57	Luis Aparicio/25	15.00
59	Al Kaline/25	40.00
60	George Kell/25	20.00
66	Rollie Fingers/25	15.00
67	Steve Carlton/25	20.00
68	Robin Roberts/25	20.00
69	Ralph Kiner/25	35.00
72	Gaylord Perry/15	15.00
74	Lou Brock/25	35.00
82	Luis Aparicio/25	15.00
84	Al Kaline/25	40.00
91	Rollie Fingers/25	15.00
92	Steve Carlton/25	20.00
93	Wade Boggs/Yanks/25	30.00
94	Wade Boggs/Sox/25	30.00
97	Gaylord Perry/25	15.00
99	Lou Brock/25	35.00

Signature Materials Bronze

NM/M

Production 5-50
No pricing 20 or less.
Gold: .75-1.5X
Production 5-25
Platinum: No Pricing
Production One Set
Silver: .75-1X
Production 5-50
Framed Black: No Pricing
Production 5-10
Framed Blue: .75-1.5X
Production 5-25
Framed Green: No Pricing
Production 1-10
Framed Red: .75-1.5X
Production 1-25
#53-99 are found in DK Update

#	Player	Price
2	Brooks Robinson/Bat-Jsy/25	50.00
3	Jim Palmer/Jsy-Pants/25	40.00
6	Duke Snider/Jsy-Pants/25	40.00
8	Don Sutton/Jsy-Jsy/25	30.00
10	Fergie Jenkins/Pants-Pants/25	30.00
13	Bob Feller/Pants-Pants/50	35.00
18	Rod Carew/Bat-Jsy/50	40.00
19	Harmon Killebrew/Bat-Jsy/50	50.00
21	Gary Carter/Bat-Jsy/25	25.00
27	Juan Marichal/Pants-Pants/25	40.00
28	Willie McCovey/Jsy-Pants/25	50.00
29	Stan Musial/Bat-Bat/25	85.00
30	Ozzie Smith/Bat-Pants/25	75.00
31	Dennis Eckersley/Jsy-Jsy/25	35.00
32	Phil Niekro/Bat-Jsy/25	30.00
33	Jim Palmer/Jsy-Pants/25	40.00
35	Duke Snider/Jsy-Pants/25	40.00
36	Don Sutton/Jsy-Jsy/25	30.00
40	Bob Feller/Pants-Pants/50	35.00
43	Harmon Killebrew/Bat-Jsy/50	40.00
44	Gary Carter/Bat-Jsy/25	25.00
47	Ozzie Smith/Bat-Pants/25	75.00
48	Dennis Eckersley/Jsy-Jsy/25	25.00
49	Fergie Jenkins/Pants-Pants/25	30.00
50	Brooks Robinson/Bat-Jsy/25	50.00
61	Robin Yount/Bat-Jsy/25	50.00
66	Rollie Fingers/Jsy-Jsy/50	15.00
72	Gaylord Perry/Jsy/50	15.00
74	Lou Brock/Jsy-Jsy/50	30.00
80	Rod Carew/Bat-Jsy/25	25.00
99	Lou Brock/Bat-Jsy/25	40.00

Materials Bronze

NM/M

Production 10-200
No pricing 20 or less.
Gold: .75-1.5X
Production 25-50
Silver: .75-1.5X
Production 25-100
Platinum: No Pricing
Production One Set
Framed Black: No Pricing
Production 10 Sets
Framed Blue: .75-1.5X
Production 50 Sets
Framed Green:
Production 25 Sets
Framed Red: .75-1.5X
Production 25-100
#302-450 are found in DK Update

#	Player	Price
1	Garret Anderson/Bat-Jsy/200	5.00
2	Vladimir Guerrero/Bat-Jsy/200	10.00
4	Troy Glaus/Bat-Jsy/200	5.00
5	Tim Salmon/Bat-Jsy/200	5.00
7	Chone Figgins/Bat-Jsy/200	5.00
10	Tony Percival/Jsy-Jsy/200	5.00
12	Brandon Webb/Bat-Pants/200	5.00
13	Richie Sexson/Bat-Bat/200	8.00
17	Luis Gonzalez/Jsy-Jsy/200	5.00
18	Rafael Furcal/Bat-Jsy/200	5.00
19	Andruw Jones/Bat-Jsy/200	8.00
21	John Smoltz/Jsy-Jsy/200	8.00
24	J.D. Drew/Bat-Bat/200	5.00
25	Chipper Jones/Bat-Jsy/200	10.00
27	Rafael Palmeiro/Bat-Jsy/200	8.00
28	Miguel Tejada/Bat-Jsy/200	10.00
29	Javy Lopez/Bat-Jsy/200	10.00
30	Luis Matos/Jsy-Jsy/100	5.00
31	Larry Bigbie/Jsy-Jsy/200	5.00
32	Rodrigo Lopez/Jsy-Jsy/200	5.00
34	Melvin Mora/Bat-Jsy/200	5.00
36	Manny Ramirez/Bat-Jsy/200	10.00
38	Trot Nixon/Bat-Bat/200	10.00
39	Curt Schilling/Bat-Jsy/200	10.00
41	Pedro Martinez/Bat-Jsy/200	10.00
42	Johnny Damon/Bat-Bat/200	15.00
43	Kevin Youkilis/Bat-Bat/200	5.00
46	David Ortiz/Bat-Jsy/200	10.00
47	Kerry Wood/Jsy-Pants/200	10.00
48	Mark Prior/Bat-Jsy/200	8.00

49	Aramis Ramirez/ Bat-Jsy/200	8.00
50	Greg Maddux/ Bat-Jsy/100	15.00
51	Carlos Zambrano/ Jsy-Jsy/200	8.00
52	Derrek Lee/ Bat-Bat/200	8.00
54	Moises Alou/ Bat-Bat/200	8.00
56	Sammy Sosa/ Bat-Jsy/200	10.00
57	Nomar Garciaparra/ Bat-Bat/200	10.00
60	Magglio Ordonez/ Bat-Jsy/200	5.00
61	Carlos Lee/ Bat-Jsy/200	5.00
62	Joe Crede/Bat-Bat/200	5.00
65	Frank Thomas/ Bat-Jsy/200	8.00
69	Adam Dunn/ Bat-Jsy/200	8.00
70	Austin Kearns/ Bat-Bat/200	5.00
74	Sean Casey/ Jsy-Pants/200	5.00
76	C.C. Sabathia/ Jsy-Jsy/200	5.00
77	Jody Gerut/ Bat-Jsy/200	5.00
78	Omar Vizquel/ Bat-Jsy/200	5.00
79	Victor Martinez/ Bat-Jsy/200	5.00
80	Matt Lawton/ Bat-Bat/200	5.00
84	Todd Helton/ Bat-Jsy/200	8.00
85	Preston Wilson/ Bat-Jsy/200	5.00
90	Ivan Rodriguez/ Bat-Jsy/200	8.00
92	Brandon Inge/ Bat-Jsy/200	5.00
94	Dontrelle Willis/ Jsy-Jsy/200	5.00
95	Miguel Cabrera/ Bat-Jsy/200	10.00
96	Josh Beckett/ Bat-Bat/100	5.00
97	Mike Lowell/ Bat-Jsy/100	5.00
98	Luis Castillo/ Bat-Bat/200	5.00
99	Juan Pierre/ Bat-Bat/200	5.00
100	Paul LoDuca/ Bat-Bat/200	5.00
102	Craig Biggio/ Bat-Pants/200	5.00
103	Lance Berkman/ Bat-Jsy/200	5.00
104	Roy Oswalt/ Bat-Jsy/200	5.00
105	Roger Clemens/ Bat-Jsy/200	15.00
106	Jeff Kent/Bat-Jsy/100	5.00
108	Jeff Bagwell/ Bat-Jsy/200	8.00
109	Carlos Beltran/ Bat-Jsy/200	8.00
110	Angel Berroa/ Bat-Bat/200	5.00
111	Mike Sweeney/ Bat-Jsy/200	5.00
112	Jeremy Affeldt/ Pants-Pants/200	5.00
114	Juan Gonzalez/ Bat-Jsy/200	8.00
116	Shawn Green/ Bat-Jsy/200	5.00
118	Adrian Beltre/ Bat-Jsy/200	8.00
119	Hideo Nomo/ Bat-Jsy/200	8.00
123	Scott Podsednik/ Jsy-Jsy/200	5.00
124	Ben Sheets/ Bat-Pants/200	8.00
125	Lyle Overbay/ Jsy-Jsy/200	5.00
126	Junior Spivey/ Jsy-Jsy/200	5.00
127	Bill Hall/Bat-Jsy/200	5.00
129	Jacque Jones/ Jsy-Jsy/200	5.00
130	Torii Hunter/ Bat-Jsy/200	5.00
131	Johan Santana/ Jsy-Jsy/200	10.00
132	Lew Ford/Bat-Jsy/200	5.00
136	Jose Vidro/ Bat-Jsy/200	5.00
138	Brad Wilkerson/ Bat-Bat/100	5.00
139	Nick Johnson/ Bat-Bat/100	5.00
140	Livan Hernandez/ Jsy-Jsy/25	5.00
141	Tom Glavine/ Bat-Bat/200	8.00
143	Jose Reyes/ Bat-Jsy/200	6.00
144	Al Leiter/Jsy-Jsy/200	5.00
145	Mike Piazza/ Jsy-Jsy/100	15.00
146	Kazuo Matsui/ Bat-Jsy/200	8.00
147	Richard Hidalgo/ Bat-Bat/200	5.00
149	Mariano Rivera/ Jsy-Jsy/100	8.00
150	Mike Mussina/ Bat-Jsy/200	8.00
153	Jorge Posada/ Bat-Jsy/200	8.00
154	Jason Giambi/ Bat-Jsy/200	5.00
155	Gary Sheffield/ Bat-Jsy/200	8.00
158	Kevin Brown/ Bat-Bat/100	5.00
160	Esteban Loaiza/ Bat-Bat/100	5.00
161	Hideki Matsui/ Jsy-Pants/200	20.00
162	Eric Chavez/ Bat-Jsy/200	5.00
163	Mark Mulder/ Bat-Bat/25	10.00
164	Barry Zito/Bat-Jsy/200	5.00
165	Tim Hudson/ Bat-Jsy/200	8.00
166	Jermaine Dye/ Bat-Jsy/200	5.00
168	Bobby Crosby/ Jsy-Jsy/200	8.00
171	Jim Thome/ Bat-Jsy/200	8.00
172	Bobby Abreu/ Jsy-Jsy/200	8.00
173	Kevin Millwood/ Jsy-Jsy/200	5.00
178	Craig Wilson/ Bat-Jsy/200	5.00
180	Jack Wilson/ Bat-Bat/200	5.00
181	Jose Castillo/ Bat-Bat/200	5.00
184	Jason Bay/ Bat-Jsy/200	5.00
185	Sean Burroughs/ Bat-Jsy/200	8.00
187	Brian Giles/ Bat-Bat/200	5.00
193	Trevor Hoffman/ Jsy-Jsy/200	5.00
199	J.T. Snow/Jsy-Jsy/25	5.00
200	A.J. Pierzynski/ Jsy-Jsy/100	5.00
201	Edgar Martinez/ Bat-Bat/200	5.00
204	Bret Boone/ Jsy-Jsy/200	5.00
208	Jamie Moyer/ Jsy-Jsy/50	5.00
209	Jim Edmonds/ Bat-Jsy/200	8.00
210	Scott Rolen/ Bat-Jsy/200	10.00
211	Edgar Renteria/ Bat-Jsy/200	8.00
212	Dan Haren/ Bat-Jsy/100	5.00
213	Matt Morris/ Bat-Jsy/100	5.00
214	Albert Pujols/ Jsy-Jsy/200	20.00
215	Larry Walker/ Bat-Jsy/200	8.00
220	Aubrey Huff/ Bat-Bat/100	5.00
221	Carl Crawford/ Jsy-Jsy/200	5.00
222	Rocco Baldelli/ Bat-Jsy/200	5.00
223	Fred McGriff/ Bat-Jsy/200	5.00
224	Dewon Brazelton/ Jsy-Jsy/200	5.00
225	B.J. Upton/Bat-Bat/200	8.00
226	Joey Gathright/ Bat-Jsy/200	5.00
228	Hank Blalock/ Bat-Jsy/100	8.00
229	Mark Teixeira/ Bat-Jsy/200	8.00
230	Michael Young/ Bat-Jsy/200	5.00
232	Laynce Nix/ Bat-Jsy/200	5.00
233	Alfonso Soriano/ Bat-Jsy/200	8.00
234	Rafael Palmeiro/ Bat-Jsy/200	8.00
235	Kevin Mench/ Bat-Jsy/200	5.00
236	David Dellucci/ Jsy-Jsy/200	8.00
237	Francisco Cordero/ Jsy-Jsy/200	5.00
239	Roy Halladay/ Jsy-Jsy/200	5.00
240	Carlos Delgado/ Bat-Jsy/200	5.00
242	Vernon Wells/ Bat-Jsy/200	5.00
267	Larry Walker/ Jsy-Jsy/200	8.00
268	Ivan Rodriguez/ Bat-Jsy/200	8.00
269	Brad Penny/ Bat-Jsy/200	5.00
270	Carlos Beltran/ Bat-Jsy/200	8.00
271	Paul LoDuca/ Bat-Jsy/200	5.00
273	Nomar Garciaparra/ Bat-Bat/100	10.00
274	Esteban Loiaza/ Bat-Bat/100	5.00
275	Richard Hidalgo/ Jkt-Pants/200	5.00
276	John Olerud/ Bat-Jsy/200	5.00
277	Greg Maddux/ Jsy-Jsy/200	12.00
278	Roger Clemens/ Bat-Jsy/200	15.00
279	Alfonso Soriano/ Bat-Jsy/200	8.00
280	Dale Murphy/ Jsy-Jsy/200	8.00
281	Cal Ripken Jr./ Bat-Jsy/200	30.00
282	Dwight Evans/ Bat-Jsy/200	8.00
283	Ron Santo/ Bat-Bat/200	10.00
284	Andre Dawson/ Bat-Jsy/100	8.00
285	Harold Baines/ Bat-Jsy/200	8.00
286	Jack Morris/ Jsy-Jsy/100	8.00
287	Kirk Gibson/ Bat-Jsy/200	5.00
288	Bo Jackson/ Bat-Jsy/200	10.00
289	Orel Hershiser/ Jsy-Jsy/50	8.00
291	Tony Oliva/ Bat-Jsy/200	10.00
292	Darryl Strawberry/ Bat-Jsy/100	8.00
293	Roger Maris/ Bat-Jsy/200	50.00
294	Don Mattingly/ Bat-Jsy/100	25.00
295	Rickey Henderson/ Bat-Jsy/100	10.00
297	Dave Parker/ Bat-Jsy/200	8.00
298	Steve Garvey/ Bat-Jsy/200	8.00
299	Matt Williams/ Jsy-Jsy/200	8.00
300	Keith Hernandez/ Bat-Jsy/200	8.00
302	Vladimir Guerrero/ Jsy-Jsy/200	10.00
303	Garret Anderson/ Bat-Jsy/200	5.00
307	Luis Gonzalez/ Jsy-Jsy/200	5.00
310	Shawn Green/ Bat-Bat/200	5.00
311	Troy Glaus/ Bat-Jsy/200	5.00
314	Chipper Jones/ Jsy-Jsy/100	10.00
315	Johnny Estrada/	
316	Andruw Jones/ Bat-Jsy/200	8.00
319	Jay Gibbons/ Bat-Bat/200	5.00
320	Melvin Mora/ Jsy-Jsy/200	5.00
321	Rafael Palmeiro/ Bat-Jsy/200	8.00
323	David Ortiz/ Bat-Jsy/200	10.00
324	Manny Ramirez/ Bat-Jsy/200	10.00
327	Curt Schilling/ Jsy-Jsy/200	10.00
328	Sammy Sosa/ Bat-Jsy/100	10.00
329	Mark Prior/ Bat-Jsy/200	8.00
330	Greg Maddux/ Jsy-Jsy/25	15.00
332	Frank Thomas/ Bat-Pants/200	10.00
333	Mark Buehrle/ Bat-Jsy/200	5.00
336	Sean Casey/ Bat-Jsy/200	5.00
337	Adam Dunn/ Bat-Jsy/200	8.00
339	Travis Hafner/ Bat-Jsy/100	5.00
340	Victor Martinez/ Bat-Jsy/100	5.00
341	Cliff Lee/Jsy-Jsy/200	5.00
342	Todd Helton/ Bat-Jsy/25	8.00
343	Preston Wilson/ Jsy-Jsy/200	5.00
344	Ivan Rodriguez/ Bat-Jsy/200	8.00
347	Miguel Cabrera/ Bat-Jsy/200	10.00
348	Jeff Bagwell/ Bat-Jsy/200	8.00
349	Andy Pettitte/ Bat-Jsy/200	8.00
350	Roger Clemens/ Bat-Jsy/100	15.00
351	Ken Harvey/ Jsy-Jsy/200	5.00
353	Hideo Nomo/ Bat-Jsy/200	8.00
354	Kazuhisa Ishii/ Jsy-Jsy/200	5.00
355	Edwin Jackson/ Jsy-Jsy/200	5.00
356	J.D. Drew/Bat-Bat/200	5.00
357	Jeff Kent/Bat-Bat/25	5.00
358	Geoff Jenkins/ Jsy-Pants/200	5.00
359	Carlos Lee/ Bat-Bat/200	5.00
360	Shannon Stewart/ Jsy-Jsy/200	5.00
362	Johan Santana/ Jsy-Jsy/100	10.00
363	Mike Piazza/ Jsy-Jsy/100	12.00
364	Kazuo Matsui/ Jsy-Jsy/100	5.00
366	Pedro Martinez/ Bat-Bat/100	10.00
368	Hideki Matsui/ Bat-Jsy/100	20.00
369	Bernie Williams/ Bat-Jsy/200	8.00
370	Gary Sheffield/ Bat-Jsy/100	8.00
371	Randy Johnson/ Bat-Bat/25	10.00
378	Mark Mulder/ Bat-Bat/50	8.00
380	Eric Chavez/ Jsy-Jsy/100	5.00
382	Marlon Byrd/ Bat-Jsy/200	5.00
383	Pat Burrell/Jsy-Jsy/200	5.00
385	Jim Thome/ Bat-Bat/200	5.00
386	Jason Bay/Bat-Jsy/1	
388	Moises Alou/ Bat-Bat/200	5.00
393	Adrian Beltre/ Bat-Bat/50	5.00
394	Richie Sexson/ Bat-Bat/200	5.00
397	Albert Pujols/ Bat-Jsy/200	20.00
398	Scott Rolen/ Bat-Jsy/200	10.00
401	Delmon Young/ Bat-Bat/200	5.00
402	Aubrey Huff/ Bat-Bat/50	5.00
403	Alfonso Soriano/ Bat-Jsy/200	8.00

ABBREVIATIONS

SP - Short Print

404	Hank Blalock/ Bat-Jsy/200	5.00
405	Richard Hidalgo/ Bat-Bat/200	5.00
406	Vernon Wells/ Jsy-Jsy/200	5.00
407	Orlando Hudson/ Bat-Bat/200	5.00
412	Jose Vidro/Bat-Jsy/5	5.00
415	Miguel Tejada/ Jsy-Jsy/200	8.00
416	Gary Sheffield/ Bat-Bat/200	8.00
417	Curt Schilling/ Jsy-Jsy/200	10.00
418	Rafael Palmeiro/ Bat-Pants/50	8.00
419	Scott Rolen/ Bat-Jsy/200	10.00
420	Aramis Ramirez/ Jsy-Jsy/200	8.00
421	Vladimir Guerrero/ Bat-Bat/200	10.00
422	Steve Finley/ Jsy-Jsy/200	5.00
423	Roger Clemens/ Bat-Jsy/200	15.00
424	Mike Piazza/ Jsy-Jsy/200	12.00
425	Ivan Rodriguez/ Bat-Jsy/200	8.00
426	David Justice/ Jsy-Jsy/200	5.00
427	Mark Grace/ Bat-Jsy/25	8.00
428	Alan Trammell/ Bat-Jsy/100	5.00
430	Dwight Gooden/ Bat-Jsy/200	5.00
431	Deion Sanders/ Bat-Jsy/200	8.00
432	Joe Torre/Bat-Bat/100	5.00
433	Jose Canseco/ Jsy-Jsy/200	8.00
434	Tony Gwynn/ Bat-Pants/200	10.00
435	Will Clark/Bat-Jsy/100	8.00
437	Nolan Ryan/ Bat-Jsy/50	15.00
438	Billy Martin/ Jsy-Pants/200	10.00
439	Carlos Delgado/ Bat-Bat/100	5.00
440	Magglio Ordonez/ Bat-Bat/200	5.00
441	Sammy Sosa/ Bat-Bat/25	10.00
449	Ryne Sandberg/ Bat-Jsy/100	10.00

Recollection Autographs Gold

NM/M

No Pricing
Production One Set

Silver:	No Pricing
Production One Set	
Platinum:	No Pricing
Production One Set	

Signature Bronze

NM/M

Production 1-100
No pricing 20 or less.

Black:	No Pricing
Production One Set	
Gold:	.75-1.5X
Production 1-50	
Silver:	.75-1.5X
Production 1-100	
Platinum:	No Pricing
Production One Set	
Framed Blue:	.75-1.5X
Production 1-50	
Framed Green:	.75-1.5X
Production 1-25	
Framed Red:	.75-1.5X
Production 1-100	

#303-450 found in DK Update

3	Jose Guillen/100	15.00
5	Tim Salmon/100	20.00
6	Casey Kotchman/100	15.00
7	Chone Figgins/100	15.00
8	Robb Quinlan/100	8.00
9	Francisco Rodriguez/ 50	40.00
10	Troy Percival/50	10.00
14	Shea Hillenbrand/100	10.00
15	Chad Tracy/100	10.00
16	Alex Cintron/100	8.00
22	Adam LaRoche/100	10.00
23	Russ Ortiz/100	12.00
26	Nick Green/100	8.00

30	Luis Matos/100	10.00
31	Larry Bigbie/100	10.00
32	Rodrigo Lopez/100	15.00
33	Brian Roberts/100	25.00
34	Melvin Mora/100	15.00
40	Keith Foulke/50	40.00
43	Kevin Youkilis/100	10.00
44	Orlando Cabrera/50	20.00
45	Abe Alvarez/100	8.00
51	Carlos Zambrano/50	30.00
58	Todd Walker/50	15.00
59	Angel Guzman/100	15.00
61	Carlos Lee/100	15.00
73	Ryan Wagner/100	10.00
75	Danny Graves/100	12.00
76	C.C. Sabathia/50	20.00
77	Jody Gerut/100	8.00
79	Victor Martinez/50	20.00
82	Kazuhito Tadano/ 100	20.00
83	Travis Hafner/100	15.00
89	Jeremy Bonderman/ 100	15.00
92	Brandon Inge/100	10.00
101	Guillermo Mota/50	10.00
107	Morgan Ensberg/100	10.00
112	Jeremy Affeldt/100	10.00
117	Milton Bradley/100	15.00
122	Brad Penny/100	15.00
123	Scott Podsednik/50	15.00
125	Lyle Overbay/100	12.00
127	Bill Hall/100	10.00
132	Lew Ford/100	15.00
135	Jason Kubel/100	15.00
137	Chad Cordero/100	10.00
140	Livan Hernandez/25	15.00
156	Bubba Crosby/100	10.00
159	Tom Gordon/25	20.00
160	Esteban Loaiza/100	10.00
166	Jermaine Dye/50	15.00
167	Octavio Dotel/50	15.00
168	Bobby Crosby/100	20.00
174	Mike Lieberthal/100	12.00
177	Randy Wolf/100	10.00
178	Craig Wilson/100	10.00
180	Jack Wilson/100	12.00
181	Jose Castillo/100	10.00
184	Jason Bay/100	15.00
186	Jay Payton/50	10.00
189	Jake Peavy/50	30.00
194	Freddy Guzman/100	8.00
197	Todd Linden/50	10.00
198	Merkin Valdez/100	10.00
203	Raul Ibanez/100	10.00
206	Miguel Olivo/100	8.00
207	Bucky Jacobsen/100	12.00
208	Jamie Moyer/50	15.00
212	Dan Haren/100	12.00
219	Jeff Suppan/100	10.00
220	Aubrey Huff/50	15.00
221	Carl Crawford/25	20.00
224	Dewon Brazelton/100	8.00
226	Joey Gathright/100	10.00
227	Scott Kazmir/25	25.00
230	Michael Young/50	20.00
231	Adrian Gonzalez/100	10.00
232	Laynce Nix/100	15.00
236	David Dellucci/100	20.00
237	Francisco Cordero/ 100	15.00
241	Alexis Rios/100	15.00
248	Dioner Navarro/100	15.00
253	Yhency Brazoban/ 100	10.00
257	Scott Proctor/100	8.00
260	Matt Peterson/100	8.00
269	Brad Penny/50	10.00
272	Orlando Cabrera/50	10.00
274	Esteban Loaiza/100	10.00
284	Andre Dawson/50	20.00
285	Harold Baines/100	15.00
286	Jack Morris/100	10.00
290	Maury Wills/100	15.00
292	Darryl Strawberry/100	15.00
297	Dave Parker/100	20.00
299	Matt Williams/25	25.00
303	Garret Anderson/100	15.00
304	Dallas McPherson/ 100	10.00
305	Orlando Cabrera/25	10.00
306	Steve Finley/50	10.00
313	Russ Ortiz/50	10.00
315	Johnny Estrada/100	8.00
318	Danny Kolb/50	8.00
319	Jay Gibbons/50	8.00
320	Melvin Mora/50	10.00
325	Edgar Renteria/50	15.00
333	Mark Buehrle/50	20.00
336	Sean Casey/25	15.00
339	Travis Hafner/50	15.00
340	Victor Martinez/50	10.00
341	Cliff Lee/100	10.00
343	Preston Wilson/50	15.00
351	Ken Harvey/100	8.00

355	Edwin Jackson/100	8.00
359	Carlos Lee/100	10.00
360	Shannon Stewart/25	15.00
361	Joe Nathan/100	15.00
376	Eric Byrnes/100	8.00
377	Rich Harden/100	15.00
378	Mark Mulder/25	20.00
380	Eric Chavez/25	15.00
382	Marlon Byrd/100	8.00
384	Brett Myers/100	10.00
386	Jason Bay/50	15.00
387	Jake Peavy/50	25.00
402	Aubrey Huff/50	15.00
407	Orlando Hudson/25	15.00
410	Jose Guillen/25	15.00
429	Bert Blyleven/50	10.00
430	Dwight Gooden/50	15.00
436	Marty Marion/50	15.00

Signature Materials Bronze

NM/M

Production 1-200
No pricing 20 or less.

Platinum:	No Pricing
Production One Set	
Framed Black:	No Pricing
Production 1-10	
Framed Blue:	No Pricing
Production 1-50	
Framed Green:	1-2X
Production 1-25	
Framed Red:	.75-1.5X
Production 1-100	

1	Garret Anderson/ Bat-Jsy/25	25.00
7	Chone Figgins/ Bat-Jsy/200	15.00
18	Rafael Furcal/ Bat-Jsy/50	20.00
19	Andruw Jones/ Bat-Jsy/25	35.00
31	Larry Bigbie/ Jsy-Jsy/200	15.00
32	Rodrigo Lopez/ Jsy-Jsy/200	15.00
38	Trot Nixon/ Jsy-Jsy/100	30.00
46	David Ortiz/ Bat-Jsy/100	50.00
48	Mark Prior/ Bat-Jsy/25	40.00
49	Aramis Ramirez/ Bat-Jsy/25	25.00
51	Carlos Zambrano/ Jsy-Jsy/200	25.00
52	Derrek Lee/ Bat-Bat/25	20.00
61	Carlos Lee/ Bat-Jsy/100	10.00
76	C.C. Sabathia/ Jsy-Jsy/100	20.00
78	Omar Vizquel/ Jsy-Jsy/25	40.00
95	Miguel Cabrera/ Bat-Jsy/25	50.00
109	Carlos Beltran/ Bat-Jsy/100	40.00
112	Jeremy Affeldt/ Pants-Pants/100	10.00
127	Bill Hall/Bat-Bat/100	10.00
129	Jacque Jones/ Bat-Jsy/50	20.00
131	Johan Santana/ Jsy-Jsy/50	40.00
132	Lew Ford/Bat-Jsy/200	15.00
139	Nick Johnson/ Bat-Bat/50	12.00
153	Jorge Posada/ Bat-Jsy/25	40.00
162	Eric Chavez/ Bat-Jsy/25	25.00
178	Craig Wilson/ Bat-Jsy/200	15.00
185	Sean Burroughs/ Bat-Jsy/100	10.00
201	Edgar Martinez/ Bat-Bat/25	40.00
211	Edgar Renteria/ Jsy-Jsy/50	30.00
221	Carl Crawford/ Jsy-Jsy/200	15.00
229	Mark Teixeira/ Bat-Jsy/25	40.00
230	Michael Young/ Bat-Jsy/100	20.00
232	Laynce Nix/ Bat-Jsy/200	12.00
233	Alfonso Soriano/ Bat-Jsy/25	50.00
239	Roy Halladay/ Jsy-Jsy/25	25.00

269	Brad Penny/ Bat-Jsy/100	10.00
280	Dale Murphy/ Jsy-Jsy/50	35.00
282	Dwight Evans/ Bat-Jsy/50	25.00
283	Ron Santo/ Bat-Bat/100	35.00
284	Andre Dawson/ Bat-Jsy/100	25.00
286	Jack Morris/ Jsy-Jsy/100	20.00
287	Kirk Gibson/ Bat-Jsy/25	40.00
289	Orel Hershiser/ Jsy-Jsy/100	35.00
291	Tony Oliva/ Bat-Jsy/100	25.00
294	Don Mattingly/ Bat-Jsy/25	90.00
297	Dave Parker/ Bat-Jsy/100	25.00
298	Steve Garvey/ Bat-Jsy/50	25.00
300	Keith Hernandez/ Bat-Jsy/100	20.00
303	Garret Anderson/ Bat-Jsy/50	20.00
315	Johnny Estrada/ Jsy-Jsy/50	12.00
319	Jay Gibbons/ Bat-Bat/50	12.00
320	Melvin Mora/ Jsy-Jsy/50	15.00
323	David Ortiz/ Jsy-Jsy/25	50.00
333	Mark Buehrle/ Jsy-Jsy/25	25.00
339	Travis Hafner/ Jsy-Jsy/25	25.00
340	Victor Martinez/ Jsy-Jsy/25	20.00
341	Cliff Lee/Jsy-Jsy/25	15.00
343	Preston Wilson/ Bat-Jsy/25	20.00
351	Ken Harvey/ Jsy-Jsy/25	12.00
382	Marlon Byrd/ Bat-Jsy/50	12.00
401	Delmon Young/ Bat-Bat/25	25.00
407	Orlando Hudson/ Bat-Jsy/25	12.00
419	Scott Rolen/ Bat-Jsy/25	30.00
428	Alan Trammell/ Bat-Jsy/25	25.00
430	Dwight Gooden/ Bat-Jsy/25	25.00
434	Tony Gwynn/ Bat-Jsy/25	40.00

Signature Materials Gold

NM/M

Production 1-50

7	Chone Figgins/ Bat-Jsy/50	20.00
18	Rafael Furcal/ Bat-Jsy/25	30.00
31	Larry Bigbie/ Jsy-Jsy/50	20.00
32	Rodrigo Lopez/ Jsy-Jsy/50	20.00
46	David Ortiz/ Bat-Jsy/50	60.00
49	Aramis Ramirez/ Bat-Jsy/25	35.00
51	Carlos Zambrano/ Jsy-Jsy/50	35.00
76	C.C. Sabathia/ Jsy-Jsy/25	25.00
104	Roy Oswalt/ Jsy-Jsy/50	30.00
112	Jeremy Affeldt/ Pants-Pants/25	15.00
127	Bill Hall/Bat-Bat/50	15.00
129	Jacque Jones/ Bat-Jsy/50	20.00
132	Lew Ford/Bat-Jsy/50	20.00
178	Craig Wilson/ Bat-Jsy/50	20.00
221	Carl Crawford/ Jsy-Jsy/50	20.00
230	Michael Young/ Bat-Jsy/50	25.00
269	Brad Penny/ Bat-Jsy/50	15.00
280	Dale Murphy/ Jsy-Jsy/25	50.00
282	Dwight Evans/ Bat-Jsy/25	30.00

283	Ron Santo/ Bat-Bat/50	45.00
284	Andre Dawson/ Bat-Jsy/50	30.00
285	Harold Baines/ Bat-Jsy/50	25.00
286	Jack Morris/ Jsy-Jsy/50	25.00
291	Tony Oliva/ Bat-Jsy/50	30.00
297	Dave Parker/ Bat-Jsy/50	30.00
299	Matt Williams/ Jsy-Jsy/25	35.00

Signature Materials
Silver

NM/M

Production 1-100

7	Chone Figgins/ Bat-Jsy/100	15.00
18	Rafael Furcal/ Bat-Jsy/25	30.00
31	Larry Bigbie/ Jsy-Jsy/100	15.00
32	Rodrigo Lopez/ Jsy-Jsy/100	15.00
46	David Ortiz/ Bat-Jsy/50	60.00
49	Aramis Ramirez/ Bat-Jsy/50	35.00
51	Carlos Zambrano/ Jsy-Jsy/100	30.00
61	Carlos Lee/ Bat-Jsy/100	10.00
76	C.C. Sabathia/ Jsy-Jsy/100	20.00
104	Roy Oswalt/ Jsy-Jsy/50	30.00
112	Jeremy Affeldt/ Pants-Pants/100	10.00
127	Bill Hall/Bat-Bat/100	10.00
129	Jacque Jones/ Bat-Jsy/50	20.00
132	Lew Ford/ Bat-Jsy/100	15.00
178	Craig Wilson/ Bat-Jsy/100	15.00
221	Carl Crawford/ Jsy-Jsy/100	15.00
230	Michael Young/ Bat-Jsy/50	25.00
232	Laynce Nix/ Bat-Jsy/100	15.00
269	Brad Penny/ Bat-Jsy/50	15.00
280	Dale Murphy/ Jsy-Jsy/25	50.00
282	Dwight Evans/ Bat-Jsy/25	30.00
283	Ron Santo/ Bat-Bat/50	45.00
284	Andre Dawson/ Bat-Jsy/50	30.00
285	Harold Baines/ Bat-Jsy/50	25.00
286	Jack Morris/ Jsy-Jsy/50	25.00
291	Tony Oliva/ Bat-Jsy/50	30.00
297	Dave Parker/ Bat-Jsy/50	30.00
298	Steve Garvey/ Bat-Jsy/25	30.00
299	Matt Williams/ Jsy-Jsy/25	35.00
300	Keith Hernandez/ Bat-Jsy/50	25.00

Team Timeline

NM/M

Complete Set (25): 65.00
Common Duo: 1.50
Inserted 1:21
#26-30 found in DK Update

1	Albert Pujols, Scott Rolen	6.00
2	Roger Clemens, Andy Pettitte	6.00
3	Tim Hudson, Mark Mulder	1.50
4	Hank Blalock, Mark Teixeira	2.00
5	Miguel Cabrera, Mike Lowell	2.00
6	Greg Maddux, Sammy Sosa	4.00
7	Miguel Tejada, Cal Ripken Jr.	8.00
8	Vladimir Guerrero, Reggie Jackson	3.00
9	Mike Schmidt, Jim Thome	4.00
10	Chipper Jones, Greg Maddux	4.00
11	George Brett, Ken Harvey	5.00
12	Don Mattingly, Hideki Matsui	5.00
13	Torii Hunter, Johan Santana	2.00
14	Carlos Delgado, Vernon Wells	1.50
15	Todd Helton, Larry Walker	2.00
16	Duke Snider, Adrian Beltre	2.00
17	Al Kaline, Ivan Rodriguez	3.00
18	Rafael Palmeiro, Eddie Murray	2.00
19	Manny Ramirez, Carl Yastrzemski	3.00
20	Ralph Kiner, Jason Bay	1.50
21	Johnny Bench, Adam Dunn	3.00
22	Robin Yount, Lyle Overbay	4.00
23	Nolan Ryan, Randy Johnson	8.00
24	Gary Carter, Mike Piazza	4.00
25	Carlton Fisk, Frank Thomas	3.00
26	Nolan Ryan, Mike Piazza	8.00
27	Roger Clemens, Jeff Bagwell	8.00
28	Cal Ripken Jr., Sammy Sosa	8.00
29	Willie Mays, Jim Thorpe	8.00
30	Albert Pujols, Stan Musial	8.00

Team Timeline
Materials Bat

NM/M

Production 25-100

2	Roger Clemens, Andy Pettitte/50	25.00
5	Miguel Cabrera, Mike Lowell/100	15.00
8	Vladimir Guerrero, Reggie Jackson/75	20.00
9	Mike Schmidt, Jim Thome/50	30.00
12	Don Mattingly, Hideki Matsui/50	50.00
15	Todd Helton, Larry Walker/100	10.00
17	Al Kaline, Ivan Rodriguez/25	30.00
18	Rafael Palmeiro, Eddie Murray/100	15.00
21	Johnny Bench, Adam Dunn/100	15.00
22	Robin Yount, Lyle Overbay/100	20.00
23	Nolan Ryan, Randy Johnson/25	40.00

Team Timeline
Materials Jersey

NM/M

Common Duo: 8.00
Production 100 Sets
Prime: No Pricing
Production One Set
#26-30 found in DK Update

1	Albert Pujols, Scott Rolen	40.00
2	Roger Clemens, Andy Pettitte	25.00
3	Tim Hudson, Mark Mulder	8.00
4	Hank Blalock, Mark Teixeira	10.00
7	Miguel Tejada, Cal Ripken Jr.	40.00
8	Vladimir Guerrero, Reggie Jackson	15.00
9	Mike Schmidt/Jkt, Jim Thome	30.00
10	Chipper Jones, Greg Maddux	20.00
12	Don Mattingly/Jkt, Hideki Matsui	50.00
14	Carlos Delgado, Vernon Wells	8.00
15	Todd Helton, Larry Walker	10.00
16	Duke Snider, Adrian Beltre	10.00
18	Rafael Palmeiro, Eddie Murray	15.00
19	Manny Ramirez, Carl Yastrzemski	25.00
21	Johnny Bench, Adam Dunn	15.00
22	Robin Yount, Lyle Overbay	15.00
24	Gary Carter, Mike Piazza	15.00
25	Carlton Fisk, Frank Thomas	15.00
26	Nolan Ryan, Mike Piazza	30.00
27	Roger Clemens, Jeff Bagwell	20.00
30	Albert Pujols, Stan Musial	40.00

Timeline

NM/M

Complete Set (25): 50.00
Common Player: 1.50
Inserted 1:21
#26-30 found in DK Update

1	Roger Clemens	6.00
2	Nolan Ryan	8.00
3	Carlos Beltran	3.00
4	Ivan Rodriguez	3.00
5	Jim Thome	3.00
6	Mike Piazza	4.00
7	Miguel Tejada	3.00
8	Rafael Palmeiro	2.00
9	Greg Maddux	4.00
10	Tom Glavine	1.50
11	Vladimir Guerrero	3.00
12	Curt Schilling	3.00
13	Mike Mussina	2.00
14	Rickey Henderson	2.00
15	Scott Rolen	3.00
16	Alfonso Soriano	3.00
17	Gary Sheffield	2.00
18	Carlton Fisk	2.00
19	Aramis Ramirez	2.00
20	Mark Grace	1.50
21	Jason Giambi	1.50
22	Juan Gonzalez	1.50
23	Brad Penny	1.50
24	Nomar Garciaparra	4.00
25	Larry Walker	2.00
26	Curt Schilling	2.00
27	Reggie Jackson	2.00
28	Gary Carter	1.50
29	Roger Clemens	6.00
30	Nolan Ryan	8.00

Timeline Materials Bat

NM/M

Production 25-100

1	Roger Clemens	30.00
2	Nolan Ryan	50.00
3	Carlos Beltran	10.00
4	Ivan Rodriguez	10.00
5	Jim Thome	20.00
8	Rafael Palmeiro	10.00
9	Greg Maddux	30.00
10	Tom Glavine	10.00
11	Vladimir Guerrero	15.00
12	Curt Schilling	20.00
13	Mike Mussina	10.00
14	Rickey Henderson	10.00
15	Scott Rolen	20.00
17	Gary Sheffield	10.00
18	Carlton Fisk	10.00
19	Aramis Ramirez	10.00
20	Mark Grace	10.00
22	Juan Gonzalez	10.00
25	Larry Walker	10.00

Timeline Materials
Jersey

NM/M

Production 50-200
Prime: No Pricing
Production One Set
#26-30 found in DK Update

1	Roger Clemens	15.00
2	Nolan Ryan	25.00
3	Carlos Beltran	10.00
4	Ivan Rodriguez	8.00
6	Mike Piazza	15.00
7	Miguel Tejada	10.00
8	Rafael Palmeiro	10.00
9	Greg Maddux	15.00
11	Vladimir Guerrero	15.00
12	Curt Schilling	10.00
13	Mike Mussina	10.00
14	Rickey Henderson	10.00
15	Scott Rolen	15.00
16	Alfonso Soriano	10.00
18	Carlton Fisk	10.00
19	Aramis Ramirez	10.00
21	Jason Giambi	8.00
22	Juan Gonzalez	8.00
26	Curt Schilling	10.00
27	Reggie Jackson	10.00
28	Gary Carter	8.00
29	Roger Clemens	15.00
30	Nolan Ryan	25.00

Update B/W

B/W: 1X
Inserted 1:2

Update Silver B/W

Silvers: 4-8X
Production 50 Sets

Update Gallery of Stars

NM/M

Complete Set (25): 30.00
Common Player: 1.50
Inserted 1:8

1	Andre Dawson	1.50
2	Bob Feller	2.00
3	Bobby Doerr	1.50
4	C.C. Sabathia	1.50
5	Carl Crawford	1.50
6	Dale Murphy	2.00
7	Danny Kolb	1.50
8	Darryl Strawberry	1.50
9	Dave Parker	1.50
10	David Ortiz	3.00
11	Dwight Gooden	1.50
12	Garret Anderson	1.50
13	Jack Morris	1.50
14	Jacque Jones	1.50
15	Jim Palmer	2.00
16	Johan Santana	3.00
17	Ken Harvey	1.50
18	Lyle Overbay	1.50
19	Marty Marion	1.50
20	Melvin Mora	1.50
21	Michael Young	1.50
22	Miguel Cabrera	3.00
23	Preston Wilson	1.50
24	Sean Casey	1.50
25	Victor Martinez	1.50

Update Gallery of
Stars Bat

NM/M

Production 50-200

1	Andre Dawson/50	8.00
3	Bobby Doerr/100	4.00
6	Dale Murphy/100	8.00
8	Darryl Strawberry/100	4.00
9	Dave Parker/200	4.00
10	David Ortiz/200	10.00
11	Dwight Gooden/100	4.00
12	Garret Anderson/100	4.00
18	Lyle Overbay/50	4.00
21	Michael Young/200	4.00
22	Miguel Cabrera/100	8.00
23	Preston Wilson/200	4.00
24	Sean Casey/200	4.00

Update Gallery of Star
Combo

NM/M

Production 50-200: 5.00
Prime: No Pricing
Production One Set

1	Andre Dawson/100	10.00
3	Bobby Doerr/100	8.00
4	C.C. Sabathia/100	5.00
6	Dale Murphy/100	10.00
9	Dave Parker/200	5.00
10	David Ortiz/200	12.00
11	Dwight Gooden/100	6.00
12	Garret Anderson/100	6.00
14	Jacque Jones/50	5.00
15	Jim Palmer/50	8.00
18	Lyle Overbay/50	5.00
21	Michael Young/200	5.00
22	Miguel Cabrera/200	10.00
23	Preston Wilson/200	5.00
24	Sean Casey/200	5.00

Update Gallery of
Stars Jersey

NM/M

Production 25-100

Prime: No pricing
Production One Set
1	Andre Dawson/100	6.00
2	Bob Feller/50	8.00
3	Bobby Doerr/100	6.00
4	C.C. Sabathia/100	4.00
5	Carl Crawford/100	4.00
6	Dale Murphy/100	8.00
8	Darryl Strawberry/25	6.00
9	Dave Parker/100	4.00
10	David Ortiz/100	8.00
11	Dwight Gooden/25	4.00
12	Garret Anderson/100	4.00
13	Jack Morris/100	4.00
14	Jacque Jones/100	4.00
15	Jim Parker/50	6.00
17	Ken Harvey/100	4.00
18	Lyle Overbay/100	4.00
20	Melvin Mora/100	4.00
21	Michael Young/100	4.00
22	Miguel Cabrera/100	8.00
23	Preston Wilson/100	4.00
24	Sean Casey/100	4.00
25	Victor Martinez/25	6.00

Update Gallery of Stars Autograph

NM/M
Production 5-100
1	Andre Dawson/100	15.00
2	Bob Feller/100	25.00
3	Bobby Doerr/100	15.00
4	C.C. Sabathia/25	20.00
5	Carl Crawford/100	12.00
6	Dale Murphy/100	20.00
7	Danny Kolb/10	10.00
8	Darryl Strawberry/100	15.00
9	Dave Parker/100	12.00
11	Dwight Gooden/100	15.00
13	Jack Morris/100	12.00
14	Jacque Jones/50	10.00
17	Ken Harvey/100	8.00
18	Lyle Overbay/50	10.00
19	Marty Marion/25	20.00
20	Melvin Mora/100	12.00
25	Victor Martinez/100	12.00

Update Gallery of Stars Bat Autograph

NM/M
Production 5-200
1	Andre Dawson/25	25.00
5	Bobby Doerr/200	15.00
9	Dave Parker/200	15.00
11	Dwight Gooden/100	20.00
12	Garret Anderson/100	15.00
14	Jacque Jones/100	15.00
17	Ken Harvey/25	12.00
21	Michael Young/100	15.00
22	Miguel Cabrera/50	35.00
24	Sean Casey/50	20.00

Update Gallery of Stars Combo Autograph

NM/M
Production 25-200
Prime: No Pricing
Production One Set
1	Andre Dawson/50	25.00
3	Bobby Doerr/200	20.00
6	Dale Murphy/50	30.00
9	Dave Parker/50	15.00
10	David Ortiz/50	40.00
11	Dwight Gooden/100	20.00
12	Garret Anderson/50	20.00
14	Jacque Jones/50	20.00
15	Jim Palmer/25	25.00
17	Ken Harvey/25	15.00
21	Michael Young/50	20.00
22	Miguel Cabrera/50	35.00
24	Sean Casey/25	20.00
25	Victor Martinez/100	20.00

Update Gallery of Stars Jersey Autograph

NM/M
Prime: No Pricing
Production One Set
1	Andre Dawson/50	25.00
2	Bob Feller/50	30.00
3	Bobby Doerr/100	15.00
4	C.C. Sabathia/100	15.00
5	Carl Crawford/50	15.00
6	Dale Murphy/50	25.00
9	Dave Parker/100	15.00
10	David Ortiz/50	40.00
11	Dwight Gooden/50	20.00
12	Garret Anderson/50	20.00
13	Jack Morris/50	15.00
14	Jacque Jones/25	20.00

15	Jim Palmer/25	25.00
17	Ken Harvey/100	8.00
18	Lyle Overbay/100	10.00
19	Marty Marion/25	20.00
20	Melvin Mora/100	15.00
24	Sean Casey/25	20.00
25	Victor Martinez/100	20.00

Update HOF Sluggers

NM/M
Common Player: 2.00
1	Duke Snider	2.00
2	Eddie Murray	2.00
3	Frank Robinson	2.00
4	George Brett	5.00
5	Harmon Killebrew	3.00
6	Mike Schmidt	5.00
7	Reggie Jackson	3.00
8	Roberto Clemente	6.00
9	Stan Musial	4.00
10	Willie Mays	5.00

Update HOF Sluggers Jersey

NM/M
Production 5-50
1	Duke Snider/ Pants/25	10.00
2	Eddie Murray/50	10.00
5	Harmon Killebrew/25	15.00
6	Mike Schmidt/50	15.00
7	Reggie Jackson/ Pants/50	8.00
9	Stan Musial/ Pants/25	20.00
10	Willie Mays/ Pants/50	25.00

Update Masters of the Game

NM/M
Common Player: 2.00
1	Albert Pujols	4.00
2	Cal Ripken Jr.	6.00
3	Don Mattingly	4.00
4	Greg Maddux	3.00
5	Jim Thorpe	4.00
6	Nolan Ryan	5.00
7	Randy Johnson	4.00
8	Roberto Clemente	6.00
9	Roger Clemens	5.00
10	Willie Mays	4.00

Update Masters of the Game Jersey

NM/M
Production 25-50
1	Albert Pujols/50	20.00
2	Cal Ripken Jr./50	30.00
3	Don Mattingly/25	20.00
4	Greg Maddux/50	20.00
5	Jim Thorpe/25	250.00
6	Nolan Ryan/50	20.00
7	Randy Johnson/25	10.00
9	Roger Clemens/50	10.00
10	Willie Mays Pants/25	30.00

2005 Donruss Elite

NM/M
Complete Set (200):
Common Player (1-150): .25
Common SP (151-170): 3.00
Production 1,250
Common Auto. (171-200): 8.00
Production 500 to 1,500
Pack (5): 5.00
Box (20): 90.00
| 1 | Bartolo Colon | .25 |

2	Casey Kotchman	.25
3	Chone Figgins	.25
4	Darin Erstad	.25
5	Garret Anderson	.40
6	Jose Guillen	.25
7	Vladimir Guerrero	.75
8	Luis Gonzalez	.25
9	Randy Johnson	.75
10	Troy Glaus	.40
11	Andruw Jones	.40
12	Chipper Jones	.75
13	J.D. Drew	.25
14	John Smoltz	.40
15	Johnny Estrada	.25
16	Marcus Giles	.25
17	Rafael Furcal	.25
18	Javy Lopez	.40
19	Jay Gibbons	.25
20	Melvin Mora	.25
21	Miguel Tejada	.50
22	Rafael Palmeiro	.50
23	Sidney Ponson	.25
24	Curt Schilling	.75
25	David Ortiz	.75
26	Derek Lowe	.25
27	Jason Varitek	.40
28	Johnny Damon	.75
29	Manny Ramirez	.75
30	Pedro Martinez	.75
31	Aramis Ramirez	.40
32	Carlos Zambrano	.40
33	Corey Patterson	.25
34	Derrek Lee	.50
35	Greg Maddux	1.00
36	Kerry Wood	.40
37	Mark Prior	.75
38	Moises Alou	.40
39	Nomar Garciaparra	1.00
40	Sammy Sosa	1.00
41	Carlos Lee	.25
42	Frank Thomas	.50
43	Jermaine Dye	.25
44	Magglio Ordonez	.25
45	Mark Buehrle	.25
46	Paul Konerko	.25
47	Adam Dunn	.50
48	Austin Kearns	.25
49	Barry Larkin	.40
50	Ken Griffey Jr.	1.00
51	Sean Casey	.25
52	C.C. Sabathia	.25
53	Cliff Lee	.25
54	Travis Hafner	.25
55	Victor Martinez	.25
56	Jeromy Burnitz	.25
57	Preston Wilson	.25
58	Todd Helton	.25
59	Brandon Inge	.25
60	Ivan Rodriguez	.50
61	Jeremy Bonderman	.25
62	Troy Percival	.25
63	Dontrelle Willis	.40
64	Josh Beckett	.40
65	Juan Pierre	.25
66	Miguel Cabrera	.75
67	Mike Lowell	.25
68	Paul LoDuca	.25
69	Andy Pettitte	.40
70	Brad Ausmus	.25
71	Carlos Beltran	.50
72	Craig Biggio	.40
73	Jeff Bagwell	.50
74	Lance Berkman	.40
75	Roger Clemens	2.00
76	Roy Oswalt	.25
77	Juan Gonzalez	.25
78	Mike Sweeney	.25
79	Zack Greinke	.25
80	Adrian Beltre	.25
81	Hideo Nomo	.25
82	Jeff Kent	.25
83	Milton Bradley	.25
84	Shawn Green	.25

85	Steve Finley	.25
86	Ben Sheets	.25
87	Lyle Overbay	.25
88	Scott Podsednik	.25
89	Lew Ford	.25
90	Shannon Stewart	.25
91	Torii Hunter	.25
92	David Wright	.75
93	Jose Reyes	.50
94	Kazuo Matsui	.25
95	Mike Piazza	1.00
96	Tom Glavine	.40
97	Alex Rodriguez	1.50
98	Bernie Williams	.40
99	Derek Jeter	2.00
100	Gary Sheffield	.50
101	Hideki Matsui	1.50
102	Jason Giambi	.25
103	Kevin Brown	.25
104	Mike Mussina	.40
105	Barry Zito	.25
106	Bobby Crosby	.40
107	Eric Chavez	.40
108	Jason Kendall	.25
109	Mark Mulder	.40
110	Bobby Abreu	.40
111	Jim Thome	.75
112	Kevin Millwood	.25
113	Pat Burrell	.25
114	Craig Wilson	.25
115	Jack Wilson	.25
116	Jason Bay	.40
117	Brian Giles	.25
118	Khalil Greene	.40
119	Mark Loretta	.25
120	Ryan Klesko	.25
121	Sean Burroughs	.25
122	Edgardo Alfonzo	.25
123	J.T. Snow	.25
124	Jason Schmidt	.25
125	Omar Vizquel	.25
126	Ichiro Suzuki	1.50
127	Jamie Moyer	.25
128	Bret Boone	.25
129	Richie Sexson	.40
130	Albert Pujols	2.00
131	Edgar Renteria	.40
132	Jeff Suppan	.25
133	Jim Edmonds	.40
134	Larry Walker	.40
135	Scott Rolen	.75
136	Aubrey Huff	.25
137	B.J. Upton	.25
138	Carl Crawford	.25
139	Rocco Baldelli	.25
140	Alfonso Soriano	.75
141	Hank Blalock	.40
142	Kenny Rogers	.25
143	Laynce Nix	.25
144	Mark Teixeira	.50
145	Michael Young	.25
146	Carlos Delgado	.40
147	Eric Hinske	.25
148	Roy Halladay	.25
149	Vernon Wells	.25
150	Jose Vidro	.25
151	Bob Gibson	3.00
152	Brooks Robinson	3.00
153	Cal Ripken Jr.	10.00
154	Carl Yastrzemski	4.00
155	Don Mattingly	5.00
156	Eddie Murray	3.00
157	Ernie Banks	4.00
158	Frank Robinson	3.00
159	George Brett	5.00
160	Harmon Killebrew	4.00
161	Johnny Bench	4.00
162	Mike Schmidt	5.00
163	Nolan Ryan	6.00
164	Paul Molitor	4.00
165	Stan Musial	5.00
166	Steve Carlton	3.00
167	Tony Gwynn	4.00
168	Warren Spahn	4.00
169	Willie Mays	6.00
170	Willie McCovey	3.00
171	Miguel Negron/ AU/1500 RC	8.00
172	Mike Morse/ AU/1000 RC	15.00
173	Wladimir Balentien/ AU/1500 RC	10.00
174	Alberto Concepcion/ AU/651 RC	10.00
175	Ubaldo Jimenez/ AU/500 RC	10.00
176	Justin Verlander/ AU/500 RC	50.00
177	Ryan Speier/ AU/1000 RC	8.00
178	Geovany Soto/ AU/500 RC	15.00
179	Mark McLemore/ AU/1200 RC	8.00

180	Ambiorix Burgos/ AU/599 RC	8.00
181	Chris Roberson/ AU/1000 RC	10.00
182	Colter Bean/ AU/625 RC	10.00
183	Erick Threets/ AU/500 RC	8.00
184	Carlos Ruiz/ AU/1000 RC	15.00
186	Jared Gothreaux/ AU/1500 RC	10.00
187	Luis Hernandez/ AU/1000 RC	8.00
188	Agustin Montero/ 1000 RC	2.00
189	Paulino Reynoso/ 1000 RC	2.00
190	Garrett Jones/ AU/500 RC	8.00
191	Sean Thompson/ AU/500 RC	8.00
192	Matt Lindstrom/ AU/1500 RC	8.00
193	Nate McLouth/ AU/500 RC	10.00
194	Luke Scott/ AU/671 RC	25.00
195	Keith Hattig/AU/500	10.00
196	Jason Hammel/ AU/1500 RC	10.00
197	Danny Rueckel/ AU/671 RC	8.00
198	Justin Wechsler/ AU/500 RC	8.00
199	Chris Resop/ AU/500 RC	15.00
200	Jeff Miller/AU/500 RC	10.00

Aspirations

Cards (1-150) print run

61-99:	4-8X
(1-150) p/r 41-60:	6-10X
(1-150) p/r 21-40:	8-15X
(151-170) p/r 36-80:	1.5-3X
Autos (171-200) p/r	
40-99:	.5-1.5X

No pricing production 20 or less.
Production 15-99

Status

Cards (1-150) print run

61-81:	4-8X
(1-150) p/r 41-60:	6-10X
(1-150) p/r 21-40:	8-15X
(151-170) p/r 36-81:	1.5-3X
Autos (171-200) p/r	
40-81:	.5-1.5X

No pricing production 20 or less.
Production 1-81

Status Gold

Gold (1-150):	10-20X
Gold (151-170):	3-5X
Gold (171-200):	No Pricing
Production 24 Sets	

Turn of the Century

Stars (1-150):	2-3X
Production 750	
(151-170):	1X
Production 250	
Rookies (171-200):	.25-1X
Production 500	

Back 2 Back Jacks

		NM/M
Production 25-200		
1	Adam Dunn/200	8.00
3	Albert Pujols/100	15.00
4	Babe Ruth/50	160.00
5	Cal Ripken Jr./100	30.00
6	David Ortiz/200	10.00
7	Eddie Murray/150	8.00
8	Ernie Banks/50	15.00
9	Frank Robinson/50	8.00
10	Gary Sheffield/200	5.00
11	George Foster/125	5.00
12	Don Mattingly/10	15.00
13	Hideki Matsui/25	30.00
14	Jason Giambi/50	5.00
16	Jim Rice/125	8.00
17	Jim Thome/200	8.00
18	Johnny Bench/125	10.00
19	Lance Berkman/200	5.00
20	Manny Ramirez/200	8.00
21	Mike Piazza/200	10.00
22	Mike Schmidt/125	15.00
23	Rafael Palmeiro/200	8.00
24	Reggie Jackson/125	10.00
25	Sammy Sosa/100	10.00
26	Scott Rolen/200	8.00
27	Stan Musial/125	15.00
28	Willie Mays/50	40.00

29	Kirk Gibson/125	5.00
30	Will Clark/125	5.00
31	Willie Mays, Sammy Sosa/50	50.00
32	Eddie Murray, Mike Piazza/50	20.00
33	Mike Schmidt, Jim Thome/50	30.00
34	Rafael Palmeiro, Kirk Gibson/50	10.00
35	Jim Rice, Manny Ramirez/50	15.00
36	Adrian Beltre, Will Clark/50	15.00
37	Reggie Jackson, David Ortiz/50	15.00
38	Johnny Bench, Adam Dunn/50	20.00

Back 2 Back Jacks Combos

		NM/M
1	Adam Dunn/ Bat-Jsy/100	10.00
2	Adrian Beltre/ Bat-Jsy/100	8.00
5	Cal Ripken Jr./ Bat-Jsy/50	40.00
6	David Ortiz/ Bat-Jsy/50	12.00
7	Eddie Murray/ Bat-Jsy/50	10.00
8	Ernie Banks/ Bat-Jsy/10	20.00
10	Gary Sheffield/ Bat-Jsy/100	8.00
11	George Foster/ Bat-Jsy/50	8.00
12	Don Mattingly/ Bat-Jsy/50	20.00
13	Hideki Matsui/ Bat-Jsy/25	40.00
14	Jason Giambi/ Bat-Jsy/50	8.00
15	Jim Edmonds/ Bat-Jsy/100	10.00
17	Jim Thome/ Bat-Jsy/100	8.00
18	Johnny Bench/ Bat-Jsy/50	15.00
19	Lance Berkman/ Bat-Jsy/100	8.00
20	Manny Ramirez/ Bat-Jsy/50	12.00
21	Mike Piazza/ Bat-Jsy/50	15.00
22	Mike Schmidt/ Bat-Jsy/50	20.00
23	Rafael Palmeiro/ Bat-Jsy/50	10.00
24	Reggie Jackson/ Bat-Jsy/50	15.00
25	Sammy Sosa/ Bat-Jsy/100	15.00
26	Scott Rolen/ Bat-Jsy/50	12.00
27	Stan Musial/ Bat-Pants/50	25.00
28	Willie Mays/ Bat-Jsy/50	60.00
29	Kirk Gibson/ Bat-Jsy/50	10.00
30	Will Clark/Bat-Jsy/50	12.00
32	Eddie Murray, Mike Piazza/25	30.00
33	Mike Schmidt, Jim Thome/25	50.00
34	Rafael Palmeiro, Kirk Gibson/25	20.00
35	Jim Rice, Manny Ramirez/50	25.00
36	Adrian Beltre, Will Clark/50	15.00
37	Reggie Jackson, David Ortiz/50	30.00
38	Johnny Bench, Adam Dunn/25	30.00
40	Cal Ripken Jr., Albert Pujols/25	100.00

Career Best

	NM/M
Common Player:	1.00

Production 1,500 Sets Black:		1-2X
Production 150 Sets Blue:		1-2X
Production 250 Sets Gold:		1-1.5X
Production 500 Sets		
1	Adam Dunn	1.50
2	Adrian Beltre	1.00
3	Albert Pujols	4.00
4	Andruw Jones	1.50
5	Ben Sheets	1.00
6	Bo Jackson	2.00
7	Brooks Robinson	2.00
8	Cal Ripken Jr.	6.00
9	Dale Murphy	1.50
10	Don Mattingly	3.00
11	Eddie Murray	1.50
12	George Brett	3.00
13	Hank Blalock	1.50
14	Ichiro Suzuki	3.00
15	Jim Thome	1.50
16	Kerry Wood	1.50
17	Lance Berkman	1.00
18	Mark Prior	2.00
19	Mark Teixeira	1.50
20	Mike Schmidt	3.00
21	Pedro Martinez	2.00
22	Randy Johnson	2.00
23	Rickey Henderson	1.50
24	Sammy Sosa	3.00
25	Tony Gwynn	2.00

Career Best Bats

		NM/M
Production 50-250		
1	Adam Dunn/250	8.00
2	Adrian Beltre/250	5.00
3	Albert Pujols/250	15.00
4	Andruw Jones/250	5.00
5	Ben Sheets/250	5.00
6	Bo Jackson/250	10.00
7	Brooks Robinson/250	8.00
8	Cal Ripken Jr./150	25.00
9	Dale Murphy/150	10.00
10	Don Mattingly/250	12.00
11	Eddie Murray/250	8.00
12	George Brett/250	15.00
13	Hank Blalock/250	8.00
15	Jim Thome/100	8.00
16	Kerry Wood/100	8.00
17	Lance Berkman/250	5.00
18	Mark Prior/150	6.00
19	Mark Teixeira/250	8.00
20	Mike Schmidt/250	12.00
21	Pedro Martinez/100	8.00
22	Randy Johnson/100	10.00
23	Rickey Henderson/ 250	8.00
24	Sammy Sosa/100	10.00
25	Tony Gwynn/100	10.00

Career Best Combos

		NM/M
Production 25-150		10.00
1	Adam Dunn/ Bat-Jsy/150	10.00
2	Adrian Beltre/ Bat-Jsy/150	8.00
3	Albert Pujols/ Bat-Jsy/150	20.00
4	Andruw Jones/ Bat-Jsy/150	8.00
5	Ben Sheets/ Bat-Jsy/150	8.00
6	Bo Jackson/ Bat-Jsy/25	20.00
7	Brooks Robinson/ Bat-Jsy/25	20.00
8	Cal Ripken Jr./ Bat-Jsy/25	40.00
9	Dale Murphy/ Bat-Jsy/25	10.00
10	Don Mattingly/ Bat-Jsy/25	20.00
11	Eddie Murray/ Bat-Jsy/25	12.00
12	George Brett/ Bat-Jsy/25	25.00
13	Hank Blalock/ Bat-Jsy/150	10.00
15	Jim Thome/ Bat-Jsy/150	10.00
16	Kerry Wood/ Bat-Pants/150	10.00
17	Lance Berkman/ Bat-Jsy/150	8.00
18	Mark Prior/ Bat-Jsy/150	8.00
19	Mark Teixeira/ Bat-Jsy/150	12.00
21	Pedro Martinez/ Bat-Jsy/125	10.00

23	Rickey Henderson/ Bat-Jsy/25	15.00
24	Sammy Sosa/ Bat-Jsy/150	12.00
25	Tony Gwynn/ Bat-Jsy/25	15.00

Career Best Jerseys

		NM/M
Production 100-250		
1	Adam Dunn/250	8.00
2	Adrian Beltre/250	5.00
3	Albert Pujols/250	15.00
4	Andruw Jones/250	5.00
5	Ben Sheets/250	5.00
6	Bo Jackson/250	10.00
7	Brooks Robinson/50	10.00
8	Cal Ripken Jr./150	25.00
9	Dale Murphy/100	10.00
10	Don Mattingly/150	12.00
11	Eddie Murray/100	8.00
12	George Brett/100	15.00
13	Hank Blalock/250	8.00
15	Jim Thome/250	8.00
16	Kerry Wood/250	8.00
17	Lance Berkman/250	5.00
18	Mark Prior/250	6.00
19	Mark Teixeira/250	8.00
20	Mike Schmidt/250	12.00
21	Pedro Martinez/250	8.00
22	Randy Johnson/100	10.00
23	Rickey Henderson/50	10.00
24	Sammy Sosa/250	10.00
25	Tony Gwynn/250	10.00

Face 2 Face

		NM/M
Complete Set (20):		35.00
Common Duo:		
Production 1,500 Sets Black:		1-1.5X
Production 500 Sets Gold:		1-2X
Production 250 Sets Red:		1X
Production 750 Sets		
1	Roger Clemens, Scott Rolen	3.00
2	Greg Maddux, Jeff Bagwell	3.00
3	Mark Prior, Mike Piazza	3.00
4	Mike Mussina, Ivan Rodriguez	2.00
5	Josh Beckett, Sammy Sosa	2.00
6	Roy Oswalt, Miguel Cabrera	2.00
7	Roger Clemens, Albert Pujols	4.00
8	Pedro Martinez, Vladimir Guerrero	2.00
9	Randy Johnson, Jim Edmonds	2.00
10	Curt Schilling, Derek Jeter	4.00
11	Kerry Wood, Lance Berkman	1.50
12	Tim Hudson, Garret Anderson	1.00
13	Pedro Martinez, Gary Sheffield	2.00
14	Barry Zito, Magglio Ordonez	1.00
15	Kerry Wood, Shawn Green	1.50
16	Mike Mussina, Miguel Tejada	2.00
17	Randy Johnson, Albert Pujols	4.00
18	Nolan Ryan, George Brett	4.00

19	Tom Seaver, Mike Schmidt	3.00
20	Jim Palmer, Harmon Killebrew	2.00

Face 2 Face Bats

NM/M

Production 25-150

3	Mark Prior, Mike Piazza/10	8.00
4	Mike Mussina, Ivan Rodriguez/100	8.00
5	Josh Beckett, Sammy Sosa/50	10.00
6	Roy Oswalt, Miguel Cabrera/100	10.00
8	Pedro Martinez, Vladimir Guerrero/50	10.00
9	Randy Johnson, Jim Edmonds/50	10.00
11	Kerry Wood, Lance Berkman/150	8.00
12	Tim Hudson, Garret Anderson/150	8.00
13	Pedro Martinez, Gary Sheffield/150	10.00
14	Barry Zito, Magglio Ordonez/50	8.00
15	Kerry Wood, Shawn Green/150	8.00
18	Nolan Ryan, George Brett/100	25.00
19	Tom Seaver, Mike Schmidt/150	15.00

Face 2 Face Combos

NM/M

Production 25-250

1	Roger Clemens/Jsy, Scott Rolen/Bat/100	15.00
2	Greg Maddux/Jsy, Jeff Bagwell/Bat/100	10.00
3	Mark Prior/Jsy, Mike Piazza/Bat/250	8.00
4	Mike Mussina/Jsy, Ivan Rodriguez/ Bat/250	8.00
5	Josh Beckett/Jsy, Sammy Sosa/Bat/250	10.00
6	Roy Oswalt/Jsy, Miguel Cabrera/ Bat/250	8.00
8	Pedro Martinez/Jsy, Vladimir Guerrero/ Bat/75	10.00
11	Kerry Wood/Bat, Lance Berkman/ Jsy/250	8.00
12	Tim Hudson/Jsy, Garret Anderson/ Bat/100	8.00
13	Pedro Martinez/Bat, Gary Sheffield/Jsy/75	12.00
14	Barry Zito/Jsy, Magglio Ordonez/ Bat/250	8.00
15	Kerry Wood/Jsy, Shawn Green/Bat/250	8.00
16	Mike Mussina/Jsy, Miguel Tejada/ Bat/250	10.00
19	Tom Seaver/Jsy, Mike Schmidt/Bat/50	20.00

Face 2 Face Jerseys

NM/M

Production 25-200

1	Roger Clemens, Scott Rolen/200	15.00
2	Greg Maddux, Jeff Bagwell/75	10.00
3	Mark Prior, Mike Piazza/200	8.00
4	Mike Mussina, Ivan Rodriguez/200	8.00
5	Josh Beckett, Sammy Sosa/200	12.00
6	Roy Oswalt, Miguel Cabrera/200	8.00
7	Roger Clemens, Albert Pujols/200	20.00
8	Pedro Martinez, Vladimir Guerrero/75	10.00
11	Kerry Wood, Lance Berkman/200	8.00
12	Tim Hudson, Garret Anderson/75	8.00
13	Pedro Martinez, Gary Sheffield/75	10.00
14	Barry Zito, Magglio Ordonez/200	8.00
15	Kerry Wood, Shawn Green/200	8.00

16	Mike Mussina, Miguel Tejada/200	10.00
17	Randy Johnson, Albert Pujols/75	20.00
19	Tom Seaver, Mike Schmidt/50	20.00

Passing the Torch

NM/M

Common Player:	1.50
1-30 Production 1,000	
31-45 Production 500	
Black:	2-3X
1-30 Production 50	
31-45 Production 25	
Gold:	1-2X
1-30 Production 50	
31-45 Production 50	
Green:	1-1.5X
1-30 Production 250	
31-45 Production 125	
Red:	1X
1-30 Production 500	
31-45 Production 250	

1	Adrian Beltre	1.50
2	Albert Pujols	5.00
3	Alex Rodriguez	4.00
4	Andruw Jones	1.50
5	Babe Ruth	6.00
6	Ben Sheets	1.50
7	Brooks Robinson	2.00
8	Cal Ripken Jr.	8.00
9	Carl Yastrzemski	3.00
10	Dale Murphy	2.00
11	David Ortiz	2.00
12	Derek Jeter	5.00
13	Don Mattingly	4.00
14	George Brett	4.00
15	Greg Maddux	3.00
16	Hank Blalock	1.50
17	Jeff Bagwell	1.50
18	Johnny Bench	3.00
19	Magglio Ordonez	1.50
20	Mark Prior	2.00
21	Mark Teixeira	2.00
22	Miguel Cabrera	2.00
23	Mike Schmidt	3.00
24	Nolan Ryan	6.00
25	Pedro Martinez	2.00
26	Sammy Sosa	3.00
27	Scott Rolen	2.00
28	Tom Seaver	2.00
29	Vladimir Guerrero	2.00
30	Willie Mays	4.00
31	Carlton Fisk, Magglio Ordonez	3.00
32	Nolan Ryan, Ben Sheets	8.00
33	Babe Ruth, Alex Rodriguez	8.00
34	Cal Ripken Jr., B.J. Upton	10.00
35	Willie Mays, Andruw Jones	5.00
36	George Brett, Hank Blalock	5.00
37	Greg Maddux, Whitey Ford	4.00
38	Harmon Killebrew, Mark Prior	3.00
39	Tom Seaver, Mark Prior	5.00
40	Don Mattingly, Mark Teixeira	5.00
41	Stan Musial, Carlos Beltran	5.00
42	Dale Murphy, Lance Berkman	3.00
43	Willie McCovey, Jeff Bagwell	3.00
44	Andre Dawson, Miguel Cabrera	3.00
45	Brooks Robinson, Scott Rolen	4.00

Passing the Torch Autographs

NM/M

Production 5-100

1	Adrian Beltre/75	15.00
2	Ben Sheets/75	15.00
7	Brooks Robinson/100	25.00

10	Dale Murphy/100	20.00
13	Don Mattingly/50	50.00
18	Johnny Bench/25	50.00
19	Magglio Ordonez/75	10.00
20	Mark Prior/25	40.00
21	Mark Teixeira/75	25.00
22	Miguel Cabrera/75	25.00
23	Mike Schmidt/25	50.00
27	Scott Rolen/25	40.00
28	Tom Seaver/25	50.00
31	Carlton Fisk, Magglio Ordonez/25	50.00
44	Andre Dawson, Miguel Cabrera/25	50.00
45	Brooks Robinson, Scott Rolen/25	75.00

Passing the Torch Bats

NM/M

Production 25-250

1	Adrian Beltre/250	4.00
2	Albert Pujols/250	15.00
4	Andruw Jones/250	4.00
6	Ben Sheets/250	4.00
7	Brooks Robinson/ 150	10.00
8	Cal Ripken Jr./150	25.00
9	Carl Yastrzemski/150	10.00
10	Dale Murphy/150	6.00
11	David Ortiz/250	8.00
13	Don Mattingly/150	10.00
14	George Brett/150	10.00
16	Hank Blalock/250	4.00
17	Jeff Bagwell/250	6.00
18	Johnny Bench/150	10.00
19	Magglio Ordonez/250	4.00
20	Mark Prior/250	10.00
21	Mark Teixeira/250	6.00
22	Miguel Cabrera/250	8.00
23	Mike Schmidt/150	10.00
24	Nolan Ryan/50	20.00
25	Pedro Martinez/150	8.00
26	Sammy Sosa/250	8.00
27	Scott Rolen/250	8.00
28	Tom Seaver/150	8.00
29	Vladimir Guerrero/250	8.00
30	Willie Mays/50	30.00
31	Carlton Fisk, Magglio Ordonez/250	6.00
32	Nolan Ryan, Ben Sheets/50	35.00
34	Cal Ripken Jr., B.J. Upton/50	50.00
35	Willie Mays, Andruw Jones/50	35.00
36	George Brett, Hank Blalock/150	15.00
39	Tom Seaver, Mark Prior/25	20.00
40	Don Mattingly, Mark Teixeira/150	15.00
42	Dale Murphy, Lance Berkman/50	12.00
43	Willie McCovey, Jeff Bagwell/25	20.00
44	Andre Dawson, Miguel Cabrera/150	10.00
45	Brooks Robinson, Scott Rolen/150	15.00

Passing the Torch Jerseys

NM/M

Production 25-250

1	Adrian Beltre/250	4.00
2	Albert Pujols/250	15.00
4	Andruw Jones/250	4.00
5	Babe Ruth.Pants/25	
6	Ben Sheets/250	4.00
7	Brooks Robinson/25	
8	Cal Ripken Jr./250	20.00
9	Carl Yastrzemski/ Pants/50	10.00
10	Dale Murphy/250	6.00
11	David Ortiz/250	8.00
13	Don Mattingly/150	10.00
14	George Brett/50	12.00
15	Greg Maddux/250	4.00
16	Hank Blalock/250	4.00
17	Jeff Bagwell/250	6.00
18	Johnny Bench/ Pants/150	10.00
19	Magglio Ordonez/250	4.00
20	Mark Prior/250	8.00
21	Mark Teixeira/250	6.00
22	Miguel Cabrera/250	8.00
23	Mike Schmidt/150	10.00
24	Nolan Ryan/50	20.00
25	Pedro Martinez/250	8.00
26	Sammy Sosa/250	8.00
27	Scott Rolen/250	8.00
28	Tom Seaver/50	8.00

29	Vladimir Guerrero/250	8.00
31	Carlton Fisk, Magglio Ordonez/50	8.00
32	Nolan Ryan, Ben Sheets/50	35.00
34	Cal Ripken Jr., B.J. Upton/50	50.00
35	Willie Mays, Andruw Jones/50	35.00
36	George Brett, Hank Blalock/50	15.00
39	Tom Seaver, Mark Prior/25	20.00
40	Don Mattingly, Mark Teixeira/100	15.00
42	Dale Murphy, Lance Berkman/150	10.00
43	Willie McCovey, Jeff Bagwell/50	15.00
44	Andre Dawson, Miguel Cabrera/150	10.00

Recollection Autographs

Production 10-25

Teams

NM/M

Common Card:	
Production 1,500 Sets	
Black:	1-2X
Production 250 Sets	
Blue:	1X
Production 1,000 Sets	
Gold:	2-3X
Production 100 Sets	
Green:	1-1.5X
Production 750 Sets	
Red:	1-1.5X
Production 500 Sets	

1	Manny Ramirez, Pedro Martinez, David Ortiz	4.00
2	Albert Pujols, Scott Rolen, Jim Edmonds	4.00
3	Roger Clemens, Jeff Bagwell, Lance Berkman, Craig Biggio	4.00
4	Miguel Cabrera, Josh Beckett, Mike Lowell	2.00
5	Kerry Wood, Mark Prior, Sammy Sosa, Greg Maddux	4.00
6	Adrian Beltre, Shawn Green, Hideo Nomo, Kazuhisa Ishii	2.00
7	Cal Ripken Jr., Eddie Murray, Jim Palmer	8.00
8	George Brett, Bo Jackson, Frank White	4.00
9	Roger Clemens, Mike Mussina, Alfonso Soriano, Bernie Williams	4.00
10	Tom Glavine, Greg Maddux, Ryan Klesko, David Justice	4.00

Teams Bats

NM/M

Production 50-100

1	Manny Ramirez, Pedro Martinez, David Ortiz/100	20.00

2 Albert Pujols, Scott Rolen, Jim Edmonds/100 — 40.00
3 Roger Clemens, Jeff Bagwell, Lance Berkman, Craig Biggio/50 — 35.00
4 Miguel Cabrera, Josh Beckett, Mike Lowell/100 — 10.00
6 Adrian Beltre, Shawn Green, Hideo Nomo, Kazuhisa Ishii/50 — 20.00
8 George Brett, Bo Jackson, Frank White/100 — 25.00

Teams Jerseys

NM/M
Production 50-150
1 Manny Ramirez, Pedro Martinez, David Ortiz/150 — 20.00
2 Albert Pujols, Scott Rolen, Jim Edmonds/150 — 30.00
3 Roger Clemens, Jeff Bagwell, Lance Berkman, Craig Biggio/150 — 25.00
4 Miguel Cabrera, Josh Beckett, Mike Lowell/50 — 15.00
5 Kerry Wood, Mark Prior, Sammy Sosa, Greg Maddux/150 — 25.00
6 Adrian Beltre, Shawn Green, Hideo Nomo, Kazuhisa Ishii/50 — 20.00
7 Cal Ripken Jr., Eddie Murray, Jim Palmer/100 — 35.00
9 Roger Clemens, Mike Mussina, Alfonso Soriano, Bernie Williams/100 — 25.00
10 Tom Glavine, Greg Maddux, Ryan Klesko, David Justice/100 — 30.00

Throwback Threads

NM/M
Production 10-200
1 Albert Pujols/200 — 15.00
3 Bert Blyleven/200 — 4.00
4 Bobby Doerr/ Pants/200 — 6.00
6 Cal Ripken Jr./150 — 25.00
7 Carl Yastrzemski/ Pants/150 — 12.00
8 Dale Murphy/150 — 8.00
9 Dennis Eckersley/50 — 8.00
10 Don Mattingly/200 — 10.00
11 Don Sutton/100 — 4.00
13 Early Wynn/50 — 6.00
14 Eddie Murray/100 — 8.00
16 Greg Maddux/150 — 8.00
17 Harmon Killebrew/100 — 8.00
19 Hoyt Wilhelm/50 — 6.00
19 Jim Edmonds/200 — 8.00
21 Lou Boudreau/100 — 8.00
22 Lou Brock/100 — 8.00
23 Miguel Cabrera/200 — 8.00
24 Mike Mussina/150 — 8.00
25 Mike Piazza/150 — 8.00
26 Mike Schmidt/150 — 15.00
27 Nolan Ryan/50 — 20.00
28 Phil Niekro/100 — 6.00
29 Randy Johnson/150 — 8.00
30 Rickey Henderson/ 150 — 8.00
31 Sammy Sosa/150 — 8.00
32 Scott Rolen/200 — 8.00
34 Steve Carlton/150 — 8.00
36 Tommy John/150 — 6.00
37 Vladimir Guerrero/ 200 — 8.00
38 Whitey Ford/25 — 15.00
39 Willie Mays/50 — 40.00
40 Willie McCovey/150 — 8.00
46 Lou Brock, Rickey Henderson/ 100 — 15.00
49 Bo Jackson, Deion Sanders/150 — 15.00
50 Nolan Ryan, Curt Schilling/100 — 25.00
51 Don Sutton, Greg Maddux/100 — 15.00
52 Harmon Killebrew, Rafael Palmeiro/100 — 15.00
53 Dale Murphy, Dwight Evans/150 — 12.00

55 Carl Yastrzemski, Vladimir Guerrero/50 — 15.00
56 Eddie Murray, Mike Piazza/100 — 12.00
57 Johnny Bench, Ivan Rodriguez/50 — 12.00
58 Jim Palmer, Tim Hudson/50 — 10.00
59 Cal Ripken Jr., Hank Blalock/50 — 35.00
60 Jim Rice, Manny Ramirez/100 — 12.00

Throwback Threads Autographs

NM/M
Production 5-100
Prime: No Pricing
Production 1-10
3 Bert Blyleven/100 — 15.00
4 Bobby Doerr/ Pants/100 — 20.00
5 Brooks Robinson/50 — 30.00
8 Dale Murphy/100 — 25.00
9 Dennis Eckersley/75 — 20.00
11 Don Sutton/50 — 20.00
17 Harmon Killebrew/75 — 30.00
20 Jim Palmer/75 — 15.00
22 Lou Brock/Jkt/75 — 30.00
23 Miguel Cabrera/75 — 30.00

Throwback Threads Prime

Production 1-25

2005 Donruss Greats

NM/M
Complete Set (150): — 50.00
Common Player: — .50
Pack (5): — 9.00
Box (15): — 120.00
1 Al Kaline — .75
2 Alan Trammell — .50
3 Andre Dawson — .50
4 Barry Larkin — .75
5 Bert Blyleven — .50
6 Billy Williams — .50
7 Bo Jackson — 1.00
8 Bob Feller — .75
9 Bobby Doerr — .50
10 Brooks Robinson — 1.00
11 Cal Ripken Jr. — 4.00
12 Dale Murphy — .50
13 Darryl Strawberry — .50
14 Dave Parker — .50
15 Dave Stewart — .50
16 David Cone — .50
17 Dennis Eckersley — .50
18 Don Larsen — .50
19 Don Mattingly — 2.00
20 Don Sutton — .50
21 Duke Snider — 1.00
22 Dwight Evans — .50
23 Dwight Gooden — .50
24 Earl Weaver — .50
25 Fergie Jenkins — .50
26 Frank Robinson — 1.00
27 Fred Lynn — .50
28 Gary Carter — .50
29 Gaylord Perry — .50
30 George Brett — 2.50
31 George Foster — .50
32 George Kell — .50
33 Harmon Killebrew — 1.50
34 Harold Baines — .50
35 Harold Reynolds — .50
36 Jack Morris — .50
37 Jim Abbott — .50
38 Jim Bunning — .50
39 Jim Palmer — .50
40 Jim Rice — .50
41 Jim Leyritz — .50
42 Joe Morgan — .50
43 John Kruk — .50
44 Johnny Bench — 2.00
45 Johnny Podres — .50
46 Jose Canseco — 1.00
47 Juan Marichal — .50
48 Keith Hernandez — .50
49 Kent Hrbek — .50
50 Kirby Puckett — 2.00
51 Lee Smith — .50
52 Lenny Dykstra — .50
53 Luis Aparicio — .50
54 Luis Tiant — .50
55 Mark Grace — .50
56 Marty Marion — .50
57 Matt Williams — .50
58 Maury Wills — .50
59 Mike Schmidt — 2.00
60 Minnie Minoso — .50
61 Nolan Ryan — 3.00

62 Ozzie Smith — 1.00
63 Paul Molitor — .75
64 Phil Rizzuto — .75
65 Ralph Kiner — .50
66 Randy Jones — .50
67 Red Schoendienst — .50
68 Rich "Goose" Gossage — .50
69 Rob Dibble — .50
70 Robin Roberts — .50
71 Rod Carew — .50
72 Rollie Fingers — .50
73 Ron Guidry — .50
74 Ron Santo — .50
75 Ryne Sandberg — 2.00
76 Stan Musial — 2.00
77 Steve Carlton — .50
78 Steve Garvey — .50
79 Steve Stone — .50
80 Terry Pendleton — .50
81 Terry Steinbach — .50
82 Tom Seaver — 1.00
83 Tommy John — .50
84 Tony Gwynn — 1.00
85 Tony Oliva — .50
86 Whitey Ford — 1.00
87 Will Clark — .75
88 Willie Mays — 3.00
89 Willie McCovey — 1.00
90 Roberto Clemente — 2.50
91 Roger Maris — 2.00
92 Bob Gibson — .75
93 Carl Yastrzemski — 1.50
94 Jim "Catfish" Hunter — .50
95 Warren Spahn — 1.00
96 Reggie Jackson — 1.00
97 Lou Brock — .75
98 Joe Morgan — .50
99 Carlton Fisk — .50
100 Eddie Murray — .50
101 Roger Clemens — 3.00
102 Greg Maddux — 2.00
103 Derek Jeter — 3.00
104 Albert Pujols — 3.00
105 Ken Griffey Jr. — 2.00
106 Alex Rodriguez — 3.00
107 Mike Piazza — 1.50
108 Manny Ramirez — 1.00
109 Sammy Sosa — 1.00
110 Rafael Palmeiro — .75
111 Randy Johnson — 1.00
112 Vladimir Guerrero — 1.00
113 Ichiro Suzuki — 2.00
114 David Ortiz — 1.00
115 Miguel Cabrera — 1.00
116 Frank Thomas — 1.00
117 Pedro Martinez — 1.00
118 Chipper Jones — 1.00
119 Todd Helton — .75
120 Alfonso Soriano — 1.00
121 Ivan Rodriguez — .75
122 Carlos Delgado — .75
123 Carlos Beltran — .75
124 Jeff Kent — .50
125 Curt Schilling — .75
126 Derrek Lee — .75
127 Jason Bay — .50
128 Mark Teixeira — .75
129 Craig Biggio — .50
130 Miguel Tejada — .50
131 Johan Santana — .75
132 Jim Thome — .75
133 Tim Hudson — .50
134 Barry Zito — .50
135 Mark Mulder — .50
136 Hideki Matsui — 2.00
137 John Smoltz — .50
138 Mark Prior — .75
139 Andruw Jones — .75
140 Adam Dunn — .75
141 Prince Fielder — 4.00
142 Tadahito Iguchi RC — 2.00
143 Randy Johnson — 1.00
144 Pedro Martinez — 1.00
145 Alex Rodriguez — 3.00
146 Roger Clemens — 3.00
147 Vladimir Guerrero — 1.00
148 Greg Maddux — 2.00
149 Ken Griffey Jr. — 2.00
150 Roger Clemens — 3.00

Gold Holofoil

Gold Holofoil: — 3-4X
Production 100 Sets

Platinum Holofoil

Platinum Holofoil: — 3-5X
Production 50 Sets

Silver Holofoil

Silver Holofoil: — 1-2X
Inserted 1:3

Dodger Blues Brooklyn Material

NM/M
Common Player: — 10.00
Prime: — No Pricing
Production 10
1 Sandy Koufax/43 — 140.00
2 Duke Snider/27 — 40.00
3 Burleigh Grimes — 40.00
4 Tommy Lasorda — 10.00

Dodger Blues Brooklyn Signature Material

NM/M
1 Sandy Koufax/37 — 300.00

Dodger Blues LA Material

NM/M
Common Player: — 10.00
Prime: — No Pricing
Production 1-10
1 Sandy Koufax/43 — 140.00
2 Duke Snider/55 — 35.00
4 Tommy Lasorda — 10.00
5 Orel Hershiser — 10.00
6 Don Sutton — 10.00

Dodger Blues LA Signature Material

NM/M
Production 10-37
Prime: — No Pricing
Production 1-5
1 Sandy Koufax/37 — 300.00

Hall of Fame Souvenirs

NM/M
Common Player: — 2.00
1 Willie Mays Giants — 4.00
2 Hank Aaron Mil — 4.00
3 Hank Aaron Atl — 4.00
4 Willie Mays Mets — 4.00
5 Nolan Ryan — 6.00
6 Roberto Clemente/ Kneeling — 4.00
7 Nellie Fox — 2.00
8 Pee Wee Reese — 3.00
9 Babe Ruth — 6.00
10 Bobby Doerr — 2.00
11 Brooks Robinson — 3.00
12 Carlton Fisk — 3.00
13 Eddie Murray — 3.00
14 Ernie Banks — 4.00
15 Frank Robinson — 3.00
16 Gary Carter — 2.00
17 Hack Wilson — 2.00
18 Harmon Killebrew — 4.00
19 Joe Morgan — 2.00
20 Kirby Puckett — 4.00
21 Lou Brock — 3.00
22 Orlando Cepeda — 2.00
23 Red Schoendienst — 2.00
24 Richie Ashburn — 2.00
25 Stan Musial — 5.00
26 Roberto Clemente/ Standing — 6.00
27 Wade Boggs/Sox — 3.00
28 Wade Boggs/Yanks — 3.00

Hall of Fame Souvenirs Material Bat

NM/M
Common Player: — 10.00
1 Willie Mays — 25.00
2 Hank Aaron — 25.00
3 Hank Aaron — 25.00
4 Willie Mays — 25.00
5 Nolan Ryan/30 — 25.00
6 Roberto Clemente — 40.00
7 Nellie Fox — 10.00
8 Pee Wee Reese — 10.00
9 Babe Ruth — 140.00
11 Brooks Robinson — 10.00
12 Carlton Fisk — 10.00
13 Eddie Murray — 10.00
14 Ernie Banks — 15.00
15 Frank Robinson — 8.00
16 Gary Carter — 8.00
17 Hack Wilson — 30.00
18 Harmon Killebrew — 10.00
19 Joe Morgan — 8.00
20 Kirby Puckett — 10.00
21 Lou Brock — 8.00
22 Orlando Cepeda — 8.00
23 Red Schoendienst — 8.00

24	Richie Ashburn	8.00
25	Stan Musial	20.00
26	Roberto Clemente	40.00
27	Wade Boggs	10.00
28	Wade Boggs	10.00

HOF Souvenirs Material Combo

NM/M

Common Combo:		10.00
1	Willie Mays Giants	50.00
2	Hank Aaron Mil	50.00
3	Hank Aaron Atl	50.00
4	Willie Mays/25	50.00
5	Nolan Ryan/25	40.00
8	Pee Wee Reese/38	25.00
9	Babe Ruth/50	300.00
10	Bobby Doerr	10.00
11	Brooks Robinson/29	20.00
12	Carlton Fisk	10.00
13	Eddie Murray	10.00
14	Ernie Banks	20.00
16	Gary Carter	10.00
18	Harmon Killebrew	15.00
23	Red Schoendienst	10.00
26	Roberto Clemente	75.00
27	Wade Boggs	15.00
28	Wade Boggs	25.00

HOF Souvenirs Material Jersey

NM/M

Common Player:		10.00
1	Willie Mays/25	40.00
2	Hank Aaron/25	40.00
3	Hank Aaron/25	40.00
4	Willie Mays/25	40.00
5	Nolan Ryan/25	25.00
9	Babe Ruth/25	225.00
10	Bobby Doerr	10.00
12	Carlton Fisk	10.00
24	Richie Ashburn	10.00
25	Stan Musial	25.00
27	Wade Boggs	12.00

Hall of Fame Souvenirs Signature

No Pricing

HOF Souvenirs Signature Material Bat

NM/M

No pricing production 22 or less.

10	Bobby Doerr	20.00
11	Brooks Robinson	30.00
12	Carlton Fisk	30.00
15	Frank Robinson	20.00
16	Gary Carter	20.00
18	Harmon Killebrew	30.00
19	Joe Morgan	20.00
20	Kirby Puckett/52	90.00
21	Lou Brock	25.00
22	Orlando Cepeda	20.00
23	Red Schoendienst	25.00
25	Stan Musial/50	60.00

HOF Souvenirs Signature Material Combo

NM/M

Common Signature:		20.00
10	Bobby Doerr	20.00
11	Brooks Robinson	40.00
12	Carlton Fisk/50	40.00
15	Frank Robinson/39	30.00
16	Gary Carter	20.00
18	Harmon Killebrew	30.00
19	Joe Morgan/23	25.00
20	Kirby Puckett/45	125.00
22	Orlando Cepeda	25.00
25	Stan Musial	80.00
27	Wade Boggs/50	40.00
28	Wade Boggs/31	40.00

HOF Souvenirs Signature Material Jersey

NM/M

Common Signature:		20.00
10	Bobby Doerr	20.00
11	Brooks Robinson	40.00
12	Carlton Fisk	30.00
15	Frank Robinson	30.00
16	Gary Carter/63	20.00
18	Harmon Killebrew	30.00
22	Orlando Cepeda/68	20.00
23	Red Schoendienst	25.00
25	Stan Musial	65.00

27	Wade Boggs/50	40.00
28	Wade Boggs/3	40.00

Redbirds Material

NM/M

Common Player:		8.00
Prime:		No Pricing

Production 1-25

1	Stan Musial/ w/Glove/Jsy T2	35.00
2	Ozzie Smith/Jkt T4	20.00
3	Enos Slaughter/ Jsy T4	15.00
4	Frankie Frisch/Jkt T3	20.00
5	Lou Brock/Jsy T2	15.00
6	Bob Gibson/Jsy T2	15.00
7	Ken Boyer/Jsy T3	25.00
8	Lee Smith/Jsy T4	8.00
9	Albert Pujols/Jsy T2	30.00
10	Stan Musial/ w/Bant Pants T2	35.00

Redbirds Signature Material

NM/M

Production 5-50

Prime:	No Pricing

Production 1-5

8	Lee Smith/50	20.00

Signature Gold HoloFoil

NM/M

Tier 1 Production 1-50
Tier 2 Production 51-100
Tier 3 Production 101-250
Tier 4 Production 251-800
Tier 5 Production 801-1200
Tier 6 Production 1201-2000
Cards are not serial numbered.

1	Al Kaline T2	30.00
2	Alan Trammell T3	15.00
3	Andre Dawson T5	10.00
4	Barry Larkin T2/55	30.00
5	Bert Blyleven T4	10.00
6	Billy Williams T2/55	15.00
7	Bo Jackson T1/35	50.00
8	Bob Feller T6	15.00
9	Bobby Doerr T5	20.00
10	Brooks Robinson T2	30.00
11	Cal Ripken Jr. T3	120.00
12	Dale Murphy T3	20.00
13	Darryl Strawberry T6	15.00
14	Dave Parker T3	10.00
15	Dave Stewart T4	10.00
16	David Cone T2	10.00
17	Dennis Eckersley T2	20.00
18	Don Larsen T4	10.00
19	Don Mattingly T1/45	75.00
20	Don Sutton T3	15.00
21	Duke Snider T2/55	25.00
22	Dwight Evans T3	15.00
23	Dwight Gooden T4	15.00
24	Earl Weaver T4	15.00
25	Fergie Jenkins T3	15.00
26	Frank Robinson T2	25.00
27	Fred Lynn T4	10.00
28	Gary Carter T2/55	15.00
29	Gaylord Perry T3	15.00
30	George Brett T1/35	75.00
31	George Foster T5	10.00
32	George Kell T6	15.00
33	Harmon Killebrew T2/55	30.00
34	Harold Baines T4	10.00
35	Harold Reynolds T4	10.00
36	Jack Morris T5	10.00
37	Jim Abbott T4	10.00
38	Jim Bunning T2	25.00
39	Jim Palmer T3	15.00
40	Jim Rice T2	20.00
41	Jim Leyritz T3	10.00
42	Joe Morgan T1/35	20.00
43	John Kruk T2	20.00
44	Johnny Bench T1/35	50.00
45	Johnny Podres T6	10.00
46	Jose Canseco T1/45	35.00
47	Juan Marichal T2	20.00
48	Keith Hernandez T5	15.00
49	Kent Hrbek T5	10.00
50	Kirby Puckett T1/35	85.00
51	Lee Smith T5	10.00
52	Lenny Dykstra T4	10.00
53	Luis Aparicio T3	15.00
54	Luis Tiant T3	15.00
55	Mark Grace T1/45	25.00
56	Marty Marion T5	15.00
57	Matt Williams T5	15.00
58	Maury Wills T5	15.00
59	Mike Schmidt T1/35	50.00
60	Minnie Minoso T5	15.00
61	Nolan Ryan T2/75	80.00
62	Ozzie Smith T2/55	40.00

63	Paul Molitor T2/55	30.00
64	Phil Rizzuto T2/55	30.00
65	Ralph Kiner T5	25.00
66	Randy Jones T4	10.00
67	Red Schoendienst T3	10.00
68	Rich "Goose" Gossage T3	10.00
69	Rob Dibble T4	30.00
70	Robin Roberts T2	30.00
71	Rod Carew T2/55	25.00
72	Rollie Fingers T3	15.00
73	Ron Guidry T3	25.00
74	Ron Santo T3	20.00
75	Ryne Sandberg T1/35	60.00
76	Stan Musial T1/35	20.00
77	Steve Carlton T2	15.00
78	Steve Garvey T3	15.00
79	Steve Stone T5	15.00
81	Terry Steinbach T3	10.00
82	Tom Seaver T1/35	40.00
83	Tommy John T6	10.00
84	Tony Gwynn T1/45	40.00
85	Tony Oliva T5	15.00
86	Whitey Ford T1/35	40.00
87	Will Clark T2/55	25.00
88	Willie Mays T2	150.00
89	Willie McCovey T1/45	35.00

Signature Platinum HoloFoil

NM/M

Production 1-50
Cards are not serial #'d.

3	Andre Dawson	15.00
5	Bert Blyleven	15.00
8	Bob Feller	25.00
9	Bobby Doerr	20.00
13	Darryl Strawberry	15.00
14	Dave Parker	15.00
18	Don Larsen	30.00
23	Dwight Gooden	20.00
25	Fergie Jenkins	25.00
27	Fred Lynn	15.00
31	George Foster	15.00
32	George Kell	25.00
34	Harold Baines	20.00
35	Harold Reynolds	15.00
36	Jack Morris	15.00
39	Jim Palmer	25.00
45	Johnny Podres	20.00
48	Keith Hernandez	15.00
49	Kent Hrbek	20.00
51	Lee Smith	20.00
52	Lenny Dykstra	20.00
54	Luis Tiant	20.00
56	Marty Marion	25.00
57	Matt Williams	20.00
58	Maury Wills	20.00
60	Minnie Minoso	20.00
65	Ralph Kiner	40.00
66	Randy Jones	15.00
67	Red Schoendienst	25.00
69	Rob Dibble	15.00
74	Ron Santo	30.00
79	Steve Stone	20.00
81	Terry Steinbach	15.00
83	Tommy John	15.00
85	Tony Oliva	20.00

Souvenirs

NM/M

Common Player:		2.00
1	Jim Thorpe	4.00
2	Joe Carter	2.00
3	Will Clark	3.00
4	Cal Ripken Jr.	6.00
5	Dwight Evans	2.00
6	George Foster	2.00
7	Steve Leyritz	2.00
8	Don Mattingly	4.00
9	Deion Sanders	3.00
10	Ron Santo	3.00
11	Alan Trammell	2.00
12	Robin Ventura	2.00
13	Matt Williams	3.00

Souvenirs Material Bat

NM/M

Common Player:		5.00
2	Joe Carter	5.00
3	Will Clark	8.00
5	Dwight Evans	5.00
6	George Foster	5.00
7	Steve Garvey	5.00
8	Don Mattingly	15.00
9	Deion Sanders	8.00
10	Ron Santo	8.00
11	Alan Trammell	8.00
12	Robin Ventura	5.00
13	Matt Williams	5.00

Souvenirs Material Combo

NM/M

Common Combo:		
2	Joe Carter/50	10.00
3	Will Clark	12.00
9	Deion Sanders	12.00
11	Alan Trammell	10.00
13	Matt Williams	10.00

Souvenirs Material Jersey

NM/M

Common Player:		5.00
1	Jim Thorpe	120.00
3	Will Clark	10.00
4	Cal Ripken Jr.	25.00
9	Deion Sanders	10.00
11	Alan Trammell/68	10.00
12	Robin Ventura/48	5.00
13	Matt Williams	8.00

Souvenirs Signature

NM/M

Common Auto.:		15.00
3	Will Clark	25.00
5	Dwight Evans/25	20.00
7	Steve Garvey	15.00
10	Ron Santo	25.00
11	Alan Trammell	20.00

Souvenirs Signature Material Bat

NM/M

Common Player:		15.00
3	Will Clark	25.00
5	Dwight Evans	20.00
7	Steve Garvey	15.00
10	Ron Santo	25.00
11	Alan Trammell	20.00
12	Robin Ventura	15.00

Souvenirs Signature Material Combo

NM/M

Common Player:		20.00
3	Will Clark	30.00
7	Steve Garvey	20.00
11	Alan Trammell	20.00

Souvenirs Signature Material Jersey

NM/M

Common Player:		15.00
3	Will Clark	25.00
5	Dwight Evans	25.00
7	Steve Garvey	15.00
11	Alan Trammell	20.00

Sox Nation Material

NM/M

Common Player:		10.00
Prime:		No Pricing

Production 1-10

1	Ted Williams	75.00
2	Bobby Doerr	20.00
3	Roger Clemens/55	40.00
4	Carl Yastrzemski	25.00
5	Carl Yastrzemski	25.00
6	Jim Rice	15.00
7	Jim Rice	15.00
8	Joe Cronin	15.00
9	Joe Cronin	15.00
10	Carlton Fisk	20.00
11	Fred Lynn	10.00
12	Wade Boggs	25.00
13	Wade Boggs/55	25.00

Sox Nation Signature Material

NM/M

Prime:	No Pricing

Production 1-5

2	Bobby Doerr/50	25.00
6	Jim Rice/50	25.00
7	Jim Rice/50	25.00
11	Fred Lynn/50	15.00

Yankee Clippings Material

NM/M

Common Player:		8.00
Prime:		No Pricing

Production 1-33

2	Babe Ruth	300.00
3	Billy Martin	40.00
4	Billy Martin	40.00

#	Player	Price
5	Bobby Murcer	15.00
6	Bucky Dent	10.00
7	Jim "Catfish" Hunter	15.00
8	Jim "Catfish" Hunter	15.00
9	Darryl Strawberry	8.00
10	Dave Righetti	8.00
11	Dave Winfield	10.00
12	Deion Sanders	15.00
13	Deion Sanders	15.00
14	Don Mattingly	35.00
15	Elston Howard	15.00
16	Graig Nettles	10.00
17	Roger Clemens/43	50.00
18	Luis Tiant	8.00
19	Mickey Rivers	15.00
20	Phil Rizzuto	15.00
21	Reggie Jackson	20.00
22	Rickey Henderson	15.00
23	Roger Maris	50.00
24	Roger Maris	50.00
25	Ron Guidry	15.00
26	Sparky Lyle	8.00
27	Phil Niekro	20.00
28	Tommy John	20.00
29	Whitey Ford	40.00
30	Yogi Berra	60.00

Yankee Clippings Signature Material

NM/M
Prime: No Pricing
Production 1-5

#	Player	Price
9	Darryl Strawberry/25	30.00
18	Luis Tiant/50	30.00
20	Phil Rizzuto/25	60.00
25	Ron Guidry/25	50.00
28	Tommy John/25	30.00

2005 Donruss Leather & Lumber

NM/M
Complete Set (177):
Common Player (1-150): .25
Common Auto. (151-175): 8.00
Production 256
Card #176 doesn't exist.
Pack (5): 7.00
Box (18): 100.00

#	Player	Price
1	Adam Dunn	.50
2	Adrian Beltre	.40
3	Akinori Otsuka	.25
4	Al Leiter	.25
5	Albert Pujols	2.00
6	Alex Rodriguez	1.50
7	Alfonso Soriano	.75
8	Andy Pettitte	.40
9	Aramis Ramirez	.40
10	Aubrey Huff	.25
11	Austin Kearns	.25
12	Barry Larkin	.40
13	Barry Zito	.40
14	Bartolo Colon	.25
15	Bernie Williams	.40
16	Bobby Abreu	.40
17	Bobby Crosby	.40
18	Brad Penny	.25
19	Brian Giles	.25
20	C.C. Sabathia	.25
21	Carl Crawford	.25
22	Carl Pavano	.25
23	Carlos Beltran	.50
24	Carlos Delgado	.40
25	Carlos Lee	.40
26	Carlos Zambrano	.40
27	Casey Kotchman	.25
28	Chipper Jones	.75
29	Chone Figgins	.40
30	Craig Biggio	.40
31	Craig Monroe	.25
32	Cristian Guzman	.25
33	Curt Schilling	.75
34	Danny Haren	.25
35	Darin Erstad	.25
36	David Dellucci	.25
37	David Ortiz	.75
38	David Wells	.25
39	Derek Jeter	2.00
40	Dontrelle Willis	.40
41	Edgar Renteria	.40
42	Eric Gagne	.40
43	Frank Thomas	.50
44	Garret Anderson	.40
45	Gary Sheffield	.50
46	Geoff Jenkins	.25
47	Greg Maddux	1.50
48	Hideo Nomo	.40
49	Ichiro Suzuki	1.50
50	Ivan Rodriguez	.50
51	J.D. Drew	.25
52	Jake Peavy	.40
53	Jamie Moyer	.25
54	Jason Giambi	.40
55	Jason Kendall	.25
56	Jason Schmidt	.40
57	Jason Varitek	.40
58	Javy Lopez	.40
59	Jay Gibbons	.25
60	Jeff Bagwell	.50
61	Jeff Bagwell	.25
62	Jeremy Bonderman	.25
63	Jermaine Dye	.40
64	Jim Edmonds	.40
65	Jim Thome	.50
66	Joe Nathan	.25
67	Johan Santana	.50
68	John Olerud	.25
69	John Smoltz	.40
70	Johnny Damon	.75
71	Johnny Estrada	.25
72	Jose Reyes	.50
73	Jose Vidro	.25
74	Josh Beckett	.40
75	Juan Pierre	.25
76	Junior Spivey	.25
77	Justin Morneau	.40
78	Kazuhisa Ishii	.25
79	Kazuo Matsui	.25
80	Ken Griffey Jr.	1.50
81	Kerry Wood	.40
82	Kevin Brown	.25
83	Kevin Millwood	.40
84	Khalil Greene	.25
85	Lance Berkman	.40
86	Larry Walker	.40
87	Laynce Nix	.25
88	Lyle Overbay	.25
89	Magglio Ordonez	.40
90	Manny Ramirez	.50
91	Marcus Giles	.25
92	Mark Loretta	.25
93	Mark Mulder	.40
94	Mark Prior	.50
95	Mark Teixeira	.40
96	Melvin Mora	.25
97	Michael Young	.25
98	Miguel Tejada	.50
99	Mike Lieberthal	.25
100	Mike Lowell	.25
101	Mike Mussina	.40
102	Mike Piazza	1.00
103	Milton Bradley	.25
104	Moises Alou	.40
105	Morgan Ensberg	.25
106	Nomar Garciaparra	1.00
107	Omar Vizquel	.25
108	Paul Konerko	.40
109	Paul LoDuca	.25
110	Pedro Martinez	.75
111	Rafael Furcal	.25
112	Rafael Palmeiro	.40
113	Randy Johnson	.75
114	Richie Sexson	.40
115	Rocco Baldelli	.25
116	Roger Clemens	2.00
117	Roy Halladay	.40
118	Sammy Sosa	.75
119	Scott Podsednik	.25
120	Scott Rolen	.75
121	Sean Burroughs	.25
122	Sean Casey	.25
123	Shannon Stewart	.25
124	Shawn Green	.40
125	Steve Finley	.25
126	Tim Hudson	.40
127	Tim Salmon	.50
128	Todd Helton	.50
129	Tom Glavine	.40
130	Torii Hunter	.40
131	Travis Hafner	.40
132	Troy Glaus	.40
133	Troy Percival	.25
134	Vernon Wells	.40
135	Victor Martinez	.40
136	Vladimir Guerrero	.75
137	Andre Dawson	.40
138	Brooks Robinson	.75
139	Cal Ripken Jr.	3.00
140	Dale Murphy	.50
141	Darryl Strawberry	.40
142	George Brett	2.00
143	Harmon Killebrew	1.00
144	Jim Palmer	.50
145	Lou Brock	.75
146	Mike Schmidt	2.00
147	Nolan Ryan	2.00
148	Steve Carlton	.50
149	Tony Gwynn	1.00
150	Willie Mays	2.00
151	Agustin Montero RC	10.00
152	Carlos Ruiz RC	15.00
153	Casey Rogowski RC	8.00
154	Chris Resop RC	15.00
155	Chris Roberson RC	15.00
156	Colter Bean RC	15.00
157	Danny Rueckel RC	8.00
158	David Gassner RC	15.00
159	Geovany Soto RC	15.00
160	John Hattig Jr. RC	8.00
161	Justin Wechsler RC	10.00
162	Luke Scott RC	25.00
163	Mark McLemore RC	10.00
164	Miguel Negron RC	8.00
165	Mike Morse RC	20.00
166	Nate McLouth RC	8.00
167	Philip Humber RC	20.00
168	Randy Messenger RC	8.00
169	Raul Tablado RC	8.00
170	Russel Rohlicek RC	8.00
171	Ryan Speier RC	8.00
172	Scott Munter RC	10.00
173	Sean Thompson RC	10.00
174	Sean Tracey RC	10.00
175	Wladimir Balentien RC	25.00
177	Norihiro Nakamura/128 RC	75.00

Gold

Gold (1-150): 4-8X
Production 50 Sets

Silver

Silver (1-150): 3-5X
Production 100 Sets

Platinum

Platinum: No Pricing
Production One Set

Big Bang

NM/M
Common Player: 1.50
Production 2,000 Sets
Gold: 1-2X
Production 100 Sets
Silver: 1-2X
Production 200 Sets
Platinum: No Pricing
Production One Set

#	Player	Price
1	Adam Dunn	2.00
2	Adrian Beltre	1.50
3	Albert Pujols	6.00
4	Alex Rodriguez	5.00
5	Chipper Jones	2.00
6	Dale Murphy	2.00
7	Darryl Strawberry	1.50
8	Dave Parker	1.50
9	David Ortiz	2.00
10	Duke Snider	2.00
11	Frank Robinson	2.00
12	Gary Sheffield	1.50
13	George Foster	1.50
14	Harmon Killebrew	3.00
15	Jim Edmonds	2.00
16	Jim Rice	1.50
17	Jim Thome	2.00
18	Ken Griffey Jr.	4.00
19	Manny Ramirez	2.00
20	Matt Williams	1.50
21	Mike Piazza	3.00
22	Mike Schmidt	5.00
23	Rafael Palmeiro	2.00
24	Sammy Sosa	3.00
25	Ted Williams	5.00

Big Bang Bat

NM/M
Production 50-250

#	Player	Price
3	Albert Pujols/250	15.00
8	Dave Parker/250	4.00
9	David Ortiz/250	8.00
11	Frank Robinson/100	8.00
13	George Foster/250	4.00
16	Jim Rice/50	6.00
19	Manny Ramirez/250	8.00
22	Mike Schmidt/100	15.00
23	Rafael Palmeiro/250	6.00
24	Sammy Sosa/250	8.00
25	Ted Williams/100	60.00

Big Bang Combos

NM/M
Production 25-100
Prime: No Pricing
Production 5 Sets

#	Player	Price
1	Adam Dunn/Bat-Jsy/25	12.00
2	Adrian Beltre/Bat-Jsy/25	8.00
3	Albert Pujols/Bat-Jsy/100	25.00
7	Darryl Strawberry/Jsy-Pants/100	8.00
8	Dave Parker/Bat-Jsy/100	8.00
9	David Ortiz/Bat-Jsy/100	15.00
15	Jim Edmonds/Jsy-Jsy/100	10.00
16	Jim Rice/Jsy-Jsy-Jsy/100	10.00
19	Manny Ramirez/Bat-Jsy/100	12.00
20	Matt Williams/Jsy-Jsy/100	8.00
21	Mike Piazza/Bat-Jsy/50	15.00
22	Mike Schmidt/Bat-Jsy/100	20.00
23	Rafael Palmeiro/Bat-Jsy/100	10.00
24	Sammy Sosa/Bat-Jsy/100	12.00

Big Bang Jersey

NM/M
Production 25-250
Prime: No Pricing
Production 5 Sets

#	Player	Price
1	Adam Dunn/250	6.00
3	Albert Pujols/250	15.00
5	Chipper Jones/250	8.00
6	Dale Murphy/250	8.00
7	Darryl Strawberry/Pants/250	6.00
8	Dave Parker/250	4.00
9	David Ortiz/250	8.00
10	Duke Snider/25	12.00
12	Gary Sheffield/250	6.00
14	Harmon Killebrew/100	10.00
15	Jim Edmonds/250	6.00
16	Jim Rice Pants/250	6.00
17	Jim Thome/250	8.00
19	Manny Ramirez/100	8.00
20	Matt Williams/250	6.00
21	Mike Piazza/250	10.00
22	Mike Schmidt/100	15.00
23	Rafael Palmeiro/Pants/250	6.00
24	Sammy Sosa/250	8.00
25	Ted Williams/Jkt/250	40.00

Big Bang Signatures

No Pricing
Production 1-10

Game Ball Signatures

NM/M
Production 1-50

#	Player	Price
1	Ben Grieve/50	10.00
3	Eli Marrero/24	12.00
4	Jeff Fassero/24	25.00
5	Jose Guillen/47	25.00
7	Mark Grudzielanek/23	30.00
8	Mike Lowell/23	
9	Paul Konerko/45	25.00
10	Willie Mays/1	

Great Gloves

NM/M
Common Player: 1.50
Production 2,000 Sets
Gold: 2-3X
Production 50 Sets
Silver: 1-2X
Production 100 Sets
Platinum: No Pricing
Production One Set

#	Player	Price
1	Austin Kearns	1.50
2	Gary Carter	2.00
3	Ivan Rodriguez	2.00
4	Mark Grace	2.00
5	Mark Teixeira	2.00
6	Mike Schmidt	5.00
7	Omar Vizquel	1.50
8	Scott Rolen	3.00
9	Tony Gwynn	3.00
10	Willie Mays	5.00

Great Gloves Fielding Glove

NM/M

Production 25 Sets

#	Player	NM/M
1	Austin Kearns/25	10.00
2	Gary Carter/25	20.00
3	Ivan Rodriguez/25	15.00
4	Mark Grace/25	20.00
5	Mark Teixeira/25	15.00
6	Mike Schmidt/25	40.00
9	Tony Gwynn/25	20.00

Great Gloves Jersey

NM/M

Prime: No Pricing
Production 25-50
Production 5 Sets

#	Player	NM/M
1	Austin Kearns/50	8.00
2	Gary Carter/50	8.00
3	Ivan Rodriguez/50	8.00
4	Mark Grace/50	10.00
5	Mark Teixeira/50	8.00
6	Mike Schmidt/50	20.00
7	Omar Vizquel/50	8.00
8	Scott Rolen/50	10.00
9	Tony Gwynn/50	12.00
10	Willie Mays/25	40.00

Hitters Inc.

NM/M

Common Player: 1.50
Production 2,000 Sets
Gold: 2-3X
Production 50 Sets
Silver: 1-2X
Production 100 Sets
Platinum: No Pricing
Production One Set

#	Player	NM/M
1	Albert Pujols	6.00
2	Alfonso Soriano	2.00
3	Cal Ripken Jr.	8.00
4	Don Mattingly	5.00
5	Dwight Evans	1.50
6	George Brett	5.00
7	Hank Blalock	1.50
8	Ichiro Suzuki	5.00
9	Ivan Rodriguez	2.00
10	Jack Wilson	1.50
11	Keith Hernandez	1.50
12	Larry Walker	2.00
13	Lou Brock	2.00
14	Lyle Overbay	1.50
15	Michael Young	1.50
16	Paul Molitor	2.00
17	Rod Carew	2.00
18	Sean Casey	1.50
19	Steve Garvey	1.50
20	Todd Helton	2.00
21	Tony Gwynn	3.00
22	Travis Hafner	1.50
23	Ted Williams	6.00
24	Wade Boggs	2.00
25	Willie Mays	5.00

Hitters Inc. Bat

NM/M

Production 25-100

#	Player	NM/M
1	Albert Pujols/100	15.00
2	Alfonso Soriano/50	6.00
3	Cal Ripken Jr./100	25.00
4	Don Mattingly/100	15.00
5	Dwight Evans/100	6.00
6	George Brett/50	15.00
7	Hank Blalock/50	6.00
9	Ivan Rodriguez/100	6.00
10	Jack Wilson/100	4.00
12	Larry Walker/100	6.00
13	Lou Brock/100	8.00
15	Michael Young/100	4.00
16	Paul Molitor/100	8.00
17	Rod Carew/100	8.00
18	Sean Casey/100	4.00
19	Steve Garvey/100	6.00
21	Tony Gwynn/100	10.00
23	Ted Williams/50	60.00
24	Wade Boggs/100	8.00
25	Willie Mays/25	40.00

Hitters Inc. Jersey

NM/M

Production 25-100

#	Player	NM/M
1	Albert Pujols/100	15.00
2	Alfonso Soriano/100	6.00
3	Cal Ripken Jr./100	25.00
4	Don Mattingly/100	15.00
5	Dwight Evans/100	6.00
6	George Brett/100	
7	Hank Blalock/100	4.00
9	Ivan Rodriguez/100	6.00
10	Jack Wilson/100	4.00
12	Larry Walker/100	6.00
13	Lou Brock/50	8.00
14	Lyle Overbay/100	4.00
16	Paul Molitor/100	8.00
17	Rod Carew/100	8.00
18	Sean Casey/100	4.00
19	Steve Garvey/100	6.00
20	Todd Helton/100	8.00
21	Tony Gwynn/100	10.00
22	Travis Hafner/100	4.00
23	Ted Williams/Jkt/100	40.00
24	Wade Boggs/100	8.00
25	Willie Mays/25	40.00

Hitters Inc. Signatures

No Pricing
Production 5-10

Hitters Inc. Sig. Bat

NM/M

Production 5-25

#	Player	NM/M
5	Dwight Evans/25	20.00
7	Hank Blalock/25	25.00
10	Jack Wilson/25	15.00
13	Lou Brock/25	30.00
15	Michael Young/25	20.00
18	Sean Casey/25	15.00
19	Steve Garvey/25	30.00

Hitters Inc. Sig. Jersey

NM/M

Production 5-25

#	Player	NM/M
5	Dwight Evans/25	20.00
7	Hank Blalock/25	25.00
10	Jack Wilson/25	15.00
13	Lou Brock/25	30.00
14	Lyle Overbay/25	15.00
18	Sean Casey/25	15.00
19	Steve Garvey/25	30.00
22	Travis Hafner/25	20.00

Leather Cuts

NM/M

Production 1-128

#	Player	NM/M
1	Al Kaline/5	
2	Andre Dawson/128	15.00
3	Bert Blyleven/128	15.00
4	Lee Smith/32	15.00
5	Billy Williams/64	15.00
6	Bob Feller/128	25.00
7	Joe Pepitone/128	20.00
8	Bobby Doerr/128	15.00
9	Juan Marichal/112	20.00
12	Dale Murphy/96	25.00
13	Darryl Strawberry/128	15.00
14	Johnny Podres/128	20.00
18	Duke Snider/128	25.00
20	Dwight Gooden/128	15.00
21	Fergie Jenkins/96	15.00
23	Fred Lynn/128	15.00
24	Justin Morneau/128	20.00
25	Gaylord Perry/128	15.00
27	George Foster/128	15.00
28	Harmon Killebrew/64	30.00
29	Jack Morris/128	15.00
30	Jim Palmer/128	15.00
31	Jim Rice/128	15.00
33	John Kruk/128	20.00
34	Randy Jones/128	15.00
35	Keith Hernandez/128	15.00
36	Lenny Dykstra/128	15.00
37	Lou Brock/64	35.00
38	Luis Aparicio/128	15.00
39	Lyle Overbay/128	10.00
40	Maury Wills/128	15.00
41	Earl Weaver/128	15.00
42	Miguel Cabrera/64	40.00
44	Monte Irvin/96	20.00
47	Red Schoendienst/128	15.00
48	Rich "Goose" Gossage/128	20.00
50	Minnie Minoso/128	20.00
51	Sean Casey/64	15.00
54	Steve Stone/128	15.00
57	Victor Martinez/128	15.00
61	Lee Smith/128	15.00

Leather Cuts Bat

NM/M

Production 6-128

#	Player	NM/M
1	Al Kaline/58	40.00
10	Cal Ripken Jr./60	125.00
13	Darryl Strawberry/96	20.00
19	Dwight Evans/128	25.00
20	Dwight Gooden/128	15.00
22	Frank Robinson/40	25.00
27	George Foster/128	15.00
31	Jim Rice/32	25.00
36	Lenny Dykstra/128	15.00
37	Lou Brock/128	30.00
38	Luis Aparicio/128	15.00
39	Lyle Overbay/128	10.00
51	Sean Casey/32	15.00
55	Tommy John/128	15.00
57	Victor Martinez/128	15.00

Leather Cuts Jersey

NM/M

Production 1-128

#	Player	NM/M
2	Andre Dawson/128	20.00
3	Bert Blyleven/128	15.00
4	Lee Smith/96	15.00
8	Bobby Doerr/ Pants/128	20.00
9	Juan Marichal/112	20.00
10	Cal Ripken Jr./60	125.00
12	Dale Murphy/96	25.00
13	Darryl Strawberry/96	20.00
15	Dave Righetti/48	20.00
16	David Cone/120	15.00
19	Dwight Evans/44	30.00
20	Dwight Gooden/128	15.00
21	Fergie Jenkins/ Pants/96	15.00
23	Fred Lynn/96	15.00
25	Gaylord Perry/128	15.00
28	Harmon Killebrew/32	40.00
29	Jack Morris/64	15.00
31	Jim Rice Pants/128	20.00
33	John Kruk/128	20.00
35	Keith Hernandez/32	20.00
36	Lenny Dykstra/128	15.00
38	Luis Aparicio/128	15.00
39	Lyle Overbay/128	10.00
42	Miguel Cabrera/64	40.00
51	Sean Casey/32	15.00
55	Tommy John/128	15.00
57	Victor Martinez/128	15.00

Lumber Cuts

NM/M

Production 1-128

#	Player	NM/M
1	Al Kaline/6	
2	Andre Dawson/128	15.00
3	Bert Blyleven/128	15.00
4	Lee Smith/32	20.00
5	Billy Williams/64	20.00
6	Bob Feller/128	25.00
7	Joe Pepitone/128	20.00
8	Bobby Doerr/128	20.00
9	Juan Marichal/112	20.00
12	Dale Murphy/96	25.00
13	Darryl Strawberry/128	15.00
14	Johnny Podres/128	15.00
18	Duke Snider/128	25.00
20	Dwight Gooden/128	15.00
21	Fergie Jenkins/96	15.00
23	Fred Lynn/128	15.00
24	Justin Morneau/128	15.00
25	Gaylord Perry/128	15.00
27	George Foster/128	15.00
28	Harmon Killebrew/64	30.00
29	Jack Morris/128	15.00
31	Jim Palmer/128	15.00
33	John Kruk/128	15.00
34	Randy Jones/128	15.00
35	Keith Hernandez/128	15.00
36	Lenny Dykstra/128	15.00
37	Lou Brock/64	35.00
38	Luis Aparicio/128	15.00
39	Lyle Overbay/128	10.00
40	Maury Wills/128	15.00
41	Earl Weaver/128	15.00
42	Miguel Cabrera/128	40.00
44	Monte Irvin/96	20.00
46	Kent Hrbek/128	15.00
47	Red Schoendienst/128	20.00
48	Rich "Goose" Gossage/128	15.00
50	Minnie Minoso/128	20.00
51	Sean Casey/64	15.00
54	Steve Stone/128	15.00
55	Tommy John/128	15.00
57	Victor Martinez/128	15.00
61	Lee Smith/128	15.00

Lumber Cuts Bat

NM/M

Production 6-128

#	Player	NM/M
1	Al Kaline	40.00
10	Cal Ripken Jr./60	125.00
13	Darryl Strawberry/96	20.00
19	Dwight Evans/128	25.00
20	Dwight Gooden/128	15.00
22	Frank Robinson/40	25.00
23	Fred Lynn/96	15.00
27	George Foster/128	15.00
31	Jim Rice/32	25.00
36	Lenny Dykstra/128	15.00
37	Lou Brock/128	30.00
38	Luis Aparicio/128	15.00
39	Lyle Overbay/128	10.00
51	Sean Casey/32	15.00
55	Tommy John/128	15.00
57	Victor Martinez/128	15.00

Lumber Cuts Jersey

NM/M

Production 7-128

#	Player	NM/M
2	Andre Dawson/128	20.00
3	Bert Blyleven/128	15.00
4	Lee Smith/96	15.00
8	Bobby Doerr/ Pants/128	20.00
9	Juan Marichal/112	20.00
10	Cal Ripken Jr./60	125.00
12	Dale Murphy/96	25.00
13	Darryl Strawberry/96	20.00
15	Dave Righetti/48	20.00
16	David Cone/120	15.00
19	Dwight Evans/44	30.00
20	Dwight Gooden/128	15.00
21	Fergie Jenkins/ Pants/96	15.00
23	Fred Lynn/96	15.00
25	Gaylord Perry/128	15.00
28	Harmon Killebrew/32	40.00
29	Jack Morris/64	15.00
31	Jim Rice Pants/128	20.00
33	John Kruk/128	20.00
35	Keith Hernandez/32	20.00
36	Lenny Dykstra/128	15.00
38	Luis Aparicio/128	15.00
39	Lyle Overbay/128	10.00
42	Miguel Cabrera/64	40.00
51	Sean Casey/32	15.00
55	Tommy John/128	15.00
57	Victor Martinez/128	15.00

Lumber/Leather

NM/M

Common Player: 1.50
Production 2,000 Sets
Gold: 2-3X
Production 50 Sets
Silver: 1-2X
Production 100 Sets
Platinum: No Pricing
Production One Set

#	Player	NM/M
1	Albert Pujols	6.00
2	Alex Rodriguez	5.00
3	Alfonso Soriano	2.00
4	Cal Ripken Jr.	8.00
5	Carlos Lee	2.00
6	Derek Jeter	6.00
7	Don Mattingly	5.00
8	Ichiro Suzuki	4.00
9	Ivan Rodriguez	2.00
10	Jack Wilson	1.50
11	Josh Beckett	1.50
12	Ken Griffey Jr.	4.00
13	Lance Berkman	1.50
14	Magglio Ordonez	1.50
15	Mark Grace	2.00
16	Mark Prior	2.00
17	Mark Teixeira	2.00
18	Mike Schmidt	4.00
19	Nolan Ryan	6.00
20	Nomar Garciaparra	3.00
21	Paul LoDuca	1.50
22	Rafael Palmeiro	2.00
23	Randy Johnson	2.00
24	Richie Sexson	2.00
25	Rickey Henderson	2.00
26	Roger Clemens	6.00
27	Ryan Klesko	1.50
28	Stan Musial	3.00
29	Steve Carlton	2.00
30	Tim Hudson	2.00
31	Tony Gwynn	2.00
32	Travis Hafner	1.50
33	Victor Martinez	1.50
34	Wade Boggs	2.00
35	Willie Mays	5.00

Lumber/Leather Barrel

No Pricing
Production One Set

L/L Barrel-Jersey

No Pricing
Production One Set

L/L Bat-Btg Glove

NM/M

Production 1-25

#	Player	NM/M
3	Alfonso Soriano/25	15.00
4	Cal Ripken Jr./1	
7	Carlos Lee/25	12.00
9	Don Mattingly/25	40.00
11	Ivan Rodriguez/25	15.00
13	Lance Berkman/25	15.00
14	Magglio Ordonez/25	10.00
18	Mike Schmidt/25	40.00
21	Paul LoDuca/25	10.00
22	Rafael Palmeiro/25	15.00
24	Richie Sexson/25	15.00
25	Rickey Henderson/25	20.00

27	Ryan Klesko/25	10.00
31	Tony Gwynn/25	20.00
34	Wade Boggs/10	

L/L Bat-Fielding Glove

NM/M

Production 5-25

1	Albert Pujols/5	
5	Carlos Lee/25	12.00
9	Ivan Rodriguez/25	15.00
10	Jack Wilson/25	10.00
13	Lance Berkman/25	15.00
15	Mark Grace/25	20.00
16	Mark Prior/25	20.00
18	Mike Schmidt/25	40.00
21	Paul LoDuca/25	10.00
22	Rafael Palmeiro/25	15.00
24	Richie Sexson/25	15.00
27	Ryan Klesko/25	10.00
29	Steve Carlton/25	15.00
30	Tim Hudson/25	15.00
31	Tony Gwynn/25	20.00
33	Victor Martinez/10	

Lumber/Leather Bat-Spikes

NM/M

Production 1-25

1	Albert Pujols/25	40.00
5	Carlos Lee/25	12.00
9	Ivan Rodriguez/25	15.00
11	Josh Beckett/25	12.00
13	Lance Berkman/25	15.00
14	Magglio Ordonez/25	10.00
16	Mark Prior/25	20.00
21	Paul LoDuca/25	10.00
24	Richie Sexson/25	15.00
25	Rickey Henderson/25	20.00
27	Ryan Klesko/25	10.00
30	Tim Hudson/25	15.00
31	Tony Gwynn/25	20.00

Materials Barrel

No Pricing

Production 1-4

Materials Bat

NM/M

Production 25-250

1	Adam Dunn/250	6.00
2	Adrian Beltre/100	4.00
5	Albert Pujols/250	15.00
7	Alfonso Soriano/100	6.00
9	Andy Pettitte/100	6.00
9	Aramis Ramirez/100	6.00
10	Aubrey Huff/250	4.00
11	Austin Kearns/100	4.00
12	Barry Larkin/200	6.00
13	Barry Zito/25	8.00
15	Bernie Williams/250	6.00
18	Brad Penny/75	4.00
19	Brian Giles/50	6.00
23	Carlos Beltran/100	8.00
24	Carlos Delgado/250	4.00
25	Carlos Lee/150	4.00
27	Casey Kotchman/250	4.00
29	Chone Figgins/250	6.00
30	Craig Biggio/250	6.00
31	Craig Monroe/250	4.00
33	Curt Schilling/100	8.00
35	Darin Erstad/250	4.00
37	David Ortiz/250	8.00
40	Dontrelle Willis/250	6.00
43	Frank Thomas/50	8.00
44	Garret Anderson/250	4.00
46	Geoff Jenkins/50	4.00
47	Greg Maddux/250	10.00
49	J.D. Drew/250	4.00
57	Jason Varitek/100	6.00
58	Javy Lopez/250	4.00
59	Jay Gibbons/250	4.00
60	Jeff Bagwell/250	4.00
61	Jeff Kent/250	4.00
68	John Olerud/250	4.00
72	Jose Reyes/250	6.00
73	Jose Vidro/250	4.00
75	Juan Pierre/250	4.00
81	Kerry Wood/100	6.00
82	Kevin Brown/100	4.00
85	Lance Berkman/250	4.00
87	Laynce Nix/250	4.00
89	Magglio Ordonez/250	4.00
90	Manny Ramirez/100	8.00
94	Mark Prior/250	6.00
97	Michael Young/250	4.00
104	Moises Alou/250	4.00
106	Nomar Garciaparra/100	8.00
109	Paul LoDuca/250	4.00
111	Rafael Furcal/250	4.00
112	Rafael Palmeiro/250	6.00
114	Richie Sexson/250	4.00
115	Rocco Baldelli/250	8.00
118	Sammy Sosa/100	4.00
122	Sean Casey/100	4.00
123	Shannon Stewart/50	4.00
124	Shawn Green/250	4.00
126	Tim Hudson/50	6.00
127	Tim Salmon/250	4.00
129	Tom Glavine/250	4.00
130	Torii Hunter/250	4.00
132	Troy Glaus/250	4.00
138	Brooks Robinson/100	8.00
139	Cal Ripken Jr./50	30.00
145	Lou Brock/100	8.00
146	Mike Schmidt/50	15.00
147	Nolan Ryan/100	25.00
149	Tony Gwynn/100	10.00
150	Willie Mays/25	40.00

Materials Jersey

NM/M

Production 20-250

1	Adam Dunn/150	6.00
5	Albert Pujols/250	15.00
7	Alfonso Soriano/150	6.00
8	Andy Pettitte/150	6.00
9	Aramis Ramirez/250	4.00
10	Aubrey Huff/250	4.00
12	Barry Larkin/250	6.00
13	Barry Zito/150	4.00
15	Bernie Williams/150	6.00
16	Bobby Abreu/250	4.00
17	Bobby Crosby/150	4.00
20	C.C. Sabathia/250	4.00
21	Carl Crawford/200	4.00
26	Carlos Zambrano/250	6.00
27	Casey Kotchman/140	4.00
28	Chipper Jones/250	8.00
29	Chone Figgins/200	4.00
30	Craig Biggio/200	6.00
33	Curt Schilling/250	8.00
35	Darin Erstad/150	4.00
36	David Dellucci/250	4.00
37	David Ortiz/250	8.00
40	Dontrelle Willis/250	4.00
43	Frank Thomas/Pants/150	8.00
44	Garret Anderson/250	4.00
45	Gary Sheffield/250	6.00
46	Geoff Jenkins/250	4.00
47	Greg Maddux/25	15.00
50	Hideo Nomo/250	6.00
53	Ivan Rodriguez/150	6.00
54	Jamie Moyer/50	6.00
57	Jason Giambi/250	4.00
57	Jason Varitek/100	10.00
58	Javy Lopez/150	4.00
59	Jay Gibbons/75	4.00
60	Jeff Bagwell/250	6.00
62	Jeremy Bonderman/150	4.00
64	Jim Edmonds/250	6.00
65	Jim Thome/150	4.00
67	Johan Santana/250	8.00
69	John Smoltz/250	6.00
70	Johnny Damon/250	8.00
71	Johnny Estrada/250	4.00
72	Jose Reyes/150	4.00
73	Jose Vidro/150	4.00
74	Josh Beckett/50	4.00
76	Junior Spivey/250	4.00
77	Justin Morneau/250	6.00
78	Kazuhisa Ishii/250	4.00
79	Kazuo Matsui/150	4.00
81	Kerry Wood/Pants/150	6.00
85	Lance Berkman/250	4.00
86	Larry Walker/250	4.00
87	Laynce Nix/250	4.00
88	Lyle Overbay/200	4.00
90	Manny Ramirez/250	8.00
91	Marcus Giles/150	4.00
94	Mark Prior/250	6.00
95	Mark Teixeira/250	4.00
96	Melvin Mora/100	4.00
97	Michael Young/25	8.00
98	Miguel Tejada/250	6.00
100	Mike Lowell/250	4.00
101	Mike Mussina/250	6.00
102	Mike Piazza/250	8.00
105	Morgan Ensberg/150	4.00
108	Paul Konerko/150	4.00
111	Rafael Furcal/150	4.00
112	Rafael Palmeiro/150	6.00
115	Rocco Baldelli/250	4.00
116	Roger Clemens/150	10.00
117	Roy Halladay/150	4.00
119	Scott Podsednik/250	4.00
120	Scott Rolen/250	4.00
121	Sean Burroughs/150	4.00
122	Sean Casey/250	4.00
123	Shannon Stewart/150	4.00
128	Todd Helton/250	6.00
130	Torii Hunter/250	4.00
131	Travis Hafner/250	6.00
134	Vernon Wells/250	4.00
135	Victor Martinez/150	4.00
136	Vladimir Guerrero/250	8.00
137	Andre Dawson/50	8.00
139	Cal Ripken Jr./250	20.00
140	Dale Murphy/250	6.00
141	Darryl Strawberry/Pants/150	4.00
143	Harmon Killebrew/100	8.00
144	Jim Palmer/Pants/20	
145	Lou Brock/Jkt/250	8.00
146	Mike Schmidt/50	15.00
147	Nolan Ryan/250	15.00
148	Steve Carlton/25	10.00
149	Tony Gwynn/250	8.00
150	Willie Mays/Pants/25	40.00

Naturals Barrel

No Pricing

Production 1-3

Naturals Bat

NM/M

Production 25-100

1	Andruw Jones/100	6.00
2	Bernie Williams/100	6.00
3	Brooks Robinson/100	8.00
4	Cal Ripken Jr./100	25.00
5	Casey Kotchman/100	4.00
6	Craig Biggio/100	6.00
7	Craig Wilson/100	4.00
8	David Ortiz/100	10.00
9	Eddie Murray/100	8.00
10	Javy Lopez/100	4.00
11	Jeff Bagwell/100	4.00
12	Lance Berkman/100	4.00
13	Magglio Ordonez/100	4.00
14	Michael Young/100	4.00
15	Rafael Palmeiro/100	4.00
16	Reggie Jackson/100	8.00
17	Rickey Henderson/100	8.00
18	Rocco Baldelli/100	4.00
19	Sammy Sosa/100	8.00
20	Shawn Green/100	4.00
21	Ted Williams/50	50.00
22	Tony Gwynn/100	10.00
23	Wade Boggs/100	8.00
24	Will Clark/100	8.00
25	Willie Mays/25	40.00

Naturals Combos

NM/M

Production 25-100

Prime: No Pricing

Production Five Sets

1	Andruw Jones/Bat-Jsy/100	8.00
2	Bernie Williams/Bat-Jsy/100	8.00
3	Brooks Robinson/Bat-Jsy/25	15.00
4	Cal Ripken Jr./Bat-Jsy/100	30.00
5	Casey Kotchman/Bat-Jsy/100	6.00
6	Craig Biggio/Bat-Jsy/100	8.00
7	Craig Wilson/Bat-Jsy/100	6.00
8	David Ortiz/Bat-Jsy/100	12.00
9	Eddie Murray/Bat-Jsy/100	10.00
10	Javy Lopez/Bat-Jsy/100	6.00
11	Jeff Bagwell/Bat-Jsy/100	8.00
12	Lance Berkman/Bat-Jsy/100	6.00
13	Magglio Ordonez/Bat-Jsy/25	8.00
14	Michael Young/Bat-Jsy/100	6.00
15	Rafael Palmeiro/Bat-Jsy/100	8.00
16	Reggie Jackson/Bat-Jsy/100	12.00
17	Rickey Henderson/Bat-Jkt/100	10.00
18	Rocco Baldelli/Bat-Jsy/100	6.00
19	Sammy Sosa/Bat-Jsy/100	10.00
20	Shawn Green/Bat-Jsy/100	6.00
21	Ted Williams/Bat-Jkt/50	60.00
22	Tony Gwynn/Bat-Jsy/100	12.00
23	Wade Boggs/Bat-Jsy/100	10.00
24	Will Clark/Bat-Jsy/50	10.00
25	Willie Mays/Bat-Jsy/25	50.00

Naturals

NM/M

Common Player: 1.50
Production 2,000 Sets
Gold: 2-3X
Production 50 Sets
Silver: 1-2X
Production 100 Sets
Platinum: No Pricing
Production One Set

1	Andruw Jones	2.00
2	Bernie Williams	1.50
3	Brooks Robinson	2.00
4	Cal Ripken Jr.	8.00
5	Casey Kotchman	1.50
6	Craig Biggio	2.00
7	Craig Wilson	1.50
8	David Ortiz	3.00
9	Eddie Murray	2.00
10	Javy Lopez	1.50
11	Jeff Bagwell	2.00
12	Lance Berkman	1.50
13	Magglio Ordonez	1.50
14	Michael Young	1.50
15	Rafael Palmeiro	2.00
16	Reggie Jackson	2.00
17	Rickey Henderson	2.00
18	Rocco Baldelli	1.50
19	Sammy Sosa	4.00
20	Shawn Green	1.50
21	Ted Williams	6.00
22	Tony Gwynn	3.00
23	Wade Boggs	2.00
24	Will Clark	2.00
25	Willie Mays	5.00

Naturals Jersey

NM/M

Production 25-100

Prime: No Pricing

Production 5 Sets

1	Andruw Jones/100	6.00
2	Bernie Williams/100	6.00
4	Cal Ripken Jr./100	25.00
5	Casey Kotchman/100	4.00
6	Craig Biggio/100	4.00
7	Craig Wilson/100	4.00
8	David Ortiz/100	10.00
9	Eddie Murray/100	8.00
10	Javy Lopez/100	4.00
11	Jeff Bagwell/100	6.00
12	Lance Berkman/100	4.00
13	Magglio Ordonez/50	4.00
14	Michael Young/50	4.00
15	Rafael Palmeiro/100	6.00
16	Reggie Jackson/100	8.00
17	Rickey Henderson/Jkt/100	8.00
18	Rocco Baldelli/100	4.00
19	Sammy Sosa/100	8.00
20	Shawn Green/100	4.00
21	Ted Williams/Jkt/100	40.00
22	Tony Gwynn/100	10.00
23	Wade Boggs/100	8.00
24	Will Clark/50	8.00
25	Willie Mays/25	40.00

Rivals

NM/M

Common Duo: 1.50
Production 2,000 Sets
Gold: 2-3X
Production 50 Sets
Silver: 1-2X
Production 100 Sets
Platinum: No Pricing
Production One Set

1	Ichiro Suzuki, Hideki Matsui	5.00
2	Mark Mulder, Vladimir Guerrero	2.00
3	Tim Hudson, Mark Teixeira	2.00
4	Roger Clemens, Albert Pujols	6.00
5	Greg Maddux, Jeff Bagwell	4.00
6	Randy Johnson, Adrian Beltre	3.00
7	Kerry Wood, Larry Walker	2.00
8	Mike Mussina, Manny Ramirez	2.00
9	C.C. Sabathia, Torii Hunter	1.50
10	Josh Beckett, Chipper Jones	2.00
11	Derek Jeter, Miguel Tejada	6.00
12	Alex Rodriguez, Hank Blalock	5.00
13	Carlos Beltran, Sammy Sosa	3.00

14	Mark Prior, Jim Thome	2.00
15	Miguel Cabrera, Andruw Jones	2.00
16	Johan Santana, Magglio Ordonez	2.00
17	Josh Beckett, Craig Biggio	2.00
18	Adam Dunn, Shawn Green	2.00
19	J. Morris, Rod Carew	2.00
20	Jim Palmer, Paul Molitor	2.00
21	Mike Schmidt, George Brett	5.00
22	Cal Ripken Jr., Don Mattingly	8.00
23	Bob Gibson, Ernie Banks	4.00
24	Eddie Murray, Bert Blyleven	3.00
25	Warren Spahn, Willie Mays	6.00

Rivals Bat

NM/M

Production 50-100

3	Tim Hudson, Mark Teixeira/50	10.00
4	Roger Clemens, Albert Pujols/100	25.00
5	Greg Maddux, Jeff Bagwell/100	15.00
7	Kerry Wood, Larry Walker/100	15.00
10	Josh Beckett, Chipper Jones/50	15.00
13	Carlos Beltran, Sammy Sosa/100	15.00
14	Mark Prior, Jim Thome/50	15.00
18	Adam Dunn, Shawn Green/100	10.00
21	Mike Schmidt, George Brett	20.00
22	Cal Ripken Jr., Don Mattingly/100	30.00

Rivals Jersey

NM/M

Production 50-250
Prime: No Pricing
Production Five Sets

2	Mark Mulder, Vladimir Guerrero/100	10.00
3	Tim Hudson, Mark Teixeira/250	10.00
4	Roger Clemens, Albert Pujols/100	20.00
5	Greg Maddux, Jeff Bagwell/250	10.00
7	Kerry Wood, Larry Walker/250	8.00
9	C.C. Sabathia, Torii Hunter/150	6.00
10	Josh Beckett/Pants, Chipper Jones/150	10.00
13	Carlos Beltran, Sammy Sosa/250	10.00
14	Mark Prior, Jim Thome/250	10.00
15	Miguel Cabrera, Andruw Jones/250	10.00
16	Johan Santana, Magglio Ordonez/100	10.00
18	Adam Dunn, Shawn Green/100	10.00
19	J. Morris, Rod Carew/250	10.00
21	Mike Schmidt, George Brett/100	15.00
22	Cal Ripken Jr., Don Mattingly/100	40.00
23	Bob Gibson, Ernie Banks/50	15.00
24	Eddie Murray, Bert Blyleven	10.00
25	Warren Spahn/Pant, Willie Mays/Pant/50	60.00

Signatures Gold

NM/M

Production 5-100
Platinum: No Pricing
Production One Set

1	Adam Dunn/25	35.00
2	Adrian Beltre/25	25.00
3	Akinori Otsuka/50	30.00
10	Aubrey Huff/50	15.00
11	Austin Kearns/25	15.00
17	Bobby Crosby/100	15.00
18	Brad Penny/10	15.00
25	Carlos Lee/100	15.00
26	Carlos Zambrano/100	25.00
27	Casey Kotchman/100	10.00
29	Chone Figgins/100	15.00
31	Craig Monroe/100	10.00
34	Danny Haren/100	10.00
36	David Dellucci/100	15.00
52	Jake Peavy/100	25.00
53	Jamie Moyer/100	15.00
59	Jay Gibbons/100	10.00
62	Jeremy Bonderman/100	10.00
63	Jermaine Dye/100	12.00
66	Joe Nathan/100	15.00
71	Johnny Estrada/50	10.00
87	Laynce Nix/100	10.00
88	Lyle Overbay/100	10.00
92	Mark Loretta/100	15.00
99	Mike Lieberthal/100	10.00
103	Milton Bradley/100	12.00
105	Morgan Ensberg/100	12.00
111	Rafael Furcal/50	15.00
117	Roy Halladay/25	25.00
119	Scott Podsednik/50	15.00
121	Sean Burroughs/100	8.00
122	Sean Casey/25	15.00
123	Shannon Stewart/100	8.00
125	Steve Finley/50	15.00
126	Tim Hudson/25	30.00
127	Tim Salmon/100	15.00
130	Torii Hunter/25	20.00
131	Travis Hafner/100	12.00
133	Troy Percival/50	15.00
134	Vernon Wells/25	15.00
135	Victor Martinez/100	15.00
137	Andre Dawson/100	15.00
138	Brooks Robinson/25	30.00
140	Dale Murphy/25	25.00
141	Darryl Strawberry/100	15.00
143	Harmon Killebrew/50	30.00
144	Jim Palmer/25	20.00
145	Lou Brock/25	30.00
146	Mike Schmidt/25	60.00
148	Steve Carlton/25	25.00
149	Tony Gwynn/25	50.00

Signatures Lumber Cuts

NM/M

Production 256 Sets

151	Agustin Montero	8.00
152	Carlos Ruiz	8.00
153	Casey Rogowski	10.00
154	Chris Resop	15.00
155	Chris Roberson	10.00
156	Colter Bean	10.00
157	Danny Rueckel	8.00
158	David Gassner	8.00
159	Geovany Soto	15.00
160	John Hattig Jr.	8.00
161	Justin Wechsler	8.00
162	Luke Scott	15.00
163	Mark McLemore	8.00
164	Miguel Negron	8.00
165	Mike Morse	40.00
166	Nate McLouth/254	10.00
167	Philip Humber	20.00
168	Randy Messenger	8.00
169	Raul Tablado	8.00
170	Russel Rohlicek	8.00
171	Ryan Speier	8.00
172	Scott Munter	12.00
173	Sean Thompson	10.00
174	Sean Tracey	10.00
175	Wladimir Balentien	20.00
177	Norihiro Nakamura/128	75.00

2005 Donruss Sig.

NM/M

Complete Set (159):
Common Player (1-150): 1.00
Common Dual Auto. (151-156):
Triple Auto. (157-158):
Inserted 1:51
Quad Auto. (#159): No Pricing
Inserted 1:626
Pack (5): 60.00
Box (4): 200.00

1	Scot Shields	1.00
2	Tim Salmon	1.50
3	Chone Figgins	1.00
4	Dallas McPherson	1.00
5	John Lackey	1.00
6	Ervin Santana	1.00
7	Casey Kotchman	1.00
8	Steve Finley	1.00
9	Brandon Webb	1.00
10	Chad Tracy	1.00
11	Russ Ortiz	1.00
12	Alex Cintron	1.00
13	Marcus Giles	1.00
14	Ichiro Suzuki	5.00
15	Tadahito Iguchi RC	4.00
16	Chipper Jones	2.50
17	Cal Ripken Jr.	6.00
18	Rick Dempsey	1.00
19	Adam Loewen	1.00
20	Eric Byrnes	1.00
21	Luis Matos	1.00
22	Miguel Tejada	1.50
23	Brooks Robinson	3.00
24	Kevin Youkilis	1.50
25	Keith Foulke	1.00
26	Trot Nixon	1.00
27	Edgar Renteria	1.00
28	Luis Tiant	1.00
29	Todd Walker	1.00
30	Mark Grace	2.00
31	Steve Stone	1.00
32	Ron Santo	2.00
33	Mike Wuertz	1.00
34	Russel Rohlicek RC	2.00
35	Ryne Sandberg	4.00
36	Andre Dawson	1.50
37	Aramis Ramirez	1.50
38	Derrek Lee	2.00
39	Paulino Reynoso RC	1.50
40	Jose Contreras	1.00
41	Freddy Garcia	1.00
42	Mark Buehrle	1.50
43	Bubba Nelson	1.00
44	Eric Davis	1.00
45	Adam Dunn	2.00
46	Travis Hafner	1.50
47	Larry Bigbie	1.00
48	Todd Helton	2.00
49	Chris Shelton	1.00
50	Willie Mays	5.00
51	Craig Monroe	1.00
52	Ivan Rodriguez	2.00
53	Miguel Cabrera	2.50
54	Chris Resop RC	1.50
55	Paul LoDuca	1.00
56	Luke Scott RC	3.00
57	Brandon Backe	1.00
58	Mark McLemore RC	1.50
59	Devon Lowery RC	1.50
60	Jeremy Affeldt	1.00
61	Duke Snider	2.00
62	Johnny Podres	1.00
63	Rickie Weeks	1.50
64	Ben Sheets	1.50
65	Carlos Lee	1.50
66	Lew Ford	1.00
67	Travis Bowyer RC	1.50
68	Garrett Jones RC	1.50
69	Joe Nathan	1.00
70	Kent Hrbek	1.50
71	J.D. Durbin	1.00
72	Shannon Stewart	1.00
73	Torii Hunter	1.00
74	Kirby Puckett	4.00
75	Danny Graves	1.00
76	Jae Weong Seo	1.00
77	Matt Lindstrom RC	1.50
78	Dwight Gooden	1.50
79	Carlos Beltran	2.00
80	Mike Piazza	3.00
81	Tom Gordon	1.00
82	Adam LaRoche	1.00
83	Dave Righetti	1.00
84	Joe Pepitone	1.00
85	Gary Sheffield	2.00
86	Jim Leyritz	1.00
87	Rich "Goose" Gossage	1.00
88	Don Larsen	1.00
89	Bernie Williams	1.50
90	Jorge Posada	2.00
91	Octavio Dotel	1.00
92	Rollie Fingers	1.00
93	Dennis Eckersley	1.50
94	Rich Harden	1.00
95	Art Howe	1.00
96	Jose Canseco	2.00
97	Barry Zito	1.50
98	Eric Chavez	1.50
99	Rickey Henderson	1.50
100	Chris Roberson RC	1.50
101	Eude Brito RC	1.00
102	Randy Wolf	1.00
103	Mike Lieberthal	1.00
104	John Kruk	1.00
105	Lenny Dykstra	1.00
106	Carlos Ruiz RC	1.50
107	Bobby Abreu	1.50
108	Bill Madlock	1.00
109	Mike Johnston	1.00
110	Ian Snell	1.00
111	Freddy Sanchez	1.00
112	Jose Castillo	1.00
113	Jeff Miller RC	1.50
114	John Candelaria	1.00
115	Jason Bay	1.50
116	Mark Loretta	1.00
117	Sean Thompson RC	1.50
118	Akinori Otsuka	1.00
119	Omar Vizquel	1.00
120	Will Clark	1.50
121	Clint Nageotte	1.00
122	J.J. Putz	1.00
123	Raul Ibanez	1.00
124	Wladimir Balentien RC	3.00
125	Jamie Moyer	1.00
126	Adrian Beltre	1.00
127	Richie Sexson	1.50
128	Edgar Martinez	1.00
129	Jeff Suppan	1.00
130	Marty Marion	1.00
131	Keith Hernandez	1.00
132	Ozzie Smith	4.00
133	Mark Mulder	1.00
134	Lee Smith	1.00
135	Jim Edmonds	1.50
136	Nomar Garciaparra	2.50
137	Delmon Young	1.50
138	Jason Hammel RC	1.50
139	Agustin Montero RC	1.50
140	Francisco Cordero	1.00
141	Michael Young	1.00
142	Al Oliver	1.00
143	David Dellucci	1.00
144	Nolan Ryan	6.00
145	Rafael Palmeiro	1.50
146	Alexis Rios	1.00
147	Jose Guillen	1.00
148	Danny Rueckel RC	1.00
149	Jose Vidro	1.00
150	Preston Wilson	1.00
151	Rickie Weeks, Prince Fielder	100.00
152	Hayden Penn, Adam Loewen	20.00
153	Akinori Otsuka, Keiichi Yabu RC	25.00
154	Brandon McCarthy, Anibal Sanchez RC	30.00
157	Jeff Niemann, Justin Verlander, Philip Humber RC	50.00
158	Wladimir Balentien, Ambiorix Concepcion, Miguel Negron RC	25.00
159	Justin Verlander, Jeff Niemann, Tony Pena, Ubaldo Jimenez	80.00

Autograph Gold MS

NM/M

Production 5-50

1	Scot Shields/50	10.00
2	Tim Salmon/50	15.00
3	Chone Figgins/50	15.00
4	Dallas McPherson/50	10.00
5	John Lackey/50	20.00
6	Ervin Santana/50	20.00
9	Brandon Webb/50	20.00
10	Chad Tracy/50	10.00
11	Russ Ortiz/50	10.00
12	Alex Cintron/50	10.00
17	Cal Ripken Jr./50	100.00
18	Rick Dempsey/50	10.00
19	Adam Loewen/50	10.00
20	Eric Byrnes/50	10.00
21	Luis Matos/50	10.00
24	Kevin Youkilis/50	15.00
25	Keith Foulke/50	10.00
26	Trot Nixon/50	20.00
27	Edgar Renteria/50	20.00
28	Luis Tiant/50	20.00
29	Todd Walker/50	10.00
30	Mark Grace/25	25.00
31	Steve Stone/50	20.00
32	Ron Santo/50	35.00
34	Russel Rohlicek/50	10.00
35	Ryne Sandberg/50	75.00
43	Bubba Nelson/50	10.00
47	Larry Bigbie/50	15.00
49	Chris Shelton/43	15.00
53	Miguel Cabrera/50	30.00
54	Chris Resop/50	10.00
56	Luke Scott/25	40.00
59	Devon Lowery/50	10.00
61	Duke Snider/50	35.00
62	Johnny Podres/25	25.00
63	Rickie Weeks/50	20.00
64	Ben Sheets/50	20.00
66	Lew Ford/50	10.00
67	Travis Bowyer/50	10.00
68	Garrett Jones/50	10.00
69	Joe Nathan/50	15.00
70	Kent Hrbek/25	20.00
71	J.D. Durbin/50	10.00
75	Danny Graves/50	10.00
76	Jae Weong Seo/50	20.00
77	Matt Lindstrom/50	10.00
81	Tom Gordon/50	15.00
82	Adam LaRoche/50	20.00
83	Dave Righetti/50	10.00
84	Joe Pepitone/25	25.00
85	Gary Sheffield/50	25.00
86	Jim Leyritz/25	25.00

87	Rich "Goose"	
	Gossage/25	20.00
88	Don Larsen/25	25.00
91	Octavio Dotel/25	10.00
92	Rollie Fingers/50	20.00
93	Dennis Eckersley/50	25.00
94	Rich Harden/50	20.00
97	Barry Zito/50	20.00
100	Chris Roberson/50	10.00
101	Eude Brito/50	10.00
102	Randy Wolf/50	10.00
103	Mike Lieberthal/50	15.00
104	John Kruk/25	25.00
106	Carlos Ruiz/50	10.00
110	Ian Snell/34	15.00
116	Mark Loretta/50	15.00
117	Sean Thompson/50	10.00
119	Omar Vizquel/50	25.00
121	Clint Nageotte/50	10.00
122	J.J. Putz/50	10.00
123	Raul Ibanez/50	10.00
124	Wladimir Balentien/	
	50	20.00
125	Jamie Moyer/25	15.00
129	Jeff Suppan/50	15.00
130	Marty Marion/50	20.00
131	Keith Hernandez/52	20.00
132	Ozzie Smith/50	50.00
133	Mark Mulder/50	20.00
137	Delmon Young/25	35.00
139	Agustin Montero/50	10.00
140	Francisco Cordero/50	10.00
142	Al Oliver/25	20.00
143	David Dellucci/25	15.00
146	Alexis Rios/50	15.00
147	Jose Guillen/50	15.00
148	Danny Rueckel/50	10.00

Autograph Material Bat Gold
NM/M
Production 1-50
Platinum: No Pricing
Production 1-25

3	Chone Figgins/50	20.00
7	Casey Kotchman/25	20.00
24	Kevin Youkilis/25	20.00
65	Carlos Lee/25	20.00
108	Bill Madlock/50	15.00
111	Freddy Sanchez/42	20.00
119	Omar Vizquel/50	25.00
146	Alexis Rios/50	20.00

Autograph Material Bat Silver
NM/M
Cards are not serial numbered.

3	Chone Figgins/50	20.00
108	Bill Madlock	15.00
119	Omar Vizquel	15.00

Autograph Material Button Platinum
No Pricing
Production 1-6

Autograph Material Combo Gold
NM/M
Production 1-46
Platinum: No Pricing
Production 1-25

17	Cal Ripken Jr./46	125.00
30	Mark Grace/25	40.00

Autograph Material Combo Silver
NM/M
Cards are not serial numbered.

17	Cal Ripken Jr./100	100.00
30	Mark Grace/25	35.00

Auto. Material Jersey Number Platinum
NM/M
Production 1-25

9	Brandon Webb/25	20.00
26	Trot Nixon/25	20.00
57	Brandon Backe/25	15.00
76	Jae Weong Seo/25	20.00
93	Dennis Eckersley/25	25.00

Autograph Material Jersey Position Gold
NM/M
Production 1-50

9	Brandon Webb/50	15.00
21	Luis Matos/50	15.00
26	Trot Nixon/50	20.00
30	Mark Grace/25	30.00
57	Brandon Backe/50	10.00
76	Jae Weong Seo/50	20.00
93	Dennis Eckersley/25	25.00

Autograph Material Jersey Silver
NM/M
Cards are not serial numbered.

21	Luis Matos	10.00
26	Trot Nixon/71	20.00
30	Mark Grace	20.00
60	Jeremy Affeldt/36	10.00
76	Jae Weong Seo/86	20.00
93	Dennis Eckersley/25	25.00
104	John Kruk/75	20.00
130	Marty Marion/38	20.00

Autograph Platinum MS
NM/M
Production 1-25

1	Scot Shields/25	15.00
2	Tim Salmon/25	20.00
3	Chone Figgins/25	20.00
4	Dallas McPherson/25	15.00
6	Ervin Santana/25	25.00
9	Brandon Webb/25	20.00
10	Chad Tracy/25	15.00
11	Russ Ortiz/25	15.00
12	Alex Cintron/25	15.00
17	Cal Ripken Jr./25	125.00
18	Rick Dempsey/25	15.00
19	Adam Loewen/25	15.00
20	Eric Byrnes/25	15.00
21	Luis Matos/25	15.00
24	Kevin Youkilis/25	20.00
25	Keith Foulke/25	25.00
26	Trot Nixon/25	25.00
27	Edgar Renteria/25	15.00
29	Todd Walker/25	15.00
31	Steve Stone/25	25.00
32	Ron Santo/25	40.00
34	Russel Rohlicek/25	10.00
35	Ryne Sandberg/25	90.00
43	Bubba Nelson/25	15.00
47	Larry Bigbie/25	15.00
54	Chris Resop/25	10.00
59	Devon Lowery/25	40.00
61	Rickie Weeks/25	25.00
66	Lew Ford/25	10.00
67	Travis Bowyer/25	10.00
68	Garrett Jones/25	10.00
69	Joe Nathan/25	20.00
71	J.D. Durbin/25	15.00
75	Danny Graves/25	10.00
76	Jae Weong Seo/25	25.00
77	Matt Lindstrom/25	15.00
81	Tom Gordon/25	15.00
83	Dave Righetti/25	25.00
85	Gary Sheffield/25	25.00
91	Octavio Dotel/25	10.00
92	Rollie Fingers/25	25.00
94	Rich Harden/25	25.00
97	Barry Zito/25	25.00
100	Chris Roberson/25	10.00
101	Eude Brito/25	15.00
102	Randy Wolf/25	15.00
103	Mike Lieberthal/25	20.00
106	Carlos Ruiz/25	15.00
110	Ian Snell/25	15.00
116	Mark Loretta/25	20.00
117	Sean Thompson/25	15.00
119	Omar Vizquel/25	30.00
121	Clint Nageotte/25	10.00
122	J.J. Putz/25	15.00
123	Raul Ibanez/25	15.00
124	Wladimir Balentien/	
	25	20.00
129	Jeff Suppan/25	20.00
130	Marty Marion/25	25.00
131	Keith Hernandez/25	25.00
132	Ozzie Smith/25	60.00
139	Agustin Montero/25	10.00
140	Francisco Cordero/25	15.00
146	Alexis Rios/25	20.00
147	Jose Guillen/25	15.00
148	Danny Rueckel/25	15.00

Autograph Silver
NM/M
Cards are not serial numbered.

1	Scot Shields	8.00
2	Tim Salmon	10.00
3	Chone Figgins	10.00
4	Dallas McPherson	8.00
5	John Lackey	15.00
6	Ervin Santana/25	25.00
9	Brandon Webb	15.00
10	Chad Tracy	8.00
11	Russ Ortiz	8.00
12	Alex Cintron	5.00
17	Cal Ripken Jr.	85.00
18	Rick Dempsey	8.00
19	Adam Loewen	8.00
20	Eric Byrnes	8.00
24	Kevin Youkilis	15.00
25	Keith Foulke	15.00
26	Trot Nixon	15.00
27	Edgar Renteria	15.00
28	Luis Tiant	15.00
29	Todd Walker	8.00
30	Mark Grace	20.00
31	Steve Stone	15.00
32	Ron Santo	25.00
33	Mike Wuertz	10.00
34	Russel Rohlicek/60	10.00
35	Ryne Sandberg	50.00
39	Paulino Reynoso/86	10.00
43	Bubba Nelson	8.00
47	Larry Bigbie/92	10.00
53	Miguel Cabrera	20.00
54	Chris Resop	8.00
56	Luke Scott	20.00
58	Mark McLemore/43	15.00
59	Devon Lowery	8.00
61	Duke Snider	25.00
62	Johnny Podres/99	20.00
63	Rickie Weeks	15.00
64	Ben Sheets	15.00
66	Lew Ford	8.00
67	Travis Bowyer	8.00
68	Garrett Jones	8.00
69	Joe Nathan	10.00
70	Kent Hrbek	15.00
71	J.D. Durbin/39	10.00
75	Danny Graves	5.00
76	Jae Weong Seo	15.00
77	Matt Lindstrom	8.00
79	Carlos Beltran/37	25.00
81	Tom Gordon	10.00
82	Adam LaRoche/53	15.00
83	Dave Righetti	15.00
84	Joe Pepitone	20.00
85	Gary Sheffield	20.00
86	Jim Leyritz/93	15.00
87	Rich "Goose"	
	Gossage/65	15.00
91	Octavio Dotel	8.00
92	Rollie Fingers	15.00
94	Rich Harden	15.00
97	Barry Zito/26	25.00
100	Chris Roberson	8.00
101	Eude Brito	8.00
102	Randy Wolf	8.00
103	Mike Lieberthal	15.00
104	John Kruk	15.00
109	Mike Johnston	10.00
113	Jeff Miller/49	10.00
114	John Candelaria/43	20.00
116	Mark Loretta	10.00
117	Sean Thompson	8.00
118	Akinori Otsuka/52	20.00
119	Omar Vizquel/100	20.00
121	Clint Nageotte	5.00
122	J.J. Putz	5.00
123	Raul Ibanez	8.00
124	Wladimir Balentien	15.00
125	Jamie Moyer	10.00
129	Jeff Suppan	15.00
130	Marty Marion	15.00
131	Keith Hernandez	15.00
132	Ozzie Smith/94	40.00
133	Mark Mulder	10.00
137	Delmon Young/99	25.00
138	Jason Hammel/57	10.00
139	Agustin Montero	8.00
140	Francisco Cordero	8.00
144	Nolan Ryan/62	80.00
146	Alexis Rios	10.00
147	Jose Guillen	10.00
148	Danny Rueckel	8.00
149	Jose Vidro/18	

Auto. Silver Notation
NM/M
Cards are not serial numbered.

11	Russ Ortiz/84	12.00
17	Cal Ripken Jr./25	125.00
81	Tom Gordon	10.00
105	Lenny Dykstra/41	15.00
131	Keith Hernandez/34	15.00
147	Jose Guillen	8.00

Club Autograph Barrel
Production 1-4

Club Autograph Bat
NM/M
Cards are not serial numbered.

1	Paul O'Neill/32	35.00
2	Alan Trammell/70	20.00
3	Barry Larkin	20.00
4	Carlton Fisk/34	35.00
5	Dale Murphy/100	20.00
6	Frank Thomas	35.00
7	Magglio Ordonez	15.00
8	Mark Teixeira/100	25.00
10	Omar Vizquel	20.00
11	Steve Garvey	15.00

Hall of Fame
NM/M
Common Player: 2.00
Inserted 1:3

1	Al Kaline	4.00
2	Billy Williams	2.00
3	Bobby Doerr	2.00
4	Gaylord Perry	2.00
5	George Brett	6.00
6	Hank Aaron	6.00
7	Mike Schmidt	5.00
8	Nolan Ryan	8.00
9	Robin Roberts	2.00
10	Phil Niekro	2.00
11	Phil Rizzuto	4.00
12	Ralph Kiner	3.00
13	Rod Carew	3.00
14	Ryne Sandberg	6.00
15	Stan Musial	5.00
16	Steve Carlton	3.00
17	Tom Seaver	4.00
18	Willie McCovey	4.00
19	Willie Mays	6.00
20	Duke Snider	4.00
21	Rollie Fingers	2.00
22	Monte Irvin	3.00
23	Ozzie Smith	5.00
24	Johnny Bench	5.00
25	Luis Aparicio	2.00
26	Whitey Ford	4.00
27	Orlando Cepeda	3.00
28	Jim Bunning	2.00
29	Earl Weaver	2.00
30	Frank Robinson	3.00
31	Babe Ruth	8.00
32	Yogi Berra	4.00
33	Wade Boggs	3.00
34	Ted Williams	6.00
35	Roberto Clemente	6.00
36	Nellie Fox	3.00
37	Joe Morgan	3.00
38	Harmon Killebrew	4.00
39	Carlton Fisk	3.00
40	Babe Ruth	8.00

Hall of Fame Auto.
NM/M
Cards are not serial numbered.

1	Al Kaline/82	40.00
2	Billy Williams/42	20.00
3	Bobby Doerr/25	25.00
4	Gaylord Perry	15.00
8	Nolan Ryan/	100.00
9	Robin Roberts	15.00
11	Phil Rizzuto	35.00
14	Ryne Sandberg/55	60.00
15	Stan Musial/56	60.00
18	Willie McCovey	25.00
20	Duke Snider	35.00
21	Rollie Fingers	15.00
22	Monte Irvin	20.00
24	Johnny Bench	40.00
27	Orlando Cepeda	25.00
28	Jim Bunning/25	25.00

Hall of Fame Auto. Bat
NM/M
Cards are not serial numbered.

12	Ralph Kiner/97	40.00
25	Luis Aparicio/100	20.00
33	Wade Boggs/56	30.00

Hall of Fame Autograph Combo
NM/M
Cards are not serial numbered.

14	Ryne Sandberg/100	75.00
15	Stan Musial/100	75.00
16	Steve Carlton/50	25.00
17	Tom Seaver/50	50.00
18	Willie McCovey/50	40.00

Hall of Fame Autograph Jersey
NM/M
Cards are not serial numbered.

1	Al Kaline/20	
2	Billy Williams/35	25.00
4	Gaylord Perry/100	20.00
6	Hank Aaron/25	200.00
8	Nolan Ryan/50	100.00
11	Phil Rizzuto/100	40.00
14	Ryne Sandberg/35	75.00
15	Stan Musial/50	75.00
16	Steve Carlton/25	30.00
17	Tom Seaver/25	50.00

18	Willie McCovey/25	40.00
21	Rollie Fingers/84	20.00
24	Johnny Bench/100	50.00
26	Whitey Ford/33	40.00

Hall of Fame Autograph MS

NM/M

Production 1-25

2	Billy Williams/25	25.00
4	Gaylord Perry/25	20.00
8	Nolan Ryan/25	100.00
9	Robin Roberts/25	20.00
20	Duke Snider/25	40.00
21	Rollie Fingers/25	20.00
22	Monte Irvin/25	25.00
23	Ozzie Smith/25	60.00
24	Johnny Bench/25	60.00
26	Whitey Ford/25	40.00
27	Orlando Cepeda/25	30.00
28	Jim Bunning/25	25.00
29	Earl Weaver/25	20.00

Hall of Fame Bat

Cards are not serial numbered.

Hall of Fame Combo

NM/M

Cards are not serial numbered.

6	Hank Aaron	40.00
34	Ted Williams	60.00

Hall of Fame Jersey

NM/M

Cards are not serial numbered.

2	Billy Williams/25	8.00
3	Bobby Doerr/100	10.00
4	Gaylord Perry	8.00
6	Hank Aaron	25.00
8	Nolan Ryan/30	40.00
10	Phil Niekro	10.00
11	Phil Rizzuto	15.00
13	Rod Carew	12.00
15	Stan Musial/66	20.00
16	Steve Carlton	10.00
19	Willie Mays	25.00
21	Rollie Fingers/33	8.00
23	Ozzie Smith/47	20.00
24	Johnny Bench/51	15.00
34	Ted Williams	40.00

HOF Combos Auto.

NM/M

Cards are not serial numbered.

41	Harmon Killebrew, Rod Carew/25	80.00
42	Ryne Sandberg, Wade Boggs/100	70.00
43	Nolan Ryan, George Brett/36	120.00
44	Phil Rizzuto, Steve Carlton/100	50.00
45	Tom Seaver, Rollie Fingers/100	40.00
46	Jim Palmer, Joe Morgan/25	40.00
47	Bobby Doerr, Willie McCovey/51	40.00
48	Harmon Killebrew, Luis Aparicio/25	65.00
49	Duke Snider, Al Kaline/25	75.00
50	Frank Robinson, Jim Palmer/25	40.00
51	Bobby Doerr, Carlton Fisk/25	50.00
52	Joe Morgan, Johnny Bench/25	75.00
53	Duke Snider, Don Sutton/100	50.00
54	Phil Rizzuto, Whitey Ford/57	60.00
55	Johnny Bench, Carlton Fisk/25	75.00
57	Steve Carlton, Whitey Ford/25	50.00
58	Jim Palmer, Tom Seaver/32	50.00
59	Reggie Jackson, Rollie Fingers/49	60.00
60	Duke Snider, Stan Musial	85.00

HOF Quads Autograph

NM/M

Cards are not serial numbered.

72	Jim Bunning, Mike Schmidt, Robin Roberts, Steve Carlton/38	100.00
74	Billy Williams, Lou Brock, Monte Irvin, Ralph Kiner/41	100.00

75	Fergie Jenkins, Gaylord Perry, Tom Seaver, Bob Gibson/50	100.00
76	Nolan Ryan, Don Sutton, Tom Seaver, Steve Carlton/50	80.00

HOF Six Autograph

No Pricing

HOF Trios Autograph

NM/M

Cards are not serial numbered.

64	Joe Morgan, Ryne Sandberg, Bobby Doerr/63	85.00
65	Ozzie Smith, Phil Rizzuto, Luis Aparicio/50	100.00
67	Ralph Kiner, Frank Robinson, Reggie Jackson/25	85.00
68	Gaylord Perry, Bob Gibson, Fergie Jenkins/50	75.00
69	Bob Gibson, Stan Musial, Ozzie Smith/100	140.00

INKcredible Combos

NM/M

Cards are not serial numbered.

1	Francisco Rodriguez, Troy Percival	25.00
2	Francisco Rodriguez, Scot Shields	15.00
3	Scot Shields, Troy Percival	15.00
6	Paul Molitor, Rickie Weeks/28	25.00
9	Ron Cey, Ron Santo/25	50.00
11	Don Sutton, Steve Garvey/100	30.00
12	Billy Ripken, Cal Ripken Jr.	90.00
13	Jim Palmer, Rick Dempsey/100	25.00
15	Mark Loretta, Sean Burroughs	10.00
17	Brett Myers, Randy Wolf	10.00
19	Justin Morneau, Kent Hrbek/36	25.00
20	Frank Thomas, Paul Konerko/50	50.00
21	Luis Aparicio, Minnie Minoso	20.00
22	Cal Ripken Jr., Tony Gwynn/100	125.00
24	Jose Guillen, Tim Salmon	10.00
25	Dallas McPherson, Kevin Youkilis	15.00
26	Esteban Loaiza, Jose Guillen	10.00
31	Jason Kubel, Lew Ford	10.00
32	Danny Graves, Matt Lindstrom	10.00
33	Garret Anderson, Tim Salmon	25.00
34	Clint Nageotte, J.J. Putz	10.00

INKredible Quads

NM/M

Cards are not serial numbered.

60	Jose Guillen, Esteban Loaiza, Marlon Byrd, Junior Spivey	50.00
61	Marlon Byrd, Jose Guillen, Livan Hernandez, Esteban Loaiza	50.00
63	Dwight Evans, Jim Rice, Luis Tiant, Carlton Fisk/73	100.00
65	Hideo Nomo, Shigetoshi Hasegawa, Akinori Otsuka, So Taguchi/45	300.00

INKcredible Six

NM/M

Cards are not serial numbered.

67	St. Louis Cardinals	240.00

INKcredible Trios

NM/M

Cards are not serial numbered.

35	Scot Shields, Troy Percival, Francisco Rodriguez	30.00
36	Barry Zito, Mark Mulder, Tim Hudson/37	80.00

38	Roy Halladay, Vernon Wells, Alex Rios/39	40.00
40	Duke Snider, Johnny Podres, Maury Wills/100	60.00
42	Keith Hernandez, Lenny Dykstra, Jesse Orosco/80	40.00
43	Esteban Loaiza, Jose Guillen, Paul Byrd	30.00
44	Cal Ripken Jr., Jim Palmer, Rick Dempsey/80	150.00
45	Brett Myers, Randy Wolf, Mike Lieberthal	30.00
46	Jacque Jones, Lew Ford, Jason Kubel/91	30.00
47	Randy Jones, Ozzie Smith, Rollie Fingers/36	80.00
48	Ron Guidry, "Goose" Gossage, Luis Tiant	40.00
49	Ron Guidry, 'Goose' Gossage, Dave Righetti	40.00
50	Ozzie Smith, Cal Ripken Jr., Alan Trammell/99	180.00
51	Wade Boggs, Ryne Sandberg, Tony Gwynn/95	140.00
52	Earl Weaver, Cal Ripken Jr., Frank Robinson/38	150.00
53	Harmon Killebrew, Kent Hrbek/28 Rod Carew,	100.00
54	Minnie Minoso, Luis Aparicio, Carlton Fisk/25	60.00

K-Force

NM/M

Inserted 1:7

1	Nolan Ryan	8.00
2	Steve Carlton	3.00
3	Roger Clemens	8.00
4	Randy Johnson	4.00
5	Tom Seaver	4.00
6	Don Sutton	2.00
7	Gaylord Perry	2.00
8	Fergie Jenkins	2.00
9	Bob Gibson	4.00
10	Greg Maddux	4.00
11	David Cone	2.00
12	Bob Feller	3.00
13	Johan Santana	4.00
14	Roy Halladay	3.00
15	Juan Marichal	3.00

K-Force Autograph

NM/M

Cards are not serial numbered.

1	Nolan Ryan	75.00
2	Steve Carlton/33	20.00
6	Don Sutton	10.00
7	Gaylord Perry/75	15.00
8	Fergie Jenkins/55	20.00
10	Greg Maddux/55	80.00
11	David Cone	10.00
12	Bob Feller/39	25.00
13	Johan Santana/55	30.00
15	Juan Marichal	15.00

K-Force Autograph Material

NM/M

Cards are not serial numbered.

1	Nolan Ryan/100	90.00
2	Steve Carlton	15.00
6	Don Sutton/80	15.00
7	Gaylord Perry/50	20.00
8	Fergie Jenkins/41	25.00
9	Bob Gibson/41	40.00
10	Greg Maddux/25	90.00
11	David Cone	15.00
12	Bob Feller/30	25.00
15	Juan Marichal/58	20.00

K-Force Autograph MS

NM/M

Production 1-25

1	Nolan Ryan/25	100.00
2	Steve Carlton/25	20.00
6	Don Sutton/25	20.00
7	Gaylord Perry/25	25.00
8	Fergie Jenkins/25	25.00
10	Greg Maddux/25	90.00
11	David Cone/25	15.00
12	Bob Feller/25	25.00
13	Johan Santana/25	40.00
15	Juan Marichal/25	25.00

Milestone Marks

NM/M

Common Player: 2.00

Inserted 1:10

1	Duke Snider	4.00
2	Nolan Ryan	8.00
3	Gaylord Perry	2.00
4	Johnny Bench	4.00
5	Willie McCovey	3.00
6	Stan Musial	5.00
7	Randi Johnson	4.00
9	Gary Carter	3.00
10	Tony Gwynn	4.00

Milestone Marks Auto.

NM/M

Cards are not serial numbered.

1	Duke Snider	25.00
2	Nolan Ryan	75.00
3	Gaylord Perry	15.00
4	Johnny Bench	30.00
5	Willie McCovey/44	30.00
6	Stan Musial	50.00
10	Tony Gwynn/6	2.00

Milestone Marks Autograph Material Bat

Cards are not serial numbered.

Milestone Marks Autograph Material Combo

NM/M

Inserted 1:210

Cards are not serial numbered.

7	Randy Johnson/25	75.00
10	Tony Gwynn	30.00

Milestone Marks Auto. Material Jersey

NM/M

Cards are not serial numbered.

3	Gaylord Perry/100	10.00
5	Willie McCovey	30.00
10	Tony Gwynn/75	30.00

Milestone Marks Autograph MS

NM/M

Production 20-25

1	Duke Snider/25	40.00
2	Nolan Ryan/25	100.00
3	Gaylord Perry/25	20.00
4	Johnny Bench/25	40.00
5	Willie McCovey/25	35.00
6	Stan Musial/25	80.00
10	Tony Gwynn/25	50.00

Notable Nicknames

NM/M

Production 100 Sets

Master Series: No Pricing

GM	Greg Maddux Bulldog	300.00
IR	Ivan Rodriguez Pudge	
OS	Ozzie Smith Wizard	60.00

Stamps Autograph Centennial

NM/M

Production 3-81

Pro Ball: .75-1X

Production 3-81

2	Cal Ripken Jr./50	125.00
4	Duke Snider/81	30.00
6	Orlando Cepeda/48	25.00
7	Don Larsen/50	25.00
10	Cal Ripken Jr./50	125.00

Stamps Autograph Material Centennial

NM/M

Production 2-50

Pro Ball: .75-1X

Production 1-50

2	Cal Ripken Jr./50	140.00
10	Cal Ripken Jr./50	140.00

Stamps Centennial Autograph

No Pricing

Production 1-2

Stamps Material Centennial

		NM/M
Production 40-100		
Pro Ball:		.75-1X
Production 40-100		
2	Cal Ripken Jr./50	40.00
5	Harmon Killebrew/70	15.00
8	Adrian Beltre/100	8.00
10	Cal Ripken Jr./50	40.00
11	Jim Thorpe/68	140.00
12	Willie Mays/100	40.00
13	Roger Maris/100	40.00

Stars Autograph

		NM/M
Cards are not serial numbered.		
1	Mark Teixeira/42	30.00
2	Scott Rolen	25.00
3	Roy Oswalt/85	20.00
5	Morgan Ensberg	15.00
6	Mark Grace/86	25.00
7	Gary Sheffield/82	25.00
8	Sean Casey	15.00
10	Ryne Sandberg	50.00

Stars Autograph Material Bat

		NM/M
Cards are not serial numbered.		
1	Mark Teixeira/100	25.00
3	Roy Oswalt	15.00
4	Hideo Nomo/36	200.00
6	Mark Grace	25.00
7	Gary Sheffield	25.00
11	Stan Musial/38	75.00
12	Joe Torre/44	40.00
13	Wade Boggs/40	30.00
14	Barry Larkin	25.00
15	Dale Murphy/100	25.00

Stars Autograph Material Jersey

		NM/M
Cards are not serial numbered.		
2	Scott Rolen	25.00
4	Hideo Nomo/50	200.00
6	Mark Grace/43	35.00
7	Gary Sheffield/43	30.00
8	Sean Casey/52	20.00
11	Stan Musial/44	80.00
12	Joe Torre/50	40.00
15	Dale Murphy	25.00

Stars Autograph MS

		NM/M
Production 1-25		
1	Mark Teixeira/25	35.00
2	Scott Rolen/25	35.00
3	Roy Oswalt/25	35.00
5	Morgan Ensberg/25	20.00
6	Mark Grace/25	40.00
7	Gary Sheffield/25	40.00
8	Sean Casey/25	20.00
10	Ryne Sandberg/25	75.00
14	Barry Larkin/25	35.00

Stats Autograph

		NM/M
Cards are not serial numbered.		
4	Alfonso Soriano	25.00
9	Miguel Cabrera	30.00
10	Mark Teixeira/41	30.00

Stats Autograph Material Bat

		NM/M
Cards are not serial numbered.		
4	Alfonso Soriano	25.00
5	Don Mattingly/25	75.00
10	Mark Teixeira	25.00

Stats Autograph Material Combo

		NM/M
Cards are not serial numbered.		
1	Tony Gwynn	30.00
4	Alfonso Soriano/25	30.00

Stats Autograph Material Jersey

		NM/M
Cards are not serial numbered.		
1	Tony Gwynn/25	50.00
2	Johan Santana/100	30.00
3	Orel Hershiser/25	25.00
8	Victor Martinez/25	25.00

Stats Autograph MS

		NM/M
Production 1-25		
1	Tony Gwynn/25	50.00
2	Johan Santana/25	40.00
3	Orel Hershiser/25	25.00
4	Alfonso Soriano/25	30.00
5	Don Mattingly/25	75.00
8	Victor Martinez/25	25.00
9	Miguel Cabrera/25	40.00
10	Mark Teixeira/25	35.00

2005 Donruss Studio

		NM/M
Complete Set (300):		
Common Player:		.25
Pack (6):		4.00
Box (24):		90.00
1	Casey Kotchman	.25
2	Chone Figgins	.25
3	Dallas McPherson	.25
4	Darin Erstad	.25
5	Ervin Santana	.25
6	Garret Anderson	.40
7	Norihiro Nakamura RC	2.00
8	John Lackey	.25
9	Orlando Cabrera	.25
10	Robb Quinlan	.25
11	Steve Finley	.25
12	Tim Salmon	.25
13	Vladimir Guerrero	.75
14	Brandon Webb	.25
15	Craig Counsell	.25
16	Javier Vazquez	.25
17	Luis Gonzalez	.25
18	Tony Pena RC	.40
19	Russ Ortiz	.25
20	Scott Hairston	.25
21	Shawn Green	.25
22	Jose Cruz Jr.	.25
23	Troy Glaus	.40
24	Adam LaRoche	.25
25	Andruw Jones	.50
26	Chipper Jones	.75
27	Danny Kolb	.25
28	John Smoltz	.40
29	Johnny Estrada	.25
30	Marcus Giles	.25
31	Nick Green	.25
32	Rafael Furcal	.25
33	Tim Hudson	.40
34	Brian Roberts	.25
35	Javy Lopez	.25
36	Jay Gibbons	.25
37	Melvin Mora	.25
38	Miguel Tejada	.50
39	Rafael Palmeiro	.50
40	Rodrigo Lopez	.25
41	Sidney Ponson	.25
42	Abe Alvarez	.25
43	Bill Mueller	.25
44	Curt Schilling	.75
45	David Ortiz	.75
46	David Wells	.25
47	Edgar Renteria	.25
48	Jason Varitek	.50
49	Jay Payton	.25
50	Johnny Damon	.75
51	Juan Cedeno	.25
52	Manny Ramirez	.75
53	Matt Clement	.25
54	Trot Nixon	.25
55	Wade Miller	.25
56	Aramis Ramirez	.40
57	Carlos Zambrano	.40
58	Corey Patterson	.25
59	Derrek Lee	.50
60	Greg Maddux	1.50
61	Kerry Wood	.40
62	Mark Prior	.75
63	Nomar Garciaparra	.75
64	Sammy Sosa	1.00
65	Todd Walker	.25
66	A.J. Pierzynski	.25
67	Aaron Rowand	.25
68	Frank Thomas	.50
69	Freddy Garcia	.25
70	Jermaine Dye	.25
71	Mark Buehrle	.40
72	Paul Konerko	.40
73	Tadahito Iguchi RC	3.00
74	Pedro Lopez RC	.40
75	Scott Podsednik	.25
76	Shingo Takatsu	.25
77	Adam Dunn	.50
78	Austin Kearns	.25
79	Barry Larkin	.50
80	Bubba Nelson	.25
81	Danny Graves	.25
82	Eric Milton	.25
83	Ken Griffey Jr.	1.50
84	Ryan Wagner	.25
85	Sean Casey	.25
86	C.C. Sabathia	.25
87	Cliff Lee	.25
88	Fausto Carmona	.25
89	Grady Sizemore	.40
90	Jake Westbrook	.25
91	Jody Gerut	.25
92	Juan Gonzalez	.40
93	Kazuhito Tadano	.25
94	Travis Hafner	.25
95	Victor Martinez	.25
96	Charles Johnson	.25
97	Clint Barmes	.25
98	Cory Sullivan	.25
99	Jeff Baker	.25
100	Jeff Francis	.25
101	Jeff Salazar	.25
102	Jeromy Burnitz	.25
103	Joe Kennedy	.25
104	Matt Holliday	.50
105	Preston Wilson	.25
106	Todd Helton	.50
107	Ubaldo Jimenez RC	.40
108	Brandon Inge	.25
109	Carlos Guillen	.25
110	Carlos Pena	.25
111	Craig Monroe	.25
112	Ivan Rodriguez	.50
113	Jeremy Bonderman	.25
114	Justin Verlander RC	2.00
115	Magglio Ordonez	.25
116	Troy Percival	.25
117	Vance Wilson	.25
118	A.J. Burnett	.25
119	Al Leiter	.25
120	Dontrelle Willis	.40
121	Josh Beckett	.40
122	Juan Pierre	.25
123	Miguel Cabrera	.75
124	Mike Lowell	.25
125	Paul LoDuca	.25
126	Randy Messenger RC	.40
127	Yorman Bazardo RC	.40
128	Andy Pettitte	.40
129	Brad Lidge	.25
130	Chris Burke	.25
131	Craig Biggio	.40
132	Fernando Nieve	.25
133	Jason Lane	.25
134	Jeff Bagwell	.50
135	Lance Berkman	.40
136	Morgan Ensberg	.25
137	Roger Clemens	2.00
138	Roy Oswalt	.25
139	Ambiorix Burgos RC	.40
140	David DeJesus	.25
141	Jeremy Affeldt	.25
142	Jose Lima	.25
143	Ken Harvey	.25
144	Mike MacDougal	.25
145	Mike Sweeney	.25
146	Terrence Long	.25
147	Zack Greinke	.25
148	Brad Penny	.25
149	Derek Lowe	.25
150	Dioner Navarro	.25
151	Edwin Jackson	.25
152	Eric Gagne	.25
153	Hee Seop Choi	.25
154	Hideo Nomo	.50
155	J.D. Drew	.40
156	Jeff Kent	.25
157	Jeff Weaver	.25
158	Milton Bradley	.25
159	Yhency Brazoban	.25
160	Ben Sheets	.40
161	Bill Hall	.25
162	Carlos Lee	.25
163	Gustavo Chacin	.25
164	Geoff Jenkins	.25
165	Jose Capellan	.25
166	Lyle Overbay	.25
167	Rickie Weeks	.40
168	Jacque Jones	.25
169	Joe Mauer	.50
170	Joe Nathan	.25
171	Johan Santana	.50
172	Justin Morneau	.40
173	Lew Ford	.25
174	Michael Cuddyer	.25
175	Shannon Stewart	.25
176	Torii Hunter	.25
177	Brad Radke	.25
178	Ambiorix Concepcion RC	.40
179	Carlos Beltran	.50
180	David Wright	.75
181	Jose Reyes	.50
182	Kazuo Matsui	.25
183	Kris Benson	.25
184	Mike Piazza	1.00
185	Pedro Martinez	.75
186	Philip Humber RC	1.00
187	Tom Glavine	.40
188	Alex Rodriguez	1.50
189	Carl Pavano	.25
190	Derek Jeter	2.00
191	Yuniesky Betancourt RC	1.00
192	Hideki Matsui	1.50
193	Jorge Posada	.40
194	Kevin Brown	.25
195	Mariano Rivera	.40
196	Mike Mussina	.40
197	Randy Johnson	.75
198	Scott Proctor	.25
199	Tom Gordon	.25
200	Barry Zito	.40
201	Bobby Crosby	.40
202	Danny Haren	.25
203	Eric Chavez	.40
204	Keiichi Yabu RC	.40
205	Jason Kendall	.25
206	Joe Blanton	.25
207	Mark Kotsay	.25
208	Nick Swisher	.25
209	Octavio Dotel	.25
210	Rich Harden	.40
211	Billy Wagner	.25
212	Bobby Abreu	.40
213	Chase Utley	.50
214	Gavin Floyd	.25
215	Jim Thome	.50
216	Jimmy Rollins	.50
217	Jon Lieber	.25
218	Kenny Lofton	.25
219	Mike Lieberthal	.25
220	Pat Burrell	.25
221	Randy Wolf	.25
222	Craig Wilson	.25
223	Jack Wilson	.25
224	Jason Bay	.40
225	John Van Benschoten	.25
226	Jose Castillo	.25
227	Kip Wells	.25
228	Matt Lawton	.25
229	Akinori Otsuka	.25
230	Brian Giles	.25
231	Freddy Guzman	.25
232	Jake Peavy	.40
233	Khalil Greene	.40
234	Mark Loretta	.25
235	Sean Burroughs	.25
236	Trevor Hoffman	.25
237	Woody Williams	.25
238	Armando Benitez	.25
239	Edgardo Alfonzo	.25
240	Erick Threets RC	.40
241	Jason Schmidt	.40
242	Marquis Grissom	.25
243	Merkin Valdez	.25
244	Michael Tucker	.25
245	Moises Alou	.40
246	Omar Vizquel	.25
247	Adrian Beltre	.40
248	Bret Boone	.25
249	Bucky Jacobsen	.25
250	Clint Nageotte	.25
251	Ichiro Suzuki	1.50
252	J.J. Putz	.25
253	Jeremy Reed	.25
254	Miguel Olivo	.25
255	Mike Morse RC	2.00
256	Richie Sexson	.40
257	Wladimir Balentien RC	1.00
258	Albert Pujols	2.00
259	Jason Isringhausen	.25
260	Jeff Suppan	.25
261	Jim Edmonds	.40
262	Larry Walker	.40
263	Mark Mulder	.40
264	Rick Ankiel	.25
265	Scott Rolen	.75
266	Yadier Molina	.25
267	Aubrey Huff	.25
268	B.J. Upton	.25
269	Carl Crawford	.25
270	Chris Seddon RC	.40
271	Delmon Young	.25
272	Dewon Brazelton	.25
273	Jeff Niemann RC	1.00
274	Rocco Baldelli	.25
275	Scott Kazmir	.25
276	Adrian Gonzalez	.25
277	Alfonso Soriano	.75
278	Francisco Cordero	.25
279	Hank Blalock	.40
280	Kameron Loe	.25
281	Kenny Rogers	.25
282	Laynce Nix	.25
283	Mark Teixeira	.40
284	Michael Young	.25
285	Corey Koskie	.25
286	David Bush	.25
287	Frank Catalanotto	.25
288	Gabe Gross	.25
289	Raul Tablado RC	.40
290	Roy Halladay	.40
291	Shea Hillenbrand	.25
292	Vernon Wells	.25

293	Chad Cordero	.25
294	Cristian Guzman	.25
295	Jose Guillen	.25
296	Jose Vidro	.25
297	Josh Karp	.25
298	Livan Hernandez	.25
299	Nick Johnson	.25
300	Vinny Castilla	.25

Proofs Gold
Stars: 8-12X
Production 25 Sets

Proofs Platinum
No Pricing
Production 10 Sets

Proofs Silver
Stars: 3-5X
Production 100 Sets

Autographs
No Pricing

Diamond Cuts
NM/M
Common Player: 1.00
Production 1,250 Sets
Die-cut: 1-1.5X
Production 250 Sets
Die-cut Gold: 1.5-3X
Production 75 Sets

1	Roger Clemens	4.00
2	Manny Ramirez	1.50
3	Francisco Rodriguez	1.00
4	Brian Roberts	1.00
5	Javy Lopez	1.00
6	Vernon Wells	1.00
7	Johan Santana	1.50
8	Torii Hunter	1.00
9	Mike Mussina	1.50
10	Sammy Sosa	2.50
11	Ryan Wagner	1.00
12	Jack Wilson	1.00
13	Ichiro Suzuki	3.00
14	Greg Maddux	3.00
15	Albert Pujols	4.00
16	Jeremy Bonderman	1.00
17	Johnny Estrada	1.00
18	Mark Buehrle	1.00
19	Jorge Posada	1.00
20	Carl Crawford	1.00
21	Paul Konerko	1.00
22	Victor Martinez	1.00
23	Jose Vidro	1.00
24	Jim Thome	1.50
25	Andruw Jones	1.50

Diamond Cuts Bat
NM/M
Production 5-300

1	Roger Clemens/50	15.00
2	Manny Ramirez/200	8.00
5	Javy Lopez/300	4.00
8	Torii Hunter/300	4.00
10	Sammy Sosa/300	15.00
12	Jack Wilson/300	4.00
14	Greg Maddux/225	15.00
15	Albert Pujols/300	15.00
21	Paul Konerko/50	6.00
22	Victor Martinez/300	4.00
23	Jose Vidro/300	4.00
25	Andruw Jones/300	6.00

Diamond Cuts Combo
NM/M
Production 5-50
Prime: No Pricing
Production 10 Sets

1	Roger Clemens/ Bat-Jsy/50	20.00
2	Manny Ramirez/ Bat-Jsy/50	12.00
3	Freddy Rodriguez/ Jsy-Jsy/50	10.00
5	Javy Lopez/ Bat-Jsy/50	8.00
6	Vernon Wells/ Jsy-Jsy/50	8.00
8	Torii Hunter/ Bat-Jsy/50	8.00
10	Sammy Sosa/ Jsy-Jsy/50	12.00
11	Ryan Wagner/ Jsy-Jsy/50	8.00
12	Jack Wilson/ Bat-Jsy/50	8.00
14	Greg Maddux/ Bat-Jsy/50	15.00
15	Albert Pujols/ Bat-Jsy/50	30.00
17	Johnny Estrada/ Fld Glve-Jsy/50	10.00
21	Paul Konerko/ Jsy-Jsy/50	10.00
22	Victor Martinez/ Bat-Jsy/50	10.00
23	Jose Vidro/Bat-Jsy/50	8.00
24	Jim Thome/ Jsy-Jsy/45	12.00
25	Andruw Jones/ Bat-Jsy/50	10.00

Diamond Cuts Jersey
NM/M
Production 15-250
Prime: No Pricing
Production 5-10

1	Roger Clemens/125	10.00
2	Manny Ramirez/250	8.00
3	Francisco Rodriguez/250	4.00
4	Brian Roberts/250	6.00
5	Javy Lopez/250	4.00
6	Vernon Wells/250	4.00
7	Johan Santana/175	8.00
8	Torii Hunter/250	4.00
9	Mike Mussina/250	6.00
10	Sammy Sosa/250	8.00
11	Ryan Wagner/250	4.00
12	Jack Wilson/15	
14	Greg Maddux/250	8.00
15	Albert Pujols/250	20.00
16	Jeremy Bonderman/250	4.00
17	Johnny Estrada/250	4.00
18	Mark Buehrle/250	4.00
19	Jorge Posada/250	4.00
20	Carl Crawford/250	4.00
21	Paul Konerko/250	4.00
22	Victor Martinez/250	4.00
23	Jose Vidro/175	4.00
24	Jim Thome/250	6.00
25	Andruw Jones/250	6.00

Diamond Cuts Signature Combo
NM/M
Production 25-50
Prime: No Pricing
Production 10 Sets

3	Freddy Rodriguez/ Jsy-Jsy/25	40.00
6	Vernon Wells/ Jsy-Jsy/25	25.00
8	Torii Hunter/ Bat-Jsy/25	20.00
11	Ryan Wagner/ Jsy-Jsy/25	15.00
12	Jack Wilson/ Bat-Jsy/25	20.00
16	Jeremy Bonderman/ Jsy-Jsy/25	20.00
17	Johnny Estrada/ Fld Glv-Jsy/50	15.00
21	Paul Konerko/ Jsy-Jsy/25	25.00

Heritage
NM/M
Common Player: 1.00
Production 1,000 Sets
Die-cut: 1-1.5X
Production 200 Sets
Die-cut Gold: 2-3X
Production 50 Sets

1	Rickey Henderson	1.50
2	Jeff Bagwell	1.50
3	Steve Garvey	1.00
4	Albert Pujols	5.00
5	Don Mattingly	4.00
6	Frank Thomas	1.50
7	Tony Gwynn	2.00
8	Gary Sheffield	1.50
9	Dale Murphy	1.50
10	Kerry Wood	1.50
11	Cal Ripken Jr.	6.00
12	Miguel Cabrera	2.00
13	Dwight Gooden	1.00
14	Barry Zito	1.00
15	Darryl Strawberry	1.00

Heritage Bat
NM/M
Production 150 Sets

1	Rickey Henderson	8.00
2	Jeff Bagwell	6.00
3	Steve Garvey	4.00
4	Albert Pujols	15.00
5	Don Mattingly	10.00
6	Frank Thomas	6.00
7	Tony Gwynn	8.00
8	Gary Sheffield	6.00
9	Dale Murphy	6.00
11	Cal Ripken Jr.	20.00
12	Miguel Cabrera	6.00
13	Dwight Gooden	4.00
15	Darryl Strawberry	4.00

Heritage Combo
NM/M
Production 10-50
Prime: No Pricing
Production 10 Sets

1	Rickey Henderson/ Bat-Jsy/50	15.00
2	Jeff Bagwell/ Bat-Jsy/50	10.00
3	Steve Garvey/ Bat-Jsy/50	10.00
4	Albert Pujols/ Bat-Jsy/50	25.00
5	Don Mattingly/ Bat-Jsy/50	20.00
6	Frank Thomas/ Bat-Jsy/50	10.00
7	Tony Gwynn/ Bat-Jsy/50	15.00
8	Gary Sheffield/ Bat-Jsy/50	10.00
9	Dale Murphy/ Bat-Jsy/50	12.00
10	Kerry Wood/ Jsy-Pants/25	10.00
11	Cal Ripken Jr./ Bat-Jsy/50	4.00
12	Miguel Cabrera/ Bat-Jsy/50	12.00
13	Dwight Gooden/ Bat-Jsy/50	10.00
15	Darryl Strawberry/ Bat-Jsy/50	10.00

Heritage Jersey
NM/M
Production 50-250
Prime: No Pricing
Production 10 Sets

1	Rickey Henderson/250	8.00
2	Jeff Bagwell/250	6.00
3	Steve Garvey/250	4.00
4	Albert Pujols/250	15.00
5	Don Mattingly/250	12.00
6	Frank Thomas/250	6.00
7	Tony Gwynn/250	8.00
9	Dale Murphy/250	6.00
10	Kerry Wood/250	6.00
11	Cal Ripken Jr./250	20.00
12	Miguel Cabrera/250	8.00
13	Dwight Gooden/250	4.00
14	Barry Zito/250	4.00
15	Darryl Strawberry/250	4.00

Heritage Sig. Combo
NM/M
Production 10-50
Prime: No Pricing
Production 5-10

3	Steve Garvey/ Bat-Jsy/25	25.00
5	Don Mattingly/ Bat-Jsy/25	75.00
9	Dale Murphy/ Bat-Jsy/25	40.00
11	Cal Ripken Jr./ Bat-Jsy/25	160.00
12	Miguel Cabrera/ Bat-Jsy/25	50.00
13	Dwight Gooden/ Bat-Jsy/25	25.00
15	Darryl Strawberry/ Bat-Jsy/25	25.00

Heroes of the Hall
NM/M
Common Player: 2.00
Production 350 Sets
Die-cut: 1-1.5X
Production 75 Sets
Die-cut Gold: 2-3X
Production 25 Sets

1	Luis Aparicio	2.00
2	Dennis Eckersley	2.00
3	Brooks Robinson	4.00
4	Carlton Fisk	4.00
5	Tom Seaver	4.00
6	Paul Molitor	4.00
7	Rod Carew	3.00
8	George Brett	6.00
9	Nolan Ryan	8.00
10	Mike Schmidt	6.00
11	Willie Mays	6.00
12	Gary Carter	2.00
13	Lou Brock	2.00
14	Steve Carlton	2.00
15	Harmon Killebrew	2.00

Heroes of the Hall Bat
NM/M
Production 100-150

1	Luis Aparicio/150	4.00
3	Brooks Robinson/150	8.00
4	Carlton Fisk/150	6.00
6	Paul Molitor/150	8.00
8	George Brett/150	12.00
10	Mike Schmidt/125	15.00
11	Willie Mays/100	35.00
12	Gary Carter/125	6.00
13	Lou Brock/150	6.00
15	Harmon Killebrew/150	8.00

Heroes of the Hall Combo
NM/M
Production 25-50
Prime: No Pricing
Production 5-10

1	Luis Aparicio/ Bat-Jsy/50	10.00
2	Dennis Eckersley/ Jsy-Jsy/50	10.00
3	Brooks Robinson/ Bat-Jsy/50	15.00
4	Carlton Fisk/ Bat-Jsy/50	12.00
5	Tom Seaver/ Jsy-Pants/50	15.00
6	Paul Molitor/ Bat-Jsy/50	15.00
7	Rod Carew/ Bat-Jsy/50	12.00
8	George Brett/ Bat-Jsy/50	20.00
9	Nolan Ryan/ Bat-Jsy/50	25.00
10	Mike Schmidt/ Bat-Jsy/50	20.00
11	Willie Mays/ Bat-Jsy/25	60.00
12	Gary Carter/ Jsy-Pants/50	10.00
13	Lou Brock/Bat-Jkt/50	15.00
15	Harmon Killebrew/ Bat-Jsy/50	15.00

Heroes of the Hall Jersey
NM/M
Production 50-150
Prime: No Pricing
Production 5-10

1	Luis Aparicio/150	4.00
2	Dennis Eckersley/150	6.00
3	Brooks Robinson/50	10.00
4	Carlton Fisk/150	6.00
5	Tom Seaver/150	8.00
6	Paul Molitor/150	8.00
7	Rod Carew/150	6.00
8	George Brett/150	12.00
9	Nolan Ryan/100	20.00
10	Mike Schmidt/100	15.00
11	Willie Mays/50	40.00
12	Gary Carter/150	6.00
14	Steve Carlton/150	4.00
15	Harmon Killebrew/150	8.00

Heroes of the Hall Signature Combo
NM/M
Production 5-50
Prime: No Pricing
Production 5-10

1	Luis Aparicio/ Bat-Jsy/50	20.00
2	Dennis Eckersley/ Jsy-Pants/25	30.00
4	Carlton Fisk/ Bat-Jsy/25	40.00
6	Paul Molitor/ Bat-Jsy/25	35.00
14	Steve Carlton/ Bat-Jsy/25	35.00
15	Harmon Killebrew/ Bat-Jsy/25	35.00

Masterstrokes
NM/M
Common Player: 1.50
Production 750 Sets
Die-cut: 1-1.5X
Production 150 Sets
Die-cut Gold: 1.5-2X
Production 50 Sets

1	Hideki Matsui	6.00
2	David Ortiz	3.00
3	Aramis Ramirez	2.00
4	Lance Berkman	1.50
5	Ichiro Suzuki	6.00
6	Mike Piazza	4.00
7	Ivan Rodriguez	2.00
8	Hideo Nomo	2.00

#	Player	Price
9	Jeff Bagwell	2.00
10	Travis Hafner	1.50
11	Casey Kotchman	1.50
12	Jim Edmonds	2.00
13	Michael Young	1.50
14	Lyle Overbay	1.50
15	Eric Chavez	2.00
16	Jason Bay	1.50
17	Hank Blalock	2.00
18	Frank Thomas	2.00
19	Craig Biggio	2.00
20	Miguel Cabrera	3.00
21	Vladimir Guerrero	3.00
22	Sammy Sosa	4.00
23	Chipper Jones	3.00
24	Rafael Palmeiro	2.00
25	Adam Dunn	2.00

Masterstrokes Bat

NM/M

Production 25-250

#	Player	Price
1	Hideki Matsui/25	30.00
2	David Ortiz/250	8.00
3	Aramis Ramirez/35	8.00
4	Lance Berkman/250	4.00
6	Mike Piazza/100	10.00
7	Ivan Rodriguez/250	6.00
9	Jeff Bagwell/250	6.00
10	Travis Hafner/250	4.00
11	Casey Kotchman/250	4.00
13	Michael Young/250	4.00
14	Lyle Overbay/250	4.00
16	Jason Bay/250	4.00
17	Hank Blalock/50	6.00
18	Frank Thomas/250	6.00
19	Craig Biggio/250	6.00
20	Miguel Cabrera/250	6.00
21	Vladimir Guerrero/250	8.00
22	Sammy Sosa/200	8.00
23	Chipper Jones/250	6.00
25	Adam Dunn/250	6.00

Masterstrokes Combo

NM/M

Production 15-50

Prime: No Pricing

Production 10 Sets

#	Player	Price
2	David Ortiz/Bat-Jsy/50	15.00
3	Aramis Ramirez/Jsy-Jsy/50	10.00
4	Lance Berkman/Bat-Jsy/50	8.00
6	Mike Piazza/Jsy-Jsy/50	15.00
7	Ivan Rodriguez/Bat-Jsy/50	10.00
8	Hideo Nomo/Jsy-Jsy/50	12.00
9	Jeff Bagwell/Bat-Jsy/50	10.00
10	Travis Hafner/Bat-Jsy/50	8.00
11	Casey Kotchman/Bat-Jsy/50	8.00
12	Jim Edmonds/Jsy-Jsy/50	10.00
13	Michael Young/Bat-Jsy/50	10.00
14	Lyle Overbay/Bat-Jsy/50	8.00
15	Eric Chavez/Bat-Jsy/50	10.00
16	Jason Bay/Bat-Jsy/50	8.00
17	Hank Blalock/Jsy-Jsy/50	10.00
18	Frank Thomas/Bat-Jsy/50	12.00
19	Craig Biggio/Bat-Jsy/50	10.00
20	Miguel Cabrera/Bat-Jsy/50	15.00
21	Vladimir Guerrero/Bat-Jsy/50	15.00
22	Sammy Sosa/Bat-Jsy/50	15.00
23	Chipper Jones/Bat-Jsy/50	12.00
24	Rafael Palmeiro/Bat-Pants/50	12.00
25	Adam Dunn/Bat-Jsy/50	10.00

Masterstrokes Jersey

NM/M

Production 40-250

Prime: No Pricing

Production 10 Sets

#	Player	Price
1	Hideki Matsui/250	20.00
2	David Ortiz/250	8.00
3	Aramis Ramirez/250	6.00
4	Lance Berkman/250	4.00
6	Mike Piazza/250	8.00
7	Ivan Rodriguez/250	6.00
8	Hideo Nomo/250	6.00
9	Jeff Bagwell/250	6.00
10	Travis Hafner/200	4.00
11	Casey Kotchman/250	4.00
12	Jim Edmonds/250	6.00
13	Michael Young/150	4.00
14	Lyle Overbay/250	4.00
15	Eric Chavez/250	4.00
16	Jason Bay/150	4.00
17	Hank Blalock/250	6.00
18	Frank Thomas/250	6.00
19	Craig Biggio/250	6.00
20	Miguel Cabrera/250	6.00
21	Vladimir Guerrero/50	10.00
22	Sammy Sosa/250	8.00
23	Chipper Jones/225	6.00
24	Rafael Palmeiro/40	8.00
25	Adam Dunn/250	6.00

Masterstrokes Signature Combo

NM/M

Production 5-50

Prime: No Pricing

Production 5-10

#	Player	Price
10	Travis Hafner/Bat-Jsy/	25.00
11	Casey Kotchman/Bat-Jsy/	20.00
14	Lyle Overbay/Bat-Jsy/	12.00
15	Eric Chavez/Bat-Jsy/25	25.00
16	Jason Bay/Bat-Jsy/	25.00
17	Hank Blalock/Jsy-Jsy/25	30.00
20	Miguel Cabrera/Jsy-Jsy/25	50.00

Portraits Zenith White

NM/M

Common Player:		2.00
Production 70 Sets		
Parallel #'d 40-60:		.75-1X
Parallel #'d 20-35:		.75-1.5X
No pricing 15 or less.		

#	Player	Price
1	Ozzie Smith	6.00
2	Derek Jeter	8.00
3	Eric Chavez	2.00
4	Duke Snider	4.00
5	Albert Pujols	8.00
6	Stan Musial	6.00
7	Ivan Rodriguez	2.00
8	Cal Ripken Jr.	15.00
9	Hank Blalock	2.00
10	Chipper Jones	3.00
11	Gary Sheffield	2.00
12	Alfonso Soriano	3.00
13	Carl Crawford	2.00
14	Lou Brock	4.00
15	Jim Edmonds	3.00
16	Bo Jackson	4.00
17	Todd Helton	3.00
18	Javy Lopez	2.00
19	Tony Gwynn	5.00
20	Mark Mulder	2.00
21	Sammy Sosa	4.00
22	Roger Clemens	6.00
23	Don Mattingly	8.00
24	Willie Mays	8.00
25	Andruw Jones	3.00
26	Steve Garvey	2.00
27	Scott Rolen	3.00
28	George Brett	8.00
29	Rod Carew	4.00
30	Ken Griffey Jr.	6.00
31	Mike Piazza	5.00
32	Steve Carlton	3.00
33	Larry Walker	3.00
34	Kerry Wood	2.00
35	Frank Thomas	3.00
36	Lance Berkman	2.00
37	Nomar Garciaparra	4.00
38	Curt Schilling	3.00
39	Carl Yastrzemski	6.00
40	Mark Grace	3.00
41	Tom Seaver	4.00
42	Mariano Rivera	3.00
43	Carlos Beltran	3.00
44	Reggie Jackson	4.00
45	Pedro Martinez	4.00
46	Richie Sexson	2.00
47	Tom Glavine	2.00
48	Torii Hunter	2.00
49	Ron Guidry	2.00
50	Michael Young	2.00
51	Ichiro Suzuki	6.00
52	C.C. Sabathia	2.00
53	Johnny Bench	4.00
54	Mark Teixeira	3.00
55	Hideki Matsui	6.00
56	Mike Mussina	3.00
57	Johan Santana	3.00
58	Fergie Jenkins	2.00
59	Hideo Nomo	3.00
60	Nolan Ryan	10.00
61	Whitey Ford	4.00
62	Jim Thome	3.00
63	Gary Carter	3.00
64	Randy Johnson	3.00
65	Vladimir Guerrero	3.00
66	Harmon Killebrew	4.00
67	Tim Hudson	3.00
68	Josh Beckett	2.00
69	Eddie Murray	4.00
70	Greg Maddux	5.00
71	J.D. Drew	2.00
72	Bob Feller	4.00
73	Adrian Beltre	2.00
74	Wade Boggs	4.00
75	Barry Zito	2.00
76	David Ortiz	3.00
77	Mike Schmidt	8.00
78	Miguel Cabrera	4.00
79	Carlos Delgado	2.00
80	Andre Dawson	2.00
81	Garret Anderson	2.00
82	Rickey Henderson	3.00
83	Shawn Green	2.00
84	Dale Murphy	3.00
85	Alex Rodriguez	6.00
86	Mark Prior	3.00
87	Paul Molitor	4.00
88	Jeff Bagwell	3.00
89	Eric Gagne	2.00
90	Troy Glaus	2.00
91	Robin Yount	4.00
92	Miguel Tejada	3.00
93	Kirk Gibson	2.00
94	Manny Ramirez	3.00
95	Rafael Palmeiro	3.00
96	Maury Wills	2.00
97	Craig Biggio	2.00
98	Jim Palmer	3.00
99	Adam Dunn	3.00
100	Carlton Fisk	3.00

Private Signings Gold

NM/M

Common Autograph: 8.00

Production 50 Sets

#	Player	Price
1	Casey Kotchman	20.00
2	Chone Figgins	10.00
5	Ervin Santana	10.00
6	Garret Anderson	15.00
9	Orlando Cabrera	15.00
10	Robb Quinlan	8.00
11	Steve Finley	15.00
12	Tim Salmon	15.00
14	Brandon Webb	10.00
18	Tony Pena	10.00
19	Russ Ortiz	10.00
24	Adam LaRoche	12.00
27	Danny Kolb	10.00
29	Johnny Estrada	10.00
31	Nick Green	8.00
32	Rafael Furcal	15.00
34	Brian Roberts	20.00
36	Jay Gibbons	10.00
40	Rodrigo Lopez	10.00
47	Edgar Renteria	25.00
49	Jay Payton	10.00
51	Juan Cedeno	8.00
53	Matt Clement	30.00
54	Trot Nixon	20.00
55	Wade Miller	10.00
57	Carlos Zambrano	25.00
59	Derrek Lee	40.00
65	Todd Walker	12.00
70	Jermaine Dye	15.00
71	Mark Buehrle	25.00
72	Paul Konerko	15.00
76	Shingo Takatsu	20.00
78	Austin Kearns	10.00
80	Bubba Nelson	8.00
81	Danny Graves	8.00
84	Ryan Wagner	8.00
87	Cliff Lee	10.00
88	Fausto Carmona	8.00
92	Jody Gerut	10.00
93	Kazuhito Tadano	8.00
94	Travis Hafner	15.00
98	Cory Sullivan	8.00
101	Jeff Salazar	8.00
103	Joe Kennedy	8.00
108	Brandon Inge	10.00
111	Craig Monroe	8.00
113	Jeremy Bonderman	15.00
116	Troy Percival	15.00
117	Vance Wilson	8.00
123	Miguel Cabrera	35.00
127	Yorman Bazardo	8.00
133	Jason Lane	8.00
136	Morgan Ensberg	15.00
141	Jeremy Affeldt	8.00
143	Ken Harvey	8.00
148	Brad Penny	10.00
150	Dioner Navarro	15.00
151	Edwin Jackson	10.00
158	Milton Bradley	12.00
159	Yhency Brazoban	8.00
161	Bill Hall	10.00
162	Carlos Lee	15.00
166	Lyle Overbay	8.00
168	Jacque Jones	8.00
170	Joe Nathan	12.00
173	Lew Ford	10.00
175	Shannon Stewart	10.00
191	Yuniesky Betancourt	30.00
198	Scott Proctor	10.00
199	Tom Gordon	12.00
201	Bobby Crosby	20.00
202	Danny Haren	10.00
209	Octavio Dotel	10.00
210	Rich Harden	15.00
219	Mike Lieberthal	15.00
221	Randy Wolf	8.00
222	Craig Wilson	8.00
223	Jack Wilson	10.00
224	Jason Bay	15.00
226	Jose Castillo	10.00
229	Akinori Otsuka	20.00
231	Freddy Guzman	8.00
232	Jake Peavy	30.00
234	Mark Loretta	12.00
235	Sean Burroughs	8.00
243	Merkin Valdez	10.00
246	Omar Vizquel	8.00
249	Bucky Jacobsen	10.00
250	Clint Nageotte	15.00
252	J.J. Putz	15.00
254	Miguel Olivo	8.00
260	Jeff Suppan	12.00
266	Yadier Molina	12.00
267	Aubrey Huff	12.00
268	B.J. Upton	20.00
269	Carl Crawford	20.00
271	Delmon Young	25.00
272	Dewon Brazelton	10.00
276	Adrian Gonzalez	10.00
278	Francisco Cordero	10.00
280	Kameron Loe	10.00
282	Laynce Nix	10.00
284	Michael Young	15.00
291	Shea Hillenbrand	12.00
293	Chad Cordero	12.00
295	Jose Guillen	12.00
297	Josh Karp	8.00
298	Livan Hernandez	15.00
299	Nick Johnson	15.00

Private Signings Silver

NM/M

Common Autograph: 8.00

Production 100 Sets

#	Player	Price
1	Casey Kotchman	15.00
2	Chone Figgins	8.00
5	Ervin Santana	8.00
9	Orlando Cabrera	12.00
12	Tim Salmon	12.00
18	Tony Pena	8.00
19	Russ Ortiz	8.00
24	Adam LaRoche	10.00
27	Danny Kolb	8.00
31	Nick Green	8.00
34	Brian Roberts	15.00
36	Jay Gibbons	8.00
49	Jay Payton	8.00
51	Juan Cedeno	8.00
55	Wade Miller	8.00
57	Carlos Zambrano	20.00
65	Todd Walker	10.00
70	Jermaine Dye	12.00
80	Bubba Nelson	8.00
81	Danny Graves	8.00
84	Ryan Wagner	8.00
87	Cliff Lee	8.00
88	Fausto Carmona	8.00
91	Jody Gerut	8.00
94	Travis Hafner	12.00
98	Cory Sullivan	8.00
101	Jeff Salazar	8.00
103	Joe Kennedy	8.00
108	Brandon Inge	8.00
111	Craig Monroe	8.00
113	Jeremy Bonderman	12.00
117	Vance Wilson	8.00
127	Yorman Bazardo	8.00
127	Yorman Bazardo	8.00
133	Jason Lane	8.00
136	Morgan Ensberg	12.00
141	Jeremy Affeldt	8.00
143	Ken Harvey	8.00
150	Dioner Navarro	12.00
151	Edwin Jackson	8.00
158	Milton Bradley	8.00
159	Yhency Brazoban	8.00
161	Bill Hall	8.00
162	Carlos Lee	12.00
166	Lyle Overbay	8.00
170	Joe Nathan	10.00
173	Lew Ford	8.00

191	Yuniesky Betancourt	25.00
198	Scott Proctor	8.00
201	Bobby Crosby	10.00
202	Danny Haren	8.00
209	Octavio Dotel	8.00
210	Rich Harden	12.00
219	Mike Lieberthal	12.00
221	Randy Wolf	8.00
222	Craig Wilson	8.00
223	Jack Wilson	8.00
224	Jason Bay	10.00
226	Jose Castillo	8.00
231	Freddy Guzman	8.00
232	Jake Peavy	25.00
234	Mark Loretta	10.00
250	Clint Nageotte	8.00
252	J.J. Putz	8.00
260	Jeff Suppan	10.00
276	Adrian Gonzalez	8.00
278	Francisco Cordero	8.00
280	Kameron Loe	8.00
282	Laynce Nix	8.00
291	Shea Hillenbrand	10.00
293	Chad Cordero	10.00
295	Jose Guillen	10.00
297	Josh Karp	8.00
298	Livan Hernandez	12.00

Spirit of the Game

NM/M

Common Player:		1.50
Production 600 Sets		
Die-cut:		1-1.5X
Production 125 Sets		
Die-cut Gold:		2-4X
Production 25 Sets		
1	Mark Prior	3.00
2	Sean Casey	1.50
3	Ichiro Suzuki	6.00
4	Andruw Jones	2.00
5	Francisco Cordero	1.50
6	Ben Sheets	2.00
7	Rocco Baldelli	1.50
8	Rafael Furcal	1.50
9	Angel Berroa	1.50
10	Roy Oswalt	1.50
11	Jose Reyes	1.50
12	Shannon Stewart	1.50
13	Greg Maddux	5.00
14	Alfonso Soriano	3.00
15	Curt Schilling	3.00
16	Jody Gerut	1.50
17	Brandon Webb	1.50
18	Josh Beckett	2.00
19	Laynce Nix	1.50
20	Scott Rolen	3.00

Spirit of the Game Bat

NM/M

Production 75-300

1	Mark Prior/300	6.00
4	Andruw Jones/300	6.00
6	Ben Sheets/300	4.00
7	Rocco Baldelli/300	4.00
8	Rafael Furcal/300	4.00
9	Angel Berroa/300	4.00
11	Jose Reyes/300	4.00
12	Shannon Stewart/75	4.00
13	Greg Maddux/300	8.00
14	Alfonso Soriano/225	6.00
16	Jody Gerut/300	4.00
17	Brandon Webb/300	4.00
19	Laynce Nix/300	4.00

Spirit of the Game Combo

NM/M

Production 50 Sets		
Prime:		No Pricing
Production 10 Sets		
1	Mark Prior/Bat-Jsy	12.00
2	Sean Casey/Jsy-Jsy	6.00
4	Andruw Jones/Bat-Jsy	8.00
6	Ben Sheets/Bat-Jsy	6.00
7	Rocco Baldelli/Bat-Jsy	6.00
8	Rafael Furcal/Bat-Jsy	6.00
10	Roy Oswalt/Bat-Jsy	8.00
11	Jose Reyes/Bat-Jsy	8.00
12	Shannon Stewart/Jsy-Jsy	6.00
13	Greg Maddux/Bat-Jsy	15.00
14	Alfonso Soriano/Jsy-Jsy	12.00
15	Curt Schilling/Bat-Jsy	12.00
16	Jody Gerut/Bat-Jsy	6.00
19	Laynce Nix/Bat-Jsy	6.00
20	Scott Rolen/Bat-Jsy	12.00

Spirit of the Game Jersey

NM/M

Production 125-250

Prime:		No Pricing
Production 10 Sets		
1	Mark Prior/250	6.00
2	Sean Casey/250	4.00
4	Andruw Jones/250	6.00
5	Francisco Cordero/250	4.00
6	Ben Sheets/250	4.00
7	Rocco Baldelli/250	4.00
8	Rafael Furcal/250	4.00
10	Roy Oswalt/250	4.00
11	Jose Reyes/250	4.00
12	Shannon Stewart/250	4.00
13	Greg Maddux/250	8.00
14	Alfonso Soriano/250	6.00
15	Curt Schilling/250	6.00
16	Jody Gerut/125	4.00
18	Josh Beckett/250	4.00
19	Laynce Nix/250	4.00
20	Scott Rolen/250	6.00

Spirit of the Game Signature Combo

NM/M

Production 10-25		
Prime:		No Pricing
Production 5-10		
2	Sean Casey/Jsy-Jsy/25	20.00
8	Rafael Furcal/Bat-Jsy/25	25.00
12	Shannon Stewart/Jsy-Jsy/25	20.00
16	Jody Gerut/Bat-Jsy/25	15.00
19	Laynce Nix/Bat-Jsy/25	15.00

Stars

NM/M

Common Player:		1.00
Inserted 1:6		
Gold:		1-2X
Production 500 Sets		
Platinum:		2-4X
Production 50 Sets		
1	Carlos Beltran	1.50
2	Sean Casey	1.00
3	Ichiro Suzuki	3.00
4	Vladimir Guerrero	1.50
5	Tim Hudson	1.50
6	Alex Rodriguez	4.00
7	Miguel Tejada	1.50
8	Curt Schilling	1.50
9	Roger Clemens	4.00
10	Ben Sheets	1.00
11	Todd Helton	1.50
12	Mark Mulder	1.00
13	Scott Podsednik	1.00
14	Victor Martinez	1.00
15	Mark Prior	1.50
16	Ivan Rodriguez	1.50
17	Dontrelle Willis	1.00
18	Andy Pettitte	1.00
19	Khalil Greene	1.50
20	Jeff Kent	1.00
21	Paul Konerko	1.00
22	Joe Mauer	1.50
23	Bobby Crosby	1.00
24	Pedro Martinez	2.00
25	John Smoltz	1.00
26	Derek Jeter	4.00
27	Moises Alou	1.00
28	Rich Harden	1.00
29	Jim Thome	1.50
30	Jason Bay	2.00
31	Aramis Ramirez	3.00
32	Carlos Lee	1.00
33	B.J. Upton	1.00
34	Nomar Garciaparra	1.00
35	Ken Griffey Jr.	1.00
36	Darin Erstad	1.00
37	Larry Walker	1.00
38	Jose Vidro	1.00
39	Zack Greinke	1.00
40	Michael Young	1.00
41	David Wright	2.00
42	Albert Pujols	4.00
43	Vernon Wells	1.00
44	Mark Teixeira	1.50
45	Jacque Jones	1.00
46	Brian Giles	1.00
47	Austin Kearns	1.00
48	Omar Vizquel	1.00
49	Randy Johnson	1.50
50	Jason Varitek	1.50

2005 Donruss Throwback Threads

NM/M

Complete Set (300):		
Common Player:		.20
Pack (5):		3.00
Box (24):		65.00
1	Luis Castillo	.20
2	Derek Jeter	1.50
3	Eric Chavez	.20
4	Angel Berroa	.20
5	Jeff Bagwell	.40
6	J.T. Snow	.20
7	Craig Biggio	.30
8	Michael Barrett	.20
9	Hank Blalock	.40
10	Chipper Jones	.50
11	Jacque Jones	.20
12	Mark Teixeira	.50
13	Omar Vizquel	.20
14	Paul LoDuca	.20
15	Jim Edmonds	.30
16	Aramis Ramirez	.30
17	Lance Berkman	.30
18	Javy Lopez	.30
19	Adam LaRoche	.20
20	Jorge Posada	.40
21	Sean Casey	.20
22	Mark Prior	.40
23	Phil Nevin	.20
24	Manny Ramirez	.50
25	Andruw Jones	.40
26	Matt Lawton	.20
27	Vladimir Guerrero	.50
28	Austin Kearns	.20
29	John Smoltz	.40
30	Ken Griffey Jr.	1.00
31	Mike Piazza	.75
32	Jason Jennings	.20
33	Jason Varitek	.40
34	David Ortiz	.50
35	Mike Mussina	.40
36	Joe Nathan	.20
37	Kenny Rogers	.20
38	Carlos Zambrano	.30
39	Eric Byrnes	.20
40	Clint Barmes	.20
41	Danny Kolb	.20
42	Mariano Rivera	.40
43	Joey Gathright	.20
44	Adam Dunn	.40
45	Carlos Lee	.20
46	Yhency Brazoban	.20
47	Roy Oswalt	.30
48	Torii Hunter	.20
49	Scott Podsednik	.20
50	Jason Hammel RC	.20
51	Ichiro Suzuki	1.00
52	C.C. Sabathia	.20
53	Bobby Abreu	.40
54	Jon Garland	.20
55	Brandon Webb	.20
56	Mark Buehrle	.30
57	Johan Santana	.50
58	Mike Sweeney	.20
59	Tadahito Iguchi RC	1.50
60	Edgar Renteria	.20
61	Aaron Rowand	.20
62	Craig Wilson	.20
63	J.D. Drew	.30
64	Bobby Crosby	.40
65	Justin Morneau	.50
66	Scott Rolen	.20
67	Jose Vidro	.20
68	Carlos Beltran	.40
69	Jeff Weaver	.20
70	Jason Schmidt	.30
71	Brad Wilkerson	.20
72	Yuniesky Betancourt RC	1.50
73	Octavio Dotel	.20
74	Mike Cameron	.20
75	Barry Zito	.40
76	Woody Williams	.20
77	Russel Rohlicek RC	.40
78	Mark Kotsay	.20
79	Jeff Suppan	.20
80	Eric Gagne	.40
81	Tim Salmon	.40
82	Troy Glaus	.40
83	Kevin Mench	.20
84	Ivan Rodriguez	.40
85	Sean Burroughs	.20
86	Dallas McPherson	.20
87	Jamie Moyer	.20
88	Orlando Cabrera	.20
89	Wladimir Balentien RC	1.00
90	Philip Humber RC	1.00
91	Francisco Cordero	.20
92	Danny Graves	.20
93	Bucky Jacobsen	.20
94	Cliff Lee	.20
95	Oliver Perez	.20
96	Jake Peavy	.30
97	Doug Mientkiewicz	.20
98	Brad Radke	.20
99	Jeremy Reed	.20
100	Garret Anderson	.30
101	Rafael Furcal	.20
102	Jack Wilson	.20
103	Bernie Williams	.20
104	Josh Beckett	.20
105	Albert Pujols	1.50
106	Ubaldo Jimenez RC	.40
107	Richard Hidalgo	.20
108	Luke Scott RC	1.00
109	Hideo Nomo	.40
110	Vernon Wells	.30
111	Richie Sexson	.40
112	Chad Cordero	.20
113	Alex Rodriguez	1.50
114	Paul Konerko	.30
115	Carlos Guillen	.20
116	Francisco Rodriguez	.20
117	Johnny Damon	.50
118	David Wright	1.00
119	Lyle Overbay	.20
120	Brian Roberts	.20
121	Sammy Sosa	1.00
122	Roger Clemens	1.50
123	Rickie Weeks	.50
124	Larry Bigbie	.20
125	Rafael Palmeiro	.40
126	Jason Giambi	.30
127	Hideki Matsui	1.00
128	Brad Lidge	.20
129	Jeremy Affeldt	.20
130	Mike MacDougal	.20
131	Troy Percival	.20
132	Matt Morris	.20
133	David Gassner RC	.40
134	Kerry Wood	.40
135	Dontrelle Willis	.40
136	Michael Young	.30
137	Andy Pettitte	.40
138	Kris Benson	.20
139	Miguel Negron RC	.40
140	Rich Harden	.40
141	Bret Boone	.20
142	Danny Rueckel RC	.40
143	Jeff Niemann RC	1.00
144	Randy Messenger RC	.40
145	Pedro Martinez	.50
146	Kazuhisa Ishii	.20
147	Carlos Delgado	.30
148	Tom Glavine	.30
149	Russ Ortiz	.20
150	Gavin Floyd	.20
151	Randy Johnson	.50
152	Prince Fielder	10.00
153	Nomar Garciaparra	.75
154	Pat Burrell	.30
155	Melvin Mora	.20
156	Jose Reyes	.50
157	Trot Nixon	.20
158	B.J. Upton	.20
159	Jody Gerut	.20
160	Juan Pierre	.40
161	Miguel Tejada	.40
162	Barry Larkin	.40
163	Carl Crawford	.20
164	Ben Sheets	.30
165	Tim Hudson	.40
166	Darin Erstad	.20
167	Todd Helton	.40
168	Luis Gonzalez	.30
169	Mark Mulder	.20
170	David Dellucci	.20
171	Marcus Giles	.20
172	Shannon Stewart	.20
173	Zack Greinke	.20
174	Miguel Cabrera	.50
175	Nick Johnson	.20
176	Derrek Lee	.50
177	Jim Thome	.40
178	Ken Harvey	.20
179	Ambiorix Concepcion RC	.40
180	Roy Halladay	.30
181	Larry Walker	.40
182	Greg Maddux	1.00
183	Frank Thomas	.50
184	Travis Hafner	.30
185	Matt Holliday	.50
186	Victor Martinez	.20
187	Jason Isringhausen	.20
188	Bill Mueller	.20
189	Dewon Brazelton	.20
190	Adrian Beltre	.40
191	Tim Wakefield	.20
192	Alexis Rios	.20
193	Alfonso Soriano	.50
194	Fernando Vina	.20
195	Armando Benitez	.20
196	Bartolo Colon	.30
197	A.J. Burnett	.20
198	Milton Bradley	.20
199	Brad Penny	.20
200	Rocco Baldelli	.20
201	Curt Schilling	.20
202	Ryan Wagner	.20
203	Preston Wilson	.20
204	Akinori Otsuka	.20
205	Bill McCarthy RC	.40

206	Edgardo Alfonzo	.20
207	Mike Lieberthal	.20
208	Shea Hillenbrand	.20
209	Tom Gordon	.20
210	Kip Wells	.20
211	Frank Catalanotto	.20
212	Casey Kotchman	.20
213	Justin Verlander RC	1.50
214	Brandon Inge	.20
215	Terrmel Sledge	.20
216	Gary Sheffield	.40
217	Steve Finley	.20
218	Kenny Lofton	.20
219	Chris Carpenter	.30
220	Danny Haren	.20
221	Brett Myers	.20
222	Joe Mauer	.50
223	David Wells	.20
224	Brian Giles	.20
225	Moises Alou	.30
226	Casey Rogowski RC	.40
227	Chase Utley	.50
228	Corey Koskie	.20
229	Derek Lowe	.20
230	Erick Threets RC	.40
231	Grady Sizemore	.40
232	Jason Lane	.20
233	Jeremy Bonderman	.20
234	Livan Hernandez	.20
235	Ryan Klesko	.20
236	Sidney Ponson	.20
237	Jimmy Rollins	.40
238	Eric Milton	.20
239	Shingo Takatsu	.20
240	Scott Kazmir	.20
241	Shawn Green	.30
242	Nick Swisher	.20
243	Shawn Chacon	.20
244	Javier Vazquez	.20
245	Mark Loretta	.20
246	Dmitri Young	.20
247	Charles Johnson	.20
248	Magglio Ordonez	.30
249	Sean Thompson RC	.40
250	Jared Gothreaux RC	.40
251	Kevin Millwood	.20
252	Mike Lowell	.20
253	Cristian Guzman	.20
254	Nate McLouth RC	.40
255	Delmon Young	.40
256	Jeromy Burnitz	.20
257	Garrett Atkins	.20
258	Junior Spivey	.20
259	Morgan Ensberg	.20
260	Chone Figgins	.20
261	Hayden Penn RC	.50
262	Jason Bay	.20
263	Jose Cruz Jr.	.20
264	Khalil Greene	.40
265	Ray Durham	.20
266	Juan Gonzalez	.40
267	Jeff Kent	.20
268	Dioner Navarro	.20
269	Rodrigo Lopez	.20
270	Geoff Jenkins	.20
271	Jermaine Dye	.20
272	Orlando Hudson	.20
273	Jose Lima	.20
274	Jeff Francis	.20
275	Luis Matos	.20
276	Jason Kendall	.20
277	Mike Hampton	.20
278	Al Kaline	.75
279	Bert Blyleven	.20
280	Bill Madlock	.20
281	Cal Ripken Jr.	3.00
282	Dale Murphy	.50
283	Gary Carter	.50
284	George Brett	2.00
285	Harmon Killebrew	1.00
286	Harold Baines	.40
287	John Kruk	.50
288	Keith Hernandez	.40
289	Willie Mays	3.00
290	Matt Williams	.20
291	Nolan Ryan	2.50
292	Paul Molitor	.50
293	Reggie Jackson	.75
294	Rickey Henderson	.50
295	Ron Cey	.20
296	Ryne Sandberg	1.00
297	Ted Williams	2.50
298	Tom Seaver	.50
299	Tony Gwynn	.75
300	Babe Ruth/SP	20.00

Century Stars

		NM/M
Common Player:		1.00
Spectrum:		1.5-3X
Production 100 Sets		
1	Bobby Doerr	1.00
2	Derek Jeter	4.00
3	Harmon Killebrew	1.50
4	Paul Molitor	1.50
5	Brooks Robinson	1.50
6	Steve Garvey	1.00
7	Ivan Rodriguez	1.00
8	Carl Yastrzemski	2.50
9	Nomar Garciaparra	2.00
10	Miguel Tejada	1.00
11	Edgar Martinez	1.00
12	Kevin Brown	1.00
13	Alex Rodriguez	3.00
14	Carlton Fisk	1.00
15	Craig Biggio	1.00
16	Dwight Gooden	1.00
17	Jim Palmer	1.00
18	Ken Griffey Jr.	2.00
19	Bob Feller	1.50
20	Don Sutton	1.00
21	Al Kaline	1.50
22	Roger Clemens	4.00
23	Kirk Gibson	1.00
24	Willie Mays	3.00
25	Frank Robinson	1.00
26	Randy Johnson	1.50
27	Jim "Catfish" Hunter	1.00
28	Austin Kearns	1.00
29	John Smoltz	1.00
30	Nolan Ryan	4.00
31	Duke Snider	1.50
32	Bernie Williams	1.00
33	David Wells	1.00
34	Bo Jackson	1.50
35	Mike Mussina	1.00
36	Gaylord Perry	1.00
37	Andre Dawson	1.00
38	Curt Schilling	1.50
39	Darryl Strawberry	1.00
40	Willie McCovey	1.00
41	Tom Seaver	1.50
42	Mariano Rivera	1.00
43	Dennis Eckersley	1.00
44	David Cone	1.00
45	Bret Boone	1.00
46	Will Clark	1.00
47	Jack Morris	1.00
48	Ichiro Suzuki	3.00
49	Alan Trammell	1.00
50	Cal Ripken Jr.	4.00

Century Stars Material

		NM/M
Common Player:		4.00
Production 20-50		
Prime:		No Pricing
Production Five Sets		
1	Bobby Doerr/Pants/50	8.00
3	Harmon Killebrew/Jsy/50	15.00
4	Paul Molitor/Jsy/50	10.00
5	Brooks Robinson/Bat/50	10.00
6	Steve Garvey/Jsy/50	4.00
7	Ivan Rodriguez/Jsy/50	8.00
8	Carl Yastrzemski/Jsy/50	15.00
10	Miguel Tejada/Jsy/50	6.00
11	Edgar Martinez/Jsy/50	6.00
12	Kevin Brown/Jsy/50	4.00
14	Carlton Fisk/Jsy/50	8.00
15	Craig Biggio/Jsy/50	8.00
16	Dwight Gooden/Jsy/50	4.00
17	Jim Palmer/Jsy/50	6.00
20	Don Sutton/Jsy/50	4.00
21	Al Kaline/Bat/50	15.00
22	Roger Clemens/Jsy/50	15.00
23	Kirk Gibson/Jsy/50	4.00
25	Frank Robinson/Bat/50	6.00
26	Randy Johnson/Jsy/50	8.00
28	Austin Kearns/Jsy/50	4.00
29	John Smoltz/Jsy/50	8.00
30	Nolan Ryan/Jkt/50	25.00
32	Bernie Williams/Jsy/50	6.00
33	David Wells/Jsy/50	4.00
34	Bo Jackson/Jsy/50	10.00
35	Mike Mussina/Jsy/50	8.00
36	Gaylord Perry/Jsy/50	6.00
37	Andre Dawson/Jsy/50	6.00
38	Curt Schilling/Jsy/50	8.00
39	Darryl Strawberry/Jsy/50	6.00
40	Willie McCovey/Jsy/50	8.00
42	Mariano Rivera/Jsy/50	10.00
43	Dennis Eckersley/Jsy/50	6.00
44	David Cone/Jsy/50	4.00
45	Bret Boone/Jsy/50	4.00
47	Jack Morris/Jsy/50	4.00
49	Alan Trammell/Jsy/50	6.00
50	Cal Ripken Jr./Jsy/50	30.00

Century Stars Signatrue Material

No Pricing
Production 10 Sets
Prime: No Pricing
Production Five Sets

Dynasty

		NM/M
Common Trio:		2.00
Spectrum:		1.25X
Production 100 Sets		
1	Reggie Jackson, Jim "Catfish" Hunter, Sparky Lyle	2.00
2	Cal Ripken Jr., Jim Palmer, Eddie Murray	8.00
3	Dwight Gooden, Gary Carter, Darryl Strawberry	2.00
4	Rickey Henderson, Dennis Eckersley, Jose Canseco	2.00
5	Chipper Jones, Greg Maddux, David Justice	3.00
6	Roger Clemens, Alfonso Soriano, Bernie Williams	6.00
7	Randy Johnson, Curt Schilling, Matt Williams	3.00
8	Troy Glaus, Garret Anderson, Francisco Rodriguez	2.00
9	Josh Beckett, Miguel Cabrera, Mike Lowell	2.00
10	Curt Schilling, Manny Ramirez, Jason Varitek	8.00

Dynasty Material

		NM/M
Production 20-50		
Prime:		No Pricing
Production Five Sets		
1	Reggie Jackson/Pants, Jim "Catfish" Hunter/Pants, Sparky Lyle/Pants/50	20.00
2	Cal Ripken Jr./Jsy, Jim Palmer/Jsy, Eddie Murray/Jsy/50	40.00
3	Dwight Gooden/Jsy, Gary Carter/Jsy, Darryl Strawberry/Pants/20	15.00
4	Rickey Henderson/Jsy, Dennis Eckersley/Pants, Jose Canseco/Jsy/50	35.00
5	Chipper Jones/Jsy, Greg Maddux/Jsy, David Justice/Jsy/50	25.00
6	Roger Clemens/Jsy, Alfonso Soriano/Jsy, Bernie Williams/Jsy/50	30.00
7	Randy Johnson/Jsy, Curt Schilling/Jsy, Matt Williams/Jsy/50	20.00
8	Troy Glaus/Jsy, Garret Anderson/Jsy, Francisco Rodriguez/Jsy/50	15.00
9	Josh Beckett/Jsy, Miguel Cabrera/Jsy, Mike Lowell/Jsy/20	
10	Curt Schilling/Jsy, Manny Ramirez/Jsy, Jason Varitek/Jsy/50	40.00

Generations

		NM/M
Common Player:		2.00
Spectrum:		1-2.5X
Production 100 Sets		
1	Duke Snider, Reggie Jackson, Sammy Sosa	2.00
2	Rod Carew, John Kruk, Eric Chavez	2.00
3	Bo Jackson, Deion Sanders, Brian Jordan	3.00
4	Brett George, Tony Gwynn, Todd Helton	4.00
5	Babe Ruth, Ted Williams, Willie Mays	5.00
6	Rickey Henderson, Lenny Dykstra, Ichiro Suzuki	3.00
7	Keith Hernandez, Don Mattingly, Casey Kotchman	3.00
8	Wade Boggs, Mark Grace, Hank Blalock	2.00
9	Gary Carter, Ivan Rodriguez, Victor Martinez	2.00
10	Gaylord Perry, Morris, Greg Maddux	2.00
11	Joe Morgan, Ryne Sandberg, Alfonso Soriano	3.00
12	Juan Marichal, Luis Tiant, Pedro Martinez	2.00
13	Stan Musial, Carl Yastrzemski, Lance Berkman	3.00
14	Johnny Bench, Carlton Fisk, Mike Piazza	3.00
15	Harmon Killebrew, Cal Ripken Jr., Albert Pujols	5.00
16	Frank Robinson, Andre Dawson, Gary Sheffield	2.00
17	Bob Feller, Roger Clemens, Kerry Wood	4.00
18	Steve Carlton, Tom Glavine, Barry Zito	2.00
19	Murray, Rafael Palmeiro, Mark Teixeira	2.00
20	Brooks Robinson, Mike Schmidt, Scott Rolen	3.00
21	Luis Aparicio, Omar Vizquel, Rafael Furcal	2.00
22	Don Sutton, David Cone, Roy Oswalt	2.00
23	Fred Lynn, Dale Murphy, Jim Edmonds	2.00
24	Ozzie, Barry Larkin, B.J. Upton	3.00
25	Gibson, Nolan Ryan, Mark Prior	4.00

Generations Material

		NM/M
Production 20-50		
Prime:		No Pricing
Production 10 Sets		
2	Rod Carew/Jsy, John Kruk/Jsy, Eric Chavez/Jsy/50	15.00
3	Bo Jackson/Jsy, Deion Sanders/Jsy, Brian Jordan/Jsy/50	25.00
4	Brett George/Jsy, Tony Gwynn/Jsy, Todd Helton/Jsy/50	25.00
7	Keith Hernandez/Jsy, Don Mattingly/Pants, Casey Kotchman/Jsy/20	30.00
8	Wade Boggs/Jsy, Mark Grace/Jsy, Hank Blalock/Jsy/50	15.00
9	Gary Carter/Jsy, Ivan Rodriguez/Jsy, Victor Martinez/Jsy/50	15.00
10	Gaylord Perry/Jsy, Morris/Jsy, Greg Maddux/Jsy/50	25.00
11	Joe Morgan/Jsy, Ryne Sandberg/Jsy, Alfonso Soriano/Jsy/50	35.00
12	Juan Marichal/Pants, Luis Tiant/Pants, Pedro Martinez/Jsy/50	20.00
13	Johnny Bench/Pants, Carlton Fisk/Jsy, Mike Piazza/Jsy/50	20.00
15	Harmon Killebrew/Jsy, Cal Ripken Jr./Jsy, Albert Pujols/Jsy/50	50.00
16	Frank Robinson/Bat, Andre Dawson/Jsy, Gary Sheffield/Jsy/20	15.00
17	Bob Feller/Pants, Roger Clemens/Jsy, Kerry Wood/Jsy/50	50.00
18	Steve Carlton/Jsy, Tom Glavine/Jsy, Barry Zito/Jsy/50	20.00
19	Murray/Jsy, Rafael Palmeiro/Jsy, Mark Teixeira/Jsy/50	20.00

Material Bat

		NM/M
Common Player:		4.00
Production 5-250		
1	Luis Castillo/250	4.00
4	Angel Berroa/250	4.00
5	Jeff Bagwell/250	6.00
7	Craig Biggio/250	6.00
14	Paul LoDuca/250	4.00
17	Lance Berkman/250	4.00
18	Javy Lopez/250	4.00
21	Sean Casey/50	6.00
25	Andruw Jones/250	6.00
26	Matt Lawton/250	4.00
28	Austin Kearns/250	4.00
32	Jason Jennings/250	4.00
33	Jason Varitek/50	12.00
34	David Ortiz/250	8.00
43	Joey Gathright/250	4.00
48	Torii Hunter/250	4.00
55	Brandon Webb/250	4.00
58	Mike Sweeney/250	4.00
62	Craig Wilson/250	4.00
63	J.D. Drew/250	4.00
67	Jose Vidro/250	4.00
68	Carlos Beltran/250	6.00
81	Tim Salmon/250	4.00
82	Troy Glaus/250	4.00
83	Kevin Mench/250	4.00
101	Rafael Furcal/150	4.00
102	Jack Wilson/250	4.00
103	Bernie Williams/250	4.00
107	Richard Hidalgo/250	4.00
111	Richie Sexson/100	6.00
121	Sammy Sosa/50	8.00
123	Rickie Weeks/25	6.00
125	Rafael Palmeiro/250	6.00
135	Dontrelle Willis/50	6.00
136	Michael Young/250	4.00
141	Bret Boone/50	6.00
147	Carlos Delgado/250	4.00
148	Tom Glavine/250	4.00
153	Nomar Garciaparra/ 150	8.00
154	Pat Burrell/150	4.00
156	Jose Reyes/50	6.00
157	Trot Nixon/25	
158	B.J. Upton/250	6.00
159	Jody Gerut/250	4.00
160	Juan Pierre/250	4.00
162	Barry Larkin/100	6.00
164	Ben Sheets/250	4.00
165	Tim Hudson/50	6.00
166	Darin Erstad/250	4.00
168	Luis Gonzalez/25	6.00
169	Mark Mulder/35	6.00
174	Miguel Cabrera/50	10.00
175	Nick Johnson/250	4.00
176	Derrek Lee/50	8.00
192	Alex Rios/50	4.00
197	A.J. Burnett/250	4.00
200	Rocco Baldelli/250	4.00
203	Preston Wilson/150	4.00
206	Edgardo Alfonzo/250	4.00
212	Casey Kotchman/250	4.00
215	Terrmel Sledge/250	4.00
218	Kenny Lofton/150	4.00
224	Brian Giles/35	6.00
225	Moises Alou/250	6.00
232	Jason Lane/250	4.00
235	Ryan Klesko/250	4.00
241	Shawn Green/250	4.00
247	Charles Johnson/250	4.00
248	Magglio Ordonez/250	4.00
252	Mike Lowell/250	4.00
255	Delmon Young/250	4.00
259	Morgan Ensberg/250	6.00
260	Chone Figgins/250	4.00
262	Jason Bay/175	6.00
265	Ray Durham/200	6.00
266	Juan Gonzalez/250	6.00
267	Jeff Kent/250	4.00
272	Orlando Hudson/250	4.00
280	Bill Madlock/100	4.00
281	Cal Ripken Jr./150	25.00
283	Gary Carter/25	8.00
284	George Brett/25	25.00
286	Harold Baines/50	6.00
288	Keith Hernandez/25	8.00
289	Willie Mays/25	35.00
291	Nolan Ryan/50	25.00
292	Paul Molitor/150	6.00
293	Reggie Jackson/25	10.00
294	Rickey Henderson/250	8.00
296	Ryne Sandberg/25	15.00
297	Ted Williams/25	50.00
299	Tony Gwynn/50	10.00
300	Babe Ruth/25	180.00

Material Combo

	NM/M
Common Player:	6.00
Production 10-100	

Prime: 1-2X
Production 5-40
No pricing 20 or less.

1	Luis Castillo/ Bat-Jsy/90	6.00
3	Eric Chavez/ Bat-Jsy/25	8.00
5	Jeff Bagwell/ Bat-Jsy/100	8.00
7	Craig Biggio/ Bat-Jsy/25	10.00
12	Mark Teixeira/ Bat-Jsy/25	10.00
17	Lance Berkman/ Bat-Jsy/100	6.00
21	Sean Casey/ Bat-Jsy/50	6.00
22	Mark Prior/Bat-Jsy/25	10.00
25	Andruw Jones/ Bat-Jsy/100	8.00
32	Jason Jennings/ Bat-Jsy/100	6.00
34	David Ortiz/ Bat-Jsy/25	20.00
43	Joey Gathright/ Bat-Jsy/50	6.00
55	Brandon Webb/ Bat-Pants/100	6.00
58	Mike Sweeney/ Bat-Jsy/50	6.00
62	Craig Wilson/ Bat-Jsy/100	6.00
67	Jose Vidro/ Bat-Jsy/100	6.00
83	Kevin Mench/ Bat-Jsy/100	6.00
101	Rafael Furcal/ Bat-Jsy/100	6.00
103	Bernie Williams/ Bat-Jsy/50	8.00
104	Josh Beckett/ Bat-Jsy/25	8.00
110	Vernon Wells/ Hat-Jsy/100	6.00
124	Larry Bigbie/ Jsy-Jsy/100	6.00
126	Jason Giambi/ Jsy-Jsy/100	8.00
136	Michael Young/ Bat-Jsy/50	8.00
146	Kazuhisa Ishii/ Hat-Jsy/25	10.00
154	Pat Burrell/Bat-Jsy/50	8.00
156	Jose Reyes/ Bat-Jsy/25	8.00
157	Trot Nixon/Bat-Jsy/25	10.00
160	Juan Pierre/ Bat-Fld Glv/95	6.00
164	Ben Sheets/ Bat-Jsy/100	8.00
168	Luis Gonzalez/ Jsy-Jsy/100	6.00
171	Marcus Giles/ Hat-Jsy/50	6.00
172	Shannon Stewart/ Jsy-Jsy/30	6.00
174	Miguel Cabrera/ Bat-Jsy/25	12.00
180	Roy Halladay/ Jsy-Jsy/85	8.00
183	Frank Thomas/ Bat-Jsy/15	15.00
186	Victor Martinez/ Fld Glv-Jsy/40	8.00
197	A.J. Burnett/ Bat-Jsy/100	6.00
200	Rocco Baldelli/ Bat-Jsy/100	6.00
201	Curt Schilling/ Bat-Jsy/85	12.00
202	Ryan Wagner/ Jsy-Jsy/100	6.00
203	Preston Wilson/ Bat-Jsy/85	6.00
212	Casey Kotchman/ Bat-Jsy/100	6.00
218	Kenny Lofton/ Bat-Fld Glv/100	6.00
232	Jason Lane/ Bat-Hat/50	6.00
235	Ryan Klesko/ Hat-Jsy/100	6.00
252	Mike Lowell/ Bat-Jsy/100	6.00
257	Garrett Atkins/ Jsy-Jsy/100	6.00
259	Morgan Ensberg/ Hat-Jsy/100	8.00
260	Chone Figgins/ Bat-Jsy/65	6.00
262	Jason Bay/Bat-Jsy/40	8.00
272	Orlando Hudson/ Bat-Jsy/40	6.00
275	Luis Matos/Jsy-Jsy/50	6.00
281	Cal Ripken Jr./ Bat-Jsy/50	40.00
283	Gary Carter/ Jsy-Pants/25	15.00
284	George Brett/ Bat-Jsy/25	30.00
286	Harold Baines/ Bat-Jsy/50	10.00
288	Keith Hernandez/ Bat-Jsy/25	10.00
289	Willie Mays/ Bat-Pants/25	50.00
291	Nolan Ryan/ Bat-Jsy/25	25.00
292	Paul Molitor/ Bat-Jsy/25	15.00
293	Reggie Jackson/ Bat-Jsy/25	15.00
294	Rickey Henderson/ Bat-Jsy/25	15.00
296	Ryne Sandberg/ Bat-Jsy/25	25.00
297	Ted Williams/ Bat-Jsy/25	75.00
298	Tom Seaver/ Jsy-Pants/25	15.00
299	Tony Gwynn/ Jsy-Pants/50	15.00
300	Babe Ruth/ Bat-Jsy/25	375.00

Material Jersey

		NM/M
Common Player:		4.00
Production 5-250		
Prime:		1-2X
Production 10-100		
No pricing 20 or less.		
1	Luis Castillo/45	4.00
3	Eric Chavez/250	4.00
5	Jeff Bagwell/250	6.00
6	J.T. Snow/250	4.00
7	Craig Biggio/50	6.00
9	Hank Blalock/25	6.00
10	Chipper Jones/250	8.00
11	Jacque Jones/250	4.00
12	Mark Teixeira/150	6.00
15	Jim Edmonds/250	6.00
16	Aramis Ramirez/250	6.00
17	Lance Berkman/250	4.00
18	Javy Lopez/250	4.00
20	Jorge Posada/250	6.00
21	Sean Casey/250	4.00
22	Mark Prior/50	4.00
23	Phil Nevin/50	4.00
24	Manny Ramirez/250	8.00
25	Andruw Jones/250	6.00
27	Vladimir Guerrero/250	8.00
28	Austin Kearns/250	4.00
29	John Smoltz/250	8.00
31	Mike Piazza/250	8.00
32	Jason Jennings/250	4.00
34	David Ortiz/250	10.00
35	Mike Mussina/250	6.00
36	Carlos Zambrano/250	6.00
42	Mariano Rivera/250	8.00
43	Joey Gathright/100	4.00
44	Adam Dunn/250	6.00
47	Roy Oswalt/250	4.00
48	Torii Hunter/100	4.00
52	C.C. Sabathia/250	4.00
53	Bobby Abreu/250	4.00
56	Mark Buehrle/250	4.00
57	Johan Santana/250	6.00
58	Mike Sweeney/75	4.00
62	Craig Wilson/250	4.00
64	Bobby Crosby/100	6.00
66	Scott Rolen/250	6.00
67	Jose Vidro/75	4.00
74	Mike Cameron/250	4.00
75	Barry Zito/250	4.00
83	Kevin Mench/250	4.00
84	Ivan Rodriguez/250	6.00
87	Jamie Moyer/50	4.00
91	Francisco Cordero/250	4.00
94	Cliff Lee/250	4.00
98	Brad Radke/250	4.00
100	Garret Anderson/50	4.00
101	Rafael Furcal/100	4.00
102	Jack Wilson/15	
103	Bernie Williams/250	6.00
104	Josh Beckett/250	6.00
105	Albert Pujols/250	15.00
109	Hideo Nomo/250	8.00
110	Vernon Wells/250	4.00
114	Paul Konerko/250	4.00
116	Francisco Rodriguez/ 250	4.00
117	Johnny Damon/250	8.00
118	David Wright/250	10.00
119	Lyle Overbay/250	4.00
120	Brian Roberts/100	4.00
122	Roger Clemens/100	12.00
124	Larry Bigbie/200	4.00
125	Rafael Palmeiro/250	6.00
126	Jason Giambi/250	6.00
127	Hideki Matsui/250	15.00
134	Kerry Wood/250	6.00
135	Dontrelle Willis/250	6.00
136	Michael Young/250	4.00
137	Andy Pettitte/250	6.00
141	Bret Boone/250	4.00
146	Kazuhisa Ishii/250	4.00
147	Carlos Delgado/250	4.00
148	Tom Glavine/250	8.00
154	Pat Burrell/250	4.00
155	Melvin Mora/250	4.00
156	Jose Reyes/200	6.00
157	Trot Nixon/250	4.00
158	B.J. Upton/250	4.00
159	Jody Gerut/100	4.00
161	Miguel Tejada/35	8.00
162	Barry Larkin/40	4.00
163	Carl Crawford/40	4.00
164	Ben Sheets/250	6.00
166	Darin Erstad/25	6.00
167	Todd Helton/150	6.00
168	Luis Gonzalez/250	4.00
170	David Dellucci/150	4.00
172	Shannon Stewart/250	4.00
174	Miguel Cabrera/100	8.00
176	Derrek Lee/250	6.00
177	Jim Thome/250	6.00
178	Ken Harvey/150	4.00
180	Roy Halladay/250	4.00
182	Greg Maddux/250	8.00
186	Victor Martinez/250	4.00
189	Dewon Brazelton/250	4.00
190	Adrian Beltre/250	4.00
193	Alfonso Soriano/250	8.00
197	A.J. Burnett/250	4.00
200	Rocco Baldelli/250	8.00
201	Curt Schilling/250	4.00
202	Ryan Wagner/250	4.00
203	Preston Wilson/250	4.00
211	Frank Catalanotto/250	4.00
212	Casey Kotchman/250	4.00
214	Brandon Inge/250	4.00
221	Brett Myers/50	4.00
232	Jason Lane/95	4.00
233	Jeremy Bonderman/ 250	4.00
234	Livan Hernandez/250	4.00
235	Ryan Klesko/250	4.00
237	Jimmy Rollins/35	6.00
252	Mike Lowell/250	4.00
257	Garrett Atkins/250	4.00
258	Junior Spivey/250	4.00
259	Morgan Ensberg/150	4.00
260	Chone Figgins/250	4.00
262	Jason Bay/250	6.00
269	Rodrigo Lopez/250	4.00
270	Geoff Jenkins/250	4.00
275	Luis Matos/250	4.00
279	Bert Blyleven/50	6.00
281	Cal Ripken Jr./50	30.00
282	Dale Murphy/25	10.00
283	Gary Carter/50	8.00
284	George Brett/50	15.00
285	Harmon Killebrew/25	15.00
286	Harold Baines/50	6.00
287	John Kruk/25	8.00
289	Willie Mays Pants/25	40.00
290	Matt Williams/50	4.00
291	Nolan Ryan/50	25.00
292	Paul Molitor/50	10.00
293	Reggie Jackson/25	8.00
294	Rickey Henderson/50	10.00
295	Ron Cey/50	6.00
296	Ryne Sandberg/50	15.00
297	Ted Williams/25	60.00
298	Tom Seaver/25	15.00
299	Tony Gwynn/50	12.00
300	Babe Ruth/25	200.00

Player Timelines

		NM/M
Common Player:		1.00
Spectrum:		1-2.5X
Production 100 Sets		
1	Dale Murphy	2.00
2	Greg Maddux	3.00
3	Tom Glavine	2.00
4	David Ortiz	3.00
5	Bo Jackson	2.00
6	Lyle Overbay	1.00
7	Tommy John	1.00
8	Shawn Green	1.00
9	Aramis Ramirez	1.50
10	Javy Lopez	1.00
11	Vladimir Guerrero	3.00
12	Travis Hafner	1.00
13	Junior Spivey	1.00
14	Alfonso Soriano	2.00
15	Andre Dawson	1.00
16	Sammy Sosa	3.00
17	Andy Pettitte	1.50
18	Jim Edmonds	1.50
19	Willie McCovey	2.00

20	Scott Rolen	2.00
21	Jermaine Dye	1.00
22	Pedro Martinez	2.50
23	Don Sutton	1.00
24	Randy Johnson	2.00
25	Nolan Ryan	3.00
26	Dennis Eckersley	1.00
27	Reggie Jackson	2.00
28	Deion Sanders	1.00
29	Curt Schilling	2.00
30	Rickey Henderson	1.00
31	Mike Piazza	2.00
32	Gary Carter	1.00
33	Roberto Alomar	1.00
34	Hideo Nomo	1.00
35	Andres Galarraga	1.00
36	Juan Gonzalez	1.00
37	Roger Clemens	4.00
38	Jeff Kent	1.00
39	Steve Carlton	1.00
40	Wade Boggs	1.50

Player Timeline Mat.

NM/M

Production 25-250

1	Dale Murphy/50	10.00
2	Greg Maddux/100	10.00
3	Tom Glavine/50	8.00
4	David Ortiz/250	10.00
5	Bo Jackson/100	12.00
6	Lyle Overbay/250	4.00
7	Tommy John/Pants/250	4.00
8	Shawn Green/100	4.00
9	Aramis Ramirez/250	6.00
10	Javy Lopez/100	4.00
11	Vladimir Guerrero/25	15.00
12	Travis Hafner/25	8.00
13	Junior Spivey/250	4.00
14	Alfonso Soriano/100	6.00
16	Sammy Sosa/250	8.00
17	Andy Pettitte/100	8.00
18	Jim Edmonds/100	8.00
19	Willie McCovey/Pants/250	12.00
20	Scott Rolen/50	10.00
21	Jermaine Dye/100	4.00
22	Pedro Martinez/50	12.00
23	Don Sutton/25	10.00
24	Randy Johnson/25	15.00
25	Nolan Ryan/Jkt/50	40.00
27	Reggie Jackson/Pants/250	15.00
28	Deion Sanders/25	15.00
29	Curt Schilling/50	10.00
30	Rickey Henderson/Pants/100	15.00
31	Mike Piazza/50	15.00
32	Gary Carter Pants/50	10.00
33	Roberto Alomar/250	8.00
34	Hideo Nomo/50	15.00
35	Andres Galarraga/250	6.00
36	Juan Gonzalez/25	8.00
37	Roger Clemens/25	30.00
38	Jeff Kent/50	6.00

Player Timelines Signature Material

NM/M

Production 5-50

Prime: No Pricing

Production 5-10

1	Dale Murphy/50	30.00
6	Lyle Overbay/50	12.00
7	Tommy John/Pants/50	15.00
12	Travis Hafner/50	20.00
13	Junior Spivey/50	12.00
15	Andre Dawson/25	25.00
21	Jermaine Dye/50	15.00
23	Don Sutton/25	20.00
32	Gary Carter/Pants/50	20.00
36	Juan Gonzalez/25	40.00

Polo Grounds 85 HIT Long Fly

NM/M

Common Player: 1.50
Production 85 Sets
Parallel #'d 40-75: .75-1.5X
Parallel #'d 20-35: 1-2X
No pricing 15 or less.

1	Ken Griffey Jr.	4.00
2	Roger Clemens	6.00
3	Barry Zito	2.00
4	Alex Rodriguez	5.00
5	Melvin Mora	1.50
6	Kevin Brown	1.50
7	Chipper Jones	3.00
8	Scott Kazmir	2.00
9	Kip Wells	1.50
10	Khalil Greene	2.00

11	Kevin Millwood	1.50
12	Kerry Wood	2.00
13	Mark Kotsay	1.50
14	Jeff Bagwell	2.00
15	Hank Blalock	2.00
16	Scott Rolen	2.00
17	Lance Berkman	2.00
18	Mike Mussina	2.00
19	Jim Edmonds	2.00
20	Jorge Posada	2.00
21	Curt Schilling	3.00
22	Vernon Wells	1.50
23	Pedro Martinez	3.00
24	Jeremy Reed	1.50
25	Hideki Matsui	4.00
26	Steve Finley	1.50
27	Gavin Floyd	1.50
28	Darin Erstad	1.50
29	Bernie Williams	2.00
30	Mark Mulder	2.00
31	Rafael Palmeiro	2.00
32	Andruw Jones	2.00
33	Roy Halladay	2.00
34	Dontrelle Willis	2.00
35	Bret Boone	1.50
36	Andy Pettitte	2.00
37	Vladimir Guerrero	3.00
38	Randy Johnson	3.00
39	Michael Young	2.00
40	Frank Thomas	2.00
41	Todd Helton	2.00
42	Johan Santana	3.00
43	Mark Teixeira	2.00
44	Justin Morneau	1.50
45	Brad Radke	1.50
46	Dallas McPherson	1.50
47	Tim Hudson	1.50
48	Carl Crawford	1.50
49	Eric Gagne	2.00
50	Mark Prior	3.00
51	Tom Glavine	2.00
52	Craig Biggio	2.00
53	John Smoltz	2.00
54	Manny Ramirez	3.00
55	Ivan Rodriguez	2.00
56	Gary Sheffield	2.00
57	Josh Beckett	2.00
58	Miguel Tejada	2.00
59	Bobby Abreu	2.00
60	Ichiro Suzuki	4.00
61	Sammy Sosa	2.50
62	Garret Anderson	2.00
63	Sean Casey	1.50
64	Troy Glaus	2.00
65	Larry Walker	2.00
66	Alfonso Soriano	2.00
67	Luis Gonzalez	2.00
68	Eric Chavez	2.00
69	Adrian Beltre	2.00
70	Miguel Cabrera	3.00
71	Carlos Beltran	2.00
72	Jim Thome	2.00
73	David Ortiz	3.00
74	Adam Dunn	2.00
75	Jacque Jones	1.50
76	Shawn Green	1.50
77	Victor Martinez	1.50
78	Torii Hunter	1.50
79	Carlos Lee	1.50
80	C.C. Sabathia	1.50
81	Joe Mauer	2.00
82	Kris Benson	1.50
83	Zack Greinke	1.50
84	Greg Maddux	4.00
85	David Wright	4.00
86	Mike Piazza	4.00
87	Johnny Damon	3.00
88	Derek Jeter	6.00
89	B.J. Upton	1.50
90	Albert Pujols	6.00
91	Cal Ripken Jr.	6.00
92	Nolan Ryan	5.00
93	George Brett	5.00
94	Don Mattingly	4.00
95	Ryne Sandberg	4.00
96	Rickey Henderson	3.00
97	Robin Yount	3.00
98	Mike Schmidt	4.00
99	Tony Gwynn	3.00
100	Willie Mays	5.00

Signature Marks

NM/M

Production 5-1,000

4	Angel Berroa/25	12.00
19	Adam LaRoche/50	20.00
36	Joe Nathan/25	20.00
38	Carlos Zambrano/25	30.00
39	Eric Byrnes/50	10.00
41	Danny Kolb/25	10.00
45	Carlos Lee/25	20.00
49	Scott Podsednik/20	20.00
52	C.C. Sabathia/25	15.00
56	Mark Buehrle/25	30.00
62	Craig Wilson/25	10.00

64	Bobby Crosby/100	15.00
67	Jose Vidro/25	15.00
73	Octavio Dotel/25	12.00
77	Russel Rohlicek/250	5.00
81	Tim Salmon/50	20.00
85	Sean Burroughs/25	10.00
87	Jamie Moyer/25	15.00
88	Orlando Cabrera/25	20.00
90	Philip Humber/50	20.00
91	Francisco Cordero/50	10.00
92	Danny Graves/25	10.00
93	Bucky Jacobsen/64	8.00
94	Cliff Lee/50	10.00
96	Jake Peavy/25	35.00
101	Rafael Furcal/25	20.00
102	Jack Wilson/100	10.00
108	Luke Scott/250	15.00
110	Vernon Wells/25	15.00
112	Chad Cordero/25	15.00
114	Paul Konerko/20	20.00
116	Francisco Rodriguez/25	20.00
118	David Wright/25	85.00
119	Lyle Overbay/25	10.00
120	Brian Roberts/100	15.00
124	Larry Bigbie/75	8.00
129	Jeremy Affeldt/50	8.00
131	Troy Percival/25	15.00
133	David Gassner/1,000	5.00
136	Michael Young/25	20.00
139	Miguel Negron/250	5.00
140	Rich Harden/50	25.00
142	Danny Rueckel/250	5.00
144	Randy Messenger/500	5.00
149	Russ Ortiz/25	15.00
157	Trot Nixon/25	25.00
158	B.J. Upton/25	20.00
159	Jody Gerut/25	10.00
170	David Dellucci/50	15.00
172	Shannon Stewart/25	15.00
175	Nick Johnson/25	15.00
176	Derrek Lee/25	40.00
178	Ken Harvey/25	8.00
179	Ambiorix Concepcion/500	8.00
184	Travis Hafner/50	15.00
189	Dewon Brazelton/66	8.00
192	Alexis Rios/25	15.00
198	Milton Bradley/100	12.00
199	Brad Penny/25	15.00
202	Ryan Wagner/25	10.00
204	Akinori Otsuka/25	20.00
207	Mike Lieberthal/25	10.00
208	Shea Hillenbrand/25	20.00
209	Tom Gordon/25	20.00
212	Casey Kotchman/100	10.00
213	Justin Verlander/50	40.00
220	Danny Haren/25	20.00
226	Casey Rogowski/250	5.00
230	Erick Threets/500	5.00
232	Jason Lane/25	10.00
233	Jeremy Bonderman/50	15.00
234	Livan Hernandez/25	15.00
239	Shingo Takatsu/25	20.00
245	Mark Loretta/25	20.00
250	Jared Gothreaux/1,000	5.00
254	Nate McLouth/1,000	8.00
258	Junior Spivey/25	10.00
259	Morgan Ensberg/25	20.00
260	Chone Figgins/50	10.00
262	Jason Bay/186	15.00
268	Dioner Navarro/75	15.00
271	Jermaine Dye/25	15.00
272	Orlando Hudson/100	8.00
275	Luis Matos/50	10.00
279	Bert Blyleven/25	15.00
280	Bill Madlock/25	15.00
281	Cal Ripken Jr./25	150.00
282	Dale Murphy/25	30.00
286	Harold Baines/25	15.00
288	Keith Hernandez/25	15.00
290	Matt Williams/25	30.00

Throwback Collection

NM/M

Common Player: 1.00
Spectrum: 1-2.5X
Production 100 Sets

1	Billy Martin	2.00
2	Tony Gwynn	2.00
3	Babe Ruth	4.00
4	Angel Berroa	1.00
5	Jeff Bagwell	1.50
6	Tony Oliva	1.00
7	Ivan Rodriguez	1.50
8	Gary Carter	1.50
9	Ted Williams	4.00
10	Chipper Jones	2.00
11	Al Oliver	1.00
12	Roberto Alomar	1.00
13	Omar Vizquel	1.00
14	Ernie Banks	2.00

15	Carlos Beltran	1.50
16	Garret Anderson	1.00
17	Mark Grace	1.00
18	Jason Giambi	1.00
19	Dave Righetti	1.00
20	Mike Schmidt	3.00
21	Roger Clemens	4.00
22	Juan Gonzalez	1.50
23	Carlos Delgado	1.00
24	Manny Ramirez	2.00
25	Jim Thome	1.50
26	Wade Boggs	2.00
27	Luis Tiant	1.00
28	Kerry Wood	1.50
29	Rod Carew	1.50
30	Dwight Evans	1.00
31	Mike Piazza	2.00
32	Billy Williams	1.00
33	Larry Walker	1.00
34	Nolan Ryan	4.00
35	Edgar Renteria	1.00
36	Greg Maddux	2.50
37	Gaylord Perry	1.00
38	Curt Schilling	1.00
39	Dave Parker	1.00
40	Andruw Jones	1.50
41	Orlando Cepeda	1.50
42	Fergie Jenkins	1.00
43	Kirby Puckett	2.00
44	Reggie Jackson	2.00
45	Bob Gibson	2.00
46	Rickey Henderson	2.00
47	Lee Smith	1.00
48	Lou Brock	1.50
49	Fred Lynn	1.00
50	Lance Berkman	1.00
51	Shawn Green	1.00
52	Hoyt Wilhelm	1.00
53	Sammy Sosa	2.50
54	Tim Hudson	1.50
55	Matt Williams	1.00
56	Marty Marion	1.00
57	Eric Chavez	1.00
58	Rafael Palmeiro	1.50
59	Randy Johnson	2.00
60	David Ortiz	2.00
61	Hank Blalock	1.00
62	Jim Rice	1.00
63	Mark Mulder	1.50
64	Kazuo Matsui	1.00
65	Pedro Martinez	2.00
66	Sean Casey	1.00
67	Carlos Lee	1.00
68	Stan Musial	3.00
69	Fred McGriff	1.00
70	Darryl Strawberry	1.00
71	Tommy John	1.00
72	Hideo Nomo	1.00
73	Johnny Bench	2.00
74	Cal Ripken Jr.	5.00
75	Harold Baines	1.00

Throwback Collection Material

NM/M

Production 5-500
Prime: 1-2X
Production 5-25
No pricing 20 or less.

1	Billy Martin/Pants/250	8.00
2	Tony Gwynn/Jsy/250	8.00
4	Angel Berroa/Pants/100	4.00
5	Jeff Bagwell/Jsy/250	6.00
6	Tony Oliva/Jsy/250	4.00
7	Ivan Rodriguez/Jsy/500	6.00
8	Gary Carter/Pants/250	4.00
10	Chipper Jones/Jsy/250	6.00
11	Al Oliver/Jsy/250	4.00
12	Roberto Alomar/Jsy/500	6.00
13	Omar Vizquel/Jsy/250	4.00
15	Carlos Beltran/Jsy/100	6.00
16	Garret Anderson/Jsy/50	4.00
17	Mark Grace/Jsy/250	6.00
18	Jason Giambi/Jsy/500	4.00
19	Dave Righetti/Jsy/250	4.00
21	Roger Clemens/Jsy/250	10.00
22	Juan Gonzalez/Jsy/150	4.00
23	Carlos Delgado/Jsy/150	4.00
24	Manny Ramirez/Jsy/500	10.00
25	Jim Thome/Jsy/500	6.00
26	Wade Boggs/Jsy/250	6.00
27	Luis Tiant/Pants/500	4.00
28	Kerry Wood/Jsy/50	4.00

29	Rod Carew/Jkt/250	6.00
30	Dwight Evans/Jsy/50	6.00
31	Mike Piazza/Jsy/250	8.00
32	Billy Williams/Jsy/100	4.00
33	Larry Walker/Jsy/500	4.00
34	Nolan Ryan/ Pants/100	15.00
35	Edgar Renteria/ Jsy/500	4.00
36	Greg Maddux/Jsy/375	8.00
37	Gaylord Perry/ Jsyu/250	4.00
38	Curt Schilling/Jsy/500	4.00
39	Dave Parker/Jsy/50	4.00
40	Andruw Jones/ Jsy/500	4.00
41	Orlando Cepeda/ Pants/250	4.00
42	Fergie Jenkins/ Jsy/250	4.00
43	Kirby Puckett/Jsy/400	6.00
44	Reggie Jackson/ Jsy/250	6.00
45	Bob Gibson/Jsy/100	8.00
46	Rickey Henderson/ Jsy/500	6.00
47	Lee Smith/Jsy/250	4.00
49	Fred Lynn/Jsy/250	4.00
50	Lance Berkman/ Jsy/500	4.00
51	Shawn Green/Jsy/500	4.00
52	Hoyt Wilhelm/Jsy/250	4.00
53	Sammy Sosa/Jsy/500	8.00
54	Tim Hudson/Jsy/500	4.00
55	Matt Williams/Jsy/250	4.00
57	Eric Chavez/Jsy/500	4.00
58	Rafael Palmeiro/ Jsy/500	6.00
59	Randy Johnson/ Jsy/250	6.00
60	David Ortiz/Jsy/500	8.00
61	Hank Blalock/Jsy/50	4.00
62	Jim Rice/Pants/250	4.00
63	Mark Mulder/Jsy/100	4.00
64	Kazuo Matsui/Jsy/500	4.00
65	Pedro Martinez/ Jsy/250	6.00
66	Sean Casey/Jsy/500	4.00
67	Carlos Lee/Jsy/500	4.00
68	Stan Musial/ Pants/100	20.00
69	Fred McGriff/Jsy/500	4.00
70	Darryl Strawberry/ Jsy/250	4.00
71	Tommy John/Jsy/250	4.00
72	Hideo Nomo/Jsy/500	6.00
73	Johnny Bench/ Pants/100	8.00
74	Cal Ripken Jr./ Jsy/250	20.00
75	Harold Baines/ Jsy/250	4.00

Throwback Collection Material Combo

NM/M

Production 5-100

1	Billy Martin/ Jsy-Pants/100	10.00
2	Tony Gwynn/ Jsy-Pants/100	12.00
4	Angel Berroa/ Bat-Pants/100	4.00
5	Jeff Bagwell/ Jsy-Pants/100	8.00
6	Tony Oliva/ Bat-Jsy/100	6.00
7	Ivan Rodriguez/ Chest Prot-Jsy/100	8.00
8	Gary Carter/ Jsy-Pants/100	4.00
10	Chipper Jones/ Bat-Jsy/100	8.00
11	Al Oliver/Bat-Jsy/100	6.00
12	Roberto Alomar/ Bat-Jsy/100	8.00
13	Omar Vizquel/ Bat-Jsy/100	6.00
15	Carlos Beltran/ Bat-Jsy/100	8.00
17	Mark Grace/ Bat-Jsy/100	10.00
18	Jason Giambi/ Jsy-Jsy/100	6.00
19	Dave Righetti/ Jsy-Jsy/100	6.00
21	Roger Clemens/ Jsy-Jsy/100	15.00
22	Juan Gonzalez/ Bat-Jsy/100	6.00
23	Carlos Delgado/ Bat-Jsy/100	4.00
26	Wade Boggs/ Bat-Jsy/100	10.00
29	Rod Carew/ Jkt-Jsy/100	10.00
33	Larry Walker/ Jsy-Jsy/100	6.00
34	Nolan Ryan/ Bat-Pants/100	20.00
36	Greg Maddux/ Jsy-Jsy/100	12.00
38	Curt Schilling/ Jsy-Jsy/100	6.00
40	Andruw Jones/ Bat-Jsy/100	8.00
41	Orlando Cepeda/ Bat-Pants/100	8.00
43	Kirby Puckett/ Bat-Jsy/100	12.00
44	Reggie Jackson/ Bat-Jsy/100	10.00
46	Rickey Henderson/ Bat-Jsy/100	10.00
47	Lee Smith/ Jsy-Jsy/100	6.00
49	Fred Lynn/ Bat-Jsy/100	4.00
50	Lance Berkman/ Bat-Jsy/100	4.00
51	Shawn Green/ Bat-Jsy/100	4.00
52	Hoyt Wilhelm/ Jsy-Jsy/100	4.00
53	Sammy Sosa/ Hat-Jsy/100	8.00
54	Tim Hudson/ Jsy-Jsy/100	4.00
57	Eric Chavez/ Jsy-Jsy/100	6.00
58	Rafael Palmeiro/ Bat-Jsy/100	8.00
59	Randy Johnson/ Jsy-Pants/100	10.00
60	David Ortiz/ Bat-Jsy/100	10.00
61	Hank Blalock/ Jsy-Jsy/100	6.00
62	Jim Rice/ Jsy-Pants/100	6.00
64	Kazuo Matsui/ Bat-Jsy/100	4.00
65	Pedro Martinez/ Jsy-Jsy/100	8.00
66	Sean Casey/ Jsy-Jsy/100	4.00
67	Carlos Lee/ Hat-Jsy/100	4.00
69	Fred McGriff/ Bat-Jsy/100	8.00
70	Darryl Strawberry/ Bat-Jsy/100	6.00
71	Tommy John/ Bat-Jsy/100	4.00
72	Hideo Nomo/ Jsy-Jsy/100	10.00
73	Johnny Bench/ Bat-Pants/100	12.00
74	Cal Ripken Jr./ Bat-Jsy/100	30.00
75	Harold Baines/ Bat-Jsy/100	4.00

Throwback Collection Signature Material

NM/M

Production 5-50

2	Tony Gwynn/Jsy/50	40.00
4	Angel Berroa/ Pants/50	10.00
6	Tony Oliva/Jsy/50	20.00
8	Gary Carter/Pants/50	20.00
12	Roberto Alomar/ Jsy/50	30.00
13	Omar Vizquel/Jsy/50	30.00
15	Carlos Beltran/ Jsy/50	30.00
17	Mark Grace/Jsy/50	30.00
19	Dave Righetti/Jsy/50	20.00
26	Wade Boggs/Jsy/50	35.00
27	Luis Tiant/Pants/50	20.00
29	Rod Carew/Jkt/50	30.00
30	Dwight Evans/Jsy/50	25.00
32	Billy Williams/Jsy/50	20.00
35	Edgar Renteria/ Jsy/50	20.00
37	Gaylord Perry/Jsy/50	15.00
39	Dave Parker/Jsy/50	20.00
41	Orlando Cepeda/ Pants/25	25.00
42	Fergie Jenkins/ Jsy/50	20.00
44	Reggie Jackson/ Jsy/25	50.00
45	Bob Gibson/Jsy/50	40.00
49	Fred Lynn/Jsy/50	20.00
54	Tim Hudson/Jsy/25	25.00
55	Matt Williams/Jsy/50	30.00
57	Eric Chavez/Jsy/50	20.00
62	Jim Rice/Pants/50	25.00
63	Mark Mulder/Jsy/50	20.00
66	Sean Casey/Jsy/50	20.00
67	Carlos Lee/Jsy/50	20.00
68	Stan Musial/ Pants/25	75.00
70	Darryl Strawberry/ Jsy/50	20.00
71	Tommy John/Jsy/50	15.00
75	Harold Baines/ Jsy/50	15.00

Throwback Collection Sig. Material Combo

NM/M

Production 5-25

2	Tony Gwynn/ Jsy-Pants/25	50.00
4	Angel Berroa/ Bat-Pants/25	15.00
6	Tony Oliva/ Bat-Jsy/25	25.00
8	Gary Carter/ Jsy-Pants/25	25.00
12	Roberto Alomar/ Bat-Jsy/25	40.00
15	Carlos Beltran/ Bat-Jsy/25	35.00
17	Mark Grace/ Bat-Jsy/25	35.00
19	Dave Righetti/ Jsy-Jsy/25	25.00
26	Wade Boggs/ Bat-Jsy/25	40.00
29	Rod Carew/ Jkt-Jsy/25	40.00
44	Reggie Jackson/ Bat-Jsy/25	50.00
49	Fred Lynn/ Bat-Jsy/25	25.00
62	Jim Rice/ Jsy-Pants/25	30.00
67	Carlos Lee/ Hat-Jsy/25	25.00
68	Stan Musial/ Bat-Pants/25	75.00
70	Darryl Strawberry/ Jsy-Jsy/25	20.00
75	Harold Baines/ Bat-Jsy/25	20.00

Century Proof Blue

Blue (1-299): 3-6X
Production 150 Sets

Century Proof Gold

Gold (1-299): 3-6X
Production 100 Sets

Century Proof Green

Green (1-299): 3-6X

Century Proof Platinum Blue

No Pricing
Production 10 Sets

2005 Donruss Timeless Treasures

NM/M

Complete Set (100):		
Common Player:		1.50
Production 799 Sets		
Tin (4):		100.00
1	David Ortiz	3.00
2	Derek Jeter	8.00
3	Edgar Renteria	2.00
4	Paul Molitor	3.00
5	Jeff Bagwell	2.00
6	Melvin Mora	1.50
7	Bobby Crosby	1.50
8	Cal Ripken Jr.	10.00
9	Hank Blalock	2.00
10	Hideo Nomo	2.00
11	Gary Sheffield	2.00
12	Alfonso Soriano	3.00
13	Carl Crawford	1.50
14	Paul Konerko	1.50
15	Jim Edmonds	2.00
16	Garret Anderson	1.50
17	Lance Berkman	1.50
18	Javy Lopez	1.50
19	Tony Gwynn	3.00
20	Mark Mulder	1.50
21	Sammy Sosa	5.00
22	Roger Clemens	8.00
23	Mark Teixeira	2.00
24	Miguel Cabrera	3.00
25	Jim Thome	3.00
26	Mike Piazza	4.00
27	Vladimir Guerrero	3.00
28	Austin Kearns	1.50
29	Rod Carew	3.00
30	Ken Griffey Jr.	5.00
31	Mike Piazza	4.00
32	David Wright	3.00
33	Jason Varitek	2.00
34	Kerry Wood	3.00
35	Frank Thomas	2.00
36	Mark Prior	3.00
37	Mike Mussina	2.00
38	Curt Schilling	3.00
39	Greg Maddux	4.00
40	Miguel Tejada	3.00
41	Tom Seaver	3.00
42	Mariano Rivera	2.00
43	Jason Giambi	1.50
44	Roy Oswalt	1.50
45	Pedro Martinez	3.00
46	Jeff Niemann RC	5.00
47	Tom Glavine	1.50
48	Torii Hunter	1.50
49	Scott Rolen	3.00
50	Curt Schilling	3.00
51	Randy Johnson	3.00
52	C.C. Sabathia	1.50
53	Rafael Palmeiro	2.00
54	Jake Peavy	2.00
55	Hideki Matsui	6.00
56	Ichiro Suzuki	6.00
57	Johan Santana	3.00
58	Todd Helton	2.00
59	Justin Verlander RC	8.00
60	Kazuo Matsui	1.50
61	Rafael Palmeiro	2.00
62	Sean Casey	1.50
63	Nolan Ryan	8.00
64	Magglio Ordonez	1.50
65	Craig Biggio	2.00
66	Vernon Wells	1.50
67	Manny Ramirez	3.00
68	Aramis Ramirez	2.00
69	Omar Vizquel	1.50
70	Eric Gagne	1.50
71	Troy Glaus	2.00
72	Carlton Fisk	2.00
73	Victor Martinez	1.50
74	Adrian Beltre	2.00
75	Barry Zito	1.50
76	Josh Beckett	2.00
77	Michael Young	1.50
78	Eric Chavez	1.50
79	Hideo Nomo	2.00
80	Andruw Jones	2.00
81	Ivan Rodriguez	2.00
82	Don Mattingly	6.00
83	Larry Walker	2.00
84	Philip Humber RC	5.00
85	Juan Gonzalez	1.50
86	Tim Hudson	2.00
87	Alex Rodriguez	6.00
88	Greg Maddux	4.00
89	J.D. Drew	2.00
90	Shawn Green	1.50
91	Roger Clemens	8.00
92	Nomar Garciaparra	4.00
93	Andy Pettitte	2.00
94	Khalil Greene	1.50
95	Mike Schmidt	5.00
96	Carlos Beltran	2.00
97	Mike Mussina	2.00
98	Ben Sheets	1.50
99	Chipper Jones	3.00
100	Albert Pujols	8.00

Bronze

Bronze: 1-2X
Production 100 Sets

Gold

Gold: 3-5X
Production 25 Sets

Platinum

No Pricing
Production One Set

Silver

Gold: 2-3X
Production 50 Sets

Award Materials Number

NM/M

Production 1-29
Prime: No Pricing
Production 1-5

9	Jim Palmer/Pants/22	12.00
10	Rod Carew/Jsy/29	15.00
12	Mike Schmidt/Jsy/20	25.00
13	Robin Yount/Jsy/19	25.00
15	Roger Clemens/ Jsy/21	25.00

Award Material Signature Number

No Pricing
Production 1-5

Award Material Signature Year

NM/M

Production 1-25
Prime: No Pricing
Production 1-5

6	Johnny Bench/Jsy/25	60.00
9	Jim Palmer/Pants/25	35.00
10	Rod Carew/Jsy/25	50.00
12	Mike Schmidt/Jsy/25	75.00
14	Dale Murphy/Jsy/25	50.00

Award Materials Year

NM/M

Production 1-99

1	Lou Boudreau/Jsy/48	20.00
2	Roger Maris/Pants/61	40.00
6	Johnny Bench/Jsy/72	15.00
9	Jim Palmer/Pants/76	10.00
10	Rod Carew/Jsy/77	10.00
12	Mike Schmidt/Jsy/81	20.00
13	Robin Yount/Jsy/89	15.00
14	Dale Murphy/Jsy/83	10.00
15	Roger Clemens/Jsy/86	20.00
16	Cal Ripken Jr./Jsy/91	40.00
17	Tom Glavine/Jsy/91	8.00
18	Frank Thomas/Jsy/94	10.00
19	Jeff Bagwell/Pants/94	8.00
20	Randy Johnson/Jsy/95	10.00
21	Pedro Martinez/Jsy/97	10.00
22	Ivan Rodriguez/Jsy/99	10.00

Game Day Materials

NM/M

Production 5-100

1	Rod Carew/Hat/25	20.00
2	Kirby Puckett/Bat/100	15.00
5	Nellie Fox/Bat/25	60.00
6	Vladimir Guerrero/Fld Glv/25	15.00
7	Tony Gwynn/Jsy/100	15.00
8	Rickey Henderson/Bat/100	10.00
9	David Ortiz/Hat/100	15.00
10	Carlos Beltran/Jsy/50	10.00

Game Day Material Sig.

NM/M

Production 3-25

7	Tony Gwynn/Jsy/25	50.00

Gamers NY

NM/M

Production 25 Sets

1	Jim Thorpe/Jsy/25	450.00
2	Willie Mays/Jsy-Pants/25	75.00
3	Nolan Ryan/Bat-Jsy/25	65.00

Gamers NY Signatures

NM/M

Production 25 Sets

2	Willie Mays/Jsy-Pants/25	250.00
3	Nolan Ryan/Bat-Jsy/25	125.00

HOF Cuts

No Pricing
Production 1-10

HOF Cuts Materials

No Pricing
Production 1-10

HOF Materials Barrel

Production One Set

HOF Materials Bat

NM/M

Production 5-50

1	Pee Wee Reese/25	20.00
3	Harmon Killebrew/25	20.00
4	Hack Wilson/50	65.00
5	Brooks Robinson/50	20.00
6	Stan Musial/50	30.00
8	Carl Yastrzemski/50	20.00
9	Ted Williams/50	50.00
11	Luis Aparicio/25	15.00
12	Bobby Doerr/25	15.00
14	Ernie Banks/50	20.00
15	Ralph Kiner/25	20.00
20	Mike Schmidt/50	20.00
21	Roberto Clemente/50	75.00
24	Willie Mays/50	40.00
25	Willie Stargell/25	25.00
26	Frank Robinson/50	10.00
28	Reggie Jackson/50	15.00
30	Orlando Cepeda/50	10.00
34	Nolan Ryan/50	30.00
35	George Brett/50	25.00
39	Nellie Fox/50	40.00
43	Johnny Bench/50	20.00
44	Hank Aaron/50	40.00
50	Al Kaline/50	20.00

HOF Materials Combos

NM/M

Production 1-25
Prime: No Pricing
Production 1-5

3	Warren Killebrew/Bat-Jsy/25	25.00
5	Brooks Robinson/Bat-Jsy/25	30.00
6	Stan Musial/Bat-Jsy/25	40.00
8	Carl Yastrzemski/Bat-Jsy/25	30.00
9	Ted Williams/Bat-Jsy/25	85.00
12	Bobby Doerr/Bat-Pants/25	15.00
14	Ernie Banks/Bat-Jsy/25	25.00
18	Willie McCovey/Jsy-Pants/25	25.00
20	Mike Schmidt/Bat-Jsy/25	30.00
24	Willie Mays/Bat-Jsy/25	75.00
25	Willie Stargell/Bat-Jsy/25	30.00
28	Reggie Jackson/Jsy-Pants/25	30.00
29	Warren Spahn/Jsy-Pants/25	30.00
34	Nolan Ryan/Jsy-Pants/25	50.00
35	George Brett/Bat-Jsy/25	30.00
43	Johnny Bench/Bat-Jsy/25	25.00
44	Hank Aaron/Bat-Jsy/25	60.00

HOF Materials Hat

No Pricing

HOF Materials Jersey

NM/M

Production 1-100
Prime: No Pricing
Production 1-5

3	Harmon Killebrew/100	15.00
5	Brooks Robinson/50	15.00
6	Stan Musial/100	25.00
8	Carl Yastrzemski/100	15.00
9	Ted Williams/100	60.00
14	Ernie Banks/100	15.00
16	Whitey Ford/100	15.00
17	Duke Snider/25	20.00
18	Willie McCovey/25	20.00
20	Mike Schmidt/50	25.00
22	Jim Palmer/50	12.00
23	Enos Slaughter/25	15.00
24	Willie Mays/100	40.00
25	Willie Stargell/50	20.00
28	Reggie Jackson/25	25.00
29	Warren Spahn/25	25.00
31	Hoyt Wilhelm/50	10.00
32	Sandy Koufax/25	250.00
33	Hal Newhouser/50	10.00
34	Nolan Ryan/50	30.00
35	George Brett/50	25.00
37	Jim "Catfish" Hunter/25	15.00
38	Frankie Frisch/Jkt/50	15.00
40	Lou Boudreau/25	15.00
43	Johnny Bench/50	15.00
44	Hank Aaron/100	40.00
45	Joe Cronin/50	20.00
49	Early Wynn/50	15.00

HOF Materials Jersey Number

NM/M

Production 1-44

18	Willie McCovey/44	15.00
20	Mike Schmidt/20	30.00
22	Jim Palmer/22	12.00
24	Willie Mays/24	65.00
28	Reggie Jackson/44	15.00
29	Warren Spahn/21	25.00
31	Hoyt Wilhelm/31	10.00
32	Sandy Koufax/32	250.00
34	Nolan Ryan/34	30.00
37	Jim "Catfish" Hunter/29	15.00
44	Hank Aaron/44	50.00
49	Early Wynn/24	15.00

HOF Materials Pants

NM/M

Production 1-50

6	Stan Musial/50	30.00
8	Carl Yastrzemski/50	20.00
12	Bobby Doerr/50	10.00
17	Duke Snider/25	20.00
18	Willie McCovey/50	15.00
19	Bob Feller/50	20.00
22	Jim Palmer/25	10.00
24	Willie Mays/50	40.00
29	Warren Spahn/25	25.00
30	Orlando Cepeda/50	10.00
34	Nolan Ryan/50	25.00
42	Burleigh Grimes/50	75.00
43	Johnny Bench/50	15.00
45	Joe Cronin/50	20.00
46	Fergie Jenkins/50	15.00

HOF Materials Sig. Bat

NM/M

Production 1-25

3	Harmon Killebrew/25	50.00
5	Brooks Robinson/25	50.00
6	Stan Musial/25	85.00
11	Luis Aparicio/25	25.00
12	Bobby Doerr/25	25.00
15	Ralph Kiner/25	50.00
20	Mike Schmidt/25	75.00
24	Willie Mays/25	240.00
26	Frank Robinson/25	40.00
30	Orlando Cepeda/25	25.00
34	Nolan Ryan/25	120.00
43	Johnny Bench/25	60.00
50	Al Kaline/25	50.00

HOF Materials Signature Combos

NM/M

Production 1-25
Prime: No Pricing
Production 1-5

3	Harmon Killebrew/Bat-Jsy/25	65.00
5	Brooks Robinson/Bat-Jsy/25	65.00
6	Stan Musial/Bat-Jsy/25	100.00
12	Bobby Doerr/Bat-Pants/25	30.00
18	Willie McCovey/Jsy-Pants/25	60.00
20	Mike Schmidt/Bat-Jsy/25	85.00
24	Willie Mays/Bat-Jsy/25	250.00
30	Orlando Cepeda/Bat-Pants/25	30.00
34	Nolan Ryan/Jsy-Pants/25	120.00
43	Johnny Bench/Bat-Jsy/25	60.00

HOF Materials Signature Hat

Production 5-10

HOF Materials Signature Jersey

NM/M

Production 1-25
Prime: No Pricing
Production 1-5

3	Harmon Killebrew/25	50.00
5	Brooks Robinson/25	50.00
6	Stan Musial/25	85.00
17	Duke Snider/25	40.00
18	Willie McCovey/25	50.00
20	Mike Schmidt/25	75.00
22	Jim Palmer/25	40.00
24	Willie Mays/25	240.00
34	Nolan Ryan/25	120.00
43	Johnny Bench/25	60.00

HOF Materials Signature Pants

NM/M

Production 1-50

6	Stan Musial/25	85.00
12	Bobby Doerr/25	25.00
17	Duke Snider/25	40.00
18	Willie McCovey/25	50.00
22	Jim Palmer/25	40.00
24	Willie Mays/25	240.00
30	Orlando Cepeda/25	25.00
34	Nolan Ryan/25	120.00
43	Johnny Bench/25	60.00
46	Fergie Jenkins/25	30.00

HOF Silver

NM/M

Common Player:	4.00

Production 500 Sets

Gold:	2-4X

Production 25 Sets

Platinum:	No Pricing

Production One Set

1	Pee Wee Reese	4.00
2	Red Schoendienst	4.00
3	Harmon Killebrew	5.00
4	Hack Wilson	5.00
5	Brooks Robinson	5.00
6	Stan Musial	6.00
7	Al Simmons	4.00
8	Carl Yastrzemski	5.00
9	Ted Williams	8.00
10	Phil Rizzuto	4.00
11	Luis Aparicio	4.00
12	Bobby Doerr	4.00
13	Bob Lemon	4.00
14	Ernie Banks	5.00
15	Ralph Kiner	4.00
16	Whitey Ford	4.00
17	Duke Snider	4.00
18	Willie McCovey	4.00
19	Bob Feller	5.00
20	Mike Schmidt	6.00
21	Roberto Clemente	8.00
22	Jim Palmer	4.00
23	Enos Slaughter	4.00
24	Willie Mays	8.00
25	Willie Stargell	4.00
26	Frank Robinson	4.00
27	Carl Hubbell	4.00
28	Reggie Jackson	4.00
29	Warren Spahn	5.00
30	Orlando Cepeda	4.00
31	Hoyt Wilhelm	4.00
32	Sandy Koufax	15.00
33	Hal Newhouser	4.00
34	Nolan Ryan	8.00
35	George Brett	4.00
36	Bill Dickey	4.00
37	Jim "Catfish" Hunter	4.00
38	Frankie Frisch	4.00
39	Nellie Fox	4.00
40	Lou Boudreau	4.00
41	Hank Greenberg	5.00
42	Burleigh Grimes	4.00
43	Johnny Bench	5.00
44	Hank Aaron	8.00
45	Joe Cronin	4.00
46	Fergie Jenkins	4.00
47	Luke Appling	4.00
48	Yogi Berra	5.00
49	Early Wynn	4.00
50	Al Kaline	5.00

Home Road Gamers Duos

NM/M

Production 1-100
Prime: No Pricing
Production 1-10

3	Babe Ruth/Jsy-Jsy/25	450.00
4	Paul Molitor/Jsy-Pants/100	15.00
7	Ivan Rodriguez/Jsy-Jsy/100	10.00
9	Ted Williams/Jsy-Jsy/25	85.00
10	Andre Dawson/Jsy-Jsy/25	15.00
11	Darryl Strawberry/Jsy-Jsy/25	12.00
14	Ernie Banks/Jsy-Jsy/25	30.00
15	Jim Edmonds/Jsy-Jsy/25	15.00
16	Bo Jackson/Jsy-Jsy/25	20.00
17	Mark Grace/Jsy-Jsy/100	15.00
18	Albert Pujols/Jsy-Jsy/100	25.00
19	Tony Gwynn/Jsy-Jsy/100	15.00
20	Cal Ripken Jr./Jsy-Jsy/100	40.00
21	Chipper Jones/Jsy-Jsy/50	15.00

23	Don Mattingly/ Jsy-Jsy/100	25.00
24	Willie Mays/ Jsy-Jsy/25	80.00
25	Tony Oliva/ Jsy-Jsy/50	10.00
28	Reggie Jackson/ Jsy-Jsy/100	15.00
29	Rod Carew/ Jsy-Jsy/100	15.00
30	Harmon Killebrew/ Jsy-Jsy/25	25.00
32	Nolan Ryan/ Jsy-Jsy/100	30.00
33	Eddie Murray/ Jsy-Jsy/100	15.00
35	Rickey Henderson/ Jsy-Jsy/50	15.00
36	Jim Rice/Jsy-Jsy/50	12.00
37	Hoyt Wilhelm/ Jsy-Jsy/50	10.00
38	Curt Schilling/ Jsy-Jsy/100	10.00
42	Greg Maddux/ Jsy-Jsy/100	15.00
43	Dennis Eckersley/ Jsy-Jsy/100	10.00
44	Willie McCovey/ Jsy-Pants/100	15.00
45	Willie Stargell/ Jsy-Jsy/50	20.00
46	Mike Mussina/ Jsy-Pants/50	15.00
47	Gary Carter/ Jsy-Jsy/50	15.00
48	Dale Murphy/ Jsy-Jsy/50	15.00
49	Mike Piazza/ Jsy-Jsy/50	20.00
50	Jim Palmer/ Jsy-Pants/100	10.00

Home Road Gamers Signature Duos

NM/M

Production 1-25

4	Paul Molitor/ Jsy-Pants/25	60.00
11	Darryl Strawberry/ Jsy-Jsy/25	30.00
17	Mark Grace/ Jsy-Jsy/50	50.00
19	Tony Gwynn/ Jsy-Jsy/50	50.00
23	Don Mattingly/ Jsy-Jsy/25	80.00
29	Rod Carew/ Jsy-Jsy/50	50.00
30	Harmon Killebrew/ Jsy-Jsy/50	50.00
36	Jim Rice/Jsy-Jsy/25	35.00
43	Dennis Eckersley/ Jsy-Jsy/25	30.00
44	Willie McCovey/ Jsy-Pants/25	50.00
47	Gary Carter/ Jsy-Jsy/25	30.00
48	Dale Murphy/ Jsy-Jsy/25	50.00
50	Jim Palmer/ Jsy-Pants/25	40.00

Home Road Gamer Signature Trios

NM/M

Production 1-25

Prime: No Pricing

Production 1-5

11	Darryl Strawberry/ Fld Glv-Jsy-Jsy/25	40.00
17	Mark Grace/ Bat-Jsy-Jsy/25	60.00
19	Tony Gwynn/ Jsy-Jsy-Jsy/25	70.00
23	Don Mattingly/ Bat-Jsy-Jsy/25	90.00
25	Tony Oliva/ Bat-Jsy-Jsy/25	35.00
29	Rod Carew/ Bat-Jsy-Jsy/25	60.00
30	Harmon Killebrew/ Bat-Jsy-Jsy/25	70.00
36	Jim Rice/ Bat-Jsy-Jsy/25	40.00

Home Road Gamers Trios

NM/M

Production 1-100

Prime: No Pricing

Production 1-10

4	Paul Molitor/ Bat-Jsy-Pants/100	25.00

7	Ivan Rodriguez/ Jsy-Jsy/100	15.00
9	Ted Williams/ Bat-Jsy/25	120.00
11	Darryl Strawberry/ Fld Glv-Jsy-Jsy/25	20.00
14	Ernie Banks/ Bat-Jsy-Jsy/25	40.00
15	Jim Edmonds/ Bat-Jsy-Jsy/25	25.00
17	Mark Grace/ Bat-Jsy-Jsy/100	20.00
18	Albert Pujols/ Bat-Jsy-Jsy/100	40.00
19	Tony Gwynn/ Jsy-Jsy/100	25.00
20	Cal Ripken Jr./ Jsy-Jsy/100	60.00
21	Chipper Jones/ Bat-Jsy-Jsy/25	20.00
23	Don Mattingly/ Bat-Jsy-Jsy/100	30.00
24	Willie Mays/ Bat-Jsy-Jsy/25	75.00
25	Tony Oliva/ Bat-Jsy-Jsy/25	20.00
28	Reggie Jackson/ Bat-Jsy-Jsy/100	20.00
29	Rod Carew/ Bat-Jsy-Jsy/100	20.00
30	Harmon Killebrew/ Bat-Jsy-Jsy/35	35.00
32	Nolan Ryan/ Jkt-Jsy-Jsy/100	35.00
33	Eddie Murray/ Jsy-Jsy-Pants/100	20.00
35	Rickey Henderson/ Bat-Jsy-Jsy/100	20.00
36	Jim Rice/ Bat-Jsy-Jsy/25	20.00
38	Curt Schilling/ Bat-Jsy-Jsy/50	15.00
44	Willie McCovey/ Bat-Jsy-Pants/100	20.00
45	Willie Stargell/ Bat-Jsy-Jsy/25	25.00
46	Mike Mussina/ Bat-Jsy-Pants/25	35.00
47	Gary Carter/ Bat-Jsy-Jsy/50	25.00
48	Dale Murphy/ Bat-Jsy-Jsy/25	30.00
49	Mike Piazza/ Jsy-Jsy-Jsy/25	35.00

Home Run Materials

NM/M

Production 1-100

1	Ernie Banks/Bat/60	15.00
2	Roger Maris/Bat/61	50.00
4	Johnny Bench/ Pants/71	10.00
5	Harmon Killebrew/ Bat/75	10.00
6	Jose Canseco/Bat/25	15.00
8	Sammy Sosa/ Jsy/100	10.00
9	Jim Thome/Jsy/50	10.00
10	Rafael Palmeiro/ Jsy/50	8.00

Home Run Materials Signature

NM/M

Production 3-25

1	Ernie Banks/Bat/25	60.00
4	Johnny Bench/ Pants/25	60.00
5	Harmon Killebrew/ Bat/25	50.00

Material Ink Bat

No Pricing

Production 1-10

Material Ink Combos

NM/M

Production 1-25

Prime: No Pricing

Production 1-5

2	Fred Lynn/ Bat-Jsy/25	35.00
8	Gary Carter/ Bat-Jsy/25	30.00
10	Andre Dawson/ Bat-Jsy/25	30.00
11	Luis Aparicio/ Bat-Jsy/25	30.00
14	Darryl Strawberry/ Bat-Jsy/25	30.00
27	Carlton Fisk/ Bat-Jsy/25	40.00
37	Miguel Cabrera/ Bat-Jsy/25	50.00

39	Dave Parker/ Bat-Jsy/25	25.00
48	Mark Grace/ Bat-Jsy/25	40.00

Material Ink Jersey

NM/M

Production 1-50

2	Fred Lynn/50	15.00
3	Dale Murphy/50	30.00
4	Paul Molitor/50	30.00
5	Alan Trammell/50	15.00
8	Gary Carter/50	20.00
10	Andre Dawson/50	20.00
11	Luis Aparicio/50	15.00
14	Darryl Strawberry/50	15.00
18	Kirk Gibson/50	20.00
20	Don Sutton/25	20.00
23	Don Mattingly/Jkt/25	75.00
24	Tony Perez/25	20.00
27	Carlton Fisk/25	40.00
29	Fred McGriff/25	40.00
30	John Kruk/25	50.00
32	Dwight Evans/50	20.00
33	Gary Sheffield/25	50.00
34	Bo Jackson/25	65.00
36	Gaylord Perry/50	20.00
39	Dave Parker/25	20.00
42	Harmon Killebrew/50	50.00
43	Dennis Eckersley/25	25.00
44	Willie McCovey/25	50.00
46	Luis Tiant/50	20.00
48	Mark Grace/25	40.00

Material Ink Jersey Number

NM/M

Production 1-44

2	Fred Lynn/19	30.00
14	Darryl Strawberry/44	20.00
20	Don Sutton/20	25.00
22	Mark Prior/22	50.00
23	Don Mattingly/ Jkt/23	80.00
24	Tony Perez/34	30.00
27	Carlton Fisk/27	40.00
29	Fred McGriff/29	40.00
30	John Kruk/29	50.00
32	Dwight Evans/24	35.00
36	Gaylord Perry/36	20.00
40	Mark Teixeira/23	40.00
43	Dennis Eckersley/43	20.00
44	Willie McCovey/44	40.00
46	Luis Tiant/27	25.00

Milestone Material Number

NM/M

Production 1-31

2	Nolan Ryan/Jsy/30	35.00
10	Greg Maddux/ Jsy/31	20.00

Milestone Material Year

NM/M

Production 10-25

Prime: No Pricing

Production 1-10

1	Roger Maris/ Pants/25	40.00
2	Nolan Ryan/Jsy/25	30.00
5	Steve Garvey/Jsy/25	10.00
6	Wade Boggs/Jsy/25	20.00
7	Tony Gwynn/Jsy/25	20.00
8	Sammy Sosa/Jsy/25	20.00
9	Randy Johnson/ Jsy/25	15.00
10	Greg Maddux/ Jsy/25	20.00

No-Hitters

NM/M

Production 3-25

7	Dennis Eckersley, Bert Blyleven/25	35.00
8	Juan Marichal, Gaylord Perry/25	35.00
9	Jim Palmer, Bob Gibson/25	40.00

Salutations Signature

NM/M

Production 1-24

1	Al Kaline/24	70.00
5	Dale Murphy/24	50.00
7	Duke Snider/24	50.00
11	Johnny Bench/24	60.00
19	Steve Carlton/24	40.00

Signature Bronze

NM/M

Production 10-100

Platinum: No Pricing

Production One Set

3	Edgar Renteria/50	30.00
4	Paul Molitor/100	25.00
7	Bobby Crosby/25	25.00
8	Cal Ripken Jr./25	200.00
9	Hank Blalock/50	20.00
11	Gary Sheffield/50	35.00
12	Alfonso Soriano/25	25.00
14	Paul Konerko/50	20.00
15	Jim Edmonds/50	20.00
16	Garret Anderson/50	20.00
19	Tony Gwynn/100	40.00
23	Mark Teixeira/50	30.00
24	Miguel Cabrera/50	30.00
28	Austin Kearns/50	15.00
29	Rod Carew/100	25.00
32	David Wright/25	75.00
34	Kerry Wood/50	35.00
36	Mark Prior/100	40.00
41	Tom Seaver/100	40.00
44	Roy Oswalt/25	20.00
46	Jeff Niemann/100	35.00
48	Torii Hunter/50	20.00
49	Scott Rolen/50	40.00
52	C.C. Sabathia/25	25.00
53	Rafael Palmeiro/25	50.00
57	Johan Santana/50	40.00
59	Justin Verlander/100	30.00
61	Rafael Palmeiro/25	50.00
62	Sean Casey/25	20.00
63	Nolan Ryan/100	85.00
64	Magglio Ordonez/50	15.00
65	Craig Biggio/50	30.00
66	Vernon Wells/25	20.00
67	Manny Ramirez/25	50.00
69	Omar Vizquel/50	40.00
72	Carlton Fisk/100	25.00
73	Victor Martinez/50	15.00
74	Adrian Beltre/50	25.00
75	Barry Zito/50	20.00
76	Josh Beckett/25	35.00
77	Michael Young/50	20.00
78	Eric Chavez/50	15.00
82	Don Mattingly/100	60.00
84	Philip Humber/100	25.00
85	Juan Gonzalez/50	25.00
86	Tim Hudson/50	30.00
90	Shawn Green/25	30.00
95	Mike Schmidt/100	50.00
98	Ben Sheets/25	25.00
99	Chipper Jones/25	60.00

Signature Gold

NM/M

Production 3-25

4	Paul Molitor/25	35.00
19	Tony Gwynn/25	50.00
20	Mark Mulder/25	30.00
29	Rod Carew/25	35.00
36	Mark Prior/25	50.00
41	Tom Seaver/25	40.00
63	Nolan Ryan/25	120.00
72	Carlton Fisk/25	35.00
82	Don Mattingly/25	80.00
95	Mike Schmidt/25	85.00

Signature Silver

NM/M

Production 5-50

3	Edgar Renteria/25	40.00
4	Paul Molitor/50	30.00
9	Hank Blalock/25	25.00
11	Gary Sheffield/25	40.00
12	Alfonso Soriano/25	35.00
14	Paul Konerko/25	25.00
15	Jim Edmonds/25	35.00
16	Garret Anderson/25	25.00
19	Tony Gwynn/50	60.00
20	Mark Mulder/50	25.00
23	Mark Teixeira/25	40.00
24	Miguel Cabrera/25	40.00
28	Austin Kearns/25	20.00
29	Rod Carew/25	30.00
34	Kerry Wood/25	40.00
36	Mark Prior/25	40.00
41	Tom Seaver/50	50.00
46	Jeff Niemann/50	40.00
48	Torii Hunter/25	25.00
49	Scott Rolen/50	50.00
57	Johan Santana/50	50.00
59	Justin Verlander/50	35.00
63	Nolan Ryan/50	100.00
64	Magglio Ordonez/25	20.00
65	Craig Biggio/25	35.00
69	Omar Vizquel/25	40.00
72	Carlton Fisk/50	25.00
73	Victor Martinez/25	20.00
74	Adrian Beltre/25	25.00
75	Barry Zito/25	20.00

77	Michael Young/25	20.00
78	Eric Chavez/25	20.00
82	Don Mattingly/50	60.00
84	Philip Humber/50	30.00
85	Juan Gonzalez/25	30.00
86	Tim Hudson/25	40.00
95	Mike Schmidt/50	65.00

World Series Materials

NM/M

Production 1-100
1	Frank Robinson/Bat/100	10.00
3	Carl Yastrzemski/Bat/100	25.00
4	Jack Morris/Jsy/50	8.00
5	Wade Boggs/Bat/100	12.00
8	Andruw Jones/Jsy/100	8.00
10	Darryl Strawberry/Jsy/25	10.00

2005 Donruss Zenith

NM/M

Complete Set (250):		50.00
Common Player:		.25
Hobby Pack (5):		5.00
Hobby Box (18):		80.00
1	Curt Schilling	.50
2	Jim Edmonds	.40
3	Ichiro Suzuki	1.50
4	Jody Gerut	.25
5	Carlos Beltran	.50
6	Miguel Tejada	.50
7	Ted Lilly	.25
8	Bobby Abreu	.40
9	Mark Teixeira	.50
10	Manny Ramirez	.75
11	Eric Gagne	.40
12	Adrian Beltre	.40
13	Dmitri Young	.25
14	Alfonso Soriano	.50
15	Vladimir Guerrero	.75
16	Carl Crawford	.25
17	David Ortiz	.50
18	Jose Guillen	.25
19	Miguel Cabrera	.75
20	Alex Rodriguez	2.00
21	Brad Lidge	.25
22	Francisco Rodriguez	.25
23	Carlos Lee	.25
24	Ben Sheets	.40
25	Jason Schmidt	.25
26	Cesar Izturis	.25
27	Corey Patterson	.25
28	Marcus Giles	.25
29	Melvin Mora	.25
30	Yadier Molina	.25
31	Juan Pierre	.25
32	Aubrey Huff	.25
33	Rafael Furcal	.25
34	David Dellucci	.25
35	Jake Peavy	.40
36	Aramis Ramirez	.25
37	Javy Lopez	.25
38	Aaron Rowand	.25
39	Raul Ibanez	.25
40	Jason Bay	.40
41	Michael Young	.25
42	Ivan Rodriguez	.50
43	Derrek Lee	.50
44	Adam Dunn	.50
45	Eric Chavez	.40
46	Pedro Martinez	.75
47	Roy Oswalt	.40
48	Kevin Millwood	.25
49	Carlos Delgado	.40
50	Derek Jeter	2.00
51	Johnny Damon	.50
52	Richie Sexson	.40
53	Nomar Garciaparra	.75
54	Edgar Renteria	.25
55	Carl Pavano	.25
56	Tim Wakefield	.25
57	Michael Barrett	.25
58	Johnny Estrada	.25
59	Jeff Kent	.25
60	Mark Loretta	.25
61	Greg Maddux	1.00
62	Hank Blalock	.40
63	Moises Alou	.40
64	Brad Radke	.25
65	Brad Wilkerson	.25
66	Sean Casey	.25
67	Oliver Perez	.40
68	Scott Hatteberg	.25
69	Mike Lowell	.25
70	Kazuo Matsui	.25
71	Mark Prior	.50
72	Hideki Matsui	1.50
73	Geoff Jenkins	.25
74	Gary Sheffield	.50
75	A.J. Burnett	.25
76	Vernon Wells	.25

77	Kenny Rogers	.25
78	Jose Reyes	.50
79	Victor Martinez	.25
80	Jorge Posada	.40
81	Rich Harden	.25
82	Travis Hafner	.25
83	Bret Boone	.25
84	Chipper Jones	.75
85	Bartolo Colon	.25
86	Scott Podsednik	.25
87	Coco Crisp	.25
88	Luis Castillo	.25
89	John Smoltz	.40
90	Andruw Jones	.50
91	Milton Bradley	.25
92	Torii Hunter	.25
93	Shawn Green	.40
94	Paul Konerko	.40
95	David Wells	.25
96	Scott Rolen	.50
97	Rodrigo Lopez	.25
98	Garret Anderson	.40
99	Tim Hudson	.40
100	Sammy Sosa	.75
101	Jason Varitek	.50
102	Lance Berkman	.40
103	Troy Glaus	.40
104	Carlos Guillen	.25
105	Jeff Bagwell	.50
106	Phil Nevin	.25
107	Freddy Garcia	.25
108	Jake Westbrook	.25
109	Marquis Grissom	.25
110	Johan Santana	.75
111	Kerry Wood	.40
112	Jose Vidro	.25
113	Mike Mussina	.40
114	Josh Beckett	.40
115	Matt Lawton	.25
116	Craig Biggio	.40
117	Reggie Sanders	.25
118	Jason Kendall	.25
119	Larry Walker	.40
120	Roger Clemens	2.00
121	C.C. Sabathia	.25
122	Javier Vazquez	.25
123	Barry Zito	.40
124	Jon Lieber	.25
125	Kris Benson	.25
126	Jacque Jones	.25
127	Ray Durham	.25
128	Mark Kotsay	.25
129	Jack Wilson	.25
130	Bobby Crosby	.25
131	Todd Helton	.50
132	Lyle Overbay	.25
133	Jon Garland	.25
134	Roy Halladay	.40
135	Orlando Cabrera	.25
136	Danny Kolb	.25
137	Austin Kearns	.25
138	Paul LoDuca	.25
139	Magglio Ordonez	.40
140	Rafael Palmeiro	.50
141	Omar Vizquel	.25
142	Mike Piazza	1.00
143	Mark Mulder	.40
144	Dontrelle Willis	.40
145	Tom Glavine	.40
146	Khalil Greene	.40
147	Ken Griffey Jr.	1.50
148	Mike Sweeney	.25
149	Trot Nixon	.25
150	Randy Johnson	.75
151	Doug Mientkiewicz	.25
152	Jeromy Burnitz	.25
153	Brandon Webb	.25
154	Kevin Brown	.25
155	Carlos Zambrano	.40
156	Shingo Takatsu	.25
157	Erubiel Durazo	.25
158	Jason Isringhausen	.25
159	Corey Koskie	.25
160	Aaron Boone	.25
161	Joe Nathan	.25
162	Nick Johnson	.25
163	Michael Tucker	.25
164	Chris Carpenter	.25
165	Preston Wilson	.25
166	J.T. Snow	.25
167	Hideo Nomo	.40
168	Miguel Olivo	.25
169	Jarrod Washburn	.25
170	Derek Lowe	.25
171	Eric Milton	.25
172	Andy Pettitte	.40
173	Jason Giambi	.40
174	Richard Hidalgo	.25
175	Jayson Werth	.25
176	Juan Gonzalez	.25
177	Rocco Baldelli	.25
178	Steve Finley	.25
179	Frank Thomas	.75
180	Kenny Lofton	.25
181	Randy Winn	.25

182	Brandon McCarthy RC	1.50
183	Lew Ford	.25
184	Mike Cameron	.25
185	Carlos Pena	.25
186	Brian Roberts	.25
187	Jeremy Bonderman	.25
188	Luis Gonzalez	.25
189	J.D. Drew	.25
190	Frank Catalanotto	.25
191	John Buck	.25
192	Pat Burrell	.25
193	Ryan Klesko	.25
194	Jermaine Dye	.25
195	Mariano Rivera	.40
196	Angel Berroa	.25
197	Carlos Zambrano	.25
198	Joel Pineiro	.25
199	Jay Gibbons	.25
200	Albert Pujols	2.00
201	Billy Wagner	.25
202	Darin Erstad	.25
203	Jim Thome	.50
204	Adam LaRoche	.25
205	Cliff Floyd	.25
206	Grady Sizemore	.50
207	Garrett Atkins	.25
208	Philip Humber RC	1.00
209	Zack Greinke	.25
210	Wladimir Balentien RC	1.00
211	Ubaldo Jimenez RC	.50
212	Dallas McPherson	.25
213	Justin Verlander RC	3.00
214	Justin Morneau	.50
215	Chase Utley	.50
216	Casey Kotchman	.25
217	Tadahito Iguchi RC	3.00
218	Hanley Ramirez	.50
219	Scott Kazmir	.25
220	J.J. Hardy	.25
221	Ambiorix Concepcion RC	.50
222	Jeff Niemann RC	1.00
223	David Wright	1.00
224	Joe Mauer	.50
225	Rickie Weeks	.25
226	Yuniesky Betancourt RC	1.00
227	Brady Clark	.25
228	Keiichi Yabu RC	.50
229	Delmon Young	.50
230	Nick Swisher	.25
231	George Brett	1.00
232	Ryne Sandberg	1.00
233	Mike Schmidt	1.00
234	Tony Gwynn	.75
235	Rickey Henderson	.50
236	Ozzie Smith	1.00
237	Reggie Jackson	.75
238	Steve Carlton	.40
239	Robin Yount	1.00
240	Tom Seaver	.50
241	Ted Williams	1.50
242	Don Mattingly	1.00
243	Mark Grace	.40
244	Rod Carew	.40
245	Willie Mays	1.50
246	Gary Carter	.40
247	Wade Boggs	.50
248	Dale Murphy	.40
249	Nolan Ryan	2.00
250	Cal Ripken Jr.	3.00

Artist's Proofs Gold

Gold AP (1-250):	5-10X
Production 50 Sets	

Artist's Proofs Silver

Silver AP (1-250):	3-5X
Inserted 1:16	

Museum Collection

Museum (1-250):	2-3X
Inserted 1:3	

Epix Orange Play

NM/M

Common Player:	1.50
Production 750 Sets	
Black Game:	1-2X
Production 75 Sets	
Black Moment:	2-3X
Production 25 Sets	
Black Play:	1X
Production 100 Sets	
Black Season:	1-2X
Production 50 Sets	
Blue Game:	1X
Production 350	
Blue Moment:	1X
Production 150 Sets	
Blue Play:	1X
Production 500 Sets	
Blue Season:	1X
Production 250 Sets	

Emerald Game:	1X
Production 100 Sets	
Emerald Moment:	1-2X
Production 50 Sets	
Emerald Play:	1X
Production 150 Sets	
Emerald Season:	1X
Production 75 Sets	
Orange Game:	1X
Production 500 Sets	
Orange Moment:	1X
Production 250 Sets	
Orange Season:	1X
Production 350 Sets	
Purple Game:	1X
Production 250 Sets	
Purple Moment:	1X
Production 100 Sets	
Purple Play:	1X
Production 350 Sets	
Purple Season:	1X
Production 150 Sets	
Red Game:	1X
Production 150 Sets	
Red Moment:	1-2X
Production 50 Sets	
Red Play:	1X
Production 250 Sets	
Red Season:	1X
Production 100 Sets	
1	Vladimir Guerrero	3.00
2	Alex Rodriguez	6.00
3	Johan Santana	3.00
4	Todd Helton	2.00
5	Mark Teixeira	2.00
6	Manny Ramirez	3.00
7	Scott Rolen	2.00
8	Gary Sheffield	2.00
9	Miguel Cabrera	3.00
10	Jim Thome	2.00
11	Eric Chavez	1.50
12	Roger Clemens	6.00
13	Pedro Martinez	3.00
14	Roy Oswalt	1.50
15	Carlos Delgado	1.50
16	Nomar Garciaparra	2.00
17	Hideki Matsui	5.00
18	Shawn Green	1.50
19	Greg Maddux	4.00
20	Ted Williams	6.00
21	Don Mattingly	5.00
22	Cal Ripken Jr.	10.00
23	George Brett	6.00
24	Nolan Ryan	8.00
25	Willie Mays	6.00

Mozaics

NM/M

Common Trio:		1.00
Inserted 1:8		
1	Pedro Martinez, Carlos Beltran, Tom Glavine	2.00
2	Albert Pujols, Jim Edmonds, Mark Mulder	5.00
3	Sammy Sosa, Miguel Tejada, Rafael Palmeiro	2.00
4	Mark Teixeira, Hank Blalock, Michael Young	2.00
5	Andruw Jones, Rafael Furcal, Johnny Estrada	1.50
6	Bobby Crosby, Eric Chavez, Barry Zito	1.00
7	Shawn Green, Troy Glaus, Luis Gonzalez	1.00
8	Austin Kearns, Adam Dunn, Sean Casey	1.00
9	Jim Thome, Bobby Abreu, Pat Burrell	1.50
10	Lance Berkman, Jeff Bagwell, Craig Biggio	1.50
11	Orlando Cabrera, Steve Finley, Darin Erstad	1.00
12	J.D. Drew, Jeff Kent, Milton Bradley	1.00
13	Dontrelle Willis, Mike Lowell, A.J. Burnett	1.00
14	Adrian Beltre, Jeremy Reed, Richie Sexson	1.00
15	Joe Mauer, Justin Morneau, Jacque Jones	1.00
16	Gary Sheffield, Hideki Matsui, Mike Mussina	4.00

Mozaics Materials Single

		NM/M
	Common Player:	4.00
1	Pedro Martinez/Jsy	6.00
2	Albert Pujols/Bat	15.00
3	Miguel Tejada/Jsy	6.00
4	Mark Teixeira/Bat	6.00
5	Andruw Jones/Bat	6.00
7	Luis Gonzalez/Bat	4.00
8	Adam Dunn/Bat	6.00
9	Bobby Abreu/Jsy	4.00
10	Craig Biggio/Bat	4.00
11	Darin Erstad/Bat	4.00
12	J.D. Drew/Bat	4.00
13	A.J. Burnett/Bat	4.00
14	Richie Sexson/Bat	4.00
15	Jacque Jones/Bat	4.00
16	Gary Sheffield/Fld Glv	6.00

Mozaics Materials Triple Jerseys

NM/M
Production 5-100
Prime: No Pricing
Production 5-10

4	Mark Teixeira, Hank Blalock, Michael Young/100	10.00
6	Bobby Crosby, Eric Chavez, Barry Zito/25	10.00
8	Austin Kearns, Adam Dunn, Sean Casey/100	10.00
9	Jim Thome, Bobby Abreu, Pat Burrell/100	10.00
10	Lance Berkman, Jeff Bagwell, Craig Biggio/100	10.00
16	Gary Sheffield, Hideki Matsui, Mike Mussina/50	25.00

Positions

NM/M
Common Card: 4.00
Inserted 1:21
Gold: 1-2X
Production 100 Sets

1	Randy Johnson, Mark Prior, Roger Clemens	4.00
2	Ivan Rodriguez, Mike Piazza, Victor Martinez	2.00
3	Albert Pujols, Todd Helton, David Ortiz	5.00
4	Marcus Giles, Mark Loretta, Bret Boone	1.00
5	Scott Rolen, Aramis Ramirez, Chipper Jones	2.00
6	Kazuo Matsui, Miguel Tejada, Michael Young	1.50
7	Brian Giles, Manny Ramirez, Shannon Stewart	2.00
8	Rocco Baldelli, Andruw Jones, Vernon Wells	1.50
9	Miguel Cabrera, Lance Berkman, Vladimir Guerrero	2.00

Positions Materials Single

		NM/M
	Common Player:	4.00
1	Mark Prior/Bat	6.00
2	Ivan Rodriguez/Bat	6.00
3	Albert Pujols/Bat	15.00
4	Bret Boone/Jsy	4.00
5	Chipper Jones/Bat	6.00
6	Kazuo Matsui/Jsy	4.00
7	Manny Ramirez/Bat	6.00
8	Andruw Jones/Bat	6.00
9	Lance Berkman/Bat	4.00

Positions Materials Triple Jersey

NM/M
Production 5-100

2	Ivan Rodriguez, Mike Piazza, Victor Martinez/50	15.00
3	Albert Pujols, Todd Helton, David Ortiz/50	25.00
5	Scott Rolen, Aramis Ramirez, Chipper Jones/100	15.00
6	Kazuo Matsui, Miguel Tejada, Michael Young/75	10.00
8	Rocco Baldelli, Andruw Jones, Vernon Wells/100	10.00
9	Miguel Cabrera, Lance Berkman, Vladimir Guerrero/100	15.00

Positions Material Triple Jersey Prime

NM/M
Production 5-25

2	Ivan Rodriguez, Mike Piazza, Victor Martinez/25	35.00
5	Scott Rolen, Aramis Ramirez, Chipper Jones/25	35.00
6	Kazuo Matsui, Miguel Tejada, Michael Young/25	25.00
7	Brian Giles, Manny Ramirez, Shannon Stewart/25	20.00
8	Rocco Baldelli, Andruw Jones, Vernon Wells/25	25.00
9	Miguel Cabrera, Lance Berkman, Vladimir Guerrero/25	35.00

Red Hot

NM/M
Common Player:
Inserted 1:16

1	Scott Rolen	1.50
2	Johan Santana	1.50
3	Josh Beckett	1.00
4	Aubrey Huff	1.00
5	Alfonso Soriano	1.50
6	Jeff Bagwell	1.50
7	Ted Williams	5.00
8	Mark Prior	1.50
9	Todd Helton	1.50
10	Vladimir Guerrero	2.00

Red Hot Bats

NM/M
Production 50-150

1	Scott Rolen/150	6.00
4	Aubrey Huff/150	4.00
5	Alfonso Soriano/150	6.00
6	Jeff Bagwell/150	6.00
7	Ted Williams/50	40.00
8	Mark Prior/150	6.00
9	Todd Helton/150	6.00
10	Vladimir Guerrero/150	8.00

Red Hot Jerseys

NM/M
Production 25-300

1	Scott Rolen/150	6.00
2	Johan Santana/150	6.00
3	Josh Beckett/300	4.00
4	Aubrey Huff/25	6.00
5	Alfonso Soriano/150	6.00
6	Jeff Bagwell/300	6.00
7	Ted Williams/50	60.00
8	Mark Prior/250	6.00
9	Todd Helton/165	6.00
10	Vladimir Guerrero/150	8.00

Red Hot Jerseys Prime

NM/M
Production 1-25

1	Scott Rolen/25	20.00
2	Johan Santana/25	20.00
3	Josh Beckett/25	15.00
4	Aubrey Huff/25	10.00
5	Alfonso Soriano/25	15.00
6	Jeff Bagwell/25	20.00
7	Mark Prior/25	20.00
8	Todd Helton/25	20.00
10	Vladimir Guerrero/25	25.00

Roll Call Autographs

NM/M
Inserted 1:24

1	Hanley Ramirez	20.00
2	Sean Tracey	8.00
3	Justin Wechsler	8.00
4	Matt Lindstrom	6.00
5	Garrett Jones	8.00
6	Ambiorix Concepcion	8.00
7	Casey Rogowski	8.00
8	Kelly Shoppach	6.00
9	Sean Thompson	8.00
10	Jeff Miller	6.00
11	Chris Resop	10.00
12	Justin Verlander	25.00
13	Geovany Soto	8.00
14	Paulino Reynoso	6.00
15	Chris Roberson	8.00
16	Justin Leone	6.00
17	Jeff Niemann	15.00
18	Mark Woodyard	6.00
19	Raul Tablado	8.00
20	Norihiro Nakamura	40.00
21	Tony Pena	8.00
22	Wladimir Balentien	10.00
23	Miguel Negron	6.00
24	Eude Brito	8.00
25	Ubaldo Jimenez	6.00
26	Mike Morse	10.00
27	Devon Lowery	6.00
28	Philip Humber	12.00
29	Nate McLouth	10.00
30	Jason Hammel	8.00

Spellbound

NM/M
Common Maddux (1-4): 3.00
Common Clemens (5-9): 4.00
Common A-Rod (10-13): 4.00
Common Pujols (14-19): 4.00
Inserted 1:11

1	Greg Maddux/G	3.00
2	Greg Maddux/R	3.00
3	Greg Maddux/E	3.00
4	Greg Maddux/G	3.00
5	Roger Clemens/R	4.00
6	Roger Clemens/O	4.00
7	Roger Clemens/G	4.00
8	Roger Clemens/E	4.00
9	Roger Clemens/R	4.00
10	Alex Rodriguez/A	4.00
11	Alex Rodriguez/L	4.00
12	Alex Rodriguez/E	4.00
13	Alex Rodriguez/X	4.00
14	Albert Pujols/A	4.00
15	Albert Pujols/L	4.00
16	Albert Pujols/B	4.00
17	Albert Pujols/E	4.00
18	Albert Pujols/R	4.00
19	Albert Pujols/T	4.00

Spellbound Jerseys

NM/M
Production 150-250

1	Greg Maddux G/150	12.00
2	Greg Maddux R/150	12.00
3	Greg Maddux E/150	12.00
4	Greg Maddux G/150	12.00
5	Roger Clemens R/150	15.00
6	Roger Clemens O/150	15.00
7	Roger Clemens G/150	15.00
8	Roger Clemens E/150	15.00
9	Roger Clemens R/150	15.00
14	Albert Pujols A/250	15.00
15	Albert Pujols L/250	15.00
16	Albert Pujols B/250	15.00
17	Albert Pujols E/250	15.00
18	Albert Pujols R/250	15.00
19	Albert Pujols T/250	15.00

Spellbound Jerseys Prime

NM/M
Production 10-25

5	Roger Clemens R/25	40.00
6	Roger Clemens O/25	40.00
7	Roger Clemens G/25	40.00
8	Roger Clemens E/25	40.00
9	Roger Clemens R/25	40.00

Team Zenith

NM/M
Common Player:
Inserted 1:31
Gold: 1-2X
Production 100 Sets

1	Ichiro Suzuki	5.00
2	Jim Edmonds	2.00
3	Hideki Matsui	5.00
4	Alex Rodriguez	5.00
5	Derek Jeter	6.00
6	Alfonso Soriano	2.00
7	Jim Thome	2.00
8	Jorge Posada	1.50
9	Barry Zito	1.50
10	Curt Schilling	2.00
11	Willie Mays	4.00

Team Zenith Bats

NM/M
Production 15-25

3	Hideki Matsui/50	25.00
7	Jim Thome/150	6.00
8	Jorge Posada/25	8.00
11	Willie Mays/25	70.00

Team Zenith Jerseys

NM/M
Production 15-300

3	Hideki Matsui/165	20.00
7	Jim Thome/175	6.00
8	Jorge Posada/300	6.00
9	Barry Zito/150	4.00
10	Curt Schilling/150	6.00
11	Willie Mays/175	30.00

Team Zenith Jerseys Prime

NM/M
Production 25 Sets

2	Jim Edmonds/25	15.00
6	Alfonso Soriano/25	15.00
7	Jim Thome/25	20.00
8	Jorge Posada/25	15.00
9	Barry Zito/25	15.00
10	Curt Schilling/25	20.00

White Hot

NM/M
Common Player:
Inserted 1:65

1	Scott Rolen	2.00
2	Johan Santana	2.00
3	Josh Beckett	1.50
4	Aubrey Huff	1.50
5	Alfonso Soriano	2.00
6	Jeff Bagwell	2.00
7	Ted Williams	6.00
8	Mark Prior	2.00
9	Todd Helton	2.00
10	Vladimir Guerrero	2.00

White Hot Bats

NM/M
Production 50 Sets

1	Scott Rolen/50	8.00
4	Aubrey Huff/50	4.00
5	Alfonso Soriano/50	6.00
6	Jeff Bagwell/50	6.00
7	Ted Williams/50	40.00
8	Mark Prior/50	8.00
9	Todd Helton/50	6.00
10	Vladimir Guerrero/50	8.00

White Hot Jerseys

NM/M
Production 1-200
Prime: No Pricing
Production 1-10

1	Scott Rolen/50	8.00
2	Johan Santana/50	8.00
3	Josh Beckett/185	4.00
5	Alfonso Soriano/50	6.00
6	Jeff Bagwell/200	6.00
8	Mark Prior/200	6.00
9	Todd Helton/151	6.00
10	Vladimir Guerrero/50	8.00

Z-Batgraphs

NM/M
Production 1-100

7	Craig Wilson/100	12.00
9	Nick Johnson/100	15.00
11	Dontrelle Willis/25	40.00
24	Angel Berroa/100	8.00
39	Magglio Ordonez/100	10.00
44	Jack Wilson/25	15.00
52	Paul Molitor/25	40.00
55	Ryne Sandberg/25	65.00
57	Casey Kotchman/50	20.00
69	Chone Figgins/50	20.00
73	Victor Martinez/25	25.00
90	Mark Prior/25	50.00
97	Michael Young/100	15.00
91	Dale Murphy/100	20.00
97	Carlos Lee/50	20.00
99	Mark Teixeira/25	40.00

Z-Bats

		NM/M
	Common Player:	4.00
3	Rickey Henderson	8.00
4	Andy Pettitte	4.00
7	Craig Wilson	4.00
9	Nick Johnson	4.00
10	Bernie Williams	6.00
11	Dontrelle Willis	6.00
12	Kenny Lofton	4.00
13	Tom Glavine	4.00
14	Kazuo Matsui/SP	6.00
15	Morgan Ensberg/SP	6.00
16	Mike Piazza	8.00
17	Trot Nixon/SP	4.00
18	Ryan Klesko/SP	4.00
19	B.J. Upton	6.00
21	Omar Vizquel	4.00
22	Shannon Stewart	4.00

23	Preston Wilson	4.00
24	Angel Berroa	4.00
26	Brandon Webb	4.00
27	Rafael Palmeiro	6.00
28	Mike Sweeney	4.00
29	Magglio Ordonez	4.00
30	Cal Ripken Jr.	25.00
31	Johnny Estrada	4.00
32	Austin Kearns	4.00
33	Nolan Ryan	20.00
34	Orlando Cabrera	4.00
35	Roy Oswalt	4.00
37	Lyle Overbay	4.00
39	Jack Wilson	4.00
40	Jacque Jones	4.00
44	Tony Gwynn	8.00
46	Geoff Jenkins	4.00
47	Bo Jackson	8.00
48	Luis Gonzalez	4.00
50	Craig Biggio	4.00
51	Josh Beckett	6.00
52	Paul Molitor	4.00
55	Ryne Sandberg	10.00
56	Jeff Bagwell	6.00
57	Casey Kotchman	4.00
58	Chipper Jones	6.00
60	Paul Konerko	6.00
61	Kevin Mench	4.00
62	David Wright	10.00
64	Andruw Jones	6.00
65	Garret Anderson	4.00
66	Jorge Posada	6.00
68	Travis Hafner	4.00
69	Victor Martinez	4.00
70	Vernon Wells	4.00
71	A.J. Burnett	4.00
73	Mark Prior	6.00
74	Mike Lowell	4.00
76	Brad Wilkerson	4.00
79	Moises Alou	4.00
81	Hank Blalock	4.00
82	J.D. Drew	4.00
83	Reggie Jackson/SP	8.00
84	Mark Buehrle/SP	6.00
87	Adam Dunn	6.00
88	Derrek Lee	6.00
90	Michael Young	4.00
91	Dale Murphy	6.00
92	Aramis Ramirez	4.00
95	Aubrey Huff	4.00
96	Ben Sheets	4.00
97	Carlos Lee	4.00
98	Miguel Cabrera	6.00
99	Mark Teixeira	6.00
100	Albert Pujols	15.00

Z-Combos

NM/M

Production 1-150
Cards are bat/jsy unless noted.

3	Rickey Henderson/100	12.00
7	Craig Wilson/150	6.00
10	Bernie Williams/150	8.00
11	Dontrelle Willis/25	10.00
14	Kazuo Matsui/50	8.00
19	B.J. Upton/25	10.00
24	Angel Berroa/Bat-Pants/100	6.00
26	Brandon Webb/Bat-Pants/100	6.00
30	Cal Ripken Jr./100	30.00
33	Nolan Ryan/100	40.00
44	Tony Gwynn/100	12.00
47	Bo Jackson/100	12.00
50	Craig Biggio/50	10.00
52	Paul Molitor/50	12.00
53	Kerry Wood/25	10.00
54	Lew Ford/25	6.00
55	Ryne Sandberg/100	20.00
56	Jeff Bagwell/50	10.00
57	Casey Kotchman/50	8.00
58	Chipper Jones/100	10.00
59	Chone Figgins/100	6.00
61	Kevin Mench/100	6.00
64	Andruw Jones/100	10.00
69	Victor Martinez/100	8.00
71	A.J. Burnett/100	6.00
73	Mark Prior/100	10.00
81	Hank Blalock/100	8.00
87	Adam Dunn/25	10.00
88	Derrek Lee/25	12.00
90	Michael Young/100	6.00
91	Dale Murphy/100	10.00
99	Mark Teixeira/Bat-Hat/100	12.00

Z-Combos Prime

NM/M

Production 1-25
All are bat/patch.

3	Rickey Henderson/25	25.00
7	Craig Wilson/25	10.00
10	Bernie Williams/25	15.00
11	Dontrelle Willis/25	15.00
14	Kazuo Matsui/25	10.00
19	B.J. Upton/25	15.00
27	Rafael Palmeiro/25	15.00
30	Cal Ripken Jr./25	65.00
33	Nolan Ryan/25	50.00
44	Tony Gwynn/25	25.00
47	Bo Jackson/25	25.00
55	Ryne Sandberg/25	35.00
56	Jeff Bagwell/25	15.00
57	Casey Kotchman/25	15.00
58	Chipper Jones/25	20.00
61	Kevin Mench/25	10.00
64	Andruw Jones/25	20.00
65	Garret Anderson/25	15.00
69	Victor Martinez/25	15.00
71	A.J. Burnett/25	10.00
73	Mark Prior/25	20.00
74	Mike Lowell/25	15.00
81	Hank Blalock/25	15.00
87	Adam Dunn/25	15.00
88	Derrek Lee/25	20.00
90	Michael Young/25	15.00
91	Dale Murphy/25	20.00
96	Ben Sheets/25	15.00
99	Mark Teixeira/25	25.00

Z-Graphs

NM/M

Production 1-250

1	Danny Haren/250	10.00
2	Dallas McPherson/250	12.00
5	Jeremy Bonderman/200	15.00
7	Craig Wilson/250	8.00
8	Adam LaRoche/250	12.00
9	Nick Johnson/250	10.00
11	Dontrelle Willis/25	25.00
15	Morgan Ensberg/250	10.00
17	Trot Nixon/100	20.00
19	B.J. Upton/50	20.00
20	Brian Roberts/250	15.00
21	Omar Vizquel/100	20.00
22	Shannon Stewart/100	10.00
24	Angel Berroa/250	8.00
26	Brandon Webb/100	10.00
29	Magglio Ordonez/100	12.00
30	Cal Ripken Jr./100	90.00
31	Johnny Estrada/50	10.00
32	Austin Kearns/100	10.00
33	Nolan Ryan/34	80.00
34	Orlando Cabrera/25	10.00
35	Roy Oswalt/100	15.00
36	Roy Halladay/50	20.00
38	Bobby Crosby/50	20.00
39	Jack Wilson/25	10.00
40	Jacque Jones/100	12.00
41	Eric Byrnes/250	8.00
44	Tony Gwynn/25	40.00
52	Paul Molitor/25	30.00
55	Ryne Sandberg/25	50.00
57	Casey Kotchman/100	12.00
60	Paul Konerko/100	20.00
62	David Wright/100	60.00
63	Milton Bradley/100	12.00
67	Rich Harden/250	15.00
68	Travis Hafner/250	10.00
69	Victor Martinez/25	15.00
70	Vernon Wells/25	15.00
72	Francisco Rodriguez/100	20.00
73	Mark Prior/25	40.00
75	Sean Casey/50	15.00
77	Carlos Zambrano/50	20.00
80	Livan Hernandez/100	12.00
84	Mark Buehrle/100	15.00
85	Keith Foulke/100	20.00
86	Edgar Renteria/50	15.00
88	Derrek Lee/25	25.00
89	Joe Nathan/100	10.00
90	Michael Young/50	15.00
91	Dale Murphy/100	20.00
93	Francisco Cordero/100	8.00
94	Jake Peavy/100	20.00
95	Aubrey Huff/100	10.00
96	Ben Sheets/100	20.00
97	Carlos Lee/25	15.00
98	Miguel Cabrera/25	40.00
99	Mark Teixeira/25	40.00

Z-Jerseygraphs

NM/M

Production 1-100

5	Jeremy Bonderman/100	20.00
7	Craig Wilson/100	10.00
11	Dontrelle Willis/25	35.00
15	Morgan Ensberg/25	20.00
17	Trot Nixon/50	25.00
19	B.J. Upton/25	25.00
20	Brian Roberts/100	20.00
22	Shannon Stewart/100	15.00
31	Johnny Estrada/100	10.00
35	Roy Oswalt/20	25.00
36	Roy Halladay/25	25.00
37	Lyle Overbay/25	15.00
38	Bobby Crosby/25	25.00
40	Jacque Jones/100	15.00
44	Tony Gwynn/25	50.00
52	Paul Molitor/25	35.00
55	Ryne Sandberg/25	65.00
57	Casey Kotchman/50	25.00
60	Chone Figgins/50	20.00
60	Paul Konerko/25	35.00
69	Travis Hafner/50	20.00
69	Victor Martinez/25	25.00
72	Vernon Wells/25	20.00
72	Francisco Rodriguez/100	25.00
73	Mark Prior/25	50.00
75	Sean Casey/25	50.00
84	Livan Hernandez/100	15.00
88	Mark Buehrle/100	15.00
88	Derrek Lee/100	30.00
90	Michael Young/100	20.00
91	Dale Murphy/100	30.00
93	Francisco Cordero/100	12.00
95	Aubrey Huff/5	25.00
96	Ben Sheets/25	25.00
99	Mark Teixeira/25	50.00

Z-Jerseygraphs Prime

NM/M

Production 1-25

5	Jeremy Bonderman/25	35.00
7	Craig Wilson/25	20.00
11	Dontrelle Willis/25	50.00
17	Trot Nixon/25	40.00
19	B.J. Upton/25	35.00
20	Brian Roberts/25	40.00
22	Shannon Stewart/25	25.00
24	Angel Berroa/25	20.00
31	Johnny Estrada/25	20.00
32	Austin Kearns/25	20.00
35	Roy Oswalt/25	35.00
36	Roy Halladay/25	45.00
40	Jacque Jones/25	25.00
41	Eric Byrnes/25	20.00
44	Tony Gwynn/25	65.00
52	Paul Molitor/25	50.00
55	Ryne Sandberg/25	80.00
57	Casey Kotchman/25	30.00
60	Paul Konerko/25	50.00
68	Travis Hafner/25	35.00
69	Victor Martinez/25	35.00
70	Vernon Wells/25	30.00
72	Francisco Rodriguez/25	40.00
73	Mark Prior/25	60.00
75	Sean Casey/25	30.00
77	Carlos Zambrano/25	30.00
80	Livan Hernandez/25	25.00
84	Mark Buehrle/25	30.00
88	Derrek Lee/25	50.00
90	Michael Young/25	30.00
91	Dale Murphy/25	40.00
93	Francisco Cordero/25	20.00
95	Aubrey Huff/25	25.00
96	Ben Sheets/25	35.00
98	Miguel Cabrera/25	50.00
99	Mark Teixeira/25	60.00

Z-Jerseys

NM/M

Common Player: 4.00

1	Danny Haren	6.00
3	Rickey Henderson	8.00
4	Andy Pettitte	4.00
5	Jeremy Bonderman	4.00
6	Pat Burrell	4.00
7	Craig Wilson	4.00
10	Bernie Williams	6.00
11	Dontrelle Willis	6.00
13	Tom Glavine	4.00
14	Kazuo Matsui	8.00
16	Mike Piazza	8.00
17	Trot Nixon	4.00
18	Ryan Klesko	4.00
19	B.J. Upton	4.00
20	Brian Roberts	4.00
21	Omar Vizquel	4.00
22	Shannon Stewart	4.00
23	Preston Wilson	4.00
25	Garrett Atkins	4.00
27	Rafael Palmeiro	6.00
28	Mike Sweeney	4.00
29	Magglio Ordonez	4.00
30	Cal Ripken Jr.	25.00
32	Austin Kearns	4.00
33	Nolan Ryan	20.00
34	Orlando Cabrera	4.00
35	Roy Oswalt	4.00
36	Roy Halladay	6.00
37	Lyle Overbay	4.00
39	Jack Wilson	4.00
40	Jacque Jones	4.00
41	Eric Byrnes	4.00
42	Barry Zito	4.00
43	C.C. Sabathia	4.00
44	Tony Gwynn	8.00
45	Mike Cameron	4.00
46	Geoff Jenkins	4.00
47	Bo Jackson	8.00
48	Luis Gonzalez	4.00
49	Johnny Damon	6.00
50	Craig Biggio	6.00
51	Josh Beckett	4.00
52	Paul Molitor	8.00
53	Kerry Wood	4.00
54	Lew Ford	4.00
55	Ryne Sandberg	10.00
56	Jeff Bagwell	6.00
57	Casey Kotchman	4.00
58	Chipper Jones	8.00
59	Chone Figgins	4.00
60	Paul Konerko	6.00
61	Kevin Mench	4.00
62	David Wright	10.00
64	Andruw Jones	6.00
65	Garret Anderson	4.00
66	Jorge Posada	6.00
68	Travis Hafner	4.00
69	Victor Martinez	4.00
70	Vernon Wells	4.00
71	A.J. Burnett	4.00
72	Francisco Rodriguez	4.00
73	Mark Prior	6.00
74	Mike Lowell	4.00
75	Sean Casey	4.00
77	Carlos Zambrano	4.00
78	Brad Radke	4.00
79	Moises Alou	4.00
80	Livan Hernandez	4.00
81	Hank Blalock	4.00
82	J.D. Drew	4.00
83	Reggie Jackson	8.00
84	Mark Buehrle	6.00
86	Edgar Renteria	4.00
87	Adam Dunn	6.00
88	Derrek Lee	6.00
90	Michael Young	4.00
91	Dale Murphy	6.00
92	Aramis Ramirez	4.00
93	Francisco Cordero	4.00
95	Aubrey Huff	4.00
96	Ben Sheets	4.00
97	Carlos Lee	4.00
98	Miguel Cabrera	8.00
99	Mark Teixeira	4.00
100	Albert Pujols	15.00

Z-Jerseys Prime

NM/M

Production 1-150

3	Rickey Henderson/150	15.00
4	Andy Pettitte/100	10.00
5	Jeremy Bonderman/150	8.00
6	Pat Burrell/150	8.00
7	Craig Wilson/150	8.00
10	Bernie Williams/150	10.00
11	Dontrelle Willis/100	10.00
14	Kazuo Matsui/150	12.00
17	Trot Nixon/25	8.00
18	Ryan Klesko/150	8.00
19	B.J. Upton/50	10.00
22	Shannon Stewart/150	8.00
23	Preston Wilson/150	8.00
25	Garrett Atkins/150	8.00
27	Rafael Palmeiro/150	10.00
28	Mike Sweeney/150	8.00
30	Cal Ripken Jr./25	50.00
31	Johnny Estrada/100	8.00
32	Austin Kearns/150	8.00
33	Nolan Ryan/100	30.00
35	Roy Oswalt/100	10.00
36	Roy Halladay/150	10.00
37	Lyle Overbay/100	8.00
40	Jacque Jones/100	8.00
41	Eric Byrnes/50	8.00
42	Barry Zito/50	10.00
43	C.C. Sabathia/150	8.00
44	Tony Gwynn/150	15.00
45	Mike Cameron/150	8.00
46	Geoff Jenkins/50	10.00
47	Bo Jackson/100	20.00
48	Luis Gonzalez/150	8.00
49	Johnny Damon/25	20.00
51	Josh Beckett/150	10.00
52	Paul Molitor/70	15.00
54	Lew Ford/150	8.00
55	Ryne Sandberg/50	25.00
56	Jeff Bagwell/150	12.00

57	Casey Kotchman/50	10.00
58	Chipper Jones/150	15.00
60	Paul Konerko/150	10.00
61	Kevin Mench/150	8.00
64	Andruw Jones/150	12.00
65	Garret Anderson/25	12.00
66	Jorge Posada/50	12.00
68	Travis Hafner/100	10.00
69	Victor Martinez/25	12.00
70	Vernon Wells/150	10.00
71	A.J. Burnett/150	10.00
72	Francisco Rodriguez/100	8.00
73	Mark Prior/50	15.00
74	Mike Lowell/150	8.00
75	Sean Casey/150	8.00
77	Carlos Zambrano/100	10.00
78	Brad Radke/150	8.00
80	Livan Hernandez/50	10.00
81	Hank Blalock/100	10.00
83	Reggie Jackson/150	15.00
84	Mark Buehrle/50	12.00
87	Adam Dunn/150	10.00
88	Derek Lee/50	15.00
90	Michael Young/50	10.00
91	Dale Murphy/50	20.00
92	Aramis Ramirez/100	10.00
93	Francisco Cordero/50	10.00
95	Aubrey Huff/50	8.00
96	Ben Sheets/150	10.00
98	Miguel Cabrera/150	15.00
99	Mark Teixeira/100	15.00

Z-Team

		NM/M
Common Player:		
Inserted 1:11		
Gold:		1-2X
Production 100 Sets		
1	Albert Pujols	5.00
2	Carlos Beltran	1.50
3	Randy Johnson	2.00
4	Miguel Tejada	1.50
5	Ichiro Suzuki	4.00
6	Eric Gagne	1.00
7	Adrian Beltre	1.00
8	Alfonso Soriano	1.50
9	Jim Edmonds	1.50
10	David Ortiz	2.00
11	Curt Schilling	2.00
12	Mariano Rivera	1.50
13	Derek Jeter	5.00
14	Ivan Rodriguez	1.50
15	Johnny Damon	2.00
16	Mark Prior	1.50
17	Vernon Wells	1.00
18	Chipper Jones	2.00
19	Torii Hunter	1.00
20	Tim Hudson	1.50
21	Lance Berkman	1.00
22	Troy Glaus	1.00
23	Mike Piazza	2.50
24	Mark Mulder	1.00
25	Ken Griffey Jr.	3.00

E

2000 E-X

		NM/M
Complete Set (90):		80.00
Common Player:		.25
Common Prospect (61-90):		3.00
Production 3,499 Sets		
Pack:		2.75
Box:		50.00
1	Alex Rodriguez	2.50
2	Jeff Bagwell	1.00
3	Mike Piazza	2.00
4	Tony Gwynn	1.50
5	Ken Griffey Jr.	2.00
6	Juan Gonzalez	.40
7	Vladimir Guerrero	1.00
8	Cal Ripken Jr.	3.00
9	Mo Vaughn	.25
10	Chipper Jones	1.50
11	Derek Jeter	3.00
12	Nomar Garciaparra	1.50
13	Mark McGwire	2.50
14	Sammy Sosa	1.50
15	Pedro Martinez	1.00
16	Greg Maddux	1.50
17	Frank Thomas	.75
18	Shawn Green	.50
19	Carlos Beltran	.50
20	Roger Clemens	1.75
21	Randy Johnson	1.00
22	Bernie Williams	.25

23	Carlos Delgado	.50
24	Manny Ramirez	.75
25	Freddy Garcia	.25
26	Barry Bonds	3.00
27	Tim Hudson	.40
28	Larry Walker	.25
29	Raul Mondesi	.25
30	Ivan Rodriguez	.65
31	Magglio Ordonez	.25
32	Scott Rolen	.65
33	Mike Mussina	.40
34	J.D. Drew	.40
35	Tom Glavine	.50
36	Barry Larkin	.25
37	Jim Thome	.65
38	Erubiel Durazo	.25
39	Curt Schilling	.50
40	Orlando Hernandez	.65
41	Rafael Palmeiro	.25
42	Gabe Kapler	.25
43	Mark Grace	.25
44	Jeff Cirillo	.25
45	Jeromy Burnitz	.25
46	Sean Casey	.35
47	Kevin Millwood	.25
48	Vinny Castilla	.25
49	Jose Canseco	.50
50	Roberto Alomar	.30
51	Craig Biggio	.25
52	Preston Wilson	.25
53	Jeff Weaver	.25
54	Robin Ventura	.25
55	Ben Grieve	.25
56	Troy Glaus	.65
57	Jacque Jones	.25
58	Brian Giles	.25
59	Kevin Brown	.25
60	Todd Helton	.65
61	Ben Petrick	3.00
62	Chad Hermansen	3.00
63	Kevin Barker	3.00
64	Matt LeCroy	3.00
65	Brad Penny	4.00
66	D.T. Cromer	3.00
67	Steve Lomasney	3.00
68	Cole Liniak	3.00
69	B.J. Ryan	3.00
70	Wilton Veras	3.00
71	Aaron McNeal RC	4.00
72	Nick Johnson	4.00
73	Adam Piatt	3.00
74	Adam Kennedy	3.00
75	Cesar King	3.00
76	Peter Bergeron	3.00
77	Rob Bell	3.00
78	Wily Pena	4.00
79	Ruben Mateo	3.00
80	Kip Wells	3.00
81	Alex Escobar	3.00
82	Danys Baez RC	5.00
83	Travis Dawkins	3.00
84	Mark Quinn	3.00
85	Jimmy Anderson	3.00
86	Rick Ankiel	4.00
87	Alfonso Soriano	5.00
88	Pat Burrell	4.00
89	Eric Munson	3.00
90	Josh Beckett	4.00

Essential Credentials Future

		NM/M
Common Player:		10.00
1	Alex Rodriguez/60	75.00
2	Jeff Bagwell/59	30.00
3	Mike Piazza/58	50.00
4	Tony Gwynn/57	50.00
5	Ken Griffey Jr./56	50.00
6	Juan Gonzalez/55	15.00
7	Vladimir Guerrero/54	20.00
8	Cal Ripken Jr./53	85.00
9	Mo Vaughn/52	10.00
10	Chipper Jones/51	30.00
11	Derek Jeter/50	85.00
12	Nomar Garciaparra/49	45.00
13	Mark McGwire/48	75.00
14	Sammy Sosa/47	50.00
15	Pedro Martinez/46	30.00
16	Greg Maddux/45	50.00
17	Frank Thomas/44	20.00
18	Shawn Green/43	10.00
19	Carlos Beltran/42	10.00
20	Roger Clemens/41	60.00
21	Randy Johnson/40	30.00
22	Bernie Williams/39	10.00
23	Carlos Delgado/38	15.00
24	Manny Ramirez/37	20.00
25	Freddy Garcia/36	10.00
26	Barry Bonds/35	90.00

27	Tim Hudson/34	20.00
28	Larry Walker/33	10.00
29	Raul Mondesi/32	10.00
30	Ivan Rodriguez/31	15.00
31	Magglio Ordonez/30	10.00
32	Scott Rolen/29	20.00
33	Mike Mussina/28	25.00
34	J.D. Drew/27	20.00
35	Tom Glavine/26	25.00
36	Barry Larkin/25	15.00
37	Jim Thome/24	30.00
38	Erubiel Durazo23	15.00
39	Curt Schilling/22	25.00
40	Orlando Hernandez/21	15.00
41	Rafael Palmeiro/20	40.00
42	Gabe Kapler/19	15.00
43	Mark Grace/18	15.00
44	Jeff Cirillo/17	15.00
45	Jeromy Burnitz/16	15.00
46	Sean Casey/15	15.00
47	Kevin Millwood/14	20.00
48	Vinny Castilla/13	20.00
49	Jose Canseco/12	40.00
50	Roberto Alomar/11	50.00
51	Craig Biggio/10	50.00
61	Ben Petrick/30	10.00
62	Chad Hermansen/29	10.00
63	Kevin Barker/28	10.00
64	Matt LeCroy/27	10.00
65	Brad Penny/26	10.00
66	D.T. Cromer/25	10.00
67	Steve Lomasney/24	10.00
68	Cole Liniak/23	10.00
69	B.J. Ryan/22	10.00
70	Wilton Veras/21	10.00
71	Aaron McNeal/20	15.00
72	Nick Johnson/19	25.00
73	Adam Piatt/18	15.00
74	Adam Kennedy/17	15.00
75	Cesar King/16	15.00
76	Peter Bergeron/15	15.00
77	Rob Bell/14	15.00
78	Wily Pena/13	15.00
79	Ruben Mateo/12	15.00
80	Kip Wells/11	15.00
81	Alex Escobar/10	20.00

Essential Credentials Now

		NM/M
Common Player:		8.00
20	Roger Clemens/20	50.00
21	Randy Johnson/21	30.00
22	Bernie Williams/22	10.00
23	Carlos Delgado/23	25.00
24	Manny Ramirez/24	30.00
25	Freddy Garcia/25	10.00
26	Barry Bonds/26	75.00
27	Tim Hudson/27	15.00
28	Larry Walker/28	10.00
29	Raul Mondesi/29	15.00
30	Ivan Rodriguez/30	15.00
31	Magglio Ordonez/31	10.00
32	Scott Rolen/32	20.00
33	Mike Mussina/33	15.00
34	J.D. Drew/34	20.00
35	Tom Glavine/35	20.00
36	Barry Larkin/36	15.00
37	Jim Thome/37	25.00
38	Erubiel Durazo/38	8.00
39	Curt Schilling/39	20.00
40	Orlando Hernandez/40	8.00
41	Rafael Palmeiro/41	15.00
42	Gabe Kapler/42	8.00
43	Mark Grace/43	8.00
44	Jeff Cirillo/44	8.00
45	Jeromy Burnitz/45	8.00
46	Sean Casey/46	8.00
47	Kevin Millwood/47	8.00
48	Vinny Castilla/48	8.00
49	Jose Canseco/49	15.00
50	Roberto Alomar/50	12.00
51	Craig Biggio/51	10.00
52	Preston Wilson/52	8.00
53	Jeff Weaver/53	8.00
54	Robin Ventura/54	8.00
55	Ben Grieve/55	8.00
56	Troy Glaus/56	15.00
57	Jacque Jones/57	12.00
58	Brian Giles/58	8.00
59	Kevin Brown/59	8.00
60	Todd Helton/60	20.00
74	Cesar King/15	15.00
75	Cesar King/15	15.00
76	Peter Bergeron/16	15.00
77	Rob Bell/17	15.00
78	Wily Pena/18	15.00
79	Ruben Mateo/19	15.00
80	Kip Wells/20	15.00
81	Alex Escobar/21	15.00
82	Danys Baez/22	15.00

83	Travis Dawkins/23	15.00
84	Mark Quinn/24	15.00
85	Jimmy Anderson/25	15.00
86	Rick Ankiel/26	15.00
87	Alfonso Soriano/27	60.00
88	Pat Burrell/28	30.00
89	Eric Munson/29	15.00
90	Josh Beckett/30	20.00

Autographics

	NM/M
Common Player:	5.00
Inserted 1:24	
Bob Abreu	15.00
Moises Alou	15.00
Rick Ankiel	6.00
Michael Barrett	5.00
Josh Beckett	25.00
Rob Bell	5.00
Adrian Beltre	15.00
Carlos Beltran	15.00
Wade Boggs	25.00
Barry Bonds	150.00
Kent Bottenfield	5.00
Milton Bradley	10.00
Pat Burrell	20.00
Chris Carpenter	20.00
Sean Casey	15.00
Eric Chavez	15.00
Will Clark	25.00
Johnny Damon	20.00
Mike Darr	5.00
Ben Davis	5.00
Russ Davis	5.00
Carlos Delgado	20.00
Jason Dewey	5.00
Octavio Dotel	5.00
J.D. Drew	15.00
Ray Durham	8.00
Damion Easley	6.00
Kelvim Escobar	5.00
Carlos Febles	6.00
Freddy Garcia	10.00
Jeremy Giambi	10.00
Todd Greene	5.00
Jason Grilli	5.00
Vladimir Guerrero	30.00
Tony Gwynn	40.00
Jerry Hairston Jr.	10.00
Mike Hampton	8.00
Todd Helton	20.00
Trevor Hoffman	10.00
Tim Hudson	15.00
John Jaha	5.00
Derek Jeter	100.00
D'Angelo Jimenez	5.00
Randy Johnson	60.00
Jason Kendall	10.00
Adam Kennedy	8.00
Cesar King	5.00
Paul Konerko	15.00
Mark Kotsay	6.00
Ray Lankford	6.00
Jason LaRue	6.00
Matt Lawton	10.00
Carlos Lee	8.00
Mike Lieberthal	8.00
Cole Liniak	5.00
Steve Lomasney	5.00
Jose Macias	5.00
Greg Maddux	60.00
Edgar Martinez	15.00
Pedro Martinez	75.00
Ruben Mateo	8.00
Gary Matthews Jr.	8.00
Aaron McNeal	5.00
Raul Mondesi	5.00
Orber Moreno	5.00
Warren Morris	5.00
Eric Munson	8.00
Heath Murray	5.00
Mike Mussina	30.00
Joe Nathan	5.00
Rafael Palmeiro	25.00
Jim Parque	6.00
Angel Pena	5.00
Wily Pena	10.00
Pokey Reese	5.00
Matt Riley	5.00
Cal Ripken Jr.	85.00
Alex Rodriguez	75.00
Scott Rolen	20.00
Jimmy Rollins	20.00
B.J. Ryan	5.00
Randall Simon	8.00
Chris Singleton	5.00

Alfonso Soriano	30.00
Shannon Stewart	10.00
Mike Sweeney	8.00
Miguel Tejada	20.00
Frank Thomas	25.00
Wilton Veras	5.00
Billy Wagner	12.00
Jeff Weaver	8.00
Rondell White	8.00
Scott Williamson	8.00
Randy Wolf	8.00
Jaret Wright	5.00
Ed Yarnall	5.00
Kevin Young	10.00

E-Xceptional Red

	NM/M
Complete Set (15):	100.00
Common Player:	3.00
Inserted 1:14	
Blue:	2-3X
Inserted 1:288	
Green:	1-1.5X
Production 999 Sets	
1 Ken Griffey Jr.	8.00
2 Derek Jeter	15.00
3 Nomar Garciaparra	6.00
4 Mark McGwire	10.00
5 Sammy Sosa	6.00
6 Mike Piazza	8.00
7 Alex Rodriguez	10.00
8 Cal Ripken Jr.	15.00
9 Chipper Jones	6.00
10 Pedro Martinez	4.00
11 Jeff Bagwell	4.00
12 Greg Maddux	6.00
13 Roger Clemens	7.00
14 Tony Gwynn	5.00
15 Frank Thomas	4.00

E-Xciting

	NM/M
Complete Set (10):	25.00
Common Player:	1.00
Inserted 1:24	
1 Mark McGwire	6.00
2 Ken Griffey Jr.	4.00
3 Randy Johnson	2.00
4 Sammy Sosa	3.00
5 Manny Ramirez	2.00
6 Jose Canseco	1.00
7 Derek Jeter	6.00
8 Scott Rolen	1.50
9 Juan Gonzalez	1.25
10 Barry Bonds	6.00

E-Xplosive

	NM/M
Complete Set (20):	90.00
Common Player:	2.00
Production 2,499 Sets	

1 Tony Gwynn	6.00
2 Alex Rodriguez	10.00
3 Pedro Martinez	5.00
4 Sammy Sosa	6.00
5 Cal Ripken Jr.	15.00
6 Adam Piatt	2.00
7 Pat Burrell	2.50
8 J.D. Drew	2.50
9 Mike Piazza	8.00
10 Shawn Green	2.50
11 Troy Glaus	4.00
12 Randy Johnson	5.00
13 Juan Gonzalez	2.50
14 Chipper Jones	6.00
15 Ivan Rodriguez	4.00
16 Nomar Garciaparra	6.00
17 Ken Griffey Jr.	8.00
18 Nick Johnson	2.50
19 Mark McGwire	10.00
20 Frank Thomas	5.00

Generation E-X

	NM/M
Complete Set (15):	20.00
Common Player:	1.00
Inserted 1:8	
1 Rick Ankiel	1.00
2 Josh Beckett	1.50
3 Carlos Beltran	2.00
4 Pat Burrell	2.00
5 Freddy Garcia	1.00
6 Alex Rodriguez	5.00
7 Derek Jeter	6.00
8 Tim Hudson	1.50
9 Shawn Green	1.50
10 Eric Munson	1.00
11 Adam Piatt	1.00
12 Adam Kennedy	1.00
13 Nick Johnson	1.00
14 Alfonso Soriano	2.00
15 Nomar Garciaparra	4.00

Genuine Coverage

	NM/M
Common Player:	5.00
Inserted 1:144	
1 Alex Rodriguez	40.00
2 Tom Glavine	10.00
3 Cal Ripken Jr.	50.00
4 Edgar Martinez	5.00
5 Raul Mondesi	5.00
6 Carlos Beltran	5.00
7 Chipper Jones	25.00
8 Barry Bonds	50.00
9 Heath Murray	5.00
10 Tim Hudson	10.00
11 Mike Mussina	10.00
12 Derek Jeter	50.00

2001 E-X

	NM/M
Complete Set (130):	100.00
Common Player:	.25
Common SP (101-130):	4.00
Production Listed	
Pack (5):	4.00
Box (24):	80.00
1 Jason Kendall	.25
2 Derek Jeter	3.00
3 Greg Vaughn	.25
4 Eric Chavez	.40

5 Nomar Garciaparra	2.00
6 Roberto Alomar	.50
7 Barry Larkin	.25
8 Matt Lawton	.25
9 Larry Walker	.25
10 Chipper Jones	1.50
11 Scott Rolen	.75
12 Carlos Lee	.25
13 Adrian Beltre	.40
14 Ben Grieve	.25
15 Mike Sweeney	.25
16 John Olerud	.25
17 Gabe Kapler	.25
18 Brian Giles	.25
19 Luis Gonzalez	.40
20 Sammy Sosa	2.00
21 Roger Clemens	1.75
22 Vladimir Guerrero	1.00
23 Ken Griffey Jr.	2.00
24 Mark McGwire	2.50
25 Orlando Hernandez	.25
26 Shannon Stewart	.25
27 Fred McGriff	.25
28 Lance Berkman	.25
29 Carlos Delgado	.75
30 Mike Piazza	2.00
31 Juan Encarnacion	.25
32 David Justice	.25
33 Greg Maddux	1.50
34 Frank Thomas	1.00
35 Jason Giambi	.75
36 Ruben Mateo	.25
37 Todd Helton	1.00
38 Jim Edmonds	.25
39 Steve Finley	.25
40 Tom Glavine	.40
41 Mo Vaughn	.25
42 Phil Nevin	.25
43 Richie Sexson	.25
44 Craig Biggio	.25
45 Kerry Wood	.50
46 Pat Burrell	.60
47 Edgar Martinez	.25
48 Jim Thome	.25
49 Jeff Bagwell	1.00
50 Bernie Williams	.45
51 Andruw Jones	1.00
52 Gary Sheffield	.40
53 Johnny Damon	.40
54 Rondell White	.25
55 J.D. Drew	.50
56 Tony Batista	.25
57 Paul Konerko	.25
58 Rafael Palmeiro	.75
59 Cal Ripken Jr.	3.00
60 Darin Erstad	.60
61 Ivan Rodriguez	.75
62 Barry Bonds	3.00
63 Edgardo Alfonzo	.25
64 Ellis Burks	.25
65 Mike Lieberthal	.25
66 Robin Ventura	.25
67 Richard Hidalgo	.25
68 Magglio Ordonez	.40
69 Kazuhiro Sasaki	.25
70 Miguel Tejada	.50
71 David Wells	.25
72 Troy Glaus	1.00
73 Jose Vidro	.25
74 Shawn Green	.50
75 Barry Zito	.50
76 Jermaine Dye	.25
77 Geoff Jenkins	.25
78 Jeff Kent	.25
79 Al Leiter	.25
80 Deivi Cruz	.25
81 Eric Karros	.25
82 Albert Belle	.25
83 Pedro Martinez	1.00
84 Raul Mondesi	.25
85 Preston Wilson	.25
86 Rafael Furcal	.25
87 Rick Ankiel	.25

88 Randy Johnson	1.00
89 Kevin Brown	.25
90 Sean Casey	.35
91 Mike Mussina	.50
92 Alex Rodriguez	2.50
93 Andres Galarraga	.25
94 Juan Gonzalez	1.00
95 Manny Ramirez	1.00
96 Mark Grace	.35
97 Carl Everett	.25
98 Tony Gwynn	1.50
99 Mike Hampton	.25
100 Ken Caminiti	.25
101 Jason Hart/1749	4.00
102 Corey Patterson/1199	5.00
103 Timo Perez/1999	4.00
104 Marcus Giles/1999	4.00
105 Ichiro Suzuki/1999 RC	50.00
106 Aubrey Huff/1499	8.00
107 Joe Crede/1999	5.00
108 Larry Barnes/1499	4.00
109 Esix Snead/1499 RC	4.00
110 Kenny Kelly/2249	4.00
111 Justin Miller/2249	4.00
112 Jack Cust/1999	4.00
113 Xavier Nady/999	4.00
114 Eric Munson/1499	4.00
115 Elpidio Guzman/1749 RC	4.00
116 Juan Pierre/2189	4.00
117 Winston Abreu/1749 RC	4.00
118 Keith Ginter/1999	4.00
119 Jace Brewer/2699	4.00
120 Paxton Crawford/2249	4.00
121 Jason Tyner/2249	4.00
122 Tike Redman/1999	4.00
123 John Riedling/2499	4.00
124 Jose Ortiz/1499	4.00
125 Oswaldo Mairena/2499	4.00
126 Eric Byrnes/2249	4.00
127 Brian Cole/999	4.00
128 Adam Piatt/2249	4.00
129 Nate Rolison/2499	4.00
130 Keith McDonald/2249	4.00

Essential Credentials

	NM/M
Stars (1-100):	3-6X
Production 299	
Common (101-130):	10.00
Minor Stars (101-130):	15.00
Production 29	
(See 2001 E-X for checklist and base card values.)	

Base Inks

	NM/M
Random Inserts	
Derek Jeter/AU/500	110.00

Behind the Numbers

	NM/M
Common Player:	5.00
Inserted 1:33	
1BN Johnny Bench	10.00
2BN Wade Boggs	15.00
3BN George Brett	20.00

4BN	Lou Brock	5.00
5BN	Rollie Fingers	5.00
6BN	Carlton Fisk	10.00
7BN	Reggie Jackson	10.00
8BN	Al Kaline	10.00
10BN	Willie McCovey	5.00
11BN	Paul Molitor	10.00
12BN	Eddie Murray	10.00
13BN	Jim Palmer	5.00
14BN	Ozzie Smith	15.00
15BN	Nolan Ryan	30.00
16BN	Mike Schmidt	20.00
17BN	Tom Seaver	10.00
18BN	Dave Winfield	5.00
19BN	Ted Williams	75.00
20BN	Robin Yount	10.00
21BN	Brady Anderson	5.00
22BN	Rick Ankiel	5.00
23BN	Albert Belle	5.00
24BN	Adrian Beltre	7.50
25BN	Barry Bonds	30.00
26BN	Eric Chavez	5.00
27BN	J.D. Drew	6.00
28BN	Darin Erstad	5.00
29BN	Troy Glaus	6.00
30BN	Mark Grace	6.00
31BN	Ben Grieve	5.00
32BN	Tony Gwynn	15.00
33BN	Todd Helton	10.00
34BN	Derek Jeter	30.00
35BN	Jeff Kent	5.00
36BN	Jason Kendall	5.00
37BN	Greg Maddux	15.00
38BN	John Olerud	5.00
39BN	Cal Ripken Jr.	30.00
40BN	Chipper Jones	15.00
41BN	John Smoltz	5.00
42BN	Frank Thomas	10.00
43BN	Robin Ventura	5.00
44BN	Bernie Williams	6.00

Behind the Numbers Autograph

NM/M

Quantity produced listed

2BN	Wade Boggs/26	150.00
4BN	Lou Brock/20	100.00
5BN	Rollie Fingers/34	50.00
6BN	Carlton Fisk/27	125.00
7BN	Reggie Jackson/44	80.00
10BN	Willie McCovey/44	80.00
12BN	Eddie Murray/33	100.00
13BN	Jim Palmer/22	100.00
15BN	Nolan Ryan/34	350.00
16BN	Mike Schmidt/20	200.00
17BN	Tom Seaver/41	80.00
18BN	Dave Winfield/31	60.00
20BN	Robin Yount/19	180.00
22BN	Rick Ankiel/66	20.00
23BN	Albert Belle/88	20.00
24BN	Adrian Beltre/29	25.00
25BN	Barry Bonds/25	250.00
28BN	Darin Erstad/17	80.00
29BN	Troy Glaus/25	80.00
30BN	Mark Grace/17	100.00
32BN	Tony Gwynn/19	150.00
33BN	Todd Helton/17	125.00
35BN	Jeff Kent/2	50.00
36BN	Jason Kendall/18	40.00
37BN	Greg Maddux/29	250.00
41BN	John Smoltz/29	40.00
42BN	Frank Thomas/35	75.00
44BN	Bernie Williams/51	75.00

Derek Jeter Monumental Moments

NM/M

| 2DJMM | Derek Jeter (Edition of 1,996.) | 5.00 |

| 2DJMM | Derek Jeter (Autographed edition of 96.) | 80.00 |

E-Xtra Innings

NM/M

Complete Set (10):		30.00
Common Player:		2.00
Inserted 1:20 R		
1XI	Mark McGwire	5.00
2XI	Sammy Sosa	4.00
3XI	Chipper Jones	3.00
4XI	Mike Piazza	4.00
5XI	Cal Ripken Jr.	6.00
6XI	Ken Griffey Jr.	4.00
7XI	Alex Rodriguez	5.00
8XI	Vladimir Guerrero	2.00
9XI	Nomar Garciaparra	4.00
10XI	Derek Jeter	6.00

Prospects Autograph

NM/M

Common Autograph:		8.00
Prod. #'s Listed		
101	Jason Hart/250	8.00
102	Corey Patterson/800	15.00
103	Timoniel Perez/1000	8.00
104	Marcus Giles/500	10.00
106	Aubrey Huff/500	15.00
107	Joe Crede/500	10.00
108	Larry Barnes/500	8.00
109	Esix Snead/500	8.00
110	Kenny Kelly/250	8.00
111	Justin Miller/250	8.00
112	Jack Cust/1000	10.00
113	Xavier Nady/1000	10.00
114	Eric Munson/1500	8.00
115	Elpidio Guzman/250	8.00
116	Juan Pierre/810	10.00
117	Winston Abreu/250	8.00
118	Keith Ginter/500	8.00
119	Jace Brewer/300	8.00
120	Paxton Crawford/250	8.00
121	Jason Tyner/250	8.00
122	Tike Redman/250	8.00
123	John Riedling/500	8.00
124	Jose Ortiz/500	8.00
125	Oswaldo Mairena/500	8.00
126	Eric Byrnes/250	8.00
127	Brian Cole/2000	8.00
128	Adam Piatt/250	8.00
129	Nate Rolison/500	8.00
130	Keith McDonald/250	8.00

Wall of Fame

NM/M

Common Player:		4.00
Inserted 1:24		
1WF	Robin Yount	8.00

2WF	Paul Molitor	8.00
3WF	Geoff Jenkins	4.00
4WF	Mark McGwire	15.00
5WF	Sammy Sosa	12.00
6WF	Greg Maddux	10.00
7WF	Mike Piazza	12.00
8WF	Cal Ripken Jr.	20.00
9WF	Todd Helton	8.00
10WF	Ken Griffey Jr.	12.00
11WF	Alex Rodriguez	15.00
12WF	Vladimir Guerrero	8.00
13WF	Jeff Bagwell	8.00
14WF	Ivan Rodriguez	6.00
15WF	Juan Gonzalez	8.00
16WF	Barry Bonds	20.00
17WF	Derek Jeter	20.00
18WF	Chipper Jones	10.00
19WF	Frank Thomas	8.00
20WF	Tony Gwynn	10.00
21WF	Nomar Garciaparra	12.00
22WF	Manny Ramirez	8.00
23WF	Andruw Jones	8.00
24WF	Scott Rolen	6.00
25WF	Jason Kendall	4.00
26WF	Roger Clemens	15.00
27WF	Troy Glaus	6.00
28WF	Pedro Martinez	8.00
29WF	Jason Giambi	5.00
30WF	Pat Burrell	5.00

F

1993 Finest

NM/M

Complete Set (199):		75.00
Common Player:		.50
Refractors:		40-50X
Pack (6):		15.00
Wax Box (18):		300.00
1	Dave Justice	.50
2	Lou Whitaker	.50
3	Bryan Harvey	.50
4	Carlos Garcia	.50
5	Sid Fernandez	.50
6	Brett Butler	.50
7	Scott Cooper	.50
8	B.J. Surhoff	.50
9	Steve Finley	.50
10	Curt Schilling	2.00
11	Jeff Bagwell	4.00
12	Alex Cole	.50
13	John Olerud	.50
14	John Smiley	.50
15	Bip Roberts	.50
16	Albert Belle	.50
17	Duane Ward	.50
18	Alan Trammell	.50
19	Andy Benes	.50
20	Reggie Sanders	.50
21	Todd Zeile	.50
22	Rick Aguilera	.50
23	Dave Hollins	.50
24	Jose Rijo	.50
25	Matt Williams	.50
26	Sandy Alomar	.50
27	Alex Fernandez	.50
28	Ozzie Smith	6.00
29	Ramon Martinez	.50
30	Bernie Williams	.50
31	Gary Sheffield	1.00
32	Eric Karros	.50
33	Frank Viola	.50
34	Kevin Young	.50
35	Ken Hill	.50
36	Tony Fernandez	.50
37	Tim Wakefield	.50
38	John Kruk	.50
39	Chris Sabo	.50
40	Marquis Grissom	.50

41	Glenn Davis	.50
42	Jeff Montgomery	.50
43	Kenny Lofton	.50
44	John Burkett	.50
45	Darryl Hamilton	.50
46	Jim Abbott	.50
47	Ivan Rodriguez	3.00
48	Eric Young	.50
49	Mitch Williams	.50
50	Harold Reynolds	.50
51	Brian Harper	.50
52	Rafael Palmeiro	3.00
53	Bret Saberhagen	.50
54	Jeff Conine	.50
55	Ivan Calderon	.50
56	Juan Guzman	.50
57	Carlos Baerga	.50
58	Charles Nagy	.50
59	Wally Joyner	.50
60	Charlie Hayes	.50
61	Shane Mack	.50
62	Pete Harnisch	.50
63	George Brett	8.00
64	Lance Johnson	.50
65	Ben McDonald	.50
66	Bobby Bonilla	.50
67	Terry Steinbach	.50
68	Ron Gant	.50
69	Doug Jones	.50
70	Paul Molitor	4.00
71	Brady Anderson	.50
72	Chuck Finley	.50
73	Mark Grace	.75
74	Mike Devereaux	.50
75	Tony Phillips	.50
76	Chuck Knoblauch	.50
77	Tony Gwynn	6.00
78	Kevin Appier	.50
79	Sammy Sosa	6.00
80	Mickey Tettleton	.50
81	Felix Jose	.50
82	Mark Langston	.50
83	Gregg Jefferies	.50
84	Andre Dawson/AS	1.00
85	Greg Maddux/AS	6.00
86	Rickey Henderson/AS	4.00
87	Tom Glavine/AS	2.50
88	Roberto Alomar/AS	1.00
89	Darryl Strawberry/AS	.50
90	Wade Boggs/AS	6.00
91	Bo Jackson/AS	1.00
92	Mark McGwire/AS	6.00
93	Robin Ventura/AS	.50
94	Joe Carter/AS	.50
95	Lee Smith/AS	.50
96	Cal Ripken, Jr./AS	10.00
97	Larry Walker/AS	.50
98	Don Mattingly/AS	8.00
99	Jose Canseco/AS	2.50
100	Dennis Eckersley/AS	3.00
101	Terry Pendleton/AS	.50
102	Frank Thomas/AS	4.00
103	Barry Bonds/AS	10.00
104	Roger Clemens/AS	8.00
105	Ryne Sandberg/AS	6.00
106	Fred McGriff/AS	.50
107	Nolan Ryan/AS	10.00
108	Will Clark/AS	.50
109	Pat Listach/AS	.50
110	Ken Griffey Jr./AS	6.00
111	Cecil Fielder/AS	.50
112	Kirby Puckett/AS	6.00
113	Dwight Gooden/AS	.50
114	Barry Larkin/AS	.50
115	David Cone/AS	.50
116	Juan Gonzalez/AS	2.50
117	Kent Hrbek	.50
118	Tim Wallach	.50
119	Craig Biggio	.50
120	Bobby Kelly	.50
121	Greg Olson	.50
122	Eddie Murray	4.00
123	Wil Cordero	.50
124	Jay Buhner	.50
125	Carlton Fisk	4.00
126	Eric Davis	.50
127	Doug Drabek	.50
128	Ozzie Guillen	.50
129	John Wetteland	.50
130	Andres Galarraga	.50
131	Ken Caminiti	.50
132	Tom Candiotti	.50
133	Pat Borders	.50
134	Kevin Brown	.50
135	Travis Fryman	.50
136	Kevin Mitchell	.50
137	Greg Swindell	.50
138	Benny Santiago	.50
139	Reggie Jefferson	.50
140	Chris Bosio	.50
141	Deion Sanders	.60
142	Scott Erickson	.50
143	Howard Johnson	.50
144	Orestes Destrade	.50

145	Jose Guzman	.50
146	Chad Curtis	.50
147	Cal Eldred	.50
148	Willie Greene	.50
149	Tommy Greene	.50
150	Erik Hanson	.50
151	Bob Welch	.50
152	John Jaha	.50
153	Harold Baines	.50
154	Randy Johnson	4.00
155	Al Martin	.50
156	J.T. Snow RC	1.50
157	Mike Mussina	2.50
158	Ruben Sierra	.50
159	Dean Palmer	.50
160	Steve Avery	.50
161	Julio Franco	.50
162	Dave Winfield	4.00
163	Tim Salmon	.50
164	Tom Henke	.50
165	Mo Vaughn	.50
166	John Smoltz	.50
167	Danny Tartabull	.50
168	Delino DeShields	.50
169	Charlie Hough	.50
170	Paul O'Neill	.50
171	Darren Daulton	.50
172	Jack McDowell	.50
173	Junior Felix	.50
174	Jimmy Key	.50
175	George Bell	.50
176	Mike Stanton	.50
177	Len Dykstra	.50
178	Norm Charlton	.50
179	Eric Anthony	.50
180	Bob Dibble	.50
181	Otis Nixon	.50
182	Randy Myers	.50
183	Tim Raines	.50
184	Orel Hershiser	.50
185	Andy Van Slyke	.50
186	Mike Lansing RC	1.00
187	Ray Lankford	.50
188	Mike Morgan	.50
189	Moises Alou	.50
190	Edgar Martinez	.50
191	John Franco	.50
192	Robin Yount	5.00
193	Bob Tewksbury	.50
194	Jay Bell	.50
195	Luis Gonzalez	.50
196	Dave Fleming	.50
197	Mike Greenwell	.50
198	David Nied	.50
199	Mike Piazza	10.00

Refractors

		NM/M
Common Player:		15.00
1	Dave Justice	15.00
2	Lou Whitaker	15.00
3	Bryan Harvey/SP	45.00
4	Carlos Garcia	15.00
5	Sid Fernandez	15.00
6	Brett Butler	15.00
7	Scott Cooper	15.00
8	B.J. Surhoff	15.00
9	Steve Finley	15.00
10	Curt Schilling	50.00
11	Jeff Bagwell	100.00
12	Alex Cole	15.00
13	John Olerud	15.00
14	John Smiley	15.00
15	Bip Roberts	15.00
16	Albert Belle	15.00
17	Duane Ward	15.00
18	Alan Trammell	15.00
19	Andy Benes	15.00
20	Reggie Sanders	15.00
21	Todd Zeile	15.00
22	Rick Aguilera	15.00
23	Dave Hollins	15.00
24	Jose Rijo	15.00
25	Matt Williams	15.00
26	Sandy Alomar	15.00
27	Alex Fernandez	15.00
28	Ozzie Smith	100.00
29	Ramon Martinez	15.00
30	Bernie Williams	15.00
31	Gary Sheffield	40.00
32	Eric Karros	15.00
33	Frank Viola	15.00
34	Kevin Young	15.00
35	Ken Hill	15.00
36	Tony Fernandez	15.00
37	Tim Wakefield	15.00
38	John Kruk	15.00
39	Chris Sabo/SP	75.00
40	Marquis Grissom	15.00
41	Glenn Davis/SP	50.00
42	Jeff Montgomery	15.00
43	Kenny Lofton	15.00
44	John Burkett	15.00
45	Darryl Hamilton	15.00

46	Jim Abbott	15.00
47	Ivan Rodriguez	150.00
48	Eric Young	15.00
49	Mitch Williams	15.00
50	Harold Reynolds	15.00
51	Brian Harper	15.00
52	Rafael Palmeiro	75.00
53	Bret Saberhagen	15.00
54	Jeff Conine	15.00
55	Ivan Calderon	15.00
56	Juan Guzman	15.00
57	Carlos Baerga	15.00
58	Charles Nagy	15.00
59	Wally Joyner	15.00
60	Charlie Hayes	15.00
61	Shane Mack	15.00
62	Pete Harnisch	15.00
63	George Brett	125.00
64	Lance Johnson	15.00
65	Ben McDonald	15.00
66	Bobby Bonilla	15.00
67	Terry Steinbach	15.00
68	Ron Gant	15.00
69	Doug Jones	15.00
70	Paul Molitor	100.00
71	Brady Anderson	15.00
72	Chuck Finley	15.00
73	Mark Grace	15.00
74	Mike Devereaux	15.00
75	Tony Phillips	15.00
76	Chuck Knoblauch	15.00
77	Tony Gwynn	100.00
78	Kevin Appier	15.00
79	Sammy Sosa	150.00
80	Mickey Tettleton	15.00
81	Felix Jose	15.00
82	Mark Langston	15.00
83	Gregg Jefferies	15.00
84	Andre Dawson/AS	35.00
85	Greg Maddux/AS	150.00
86	Rickey Henderson/AS	125.00
87	Tom Glavine/AS	15.00
88	Roberto Alomar/AS	45.00
89	Darryl Strawberry/ AS	15.00
90	Wade Boggs/AS	100.00
91	Bo Jackson/AS	60.00
92	Mark McGwire/AS	200.00
93	Robin Ventura/AS	15.00
94	Joe Carter/AS/SP	50.00
95	Lee Smith/AS	15.00
96	Cal Ripken, Jr./AS	500.00
97	Larry Walker/AS/SP	100.00
98	Don Mattingly/AS	100.00
99	Jose Canseco/AS	50.00
100	Dennis Eckersley/AS	75.00
101	Terry Pendleton/AS	15.00
102	Frank Thomas/ AS/SP	200.00
103	Barry Bonds/AS	300.00
104	Roger Clemens/AS	200.00
105	Ryne Sandberg/AS	125.00
106	Fred McGriff/AS	15.00
107	Nolan Ryan/AS	500.00
108	Will Clark/AS/SP	75.00
109	Pat Listach/AS	15.00
110	Ken Griffey Jr./AS	450.00
111	Cecil Fielder/AS	15.00
112	Kirby Puckett/AS	100.00
113	Dwight Gooden/AS	15.00
114	Barry Larkin/AS	15.00
115	David Cone/AS	15.00
116	Juan Gonzalez/ AS/SP	150.00
117	Kent Hrbek	15.00
118	Tim Wallach	15.00
119	Craig Biggio	15.00
120	Bobby Kelly	15.00
121	Greg Olson	15.00
122	Eddie Murray	100.00
123	Wil Cordero	15.00
124	Jay Buhner	15.00
125	Carlton Fisk	75.00
126	Eric Davis	15.00
127	Doug Drabek	15.00
128	Ozzie Guillen	15.00
129	John Wetteland	15.00
130	Andres Galarraga	15.00
131	Ken Caminiti	15.00
132	Tom Candiotti	15.00
133	Pat Borders	15.00
134	Kevin Brown	15.00
135	Travis Fryman	15.00
136	Kevin Mitchell	15.00
137	Greg Swindell	15.00

Abbreviations

AS - All-Star
SP - Short Print

138	Benny Santiago	15.00
139	Reggie Jefferson	15.00
140	Chris Bosio	15.00
141	Deion Sanders	15.00
142	Scott Erickson	15.00
143	Howard Johnson	15.00
144	Orestes Destrade	15.00
145	Jose Guzman	15.00
146	Chad Curtis	15.00
147	Cal Eldred	15.00
148	Willie Greene/SP	75.00
149	Tommy Greene	15.00
150	Erik Hanson	15.00
151	Bob Welch	15.00
152	John Jaha	15.00
153	Harold Baines	15.00
154	Randy Johnson	100.00
155	Al Martin	15.00
156	J.T. Snow	15.00
157	Mike Mussina	45.00
158	Ruben Sierra	15.00
159	Dean Palmer	15.00
160	Steve Avery	15.00
161	Julio Franco	15.00
162	Dave Winfield	100.00
163	Tim Salmon/SP	50.00
164	Tom Henke	15.00
165	Mo Vaughn	15.00
166	John Smoltz	15.00
167	Danny Tartabull	15.00
168	Delino DeShields	15.00
169	Charlie Hough	15.00
170	Paul O'Neill	15.00
171	Darren Daulton	15.00
172	Jack McDowell	15.00
173	Junior Felix	15.00
174	Jimmy Key	15.00
175	George Bell	15.00
176	Mike Stanton	15.00
177	Len Dykstra	15.00
178	Norm Charlton	15.00
179	Eric Anthony	15.00
180	Bob Dibble	15.00
181	Otis Nixon	15.00
182	Randy Myers	15.00
183	Tim Raines	15.00
184	Orel Hershiser	15.00
185	Andy Van Slyke	15.00
186	Mike Lansing	15.00
187	Ray Lankford	15.00
188	Mike Morgan	15.00
189	Moises Alou	15.00
190	Edgar Martinez	15.00
191	John Franco	15.00
192	Robin Yount	90.00
193	Bob Tewksbury	15.00
194	Jay Bell	15.00
195	Luis Gonzalez	15.00
196	Dave Fleming	15.00
197	Mike Greenwell	15.00
198	David Nied	15.00
199	Mike Piazza	250.00

1993 Finest Promos

		NM/M
Complete Set (3):		25.00
Complete Set, Refractors (3):		1,500
88	Roberto Alomar	3.50
88r	Roberto Alomar (Refractor)	300.00
98	Don Mattingly	10.00
98r	Don Mattingly (Refractor)	500.00
107	Nolan Ryan	15.00
107r	Nolan Ryan (Refractor)	750.00

Jumbo All-Stars

	NM/M
Complete Set (33):	185.00
Common Player:	2.00

84	Andre Dawson	2.50
85	Greg Maddux	10.00
86	Rickey Henderson	7.50
87	Tom Glavine	3.00
88	Roberto Alomar	3.00
89	Darryl Strawberry	2.00
90	Wade Boggs	10.00
91	Bo Jackson	2.00
92	Mark McGwire	20.00
93	Robin Ventura	2.00
94	Joe Carter	2.00
95	Lee Smith	2.00
96	Cal Ripken, Jr.	30.00
97	Larry Walker	2.00
98	Don Mattingly	12.00
99	Jose Canseco	3.50
100	Dennis Eckersley	6.00
101	Terry Pendleton	2.00
102	Frank Thomas	7.50
103	Barry Bonds	30.00
104	Roger Clemens	12.00
105	Ryne Sandberg	10.00
106	Fred McGriff	2.00
107	Nolan Ryan	30.00
108	Will Clark	2.50
109	Pat Listach	2.00
110	Ken Griffey Jr.	15.00
111	Cecil Fielder	2.00
112	Kirby Puckett	10.00
113	Dwight Gooden	2.00
114	Barry Larkin	2.00
115	David Cone	2.00
116	Juan Gonzalez	7.50

1994 Finest

		NM/M
Complete Set (440):		40.00
Common Player:		.15
Refractors:		3X
Series 1 or 2 Pack (7):		1.50
Series 1 or 2 Box (24):		25.00
1	Mike Piazza	3.00
2	Kevin Stocker	.15
3	Greg McMichael	.15
4	Jeff Conine	.15
5	Rene Arocha	.15
6	Aaron Sele	.15
7	Brent Gates	.15
8	Chuck Carr	.15
9	Kirk Rueter	.15
10	Mike Lansing	.15
11	Al Martin	.15
12	Jason Bere	.15
13	Troy Neel	.15
14	Armando Reynoso	.15
15	Jeromy Burnitz	.15
16	Rich Amaral	.15
17	David McCarty	.15
18	Tim Salmon	.15
19	Steve Cooke	.15
20	Wil Cordero	.15

No.	Player	Price	No.	Player	Price	No.	Player	Price	No.	Player	Price
21	Kevin Tapani	.15	125	Devon White	.15	229	Marquis Grissom	.15	333	Reggie Jefferson	.15
22	Deion Sanders	.15	126	Ivan Rodriguez	1.25	230	Barry Bonds	5.00	334	Kevin McReynolds	.15
23	Jose Offerman	.15	127	Don Slaught	.15	231	Carlos Baerga	.15	335	Arthur Rhodes	.15
24	Mark Langston	.15	128	John Valentin	.15	232	Ken Griffey Jr.	3.00	336	Brian Hunter	.15
25	Ken Hill	.15	129	Jaime Navarro	.15	233	Dave Justice	.15	337	Tom Browning	.15
26	Alex Fernandez	.15	130	Dave Magadan	.15	234	Bobby Bonilla	.15	338	Pedro Munoz	.15
27	Jeff Blauser	.15	131	Brady Anderson	.15	235	Cal Ripken	5.00	339	Billy Ripken	.15
28	Royce Clayton	.15	132	Juan Guzman	.15	236	Sammy Sosa	2.50	340	Gene Harris	.15
29	Brad Ausmus	.15	133	John Wetteland	.15	237	Len Dykstra	.15	341	Fernando Vina	.15
30	Ryan Bowen	.15	134	Dave Stewart	.15	238	Will Clark	.15	342	Sean Berry	.15
31	Steve Finley	.15	135	Scott Servais	.15	239	Paul Molitor	1.50	343	Pedro Astacio	.15
32	Charlie Hayes	.15	136	Ozzie Smith	2.50	240	Barry Larkin	.15	344	B.J. Surhoff	.15
33	Jeff Kent	.15	137	Darrin Fletcher	.15	241	Bo Jackson	.35	345	Doug Drabek	.15
34	Mike Henneman	.15	138	Jose Mesa	.15	242	Mitch Williams	.15	346	Jody Reed	.15
35	Andres Galarraga	.15	139	Wilson Alvarez	.15	243	Ron Darling	.15	347	Ray Lankford	.15
36	Wayne Kirby	.15	140	Pete Incaviglia	.15	244	Darryl Kile	.15	348	Steve Farr	.15
37	Joe Oliver	.15	141	Chris Hoiles	.15	245	Geronimo Berroa	.15	349	Eric Anthony	.15
38	Terry Steinbach	.15	142	Darryl Hamilton	.15	246	Gregg Olson	.15	350	Pete Smith	.15
39	Ryan Thompson	.15	143	Chuck Finley	.15	247	Brian Harper	.15	351	Lee Smith	.15
40	Luis Alicea	.15	144	Archi Cianfrocco	.15	248	Rheal Cormier	.15	352	Mariano Duncan	.15
41	Randy Velarde	.15	145	Bill Wegman	.15	249	Rey Sanchez	.15	353	Doug Strange	.15
42	Bob Tewksbury	.15	146	Joey Cora	.15	250	Jeff Fassero	.15	354	Tim Bogar	.15
43	Reggie Sanders	.15	147	Darrell Whitmore	.15	251	Sandy Alomar	.15	355	Dave Weathers	.15
44	Brian Williams	.15	148	David Hulse	.15	252	Chris Bosio	.15	356	Eric Karros	.15
45	Joe Orsulak	.15	149	Jim Abbott	.15	253	Andy Stankiewicz	.15	357	Randy Myers	.15
46	Jose Lind	.15	150	Curt Schilling	.40	254	Harold Baines	.15	358	Chad Curtis	.15
47	Dave Hollins	.15	151	Bill Swift	.15	255	Andy Ashby	.15	359	Steve Avery	.15
48	Graeme Lloyd	.15	152	Tommy Greene	.15	256	Tyler Green	.15	360	Brian Jordan	.15
49	Jim Gott	.15	153	Roberto Mejia	.15	257	Kevin Brown	.15	361	Tim Wallach	.15
50	Andre Dawson	.40	154	Edgar Martinez	.15	258	Mo Vaughn	.15	362	Pedro Martinez	1.50
51	Steve Buechele	.15	155	Roger Pavlik	.15	259	Mike Harkey	.15	363	Bip Roberts	.15
52	David Cone	.15	156	Randy Tomlin	.15	260	Dave Henderson	.15	364	Lou Whitaker	.15
53	Ricky Gutierrez	.15	157	J.T. Snow	.15	261	Kent Hrbek	.15	365	Luis Polonia	.15
54	Lance Johnson	.15	158	Bob Welch	.15	262	Darrin Jackson	.15	366	Benny Santiago	.15
55	Tino Martinez	.15	159	Alan Trammell	.15	263	Bob Wickman	.15	367	Brett Butler	.15
56	Phil Hiatt	.15	160	Ed Sprague	.15	264	Spike Owen	.15	368	Shawon Dunston	.15
57	Carlos Garcia	.15	161	Ben McDonald	.15	265	Todd Jones	.15	369	Kelly Stinnett	.15
58	Danny Darwin	.15	162	Derrick May	.15	266	Pat Borders	.15	370	Chris Turner	.15
59	Dante Bichette	.15	163	Roberto Kelly	.15	267	Tom Glavine	.45	371	Ruben Sierra	.15
60	Scott Kamieniecki	.15	164	Bryan Harvey	.15	268	Dave Nilsson	.15	372	Greg Harris	.15
61	Orlando Merced	.15	165	Ron Gant	.15	269	Rich Batchelor	.15	373	Xavier Hernandez	.15
62	Brian McRae	.15	166	Scott Erickson	.15	270	Delino DeShields	.15	374	Howard Johnson	.15
63	Pat Kelly	.15	167	Anthony Young	.15	271	Felix Fermin	.15	375	Duane Ward	.15
64	Tom Henke	.15	168	Scott Cooper	.15	272	Orestes Destrade	.15	376	Roberto Hernandez	.15
65	Jeff King	.15	169	Rod Beck	.15	273	Mickey Morandini	.15	377	Scott Leius	.15
66	Mike Mussina	.75	170	John Franco	.15	274	Otis Nixon	.15	378	Dave Valle	.15
67	Tim Pugh	.15	171	Gary DiSarcina	.15	275	Ellis Burks	.15	379	Sid Fernandez	.15
68	Robby Thompson	.15	172	Dave Fleming	.15	276	Greg Gagne	.15	380	Doug Jones	.15
69	Paul O'Neill	.15	173	Wade Boggs	2.50	277	John Doherty	.15	381	Zane Smith	.15
70	Hal Morris	.15	174	Kevin Appier	.15	278	Julio Franco	.15	382	Craig Biggio	.15
71	Ron Karkovice	.15	175	Jose Bautista	.15	279	Bernie Williams	.15	383	Rick White	.15
72	Joe Girardi	.15	176	Wally Joyner	.15	280	Rick Aguilera	.15	384	Tom Pagnozzi	.15
73	Eduardo Perez	.15	177	Dean Palmer	.15	281	Mickey Tettleton	.15	385	Chris James	.15
74	Raul Mondesi	.15	178	Tony Phillips	.15	282	David Nied	.15	386	Bret Boone	.15
75	Mike Gallego	.15	179	John Smiley	.15	283	Johnny Ruffin	.15	387	Jeff Montgomery	.15
76	Mike Stanley	.15	180	Charlie Hough	.15	284	Dan Wilson	.15	388	Chad Kreuter	.15
77	Kevin Roberson	.15	181	Scott Fletcher	.15	285	Omar Vizquel	.15	389	Greg Hibbard	.15
78	Mark McGwire	4.00	182	Todd Van Poppel	.15	286	Willie Banks	.15	390	Mark Grace	.15
79	Pat Listach	.15	183	Mike Blowers	.15	287	Erik Pappas	.15	391	Phil Leftwich	.15
80	Eric Davis	.15	184	Willie McGee	.15	288	Cal Eldred	.15	392	Don Mattingly	2.75
81	Mike Bordick	.15	185	Paul Sorrento	.15	289	Bobby Witt	.15	393	Ozzie Guillen	.15
82	Dwight Gooden	.15	186	Eric Young	.15	290	Luis Gonzalez	.15	394	Gary Gaetti	.15
83	Mike Moore	.15	187	Bret Barberie	.15	291	Greg Pirkl	.15	395	Erik Hanson	.15
84	Phil Plantier	.15	188	Manuel Lee	.15	292	Alex Cole	.15	396	Scott Brosius	.15
85	Darren Lewis	.15	189	Jeff Branson	.15	293	Ricky Bones	.15	397	Tom Gordon	.15
86	Rick Wilkins	.15	190	Jim Deshaies	.15	294	Denis Boucher	.15	398	Bill Gullickson	.15
87	Darryl Strawberry	.15	191	Ken Caminiti	.15	295	John Burkett	.15	399	Matt Mieske	.15
88	Rob Dibble	.15	192	Tim Raines	.15	296	Steve Trachsel	.15	400	Pat Hentgen	.15
89	Greg Vaughn	.15	193	Joe Grahe	.15	297	Ricky Jordan	.15	401	Walt Weiss	.15
90	Jeff Russell	.15	194	Hipolito Pichardo	.15	298	Mark Dewey	.15	402	Greg Blosser	.15
91	Mark Lewis	.15	195	Denny Neagle	.15	299	Jimmy Key	.15	403	Stan Javier	.15
92	Gregg Jefferies	.15	196	Jeff Gardner	.15	300	Mike MacFarlane	.15	404	Doug Henry	.15
93	Jose Guzman	.15	197	Mike Benjamin	.15	301	Tim Belcher	.15	405	Ramon Martinez	.15
94	Kenny Rogers	.15	198	Milt Thompson	.15	302	Carlos Reyes	.15	406	Frank Viola	.15
95	Mark Lemke	.15	199	Bruce Ruffin	.15	303	Greg Harris	.15	407	Mike Hampton	.15
96	Mike Morgan	.15	200	Chris Hammond	.15	304	Brian Anderson RC	.15	408	Andy Van Slyke	.15
97	Andujar Cedeno	.15	201	Tony Gwynn	2.50	305	Terry Mulholland	.15	409	Bobby Ayala	.15
98	Orel Hershiser	.15	202	Robin Ventura	.15	306	Felix Jose	.15	410	Todd Zeile	.15
99	Greg Swindell	.15	203	Frank Thomas	1.50	307	Darren Holmes	.15	411	Jay Bell	.15
100	John Smoltz	.15	204	Kirby Puckett	2.50	308	Jose Rijo	.15	412	Denny Martinez	.15
101	Pedro Martinez	.15	205	Roberto Alomar	.30	309	Paul Wagner	.15	413	Mark Portugal	.15
102	Jim Thome	1.00	206	Dennis Eckersley	1.25	310	Bob Scanlan	.15	414	Bobby Munoz	.15
103	David Segui	.15	207	Joe Carter	.15	311	Mike Jackson	.15	415	Kirt Manwaring	.15
104	Charles Nagy	.15	208	Albert Belle	2.50	312	Jose Vizcaino	.15	416	John Kruk	.15
105	Shane Mack	.15	209	Greg Maddux	2.50	313	Rob Butler	.15	417	Trevor Hoffman	.15
106	John Jaha	.15	210	Ryne Sandberg	2.50	314	Kevin Seitzer	.15	418	Chris Sabo	.15
107	Tom Candiotti	.15	211	Juan Gonzalez	.75	315	Geronimo Pena	.15	419	Bret Saberhagen	.15
108	David Wells	.15	212	Jeff Bagwell	1.50	316	Hector Carrasco	.15	420	Chris Nabholz	.15
109	Bobby Jones	.15	213	Randy Johnson	1.50	317	Eddie Murray	1.50	421	James Mouton	.15
110	Bob Hamelin	.15	214	Matt Williams	.15	318	Roger Salkeld	.15	422	Tony Tarasco	.15
111	Bernard Gilkey	.15	215	Dave Winfield	1.50	319	Todd Hundley	.15	423	Carlos Delgado	.75
112	Chili Davis	.15	216	Larry Walker	.15	320	Danny Jackson	.15	424	Rondell White	.15
113	Todd Stottlemyre	.15	217	Roger Clemens	2.75	321	Kevin Young	.15	425	Javier Lopez	.15
114	Derek Bell	.15	218	Kenny Lofton	.15	322	Mike Greenwell	.15	426	Chan Ho Park RC	1.00
115	Mark McLemore	.15	219	Cecil Fielder	.15	323	Kevin Mitchell	.15	427	Cliff Floyd	.15
116	Mark Whiten	.15	220	Darren Daulton	.15	324	Chuck Knoblauch	.15	428	Dave Staton	.15
117	Mike Devereaux	.15	221	John Olerud	.15	325	Danny Tartabull	.15	429	J.R. Phillips	.15
118	Terry Pendleton	.15	222	Jose Canseco	.75	326	Vince Coleman	.15	430	Manny Ramirez	1.50
119	Pat Meares	.15	223	Rickey Henderson	1.50	327	Marvin Freeman	.15	431	Kurt Abbott	.15
120	Pete Harnisch	.15	224	Fred McGriff	.15	328	Andy Benes	.15	432	Melvin Nieves	.15
121	Moises Alou	.15	225	Gary Sheffield	.50	329	Mike Kelly	.15	433	Alex Gonzalez	.15
122	Jay Buhner	.15	226	Jack McDowell	.15	330	Karl Rhodes	.15	434	Rick Helling	.15
123	Wes Chamberlain	.15	227	Rafael Palmeiro	1.25	331	Allen Watson	.15	435	Danny Bautista	.15
124	Mike Perez	.15	228	Travis Fryman	.15	332	Damion Easley	.15	436	Matt Walbeck	.15

437	Ryan Klesko	.15
438	Steve Karsay	.15
439	Salomon Torres	.15
440	Scott Ruffcorn	.15

1994 Finest Bronze

		NM/M
Complete Set (3):		40.00
Common Player:		10.00
1	Barry Bonds	20.00
2	Ken Griffey Jr.	15.00
3	Frank Thomas	10.00

1994 Finest Pre-Production

		NM/M
Complete Set (40):		35.00
Common Player:		1.00
22	Deion Sanders	1.00
23	Jose Offerman	1.00
26	Alex Fernandez	1.00
31	Steve Finley	1.00
35	Andres Galarraga	1.00
43	Reggie Sanders	1.00
47	Dave Hollins	1.00
52	David Cone	1.00
59	Dante Bichette	1.00
61	Orlando Merced	1.00
62	Brian McRae	1.00
66	Mike Mussina	2.50
76	Mike Stanley	1.00
78	Mark McGwire	6.00
79	Pat Listach	1.00
82	Dwight Gooden	1.00
84	Phil Plantier	1.00
90	Jeff Russell	1.00
92	Gregg Jefferies	1.00
93	Jose Guzman	1.00
100	John Smoltz	1.00
102	Jim Thome	3.00
121	Moises Alou	1.00
125	Devon White	1.00
126	Ivan Rodriguez	3.00
130	Dave Magadan	1.00
136	Ozzie Smith	4.00
141	Chris Hoiles	1.00
149	Jim Abbott	1.00
151	Bill Swift	1.00
154	Edgar Martinez	1.00
157	J.T. Snow	1.00
159	Alan Trammell	1.00
163	Roberto Kelly	1.00
166	Scott Erickson	1.00
168	Scott Cooper	1.00
169	Rod Beck	1.00
177	Dean Palmer	1.00
182	Todd Van Poppel	1.00
185	Paul Sorrento	1.00

Refractors

		NM/M
Complete Set (440):		300.00
Common Player:		1.00
Stars/Rookies:		3X

(See 1994 Finest for checklist and base card prices.)

1994 Finest Superstar Jumbos

		NM/M
Complete Set (80):		140.00
Common Player:		1.00
1	Mike Piazza	12.50
2	Kevin Stocker	1.00
3	Greg McMichael	1.00
4	Jeff Conine	1.00
5	Rene Arocha	1.00
6	Aaron Sele	1.00
7	Brent Gates	1.00
8	Chuck Carr	1.00
9	Kirk Rueter	1.00
10	Mike Lansing	1.00
11	Al Martin	1.00
12	Jason Bere	1.00
13	Troy Neel	1.00
14	Armando Reynoso	1.00
15	Jeromy Burnitz	1.00
16	Rich Amaral	1.00
17	David McCarty	1.00
18	Tim Salmon	1.00
19	Steve Cooke	1.00
20	Wil Cordero	1.00
201	Tony Gwynn	7.50
202	Robin Ventura	1.00
203	Frank Thomas	6.00
204	Kirby Puckett	7.50
205	Roberto Alomar	2.00
206	Dennis Eckersley	5.00
207	Joe Carter	1.00
208	Albert Belle	1.00
209	Greg Maddux	7.50
210	Ryne Sandberg	7.50
211	Juan Gonzalez	3.00
212	Jeff Bagwell	6.00
213	Randy Johnson	6.00
214	Matt Williams	1.00
215	Dave Winfield	6.00
216	Larry Walker	1.00
217	Roger Clemens	10.00
218	Kenny Lofton	1.00
219	Cecil Fielder	1.00
220	Darren Daulton	1.00
221	John Olerud	1.00
222	Jose Canseco	4.00
223	Rickey Henderson	6.00
224	Fred McGriff	1.00
225	Gary Sheffield	2.00
226	Jack McDowell	1.00
227	Rafael Palmeiro	5.00
228	Travis Fryman	1.00
229	Marquis Grissom	1.00
230	Barry Bonds	20.00
231	Carlos Baerga	1.00
232	Ken Griffey Jr.	12.50
233	Dave Justice	1.00
234	Bobby Bonilla	1.00
235	Cal Ripken	20.00
236	Sammy Sosa	7.50
237	Len Dykstra	1.00
238	Will Clark	1.00
239	Paul Molitor	6.00
240	Barry Larkin	1.00
421	James Mouton	1.00
422	Tony Tarasco	1.00
423	Carlos Delgado	3.00
424	Rondell White	1.00
425	Javier Lopez	1.00
426	Chan Ho Park	1.00
427	Cliff Floyd	1.00
428	Dave Staton	1.00

429	J.R. Phillips	1.00
430	Manny Ramirez	6.00
431	Kurt Abbott	1.00
432	Melvin Nieves	1.00
433	Alex Gonzalez	1.00
434	Rick Helling	1.00
435	Danny Bautista	1.00
436	Matt Walbeck	1.00
437	Ryan Klesko	1.00
438	Steve Karsay	1.00
439	Salomon Torres	1.00
440	Scott Ruffcorn	1.00

1994 Finest Superstar Sampler

		NM/M
Complete Set (45):		400.00
Common Player:		4.00
1	Mike Piazza	35.00
18	Tim Salmon	4.00
35	Andres Galarraga	4.00
74	Raul Mondesi	4.00
92	Gregg Jefferies	4.00
201	Tony Gwynn	20.00
203	Frank Thomas	15.00
204	Kirby Puckett	20.00
205	Roberto Alomar	6.00
207	Joe Carter	4.00
208	Albert Belle	4.00
209	Greg Maddux	20.00
210	Ryne Sandberg	20.00
211	Juan Gonzalez	7.50
212	Jeff Bagwell	15.00
213	Randy Johnson	15.00
214	Matt Williams	4.00
216	Larry Walker	4.00
217	Roger Clemens	30.00
219	Cecil Fielder	4.00
220	Darren Daulton	4.00
221	John Olerud	4.00
222	Jose Canseco	7.50
224	Fred McGriff	4.00
225	Gary Sheffield	6.00
226	Jack McDowell	4.00
227	Rafael Palmeiro	12.00
229	Marquis Grissom	4.00
230	Barry Bonds	65.00
231	Carlos Baerga	4.00
232	Ken Griffey Jr.	35.00
233	Dave Justice	4.00
234	Bobby Bonilla	4.00
235	Cal Ripken Jr.	65.00
237	Len Dykstra	4.00
238	Will Clark	4.00
239	Paul Molitor	15.00
240	Barry Larkin	4.00
258	Mo Vaughn	4.00
267	Tom Glavine	7.50
390	Mark Grace	4.00
392	Don Mattingly	30.00
408	Andy Van Slyke	4.00
427	Cliff Floyd	4.00
430	Manny Ramirez	15.00

1995 Finest

	NM/M
Complete Set (220):	75.00

Common Player:		.25
Refractors:		5X
Series 1 or 2 Pack (7):		2.00
Series 1 or 2 Wax		
Box (24):		30.00
1	Raul Mondesi	.25
2	Kurt Abbott	.25
3	Chris Gomez	.25
4	Manny Ramirez	1.50
5	Rondell White	.25
6	William Van Landingham	.25
7	Jon Lieber	.25
8	Ryan Klesko	.25
9	John Hudek	.25
10	Joey Hamilton	.25
11	Bob Hamelin	.25
12	Brian Anderson	.25
13	Mike Lieberthal	.25
14	Rico Brogna	.25
15	Rusty Greer	.25
16	Carlos Delgado	1.00
17	Jim Edmonds	.65
18	Steve Trachsel	.25
19	Matt Walbeck	.25
20	Armando Benitez	.25
21	Steve Karsay	.25
22	Jose Oliva	.25
23	Cliff Floyd	.25
24	Kevin Foster	.25
25	Javier Lopez	.25
26	Jose Valentin	.25
27	James Mouton	.25
28	Hector Carrasco	.25
29	Orlando Miller	.25
30	Garret Anderson	.25
31	Marvin Freeman	.25
32	Brett Butler	.25
33	Roberto Kelly	.25
34	Rod Beck	.25
35	Jose Rijo	.25
36	Edgar Martinez	.25
37	Jim Thome	.65
38	Rick Wilkins	.25
39	Wally Joyner	.25
40	Wil Cordero	.25
41	Tommy Greene	.25
42	Travis Fryman	.25
43	Don Slaught	.25
44	Brady Anderson	.25
45	Matt Williams	.25
46	Rene Arocha	.25
47	Rickey Henderson	1.50
48	Mike Mussina	.75
49	Greg McMichael	.25
50	Jody Reed	.25
51	Tino Martinez	.25
52	Dave Clark	.25
53	John Valentin	.25
54	Bret Boone	.25
55	Walt Weiss	.25
56	Kenny Lofton	.25
57	Scott Leius	.25
58	Eric Karros	.25
59	John Olerud	.25
60	Chris Hoiles	.25
61	Sandy Alomar	.25
62	Tim Wallach	.25
63	Cal Eldred	.25
64	Tom Glavine	.50
65	Mark Grace	.25
66	Rey Sanchez	.25
67	Bobby Ayala	.25
68	Dante Bichette	.25
69	Andres Galarraga	.25
70	Chuck Carr	.25
71	Bobby Witt	.25
72	Steve Avery	.25
73	Bobby Jones	.25
74	Delino DeShields	.25
75	Kevin Tapani	.25
76	Randy Johnson	1.50
77	David Nied	.25
78	Pat Hentgen	.25
79	Tim Salmon	.25
80	Todd Zeile	.25
81	John Wetteland	.25
82	Albert Belle	.25
83	Ben McDonald	.25
84	Bobby Munoz	.25
85	Bip Roberts	.25
86	Mo Vaughn	.25
87	Chuck Finley	.25
88	Chuck Knoblauch	.25
89	Frank Thomas	1.50
90	Danny Tartabull	.25
91	Dean Palmer	.25
92	Len Dykstra	.25
93	J.R. Phillips	.25
94	Tom Candiotti	.25
95	Marquis Grissom	.25
96	Barry Larkin	.25
97	Bryan Harvey	.25
98	Dave Justice	.25

99	David Cone	.25
100	Wade Boggs	2.50
101	Jason Bere	.25
102	Hal Morris	.25
103	Fred McGriff	.25
104	Bobby Bonilla	.25
105	Jay Buhner	.25
106	Allen Watson	.25
107	Mickey Tettleton	.25
108	Kevin Appier	.25
109	Ivan Rodriguez	1.00
110	Carlos Garcia	.25
111	Andy Benes	.25
112	Eddie Murray	1.50
113	Mike Piazza	3.50
114	Greg Vaughn	1.50
115	Paul Molitor	1.50
116	Terry Steinbach	.25
117	Jeff Bagwell	1.50
118	Ken Griffey Jr.	3.50
119	Gary Sheffield	.75
120	Cal Ripken Jr.	5.00
121	Jeff Kent	.25
122	Jay Bell	.25
123	Will Clark	.25
124	Cecil Fielder	.25
125	Alex Fernandez	.25
126	Don Mattingly	3.00
127	Reggie Sanders	.25
128	Moises Alou	.25
129	Craig Biggio	.25
130	Eddie Williams	.25
131	John Franco	.25
132	John Kruk	.25
133	Jeff King	.25
134	Royce Clayton	.25
135	Doug Drabek	.25
136	Ray Lankford	.25
137	Roberto Alomar	.50
138	Todd Hundley	.25
139	Alex Cole	.25
140	Shawon Dunston	.25
141	John Roper	.25
142	Mark Langston	.25
143	Tom Pagnozzi	.25
144	Wilson Alvarez	.25
145	Scott Cooper	.25
146	Kevin Mitchell	.25
147	Mark Whiten	.25
148	Jeff Conine	.25
149	Chili Davis	.25
150	Luis Gonzalez	.25
151	Juan Guzman	.25
152	Mike Greenwell	.25
153	Mike Henneman	.25
154	Rick Aguilera	.25
155	Dennis Eckersley	1.00
156	Darrin Fletcher	.25
157	Darren Lewis	.25
158	Juan Gonzalez	.75
159	Dave Hollins	.25
160	Jimmy Key	.25
161	Roberto Hernandez	.25
162	Randy Myers	.25
163	Joe Carter	.25
164	Darren Daulton	.25
165	Mike MacFarlane	.25
166	Bret Saberhagen	.25
167	Kirby Puckett	2.50
168	Lance Johnson	.25
169	Mark McGwire	4.00
170	Jose Canseco	.75
171	Mike Stanley	.25
172	Lee Smith	.25
173	Robin Ventura	.25
174	Greg Gagne	.25
175	Brian McRae	.25
176	Mike Bordick	.25
177	Rafael Palmeiro	1.00
178	Kenny Rogers	.25
179	Chad Curtis	.25
180	Devon White	.25
181	Paul O'Neill	.25
182	Ken Caminiti	.25
183	Dave Nilsson	.25
184	Tim Naehring	.25
185	Roger Clemens	3.00
186	Otis Nixon	.25
187	Tim Raines	.25
188	Dennis Martinez	.25
189	Pedro Martinez	1.50
190	Jim Abbott	.25
191	Ryan Thompson	.25
192	Barry Bonds	5.00
193	Joe Girardi	.25
194	Steve Finley	.25
195	John Jaha	.25
196	Tony Gwynn	2.50
197	Sammy Sosa	2.50
198	John Burkett	.25
199	Carlos Baerga	.25
200	Ramon Martinez	.25
201	Aaron Sele	.25
202	Eduardo Perez	.25
203	Alan Trammell	.25
204	Orlando Merced	.25
205	Deion Sanders	.35
206	Robb Nen	.25
207	Jack McDowell	.25
208	Ruben Sierra	.25
209	Bernie Williams	.25
210	Kevin Seitzer	.25
211	Charles Nagy	.25
212	Tony Phillips	.25
213	Greg Maddux	2.50
214	Jeff Montgomery	.25
215	Larry Walker	.25
216	Andy Van Slyke	.25
217	Ozzie Smith	2.50
218	Geronimo Pena	.25
219	Gregg Jefferies	.25
220	Lou Whitaker	.25

Refractors

Complete Set (220): 400.00
Common Player: 1.00
Stars: 5X
(See 1995 Finest for checklist and base card values.)

Bronze League Leaders

NM/M
Complete Set (6): 20.00
Common Player: 2.50

1	Matt Williams	2.50
2	Tony Gwynn	6.50
3	Jeff Bagwell	5.00
4	Ken Griffey Jr.	9.00
5	Paul O'Neill	2.50
6	Frank Thomas	5.00

Flame Throwers

NM/M
Complete Set (9): 20.00
Common Player: 1.50

1	Jason Bere	1.50
2	Roger Clemens	8.00
3	Juan Guzman	1.50
4	John Hudek	1.50
5	Randy Johnson	5.00
6	Pedro Martinez	4.00
7	Jose Rijo	1.50
8	Bret Saberhagen	1.50
9	John Wetteland	1.50

Power Kings

NM/M
Complete Set (18): 35.00
Common Player: .75

1	Bob Hamelin	.75
2	Raul Mondesi	.75
3	Ryan Klesko	.75
4	Carlos Delgado	1.50
5	Manny Ramirez	3.00

6	Mike Piazza	5.00
7	Jeff Bagwell	3.00
8	Mo Vaughn	.75
9	Frank Thomas	3.00
10	Ken Griffey Jr.	5.00
11	Albert Belle	.75
12	Sammy Sosa	4.00
13	Dante Bichette	.75
14	Gary Sheffield	.75
15	Matt Williams	.75
16	Fred McGriff	.75
17	Barry Bonds	7.50
18	Cecil Fielder	.75

Update

NM/M
Complete Set (110): 20.00
Common Player: .25
Refractors: 5X
Wax Pack (7): 1.25
Wax Box (24): 20.00

221	Chipper Jones	2.50
222	Benji Gil	.25
223	Tony Phillips	.25
224	Trevor Wilson	.25
225	Tony Tarasco	.25
226	Roberto Petagine	.25
227	Mike MacFarlane	.25
228	Hideo Nomo RC	3.00
229	Mark McLemore	.25
230	Ron Gant	.25
231	Andujar Cedeno	.25
232	Mike Mimbs RC	.25
233	Jim Abbott	.25
234	Ricky Bones	.25
235	Marty Cordova	.25
236	Mark Johnson	.25
237	Marquis Grissom	.25
238	Tom Henke	.25
239	Terry Pendleton	.25
240	John Wetteland	.25
241	Lee Smith	.25
242	Jaime Navarro	.25
243	Luis Alicea	.25
244	Scott Cooper	.25
245	Gary Gaetti	.25
246	Edgardo Alfonzo	.25
247	Brad Clontz	.25
248	Dave Mlicki	.25
249	Dave Winfield	1.50
250	Mark Grudzielanek RC	.50
251	Alex Gonzalez	.25
252	Kevin Brown	.25
253	Esteban Loaiza	.25
254	Vaughn Eshelman	.25
255	Bill Swift	.25
256	Brian McRae	.25
257	Bobby Higginson RC	.50
258	Jack McDowell	.25
259	Scott Stahoviak	.25
260	Jon Nunnally	.25
261	Charlie Hayes	.25
262	Jacob Brumfield	.25
263	Chad Curtis	.25
264	Heathcliff Slocumb	.25
265	Mark Whiten	.25
266	Mickey Tettleton	.25
267	Jose Mesa	.25
268	Doug Jones	.25
269	Trevor Hoffman	.25
270	Paul Sorrento	.25
271	Shane Andrews	.25
272	Brett Butler	.25
273	Curtis Goodwin	.25
274	Larry Walker	.25
275	Phil Plantier	.25
276	Ken Hill	.25
277	Vinny Castilla	.25
278	Billy Ashley	.25
279	Derek Jeter	6.00
280	Bob Tewksbury	.25
281	Jose Offerman	.25
282	Glenallen Hill	.25
283	Tony Fernandez	.25
284	Mike Devereaux	.25
285	John Burkett	.25
286	Geronimo Berroa	.25
287	Quilvio Veras	.25
288	Jason Bates	.25
289	Lee Tinsley	.25
290	Derek Bell	.25
291	Jeff Fassero	.25
292	Ray Durham	.25
293	Chad Ogea	.25
294	Bill Pulsipher	.25
295	Phil Nevin	.25
296	Carlos Perez RC	.25
297	Roberto Kelly	.25
298	Tim Wakefield	.25
299	Jeff Manto	.25
300	Brian Hunter	.25
301	C.J. Nitkowski	.25
302	Dustin Hermanson	.25
303	John Mabry	.25
304	Orel Hershiser	.25
305	Ron Villone	.25
306	Sean Bergman	.25
307	Tom Goodwin	.25
308	Al Reyes	.25
309	Todd Stottlemyre	.25
310	Rich Becker	.25
311	Joey Cora	.25
312	Ed Sprague	.25
313	John Smoltz	.25
314	Frank Castillo	.25
315	Chris Hammond	.25
316	Ismael Valdes	.25
317	Pete Harnisch	.25
318	Bernard Gilkey	.25
319	John Kruk	.25
320	Marc Newfield	.25
321	Brian Johnson	.25
322	Mark Portugal	.25
323	David Hulse	.25
324	Luis Ortiz	.25
325	Mike Benjamin	.25
326	Brian Jordan	.25
327	Shawn Green	.75
328	Joe Oliver	.25
329	Felipe Lira	.25
330	Andre Dawson	.75

Update Refractors

NM/M
Complete Set (110): 100.00
Common Player: 1.00
Stars: 5X
(See 1995 Finest Update for checklist and base card values.)

1996 Finest

NM/M
Complete Set (359): 300.00

Bronze Set (220):	60.00
Common Bronze:	.15
Silver Set (91):	90.00
Typical Silver:	.50
Gold Set (47):	200.00
Typical Gold:	1.50
Series 1 Pack (6):	1.50
Series 1 Wax Box (24):	30.00
Series 2 Pack (6):	1.50
Series 2 Wax Box (24):	30.00

No.	Player	Value
1	Greg Maddux/S	3.00
2	Bernie Williams/S	.50
3	Ivan Rodriguez/S	1.50
4	Marty Cordova/S	2.00
5	Roberto Hernandez	.15
6	Tony Gwynn/S	7.50
7	Barry Larkin/S	.50
8	Terry Pendleton	.15
9	Albert Belle/G	2.00
10	Ray Lankford/S	.50
11	Mike Piazza/S	4.00
12	Ken Caminiti	.15
13	Larry Walker/S	.50
14	Matt Williams/S	.50
15	Dan Miceli	.15
16	Chipper Jones	2.00
17	John Wetteland	.15
18	Kirby Puckett/G	7.50
19	Tim Naehring	.15
20	Karim Garcia/G	2.00
21	Eddie Murray	1.25
22	Tim Salmon/S	.50
23	Kevin Appier	.15
24	Ken Griffey Jr.	3.00
25	Cal Ripken Jr./G	15.00
26	Brian McRae	.15
27	Pedro Martinez	1.25
28	Brian Jordan	.15
29	Mike Fetters	.15
30	Carlos Delgado	.65
31	Shane Reynolds	.15
32	Terry Steinbach	.15
33	Hideo Nomo/S	2.50
34	Mark Leiter	.15
35	Edgar Martinez/S	.50
36	David Segui	.15
37	Gregg Jefferies/S	.50
38	Bill Pulsipher/S	.50
39	Ryne Sandberg/G	7.50
40	Fred McGriff	.15
41	Shawn Green/S	.75
42	Jeff Bagwell/S	5.00
43	Jim Abbott/S	.50
44	Glenallen Hill	.15
45	Brady Anderson	.15
46	Roger Clemens/S	3.50
47	Jim Thome	.60
48	Frank Thomas	1.25
49	Chuck Knoblauch	.15
50	Lenny Dykstra	.15
51	Jason Isringhausen/G	2.00
52	Rondell White/S	.15
53	Tom Pagnozzi	.15
54	Dennis Eckersley/S	1.50
55	Ricky Bones	.15
56	David Justice	.15
57	Steve Avery	.15
58	Robby Thompson	.15
59	Hideo Nomo/S	1.00
60	Gary Sheffield/S	.75
61	Tony Gwynn	2.00
62	Will Clark/S	.50
63	Denny Neagle	.15
64	Mo Vaughn/G	2.00
65	Bret Boone/S	.50
66	Dante Bichette/S	2.00
67	Robin Ventura	.15
68	Rafael Palmeiro/S	1.50
69	Carlos Baerga/S	.50
70	Kevin Seitzer	.15
71	Ramon Martinez	.15
72	Tom Glavine/S	1.00
73	Garret Anderson/S	.50
74	Mark McGwire/S	12.00
75	Brian Hunter	.15
76	Alan Benes	.15
77	Randy Johnson/S	2.00
78	Jeff King/S	.50
79	Kirby Puckett/S	3.00
80	Ozzie Guillen	.15
81	Kenny Lofton/S	2.00
82	Benji Gil	.15
83	Jim Edmonds/G	2.00
84	Cecil Fielder/S	.50
85	Todd Hundley	.15
86	Reggie Sanders/S	.50
87	Pat Hentgen	.15
88	Ryan Klesko/S	.50
89	Chuck Finley	.15
90	Mike Mussina/G	2.50
91	John Valentin/S	.50
92	Derek Jeter	4.00
93	Paul O'Neill	.15
94	Darrin Fletcher	.15
95	Manny Ramirez/S	2.00
96	Delino DeShields	.15
97	Tim Salmon	.15
98	John Olerud	.15
99	Vinny Castilla/S	.50
100	Jeff Conine/G	2.00
101	Tim Wakefield	.15
102	Johnny Damon/S	3.50
103	Dave Stevens	.15
104	Orlando Merced	.15
105	Barry Bonds/G	15.00
106	Jay Bell	.15
107	John Burkett	.15
108	Chris Hoiles	.15
109	Carlos Perez/S	.50
110	Dave Nilsson	.15
111	Rod Beck	.15
112	Craig Biggio/S	.50
113	Mike Piazza	3.00
114	Mark Langston	.15
115	Juan Gonzalez/S	1.00
116	Rico Brogna	.15
117	Jose Canseco/S	3.00
118	Tom Goodwin	.15
119	Bryan Rekar	.15
120	David Cone	.15
121	Ray Durham/S	.50
122	Andy Pettitte	.40
123	Chili Davis	.15
124	John Smoltz	.15
125	Heathcliff Slocumb	.15
126	Dante Bichette	.15
127	C.J. Nitkowski/S	.50
128	Alex Gonzalez	.15
129	Jeff Montgomery	.15
130	Raul Mondesi/S	.50
131	Denny Martinez	.15
132	Mel Rojas	.15
133	Derek Bell	.15
134	Trevor Hoffman	.15
135	Ken Griffey Jr./G	9.00
136	Darren Daulton	.15
137	Pete Schourek	.15
138	Phil Nevin	.15
139	Andres Galarraga	.15
140	Chad Fonville	.15
141	Chipper Jones/G	7.50
142	Lee Smith/S	.50
143	Joe Carter/S	.50
144	J.T. Snow	.15
145	Greg Maddux/S	7.50
146	Barry Bonds	4.00
147	Orel Hershiser	.15
148	Quilvio Veras	.15
149	Will Clark	.15
150	Jose Rijo	.15
151	Mo Vaughn/S	.50
152	Travis Fryman	.15
153	Frank Rodriguez/S	.50
154	Alex Fernandez	.15
155	Wade Boggs	2.00
156	Troy Percival	.15
157	Moises Alou	.15
158	Javy Lopez	.15
159	Jason Giambi	.50
160	Steve Finley/S	.50
161	Jeff Bagwell/S	2.00
162	Mark McGwire	3.50
163	Eric Karros	.15
164	Jay Buhner/G	2.00
165	Cal Ripken Jr./S	6.00
166	Mickey Tettleton	.15
167	Barry Larkin	.15
168	Lyle Mouton/S	.50
169	Ruben Sierra	.15
170	Bill Swift	.15
171	Sammy Sosa/S	3.00
172	Chad Curtis	.15
173	Dean Palmer	.15
174	John Franco/S	.50
175	Bobby Bonilla	.15
176	Greg Colbrunn	.15
177	Jose Mesa	.15
178	Mike Greenwell	.15
179	Greg Vaughn/S	.50
180	Mark Wohlers/S	.50
181	Doug Drabek	.15
182	Paul O'Neill/S	.50
183	Wilson Alvarez	.15
184	Marty Cordova	.15
185	Hal Morris	.15
186	Frank Thomas/G	6.00
187	Carlos Garcia	.15
188	Albert Belle/S	.50
189	Mark Grace/S	.50
190	Marquis Grissom	.15
191	Checklist	.15
192	Chipper Jones/G	7.50
193	Will Clark	.15
194	Paul Molitor	1.25
195	Kenny Rogers	.15
196	Reggie Sanders	.15
197	Roberto Alomar/S	2.50
198	Dennis Eckersley/G	4.00
199	Raul Mondesi	.15
200	Lance Johnson	.15
201	Alvin Mormon	.15
202	George Arias/G	2.00
203	Jack McDowell	.15
204	Randy Myers	.15
205	Harold Baines	.15
206	Marty Cordova	.15
207	Rich Nomer RC	.15
208	Al Leiter	.15
209	Greg Gagne	.15
210	Ben McDonald	.15
211	Ernie Young/S	.50
212	Terry Adams	.15
213	Paul Sorrento	.15
214	Albert Belle	.15
215	Mike Blowers	.15
216	Jim Edmonds	.15
217	Felipe Crespo	.15
218	Fred McGriff/S	.50
219	Shawon Dunston	.15
220	Jimmy Haynes	.15
221	Jose Canseco	.50
222	Eric Davis	.15
223	Kimera Bartee/S	.50
224	Tim Raines	.15
225	Tony Phillips	.15
226	Charlie Hayes	.15
227	Eric Owens	.15
228	Roberto Alomar	.30
229	Rickey Henderson/S	2.00
230	Sterling Hitchcock/S	.50
231	Bernard Gilkey/S	.50
232	Hideo Nomo/G	2.50
233	Kenny Lofton	.15
234	Ryne Sandberg/S	3.00
235	Greg Maddux/S	3.00
236	Mark McGwire	3.50
237	Jay Buhner	.15
238	Craig Biggio	.15
239	Todd Stottlemyre/S	.50
240	Barry Bonds	4.00
241	Jason Kendall/S	.50
242	Paul O'Neill/S	.50
243	Chris Snopek/S	2.00
244	Ron Gant	.15
245	Paul Wilson	.15
246	Todd Hollandsworth	.15
247	Todd Zeile	.15
248	David Justice	.15
249	Tim Salmon/G	2.00
250	Moises Alou	.15
251	Bob Wolcott	.15
252	David Wells	.15
253	Juan Gonzalez	.65
254	Andres Galarraga	.15
255	Dave Hollins	.15
256	Devon White/S	.50
257	Sammy Sosa	2.00
258	Ivan Rodriguez	.75
259	Bip Roberts	.15
260	Tino Martinez	.15
261	Chuck Knoblauch/S	.50
262	Mike Stanley	.15
263	Wally Joyner/S	.50
264	Butch Huskey	.15
265	Jeff Conine	.15
266	Matt Williams/G	2.00
267	Mark Grace	.15
268	Jason Schmidt	.15
269	Otis Nixon	.15
270	Randy Johnson/G	5.00
271	Kirby Puckett	2.00
272	Andy Fox RC	.50
273	Andy Benes	.15
274	Sean Berry/S	.50
275	Mike Piazza	3.00
276	Rey Ordonez	.15
277	Benito Santiago/S	.50
278	Gary Gaetti	.15
279	Paul Molitor/S	5.00
280	Robin Ventura	.15
281	Cal Ripken Jr.	4.00
282	Carlos Baerga	.15
283	Roger Cedeno	.15
284	Chad Mottola/S	.50
285	Terrell Wade	.15
286	Kevin Brown	.15
287	Rafael Palmeiro	1.00
288	Mo Vaughn	.15
289	Dante Bichette/S	.50
290	Cecil Fielder/G	2.00
291	Doc Gooden	.50
292	Bob Tewksbury	.15
293	Kevin Mitchell/S	.50
294	Livan Hernandez/G RC	2.00
295	Russ Davis/S	.50
296	Chan Ho Park/S	.50
297	T.J. Mathews	.15
298	Manny Ramirez	1.25
299	Jeff Bagwell	1.25
300	Marty Janzen/G RC	2.00
301	Wade Boggs	2.00
302	Larry Walker/S	.50
303	Steve Gibralter	.15
304	B.J. Surhoff	.15
305	Ken Griffey Jr./S	4.00
306	Royce Clayton	.15
307	Sal Fasano	.15
308	Ron Gant/G	2.00
309	Gary Sheffield	.40
310	Ken Hill	.15
311	Joe Girardi	.15
312	Matt Lawton RC	.15
313	Billy Wagner/S	.50
314	Julio Franco	.15
315	Joe Carter	.15
316	Brooks Kieschnick	.15
317	Mike Grace/S RC	.50
318	Heathcliff Slocumb	.15
319	Barry Larkin	.15
320	Tony Gwynn	2.00
321	Ryan Klesko/G	2.00
322	Frank Thomas	1.25
323	Edgar Martinez	.15
324	Jermaine Dye/G	2.00
325	Henry Rodriguez	.15
326	Marvin Benard RC	.50
327	Kenny Lofton/S	.50
328	Derek Bell/S	.50
329	Ugueth Urbina	.15
330	Jason Giambi/G	3.00
331	Roger Salkeld	.15
332	Edgar Renteria	.15
333	Ryan Klesko	.15
334	Ray Lankford	.15
335	Edgar Martinez/G	2.00
336	Justin Thompson	.15
337	Gary Sheffield/S	.75
338	Rey Ordonez/G	2.00
339	Mark Clark	.15
340	Ruben Rivera	.15
341	Mark Grace/S	.50
342	Matt Williams	.15
343	Francisco Cordova RC	.25
344	Cecil Fielder	.50
345	Andres Galarraga/S	.50
346	Brady Anderson/S	.50
347	Sammy Sosa/G	7.50
348	Mark Grudzielanek	.15
349	Ron Coomer	.15
350	Derek Jeter/S	6.00
351	Rich Aurilia	.15
352	Jose Herrera	.15
353	Jay Buhner/S	.50
354	Juan Gonzalez/S	2.50
355	Craig Biggio/G	2.00
356	Tony Clark	.15
357	Tino Martinez/S	.50
358	Dan Naulty RC	.15
359	Checklist	.15

Refractors

	NM/M
Complete Set (359):	900.00
Bronze Set (220):	300.00
Common Bronze:	1.00
Bronze Stars:	4X
Silver Set (91):	250.00
Typical Silver:	2.00
Silver Stars:	2.5X
Gold Set (48):	600.00
Typical Gold:	6.00
Gold Stars:	2X

(See 1996 Finest for checklist and base card values.)

1997 Finest

	NM/M
Complete Set (350):	200.00
Bronze Set (200):	15.00
Common Bronze:	.15
Silver Set (100):	75.00
Typical Silver:	.50
Embossed Silvers:	2X
Gold Set (50):	150.00
Typical Gold:	2.00
Embossed Die-Cut Golds:	1.5X

Series 1 or 2 Pack (6): 1.50
Series 1 or 2 Wax
  Box (24): 25.00

1	Barry Bonds/B	2.00
2	Ryne Sandberg/B	.75
3	Brian Jordan/B	.15
4	Rocky Coppinger/B	.15
5	Dante Bichette/B	.15
6	Al Martin/B	.15
7	Charles Nagy/B	.15
8	Otis Nixon/B	.15
9	Mark Johnson/B	.15
10	Jeff Bagwell/B	.60
11	Ken Hill/B	.15
12	Willie Adams/B	.15
13	Raul Mondesi/B	.15
14	Reggie Sanders/B	.15
15	Derek Jeter/B	2.00
16	Jermaine Dye/B	.15
17	Edgar Renteria/B	.15
18	Travis Fryman/B	.15
19	Roberto Hernandez/B	.15
20	Sammy Sosa/B	.75
21	Garret Anderson/B	.15
22	Rey Ordonez/B	.15
23	Glenallen Hill/B	.15
24	Dave Nilsson/B	.15
25	Kevin Brown/B	.15
26	Brian McRae/B	.15
27	Joey Hamilton/B	.15
28	Jamey Wright/B	.15
29	Frank Thomas/B	.60
30	Mark McGwire/B	1.50
31	Ramon Martinez/B	.15
32	Jaime Bluma/B	.15
33	Frank Rodriguez/B	.15
34	Andy Benes/B	.15
35	Jay Buhner/B	.15
36	Justin Thompson/B	.15
37	Darin Erstad/B	.30
38	Gregg Jefferies/B	.15
39	Jeff D'Amico/B	.15
40	Pedro Martinez/B	.60
41	Nomar Garciaparra/B	.75
42	Jose Valentin/B	.15
43	Pat Hentgen/B	.15
44	Will Clark/B	.15
45	Bernie Williams/B	.15
46	Luis Castillo/B	.15
47	B.J. Surhoff/B	.15
48	Greg Gagne/B	.15
49	Pete Schourek/B	.15
50	Mike Piazza/B	1.00
51	Dwight Gooden/B	.15
52	Javy Lopez/B	.15
53	Chuck Finley/B	.15
54	James Baldwin/B	.15
55	Jack McDowell/B	.15
56	Royce Clayton/B	.15
57	Carlos Delgado/B	.35
58	Neifi Perez/B	.15
59	Eddie Taubensee/B	.15
60	Rafael Palmeiro/B	.50
61	Marty Cordova/B	.15
62	Wade Boggs/B	.75
63	Rickey Henderson/B	.60
64	Mike Hampton/B	.15
65	Troy Percival/B	.15
66	Barry Larkin/B	.15
67	Jermaine Allensworth/B	.15
68	Mark Clark/B	.15
69	Mike Lansing/B	.15
70	Mark Grudzielanek/B	.15
71	Todd Stottlemyre/B	.15
72	Juan Guzman/B	.15
73	John Burkett/B	.15
74	Wilson Alvarez/B	.15
75	Ellis Burks/B	.15
76	Bobby Higginson/B	.15
77	Ricky Bottalico/B	.15
78	Omar Vizquel/B	.15
79	Paul Sorrento/B	.15
80	Denny Neagle/B	.15
81	Roger Pavlik/B	.15
82	Mike Lieberthal/B	.15
83	Devon White/B	.15
84	John Olerud/B	.15
85	Kevin Appier/B	.15
86	Joe Girardi/B	.15
87	Paul O'Neill/B	.15
88	Mike Sweeney/B	.15
89	John Smiley/B	.15
90	Ivan Rodriguez/B	.50
91	Randy Myers/B	.15
92	Bip Roberts/B	.15
93	Jose Mesa/B	.15
94	Paul Wilson/B	.15
95	Mike Mussina/B	.30
96	Ben McDonald/B	.15
97	John Mabry/B	.15
98	Tom Goodwin/B	.15
99	Edgar Martinez/B	.15
100	Andruw Jones/B	.60
101	Jose Canseco/S	.75
102	Billy Wagner/S	.50
103	Dante Bichette/S	.50
104	Curt Schilling/S	1.00
105	Dean Palmer/S	.50
106	Larry Walker/S	.50
107	Bernie Williams/S	.50
108	Chipper Jones/S	2.00
109	Gary Sheffield/S	1.00
110	Randy Johnson/S	1.50
111	Roberto Alomar/S	.75
112	Todd Walker/S	.50
113	Sandy Alomar/S	.50
114	John Jaha/S	.50
115	Ken Caminiti/S	.50
116	Ryan Klesko/S	.50
117	Mariano Rivera/S	.75
118	Jason Giambi/S	1.00
119	Lance Johnson/S	.50
120	Robin Ventura/S	.50
121	Todd Hollandsworth/S	.50
122	Johnny Damon/S	.75
123	William Van Landingham/S	.50
124	Jason Kendall/S	.50
125	Vinny Castilla/S	.50
126	Harold Baines/S	.50
127	Joe Carter/S	.50
128	Craig Biggio/S	.50
129	Tony Clark/S	.50
130	Ron Gant/S	.50
131	David Segui/S	.50
132	Steve Trachsel/S	.50
133	Scott Rolen/S	1.00
134	Mike Stanley/S	.50
135	Cal Ripken Jr./S	5.00
136	John Smoltz/S	.50
137	Bobby Jones/S	.50
138	Manny Ramirez/S	1.50
139	Ken Griffey Jr./S	3.00
140	Chuck Knoblauch/S	.50
141	Mark Grace/S	.50
142	Chris Snopek/S	.50
143	Hideo Nomo/S	.75
144	Tim Salmon/S	.50
145	David Cone/S	.50
146	Eric Young/S	.50
147	Jeff Brantley/S	.50
148	Jim Thome/S	1.00
149	Trevor Hoffman/S	.50
150	Juan Gonzalez/S	.75
151	Mike Piazza/G	8.00
152	Ivan Rodriguez/G	4.00
153	Mo Vaughn/G	2.00
154	Brady Anderson/G	2.00
155	Mark McGwire/G	8.00
156	Rafael Palmeiro/G	4.00
157	Barry Larkin/G	2.00
158	Greg Maddux/G	7.50
159	Jeff Bagwell/G	5.00
160	Frank Thomas/G	6.00
161	Ken Caminiti/G	2.00
162	Andruw Jones/G	5.00
163	Dennis Eckersley/G	4.00
164	Jeff Conine/G	2.00
165	Jim Edmonds/G	2.00
166	Derek Jeter/G	12.00
167	Vladimir Guerrero/G	6.00
168	Sammy Sosa/G	5.00
169	Tony Gwynn/G	6.00
170	Andres Galarraga/G	2.00
171	Todd Hundley/G	2.00
172	Jay Buhner/G	2.00
173	Paul Molitor/G	6.00
174	Kenny Lofton/G	2.00
175	Barry Bonds/G	12.00
176	Gary Sheffield/G	.35
177	Dmitri Young/S	.15
178	Jay Bell/S	.15
179	David Wells/S	.15
180	Walt Weiss/S	.15
181	Paul Molitor/S	.60
182	Jose Guillen/S	.15
183	Al Leiter/S	.15
184	Mike Fetters/S	.15
185	Mark Langston/S	.15
186	Fred McGriff/S	.15
187	Darrin Fletcher/B	.15
188	Brant Brown/B	.15
189	Geronimo Berroa/B	.15
190	Jim Thome/B	.50
191	Jose Vizcaino/B	.15
192	Andy Ashby/B	.15
193	Rusty Greer/B	.15
194	Brian Hunter/B	.15
195	Chris Hoiles/B	.15
196	Orlando Merced/B	.15
197	Brett Butler/B	.15
198	Derek Bell/B	.15
199	Bobby Bonilla/B	.15
200	Alex Ochoa/B	.15
201	Wally Joyner/B	.15
202	Mo Vaughn/B	.15
203	Doug Drabek/B	.15
204	Tino Martinez/B	.15
205	Roberto Alomar/B	.30
206	Brian Giles/B RC	.75
207	Todd Worrell/B	.15
208	Alan Benes/B	.15
209	Jim Leyritz/B	.15
210	Darryl Hamilton/B	.15
211	Jimmy Key/B	.15
212	Juan Gonzalez/B	.35
213	Vinny Castilla/B	.15
214	Chuck Knoblauch/B	.15
215	Tony Phillips/B	.15
216	Jeff Cirillo/B	.15
217	Carlos Garcia/B	.15
218	Brooks Kieschnick/B	.15
219	Marquis Grissom/B	.15
220	Dan Wilson/B	.15
221	Greg Vaughn/B	.15
222	John Wetteland/B	.15
223	Andres Galarraga/B	.15
224	Ozzie Guillen/B	.15
225	Kevin Elster/B	.15
226	Bernard Gilkey/B	.15
227	Mike MacFarlane/B	.15
228	Heathcliff Slocumb/B	.15
229	Wendell Magee Jr./B	.15
230	Carlos Baerga/B	.15
231	Kevin Seitzer/B	.15
232	Henry Rodriguez/B	.15
233	Roger Clemens/B	1.00
234	Mark Wohlers/B	.15
235	Eddie Murray/B	.60
236	Todd Zeile/B	.15
237	J.T. Snow/B	.15
238	Ken Griffey Jr./B	1.00
239	Sterling Hitchcock/B	.15
240	Albert Belle/B	.15
241	Terry Steinbach/B	.15
242	Robb Nen/B	.15
243	Mark McLemore/B	.15
244	Jeff King/B	.15
245	Tony Clark/B	.15
246	Tim Salmon/B	.15
247	Benito Santiago/B	.15
248	Robin Ventura/B	.15
249	Bubba Trammell/B RC	.15
250	Chili Davis/B	.15
251	John Valentin/B	.15
252	Cal Ripken Jr./B	2.00
253	Matt Williams/B	.15
254	Jeff Kent/B	.15
255	Eric Karros/B	.15
256	Ray Lankford/B	.15
257	Ed Sprague/B	.15
258	Shane Reynolds/B	.15
259	Jaime Navarro/B	.15
260	Eric Davis/B	.15
261	Orel Hershiser/B	.15
262	Mark Grace/B	.15
263	Rod Beck/B	.15
264	Ismael Valdes/B	.15
265	Manny Ramirez/B	.60
266	Ken Caminiti/B	.15
267	Tim Naehring/B	.15
268	Jose Rosado/B	.15
269	Greg Colbrunn/B	.15
270	Dean Palmer/B	.15
271	David Justice/B	.15
272	Scott Spiezio/B	.15
273	Chipper Jones/B	.75
274	Mel Rojas/B	.15
275	Bartolo Colon/B	.15
276	Darin Erstad/S	1.00
277	Sammy Sosa/S	2.00
278	Rafael Palmeiro/S	1.00
279	Frank Thomas/S	1.50
280	Ruben Rivera/S	.50
281	Hal Morris/S	.15
282	Jay Buhner/S	.50
283	Kenny Lofton/S	.50
284	Jose Canseco/S	.75
285	Alex Fernandez/S	.50
286	Todd Helton/S	1.25
287	Andy Pettitte/S	1.00
288	John Franco/S	.50
289	Ivan Rodriguez/S	1.25
290	Ellis Burks/S	.50
291	Julio Franco/S	.50
292	Mike Piazza/S	3.00
293	Brian Jordan/S	.50
294	Greg Maddux/S	2.00
295	Bob Abreu/S	.50
296	Rondell White/S	.50
297	Moises Alou/S	.50
298	Tony Gwynn/S	2.00
299	Deion Sanders/S	.50
300	Jeff Montgomery/S	.50
301	Ray Durham/S	.50
302	John Wasdin/S	.50
303	Ryne Sandberg/S	2.00
304	Delino DeShields/S	.50
305	Mark McGwire/S	4.00
306	Andruw Jones/S	1.50
307	Kevin Orie/S	.50
308	Matt Williams/S	.50
309	Karim Garcia/S	.50
310	Derek Jeter/S	5.00
311	Mo Vaughn/S	.50
312	Brady Anderson/S	.50
313	Barry Bonds/S	5.00
314	Steve Finley/S	.50
315	Vladimir Guerrero/S	1.50
316	Matt Morris/S	.50
317	Tom Glavine/S	1.00
318	Jeff Bagwell/S	1.50
319	Albert Belle/S	.50
320	Hideki Irabu/S RC	1.00
321	Andres Galarraga/S	.50
322	Cecil Fielder/S	.50
323	Barry Larkin/S	.50
324	Todd Hundley/S	.50
325	Fred McGriff/S	.50
326	Gary Sheffield/G	3.00
327	Craig Biggio/G	2.00
328	Raul Mondesi/G	2.00
329	Edgar Martinez/G	2.00
330	Chipper Jones/G	8.00
331	Bernie Williams/G	2.00
332	Juan Gonzalez/G	3.00
333	Ron Gant/G	2.00
334	Cal Ripken Jr./G	12.00
335	Larry Walker/G	2.00
336	Matt Williams/G	2.00
337	Jose Cruz Jr./G	2.00
338	Joe Carter/G	2.00
339	Wilton Guerrero/G	2.00
340	Cecil Fielder/G	2.00
341	Todd Walker/G	2.00
342	Ken Griffey Jr./G	10.00
343	Ryan Klesko/G	2.00
344	Roger Clemens/G	10.00
345	Hideo Nomo/G	3.00
346	Dante Bichette/G	2.00
347	Albert Belle/G	2.00
348	Randy Johnson/G	6.00
349	Manny Ramirez/G	6.00
350	Jim Smoltz/G	2.00

1997 Finest Samples

		NM/M
Complete Set (5):		15.00
Common Player:		2.00
1	Barry Bonds	3.50
15	Derek Jeter	3.50
30	Mark McGwire	3.00
143	Hideo Nomo	2.50
159	Jeff Bagwell	2.50

Refractors

	NM/M
Common Bronze:	2.00
Bronze Stars:	6X
Typical Silver:	3.00
Silver Stars:	3X
Typical Gold:	8.00
Gold Stars:	2X
Typical Embossed Silver:	7.50
Embossed Silver Stars:	7X
Typical Embossed Gold:	20.00
Embossed Gold Stars:	5X

(See 1997 Finest for cheklist and base card values.)

Embossed

NM/M
Common Embossed Silver: 1.00
Embossed Silver Stars: 2X
Common Embossed Gold: 3.00
Embossed/Die-Cut
Gold Stars: 1.5X
(See 1997 Finest for checklist and base card values.)

1998 Finest

NM/M
Complete Set (275): 30.00
Common Player: .15
Pack (6): 1.50
Wax Box (24): 25.00
Jumbo Pack (13): 2.50
Jumbo Box (12): 25.00
1 Larry Walker .15
2 Andruw Jones .75
3 Ramon Martinez .15
4 Geronimo Berroa .15
5 David Justice .15
6 Rusty Greer .15
7 Chad Ogea .15
8 Tom Goodwin .15
9 Tino Martinez .15
10 Jose Guillen .15
11 Jeffrey Hammonds .15
12 Brian McRae .15
13 Jeremi Gonzalez .15
14 Craig Counsell .15
15 Mike Piazza 1.50
16 Greg Maddux 1.00
17 Todd Greene .15
18 Rondell White .15
19 Kirk Rueter .15
20 Tony Clark .15
21 Brad Radke .15
22 Jaret Wright .15
23 Carlos Delgado .50
24 Dustin Hermanson .15
25 Gary Sheffield .40
26 Jose Canseco .35
27 Kevin Young .15
28 David Wells .15
29 Mariano Rivera .25
30 Reggie Sanders .15
31 Mike Cameron .15
32 Bobby Witt .15
33 Kevin Orie .15
34 Royce Clayton .15
35 Edgar Martinez .15
36 Neifi Perez .15
37 Kevin Appier .15
38 Darryl Hamilton .15
39 Michael Tucker .15
40 Roger Clemens 1.25
41 Carl Everett .15
42 Mike Sweeney .15
43 Pat Meares .15

44 Brian Giles .15
45 Matt Morris .15
46 Jason Dickson .15
47 Rich Loiselle .15
48 Joe Girardi .15
49 Steve Trachsel .15
50 Ben Grieve .15
51 Jose Vizcaino .15
52 Hideki Irabu .15
53 J.T. Snow .15
54 Mike Hampton .15
55 Dave Nilsson .15
56 Alex Fernandez .15
57 Brett Tomko .15
58 Wally Joyner .15
59 Kelvim Escobar .15
60 Roberto Alomar .30
61 Todd Jones .15
62 Paul O'Neill .15
63 Jamie Moyer .15
64 Mark Wohlers .15
65 Jose Cruz Jr. .15
66 Troy Percival .15
67 Rick Reed .15
68 Will Clark .15
69 Jamey Wright .15
70 Mike Mussina .35
71 David Cone .15
72 Ryan Klesko .15
73 Scott Hatteberg .15
74 James Baldwin .15
75 Tony Womack .15
76 Carlos Perez .15
77 Charles Nagy .15
78 Jeromy Burnitz .15
79 Shane Reynolds .15
80 Cliff Floyd .15
81 Jason Kendall .15
82 Chad Curtis .15
83 Matt Karchner .15
84 Ricky Bottalico .15
85 Sammy Sosa 1.00
86 Javy Lopez .15
87 Jeff Kent .15
88 Shawn Green .25
89 Devon White .15
90 Tony Gwynn 1.00
91 Bob Tewksbury .15
92 Derek Jeter 2.50
93 Eric Davis .15
94 Jeff Fassero .15
95 Denny Neagle .15
96 Ismael Valdes .15
97 Tim Salmon .15
98 Mark Grudzielanek .15
99 Curt Schilling .35
100 Ken Griffey Jr. 1.50
101 Edgardo Alfonzo .15
102 Vinny Castilla .15
103 Jose Rosado .15
104 Scott Erickson .15
105 Alan Benes .15
106 Shannon Stewart .15
107 Delino DeShields .15
108 Mark Loretta .15
109 Todd Hundley .15
110 Chuck Knoblauch .15
111 Quinton McCracken .15
112 F.P. Santangelo .15
113 Gerald Williams .15
114 Omar Vizquel .15
115 John Valentin .15
116 Damion Easley .15
117 Matt Lawton .15
118 Jim Thome .60
119 Sandy Alomar .15
120 Albert Belle .60
121 Chris Stynes .15
122 Butch Huskey .15
123 Shawn Estes .15
124 Terry Adams .15
125 Ivan Rodriguez .60
126 Ron Gant .15
127 John Mabry .15
128 Jeff Shaw .15
129 Jeff Montgomery .15
130 Justin Thompson .15
131 Livan Hernandez .15
132 Ugueth Urbina .15
133 Doug Glanville .15
134 Troy O'Leary .15
135 Cal Ripken Jr. 2.50
136 Quilvio Veras .15
137 Pedro Astacio .15
138 Willie Greene .15
139 Lance Johnson .15
140 Nomar Garciaparra 1.00
141 Jose Offerman .15
142 Scott Rolen .60
143 Derek Bell .15
144 Johnny Damon .35
145 Mark McGwire 2.00
146 Chan Ho Park .15
147 Edgar Renteria .15
148 Eric Young .15
149 Craig Biggio .15

150 Checklist 1-150 .15
151 Frank Thomas .75
152 John Wetteland .15
153 Mike Lansing .15
154 Pedro Martinez .75
155 Rico Brogna .15
156 Kevin Brown .15
157 Alex Rodriguez 2.00
158 Wade Boggs 1.00
159 Richard Hidalgo .15
160 Mark Grace .15
161 Jose Mesa .15
162 John Olerud .15
163 Tim Belcher .15
164 Chuck Finley .15
165 Brian Hunter .15
166 Joe Carter .15
167 Stan Javier .15
168 Jay Bell .15
169 Ray Lankford .15
170 John Smoltz .15
171 Ed Sprague .15
172 Jason Giambi .50
173 Todd Walker .15
174 Paul Konerko .15
175 Rey Ordonez .15
176 Dante Bichette .15
177 Bernie Williams .15
178 Jon Nunnally .15
179 Rafael Palmeiro .60
180 Jay Buhner .15
181 Devon White .15
182 Jeff D'Amico .15
183 Walt Weiss .15
184 Scott Spiezio .15
185 Moises Alou .15
186 Carlos Baerga .15
187 Todd Zeile .15
188 Gregg Jefferies .15
189 Mo Vaughn .15
190 Terry Steinbach .15
191 Ray Durham .15
192 Robin Ventura .15
193 Jeff Reed .15
194 Ken Caminiti .15
195 Eric Karros .15
196 Wilson Alvarez .15
197 Gary Gaetti .15
198 Andres Galarraga .15
199 Alex Gonzalez .15
200 Garret Anderson .15
201 Andy Benes .15
202 Harold Baines .15
203 Ron Coomer .15
204 Dean Palmer .15
205 Reggie Jefferson .15
206 John Burkett .15
207 Jermaine Allensworth .15
208 Bernard Gilkey .15
209 Jeff Bagwell .75
210 Kenny Lofton .15
211 Bobby Jones .15
212 Bartolo Colon .15
213 Jim Edmonds .15
214 Pat Hentgen .15
215 Matt Williams .15
216 Bob Abreu .15
217 Jorge Posada .15
218 Marty Cordova .15
219 Ken Hill .15
220 Steve Finley .15
221 Jeff King .15
222 Quinton McCracken .15
223 Matt Stairs .15
224 Darin Erstad .35
225 Fred McGriff .15
226 Marquis Grissom .15
227 Doug Glanville .15
228 Tom Glavine .35
229 John Franco .15
230 Darren Bragg .15
231 Barry Larkin .15
232 Trevor Hoffman .15
233 Brady Anderson .15
234 Al Martin .15
235 B.J. Surhoff .15
236 Ellis Burks .15
237 Randy Johnson .75
238 Mark Clark .15
239 Tony Saunders .15
240 Hideo Nomo .40
241 Brad Fullmer .15
242 Chipper Jones 1.00
243 Jose Valentin .15
244 Manny Ramirez .75
245 Derrek Lee .50
246 Jimmy Key .15
247 Tim Naehring .15
248 Bobby Higginson .15
249 Charles Johnson .15
250 Chili Davis .15
251 Tom Gordon .15
252 Mike Lieberthal .15
253 Billy Wagner .15
254 Juan Guzman .15
255 Todd Stottlemyre .15

256 Brian Jordan .15
257 Barry Bonds 2.50
258 Dan Wilson .15
259 Paul Molitor .75
260 Juan Gonzalez .40
261 Francisco Cordova .15
262 Cecil Fielder .15
263 Travis Lee .15
264 Kevin Tapani .15
265 Raul Mondesi .15
266 Travis Fryman .15
267 Armando Benitez .15
268 Pokey Reese .15
269 Rick Aguilera .15
270 Andy Pettitte .35
271 Jose Vizcaino .15
272 Kerry Wood .40
273 Vladimir Guerrero .75
274 John Smiley .15
275 Checklist 151-275 .15

Refractors

NM/M
Complete Set (275): 200.00
Common Player: 1.00
Stars/Rookies: 4X
(See 1998 Finest for checklist and base card values.)

No-Protector

NM/M
Complete Set (275): 150.00
Common Player: .50
Stars/Rookies: 2.5X
(See 1998 Finest for checklist and base card values.)

No-Protector Refractor

NM/M
Complete Set (275): 400.00
Common Player: 2.00
Stars/Rookies: 8X
(See 1998 Finest for checklist and base card values.)

Pre-Production

NM/M
Complete Set (5): 8.00
Common Player: 1.00
1 Nomar Garciaparra 2.25
2 Mark McGwire 3.00
3 Ivan Rodriguez 2.00
4 Ken Griffey Jr. 2.50
5 Roger Clemens 2.25

Centurions

NM/M
Complete Set (20): 75.00
Common Player: 1.50
Production 500 Sets
Refractors (75 Sets): 4X
C1 Andruw Jones 4.50
C2 Vladimir Guerrero 4.50
C3 Nomar Garciaparra 6.00
C4 Scott Rolen 3.50
C5 Ken Griffey Jr. 8.00
C6 Jose Cruz Jr. 1.50
C7 Barry Bonds 12.00
C8 Mark McGwire 10.00
C9 Juan Gonzalez 2.50
C10 Jeff Bagwell 4.50
C11 Frank Thomas 4.50
C12 Paul Konerko 2.00
C13 Alex Rodriguez 10.00
C14 Mike Piazza 8.00
C15 Travis Lee 1.50
C16 Chipper Jones 6.00
C17 Larry Walker 1.50
C18 Mo Vaughn 1.50
C19 Livan Hernandez 1.50
C20 Jaret Wright 1.50

Jumbo

	NM/M
Complete Set (16):	30.00
Common Player:	1.00
Refractors:	1.5X

FIRST SERIES

1	Mark McGwire	4.00
2	Cal Ripken Jr.	5.00
3	Nomar Garciaparra	2.00
4	Mike Piazza	3.00
5	Greg Maddux	2.00
6	Jose Cruz Jr.	1.00
7	Roger Clemens	2.50
8	Ken Griffey Jr.	3.00

SECOND SERIES

1	Frank Thomas	1.50
2	Bernie Williams	1.00
3	Randy Johnson	1.50
4	Chipper Jones	2.00
5	Manny Ramirez	1.50
6	Barry Bonds	5.00
7	Juan Gonzalez	1.25
8	Jeff Bagwell	1.50

Mystery Finest

	NM/M
Complete Set (50):	125.00
Common Player:	1.50
Refractors:	4X

M1	Frank Thomas, Ken Griffey Jr.	3.00
M2	Frank Thomas, Mike Piazza	3.00
M3	Frank Thomas, Mark McGwire	4.00
M4	Frank Thomas, Frank Thomas	2.00
M5	Ken Griffey Jr., Mike Piazza	3.00
M6	Ken Griffey Jr., Mark McGwire	4.00
M7	Ken Griffey Jr., Ken Griffey Jr.	4.00
M8	Mike Piazza, Mark McGwire	4.00
M9	Mike Piazza, Mike Piazza	4.00
M10	Mark McGwire, Mark McGwire	6.00
M11	Nomar Garciaparra, Jose Cruz Jr.	2.50
M12	Nomar Garciaparra, Derek Jeter	5.00
M13	Nomar Garciaparra, Andruw Jones	2.50
M14	Nomar Garciaparra, Nomar Garciaparra	3.00
M15	Jose Cruz Jr., Derek Jeter	5.00
M16	Jose Cruz Jr., Andruw Jones	1.50
M17	Jose Cruz Jr., Jose Cruz Jr.	1.50
M18	Derek Jeter, Andruw Jones	5.00
M19	Derek Jeter, Derek Jeter	7.50
M20	Andruw Jones, Andruw Jones	2.00
M21	Cal Ripken Jr., Tony Gwynn	5.00
M22	Cal Ripken Jr., Barry Bonds	5.00
M23	Cal Ripken Jr., Greg Maddux	5.00
M24	Cal Ripken Jr., Cal Ripken Jr.	7.50
M25	Tony Gwynn, Barry Bonds	5.00
M26	Tony Gwynn, Greg Maddux	2.50
M27	Tony Gwynn, Tony Gwynn	3.00
M28	Barry Bonds, Greg Maddux	5.00
M29	Barry Bonds, Barry Bonds	7.50
M30	Greg Maddux, Greg Maddux	3.00
M31	Juan Gonzalez, Larry Walker	1.50
M32	Juan Gonzalez, Andres Galarraga	1.50
M33	Juan Gonzalez, Chipper Jones	2.50
M34	Juan Gonzalez, Juan Gonzalez	1.50
M35	Larry Walker, Andres Galarraga	1.50
M36	Larry Walker, Chipper Jones	2.50
M37	Larry Walker, Larry Walker	1.50
M38	Andres Galarraga, Chipper Jones	2.50
M39	Andres Galarraga, Andres Galarraga	1.50
M40	Chipper Jones, Chipper Jones	3.00
M41	Gary Sheffield, Sammy Sosa	3.00
M42	Gary Sheffield, Jeff Bagwell	1.50
M43	Gary Sheffield, Tino Martinez	1.50
M44	Gary Sheffield, Gary Sheffield	2.00
M45	Sammy Sosa, Jeff Bagwell	3.00
M46	Sammy Sosa, Tino Martinez	3.00
M47	Sammy Sosa, Sammy Sosa	3.00
M48	Jeff Bagwell, Tino Martinez	1.50
M49	Jeff Bagwell, Jeff Bagwell	2.00
M50	Tino Martinez, Tino Martinez	1.50

Mystery Finest 2

	NM/M
Complete Set (40):	100.00
Common Player:	1.50
Refractors:	4X

M1	Nomar Garciaparra, Frank Thomas	3.50
M2	Nomar Garciaparra, Albert Belle	3.50
M3	Nomar Garciaparra, Scott Rolen	3.50
M4	Frank Thomas, Albert Belle	2.50
M5	Frank Thomas, Scott Rolen	2.50
M6	Albert Belle, Scott Rolen	1.50
M7	Ken Griffey Jr., Jose Cruz	4.00
M8	Ken Griffey Jr., Alex Rodriguez	6.00
M9	Ken Griffey Jr., Roger Clemens	4.50
M10	Jose Cruz, Alex Rodriguez	6.00
M11	Jose Cruz, Roger Clemens	3.00
M12	Alex Rodriguez, Roger Clemens	6.00
M13	Travis Lee, Barry Bonds	6.00
M14	Mike Piazza, Derek Jeter	6.00
M15	Mike Piazza, Bernie Williams	5.00
M16	Barry Bonds, Derek Jeter	6.50
M17	Barry Bonds, Bernie Williams	4.00
M18	Derek Jeter, Bernie Williams	6.00
M19	Mark McGwire, Jeff Bagwell	4.50
M20	Mark McGwire, Mo Vaughn	5.00
M21	Mark McGwire, Jim Thome	5.00
M22	Jeff Bagwell, Mo Vaughn	2.00
M23	Jeff Bagwell, Jim Thome	1.50
M24	Mo Vaughn, Jim Thome	1.50
M25	Juan Gonzalez, Travis Lee	1.50
M26	Juan Gonzalez, Ben Grieve	1.50
M27	Juan Gonzalez, Fred McGriff	1.50
M28	Travis Lee, Ben Grieve	1.50
M29	Travis Lee, Fred McGriff	1.50
M30	Ben Grieve, Fred McGriff	1.50
M31	Albert Belle, Albert Belle	1.50
M32	Scott Rolen, Scott Rolen	2.00
M33	Alex Rodriguez, Alex Rodriguez	6.00
M34	Roger Clemens, Roger Clemens	4.00
M35	Bernie Williams, Bernie Williams	1.50
M36	Mo Vaughn, Mo Vaughn	1.50
M37	Jim Thome, Jim Thome	2.00
M38	Travis Lee, Travis Lee	1.50
M39	Fred McGriff, Fred McGriff	1.50
M40	Ben Grieve, Ben Grieve	1.50

Mystery Finest Jumbo

	NM/M
Complete Set (3):	12.50
Common Card:	4.00
Refractor:	1.5X

1	Ken Griffey Jr., Alex Rodriguez	4.00
2	Derek Jeter, Bernie Williams	5.00
3	Mark McGwire, Jeff Bagwell	4.00

Power Zone

	NM/M
Complete Set (20):	25.00
Common Player:	.50

1	Ken Griffey Jr.	3.00
2	Jeff Bagwell	2.00
3	Jose Cruz Jr.	.50
4	Barry Bonds	5.00
5	Mark McGwire	4.00
6	Jim Thome	1.50
7	Mo Vaughn	.50
8	Gary Sheffield	1.00
9	Andres Galarraga	.50
10	Nomar Garciaparra	2.50
11	Rafael Palmeiro	1.50
12	Sammy Sosa	2.50
13	Jay Buhner	.50
14	Tony Clark	.50
15	Mike Piazza	3.00
16	Larry Walker	.50
17	Albert Belle	.50
18	Tino Martinez	.50
19	Juan Gonzalez	1.25
20	Frank Thomas	2.00

Stadium Stars

	NM/M
Complete Set (24):	95.00
Common Player:	1.00

SS1	Ken Griffey Jr.	8.00
SS2	Alex Rodriguez	10.00
SS3	Mo Vaughn	1.00
SS4	Nomar Garciaparra	6.00
SS5	Frank Thomas	4.50
SS6	Albert Belle	1.00
SS7	Derek Jeter	12.00
SS8	Chipper Jones	6.00
SS9	Cal Ripken Jr.	12.00
SS10	Jim Thome	3.00
SS11	Mike Piazza	8.00
SS12	Juan Gonzalez	2.50
SS13	Jeff Bagwell	4.50
SS14	Sammy Sosa	6.00
SS15	Jose Cruz Jr.	1.00
SS16	Gary Sheffield	2.00
SS17	Larry Walker	1.00
SS18	Tony Gwynn	6.00
SS19	Mark McGwire	10.00
SS20	Barry Bonds	12.00
SS21	Tino Martinez	1.00
SS22	Manny Ramirez	4.50
SS23	Ken Caminiti	1.00
SS24	Andres Galarraga	1.00

The Man

	NM/M
Complete Set (20):	125.00
Common Player:	1.50
Refractors:	3X

TM1	Ken Griffey Jr.	10.00
TM2	Barry Bonds	15.00
TM3	Frank Thomas	6.00
TM4	Chipper Jones	7.50
TM5	Cal Ripken Jr.	15.00
TM6	Nomar Garciaparra	7.50
TM7	Mark McGwire	12.50
TM8	Mike Piazza	10.00
TM9	Derek Jeter	15.00
TM10	Alex Rodriguez	12.50
TM11	Jose Cruz Jr.	1.50
TM12	Larry Walker	1.50
TM13	Jeff Bagwell	6.00
TM14	Tony Gwynn	7.50
TM15	Travis Lee	2.00
TM16	Juan Gonzalez	6.00
TM17	Scott Rolen	4.50
TM18	Randy Johnson	6.00
TM19	Roger Clemens	9.00
TM20	Greg Maddux	7.50

1999 Finest

	NM/M
Complete Set (300):	80.00
Complete Series 1 (150):	30.00
Complete Series 2 (150):	50.00
Common Player:	.15
Common SP	
(101-150, 251-300):	.50
Pack (6):	1.50
Wax Box (24):	30.00

1	Darin Erstad	.35
2	Javy Lopez	.15
3	Vinny Castilla	.15
4	Jim Thome	.60
5	Tino Martinez	.15
6	Mark Grace	.15
7	Shawn Green	.40
8	Dustin Hermanson	.15
9	Kevin Young	.15
10	Tony Clark	.15
11	Scott Brosius	.15
12	Craig Biggio	.15
13	Brian McRae	.15
14	Chan Ho Park	.15
15	Manny Ramirez	1.00
16	Chipper Jones	1.50
17	Rico Brogna	.15
18	Quinton McCracken	.15
19	J.T. Snow Jr.	.15
20	Tony Gwynn	1.50
21	Juan Guzman	.15
22	John Valentin	.15
23	Rick Helling	.15
24	Sandy Alomar	.15
25	Frank Thomas	1.00
26	Jorge Posada	.15
27	Dmitri Young	.15
28	Rick Reed	.15
29	Kevin Tapani	.15
30	Troy Glaus	.75
31	Kenny Rogers	.15
32	Jeromy Burnitz	.15
33	Mark Grudzielanek	.15
34	Mike Mussina	.50
35	Scott Rolen	.75
36	Neifi Perez	.15
37	Brad Radke	.15
38	Darryl Strawberry	.15
39	Robb Nen	.15
40	Moises Alou	.15
41	Eric Young	.15
42	Livan Hernandez	.15
43	John Wetteland	.15
44	Matt Lawton	.15
45	Ben Grieve	.15
46	Fernando Tatis	.15
47	Travis Fryman	.15
48	David Segui	.15
49	Bob Abreu	.15
50	Nomar Garciaparra	1.50
51	Paul O'Neill	.15
52	Jeff King	.15
53	Francisco Cordova	.15
54	John Olerud	.15
55	Vladimir Guerrero	1.00
56	Fernando Vina	.15
57	Shane Reynolds	.15
58	Chuck Finley	.15
59	Rondell White	.15
60	Greg Vaughn	.15
61	Ryan Minor	.15
62	Tom Gordon	.15
63	Damion Easley	.15
64	Ray Durham	.15
65	Orlando Hernandez	.15
66	Bartolo Colon	.15
67	Jaret Wright	.15
68	Royce Clayton	.15
69	Tim Salmon	.15
70	Mark McGwire	2.50
71	Alex Gonzalez	.15
72	Tom Glavine	.40
73	David Justice	.15
74	Omar Vizquel	.15
75	Juan Gonzalez	.50
76	Bobby Higginson	.15
77	Todd Walker	.15
78	Dante Bichette	.15
79	Kevin Millwood	.15
80	Roger Clemens	1.75
81	Kerry Wood	.50
82	Cal Ripken Jr.	3.00
83	Jay Bell	.15
84	Barry Bonds	3.00
85	Alex Rodriguez	2.50
86	Doug Glanville	.15
87	Jason Kendall	.15
88	Sean Casey	.25
89	Aaron Sele	.15
90	Derek Jeter	3.00
91	Andy Ashby	.15
92	Rusty Greer	.15
93	Rod Beck	.15
94	Matt Williams	.15
95	Mike Piazza	2.00
96	Wally Joyner	.15
97	Barry Larkin	.15
98	Eric Milton	.15
99	Gary Sheffield	.50
100	Greg Maddux	1.50
101	Ken Griffey Jr.	4.00
102	Frank Thomas	2.00
103	Nomar Garciaparra	3.00
104	Mark McGwire	5.00
105	Alex Rodriguez	5.00
106	Tony Gwynn	3.00
107	Juan Gonzalez	.75
108	Jeff Bagwell	2.00
109	Sammy Sosa	3.00
110	Vladimir Guerrero	2.00
111	Roger Clemens	3.50
112	Barry Bonds	6.00
113	Darin Erstad	.50
114	Mike Piazza	4.00
115	Derek Jeter	6.00
116	Chipper Jones	3.00
117	Larry Walker	.50
118	Scott Rolen	1.50
119	Cal Ripken Jr.	6.00
120	Greg Maddux	3.00
121	Troy Glaus	1.50
122	Ben Grieve	.50
123	Ryan Minor	.50
124	Kerry Wood	.50
125	Travis Lee	.50
126	Adrian Beltre	.50
127	Brad Fullmer	.50
128	Aramis Ramirez	.50
129	Eric Chavez	.50
130	Todd Helton	.75
131	Pat Burrell RC	4.00
132	Ryan Mills RC	.50
133	Austin Kearns RC	3.00
134	Josh McKinley RC	.50
135	Adam Everett RC	.75
136	Marlon Anderson	.50
137	Bruce Chen	.50
138	Matt Clement	.50
139	Alex Gonzalez	.50
140	Roy Halladay	.50
141	Calvin Pickering	.50
142	Randy Wolf	.50
143	Ryan Anderson	.50
144	Ruben Mateo	.50
145	Alex Escobar RC	.50
146	Jeremy Giambi	.50
147	Lance Berkman	.50
148	Michael Barrett	.50
149	Preston Wilson	.50
150	Gabe Kapler	.50
151	Roger Clemens	1.75
152	Jay Buhner	.15
153	Brad Fullmer	.15
154	Ray Lankford	.15
155	Jim Edmonds	.15
156	Jason Giambi	.60
157	Bret Boone	.15
158	Jeff Cirillo	.15
159	Rickey Henderson	1.00
160	Edgar Martinez	.15
161	Ron Gant	.15
162	Mark Kotsay	.15
163	Trevor Hoffman	.15
164	Jason Schmidt	.15
165	Brett Tomko	.15
166	David Ortiz	.50
167	Dean Palmer	.15
168	Hideki Irabu	.15
169	Mike Cameron	.15
170	Pedro Martinez	1.00
171	Tom Goodwin	.15
172	Brian Hunter	.15
173	Al Leiter	.15
174	Charles Johnson	.15
175	Curt Schilling	.50
176	Robin Ventura	.15
177	Travis Lee	.15
178	Jeff Shaw	.15
179	Ugueth Urbina	.15
180	Roberto Alomar	.30
181	Cliff Floyd	.15
182	Adrian Beltre	.25
183	Tony Womack	.15
184	Brian Jordan	.15
185	Randy Johnson	1.00
186	Mickey Morandini	.15
187	Todd Hundley	.15
188	Jose Valentin	.15
189	Eric Davis	.15
190	Ken Caminiti	.15
191	David Wells	.15
192	Ryan Klesko	.15
193	Garret Anderson	.15
194	Eric Karros	.15
195	Ivan Rodriguez	.75
196	Aramis Ramirez	.15
197	Mike Lieberthal	.15
198	Will Clark	.15
199	Rey Ordonez	.15
200	Ken Griffey Jr.	2.00
201	Jose Guillen	.15
202	Scott Erickson	.15
203	Paul Konerko	.15
204	Johnny Damon	.40
205	Larry Walker	.15
206	Denny Neagle	.15
207	Jose Offerman	.15
208	Andy Pettitte	.30
209	Bobby Jones	.15
210	Kevin Brown	.15
211	John Smoltz	.15
212	Henry Rodriguez	.15
213	Tim Belcher	.15
214	Carlos Delgado	.50
215	Andruw Jones	1.00
216	Andy Benes	.15
217	Fred McGriff	.15
218	Edgar Renteria	.15
219	Miguel Tejada	.25
220	Bernie Williams	.15
221	Justin Thompson	.15
222	Marty Cordova	.15
223	Delino DeShields	.15
224	Ellis Burks	.15
225	Kenny Lofton	.15
226	Steve Finley	.15
227	Eric Chavez	.25
228	Jose Cruz Jr.	.15
229	Marquis Grissom	.15
230	Jeff Bagwell	1.00
231	Jose Canseco	.50
232	Edgardo Alfonzo	.15
233	Richie Sexson	.15
234	Jeff Kent	.15
235	Rafael Palmeiro	.75
236	David Cone	.15
237	Gregg Jefferies	.15
238	Mike Lansing	.15
239	Mariano Rivera	.25
240	Albert Belle	.15
241	Chuck Knoblauch	.15
242	Derek Bell	.15
243	Pat Hentgen	.15
244	Andres Galarraga	.15
245	Mo Vaughn	.15
246	Wade Boggs	1.50
247	Devon White	.15
248	Todd Helton	.75
249	Raul Mondesi	.15
250	Sammy Sosa	1.50
251	Nomar Garciaparra	3.00
252	Mark McGwire	5.00
253	Alex Rodriguez	5.00
254	Juan Gonzalez	.75
255	Vladimir Guerrero	2.00
256	Ken Griffey Jr.	4.00
257	Mike Piazza	4.00
258	Derek Jeter	6.00
259	Albert Belle	.50
260	Greg Vaughn	.50
261	Sammy Sosa	3.00
262	Greg Maddux	3.00
263	Frank Thomas	2.00
264	Mark Grace	.50
265	Ivan Rodriguez	1.25
266	Roger Clemens	3.50
267	Mo Vaughn	.50
268	Jim Thome	.75
269	Darin Erstad	.65
270	Chipper Jones	2.50
271	Larry Walker	.50
272	Cal Ripken Jr.	6.00
273	Scott Rolen	1.25
274	Randy Johnson	2.00
275	Tony Gwynn	2.50
276	Barry Bonds	6.00
277	Sean Burroughs RC	1.50
278	J.M. Gold RC	.50
279	Carlos Lee	.50
280	George Lombard	.50
281	Carlos Beltran	1.50
282	Fernando Seguignol	.50
283	Eric Chavez	.65
284	Carlos Pena RC	3.00
285	Corey Patterson RC	2.00
286	Alfonso Soriano RC	12.00
287	Nick Johnson RC	2.00
288	Jorge Toca RC	.50
289	A.J. Burnett RC	1.00
290	Andy Brown RC	.50
291	Doug Mientkiewicz RC	1.00
292	Bobby Seay RC	.50
293	Chip Ambres RC	.50
294	C.C. Sabathia RC	2.50
295	Choo Freeman RC	1.00
296	Eric Valent RC	.50
297	Matt Belisle RC	.50
298	Jason Tyner RC	.50
299	Masao Kida RC	.50
300	Hank Aaron,	
	Mark McGwire	3.00

Refractors

	NM/M
Complete Set (300):	750.00
Common Player:	1.00
Stars:	6X
SP's:	3X

(See 1999 Finest for checklist and base card values.)

Gold Refractors

	NM/M
Common Player:	3.00
Stars:	15X
SP's:	10X

(See 1999 Finest for checklist and base card values.)

Complements

	NM/M
Complete Set (7):	25.00
Common Player:	2.50
Inserted 1:56	
Dual-Refractors:	2X
Inserted 1:168	
1	Mike Piazza,
	Ivan Rodriguez	4.00
2	Tony Gwynn,
	Wade Boggs	3.00
3	Kerry Wood,
	Roger Clemens	3.50
4	Juan Gonzalez,
	Sammy Sosa	3.00
5	Derek Jeter,
	Nomar Garciaparra	6.00
6	Mark McGwire,
	Frank Thomas	5.00
7	Vladimir Guerrero,
	Andruw Jones	2.50

Double Feature

	NM/M
Complete Set (7):	30.00
Common Player:	2.00
Dual-Refractors:	2X
1	Ken Griffey Jr.,
	Alex Rodriguez	10.00
2	Chipper Jones,
	Andruw Jones	6.00

3 Darin Erstad, Mo Vaughn 2.00
4 Craig Biggio, Jeff Bagwell 4.00
5 Ben Grieve, Eric Chavez 2.00
6 Albert Belle, Cal Ripken Jr. 10.00
7 Scott Rolen, Pat Burrell 3.00

Franchise Records

		NM/M
Complete Set (10):		35.00
Common Player:		2.00
Refractors:		3X
1	Frank Thomas	2.50
2	Ken Griffey Jr.	5.00
3	Mark McGwire	6.00
4	Juan Gonzalez	2.00
5	Nomar Garciaparra	3.00
6	Mike Piazza	5.00
7	Cal Ripken Jr.	7.50
8	Sammy Sosa	3.00
9	Barry Bonds	7.50
10	Tony Gwynn	3.00

Future's Finest

		NM/M
Complete Set (10):		35.00
Common Player:		2.00
1	Pat Burrell	10.00
2	Troy Glaus	12.50
3	Eric Chavez	3.00
4	Ryan Anderson	2.00
5	Ruben Mateo	2.00
6	Gabe Kapler	2.00
7	Alex Gonzalez	2.00
8	Michael Barrett	2.00
9	Lance Berkman	2.00
10	Fernando Seguignol	2.00

Hank Aaron Award Contenders

		NM/M
Complete Set (9):		20.00
Common Player:		2.00
Refractors:		3X
1	Juan Gonzalez	2.00

2 Vladimir Guerrero 2.50
3 Nomar Garciaparra 3.00
4 Albert Belle 2.00
5 Frank Thomas 2.50
6 Sammy Sosa 3.00
7 Alex Rodriguez 5.00
8 Ken Griffey Jr. 4.00
9 Mark McGwire 5.00

Leading Indicators

		NM/M
Complete Set (10):		20.00
Common Player:		.50
Inserted 1:24		
L1	Mark McGwire	5.00
L2	Sammy Sosa	3.00
L3	Ken Griffey Jr.	4.00
L4	Greg Vaughn	.50
L5	Albert Belle	.50
L6	Juan Gonzalez	.75
L7	Andres Galarraga	.50
L8	Alex Rodriguez	5.00
L9	Barry Bonds	6.00
L10	Jeff Bagwell	1.50

Milestones

		NM/M
Complete Set (40):		125.00
Common Hits (1-10):		.50
Common Homeruns (11-20):		2.00
Common RBI (21-30):		1.00
Common Doubles (31-40):		2.00
1	Tony Gwynn	1.50
2	Cal Ripken Jr.	3.00
3	Wade Boggs	1.50
4	Ken Griffey Jr.	2.00
5	Frank Thomas	1.00
6	Barry Bonds	3.00
7	Travis Lee	.50
8	Alex Rodriguez	2.50
9	Derek Jeter	3.00
10	Vladimir Guerrero	1.00
11	Mark McGwire	8.00
12	Ken Griffey Jr.	7.00
13	Vladimir Guerrero	4.00
14	Alex Rodriguez	8.00
15	Barry Bonds	10.00
16	Sammy Sosa	5.00
17	Albert Belle	2.00
18	Frank Thomas	4.00
19	Jose Canseco	2.00
20	Mike Piazza	7.00
21	Jeff Bagwell	2.00
22	Barry Bonds	6.00
23	Ken Griffey Jr.	4.00
24	Albert Belle	1.00
25	Juan Gonzalez	1.50
26	Vinny Castilla	1.00
27	Mark McGwire	5.00
28	Alex Rodriguez	5.00
29	Nomar Garciaparra	3.00

30 Frank Thomas 2.50
31 Barry Bonds 10.00
32 Albert Belle 2.00
33 Ben Grieve 2.00
34 Craig Biggio 2.00
35 Vladimir Guerrero 4.00
36 Nomar Garciaparra 5.00
37 Alex Rodriguez 7.00
38 Derek Jeter 10.00
39 Ken Griffey Jr. 7.00
40 Brad Fullmer 2.00

Peel & Reveal

		NM/M
Complete Set (20):		40.00
Common Player:		1.00
Hyperplaid:		1.5X
Stadium Stars:		2.5X
1	Kerry Wood	1.50
2	Mark McGwire	5.00
3	Sammy Sosa	3.00
4	Ken Griffey Jr.	4.00
5	Nomar Garciaparra	3.00
6	Greg Maddux	3.00
7	Derek Jeter	6.00
8	Andres Galarraga	1.00
9	Alex Rodriguez	5.00
10	Frank Thomas	2.00
11	Roger Clemens	3.50
12	Juan Gonzalez	1.50
13	Ben Grieve	1.00
14	Jeff Bagwell	2.00
15	Todd Helton	2.00
16	Chipper Jones	3.00
17	Barry Bonds	6.00
18	Travis Lee	1.00
19	Vladimir Guerrero	2.00
20	Pat Burrell	1.50

Prominent Figures

		NM/M
Complete Set (50):		250.00
Common Home Runs (1-10); #'d to 70:		3.00
Common Slugging % (11-20); #'d to 847:		1.00
Common Batting Ave. (21-30); #'d to 424:		1.75
Common RBIs (31-40); #'d to 190:		2.00
Common Total Bases (41-50); #'d to 457:		1.75
1	Mark McGwire (HR)	25.00
2	Sammy Sosa (HR)	10.00
3	Ken Griffey Jr. (HR)	15.00
4	Mike Piazza (HR)	15.00
5	Juan Gonzalez (HR)	15.00
6	Greg Vaughn (HR)	3.00
7	Alex Rodriguez (HR)	25.00
8	Manny Ramirez (HR)	7.50

9 Jeff Bagwell (HR) 7.50
10 Andres Galarraga (HR) 3.00
11 Mark McGwire (S%) 6.00
12 Sammy Sosa (S%) 5.00
13 Juan Gonzalez (S%) 2.50
14 Ken Griffey Jr. (S%) 5.00
15 Barry Bonds (S%) 7.50
16 Greg Vaughn (S%) 1.00
17 Larry Walker (S%) 1.00
18 Andres Galarraga (S%) 1.00
19 Jeff Bagwell (S%) 2.50
20 Albert Belle (S%) 1.00
21 Tony Gwynn (BA) 5.00
22 Mike Piazza (BA) 6.00
23 Larry Walker (BA) 1.75
24 Alex Rodriguez (BA) 7.50
25 John Olerud (BA) 1.75
26 Frank Thomas (BA) 3.50
27 Bernie Williams (BA) 1.75
28 Chipper Jones (BA) 5.00
29 Jim Thome (BA) 2.50
30 Barry Bonds (BA) 9.00
31 Juan Gonzalez (RBI) 3.00
32 Sammy Sosa (RBI) 9.00
33 Mark McGwire (RBI) 20.00
34 Albert Belle (RBI) 2.00
35 Ken Griffey Jr. (RBI) 15.00
36 Jeff Bagwell (RBI) 6.00
37 Chipper Jones (RBI) 9.00
38 Vinny Castilla (RBI) 2.00
39 Alex Rodriguez (RBI) 20.00
40 Andres Galarraga (RBI) 2.00
41 Sammy Sosa (TB) 6.00
42 Mark McGwire (TB) 7.50
43 Albert Belle (TB) 1.75
44 Ken Griffey Jr. (TB) 6.00
45 Jeff Bagwell (TB) 3.50
46 Juan Gonzalez (TB) 3.50
47 Barry Bonds (TB) 9.00
48 Vladimir Guerrero (TB) 3.50
49 Larry Walker (TB) 1.75
50 Alex Rodriguez (TB) 7.50

Split Screen

		NM/M
Complete Set (14):		30.00
Common Card:		1.00
Dual-Refractor:		2X
1	Mark McGwire, Sammy Sosa	4.00
2	Ken Griffey Jr., Alex Rodriguez	4.00
3	Nomar Garciaparra, Derek Jeter	5.00
4	Barry Bonds, Albert Belle	4.00
5	Cal Ripken Jr., Tony Gwynn	4.00
6	Manny Ramirez, Juan Gonzalez	1.50
7	Frank Thomas, Andres Galarraga	1.50
8	Scott Rolen, Chipper Jones	2.00
9	Ivan Rodriguez, Mike Piazza	3.00
10	Kerry Wood, Roger Clemens	2.50
11	Greg Maddux, Tom Glavine	2.00
12	Troy Glaus, Eric Chavez	1.50
13	Ben Grieve, Todd Helton	1.00
14	Travis Lee, Pat Burrell	2.50

Team Finest

	NM/M
Complete Set (20):	25.00
Common Blue:	1.00
Production 1,500 Sets	
Blue Refractors:	3X
Production 150 Sets	
Reds:	1.5X
Production 500 Sets	
Red Refractors:	7X
Production 50 Sets	
Golds:	2X

Production 250 Sets		
Gold Refractors:	10X	
Production 25 Sets		
1	Greg Maddux	2.50
2	Mark McGwire	4.50
3	Sammy Sosa	2.50
4	Juan Gonzalez	1.25
5	Alex Rodriguez	4.50
6	Travis Lee	1.00
7	Roger Clemens	2.75
8	Darin Erstad	1.25
9	Todd Helton	1.75
10	Mike Piazza	3.50
11	Kerry Wood	1.25
12	Ken Griffey Jr.	3.50
13	Frank Thomas	2.00
14	Jeff Bagwell	2.00
15	Nomar Garciaparra	2.50
16	Derek Jeter	6.00
17	Chipper Jones	2.50
18	Barry Bonds	6.00
19	Tony Gwynn	2.50
20	Ben Grieve	1.00

2000 Finest

MARK GRACE

	NM/M
Complete Set (286):	250.00
Complete Series 1 (147)	175.00
Complete Series 2 (140)	125.00
Common Player:	.25
Common Rookie (101-120):	4.00
Production 2,000	
Common Rookie (247-266)	4.00
Production 3,000	
Common Counterpart	
(267-276)	.75
Inserted 1:8	
Common Gem (136-145):	1.50
Inserted 1:24	
Pack (6):	2.00
Series 1 & 2 Box (24):	40.00

1	Nomar Garciaparra	2.00
2	Chipper Jones	1.50
3	Erubiel Durazo	.25
4	Robin Ventura	.25
5	Garret Anderson	.25
6	Dean Palmer	.25
7	Mariano Rivera	.35
8	Rusty Greer	.25
9	Jim Thome	.25
10	Jeff Bagwell	1.00
11	Jason Giambi	.75
12	Jeromy Burnitz	.25
13	Mark Grace	.35
14	Russ Ortiz	.25
15	Kevin Brown	.25
16	Kevin Millwood	.25
17	Scott Williamson	.25
18	Orlando Hernandez	.25
19	Todd Walker	.25
20	Carlos Beltran	.50
21	Ruben Rivera	.25
22	Curt Schilling	.40
23	Brian Giles	.25
24	Eric Karros	.25
25	Preston Wilson	.25
26	Al Leiter	.25
27	Juan Encarnacion	.40
28	Tim Salmon	.25
29	B.J. Surhoff	.25
30	Bernie Williams	.45
31	Lee Stevens	.25
32	Pokey Reese	.25
33	Mike Sweeney	.25
34	Corey Koskie	.25
35	Roberto Alomar	.40
36	Tim Hudson	.40
37	Tom Glavine	.25
38	Jeff Kent	.25
39	Mike Lieberthal	.25
40	Barry Larkin	.25
41	Paul O'Neill	.25
42	Rico Brogna	.25
43	Brian Daubach	.25
44	Rich Aurilia	.25

45	Vladimir Guerrero	1.00
46	Luis Castillo	.25
47	Bartolo Colon	.25
48	Kevin Appier	.25
49	Mo Vaughn	.25
50	Alex Rodriguez	2.50
51	Randy Johnson	1.00
52	Kris Benson	.25
53	Tony Clark	.25
54	Chad Allen	.25
55	Larry Walker	.25
56	Freddy Garcia	.25
57	Paul Konerko	.35
58	Edgardo Alfonzo	.25
59	Brady Anderson	.25
60	Derek Jeter	3.00
61	Mike Hampton	.25
62	Jeff Cirillo	.25
63	Shannon Stewart	.25
64	Greg Maddux	1.50
65	Mark McGwire	2.50
66	Gary Sheffield	.50
67	Kevin Young	.25
68	Tony Gwynn	1.50
69	Rey Ordonez	.25
70	Cal Ripken Jr.	3.00
71	Todd Helton	1.00
72	Brian Jordan	.25
73	Jose Canseco	.50
74	Luis Gonzalez	.40
75	Barry Bonds	3.00
76	Jermaine Dye	.25
77	Jose Offerman	.25
78	Magglio Ordonez	.40
79	Fred McGriff	.25
80	Ivan Rodriguez	.60
81	Josh Hamilton	.50
82	Vernon Wells	.25
83	Mark Mulder	.35
84	John Patterson	.25
85	Nick Johnson	.50
86	Pablo Ozuna	.25
87	A.J. Burnett	.25
88	Jack Cust	.25
89	Adam Piatt	.25
90	Rob Ryan	.25
91	Sean Burroughs	.35
92	D'Angelo Jimenez	.25
93	Chad Hermansen	.25
94	Rob Fick	.25
95	Ruben Mateo	.25
96	Alex Escobar	.25
97	Willi Mo Pena	.25
98	Corey Patterson	.50
99	Eric Munson	.25
100	Pat Burrell	.75
101	Michael Tejera RC	4.00
102	Bobby Bradley RC	4.00
103	Larry Bigbie RC	6.00
104	B.J. Garbe RC	4.00
105	Josh Kalinowski RC	4.00
106	Brett Myers RC	15.00
107	Chris Mears RC	4.00
108	Aaron Rowand RC	10.00
109	Corey Myers RC	4.00
110	John Sneed RC	4.00
111	Ryan Christensen RC	4.00
112	Kyle Snyder RC	4.00
113	Mike Paradis RC	4.00
114	Chance Caple RC	4.00
115	Ben Christensen RC	4.00
116	Brad Baker RC	4.00
117	Rob Purvis RC	4.00
118	Rick Asadoorian RC	4.00
119	Ruben Salazar RC	4.00
120	Julio Zuleta RC	4.00
121	Ken Griffey Jr.,	
	Alex Rodriguez	4.00
122	Nomar Garciaparra,	
	Derek Jeter	5.00
123	Mark McGwire,	
	Sammy Sosa	4.00
124	Randy Johnson,	
	Pedro Martinez	2.00
125	Mike Piazza,	
	Ivan Rodriguez	3.00
126	Manny Ramirez,	
	Roberto Alomar	2.00
127	Chipper Jones,	
	Andruw Jones	3.00
128	Cal Ripken Jr.,	
	Tony Gwynn	5.00
129	Jeff Bagwell,	
	Craig Biggio	1.50
130	Vladimir Guerrero,	
	Barry Bonds	5.00
131	Andruw Soriano,	
	Nick Johnson	2.00
132	Josh Hamilton,	
	Pat Burrell	1.50
133	Corey Patterson,	
	Ruben Mateo	.75
134	Larry Walker,	
	Todd Helton	1.50
135	Edgardo Alfonzo,	
	Rey Ordonez	.75

136	Derek Jeter	10.00
137	Alex Rodriguez	8.00
138	Chipper Jones	5.00
139	Mike Piazza	6.00
140	Mark McGwire	8.00
141	Ivan Rodriguez	2.00
142	Cal Ripken Jr.	10.00
143	Vladimir Guerrero	3.00
144	Randy Johnson	3.00
145	Jeff Bagwell	3.00
146	Ken Griffey Jr./Field	1.50
146a	Ken Griffey Jr./Press	1.50
147	Andruw Jones	1.00
148	Kerry Wood	.50
149	Jim Edmonds	.25
150	Pedro Martinez	1.00
151	Warren Morris	.25
152	Trevor Hoffman	.25
153	Eric Young	.25
154	Andy Pettitte	.40
155	Frank Thomas	1.00
156	Damion Easley	.25
157	Cliff Floyd	.25
158	Ben Davis	.25
159	John Valentin	.25
160	Rafael Palmeiro	.65
161	Andy Ashby	.25
162	J.D. Drew	.40
163	Jay Bell	.25
164	Adam Kennedy	.25
165	Manny Ramirez	1.00
166	John Halama	.25
167	Octavio Dotel	.25
168	Darin Erstad	.40
169	Jose Lima	.25
170	Andres Galarraga	.25
171	Scott Rolen	.75
172	Delino DeShields	.25
173	J.T. Snow Jr.	.25
174	Tony Womack	.25
175	John Olerud	.25
176	Jason Kendall	.25
177	Carlos Lee	.25
178	Eric Milton	.25
179	Jeff Cirillo	.25
180	Gabe Kapler	.25
181	Greg Vaughn	.25
182	Denny Neagle	.25
183	Tino Martinez	.25
184	Doug Mientkiewicz	.25
185	Juan Gonzalez	1.00
186	Ellis Burks	.25
187	Mike Hampton	.25
188	Royce Clayton	.25
189	Mike Mussina	.50
190	Carlos Delgado	.50
191	Ben Grieve	.25
192	Fernando Tatis	.25
193	Matt Williams	.25
194	Rondell White	.25
195	Shawn Green	.50
196	Justin Thompson	.25
197	Troy Glaus	1.00
198	Roger Cedeno	.25
199	Ray Lankford	.25
200	Sammy Sosa	2.00
201	Kenny Lofton	.25
202	Edgar Martinez	.25
203	Mark Kotsay	.25
204	David Wells	.25
205	Craig Biggio	.25
206	Ray Durham	.25
207	Troy O'Leary	.25
208	Rickey Henderson	.75
209	Bob Abreu	.25
210	Neifi Perez	.25
211	Carlos Febles	.25
212	Chuck Knoblauch	.25
213	Moises Alou	.25
214	Omar Vizquel	.25
215	Vinny Castilla	.25
216	Javy Lopez	.25
217	Johnny Damon	.40
218	Roger Clemens	1.75
219	Miguel Tejada	.40
220	Deion Sanders	.35
221	Matt Lawton	.25
222	Albert Belle	.25
223	Adrian Beltre	.50
224	Dante Bichette	.25
225	Raul Mondesi	.25
226	Mike Piazza	2.00
227	Brad Penny	.25
228	Kip Wells	.25
229	Adam Everett	.25
230	Eddie Yarnall	.25
231	Matt LeCroy	.25
232	Ryan Anderson	.25
233	Rick Ankiel	.25
234	Daryle Ward	.25
235	Rafael Furcal	.25
236	Dee Brown	.25
237	Travis Dawkins	.25
238	Eric Valent	.25
239	Peter Bergeron	.25
240	Alfonso Soriano	1.50

241	John Patterson	.25
242	Jorge Toca	.25
243	Ryan Anderson	.25
244	Jason Dallaero	.25
245	Jason Grilli	.25
246	Chad Hermansen	.25
247	Scott Downs RC	4.00
248	Keith Reed RC	4.00
249	Edgar Cruz RC	4.00
250	Wes Anderson RC	4.00
251	Lyle Overbay RC	10.00
252	Mike Lamb RC	4.00
253	Vince Faison RC	4.00
254	Chad Alexander RC	4.00
255	Chris Wakeland RC	4.00
256	Aaron McNeal RC	4.00
257	Tomokazu Ohka RC	4.00
258	Ty Howington RC	6.00
259	Javier Colina RC	4.00
260	Jason Jennings RC	4.00
261	Ramon Santiago RC	4.00
262	Johan Santana RC	80.00
263	Quincey Foster RC	4.00
264	Junior Brignac RC	4.00
265	Rico Washington RC	4.00
266	Scott Sobkowiak RC	4.00
267	Pedro Martinez,	
	Rick Ankiel	2.00
268	Manny Ramirez,	
	Vladimir Guerrero	2.00
269	A.J. Burnett,	
	Mark Mulder	.75
270	Mike Piazza,	
	Eric Munson	2.50
271	Josh Hamilton,	
	Corey Patterson	1.00
272	Ken Griffey Jr.,	
	Sammy Sosa	3.00
273	Derek Jeter,	
	Alfonso Soriano	5.00
274	Mark McGwire,	
	Pat Burrell	4.00
275	Chipper Jones,	
	Cal Ripken Jr.	5.00
276	Nomar Garciaparra,	
	Alex Rodriguez	4.00
277	Pedro Martinez	3.00
278	Tony Gwynn	5.00
279	Barry Bonds	10.00
280	Juan Gonzalez	3.00
281	Larry Walker	1.50
282	Nomar Garciaparra	8.00
283	Ken Griffey Jr.	6.00
284	Manny Ramirez	3.00
285	Shawn Green	2.00
286	Sammy Sosa	6.00

Refractor

Stars (1-100):	5-10X
Inserted 1:24	
Rookies (101-120,247-266):	.5-1X
Production 500 Sets	
Features (121-135):	2-3X
Inserted 1:96	
Counterparts (267-276):	2-3X
Inserted 1:96	
Gems (136-145,277-286):	2-3X
Inserted 1:288	

Gold Refractor

Stars (1-100):	20-40X
Inserted 1:240	
Rookies (101-120, 247-266):	1-2X
Production 100 Sets	
Features:	4-8X
Inserted 1:960	
Counterparts:	4-8X
Inserted 1:960	
Gems:	5-10X
Inserted 1:2,880	

Ballpark Bounties

Scott Rolen

	NM/M
Complete Set (30):	85.00
Complete Series 1 (15):	45.00

Complete Series 2 (15): 45.00
Common Player: 1.50
Inserted 1:24

1	Chipper Jones	5.00
2	Mike Piazza	6.00
3	Vladimir Guerrero	3.00
4	Sammy Sosa	6.00
5	Nomar Garciaparra	6.00
6	Manny Ramirez	3.00
7	Jeff Bagwell	3.00
8	Scott Rolen	2.00
9	Carlos Beltran	2.50
10	Pedro Martinez	3.00
11	Greg Maddux	5.00
12	Josh Hamilton	2.00
13	Adam Piatt	1.50
14	Pat Burrell	2.00
15	Alfonso Soriano	3.00
16	Alex Rodriguez	8.00
17	Derek Jeter	10.00
18	Cal Ripken Jr.	10.00
19	Larry Walker	1.50
20	Barry Bonds	10.00
21	Ken Griffey Jr.	6.00
22	Mark McGwire	8.00
23	Ivan Rodriguez	2.00
24	Andruw Jones	2.50
25	Todd Helton	2.50
26	Randy Johnson	3.00
27	Ruben Mateo	1.50
28	Corey Patterson	1.50
29	Sean Burroughs	1.50
30	Eric Munson	1.50

Dream Cast

NM/M
Complete Set (10): 40.00
Common Player: 2.00
Inserted 1:36

1	Mark McGwire	8.00
2	Roberto Alomar	2.00
3	Chipper Jones	5.00
4	Derek Jeter	10.00
5	Barry Bonds	10.00
6	Ken Griffey Jr.	6.00
7	Sammy Sosa	6.00
8	Mike Piazza	6.00
9	Pedro Martinez	3.00
10	Randy Johnson	3.00

Finest Moments

NM/M
Complete Set (4): 6.00
Common Player: 1.00
Inserted 1:9
Refractor: 1-2X
Inserted 1:20

1	Chipper Jones	3.00
2	Ivan Rodriguez	1.50
3	Tony Gwynn	3.00
4	Wade Boggs	3.00

For The Record

FOR THE RECORD CHIPPER JONES Atlanta Braves

NM/M
Complete Set (30): 300.00
Common Player: 8.00

1A	Derek Jeter/318	20.00
1B	Derek Jeter/408	20.00
1C	Derek Jeter/314	20.00
2A	Mark McGwire/330	15.00
2B	Mark McGwire/402	15.00
2C	Mark McGwire/330	15.00
3A	Ken Griffey Jr./331	10.00
3B	Ken Griffey Jr./405	10.00
3C	Ken Griffey Jr./327	10.00
4A	Alex Rodriguez/331	15.00
4B	Alex Rodriguez/405	15.00
4C	Alex Rodriguez/327	15.00
5A	Nomar Garciaparra/310	10.00
5B	Nomar Garciaparra/390	10.00
5C	Nomar Garciaparra/302	10.00
6A	Cal Ripken Jr./333	20.00
6B	Cal Ripken Jr./410	20.00
6C	Cal Ripken Jr./318	20.00
7A	Sammy Sosa/355	10.00
7B	Sammy Sosa/400	10.00
7C	Sammy Sosa/353	10.00
8A	Manny Ramirez/325	8.00
8B	Manny Ramirez/410	8.00
8C	Manny Ramirez/325	8.00
9A	Mike Piazza/338	10.00
9B	Mike Piazza/410	10.00
9C	Mike Piazza/338	10.00
10A	Chipper Jones/335	9.00
10B	Chipper Jones/401	9.00
10C	Chipper Jones/330	9.00

Gems Oversized

ALEX RODRIGUEZ

NM/M
Complete Set (20): 50.00
Common Player: 1.00
Inserted 1:Box

1	Derek Jeter	6.00
2	Alex Rodriguez	5.00
3	Chipper Jones	3.00
4	Mike Piazza	4.00
5	Mark McGwire	5.00
6	Ivan Rodriguez	1.25
7	Cal Ripken Jr.	6.00
8	Vladimir Guerrero	2.00
9	Randy Johnson	2.00
10	Jeff Bagwell	2.00
11	Nomar Garciaparra	4.00
12	Ken Griffey Jr.	4.00
13	Manny Ramirez	2.00
14	Shawn Green	1.50
15	Sammy Sosa	4.00
16	Pedro Martinez	2.00
17	Tony Gwynn	2.00
18	Barry Bonds	6.00
19	Juan Gonzalez	1.50
20	Larry Walker	1.00

Going the Distance

GOING THE DISTANCE MIKE PIAZZA

NM/M
Complete Set (12): 45.00
Common Player: 3.00
Inserted 1:24

1	Tony Gwynn	3.50
2	Alex Rodriguez	6.00
3	Derek Jeter	8.00
4	Chipper Jones	3.50
5	Nomar Garciaparra	4.00
6	Sammy Sosa	4.00
7	Ken Griffey Jr.	4.00
8	Vladimir Guerrero	3.00
9	Mark McGwire	6.00
10	Mike Piazza	4.00
11	Manny Ramirez	3.00
12	Cal Ripken Jr.	8.00

Moments Autographs

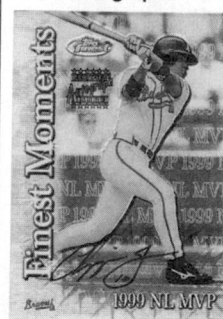

1999 NL MVP

NM/M
Common Autograph: 25.00
Inserted 1:425

1	Chipper Jones	50.00
2	Ivan Rodriguez	25.00
3	Tony Gwynn	50.00
4	Wade Boggs	25.00

2001 Finest

NM/M
Complete Set (140): 250.00
Common Player: .25
Common Standout Veteran (10): 5.00
Production 1999
Common Rookie (111-140): 4.00
Production 999
Pack (6): 8.00
Box (20): 140.00

1	Mike Piazza/SV	10.00
2	Andruw Jones	1.00
3	Jason Giambi	.75
4	Fred McGriff	.25
5	Vladimir Guerrero/SV	6.00
6	Adrian Gonzalez	.25
7	Pedro Martinez	1.00
8	Mike Lieberthal	.25
9	Warren Morris	.25
10	Juan Gonzalez	1.00
11	Jose Canseco	.50
12	Jose Valentin	.25
13	Jeff Cirillo	.25
14	Pokey Reese	.25
15	Scott Rolen	.75
16	Greg Maddux	1.50
17	Carlos Delgado	.50
18	Rick Ankiel	.25
19	Steve Finley	.25
20	Shawn Green	.40
21	Orlando Cabrerra	.25
22	Roberto Alomar	.45
23	John Olerud	.25
24	Albert Belle	.35
25	Edgardo Alfonzo	.25
26	Rafael Palmeiro	.75
27	Mike Sweeney	.25
28	Bernie Williams	.35
29	Larry Walker	.25
30	Barry Bonds/SV	15.00
31	Orlando Hernandez	.25
32	Randy Johnson	1.00
33	Shannon Stewart	.25
34	Mark Grace	.35
35	Alex Rodriguez/SV	12.00
36	Tino Martinez	.25
37	Carlos Febles	.25
38	Al Leiter	.25
39	Omar Vizquel	.25
40	Chuck Knoblauch	.25
41	Tim Salmon	.40
42	Brian Jordan	.25
43	Edgar Renteria	.25
44	Preston Wilson	.25
45	Mariano Rivera	.40
46	Gabe Kapler	.25
47	Jason Kendall	.25
48	Rickey Henderson	.75
49	Luis Gonzalez	.40
50	Tom Glavine	.40
51	Jeromy Burnitz	.25
52	Garret Anderson	.25
53	Craig Biggio	.25
54	Vinny Castilla	.25
55	Jeff Kent	.25
56	Gary Sheffield	.50
57	Jorge Posada	.40
58	Sean Casey	.40
59	Johnny Damon	.40
60	Dean Palmer	.25
61	Todd Helton	1.00
62	Barry Larkin	.25
63	Robin Ventura	.25
64	Kenny Lofton	.25
65	Sammy Sosa/SV	10.00
66	Rafael Furcal	.25
67	Jay Bell	.25
68	J.T. Snow Jr.	.25
69	Jose Vidro	.25
70	Ivan Rodriguez	.75
71	Jermaine Dye	.25
72	Chipper Jones/SV	8.00
73	Fernando Vina	.25
74	Ben Grieve	.25
75	Mark McGwire/SV	12.00
76	Matt Williams	.25
77	Mark Grudzielanek	.25
78	Mike Hampton	.25
79	Brian Giles	.25
80	Tony Gwynn	1.50
81	Carlos Beltran	.50
82	Ray Durham	.25
83	Brad Radke	.25
84	David Justice	.25
85	Frank Thomas	1.00
86	Todd Zeile	.25
87	Pat Burrell	.75
88	Jim Thome	.25
89	Greg Vaughn	.25
90	Ken Griffey Jr./SV	10.00
91	Mike Mussina	.40

92	Magglio Ordonez	.40
93	Bobby Abreu	.25
94	Alex Gonzalez	.25
95	Kevin Brown	.25
96	Jay Buhner	.25
97	Roger Clemens	2.00
98	Nomar Garciaparra/SV	10.00
99	Derek Lee	.25
100	Derek Jeter/SV	15.00
101	Adrian Beltre	.45
102	Geoff Jenkins	.25
103	Javy Lopez	.25
104	Raul Mondesi	.25
105	Troy Glaus	1.00
106	Jeff Bagwell	1.00
107	Eric Karros	.25
108	Mo Vaughn	.25
109	Cal Ripken Jr.	3.00
110	Manny Ramirez	1.00
111	Scott Heard	4.00
112	Luis Montanez RC	5.00
113	Ben Diggins RC	4.00
114	Shaun Boyd RC	4.00
115	Sean Burnett RC	4.00
116	Carmen Cali RC	4.00
117	Derek Thompson RC	4.00
118	David Parrish RC	4.00
119	Dominic Rich RC	4.00
120	Chad Petty RC	4.00
121	Steve Smyth RC	4.00
122	John Lackey	4.00
123	Matt Galante RC	4.00
124	Danny Borrell RC	4.00
125	Bob Keppel RC	4.00
126	Justin Wayne RC	8.00
127	J.R. House	4.00
128	Brian Sellier RC	4.00
129	Dan Moylan RC	4.00
130	Scott Pratt RC	4.00
131	Victor Hall RC	4.00
132	Joel Pineiro	8.00
133	Josh Axelson RC	4.00
134	Jose Reyes RC	200.00
135	Greg Runser RC	4.00
136	Bryan Hebson RC	4.00
137	Sammy Serrano RC	4.00
138	Kevin Joseph RC	4.00
139	Juan Richardson RC	8.00
140	Mark Fischer RC	4.00

Refractors

Stars (1-110): 4-8X
Production 499
SP's: .5-1.5X
Production 399
Cards (111-140): 1-2X
Production 241

Autographed

		NM/M
	Common Player:	5.00
	Inserted 1:22	
MB	Milton Bradley	10.00
SB	Sean Burnett	5.00
BKC	Brian Cole	5.00
JC	Joe Crede	6.00
BD	Ben Diggins	5.00
CD	Chad Durham	5.00
TF	Troy Farnsworth	5.00
RF	Rafael Furcal	8.00
KG	Keith Ginter	5.00
AG	Adrian Gonzalez	15.00
JHH	Josh Hamilton	40.00
JH	Jason Hart	5.00
JRH	J.R. House	5.00
AH	Adam Hyzdu	5.00
DKC	David Kelton	5.00
AK	Adam Kennedy	5.00
DK	David Krynzel	8.00
ML	Mike Lamb	5.00
TL	Terrence Long	5.00
KM	Kevin Mench	5.00
BM	Ben Molina	5.00
JM	Justin Morneau	100.00
CM	Chad Mottola	5.00
JO	Jose Ortiz	5.00
DP	David Parrish	5.00
DCP	Corey Patterson	15.00
JP	Jay Payton	6.00

CP	Carlos Pena	8.00
AP	Albert Pujols	400.00
MQ	Mark Quinn	5.00
MR	Mark Redman	5.00
BS	Ben Sheets	15.00
JS	Juan Silvestre	5.00
JNS	Jamal Strong	5.00
BZ	Barry Zito	20.00

All-Stars

		NM/M
	Complete Set (10):	30.00
	Common Player:	2.00
	Inserted 1:10	
	Refractors:	1.5-2X
	Inserted 1:40	
1	Mark McGwire	5.00
2	Derek Jeter	6.00
3	Alex Rodriguez	5.00
4	Chipper Jones	3.00
5	Nomar Garciaparra	4.00
6	Sammy Sosa	4.00
7	Mike Piazza	4.00
8	Barry Bonds	6.00
9	Vladimir Guerrero	2.00
10	Ken Griffey Jr.	4.00

Moments

		NM/M
	Complete Set (25):	45.00
	Common Player:	1.00
	Inserted 1:12	
	Refractors:	1.5-2X
	Inserted 1:40	
1	Pat Burrell	2.00
2	Adam Kennedy	1.00
3	Mike Lamb	1.00
4	Rafael Furcal	1.00
5	Terrence Long	1.00
6	Jay Payton	1.00
7	Mark Quinn	1.00
8	Ben Molina	1.00
9	Kazuhiro Sasaki	1.00
10	Mark Redman	1.00
11	Barry Bonds	8.00
12	Alex Rodriguez	6.00
13	Roger Clemens	5.00
14	Jim Edmonds	1.00
15	Jason Giambi	2.00
16	Todd Helton	2.50
17	Troy Glaus	2.50
18	Carlos Delgado	2.00
19	Darin Erstad	2.00
20	Cal Ripken Jr.	8.00
21	Paul Molitor	3.00
22	Robin Yount	2.50
23	George Brett	5.00
24	Dave Winfield	2.50
25	Wade Boggs	3.00

Moments Autographs

		NM/M
	Inserted 1:250	
BB	Barry Bonds	180.00
GB	George Brett	75.00
JG	Jason Giambi	25.00
TG	Troy Glaus	20.00
TH	Todd Helton	30.00
PM	Paul Molitor	30.00
EM	Eddie Murray	20.00
CR	Cal Ripken Jr.	125.00
DW	Dave Winfield	20.00
RY	Robin Yount	50.00

Origins

		NM/M
	Complete Set (15):	18.00
	Common Player:	1.00
	Inserted 1:7	
	Refractors:	1.5-2X
	Inserted 1:40	
1	Derek Jeter	5.00
2	Jason Kendall	1.00
3	Jose Vidro	1.00
4	Preston Wilson	1.00
5	Jim Edmonds	1.00
6	Vladimir Guerrero	2.00
7	Andruw Jones	1.50
8	Scott Rolen	1.50
9	Edgardo Alfonzo	1.00
10	Mike Sweeney	1.00
11	Alex Rodriguez	4.00
12	Jermaine Dye	1.00
13	Charles Johnson	1.00
14	Darren Dreifort	1.00
15	Neifi Perez	1.00

2002 Finest

		NM/M
	Complete Set (110):	125.00
	Common Player:	.25
	Common SP Auto. (101-110):	8.00
	Pack (5):	4.00
	Box (18):	60.00
1	Mike Mussina	.50
2	Steve Sparks	.25
3	Randy Johnson	1.00
4	Orlando Cabrera	.25
5	Jeff Kent	.25
6	Carlos Delgado	.75
7	Ivan Rodriguez	.75
8	Jose Cruz	.25
9	Jason Giambi	.75
10	Brad Penny	.25
11	Moises Alou	.25
12	Mike Piazza	2.00
13	Ben Grieve	.25
14	Derek Jeter	3.00
15	Roy Oswalt	.40
16	Pat Burrell	.65

17	Preston Wilson	.25
18	Kevin Brown	.25
19	Barry Bonds	3.00
20	Phil Nevin	.25
21	Juan Gonzalez	1.00
22	Carlos Beltran	.60
23	Chipper Jones	1.50
24	Curt Schilling	.50
25	Jorge Posada	.40
26	Alfonso Soriano	1.00
27	Cliff Floyd	.25
28	Rafael Palmeiro	.75
29	Terrence Long	.25
30	Ken Griffey Jr.	2.00
31	Jason Kendall	.25
32	Jose Vidro	.25
33	Jermaine Dye	.25
34	Bobby Higginson	.25
35	Albert Pujols	2.50
36	Miguel Tejada	.40
37	Jim Edmonds	.25
38	Barry Zito	.40
39	Jimmy Rollins	.50
40	Rafael Furcal	.25
41	Omar Vizquel	.25
42	Kazuhiro Sasaki	.25
43	Brian Giles	.25
44	Darin Erstad	.50
45	Mariano Rivera	.40
46	Troy Percival	.25
47	Mike Sweeney	.25
48	Vladimir Guerrero	1.00
49	Troy Glaus	1.00
50	Hideo Nomo	.65
51	Edgardo Alfonzo	.25
52	Roger Clemens	1.75
53	Eric Chavez	.40
54	Alex Rodriguez	2.50
55	Cristian Guzman	.25
56	Jeff Bagwell	1.00
57	Bernie Williams	.40
58	Kerry Wood	.60
59	Ryan Klesko	.25
60	Ichiro Suzuki	2.00
61	Larry Walker	.25
62	Nomar Garciaparra	2.00
63	Craig Biggio	.25
64	J.D. Drew	.40
65	Juan Pierre	.25
66	Roberto Alomar	.50
67	Luis Gonzalez	.40
68	Bud Smith	.25
69	Magglio Ordonez	.50
70	Scott Rolen	1.00
71	Tsuyoshi Shinjo	.25
72	Reggie Sanders	.25
73	Garret Anderson	.25
74	Tim Hudson	.40
75	Adam Dunn	.75
76	Gary Sheffield	.50
77	Johnny Damon	.40
78	Todd Helton	1.00
79	Geoff Jenkins	.25
80	Shawn Green	.40
81	C.C. Sabathia	.25
82	Kazuhisa Ishii RC	3.00
83	Rich Aurilia	.25
84	Mike Hampton	.25
85	Ben Sheets	.25
86	Andruw Jones	1.00
87	Richie Sexson	.25
88	Jim Thome	.25
89	Sammy Sosa	2.00
90	Greg Maddux	1.50
91	Pedro Martinez	1.00
92	Jeromy Burnitz	.25
93	Raul Mondesi	.25
94	Bret Boone	.25
95	Jerry Hairston Jr.	.25
96	Carlos Pena	.25
97	Juan Cruz	.25
98	Morgan Ensberg	.25
99	Nathan Haynes	.25
100	Xavier Nady	.25
101	Nic Jackson/Auto. RC	10.00
102	Mauricio Lara/Auto. RC	8.00
103	Freddy Sanchez/Auto. RC	20.00
104	Clint Nageotte/Auto. RC	15.00
105	Beltran Perez/Auto. RC	8.00
106	Garrett Gentry/Auto. RC	8.00
107	Chad Qualls/Auto. RC	8.00
108	Jason Bay/Auto. RC	65.00
109	Michael Hill/Auto. RC	8.00
110	Brian Tallet/Auto.	10.00

Refractors

Star Refractors: 2-5X
Numbered to 499
X-Fractors: 3-6X
Numbered to 299

X-Fractor Protector: 5-10X
X-Fract. Protector (101-110): 1-2X
Numbered to 99

Bat Relics

	NM/M
Common Player:	5.00
Inserted 1:72	
BB Barry Bonds	25.00
BBO Bret Boone	5.00
NG Nomar Garciaparra	15.00
LG Luis Gonzalez	5.00
TG Tony Gwynn	10.00
TH Todd Helton	8.00
AJ Andruw Jones	5.00
CJ Chipper Jones	10.00
MP Mike Piazza	10.00
AP Albert Pujols	20.00
AR Alex Rodriguez	10.00
IR Ivan Rodriguez	8.00
TS Tsuyoshi Shinjo	5.00
AS Alfonso Soriano	8.00
BW Bernie Williams	8.00

Moments Autographs

	NM/M
Common Autograph:	10.00
Inserted 1:18	
LA Luis Aparicio	15.00
YB Yogi Berra	30.00
JB Jim Bunning	10.00
BG Bob Gibson	25.00
GG Rich "Goose" Gossage	10.00
FJ Fergie Jenkins	15.00
DL Don Larsen	15.00
DM Don Mattingly	75.00
GP Gaylord Perry	10.00
BR Bobby Richardson	10.00
BRO Brooks Robinson	35.00
JS Johnny Sain	10.00
MS Mike Schmidt	50.00
RS Red Schoendienst	10.00
BT Bobby Thomson	15.00

Team Topps Legends

Common Autograph

Uniform Relics

	NM/M
Common Player:	5.00

Inserted 1:24

RA	Roberto Alomar	8.00
JB	Jeff Bagwell	8.00
BB	Barry Bonds	20.00
BBO	Bret Boone	5.00
CD	Carlos Delgado	8.00
LG	Luis Gonzalez	5.00
MG	Mark Grace	8.00
SG	Shawn Green	5.00
TG	Tony Gwynn	10.00
TH	Todd Helton	8.00
RH	Rickey Henderson	15.00
AJ	Andruw Jones	8.00
CJ	Chipper Jones	10.00
GM	Greg Maddux	10.00
PM	Pedro Martinez	10.00
HN	Hideo Nomo	20.00
RP	Rafael Palmeiro	10.00
MP	Mike Piazza	10.00
AR	Alex Rodriguez	10.00
IR	Ivan Rodriguez	8.00
CS	Curt Schilling	10.00
TS	Tsuyoshi Shinjo	5.00
FT	Frank Thomas	8.00
LW	Larry Walker	5.00

2003 Finest

	NM/M
Complete Set (110):	
Common Player:	.25
Common Auto. (101-110):	10.00
Pack (5):	5.00
Box (18):	75.00
1 Sammy Sosa	2.00
2 Paul Konerko	.25
3 Todd Helton	.75
4 Mike Lowell	.25
5 Lance Berkman	.25
6 Kazuhisa Ishii	.25
7 A.J. Pierzynski	.25
8 Jose Vidro	.25
9 Roberto Alomar	.40
10 Derek Jeter	3.00
11 Barry Zito	.50
12 Jimmy Rollins	.25
13 Brian Giles	.25
14 Ryan Klesko	.25
15 Rich Aurilia	.25
16 Jim Edmonds	.25
17 Aubrey Huff	.25
18 Ivan Rodriguez	.65
19 Eric Hinske	.25
20 Barry Bonds	3.00
21 Darin Erstad	.60
22 Curt Schilling	.50
23 Andruw Jones	.75
24 Jay Gibbons	.25
25 Nomar Garciaparra	1.50
26 Kerry Wood	.60
27 Magglio Ordonez	.50
28 Austin Kearns	.50
29 Jason Jennings	.25
30 Jason Giambi	.50
31 Tim Hudson	.40
32 Edgar Martinez	.25
33 Carl Crawford	.25
34 Hee Seop Choi	15.00
35 Vladimir Guerrero	.75
36 Jeff Kent	.25
37 John Smoltz	.25
38 Frank Thomas	.75
39 Cliff Floyd	.25
40 Mike Piazza	1.50
41 Mark Prior	.75
42 Tim Salmon	.40
43 Shawn Green	.50
44 Bernie Williams	.40
45 Jim Thome	.25
46 John Olerud	.25
47 Orlando Hudson	.25
48 Mark Teixeira	.75
49 Gary Sheffield	.50

---

50 Ichiro Suzuki	2.00
51 Tom Glavine	.40
52 Torii Hunter	.25
53 Craig Biggio	.25
54 Carlos Beltran	.75
55 Bartolo Colon	.25
56 Jorge Posada	.35
57 Pat Burrell	.65
58 Edgar Renteria	.25
59 Rafael Palmeiro	.65
60 Alfonso Soriano	.75
61 Brandon Phillips	.25
62 Luis Gonzalez	.40
63 Manny Ramirez	.75
64 Garret Anderson	.25
65 Ken Griffey Jr.	1.50
66 A.J. Burnett	.25
67 Mike Sweeney	.25
68 Doug Mientkiewicz	.25
69 Eric Chavez	.50
70 Adam Dunn	.75
71 Shea Hillenbrand	.25
72 Troy Glaus	.75
73 Rodrigo Lopez	.25
74 Moises Alou	.25
75 Chipper Jones	1.00
76 Bobby Abreu	.25
77 Mark Mulder	.40
78 Kevin Brown	.25
79 Josh Beckett	.50
80 Larry Walker	.25
81 Randy Johnson	.75
82 Greg Maddux	1.00
83 Johnny Damon	.40
84 Omar Vizquel	.25
85 Jeff Bagwell	.75
86 Carlos Pena	.25
87 Roy Oswalt	.40
88 Richie Sexson	.25
89 Roger Clemens	1.25
90 Miguel Tejada	.40
91 Vicente Padilla	.25
92 Phil Nevin	.25
93 Edgardo Alfonzo	.25
94 Bret Boone	.25
95 Albert Pujols	2.00
96 Carlos Delgado	.50
97 Marlon Byrd	.25
98 Scott Rolen	.75
99 Pedro J. Martinez	.75
100 Alex Rodriguez	2.00
101 Adam LaRoche	15.00
102 Andy Marte RC	40.00
103 Daryl Clark RC	10.00
104 J.D. Durbin RC	10.00
105 Craig Brazell RC	15.00
106 Brian Burgamy RC	10.00
107 Tyler Johnson RC	10.00
108 Joey Gomes	10.00
109 Bryan Bullington RC	15.00
110 Byron Gettis RC	10.00

Refractors

Stars (1-100): 2-4X
Rookie Autos. (101-110): .75-1.5X
Inserted 1:6

X-Fractors

Stars (1-100): 5-10X
Rookie Autos. (101-110): 1-2.5X
Production 99 Sets
X-Fractor Golds (1-100): 3-6X
Golds Rk Autos. (101-110): 1-2X
Production 199 Sets

Bat Relics

	NM/M
Common Player:	8.00
Inserted 1:6	
JB	Jeff Bagwell	8.00
LB	Lance Berkman	8.00
WB	Wade Boggs	8.00
BB	Barry Bonds	20.00
RC	Rod Carew	10.00
RCL	Roger Clemens	15.00
AD	Adam Dunn	8.00
NG	Nomar Garciaparra	20.00
TH	Todd Helton	8.00
RH	Rickey Henderson	10.00
CJ	Chipper Jones	10.00
AK	Austin Kearns	8.00
GM	Greg Maddux	15.00
PM	Paul Molitor	8.00

DM	Dale Murphy	15.00
RP	Rafael Palmeiro	8.00
MP	Mike Piazza	15.00
KP	Kirby Puckett	15.00
AP	Albert Pujols	15.00
MR	Manny Ramirez	8.00
CR	Cal Ripken Jr.	35.00
AR	Alex Rodriguez	12.00
IR	Ivan Rodriguez	8.00
MS	Mike Schmidt	20.00
AS	Alfonso Soriano	10.00
MT	Miguel Tejada	8.00
JT	Jim Thome	10.00

Moments Autographs

	NM/M
Common Player:	10.00
EB Ernie Banks	60.00
PB Paul Blair	10.00
LB Lou Brock	25.00
GC Gary Carter	15.00
OC Orlando Cepeda	15.00
GF George Foster	15.00
GG Rich "Goose" Gossage	15.00
KH Keith Hernandez	15.00
DL Don Larsen	15.00
WMA Willie Mays	150.00
JP Jim Palmer	15.00
GP Gaylord Perry	15.00
JS Johnny Sain	10.00

Team Topps Legends Autograph

	NM/M
Common Autograph:	10.00
Luis Aparicio	15.00
Paul Blair	10.00
Lou Brock	25.00
Rich "Goose" Gossage	15.00
Al Kaline	35.00
Don Larsen	20.00
Vern Law	12.00
Stan Musial	75.00
Brooks Robinson	

Uniform Relics

	NM/M
Common Player:	5.00
BB Barry Bonds	20.00
EC Eric Chavez	5.00
AD Adam Dunn	10.00
LG Luis Gonzalez	5.00
TH Todd Helton	8.00
RJ Randy Johnson	8.00
AJ Andruw Jones	8.00
CJ Chipper Jones	10.00
GM Greg Maddux	12.00
WM Willie Mays	30.00
MM Mark Mulder	6.00
RO Roy Oswalt	5.00
RP Rafael Palmeiro	8.00
MP Mike Piazza	12.00
AP Albert Pujols	15.00
MR Manny Ramirez	15.00
AR Alex Rodriguez	15.00
CS Curt Schilling	8.00
AS Alfonso Soriano	10.00
SS Sammy Sosa	15.00
MSW Mike Sweeney	5.00
LW Larry Walker	5.00

2004 Finest

	NM/M
Complete Set (122):	
Common Player:	.40
Common Star Relic (101-110):	8.00
Inserted 1:42	

TRAVIS BLACKLEY

Common FYP Autograph
(111-122): 10.00
Inserted 1:18
Pack (5): 6.00
Box (18): 85.00
Mini-Box (6): 30.00

1	Juan Pierre	.40
2	Derek Jeter	3.00
3	Garret Anderson	.50
4	Javy Lopez	.50
5	Corey Patterson	.50
6	Todd Helton	.75
7	Roy Oswalt	.50
8	Shawn Green	.40
9	Vladimir Guerrero	1.00
10	Jorge Posada	.50
11	Jason Kendall	.40
12	Scott Rolen	1.00
13	Randy Johnson	1.00
14	Bill Mueller	.40
15	Magglio Ordonez	.50
16	Larry Walker	.50
17	Lance Berkman	.50
18	Richie Sexson	.75
19	Orlando Cabrera	.40
20	Alfonso Soriano	1.00
21	Kevin Millwood	.50
22	Edgar Martinez	.50
23	Aubrey Huff	.40
24	Carlos Delgado	.75
25	Vernon Wells	.40
26	Mark Teixeira	.40
27	Troy Glaus	.50
28	Jeff Kent	.50
29	Hideo Nomo	.50
30	Torii Hunter	.50
31	Hank Blalock	.50
32	Brandon Webb	.40
33	Tony Batista	.40
34	Bret Boone	.50
35	Ryan Klesko	.50
36	Barry Zito	.50
37	Aaron Boone	.40
38	Geoff Jenkins	.50
39	Jeff Bagwell	.75
40	Dontrelle Willis	.50
41	Adam Dunn	.75
42	Mark Buehrle	.40
43	Esteban Loaiza	.40
44	Angel Berroa	.40
45	Ivan Rodriguez	.75
46	Jose Vidro	.40
47	Mark Mulder	.50
48	Marlon Byrd	.40
49	Jim Edmonds	.50
50	Eric Gagne	.50
51	Marcus Giles	.40
52	Curt Schilling	.75
53	Ken Griffey Jr.	1.50
54	Jason Schmidt	.50
55	Miguel Tejada	.50
56	Dmitri Young	.40
57	Mike Lowell	.50
58	Mike Sweeney	.40
59	Scott Podsednik	.75
60	Miguel Cabrera	1.00
61	Johan Santana	.40
62	Bernie Williams	.50
63	Eric Chavez	.50
64	Bobby Abreu	.50
65	Brian Giles	.50
66	Michael Young	.40
67	Paul LoDuca	.40
68	Austin Kearns	.40
69	Jody Gerut	.40
70	Kerry Wood	1.00
71	Luis Matos	.40
72	Greg Maddux	1.50
73	Alex Rodriguez	4.00
74	Mike Lieberthal	.40
75	Jim Thome	1.00
76	Javier Vazquez	.40
77	Bartolo Colon	.50

78	Manny Ramirez	.75
79	Jacque Jones	.40
80	Johnny Damon	.40
81	Carlos Beltran	.75
82	C.C. Sabathia	.40
83	Preston Wilson	.40
84	Luis Castillo	.40
85	Kevin Brown	.50
86	Shannon Stewart	.40
87	Cliff Floyd	.40
88	Mike Mussina	.50
89	Rafael Furcal	.40
90	Roy Halladay	.50
91	Frank Thomas	.75
92	Melvin Mora	.40
93	Andruw Jones	.75
94	Luis Gonzalez	.50
95	David Ortiz	.75
96	Gary Sheffield	.50
97	Tim Hudson	.50
98	Phil Nevin	.40
99	Ichiro Suzuki	2.00
100	Albert Pujols	2.50
101	Nomar Garciaparra	15.00
102	Sammy Sosa	15.00
103	Josh Beckett	8.00
104	Jason Giambi	8.00
105	Rocco Baldelli	8.00
106	Jose Reyes	8.00
107	Chipper Jones	10.00
108	Pedro J. Martinez	10.00
109	Mike Piazza	8.00
110	Mark Prior	8.00
111	Craig Ansman RC	10.00
112	Jeff Allison	15.00
113	David Murphy	15.00
114	Jason Hirsh	20.00
115	Matt Moses	20.00
116	Estee Harris RC	10.00
117	Logan Kensing RC	10.00
118	Lastings Milledge	60.00
119	Merkin Valdez RC	15.00
120	Travis Blackley RC	15.00
121	Vito Chiaravalloti RC	15.00
122	Dioner Navarro RC	25.00

Refractor

Refractor (1-100):	2-4X
Inserted 1:6	
Refractor (101-110):	1-2X
Inserted 1:156	
Refractor (111-122):	1-2X
Inserted 1:132	

Gold Refractor

Gold Refractor (1-100):	6-12X
Gold Refr. (101-110):	1.5-2X
Gold Refr. (111-122):	2-4X
Production 50 Sets	

Uncirculated X-Fractor

CURT SCHILLING

Stars (1-100):	4-8X
Relics (101-110):	1-2X
Autographs (111-122):	1-2X
Inserted as a box topper.	
Production 139 Sets	

Moments Autographs

	NM/M
Common Autograph:	10.00
JA	Jim Abbott	15.00
VB	Vida Blue	12.00
OC	Orlando Cepeda	12.00
LD	Lenny Dykstra	10.00
GS	George Foster	10.00
EK	Ed Kranepool	10.00
WM	Willie Mays	100.00

Padres Patches Dodgers to World Series Championship

FINEST MOMENTS

JIM PODRES

JP	Johnny Podres	10.00
DS	Duke Snider	40.00
RY	Robin Yount	75.00

Relics

MARLON BYRD

AUTHENTIC GAME-WORN JERSEY

		NM/M
Common Player:		4.00
JB	Jeff Bagwell	8.00
RB1	Rocco Baldelli/Jsy	6.00
RB3	Rocco Baldelli/Jsy	6.00
JPB1	Josh Beckett	8.00
LB1	Lance Berkman/Bat	5.00
LB2	Lance Berkman/Jsy	5.00
AB	Angel Berroa	4.00
HB1	Hank Blalock/Bat	8.00
HB2	Hank Blalock/Jsy	8.00
PB	Pat Burrell	10.00
SB	Sean Burroughs	5.00
MB	Marlon Byrd	4.00
MC	Miguel Cabrera	10.00
EC	Eric Chavez	6.00
AD	Adam Dunn	8.00
DE	Darin Erstad	4.00
NG	Nomar Garciaparra	12.00
TG	Troy Glaus	6.00
AG	Adrian Gonzalez	4.00
LG	Luis Gonzalez	4.00
SG	Shawn Green	4.00
VG	Vladimir Guerrero	8.00
CG	Cristian Guzman	4.00
RH	Rich Harden	5.00
TH1	Todd Helton/Bat	8.00
TH2	Todd Helton/Jsy	8.00
TH	Tim Hudson	5.00
TKH1	Torii Hunter/Bat	6.00
TKH2	Torii Hunter/Jsy	6.00
KI	Kazuhisa Ishii	4.00
RJ	Randy Johnson	8.00
AJ	Andruw Jones	6.00
JL	Javy Lopez	6.00
DL	Derek Lowe	4.00
ML1	Mike Lowell/Jsy	5.00
ML2	Mike Lowell/Jsy	5.00
GM	Greg Maddux	10.00
KM	Kevin Millwood	6.00
MM	Mark Mulder	4.00
BM1	Brett Myers/Jsy	4.00
BM2	Brett Myers/Jsy	4.00
MO1	Magglio Ordonez/Jsy	6.00
MO2	Magglio Ordonez/Bat	6.00
RP1	Rafael Palmeiro/Bat	8.00
RP2	Rafael Palmeiro/Jsy	8.00
RP3	Rafael Palmeiro/Jsy	8.00
AP	Andy Pettitte	6.00
JP	Juan Pierre	4.00
MP	Mark Prior	10.00
AP1	Albert Pujols/Jsy	15.00
AP2	Albert Pujols/Bat	15.00
JR1	Jose Reyes/Jsy	8.00
JR2	Jose Reyes/Bat	8.00
JR3	Jose Reyes/Jsy	8.00

MR	Mariano Rivera	10.00
AR1	Alex Rodriguez/ Rangers	10.00
AR2	Alex Rodriguez/ Yankees	20.00
IR1	Ivan Rodriguez/Jsy	4.00
IR2	Ivan Rodriguez/Jsy	8.00
IR3	Ivan Rodriguez/Bat	8.00
SR	Scott Rolen	8.00
CCS	C.C. Sabathia	6.00
KS	Kazuhiro Sasaki	4.00
CS	Curt Schilling	6.00
GS	Gary Sheffield	6.00
JS	John Smoltz	8.00
AS	Alfonso Soriano	8.00
SS	Sammy Sosa	12.00
MT1	Miguel Tejada/Bat	6.00
MT2	Miguel Tejada/Jsy	6.00
FT	Frank Thomas	8.00
JT	Jim Thome	10.00
LW	Larry Walker	4.00
VW	Vernon Wells	5.00
BW	Bernie Williams	6.00
DW	Dontrelle Willis	6.00
PW	Preston Wilson	4.00
KW1	Kerry Wood/Jsy	10.00
KW2	Kerry Wood/Bat	10.00
DY	Delmon Young	8.00
BZ	Barry Zito	8.00

2005 Finest

MATT CAMPBELL

292 /770

TOPPS CERTIFIED AUTOGRAPH ISSUE

	NM/M
Complete Set (166):	
Common Player:	.40
Common Auto. (141-156):	10.00
Production 970, unless noted.	
Pack (5):	10.00
Box (18):	150.00

1	Alexis Rios	.40
2	Hank Blalock	.50
3	Bobby Abreu	.50
4	Curt Schilling	1.00
5	Albert Pujols	3.00
6	Aaron Rowand	.40
7	B.J. Upton	.50
8	Andruw Jones	.75
9	Jeff Francis	.40
10	Sammy Sosa	1.50
11	Aramis Ramirez	.75
12	Carl Pavano	.40
13	Bartolo Colon	.40
14	Greg Maddux	2.00
15	Scott Kazmir	.50
16	Melvin Mora	.40
17	Brandon Backe	.40
18	Bobby Crosby	.40
19	Carlos Lee	.50
20	Carl Crawford	.50
21	Brian Giles	.40
22	Jeff Bagwell	.75
23	J.D. Drew	.50
24	C.C. Sabathia	.40
25	Alfonso Soriano	1.00
26	Chipper Jones	1.00
27	Austin Kearns	.40
28	Carlos Delgado	.75
29	Jack Wilson	.40
30	Dmitri Young	.40
31	Carlos Guillen	.40
32	Jim Thome	1.00
33	Eric Chavez	.50
34	Jason Schmidt	.50
35	Brad Radke	.40
36	Frank Thomas	.75
37	Darin Erstad	.40
38	Javier Vazquez	.40
39	Garret Anderson	.50
40	David Ortiz	1.00
41	Javy Lopez	.40
42	Geoff Jenkins	.40
43	Jose Vidro	.40
44	Aubrey Huff	.40

45	Bernie Williams	.50
46	Dontrelle Willis	.50
47	Jim Edmonds	.50
48	Ivan Rodriguez	.75
49	Gary Sheffield	.50
50	Alex Rodriguez	2.50
51	John Buck	.40
52	Andy Pettitte	.50
53	Ichiro Suzuki	2.50
54	Johnny Estrada	.40
55	Jake Peavy	.50
56	Carlos Zambrano	.50
57	Jose Reyes	.75
58	Bret Boone	.40
59	Jason Bay	.50
60	David Wright	1.50
61	Jeromy Burnitz	.40
62	Corey Patterson	.50
63	Juan Pierre	.40
64	Zack Greinke	.40
65	Mike Lowell	.40
66	Ken Griffey Jr.	2.00
67	Marcus Giles	.40
68	Edgar Renteria	.50
69	Ken Harvey	.40
70	Pedro Martinez	1.00
71	Johnny Damon	1.00
72	Lyle Overbay	.50
73	Mike Maroth	.40
74	Jorge Posada	.50
75	Carlos Beltran	.75
76	Mark Buehrle	.50
77	Khalil Greene	.40
78	Josh Beckett	.50
79	Mark Loretta	.40
80	Rafael Palmeiro	.75
81	Justin Morneau	.75
82	Rocco Baldelli	.50
83	Ben Sheets	.50
84	Kerry Wood	.50
85	Miguel Tejada	.75
86	Magglio Ordonez	.50
87	Livan Hernandez	.40
88	Kazuo Matsui	.40
89	Manny Ramirez	1.00
90	Hideki Matsui	2.00
91	Jeff Kent	.50
92	Matt Lawton	.40
93	Richie Sexson	.50
94	Mike Mussina	.75
95	Adam Dunn	.75
96	Johan Santana	.75
97	Nomar Garciaparra	1.50
98	Michael Young	.40
99	Victor Martinez	.50
100	Barry Bonds	3.00
101	Oliver Perez	.40
102	Randy Johnson	1.00
103	Mark Mulder	.40
104	Pat Burrell	.40
105	Mike Sweeney	.40
106	Mark Teixeira	.75
107	Paul LoDuca	.40
108	Jon Lieber	.40
109	Mike Piazza	1.50
110	Roger Clemens	3.00
111	Rafael Furcal	.50
112	Troy Glaus	.50
113	Miguel Cabrera	1.00
114	Randy Wolf	.40
115	Lance Berkman	.75
116	Mark Prior	.75
117	Rich Harden	.50
118	Preston Wilson	.40
119	Roy Oswalt	.50
120	Luis Gonzalez	.50
121	Ronnie Belliard	.40
122	Sean Casey	.50
123	Barry Zito	.50
124	Larry Walker	.50
125	Derek Jeter	3.00
126	Tim Hudson	.50
127	Tom Glavine	.50
128	Scott Rolen	1.00
129	Torii Hunter	.50
130	Paul Konerko	.75
131	Shawn Green	.40
132	Travis Hafner	.50
133	Vernon Wells	.50
134	Sidney Ponson	.40
135	Vladimir Guerrero	1.00
136	Mark Kotsay	.40
137	Todd Helton	.75
138	Adrian Beltre	.50
139	Wily Mo Pena	.40
140	Joe Mauer	.75
141	Brian Stavisky RC	10.00
142	Nate McLouth RC	15.00
143	Glen Perkins/375 RC	20.00
144	Chip Cannon RC	15.00
145	Shane Costa RC	10.00
146	Wes Swackhamer RC	10.00
147	Kevin Melillo RC	15.00
148	Billy Butler RC	60.00

149	Landon Powell RC	15.00
150	Scott Mathieson RC	10.00
151	Chris Roberson RC	10.00
152	Chad Orvella/375 RC	15.00
153	Eric Nielsen RC	10.00
154	Matt Campbell RC	10.00
155	Mike Rogers RC	10.00
156	Melky Cabrera RC	40.00
157	Nolan Ryan	4.00
158	Bo Jackson	1.00
159	Wade Boggs	1.00
160	Andre Dawson	.75
161	Dave Winfield	1.00
162	Reggie Jackson	1.00
163	David Justice	.50
164	Dale Murphy	1.00
165	Paul O'Neill	.75
166	Tom Seaver	1.50

Refractors
Refrac. (1-140, 157-166): 2-4X
Autograph (141-156): .5-1X
Production 399 Sets

Refractors Black
Refrac. (1-140, 157-166): 4-8X
Autograph (141-156): 1-2X
Production 99 Sets

Refractors Blue

Refrac. (1-140, 157-166): 2-4X
Autograph (141-156): .5-1X
Production 299 Sets

Refractors Gold
Refrac. (1-140, 157-166): 5-10X
Autograph (141-156): 2-4X
Production 49 Sets

Refractors Green
Refrac. (1-140, 157-166): 2-4X
Autograph (141-156): .5-1.5X
Production 199 Sets

Refractors White Framed
No Pricing
Production One Set

X-Fractor
Refrac. (1-140, 157-166): 2-4X
Autograph (141-156): .5-1X
Production 250 Sets

X-Fractor Black
Refrac. (1-140, 157-166): 8-15X
Autograph (141-156): No Pricing
Production 25 Sets

X-Fractor Blue
Refrac. (1-140, 157-166): 3-5X
Autograph (141-156): .5-1.5X
Production 150 Sets

X-Fractor Gold
No Pricing
Production 10 Sets

X-Fractor Green
Refrac. (1-140, 157-166): 5-10X
Autograph (141-156): 1.5-3X
Production 50 Sets

X-Fractor White Framed
No Pricing
Production One Set

Super Fractor
No Pricing
Production One Set

Printing Plates

No Pricing
Production one set for each color.

Autographs

		NM/M
X-Fractor:		1.5-2X
Production 25 Sets		
JB	Jason Bay	25.00
CB	Carlos Beltran	30.00
BB	Barry Bonds	280.00
MB	Milton Bradley	15.00
EC	Eric Chavez	20.00
JE	Johnny Estrada	15.00
EG	Eric Gagne	30.00
KM	Kevin Millar	35.00
DO	David Ortiz	50.00
MR	Mariano Rivera	60.00
JS	Johan Santana	40.00
GS	Gary Sheffield	30.00
AS	Alfonso Soriano	30.00
JST	Jacob Stevens	10.00
DW	David Wright	80.00

Alex Rodriguez Finest Moments Autograph
	NM/M
Production 13 Sets	
A-Rod Auto. 1-49:	150.00

Alex Rodriguez Finest Moments
	NM/M
A-Rod 1-49:	10.00
Production 190 Sets	

Finest Moment Autographs
No Pricing
Production 50

2 of a Kind Autographs
No Pricing
Production 13

2006 Finest
	NM/M
Complete Set (155):	
Common Player:	.40
Common Auto. (141-155):	10.00
Pack (5):	9.00
Box (18):	150.00
1 Vladimir Guerrero	1.00
2 Troy Glaus	.50
3 Andruw Jones	1.00
4 Miguel Tejada	.75

5	Manny Ramirez	1.00
6	Curt Schilling	1.00
7	Mark Prior	.75
8	Kerry Wood	.50
9	Tadahito Iguchi	.40
10	Freddy Garcia	.40
11	Ryan Howard	1.50
12	Mark Buehrle	.50
13	Wily Mo Pena	.40
14	C.C. Sabathia	.40
15	Garret Anderson	.40
16	Shawn Green	.40
17	Rafael Furcal	.40
18	Jeff Francoeur	.40
19	Ken Griffey Jr.	2.00
20	Derrek Lee	.75
21	Paul Konerko	.75
22	Rickie Weeks	.50
23	Magglio Ordonez	.40
24	Juan Pierre	.40
25	Felix Hernandez	1.00
26	Roger Clemens	3.00
27	Zack Greinke	.40
28	Johan Santana	1.00
29	Jose Reyes	.75
30	Bobby Crosby	.40
31	Jason Schmidt	.40
32	Khalil Greene	.40
33	Richie Sexson	.50
34	Mark Mulder	.50
35	Mark Teixeira	.75
36	Nick Johnson	.40
37	Vernon Wells	.50
38	Scott Kazmir	.40
39	Jim Edmonds	.50
40	Adrian Beltre	.40
41	Dan Johnson	.40
42	Carlos Lee	.50
43	Lance Berkman	.75
44	Josh Beckett	.50
45	Morgan Ensberg	.40
46	Garrett Atkins	.40
47	Chase Utley	.50
48	Joe Mauer	.75
49	Travis Hafner	.75
50	Alex Rodriguez	3.00
51	Austin Kearns	.40
52	Scott Podsednik	.50
53	Jose Contreras	.40
54	Greg Maddux	2.00
55	Hideki Matsui	2.00
56	Matt Clement	.40
57	Javy Lopez	.40
58	Tim Hudson	.50
59	Luis Gonzalez	.40
60	Bartolo Colon	.50
61	Marcus Giles	.40
62	Justin Morneau	.75
63	Nomar Garciaparra	1.00
64	Robinson Cano	1.00
65	Ervin Santana	.40
66	Brady Clark	.40
67	Edgar Renteria	.40
68	Jon Garland	.40
69	Felipe Lopez	.40
70	Ivan Rodriguez	.75
71	Dontrelle Willis	.50
72	Carlos Guillen	.40
73	J.D. Drew	.40
74	Rich Harden	.40
75	Albert Pujols	3.00
76	Livan Hernandez	.40
77	Roy Halladay	.50
78	Hank Blalock	.50
79	David Wright	1.50
80	Jimmy Rollins	.50
81	John Smoltz	.50
82	Miguel Cabrera	1.00
83	David DeJesus	.40
84	Torii Hunter	.50
85	Adam Dunn	.75
86	Randy Johnson	1.00
87	Roy Oswalt	.50

88	Bobby Abreu	.50
89	Rocco Baldelli	.40
90	Ichiro Suzuki	2.00
91	Jorge Cantu	.40
92	Jack Wilson	.40
93	Jose Vidro	.40
94	Kevin Millwood	.50
95	David Ortiz	1.00
96	Victor Martinez	.50
97	Jeremy Bonderman	.40
98	Todd Helton	.75
99	Carlos Beltran	.75
100	Barry Bonds	3.00
101	Jeff Kent	.50
102	Mike Sweeney	.40
103	Ben Sheets	.50
104	Melvin Mora	.40
105	Gary Sheffield	.75
106	Craig Wilson	.40
107	Chris Carpenter	.75
108	Michael Young	.40
109	Gustavo Chacin	.40
110	Chipper Jones	1.00
111	Mark Loretta	.40
112	Andy Pettitte	.50
113	Carlos Delgado	.75
114	Pat Burrell	.50
115	Jason Bay	.50
116	Brian Roberts	.50
117	Joe Crede	.40
118	Jake Peavy	.50
119	Aubrey Huff	.40
120	Pedro Martinez	1.00
121	Jorge Posada	.50
122	Barry Zito	.50
123	Scott Rolen	.75
124	Brett Myers	.40
125	Derek Jeter	3.00
126	Eric Chavez	.50
127	Carl Crawford	.50
128	Jim Thome	1.00
129	Johnny Damon	1.00
130	Alfonso Soriano	.75
131	Clint Barmes	.40
132	Dustin Nippert	1.00
133	Hanley Ramirez	2.00
134	Matt Capps	1.00
135	Miguel Perez	1.00
136	Tom Gorzelanny	1.00
137	Charlton Jimerson	1.00
138	Bryan Bullington	1.00
139	Kenji Johjima RC	4.00
140	Craig Hansen RC	3.00
141	Craig Breslow RC	15.00
142	Adam Wainwright	20.00
143	Joey Devine RC	15.00
144	Hong-Chih Kuo	40.00
145	Jason Botts	15.00
146	Josh Johnson	15.00
147	Jason Bergmann RC	15.00
148	Scott Olsen	15.00
149	Darrell Rasner	15.00
150	Daniel Ortmeier	15.00
151	Chuck James	20.00
152	Ryan Garko	20.00
153	Nelson Cruz	15.00
154	Anthony Lerew	10.00
155	Francisco Liriano	35.00

Refractor
Stars (1-140): 2-4X
Autos. (141-155): .5-1X
Production 399 Sets

Black Refractor
Stars (1-140): 4-8X
Autos. (141-155): 1-2X
Production 99 Sets

Blue Refractor
Stars (1-140): 2-5X
Autos. (141-155): .75-1X
Production 299 Sets

Gold Refractor
Stars (1-140): 6-12X
Autos. (141-155): 2-3X
Production 49 Sets

Green Refractor
Stars (1-140): 2-5X
Autos. (141-155): .75-1.5X
Production 199 Sets

SuperFractor
No Pricing
Production One Set

White Framed Refractor
No Pricing
Production One Set

Black X-Fractor
Stars (1-140): 8-15X
Autos. (141-155): No Pricing
Production 25 Sets

Blue X-Fractor
Stars (1-140): 3-5X
Autos. (141-155): 1-1.5X
Production 150 Sets

Gold X-Fractor
No Pricing
Production 10 Sets

Green X-Fractor
Stars (1-140): 6-12X
Autos. (141-155): 2-3X
Production 50 Sets

X-Fractor
Stars (1-140): 2-5X
Autos. (141-155): .75-1X
Production 250 Sets

Autographs
NM/M
JB	Jason Bay	25.00
MC	Miguel Cabrera	40.00
RC	Robinson Cano	50.00
EC	Eric Chavez	20.00
MG	Marcus Giles	15.00
VG	Vladimir Guerrero	50.00
JG	Jose Guillen	12.00
RH	Rich Harden	20.00
KJ	Kenji Johjima	80.00
AJ	Andruw Jones	40.00
CJ	Chipper Jones	60.00
DL	Derrek Lee	30.00
RO	Roy Oswalt	25.00
AR	Alex Rodriguez	160.00
GS	Gary Sheffield	30.00
DWI	Dontrelle Willis	25.00
CW	Craig Wilson	10.00
DW	David Wright	60.00

Barry Bonds Finest Moments Autographs
No Pricing

Barry Bonds Finest Moments

NM/M
Common Bonds: 10.00
Production 425 Sets
Gold Refractor: 1-2X
Production 199 Sets

Mickey Mantle Finest Moments

NM/M
Common Mantle: 10.00
Production 850 Sets
Refractor: 1X
Production 399 Sets
Blue Refractor: 1-1.5X
Production 299 Sets
Green Refractor: 1-2X
Production 199 Sets
Black Refractor: 1.5-3X
Production 99 Sets
Gold Refractor: 3-4X
Production 49 Sets
X-Fractor: 1-1.5X
Production 250 Sets
Blue X-Fractor: 1-2X
Production 150 Sets
Green X-Fractor: 3-4X
Production 50 Sets
Black X-Fractor: 4-6X
Production 25 Sets
Gold X-Fractor: No Pricing
Production 10 Sets

Mickey Mantle Finest Moments Cut Signature
No Pricing
Production One Set

2007 Finest

NM/M
Complete Set (165):
Common Player (1-135): .25
Common RC (136-150): 1.00
Common RC Auto.
  (151-165): 10.00
Pack (5): 8.00
Box (18): 125.00

1	David Wright	2.00
2	Jered Weaver	.50
3	Chipper Jones	1.00
4	Magglio Ordonez	.50
5	Ben Sheets	.50
6	Nick Johnson	.25
7	Melvin Mora	.25
8	Chien-Ming Wang	1.00
9	Andre Ethier	.50
10	Carlos Beltran	1.00
11	Ryan Zimmerman	1.00
12	Troy Glaus	.50
13	Hanley Ramirez	.75
14	Mark Buehrle	.50
15	Dan Uggla	.50
16	Richie Sexson	.75
17	Scott Kazmir	.50
18	Garrett Atkins	.25
19	Matt Cain	.50
20	Jorge Posada	.50
21	Brett Myers	.25
22	Jeff Francoeur	.50
23	Scott Rolen	1.00
24	Derrek Lee	.75
25	Manny Ramirez	1.00
26	Johnny Damon	1.00
27	Mark Teixeira	1.00
28	Mark Prior	.75
29	Victor Martinez	.50
30	Greg Maddux	2.00
31	Prince Fielder	1.50
32	Jeremy Bonderman	.50
33	Paul LoDuca	.25
34	Brandon Webb	.50
35	Robinson Cano	1.00
36	Josh Beckett	.50
37	David DeJesus	.25
38	Kenny Rogers	.25
39	Jim Thome	1.00
40	Brian McCann	.50
41	Lance Berkman	.50
42	Adam Dunn	.75
43	Rocco Baldelli	.50
44	Brian Roberts	.50
45	Vladimir Guerrero	1.00
46	Dontrelle Willis	.50
47	Eric Chavez	.50
48	Carlos Zambrano	.50
49	Ivan Rodriguez	1.00
50	Alex Rodriguez	3.00
51	Curt Schilling	1.00
52	Carlos Delgado	.75
53	Matt Holliday	.75
54	Mark Teahen	.25
55	Frank Thomas	1.00
56	Grady Sizemore	.75
57	Aramis Ramirez	.50
58	Rafael Furcal	.50
59	David Ortiz	1.00
60	Paul Konerko	.50
61	Barry Zito	.50
62	Travis Hafner	.50
63	Nick Swisher	.50
64	Johan Santana	1.00
65	Miguel Tejada	.75
66	Carl Crawford	.50
67	Kenji Johjima	.50
68	Derek Jeter	3.00
69	Francisco Liriano	.50
70	Ken Griffey Jr.	2.00
71	Pat Burrell	.50
72	Adrian Gonzalez	.25
73	Miguel Cabrera	1.00
74	Albert Pujols	3.00
75	Justin Verlander	.75
76	Carlos Lee	.50
77	John Smoltz	.50
78	Orlando Hudson	.25
79	Joe Mauer	.50
80	Freddy Sanchez	.25
81	Bobby Abreu	.50
82	Pedro Martinez	1.00
83	Vernon Wells	.50
84	Justin Morneau	.75
85	Bill Hall	.50
86	Jason Schmidt	.50
87	Michael Young	.50
88	Tadahito Iguchi	.25
89	Kevin Millwood	.50
90	Randy Johnson	1.00
91	Roy Halladay	.50
92	Mike Lowell	.25
93	Jake Peavy	.50
94	Jason Varitek	.75
95	Todd Helton	.75
96	Mark Loretta	.25
97	Gary Matthews	.25
98	Ryan Howard	2.00
99	Jose Reyes	1.00
100	Chris Carpenter	.50
101	Hideki Matsui	2.00
102	Brian Giles	.25
103	Torii Hunter	.50
104	Rich Harden	.25
105	Ichiro Suzuki	2.00
106	Chase Utley	1.00
107	Nicholas Markakis	.50
108	Marcus Giles	.25
109	Gary Sheffield	.75
110	Jim Edmonds	.50
111	Brandon Phillips	.25
112	Roy Oswalt	.50
113	Jeff Kent	.50
114	Jason Bay	.50
115	Raul Ibanez	.25
116	Stephen Drew	.50
117	Hank Blalock	.50
118	Tom Glavine	.50
119	Andruw Jones	.75
120	Alfonso Soriano	1.00
121	Mariano Rivera	.50
122	Garret Anderson	.25
123	Erik Bedard	.50
124	Huston Street	.25
125	Austin Kearns	.50
126	Jermaine Dye	.25
127	C.C. Sabathia	.25
128	Joe Nathan	.25
129	Craig Monroe	.25
130	Aubrey Huff	.25
131	Billy Wagner	.25
132	Jorge Cantu	.25
133	Trevor Hoffman	.25
134	Ronnie Belliard	.25
135	B.J. Ryan	.25
136	Adam Lind (RC)	1.00
137	Hector Gimenez (RC)	1.00
138	Shawn Riggans (RC)	1.00
139	Joaquin Arias (RC)	1.00
140	Drew Anderson (RC)	1.00
141	Mike Rabelo RC	1.00
142	Chris Narveson (RC)	1.00
143	Ryan Feierabend (RC)	1.00
144	Vinny Rottino (RC)	2.00
145	Jon Knott (RC)	1.00
146	Oswaldo Navarro RC	1.00
147	Brian Stokes (RC)	1.00
148	Glen Perkins (RC)	1.00

149	Mitch Maier (RC)	1.00
150	Delmon Young (RC)	2.00
151	Andrew Miller RC	50.00
152	Troy Tulowitzki (RC)	40.00
153	Philip Humber (RC)	20.00
154	Kevin Kouzmanoff (RC)	20.00
155	Michael Bourn (RC)	15.00
156	Miguel Montero (RC)	15.00
157	David Murphy (RC)	15.00
158	Ryan Sweeney (RC)	15.00
159	Jeff Baker (RC)	10.00
160	Jeff Salazar (RC)	10.00
161	Jose Garcia (RC)	10.00
162	Josh Fields (RC)	10.00
163	Delwyn Young (RC)	15.00
164	Fred Lewis (RC)	15.00
165	Scott Moore (RC)	15.00

Printing Plates
Production one set per color.

SuperFractor
Production One Set

X-Fractor
X-Fractor (1-135):	10-20X
RC Autos.:	No Pricing
Production 25 Sets	

Gold Refractor
Gold Refractor (1-150):	5-10X
Production 50	
RC Autos.:	2X
Production 49	

Black Refractor
Black Refractor (1-150):	4-8X
RC Autos.:	1.5X
Production 99 Sets	

Green Refractor
Green Refractor (1-150):	2-5X
RC Autos.:	1-1.5X
Production 199 Sets	

Blue Refractor
Blue Refractor (1-150):	2-5X
Production 399 Sets	
RC Autos.:	.75-1X
Production 299	

Refractor
Refractor (1-150):	2-4X
RC Autographs:	.5-1X
Production 399 only autos. serial #'d.	

Rookies Finest Moments Autograph

		NM/M
Common Autograph:		10.00
Refractors:		No Pricing
Production 25 Sets		
DO	David Ortiz	50.00
DW	David Wright	75.00
JN	Joe Nathan	10.00
AR	Alex Rodriguez	125.00
TH	Travis Hafner	20.00
RH	Ryan Howard	100.00
AS	Anibal Sanchez	20.00
BP	Brandon Phillips	10.00
CH	Cole Hamels	40.00
DWW	Dontrelle Willis	20.00
LM	Lastings Milledge	25.00
RC	Robinson Cano	50.00
MN	Michael Napoli	20.00
DU	Dan Uggla	15.00
BW	Brad Wilkerson	10.00
MC	Melky Cabrera	35.00
AW	Adam Wainwright	30.00
CQ	Carlos Quentin	15.00

RJH	Rich Hill	30.00
YP	Yusmeiro Petit	15.00
FC	Fausto Carmona	15.00
CJ	Chuck James	20.00
JM	Justin Morneau	25.00
RZ	Ryan Zimmerman	35.00
RM	Russell Martin	15.00
JP	Jonathan Papelbon	50.00
HR	Hanley Ramirez	20.00
MTC	Matt Cain	25.00
DY	Delmon Young	30.00

Dual Rookies Finest Moments Autograph
		NM/M
Refractors:		No Pricing
Production 25 Sets		
VR	Justin Verlander, Hanley Ramirez	60.00
US	Dan Uggla, Anibal Sanchez	25.00
RP	Mariano Rivera, Jorge Posada	80.00
OP	Roy Oswalt, Mark Prior	40.00
UW	Chase Utley, David Wright	100.00
CY	Robinson Cano, Michael Young	50.00
HR	Travis Hafner, Manny Ramirez	40.00
WW	Chien-Ming Wang, Brandon Webb	175.00
JH	Chuck James, Cole Hamels	40.00
MNA	Russell Martin, Michael Napoli	20.00
PO	Yusmeiro Petit, Scott Olsen	20.00
PP	Jonathan Papelbon, Dustin Pedroia	75.00
CC	Eric Chavez, Miguel Cabrera	40.00
UG	Dan Uggla, Marcus Giles	15.00
CK	Nelson Cruz, Matthew Kemp	25.00
HJ	Rich Hill, Josh Johnson	30.00
HM	Cole Hamels, Brett Myers	60.00
MC	Lastings Milledge, Melky Cabrera	35.00
CR	Matt Cain, Anthony Reyes	25.00
ZC	Joel Zumaya, Fausto Carmona	20.00
BM	Jason Bay, Justin Morneau	35.00
MG	Russell Martin, Ryan Garko	25.00
MN	Kendry Morales, Michael Napoli	25.00
MK	Lastings Milledge, Matthew Kemp	30.00
RU	Hanley Ramirez, Dan Uggla	40.00

A-Rod Road to 500
	NM/M
Common A-Rod (26-50):	2.00
Inserted 2:Box	

Ryan Howard HR History

	NM/M
Common Howard (1-58):	4.00
Inserted 2:Box	
Production 459 Sets	
Refractor:	1.5-2X
Production 149 Sets	
X-Fractor:	2-4X
Production 50 Sets	
Gold Refractor:	No Pricing
Production One Set	

Mantle Cut Signature
Production One
Rookies Finest Moments

Melky Cabrera
Rookie Robbery

		NM/M
Common Player:		.50
Refractor:		2-3X
Blue Refractor:		2-4X
Production 299 Sets		
Green Refractor:		2-4X
Production 199 Sets		
Black Refractor:		4-6X
Production 99 Sets		
Gold Refractor:		4-8X
Production 50 Sets		
X-Fractor:		10-15X
Production 25 Sets		
AD	Adam Dunn	1.00
AJ	Andruw Jones	1.50
AP	Albert Pujols	4.00
AR	Alex Rodriguez	4.00
CB	Carlos Beltran	1.50
CC	Carl Crawford	.50
CJ	Chipper Jones	1.50
DJ	Derek Jeter	4.00
DL	Derrek Lee	1.50
DO	David Ortiz	1.50
DW	David Wright	2.50
DWW	Dontrelle Willis	.50
HM	Hideki Matsui	2.50
IS	Ichiro Suzuki	2.50
JB	Jason Bay	1.00
JM	Joe Mauer	1.00
JR	Jose Reyes	2.00
KG	Ken Griffey Jr.	3.00
MC	Miguel Cabrera	1.50
MP	Mike Piazza	2.00
MR	Manny Ramirez	1.50
MT	Miguel Tejada	1.00
NG	Nomar Garciaparra	1.50
RH	Ryan Howard	3.00
VG	Vladimir Guerrero	1.50
AS	Anibal Sanchez	.50
JP	Jonathan Papelbon	1.50
DU	Dan Uggla	1.00
HR	Hanley Ramirez	1.00
JV	Justin Verlander	1.00
FL	Francisco Liriano	1.00
SD	Stephen Drew	1.00
JW	Jered Weaver	1.00
JS	Jeremy Sowers	.50
KJ	Kenji Johjima	1.00
MCA	Melky Cabrera	1.00
NM	Nicholas Markakis	1.00
PF	Prince Fielder	2.00
RM	Russell Martin	.50
AE	Andre Ethier	1.00
MK	Matthew Kemp	1.00
JH	Jason Hirsh	.50
CH	Cole Hamels	2.00
JBA	Josh Barfield	.50
IK	Ian Kinsler	.50
AW	Adam Wainwright	1.00
JST	Brian Stokes	.50
MN	Michael Napoli	.50
CQ	Carlos Quentin	1.00
NC	Nelson Cruz	.50

Rookie Redemption
		NM/M
Complete Set (10):		
Common Card:		
Inserted 1:3 Mini Box		
1	Hideki Okajima RC	15.00
2	Elijah Dukes RC	10.00
3	Akinori Iwamura RC	20.00
4	Tim Lincecum RC	40.00
5	Daisuke Matsuzaka RC	40.00
6	Ryan Braun (RC)	25.00
7	Daisuke Matsuzaka, Hideki Okajima	15.00

JOBA CHAMBERLAIN
NEW YORK YANKEES™

8	Justin Upton RC	30.00
9	Phil Hughes (RC)	25.00
10	Joba Chamberlain/ Auto. RC	140.00

1993 Flair

		NM/M
Complete Set (300):		15.00
Common Player:		.10
Pack (10):		1.50
Wax Box (24):		20.00
1	Steve Avery	.10
2	Jeff Blauser	.10
3	Ron Gant	.10
4	Tom Glavine	.25
5	Dave Justice	.10
6	Mark Lemke	.10
7	Greg Maddux	1.00
8	Fred McGriff	.10
9	Terry Pendleton	.10
10	Deion Sanders	.15
11	John Smoltz	.10
12	Mike Stanton	.10
13	Steve Buechele	.10
14	Mark Grace	.10
15	Greg Hibbard	.10
16	Derrick May	.10
17	Chuck McElroy	.10
18	Mike Morgan	.10
19	Randy Myers	.10
20	Ryne Sandberg	1.00
21	Dwight Smith	.10
22	Sammy Sosa	1.00
23	Jose Vizcaino	.10
24	Tim Belcher	.10
25	Rob Dibble	.10
26	Roberto Kelly	.10
27	Barry Larkin	.10
28	Kevin Mitchell	.10
29	Hal Morris	.10
30	Joe Oliver	.10
31	Jose Rijo	.10
32	Bip Roberts	.10
33	Chris Sabo	.10
34	Reggie Sanders	.10
35	Dante Bichette	.10
36	Willie Blair	.10
37	Jerald Clark	.10
38	Alex Cole	.10
39	Andres Galarraga	.10
40	Joe Girardi	.10
41	Charlie Hayes	.10
42	Chris Jones	.10
43	David Nied	.10
44	Eric Young	.10
45	Alex Arias	.10
46	Jack Armstrong	.10
47	Bret Barberie	.10
48	Chuck Carr	.10
49	Jeff Conine	.10
50	Orestes Destrade	.10

#	Player	Price
51	Chris Hammond	.10
52	Bryan Harvey	.10
53	Benito Santiago	.10
54	Gary Sheffield	.35
55	Walt Weiss	.10
56	Eric Anthony	.10
57	Jeff Bagwell	.75
58	Craig Biggio	.10
59	Ken Caminiti	.10
60	Andujar Cedeno	.10
61	Doug Drabek	.10
62	Steve Finley	.10
63	Luis Gonzalez	.10
64	Pete Harnisch	.10
65	Doug Jones	.10
66	Darryl Kile	.10
67	Greg Swindell	.10
68	Brett Butler	.10
69	Jim Gott	.10
70	Orel Hershiser	.10
71	Eric Karros	.10
72	Pedro Martinez	.75
73	Ramon Martinez	.10
74	Roger McDowell	.10
75	Mike Piazza	1.50
76	Jody Reed	.10
77	Tim Wallach	.10
78	Moises Alou	.10
79	Greg Colbrunn	.10
80	Wil Cordero	.10
81	Delino DeShields	.10
82	Jeff Fassero	.10
83	Marquis Grissom	.10
84	Ken Hill	.10
85	Mike Lansing RC	.25
86	Dennis Martinez	.10
87	Larry Walker	.10
88	John Wetteland	.10
89	Bobby Bonilla	.10
90	Vince Coleman	.10
91	Dwight Gooden	.10
92	Todd Hundley	.10
93	Howard Johnson	.10
94	Eddie Murray	.75
95	Joe Orsulak	.10
96	Bret Saberhagen	.10
97	Darren Daulton	.10
98	Mariano Duncan	.10
99	Len Dykstra	.10
100	Jim Eisenreich	.10
101	Tommy Greene	.10
102	Dave Hollins	.10
103	Pete Incaviglia	.10
104	Danny Jackson	.10
105	John Kruk	.10
106	Terry Mulholland	.10
107	Curt Schilling	.25
108	Mitch Williams	.10
109	Stan Belinda	.10
110	Jay Bell	.10
111	Steve Cooke	.10
112	Carlos Garcia	.10
113	Jeff King	.10
114	Al Martin	.10
115	Orlando Merced	.10
116	Don Slaught	.10
117	Andy Van Slyke	.10
118	Tim Wakefield	.10
119	Rene Arocha RC	.10
120	Bernard Gilkey	.10
121	Gregg Jefferies	.10
122	Ray Lankford	.10
123	Donovan Osborne	.10
124	Tom Pagnozzi	.10
125	Erik Pappas	.10
126	Geronimo Pena	.10
127	Lee Smith	.10
128	Ozzie Smith	1.00
129	Bob Tewksbury	.10
130	Mark Whiten	.10
131	Derek Bell	.10
132	Andy Benes	.10
133	Tony Gwynn	1.00
134	Gene Harris	.10
135	Trevor Hoffman	.10
136	Phil Plantier	.10
137	Rod Beck	.10
138	Barry Bonds	2.50
139	John Burkett	.10
140	Will Clark	.10
141	Royce Clayton	.10
142	Mike Jackson	.10
143	Darren Lewis	.10
144	Kirt Manwaring	.10
145	Willie McGee	.10
146	Bill Swift	.10
147	Robby Thompson	.10
148	Matt Williams	.10
149	Brady Anderson	.10
150	Mike Devereaux	.10
151	Chris Hoiles	.10
152	Ben McDonald	.10
153	Mark McLemore	.10
154	Mike Mussina	.40

#	Player	Price
155	Gregg Olson	.10
156	Harold Reynolds	.10
157	Cal Ripken, Jr.	2.50
158	Rick Sutcliffe	.10
159	Fernando Valenzuela	.10
160	Roger Clemens	1.25
161	Scott Cooper	.10
162	Andre Dawson	.30
163	Scott Fletcher	.10
164	Mike Greenwell	.10
165	Greg Harris	.10
166	Billy Hatcher	.10
167	Jeff Russell	.10
168	Mo Vaughn	.10
169	Frank Viola	.10
170	Chad Curtis	.10
171	Chili Davis	.10
172	Gary DiSarcina	.10
173	Damion Easley	.10
174	Chuck Finley	.10
175	Mark Langston	.10
176	Luis Polonia	.10
177	Tim Salmon	.10
178	Scott Sanderson	.10
179	J.T. Snow RC	.50
180	Wilson Alvarez	.10
181	Ellis Burks	.10
182	Joey Cora	.10
183	Alex Fernandez	.10
184	Ozzie Guillen	.10
185	Roberto Hernandez	.10
186	Bo Jackson	.20
187	Lance Johnson	.10
188	Jack McDowell	.10
189	Frank Thomas	.75
190	Robin Ventura	.10
191	Carlos Baerga	.10
192	Albert Belle	.10
193	Wayne Kirby	.10
194	Derek Lilliquist	.10
195	Kenny Lofton	.10
196	Carlos Martinez	.10
197	Jose Mesa	.10
198	Eric Plunk	.10
199	Paul Sorrento	.10
200	John Doherty	.10
201	Cecil Fielder	.10
202	Travis Fryman	.10
203	Kirk Gibson	.10
204	Mike Henneman	.10
205	Chad Kreuter	.10
206	Scott Livingstone	.10
207	Tony Phillips	.10
208	Mickey Tettleton	.10
209	Alan Trammell	.10
210	David Wells	.10
211	Lou Whitaker	.10
212	Kevin Appier	.10
213	George Brett	1.25
214	David Cone	.10
215	Tom Gordon	.10
216	Phil Hiatt	.10
217	Felix Jose	.10
218	Wally Joyner	.10
219	Jose Lind	.10
220	Mike Macfarlane	.10
221	Brian McRae	.10
222	Jeff Montgomery	.10
223	Cal Eldred	.10
224	Darryl Hamilton	.10
225	John Jaha	.10
226	Pat Listach	.10
227	Graeme Lloyd RC	.10
228	Kevin Reimer	.10
229	Bill Spiers	.10
230	B.J. Surhoff	.10
231	Greg Vaughn	.10
232	Robin Yount	.75
233	Rick Aguilera	.10
234	Jim Deshaies	.10
235	Brian Harper	.10
236	Kent Hrbek	.10
237	Chuck Knoblauch	.10
238	Shane Mack	.10
239	David McCarty	.10
240	Pedro Munoz	.10
241	Mike Pagliarulo	.10
242	Kirby Puckett	1.00
243	Dave Winfield	.75
244	Jim Abbott	.10
245	Wade Boggs	1.00
246	Pat Kelly	.10
247	Jimmy Key	.10
248	Jim Leyritz	.10
249	Don Mattingly	1.25
250	Matt Nokes	.10
251	Paul O'Neill	.10
252	Mike Stanley	.10
253	Danny Tartabull	.10
254	Bob Wickman	.10
255	Bernie Williams	.10
256	Mike Bordick	.10
257	Dennis Eckersley	.60
258	Brent Gates	.10

#	Player	Price
259	Goose Gossage	.10
260	Rickey Henderson	.75
261	Mark McGwire	2.00
262	Ruben Sierra	.10
263	Terry Steinbach	.10
264	Bob Welch	.10
265	Bobby Witt	.10
266	Rich Amaral	.10
267	Chris Bosio	.10
268	Jay Buhner	.10
269	Norm Charlton	.10
270	Ken Griffey Jr.	1.50
271	Erik Hanson	.10
272	Randy Johnson	.75
273	Edgar Martinez	.10
274	Tino Martinez	.10
275	Dave Valle	.10
276	Omar Vizquel	.10
277	Kevin Brown	.10
278	Jose Canseco	.45
279	Julio Franco	.10
280	Juan Gonzalez	.40
281	Tom Henke	.10
282	David Hulse	.10
283	Rafael Palmeiro	.65
284	Dean Palmer	.10
285	Ivan Rodriguez	.65
286	Nolan Ryan	2.50
287	Roberto Alomar	.25
288	Pat Borders	.10
289	Joe Carter	.10
290	Juan Guzman	.10
291	Pat Hentgen	.10
292	Paul Molitor	.75
293	John Olerud	.10
294	Ed Sprague	.10
295	Dave Stewart	.10
296	Duane Ward	.10
297	Devon White	.10
298	Checklist	.05
299	Checklist	.05
300	Checklist	.05

1993 Flair Promos

		NM/M
Complete Set (8):		200.00
Common Player:		10.00
(1)	Will Clark	10.00
(2)	Darren Daulton	10.00
(3)	Andres Galarraga	10.00
(4)	Bryan Harvey	10.00
(5)	David Justice	10.00
(6)	Jody Reed	10.00
(7)	Nolan Ryan	100.00
(8)	Sammy Sosa	60.00

Wave of the Future

	NM/M
Complete Set (20):	6.00
Common Player:	.15

#	Player	Price
1	Jason Bere	.15
2	Jeremy Burnitz	.15
3	Russ Davis	.15
4	Jim Edmonds	.25
5	Cliff Floyd	.15
6	Jeffrey Hammonds	.15
7	Trevor Hoffman	.15
8	Domingo Jean	.15
9	David McCarty	.15
10	Bobby Munoz	.15
11	Brad Pennington	.15
12	Mike Piazza	3.00
13	Manny Ramirez	2.00
14	John Roper	.15
15	Tim Salmon	.25
16	Aaron Sele	.15
17	Allen Watson	.15
18	Rondell White	.15
19	Darell Whitmore	.15
20	Nigel Wilson	.15

1994 Flair

	NM/M
Complete Set (450):	60.00
Common Player:	.10
Series 1 Pack (10):	1.50
Series 1 Box (24):	20.00
Series 2 Pack (10):	3.00
Series 2 Box (24):	50.00

#	Player	Price
1	Harold Baines	.10
2	Jeffrey Hammonds	.10
3	Chris Hoiles	.10
4	Ben McDonald	.10
5	Mark McLemore	.10
6	Jamie Moyer	.10
7	Jim Poole	.10
8	Cal Ripken, Jr.	3.00
9	Chris Sabo	.10
10	Scott Bankhead	.10
11	Scott Cooper	.10
12	Danny Darwin	.10
13	Andre Dawson	.30
14	Billy Hatcher	.10
15	Aaron Sele	.10
15a	Aaron Sele/OPS	2.00
16	John Valentin	.10
17	Dave Valle	.10
18	Mo Vaughn	.10
19	Brian Anderson RC	.50
20	Gary DiSarcina	.10
21	Jim Edmonds	.10
22	Chuck Finley	.10
23	Bo Jackson	.20
24	Mark Leiter	.10
25	Greg Myers	.10
26	Eduardo Perez	.10
27	Tim Salmon	.10
28	Wilson Alvarez	.10
29	Jason Bere	.10
30	Alex Fernandez	.10
31	Ozzie Guillen	.10
32	Joe Hall	.10
33	Darrin Jackson	.10
34	Kirk McCaskill	.10
35	Tim Raines	.10
36	Frank Thomas	1.00
37	Carlos Baerga	.10
38	Albert Belle	.10
39	Mark Clark	.10
40	Wayne Kirby	.10
41	Dennis Martinez	.10
42	Charles Nagy	.10
43	Manny Ramirez	1.00
44	Paul Sorrento	.10
45	Jim Thome	.65
46	Eric Davis	.10
47	John Doherty	.10
48	Junior Felix	.10
49	Cecil Fielder	.10
50	Kirk Gibson	.10
51	Mike Moore	.10
52	Tony Phillips	.10

#	Player	Price
53	Alan Trammell	.10
54	Kevin Appier	.10
55	Stan Belinda	.10
56	Vince Coleman	.10
57	Greg Gagne	.10
58	Bob Hamelin	.10
59	Dave Henderson	.10
60	Wally Joyner	.10
61	Mike Macfarlane	.10
62	Jeff Montgomery	.10
63	Ricky Bones	.10
64	Jeff Bronkey	.10
65	Alex Diaz	.10
66	Cal Eldred	.10
67	Darryl Hamilton	.10
68	John Jaha	.10
69	Mark Kiefer	.10
70	Kevin Seitzer	.10
71	Turner Ward	.10
72	Rich Becker	.10
73	Scott Erickson	.10
74	Keith Garagozzo	.10
75	Kent Hrbek	.10
76	Scott Leius	.10
77	Kirby Puckett	1.50
78	Matt Walbeck	.10
79	Dave Winfield	1.00
80	Mike Gallego	.10
81	Xavier Hernandez	.10
82	Jimmy Key	.10
83	Jim Leyritz	.10
84	Don Mattingly	1.75
85	Matt Nokes	.10
86	Paul O'Neill	.10
87	Melido Perez	.10
88	Danny Tartabull	.10
89	Mike Bordick	.10
90	Ron Darling	.10
91	Dennis Eckersley	.75
92	Stan Javier	.10
93	Steve Karsay	.10
94	Mark McGwire	2.50
95	Troy Neel	.10
96	Terry Steinbach	.10
97	Bill Taylor	.10
98	Eric Anthony	.10
99	Chris Bosio	.10
100	Tim Davis	.10
101	Felix Fermin	.10
102	Dave Fleming	.10
103	Ken Griffey Jr.	2.00
104	Greg Hibbard	.10
105	Reggie Jefferson	.10
106	Tino Martinez	.10
107	Jack Armstrong	.10
108	Will Clark	.10
109	Juan Gonzalez	.50
110	Rick Helling	.10
111	Tom Henke	.10
112	David Hulse	.10
113	Manuel Lee	.10
114	Doug Strange	.10
115	Roberto Alomar	.25
116	Joe Carter	.10
117	Carlos Delgado	.50
118	Pat Hentgen	.10
119	Paul Molitor	1.00
120	John Olerud	.10
121	Dave Stewart	.10
122	Todd Stottlemyre	.10
123	Mike Timlin	.10
124	Jeff Blauser	.10
125	Tom Glavine	.30
126	Dave Justice	.10
127	Mike Kelly	.10
128	Ryan Klesko	.10
129	Javier Lopez	.10
130	Greg Maddux	1.50
131	Fred McGriff	.10
132	Kent Mercker	.10
133	Mark Wohlers	.10
134	Willie Banks	.10
135	Steve Buechele	.10
136	Shawon Dunston	.10
137	Jose Guzman	.10
138	Glenallen Hill	.10
139	Randy Myers	.10
140	Karl Rhodes	.10
141	Ryne Sandberg	1.50
142	Steve Trachsel	.10
143	Bret Boone	.10
144	Tom Browning	.10
145	Hector Carrasco	.10
146	Barry Larkin	.10
147	Hal Morris	.10
148	Jose Rijo	.10
149	Reggie Sanders	.10
150	John Smiley	.10
151	Dante Bichette	.10
152	Ellis Burks	.10
153	Joe Girardi	.10
154	Mike Harkey	.10
155	Roberto Mejia	.10
156	Marcus Moore	.10
157	Armando Reynoso	.10
158	Bruce Ruffin	.10
159	Eric Young	.10
160	Kurt Abbott RC	.10
161	Jeff Conine	.10
162	Orestes Destrade	.10
163	Chris Hammond	.10
164	Bryan Harvey	.10
165	Dave Magadan	.10
166	Gary Sheffield	.40
167	David Weathers	.10
168	Andujar Cedeno	.10
169	Tom Edens	.10
170	Luis Gonzalez	.10
171	Pete Harnisch	.10
172	Todd Jones	.10
173	Darryl Kile	.10
174	James Mouton	.10
175	Scott Servais	.10
176	Mitch Williams	.10
177	Pedro Astacio	.10
178	Orel Hershiser	.10
179	Raul Mondesi	.10
180	Jose Offerman	.10
181	Chan Ho Park RC	1.00
182	Mike Piazza	2.00
183	Cory Snyder	.10
184	Tim Wallach	.10
185	Todd Worrell	.10
186	Sean Berry	.10
187	Wil Cordero	.10
188	Darrin Fletcher	.10
189	Cliff Floyd	.10
190	Marquis Grissom	.10
191	Rod Henderson	.10
192	Ken Hill	.10
193	Pedro Martinez	1.00
194	Kirk Rueter	.10
195	Jeromy Burnitz	.10
196	John Franco	.10
197	Dwight Gooden	.10
198	Todd Hundley	.10
199	Bobby Jones	.10
200	Jeff Kent	.10
201	Mike Maddux	.10
202	Ryan Thompson	.10
203	Jose Vizcaino	.10
204	Darren Daulton	.10
205	Len Dykstra	.10
206	Jim Eisenreich	.10
207	Dave Hollins	.10
208	Danny Jackson	.10
209	Doug Jones	.10
210	Jeff Juden	.10
211	Ben Rivera	.10
212	Kevin Stocker	.10
213	Milt Thompson	.10
214	Jay Bell	.10
215	Steve Cooke	.10
216	Mark Dewey	.10
217	Al Martin	.10
218	Orlando Merced	.10
219	Don Slaught	.10
220	Zane Smith	.10
221	Rick White	.10
222	Kevin Young	.10
223	Rene Arocha	.10
224	Rheal Cormier	.10
225	Brian Jordan	.10
226	Ray Lankford	.10
227	Mike Perez	.10
228	Ozzie Smith	1.50
229	Mark Whiten	.10
230	Todd Zeile	.10
231	Derek Bell	.10
232	Archi Cianfrocco	.10
233	Ricky Gutierrez	.10
234	Trevor Hoffman	.10
235	Phil Plantier	.10
236	Dave Staton	.10
237	Wally Whitehurst	.10
238	Todd Benzinger	.10
239	Barry Bonds	3.00
240	John Burkett	.10
241	Royce Clayton	.10
242	Bryan Hickerson	.10
243	Mike Jackson	.10
244	Darren Lewis	.10
245	Kirt Manwaring	.10
246	Mark Portugal	.10
247	Salomon Torres	.10
248	Checklist	.10
249	Checklist	.10
250	Checklist	.10
251	Brady Anderson	.10
252	Mike Devereaux	.10
253	Sid Fernandez	.10
254	Leo Gomez	.10
255	Mike Mussina	.40
256	Mike Oquist	.10
257	Rafael Palmeiro	.75
258	Lee Smith	.10
259	Damon Berryhill	.10
260	Wes Chamberlain	.10
261	Roger Clemens	1.75
262	Gar Finnvold	.10
263	Mike Greenwell	.10
264	Tim Naehring	.10
265	Otis Nixon	.10
266	Ken Ryan	.10
267	Chad Curtis	.10
268	Chili Davis	.10
269	Damion Easley	.10
270	Jorge Fabregas	.10
271	Mark Langston	.10
272	Phil Leftwich	.10
273	Harold Reynolds	.10
274	J.T. Snow	.10
275	Joey Cora	.10
276	Julio Franco	.10
277	Roberto Hernandez	.10
278	Lance Johnson	.10
279	Ron Karkovice	.10
280	Jack McDowell	.10
281	Robin Ventura	.10
282	Sandy Alomar Jr.	.10
283	Kenny Lofton	.10
284	Jose Mesa	.10
285	Jack Morris	.10
286	Eddie Murray	1.00
287	Chad Ogea	.10
288	Eric Plunk	.10
289	Paul Shuey	.10
290	Omar Vizquel	.10
291	Danny Bautista	.10
292	Travis Fryman	.10
293	Greg Gohr	.10
294	Chris Gomez	.10
295	Mickey Tettleton	.10
296	Lou Whitaker	.10
297	David Cone	.10
298	Gary Gaetti	.10
299	Tom Gordon	.10
300	Felix Jose	.10
301	Jose Lind	.10
302	Brian McRae	.10
303	Mike Fetters	.10
304	Brian Harper	.10
305	Pat Listach	.10
306	Matt Mieske	.10
307	Dave Nilsson	.10
308	Jody Reed	.10
309	Greg Vaughn	.10
310	Bill Wegman	.10
311	Rick Aguilera	.10
312	Alex Cole	.10
313	Denny Hocking	.10
314	Chuck Knoblauch	.10
315	Shane Mack	.10
316	Pat Meares	.10
317	Kevin Tapani	.10
318	Jim Abbott	.10
319	Wade Boggs	1.00
320	Sterling Hitchcock	.10
321	Pat Kelly	.10
322	Terry Mulholland	.10
323	Luis Polonia	.10
324	Mike Stanley	.10
325	Bob Wickman	.10
326	Bernie Williams	.10
327	Mark Acre	.10
328	Geronimo Berroa	.10
329	Scott Brosius	.10
330	Brent Gates	.10
331	Rickey Henderson	1.00
332	Carlos Reyes	.10
333	Ruben Sierra	.10
334	Bobby Witt	.10
335	Bobby Ayala	.10
336	Jay Buhner	.10
337	Randy Johnson	1.00
338	Edgar Martinez	.10
339	Bill Risley	.10
340	Alex Rodriguez RC	40.00
341	Roger Salkeld	.10
342	Dan Wilson	.10
343	Kevin Brown	.10
344	Jose Canseco	.45
345	Dean Palmer	.10
346	Ivan Rodriguez	.75
347	Kenny Rogers	.10
348	Pat Borders	.10
349	Juan Guzman	.10
350	Ed Sprague	.10
351	Devon White	.10
352	Steve Avery	.10
353	Roberto Kelly	.10
354	Mark Lemke	.10
355	Greg McMichael	.10
356	Terry Pendleton	.10
357	John Smoltz	.10
358	Mike Stanton	.10
359	Tony Tarasco	.10
360	Mark Grace	.10
361	Derrick May	.10
362	Rey Sanchez	.10
363	Sammy Sosa	1.50
364	Rick Wilkins	.10
365	Jeff Brantley	.10
366	Tony Fernandez	.10
367	Chuck McElroy	.10
368	Kevin Mitchell	.10
369	John Roper	.10
370	Johnny Ruffin	.10
371	Deion Sanders	.15
372	Marvin Freeman	.10
373	Andres Galarraga	.10
374	Charlie Hayes	.10
375	Nelson Liriano	.10
376	David Nied	.10
377	Walt Weiss	.10
378	Bret Barberie	.10
379	Jerry Browne	.10
380	Chuck Carr	.10
381	Greg Colbrunn	.10
382	Charlie Hough	.10
383	Kurt Miller	.10
384	Benito Santiago	.10
385	Jeff Bagwell	1.00
386	Craig Biggio	.10
387	Ken Caminiti	.10
388	Doug Drabek	.10
389	Steve Finley	.10
390	John Hudek	.10
391	Orlando Miller	.10
392	Shane Reynolds	.10
393	Brett Butler	.10
394	Tom Candiotti	.10
395	Delino DeShields	.10
396	Kevin Gross	.10
397	Eric Karros	.10
398	Ramon Martinez	.10
399	Henry Rodriguez	.10
400	Moises Alou	.10
401	Jeff Fassero	.10
402	Mike Lansing	.10
403	Mel Rojas	.10
404	Larry Walker	.10
405	John Wetteland	.10
406	Gabe White	.10
407	Bobby Bonilla	.10
408	Josias Manzanillo	.10
409	Bret Saberhagen	.10
410	David Segui	.10
411	Mariano Duncan	.10
412	Tommy Greene	.10
413	Billy Hatcher	.10
414	Ricky Jordan	.10
415	John Kruk	.10
416	Bobby Munoz	.10
417	Curt Schilling	.30
418	Fernando Valenzuela	.10
419	David West	.10
420	Carlos Garcia	.10
421	Brian Hunter	.10
422	Jeff King	.10
423	Jon Lieber	.10
424	Ravelo Manzanillo	.10
425	Denny Neagle	.10
426	Andy Van Slyke	.10
427	Bryan Eversgerd	.10
428	Bernard Gilkey	.10
429	Gregg Jefferies	.10
430	Tom Pagnozzi	.10
431	Bob Tewksbury	.10
432	Allen Watson	.10
433	Andy Ashby	.10
434	Andy Benes	.10
435	Donnie Elliott	.10
436	Tony Gwynn	1.50
437	Joey Hamilton	.10
438	Tim Hyers	.10
439	Luis Lopez	.10
440	Bip Roberts	.10
441	Scott Sanders	.10
442	Rod Beck	.10
443	Dave Burba	.10
444	Darryl Strawberry	.10
445	Bill Swift	.10
446	Robby Thompson	.10
447	William Van Landingham RC	.10
448	Matt Williams	.10
449	Checklist	.10
450	Checklist	.10

Hot Gloves

	NM/M
Complete Set (10):	40.00

Common Player:	2.00
1 Barry Bonds	10.00
2 Will Clark	2.00
3 Ken Griffey Jr.	7.50
4 Kenny Lofton	2.00
5 Greg Maddux	5.00
6 Don Mattingly	6.50
7 Kirby Puckett	5.00
8 Cal Ripken, Jr.	10.00
9 Tim Salmon	2.00
10 Matt Williams	2.00

Hot Numbers

	NM/M
Complete Set (10):	15.00
Common Player:	.50
1 Roberto Alomar	1.00
2 Carlos Baerga	.50
3 Will Clark	.50
4 Fred McGriff	.50
5 Paul Molitor	3.00
6 John Olerud	.50
7 Mike Piazza	4.50
8 Cal Ripken, Jr.	6.00
9 Ryne Sandberg	4.00
10 Frank Thomas	3.00

Infield Power

	NM/M
Complete Set (10):	5.00
Common Player:	.25
1 Jeff Bagwell	.75
2 Will Clark	.25
3 Darren Daulton	.25
4 Don Mattingly	1.25
5 Fred McGriff	.25
6 Rafael Palmeiro	.65
7 Mike Piazza	1.50
8 Cal Ripken, Jr.	2.50
9 Frank Thomas	.75
10 Matt Williams	.25

Outfield Power

	NM/M
Complete Set (10):	5.00
Common Player:	.30
1 Albert Belle	.30
2 Barry Bonds	2.00
3 Joe Carter	.30
4 Len Dykstra	.30
5 Juan Gonzalez	.45
6 Ken Griffey Jr.	1.50
7 Dave Justice	.30
8 Kirby Puckett	1.00
9 Tim Salmon	.30
10 Dave Winfield	.75

Wave of the Future 1

	NM/M
Complete Set (10):	6.00

Common Player:	.25
1 Kurt Abbott	.25
2 Carlos Delgado	5.00
3 Steve Karsay	.25
4 Ryan Klesko	.25
5 Javier Lopez	.25
6 Raul Mondesi	.25
7 James Mouton	.25
8 Chan Ho Park	.25
9 Dave Staton	.25
10 Rick White	.25

Wave of the Future 2

	NM/M
Complete Set (10):	22.50
Common Player:	.50
1 Mark Acre	.50
2 Chris Gomez	.50
3 Joey Hamilton	.50
4 John Hudek	.50
5 Jon Lieber	.50
6 Matt Mieske	.50
7 Orlando Miller	.50
8 Alex Rodriguez	20.00
9 Tony Tarasco	.50
10 Bill Van Landingham	.50

1995 Flair

	NM/M
Complete Set (432):	30.00
Common Player:	.10
Series 1 or 2 Pack (9):	1.00
Series 1 or 2 Wax Box (24):	15.00
1 Brady Anderson	.10
2 Harold Baines	.10
3 Leo Gomez	.10
4 Alan Mills	.10
5 Jamie Moyer	.10
6 Mike Mussina	.40
7 Mike Oquist	.10
8 Arthur Rhodes	.10
9 Cal Ripken Jr.	3.00
10 Roger Clemens	1.75
11 Scott Cooper	.10
12 Mike Greenwell	.10
13 Aaron Sele	.10
14 John Valentin	.10
15 Mo Vaughn	.10
16 Chad Curtis	.10
17 Gary DiSarcina	.10
18 Chuck Finley	.10
19 Andrew Lorraine	.10
20 Spike Owen	.10
21 Tim Salmon	.10
22 J.T. Snow	.10
23 Wilson Alvarez	.10
24 Jason Bere	.10
25 Ozzie Guillen	.10
26 Mike LaValliere	.10
27 Frank Thomas	1.00
28 Robin Ventura	.10
29 Carlos Baerga	.10
30 Albert Belle	.10
31 Jason Grimsley	.10
32 Dennis Martinez	.10
33 Eddie Murray	1.00
34 Charles Nagy	.10
35 Manny Ramirez	1.00
36 Paul Sorrento	.10
37 John Doherty	.10
38 Cecil Fielder	.10
39 Travis Fryman	.10
40 Chris Gomez	.10
41 Tony Phillips	.10
42 Lou Whitaker	.10
43 David Cone	.10
44 Gary Gaetti	.10
45 Mark Gubicza	.10
46 Bob Hamelin	.10
47 Wally Joyner	.10
48 Rusty Meacham	.10
49 Jeff Montgomery	.10
50 Ricky Bones	.10
51 Cal Eldred	.10
52 Pat Listach	.10
53 Matt Mieske	.10
54 Dave Nilsson	.10
55 Greg Vaughn	.10
56 Bill Wegman	.10
57 Chuck Knoblauch	.10
58 Scott Leius	.10

59 Pat Mahomes	.10
60 Pat Meares	.10
61 Pedro Munoz	.10
62 Kirby Puckett	1.50
63 Wade Boggs	1.00
64 Jimmy Key	.10
65 Jim Leyritz	.10
66 Don Mattingly	1.75
67 Paul O'Neill	.10
68 Melido Perez	.10
69 Danny Tartabull	.10
70 John Briscoe	.10
71 Scott Brosius	.10
72 Ron Darling	.10
73 Brent Gates	.10
74 Rickey Henderson	1.00
75 Stan Javier	.10
76 Mark McGwire	2.50
77 Todd Van Poppel	.10
78 Bobby Ayala	.10
79 Mike Blowers	.10
80 Jay Buhner	.10
81 Ken Griffey Jr.	2.00
82 Randy Johnson	1.00
83 Tino Martinez	.10
84 Jeff Nelson	.10
85 Alex Rodriguez	2.50
86 Will Clark	.10
87 Jeff Frye	.10
88 Juan Gonzalez	.50
89 Rusty Greer	.10
90 Darren Oliver	.10
91 Dean Palmer	.10
92 Ivan Rodriguez	.75
93 Matt Whiteside	.10
94 Roberto Alomar	.25
95 Joe Carter	.10
96 Tony Castillo	.10
97 Juan Guzman	.10
98 Pat Hentgen	.10
99 Mike Huff	.10
100 John Olerud	.10
101 Woody Williams	.10
102 Roberto Kelly	.10
103 Ryan Klesko	.10
104 Javier Lopez	.10
105 Greg Maddux	1.50
106 Fred McGriff	.10
107 Jose Oliva	.10
108 John Smoltz	.10
109 Tony Tarasco	.10
110 Mark Wohlers	.10
111 Jim Bullinger	.10
112 Shawon Dunston	.10
113 Derrick May	.10
114 Randy Myers	.10
115 Karl Rhodes	.10
116 Rey Sanchez	.10
117 Steve Trachsel	.10
118 Eddie Zambrano	.10
119 Bret Boone	.10
120 Brian Dorsett	.10
121 Hal Morris	.10
122 Jose Rijo	.10
123 John Roper	.10
124 Reggie Sanders	.10
125 Pete Schourek	.10
126 John Smiley	.10
127 Ellis Burks	.10
128 Vinny Castilla	.10
129 Marvin Freeman	.10
130 Andres Galarraga	.10
131 Mike Munoz	.10
132 David Nied	.10
133 Bruce Ruffin	.10
134 Walt Weiss	.10
135 Eric Young	.10
136 Greg Colbrunn	.10
137 Jeff Conine	.10
138 Jeremy Hernandez	.10
139 Charles Johnson	.10
140 Robb Nen	.10
141 Gary Sheffield	.40
142 Dave Weathers	.10
143 Jeff Bagwell	1.00
144 Craig Biggio	.10
145 Tony Eusebio	.10
146 Luis Gonzalez	.10
147 John Hudek	.10
148 Darryl Kile	.10
149 Dave Veres	.10
150 Billy Ashley	.10
151 Pedro Astacio	.10
152 Rafael Bournigal	.10
153 Delino DeShields	.10
154 Raul Mondesi	.10
155 Mike Piazza	2.00
156 Rudy Seanez	.10
157 Ismael Valdes	.10
158 Tim Wallach	.10
159 Todd Worrell	.10
160 Moises Alou	.10
161 Cliff Floyd	.10
162 Gil Heredia	.10

163 Mike Lansing	.10
164 Pedro Martinez	1.00
165 Kirk Rueter	.10
166 Tim Scott	.10
167 Jeff Shaw	.10
168 Rondell White	.10
169 Bobby Bonilla	.10
170 Rico Brogna	.10
171 Todd Hundley	.10
172 Jeff Kent	.10
173 Jim Lindeman	.10
174 Joe Orsulak	.10
175 Bret Saberhagen	.10
176 Toby Borland	.10
177 Darren Daulton	.10
178 Lenny Dykstra	.10
179 Jim Eisenreich	.10
180 Tommy Greene	.10
181 Tony Longmire	.10
182 Bobby Munoz	.10
183 Kevin Stocker	.10
184 Jay Bell	.10
185 Steve Cooke	.10
186 Ravelo Manzanillo	.10
187 Al Martin	.10
188 Denny Neagle	.10
189 Don Slaught	.10
190 Paul Wagner	.10
191 Rene Arocha	.10
192 Bernard Gilkey	.10
193 Jose Oquendo	.10
194 Tom Pagnozzi	.10
195 Ozzie Smith	1.50
196 Allen Watson	.10
197 Mark Whiten	.10
198 Andy Ashby	.10
199 Donnie Elliott	.10
200 Bryce Florie	.10
201 Tony Gwynn	1.50
202 Trevor Hoffman	.10
203 Brian Johnson	.10
204 Tim Mauser	.10
205 Bip Roberts	.10
206 Rod Beck	.10
207 Barry Bonds	3.00
208 Royce Clayton	.10
209 Darren Lewis	.10
210 Mark Portugal	.10
211 Kevin Rogers	.10
212 William Van Landingham	.10
213 Matt Williams	.10
214 Checklist	.10
215 Checklist	.10
216 Checklist	.10
217 Bret Barberie	.10
218 Armando Benitez	.10
219 Kevin Brown	.10
220 Sid Fernandez	.10
221 Chris Hoiles	.10
222 Doug Jones	.10
223 Ben McDonald	.10
224 Rafael Palmeiro	.75
225 Andy Van Slyke	.10
226 Jose Canseco	.40
227 Vaughn Eshelman	.10
228 Mike Macfarlane	.10
229 Tim Naehring	.10
230 Frank Rodriguez	.10
231 Lee Tinsley	.10
232 Mark Whiten	.10
233 Garret Anderson	.10
234 Chili Davis	.10
235 Jim Edmonds	.10
236 Mark Langston	.10
237 Troy Percival	.10
238 Tony Phillips	.10
239 Lee Smith	.10
240 Jim Abbott	.10
241 James Baldwin	.10
242 Mike Devereaux	.10
243 Ray Durham	.10
244 Alex Fernandez	.10
245 Roberto Hernandez	.10
246 Lance Johnson	.10
247 Ron Karkovice	.10
248 Tim Raines	.10
249 Sandy Alomar Jr.	.10
250 Orel Hershiser	.10
251 Julian Tavarez	.10
252 Jim Thome	.65
253 Omar Vizquel	.10
254 Dave Winfield	1.00
255 Chad Curtis	.10
256 Kirk Gibson	.10
257 Mike Henneman	.10
258 Bob Higginson RC	.25
259 Felipe Lira	.10
260 Rudy Pemberton	.10
261 Alan Trammell	.10
262 Kevin Appier	.10
263 Pat Borders	.10
264 Tom Gordon	.10
265 Jose Lind	.10

266	Jon Nunnally	.10
267	Dilson Torres	.10
268	Michael Tucker	.10
269	Jeff Cirillo	.10
270	Darryl Hamilton	.10
271	David Hulse	.10
272	Mark Kiefer	.10
273	Graeme Lloyd	.10
274	Joe Oliver	.10
275	Al Reyes	.10
276	Kevin Seitzer	.10
277	Rick Aguilera	.10
278	Marty Cordova	.10
279	Scott Erickson	.10
280	LaTroy Hawkins	.10
281	Brad Radke	.10
282	Kevin Tapani	.10
283	Tony Fernandez	.10
284	Sterling Hitchcock	.10
285	Pat Kelly	.10
286	Jack McDowell	.10
287	Andy Pettitte	.30
288	Mike Stanley	.10
289	John Wetteland	.10
290	Bernie Williams	.10
291	Mark Acre	.10
292	Geronimo Berroa	.10
293	Dennis Eckersley	.75
294	Steve Ontiveros	.10
295	Ruben Sierra	.10
296	Terry Steinbach	.10
297	Dave Stewart	.10
298	Todd Stottlemyre	.10
299	Darren Bragg	.10
300	Joey Cora	.10
301	Edgar Martinez	.10
302	Bill Risley	.10
303	Ron Villone	.10
304	Dan Wilson	.10
305	Benji Gil	.10
306	Wilson Heredia	.10
307	Mark McLemore	.10
308	Otis Nixon	.10
309	Kenny Rogers	.10
310	Jeff Russell	.10
311	Mickey Tettleton	.10
312	Bob Tewksbury	.10
313	David Cone	.10
314	Carlos Delgado	.50
315	Alex Gonzalez	.10
316	Shawn Green	.40
317	Paul Molitor	1.00
318	Ed Sprague	.10
319	Devon White	.10
320	Steve Avery	.10
321	Jeff Blauser	.10
322	Brad Clontz	.10
323	Tom Glavine	.30
324	Marquis Grissom	.10
325	Chipper Jones	1.50
326	Dave Justice	.10
327	Mark Lemke	.10
328	Kent Mercker	.10
329	Jason Schmidt	.10
330	Steve Buechele	.10
331	Kevin Foster	.10
332	Mark Grace	.10
333	Brian McRae	.10
334	Sammy Sosa	1.50
335	Ozzie Timmons	.10
336	Rick Wilkins	.10
337	Hector Carrasco	.10
338	Ron Gant	.10
339	Barry Larkin	.10
340	Deion Sanders	.15
341	Benito Santiago	.10
342	Roger Bailey	.10
343	Jason Bates	.10
344	Dante Bichette	.10
345	Joe Girardi	.10
346	Bill Swift	.10
347	Mark Thompson	.10
348	Larry Walker	.10
349	Kurt Abbott	.10
350	John Burkett	.10
351	Chuck Carr	.10
352	Andre Dawson	.30
353	Chris Hammond	.10
354	Charles Johnson	.10
355	Terry Pendleton	.10
356	Quilvio Veras	.10
357	Derek Bell	.10
358	Jim Dougherty	.10
359	Doug Drabek	.10
360	Todd Jones	.10
361	Orlando Miller	.10
362	James Mouton	.10
363	Phil Plantier	.10
364	Shane Reynolds	.10
365	Todd Hollandsworth	.10
366	Eric Karros	.10
367	Ramon Martinez	.10
368	Hideo Nomo RC	3.00
369	Jose Offerman	.10

370	Antonio Osuna	.10
371	Todd Williams	.10
372	Shane Andrews	.10
373	Wil Cordero	.10
374	Jeff Fassero	.10
375	Darrin Fletcher	.10
376	Mark Grudzielanek RC	.50
377	Carlos Perez RC	.25
378	Mel Rojas	.10
379	Tony Tarasco	.10
380	Edgardo Alfonzo	.10
381	Brett Butler	.10
382	Carl Everett	.10
383	John Franco	.10
384	Pete Harnisch	.10
385	Bobby Jones	.10
386	Dave Mlicki	.10
387	Jose Vizcaino	.10
388	Ricky Bottalico	.10
389	Tyler Green	.10
390	Charlie Hayes	.10
391	Dave Hollins	.10
392	Gregg Jefferies	.10
393	Michael Mimbs RC	.10
394	Mickey Morandini	.10
395	Curt Schilling	.30
396	Heathcliff Slocumb	.10
397	Jason Christiansen	.10
398	Midre Cummings	.10
399	Carlos Garcia	.10
400	Mark Johnson	.10
401	Jeff King	.10
402	Jon Lieber	.10
403	Esteban Loaiza	.10
404	Orlando Merced	.10
405	Gary Wilson RC	.10
406	Scott Cooper	.10
407	Tom Henke	.10
408	Ken Hill	.10
409	Danny Jackson	.10
410	Brian Jordan	.10
411	Ray Lankford	.10
412	John Mabry	.10
413	Todd Zeile	.10
414	Andy Benes	.10
415	Andres Berumen	.10
416	Ken Caminiti	.10
417	Andujar Cedeno	.10
418	Steve Finley	.10
419	Joey Hamilton	.10
420	Dustin Hermanson	.10
421	Melvin Nieves	.10
422	Roberto Petagine	.10
423	Eddie Williams	.10
424	Glenallen Hill	.10
425	Kirt Manwaring	.10
426	Terry Mulholland	.10
427	J.R. Phillips	.10
428	Joe Rosselli	.10
429	Robby Thompson	.10
430	Checklist	.10
431	Checklist	.10
432	Checklist	.10

Cal Ripken, Jr. Enduring Flair

		NM/M
Complete Set (15):		40.00
Common Card:		4.00
1	Rookie Of The Year	4.00
2	1st MVP Season	4.00
3	World Series Highlight	4.00
4	Family Tradition	4.00
5	8,243 Consecutive Innings	4.00
6	95 Consecutive Errorless Games	4.00
7	All-Star MVP	4.00
8	1,000th RBI	4.00
9	287th Home Run	4.00
10	2,000th Consecutive Game	4.00
11	Record-tying Game	6.00
12	Record-breaking Game	6.00
13	Defensive Prowess	6.00
14	Literacy Work	6.00
15	2,153 and Counting	6.00

Hot Gloves

		NM/M
Complete Set (12):		35.00
Common Player:		1.25
1	Roberto Alomar	2.00
2	Barry Bonds	10.00
3	Ken Griffey Jr.	7.50
4	Marquis Grissom	1.25
5	Barry Larkin	1.25
6	Darren Lewis	1.25
7	Kenny Lofton	1.25
8	Don Mattingly	6.00
9	Cal Ripken Jr.	10.00
10	Ivan Rodriguez	2.50
11	Devon White	1.25
12	Matt Williams	1.25

Hot Numbers

		NM/M
Complete Set (10):		10.00
Common Player:		1.00
1	Jeff Bagwell	1.00
2	Albert Belle	1.00
3	Barry Bonds	2.25
4	Ken Griffey Jr.	2.00
5	Kenny Lofton	.50
6	Greg Maddux	1.25
7	Mike Piazza	2.00
8	Cal Ripken Jr.	2.25
9	Frank Thomas	1.00
10	Matt Williams	.50

Infield Power

		NM/M
Complete Set (10):		4.00
Common Player:		.25
1	Jeff Bagwell	.75
2	Darren Daulton	.25
3	Cecil Fielder	.25
4	Andres Galarraga	.25
5	Fred McGriff	.25
6	Rafael Palmeiro	.65
7	Mike Piazza	1.50
8	Frank Thomas	1.00
9	Mo Vaughn	.25
10	Matt Williams	.25

Outfield Power

		NM/M
Complete Set (10):		4.00
Common Player:		.25

1	Albert Belle	.25
2	Dante Bichette	.25
3	Barry Bonds	2.00
4	Jose Canseco	.50
5	Joe Carter	.25
6	Juan Gonzalez	.50
7	Ken Griffey Jr.	1.00
8	Kirby Puckett	.75
9	Gary Sheffield	.50
10	Ruben Sierra	.25

Today's Spotlight

		NM/M
Complete Set (12):		15.00
Common Player:		1.00
1	Jeff Bagwell	3.00
2	Jason Bere	1.00
3	Cliff Floyd	1.00
4	Chuck Knoblauch	1.00
5	Kenny Lofton	1.00
6	Javier Lopez	1.00
7	Raul Mondesi	1.00
8	Mike Mussina	1.50
9	Mike Piazza	5.00
10	Manny Ramirez	3.00
11	Tim Salmon	1.00
12	Frank Thomas	3.00

Wave Of The Future

		NM/M
Complete Set (10):		7.50
Common Player:		.35
1	Jason Bates	.25
2	Armando Benitez	.25
3	Marty Cordova	.25
4	Ray Durham	.25
5	Vaughn Eshelman	.25
6	Carl Everett	.25
7	Shawn Green	1.50
8	Dustin Hermanson	.25
9	Chipper Jones	4.00
10	Hideo Nomo	1.50

1996 Flair

		NM/M
Complete Set (400):		50.00
Common Player:		.15
Pack (9):		3.00
Wax Box (18):		40.00
1	Roberto Alomar	.30
2	Brady Anderson	.15
3	Bobby Bonilla	.15
4	Scott Erickson	.15
5	Jeffrey Hammonds	.15
6	Jimmy Haynes	.15
7	Chris Hoiles	.15
8	Kent Mercker	.15
9	Mike Mussina	.50
10	Randy Myers	.15
11	Rafael Palmeiro	.75

No.	Player	Price
12	Cal Ripken Jr.	3.00
(12p)	Cal Ripken Jr./OPS (No card #.)	3.00
13	B.J. Surhoff	.15
14	David Wells	.15
15	Jose Canseco	.50
16	Roger Clemens	1.75
17	Wil Cordero	.15
18	Tom Gordon	.15
19	Mike Greenwell	.15
20	Dwayne Hosey	.15
21	Jose Malave	.15
22	Tim Naehring	.15
23	Troy O'Leary	.15
24	Aaron Sele	.15
25	Heathcliff Slocumb	.15
26	Mike Stanley	.15
27	Jeff Suppan	.15
28	John Valentin	.15
29	Mo Vaughn	.15
30	Tim Wakefield	.15
31	Jim Abbott	.15
32	Garret Anderson	.15
33	George Arias	.15
34	Chili Davis	.15
35	Gary DiSarcina	.15
36	Jim Edmonds	.15
37	Chuck Finley	.15
38	Todd Greene	.15
39	Mark Langston	.15
40	Troy Percival	.15
41	Tim Salmon	.15
42	Lee Smith	.15
43	J.T. Snow	.15
44	Randy Velarde	.15
45	Tim Wallach	.15
46	Wilson Alvarez	.15
47	Harold Baines	.15
48	Jason Bere	.15
49	Ray Durham	.15
50	Alex Fernandez	.15
51	Ozzie Guillen	.15
52	Roberto Hernandez	.15
53	Ron Karkovice	.15
54	Darren Lewis	.15
55	Lyle Mouton	.15
56	Tony Phillips	.15
57	Chris Snopek	.15
58	Kevin Tapani	.15
59	Danny Tartabull	.15
60	Frank Thomas	1.00
61	Robin Ventura	.15
62	Sandy Alomar	.15
63	Carlos Baerga	.15
64	Albert Belle	.15
65	Julio Franco	.15
66	Orel Hershiser	.15
67	Kenny Lofton	.15
68	Dennis Martinez	.15
69	Jack McDowell	.15
70	Jose Mesa	.15
71	Eddie Murray	1.00
72	Charles Nagy	.15
73	Tony Pena	.15
74	Manny Ramirez	1.00
75	Julian Tavarez	.15
76	Jim Thome	.65
77	Omar Vizquel	.15
78	Chad Curtis	.15
79	Cecil Fielder	.15
80	Travis Fryman	.15
81	Chris Gomez	.15
82	Bob Higginson	.15
83	Mark Lewis	.15
84	Felipe Lira	.15
85	Alan Trammell	.15
86	Kevin Appier	.15
87	Johnny Damon	.50
88	Tom Goodwin	.15
89	Mark Gubicza	.15
90	Bob Hamelin	.15
91	Keith Lockhart	.15
92	Jeff Montgomery	.15
93	Jon Nunnally	.15
94	Bip Roberts	.15
95	Michael Tucker	.15
96	Joe Vitiello	.15
97	Ricky Bones	.15
98	Chuck Carr	.15
99	Jeff Cirillo	.15
100	Mike Fetters	.15
101	John Jaha	.15
102	Mike Matheny	.15
103	Ben McDonald	.15
104	Matt Mieske	.15
105	Dave Nilsson	.15
106	Kevin Seitzer	.15
107	Steve Sparks	.15
108	Jose Valentin	.15
109	Greg Vaughn	.15
110	Rick Aguilera	.15
111	Rich Becker	.15
112	Marty Cordova	.15
113	LaTroy Hawkins	.15
114	Dave Hollins	.15
115	Roberto Kelly	.15
116	Chuck Knoblauch	.15
117	Matt Lawton RC	.50
118	Pat Meares	.15
119	Paul Molitor	1.00
120	Kirby Puckett	1.50
121	Brad Radke	.15
122	Frank Rodriguez	.15
123	Scott Stahoviak	.15
124	Matt Walbeck	.15
125	Wade Boggs	1.00
126	David Cone	.15
127	Joe Girardi	.15
128	Dwight Gooden	.15
129	Derek Jeter	3.00
130	Jimmy Key	.15
131	Jim Leyritz	.15
132	Tino Martinez	.15
133	Paul O'Neill	.15
134	Andy Pettitte	.40
135	Tim Raines	.15
136	Ruben Rivera	.15
137	Kenny Rogers	.15
138	Ruben Sierra	.15
139	John Wetteland	.15
140	Bernie Williams	.15
141	Tony Batista RC	.50
142	Allen Battle	.15
143	Geronimo Berroa	.15
144	Mike Bordick	.15
145	Scott Brosius	.15
146	Steve Cox	.15
147	Brent Gates	.15
148	Jason Giambi	.65
149	Doug Johns	.15
150	Mark McGwire	2.50
151	Pedro Munoz	.15
152	Ariel Prieto	.15
153	Terry Steinbach	.15
154	Todd Van Poppel	.15
155	Bobby Ayala	.15
156	Chris Bosio	.15
157	Jay Buhner	.15
158	Joey Cora	.15
159	Russ Davis	.15
160	Ken Griffey Jr.	2.00
161	Sterling Hitchcock	.15
162	Randy Johnson	1.00
163	Edgar Martinez	.15
164	Alex Rodriguez	2.50
165	Paul Sorrento	.15
166	Dan Wilson	.15
167	Will Clark	.15
168	Benji Gil	.15
169	Juan Gonzalez	.50
170	Rusty Greer	.15
171	Kevin Gross	.15
172	Darryl Hamilton	.15
173	Mike Henneman	.15
174	Ken Hill	.15
175	Mark McLemore	.15
176	Dean Palmer	.15
177	Roger Pavlik	.15
178	Ivan Rodriguez	.75
179	Mickey Tettleton	.15
180	Bobby Witt	.15
181	Joe Carter	.15
182	Felipe Crespo	.15
183	Alex Gonzalez	.15
184	Shawn Green	.40
185	Juan Guzman	.15
186	Erik Hanson	.15
187	Pat Hentgen	.15
188	Sandy Martinez RC	.15
189	Otis Nixon	.15
190	John Olerud	.15
191	Paul Quantrill	.15
192	Bill Risley	.15
193	Ed Sprague	.15
194	Steve Avery	.15
195	Mark Blauser	.15
196	Brad Clontz	.15
197	Jermaine Dye	.15
198	Tom Glavine	.40
199	Marquis Grissom	.15
200	Chipper Jones	1.50
201	David Justice	.15
202	Ryan Klesko	.15
203	Mark Lemke	.15
204	Javier Lopez	.15
205	Greg Maddux	1.50
206	Fred McGriff	.15
207	Greg McMichael	.15
208	Wonderful Monds	.15
209	Jason Schmidt	.15
210	John Smoltz	.15
211	Mark Wohlers	.15
212	Jim Bullinger	.15
213	Frank Castillo	.15
214	Kevin Foster	.15
215	Luis Gonzalez	.15
216	Mark Grace	.15
217	Robin Jennings RC	.15
218	Doug Jones	.15
219	Dave Magadan	.15
220	Brian McRae	.15
221	Jaime Navarro	.15
222	Rey Sanchez	.15
223	Ryne Sandberg	1.50
224	Scott Servais	.15
225	Sammy Sosa	1.50
226	Ozzie Timmons	.15
227	Bret Boone	.15
228	Jeff Branson	.15
229	Jeff Brantley	.15
230	Dave Burba	.15
231	Vince Coleman	.15
232	Steve Gibralter	.15
233	Mike Kelly	.15
234	Barry Larkin	.15
235	Hal Morris	.15
236	Mark Portugal	.15
237	Jose Rijo	.15
238	Reggie Sanders	.15
239	Pete Schourek	.15
240	John Smiley	.15
241	Eddie Taubensee	.15
242	Jason Bates	.15
243	Dante Bichette	.15
244	Ellis Burks	.15
245	Vinny Castilla	.15
246	Andres Galarraga	.15
247	Darren Holmes	.15
248	Curt Leskanic	.15
249	Steve Reed	.15
250	Kevin Ritz	.15
251	Bret Saberhagen	.15
252	Bill Swift	.15
253	Larry Walker	.15
254	Walt Weiss	.15
255	Eric Young	.15
256	Kurt Abbott	.15
257	Kevin Brown	.15
258	John Burkett	.15
259	Greg Colbrunn	.15
260	Jeff Conine	.15
261	Andre Dawson	.40
262	Chris Hammond	.15
263	Charles Johnson	.15
264	Al Leiter	.15
265	Robb Nen	.15
266	Terry Pendleton	.15
267	Pat Rapp	.15
268	Gary Sheffield	.50
269	Quilvio Veras	.15
270	Devon White	.15
271	Bob Abreu	.15
272	Jeff Bagwell	1.00
273	Derek Bell	.15
274	Sean Berry	.15
275	Craig Biggio	.15
276	Doug Drabek	.15
277	Tony Eusebio	.15
278	Richard Hidalgo	.15
279	Brian Hunter	.15
280	Todd Jones	.15
281	Derrick May	.15
282	Orlando Miller	.15
283	James Mouton	.15
284	Shane Reynolds	.15
285	Greg Swindell	.15
286	Mike Blowers	.15
287	Brett Butler	.15
288	Tom Candiotti	.15
289	Roger Cedeno	.15
290	Delino DeShields	.15
291	Greg Gagne	.15
292	Karim Garcia	.15
293	Todd Hollandsworth	.15
294	Eric Karros	.15
295	Ramon Martinez	.15
296	Raul Mondesi	.15
297	Hideo Nomo	.50
298	Mike Piazza	2.00
299	Ismael Valdes	.15
300	Todd Worrell	.15
301	Moises Alou	.15
302	Shane Andrews	.15
303	Yamil Benitez	.15
304	Jeff Fassero	.15
305	Darrin Fletcher	.15
306	Cliff Floyd	.15
307	Mark Grudzielanek	.15
308	Mike Lansing	.15
309	Pedro Martinez	1.00
310	Ryan McGuire	.15
311	Carlos Perez	.15
312	Mel Rojas	.15
313	David Segui	.15
314	Rondell White	.15
315	Edgardo Alfonzo	.15
316	Rico Brogna	.15
317	Carl Everett	.15
318	John Franco	.15
319	Bernard Gilkey	.15
320	Todd Hundley	.15
321	Jason Isringhausen	.15
322	Lance Johnson	.15
323	Bobby Jones	.15
324	Jeff Kent	.15
325	Rey Ordonez	.15
326	Bill Pulsipher	.15
327	Jose Vizcaino	.15
328	Paul Wilson	.15
329	Ricky Bottalico	.15
330	Darren Daulton	.15
331	David Doster RC	.15
332	Lenny Dykstra	.15
333	Jim Eisenreich	.15
334	Sid Fernandez	.15
335	Gregg Jefferies	.15
336	Mickey Morandini	.15
337	Benito Santiago	.15
338	Curt Schilling	.40
339	Kevin Stocker	.15
340	David West	.15
341	Mark Whiten	.15
342	Todd Zeile	.15
343	Jay Bell	.15
344	John Ericks	.15
345	Carlos Garcia	.15
346	Charlie Hayes	.15
347	Jason Kendall	.15
348	Jeff King	.15
349	Mike Kingery	.15
350	Al Martin	.15
351	Orlando Merced	.15
352	Dan Miceli	.15
353	Denny Neagle	.15
354	Alan Benes	.15
355	Andy Benes	.15
356	Royce Clayton	.15
357	Dennis Eckersley	.75
358	Gary Gaetti	.15
359	Ron Gant	.15
360	Brian Jordan	.15
361	Ray Lankford	.15
362	John Mabry	.15
363	T.J. Mathews	.15
364	Mike Morgan	.15
365	Donovan Osborne	.15
366	Tom Pagnozzi	.15
367	Ozzie Smith	1.50
368	Todd Stottlemyre	.15
369	Andy Ashby	.15
370	Brad Ausmus	.15
371	Ken Caminiti	.15
372	Andujar Cedeno	.15
373	Steve Finley	.15
374	Tony Gwynn	1.50
375	Joey Hamilton	.15
376	Rickey Henderson	1.00
377	Trevor Hoffman	.15
378	Wally Joyner	.15
379	Marc Newfield	.15
380	Jody Reed	.15
381	Bob Tewksbury	.15
382	Fernando Valenzuela	.15
383	Rod Beck	.15
384	Barry Bonds	3.00
385	Mark Carreon	.15
386	Shawon Dunston	.15
387	Osvaldo Fernandez RC	.40
388	Glenallen Hill	.15
389	Stan Javier	.15
390	Mark Leiter	.15
391	Kirt Manwaring	.15
392	Robby Thompson	.15
393	William Van Landingham	.15
394	Allen Watson	.15
395	Matt Williams	.15
396	Checklist	.15
397	Checklist	.15
398	Checklist	.15
399	Checklist	.15
400	Checklist	.15

Diamond Cuts

	NM/M
Complete Set (12):	25.00
Common Player:	1.00
1 Jeff Bagwell	2.50
2 Albert Belle	1.00
3 Barry Bonds	6.00
4 Juan Gonzalez	1.25
5 Ken Griffey Jr.	4.00

6	Greg Maddux	3.00
7	Eddie Murray	2.50
8	Mike Piazza	4.00
9	Cal Ripken Jr.	6.00
10	Frank Thomas	2.50
11	Mo Vaughn	1.00
12	Matt Williams	1.00

Hot Gloves

NM/M

Complete Set (10): 60.00
Common Player: 3.00

1	Roberto Alomar	4.00
2	Barry Bonds	15.00
3	Will Clark	3.00
4	Ken Griffey Jr.	10.00
5	Kenny Lofton	3.00
6	Greg Maddux	7.50
7	Mike Piazza	10.00
8	Cal Ripken Jr.	15.00
9	Ivan Rodriguez	6.00
10	Matt Williams	3.00

Powerline

NM/M

Complete Set (10): 6.00
Common Player: .25

1	Albert Belle	.25
2	Barry Bonds	2.00
3	Juan Gonzalez	.35
4	Ken Griffey Jr.	.75
5	Mark McGwire	1.00
6	Mike Piazza	.75
7	Manny Ramirez	.50
8	Sammy Sosa	.65
9	Frank Thomas	.50
10	Matt Williams	.25

1996 Flair Promotional Sheet

NM/M

Complete Sheet: 5.00
Manny Ramirez,
Cal Ripken Jr.,
Matt Williams,
Information Card

Wave of the Future

NM/M

Complete Set (20): 30.00
Common Player: 2.00

1	Bob Abreu	3.00
2	George Arias	2.00
3	Tony Batista	2.00
4	Alan Benes	2.00
5	Yamil Benitez	2.00
6	Steve Cox	2.00
7	David Doster	2.00
8	Jermaine Dye	2.00
9	Osvaldo Fernandez	2.00
10	Karim Garcia	3.00
11	Steve Gibralter	2.00
12	Todd Greene	2.00
13	Richard Hidalgo	2.00
14	Robin Jennings	2.00
15	Jason Kendall	2.00
16	Jose Malave	2.00
17	Wonderful Monds	2.00
18	Rey Ordonez	2.00
19	Ruben Rivera	2.00
20	Paul Wilson	2.00

1997 Flair Showcase Row 2 (Style)

NM/M

Complete Set (180): 15.00
Common Showtime (1-60): .15
Common Showpiece (61-120): .25
Common Showstopper (121-180): .20
A-Rod Glove Exchange: 125.00
Pack (5): 2.00
Wax Box (24): 35.00

1	Andruw Jones	1.25
2	Derek Jeter	3.00
3	Alex Rodriguez	2.25
4	Paul Molitor	1.25
5	Jeff Bagwell	1.25
6	Scott Rolen	1.00
7	Kenny Lofton	.15
8	Cal Ripken Jr.	3.00
9	Brady Anderson	.15
10	Chipper Jones	1.50
11	Todd Greene	.15
12	Todd Walker	.15
13	Billy Wagner	.15
14	Craig Biggio	.15
15	Kevin Orie	.15
16	Hideo Nomo	.65
17	Kevin Appier	.15
18	Bubba Trammell RC	.25
19	Juan Gonzalez	.65
20	Randy Johnson	1.25
21	Roger Clemens	1.75
22	Johnny Damon	.35
23	Ryne Sandberg	1.50
24	Ken Griffey Jr.	2.00
25	Barry Bonds	3.00
26	Nomar Garciaparra	1.50
27	Vladimir Guerrero	1.25
28	Ron Gant	.15
29	Joe Carter	.15
30	Tim Salmon	.15
31	Mike Piazza	2.00
32	Barry Larkin	.15
33	Manny Ramirez	1.25
34	Sammy Sosa	1.50
35	Frank Thomas	1.25
36	Melvin Nieves	.15
37	Tony Gwynn	1.50
38	Gary Sheffield	.35
39	Darin Erstad	.50
40	Ken Caminiti	.15
41	Jermaine Dye	.15
42	Mo Vaughn	.15
43	Raul Mondesi	.15
44	Greg Maddux	1.50
45	Chuck Knoblauch	.15
46	Andy Pettitte	.50
47	Deion Sanders	.25
48	Albert Belle	.15
49	Jamey Wright	.15
50	Rey Ordonez	.15
51	Bernie Williams	.15
52	Mark McGwire	2.25
53	Mike Mussina	.50
54	Bob Abreu	.20
55	Reggie Sanders	.15
56	Brian Jordan	.15
57	Ivan Rodriguez	1.00
58	Roberto Alomar	.30
59	Tim Naehring	.15
60	Edgar Renteria	.15
61	Dean Palmer	.25
62	Benito Santiago	.25
63	David Cone	.25
64	Carlos Delgado	.75
65	Brian Giles RC	.75
66	Alex Ochoa	.25
67	Rondell White	.25
68	Robin Ventura	.25
69	Eric Karros	.25
70	Jose Valentin	.25
71	Rafael Palmeiro	1.00
72	Chris Snopek	.25
73	David Justice	.25
74	Tom Glavine	.45
75	Rudy Pemberton	.25
76	Larry Walker	.25
77	Jim Thome	.75
78	Charles Johnson	.25
79	Dante Powell	.25
80	Derrek Lee	.75
81	Jason Kendall	.25
82	Todd Hollandsworth	.25
83	Bernard Gilkey	.25
84	Mel Rojas	.25
85	Dmitri Young	.25
86	Bret Boone	.25
87	Pat Hentgen	.25
88	Bobby Bonilla	.25
89	John Wetteland	.25
90	Todd Hundley	.25
91	Wilton Guerrero	.25
92	Geronimo Berroa	.25
93	Al Martin	.25
94	Danny Tartabull	.25
95	Brian McRae	.25
96	Steve Finley	.25
97	Todd Stottlemyre	.25
98	John Smoltz	.25
99	Matt Williams	.25
100	Eddie Murray	1.25
101	Henry Rodriguez	.25
102	Marty Cordova	.25
103	Juan Guzman	.25
104	Chili Davis	.25
105	Eric Young	.25
106	Jeff Abbott	.25
107	Shannon Stewart	.25
108	Rocky Coppinger	.25
109	Jose Canseco	.65
110	Dante Bichette	.25
111	Dwight Gooden	.25
112	Scott Brosius	.25
113	Steve Avery	.25
114	Andres Galarraga	.25
115	Sandy Alomar Jr.	.25
116	Ray Lankford	.25
117	Jorge Posada	.25
118	Ryan Klesko	.25
119	Jay Buhner	.25
120	Jose Guillen	.25
121	Paul O'Neill	.20
122	Jimmy Key	.20
123	Hal Morris	.20
124	Travis Fryman	.20
125	Jim Edmonds	.20
126	Jeff Cirillo	.20
127	Fred McGriff	.20
128	Alan Benes	.20
129	Derek Bell	.20
130	Tony Graffanino	.20
131	Shawn Green	.40
132	Denny Neagle	.20
133	Alex Fernandez	.20
134	Mickey Morandini	.20
135	Royce Clayton	.20
136	Jose Mesa	.20
137	Edgar Martinez	.20
138	Curt Schilling	.40
139	Lance Johnson	.20
140	Andy Benes	.20
141	Charles Nagy	.20
142	Mariano Rivera	.40
143	Mark Wohlers	.20
144	Ken Hill	.20
145	Jay Bell	.20
146	Bob Higginson	.20
147	Mark Grudzielanek	.20
148	Ray Durham	.20
149	John Olerud	.20
150	Joey Hamilton	.20
151	Trevor Hoffman	.20
152	Dan Wilson	.20
153	J.T. Snow	.20
154	Marquis Grissom	.20
155	Yamil Benitez	.20
156	Rusty Greer	.20
157	Darryl Kile	.20
158	Ismael Valdes	.20
159	Jeff Conine	.20
160	Darren Daulton	.20
161	Chan Ho Park	.20
162	Troy Percival	.20
163	Wade Boggs	1.50
164	Dave Nilsson	.20
165	Vinny Castilla	.20
166	Kevin Brown	.20
167	Dennis Eckersley	1.00
168	Wendell Magee Jr.	.20
169	John Jaha	.20
170	Garret Anderson	.20
171	Jason Giambi	.75
172	Mark Grace	.15
173	Tony Clark	.20
174	Moises Alou	.20
175	Brett Butler	.20
176	Cecil Fielder	.20
177	Chris Widger	.20
178	Doug Drabek	.20
179	Ellis Burks	.20
180	Shigetosi Hasegawa	.20

Row 1 (Grace)

NM/M

Complete Set (180): 50.00
Common Showstopper (1-60): .35
Stars: 1.5X
Common Showtime (#61-120): .25
Stars: 1X
Common Showpiece (#121-180): .60
Stars: 1.5X

(See 1997 Flair Showcase Row 2 for checklist and base card values.)

Row 0 (Showcase)

NM/M

Complete Set (180): 200.00
Common Showpiece (1-60): 1.50
Stars: 2X

Common Showstopper
(61-120): .75
Stars: 4X
Common Showtime
(121-180): .35
Stars: 3X
(See 1997 Flair Showcase Row 2 for checklist and base card values.)

Legacy Collection
NM/M
Common Player: 10.00
Stars: 25X
(See 1997 Flair Showcase Row 2 for checklist and base card values.)

Legacy Masterpiece

KEN GRIFFEY Jr.
SEATTLE MARINERS • OUTFIELD

NM/M
Common Player: 100.00
(Star values undetermined.)

Diamond Cuts

		NM/M
Complete Set (20):		55.00
Common Player:		1.50
1	Jeff Bagwell	3.00
2	Albert Belle	1.50
3	Ken Caminiti	1.50
4	Juan Gonzalez	2.00
5	Ken Griffey Jr.	4.50
6	Tony Gwynn	4.00
7	Todd Hundley	1.50
8	Andruw Jones	3.00
9	Chipper Jones	4.00
10	Greg Maddux	4.00
11	Mark McGwire	5.00
12	Mike Piazza	4.50
13	Derek Jeter	6.00
14	Manny Ramirez	3.00
15	Cal Ripken Jr.	6.00
16	Alex Rodriguez	5.00
17	Frank Thomas	3.00
18	Mo Vaughn	1.50
19	Bernie Williams	1.50
20	Matt Williams	1.50
Complete Set (15):		125.00
Common Player:		2.50
1	Roberto Alomar	3.00
2	Barry Bonds	20.00
3	Juan Gonzalez	6.00

ABBREVIATIONS
OPS - Overprinted
"Promotional Sample"

4	Ken Griffey Jr.	15.00
5	Marquis Grissom	2.50
6	Derek Jeter	20.00
7	Chipper Jones	12.00
8	Barry Larkin	2.50
9	Kenny Lofton	2.50
10	Greg Maddux	12.00
11	Mike Piazza	15.00
12	Cal Ripken Jr.	20.00
13	Alex Rodriguez	17.50
14	Ivan Rodriguez	7.50
15	Frank Thomas	10.00

Promo Strip

NM/M
Complete Strip (3): 5.00
ROW0 Alex Rodriguez (Showcase)
ROW1 Alex Rodriguez (Grace)
ROW2 Alex Rodriguez (Style)

Wave of the Future
NM/M
Complete Set (27):		10.00
Common Player:		.25
1	Todd Greene	.25
2	Andruw Jones	1.50
3	Randall Simon	.25
4	Wady Almonte	.25
5	Pat Cline	.25
6	Jeff Abbott	.25
7	Justin Towle	.25
8	Richie Sexson	.25
9	Bubba Trammell	.25
10	Bob Abreu	.35
11	David Arias (Last name actually Ortiz.)	9.00
12	Todd Walker	.25
13	Orlando Cabrera	.25
14	Vladimir Guerrero	1.50
15	Ricky Ledee	.25
16	Jorge Posada	.25
17	Ruben Rivera	.25
18	Scott Spiezio	.25
19	Scott Rolen	1.00
20	Emil Brown	.25
21	Jose Guillen	.25
22	T.J. Staton	.25
23	Elieser Marrero	.25
24	Fernando Tatis	.25
25	Ryan Jones	.25
WF1	Hideki Irabu	.25
WF2	Jose Cruz Jr.	.25

1998 Flair Showcase
Row 3

NM/M
Complete Set (120):		20.00
Common Player (1-30):		.25
Common Player (31-60):		.25
Common Player (61-90):		.35
Common Player (91-120):		.45
Pack (5):		2.50
Wax Box (24):		45.00
1	Ken Griffey Jr.	2.00
2	Travis Lee	.25
3	Frank Thomas	1.25
4	Ben Grieve	.25
5	Nomar Garciaparra	1.50
6	Jose Cruz Jr.	.25
7	Alex Rodriguez	2.50
8	Cal Ripken Jr.	3.00

9	Mark McGwire	2.50
10	Chipper Jones	1.50
11	Paul Konerko	.40
12	Todd Helton	1.00
13	Greg Maddux	1.50
14	Derek Jeter	3.00
15	Jaret Wright	.25
16	Livan Hernandez	.25
17	Mike Piazza	2.00
18	Juan Encarnacion	.25
19	Tony Gwynn	1.50
20	Scott Rolen	1.00
21	Roger Clemens	1.75
22	Tony Clark	.25
23	Albert Belle	.25
24	Mo Vaughn	.25
25	Andruw Jones	1.25
26	Jason Dickson	.25
27	Fernando Tatis	.25
28	Ivan Rodriguez	.75
29	Ricky Ledee	.25
30	Darin Erstad	.50
31	Brian Rose	.25
32	Magglio Ordonez RC	3.00
33	Larry Walker	.25
34	Bobby Higginson	.25
35	Chili Davis	.25
36	Barry Bonds	3.00
37	Vladimir Guerrero	1.25
38	Jeff Bagwell	1.25
39	Kenny Lofton	.25
40	Ryan Klesko	.25
41	Mike Cameron	.25
42	Charles Johnson	.25
43	Andy Pettitte	.40
44	Juan Gonzalez	1.25
45	Tim Salmon	.25
46	Hideki Irabu	.25
47	Paul Molitor	1.25
48	Edgar Renteria	.25
49	Manny Ramirez	1.25
50	Jim Edmonds	.25
51	Bernie Williams	.25
52	Roberto Alomar	.40
53	David Justice	.25
54	Rey Ordonez	.25
55	Ken Caminiti	.25
56	Jose Guillen	.25
57	Randy Johnson	1.25
58	Brady Anderson	.25
59	Hideo Nomo	.50
60	Tino Martinez	.25
61	John Smoltz	.35
62	Joe Carter	.35
63	Matt Williams	.35
64	Robin Ventura	.35
65	Barry Larkin	.35
66	Dante Bichette	.35
67	Travis Fryman	.35
68	Gary Sheffield	.60
69	Eric Karros	.35
70	Matt Stairs	.35
71	Al Martin	.35
72	Jay Buhner	.35
73	Ray Lankford	.35
74	Carlos Delgado	.65
75	Edgardo Alfonzo	.35
76	Rondell White	.35
77	Chuck Knoblauch	.35
78	Raul Mondesi	.35
79	Johnny Damon	.60
80	Matt Morris	.35
81	Tom Glavine	.60
82	Kevin Brown	.35
83	Garret Anderson	.35
84	Mike Mussina	.40
85	Pedro Martinez	1.25
86	Craig Biggio	.35
87	Darryl Kile	.35
88	Rafael Palmeiro	.75
89	Jim Thome	.60
90	Andres Galarraga	.35
91	Sammy Sosa	1.50
92	Willie Greene	.45
93	Vinny Castilla	.45
94	Justin Thompson	.45
95	Jeff King	.45
96	Jeff Cirillo	.45
97	Mark Grudzielanek	.45
98	Brad Radke	.45
99	John Olerud	.45
100	Curt Schilling	.65
101	Steve Finley	.45
102	J.T. Snow	.45
103	Edgar Martinez	.45
104	Wilson Alvarez	.45
105	Rusty Greer	.45
106	Pat Hentgen	.45
107	David Cone	.45
108	Fred McGriff	.45
109	Jason Giambi	.75
110	Tony Womack	.45
111	Bernard Gilkey	.45
112	Alan Benes	.45

113	Mark Grace	.45
114	Reggie Sanders	.45
115	Moises Alou	.45
116	John Jaha	.45
117	Henry Rodriguez	.45
118	Dean Palmer	.45
119	Mike Lieberthal	.45
120	Shawn Estes	.45

Row 2

NM/M
Complete Set (120): 40.00
Common Player: .50
Stars: 1.5-2X

Row 1
(See 1998 Flair Showcase Row 3 for checklist and base card values.)
Complete Set (1-120): 100.00
Commons (1-30): 1.00
Stars: 2X
Commons (31-60): 1.25
Stars: 3X
Commons (61-90): .35
Stars: 1X
Commons (91-120): .75
Stars: 1.5X

Row 0
(See 1998 Flair Showcase Row 3 for checklist and base cards values.)
Complete Set (120): 350.00
Common Player (1-30): 5.00
Stars: 10X
Common Player (31-60): 3.00
Stars: 8X
Common Player (61-90): 2.00
Stars: 6X
Common Player (91-120): 1.00
Stars: 4X
(See 1998 Flair Showcase Row 3 for checklist and base card values.)

Legacy Masterpiece

NM/M
Common Player: 50.00
(Values Undetermined)

Legacy Collection
NM/M
Common Player: 7.50
Stars: 25X

(See 1998 Flair Showcase
Row 3 for checklist and base card
values.)

Perfect 10

		NM/M
Complete Set (10):		1,600
Common Player:		100.00
1	Ken Griffey Jr.	200.00
2	Cal Ripken Jr.	300.00
3	Frank Thomas	125.00
4	Mike Piazza	200.00
5	Greg Maddux	150.00
6	Nomar Garciaparra	150.00
7	Mark McGwire	250.00
8	Scott Rolen	100.00
9	Alex Rodriguez	250.00
10	Roger Clemens	175.00

Promo Strip

	NM/M
Complete Promo Strip:	5.00
Cal Ripken Jr.	

Wave of the Future

		NM/M
Complete Set (12):		10.00
Common Player:		.50
WF1	Travis Lee	.50
WF2	Todd Helton	5.00
WF3	Ben Grieve	.50
WF4	Juan Encarnacion	.50
WF5	Brad Fullmer	.50
WF6	Ruben Rivera	.50
WF7	Paul Konerko	.75
WF8	Derrek Lee	1.50
WF9	Mike Lowell	.50
WF10	Magglio Ordonez	2.00
WF11	Rich Butler	.50
WF12	Eli Marrero	.50

1999 Flair Showcase
Row 3 (Power)

		NM/M
Complete Set (144):		25.00
Common Player:		.25
Pack (5):		3.00
Wax Box (24):		45.00
1	Mark McGwire	2.50
2	Sammy Sosa	1.50
3	Ken Griffey Jr.	2.00
4	Chipper Jones	1.50
5	Ben Grieve	.25

6	J.D. Drew	.75
7	Jeff Bagwell	1.00
8	Cal Ripken Jr.	3.00
9	Tony Gwynn	1.50
10	Nomar Garciaparra	1.50
11	Travis Lee	.35
12	Troy Glaus	.75
13	Mike Piazza	2.00
14	Alex Rodriguez	2.50
15	Kevin Brown	.25
16	Darin Erstad	.50
17	Scott Rolen	.50
18	Micah Bowie RC	.25
19	Juan Gonzalez	.50
20	Kerry Wood	.50
21	Roger Clemens	1.75
22	Derek Jeter	3.00
23	Pat Burrell RC	3.00
24	Tim Salmon	.25
25	Barry Bonds	3.00
26	Roosevelt Brown RC	.25
27	Vladimir Guerrero	1.00
28	Randy Johnson	1.00
29	Mo Vaughn	.25
30	Fernando Seguignol	.25
31	Greg Maddux	1.50
32	Tony Clark	.25
33	Eric Chavez	.40
34	Kris Benson	.25
35	Frank Thomas	1.00
36	Mario Encarnacion	.25
37	Gabe Kapler	.25
38	Jeremy Giambi	.25
39	Peter Tucci RC	.25
40	Manny Ramirez	1.00
41	Albert Belle	.25
42	Warren Morris	.25
43	Michael Barrett	.25
44	Andruw Jones	1.00
45	Carlos Delgado	.60
46	Jaret Wright	.25
47	Juan Encarnacion	.25
48	Scott Hunter	.25
49	Tino Martinez	.25
50	Craig Biggio	.60
51	Jim Thome	.60
52	Vinny Castilla	.25
53	Tom Glavine	.40
54	Bob Higginson	.25
55	Moises Alou	.25
56	Robin Ventura	.25
57	Bernie Williams	.25
58	Pedro J. Martinez	1.00
59	Greg Vaughn	.25
60	Ray Lankford	.25
61	Jose Canseco	.40
62	Ivan Rodriguez	.75
63	Shawn Green	.40
64	Rafael Palmeiro	.75
65	Ellis Burks	.25
66	Jason Kendall	.25
67	David Wells	.25
68	Rondell White	.25
69	Gary Sheffield	.40
70	Ken Caminiti	.25
71	Cliff Floyd	.25
72	Larry Walker	.25
73	Bartolo Colon	.25
74	Barry Larkin	.25
75	Calvin Pickering	.25
76	Jim Edmonds	.25
77	Henry Rodriguez	.25
78	Roberto Alomar	.40
79	Andres Galarraga	.25
80	Richie Sexson	.25
81	Todd Helton	.75
82	Damion Easley	.25
83	Livan Hernandez	.25
84	Carlos Beltran	.60
85	Todd Hundley	.25
86	Todd Walker	.25
87	Scott Brosius	.25
88	Bob Abreu	.25

89	Corey Koskie	.25
90	Ruben Rivera	.25
91	Edgar Renteria	.25
92	Quinton McCracken	.25
93	Bernard Gilkey	.25
94	Shannon Stewart	.25
95	Dustin Hermanson	.25
96	Mike Caruso	.25
97	Alex Gonzalez	.25
98	Raul Mondesi	.25
99	David Cone	.25
100	Curt Schilling	.40
101	Brian Giles	.25
102	Edgar Martinez	.25
103	Rolando Arrojo	.25
104	Derek Bell	.25
105	Denny Neagle	.25
106	Marquis Grissom	.25
107	Bret Boone	.25
108	Mike Mussina	.50
109	John Smoltz	.25
110	Brett Tomko	.25
111	David Justice	.25
112	Andy Pettitte	.40
113	Eric Karros	.25
114	Dante Bichette	.25
115	Jeromy Burnitz	.25
116	Paul Konerko	.40
117	Steve Finley	.25
118	Ricky Ledee	.25
119	Edgardo Alfonzo	.25
120	Dean Palmer	.25
121	Rusty Greer	.25
122	Luis Gonzalez	.25
123	Randy Winn	.25
124	Jeff Kent	.25
125	Doug Glanville	.25
126	Justin Thompson	.25
127	Bret Saberhagen	.25
128	Wade Boggs	1.50
129	Al Leiter	.25
130	Paul O'Neill	.25
131	Chan Ho Park	.25
132	Johnny Damon	.60
133	Darryl Kile	.25
134	Reggie Sanders	.25
135	Kevin Millwood	.25
136	Charles Johnson	.25
137	Ray Durham	.25
138	Rico Brogna	.25
139	Matt Williams	.25
140	Sandy Alomar	.25
141	Jeff Cirillo	.25
142	Devon White	.25
143	Andy Benes	.25
144	Mike Stanley	.25
	Checklist Card	.05

Row 2 (Passion)

	NM/M
Complete Set (144):	65.00
Common Player:	.25
Showdown (1-48):	2X
Showpiece (49-96):	1X
Showtime (97-144):	1X
(See 1999 Flair Showcase	
Row 3 for checklist and base card	
values.)	

Row 1 (Showcase)

	NM/M
Complete Set (144):	300.00
Common Showpiece (1-48):	2.00
Showpiece Stars:	5X
Common Showtime (49-96):	1.00
Showtime Stars:	3X
Common Showdown	
(97-144):	.50
Showdown Stars:	2X
(See 1999 Flair Showcase	
Row 1 for checklist and base card	
values.)	

Legacy Masterpiece

	NM/M
Common Legacy:	6.00
Legacy Stars:	20X
Common Masterpiece:	50.00
(See 1999 Flair Showcase for	
checklist.)	

Measure of Greatness

		NM/M
Complete Set (15):		100.00
Common Player:		3.00
Production 500 Sets		
1	Roger Clemens	7.50
2	Nomar Garciaparra	6.50
3	Juan Gonzalez	3.00
4	Ken Griffey Jr.	9.00
5	Vladimir Guerrero	5.00
6	Tony Gwynn	6.50
7	Derek Jeter	15.00
8	Chipper Jones	6.50
9	Mark McGwire	12.50
10	Mike Piazza	9.00
11	Manny Ramirez	5.00
12	Cal Ripken Jr.	15.00
13	Alex Rodriguez	12.50
14	Sammy Sosa	6.50
15	Frank Thomas	5.00

Wave of the Future

		NM/M
Complete Set (15):		40.00
Common Player:		1.50
Production 1,000 Sets		
1	Kerry Wood	4.00
2	Ben Grieve	1.50
3	J.D. Drew	4.00
4	Juan Encarnacion	1.50
5	Travis Lee	2.00
6	Todd Helton	7.50
7	Troy Glaus	7.50
8	Ricky Ledee	1.50
9	Eric Chavez	2.00
10	Ben Davis	1.50
11	George Lombard	1.50
12	Jeremy Giambi	1.50
13	Roosevelt Brown	1.50
14	Pat Burrell	6.00
15	Preston Wilson	1.50

2003 Flair
Greats of the Game

	NM/M
Complete Set (95):	35.00
Common Player:	.40

Pack (5): 6.00
Box (20): 100.00

1	Ozzie Smith	1.00
2	Red Schoendienst	.40
3	Harmon Killebrew	1.50
4	Ralph Kiner	.40
5	Johnny Bench	2.00
6	Al Kaline	1.00
7	Bobby Doerr	.40
8	Cal Ripken Jr.	4.00
9	Enos Slaughter	.40
10	Phil Rizzuto	1.00
11	Luis Aparicio	.40
12	Pee Wee Reese	.40
13	Richie Ashburn	.40
14	Ernie Banks	2.00
15	Earl Weaver	.40
16	Whitey Ford	1.50
17	Brooks Robinson	1.00
18	Lou Boudreau	.40
19	Robin Yount	1.00
20	Mike Schmidt	2.50
21	Bob Lemon	.40
22	Stan Musial	2.50
23	Joe Morgan	.60
24	Early Wynn	.40
25	Willie Stargell	.75
26	Yogi Berra	2.00
27	Juan Marichal	.40
28	Rick Ferrell	.40
29	Rod Carew	.75
30	Jim Bunning	.40
31	Ferguson Jenkins	.40
32	Steve Carlton	.75
33	Larry Doby	.40
34	Nolan Ryan	4.00
35	Phil Niekro	.40
36	Billy Williams	.40
37	Hal Newhouser	.40
38	Bob Feller	.75
39	Lou Brock	.75
40	Monte Irvin	.75
41	Eddie Mathews	1.00
42	Rollie Fingers	.40
43	Gaylord Perry	.40
44	Reggie Jackson	1.50
45	Bob Gibson	1.00
46	Robin Roberts	.40
47	Tom Seaver	1.00
48	Willie McCovey	.40
49	Hoyt Wilhelm	.40
50	George Kell	.40
51	Warren Spahn	1.00
52	Jim "Catfish" Hunter	.40
53	Dom DiMaggio	.40
54	Joe Medwick	.40
55	Johnny Pesky	.40
56	Steve Garvey	.40
57	Harry Heilmann	.40
58	Dave Winfield	.75
59	Andre Dawson	.40
60	Jimmie Foxx	1.00
61	Buddy Bell	.40
62	Gabby Hartnett	.40
63	Babe Ruth	4.00
64	Dizzy Dean	1.50
65	Hank Greenberg	.40
66	Don Drysdale	.75
67	Gary Carter	.40
68	Wade Boggs	.75
69	Tony Perez	.40
70	Mickey Cochrane	.75
71	Bill Dickey	.40
72	George Brett	3.00
73	Honus Wagner	3.00
74	George Sisler	1.00
75	Walter Johnson	2.00
76	Ron Santo	.40
77	Roy Campanella	1.00
78	Roger Maris	2.50
79	Kirby Puckett	2.50
80	Alan Trammell	.40
81	Don Mattingly	4.00
82	Ty Cobb	3.00
83	Lou Gehrig	3.00
84	Jackie Robinson	3.00
85	Billy Martin	.75
86	Paul Molitor	.75
87	Duke Snider	1.00
88	Thurman Munson	1.50
89	Luke Appling	.40
90	Ernie Lombardi	.40
91	Rube Waddell	.40
92	Travis Jackson	.40
93	Joe Sewell	.40
94	King Kelly	.40
95	Heinie Manush	.40

Common Home Team
(96-133): 2.00

96HT	Bobby Doerr	2.00
97HT	Johnny Pesky	2.00
98HT	Wade Boggs	3.00
99HT	Tony Conigliaro	2.00
100HT	Carlton Fisk	3.00
101HT	Rico Petrocelli	2.00
102HT	Jim Rice	2.00
103HT	Al Lopez	2.00
104HT	Pee Wee Reese	2.00
105HT	Tommy Lasorda	2.00
106HT	Gil Hodges	3.00
107HT	Jackie Robinson	6.00
108HT	Duke Snider	4.00
109HT	Don Drysdale	4.00
110HT	Steve Garvey	2.00
111HT	Hoyt Wilhelm	2.00
112HT	Juan Marichal	3.00
113HT	Monte Irvin	3.00
114HT	Willie McCovey	3.00
115HT	Travis Jackson	2.00
116HT	Bobby Bonds	2.00
117HT	Orlando Cepeda	2.00
118HT	Whitey Ford	4.00
119HT	Phil Rizzuto	4.00
120HT	Reggie Jackson	4.00
121HT	Yogi Berra	5.00
122HT	Roger Maris	6.00
123HT	Don Mattingly	10.00
124HT	Babe Ruth	10.00
125HT	Dave Winfield	3.00
126HT	Bob Gibson	4.00
127HT	Enos Slaughter	2.00
128HT	Joe Medwick	2.00
129HT	Lou Brock	3.00
130HT	Ozzie Smith	5.00
131HT	Stan Musial	6.00
132HT	Steve Carlton	3.00
133HT	Dizzy Dean	4.00

Ballpark Heroes

		NM/M
Complete Set (9):		25.00
Common Player:		2.00
Inserted 1:10		
1BH	Nolan Ryan	5.00
2BH	Babe Ruth	5.00
3BH	Honus Wagner	3.00
4BH	Ty Cobb	4.00
5BH	Ernie Banks	3.00
6BH	Mike Schmidt	3.00
7BH	Duke Snider	2.00
8BH	Cal Ripken Jr.	5.00
9BH	Stan Musial	3.00

Classic Numbers

		NM/M
Complete Set (13):		50.00
Common Player:		3.00
Inserted 1:20		
1CN	Jackie Robinson	6.00
2CN	Willie McCovey	3.00
3CN	Brooks Robinson	5.00
4CN	Reggie Jackson	6.00
5CN	Ozzie Smith	6.00
6CN	Johnny Bench	6.00
7CN	Yogi Berra	6.00
8CN	Cal Ripken Jr.	10.00
9CN	George Brett	8.00
10CN	Thurman Munson	5.00
11CN	Nolan Ryan	3.00
12CN	Nolan Ryan	10.00
13CN	Steve Carlton	3.00

Classic Numbers Game-Used

	NM/M
Common Player:	10.00
Inserted 1:24	
Willie McCovey	12.00
George Brett	20.00
Joe Morgan	10.00
Yogi Berra	20.00
Cal Ripken Jr.	25.00
Nolan Ryan	35.00
Ozzie Smith	15.00
Johnny Bench	15.00
Ryne Sandberg	25.00
Thurman Munson	20.00
Steve Carlton	10.00

Classic Numbers Dual-Side

	NM/M
Common Card:	25.00
Production 250 Sets	
Yogi Berra,	
Thurman Munson	45.00
Nolan Ryan,	
Steve Carlton	65.00
Johnny Bench,	
Thurman Munson	35.00
Cal Ripken Jr.,	
Ozzie Smith	60.00
Joe Morgan,	
Ryne Sandberg	35.00
Willie McCovey,	
Johnny Bench	25.00
Yogi Berra,	
Cal Ripken Jr.	50.00
George Brett,	
Nolan Ryan	75.00

HOF Postmark

	NM/M
Production 2,002	
Ozzie Smith	20.00
Ozzie Smith/	
Auto./202	100.00

Bat Rack Triple

	NM/M
Common Card:	15.00
Production 300	
Eddie Murray,	
Cal Ripken Jr.,	
Brooks Robinson	75.00
Ryne Sandberg,	
Ron Santo,	
Billy Williams,	
Johnny Bench,	45.00
Joe Morgan,	
Tony Perez	35.00
Eddie Mathews,	
Paul Molitor,	
Robin Yount	40.00
Tommie Agee, Jerry Grote,	
Bud Harrelson	15.00
Reggie Jackson,	
Don Mattingly,	
Dave Winfield	45.00
Dave Parker,	
Willie Stargell	20.00

Bat Rack Quad

	NM/M
Common Card:	50.00

Numbered to 150.

	NM/M
Don Mattingly, Joe Morgan,	
Cal Ripken Jr.,	
Brooks Robinson	90.00
Ryne Sandberg,	
Ron Santo, Billy Williams,	
Andre Dawson	60.00
Dave Winfield,	
Cal Ripken Jr.,	
Paul Molitor,	
Robin Yount	80.00
Eddie Murray,	
Eddie Mathews,	
Reggie Jackson,	
Willie McCovey	50.00

Cut of History

	NM/M
Common Player:	5.00
Inserted 1:10	
Paul O'Neill	5.00
Dennis Eckersley	8.00
Jim Palmer	6.00
Graig Nettles	8.00
Frank Baker	30.00
Wade Boggs	8.00
Roger Maris	60.00
Jim "Catfish" Hunter	8.00
Alan Trammell	12.00
Eddie Murray	20.00
Steve Carlton	10.00
Tom Seaver	8.00
Gary Carter	8.00
Phil Niekro	6.00
Luis Aparicio	8.00
Reggie Jackson	12.00
Fergie Jenkins	8.00
Kirby Puckett	15.00
Billy Martin	15.00
Joe Medwick	25.00
Buddy Bell	5.00
Early Wynn	10.00
Cal Ripken Jr.	25.00
Hoyt Wilhelm	8.00
Willie McCovey	10.00

Cut of History Autograph

	NM/M
Common Player:	
Alan Trammell/211	25.00
Steve Carlton/506	30.00
Cal Ripken Jr/155	150.00
Johnny Bench/161	50.00

Greats of the Grain

		NM/M
Production 50 Sets		
1GOG	Ty Cobb	100.00
2GOG	Mike Schmidt	50.00
3GOG	Babe Ruth	140.00
4GOG	Lou Gehrig	80.00
5GOG	George Brett	160.00
6GOG	Stan Musial	75.00
7GOG	Don Mattingly	110.00
8GOG	Cal Ripken Jr.	100.00
9GOG	Eddie Mathews	75.00

Home Team Cut

	NM/M
Common Player:	8.00
Patch:	2-5X
Production 25 Sets	
Wade Boggs	15.00
Carlton Fisk	20.00
Jim Rice	15.00
Pee Wee Reese	15.00
Duke Snider	20.00
Steve Garvey	10.00
Tommy Lasorda	15.00
Juan Marichal	10.00
Bobby Bonds	8.00
Willie McCovey	10.00
Billy Martin	15.00
Roger Maris	65.00
Reggie Jackson	15.00
Dave Winfield	12.00
Red Schoendienst	8.00
Ozzie Smith	35.00
Joe Medwick	25.00

Sweet Swatch Jersey

	NM/M
Common Player:	15.00
Jerry Coleman/528	20.00
Ryne Sandberg/374	25.00
Johnny Bench/410	20.00
Paul Molitor/592	15.00
Cal Ripken Jr/557	45.00
Gil Hodges/545	20.00
Carlton Fisk/1,200	15.00
Nolan Ryan/590	40.00
Tom Seaver/385	20.00
Don Mattingly/880	35.00
Jose Canseco/1,329	15.00
George Brett/384	30.00
Jim Palmer/335	15.00
Kirby Puckett/445	20.00
Juan Marichal/335	15.00
Robin Yount/340	25.00
Andre Dawson/335	15.00

Sweet Swatch Bat

	NM/M
Common Player:	15.00
Cal Ripken Jr/305	40.00
George Brett/320	30.00
Johnny Bench/175	20.00
Reggie Jackson/155	20.00
Don Mattingly/340	40.00
Willie McCovey/155	15.00
Jose Canseco/155	25.00
Kirby Puckett/251	30.00
Orlando Cepeda/165	15.00
Hank Greenberg	
Eddie Mathews/185	40.00
Pee Wee Reese/165	30.00
Andre Dawson/310	15.00

Sweet Swatch Jersey Autograph

	NM/M
Common Autograph:	
Cal Ripken Jr/40	240.00
Johnny Bench/40	130.00
Alan Trammell/40	75.00
Tony Kubek	

2003 Flair

	NM/M
Complete Set (125):	
Common Player:	.25
Common SP (91-125):	4.00
Production 500	
Pack (5):	3.50
Box (20):	50.00
1 Hideo Nomo	.60
2 Derek Jeter	3.00
3 Junior Spivey	.25
4 Rich Aurilia	.25
5 Luis Gonzalez	.35
6 Sean Burroughs	.25
7 Pedro J. Martinez	1.00
8 Randy Winn	.25
9 Carlos Delgado	.50
10 Pat Burrell	.50
11 Barry Larkin	.25
12 Roberto Alomar	.40
13 Tony Batista	.25
14 Barry Bonds	3.00

15 Craig Biggio	.25
16 Ivan Rodriguez	.65
17 Javier Vazquez	.25
18 Joe Borchard	.25
19 Josh Phelps	.25
20 Omar Vizquel	.25
21 Tom Glavine	.40
22 Darin Erstad	.50
23 Hee Seop Choi	.25
24 Roger Clemens	1.75
25 Michael Cuddyer	.25
26 Mike Sweeney	.25
27 Phil Nevin	.25
28 Torii Hunter	.25
29 Vladimir Guerrero	1.00
30 Ellis Burks	.25
31 Jimmy Rollins	.50
32 Ken Griffey Jr.	2.00
33 Magglio Ordonez	.40
34 Mark Prior	1.00
35 Mike Lieberthal	.25
36 Jorge Posada	.30
37 Rodrigo Lopez	.25
38 Todd Helton	1.00
39 Adam Kennedy	.25
40 Curt Schilling	.40
41 Jim Thome	.25
42 Josh Beckett	.25
43 Carlos Pena	.25
44 Jason Kendall	.25
45 Sammy Sosa	2.00
46 Scott Rolen	.75
47 Alex Rodriguez	2.50
48 Aubrey Huff	.25
49 Bobby Abreu	.25
50 Jeff Kent	.25
51 Joe Randa	.25
52 Lance Berkman	.25
53 Orlando Cabrera	.25
54 Richie Sexson	.25
55 Albert Pujols	2.00
56 Alfonso Soriano	.50
57 Greg Maddux	1.50
58 Jason Giambi	.75
59 Jeff Bagwell	1.00
60 Kerry Wood	.50
61 Manny Ramirez	1.00
62 Eric Chavez	.40
63 Preston Wilson	.25
64 Shawn Green	.50
65 Shea Hillenbrand	.25
66 Austin Kearns	.75
67 Cliff Floyd	.25
68 Edgardo Alfonzo	.25
69 J.D. Drew	.40
70 Larry Walker	.25
71 Mike Piazza	2.00
72 Andruw Jones	.75
73 Ben Grieve	.25
74 Eric Hinske	.25
75 Geoff Jenkins	.25
76 Kazuhiro Sasaki	.25
77 Matt Morris	.25
78 Miguel Tejada	.40
79 Aramis Ramirez	.25
80 Troy Glaus	1.00
81 Ichiro Suzuki	2.00
82 Mark Teixeira	.50
83 Nomar Garciaparra	2.00
84 Chipper Jones	1.50
85 Frank Thomas	1.00
86 Paul LoDuca	.25
87 Bernie Williams	.35
88 Adam Dunn	.75
89 Randy Johnson	1.00
90 Barry Zito	.40
91 Lew Ford RC	8.00
92 Joe Valentine RC	3.00
93 Jhonny Peralta RC	4.00
94 Hideki Matsui RC	20.00
95 Francisco Rosario RC	3.00
96 Adam LaRoche RC	4.00
97 Josh Hall RC	6.00
98 Chien-Ming Wang RC	25.00
99 Josh Willingham RC	6.00
100 Guillermo Quiroz RC	6.00
101 Terrmel Sledge RC	3.00
102 Prentice Redman RC	3.00
103 Matt Bruback RC	3.00
104 Alejandro Machado RC	3.00
105 Shane Victorino RC	6.00
106 Chris Waters RC	3.00
107 Jose Contreras RC	8.00
108 Pete LaForest RC	3.00
109 Nook Logan RC	3.00
110 Hector Luna RC	8.00
111 Daniel Cabrera RC	6.00
112 Matt Kata RC	6.00
113 Rontrez Johnson RC	6.00
114 Josh Stewart RC	8.00
115 Michael Hessman RC	3.00
116 Felix Sanchez RC	6.00
117 Michel Hernandez RC	3.00
118 Arnaldo Munoz RC	3.00
119 Ian Ferguson RC	3.00
120 Clint Barmes RC	6.00

121 Brian Stokes RC	3.00
122 Craig Brazell RC	6.00
123 John Webb	3.00
124 Tim Olson RC	6.00
125 Jeremy Bonderman	10.00

Row 1

Stars (1-90):	5-10X
Rookies (91-125):	.75-1.5X
Production 150 Sets	
Row 2:	No Pricing
Production 25 Sets	

Diamond Cuts

	NM/M
Common Player:	4.00
Inserted 1:10	
Golds:	1-2X
Production 100 Sets	
1DC Alex Rodriguez	12.00
2DC Roberto Alomar	4.00
3DC Scott Rolen	5.00
4DC Alfonso Soriano	6.00
5DC Chipper Jones	7.50
6DC Pat Burrell	5.00
7DC Derek Jeter	15.00
8DC Mike Piazza	10.00
9DC J.D. Drew	4.00
10DC Vladimir Guerrero	6.00
11DC Greg Maddux	7.50
12DC Barry Zito	4.00
13DC Troy Glaus	5.00
14DC Roy Oswalt	4.00
15DC Roger Clemens	9.00

Hot Numbers

	NM/M
Common Player:	15.00
Production 100 Sets	
1HN Alex Rodriguez	35.00
2HN Roberto Alomar	20.00
3HN Scott Rolen	15.00
4HN Alfonso Soriano	30.00
5HN Chipper Jones	25.00
6HN Pat Burrell	25.00
7HN Derek Jeter	40.00
8HN Mike Piazza	30.00
9HN J.D. Drew	15.00
10HN Vladimir Guerrero	20.00
11HN Greg Maddux	30.00
12HN Barry Zito	15.00
13HN Troy Glaus	15.00
14HN Roy Oswalt	15.00
15HN Roger Clemens	

Hot Numbers Dual

Production 25 Sets: No Pricing

Power Tools

	NM/M
Common Player:	5.00
Production 500 Sets	
Golds:	1-1.5X
Production 100 Sets	
1PT Nomar Garciaparra	15.00
2PT Derek Jeter	25.00
3PT Sammy Sosa	12.00
4PT Miguel Tejada	5.00
5PT Austin Kearns	10.00
6PT Jason Giambi	8.00
7PT Adam Dunn	8.00
8PT Jim Thome	8.00
9PT Lance Berkman	6.00
10PT Alfonso Soriano	15.00
12PT Alex Rodriguez	15.00
13PT Mike Piazza	10.00
14PT Bernie Williams	10.00
15PT Jeff Bagwell	8.00
16PT Andruw Jones	5.00
17PT Scott Rolen	12.00
19PT Juan Gonzalez	6.00

Power Tools - Dual

	NM/M
Common Duo:	
Production 200 Sets	
1PTD Nomar Garciaparra,	
Derek Jeter	40.00
2PTD Pat Burrell, Jim Thome	
3PTD Adam Dunn,	
Austin Kearns	25.00

4PTD Jim Thome,	
Sammy Sosa	15.00
5PTD Alex Rodriguez,	
Nomar Garciaparra	20.00
6PTD Jason Giambi,	
Bernie Williams	15.00
7PTD Derek Jeter,	
Alfonso Soriano	25.00
8PTD Lance Berkman,	
Jeff Bagwell	10.00
9PTD Miguel Tejada,	
Alex Rodriguez	20.00
10PTD Jason Giambi,	
Mike Piazza	20.00

Sweet Swatch

	NM/M
Common Player:	5.00
Production 250 Sets	
Derek Jeter	20.00
Sammy Sosa	15.00
Hideo Nomo	20.00
Vladimir Guerrero	6.00
Jason Giambi	8.00
Nomar Garciaparra	15.00
Randy Johnson	12.00
Miguel Tejada	5.00
Pedro J. Martinez	10.00
Adam Dunn	8.00
Roger Clemens	15.00
Mark Prior	10.00
Chipper Jones	10.00
Alex Rodriguez	15.00
Bernie Williams	6.00
Lance Berkman	6.00
Kazuhiro Sasaki	6.00
Alfonso Soriano	12.00

Sweet Swatch Patch

	NM/M
Common Player:	15.00
Production 50 Sets	
Sammy Sosa	50.00
Hideo Nomo	50.00
Jason Giambi	20.00
Nomar Garciaparra	45.00
Randy Johnson	40.00
Miguel Tejada	15.00
Pedro J. Martinez	40.00
Adam Dunn	35.00
Roger Clemens	50.00
Mark Prior	25.00
Alex Rodriguez	45.00
Bernie Williams	20.00
Kazuhiro Sasaki	30.00
Alfonso Soriano	35.00

Sweet Swatch Oversized

	NM/M
Common Player:	6.00

1:Hobby Box
Masterpiece One-of-One's exist.

Derek Jeter/150	20.00
Sammy Sosa/279	15.00
Hideo Nomo/970	12.00
Jason Giambi/350	15.00
Nomar Garciaparra/ 727	15.00
Randy Johnson/274	15.00
Miguel Tejada/518	6.00
Pedro Martinez/1,480	10.00
Adam Dunn/1,090	8.00
Roger Clemens/97	25.00
Mark Prior/1,195	10.00
Chipper Jones/80	15.00
Alex Rodriguez/150	15.00
Bernie Williams/1,420	8.00
Lance Berkman/1,465	6.00
Kazuhiro Sasaki/505	10.00
Alfonso Soriano	

Sweet Swatch Patch Oversized

	NM/M
Common Player:	15.00
Derek Jeter/35	75.00
Sammy Sosa/190	40.00
Hideo Nomo/114	50.00
Vladimir Guerrero/ 290	35.00
Nomar Garciaparra/ 124	40.00
Randy Johnson/46	
Miguel Tejada/183	15.00
Pedro Martinez/185	40.00
Adam Dunn/130	30.00
Mark Prior/290	25.00
Chipper Jones/284	25.00
Alex Rodriguez/298	40.00
Bernie Williams/123	25.00
Lance Berkman/287	25.00

Sweet Swatch Dual Oversized

Production 25 Sets: No Pricing

Sweet Swatch Autograph Oversized

	NM/M
Common Player:	
Golds:	1.5-2X

Production 25, Jeter 50
Masterpiece One-of-Ones exist.

Derek Jeter/312	90.00
Randy Johnson/218	60.00
Adam Dunn/218	30.00
Jeff Bagwell/218	40.00

Wave of the Future

	NM/M
Common Player:	3.00

Production 500 Sets

Golds:	1-2X

Production 100 Sets

1WOF	Francisco Rodriguez	3.00
2WOF	Carl Crawford	4.00
3WOF	Austin Kearns	10.00
4WOF	Hank Blalock	8.00
5WOF	Marlon Byrd	3.00
6WOF	Michael Restovich	3.00
7WOF	Joe Borchard	3.00
8WOF	Sean Burroughs	4.00
9WOF	Aubrey Huff	3.00
10WOF	Josh Phelps	5.00

2006 Flair Showcase

Jason Bay
Pittsburgh Pirates / Outfield

	NM/M
Complete Set (200):	
Common Player (1-100):	.50

Common Player (101-150):	1.50
Inserted 1:4 Hobby	
Common Player (151-200):	2.00
Inserted 1:8 Hobby	
Pack (5):	5.00
Box (18):	80.00
1	Jeremy Hermida (RC)	1.50
2	Albert Pujols	3.00
3	Ryan Shealy (RC)	.50
4	Mark Prior	.75
5	Chuck James (RC)	1.00
6	Shawn Green	.50
7	Rickie Weeks	.50
8	Roy Halladay	.75
9	Luis Gonzalez	.50
10	David Ortiz	1.50
11	Josh Beckett	.50
12	Gary Sheffield	.75
13	Jose Reyes	.75
14	Brandon Watson (RC)	.50
15	Tadahito Iguchi	.50
16	Rich Harden	.50
17	Skip Schumaker (RC)	.50
18	Vladimir Guerrero	1.00
19	Chris Carpenter	.75
20	Brian Roberts	.50
21	Roy Oswalt	.50
22	Ben Johnson (RC)	.50
23	Todd Helton	.75
24	Wilbert Nieves (RC)	.50
25	Michael Young	.50
26	A.J. Burnett	.50
27	J.D. Drew	.50
28	Adrian Beltre	.50
29	Tim Hudson	.50
30	Jake Peavy	.50
31	Magglio Ordonez	.50
32	Brad Wilkerson	.50
33	Ryan Freel	.50
34	Javier Vazquez	.50
35	Tom Glavine	.50
36	Jason Bergmann RC	1.00
37	Marcus Giles	.50
38	Jim Thome	1.00
39	Ichiro Suzuki	2.00
40	Jeff Harris RC	.75
41	Miguel Cabrera	1.00
42	Nomar Garciaparra	1.00
43	Brian Giles	.50
44	Jeremy Accardo RC	1.00
45	Taylor Buchholz (RC)	.50
46	Mike Jacobs	.50
47	Chris Denorfia (RC)	.50
48	Ivan Rodriguez	.75
49	Mike Piazza	1.50
50	Curt Schilling	1.00
51	Kelly Stoppach (RC)	.50
52	Jason Kubel (RC)	.50
53	Craig Biggio	.75
54	Livan Hernandez	.50
55	Joe Mauer	.75
56	Scott Feldman RC	1.00
57	Garret Anderson	.50
58	Steve Stemle RC	1.00
59	Boof Bonser (RC)	.50
60	Jose Guillen	.50
61	Rafael Furcal	.50
62	John Van Benschoten (RC)	.50
63	Dontrelle Willis	.75
64	Jose Vidro	.50
65	David Wright	2.00
66	Alfonso Soriano	1.00
67	Scott Podsednik	.50
68	Felix Hernandez	.75
69	Richie Sexson	.50
70	Jeff Francoeur	.50
71	Conor Jackson	.50
72	Javy Lopez	.50
73	Jonathan Papelbon (RC)	6.00
74	Frank Thomas	.75
75	Greg Maddux	2.00
76	Josh Rupe (RC)	.50
77	Eric Chavez	.50
78	Ben Sheets	.50
79	Chase Utley	.75
80	Derrek Lee	.75
81	Manny Ramirez	1.00
82	Pedro Martinez	1.00
83	Hideki Matsui	2.00
84	Jeremy Bonderman	.50
85	Ronny Cedeno	.50
86	Trevor Hoffman	.50
87	Mark Buehrle	.50
88	Jason Bay	.75
89	Reggie Sanders	.50
90	Brian Anderson (RC)	.50
91	Travis Hafner	.75
92	Carlos Beltran	.75
93	Cody Ross (RC)	.50
94	Melvin Mora	.50
95	Chris Duffy	.50
96	Vernon Wells	.50

97	Bartolo Colon	.50
98	Aubrey Huff	.50
99	Paul Konerko	.50
100	Cesar Izturis	.50
101	Josh Willingham (RC)	1.50
102	Matt Cain (RC)	2.00
103	Macay McBride (RC)	1.50
104	Jeff Mathis	1.50
105	Alex Rodriguez	8.00
106	Justin Morneau	2.00
107	Felipe Lopez	1.50
108	Justin Verlander (RC)	8.00
109	Ryan Howard	5.00
110	Mike Sweeney	1.50
111	Scott Rolen	3.00
112	Hank Blalock	1.50
113	Kerry Wood	1.50
114	B.J. Ryan	1.50
115	Garrett Atkins	1.50
116	Carlos Delgado	2.50
117	Zack Greinke	1.50
118	Chad Cordero	1.50
119	Julio Lugo	1.50
120	Bobby Crosby	1.50
121	Barry Zito	1.50
122	Jhonny Peralta	1.50
123	Miguel Tejada	2.50
124	Grady Sizemore	2.00
125	Derek Jeter	10.00
126	Cliff Lee	1.50
127	Khalil Greene	1.50
128	Lance Berkman	2.00
129	Huston Street	1.50
130	Jermaine Dye	1.50
131	Chone Figgins	1.50
132	Torii Hunter	2.00
133	Jorge Cantu	1.50
134	Jason Giambi	3.00
135	Johan Santana	3.00
136	Chad Tracy	1.50
137	Troy Glaus	2.00
138	Moises Alou	2.00
139	Jason Schmidt	2.00
140	Ken Griffey Jr.	8.00
141	Jason Varitek	3.00
142	John Smoltz	2.50
143	Andy Pettitte	2.00
144	Jeff Kent	2.00
145	Coco Crisp	2.00
146	Jonny Gomes	1.50
147	Aaron Rowand	1.50
148	Mike Mussina	2.50
149	Johnny Damon	4.00
150	Edgar Renteria	1.50
151	Scott Kazmir	2.00
152	Lyle Overbay	2.00
153	Placido Polanco	2.00
154	Mariano Rivera	3.00
155	Hanley Ramirez (RC)	3.00
156	Morgan Ensberg	2.00
157	Kenny Rogers	2.00
158	Brad Lidge	2.00
159	A.J. Pierzynski	2.00
160	Aramis Ramirez	3.00
161	Mark Teixeira	3.00
162	Carl Crawford	3.00
163	Ryan Zimmerman (RC)	10.00
164	Adam Dunn	3.00
165	Joe Nathan	2.00
166	Juan Pierre	2.00
167	Pat Burrell	3.00
168	Carlos Lee	2.00
169	Billy Wagner	2.00
170	Prince Fielder (RC)	10.00
171	Randy Johnson	4.00
172	Andruw Jones	4.00
173	Francisco Rodriguez	2.00
174	Robinson Cano	3.00
175	Matt Holliday	2.00
176	Jim Edmonds	3.00
177	Josh Barfield (RC)	2.00
178	Chipper Jones	4.00
179	Bobby Jenks	2.00
180	Carlos Zambrano	3.00
181	Bobby Abreu	2.00
182	Brandon Webb	2.00
183	Kevin Millwood	2.00
184	Zachary Duke	2.00
185	Randy Winn	2.00
186	Eric Gagne	2.00
187	Kenji Johjima RC	10.00
188	John Patterson	2.00
189	Mark Loretta	2.00
190	Anderson Hernandez (RC)	2.00
191	Chris Resop (RC)	2.00
192	Ian Kinsler (RC)	2.00
193	Francisco Liriano (RC)	8.00
194	Noah Lowry	2.00
195	Brett Myers	2.00
196	Rocco Baldelli	2.00
197	Cliff Floyd	2.00
198	Sean Casey	2.00

199	Geoff Jenkins	2.00
200	Clint Barmes	2.00

Legacy Blue

Blue (1-100):	2-4X
Blue (101-150):	1-1.5X
Blue (151-200):	1X

Production 150 Sets

Legacy Emerald

Jeremy Bonderman
Detroit Tigers/Pitcher

Emerald (1-100):	2-4X
Emerald (101-150):	1-1.5X
Emerald (151-200):	1X

Production 150 Sets

Printing Plates

No Pricing
Production one set per color.

Autographics

		NM/M
Common Autograph:		8.00
BA	Bronson Arroyo	20.00
JB	Jason Bay	20.00
HB	Hank Blalock	10.00
BO	Jeremy Bonderman	20.00
SC	Sean Casey/SP	15.00
GC	Gustavo Chacin	10.00
BC	Brandon Claussen	10.00
CH	Chad Cordero	8.00
CO	Craig Counsell	10.00
CA	Carl Crawford	15.00
CC	Coco Crisp	15.00
KG	Ken Griffey Jr./SP	75.00
JG	Jose Guillen	8.00
TH	Travis Hafner/SP	15.00
AH	Aaron Harang	15.00
LH	Livan Hernandez	8.00
CI	Cesar Izturis	8.00
MK	Mark Kotsay	8.00
CL	Cliff Lee	8.00
DL	Derrek Lee/43	
JM	Justin Morneau	20.00
XN	Xavier Nady	10.00
RO	Roy Oswalt	20.00
WP	Wily Mo Pena	15.00
JH	Jhonny Peralta	10.00
JP	Joel Pineiro	10.00
RA	Aramis Ramirez	15.00
AR	Aaron Rowand	15.00
CU	Chase Utley/SP/100	25.00
JV	Javier Vazquez/SP	8.00
OV	Omar Vizquel	30.00
RZ	Ryan Zimmerman	50.00

Fresh Ink

		NM/M
Common Auto.:		10.00
GA	Garrett Atkins	10.00
CB	Clint Barmes/SP	10.00
JB	Joe Blanton	10.00
MC	Miguel Cabrera/SP	25.00
MA	Matt Cain/SP	25.00
BC	Bobby Crosby	10.00
DD	David DeJesus	15.00
GF	Gavin Floyd	15.00
JG	Jonny Gomes	15.00
KG	Khalil Greene/SP	25.00
ZG	Zack Greinke	10.00
HA	Rich Harden	15.00
DH	Danny Haren	10.00

RH	Rich Hill	30.00
TI	Tadahito Iguchi	40.00
SK	Scott Kazmir	15.00
CK	Casey Kotchman	10.00
NL	Noah Lowry	20.00
VM	Victor Martinez	15.00
BM	Brandon McCarthy	10.00
OP	Odalis Perez	10.00
RE	Jeremy Reed	10.00
BR	Brian Roberts	15.00
ES	Ervin Santana	15.00
JS	Johan Santana/SP	50.00
CS	Chris Shelton	15.00
HS	Huston Street	15.00
MT	Mark Teahen	10.00
DW	Dontrelle Willis	15.00
WR	David Wright/SP/100	60.00
KY	Kevin Youkilis	15.00
MY	Michael Young/SP/100	20.00

Hot Gloves

NM/M
Common Player: 10.00
Inserted 1:108 Hobby

1	Derrek Lee	15.00
2	Andruw Jones	15.00
3	Bobby Abreu	10.00
4	Luis Castillo	10.00
5	Mike Matheny	10.00
6	Cesar Izturis	10.00
7	Craig Biggio	15.00
8	Darin Erstad	10.00
9	Derek Jeter	40.00
10	Eric Chavez	10.00
11	Greg Maddux	40.00
12	Ichiro Suzuki	35.00
13	Ivan Rodriguez	15.00
14	J.T. Snow	15.00
15	Jim Edmonds	15.00
16	Steve Finley	10.00
17	Kenny Rogers	10.00
18	Jason Varitek	20.00
19	Ken Griffey Jr.	40.00
20	Mark Teixeira	15.00
21	Orlando Hudson	10.00
22	Mike Hampton	10.00
23	Mike Mussina	15.00
24	Vernon Wells	15.00
25	Omar Vizquel	10.00
26	Alex Rodriguez	40.00
27	Mike Cameron	15.00
28	Scott Rolen	25.00
29	Todd Helton	15.00
30	Torii Hunter	15.00

Hot Numbers

NM/M
Common Player: 1.50
Inserted 1:6 Hobby

1	Albert Pujols	8.00
2	Alex Rodriguez	8.00
3	Andruw Jones	3.00
4	Bobby Abreu	1.50
5	Chipper Jones	3.00
6	Curt Schilling	3.00
7	David Ortiz	3.00
8	David Wright	5.00
9	Derek Jeter	8.00
10	Derrek Lee	3.00
11	Eric Gagne	1.50
12	Greg Maddux	5.00
13	Hideki Matsui	5.00
14	Ichiro Suzuki	5.00
15	Ivan Rodriguez	2.00
16	Johan Santana	2.00
17	Johnny Damon	3.00
18	Ken Griffey Jr.	5.00
19	Manny Ramirez	3.00
20	Mark Prior	2.00
21	Mark Teixeira	2.00
22	Miguel Cabrera	3.00
23	Miguel Tejada	2.00
24	Pedro Martinez	3.00
25	Randy Johnson	3.00
26	Rickie Weeks	1.50
27	Roger Clemens	6.00
28	Todd Helton	2.00
29	Torii Hunter	1.50
30	Vladimir Guerrero	3.00

Lettermen

No Pricing
Production 3-9

Showcase Signatures

NM/M
Production 35 Sets

JE	Jeremy Bonderman	30.00
SC	Sean Casey	20.00
CD	Chad Cordero	10.00
JG	Jose Guillen	10.00
AH	Aaron Harang	20.00
HA	Rich Harden	30.00
CI	Cesar Izturis	10.00
XN	Xavier Nady	20.00
RO	Roy Oswalt	20.00
WM	Wily Mo Pena	20.00
PE	Jhonny Peralta	15.00
BR	Brian Roberts	30.00
CS	Chris Shelton	20.00
KY	Kevin Youkilis	20.00
RZ	Ryan Zimmerman	65.00

Stitches

NM/M
Common Player: 4.00
Inserted 1:9

BA	Bobby Abreu	4.00
MA	Moises Alou	6.00
RB	Rocco Baldelli	6.00
JO	Josh Beckett	6.00
CB	Carlos Beltran	8.00
AB	Adrian Beltre	4.00
LB	Lance Berkman	4.00
HB	Hank Blalock	6.00
BO	Jeremy Bonderman	6.00
MB	Mark Buehrle	4.00
MC	Miguel Cabrera	10.00
RC	Robinson Cano	12.00
JC	Jorge Cantu	6.00
EC	Eric Chavez	6.00
CO	Michael Collins	4.00
CA	Carl Crawford	6.00
BC	Bobby Crosby	4.00
JD	Johnny Damon	10.00
CD	Carlos Delgado	6.00
DR	J.D. Drew	6.00
AD	Adam Dunn	6.00
JE	Jim Edmonds	6.00
RF	Rafael Furcal	6.00
EG	Eric Gagne	6.00
FG	Freddy Garcia	4.00
JG	Jason Giambi	8.00
BG	Brian Giles	4.00
TG	Tom Glavine	6.00
LG	Luis Gonzalez	4.00
GR	Khalil Greene	4.00
KG	Ken Griffey Jr.	10.00
VG	Vladimir Guerrero	8.00
TR	Travis Hafner	6.00
RH	Roy Halladay	6.00
RI	Rich Harden	4.00
HA	J.J. Hardy	4.00
TH	Todd Helton	8.00
HO	Trevor Hoffman	6.00
MH	Matt Holliday	8.00
HU	Tim Hudson	6.00
TO	Torii Hunter	6.00
DJ	Derek Jeter	20.00
RJ	Randy Johnson	8.00
AJ	Andruw Jones	6.00
CJ	Chipper Jones	8.00
JJ	Jacque Jones	4.00
SK	Scott Kazmir	6.00
JK	Jeff Kent	6.00
CL	Carlos Lee	4.00
DL	Derrek Lee	8.00
PL	Paul LoDuca	4.00
JL	Javy Lopez	4.00
GM	Greg Maddux	10.00
PM	Pedro Martinez	10.00
KM	Kazuo Matsui	6.00
DM	Daisuke Matsuzaka	125.00
JM	Joe Mauer	8.00
KE	Kevin Millwood	4.00
MM	Mike Mussina	8.00
TN	Trot Nixon	8.00
DO	David Ortiz	10.00
JP	Jake Peavy	6.00
AN	Andy Pettitte	6.00
MI	Mike Piazza	10.00
MP	Mark Prior	6.00
AP	Albert Pujols	20.00
AR	Aramis Ramirez	6.00
MR	Manny Ramirez	8.00
RE	Jeremy Reed	4.00
JR	Jose Reyes	10.00
BR	Brian Roberts	4.00
FR	Francisco Rodriguez	4.00
IR	Ivan Rodriguez	8.00
SR	Scott Rolen	4.00
CC	C.C. Sabathia	4.00
JS	Johan Santana	8.00
CS	Curt Schilling	8.00
JA	Jason Schmidt	6.00
RS	Richie Sexson	6.00
BS	Ben Sheets	4.00
GS	Gary Sheffield	6.00
SM	John Smoltz	8.00
AS	Alfonso Soriano	8.00
SW	Mike Sweeney	4.00
MT	Mark Teixeira	8.00
TE	Miguel Tejada	8.00
FT	Frank Thomas	10.00
JT	Jim Thome	8.00
JU	Juan Uribe	4.00
JV	Jason Varitek	10.00
OV	Omar Vizquel	6.00
RW	Rickie Weeks	6.00
VW	Vernon Wells	6.00
DW	Dontrelle Willis	6.00
PW	Preston Wilson	4.00
KW	Kerry Wood	6.00
WR	David Wright	15.00
MY	Michael Young	6.00
BZ	Barry Zito	4.00

Wave of the Future

NM/M
Common Player: 1.00
Inserted 1:2

WF-1	Jeremy Hermida	1.00
WF-2	Kelly Stoppach	1.00
WF-3	Adam Wainwright	1.00
WF-4	Ryan Zimmerman	4.00
WF-5	Josh Willingham	1.00
WF-6	Brandon McCarthy	1.00
WF-7	Conor Jackson	1.00
WF-8	Grady Sizemore	1.50
WF-9	Curtis Granderson	1.00
WF-10	Jose Capellan	1.00
WF-11	Mike Jacobs	1.00
WF-12	Gavin Floyd	1.00
WF-13	Hanley Ramirez	1.50
WF-14	Jason Kubel	1.00
WF-15	Nate McLouth	1.50
WF-16	Felix Hernandez	1.50
WF-17	Jeff Francoeur	1.00
WF-18	Wilbert Nieves	1.00
WF-19	Cody Ross	1.00
WF-20	Justin Verlander	5.00
WF-21	Ben Johnson	1.00
WF-22	Guillermo Quiroz	1.00
WF-23	Jonathan Papelbon	4.00
WF-24	Prince Fielder	4.00
WF-25	Rickie Weeks	1.50
WF-26	Robinson Cano	2.00
WF-27	Kenji Johjima	4.00
WF-28	Anderson Hernandez	1.00
WF-29	Yuniesky Betancourt	1.00
WF-30	Zachary Duke	1.00

WBC Classic Moments

NM/M
Common Player: 1.50
Inserted 1:8

CM-1	Adam Stern	1.50
CM-2	Jason Bay	2.00
CM-3	Wei Wang	1.50
CM-4	Yung-Chi Chen	3.00
CM-5	Pedro Luis Lazo	1.50
CM-6	Yoandy Garlobo	1.50
CM-7	Ormari Romero	1.50
CM-8	Frederich Cepeda	1.50
CM-9	Yulieski Gourriel	1.50
CM-10	Yadel Marti	1.50
CM-11	David Ortiz	2.50
CM-12	Albert Pujols	5.00
CM-13	Adrian Beltre	1.50
CM-14	Alberto Castillo	1.50
CM-15	Odalis Perez	1.50
CM-16	Jason Grilli	1.50
CM-17	Daisuke Matsuzaka	5.00
CM-18	Sadaharu Oh	10.00
CM-19	Nobuhiko Matsunaka	3.00
CM-20	Ichiro Suzuki	5.00
CM-21	Akinori Otsuka	3.00
CM-22	Koji Uehara	3.00
CM-23	Kosuke Fukudome	5.00
CM-24	Daisuke Matsuzaka	5.00
CM-25	Ichiro Suzuki	5.00
CM-26	Seung-Yeop Lee	2.00
CM-27	Seung-Yeop Lee	2.00
CM-28	Jong Beom Lee	1.50
CM-29	Jae Weong Seo	1.50
CM-30	Chan Ho Park	1.50
CM-31	Hee Seop Choi	1.50
CM-32	Jorge Cantu	1.50
CM-33	Oliver Perez	1.50
CM-34	Vinny Castilla	1.50
CM-35	Esteban Loaiza	1.50
CM-36	Shairon Martis	1.50
CM-37	Bernie Williams	2.00
CM-38	Javier Vazquez	1.50
CM-39	Carlos Beltran	2.00
CM-40	Bernie Williams	2.00
CM-41	Roger Clemens	5.00
CM-42	Ken Griffey Jr.	5.00
CM-43	Alex Rodriguez	5.00
CM-44	Derrek Lee	2.00
CM-45	Derek Jeter	5.00
CM-46	Chipper Jones	2.00
CM-47	Miguel Cabrera	2.00
CM-48	Francisco Rodriguez	1.50
CM-49	Victor Martinez	1.50
CM-50	Freddy Garcia	1.50

1981 Fleer

NM/M
Complete Set (660): 30.00
Common Player: .05
Wax Pack (17): 1.75
Wax Box (38): 50.00
Vending Box (500): 20.00

1	Pete Rose	2.25
2	Larry Bowa	.04
3	Manny Trillo	.05
4	Bob Boone	.04
5a	Mike Schmidt/Portrait	2.00
5b	Mike Schmidt/Btg	1.50
6a	Steve Carlton ("Lefty" on front.)	.70

Card	Player	Price
6b	Steve Carlton (Pitcher of the Year on front, date 1066 on back.)	1.50
6c	Steve Carlton (Pitcher of the Year on front, date 1966 on back.)	2.00
7a	Tug McGraw (Game Saver on front.)	.40
7b	Tug McGraw (Pitcher on front.)	.06
8	Larry Christenson	.05
9	Bake McBride	.05
10	Greg Luzinski	.06
11	Ron Reed	.05
12	Dickie Noles	.05
13	Keith Moreland RC	.11
14	Bob Walk RC	.06
15	Lonnie Smith	.05
16	Dick Ruthven	.05
17	Sparky Lyle	.06
18	Greg Gross	.05
19	Garry Maddox	.06
20	Nino Espinosa	.05
21	George Vukovich	.05
22	John Vukovich	.05
23	Ramon Aviles	.05
24a	Kevin Saucier (Ken Saucier on back.)	.08
24b	Kevin Saucier (Kevin Saucier on back.)	.40
25	Randy Lerch	.05
26	Del Unser	.05
27	Tim McCarver	.11
28a	George Brett/Btg	1.50
28b	George Brett/Portrait	1.50
29a	Willie Wilson/Portrait	.40
29b	Willie Wilson/Btg	.11
30	Paul Splittorff	.05
31	Dan Quisenberry	.06
32a	Amos Otis/Btg	.40
32b	Amos Otis/Portrait	.08
33	Steve Busby	.05
34	U.L. Washington	.05
35	Dave Chalk	.05
36	Darrell Porter	.05
37	Marty Pattin	.05
38	Larry Gura	.05
39	Renie Martin	.05
40	Rich Gale	.05
41a	Hal McRae (Dark blue "Royals" on front.)	.30
41b	Hal McRae (Light blue "Royals" on front.)	.08
42	Dennis Leonard	.05
43	Willie Aikens	.05
44	Frank White	.05
45	Clint Hurdle	.05
46	John Wathan	.05
47	Pete LaCock	.05
48	Rance Mulliniks	.05
49	Jeff Twitty	.05
50	Jamie Quirk	.05
51	Art Howe	.05
52	Ken Forsch	.05
53	Vern Ruhle	.05
54	Joe Niekro	.04
55	Frank LaCorte	.05
56	J.R. Richard	.05
57	Nolan Ryan	3.00
58	Enos Cabell	.05
59	Cesar Cedeno	.04
60	Jose Cruz	.05
61	Bill Virdon	.05
62	Terry Puhl	.05
63	Joaquin Andujar	.05
64	Alan Ashby	.05
65	Joe Sambito	.05
66	Denny Walling	.05
67	Jeff Leonard	.05
68	Luis Pujols	.05
69	Bruce Bochy	.05
70	Rafael Landestoy	.05
71	Dave Smith RC	.05
72	Danny Heep RC	.05
73	Julio Gonzalez	.05
74	Craig Reynolds	.05
75	Gary Woods	.05
76	Dave Bergman	.05
77	Randy Niemann	.05
78	Joe Morgan	.70
79a	Reggie Jackson/Portrait	2.00
79b	Reggie Jackson/Btg	1.50
80	Bucky Dent	.08
81	Tommy John	.08
82	Luis Tiant	.05
83	Rick Cerone	.05
84	Dick Howser	.05
85	Lou Piniella	.08
86	Ron Davis	.05
87a	Graig Nettles (Craig on back.)	3.50
87b	Graig Nettles (Graig on back.)	.11
88	Ron Guidry	.08
89	Rich Gossage	.08
90	Rudy May	.05
91	Gaylord Perry	.60
92	Eric Soderholm	.05
93	Bob Watson	.05
94	Bobby Murcer	.08
95	Bobby Brown	.05
96	Jim Spencer	.05
97	Tom Underwood	.05
98	Oscar Gamble	.05
99	Johnny Oates	.05
100	Fred Stanley	.05
101	Ruppert Jones	.05
102	Dennis Werth	.05
103	Joe Lefebvre	.05
104	Brian Doyle	.05
105	Aurelio Rodriguez	.05
106	Doug Bird	.05
107	Mike Griffin	.05
108	Tim Lollar	.05
109	Willie Randolph	.05
110	Steve Garvey	.25
111	Reggie Smith	.06
112	Don Sutton	.60
113	Burt Hooton	.05
114a	Davy Lopes (Davey) (No finger on back.)	.05
114b	Davy Lopes (Davey) (Small finger on back.)	.40
115	Dusty Baker	.04
116	Tom Lasorda	.08
117	Bill Russell	.06
118	Jerry Reuss	.05
119	Terry Forster	.05
120a	Bob Welch (Bob on back.)	.08
120b	Bob Welch (Robert)	.40
121	Don Stanhouse	.05
122	Rick Monday	.05
123	Derrel Thomas	.05
124	Joe Ferguson	.05
125	Rick Sutcliffe	.08
126a	Ron Cey (Ron finger on back.)	.06
126b	Ron Cey (Small finger on back.)	.40
127	Dave Goltz	.05
128	Jay Johnstone	.05
129	Steve Yeager	.05
130	Gary Weiss	.05
131	Mike Scioscia RC	.40
132	Vic Davalillo	.05
133	Doug Rau	.05
134	Pepe Frias	.05
135	Mickey Hatcher	.05
136	Steve Howe RC	.08
137	Robert Castillo	.05
138	Gary Thomasson	.05
139	Rudy Law	.05
140	Fernando Valenzuela RC	1.25
141	Manny Mota	.05
142	Gary Carter	.70
143	Steve Rogers	.05
144	Warren Cromartie	.05
145	Andre Dawson	.30
146	Larry Parrish	.05
147	Rowland Office	.05
148	Ellis Valentine	.05
149	Dick Williams	.05
150	Bill Gullickson RC	.11
151	Elias Sosa	.05
152	John Tamargo	.05
153	Chris Speier	.05
154	Ron LeFlore	.05
155	Rodney Scott	.05
156	Stan Bahnsen	.05
157	Bill Lee	.06
158	Fred Norman	.05
159	Woodie Fryman	.05
160	Dave Palmer	.05
161	Jerry White	.05
162	Roberto Ramos	.05
163	John D'Acquisto	.05
164	Tommy Hutton	.05
165	Charlie Lea RC	.11
166	Scott Sanderson	.05
167	Ken Macha	.05
168	Tony Bernazard	.05
169	Jim Palmer	.70
170	Steve Stone	.08
171	Mike Flanagan	.05
172	Al Bumbry	.05
173	Doug DeCinces	.05
174	Scott McGregor	.05
175	Mark Belanger	.05
176	Tim Stoddard	.05
177a	Rick Dempsey (No finger on front.)	.05
177b	Rick Dempsey (Small finger on front.)	.40
178	Earl Weaver	.20
179	Tippy Martinez	.05
180	Dennis Martinez	.06
181	Sammy Stewart	.05
182	Rich Dauer	.05
183	Lee May	.05
184	Eddie Murray	.70
185	Benny Ayala	.05
186	John Lowenstein	.05
187	Gary Roenicke	.05
188	Ken Singleton	.06
189	Dan Graham	.05
190	Terry Crowley	.05
191	Kiko Garcia	.05
192	Dave Ford	.05
193	Mark Corey	.05
194	Lenn Sakata	.05
195	Doug DeCinces	.05
196	Johnny Bench	.70
197	Dave Concepcion	.04
198	Ray Knight	.04
199	Ken Griffey	.08
200	Tom Seaver	.70
201	Dave Collins	.05
202	George Foster	.04
203	Junior Kennedy	.05
204	Frank Pastore	.05
205	Dan Driessen	.06
206	Hector Cruz	.05
207	Paul Moskau	.05
208	Charlie Leibrandt RC	.20
209	Harry Spilman	.05
210	Joe Price RC	.05
211	Tom Hume	.05
212	Joe Nolan	.05
213	Doug Bair	.05
214	Mario Soto	.05
215a	Bill Bonham (No finger on back.)	.05
215b	Bill Bonham (Small finger on back.)	.40
216a	George Foster (Slugger on front.)	.20
216b	George Foster (Outfield on front.)	.11
217	Paul Householder	.05
218	Ron Oester	.05
219	Sam Mejias	.05
220	Sheldon Burnside	.05
221	Carl Yastrzemski	.70
222	Jim Rice	.30
223	Fred Lynn	.04
224	Carlton Fisk	.70
225	Rick Burleson	.05
226	Dennis Eckersley	.60
227	Butch Hobson	.05
228	Tom Burgmeier	.05
229	Garry Hancock	.05
230	Don Zimmer	.05
231	Steve Renko	.05
232	Dwight Evans	.04
233	Mike Torrez	.05
234	Bob Stanley	.05
235	Jim Dwyer	.05
236	Dave Stapleton	.05
237	Glenn Hoffman	.05
238	Jerry Remy	.05
239	Dick Drago	.05
240	Bill Campbell	.05
241	Tony Perez	.60
242	Phil Niekro	.60
243	Dale Murphy	.25
244	Bob Horner	.04
245	Jeff Burroughs	.05
246	Rick Camp	.05
247	Bob Cox	.20
248	Bruce Benedict	.05
249	Gene Garber	.05
250	Jerry Royster	.05
251a	Gary Matthews (No finger on back.)	.05
251b	Gary Matthews (Small finger on back.)	.40
252	Chris Chambliss	.05
253	Luis Gomez	.05
254	Bill Nahorodny	.05
255	Doyle Alexander	.05
256	Brian Asselstine	.05
257	Biff Pocoroba	.05
258	Mike Lum	.05
259	Charlie Spikes	.05
260	Glenn Hubbard	.06
261	Tommy Boggs	.05
262	Al Hrabosky	.05
263	Rick Matula	.05
264	Preston Hanna	.05
265	Larry Bradford	.05
266	Rafael Ramirez RC	.05
267	Larry McWilliams	.05
268	Rod Carew	.70
269	Bobby Grich	.04
270	Carney Lansford	.05
271	Don Baylor	.04
272	Joe Rudi	.05
273	Dan Ford	.05
274	Jim Fregosi	.06
275	Dave Frost	.05
276	Frank Tanana	.05
277	Dickie Thon	.05
278	Jason Thompson	.05
279	Rick Miller	.05
280	Bert Campaneris	.05
281	Tom Donohue	.05
282	Brian Downing	.05
283	Fred Patek	.05
284	Bruce Kison	.05
285	Dave LaRoche	.05
286	Don Aase	.05
287	Jim Barr	.05
288	Alfredo Martinez	.05
289	Larry Harlow	.05
290	Andy Hassler	.05
291	Dave Kingman	.04
292	Bill Buckner	.04
293	Rick Reuschel	.05
294	Bruce Sutter	.60
295	Jerry Martin	.05
296	Scot Thompson	.05
297	Ivan DeJesus	.05
298	Steve Dillard	.05
299	Dick Tidrow	.05
300	Randy Martz	.05
301	Lenny Randle	.05
302	Lynn McGlothen	.05
303	Cliff Johnson	.05
304	Tim Blackwell	.05
305	Dennis Lamp	.05
306	Bill Caudill	.05
307	Carlos Lezcano	.05
308	Jim Tracy	.06
309	Doug Capilla	.05
310	Willie Hernandez	.05
311	Mike Vail	.05
312	Mike Krukow	.05
313	Barry Foote	.05
314	Larry Biittner	.05
315	Mike Tyson	.05
316	Lee Mazzilli	.05
317	John Stearns	.05
318	Alex Trevino	.05
319	Craig Swan	.05
320	Frank Taveras	.05
321	Steve Henderson	.05
322	Neil Allen	.05
323	Mark Bomback	.05
324	Mike Jorgensen	.05
325	Joe Torre	.20
326	Elliott Maddox	.05
327	Pete Falcone	.05
328	Ray Burris	.05
329	Claudell Washington	.05
330	Doug Flynn	.05
331	Joel Youngblood	.05
332	Bill Almon	.05
333	Tom Hausman	.05
334	Pat Zachry	.05
335	Jeff Reardon RC	1.50
336	Wally Backman RC	.11
337	Dan Norman	.05
338	Jerry Morales	.05
339	Ed Farmer	.05
340	Bob Molinaro	.05
341	Todd Cruz	.05
342a	Britt Burns RC (No finger on front.)	.08
342b	Britt Burns RC (Small finger on front.)	.40
343	Kevin Bell	.05
344	Tony LaRussa	.20
345	Steve Trout	.05
346	Harold Baines RC	2.25
347	Richard Wortham	.05
348	Wayne Nordhagen	.05
349	Mike Squires	.05
350	Lamar Johnson	.05
351	Rickey Henderson	2.00
352	Francisco Barrios	.05
353	Thad Bosley	.05
354	Chet Lemon	.05
355	Bruce Kimm	.05
356	Richard Dotson RC	.05
357	Jim Morrison	.05
358	Mike Proly	.05
359	Greg Pryor	.05
360	Dave Parker	.04
361	Omar Moreno	.05
362a	Kent Tekulve (1071 Waterbury on back)	.11
362b	Kent Tekulve (1971 Waterbury on back)	.40
363	Willie Stargell	.70
364	Phil Garner	.05
365	Ed Ott	.05
366	Don Robinson	.05
367	Chuck Tanner	.05
368	Jim Rooker	.05
369	Dale Berra	.05
370	Jim Bibby	.05
371	Steve Nicosia	.05
372	Mike Easler	.05

373	Bill Robinson	.05
374	Lee Lacy	.05
375	John Candelaria	.05
376	Manny Sanguillen	.05
377	Rick Rhoden	.05
378	Grant Jackson	.05
379	Tim Foli	.05
380	Rod Scurry **RC**	.05
381	Bill Madlock	.04
382a	Kurt Bevacqua (Photo reversed, backwards "P" on cap.)	.11
382b	Kurt Bevacqua (Correct photo.)	.40
383	Bert Blyleven	.08
384	Eddie Solomon	.05
385	Enrique Romo	.05
386	John Milner	.05
387	Mike Hargrove	.05
388	Jorge Orta	.05
389	Toby Harrah	.06
390	Tom Veryzer	.05
391	Miguel Dilone	.05
392	Dan Spillner	.05
393	Jack Brohamer	.05
394	Wayne Garland	.05
395	Sid Monge	.05
396	Rick Waits	.05
397	Joe Charboneau **RC**	.40
398	Gary Alexander	.05
399	Jerry Dybzinski	.05
400	Mike Stanton	.05
401	Mike Paxton	.05
402	Gary Gray	.05
403	Rick Manning	.05
404	Bo Diaz	.05
405	Ron Hassey	.05
406	Ross Grimsley	.05
407	Victor Cruz	.05
408	Len Barker	.05
409	Bob Bailor	.05
410	Otto Velez	.05
411	Ernie Whitt	.05
412	Jim Clancy	.05
413	Barry Bonnell	.05
414	Dave Stieb	.04
415	Damaso Garcia **RC**	.08
416	John Mayberry	.05
417	Roy Howell	.05
418	Dan Ainge **RC**	2.25
419a	Jesse Jefferson (Pirates on back.)	.08
419b	Jesse Jefferson (Blue Jays on back.)	.40
420	Joey McLaughlin	.05
421	Lloyd Moseby **RC**	.08
422	Al Woods	.05
423	Garth Iorg	.05
424	Doug Ault	.05
425	Ken Schrom **RC**	.05
426	Mike Willis	.05
427	Steve Braun	.05
428	Bob Davis	.05
429	Jerry Garvin	.05
430	Alfredo Griffin	.05
431	Bob Mattick	.05
432	Vida Blue	.04
433	Jack Clark	.04
434	Willie McCovey	.70
435	Mike Ivie	.05
436a	Darrel Evans (Darrel on front.)	.11
436b	Darrell Evans (Darrell on front.)	.40
437	Terry Whitfield	.05
438	Rennie Stennett	.05
439	John Montefusco	.05
440	Jim Wohlford	.05
441	Bill North	.05
442	Milt May	.05
443	Max Venable	.05
444	Ed Whitson	.05
445	Al Holland **RC**	.05
446	Randy Moffitt	.05
447	Bob Knepper	.06
448	Gary Lavelle	.05
449	Greg Minton	.05
450	Johnnie LeMaster	.05
451	Larry Herndon	.05
452	Rich Murray	.05
453	Joe Pettini	.05
454	Allen Ripley	.05
455	Dennis Littlejohn	.05
456	Tom Griffin	.05
457	Alan Hargesheimer	.05
458	Joe Strain	.05
459	Steve Kemp	.05
460	Sparky Anderson	.20
461	Alan Trammell	.04
462	Mark Fidrych	.05
463	Lou Whitaker	.04
464	Dave Rozema	.05
465	Milt Wilcox	.05
466	Champ Summers	.05

467	Lance Parrish	.04
468	Dan Petry	.05
469	Pat Underwood	.05
470	Rick Peters	.05
471	Al Cowens	.05
472	John Wockenfuss	.05
473	Tom Brookens	.05
474	Richie Hebner	.05
475	Jack Morris	.04
476	Jim Lentine	.05
477	Bruce Robbins	.05
478	Mark Wagner	.05
479	Tim Corcoran	.05
480a	Stan Papi (Pitcher on front.)	.11
480b	Stan Papi (Shortstop on front.)	.40
481	Kirk Gibson **RC**	3.75
482	Dan Schatzeder	.05
483	Amos Otis	.04
484	Dave Winfield	.70
485	Rollie Fingers	.60
486	Gene Richards	.05
487	Randy Jones	.05
488	Ozzie Smith	1.50
489	Gene Tenace	.05
490	Bill Fahey	.05
491	John Curtis	.05
492	Dave Cash	.05
493a	Tim Flannery (Photo reversed, batting righty.)	.11
493b	Tim Flannery (Photo correct, batting lefty.)	.40
494	Jerry Mumphrey	.05
495	Bob Shirley	.05
496	Steve Mura	.05
497	Eric Rasmussen	.05
498	Broderick Perkins	.05
499	Barry Evans	.05
500	Chuck Baker	.05
501	Luis Salazar **RC**	.06
502	Gary Lucas	.05
503	Mike Armstrong	.05
504	Jerry Turner	.05
505	Dennis Kinney	.05
506	Willy Montanez (Willie)	.05
507	Gorman Thomas	.05
508	Ben Oglivie	.05
509	Larry Hisle	.05
510	Sal Bando	.05
511	Robin Yount	.70
512	Mike Caldwell	.05
513	Sixto Lezcano	.05
514a	Jerry Augustine (Billy Travers photo.)	.11
514b	Billy Travers (Correct name with photo.)	.40
515	Paul Molitor	.70
516	Moose Haas	.05
517	Bill Castro	.05
518	Jim Slaton	.05
519	Lary Sorensen	.05
520	Bob McClure	.05
521	Charlie Moore	.05
522	Jim Gantner	.05
523	Reggie Cleveland	.05
524	Don Money	.05
525	Billy Travers	.05
526	Buck Martinez	.05
527	Dick Davis	.05
528	Ted Simmons	.05
529	Garry Templeton	.05
530	Ken Reitz	.05
531	Tony Scott	.05
532	Ken Oberkfell	.05
533	Bob Sykes	.05
534	Keith Smith	.05
535	John Littlefield	.05
536	Jim Kaat	.04
537	Bob Forsch	.05
538	Mike Phillips	.05
539	Terry Landrum **RC**	.05
540	Leon Durham **RC**	.08
541	Terry Kennedy	.05
542	George Hendrick	.05
543	Dane Iorg	.05
544	Mark Littell (Photo actually Jeff Little.)	.05
545	Keith Hernandez	.05
546	Silvio Martinez	.05
547a	Pete Vuckovich (Photo actually Don Hood.)	.11
547b	Don Hood (Correct name with photo.)	.40
548	Bobby Bonds	.08
549	Mike Ramsey	.05
550	Tom Herr	.05
551	Roy Smalley	.05
552	Jerry Koosman	.05
553	Ken Landreaux	.05
554	John Castino	.05
555	Doug Corbett	.05
556	Bombo Rivera	.05
557	Ron Jackson	.05

558	Butch Wynegar	.05
559	Hosken Powell	.05
560	Pete Redfern	.05
561	Roger Erickson	.05
562	Glenn Adams	.05
563	Rick Sofield	.05
564	Geoff Zahn	.05
565	Pete Mackanin	.05
566	Mike Cubbage	.05
567	Darrell Jackson	.05
568	Dave Edwards	.05
569	Rob Wilfong	.05
570	Sal Butera	.05
571	Jose Morales	.05
572	Rick Langford	.05
573	Mike Norris	.05
574	Rickey Henderson	2.00
575	Tony Armas	.05
576	Dave Revering	.05
577	Jeff Newman	.05
578	Bob Lacey	.05
579	Brian Kingman (Photo actually Alan Wirth.)	.05
580	Mitchell Page	.05
581	Billy Martin	.20
582	Rob Picciolo	.05
583	Mike Heath	.05
584	Mickey Klutts	.05
585	Orlando Gonzalez	.05
586	Mike Davis **RC**	.05
587	Wayne Gross	.05
588	Matt Keough	.05
589	Steve McCatty	.05
590	Dwayne Murphy	.05
591	Mario Guerrero	.05
592	Dave McKay	.05
593	Jim Essian	.05
594	Dave Heaverlo	.05
595	Maury Wills	.08
596	Juan Beniquez	.05
597	Rodney Craig	.05
598	Jim Anderson	.05
599	Floyd Bannister	.05
600	Bruce Bochte	.05
601	Julio Cruz	.05
602	Ted Cox	.05
603	Dan Meyer	.05
604	Larry Cox	.05
605	Bill Stein	.05
606	Steve Garvey	.25
607	Dave Roberts	.05
608	Leon Roberts	.05
609	Reggie Walton	.05
610	Dave Edler	.05
611	Larry Milbourne	.05
612	Kim Allen	.05
613	Mario Mendoza	.05
614	Tom Paciorek	.05
615	Glenn Abbott	.05
616	Joe Simpson	.05
617	Mickey Rivers	.05
618	Jim Kern	.05
619	Jim Sundberg	.05
620	Richie Zisk	.06
621	Jon Matlack	.06
622	Fergie Jenkins	.60
623	Pat Corrales	.05
624	Ed Figueroa	.05
625	Buddy Bell	.04
626	Al Oliver	.04
627	Doc Medich	.05
628	Bump Wills	.05
629	Rusty Staub	.04
630	Pat Putnam	.05
631	John Grubb	.05
632	Danny Darwin	.05
633	Ken Clay	.05
634	Jim Norris	.05
635	John Butcher	.05
636	Dave Roberts	.05
637	Billy Sample	.05
638	Carl Yastrzemski	.70
639	Cecil Cooper	.05
640	Mike Schmidt	1.50
641a	Checklist 1-50 (41 Hal McRae.)	.08
641b	Checklist 1-50 (41 Hal McRae Double Threat)	.08
642	Checklist 51-109	.05
643	Checklist 110-168	.05
644a	Checklist 169-220 (202 George Foster)	.08
644b	Checklist 169-220 (202 George Foster "Slugger")	.08
(645a)	Larry Bowa, Pete Rose, Mike Schmidt Triple Threat (No number on back.)	1.50
645b	Pete Rose, Larry Bowa, Mike Schmidt Triple Threat (Number on back.)	1.50
646	Checklist 221-267	.05
647	Checklist 268-315	.05
648	Checklist 316-359	.05

649	Checklist 360-408	.05
650	Reggie Jackson	1.50
651	Checklist 409-458	.05
652a	Checklist 459-509 (483 Aurelio Lopez)	.08
652b	Checklist 459-506 (No 483.)	.08
653	Willie Wilson	.04
654a	Checklist 507-550 (514 Jerry Augustine)	.08
654b	Checklist 507-550 (514 Billy Travers)	.08
655	George Brett	2.25
656	Checklist 551-593	.05
657	Tug McGraw	.05
658	Checklist 594-637	.05
659a	Checklist 640-660 (Last number on front is 551.)	.08
659b	Checklist 640-660 (Last number on front is 483.)	.11
660a	Steve Carlton (Date 1066 on back.)	.70
660b	Steve Carlton (Date 1966 on back.)	1.50

1982 Fleer

Tom Herr
CARDINALS • SECOND BASE

	NM/M
Complete Set (660):	45.00
Common Player:	.05
Wax Pack (15):	3.00
Wax Box (36):	85.00
Cello Pack (28):	4.00
Cello Box (24):	85.00
Vending Box (500):	40.00

1	Dusty Baker	.05
2	Robert Castillo	.05
3	Ron Cey	.05
4	Terry Forster	.05
5	Steve Garvey	.30
6	Dave Goltz	.05
7	Pedro Guerrero	.05
8	Burt Hooton	.05
9	Steve Howe	.05
10	Jay Johnstone	.05
11	Ken Landreaux	.05
12	Davey Lopes	.05
13	Mike Marshall **RC**	.15
14	Bobby Mitchell	.05
15	Rick Monday	.05
16	Tom Niedenfuer **RC**	.05
17	Ted Power **RC**	.05
18	Jerry Reuss	.05
19	Ron Roenicke	.05
20	Bill Russell	.05
21	Steve Sax **RC**	.45
22	Mike Scioscia	.05
23	Reggie Smith	.05
24	Dave Stewart **RC**	1.50
25	Rick Sutcliffe	.05
26	Derrel Thomas	.05
27	Fernando Valenzuela	.10
28	Bob Welch	.05
29	Steve Yeager	.05
30	Bobby Brown	.05
31	Rick Cerone	.05
32	Ron Davis	.05
33	Bucky Dent	.10
34	Barry Foote	.05
35	George Frazier	.05
36	Oscar Gamble	.05
37	Rich Gossage	.10
38	Ron Guidry	.10
39	Reggie Jackson	1.50
40	Tommy John	.10
41	Rudy May	.05
42	Larry Milbourne	.05
43	Jerry Mumphrey	.05
44	Bobby Murcer	.10
45	Gene Nelson **RC**	.05
46	Graig Nettles	.10
47	Johnny Oates	.05
48	Lou Piniella	.10
49	Willie Randolph	.05

No.	Player	Value	No.	Player	Value	No.	Player	Value	No.	Player	Value
50	Rick Reuschel	.05	154	Gorman Thomas	.05	257	Dick Ruthven	.05	361	Bert Blyleven	.10
51	Dave Revering	.05	155	Robin Yount	1.00	258	Mike Schmidt	2.00	362	Joe Charboneau	.10
52	Dave Righetti RC	.45	156	Pete Vukovich	.05	259	Lonnie Smith	.05	363	John Denny	.05
53	Aurelio Rodriguez	.05	157	Benny Ayala	.05	260	Manny Trillo	.05	364	Bo Diaz	.05
54	Bob Watson	.05	158	Mark Belanger	.05	261	Del Unser	.05	365	Miguel Dilone	.05
55	Dennis Werth	.05	159	Al Bumbry	.05	262	George Vukovich	.05	366	Jerry Dybzinski	.05
56	Dave Winfield	1.00	160	Terry Crowley	.05	263	Tom Brookens	.05	367	Wayne Garland	.05
57	Johnny Bench	1.00	161	Rich Dauer	.05	264	George Cappuzzello	.05	368	Mike Hargrove	.05
58	Bruce Berenyi	.05	162	Doug DeCinces	.05	265	Marty Castillo	.05	369	Toby Harrah	.05
59	Larry Biittner	.05	163	Rick Dempsey	.05	266	Al Cowens	.05	370	Ron Hassey	.05
60	Scott Brown	.05	164	Jim Dwyer	.05	267	Kirk Gibson	.05	371	Von Hayes RC	.25
61	Dave Collins	.05	165	Mike Flanagan	.05	268	Richie Hebner	.05	372	Pat Kelly	.05
62	Geoff Combe	.05	166	Dave Ford	.05	269	Ron Jackson	.05	373	Duane Kuiper	.05
63	Dave Concepcion	.05	167	Dan Graham	.05	270	Lynn Jones	.05	374	Rick Manning	.05
64	Dan Driessen	.05	168	Wayne Krenchicki	.05	271	Steve Kemp	.05	375	Sid Monge	.05
65	Joe Edelen	.05	169	John Lowenstein	.05	272	Rick Leach RC	.25	376	Jorge Orta	.05
66	George Foster	.05	170	Dennis Martinez	.05	273	Aurelio Lopez	.05	377	Dave Rosello	.05
67	Ken Griffey	.05	171	Tippy Martinez	.05	274	Jack Morris	.05	378	Dan Spillner	.05
68	Paul Householder	.05	172	Scott McGregor	.05	275	Kevin Saucier	.05	379	Mike Stanton	.05
69	Tom Hume	.05	173	Jose Morales	.05	276	Lance Parrish	.05	380	Andre Thornton	.05
70	Junior Kennedy	.05	174	Eddie Murray	1.00	277	Rick Peters	.05	381	Tom Veryzer	.05
71	Ray Knight	.05	175	Jim Palmer	1.00	278	Dan Petry	.05	382	Rick Waits	.05
72	Mike LaCoss	.05	176	Cal Ripken, Jr. RC	40.00	279	David Rozema	.05	383	Doyle Alexander	.05
73	Rafael Landestoy	.05	177	Gary Roenicke	.05	280	Stan Papi	.05	384	Vida Blue	.05
74	Charlie Leibrandt	.05	178	Lenn Sakata	.05	281	Dan Schatzeder	.05	385	Fred Breining	.05
75	Sam Mejias	.05	179	Ken Singleton	.05	282	Champ Summers	.05	386	Enos Cabell	.05
76	Paul Moskau	.05	180	Sammy Stewart	.05	283	Alan Trammell	.05	387	Jack Clark	.05
77	Joe Nolan	.05	181	Tim Stoddard	.05	284	Lou Whitaker	.05	388	Darrell Evans	.05
78	Mike O'Berry	.05	182	Steve Stone	.05	285	Milt Wilcox	.05	389	Tom Griffin	.05
79	Ron Oester	.05	183	Stan Bahnsen	.05	286	John Wockenfuss	.05	390	Larry Herndon	.05
80	Frank Pastore	.05	184	Ray Burris	.05	287	Gary Allenson	.05	391	Al Holland	.05
81	Joe Price	.05	185	Gary Carter	1.00	288	Tom Burgmeier	.05	392	Gary Lavelle	.05
82	Tom Seaver	1.00	186	Warren Cromartie	.05	289	Bill Campbell	.05	393	Johnnie LeMaster	.05
83	Mario Soto	.05	187	Andre Dawson	.50	290	Mark Clear	.05	394	Jerry Martin	.05
84	Mike Vail	.05	188	Terry Francona RC	.05	291	Steve Crawford	.05	395	Milt May	.05
85	Tony Armas	.05	189	Woodie Fryman	.05	292	Dennis Eckersley	.75	396	Greg Minton	.05
86	Shooty Babitt	.05	190	Bill Gullickson	.05	293	Dwight Evans	.05	397	Joe Morgan	1.00
87	Dave Beard	.05	191	Grant Jackson	.05	294	Rich Gedman RC	.10	398	Joe Pettini	.05
88	Rick Bosetti	.05	192	Wallace Johnson	.05	295	Garry Hancock	.05	399	Alan Ripley	.05
89	Keith Drumright	.05	193	Charlie Lea	.05	296	Glenn Hoffman	.05	400	Billy Smith	.05
90	Wayne Gross	.05	194	Bill Lee	.05	297	Bruce Hurst	.05	401	Rennie Stennett	.05
91	Mike Heath	.05	195	Jerry Manuel	.05	298	Carney Lansford	.05	402	Ed Whitson	.05
92	Rickey Henderson	1.00	196	Brad Mills	.05	299	Rick Miller	.05	403	Jim Wohlford	.05
93	Cliff Johnson	.05	197	John Milner	.05	300	Reid Nichols	.05	404	Willie Aikens	.05
94	Jeff Jones	.05	198	Rowland Office	.05	301	Bob Ojeda RC	.25	405	George Brett	2.00
95	Matt Keough	.05	199	David Palmer	.05	302	Tony Perez	.75	406	Ken Brett	.05
96	Brian Kingman	.05	200	Larry Parrish	.05	303	Chuck Rainey	.05	407	Dave Chalk	.05
97	Mickey Klutts	.05	201	Mike Phillips	.05	304	Jerry Remy	.05	408	Rich Gale	.05
98	Rick Langford	.05	202	Tim Raines	.25	305	Jim Rice	.50	409	Cesar Geronimo	.05
99	Steve McCatty	.05	203	Bobby Ramos	.05	306	Joe Rudi	.05	410	Larry Gura	.05
100	Dave McKay	.05	204	Jeff Reardon	.05	307	Bob Stanley	.05	411	Clint Hurdle	.05
101	Dwayne Murphy	.05	205	Steve Rogers	.05	308	Dave Stapleton	.05	412	Mike Jones	.05
102	Jeff Newman	.05	206	Scott Sanderson	.05	309	Frank Tanana	.05	413	Dennis Leonard	.05
103	Mike Norris	.05	207	Rodney Scott (Photo actually Tim Raines.)	.10	310	Mike Torrez	.05	414	Renie Martin	.05
104	Bob Owchinko	.05	208	Elias Sosa	.05	311	John Tudor	.05	415	Lee May	.05
105	Mitchell Page	.05	209	Chris Speier	.05	312	Carl Yastrzemski	1.00	416	Hal McRae	.05
106	Rob Picciolo	.05	210	Tim Wallach RC	1.00	313	Buddy Bell	.05	417	Darryl Motley	.05
107	Jim Spencer	.05	211	Jerry White	.05	314	Steve Comer	.05	418	Rance Mulliniks	.05
108	Fred Stanley	.05	212	Alan Ashby	.05	315	Danny Darwin	.05	419	Amos Otis	.05
109	Tom Underwood	.05	213	Cesar Cedeno	.05	316	John Ellis	.05	420	Ken Phelps RC	.05
110	Joaquin Andujar	.05	214	Jose Cruz	.05	317	John Grubb	.05	421	Jamie Quirk	.05
111	Steve Braun	.05	215	Kiko Garcia	.05	318	Rick Honeycutt	.05	422	Dan Quisenberry	.05
112	Bob Forsch	.05	216	Phil Garner	.05	319	Charlie Hough	.05	423	Paul Splittorff	.05
113	George Hendrick	.05	217	Danny Heep	.05	320	Fergie Jenkins	.75	424	U.L. Washington	.05
114	Keith Hernandez	.05	218	Art Howe	.05	321	John Henry Johnson	.05	425	John Wathan	.05
115	Tom Herr	.05	219	Bob Knepper	.05	322	Jim Kern	.05	426	Frank White	.05
116	Dane Iorg	.05	220	Frank LaCorte	.05	323	Jon Matlack	.05	427	Willie Wilson	.05
117	Jim Kaat	.10	221	Joe Niekro	.05	324	Doc Medich	.05	428	Brian Asselstine	.05
118	Tito Landrum	.05	222	Joe Pittman	.05	325	Mario Mendoza	.05	429	Bruce Benedict	.05
119	Sixto Lezcano	.05	223	Terry Puhl	.05	326	Al Oliver	.05	430	Tom Boggs	.05
120	Mark Littell	.05	224	Luis Pujols	.05	327	Pat Putnam	.05	431	Larry Bradford	.05
121	John Martin	.05	225	Craig Reynolds	.05	328	Mickey Rivers	.05	432	Rick Camp	.05
122	Silvio Martinez	.05	226	J.R. Richard	.05	329	Leon Roberts	.05	433	Chris Chambliss	.05
123	Ken Oberkfell	.05	227	Dave Roberts	.05	330	Billy Sample	.05	434	Gene Garber	.05
124	Darrell Porter	.05	228	Vern Ruhle	.05	331	Bill Stein	.05	435	Preston Hanna	.05
125	Mike Ramsey	.05	229	Nolan Ryan	3.00	332	Jim Sundberg	.05	436	Bob Horner	.05
126	Orlando Sanchez	.05	230	Joe Sambito	.05	333	Mark Wagner	.05	437	Glenn Hubbard	.05
127	Bob Shirley	.05	231	Tony Scott	.05	334	Bump Wills	.05	438a	Al Hrabosky (All Hrabosky, 5'1" on back.)	4.50
128	Lary Sorensen	.05	232	Dave Smith	.05	335	Bill Almon	.05	438b	Al Hrabosky (Al Hrabosky, 5'1" on back.)	1.00
129	Bruce Sutter	.75	233	Harry Spilman	.05	336	Harold Baines	.05	438c	Al Hrabosky (Al Hrabosky, 5'10" on back.)	.25
130	Bob Sykes	.05	234	Don Sutton	.75	337	Ross Baumgarten	.05	439	Rufino Linares	.05
131	Garry Templeton	.05	235	Dickie Thon	.05	338	Tony Bernazard	.05	440	Rick Mahler RC	.05
132	Gene Tenace	.05	236	Denny Walling	.05	339	Britt Burns	.05	441	Ed Miller	.05
133	Jerry Augustine	.05	237	Gary Woods	.05	340	Richard Dotson	.05	442	John Montefusco	.05
134	Sal Bando	.05	238	Luis Aguayo RC	.05	341	Jim Essian	.05	443	Dale Murphy	.50
135	Mark Brouhard	.05	239	Ramon Aviles	.05	342	Ed Farmer	.05	444	Phil Niekro	.75
136	Mike Caldwell	.05	240	Bob Boone	.05	343	Carlton Fisk	1.00	445	Gaylord Perry	.75
137	Reggie Cleveland	.05	241	Larry Bowa	.05	344	Kevin Hickey	.05	446	Biff Pocoroba	.05
138	Cecil Cooper	.05	242	Warren Brusstar	.05	345	Lamarr Hoyt (LaMarr)	.05	447	Rafael Ramirez	.05
139	Jamie Easterly	.05	243	Steve Carlton	1.00	346	Lamar Johnson	.05	448	Jerry Royster	.05
140	Marshall Edwards	.05	244	Larry Christenson	.05	347	Jerry Koosman	.05	449	Claudell Washington	.05
141	Rollie Fingers	.75	245	Dick Davis	.05	348	Rusty Kuntz	.05	450	Don Aase	.05
142	Jim Gantner	.05	246	Greg Gross	.05	349	Dennis Lamp	.05	451	Don Baylor	.05
143	Moose Haas	.05	247	Sparky Lyle	.05	350	Ron LeFlore	.05	452	Juan Beniquez	.05
144	Larry Hisle	.05	248	Garry Maddox	.05	351	Chet Lemon	.05	453	Rick Burleson	.05
145	Roy Howell	.05	249	Gary Matthews	.05	352	Greg Luzinski	.05	454	Bert Campaneris	.05
146	Rickey Keeton	.05	250	Bake McBride	.05	353	Bob Molinaro	.05	455	Rod Carew	1.00
147	Randy Lerch	.05	251	Tug McGraw	.05	354	Jim Morrison	.05	456	Bob Clark	.05
148	Paul Molitor	1.00	252	Keith Moreland	.05	355	Wayne Nordhagen	.05	457	Brian Downing	.05
149	Don Money	.05	253	Dickie Noles	.05	356	Greg Pryor	.05	458	Dan Ford	.05
150	Charlie Moore	.05	254	Mike Proly	.05	357	Mike Squires	.05	459	Ken Forsch	.05
151	Ben Oglivie	.05	255	Ron Reed	.05	358	Steve Trout	.05			
152	Ted Simmons	.05	256	Pete Rose	2.50	359	Alan Bannister	.05			
153	Jim Slaton	.05				360	Len Barker	.05			

460	Dave Frost	.05
461	Bobby Grich	.05
462	Larry Harlow	.05
463	John Harris	.05
464	Andy Hassler	.05
465	Butch Hobson	.05
466	Jesse Jefferson	.05
467	Bruce Kison	.05
468	Fred Lynn	.05
469	Angel Moreno	.05
470	Ed Ott	.05
471	Fred Patek	.05
472	Steve Renko	.05
473	Mike Witt RC	.10
474	Geoff Zahn	.05
475	Gary Alexander	.05
476	Dale Berra	.05
477	Kurt Bevacqua	.05
478	Jim Bibby	.05
479	John Candelaria	.05
480	Victor Cruz	.05
481	Mike Easler	.05
482	Tim Foli	.05
483	Lee Lacy	.05
484	Vance Law	.05
485	Bill Madlock	.05
486	Willie Montanez	.05
487	Omar Moreno	.05
488	Steve Nicosia	.05
489	Dave Parker	.05
490	Tony Pena	.05
491	Pascual Perez	.05
492	Johnny Ray RC	.05
493	Rick Rhoden	.05
494	Bill Robinson	.05
495	Don Robinson	.05
496	Enrique Romo	.05
497	Rod Scurry	.05
498	Eddie Solomon	.05
499	Willie Stargell	1.00
500	Kent Tekulve	.05
501	Jason Thompson	.05
502	Glenn Abbott	.05
503	Jim Anderson	.05
504	Floyd Bannister	.05
505	Bruce Bochte	.05
506	Jeff Burroughs	.05
507	Bryan Clark	.05
508	Ken Clay	.05
509	Julio Cruz	.05
510	Dick Drago	.05
511	Gary Gray	.05
512	Dan Meyer	.05
513	Jerry Narron	.05
514	Tom Paciorek	.05
515	Casey Parsons	.05
516	Lenny Randle	.05
517	Shane Rawley	.05
518	Joe Simpson	.05
519	Richie Zisk	.05
520	Neil Allen	.05
521	Bob Bailor	.05
522	Hubie Brooks	.05
523	Mike Cubbage	.05
524	Pete Falcone	.05
525	Doug Flynn	.05
526	Tom Hausman	.05
527	Ron Hodges	.05
528	Randy Jones	.05
529	Mike Jorgensen	.05
530	Dave Kingman	.05
531	Ed Lynch	.05
532	Mike Marshall	.05
533	Lee Mazzilli	.05
534	Dyar Miller	.05
535	Mike Scott	.05
536	Rusty Staub	.05
537	John Stearns	.05
538	Craig Swan	.05
539	Frank Taveras	.05
540	Alex Trevino	.05
541	Ellis Valentine	.05
542	Mookie Wilson	.05
543	Joel Youngblood	.05
544	Pat Zachry	.05
545	Glenn Adams	.05
546	Fernando Arroyo	.05
547	John Verhoeven	.05
548	Sal Butera	.05
549	John Castino	.05
550	Don Cooper	.05
551	Doug Corbett	.05
552	Dave Engle	.05
553	Roger Erickson	.05
554	Danny Goodwin	.05
555a	Darrell Jackson (Black cap.)	.65
555b	Darrell Jackson (Red cap w/speck of white.)	3.00
555c	Darrell Jackson (Red cap w/white T.)	.10
556	Pete Mackanin	.05
557	Jack O'Connor	.05
558	Hosken Powell	.05
559	Pete Redfern	.05
560	Roy Smalley	.05
561	Chuck Baker	.05
562	Gary Ward	.05
563	Rob Wilfong	.05
564	Al Williams	.05
565	Butch Wynegar	.05
566	Randy Bass	.05
567	Juan Bonilla	.05
568	Danny Boone	.05
569	John Curtis	.05
570	Juan Eichelberger	.05
571	Barry Evans	.05
572	Tim Flannery	.05
573	Ruppert Jones	.05
574	Terry Kennedy	.05
575	Joe Lefebvre	.05
576a	John Littlefield (Pitching lefty.)	80.00
576b	John Littlefield (Pitching righty.)	.05
577	Gary Lucas	.05
578	Steve Mura	.05
579	Broderick Perkins	.05
580	Gene Richards	.05
581	Luis Salazar	.05
582	Ozzie Smith	1.50
583	John Urrea	.05
584	Chris Welsh	.05
585	Rick Wise	.05
586	Doug Bird	.05
587	Tim Blackwell	.05
588	Bobby Bonds	.10
589	Bill Buckner	.05
590	Bill Caudill	.05
591	Hector Cruz	.05
592	Jody Davis RC	.10
593	Ivan DeJesus	.05
594	Steve Dillard	.05
595	Leon Durham	.05
596	Rawly Eastwick	.05
597	Steve Henderson	.05
598	Mike Krukow	.05
599	Mike Lum	.05
600	Randy Martz	.05
601	Jerry Morales	.05
602	Ken Reitz	.05
603a	Lee Smith RC (Cubs logo reversed on back.)	2.50
603b	Lee Smith RC (Corrected)	2.50
604	Dick Tidrow	.05
605	Jim Tracy	.05
606	Mike Tyson	.05
607	Ty Waller	.05
608	Danny Ainge	.05
609	Jorge Bell RC	1.00
610	Mark Bomback	.05
611	Barry Bonnell	.05
612	Jim Clancy	.05
613	Damaso Garcia	.05
614	Jerry Garvin	.05
615	Alfredo Griffin	.05
616	Garth Iorg	.05
617	Luis Leal	.05
618	Ken Macha	.05
619	Jim Mayberry	.05
620	Joey McLaughlin	.05
621	Lloyd Moseby	.05
622	Dave Stieb	.05
623	Jackson Todd	.05
624	Willie Upshaw (RC)	.05
625	Otto Velez	.05
626	Ernie Whitt	.05
627	Al Woods	.05
628	1981 All-Star Game	.05
629	Bucky Dent, Frank White All-Star Infielders	.05
630	Dave Concepcion, Dan Driessen, George Foster Big Red Machine	.10
631	Bruce Sutter Top N.L. Relief Pitcher	.30
632	Steve Carlton, Carlton Fisk Steve & Carlton	.25
633	Carl Yastrzemski 3000th Game, May 25, 1981	.35
634	Johnny Bench, Tom Seaver Dynamic Duo	.30
635	Gary Carter, Fernando Valenzuela West Meets East	.20
636a	Fernando Valenzuela N.L. Strikeout King ("...led the National League...")	.50
636b	Fernando Valenzuela N.L. Strikeout King ("... led the National League...")	.25
637	Mike Schmidt Home Run King	.50
638	Gary Carter, Dave Parker N.L. All-Stars	.25
639	Len Barker, Bo Diaz Perfect Game!	.05
640	Pete Rose, Pete Rose, Jr. (Re-Pete)	2.00
641	Steve Carlton, Mike Schmidt, Lonnie Smith Phillies' Finest	.50
642	Dwight Evans, Fred Lynn Red Sox Reunion	.10
643	Rickey Henderson Most Hits and Runs	1.00
644	Rollie Fingers Most Saves 1981 A.L.	.15
645	Tom Seaver Most 1981 Wins	.25
646a	Reggie Jackson, Dave Winfield Yankee Powerhouse (Comma after "outfielder" on back.)	1.50
646b	Reggie Jackson, Dave Winfield Yankee Powerhouse (No comma.)	2.00
647	Checklist 1-56	.05
648	Checklist 57-109	.05
649	Checklist 110-156	.05
650	Checklist 157-211	.05
651	Checklist 212-262	.05
652	Checklist 263-312	.05
653	Checklist 313-358	.05
654	Checklist 359-403	.05
655	Checklist 404-449	.05
656	Checklist 450-501	.05
657	Checklist 502-544	.05
658	Checklist 545-585	.05
659	Checklist 586-627	.05
660	Checklist 628-646	.05

1983 Fleer

Reggie Smith — FIRST BASE

	NM/M
Complete Set (660):	40.00
Common Player:	.05
Wax Pack (15):	3.00
Wax Box (38):	100.00
Cello Pack (28):	4.00
Cello Box (24):	80.00
Vending Box (500):	35.00

1	Joaquin Andujar	.05
2	Doug Bair	.05
3	Steve Braun	.05
4	Glenn Brummer	.05
5	Bob Forsch	.05
6	David Green	.05
7	George Hendrick	.05
8	Keith Hernandez	.05
9	Tom Herr	.05
10	Dane Iorg	.05
11	Jim Kaat	.10
12	Jeff Lahti	.05
13	Tito Landrum	.05
14	Dave LaPoint RC	.05
15	Willie McGee RC	1.50
16	Steve Mura	.05
17	Ken Oberkfell	.05
18	Darrell Porter	.05
19	Mike Ramsey	.05
20	Gene Roof	.05
21	Lonnie Smith	.05
22	Ozzie Smith	1.50
23	John Stuper	.05
24	Bruce Sutter	.65
25	Gene Tenace	.05
26	Jerry Augustine	.05
27	Dwight Bernard	.05
28	Mark Brouhard	.05
29	Mike Caldwell	.05
30	Cecil Cooper	.05
31	Jamie Easterly	.05
32	Marshall Edwards	.05
33	Rollie Fingers	.65
34	Jim Gantner	.05
35	Moose Haas	.05
36	Roy Howell	.05
37	Peter Ladd	.05
38	Bob McClure	.05
39	Doc Medich	.05
40	Paul Molitor	.75
41	Don Money	.05
42	Charlie Moore	.05
43	Ben Oglivie	.05
44	Ed Romero	.05
45	Ted Simmons	.05
46	Jim Slaton	.05
47	Don Sutton	.65
48	Gorman Thomas	.05
49	Pete Vuckovich	.05
50	Ned Yost	.05
51	Robin Yount	.75
52	Benny Ayala	.05
53	Bob Bonner	.05
54	Al Bumbry	.05
55	Terry Crowley	.05
56	Storm Davis RC	.10
57	Rich Dauer	.05
58	Rick Dempsey	.05
59	Jim Dwyer	.05
60	Mike Flanagan	.05
61	Dan Ford	.05
62	Glenn Gulliver	.05
63	John Lowenstein	.05
64	Dennis Martinez	.05
65	Tippy Martinez	.05
66	Scott McGregor	.05
67	Eddie Murray	.75
68	Joe Nolan	.05
69	Jim Palmer	.75
70	Cal Ripken, Jr.	6.00
71	Gary Roenicke	.05
72	Lenn Sakata	.05
73	Ken Singleton	.05
74	Sammy Stewart	.05
75	Tim Stoddard	.05
76	Don Aase	.05
77	Don Baylor	.05
78	Juan Beniquez	.05
79	Bob Boone	.05
80	Rick Burleson	.05
81	Rod Carew	.75
82	Bobby Clark	.05
83	Doug Corbett	.05
84	John Curtis	.05
85	Doug DeCinces	.05
86	Brian Downing	.05
87	Joe Ferguson	.05
88	Tim Foli	.05
89	Ken Forsch	.05
90	Dave Goltz	.05
91	Bobby Grich	.05
92	Andy Hassler	.05
93	Reggie Jackson	1.50
94	Ron Jackson	.05
95	Tommy John	.10
96	Bruce Kison	.05
97	Fred Lynn	.05
98	Ed Ott	.05
99	Steve Renko	.05
100	Luis Sanchez	.05
101	Rob Wilfong	.05
102	Mike Witt	.05
103	Geoff Zahn	.05
104	Willie Aikens	.05
105	Mike Armstrong	.05
106	Vida Blue	.05
107	Bud Black RC	.50
108	George Brett	2.00
109	Bill Castro	.05
110	Onix Concepcion	.05
111	Dave Frost	.05
112	Cesar Geronimo	.05
113	Larry Gura	.05
114	Steve Hammond	.05
115	Don Hood	.05
116	Dennis Leonard	.05
117	Jerry Martin	.05
118	Lee May	.05
119	Hal McRae	.05
120	Amos Otis	.05
121	Greg Pryor	.05
122	Dan Quisenberry	.05
123	Don Slaught RC	.20
124	Paul Splittorff	.05
125	U.L. Washington	.05
126	John Wathan	.05
127	Frank White	.05
128	Willie Wilson	.05
129	Steve Bedrosian	.05
130	Bruce Benedict	.05
131	Tommy Boggs	.05
132	Brett Butler	.05
133	Rick Camp	.05
134	Chris Chambliss	.05
135	Ken Dayley	.05
136	Gene Garber	.05
137	Terry Harper	.05
138	Bob Horner	.05

No.	Player	Value
139	Glenn Hubbard	.05
140	Rufino Linares	.05
141	Rick Mahler	.05
142	Dale Murphy	.50
143	Phil Niekro	.65
144	Pascual Perez	.05
145	Biff Pocoroba	.05
146	Rafael Ramirez	.05
147	Jerry Royster	.05
148	Ken Smith	.05
149	Bob Walk	.05
150	Claudell Washington	.05
151	Bob Watson	.05
152	Larry Whisenton	.05
153	Porfirio Altamirano	.05
154	Marty Bystrom	.05
155	Steve Carlton	.75
156	Larry Christenson	.05
157	Ivan DeJesus	.05
158	John Denny	.05
159	Bob Dernier	.05
160	Bo Diaz	.05
161	Ed Farmer	.05
162	Greg Gross	.05
163	Mike Krukow	.05
164	Garry Maddox	.05
165	Gary Matthews	.05
166	Tug McGraw	.05
167	Bob Molinaro	.05
168	Sid Monge	.05
169	Ron Reed	.05
170	Bill Robinson	.05
171	Pete Rose	3.00
172	Dick Ruthven	.05
173	Mike Schmidt	2.00
174	Manny Trillo	.05
175	Ozzie Virgil	.05
176	George Vukovich	.05
177	Gary Allenson	.05
178	Luis Aponte	.05
179	Wade Boggs RC	10.00
180	Tom Burgmeier	.05
181	Mark Clear	.05
182	Dennis Eckersley	.65
183	Dwight Evans	.05
184	Rich Gedman	.05
185	Glenn Hoffman	.05
186	Bruce Hurst	.05
187	Carney Lansford	.05
188	Rick Miller	.05
189	Reid Nichols	.05
190	Bob Ojeda	.05
191	Tony Perez	.65
192	Chuck Rainey	.05
193	Jerry Remy	.05
194	Jim Rice	.35
195	Bob Stanley	.05
196	Dave Stapleton	.05
197	Mike Torrez	.05
198	John Tudor	.05
199	Julio Valdez	.05
200	Carl Yastrzemski	.75
201	Dusty Baker	.05
202	Joe Beckwith	.05
203	Greg Brock (RC) RC	.05
204	Ron Cey	.05
205	Terry Forster	.05
206	Steve Garvey	.30
207	Pedro Guerrero	.05
208	Burt Hooton	.05
209	Steve Howe	.05
210	Ken Landreaux	.05
211	Mike Marshall	.05
212	Candy Maldonado RC	.05
213	Rick Monday	.05
214	Tom Niedenfuer	.05
215	Jorge Orta	.05
216	Jerry Reuss	.05
217	Ron Roenicke	.05
218	Vicente Romo	.05
219	Bill Russell	.05
220	Steve Sax	.05
221	Mike Scioscia	.05
222	Dave Stewart	.05
223	Derrel Thomas	.05
224	Fernando Valenzuela	.05
225	Bob Welch	.05
226	Ricky Wright	.05
227	Steve Yeager	.05
228	Bill Almon	.05
229	Harold Baines	.05
230	Salome Barojas	.05
231	Tony Bernazard	.05
232	Britt Burns	.05
233	Richard Dotson	.05
234	Ernesto Escarrega	.05
235	Carlton Fisk	.75
236	Jerry Hairston Sr.	.05
237	Kevin Hickey	.05
238	LaMarr Hoyt	.05
239	Steve Kemp	.05
240	Jim Kern	.05
241	Ron Kittle RC	.25
242	Jerry Koosman	.05
243	Dennis Lamp	.05
244	Rudy Law	.05
245	Vance Law	.05
246	Ron LeFlore	.05
247	Greg Luzinski	.05
248	Tom Paciorek	.05
249	Aurelio Rodriguez	.05
250	Mike Squires	.05
251	Steve Trout	.05
252	Jim Barr	.05
253	Dave Bergman	.05
254	Fred Breining	.05
255	Bob Brenly	.05
256	Jack Clark	.05
257	Chili Davis	.05
258	Darrell Evans	.05
259	Alan Fowlkes	.05
260	Rich Gale	.05
261	Atlee Hammaker	.05
262	Al Holland	.05
263	Duane Kuiper	.05
264	Bill Laskey	.05
265	Gary Lavelle	.05
266	Johnnie LeMaster	.05
267	Renie Martin	.05
268	Milt May	.05
269	Greg Minton	.05
270	Joe Morgan	.75
271	Tom O'Malley	.05
272	Reggie Smith	.05
273	Guy Sularz	.05
274	Champ Summers	.05
275	Max Venable	.05
276	Jim Wohlford	.05
277	Ray Burris	.05
278	Gary Carter	.75
279	Warren Cromartie	.05
280	Andre Dawson	.40
281	Terry Francona	.05
282	Doug Flynn	.05
283	Woody Fryman	.05
284	Bill Gullickson	.05
285	Wallace Johnson	.05
286	Charlie Lea	.05
287	Randy Lerch	.05
288	Brad Mills	.05
289	Dan Norman	.05
290	Al Oliver	.05
291	David Palmer	.05
292	Tim Raines	.05
293	Jeff Reardon	.05
294	Steve Rogers	.05
295	Scott Sanderson	.05
296	Dan Schatzeder	.05
297	Bryn Smith	.05
298	Chris Speier	.05
299	Tim Wallach	.05
300	Jerry White	.05
301	Joel Youngblood	.05
302	Ross Baumgarten	.05
303	Dale Berra	.05
304	John Candelaria	.05
305	Dick Davis	.05
306	Mike Easler	.05
307	Richie Hebner	.05
308	Lee Lacy	.05
309	Bill Madlock	.05
310	Larry McWilliams	.05
311	John Milner	.05
312	Omar Moreno	.05
313	Jim Morrison	.05
314	Steve Nicosia	.05
315	Dave Parker	.05
316	Tony Pena	.05
317	Johnny Ray	.05
318	Rick Rhoden	.05
319	Don Robinson	.05
320	Enrique Romo	.05
321	Manny Sarmiento	.05
322	Rod Scurry	.05
323	Jim Smith	.05
324	Willie Stargell	.75
325	Jason Thompson	.05
326	Kent Tekulve	.05
327a	Tom Brookens (Narrow (1/4") brown box at bottom on back.)	.45
327b	Tom Brookens (Wide (1-1/4") brown box at bottom on back.)	.05
328	Enos Cabell	.05
329	Kirk Gibson	.05
330	Larry Herndon	.05
331	Mike Ivie	.05
332	Howard Johnson RC	1.00
333	Lynn Jones	.05
334	Rick Leach	.05
335	Chet Lemon	.05
336	Jack Morris	.05
337	Lance Parrish	.05
338	Larry Pashnick	.05
339	Dan Petry	.05
340	Dave Rozema	.05
341	Dave Rucker	.05
342	Elias Sosa	.05
343	Dave Tobik	.05
344	Alan Trammell	.05
345	Jerry Turner	.05
346	Jerry Ujdur	.05
347	Pat Underwood	.05
348	Lou Whitaker	.05
349	Milt Wilcox	.05
350	Glenn Wilson RC	.05
351	John Wockenfuss	.05
352	Kurt Bevacqua	.05
353	Juan Bonilla	.05
354	Floyd Chiffer	.05
355	Luis DeLeon	.05
356	Dave Dravecky RC	.30
357	Dave Edwards	.05
358	Juan Eichelberger	.05
359	Tim Flannery	.05
360	Tony Gwynn RC	15.00
361	Ruppert Jones	.05
362	Terry Kennedy	.05
363	Joe Lefebvre	.05
364	Sixto Lezcano	.05
365	Tim Lollar	.05
366	Gary Lucas	.05
367	John Montefusco	.05
368	Broderick Perkins	.05
369	Joe Pittman	.05
370	Gene Richards	.05
371	Luis Salazar	.05
372	Eric Show RC	.05
373	Garry Templeton	.05
374	Chris Welsh	.05
375	Alan Wiggins	.05
376	Rick Cerone	.05
377	Dave Collins	.05
378	Roger Erickson	.05
379	George Frazier	.05
380	Oscar Gamble	.05
381	Goose Gossage	.10
382	Ken Griffey	.05
383	Ron Guidry	.10
384	Dave LaRoche	.05
385	Rudy May	.05
386	John Mayberry	.05
387	Lee Mazzilli	.05
388	Mike Morgan	.05
389	Jerry Mumphrey	.05
390	Bobby Murcer	.10
391	Graig Nettles	.10
392	Lou Piniella	.10
393	Willie Randolph	.05
394	Shane Rawley	.05
395	Dave Righetti	.05
396	Andre Robertson	.05
397	Roy Smalley	.05
398	Dave Winfield	.75
399	Butch Wynegar	.05
400	Chris Bando	.05
401	Alan Bannister	.05
402	Len Barker	.05
403	Tom Brennan	.05
404	Carmelo Castillo RC	.05
405	Miguel Dilone	.05
406	Jerry Dybzinski	.05
407	Mike Fischlin	.05
408	Ed Glynn (Photo actually Bud Anderson.)	.05
409	Mike Hargrove	.05
410	Toby Harrah	.05
411	Ron Hassey	.05
412	Von Hayes	.05
413	Rick Manning	.05
414	Bake McBride	.05
415	Larry Milbourne	.05
416	Bill Nahorodny	.05
417	Jack Perconte	.05
418	Larry Sorensen	.05
419	Dan Spillner	.05
420	Rick Sutcliffe	.05
421	Andre Thornton	.05
422	Rick Waits	.05
423	Eddie Whitson	.05
424	Jesse Barfield	.05
425	Barry Bonnell	.05
426	Jim Clancy	.05
427	Damaso Garcia	.05
428	Jerry Garvin	.05
429	Alfredo Griffin	.05
430	Garth Iorg	.05
431	Roy Lee Jackson	.05
432	Luis Leal	.05
433	Buck Martinez	.05
434	Joey McLaughlin	.05
435	Lloyd Moseby	.05
436	Rance Mulliniks	.05
437	Dale Murray	.05
438	Wayne Nordhagen	.05
439	Gene Petralli RC	.05
440	Hosken Powell	.05
441	Dave Stieb	.05
442	Willie Upshaw	.05
443	Ernie Whitt	.05
444	Al Woods	.05
445	Alan Ashby	.05
446	Jose Cruz	.05
447	Kiko Garcia	.05
448	Phil Garner	.05
449	Danny Heep	.05
450	Art Howe	.05
451	Bob Knepper	.05
452	Alan Knicely	.05
453	Ray Knight	.05
454	Frank LaCorte	.05
455	Mike LaCoss	.05
456	Randy Moffitt	.05
457	Joe Niekro	.05
458	Terry Puhl	.05
459	Luis Pujols	.05
460	Craig Reynolds	.05
461	Bert Roberge	.05
462	Vern Ruhle	.05
463	Nolan Ryan	4.00
464	Joe Sambito	.05
465	Tony Scott	.05
466	Dave Smith	.05
467	Harry Spilman	.05
468	Dickie Thon	.05
469	Denny Walling	.05
470	Larry Andersen	.05
471	Floyd Bannister	.05
472	Jim Beattie	.05
473	Bruce Bochte	.05
474	Manny Castillo	.05
475	Bill Caudill	.05
476	Bryan Clark	.05
477	Al Cowens	.05
478	Julio Cruz	.05
479	Todd Cruz	.05
480	Gary Gray	.05
481	Dave Henderson	.05
482	Mike Moore RC	.65
483	Gaylord Perry	.65
484	Dave Revering	.05
485	Joe Simpson	.05
486	Mike Stanton	.05
487	Rick Sweet	.05
488	Ed Vande Berg RC	.05
489	Richie Zisk	.05
490	Doug Bird	.05
491	Larry Bowa	.05
492	Bill Buckner	.05
493	Bill Campbell	.05
494	Jody Davis	.05
495	Leon Durham	.05
496	Steve Henderson	.05
497	Willie Hernandez	.05
498	Fergie Jenkins	.65
499	Jay Johnstone	.05
500	Junior Kennedy	.05
501	Randy Martz	.05
502	Jerry Morales	.05
503	Keith Moreland	.05
504	Dickie Noles	.05
505	Mike Proly	.05
506	Allen Ripley	.05
507	Ryne Sandberg RC	10.00
508	Lee Smith	1.00
509	Pat Tabler	.05
510	Dick Tidrow	.05
511	Bump Wills	.05
512	Gary Woods	.05
513	Tony Armas	.05
514	Dave Beard	.05
515	Jeff Burroughs	.05
516	John D'Acquisto	.05
517	Wayne Gross	.05
518	Mike Heath	.05
519	Rickey Henderson	.75
520	Cliff Johnson	.05
521	Matt Keough	.05
522	Brian Kingman	.05
523	Rick Langford	.05
524	Davey Lopes	.05
525	Steve McCatty	.05
526	Dave McKay	.05
527	Dan Meyer	.05
528	Dwayne Murphy	.05
529	Jeff Newman	.05
530	Mike Norris	.05
531	Bob Owchinko	.05
532	Joe Rudi	.05
533	Jimmy Sexton	.05
534	Fred Stanley	.05
535	Tom Underwood	.05
536	Neil Allen	.05
537	Wally Backman	.05
538	Bob Bailor	.05
539	Hubie Brooks	.05
540	Carlos Diaz	.05
541	Pete Falcone	.05
542	George Foster	.05
543	Ron Gardenhire	.05
544	Brian Giles	.05
545	Ron Hodges	.05
546	Randy Jones	.05
547	Mike Jorgensen	.05
548	Dave Kingman	.05

#	Player	Price
549	Ed Lynch	.05
550	Jesse Orosco	.05
551	Rick Ownbey	.05
552	Charlie Puleo RC	.05
553	Gary Rajsich	.05
554	Mike Scott	.05
555	Rusty Staub	.05
556	John Stearns	.05
557	Craig Swan	.05
558	Ellis Valentine	.05
559	Tom Veryzer	.05
560	Mookie Wilson	.05
561	Pat Zachry	.05
562	Buddy Bell	.05
563	John Butcher	.05
564	Steve Comer	.05
565	Danny Darwin	.05
566	Bucky Dent	.05
567	John Grubb	.05
568	Rick Honeycutt	.05
569	Dave Hostetler	.05
570	Charlie Hough	.05
571	Lamar Johnson	.05
572	Jon Matlack	.05
573	Paul Mirabella	.05
574	Larry Parrish	.05
575	Mike Richardt	.05
576	Mickey Rivers	.05
577	Billy Sample	.05
578	Dave Schmidt RC	.05
579	Bill Stein	.05
580	Jim Sundberg	.05
581	Frank Tanana	.05
582	Mark Wagner	.05
583	George Wright	.05
584	Johnny Bench	.75
585	Bruce Berenyi	.05
586	Larry Biittner	.05
587	Cesar Cedeno	.05
588	Dave Concepcion	.05
589	Dan Driessen	.05
590	Greg Harris	.05
591	Ben Hayes	.05
592	Paul Householder	.05
593	Tom Hume	.05
594	Wayne Krenchicki	.05
595	Rafael Landestoy	.05
596	Charlie Leibrandt	.05
597	Eddie Milner RC	.05
598	Ron Oester	.05
599	Frank Pastore	.05
600	Joe Price	.05
601	Tom Seaver	.75
602	Bob Shirley	.05
603	Mario Soto	.05
604	Alex Trevino	.05
605	Mike Vail	.05
606	Duane Walker	.05
607	Tom Brunansky	.05
608	Bobby Castillo	.05
609	John Castino	.05
610	Ron Davis	.05
611	Lenny Faedo	.05
612	Terry Felton	.05
613	Gary Gaetti RC	.35
614	Mickey Hatcher	.05
615	Brad Havens	.05
616	Kent Hrbek	.05
617	Randy S. Johnson	.05
618	Tim Laudner	.05
619	Jeff Little	.05
620	Bob Mitchell	.05
621	Jack O'Connor	.05
622	John Pacella	.05
623	Pete Redfern	.05
624	Jesus Vega	.05
625	Frank Viola RC	1.00
626	Ron Washington	.05
627	Gary Ward	.05
628	Al Williams	.05
629	Mark Clear, Dennis Eckersley, Carl Yastrzemski Red Sox All-Stars	.25
630	Terry Bulling, Gaylord Perry 300 Career Wins	.10
631	Dave Concepcion, Manny Trillo Pride of Venezuela	.10
632	Buddy Bell, Robin Yount All-Star Infielders	.20
633	Kent Hrbek, Dave Winfield Mr. Vet & Mr. Rookie	.25
634	Pete Rose, Willie Stargell Fountain of Youth	.40
635	Toby Harrah, Andre Thornton Big Chiefs	.05
636	Lonnie Smith, Ozzie Smith "Smith Bros."	.05
637	Gary Carter, Bo Diaz Base Stealers' Threat	.10
638	Gary Carter, Carlton Fisk All-Star Catchers	.15
639	Rickey Henderson (In Action)	.50
640	Reggie Jackson, Ben Oglivie Home Run Threats	.25
641	Joel Youngblood Two Teams - Same Day	.05
642	Len Barker, Ron Hassey Last Perfect Game	.05
643	Vida Blue Blue	.05
644	Bud Black Black &	.05
645	Reggie Jackson Power	.30
646	Rickey Henderson Speed &	.30
647	Checklist 1-51	.05
648	Checklist 52-103	.05
649	Checklist 104-152	.05
650	Checklist 153-200	.05
651	Checklist 201-251	.05
652	Checklist 252-301	.05
653	Checklist 302-351	.05
654	Checklist 352-399	.05
655	Checklist 400-444	.05
656	Checklist 445-489	.05
657	Checklist 490-535	.05
658	Checklist 536-583	.05
659	Checklist 584-628	.05
660	Checklist 629-646	.05

1984 Fleer

Kent Hrbek
FIRST BASE

	NM/M
Complete Set (660):	40.00
Common Player:	.05
Wax Pack (15):	2.50
Wax Box (36):	75.00
Cello Pack (28):	4.50
Cello Box (24):	85.00
Vending Box (500):	40.00

#	Player	Price
1	Mike Boddicker	.05
2	Al Bumbry	.05
3	Todd Cruz	.05
4	Rich Dauer	.05
5	Storm Davis	.05
6	Rick Dempsey	.05
7	Jim Dwyer	.05
8	Mike Flanagan	.05
9	Dan Ford	.05
10	John Lowenstein	.05
11	Dennis Martinez	.05
12	Tippy Martinez	.05
13	Scott McGregor	.05
14	Eddie Murray	1.00
15	Joe Nolan	.05
16	Jim Palmer	1.00
17	Cal Ripken, Jr.	4.00
18	Gary Roenicke	.05
19	Lenn Sakata	.05
20	John Shelby RC	.05
21	Ken Singleton	.05
22	Sammy Stewart	.05
23	Tim Stoddard	.05
24	Marty Bystrom	.05
25	Steve Carlton	1.00
26	Ivan DeJesus	.05
27	John Denny	.05
28	Bob Dernier	.05
29	Bo Diaz	.05
30	Kiko Garcia	.05
31	Greg Gross	.05
32	Kevin Gross RC	.05
33	Von Hayes	.05
34	Willie Hernandez	.05
35	Al Holland	.05
36	Charles Hudson RC	.05
37	Joe Lefebvre	.05
38	Sixto Lezcano	.05
39	Garry Maddox	.05
40	Gary Matthews	.05
41	Len Matuszek	.05
42	Tug McGraw	.05
43	Joe Morgan	1.00
44	Tony Perez	.75
45	Ron Reed	.05
46	Pete Rose	3.00
47	Juan Samuel RC	.25
48	Mike Schmidt	2.50
49	Ozzie Virgil	.05
50	Juan Agosto RC	.05
51	Harold Baines	.05
52	Floyd Bannister	.05
53	Salome Barojas	.05
54	Britt Burns	.05
55	Julio Cruz	.05
56	Richard Dotson	.05
57	Jerry Dybzinski	.05
58	Carlton Fisk	1.00
59	Scott Fletcher	.05
60	Jerry Hairston Sr.	.05
61	Kevin Hickey	.05
62	Marc Hill	.05
63	LaMarr Hoyt	.05
64	Ron Kittle	.05
65	Jerry Koosman	.05
66	Dennis Lamp	.05
67	Rudy Law	.05
68	Vance Law	.05
69	Greg Luzinski	.05
70	Tom Paciorek	.05
71	Mike Squires	.05
72	Dick Tidrow	.05
73	Greg Walker RC	.05
74	Glenn Abbott	.05
75	Howard Bailey	.05
76	Doug Bair	.05
77	Juan Berenguer	.05
78	Tom Brookens	.05
79	Enos Cabell	.05
80	Kirk Gibson	.05
81	John Grubb	.05
82	Larry Herndon	.05
83	Wayne Krenchicki	.05
84	Rick Leach	.05
85	Chet Lemon	.05
86	Aurelio Lopez	.05
87	Jack Morris	.05
88	Lance Parrish	.05
89	Dan Petry	.05
90	Dave Rozema	.05
91	Alan Trammell	.05
92	Lou Whitaker	.05
93	Milt Wilcox	.05
94	Glenn Wilson	.05
95	John Wockenfuss	.05
96	Dusty Baker	.05
97	Joe Beckwith	.05
98	Greg Brock	.05
99	Jack Fimple	.05
100	Pedro Guerrero	.05
101	Rick Honeycutt	.05
102	Burt Hooton	.05
103	Steve Howe	.05
104	Ken Landreaux	.05
105	Mike Marshall	.05
106	Rick Monday	.05
107	Jose Morales	.05
108	Tom Niedenfuer	.05
109	Alejandro Pena RC	.05
110	Jerry Reuss	.05
111	Bill Russell	.05
112	Steve Sax	.05
113	Mike Scioscia	.05
114	Derrel Thomas	.05
115	Fernando Valenzuela	.05
116	Bob Welch	.05
117	Steve Yeager	.05
118	Pat Zachry	.05
119	Don Baylor	.05
120	Bert Campaneris	.05
121	Rick Cerone	.05
122	Ray Fontenot RC	.05
123	George Frazier	.05
124	Oscar Gamble	.05
125	Goose Gossage	.10
126	Ken Griffey	.05
127	Ron Guidry	.10
128	Jay Howell	.05
129	Steve Kemp	.05
130	Matt Keough	.05
131	Don Mattingly RC	20.00
132	John Montefusco	.05
133	Omar Moreno	.05
134	Dale Murray	.05
135	Graig Nettles	.05
136	Lou Piniella	.10
137	Willie Randolph	.05
138	Shane Rawley	.05
139	Dave Righetti	.05
140	Andre Robertson	.05
141	Bob Shirley	.05
142	Roy Smalley	.05
143	Dave Winfield	1.00
144	Butch Wynegar	.05
145	Jim Acker (RC) RC	.05
146	Doyle Alexander	.05
147	Jesse Barfield	.05
148	George Bell	.05
149	Barry Bonnell	.05
150	Jim Clancy	.05
151	Dave Collins	.05
152	Tony Fernandez RC	.50
153	Damaso Garcia	.05
154	Dave Geisel	.05
155	Jim Gott	.05
156	Alfredo Griffin	.05
157	Garth Iorg	.05
158	Roy Lee Jackson	.05
159	Cliff Johnson	.05
160	Luis Leal	.05
161	Buck Martinez	.05
162	Joey McLaughlin	.05
163	Randy Moffitt	.05
164	Lloyd Moseby	.05
165	Rance Mulliniks	.05
166	Jorge Orta	.05
167	Dave Stieb	.05
168	Willie Upshaw	.05
169	Ernie Whitt	.05
170	Len Barker	.05
171	Steve Bedrosian	.05
172	Bruce Benedict	.05
173	Brett Butler	.05
174	Rick Camp	.05
175	Chris Chambliss	.05
176	Ken Dayley	.05
177	Pete Falcone	.05
178	Terry Forster	.05
179	Gene Garber	.05
180	Terry Harper	.05
181	Bob Horner	.05
182	Glenn Hubbard	.05
183	Randy Johnson	.05
184	Craig McMurtry RC	.05
185	Donnie Moore	.05
186	Dale Murphy	.60
187	Phil Niekro	.75
188	Pascual Perez	.05
189	Biff Pocoroba	.05
190	Rafael Ramirez	.05
191	Jerry Royster	.05
192	Claudell Washington	.05
193	Bob Watson	.05
194	Jerry Augustine	.05
195	Mark Brouhard	.05
196	Mike Caldwell	.05
197	Tom Candiotti RC	.25
198	Cecil Cooper	.05
199	Rollie Fingers	.75
200	Jim Gantner	.05
201	Bob L. Gibson	.05
202	Moose Haas	.05
203	Roy Howell	.05
204	Pete Ladd	.05
205	Rick Manning	.05
206	Bob McClure	.05
207	Paul Molitor	1.00
208	Don Money	.05
209	Charlie Moore	.05
210	Ben Oglivie	.05
211	Chuck Porter	.05
212	Ed Romero	.05
213	Ted Simmons	.05
214	Jim Slaton	.05
215	Don Sutton	.75
216	Tom Tellmann	.05
217	Pete Vuckovich	.05
218	Ned Yost	.05
219	Robin Yount	1.00
220	Alan Ashby	.05
221	Kevin Bass	.05
222	Jose Cruz	.05
223	Bill Dawley RC	.05
224	Frank DiPino	.05
225	Bill Doran RC	.05
226	Phil Garner	.05
227	Art Howe	.05
228	Bob Knepper	.05
229	Ray Knight	.05
230	Frank LaCorte	.05
231	Mike LaCoss	.05
232	Mike Madden	.05
233	Jerry Mumphrey	.05
234	Joe Niekro	.05
235	Terry Puhl	.05
236	Luis Pujols	.05
237	Craig Reynolds	.05
238	Vern Ruhle	.05
239	Nolan Ryan	4.00
240	Mike Scott	.05
241	Tony Scott	.05
242	Dave Smith	.05
243	Dickie Thon	.05
244	Denny Walling	.05
245	Dale Berra	.05
246	Jim Bibby	.05
247	John Candelaria	.05
248	Jose DeLeon RC	.05
249	Mike Easler	.05
250	Cecilio Guante	.05
251	Richie Hebner	.05
252	Lee Lacy	.05

No.	Player	Value
253	Bill Madlock	.05
254	Milt May	.05
255	Lee Mazzilli	.05
256	Larry McWilliams	.05
257	Jim Morrison	.05
258	Dave Parker	.05
259	Tony Pena	.05
260	Johnny Ray	.05
261	Rick Rhoden	.05
262	Don Robinson	.05
263	Manny Sarmiento	.05
264	Rod Scurry	.05
265	Kent Tekulve	.05
266	Gene Tenace	.05
267	Jason Thompson	.05
268	Lee Tunnell RC	.05
269	Marvell Wynne RC	.05
270	Ray Burris	.05
271	Gary Carter	1.00
272	Warren Cromartie	.05
273	Andre Dawson	.30
274	Doug Flynn	.05
275	Terry Francona	.05
276	Bill Gullickson	.05
277	Bob James	.05
278	Charlie Lea	.05
279	Bryan Little	.05
280	Al Oliver	.05
281	Tim Raines	.05
282	Bobby Ramos	.05
283	Jeff Reardon	.05
284	Steve Rogers	.05
285	Scott Sanderson	.05
286	Dan Schatzeder	.05
287	Bryn Smith	.05
288	Chris Speier	.05
289	Manny Trillo	.05
290	Mike Vail	.05
291	Tim Wallach	.05
292	Chris Welsh	.05
293	Jim Wohlford	.05
294	Kurt Bevacqua	.05
295	Juan Bonilla	.05
296	Bobby Brown	.05
297	Luis DeLeon	.05
298	Dave Dravecky	.05
299	Tim Flannery	.05
300	Steve Garvey	.25
301	Tony Gwynn	2.00
302	Andy Hawkins RC	.10
303	Ruppert Jones	.05
304	Terry Kennedy	.05
305	Tim Lollar	.05
306	Gary Lucas	.05
307	Kevin McReynolds RC	.25
308	Sid Monge	.05
309	Mario Ramirez	.05
310	Gene Richards	.05
311	Luis Salazar	.05
312	Eric Show	.05
313	Elias Sosa	.05
314	Garry Templeton	.05
315	Mark Thurmond RC	.05
316	Ed Whitson	.05
317	Alan Wiggins	.05
318	Neil Allen	.05
319	Joaquin Andujar	.05
320	Steve Braun	.05
321	Glenn Brummer	.05
322	Bob Forsch	.05
323	David Green	.05
324	George Hendrick	.05
325	Tom Herr	.05
326	Dane Iorg	.05
327	Jeff Lahti	.05
328	Dave LaPoint	.05
329	Willie McGee	.05
330	Ken Oberkfell	.05
331	Darrell Porter	.05
332	Jamie Quirk	.05
333	Mike Ramsey	.05
334	Floyd Rayford	.05
335	Lonnie Smith	.05
336	Ozzie Smith	2.00
337	John Stuper	.05
338	Bruce Sutter	.75
339	Andy Van Slyke RC	1.00
340	Dave Von Ohlen	.05
341	Willie Aikens	.05
342	Mike Armstrong	.05
343	Bud Black	.05
344	George Brett	2.50
345	Onix Concepcion	.05
346	Keith Creel	.05
347	Larry Gura	.05
348	Don Hood	.05
349	Dennis Leonard	.05
350	Hal McRae	.05
351	Amos Otis	.05
352	Gaylord Perry	.75
353	Greg Pryor	.05
354	Dan Quisenberry	.05
355	Steve Renko	.05
356	Leon Roberts	.05
357	Pat Sheridan RC	.05
358	Joe Simpson	.05
359	Don Slaught	.05
360	Paul Splittorff	.05
361	U.L. Washington	.05
362	John Wathan	.05
363	Frank White	.05
364	Willie Wilson	.05
365	Jim Barr	.05
366	Dave Bergman	.05
367	Fred Breining	.05
368	Bob Brenly	.05
369	Jack Clark	.05
370	Chili Davis	.05
371	Mark Davis	.05
372	Darrell Evans	.05
373	Atlee Hammaker	.05
374	Mike Krukow	.05
375	Duane Kuiper	.05
376	Bill Laskey	.05
377	Gary Lavelle	.05
378	Johnnie LeMaster	.05
379	Jeff Leonard	.05
380	Randy Lerch	.05
381	Renie Martin	.05
382	Andy McGaffigan	.05
383	Greg Minton	.05
384	Tom O'Malley	.05
385	Max Venable	.05
386	Brad Wellman	.05
387	Joel Youngblood	.05
388	Gary Allenson	.05
389	Luis Aponte	.05
390	Tony Armas	.05
391	Doug Bird	.05
392	Wade Boggs	2.00
393	Dennis Boyd RC	.05
394	Mike Brown	.05
395	Mark Clear	.05
396	Dennis Eckersley	.75
397	Dwight Evans	.05
398	Rich Gedman	.05
399	Glenn Hoffman	.05
400	Bruce Hurst	.05
401	John Henry Johnson	.05
402	Ed Jurak	.05
403	Rick Miller	.05
404	Jeff Newman	.05
405	Reid Nichols	.05
406	Bob Ojeda	.05
407	Jerry Remy	.05
408	Jim Rice	.05
409	Bob Stanley	.05
410	Dave Stapleton	.05
411	John Tudor	.05
412	Carl Yastrzemski	1.50
413	Buddy Bell	.05
414	Larry Biittner	.05
415	John Butcher	.05
416	Danny Darwin	.05
417	Bucky Dent	.05
418	Dave Hostetler	.05
419	Charlie Hough	.05
420	Bobby Johnson	.05
421	Odell Jones	.05
422	Jon Matlack	.05
423	Pete O'Brien RC	.05
424	Larry Parrish	.05
425	Mickey Rivers	.05
426	Billy Sample	.05
427	Dave Schmidt	.05
428	Mike Smithson RC	.05
429	Bill Stein	.05
430	Dave Stewart	.05
431	Jim Sundberg	.05
432	Frank Tanana	.05
433	Dave Tobik	.05
434	Wayne Tolleson	.05
435	George Wright	.05
436	Bill Almon	.05
437	Keith Atherton RC	.05
438	Dave Beard	.05
439	Tom Burgmeier	.05
440	Jeff Burroughs	.05
441	Chris Codiroli RC	.05
442	Tim Conroy RC	.05
443	Mike Davis	.05
444	Wayne Gross	.05
445	Garry Hancock	.05
446	Mike Heath	.05
447	Rickey Henderson	1.00
448	Don Hill RC	.05
449	Bob Kearney	.05
450	Bill Krueger	.05
451	Rick Langford	.05
452	Carney Lansford	.05
453	Davey Lopes	.05
454	Steve McCatty	.05
455	Dan Meyer	.05
456	Dwayne Murphy	.05
457	Mike Norris	.05
458	Ricky Peters	.05
459	Tony Phillips	.05
460	Tom Underwood	.05
461	Mike Warren	.05
462	Johnny Bench	1.50
463	Bruce Berenyi	.05
464	Dann Bilardello	.05
465	Cesar Cedeno	.05
466	Dave Concepcion	.05
467	Dan Driessen	.05
468	Nick Esasky RC	.05
469	Rich Gale	.05
470	Ben Hayes	.05
471	Paul Householder	.05
472	Tom Hume	.05
473	Alan Knicely	.05
474	Eddie Milner	.05
475	Ron Oester	.05
476	Kelly Paris	.05
477	Frank Pastore	.05
478	Ted Power	.05
479	Joe Price	.05
480	Charlie Puleo	.05
481	Gary Redus RC	.05
482	Bill Scherrer	.05
483	Mario Soto	.05
484	Alex Trevino	.05
485	Duane Walker	.05
486	Larry Bowa	.05
487	Warren Brusstar	.05
488	Bill Buckner	.05
489	Bill Campbell	.05
490	Ron Cey	.05
491	Jody Davis	.05
492	Leon Durham	.05
493	Mel Hall	.05
494	Fergie Jenkins	.75
495	Jay Johnstone	.05
496	Craig Lefferts RC	.10
497	Carmelo Martinez RC	.05
498	Jerry Morales	.05
499	Keith Moreland	.05
500	Dickie Noles	.05
501	Mike Proly	.05
502	Chuck Rainey	.05
503	Dick Ruthven	.05
504	Ryne Sandberg	2.00
505	Lee Smith	.05
506	Steve Trout	.05
507	Gary Woods	.05
508	Juan Beniquez	.05
509	Bob Boone	.05
510	Rick Burleson	.05
511	Rod Carew	1.00
512	Bobby Clark	.05
513	John Curtis	.05
514	Doug DeCinces	.05
515	Brian Downing	.05
516	Tim Foli	.05
517	Ken Forsch	.05
518	Bobby Grich	.05
519	Andy Hassler	.05
520	Reggie Jackson	1.50
521	Ron Jackson	.05
522	Tommy John	.10
523	Bruce Kison	.05
524	Steve Lubratich	.05
525	Fred Lynn	.05
526	Gary Pettis (RC) RC	.05
527	Luis Sanchez	.05
528	Daryl Sconiers	.05
529	Ellis Valentine	.05
530	Rob Wilfong	.05
531	Mike Witt	.05
532	Geoff Zahn	.05
533	Bud Anderson	.05
534	Chris Bando	.05
535	Alan Bannister	.05
536	Bert Blyleven	.10
537	Tom Brennan	.05
538	Jamie Easterly	.05
539	Juan Eichelberger	.05
540	Jim Essian	.05
541	Mike Fischlin	.05
542	Julio Franco	.05
543	Mike Hargrove	.05
544	Toby Harrah	.05
545	Ron Hassey	.05
546	Neal Heaton RC	.05
547	Bake McBride	.05
548	Broderick Perkins	.05
549	Lary Sorensen	.05
550	Dan Spillner	.05
551	Rick Sutcliffe	.05
552	Pat Tabler	.05
553	Gorman Thomas	.05
554	Andre Thornton	.05
555	George Vukovich	.05
556	Darrell Brown	.05
557	Tom Brunansky	.05
558	Randy Bush RC	.05
559	Bobby Castillo	.05
560	John Castino	.05
561	Ron Davis	.05
562	Dave Engle	.05
563	Lenny Faedo	.05
564	Pete Filson	.05
565	Gary Gaetti	.05
566	Mickey Hatcher	.05
567	Kent Hrbek	.05
568	Rusty Kuntz	.05
569	Tim Laudner	.05
570	Rick Lysander	.05
571	Bobby Mitchell	.05
572	Ken Schrom	.05
573	Ray Smith	.05
574	Tim Teufel RC	.05
575	Frank Viola	.05
576	Gary Ward	.05
577	Ron Washington	.05
578	Len Whitehouse	.05
579	Al Williams	.05
580	Bob Bailor	.05
581	Mark Bradley	.05
582	Hubie Brooks	.05
583	Carlos Diaz	.05
584	George Foster	.05
585	Brian Giles	.05
586	Danny Heep	.05
587	Keith Hernandez	.05
588	Ron Hodges	.05
589	Scott Holman	.05
590	Dave Kingman	.05
591	Ed Lynch	.05
592	Jose Oquendo RC	.05
593	Jesse Orosco	.05
594	Junior Ortiz RC	.05
595	Tom Seaver	1.00
596	Doug Sisk RC	.05
597	Rusty Staub	.05
598	John Stearns	.05
599	Darryl Strawberry	.25
600	Craig Swan	.05
601	Walt Terrell RC	.05
602	Mike Torrez	.05
603	Mookie Wilson	.05
604	Jamie Allen	.05
605	Jim Beattie	.05
606	Tony Bernazard	.05
607	Manny Castillo	.05
608	Bill Caudill	.05
609	Bryan Clark	.05
610	Al Cowens	.05
611	Dave Henderson	.05
612	Steve Henderson	.05
613	Orlando Mercado	.05
614	Mike Moore	.05
615	Ricky Nelson	.05
616	Spike Owen RC	.10
617	Pat Putnam	.05
618	Ron Roenicke	.05
619	Mike Stanton	.05
620	Bob Stoddard	.05
621	Rick Sweet	.05
622	Roy Thomas	.05
623	Ed Vande Berg	.05
624	Matt Young RC	.05
625	Richie Zisk	.05
626	Fred Lynn '83 All-Star Game Record Breaker	.05
627	Manny Trillo '83 All-Star Game Record Breaker	.05
628	Steve Garvey N.L. Iron Man	.10
629	Rod Carew A.L. Batting Runner-Up	.15
630	Wade Boggs A.L. Batting Champion	.50
631	Tim Raines Letting Go Of The Raines	.10
632	Al Oliver Double Trouble	.05
633	Steve Sax All-Star Second Base	.05
634	Dickie Thon All-Star Shortstop	.05
635	Tippy Martinez, Dan Quisenberry Ace Firemen	.05
636	Joe Morgan, Tony Perez, Pete Rose Reds Reunited	.75
637	Bob Boone, Lance Parrish Backstop Stars	.05
638	George Brett, Gaylord Perry The Pine Tar Incident, 7/24/83	.25
639	Bob Forsch, Dave Righetti, Mike Warren 1983 No-Hitters	.05
640	Johnny Bench, Carl Yastrzemski Retiring Superstars	.50
641	Gaylord Perry Going Out In Style	.05
642	Steve Carlton 300 Club & Strikeout Record	.10
643	Joe Altobelli, Paul Owens The Managers	.05
644	Rick Dempsey The MVP	.05
645	Mike Boddicker The Rookie Winner	.05

646	Scott McGregor The Clincher	.05
647	Joe Altobelli Checklist: Orioles/Royals	.05
648	Paul Owens Checklist: Phillies/Giants	.05
649	Tony LaRussa Checklist: White Sox/Red Sox	.05
650	Sparky Anderson Checklist: Tigers/Rangers	.10
651	Tommy Lasorda Checklist: Dodgers/A's	.10
652	Billy Martin Checklist: Yankees/Reds	.05
653	Bobby Cox Checklist: Blue Jays/Cubs	.10
654	Joe Torre Checklist: Braves/Angels	.10
655	Rene Lacheman Checklist: Brewers/Indians	.05
656	Bob Lillis Checklist: Astros/Twins	.05
657	Chuck Tanner Checklist: Pirates/Mets	.05
658	Bill Virdon Checklist: Expos/Mariners	.05
659	Dick Williams Checklist: Padres/Specials	.05
660	Whitey Herzog Checklist: Cardinals/Specials	.05

Update

Brett Butler
OUTFIELD

		NM/M
	Complete Set (132):	300.00
	Common Player:	.25
1	Willie Aikens	.25
2	Luis Aponte	.25
3	Mark Bailey	.25
4	Bob Bailor	.25
5	Dusty Baker	.25
6	Steve Balboni	.25
7	Alan Bannister	.25
8	Marty Barrett	.25
9	Dave Beard	.25
10	Joe Beckwith	.25
11	Dave Bergman	.25
12	Tony Bernazard	.25
13	Bruce Bochte	.25
14	Barry Bonnell	.25
15	Phil Bradley	.25
16	Fred Breining	.25
17	Mike Brown	.25
18	Bill Buckner	.25
19	Ray Burris	.25
20	John Butcher	.25
21	Brett Butler	.25
22	Enos Cabell	.25
23	Bill Campbell	.25
24	Bill Caudill	.25
25	Bobby Clark	.25
26	Bryan Clark	.25
27	Roger Clemens RC	250.00
28	Jaime Cocanower	.25
29	Ron Darling RC	1.00
30	Alvin Davis RC	.25
31	Bob Dernier	.25
32	Carlos Diaz	.25
33	Mike Easler	.25
34	Dennis Eckersley	4.00
35	Jim Essian	.25
36	Darrell Evans	.25
37	Mike Fitzgerald	.25
38	Tim Foli	.25
39	John Franco RC	3.00
40	George Frazier	.25
41	Rich Gale	.25
42	Barbaro Garbey	.25
43	Dwight Gooden RC	7.50
44	Goose Gossage	.40
45	Wayne Gross	.25
46	Mark Gubicza	1.00
47	Jackie Gutierrez	.25

48	Toby Harrah	.25
49	Ron Hassey	.25
50	Richie Hebner	.25
51	Willie Hernandez	.25
52	Ed Hodge	.25
53	Ricky Horton	.25
54	Art Howe	.25
55	Dane Iorg	.25
56	Brook Jacoby	.25
57	Dion James RC	.25
58	Mike Jeffcoat RC	.25
59	Ruppert Jones	.25
60	Bob Kearney	.25
61	Jimmy Key RC	1.00
62	Dave Kingman	.25
63	Brad Komminsk RC	.25
64	Jerry Koosman	.25
65	Wayne Krenchicki	.25
66	Rusty Kuntz	.25
67	Frank LaCorte	.25
68	Dennis Lamp	.25
69	Tito Landrum	.25
70	Mark Langston RC	4.00
71	Rick Leach	.25
72	Craig Lefferts	.25
73	Gary Lucas	.25
74	Jerry Martin	.25
75	Carmelo Martinez	.25
76	Mike Mason RC	.25
77	Gary Matthews	.25
78	Andy McGaffigan	.25
79	Joey McLaughlin	.25
80	Joe Morgan	5.00
81	Darryl Motley	.25
82	Graig Nettles	.40
83	Phil Niekro	3.00
84	Ken Oberkfell	.25
85	Al Oliver	.25
86	Jorge Orta	.25
87	Amos Otis	.25
88	Bob Owchinko	.25
89	Dave Parker	.25
90	Jack Perconte	.25
91	Tony Perez	3.00
92	Gerald Perry	.25
93	Kirby Puckett RC	75.00
94	Shane Rawley	.25
95	Floyd Rayford	.25
96	Ron Reed	.25
97	R.J. Reynolds	.25
98	Gene Richards	.25
99	Jose Rijo RC	1.00
100	Jeff Robinson	.25
101	Ron Romanick	.25
102	Pete Rose	10.00
103	Bret Saberhagen RC	5.00
104	Scott Sanderson	.25
105	Dick Schofield RC	.25
106	Tom Seaver	7.50
107	Jim Slaton	.25
108	Mike Smithson	.25
109	Lary Sorensen	.25
110	Tim Stoddard	.25
111	Jeff Stone	.25
112	Champ Summers	.25
113	Jim Sundberg	.25
114	Rick Sutcliffe	.35
115	Craig Swan	.25
116	Derrel Thomas	.25
117	Gorman Thomas	.25
118	Alex Trevino	.25
119	Manny Trillo	.25
120	John Tudor	.25
121	Tom Underwood	.25
122	Mike Vail	.25
123	Tom Waddell	.25
124	Gary Ward	.25
125	Terry Whitfield	.25
126	Curtis Wilkerson	.25
127	Frank Williams	.25
128	Glenn Wilson	.25
129	John Wockenfuss	.25
130	Ned Yost	.25
131	Mike Young RC	.25
132	Checklist 1-132	.10

1985 Fleer

		NM/M
	Unopened Factory Set (660):	50.00
	Complete Set (660):	40.00
	Common Player:	.05
	Wax Pack (15):	4.50
	Wax Box (36):	150.00
	Cello Pack (28):	6.00
	Cello Box (24):	150.00
	Rack Pack (45):	8.00
	Vending Box (500):	35.00
1	Doug Bair	.05
2	Juan Berenguer	.05
3	Dave Bergman	.05
4	Tom Brookens	.05
5	Marty Castillo	.05
6	Darrell Evans	.05

7	Barbaro Garbey	.05
8	Kirk Gibson	.05
9	John Grubb	.05
10	Willie Hernandez	.05
11	Larry Herndon	.05
12	Howard Johnson	.05
13	Ruppert Jones	.05
14	Rusty Kuntz	.05
15	Chet Lemon	.05
16	Aurelio Lopez	.05
17	Sid Monge	.05
18	Jack Morris	.05
19	Lance Parrish	.05
20	Dan Petry	.05
21	Dave Rozema	.05
22	Bill Scherrer	.05
23	Alan Trammell	.05
24	Lou Whitaker	.05
25	Milt Wilcox	.05
26	Kurt Bevacqua	.05
27	Greg Booker RC	.05
28	Bobby Brown	.05
29	Luis DeLeon	.05
30	Dave Dravecky	.05
31	Tim Flannery	.05
32	Steve Garvey	.40
33	Goose Gossage	.10
34	Tony Gwynn	2.00
35	Greg Harris	.05
36	Andy Hawkins	.05
37	Terry Kennedy	.05
38	Craig Lefferts	.05
39	Tim Lollar	.05
40	Carmelo Martinez	.05
41	Kevin McReynolds	.05
42	Graig Nettles	.05
43	Luis Salazar	.05
44	Eric Show	.05
45	Garry Templeton	.05
46	Mark Thurmond	.05
47	Ed Whitson	.05
48	Alan Wiggins	.05
49	Rich Bordi	.05
50	Larry Bowa	.05
51	Warren Brusstar	.05
52	Ron Cey	.05
53	Henry Cotto RC	.05
54	Jody Davis	.05
55	Bob Dernier	.05
56	Leon Durham	.05
57	Dennis Eckersley	.75
58	George Frazier	.05
59	Richie Hebner	.05
60	Dave Lopes	.05
61	Gary Matthews	.05
62	Keith Moreland	.05
63	Rick Reuschel	.05
64	Dick Ruthven	.05
65	Ryne Sandberg	2.00
66	Scott Sanderson	.05
67	Lee Smith	.05
68	Tim Stoddard	.05
69	Rick Sutcliffe	.05
70	Steve Trout	.05
71	Gary Woods	.05
72	Wally Backman	.05
73	Bruce Berenyi	.05
74	Hubie Brooks	.05
75	Kelvin Chapman	.05
76	Ron Darling	.05
77	Sid Fernandez	.05
78	Mike Fitzgerald	.05
79	George Foster	.05
80	Brent Gaff	.05
81	Ron Gardenhire	.05
82	Dwight Gooden RC	.25
83	Tom Gorman	.05
84	Danny Heep	.05
85	Keith Hernandez	.05
86	Ray Knight	.05
87	Ed Lynch	.05
88	Jose Oquendo	.05
89	Jesse Orosco	.05

90	Rafael Santana RC	.05
91	Doug Sisk	.05
92	Rusty Staub	.05
93	Darryl Strawberry	.10
94	Walt Terrell	.05
95	Mookie Wilson	.05
96	Jim Acker	.05
97	Willie Aikens	.05
98	Doyle Alexander	.05
99	Jesse Barfield	.05
100	George Bell	.05
101	Jim Clancy	.05
102	Dave Collins	.05
103	Tony Fernandez	.05
104	Damaso Garcia	.05
105	Jim Gott	.05
106	Alfredo Griffin	.05
107	Garth Iorg	.05
108	Roy Lee Jackson	.05
109	Cliff Johnson	.05
110	Jimmy Key	.05
111	Dennis Lamp	.05
112	Rick Leach	.05
113	Luis Leal	.05
114	Buck Martinez	.05
115	Lloyd Moseby	.05
116	Rance Mulliniks	.05
117	Dave Stieb	.05
118	Willie Upshaw	.05
119	Ernie Whitt	.05
120	Mike Armstrong	.05
121	Don Baylor	.05
122	Marty Bystrom	.05
123	Rick Cerone	.05
124	Joe Cowley	.05
125	Brian Dayett	.05
126	Tim Foli	.05
127	Ray Fontenot	.05
128	Ken Griffey	.05
129	Ron Guidry	.10
130	Toby Harrah	.05
131	Jay Howell	.05
132	Steve Kemp	.05
133	Don Mattingly	2.50
134	Bobby Meacham	.05
135	John Montefusco	.05
136	Omar Moreno	.05
137	Dale Murray	.05
138	Phil Niekro	.75
139	Mike Pagliarulo RC	.20
140	Willie Randolph	.05
141	Dennis Rasmussen	.05
142	Dave Righetti	.05
143	Jose Rijo	.05
144	Andre Robertson	.05
145	Bob Shirley	.05
146	Dave Winfield	1.00
147	Butch Wynegar	.05
148	Gary Allenson	.05
149	Tony Armas	.05
150	Marty Barrett	.05
151	Wade Boggs	2.00
152	Dennis Boyd	.05
153	Bill Buckner	.05
154	Mark Clear	.05
155	Roger Clemens	40.00
156	Steve Crawford	.05
157	Mike Easler	.05
158	Dwight Evans	.05
159	Rich Gedman	.05
160	Jackie Gutierrez	.05
161	Bruce Hurst	.05
162	John Henry Johnson	.05
163	Rick Miller	.05
164	Reid Nichols	.05
165	Al Nipper RC	.05
166	Bob Ojeda	.05
167	Jerry Remy	.05
168	Jim Rice	.25
169	Bob Stanley	.05
170	Mike Boddicker	.05
171	Al Bumbry	.05
172	Todd Cruz	.05
173	Rich Dauer	.05
174	Storm Davis	.05
175	Rick Dempsey	.05
176	Jim Dwyer	.05
177	Mike Flanagan	.05
178	Dan Ford	.05
179	Wayne Gross	.05
180	John Lowenstein	.05
181	Dennis Martinez	.05
182	Tippy Martinez	.05
183	Scott McGregor	.05
184	Eddie Murray	1.00
185	Joe Nolan	.05
186	Floyd Rayford	.05
187	Cal Ripken, Jr.	4.00
188	Gary Roenicke	.05
189	Lenn Sakata	.05
190	John Shelby	.05
191	Ken Singleton	.05
192	Sammy Stewart	.05
193	Bill Swaggerty	.05

#	Player	Price	#	Player	Price	#	Player	Price	#	Player	Price
194	Tom Underwood	.05	298	Doug Corbett	.05	402	Bryan Little	.05	506	Juan Agosto	.05
195	Mike Young	.05	299	Doug DeCinces	.05	403	Gary Lucas	.05	507	Harold Baines	.05
196	Steve Balboni	.05	300	Brian Downing	.05	404	David Palmer	.05	508	Floyd Bannister	.05
197	Joe Beckwith	.05	301	Ken Forsch	.05	405	Tim Raines	.05	509	Britt Burns	.05
198	Bud Black	.05	302	Bobby Grich	.05	406	Mike Ramsey	.05	510	Julio Cruz	.05
199	George Brett	2.50	303	Reggie Jackson	2.00	407	Jeff Reardon	.05	511	Richard Dotson	.05
200	Onix Concepcion	.05	304	Tommy John	.10	408	Steve Rogers	.05	512	Jerry Dybzinski	.05
201	Mark Gubicza RC	.50	305	Curt Kaufman	.05	409	Dan Schatzeder	.05	513	Carlton Fisk	1.00
202	Larry Gura	.05	306	Brian Kison	.05	410	Bryn Smith	.05	514	Scott Fletcher	.05
203	Mark Huismann	.05	307	Fred Lynn	.05	411	Mike Stenhouse	.05	515	Jerry Hairston Sr.	.05
204	Dane Iorg	.05	308	Gary Pettis	.05	412	Tim Wallach	.05	516	Marc Hill	.05
205	Danny Jackson	.05	309	Ron Romanick RC	.05	413	Jim Wohlford	.05	517	LaMarr Hoyt	.05
206	Charlie Leibrandt	.05	310	Luis Sanchez	.05	414	Bill Almon	.05	518	Ron Kittle	.05
207	Hal McRae	.05	311	Dick Schofield	.05	415	Keith Atherton	.05	519	Rudy Law	.05
208	Darryl Motley	.05	312	Daryl Sconiers	.05	416	Bruce Bochte	.05	520	Vance Law	.05
209	Jorge Orta	.05	313	Jim Slaton	.05	417	Tom Burgmeier	.05	521	Greg Luzinski	.05
210	Greg Pryor	.05	314	Derrel Thomas	.05	418	Ray Burris	.05	522	Gene Nelson	.05
211	Dan Quisenberry	.05	315	Rob Wilfong	.05	419	Bill Caudill	.05	523	Tom Paciorek	.05
212	Bret Saberhagen	.25	316	Mike Witt	.05	420	Chris Codiroli	.05	524	Ron Reed	.05
213	Pat Sheridan	.05	317	Geoff Zahn	.05	421	Tim Conroy	.05	525	Bert Roberge	.05
214	Don Slaught	.05	318	Len Barker	.05	422	Mike Davis	.05	526	Tom Seaver	1.00
215	U.L. Washington	.05	319	Steve Bedrosian	.05	423	Jim Essian	.05	527	Roy Smalley	.05
216	John Wathan	.05	320	Bruce Benedict	.05	424	Mike Heath	.05	528	Dan Spillner	.05
217	Frank White	.05	321	Rick Camp	.05	425	Rickey Henderson	1.00	529	Mike Squires	.05
218	Willie Wilson	.05	322	Chris Chambliss	.05	426	Donnie Hill	.05	530	Greg Walker	.05
219	Neil Allen	.05	323	Jeff Dedmon RC	.05	427	Dave Kingman	.05	531	Cesar Cedeno	.05
220	Joaquin Andujar	.05	324	Terry Forster	.05	428	Bill Krueger	.05	532	Dave Concepcion	.05
221	Steve Braun	.05	325	Gene Garber	.05	429	Carney Lansford	.05	533	Eric Davis RC	2.00
222	Danny Cox	.05	326	Albert Hall RC	.05	430	Steve McCatty	.05	534	Nick Esasky	.05
223	Bob Forsch	.05	327	Terry Harper	.05	431	Joe Morgan	1.00	535	Tom Foley	.05
224	David Green	.05	328	Bob Horner	.05	432	Dwayne Murphy	.05	536	John Franco	.05
225	George Hendrick	.05	329	Glenn Hubbard	.05	433	Tony Phillips	.05	537	Brad Gulden	.05
226	Tom Herr	.05	330	Randy Johnson	.05	434	Lary Sorensen	.05	538	Tom Hume	.05
227	Ricky Horton RC	.05	331	Brad Komminsk	.05	435	Mike Warren	.05	539	Wayne Krenchicki	.05
228	Art Howe	.05	332	Rick Mahler	.05	436	Curt Young RC	.05	540	Andy McGaffigan	.05
229	Mike Jorgensen	.05	333	Craig McMurtry	.05	437	Luis Aponte	.05	541	Eddie Milner	.05
230	Kurt Kepshire	.05	334	Donnie Moore	.05	438	Chris Bando	.05	542	Ron Oester	.05
231	Jeff Lahti	.05	335	Dale Murphy	.40	439	Tony Bernazard	.05	543	Bob Owchinko	.05
232	Tito Landrum	.05	336	Ken Oberkfell	.05	440	Bert Blyleven	.10	544	Dave Parker	.05
233	Dave LaPoint	.05	337	Pascual Perez	.05	441	Brett Butler	.05	545	Frank Pastore	.05
234	Willie McGee	.05	338	Gerald Perry	.05	442	Ernie Camacho	.05	546	Tony Perez	.75
235	Tom Nieto RC	.05	339	Rafael Ramirez	.05	443	Joe Carter	.25	547	Ted Power	.05
236	Terry Pendleton RC	1.00	340	Jerry Royster	.05	444	Carmelo Castillo	.05	548	Joe Price	.05
237	Darrell Porter	.05	341	Alex Trevino	.05	445	Jamie Easterly	.05	549	Gary Redus	.05
238	Dave Rucker	.05	342	Claudell Washington	.05	446	Steve Farr RC	.05	550	Pete Rose	3.00
239	Lonnie Smith	.05	343	Alan Ashby	.05	447	Mike Fischlin	.05	551	Jeff Russell	.05
240	Ozzie Smith	2.00	344	Mark Bailey RC	.05	448	Julio Franco	.05	552	Mario Soto	.05
241	Bruce Sutter	.75	345	Kevin Bass	.05	449	Mel Hall	.05	553	Jay Tibbs RC	.05
242	Andy Van Slyke	.05	346	Enos Cabell	.05	450	Mike Hargrove	.05	554	Duane Walker	.05
243	Dave Von Ohlen	.05	347	Jose Cruz	.05	451	Neal Heaton	.05	555	Alan Bannister	.05
244	Larry Andersen	.05	348	Bill Dawley	.05	452	Brook Jacoby	.05	556	Buddy Bell	.05
245	Bill Campbell	.05	349	Frank DiPino	.05	453	Mike Jeffcoat RC	.05	557	Danny Darwin	.05
246	Steve Carlton	1.00	350	Bill Doran	.05	454	Don Schulze RC	.05	558	Charlie Hough	.05
247	Tim Corcoran	.05	351	Phil Garner	.05	455	Roy Smith	.05	559	Bobby Jones	.05
248	Ivan DeJesus	.05	352	Bob Knepper	.05	456	Pat Tabler	.05	560	Odell Jones	.05
249	John Denny	.05	353	Mike LaCoss	.05	457	Andre Thornton	.05	561	Jeff Kunkel RC	.05
250	Bo Diaz	.05	354	Jerry Mumphrey	.05	458	George Vukovich	.05	562	Mike Mason RC	.05
251	Greg Gross	.05	355	Joe Niekro	.05	459	Tom Waddell	.05	563	Pete O'Brien	.05
252	Kevin Gross	.05	356	Terry Puhl	.05	460	Jerry Willard	.05	564	Larry Parrish	.05
253	Von Hayes	.05	357	Craig Reynolds	.05	461	Dale Berra	.05	565	Mickey Rivers	.05
254	Al Holland	.05	358	Vern Ruhle	.05	462	John Candelaria	.05	566	Billy Sample	.05
255	Charles Hudson	.05	359	Nolan Ryan	4.00	463	Jose DeLeon	.05	567	Dave Schmidt	.05
256	Jerry Koosman	.05	360	Joe Sambito	.05	464	Doug Frobel	.05	568	Donnie Scott	.05
257	Joe Lefebvre	.05	361	Mike Scott	.05	465	Cecilio Guante	.05	569	Dave Stewart	.05
258	Sixto Lezcano	.05	362	Dave Smith	.05	466	Brian Harper	.05	570	Frank Tanana	.05
259	Garry Maddox	.05	363	Julio Solano RC	.05	467	Lee Lacy	.05	571	Wayne Tolleson	.05
260	Len Matuszek	.05	364	Dickie Thon	.05	468	Bill Madlock	.05	572	Gary Ward	.05
261	Tug McGraw	.05	365	Denny Walling	.05	469	Lee Mazzilli	.05	573	Curtis Wilkerson	.05
262	Al Oliver	.05	366	Dave Anderson	.05	470	Larry McWilliams	.05	574	George Wright	.05
263	Shane Rawley	.05	367	Bob Bailor	.05	471	Jim Morrison	.05	575	Ned Yost	.05
264	Juan Samuel	.05	368	Greg Brock	.05	472	Tony Pena	.05	576	Mark Brouhard	.05
265	Mike Schmidt	2.50	369	Carlos Diaz	.05	473	Johnny Ray	.05	577	Mike Caldwell	.05
266	Jeff Stone RC	.05	370	Pedro Guerrero	.05	474	Rick Rhoden	.05	578	Bobby Clark	.05
267	Ozzie Virgil	.05	371	Orel Hershiser RC	3.00	475	Don Robinson	.05	579	Jaime Cocanower	.05
268	Glenn Wilson	.05	372	Rick Honeycutt	.05	476	Rod Scurry	.05	580	Cecil Cooper	.05
269	John Wockenfuss	.05	373	Burt Hooton	.05	477	Kent Tekulve	.05	581	Rollie Fingers	.75
270	Darrell Brown	.05	374	Ken Howell RC	.05	478	Jason Thompson	.05	582	Jim Gantner	.05
271	Tom Brunansky	.05	375	Ken Landreaux	.05	479	John Tudor	.05	583	Moose Haas	.05
272	Randy Bush	.05	376	Candy Maldonado	.05	480	Lee Tunnell	.05	584	Dion James	.05
273	John Butcher	.05	377	Mike Marshall	.05	481	Marvell Wynne	.05	585	Pete Ladd	.05
274	Bobby Castillo	.05	378	Tom Niedenfuer	.05	482	Salome Barojas	.05	586	Rick Manning	.05
275	Ron Davis	.05	379	Alejandro Pena	.05	483	Dave Beard	.05	587	Bob McClure	.05
276	Dave Engle	.05	380	Jerry Reuss	.05	484	Jim Beattie	.05	588	Paul Molitor	1.00
277	Pete Filson	.05	381	R.J. Reynolds RC	.05	485	Barry Bonnell	.05	589	Charlie Moore	.05
278	Gary Gaetti	.05	382	German Rivera	.05	486	Phil Bradley RC	.05	590	Ben Oglivie	.05
279	Mickey Hatcher	.05	383	Bill Russell	.05	487	Al Cowens	.05	591	Chuck Porter	.05
280	Ed Hodge	.05	384	Steve Sax	.05	488	Alvin Davis	.05	592	Randy Ready RC	.05
281	Kent Hrbek	.05	385	Mike Scioscia	.05	489	Dave Henderson	.05	593	Ed Romero	.05
282	Houston Jimenez	.05	386	Franklin Stubbs RC	.05	490	Steve Henderson	.05	594	Bill Schroeder	.05
283	Tim Laudner	.05	387	Fernando Valenzuela	.05	491	Bob Kearney	.05	595	Ray Searage	.05
284	Rick Lysander	.05	388	Bob Welch	.05	492	Mark Langston	.15	596	Ted Simmons	.05
285	Dave Meier	.05	389	Terry Whitfield	.05	493	Larry Milbourne	.05	597	Jim Sundberg	.05
286	Kirby Puckett	8.00	390	Steve Yeager	.05	494	Paul Mirabella	.05	598	Don Sutton	.75
287	Pat Putnam	.05	391	Pat Zachry	.05	495	Mike Moore	.05	599	Tom Tellmann	.05
288	Ken Schrom	.05	392	Fred Breining	.05	496	Edwin Nunez	.05	600	Rick Waits	.05
289	Mike Smithson	.05	393	Gary Carter	1.00	497	Spike Owen	.05	601	Robin Yount	1.00
290	Tim Teufel	.05	394	Andre Dawson	.25	498	Jack Perconte	.05	602	Dusty Baker	.05
291	Frank Viola	.05	395	Miguel Dilone	.05	499	Ken Phelps	.05	603	Bob Brenly	.05
292	Ron Washington	.05	396	Dan Driessen	.05	500	Jim Presley RC	.05	604	Jack Clark	.05
293	Don Aase	.05	397	Doug Flynn	.05	501	Mike Stanton	.05	605	Chili Davis	.05
294	Juan Beniquez	.05	398	Terry Francona	.05	502	Bob Stoddard	.05	606	Mark Davis	.05
295	Bob Boone	.05	399	Bill Gullickson	.05	503	Gorman Thomas	.05	607	Dan Gladden RC	.25
296	Mike Brown	.05	400	Bob James	.05	504	Ed Vande Berg	.05	608	Atlee Hammaker	.05
297	Rod Carew	1.00	401	Charlie Lea	.05	505	Matt Young	.05	609	Mike Krukow	.05

610	Duane Kuiper	.05
611	Bob Lacey	.05
612	Bill Laskey	.05
613	Gary Lavelle	.05
614	Johnnie LeMaster	.05
615	Jeff Leonard	.05
616	Randy Lerch	.05
617	Greg Minton	.05
618	Steve Nicosia	.05
619	Gene Richards	.05
620	Jeff Robinson RC	.05
621	Scot Thompson	.05
622	Manny Trillo	.05
623	Brad Wellman	.05
624	Frank Williams RC	.05
625	Joel Youngblood	.05
626	Cal Ripken, Jr./IA	1.00
627	Mike Schmidt/IA	.50
628	Sparky Anderson	.05
629	Rickey Henderson, Dave Winfield	.50
630	Ryne Sandberg, Mike Schmidt	1.00
631	Gary Carter, Steve Garvey, Ozzie Smith, Darryl Strawberry	.25
632	Gary Carter, Charlie Lea	.10
633	Steve Garvey, Goose Gossage	.10
634	Dwight Gooden, Juan Samuel	.05
635	Willie Upshaw	.05
636	Lloyd Moseby	.05
637	Al Holland Holland	.05
638	Lee Tunnell Tunnell	.05
639	Reggie Jackson/IA	.50
640	Pete Rose/IA	.75
641	Cal Ripken, Jr., Cal Ripken, Sr.	1.00
642	Cubs Team	.10
643	Jack Morris, David Palmer, Mike Witt	.05
644	Willie Lozado, Vic Mata	.05
645	Kelly Gruber, Randy O'Neal RC	.15
646	Jose Roman, Joel Skinner RC	.05
647	Steve Kiefer, Danny Tartabull RC	.50
648	Rob Deer, Alejandro Sanchez RC	.25
649	Shawon Dunston, Bill Hatcher RC	1.00
650	Mike Bielecki, Ron Robinson RC	.10
651	Zane Smith, Paul Zuvella RC	.10
652	Glenn Davis, Joe Hesketh RC	.20
653	Steve Jeltz, John Russell RC	.10
654	Checklist 1-95	.05
655	Checklist 96-195	.05
656	Checklist 196-292	.05
657	Checklist 293-391	.05
658	Checklist 392-481	.05
659	Checklist 482-575	.05
660	Checklist 576-660	.05

Update

		NM/M
Complete Set (132):		5.00
Common Player:		.10
1	Don Aase	.10
2	Bill Almon	.10
3	Dusty Baker	.10
4	Dale Berra	.10
5	Karl Best	.10
6	Tim Birtsas	.10
7	Vida Blue	.10
8	Rich Bordi	.10

9	Daryl Boston	.10
10	Hubie Brooks	.10
11	Chris Brown	.10
12	Tom Browning	.10
13	Al Bumbry	.10
14	Tim Burke	.10
15	Ray Burris	.10
16	Jeff Burroughs	.10
17	Ivan Calderon	.10
18	Jeff Calhoun	.10
19	Bill Campbell	.10
20	Don Carman	.10
21	Gary Carter	.50
22	Bobby Castillo	.10
23	Bill Caudill	.10
24	Rick Cerone	.10
25	Jack Clark	.10
26	Pat Clements	.10
27	Stewart Cliburn	.10
28	Vince Coleman	.10
29	Dave Collins	.10
30	Fritz Connally	.10
31	Henry Cotto	.10
32	Danny Darwin	.10
33	Darren Daulton RC	1.00
34	Jerry Davis	.10
35	Brian Dayett	.10
36	Ken Dixon	.10
37	Tommy Dunbar	.10
38	Mariano Duncan	.10
39	Bob Fallon	.10
40	Brian Fisher	.10
41	Mike Fitzgerald	.10
42	Ray Fontenot	.10
43	Greg Gagne	.10
44	Oscar Gamble	.10
45	Jim Gott	.10
46	David Green	.10
47	Alfredo Griffin	.10
48	Ozzie Guillen RC	2.00
49	Toby Harrah	.10
50	Ron Hassey	.10
51	Rickey Henderson	3.00
52	Steve Henderson	.10
53	George Hendrick	.10
54	Teddy Higuera	.10
55	Al Holland	.10
56	Burt Hooton	.10
57	Jay Howell	.10
58	LaMarr Hoyt	.10
59	Tim Hulett	.10
60	Bob James	.10
61	Cliff Johnson	.10
62	Howard Johnson	.10
63	Ruppert Jones	.10
64	Steve Kemp	.10
65	Bruce Kison	.10
66	Mike LaCoss	.10
67	Lee Lacy	.10
68	Dave LaPoint	.10
69	Gary Lavelle	.10
70	Vance Law	.10
71	Manny Lee	.10
72	Sixto Lezcano	.10
73	Tim Lollar	.10
74	Urbano Lugo	.10
75	Fred Lynn	.10
76	Steve Lyons	.10
77	Mickey Mahler	.10
78	Ron Mathis	.10
79	Len Matuszek	.10
80	Oddibe McDowell	.10
81	Roger McDowell	.10
82	Donnie Moore	.10
83	Ron Musselman	.10
84	Al Oliver	.10
85	Joe Orsulak	.10
86	Dan Pasqua	.10
87	Chris Pittaro	.10
88	Rick Reuschel	.10
89	Earnie Riles	.10
90	Jerry Royster	.10
91	Dave Rozema	.10
92	Dave Rucker	.10
93	Vern Ruhle	.10
94	Mark Salas	.10
95	Luis Salazar	.10
96	Joe Sambito	.10
97	Billy Sample	.10
98	Alex Sanchez	.10
99	Calvin Schiraldi	.10
100	Rick Schu	.10
101	Larry Sheets	.10
102	Ron Shepherd	.10
103	Nelson Simmons	.10
104	Don Slaught	.10
105	Roy Smalley	.10
106	Lonnie Smith	.10
107	Nate Snell (RC)	.10
108	Lary Sorensen	.10
109	Chris Speier	.10
110	Mike Stenhouse	.10
111	John Stoddard	.10
112	John Stuper	.10
113	Jim Sundberg	.10

114	Bruce Sutter	.40
115	Don Sutton	.50
116	Bruce Tanner	.10
117	Kent Tekulve	.10
118	Walt Terrell	.10
119	Mickey Tettleton RC	1.00
120	Rich Thompson	.10
121	Louis Thornton	.10
122	Alex Trevino	.10
123	John Tudor	.10
124	Jose Uribe	.10
125	Dave Valle	.10
126	Dave Von Ohlen	.10
127	Curt Wardle	.10
128	U.L. Washington	.10
129	Ed Whitson	.10
130	Herm Winningham	.10
131	Rich Yett	.10
132	Checklist	.10

1986 Fleer

		NM/M
Unopened Fact. Set (660):		30.00
Complete Set (660):		25.00
Common Player:		.05
Wax Pack (15):		1.50
Wax Box (36):		45.00
Cello Pack (28):		2.00
Cello Box (24):		40.00
Rack Pack (45):		4.00
Rack Box (24):		65.00
1	Steve Balboni	.05
2	Joe Beckwith	.05
3	Buddy Biancalana	.05
4	Bud Black	.05
5	George Brett	2.00
6	Onix Concepcion	.05
7	Steve Farr	.05
8	Mark Gubicza	.05
9	Dane Iorg	.05
10	Danny Jackson	.05
11	Lynn Jones	.05
12	Mike Jones	.05
13	Charlie Leibrandt	.05
14	Hal McRae	.05
15	Omar Moreno	.05
16	Darryl Motley	.05
17	Jorge Orta	.05
18	Dan Quisenberry	.05
19	Bret Saberhagen	.05
20	Pat Sheridan	.05
21	Lonnie Smith	.05
22	Jim Sundberg	.05
23	John Wathan	.05
24	Frank White	.05
25	Willie Wilson	.05
26	Joaquin Andujar	.05
27	Steve Braun	.05
28	Bill Campbell	.05
29	Cesar Cedeno	.05
30	Jack Clark	.05
31	Vince Coleman	.05
32	Danny Cox	.05
33	Ken Dayley	.05
34	Ivan DeJesus	.05
35	Bob Forsch	.05
36	Brian Harper	.05
37	Tom Herr	.05
38	Ricky Horton	.05
39	Kurt Kepshire	.05
40	Jeff Lahti	.05
41	Tito Landrum	.05
42	Willie McGee	.05
43	Tom Nieto	.05
44	Terry Pendleton	.05
45	Darrell Porter	.05
46	Ozzie Smith	1.50
47	John Tudor	.05
48	Andy Van Slyke	.05
49	Todd Worrell RC	.25
50	Jim Acker	.05
51	Doyle Alexander	.05
52	Jesse Barfield	.05

53	George Bell	.05
54	Jeff Burroughs	.05
55	Bill Caudill	.05
56	Jim Clancy	.05
57	Tony Fernandez	.05
58	Tom Filer	.05
59	Damaso Garcia	.05
60	Tom Henke	.05
61	Garth Iorg	.05
62	Cliff Johnson	.05
63	Jimmy Key	.05
64	Dennis Lamp	.05
65	Gary Lavelle	.05
66	Buck Martinez	.05
67	Lloyd Moseby	.05
68	Rance Mulliniks	.05
69	Al Oliver	.05
70	Dave Stieb	.05
71	Louis Thornton	.05
72	Willie Upshaw	.05
73	Ernie Whitt	.05
74	Rick Aguilera RC	.75
75	Wally Backman	.05
76	Gary Carter	1.00
77	Ron Darling	.05
78	Len Dykstra RC	2.00
79	Sid Fernandez	.05
80	George Foster	.05
81	Dwight Gooden	.05
82	Tom Gorman	.05
83	Danny Heep	.05
84	Keith Hernandez	.05
85	Howard Johnson	.05
86	Ray Knight	.05
87	Terry Leach	.05
88	Ed Lynch	.05
89	Roger McDowell	.05
90	Jesse Orosco	.05
91	Tom Paciorek	.05
92	Ronn Reynolds	.05
93	Rafael Santana	.05
94	Doug Sisk	.05
95	Rusty Staub	.05
96	Darryl Strawberry	.05
97	Mookie Wilson	.05
98	Neil Allen	.05
99	Don Baylor	.05
100	Dale Berra	.05
101	Rich Bordi	.05
102	Marty Bystrom	.05
103	Joe Cowley	.05
104	Brian Fisher RC	.05
105	Ken Griffey	.05
106	Ron Guidry	.10
107	Ron Hassey	.05
108	Rickey Henderson	1.00
109	Don Mattingly	2.00
110	Bobby Meacham	.05
111	John Montefusco	.05
112	Phil Niekro	.75
113	Mike Pagliarulo	.05
114	Dan Pasqua	.05
115	Willie Randolph	.05
116	Dave Righetti	.05
117	Andre Robertson	.05
118	Billy Sample	.05
119	Bob Shirley	.05
120	Ed Whitson	.05
121	Dave Winfield	1.00
122	Butch Wynegar	.05
123	Dave Anderson	.05
124	Bob Bailor	.05
125	Greg Brock	.05
126	Enos Cabell	.05
127	Bobby Castillo	.05
128	Carlos Diaz	.05
129	Mariano Duncan	.05
130	Pedro Guerrero	.05
131	Orel Hershiser	.05
132	Rick Honeycutt	.05
133	Ken Howell	.05
134	Ken Landreaux	.05
135	Bill Madlock	.05
136	Candy Maldonado	.05
137	Mike Marshall	.05
138	Len Matuszek	.05
139	Tom Niedenfuer	.05
140	Alejandro Pena	.05
141	Jerry Reuss	.05
142	Bill Russell	.05
143	Steve Sax	.05
144	Mike Scioscia	.05
145	Fernando Valenzuela	.05
146	Bob Welch	.05
147	Terry Whitfield	.05
148	Juan Beniquez	.05
149	Bob Boone	.05
150	John Candelaria	.05
151	Rod Carew	1.00
152	Stewart Cliburn RC	.05
153	Doug DeCinces	.05
154	Brian Downing	.05
155	Ken Forsch	.05
156	Craig Gerber	.05

No.	Player	Price	No.	Player	Price	No.	Player	Price	No.	Player	Price
157	Bobby Grich	.05	261	Randy St. Claire	.05	365	Bob Dernier	.05	470	Edwin Nunez	.05
158	George Hendrick	.05	262	Scot Thompson	.05	366	Shawon Dunston	.05	471	Spike Owen	.05
159	Al Holland	.05	263	Tim Wallach	.05	367	Leon Durham	.05	472	Jack Perconte	.05
160	Reggie Jackson	1.50	264	U.L. Washington	.05	368	Dennis Eckersley	.75	473	Jim Presley	.05
161	Ruppert Jones	.05	265	Mitch Webster RC	.05	369	Ray Fontenot	.05	474	Donnie Scott	.05
162	Urbano Lugo RC	.05	266	Herm Winningham RC	.05	370	George Frazier	.05	475	Bill Swift	.05
163	Kirk McCaskill RC	.25	267	Floyd Youmans RC	.05	371	Bill Hatcher	.05	476	Danny Tartabull	.05
164	Donnie Moore	.05	268	Don Aase	.05	372	Dave Lopes	.05	477	Gorman Thomas	.05
165	Gary Pettis	.05	269	Mike Boddicker	.05	373	Gary Matthews	.05	478	Roy Thomas	.05
166	Ron Romanick	.05	270	Rich Dauer	.05	374	Ron Meredith	.05	479	Ed Vande Berg	.05
167	Dick Schofield	.05	271	Storm Davis	.05	375	Keith Moreland	.05	480	Frank Wills	.05
168	Daryl Sconiers	.05	272	Rick Dempsey	.05	376	Reggie Patterson	.05	481	Matt Young	.05
169	Jim Slaton	.05	273	Ken Dixon	.05	377	Dick Ruthven	.05	482	Ray Burris	.05
170	Don Sutton	.75	274	Jim Dwyer	.05	378	Ryne Sandberg	1.50	483	Jaime Cocanower	.05
171	Mike Witt	.05	275	Mike Flanagan	.05	379	Scott Sanderson	.05	484	Cecil Cooper	.05
172	Buddy Bell	.05	276	Wayne Gross	.05	380	Lee Smith	.05	485	Danny Darwin	.05
173	Tom Browning	.05	277	Lee Lacy	.05	381	Lary Sorensen	.05	486	Rollie Fingers	.75
174	Dave Concepcion	.05	278	Fred Lynn	.05	382	Chris Speier	.05	487	Jim Gantner	.05
175	Eric Davis	.05	279	Tippy Martinez	.05	383	Rick Sutcliffe	.05	488	Bob Gibson	.05
176	Bo Diaz	.05	280	Dennis Martinez	.05	384	Steve Trout	.05	489	Moose Haas	.05
177	Nick Esasky	.05	281	Scott McGregor	.05	385	Gary Woods	.05	490	Teddy Higuera RC	.05
178	John Franco	.05	282	Eddie Murray	1.00	386	Bert Blyleven	.10	491	Paul Householder	.05
179	Tom Hume	.05	283	Floyd Rayford	.05	387	Tom Brunansky	.05	492	Pete Ladd	.05
180	Wayne Krenchicki	.05	284	Cal Ripken, Jr.	3.00	388	Randy Bush	.05	493	Rick Manning	.05
181	Andy McGaffigan	.05	285	Gary Roenicke	.05	389	John Butcher	.05	494	Bob McClure	.05
182	Eddie Milner	.05	286	Larry Sheets	.05	390	Ron Davis	.05	495	Paul Molitor	1.00
183	Ron Oester	.05	287	John Shelby	.05	391	Dave Engle	.05	496	Charlie Moore	.05
184	Dave Parker	.05	288	Nate Snell	.05	392	Frank Eufemia	.05	497	Ben Oglivie	.05
185	Frank Pastore	.05	289	Sammy Stewart	.05	393	Pete Filson	.05	498	Randy Ready	.05
186	Tony Perez	.75	290	Alan Wiggins	.05	394	Gary Gaetti	.05	499	Earnie Riles RC	.05
187	Ted Power	.05	291	Mike Young	.05	395	Greg Gagne	.05	500	Ed Romero	.05
188	Joe Price	.05	292	Alan Ashby	.05	396	Mickey Hatcher	.05	501	Bill Schroeder	.05
189	Gary Redus	.05	293	Mark Bailey	.05	397	Kent Hrbek	.05	502	Ray Searage	.05
190	Ron Robinson	.05	294	Kevin Bass	.05	398	Tim Laudner	.05	503	Ted Simmons	.05
191	Pete Rose	2.50	295	Jeff Calhoun	.05	399	Rick Lysander	.05	504	Pete Vuckovich	.05
192	Mario Soto	.05	296	Jose Cruz	.05	400	Dave Meier	.05	505	Rick Waits	.05
193	John Stuper	.05	297	Glenn Davis	.05	401	Kirby Puckett	1.50	506	Robin Yount	1.00
194	Jay Tibbs	.05	298	Bill Dawley	.05	402	Mark Salas	.05	507	Len Barker	.05
195	Dave Van Gorder	.05	299	Frank DiPino	.05	403	Ken Schrom	.05	508	Steve Bedrosian	.05
196	Max Venable	.05	300	Bill Doran	.05	404	Roy Smalley	.05	509	Bruce Benedict	.05
197	Juan Agosto	.05	301	Phil Garner	.05	405	Mike Smithson	.05	510	Rick Camp	.05
198	Harold Baines	.05	302	Jeff Heathcock RC	.05	406	Mike Stenhouse	.05	511	Rick Cerone	.05
199	Floyd Bannister	.05	303	Charlie Kerfeld RC	.05	407	Tim Teufel	.05	512	Chris Chambliss	.05
200	Britt Burns	.05	304	Bob Knepper	.05	408	Frank Viola	.05	513	Jeff Dedmon	.05
201	Julio Cruz	.05	305	Ron Mathis	.05	409	Ron Washington	.05	514	Terry Forster	.05
202	Joel Davis RC	.05	306	Jerry Mumphrey	.05	410	Keith Atherton	.05	515	Gene Garber	.05
203	Richard Dotson	.05	307	Jim Pankovits	.05	411	Dusty Baker	.05	516	Terry Harper	.05
204	Carlton Fisk	1.00	308	Terry Puhl	.05	412	Tim Birtsas RC	.05	517	Bob Horner	.05
205	Scott Fletcher	.05	309	Craig Reynolds	.05	413	Bruce Bochte	.05	518	Glenn Hubbard	.05
206	Ozzie Guillen	.05	310	Nolan Ryan	3.00	414	Chris Codiroli	.05	519	Joe Johnson RC	.05
207	Jerry Hairston Sr.	.05	311	Mike Scott	.05	415	Dave Collins	.05	520	Brad Komminsk	.05
208	Tim Hulett	.05	312	Dave Smith	.05	416	Mike Davis	.05	521	Rick Mahler	.05
209	Bob James	.05	313	Dickie Thon	.05	417	Alfredo Griffin	.05	522	Dale Murphy	.30
210	Ron Kittle	.05	314	Denny Walling	.05	418	Mike Heath	.05	523	Ken Oberkfell	.05
211	Rudy Law	.05	315	Kurt Bevacqua	.05	419	Steve Henderson	.05	524	Pascual Perez	.05
212	Bryan Little	.05	316	Al Bumbry	.05	420	Donnie Hill	.05	525	Gerald Perry	.05
213	Gene Nelson	.05	317	Jerry Davis	.05	421	Jay Howell	.05	526	Rafael Ramirez	.05
214	Reid Nichols	.05	318	Luis DeLeon	.05	422	Tommy John	.10	527	Steve Shields RC	.05
215	Luis Salazar	.05	319	Dave Dravecky	.05	423	Dave Kingman	.05	528	Zane Smith	.05
216	Tom Seaver	1.00	320	Tim Flannery	.05	424	Bill Krueger	.05	529	Bruce Sutter	.75
217	Dan Spillner	.05	321	Steve Garvey	.30	425	Rick Langford	.05	530	Milt Thompson RC	.05
218	Bruce Tanner	.05	322	Goose Gossage	.05	426	Carney Lansford	.05	531	Claudell Washington	.05
219	Greg Walker	.05	323	Tony Gwynn	1.50	427	Steve McCatty	.05	532	Paul Zuvella	.05
220	Dave Wehrmeister	.05	324	Andy Hawkins	.05	428	Dwayne Murphy	.05	533	Vida Blue	.05
221	Juan Berenguer	.05	325	LaMarr Hoyt	.05	429	Steve Ontiveros RC	.05	534	Bob Brenly	.05
222	Dave Bergman	.05	326	Roy Lee Jackson	.05	430	Tony Phillips	.05	535	Chris Brown RC	.05
223	Tom Brookens	.05	327	Terry Kennedy	.05	431	Jose Rijo	.05	536	Chili Davis	.05
224	Darrell Evans	.05	328	Craig Lefferts	.05	432	Mickey Tettleton	.05	537	Mark Davis	.05
225	Barbaro Garbey	.05	329	Carmelo Martinez	.05	433	Luis Aguayo	.05	538	Rob Deer	.05
226	Kirk Gibson	.05	330	Lance McCullers RC	.05	434	Larry Andersen	.05	539	Dan Driessen	.05
227	John Grubb	.05	331	Kevin McReynolds	.05	435	Steve Carlton	1.00	540	Scott Garrelts	.05
228	Willie Hernandez	.05	332	Graig Nettles	.05	436	Don Carman RC	.05	541	Dan Gladden	.05
229	Larry Herndon	.05	333	Jerry Royster	.05	437	Tim Corcoran	.05	542	Jim Gott	.05
230	Chet Lemon	.05	334	Eric Show	.05	438	Darren Daulton	.05	543	David Green	.05
231	Aurelio Lopez	.05	335	Tim Stoddard	.05	439	John Denny	.05	544	Atlee Hammaker	.05
232	Jack Morris	.05	336	Garry Templeton	.05	440	Tom Foley	.05	545	Mike Jeffcoat	.05
233	Randy O'Neal	.05	337	Mark Thurmond	.05	441	Greg Gross	.05	546	Mike Krukow	.05
234	Lance Parrish	.05	338	Ed Wojna	.05	442	Kevin Gross	.05	547	Dave LaPoint	.05
235	Dan Petry	.05	339	Tony Armas	.05	443	Von Hayes	.05	548	Jeff Leonard	.05
236	Alex Sanchez	.05	340	Marty Barrett	.05	444	Charles Hudson	.05	549	Greg Minton	.05
237	Bill Scherrer	.05	341	Wade Boggs	1.50	445	Garry Maddox	.05	550	Alex Trevino	.05
238	Nelson Simmons	.05	342	Dennis Boyd	.05	446	Shane Rawley	.05	551	Manny Trillo	.05
239	Frank Tanana	.05	343	Bill Buckner	.05	447	Dave Rucker	.05	552	Jose Uribe RC	.05
240	Walt Terrell	.05	344	Mark Clear	.05	448	John Russell	.05	553	Brad Wellman	.05
241	Alan Trammell	.05	345	Roger Clemens	2.00	449	Juan Samuel	.05	554	Frank Williams	.05
242	Lou Whitaker	.05	346	Steve Crawford	.05	450	Mike Schmidt	2.00	555	Joel Youngblood	.05
243	Milt Wilcox	.05	347	Mike Easler	.05	451	Rick Schu	.05	556	Alan Bannister	.05
244	Hubie Brooks	.05	348	Dwight Evans	.05	452	Dave Shipanoff	.05	557	Glenn Brummer	.05
245	Tim Burke RC	.05	349	Rich Gedman	.05	453	Dave Stewart	.05	558	Steve Buechele RC	.05
246	Andre Dawson	.35	350	Jackie Gutierrez	.05	454	Jeff Stone	.05	559	Jose Guzman RC	.05
247	Mike Fitzgerald	.05	351	Glenn Hoffman	.05	455	Kent Tekulve	.05	560	Toby Harrah	.05
248	Terry Francona	.05	352	Bruce Hurst	.05	456	Ozzie Virgil	.05	561	Greg Harris	.05
249	Bill Gullickson	.05	353	Bruce Kison	.05	457	Glenn Wilson	.05	562	Dwayne Henry RC	.05
250	Joe Hesketh	.05	354	Tim Lollar	.05	458	Jim Beattie	.05	563	Burt Hooton	.05
251	Bill Laskey	.05	355	Steve Lyons	.05	459	Karl Best	.05	564	Charlie Hough	.05
252	Vance Law	.05	356	Al Nipper	.05	460	Barry Bonnell	.05	565	Mike Mason	.05
253	Charlie Lea	.05	357	Bob Ojeda	.05	461	Phil Bradley	.05	566	Oddibe McDowell RC	.05
254	Gary Lucas	.05	358	Jim Rice	.30	462	Ivan Calderon RC	.05	567	Dickie Noles	.05
255	David Palmer	.05	359	Bob Stanley	.05	463	Al Cowens	.05	568	Pete O'Brien	.05
256	Tim Raines	.05	360	Mike Trujillo	.05	464	Alvin Davis	.05	569	Larry Parrish	.05
257	Jeff Reardon	.05	361	Thad Bosley	.05	465	Dave Henderson	.05	570	Dave Rozema	.05
258	Bert Roberge	.05	362	Warren Brusstar	.05	466	Bob Kearney	.05	571	Dave Schmidt	.05
259	Dan Schatzeder	.05	363	Ron Cey	.05	467	Mark Langston	.05	572	Don Slaught	.05
260	Bryn Smith	.05	364	Jody Davis	.05	468	Bob Long	.05	573	Wayne Tolleson	.05
						469	Mike Moore	.05	574	Duane Walker	.05
									575	Gary Ward	.05

576	Chris Welsh	.05
577	Curtis Wilkerson	.05
578	George Wright	.05
579	Chris Bando	.05
580	Tony Bernazard	.05
581	Brett Butler	.05
582	Ernie Camacho	.05
583	Joe Carter	.05
584	Carmello Castillo (Carmelo)	.05
585	Jamie Easterly	.05
586	Julio Franco	.05
587	Mel Hall	.05
588	Mike Hargrove	.05
589	Neal Heaton	.05
590	Brook Jacoby	.05
591	Otis Nixon RC	.25
592	Jerry Reed	.05
593	Vern Ruhle	.05
594	Pat Tabler	.05
595	Rich Thompson	.05
596	Andre Thornton	.05
597	Dave Von Ohlen	.05
598	George Vukovich	.05
599	Tom Waddell	.05
600	Curt Wardle	.05
601	Jerry Willard	.05
602	Bill Almon	.05
603	Mike Bielecki	.05
604	Sid Bream	.05
605	Mike Brown	.05
606	Pat Clements RC	.05
607	Jose DeLeon	.05
608	Denny Gonzalez	.05
609	Cecilio Guante	.05
610	Steve Kemp	.05
611	Sam Khalifa	.05
612	Lee Mazzilli	.05
613	Larry McWilliams	.05
614	Jim Morrison	.05
615	Joe Orsulak RC	.25
616	Tony Pena	.05
617	Johnny Ray	.05
618	Rick Reuschel	.05
619	R.J. Reynolds	.05
620	Rick Rhoden	.05
621	Don Robinson	.05
622	Jason Thompson	.05
623	Lee Tunnell	.05
624	Jim Winn	.05
625	Marvell Wynne	.05
626	Dwight Gooden/IA	.05
627	Don Mattingly/IA	.50
628	Pete Rose (4,192 Hits)	1.00
629	Rod Carew (3,000 Hits)	.25
630	Phil Niekro, Tom Seaver (300 Wins)	.25
631	Don Baylor Ouch!	.05
632	Tim Raines, Darryl Strawberry	.05
633	Cal Ripken, Jr., Alan Trammell	1.00
634	Wade Boggs, George Brett	1.00
635	Bob Horner, Dale Murphy	.25
636	Vince Coleman, Willie McGee	.25
637	Vince Coleman	.05
638	Dwight Gooden, Pete Rose	.50
639	Wade Boggs, Don Mattingly	1.00
640	Steve Garvey, Dale Murphy, Dave Parker	.25
641	Dwight Gooden, Fernando Valenzuela	.10
642	Jimmy Key, Dave Stieb	.05
643	Carlton Fisk, Rich Gedman	.10
644	Benito Santiago, Gene Walter RC	1.00
645	Colin Ward, Mike Woodard RC	.10
646	Kal Daniels, Paul O'Neill RC	2.00
647	Andres Galarraga, Fred Toliver RC	3.00
648	Curt Ford, Bob Kipper RC	.10
649	Jose Canseco, Eric Plunk RC	5.00
650	Mark McLemore, Gus Polidor RC	.75
651	Mickey Brantley, Rob Woodward RC	.10
652	Mark Funderburk, Billy Joe Robidoux RC	.10
653	Cecil Fielder, Cory Snyder RC	1.50
654	Checklist 1-97	.05
655	Checklist 98-196	.05
656	Checklist 197-291	.05
657	Checklist 292-385	.05
658	Checklist 386-482	.05
659	Checklist 483-578	.05
660	Checklist 579-660	.05

Update

NM/M

Unopened Fact. Set (132):		40.00
Complete Set (132):		30.00
Common Player:		.05
1	Mike Aldrete	.05
2	Andy Allanson	.05
3	Neil Allen	.05
4	Joaquin Andujar	.05
5	Paul Assenmacher	.05
6	Scott Bailes	.05
7	Jay Baller	.05
8	Scott Bankhead	.05
9	Bill Bathe	.05
10	Don Baylor	.05
11	Billy Beane	.05
12	Steve Bedrosian	.05
13	Juan Beniquez	.05
14	Barry Bonds RC	25.00
15	Bobby Bonilla RC	1.00
16	Rich Bordi	.05
17	Bill Campbell	.05
18	Tom Candiotti	.05
19	John Cangelosi	.05
20	Jose Canseco	4.00
21	Chuck Cary	.05
22	Juan Castillo	.05
23	Rick Cerone	.05
24	John Cerutti	.05
25	Will Clark RC	1.00
26	Mark Clear	.05
27	Darnell Coles	.05
28	Dave Collins	.05
29	Tim Conroy	.05
30	Ed Correa	.05
31	Joe Cowley	.05
32	Bill Dawley	.05
33	Rob Deer	.05
34	John Denny	.05
35	Jim DeShaies	.05
36	Doug Drabek RC	1.00
37	Mike Easler	.05
38	Mark Eichhorn	.05
39	Dave Engle	.05
40	Mike Fischlin	.05
41	Scott Fletcher	.05
42	Terry Forster	.05
43	Terry Francona	.05
44	Andres Galarraga	.50
45	Lee Guetterman	.05
46	Bill Gullickson	.05
47	Jackie Gutierrez	.05
48	Moose Haas	.05
49	Billy Hatcher	.05
50	Mike Heath	.05
51	Guy Hoffman	.05
52	Tom Hume	.05
53	Pete Incaviglia RC	.50
54	Dane Iorg	.05
55	Chris James	.05
56	Stan Javier	.05
57	Tommy John	.15
58	Tracy Jones	.05
59	Wally Joyner RC	1.00
60	Wayne Krenchicki	.05
61	John Kruk RC	1.00
62	Mike LaCoss	.05
63	Pete Ladd	.05
64	Dave LaPoint	.05
65	Mike LaValliere	.05
66	Rudy Law	.05
67	Dennis Leonard	.05
68	Steve Lombardozzi	.05
69	Aurelio Lopez	.05
70	Mickey Mahler	.05
71	Candy Maldonado	.05
72	Roger Mason	.05
73	Greg Mathews	.05
74	Andy McGaffigan	.05
75	Joel McKeon	.05
76	Kevin Mitchell RC	.50
77	Bill Mooneyham	.05
78	Omar Moreno	.05
79	Jerry Mumphrey	.05
80	Al Newman	.05
81	Phil Niekro	.50
82	Randy Niemann	.05
83	Juan Nieves	.05
84	Bob Ojeda	.05
85	Rick Ownbey	.05
86	Tom Paciorek	.05
87	David Palmer	.05
88	Jeff Parrett	.05
89	Pat Perry	.05
90	Dan Plesac	.05
91	Darrell Porter	.05
92	Luis Quinones	.05
93	Rey Quinonez	.05
94	Gary Redus	.05
95	Jeff Reed	.05
96	Bip Roberts	.05
97	Billy Joe Robidoux	.05
98	Gary Roenicke	.05
99	Ron Roenicke	.05
100	Angel Salazar	.05
101	Joe Sambito	.05
102	Billy Sample	.05
103	Dave Schmidt	.05
104	Ken Schrom	.05
105	Ruben Sierra RC	.75
106	Ted Simmons	.05
107	Sammy Stewart	.05
108	Kurt Stillwell	.05
109	Dale Sveum	.05
110	Tim Teufel	.05
111	Bob Tewksbury	.05
112	Andres Thomas	.05
113	Jason Thompson	.05
114	Milt Thompson	.05
115	Rob Thompson	.05
116	Jay Tibbs	.05
117	Fred Toliver	.05
118	Wayne Tolleson	.05
119	Alex Trevino	.05
120	Manny Trillo	.05
121	Ed Vande Berg	.05
122	Ozzie Virgil	.05
123	Tony Walker	.05
124	Gene Walter	.05
125	Duane Ward	.05
126	Jerry Willard	.05
127	Mitch Williams	.05
128	Reggie Williams	.05
129	Bobby Witt	.05
130	Marvell Wynne	.05
131	Steve Yeager	.05
132	Checklist	.05

1987 Fleer

NM/M

Unopened Fact. Set (672):		65.00
Complete Set (660):		50.00
Common Player:		.05
Wax Pack (15/17):		3.00
Wax Box (36):		100.00
Cello Pack (28):		5.00
Cello Box (24):		100.00
Rack Pack (51):		8.00
Rack Box (24):		160.00
1	Rick Aguilera	.05
2	Richard Anderson	.05
3	Wally Backman	.05
4	Gary Carter	.75
5	Ron Darling	.05
6	Len Dykstra	.05
7	Kevin Elster RC	.15
8	Sid Fernandez	.05
9	Dwight Gooden	.05
10	Ed Hearn RC	.05
11	Danny Heep	.05
12	Keith Hernandez	.05
13	Howard Johnson	.05
14	Ray Knight	.05
15	Lee Mazzilli	.05
16	Roger McDowell	.05
17	Kevin Mitchell	.05
18	Randy Niemann	.05
19	Bob Ojeda	.05
20	Jesse Orosco	.05
21	Rafael Santana	.05
22	Doug Sisk	.05
23	Darryl Strawberry	.05
24	Tim Teufel	.05
25	Mookie Wilson	.05
26	Tony Armas	.05
27	Marty Barrett	.05
28	Don Baylor	.05
29	Wade Boggs	1.00
30	Oil Can Boyd	.05
31	Bill Buckner	.05
32	Roger Clemens	2.00
33	Steve Crawford	.05
34	Dwight Evans	.05
35	Rich Gedman	.05
36	Dave Henderson	.05
37	Bruce Hurst	.05
38	Tim Lollar	.05
39	Al Nipper	.05
40	Spike Owen	.05
41	Jim Rice	.30
42	Ed Romero	.05
43	Joe Sambito	.05
44	Calvin Schiraldi	.05
45	Tom Seaver	.75
46	Jeff Sellers RC	.05
47	Bob Stanley	.05
48	Sammy Stewart	.05
49	Larry Andersen	.05
50	Alan Ashby	.05
51	Kevin Bass	.05
52	Jeff Calhoun	.05
53	Jose Cruz	.05
54	Danny Darwin	.05
55	Glenn Davis	.05
56	Jim Deshaies RC	.10
57	Bill Doran	.05
58	Phil Garner	.05
59	Billy Hatcher	.05
60	Charlie Kerfeld	.05
61	Bob Knepper	.05
62	Dave Lopes	.05
63	Aurelio Lopez	.05
64	Jim Pankovits	.05
65	Terry Puhl	.05
66	Craig Reynolds	.05
67	Nolan Ryan	3.00
68	Mike Scott	.05
69	Dave Smith	.05
70	Dickie Thon	.05
71	Tony Walker	.05
72	Denny Walling	.05
73	Bob Boone	.05
74	Rick Burleson	.05
75	John Candelaria	.05
76	Doug Corbett	.05
77	Doug DeCinces	.05
78	Brian Downing	.05
79	Chuck Finley RC	1.00
80	Terry Forster	.05
81	Bobby Grich	.05
82	George Hendrick	.05
83	Jack Howell	.05
84	Reggie Jackson	1.00
85	Ruppert Jones	.05
86	Wally Joyner	.05
87	Gary Lucas	.05
88	Kirk McCaskill	.05
89	Donnie Moore	.05
90	Gary Pettis	.05
91	Vern Ruhle	.05
92	Dick Schofield	.05
93	Don Sutton	.65
94	Rob Wilfong	.05
95	Mike Witt	.05
96	Doug Drabek	.05
97	Mike Easler	.05
98	Mike Fischlin	.05
99	Brian Fisher	.05
100	Ron Guidry	.10
101	Rickey Henderson	.75
102	Tommy John	.10
103	Ron Kittle	.05
104	Don Mattingly	2.00
105	Bobby Meacham	.05
106	Joe Niekro	.05
107	Mike Pagliarulo	.05
108	Dan Pasqua	.05
109	Willie Randolph	.05
110	Dennis Rasmussen	.05
111	Dave Righetti	.05
112	Gary Roenicke	.05
113	Rod Scurry	.05
114	Bob Shirley	.05
115	Joel Skinner	.05
116	Tim Stoddard	.05
117	Bob Tewksbury RC	.35

No.	Player	Value
118	Wayne Tolleson	.05
119	Claudell Washington	.05
120	Dave Winfield	.75
121	Steve Buechele	.05
122	Ed Correa RC	.05
123	Scott Fletcher	.05
124	Jose Guzman	.05
125	Toby Harrah	.05
126	Greg Harris	.05
127	Charlie Hough	.05
128	Pete Incaviglia	.05
129	Mike Mason	.05
130	Oddibe McDowell	.05
131	Dale Mohorcic RC	.05
132	Pete O'Brien	.05
133	Tom Paciorek	.05
134	Larry Parrish	.05
135	Geno Petralli	.05
136	Darrell Porter	.05
137	Jeff Russell	.05
138	Ruben Sierra	.05
139	Don Slaught	.05
140	Gary Ward	.05
141	Curtis Wilkerson	.05
142	Mitch Williams RC	.10
143	Bobby Witt RC	.10
144	Dave Bergman	.05
145	Tom Brookens	.05
146	Bill Campbell	.05
147	Chuck Cary RC	.05
148	Darnell Coles	.05
149	Dave Collins	.05
150	Darrell Evans	.05
151	Kirk Gibson	.05
152	John Grubb	.05
153	Willie Hernandez	.05
154	Larry Herndon	.05
155	Eric King RC	.05
156	Chet Lemon	.05
157	Dwight Lowry	.05
158	Jack Morris	.05
159	Randy O'Neal	.05
160	Lance Parrish	.05
161	Dan Petry	.05
162	Pat Sheridan	.05
163	Jim Slaton	.05
164	Frank Tanana	.05
165	Walt Terrell	.05
166	Mark Thurmond	.05
167	Alan Trammell	.05
168	Lou Whitaker	.05
169	Luis Aguayo	.05
170	Steve Bedrosian	.05
171	Don Carman	.05
172	Darren Daulton	.05
173	Greg Gross	.05
174	Kevin Gross	.05
175	Von Hayes	.05
176	Charles Hudson	.05
177	Tom Hume	.05
178	Steve Jeltz	.05
179	Mike Maddux RC	.05
180	Shane Rawley	.05
181	Gary Redus	.05
182	Ron Roenicke	.05
183	Bruce Ruffin RC	.10
184	John Russell	.05
185	Juan Samuel	.05
186	Dan Schatzeder	.05
187	Mike Schmidt	2.00
188	Rick Schu	.05
189	Jeff Stone	.05
190	Kent Tekulve	.05
191	Milt Thompson	.05
192	Glenn Wilson	.05
193	Buddy Bell	.05
194	Tom Browning	.05
195	Sal Butera	.05
196	Dave Concepcion	.05
197	Kal Daniels	.05
198	Eric Davis	.05
199	John Denny	.05
200	Bo Diaz	.05
201	Nick Esasky	.05
202	John Franco	.05
203	Bill Gullickson	.05
204	Barry Larkin RC	2.00
205	Eddie Milner	.05
206	Rob Murphy RC	.05
207	Ron Oester	.05
208	Dave Parker	.05
209	Tony Perez	.65
210	Ted Power	.05
211	Joe Price	.05
212	Ron Robinson	.05
213	Pete Rose	2.50
214	Mario Soto	.05
215	Kurt Stillwell RC	.05
216	Max Venable	.05
217	Chris Welsh	.05
218	Carl Willis RC	.05
219	Jesse Barfield	.05
220	George Bell	.05
221	Bill Caudill	.05
222	John Cerutti RC	.05
223	Jim Clancy	.05
224	Mark Eichhorn RC	.10
225	Tony Fernandez	.05
226	Damaso Garcia	.05
227	Kelly Gruber	.05
228	Tom Henke	.05
229	Garth Iorg	.05
230	Cliff Johnson	.05
231	Joe Johnson	.05
232	Jimmy Key	.05
233	Dennis Lamp	.05
234	Rick Leach	.05
235	Buck Martinez	.05
236	Lloyd Moseby	.05
237	Rance Mulliniks	.05
238	Dave Stieb	.05
239	Willie Upshaw	.05
240	Ernie Whitt	.05
241	Andy Allanson RC	.05
242	Scott Bailes RC	.05
243	Chris Bando	.05
244	Tony Bernazard	.05
245	John Butcher	.05
246	Brett Butler	.05
247	Ernie Camacho	.05
248	Tom Candiotti	.05
249	Joe Carter	.05
250	Carmen Castillo	.05
251	Julio Franco	.05
252	Mel Hall	.05
253	Brook Jacoby	.05
254	Phil Niekro	.65
255	Otis Nixon	.05
256	Dickie Noles	.05
257	Bryan Oelkers	.05
258	Ken Schrom	.05
259	Don Schulze	.05
260	Cory Snyder	.05
261	Pat Tabler	.05
262	Andre Thornton	.05
263	Rich Yett RC	.05
264	Mike Aldrete RC	.05
265	Juan Berenguer	.05
266	Vida Blue	.05
267	Bob Brenly	.05
268	Chris Brown	.05
269	Will Clark	.05
270	Chili Davis	.05
271	Mark Davis	.05
272	Kelly Downs RC	.05
273	Scott Garrelts	.05
274	Dan Gladden	.05
275	Mike Krukow	.05
276	Randy Kutcher RC	.05
277	Mike LaCoss	.05
278	Jeff Leonard	.05
279	Candy Maldonado	.05
280	Roger Mason	.05
281	Bob Melvin	.05
282	Greg Minton	.05
283	Jeff Robinson	.05
284	Harry Spilman	.05
285	Rob Thompson RC	.05
286	Jose Uribe	.05
287	Frank Williams	.05
288	Joel Youngblood	.05
289	Jack Clark	.05
290	Vince Coleman	.05
291	Tim Conroy	.05
292	Danny Cox	.05
293	Ken Dayley	.05
294	Curt Ford	.05
295	Bob Forsch	.05
296	Tom Herr	.05
297	Ricky Horton	.05
298	Clint Hurdle	.05
299	Jeff Lahti	.05
300	Steve Lake	.05
301	Tito Landrum	.05
302	Mike LaValliere RC	.05
303	Greg Mathews RC	.05
304	Willie McGee	.05
305	Jose Oquendo	.05
306	Terry Pendleton	.05
307	Pat Perry	.05
308	Ozzie Smith	1.50
309	Ray Soff	.05
310	John Tudor	.05
311	Andy Van Slyke	.05
312	Todd Worrell	.05
313	Dann Bilardello	.05
314	Hubie Brooks	.05
315	Tim Burke	.05
316	Andre Dawson	.35
317	Mike Fitzgerald	.05
318	Tom Foley	.05
319	Andres Galarraga	.05
320	Joe Hesketh	.05
321	Wallace Johnson	.05
322	Wayne Krenchicki	.05
323	Vance Law	.05
324	Dennis Martinez	.05
325	Bob McClure	.05
326	Andy McGaffigan	.05
327	Al Newman RC	.05
328	Tim Raines	.05
329	Jeff Reardon	.05
330	Luis Rivera RC	.05
331	Bob Sebra RC	.05
332	Bryn Smith	.05
333	Jay Tibbs	.05
334	Tim Wallach	.05
335	Mitch Webster	.05
336	Jim Wohlford	.05
337	Floyd Youmans	.05
338	Chris Bosio RC	.25
339	Glenn Braggs RC	.05
340	Rick Cerone	.05
341	Mark Clear	.05
342	Bryan Clutterbuck RC	.05
343	Cecil Cooper	.05
344	Rob Deer	.05
345	Jim Gantner	.05
346	Ted Higuera	.05
347	John Henry Johnson	.05
348	Tim Leary	.05
349	Rick Manning	.05
350	Paul Molitor	.75
351	Charlie Moore	.05
352	Juan Nieves	.05
353	Ben Oglivie	.05
354	Dan Plesac RC	.10
355	Ernest Riles	.05
356	Billy Joe Robidoux	.05
357	Bill Schroeder	.05
358	Dale Sveum RC	.05
359	Gorman Thomas	.05
360	Bill Wegman	.05
361	Robin Yount	.75
362	Steve Balboni	.05
363	Scott Bankhead RC	.05
364	Buddy Biancalana	.05
365	Bud Black	.05
366	George Brett	2.00
367	Steve Farr	.05
368	Mark Gubicza	.05
369	Bo Jackson	.75
370	Danny Jackson	.05
371	Mike Kingery RC	.05
372	Rudy Law	.05
373	Charlie Leibrandt	.05
374	Dennis Leonard	.05
375	Hal McRae	.05
376	Jorge Orta	.05
377	Jamie Quirk	.05
378	Dan Quisenberry	.05
379	Bret Saberhagen	.05
380	Angel Salazar	.05
381	Lonnie Smith	.05
382	Jim Sundberg	.05
383	Frank White	.05
384	Willie Wilson	.05
385	Joaquin Andujar	.05
386	Doug Bair	.05
387	Dusty Baker	.05
388	Bruce Bochte	.05
389	Jose Canseco	.65
390	Chris Codiroli	.05
391	Mike Davis	.05
392	Alfredo Griffin	.05
393	Moose Haas	.05
394	Donnie Hill	.05
395	Jay Howell	.05
396	Dave Kingman	.05
397	Carney Lansford	.05
398	David Leiper RC	.05
399	Bill Mooneyham RC	.05
400	Dwayne Murphy	.05
401	Steve Ontiveros	.05
402	Tony Phillips	.05
403	Eric Plunk	.05
404	Jose Rijo	.05
405	Terry Steinbach RC	.50
406	Dave Stewart	.05
407	Mickey Tettleton	.05
408	Dave Von Ohlen	.05
409	Jerry Willard	.05
410	Curt Young	.05
411	Bruce Bochy	.05
412	Dave Dravecky	.05
413	Tim Flannery	.05
414	Steve Garvey	.25
415	Goose Gossage	.10
416	Tony Gwynn	1.50
417	Andy Hawkins	.05
418	LaMarr Hoyt	.05
419	Terry Kennedy	.05
420	John Kruk	.05
421	Dave LaPoint	.05
422	Craig Lefferts	.05
423	Carmelo Martinez	.05
424	Lance McCullers	.05
425	Kevin McReynolds	.05
426	Graig Nettles	.05
427	Bip Roberts	.05
428	Jerry Royster	.05
429	Benito Santiago	.05
430	Eric Show	.05
431	Bob Stoddard	.05
432	Garry Templeton	.05
433	Gene Walter	.05
434	Ed Whitson	.05
435	Marvell Wynne	.05
436	Dave Anderson	.05
437	Greg Brock	.05
438	Enos Cabell	.05
439	Mariano Duncan	.05
440	Pedro Guerrero	.05
441	Orel Hershiser	.05
442	Rick Honeycutt	.05
443	Ken Howell	.05
444	Ken Landreaux	.05
445	Bill Madlock	.05
446	Mike Marshall	.05
447	Len Matuszek	.05
448	Tom Niedenfuer	.05
449	Alejandro Pena	.05
450	Dennis Powell	.05
451	Jerry Reuss	.05
452	Bill Russell	.05
453	Steve Sax	.05
454	Mike Scioscia	.05
455	Franklin Stubbs	.05
456	Alex Trevino	.05
457	Fernando Valenzuela	.05
458	Ed Vande Berg	.05
459	Bob Welch	.05
460	Reggie Williams RC	.05
461	Don Aase	.05
462	Juan Beniquez	.05
463	Mike Boddicker	.05
464	Juan Bonilla	.05
465	Rich Bordi	.05
466	Storm Davis	.05
467	Rick Dempsey	.05
468	Ken Dixon	.05
469	Jim Dwyer	.05
470	Mike Flanagan	.05
471	Jackie Gutierrez	.05
472	Brad Havens	.05
473	Lee Lacy	.05
474	Fred Lynn	.05
475	Scott McGregor	.05
476	Eddie Murray	.75
477	Tom O'Malley	.05
478	Cal Ripken, Jr.	3.00
479	Larry Sheets	.05
480	John Shelby	.05
481	Nate Snell	.05
482	Jim Traber	.05
483	Mike Young	.05
484	Neil Allen	.05
485	Harold Baines	.05
486	Floyd Bannister	.05
487	Daryl Boston	.05
488	Ivan Calderon	.05
489	John Cangelosi RC	.05
490	Steve Carlton	.75
491	Joe Cowley	.05
492	Julio Cruz	.05
493	Bill Dawley	.05
494	Jose DeLeon	.05
495	Richard Dotson	.05
496	Carlton Fisk	.75
497	Ozzie Guillen	.05
498	Jerry Hairston Sr.	.05
499	Ron Hassey	.05
500	Tim Hulett	.05
501	Bob James	.05
502	Steve Lyons	.05
503	Joel McKeon RC	.05
504	Gene Nelson	.05
505	Dave Schmidt	.05
506	Ray Searage	.05
507	Bobby Thigpen RC	.15
508	Greg Walker	.05
509	Jim Acker	.05
510	Doyle Alexander	.05
511	Paul Assenmacher RC	.05
512	Bruce Benedict	.05
513	Chris Chambliss	.05
514	Jeff Dedmon	.05
515	Gene Garber	.05
516	Ken Griffey	.05
517	Terry Harper	.05
518	Bob Horner	.05
519	Glenn Hubbard	.05
520	Rick Mahler	.05
521	Omar Moreno	.05
522	Dale Murphy	.35
523	Ken Oberkfell	.05
524	Ed Olwine	.05
525	David Palmer	.05
526	Rafael Ramirez	.05
527	Billy Sample	.05
528	Ted Simmons	.05
529	Zane Smith	.05
530	Bruce Sutter	.65
531	Andres Thomas RC	.05
532	Ozzie Virgil	.05
533	Allan Anderson RC	.05

534	Keith Atherton	.05
535	Billy Beane	.05
536	Bert Blyleven	.10
537	Tom Brunansky	.05
538	Randy Bush	.05
539	George Frazier	.05
540	Gary Gaetti	.05
541	Greg Gagne	.05
542	Mickey Hatcher	.05
543	Neal Heaton	.05
544	Kent Hrbek	.05
545	Roy Lee Jackson	.05
546	Tim Laudner	.05
547	Steve Lombardozzi	.05
548	Mark Portugal RC	.10
549	Kirby Puckett	1.50
550	Jeff Reed	.05
551	Mark Salas	.05
552	Roy Smalley	.05
553	Mike Smithson	.05
554	Frank Viola	.05
555	Thad Bosley	.05
556	Ron Cey	.05
557	Jody Davis	.05
558	Ron Davis	.05
559	Bob Dernier	.05
560	Frank DiPino	.05
561	Shawon Dunston	.05
562	Leon Durham	.05
563	Dennis Eckersley	.65
564	Terry Francona	.05
565	Dave Gumpert	.05
566	Guy Hoffman	.05
567	Ed Lynch	.05
568	Gary Matthews	.05
569	Keith Moreland	.05
570	Jamie Moyer RC	.05
571	Jerry Mumphrey	.05
572	Ryne Sandberg	1.00
573	Scott Sanderson	.05
574	Lee Smith	.05
575	Chris Speier	.05
576	Rick Sutcliffe	.05
577	Manny Trillo	.05
578	Steve Trout	.05
579	Karl Best	.05
580	Scott Bradley	.05
581	Phil Bradley	.05
582	Mickey Brantley	.05
583	Mike Brown	.05
584	Alvin Davis	.05
585	Lee Guetterman RC	.05
586	Mark Huismann	.05
587	Bob Kearney	.05
588	Pete Ladd	.05
589	Mark Langston	.05
590	Mike Moore	.05
591	Mike Morgan	.05
592	John Moses	.05
593	Ken Phelps	.05
594	Jim Presley	.05
595	Rey Quinonez (Quinones) RC	.05
596	Harold Reynolds	.05
597	Billy Swift	.05
598	Danny Tartabull	.05
599	Steve Yeager	.05
600	Matt Young	.05
601	Bill Almon	.05
602	Rafael Belliard RC	.05
603	Mike Bielecki	.05
604	Barry Bonds	40.00
605	Bobby Bonilla	.05
606	Sid Bream	.05
607	Mike Brown	.05
608	Pat Clements	.05
609	Mike Diaz RC	.05
610	Cecilio Guante	.05
611	Barry Jones RC	.05
612	Bob Kipper	.05
613	Larry McWilliams	.05
614	Jim Morrison	.05
615	Joe Orsulak	.05
616	Junior Ortiz	.05
617	Tony Pena	.05
618	Johnny Ray	.05
619	Rick Reuschel	.05
620	R.J. Reynolds	.05
621	Rick Rhoden	.05
622	Don Robinson	.05
623	Bob Walk	.05
624	Jim Winn	.05
625	Jose Canseco, Pete Incaviglia	.15
626	Phil Niekro, Don Sutton	.25
627	Don Aase, Dave Righetti	.05
628	Jose Canseco, Wally Joyner	.15
629	Gary Carter, Dwight Gooden, Keith Hernandez, Darryl Strawberry	.15
630	Mike Krukow, Mike Scott	.05
631	John Franco, Fernando Valenzuela	.05
632	Bob Horner	.05
633	Jose Canseco, Kirby Puckett, Jim Rice	.25
634	Gary Carter, Roger Clemens	.50
635	Steve Carlton	.15
636	Glenn Davis, Eddie Murray	.15
637	Wade Boggs, Keith Hernandez	.25
638	Don Mattingly, Darryl Strawberry	.50
639	Dave Parker, Ryne Sandberg	.25
640	Roger Clemens, Dwight Gooden	.50
641	Charlie Hough, Mike Witt	.05
642	Tim Raines, Juan Samuel	.05
643	Harold Baines, Jesse Barfield	.05
644	Dave Clark, Greg Swindell RC	.35
645	Ron Karkovice, Russ Morman RC	.25
646	Willie Fraser, Devon White RC	1.00
647	Jerry Browne, Mike Stanley RC	.25
648	Phil Lombardi, Dave Magadan RC	.20
649	Ralph Bryant, Jose Gonzalez RC	.10
650	Randy Asadoor, Jimmy Jones RC	.10
651	Marvin Freeman, Tracy Jones RC	.10
652	Kevin Seitzer, John Stefero	.25
653	Steve Fireovid, Rob Nelson RC	.10
654	Checklist 1-95	.05
655	Checklist 96-192	.05
656	Checklist 193-288	.05
657	Checklist 289-384	.05
658	Checklist 385-483	.05
659	Checklist 484-578	.05
660	Checklist 579-660	.05

Update

Steve Carlton PITCHER

		NM/M
	Complete Set (132):	9.00
	Common Player:	.05
1	Scott Bankhead	.05
2	Eric Bell	.05
3	Juan Beniquez	.05
4	Juan Berenguer	.05
5	Mike Birkbeck	.05
6	Randy Bockus	.05
7	Rod Booker	.05
8	Thad Bosley	.05
9	Greg Brock	.05
10	Bob Brower	.05
11	Chris Brown	.05
12	Jerry Browne	.05
13	Ralph Bryant	.05
14	DeWayne Buice	.05
15	Ellis Burks	.05
16	Casey Candaele	.05
17	Steve Carlton	.50
18	Juan Castillo	.05
19	Chuck Crim	.05
20	Mark Davidson	.05
21	Mark Davis	.05
22	Storm Davis	.05
23	Bill Dawley	.05
24	Andre Dawson	.30
25	Brian Dayett	.05

26	Rick Dempsey	.05
27	Ken Dowell	.05
28	Dave Dravecky	.05
29	Mike Dunne	.05
30	Dennis Eckersley	.40
31	Cecil Fielder	.05
32	Brian Fisher	.05
33	Willie Fraser	.05
34	Ken Gerhart	.05
35	Jim Gott	.05
36	Dan Gladden	.05
37	Mike Greenwell	.05
38	Cecilio Guante	.05
39	Albert Hall	.05
40	Atlee Hammaker	.05
41	Mickey Hatcher	.05
42	Mike Heath	.05
43	Neal Heaton	.05
44	Mike Henneman	.05
45	Guy Hoffman	.05
46	Charles Hudson	.05
47	Chuck Jackson	.05
48	Mike Jackson	.05
49	Reggie Jackson	.75
50	Chris James	.05
51	Dion James	.05
52	Stan Javier	.05
53	Stan Jefferson	.05
54	Jimmy Jones	.05
55	Tracy Jones	.05
56	Terry Kennedy	.05
57	Mike Kingery	.05
58	Ray Knight	.05
59	Gene Larkin	.05
60	Mike LaValliere	.05
61	Jack Lazorko	.05
62	Terry Leach	.05
63	Rick Leach	.05
64	Craig Lefferts	.05
65	Jim Lindeman	.05
66	Bill Long	.05
67	Mike Loynd	.05
68	Greg Maddux RC	6.00
69	Bill Madlock	.05
70	Dave Magadan	.05
71	Joe Magrane	.05
72	Fred Manrique	.05
73	Mike Mason	.05
74	Lloyd McClendon	.05
75	Fred McGriff	.05
76	Mark McGwire	3.00
77	Mark McLemore	.05
78	Kevin McReynolds	.05
79	Dave Meads	.05
80	Greg Minton	.05
81	John Mitchell	.05
82	Kevin Mitchell	.05
83	John Morris	.05
84	Jeff Musselman	.05
85	Randy Myers	.05
86	Gene Nelson	.05
87	Joe Niekro	.05
88	Tom Nieto	.05
89	Reid Nichols	.05
90	Matt Nokes	.05
91	Dickie Noles	.05
92	Edwin Nunez	.05
93	Jose Nunez	.05
94	Paul O'Neill	.05
95	Jim Paciorek	.05
96	Lance Parrish	.05
97	Bill Pecota	.05
98	Tony Pena	.05
99	Luis Polonia	.05
100	Randy Ready	.05
101	Jeff Reardon	.05
102	Gary Redus	.05
103	Rick Rhoden	.05
104	Wally Ritchie	.05
105	Jeff Robinson	.05
106	Mark Salas	.05
107	Dave Schmidt	.05
108	Kevin Seitzer	.05
109	John Shelby	.05
110	John Smiley	.05
111	Lary Sorensen	.05
112	Chris Speier	.05
113	Randy St. Claire	.05
114	Jim Sundberg	.05
115	B.J. Surhoff	.05
116	Greg Swindell	.05
117	Danny Tartabull	.05
118	Dorn Taylor	.05
119	Lee Tunnell	.05
120	Ed Vande Berg	.05
121	Andy Van Slyke	.05
122	Gary Ward	.05
123	Devon White	.05
124	Alan Wiggins	.05
125	Bill Wilkinson	.05
126	Jim Winn	.05
127	Frank Williams	.05
128	Ken Williams	.05
129	Matt Williams RC	1.00

130	Herm Winningham	.05
131	Matt Young	.05
132	Checklist 1-132	.05

Glossy Tin

	NM/M
Unopened Set (672):	75.00
Complete Set (672):	50.00
Common Player:	.10

(Single star cards valued at .75-1X regular-issue 1987 Fleer.)

Update Glossy Tin

	NM/M
Unopened Set (132):	12.00
Complete Set (132):	7.50
Common Player:	.10

(Star cards valued at .75-1X regular version 1987 Fleer updates.)

1988 Fleer

Alan Trammell SHORTSTOP

		NM/M
	Retail Factory Set (672):	12.00
	Hobby Factory Set (672):	10.00
	Complete Set (660):	8.00
	Common Player:	.05
	Wax Pack (15):	.75
	Wax Box (36):	12.00
	Cello Pack (28):	1.25
	Cello Box (24):	16.00
1	Keith Atherton	.05
2	Don Baylor	.05
3	Juan Berenguer	.05
4	Bert Blyleven	.10
5	Tom Brunansky	.05
6	Randy Bush	.05
7	Steve Carlton	.50
8	Mark Davidson RC	.05
9	George Frazier	.05
10	Gary Gaetti	.05
11	Greg Gagne	.05
12	Dan Gladden	.05
13	Kent Hrbek	.05
14	Gene Larkin RC	.05
15	Tim Laudner	.05
16	Steve Lombardozzi	.05
17	Al Newman	.05
18	Joe Niekro	.05
19	Kirby Puckett	.65
20	Jeff Reardon	.05
21a	Dan Schatzader (Incorrect spelling.)	.10
21b	Dan Schatzeder (Correct spelling.)	.05
22	Roy Smalley	.05
23	Mike Smithson	.05
24	Les Straker RC	.05
25	Frank Viola	.05
26	Jack Clark	.05
27	Vince Coleman	.05
28	Danny Cox	.05
29	Bill Dawley	.05
30	Ken Dayley	.05
31	Doug DeCinces	.05
32	Curt Ford	.05
33	Bob Forsch	.05
34	David Green	.05
35	Tom Herr	.05
36	Ricky Horton	.05
37	Lance Johnson RC	.25

#	Player	Price		#	Player	Price		#	Player	Price		#	Player	Price
38	Steve Lake	.05		139	Terry Leach	.05		243	Dave Parker	.05		347	Oil Can Boyd	.05
39	Jim Lindeman	.05		140	Barry Lyons RC	.05		244	Pat Perry	.05		348	Ellis Burks	.05
40	Joe Magrane RC	.10		141	Dave Magadan	.05		245	Ted Power	.05		349	Roger Clemens	.75
41	Greg Mathews	.05		142	Roger McDowell	.05		246	Dennis Rasmussen	.05		350	Steve Crawford	.05
42	Willie McGee	.05		143	Kevin McReynolds	.05		247	Ron Robinson	.05		351	Dwight Evans	.05
43	John Morris	.05		144	Keith Miller RC	.05		248	Kurt Stillwell	.05		352	Wes Gardner RC	.05
44	Jose Oquendo	.05		145	John Mitchell RC	.05		249	Jeff Treadway RC	.05		353	Rich Gedman	.05
45	Tony Pena	.05		146	Randy Myers	.05		250	Frank Williams	.05		354	Mike Greenwell	.05
46	Terry Pendleton	.05		147	Bob Ojeda	.05		251	Steve Balboni	.05		355	Sam Horn RC	.05
47	Ozzie Smith	.65		148	Jesse Orosco	.05		252	Bud Black	.05		356	Bruce Hurst	.05
48	John Tudor	.05		149	Rafael Santana	.05		253	Thad Bosley	.05		357	John Marzano RC	.05
49	Lee Tunnell	.05		150	Doug Sisk	.05		254	George Brett	.75		358	Al Nipper	.05
50	Todd Worrell	.05		151	Darryl Strawberry	.05		255	John Davis RC	.05		359	Spike Owen	.05
51	Doyle Alexander	.05		152	Tim Teufel	.05		256	Steve Farr	.05		360	Jody Reed RC	.15
52	Dave Bergman	.05		153	Gene Walter	.05		257	Gene Garber	.05		361	Jim Rice	.20
53	Tom Brookens	.05		154	Mookie Wilson	.05		258	Jerry Gleaton	.05		362	Ed Romero	.05
54	Darrell Evans	.05		155	Jay Aldrich RC	.05		259	Mark Gubicza	.10		363	Kevin Romine	.05
55	Kirk Gibson	.05		156	Chris Bosio	.05		260	Bo Jackson	.05		364	Joe Sambito	.05
56	Mike Heath	.05		157	Glenn Braggs	.05		261	Danny Jackson	.05		365	Calvin Schiraldi	.05
57	Mike Henneman	.05		158	Greg Brock	.05		262	Ross Jones RC	.05		366	Jeff Sellers	.05
58	Willie Hernandez	.05		159	Juan Castillo	.05		263	Charlie Leibrandt	.05		367	Bob Stanley	.05
59	Larry Herndon	.05		160	Mark Clear	.05		264	Bill Pecota RC	.05		368	Scott Bankhead	.05
60	Eric King	.05		161	Cecil Cooper	.05		265	Melido Perez RC	.05		369	Phil Bradley	.05
61	Chet Lemon	.05		162	Chuck Crim RC	.05		266	Jamie Quirk	.05		370	Scott Bradley	.05
62	Scott Lusader RC	.05		163	Rob Deer	.05		267	Dan Quisenberry	.05		371	Mickey Brantley	.05
63	Bill Madlock	.05		164	Mike Felder	.05		268	Bret Saberhagen	.05		372	Mike Campbell RC	.05
64	Jack Morris	.05		165	Jim Gantner	.05		269	Angel Salazar	.05		373	Alvin Davis	.05
65	Jim Morrison	.05		166	Ted Higuera	.05		270	Kevin Seitzer	.05		374	Lee Guetterman	.05
66	Matt Nokes	.05		167	Steve Kiefer	.05		271	Danny Tartabull	.05		375	Dave Hengel RC	.05
67	Dan Petry	.05		168	Rick Manning	.05		272	Gary Thurman RC	.05		376	Mike Kingery	.05
68a	Jeff Robinson RC (Born 12-13-60 on back.)	.25		169	Paul Molitor	.50		273	Frank White	.05		377	Mark Langston	.05
68b	Jeff Robinson RC (Born 12/14/61 on back.)	.10		170	Juan Nieves	.05		274	Willie Wilson	.05		378	Edgar Martinez RC	1.00
69	Pat Sheridan	.05		171	Dan Plesac	.05		275	Tony Bernazard	.05		379	Mike Moore	.05
70	Nate Snell	.05		172	Earnest Riles	.05		276	Jose Canseco	.30		380	Mike Morgan	.05
71	Frank Tanana	.05		173	Bill Schroeder	.05		277	Mike Davis	.05		381	John Moses	.05
72	Walt Terrell	.05		174	Steve Stanicek RC	.05		278	Storm Davis	.05		382	Donnell Nixon RC	.05
73	Mark Thurmond	.05		175	B.J. Surhoff	.05		279	Dennis Eckersley	.40		383	Edwin Nunez	.05
74	Alan Trammell	.05		176	Dale Sveum	.05		280	Alfredo Griffin	.05		384	Ken Phelps	.05
75	Lou Whitaker	.05		177	Bill Wegman	.05		281	Rick Honeycutt	.05		385	Jim Presley	.05
76	Mike Aldrete	.05		178	Robin Yount	.50		282	Jay Howell	.05		386	Rey Quinones	.05
77	Bob Brenly	.05		179	Hubie Brooks	.05		283	Reggie Jackson	.65		387	Jerry Reed	.05
78	Will Clark	.05		180	Tim Burke	.05		284	Dennis Lamp	.05		388	Harold Reynolds	.05
79	Chili Davis	.05		181	Casey Candaele	.05		285	Carney Lansford	.05		389	Dave Valle	.05
80	Kelly Downs	.05		182	Mike Fitzgerald	.05		286	Mark McGwire	.85		390	Bill Wilkinson RC	.05
81	Dave Dravecky	.05		183	Tom Foley	.05		287	Dwayne Murphy	.05		391	Harold Baines	.05
82	Scott Garrelts	.05		184	Andres Galarraga	.05		288	Gene Nelson	.05		392	Floyd Bannister	.05
83	Atlee Hammaker	.05		185	Neal Heaton	.05		289	Steve Ontiveros	.05		393	Daryl Boston	.05
84	Dave Henderson	.05		186	Wallace Johnson	.05		290	Tony Phillips	.05		394	Ivan Calderon	.05
85	Mike Krukow	.05		187	Vance Law	.05		291	Eric Plunk	.05		395	Jose DeLeon	.05
86	Mike LaCoss	.05		188	Dennis Martinez	.05		292	Luis Polonia RC	.15		396	Richard Dotson	.05
87	Craig Lefferts	.05		189	Bob McClure	.05		293	Rick Rodriguez RC	.05		397	Carlton Fisk	.50
88	Jeff Leonard	.05		190	Andy McGaffigan	.05		294	Terry Steinbach	.05		398	Ozzie Guillen	.05
89	Candy Maldonado	.05		191	Reid Nichols	.05		295	Dave Stewart	.05		399	Ron Hassey	.05
90	Ed Milner	.05		192	Pascual Perez	.05		296	Curt Young	.05		400	Donnie Hill	.05
91	Bob Melvin	.05		193	Tim Raines	.05		297	Luis Aguayo	.05		401	Bob James	.05
92	Kevin Mitchell	.05		194	Jeff Reed	.05		298	Steve Bedrosian	.05		402	Dave LaPoint	.05
93	Jon Perlman RC	.05		195	Bob Sebra	.05		299	Jeff Calhoun	.05		403	Bill Lindsey RC	.05
94	Rick Reuschel	.05		196	Bryn Smith	.05		300	Don Carman	.05		404	Bill Long RC	.05
95	Don Robinson	.05		197	Randy St. Claire	.05		301	Todd Frohwirth RC	.05		405	Steve Lyons	.05
96	Chris Speier	.05		198	Tim Wallach	.05		302	Greg Gross	.05		406	Fred Manrique RC	.05
97	Harry Spilman	.05		199	Mitch Webster	.05		303	Kevin Gross	.05		407	Jack McDowell RC	.25
98	Robbie Thompson	.05		200	Herm Winningham	.05		304	Von Hayes	.05		408	Gary Redus	.05
99	Jose Uribe	.05		201	Floyd Youmans	.05		305	Keith Hughes RC	.05		409	Ray Searage	.05
100	Mark Wasinger RC	.05		202	Brad Arnsberg RC	.05		306	Mike Jackson RC	.05		410	Bobby Thigpen	.05
101	Matt Williams	.05		203	Rick Cerone	.05		307	Chris James	.05		411	Greg Walker	.05
102	Jesse Barfield	.05		204	Pat Clements	.05		308	Steve Jeltz	.05		412	Kenny Williams RC	.05
103	George Bell	.05		205	Henry Cotto	.05		309	Mike Maddux	.05		413	Jim Winn	.05
104	Juan Beniquez	.05		206	Mike Easler	.05		310	Lance Parrish	.05		414	Jody Davis	.05
105	John Cerutti	.05		207	Ron Guidry	.10		311	Shane Rawley	.05		415	Andre Dawson	.25
106	Jim Clancy	.05		208	Bill Gullickson	.05		312	Wally Ritchie RC	.05		416	Brian Dayett	.05
107	Rob Ducey RC	.05		209	Rickey Henderson	.50		313	Bruce Ruffin	.05		417	Bob Dernier	.05
108	Mark Eichhorn	.05		210	Charles Hudson	.05		314	Juan Samuel	.05		418	Frank DiPino	.05
109	Tony Fernandez	.05		211	Tommy John	.10		315	Mike Schmidt	.75		419	Shawon Dunston	.05
110	Cecil Fielder	.05		212	Roberto Kelly RC	.25		316	Rick Schu	.05		420	Leon Durham	.05
111	Kelly Gruber	.05		213	Ron Kittle	.05		317	Jeff Stone	.05		421	Les Lancaster RC	.10
112	Tom Henke	.05		214	Don Mattingly	.75		318	Kent Tekulve	.05		422	Ed Lynch	.05
113	Garth Iorq (Iorg)	.05		215	Bobby Meacham	.05		319	Milt Thompson	.05		423	Greg Maddux	.75
114	Jimmy Key	.05		216	Mike Pagliarulo	.05		320	Glenn Wilson	.05		424	Dave Martinez	.05
115	Rick Leach	.05		217	Dan Pasqua	.05		321	Rafael Belliard	.05		425a	Keith Moreland (Bunting, photo actually Jody Davis.)	2.00
116	Manny Lee	.05		218	Willie Randolph	.05		322	Barry Bonds	1.00		425b	Keith Moreland (Standing upright, correct photo.)	.05
117	Nelson Liriano RC	.05		219	Rick Rhoden	.05		323	Bobby Bonilla	.05		426	Jamie Moyer	.05
118	Fred McGriff	.05		220	Dave Righetti	.05		324	Sid Bream	.05		427	Jerry Mumphrey	.05
119	Lloyd Moseby	.05		221	Jerry Royster	.05		325	John Cangelosi	.05		428	Paul Noce RC	.05
120	Rance Mulliniks	.05		222	Tim Stoddard	.05		326	Mike Diaz	.05		429	Rafael Palmeiro	.40
121	Jeff Musselman	.05		223	Wayne Tolleson	.05		327	Doug Drabek	.05		430	Wade Rowdon	.05
122	Jose Nunez RC	.05		224	Gary Ward	.05		328	Mike Dunne RC	.05		431	Ryne Sandberg	.65
123	Dave Stieb	.05		225	Claudell Washington	.05		329	Brian Fisher	.05		432	Scott Sanderson	.05
124	Willie Upshaw	.05		226	Dave Winfield	.50		330	Brett Gideon RC	.05		433	Lee Smith	.05
125	Duane Ward	.05		227	Buddy Bell	.05		331	Terry Harper	.05		434	Jim Sundberg	.05
126	Ernie Whitt	.05		228	Tom Browning	.05		332	Bob Kipper	.05		435	Rick Sutcliffe	.05
127	Rick Aguilera	.05		229	Dave Concepcion	.05		333	Mike LaValliere	.05		436	Manny Trillo	.05
128	Wally Backman	.05		230	Kal Daniels	.05		334	Jose Lind RC	.15		437	Juan Agosto	.05
129	Mark Carreon RC	.10		231	Eric Davis	.05		335	Junior Ortiz	.05		438	Larry Andersen	.05
130	Gary Carter	.50		232	Bo Diaz	.05		336	Vicente Palacios RC	.05		439	Alan Ashby	.05
131	David Cone	.05		233	Nick Esasky	.05		337	Bob Patterson RC	.05		440	Kevin Bass	.05
132	Ron Darling	.05		234	John Franco	.05		338	Al Pedrique RC	.05		441	Ken Caminiti RC	.25
133	Len Dykstra	.05		235	Guy Hoffman	.05		339	R.J. Reynolds	.05		442	Rocky Childress RC	.05
134	Sid Fernandez	.05		236	Tom Hume	.05		340	John Smiley	.05		443	Jose Cruz	.05
135	Dwight Gooden	.05		237	Tracy Jones	.05		341	Andy Van Slyke	.05		444	Danny Darwin	.05
136	Keith Hernandez	.05		238	Bill Landrum RC	.05		342	Bob Walk	.05		445	Glenn Davis	.05
137	Gregg Jefferies RC	.50		239	Barry Larkin	.05		343	Marty Barrett	.05		446	Jim Deshaies	.05
138	Howard Johnson	.05		240	Terry McGriff	.05		344	Todd Benzinger RC	.05				
				241	Rob Murphy	.05		345	Wade Boggs	.65				
				242	Ron Oester	.05		346	Tom Bolton RC	.05				

#	Player	Value
447	Bill Doran	.05
448	Ty Gainey	.05
449	Billy Hatcher	.05
450	Jeff Heathcock	.05
451	Bob Knepper	.05
452	Rob Mallicoat RC	.05
453	Dave Meads RC	.05
454	Craig Reynolds	.05
455	Nolan Ryan	1.00
456	Mike Scott	.05
457	Dave Smith	.05
458	Denny Walling	.05
459	Robbie Wine RC	.05
460	Gerald Young RC	.05
461	Bob Brower	.05
462a	Jerry Browne (White player, photo actually Bob Brower.)	2.00
462b	Jerry Browne (Black player, correct photo.)	.05
463	Steve Buechele	.05
464	Edwin Correa	.05
465	Cecil Espy RC	.05
466	Scott Fletcher	.05
467	Jose Guzman	.05
468	Greg Harris	.05
469	Charlie Hough	.05
470	Pete Incaviglia	.05
471	Paul Kilgus RC	.05
472	Mike Loynd	.05
473	Oddibe McDowell	.05
474	Dale Mohorcic	.05
475	Pete O'Brien	.05
476	Larry Parrish	.05
477	Geno Petralli	.05
478	Jeff Russell	.05
479	Ruben Sierra	.05
480	Mike Stanley	.05
481	Curtis Wilkerson	.05
482	Mitch Williams	.05
483	Bobby Witt	.05
484	Tony Armas	.05
485	Bob Boone	.05
486	Bill Buckner	.05
487	DeWayne Buice RC	.05
488	Brian Downing	.05
489	Chuck Finley	.05
490	Willie Fraser	.05
491	Jack Howell	.05
492	Ruppert Jones	.05
493	Wally Joyner	.05
494	Jack Lazorko	.05
495	Gary Lucas	.05
496	Kirk McCaskill	.05
497	Mark McLemore	.05
498	Darrell Miller	.05
499	Greg Minton	.05
500	Donnie Moore	.05
501	Gus Polidor	.05
502	Johnny Ray	.05
503	Mark Ryal	.05
504	Dick Schofield	.05
505	Don Sutton	.40
506	Devon White	.05
507	Mike Witt	.05
508	Dave Anderson	.05
509	Tim Belcher	.05
510	Ralph Bryant	.15
511	Tim Crews RC	.05
512	Mike Devereaux RC	.10
513	Mariano Duncan	.05
514	Pedro Guerrero	.05
515	Jeff Hamilton	.05
516	Mickey Hatcher	.05
517	Brad Havens	.05
518	Orel Hershiser	.05
519	Shawn Hillegas RC	.05
520	Ken Howell	.05
521	Tim Leary	.05
522	Mike Marshall	.05
523	Steve Sax	.05
524	Mike Scioscia	.05
525	Mike Sharperson	.05
526	John Shelby	.05
527	Franklin Stubbs	.05
528	Fernando Valenzuela	.05
529	Bob Welch	.05
530	Matt Young	.05
531	Jim Acker	.05
532	Paul Assenmacher	.05
533	Jeff Blauser RC	.10
534	Joe Boever RC	.05
535	Martin Clary	.05
536	Kevin Coffman RC	.05
537	Jeff Dedmon	.05
538	Ron Gant RC	.50
539	Tom Glavine RC	2.00
540	Ken Griffey	.05
541	Al Hall	.05
542	Glenn Hubbard	.05
543	Dion James	.05
544	Dale Murphy	.20
545	Ken Oberkfell	.05
546	David Palmer	.05
547	Gerald Perry	.05
548	Charlie Puleo	.05
549	Ted Simmons	.05
550	Zane Smith	.05
551	Andres Thomas	.05
552	Ozzie Virgil	.05
553	Don Aase	.05
554	Jeff Ballard RC	.05
555	Eric Bell	.05
556	Mike Boddicker	.05
557	Ken Dixon	.05
558	Jim Dwyer	.05
559	Ken Gerhart	.05
560	Rene Gonzales RC	.05
561	Mike Griffin	.05
562	John Hayban (Habyan)	.05
563	Terry Kennedy	.05
564	Ray Knight	.05
565	Lee Lacy	.05
566	Fred Lynn	.05
567	Eddie Murray	.50
568	Tom Niedenfuer	.05
569	Bill Ripken RC	.05
570	Cal Ripken, Jr.	1.00
571	Dave Schmidt	.05
572	Larry Sheets	.05
573	Pete Stanicek RC	.05
574	Mark Williamson RC	.05
575	Mike Young	.05
576	Shawn Abner	.05
577	Greg Booker	.05
578	Chris Brown	.05
579	Keith Comstock RC	.05
580	Joey Cora RC	.05
581	Mark Davis	.05
582	Tim Flannery	.05
583	Goose Gossage	.05
584	Mark Grant	.05
585	Tony Gwynn*	.65
586	Andy Hawkins	.05
587	Stan Jefferson	.05
588	Jimmy Jones	.05
589	John Kruk	.05
590	Shane Mack RC	.10
591	Carmelo Martinez	.05
592	Lance McCullers	.05
593	Eric Nolte RC	.05
594	Randy Ready	.05
595	Luis Salazar	.05
596	Benito Santiago	.05
597	Eric Show	.05
598	Garry Templeton	.05
599	Ed Whitson	.05
600	Scott Bailes	.05
601	Chris Bando	.05
602	Jay Bell RC	.50
603	Brett Butler	.05
604	Tom Candiotti	.05
605	Joe Carter	.05
606	Carmen Castillo	.05
607	Brian Dorsett RC	.05
608	John Farrell RC	.05
609	Julio Franco	.05
610	Mel Hall	.05
611	Tommy Hinzo RC	.05
612	Brook Jacoby	.05
613	Doug Jones RC	.10
614	Ken Schrom	.05
615	Cory Snyder	.05
616	Sammy Stewart	.05
617	Greg Swindell	.05
618	Pat Tabler	.05
619	Ed Vande Berg	.05
620	Eddie Williams RC	.05
621	Rich Yett	.05
622	Wally Joyner, Cory Snyder	.10
623	George Bell, Pedro Guerrero	.05
624	Jose Canseco, Mark McGwire	.50
625	Dan Plesac, Dave Righetti	.05
626	Jack Morris, Bret Saberhagen, Mike Witt	.05
627	Steve Bedrosian, John Franco	.05
628	Ryne Sandberg, Ozzie Smith	.50
629	Mark McGwire	.50
630	Todd Benzinger, Ellis Burks, Mike Greenwell	.10
631	Tony Gwynn, Tim Raines	.20
632	Orel Hershiser, Mike Scott	.05
633	Mark McGwire, Pat Tabler	.50
634	Tony Gwynn, Vince Coleman	.15
635	Tony Fernandez, Cal Ripken, Jr., Alan Trammell	.40
636	Gary Carter, Mike Schmidt	.40
637	Eric Davis	.05
638	Matt Nokes, Kirby Puckett	.25
639	Keith Hernandez, Dale Murphy	.10
640	Bill Ripken, Cal Ripken, Jr.	.50
641	Mark Grace, Darrin Jackson RC	1.00
642	Damon Berryhill, Jeff Montgomery RC	.20
643	Felix Fermin, Jessie Reid RC	.05
644	Greg Myers, Greg Tabor RC	.05
645	Jim Eppard, Joey Meyer	.05
646	Adam Peterson, Randy Velarde RC	.10
647	Chris Gwynn, Peter Smith RC	.15
648	Greg Jelks, Tom Newell RC	.05
649	Mario Diaz, Clay Parker RC	.05
650	Jack Savage, Todd Simmons RC	.05
651	John Burkett, Kirt Manwaring RC	.30
652	Dave Otto, Walt Weiss RC	.25
653	Randell Byers (Randall), Jeff King RC	.25
654a	Checklist 1-101 (21 is Schatzeder)	.10
654b	Checklist 1-101 (21 is Schatzeder)	.05
655	Checklist 102-201	.05
656	Checklist 202-296	.05
657	Checklist 297-390	.05
658	Checklist 391-483	.05
659	Checklist 484-575	.05
660	Checklist 576-660	.05

Update

Kirk Gibson
OUTFIELD
Dodgers
22
FLEER

	NM/M
Complete Set (132):	5.00
Common Player:	.05

#	Player	Value
1	Jose Bautista	.05
2	Joe Orsulak	.05
3	Doug Sisk	.05
4	Craig Worthington	.05
5	Mike Boddicker	.05
6	Rick Cerone	.05
7	Larry Parrish	.05
8	Lee Smith	.10
9	Mike Smithson	.05
10	John Trautwein	.05
11	Sherman Corbett	.05
12	Chili Davis	.05
13	Jim Eppard	.05
14	Bryan Harvey	.05
15	John Davis	.05
16	Dave Gallagher	.05
17	Ricky Horton	.05
18	Dan Pasqua	.05
19	Melido Perez	.05
20	Jose Segura	.05
21	Andy Allanson	.05
22	Jon Perlman	.05
23	Domingo Ramos	.05
24	Rick Rodriguez	.05
25	Willie Upshaw	.05
26	Paul Gibson	.05
27	Don Heinkel	.05
28	Ray Knight	.05
29	Gary Pettis	.05
30	Luis Salazar	.05
31	Mike MacFarlane	.05
32	Jeff Montgomery	.05
33	Ted Power	.05
34	Israel Sanchez	.05
35	Kurt Stillwell	.05
36	Pat Tabler	.05
37	Don August	.05
38	Darryl Hamilton	.05
39	Jeff Leonard	.05
40	Joey Meyer	.05
41	Allan Anderson	.05
42	Brian Harper	.05
43	Tom Herr	.05
44	Charlie Lea	.05
45	John Moses	.05
46	John Candelaria	.05
47	Jack Clark	.05
48	Richard Dotson	.05
49	Al Leiter (RC)	.05
50	Rafael Santana	.05
51	Don Slaught	.05
52	Todd Burns (RC)	.05
53	Dave Henderson	.05
54	Doug Jennings (RC)	.05
55	Dave Parker	.05
56	Walt Weiss	.05
57	Bob Welch	.05
58	Henry Cotto	.05
59	Marion Diaz (Mario)	.05
60	Mike Jackson	.05
61	Bill Swift	.05
62	Jose Cecena	.05
63	Ray Hayward	.05
64	Jim Steels	.05
65	Pat Borders	.05
66	Sil Campusano	.05
67	Mike Flanagan	.05
68	Todd Stottlemyre	.05
69	David Wells	.05
70	Jose Alvarez	.05
71	Paul Runge	.05
72	Cesar Jimenez (German)	.05
73	Pete Smith	.05
74	John Smoltz RC	1.50
75	Damon Berryhill	.05
76	Goose Gossage	.05
77	Mark Grace	.10
78	Darrin Jackson	.05
79	Vance Law	.05
80	Jeff Pico	.05
81	Gary Varsho	.05
82	Tim Birtsas	.05
83	Rob Dibble	.05
84	Danny Jackson	.05
85	Paul O'Neill	.05
86	Jose Rijo	.05
87	Chris Sabo RC	.25
88	John Fishel	.05
89	Craig Biggio RC	2.00
90	Terry Puhl	.05
91	Rafael Ramirez	.05
92	Louie Meadows	.05
93	Kirk Gibson	.05
94	Alfredo Griffin	.05
95	Jay Howell	.05
96	Jesse Orosco	.05
97	Alejandro Pena	.05
98	Tracy Woodson	.05
99	John Dopson	.05
100	Brian Holman	.05
101	Rex Hudler	.05
102	Jeff Parrett	.05
103	Nelson Santovenia	.05
104	Kevin Elster	.05
105	Jeff Innis	.05
106	Mackey Sasser	.05
107	Phil Bradley	.05
108	Danny Clay	.05
109	Greg Harris	.05
110	Ricky Jordan	.05
111	David Palmer	.05
112	Jim Gott	.05
113	Tommy Gregg (Photo actually Randy Milligan.)	
114	Barry Jones	.05
115	Randy Milligan	.05
116	Luis Alicea	.05
117	Tom Brunansky	.05
118	John Costello	.05
119	Jose DeLeon	.05
120	Bob Horner	.05
121	Scott Terry	.05
122	Roberto Alomar RC	1.50
123	Dave Leiper	.05
124	Keith Moreland	.05
125	Mark Parent	.05
126	Dennis Rasmussen	.05
127	Randy Bockus	.05
128	Brett Butler	.05
129	Donell Nixon	.05
130	Earnest Riles	.05
131	Roger Samuels	.05
132	Checklist	.05

Glossy Tin

	NM/M
Complete Set (672):	20.00
Common Player:	.15

(Star cards valued 1-1.5X regular-issue 1988 Fleer.)

Update Glossy Tin

	NM/M
Complete Set (132):	9.00
Common Player:	.15

(Star cards valued about 2X regular-issue1988 Fleer Updates.)

1989 Fleer

KEVIN ROMINE
OUTFIELD

FLEER

	NM/M
Retail Factory Set (660):	17.50
Hobby Factory Set (672):	20.00
Complete Set (660):	15.00
Common Player:	.05
Wax Pack (15):	1.00
Wax Box (36):	25.00
Cello Pack (36):	1.50
Cello Box (24):	20.00
Rack Pack (42+1):	1.50
Rack Box (24):	25.00

1	Don Baylor	.05
2	Lance Blankenship RC	.05
3	Todd Burns RC	.05
4	Greg Cadaret	.05
5	Jose Canseco	.35
6	Storm Davis	.05
7	Dennis Eckersley	.35
8	Mike Gallego	.05
9	Ron Hassey	.05
10	Dave Henderson	.05
11	Rick Honeycutt	.05
12	Glenn Hubbard	.05
13	Stan Javier	.05
14	Doug Jennings RC	.05
15	Felix Jose RC	.05
16	Carney Lansford	.05
17	Mark McGwire	.65
18	Gene Nelson	.05
19	Dave Parker	.05
20	Eric Plunk	.05
21	Luis Polonia	.05
22	Terry Steinbach	.05
23	Dave Stewart	.05
24	Walt Weiss	.05
25	Bob Welch	.05
26	Curt Young	.05
27	Rick Aguilera	.05
28	Wally Backman	.05
29	Mark Carreon	.05
30	Gary Carter	.40
31	David Cone	.05
32	Ron Darling	.05
33	Len Dykstra	.05
34	Kevin Elster	.05
35	Sid Fernandez	.05
36	Dwight Gooden	.05
37	Keith Hernandez	.05
38	Gregg Jefferies	.05
39	Howard Johnson	.05
40	Terry Leach	.05
41	Dave Magadan	.05
42	Bob McClure	.05
43	Roger McDowell	.05
44	Kevin McReynolds	.05
45	Keith Miller	.05
46	Randy Myers	.05
47	Bob Ojeda	.05
48	Mackey Sasser	.05
49	Darryl Strawberry	.05
50	Tim Teufel	.05
51	Dave West RC	.05
52	Mookie Wilson	.05
53	Dave Anderson	.05
54	Tim Belcher	.05
55	Mike Davis	.05

56	Mike Devereaux	.05
57	Kirk Gibson	.05
58	Alfredo Griffin	.05
59	Chris Gwynn	.05
60	Jeff Hamilton	.05
61a	Danny Heep(Home: San Antonio, TX)	.25
61b	Danny Heep (Home: Lake Hills, TX)	.05
62	Orel Hershiser	.05
63	Brian Holton	.05
64	Jay Howell	.05
65	Tim Leary	.05
66	Mike Marshall	.05
67	Ramon Martinez RC	.25
68	Jesse Orosco	.05
69	Alejandro Pena	.05
70	Steve Sax	.05
71	Mike Scioscia	.05
72	Mike Sharperson	.05
73	John Shelby	.05
74	Franklin Stubbs	.05
75	John Tudor	.05
76	Fernando Valenzuela	.05
77	Tracy Woodson	.05
78	Marty Barrett	.05
79	Todd Benzinger	.05
80	Mike Boddicker	.05
81	Wade Boggs	.50
82	"Oil Can" Boyd	.05
83	Ellis Burks	.05
84	Rick Cerone	.05
85	Roger Clemens	.60
86	Steve Curry RC	.05
87	Dwight Evans	.05
88	Wes Gardner	.05
89	Rich Gedman	.05
90	Mike Greenwell	.05
91	Bruce Hurst	.05
92	Dennis Lamp	.05
93	Spike Owen	.05
94	Larry Parrish	.05
95	Carlos Quintana RC	.05
96	Jody Reed	.05
97	Jim Rice	.25
98a	Kevin Romine (Batting follow-thru, photo actually Randy Kutcher.)	.25
98b	Kevin Romine (Arms crossed on chest, correct photo.)	.25
99	Lee Smith	.05
100	Mike Smithson	.05
101	Bob Stanley	.05
102	Allan Anderson	.05
103	Keith Atherton	.05
104	Juan Berenguer	.05
105	Bert Blyleven	.10
106	Eric Bullock RC	.05
107	Randy Bush	.05
108	John Christensen	.05
109	Mark Davidson	.05
110	Gary Gaetti	.05
111	Greg Gagne	.05
112	Dan Gladden	.05
113	German Gonzalez RC	.05
114	Brian Harper	.05
115	Tom Herr	.05
116	Kent Hrbek	.05
117	Gene Larkin	.05
118	Tim Laudner	.05
119	Charlie Lea	.05
120	Steve Lombardozzi	.05
121a	John Moses (Home: Phoenix, AZ)	.25
121b	John Moses (Home: Tempe, AZ)	.05
122	Al Newman	.05
123	Mark Portugal	.05
124	Kirby Puckett	.50
125	Jeff Reardon	.05
126	Fred Toliver	.05
127	Frank Viola	.05
128	Doyle Alexander	.05
129	Dave Bergman	.05
130a	Tom Brookens (Mike Heath stats on back.)	.50
130b	Tom Brookens (Correct stats on back.)	.05
131	Paul Gibson RC	.05
132a	Mike Heath (Tom Brookens stats on back.)	.50
132b	Mike Heath (Correct stats on back.)	.05
133	Don Heinkel RC	.05
134	Mike Henneman	.05
135	Guillermo Hernandez	.05
136	Eric King	.05
137	Chet Lemon	.05
138	Fred Lynn	.05
139	Jack Morris	.05
140	Matt Nokes	.05
141	Gary Pettis	.05
142	Ted Power	.05

143	Jeff Robinson	.05
144	Luis Salazar	.05
145	Steve Searcy RC	.05
146	Pat Sheridan	.05
147	Frank Tanana	.05
148	Alan Trammell	.05
149	Walt Terrell	.05
150	Jim Walewander	.05
151	Lou Whitaker	.05
152	Tim Birtsas	.05
153	Tom Browning	.05
154	Keith Brown RC	.05
155	Norm Charlton RC	.15
156	Dave Concepcion	.05
157	Kal Daniels	.05
158	Eric Davis	.05
159	Bo Diaz	.05
160	Rob Dibble	.05
161	Nick Esasky	.05
162	John Franco	.05
163	Danny Jackson	.05
164	Barry Larkin	.05
165	Rob Murphy	.05
166	Paul O'Neill	.05
167	Jeff Reed	.05
168	Jose Rijo	.05
169	Ron Robinson	.05
170	Chris Sabo	.05
171	Candy Sierra RC	.05
172	Van Snider RC	.05
173a	Jeff Treadway (Blue "target" above head.)	75.00
173b	Jeff Treadway (No "target.")	.05
174	Frank Williams	.05
175	Herm Winningham	.05
176	Jim Adduci	.05
177	Don August	.05
178	Mike Birkbeck	.05
179	Chris Bosio	.05
180	Glenn Braggs	.05
181	Greg Brock	.05
182	Mark Clear	.05
183	Chuck Crim	.05
184	Rob Deer	.05
185	Tom Filer	.05
186	Jim Gantner	.05
187	Darryl Hamilton	.05
188	Ted Higuera	.05
189	Odell Jones	.05
190	Jeffrey Leonard	.05
191	Joey Meyer	.05
192	Paul Mirabella	.05
193	Paul Molitor	.40
194	Charlie O'Brien	.05
195	Dan Plesac	.05
196	Gary Sheffield RC	1.00
197	B.J. Surhoff	.05
198	Dale Sveum	.05
199	Bill Wegman	.05
200	Robin Yount	.40
201	Rafael Belliard	.05
202	Barry Bonds	.75
203	Bobby Bonilla	.05
204	Sid Bream	.05
205	Benny Distefano	.05
206	Doug Drabek	.05
207	Mike Dunne	.05
208	Felix Fermin	.05
209	Brian Fisher	.05
210	Jim Gott	.05
211	Bob Kipper	.05
212	Bob LaPoint	.05
213	Mike LaValliere	.05
214	Jose Lind	.05
215	Junior Ortiz	.05
216	Vicente Palacios	.05
217	Tom Prince (RC)	.05
218	Gary Redus	.05
219	R.J. Reynolds	.05
220	Jeff Robinson	.05
221	John Smiley	.05
222	Andy Van Slyke	.05
223	Bob Walk	.05
224	Glenn Wilson	.05
225	Jesse Barfield	.05
226	George Bell	.05
227	Pat Borders	.05
228	John Cerutti	.05
229	Jim Clancy	.05
230	Mark Eichhorn	.05
231	Tony Fernandez	.05
232	Cecil Fielder	.05
233	Mike Flanagan	.05
234	Kelly Gruber	.05
235	Tom Henke	.05
236	Jimmy Key	.05
237	Rick Leach	.05
238	Manny Lee	.05
239	Nelson Liriano	.05
240	Fred McGriff	.05
241	Lloyd Moseby	.05
242	Rance Mulliniks	.05
243	Jeff Musselman	.05

244	Dave Stieb	.05
245	Todd Stottlemyre	.05
246	Duane Ward	.05
247	David Wells	.05
248	Ernie Whitt	.05
249	Luis Aguayo	.05
250a	Neil Allen (Home: Sarasota, FL)	.25
250b	Neil Allen (Home: Syosset, NY)	.05
251	John Candelaria	.05
252	Jack Clark	.05
253	Richard Dotson	.05
254	Rickey Henderson	.40
255	Tommy John	.10
256	Roberto Kelly	.05
257	Al Leiter	.05
258	Don Mattingly	.60
259	Dale Mohorcic	.05
260	Hal Morris RC	.25
261	Scott Nielsen	.05
262	Mike Pagliarulo	.05
263	Hipolito Pena RC	.05
264	Ken Phelps	.05
265	Willie Randolph	.05
266	Rick Rhoden	.05
267	Dave Righetti	.05
268	Rafael Santana	.05
269	Steve Shields	.05
270	Joel Skinner	.05
271	Don Slaught	.05
272	Claudell Washington	.05
273	Gary Ward	.05
274	Dave Winfield	.40
275	Luis Aquino	.05
276	Floyd Bannister	.05
277	George Brett	.60
278	Bill Buckner	.05
279	Nick Capra RC	.05
280	Jose DeJesus RC	.05
281	Steve Farr	.05
282	Jerry Gleaton	.05
283	Mark Gubicza	.05
284	Tom Gordon RC	.25
285	Bo Jackson	.10
286	Charlie Leibrandt	.05
287	Mike Macfarlane RC	.10
288	Jeff Montgomery	.05
289	Bill Pecota	.05
290	Jamie Quirk	.05
291	Bret Saberhagen	.05
292	Kevin Seitzer	.05
293	Kurt Stillwell	.05
294	Pat Tabler	.05
295	Danny Tartabull	.05
296	Gary Thurman	.05
297	Frank White	.05
298	Willie Wilson	.05
299	Roberto Alomar	.20
300	Sandy Alomar, Jr. RC	.25
301	Chris Brown	.05
302	Mike Brumley	.05
303	Mark Davis	.05
304	Mark Grant	.05
305	Tony Gwynn	.50
306	Greg Harris RC	.05
307	Andy Hawkins	.05
308	Jimmy Jones	.05
309	John Kruk	.05
310	Dave Leiper	.05
311	Carmelo Martinez	.05
312	Lance McCullers	.05
313	Keith Moreland	.05
314	Dennis Rasmussen	.05
315	Randy Ready	.05
316	Benito Santiago	.05
317	Eric Show	.05
318	Todd Simmons	.05
319	Garry Templeton	.05
320	Dickie Thon	.05
321	Ed Whitson	.05
322	Marvell Wynne	.05
323	Mike Aldrete	.05
324	Brett Butler	.05
325	Will Clark	.05
326	Kelly Downs	.05
327	Dave Dravecky	.05
328	Scott Garrelts	.05
329	Atlee Hammaker	.05
330	Charlie Hayes RC	.10
331	Mike Krukow	.05
332	Craig Lefferts	.05
333	Candy Maldonado	.05
334	Kirt Manwaring	.05
335	Bob Melvin	.05
336	Kevin Mitchell	.05
337	Donell Nixon	.05
338	Tony Perezchica RC	.05
339	Joe Price	.05
340	Rick Reuschel	.05
341	Earnest Riles	.05
342	Don Robinson	.05
343	Chris Speier	.05
344	Robby Thompson	.05

345	Jose Uribe	.05
346	Matt Williams	.05
347	Trevor Wilson RC	.15
348	Juan Agosto	.05
349	Larry Andersen	.05
350a	Alan Ashby ("Throws Right")	.25
350b	Alan Ashby ("Throws Right")	.05
351	Kevin Bass	.05
352	Buddy Bell	.05
353	Craig Biggio	.05
354	Danny Darwin	.05
355	Glenn Davis	.05
356	Jim Deshaies	.05
357	Bill Doran	.05
358	John Fishel RC	.05
359	Billy Hatcher	.05
360	Bob Knepper	.05
361	Louie Meadows RC	.05
362	Dave Meads	.05
363	Jim Pankovits	.05
364	Terry Puhl	.05
365	Rafael Ramirez	.05
366	Craig Reynolds	.05
367	Mike Scott	.05
368	Nolan Ryan	.75
369	Dave Smith	.05
370	Gerald Young	.05
371	Hubie Brooks	.05
372	Tim Burke	.05
373	John Dopson RC	.05
374	Mike Fitzgerald	.05
375	Tom Foley	.05
376	Andres Galarraga	.05
377	Neal Heaton	.05
378	Joe Hesketh	.05
379	Brian Holman RC	.05
380	Rex Hudler	.05
381a	Randy Johnson RC (Marlboro ad on scoreboard.)	40.00
381b	Randy Johnson (Ad partially obscured.)	10.00
381c	Randy Johnson RC (Ad completely blacked out.)	3.00
382	Wallace Johnson	.05
383	Tracy Jones	.05
384	Dave Martinez	.05
385	Dennis Martinez	.05
386	Andy McGaffigan	.05
387	Otis Nixon	.05
388	Johnny Paredes RC	.05
389	Jeff Parrett	.05
390	Pascual Perez	.05
391	Tim Raines	.05
392	Luis Rivera	.05
393	Nelson Santovenia RC	.05
394	Bryn Smith	.05
395	Tim Wallach	.05
396	Andy Allanson	.05
397	Rod Allen RC	.05
398	Scott Bailes	.05
399	Tom Candiotti	.05
400	Joe Carter	.05
401	Carmen Castillo	.05
402	Dave Clark	.05
403	John Farrell	.05
404	Julio Franco	.05
405	Don Gordon	.05
406	Mel Hall	.05
407	Brad Havens	.05
408	Brook Jacoby	.05
409	Doug Jones	.05
410	Jeff Kaiser RC	.05
411	Luis Medina RC	.05
412	Cory Snyder	.05
413	Greg Swindell	.05
414	Ron Tingley RC	.05
415	Willie Upshaw	.05
416	Ron Washington	.05
417	Rich Yett	.05
418	Damon Berryhill	.05
419	Mike Bielecki	.05
420	Doug Dascenzo RC	.05
421	Jody Davis	.05
422	Andre Dawson	.25
423	Frank DiPino	.05
424	Shawon Dunston	.05
425	"Goose" Gossage	.10
426	Mark Grace	.05
427	Mike Harkey RC	.05
428	Darrin Jackson	.05
429	Les Lancaster	.05
430	Vance Law	.05
431	Greg Maddux	.50
432	Jamie Moyer	.05
433	Al Nipper	.05
434	Rafael Palmeiro	.35
435	Pat Perry	.05
436	Jeff Pico RC	.05
437	Ryne Sandberg	.50
438	Calvin Schiraldi	.05

439	Rick Sutcliffe	.05
440a	Manny Trillo ("Throws Rig")	.35
440b	Manny Trillo ("Throws Right")	.05
441	Gary Varsho RC	.05
442	Mitch Webster	.05
443	Luis Alicea	.05
444	Tom Brunansky	.05
445	Vince Coleman	.05
446	John Costello RC	.05
447	Danny Cox	.05
448	Ken Dayley	.05
449	Jose DeLeon	.05
450	Curt Ford	.05
451	Pedro Guerrero	.05
452	Bob Horner	.05
453	Tim Jones RC	.05
454	Steve Lake	.05
455	Joe Magrane	.05
456	Greg Mathews	.05
457	Willie McGee	.05
458	Larry McWilliams	.05
459	Jose Oquendo	.05
460	Tony Pena	.05
461	Terry Pendleton	.05
462	Steve Peters RC	.05
463	Ozzie Smith	.50
464	Scott Terry	.05
465	Denny Walling	.05
466	Todd Worrell	.05
467	Tony Armas	.05
468	Dante Bichette RC	.25
469	Bob Boone	.05
470	Terry Clark RC	.05
471	Stew Cliburn	.05
472	Mike Cook RC	.05
473	Sherman Corbett RC	.05
474	Chili Davis	.05
475	Brian Downing	.05
476	Jim Eppard	.05
477	Chuck Finley	.05
478	Willie Fraser	.05
479	Bryan Harvey	.05
480	Jack Howell	.05
481	Wally Joyner	.05
482	Jack Lazorko	.05
483	Kirk McCaskill	.05
484	Mark McLemore	.05
485	Greg Minton	.05
486	Dan Petry	.05
487	Johnny Ray	.05
488	Dick Schofield	.05
489	Devon White	.05
490	Mike Witt	.05
491	Harold Baines	.05
492	Daryl Boston	.05
493	Ivan Calderon	.05
494	Mike Diaz	.05
495	Carlton Fisk	.40
496	Dave Gallagher RC	.05
497	Ozzie Guillen	.05
498	Shawn Hillegas	.05
499	Lance Johnson	.05
500	Barry Jones	.05
501	Bill Long	.05
502	Steve Lyons	.05
503	Fred Manrique	.05
504	Jack McDowell	.05
505	Donn Pall RC	.05
506	Kelly Paris	.05
507	Dan Pasqua	.05
508	Ken Patterson RC	.05
509	Melido Perez	.05
510	Jerry Reuss	.05
511	Mark Salas	.05
512	Bobby Thigpen	.05
513	Mike Woodard	.05
514	Bob Brower	.05
515	Steve Buechele	.05
516	Jose Cecena RC	.05
517	Cecil Espy	.05
518	Scott Fletcher	.05
519	Cecilio Guante	.05
520	Jose Guzman	.05
521	Ray Hayward	.05
522	Charlie Hough	.05
523	Pete Incaviglia	.05
524	Mike Jeffcoat	.05
525	Paul Kilgus	.05
526	Chad Kreuter RC	.15
527	Jeff Kunkel	.05
528	Oddibe McDowell	.05
529	Pete O'Brien	.05
530	Geno Petralli	.05
531	Jeff Russell	.05
532	Ruben Sierra	.05
533	Mike Stanley	.05
534	Ed Vande Berg	.05
535	Curtis Wilkerson	.05
536	Mitch Williams	.05
537	Bobby Witt	.05
538	Steve Balboni	.05
539	Scott Bankhead	.05

540	Scott Bradley	.05
541	Mickey Brantley	.05
542	Jay Buhner	.05
543	Mike Campbell	.05
544	Darnell Coles	.05
545	Henry Cotto	.05
546	Alvin Davis	.05
547	Mario Diaz	.05
548	Ken Griffey Jr. RC	6.00
549	Erik Hanson RC	.05
550	Mike Jackson	.05
551	Mark Langston	.05
552	Edgar Martinez	.05
553	Bill McGuire RC	.05
554	Mike Moore	.05
555	Jim Presley	.05
556	Rey Quinones	.05
557	Jerry Reed	.05
558	Harold Reynolds	.05
559	Mike Schooler RC	.05
560	Bill Swift	.05
561	Dave Valle	.05
562	Steve Bedrosian	.05
563	Phil Bradley	.05
564	Don Carman	.05
565	Bob Dernier	.05
566	Marvin Freeman	.05
567	Todd Frohwirth	.05
568	Greg Gross	.05
569	Kevin Gross	.05
570	Greg Harris	.05
571	Von Hayes	.05
572	Chris James	.05
573	Steve Jeltz	.05
574	Ron Jones RC	.05
575	Ricky Jordan RC	.05
576	Mike Maddux	.05
577	David Palmer	.05
578	Lance Parrish	.05
579	Shane Rawley	.05
580	Bruce Ruffin	.05
581	Juan Samuel	.05
582	Mike Schmidt	.60
583	Kent Tekulve	.05
584	Milt Thompson	.05
585	Jose Alvarez RC	.05
586	Paul Assenmacher	.05
587	Bruce Benedict	.05
588	Jeff Blauser	.05
589	Terry Blocker RC	.05
590	Ron Gant	.05
591	Tom Glavine	.30
592	Tommy Gregg	.05
593	Albert Hall	.05
594	Dion James	.05
595	Rick Mahler	.05
596	Dale Murphy	.25
597	Gerald Perry	.05
598	Charlie Puleo	.05
599	Ted Simmons	.05
600	Pete Smith	.05
601	Zane Smith	.05
602	John Smoltz	.50
603	Bruce Sutter	.35
604	Andres Thomas	.05
605	Ozzie Virgil	.05
606	Brady Anderson	.05
607	Jeff Ballard	.05
608	Jose Bautista RC	.05
609	Ken Gerhart	.05
610	Terry Kennedy	.05
611	Eddie Murray	.40
612	Carl Nichols	.05
613	Tom Niedenfuer	.05
614	Joe Orsulak	.05
615	Oswaldo Peraza RC (Oswald)	.05
616a	Bill Ripken (Vulgarity on bat knob.)	8.00
616b	Bill Ripken (Scribble over vulgarity.)	6.00
616c	Bill Ripken (Black box over vulgarity.)	.10
616d	Bill Ripken (Vulgarity whited out.(Many fake "white out" cards exist, created by erasures.)	250.00
616e	Billy Ripken (Strip cut out of bottom of card.)	.10
617	Cal Ripken, Jr.	.75
618	Dave Schmidt	.05
619	Rick Schu	.05
620	Larry Sheets	.05
621	Doug Sisk	.05
622	Pete Stanicek	.05
623	Mickey Tettleton	.05
624	Jay Tibbs	.05
625	Jim Traber	.05
626	Mark Williamson	.05
627	Craig Worthington RC	.05
628	Jose Canseco	.20
629	Tom Browning	.05
630	Roberto Alomar, Sandy Alomar, Jr.	.20

631	Will Clark, Rafael Palmeiro	.10
632	Will Clark, Darryl Strawberry	.05
633	Wade Boggs, Carney Lansford	.25
634	Jose Canseco, Mark McGwire, Terry Steinbach	.40
635	Mark Davis, Dwight Gooden	.05
636	David Cone, Danny Jackson	.05
637	Bobby Bonilla, Chris Sabo	.05
638	Andres Galarraga, Gerald Perry	.05
639	Eric Davis, Cameron Drew, Steve Wilson RC	.05
640	Kevin Brown, Kevin Reimer RC	.30
641	Jerald Clark, Brad Pounders RC	.05
642	Mike Capel, Drew Hall RC	.05
643	Joe Girardi, Rolando Roomes RC	.20
644	Marty Brown, Lenny Harris RC	.15
645	Luis de los Santos, Jim Campbell RC	.05
646	Miguel Garcia, Randy Kramer RC	.05
647	Torey Lovullo, Robert Palacios RC	.05
648	Jim Corsi, Bob Milacki RC	.05
649	Grady Hall, Mike Rochford RC	.05
650	Vance Lovelace, Terry Taylor RC	.05
651	Dennis Cook, Ken Hill RC	.20
652	Scott Service, Shane Turner RC	.05
653	Checklist 1-101	.05
654	Checklist 102-200	.05
655	Checklist 201-298	.05
656	Checklist 299-395	.05
657	Checklist 396-490	.05
658	Checklist 491-584	.05
659	Checklist 585-660	.05
660		

Update

ROBIN VENTURA
THIRD BASE

	NM/M
Complete Set (132):	6.00
Common Player:	.05

1	Phil Bradley	.05
2	Mike Devereaux	.05
3	Steve Finley	.05
4	Kevin Hickey	.05
5	Brian Holton	.05
6	Bob Milacki	.05
7	Randy Milligan	.05
8	John Dopson	.05
9	Nick Esasky	.05
10	Rob Murphy	.05
11	Jim Abbott	.05
12	Bert Blyleven	.10
13	Jeff Manto	.05
14	Bob McClure	.05
15	Lance Parrish	.05
16	Lee Stevens	.05
17	Claudell Washington	.05
18	Mark Davis	.05
19	Eric King	.05
20	Ron Kittle	.05
21	Matt Merullo	.05
22	Steve Rosenberg	.05
23	Robin Ventura	.25
24	Keith Atherton	.05
25	Joey (Albert) Belle RC	1.00

26 Jerry Browne .05
27 Felix Fermin .05
28 Brad Komminsk .05
29 Pete O'Brien .05
30 Mike Brumley .05
31 Tracy Jones .05
32 Mike Schwabe .05
33 Gary Ward .05
34 Frank Williams .05
35 Kevin Appier RC .25
36 Bob Boone .05
37 Luis de los Santos .05
38 Jim Eisenreich .05
39 Jaime Navarro RC .05
40 Bill Spiers .05
41 Greg Vaughn RC .25
42 Randy Veres .05
43 Wally Backman .05
44 Shane Rawley .05
45 Steve Balboni .05
46 Jesse Barfield .05
47 Alvaro Espinoza .05
48 Bob Geren .05
49 Mel Hall .05
50 Andy Hawkins .05
51 Hensley Meulens .05
52 Steve Sax .05
53 Deion Sanders RC .75
54 Rickey Henderson .40
55 Mike Moore .05
56 Tony Phillips .05
57 Greg Briley .05
58 Gene Harris .05
59 Randy Johnson 2.00
60 Jeffrey Leonard .05
61 Dennis Powell .05
62 Omar Vizquel .05
63 Kevin Brown .05
64 Julio Franco .05
65 Jamie Moyer .05
66 Rafael Palmeiro .35
67 Nolan Ryan 1.00
68 Francisco Cabrera .05
69 Junior Felix .05
70 Al Leiter .05
71 Alex Sanchez .05
72 Geronimo Berroa .05
73 Derek Lilliquist .05
74 Lonnie Smith .05
75 Jeff Treadway .05
76 Paul Kilgus .05
77 Lloyd McClendon .05
78 Scott Sanderson .05
79 Dwight Smith .05
80 Jerome Walton .05
81 Mitch Williams .05
82 Steve Wilson .05
83 Todd Benzinger .05
84 Ken Griffey .05
85 Rick Mahler .05
86 Rolando Roomes .05
87 Scott Scudder .05
88 Jim Clancy .05
89 Rick Rhoden .05
90 Dan Schatzeder .05
91 Mike Morgan .05
92 Eddie Murray .40
93 Willie Randolph .05
94 Ray Searage .05
95 Mike Aldrete .05
96 Kevin Gross .05
97 Mark Langston .05
98 Spike Owen .05
99 Zane Smith .05
100 Don Aase .05
101 Barry Lyons .05
102 Juan Samuel .05
103 Wally Whitehurst .05
104 Dennis Cook .05
105 Len Dykstra .05
106 Charlie Hayes .05
107 Tommy Herr .05
108 Ken Howell .05
109 John Kruk .05
110 Roger McDowell .05
111 Terry Mulholland .05
112 Jeff Parrett .05
113 Neal Heaton .05
114 Jeff King .05
115 Randy Kramer .05
116 Bill Landrum .05
117 Cris Carpenter .05
118 Frank DiPino .05
119 Ken Hill .05
120 Dan Quisenberry .05
121 Milt Thompson .05
122 Todd Zeile RC .25
123 Jack Clark .05
124 Bruce Hurst .05
125 Mark Parent .05
126 Bip Roberts .05
127 Jeff Brantley .05
128 Terry Kennedy .05
129 Mike LaCoss .05

130 Greg Litton .05
131 Mike Schmidt .65
132 Checklist .05

Glossy Tin

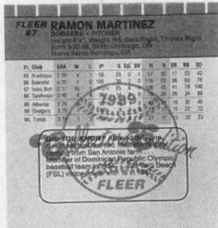

	NM/M
Unopened Set (672):	75.00
Complete Set (672):	50.00
Common Player:	.25

(Star cards valued at 3-4X
regular 1989 Fleer cards.)

1990 Fleer

	NM/M
Factory Hobby Set (672):	12.50
Retail Hobby Set (660):	12.00
Complete Set (660):	10.00
Common Player:	.05
Wax Pack (15):	.50
Wax Box (36):	10.00
Cello Pack (33):	1.00
Cello Box (24):	12.00

1 Lance Blankenship .05
2 Todd Burns .05
3 Jose Canseco .30
4 Jim Corsi .05
5 Storm Davis .05
6 Dennis Eckersley .35
7 Mike Gallego .05
8 Ron Hassey .05
9 Dave Henderson .05
10 Rickey Henderson .40
11 Rick Honeycutt .05
12 Stan Javier .05
13 Felix Jose .05
14 Carney Lansford .05
15 Mark McGwire .65
16 Mike Moore .05
17 Gene Nelson .05
18 Dave Parker .05
19 Tony Phillips .05
20 Terry Steinbach .05
21 Dave Stewart .05
22 Walt Weiss .05
23 Bob Welch .05
24 Curt Young .05
25 Paul Assenmacher .05
26 Damon Berryhill .05
27 Mike Bielecki .05
28 Kevin Blankenship .05
29 Andre Dawson .25
30 Shawon Dunston .05
31 Joe Girardi .05
32 Mark Grace .05
33 Mike Harkey .05
34 Paul Kilgus .05
35 Les Lancaster .05
36 Vance Law .05
37 Greg Maddux .50
38 Lloyd McClendon .05
39 Jeff Pico .05

40 Ryne Sandberg .50
41 Scott Sanderson .05
42 Dwight Smith .05
43 Rick Sutcliffe .05
44 Jerome Walton RC .05
45 Mitch Webster .05
46 Curt Wilkerson .05
47 Dean Wilkins RC .05
48 Mitch Williams .05
49 Steve Wilson .05
50 Steve Bedrosian .05
51 Mike Benjamin RC .05
52 Jeff Brantley RC .10
53 Brett Butler .05
54 Will Clark .05
55 Kelly Downs .05
56 Scott Garrelts .05
57 Atlee Hammaker .05
58 Terry Kennedy .05
59 Mike LaCoss .05
60 Craig Lefferts .05
61 Greg Litton RC .05
62 Candy Maldonado .05
63 Kirt Manwaring .05
64 Randy McCament RC .05
65 Kevin Mitchell .05
66 Donell Nixon .05
67 Ken Oberkfell .05
68 Rick Reuschel .05
69 Ernest Riles .05
70 Don Robinson .05
71 Pat Sheridan .05
72 Chris Speier .05
73 Robby Thompson .05
74 Jose Uribe .05
75 Matt Williams .05
76 George Bell .05
77 Pat Borders .05
78 John Cerutti .05
79 Junior Felix RC .05
80 Tony Fernandez .05
81 Mike Flanagan .05
82 Mauro Gozzo RC .05
83 Kelly Gruber .05
84 Tom Henke .05
85 Jimmy Key .05
86 Manny Lee .05
87 Nelson Liriano .05
88 Lee Mazzilli .05
89 Fred McGriff .05
90 Lloyd Moseby .05
91 Rance Mulliniks .05
92 Alex Sanchez .05
93 Dave Steib .05
94 Todd Stottlemyre .05
95 Duane Ward .05
96 David Wells .05
97 Ernie Whitt .05
98 Frank Wills .05
99 Mookie Wilson .05
100 Kevin Appier .05
101 Luis Aquino .05
102 Bob Boone .05
103 George Brett .60
104 Jose DeJesus .05
105 Luis de los Santos .05
106 Jim Eisenreich .05
107 Steve Farr .05
108 Tom Gordon .05
109 Mark Gubicza .05
110 Bo Jackson .10
111 Terry Leach .05
112 Charlie Leibrandt .05
113 Rick Luecken RC .05
114 Mike Macfarlane .05
115 Jeff Montgomery .05
116 Bret Saberhagen .05
117 Kevin Seitzer .05
118 Kurt Stillwell .05
119 Pat Tabler .05
120 Danny Tartabull .05
121 Gary Thurman .05
122 Frank White .05
123 Willie Wilson .05
124 Matt Winters RC .05
125 Jim Abbott .05
126 Tony Armas .05
127 Dante Bichette .05
128 Bert Blyleven .10
129 Chili Davis .05
130 Brian Downing .05
131 Mike Fetters RC .05
132 Chuck Finley .05
133 Willie Fraser .05
134 Bryan Harvey .05
135 Jack Howell .05
136 Wally Joyner .05
137 Jeff Manto RC .05
138 Kirk McCaskill .05
139 Bob McClure .05
140 Greg Minton .05
141 Lance Parrish .05
142 Dan Petry .05
143 Johnny Ray .05

144 Dick Schofield .05
145 Lee Stevens RC .05
146 Claudell Washington .05
147 Devon White .05
148 Mike Witt .05
149 Roberto Alomar .20
150 Sandy Alomar, Jr. .05
151 Andy Benes .05
152 Jack Clark .05
153 Pat Clements .05
154 Joey Cora .05
155 Mark Davis .05
156 Mark Grant .05
157 Tony Gwynn .50
158 Greg Harris .05
159 Bruce Hurst .05
160 Darrin Jackson .05
161 Chris James .05
162 Carmelo Martinez .05
163 Mike Pagliarulo .05
164 Mark Parent .05
165 Dennis Rasmussen .05
166 Bip Roberts .05
167 Benito Santiago .05
168 Calvin Schiraldi .05
169 Eric Show .05
170 Garry Templeton .05
171 Ed Whitson .05
172 Brady Anderson .05
173 Jeff Ballard .05
174 Phil Bradley .05
175 Mike Devereaux .05
176 Steve Finley .05
177 Pete Harnisch .05
178 Kevin Hickey .05
179 Brian Holton .05
180 Ben McDonald RC .15
181 Bob Melvin .05
182 Bob Milacki .05
183 Randy Milligan .05
184 Gregg Olson .05
185 Joe Orsulak .05
186 Bill Ripken .05
187 Cal Ripken, Jr. .75
188 Dave Schmidt .05
189 Larry Sheets .05
190 Mickey Tettleton .05
191 Mark Thurmond .05
192 Jay Tibbs .05
193 Jim Traber .05
194 Mark Williamson .05
195 Craig Worthington .05
196 Don Aase .05
197 Blaine Beatty RC .05
198 Mark Carreon .05
199 Gary Carter .40
200 David Cone .05
201 Ron Darling .05
202 Kevin Elster .05
203 Sid Fernandez .05
204 Dwight Gooden .05
205 Keith Hernandez .05
206 Jeff Innis RC .05
207 Gregg Jefferies .05
208 Howard Johnson .05
209 Barry Lyons .05
210 Dave Magadan .05
211 Kevin McReynolds .05
212 Jeff Musselman .05
213 Randy Myers .05
214 Bob Ojeda .05
215 Juan Samuel .05
216 Mackey Sasser .05
217 Darryl Strawberry .05
218 Tim Teufel .05
219 Frank Viola .05
220 Juan Agosto .05
221 Larry Anderson .05
222 Eric Anthony RC .10
223 Kevin Bass .05
224 Craig Biggio .05
225 Ken Caminiti .05
226 Jim Clancy .05
227 Danny Darwin .05
228 Glenn Davis .05
229 Jim Deshaies .05
230 Bill Doran .05
231 Bob Forsch .05
232 Brian Meyer .05
233 Terry Puhl .05
234 Rafael Ramirez .05
235 Rick Rhoden .05
236 Dan Schatzeder .05
237 Mike Scott .05
238 Dave Smith .05
239 Alex Trevino .05
240 Glenn Wilson .05
241 Gerald Young .05
242 Tom Brunansky .05
243 Cris Carpenter .05
244 Alex Cole RC .05
245 Vince Coleman .05
246 John Costello .05
247 Ken Dayley .05

#	Player	Price
248	Jose DeLeon	.05
249	Frank DiPino	.05
250	Pedro Guerrero	.05
251	Ken Hill	.05
252	Joe Magrane	.05
253	Willie McGee	.05
254	John Morris	.05
255	Jose Oquendo	.05
256	Tony Pena	.05
257	Terry Pendleton	.05
258	Ted Power	.05
259	Dan Quisenberry	.05
260	Ozzie Smith	.50
261	Scott Terry	.05
262	Milt Thompson	.05
263	Denny Walling	.05
264	Todd Worrell	.05
265	Todd Zeile	.05
266	Marty Barrett	.05
267	Mike Boddicker	.05
268	Wade Boggs	.50
269	Ellis Burks	.05
270	Rick Cerone	.05
271	Roger Clemens	.60
272	John Dopson	.05
273	Nick Esasky	.05
274	Dwight Evans	.05
275	Wes Gardner	.05
276	Rich Gedman	.05
277	Mike Greenwell	.05
278	Danny Heep	.05
279	Eric Hetzel	.05
280	Dennis Lamp	.05
281	Rob Murphy	.05
282	Joe Price	.05
283	Carlos Quintana	.05
284	Jody Reed	.05
285	Luis Rivera	.05
286	Kevin Romine	.05
287	Lee Smith	.05
288	Mike Smithson	.05
289	Bob Stanley	.05
290	Harold Baines	.05
291	Kevin Brown	.05
292	Steve Buechele	.05
293	Scott Coolbaugh RC	.05
294	Jack Daugherty RC	.05
295	Cecil Espy	.05
296	Julio Franco	.05
297	Juan Gonzalez RC	2.00
298	Cecilio Guante	.05
299	Drew Hall	.05
300	Charlie Hough	.05
301	Pete Incaviglia	.05
302	Mike Jeffcoat	.05
303	Chad Kreuter	.05
304	Jeff Kunkel	.05
305	Rick Leach	.05
306	Fred Manrique	.05
307	Jamie Moyer	.05
308	Rafael Palmeiro	.35
309	Geno Petralli	.05
310	Kevin Reimer	.05
311	Kenny Rogers RC	.10
312	Jeff Russell	.05
313	Nolan Ryan	.75
314	Ruben Sierra	.05
315	Bobby Witt	.05
316	Chris Bosio	.05
317	Glenn Braggs	.05
318	Greg Brock	.05
319	Chuck Crim	.05
320	Rob Deer	.05
321	Mike Felder	.05
322	Tom Filer	.05
323	Tony Fossas RC	.05
324	Jim Gantner	.05
325	Darryl Hamilton	.05
326	Ted Higuera	.05
327	Mark Knudson	.05
328	Bill Krueger	.05
329	Tim McIntosh RC	.05
330	Paul Molitor	.40
331	Jaime Navarro	.05
332	Charlie O'Brien	.05
333	Jeff Peterek RC	.05
334	Dan Plesac	.05
335	Jerry Reuss	.05
336	Gary Sheffield	.35
337	Bill Spiers RC	.05
338	B.J. Surhoff	.05
339	Greg Vaughn	.05
340	Robin Yount	.40
341	Hubie Brooks	.05
342	Tim Burke	.05
343	Mike Fitzgerald	.05
344	Tom Foley	.05
345	Andres Galarraga	.05
346	Damaso Garcia	.05
347	Marquis Grissom RC	.50
348	Kevin Gross	.05
349	Joe Hesketh	.05
350	Jeff Huson RC	.05
351	Wallace Johnson	.05
352	Mark Langston	.05
353a	Dave Martinez (Yellow 90.)	6.00
353b	Dave Martinez (Red 90.)	.05
354	Dennis Martinez	.05
355	Andy McGaffigan	.05
356	Otis Nixon	.05
357	Spike Owen	.05
358	Pascual Perez	.05
359	Tim Raines	.05
360	Nelson Santovenia	.05
361	Bryn Smith	.05
362	Zane Smith	.05
363	Larry Walker RC	.75
364	Tim Wallach	.05
365	Rick Aguilera	.05
366	Allan Anderson	.05
367	Wally Backman	.05
368	Doug Baker	.05
369	Juan Berenguer	.05
370	Randy Bush	.05
371	Carmen Castillo	.05
372	Mike Dyer RC	.05
373	Gary Gaetti	.05
374	Greg Gagne	.05
375	Dan Gladden	.05
376	German Gonzalez	.05
377	Brian Harper	.05
378	Kent Hrbek	.05
379	Gene Larkin	.05
380	Tim Laudner	.05
381	John Moses	.05
382	Al Newman	.05
383	Kirby Puckett	.50
384	Shane Rawley	.05
385	Jeff Reardon	.05
386	Roy Smith	.05
387	Gary Wayne RC	.05
388	Dave West	.05
389	Tim Belcher	.05
390	Tim Crews	.05
391	Mike Davis	.05
392	Rick Dempsey	.05
393	Kirk Gibson	.05
394	Jose Gonzalez	.05
395	Alfredo Griffin	.05
396	Jeff Hamilton	.05
397	Lenny Harris	.05
398	Mickey Hatcher	.05
399	Orel Hershiser	.05
400	Jay Howell	.05
401	Mike Marshall	.05
402	Ramon Martinez	.05
403	Mike Morgan	.05
404	Eddie Murray	.40
405	Alejandro Pena	.05
406	Willie Randolph	.05
407	Mike Scioscia	.05
408	Ray Searage	.05
409	Fernando Valenzuela	.05
410	Jose Vizcaino RC	.10
411	John Wetteland RC	.20
412	Jack Armstrong	.05
413	Todd Benzinger	.05
414	Tim Birtsas	.05
415	Tom Browning	.05
416	Norm Charlton	.05
417	Eric Davis	.05
418	Rob Dibble	.05
419	John Franco	.05
420	Ken Griffey Sr.	.05
421	Chris Hammond RC	.15
422	Danny Jackson	.05
423	Barry Larkin	.05
424	Tim Leary	.05
425	Rick Mahler	.05
426	Joe Oliver RC	.05
427	Paul O'Neill	.05
428	Luis Quinones	.05
429	Jeff Reed	.05
430	Jose Rijo	.05
431	Ron Robinson	.05
432	Rolando Roomes	.05
433	Chris Sabo	.05
434	Scott Scudder RC	.05
435	Herm Winningham	.05
436	Steve Balboni	.05
437	Jesse Barfield	.05
438	Mike Blowers RC	.05
439	Tom Brookens	.05
440	Greg Cadaret	.05
441	Alvaro Espinoza	.05
442	Bob Geren RC	.05
443	Lee Guetterman	.05
444	Mel Hall	.05
445	Andy Hawkins	.05
446	Roberto Kelly	.05
447	Don Mattingly	.60
448	Lance McCullers	.05
449	Hensley Meulens	.05
450	Dale Mohorcic	.05
451	Clay Parker	.05
452	Eric Plunk	.05
453	Dave Righetti	.05
454	Deion Sanders	.10
455	Steve Sax	.05
456	Don Slaught	.05
457	Walt Terrell	.05
458	Dave Winfield	.40
459	Jay Bell	.05
460	Rafael Belliard	.05
461	Barry Bonds	.75
462	Bobby Bonilla	.05
463	Sid Bream	.05
464	Benny Distefano	.05
465	Doug Drabek	.05
466	Jim Gott	.05
467	Billy Hatcher	.05
468	Neal Heaton	.05
469	Jeff King	.05
470	Bob Kipper	.05
471	Randy Kramer	.05
472	Bill Landrum	.05
473	Mike LaValliere	.05
474	Jose Lind	.05
475	Junior Ortiz	.05
476	Gary Redus	.05
477	Rick Reed RC	.05
478	R.J. Reynolds	.05
479	Jeff Robinson	.05
480	John Smiley	.05
481	Andy Van Slyke	.05
482	Bob Walk	.05
483	Andy Allanson	.05
484	Scott Bailes	.05
485	Albert Belle	.05
486	Bud Black	.05
487	Jerry Browne	.05
488	Tom Candiotti	.05
489	Joe Carter	.05
490	David Clark	.05
491	John Farrell	.05
492	Felix Fermin	.05
493	Brook Jacoby	.05
494	Dion James	.05
495	Doug Jones	.05
496	Brad Komminsk	.05
497	Rod Nichols	.05
498	Pete O'Brien	.05
499	Steve Olin RC	.05
500	Jesse Orosco	.05
501	Joel Skinner	.05
502	Cory Snyder	.05
503	Greg Swindell	.05
504	Rich Yett	.05
505	Scott Bankhead	.05
506	Scott Bradley	.05
507	Greg Briley	.05
508	Jay Buhner	.05
509	Darnell Coles	.05
510	Keith Comstock	.05
511	Henry Cotto	.05
512	Alvin Davis	.05
513	Ken Griffey Jr.	.65
514	Erik Hanson	.05
515	Gene Harris	.05
516	Brian Holman	.05
517	Mike Jackson	.05
518	Randy Johnson	.40
519	Jeffrey Leonard	.05
520	Edgar Martinez	.05
521	Dennis Powell	.05
522	Jim Presley	.05
523	Jerry Reed	.05
524	Harold Reynolds	.05
525	Mike Schooler	.05
526	Bill Swift	.05
527	David Valle	.05
528	Omar Vizquel	.05
529	Ivan Calderon	.05
530	Carlton Fisk	.40
531	Scott Fletcher	.05
532	Dave Gallagher	.05
533	Ozzie Guillen	.05
534	Greg Hibbard RC	.05
535	Shawn Hillegas	.05
536	Lance Johnson	.05
537	Eric King	.05
538	Ron Kittle	.05
539	Steve Lyons	.05
540	Carlos Martinez	.05
541	Tom McCarthy RC	.05
542	Matt Merullo RC	.05
543	Donn Pall	.05
544	Dan Pasqua	.05
545	Ken Patterson	.05
546	Melido Perez	.05
547	Steve Rosenberg	.05
548	Sammy Sosa RC	5.00
549	Bobby Thigpen	.05
550	Robin Ventura	.05
551	Greg Walker	.05
552	Don Carman	.05
553	Pat Combs RC	.05
554	Dennis Cook	.05
555	Darren Daulton	.05
556	Len Dykstra	.05
557	Curt Ford	.05
558	Charlie Hayes	.05
559	Von Hayes	.05
560	Tom Herr	.05
561	Ken Howell	.05
562	Steve Jeltz	.05
563	Ron Jones	.05
564	Ricky Jordan	.05
565	John Kruk	.05
566	Steve Lake	.05
567	Roger McDowell	.05
568	Terry Mulholland	.05
569	Dwayne Murphy	.05
570	Jeff Parrett	.05
571	Randy Ready	.05
572	Bruce Ruffin	.05
573	Dickie Thon	.05
574	Jose Alvarez	.05
575	Geronimo Berroa	.05
576	Jeff Blauser	.05
577	Joe Boever	.05
578	Marty Clary	.05
579	Jody Davis	.05
580	Mark Eichhorn	.05
581	Darrell Evans	.05
582	Ron Gant	.05
583	Tom Glavine	.25
584	Tommy Greene RC	.05
585	Tommy Gregg	.05
586	Dave Justice RC	.40
587	Mark Lemke	.05
588	Derek Lilliquist	.05
589	Oddibe McDowell	.05
590	Kent Mercker RC	.05
591	Dale Murphy	.20
592	Gerald Perry	.05
593	Lonnie Smith	.05
594	Pete Smith	.05
595	John Smoltz	.05
596	Mike Stanton RC	.05
597	Andres Thomas	.05
598	Jeff Treadway	.05
599	Doyle Alexander	.05
600	Dave Bergman	.05
601	Brian Dubois RC	.05
602	Paul Gibson	.05
603	Mike Heath	.05
604	Mike Henneman	.05
605	Guillermo Hernandez	.05
606	Shawn Holman RC	.05
607	Tracy Jones	.05
608	Chet Lemon	.05
609	Fred Lynn	.05
610	Jack Morris	.05
611	Matt Nokes	.05
612	Gary Pettis	.05
613	Kevin Ritz RC	.05
614	Jeff Robinson	.05
615	Steve Searcy	.05
616	Frank Tanana	.05
617	Alan Trammell	.05
618	Gary Ward	.05
619	Lou Whitaker	.05
620	Frank Williams	.05
621a	George Brett Players of the Decade - 1980 (... 10 .390 hitting ...)	1.00
621b	George Brett Players of the Decade - 1980	.25
622	Fernando Valenzuela Players of the Decade - 1981	.05
623	Dale Murphy Players of the Decade - 1982	.05
624a	Cal Ripken, Jr. Players of the Decade - 1983 (Ripken)	1.50
624b	Cal Ripken, Jr. Players of the Decade - 1983	.30
625	Ryne Sandberg Players of the Decade - 1984	.25
626	Don Mattingly Players of the Decade - 1985	.30
627	Roger Clemens Players of the Decade - 1986	.30
628	George Bell Players of the Decade - 1987	.05
629	Jose Canseco Players of the Decade - 1988	.10
630a	Will Clark Players of the Decade - 1989 (Total bases 32.)	.35
630b	Will Clark Players of the Decade - 1989 (Total bases 321.)	.05
631	Mark Davis, Mitch Williams	.05
632	Wade Boggs, Mike Greenwell	.15
633	Mark Gubicza, Jeff Russell	.05
634	Tony Fernandez, Cal Ripken Jr.	.30

635	Kirby Puckett, Bo Jackson	.20
636	Mike Scott, Nolan Ryan	.30
637	Will Clark, Kevin Mitchell	.05
638	Don Mattingly, Mark McGwire	.65
639	Howard Johnson, Ryne Sandberg	.20
640	Rudy Seanez, Colin Charland **RC**	.05
641	George Canale, Kevin Maas **RC**	.10
642	Kelly Mann, Dave Hansen **RC**	.05
643	Greg Smith, Stu Tate **RC**	.05
644	Tom Drees, Dan Howitt **RC**	.05
645	Mike Roesler, Derrick May **RC**	.05
646	Scott Hemond, Mark Gardner **RC**	.10
647	John Orton, Scott Leius **RC**	.10
648	Rich Monteleone, Dana Williams **RC**	.05
649	Mike Huff, Steve Frey **RC**	.05
650	Chuck McElroy, Moises Alou **RC**	.50
651	Bobby Rose, Mike Hartley **RC**	.10
652	Matt Kinzer, Wayne Edwards **RC**	.05
653	Delino DeShields, Jason Grimsley **RC**	.15
654	Athletics, Cubs, Giants & Blue Jays (Checklist)	
655	Royals, Angels, Padres & Orioles (Checklist)	
656	Mets, Astros, Cardinals & Red Sox (Checklist)	
657	Rangers, Brewers, Expos & Twins (Checklist)	
658	Dodgers, Reds, Yankees & Pirates (Checklist)	.05
659	Indians, Mariners, White Sox & Phillies (Checklist)	.05
660	Braves, Tigers & Special Cards (Checklist)	.05

Update

NM/M

Complete Set (132): 3.00
Common Player: .05

1	Steve Avery	.05
2	Francisco Cabrera	.05
3	Nick Esasky	.05
4	Jim Kremers	.05
5	Greg Olson	.05
6	Jim Presley	.05
7	Shawn Boskie	.05
8	Joe Kraemer	.05
9	Luis Salazar	.05
10	Hector Villanueva	.05
11	Glenn Braggs	.05
12	Mariano Duncan	.05
13	Billy Hatcher	.05
14	Tim Layana	.05
15	Hal Morris	.05
16	Javier Ortiz	.05
17	Dave Rohde	.05
18	Eric Yelding	.05
19	Hubie Brooks	.05
20	Kal Daniels	.05
21	Dave Hansen	.05
22	Mike Hartley	.05
23	Stan Javier	.05
24	Jose Offerman	.05
25	Juan Samuel	.05
26	Dennis Boyd	.05
27	Delino DeShields	.05
28	Steve Frey	.05
29	Mark Gardner	.05
30	Chris Nabholz	.05
31	Bill Sampen	.05
32	Dave Schmidt	.05
33	Daryl Boston	.05
34	Chuck Carr	.05
35	John Franco	.05
36	Todd Hundley **RC**	.25
37	Julio Machado	.05
38	Alejandro Pena	.05
39	Darren Reed	.05
40	Kelvin Torve	.05
41	Darrel Akerfelds	.05
42	Jose DeJesus	.05
43	Dave Hollins	.05
44	Carmelo Martinez	.05
45	Brad Moore	.05
46	Dale Murphy	.15
47	Wally Backman	.05
48	Stan Belinda	.05
49	Bob Patterson	.05
50	Ted Power	.05
51	Don Slaught	.05
52	Geronimo Pena	.05
53	Lee Smith	.05
54	John Tudor	.05
55	Joe Carter	.05
56	Tom Howard	.05
57	Craig Lefferts	.05
58	Rafael Valdez	.05
59	Dave Anderson	.05
60	Kevin Bass	.05
61	John Burkett	.05
62	Gary Carter	.40
63	Rick Parker	.05
64	Trevor Wilson	.05
65	Chris Hoiles	.05
66	Tim Hulett	.05
67	Dave Johnson	.05
68	Curt Schilling	.35
69	David Segui	.05
70	Tom Brunansky	.05
71	Greg Harris	.05
72	Dana Kiecker	.05
73	Tim Naehring	.05
74	Tony Pena	.05
75	Jeff Reardon	.05
76	Jerry Reed	.05
77	Mark Eichhorn	.05
78	Mark Langston	.05
79	John Orton	.05
80	Luis Polonia	.05
81	Dave Winfield	.40
82	Cliff Young	.05
83	Wayne Edwards	.05
84	Alex Fernandez	.05
85	Craig Grebeck	.05
86	Scott Radinsky	.05
87	Frank Thomas	2.00
88	Beau Allred	.05
89	Sandy Alomar, Jr.	.05
90	Carlos Baerga **RC**	.10
91	Kevin Bearse	.05
92	Chris James	.05
93	Candy Maldonado	.05
94	Jeff Manto	.05
95	Cecil Fielder	.05
96	Travis Fryman **RC**	.25
97	Lloyd Moseby	.05
98	Edwin Nunez	.05
99	Tony Phillips	.05
100	Larry Sheets	.05
101	Mark Davis	.05
102	Storm Davis	.05
103	Gerald Perry	.05
104	Terry Shumpert	.05
105	Edgar Diaz	.05
106	Dave Parker	.05
107	Tim Drummond	.05
108	Junior Ortiz	.05
109	Park Pittman	.05
110	Kevin Tapani	.05
111	Oscar Azocar	.05
112	Jim Leyritz	.05
113	Kevin Maas	.05
114	Alan Mills	.05
115	Matt Nokes	.05
116	Pascual Perez	.05
117	Ozzie Canseco	.05
118	Scott Sanderson	.05
119	Tino Martinez	.05
120	Jeff Schaefer	.05
121	Matt Young	.05
122	Brian Bohanon	.05
123	Jeff Huson	.05
124	Ramon Manon	.05
125	Gary Mielke	.05
126	Willie Blair	.05
127	Glenallen Hill	.05
128	John Olerud **RC**	.35
129	Luis Sojo	.05
130	Mark Whiten	.05
131	Nolan Ryan Three Decades of No Hitters	1.00
132	Checklist	.05

1991 Fleer

NM/M

Unopened Factory Set (732): 12.00
Complete Set (720): 10.00
Common Player: .05
Wax Pack (15): .50
Wax Box (36): 12.50
Jumbo Wax Pack (53): 1.25
Jumbo Wax Box (24): 20.00
Cello Pack (30): 1.00
Cello Box (24): 16.00

1	Troy Afenir **RC**	.05
2	Harold Baines	.05
3	Lance Blankenship	.05
4	Todd Burns	.05
5	Jose Canseco	.30
6	Dennis Eckersley	.35
7	Mike Gallego	.05
8	Ron Hassey	.05
9	Dave Henderson	.05
10	Rickey Henderson	.40
11	Rick Honeycutt	.05
12	Doug Jennings	.05
13	Joe Klink **RC**	.05
14	Carney Lansford	.05
15	Darren Lewis **RC**	.05
16	Willie McGee	.05
17a	Mark McGwire (Six-line career summary.)	.65
17b	Mark McGwire (Seven-line career summary.)	.65
18	Mike Moore	.05
19	Gene Nelson	.05
20	Dave Otto	.05
21	Jamie Quirk	.05
22	Willie Randolph	.05
23	Scott Sanderson	.05
24	Terry Steinbach	.05
25	Dave Stewart	.05
26	Walt Weiss	.05
27	Bob Welch	.05
28	Curt Young	.05
29	Wally Backman	.05
30	Stan Belinda **RC**	.05
31	Jay Bell	.05
32	Rafael Belliard	.05
33	Barry Bonds	.75
34	Bobby Bonilla	.05
35	Sid Bream	.05
36	Doug Drabek	.05
37	Carlos Garcia **RC**	.10
38	Neal Heaton	.05
39	Jeff King	.05
40	Bob Kipper	.05
41	Bill Landrum	.05
42	Mike LaValliere	.05
43	Jose Lind	.05
44	Carmelo Martinez	.05
45	Bob Patterson	.05
46	Ted Power	.05
47	Gary Redus	.05
48	R.J. Reynolds	.05
49	Don Slaught	.05
50	John Smiley	.05
51	Zane Smith	.05
52	Randy Tomlin **RC**	.10
53	Andy Van Slyke	.05
54	Bob Walk	.05
55	Jack Armstrong	.05
56	Todd Benzinger	.05
57	Glenn Braggs	.05
58	Keith Brown	.05
59	Tom Browning	.05
60	Norm Charlton	.05
61	Eric Davis	.05
62	Rob Dibble	.05
63	Bill Doran	.05
64	Mariano Duncan	.05
65	Chris Hammond	.05
66	Billy Hatcher	.05
67	Danny Jackson	.05
68	Barry Larkin	.05
69	Tim Layana **RC**	.05
70	Terry Lee **RC**	.05
71	Rick Mahler	.05
72	Hal Morris	.05
73	Randy Myers	.05
74	Ron Oester	.05
75	Joe Oliver	.05
76	Paul O'Neill	.05
77	Luis Quinones	.05
78	Jeff Reed	.05
79	Jose Rijo	.05
80	Chris Sabo	.05
81	Scott Scudder	.05
82	Herm Winningham	.05
83	Larry Andersen	.05
84	Marty Barrett	.05
85	Mike Boddicker	.05
86	Wade Boggs	.50
87	Tom Bolton	.05
88	Tom Brunansky	.05
89	Ellis Burks	.05
90	Roger Clemens	.55
91	Scott Cooper	.05
92	John Dopson	.05
93	Dwight Evans	.05
94	Wes Gardner	.05
95	Jeff Gray **RC**	.05
96	Mike Greenwell	.05
97	Greg Harris	.05
98	Daryl Irvine **RC**	.05
99	Dana Kiecker **RC**	.05
100	Randy Kutcher	.05
101	Dennis Lamp	.05
102	Mike Marshall	.05
103	John Marzano	.05
104	Rob Murphy	.05
105a	Tim Naehring **RC** (Seven-line career summary.)	.05
105b	Tim Naehring **RC** (Nine-line career summary.)	.05
106	Tony Pena	.05
107	Phil Plantier **RC**	.05
108	Carlos Quintana	.05
109	Jeff Reardon	.05
110	Jerry Reed	.05
111	Jody Reed	.05
112	Luis Rivera	.05
113a	Kevin Romine (One-line career summary.)	.05
113b	Kevin Romine (Two-line career summary.)	.05
114	Phil Bradley	.05
115	Ivan Calderon	.05
116	Wayne Edwards	.05
117	Alex Fernandez	.05
118	Carlton Fisk	.40
119	Scott Fletcher	.05
120	Craig Grebeck **RC**	.05
121	Ozzie Guillen	.05
122	Greg Hibbard	.05
123	Lance Johnson	.05
124	Barry Jones	.05
125a	Ron Karkovice (Two-line career summary.)	.05
125b	Ron Karkovice (One-line career summary.)	.05
126	Eric King	.05
127	Steve Lyons	.05
128	Carlos Martinez	.05
129	Jack McDowell	.05
130	Donn Pall	.05
131	Dan Pasqua	.05
132	Ken Patterson	.05
133	Melido Perez	.05
134	Adam Peterson	.05
135	Scott Radinsky **RC**	.05
136	Sammy Sosa	.50
137	Bobby Thigpen	.05
138	Frank Thomas	.40
139	Robin Ventura	.05
140	Daryl Boston	.05
141	Chuck Carr **RC**	.05
142	Mark Carreon	.05
143	David Cone	.05
144	Ron Darling	.05
145	Kevin Elster	.05
146	Sid Fernandez	.05
147	John Franco	.05
148	Dwight Gooden	.05
149	Tom Herr	.05
150	Todd Hundley	.05
151	Gregg Jefferies	.05
152	Howard Johnson	.05
153	Dave Magadan	.05
154	Kevin McReynolds	.05
155	Keith Miller	.05
156	Bob Ojeda	.05
157	Tom O'Malley	.05
158	Alejandro Pena	.05
159	Darren Reed **RC**	.05

555	Mark Davis	.05
556	Storm Davis	.05
557	Jim Eisenreich	.05
558	Steve Farr	.05
559	Tom Gordon	.05
560	Mark Gubicza	.05
561	Bo Jackson	.10
562	Mike Macfarlane	.05
563	Brian McRae RC	.10
564	Jeff Montgomery	.05
565	Bill Pecota	.05
566	Gerald Perry	.05
567	Bret Saberhagen	.05
568	Jeff Schulz RC	.05
569	Kevin Seitzer	.05
570	Terry Shumpert RC	.05
571	Kurt Stillwell	.05
572	Danny Tartabull	.05
573	Gary Thurman	.05
574	Frank White	.05
575	Willie Wilson	.05
576	Chris Bosio	.05
577	Greg Brock	.05
578	George Canale	.05
579	Chuck Crim	.05
580	Rob Deer	.05
581	Edgar Diaz RC	.05
582	Tom Edens RC	.05
583	Mike Felder	.05
584	Jim Gantner	.05
585	Darryl Hamilton	.05
586	Ted Higuera	.05
587	Mark Knudson	.05
588	Bill Krueger	.05
589	Tim McIntosh	.05
590	Paul Mirabella	.05
591	Paul Molitor	.40
592	Jaime Navarro	.05
593	Dave Parker	.05
594	Dan Plesac	.05
595	Ron Robinson	.05
596	Gary Sheffield	.30
597	Bill Spiers	.05
598	B.J. Surhoff	.05
599	Greg Vaughn	.05
600	Randy Veres	.05
601	Robin Yount	.40
602a	Rick Aguilera (Five-line career summary.)	.05
602b	Rick Aguilera (Four-line career summary.)	.05
603	Allan Anderson	.05
604	Juan Berenguer	.05
605	Randy Bush	.05
606	Carmen Castillo	.05
607	Tim Drummond	.05
608	Scott Erickson RC	.10
609	Gary Gaetti	.05
610a	Greg Gagne (Horizontal lines under 82 Ft. Lauderdale, 84 Toledo and 87 Twins.)	.05
610b	Greg Gagne (Horizontal lines under 82 Orlando, 84 Twins and 88 Twins.)	.05
611	Dan Gladden	.05
612	Mark Guthrie	.05
613	Brian Harper	.05
614	Kent Hrbek	.05
615	Gene Larkin	.05
616	Terry Leach	.05
617	Nelson Liriano	.05
618	Shane Mack	.05
619	John Moses	.05
620	Pedro Munoz RC	.05
621	Al Newman	.05
622	Junior Ortiz	.05
623	Kirby Puckett	.50
624	Roy Smith	.05
625	Kevin Tapani	.05
626	Gary Wayne	.05
627	David West	.05
628	Cris Carpenter	.05
629	Vince Coleman	.05
630	Ken Dayley	.05
631	Jose DeLeon	.05
632	Frank DiPino	.05
633	Bernard Gilkey RC	.25
634	Pedro Guerrero	.05
635	Ken Hill	.05
636	Felix Jose	.05
637	Ray Lankford RC	.25
638	Joe Magrane	.05
639	Tom Niedenfuer	.05
640	Jose Oquendo	.05
641	Tom Pagnozzi	.05
642	Terry Pendleton	.05
643	Mike Perez RC	.05
644	Bryn Smith	.05
645	Lee Smith	.05
646	Ozzie Smith	.50
647	Scott Terry	.05
648	Bob Tewksbury	.05
649	Milt Thompson	.05
650	John Tudor	.05
651	Denny Walling	.05
652	Craig Wilson RC	.05
653	Todd Worrell	.05
654	Todd Zeile	.05
655	Oscar Azocar RC	.05
656	Steve Balboni	.05
657	Jesse Barfield	.05
658	Greg Cadaret	.05
659	Chuck Cary	.05
660	Rick Cerone	.05
661	Dave Eiland	.05
662a	Alvaro Espinoza (No 1979-80 stats.)	.05
662b	Alvaro Espinoza (1979-80 stats included)	.05
663	Bob Geren	.05
664	Lee Guetterman	.05
665	Mel Hall	.05
666a	Andy Hawkins (No 1978 stats.)	.05
666b	Andy Hawkins (1978 stats included)	.05
667	Jimmy Jones	.05
668	Roberto Kelly	.05
669	Dave LaPoint	.05
670	Tim Leary	.05
671	Jim Leyritz RC	.10
672	Kevin Maas	.05
673	Don Mattingly	.60
674	Matt Nokes	.05
675	Pascual Perez	.05
676	Eric Plunk	.05
677	Dave Righetti	.05
678	Jeff Robinson	.05
679	Steve Sax	.05
680	Mike Witt	.05
681	Steve Avery	.05
682	Mike Bell	.05
683	Jeff Blauser	.05
684	Francisco Cabrera	.05
685	Tony Castillo	.05
686	Marty Clary	.05
687	Nick Esasky	.05
688	Ron Gant	.05
689	Tom Glavine	.25
690	Mark Grant	.05
691	Tommy Gregg	.05
692	Dwayne Henry	.05
693	Dave Justice	.05
694	Jimmy Kremers RC	.05
695	Charlie Leibrandt	.05
696	Mark Lemke	.05
697	Oddibe McDowell	.05
698	Greg Olson RC	.05
699	Jeff Parrett	.05
700	Jim Presley	.05
701	Victor Rosario RC	.05
702	Lonnie Smith	.05
703	Pete Smith	.05
704	John Smoltz	.05
705	Mike Stanton	.05
706	Andres Thomas	.05
707	Jeff Treadway	.05
708	Jim Vatcher RC	.05
709	Ryne Sandberg, Cecil Fielder	.10
710	Barry Bonds, Ken Griffey Jr.	.65
711	Bobby Bonilla, Barry Larkin	.05
712	Bobby Thigpen, John Franco	.05
713	Andre Dawson, Ryne Sandberg	.10
714	Athletics, Pirates, Reds, Red Sox Checklists	.05
715	Dodgers	.05
716	Expos, Giants, Rangers, Angels Checklists	.05
717	Tigers, Indians, Phillies, Cubs Checklists	.05
718	Checklists (Mariners, Orioles, Astros, Padres)	.05
719	Royals, Brewers, Twins, Cardinals Checklists	.05
720	Checklists (Yankees, Braves, Super Stars)	.05

Update

		NM/M
Complete Set (132):		3.00
Common Player:		.05
1	Glenn Davis	.05
2	Dwight Evans	.05
3	Jose Mesa	.05
4	Jack Clark	.05
5	Danny Darwin	.05
6	Steve Lyons	.05
7	Mo Vaughn	.05
8	Floyd Bannister	.05
9	Gary Gaetti	.05
10	Dave Parker	.05
11	Joey Cora	.05

12	Charlie Hough	.05
13	Matt Merullo	.05
14	Warren Newson	.05
15	Tim Raines	.05
16	Albert Belle	.05
17	Glenallen Hill	.05
18	Shawn Hillegas	.05
19	Mark Lewis	.05
20	Charles Nagy	.05
21	Mark Whiten	.05
22	John Cerutti	.05
23	Rob Deer	.05
24	Mickey Tettleton	.05
25	Warren Cromartie	.05
26	Kirk Gibson	.05
27	David Howard	.05
28	Brent Mayne	.05
29	Dante Bichette	.05
30	Mark Lee	.05
31	Julio Machado	.05
32	Edwin Nunez	.05
33	Willie Randolph	.05
34	Franklin Stubbs	.05
35	Bill Wegman	.05
36	Chili Davis	.05
37	Chuck Knoblauch	.05
38	Scott Leius	.05
39	Jack Morris	.05
40	Mike Pagliarulo	.05
41	Lenny Webster	.05
42	John Habyan	.05
43	Steve Howe	.05
44	Jeff Johnson	.05
45	Scott Kamieniecki	.05
46	Pat Kelly	.05
47	Hensley Meulens	.05
48	Wade Taylor	.05
49	Bernie Williams	.20
50	Kirk Dressendorfer	.05
51	Ernest Riles	.05
52	Rich DeLucia	.05
53	Tracy Jones	.05
54	Bill Krueger	.05
55	Alonzo Powell	.05
56	Jeff Schaefer	.05
57	Russ Swan	.05
58	John Barfield	.05
59	Rich Gossage	.10
60	Jose Guzman	.05
61	Dean Palmer	.05
62	Ivan Rodriguez RC	1.50
63	Roberto Alomar	.20
64	Tom Candiotti	.05
65	Joe Carter	.05
66	Ed Sprague	.05
67	Pat Tabler	.05
68	Mike Timlin	.05
69	Devon White	.05
70	Rafael Belliard	.05
71	Juan Berenguer	.05
72	Sid Bream	.05
73	Marvin Freeman	.05
74	Kent Mercker	.05
75	Otis Nixon	.05
76	Terry Pendleton	.05
77	George Bell	.05
78	Danny Jackson	.05
79	Chuck McElroy	.05
80	Gary Scott	.05
81	Heathcliff Slocumb	.05
82	Dave Smith	.05
83	Rick Wilkins	.05
84	Freddie Benavides	.05
85	Ted Power	.05
86	Mo Sanford	.05
87	Jeff Bagwell RC	2.00
88	Steve Finley	.05
89	Pete Harnisch	.05
90	Darryl Kile	.05
91	Brett Butler	.05
92	John Candelaria	.05
93	Gary Carter	.40
94	Kevin Gross	.05

95	Bob Ojeda	.05
96	Darryl Strawberry	.05
97	Ivan Calderon	.05
98	Ron Hassey	.05
99	Gilberto Reyes	.05
100	Hubie Brooks	.05
101	Rick Cerone	.05
102	Vince Coleman	.05
103	Jeff Innis	.05
104	Pete Schourek	.05
105	Andy Ashby	.05
106	Wally Backman	.05
107	Darrin Fletcher	.05
108	Tommy Greene	.05
109	John Morris	.05
110	Mitch Williams	.05
111	Lloyd McClendon	.05
112	Orlando Merced	.05
113	Vicente Palacios	.05
114	Gary Varsho	.05
115	John Wehner	.05
116	Rex Hudler	.05
117	Tim Jones	.05
118	Geronimo Pena	.05
119	Gerald Perry	.05
120	Larry Andersen	.05
121	Jerald Clark	.05
122	Scott Coolbaugh	.05
123	Tony Fernandez	.05
124	Darrin Jackson	.05
125	Fred McGriff	.05
126	Jose Mota	.05
127	Tim Teufel	.05
128	Bud Black	.05
129	Mike Felder	.05
130	Willie McGee	.05
131	Dave Righetti	.05
132	Checklist	.05

1992 Fleer

		NM/M
Unopened Factory Set (732):		17.50
Complete Set (720):		8.00
Common Player:		.05
Wax Pack (15):		.45
Wax Box (36):		10.00
Cello Pack (35):		1.00
Cello Box (24):		16.00
1	Brady Anderson	.05
2	Jose Bautista	.05
3	Juan Bell	.05
4	Glenn Davis	.05
5	Mike Devereaux	.05
6	Dwight Evans	.05
7	Mike Flanagan	.05
8	Leo Gomez	.05
9	Chris Hoiles	.05
10	Sam Horn	.05
11	Tim Hulett	.05
12	Dave Johnson	.05
13	Chito Martinez RC	.05
14	Ben McDonald	.05
15	Bob Melvin	.05
16	Luis Mercedes RC	.10
17	Jose Mesa	.05
18	Bob Milacki	.05
19	Randy Milligan	.05
20	Mike Mussina	.30
21	Gregg Olson	.05
22	Joe Orsulak	.05
23	Jim Poole	.05
24	Arthur Rhodes RC	.10
25	Billy Ripken	.05
26	Cal Ripken, Jr.	1.00
27	David Segui	.05
28	Roy Smith	.05
29	Anthony Telford	.05
30	Mark Williamson	.05
31	Craig Worthington	.05
32	Wade Boggs	.55
33	Tom Bolton	.05
34	Tom Brunansky	.05

#	Player	Price	#	Player	Price	#	Player	Price	#	Player	Price
35	Ellis Burks	.05	139	Pete Incaviglia	.05	243	Scott Sanderson	.05	347	Mookie Wilson	.05
36	Jack Clark	.05	140	Mark Leiter RC	.05	244	Steve Sax	.05	348	Eddie Zosky	.05
37	Roger Clemens	.60	141	Scott Livingstone RC	.10	245	Wade Taylor RC	.05	349	Steve Avery	.05
38	Danny Darwin	.05	142	Lloyd Moseby	.05	246	Randy Velarde	.05	350	Mike Bell	.05
39	Mike Greenwell	.05	143	Tony Phillips	.05	247	Bernie Williams	.05	351	Rafael Belliard	.05
40	Joe Hesketh	.05	144	Mark Salas	.05	248	Troy Afenir	.05	352	Juan Berenguer	.05
41	Daryl Irvine	.05	145	Frank Tanana	.05	249	Harold Baines	.05	353	Jeff Blauser	.05
42	Dennis Lamp	.05	146	Walt Terrell	.05	250	Lance Blankenship	.05	354	Sid Bream	.05
43	Tony Pena	.05	147	Mickey Tettleton	.05	251	Mike Bordick RC	.10	355	Francisco Cabrera	.05
44	Phil Plantier	.05	148	Alan Trammell	.05	252	Jose Canseco	.30	356	Marvin Freeman	.05
45	Carlos Quintana	.05	149	Lou Whitaker	.05	253	Steve Chitren	.05	357	Ron Gant	.05
46	Jeff Reardon	.05	150	Kevin Appier	.05	254	Ron Darling	.05	358	Tom Glavine	.30
47	Jody Reed	.05	151	Luis Aquino	.05	255	Dennis Eckersley	.45	359	Brian Hunter RC	.05
48	Luis Rivera	.05	152	Todd Benzinger	.05	256	Mike Gallego	.05	360	Dave Justice	.05
49	Mo Vaughn	.05	153	Mike Boddicker	.05	257	Dave Henderson	.05	361	Charlie Leibrandt	.05
50	Jim Abbott	.05	154	George Brett	.60	258	Rickey Henderson	.50	362	Mark Lemke	.05
51	Kyle Abbott	.05	155	Storm Davis	.05	259	Rick Honeycutt	.05	363	Kent Mercker	.05
52	Ruben Amaro Jr. RC	.05	156	Jim Eisenreich	.05	260	Brook Jacoby	.05	364	Keith Mitchell RC	.05
53	Scott Bailes	.05	157	Kirk Gibson	.05	261	Carney Lansford	.05	365	Greg Olson	.05
54	Chris Beasley RC	.05	158	Tom Gordon	.05	262	Mark McGwire	.75	366	Terry Pendleton	.05
55	Mark Eichhorn	.05	159	Mark Gubicza	.05	263	Mike Moore	.05	367	Armando Reynoso RC	.05
56	Mike Fetters	.05	160	David Howard RC	.05	264	Gene Nelson	.05	368	Deion Sanders	.10
57	Chuck Finley	.05	161	Mike Macfarlane	.05	265	Jamie Quirk	.05	369	Lonnie Smith	.05
58	Gary Gaetti	.05	162	Brent Mayne	.05	266	Joe Slusarski RC	.10	370	Pete Smith	.05
59	Dave Gallagher	.05	163	Brian McRae	.05	267	Terry Steinbach	.05	371	John Smoltz	.05
60	Donnie Hill	.05	164	Jeff Montgomery	.05	268	Dave Stewart	.05	372	Mike Stanton	.05
61	Bryan Harvey	.05	165	Bill Pecota	.05	269	Todd Van Poppel	.05	373	Jeff Treadway	.05
62	Wally Joyner	.05	166	Harvey Pulliam RC	.05	270	Walt Weiss	.05	374	Mark Wohlers RC	.05
63	Mark Langston	.05	167	Bret Saberhagen	.05	271	Bob Welch	.05	375	Paul Assenmacher	.05
64	Kirk McCaskill	.05	168	Kevin Seitzer	.05	272	Curt Young	.05	376	George Bell	.05
65	John Orton	.05	169	Terry Shumpert	.05	273	Scott Bradley	.05	377	Shawn Boskie	.05
66	Lance Parrish	.05	170	Kurt Stillwell	.05	274	Greg Briley	.05	378	Frank Castillo RC	.05
67	Luis Polonia	.05	171	Danny Tartabull	.05	275	Jay Buhner	.05	379	Andre Dawson	.25
68	Bobby Rose	.05	172	Gary Thurman	.05	276	Henry Cotto	.05	380	Shawon Dunston	.05
69	Dick Schofield	.05	173	Dante Bichette	.05	277	Alvin Davis	.05	381	Mark Grace	.05
70	Luis Sojo	.05	174	Kevin Brown	.05	278	Rich DeLucia	.05	382	Mike Harkey	.05
71	Lee Stevens	.05	175	Chuck Crim	.05	279	Ken Griffey Jr.	.65	383	Danny Jackson	.05
72	Dave Winfield	.50	176	Jim Gantner	.05	280	Erik Hanson	.05	384	Les Lancaster	.05
73	Cliff Young	.05	177	Darryl Hamilton	.05	281	Brian Holman	.05	385	Cedric Landrum RC	.05
74	Wilson Alvarez	.05	178	Ted Higuera	.05	282	Mike Jackson	.05	386	Greg Maddux	.55
75	Esteban Beltre RC	.05	179	Darren Holmes	.05	283	Randy Johnson	.50	387	Derrick May	.05
76	Joey Cora	.05	180	Mark Lee	.05	284	Tracy Jones	.05	388	Chuck McElroy	.05
77	Brian Drahman RC	.05	181	Julio Machado	.05	285	Bill Krueger	.05	389	Ryne Sandberg	.55
78	Alex Fernandez	.05	182	Paul Molitor	.50	286	Edgar Martinez	.05	390	Heathcliff Slocumb RC	.10
79	Carlton Fisk	.50	183	Jaime Navarro	.05	287	Tino Martinez	.05	391	Dave Smith	.05
80	Scott Fletcher	.05	184	Edwin Nunez	.05	288	Rob Murphy	.05	392	Dwight Smith	.05
81	Craig Grebeck	.05	185	Dan Plesac	.05	289	Pete O'Brien	.05	393	Rick Sutcliffe	.05
82	Ozzie Guillen	.05	186	Willie Randolph	.05	290	Alonzo Powell	.05	394	Hector Villanueva	.05
83	Greg Hibbard	.05	187	Ron Robinson	.05	291	Harold Reynolds	.05	395	Chico Walker RC	.05
84	Charlie Hough	.05	188	Gary Sheffield	.30	292	Mike Schooler	.05	396	Jerome Walton	.05
85	Mike Huff	.05	189	Bill Spiers	.05	293	Russ Swan	.05	397	Rick Wilkins RC	.15
86	Bo Jackson	.10	190	B.J. Surhoff	.05	294	Bill Swift	.05	398	Jack Armstrong	.05
87	Lance Johnson	.05	191	Dale Sveum	.05	295	Dave Valle	.05	399	Freddie Benavides RC	.05
88	Ron Karkovice	.05	192	Greg Vaughn	.05	296	Omar Vizquel	.05	400	Glenn Braggs	.05
89	Jack McDowell	.05	193	Bill Wegman	.05	297	Gerald Alexander	.05	401	Tom Browning	.05
90	Matt Merullo	.05	194	Robin Yount	.50	298	Brad Arnsberg	.05	402	Norm Charlton	.05
91	Warren Newson RC	.05	195	Rick Aguilera	.05	299	Kevin Brown	.05	403	Eric Davis	.05
92	Donn Pall	.05	196	Allan Anderson	.05	300	Jack Daugherty	.05	404	Rob Dibble	.05
93	Dan Pasqua	.05	197	Steve Bedrosian	.05	301	Mario Diaz	.05	405	Bill Doran	.05
94	Ken Patterson	.05	198	Randy Bush	.05	302	Brian Downing	.05	406	Mariano Duncan	.05
95	Melido Perez	.05	199	Larry Casian	.05	303	Julio Franco	.05	407	Kip Gross RC	.05
96	Scott Radinsky	.05	200	Chili Davis	.05	304	Juan Gonzalez	.25	408	Chris Hammond	.05
97	Tim Raines	.05	201	Scott Erickson	.05	305	Rich Gossage	.10	409	Billy Hatcher	.05
98	Sammy Sosa	.55	202	Greg Gagne	.05	306	Jose Guzman	.05	410	Chris Jones RC	.05
99	Bobby Thigpen	.05	203	Dan Gladden	.05	307	Jose Hernandez RC	.05	411	Barry Larkin	.05
100	Frank Thomas	.50	204	Brian Harper	.05	308	Jeff Huson	.05	412	Hal Morris	.05
101	Robin Ventura	.05	205	Kent Hrbek	.05	309	Mike Jeffcoat	.05	413	Randy Myers	.05
102	Mike Aldrete	.05	206	Chuck Knoblauch	.05	310	Terry Mathews RC	.05	414	Joe Oliver	.05
103	Sandy Alomar, Jr.	.05	207	Gene Larkin	.05	311	Rafael Palmeiro	.45	415	Paul O'Neill	.05
104	Carlos Baerga	.05	208	Terry Leach	.05	312	Dean Palmer	.05	416	Ted Power	.05
105	Albert Belle	.05	209	Scott Leius	.05	313	Geno Petralli	.05	417	Luis Quinones	.05
106	Willie Blair	.05	210	Shane Mack	.05	314	Gary Pettis	.05	418	Jeff Reed	.05
107	Jerry Browne	.05	211	Jack Morris	.05	315	Kevin Reimer	.05	419	Jose Rijo	.05
108	Alex Cole	.05	212	Pedro Munoz	.05	316	Ivan Rodriguez	.45	420	Chris Sabo	.05
109	Felix Fermin	.05	213	Denny Neagle RC	.10	317	Kenny Rogers	.05	421	Reggie Sanders	.05
110	Glenallen Hill	.05	214	Al Newman	.05	318	Wayne Rosenthal RC	.05	422	Scott Scudder	.05
111	Shawn Hillegas	.05	215	Junior Ortiz	.05	319	Jeff Russell	.05	423	Glenn Sutko	.05
112	Chris James	.05	216	Mike Pagliarulo	.05	320	Nolan Ryan	1.00	424	Eric Anthony	.05
113	Reggie Jefferson	.05	217	Kirby Puckett	.55	321	Ruben Sierra	.05	425	Jeff Bagwell	.50
114	Doug Jones	.05	218	Paul Sorrento	.05	322	Jim Acker	.05	426	Craig Biggio	.05
115	Eric King	.05	219	Kevin Tapani	.05	323	Roberto Alomar	.20	427	Ken Caminiti	.05
116	Mark Lewis	.05	220	Lenny Webster	.05	324	Derek Bell	.05	428	Casey Candaele	.05
117	Carlos Martinez	.05	221	Jesse Barfield	.05	325	Pat Borders	.05	429	Mike Capel	.05
118	Charles Nagy	.05	222	Greg Cadaret	.05	326	Tom Candiotti	.05	430	Andujar Cedeno	.05
119	Rod Nichols	.05	223	Dave Eiland	.05	327	Joe Carter	.05	431	Jim Corsi	.05
120	Steve Olin	.05	224	Alvaro Espinoza	.05	328	Rob Ducey	.05	432	Mark Davidson	.05
121	Jesse Orosco	.05	225	Steve Farr	.05	329	Kelly Gruber	.05	433	Steve Finley	.05
122	Rudy Seanez	.05	226	Bob Geren	.05	330	Juan Guzman RC	.25	434	Luis Gonzalez	.05
123	Joel Skinner	.05	227	Lee Guetterman	.05	331	Tom Henke	.05	435	Pete Harnisch	.05
124	Greg Swindell	.05	228	John Habyan	.05	332	Jimmy Key	.05	436	Dwayne Henry	.05
125	Jim Thome	.50	229	Mel Hall	.05	333	Manny Lee	.05	437	Xavier Hernandez	.05
126	Mark Whiten	.05	230	Steve Howe	.05	334	Al Leiter	.05	438	Jimmy Jones	.05
127	Scott Aldred	.05	231	Mike Humphreys RC	.05	335	Bob MacDonald RC	.05	439	Darryl Kile RC	.05
128	Andy Allanson	.05	232	Scott Kamieniecki RC	.10	336	Candy Maldonado	.05	440	Rob Mallicoat RC	.05
129	John Cerutti	.05	233	Pat Kelly	.05	337	Rance Mulliniks	.05	441	Andy Mota RC	.05
130	Milt Cuyler	.05	234	Roberto Kelly	.05	338	Greg Myers	.05	442	Al Osuna	.05
131	Mike Dalton RC	.05	235	Tim Leary	.05	339	John Olerud	.05	443	Mark Portugal	.05
132	Rob Deer	.05	236	Kevin Maas	.05	340	Ed Sprague RC	.10	444	Scott Servais RC	.10
133	Cecil Fielder	.05	237	Don Mattingly	.60	341	Dave Stieb	.05	445	Mike Simms	.05
134	Travis Fryman	.05	238	Hensley Meulens	.05	342	Todd Stottlemyre	.05	446	Gerald Young	.05
135	Dan Gakeler RC	.05	239	Matt Nokes	.05	343	Mike Timlin RC	.10	447	Tim Belcher	.05
136	Paul Gibson	.05	240	Pascual Perez	.05	344	Duane Ward	.05	448	Brett Butler	.05
137	Bill Gullickson	.05	241	Eric Plunk	.05	345	David Wells	.05	449	John Candelaria	.05
138	Mike Henneman	.05	242	John Ramos RC	.05	346	Devon White	.05	450	Gary Carter	.50

451	Dennis Cook	.05
452	Tim Crews	.05
453	Kal Daniels	.05
454	Jim Gott	.05
455	Alfredo Griffin	.05
456	Kevin Gross	.05
457	Chris Gwynn	.05
458	Lenny Harris	.05
459	Orel Hershiser	.05
460	Jay Howell	.05
461	Stan Javier	.05
462	Eric Karros	.05
463	Ramon Martinez	.05
464	Roger McDowell	.05
465	Mike Morgan	.05
466	Eddie Murray	.50
467	Jose Offerman	.05
468	Bob Ojeda	.05
469	Juan Samuel	.05
470	Mike Scioscia	.05
471	Darryl Strawberry	.05
472	Bret Barberie RC	.10
473	Brian Barnes	.05
474	Eric Bullock	.05
475	Ivan Calderon	.05
476	Delino DeShields	.05
477	Jeff Fassero RC	.10
478	Mike Fitzgerald	.05
479	Steve Frey	.05
480	Andres Galarraga	.05
481	Mark Gardner	.05
482	Marquis Grissom	.05
483	Chris Haney RC	.05
484	Barry Jones	.05
485	Dave Martinez	.05
486	Dennis Martinez	.05
487	Chris Nabholz	.05
488	Spike Owen	.05
489	Gilberto Reyes	.05
490	Mel Rojas	.05
491	Scott Ruskin	.05
492	Bill Sampen	.05
493	Larry Walker	.05
494	Tim Wallach	.05
495	Daryl Boston	.05
496	Hubie Brooks	.05
497	Tim Burke	.05
498	Mark Carreon	.05
499	Tony Castillo	.05
500	Vince Coleman	.05
501	David Cone	.05
502	Kevin Elster	.05
503	Sid Fernandez	.05
504	John Franco	.05
505	Dwight Gooden	.05
506	Todd Hundley	.05
507	Jeff Innis	.05
508	Gregg Jefferies	.05
509	Howard Johnson	.05
510	Dave Magadan	.05
511	Terry McDaniel RC	.05
512	Kevin McReynolds	.05
513	Keith Miller	.05
514	Charlie O'Brien	.05
515	Mackey Sasser	.05
516	Pete Schourek RC	.05
517	Julio Valera	.05
518	Frank Viola	.05
519	Wally Whitehurst	.05
520	Anthony Young RC	.05
521	Andy Ashby RC	.10
522	Kim Batiste RC	.05
523	Joe Boever	.05
524	Wes Chamberlain	.05
525	Pat Combs	.05
526	Danny Cox	.05
527	Darren Daulton	.05
528	Jose DeJesus	.05
529	Len Dykstra	.05
530	Darrin Fletcher	.05
531	Tommy Greene	.05
532	Jason Grimsley	.05
533	Charlie Hayes	.05
534	Von Hayes	.05
535	Dave Hollins	.05
536	Ricky Jordan	.05
537	John Kruk	.05
538	Jim Lindeman	.05
539	Mickey Morandini	.05
540	Terry Mulholland	.05
541	Dale Murphy	.20
542	Randy Ready	.05
543	Wally Ritchie	.05
544	Bruce Ruffin	.05
545	Steve Searcy	.05
546	Dickie Thon	.05
547	Mitch Williams	.05
548	Stan Belinda	.05
549	Jay Bell	.05
550	Barry Bonds	1.00
551	Bobby Bonilla	.05
552	Steve Buechele	.05
553	Doug Drabek	.05
554	Neal Heaton	.05

555	Jeff King	.05
556	Bob Kipper	.05
557	Bill Landrum	.05
558	Mike LaValliere	.05
559	Jose Lind	.05
560	Lloyd McClendon	.05
561	Orlando Merced	.05
562	Bob Patterson	.05
563	Joe Redfield RC	.05
564	Gary Redus	.05
565	Rosario Rodriguez	.05
566	Don Slaught	.05
567	John Smiley	.05
568	Zane Smith	.05
569	Randy Tomlin	.05
570	Andy Van Slyke	.05
571	Gary Varsho	.05
572	Bob Walk	.05
573	John Wehner RC	.05
574	Juan Agosto	.05
575	Cris Carpenter	.05
576	Jose DeLeon	.05
577	Rich Gedman	.05
578	Bernard Gilkey	.05
579	Pedro Guerrero	.05
580	Ken Hill	.05
581	Rex Hudler	.05
582	Felix Jose	.05
583	Ray Lankford	.05
584	Omar Olivares	.05
585	Jose Oquendo	.05
586	Tom Pagnozzi	.05
587	Geronimo Pena	.05
588	Mike Perez	.05
589	Gerald Perry	.05
590	Bryn Smith	.05
591	Lee Smith	.05
592	Ozzie Smith	.55
593	Scott Terry	.05
594	Bob Tewksbury	.05
595	Milt Thompson	.05
596	Todd Zeile	.05
597	Larry Andersen	.05
598	Oscar Azocar	.05
599	Andy Benes	.05
600	Ricky Bones RC	.05
601	Jerald Clark	.05
602	Pat Clements	.05
603	Paul Faries	.05
604	Tony Fernandez	.05
605	Tony Gwynn	.55
606	Greg Harris	.05
607	Thomas Howard	.05
608	Bruce Hurst	.05
609	Darrin Jackson	.05
610	Tom Lampkin	.05
611	Craig Lefferts	.05
612	Jim Lewis RC	.05
613	Mike Maddux	.05
614	Fred McGriff	.05
615	Jose Melendez RC	.05
616	Jose Mota RC	.05
617	Dennis Rasmussen	.05
618	Bip Roberts	.05
619	Rich Rodriguez	.05
620	Benito Santiago	.05
621	Craig Shipley RC	.05
622	Tim Teufel	.05
623	Kevin Ward RC	.05
624	Ed Whitson	.05
625	Dave Anderson	.05
626	Kevin Bass	.05
627	Rod Beck RC	.10
628	Bud Black	.05
629	Jeff Brantley	.05
630	John Burkett	.05
631	Will Clark	.05
632	Royce Clayton	.05
633	Steve Decker	.05
634	Kelly Downs	.05
635	Mike Felder	.05
636	Scott Garrelts	.05
637	Eric Gunderson	.05
638	Bryan Hickerson RC	.05
639	Darren Lewis	.05
640	Greg Litton	.05
641	Kirt Manwaring	.05
642	Paul McClellan RC	.05
643	Willie McGee	.05
644	Kevin Mitchell	.05
645	Francisco Olivares	.05
646	Mike Remlinger RC	.10
647	Dave Righetti	.05
648	Robby Thompson	.05
649	Jose Uribe	.05
650	Matt Williams	.05
651	Trevor Wilson	.05
652	Tom Goodwin	.05
653	Terry Bross	.05
654	Mike Christopher RC	.05
655	Kenny Lofton	.05
656	Chris Cron RC	.05
657	Willie Banks	.05
658	Pat Rice RC	.05

659a	Rob Mauer RC (Last name misspelled.)	.75
659b	Rob Maurer RC (Corrected)	.05
660	Don Harris	.05
661	Henry Rodriguez	.05
662	Cliff Brantley RC	.05
663	Mike Linskey RC	.05
664	Gary Disarcina	.05
665	Gil Heredia RC	.10
666	Vinny Castilla RC	.50
667	Paul Abbott	.05
668	Monty Fariss	.05
669	Jarvis Brown RC	.05
670	Wayne Kirby RC	.05
671	Scott Brosius RC	.05
672	Bob Hamelin	.05
673	Joel Johnston RC	.05
674	Tim Spehr RC	.05
675	Jeff Gardner RC	.05
676	Rico Rossy RC	.05
677	Roberto Hernandez RC	.20
678	Ted Wood RC	.05
679	Cal Eldred	.05
680	Sean Berry	.05
681	Rickey Henderson	.20
682	Nolan Ryan	.25
683	Dennis Martinez	.05
684	Wilson Alvarez	.05
685	Joe Carter	.05
686	Dave Winfield	.20
687	David Cone	.05
688	Jose Canseco	.15
689	Howard Johnson	.05
690	Julio Franco	.05
691	Terry Pendleton	.05
692	Cecil Fielder	.05
693	Scott Erickson	.05
694	Tom Glavine	.05
695	Dennis Martinez	.05
696	Bryan Harvey	.05
697	Lee Smith	.05
698	Roberto & Sandy Alomar, Roberto & Sandy Alomar	.10
699	Bobby Bonilla, Will Clark	.05
700	Mark Wohlers, Kent Mercker, Alejandro Pena	.05
701	Chris Jones, Bo Jackson, Gregg Olson, Frank Thomas	.05
702	Brett Butler, Paul Molitor	.10
703	Cal Ripken Jr., Joe Carter	.20
704	Barry Larkin, Kirby Puckett	.15
705	Mo Vaughn, Cecil Fielder	.05
706	Ramon Martinez, Ozzie Guillen	.05
707	Harold Baines, Wade Boggs	.20
708	Robin Yount	.35
709	Ken Griffey Jr.	.60
710	Nolan Ryan	.75
711	Cal Ripken, Jr.	.75
712	Frank Thomas	.50
713	Dave Justice	.05
714	Checklist 1-101	.05
715	Checklist 102-194	.05
716	Checklist 195-296	.05
717	Checklist 297-397	.05
718	Checklist 398-494	.05
719	Checklist 495-596	.05
720a	Checklist 597-720 (659 Rob Decker)	.05
720b	Checklist 597-720 (659 Rob Maurer)	.05

All-Stars

		NM/M
Complete Set (24):		8.00
Common Player:		.10
1	Felix Jose	.10
2	Tony Gwynn	1.25
3	Barry Bonds	3.00
4	Bobby Bonilla	.10
5	Mike LaValliere	.10
6	Tom Glavine	.40
7	Ramon Martinez	.10
8	Lee Smith	.10
9	Mickey Tettleton	.10
10	Scott Erickson	.10
11	Frank Thomas	.75
12	Danny Tartabull	.10
13	Will Clark	.10
14	Ryne Sandberg	1.25
15	Terry Pendleton	.10
16	Barry Larkin	.10
17	Rafael Palmeiro	.65
18	Julio Franco	.10
19	Robin Ventura	.10
20	Cal Ripken, Jr.	3.00
21	Joe Carter	.10
22	Kirby Puckett	1.25
23	Ken Griffey Jr.	2.25
24	Jose Canseco	.50

Lumber Co.

		NM/M
Complete Set (9):		5.00
Common Player:		.25
1	Cecil Fielder	.25
2	Mickey Tettleton	.25
3	Darryl Strawberry	.25
4	Ryne Sandberg	1.00
5	Jose Canseco	.40
6	Matt Williams	.25
7	Cal Ripken, Jr.	2.00
8	Barry Bonds	2.00
9	Ron Gant	.25

Roger Clemens

		NM/M
Complete Set (15):		6.00
Common Card:		.50
Autographed Card:		40.00
1	Quiet Storm	.50
2	Courted by the Mets and Twins	.50
3	The Show	.50
4	A Rocket Launched	.50
5	Time of Trial	.50
6	Break Through	.50
7	Play it Again Roger	.50
8	Business as Usual	.50
9	Heee's Back	.50
10	Blood, Sweat and Tears	.50
11	Prime of Life	.50
12	Man for Every Season	.50
13	Cooperstown Bound	1.50

		NM/M
14	The Heat of the Moment	1.50
15	Final Words	1.50

Rookie Sensations

ROOKIE SENSATIONS

TODD VAN POPPEL
ATHLETICS

		NM/M
Complete Set (20):		13.50
Common Player:		.35
1	Frank Thomas	6.00
2	Todd Van Poppel	.35
3	Orlando Merced	.35
4	Jeff Bagwell	6.00
5	Jeff Fassero	.35
6	Darren Lewis	.35
7	Milt Cuyler	.35
8	Mike Timlin	.35
9	Brian McRae	.35
10	Chuck Knoblauch	.35
11	Rich DeLucia	.35
12	Ivan Rodriguez	4.50
13	Juan Guzman	.35
14	Steve Chitren	.35
15	Mark Wohlers	.35
16	Wes Chamberlain	.35
17	Ray Lankford	.35
18	Chito Martinez	.35
19	Phil Plantier	.35
20	Scott Leius	.35

Smoke 'N Heat

		NM/M
Complete Set (12):		7.50
Common Player:		.25
1	Lee Smith	.25
2	Jack McDowell	.25
3	David Cone	.25
4	Roger Clemens	2.00
5	Nolan Ryan	3.00
6	Scott Erickson	.25
7	Tom Glavine	.50
8	Dwight Gooden	.25
9	Andy Benes	.25
10	Steve Avery	.25
11	Randy Johnson	1.00
12	Jim Abbott	.25

Team Leaders

		NM/M
Complete Set (20):		10.00
Common Player:		.50
1	Don Mattingly	2.00
2	Howard Johnson	.50
3	Chris Sabo	.50
4	Carlton Fisk	1.25
5	Kirby Puckett	1.50
6	Cecil Fielder	.50
7	Tony Gwynn	1.50
8	Will Clark	.50
9	Bobby Bonilla	.50
10	Len Dykstra	.50
11	Tom Glavine	.75
12	Rafael Palmeiro	1.00
13	Wade Boggs	1.50
14	Joe Carter	.50
15	Ken Griffey Jr.	2.50
16	Darryl Strawberry	.50
17	Cal Ripken, Jr.	3.00
18	Danny Tartabull	.50
19	Jose Canseco	.75
20	Andre Dawson	.50

Update

		NM/M
Complete Set (136):		60.00
Common Player:		.05
H1	Ken Griffey Jr.	1.50
H2	Robin Yount	.50
H3	Jeff Reardon	.10
H4	Cecil Fielder	.05
1	Todd Frohwirth	.05
2	Alan Mills	.05

RYAN THOMPSON
OUTFIELD

3	Rick Sutcliffe	.05
4	John Valentin RC	.25
5	Frank Viola	.05
6	Bob Zupcic	.05
7	Mike Butcher	.05
8	Chad Curtis RC	.50
9	Damion Easley RC	.25
10	Tim Salmon	.50
11	Julio Valera	.05
12	George Bell	.05
13	Roberto Hernandez	.05
14	Shawn Jeter	.05
15	Thomas Howard	.05
16	Jesse Levis	.05
17	Kenny Lofton	.05
18	Paul Sorrento	.05
19	Rico Brogna	.05
20	John Doherty	.05
21	Dan Gladden	.05
22	Buddy Groom	.05
23	Shawn Hare	.05
24	John Kiely	.05
25	Kurt Knudsen	.05
26	Gregg Jefferies	.05
27	Wally Joyner	.05
28	Kevin Koslofski	.05
29	Kevin McReynolds	.05
30	Rusty Meacham	.05
31	Keith Miller	.05
32	Hipolito Pichardo	.05
33	James Austin	.05
34	Scott Fletcher	.05
35	John Jaha RC	.05
36	Pat Listach	.05
37	Dave Nilsson	.05
38	Kevin Seitzer	.05
39	Tom Edens	.05
40	Pat Mahomes	.05
41	John Smiley	.05
42	Charlie Hayes	.05
43	Sam Militello	.05
44	Andy Stankiewicz	.05
45	Danny Tartabull	.05
46	Bob Wickman	.05
47	Jerry Browne	.05
48	Kevin Campbell	.05
49	Vince Horsman	.05
50	Troy Neel	.05
51	Ruben Sierra	.05
52	Bruce Walton	.05
53	Willie Wilson	.05
54	Bret Boone	.50
55	Dave Fleming	.05
56	Kevin Mitchell	.05
57	Jeff Nelson RC	.05
58	Shane Turner	.05
59	Jose Canseco	.65
60	Jeff Frye RC	.05
61	Damilo Leon	.05
62	Roger Pavlik	.05
63	David Cone	.05
64	Pat Hentgen	.05
65	Randy Knorr	.05
66	Jack Morris	.05
67	Dave Winfield	1.00
68	David Nied RC	.05
69	Otis Nixon	.05
70	Alejandro Pena	.05
71	Jeff Reardon	.05
72	Alex Arias	.05
73	Jim Bullinger	.05
74	Mike Morgan	.05
75	Rey Sanchez	.05
76	Bob Scanlan	.05
77	Sammy Sosa	3.00
78	Scott Bankhead	.05
79	Tim Belcher	.05
80	Steve Foster	.05
81	Willie Greene	.05
82	Bip Roberts	.05
83	Scott Ruskin	.05
84	Greg Swindell	.05

85	Juan Guerrero	.05
86	Butch Henry	.05
87	Doug Jones	.05
88	Brian Williams	.05
89	Tom Candiotti	.05
90	Eric Davis	.05
91	Carlos Hernandez	.05
92	Mike Piazza RC	45.00
93	Mike Sharperson	.05
94	Eric Young	.05
95	Moises Alou	.05
96	Greg Colbrunn	.05
97	Wil Cordero	.05
98	Ken Hill	.05
99	John Vander Wal	.05
100	John Wetteland	.05
101	Bobby Bonilla	.05
102	Eric Hilman	.05
103	Pat Howell	.05
104	Jeff Kent RC	15.00
105	Dick Schofield	.05
106	Ryan Thompson RC	.05
107	Chico Walker	.05
108	Juan Bell	.05
109	Mariano Duncan	.05
110	Jeff Grotewold	.05
111	Ben Rivera	.05
112	Curt Schilling	.65
113	Victor Cole	.05
114	Al Martin	.05
115	Roger Mason	.05
116	Blas Minor	.05
117	Tim Wakefield	4.00
118	Mark Clark RC	.05
119	Rheal Cormier	.05
120	Donovan Osborne	.05
121	Todd Worrell	.05
122	Jeremy Hernandez	.05
123	Randy Myers	.05
124	Frank Seminara	.05
125	Gary Sheffield	.75
126	Dan Walters	.05
127	Steve Hosey	.05
128	Mike Jackson	.05
129	Jim Pena	.05
130	Cory Snyder	.05
131	Bill Swift	.05
132	Checklist	.05

1993 Fleer

BRETT BUTLER • LOS ANGELES DODGERS • OF

		NM/M
Complete Set (720):		10.00
Common Player:		.05
Series 1 or 2 Pack (15):		.50
Series 1 or 2 Box (36):		12.50
1	Steve Avery	.05
2	Sid Bream	.05
3	Ron Gant	.05
4	Tom Glavine	.25
5	Brian Hunter	.05
6	Ryan Klesko	.05
7	Charlie Leibrandt	.05
8	Kent Mercker	.05
9	David Nied	.05
10	Otis Nixon	.05
11	Greg Olson	.05
12	Terry Pendleton	.05
13	Deion Sanders	.10
14	John Smoltz	.05
15	Mike Stanton	.05
16	Mark Wohlers	.05
17	Paul Assenmacher	.05
18	Steve Buechele	.05
19	Shawon Dunston	.05
20	Mark Grace	.05
21	Derrick May	.05
22	Chuck McElroy	.05
23	Mike Morgan	.05
24	Rey Sanchez	.05
25	Ryne Sandberg	.60
26	Bob Scanlan	.05
27	Sammy Sosa	.60
28	Rick Wilkins	.05

29	Bobby Ayala RC	.05
30	Tim Belcher	.05
31	Jeff Branson RC	.05
32	Norm Charlton	.05
33	Steve Foster RC	.05
34	Willie Greene	.05
35	Chris Hammond	.05
36	Milt Hill	.05
37	Hal Morris	.05
38	Joe Oliver	.05
39	Paul O'Neill	.05
40	Tim Pugh RC	.05
41	Jose Rijo	.05
42	Bip Roberts	.05
43	Chris Sabo	.05
44	Reggie Sanders	.05
45	Eric Anthony	.05
46	Jeff Bagwell	.50
47	Craig Biggio	.05
48	Joe Boever	.05
49	Casey Candaele	.05
50	Steve Finley	.05
51	Luis Gonzalez	.05
52	Pete Harnisch	.05
53	Xavier Hernandez	.05
54	Doug Jones	.05
55	Eddie Taubensee	.05
56	Brian Williams	.05
57	Pedro Astacio RC	.10
58	Todd Benzinger	.05
59	Brett Butler	.05
60	Tom Candiotti	.05
61	Lenny Harris	.05
62	Carlos Hernandez	.05
63	Orel Hershiser	.05
64	Eric Karros	.05
65	Ramon Martinez	.05
66	Jose Offerman	.05
67	Mike Scioscia	.05
68	Mike Sharperson	.05
69	Eric Young RC	.10
70	Moises Alou	.05
71	Ivan Calderon	.05
72	Archi Cianfrocco RC	.05
73	Wil Cordero	.05
74	Delino DeShields	.05
75	Mark Gardner	.05
76	Ken Hill	.05
77	Tim Laker RC	.05
78	Chris Nabholz	.05
79	Mel Rojas	.05
80	John Vander Wal RC	.10
81	Larry Walker	.05
82	Tim Wallach	.05
83	John Wetteland	.05
84	Bobby Bonilla	.05
85	Daryl Boston	.05
86	Sid Fernandez	.05
87	Eric Hillman RC	.05
88	Todd Hundley	.05
89	Howard Johnson	.05
90	Jeff Kent	.05
91	Eddie Murray	.50
92	Bill Pecota	.05
93	Bret Saberhagen	.05
94	Dick Schofield	.05
95	Pete Schourek	.05
96	Anthony Young	.05
97	Ruben Amaro Jr.	.05
98	Juan Bell	.05
99	Wes Chamberlain	.05
100	Darren Daulton	.05
101	Mariano Duncan	.05
102	Mike Hartley	.05
103	Ricky Jordan	.05
104	John Kruk	.05
105	Mickey Morandini	.05
106	Terry Mulholland	.05
107	Ben Rivera RC	.05
108	Curt Schilling	.25
109	Keith Shepherd RC	.05
110	Stan Belinda	.05
111	Jay Bell	.05
112	Barry Bonds	1.00
113	Jeff King	.05
114	Mike LaValliere	.05
115	Jose Lind	.05
116	Roger Mason	.05
117	Orlando Merced	.05
118	Bob Patterson	.05
119	Don Slaught	.05
120	Zane Smith	.05
121	Randy Tomlin	.05
122	Andy Van Slyke	.05
123	Tim Wakefield RC	.10
124	Rheal Cormier	.05
125	Bernard Gilkey	.05
126	Felix Jose	.05
127	Ray Lankford	.05
128	Bob McClure	.05
129	Donovan Osborne	.05
130	Tom Pagnozzi	.05
131	Geronimo Pena	.05
132	Mike Perez	.05

#	Player	Value		#	Player	Value		#	Player	Value		#	Player	Value
133	Lee Smith	.05		237	Tom Gordon	.05		341	Duane Ward	.05		440	Al Osuna	.05
134	Bob Tewksbury	.05		238	Gregg Jefferies	.05		342	Devon White	.05		441	Mark Portugal	.05
135	Todd Worrell	.05		239	Wally Joyner	.05		343	Dave Winfield	.50		442	Scott Servais	.05
136	Todd Zeile	.05		240	Kevin Koslofski RC	.05		344	Edgar Martinez	.05		443	John Candelaria	.05
137	Jerald Clark	.05		241	Mike Macfarlane	.05		345	Cecil Fielder	.05		444	Tim Crews	.05
138	Tony Gwynn	.60		242	Brian McRae	.05		346	Kenny Lofton	.05		445	Eric Davis	.05
139	Greg Harris	.05		243	Rusty Meacham	.05		347	Jack Morris	.05		446	Tom Goodwin	.05
140	Jeremy Hernandez	.05		244	Keith Miller	.05		348	Roger Clemens	.35		447	Jim Gott	.05
141	Darrin Jackson	.05		245	Jeff Montgomery	.05		349	Fred McGriff	.05		448	Kevin Gross	.05
142	Mike Maddux	.05		246	Hipolito Pichardo RC	.05		350	Barry Bonds	.60		449	Dave Hansen	.05
143	Fred McGriff	.05		247	Ricky Bones	.05		351	Gary Sheffield	.05		450	Jay Howell	.05
144	Jose Melendez	.05		248	Cal Eldred	.05		352	Darren Daulton	.05		451	Roger McDowell	.05
145	Rich Rodriguez	.05		249	Mike Fetters	.05		353	Dave Hollins	.05		452	Bob Ojeda	.05
146	Frank Seminara	.05		250	Darryl Hamilton	.05		354	Pedro Martinez, Ramon Martinez	.25		453	Henry Rodriguez	.05
147	Gary Sheffield	.35		251	Doug Henry	.05		355	Ivan Rodriguez, Kirby Puckett	.25		454	Darryl Strawberry	.05
148	Kurt Stillwell	.05		252	John Jaha	.05		356	Ryne Sandberg, Gary Sheffield	.20		455	Mitch Webster	.05
149	Dan Walters RC	.05		253	Pat Listach	.05		357	Roberto Alomar, Chuck Knoblauch, Carlos Baerga	.05		456	Steve Wilson	.05
150	Rod Beck	.05		254	Paul Molitor	.50		358	Checklist	.05		457	Brian Barnes	.05
151	Bud Black	.05		255	Jaime Navarro	.05		359	Checklist	.05		458	Sean Berry	.05
152	Jeff Brantley	.05		256	Kevin Seitzer	.05		360	Checklist	.05		459	Jeff Fassero	.05
153	John Burkett	.05		257	B.J. Surhoff	.05		361	Rafael Belliard	.05		460	Darrin Fletcher	.05
154	Will Clark	.05		258	Greg Vaughn	.05		362	Damon Berryhill	.05		461	Marquis Grissom	.05
155	Royce Clayton	.05		259	Bill Wegman	.05		363	Mike Bielecki	.05		462	Dennis Martinez	.05
156	Mike Jackson	.05		260	Robin Yount	.50		364	Jeff Blauser	.05		463	Spike Owen	.05
157	Darren Lewis	.05		261	Rick Aguilera	.05		365	Francisco Cabrera	.05		464	Matt Stairs	.05
158	Kirt Manwaring	.05		262	Chili Davis	.05		366	Marvin Freeman	.05		465	Sergio Valdez	.05
159	Willie McGee	.05		263	Scott Erickson	.05		367	Dave Justice	.05		466	Kevin Bass	.05
160	Cory Snyder	.05		264	Greg Gagne	.05		368	Mark Lemke	.05		467	Vince Coleman	.05
161	Bill Swift	.05		265	Mark Guthrie	.05		369	Alejandro Pena	.05		468	Mark Dewey	.05
162	Trevor Wilson	.05		266	Brian Harper	.05		370	Jeff Reardon	.05		469	Kevin Elster	.05
163	Brady Anderson	.05		267	Kent Hrbek	.05		371	Lonnie Smith	.05		470	Tony Fernandez	.05
164	Glenn Davis	.05		268	Terry Jorgensen	.05		372	Pete Smith	.05		471	John Franco	.05
165	Mike Devereaux	.05		269	Gene Larkin	.05		373	Shawn Boskie	.05		472	Dave Gallagher	.05
166	Todd Frohwirth	.05		270	Scott Leius	.05		374	Jim Bullinger	.05		473	Paul Gibson	.05
167	Leo Gomez	.05		271	Pat Mahomes	.05		375	Frank Castillo	.05		474	Dwight Gooden	.05
168	Chris Hoiles	.05		272	Pedro Munoz	.05		376	Doug Dascenzo	.05		475	Lee Guetterman	.05
169	Ben McDonald	.05		273	Kirby Puckett	.60		377	Andre Dawson	.25		476	Jeff Innis	.05
170	Randy Milligan	.05		274	Kevin Tapani	.05		378	Mike Harkey	.05		477	Dave Magadan	.05
171	Alan Mills	.05		275	Carl Willis	.05		379	Greg Hibbard	.05		478	Charlie O'Brien	.05
172	Mike Mussina	.30		276	Steve Farr	.05		380	Greg Maddux	.60		479	Willie Randolph	.05
173	Gregg Olson	.05		277	John Habyan	.05		381	Ken Patterson	.05		480	Mackey Sasser	.05
174	Arthur Rhodes	.05		278	Mel Hall	.05		382	Jeff Robinson	.05		481	Ryan Thompson	.05
175	David Segui	.05		279	Charlie Hayes	.05		383	Luis Salazar	.05		482	Chico Walker	.05
176	Ellis Burks	.05		280	Pat Kelly	.05		384	Dwight Smith	.05		483	Kyle Abbott	.05
177	Roger Clemens	.65		281	Don Mattingly	.65		385	Jose Vizcaino	.05		484	Bob Ayrault	.05
178	Scott Cooper	.05		282	Sam Militello	.05		386	Scott Bankhead	.05		485	Kim Batiste	.05
179	Danny Darwin	.05		283	Matt Nokes	.05		387	Tom Browning	.05		486	Cliff Brantley	.05
180	Tony Fossas	.05		284	Melido Perez	.05		388	Darnell Coles	.05		487	Jose DeLeon	.05
181	Paul Quantrill RC	.10		285	Andy Stankiewicz	.05		389	Rob Dibble	.05		488	Len Dykstra	.05
182	Jody Reed	.05		286	Danny Tartabull	.05		390	Bill Doran	.05		489	Tommy Greene	.05
183	John Valentin RC	.10		287	Randy Velarde	.05		391	Dwayne Henry	.05		490	Jeff Grotewold	.05
184	Mo Vaughn	.05		288	Bob Wickman	.05		392	Cesar Hernandez	.05		491	Dave Hollins	.05
185	Frank Viola	.05		289	Bernie Williams	.05		393	Roberto Kelly	.05		492	Danny Jackson	.05
186	Bob Zupcic	.05		290	Lance Blankenship	.05		394	Barry Larkin	.05		493	Stan Javier	.05
187	Jim Abbott	.05		291	Mike Bordick	.05		395	Dave Martinez	.05		494	Tom Marsh	.05
188	Gary DiSarcina	.05		292	Jerry Browne	.05		396	Kevin Mitchell	.05		495	Greg Matthews	.05
189	Damion Easley RC	.10		293	Dennis Eckersley	.40		397	Jeff Reed	.05		496	Dale Murphy	.15
190	Junior Felix	.05		294	Rickey Henderson	.50		398	Scott Ruskin	.05		497	Todd Pratt RC	.05
191	Chuck Finley	.05		295	Vince Horsman RC	.05		399	Greg Swindell	.05		498	Mitch Williams	.05
192	Joe Grahe	.05		296	Mark McGwire	.85		400	Dan Wilson	.05		499	Danny Cox	.05
193	Bryan Harvey	.05		297	Jeff Parrett	.05		401	Andy Ashby	.05		500	Doug Drabek	.05
194	Mark Langston	.05		298	Ruben Sierra	.05		402	Freddie Benavides	.05		501	Carlos Garcia	.05
195	John Orton	.05		299	Terry Steinbach	.05		403	Dante Bichette	.05		502	Lloyd McClendon	.05
196	Luis Polonia	.05		300	Walt Weiss	.05		404	Willie Blair	.05		503	Denny Neagle	.05
197	Tim Salmon	.05		301	Bob Welch	.05		405	Denis Boucher	.05		504	Gary Redus	.05
198	Luis Sojo	.05		302	Willie Wilson	.05		406	Vinny Castilla	.05		505	Bob Walk	.05
199	Wilson Alvarez	.05		303	Bobby Witt	.05		407	Braulio Castillo	.05		506	John Wehner	.05
200	George Bell	.05		304	Bret Boone	.05		408	Alex Cole	.05		507	Luis Alicea	.05
201	Alex Fernandez	.05		305	Jay Buhner	.05		409	Andres Galarraga	.05		508	Mark Clark	.05
202	Craig Grebeck	.05		306	Dave Fleming	.05		410	Joe Girardi	.05		509	Pedro Guerrero	.05
203	Ozzie Guillen	.05		307	Ken Griffey Jr.	.75		411	Butch Henry	.05		510	Rex Hudler	.05
204	Lance Johnson	.05		308	Erik Hanson	.05		412	Darren Holmes	.05		511	Brian Jordan	.05
205	Ron Karkovice	.05		309	Edgar Martinez	.05		413	Calvin Jones	.05		512	Omar Olivares	.05
206	Kirk McCaskill	.05		310	Tino Martinez	.05		414	Steve Reed RC	.05		513	Jose Oquendo	.05
207	Jack McDowell	.05		311	Jeff Nelson	.05		415	Kevin Ritz	.05		514	Gerald Perry	.05
208	Scott Radinsky	.05		312	Dennis Powell	.05		416	Jim Tatum RC	.05		515	Bryn Smith	.05
209	Tim Raines	.05		313	Mike Schooler	.05		417	Jack Armstrong	.05		516	Craig Wilson	.05
210	Frank Thomas	.50		314	Russ Swan	.05		418	Bret Barberie	.05		517	Tracy Woodson	.05
211	Robin Ventura	.05		315	Dave Valle	.05		419	Ryan Bowen	.05		518	Larry Anderson	.05
212	Sandy Alomar Jr.	.05		316	Omar Vizquel	.05		420	Cris Carpenter	.05		519	Andy Benes	.05
213	Carlos Baerga	.05		317	Kevin Brown	.05		421	Chuck Carr	.05		520	Jim Deshaies	.05
214	Dennis Cook	.05		318	Todd Burns	.05		422	Scott Chiamparino	.05		521	Bruce Hurst	.05
215	Thomas Howard	.05		319	Jose Canseco	.35		423	Jeff Conine	.05		522	Randy Myers	.05
216	Mark Lewis	.05		320	Julio Franco	.05		424	Jim Corsi	.05		523	Benito Santiago	.05
217	Derek Lilliquist	.05		321	Jeff Frye	.05		425	Steve Decker	.05		524	Tim Scott	.05
218	Kenny Lofton	.05		322	Juan Gonzalez	.30		426	Chris Donnels	.05		525	Tim Teufel	.05
219	Charles Nagy	.05		323	Jose Guzman	.05		427	Monty Fariss	.05		526	Mike Benjamin	.05
220	Steve Olin	.05		324	Jeff Huson	.05		428	Bob Natal	.05		527	Dave Burba	.05
221	Paul Sorrento	.05		325	Dean Palmer	.05		429	Pat Rapp RC	.05		528	Craig Colbert	.05
222	Jim Thome	.40		326	Kevin Reimer	.05		430	Dave Weathers	.05		529	Mike Felder	.05
223	Mark Whiten	.05		327	Ivan Rodriguez	.40		431	Nigel Wilson RC	.05		530	Bryan Hickerson	.05
224	Milt Cuyler	.05		328	Kenny Rogers	.05		432	Ken Caminiti	.05		531	Chris James	.05
225	Rob Deer	.05		329	Dan Smith	.05		433	Andujar Cedeno	.05		532	Mark Leonard	.05
226	John Doherty RC	.05		330	Roberto Alomar	.20		434	Tom Edens	.05		533	Greg Litton	.05
227	Cecil Fielder	.05		331	Derek Bell	.05		435	Juan Guerrero	.05		534	Francisco Oliveras	.05
228	Travis Fryman	.05		332	Pat Borders	.05		436	Pete Incaviglia	.05		535	John Patterson	.05
229	Mike Henneman	.05		333	Joe Carter	.05		437	Jimmy Jones	.05		536	Jim Pena	.05
230	John Kiely RC	.05		334	Kelly Gruber	.05		438	Darryl Kile	.05		537	Dave Righetti	.05
231	Kurt Knudsen RC	.05		335	Tom Henke	.05		439	Rob Murphy	.05		538	Robby Thompson	.05
232	Scott Livingstone	.05		336	Jimmy Key	.05						539	Jose Uribe	.05
233	Tony Phillips	.05		337	Manuel Lee	.05						540	Matt Williams	.05
234	Mickey Tettleton	.05		338	Candy Maldonado	.05						541	Storm Davis	.05
235	Kevin Appier	.05		339	John Olerud	.05						542	Sam Horn	.05
236	George Brett	.65		340	Todd Stottlemyre	.05						543	Tim Hulett	.05

544	Craig Lefferts	.05
545	Chito Martinez	.05
546	Mark McLemore	.05
547	Luis Mercedes	.05
548	Bob Milacki	.05
549	Joe Orsulak	.05
550	Billy Ripken	.05
551	Cal Ripken, Jr.	1.00
552	Rick Sutcliffe	.05
553	Jeff Tackett	.05
554	Wade Boggs	.60
555	Tom Brunansky	.05
556	Jack Clark	.05
557	John Dopson	.05
558	Mike Gardiner	.05
559	Mike Greenwell	.05
560	Greg Harris	.05
561	Billy Hatcher	.05
562	Joe Hesketh	.05
563	Tony Pena	.05
564	Phil Plantier	.05
565	Luis Rivera	.05
566	Herm Winningham	.05
567	Matt Young	.05
568	Bert Blyleven	.05
569	Mike Butcher	.05
570	Chuck Crim	.05
571	Chad Curtis RC	.15
572	Tim Fortugno	.05
573	Steve Frey	.05
574	Gary Gaetti	.05
575	Scott Lewis	.05
576	Lee Stevens	.05
577	Ron Tingley	.05
578	Julio Valera	.05
579	Shawn Abner	.05
580	Joey Cora	.05
581	Chris Cron	.05
582	Carlton Fisk	.50
583	Roberto Hernandez	.05
584	Charlie Hough	.05
585	Terry Leach	.05
586	Donn Pall	.05
587	Dan Pasqua	.05
588	Steve Sax	.05
589	Bobby Thigpen	.05
590	Albert Belle	.05
591	Felix Fermin	.05
592	Glenallen Hill	.05
593	Brook Jacoby	.05
594	Reggie Jefferson	.05
595	Carlos Martinez	.05
596	Jose Mesa	.05
597	Rod Nichols	.05
598	Junior Ortiz	.05
599	Eric Plunk	.05
600	Ted Power	.05
601	Scott Scudder	.05
602	Kevin Wickander	.05
603	Skeeter Barnes	.05
604	Mark Carreon	.05
605	Dan Gladden	.05
606	Bill Gullickson	.05
607	Chad Kreuter	.05
608	Mark Leiter	.05
609	Mike Munoz	.05
610	Rich Rowland	.05
611	Frank Tanana	.05
612	Walt Terrell	.05
613	Alan Trammell	.05
614	Lou Whitaker	.05
615	Luis Aquino	.05
616	Mike Boddicker	.05
617	Jim Eisenreich	.05
618	Mark Gubicza	.05
619	David Howard	.05
620	Mike Magnante	.05
621	Brent Mayne	.05
622	Kevin McReynolds	.05
623	Eddie Pierce RC	.05
624	Bill Sampen	.05
625	Steve Shifflett	.05
626	Gary Thurman	.05
627	Curtis Wikerson	.05
628	Chris Bosio	.05
629	Scott Fletcher	.05
630	Jim Gantner	.05
631	Dave Nilsson	.05
632	Jesse Orosco	.05
633	Dan Plesac	.05
634	Ron Robinson	.05
635	Bill Spiers	.05
636	Franklin Stubbs	.05
637	Willie Banks	.05
638	Randy Bush	.05
639	Chuck Knoblauch	.05
640	Shane Mack	.05
641	Mike Pagliarulo	.05
642	Jeff Reboulet	.05
643	John Smiley	.05
644	Mike Trombley RC	.05
645	Gary Wayne	.05
646	Lenny Webster	.05
647	Tim Burke	.05
648	Mike Gallego	.05
649	Dion James	.05

650	Jeff Johnson	.05
651	Scott Kamieniecki	.05
652	Kevin Maas	.05
653	Rich Monteleone	.05
654	Jerry Nielsen	.05
655	Scott Sanderson	.05
656	Mike Stanley	.05
657	Gerald Williams	.05
658	Curt Young	.05
659	Harold Baines	.05
660	Kevin Campbell	.05
661	Ron Darling	.05
662	Kelly Downs	.05
663	Eric Fox	.05
664	Dave Henderson	.05
665	Rick Honeycutt	.05
666	Mike Moore	.05
667	Jamie Quirk	.05
668	Jeff Russell	.05
669	Dave Stewart	.05
670	Greg Briley	.05
671	Dave Cochrane	.05
672	Henry Cotto	.05
673	Rich DeLucia	.05
674	Brian Fisher	.05
675	Mark Grant	.05
676	Randy Johnson	.50
677	Tim Leary	.05
678	Pete O'Brien	.05
679	Lance Parrish	.05
680	Harold Reynolds	.05
681	Shane Turner	.05
682	Jack Daugherty	.05
683	David Hulse RC	.05
684	Terry Mathews	.05
685	Al Newman	.05
686	Edwin Nunez	.05
687	Rafael Palmeiro	.40
688	Roger Pavlik	.05
689	Geno Petralli	.05
690	Nolan Ryan	1.00
691	David Cone	.05
692	Alfredo Griffin	.05
693	Juan Guzman	.05
694	Pat Hentgen	.05
695	Randy Knorr	.05
696	Bob MacDonald	.05
697	Jack Morris	.05
698	Ed Sprague	.05
699	Dave Stieb	.05
700	Pat Tabler	.05
701	Mike Timlin	.05
702	David Wells	.05
703	Eddie Zosky	.05
704	Gary Sheffield	.05
705	Darren Daulton	.05
706	Marquis Grissom	.05
707	Greg Maddux	.10
708	Bill Swift	.05
709	Juan Gonzalez	.15
710	Mark McGwire	.50
711	Cecil Fielder	.05
712	Albert Belle	.05
713	Joe Carter	.05
714	Frank Thomas, Cecil Fielder	.10
715	Larry Walker, Darren Daulton	.05
716	Edgar Martinez, Robin Ventura	.05
717	Roger Clemens, Dennis Eckersley	.25
718	Checklist	.05
719	Checklist	.05
720	Checklist	.05

All-Stars

Complete Set A.L. (12):		6.00
Complete Set N.L. (12):		3.75
Common Player:		.15

NATIONAL LEAGUE

1	Fred McGriff	.15
2	Delino DeShields	.15
3	Gary Sheffield	.40
4	Barry Larkin	.15
5	Felix Jose	.15
6	Larry Walker	.15
7	Barry Bonds	2.50
8	Andy Van Slyke	.15
9	Darren Daulton	.15
10	Greg Maddux	.75
11	Tom Glavine	.25
12	Lee Smith	.15

AMERICAN LEAGUE

1	Frank Thomas	.85
2	Roberto Alomar	.40
3	Edgar Martinez	.15
4	Pat Listach	.15
5	Cecil Fielder	.15
6	Juan Gonzalez	.40
7	Ken Griffey Jr.	2.00
8	Joe Carter	.15
9	Kirby Puckett	1.00
10	Brian Harper	.15
11	Dave Fleming	.15
12	Jack McDowell	.15

Golden Moments

DAVE WINFIELD
GOLDEN MOMENTS

		NM/M
Complete Set (6):		4.00
Common Player:		.25
SERIES 1		2.00
(1)	George Brett	1.50
(2)	Mickey Morandini	.25
(3)	Dave Winfield	.50
SERIES 2		2.00
(1)	Dennis Eckersley	.40
(2)	Bip Roberts	.25
(3)	Frank Thomas, Juan Gonzalez	1.50

Major League Prospects

		NM/M
Complete Set (36):		7.50
Common Player:		.15
SERIES 1		5.00
1	Melvin Nieves	.15
2	Sterling Hitchcock	.15
3	Tim Costo	.15
4	Manny Alexander	.15
5	Alan Embree	.15
6	Kevin Young	.15
7	J.T. Snow	.15
8	Russ Springer	.15
9	Billy Ashley	.15
10	Kevin Rogers	.15
11	Steve Hosey	.15
12	Eric Wedge	.15
13	Mike Piazza	3.50
14	Jesse Levis	.15
15	Rico Brogna	.15
16	Alex Arias	.15
17	Rod Brewer	.15
18	Troy Neel	.15
SERIES 2		2.50
1	Scooter Tucker	.15
2	Kerry Woodson	.15
3	Greg Colbrunn	.15
4	Pedro Martinez	1.50
5	Dave Silvestri	.15
6	Kent Bottenfield	.15
7	Rafael Bournigal	.15
8	J.T. Bruett	.15
9	Dave Mlicki	.15
10	Paul Wagner	.15
11	Mike Williams	.15
12	Henry Mercedes	.15
13	Scott Taylor	.15
14	Dennis Moeller	.15
15	Javier Lopez	.15
16	Steve Cooke	.15
17	Pete Young	.15
18	Ken Ryan	.15

ProVisions

GARY
SHEFFIELD

Golden Moments

		NM/M
Complete Set (6):		3.00
Common Player:		.40
SERIES 1		2.00
1	Roberto Alomar	.65
2	Dennis Eckersley	1.00
3	Gary Sheffield	.75
SERIES 2		1.00
1	Andy Van Slyke	.40
2	Tom Glavine	.75
3	Cecil Fielder	.40

Rookie Sensations

ROOKIE
KENNY
LOFTON

		NM/M
Complete Set (20):		6.25
Common Player:		.25
SERIES 1		3.00
1	Kenny Lofton	.50
2	Cal Eldred	.25
3	Pat Listach	.25
4	Roberto Hernandez	.25
5	Dave Fleming	.25
6	Eric Karros	.25
7	Reggie Sanders	.25
8	Derrick May	.25
9	Mike Perez	.25
10	Donovan Osborne	.25
SERIES 2		2.00
1	Moises Alou	.50
2	Pedro Astacio	.25
3	Jim Austin	.25
4	Chad Curtis	.25
5	Gary DiSarcina	.25
6	Scott Livingstone	.25
7	Sam Militello	.25
8	Arthur Rhodes	.25
9	Tim Wakefield	.35
10	Bob Zupcic	.25

Team Leaders

		NM/M
Complete Set (20):		12.50
Common Player:		.40
SERIES 1		10.00
1	Kirby Puckett	1.25
2	Mark McGwire	3.00
3	Pat Listach	.40
4	Roger Clemens	1.50
5	Frank Thomas	1.00
6	Carlos Baerga	.40
7	Brady Anderson	.40
8	Juan Gonzalez	.50
9	Roberto Alomar	.60
10	Ken Griffey Jr.	2.00
SERIES 2		4.00
1	Will Clark	.40
2	Terry Pendleton	.40
3	Ray Lankford	.40
4	Eric Karros	.40

5	Gary Sheffield	.75
6	Ryne Sandberg	1.25
7	Marquis Grissom	.40
8	John Kruk	.40
9	Jeff Bagwell	1.00
10	Andy Van Slyke	.40

Tom Glavine Career Highlights

	NM/M
Complete Set (15):	5.00
Autographed Card:	30.00
1-15 Tom Glavine	.50

Final Edition

	NM/M
Complete Set (310):	7.50
Common Player:	.05
1	Steve Bedrosian	.05
2	Jay Howell	.05
3	Greg Maddux	.65
4	Greg McMichael RC	.05
5	Tony Tarasco RC	.05
6	Jose Bautista	.05
7	Jose Guzman	.05
8	Greg Hibbard	.05
9	Candy Maldonado	.05
10	Randy Myers	.05
11	Matt Walbeck RC	.05
12	Turk Wendell	.05
13	Willie Nelson	.05
14	Greg Cadaret	.05
15	Roberto Kelly	.05
16	Randy Milligan	.05
17	Kevin Mitchell	.05
18	Jeff Reardon	.05
19	John Roper	.05
20	John Smiley	.05
21	Andy Ashby	.05
22	Dante Bichette	.05
23	Willie Blair	.05
24	Pedro Castellano	.05
25	Vinny Castilla	.05
26	Jerald Clark	.05
27	Alex Cole	.05
28	Scott Fredrickson RC	.05
29	Jay Gainer RC	.05
30	Andres Galarraga	.05
31	Joe Girardi	.05
32	Ryan Hawblitzel	.05
33	Charlie Hayes	.05
34	Darren Holmes	.05
35	Chris Jones	.05
36	David Nied	.05
37	J. Owens RC	.05
38	Lance Painter RC	.05
39	Jeff Parrett	.05
40	Steve Reed RC	.05
41	Armando Reynoso	.05
42	Bruce Ruffin	.05
43	Danny Sheaffer RC	.05
44	Keith Shepherd	.05
45	Jim Tatum	.05
46	Gary Wayne	.05
47	Eric Young	.05
48	Luis Aquino	.05
49	Alex Arias	.05
50	Jack Armstrong	.05
51	Bret Barberie	.05
52	Geronimo Berroa	.05
53	Ryan Bowen	.05
54	Greg Briley	.05
55	Chris Carpenter	.05
56	Chuck Carr	.05
57	Jeff Conine	.05
58	Jim Corsi	.05
59	Orestes Destrade	.05
60	Junior Felix	.05
61	Chris Hammond	.05
62	Bryan Harvey	.05
63	Charlie Hough	.05
64	Joe Klink	.05
65	Richie Lewis RC	.05
66	Mitch Lyden RC	.05
67	Bob Natal	.05
68	Scott Pose RC	.05
69	Rich Renteria	.05
70	Benito Santiago	.05
71	Gary Sheffield	.15
72	Matt Turner RC	.05
73	Walt Weiss	.05
74	Darrell Whitmore RC	.05
75	Nigel Wilson	.05
76	Kevin Bass	.05
77	Doug Drabek	.05
78	Tom Edens	.05
79	Chris James	.05
80	Greg Swindell	.05
81	Omar Daal RC	.05
82	Raul Mondesi	.05
83	Jody Reed	.05
84	Cory Snyder	.05
85	Rick Trlicek	.05
86	Tim Wallach	.05
87	Todd Worrell	.05
88	Tavo Alvarez	.05
89	Frank Bolick	.05
90	Kent Bottenfield	.05
91	Greg Colbrunn	.05
92	Cliff Floyd	.05
93	Lou Frazier RC	.05
94	Mike Gardiner	.05
95	Mike Lansing RC	.25
96	Bill Risley	.05
97	Jeff Shaw	.05
98	Kevin Baez	.05
99	Tim Bogar RC	.05
100	Jeromy Burnitz	.05
101	Mike Draper	.05
102	Darrin Jackson	.05
103	Mike Maddux	.05
104	Joe Orsulak	.05
105	Doug Saunders	.05
106	Frank Tanana	.05
107	Dave Telgheder	.05
108	Larry Anderson	.05
109	Jim Eisenreich	.05
110	Pete Incaviglia	.05
111	Danny Jackson	.05
112	David West	.05
113	Al Martin	.05
114	Blas Minor	.05
115	Dennis Moeller	.05
116	Will Pennyfeather	.05
117	Rich Robertson	.05
118	Ben Shelton	.05
119	Lonnie Smith	.05
120	Freddie Toliver	.05
121	Paul Wagner	.05
122	Kevin Young	.05
123	Rene Arocha RC	.05
124	Gregg Jefferies	.05
125	Paul Kilgus	.05
126	Les Lancaster	.05
127	Joe Magrane	.05
128	Rob Murphy	.05
129	Erik Pappas	.05
130	Stan Royer	.05
131	Ozzie Smith	.65
132	Tom Urbani	.05
133	Mark Whiten	.05
134	Derek Bell	.05
135	Doug Brocail	.05
136	Phil Clark	.05
137	Mark Ettles RC	.05
138	Jeff Gardner	.05
139	Pat Gomez RC	.05
140	Ricky Gutierrez	.05
141	Gene Harris	.05
142	Kevin Higgins RC	.05
143	Trevor Hoffman	.05
144	Phil Plantier	.05
145	Kerry Taylor RC	.05
146	Guillermo Velasquez	.05
147	Wally Whitehurst	.05
148	Tim Worrell RC	.05
149	Todd Benzinger	.05
150	Barry Bonds	2.00
151	Greg Brummett	.05
152	Mark Carreon	.05
153	Dave Martinez	.05
154	Jeff Reed	.05
155	Kevin Rogers	.05
156	Harold Baines	.05
157	Damon Buford	.05
158	Paul Carey RC	.05
159	Jeffrey Hammonds	.05
160	Jamie Moyer	.05
161	Sherman Obando RC	.05
162	John O'Donoghue RC	.05
163	Brad Pennington	.05
164	Jim Poole	.05
165	Harold Reynolds	.05
166	Fernando Valenzuela	.05
167	Jack Voight RC	.05
168	Mark Williamson	.05
169	Scott Bankhead	.05
170	Greg Blosser	.05
171	Jim Byrd RC	.05
172	Ivan Calderon	.05
173	Andre Dawson	.25
174	Scott Fletcher	.05
175	Jose Melendez	.05
176	Carlos Quintana	.05
177	Jeff Russell	.05
178	Aaron Sele	.05
179	Rod Correia RC	.05
180	Chili Davis	.05
181	Jim Edmonds RC	3.00
182	Rene Gonzales	.05
183	Hilly Hathaway RC	.05
184	Torey Lovullo	.05
185	Greg Myers	.05
186	Gene Nelson	.05
187	Troy Percival	.05
188	Scott Sanderson	.05
189	Darryl Scott RC	.05
190	J.T. Snow RC	.50
191	Russ Springer	.05
192	Jason Bere	.05
193	Rodney Bolton	.05
194	Ellis Burks	.05
195	Bo Jackson	.15
196	Mike LaValliere	.05
197	Scott Ruffcorn	.05
198	Jeff Schwartz RC	.05
199	Jerry DiPoto	.05
200	Alvaro Espinoza	.05
201	Wayne Kirby	.05
202	Tom Kramer RC	.05
203	Jesse Levis	.05
204	Manny Ramirez	.50
205	Jeff Treadway	.05
206	Bill Wertz RC	.05
207	Cliff Young	.05
208	Matt Young	.05
209	Kirk Gibson	.05
210	Greg Gohr	.05
211	Bill Krueger	.05
212	Bob MacDonald	.05
213	Mike Moore	.05
214	David Wells	.05
215	Billy Brewer RC	.05
216	David Cone	.05
217	Greg Gagne	.05
218	Mark Gardner	.05
219	Chris Haney	.05
220	Phil Hiatt	.05
221	Jose Lind	.05
222	Juan Bell	.05
223	Tom Brunansky	.05
224	Mike Ignasiak	.05
225	Joe Kmak	.05
226	Tom Lampkin	.05
227	Graeme Lloyd RC	.05
228	Carlos Maldonado	.05
229	Matt Mieske	.05
230	Angel Miranda	.05
231	Troy O'Leary RC	.10
232	Kevin Reimer	.05
233	Larry Casian	.05
234	Jim Deshaies	.05
235	Eddie Guardado RC	.10
236	Chip Hale	.05
237	Mike Maksudian RC	.05
238	David McCarty	.05
239	Pat Meares RC	.05
240	George Tsamis RC	.05
241	Dave Winfield	.50
242	Jim Abbott	.05
243	Wade Boggs	.65
244	Andy Cook RC	.05
245	Russ Davis RC	.10
246	Mike Humphreys	.05
247	Jimmy Key	.05
248	Jim Leyritz	.05
249	Bobby Munoz	.05
250	Paul O'Neill	.05
251	Spike Owen	.05
252	Dave Silvestri	.05
253	Marcos Armas RC	.05
254	Brent Gates	.05
255	Goose Gossage	.25
256	Scott Lydy RC	.05
257	Henry Mercedes	.05
258	Mike Mohler RC	.05
259	Troy Neel	.05
260	Edwin Nunez	.05
261	Craig Paquette	.05
262	Kevin Seitzer	.05
263	Rich Amaral	.05
264	Mike Blowers	.05
265	Chris Bosio	.05
266	Norm Charlton	.05
267	Jim Converse RC	.05
268	John Cummings RC	.05
269	Mike Felder	.05
270	Mike Hampton	.05
271	Bill Haselman	.05
272	Dwayne Henry	.05
273	Greg Litton	.05
274	Mackey Sasser	.05
275	Lee Tinsley	.05
276	David Wainhouse	.05
277	Jeff Bronkey RC	.05
278	Benji Gil	.05
279	Tom Henke	.05
280	Charlie Leibrandt	.05
281	Robb Nen	.05
282	Bill Ripken	.05
283	Jon Shave RC	.05
284	Doug Strange	.05
285	Matt Whiteside RC	.05
286	Scott Brow RC	.05
287	Willie Canate RC	.05
288	Tony Castillo	.05
289	Domingo Cedeno RC	.05
290	Darnell Coles	.05
291	Danny Cox	.05
292	Mark Eichhorn	.05
293	Tony Fernandez	.05
294	Al Leiter	.05
295	Paul Molitor	.50
296	Dave Stewart	.05
297	Woody Williams RC	.05
298	Checklist	.05
299	Checklist	.05
300	Checklist	.05

DIAMOND TRIBUTE

1DT	Wade Boggs	.65
2DT	George Brett	.75
3DT	Andre Dawson	.25
4DT	Carlton Fisk	.50
5DT	Paul Molitor	.50
6DT	Nolan Ryan	2.00
7DT	Lee Smith	.05
8DT	Ozzie Smith	.65
9DT	Dave Winfield	.50
10DT	Robin Yount	.50

1994 Fleer

	NM/M
Complete Set (720):	12.50
Common Player:	.05
Pack (15):	.50
Wax Box (36):	12.50
1	Brady Anderson	.05
2	Harold Baines	.05
3	Mike Devereaux	.05
4	Todd Frohwirth	.05
5	Jeffrey Hammonds	.05
6	Chris Hoiles	.05
7	Tim Hulett	.05
8	Ben McDonald	.05
9	Mark McLemore	.05
10	Alan Mills	.05
11	Jamie Moyer	.05
12	Mike Mussina	.40
13	Gregg Olson	.05
14	Mike Pagliarulo	.05
15	Brad Pennington	.05
16	Jim Poole	.05
17	Harold Reynolds	.05
18	Arthur Rhodes	.05
19	Cal Ripken, Jr.	2.00
20	David Segui	.05
21	Rick Sutcliffe	.05
22	Fernando Valenzuela	.05
23	Jack Voigt	.05
24	Mark Williamson	.05
25	Scott Bankhead	.05
26	Roger Clemens	1.00
27	Scott Cooper	.05
28	Danny Darwin	.05
29	Andre Dawson	.25
30	Rob Deer	.05
31	John Dopson	.05
32	Scott Fletcher	.05
33	Mike Greenwell	.05
34	Greg Harris	.05
35	Billy Hatcher	.05
36	Bob Melvin	.05

#	Player	Price		#	Player	Price		#	Player	Price		#	Player	Price
37	Tony Pena	.05		140	Bob MacDonald	.05		244	Spike Owen	.05		348	Devon White	.05
38	Paul Quantrill	.05		141	Mike Moore	.05		245	Melido Perez	.05		349	Woody Williams	.05
39	Carlos Quintana	.05		142	Tony Phillips	.05		246	Lee Smith	.05		350	Steve Avery	.05
40	Ernest Riles	.05		143	Mickey Tettleton	.05		247	Mike Stanley	.05		351	Steve Bedrosian	.05
41	Jeff Russell	.05		144	Alan Trammell	.05		248	Danny Tartabull	.05		352	Rafael Belliard	.05
42	Ken Ryan	.05		145	David Wells	.05		249	Randy Velarde	.05		353	Damon Berryhill	.05
43	Aaron Sele	.05		146	Lou Whitaker	.05		250	Bob Wickman	.05		354	Jeff Blauser	.05
44	John Valentin	.05		147	Kevin Appier	.05		251	Bernie Williams	.20		355	Sid Bream	.05
45	Mo Vaughn	.05		148	Stan Belinda	.05		252	Mike Aldrete	.05		356	Francisco Cabrera	.05
46	Frank Viola	.05		149	George Brett	1.00		253	Marcos Armas	.05		357	Marvin Freeman	.05
47	Bob Zupcic	.05		150	Billy Brewer	.05		254	Lance Blankenship	.05		358	Ron Gant	.05
48	Mike Butcher	.05		151	Hubie Brooks	.05		255	Mike Bordick	.05		359	Tom Glavine	.25
49	Rod Correia	.05		152	David Cone	.05		256	Scott Brosius	.05		360	Jay Howell	.05
50	Chad Curtis	.05		153	Gary Gaetti	.05		257	Jerry Browne	.05		361	Dave Justice	.05
51	Chili Davis	.05		154	Greg Gagne	.05		258	Ron Darling	.05		362	Ryan Klesko	.05
52	Gary DiSarcina	.05		155	Tom Gordon	.05		259	Kelly Downs	.05		363	Mark Lemke	.05
53	Damion Easley	.05		156	Mark Gubicza	.05		260	Dennis Eckersley	.60		364	Javier Lopez	.05
54	Jim Edmonds	.05		157	Chris Gwynn	.05		261	Brent Gates	.05		365	Greg Maddux	.85
55	Chuck Finley	.05		158	John Habyan	.05		262	Goose Gossage	.05		366	Fred McGriff	.05
56	Steve Frey	.05		159	Chris Haney	.05		263	Scott Hemond	.05		367	Greg McMichael	.05
57	Rene Gonzales	.05		160	Phil Hiatt	.05		264	Dave Henderson	.05		368	Kent Mercker	.05
58	Joe Grahe	.05		161	Felix Jose	.05		265	Rick Honeycutt	.05		369	Otis Nixon	.05
59	Hilly Hathaway	.05		162	Wally Joyner	.05		266	Vince Horsman	.05		370	Greg Olson	.05
60	Stan Javier	.05		163	Jose Lind	.05		267	Scott Lydy	.05		371	Bill Pecota	.05
61	Mark Langston	.05		164	Mike Macfarlane	.05		268	Mark McGwire	1.50		372	Terry Pendleton	.05
62	Phil Leftwich	.05		165	Mike Magnante	.05		269	Mike Mohler	.05		373	Deion Sanders	.05
63	Torey Lovullo	.05		166	Brent Mayne	.05		270	Troy Neel	.05		374	Pete Smith	.05
64	Joe Magrane	.05		167	Brian McRae	.05		271	Edwin Nunez	.05		375	John Smoltz	.05
65	Greg Myers	.05		168	Kevin McReynolds	.05		272	Craig Paquette	.05		376	Mike Stanton	.05
66	Ken Patterson	.05		169	Keith Miller	.05		273	Ruben Sierra	.05		377	Tony Tarasco	.05
67	Eduardo Perez	.05		170	Jeff Montgomery	.05		274	Terry Steinbach	.05		378	Mark Wohlers	.05
68	Luis Polonia	.05		171	Hipolito Pichardo	.05		275	Todd Van Poppel	.05		379	Jose Bautista	.05
69	Tim Salmon	.20		172	Rico Rossy	.05		276	Bob Welch	.05		380	Shawn Boskie	.05
69a	Tim Salmon/OPS	2.00		173	Juan Bell	.05		277	Bobby Witt	.05		381	Steve Buechele	.05
70	J.T. Snow	.05		174	Ricky Bones	.05		278	Rich Amaral	.05		382	Frank Castillo	.05
71	Ron Tingley	.05		175	Cal Eldred	.05		279	Mike Blowers	.05		383	Mark Grace	.10
72	Julio Valera	.05		176	Mike Fetters	.05		280	Bret Boone	.05		384	Jose Guzman	.05
73	Wilson Alvarez	.05		177	Darryl Hamilton	.05		281	Chris Bosio	.05		385	Mike Harkey	.05
74	Tim Belcher	.05		178	Doug Henry	.05		282	Jay Buhner	.05		386	Greg Hibbard	.05
75	George Bell	.05		179	Mike Ignasiak	.05		283	Norm Charlton	.05		387	Glenallen Hill	.05
76	Jason Bere	.05		180	John Jaha	.05		284	Mike Felder	.05		388	Steve Lake	.05
77	Rod Bolton	.05		181	Pat Listach	.05		285	Dave Fleming	.05		389	Derrick May	.05
78	Ellis Burks	.05		182	Graeme Lloyd	.05		286	Ken Griffey Jr.	1.25		390	Chuck McElroy	.05
79	Joey Cora	.05		183	Matt Mieske	.05		287	Erik Hanson	.05		391	Mike Morgan	.05
80	Alex Fernandez	.05		184	Angel Miranda	.05		288	Bill Haselman	.05		392	Randy Myers	.05
81	Craig Grebeck	.05		185	Jaime Navarro	.05		289	Brad Holman RC	.05		393	Dan Plesac	.05
82	Ozzie Guillen	.05		186	Dave Nilsson	.05		290	Randy Johnson	.75		394	Kevin Roberson	.05
83	Roberto Hernandez	.05		187	Troy O'Leary	.05		291	Tim Leary	.05		395	Rey Sanchez	.05
84	Bo Jackson	.10		188	Jesse Orosco	.05		292	Greg Litton	.05		396	Ryne Sandberg	.85
85	Lance Johnson	.05		189	Kevin Reimer	.05		293	Dave Magadan	.05		397	Bob Scanlan	.05
86	Ron Karkovice	.05		190	Kevin Seitzer	.05		294	Edgar Martinez	.05		398	Dwight Smith	.05
87	Mike LaValliere	.05		191	Bill Spiers	.05		295	Tino Martinez	.05		399	Sammy Sosa	1.25
88	Kirk McCaskill	.05		192	B.J. Surhoff	.05		296	Jeff Nelson	.05		400	Jose Vizcaino	.05
89	Jack McDowell	.05		193	Dickie Thon	.05		297	Erik Plantenberg RC	.05		401	Rick Wilkins	.05
90	Warren Newson	.05		194	Jose Valentin	.05		298	Mackey Sasser	.05		402	Willie Wilson	.05
91	Dan Pasqua	.05		195	Greg Vaughn	.05		299	Brian Turang RC	.05		403	Eric Yelding	.05
92	Scott Radinsky	.05		196	Bill Wegman	.05		300	Dave Valle	.05		404	Bobby Ayala	.05
93	Tim Raines	.05		197	Robin Yount	.75		301	Omar Vizquel	.05		405	Jeff Branson	.05
94	Steve Sax	.05		198	Rick Aguilera	.05		302	Brian Bohanon	.05		406	Tom Browning	.05
95	Jeff Schwarz	.05		199	Willie Banks	.05		303	Kevin Brown	.05		407	Jacob Brumfield	.05
96	Frank Thomas	.75		200	Bernardo Brito	.05		304	Jose Canseco	.40		408	Tim Costo	.05
97	Robin Ventura	.05		201	Larry Casian	.05		305	Mario Diaz	.05		409	Rob Dibble	.05
98	Sandy Alomar, Jr.	.05		202	Scott Erickson	.05		306	Julio Franco	.05		410	Willie Greene	.05
99	Carlos Baerga	.05		203	Eddie Guardado	.05		307	Juan Gonzalez	.75		411	Thomas Howard	.05
100	Albert Belle	.05		204	Mark Guthrie	.05		308	Tom Henke	.05		412	Roberto Kelly	.05
101	Mark Clark	.05		205	Chip Hale	.05		309	David Hulse	.05		413	Bill Landrum	.05
102	Jerry DiPoto	.05		206	Brian Harper	.05		310	Manuel Lee	.05		414	Barry Larkin	.05
103	Alvaro Espinoza	.05		207	Mike Hartley	.05		311	Craig Lefferts	.05		415	Larry Luebbers RC	.05
104	Felix Fermin	.05		208	Kent Hrbek	.05		312	Charlie Leibrandt	.05		416	Kevin Mitchell	.05
105	Jeremy Hernandez	.05		209	Terry Jorgensen	.05		313	Rafael Palmeiro	.75		417	Hal Morris	.05
106	Reggie Jefferson	.05		210	Chuck Knoblauch	.05		314	Dean Palmer	.05		418	Joe Oliver	.05
107	Wayne Kirby	.05		211	Gene Larkin	.05		315	Roger Pavlik	.05		419	Tim Pugh	.05
108	Tom Kramer	.05		212	Shane Mack	.05		316	Dan Peltier	.05		420	Jeff Reardon	.05
109	Mark Lewis	.05		213	David McCarty	.05		317	Geno Petralli	.05		421	Jose Rijo	.05
110	Derek Lilliquist	.05		214	Pat Meares	.05		318	Gary Redus	.05		422	Bip Roberts	.05
111	Kenny Lofton	.05		215	Pedro Munoz	.05		319	Ivan Rodriguez	.65		423	John Roper	.05
112	Candy Maldonado	.05		216	Derek Parks	.05		320	Kenny Rogers	.05		424	Johnny Ruffin	.05
113	Jose Mesa	.05		217	Kirby Puckett	.85		321	Nolan Ryan	2.00		425	Chris Sabo	.05
114	Jeff Mutis	.05		218	Jeff Reboulet	.05		322	Doug Strange	.05		426	Juan Samuel	.05
115	Charles Nagy	.05		219	Kevin Tapani	.05		323	Matt Whiteside	.05		427	Reggie Sanders	.05
116	Bob Ojeda	.05		220	Mike Trombley	.05		324	Roberto Alomar	.30		428	Scott Service	.05
117	Junior Ortiz	.05		221	George Tsamis	.05		325	Pat Borders	.05		429	John Smiley	.05
118	Eric Plunk	.05		222	Carl Willis	.05		326	Joe Carter	.05		430	Jerry Spradlin RC	.05
119	Manny Ramirez	.75		223	Dave Winfield	.75		327	Tony Castillo	.05		431	Kevin Wickander	.05
120	Paul Sorrento	.05		224	Jim Abbott	.05		328	Darnell Coles	.05		432	Freddie Benavides	.05
121	Jim Thome	.60		225	Paul Assenmacher	.05		329	Danny Cox	.05		433	Dante Bichette	.05
122	Jeff Treadway	.05		226	Wade Boggs	.85		330	Mark Eichhorn	.05		434	Willie Blair	.05
123	Bill Wertz	.05		227	Russ Davis	.05		331	Tony Fernandez	.05		435	Daryl Boston	.05
124	Skeeter Barnes	.05		228	Steve Farr	.05		332	Alfredo Griffin	.05		436	Kent Bottenfield	.05
125	Milt Cuyler	.05		229	Mike Gallego	.05		333	Juan Guzman	.05		437	Vinny Castilla	.05
126	Eric Davis	.05		230	Paul Gibson	.05		334	Rickey Henderson	.75		438	Jerald Clark	.05
127	John Doherty	.05		231	Steve Howe	.05		335	Pat Hentgen	.05		439	Alex Cole	.05
128	Cecil Fielder	.05		232	Dion James	.05		336	Randy Knorr	.05		440	Andres Galarraga	.05
129	Travis Fryman	.05		233	Domingo Jean	.05		337	Al Leiter	.05		441	Joe Girardi	.05
130	Kirk Gibson	.05		234	Scott Kamieniecki	.05		338	Paul Molitor	.75		442	Greg Harris	.05
131	Dan Gladden	.05		235	Pat Kelly	.05		339	Jack Morris	.05		443	Charlie Hayes	.05
132	Greg Gohr	.05		236	Jimmy Key	.05		340	John Olerud	.05		444	Darren Holmes	.05
133	Chris Gomez	.05		237	Jim Leyritz	.05		341	Dick Schofield	.05		445	Chris Jones	.05
134	Bill Gullickson	.05		238	Kevin Maas	.05		342	Ed Sprague	.05		446	Roberto Mejia	.05
135	Mike Henneman	.05		239	Don Mattingly	1.00		343	Dave Stewart	.05		447	David Nied	.05
136	Kurt Knudsen	.05		240	Rich Monteleone	.05		344	Todd Stottlemyre	.05		448	J. Owens	.05
137	Chad Kreuter	.05		241	Bobby Munoz	.05		345	Mike Timlin	.05		449	Jeff Parrett	.05
138	Bill Krueger	.05		242	Matt Nokes	.05		346	Duane Ward	.05		450	Steve Reed	.05
139	Scott Livingstone	.05		243	Paul O'Neill	.05		347	Turner Ward	.05		451	Armando Reynoso	.05

#	Player	Price
452	Bruce Ruffin	.05
453	Mo Sanford	.05
454	Danny Sheaffer	.05
455	Jim Tatum	.05
456	Gary Wayne	.05
457	Eric Young	.05
458	Luis Aquino	.05
459	Alex Arias	.05
460	Jack Armstrong	.05
461	Bret Barberie	.05
462	Ryan Bowen	.05
463	Chuck Carr	.05
464	Jeff Conine	.05
465	Henry Cotto	.05
466	Orestes Destrade	.05
467	Chris Hammond	.05
468	Bryan Harvey	.05
469	Charlie Hough	.05
470	Joe Klink	.05
471	Richie Lewis	.05
472	Bob Natal RC	.05
473	Pat Rapp RC	.05
474	Rich Renteria RC	.10
475	Rich Rodriguez	.05
476	Benito Santiago	.05
477	Gary Sheffield	.35
478	Matt Turner	.05
479	David Weathers	.05
480	Walt Weiss	.05
481	Darrell Whitmore	.05
482	Eric Anthony	.05
483	Jeff Bagwell	.75
484	Kevin Bass	.05
485	Craig Biggio	.05
486	Ken Caminiti	.05
487	Andujar Cedeno	.05
488	Chris Donnels	.05
489	Doug Drabek	.05
490	Steve Finley	.05
491	Luis Gonzalez	.25
492	Pete Harnisch	.05
493	Xavier Hernandez	.05
494	Doug Jones	.05
495	Todd Jones	.05
496	Darryl Kile	.05
497	Al Osuna	.05
498	Mark Portugal	.05
499	Scott Servais	.05
500	Greg Swindell	.05
501	Eddie Taubensee	.05
502	Jose Uribe	.05
503	Brian Williams	.05
504	Billy Ashley	.05
505	Pedro Astacio	.05
506	Brett Butler	.05
507	Tom Candiotti	.05
508	Omar Daal	.05
509	Jim Gott	.05
510	Kevin Gross	.05
511	Dave Hansen	.05
512	Carlos Hernandez	.05
513	Orel Hershiser	.05
514	Eric Karros	.05
515	Pedro Martinez	.75
516	Ramon Martinez	.05
517	Roger McDowell	.05
518	Raul Mondesi	.05
519	Jose Offerman	.05
520	Mike Piazza	1.25
521	Jody Reed	.05
522	Henry Rodriguez	.05
523	Mike Sharperson	.05
524	Cory Snyder	.05
525	Darryl Strawberry	.05
526	Rick Trlicek	.05
527	Tim Wallach	.05
528	Mitch Webster	.05
529	Steve Wilson	.05
530	Todd Worrell	.05
531	Moises Alou	.05
532	Brian Barnes	.05
533	Sean Berry	.05
534	Greg Colbrunn	.05
535	Delino DeShields	.05
536	Jeff Fassero	.05
537	Darrin Fletcher	.05
538	Cliff Floyd	.05
539	Lou Frazier	.05
540	Marquis Grissom	.05
541	Butch Henry	.05
542	Ken Hill	.05
543	Mike Lansing	.05
544	Brian Looney RC	.05
545	Dennis Martinez	.05
546	Chris Nabholz	.05
547	Randy Ready	.05
548	Mel Rojas	.05
549	Kirk Rueter	.05
550	Tim Scott	.05
551	Jeff Shaw	.05
552	Tim Spehr	.05
553	John VanderWal	.05
554	Larry Walker	.05
555	John Wetteland	.05
556	Rondell White	.05
557	Tim Bogar	.05
558	Bobby Bonilla	.05
559	Jeromy Burnitz	.05
560	Sid Fernandez	.05
561	John Franco	.05
562	Dave Gallagher	.05
563	Dwight Gooden	.05
564	Eric Hillman	.05
565	Todd Hundley	.05
566	Jeff Innis	.05
567	Darrin Jackson	.05
568	Howard Johnson	.05
569	Bobby Jones	.05
570	Jeff Kent	.05
571	Mike Maddux	.05
572	Jeff McKnight	.05
573	Eddie Murray	.75
574	Charlie O'Brien	.05
575	Joe Orsulak	.05
576	Bret Saberhagen	.05
577	Pete Schourek	.05
578	Dave Telgheder	.05
579	Ryan Thompson	.05
580	Anthony Young	.05
581	Ruben Amaro	.05
582	Larry Andersen	.05
583	Kim Batiste	.05
584	Wes Chamberlain	.05
585	Darren Daulton	.05
586	Mariano Duncan	.05
587	Len Dykstra	.05
588	Jim Eisenreich	.05
589	Tommy Greene	.05
590	Dave Hollins	.05
591	Pete Incaviglia	.05
592	Danny Jackson	.05
593	Ricky Jordan	.05
594	John Kruk	.05
595	Roger Mason	.05
596	Mickey Morandini	.05
597	Terry Mulholland	.05
598	Todd Pratt	.05
599	Ben Rivera	.05
600	Curt Schilling	.25
601	Kevin Stocker	.05
602	Milt Thompson	.05
603	David West	.05
604	Mitch Williams	.05
605	Jay Bell	.05
606	Dave Clark	.05
607	Steve Cooke	.05
608	Tom Foley	.05
609	Carlos Garcia	.05
610	Joel Johnston	.05
611	Jeff King	.05
612	Al Martin	.05
613	Lloyd McClendon	.05
614	Orlando Merced	.05
615	Blas Minor	.05
616	Denny Neagle	.05
617	Mark Petkovsek RC	.05
618	Tom Prince	.05
619	Don Slaught	.05
620	Zane Smith	.05
621	Randy Tomlin	.05
622	Andy Van Slyke	.05
623	Paul Wagner	.05
624	Tim Wakefield	.05
625	Bob Walk	.05
626	Kevin Young	.05
627	Luis Alicea	.05
628	Rene Arocha	.05
629	Rod Brewer	.05
630	Rheal Cormier	.05
631	Bernard Gilkey	.05
632	Lee Guetterman	.05
633	Gregg Jefferies	.05
634	Brian Jordan	.05
635	Les Lancaster	.05
636	Ray Lankford	.05
637	Rob Murphy	.05
638	Omar Olivares	.05
639	Jose Oquendo	.05
640	Donovan Osborne	.05
641	Tom Pagnozzi	.05
642	Erik Pappas	.05
643	Geronimo Pena	.05
644	Mike Perez	.05
645	Gerald Perry	.05
646	Ozzie Smith	.85
647	Bob Tewksbury	.05
648	Allen Watson	.05
649	Mark Whiten	.05
650	Tracy Woodson	.05
651	Todd Zeile	.05
652	Andy Ashby	.05
653	Brad Ausmus	.05
654	Billy Bean	.05
655	Derek Bell	.05
656	Andy Benes	.05
657	Doug Brocail	.05
658	Jarvis Brown	.05
659	Archi Cianfrocco	.05
660	Phil Clark	.05
661	Mark Davis	.05
662	Jeff Gardner	.05
663	Pat Gomez	.05
664	Ricky Gutierrez	.05
665	Tony Gwynn	.85
666	Gene Harris	.05
667	Kevin Higgins	.05
668	Trevor Hoffman	.05
669	Pedro A. Martinez RC	.05
670	Tim Mauser	.05
671	Melvin Nieves	.05
672	Phil Plantier	.05
673	Frank Seminara	.05
674	Craig Shipley	.05
675	Kerry Taylor	.05
676	Tim Teufel	.05
677	Guillermo Velasquez	.05
678	Wally Whitehurst	.05
679	Tim Worrell	.05
680	Rod Beck	.05
681	Mike Benjamin	.05
682	Todd Benzinger	.05
683	Bud Black	.05
684	Barry Bonds	2.00
685	Jeff Brantley	.05
686	Dave Burba	.05
687	John Burkett	.05
688	Mark Carreon	.05
689	Will Clark	.10
690	Royce Clayton	.05
691	Bryan Hickerson	.05
692	Mike Jackson	.05
693	Darren Lewis	.05
694	Kirt Manwaring	.05
695	Dave Martinez	.05
696	Willie McGee	.05
697	John Patterson	.05
698	Jeff Reed	.05
699	Kevin Rogers	.05
700	Scott Sanderson	.05
701	Steve Scarsone	.05
702	Billy Swift	.05
703	Robby Thompson	.05
704	Matt Williams	.05
705	Trevor Wilson	.05
706	Fred McGriff, Ron Gant, Dave Justice	.10
707	Paul Molitor, John Olerud	.10
708	Mike Mussina, Jack McDowell	.10
709	Lou Whitaker, Alan Trammell	.10
710	Rafael Palmeiro, Juan Gonzalez	.20
711	Brett Butler, Tony Gwynn	.10
712	Kirby Puckett, Chuck Knoblauch	.20
713	Mike Piazza, Eric Karros	.25
714	Checklist	.05
715	Checklist	.05
716	Checklist	.05
717	Checklist	.05
718	Checklist	.05
719	Checklist	.05
720	Checklist	.05

#	Player	Price
10	Ken Griffey Jr.	1.50
11	Pat Hentgen	.10
12	Randy Johnson	.60
13	Jimmy Key	.10
14	Mark Langston	.10
15	Jack McDowell	.10
16	Paul Molitor	.60
17	Jeff Montgomery	.10
18	Mike Mussina	.40
19	John Olerud	.10
20	Kirby Puckett	.75
21	Cal Ripken, Jr.	2.00
22	Ivan Rodriguez	.50
23	Frank Thomas	.65
24	Greg Vaughn	.10
25	Duane Ward	.10
26	Steve Avery	.10
27	Rod Beck	.10
28	Jay Bell	.10
29	Andy Benes	.10
30	Jeff Blauser	.10
31	Barry Bonds	2.00
32	Bobby Bonilla	.10
33	John Burkett	.10
34	Darren Daulton	.10
35	Andres Galarraga	.10
36	Tom Glavine	.30
37	Mark Grace	.25
38	Marquis Grissom	.10
39	Tony Gwynn	.75
40	Bryan Harvey	.10
41	Dave Hollins	.10
42	Dave Justice	.10
43	Darryl Kile	.10
44	John Kruk	.10
45	Barry Larkin	.10
46	Terry Mulholland	.10
47	Mike Piazza	1.50
48	Ryne Sandberg	.75
49	Gary Sheffield	.30
50	John Smoltz	.10

All-Rookie Team

		NM/M
Complete Set (9):		3.00
Common Player:		.25
Exchange Card:		.25
1	Kurt Abbott	.25
2	Rich Becker	.25
3	Carlos Delgado	2.00
4	Jorge Fabregas	.25
5	Bob Hamelin	.25
6	John Hudek	.25
7	Tim Hyers	.25
8	Luis Lopez	.25
9	James Mouton	.25

Award Winners

		NM/M
Complete Set (6):		4.50
Common Player:		.25
1	Frank Thomas	.75
2	Barry Bonds	2.00
3	Jack McDowell	.25
4	Greg Maddux	1.00
5	Tim Salmon	.50
6	Mike Piazza	1.50

Golden Moments

		NM/M
Complete Set (10):		5.00
Common Player:		.10
1	Mark Whiten	.10
2	Carlos Baerga	.10
3	Dave Winfield	.50
4	Ken Griffey Jr.	1.50
5	Bo Jackson	.25
6	George Brett	1.00
7	Nolan Ryan	2.00
8	Fred McGriff	.10
9	Frank Thomas	.75
10	Chris Bosio, Jim Abbott, Darryl Kile	.10

League Leaders

		NM/M
Complete Set (12):		3.00
Common Player:		.10
1	John Olerud	.10
2	Albert Belle	.10
3	Rafael Palmeiro	.75
4	Kenny Lofton	.10

All-Stars

		NM/M
Complete Set (50):		10.00
Common Player:		.10
1	Roberto Alomar	.20
2	Carlos Baerga	.10
3	Albert Belle	.10
4	Wade Boggs	.75
5	Joe Carter	.10
6	Scott Cooper	.10
7	Cecil Fielder	.10
8	Travis Fryman	.10
9	Juan Gonzalez	.60

32	Dave Staton	.10
33	Salomon Torres	.10
34	Steve Trachsel	.10
35	Chris Turner	.10

ProVisions

		NM/M
Complete Set (9):		4.00
Common Player:		.25
1	Darren Daulton	.25
2	John Olerud	.25
3	Matt Williams	.25
4	Carlos Baerga	.25
5	Ozzie Smith	1.00
6	Juan Gonzalez	.75
7	Jack McDowell	.25
8	Mike Piazza	2.00
9	Tony Gwynn	1.00

Rookie Sensations

		NM/M
Complete Set (20):		6.00
Common Player:		.25
1	Rene Arocha	.25
2	Jason Bere	.25
3	Jeromy Burnitz	.25
4	Chuck Carr	.25
5	Jeff Conine	.25
6	Steve Cooke	.25
7	Cliff Floyd	.25
8	Jeffrey Hammonds	.25
9	Wayne Kirby	.25
10	Mike Lansing	.25
11	Al Martin	.25
12	Greg McMichael	.25
13	Troy Neel	.25
14	Mike Piazza	4.00
15	Armando Reynoso	.25
16	Kirk Rueter	.25
17	Tim Salmon	1.00
18	Aaron Sele	.25
19	J.T. Snow	.25
20	Kevin Stocker	.25

Tim Salmon A.L. Rookie of the Year

		NM/M
Complete Set (15):		12.50
Common Salmon:		1.00
Autograph/2,000:		15.00

Smoke N' Heat

		NM/M
Complete Set (12):		10.00
Common Player:		.20
1	Roger Clemens	3.50
2	David Cone	.20
3	Juan Guzman	.20
4	Pete Harnisch	.20
5	Randy Johnson	2.00

6	Mark Langston	.20
7	Greg Maddux	2.50
8	Mike Mussina	.75
9	Jose Rijo	.20
10	Nolan Ryan	4.50
11	Curt Schilling	.75
12	John Smoltz	.25

Team Leaders

		NM/M
Complete Set (28):		7.50
Common Player:		.10
1	Cal Ripken, Jr.	2.00
2	Mo Vaughn	.10
3	Tim Salmon	.15
4	Frank Thomas	.50
5	Carlos Baerga	.10
6	Cecil Fielder	.10
7	Brian McRae	.10
8	Greg Vaughn	.10
9	Kirby Puckett	.65
10	Don Mattingly	.75
11	Mark McGwire	1.50
12	Ken Griffey Jr.	1.00
13	Juan Gonzalez	.50
14	Paul Molitor	.50
15	Dave Justice	.10
16	Ryne Sandberg	.65
17	Barry Larkin	.10
18	Andres Galarraga	.10
19	Gary Sheffield	.25
20	Jeff Bagwell	.50
21	Mike Piazza	1.00
22	Marquis Grissom	.10
23	Bobby Bonilla	.10
24	Len Dykstra	.10
25	Jay Bell	.10
26	Gregg Jefferies	.10
27	Tony Gwynn	.65
28	Will Clark	.15

Update

		NM/M
Complete Set (210):		50.00
Common Player:		.05
1	Mark Eichhorn	.05
2	Sid Fernandez	.05
3	Leo Gomez	.05
4	Mike Oquist	.05
5	Rafael Palmeiro	.60
6	Chris Sabo	.05
7	Dwight Smith	.05
8	Lee Smith	.05
9	Damon Berryhill	.05
10	Wes Chamberlain	.05
11	Gar Finnvold	.05
12	Chris Howard	.05
13	Tim Naehring	.05
14	Otis Nixon	.05
15	Brian Anderson	.05
16	Jorge Fabregas	.05

5	Jack McDowell	.10
6	Kevin Appier	.10
7	Andres Galarraga	.10
8	Barry Bonds	2.00
9	Len Dykstra	.10
10	Chuck Carr	.10
11	Tom Glavine	.30
12	Greg Maddux	1.00

Lumber Co.

		NM/M
Complete Set (10):		7.50
Common Player:		.40
1	Albert Belle	.40
2	Barry Bonds	2.50
3	Ron Gant	.40
4	Juan Gonzalez	1.00
5	Ken Griffey Jr.	2.00
6	Dave Justice	.40
7	Fred McGriff	.40
8	Rafael Palmeiro	.75
9	Frank Thomas	1.25
10	Matt Williams	.40

Major League Prospects

		NM/M
Complete Set (35):		4.00
Common Player:		.10
1	Kurt Abbott	.10
2	Brian Anderson	.10
3	Rich Aude	.10
4	Cory Bailey	.10
5	Danny Bautista	.10
6	Marty Cordova	.10
7	Tripp Cromer	.10
8	Midre Cummings	.10
9	Carlos Delgado	1.50
10	Steve Dreyer	.10
11	Steve Dunn	.10
12	Jeff Granger	.10
13	Tyrone Hill	.10
14	Denny Hocking	.10
15	John Hope	.10
16	Butch Huskey	.10
17	Miguel Jimenez	.10
18	Chipper Jones	2.50
19	Steve Karsay	.10
20	Mike Kelly	.10
21	Mike Lieberthal	.20
22	Albie Lopez	.10
23	Jeff McNeely	.10
24	Dan Miceli	.10
25	Nate Minchey	.10
26	Marc Newfield	.10
27	Darren Oliver	.10
28	Luis Ortiz	.10
29	Curtis Pride	.10
30	Roger Salkeld	.10
31	Scott Sanders	.10

17	Rex Hudler	.05
18	Bo Jackson	.15
19	Mark Leiter	.05
20	Spike Owen	.05
21	Harold Reynolds	.05
22	Chris Turner	.05
23	Dennis Cook	.05
24	Jose DeLeon	.05
25	Julio Franco	.05
26	Joe Hall	.05
27	Darrin Jackson	.05
28	Dane Johnson	.05
29	Norberto Martin	.05
30	Scott Sanderson	.05
31	Jason Grimsley	.05
32	Dennis Martinez	.05
33	Jack Morris	.05
34	Eddie Murray	.75
35	Chad Ogea	.05
36	Tony Pena	.05
37	Paul Shuey	.05
38	Omar Vizquel	.05
39	Danny Bautista	.05
40	Tim Belcher	.05
41	Joe Boever	.05
42	Storm Davis	.05
43	Junior Felix	.05
44	Mike Gardiner	.05
45	Buddy Groom	.05
46	Juan Samuel	.05
47	Vince Coleman	.05
48	Bob Hamelin	.05
49	Dave Henderson	.05
50	Rusty Meacham	.05
51	Terry Shumpert	.05
52	Jeff Bronkey	.05
53	Alex Diaz	.05
54	Brian Harper	.05
55	Jose Mercedes	.05
56	Jody Reed	.05
57	Bob Scanlan	.05
58	Turner Ward	.05
59	Rich Becker	.05
60	Alex Cole	.05
61	Denny Hocking	.05
62	Scott Leius	.05
63	Pat Mahomes	.05
64	Carlos Pulido	.05
65	Dave Stevens	.05
66	Matt Walbeck	.05
67	Xavier Hernandez	.05
68	Sterling Hitchcock	.05
69	Terry Mulholland	.05
70	Luis Polonia	.05
71	Gerald Williams	.05
72	Mark Acre	.05
73	Geronimo Berroa	.05
74	Rickey Henderson	.75
75	Stan Javier	.05
76	Steve Karsay	.05
77	Carlos Reyes	.05
78	Bill Taylor	.05
79	Eric Anthony	.05
80	Bobby Ayala	.05
81	Tim Davis	.05
82	Felix Fermin	.05
83	Reggie Jefferson	.05
84	Keith Mitchell	.05
85	Bill Risley	.05
86	Alex Rodriguez **RC**	40.00
87	Roger Salkeld	.05
88	Dan Wilson	.05
89	Cris Carpenter	.05
90	Will Clark	.10
91	Jeff Frye	.05
92	Rick Helling	.05
93	Chris James	.05
94	Oddibe McDowell	.05
95	Billy Ripken	.05
96	Carlos Delgado	.60
97	Alex Gonzalez	.05
98	Shawn Green	.50
99	Darren Hall	.05
100	Mike Huff	.05
101	Mike Kelly	.05
102	Roberto Kelly	.05
103	Charlie O'Brien	.05
104	Jose Oliva	.05
105	Gregg Olson	.05
106	Willie Banks	.05
107	Jim Bullinger	.05
108	Chuck Crim	.05
109	Shawon Dunston	.05
110	Karl Rhodes	.05
111	Steve Trachsel	.05
112	Anthony Young	.05
113	Eddie Zambrano	.05
114	Bret Boone	.05
115	Jeff Brantley	.05
116	Hector Carrasco	.05
117	Tony Fernandez	.05
118	Tim Fortugno	.05
119	Erik Hanson	.05
120	Chuck McElroy	.05

121	Deion Sanders	.05
122	Ellis Burks	.05
123	Marvin Freeman	.05
124	Mike Harkey	.05
125	Howard Johnson	.05
126	Mike Kingery	.05
127	Nelson Liriano	.05
128	Marcus Moore	.05
129	Mike Munoz	.05
130	Kevin Ritz	.05
131	Walt Weiss	.05
132	Kurt Abbott	.05
133	Jerry Browne	.05
134	Greg Colbrunn	.05
135	Jeremy Hernandez	.05
136	Dave Magadan	.05
137	Kurt Miller	.05
138	Robb Nen	.05
139	Jesus Taverez	.05
140	Sid Bream	.05
141	Tom Edens	.05
142	Tony Eusebio	.05
143	John Hudek	.05
144	Brian Hunter	.05
145	Orlando Miller	.05
146	James Mouton	.05
147	Shane Reynolds	.05
148	Rafael Bournigal	.05
149	Delino DeShields	.05
150	Garey Ingram	.05
151	Chan Ho Park	.05
152	Wil Cordero	.05
153	Pedro Martinez	.75
154	Randy Milligan	.05
155	Lenny Webster	.05
156	Rico Brogna	.05
157	Josias Manzanillo	.05
158	Kevin McReynolds	.05
159	Mike Remlinger	.05
160	David Segui	.05
161	Pete Smith	.05
162	Kelly Stinnett	.05
163	Jose Vizcaino	.05
164	Billy Hatcher	.05
165	Doug Jones	.05
166	Mike Lieberthal	.05
167	Tony Longmire	.05
168	Bobby Munoz	.05
169	Paul Quantrill	.05
170	Heathcliff Slocumb	.05
171	Fernando Valenzuela	.05
172	Mark Dewey	.05
173	Brian Hunter	.05
174	Jon Lieber	.05
175	Ravelo Manzanillo	.05
176	Dan Miceli	.05
177	Rick White	.05
178	Bryan Eversgerd	.05
179	John Habyan	.05
180	Terry McGriff	.05
181	Vicente Palacios	.05
182	Rich Rodriguez	.05
183	Rick Sutcliffe	.05
184	Donnie Elliott	.05
185	Joey Hamilton	.05
186	Tim Hyers	.05
187	Luis Lopez	.05
188	Ray McDavid	.05
189	Bip Roberts	.05
190	Scott Sanders	.05
191	Eddie Williams	.05
192	Steve Frey	.05
193	Pat Gomez	.05
194	Rich Monteleone	.05
195	Mark Portugal	.05
196	Darryl Strawberry	.05
197	Salomon Torres	.05
198	W. Van Landingham	.05
199	Checklist	.05
200	Checklist	.05

DIAMOND TRIBUTE

DT1	Barry Bonds	2.00
DT2	Joe Carter	.05
DT3	Will Clark	.10
DT4	Roger Clemens	1.50
DT5	Tony Gwynn	1.00
DT6	Don Mattingly	1.50
DT7	Fred McGriff	.05
DT8	Eddie Murray	.75
DT9	Kirby Puckett	1.00
DT10	Cal Ripken Jr.	2.00

1995 Fleer

		NM/M
Complete Set (600):		15.00
Common Player:		.05
Pack (12):		.75
Wax Box (36):		17.50
1	Brady Anderson	.05
2	Harold Baines	.05
3	Damon Buford	.05
4	Mike Devereaux	.05
5	Mark Eichhorn	.05
6	Sid Fernandez	.05

7	Leo Gomez	.05
8	Jeffrey Hammonds	.05
9	Chris Hoiles	.05
10	Rick Krivda	.05
11	Ben McDonald	.05
12	Mark McLemore	.05
13	Alan Mills	.05
14	Jamie Moyer	.05
15	Mike Mussina	.40
16	Mike Oquist	.05
17	Rafael Palmeiro	.65
18	Arthur Rhodes	.05
19	Cal Ripken, Jr.	2.50
20	Chris Sabo	.05
21	Lee Smith	.05
22	Jack Voight	.05
23	Damon Berryhill	.05
24	Tom Brunansky	.05
25	Wes Chamberlain	.05
26	Roger Clemens	1.25
27	Scott Cooper	.05
28	Andre Dawson	.25
29	Gar Finnvold	.05
30	Tony Fossas	.05
31	Mike Greenwell	.05
32	Joe Hesketh	.05
33	Chris Howard	.05
34	Chris Nabholz	.05
35	Tim Naehring	.05
36	Otis Nixon	.05
37	Carlos Rodriguez	.05
38	Rich Rowland	.05
39	Ken Ryan	.05
40	Aaron Sele	.05
41	John Valentin	.05
42	Mo Vaughn	.05
43	Frank Viola	.05
44	Danny Bautista	.05
45	Joe Boeven	.05
46	Milt Cuyler	.05
47	Storm Davis	.05
48	John Doherty	.05
49	Junior Felix	.05
50	Cecil Fielder	.05
51	Travis Fryman	.05
52	Mike Gardiner	.05
53	Kirk Gibson	.05
54	Chris Gomez	.05
55	Buddy Groom	.05
56	Mike Henneman	.05
57	Chad Kreuter	.05
58	Mike Moore	.05
59	Tony Phillips	.05
60	Juan Samuel	.05
61	Mickey Tettleton	.05
62	Alan Trammell	.05
63	David Wells	.05
64	Lou Whitaker	.05
65	Jim Abbott	.05
66	Joe Ausanio	.05
67	Wade Boggs	1.00
68	Mike Gallego	.05
69	Xavier Hernandez	.05
70	Sterling Hitchcock	.05
71	Steve Howe	.05
72	Scott Kamieniecki	.05
73	Pat Kelly	.05
74	Jimmy Key	.05
75	Jim Leyritz	.05
76	Don Mattingly	1.25
77	Terry Mulholland	.05
78	Paul O'Neill	.05
79	Melido Perez	.05
80	Luis Polonia	.05
81	Mike Stanley	.05
82	Danny Tartabull	.05
83	Randy Velarde	.05
84	Bob Wickman	.05
85	Bernie Williams	.10
86	Gerald Williams	.05
87	Roberto Alomar	.10
88	Pat Borders	.05
89	Joe Carter	.05

90	Tony Castillo	.05
91	Brad Cornett	.05
92	Carlos Delgado	.50
93	Alex Gonzalez	.05
94	Shawn Green	.40
95	Juan Guzman	.05
96	Darren Hall	.05
97	Pat Hentgen	.05
98	Mike Huff	.05
99	Randy Knorr	.05
100	Al Leiter	.05
101	Paul Molitor	.75
102	John Olerud	.05
103	Dick Schofield	.05
104	Ed Sprague	.05
105	Dave Stewart	.05
106	Todd Stottlemyre	.05
107	Devon White	.05
108	Woody Williams	.05
109	Wilson Alvarez	.05
110	Paul Assenmacher	.05
111	Jason Bere	.05
112	Dennis Cook	.05
113	Joey Cora	.05
114	Jose DeLeon	.05
115	Alex Fernandez	.05
116	Julio Franco	.05
117	Craig Graboeck	.05
118	Ozzie Guillen	.05
119	Roberto Hernandez	.05
120	Darrin Jackson	.05
121	Lance Johnson	.05
122	Ron Karkovice	.05
123	Mike LaValliere	.05
124	Norberto Martin	.05
125	Kirk McCaskill	.05
126	Jack McDowell	.05
127	Tim Raines	.05
128	Frank Thomas	.75
129	Robin Ventura	.05
130	Sandy Alomar Jr.	.05
131	Carlos Baerga	.05
132	Albert Belle	.05
133	Mark Clark	.05
134	Alvaro Espinoza	.05
135	Jason Grimsley	.05
136	Wayne Kirby	.05
137	Kenny Lofton	.05
138	Albie Lopez	.05
139	Dennis Martinez	.05
140	Jose Mesa	.05
141	Eddie Murray	.75
142	Charles Nagy	.05
143	Tony Pena	.05
144	Eric Plunk	.05
145	Manny Ramirez	.75
146	Jeff Russell	.05
147	Paul Shuey	.05
148	Paul Sorrento	.05
149	Jim Thome	.65
150	Omar Vizquel	.05
151	Dave Winfield	.75
152	Kevin Appier	.05
153	Billy Brewer	.05
154	Vince Coleman	.05
155	David Cone	.05
156	Gary Gaetti	.05
157	Greg Gagne	.05
158	Tom Gordon	.05
159	Mark Gubicza	.05
160	Bob Hamelin	.05
161	Dave Henderson	.05
162	Felix Jose	.05
163	Wally Joyner	.05
164	Jose Lind	.05
165	Mike Macfarlane	.05
166	Mike Magnante	.05
167	Brent Mayne	.05
168	Brian McRae	.05
169	Rusty Meacham	.05
170	Jeff Montgomery	.05
171	Hipolito Pichardo	.05
172	Terry Shumpert	.05
173	Michael Tucker	.05
174	Ricky Bones	.05
175	Jeff Cirillo RC	.30
176	Alex Diaz	.05
177	Cal Eldred	.05
178	Mike Fetters	.05
179	Darryl Hamilton	.05
180	Brian Harper	.05
181	Jon Jaha	.05
182	Pat Listach	.05
183	Graeme Lloyd	.05
184	Jose Mercedes	.05
185	Matt Mieske	.05
186	Dave Nilsson	.05
187	Jody Reed	.05
188	Bob Scanlan	.05
189	Kevin Seitzer	.05
190	Bill Spiers	.05
191	B.J. Surhoff	.05
192	Jose Valentin	.05
193	Greg Vaughn	.05
194	Turner Ward	.05
195	Bill Wegman	.05

196	Rick Aguilera	.05
197	Rich Becker	.05
198	Alex Cole	.05
199	Marty Cordova	.05
200	Steve Dunn	.05
201	Scott Erickson	.05
202	Mark Guthrie	.05
203	Chip Hale	.05
204	LaTroy Hawkins	.05
205	Denny Hocking	.05
206	Chuck Knoblauch	.05
207	Scott Leius	.05
208	Shane Mack	.05
209	Pat Mahomes	.05
210	Pat Meares	.05
211	Pedro Munoz	.05
212	Kirby Puckett	1.00
213	Jeff Reboulet	.05
214	Dave Stevens	.05
215	Kevin Tapani	.05
216	Matt Walbeck	.05
217	Carl Willis	.05
218	Brian Anderson	.05
219	Chad Curtis	.05
220	Chili Davis	.05
221	Gary DiSarcina	.05
222	Damion Easley	.05
223	Jim Edmonds	.05
224	Chuck Finley	.05
225	Joe Grahe	.05
226	Rex Hudler	.05
227	Bo Jackson	.10
228	Mark Langston	.05
229	Phil Leftwich	.05
230	Mark Leiter	.05
231	Spike Owen	.05
232	Bob Patterson	.05
233	Troy Percival	.05
234	Eduardo Perez	.05
235	Tim Salmon	.10
236	J.T. Snow	.05
237	Chris Turner	.05
238	Mark Acre	.05
239	Geronimo Berroa	.05
240	Mike Bordick	.05
241	John Briscoe	.05
242	Scott Brosius	.05
243	Ron Darling	.05
244	Dennis Eckersley	.65
245	Brent Gates	.05
246	Rickey Henderson	.75
247	Stan Javier	.05
248	Steve Karsay	.05
249	Mark McGwire	2.00
250	Troy Neel	.05
251	Steve Ontiveros	.05
252	Carlos Reyes	.05
253	Ruben Sierra	.05
254	Terry Steinbach	.05
255	Bill Taylor	.05
256	Todd Van Poppel	.05
257	Bobby Witt	.05
258	Rich Amaral	.05
259	Eric Anthony	.05
260	Bobby Ayala	.05
261	Mike Blowers	.05
262	Chris Bosio	.05
263	Jay Buhner	.05
264	John Cummings	.05
265	Tim Davis	.05
266	Felix Fermin	.05
267	Dave Fleming	.05
268	Goose Gossage	.05
269	Ken Griffey Jr.	1.50
270	Reggie Jefferson	.05
271	Randy Johnson	.75
272	Edgar Martinez	.05
273	Tino Martinez	.05
274	Greg Pirkl	.05
275	Bill Risley	.05
276	Roger Salkeld	.05
277	Luis Sojo	.05
278	Mac Suzuki	.05
279	Dan Wilson	.05
280	Kevin Brown	.05
281	Jose Canseco	.40
282	Cris Carpenter	.05
283	Will Clark	.10
284	Jeff Frye	.05
285	Juan Gonzalez	.65
286	Rick Helling	.05
287	Tom Henke	.05
288	David Hulse	.05
289	Chris James	.05
290	Manuel Lee	.05
291	Oddibe McDowell	.05
292	Dean Palmer	.05
293	Roger Pavlik	.05

ABBREVIATIONS

OPS - Overprinted
"Promotional Sample"

294	Bill Ripken	.05
295	Ivan Rodriguez	.65
296	Kenny Rogers	.05
297	Doug Strange	.05
298	Matt Whiteside	.05
299	Steve Avery	.05
300	Steve Bedrosian	.05
301	Rafael Belliard	.05
302	Jeff Blauser	.05
303	Dave Gallagher	.05
304	Tom Glavine	.30
305	Dave Justice	.05
306	Mike Kelly	.05
307	Roberto Kelly	.05
308	Ryan Klesko	.05
309	Mark Lemke	.05
310	Javier Lopez	.05
311	Greg Maddux	1.00
312	Fred McGriff	.05
313	Greg McMichael	.05
314	Kent Mercker	.05
315	Charlie O'Brien	.05
316	Jose Oliva	.05
317	Terry Pendleton	.05
318	John Smoltz	.05
319	Mike Stanton	.05
320	Tony Tarasco	.05
321	Terrell Wade	.05
322	Mark Wohlers	.05
323	Kurt Abbott	.05
324	Luis Aquino	.05
325	Bret Barberie	.05
326	Ryan Bowen	.05
327	Jerry Browne	.05
328	Chuck Carr	.05
329	Matias Carrillo	.05
330	Greg Colbrunn	.05
331	Jeff Conine	.05
332	Mark Gardner	.05
333	Chris Hammond	.05
334	Bryan Harvey	.05
335	Richie Lewis	.05
336	Dave Magadan	.05
337	Terry Mathews	.05
338	Robb Nen	.05
339	Yorkis Perez	.05
340	Pat Rapp	.05
341	Benito Santiago	.05
342	Gary Sheffield	.40
343	Dave Weathers	.05
344	Moises Alou	.05
345	Sean Berry	.05
346	Wil Cordero	.05
347	Joe Eischen	.05
348	Jeff Fassero	.05
349	Darrin Fletcher	.05
350	Cliff Floyd	.05
351	Marquis Grissom	.05
352	Butch Henry	.05
353	Gil Heredia	.05
354	Ken Hill	.05
355	Mike Lansing	.05
356	Pedro Martinez	.75
357	Mel Rojas	.05
358	Kirk Rueter	.05
359	Tim Scott	.05
360	Jeff Shaw	.05
361	Larry Walker	.05
362	Lenny Webster	.05
363	John Wetteland	.05
364	Rondell White	.05
365	Bobby Bonilla	.05
366	Rico Brogna	.05
367	Jeromy Burnitz	.05
368	John Franco	.05
369	Dwight Gooden	.05
370	Todd Hundley	.05
371	Jason Jacome	.05
372	Bobby Jones	.05
373	Jeff Kent	.05
374	Jim Lindeman	.05
375	Josias Manzanillo	.05
376	Roger Mason	.05
377	Kevin McReynolds	.05
378	Joe Orsulak	.05
379	Bill Pulsipher	.05
380	Bret Saberhagen	.05
381	David Segui	.05
382	Pete Smith	.05
383	Kelly Stinnett	.05
384	Ryan Thompson	.05
385	Jose Vizcaino	.05
386	Toby Borland	.05
387	Ricky Bettalico	.05
388	Darren Daulton	.05
389	Mariano Duncan	.05
390	Len Dykstra	.05
391	Jim Eisenreich	.05
392	Tommy Greene	.05
393	Dave Hollins	.05
394	Pete Incaviglia	.05
395	Danny Jackson	.05
396	Doug Jones	.05
397	Ricky Jordan	.05
398	John Kruk	.05
399	Mike Lieberthal	.05

400	Tony Longmire	.05
401	Mickey Morandini	.05
402	Bobby Munoz	.05
403	Curt Schilling	.25
404	Heathcliff Slocumb	.05
405	Kevin Stocker	.05
406	Fernando Valenzuela	.05
407	David West	.05
408	Willie Banks	.05
409	Jose Bautista	.05
410	Steve Buechele	.05
411	Jim Bullinger	.05
412	Chuck Crim	.05
413	Shawon Dunston	.05
414	Kevin Foster	.05
415	Mark Grace	.10
416	Jose Hernandez	.05
417	Glenallen Hill	.05
418	Brooks Kieschnick	.05
419	Derrick May	.05
420	Randy Myers	.05
421	Dan Plesac	.05
422	Karl Rhodes	.05
423	Rey Sanchez	.05
424	Sammy Sosa	1.50
425	Steve Trachsel	.05
426	Rick Wilkins	.05
427	Anthony Young	.05
428	Eddie Zambrano	.05
429	Bret Boone	.05
430	Jeff Branson	.05
431	Jeff Brantley	.05
432	Hector Carrasco	.05
433	Brian Dorsett	.05
434	Tony Fernandez	.05
435	Tim Fortugno	.05
436	Erik Hanson	.05
437	Thomas Howard	.05
438	Kevin Jarvis	.05
439	Barry Larkin	.05
440	Chuck McElroy	.05
441	Kevin Mitchell	.05
442	Hal Morris	.05
443	Jose Rijo	.05
444	John Roper	.05
445	Johnny Ruffin	.05
446	Deion Sanders	.05
447	Reggie Sanders	.05
448	Pete Schourek	.05
449	John Smiley	.05
450	Eddie Taubensee	.05
451	Jeff Bagwell	.75
452	Kevin Bass	.05
453	Craig Biggio	.05
454	Ken Caminiti	.05
455	Andujar Cedeno	.05
456	Doug Drabek	.05
457	Tony Eusebio	.05
458	Mike Felder	.05
459	Steve Finley	.05
460	Luis Gonzalez	.10
461	Mike Hampton	.05
462	Pete Harnisch	.05
463	John Hudek	.05
464	Todd Jones	.05
465	Darryl Kile	.05
466	James Mouton	.05
467	Shane Reynolds	.05
468	Scott Servais	.05
469	Greg Swindell	.05
470	Dave Veres	.05
471	Brian Williams	.05
472	Jay Bell	.05
473	Jacob Brumfield	.05
474	Dave Clark	.05
475	Steve Cooke	.05
476	Midre Cummings	.05
477	Mark Dewey	.05
478	Tom Foley	.05
479	Carlos Garcia	.05
480	Jeff King	.05
481	Jon Lieber	.05
482	Ravelo Manzanillo	.05
483	Al Martin	.05
484	Orlando Merced	.05
485	Danny Miceli	.05
486	Denny Neagle	.05
487	Lance Parrish	.05
488	Don Slaught	.05
489	Zane Smith	.05
490	Andy Van Slyke	.05
491	Paul Wagner	.05
492	Rick White	.05
493	Luis Alicea	.05
494	Rene Arocha	.05
495	Rheal Cormier	.05
496	Bryan Eversgerd	.05
497	Bernard Gilkey	.05
498	John Habyan	.05
499	Gregg Jefferies	.05
500	Brian Jordan	.05
501	Ray Lankford	.05
502	John Mabry	.05
503	Terry McGriff	.05
504	Tom Pagnozzi	.05
505	Vicente Palacios	.05

506	Geronimo Pena	.05
507	Gerald Perry	.05
508	Rich Rodriguez	.05
509	Ozzie Smith	1.00
510	Bob Tewksbury	.05
511	Allen Watson	.05
512	Mark Whiten	.05
513	Todd Zeile	.05
514	Dante Bichette	.05
515	Willie Blair	.05
516	Ellis Burks	.05
517	Marvin Freeman	.05
518	Andres Galarraga	.05
519	Joe Girardi	.05
520	Greg Harris	.05
521	Charlie Hayes	.05
522	Mike Kingery	.05
523	Nelson Liriano	.05
524	Mike Munoz	.05
525	David Nied	.05
526	Steve Reed	.05
527	Kevin Ritz	.05
528	Bruce Ruffin	.05
529	John Vander Wal	.05
530	Walt Weiss	.05
531	Eric Young	.05
532	Billy Ashley	.05
533	Pedro Astacio	.05
534	Rafael Bournigal	.05
535	Brett Butler	.05
536	Tom Candiotti	.05
537	Omar Daal	.05
538	Delino DeShields	.05
539	Darren Dreifort	.05
540	Kevin Gross	.05
541	Orel Hershiser	.05
542	Garey Ingram	.05
543	Eric Karros	.05
544	Ramon Martinez	.05
545	Raul Mondesi	.05
546	Chan Ho Park	.05
547	Mike Piazza	1.50
548	Henry Rodriguez	.05
549	Rudy Seanez	.05
550	Ismael Valdes	.05
551	Tim Wallach	.05
552	Todd Worrell	.05
553	Andy Ashby	.05
554	Brad Ausmus	.05
555	Derek Bell	.05
556	Andy Benes	.05
557	Phil Clark	.05
558	Donnie Elliott	.05
559	Ricky Gutierrez	.05
560	Tony Gwynn	1.00
561	Joey Hamilton	.05
562	Trevor Hoffman	.05
563	Luis Lopez	.05
564	Pedro Martinez	.05
565	Tim Mauser	.05
566	Phil Plantier	.05
567	Bip Roberts	.05
568	Scott Sanders	.05
569	Craig Shipley	.05
570	Jeff Tabaka	.05
571	Eddie Williams	.05
572	Rod Beck	.05
573	Mike Benjamin	.05
574	Barry Bonds	2.50
575	Dave Burba	.05
576	John Burkett	.05
577	Mark Carreon	.05
578	Royce Clayton	.05
579	Steve Frey	.05
580	Bryan Hickerson	.05
581	Mike Jackson	.05
582	Darren Lewis	.05
583	Kirt Manwaring	.05
584	Rich Monteleone	.05
585	John Patterson	.05
586	J.R. Phillips	.05
587	Mark Portugal	.05
588	Joe Rosselli	.05
589	Darryl Strawberry	.05
590	Bill Swift	.05
591	Robby Thompson	.05
592	William Van Landingham	.05
593	Matt Williams	.05
594	Checklist	.05
595	Checklist	.05
596	Checklist	.05
597	Checklist	.05
598	Checklist	.05
599	Checklist	.05
600	Checklist	.05

All-Stars

		NM/M
Complete Set (25):		8.00
Common Card:		.20
1	Ivan Rodriguez, Mike Piazza	.75
2	Frank Thomas, Gregg Jefferies	.50

Kenny Lofton OF

3	Roberto Alomar, Mariano Duncan	.40
4	Wade Boggs, Matt Williams	.65
5	Cal Ripken, Jr., Ozzie Smith	1.50
6	Joe Carter, Barry Bonds	1.50
7	Ken Griffey Jr., Tony Gwynn	.75
8	Kirby Puckett, Dave Justice	.65
9	Jimmy Key, Greg Maddux	.65
10	Chuck Knoblauch, Wil Cordero	.20
11	Scott Cooper, Ken Caminiti	.20
12	Will Clark, Carlos Garcia	.50
13	Paul Molitor, Jeff Bagwell	.50
14	Travis Fryman, Craig Biggio	.20
15	Mickey Tettleton, Fred McGriff	.20
16	Kenny Lofton, Moises Alou	.20
17	Albert Belle, Marquis Grissom	.20
18	Paul O'Neill, Dante Bichette	.20
19	David Cone, Ken Hill	.20
20	Mike Mussina, Doug Drabek	.50
21	Randy Johnson, John Hudek	.50
22	Pat Hentgen, Danny Jackson	.20
23	Wilson Alvarez, Rod Beck	.20
24	Lee Smith, Randy Myers	.20
25	Jason Bere, Doug Jones	.20

All-Fleer 9

		NM/M
Complete Set (9):		4.00
Common Player:		.25
1	Mike Piazza	1.00
2	Frank Thomas	.50
3	Roberto Alomar	.40
4	Cal Ripken Jr.	2.50
5	Matt Williams	.25
6	Barry Bonds	2.50
7	Ken Griffey Jr.	1.00
8	Tony Gwynn	.65
9	Greg Maddux	.65

All-Rookies

		NM/M
Complete Set (9):		1.50
Common Player:		.25
Trade card: 2X		.12
1	Edgardo Alfonzo	.25
2	Jason Bates	.25
3	Brian Boehringer	.25
4	Darren Bragg	.25
5	Brad Clontz	.25
6	Jim Dougherty	.25

7 Todd Hollandsworth .25
8 Rudy Pemberton .25
9 Frank Rodriguez .25

Award Winners

		NM/M
Complete Set (6):		4.00
Common Player:		.25
1	Frank Thomas	1.50
2	Jeff Bagwell	1.50
3	David Cone	.25
4	Greg Maddux	2.00
5	Bob Hamelin	.25
6	Raul Mondesi	.25

League Leaders

		NM/M
Complete Set (10):		4.00
Common Player:		.25
1	Paul O'Neill	.25
2	Ken Griffey Jr.	1.50
3	Kirby Puckett	.75
4	Jimmy Key	.25
5	Randy Johnson	.65
6	Tony Gwynn	.75
7	Matt Williams	.25
8	Jeff Bagwell	.50
9	Greg Maddux, Ken Hill	.75
10	Andy Benes	.25

Lumber Company

		NM/M
Complete Set (10):		12.00
Common Player:		.40
1	Jeff Bagwell	1.50
2	Albert Belle	.40
3	Barry Bonds	3.50
4	Jose Canseco	.75
5	Joe Carter	.40
6	Ken Griffey Jr.	2.50
7	Fred McGriff	.40
8	Kevin Mitchell	.40
9	Frank Thomas	1.75
10	Matt Williams	.40

Major League Prospects

		NM/M
Complete Set (10):		6.00
Common Player:		.25
1	Garret Anderson	.50
2	James Baldwin	.25
3	Alan Benes	.25
4	Armando Benitez	.25
5	Ray Durham	.25
6	Brian Hunter	.25
7a	Derek Jeter (No licensor logos on back.)	4.00
7b	Derek Jeter (Licensor logos on back.)	4.00
8	Charles Johnson	.25
9	Orlando Miller	.25
10	Alex Rodriguez	3.00

Pro-Visions

		NM/M
Complete Set (6):		2.00
Common Player:		.25
1	Mike Mussina	.40
2	Raul Mondesi	.25

3 Jeff Bagwell .75
4 Greg Maddux 1.00
5 Tim Salmon .25
6 Manny Ramirez .75

Rookie Sensations

		NM/M
Complete Set (20):		5.00
Common Player:		.25
1	Kurt Abbott	.25
2	Rico Brogna	.25
3	Hector Carrasco	.25
4	Kevin Foster	.25
5	Chris Gomez	.25
6	Darren Hall	.25
7	Bob Hamelin	.25
8	Joey Hamilton	.25
9	John Hudek	.25
10	Ryan Klesko	.25
11	Javier Lopez	.25
12	Matt Mieske	.25
13	Raul Mondesi	.25
14	Manny Ramirez	4.00
15	Shane Reynolds	.25
16	Bill Risley	.25
17	Johnny Ruffin	.25
18	Steve Trachsel	.25
19	William Van Landingham	.25
20	Rondell White	.25

Team Leaders

		NM/M
Complete Set (28):		50.00
Common Card:		.50
1	Cal Ripken, Jr., Mike Mussina	7.50
2	Mo Vaughn, Roger Clemens	4.50
3	Tim Salmon, Chuck Finley	.75
4	Frank Thomas, Jack McDowell	2.50
5	Albert Belle, Dennis Martinez	.50
6	Cecil Fielder, Mike Moore	.50
7	Bob Hamelin, David Cone	.50
8	Greg Vaughn, Ricky Bones	.50
9	Kirby Puckett, Rick Aguilera	3.00
10	Don Mattingly, Jimmy Key	4.50
11	Ruben Sierra, Dennis Eckersley	1.50
12	Ken Griffey Jr., Randy Johnson	6.00
13	Jose Canseco, Kenny Rogers	1.00
14	Joe Carter, Pat Hentgen	.50
15	Dave Justice, Greg Maddux	3.00
16	Sammy Sosa, Steve Trachsel	5.00
17	Kevin Mitchell, Jose Rijo	.50
18	Dante Bichette, Bruce Ruffin	.50
19	Jeff Conine, Robb Nen	.50
20	Jeff Bagwell, Doug Drabek	2.50
21	Mike Piazza, Ramon Martinez	5.00
22	Moises Alou, Ken Hill	.50
23	Bobby Bonilla, Bret Saberhagen	.50
24	Darren Daulton, Danny Jackson	.50
25	Jay Bell, Zane Smith	.50
26	Gregg Jefferies, Bob Tewksbury	.50
27	Tony Gwynn, Andy Benes	3.00
28	Matt Williams, Rod Beck	.50

Update

		NM/M
Complete Set (200):		7.00
Common Player:		.05
Pack (12):		.50
Wax Box (36):		7.50
1	Manny Alexander	.05
2	Bret Barberie	.05
3	Armando Benitez	.05
4	Kevin Brown	.05
5	Doug Jones	.05
6	Sherman Obando	.05
7	Andy Van Slyke	.05
8	Stan Belinda	.05
9	Jose Canseco	.30
10	Vaughn Eshelman	.05
11	Mike Macfarlane	.05
12	Troy O'Leary	.05
13	Steve Rodriguez	.05
14	Lee Tinsley	.05
15	Tim Vanegmond	.05
16	Mark Whiten	.05
17	Sean Bergman	.05
18	Chad Curtis	.05
19	John Flaherty	.05
20	Bob Higginson RC	.15
21	Felipe Lira	.05
22	Shannon Penn	.05
23	Todd Steverson	.05
24	Sean Whiteside	.05
25	Tony Fernandez	.05
26	Jack McDowell	.05
27	Andy Petitte	.15
28	John Wetteland	.05
29	David Cone	.05
30	Mike Timlin	.05
31	Duane Ward	.05
32	Jim Abbott	.05
33	James Baldwin	.05
34	Mike Devereaux	.05
35	Ray Durham	.05
36	Tim Fortugno	.05
37	Scott Ruffcorn	.05
38	Chris Sabo	.05
39	Paul Assenmacher	.05
40	Bud Black	.05
41	Orel Hershiser	.05
42	Julian Tavarez	.05
43	Dave Winfield	.60
44	Pat Borders	.05
45	Melvin Bunch RC	.05
46	Tom Goodwin	.05
47	Jon Nunnally	.05
48	Joe Randa	.05
49	Dilson Torres RC	.05
50	Joe Vitiello	.05
51	David Hulse	.05
52	Scott Karl	.05
53	Mark Kiefer	.05
54	Derrick May	.05
55	Joe Oliver	.05
56	Al Reyes	.05
57	Steve Sparks RC	.05
58	Jerald Clark	.05
59	Eddie Guardado	.05
60	Kevin Maas	.05
61	David McCarty	.05
62	Brad Radke RC	.50
63	Scott Stahoviak	.05
64	Garret Anderson	.05
65	Shawn Boskie	.05
66	Mike James	.05
67	Tony Phillips	.05
68	Lee Smith	.05
69	Mitch Williams	.05
70	Jim Corsi	.05
71	Mark Harkey	.05
72	Dave Stewart	.05
73	Todd Stottlemyre	.05
74	Joey Cora	.05
75	Chad Kreuter	.05
76	Jeff Nelson	.05
77	Alex Rodriguez	2.00
78	Ron Villone	.05
79	Bob Wells RC	.05
80	Jose Alberro RC	.05
81	Terry Burrows	.05
82	Kevin Gross	.05
83	Wilson Heredia	.05
84	Mark McLemore	.05
85	Otis Nixon	.05
86	Jeff Russell	.05
87	Mickey Tettleton	.05
88	Bob Tewksbury	.05
89	Pedro Borbon	.05
90	Marquis Grissom	.05
91	Chipper Jones	.75
92	Mike Mordecai	.05
93	Jason Schmidt	.15
94	John Burkett	.05
95	Andre Dawson	.25
96	Matt Dunbar RC	.05
97	Charles Johnson	.05
98	Terry Pendleton	.05
99	Rich Scheid	.05
100	Quilvio Veras	.05
101	Bobby Witt	.05
102	Eddie Zosky	.05
103	Shane Andrews	.05
104	Reid Cornelius	.05
105	Chad Fonville RC	.05
106	Mark Grudzielanek RC	.25
107	Roberto Kelly	.05
108	Carlos Perez RC	.05
109	Tony Tarasco	.05
110	Brett Butler	.05
111	Carl Everett	.05
112	Pete Harnisch	.05
113	Doug Henry	.05
114	Kevin Lomon	.05
115	Blas Minor	.05
116	Dave Mlicki	.05
117	Ricky Otero RC	.05
118	Norm Charlton	.05
119	Tyler Green	.05
120	Gene Harris	.05
121	Charlie Hayes	.05
122	Gregg Jefferies	.05
123	Michael Mimbs RC	.05
124	Paul Quantrill	.05
125	Frank Castillo	.05
126	Brian McRae	.05
127	Jaime Navarro	.05
128	Mike Perez	.05
129	Tanyon Sturtze	.05
130	Ozzie Timmons	.05

131	John Courtright	.05
132	Ron Gant	.05
133	Xavier Hernandez	.05
134	Brian Hunter	.05
135	Benito Santiago	.05
136	Pete Smith	.05
137	Scott Sullivan	.05
138	Derek Bell	.05
139	Doug Brocail	.05
140	Ricky Gutierrez	.05
141	Pedro Martinez	.05
142	Orlando Miller	.05
143	Phil Plantier	.05
144	Craig Shipley	.05
145	Rich Aude	.05
146	Jason Christiansen RC	.05
147	Freddy Garcia RC	.25
148	Jim Gott	.05
149	Mark Johnson RC	.05
150	Esteban Loaiza	.05
151	Dan Plesac	.05
152	Gary Wilson RC	.05
153	Allen Battle	.05
154	Terry Bradshaw	.05
155	Scott Cooper	.05
156	Tripp Cromer	.05
157	John Frascatore	.05
158	John Habyan	.05
159	Tom Henke	.05
160	Ken Hill	.05
161	Danny Jackson	.05
162	Donovan Osborne	.05
163	Tom Urbani	.05
164	Roger Bailey	.05
165	Jorge Brito RC	.05
166	Vinny Castilla	.05
167	Darren Holmes	.05
168	Roberto Mejia	.05
169	Bill Swift	.05
170	Mark Thompson	.05
171	Larry Walker	.05
172	Greg Hansell	.05
173	Dave Hansen	.05
174	Carlos Hernandez	.05
175	Hideo Nomo RC	2.00
176	Jose Offerman	.05
177	Antonio Osuna	.05
178	Reggie Williams	.05
179	Todd Williams	.05
180	Andres Berumen	.05
181	Ken Caminiti	.05
182	Andujar Cedeno	.05
183	Steve Finley	.05
184	Bryce Florie	.05
185	Dustin Hermanson	.05
186	Ray Holbert	.05
187	Melvin Nieves	.05
188	Roberto Petagine	.05
189	Jody Reed	.05
190	Fernando Valenzuela	.05
191	Brian Williams	.05
192	Mark Dewey	.05
193	Glenallen Hill	.05
194	Chris Hook RC	.05
195	Terry Mulholland	.05
196	Steve Scarsone	.05
197	Trevor Wilson	.05
198	Checklist	.05
199	Checklist	.05
200	Checklist	.05

Update Diamond Tribute

		NM/M
Complete Set (10):		6.00
Common Player:		.25
1	Jeff Bagwell	.75
2	Albert Belle	.25
3	Barry Bonds	3.00
4	David Cone	.25
5	Dennis Eckersley	.50
6	Ken Griffey Jr.	1.50
7	Rickey Henderson	.60
8	Greg Maddux	1.00
9	Frank Thomas	.75
10	Matt Williams	.25

Update Smooth Leather

		NM/M
Complete Set (10):		7.50
Common Player:		.25
1	Roberto Alomar	.50
2	Barry Bonds	2.50
3	Ken Griffey Jr.	1.50
4	Marquis Grissom	.25
5	Darren Lewis	.25
6	Kenny Lofton	.25
7	Don Mattingly	1.00
8	Cal Ripken Jr.	2.50
9	Ivan Rodriguez	.75
10	Matt Williams	.25

Update Rookie Update

		NM/M
Complete Set (10):		4.00
Common Player:		.10
1	Shane Andrews	.10
2	Ray Durham	.10
3	Shawn Green	.40
4	Charles Johnson	.10
5	Chipper Jones	1.50
6	Esteban Loaiza	.10
7	Hideo Nomo	1.00
8	Jon Nunnally	.10
9	Alex Rodriguez	2.00
10	Julian Tavarez	.10

Update Soaring Stars

		NM/M
Complete Set (9):		3.50
Common Player:		.15
1	Moises Alou	.35
2	Jason Bere	.25
3	Jeff Conine	.25
4	Cliff Floyd	.25
5	Pat Hentgen	.25
6	Kenny Lofton	.25
7	Raul Mondesi	.25
8	Mike Piazza	3.00
9	Tim Salmon	.35

Update Headliners

		NM/M
Complete Set (20):		8.00
Common Player:		.10
1	Jeff Bagwell	.50
2	Albert Belle	.15
3	Barry Bonds	3.00
4	Jose Canseco	.40
5	Joe Carter	.15
6	Will Clark	.25
7	Roger Clemens	2.00
8	Lenny Dykstra	.15
9	Cecil Fielder	.15
10	Juan Gonzalez	.40
11	Ken Griffey Jr.	2.00
12	Kenny Lofton	.15
13	Greg Maddux	.75

14	Fred McGriff	.15
15	Mike Piazza	1.50
16	Kirby Puckett	.75
17	Tim Salmon	.15
18	Frank Thomas	.50
19	Mo Vaughn	.15
20	Matt Williams	.15

1996 Fleer

		NM/M
Complete Set (600):		20.00
Common Player:		.05
Complete Tiffany Set (600):		100.00
Tiffanies:		2X
Pack (11):		.75
Wax Box (36):		16.00
1	Manny Alexander	.05
2	Brady Anderson	.05
3	Harold Baines	.05
4	Armando Benitez	.05
5	Bobby Bonilla	.05
6	Kevin Brown	.05
7	Scott Erickson	.05
8	Curtis Goodwin	.05
9	Jeffrey Hammonds	.05
10	Jimmy Haynes	.05
11	Chris Hoiles	.05
12	Doug Jones	.05
13	Rick Krivda	.05
14	Jeff Manto	.05
15	Ben McDonald	.05
16	Jamie Moyer	.05
17	Mike Mussina	.50
18	Jesse Orosco	.05
19	Rafael Palmeiro	.65
20	Cal Ripken Jr.	2.50
20(p)	Cal Ripken Jr./OPS	2.50
21	Rick Aguilera	.05
22	Luis Alicea	.05
23	Stan Belinda	.05
24	Jose Canseco	.50
25	Roger Clemens	1.25
26	Vaughn Eshelman	.05
27	Mike Greenwell	.05
28	Erik Hanson	.05
29	Dwayne Hosey	.05
30	Mike Macfarlane	.05
31	Tim Naehring	.05
32	Troy O'Leary	.05
33	Aaron Sele	.05
34	Zane Smith	.05
35	Jeff Suppan	.05
36	Lee Tinsley	.05
37	John Valentin	.05
38	Mo Vaughn	.05
39	Tim Wakefield	.05
40	Jim Abbott	.05
41	Brian Anderson	.05
42	Garret Anderson	.05
43	Chili Davis	.05

44	Gary DiSarcina	.05
45	Damion Easley	.05
46	Jim Edmonds	.05
47	Chuck Finley	.05
48	Todd Greene	.05
49	Mike Harkey	.05
50	Mike James	.05
51	Mark Langston	.05
52	Greg Myers	.05
53	Orlando Palmeiro	.05
54	Bob Patterson	.05
55	Troy Percival	.05
56	Tony Phillips	.05
57	Tim Salmon	.10
58	Lee Smith	.05
59	J.T. Snow	.05
60	Randy Velarde	.05
61	Wilson Alvarez	.05
62	Luis Andujar RC	.05
63	Jason Bere	.05
64	Ray Durham	.05
65	Alex Fernandez	.05
66	Ozzie Guillen	.05
67	Roberto Hernandez	.05
68	Lance Johnson	.05
69	Matt Karchner	.05
70	Ron Karkovice	.05
71	Norberto Martin	.05
72	Dave Martinez	.05
73	Kirk McCaskill	.05
74	Lyle Mouton	.05
75	Tim Raines	.05
76	Mike Sirotka RC	.05
77	Frank Thomas	.75
78	Larry Thomas	.05
79	Robin Ventura	.05
80	Sandy Alomar Jr.	.05
81	Paul Assenmacher	.05
82	Carlos Baerga	.05
83	Albert Belle	.05
84	Mark Clark	.05
85	Alan Embree	.05
86	Alvaro Espinoza	.05
87	Orel Hershiser	.05
88	Ken Hill	.05
89	Kenny Lofton	.05
90	Dennis Martinez	.05
91	Jose Mesa	.05
92	Eddie Murray	.75
93	Charles Nagy	.05
94	Chad Ogea	.05
95	Tony Pena	.05
96	Herb Perry	.05
97	Eric Plunk	.05
98	Jim Poole	.05
99	Manny Ramirez	.75
100	Paul Sorrento	.05
101	Julian Travarez	.05
102	Jim Thome	.60
103	Omar Vizquel	.05
104	Dave Winfield	.75
105	Danny Bautista	.05
106	Joe Boever	.05
107	Chad Curtis	.05
108	John Doherty	.05
109	Cecil Fielder	.05
110	John Flaherty	.05
111	Travis Fryman	.05
112	Chris Gomez	.05
113	Bob Higginson	.05
114	Mark Lewis	.05
115	Jose Lima	.05
116	Felipe Lira	.05
117	Brian Maxcy	.05
118	C.J. Nitkowski	.05
119	Phil Plantier	.05
120	Clint Sodowsky	.05
121	Alan Trammell	.05
122	Lou Whitaker	.05
123	Kevin Appier	.05
124	Johnny Damon	.35
125	Gary Gaetti	.05
126	Tom Goodwin	.05
127	Tom Gordon	.05
128	Mark Gubicza	.05
129	Bob Hamelin	.05
130	David Howard	.05
131	Jason Jacome	.05
132	Wally Joyner	.05
133	Keith Lockhart	.05
134	Brent Mayne	.05
135	Jeff Montgomery	.05
136	Jon Nunnally	.05
137	Juan Samuel	.05
138	Mike Sweeney RC	.50
139	Michael Tucker	.05
140	Joe Vitiello	.05
141	Ricky Bones	.05
142	Chuck Carr	.05
143	Jeff Cirillo	.05
144	Mike Fetters	.05
145	Darryl Hamilton	.05
146	David Hulse	.05
147	John Jaha	.05

No	Player	Value
148	Scott Karl	.05
149	Mark Kiefer	.05
150	Pat Listach	.05
151	Mark Loretta	.05
152	Mike Matheny	.05
153	Matt Mieske	.05
154	Dave Nilsson	.05
155	Joe Oliver	.05
156	Al Reyes	.05
157	Kevin Seitzer	.05
158	Steve Sparks	.05
159	B.J. Surhoff	.05
160	Jose Valentin	.05
161	Greg Vaughn	.05
162	Fernando Vina	.05
163	Rich Becker	.05
164	Ron Coomer	.05
165	Marty Cordova	.05
166	Chuck Knoblauch	.05
167	Matt Lawton RC	.30
168	Pat Meares	.05
169	Paul Molitor	.75
170	Pedro Munoz	.05
171	Jose Parra	.05
172	Kirby Puckett	1.00
173	Brad Radke	.05
174	Jeff Reboulet	.05
175	Rich Robertson	.05
176	Frank Rodriguez	.05
177	Scott Stahoviak	.05
178	Dave Stevens	.05
179	Matt Walbeck	.05
180	Wade Boggs	1.00
181	David Cone	.05
182	Tony Fernandez	.05
183	Joe Girardi	.05
184	Derek Jeter	2.50
185	Scott Kamieniecki	.05
186	Pat Kelly	.05
187	Jim Leyritz	.05
188	Tino Martinez	.05
189	Don Mattingly	1.25
190	Jack McDowell	.05
191	Jeff Nelson	.05
192	Paul O'Neill	.05
193	Melido Perez	.05
194	Andy Pettitte	.30
195	Mariano Rivera	.15
196	Ruben Sierra	.05
197	Mike Stanley	.05
198	Darryl Strawberry	.05
199	John Wetteland	.05
200	Bob Wickman	.05
201	Bernie Williams	.10
202	Mark Acre	.05
203	Geronimo Berroa	.05
204	Mike Bordick	.05
205	Scott Brosius	.05
206	Dennis Eckersley	.65
207	Brent Gates	.05
208	Jason Giambi	.60
209	Rickey Henderson	.75
210	Jose Herrera	.05
211	Stan Javier	.05
212	Doug Johns	.05
213	Mark McGwire	2.00
214	Steve Ontiveros	.05
215	Craig Paquette	.05
216	Ariel Prieto	.05
217	Carlos Reyes	.05
218	Terry Steinbach	.05
219	Todd Stottlemyre	.05
220	Danny Tartabull	.05
221	Todd Van Poppel	.05
222	John Wasdin	.05
223	George Williams	.05
224	Steve Wojciechowski	.05
225	Rich Amaral	.05
226	Bobby Ayala	.05
227	Tim Belcher	.05
228	Andy Benes	.05
229	Chris Bosio	.05
230	Darren Bragg	.05
231	Jay Buhner	.05
232	Norm Charlton	.05
233	Vince Coleman	.05
234	Joey Cora	.05
235	Russ Davis	.05
236	Alex Diaz	.05
237	Felix Fermin	.05
238	Ken Griffey Jr.	1.75
239	Sterling Hitchcock	.05
240	Randy Johnson	.75
241	Edgar Martinez	.05
242	Bill Risley	.05
243	Alex Rodriguez	2.00
244	Luis Sojo	.05
245	Dan Wilson	.05
246	Bob Wolcott	.05
247	Will Clark	.10
248	Jeff Frye	.05
249	Benji Gil	.05
250	Juan Gonzalez	.65
251	Rusty Greer	.05
252	Kevin Gross	.05
253	Roger McDowell	.05
254	Mark McLemore	.05
255	Otis Nixon	.05
256	Luis Ortiz	.05
257	Mike Pagliarulo	.05
258	Dean Palmer	.05
259	Roger Pavlik	.05
260	Ivan Rodriguez	.65
261	Kenny Rogers	.05
262	Jeff Russell	.05
263	Mickey Tettleton	.05
264	Bob Tewksbury	.05
265	Dave Valle	.05
266	Matt Whiteside	.05
267	Roberto Alomar	.10
268	Joe Carter	.05
269	Tony Castillo	.05
270	Domingo Cedeno	.05
271	Timothy Crabtree	.05
272	Carlos Delgado	.60
273	Alex Gonzalez	.05
274	Shawn Green	.20
275	Juan Guzman	.05
276	Pat Hentgen	.05
277	Al Leiter	.05
278	Sandy Martinez RC	.05
279	Paul Menhart	.05
280	John Olerud	.05
281	Paul Quantrill	.05
282	Ken Robinson	.05
283	Ed Sprague	.05
284	Mike Timlin	.05
285	Steve Avery	.05
286	Rafael Belliard	.05
287	Jeff Blauser	.05
288	Pedro Borbon	.05
289	Brad Clontz	.05
290	Mike Devereaux	.05
291	Tom Glavine	.25
292	Marquis Grissom	.05
293	Chipper Jones	1.00
294	David Justice	.05
295	Mike Kelly	.05
296	Ryan Klesko	.05
297	Mark Lemke	.05
298	Javier Lopez	.05
299	Greg Maddux	1.00
300	Fred McGriff	.05
301	Greg McMichael	.05
302	Kent Mercker	.05
303	Mike Mordecai	.05
304	Charlie O'Brien	.05
305	Eduardo Perez	.05
306	Luis Polonia	.05
307	Jason Schmidt	.05
308	John Smoltz	.05
309	Terrell Wade	.05
310	Mark Wohlers	.05
311	Scott Bullett	.05
312	Jim Bullinger	.05
313	Larry Casian	.05
314	Frank Castillo	.05
315	Shawon Dunston	.05
316	Kevin Foster	.05
317	Matt Franco	.05
318	Luis Gonzalez	.10
319	Mark Grace	.10
320	Jose Hernandez	.05
321	Mike Hubbard	.05
322	Brian McRae	.05
323	Randy Myers	.05
324	Jaime Navarro	.05
325	Mark Parent	.05
326	Mike Perez	.05
327	Rey Sanchez	.05
328	Ryne Sandberg	1.00
329	Scott Servais	.05
330	Sammy Sosa	1.50
331	Ozzie Timmons	.05
332	Steve Trachsel	.05
333	Todd Zeile	.05
334	Bret Boone	.10
335	Jeff Branson	.05
336	Jeff Brantley	.05
337	Dave Burba	.05
338	Hector Carrasco	.05
339	Mariano Duncan	.05
340	Ron Gant	.05
341	Lenny Harris	.05
342	Xavier Hernandez	.05
343	Thomas Howard	.05
344	Mike Jackson	.05
345	Barry Larkin	.05
346	Darren Lewis	.05
347	Hal Morris	.05
348	Eric Owens	.05
349	Mark Portugal	.05
350	Jose Rijo	.05
351	Reggie Sanders	.05
352	Benito Santiago	.05
353	Pete Schourek	.05
354	John Smiley	.05
355	Eddie Taubensee	.05
356	Jerome Walton	.05
357	David Wells	.05
358	Roger Bailey	.05
359	Jason Bates	.05
360	Dante Bichette	.05
361	Ellis Burks	.05
362	Vinny Castilla	.05
363	Andres Galarraga	.05
364	Darren Holmes	.05
365	Mike Kingery	.05
366	Curt Leskanic	.05
367	Quinton McCracken	.05
368	Mike Munoz	.05
369	David Nied	.05
370	Steve Reed	.05
371	Bryan Rekar	.05
372	Kevin Ritz	.05
373	Bruce Ruffin	.05
374	Bret Saberhagen	.05
375	Bill Swift	.05
376	John Vander Wal	.05
377	Larry Walker	.05
378	Walt Weiss	.05
379	Eric Young	.05
380	Kurt Abbott	.05
381	Alex Arias	.05
382	Jerry Browne	.05
383	John Burkett	.05
384	Greg Colbrunn	.05
385	Jeff Conine	.05
386	Andre Dawson	.35
387	Chris Hammond	.05
388	Charles Johnson	.05
389	Terry Mathews	.05
390	Robb Nen	.05
391	Joe Orsulak	.05
392	Terry Pendleton	.05
393	Pat Rapp	.05
394	Gary Sheffield	.45
395	Jesus Tavarez	.05
396	Marc Valdes	.05
397	Quilvio Veras	.05
398	Randy Veres	.05
399	Devon White	.05
400	Jeff Bagwell	.75
401	Derek Bell	.05
402	Craig Biggio	.05
403	John Cangelosi	.05
404	Jim Dougherty	.05
405	Doug Drabek	.05
406	Tony Eusebio	.05
407	Ricky Gutierrez	.05
408	Mike Hampton	.05
409	Dean Hartgraves	.05
410	John Hudek	.05
411	Brian Hunter	.05
412	Todd Jones	.05
413	Darryl Kile	.05
414	Dave Magadan	.05
415	Derrick May	.05
416	Orlando Miller	.05
417	James Mouton	.05
418	Shane Reynolds	.05
419	Greg Swindell	.05
420	Jeff Tabaka	.05
421	Dave Veres	.05
422	Billy Wagner	.05
423	Donne Wall RC	.05
424	Rick Wilkins	.05
425	Billy Ashley	.05
426	Mike Blowers	.05
427	Brett Butler	.05
428	Tom Candiotti	.05
429	Juan Castro	.05
430	John Cummings	.05
431	Delino DeShields	.05
432	Joey Eischen	.05
433	Chad Fonville	.05
434	Greg Gagne	.05
435	Dave Hansen	.05
436	Carlos Hernandez	.05
437	Todd Hollandsworth	.05
438	Eric Karros	.05
439	Roberto Kelly	.05
440	Ramon Martinez	.05
441	Raul Mondesi	.05
442	Hideo Nomo	.65
443	Antonio Osuna	.05
444	Chan Ho Park	.05
445	Mike Piazza	1.75
446	Felix Rodriguez	.05
447	Kevin Tapani	.05
448	Ismael Valdes	.05
449	Todd Worrell	.05
450	Moises Alou	.05
451	Shawn Andrews	.05
452	Yamil Benitez	.05
453	Sean Berry	.05
454	Wil Cordero	.05
455	Jeff Fassero	.05
456	Darrin Fletcher	.05
457	Cliff Floyd	.05
458	Mark Grudzielanek	.05
459	Gil Heredia	.05
460	Tim Laker	.05
461	Mike Lansing	.05
462	Pedro Martinez	.75
463	Carlos Perez	.05
464	Curtis Pride	.05
465	Mel Rojas	.05
466	Kirk Rueter	.05
467	F.P. Santangelo RC	.05
468	Tim Scott	.05
469	David Segui	.05
470	Tony Tarasco	.05
471	Rondell White	.05
472	Edgardo Alfonzo	.05
473	Tim Bogar	.05
474	Rico Brogna	.05
475	Damon Buford	.05
476	Paul Byrd	.05
477	Carl Everett	.10
478	John Franco	.05
479	Todd Hundley	.05
480	Butch Huskey	.05
481	Jason Isringhausen	.05
482	Bobby Jones	.05
483	Chris Jones	.05
484	Jeff Kent	.10
485	Dave Mlicki	.05
486	Robert Person	.05
487	Bill Pulsipher	.05
488	Kelly Stinnett	.05
489	Ryan Thompson	.05
490	Jose Vizcaino	.05
491	Howard Battle	.05
492	Toby Borland	.05
493	Ricky Bottalico	.05
494	Darren Daulton	.05
495	Lenny Dykstra	.05
496	Jim Eisenreich	.05
497	Sid Fernandez	.05
498	Tyler Green	.05
499	Charlie Hayes	.05
500	Gregg Jefferies	.05
501	Kevin Jordan	.05
502	Tony Longmire	.05
503	Tom Marsh	.05
504	Michael Mimbs	.05
505	Mickey Morandini	.05
506	Gene Schall	.05
507	Curt Schilling	.25
508	Heathcliff Slocumb	.05
509	Kevin Stocker	.05
510	Andy Van Slyke	.05
511	Lenny Webster	.05
512	Mark Whiten	.05
513	Mike Williams	.05
514	Jay Bell	.05
515	Jacob Brumfield	.05
516	Jason Christiansen	.05
517	Dave Clark	.05
518	Midre Cummings	.05
519	Angelo Encarnacion	.05
520	John Ericks	.05
521	Carlos Garcia	.05
522	Mark Johnson	.05
523	Jeff King	.05
524	Nelson Liriano	.05
525	Esteban Loaiza	.05
526	Al Martin	.05
527	Orlando Merced	.05
528	Dan Miceli	.05
529	Ramon Morel	.05
530	Denny Neagle	.05
531	Steve Parris	.05
532	Dan Plesac	.05
533	Don Slaught	.05
534	Paul Wagner	.05
535	John Wehner	.05
536	Kevin Young	.05
537	Allen Battle	.05
538	David Bell	.05
539	Alan Benes	.05
540	Scott Cooper	.05
541	Tripp Cromer	.05
542	Tony Fossas	.05
543	Bernard Gilkey	.05
544	Tom Henke	.05
545	Brian Jordan	.05
546	Ray Lankford	.05
547	John Mabry	.05
548	T.J. Mathews	.05
549	Mike Morgan	.05
550	Jose Oliva	.05
551	Jose Oquendo	.05
552	Donovan Osborne	.05
553	Tom Pagnozzi	.05
554	Mark Petkovsek	.05
555	Danny Sheaffer	.05
556	Ozzie Smith	1.00
557	Mark Sweeney	.05
558	Allen Watson	.05
559	Andy Ashby	.05
560	Brad Ausmus	.05
561	Willie Blair	.05
562	Ken Caminiti	.05
563	Andujar Cedeno	.05

564	Glenn Dishman	.05
565	Steve Finley	.05
566	Bryce Florie	.05
567	Tony Gwynn	1.00
568	Joey Hamilton	.05
569	Dustin Hermanson	.05
570	Trevor Hoffman	.05
571	Brian Johnson	.05
572	Marc Kroon	.05
573	Scott Livingstone	.05
574	Marc Newfield	.05
575	Melvin Nieves	.05
576	Jody Reed	.05
577	Bip Roberts	.05
578	Scott Sanders	.05
579	Fernando Valenzuela	.05
580	Eddie Williams	.05
581	Rod Beck	.05
582	Marvin Benard RC	.10
583	Barry Bonds	2.50
584	Jamie Brewington	.05
585	Mark Carreon	.05
586	Royce Clayton	.05
587	Shawn Estes	.05
588	Glenallen Hill	.05
589	Mark Leiter	.05
590	Kirt Manwaring	.05
591	David McCarty	.05
592	Terry Mulholland	.05
593	John Patterson	.05
594	J.R. Phillips	.05
595	Deion Sanders	.05
596	Steve Scarsone	.05
597	Robby Thompson	.05
598	Sergio Valdez	.05
599	William Van Landingham	.05
600	Matt Williams	.05

1996 Fleer Tiffany

	NM/M
Complete Set (600):	100.00
Common Player:	.15
Stars:	2X

(See 1996 Fleer for checklist and base card values.)

1996 Fleer Baseball '96

	NM/M
Complete Set (180):	27.00
Common Player:	.09

Atlanta Braves Team Set: 4.00

1	Steve Avery	.10
2	Jeff Blauser	.10
3	Brad Clontz	.10
4	Tom Glavine	.35
5	Marquis Grissom	.10
6	Chipper Jones	1.25
7	David Justice	.10
8	Ryan Klesko	.10
9	Mark Lemke	.10
10	Javier Lopez	.10
11	Greg Maddux	1.25
12	Fred McGriff	.10
13	Greg McMichael	.10
14	Eddie Perez	.10
15	Jason Schmidt	.10
16	John Smoltz	.10
17	Terrell Wade	.10
18	Mark Wohlers	.10
19	Logo Card	.10
20	Checklist	.10

Baltimore Orioles Team Set: 5.00

1	Roberto Alomar	.20
2	Brady Anderson	.10
3	Armando Benitez	.10
4	Bobby Bonilla	.10
5	Scott Erickson	.10
6	Jeffrey Hammonds	.10
7	Jimmy Haynes	.10
8	Chris Hoiles	.10
9	Rick Krivda	.10
10	Kent Mercker	.10
11	Mike Mussina	.45
12	Randy Myers	.10
13	Jesse Orosco	.10
14	Rafael Palmeiro	.75
15	Cal Ripken Jr.	2.50
16	B.J. Surhoff	.10
17	Tony Tarasco	.10
18	David Wells	.10
19	Logo Card	.10
20	Checklist	.10

Boston Red Sox Team Set: 3.00

1	Stan Belinda	.10
2	Jose Canseco	.50
3	Roger Clemens	2.00
4	Wil Cordero	.10
5	Vaughn Eshelman	.10
6	Tom Gordon	.10
7	Mike Greenwell	.10
8	Dwayne Hosey	.10
9	Kevin Mitchell	.10
10	Tim Naehring	.10
11	Troy O'Leary	.10
12	Aaron Sele	.10
13	Heathcliff Slocumb	.10
14	Mike Stanley	.10
15	Jeff Suppan	.10
16	John Valentin	.10
17	Mo Vaughn	.10
18	Tim Wakefield	.10
19	Logo Card	.10
20	Checklist	.10

Chicago Cubs Team Set: 4.00

1	Terry Adams	.10
2	Jim Bullinger	.10
3	Frank Castillo	.10
4	Kevin Foster	.10
5	Leo Gomez	.10
6	Luis Gonzalez	.20
7	Mark Grace	.15
8	Jose Hernandez	.10
9	Robin Jennings RC	.10
10	Doug Jones	.10
11	Brooks Kieschnick	.10
12	Brian McRae	.10
13	Jaime Navarro	.10
14	Rey Sanchez	.10
15	Ryne Sandberg	1.25
16	Scott Servais	.10
17	Sammy Sosa	1.50
18	Steve Trachsel	.10
19	Logo Card	.10
20	Checklist	.10

Chicago White Sox Team Set: 4.00

1	Wilson Alvarez	.10
2	Harold Baines	.10
3	Jason Bere	.10
4	Ray Durham	.10
5	Alex Fernandez	.10
6	Ozzie Guillen	.10
7	Roberto Hernandez	.10
8	Matt Karchner	.10
9	Ron Karkovice	.10
10	Darren Lewis	.10
11	Dave Martinez	.10
12	Lyle Mouton	.10
13	Tony Phillips	.10
14	Chris Snopek	.10
15	Kevin Tapani	.10
16	Danny Tartabull	.10
17	Frank Thomas	1.00
18	Robin Ventura	.10
19	Logo Card	.10
20	Checklist	.10

Cleveland Indians Team Set: 4.00

1	Sandy Alomar Jr.	.10
2	Paul Assenmacher	.10
3	Carlos Baerga	.10
4	Albert Belle	.09
5	Orel Hershiser	.10
7	Kenny Lofton	.10
7	Dennis Martinez	.10
8	Jose Mesa	.10
9	Eddie Murray	1.00
10	Charles Nagy	.10
11	Tony Pena	.10
12	Herb Perry	.10
13	Eric Plunk	.10
14	Jim Poole	.10
15	Manny Ramirez	1.00
16	Julian Tavarez	.10
17	Jim Thome	.75
18	Omar Vizquel	.10
19	Logo Card	.10
20	Checklist	.10

Colorado Rockies Team Set: 2.75

1	Jason Bates	.10
2	Dante Bichette	.10
3	Ellis Burks	.10
4	Vinny Castilla	.10
5	Andres Galarraga	.10
6	Darren Holmes	.10
7	Curt Leskanic	.10
8	Quinton McCracken	.10
9	Mike Munoz	.10
10	Jayhawk Owens	.10
11	Steve Reed	.10
12	Kevin Ritz	.10
13	Bret Saberhagen	.10
14	Bill Swift	.10
15	John Vander Wal	.10
16	Larry Walker	.10
17	Walt Weiss	.10
18	Eric Young	.10
19	Logo Card	.10
20	Checklist	.10

L.A. Dodgers Team Set: 4.00

1	Mike Blowers	.10
2	Brett Butler	.10
3	Tom Candiotti	.10
4	Roger Cedeno	.10
5	Delino DeShields	.10
6	Chad Fonville	.10
7	Greg Gagne	.10
8	Karim Garcia	.15
9	Todd Hollandsworth	.10
10	Eric Karros	.10
11	Ramon Martinez	.10
12	Raul Mondesi	.10
13	Hideo Nomo	.75
14	Antonio Osuna	.10
15	Chan Ho Park	.10
16	Mike Piazza	2.00
17	Ismael Valdes	.10
18	Todd Worrell	.10
19	Logo Card	.10
20	Checklist	.10

Texas Rangers Team Set: 2.75

1	Mark Brandenburg	.10
2	Damon Buford	.10
3	Will Clark	.15
4	Kevin Elster	.10
5	Benji Gil	.10
6	Juan Gonzalez	.75
7	Rusty Greer	.10
8	Kevin Gross	.10
9	Darryl Hamilton	.10
10	Ken Hill	.10
11	Mark McLemore	.10
12	Dean Palmer	.10
13	Roger Pavlik	.10
14	Ivan Rodriguez	.75
15	Mickey Tettleton	.10
16	Dave Valle	.10
17	Ed Vosberg	.10
18	Matt Whiteside	.10
19	Logo Card	.10
20	Checklist	.10

Checklists

	NM/M
Complete Set (10):	5.00
Common Player:	.25

1	Barry Bonds	2.00
2	Ken Griffey Jr.	1.00
3	Chipper Jones	.75
4	Greg Maddux	.75
5	Mike Piazza	1.00
6	Manny Ramirez	.60
7	Cal Ripken Jr.	2.00
8	Frank Thomas	.60
9	Mo Vaughn	.25
10	Matt Williams	.25

Golden Memories

	NM/M
Complete Set (10):	6.00
Common Player:	.10

1	Albert Belle	.10
2	Barry Bonds, Sammy Sosa	1.50
3	Greg Maddux	1.00

4	Edgar Martinez	.10
5	Ramon Martinez	.10
6	Mark McGwire	1.50
7	Eddie Murray	.75
8	Cal Ripken Jr.	2.00
9	Frank Thomas	.75
10	Alan Trammell, Lou Whitaker	.15

Lumber Company

	NM/M
Complete Set (12):	12.50
Common Player:	.50

1	Albert Belle	.50
2	Dante Bichette	.50
3	Barry Bonds	3.00
4	Ken Griffey Jr.	1.50
5	Mark McGwire	2.00
6	Mike Piazza	1.50
7	Manny Ramirez	1.00
8	Tim Salmon	.60
9	Sammy Sosa	1.25
10	Frank Thomas	1.00
11	Mo Vaughn	.50
12	Matt Williams	.50

Post-Season Glory

	NM/M
Complete Set (5):	1.50
Common Player:	.15

1	Tom Glavine	.25
2	Ken Griffey Jr.	1.00
3	Orel Hershiser	.15
4	Randy Johnson	.50
5	Jim Thome	.50

Prospects

	NM/M
Complete Set (10):	1.00
Common Player:	.15

1	Yamil Benitez	.15
2	Roger Cedeno	.15
3	Tony Clark	.15
4	Micah Franklin	.15
5	Karim Garcia	.30
6	Todd Greene	.15
7	Alex Ochoa	.15
8	Ruben Rivera	.15
9	Chris Snopek	.15
10	Shannon Stewart	.15

Road Warriors

	NM/M
Complete Set (10):	9.00
Common Player:	.35

1	Derek Bell	.40
2	Tony Gwynn	1.25
3	Greg Maddux	1.25
4	Mark McGwire	2.50
5	Mike Piazza	2.00
6	Manny Ramirez	1.00

7	Tim Salmon	.50
8	Frank Thomas	1.00
9	Mo Vaughn	.40
10	Matt Williams	.40

Rookie Sensations

		NM/M
Complete Set (15):		5.00
Common Player:		.25
1	Garret Anderson	.40
2	Marty Cordova	.25
3	Johnny Damon	1.00
4	Ray Durham	.25
5	Carl Everett	.25
6	Shawn Green	.50
7	Brian Hunter	.25
8	Jason Isringhausen	.25
9	Charles Johnson	.25
10	Chipper Jones	2.00
11	John Mabry	.25
12	Hideo Nomo	.50
13	Troy Percival	.25
14	Andy Pettitte	.50
15	Quilvio Veras	.25

Smoke 'N Heat

		NM/M
Complete Set (10):		4.00
Common Player:		.15
1	Kevin Appier	.15
2	Roger Clemens	1.50
3	David Cone	.15
4	Chuck Finley	.15
5	Randy Johnson	.75
6	Greg Maddux	1.00
7	Pedro Martinez	.75
8	Hideo Nomo	.50
9	John Smoltz	.30
10	Todd Stottlemyre	.15

Team Leaders

		NM/M
Complete Set (28):		30.00
Common Player:		.50
1	Cal Ripken Jr.	6.00
2	Mo Vaughn	.50
3	Jim Edmonds	1.00
4	Frank Thomas	2.00
5	Kenny Lofton	.50

6	Travis Fryman	.50
7	Gary Gaetti	.50
8	B.J. Surhoff	.50
9	Kirby Puckett	2.50
10	Don Mattingly	3.00
11	Mark McGwire	4.00
12	Ken Griffey Jr.	3.00
13	Juan Gonzalez	1.00
14	Joe Carter	.50
15	Greg Maddux	2.50
16	Sammy Sosa	.50
17	Barry Larkin	.50
18	Dante Bichette	.50
19	Jeff Conine	.50
20	Jeff Bagwell	2.00
21	Mike Piazza	3.00
22	Rondell White	.50
23	Rico Brogna	.50
24	Darren Daulton	.50
25	Jeff King	.50
26	Ray Lankford	.50
27	Tony Gwynn	2.50
28	Barry Bonds	6.00

Tomorrow's Legends

		NM/M
Complete Set (10):		3.50
Common Player:		.25
1	Garret Anderson	.25
2	Jim Edmonds	.50
3	Brian Hunter	.25
4	Jason Isringhausen	.25
5	Charles Johnson	.25
6	Chipper Jones	2.00
7	Ryan Klesko	.25
8	Hideo Nomo	1.00
9	Manny Ramirez	1.50
10	Rondell White	.25

Zone

		NM/M
Complete Set (12):		20.00
Common Player:		.75
1	Albert Belle	.75
2	Barry Bonds	6.00
3	Ken Griffey Jr.	4.00
4	Tony Gwynn	3.00
5	Randy Johnson	2.00
6	Kenny Lofton	.75
7	Greg Maddux	3.00
8	Edgar Martinez	.75
9	Mike Piazza	4.00
10	Frank Thomas	2.00
11	Mo Vaughn	.75
12	Matt Williams	.75

Update

		NM/M
Complete Set (250):		12.00
Common Player:		.05

Complete Tiffany Set (250):		40.00
Tiffany Stars:		2X
Pack (11):		1.00
Wax Box (24):		15.00
1	Roberto Alomar	.10
2	Mike Devereaux	.05
3	Scott McClain RC	.05
4	Roger McDowell	.05
5	Kent Mercker	.05
6	Jimmy Myers	.05
7	Randy Myers	.05
8	B.J. Surhoff	.05
9	Tony Tarasco	.05
10	David Wells	.05
11	Wil Cordero	.05
12	Tom Gordon	.05
13	Reggie Jefferson	.05
14	Jose Malave	.05
15	Kevin Mitchell	.05
16	Jamie Moyer	.05
17	Heathcliff Slocumb	.05
18	Mike Stanley	.05
19	George Arias	.05
20	Jorge Fabregas	.05
21	Don Slaught	.05
22	Randy Velarde	.05
23	Harold Baines	.05
24	Mike Cameron RC	.75
25	Darren Lewis	.05
26	Tony Phillips	.05
27	Bill Simas	.05
28	Chris Snopek	.05
29	Kevin Tapani	.05
30	Danny Tartabull	.05
31	Julio Franco	.05
32	Jack McDowell	.05
33	Kimera Bartee	.05
34	Mark Lewis	.05
35	Melvin Nieves	.05
36	Mark Parent	.05
37	Eddie Williams	.05
38	Tim Belcher	.05
39	Sal Fasano	.05
40	Chris Haney	.05
41	Mike Macfarlane	.05
42	Jose Offerman	.05
43	Joe Randa	.05
44	Bip Roberts	.05
45	Chuck Carr	.05
46	Bobby Hughes	.05
47	Graeme Lloyd	.05
48	Ben McDonald	.05
49	Kevin Wickander	.05
50	Rick Aguilera	.05
51	Mike Durant	.05
52	Chip Hale	.05
53	LaTroy Hawkins	.05
54	Dave Hollins	.05
55	Roberto Kelly	.05
56	Paul Molitor	.75
57	Dan Naulty RC	.05
58	Mariano Duncan	.05
59	Andy Fox RC	.05
60	Joe Girardi	.05
61	Dwight Gooden	.05
62	Jimmy Key	.05
63	Matt Luke RC	.05
64	Tino Martinez	.05
65	Jeff Nelson	.05
66	Tim Raines	.05
67	Ruben Rivera	.05
68	Kenny Rogers	.05
69	Gerald Williams	.05
70	Tony Batista RC	.50
71	Allen Battle	.05
72	Jim Corsi	.05
73	Steve Cox	.05
74	Pedro Munoz	.05
75	Phil Plantier	.05
76	Scott Spiezio	.05
77	Ernie Young	.05
78	Russ Davis	.05
79	Sterling Hitchcock	.05
80	Edwin Hurtado	.05
81	Raul Ibanez RC	.05
82	Mike Jackson	.05
83	Ricky Jordan	.05
84	Paul Sorrento	.05
85	Doug Strange	.05
86	Mark Brandenburg	.05
87	Damon Buford	.05
88	Kevin Elster	.05
89	Darryl Hamilton	.05
90	Ken Hill	.05
91	Ed Vosberg	.05
92	Craig Worthington	.05
93	Tilson Brito	.05
94	Giovanni Carrara	.05
95	Felipe Crespo	.05
96	Erik Hanson	.05
97	Marty Janzen RC	.05
98	Otis Nixon	.05
99	Charlie O'Brien	.05
100	Robert Perez	.05

101	Paul Quantrill	.05
102	Bill Risley	.05
103	Juan Samuel	.05
104	Jermaine Dye	.05
105	Wonderful Monds	.05
106	Dwight Smith	.05
107	Jerome Walton	.05
108	Terry Adams	.05
109	Leo Gomez	.05
110	Robin Jennings RC	.05
111	Doug Jones	.05
112	Brooks Kieschnick	.05
113	Dave Magadan	.05
114	Jason Maxwell RC	.05
115	Rodney Myers	.05
116	Eric Anthony	.05
117	Vince Coleman	.05
118	Eric Davis	.05
119	Steve Gibralter	.05
120	Curtis Goodwin	.05
121	Willie Greene	.05
122	Mike Kelly	.05
123	Marcus Moore	.05
124	Chad Mottola	.05
125	Chris Sabo	.05
126	Roger Salkeld	.05
127	Pedro Castellano	.05
128	Trenidad Hubbard	.05
129	Jayhawk Owens	.05
130	Jeff Reed	.05
131	Kevin Brown	.05
132	Al Leiter	.05
133	Matt Mantei RC	.05
134	Dave Weathers	.05
135	Devon White	.05
136	Bob Abreu	.05
137	Sean Berry	.05
138	Doug Brocail	.05
139	Richard Hidalgo	.05
140	Alvin Morman	.05
141	Mike Blowers	.05
142	Roger Cedeno	.05
143	Greg Gagne	.05
144	Karim Garcia	.10
145	Wilton Guerrero RC	.05
146	Israel Alcantara RC	.05
147	Omar Daal	.05
148	Ryan McGuire	.05
149	Sherman Obando	.05
150	Jose Paniagua	.05
151	Henry Rodriguez	.05
152	Andy Stankiewicz	.05
153	Dave Veres	.05
154	Juan Acevedo	.05
155	Mark Clark	.05
156	Bernard Gilkey	.05
157	Pete Harnisch	.05
158	Lance Johnson	.05
159	Brent Mayne	.05
160	Rey Ordonez	.05
161	Kevin Roberson	.05
162	Paul Wilson	.05
163	David Doster RC	.05
164	Mike Grace RC	.05
165	Rich Hunter RC	.05
166	Pete Incaviglia	.05
167	Mike Lieberthal	.05
168	Terry Mulholland	.05
169	Ken Ryan	.05
170	Benito Santiago	.05
171	Kevin Sefcik RC	.05
172	Lee Tinsley	.05
173	Todd Zeile	.05
174	Francisco Cordova RC	.05
175	Danny Darwin	.05
176	Charlie Hayes	.05
177	Jason Kendall	.05
178	Mike Kingery	.05
179	Jon Lieber	.05
180	Zane Smith	.05
181	Luis Alicea	.05
182	Cory Bailey	.05
183	Andy Benes	.05
184	Pat Borders	.05
185	Mike Busby RC	.05
186	Royce Clayton	.05
187	Dennis Eckersley	.65
188	Gary Gaetti	.05
189	Ron Gant	.05
190	Aaron Holbert	.05
191	Willie McGee	.05
192	Miguel Mejia RC	.05
193	Jeff Parrett	.05
194	Todd Stottlemyre	.05
195	Sean Bergman	.05
196	Archi Cianfrocco	.05
197	Rickey Henderson	.75
198	Wally Joyner	.05
199	Craig Shipley	.05
200	Bob Tewksbury	.05
201	Tim Worrell	.05
202	Rich Aurilia RC	.05
203	Doug Creek	.05
204	Shawon Dunston	.05
205	Osvaldo Fernandez RC	.05
206	Mark Gardner	.05

207	Stan Javier	.05
208	Marcus Jensen	.05
209	Chris Singleton RC	.05
210	Allen Watson	.05
211	Jeff Bagwell	.75
212	Derek Bell	.05
213	Albert Belle	.05
214	Wade Boggs	1.00
215	Barry Bonds	2.00
216	Jose Canseco	.50
217	Marty Cordova	.05
218	Jim Edmonds	.05
219	Cecil Fielder	.05
220	Andres Galarraga	.65
221	Juan Gonzalez	.65
222	Mark Grace	.10
223	Ken Griffey Jr.	1.50
224	Tony Gwynn	1.00
225	Jason Isringhausen	.05
226	Derek Jeter	2.00
227	Randy Johnson	.75
228	Chipper Jones	1.00
229	Ryan Klesko	.05
230	Barry Larkin	.05
231	Kenny Lofton	.05
232	Greg Maddux	1.00
233	Raul Mondesi	.05
234	Hideo Nomo	.65
235	Mike Piazza	1.50
236	Manny Ramirez	.75
237	Cal Ripken Jr.	2.00
238	Tim Salmon	.10
239	Ryne Sandberg	1.00
240	Reggie Sanders	.05
241	Gary Sheffield	.30
242	Sammy Sosa	1.25
243	Frank Thomas	.75
244	Mo Vaughn	.05
245	Matt Williams	.05
246	Checklist	.05
247	Checklist	.05
248	Checklist	.05
249	Checklist	.05
250	Checklist	.05

Update Tiffany

	NM/M
Complete Set (250):	45.00
Common Player:	.15
Glossy Stars:	2X

(See 1996 Fleer Update for checklist and base card values.)

Update Diamond Tribute

	NM/M
Complete Set (10):	50.00
Common Player:	4.00
1 Wade Boggs	6.00
2 Barry Bonds	10.00
3 Ken Griffey Jr.	7.50
4 Tony Gwynn	6.00
5 Rickey Henderson	4.00
6 Greg Maddux	6.00
7 Eddie Murray	4.00
8 Cal Ripken Jr.	10.00
9 Ozzie Smith	6.00
10 Frank Thomas	5.00

Update Headliners

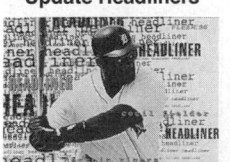

	NM/M
Complete Set (20):	20.00

Common Player:		.25
1	Roberto Alomar	.50
2	Jeff Bagwell	1.00
3	Albert Belle	.25
4	Barry Bonds	3.50
5	Cecil Fielder	.25
6	Juan Gonzalez	.75
7	Ken Griffey Jr.	2.25
8	Tony Gwynn	1.50
9	Randy Johnson	1.00
10	Chipper Jones	1.50
11	Ryan Klesko	.25
12	Kenny Lofton	.25
13	Greg Maddux	1.50
14	Hideo Nomo	.75
15	Mike Piazza	2.25
16	Manny Ramirez	1.00
17	Cal Ripken Jr.	3.50
18	Tim Salmon	.40
19	Frank Thomas	1.00
20	Matt Williams	.05

Update New Horizons

		NM/M
Complete Set (20):		2.00
Common Player:		.25
1	Bob Abreu	.45
2	George Arias	.25
3	Tony Batista	.25
4	Steve Cox	.25
5	David Doster	.25
6	Jermaine Dye	.25
7	Andy Fox	.25
8	Mike Grace	.25
9	Todd Greene	.25
10	Wilton Guerrero	.25
11	Richard Hidalgo	.25
12	Raul Ibanez	.25
13	Robin Jennings	.25
14	Marcus Jensen	.25
15	Jason Kendall	.35
16	Brooks Kieschnick	.25
17	Ryan McGuire	.25
18	Miguel Mejia	.25
19	Rey Ordonez	.25
20	Paul Wilson	.25

Update Smooth Leather

		NM/M
Complete Set (10):		7.00
Common Player:		.40
1	Roberto Alomar	.50
1p	Roberto Alomar (Promo)	2.00
2	Barry Bonds	2.50
3	Will Clark	.45
4	Ken Griffey Jr.	1.75
5	Kenny Lofton	.40
6	Greg Maddux	1.00
7	Raul Mondesi	.40
8	Rey Ordonez	.40
9	Cal Ripken Jr.	2.50
9p	Cal Ripken Jr. (Promo)	6.00
10	Matt Williams	.40

Update Soaring Stars

	NM/M
Complete Set (10):	6.00
Common Player:	.25

1	Jeff Bagwell	.75
2	Barry Bonds	2.00
3	Juan Gonzalez	.75
4	Ken Griffey Jr.	1.50
5	Chipper Jones	1.00
6	Greg Maddux	1.00
7	Mike Piazza	1.50
8	Manny Ramirez	.75
9	Frank Thomas	.75
10	Matt Williams	.25

1997 Fleer

	NM/M
Complete Set (761):	100.00
Complete Series 1 Set (500):	30.00
Complete Series 2 Set (261):	70.00
Common Player:	.05
Complete Tiffany Set (1-761):	500.00
Tiffany Stars/RC's:	8X
A. Jones Circa AU/200:	35.00
Series 2 Pack (10):	3.00
Series 2 Wax Box (36):	90.00

1	Roberto Alomar	.10
2	Brady Anderson	.05
3	Bobby Bonilla	.05
4	Rocky Coppinger	.05
5	Cesar Devarez	.05
6	Scott Erickson	.05
7	Jeffrey Hammonds	.05
8	Chris Hoiles	.05
9	Eddie Murray	1.00
10	Mike Mussina	.40
11	Randy Myers	.05
12	Rafael Palmeiro	.75
13	Cal Ripken Jr.	2.50
14	B.J. Surhoff	.05
15	David Wells	.05
16	Todd Zeile	.05
17	Darren Bragg	.05
18	Jose Canseco	.40
19	Roger Clemens	1.75
20	Wil Cordero	.05
21	Jeff Frye	.05
22	Nomar Garciaparra	1.75
23	Tom Gordon	.05
24	Mike Greenwell	.05
25	Reggie Jefferson	.05
26	Jose Malave	.05
27	Tim Naehring	.05
28	Troy O'Leary	.05
29	Heathcliff Slocumb	.05
30	Mike Stanley	.05
31	John Valentin	.05
32	Mo Vaughn	.05
33	Tim Wakefield	.05
34	Garret Anderson	.05
35	George Arias	.05
36	Shawn Boskie	.05

37	Chili Davis	.05
38	Jason Dickson	.05
39	Gary DiSarcina	.05
40	Jim Edmonds	.05
41	Darin Erstad	.10
42	Jorge Fabregas	.05
43	Chuck Finley	.05
44	Todd Greene	.05
45	Mike Holtz RC	.05
46	Rex Hudler	.05
47	Mike James	.05
48	Mark Langston	.05
49	Troy Percival	.05
50	Tim Salmon	.15
51	Jeff Schmidt	.05
52	J.T. Snow	.05
53	Randy Velarde	.05
54	Wilson Alvarez	.05
55	Harold Baines	.05
56	James Baldwin	.05
57	Jason Bere	.05
58	Mike Cameron	.05
59	Ray Durham	.05
60	Alex Fernandez	.05
61	Ozzie Guillen	.05
62	Roberto Hernandez	.05
63	Ron Karkovice	.05
64	Darren Lewis	.05
65	Dave Martinez	.05
66	Lyle Mouton	.05
67	Greg Norton	.05
68	Tony Phillips	.05
69	Chris Snopek	.05
70	Kevin Tapani	.05
71	Danny Tartabull	.05
72	Frank Thomas	1.00
73	Robin Ventura	.05
74	Sandy Alomar Jr.	.05
75	Albert Belle	.05
76	Mark Carreon	.05
77	Julio Franco	.05
78	Brian Giles RC	1.00
79	Orel Hershiser	.05
80	Kenny Lofton	.05
81	Dennis Martinez	.05
82	Jack McDowell	.05
83	Jose Mesa	.05
84	Charles Nagy	.05
85	Chad Ogea	.05
86	Eric Plunk	.05
87	Manny Ramirez	1.00
88	Kevin Seitzer	.05
89	Julian Tavarez	.05
90	Jim Thome	.65
91	Jose Vizcaino	.05
92	Omar Vizquel	.05
93	Brad Ausmus	.05
94	Kimera Bartee	.05
95	Raul Casanova	.05
96	Tony Clark	.05
97	John Cummings	.05
98	Travis Fryman	.05
99	Bob Higginson	.05
100	Mark Lewis	.05
101	Felipe Lira	.05
102	Phil Nevin	.05
103	Melvin Nieves	.05
104	Curtis Pride	.05
105	A.J. Sager	.05
106	Ruben Sierra	.05
107	Justin Thompson	.05
108	Alan Trammell	.05
109	Kevin Appier	.05
110	Tim Belcher	.05
111	Jaime Bluma	.05
112	Johnny Damon	.35
113	Tom Goodwin	.05
114	Chris Haney	.05
115	Keith Lockhart	.05
116	Mike Macfarlane	.05
117	Jeff Montgomery	.05
118	Jose Offerman	.05
119	Craig Paquette	.05
120	Joe Randa	.05
121	Bip Roberts	.05
122	Jose Rosado	.05
123	Mike Sweeney	.05
124	Michael Tucker	.05
125	Jeromy Burnitz	.05
126	Jeff Cirillo	.05
127	Jeff D'Amico	.05
128	Mike Fetters	.05
129	John Jaha	.05
130	Scott Karl	.05
131	Jesse Levis	.05
132	Mark Loretta	.05
133	Mike Matheny	.05
134	Ben McDonald	.05
135	Matt Mieske	.05
136	Marc Newfield	.05
137	Dave Nilsson	.05
138	Jose Valentin	.05
139	Fernando Vina	.05
140	Bob Wickman	.05

No.	Name	Value	No.	Name	Value	No.	Name	Value	No.	Name	Value
141	Gerald Williams	.05	245	Otis Nixon	.05	349	Darryl Kile	.05	453	Todd Stottlemyre	.05
142	Rick Aguilera	.05	246	Charlie O'Brien	.05	350	Derrick May	.05	454	Mark Sweeney	.05
143	Rich Becker	.05	247	John Olerud	.05	351	Orlando Miller	.05	455	Dmitri Young	.05
144	Ron Coomer	.05	248	Robert Perez	.05	352	James Mouton	.05	456	Andy Ashby	.05
145	Marty Cordova	.05	249	Ed Sprague	.05	353	Shane Reynolds	.05	457	Ken Caminiti	.05
146	Roberto Kelly	.05	250	Mike Timlin	.05	354	Billy Wagner	.05	458	Archi Cianfrocco	.05
147	Chuck Knoblauch	.05	251	Steve Avery	.05	355	Donne Wall	.05	459	Steve Finley	.05
148	Matt Lawton	.05	252	Jeff Blauser	.05	356	Mike Blowers	.05	460	John Flaherty	.05
149	Pat Meares	.05	253	Brad Clontz	.05	357	Brett Butler	.05	461	Chris Gomez	.05
150	Travis Miller	.05	254	Jermaine Dye	.05	358	Roger Cedeno	.05	462	Tony Gwynn	1.50
151	Paul Molitor	1.00	255	Tom Glavine	.30	359	Chad Curtis	.05	463	Joey Hamilton	.05
152	Greg Myers	.05	256	Marquis Grissom	.05	360	Delino DeShields	.05	464	Rickey Henderson	1.00
153	Dan Naulty	.05	257	Andruw Jones	1.00	361	Greg Gagne	.05	465	Trevor Hoffman	.05
154	Kirby Puckett	1.50	258	Chipper Jones	1.50	362	Karim Garcia	.10	466	Brian Johnson	.05
155	Brad Radke	.05	259	David Justice	.05	363	Wilton Guerrero	.05	467	Wally Joyner	.05
156	Frank Rodriguez	.05	260	Ryan Klesko	.05	364	Todd Hollandsworth	.05	468	Jody Reed	.05
157	Scott Stahoviak	.05	261	Mark Lemke	.05	365	Eric Karros	.05	469	Scott Sanders	.05
158	Dave Stevens	.05	262	Javier Lopez	.05	366	Ramon Martinez	.05	470	Bob Tewksbury	.05
159	Matt Walbeck	.05	263	Greg Maddux	1.50	367	Raul Mondesi	.05	471	Fernando Valenzuela	.05
160	Todd Walker	.05	264	Fred McGriff	.05	368	Hideo Nomo	.75	472	Greg Vaughn	.05
161	Wade Boggs	1.50	265	Greg McMichael	.05	369	Antonio Osuna	.05	473	Tim Worrell	.05
162	David Cone	.05	266	Denny Neagle	.05	370	Chan Ho Park	.05	474	Rich Aurilia	.05
163	Mariano Duncan	.05	267	Terry Pendleton	.05	371	Mike Piazza	2.00	475	Rod Beck	.05
164	Cecil Fielder	.05	268	Eddie Perez	.05	372	Ismael Valdes	.05	476	Marvin Benard	.05
165	Joe Girardi	.05	269	John Smoltz	.05	373	Todd Worrell	.05	477	Barry Bonds	2.50
166	Dwight Gooden	.05	270	Terrell Wade	.05	374	Moises Alou	.05	478	Jay Canizaro	.05
167	Charlie Hayes	.05	271	Mark Wohlers	.05	375	Shane Andrews	.05	479	Shawon Dunston	.05
168	Derek Jeter	2.50	272	Terry Adams	.05	376	Yamil Benitez	.05	480	Shawn Estes	.05
169	Jimmy Key	.05	273	Brant Brown	.05	377	Jeff Fassero	.05	481	Mark Gardner	.05
170	Jim Leyritz	.05	274	Leo Gomez	.05	378	Darrin Fletcher	.05	482	Glenallen Hill	.05
171	Tino Martinez	.05	275	Luis Gonzalez	.10	379	Cliff Floyd	.05	483	Stan Javier	.05
172	Ramiro Mendoza RC	.10	276	Mark Grace	.10	380	Mark Grudzielanek	.05	484	Marcus Jensen	.05
173	Jeff Nelson	.05	277	Tyler Houston	.05	381	Mike Lansing	.05	485	Bill Mueller RC	1.50
174	Paul O'Neill	.05	278	Robin Jennings	.05	382	Barry Manuel	.05	486	William Van Landingham	.05
175	Andy Pettitte	.35	279	Brooks Kieschnick	.05	383	Pedro Martinez	1.00	487	Allen Watson	.05
176	Mariano Rivera	.15	280	Brian McRae	.05	384	Henry Rodriguez	.05	488	Rick Wilkins	.05
177	Ruben Rivera	.05	281	Jaime Navarro	.05	385	Mel Rojas	.05	489	Matt Williams	.05
178	Kenny Rogers	.05	282	Ryne Sandberg	1.50	386	F.P. Santangelo	.05	489p	Matt Williams/OPS	1.50
179	Darryl Strawberry	.05	283	Scott Servais	.05	387	David Segui	.05	490	Desi Wilson	.05
180	John Wetteland	.05	284	Sammy Sosa	1.75	388	Ugueth Urbina	.05	491	Albert Belle Checklist	
181	Bernie Williams	.10	285	Dave Swartzbaugh RC	.05	389	Rondell White	.05	492	Ken Griffey Jr. Checklist	.85
182	Willie Adams	.05	286	Amaury Telemaco	.05	390	Edgardo Alfonzo	.05	493	Andruw Jones Checklist	.40
183	Tony Batista	.05	287	Steve Trachsel	.05	391	Carlos Baerga	.05	494	Chipper Jones Checklist	.60
184	Geronimo Berroa	.05	288	Pedro Valdes RC	.05	392	Mark Clark	.05	495	Mark McGwire Checklist	1.00
185	Mike Bordick	.05	289	Turk Wendell	.05	393	Alvaro Espinoza	.05	496	Paul Molitor Checklist	.45
186	Scott Brosius	.05	290	Bret Boone	.05	394	John Franco	.05	497	Mike Piazza Checklist	.85
187	Bobby Chouinard	.05	291	Jeff Branson	.05	395	Bernard Gilkey	.05	498	Cal Ripken Jr. Checklist	1.25
188	Jim Corsi	.05	292	Jeff Brantley	.05	396	Pete Harnisch	.05	499	Alex Rodriguez Checklist	1.00
189	Brent Gates	.05	293	Eric Davis	.05	397	Todd Hundley	.05	500	Frank Thomas Checklist	.45
190	Jason Giambi	.50	294	Willie Greene	.05	398	Butch Huskey	.05	501	Kenny Lofton	.05
191	Jose Herrera	.05	295	Thomas Howard	.05	399	Jason Isringhausen	.05	502	Carlos Perez	.05
192	Damon Mashore RC	.05	296	Barry Larkin	.05	400	Lance Johnson	.05	503	Tim Raines	.05
193	Mark McGwire	2.25	297	Kevin Mitchell	.05	401	Bobby Jones	.05	504	Danny Patterson RC	.05
194	Mike Mohler	.05	298	Hal Morris	.05	402	Alex Ochoa	.05	505	Derrick May	.05
195	Scott Spiezio	.05	299	Chad Mottola	.05	403	Rey Ordonez	.05	506	Dave Hollins	.05
196	Terry Steinbach	.05	300	Joe Oliver	.05	404	Robert Person	.05	507	Felipe Crespo	.05
197	Bill Taylor	.05	301	Mark Portugal	.05	405	Paul Wilson	.05	508	Brian Banks	.05
198	John Wasdin	.05	302	Roger Salkeld	.05	406	Matt Beech	.05	509	Jeff Kent	.05
199	Steve Wojciechowski	.05	303	Reggie Sanders	.05	407	Ron Blazier	.05	510	Bubba Trammell RC	.25
200	Ernie Young	.05	304	Pete Schourek	.05	408	Ricky Bottalico	.05	511	Robert Person	.05
201	Rich Amaral	.05	305	John Smiley	.05	409	Lenny Dykstra	.05	512	David Arias RC (Ortiz)	40.00
202	Jay Buhner	.05	306	Eddie Taubensee	.05	410	Jim Eisenreich	.05	513	Ryan Jones	.05
203	Norm Charlton	.05	307	Dante Bichette	.05	411	Bobby Estalella	.05	514	David Justice	.05
204	Joey Cora	.05	308	Ellis Burks	.05	412	Mike Grace	.05	515	Will Cunnane	.05
205	Russ Davis	.05	309	Vinny Castilla	.05	413	Gregg Jefferies	.05	516	Russ Johnson	.05
206	Ken Griffey Jr.	2.00	310	Andres Galarraga	.05	414	Mike Lieberthal	.05	517	John Burkett	.05
207	Sterling Hitchcock	.05	311	Curt Leskanic	.05	415	Wendell Magee Jr.	.05	518	Robinson Checo RC	.05
208	Brian Hunter	.05	312	Quinton McCracken	.05	416	Mickey Morandini	.05	519	Ricardo Rincon RC	.05
209	Raul Ibanez	.05	313	Neifi Perez	.05	417	Ricky Otero	.05	520	Woody Williams	.05
210	Randy Johnson	1.00	314	Jeff Reed	.05	418	Scott Rolen	.75	521	Rick Helling	.05
211	Edgar Martinez	.05	315	Steve Reed	.05	419	Ken Ryan	.05	522	Jorge Posada	.05
212	Jamie Moyer	.05	316	Armando Reynoso	.05	420	Benito Santiago	.05	523	Kevin Orie	.05
213	Alex Rodriguez	2.25	317	Kevin Ritz	.05	421	Curt Schilling	.25	524	Fernando Tatis RC	.15
214	Paul Sorrento	.05	318	Bruce Ruffin	.05	422	Kevin Sefcik	.05	525	Jermaine Dye	.05
215	Matt Wagner	.05	319	Larry Walker	.05	423	Jermaine Allensworth	.05	526	Brian Hunter	.05
216	Bob Wells	.05	320	Walt Weiss	.05	424	Trey Beamon	.05	527	Greg McMichael	.05
217	Dan Wilson	.05	321	Jamey Wright	.05	425	Jay Bell	.05	528	Matt Wagner	.05
218	Damon Buford	.05	322	Eric Young	.05	426	Francisco Cordova	.05	529	Richie Sexson	.05
219	Will Clark	.10	323	Kurt Abbott	.05	427	Carlos Garcia	.05	530	Scott Ruffcorn	.05
220	Kevin Elster	.05	324	Alex Arias	.05	428	Mark Johnson	.05	531	Luis Gonzalez	.10
221	Juan Gonzalez	.75	325	Kevin Brown	.05	429	Jason Kendall	.05	532	Mike Johnson	.05
222	Rusty Greer	.05	326	Luis Castillo	.05	430	Jeff King	.05	533	Mark Petkovsek	.05
223	Kevin Gross	.05	327	Greg Colbrunn	.05	431	Jon Lieber	.05	534	Doug Drabek	.05
224	Darryl Hamilton	.05	328	Jeff Conine	.05	432	Al Martin	.05	535	Jose Canseco	.40
225	Mike Henneman	.05	329	Andre Dawson	.25	433	Orlando Merced	.05	536	Bobby Bonilla	.05
226	Ken Hill	.05	330	Charles Johnson	.05	434	Ramon Morel	.05	537	J.T. Snow	.05
227	Mark McLemore	.05	331	Al Leiter	.05	435	Matt Ruebel	.05	538	Shawon Dunston	.05
228	Darren Oliver	.05	332	Ralph Milliard	.05	436	Jason Schmidt	.05	539	John Ericks	.05
229	Dean Palmer	.05	333	Robb Nen	.05	437	Marc Wilkins RC	.05	540	Terry Steinbach	.05
230	Roger Pavlik	.05	334	Pat Rapp	.05	438	Alan Benes	.05	541	Jay Bell	.05
231	Ivan Rodriguez	.75	335	Edgar Renteria	.05	439	Andy Benes	.05	542	Joe Borowski	.05
232	Mickey Tettleton	.05	336	Gary Sheffield	.35	440	Royce Clayton	.05	543	David Wells	.05
233	Bobby Witt	.05	337	Devon White	.05	441	Dennis Eckersley	.65	544	Justin Towle RC	.10
234	Jacob Brumfield	.05	338	Bob Abreu	.05	442	Gary Gaetti	.05	545	Mike Blowers	.05
235	Joe Carter	.05	339	Jeff Bagwell	1.00	443	Ron Gant	.05	546	Shannon Stewart	.05
236	Tim Crabtree	.05	340	Derek Bell	.05	444	Aaron Holbert	.05	547	Rudy Pemberton	.05
237	Carlos Delgado	.50	341	Sean Berry	.05	445	Brian Jordan	.05			
238	Huck Flener	.05	342	Craig Biggio	.05	446	Ray Lankford	.05			
239	Alex Gonzalez	.05	343	Doug Drabek	.05	447	John Mabry	.05			
240	Shawn Green	.20	344	Tony Eusebio	.05	448	T.J. Mathews	.05			
241	Juan Guzman	.05	345	Ricky Gutierrez	.05	449	Willie McGee	.05			
242	Pat Hentgen	.05	346	Mike Hampton	.05	450	Donovan Osborne	.05			
243	Marty Janzen	.05	347	Brian Hunter	.05	451	Tom Pagnozzi	.05			
244	Sandy Martinez	.05	348	Todd Jones	.05	452	Ozzie Smith	1.50			

548	Bill Swift	.05
549	Osvaldo Fernandez	.05
550	Eddie Murray	1.00
551	Don Wengert	.05
552	Brad Ausmus	.05
553	Carlos Garcia	.05
554	Jose Guillen	.05
555	Rheal Cormier	.05
556	Doug Brocail	.05
557	Rex Hudler	.05
558	Armando Benitez	.05
559	Elieser Marrero	.05
560	Ricky Ledee RC	.25
561	Bartolo Colon	.05
562	Quilvio Veras	.05
563	Alex Fernandez	.05
564	Darren Dreifort	.05
565	Benji Gil	.05
566	Kent Mercker	.05
567	Glendon Rusch	.05
568	Ramon Tatis RC	.05
569	Roger Clemens	1.75
570	Mark Lewis	.05
571	Emil Brown RC	.05
572	Jaime Navarro	.05
573	Sherman Obando	.05
574	John Wasdin	.05
575	Calvin Maduro	.05
576	Todd Jones	.05
577	Orlando Merced	.05
578	Cal Eldred	.05
579	Mark Gubicza	.05
580	Michael Tucker	.05
581	Tony Saunders RC	.05
582	Garvin Alston	.05
583	Joe Roa	.05
584	Brady Raggio RC	.05
585	Jimmy Key	.05
586	Marc Sagmoen RC	.05
587	Jim Bullinger	.05
588	Yorkis Perez	.05
589	Jose Cruz Jr. RC	.75
590	Mike Stanton	.05
591	Deivi Cruz RC	.25
592	Steve Karsay	.05
593	Mike Trombley	.05
594	Doug Glanville	.05
595	Scott Sanders	.05
596	Thomas Howard	.05
597	T.J. Staton	.05
598	Garrett Stephenson	.05
599	Rico Brogna	.05
600	Albert Belle	.05
601	Jose Vizcaino	.05
602	Chili Davis	.05
603	Shane Mack	.05
604	Jim Eisenreich	.05
605	Todd Zeile	.05
606	Brian Boehringer	.05
607	Paul Shuey	.05
608	Kevin Tapani	.05
609	John Wetteland	.05
610	Jim Leyritz	.05
611	Ray Montgomery	.05
612	Doug Bochtler	.05
613	Wady Almonte	.05
614	Danny Tartabull	.05
615	Orlando Miller	.05
616	Bobby Ayala	.05
617	Tony Graffanino	.05
618	Marc Valdes	.05
619	Ron Villone	.05
620	Derrek Lee	.05
621	Greg Colbrunn	.05
622	Felix Heredia RC	.10
623	Carl Everett	.05
624	Mark Thompson	.05
625	Jeff Granger	.05
626	Damian Jackson	.05
627	Mark Leiter	.05
628	Chris Holt	.05
629	Dario Veras RC	.05
630	Dave Burba	.05
631	Darryl Hamilton	.05
632	Mark Acre	.05
633	Fernando Hernandez	.05
634	Terry Mulholland	.05
635	Dustin Hermanson	.05
636	Delino DeShields	.05
637	Steve Avery	.05
638	Tony Womack RC	.10
639	Mark Whiten	.05
640	Marquis Grissom	.05
641	Xavier Hernandez	.05
642	Eric Davis	.05
643	Bob Tewksbury	.05
644	Dante Powell	.05
645	Carlos Castillo	.05
646	Chris Widger	.05
647	Moises Alou	.05
648	Pat Listach	.05
649	Edgar Ramos	.05
650	Deion Sanders	.05
651	John Olerud	.05

652	Todd Dunwoody	.05
653	Randall Simon RC	.10
654	Dan Carlson	.05
655	Matt Williams	.05
656	Jeff King	.05
657	Luis Alicea	.05
658	Brian Moehler	.05
659	Ariel Prieto	.05
660	Kevin Elster	.05
661	Mark Hutton	.05
662	Aaron Sele	.05
663	Graeme Lloyd	.05
664	John Burke	.05
665	Mel Rojas	.05
666	Sid Fernandez	.05
667	Pedro Astacio	.05
668	Jeff Abbott	.05
669	Darren Daulton	.05
670	Mike Bordick	.05
671	Sterling Hitchcock	.05
672	Damion Easley	.05
673	Armando Reynoso	.05
674	Pat Cline	.05
675	Orlando Cabrera RC	.50
676	Alan Embree	.05
677	Brian Bevil	.05
678	David Weathers	.05
679	Cliff Floyd	.05
680	Joe Randa	.05
681	Bill Haselman	.05
682	Jeff Fassero	.05
683	Matt Morris	.05
684	Mark Portugal	.05
685	Lee Smith	.05
686	Pokey Reese	.05
687	Benito Santiago	.05
688	Brian Johnson	.05
689	Brent Brede RC	.05
690	Shigetosi Hasegawa	.05
691	Julio Santana	.05
692	Steve Kline	.05
693	Julian Tavarez	.05
694	John Hudek	.05
695	Manny Alexander	.05
696	Roberto Alomar	.10
697	Jeff Bagwell	.45
698	Barry Bonds	1.25
699	Ken Caminiti	.05
700	Juan Gonzalez	.35
701	Ken Griffey Jr.	.85
702	Tony Gwynn	.60
703	Derek Jeter	1.25
704	Andruw Jones	.45
705	Chipper Jones	.60
706	Barry Larkin	.05
707	Greg Maddux	.60
708	Mark McGwire	1.00
709	Paul Molitor	.45
710	Hideo Nomo	.35
711	Andy Pettitte	.30
712	Mike Piazza	.85
713	Manny Ramirez	.45
714	Cal Ripken Jr.	1.25
715	Alex Rodriguez	1.00
716	Ryne Sandberg	.60
717	John Smoltz	.05
718	Frank Thomas	.50
719	Mo Vaughn	.25
720	Bernie Williams	.10
721	Tim Salmon Checklist	.05
722	Greg Maddux Checklist	.60
723	Cal Ripken Jr. Checklist	1.25
724	Mo Vaughn Checklist	.05
725	Ryne Sandberg Checklist	.45
726	Frank Thomas Checklist	.50
727	Barry Larkin Checklist	.05
728	Manny Ramirez Checklist	.45
729	Andres Galarraga Checklist	.05
730	Tony Clark Checklist	.05
731	Gary Sheffield Checklist	.20
732	Jeff Bagwell Checklist	.40
733	Kevin Appier Checklist	.05
734	Mike Piazza Checklist	.85
735	Jeff Cirillo Checklist	.05
736	Paul Molitor Checklist	.40
737	Henry Rodriguez Checklist	.05
738	Todd Hundley Checklist	.05
739	Derek Jeter Checklist	1.25
740	Mark McGwire Checklist	1.00
741	Curt Schilling Checklist	.15
742	Jason Kendall Checklist	.05
743	Tony Gwynn Checklist	.60
744	Barry Bonds Checklist	1.25
745	Ken Griffey Jr. Checklist	.85

746	Brian Jordan Checklist	.05
747	Juan Gonzalez Checklist	.40
748	Joe Carter Checklist	.05
749	Arizona Diamondbacks	.05
750	Tampa Bay Devil Rays	.05
751	Hideki Irabu RC	.15
752	Jeremi Gonzalez RC	.15
753	Mario Valdez RC	.05
754	Aaron Boone	.05
755	Brett Tomko	.05
756	Jaret Wright RC	1.00
757	Ryan McGuire	.05
758	Jason McDonald	.05
759	Adrian Brown RC	.05
760	Keith Foulke RC	.25
761	Checklist	.05

Tiffany

	NM/M
Complete Set (761):	500.00
Common Player:	1.00
Stars/Rcs:	8X

(See 1997 Fleer for checklist
and base card values.)

512	David Arias (Ortiz)	140.00

Bleacher Blasters

		NM/M
Complete Set (10):		40.00
Common Player:		1.50
1	Albert Belle	1.50
2	Barry Bonds	10.00
3	Juan Gonzalez	2.00
4	Ken Griffey Jr.	6.00
5	Mark McGwire	8.00
6	Mike Piazza	6.00
7	Alex Rodriguez	8.00
8	Frank Thomas	4.00
9	Mo Vaughn	1.50
10	Matt Williams	1.50

Decade of Excellence

		NM/M
Complete Set (12):		35.00
Common Player:		1.50
Rare Tradition:		12X
1	Wade Boggs	4.50
2	Barry Bonds	9.00
3	Roger Clemens	6.00
4	Tony Gwynn	4.50
5	Rickey Henderson	3.00
6	Greg Maddux	4.50
7	Mark McGwire	6.00
8	Paul Molitor	3.00
9	Eddie Murray	3.00
10	Cal Ripken Jr.	9.00
11	Ryne Sandberg	4.50
12	Matt Williams	1.50

Diamond Tribute

		NM/M
Complete Set (12):		120.00
Common Player:		3.00
1	Albert Belle	3.00
2	Barry Bonds	20.00
3	Juan Gonzalez	5.00
4	Ken Griffey Jr.	12.50
5	Tony Gwynn	10.00
6	Greg Maddux	10.00
7	Mark McGwire	15.00
8	Eddie Murray	8.00
9	Mike Piazza	12.50
10	Cal Ripken Jr.	20.00
11	Alex Rodriguez	15.00
12	Frank Thomas	8.00

Golden Memories

		NM/M
Complete Set (10):		6.00
Common Player:		.25
1	Barry Bonds	2.00
2	Dwight Gooden	.25
3	Todd Hundley	.25
4	Mark McGwire	1.50
5	Paul Molitor	.75
6	Eddie Murray	.75
7	Hideo Nomo	.50
8	Mike Piazza	1.25
9	Cal Ripken Jr.	2.00
10	Ozzie Smith	1.00

Goudey Greats

		NM/M
Complete Set (15):		20.00
Common Player:		.50
Foils:		15X
1	Barry Bonds	4.00
2	Ken Griffey Jr.	3.00
3	Tony Gwynn	2.00
4	Derek Jeter	4.00
5	Chipper Jones	2.00
6	Kenny Lofton	.50
7	Greg Maddux	2.00
8	Mark McGwire	3.50
9	Eddie Murray	1.50
10	Mike Piazza	3.00
11	Cal Ripken Jr.	4.00
12	Alex Rodriguez	3.50
13	Ryne Sandberg	2.00
14	Frank Thomas	1.50
15	Mo Vaughn	.50

Headliners

		NM/M
Complete Set (20):		5.00
Common Player:		.10
1	Jeff Bagwell	.25
2	Albert Belle	.10
3	Barry Bonds	1.00
4	Ken Caminiti	.10
5	Juan Gonzalez	.20
6	Ken Griffey Jr.	.60
7	Tony Gwynn	.40
8	Derek Jeter	1.00
9	Andruw Jones	.25
10	Chipper Jones	.40
11	Greg Maddux	.40
12	Mark McGwire	.75
13	Paul Molitor	.25
14	Eddie Murray	.25
15	Mike Piazza	.60

16	Cal Ripken Jr.	1.00
17	Alex Rodriguez	.75
18	Ryne Sandberg	.40
19	John Smoltz	.20
20	Frank Thomas	.25

Lumber Company

		NM/M
Complete Set (18):		45.00
Common Player:		1.00
1	Brady Anderson	1.00
2	Jeff Bagwell	3.00
3	Albert Belle	1.00
4	Barry Bonds	8.00
5	Jay Buhner	1.00
6	Ellis Burks	1.00
7	Andres Galarraga	1.00
8	Juan Gonzalez	2.00
9	Ken Griffey Jr.	5.00
10	Todd Hundley	1.00
11	Ryan Klesko	1.00
12	Mark McGwire	6.00
13	Mike Piazza	5.00
14	Alex Rodriguez	6.00
15	Gary Sheffield	2.00
16	Sammy Sosa	4.00
17	Frank Thomas	3.00
18	Mo Vaughn	1.00

New Horizons

		NM/M
Complete Set (15):		2.00
Common Player:		.05
1	Bob Abreu	.10
2	Jose Cruz Jr.	.05
3	Darin Erstad	.10
4	Nomar Garciaparra	.75
5	Vladimir Guerrero	.60
6	Wilton Guerrero	.05
7	Jose Guillen	.05
8	Hideki Irabu	.05
9	Andruw Jones	.60
10	Kevin Orie	.05
11	Scott Rolen	.50
12	Scott Spiezio	.05
13	Bubba Trammell	.05
14	Todd Walker	.05
15	Dmitri Young	.05

Night & Day

		NM/M
Complete Set (10):		45.00
Common Player:		1.00
1	Barry Bonds	12.00
2	Ellis Burks	1.00
3	Juan Gonzalez	2.00
4	Ken Griffey Jr.	6.00
5	Mark McGwire	7.50
6	Mike Piazza	6.00
7	Manny Ramirez	4.00
8	Alex Rodriguez	8.00
9	John Smoltz	2.00
10	Frank Thomas	4.00

Rookie Sensations

		NM/M
Complete Set (20):		6.00
Common Player:		.25
1	Jermaine Allensworth	.25
2	James Baldwin	.25

3	Alan Benes	.25
4	Jermaine Dye	.25
5	Darin Erstad	.50
6	Todd Hollandsworth	.25
7	Derek Jeter	2.50
8	Jason Kendall	.25
9	Alex Ochoa	.25
10	Rey Ordonez	.25
11	Edgar Renteria	.25
12	Bob Abreu	.50
13	Nomar Garciaparra	1.50
14	Wilton Guerrero	.25
15	Andruw Jones	1.00
16	Wendell Magee	.25
17	Neifi Perez	.25
18	Scott Rolen	.75
19	Scott Spiezio	.25
20	Todd Walker	.25

Soaring Stars

		NM/M
Complete Set (12):		10.00
Common Player:		.25
Glowing:		6X
1	Albert Belle	.25
2	Barry Bonds	2.00
3	Juan Gonzalez	.50
4	Ken Griffey Jr.	1.25
5	Derek Jeter	2.00
6	Andruw Jones	.60
7	Chipper Jones	1.00
8	Greg Maddux	1.00
9	Mark McGwire	1.50
10	Mike Piazza	1.25
11	Alex Rodriguez	1.50
12	Frank Thomas	.75

Team Leaders

		NM/M
Complete Set (28):		25.00
Common Player:		.25
1	Cal Ripken Jr.	5.00
2	Mo Vaughn	.25
3	Jim Edmonds	.40
4	Frank Thomas	1.50
5	Albert Belle	.25
6	Bob Higginson	.25
7	Kevin Appier	.25
8	John Jaha	.25

9	Paul Molitor	1.50
10	Andy Pettitte	.65
11	Mark McGwire	4.00
12	Ken Griffey Jr.	3.00
13	Juan Gonzalez	.75
14	Pat Hentgen	.25
15	Chipper Jones	2.00
16	Mark Grace	.35
17	Barry Larkin	.25
18	Ellis Burks	.25
19	Gary Sheffield	.60
20	Jeff Bagwell	1.50
21	Mike Piazza	3.00
22	Henry Rodriguez	.25
23	Todd Hundley	.25
24	Curt Schilling	.60
25	Jeff King	.25
26	Brian Jordan	.25
27	Tony Gwynn	1.50
28	Barry Bonds	5.00

Zone

		NM/M
Complete Set (20):		80.00
Common Player:		1.50
1	Jeff Bagwell	5.00
2	Albert Belle	1.50
3	Barry Bonds	15.00
4	Ken Caminiti	1.50
5	Andres Galarraga	1.50
6	Juan Gonzalez	2.50
7	Ken Griffey Jr.	8.00
8	Tony Gwynn	6.00
9	Chipper Jones	6.00
10	Greg Maddux	6.00
11	Mark McGwire	10.00
12	Dean Palmer	1.50
13	Andy Pettitte	3.00
14	Mike Piazza	8.00
15	Alex Rodriguez	12.00
16	Gary Sheffield	2.50
17	John Smoltz	2.50
18	Frank Thomas	5.00
19	Jim Thome	4.00
20	Matt Williams	1.50

1998 Fleer

		NM/M
Complete Set (600):		65.00
Complete Series 1 (350):		40.00
Complete Series 2 (250):		25.00
Common Player:		.05
Series 1 or 2 Pack (10):		1.00
Series 1 or 2 Wax Box (36):		20.00
1	Ken Griffey Jr.	1.50
2	Derek Jeter	2.50
3	Gerald Williams	.05
4	Carlos Delgado	.50
5	Nomar Garciaparra	1.50

6	Gary Sheffield	.30
7	Jeff King	.05
8	Cal Ripken Jr.	2.50
9	Matt Williams	.05
10	Chipper Jones	1.00
11	Chuck Knoblauch	.05
12	Mark Grudzielanek	.05
13	Edgardo Alfonzo	.05
14	Andres Galarraga	.05
15	Tim Salmon	.15
16	Reggie Sanders	.05
17	Tony Clark	.05
18	Jason Kendall	.05
19	Juan Gonzalez	.65
20	Ben Grieve	.10
21	Roger Clemens	1.25
22	Raul Mondesi	.05
23	Robin Ventura	.05
24	Derek Lee	.05
25	Mark McGwire	2.00
26	Luis Gonzalez	.10
27	Kevin Brown	.05
28	Kirk Rueter	.05
29	Bobby Estalella	.05
30	Shawn Green	.35
31	Greg Maddux	1.00
32	Jorge Velandia	.05
33	Larry Walker	.05
34	Joey Cora	.05
35	Frank Thomas	.85
36	Curtis King RC	.05
37	Aaron Boone	.05
38	Curt Schilling	.25
39	Bruce Aven	.05
40	Ben McDonald	.05
41	Andy Ashby	.05
42	Jason McDonald	.05
43	Eric Davis	.05
44	Mark Grace	.10
45	Pedro Martinez	.75
46	Lou Collier	.05
47	Chan Ho Park	.05
48	Shane Halter	.05
49	Brian Hunter	.05
50	Jeff Bagwell	.75
51	Bernie Williams	.10
52	J.T. Snow	.05
53	Todd Greene	.05
54	Shannon Stewart	.05
55	Darren Bragg	.05
56	Fernando Tatis	.05
57	Darryl Kile	.05
58	Chris Stynes	.05
59	Javier Valentin	.05
60	Brian McRae	.05
61	Tom Evans	.05
62	Randall Simon	.05
63	Darrin Fletcher	.05
64	Jaret Wright	.05
65	Luis Ordaz	.05
66	Jose Canseco	.40
67	Edgar Renteria	.05
68	Jay Buhner	.05
69	Paul Konerko	.10
70	Adrian Brown	.05
71	Chris Carpenter	.05
72	Mike Lieberthal	.05
73	Dean Palmer	.05
74	Jorge Fabregas	.05
75	Stan Javier	.05
76	Damion Easley	.05
77	David Cone	.05
78	Aaron Sele	.05
79	Antonio Alfonseca	.05
80	Bobby Jones	.05
81	David Justice	.05
82	Jeffrey Hammonds	.05
83	Doug Glanville	.05
84	Jason Dickson	.05
85	Brad Radke	.05
86	David Segui	.05
87	Greg Vaughn	.05
88	Mike Cather RC	.05
89	Alex Fernandez	.05
90	Billy Taylor	.05
91	Jason Schmidt	.05
92	Mike DeJean RC	.05
93	Domingo Cedeno	.05
94	Jeff Cirillo	.05
95	Manny Aybar RC	.10
96	Jaime Navarro	.05
97	Dennis Reyes	.05
98	Barry Larkin	.05
99	Troy O'Leary	.05
100	Alex Rodriguez	2.00
100p	Alex Rodriguez/OPS	2.00
101	Pat Hentgen	.05
102	Bubba Trammell	.06
103	Glendon Rusch	.05
104	Kenny Lofton	.05
105	Craig Biggio	.05
106	Kelvim Escobar	.05
107	Mark Kotsay	.05
108	Rondell White	.05

#	Player	Value	#	Player	Value	#	Player	Value	#	Player	Value
109	Darren Oliver	.05	215	Heath Murray	.05	321	Jeff Bagwell	.60	421	Felix Rodriguez	.05
110	Jim Thome	.65	216	Jose Vidro	.05	322	Albert Belle	.15	422	Bip Roberts	.05
111	Rich Becker	.05	217	Jim Edmonds	.05	323	Barry Bonds	1.50	423	Ken Hill	.05
112	Chad Curtis	.05	218	Shawon Dunston	.05	324	Jay Buhner	.15	424	Jermaine Allensworth	.05
113	Dave Hollins	.05	219	Homer Bush	.05	325	Tony Clark	.15	425	Esteban Yan	.05
114	Bill Mueller	.05	220	Midre Cummings	.05	326	Jose Cruz Jr.	.15	426	Scott Karl	.05
115	Antone Williamson	.05	221	Tony Saunders	.05	327	Andres Galarraga	.15	427	Sean Berry	.05
116	Tony Womack	.05	222	Jeromy Burnitz	.05	328	Juan Gonzalez	.30	428	Rafael Medina	.05
117	Randy Myers	.05	223	Enrique Wilson	.05	329	Ken Griffey Jr.	.85	429	Javier Vazquez	.05
118	Rico Brogna	.05	224	Chili Davis	.05	330	Andruw Jones	.60	430	Rickey Henderson	.75
119	Pat Watkins	.05	225	Jerry DiPoto	.05	331	Tino Martinez	.15	431	Adam Butler RC	.05
120	Eli Marrero	.05	226	Dante Powell	.05	332	Mark McGwire	1.00	432	Todd Stottlemyre	.05
121	Jay Bell	.05	227	Javier Lopez	.05	333	Rafael Palmeiro	.50	433	Yamil Benitez	.05
122	Kevin Tapani	.05	228	Kevin Polcovich RC	.10	334	Mike Piazza	.85	434	Sterling Hitchcock	.05
123	Todd Erdos RC	.10	229	Deion Sanders	.05	335	Manny Ramirez	.65	435	Paul Sorrento	.05
124	Neifi Perez	.05	230	Jimmy Key	.05	336	Alex Rodriguez	1.00	436	Bobby Ayala	.05
125	Todd Hundley	.05	231	Rusty Greer	.05	337	Frank Thomas	.65	437	Tim Raines	.05
126	Jeff Abbott	.05	232	Reggie Jefferson	.05	338	Jim Thome	.65	438	Chris Hoiles	.05
127	Todd Zeile	.05	233	Ron Coomer	.05	339	Mo Vaughn	.15	439	Rod Beck	.05
128	Travis Fryman	.05	234	Bobby Higginson	.05	340	Larry Walker	.15	440	Donnie Sadler	.05
129	Sandy Alomar	.05	235	Magglio Ordonez RC	2.00	341	Jose Cruz Jr. Checklist	.15	441	Charles Johnson	.05
130	Fred McGriff	.05	236	Miguel Tejada	.25	342	Ken Griffey Jr.		442	Russ Ortiz	.05
131	Richard Hidalgo	.05	237	Rick Gorecki	.05		Checklist	.65	443	Pedro Astacio	.05
132	Scott Spiezio	.05	238	Charles Johnson	.05	343	Derek Jeter Checklist	1.00	444	Wilson Alvarez	.05
133	John Valentin	.05	239	Lance Johnson	.05	344	Andruw Jones		445	Mike Blowers	.05
134	Quilvio Veras	.05	240	Derek Bell	.05		Checklist	.40	446	Todd Zeile	.05
135	Mike Lansing	.05	241	Will Clark	.10	345	Chipper Jones		447	Mel Rojas	.05
136	Paul Molitor	.75	242	Brady Raggio	.05		Checklist	.50	448	F.P. Santangelo	.05
137	Randy Johnson	.75	243	Orel Hershiser	.05	346	Greg Maddux Checklist	.50	449	Dmitri Young	.05
138	Harold Baines	.05	244	Vladimir Guerrero	.75	347	Mike Piazza Checklist	.65	450	Brian Anderson	.05
139	Doug Jones	.05	245	John LeRoy	.05	348	Cal Ripken Jr.		451	Cecil Fielder	.05
140	Abraham Nunez	.05	246	Shawn Estes	.05		Checklist	1.00	452	Roberto Hernandez	.05
141	Alan Benes	.05	247	Brett Tomko	.05	349	Alex Rodriguez		453	Todd Walker	.05
142	Matt Perisho	.05	248	Dave Nilsson	.05		Checklist	.75	454	Tyler Green	.05
143	Chris Clemons	.05	249	Edgar Martinez	.05	350	Frank Thomas		455	Jorge Posada	.05
144	Andy Pettitte	.30	250	Tony Gwynn	1.00		Checklist	.45	456	Geronimo Berroa	.05
145	Jason Giambi	.40	251	Mark Bellhorn	.05	351	Mo Vaughn	.05	457	Jose Silva	.05
146	Moises Alou	.05	252	Jed Hansen	.05	352	Andres Galarraga	.05	458	Bobby Bonilla	.05
147	Chad Fox RC	.05	253	Butch Huskey	.05	353	Roberto Alomar	.10	459	Walt Weiss	.05
148	Felix Martinez	.05	254	Eric Young	.05	354	Darin Erstad	.10	460	Darren Dreifort	.05
149	Carlos Mendoza RC	.05	255	Vinny Castilla	.05	355	Albert Belle	.05	461	B.J. Surhoff	.05
150	Scott Rolen	.65	256	Hideki Irabu	.05	356	Matt Williams	.05	462	Quinton McCracken	.05
151	Jose Cabrera RC	.05	257	Mike Cameron	.05	357	Darryl Kile	.05	463	Derek Lowe	.05
152	Justin Thompson	.05	258	Juan Encarnacion	.05	358	Kenny Lofton	.05	464	Jorge Fabregas	.05
153	Ellis Burks	.05	259	Brian Rose	.05	359	Orel Hershiser	.05	465	Joey Hamilton	.05
154	Pokey Reese	.05	260	Brad Ausmus	.05	360	Bob Abreu	.05	466	Brian Jordan	.05
155	Bartolo Colon	.05	261	Dan Serafini	.05	361	Chris Widger	.05	467	Allen Watson	.05
156	Ray Durham	.05	262	Willie Greene	.05	362	Glenallen Hill	.05	468	John Jaha	.05
157	Ugueth Urbina	.05	263	Troy Percival	.05	363	Chili Davis	.05	469	Heathcliff Slocumb	.05
158	Tom Goodwin	.05	264	Jeff Wallace RC	.05	364	Kevin Brown	.05	470	Gregg Jefferies	.05
159	David Dellucci RC	.25	265	Richie Sexson	.05	365	Marquis Grissom	.05	471	Scott Brosius	.05
160	Rod Beck	.05	266	Rafael Palmeiro	.65	366	Livan Hernandez	.05	472	Chad Ogea	.05
161	Ramon Martinez	.05	267	Brad Fullmer	.05	367	Moises Alou	.05	473	A.J. Hinch	.05
162	Joe Carter	.05	268	Jeremi Gonzalez	.05	368	Matt Lawton	.05	474	Bobby Smith	.05
163	Kevin Orie	.05	269	Rob Stanifer RC	.05	369	Rey Ordonez	.05	475	Brian Moehler	.05
164	Trevor Hoffman	.05	270	Mickey Morandini	.05	370	Kenny Rogers	.05	476	DaRond Stovall	.05
165	Emil Brown	.05	271	Andruw Jones	.75	371	Lee Stevens	.05	477	Kevin Young	.05
166	Robb Nen	.05	272	Royce Clayton	.05	372	Wade Boggs	1.00	478	Jeff Suppan	.05
167	Paul O'Neill	.05	273	Takashi Kashiwada	.05	373	Luis Gonzalez	.05	479	Marty Cordova	.05
168	Ryan Long	.05	274	Steve Woodard RC	.10	374	Jeff Conine	.05	480	John Halama RC	.25
169	Ray Lankford	.05	275	Jose Cruz Jr.	.05	375	Esteban Loaiza	.05	481	Bubba Trammell	.05
170	Ivan Rodriguez	.65	276	Keith Foulke	.05	376	Jose Canseco	.40	482	Mike Caruso	.05
171	Rick Aguilera	.05	277	Brad Rigby	.05	377	Henry Rodriguez	.05	483	Eric Karros	.05
172	Deivi Cruz	.05	278	Tino Martinez	.05	378	Dave Burba	.05	484	Jamey Wright	.05
173	Ricky Bottalico	.05	279	Todd Jones	.05	379	Todd Hollandsworth	.05	485	Mike Sweeney	.05
174	Garret Anderson	.05	280	John Wetteland	.05	380	Ron Gant	.05	486	Aaron Sele	.05
175	Jose Vizcaino	.05	281	Alex Gonzalez	.05	381	Pedro Martinez	.75	487	Cliff Floyd	.05
176	Omar Vizquel	.05	282	Ken Cloude	.05	382	Ryan Klesko	.05	488	Jeff Brantley	.05
177	Jeff Blauser	.05	283	Jose Guillen	.05	383	Derrek Lee	.05	489	Jim Leyritz	.05
178	Orlando Cabrera	.05	284	Danny Clyburn	.05	384	Doug Glanville	.05	490	Denny Neagle	.05
179	Russ Johnson	.05	285	David Ortiz	.05	385	David Wells	.05	491	Travis Fryman	.05
180	Matt Stairs	.05	286	John Thomson	.05	386	Ken Caminiti	.05	492	Carlos Baerga	.05
181	Will Cunnane	.05	287	Kevin Appier	.05	387	Damon Hollins	.05	493	Eddie Taubensee	.05
182	Adam Riggs	.05	288	Ismael Valdes	.05	388	Manny Ramirez	.75	494	Darryl Strawberry	.05
183	Matt Morris	.05	289	Gary DiSarcina	.05	389	Mike Mussina	.45	495	Brian Johnson	.05
184	Mario Valdez	.05	290	Todd Dunwoody	.05	390	Jay Bell	.05	496	Randy Myers	.05
185	Larry Sutton	.05	291	Wally Joyner	.05	391	Mike Piazza	1.50	497	Jeff Blauser	.05
186	Marc Pisciotta RC	.05	292	Charles Nagy	.05	392	Mike Lansing	.05	498	Jason Wood	.05
187	Dan Wilson	.05	293	Jeff Shaw	.05	393	Mike Hampton	.05	499	Rolando Arrojo RC	.25
188	John Franco	.05	294	Kevin Millwood RC	1.00	394	Geoff Jenkins	.05	500	Johnny Damon	.05
189	Darren Daulton	.05	295	Rigo Beltran RC	.05	395	Jimmy Haynes	.05	501	Jose Mercedes	.05
190	Todd Helton	.75	296	Jeff Frye	.05	396	Scott Servais	.05	502	Tony Batista	.05
191	Brady Anderson	.05	297	Oscar Henriquez	.05	397	Kent Mercker	.05	503	Mike Piazza	1.50
192	Ricardo Rincon	.05	298	Mike Thurman	.05	398	Jeff Kent	.05	504	Hideo Nomo	.65
193	Kevin Stocker	.05	299	Garrett Stephenson	.05	399	Kevin Elster	.05	505	Chris Gomez	.05
194	Jose Valentin	.05	300	Barry Bonds	2.50	400	Masato Yoshii RC	.50	506	Jesus Sanchez RC	.05
195	Ed Sprague	.05	301	Roger Clemens	.75	401	Jose Vizcaino	.05	507	Al Martin	.05
196	Ryan McGuire	.05	302	David Cone	.05	402	Javier Martinez	.05	508	Brian Edmondson	.05
197	Scott Eyre RC	.05	303	Hideki Irabu	.05	403	David Segui	.05	509	Joe Girardi	.05
198	Steve Finley	.05	304	Randy Johnson	.40	404	Tony Saunders	.05	510	Shayne Bennett	.05
199	T.J. Mathews	.05	305	Greg Maddux	.50	405	Karim Garcia	.05	511	Joe Carter	.05
200	Mike Piazza	1.50	306	Pedro Martinez	.35	406	Armando Benitez	.05	512	Dave Mlicki	.05
201	Mark Wohlers	.05	307	Mike Mussina	.25	407	Joe Randa	.05	513	Rich Butler RC	.10
202	Brian Giles	.05	308	Andy Pettitte	.15	408	Vic Darensbourg	.05	514	Dennis Eckersley	.65
203	Eduardo Perez	.05	309	Curt Schilling	.10	409	Sean Casey	.20	515	Travis Lee	.10
204	Shigetosi Hasegawa	.05	310	John Smoltz	.05	410	Eric Milton	.05	516	John Mabry	.05
205	Mariano Rivera	.15	311	Roger Clemens	1.00	411	Trey Moore	.05	517	Jose Mesa	.05
206	Jose Rosado	.05	312	Jose Cruz Jr.	.25	412	Mike Stanley	.05	518	Phil Nevin	.05
207	Michael Coleman	.05	313	Nomar Garciaparra	1.00	413	Tom Gordon	.05	519	Raul Casanova	.05
208	James Baldwin	.05	314	Ken Griffey Jr.	1.00	414	Hal Morris	.05	520	Mike Fetters	.05
209	Russ Davis	.05	315	Tony Gwynn	.75	415	Braden Looper	.05	521	Gary Sheffield	.30
210	Billy Wagner	.05	316	Hideki Irabu	.25	416	Mike Kelly	.05	522	Terry Steinbach	.05
211	Sammy Sosa	1.50	317	Randy Johnson	.60	417	John Smoltz	.05	523	Steve Trachsel	.05
212	Frank Catalanotto RC	.15	318	Mark McGwire	1.50	418	Roger Cedeno	.05	524	Josh Booty	.05
213	Delino DeShields	.05	319	Curt Schilling	.35	419	Al Leiter	.05	525	Darryl Hamilton	.05
214	John Olerud	.05	320	Larry Walker	.15	420	Chuck Knoblauch	.05	526	Mark McLemore	.05

527	Kevin Stocker	.05
528	Bret Boone	.05
529	Shane Andrews	.05
530	Robb Nen	.05
531	Carl Everett	.05
532	LaTroy Hawkins	.05
533	Fernando Vina	.05
534	Michael Tucker	.05
535	Mark Langston	.05
536	Mickey Mantle	2.00
537	Bernard Gilkey	.05
538	Francisco Cordova	.05
539	Mike Bordick	.05
540	Fred McGriff	.05
541	Cliff Politte	.05
542	Jason Varitek	.05
543	Shawon Dunston	.05
544	Brian Meadows	.05
545	Pat Meares	.05
546	Carlos Perez	.05
547	Desi Relaford	.05
548	Antonio Osuna	.05
549	Devon White	.05
550	Sean Runyan	.05
551	Mickey Morandini	.05
552	Dave Martinez	.05
553	Jeff Fassero	.05
554	Ryan Jackson RC	.05
555	Stan Javier	.05
556	Jaime Navarro	.05
557	Jose Offerman	.05
558	Mike Lowell RC	.50
559	Darrin Fletcher	.05
560	Mark Lewis	.05
561	Dante Bichette	.05
562	Chuck Finley	.05
563	Kerry Wood	.35
564	Andy Benes	.05
565	Freddy Garcia	.05
566	Tom Glavine	.25
567	Jon Nunnally	.05
568	Miguel Cairo	.05
569	Shane Reynolds	.05
570	Roberto Kelly	.05
571	Jose Cruz Jr. Checklist	.25
572	Ken Griffey Jr. Checklist	.65
573	Mark McGwire Checklist	.75
574	Cal Ripken Jr. Checklist	1.00
575	Frank Thomas Checklist	.45
576	Jeff Bagwell	1.00
577	Barry Bonds	3.00
578	Tony Clark	.25
579	Roger Clemens	2.00
580	Jose Cruz Jr.	.25
581	Nomar Garciaparra	1.50
582	Juan Gonzalez	1.00
583	Ben Grieve	.25
584	Ken Griffey Jr.	2.00
585	Tony Gwynn	1.50
586	Derek Jeter	3.00
587	Randy Johnson	1.00
588	Chipper Jones	1.50
589	Greg Maddux	1.50
590	Mark McGwire	2.50
591	Andy Pettitte	.45
592	Paul Molitor	1.00
593	Cal Ripken Jr.	3.00
594	Alex Rodriguez	2.50
595	Scott Rolen	.50
596	Curt Schilling	.50
597	Frank Thomas	1.25
598	Jim Thome	.75
599	Larry Walker	.25
600	Bernie Williams	.30

Decade of Excellence

		NM/M
Complete Set (12):		35.00
Common Player:		1.00
Inserted 1:72		

Rare Traditions: 3X
Inserted 1:720

1	Roberto Alomar	1.50
2	Barry Bonds	8.00
3	Roger Clemens	5.00
4	David Cone	1.00
5	Andres Galarraga	1.00
6	Mark Grace	1.00
7	Tony Gwynn	4.00
8	Randy Johnson	3.00
9	Greg Maddux	4.00
10	Mark McGwire	6.00
11	Paul O'Neill	1.00
12	Cal Ripken Jr.	8.00

Diamond Standouts

Chipper Jones
DIAMOND STANDOUTS

		NM/M
Complete Set (20):		25.00
Common Player:		.50
1	Jeff Bagwell	1.00
2	Barry Bonds	4.00
3	Roger Clemens	2.00
4	Jose Cruz Jr.	.50
5	Andres Galarraga	.50
6	Nomar Garciaparra	2.00
7	Juan Gonzalez	.75
8	Ken Griffey Jr.	2.00
9	Derek Jeter	4.00
10	Randy Johnson	1.00
11	Chipper Jones	1.50
12	Kenny Lofton	.50
13	Greg Maddux	1.50
14	Pedro Martinez	1.00
15	Mark McGwire	3.00
16	Mike Piazza	2.00
17	Alex Rodriguez	3.00
18	Curt Schilling	.75
19	Frank Thomas	1.00
20	Larry Walker	.50

Diamond Tribute

Diamond Tribute
MIKE PIAZZA

		NM/M
Complete Set (10):		90.00
Common Player:		5.00
DT1	Jeff Bagwell	7.50
DT2	Roger Clemens	10.00
DT3	Nomar Garciaparra	10.00
DT4	Juan Gonzalez	5.00
DT5	Ken Griffey Jr.	12.00
DT6	Mark McGwire	15.00
DT7	Mike Piazza	12.00
DT8	Cal Ripken Jr.	20.00
DT9	Alex Rodriguez	15.00
DT10	Frank Thomas	7.50

In the Clutch

		NM/M
Complete Set (15):		25.00
Common Player:		.40
IC1	Jeff Bagwell	1.00
IC2	Barry Bonds	5.00
IC3	Roger Clemens	2.00
IC4	Jose Cruz Jr.	.40
IC5	Nomar Garciaparra	2.00
IC6	Juan Gonzalez	.75
IC7	Ken Griffey Jr.	2.50
IC8	Tony Gwynn	1.50
IC9	Derek Jeter	5.00
IC10	Chipper Jones	1.50
IC11	Greg Maddux	1.50

IC12	Mark McGwire	4.00
IC13	Mike Piazza	2.50
IC14	Frank Thomas	1.00
IC15	Larry Walker	.40

Lumber Company

LUMBER COMPANY
CAL RIPKEN JR.

		NM/M
Complete Set (15):		50.00
Common Player:		.70
Inserted 1:36 R		
1	Jeff Bagwell	2.50
2	Barry Bonds	8.00
3	Jose Cruz Jr.	.75
4	Nomar Garciaparra	4.00
5	Juan Gonzalez	1.50
6	Ken Griffey Jr.	5.00
7	Tony Gwynn	3.00
8	Chipper Jones	3.00
9	Tino Martinez	.75
10	Mark McGwire	6.00
11	Mike Piazza	5.00
12	Cal Ripken Jr.	8.00
13	Alex Rodriguez	6.00
14	Frank Thomas	2.50
15	Larry Walker	.75

Mantle & Sons

		NM/M
Mickey Mantle, Danny Mantle, David Mantle		3.00

Mickey Mantle Monumental Moments

MICKEY MANTLE

		NM/M
Complete Set (10):		40.00
Common Mantle:		5.00

Inserted 1:68
Gold (51 Sets): 3X

Promising Forecast

PROMISING FORECAST

		NM/M
Complete Set (20):		7.00
Common Player:		.25
Inserted 1:12		
PF1	Rolando Arrojo	.25
PF2	Sean Casey	.40
PF3	Brad Fullmer	.25
PF4	Karim Garcia	.35
PF5	Ben Grieve	.25
PF6	Todd Helton	3.00
PF7	Richard Hidalgo	.25
PF8	A.J. Hinch	.25
PF9	Paul Konerko	.35
PF10	Mark Kotsay	.25
PF11	Derrek Lee	1.00
PF12	Travis Lee	.35
PF13	Eric Milton	.25
PF14	Magglio Ordonez	.50
PF15	David Ortiz	.50
PF16	Brian Rose	.25
PF17	Miguel Tejada	.40
PF18	Jason Varitek	.35
PF19	Enrique Wilson	.25
PF20	Kerry Wood	1.00

Rookie Sensations

TODD HELTON

		NM/M
Complete Set (20):		12.00
Common Player:		.50
Inserted 1:18		
1	Mike Cameron	.50
2	Jose Cruz Jr.	.50
3	Jason Dickson	.50
4	Kelvim Escobar	.50
5	Nomar Garciaparra	3.00
6	Ben Grieve	.50
7	Vladimir Guerrero	3.00
8	Wilton Guerrero	.50
9	Jose Guillen	.50
10	Todd Helton	2.00
11	Livan Hernandez	.50
12	Hideki Irabu	.50
13	Andruw Jones	3.00
14	Matt Morris	.50
15	Magglio Ordonez	1.00
16	Neifi Perez	.50
17	Scott Rolen	2.00
18	Fernando Tatis	.50
19	Brett Tomko	.50
20	Jaret Wright	.50

The Power Game

		NM/M
Complete Set (20):		30.00
Common Player:		.50

Inserted 1:36

1	Jeff Bagwell	2.00
2	Albert Belle	.50
3	Barry Bonds	6.00
4	Tony Clark	.50
5	Roger Clemens	3.50
6	Jose Cruz Jr.	.50
7	Andres Galarraga	.50
8	Nomar Garciaparra	3.50
9	Juan Gonzalez	1.00
10	Ken Griffey Jr.	4.00
11	Randy Johnson	2.00
12	Greg Maddux	3.00
13	Pedro Martinez	2.00
14	Tino Martinez	.50
15	Mark McGwire	5.00
16	Mike Piazza	4.00
17	Curt Schilling	.75
18	Frank Thomas	2.00
19	Jim Thome	2.00
20	Larry Walker	.50

Zone

		NM/M
Complete Set (15):		130.00
Common Player:		4.00
Inserted 1:288		
1	Jeff Bagwell	7.50
2	Barry Bonds	25.00
3	Roger Clemens	10.00
4	Jose Cruz Jr.	4.00
5	Nomar Garciaparra	10.00
6	Juan Gonzalez	6.00
7	Ken Griffey Jr.	12.00
8	Tony Gwynn	9.00
9	Chipper Jones	9.00
10	Greg Maddux	9.00
11	Mark McGwire	15.00
12	Mike Piazza	12.00
13	Alex Rodriguez	20.00
14	Frank Thomas	7.50
15	Larry Walker	4.00

Vintage '63

MARK McGWIRE
St. Louis Cardinals—16

		NM/M
Complete Set (126):		20.00
Complete Series 1 (63):		10.00
Complete Series 2 (63):		10.00
Common Player:		.10
Classics (63 sets):		20X
1	Jason Dickson	.10
2	Tim Salmon	.25
3	Andruw Jones	.75
4	Chipper Jones	1.00
5	Kenny Lofton	.10
6	Greg Maddux	1.00
7	Rafael Palmeiro	.65
8	Cal Ripken Jr.	2.50
9	Nomar Garciaparra	1.25
10	Mark Grace	.10
11	Sammy Sosa	1.25
12	Frank Thomas	.75
13	Deion Sanders	.10
14	Sandy Alomar	.10
15	David Justice	.10
16	Jim Thome	.75
17	Matt Williams	.10
18	Jaret Wright	.10
19	Vinny Castilla	.10
20	Andres Galarraga	.10
21	Todd Helton	.75
22	Larry Walker	.10
23	Tony Clark	.10
24	Moises Alou	.10
25	Kevin Brown	.10
26	Charles Johnson	.10
27	Edgar Renteria	.10
28	Gary Sheffield	.50
29	Jeff Bagwell	.75
30	Craig Biggio	.10
31	Raul Mondesi	.10
32	Mike Piazza	1.50
33	Chuck Knoblauch	.10
34	Paul Molitor	.75
35	Vladimir Guerrero	.75
36	Pedro Martinez	.75
37	Todd Hundley	.10
38	Derek Jeter	2.50
39	Tino Martinez	.10
40	Paul O'Neill	.10
41	Andy Pettitte	.35
42	Mariano Rivera	.20
43	Bernie Williams	.20
44	Ben Grieve	.10
45	Scott Rolen	.65
46	Curt Schilling	.45
47	Jason Kendall	.10
48	Tony Womack	.10
49	Ray Lankford	.10
50	Mark McGwire	2.00
51	Matt Morris	.10
52	Tony Gwynn	1.00
53	Barry Bonds	2.50
54	Jay Buhner	.10
55	Ken Griffey Jr.	1.50
56	Randy Johnson	.75
57	Edgar Martinez	.10
58	Alex Rodriguez	2.00
59	Juan Gonzalez	.65
60	Rusty Greer	.10
61	Ivan Rodriguez	.65
62	Roger Clemens	1.25
63	Jose Cruz Jr.	.10
	Checklist #1-63	.10
64	Darin Erstad	.20
65	Jay Bell	.10
66	Andy Benes	.10
67	Mickey Mantle	2.00
68	Karim Garcia	.10
69	Travis Lee	.10
70	Matt Williams	.10
71	Andres Galarraga	.10
72	Tom Glavine	.35
73	Ryan Klesko	.10
74	Denny Neagle	.10
75	John Smoltz	.10
76	Roberto Alomar	.20
77	Joe Carter	.10
78	Mike Mussina	.50
79	B.J. Surhoff	.10
80	Dennis Eckersley	.65
81	Pedro Martinez	.75
82	Mo Vaughn	.10
83	Jeff Blauser	.10
84	Henry Rodriguez	.10
85	Albert Belle	.10
86	Sean Casey	.25
87	Travis Fryman	.10
88	Kenny Lofton	.10
89	Darryl Kile	.10
90	Mike Lansing	.10
91	Bobby Bonilla	.10
92	Cliff Floyd	.10
93	Livan Hernandez	.10
94	Derrek Lee	.10
95	Moises Alou	.10
96	Shane Reynolds	.10
97	Jeff Conine	.10
98	Johnny Damon	.35
99	Eric Karros	.10
100	Hideo Nomo	.65
101	Marquis Grissom	.10
102	Matt Lawton	.10
103	Todd Walker	.10
104	Gary Sheffield	.50
105	Bernard Gilkey	.10
106	Rey Ordonez	.10
107	Chili Davis	.10
108	Chuck Knoblauch	.10
109	Charles Johnson	.10
110	Rickey Henderson	.75
111	Bob Abreu	.10
112	Doug Glanville	.10
113	Gregg Jefferies	.10
114	Al Martin	.10
115	Kevin Young	.10
116	Ron Gant	.10
117	Kevin Brown	.10
118	Ken Caminiti	.10
119	Joey Hamilton	.10
120	Jeff Kent	.10
121	Wade Boggs	1.00
122	Quinton McCracken	.10
123	Fred McGriff	.10
124	Paul Sorrento	.10
125	Jose Canseco	.50
126	Randy Myers	.10
	Checklist #64-126	.10

Vintage '63 Classic

		NM/M
Complete Set (128):		650.00
Common Player:		4.00
Stars/RC's:		20X

DAVID JUSTICE
Cleveland Indians—OF

000 of 63 CLASSIC '63

(See 1998 Fleer Vintage '63 for checklistand base card values.)

1998 Fleer Update

		NM/M
Complete Set (100):		12.50
Common Player:		.05
U1	Mark McGwire	.75
U2	Sammy Sosa	.45
U3	Roger Clemens	.45
U4	Barry Bonds	1.00
U5	Kerry Wood	.20
U6	Paul Molitor	.25
U7	Ken Griffey Jr.	.50
U8	Cal Ripken Jr.	1.00
U9	David Wells	.05
U10	Alex Rodriguez	.75
U11	Angel Pena RC	.25
U12	Bruce Chen	.05
U13	Craig Wilson	.05
U14	Orlando Hernandez RC	1.50
U15	Aramis Ramirez	.10
U16	Aaron Boone	.05
U17	Bob Henley	.05
U18	Juan Guzman	.05
U19	Darryl Hamilton	.05
U20	Jay Payton	.05
U21	Jeremy Powell RC	.05
U22	Ben Davis	.05
U23	Preston Wilson	.10
U24	Jim Parque RC	.15
U25	Odalis Perez RC	.25
U26	Ron Belliard	.05
U27	Royce Clayton	.05
U28	George Lombard	.05
U29	Tony Phillips	.05
U30	Fernando Seguignol RC	.15
U31	Armando Rios RC	.10
U32	Jerry Hairston Jr. RC	.25
U33	Justin Baughman RC	.05
U34	Seth Greisinger	.05
U35	Alex Gonzalez	.05
U36	Michael Barrett	.05
U37	Carlos Beltran	.35
U38	Ellis Burks	.05
U39	Jose Jimenez	.05
U40	Carlos Guillen	.05
U41	Marlon Anderson	.05
U42	Scott Elarton	.05
U43	Glenallen Hill	.05
U44	Shane Monahan	.05
U45	Dennis Martinez	.05
U46	Carlos Febles RC	.20
U47	Carlos Perez	.05
U48	Wilton Guerrero	.05
U49	Randy Johnson	.45
U50	Brian Simmons RC	.05
U51	Carlton Loewer	.05
U52	Mark DeRosa RC	.50
U53	Tim Young RC	.05
U54	Gary Gaetti	.05
U55	Eric Chavez	.25
U56	Carl Pavano	.15
U57	Mike Stanley	.05
U58	Todd Stottlemyre	.05
U59	Gabe Kapler RC	.50
U60	Mike Jerzembeck RC	.05
U61	Mitch Meluskey RC	.15
U62	Bill Pulsipher	.05
U63	Derrick Gibson	.05
U64	John Rocker RC	.75
U65	Calvin Pickering	.05
U66	Blake Stein	.05
U67	Fernando Tatis	.05
U68	Gabe Alvarez	.05
U69	Jeffrey Hammonds	.05
U70	Adrian Beltre	.25
U71	Ryan Bradley RC	.10
U72	Edgar Clemente RC	.05
U73	Rick Croushore RC	.05
U74	Matt Clement	.15
U75	Dermal Brown	.05
U76	Paul Bako	.05
U77	Placido Polanco RC	1.00
U78	Jay Tessmer	.05
U79	Jarrod Washburn	.05
U80	Kevin Witt	.05
U81	Mike Metcalfe	.05
U82	Daryle Ward	.05
U83	Benj Sampson RC	.05
U84	Mike Kinkade RC	.20
U85	Randy Winn	.05
U86	Jeff Shaw	.05
U87	Troy Glaus RC	4.00
U88	Hideo Nomo	.35
U89	Mark Grudzielanek	.05
U90	Mike Frank RC	.05
U91	Bobby Howry RC	.10
U92	Ryan Minor RC	.15
U93	Corey Koskie RC	1.00
U94	Matt Anderson RC	.20
U95	Joe Carter	.05
U96	Paul Konerko	.15
U97	Sidney Ponson	.05
U98	Jeremy Giambi RC	.25
U99	Jeff Kubenka RC	.05
U100	J.D. Drew RC	5.00

1999 Fleer

		NM/M
Complete Set (600):		25.00
Common Player:		.05
Warning Track:		2X
Inserted 1:1 R		
Pack (10):		1.00
Wax Box (36):		25.00
1	Mark McGwire	2.00
2	Sammy Sosa	1.25
3	Ken Griffey Jr.	1.50
4	Kerry Wood	.30
5	Derek Jeter	2.50
6	Stan Musial	2.00
7	J.D. Drew	.65
7p	J.D. Drew/OPS	1.50
8	Cal Ripken Jr.	2.50
9	Alex Rodriguez	2.00
10	Travis Lee	.15
11	Andres Galarraga	.05
12	Nomar Garciaparra	1.25
13	Albert Belle	.05
14	Barry Larkin	.05
15	Dante Bichette	.05
16	Tony Clark	.05
17	Moises Alou	.05
18	Rafael Palmeiro	.65
19	Raul Mondesi	.05
20	Vladimir Guerrero	.75
21	John Olerud	.05
22	Bernie Williams	.10
23	Ben Grieve	.05
24	Scott Rolen	.65

No.	Name	Value
25	Jeromy Burnitz	.05
26	Ken Caminiti	.05
27	Barry Bonds	2.50
28	Todd Helton	.75
29	Juan Gonzalez	.65
30	Roger Clemens	1.25
31	Andruw Jones	.75
32	Mo Vaughn	.05
33	Larry Walker	.05
34	Frank Thomas	.75
35	Manny Ramirez	.75
36	Randy Johnson	.75
37	Vinny Castilla	.05
38	Juan Encarnacion	.05
39	Jeff Bagwell	.75
40	Gary Sheffield	.50
41	Mike Piazza	1.50
42	Richie Sexson	.05
43	Tony Gwynn	1.00
44	Chipper Jones	1.00
45	Jim Thome	.65
46	Craig Biggio	.05
47	Carlos Delgado	.40
48	Greg Vaughn	.05
49	Greg Maddux	1.00
50	Troy Glaus	.65
51	Roberto Alomar	.10
52	Dennis Eckersley	.60
53	Mike Caruso	.05
54	Bruce Chen	.05
55	Aaron Boone	.05
56	Bartolo Colon	.05
57	Derrick Gibson	.05
58	Brian Anderson	.05
59	Gabe Alvarez	.05
60	Todd Dunwoody	.05
61	Rod Beck	.05
62	Derek Bell	.05
63	Francisco Cordova	.05
64	Johnny Damon	.25
65	Adrian Beltre	.15
66	Garret Anderson	.05
67	Armando Benitez	.05
68	Edgardo Alfonzo	.05
69	Ryan Bradley	.05
70	Eric Chavez	.30
71	Bobby Abreu	.05
72	Andy Ashby	.05
73	Ellis Burks	.05
74	Jeff Cirillo	.05
75	Jay Buhner	.05
76	Ron Gant	.05
77	Rolando Arrojo	.05
78	Will Clark	.10
79	Chris Carpenter	.05
80	Jim Edmonds	.05
81	Tony Batista	.05
82	Shane Andrews	.05
83	Mark DeRosa	.05
84	Brady Anderson	.05
85	Tony Gordon	.05
86	Brant Brown	.05
87	Ray Durham	.05
88	Ron Coomer	.05
89	Bret Boone	.05
90	Travis Fryman	.05
91	Darryl Kile	.05
92	Paul Bako	.05
93	Cliff Floyd	.05
94	Scott Elarton	.05
95	Jeremy Giambi	.05
96	Darren Dreifort	.05
97	Marquis Grissom	.05
98	Marty Cordova	.05
99	Fernando Seguignol	.05
100	Orlando Hernandez	.05
101	Jose Cruz Jr.	.05
102	Jason Giambi	.60
103	Damion Easley	.05
104	Freddy Garcia	.05
105	Marlon Anderson	.05
106	Kevin Brown	.05
107	Joe Carter	.05
108	Russ Davis	.05
109	Brian Jordan	.05
110	Wade Boggs	1.00
111	Tom Goodwin	.05
112	Scott Brosius	.05
113	Darin Erstad	.10
114	Jay Bell	.05
115	Tom Glavine	.25
116	Pedro Martinez	.75
117	Mark Grace	.10
118	Russ Ortiz	.05
119	Magglio Ordonez	.10
120	Sean Casey	.15
121	Rafael Roque RC	.05
122	Brian Giles	.05
123	Mike Lansing	.05
124	David Cone	.05
125	Alex Gonzalez	.05
126	Carl Everett	.05
127	Jeff King	.05
128	Charles Johnson	.05
129	Geoff Jenkins	.05
130	Corey Koskie	.05
131	Brad Fullmer	.05
132	Al Leiter	.05
133	Rickey Henderson	.75
134	Rico Brogna	.05
135	Jose Guillen	.05
136	Matt Clement	.05
137	Carlos Guillen	.05
138	Orel Hershiser	.05
139	Ray Lankford	.05
140	Miguel Cairo	.05
141	Chuck Finley	.05
142	Rusty Greer	.05
143	Kelvim Escobar	.05
144	Ryan Klesko	.05
145	Andy Benes	.05
146	Eric Davis	.05
147	David Wells	.05
148	Trot Nixon	.05
149	Jose Hernandez	.05
150	Mark Johnson	.05
151	Mike Frank	.05
152	Joey Hamilton	.05
153	David Justice	.05
154	Mike Mussina	.40
155	Neifi Perez	.05
156	Luis Gonzalez	.10
157	Livan Hernandez	.05
158	Dermal Brown	.05
159	Jose Lima	.05
160	Eric Karros	.05
161	Ronnie Belliard	.05
162	Matt Lawton	.05
163	Dustin Hermanson	.05
164	Brian McRae	.05
165	Mike Kinkade	.05
166	A.J. Hinch	.05
167	Doug Glanville	.05
168	Hideo Nomo	.65
169	Jason Kendall	.05
170	Steve Finley	.05
171	Jeff Kent	.05
172	Ben Davis	.05
173	Edgar Martinez	.05
174	Eli Marrero	.05
175	Quinton McCracken	.05
176	Rick Helling	.05
177	Tom Evans	.05
178	Carl Pavano	.10
179	Todd Greene	.05
180	Omar Daal	.05
181	George Lombard	.05
182	Ryan Minor	.05
183	Troy O'Leary	.05
184	Robb Nen	.05
185	Mickey Morandini	.05
186	Robin Ventura	.05
187	Pete Harnisch	.05
188	Kenny Lofton	.05
189	Eric Milton	.05
190	Bobby Higginson	.05
191	Jamie Moyer	.05
192	Mark Kotsay	.05
193	Shane Reynolds	.05
194	Carlos Febles	.05
195	Jeff Kubenka	.05
196	Chuck Knoblauch	.05
197	Kenny Rogers	.05
198	Bill Mueller	.05
199	Shane Monahan	.05
200	Matt Morris	.05
201	Fred McGriff	.05
202	Ivan Rodriguez	.65
203	Kevin Witt	.05
204	Troy Percival	.05
205	David Dellucci	.05
206	Kevin Millwood	.05
207	Jerry Hairston Jr.	.05
208	Mike Stanley	.05
209	Henry Rodriguez	.05
210	Trevor Hoffman	.05
211	Craig Wilson	.05
212	Reggie Sanders	.05
213	Carlton Loewer	.05
214	Omar Vizquel	.05
215	Gabe Kapler	.05
216	Derrek Lee	.05
217	Billy Wagner	.05
218	Dean Palmer	.05
219	Chan Ho Park	.05
220	Fernando Vina	.05
221	Roy Halladay	.05
222	Paul Molitor	.75
223	Ugueth Urbina	.05
224	Rey Ordonez	.05
225	Ricky Ledee	.05
226	Scott Spiezio	.05
227	Wendell Magee Jr.	.05
228	Aramis Ramirez	.05
229	Brian Simmons	.05
230	Fernando Tatis	.05
231	Bobby Smith	.05
232	Aaron Sele	.05
233	Shawn Green	.20
234	Mariano Rivera	.15
235	Tim Salmon	.10
236	Andy Fox	.05
237	Denny Neagle	.05
238	John Valentin	.05
239	Kevin Tapani	.05
240	Paul Konerko	.10
241	Robert Fick	.05
242	Edgar Renteria	.05
243	Brett Tomko	.05
244	Daryle Ward	.05
245	Carlos Beltran	.30
246	Angel Pena	.05
247	Steve Woodard	.05
248	David Ortiz	.05
249	Justin Thompson	.05
250	Rondell White	.05
251	Jaret Wright	.05
252	Ed Sprague	.05
253	Jay Payton	.05
254	Mike Lowell	.05
255	Orlando Cabrera	.05
256	Jason Schmidt	.05
257	David Segui	.05
258	Paul Sorrento	.05
259	John Wetteland	.05
260	Devon White	.05
261	Odalis Perez	.05
262	Calvin Pickering	.05
263	Alex Ramirez	.05
264	Preston Wilson	.05
265	Brad Radke	.05
266	Walt Weiss	.05
267	Tim Young	.05
268	Tino Martinez	.05
269	Matt Stairs	.05
270	Curt Schilling	.25
271	Tony Womack	.05
272	Ismael Valdes	.05
273	Wally Joyner	.05
274	Armando Rios	.05
275	Andy Pettitte	.25
276	Bubba Trammell	.05
277	Todd Zeile	.05
278	Shannon Stewart	.05
279	Matt Williams	.05
280	John Rocker	.05
281	B.J. Surhoff	.05
282	Eric Young	.05
283	Dmitri Young	.05
284	John Smoltz	.05
285	Todd Walker	.05
286	Paul O'Neill	.05
287	Blake Stein	.05
288	Kevin Young	.05
289	Quilvio Veras	.05
290	Kirk Rueter	.05
291	Randy Winn	.05
292	Miguel Tejada	.05
293	J.T. Snow	.05
294	Michael Tucker	.05
295	Jay Tessmer	.05
296	Scott Erickson	.05
297	Tim Wakefield	.05
298	Jeff Abbott	.05
299	Eddie Taubensee	.05
300	Darryl Hamilton	.05
301	Kevin Orie	.05
302	Jose Offerman	.05
303	Scott Karl	.05
304	Chris Widger	.05
305	Todd Hundley	.05
306	Desi Relaford	.05
307	Sterling Hitchcock	.05
308	Delino DeShields	.05
309	Alex Gonzalez	.05
310	Justin Baughman	.05
311	Jamey Wright	.05
312	Wes Helms	.05
313	Dante Powell	.05
314	Jim Abbott	.05
315	Manny Alexander	.05
316	Harold Baines	.05
317	Danny Graves	.05
318	Sandy Alomar	.05
319	Pedro Astacio	.05
320	Jermaine Allensworth	.05
321	Matt Anderson	.05
322	Chad Curtis	.05
323	Antonio Osuna	.05
324	Brad Ausmus	.05
325	Steve Trachsel	.05
326	Mike Blowers	.05
327	Brian Bohanon	.05
328	Chris Gomez	.05
329	Valerio de los Santos	.05
330	Rich Aurilia	.05
331	Michael Barrett	.05
332	Rick Aguilera	.05
333	Adrian Brown	.05
334	Bill Spiers	.05
335	Matt Beech	.05
336	David Bell	.05
337	Juan Acevedo	.05
338	Jose Canseco	.50
339	Wilson Alvarez	.05
340	Luis Alicea	.05
341	Jason Dickson	.05
342	Mike Bordick	.05
343	Ben Ford	.05
344	Keith Lockhart	.05
345	Jason Christiansen	.05
346	Darren Bragg	.05
347	Doug Brocail	.05
348	Jeff Blauser	.05
349	James Baldwin	.05
350	Jeffrey Hammonds	.05
351	Ricky Bottalico	.05
352	Russ Branyon	.05
353	Mark Brownson	.05
354	Dave Berg	.05
355	Sean Bergman	.05
356	Jeff Conine	.05
357	Shayne Bennett	.05
358	Bobby Bonilla	.05
359	Bob Wickman	.05
360	Carlos Baerga	.05
361	Chris Fussell	.05
362	Chili Davis	.05
363	Jerry Spradlin	.05
364	Carlos Hernandez	.05
365	Roberto Hernandez	.05
366	Marvin Benard	.05
367	Ken Cloude	.05
368	Tony Fernandez	.05
369	John Burkett	.05
370	Gary DiSarcina	.05
371	Alan Benes	.05
372	Karim Garcia	.05
373	Carlos Perez	.05
374	Damon Buford	.05
375	Mark Clark	.05
376	Edgard Clemente RC	.05
377	Chad Bradford	.05
378	Frank Catalanotto	.05
379	Vic Darensbourg	.05
380	Sean Berry	.05
381	Dave Burba	.05
382	Sal Fasano	.05
383	Steve Parris	.05
384	Roger Cedeno	.05
385	Chad Fox	.05
386	Wilton Guerrero	.05
387	Dennis Cook	.05
388	Joe Girardi	.05
389	LaTroy Hawkins	.05
390	Ryan Christenson	.05
391	Paul Byrd	.05
392	Lou Collier	.05
393	Jeff Fassero	.05
394	Jim Leyritz	.05
395	Shawn Estes	.05
396	Mike Kelly	.05
397	Rich Croushore	.05
398	Royce Clayton	.05
399	Rudy Seanez	.05
400	Darrin Fletcher	.05
401	Shigetosi Hasegawa	.05
402	Bernard Gilkey	.05
403	Juan Guzman	.05
404	Jeff Frye	.05
405	Marino Santana	.05
406	Alex Fernandez	.05
407	Gary Gaetti	.05
408	Dan Miceli	.05
409	Mike Cameron	.05
410	Mike Remlinger	.05
411	Joey Cora	.05
412	Mark Gardner	.05
413	Aaron Ledesma	.05
414	Jerry Dipoto	.05
415	Ricky Gutierrez	.05
416	John Franco	.05
417	Mendy Lopez	.05
418	Hideki Irabu	.05
419	Mark Grudzielanek	.05
420	Bobby Hughes	.05
421	Pat Meares	.05
422	Jimmy Haynes	.05
423	Bob Henley	.05
424	Bobby Estalella	.05
425	Jon Lieber	.05
426	Giomar Guevara RC	.05
427	Jose Jimenez	.05
428	Deivi Cruz	.05
429	Jonathan Johnson	.05
430	Ken Hill	.05
431	Craig Grebeck	.05
432	Jose Rosado	.05
433	Danny Klassen	.05
434	Bobby Howry	.05
435	Gerald Williams	.05
436	Omar Olivares	.05
437	Chris Hoiles	.05
438	Seth Greisinger	.05
439	Scott Hatteberg	.05
440	Jeremi Gonzalez	.05
441	Wil Cordero	.05
442	Jeff Montgomery	.05
443	Chris Stynes	.05
444	Tony Saunders	.05
445	Einar Diaz	.05
446	Laril Gonzalez	.05
447	Ryan Jackson	.05
448	Mike Hampton	.05

449	Todd Hollandsworth	.05
450	Gabe White	.05
451	John Jaha	.05
452	Bret Saberhagen	.05
453	Otis Nixon	.05
454	Steve Kline	.05
455	Butch Huskey	.05
456	Mike Jerzembeck	.05
457	Wayne Gomes	.05
458	Mike Macfarlane	.05
459	Jesus Sanchez	.05
460	Al Martin	.05
461	Dwight Gooden	.05
462	Ruben Rivera	.05
463	Pat Hentgen	.05
464	Jose Valentin	.05
465	Vladimir Nunez	.05
466	Charlie Hayes	.05
467	Jay Powell	.05
468	Raul Ibanez	.05
469	Kent Mercker	.05
470	John Mabry	.05
471	Woody Williams	.05
472	Roberto Kelly	.05
473	Jim Mecir	.05
474	Dave Hollins	.05
475	Rafael Medina	.05
476	Darren Lewis	.05
477	Felix Heredia	.05
478	Brian Hunter	.05
479	Matt Mantei	.05
480	Richard Hidalgo	.05
481	Bobby Jones	.05
482	Hal Morris	.05
483	Ramiro Mendoza	.05
484	Matt Luke	.05
485	Esteban Loaiza	.05
486	Mark Loretta	.05
487	A.J. Pierzynski	.05
488	Charles Nagy	.05
489	Kevin Sefcik	.05
490	Jason McDonald	.05
491	Jeremy Powell	.05
492	Scott Servais	.05
493	Abraham Nunez	.05
494	Stan Spencer	.05
495	Stan Javier	.05
496	Jose Paniagua	.05
497	Gregg Jefferies	.05
498	Gregg Olson	.05
499	Derek Lowe	.05
500	Willis Otanez	.05
501	Brian Moehler	.05
502	Glenallen Hill	.05
503	Bobby Jones	.05
504	Greg Norton	.05
505	Mike Jackson	.05
506	Kirt Manwaring	.05
507	Eric Weaver	.05
508	Mitch Meluskey	.05
509	Todd Jones	.05
510	Mike Matheny	.05
511	Benj Sampson	.05
512	Tony Phillips	.05
513	Mike Thurman	.05
514	Jorge Posada	.05
515	Bill Taylor	.05
516	Mike Sweeney	.05
517	Jose Silva	.05
518	Mark Lewis	.05
519	Chris Peters	.05
520	Brian Johnson	.05
521	Mike Timlin	.05
522	Mark McLemore	.05
523	Dan Plesac	.05
524	Kelly Stinnett	.05
525	Sidney Ponson	.05
526	Jim Parque	.05
527	Tyler Houston	.05
528	John Thomson	.05
529	Mike Metcalfe	.05
530	Robert Person	.05
531	Marc Newfield	.05
532	Javier Vazquez	.05
533	Terry Steinbach	.05
534	Turk Wendell	.05
535	Tim Raines	.05
536	Brian Meadows	.05
537	Mike Lieberthal	.05
538	Ricardo Rincon	.05
539	Dan Wilson	.05
540	John Johnstone	.05
541	Todd Stottlemyre	.05
542	Kevin Stocker	.05
543	Ramon Martinez	.05
544	Mike Simms	.05
545	Paul Quantrill	.05
546	Matt Walbeck	.05
547	Turner Ward	.05
548	Bill Pulsipher	.05
549	Donnie Sadler	.05
550	Lance Johnson	.05
551	Bill Simas	.05
552	Jeff Reed	.05
553	Jeff Shaw	.05
554	Joe Randa	.05

555	Paul Shuey	.05
556	Mike Redmond	.05
557	Sean Runyan	.05
558	Enrique Wilson	.05
559	Scott Radinsky	.05
560	Larry Sutton	.05
561	Masato Yoshii	.05
562	David Nilsson	.05
563	Mike Trombley	.05
564	Darryl Strawberry	.05
565	Dave Mlicki	.05
566	Placido Polanco	.05
567	Yorkis Perez	.05
568	Esteban Yan	.05
569	Lee Stevens	.05
570	Steve Sinclair	.05
571	Jarrod Washburn	.05
572	Lenny Webster	.05
573	Mike Sirotka	.05
574	Jason Varitek	.05
575	Terry Mulholland	.05
576	Adrian Beltre	.10
577	Eric Chavez	.20
578	J.D. Drew	.35
579	Juan Encarnacion	.05
580	Nomar Garciaparra	.65
581	Troy Glaus	.35
582	Ben Grieve	.05
583	Vladimir Guerrero	.40
584	Todd Helton	.35
585	Derek Jeter	1.25
586	Travis Lee	.10
587	Alex Rodriguez	1.00
588	Scott Rolen	.30
589	Richie Sexson	.05
590	Kerry Wood	.20
591	Ken Griffey Jr.	.75
592	Chipper Jones	.50
593	Alex Rodriguez	1.00
594	Sammy Sosa	.65
595	Mark McGwire	1.00
596	Cal Ripken Jr.	1.25
597	Nomar Garciaparra	.65
598	Derek Jeter	1.25
599	Kerry Wood	.20
600	J.D. Drew	.40

Warning Track Collection

	NM/M
Complete Set (600):	160.00
Common Player:	.50
Stars:	2X

(See 1999 Fleer for checklist and base card values.)

Date With Destiny

	NM/M
Complete Set (10):	300.00
Common Player:	20.00
Production 100 Sets	

1	Barry Bonds	60.00
2	Roger Clemens	35.00
3	Ken Griffey Jr.	40.00
4	Tony Gwynn	30.00
5	Greg Maddux	30.00
6	Mark McGwire	50.00
7	Mike Piazza	40.00
8	Cal Ripken Jr.	60.00
9	Alex Rodriguez	50.00
10	Frank Thomas	20.00

Diamond Magic

	NM/M
Complete Set (15):	50.00
Common Player:	1.00
Inserted 1:96	
1	Barry Bonds	9.00
2	Roger Clemens	4.50
3	Nomar Garciaparra	4.50
4	Ken Griffey Jr.	5.00
5	Tony Gwynn	3.75
6	Orlando Hernandez	1.00
7	Derek Jeter	9.00
8	Randy Johnson	3.00
9	Chipper Jones	3.75
10	Greg Maddux	3.75
11	Mark McGwire	6.00
12	Alex Rodriguez	7.50
13	Sammy Sosa	4.50
14	Bernie Williams	1.50
15	Kerry Wood	2.00

Going Yard

	NM/M
Complete Set (15):	4.00
Common Player:	.10
Inserted 1:18	
1	Moises Alou	.10
2	Albert Belle	.10
3	Jose Canseco	.30
4	Vinny Castilla	.10
5	Andres Galarraga	.10
6	Juan Gonzalez	.20
7	Ken Griffey Jr.	.75
8	Chipper Jones	.50
9	Mark McGwire	1.00
10	Rafael Palmeiro	.35
11	Mike Piazza	.75
12	Alex Rodriguez	1.00
13	Sammy Sosa	.65
14	Greg Vaughn	.10
15	Mo Vaughn	.10

Golden Memories

	NM/M
Complete Set (15):	45.00
Common Player:	.75
Inserted 1:54	
1	Albert Belle	.75
2	Barry Bonds	7.50
3	Roger Clemens	4.50

4	Nomar Garciaparra	4.50
5	Juan Gonzalez	1.50
6	Ken Griffey Jr.	3.75
7	Randy Johnson	2.75
8	Greg Maddux	3.25
9	Mark McGwire	5.00
10	Mike Piazza	3.75
11	Cal Ripken Jr.	7.50
12	Alex Rodriguez	6.00
13	Sammy Sosa	4.50
14	David Wells	.75
15	Kerry Wood	2.00

Home Run Heroes

	NM/M
Complete Set (4):	7.50
Common Player:	1.50
1	Mark McGwire	3.00
2	Sammy Sosa	2.00
3	Mike Piazza	2.00
4	Nomar Garciaparra	2.00

Rookie Flashback

	NM/M
Complete Set (15):	5.00
Common Player:	.25
Inserted 1:6	
1	Matt Anderson	.25
2	Rolando Arrojo	.25
3	Adrian Beltre	.50
4	Mike Caruso	.25
5	Eric Chavez	.40
6	J.D. Drew	.75
7	Juan Encarnacion	.25
8	Brad Fullmer	.25
9	Troy Glaus	1.50
10	Ben Grieve	.25
11	Todd Helton	1.50
12	Orlando Hernandez	.25
13	Travis Lee	.40
14	Richie Sexson	.25
15	Kerry Wood	.65

Stan Musial Monumental Moments

	NM/M
Complete Set (10):	15.00
Common Musial:	2.00
Autographed Card:	60.00

Starting Nine

	NM/M
Common Player:	20.00

(Star and rookie cards valued at 200-250X base versions.)

Vintage '61

	NM/M
Complete Set (50):	7.50

Common Player: .05
Inserted 1:1

1	Mark McGwire	.75
2	Sammy Sosa	.50
3	Ken Griffey Jr.	.60
4	Kerry Wood	.25
5	Derek Jeter	1.00
6	Stan Musial	.75
7	J.D. Drew	.30
8	Cal Ripken Jr.	1.00
9	Alex Rodriguez	.75
10	Travis Lee	.10
11	Andres Galarraga	.05
12	Nomar Garciaparra	.50
13	Albert Belle	.05
14	Barry Larkin	.05
15	Dante Bichette	.05
16	Tony Clark	.05
17	Moises Alou	.05
18	Rafael Palmeiro	.30
19	Raul Mondesi	.05
20	Vladimir Guerrero	.35
21	John Olerud	.05
22	Bernie Williams	.10
23	Ben Grieve	.05
24	Scott Rolen	.30
25	Jeromy Burnitz	.05
26	Ken Caminiti	.05
27	Barry Bonds	1.00
28	Todd Helton	.35
29	Juan Gonzalez	.25
30	Roger Clemens	.50
31	Andruw Jones	.35
32	Mo Vaughn	.05
33	Larry Walker	.05
34	Frank Thomas	.35
35	Manny Ramirez	.35
36	Randy Johnson	.35
37	Vinny Castilla	.05
38	Juan Encarnacion	.05
39	Jeff Bagwell	.35
40	Gary Sheffield	.25
41	Mike Piazza	.60
42	Richie Sexson	.05
43	Tony Gwynn	.45
44	Chipper Jones	.45
45	Jim Thome	.30
46	Craig Biggio	.05
47	Carlos Delgado	.25
48	Greg Vaughn	.05
49	Greg Maddux	.45
50	Troy Glaus	.35

1999 Fleer Update

		NM/M
Complete Set (150):		20.00
Common Player:		.10
1	Rick Ankiel RC	3.00
2	Peter Bergeron RC	.25
3	Pat Burrell RC	1.50
4	Eric Munson RC	.35

5	Alfonso Soriano RC	3.00
6	Tim Hudson RC	2.00
7	Erubiel Durazo RC	.25
8	Chad Hermansen RC	.10
9	Jeff Zimmerman RC	.10
10	Jesus Pena RC	.10
11	Ramon Hernandez RC	.10
12	Trent Durrington RC	.25
13	Tony Armas Jr. RC	.10
14	Mike Fyhrie RC	.10
15	Danny Kolb RC	.25
16	Mike Porzio RC	.10
17	Will Brunson RC	.10
18	Mike Duvall RC	.10
19	Doug Mientkiewicz RC	.75
20	Gabe Molina RC	.15
21	Luis Vizcaino RC	.20
22	Robinson Cancel RC	.10
23	Brett Laxton RC	.10
24	Joe McEwing RC	.25
25	Justin Speier RC	.20
26	Kip Wells RC	.25
27	Armando Almanza RC	.10
28	Joe Davenport RC	.10
29	Yamid Haad RC	.10
30	John Halama	.10
31	Adam Kennedy	.10
32	Vicente Padilla RC	.25
33	Travis Dawkins RC	.25
34	Ryan Rupe RC	.25
35	B.J. Ryan RC	.10
36	Chance Sanford RC	.10
37	Anthony Shumaker RC	.10
38	Ryan Glynn RC	.10
39	Matt Herges RC	.20
40	Ben Molina	.10
41	Scott Williamson	.10
42	Eric Gagne RC	1.50
43	John McDonald RC	.10
44	Scott Sauerbeck RC	.10
45	Mike Venafro RC	.10
46	Edwards Guzman RC	.10
47	Richard Barker RC	.10
48	Braden Looper	.10
49	Chad Meyers RC	.10
50	Scott Strickland RC	.10
51	Billy Koch	.10
52	Dave Newhan RC	.10
53	David Riske RC	.10
54	Jose Santiago	.10
55	Miguel Del Toro RC	.10
56	Orber Moreno RC	.10
57	Dave Roberts	.10
58	Tim Byrdak RC	.10
59	David Lee RC	.10
60	Guillermo Mota RC	.15
61	Wilton Veras RC	.15
62	Joe Mays RC	.35
63	Jose Fernandez RC	.10
64	Ray King RC	.10
65	Chris Petersen RC	.10
66	Vernon Wells	.15
67	Ruben Mateo	.10
68	Ben Petrick	.10
69	Chris Tremie RC	.10
70	Lance Berkman	.10
71	Dan Smith	.10
72	Carlos Hernandez RC	.10
73	Chad Harville RC	.25
74	Damaso Marte	.10
75	Aaron Myette RC	.15
76	Willis Roberts RC	.10
77	Erik Sabel RC	.10
78	Hector Almonte RC	.10
79	Kris Benson	.10
80	Pat Daneker RC	.10
81	Freddy Garcia RC	.50
82	Byung-Hyun Kim RC	.25
83	Wily Pena RC	1.00
84	Dan Wheeler RC	.15
85	Tim Harikkala RC	.10
86	Derrin Ebert RC	.10
87	Horacio Estrada RC	.10
88	Liu Rodriguez RC	.10
89	Jordan Zimmerman RC	.10
90	A.J. Burnett RC	.40
91	Doug Davis RC	.10
92	Robert Ramsey RC	.10
93	Ryan Franklin RC	.10
94	Charlie Greene RC	.10
95	Bo Porter RC	.10
96	Jorge Toca RC	.10
97	Casey Blake RC	.20
98	Amaury Garcia RC	.10
99	Jose Molina RC	.10
100	Melvin Mora RC	1.00
101	Joe Nathan RC	.10
102	Juan Pena RC	.25
103	Dave Borkowski RC	.10
104	Eddie Gaillard RC	.10
105	Rob Radlosky RC	.10
106	Brett Hinchliffe RC	.10
107	Carlos Lee	.10
108	Rob Ryan RC	.10

109	Jeff Weaver RC	.50
110	Ed Yarnall RC	.10
111	Nelson Cruz RC	.10
112	Cleatus Davidson RC	.10
113	Tim Kubinski RC	.10
114	Sean Spencer RC	.10
115	Joe Winkelsas RC	.10
116	Chris Clapinski RC	.10
117	Tom Davey RC	.10
118	Warren Morris	.10
119	Dan Murray RC	.10
120	Jose Nieves RC	.10
121	Mark Quinn RC	.10
122	Josh Beckett RC	10.00
123	Chad Allen RC	.10
124	Mike Figga	.10
125	Beiker Graterol RC	.10
126	Aaron Scheffer RC	.10
127	Wiki Gonzalez RC	.10
128	Ramon E. Martinez	.10
129	Matt Riley RC	.25
130	Chris Woodward RC	.10
131	Albert Belle	.10
132	Roger Cedeno	.10
133	Roger Clemens	.75
134	Brian Giles	.10
135	Rickey Henderson	.60
136	Randy Johnson	.60
137	Brian Jordan	.10
138	Paul Konerko	.15
139	Hideo Nomo	.50
140	Kenny Rogers	.10
141	Wade Boggs	.65
142	Jose Canseco	.45
143	Roger Clemens	.75
144	David Cone	.10
145	Tony Gwynn	.65
146	Mark McGwire	1.00
147	Cal Ripken Jr.	1.50
148	Alex Rodriguez	1.00
149	Fernando Tatis	.10
150	Robin Ventura	.10

1999 Fleer Brilliants

	NM/M
Complete Set (175):	60.00
Common Player:	.25
Common SP (126-175):	.50
Blues (1:3):	1.5X
SP Blues (1:6)	1X
Golds:	8X
SP Golds:	3X
Production 99 Sets	
24 Karat Golds:	40X
SP's:	15X
Production 24 Sets	
Pack (5):	2.00
Wax Box (24):	32.50
1	Mark McGwire	2.50
2	Derek Jeter	3.00
3	Nomar Garciaparra	1.75
4	Travis Lee	.25
5	Jeff Bagwell	.75
6	Andres Galarraga	.25
7	Pedro Martinez	.75
8	Cal Ripken Jr.	3.00
9	Vladimir Guerrero	.75
10	Chipper Jones	1.50
11	Rusty Greer	.25
12	Omar Vizquel	.25
13	Quinton McCracken	.25
14	Jaret Wright	.25
15	Mike Mussina	.50
16	Jason Giambi	.60
17	Tony Clark	.25
18	Troy O'Leary	.25
19	Troy Percival	.25
20	Kerry Wood	.50
21	Vinny Castilla	.25
22	Chris Carpenter	.25
23	Richie Sexson	.25
24	Ken Griffey Jr.	2.00

25	Barry Bonds	3.00
26	Carlos Delgado	.60
27	Frank Thomas	.75
28	Manny Ramirez	.75
29	Shawn Green	.50
30	Mike Piazza	2.00
31	Tino Martinez	.25
32	Dante Bichette	.25
33	Scott Rolen	.65
34	Gabe Alvarez	.25
35	Raul Mondesi	.25
36	Damion Easley	.25
37	Jeff Kent	.25
38	Al Leiter	.25
39	Alex Rodriguez	2.50
40	Jeff King	.25
41	Mark Grace	.25
42	Larry Walker	.25
43	Moises Alou	.25
44	Juan Gonzalez	.65
45	Rolando Arrojo	.25
46	Tom Glavine	.45
47	Johnny Damon	.45
48	Livan Hernandez	.25
49	Craig Biggio	.25
50	Dmitri Young	.25
51	Chan Ho Park	.25
52	Todd Walker	.25
53	Derrek Lee	.25
54	Todd Helton	.75
55	Ray Lankford	.25
56	Jim Thome	.65
57	Matt Lawton	.25
58	Matt Anderson	.25
59	Jose Offerman	.25
60	Eric Karros	.25
61	Orlando Hernandez	.25
62	Ben Grieve	.25
63	Bobby Abreu	.25
64	Kevin Young	.25
65	John Olerud	.25
66	Sammy Sosa	1.75
67	Andy Ashby	.25
68	Juan Encarnacion	.25
69	Shane Reynolds	.25
70	Bernie Williams	.35
71	Mike Cameron	.25
72	Troy Glaus	.75
73	Gary Sheffield	.60
74	Jeromy Burnitz	.25
75	Mike Caruso	.25
76	Chuck Knoblauch	.25
77	Kenny Rogers	.25
78	David Cone	.25
79	Tony Gwynn	1.50
80	Aramis Ramirez	.25
81	Paul O'Neill	.25
82	Charles Nagy	.25
83	Javy Lopez	.25
84	Scott Erickson	.25
85	Trevor Hoffman	.25
86	Andruw Jones	.75
87	Ray Durham	.25
88	Jorge Posada	.25
89	Edgar Martinez	.25
90	Tim Salmon	.35
91	Bobby Higginson	.25
92	Adrian Beltre	.45
93	Jason Kendall	.25
94	Henry Rodriguez	.25
95	Greg Maddux	1.50
96	David Justice	.25
97	Ivan Rodriguez	.65
98	Curt Schilling	.45
99	Matt Williams	.25
100	Darin Erstad	.50
101	Rafael Palmeiro	.65
102	David Wells	.25
103	Barry Larkin	.25
104	Robin Ventura	.25
105	Edgar Renteria	.25
106	Andy Pettitte	.50
107	Albert Belle	.25
108	Steve Finley	.25
109	Fernando Vina	.25
110	Rondell White	.25
111	Kevin Brown	.25
112	Jose Canseco	.50
113	Roger Clemens	1.75
114	Todd Hundley	.25
115	Will Clark	.35
116	Jim Edmonds	.25
117	Randy Johnson	.75
118	Denny Neagle	.25
119	Brian Jordan	.25
120	Dean Palmer	.25
121	Roberto Alomar	.45
122	Ken Caminiti	.25
123	Brian Giles	.25
124	Todd Stottlemyre	.25
125	Mo Vaughn	.25
126	J.D. Drew	1.00
127	Ryan Minor	.50
128	Gabe Kapler	.50

129	Jeremy Giambi	.50
130	Eric Chavez	1.00
131	Ben Davis	.50
132	Rob Fick	.50
133	George Lombard	.50
134	Calvin Pickering	.50
135	Preston Wilson	.50
136	Corey Koskie	.75
137	Russell Branyan	.50
138	Bruce Chen	.50
139	Matt Clement	.75
140	Pat Burrell RC	2.50
141	Freddy Garcia RC	1.00
142	Brian Simmons	.50
143	Carlos Febles	.50
144	Carlos Guillen	.50
145	Fernando Seguignol	.50
146	Carlos Beltran	1.00
147	Edgard Clemente	.50
148	Mitch Meluskey	.50
149	Ryan Bradley	.50
150	Marlon Anderson	.50
151	A.J. Burnett RC	1.00
152	Scott Hunter RC	.50
153	Mark Johnson	.50
154	Angel Pena	.50
155	Roy Halladay	.75
156	Chad Allen RC	.50
157	Trot Nixon	.75
158	Ricky Ledee	.50
159	Gary Bennett RC	.50
160	Micah Bowie RC	.60
161	Doug Mientkiewicz	.60
162	Danny Klassen	.50
163	Willis Otanez	.50
164	Jin Ho Cho	.50
165	Mike Lowell	.60
166	Armando Rios	.50
167	Tom Evans	.50
168	Michael Barrett	.50
169	Alex Gonzalez	.50
170	Masao Kida RC	.60
171	Peter Tucci RC	.50
172	Luis Saturria	.50
173	Kris Benson	.50
174	Mario Encarnacion RC	.50
175	Roosevelt Brown RC	.50

Blue/Golds

	NM/M
Brilliants Blue Common:	.50
Brilliants Blue Stars:	1.5X
Brilliants Blue Rookies:	1X
Brilliants Gold Common:	3.00
Brilliants Gold Stars:	8X
Brilliants Gold Rookies:	3X
Brilliants 24K Gold	
Common:	10.00
Brilliants 24K Gold Stars:	40X
Brilliants 24K Gold Rookies:	15X

(See 1999 Fleer Brilliants for checklist and base card values.)

Illuminators

	NM/M
Complete Set (15):	10.00
Common Player:	.75
Inserted 1:10	
1	Kerry Wood	2.00
2	Ben Grieve	.75
3	J.D. Drew	1.50
4	Juan Encarnacion	.75
5	Travis Lee	.75
6	Todd Helton	3.00
7	Troy Glaus	2.00
8	Ricky Ledee	.75
9	Eric Chavez	1.50
10	Ben Davis	.75
11	George Lombard	.75
12	Jeremy Giambi	.75
13	Richie Sexson	.75
14	Corey Koskie	.75
15	Russell Branyan	.75

Shining Stars

Alex Rodriguez•SS

	NM/M
Complete Set (15):	30.00
Common Player:	1.50
Inserted 1:20	
Pulsars:	4X
Inserted 1:400	
1	Ken Griffey Jr.	2.50
2	Mark McGwire	3.00
3	Sammy Sosa	2.25
4	Derek Jeter	4.00
5	Nomar Garciaparra	2.25
6	Alex Rodriguez	3.00
7	Mike Piazza	2.50
8	Juan Gonzalez	1.50
9	Chipper Jones	2.00
10	Cal Ripken Jr.	4.00
11	Frank Thomas	1.50
12	Greg Maddux	2.00
13	Roger Clemens	2.25
14	Vladimir Guerrero	1.50
15	Manny Ramirez	1.50

1999 Fleer Mystique

Derek Jeter

	NM/M
Complete Set (160):	125.00
Common Player:	.20
Common SP (1-100):	.75
Common (101-150):	1.00
Production 2,999 Sets	
Common (151-160):	2.00
Production 2,500 Sets	
Pack (4):	3.00
Wax Box (24):	60.00
1	Ken Griffey Jr./SP	2.50
2	Livan Hernandez	.20
3	Jeff Kent	.20
4	Brian Jordan	.20
5	Kevin Young	.20
6	Vinny Castilla	.20
7	Orlando Hernandez/SP	.75
8	Bobby Abreu	.20
9	Vladimir Guerrero/SP	1.50
10	Chuck Knoblauch	.20
11	Nomar Garciaparra/SP	2.25
12	Jeff Bagwell	1.00
13	Todd Walker	.20
14	Johnny Damon	.45
15	Mike Caruso	.20
16	Cliff Floyd	.20
17	Andy Pettitte	.35
18	Cal Ripken Jr./SP	4.00
19	Brian Giles	.20
20	Robin Ventura	.20
21	Alex Gonzalez	.20
22	Randy Johnson	.75
23	Raul Mondesi	.20
24	Ken Caminiti	.20
25	Tom Glavine	.40
26	Derek Jeter/SP	4.00

27	Carlos Delgado	.50
28	Adrian Beltre	.35
29	Tino Martinez	.20
30	Todd Helton	1.00
31	Juan Gonzalez/SP	1.25
32	Henry Rodriguez	.20
33	Jim Thome	.65
34	Paul O'Neill	.20
35	Scott Rolen/SP	1.25
36	Rafael Palmeiro	.65
37	Will Clark	.25
38	Todd Hundley	.20
39	Andruw Jones/SP	1.50
40	Luis Rolando Arrojo	.20
41	Barry Larkin	.20
42	Tim Salmon	.25
43	Rondell White	.20
44	Curt Schilling	.40
45	Chipper Jones/SP	2.00
46	Jeromy Burnitz	.20
47	Mo Vaughn	.20
48	Tony Clark	.20
49	Fernando Tatis	.20
50	Dmitri Young	.20
51	Wade Boggs	1.50
52	Rickey Henderson	.75
53	Manny Ramirez/SP	1.50
54	Edgar Martinez	.20
55	Jason Giambi	.65
56	Jason Kendall	.20
57	Eric Karros	.20
58	Jose Canseco/SP	1.00
59	Shawn Green	.40
60	Ellis Burks	.20
61	Derek Bell	.20
62	Shannon Stewart	.20
63	Roger Clemens/SP	2.25
64	Sean Casey/SP	.75
65	Jose Offerman	.20
66	Sammy Sosa/SP	2.25
67	Frank Thomas/SP	1.50
68	Tony Gwynn/SP	2.00
69	Roberto Alomar	.35
70	Mark McGwire/SP	3.00
71	Troy Glaus	1.00
72	Ray Durham	.20
73	Jeff Cirillo	.20
74	Alex Rodriguez/SP	3.00
75	Jose Cruz Jr.	.20
76	Juan Encarnacion	.20
77	Mark Grace	.20
78	Barry Bonds/SP	4.00
79	Ivan Rodriguez/SP	1.25
80	Greg Vaughn	.20
81	Greg Maddux/SP	2.00
82	Albert Belle	.20
83	John Olerud	.20
84	Kenny Lofton	.20
85	Bernie Williams	.30
86	Matt Williams	.20
87	Ray Lankford	.20
88	Darin Erstad	.40
89	Ben Grieve	.20
90	Craig Biggio	.20
91	Dean Palmer	.20
92	Reggie Sanders	.20
93	Dante Bichette	.20
94	Pedro Martinez/SP	1.50
95	Larry Walker	.20
96	David Wells	.20
97	Travis Lee/SP	.75
98	Mike Piazza/SP	2.50
99	Mike Mussina	.45
100	Kevin Brown	.20
101	Ruben Mateo	1.00
102	Roberto Ramirez	1.00
103	Glen Barker RC	1.00
104	Clay Bellinger RC	1.00
105	Carlos Guillen	1.00
106	Scott Schoeneweis	1.00
107	Creighton Gubanich	1.00
108	Scott Williamson	1.00
109	Edwards Guzman RC	1.00
110	A.J. Burnett RC	4.00
111	Jeremy Giambi	1.00
112	Trot Nixon	1.50
113	J.D. Drew	3.00
114	Roy Halladay	1.50
115	Jose Macias RC	2.00
116	Corey Koskie	2.00
117	Ryan Rupe RC	1.50
118	Scott Hunter	1.00
119	Rob Fick	1.00
120	McKay Christensen	1.50
121	Carlos Febles	2.00
122	Gabe Kapler	1.50
123	Jeff Liefer	1.00
124	Warren Morris	1.00
125	Chris Pritchett	1.00
126	Torii Hunter	3.00
127	Armando Rios	1.00
128	Ricky Ledee	1.00
129	Kelly Dransfeldt RC	1.00
130	Jeff Zimmerman	1.50

131	Eric Chavez	2.00
132	Freddy Garcia	3.00
133	Jose Jimenez	1.00
134	Pat Burrell RC	20.00
135	Joe McEwing RC	1.50
136	Kris Benson	1.00
137	Joe Mays RC	2.00
138	Rafael Roque	1.00
139	Cristian Guzman	1.50
140	Michael Barrett	1.50
141	Doug Mientkiewicz	1.50
142	Jeff Weaver RC	4.00
143	Mike Lowell	1.50
144	Jason Phillips RC	2.00
145	Marlon Anderson	1.50
146	Brett Hinchliffe RC	1.00
147	Matt Clement	1.50
148	Terrence Long	1.00
149	Carlos Beltran	2.50
150	Preston Wilson	1.50
151	Ken Griffey Jr.	2.00
152	Mark McGwire	3.00
153	Sammy Sosa	1.50
154	Mike Piazza	2.00
155	Alex Rodriguez	3.00
156	Nomar Garciaparra	1.50
157	Cal Ripken Jr.	4.00
158	Greg Maddux	1.50
159	Derek Jeter	4.00
160	Juan Gonzalez	1.00
	Checklist Card	.10

Gold

	NM/M
Common Player:	1.00
Stars (1-100):	1.5X
Inserted 1:8	

(See 1999 Fleer Mystique for checklist and base card values.)

Masterpiece

Ken Griffey Jr. The Only 1 of 1 Masterpiece

	NM/M
Common Player:	50.00

(Because of their unique nature star Masterpiece values cannot be determined.)

Destiny

JUAN GONZALEZ 287/999

	NM/M
Complete Set (10):	35.00
Common Player:	2.00
Production 999 Sets	
1	Tony Gwynn	5.00
2	Juan Gonzalez	3.00
3	Scott Rolen	4.00
4	Nomar Garciaparra	6.00
5	Orlando Hernandez	2.00
6	Andruw Jones	4.00
7	Vladimir Guerrero	3.00
8	Darin Erstad	2.00

| 9 | Manny Ramirez | 4.00 |
| 10 | Roger Clemens | 6.00 |

Established

		NM/M
Complete Set (10):		300.00
Common Player:		15.00
Production 100 Sets		
1	Ken Griffey Jr.	30.00
2	Derek Jeter	60.00
3	Chipper Jones	20.00
4	Greg Maddux	20.00
5	Mark McGwire	45.00
6	Mike Piazza	30.00
7	Cal Ripken Jr.	60.00
8	Alex Rodriguez	45.00
9	Sammy Sosa	25.00
10	Frank Thomas	15.00

Feel the Game

	NM/M
Common Player:	10.00
Adrian Beltre/Shoe/430	15.00
J.D. Drew/Jsy/450	15.00
Juan Gonzalez/Bat Glove/415	10.00
Tony Gwynn/Jsy/435	15.00
Kevin Millwood/Jsy/435	10.00
Alex Rodriguez/Bat Glove/345	30.00
Frank Thomas/Jsy/450	15.00

Fresh Ink

	NM/M
Complete Set (26):	300.00
Common Player:	4.00
Inserted 1:48	
Roberto Alomar/500	10.00
Michael Barrett/1,000	6.00
Kris Benson/500	8.00
Micah Bowie/1,000	4.00
A.J. Burnett/500	10.00
Pat Burrell/500	15.00
Ken Caminiti/250	10.00
Jose Canseco/250	25.00
Sean Casey/1,000	8.00
Edgard Clemente/1,000	4.00
Bartolo Colon/500	8.00
J.D. Drew/400	15.00
Juan Encarnacion/1,000	4.00
Troy Glaus/400	15.00
Juan Gonzalez/250	15.00
Shawn Green/250	15.00
Tony Gwynn/250	30.00
Chipper Jones/250	30.00
Gabe Kapler/750	6.00
Barry Larkin/250	25.00
Doug Mientkiewicz/500	6.00
Alex Rodriguez/200	80.00
Scott Rolen/140	30.00
Fernando Tatis/750	4.00
Robin Ventura/500	6.00
Todd Walker/1,000	6.00

Prophetic

		NM/M
Complete Set (10):		15.00
Common Player:		1.00
Production 1,999 Sets		
1	Eric Chavez	1.50
2	J.D. Drew	2.00
3	A.J. Burnett	1.00
4	Ben Grieve	1.00
5	Gabe Kapler	1.00
6	Todd Helton	2.50
7	Troy Glaus	4.00
8	Travis Lee	1.00
9	Pat Burrell	5.00
10	Kerry Wood	1.50

2000 Fleer Focus

		NM/M
Complete Set (250):		100.00
Common Player:		.15
Common Prospect (226-250)		4.00
Production 2,999 Sets		
Common Portrait (226-250):		8.00
Portraits:		2X
Production 999 Sets		
Pack:		2.00
Wax Box (24):		35.00
1	Nomar Garciaparra	1.25
2	Adrian Beltre	.35
3	Miguel Tejada	.35
4	Joe Randa	.15
5	Larry Walker	.15
6	Jeff Weaver	.15
7	Jay Bell	.15
8	Ivan Rodriguez	.50
9	Edgar Martinez	.15
10	Desi Relaford	.15
11	Derek Jeter	2.50
12	Delino DeShields	.15
13	Craig Biggio	.15
14	Chuck Knoblauch	.15
15	Chuck Finley	.15
16	Brett Tomko	.15
17	Bobby Higginson	.15
18	Pedro Martinez	.75
19	Troy O'Leary	.15
20	Rickey Henderson	.75
21	Robb Nen	.15
22	Rolando Arrojo	.15
23	Rondell White	.15
24	Royce Clayton	.15
25	Rusty Greer	.15
26	Stan Spencer	.15
27	Steve Finley	.15
28	Tom Goodwin	.15
29	Troy Percival	.15
30	Wilton Guerrero	.15
31	Roberto Alomar	.30
32	Mike Hampton	.15
33	Michael Barrett	.15
34	Curt Schilling	.40
35	Bill Mueller	.15
36	Bernie Williams	.30
37	John Smoltz	.15
38	B.J. Surhoff	.15
39	Pete Harnisch	.15
40	Juan Encarnacion	.15
41	Derrek Lee	.15
42	Jeff Shaw	.15
43	David Cone	.15
44	Jason Christiansen	.15
45	Jeff Kent	.15
46	Randy Johnson	.75
47	Todd Walker	.15
48	Jose Lima	.15
49	Jason Giambi	.15
50	Ken Griffey Jr.	1.50
51	Bartolo Colon	.15
52	Mike Lieberthal	.15
53	Shane Reynolds	.15
54	Travis Lee	.15
55	Travis Fryman	.15
56	John Valentin	.15
57	Joey Hamilton	.15
58	Jay Buhner	.15
59	Brad Radke	.15
60	A.J. Burnett	.15
61	Roy Halladay	.25
62	Raul Mondesi	.15
63	Matt Mantei	.15
64	Mark Grace	.15
65	David Justice	.15
66	Billy Wagner	.15
67	Eric Milton	.15
68	Eric Chavez	.25
69	Doug Glanville	.15
70	Ray Durham	.15
71	Mike Sirotka	.15
72	Greg Vaughn	.15
73	Brian Jordan	.15
74	Alex Gonzalez	.15
75	Alex Rodriguez	2.00
76	David Nilsson	.15
77	Robin Ventura	.15
78	Kevin Young	.15
79	Wilson Alvarez	.15
80	Matt Williams	.15
81	Ismael Valdes	.15
82	Kenny Lofton	.15
83	Carlos Beltran	.45
84	Doug Mientkiewicz	.15
85	Wally Joyner	.15
86	J.D. Drew	.35
87	Carlos Delgado	.50
88	Tony Womack	.15
89	Eric Young	.15
90	Manny Ramirez	.75
91	Johnny Damon	.15
92	Torii Hunter	.25
93	Kenny Rogers	.15
94	Trevor Hoffman	.15
95	John Wetteland	.15
96	Ray Lankford	.15
97	Tom Glavine	.30
98	Carlos Lee	.15
99	Richie Sexson	.15
100	Carlos Febles	.15
101	Chad Allen	.15
102	Sterling Hitchcock	.15
103	Joe McEwing	.15
104	Justin Thompson	.15
105	Jim Edmonds	.15
106	Kerry Wood	.40
107	Jim Thome	.65
108	Jeremy Giambi	.15
109	Mike Piazza	1.50
110	Darryl Kile	.15
111	Darin Erstad	.30
112	Kyle Farnsworth	.15
113	Omar Vizquel	.15
114	Orber Moreno	.15
115	Al Leiter	.15
116	John Olerud	.15
117	Aaron Sele	.15
118	Chipper Jones	1.00
119	Paul Konerko	.25
120	Chris Singleton	.15
121	Fernando Vina	.15
122	Andy Ashby	.15
123	Eli Marrero	.15
124	Edgar Renteria	.15
125	Roberto Hernandez	.15
126	Andruw Jones	.75
127	Magglio Ordonez	.25
128	Bob Wickman	.15
129	Tony Gwynn	1.00
130	Mark McGwire	2.00
131	Albert Belle	.15
132	Pokey Reese	.15
133	Tony Clark	.15
134	Jeff Bagwell	.75
135	Mark Grudzielanek	.15
136	Dustin Hermanson	.15
137	Reggie Sanders	.15
138	Ryan Rupe	.15
139	Kevin Millwood	.15
140	Bret Saberhagen	.15
141	Juan Guzman	.15
142	Alex Gonzalez	.15
143	Gary Sheffield	.30
144	Roger Clemens	1.25
145	Ben Grieve	.15
146	Bobby Abreu	.15
147	Brian Giles	.15
148	Quinton McCracken	.15
149	Freddy Garcia	.15
150	Erubiel Durazo	.15
151	Sidney Ponson	.15
152	Scott Williamson	.15
153	Ken Caminiti	.15
154	Vladimir Guerrero	.75
155	Andy Pettitte	.25
156	Edwards Guzman	.15
157	Shannon Stewart	.15
158	Greg Maddux	1.00
159	Mike Stanley	.15
160	Sean Casey	.25
161	Cliff Floyd	.15
162	Devon White	.15
163	Scott Brosius	.15
164	Marlon Anderson	.15
165	Jason Kendall	.15
166	Ryan Klesko	.15
167	Sammy Sosa	1.25
168	Frank Thomas	.75
169	Geoff Jenkins	.15
170	Jason Schmidt	.15
171	Dan Wilson	.15
172	Jose Canseco	.40
173	Troy Glaus	.75
174	Mariano Rivera	.20
175	Scott Rolen	.65
176	J.T. Snow	.15
177	Rafael Palmeiro	.65
178	A.J. Hinch	.15
179	Jose Offerman	.15
180	Jeff Cirillo	.15
181	Dean Palmer	.15
182	Jose Rosado	.15
183	Armando Benitez	.15
184	Brady Anderson	.15
185	Cal Ripken Jr.	2.50
186	Barry Larkin	.15
187	Damion Easley	.15
188	Moises Alou	.15
189	Todd Hundley	.15
190	Tim Hudson	.25
191	Livan Hernandez	.15
192	Fred McGriff	.15
193	Orlando Hernandez	.25
194	Tim Salmon	.20
195	Mike Mussina	.40
196	Todd Helton	.75
197	Juan Gonzalez	.50
198	Kevin Brown	.15
199	Ugueth Urbina	.15
200	Matt Stairs	.15
201	Shawn Estes	.15
202	Gabe Kapler	.15
203	Javy Lopez	.15
204	Henry Rodriguez	.15
205	Dante Bichette	.15
206	Jeromy Burnitz	.15
207	Todd Zeile	.15
208	Rico Brogna	.15
209	Warren Morris	.15
210	David Segui	.15
211	Vinny Castilla	.15
212	Mo Vaughn	.15
213	Charles Johnson	.15
214	Neifi Perez	.15
215	Shawn Green	.40
216	Carl Pavano	.15
217	Tino Martinez	.15
218	Barry Bonds	2.50
219	David Wells	.15
220	Paul O'Neill	.15
221	Masato Yoshii	.15
222	Kris Benson	.15
223	Fernando Tatis	.15
224	Lee Stevens	.15
225	Jose Cruz Jr.	.15
226	Rick Ankiel	4.00
227	Matt Riley	4.00
228	Norm Hutchins	4.00
229	Ruben Mateo	4.00
230	Ben Petrick	4.00
231	Mario Encarnacion	6.00
232	Nick Johnson	6.00
233	Adam Piatt	6.00
234	Mike Darr	4.00
235	Chad Hermansen	4.00
236	Wily Pena	6.00
237	Octavio Dotel	6.00
238	Vernon Wells	6.00
239	Daryle Ward	4.00
240	Adam Kennedy	4.00
241	Angel Pena	4.00
242	Lance Berkman	6.00
243	Gabe Molina	4.00
244	Steve Lomasney	4.00
245	Jacob Cruz	4.00
246	Mark Quinn	4.00
247	Eric Munson	4.00
248	Alfonso Soriano	6.00
249	Kip Wells	4.00
250	Josh Beckett	6.00

ABBREVIATIONS

OPS - Overprinted
"Promotional Sample"
SP - Short Print

Green

	NM/M
Common Player:	3.00
Stars:	5-10X
Yng Stars & RC's (226-250):	1-2X

Production 300 Sets
(See 2000 Fleer Focus for checklist and base card values.)

Masterpiece

	NM/M
Common Player:	100.00

(Values undetermined due to rarity and fluctuating demand. See 2000 Fleer Focus for checklist.)

Masterpiece Errors

DAVID SEGUI
Blue Jays • First Base

		NM/M
Complete Set (25):		250.00
Common Player:		4.00
50M	Ken Griffey Jr.	100.00
202M	Gabe Kapler	8.00
203M	Javy Lopez	6.00
204M	Henry Rodriguez	4.00
205M	Dante Bichette	5.00
206M	Jeromy Burnitz	5.00
207M	Todd Zeile	4.00
208M	Rico Brogna	4.00
209M	Warren Morris	4.00
210M	David Segui	4.00
211M	Vinny Castilla	5.00
212M	Mo Vaughn	6.00
213M	Charles Johnson	5.00
214M	Neifi Perez	5.00
215M	Shawn Green	20.00
216M	Carl Pavano	4.00
217M	Tino Martinez	5.00
218M	Barry Bonds	30.00
219M	David Wells	8.00
220M	Paul O'Neill	6.00
221M	Masato Yoshii	5.00
222M	Kris Benson	8.00
223M	Fernando Tatis	6.00
224M	Lee Stevens	4.00
225M	Jose Cruz Jr.	6.00

Club 3000

		NM/M
Complete Set (3):		4.00
Common Player:		1.50
(1)	Steve Carlton	1.50
(2)	Paul Molitor	1.50
(3)	Stan Musial	1.50

Club 3000 Memorabilia

	NM/M
Steve Carlton/ Bat/325	25.00

Steve Carlton/Hat/65	75.00
Steve Carlton/Jsy/750	20.00
Steve Carlton/ Bat/Hat/Jsy/25	200.00
Paul Molitor/Bat/355	30.00
Paul Molitor/Hat/65	85.00
Paul Molitor/Jsy/975	20.00
Paul Molitor/Bat/ Jsy/100	60.00
Stan Musial/ Bat/325	50.00
Stan Musial/Hat/65	125.00
Stan Musial/Jsy/975	35.00
Stan Musial/Bat/ Jsy/100	80.00

Feel the Game

ALEX RODRIGUEZ

		NM/M
Common Player:		5.00
Inserted 1:288		
	Adrian Beltre	7.50
	Tom Glavine	10.00
	Vladimir Guerrero	15.00
	Randy Johnson	15.00
	Javy Lopez	5.00
	Alex Rodriguez	30.00
	Scott Rolen	10.00
	Cal Ripken Jr.	40.00
	Tim Salmon	6.00
	Miguel Tejada	10.00

Focal Points

		NM/M
Complete Set (15):		15.00
Common Player:		.75
Inserted 1:6		
1	Mark McGwire	2.50
2	Tony Gwynn	1.00
3	Nomar Garciaparra	2.00
4	Juan Gonzalez	.75
5	Jeff Bagwell	.75
6	Chipper Jones	1.00
7	Cal Ripken Jr.	3.00
8	Alex Rodriguez	2.50
9	Scott Rolen	.75
10	Vladimir Guerrero	.75
11	Mike Piazza	1.50
12	Frank Thomas	.75
13	Ken Griffey Jr.	1.50
14	Sammy Sosa	1.50
15	Derek Jeter	3.00

Focus Pocus

		NM/M
Complete Set (10):		12.00
Common Player:		1.00
Inserted 1:14		
1	Cal Ripken Jr.	3.00
2	Tony Gwynn	1.50
3	Nomar Garciaparra	2.00
4	Juan Gonzalez	1.00
5	Mike Piazza	2.00

6	Mark McGwire	2.50
7	Chipper Jones	1.50
8	Ken Griffey Jr.	2.00
9	Derek Jeter	3.00
10	Alex Rodriguez	2.50

Future Vision

Chad Hermansen
Pittsburgh Pirates

		NM/M
Complete Set (15):		8.00
Common Player:		.40
Inserted 1:9		
1	Rick Ankiel	.40
2	Matt Riley	.40
3	Ruben Mateo	.40
4	Ben Petrick	.40
5	Mario Encarnacion	.40
6	Octavio Dotel	.40
7	Vernon Wells	.65
8	Adam Kennedy	.40
9	Lance Berkman	.40
10	Chad Hermansen	.40
11	Mark Quinn	.40
12	Eric Munson	.40
13	Alfonso Soriano	2.00
14	Kip Wells	.40
15	Josh Beckett	.75

Fresh Ink

		NM/M
Common Player:		5.00
Inserted 1:96		
	Chad Allen	5.00
	Michael Barrett	5.00
	Josh Beckett	30.00
	Rob Bell	5.00
	Adrian Beltre	15.00
	Milton Bradley	8.00
	Rico Brogna	5.00
	Mike Cameron	8.00
	Eric Chavez	15.00
	Bruce Chen	5.00
	Johnny Damon	20.00
	Ben Davis	5.00
	J.D. Drew	15.00
	Erubiel Durazo	10.00
	Jeremy Giambi	6.00
	Jason Giambi	25.00
	Doug Glanville	6.00
	Troy Glaus	25.00
	Shawn Green	20.00
	Mike Hampton	10.00
	Tim Hudson	15.00
	John Jaha	5.00
	Derek Jeter	150.00
	D'Angelo Jimenez	5.00
	Nick Johnson	8.00
	Andruw Jones	20.00
	Jason Kendall	10.00
	Adam Kennedy	6.00
	Mike Lieberthal	8.00

	Edgar Martinez	15.00
	Aaron McNeal	5.00
	Kevin Millwood	10.00
	Mike Mussina	30.00
	Magglio Ordonez	15.00
	Eric Owens	5.00
	Rafael Palmeiro	20.00
	Wily Pena	15.00
	Adam Piatt	8.00
	Cal Ripken Jr.	100.00
	Alex Rodriguez	65.00
	Scott Rolen	20.00
	Tim Salmon	15.00
	Chris Singleton	5.00
	Mike Sweeney	10.00
	Jose Vidro	8.00
	Rondell White	8.00
	Jaret Wright	5.00

2000 Fleer Gamers

DEREK JETER
NEW YORK YANKEES • SHORTSTOP

		NM/M
Complete Set (120):		50.00
Common Player (1-90):		.15
Common (91-110):		1.00
Inserted 1:3		
Common (111-120):		1.50
Inserted 1:8		
Pack:		2.00
Wax Box:		35.00
1	Cal Ripken Jr.	2.00
2	Derek Jeter	2.00
3	Alex Rodriguez	1.50
4	Alex Gonzalez	.15
5	Nomar Garciaparra	1.25
6	Brian Giles	.15
7	Chris Singleton	.15
8	Kevin Brown	.15
9	J.D. Drew	.25
10	Raul Mondesi	.15
11	Sammy Sosa	1.25
12	Carlos Beltran	.50
13	Eric Chavez	.25
14	Gabe Kapler	.15
15	Tim Salmon	.25
16	Manny Ramirez	.75
17	Orlando Hernandez	.15
18	Jeff Kent	.25
19	Juan Gonzalez	.75
20	Moises Alou	.15
21	Jason Giambi	.50
22	Ivan Rodriguez	.60
23	Geoff Jenkins	.15
24	Ken Griffey Jr.	1.25
25	Mark McGwire	1.50
26	Jose Canseco	.40
27	Roberto Alomar	.40
28	Craig Biggio	.15
29	Scott Rolen	.65
30	Vinny Castilla	.15
31	Greg Maddux	1.00
32	Pedro J. Martinez	.75
33	Mike Piazza	1.25
34	Albert Belle	.25
35	Frank Thomas	.75
36	Bobby Abreu	.15
37	Edgar Martinez	.15
38	Pokey Reese	.15
39	Preston Wilson	.15
40	Mike Lieberthal	.15
41	Andruw Jones	.75
42	Damion Easley	.15
43	Mike Cameron	.15
44	Todd Walker	.15
45	Jason Kendall	.15
46	Sean Casey	.25
47	Corey Koskie	.15
48	Warren Morris	.15
49	Andres Galarraga	.15
50	Dean Palmer	.15
51	Jose Vidro	.15
52	Brian Jordan	.15
53	Tony Clark	.15

54	Vladimir Guerrero	.75
55	Mo Vaughn	.15
56	Richie Sexson	.15
57	Tino Martinez	.15
58	Eric Owens	.15
59	Matt Williams	.15
60	Omar Vizquel	.15
61	Rickey Henderson	.75
62	J.T. Snow	.15
63	Mark Grace	.25
64	Carlos Febles	.15
65	Paul O'Neill	.15
66	Randy Johnson	.75
67	Kenny Lofton	.15
68	Roger Cedeno	.15
69	Shawn Green	.35
70	Chipper Jones	1.00
71	Jeff Cirillo	.15
72	Robin Ventura	.15
73	Paul Konerko	.15
74	Jeromy Burnitz	.15
75	Ben Grieve	.15
76	Troy Glaus	.75
77	Jim Thome	.15
78	Bernie Williams	.25
79	Barry Bonds	2.00
80	Ray Durham	.15
81	Adrian Beltre	.15
82	Ray Lankford	.15
83	Carlos Delgado	.50
84	Erubiel Durazo	.15
85	Larry Walker	.15
86	Edgardo Alfonzo	.15
87	Rafael Palmeiro	.65
88	Magglio Ordonez	.25
89	Jeff Bagwell	.75
90	Tony Gwynn	1.00
91	Norm Hutchins	1.00
92	Derrick Turnbow **RC**	1.50
93	Matt Riley	1.00
94	David Eckstein	1.00
95	Dernell Stenson	1.00
96	Joe Crede	1.00
97	Ben Petrick	1.00
98	Eric Munson	1.00
99	Pablo Ozuna	1.00
100	Josh Beckett	3.00
101	Aaron McNeal **RC**	1.50
102	Milton Bradley	1.50
103	Alex Escobar	1.50
104	Alfonso Soriano	4.00
105	Wily Pena	1.50
106	Nick Johnson	1.50
107	Adam Piatt	1.00
108	Pat Burrell	2.00
109	Rick Ankiel	1.00
110	Vernon Wells	2.00
111	Alex Rodriguez	3.00
112	Cal Ripken Jr.	4.00
113	Mark McGwire	3.00
114	Ken Griffey Jr.	2.00
115	Mike Piazza	2.00
116	Nomar Garciaparra	3.00
117	Derek Jeter	4.00
118	Chipper Jones	1.50
119	Sammy Sosa	2.00
120	Tony Gwynn	1.50

Extra

Stars (1-90):		5-10X
Inserted 1:24		
Next Gamers (91-110):		1-2X
Inserted 1:36		
Fame Game (110-120):		1-2X
Inserted 1:36		

(See Fleer Gamers for
checklist and base card values.)

Cal to Greatness

	NM/M
Complete Set (15):	100.00
Common Ripken (1-5):	3.00
Inserted 1:9	

Common Ripken (6-10):		6.00
Inserted 1:25		
Common Ripken (11-15):		20.00
Inserted 1:144		

Change the Game

	NM/M
Complete Set (15):	50.00
Common Player:	1.50
Inserted 1:24	

1	Alex Rodriguez	6.00
2	Cal Ripken Jr.	7.50
3	Chipper Jones	3.00
4	Derek Jeter	7.50
5	Ken Griffey Jr.	4.00
6	Mark McGwire	6.00
7	Mike Piazza	4.00
8	Nomar Garciaparra	4.00
9	Sammy Sosa	4.00
10	Tony Gwynn	3.00
11	Ivan Rodriguez	1.50
12	Pedro Martinez	2.00
13	Juan Gonzalez	2.00
14	Vladimir Guerrero	2.00
15	Manny Ramirez	2.00

Determined

	NM/M
Complete Set (15):	25.00
Common Player:	.50
Inserted 1:12	

1	Nomar Garciaparra	2.50
2	Chipper Jones	2.00
3	Derek Jeter	4.00
4	Mike Piazza	2.50
5	Jeff Bagwell	1.00
6	Mark McGwire	3.00
7	Greg Maddux	2.00
8	Sammy Sosa	2.50
9	Ken Griffey Jr.	2.50
10	Alex Rodriguez	3.00
11	Tony Gwynn	2.00
12	Cal Ripken Jr.	4.00
13	Barry Bonds	4.00
14	Juan Gonzalez	1.00
15	Sean Casey	.50

Lumber

	NM/M
Common Player:	5.00

Inserted 1:36		
1	Alex Rodriguez	30.00
2	Carlos Delgado	10.00
3	Jose Vidro	5.00
4	Carlos Febles	5.00
5	J.D. Drew	7.50
6	Mike Cameron	5.00
7	Derek Jeter	40.00
8	Eric Chavez	6.00
9	Cal Ripken Jr.	40.00
10	Gabe Kapler	5.00
11	Damion Easley	5.00
12	Frank Thomas	15.00
13	Chris Singleton	5.00
14	Norm Hutchins	5.00
15	Pokey Reese	5.00
16	Rafael Palmeiro	12.00
17	Ray Durham	5.00
18	Ray Lankford	5.00
19	Roger Cedeno	5.00
20	Shawn Green	6.00
21	Wade Boggs	20.00
22	Roberto Alomar	7.50
23	Moises Alou	5.00
24	Adrian Beltre	6.00
25	Barry Bonds	40.00
26	Jason Giambi	10.00
27	Jason Kendall	5.00
28	Paul Konerko	5.00
29	Mike Lieberthal	5.00
30	Edgar Martinez	5.00
31	Raul Mondesi	5.00
32	Scott Rolen	12.00
33	Alfonso Soriano	10.00
34	Ivan Rodriguez	10.00
35	Magglio Ordonez	5.00
36	Chipper Jones	20.00
37	Sean Casey	6.00
38	Edgardo Alfonzo	5.00
39	Robin Ventura	5.00
40	Bernie Williams	6.00
41	Vladimir Guerrero	15.00
42	Tony Clark	5.00
43	Carlos Beltran	10.00
44	Warren Morris	5.00
45	Jim Thome	5.00
46	Jeromy Burnitz	5.00
47	Matt Williams	5.00
48	Erubiel Durazo	5.00

Lumber Autograph

	NM/M
Common Player:	15.00
Inserted 1:287	

1	Derek Jeter	150.00
2	Eric Chavez	20.00
3	Rafael Palmeiro	40.00
4	Shawn Green	35.00
5	Roberto Alomar	45.00
6	Paul Konerko	15.00
7	Sean Casey	15.00
8	Alex Rodriguez	80.00
9	Robin Ventura	20.00
10	Erubiel Durazo	15.00
11	Tony Clark	15.00
12	Alfonso Soriano	60.00

2000 Fleer Greats of the Game

	NM/M
Complete Set (108):	50.00

Common Player:		.50
Pack (6):		10.00
Wax Box (24):		200.00
1	Mickey Mantle	8.00
2	Gil Hodges	1.00
3	Monte Irvin	1.00
4	Satchel Paige	2.50
5	Roy Campanella	2.00
6	Richie Ashburn	1.00
7	Roger Maris	3.00
8	Ozzie Smith	2.00
9	Reggie Jackson	2.50
10	Eddie Mathews	2.50
11	Dave Righetti	.50
12	Dave Winfield	1.00
13	Lou Whitaker	.50
14	Phil Garner	.50
15	Ron Cey	.50
16	Brooks Robinson	2.50
17	Bruce Sutter	.50
18	Dave Parker	.50
19	Johnny Bench	2.50
20	Fernando Valenzuela	.50
21	George Brett	4.00
22	Paul Molitor	2.00
23	Hoyt Wilhelm	.50
24	Luis Aparicio	.50
25	Frank White	.50
26	Herb Score	.50
27	Kirk Gibson	.50
28	Mike Schmidt	3.00
29	Don Baylor	.50
30	Joe Pepitone	.50
31	Hal McRae	.50
32	Lee Smith	.50
33	Nolan Ryan	7.00
33	Nolan Ryan/OPS	5.00
34	Bill Mazeroski	.75
35	Bobby Doerr	.50
36	Duke Snider	1.00
37	Dick Groat	.50
38	Larry Doby	.50
39	Kirby Puckett	2.00
40	Steve Carlton	1.00
41	Dennis Eckersley	.50
42	Jim Bunning	.50
43	Ron Guidry	.50
44	Alan Trammell	1.00
45	Bob Feller	1.50
46	Dave Concepcion	.50
47	Dwight Evans	.50
48	Enos Slaughter	.50
49	Tom Seaver	2.50
50	Tony Oliva	1.00
51	Mel Stottlemyre	.50
52	Tommy John	.50
53	Willie McCovey	1.00
54	Red Schoendienst	.50
55	Gorman Thomas	.50
56	Ralph Kiner	1.00
57	Robin Yount	2.00
58	Andre Dawson	1.00
59	Al Kaline	2.50
60	Dom DiMaggio	.50
61	Juan Marichal	1.00
62	Jack Morris	.50
63	Warren Spahn	1.50
64	Preacher Roe	.50
65	Darrell Evans	.50
66	Jim Bouton	.50
67	Rocky Colavito	.75
68	Bob Gibson	1.50
69	Whitey Ford	1.50
70	Moose Skowron	.50
71	Boog Powell	1.00
72	Al Lopez	.50
73	Lou Brock	1.00
74	Mickey Lolich	.50
75	Rod Carew	2.00
76	Bob Lemon	.50
77	Frank Howard	.50
78	Phil Rizzuto	1.50
79	Carl Yastrzemski	2.00
80	Rico Carty	.50
81	Jim Kaat	.50
82	Bert Blyleven	.50
83	George Kell	.50
84	Jim Palmer	1.00
85	Maury Wills	1.00
86	Jim Rice	.50
87	Joe Carter	.50
88	Clete Boyer	.50
89	Yogi Berra	2.00
90	Cecil Cooper	.50
91	Davey Johnson	.50
92	Lou Boudreau	.50
93	Orlando Cepeda	1.00
94	Tommy Henrich	.50
95	Hank Bauer	.50
96	Don Larsen	1.50
97	Vida Blue	1.00
98	Ben Oglivie	.50
99	Don Mattingly	5.00
100	Dale Murphy	1.00

101	Ferguson Jenkins	1.00
102	Bobby Bonds	.75
103	Dick Allen	.50
104	Stan Musial	3.00
105	Gaylord Perry	.50
106	Willie Randolph	.50
107	Willie Stargell	1.50
108	Checklist	.50

Autographs

George Brett

	NM/M
Common Player:	10.00

Inserted 1:6

Luis Aparicio		20.00
Hank Bauer		10.00
Don Baylor		20.00
Johnny Bench		180.00
Yogi Berra		150.00
Vida Blue		20.00
Bert Blyleven		10.00
Bobby Bonds		10.00
Lou Boudreau		75.00
Jim Bouton		20.00
Clete Boyer		15.00
George Brett		
(275 or less)		180.00
Lou Brock		20.00
Jim Bunning		30.00
Rod Carew		40.00
Steve Carlton		20.00
Joe Carter/SP		75.00
Orlando Cepeda		15.00
Ron Cey		15.00
Rocky Colavito		30.00
Dave Concepcion		
(Black autograph.)		15.00
Dave Concepcion		
(Red autograph.)		15.00
Cecil Cooper		10.00
Andre Dawson		15.00
Dom DiMaggio		75.00
Bobby Doerr		15.00
Darrell Evans		15.00
Bob Feller		20.00
Whitey Ford		
(300 or less)		100.00
Phil Garner		10.00
Bob Gibson		25.00
Kirk Gibson		20.00
Dick Groat		10.00
Ron Guidry		20.00
Tommy Henrich		
(300 or less)		100.00
Frank Howard		10.00
Reggie Jackson		
(250 or less)		120.00
Ferguson Jenkins		15.00
Tommy John		10.00
Davey Johnson		15.00
Jim Kaat		15.00
Al Kaline		35.00
George Kell		15.00
Ralph Kiner		20.00
Don Larsen		25.00
Mickey Lolich		10.00
Juan Marichal		40.00
Eddie Mathews		80.00
Don Mattingly		
(300 or less)		250.00
Bill Mazeroski		20.00
Willie McCovey		80.00
Hal McRae		10.00
Paul Molitor		40.00
Jack Morris		10.00
Dale Murphy		35.00
Stan Musial		100.00
Ben Oglivie		10.00
Tony Oliva		15.00
Jim Palmer/SP		80.00
Dave Parker		15.00
Joe Pepitone		10.00
Gaylord Perry		15.00

Boog Powell		15.00
Kirby Puckett		
(200 or less)		120.00
Willie Randolph		15.00
Jim Rice		15.00
Dave Righetti		10.00
Phil Rizzuto		
(200 or less)		140.00
Brooks Robinson		30.00
Preacher Roe		15.00
Nolan Ryan		150.00
Mike Schmidt		
(175 or less)		250.00
Red Schoendienst		15.00
Herb Score		25.00
Tom Seaver		75.00
Moose Skowron		15.00
Enos Slaughter		20.00
Lee Smith		10.00
Ozzie Smith/SP		150.00
Duke Snider/SP		140.00
Warren Spahn/SP		100.00
Bruce Sutter		12.50
Gorman Thomas		10.00
Alan Trammell		20.00
Frank White		10.00
Hoyt Wilhelm		15.00
Maury Wills		15.00
Dave Winfield		150.00
Carl Yastrzemski		60.00
Robin Yount/SP		125.00

Memorable Moments Autograph

	NM/M
Common Player:	60.00
1 Ron Guidry/78	75.00
2 Nolan Ryan/99	300.00
3 Herb Score/55	40.00
4 Tom Seaver/69	180.00

Retrospection

REGGIE JACKSON

	NM/M
Complete Set (15):	75.00
Common Player:	4.00

Inserted 1:6

1	Rod Carew	4.00
2	Stan Musial	8.00
3	Nolan Ryan	15.00
4	Tom Seaver	6.00
5	Brooks Robinson	5.00
6	Al Kaline	6.00
7	Mike Schmidt	10.00
8	Thurman Munson	8.00
9	Steve Carlton	4.00
10	Roger Maris	8.00
11	Duke Snider	5.00
12	Yogi Berra	6.00
13	Carl Yastrzemski	5.00
14	Reggie Jackson	6.00
15	Johnny Bench	8.00

Yankees Clippings

	NM/M
Common Player:	20.00

Inserted 1:48

1	Mickey Mantle	200.00
2	Ron Guidry	40.00
3	Don Larsen	40.00
4	Elston Howard	40.00

5	Mel Stottlemyre	25.00
6	Don Mattingly	100.00
7	Reggie Jackson	50.00
8	Tommy John	20.00
9	Dave Winfield	25.00
10	Willie Randolph	20.00
11	Tommy Henrich	20.00
12	Billy Martin	50.00
13	Dave Righetti	20.00
14	Joe Pepitone	20.00
15	Thurman Munson	80.00

2000 Fleer Impact

Roger Clemens P

	NM/M
Complete Set (200):	15.00
Common Player:	.10
Pack (10):	1.00
Box (36):	20.00

1	Cal Ripken Jr.	1.50
2	Jose Canseco	.25
3	Manny Ramirez	.60
4	Bernie Williams	.30
5	Troy Glaus	.60
6	Jeff Bagwell	.60
7	Corey Koskie	.10
8	Barry Larkin	.10
9	Mark Quinn	.10
10	Russ Ortiz	.10
11	Tim Salmon	.15
12	Preston Wilson	.10
13	Mo Vaughn	.10
14	Ray Lankford	.10
15	Sterling Hitchcock	.10
16	Al Leiter	.10
17	Jim Morris	.10
18	Freddy Garcia	.10
19	Adrian Beltre	.20
20	Eric Chavez	.20
21	Robinson Cancel	.10
22	Edgar Renteria	.10
23	John Jaha	.10
24	Chuck Finley	.10
25	Andres Galarraga	.10
26	Paul Byrd	.10
27	John Halama	.10
28	Eric Karros	.10
29	Mike Piazza	1.00
30	Ryan Rupe	.10
31	Frank Thomas	.60
32	Randy Velarde	.10
33	Bobby Abreu	.10
34	Randy Johnson	.60
35	Matt Williams	.10
36	Tony Gwynn	.75
37	Dean Palmer	.10
38	Aaron Sele	.10
39	Rondell White	.10
40	Erubiel Durazo	.10
41	Curt Schilling	.25
42	Kip Wells	.10
43	Craig Biggio	.10
44	Tom Glavine	.25
45	Trevor Hoffman	.10
46	Greg Vaughn	.10
47	Edgar Martinez	.10
48	Magglio Ordonez	.20
49	Mark Mulder	.10
50	John Rocker	.10
51	Kenny Rogers	.10
52	Gary Sheffield	.25
53	Brian Simmons	.10
54	Tony Womack	.10
55	Ken Caminiti	.10
56	Jeff Cirillo	.10
57	Ray Durham	.10
58	Mike Lieberthal	.10
59	Ruben Mateo	.10
60	Mike Cameron	.10
61	Rusty Greer	.10
62	Alex Rodriguez	1.25
63	Robin Ventura	.10
64	Pokey Reese	.10
65	Jose Lima	.10
66	Neifi Perez	.10

67	Rafael Palmeiro	.50
68	Scott Rolen	.50
69	Mike Hampton	.10
70	Sammy Sosa	1.00
71	Mike Stanley	.10
72	Dan Wilson	.10
73	Kerry Wood	.50
74	Mike Mussina	.30
75	Masato Yoshii	.10
76	Peter Bergeron	.10
77	Carlos Delgado	.50
78	Juan Encarnacion	.10
79	Nomar Garciaparra	1.00
80	Jason Kendall	.10
81	Pedro Martinez	.60
82	Darin Erstad	.40
83	Larry Walker	.10
84	Rick Ankiel	.10
85	Scott Erickson	.10
86	Roger Clemens	.85
87	Matt Lawton	.10
88	Jon Lieber	.10
89	Shane Reynolds	.10
90	Ivan Rodriguez	.50
91	Pat Burrell	.50
92	Kent Bottenfield	.10
93	David Cone	.10
94	Mark Grace	.15
95	Paul Konerko	.10
96	Eric Milton	.10
97	Lee Stevens	.10
98	B.J. Surhoff	.10
99	Billy Wagner	.10
100	Ken Griffey Jr.	1.00
101	Randy Wolf	.10
102	Henry Rodriguez	.10
103	Carlos Beltran	.40
104	Rich Aurilia	.10
105	Chipper Jones	.75
106	Homer Bush	.10
107	Johnny Damon	.10
108	J.D. Drew	.40
109	Orlando Hernandez	.10
110	Brad Radke	.10
111	Wilton Veras	.10
112	Dmitri Young	.10
113	Jermaine Dye	.10
114	Kris Benson	.10
115	Derek Jeter	1.50
116	Cole Liniak	.10
117	Jim Thome	.10
118	Pedro Astacio	.10
119	Carlos Febles	.10
120	Darryl Kile	.10
121	Alfonso Soriano	.50
122	Michael Barrett	.10
123	Ellis Burks	.10
124	Chad Hermansen	.10
125	Trot Nixon	.10
126	Bobby Higginson	.10
127	Rick Helling	.10
128	Chris Carpenter	.10
129	Vinny Castilla	.10
130	Brian Giles	.10
131	Todd Helton	.60
132	Jason Varitek	.10
133	Rob Ducey	.10
134	Octavio Dotel	.10
135	Adam Kennedy	.10
136	Jeff Kent	.10
137	Aaron Boone	.10
138	Todd Walker	.10
139	Jeromy Burnitz	.10
140	Roberto Hernandez	.10
141	Matt LeCroy	.10
142	Ugueth Urbina	.10
143	David Wells	.10
144	Luis Gonzalez	.25
145	Andruw Jones	.50
146	Juan Gonzalez	.60
147	Moises Alou	.10
148	Michael Tejera	.10
149	Brian Jordan	.10
150	Mark McGwire	1.25
151	Shawn Green	.25
152	Jay Bell	.10
153	Fred McGriff	.10
154	Rey Ordonez	.10
155	Matt Stairs	.10
156	A.J. Burnett	.10
157	Omar Vizquel	.10
158	Damion Easley	.10
159	Dante Bichette	.10
160	Javy Lopez	.10
161	Fernando Seguignol	.10
162	Richie Sexson	.10
163	Vladimir Guerrero	.60
164	Kevin Young	.10
165	Josh Beckett	.10
166	Albert Belle	.10
167	Cliff Floyd	.10
168	Gabe Kapler	.10
169	Nick Johnson	.15
170	Raul Mondesi	.10
171	Warren Morris	.10
172	Kenny Lofton	.10

173 Reggie Sanders	.10
174 Mike Sweeney	.10
175 Robert Fick	.10
176 Barry Bonds	1.50
177 Luis Castillo	.10
178 Roger Cedeno	.10
179 Jim Edmonds	.10
180 Geoff Jenkins	.10
181 Adam Piatt	.10
182 Phil Nevin	.10
183 Roberto Alomar	.30
184 Kevin Brown	.10
185 D.T. Cromer	.10
186 Jason Giambi	.50
187 Fernando Tatis	.10
188 Brady Anderson	.10
189 Tony Clark	.10
190 Alex Fernandez	.10
191 Matt Blank	.10
192 Greg Maddux	.75
193 Kevin Millwood	.10
194 Jason Schmidt	.10
195 Shannon Stewart	.10
196 Rolando Arrojo	.10
197 Darren Dreifort	.10
198 Ben Grieve	.10
199 Bartolo Colon	.10
200 Sean Casey	.10

Autographics

	NM/M
Common Player:	5.00
Inserted 1:216	
Silvers:	1-2X
Production 250 Sets	
Golds:	1-2X
Production 50 Sets	
1 Bobby Abreu	15.00
2 Marlon Anderson	5.00
3 Rick Ankiel	8.00
4 Rob Bell	5.00
5 Carlos Beltran	25.00
6 Wade Boggs	30.00
7 Barry Bonds	200.00
8 Milton Bradley	8.00
9 Pat Burrell	25.00
10 Orlando Cabrera	10.00
11 Chris Carpenter	5.00
12 Sean Casey	8.00
13 Carlos Delgado	20.00
14 J.D. Drew	15.00
15 Ray Durham	8.00
16 Kelvim Escobar	6.00
17 Vladimir Guerrero	30.00
18 Tony Gwynn	35.00
19 Jerry Hairston Jr.	5.00
20 Todd Helton	25.00
21 Nick Johnson	8.00
22 Jason Kendall	8.00
23 Mark Kotsay	8.00
24 Cole Liniak	5.00
25 Jose Macias	5.00
26 Greg Maddux	60.00
27 Ruben Mateo	8.00
28 Ober Moreno	5.00
29 Eric Munson	8.00
30 Joe Nathan	5.00
31 Angel Pena	5.00
32 Adam Piatt	6.00
33 Matt Riley	5.00
34 Cal Ripken Jr.	100.00
35 Alex Rodriguez	75.00
36 Scott Rolen	25.00
37 Jimmy Rollins	15.00
38 B.J. Ryan	5.00
39 Alfonso Soriano	40.00
40 Frank Thomas	25.00
41 Wilton Veras	5.00
42 Billy Wagner	10.00
43 Jeff Weaver	8.00
44 Scott Williamson	6.00

Genuine Coverage

	NM/M
Common Player:	5.00
Inserted 1:720	
1 Alex Rodriguez	65.00
2 Cole Liniak	5.00
3 Barry Bonds	75.00
4 Ben Davis	5.00
5 Bobby Abreu	7.50
6 Mike Sweeney	7.50
7 Rafael Palmeiro	35.00
8 Carlos Lee	5.00
9 Glen Barker	5.00
10 Jason Giambi	30.00
11 Jacque Jones	7.50
12 Joe Nathan	5.00
13 Jason LaRue	5.00
14 Magglio Ordonez	7.50
15 Shannon Stewart	5.00
16 Matt Lawton	5.00
18 Trevor Hoffman	5.00

Mighty Fine in '99

	NM/M
Complete Set (40):	8.00
Common Player:	.15
Inserted 1:1	
1 Clay Bellinger	.15
2 Scott Brosius	.15
3 Roger Clemens	.75
4 David Cone	.15
5 Chad Curtis	.15
6 Chili Davis	.15
7 Joe Girardi	.15
8 Jason Grimsley	.15
9 Orlando Hernandez	.15
10 Hideki Irabu	.15
11 Derek Jeter	2.00
12 Chuck Knoblauch	.15
13 Ricky Ledee	.15
14 Jim Leyritz	.15
15 Tino Martinez	.15
16 Ramiro Mendoza	.15
17 Jeff Nelson	.15
18 Paul O'Neill	.15
19 Andy Pettitte	.25
20 Jorge Posada	.25
21 Mariano Rivera	.25
22 Luis Sojo	.15
23 Mike Stanton	.15
24 Allen Watson	.15
25 Bernie Williams	.30
26 Chipper Jones	.60
27 Ivan Rodriguez	.45
28 Randy Johnson	.50
29 Pedro Martinez	.50
30 Scott Williamson	.15
31 Carlos Beltran	.40
32 Mark McGwire	1.50
33 Ken Griffey Jr.	1.00
34 Robin Ventura	.15
35 Tony Gwynn	.60
36 Wade Boggs	.60
37 Cal Ripken Jr.	2.00
38 Jose Canseco	.40
39 Alex Rodriguez	1.50
40 Fernando Tatis	.15

Point of Impact

	NM/M
Complete Set (10):	20.00
Common Player:	1.00
Inserted 1:30	
1 Ken Griffey Jr.	2.00
2 Mark McGwire	3.00
3 Sammy Sosa	2.00
4 Jeff Bagwell	1.00
5 Derek Jeter	4.00
6 Chipper Jones	1.50
7 Nomar Garciaparra	2.00
8 Cal Ripken Jr.	4.00
9 Barry Bonds	4.00
10 Alex Rodriguez	3.00

2000 Fleer Mystique

	NM/M
Complete Set (175):	350.00
Common Player:	.20
Common 126-175:	6.00
Production 2,000 Sets	
Pack (5):	3.00
Box (20):	50.00
1 Derek Jeter	3.00
2 David Justice	.20
3 Kevin Brown	.20
4 Jason Giambi	.75
5 Jose Canseco	.50
6 Mark Grace	.30
7 Hideo Nomo	.65
8 Edgardo Alfonzo	.20
9 Barry Bonds	3.00
10 Pedro Martinez	1.00
11 Juan Gonzalez	1.00
12 Vladimir Guerrero	1.00
13 Chuck Finley	.20
14 Brian Jordan	.20
15 Richie Sexson	.20
16 Chan Ho Park	.20
17 Tim Hudson	.40
18 Fred McGriff	.20
19 Darin Erstad	.60
20 Chris Singleton	.20
21 Jeff Bagwell	1.00
22 David Cone	.20
23 Edgar Martinez	.20
24 Greg Maddux	1.50
25 Jim Thome	.20
26 Eric Karros	.20
27 Bobby Abreu	.20
28 Greg Vaughn	.20
29 Kevin Millwood	.20
30 Omar Vizquel	.20
31 Marquis Grissom	.20
32 Mike Lieberthal	.20
33 Gabe Kapler	.20
34 Brady Anderson	.20
35 Jeff Cirillo	.20
36 Geoff Jenkins	.20
37 Scott Rolen	.75
38 Rafael Palmeiro	.65
39 Randy Johnson	1.00
40 Barry Larkin	.20
41 Johnny Damon	.40
42 Andy Pettitte	.40
43 Mark McGwire	2.50
44 Albert Belle	.20
45 Derrick Gibson	.20
46 Corey Koskie	.20
47 Curt Schilling	.50
48 Ivan Rodriguez	.65
49 Mike Mussina	.50
50 Todd Helton	1.00
51 Matt Lawton	.20
52 Jason Kendall	.20
53 Kenny Rogers	.20
54 Cal Ripken Jr.	3.00
55 Larry Walker	.20
56 Eric Milton	.20
57 Warren Morris	.20
58 Carlos Delgado	.50
59 Kerry Wood	.65
60 Cliff Floyd	.20
61 Mike Piazza	2.00
62 Jeff Kent	.20
63 Sammy Sosa	2.00
64 Alex Fernandez	.20
65 Mike Hampton	.20
66 Livan Hernandez	.20
67 Matt Williams	.20
68 Roberto Alomar	.45
69 Jermaine Dye	.20
70 Bernie Williams	.35
71 Edgar Renteria	.20
72 Tom Glavine	.40
73 Bartolo Colon	.20
74 Jason Varitek	.20
75 Eric Chavez	.40
76 Fernando Tatis	.20
77 Adrian Beltre	.40
78 Paul Konerko	.20
79 Mike Lowell	.20
80 Robin Ventura	.20
81 Russ Ortiz	.20
82 Troy Glaus	1.00
83 Frank Thomas	1.00
84 Craig Biggio	.20
85 Orlando Hernandez	.20
86 John Olerud	.20
87 Chipper Jones	1.50
88 Manny Ramirez	1.00
89 Shawn Green	.40
90 Ben Grieve	.20
91 Vinny Castilla	.20
92 Tim Salmon	.35
93 Dante Bichette	.20
94 Ken Caminiti	.20
95 Andruw Jones	.75
96 Alex Rodriguez	2.50
97 Erubiel Durazo	.20
98 Sean Casey	.30
99 Carlos Beltran	.50
100 Paul O'Neill	.20
101 Ray Lankford	.20
102 Troy O'Leary	.20
103 Bobby Higginson	.20
104 Rondell White	.20
105 Tony Gwynn	1.50
106 Jim Edmonds	.20
107 Magglio Ordonez	.40
108 Preston Wilson	.20
109 Roger Clemens	1.75
110 Ken Griffey Jr.	2.00
111 Nomar Garciaparra	2.00
112 Juan Encarnacion	.20
113 Michael Barrett	.20
114 Matt Clement	.20
115 David Wells	.20
116 Mo Vaughn	.20
117 Mike Cameron	.20
118 Jose Lima	.20
119 Tino Martinez	.20
120 J.D. Drew	.40
121 Carl Everett	.20
122 Tony Clark	.20
123 Brad Radke	.20
124 Kevin Young	.20
125 Raul Mondesi	.20
126 Cole Liniak	6.00
127 Alfonso Soriano	8.00
128 Lance Berkman	8.00
129 Danny Young	6.00
130 Francisco Cordero	6.00
131 Rob Fick	6.00
132 Matt LeCroy	6.00
133 Adam Piatt	6.00
134 Derrick Turnbow RC	6.00
135 Mark Quinn	6.00
136 Kip Wells	6.00
137 Rob Bell	6.00
138 Brad Penny	6.00
139 Pat Burrell	10.00
140 Danys Baez RC	6.00
141 Chad Hermansen	6.00
142 Steve Lomasney	6.00
143 Peter Bergeron	6.00
144 Jimmy Anderson	6.00
145 Mike Darr	6.00
146 Jacob Cruz	6.00
147 Kazuhiro Sasaki RC	10.00
148 Ben Petrick	6.00
149 Rick Ankiel	6.00
150 Aaron McNeal RC	6.00
151 Octavio Dotel	6.00
152 Juan Pena	6.00
153 Nick Johnson	6.00
154 Wilton Veras	6.00
155 Wily Pena	6.00
156 Mark Mulder	6.00
157 Daryle Ward	6.00
158 Chad Durbin RC	6.00
159 Angel Pena	6.00
160 Dewayne Wise	6.00
161 Tarrik Brock	6.00
162 Marcus Jensen	6.00
163 Kevin Barker	6.00
164 B.J. Ryan	6.00
165 Cesar King	6.00
166 Geoff Blum	6.00
167 Ruben Mateo	6.00
168 Ramon Ortiz	6.00
169 Eric Munson	6.00
170 Josh Beckett	8.00
171 Rafael Furcal	6.00
172 Matt Riley	6.00
173 Johan Santana RC	45.00
174 Mark Johnson	6.00
175 Adam Kennedy	6.00

Gold

	NM/M
Stars (1-125):	4-8X
SP's (126-175):	1X

Inserted 1:20
(See 2000 Fleer Mystique for checklist and base card values.)

Club 3000

	NM/M
Complete Set (3):	6.00
Common Player:	1.50
Inserted 1:20	
1 Cal Ripken Jr.	5.00
2 Bob Gibson	1.50
3 Dave Winfield	1.50

Club 3000 Memorabilia

	NM/M
Cal Ripken Jr./Jsy/825	40.00
Cal Ripken Jr./Bat/265	75.00
Cal Ripken Jr./Hat/55	120.00
Cal Ripken Jr./Bat/Jsy/100	100.00
Bob Gibson/Jsy/825	20.00
Bob Gibson/Bat/265	30.00
Bob Gibson/Bat/Jsy/100	50.00
Bob Gibson/Hat/Jsy/100	
Bob Gibson/Hat/55	75.00
Dave Winfield/Jsy/825	15.00
Dave Winfield/Bat/270	25.00
Dave Winfield/Bat/Jsy/100	50.00
Dave Winfield/Hat/55	60.00

Dave Winfield Autograph Memorabilia

	NM/M
Complete Set (2):	
1 Dave Winfield/Bat/20	140.00
2 Dave Winfield/Helmet/40	125.00

Diamond Dominators

	NM/M
Complete Set (10):	15.00
Common Player:	.75
Inserted 1:5	
1 Manny Ramirez	1.00
2 Pedro Martinez	1.00
3 Sean Casey	.75
4 Vladimir Guerrero	1.00
5 Sammy Sosa	1.50
6 Nomar Garciaparra	1.50
7 Mark McGwire	2.50
8 Ken Griffey Jr.	1.50
9 Derek Jeter	3.00
10 Alex Rodriguez	2.50

Feel the Game

	NM/M
Common Player:	5.00
Inserted 1:120	
1 Tony Gwynn/Jsy	20.00
2 Alex Rodriguez/Jsy	25.00
3 Chipper Jones/Jsy	20.00
4 Cal Ripken Jr./Jsy	40.00
5 Derek Jeter/Pants	40.00
6 Alex Rodriguez/Bat	30.00
7 Frank Thomas/Bat	15.00
8 Barry Bonds/Bat	40.00
9 Carlos Beltran/Bat	5.00
10 Shawn Green/Bat	8.00
11 Michael Barrett/Bat	5.00
12 Rafael Palmeiro/Bat	10.00
13 Vladimir Guerrero/Bat	15.00
14 Pat Burrell/Bat	12.00

Fresh Ink

	NM/M
Common Player:	5.00
Inserted 1:40	
1 Chad Allen	5.00
2 Glen Barker	5.00
3 Michael Barrett	5.00
4 Josh Beckett	30.00
5 Rob Bell	5.00
6 Lance Berkman	25.00
7 Kent Bottenfield	5.00
8 Milton Bradley	8.00
9 Orlando Cabrera	10.00
10 Sean Casey	10.00
11 Roger Cedeno	6.00
12 Will Clark	25.00
13 Russ Davis	5.00
14 Carlos Delgado	15.00
15 Einar Diaz	5.00
16 J.D. Drew	10.00
17 Erubiel Durazo	10.00
18 Damion Easley	5.00
19 Carlos Febles	5.00
20 Doug Glanville	6.00
21 Alex Gonzalez	5.00
22 Tony Gwynn	40.00
23 Mike Hampton	8.00
24 Bobby Howry	5.00
25 John Jaha	5.00
26 Nick Johnson	10.00
27 Andruw Jones	20.00
28 Adam Kennedy	8.00
29 Mike Lieberthal	8.00
30 Jose Macias	5.00
31 Ruben Mateo	8.00
32 Raul Mondesi	8.00
33 Heath Murray	5.00
34 Mike Mussina	30.00
35 Hideo Nomo	250.00
36 Magglio Ordonez	15.00
37 Eric Owens	5.00
38 Adam Piatt	5.00
39 Cal Ripken Jr.	100.00
40 Tim Salmon	15.00
41 Chris Singleton	5.00
42 J.T. Snow	8.00
43 Mike Sweeney	10.00
44 Wilton Veras	5.00
45 Jose Vidro	8.00
46 Rondell White	10.00
47 Jaret Wright	5.00

High Praise

	NM/M
Complete Set (10):	18.00
Common Player:	.75
Inserted 1:20	
1 Mark McGwire	3.00
2 Ken Griffey Jr.	2.00
3 Alex Rodriguez	3.00
4 Derek Jeter	4.00
5 Sammy Sosa	2.00
6 Mike Piazza	2.00
7 Nomar Garciaparra	2.00
8 Cal Ripken Jr.	4.00
9 Tony Gwynn	1.50
10 Shawn Green	.75

Rookie I.P.O.

	NM/M
Complete Set (10):	8.00
Common Player:	.50
Inserted 1:10	
1 Josh Beckett	1.00
2 Eric Munson	.50
3 Pat Burrell	2.00
4 Alfonso Soriano	1.50
5 Rick Ankiel	.50
6 Ruben Mateo	.50
7 Mark Quinn	.50
8 Kip Wells	.50
9 Ben Petrick	.50
10 Nick Johnson	.75

Seismic Activity

	NM/M
Complete Set (10):	45.00
Common Player:	3.00
Inserted 1:40	
Richter parallel:	3-5X
Production 100 Sets	
1 Ken Griffey Jr.	5.00
2 Sammy Sosa	5.00
3 Derek Jeter	10.00
4 Mark McGwire	8.00
5 Manny Ramirez	3.00
6 Mike Piazza	5.00
7 Vladimir Guerrero	3.00
8 Chipper Jones	4.00
9 Alex Rodriguez	8.00
10 Jeff Bagwell	3.00

Supernaturals

	NM/M
Complete Set (10):	15.00
Common Player:	1.00
Inserted 1:10	
1 Alex Rodriguez	3.00
2 Chipper Jones	1.75
3 Derek Jeter	4.00
4 Ivan Rodriguez	1.00
5 Ken Griffey Jr.	2.00
6 Mark McGwire	3.00
7 Mike Piazza	2.00
8 Nomar Garciaparra	2.00
9 Sammy Sosa	2.00
10 Vladimir Guerrero	1.50

2000 Fleer Showcase

	NM/M
Complete Set (140):	200.00
Common Player (1-100):	.25
Common (101-115):	6.00
Production 1,000 Sets	
Common (116-140):	4.00
Production 2,000 Sets	
Pack (5):	2.50
Box (24):	50.00
1 Alex Rodriguez	2.50
2 Derek Jeter	3.00
3 Jeromy Burnitz	.25
4 John Olerud	.25
5 Paul Konerko	.25
6 Johnny Damon	.40
7 Curt Schilling	.50
8 Barry Larkin	.25
9 Adrian Beltre	.40
10 Scott Rolen	.75
11 Carlos Delgado	.50
12 Pedro J. Martinez	1.00
13 Todd Helton	1.00
14 Jacque Jones	.25
15 Jeff Kent	.25
16 Darin Erstad	.65
17 Juan Encarnacion	.25
18 Roger Clemens	1.75
19 Tony Gwynn	1.50
20 Nomar Garciaparra	2.00
21 Roberto Alomar	.40
22 Matt Lawton	.25
23 Rich Aurilia	.25
24 Charles Johnson	.25
25 Jim Thome	.25
26 Eric Milton	.25
27 Barry Bonds	3.00
28 Albert Belle	.25
29 Travis Fryman	.25
30 Ken Griffey Jr.	2.00
31 Phil Nevin	.25
32 Chipper Jones	1.50
33 Craig Biggio	.25
34 Mike Hampton	.25
35 Fred McGriff	.25
36 Cal Ripken Jr.	3.00
37 Manny Ramirez	1.00
38 Jose Vidro	.25
39 Trevor Hoffman	.25
40 Tom Glavine	.50
41 Frank Thomas	1.00
42 Chris Widger	.25
43 J.D. Drew	.50
44 Andres Galarraga	.25
45 Pokey Reese	.25
46 Mike Piazza	2.00
47 Kevin Young	.25
48 Sean Casey	.25
49 Carlos Beltran	.60
50 Jason Kendall	.25
51 Vladimir Guerrero	1.00
52 Jermaine Dye	.25
53 Brian Giles	.25
54 Andruw Jones	1.00
55 Richard Hidalgo	.25
56 Robin Ventura	.25
57 Ivan Rodriguez	.65
58 Greg Maddux	1.50
59 Billy Wagner	.25
60 Ruben Mateo	.25
61 Troy Glaus	1.00
62 Dean Palmer	.25
63 Eric Chavez	.40
64 Edgar Martinez	.25
65 Randy Johnson	1.00
66 Preston Wilson	.25
67 Orlando Hernandez	.25
68 Jim Edmonds	.25
69 Carl Everett	.25
70 Larry Walker	.25
71 Ron Belliard	.25
72 Sammy Sosa	2.00
73 Matt Williams	.25
74 Cliff Floyd	.25
75 Bernie Williams	.40
76 Fernando Tatis	.25
77 Steve Finley	.25
78 Jeff Bagwell	1.00
79 Edgardo Alfonzo	.25

#	Player	Price
80	Jose Canseco	.40
81	Magglio Ordonez	.40
82	Shawn Green	.40
83	Bobby Abreu	.25
84	Tony Batista	.25
85	Mo Vaughn	.25
86	Juan Gonzalez	1.00
87	Paul O'Neill	.25
88	Mark McGwire	2.50
89	Mark Grace	.35
90	Kevin Brown	.25
91	Ben Grieve	.25
92	Shannon Stewart	.25
93	Erubiel Durazo	.25
94	Antonio Alfonseca	.25
95	Jeff Cirillo	.25
96	Greg Vaughn	.25
97	Kerry Wood	.60
98	Geoff Jenkins	.25
99	Jason Giambi	.75
100	Rafael Palmeiro	.65
101	Rafael Furcal	6.00
102	Pablo Ozuna	6.00
103	Brad Penny	6.00
104	Mark Mulder	8.00
105	Adam Piatt	6.00
106	Mike Lamb RC	6.00
107	Kazuhiro Sasaki RC	15.00
108	Aaron McNeal RC	6.00
109	Pat Burrell	8.00
110	Rick Ankiel	6.00
111	Eric Munson	6.00
112	Josh Beckett	8.00
113	Adam Kennedy	6.00
114	Alex Escobar	8.00
115	Chad Hermansen	6.00
116	Kip Wells	4.00
117	Matt LeCroy	4.00
118	Julio Ramirez	4.00
119	Ben Petrick	4.00
120	Nick Johnson	6.00
121	Gookie Dawkins	4.00
122	Julio Zuleta RC	4.00
123	Alfonso Soriano	8.00
124	Keith McDonald RC	4.00
125	Kory DeHaan	4.00
126	Vernon Wells	6.00
127	Dernell Stenson	4.00
128	David Eckstein	4.00
129	Robert Fick	4.00
130	Cole Liniak	4.00
131	Mark Quinn	4.00
132	Eric Gagne	5.00
133	Wily Pena	4.00
134	Andy Thompson RC	4.00
135	Steve Sisco RC	4.00
136	Paul Rigdon RC	6.00
137	Rob Bell	4.00
138	Carlos Guillen	5.00
139	Jimmy Rollins	5.00
140	Jason Conti	4.00

Legacy

Stars (1-100): 30-50X
Prospects (101-140): 3-6X
Production 20 Sets
(See 2000 Fleer Showcase for checklist and base card values.)

Masterpiece

(Because of each card's unique nature, catalog values cannot be presented.)

Club 3000

NM/M
Common Player: 3.00
Inserted 1:24
1 Lou Brock 2.00
2 Nolan Ryan 8.00

Club 3000 Memorabilia

NM/M
Lou Brock/Jsy/680 15.00
Lou Brock/Bat/270 25.00
Lou Brock/Hat/Bat/Jsy/25 100.00
Nolan Ryan/Jsy/780 40.00
Nolan Ryan/Hat/65 120.00
Nolan Ryan/Bat/265 60.00
Nolan Ryan/Bat/Jsy/100 120.00

Consummate Prose

Consummate Prose
Sammy Sosa

NM/M
Complete Set (15): 20.00
Common Player: .50
Inserted 1:6
1 Jeff Bagwell 1.50
2 Alex Rodriguez 3.00
3 Chipper Jones 2.00
4 Derek Jeter 4.00
5 Manny Ramirez 1.50
6 Tony Gwynn 2.00
7 Sammy Sosa 2.50
8 Ivan Rodriguez 1.00
9 Greg Maddux 2.00
10 Ken Griffey Jr. 2.50
11 Rick Ankiel .50
12 Cal Ripken Jr. 4.00
13 Pedro Martinez 1.50
14 Mike Piazza 2.50
15 Mark McGwire 3.00

Feel the Game

FEEL THE GAME
Troy Glaus
ANAHEIM ANGELS THIRD BASE

NM/M
Common Player: 5.00
Inserted 1:72
1 Barry Bonds 30.00
2 Gookie Dawkins 5.00
3 Darin Erstad 8.00
4 Troy Glaus 10.00
5 Scott Rolen 10.00
6 Alex Rodriguez 25.00
7 Andruw Jones 10.00
8 Robin Ventura 5.00
9 Sean Casey 5.00
10 Cal Ripken Jr. 40.00

Final Answer

Mike Piazza

NM/M
Complete Set (10): 20.00
Common Player: 1.00

Inserted 1:10
1 Alex Rodriguez 3.00
2 Vladimir Guerrero 1.00
3 Cal Ripken Jr. 4.00
4 Sammy Sosa 2.00
5 Barry Bonds 4.00
6 Derek Jeter 4.00
7 Ken Griffey Jr. 2.00
8 Mike Piazza 2.00
9 Nomar Garciaparra 2.00
10 Mark McGwire 3.00

Fresh Ink

Jose Cruz, Jr. - Blue Jays
FreshINK

NM/M
Common Player: 5.00
Inserted 1:24
1 Rick Ankiel 8.00
2 Josh Beckett 30.00
3 Barry Bonds 200.00
4 A.J. Burnett 10.00
5 Pat Burrell 15.00
6 Ken Caminiti 8.00
7 Sean Casey 8.00
8 Jose Cruz Jr. 10.00
9 Gookie Dawkins 5.00
10 Erubiel Durazo 10.00
11 Juan Encarnacion 8.00
12 Darin Erstad 15.00
13 Rafael Furcal 15.00
14 Nomar Garciaparra 100.00
15 Jason Giambi 20.00
16 Jeremy Giambi 6.00
17 Brian Giles 15.00
18 Troy Glaus 20.00
19 Mark Grace
20 Vladimir Guerrero 30.00
21 Chad Hermansen 5.00
22 Orlando Hernandez
23 Trevor Hoffman 8.00
24 Randy Johnson 60.00
25 Andruw Jones 15.00
26 Jason Kendall 8.00
27 Paul Konerko 10.00
28 Mike Lowell 10.00
29 Aaron McNeal 5.00
30 Warren Morris 5.00
31 Paul O'Neill 20.00
32 Magglio Ordonez 10.00
33 Pablo Ozuna 5.00
34 Brad Penny 8.00
35 Ben Petrick 5.00
36 Pokey Reese 5.00
37 Cal Ripken Jr. 125.00
38 Alex Rodriguez 75.00
39 Scott Rolen 30.00
40 Jose Vidro 8.00
41 Kip Wells 5.00

License to Skill

NM/M
Complete Set (10): 25.00
Common Player: 1.50
Inserted 1:20
1 Vladimir Guerrero 2.00
2 Pedro J. Martinez 2.00
3 Nomar Garciaparra 4.00
4 Ivan Rodriguez 1.50
5 Mark McGwire 5.00
6 Derek Jeter 6.00
7 Ken Griffey Jr. 4.00
8 Randy Johnson 2.00
9 Sammy Sosa 4.00
10 Alex Rodriguez 5.00

Long Gone

NM/M
Complete Set (10): 25.00
Common Player: 2.00
Inserted 1:20
1 Sammy Sosa 4.00
2 Derek Jeter 6.00
3 Nomar Garciaparra 4.00

VLADIMIR GUERRERO
OLYMPIC STADIUM

4 Juan Gonzalez 2.00
5 Vladimir Guerrero 2.00
6 Barry Bonds 6.00
7 Jeff Bagwell 2.00
8 Alex Rodriguez 5.00
9 Ken Griffey Jr. 4.00
10 Mark McGwire 5.00

Noise of Summer

NM/M
Complete Set (10): 15.00
Common Player: 1.00
Inserted 1:10
1 Chipper Jones 1.50
2 Jeff Bagwell 1.00
3 Manny Ramirez 1.00
4 Mark McGwire 3.00
5 Ken Griffey Jr. 2.00
6 Mike Piazza 2.00
7 Pedro J. Martinez 1.00
8 Alex Rodriguez 3.00
9 Derek Jeter 4.00
10 Randy Johnson 1.00

Prospect Showcase First

Prospects (101-140): 1-2X
Production 500 Sets
(See Prospects subset in 2000 Fleer Showcase for checklist and base values.)

Sweet Sigs

SWEET SIGS

NM/M
Common Player: 10.00
Inserted 1:250
1 Nomar Garciaparra/53 150.00
2 Alex Rodriguez/67 200.00
3 Tony Gwynn 40.00
4 Roger Clemens/79 140.00
5 Scott Rolen 50.00
6 Greg Maddux 80.00
7 Jose Cruz Jr. 15.00
8 Tony Womack 10.00
9 Jay Buhner 10.00
10 Nolan Ryan 125.00

2000 Fleer Tradition

NM/M
Complete Set (450): 50.00
Common Player: .10
Complete Glossy Factory Set (500): 450.00
Complete Glossy Factory Set (455): 75.00
Glossy (1-450): 1-2X
Common Glossy (451-500): 8.00

MOISES ALOU
HOUSTON ASTROS OUTFIELD

Five Glossy (451-500) per factory set.
1,000 produced (451-500)

Pack (10):		1.50
Wax Box:		35.00
1	AL HRs	.50
2	NL HRs	.50
3	AL RBIs	.50
4	NL RBIs	.50
5	AL Avg.	.50
6	NL Avg.	.15
7	AL Wins	.20
8	NL Wins	.40
9	AL ERA	.20
10	NL ERA	.25
11	Matt Mantei	.10
12	John Rocker	.10
13	Kyle Farnsworth	.10
14	Juan Guzman	.10
15	Manny Ramirez	.75
16	Matt Riley-P, Calvin Pickering-1B	.10
17	Tony Clark	.10
18	Brian Meadows	.10
19	Orber Moreno	.10
20	Eric Karros	.10
21	Steve Woodard	.10
22	Scott Brosius	.10
23	Gary Bennett	.10
24	Jason Wood-3B, Dave Borkowski-P	.10
25	Joe McEwing	.10
26	Juan Gonzalez	.75
27	Roy Halladay	.25
28	Trevor Hoffman	.10
29	Arizona Diamondbacks	.10
30	Domingo Guzman-P, Wiki Gonzalez-C	.25
31	Bret Boone	.10
32	Nomar Garciaparra	2.00
33	Bo Porter	.10
34	Eddie Taubensee	.10
35	Pedro Astacio	.10
36	Derek Bell	.10
37	Jacque Jones	.10
38	Ricky Ledee	.10
39	Jeff Kent	.10
40	Matt Williams	.10
41	Alfonso Soriano-SS, D'Angelo Jimenez-3B	.75
42	B.J. Surhoff	.10
43	Denny Neagle	.10
44	Omar Vizquel	.10
45	Jeff Bagwell	.75
46	Mark Grudzielanek	.10
47	LaTroy Hawkins	.10
48	Orlando Hernandez	.10
49	Ken Griffey Jr.	2.00
50	Fernando Tatis	.10
51	Quilvio Veras	.10
52	Wayne Gomes	.10
53	Rick Helling	.10
54	Shannon Stewart	.10
55	Dermal Brown-OF, Mark Quinn-OF	.20
56	Randy Johnson	1.00
57	Greg Maddux	1.50
58	Mike Cameron	.10
59	Matt Anderson	.10
60	Milwaukee Brewers	.10
61	Derrek Lee	.10
62	Mike Sweeney	.10
63	Fernando Vina	.10
64	Orlando Cabrera	.20
65	Doug Glanville	.10
66	Stan Spencer	.10
67	Ray Lankford	.10
68	Kelly Dransfeldt	.10
69	Alex Gonzalez	.10
70	Russell Branyan-3B, Danny Peoples-OF	.10
71	Jim Edmonds	.10
72	Brady Anderson	.10
73	Mike Stanley	.10
74	Travis Fryman	.10
75	Carlos Febles	.10
76	Bobby Higginson	.10
77	Carlos Perez	.10
78	Steve Cox-1B, Alex Sanchez-OF	.10
79	Dustin Hermanson	.10
80	Kenny Rogers	.10
81	Miguel Tejada	.25
82	Ben Davis	.10
83	Reggie Sanders	.10
84	Eric Davis	.10
85	J.D. Drew	.45
86	Ryan Rupe	.10
87	Bobby Smith	.10
88	Jose Cruz Jr.	.10
89	Carlos Delgado	.50
90	Toronto Blue Jays	.10
91	Denny Stark-P, Gil Meche-P	.25
92	Randy Velarde	.10
93	Aaron Boone	.10
94	Javy Lopez	.10
95	Johnny Damon	.25
96	Jon Lieber	.10
97	Montreal Expos	.10
98	Mark Kotsay	.10
99	Luis Gonzalez	.25
100	Larry Walker	.10
101	Adrian Beltre	.25
102	Alex Ochoa	.10
103	Michael Barrett	.10
104	Tampa Bay Devil Rays	.10
105	Rey Ordonez	.10
106	Derek Jeter	3.00
107	Mike Lieberthal	.10
108	Ellis Burks	.10
109	Steve Finley	.10
110	Ryan Klesko	.10
111	Steve Avery	.10
112	Dave Veres	.10
113	Cliff Floyd	.10
114	Shane Reynolds	.10
115	Kevin Brown	.10
116	David Nilsson	.10
117	Mike Trombley	.10
118	Todd Walker	.10
119	John Olerud	.10
120	Chuck Knoblauch	.10
121	Nomar Garciaparra	2.00
122	Trot Nixon	.10
123	Erubiel Durazo	.10
124	Edwards Guzman	.10
125	Curt Schilling	.50
126	Brian Jordan	.10
127	Cleveland Indians	.10
128	Benito Santiago	.10
129	Frank Thomas	.75
130	Neifi Perez	.10
131	Alex Fernandez	.10
132	Jose Lima	.10
133	Jorge Toca-1B, Melvin Mora-OF	.10
134	Scott Karl	.10
135	Brad Radke	.10
136	Paul O'Neill	.10
137	Kris Benson	.10
138	Colorado Rockies	.10
139	Jason Phillips	.10
140	Robb Nen	.10
141	Ken Hill	.10
142	Charles Johnson	.10
143	Paul Konerko	.10
144	Dmitri Young	.10
145	Justin Thompson	.10
146	Mark Loretta	.10
147	Edgardo Alfonzo	.10
148	Armando Benitez	.10
149	Octavio Dotel	.10
150	Wade Boggs	1.50
151	Ramon Hernandez	.10
152	Freddy Garcia	.10
153	Edgar Martinez	.10
154	Ivan Rodriguez	.65
155	Kansas City Royals	.10
156	Cleatus Davidson-2B, Cristian Guzman-SS	.10
157	Andy Benes	.10
158	Todd Dunwoody	.10
159	Pedro Martinez	1.00
160	Mike Caruso	.10
161	Mike Sirotka	.10
162	Houston Astros	.10
163	Darryl Kile	.10
164	Chipper Jones	1.50
165	Carl Everett	.10
166	Geoff Jenkins	.10
167	Dan Perkins	.10
168	Andy Pettitte	.25
169	Francisco Cordova	.10
170	Jay Buhner	.10
171	Jay Bell	.10
172	Andruw Jones	.75
173	Bobby Howry	.10
174	Chris Singleton	.10
175	Todd Helton	.75
176	A.J. Burnett	.10
177	Marquis Grissom	.10
178	Eric Milton	.10
179	Los Angeles Dodgers	.10
180	Kevin Appier	.10
181	Brian Giles	.10
182	Tom Davey	.10
183	Mo Vaughn	.10
184	Jose Hernandez	.10
185	Jim Parque	.10
186	Derrick Gibson	.10
187	Bruce Aven	.10
188	Jeff Cirillo	.10
189	Doug Mientkiewicz	.10
190	Eric Chavez	.25
191	Al Martin	.10
192	Tom Glavine	.25
193	Butch Huskey	.10
194	Ray Durham	.10
195	Greg Vaughn	.10
196	Vinny Castilla	.10
197	Ken Caminiti	.10
198	Joe Mays	.10
199	Chicago White Sox	.10
200	Mariano Rivera	.20
201	Mark McGwire	2.50
202	Pat Meares	.10
203	Andres Galarraga	.10
204	Tom Gordon	.10
205	Henry Rodriguez	.10
206	Brett Tomko	.10
207	Dante Bichette	.10
208	Craig Biggio	.25
209	Matt Lawton	.10
210	Tino Martinez	.10
211	Aaron Myette-P, Josh Paul-C	.10
212	Warren Morris	.10
213	San Diego Padres	.10
214	Ramon E. Martinez	.10
215	Troy Percival	.10
216	Jason Johnson	.10
217	Carlos Lee	.10
218	Scott Williamson	.10
219	Jeff Weaver	.10
220	Ronnie Belliard	.10
221	Jason Giambi	.65
222	Ken Griffey Jr.	2.00
223	John Halama	.10
224	Brett Hinchliffe	.10
225	Wilson Alvarez	.10
226	Rolando Arrojo	.10
227	Ruben Mateo	.10
228	Rafael Palmeiro	.65
229	David Wells	.10
230	Eric Gagne-P, Jeff Williams-P	.10
231	Tim Salmon	.30
232	Mike Mussina	.50
233	Magglio Ordonez	.25
234	Ron Villone	.10
235	Antonio Alfonseca	.10
236	Jeromy Burnitz	.10
237	Ben Grieve	.10
238	Giomar Guevara	.10
239	Garret Anderson	.10
240	John Smoltz	.10
241	Mark Grace	.15
242	Cole Liniak-3B, Jose Molina-C	.10
243	Damion Easley	.10
244	Jeff Montgomery	.10
245	Kenny Lofton	.10
246	Masato Yoshii	.10
247	Philadelphia Phillies	.10
248	Raul Mondesi	.10
249	Marlon Anderson	.10
250	Shawn Green	.40
251	Sterling Hitchcock	.10
252	Randy Wolf-P, Anthony Shumaker-P	.10
253	Jeff Fassero	.10
254	Eli Marrero	.10
255	Cincinnati Reds	.10
256	Rick Ankiel-P, Adam Kennedy-2B	.50
257	Darin Erstad	.60
258	Albert Belle	.20
259	Bartolo Colon	.10
260	Bret Saberhagen	.10
261	Carlos Beltran	.50
262	Glenallen Hill	.10
263	Gregg Jefferies	.10
264	Matt Clement	.10
265	Miguel Del Toro	.10
266	Robinson Cancel-C, Kevin Barker-1B	.10
267	San Francisco Giants	.10
268	Kent Bottenfield	.10
269	Fred McGriff	.10
270	Chris Carpenter	.10
271	Atlanta Braves	.10
272	Wilton Veras-3B, Tomokazu Ohka-P RC	.50
273	Will Clark	.20
274	Troy O'Leary	.10
275	Sammy Sosa	2.00
276	Travis Lee	.15
277	Sean Casey	.25
278	Ron Gant	.10
279	Roger Clemens	1.75
280	Phil Nevin	.10
281	Mike Piazza	2.00
282	Mike Lowell	.10
283	Kevin Millwood	.10
284	Joe Randa	.10
285	Jeff Shaw	.10
286	Jason Varitek	.10
287	Harold Baines	.10
288	Gabe Kapler	.10
289	Chuck Finley	.10
290	Carl Pavano	.10
291	Brad Ausmus	.10
292	Brad Fullmer	.10
293	Boston Red Sox	.10
294	Bob Wickman	.10
295	Billy Wagner	.10
296	Shawn Estes	.10
297	Gary Sheffield	.40
298	Fernando Seguignol	.10
299	Omar Olivares	.10
300	Baltimore Orioles	.10
301	Matt Stairs	.10
302	Andy Ashby	.10
303	Todd Greene	.10
304	Jesse Garcia	.10
305	Kerry Wood	.50
306	Roberto Alomar	.40
307	New York Mets	.10
308	Dean Palmer	.10
309	Mike Hampton	.10
310	Devon White	.10
311	Chad Hermansen-OF, Mike Garcia-P	.10
312	Tim Hudson	.40
313	John Franco	.10
314	Jason Schmidt	.10
315	J.T. Snow	.10
316	Ed Sprague	.10
317	Chris Widger	.10
318	Ben Petrick-C, Luther Hackman-P RC	.25
319	Jose Mesa	.10
320	Jose Canseco	.50
321	John Wetteland	.10
322	Minnesota Twins	.10
323	Jeff DaVanon-OF, Brian Cooper-P	.25
324	Tony Womack	.10
325	Rod Beck	.10
326	Mickey Morandini	.10
327	Pokey Reese	.10
328	Jaret Wright	.10
329	Glen Barker	.10
330	Darren Dreifort	.10
331	Torii Hunter	.15
332	Tony Armas Jr.-P, Peter Bergeron-OF	.10
333	Hideki Irabu	.10
334	Desi Relaford	.10
335	Barry Bonds	3.00
336	Gary DiSarcina	.10
337	Gerald Williams	.10
338	John Valentin	.10
339	David Justice	.10
340	Juan Encarnacion	.10
341	Jeremy Giambi	.10
342	Chan Ho Park	.10
343	Vladimir Guerrero	1.00
344	Robin Ventura	.10
345	Bobby Abreu	.10
346	Tony Gwynn	1.50
347	Jose Jimenez	.10
348	Royce Clayton	.10
349	Kelvim Escobar	.10
350	Chicago Cubs	.10
351	Travis Dawkins-SS, Jason LaRue-C	.10
352	Barry Larkin	.10
353	Cal Ripken Jr.	3.00
353s	Cal Ripken Jr./OPS	4.00
354	Alex Rodriguez	2.50
355	Todd Stottlemyre	.10
356	Terry Adams	.10
357	Pittsburgh Pirates	.10
358	Jim Thome	.10
359	Corey Lee-P, Doug Davis-P	.10
360	Moises Alou	.10
361	Todd Hollandsworth	.10
362	Marty Cordova	.10
363	David Cone	.10
364	Joe Nathan-P, Wilson Delgado-SS	.10
365	Paul Byrd	.10

366	Edgar Renteria	.10
367	Rusty Greer	.10
368	David Segui	.10
369	New York Yankees	.50
370	Daryle Ward-OF/1B,	
	Carlos Hernandez-2B	.10
371	Troy Glaus	.75
372	Delino DeShields	.10
373	Jose Offerman	.10
374	Sammy Sosa	2.00
375	Sandy Alomar Jr.	.10
376	Masao Kida	.10
377	Richard Hidalgo	.10
378	Ismael Valdes	.10
379	Ugueth Urbina	.10
380	Darryl Hamilton	.10
381	John Jaha	.10
382	St. Louis Cardinals	.10
383	Scott Sauerbeck	.10
384	Russ Ortiz	.10
385	Jamie Moyer	.10
386	Dave Martinez	.10
387	Todd Zeile	.10
388	Anaheim Angels	.10
389	Rob Ryan-OF,	
	Nick Bierbrodt-P	.10
390	Rickey Henderson	.75
391	Alex Rodriguez	2.50
392	Texas Rangers	.10
393	Roberto Hernandez	.10
394	Tony Batista	.10
395	Oakland Athletics	.10
396	Randall Simon-1B,	
	David Cortes-P RC	.20
397	Gregg Olson	.10
398	Sidney Ponson	.10
399	Micah Bowie	.10
400	Mark McGwire	2.50
401	Florida Marlins	.10
402	Chad Allen	.10
403	Casey Blake-3B,	
	Vernon Wells-OF	.10
404	Pete Harnisch	.10
405	Preston Wilson	.10
406	Richie Sexson	.10
407	Rico Brogna	.10
408	Todd Hundley	.10
409	Wally Joyner	.10
410	Tom Goodwin	.10
411	Joey Hamilton	.10
412	Detroit Tigers	.10
413	Michael Tejera-P,	
	Ramon Castro-C	.25
414	Alex Gonzalez	.10
415	Jermaine Dye	.10
416	Jose Rosado	.10
417	Wilton Guerrero	.10
418	Rondell White	.10
419	Al Leiter	.10
420	Bernie Williams	.25
421	A.J. Hinch	.10
422	Pat Burrell	.50
423	Scott Rolen	.65
424	Jason Kendall	.10
425	Kevin Young	.10
426	Eric Owens	.10
427	Derek Jeter	1.00
428	Livan Hernandez	.10
429	Russ Davis	.10
430	Dan Wilson	.10
431	Quinton McCracken	.10
432	Homer Bush	.10
433	Seattle Mariners	.10
434	Chad Harville-P,	
	Luis Vizcaino-P	.10
435	Carlos Beltran	.45
436	Scott Williamson	.10
437	Pedro Martinez	.75
438	Randy Johnson	.75
439	Ivan Rodriguez	.60
440	Chipper Jones	.75
441	Bernie Williams	.15
442	Pedro Martinez	.50
443	Derek Jeter	1.00
444	Brian Jordan	.10
445	Todd Pratt	.10
446	Kevin Millwood	.10
447	Orlando Hernandez	.10
448	Derek Jeter	1.00
449	Chad Curtis	.10
450	Roger Clemens	.75
451	Carlos Casimiro RC	8.00
452	Adam Melhuse RC	8.00
453	Adam Bernero RC	8.00
454	Dusty Allen RC	8.00
455	Chan Perry RC	8.00
456	Damian Rolls RC	8.00
457	Josh Phelps RC	10.00
458	Barry Zito RC	25.00
459	Hector Ortiz RC	8.00
460	Juan Pierre RC	15.00
461	Jose Ortiz RC	15.00
462	Chad Zerbe RC	8.00
463	Julio Zuleta RC	8.00

464	Eric Byrnes RC	25.00
465	Wilfredo	
	Rodriguez RC	10.00
466	Wascar Serrano RC	8.00
467	Aaron McNeal RC	8.00
468	Paul Rigdon RC	8.00
469	John Snyder RC	8.00
470	J.C. Romero RC	8.00
471	Talmadge Nunnari RC	8.00
472	Mike Lamb RC	8.00
473	Ryan Kohlmeier RC	8.00
474	Rodney Lindsey RC	8.00
475	Elvis Pena RC	8.00
476	Alex Cabrera RC	10.00
477	Chris Richard RC	8.00
478	Pedro Feliz RC	10.00
479	Ross Gload RC	8.00
480	Timoniel Perez RC	8.00
481	Jason Woolf RC	8.00
482	Kenny Kelly RC	8.00
483	Sang-Hoon Lee RC	8.00
484	John Riedling RC	8.00
485	Chris Wakeland RC	8.00
486	Britt Reames RC	8.00
487	Greg LaRocca RC	8.00
488	Randy Keisler RC	8.00
489	Xavier Nady RC	20.00
490	Keith Ginter RC	10.00
491	Joey Nation RC	8.00
492	Kazuhiro Sasaki RC	8.00
493	Lesli Brea RC	8.00
494	Jace Brewer RC	8.00
495	Yohanny Valera RC	8.00
496	Adam Piatt	10.00
497	Nate Rolison	8.00
498	Aubrey Huff	10.00
499	Jason Tyner	8.00
500	Corey Patterson	10.00

Club 3000

		NM/M
Complete Set (3):		5.00
Common Player:		3.00
Inserted 1:36		
(1)	George Brett	4.00
(2)	Rod Carew	2.00
(3)	Robin Yount	2.00

Club 3000 Memorabilia

	NM/M
George Brett/Bat/250	60.00
George Brett/Hat/100	75.00
George Brett/Jsy/445	30.00
George Brett/	
Bat/Jsy/100	90.00
Rod Carew/Bat/225	30.00
Rod Carew/Hat/100	50.00
Rod Carew/Jsy/440	20.00
Rod Carew/	
Bat/Jsy/100	65.00
Robin Yount/Bat/250	40.00
Robin Yount/Hat/100	60.00
Robin Yount/Jsy/440	30.00
Robin Yount/	
Bat/Jsy/100	75.00

Dividends

	NM/M
Complete Set (15):	15.00

Common Player:		.50
Inserted 1:6		
1	Alex Rodriguez	2.50
2	Ben Grieve	.50
3	Cal Ripken Jr.	3.00
4	Chipper Jones	1.50
5	Derek Jeter	3.00
6	Frank Thomas	1.00
7	Jeff Bagwell	1.00
8	Sammy Sosa	2.00
9	Tony Gwynn	1.50
10	Scott Rolen	.75
11	Nomar Garciaparra	2.00
12	Mike Piazza	2.00
13	Mark McGwire	2.50
14	Ken Griffey Jr.	2.00
15	Juan Gonzalez	1.00

Fresh Ink

	NM/M
Common Player:	5.00
Inserted 1:144	
Rick Ankiel	8.00
Carlos Beltran	25.00
Pat Burrell	15.00
Miguel Cairo	5.00
Sean Casey	8.00
Will Clark	30.00
Mike Darr	5.00
J.D. Drew	10.00
Erubiel Durazo	10.00
Carlos Febles	6.00
Freddy Garcia	8.00
Greg Maddux	80.00
Jason Grilli	5.00
Vladimir Guerrero	35.00
Tony Gwynn	40.00
Jerry Hairston Jr.	8.00
Tim Hudson	15.00
John Jaha	5.00
D'Angelo Jimenez	5.00
Andruw Jones	20.00
Gabe Kapler	6.00
Cesar King	5.00
Jason LaRue	6.00
Mike Lieberthal	8.00
Pedro Martinez	50.00
Gary Matthews Jr.	5.00
Orber Moreno	5.00
Eric Munson	5.00
Rafael Palmeiro	35.00
Jim Parque	6.00
Willi Mo Pena	15.00
Cal Ripken Jr.	100.00
Alex Rodriguez	80.00
Tim Salmon	15.00
Chris Singleton	5.00
Alfonso Soriano	50.00
Ed Yarnall	5.00

Glossy Lumberjacks

	NM/M
Common Player:	8.00
One per factory set.	
Production listed	
1	Edgardo Alfonzo/	
	145	10.00
2	Roberto Alomar/	
	627	10.00
3	Moises Alou/529	8.00

4	Carlos Beltran/489	8.00
5	Adrian Beltre/127	10.00
7	Barry Bonds/305	40.00
9	Pat Burrell/45	25.00
10	Sean Casey/50	15.00
11	Eric Chavez/259	10.00
12	Tony Clark/70	10.00
13	Carlos Delgado/70	20.00
14	J.D. Drew/135	10.00
15	Erubiel Durazo/70	10.00
17	Carlos Febles/120	10.00
18	Jason Giambi/220	15.00
19	Shawn Green/429	10.00
20	Vladimir Guerrero/	
	809	15.00
21	Derek Jeter/180	50.00
22	Chipper Jones/725	15.00
23	Gabe Kapler/160	8.00
25	Paul Konerko/70	10.00
27	Mike Lieberthal/45	10.00
28	Edgar Martinez/211	8.00
29	Raul Mondesi/458	8.00
30	Warren Morris/35	10.00
31	Magglio Ordonez/	
	190	10.00
32	Rafael Palmeiro/	
	49	15.00
33	Pokey Reese/110	8.00
34	Cal Ripken/235	50.00
35	Alex Rodriguez/292	25.00
36	Ivan Rodriguez/602	10.00
37	Scott Rolen/502	10.00
38	Chris Singleton/68	8.00
39	Alfonso Soriano/	
	285	15.00
40	Frank Thomas/	
	489	10.00
41	Jim Thome/479	10.00
42	Robin Ventura/	
	114	10.00
43	Jose Vidro/60	10.00
44	Bernie Williams/215	10.00
45	Matt Williams/152	8.00

Grasskickers

		NM/M
Complete Set (15):		50.00
Common Player:		2.00
Inserted 1:30		
1	Tony Gwynn	3.00
2	Scott Rolen	2.00
3	Nomar Garciaparra	4.00
4	Mike Piazza	4.00
5	Mark McGwire	6.00
6	Frank Thomas	2.00
7	Cal Ripken Jr.	8.00
8	Chipper Jones	3.00
9	Greg Maddux	3.00
10	Ken Griffey Jr.	4.00
11	Juan Gonzalez	2.00
12	Derek Jeter	8.00
13	Sammy Sosa	4.00
14	Roger Clemens	3.50
15	Alex Rodriguez	6.00

Hall's Well

	NM/M
Complete Set (15):	50.00
Common Player:	1.50

Inserted 1:30
1	Mark McGwire	6.00
2	Alex Rodriguez	6.00
3	Cal Ripken Jr.	8.00
4	Chipper Jones	3.00
5	Derek Jeter	8.00
6	Frank Thomas	2.00
7	Greg Maddux	3.00
8	Juan Gonzalez	2.00
9	Ken Griffey Jr.	4.00
10	Mike Piazza	4.00
11	Nomar Garciaparra	4.00
12	Sammy Sosa	4.00
13	Roger Clemens	3.50
14	Ivan Rodriguez	1.50
15	Tony Gwynn	3.00

Japan Commemorative Sheet

NM/M
Derek Jeter,
Chipper Jones,
Pedro Martinez,
Mike Piazza,
Cal Ripken Jr.,
Ivan Rodriguez,
Sammy Sosa,
Mo Vaughn 20.00

Opening Day 2K

Mike Piazza New York Mets

NM/M
Complete Set (8):		6.00
Common Player:		.50
9	Cal Ripken Jr.	2.00
10	Alex Rodriguez	2.00
11	Mike Piazza	1.00
12	Jeff Bagwell	.75
13	Randy Johnson	.75
14	Jason Kendall	.50
15	Magglio Ordonez	.50
16	Carlos Delgado	.50

Ripken Collection

CAL RIPKEN, JR.
THIRD BASE
BALTIMORE ORIOLES

NM/M
Complete Set (10): 50.00

Common Card: 6.00
Inserted 1:30
(Inserted at the rate of 1:30 packs.)

Ten-4

NM/M
Complete Set (10):		20.00
Common Player:		2.00
Inserted 1:18		
1	Sammy Sosa	2.00
2	Nomar Garciaparra	2.00
3	Mike Piazza	2.00
4	Mark McGwire	3.00
5	Ken Griffey Jr.	2.00
6	Juan Gonzalez	1.00
7	Derek Jeter	4.00
8	Chipper Jones	1.50
9	Cal Ripken Jr.	4.00
10	Alex Rodriguez	3.00

Who To Watch

NM/M
Complete Set (15):		5.00
Common Player:		.25
Inserted 1:3		
1	Rick Ankiel	.40
2	Matt Riley	.25
3	Wilton Veras	.25
4	Ben Petrick	.25
5	Chad Hermansen	.25
6	Peter Bergeron	.25
7	Mark Quinn	.25
8	Russell Branyan	.25
9	Alfonso Soriano	1.50
10	Randy Wolf	.50
11	Ben Davis	.25
12	Jeff DaVanon	.25
13	D'Angelo Jimenez	.25
14	Vernon Wells	1.00
15	Adam Kennedy	.40

2000 Fleer Tradition Update

CHAD DURBIN
KANSAS CITY ROYALS · PITCHER

NM/M
Complete Set (149):		15.00
Common Player:		.15
1	Ken Griffey Jr.	.50
2	Cal Ripken Jr.	1.00
3	Randy Velarde	.15
4	Fred McGriff	.15
5	Derek Jeter	1.00
6	Tom Glavine	.25
7	Brent Mayne	.15
8	Alex Ochoa	.15
9	Scott Sheldon	.15
10	Randy Johnson	.35
11	Daniel Garibay RC	.15
12	Brad Fullmer	.15
13	Kazuhiro Sasaki RC	.50
14	Andy Tracy	.15
15	Bret Boone	.15
16	Chad Durbin RC	.25
17	Mark Buehrle RC	1.50
18	Julio Zuleta RC	.15
19	Jeremy Giambi	.15
20	Gene Stechschulte RC	.15
21	Lou Pote	.15
22	Darrell Einertson	.15
23	Ken Griffey Jr.	.75

24	Jeff Sparks RC	.25
25	Aaron Fultz RC	.15
26	Derek Bell	.15
27	Rob Bell	.15
28	Rob Fick	.15
29	Darryl Kile	.15
30	Clayton Andrews	.15
31	Dave Veres	.15
32	Hector Mercado RC	.15
33	Willie Morales	.15
34	Kelly Wunsch	.15
35	Hideki Irabu	.15
36	Sean DePaula	.15
37	Dewayne Wise	.15
38	Curt Schilling	.25
39	Mark Johnson	.15
40	Mike Cameron	.15
41	Scott Sheldon	.15
42	Brett Tomko	.15
43	Johan Santana RC	8.00
44	Andy Benes	.15
45	Matt LeCroy	.15
46	Ryan Klesko	.15
47	Andy Ashby	.15
48	Octavio Dotel	.15
49	Eric Byrnes RC	1.00
50	Not Issued	
51	Kenny Rogers	.15
52	Ben Weber	.15
53	Matt Blank	.15
54	Tom Goodwin	.15
55	Jim Edmonds	.15
56	Derrick Turnbow RC	.25
57	Mark Mulder	.15
58	Tarrik Brock	.15
59	Danny Young	.15
60	Fernando Vina	.15
61	Justin Brunette RC	.15
62	Jimmy Anderson	.15
63	Reggie Sanders	.15
64	Adam Kennedy	.15
65	Jesse Garcia	.15
66	Al Martin	.15
67	Kevin Walker	.15
68	Brad Penny	.15
69	B.J. Surhoff	.15
70	Geoff Blum	.15
71	Jose Jimenez	.15
72	Chuck Finley	.15
73	Valerio De Los Santos	.15
74	Terry Adams	.15
75	Rafael Furcal	.15
76	Mike Darr	.15
77	Quilvio Veras	.15
78	Armando Almanza	.15
79	Greg Vaughn	.15
80	Keith McDonald RC	.15
81	Eric Cammack	.15
82	Horacio Estrada	.15
83	Kory DeHaan	.15
84	Kevin Hodges	.15
85	Mike Lamb RC	.25
86	Shawn Green	.40
87	Dan Reichert	.15
88	Adam Piatt	.15
89	Mike Garcia	.15
90	Rodrigo Lopez RC	1.00
91	John Olerud	.15
92	Barry Zito	1.00
93	Jimmy Rollins	.25
94	Denny Neagle	.15
95	Rickey Henderson	.50
96	Adam Eaton	.15
97	Brian O'Connor	.15
98	Andy Thompson	.15
99	Jason Boyd	.15
100	Carlos Guillen	.15
101	Raul Gonzalez	.15
102	Brandon Knight RC	.25
103	Jason Maxwell	.15
104	Luis Matos RC	.50
105	Morgan Burkhart RC	.25
106	Ismael Villegas	.15
107	David Justice	.15
108	Pablo Ozuna	.15
109	Jose Canseco	.40
110	Alex Cora	.15
111	Will Clark	.25
112	Keith Luuloa	.15
113	Bruce Chen	.15
114	Adam Hyzdu	.15
115	Scott Forster	.15
116	Allen McDill	.15
117	Kevin Nicholson	.15
118	Israel Alcantara	.15
119	Juan Alvarez	.15
120	Julio Lugo	.15
121	B.J. Waszgis	.15
122	Jeff D'Amico	.15
123	Ricky Ledee	.15
124	Mark DeRosa	.15
125	Alex Cabrera RC	.50
126	Gary Matthews	.15
127	Richie Sexson	.15
128	Santiago Perez	.15
129	Rondell White	.15

130	Craig House RC	.15
131	Kevin Beirne	.15
132	Wayne Franklin	.15
133	Henry Rodriguez	.15
134	Jay Payton	.15
135	Ron Gant	.15
136	Paxton Crawford RC	.25
137	Kent Bottenfield	.15
138	Rocky Biddle RC	.15
139	Travis Lee	.15
140	Ryan Vogelsong	.15
141	Jason Conti	.15
142	Tim Drew	.15
143	John Parrish RC	.15
144	Javier Cardona RC	.15
145	Tike Redman RC	.15
146	Brian Schneider	.15
147	Pasqual Coco RC	.15
148	Lorenzo Barcelo RC	.15
149	Jace Brewer RC	.25
150	Milton Bradley	.15

Mantle Pieces

NM/M
Inserted 1:80 Sets
1 Mickey Mantle 150.00

2001 Fleer Authority

NM/M
Complete Set (150):		265.00
Common Player:		.25
Common (101-150):		3.00
Production 2,001		
Pack (5):		6.00
Box (22 + 2		
Graded Packs):		120.00
1	Mark Grace	.35
2	Paul Konerko	.25
3	Sean Casey	.35
4	Jim Thome	.75
5	Todd Helton	.25
6	Tony Clark	.25
7	Jeff Bagwell	.75
8	Mike Sweeney	.25
9	Eric Karros	.25
10	Richie Sexson	.25
11	Doug Mientkiewicz	.25
12	Ryan Klesko	.25
13	John Olerud	.25
14	Mark McGwire	2.00
15	Fred McGriff	.25
16	Rafael Palmeiro	.65
17	Carlos Delgado	.50
18	Roberto Alomar	.40
19	Craig Biggio	.25
20	Jose Vidro	.25
21	Edgardo Alfonzo	.25
22	Jeff Kent	.25
23	Bret Boone	.25
24	Rafael Furcal	.25
25	Nomar Garciaparra	1.50
26	Barry Larkin	.25
27	Cristian Guzman	.25
28	Derek Jeter	2.50
29	Miguel Tejada	.40
30	Jimmy Rollins	.40
31	Rich Aurilia	.25
32	Alex Rodriguez	2.00
33	Cal Ripken Jr.	2.50
34	Troy Glaus	.75
35	Matt Williams	.25

36	Chipper Jones	1.00
37	Jeff Cirillo	.25
38	Robin Ventura	.25
39	Eric Chavez	.35
40	Scott Rolen	.65
41	Phil Nevin	.25
42	Mike Piazza	1.50
43	Jorge Posada	.35
44	Jason Kendall	.25
45	Ivan Rodriguez	.65
46	Frank Thomas	.75
47	Edgar Martinez	.25
48	Darin Erstad	.25
49	Tim Salmon	.35
50	Luis Gonzalez	.35
51	Andruw Jones	.75
52	Carl Everett	.25
53	Manny Ramirez	.75
54	Sammy Sosa	1.50
55	Rondell White	.25
56	Magglio Ordonez	.40
57	Ken Griffey Jr.	1.50
58	Juan Gonzalez	.75
59	Larry Walker	.25
60	Bobby Higginson	.25
61	Cliff Floyd	.25
62	Preston Wilson	.25
63	Moises Alou	.25
64	Lance Berkman	.25
65	Richard Hidalgo	.25
66	Jermaine Dye	.25
67	Mark Quinn	.25
68	Shawn Green	.50
69	Gary Sheffield	.40
70	Jeromy Burnitz	.25
71	Geoff Jenkins	.25
72	Vladimir Guerrero	.75
73	Bernie Williams	.35
74	Johnny Damon	.40
75	Jason Giambi	.60
76	Bobby Abreu	.25
77	Pat Burrell	.50
78	Brian Giles	.25
79	Tony Gwynn	1.00
80	Barry Bonds	2.50
81	J.D. Drew	.40
82	Jim Edmonds	.25
83	Greg Vaughn	.25
84	Raul Mondesi	.25
85	Shannon Stewart	.25
86	Randy Johnson	.75
87	Curt Schilling	.50
88	Tom Glavine	.40
89	Greg Maddux	1.00
90	Pedro Martinez	.75
91	Kerry Wood	.50
92	David Wells	.25
93	Bartolo Colon	.25
94	Mike Hampton	.25
95	Kevin Brown	.25
96	Al Leiter	.25
97	Roger Clemens	1.75
98	Mike Mussina	.50
99	Tim Hudson	.35
100	Kazuhiro Sasaki	.25
101	Ichiro Suzuki RC	35.00
102	Albert Pujols RC	100.00
103	Drew Henson RC	5.00
104	Adam Pettyjohn	3.00
105	Adrian Hernandez RC	3.00
106	Andy Morales RC	3.00
107	Tsuyoshi Shinjo RC	4.00
108	Juan Uribe RC	3.00
109	Jack Wilson RC	5.00
110	Jason Smith RC	3.00
111	Junior Spivey RC	4.00
112	Wilson Betemit RC	4.00
113	Elpidio Guzman RC	3.00
114	Esix Snead RC	3.00
115	Winston Abreu RC	3.00
116	Jeremy Owens RC	3.00
117	Jay Gibbons RC	5.00
118	Luis Lopez RC	3.00
119	Ryan Freel RC	3.00
120	Rafael Soriano RC	4.00
121	Johnny Estrada RC	5.00
122	Bud Smith RC	3.00
123	Jackson Melian RC	3.00
124	Matt White RC	3.00
125	Travis Hafner RC	10.00
126	Morgan Ensberg RC	5.00
127	Endy Chavez RC	3.00
128	Bret Prinz RC	3.00
129	Juan Diaz RC	3.00
130	Erick Almonte RC	3.00
131	Rob Mackowiak RC	3.00
132	Carlos Valderrama RC	3.00
133	Wilkin Ruan RC	3.00
134	Angel Berroa RC	5.00
135	Henry Mateo RC	3.00
136	Bill Ortega RC	3.00
137	Billy Sylvester RC	3.00
138	Andres Torres RC	3.00
139	Nate Frese	3.00

140	Casey Fossum RC	4.00
141	Ricardo Rodriguez RC	3.00
142	Brian Roberts RC	8.00
143	Carlos Garcia RC	3.00
144	Brian Lawrence RC	4.00
145	Cory Aldridge RC	3.00
146	Mark Teixeira RC	25.00
147	Juan Cruz RC	3.00
148	Brandon Duckworth RC	3.00
149	Dewon Brazelton RC	3.00
150	Mark Prior RC	15.00

Prominence

Stars (1-100):	5-10X
Production 125	
SP's (101-150):	3-5X
Production 75	

(See 2001 Fleer Authority for checklist and base card values.)

Graded

Mark Teixeira card

Mint:	1-1.5X
NrMt+:	.8-1X
NrMt:	.4-.6X

No Multipliers for Gem Mint.
(See 2001 Fleer Authority for checklist and base card values.)

Authority Figures

		NM/M
	Complete Set (20):	75.00
	Common Card:	2.00
1AF	Mark McGwire, Albert Pujols	8.00
2AF	Kazuhiro Sasaki, Ichiro Suzuki	8.00
3AF	Derek Jeter, Drew Henson	10.00
4AF	Ken Griffey Jr., Jackson Melian	6.00
5AF	Wilson Betemit, Chipper Jones	4.50
6AF	Jeff Bagwell, Morgan Ensberg	4.00
7AF	Cal Ripken Jr., Jay Gibbons	10.00
8AF	Mike Piazza, Tsuyoshi Shinjo	6.00
9AF	Luis Gonzalez, Junior Spivey	2.00
10AF	Barry Bonds, Carlos Valderrama	10.00
11AF	Todd Helton, Juan Uribe	4.00
12AF	Roger Clemens, Adrian Hernandez	5.00
13AF	Alex Rodriguez, Travis Hafner	8.00
14AF	Scott Rolen, Johnny Estrada	3.00
15AF	Brian Giles, Rob Mackowiak	2.00
16AF	Randy Johnson, Bret Prinz	4.00
17AF	Carlos Delgado, Luis Lopez	3.00
18AF	Manny Ramirez, Juan Diaz	4.00
19AF	Mike Sweeney, Endy Chavez	2.00
20AF	Sammy Sosa, Jaisen Randolph	6.00

Derek Jeter Monumental Moments

		NM/M
MM4	Derek Jeter/2000	5.00
MM4AU	Derek Jeter/ Auto./100	100.00

Derek Jeter Reprint Autographs

		NM/M
1DJRA	Derek Jeter/500	90.00

Diamond Cuts

		NM/M
Common Player:		4.00
Inserted 1:10		
	Rick Ankiel/Shoe	4.00
	Jeff Bagwell/Jsy	8.00
	Adrian Beltre/Hat	4.00
	Craig Biggio/Bat	4.00
	Barry Bonds/Bat	35.00
	Barry Bonds/Jsy	20.00
	Barry Bonds/Pants	20.00
	Barry Bonds/Shoe	30.00
	Barry Bonds/ Wristband/100	50.00
	Kevin Brown/Hat	6.00
	Kevin Brown/Pants	4.00
	Eric Byrnes/Bat	4.00
	Sean Casey/Jsy	4.00
	Eric Chavez/Hat	6.00
	Chipper Jones/Jsy	10.00
	Chipper Jones/Bat	10.00
	Bartolo Colon/Hat	6.00
	Erubiel Durazo/Bat	4.00
	Ray Durham/Bat	4.00
	Jim Edmonds/Hat	6.00
	Jim Edmonds/Shoe	10.00
	Darin Erstad/Bat	6.00
	Carlos Febles/Bat	4.00
	Carlos Febles/Shoe	6.00
	Rafael Furcal/Hat	6.00
	Juan Gonzalez/ Bat Glove	10.00
	Juan Gonzalez/Hat	8.00
	Luis Gonzalez	6.00
	Shawn Green/ Bat Glove	10.00
	Shawn Green/Bat	6.00
	Vladimir Guerrero/Bat	8.00
	Tony Gwynn/Bat	8.00
	Mike Hampton/Hat	5.00
	Mike Hampton/Shoe	5.00
	Jerry Hairston Jr./Hat	4.00
	Jason Hart/Bat	4.00
	Todd Helton/Jsy	8.00
	Todd Helton/Pants	8.00
	Orlando Hernandez/ Bat	4.00
	Richard Hidalgo/Bat	4.00
	Richard Hidalgo/ Bat Glove	15.00
	Derek Jeter/Bat	30.00
	Derek Jeter/ Bat Glove	60.00
	Derek Jeter/Jsy	30.00
	Derek Jeter/Pants	30.00
	Derek Jeter/Shoe	40.00
	Randy Johnson/Hat	30.00
	Andruw Jones/Bat	6.00
	Andruw Jones/Hat	8.00
	Jason Kendall/Hat	6.00
	Barry Larkin/Jsy	5.00
	Matt Lawton/Hat	6.00
	Mike Lieberthal/ Bat Glove	6.00
	Kenny Lofton/Bat	4.00
	Edgar Martinez/ Bat Glove	8.00
	Pedro Martinez/Shoe	10.00
	Raul Mondesi/Bat	4.00
	Raul Mondesi/ Bat Glove	6.00
	Hideo Nomo/Bat	15.00
	Hideo Nomo/Hat	40.00
	Magglio Ordonez/ Bat Glove	8.00
	Magglio Ordonez/Hat	6.00
	David Ortiz/Bat	4.00
	Rafael Palmeiro/Bat	8.00
	Rafael Palmeiro/Hat	10.00
	Chan Ho Park/Hat	5.00
	Mike Piazza/Bat	15.00
	Mike Piazza/Jsy	15.00
	Mike Piazza/Shoe	25.00
	Albert Pujols/Pants	30.00
	Manny Ramirez/Bat	8.00
	Manny Ramirez/ Bat Glove	15.00
	Manny Ramirez/Hat	15.00
	Cal Ripken Jr./ Bat Glove	65.00
	Cal Ripken Jr./Pants	25.00
	Ivan Rodriguez/ Bat Glove	10.00
	Ivan Rodriguez/Hat	10.00
	Ivan Rodriguez/Pants	8.00
	Ivan Rodriguez/Shoe	10.00
	Scott Rolen/Hat	10.00
	Jared Sandberg/Bat	4.00
	Deion Sanders/Jsy	4.00
	Tsuyoshi Shinjo/ Wristband	10.00
	Tsuyoshi Shinjo/Bat	6.00
	J.T. Snow	4.00
	Alfonso Soriano/Hat	20.00
	Ichiro Suzuki/Bat	50.00
	Ichiro Suzuki/Hat	65.00
	Mike Sweeney/Hat	6.00
	Miguel Tejada/Hat	6.00
	Frank Thomas/Bat	8.00
	Frank Thomas/Hat	10.00
	Jim Thome/Bat	8.00
	Larry Walker/Bat	4.00
	Larry Walker/Jsy	4.00
	Bernie Williams/Bat	6.00
	Brian Giles/Pants	5.00

Seal of Approval

		NM/M
	Complete Set (15):	45.00
	Common Player:	1.50
1SA	Derek Jeter	6.00
2SA	Alex Rodriguez	5.00
3SA	Nomar Garciaparra	4.00

4SA	Cal Ripken Jr.	6.00
5SA	Mike Piazza	4.00
6SA	Mark McGwire	5.00
7SA	Tony Gwynn	3.00
8SA	Barry Bonds	6.00
9SA	Greg Maddux	3.00
10SA	Chipper Jones	3.00
11SA	Roger Clemens	3.50
12SA	Ken Griffey Jr.	4.00
13SA	Vladimir Guerrero	2.00
14SA	Sammy Sosa	4.00
15SA	Todd Helton	1.50

2001 Fleer Boston Red Sox 100th Anniversary

		NM/M
Complete Set (100):		40.00
Common Player:		.25
Pack (5):		6.00
Box (24):		125.00
1	Carl Yastrzemski	2.50
2	Mel Parnell	.25
3	Birdie Tebbetts	.25
4	Tex Hughson	.25
5	Nomar Garciaparra	4.00
6	Fred Lynn	.50
7	John Valentin	.25
8	Rico Petrocelli	.25
9	Ted Williams	5.00
10	Roger Clemens	3.00
11	Luis Aparicio	.40
12	Cy Young	1.50
13	Carlton Fisk	1.00
14	Pedro Martinez	2.00
15	Joe Dobson	.25
16	Babe Ruth	5.00
17	Doc Cramer	.25
18	Pete Runnels	.25
19	Tony Conigliaro	.25
20	Bill Monbouquette	.25
21	Boo Ferriss	.25
22	Harry Hooper	.25
23	Tony Armas	.25
24	Joe Cronin	1.00
25	Rick Ferrell	.25
26	Wade Boggs	2.25
27	Don Baylor	.25
28	Jeff Reardon	.25
29	Smokey Joe Wood	.25
30	Mo Vaughn	.40
31	Walt Dropo	.25
32	Vern Stephens	.25
33	Bernie Carbo	.25
34	George Scott	.25
35	Lefty Grove	1.00
36	Dom DiMaggio	1.00
37	Dennis Eckersley	.75
38	Johnny Pesky	.25
39	Jim Lonborg	.25
40	Jimmy Piersall	.25
41	Tris Speaker	1.50
42	Frank Malzone	.25
43	Bobby Doerr	.75
44	Jimmie Foxx	2.00
45	Tony Pena	.25
46	Billy Goodman	.25
47	Jim Rice	.25
48	Reggie Smith	.25
49	Bill Buckner	.25
50	Earl Wilson	.25
51	Rick Burleson	.25
52	George Kell	.25
53	Dick Radatz	.25
54	Dwight Evans	.25
55	Luis Tiant	.25
56	Elijah "Pumpsie" Green	.25
57	Gene Conley	.25
58	Jackie Jensen	.25
59	Mike Fornieles	.25
60	Dutch Leonard	.25
61	Jake Stahl	.25
62	Don Schwall	.25
63	Jimmy Collins	.25
64	Herb Pennock	.25
66	Carney Lansford	.25
67	Dick Stuart	.25
68	Dave Morehead	.25
69	Harry Agganis	.25
70	Lou Boudreau	.25
71	Joe Morgan	.75
72	Don Zimmer	.75
73	Tom Yawkey	.25
74	Jean Yawkey	.25
75	Origin of the Red Sox	.25
76	First Season	.25
77	World Series History	.25
78	Carl Yastrzemski	1.00
79	Carlton Fisk	.50
80	Dom DiMaggio	.50
81	Wade Boggs	.75
82	Nomar Garciaparra	2.00
83	Pedro Martinez	1.00
84	Ted Williams	2.50
85	Jim Rice	.25
86	Fred Lynn	.25
87	Mo Vaughn	.25
88	Bobby Doerr	.40
89	Bernie Carbo	.25
90	Dennis Eckersley	.35
91	Jimmy Piersall	.25
92	Luis Tiant	.25
93	Jimmy Fund Signage	.25
94	Green Monster w/Ads	.25
95	Green Monster w/All-Star logo	.25
96	Ladder shot on Green Monster	.25
97	Manual Scoreboard	.25
98	Panoramic of Fenway	.25
99	Lansdowne St.	.25
100	1999 All-Star Game	.25

Autograph Caps

		NM/M
Complete Set (18):		825.00
Common Player:		15.00
(1)	Wade Boggs	75.00
(2)	Bill Buckner	20.00
(3)	Bernie Carbo	15.00
(4)	Roger Clemens	200.00
(5)	Dom DiMaggio	30.00
(6)	Bobby Doerr	25.00
(7)	Dennis Eckersley	50.00
(8)	Dwight Evans	40.00
(9)	Carlton Fisk	125.00
(10)	Nomar Garciaparra	125.00
(11)	Jim Lonborg	20.00
(12)	Johnny Pesky	15.00
(13)	Rico Petrocelli	20.00
(14)	Jimmy Piersall	30.00
(15)	Jim Rice	40.00
(16)	Luis Tiant	30.00
(17)	Carl Yastrzemski	200.00
(18)	Don Zimmer	30.00

BoSox Signatures

		NM/M
Complete Set (16):		1,000
Common Autograph:		15.00
Inserted 1:96		
	Wade Boggs	80.00
	Bill Buckner	20.00
	Bernie Carbo	15.00
	Roger Clemens/100	200.00
	Dom DiMaggio	75.00
	Bobby Doerr	40.00
	Dwight Evans	35.00
	Carlton Fisk	80.00
	Nomar Garciaparra	100.00
	Jim Lonborg	15.00
	Fred Lynn	40.00
	Rico Petrocelli	15.00
	Jim Rice	40.00
	Luis Tiant	30.00
	Carl Yastrzemski/200	180.00

Field the Game

		NM/M
Complete Set (4):		75.00
(1)	Piece of Green Monster outfield wall	20.00
(2)	Piece of base from 100th anniver. game	20.00
(3)	Piece of baseball from 100th Anniv. game	20.00
(4)	Anniv. game	20.00

Spendid Splinters

		NM/M
Complete Set (15):		20.00
Common Player:		1.00
Inserted 1:10		
SS1	Babe Ruth	6.00
SS2	Dom DiMaggio	1.50
SS3	Carlton Fisk	2.00
SS4	Carl Yastrzemski	1.50
SS5	Nomar Garciaparra	5.00
SS6	Wade Boggs	2.50
SS7	Ted Williams	5.00
SS8	Jim Rice	1.00
SS9	Mo Vaughn	1.00
SS10	Tris Speaker	2.00
SS11	Dwight Evans	1.00
SS12	Jimmie Foxx	2.50
SS13	Bobby Doerr	1.50
SS14	Fred Lynn	1.00
SS15	Johnny Pesky	1.00

Splendid Splinters Game Bat

		NM/M
Complete Set (8):		800.00
Common Player:		15.00
Inserted 1:96		
	Babe Ruth/SP/100	400.00
	Carl Yastrzemski	75.00
	Nomar Garciaparra	30.00
	Wade Boggs	25.00
	Ted Williams/SP/100	200.00
	Jim Rice	15.00
	Dwight Evans	15.00
	Jimmie Foxx/SP/100	200.00

Threads

		NM/M
Complete Set (9):		400.00
Common Player:		15.00
Inserted 1:96		
	Wade Boggs	25.00
	Roger Clemens	50.00
	Dwight Evans	15.00
	Carlton Fisk/100	40.00

Pedro Martinez/100	40.00
Jim Rice	20.00
Ted Williams/100	180.00
Carl Yastrzemski	40.00
Don Zimmer	15.00

Yawkey's Heroes

		NM/M
Complete Set (20):		15.00
Common Player:		.50
Inserted 1:4		
1YH	Bobby Doerr	.75
2YH	Dom DiMaggio	1.00
3YH	Jim Rice	.50
4YH	Wade Boggs	1.50
5YH	Carlton Fisk	1.00
6YH	Nomar Garciaparra	3.00
7YH	Dennis Eckersley	1.00
8YH	Carl Yastrzemski	2.00
9YH	Ted Williams	4.00
10YH	Tony Conigliaro	.75
11YH	Tony Armas	.50
12YH	Joe Cronin	1.00
13YH	Mo Vaughn	.50
14YH	Johnny Pesky	.50
15YH	Jim Lonborg	.50
16YH	Luis Tiant	.50
17YH	Tony Pena	.50
18YH	Dwight Evans	.50
19YH	Fred Lynn	.75
20YH	Jimmy Piersall	.50

2001 Fleer Cal Ripken Jr. Commemoratives

		NM/M
Cal Ripken Jr. (1982 Reprint)		10.00
Cal Ripken Jr. (Autograph card.)		125.00

2001 Fleer Focus

		NM/M
Complete Set (240):		100.00
Common Player:		.15
Common Prospect (201-224):		3.00
Common Prospect (225-250):		3.00
Pack (10):		2.50
Box (24):		50.00
1	Derek Jeter	2.00
2	Manny Ramirez	.75
3	Ken Griffey Jr.	1.25
4	Ken Caminiti	.15
5	Joe Randa	.15
6	Jason Kendall	.15
7	Ron Coomer	.15
8	Rondell White	.15

9	Tino Martinez	.15
10	Nomar Garciaparra	1.25
11	Tony Batista	.15
12	Todd Stottlemyre	.15
13	Ryan Klesko	.15
14	Darin Erstad	.50
15	Todd Walker	.15
16	Al Leiter	.15
17	Carl Everett	.15
18	Bobby Abreu	.15
19	Raul Mondesi	.15
20	Vladimir Guerrero	.75
21	Mike Bordick	.15
22	Aaron Sele	.15
23	Ray Lankford	.15
24	Roger Clemens	1.00
25	Kevin Young	.15
26	Brad Radke	.15
27	Todd Hundley	.15
28	Ellis Burks	.15
29	Lee Stevens	.15
30	Eric Karros	.15
31	Darren Dreifort	.15
32	Ivan Rodriguez	.60
33	Pedro Martinez	.75
34	Travis Fryman	.15
35	Garret Anderson	.15
36	Rafael Palmeiro	.60
37	Jason Giambi	.50
38	Jeromy Burnitz	.15
39	Robin Ventura	.15
40	Derek Bell	.15
41	Carlos Guillen	.15
42	Albert Belle	.15
43	Henry Rodriguez	.15
44	Brian Jordan	.15
45	Mike Sweeney	.15
46	Ruben Rivera	.15
47	Greg Maddux	1.00
48	Corey Koskie	.15
49	Sandy Alomar Jr.	.15
50	Mike Mussina	.15
51	Tom Glavine	.25
52	Aaron Boone	.15
53	Frank Thomas	.75
54	Kenny Lofton	.15
55	Danny Graves	.15
56	Jose Valentin	.15
57	Travis Lee	.15
58	Jim Edmonds	.15
59	Jim Thome	.15
60	Steve Finley	.15
61	Shawn Green	.45
62	Lance Berkman	.15
63	Mark Quinn	.15
64	Randy Johnson	.75
65	Dmitri Young	.15
66	Andy Pettitte	.25
67	Paul O'Neill	.15
68	Gil Heredia	.15
69	Russell Branyan	.15
70	Alex Rodriguez	1.50
71	Geoff Jenkins	.15
72	Eric Chavez	.25
73	Cal Ripken Jr.	2.00
74	Mark Kotsay	.15
75	Jeff D'Amico	.15
76	Tony Womack	.15
77	Eric Milton	.15
78	Joe Girardi	.15
79	Peter Bergeron	.15
80	Miguel Tejada	.25
81	Luis Gonzalez	.25
82	Doug Glanville	.15
83	Gerald Williams	.15
84	Troy O'Leary	.15
85	Brian Giles	.15
86	Miguel Cairo	.15
87	Magglio Ordonez	.25
88	Rick Helling	.15
89	Bruce Chen	.15
90	Jason Varitek	.15
91	Mike Lieberthal	.15
92	Shawn Estes	.15
93	Rick Ankiel	.25
94	Tim Salmon	.25
95	Jacque Jones	.15
96	Johnny Damon	.25
97	Larry Walker	.15
98	Ruben Mateo	.15
99	Brad Fullmer	.15
100	Edgardo Alfonzo	.15
101	Mark Mulder	.15
102	Tony Gwynn	1.00
103	Mike Cameron	.15
104	Richie Sexson	.15
105	Barry Larkin	.15
106	Mike Piazza	1.25
107	Eric Young	.15
108	Edgar Renteria	.15
109	Todd Zeile	.15
110	Luis Castillo	.15
111	Sammy Sosa	1.25
112	David Justice	.15
113	Delino DeShields	.15
114	Mariano Rivera	.25
115	Edgar Martinez	.15
116	Ray Durham	.15
117	Brady Anderson	.15
118	Eric Owens	.15
119	Alex Gonzalez	.15
120	Jay Buhner	.15
121	Greg Vaughn	.15
122	Mike Lowell	.15
123	Marquis Grissom	.15
124	Matt Williams	.15
125	Dean Palmer	.15
126	Troy Glaus	.75
127	Bret Boone	.15
128	David Ortiz	.25
129	Glenallen Hill	.15
130	Chipper Jones	1.00
131	Tony Clark	.15
132	Terrence Long	.15
133	Chuck Finley	.15
134	Jeff Bagwell	.75
135	J.T. Snow	.15
136	Andruw Jones	.75
137	Carlos Delgado	.50
138	Mo Vaughn	.15
139	Derek Lee	.15
140	Bobby Estalella	.15
141	Kerry Wood	.60
142	Jose Vidro	.15
143	Ben Grieve	.15
144	Barry Bonds	2.00
145	Javy Lopez	.15
146	Adam Kennedy	.15
147	Jeff Cirillo	.15
148	Cliff Floyd	.15
149	Carl Pavano	.25
150	Bobby Higginson	.15
151	Kevin Brown	.15
152	Fernando Tatis	.15
153	Matt Lawton	.15
154	Damion Easley	.15
155	Curt Schilling	.25
156	Mark McGwire	1.50
157	Mark Grace	.25
158	Adrian Beltre	.30
159	Jorge Posada	.25
160	Richard Hidalgo	.15
161	Vinny Castilla	.15
162	Bernie Williams	.30
163	John Olerud	.15
164	Todd Helton	.75
165	Craig Biggio	.15
166	David Wells	.15
167	Phil Nevin	.15
168	Andres Galarraga	.15
169	Moises Alou	.15
170	Denny Neagle	.15
171	Jeffrey Hammonds	.15
172	Sean Casey	.30
173	Gary Sheffield	.40
174	Carlos Lee	.15
175	Juan Encarnacion	.15
176	Roberto Alomar	.40
177	Kenny Rogers	.15
178	Charles Johnson	.15
179	Shannon Stewart	.15
180	B.J. Surhoff	.15
181	Paul Konerko	.15
182	Jermaine Dye	.15
183	Scott Rolen	.60
184	Fred McGriff	.15
185	Juan Gonzalez	.75
186	Carlos Beltran	.40
187	Jay Payton	.15
188	Chad Hermansen	.15
189	Pat Burrell	.50
190	Omar Vizquel	.15
191	Trot Nixon	.15
192	Mike Hampton	.15
193	Kris Benson	.15
194	Gabe Kapler	.15
195	Rickey Henderson	.75
196	J.D. Drew	.45
197	Pokey Reese	.15
198	Jeff Kent	.15
199	Jose Cruz Jr.	.15
200	Preston Wilson	.15
201	Eric Munson 2,499	3.00
202	Alex Cabrera 2,499	3.00
203	Nate Rolison 2,499	3.00
204	Julio Zuleta 2,499	3.00
205	Chris Richard 2,499	3.00
206	Dernell Stenson 2,499	3.00
207	Aaron McNeal 2,499	3.00
208	Aubrey Huff 2,999	5.00
209	Mike Lamb 2,999	3.00
210	Xavier Nady 2,999	4.00
211	Joe Crede 2,999	4.00
212	Ben Petrick 3,499	3.00
213	Morgan Burkhart 3,499	3.00
214	Jason Tyner 1,999	3.00
215	Juan Pierre 1,999	5.00
216	Adam Dunn 1,999	5.00
217	Adam Piatt 1,999	3.00
218	Eric Byrnes 1,999	4.00
219	Corey Patterson 1,999	4.00
220	Kenny Kelly 1,999	3.00
221	Tike Redman 1,999	3.00
222	Luis Matos 1,999	4.00
223	Timoniel Perez 1,999	3.00
224	Vernon Wells 1,999	3.00
225	Barry Zito 4,999	5.00
226	Adam Bernero 4,999	3.00
227	Kazuhiro Sasaki 4,999	6.00
228	Oswaldo Mairena 4,999	3.00
229	Mark Buehrle 4,999	4.00
230	Ryan Dempster 4,999	3.00
231	Tim Hudson 4,999	3.00
232	Scott Downs 4,999	3.00
233	A.J. Burnett 4,999	4.00
234	Adam Eaton 4,999	3.00
235	Paxton Crawford 4,999	3.00
236	Jace Brewer 3,999	3.00
237	Jose Ortiz 3,999	3.00
238	Rafael Furcal 3,999	4.00
239	Julio Lugo 3,999	3.00
240	Tomas de la Rosa 3,999	3.00

Green

RAY DURHAM

CHICAGO WHITE SOX · SECOND BASE

		NM/M
Common Player:		1.00

Random inserts in packs.
Stated print runs listed below.

1	Derek Jeter/339	10.00
2	Manny Ramirez/351	4.00
3	Ken Griffey Jr./271	8.00
4	Ken Caminiti/303	1.00
5	Joe Randa/304	1.00
6	Jason Kendall/270	1.50
7	Ron Coomer/270	1.00
8	Rondell White/258	1.50
9	Tino Martinez/258	2.00
10	Nomar Garciaparra/372	10.00
11	Tony Batista/263	1.00
12	Todd Stottlemyre/491	1.00
13	Ryan Klesko/283	1.50
14	Darin Erstad/355	1.50
15	Todd Walker/290	1.00
16	Al Leiter/320	1.00
17	Carl Everett/300	1.00
18	Bobby Abreu/316	1.50
19	Raul Mondesi/271	1.00
20	Vladimir Guerrero/345	5.00
21	Mike Bordick/285	1.00
22	Aaron Sele/451	1.00
23	Ray Lankford/253	1.00
24	Roger Clemens/370	10.00
25	Kevin Young/258	1.00
26	Brad Radke/445	1.00
27	Todd Hundley/284	1.00
28	Ellis Burks/344	1.00
29	Lee Stevens/265	1.00
30	Eric Karros/250	1.00
31	Darren Dreifort/416	1.00
32	Ivan Rodriguez/347	4.00
33	Pedro Martinez/174	5.00
34	Travis Fryman/232	1.50
35	Garret Anderson/286	2.00
36	Rafael Palmeiro/288	3.00
37	Jason Giambi/333	5.00
38	Jeromy Burnitz/232	1.00
39	Robin Ventura/232	1.50
40	Derek Bell/266	1.00
41	Carlos Guillen/257	1.00
42	Albert Belle/281	1.00
43	Henry Rodriguez/256	1.00
44	Brian Jordan/264	1.00
45	Mike Sweeney/333	1.00
46	Ruben Rivera/208	1.00
47	Greg Maddux/300	8.00
48	Corey Koskie/300	1.00
49	Sandy Alomar Jr./289	1.00
50	Mike Mussina/379	3.00
51	Tom Glavine/340	2.00
52	Aaron Boone/285	1.00
53	Frank Thomas/328	4.00
54	Kenny Lofton/278	2.00
55	Danny Graves/256	1.00
56	Jose Valentin/273	1.00
57	Travis Lee/235	1.00
58	Jim Edmonds/295	2.00
59	Jim Thome/269	4.00
60	Steve Finley/280	1.00
61	Shawn Green/269	2.00
62	Lance Berkman/297	2.00
63	Mark Quinn/294	1.00
64	Randy Johnson/264	5.00
65	Dmitri Young/303	1.00
66	Andy Pettitte/435	2.00
67	Paul O'Neill/283	2.00
68	Gil Heredia/412	1.00
69	Russell Branyan/238	1.00
70	Alex Rodriguez/316	10.00
71	Geoff Jenkins/303	1.50
72	Eric Chavez/277	2.00
73	Cal Ripken Jr./256	15.00
74	Mark Kotsay/298	1.00
75	Jeff D'Amico/266	1.00
76	Tony Womack/271	1.00
77	Eric Milton/486	1.00
78	Joe Girardi/278	1.00
79	Peter Bergeron/245	1.00
80	Miguel Tejada/275	2.00
81	Luis Gonzalez/311	2.00
82	Doug Glanville/275	1.00
83	Gerald Williams/274	1.00
84	Troy O'Leary/261	1.00
85	Brian Giles/315	2.00
86	Miguel Cairo/261	1.00
87	Magglio Ordonez/315	2.00
88	Rick Helling/448	1.00
89	Bruce Chen/329	1.00
90	Jason Varitek/248	1.00
91	Mike Lieberthal/278	1.00
92	Shawn Estes/426	1.00
93	Rick Ankiel/350	1.00
94	Tim Salmon/290	2.00
95	Jacque Jones/285	1.00
96	Johnny Damon/327	1.50
97	Larry Walker/309	2.00
98	Ruben Mateo/291	1.00
99	Brad Fullmer/295	1.00
100	Edgardo Alfonzo/324	1.00
101	Mark Mulder/544	2.00
102	Tony Gwynn/323	5.00
103	Mike Cameron/267	1.00
104	Richie Sexson/272	2.00
105	Barry Larkin/313	2.00
106	Mike Piazza/324	8.00
107	Eric Young/297	1.00
108	Edgar Renteria/278	1.00
109	Todd Zeile/268	1.00
110	Luis Castillo/334	1.00
111	Sammy Sosa/320	10.00
112	David Justice/286	1.50
113	Delino DeShields/296	1.50
114	Mariano Rivera/285	1.50
115	Edgar Martinez/324	2.00
116	Ray Durham/280	1.00
117	Brady Anderson/257	1.00
118	Eric Owens/293	1.00
119	Alex Gonzalez/252	1.00
120	Jay Buhner/253	1.00
121	Greg Vaughn/254	1.00
122	Mike Lowell/270	1.00
123	Marquis Grissom/244	1.00
124	Matt Williams/275	1.50
125	Dean Palmer/256	1.00
126	Troy Glaus/284	1.50
127	Bret Boone/251	1.50
128	David Ortiz/282	1.00
129	Glenallen Hill/293	1.00
130	Chipper Jones/311	8.00
131	Tony Clark/274	1.00
132	Terrence Long/288	1.00
133	Chuck Finley/417	1.00
134	Jeff Bagwell/310	4.00
135	J.T. Snow/284	1.00
136	Andruw Jones/303	3.00
137	Carlos Delgado/344	3.00
138	Mo Vaughn/272	1.50
139	Derek Lee/281	1.50
140	Bobby Estalella/234	1.00
141	Kerry Wood/480	3.00
142	Jose Vidro/330	1.00
143	Ben Grieve/279	1.00
144	Barry Bonds/306	12.00
145	Javy Lopez/287	2.00
146	Adam Kennedy/266	1.00
147	Jeff Cirillo/326	1.00
148	Cliff Floyd/300	1.00
149	Carl Pavano/265	1.00
150	Bobby Higginson/300	1.00
151	Kevin Brown/258	2.00
152	Fernando Tatis/253	1.00

153	Matt Lawton/305	1.00
154	Damion Easley/259	1.00
155	Curt Schilling/381	3.00
156	Mark McGwire/305	10.00
157	Mark Grace/280	2.50
158	Adrian Beltre/290	1.50
159	Jorge Posada/287	2.00
160	Richard Hidalgo/314	1.00
161	Vinny Castilla/221	1.00
162	Bernie Williams/307	3.00
163	John Olerud/285	1.50
164	Todd Helton/372	4.00
165	Craig Biggio/268	1.50
166	David Wells/411	1.00
167	Phil Nevin/303	1.00
168	Andres Galarraga/302	1.00
169	Moises Alou/355	2.00
170	Denny Neagle/452	1.00
171	Jeffrey Hammonds/335	1.00
172	Sean Casey/315	1.00
173	Gary Sheffield/325	2.00
174	Carlos Lee/301	1.00
175	Juan Encarnacion/289	1.00
176	Roberto Alomar/310	3.00
177	Kenny Rogers/455	1.00
178	Charles Johnson/304	1.00
179	Shannon Stewart/319	1.00
180	B.J. Surhoff/291	1.00
181	Paul Konerko/298	1.00
182	Jermaine Dye/321	1.00
183	Scott Rolen/298	4.00
184	Fred McGriff/277	2.00
185	Juan Gonzalez/289	4.00
186	Carlos Beltran/247	1.50
187	Jay Payton/291	1.50
188	Chad Hermansen/185	1.00
189	Pat Burrell/260	3.00
190	Omar Vizquel/287	2.00
191	Trot Nixon/276	1.00
192	Mike Hampton/314	1.00
193	Kris Benson/385	1.00
194	Gabe Kapler/302	1.00
195	Rickey Henderson/233	3.00
196	J.D. Drew/295	2.00
197	Pokey Reese/255	1.00
198	Jeff Kent/334	1.50
199	Jose Cruz Jr./242	1.00
200	Preston Wilson/264	1.00
201	Eric Munson/252	1.00
202	Alex Cabrera/263	1.00
203	Nate Rolison/77	1.00
204	Julio Zuleta/294	1.00
205	Chris Richard/265	1.00
206	Dernell Stenson/268	1.00
207	Aaron McNeal/310	1.00
208	Aubrey Huff/287	1.00
209	Mike Lamb/278	1.00
211	Joe Crede/357	2.00
212	Ben Petrick/322	1.00
213	Morgan Burkhart/288	1.00
214	Jason Tyner/226	1.00
215	Juan Pierre/310	3.00
216	Adam Dunn/281	4.00
217	Adam Piatt/299	1.00
218	Eric Byrnes/300	1.00
219	Corey Patterson/167	2.00
220	Kenny Kelly/252	1.00
221	Tike Redman/333	1.00
222	Luis Matos/225	1.00
223	Timo Perez/286	1.00
224	Vernon Wells/243	2.00
225	Barry Zito/272	3.00
226	Adam Bernero/419	1.00
227	Kazuhiro Sasaki/18	5.00
228	Oswaldo Mairena/18	5.00
229	Mark Buehrle/421	1.50
230	Ryan Dempster/366	1.00
231	Tim Hudson/414	2.00
232	Scott Downs/529	1.00
233	A.J. Burnett/479	1.00
234	Adam Eaton/413	1.00
235	Paxton Crawford/341	1.00
237	Jose Ortiz/182	1.00
238	Rafael Furcal/295	2.00
239	Julio Lugo/283	1.00
240	Tomas De La Rosa/288	1.00

Autographics

NM/M	
Common Player:	5.00
Inserted 1:72	
Silvers:	1-1.5X

Production 250 Sets

Golds:		1-1.5X

Production 50 Sets

	Roberto Alomar	30.00
	Rick Ankiel	5.00
	Albert Belle	5.00
	Adrian Beltre	15.00
	Lance Berkman	8.00
	Barry Bonds	200.00
	Jeromy Burnitz	5.00
	Pat Burrell	10.00
	Sean Casey	8.00
	Eric Chavez	10.00
	Carlos Delgado	10.00
	J.D. Drew	10.00
	Jermaine Dye	5.00
	Jim Edmonds	10.00
	Troy Glaus	15.00
	Ben Grieve	5.00
	Tony Gwynn	30.00
	Randy Johnson	40.00
	Chipper Jones	40.00
	Mike Lamb	5.00
	Mike Lieberthal	5.00
	Terrence Long	5.00
	Greg Maddux	50.00
	Edgar Martinez	15.00
	Kevin Millwood	10.00
	Mike Mussina	25.00
	Corey Patterson	10.00
	Jay Payton	8.00
	Juan Pierre	8.00
	Brad Radke	5.00
	Scott Rolen	20.00
	Gary Sheffield	15.00
	Fernando Tatis	5.00
	Robin Ventura	5.00
	Kerry Wood	20.00

Bat Company

NM/M		
Complete Set (10):		25.00
Common Player:		1.00
Inserted 1:24		
1	Barry Bonds	5.00
2	Mark McGwire	4.00
3	Sammy Sosa	3.00
4	Ken Griffey Jr.	3.00
5	Mike Piazza	3.00
6	Derek Jeter	5.00
7	Gary Sheffield	1.00
8	Frank Thomas	1.50
9	Chipper Jones	2.00
10	Alex Rodriguez	4.00

Big Innings

NM/M		
Complete Set (25):		15.00
Common Player:		.50
Inserted 1:6		
VIP:		5-10X

Production 50 Sets

1	Rick Ankiel	.50
2	Andruw Jones	1.00
3	Brian Giles	.50
4	Derek Jeter	4.00
5	Rafael Furcal	.50
6	Richie Sexson	.50
7	Jay Payton	.50
8	Carlos Delgado	.75
9	Jermaine Dye	.50
10	Darin Erstad	.75
11	Pat Burrell	.75
12	Richard Hidalgo	.50
13	Adrian Beltre	.60
14	Todd Helton	1.00
15	Vladimir Guerrero	1.00
16	Nomar Garciaparra	2.00
17	Gabe Kapler	.50
18	Carlos Lee	.50
19	J.D. Drew	.60
20	Troy Glaus	1.00
21	Scott Rolen	1.00
22	Alex Rodriguez	3.00
23	Magglio Ordonez	.60
24	Miguel Tejada	.60
25	Ruben Mateo	.50

Diamond Vision

NM/M	
Complete Set (15):	25.00
Common Player:	1.00

Inserted 1:12

1	Derek Jeter	4.00
2	Nomar Garciaparra	2.50
3	Cal Ripken Jr.	4.00
4	Jeff Bagwell	1.50
5	Mark McGwire	3.00
6	Ken Griffey Jr.	2.50
7	Pedro Martinez	1.50
8	Carlos Delgado	1.00
9	Chipper Jones	2.00
10	Barry Bonds	4.00
11	Mike Piazza	2.50
12	Sammy Sosa	2.50
13	Alex Rodriguez	3.00
14	Frank Thomas	1.50
15	Randy Johnson	1.50

Feel the Game

NM/M	
Common Player:	5.00
Inserted 1:72	
Moises Alou	6.00
Brady Anderson	5.00
Dante Bichette	5.00
Jermaine Dye	5.00
Brian Giles	6.00
Juan Gonzalez	10.00
Rickey Henderson	15.00
Javy Lopez	6.00
Tino Martinez	6.00
Phil Nevin	5.00
Matt Stairs	5.00
Shannon Stewart	5.00
Jose Vidro	5.00

ROY Collection

NM/M		
Complete Set (25):		75.00
Common Player:		2.00
Inserted 1:24		
1	Luis Aparicio	2.00
2	Johnny Bench	3.00
3	Joe Black	2.00
4	Rod Carew	2.00
5	Orlando Cepeda	2.00
6	Carlton Fisk	2.00
7	Ben Grieve	2.00
8	Frank Howard	2.00
9	Derek Jeter	10.00
10	Fred Lynn	2.00
11	Willie Mays	8.00
12	Willie McCovey	2.00
13	Mark McGwire	8.00
14	Raul Mondesi	2.00
15	Thurman Munson	4.00
16	Eddie Murray	2.00
17	Mike Piazza	6.00
18	Cal Ripken Jr.	10.00
19	Frank Robinson	2.00
20	Jackie Robinson	8.00
21	Scott Rolen	3.00
22	Tom Seaver	2.00
23	Fernando Valenzuela	2.00
24	David Justice	2.00
25	Billy Williams	2.00

ROY Collection Memorabilia

NM/M	
Common Player:	8.00

Inserted 1:288

1	Luis Aparicio/Bat	8.00
2	Johnny Bench/Jsy	15.00
3	Orlando Cepeda/Bat	8.00
4	Carlton Fisk/Jsy	10.00
5	Ben Grieve/Jsy	8.00
6	Frank Howard/Bat	8.00
7	Derek Jeter/Jsy	50.00
8	Fred Lynn/Bat	8.00
9	Willie Mays/Jsy	60.00
10	Willie McCovey/Bat	10.00
11	Mark McGwire/Ball	50.00
12	Raul Mondesi/Bat	8.00
13	Thurman Munson/Bat	25.00
14	Eddie Murray/Jsy	10.00
15	Mike Piazza/Base	15.00
16	Cal Ripken/Jsy	50.00
17	Frank Robinson/Bat	10.00
18	Jackie Robinson/Jsy	75.00
19	Scott Rolen/Bat	15.00
20	Tom Seaver/Jsy	15.00
22	David Justice/Jsy	8.00

ROY Collection Signed Memorabilia

NM/M		
Common Player:		25.00
1	Luis Aparicio/Jsy/56	40.00
2	Johnny Bench/68	85.00
3	Orlando Cepeda/58	25.00
4	Carlton Fisk/72	50.00
5	Ben Grieve/98	25.00
6	Frank Howard/60	25.00
7	Derek Jeter/96	200.00
8	Fred Lynn/75	25.00
9	Willie Mays/Jsy/51	200.00
10	Willie McCovey/Bat/59	40.00
11	Raul Mondesi/94	25.00
12	Eddie Murray/77	50.00
13	Cal Ripken/82	275.00
14	Frank Robinson/Bat/225	50.00
15	Scott Rolen/97	50.00
16	Tom Seaver/67	90.00
18	David Justice/90	25.00

2001 Fleer Futures

Pedro Martinez

NM/M		
Complete Set (220):		20.00
Common Player:		.15
Pack (8):		1.50
Box (28):		30.00
1	Darin Erstad	.60
2	Manny Ramirez	.75
3	Darryl Kile	.15
4	Troy O'Leary	.15
5	Mark Quinn	.15
6	Brian Giles	.15
7	Randy Johnson	.75
8	Todd Walker	.15
9	Mike Piazza	1.50
10	Fred McGriff	.15
11	Sammy Sosa	1.50
12	Chan Ho Park	.15
13	John Rocker	.15
14	Luis Castillo	.15
15	Eric Chavez	.25
16	Carlos Delgado	.50

17	Sean Casey	.25
18	Corey Koskie	.15
19	John Olerud	.15
20	Nomar Garciaparra	1.50
21	Craig Biggio	.15
22	Pat Burrell	.40
23	Bengie Molina	.15
24	Jim Thome	.15
25	Rey Ordonez	.15
26	Fernando Tatis	.15
27	Eric Young	.15
28	Eric Karros	.15
29	Adam Eaton	.15
30	Brian Jordan	.15
31	Jorge Posada	.25
32	Gabe Kapler	.15
33	Keith Foulke	.15
34	Ron Coomer	.15
35	Chipper Jones	1.00
36	Miguel Tejada	.25
37	David Wells	.15
38	Carlos Lee	.15
39	Barry Bonds	2.50
40	Derrek Lee	.15
41	Tim Hudson	.25
42	Billy Koch	.15
43	Dmitri Young	.15
44	Vladimir Guerrero	.75
45	Rickey Henderson	.75
46	Jeff Bagwell	.75
47	Robert Person	.15
48	Brady Anderson	.15
49	Lance Berkman	.15
50	Mike Lieberthal	.15
51	Adam Kennedy	.15
52	Russ Branyan	.15
53	Robin Ventura	.15
54	Mark McGwire	2.00
55	Tony Gwynn	1.00
56	Matt Williams	.15
57	Jeff Cirillo	.15
58	Roger Clemens	1.25
59	Ivan Rodriguez	.65
60	Brad Radke	.15
61	Kazuhiro Sasaki	.15
62	Cal Ripken Jr.	2.50
63	Ken Caminiti	.15
64	Bobby Abreu	.15
65	Troy Glaus	.75
66	Sandy Alomar Jr.	.15
67	Jose Vidro	.15
68	Pedro Martinez	.75
69	Kevin Young	.15
70	Jay Bell	.15
71	Larry Walker	.15
72	Derek Jeter	2.50
73	Miguel Cairo	.15
74	Magglio Ordonez	.15
75	Jeromy Burnitz	.15
76	J.T. Snow	.15
77	Andres Galarraga	.15
78	Ryan Dempster	.15
79	Ken Griffey Jr.	1.50
80	Aaron Sele	.15
81	Tom Glavine	.25
82	Hideo Nomo	.65
83	Orlando Hernandez	.15
84	Tony Batista	.15
85	Aaron Boone	.15
86	Jacque Jones	.15
87	Delino DeShields	.15
88	Garret Anderson	.15
89	Fernando Seguignol	.15
90	Jim Edmonds	.15
91	Frank Thomas	.75
92	Adrian Beltre	.30
93	Ellis Burks	.15
94	Andruw Jones	.75
95	Tony Clark	.15
96	Danny Graves	.15
97	Alex Rodriguez	2.00
98	Mike Mussina	.40
99	Scott Elarton	.15
100	Jason Giambi	.50
101	Jay Payton	.15
102	Gerald Williams	.15
103	Kerry Wood	.50
104	Shawn Green	.35
105	Greg Maddux	1.00
106	Juan Encarnacion	.15
107	Bernie Williams	.30
108	Mike Lamb	.15
109	Charles Johnson	.15
110	Richie Sexson	.15
111	Jeff Kent	.15
112	Albert Belle	.15
113	Cliff Floyd	.15
114	Ben Grieve	.15
115	Tim Salmon	.25
116	Carl Pavano	.15
117	Rick Ankiel	.15
118	Dante Bichette	.15
119	Johnny Damon	.30
120	Brian Anderson	.15

121	Roberto Alomar	.40
122	Mike Hampton	.15
123	Greg Vaughn	.15
124	Carl Everett	.15
125	Moises Alou	.15
126	Jason Kendall	.15
127	Omar Vizquel	.15
128	Mark Grace	.25
129	Kevin Brown	.15
130	Phil Nevin	.15
131	Kevin Millwood	.15
132	Bobby Higginson	.15
133	Ruben Mateo	.15
134	Luis Gonzalez	.25
135	Dean Palmer	.15
136	Mariano Rivera	.25
137	Rick Helling	.15
138	Paul Konerko	.15
139	Marquis Grissom	.15
140	Robb Nen	.15
141	Javy Lopez	.15
142	Preston Wilson	.15
143	Terrence Long	.15
144	Shannon Stewart	.15
145	Barry Larkin	.15
146	Cristian Guzman	.15
147	Jay Buhner	.15
148	Jermaine Dye	.15
149	Kris Benson	.15
150	Curt Schilling	.40
151	Todd Helton	.75
152	Paul O'Neill	.15
153	Rafael Palmeiro	.65
154	Ray Durham	.15
155	Geoff Jenkins	.15
156	Livan Hernandez	.15
157	Rafael Furcal	.15
158	Juan Gonzalez	.75
159	Tino Martinez	.15
160	Raul Mondesi	.15
161	Matt Lawton	.15
162	Edgar Martinez	.15
163	Richard Hidalgo	.15
164	Scott Rolen	.65
165	Chuck Finley	.15
166	Edgardo Alfonzo	.15
167	J.D. Drew	.35
168	Trot Nixon	.15
169	Carlos Beltran	.50
170	Ryan Klesko	.15
171	Mo Vaughn	.15
172	Kenny Lofton	.15
173	Al Leiter	.15
174	Rondell White	.15
175	Mike Sweeney	.15
176	Trevor Hoffman	.15
177	Steve Finley	.15
178	Jeffrey Hammonds	.15
179	David Justice	.15
180	Gary Sheffield	.40
181	Eric Munson	.15
182	Luis Matos	.15
183	Alex Cabrera	.15
184	Randy Keisler	.15
185	Nate Rolison	.15
186	Jason Hart	.15
187	Timo Perez	.15
188	Adam Bernero	.15
189	Barry Zito	.50
190	Ryan Kohlmeier	.15
191	Joey Nation	.15
192	Oswaldo Mairena	.15
193	Aubrey Huff	.15
194	Mark Buehrle	.15
195	Jace Brewer	.15
196	Julio Zuleta	.15
197	Xavier Nady	.15
198	Vernon Wells	.25
199	Joe Crede	.15
200	Scott Downs	.15
201	Ben Petrick	.15
202	A.J. Burnett	.15
203	Esix Snead **RC**	.15
204	Dernell Stenson	.15
205	Jose Ortiz	.15
206	Paxton Crawford	.15
207	Jason Tyner	.15
208	Jimmy Rollins	.25
209	Juan Pierre	.25
210	Keith Ginter	.15
211	Adam Dunn	.40
212	Larry Barnes	.15
213	Adam Piatt	.15
214	Rodney Lindsey	.15
215	Eric Byrnes	.15
216	Julio Lugo	.15
217	Corey Patterson	.25
218	Reggie Taylor	.15
219	Kenny Kelly	.15
220	Tike Redman	.15

Black Gold

Production 499 Sets: 3-6X
(See 2001 Fleer Futures for checklist and base card values.)

Bases Loaded

		NM/M
Common Player:		4.00
Inserted 1:134		
BL1	Ken Griffey Jr.	10.00
BL2	Mark McGwire	12.00
BL3	Carlos Delgado	4.00
BL4	Chipper Jones	7.50
BL5	Nomar Garciaparra	10.00
BL6	Cal Ripken Jr.	15.00
BL7	Sammy Sosa	10.00
BL8	Jeff Bagwell	6.00
BL9	Vladimir Guerrero	6.00
BL10	Tony Gwynn	7.50
BL11	Frank Thomas	6.00
BL12	Mike Piazza	10.00
BL13	Jason Giambi	5.00
BL14	Troy Glaus	6.00
BL15	Pat Burrell	4.00

Bats to the Future

		NM/M
Complete Set (25):		60.00
Common Player:		1.00
Inserted 1:28		
1BF	Mike Schmidt	6.00
2BF	Carlton Fisk	3.00
3BF	Paul Molitor	3.00
4BF	Vladimir Guerrero	3.00
5BF	Dave Parker	1.00
6BF	Chipper Jones	5.00
7BF	Carlos Delgado	2.00
8BF	Tony Gwynn	5.00
9BF	Reggie Jackson	5.00
10BF	Eddie Murray	1.50
11BF	Robin Yount	3.00
12BF	Alan Trammell	1.00
13BF	Frank Thomas	3.00
14BF	Cal Ripken Jr.	8.00
15BF	Don Mattingly	6.00
16BF	Jim Rice	1.00
17BF	Juan Gonzalez	3.00
18BF	Todd Helton	3.00
19BF	George Brett	6.00
20BF	Barry Bonds	8.00
21BF	Kirk Gibson	1.00
22BF	Matt Williams	1.00
23BF	Dave Winfield	1.50
24BF	Ryne Sandberg	5.00
25BF	Ivan Rodriguez	2.00

Bats to the Future Game Bat

		NM/M
Common Player:		5.00
Inserted 1:114		
1BF	Mike Schmidt	25.00
2BF	Carlton Fisk	10.00
3BF	Paul Molitor	15.00
4BF	Vladimir Guerrero	8.00
5BF	Dave Parker	5.00
6BF	Chipper Jones	10.00
7BF	Chris Delgado	8.00
8BF	Tony Gwynn	10.00
9BF	Reggie Jackson	10.00
10BF	Eddie Murray	8.00
11BF	Robin Yount	15.00
12BF	Alan Trammell	5.00
13BF	Frank Thomas	8.00
14BF	Cal Ripken Jr.	30.00
15BF	Don Mattingly	30.00
16BF	Jim Rice	5.00
17BF	Juan Gonzalez	8.00
18BF	Todd Helton	8.00
19BF	George Brett	25.00
20BF	Barry Bonds	25.00
21BF	Kirk Gibson	5.00
22BF	Matt Williams	5.00
23BF	Dave Winfield	8.00
24BF	Ryne Sandberg	15.00
25BF	Ivan Rodriguez	8.00

Bats to the Future Game Bat Autograph

		NM/M
Common Autograph:		40.00
Production 50 Sets		
1BF	Mike Schmidt	150.00
2BF	Carlton Fisk	60.00
3BF	Paul Molitor	50.00
4BF	Vladimir Guerrero	80.00
5BF	Dave Parker	40.00
6BF	Chipper Jones	75.00
7BF	Carlos Delgado	50.00
8BF	Tony Gwynn	75.00
9BF	Reggie Jackson	70.00
10BF	Eddie Murray	70.00
11BF	Robin Yount	80.00
12BF	Alan Trammell	40.00
13BF	Frank Thomas	60.00
14BF	Cal Ripken Jr.	200.00
15BF	Don Mattingly	150.00
16BF	Jim Rice	40.00
17BF	Juan Gonzalez	60.00
18BF	Todd Helton	60.00
19BF	George Brett	150.00
20BF	Barry Bonds	200.00
21BF	Kirk Gibson	40.00
22BF	Matt Williams	40.00
23BF	Dave Winfield	60.00
24BF	Ryne Sandberg	125.00
25BF	Ivan Rodriguez	40.00

Characteristics

		NM/M
Complete Set (15):		20.00
Common Player:		.75
Inserted 1:9		
1C	Derek Jeter	4.00
2C	Mark McGwire	3.00
3C	Nomar Garciaparra	2.50
4C	Sammy Sosa	2.50
5C	Pedro Martinez	1.50
6C	Chipper Jones	2.00
7C	Cal Ripken Jr.	4.00
8C	Todd Helton	1.50
9C	Jim Edmonds	.75
10C	Ken Griffey Jr.	2.50
11C	Alex Rodriguez	3.00
12C	Mike Piazza	2.50
13C	Vladimir Guerrero	1.50
14C	Frank Thomas	1.50
15C	Carlos Delgado	1.00

Hot Commodities

	NM/M
Complete Set (10):	20.00
Common Player:	1.00

1HC	Mark McGwire	3.00
2HC	Ken Griffey Jr.	2.50
3HC	Derek Jeter	4.00
4HC	Cal Ripken Jr.	4.00
5HC	Chipper Jones	2.00
6HC	Barry Bonds	4.00
7HC	Mike Piazza	2.50
8HC	Sammy Sosa	2.50
9HC	Alex Rodriguez	3.00
10HC	Frank Thomas	1.00

September Call-Ups Memorabilia

		NM/M
Common Card:		4.00
Production 200 Sets		
184	Randy Keisler/Cap/Cleat	4.00
185	Nate Rolison/Bat	4.00
187	Timoniel Perez/Bat	4.00
191	Joey Nation/Glove	4.00
192	Oswaldo Mairena/Glove	4.00
195	Jace Brewer/Bat	4.00
197	Xavier Nady/Glove	6.00
199	Joe Crede/Bat	6.00
205	Jose Ortiz/Bat	4.00
208	Jimmy Rollins/Glove	6.00
210	Keith Ginter/Bat	4.00
214	Rodney Lindsey/Bat	4.00
217	Corey Patterson/Bat	8.00
218	Reggie Taylor/Bat	4.00
219	Kenny Kelly/Bat	4.00

2001 Fleer Game Time

		NM/M
Complete Set (121):		
Common Player:		.15
Common (91-121):		3.00
Production 2,000		
Pack (5):		4.00
Box (24):		80.00
1	Derek Jeter	2.00
2	Nomar Garciaparra	1.25
3	Alex Rodriguez	1.50
4	Jason Kendall	.15
5	Barry Bonds	2.00
6	David Wells	.15
7	Craig Biggio	.15
8	Adrian Beltre	.30
9	Pat Burrell	.40
10	Rafael Palmeiro	.60
11	Jim Thome	.15
12	Mike Lowell	.15
13	Trevor Hoffman	.15
14	Pokey Reese	.15
15	Juan Encarnacion	.15
16	Shawn Green	.40
17	Kerry Wood	.50
18	Richard Hidalgo	.15
19	Scott Rolen	.60
20	Jeff Kent	.15
21	Alex Gonzalez	.15
22	Matt Williams	.15
23	Mike Sweeney	.15
24	Edgar Martinez	.15
25	Sammy Sosa	1.25
26	Bobby Higginson	.15
27	Kevin Brown	.15

28	Mike Lieberthal	.15
29	Pedro J. Martinez	.75
30	Jeff Weaver	.15
31	Greg Maddux	1.00
32	Mike Hampton	.75
33	Vladimir Guerrero	.75
34	Greg Vaughn	.15
35	Manny Ramirez	.75
36	Carlos Beltran	.40
37	Eric Chavez	.25
38	Troy Glaus	.75
39	Todd Helton	.75
40	Gary Sheffield	.40
41	Brady Anderson	.15
42	Juan Gonzalez	.75
43	Tim Hudson	.30
44	Kenny Lofton	.15
45	Al Leiter	.15
46	Eric Owens	.15
47	Roberto Alomar	.40
48	Preston Wilson	.15
49	Tony Gwynn	1.00
50	Cal Ripken Jr.	2.00
51	Ben Petrick	.15
52	Jason Giambi	.50
53	Ben Grieve	.15
54	Albert Belle	.15
55	Jose Vidro	.15
56	Barry Zito	.30
57	Ivan Rodriguez	.60
58	Jeff Bagwell	.75
59	Geoff Jenkins	.15
60	Roger Clemens	1.00
61	John Olerud	.15
62	Randy Johnson	.75
63	Matt Lawton	.15
64	Mark McGwire	1.50
65	Brad Radke	.15
66	Frank Thomas	.75
67	Edgardo Alfonzo	.15
68	Brian Giles	.15
69	J.T. Snow	.15
70	Carlos Delgado	.50
71	Chipper Jones	1.00
72	Mark Quinn	.15
73	Mike Mussina	.40
74	Rick Ankiel	.15
75	Rafael Furcal	.15
76	Jim Edmonds	.15
77	Vinny Castilla	.15
78	Sean Casey	.25
79	Derrek Lee	.15
80	Mike Piazza	1.25
81	Warren Morris	.15
82	Tim Salmon	.25
83	Jeromy Burnitz	.15
84	Freddy Garcia	.15
85	Ken Griffey Jr.	1.25
86	Andruw Jones	.75
87	Darryl Kile	.15
88	Magglio Ordonez	.15
89	Bernie Williams	.30
90	Timo Perez	.15
91	Ichiro Suzuki RC	35.00
92	Larry Barnes, Darin Erstad	3.00
93	Jaisen Randolph RC	3.00
94	Paul Phillips RC	3.00
95	Esix Snead RC	3.00
96	Matt White RC	3.00
97	Ryan Freel RC	3.00
98	Winston Abreu RC	3.00
99	Junior Spivey RC	5.00
100	Randy Keisler, Roger Clemens	5.00
101	Brian Cole, Mike Piazza	4.00
102	Aubrey Huff, Chipper Jones	4.00
103	Corey Patterson, Sammy Sosa	5.00
104	Sun-Woo Kim, Pedro Martinez	4.00
105	Drew Henson RC	5.00
106	Claudio Vargas RC	3.00
107	Cesar Izturis, Rafael Furcal	3.00
108	Paxton Crawford, Pedro Martinez	4.00
109	Adrian Hernandez RC	3.00
110	Jace Brewer, Derek Jeter	8.00
111	Andy Morales RC	3.00
112	Wilson Betemit RC	5.00
113	Juan Diaz RC	3.00
114	Erick Almonte RC	4.00
115	Nick Punto RC	3.00
116	Tsuyoshi Shinjo RC	4.00
117	Jay Gibbons RC	5.00
118	Andres Torres RC	3.00
119	Alexis Gomez RC	4.00
120	Wilken Ruan RC	3.00
121	Albert Pujols RC	80.00

Next Game Extra

Cards (91-121):	2-3X
Production 200 Sets	
(See 2001 Fleer Game Time #91-121 for checklist and base card values.)	

Derek Jeter's Monumental Moments

		NM/M
Complete Set (1):		
1JM	Derek Jeter/1996	8.00
1JMS	Derek Jeter/Auto./96	80.00

Famers Lumber

		NM/M
Common Player:		8.00
Production 100 Sets		
1FL	Luis Aparicio	8.00
2FL	Hank Bauer	8.00
3FL	Paul Blair	8.00
4FL	Bobby Bonds	8.00
5FL	Orlando Cepeda	8.00
6FL	Roberto Clemente	100.00
7FL	Rocky Colavito	10.00
8FL	Bucky Dent	8.00
9FL	Bill Dickey	10.00
10FL	Larry Doby	10.00
11FL	Carlton Fisk	10.00
12FL	Hank Greenberg	25.00
13FL	Elston Howard	8.00
14FL	Frank Howard	8.00
15FL	Reggie Jackson	15.00
16FL	Harmon Killebrew	20.00
17FL	Tony Lazzeri	8.00
18FL	Roger Maris	60.00
19FL	Johnny Mize	10.00
20FL	Thurman Munson	40.00
21FL	Tony Perez	10.00
22FL	Jim Rice	8.00
23FL	Phil Rizzuto	10.00
24FL	Bill Skowron	8.00
25FL	Enos Slaughter	10.00
26FL	Duke Snider	15.00
27FL	Willie Stargell	15.00
28FL	Bill Terry	8.00
29FL	Ted Williams	100.00

Famers Lumber Autograph

		NM/M
Common Player:		40.00
Production 25 Sets		
1FLS	Hank Bauer	40.00
2FLS	Bobby Bonds	50.00
3FLS	Orlando Cepeda	50.00
4FLS	Rocky Colavito	50.00
5FLS	Bucky Dent	40.00
6FLS	Larry Doby	50.00
7FLS	Carlton Fisk	65.00
8FLS	Frank Howard	40.00
9FLS	Reggie Jackson	100.00
10FLS	Harmon Killebrew	120.00
11FLS	Tony Perez	40.00
12FLS	Jim Rice	40.00
13FLS	Phil Rizzuto	60.00
14FLS	Bill Skowron	40.00
15FLS	Enos Slaughter	40.00
16FLS	Duke Snider	75.00

Let's Play Two!

		NM/M
Complete Set (15):		30.00
Common Card:		1.50
Inserted 1:24		
1LT	Derek Jeter, Nomar Garciaparra	4.00

2LT	Mark McGwire, Sammy Sosa	3.00
3LT	Pedro J. Martinez, Randy Johnson	1.50
4LT	Vladimir Guerrero, Carlos Delgado	1.50
5LT	Mike Piazza, Roger Clemens	2.50
6LT	Alex Rodriguez, Miguel Tejada	3.00
7LT	Troy Glaus, Chipper Jones	2.00
8LT	Derek Jeter, Alex Rodriguez	4.00
9LT	Cal Ripken Jr., Derek Jeter	4.00
10LT	Jason Giambi, Mark McGwire	3.00
11LT	Jeff Bagwell, Craig Biggio	1.50
12LT	Tom Glavine, Greg Maddux	2.00
13LT	Ken Griffey Jr., Barry Bonds	4.00
14LT	Manny Ramirez, Pedro J. Martinez	1.50
15LT	Alex Rodriguez, Ivan Rodriguez	3.00

Lumber

		NM/M
Common Player:		4.00
Inserted 1:40		
1GL	Roberto Alomar	6.00
2GL	Rick Ankiel	4.00
3GL	Adrian Beltre	6.00
4GL	Barry Bonds	25.00
5GL	Kevin Brown	4.00
7GL	Ken Caminiti	4.00
8GL	Eric Chavez	5.00
9GL	Carlos Delgado	5.00
10GL	J.D. Drew	5.00
11GL	Erubiel Durazo	4.00
12GL	Carl Everett	4.00
13GL	Rafael Furcal	4.00
14GL	Brian Giles	5.00
15GL	Juan Gonzalez	6.00
16GL	Todd Helton	8.00
18GL	Randy Johnson	10.00
19GL	Chipper Jones	10.00
20GL	Pedro J. Martinez	10.00
21GL	Tino Martinez	5.00
23GL	Cal Ripken/SP/275	40.00
24GL	Ivan Rodriguez	8.00
25GL	Frank Thomas	8.00
26GL	Jim Thome	8.00
27GL	Bernie Williams	5.00
28GL	Nomar Garciaparra	15.00

New Order

		NM/M
Complete Set (20):		30.00
Common Player:		1.50
Inserted 1:12		
1NO	Derek Jeter	6.00
2NO	Nomar Garciaparra	4.00
3NO	Alex Rodriguez	5.00
4NO	Mark McGwire	5.00
5NO	Sammy Sosa	4.00
6NO	Carlos Delgado	1.50
7NO	Troy Glaus	1.50
8NO	Jason Giambi	1.50
9NO	Mike Piazza	4.00
10NO	Todd Helton	1.50
11NO	Vladimir Guerrero	2.00
12NO	Manny Ramirez	1.50
13NO	Frank Thomas	1.50
14NO	Ken Griffey Jr.	4.00
15NO	Chipper Jones	3.00

Sticktoitness

	NM/M
Complete Set (20):	15.00

Common Player:		.50
Inserted 1:8		
1S	Derek Jeter	4.00
2S	Nomar Garciaparra	3.00
3S	Alex Rodriguez	3.00
4S	Jeff Bagwell	1.00
5S	Bernie Williams	.50
6S	Eric Chavez	.60
7S	Richard Hidalgo	.50
8S	Ichiro Suzuki	2.00
9S	Troy Glaus	.75
10S	Magglio Ordonez	.50
11S	Corey Patterson	.50
12S	Todd Helton	1.00
13S	Jim Edmonds	.50
14S	Rafael Furcal	.50
15S	Mo Vaughn	.50
16S	Pat Burrell	.65
17S	Adrian Beltre	.60
18S	Andruw Jones	1.00
19S	Manny Ramirez	1.00
20S	Sean Casey	.65

Uniformity

		NM/M
Common Player:		4.00
Inserted 1:25		
1GU	Andres Galarraga	4.00
2GU	Barry Bonds	25.00
3GU	Ben Petrick	4.00
4GU	Brad Radke	4.00
5GU	Brian Jordan	4.00
6GU	Carlos Guillen	4.00
7GU	Fernando Seguignol	4.00
8GU	Fred McGriff	4.00
9GU	Gary Sheffield	5.00
10GU	Greg Maddux	15.00
11GU	Ivan Rodriguez	8.00
12GU	Jay Buhner	4.00
13GU	Jeromy Burnitz	4.00
14GU	John Olerud	4.00
15GU	Kevin Brown	4.00
16GU	Larry Walker	4.00
17GU	Magglio Ordonez	4.00
18GU	Matt Williams	4.00
19GU	Robin Ventura	4.00
20GU	Rondell White	4.00
21GU	Tony Gwynn	15.00
22GU	Troy Glaus	8.00
23GU	Vladimir Guerrero	8.00

2001 Fleer Genuine

	NM/M
Complete Set (130):	150.00
Common Player:	.25
Common (101-130):	3.00
Production 1,500	
Pack (5):	4.00
Box (24):	80.00

1	Derek Jeter	3.00
2	Nomar Garciaparra	2.00
3	Alex Rodriguez	2.50
4	Frank Thomas	1.00
5	Travis Fryman	.25
6	Gary Sheffield	.40
7	Jason Giambi	.75
8	Trevor Hoffman	.25
9	Todd Helton	1.00
10	Ivan Rodriguez	.75
11	Roberto Alomar	.40
12	Barry Zito	.40
13	Kevin Brown	.25
14	Shawn Green	.40
15	Kenny Lofton	.25
16	Jeff Weaver	.25
17	Geoff Jenkins	.25
18	Carlos Delgado	.65
19	Mark Grace	.35
20	Ken Griffey Jr.	2.00
21	David Justice	.25
22	Brian Giles	.25
23	Scott Williamson	.25
24	Richie Sexson	.25
25	John Olerud	.25
26	Sammy Sosa	2.00
27	Bobby Higginson	.25
28	Matt Lawton	.25
29	Vinny Castilla	.25
30	Alex S. Gonzalez	.25
31	Manny Ramirez	1.00
32	Brad Radke	.25
33	Cal Ripken Jr.	3.00
34	Richard Hidalgo	.25
35	Al Leiter	.25
36	Freddy Garcia	.25
37	Juan Encarnacion	.25
38	Corey Koskie	.25
39	Greg Vaughn	.25
40	Rafael Palmeiro	.65
41	Vladimir Guerrero	1.00
42	Troy Glaus	.75
43	Mike Hampton	.25
44	Jose Vidro	.25
45	Ryan Rupe	.25
46	Troy O'Leary	.25
47	Ben Petrick	.25
48	Mike Lieberthal	.25
49	Mike Sweeney	.25
50	Scott Rolen	.75
51	Albert Belle	.25
52	Mark Quinn	.25
53	Mike Piazza	2.00
54	Mark McGwire	2.50
55	Brady Anderson	.25
56	Carlos Beltran	.45
57	Michael Barrett	.25
58	Jason Kendall	.25
59	Jim Edmonds	.25
60	Matt Williams	.25
61	Pokey Reese	.25
62	Bernie Williams	.25
63	Barry Bonds	3.00
64	David Wells	.25
65	Chipper Jones	1.50
66	Jim Parque	.25
67	Derrek Lee	.25
68	Darin Erstad	.60
69	Edgar Martinez	.25
70	Kerry Wood	.60
71	Omar Vizquel	.25
72	Jeromy Burnitz	.25
73	Warren Morris	.25
74	Rick Ankiel	.25
75	Andruw Jones	1.00
76	Paul Konerko	.25
77	Mike Lowell	.25
78	Roger Clemens	1.75
79	Tim Hudson	.35
80	Rafael Furcal	.25
81	Craig Biggio	.25
82	Edgardo Alfonzo	.25
83	Pat Burrell	.50
84	Adrian Beltre	.35
85	Tony Gwynn	1.50
86	J.T. Snow	.25
87	Randy Johnson	1.00
88	Sean Casey	.35
89	Preston Wilson	.25
90	Mike Mussina	.50
91	Eric Chavez	.35
92	Tim Salmon	.25
93	Pedro Martinez	1.00
94	Darryl Kile	.25
95	Magglio Ordonez	1.50
96	Magglio Ordonez	.25
97	Jeff Bagwell	1.00
98	Timo Perez	.25
99	Jeff Kent	.25
100	Eric Owens	.25
101	Ichiro Suzuki RC	35.00
102	Elpidio Guzman RC	3.00
103	Tsuyoshi Shinjo RC	6.00
104	Travis Hafner RC	10.00

105	Larry Barnes	3.00
106	Jaisen Randolph RC	3.00
107	Paul Phillips RC	3.00
108	Erick Almonte RC	3.00
109	Nick Punto RC	3.00
110	Jack Wilson RC	3.00
111	Jeremy Owens RC	3.00
112	Esix Snead RC	3.00
113	Jay Gibbons RC	4.00
114	Adrian Hernandez RC	4.00
115	Matt White RC	3.00
116	Ryan Freel RC	3.00
117	Martin Vargas RC	3.00
118	Winston Abreu RC	3.00
119	Junior Spivey RC	5.00
120	Paxton Crawford	3.00
121	Randy Keisler	3.00
122	Juan Diaz RC	3.00
123	Aaron Rowand	3.00
124	Toby Hall	3.00
125	Brian Cole	3.00
126	Aubrey Huff	4.00
127	Corey Patterson	4.00
128	Sun-Woo Kim	3.00
129	Jace Brewer	3.00
130	Cesar Izturis	3.00

Final Cut

	NM/M
Common Player:	4.00
Inserted 1:30	
Miguel Tejada/ SP/170	6.00
Barry Bonds/SP/330	40.00
Robin Ventura	4.00
Greg Maddux	15.00
Andruw Jones/ SP/135	10.00
J.D. Drew/SP/75	10.00
Chipper Jones	10.00
Tim Salmon	4.00
Edgar Martinez/ SP/130	8.00
Troy Glaus	8.00
Frank Thomas	8.00
Pokey Reese	4.00
Larry Walker	4.00
Ivan Rodriguez/ SP/120	10.00
Scott Rolen	8.00
Cal Ripken Jr.	30.00
Tony Gwynn	10.00
Wade Boggs	10.00
George Brett	30.00
Sean Casey	4.00
Bob Gibson	6.00
Matt Williams	6.00
Robin Yount	8.00
Ron Guidry (Not officially released.)	150.00
Reggie Jackson (Not officially released.)	250.00
Don Larsen (Not officially released.)	140.00

Genuine Coverage PLUS

	NM/M
Common Player:	6.00
Production 150 Sets	

Troy Glaus		8.00
Randy Johnson		10.00
Andruw Jones		8.00
Frank Thomas		8.00
Darin Erstad		6.00
Chipper Jones		15.00
Derek Jeter		35.00
Tony Gwynn		15.00
Barry Bonds		35.00
Cal Ripken Jr.		35.00

High Interest

		NM/M
Complete Set (15):		40.00
Common Player:		1.50
Inserted 1:23		
1HI	Derek Jeter	6.00
2HI	Nomar Garciaparra	4.00
3HI	Greg Maddux	3.00
4HI	Todd Helton	2.00
5HI	Sammy Sosa	4.00
6HI	Jeff Bagwell	2.00
7HI	Jason Giambi	1.50
8HI	Frank Thomas	2.00
9HI	Andruw Jones	2.00
10HI	Jim Edmonds	1.50
11HI	Bernie Williams	1.50
12HI	Randy Johnson	2.00
13HI	Ken Griffey Jr.	4.00
14HI	Pedro Martinez	2.00
15HI	Mark McGwire	5.00

Material Issue

	NM/M
Common Player:	5.00
Inserted 1:30	
Randy Johnson	10.00
Scott Rolen	8.00
Robin Ventura	5.00
Tony Gwynn	15.00
Troy Glaus	10.00
Kevin Millwood	5.00
Chipper Jones	15.00
Tom Glavine	5.00
Pedro Martinez/ SP/60	40.00
Greg Maddux	15.00
Frank Thomas	10.00
Curt Schilling/SP/120	10.00
Edgar Martinez	5.00
Darin Erstad	5.00
J.D. Drew	5.00
Cal Ripken Jr.	30.00
Nolan Ryan	40.00
Steve Carlton	5.00

Names of the Game - Autographs

	NM/M
Common Player:	25.00

Yogi Berra	60.00
Orlando Cepeda	20.00
Rocky Colavito	60.00
Andre Dawson	20.00
Bucky Dent	20.00
Rollie Fingers	20.00
Carlton Fisk	40.00
Whitey Ford	40.00
Reggie Jackson	60.00
Randy Johnson	60.00
Chipper Jones	50.00
Harmon Killebrew	60.00
Don Mattingly	90.00
Willie McCovey	25.00
Cal Ripken Jr.	150.00
Ivan Rodriguez	50.00
Preacher Roe	35.00
Nolan Ryan	100.00
Tom Seaver	50.00
Bill Skowron	25.00
Enos Slaughter	30.00
Duke Snider	40.00

Names of the Game - Game Used

	NM/M
Common Player:	10.00
Production 50 Sets	
Yogi Berra/Bat	25.00
Orlando Cepeda/Bat	10.00
Rocky Colavito/Bat	20.00
Andre Dawson/Jsy	10.00
Bucky Dent/Bat	10.00
Rollie Fingers/Jsy	10.00
Carlton Fisk/Bat	15.00
Whitey Ford/Jsy	25.00
Jimmie Foxx/Bat	80.00
Hank Greenberg/Bat	50.00
"Catfish" Hunter/Jsy	10.00
Reggie Jackson/Jsy	20.00
Randy Johnson/Jsy	30.00
Chipper Jones/Bat	30.00
Harmon Killebrew/Bat	25.00
Tony Lazzeri/Bat	10.00
Don Mattingly/Bat	65.00
Willie McCovey/Bat	20.00
Johnny Mize/Bat	15.00
Pee Wee Reese/Jsy	15.00
Cal Ripken Jr./Bat	75.00
Phil Rizzuto/Bat	20.00
Ivan Rodriguez/Bat	25.00
Preacher Roe/Jsy	15.00
Babe Ruth/Bat	300.00
Nolan Ryan/Jsy	90.00
Tom Seaver/Jsy	25.00
Bill Skowron/Bat	10.00
Enos Slaughter/Bat	25.00
Duke Snider/Bat	25.00
Willie Stargell/Bat	15.00
Bill Terry/Bat	10.00
Ted Williams/Bat	200.00
Hack Wilson/Bat	75.00

Pennant Aggression

	NM/M
Complete Set (10):	30.00
Inserted 1:23	
1PA Derek Jeter	6.00
2PA Alex Rodriguez	5.00
3PA Nomar Garciaparra	4.00
4PA Mark McGwire	5.00
5PA Ken Griffey Jr.	4.00
6PA Mike Piazza	4.00
7PA Sammy Sosa	4.00
8PA Barry Bonds	6.00
9PA Chipper Jones	3.00
10PA Pedro Martinez	2.00

Tip of the Cap

	NM/M
Common Player:	8.00
Production 150 Sets	
Barry Bonds	40.00
Eric Chavez	8.00
Shawn Green	8.00
Vladimir Guerrero	15.00
Randy Johnson	20.00
Andruw Jones	10.00
Javy Lopez	8.00
Rafael Palmeiro	10.00
Ivan Rodriguez	10.00
Miguel Tejada	8.00
Roberto Alomar	10.00
Pedro Martinez	15.00

@ LG (At Large)

	NM/M
Complete Set (15):	50.00
Common Player:	1.50
Inserted 1:23	
1AL Derek Jeter	7.50
2AL Nomar Garciaparra	4.00
3AL Mark McGwire	6.00
4AL Pedro Martinez	3.00
5AL Tony Gwynn	3.50
6AL Roger Clemens	3.50
7AL Ivan Rodriguez	2.00
8AL Sammy Sosa	4.00
9AL Magglio Ordonez	1.50
10AL Jason Giambi	2.00
11AL Carlos Delgado	2.00
12AL Chipper Jones	3.50
13AL Mike Piazza	4.00
14AL Cal Ripken Jr.	7.50
15AL Ken Griffey Jr.	4.00

2001 Fleer Greats of the Game

	NM/M
Complete Set (137):	50.00
Common Player:	.25
Hobby Pack (5):	10.00
Hobby Box (24):	200.00
1 Roberto Clemente	2.50
2 George "Sparky" Anderson	.25
3 Babe Ruth	4.00
4 Paul Molitor	1.00
5 Don Larsen	.25
6 Cy Young	1.00
7 Billy Martin	.50
8 Lou Brock	1.00
9 Fred Lynn	.25
10 Johnny Vander Meer	.25
11 Harmon Killebrew	1.00
12 Dave Winfield	1.00
13 Orlando Cepeda	.25
14 Johnny Mize	.75
15 Walter Johnson	1.00
16 Roy Campanella	1.00
17 Monte Irvin	.50
18 Mookie Wilson	.25
19 Elston Howard	.25
20 Walter Alston	.25
21 Rollie Fingers	.25
22 Brooks Robinson	1.00
23 Hank Greenberg	1.00
24 Maury Wills	.25
25 Rich Gossage	.25
26 Leon Day	.25
27 Jimmie Foxx	2.00
28 Alan Trammell	.50
29 Dennis Martinez	.25
30 Don Drysdale	.75
31 Bob Feller	.75
32 Jackie Robinson	3.00
33 Whitey Ford	1.00
34 Enos Slaughter	.25
35 Rod Carew	.75
36 Eddie Mathews	1.00
37 Ron Cey	.25
38 Thurman Munson	1.00
39 Henry Kimbro	.25
40 Ty Cobb	3.00
41 Rocky Colavito	.50
42 Satchel Paige	1.50
43 Andre Dawson	.50
44 Phil Rizzuto	1.00
45 Roger Maris	2.50
46 Bobby Bonds	.25
47 Joe Carter	.25
48 Christy Mathewson	.75
49 Tony Lazzeri	.25
50 Gil Hodges	.25
51 Ray Dandridge	.25
52 Gaylord Perry	.25
53 Ernie Banks	2.00
54 Lou Gehrig	3.00
55 George Kell	.25
56 Wes Parker	.25
57 Sam Jethroe	.25
58 Joe Morgan	.75
59 Steve Garvey	.50
60 Joe Torre	.75
61 Roger Craig	.25
62 Warren Spahn	1.00
63 Willie McCovey	.25
64 Cool Papa Bell	1.00
65 Frank Robinson	1.00
66 Richie Allen	.25
67 Bucky Dent	.25
68 George Foster	.25
69 Hoyt Wilhelm	.25
70 Phil Niekro	.25
71 Buck Leonard	.25
72 Preacher Roe	.25
73 Yogi Berra	1.50
74 Joe Black	.25
75 Nolan Ryan	4.00
76 Pop Lloyd	.25
77 Lester Lockett	.25
78 Paul Blair	.25
79 Ryne Sandberg	2.00
80 Bill Perkins	.25
81 Frank Howard	.25
82 Hack Wilson	1.00
83 Robin Yount	1.00
84 Harry Heilmann	.25
85 Mike Schmidt	3.00
86 Vida Blue	.25
87 George Brett	3.00
88 Juan Marichal	.50
89 Tom Seaver	1.50
90 Bill Skowron	.25
91 Don Mattingly	2.00
92 Jim Bunning	.25
93 Eddie Murray	1.00
94 Tommy Lasorda	.25
95 Pee Wee Reese	.50
96 Bill Dickey	.25
97 Ozzie Smith	1.50
98 Dale Murphy	.25
99 Artie Wilson	.25
100 Bill Terry	.25
101 Jim "Catfish" Hunter	.25
102 Don Sutton	.25
103 Luis Aparicio	.25
104 Reggie Jackson	1.50
105 Ted Radcliffe	.25
106 Carl Erskine	.25
107 Johnny Bench	2.00
108 Carl Furillo	.25
109 Stan Musial	2.00
110 Carlton Fisk	.75
111 Rube Foster	.25
112 Tony Oliva	.25
113 Hank Bauer	.25
114 Jim Rice	.25
115 Willie Mays	3.00
116 Ralph Kiner	.50
117 Al Kaline	1.00
118 Billy Williams	.25
119 Buck O'Neil	.25
120 Tony Perez	.25
121 Dave Parker	.25
122 Kirk Gibson	.25
123 Lou Piniella	.25
124 Ted Williams	4.00
125 Steve Carlton	.75
126 Dizzy Dean	.25
127 Willie Stargell	.50
128 Joe Niekro	.25
129 Lloyd Waner	.25
130 Wade Boggs	2.00
131 Wilmer Fields	.25
132 Bill Mazeroski	.50
133 Duke Snider	1.00
134 Smoky Joe Williams	.25
135 Bob Gibson	1.50
136 Jim Palmer	.75
137 Oscar Charleston	.25

Autographs

	NM/M
Common Player:	10.00
Inserted 1:8	
1 Richie Allen	10.00
2 George "Sparky" Anderson	10.00
3 Luis Aparicio	10.00
4 Ernie Banks/SP/250	80.00
5 Hank Bauer	10.00
6 Johnny Bench/SP/400	80.00
7 Yogi Berra/SP/500	50.00
8 Joe Black	10.00
9 Paul Blair	10.00
9a Paul Blair/Double Signed	10.00
10 Vida Blue	10.00
11 Wade Boggs	40.00
12 Bobby Bonds	15.00
13 George Brett/SP/247	150.00
14 Lou Brock/SP/500	40.00
15 Jim Bunning	25.00
16 Rod Carew	20.00
17 Steve Carlton	25.00
18 Joe Carter	10.00
19 Orlando Cepeda	15.00
20 Ron Cey	10.00
21 Rocky Colavito	25.00
22 Roger Craig	10.00
23 Andre Dawson	15.00
24 Bucky Dent	10.00
25 Larry Doby	35.00
26 Carl Erskine	10.00
27 Bob Feller	15.00
28 Wilmer Fields	10.00
29 Rollie Fingers	10.00
30 Carlton Fisk	40.00
31 Whitey Ford	30.00
32 George Foster	10.00
33 Steve Garvey/SP/400	40.00
34 Bob Gibson	20.00
35 Kirk Gibson	20.00
36 Rich Gossage	10.00
37 Frank Howard	10.00
38 Monte Irvin	20.00

39	Reggie Jackson/ SP/400	60.00
40	Sam Jethroe	10.00
41	Al Kaline	30.00
42	George Kell	15.00
43	Harmon Killebrew	30.00
44	Ralph Kiner	20.00
45	Don Larsen	15.00
46	Tommy Lasorda/ SP/400	40.00
47	Lester Lockett	10.00
48	Fred Lynn	10.00
49	Juan Marichal	20.00
50	Dennis Martinez	10.00
51	Don Mattingly	75.00
52	Willie Mays/SP/100	450.00
53	Bill Mazeroski	20.00
54	Willie McCovey	20.00
55	Paul Molitor	25.00
56	Joe Morgan	10.00
57	Dale Murphy	30.00
58	Eddie Murray/ SP/140	200.00
59	Stan Musial/SP/525	75.00
60	Joe Niekro	10.00
61	Phil Niekro	10.00
62	Tony Oliva	10.00
63	Buck O'Neil	20.00
64	Jim Palmer/SP/600	20.00
65	Dave Parker	10.00
66	Tony Perez	20.00
67	Gaylord Perry	10.00
68	Lou Piniella	10.00
69	Ted Radcliffe	10.00
70	Jim Rice	10.00
71	Phil Rizzuto/SP/425	80.00
72	Brooks Robinson	25.00
73	Frank Robinson	20.00
74	Preacher Roe	20.00
75	Nolan Ryan SP/650	100.00
76	Ryne Sandberg	50.00
77	Mike Schmidt/ SP/213	175.00
78	Tom Seaver	50.00
79	Bill Skowron	10.00
80	Enos Slaughter	15.00
81	Ozzie Smith	50.00
82	Duke Snider/SP/600	50.00
83	Warren Spahn	40.00
84	Willie Stargell (Redemption card only, none signed.)	10.00
85	Don Sutton	10.00
86	Joe Torre/SP/500	40.00
87	Alan Trammell	15.00
88	Hoyt Wilhelm	10.00
89	Billy Williams	10.00
90	Maury Wills	10.00
91	Artie Wilson	10.00
92	Mookie Wilson	10.00
93	Dave Winfield/ SP/370	60.00
94	Robin Yount/SP/400	80.00

Dodger Blues

		NM/M
Common Player:		10.00
Inserted 1:36		
(1)	Walter Alston/Jsy	10.00
(2)	Walt Alston/Uniform	10.00
(3)	Roy Campanella/ Uniform/SP	75.00
(4)	Roger Craig/Jsy	10.00
(5)	Don Drysdale/Jsy	20.00
(6)	Carl Furillo/Jsy	10.00
(7)	Steve Garvey/Jsy	10.00
(8)	Gil Hodges/Uniform	20.00
(9)	Wes Parker/Bat	10.00
(10)	Wes Parker/Jsy	10.00
(11)	Pee Wee Reese/Jsy	15.00
(12)	Jackie Robinson/ Uniform/SP	150.00
(13)	Preacher Roe/Jsy	10.00
(14)	Duke Snider/Bat/SP	75.00
(15)	Don Sutton/Jsy	10.00

Feel the Game Classics

		NM/M
Common Player:		5.00
Inserted 1:72		
1	Luis Aparicio/Bat	5.00

2	George Brett/Jsy	30.00
3	Lou Brock/Jsy	15.00
4	Orlando Cepeda/Bat	10.00
5	Whitey Ford/Jsy	15.00
6	Hank Greenberg/Bat	40.00
7	Elston Howard/Bat	5.00
8	"Catfish" Hunter/Jsy	8.00
9	Harmon Killebrew/ Bat	15.00
10	Roger Maris/Bat	50.00
11	Eddie Mathews/Bat	15.00
12	W. McCovey/ Bat/SP/200	15.00
13	Johnny Mize/Bat	5.00
14	Paul Molitor/Jsy	10.00
15	Jim Palmer/Jsy	10.00
16	Tony Perez/Bat	5.00
17	Brooks Robinson/ Bat/144	25.00
18	Babe Ruth/Bat/250	200.00
19	Mike Schmidt/Jsy	25.00
20	Tom Seaver/Jsy	20.00
21	Enos Slaughter	10.00
22	Willie Stargell	10.00
23	Hack Wilson	10.00
24	Harry Heilmann	5.00

Retrospection Collection

MIKE SCHMIDT
Philadelphia Phillies®

		NM/M
Complete Set (10):		20.00
Common Player:		1.00
Inserted 1:6		
1	Babe Ruth	5.00
2	Stan Musial	3.00
3	Jimmie Foxx	3.00
4	Roberto Clemente	4.00
5	Ted Williams	4.00
6	Mike Schmidt	4.00
7	Cy Young	1.50
8	Satchel Paige	2.00
9	Hank Greenberg	1.50
10	Jim Bunning	1.00

2001 Fleer Legacy

MARK McGWIRE

		NM/M
Complete Set (105):		
Common Player:		.50
Common (91-105):		8.00
Production 799 Sets		
Pack (5):		8.00
Box (15 + Cap):		140.00
1	Pedro J. Martinez	1.50
2	Andruw Jones	1.50
3	Mike Hampton	.50
4	Gary Sheffield	.65
5	Barry Zito	.65
6	J.D. Drew	.75
7	Charles Johnson	.50

8	David Wells	.50
9	Kazuhiro Sasaki	.50
10	Vladimir Guerrero	1.50
11	Pat Burrell	.75
12	Ruben Mateo	.50
13	Greg Maddux	2.00
14	Sean Casey	.65
15	Craig Biggio	.50
16	Bernie Williams	.65
17	Jeff Kent	.50
18	Nomar Garciaparra	2.50
19	Cal Ripken Jr.	4.00
20	Larry Walker	.50
21	Adrian Beltre	.65
22	Johnny Damon	.75
23	Rick Ankiel	.50
24	Matt Williams	.50
25	Magglio Ordonez	.50
26	Richard Hidalgo	.50
27	Robin Ventura	.50
28	Jason Kendall	.50
29	Tony Batista	.50
30	Chipper Jones	2.00
31	Jim Thome	.50
32	Kevin Brown	.50
33	Mike Mussina	.65
34	Mark McGwire	3.00
35	Darin Erstad	.75
36	Manny Ramirez	1.50
37	Bobby Higginson	.50
38	Richie Sexson	.50
39	Jason Giambi	1.00
40	Alex Rodriguez	3.00
41	Mark Grace	.65
42	Ken Griffey Jr.	2.50
43	Moises Alou	.50
44	Edgardo Alfonzo	.50
45	Phil Nevin	.50
46	Rafael Palmeiro	1.25
47	Javy Lopez	.50
48	Juan Gonzalez	1.50
49	Jermaine Dye	.50
50	Roger Clemens	2.25
51	Barry Bonds	4.00
52	Carl Everett	.50
53	Ben Sheets	.50
54	Juan Encarnacion	.50
55	Jeromy Burnitz	.50
56	Miguel Tejada	.65
57	Ben Grieve	.50
58	Randy Johnson	1.50
59	Frank Thomas	1.50
60	Preston Wilson	.50
61	Mike Piazza	2.50
62	Brian Giles	.50
63	Carlos Delgado	1.00
64	Tom Glavine	.75
65	Roberto Alomar	.65
66	Mike Sweeney	.50
67	Orlando Hernandez	.50
68	Edgar Martinez	.50
69	Tim Salmon	.75
70	Kerry Wood	1.00
71	Jack Wilson RC	3.00
72	Matt Lawton	.50
73	Scott Rolen	1.25
74	Ivan Rodriguez	1.25
75	Steve Finley	.50
76	Barry Larkin	.50
77	Jeff Bagwell	1.50
78	Derek Jeter	4.00
79	Tony Gwynn	2.00
80	Raul Mondesi	.50
81	Rafael Furcal	.50
82	Todd Helton	1.50
83	Shawn Green	.75
84	Tim Hudson	.65
85	Jim Edmonds	.50
86	Troy Glaus	1.50
87	Sammy Sosa	2.50
88	Cliff Floyd	.50
89	Jose Vidro	.50
90	Bobby Abreu	.50
91	Drew Henson/ Auto. RC	30.00
92	Andy Morales/ Auto. RC	8.00
93	Wilson Betemit/ Auto. RC	10.00
94	Elpidio Guzman RC	8.00
95	Esix Snead RC	8.00
96	Winston Abreu RC	8.00
97	Jeremy Owens RC	8.00
99	Junior Spivey RC	15.00
100	Jaisen Randolph RC	8.00
101	Ichiro Suzuki RC	60.00
102	Albert Pujols/499 RC	160.00
102	Albert Pujols/ Auto./300 RC	750.00
103	Tsuyoshi Shinjo RC	10.00
104	Jay Gibbons RC	10.00
105	Juan Uribe RC	10.00

Ultimate Legacy

Stars (1-90):	3-5X
Rookies (91-100):	.3-.75X

Rookies (101-105):	.75-1X
Production 250 Sets	
(See 2001 Fleer Legacy for checklist and base card values.)	

Autographed MLB Fitted Cap

	NM/M
Common Player:	25.00
Inserted 1:15	
Edgardo Alfonzo	25.00
Roberto Alomar	50.00
Ernie Banks/100	100.00
Adrian Beltre	40.00
Johnny Bench/100	125.00
Lance Berkman	30.00
Yogi Berra/200	120.00
Craig Biggio	30.00
Barry Bonds	280.00
Jeromy Burnitz	25.00
Pat Burrell	30.00
Steve Carlton	40.00
Sean Casey	30.00
Orlando Cepeda	30.00
Eric Chavez	25.00
Tony Clark	25.00
Roger Clemens/100	200.00
Johnny Damon	40.00
Dom DiMaggio/200	45.00
J.D. Drew	40.00
Jermaine Dye	25.00
Darin Erstad	40.00
Carlton Fisk/150	80.00
Rafael Furcal	25.00
Nomar Garciaparra/ 150	150.00
Jason Giambi	50.00
Troy Glaus	35.00
Tom Glavine	50.00
Juan Gonzalez	50.00
Luis Gonzalez	30.00
Tony Gwynn	85.00
Drew Henson	30.00
Derek Jeter	250.00
Andruw Jones	40.00
David Justice	30.00
Paul Konerko	25.00
Don Mattingly	150.00
Willie McCovey	30.00
Paul Molitor	60.00
Stan Musial/200	125.00
Mike Mussina	50.00
Jim Palmer	25.00
Corey Patterson	40.00
Kirby Puckett/200	75.00
Cal Ripken/200	200.00
Brooks Robinson	60.00
Ivan Rodriguez	50.00
Scott Rolen	50.00
Nolan Ryan/150	200.00
Mike Schmidt/150	125.00
Tom Seaver/100	125.00
Ben Sheets	40.00
Ozzie Smith	85.00
Duke Snider	40.00
Miguel Tejada	50.00
Jim Thome	60.00
Matt Williams	25.00
Dave Winfield/150	75.00
Carl Yastrzemski/ 150	100.00
Robin Yount	100.00
Barry Zito	40.00

Hit Kings

	NM/M
Common Player:	5.00
Inserted 1:13	
Stan Musial	15.00
Barry Bonds	25.00

Corey Patterson 5.00
Shawn Green 6.00
Ralph Kiner 5.00
Troy O'Leary 5.00
Ivan Rodriguez 6.00
Jose Vidro 5.00
Carlos Beltran 8.00
Jose Canseco 6.00
Juan Encarnacion 5.00
Reggie Jackson 10.00
Ruben Mateo 5.00
Juan Pierre 5.00
Tim Salmon 5.00
Adrian Beltre 6.00
Roger Cedeno 5.00
Troy Glaus 8.00
Jason Kendall 5.00
Rick Ankiel 5.00
Andruw Jones 8.00
Jim Thome 5.00
Tony Batista 5.00
George Brett 20.00
Vladimir Guerrero 10.00
Billy Martin 5.00
Magglio Ordonez 5.00
Johnny Damon 6.00

Hit Kings Short Prints

NM/M
Common Player: 15.00
Production 100 Sets
Robin Yount 20.00
Scott Rolen 15.00
Johnny Bench 25.00
Steve Garvey 15.00
Joe Morgan 15.00
Frank Thomas 20.00
Eddie Mathews 20.00
Tony Gwynn 25.00
Roger Clemens 40.00
Wade Boggs 25.00

Hot Gloves

NM/M
Common Player: 15.00
Inserted 1:180
1HG Andruw Jones 15.00
2HG Mike Mussina 15.00
3HG Roberto Alomar 15.00
4HG Tony Gwynn 30.00
5HG Bernie Williams 15.00
6HG Ivan Rodriguez 15.00
7HG Ken Griffey Jr. 40.00
8HG Robin Ventura 15.00
9HG Cal Ripken Jr. 60.00
10HG Jeff Bagwell 20.00
11HG Mark McGwire 50.00
12HG Rafael Palmeiro 15.00
13HG Scott Rolen 15.00
14HG Barry Bonds 60.00
15HG Greg Maddux 30.00

MLB Game Issue - Base/Ball/Jersey

NM/M
Common Card: 25.00
Production 50 Sets
Derek Jeter 100.00
Cal Ripken Jr. 100.00
Todd Helton 30.00
Tony Gwynn 50.00
Chipper Jones 50.00
Frank Thomas 30.00
Barry Bonds 100.00
Troy Glaus 25.00
Pat Burrell 25.00
Scott Rolen 30.00

MLB Game Issue - Base

NM/M
Common Player: 4.00
Inserted 1:52
1GI Mark McGwire 15.00
2GI Ken Griffey Jr. 10.00
3GI Sammy Sosa 10.00
4GI Mike Piazza 10.00
5GI Alex Rodriguez 15.00
6GI Derek Jeter 20.00
7GI Cal Ripken Jr. 20.00
8GI Todd Helton 6.00
9GI Tony Gwynn 8.00
10GI Chipper Jones 8.00
11GI Frank Thomas 6.00
12GI Barry Bonds 20.00
13GI Troy Glaus 4.00
14GI Pat Burrell 4.00
15GI Scott Rolen 5.00

MLB Game Issue - Base/Ball

NM/M
Common Player: 10.00
Production 100 Sets
Mark McGwire 50.00
Ken Griffey Jr. 40.00
Sammy Sosa 40.00
Mike Piazza 40.00
Alex Rodriguez 50.00
Derek Jeter 60.00
Cal Ripken Jr. 60.00
Todd Helton 15.00
Tony Gwynn 25.00
Chipper Jones 25.00
Frank Thomas 15.00
Barry Bonds 60.00
Troy Glaus 10.00
Pat Burrell 10.00
Scott Rolen 12.50

Tailor Made

NM/M
Common Player: 4.00
Inserted 1:15
2TM Cal Ripken Jr. 40.00
3TM Orlando Cepeda 6.00
4TM Willie McCovey 6.00
5TM Dave Winfield 6.00
6TM Don Mattingly 35.00
7TM Nolan Ryan 40.00
8TM Manny Ramirez 8.00

9TM Edgardo Alfonzo 4.00
10TM Rondell White 4.00
11TM Lou Piniella 4.00
12TM Ivan Rodriguez 8.00
13TM J.D. Drew 4.00
14TM Barry Bonds 40.00
15TM Greg Maddux 15.00
16TM Rick Ankiel 4.00
17TM Carlos Delgado 8.00
18TM Kevin Brown 4.00
20TM Reggie Jackson 10.00
21TM Shawn Green 6.00
22TM Jason Kendall 4.00
23TM Rafael Palmeiro 8.00
24TM Todd Helton 8.00
25 Curt Schilling 6.00

2001 Fleer Platinum

JEFF BAGWELL
FIRST BASE

NM/M
Complete Set (301): 140.00
Common Player: .15
Common SP (251-300): 1.00
Inserted 1:6
Card #301 Production 1,500
Pack (10): 5.00
Box (24): 100.00
1 Bobby Abreu .15
2 Brad Radke .15
3 Bill Mueller .15
4 Adam Eaton .15
5 Antonio Alfonseca .15
6 Manny Ramirez .75
7 Adam Kennedy .15
8 Jose Valentin .15
9 Jaret Wright .15
10 Aramis Ramirez .15
11 Jeff Kent .15
12 Juan Encarnacion .15
13 Sandy Alomar Jr. .15
14 Joe Randa .15
15 Darryl Kile .15
16 Darren Dreifort .15
17 Matt Kinney .15
18 Pokey Reese .15
19 Ryan Klesko .15
20 Shawn Estes .15
21 Moises Alou .15
22 Edgar Renteria .15
23 Chuck Knoblauch .15
24 Carl Everett .15
25 Garret Anderson .15
26 Shane Reynolds .15
27 Billy Koch .15
28 Carlos Febles .15
29 Brian Anderson .15
30 Armando Rios .15
31 Ryan Kohlmeier .15
32 Steve Finley .15
33 Brady Anderson .15
34 Cal Ripken Jr. 2.50
35 Paul Konerko .15
36 Chuck Finley .15
37 Rick Ankiel .15
38 Mariano Rivera .25
39 Corey Koskie .15
40 Cliff Floyd .15
41 Kevin Appier .15
42 Henry Rodriguez .15
43 Mark Kotsay .15
44 Brook Fordyce .15
45 Brad Ausmus .15
46 Alfonso Soriano .50
47 Ray Lankford .15
48 Keith Foulke .15
49 Rich Aurilia .15
50 Alex Rodriguez 2.00
51 Eric Byrnes .15
52 Travis Fryman .15
53 Jeff Bagwell .75
54 Scott Rolen .65
55 Matt Lawton .15
56 Brad Fullmer .15
57 Tony Batista .15

58 Nate Rolison .15
59 Carlos Lee .15
60 Rafael Furcal .15
61 Jay Bell .15
62 Jimmy Rollins .25
63 Derrek Lee .15
64 Andres Galarraga .15
65 Derek Bell .15
66 Tim Salmon .25
67 Travis Lee .15
68 Kevin Millwood .15
69 Albert Belle .15
70 Kazuhiro Sasaki .15
71 Al Leiter .15
72 Britt Reames .15
73 Carlos Beltran .45
74 Curt Schilling .50
75 Curtis Leskanic .15
76 Jeremy Giambi .15
77 Adrian Beltre .35
78 David Segui .15
79 Mike Lieberthal .15
80 Brian Giles .15
81 Marvin Benard .15
82 Aaron Sele .15
83 Kenny Lofton .15
84 Doug Glanville .15
85 Kris Benson .15
86 Richie Sexson .15
87 Javy Lopez .15
88 Doug Mientkiewicz .15
89 Peter Bergeron .15
90 Gary Sheffield .40
91 Derek Lowe .15
92 Tom Glavine .40
93 Lance Berkman .15
94 Chris Singleton .15
95 Mike Lowell .25
96 Luis Gonzalez .30
97 Dante Bichette .15
98 Mike Sirotka .15
99 Julio Lugo .15
100 Juan Gonzalez .75
101 Craig Biggio .15
102 Armando Benitez .15
103 Greg Maddux 1.00
104 Mark Grace .25
105 John Smoltz .15
106 J.T. Snow .15
107 Al Martin .15
108 Danny Graves .15
109 Barry Bonds 2.50
110 Lee Stevens .15
111 Pedro Martinez .75
112 Shawn Green .40
113 Bret Boone .15
114 Matt Stairs .15
115 Tino Martinez .15
116 Rusty Greer .15
117 Mike Bordick .15
118 Garrett Stephenson .15
119 Edgar Martinez .15
120 Ben Grieve .15
121 Milton Bradley .15
122 Aaron Boone .15
123 Ruben Mateo .15
124 Ken Griffey Jr. 1.50
125 Russell Branyan .15
126 Shannon Stewart .15
127 Fred McGriff .15
128 Ben Petrick .15
129 Kevin Brown .15
130 B.J. Surhoff .15
131 Mark McGwire 2.00
132 Carlos Guillen .15
133 Adrian Brown .15
134 Mike Sweeney .15
135 Eric Milton .15
136 Cristian Guzman .15
137 Ellis Burks .15
138 Fernando Tatis .15
139 Ben Molina .15
140 Tony Gwynn 1.00
141 Jeromy Burnitz .15
142 Miguel Tejada .25
143 Raul Mondesi .15
144 Jeffrey Hammonds .15
145 Pat Burrell .40
146 Frank Thomas .75
147 Eric Munson .15
148 Mike Hampton .15
149 Mike Cameron .15
150 Jim Thome .15
151 Mike Mussina .50
152 Rick Helling .15
153 Ken Caminiti .15
154 John Vander Wal .15
155 Denny Neagle .15
156 Robb Nen .15
157 Jose Canseco .50
158 Mo Vaughn .15
159 Phil Nevin .15
160 Pat Hentgen .15
161 Sean Casey .25

162	Greg Vaughn	.15
163	Trot Nixon	.15
164	Roberto Hernandez	.15
165	Vinny Castilla	.15
166	Robin Ventura	.15
167	Alex Ochoa	.15
168	Orlando Hernandez	.15
169	Luis Castillo	.15
170	Quilvio Veras	.15
171	Troy O'Leary	.15
172	Livan Hernandez	.15
173	Roger Cedeno	.15
174	Jose Vidro	.15
175	John Olerud	.15
176	Richard Hidalgo	.15
177	Eric Chavez	.25
178	Fernando Vina	.15
179	Chris Stynes	.15
180	Bobby Higginson	.15
181	Bruce Chen	.15
182	Omar Vizquel	.15
183	Rey Ordonez	.15
184	Trevor Hoffman	.15
185	Jeff Cirillo	.15
186	Billy Wagner	.15
187	David Ortiz	.15
188	Tim Hudson	.40
189	Tony Clark	.15
190	Larry Walker	.15
191	Eric Owens	.15
192	Aubrey Huff	.15
193	Royce Clayton	.15
194	Todd Walker	.15
195	Rafael Palmeiro	.65
196	Todd Hundley	.15
197	Roger Clemens	1.25
198	Jeff Weaver	.15
199	Dean Palmer	.15
200	Geoff Jenkins	.15
201	Matt Clement	.15
202	David Wells	.15
203	Chan Ho Park	.15
204	Hideo Nomo	.65
205	Bartolo Colon	.15
206	John Wetteland	.15
207	Corey Patterson	.15
208	Freddy Garcia	.15
209	David Cone	.15
210	Rondell White	.15
211	Carl Pavano	.15
212	Charles Johnson	.15
213	Ron Coomer	.15
214	Matt Williams	.15
215	Jay Payton	.15
216	Nick Johnson	.15
217	Deivi Cruz	.15
218	Scott Elarton	.15
219	Neifi Perez	.15
220	Jason Isringhausen	.15
221	Jose Cruz	.15
222	Gerald Williams	.15
223	Timo Perez	.15
224	Damion Easley	.15
225	Jeff D'Amico (Photo actually Jamey Wright.)	.15
226	Preston Wilson	.15
227	Robert Person	.15
228	Jacque Jones	.15
229	Johnny Damon	.25
230	Tony Womack	.15
231	Adam Piatt	.15
232	Brian Jordan	.15
233	Ben Davis	.15
234	Kerry Wood	.50
235	Mike Piazza	1.50
236	David Justice	.15
237	Dave Veres	.15
238	Eric Young	.15
239	Juan Pierre	.15
240	Gabe Kapler	.15
241	Ryan Dempster	.15
242	Dmitri Young	.15
243	Jorge Posada	.35
244	Eric Karros	.15
245	J.D. Drew	.25
246	Todd Zeile	.15
247	Mark Quinn	.15
248	Kenny Kelly	.15
249	Jermaine Dye	.15
250	Barry Zito	.30
251	Jason Hart, Larry Barnes	1.00
252	Ichiro Suzuki, Elpidio Guzman RC	20.00
253	Tsuyoshi Shinjo, Brian Cole	3.00
254	John Barnes, Adrian Hernandez RC	1.00
255	Jason Tyner, Jace Brewer	1.00
256	Brian Buchanan, Luis Rivas	1.00
257	Brent Abernathy, Jose Ortiz	1.00

258	Marcus Giles, Keith Ginter	1.00
259	Tike Redman, Jaisen Randolph RC	1.00
260	Dane Sardinha, David Espinosa	1.00
261	Josh Beckett, Craig House	1.00
262	Jack Cust, Hiram Bocachica	1.00
263	Alex Escobar, Esix Snead RC	1.00
264	Chris Richard, Vernon Wells	1.00
265	Pedro Feliz, Xavier Nady	1.00
266	Brandon Inge, Joe Crede	1.00
267	Ben Sheets, Roy Oswalt	1.00
268	Drew Henson, Andy Morales RC	4.00
269	C.C. Sabathia, Justin Miller	1.00
270	David Eckstein, Jason Gabrowski	1.00
271	Dee Brown, Chris Wakeland	1.00
272	Junior Spivey, Alex Cintron	3.00
273	Elvis Pena, Juan Uribe RC	2.00
274	Carlos Pena, Jason Romano	1.00
275	Winston Abreu, Wilson Betemit RC	1.50
276	Jose Mieses, Nick Neugebauer	1.00
277	Shea Hillenbrand, Dernell Stenson	1.00
278	Jared Sandberg, Toby Hall	1.00
279	Jay Gibbons, Ivanon Coffie	3.00
280	Pablo Ozuna, Santiago Perez	1.00
281	Nomar Garciaparra/AS	6.00
282	Derek Jeter/AS	6.00
283	Jason Giambi/AS	2.50
284	Magglio Ordonez/AS	1.00
285	Ivan Rodriguez/AS	2.00
286	Troy Glaus/AS	2.00
287	Carlos Delgado/AS	2.00
288	Darin Erstad/AS	1.00
289	Bernie Williams/AS	2.00
290	Roberto Alomar/AS	1.50
291	Barry Larkin/AS	1.50
292	Chipper Jones/AS	4.00
293	Vladimir Guerrero/AS	3.00
294	Sammy Sosa/AS	5.00
295	Todd Helton/AS	2.00
296	Randy Johnson/AS	3.00
297	Jason Kendall/AS	1.00
298	Jim Edmonds/AS	1.50
299	Andruw Jones/AS	2.00
300	Edgardo Alfonzo/AS	1.00
301	Albert Pujols, Donaldo Mendez RC	80.00

Platinum Edition

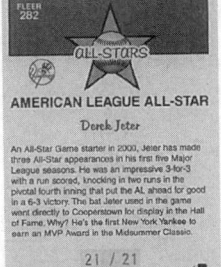

An All-Star Game starter in 2000, Jeter has made three All-Star appearances in his first five Major League seasons. He was an impressive 3-for-3 with a run scored, knocking in two runs in the pivotal fourth inning that put the AL ahead for good in a 6-3 victory. That all Jeter used in the game went directly to Cooperstown for display in the Hall of Fame. Why? He's the first New York Yankee to earn an MVP Award in the Midsummer Classic.

Cards (1-250):	4-8X
Production 201 Sets	
SP's (251-280):	8-20X
SP's (281-300):	5-10X
SP Production 21 Sets	
(See 2001 Fleer Platinum for checklist and base card values.)	

Classic Combinations

	NM/M
Common Card:	4.00
#1-10 Numbered to 250	
11-20 Numbered to 500	

21-30 Numbered to 1,000		
31-40 Numbered to 2,000		
1CC	Derek Jeter, Alex Rodriguez	20.00
2CC	Willie Mays, Willie McCovey	15.00
3CC	Lou Gehrig, Babe Ruth	20.00
4CC	Mark McGwire, Ken Griffey Jr.	15.00
5CC	Johnny Bench, Roy Campanella	10.00
6CC	Ted Williams, Nomar Garciaparra	20.00
7CC	Yogi Berra, Mike Piazza	15.00
8CC	Ernie Banks, Sammy Sosa	12.00
9CC	Nolan Ryan, Randy Johnson	25.00
10CC	Roberto Clemente, Vladimir Guerrero	15.00
11CC	Lou Gehrig, Stan Musial	15.00
12CC	Bill Mazeroski, Roberto Clemente	10.00
13CC	Ernie Banks, Alex Rodriguez	10.00
14CC	Phil Rizzuto, Derek Jeter	10.00
15CC	Mike Piazza, Johnny Bench	8.00
16CC	Mark McGwire, Sammy Sosa	10.00
17CC	Ted Williams, Tony Gwynn	12.00
18CC	Eddie Mathews, Mike Schmidt	10.00
19CC	Barry Bonds, Willie Mays	10.00
20CC	Nolan Ryan, Pedro Martinez	15.00
21CC	Barry Bonds, Ken Griffey Jr.	10.00
22CC	Willie McCovey, Reggie Jackson	5.00
23CC	Roberto Clemente, Sammy Sosa	8.00
24CC	Willie Mays, Ernie Banks	8.00
25CC	Eddie Mathews, Chipper Jones	5.00
26CC	Mike Schmidt, Brooks Robinson	6.00
27CC	Stan Musial, Mark McGwire	8.00
28CC	Ted Williams, Roger Maris	8.00
29CC	Yogi Berra, Roy Campanella	5.00
30CC	Johnny Bench, Tony Perez	5.00
31CC	Bill Mazeroski, Joe Carter	3.00
32CC	Mike Piazza, Roy Campanella	5.00
33CC	Ernie Banks, Craig Biggio	4.00
34CC	Frank Robinson, Brooks Robinson	4.00
35CC	Mike Schmidt, Scott Rolen	5.00
36CC	Roger Maris, Mark McGwire	10.00
37CC	Stan Musial, Tony Gwynn	4.00
38CC	Ted Williams, Bill Terry	6.00
39CC	Derek Jeter, Reggie Jackson	6.00
40CC	Yogi Berra, Bill Dickey	4.00

Classic Combinations
Memorabilia

	NM/M
Production 25 Sets	
1 Yogi Berra, Bill Dickey	75.00
2 Yogi Berra, Roy Campanella	100.00
3 Roberto Clemente, Vladimir Guerrero	200.00

4	Eddie Mathews, Chipper Jones	80.00
5	Willie McCovey, Reggie Jackson	75.00
6	Phil Rizzuto, Derek Jeter	180.00
7	Brooks Robinson, Frank Robinson	85.00
8	Brooks Robinson, Mike Schmidt	180.00
9	Mike Schmidt, Scott Rolen	160.00
10	Ted Williams, Bill Terry	300.00
11	Ted Williams, Tony Gwynn	375.00

Grandstand Greats

	NM/M
Complete Set (20):	25.00
Common Player:	1.00
Inserted 1:12	

1GG	Chipper Jones	2.00
2GG	Alex Rodriguez	3.00
3GG	Jeff Bagwell	1.50
4GG	Troy Glaus	1.50
5GG	Manny Ramirez	1.50
6GG	Derek Jeter	4.00
7GG	Tony Gwynn	2.00
8GG	Greg Maddux	2.00
9GG	Nomar Garciaparra	2.50
10GG	Sammy Sosa	2.50
11GG	Mike Piazza	2.50
12GG	Barry Bonds	4.00
13GG	Mark McGwire	3.00
14GG	Vladimir Guerrero	1.50
15GG	Ivan Rodriguez	1.00
16GG	Ken Griffey Jr.	2.50
17GG	Todd Helton	1.50
18GG	Cal Ripken Jr.	4.00
19GG	Pedro Martinez	1.50
20GG	Frank Thomas	1.50

Nameplates

	NM/M
Common Player:	15.00
Inserted 1:12	

Cal Ripken /19	200.00
Cal Ripken /21	200.00
Cal Ripken /23	200.00
Cal Ripken /110	100.00
Randy Johnson/99	40.00
Nolan Ryan/40	200.00
Javy Lopez/49	20.00
Frank Thomas/35	40.00
Frank Thomas/75	30.00
Frank Thomas/80	30.00
Jeffrey Hammonds/135	15.00
Larry Walker/79	15.00
Larry Walker/85	15.00
Dave Winfield/80	20.00
Vladimir Guerrero/80	25.00
Vladimir Guerrero/90	25.00
Kevin Millwood/130	15.00
Mike Mussina/91	25.00
Edgar Martinez/87	25.00
Edgar Martinez/120	20.00
Scott Rolen/65	30.00
Ivan Rodriguez/177	25.00
Manny Ramirez/75	25.00

Manny Ramirez/105	25.00
J.D. Drew/170	15.00
Greg Maddux/180	50.00
Chipper Jones/95	40.00
Carlos Beltran/90	15.00
Adrian Beltre	15.00
Matt Williams/175	15.00
Curt Schilling	20.00
Pedro Martinez/120	30.00
Robin Ventura/99	15.00
Tom Glavine/125	15.00
Tony Gwynn/35	75.00
Tony Gwynn/65	40.00
Tony Gwynn/70	40.00
Troy Glaus/85	20.00
Sean Casey/21	35.00
Darin Erstad/39	30.00
Stan Musial/30	150.00

National Patch Time

	NM/M
Common Player:	4.00
Inserted 1:24 H	
Tony Gwynn	8.00
Manny Ramirez	6.00
Freddy Garcia	4.00
Rondell White	4.00
Ivan Rodriguez	5.00
Brady Anderson	4.00
Adam Piatt	4.00
Carl Everett	4.00
Magglio Ordonez	4.00
Edgardo Alfonzo	4.00
Jason Kendall	4.00
Greg Maddux	8.00
Cal Ripken Jr.	30.00
Fred McGriff	4.00
Pedro Martinez	6.00
Roger Clemens	10.00
Wade Boggs	8.00
George Brett	15.00
Ozzie Smith	8.00
Dave Winfield	6.00
Tom Seaver	6.00
Rollie Fingers	4.00
Mike Schmidt	15.00
Eddie Murray	6.00
Nolan Ryan	30.00
Jeff Cirillo	4.00
Mike Mussina	5.00
Carl Yastrzemski	
(Not officially issued.)	

Rack Pack Autographs

	NM/M
Common Player:	5.00
Hank Aaron	
1997/90	100.00
Roger Clemens	
1998/125	100.00
Jose Cruz Jr. 1997	5.00
Bob Gibson	
1998/300	25.00
Ben Grieve 100	6.00
Tony Gwynn	
1998/125	50.00
Wes Helms 1997	5.00
Harmon Killebrew	
1998/300	30.00
Paul Konerko 135	5.00
Willie Mays	
1997/115	120.00

Willie Mays	
1998/120	120.00
Kirby Puckett	
1997/105	50.00
Brooks Robinson	
1998/40	75.00
Frank Robinson	
1998/115	20.00
Scott Rolen	
1998/150	25.00
Alex Rodriguez	
1997/94	100.00
Alex Rodriguez	
1998/150	70.00

Tickets

No Pricing

Tickets Autographs

No Pricing

20th Anniversary Reprints

	NM/M
Complete Set (18):	25.00
Common Player:	.50
Inserted 1:8	
1AR	Cal Ripken Jr.	4.00
2AR	Wade Boggs	1.50
3AR	Ryne Sandberg	1.50
4AR	Tony Gwynn	1.50
5AR	Don Mattingly	3.00
6AR	Roger Clemens	2.00
7AR	Kirby Puckett	1.50
8AR	Jose Canseco	.75
9AR	Barry Bonds	4.00
10AR	Ken Griffey Jr.	2.50
11AR	Sammy Sosa	2.50
12AR	Ivan Rodriguez	.75
13AR	Jeff Bagwell	1.00
14AR	J.D. Drew	.75
15AR	Troy Glaus	1.00
16AR	Rick Ankiel	.50
17AR	Xavier Nady	.50
18AR	Jose Ortiz	.50

2001 Fleer Platinum RC

Complete Set (300):	150.00
Common Player:	.15
Common (502-601):	1.00
Inserted 1:3 hobby	
Pack (10):	7.00
Box (24):	140.00
302	Shawn Wooten	.15
303	Todd Walker	.15
304	Brian Buchanan	.15
305	Jim Edmonds	.25
306	Jarrod Washburn	.15
307	Jose Rijo	.15
308	Tim Raines	.15
309	Matt Morris	.15
310	Troy Glaus	.50
311	Barry Larkin	.40
312	Javier Vazquez	.15
313	Placido Polanco	.15
314	Darin Erstad	.25
315	Marty Cordova	.15
316	Vladimir Guerrero	.75
317	Kerry Robinson	.15
318	Byung-Hyun Kim	.15
319	C.C. Sabathia	.15
320	Edgardo Alfonzo	.15
321	Jason Tyner	.15
322	Reggie Sanders	.15
323	Roberto Alomar	.60
324	Matt Lawton	.15
325	Brent Abernathy	.15
326	Randy Johnson	.75
327	Todd Helton	.75
328	Andy Pettitte	.40
329	Josh Beckett	.40
330	Mark DeRosa	.15

331	Jose Ortiz	.15
332	Derek Jeter	2.00
333	Toby Hall	.15
334	Wes Helms	.15
335	Jose Macias	.15
336	Bernie Williams	.60
337	Ivan Rodriguez	.75
338	Chipper Jones	1.25
339	Brandon Inge	.15
340	Jason Giambi	.75
341	Frank Catalanotto	.15
342	Andruw Jones	.50
343	Carlos Hernandez RC	.40
344	Jermaine Dye	.15
345	Mike Lamb	.15
346	Ken Caminiti	.15
347	A.J. Burnett	.15
348	Terrence Long	.15
349	Ruben Sierra	.15
350	Marcus Giles	.15
351	Wade Miller	.15
352	Mark Mulder	.25
353	Carlos Delgado	.50
354	Chris Richard	.15
355	Daryle Ward	.15
356	Brad Penny	.15
357	Vernon Wells	.25
358	Jason Johnson	.15
359	Tim Redding	.15
360	Marlon Anderson	.15
361	Carlos Pena	.15
362	Nomar Garciaparra	2.00
363	Roy Oswalt	.40
364	Todd Ritchie	.15
365	Jose Mesa	.15
366	Shea Hillenbrand	.15
367	Dee Brown	.15
368	Jason Kendall	.25
369	Vinny Castilla	.15
370	Fred McGriff	.25
371	Neifi Perez	.15
372	Xavier Nady	.15
373	Abraham Nunez	.15
374	Jon Lieber	.15
375	Paul LoDuca	.15
376	Bubba Trammell	.15
377	Brady Clark	.15
378	Joel Pineiro	.15
379	Mark Grudzielanek	.15
380	D'Angelo Jimenez	.15
381	Junior Herndon	.15
382	Magglio Ordonez	.40
383	Ben Sheets	.25
384	John Vander Wal	.15
385	Pedro Astacio	.15
386	Jose Canseco	.40
387	Jose Hernandez	.15
388	Eric Davis	.15
389	Sammy Sosa	1.25
390	Mark Buehrle	.15
391	Mark Loretta	.15
392	Andres Galarraga	.25
393	Scott Spiezio	.15
394	Joe Crede	.15
395	Luis Rivas	.15
396	David Bell	.15
397	Einar Diaz	.15
398	Adam Dunn	.75
399	A.J. Pierzynski	.15
400	Jamie Moyer	.15
401	Nick Johnson	.15
402	Freddy Garcia	4.00
403	Hideo Nomo	.50
404	Mark Mulder	.25
405	Steve Sparks	.15
406	Mariano Rivera	.25
407	Mark Buehrle, Mike Mussina	.25
408	Randy Johnson	.50
409	Randy Johnson	.50
410	Curt Schilling, Matt Morris	.25
411	Greg Maddux	.60
412	Robb Nen	.15
413	Randy Johnson	.50
414	Barry Bonds	1.00
415	Jason Giambi	.40
416	Ichiro Suzuki	2.50
417	Ichiro Suzuki	2.50
418	Alex Rodriguez	1.00
419	Bret Boone	.25
420	Ichiro Suzuki	2.50
421	Alex Rodriguez	1.00
422	Jason Giambi	.40
423	Alex Rodriguez	1.00
424	Larry Walker	.25
425	Rich Aurilia	.15
426	Barry Bonds	1.00
427	Sammy Sosa	.75
428	Jimmy Rollins, Juan Pierre	.25
429	Sammy Sosa	.75
430	Lance Berkman	.25
431	Sammy Sosa	.75

432	Carlos Delgado	.25
433	Alex Rodriguez	1.00
434	Greg Vaughn	.15
435	Albert Pujols	10.00
436	Ichiro Suzuki	2.50
437	Barry Bonds	1.00
438	Phil Nevin	.15
439	Brian Giles	.25
440	Bobby Abreu	.25
441	Jason Giambi	.40
442	Derek Jeter	1.00
443	Mike Piazza	.75
444	Vladimir Guerrero	.50
445	Corey Koskie	.15
446	Richie Sexson	.25
447	Shawn Green	.25
448	Mike Sweeney	.15
449	Jeff Bagwell	.40
450	Cliff Floyd	.15
451	Roger Cedeno	.15
452	Todd Helton	.40
453	Juan Gonzalez	.30
454	Sean Casey	.15
455	Magglio Ordonez	.25
456	Sammy Sosa	.75
457	Manny Ramirez	.40
458	Jeff Conine	.15
459	Chipper Jones	.60
460	Luis Gonzalez	.25
461	Troy Glaus	.25
462	Ivan Rodriguez	.40
463	Luis Gonzalez, Jack Cust	.25
464	Jim Thome, C.C. Sabathia	.25
465	Jason Hart, Jason Giambi	.25
466	Jeff Bagwell, Roy Oswalt	.30
467	Sammy Sosa, Corey Patterson	.50
468	Mike Piazza, Alex Escobar	.75
469	Ken Griffey Jr., Adam Dunn	.75
470	Roger Clemens, Nick Johnson	.75
471	Cliff Floyd, Josh Beckett	.15
472	Cal Ripken Jr., Jerry Hairston Jr.	.75
473	Phil Nevin, Xavier Nady	.15
474	Scott Rolen, Jimmy Rollins	.40
475	Barry Larkin, David Espinosa	.25
476	Larry Walker, Jose Ortiz	.15
477	Chipper Jones, Marcus Giles	.40
478	Craig Biggio, Keith Ginter	.15
479	Magglio Ordonez, Aaron Rowand	.25
480	Alex Rodriguez, Carlos Pena	.75
481	Derek Jeter, Alfonso Soriano	.75
482	Curt Schilling (Post Season Glory)	.20
483	(Post Season Glory)	.25
484	(Post Season Glory)	.25
485	(Post Season Glory)	.25
486	(Post Season Glory)	.25
487	(Post Season Glory)	.25
488	(Post Season Glory)	.25
489	Rudolph Giuliani (Post Season Glory)	.50
490	George Bush (Post Season Glory)	.50
491	(Post Season Glory)	.25
492	(Post Season Glory)	.25
493	(Post Season Glory)	.25
494	Derek Jeter (Post Season Glory)	.75
495	(Post Season Glory)	.25
496	(Post Season Glory)	.25
497	(Post Season Glory)	.25
498	(Post Season Glory)	.25
499	(Post Season Glory)	.25
500	(Post Season Glory)	.25
501	(Post Season Glory)	.25
502	Josh Fogg RC	1.00
503	Elpidio Guzman	1.00
504	Corky Miller RC	1.00
505	Cesar Crespo RC	1.00
506	Carlos Garcia RC	1.00
507	Carlos Valderrama RC	1.00
508	Joe Kennedy RC	1.00
509	Henry Mateo RC	1.00
510	Brandon Duckworth RC	1.00
511	Ichiro Suzuki	15.00
512	Zach Day RC	2.00
513	Ryan Freel RC	1.00
514	Brian Lawrence RC	2.00

515	Alexis Gomez RC	1.00
516	Will Ohman RC	1.00
517	Juan Diaz RC	1.00
518	Juan Moreno RC	1.00
519	Rob Mackowiak RC	1.00
520	Horacio Ramirez RC	1.50
521	Albert Pujols RC	75.00
522	Tsuyoshi Shinjo	2.50
523	Ryan Drese RC	1.00
524	Angel Berroa RC	3.00
525	Josh Towers RC	2.50
526	Junior Spivey	1.50
527	Greg Miller RC	1.00
528	Esix Snead RC	1.00
529	Mark Prior RC	8.00
530	Drew Henson	3.00
531	Brian Reith RC	1.00
532	Andres Torres RC	1.00
533	Casey Fossum RC	2.00
534	Wilmy Caceres RC	1.00
535	Matt White RC	1.00
536	Wilkin Ruan RC	1.00
537	Rick Bauer RC	1.00
538	Morgan Ensberg RC	2.00
539	Geronimo Gil RC	1.00
540	Dewon Brazelton RC	1.00
541	Johnny Estrada RC	1.50
542	Claudio Vargas RC	1.00
543	Donaldo Mendez RC	1.00
544	Kyle Lohse RC	2.00
545	Nate Frese RC	1.00
546	Christian Parker RC	1.00
547	Blaine Neal RC	1.00
548	Travis Hafner RC	4.00
549	Billy Sylvester RC	1.00
550	Adam Pettyjohn RC	1.00
551	Bill Ortega RC	1.00
552	Jose Acevedo RC	1.00
553	Steve Green RC	1.00
554	Jay Gibbons RC	2.50
555	Bert Snow RC	1.00
556	Erick Almonte RC	1.50
557	Jeremy Owens RC	1.00
558	Sean Douglass RC	1.00
559	Jason Smith RC	1.00
560	Ricardo Rodriguez RC	1.00
561	Mark Teixeira RC	15.00
562	Tyler Walker RC	1.00
563	Juan Uribe RC	1.50
564	Bud Smith RC	1.00
565	Angel Santos RC	1.00
566	Brandon Lyon RC	1.00
567	Eric Hinske RC	2.50
568	Nick Punto RC	1.00
569	Winston Abreu RC	1.00
570	Jason Phillips RC	4.00
571	Rafael Soriano RC	1.50
572	Wilson Betemit	1.00
573	Endy Chavez RC	1.00
574	Juan Cruz RC	1.00
575	Cory Aldridge RC	1.00
576	Adrian Hernandez	1.00
577	Brandon Larson RC	1.50
578	Bret Prinz RC	1.00
579	Jackson Melian RC	1.00
580	Dave Maurer RC	1.00
581	Jason Michaels RC	1.00
582	Travis Phelps RC	1.00
583	Cody Ransom RC	1.00
584	Benito Baez RC	1.00
585	Brian Roberts RC	1.00
586	Nate Teut RC	1.00
587	Jack Wilson RC	1.00
588	Willie Harris RC	1.00
589	Martin Vargas RC	1.00
590	Steve Torrealba RC	1.00
591	Stubby Clapp RC	1.00
592	Danny Wright RC	1.00
593	Mike Rivera RC	1.00
594	Luis Pineda RC	1.00
595	Lance Davis RC	1.00
596	Ramon Vazquez RC	2.00
597	Dustan Mohr RC	1.00
598	Troy Mattes RC	1.00
599	Grant Balfour RC	1.00
600	Jared Fernandez RC	1.00
601	Jorge Julio RC	2.00

E-X

131	Albert Pujols/499	300.00
132	Bud Smith/499	8.00
133	Tsuyoshi Shinjo/499 RC	10.00
134	Wilson Betemit/499 RC	8.00
135	Adrian Hernandez/499 RC	8.00
136	Jackson Melian/499	8.00
137	Jay Gibbons/499 RC	10.00
138	Johnny Estrada/499 RC	15.00
139	Morgan Ensberg/499 RC	10.00
140	Drew Henson/499 RC	20.00

Focus

241	Tsuyoshi Shinjo/999 RC	5.00
242	Wilson Betemit/999 RC	5.00
243	Jeremy Owens/999 RC	5.00
244	Drew Henson/999 RC	8.00
245	Albert Pujols/999 RC	100.00
246	Travis Hafner/999 RC	12.00
247	Ichiro Suzuki/999 RC	40.00
248	Elpidio Guzman/999 RC	6.00
249	Matt White/999 RC	6.00
250	Junior Spivey/999 RC	8.00

Futures

221	Drew Henson/2,499 RC	5.00
222	Johnny Estrada/2,499 RC	5.00
223	Elpidio Guzman/2,499 RC	3.00
224	Albert Pujols/2,499 RC	60.00
225	Wilson Betemit/2,499 RC	4.00
226	Mark Teixeira/2,499 RC	15.00
227	Tsuyoshi Shinjo/2,499 RC	5.00
228	Matt White/2,499 RC	3.00
229	Adrian Hernandez/2,499 RC	3.00
230	Ichiro Suzuki/2,499 RC	30.00

Triple Crown

301	Elpidio Guzman/2,999 RC	4.00
302	Drew Henson/2,999 RC	5.00
303	Bud Smith/2,999 RC	2.00
304	Carlos Valderrama/2,999 RC	2.00
305	Tsuyoshi Shinjo/2,999 RC	4.00
306	Ichiro Suzuki/2,999 RC	30.00
307	Jackson Melian/2,999	2.00
308	Morgan Ensberg/2,999 RC	4.00
309	Albert Pujols/2,999 RC	90.00
310	Johnny Estrada/2,999 RC	5.00

Ultra

276	Junior Spivey, Juan Uribe RC	5.00
277	Albert Pujols, Bud Smith RC	80.00
278	Ichiro Suzuki, Tsuyoshi Shinjo RC	25.00
279	Drew Henson, Jackson Melian	5.00
280	Matt White, Adrian Hernandez RC	2.00

Platinum

Cards (302-501): 4-8X
Production 201:
SP's (502-601):
Production 21 not priced.
(See 2001 Fleer Platinum RC for checklist and base card values.)

Lumberjacks

	NM/M
Common Player:	4.00

Inserted 1:1 Rack Pack

Barry Bonds	20.00
Cal Ripken Jr.	
Derek Jeter	20.00
Luis Gonzalez	4.00
Mike Sweeney	4.00
Albert Pujols	15.00
Tony Gwynn	10.00
Adam Dunn	5.00
J.D. Drew	5.00
Brian Giles	4.00
Adrian Beltre	5.00
Bret Boone	4.00
Chipper Jones	10.00
Cliff Floyd	4.00
Darin Erstad	5.00
Gary Sheffield	4.00
Manny Ramirez	8.00
Mike Piazza	12.00
Todd Helton	8.00
Ivan Rodriguez	6.00
Lance Berkman	4.00
Vladimir Guerrero	8.00
Drew Henson	6.00
Cristian Guzman	4.00
Roberto Alomar	5.00
Moises Alou	4.00
Larry Walker	5.00

Lumberjacks Autographs

	NM/M
Production 100 Sets	
Barry Bonds	200.00
J.D. Drew	40.00
Adam Dunn	60.00
Luis Gonzalez	20.00
Derek Jeter	150.00
Albert Pujols	500.00
Cal Ripken Jr.	150.00
Mike Sweeney	20.00

National Patch Time

	NM/M
Common Player:	4.00

Inserted 1:24 H

Edgardo Alfonzo	4.00
Brady Anderson	4.00
Adrian Beltre	4.00
Barry Bonds	20.00
Jeromy Burnitz	4.00
Eric Chavez	4.00
Roger Clemens	15.00
J.D. Drew	5.00
Darin Erstad	5.00
Carl Everett	4.00
Freddy Garcia	4.00
Jason Giambi	8.00
Juan Gonzalez	6.00
Mark Grace	6.00
Shawn Green	4.00
Ben Grieve	4.00
Vladimir Guerrero	8.00
Tony Gwynn	10.00
Randy Johnson	8.00
Chipper Jones	10.00
David Justice	4.00
Jeff Kent	4.00
Greg Maddux	10.00
Fred McGriff	4.00
John Olerud	4.00
Magglio Ordonez	4.00
Jorge Posada	5.00
Cal Ripken Jr.	20.00
Mariano Rivera	4.00
Ivan Rodriguez	6.00
Scott Rolen	6.00
Kazuhiro Sasaki	4.00
Aaron Sele	4.00
Gary Sheffield	4.00
John Smoltz	4.00
Frank Thomas	8.00
Mo Vaughn	4.00
Robin Ventura	4.00
Bernie Williams	5.00
Carlos Delgado	6.00
Chan Ho Park	4.00
Todd Helton	8.00
Craig Biggio	4.00
Jeff Bagwell	8.00
Paul LoDuca	4.00

Prime Numbers

	NM/M
Common Player:	8.00

Inserted 1:12 Jumbo Pack

1PN	Jeff Bagwell	15.00
2PN	Cal Ripken Jr.	50.00
3PN	Barry Bonds	50.00
4PN	Todd Helton	15.00
5PN	Derek Jeter	50.00
6PN	Tony Gwynn	20.00
7PN	Kazuhiro Sasaki	15.00
8PN	Chan Ho Park	8.00
9PN	Sean Casey	10.00
10PN	Chipper Jones	20.00
11PN	Pedro Martinez	15.00
12PN	Mike Piazza	30.00
13PN	Carlos Delgado	10.00
14PN	Craig Biggio	
15PN	Roger Clemens	25.00

Winning Combinations

	NM/M
Common Card:	3.00

Varying quantities produced

1WC	Derek Jeter, Ozzie Smith/2,000	8.00
2WC	Barry Bonds, Mark McGwire/500	10.00
3WC	Ichiro Suzuki, Albert Pujols/250	30.00
4WC	Ted Williams, Manny Ramirez/1,000	10.00
5WC	Tony Gwynn, Cal Ripken/250	15.00
6WC	Mike Piazza, Derek Jeter/500	10.00
7WC	Dave Winfield, Tony Gwynn/2,000	5.00
8WC	Hideo Nomo, Ichiro Suzuki/2,000	10.00
9WC	Cal Ripken, Ozzie Smith/1,000	10.00
10WC	Mark McGwire, Albert Pujols/2,000	10.00
11WC	Jeff Bagwell, Craig Biggio/1,000	3.00
12WC	Bobby Bonds, Barry Bonds/250	10.00
13WC	Ted Williams, Stan Musial/250	10.00
14WC	Babe Ruth, Reggie Jackson/500	15.00
15WC	Kazuhiro Sasaki, Ichiro Suzuki/500	10.00
16WC	Nolan Ryan, Roger Clemens/500	15.00
17WC	Roger Clemens, Derek Jeter/250	15.00
18WC	Ivan Rodriguez, Mike Piazza/1,000	6.00
19WC	Vladimir Guerrero, Sammy Sosa/2,000	6.00
20WC	Barry Bonds, Sammy Sosa/250	10.00
21WC	Roger Clemens, Greg Maddux/1,000	8.00
22WC	Juan Gonzalez, Manny Ramirez/2,000	3.00
23WC	Todd Helton, Jason Giambi/2,000	3.00
24WC	Jeff Bagwell, Lance Berkman/2,000	3.00
25WC	Mike Sweeney, George Brett/1,000	6.00
26WC	Luis Gonzalez, Babe Ruth/2,000	10.00
27WC	Bill Skowron, Don Mattingly/250	10.00
28WC	Yogi Berra, Cal Ripken/2,000	10.00
29WC	Pedro Martinez, Nomar Garciaparra/500	8.00
30WC	Ted Kluszewski, Frank Robinson/1,000	3.00
31WC	Curt Schilling, Randy Johnson/1,000	5.00
32WC	Ken Griffey Jr., Cal Ripken/500	10.00
33WC	Mike Piazza, Johnny Bench/1,000	6.00
34WC	Stan Musial, Albert Pujols/500	10.00
35WC	Jackie Robinson, Nellie Fox/500	8.00
36WC	Lefty Grove, Steve Carlton/250	5.00
37WC	Ty Cobb, Tony Gwynn/250	10.00

38WC	Albert Pujols, Frank Robinson/ 1,000	10.00
39WC	Ryne Sandberg, Sammy Sosa/500	10.00
40WC	Cal Ripken Jr., Lou Gehrig/250	20.00

2001 Fleer Premium

	NM/M
Complete Set (235):	
Common Player:	.15
Common SP (201-230):	4.00
Production 1,999	
Cards 231-235 are redemptions.	
Hobby Pack (8):	5.00
Hobby Box (24):	100.00
1	Cal Ripken Jr.	2.00
2	Derek Jeter	2.00
3	Edgardo Alfonzo	.15
4	Luis Castillo	.15
5	Mike Lieberthal	.15
6	Kazuhiro Sasaki	.15
7	Jeff Kent	.15
8	Eric Karros	.15
9	Tom Glavine	.40
10	Jeromy Burnitz	.15
11	Travis Fryman	.15
12	Ron Coomer	.15
13	Jeff D'Amico	.15
14	Carlos Febles	.15
15	Kevin Brown	.15
16	Deivi Cruz	.15
17	Tino Martinez	.15
18	Bobby Abreu	.15
19	Roger Clemens	1.00
20	Jeffrey Hammonds	.15
21	Peter Bergeron	.15
22	Ray Lankford	.15
23	Scott Rolen	.60
24	Jermaine Dye	.15
25	Rusty Greer	.15
26	Frank Thomas	.75
27	Jeff Bagwell	.75
28	Cliff Floyd	.15
29	Chris Singleton	.15
30	Steve Finley	.15
31	Orlando Hernandez	.15
32	Tom Goodwin	.15
33	Larry Walker	.15
34	Mike Sweeney	.15
35	Tim Hudson	.30
36	Kerry Wood	.40
37	Mike Lowell	.15
38	Andruw Jones	.75
39	Alex S. Gonzalez	.15
40	Juan Gonzalez	.75
41	J.D. Drew	.25
42	Mark McLemore	.15
43	Royce Clayton	.15
44	Paul O'Neill	.15
45	Carlos Beltran	.45
46	Phil Nevin	.15
47	Rondell White	.15
48	Gerald Williams	.15
49	Geoff Jenkins	.15
50	Marvin Benard	.15
51	Alex Rodriguez	1.50
52	Moises Alou	.15
53	Mike Lansing	.15
54	Omar Vizquel	.15
55	Eric Chavez	.30
56	Mark Quinn	.15
57	Mike Lamb	.15
58	Rick Ankiel	.15
59	Lance Berkman	.15
60	Jeff Conine	.15
61	B.J. Surhoff	.15
62	Todd Helton	.75
63	J.T. Snow	.15
64	John Vander Wal	.15
65	Johnny Damon	.25

66	Bobby Higginson	.15
67	Carlos Delgado	.40
68	Shawn Green	.35
69	Mike Redmond	.15
70	Mike Piazza	1.25
71	Adrian Beltre	.35
72	Juan Encarnacion	.15
73	Chipper Jones	1.00
74	Garret Anderson	.15
75	Paul Konerko	.15
76	Barry Larkin	.15
77	Tony Gwynn	1.00
78	Rafael Palmeiro	.60
79	Randy Johnson	.75
80	Mark Grace	.25
81	Javy Lopez	.15
82	Gabe Kapler	.15
83	Henry Rodriguez	.15
84	Raul Mondesi	.15
85	Adam Piatt	.15
86	Marquis Grissom	.15
87	Charles Johnson	.15
88	Sean Casey	.25
89	Manny Ramirez	.75
90	Curt Schilling	.40
91	Fernando Tatis	.15
92	Derek Bell	.15
93	Tony Clark	.15
94	Homer Bush	.15
95	Nomar Garciaparra	1.25
96	Vinny Castilla	.15
97	Ben Davis	.15
98	Carl Everett	.15
99	Damion Easley	.15
100	Craig Biggio	.15
101	Todd Hollandsworth	.15
102	Jay Payton	.15
103	Gary Sheffield	.35
104	Sandy Alomar Jr.	.15
105	Doug Glanville	.15
106	Barry Bonds	2.00
107	Tim Salmon	.25
108	Terrence Long	.15
109	Jorge Posada	.30
110	Jose Offerman	.15
111	Edgar Martinez	.15
112	Jeremy Giambi	.15
113	Dean Palmer	.15
114	Roberto Alomar	.35
115	Aaron Boone	.15
116	Adam Kennedy	.15
117	Joe Randa	.15
118	Jose Vidro	.15
119	Tony Batista	.15
120	Kevin Young	.15
121	Preston Wilson	.15
122	Jason Kendall	.15
123	Mark Kotsay	.15
124	Timoniel Perez	.15
125	Eric Young	.15
126	Greg Maddux	1.00
127	Richard Hidalgo	.15
128	Brian Giles	.15
129	Fred McGriff	.25
130	Troy Glaus	.75
131	Todd Walker	.15
132	Brady Anderson	.15
133	Jim Edmonds	.15
134	Ben Grieve	.15
135	Greg Vaughn	.15
136	Robin Ventura	.15
137	Sammy Sosa	1.25
138	Rich Aurilia	.15
139	Jose Valentin	.15
140	Trot Nixon	.15
141	Troy Percival	.15
142	Bernie Williams	.35
143	Warren Morris	.15
144	Jacque Jones	.15
145	Danny Bautista	.15
146	A.J. Pierzynski	.15
147	Mark McGwire	1.50
148	Rafael Furcal	.15
149	Ray Durham	.15
150	Mike Mussina	.40
151	Jay Bell	.15
152	David Wells	.15
153	Ken Caminiti	.15
154	Jim Thome	.15
155	Ivan Rodriguez	.60
156	Milton Bradley	.15
157	Ken Griffey Jr.	1.25
158	Al Leiter	.15
159	Corey Koskie	.15
160	Shannon Stewart	.15
161	Mo Vaughn	.15
162	Pedro Martinez	.75

163	Todd Hundley	.15
164	Darin Erstad	.60
165	Ruben Rivera	.15
166	Richie Sexson	.15
167	Andres Galarraga	.15
168	Darryl Kile	.15
169	Jose Cruz Jr.	.15
170	David Justice	.15
171	Vladimir Guerrero	.75
172	Jeff Cirillo	.15
173	John Olerud	.15
174	Devon White	.15
175	Ron Belliard	.15
176	Pokey Reese	.15
177	Mike Hampton	.15
178	David Ortiz	.15
179	Magglio Ordonez	.15
180	Ruben Mateo	.15
181	Carlos Lee	.15
182	Matt Williams	.15
183	Miguel Tejada	.25
184	Scott Elarton	.15
185	Bret Boone	.15
186	Pat Burrell	.40
187	Brad Radke	.15
188	Brian Jordan	.15
189	Matt Lawton	.15
190	Al Martin	.15
191	Albert Belle	.15
192	Tony Womack	.15
193	Roger Cedeno	.15
194	Travis Lee	.15
195	Dmitri Young	.15
196	Jay Buhner	.15
197	Jason Giambi	.50
198	Jason Tyner	.15
199	Ben Petrick	.15
200	Jose Canseco	.40
201	Nick Johnson	4.00
202	Jace Brewer	4.00
203	Ryan Freel RC	4.00
204	Jaisen Randolph RC	4.00
205	Marcus Giles	4.00
206	Claudio Vargas RC	4.00
207	Brian Cole	4.00
208	Scott Hodges	4.00
209	Winston Abreu RC	4.00
210	Shea Hillenbrand	4.00
211	Larry Barnes	4.00
212	Paul Phillips RC	4.00
213	Pedro Santana RC	4.00
214	Ivanon Coffie	4.00
215	Junior Spivey RC	8.00
216	Donzell McDonald	4.00
217	Vernon Wells	5.00
218	Corey Patterson	5.00
219	Sang-Hoon Lee	4.00
220	Jack Cust	4.00
221	Jason Romano	4.00
222	Jack Wilson RC	8.00
223	Adam Everett	4.00
224	Esix Snead RC	4.00
225	Jason Hart	4.00
226	Joe Lawrence	4.00
227	Brandon Inge	4.00
228	Alex Escobar	4.00
229	Abraham Nunez	4.00
230	Jared Sandberg	4.00
231	Ichiro Suzuki RC	50.00
232	Tsuyoshi Shinjo RC	6.00
233	Albert Pujols RC	100.00
234	Wilson Betemit RC	5.00
235	Drew Henson RC	6.00

Star Ruby

Stars (1-200):	5-10X
SPs (201-230):	.4-.8X
Production 125 Sets	
(See 2001 Fleer Premium for checklist and base card values.)	

A Time for Heroes

	NM/M
Complete Set (20):	30.00
Common Player:	1.00
Inserted 1:20	
Darin Erstad	1.00
Alex Rodriguez	4.00
Shawn Green	1.00
Jeff Bagwell	1.50
Sammy Sosa	3.00
Derek Jeter	5.00
Nomar Garciaparra	3.00
Carlos Delgado	1.00
Pat Burrell	1.00
Tony Gwynn	2.50
Chipper Jones	2.50
Jason Giambi	1.00
Magglio Ordonez	1.00
Troy Glaus	1.00
Ivan Rodriguez	1.00
Andruw Jones	1.50
Vladimir Guerrero	2.00
Ken Griffey Jr.	3.00
J.D. Drew	1.00
Todd Helton	1.50

A Time for Heroes Memorabilia

	NM/M
Common Player:	4.00
Inserted 1:82	
Shawn Green	5.00
Derek Jeter	25.00
Pat Burrell	5.00
Chipper Jones	10.00
Jason Giambi	8.00
Troy Glaus	6.00
Ivan Rodriguez	6.00
Andruw Jones	8.00
J.D. Drew	4.00
Todd Helton	8.00

Brother Wood

		NM/M
Common Player:		5.00
Inserted 1:108		
1BW	Vladimir Guerrero	10.00
2BW	Andruw Jones	6.00
3BW	Corey Patterson	5.00
4BW	Magglio Ordonez	5.00
5BW	Jason Giambi	8.00
6BW	Rafael Palmeiro	8.00
7BW	Eric Chavez	5.00
8BW	Pat Burrell	6.00
9BW	Adrian Beltre	5.00

Decades of Excellence

	NM/M
Complete Set (50):	140.00
Common Player:	1.00
Inserted 1:12	
Card #17 does not exist.	
Babe Ruth,	
Lou Gehrig	10.00
Lloyd Waner	1.00
Jimmie Foxx	3.00
Hank Greenberg	2.00
Ted Williams	8.00
Johnny Mize	2.00
Enos Slaughter	

Abbreviations

SP - Short Print

Jackie Robinson	6.00
Stan Musial	5.00
Duke Snider	3.00
Eddie Mathews	3.00
Roy Campanella	2.50
Yogi Berra	4.00
Pee Wee Reese	2.00
Phil Rizzuto	2.00
Al Kaline	4.00
Frank Howard	1.00
Roberto Clemente	8.00
Bob Gibson	3.00
Roger Maris	4.00
Don Drysdale	2.50
Maury Wills	1.00
Tom Seaver	2.50
Reggie Jackson	3.00
Johnny Bench	4.00
Carlton Fisk	2.50
Rod Carew	2.00
Steve Carlton	1.00
Mike Schmidt	6.00
Nolan Ryan	10.00
Rickey Henderson	3.00
Roger Clemens	5.00
Don Mattingly	6.00
George Brett	6.00
Greg Maddux	5.00
Cal Ripken Jr.	10.00
Chipper Jones	5.00
Barry Bonds	10.00
Ivan Rodriguez	2.50
Sammy Sosa,	
Mark McGwire	8.00
Ken Griffey Jr.	6.00
Tony Gwynn	4.00
Vladimir Guerrero	3.00
Shawn Green	1.00
Alex Rodriguez,	
Derek Jeter,	
Nomar Garciaparra	8.00
Pat Burrell	2.00
Rick Ankiel	1.00
Eric Chavez	1.00
Troy Glaus	2.00

Decades of Excellence Autograph

		NM/M
Common Autograph:		20.00
Production #'s listed.		
1	Rick Ankiel/99	10.00
2	Johnny Bench/67	65.00
3	Barry Bonds/86	200.00
4	George Brett/73	100.00
5	Rod Carew/67	30.00
6	Steve Carlton/65	30.00
7	Eric Chavez/98	20.00
8	Carlton Fisk/69	50.00
9	Bob Gibson/59	40.00
10	Tony Gwynn/82	50.00
11	Reggie Jackson/67	40.00
12	Chipper Jones/93	60.00
13	Al Kaline/53	80.00
14	Don Mattingly/82	100.00
15	Cal Ripken Jr./150	125.00
16	Nolan Ryan/66	125.00
17	Mike Schmidt/72	80.00
18	Tom Seaver/67	50.00
19	Enos Slaughter/38	40.00
20	Maury Wills/59	20.00

Decades of Excellence Memorabilia

		NM/M
Common Player:		8.00
Inserted 1:217 H		
1	Rick Ankiel/Jsy	8.00
2	Barry Bonds/Jsy	15.00
3	Pat Burrell/Jsy	10.00
4	Roy Campanella/	
	Bat/50	50.00
5	Eric Chavez/Bat	8.00
6	Roberto Clemente/	
	Bat/50	125.00
7	Carlton Fisk/Uni.	15.00
8	Jimmie Foxx/Bat/50	80.00
9	Shawn Green/Bat	8.00
10	Tony Gwynn/Jsy	15.00
11	Reggie Jackson/Jsy	15.00
12	Greg Maddux/Jsy	20.00

13	Roger Maris/Uni.	35.00
14	Pee Wee Reese/Jsy	8.00
15	Cal Ripken/Jsy/50	35.00
16	Ivan Rodriguez/Bat	8.00
17	Nolan Ryan/Jsy	25.00
18	Mike Schmidt/Jsy	20.00
19	Tom Seaver/Jsy	15.00
20	Duke Snider/Bat	15.00
21	Ted Williams/Jsy/50	250.00

Derek Jeter Monumental Moments

	NM/M
Numbered to 1,995.	
Autograph numbered to 95.	
DJMM Derek Jeter	8.00
DJMM Derek Jeter/	
Auto./95	80.00

Diamond Dominators

		NM/M
Common Player:		4.00
Inserted 1:51		
1DD	Troy Glaus	6.00
2DD	Darin Erstad	5.00
3DD	J.D. Drew	4.00
4DD	Barry Bonds	25.00
5DD	Roger Clemens	20.00
6DD	Vladimir Guerrero	8.00
7DD	Tony Gwynn	10.00
8DD	Greg Maddux	10.00
9DD	Cal Ripken Jr.	25.00
10DD	Ivan Rodriguez	6.00
11DD	Frank Thomas	8.00
12DD	Bernie Williams	4.00
13DD	Jeromy Burnitz	4.00
14DD	Juan Gonzalez	6.00

Diamond Dominators Patches

		NM/M
Common Player:		15.00
Production 100 Sets		
1DD	Troy Glaus	25.00
2DD	Darin Erstad	20.00
3DD	J.D. Drew	15.00
4DD	Barry Bonds	75.00
5DD	Roger Clemens	60.00
6DD	Vladimir Guerrero	25.00
7DD	Tony Gwynn	50.00
8DD	Greg Maddux	50.00
9DD	Cal Ripken Jr.	75.00
10DD	Ivan Rodriguez	20.00
11DD	Frank Thomas	25.00
12DD	Bernie Williams	20.00
13DD	Jeromy Burnitz	15.00
14DD	Juan Gonzalez	25.00

Grip It and Rip It

		NM/M
Complete Set (15):		10.00
Common Player:		.50
Inserted 1:6		
1GRP	Roger Clemens,	
	Derek Jeter	2.00
2GRP	Scott Rolen,	
	Pat Burrell	.50
3GRP	Greg Maddux,	
	Andruw Jones	1.00

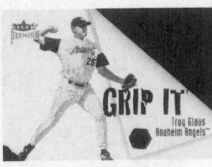

4GRP	Shannon Stewart,	
	Carlos Delgado	.50
5GRP	Shawn Estes,	
	Barry Bonds	2.00
6GRP	Cal Eldred,	
	Frank Thomas	.50
7GRP	Mark McGwire,	
	Jim Edmonds	2.00
8GRP	Jose Vidro,	
	Vladimir Guerrero	.75
9GRP	Pedro Martinez,	
	Nomar Garciaparra	1.50
10GRP	Tom Glavine,	
	Chipper Jones	1.00
11GRP	Ken Griffey Jr.,	
	Sean Casey	1.00
12GRP	Jeff Bagwell,	
	Moises Alou	.50
13GRP	Troy Glaus,	
	Darin Erstad	.50
14GRP	Mike Piazza,	
	Robin Ventura	1.00
15GRP	Eric Chavez,	
	Jason Giambi	.50

Grip It and Rip It Plus

	NM/M
Common Card:	8.00
200 Base/Bat Produced	
100 Ball/Bat Produced	
Roger Clemens,	
Derek Jeter/100	50.00
Scott Rolen,	
Pat Burrell/100	8.00
Greg Maddux,	
Andruw Jones/100	40.00
Shannon Stewart,	
Carlos Delgado/200	8.00
Shawn Estes,	
Barry Bonds/100	50.00
Cal Eldred,	
Frank Thomas/200	15.00
Mark McGwire,	
Jim Edmonds/100	60.00
Jose Vidro,	
Vladimir Guerrero/	
200	15.00
Pedro Martinez,	
Nomar Garciaparra/	
100	50.00
Tom Glavine,	
Chipper Jones/200	15.00
Ken Griffey Jr.,	
Sean Casey/200	20.00
Jeff Bagwell,	
Moises Alou/200	10.00
Troy Glaus,	
Darin Erstad/200	10.00
Mike Piazza,	
Robin Ventura/100	40.00
Eric Chavez,	
Jason Giambi/200	10.00

Home Field Advantage

	NM/M
Complete Set (15):	60.00
Common Player:	2.00
Inserted 1:72	
Mike Piazza	6.00
Derek Jeter	10.00
Ken Griffey Jr.	6.00
Carlos Delgado	2.00
Chipper Jones	5.00
Alex Rodriguez	8.00
Sammy Sosa	6.00
Scott Rolen	3.00
Nomar Garciaparra	6.00
Todd Helton	3.00
Vladimir Guerrero	3.00
Jeff Bagwell	3.00
Barry Bonds	10.00

Cal Ripken Jr.	10.00
Mark McGwire	8.00

Home Field Advantage Game Wall

		NM/M
Common Player:		6.00
Production 100 Sets		
	Mike Piazza	15.00
	Derek Jeter	25.00
	Ken Griffey Jr.	15.00
	Carlos Delgado	6.00
	Chipper Jones	10.00
	Alex Rodriguez	20.00
	Sammy Sosa	15.00
	Scott Rolen	8.00
	Nomar Garciaparra	15.00
	Todd Helton	8.00
	Vladimir Guerrero	8.00
	Jeff Bagwell	8.00
	Barry Bonds	25.00
	Cal Ripken Jr.	25.00
	Mark McGwire	20.00

Solid Performers

		NM/M
Complete Set (15):		30.00
Common Player:		1.50
Inserted 1:20		
1SP	Mark McGwire	4.00
2SP	Alex Rodriguez	4.00
3SP	Nomar Garciaparra	2.50
4SP	Derek Jeter	5.00
5SP	Vladimir Guerrero	1.50
6SP	Todd Helton	1.50
7SP	Chipper Jones	2.00
8SP	Mike Piazza	2.50
9SP	Ivan Rodriguez	1.50
10SP	Tony Gwynn	2.00
11SP	Cal Ripken Jr.	5.00
12SP	Barry Bonds	5.00
13SP	Jeff Bagwell	1.50
14SP	Ken Griffey Jr.	2.50
15SP	Sammy Sosa	2.50

Solid Performers Game Base

		NM/M
Common Player:		5.00
Production 150 Sets		
1SP	Mark McGwire	15.00
2SP	Alex Rodriguez	15.00
3SP	Nomar Garciaparra	12.00
4SP	Derek Jeter	20.00
5SP	Vladimir Guerrero	8.00
6SP	Todd Helton	8.00
7SP	Chipper Jones	10.00
8SP	Mike Piazza	12.00
9SP	Ivan Rodriguez	8.00
10SP	Tony Gwynn	10.00
11SP	Cal Ripken Jr.	20.00
12SP	Barry Bonds	20.00
13SP	Jeff Bagwell	8.00
14SP	Ken Griffey Jr.	12.00
15SP	Sammy Sosa	12.00

2001 Fleer Showcase

	NM/M
Complete Set (160):	
Common Player:	.25
Common SP (116-125):	10.00
Production 500	
Common SP (126-145):	4.00
Production 1,500	
Common SP (146-160):	4.00
Production 2,000	
Pack (5):	10.00
Box (24):	200.00
1 Tony Gwynn	1.50

2	Barry Larkin	.25
3	Chan Ho Park	.25
4	Darin Erstad	.65
5	Rafael Furcal	.25
6	Roger Cedeno	.25
7	Timo Perez	.25
8	Rick Ankiel	.25
9	Pokey Reese	.25
10	Jeromy Burnitz	.25
11	Phil Nevin	.25
12	Matt Williams	.25
13	Mike Hampton	.25
14	Fernando Tatis	.25
15	Kazuhiro Sasaki	.25
16	Jim Thome	.25
17	Geoff Jenkins	.25
18	Jeff Kent	.25
19	Tom Glavine	.40
20	Dean Palmer	.25
21	Todd Zeile	.25
22	Edgar Renteria	.25
23	Andruw Jones	1.00
24	Juan Encarnacion	.25
25	Robin Ventura	.25
26	J.D. Drew	.25
27	Ray Durham	.25
28	Richard Hidalgo	.25
29	Eric Chavez	.35
30	Rafael Palmeiro	.75
31	Steve Finley	.25
32	Jeff Weaver	.25
33	Al Leiter	.25
34	Jim Edmonds	.25
35	Garret Anderson	.25
36	Larry Walker	.25
37	Jose Vidro	.25
38	Mike Cameron	.25
39	Brady Anderson	.25
40	Mike Lowell	.25
41	Bernie Williams	.35
42	Gary Sheffield	.40
43	John Smoltz	.25
44	Mike Mussina	.40
45	Greg Vaughn	.25
46	Juan Gonzalez	.75
47	Matt Lawton	.25
48	Robb Nen	.25
49	Brad Radke	.25
50	Edgar Martinez	.25
51	Mike Bordick	.25
52	Shawn Green	.40
53	Carl Everett	.25
54	Adrian Beltre	.40
55	Kerry Wood	.50
56	Kevin Brown	.25
57	Brian Giles	.25
58	Greg Maddux	1.50
59	Preston Wilson	.25
60	Orlando Hernandez	.25
61	Ben Grieve	.25
62	Jermaine Dye	.25
63	Travis Lee	.25
64	Jose Cruz Jr.	.25
65	Rondell White	.25
66	Carlos Beltran	.45
67	Scott Rolen	.75
68	Brad Fullmer	.25
69	David Wells	.25
70	Mike Sweeney	.25
71	Barry Zito	.40
72	Tony Batista	.25
73	Curt Schilling	.40
74	Jeff Cirillo	.25
75	Edgardo Alfonzo	.25
76	John Olerud	.25
77	Carlos Lee	.25
78	Moises Alou	.25
79	Tim Hudson	.35
80	Andres Galarraga	.25
81	Roberto Alomar	.45
82	Richie Sexson	.25
83	Trevor Hoffman	.25
84	Omar Vizquel	.25

85	Jacque Jones	.25
86	J.T. Snow	.25
87	Sean Casey	.25
88	Craig Biggio	.40
89	Mariano Rivera	.35
90	Rusty Greer	.25
91	Barry Bonds	3.00
92	Pedro Martinez	1.00
93	Cal Ripken Jr.	3.00
94	Pat Burrell	.50
95	Chipper Jones	1.50
96	Magglio Ordonez	.25
97	Jeff Bagwell	1.00
98	Randy Johnson	1.00
99	Frank Thomas	1.00
100	Jason Kendall	.25
101	Nomar Garciaparra	6.00
102	Mark McGwire	8.00
103	Troy Glaus	3.00
104	Ivan Rodriguez	2.50
105	Manny Ramirez	3.00
106	Derek Jeter	10.00
107	Alex Rodriguez	8.00
108	Ken Griffey Jr.	6.00
109	Todd Helton	3.00
110	Sammy Sosa	6.00
111	Vladimir Guerrero	3.00
112	Mike Piazza	6.00
113	Roger Clemens	5.00
114	Jason Giambi	2.50
115	Carlos Delgado	2.00
116	Ichiro Suzuki RC	100.00
117	Morgan Ensberg RC	20.00
118	Carlos Valderrama RC	10.00
119	Erick Almonte RC	10.00
120	Tsuyoshi Shinjo RC	10.00
121	Albert Pujols RC	240.00
122	Wilson Betemit RC	10.00
123	Adrian Hernandez RC	10.00
124	Jackson Melian RC	10.00
125	Drew Henson RC	12.00
126	Paul Phillips RC	4.00
127	Esix Snead RC	4.00
128	Ryan Freel RC	4.00
129	Junior Spivey RC	8.00
130	Elpidio Guzman RC	6.00
131	Juan Diaz RC	4.00
132	Andres Torres RC	4.00
133	Jay Gibbons RC	10.00
134	Bill Ortega RC	4.00
135	Alexis Gomez RC	4.00
136	Wilken Ruan RC	4.00
137	Henry Mateo RC	4.00
138	Juan Uribe RC	8.00
139	Johnny Estrada RC	10.00
140	Jaisen Randolph RC	4.00
141	Eric Hinske RC	8.00
142	Jack Wilson RC	10.00
143	Cody Ransom RC	4.00
144	Nate Frese RC	4.00
145	John Grabow RC	4.00
146	Christian Parker RC	4.00
147	Brian Lawrence RC	6.00
148	Brandon Duckworth RC	4.00
149	Winston Abreu RC	4.00
150	Horacio Ramirez RC	8.00
151	Nick Maness RC	4.00
152	Blaine Neal RC	4.00
153	Billy Sylvester RC	4.00
154	David Elder RC	4.00
155	Bert Snow RC	4.00
156	Claudio Vargas RC	4.00
157	Martin Vargas RC	4.00
158	Grant Balfour RC	4.00
159	Randy Keisler RC	4.00
160	Zach Day RC	4.00

Legacy

Stars (1-100):	10-15X
Avant (101-115):	2-4X
RC's (116-125):	.75-1.5X
RC's (126-160):	1-2X
Production 50 Sets	

Autographics

	NM/M
Common Player:	5.00
Silvers:	1X
Production 250 Sets	
Golds:	1-2X
Production 50 Sets	
Roberto Alomar	30.00

Rick Ankiel	5.00
Albert Belle	8.00
Carlos Beltran	25.00
Adrian Beltre	10.00
Milton Bradley	5.00
Dee Brown	5.00
Jeromy Burnitz	5.00
Pat Burrell	10.00
Sean Casey	8.00
Joseph Crede	5.00
Jose Cruz Jr.	5.00
Ryan Dempster	5.00
J.D. Drew	10.00
Adam Dunn	15.00
Erubiel Durazo	5.00
Jermaine Dye	5.00
David Eckstein	5.00
Alex Escobar	5.00
Seth Etherton	5.00
Adam Everett	5.00
Carlos Febles	5.00
Troy Glaus	15.00
Ben Grieve	5.00
Toby Hall	5.00
Todd Helton	20.00
Shea Hillenbrand	6.00
Aubrey Huff	6.00
D'Angelo Jimenez	5.00
Paul Konerko	8.00
Mike Lamb	5.00
Matt Lawton	5.00
Derrek Lee	8.00
Mike Lieberthal	5.00
Mike Lowell	8.00
Julio Lugo	5.00
Jason Marquis	5.00
Edgar Martinez	15.00
Kevin Millwood	10.00
Eric Milton	5.00
Bengie Molina	5.00
Mike Mussina	25.00
Russ Ortiz	5.00
Corey Patterson	10.00
Jay Payton	5.00
Adam Piatt	5.00
Juan Pierre	5.00
Brad Radke	5.00
John Rocker	5.00
Alex Rodriguez	60.00
Scott Rolen	20.00
Richie Sexson	10.00
Gary Sheffield	10.00
Shannon Stewart	5.00
Miguel Tejada	25.00
Robin Ventura	5.00
Jose Vidro	5.00
Billy Wagner	8.00
Kip Wells	5.00
Rondell White	5.00
Preston Wilson	5.00
Kerry Wood	20.00
Julio Zuleta	5.00

Awards Showcase

	NM/M
Complete Set (20):	30.00
Common Player:	1.00
Inserted 1:20 Retail	
Derek Jeter	5.00
Derek Jeter	5.00
Jason Giambi	1.50
Jeff Kent	1.00
Pedro Martinez	2.00
Randy Johnson	2.00
Kazuhiro Sasaki	1.00
Rafael Furcal	1.00
Carlos Delgado	1.50
Todd Helton	2.00
Ivan Rodriguez	1.50
Darin Erstad	1.50
Bernie Williams	1.00
Greg Maddux	3.00
Jim Edmonds	1.00
Andruw Jones	2.00
Nomar Garciaparra	4.00
Todd Helton	2.00
Troy Glaus	2.00
Sammy Sosa	4.00

Awards Showcase Autographs

	NM/M
Production 25 Sets	

Johnny Bench	100.00
Yogi Berra	90.00
George Brett	200.00
Steve Carlton	60.00
Roger Clemens	180.00
Andre Dawson	40.00
Whitey Ford	80.00
Tom Glavine	50.00
Juan Gonzalez	50.00
Reggie Jackson	80.00
Randy Johnson	90.00
Chipper Jones	80.00
Harmon Killebrew	75.00
Fred Lynn	25.00
Greg Maddux	150.00
Don Mattingly	175.00
Willie McCovey	40.00
Jim Palmer	40.00
Jim Rice	25.00
Brooks Robinson	75.00
Frank Robinson	50.00
Ivan Rodriguez	50.00
Mike Schmidt	125.00
Tom Seaver	100.00
Robin Yount	

Awards Showcase Memorabilia

	NM/M
Common Player:	10.00
Production 100 Sets	
Johnny Bench	20.00
Yogi Berra	15.00
George Brett	40.00
Lou Brock	10.00
Roy Campanella	25.00
Steve Carlton	10.00
Roger Clemens	40.00
Andre Dawson	10.00
Whitey Ford	15.00
Jimmie Foxx	45.00
Kirk Gibson	10.00
Tom Glavine	10.00
Juan Gonzalez	10.00
Elston Howard	10.00
Jim "Catfish" Hunter	10.00
Reggie Jackson	20.00
Randy Johnson	15.00
Chipper Jones	10.00
Harmon Killebrew	20.00
Greg Maddux	25.00
Don Mattingly	75.00
Willie McCovey	10.00
Jim Palmer	10.00
Jim Rice	10.00
Brooks Robinson	20.00
Frank Robinson	15.00
Jackie Robinson	75.00
Ivan Rodriguez	15.00
Mike Schmidt	40.00
Tom Seaver	15.00
Willie Stargell	10.00
Ted Williams	150.00
Robin Yount	25.00

Derek Jeter's Monumental Moments

	NM/M
Production 2,000:	

MM5	Derek Jeter	8.00
	Derek Jeter/	
	Auto./100	90.00

Showcase Sticks

NM/M

Common Player:		4.00
Inserted 1:24		
	Roberto Alomar	6.00
	Adrian Beltre	5.00
	Pat Burrell	6.00
	J.D. Drew	4.00
	Juan Gonzalez	6.00
	Andruw Jones	8.00
	Chipper Jones	10.00
	Magglio Ordonez	4.00
	Ivan Rodriguez	6.00
	Scott Rolen	8.00
	Frank Thomas	8.00
	Roger Cedeno	4.00
	Shawn Green	5.00
	Richard Hidalgo	4.00
	Tony Clark	4.00
	Preston Wilson	4.00
	Barry Bonds	30.00
	Rafael Furcal	4.00
	Randy Johnson	8.00
	Vladimir Guerrero	8.00
	Al Kaline	10.00
	George Kell	4.00
	Jason Kendall	4.00
	Carlos Delgado	5.00
	Adam Piatt	4.00
	Alex Gonzalez	4.00
	Jorge Posada	6.00
	Jose Vidro	4.00
	Roger Clemens	20.00
	Steve Finley	4.00
	Reggie Jackson	8.00
	Shannon Stewart	4.00
	Rick Ankiel	4.00
	Jim Thome	8.00
	Tsuyoshi Shinjo	6.00
	Ichiro Suzuki	25.00

Sweet Sigs.

NM/M

Common Player:		10.00
Inserted 1:24		
Prices for Lumber		
Wall:		1X
Leather:		1-1.5X
	Bobby Abreu	15.00
	Wilson Betemit	10.00
	Russell Branyan	10.00
	Pat Burrell	20.00
	Eric Chavez	20.00
	Rafael Furcal	15.00
	Nomar Garciaparra	100.00
	Juan Gonzalez	35.00

Elpidio Guzman	10.00
Drew Henson	15.00
Brandon Inge	10.00
Derek Jeter	130.00
Andruw Jones	30.00
Willie Mays	180.00
Jackson Melian	10.00
Xavier Nady	10.00
Jose Ortiz	10.00
Ben Sheets	15.00
Mike Sweeney	15.00
Miguel Tejada	35.00
Albert Pujols	450.00

2001 Fleer Tradition

NM/M

Complete Set (450):	35.00
Common Player:	.15
Comp. Factory Set (485):	100.00
Pack (10):	2.00
Box (36):	55.00
1	Andres Galarraga	.15
2	Armando Rios	.15
3	Julio Lugo	.15
4	Darryl Hamilton	.15
5	Dave Veres	.15
6	Edgardo Alfonzo	.15
7	Brook Fordyce	.15
8	Eric Karros	.15
9	Neifi Perez	.15
10	Jim Edmonds	.15
11	Barry Larkin	.15
12	Trot Nixon	.15
13	Andy Pettitte	.35
14	Jose Guillen	.15
15	David Wells	.15
16	Magglio Ordonez	.15
17	David Segui	.15
18	Juan Encarnacion	.15
19	Robert Person	.15
20	Quilvio Veras	.15
21	Mo Vaughn	.15
22	B.J. Surhoff	.15
23	Ken Caminiti	.15
24	Frank Catalanotto	.15
25	Luis Gonzalez	.25
26	Pete Harnisch	.15
27	Alex Gonzalez	.15
28	Mark Quinn	.15
29	Luis Castillo	.15
30	Rick Helling	.15
31	Barry Bonds	2.00
32	Warren Morris	.15
33	Aaron Boone	.15
34	Ricky Gutierrez	.15
35	Preston Wilson	.15
36	Erubiel Durazo	.15
37	Jermaine Dye	.15
38	John Rocker	.15
39	Mark Grudzielanek	.15
40	Pedro Martinez	.75
41	Phil Nevin	.15
42	Luis Matos	.15
43	Orlando Hernandez	.15
44	Steve Cox	.15
45	James Baldwin	.15
46	Rafael Furcal	.15
47	Todd Zeile	.15
48	Elmer Dessens	.15
49	Russell Branyan	.15
50	Juan Gonzalez	.75
51	Mac Suzuki	.15
52	Adam Kennedy	.15
53	Randy Velarde	.15
54	David Bell	.15
55	Royce Clayton	.15
56	Greg Colbrunn	.15
57	Rey Ordonez	.15
58	Kevin Millwood	.15
59	Fernando Vina	.15
60	Eddie Taubensee	.15
61	Enrique Wilson	.15
62	Jay Bell	.15
63	Brian Moehler	.15
64	Brad Fullmer	.15
65	Ben Petrick	.15
66	Orlando Cabrera	.25
67	Shane Reynolds	.15
68	Mitch Meluskey	.15
69	Jeff Shaw	.15
70	Chipper Jones	1.00
71	Tomo Ohka	.15
72	Ruben Rivera	.15

73	Mike Sirotka	.15
74	Scott Rolen	.60
75	Glendon Rusch	.15
76	Miguel Tejada	.35
77	Brady Anderson	.15
78	Bartolo Colon	.15
79	Ron Coomer	.15
80	Gary DiSarcina	.15
81	Geoff Jenkins	.15
82	Billy Koch	.15
83	Mike Lamb	.15
84	Alex Rodriguez	1.50
85	Denny Neagle	.15
86	Michael Tucker	.15
87	Edgar Renteria	.15
88	Brian Anderson	.15
89	Glenallen Hill	.15
90	Aramis Ramirez	.15
91	Rondell White	.15
92	Tony Womack	.15
93	Jeffrey Hammonds	.15
94	Freddy Garcia	.15
95	Bill Mueller	.15
96	Mike Lieberthal	.15
97	Michael Barrett	.15
98	Derek Lee	.15
99	Bill Spiers	.15
100	Derek Lowe	.15
101	Javy Lopez	.15
102	Adrian Beltre	.30
103	Jim Parque	.15
104	Marquis Grissom	.15
105	Eric Chavez	.25
106	Todd Jones	.15
107	Eric Owens	.15
108	Roger Clemens	1.00
109	Denny Hocking	.15
110	Roberto Hernandez	.15
111	Albert Belle	.15
112	Troy Glaus	.75
113	Ivan Rodriguez	.60
114	Carlos Guillen	.15
115	Chuck Finley	.15
116	Dmitri Young	.15
117	Paul Konerko	.15
118	Damon Buford	.15
119	Fernando Tatis	.15
120	Larry Walker	.15
121	Jason Kendall	.15
122	Matt Williams	.15
123	Henry Rodriguez	.15
124	Placido Polanco	.15
125	Bobby Estalella	.15
126	Pat Burrell	.50
127	Mark Loretta	.15
128	Moises Alou	.15
129	Tino Martinez	.15
130	Milton Bradley	.15
131	Todd Hundley	.15
132	Keith Foulke	.15
133	Robert Fick	.15
134	Cristian Guzman	.15
135	Rusty Greer	.15
136	John Olerud	.15
137	Mariano Rivera	.25
138	Jeromy Burnitz	.15
139	Dave Burba	.15
140	Ken Griffey Jr.	1.25
141	Tony Gwynn	1.00
142	Carlos Delgado	.50
143	Edgar Martinez	.15
144	Ramon Hernandez	.15
145	Pedro Astacio	.15
146	Ray Lankford	.15
147	Mike Mussina	.40
148	Ray Durham	.15
149	Lee Stevens	.15
150	Jay Canizaro	.15
151	Adrian Brown	.15
152	Mike Piazza	1.25
153	Cliff Floyd	.15
154	Jose Vidro	.15
155	Jason Giambi	.50
156	Andruw Jones	.75
157	Robin Ventura	.15
158	Gary Sheffield	.40
159	Jeff D'Amico	.15
160	Chuck Knoblauch	.15
161	Roger Cedeno	.15
162	Jim Thome	.15
163	Peter Bergeron	.15
164	Kerry Wood	.50
165	Gabe Kapler	.15
166	Corey Koskie	.15
167	Doug Glanville	.15
168	Brent Mayne	.15
169	Scott Spiezio	.15
170	Steve Karsay	.15
171	Al Martin	.15
172	Fred McGriff	.15
173	Gabe White	.15
174	Alex Gonzalez	.15
175	Mike Darr	.15
176	Bengie Molina	.15

177	Ben Grieve	.15
178	Marlon Anderson	.15
179	Brian Giles	.15
180	Jose Valentin	.15
181	Brian Jordan	.15
182	Randy Johnson	.75
183	Ricky Ledee	.15
184	Russ Ortiz	.15
185	Mike Lowell	.15
186	Curtis Leskanic	.15
187	Bobby Abreu	.15
188	Derek Jeter	2.00
189	Lance Berkman	.15
190	Roberto Alomar	.40
191	Darin Erstad	.60
192	Richie Sexson	.15
193	Alex Ochoa	.15
194	Carlos Febles	.15
195	David Ortiz	.15
196	Shawn Green	.35
197	Mike Sweeney	.15
198	Vladimir Guerrero	.75
199	Jose Jimenez	.15
200	Travis Lee	.15
201	Rickey Henderson	.75
202	Bob Wickman	.15
203	Miguel Cairo	.15
204	Steve Finley	.15
205	Tony Batista	.15
206	Jamey Wright	.15
207	Terrence Long	.15
208	Trevor Hoffman	.15
209	John Vander Wal	.15
210	Greg Maddux	1.00
211	Tim Salmon	.25
212	Herbert Perry	.15
213	Marvin Benard	.15
214	Jose Offerman	.15
215	Jay Payton	.15
216	Jon Lieber	.15
217	Mark Kotsay	.15
218	Scott Brosius	.15
219	Scott Williamson	.15
220	Omar Vizquel	.15
221	Mike Hampton	.15
222	Richard Hidalgo	.15
223	Rey Sanchez	.15
224	Matt Lawton	.15
225	Bruce Chen	.15
226	Ryan Klesko	.15
227	Garret Anderson	.15
228	Kevin Brown	.15
229	Mike Cameron	.15
230	Tony Clark	.15
231	Curt Schilling	.40
232	Vinny Castilla	.15
233	Carl Pavano	.15
234	Eric Davis	.15
235	Darrin Fletcher	.15
236	Matt Stairs	.15
237	Octavio Dotel	.15
238	Mark Grace	.25
239	John Smoltz	.15
240	Matt Clement	.15
241	Ellis Burks	.15
242	Charles Johnson	.15
243	Jeff Bagwell	.75
244	Derek Bell	.15
245	Nomar Garciaparra	1.25
246	Jorge Posada	.35
247	Ryan Dempster	.15
248	J.T. Snow	.15
249	Eric Young	.15
250	Daryle Ward	.15
251	Joe Randa	.15
252	Travis Fryman	.15
253	Mike Williams	.15
254	Jacque Jones	.15
255	Scott Elarton	.15
256	Mark McGwire	1.50
257	Jay Buhner	.15
258	Randy Wolf	.15
259	Sammy Sosa	1.25
260	Chan Ho Park	.15
261	Damion Easley	.15
262	Rick Ankiel	.15
263	Frank Thomas	.75
264	Kris Benson	.15
265	Luis Alicea	.15
266	Jeremy Giambi	.15
267	Geoff Blum	.15
268	Joe Girardi	.15
269	Livan Hernandez	.15
270	Jeff Conine	.15
271	Danny Graves	.15
272	Craig Biggio	.15
273	Jose Canseco	.35
274	Tom Glavine	.30
275	Ruben Mateo	.15
276	Jeff Kent	.15
277	Kevin Young	.15
278	A.J. Burnett	.15
279	Dante Bichette	.15
280	Sandy Alomar Jr.	.15

281	John Wetteland	.15
282	Torii Hunter	.15
283	Jarrod Washburn	.15
284	Rich Aurilia	.15
285	Jeff Cirillo	.15
286	Fernando Seguignol	.15
287	Darren Dreifort	.15
288	Deivi Cruz	.15
289	Pokey Reese	.15
290	Garrett Stephenson	.15
291	Pat Boone	.15
292	Tim Hudson	.35
293	John Flaherty	.15
294	Shannon Stewart	.15
295	Shawn Estes	.15
296	Wilton Guerrero	.15
297	Delino DeShields	.15
298	David Justice	.15
299	Harold Baines	.15
300	Al Leiter	.15
301	Wil Cordero	.15
302	Antonio Alfonseca	.15
303	Sean Casey	.25
304	Carlos Beltran	.40
305	Brad Radke	.15
306	Jason Varitek	.15
307	Shigetosi Hasegawa	.15
308	Todd Stottlemyre	.15
309	Raul Mondesi	.15
310	Mike Bordick	.15
311	Darryl Kile	.15
312	Dean Palmer	.15
313	Johnny Damon	.30
314	Todd Helton	.75
315	Chad Hermansen	.15
316	Kevin Appier	.15
317	Greg Vaughn	.15
318	Robb Nen	.15
319	Jose Cruz Jr.	.15
320	Ron Ballard	.15
321	Bernie Williams	.35
322	Melvin Mora	.15
323	Kenny Lofton	.15
324	Armando Benitez	.15
325	Carlos Lee	.15
326	Damian Jackson	.15
327	Eric Milton	.15
328	J.D. Drew	.30
329	Byung-Hyun Kim	.15
330	Chris Stynes	.15
331	Kazuhiro Sasaki	.15
332	Troy O'Leary	.15
333	Pat Hentgen	.15
334	Brad Ausmus	.15
335	Todd Walker	.15
336	Jason Isringhausen	.15
337	Gerald Williams	.15
338	Aaron Sele	.15
339	Paul O'Neill	.15
340	Cal Ripken Jr.	2.00
341	Manny Ramirez	.75
342	Will Clark	.35
343	Mark Redman	.15
344	Bubba Trammell	.15
345	Troy Percival	.15
346	Chris Singleton	.15
347	Rafael Palmeiro	.60
348	Carl Everett	.15
349	Andy Benes	.15
350	Bobby Higginson	.15
351	Alex Cabrera	.15
352	Barry Zito	.40
353	Jace Brewer	.15
354	Paxton Crawford	.15
355	Oswaldo Mairena	.15
356	Joe Crede	.15
357	A.J. Pierzynski	.15
358	Daniel Garibay	.15
359	Jason Tyner	.15
360	Nate Rolison	.15
361	Scott Downs	.15
362	Keith Ginter	.15
363	Juan Pierre	.15
364	Adam Bernero	.15
365	Chris Richard	.15
366	Joey Nation	.15
367	Aubrey Huff	.15
368	Adam Eaton	.15
369	Jose Ortiz	.15
370	Eric Munson	.15
371	Matt Kinney	.15
372	Eric Byrnes	.15
373	Keith McDonald	.15
374	Matt Wise	.15
375	Timo Perez	.15
376	Julio Zuleta	.15
377	Jimmy Rollins	.25
378	Xavier Nady	.15
379	Ryan Kohlmeier	.15
380	Corey Patterson	.15
381	Todd Helton	.40
382	Moises Alou	.15
383	Vladimir Guerrero	.40
384	Luis Castillo	.15

385	Jeffrey Hammonds	.15
386	Nomar Garciaparra	.75
387	Carlos Delgado	.25
388	Darin Erstad	.15
389	Manny Ramirez	.40
390	Mike Sweeney	.15
391	Sammy Sosa	.75
392	Barry Bonds	1.00
393	Jeff Bagwell	.40
394	Richard Hidalgo	.15
395	Vladimir Guerrero	.40
396	Troy Glaus	.30
397	Frank Thomas	.40
398	Carlos Delgado	.25
399	David Justice	.15
400	Jason Giambi	.25
401	Randy Johnson	.40
402	Kevin Brown	.15
403	Greg Maddux	.50
404	Al Leiter	.15
405	Mike Hampton	.15
406	Pedro Martinez	.40
407	Roger Clemens	.65
408	Mike Sirotka	.15
409	Mike Mussina	.25
410	Bartolo Colon	.15
411	World Series Update	.15
412	World Series Update	.15
413	World Series Update	.15
414	World Series Update	.15
415	World Series Update	.15
416	World Series Update	.15
417	World Series Update	.15
418	World Series Update	.15
419	World Series Update	.15
420	World Series Update	.15
421	Atlanta Braves	.15
422	New York Mets	.15
423	Florida Marlins	.15
424	Philadelphia Phillies	.15
425	Montreal Expos	.15
426	St. Louis Cardinals	.15
427	Cincinnati Reds	.15
428	Chicago Cubs	.15
429	Milwaukee Brewers	.15
430	Houston Astros	.15
431	Pittsburgh Pirates	.15
432	San Francisco Giants	.15
433	Arizona Diamondbacks	.15
434	Los Angeles Dodgers	.15
435	Colorado Rockies	.15
436	San Diego Padres	.15
437	New York Yankees	.15
438	Boston Red Sox	.15
439	Baltimore Orioles	.15
440	Toronto Blue Jays	.15
441	Tampa Bay Devil Rays	.15
442	Chicago White Sox	.15
443	Cleveland Indians	.15
444	Detroit Tigers	.15
445	Kansas City Royals	.15
446	Minnesota Twins	.15
447	Seattle Mariners	.15
448	Oakland Athletics	.15
449	Anaheim Angels	.15
450	Texas Rangers	.15
451	Albert Pujols RC	70.00
452	Ichiro Suzuki RC	15.00
453	Tsuyoshi Shinjo RC	.75
454	Johnny Estrada RC	.75
455	Elpidio Guzman RC	.40
456	Adrian Hernandez RC	.30
457	Rafael Soriano RC	.75
458	Drew Henson RC	1.00
459	Juan Uribe RC	.75
460	Matt White RC	.40
461	Endy Chavez RC	.30
462	Bud Smith RC	.25
463	Morgan Ensberg RC	.75
464	Jay Gibbons RC	2.00
465	Jackson Melian RC	.30
466	Junior Spivey RC	.50
467	Juan Cruz RC	.50
468	Wilson Betemit RC	.40
469	Alexis Gomez RC	.30
470	Mark Teixeira RC	15.00
471	Erick Almonte RC	.30
472	Travis Hafner RC	5.00
473	Carlos Valderrama RC	.30
474	Brandon Duckworth RC	.75
475	Ryan Freel RC	.30
476	Wilkin Ruan RC	.30
477	Andres Torres RC	.30
478	Josh Towers RC	.50
479	Kyle Lohse RC	.75
480	Jason Michaels RC	.30
481	Alfonso Soriano	.50
482	C.C. Sabathia	.15
483	Roy Oswalt	.15
484	Ben Sheets	.15
485	Adam Dunn	.50

Diamond Tributes

		NM/M
Complete Set (30):		35.00
Common Player:		.50
Inserted 1:7		
1	Jackie Robinson	2.00
2	Mike Piazza	2.00
3	Alex Rodriguez	3.00
4	Barry Bonds	4.00
5	Nomar Garciaparra	2.00
6	Roger Clemens	1.75
7	Ivan Rodriguez	.75
8	Cal Ripken Jr.	4.00
9	Manny Ramirez	1.00
10	Chipper Jones	1.50
11	Barry Larkin	.50
12	Carlos Delgado	.75
13	J.D. Drew	.60
14	Carl Everett	.50
15	Todd Helton	1.50
16	Greg Maddux	1.50
17	Scott Rolen	.75
18	Troy Glaus	1.00
19	Brian Giles	.50
20	Jeff Bagwell	1.00
21	Sammy Sosa	2.00
22	Randy Johnson	1.00
23	Andruw Jones	1.00
24	Ken Griffey Jr.	2.00
25	Mark McGwire	3.00
26	Derek Jeter	4.00
27	Vladimir Guerrero	1.00
28	Frank Thomas	1.00
29	Pedro Martinez	1.00
30	Bernie Williams	.50

Grass Roots

		NM/M
Complete Set (15):		25.00
Common Player:		1.00
Inserted 1:18		
1	Derek Jeter	4.00
2	Greg Maddux	2.00
3	Sammy Sosa	2.50
4	Alex Rodriguez	3.00
5	Vladimir Guerrero	1.50
6	Scott Rolen	1.00
7	Frank Thomas	1.50
8	Nomar Garciaparra	2.50
9	Cal Ripken Jr.	4.00
10	Mike Piazza	2.50
11	Ivan Rodriguez	1.00
12	Chipper Jones	2.00
13	Tony Gwynn	2.00
14	Ken Griffey Jr.	2.50
15	Mark McGwire	3.00

Lumber Company

		NM/M
Complete Set (20):		25.00
Common Player:		.50
Inserted 1:12		
1	Vladimir Guerrero	1.50
2	Mo Vaughn	.50
3	Ken Griffey Jr.	2.50
4	Juan Gonzalez	1.50
5	Tony Gwynn	2.00
6	Jim Edmonds	.50

7	Jason Giambi	1.00
8	Alex Rodriguez	3.00
9	Derek Jeter	4.00
10	Darin Erstad	1.00
11	Andruw Jones	1.50
12	Cal Ripken Jr.	4.00
13	Magglio Ordonez	.50
14	Nomar Garciaparra	2.50
15	Chipper Jones	2.00
16	Sean Casey	.60
17	Shawn Green	.60
18	Mike Piazza	2.50
19	Sammy Sosa	2.50
20	Barry Bonds	4.00

Season Pass

Values Undetermined

Stitches in Time

		NM/M
Complete Set (25):		40.00
Common Player:		1.50
Inserted 1:18		
1	Henry Kimbro	1.50
2	Ernie Banks	3.00
3	James "Cool Papa" Bell	2.00
4	Joe Black	1.50
5	Roy Campanella	2.00
6	Ray Dandridge	1.50
7	Leon Day	1.50
8	Larry Doby	2.00
9	Josh Gibson	2.00
10	Elston Howard	2.00
11	Monte Irvin	2.00
12	Buck Leonard	2.00
13	Max Manning	1.50
14	Willie Mays	6.00
15	Buck O'Neil	2.00
16	Satchel Paige	3.00
17	Ted Radcliffe	2.00
18	Jackie Robinson	4.00
19	Bill Perkins	1.50
20	Andrew "Rube" Foster	2.00
21	William "Judy" Johnson	1.50
22	Oscar Charleston	1.50
23	John Henry "Pop" Lloyd	1.50
24	Artie Wilson	1.50
25	Sam Jethroe	1.50

Stitches in Time Autographs

		NM/M
Common Autograph:		20.00
2	Ernie Banks	50.00
4	Joe Black	20.00
11	Monte Irvin	30.00
14	Willie Mays	150.00
15	Buck O'Neil	30.00

ABBREVIATIONS

AS - All-Star
SP - Short Print

17	Ted Radcliffe	25.00
24	Artie Wilson	20.00

Stitches in Time Game-Used

		NM/M
	Common Card:	25.00
5	Roy Campanella	60.00
8	Larry Doby/Bat	25.00
10	Elston Howard/Bat	25.00
14	Willie Mays/Jsy	125.00
18	Jackie Robinson/Jsy	100.00

Turn Back the Clock

		NM/M
	Common Card:	8.00
	Inserted 1:352	
1	Tom Glavine	10.00
2	Greg Maddux	20.00
3	Sean Casey	8.00
4	Pokey Reese	8.00
5	Jason Giambi	15.00
6	Tim Hudson	8.00
7	Larry Walker	8.00
8	Jeffrey Hammonds	8.00
9	Scott Rolen	15.00
10	Pat Burrell	10.00
11	Chipper Jones	20.00
13	Troy Glaus	15.00
14	Tony Gwynn	20.00
15	Cal Ripken Jr.	50.00
16	Tom Glavine, Greg Maddux	75.00
17	Sean Casey, Pokey Reese	30.00
18	Chipper Jones, Greg Maddux	100.00
19	Larry Walker, Jeffrey Hammonds	30.00
20	Scott Rolen, Pat Burrell	40.00
21	Jason Giambi, Tim Hudson	40.00

Warning Track

	NM/M
Complete Set (23):	120.00
Common Player:	2.00

	Inserted 1:72	
1	Josh Gibson	5.00
2	Willie Mays	10.00
3	Mark McGwire	12.00
4	Barry Bonds	15.00
5	Jose Canseco	4.00
6	Ken Griffey Jr.	10.00
7	Cal Ripken Jr.	15.00
8	Rafael Palmeiro	5.00
9	Sammy Sosa	10.00
10	Juan Gonzalez	6.00
11	Frank Thomas	6.00
12	Jeff Bagwell	6.00
13	Gary Sheffield	2.50
14	Larry Walker	2.00
15	Mike Piazza	10.00
16	Larry Doby	4.00
17	Roy Campanella	5.00
18	Manny Ramirez	6.00
19	Chipper Jones	8.00
20	Alex Rodriguez	12.00
21	Ivan Rodriguez	5.00
22	Vladimir Guerrero	6.00
23	Nomar Garciaparra	10.00
24	Andres Galarraga	2.00
25	Jim Thome	2.00

2001 Fleer Triple Crown

		NM/M
	Complete Set (300):	25.00
	Common Player:	.15
	Pack (10):	2.00
	Box (24):	40.00
1	Derek Jeter	2.00
2	Vladimir Guerrero	.75
3	Henry Rodriguez	.15
4	Jason Giambi	.50
5	Nomar Garciaparra	1.25
6	Jeff Kent	.15
7	Garret Anderson	.15
8	Todd Helton	.75
9	Barry Bonds	2.00
10	Preston Wilson	.15
11	Troy Glaus	.75
12	Geoff Jenkins	.15
13	Jim Edmonds	.15
14	Bobby Higginson	.15
15	Mark Quinn	.15
16	Barry Larkin	.15
17	Richie Sexson	.15
18	Fernando Tatis	.15
19	John Vander Wal	.15
20	Darin Erstad	.60
21	Shawn Green	.40
22	Scott Rolen	.60
23	Tony Batista	.15
24	Phil Nevin	.15
25	Tim Salmon	.25
26	Gary Sheffield	.35

27	Ben Grieve	.15
28	Jermaine Dye	.15
29	Andres Galarraga	.15
30	Adrian Beltre	.35
31	Rafael Palmeiro	.60
32	J.T. Snow	.15
33	Edgardo Alfonzo	.15
34	Paul Konerko	.15
35	Jim Thome	.15
36	Andruw Jones	.75
37	Mike Sweeney	.15
38	Jose Cruz Jr.	.15
39	David Ortiz	.15
40	Pat Burrell	.40
41	Chipper Jones	1.00
42	Jeff Bagwell	.75
43	Raul Mondesi	.15
44	Rondell White	.15
45	Edgar Martinez	.15
46	Cal Ripken Jr.	2.00
47	Moises Alou	.15
48	Shannon Stewart	.15
49	Tino Martinez	.15
50	Jason Kendall	.15
51	Richard Hidalgo	.15
52	Albert Belle	.15
53	Jay Payton	.15
54	Cliff Floyd	.15
55	Rusty Greer	.15
56	Matt Williams	.15
57	Sammy Sosa	1.25
58	Carl Everett	.15
59	Carlos Delgado	.50
60	Jeremy Giambi	.15
61	Jose Canseco	.40
62	David Segui	.15
63	Jose Vidro	.15
64	Matt Stairs	.15
65	Travis Fryman	.15
66	Ken Griffey Jr.	1.25
67	Mike Piazza	1.25
68	Mark McGwire	1.50
69	Craig Biggio	.15
70	Eric Chavez	.25
71	Mo Vaughn	.15
72	Matt Lawton	.15
73	Miguel Tejada	.25
74	Brian Giles	.15
75	Sean Casey	.25
76	Robin Ventura	.15
77	Ivan Rodriguez	.60
78	Dean Palmer	.15
79	Frank Thomas	.75
80	Bernie Williams	.30
81	Juan Encarnacion	.15
82	John Olerud	.15
83	Rich Aurilia	.15
84	Juan Gonzalez	.15
85	Ray Durham	.15
86	Steve Finley	.15
87	Ken Caminiti	.15
88	Roberto Alomar	.40
89	Jeromy Burnitz	.15
90	J.D. Drew	.15
91	Lance Berkman	.15
92	Gabe Kapler	.15
93	Larry Walker	.15
94	Alex Rodriguez	1.50
95	Jeffrey Hammonds	.15
96	Magglio Ordonez	.15
97	David Justice	.15
98	Eric Karros	.15
99	Manny Ramirez	.75
100	Paul O'Neill	.15
101	Ron Gant	.15
102	Erubiel Durazo	.15
103	Jason Varitek	.15
104	Chan Ho Park	.15
105	Corey Koskie	.15
106	Jeff Conine	.15
107	Kevin Tapani	.15
108	Mike Lowell	.15
109	Tim Hudson	.25
110	Bobby Abreu	.15
111	Bret Boone	.15
112	David Wells	.15
113	Brian Jordan	.15
114	Mitch Meluskey	.15
115	Terrence Long	.15
116	Matt Clement	.15
117	Fernando Vina	.15
118	Luis Alicea	.15
119	Jay Bell	.15
120	Mark Grace	.25
121	Carlos Febles	.15
122	Mark Redman	.15
123	Kevin Jordan	.15
124	Pat Meares	.15
125	Mark McLemore	.15
126	Chris Singleton	.15
127	Trot Nixon	.15
128	Carlos Beltran	.40
129	Lee Stevens	.15
130	Kris Benson	.15

131	Jay Buhner	.15
132	Greg Vaughn	.15
133	Eric Young	.15
134	Tony Womack	.15
135	Roger Cedeno	.15
136	Travis Lee	.15
137	Marvin Benard	.15
138	Aaron Sele	.15
139	Rick Ankiel	.15
140	Ruben Mateo	.15
141	Randy Johnson	.75
142	Jason Tyner	.15
143	Mike Redmond	.15
144	Ron Coomer	.15
145	Scott Elarton	.15
146	Javy Lopez	.15
147	Carlos Lee	.15
148	Tony Clark	.15
149	Roger Clemens	1.00
150	Mike Lieberthal	.15
151	Shawn Estes	.15
152	Vinny Castilla	.15
153	Alex Gonzalez	.15
154	Troy Percival	.15
155	Pokey Reese	.15
156	Todd Hollandsworth	.15
157	Marquis Grissom	.15
158	Greg Maddux	1.00
159	Dante Bichette	.15
160	Hideo Nomo	.75
161	Jacque Jones	.15
162	Kevin Young	.15
163	B.J. Surhoff	.15
164	Eddie Taubensee	.15
165	Neifi Perez	.15
166	Orlando Hernandez	.15
167	Francisco Cordova	.15
168	Miguel Cairo	.15
169	Rafael Furcal	.15
170	Sandy Alomar Jr.	.15
171	Jeff Cirillo	.15
172	A.J. Pierzynski	.15
173	Fred McGriff	.15
174	Mike Mussina	.40
175	Aaron Boone	.15
176	Nick Johnson	.15
177	Kent Bottenfield	.15
178	Felipe Crespo	.15
179	Ryan Minor	.15
180	Charles Johnson	.15
181	Damion Easley	.15
182	Michael Barrett	.15
183	Doug Glanville	.15
184	Ben Davis	.15
185	Rickey Henderson	.75
186	Edgard Clemente	.15
187	Dmitri Young	.15
188	Tom Goodwin	.15
189	Mike Hampton	.15
190	Gerald Williams	.15
191	Omar Vizquel	.15
192	Ben Petrick	.15
193	Brad Radke	.15
194	Russ Davis	.15
195	Milton Bradley	.15
196	John Parrish	.15
197	Todd Hundley	.15
198	Carl Pavano	.15
199	Bruce Chen	.15
200	Royce Clayton	.15
201	Homer Bush	.15
202	Mark Grudzielanek	.15
203	Mike Lansing	.15
204	Daryle Ward	.15
205	Jeff D'Amico	.15
206	Ray Lankford	.15
207	Curt Schilling	.40
208	Pedro Martinez	.75
209	Johnny Damon	.30
210	Al Leiter	.15
211	Ruben Rivera	.15
212	Kazuhiro Sasaki	.15
213	Will Clark	.25
214	Rick Helling	.15
215	Adam Piatt	.15
216	Joe Girardi	.15
217	A.J. Burnett	.15
218	Mike Bordick	.15
219	Mike Cameron	.15
220	Tony Gwynn	1.00
221	Deivi Cruz	.15
222	Bubba Trammell	.15
223	Scott Erickson	.15
224	Kerry Wood	.50
225	Derrek Lee	.15
226	Peter Bergeron	.15
227	Chris Gomez	.15
228	Al Martin	.15
229	Brady Anderson	.15
230	Ramon Martinez	.15
231	Darryl Kile	.15
232	Devon White	.15
233	Charlie Hayes	.15
234	Aramis Ramirez	.15

235	Mike Lamb	.15
236	Tom Glavine	.30
237	Troy O'Leary	.15
238	Joe Randa	.15
239	Dustin Hermanson	.15
240	Adam Kennedy	.15
241	Jose Valentin	.15
242	Derek Bell	.15
243	Mark Kotsay	.15
244	Ron Belliard	.15
245	Warren Morris	.15
246	Ozzie Guillen	.15
247	Andy Ashby	.15
248	Jose Offerman	.15
249	Kevin Brown	.15
250	Jorge Posada	.35
251	Alex Cabrera	.15
252	Chan Perry	.15
253	Augie Ojeda	.15
254	Santiago Perez	.15
255	Grant Roberts	.15
256	Dusty Allen	.15
257	Elvis Pena	.15
258	Matt Kinney	.15
259	Timoniel Perez	.15
260	Adam Eaton	.15
261	Geraldo Guzman	.15
262	Damian Rolls	.15
263	Alfonso Soriano	.50
264	Corey Patterson	.15
265	Juan Alvarez	.15
266	Shawn Gilbert	.15
267	Adam Bernero	.15
268	Ben Weber	.15
269	Tike Redman	.15
270	Willie Morales	.15
271	Tomas De La Rosa	.15
272	Rodney Lindsey	.15
273	Carlos Casimiro	.15
274	Jim Mann	.15
275	Pasqual Coco	.15
276	Julio Zuleta	.15
277	Damon Minor	.15
278	Jose Ortiz	.15
279	Eric Munson	.15
280	Andy Thompson	.15
281	Aubrey Huff	.15
282	Chris Richard	.15
283	Ross Gload	.15
284	Travis Dawkins	.15
285	Tim Drew	.15
286	Barry Zito	.40
287	Andy Tracy	.15
288	Julio Lugo	.15
289	Matt DeWitt	.15
290	Keith McDonald	.15
291	J.C. Romero	.15
292	Adam Melhuse	.15
293	Ryan Kohlmeier	.15
294	John Bale	.15
295	Eric Cammack	.15
296	Morgan Burkhart	.15
297	Kory DeHaan	.15
298	Raul Gonzalez	.15
299	Hector Ortiz	.15
300	Talmadge Nunnari	.15

Blue

NM/M

Common Player: 3.00
Produced to # of 2000 HR's

1	Derek Jeter/15	150.00
2	Vladimir Guerrero/44	25.00
3	Henry Rodriguez/20	3.00
4	Jason Giambi/43	15.00
5	Nomar Garciaparra/21	25.00
6	Jeff Kent/33	8.00
7	Garret Anderson/35	8.00
8	Todd Helton/42	15.00
9	Barry Bonds/49	40.00
10	Preston Wilson/31	3.00
11	Troy Glaus/47	10.00
12	Geoff Jenkins/34	8.00
13	Jim Edmonds/42	10.00
14	Bobby Higginson/30	3.00
15	Mark Quinn/20	5.00
16	Barry Larkin/11	5.00
17	Richie Sexson/30	10.00
18	Fernando Tatis/18	3.00
19	John Vander Wal/24	3.00
20	Darin Erstad /25	10.00
21	Shawn Green/24	10.00
22	Scott Rolen/26	15.00
23	Tony Batista/41	3.00
24	Phil Nevin/31	3.00
25	Tim Salmon/34	5.00
26	Gary Sheffield/43	8.00
27	Ben Grieve/27	5.00
28	Jermaine Dye/33	3.00
29	Andres Galarraga/28	5.00
30	Adrian Beltre/20	8.00
31	Rafael Palmeiro/39	10.00
32	J.T. Snow/19	5.00
33	Edgardo Alfonzo/25	5.00
34	Paul Konerko/21	5.00
35	Jim Thome/37	15.00
36	Andruw Jones/36	10.00
37	Mike Sweeney/29	3.00
38	Jose Cruz Jr./31	3.00
39	David Ortiz/10	8.00
40	Pat Burrell/18	15.00
41	Chipper Jones/36	15.00
42	Jeff Bagwell/47	10.00
43	Raul Mondesi/24	5.00
44	Rondell White/13	10.00
45	Edgar Martinez/37	5.00
46	Cal Ripken Jr./15	150.00
47	Moises Alou/30	5.00
48	Shannon Stewart/21	3.00
49	Tino Martinez/16	5.00
50	Jason Kendall/14	5.00
51	Richard Hidalgo/44	3.00
52	Albert Belle/23	5.00
53	Jay Payton/17	3.00
54	Cliff Floyd/22	3.00
55	Rusty Greer/8	8.00
56	Matt Williams/12	10.00
57	Sammy Sosa/50	25.00
58	Carl Everett/34	3.00
59	Carlos Delgado/41	5.00
60	Jeremy Giambi/10	5.00
61	Jose Canseco/15	10.00
62	David Segui/19	3.00
63	Jose Vidro/24	3.00
64	Matt Stairs/21	3.00
65	Travis Fryman/22	5.00
66	Ken Griffey Jr./40	15.00
67	Mike Piazza/38	15.00
68	Mark McGwire/32	20.00
69	Craig Biggio/8	10.00
70	Eric Chavez/26	10.00
71	Mo Vaughn/36	5.00
72	Matt Lawton/13	5.00
73	Miguel Tejada/30	10.00
74	Brian Giles/35	5.00
75	Sean Casey/20	5.00
76	Robin Ventura/24	5.00
77	Ivan Rodriguez/27	8.00
78	Dean Palmer/29	3.00
79	Frank Thomas/43	10.00
80	Bernie Williams/30	8.00
81	John Encarnacion/14	5.00
82	John Olerud/14	5.00
83	Rich Aurilia/20	3.00
84	Juan Gonzalez/22	8.00
85	Ray Durham/17	5.00
86	Steve Finley/3	5.00
87	Ken Caminiti/15	5.00
88	Roberto Alomar/19	15.00
89	Jeromy Burnitz/31	3.00
90	J.D. Drew/18	8.00
91	Lance Berkman/21	8.00
92	Gabe Kapler/14	8.00
93	Larry Walker/9	10.00
94	Alex Rodriguez/41	20.00
95	Jeffrey Hammonds/20	3.00
96	Magglio Ordonez/32	5.00
97	David Justice/20	5.00
98	Eric Karros/31	3.00
99	Manny Ramirez/38	10.00
100	Paul O'Neill/18	8.00

Green

NM/M

Common Player: 1.00
Produced to # of 2000 RBI's

1	Derek Jeter/73	20.00
2	Vladimir Guerrero/123	5.00
3	Henry Rodriguez/61	1.00
4	Jason Giambi/137	5.00
5	Nomar Garciaparra/96	10.00
6	Jeff Kent/125	3.00
7	Garret Anderson/117	3.00
8	Todd Helton147	5.00
9	Barry Bonds/106	20.00
10	Preston Wilson/121	1.00
11	Troy Glaus/102	4.00
12	Geoff Jenkins/94	3.00
13	Jim Edmonds/108	4.00
14	Bobby Higginson/102	1.00
15	Mark Quinn/78	1.00
16	Barry Larkin/41	4.00
17	Richie Sexson/91	4.00
18	Fernando Tatis/64	1.00
19	John Vander Wal/94	1.00
20	Darin Erstad/100	3.00
21	Shawn Green/99	3.00
22	Scott Rolen/89	4.00
23	Tony Batista/114	1.00
24	Phil Nevin/107	1.00
25	Tim Salmon/97	1.00
26	Gary Sheffield/109	3.00
27	Ben Grieve/104	1.00
28	Jermaine Dye/118	1.00
29	Andres Galarraga/100	1.50
30	Adrian Beltre/85	1.00
31	Rafael Palmeiro/120	3.00
32	J.T. Snow/96	1.00
33	Edgardo Alfonzo/94	1.00
34	Paul Konerko/97	1.50
35	Jim Thome/106	4.00
36	Andruw Jones/104	4.00
37	Mike Sweeney/144	1.00
38	Jose Cruz Jr./76	1.00
39	David Ortiz/63	1.00
40	Pat Burrell/79	4.00
41	Chipper Jones/111	8.00
42	Jeff Bagwell/132	5.00
43	Raul Mondesi/67	2.00
44	Rondell White/61	1.50
45	Edgar Martinez/145	2.00
46	Cal Ripken Jr./56	25.00
47	Moises Alou/114	1.00
48	Shannon Stewart/69	1.00
49	Tino Martinez/91	2.00
50	Jason Kendall/58	1.00
51	Richard Hidalgo/122	1.00
52	Albert Belle/103	1.00
53	Jay Payton/62	1.00
54	Cliff Floyd/91	1.00
55	Rusty Greer/65	1.00
56	Matt Williams/47	2.00
57	Sammy Sosa/138	10.00
58	Carl Everett/108	1.00
59	Carlos Delgado/137	3.00
60	Jeremy Giambi/50	1.00
61	Jose Canseco/49	5.00
62	David Segui/103	1.00
63	Jose Vidro/97	1.00
64	Matt Stairs/81	1.00
65	Travis Fryman/106	2.00
66	Ken Griffey Jr./118	10.00
67	Mike Piazza/113	10.00
68	Mark McGwire/73	15.00
69	Craig Biggio/35	4.00
70	Eric Chavez/86	4.00
71	Mo Vaughn/117	3.00
72	Matt Lawton/88	1.00
73	Miguel Tejada/115	4.00
74	Brian Giles/123	3.00
75	Sean Casey/85	2.00
76	Robin Ventura/84	2.00
77	Ivan Rodriguez/83	5.00
78	Dean Palmer/102	1.00
79	Frank Thomas/143	5.00
80	Bernie Williams/121	4.00
81	Juan Encarnacion/72	1.00
82	John Olerud/103	3.00
83	Rich Aurilia/79	1.00
84	Juan Gonzalez/67	5.00
85	Ray Durham/75	1.00
86	Steve Finley/96	1.00
87	Ken Caminiti/45	1.00
88	Roberto Alomar/89	5.00
89	Jeromy Burnitz/98	1.00
90	J.D. Drew/57	3.00
91	Lance Berkman/67	2.00
92	Gabe Kapler/66	1.00
93	Larry Walker/51	3.00
94	Alex Rodriguez/132	15.00
95	Jeffrey Hammonds/106	1.00
96	Magglio Ordonez/126	3.00
97	David Justice/118	3.00
98	Eric Karros/106	1.00
99	Manny Ramirez/122	5.00
100	Paul O'Neill/100	2.00

Red

Common Player (1-100):
Stars: 4-8X
Produced to 2000 Bat Avg.
(See 2001 Fleer Triple Crown #1-100 for checklist and base card values.)

Autographics

NM/M

Common Autograph: 5.00
Inserted 1:72
Silvers: 1X
Production 250 Sets
Golds: 1-2X
Production 50 Sets

1	Roberto Alomar	30.00
2	Jimmy Anderson	5.00
3	Ryan Anderson	5.00
4	Rick Ankiel	5.00
5	Adrian Beltre	10.00
6	Peter Bergeron	5.00
7	Lance Berkman	8.00
8	Barry Bonds	200.00
9	Milton Bradley	5.00
10	Dee Brown	5.00
11	Roosevelt Brown	5.00
12	Pat Burrell	10.00
13	Sean Casey	8.00
14	Eric Chavez	10.00
15	Giuseppe Chiaramonte	5.00
16	Joe Crede	5.00
17	Jose Cruz Jr.	5.00
18	Carlos Delgado	10.00
19	Ryan Dempster	5.00
20	Adam Dunn	15.00
21	David Eckstein	5.00
22	Jim Edmonds	10.00
23	Troy Glaus	15.00
24	Chad Green	5.00
25	Tony Gwynn	30.00
26	Todd Helton	20.00
27	Chad Hermansen	5.00
28	Shea Hillenbrand	6.00
29	Aubrey Huff	6.00
30	Randy Johnson	40.00
31	Chipper Jones	40.00
32	Mike Lamb	5.00
33	Corey Lee	5.00
34	Steve Lomasney	5.00
35	Terrence Long	5.00
36	Julio Lugo	5.00
37	Jason Marquis	5.00
38	Bengie Molina	5.00
39	Mike Mussina	25.00
40	Pablo Ozuna	5.00
41	Corey Patterson	10.00
42	Jay Payton	6.00
43	Wily Pena	15.00
44	Josh Phelps	8.00
45	Adam Piatt	5.00
46	Matt Riley	5.00
47	Alex Rodriguez	75.00
48	Alex Sanchez	5.00
49	Gary Sheffield	10.00
50	Alfonso Soriano	40.00
51	Shannon Stewart	6.00
52	Fernando Tatis	5.00
53	Jose Vidro	5.00
54	Preston Wilson	8.00
55	Kerry Wood	25.00
56	Julio Zuleta	5.00

Crowning Achievements

NM/M

Complete Set (15): 15.00
Common Player: .50
Inserted 1:9

1	Troy Glaus	1.00
2	Mark McGwire	2.50
3	Barry Larkin, Craig Biggio	.50
4	Ken Griffey Jr.	2.00
5	Rafael Palmeiro	.75
6	Alex Rodriguez	2.50
7	Roger Clemens	1.75
8	Mike Piazza	2.00
9	Cal Ripken Jr.	3.00
10	Randy Johnson	1.00
11	Jeff Bagwell	1.00
12	Sammy Sosa	2.00
13	Greg Maddux	1.50
14	Barry Bonds	3.00
15	Fred McGriff	.50

Crowns of Gold

NM/M

Common Player: 4.00

Random inserts in Hobby packs.

Rick Ankiel/Jsy	4.00
Steve Carlton/Jsy	10.00
Roger Clemens/Jsy	40.00
Carlos Delgado/Bat	8.00
Darin Erstad/Bat	6.00
Jimmie Foxx/Bat	100.00
Todd Helton/Bat	10.00
Randy Johnson/Jsy	15.00
Frank Robinson/Bat	10.00
Gary Sheffield/Jsy	8.00
Frank Thomas/Bat	10.00
Ted Williams/Bat	200.00

Crowns of Gold Autograph

NM/M

Random inserts in Hobby packs.

Steve Carlton/Jsy/72	80.00
Roger Clemens/Jsy/98	200.00
Frank Robinson/Bat/66	80.00

Feel the Game

NM/M

Common Player:	4.00
Inserted 1:72	
Golds:	1.5-2X

Production 50 Sets

Adrian Beltre	6.00
Dante Bichette	4.00
Roger Cedeno	4.00
Ben Davis	4.00
Carlos Delgado	6.00
J.D. Drew	6.00
Jason Giambi	6.00
Brian Giles	4.00
Juan Gonzalez	8.00
Richard Hidalgo	4.00
Chipper Jones	10.00
Eric Karros	4.00
Javy Lopez	4.00
Tino Martinez	4.00
Raul Mondesi	4.00
Phil Nevin	4.00
Chan Ho Park	4.00
Ivan Rodriguez	6.00
Shannon Stewart	4.00
Frank Thomas	8.00
Jose Vidro	4.00
Matt Williams	4.00
Preston Wilson	4.00

Future Threats

NM/M

Complete Set (15):	15.00
Common Player:	.50
Inserted 1:7	
1 Derek Jeter	3.00
2 Alex Rodriguez	2.50
3 Magglio Ordonez, Shawn Green	.50
4 Larry Walker	.50
5 Vladimir Guerrero	1.00
6 Nomar Garciaparra	2.00
7 Ken Griffey Jr.	3.00
8 Barry Bonds	3.00
9 Chipper Jones	1.50
10 Todd Helton	1.00
11 Ivan Rodriguez	.75
12 Jeff Bagwell	1.00
13 Frank Thomas	1.00
14 Carlos Delgado	.65
15 Mike Piazza	2.00

Glamour Boys

NM/M

Complete Set (15):	40.00

Common Player:	1.50
Inserted 1:24	
1 Derek Jeter	6.00
2 Vladimir Guerrero	2.00
3 Scott Rolen, Jeff Bagwell	1.50
4 Sammy Sosa	4.00
5 Ken Griffey Jr.	4.00
6 Mark McGwire	5.00
7 Ivan Rodriguez	1.50
8 Mike Piazza	4.00
9 Nomar Garciaparra	4.00
10 Cal Ripken Jr.	6.00
11 Tony Gwynn	3.00
12 Barry Bonds	6.00
13 Randy Johnson	2.00
14 Alex Rodriguez	5.00
15 Pedro Martinez	2.00

2002 Fleer

NM/M

Complete Set (540):	75.00
Common Player:	.15
Pack (10):	2.00
Box (24):	40.00
1 Darin Erstad	.15
2 Randy Johnson	.25
3 Chipper Jones	.50
4 Jay Gibbons	.15
5 Nomar Garciaparra	.50
6 Sammy Sosa	.50
7 Frank Thomas	.50
8 Ken Griffey Jr.	.75
9 Jim Thome	.25
10 Todd Helton	.25
11 Jeff Weaver	.15
12 Cliff Floyd	.15
13 Jeff Bagwell	.25
14 Mike Sweeney	.15
15 Adrian Beltre	.25
16 Richie Sexson	.25
17 Brad Radke	.15
18 Vladimir Guerrero	.50
19 Mike Piazza	.50
20 Derek Jeter	1.00
21 Eric Chavez	.15
22 Pat Burrell	.15
23 Brian Giles	.15
24 Trevor Hoffman	.15
25 Barry Bonds	1.00
26 Ichiro Suzuki	.75
27 Albert Pujols	1.00
28 Ben Grieve	.15
29 Alex Rodriguez	1.00
30 Carlos Delgado	.25
31 Miguel Tejada	.25
32 Todd Hollandsworth	.15
33 Marlon Anderson	.15
34 Kerry Robinson	.15
35 Chris Richard	.15
36 Jamey Wright	.15
37 Ray Lankford	.15
38 Mike Bordick	.15
39 Danny Graves	.15
40 A.J. Pierzynski	.15
41 Shannon Stewart	.15
42 Tony Armas Jr.	.15
43 Brad Ausmus	.15
44 Alfonso Soriano	.50
45 Junior Spivey	.15
46 Brent Mayne	.15
47 Jim Thome	.15
48 Dan Wilson	.15
49 Geoff Jenkins	.15
50 Kris Benson	.15
51 Rafael Furcal	.15
52 Wiki Gonzalez	.15
53 Jeff Kent	.15
54 Curt Schilling	.40
55 Ken Harvey	.15
56 Roosevelt Brown	.15
57 David Segui	.15
58 Mario Valdez	.15
59 Adam Dunn	.50
60 Bob Howry	.15
61 Michael Barrett	.15
62 Garret Anderson	.15
63 Kelvim Escobar	.15
64 Ben Grieve	.15
65 Randy Johnson	.75
66 Jose Offerman	.15
67 Jason Kendall	.15
68 Joel Pineiro	.15
69 Alex Escobar	.15
70 Chris George	.15
71 Bobby Higginson	.15
72 Nomar Garciaparra	1.50
73 Pat Burrell	.40
74 Lee Stevens	.15
75 Felipe Lopez	.15
76 Al Leiter	.15
77 Jim Edmonds	.15
78 Al Levine	.15
79 Raul Mondesi	.15
80 Jose Valentin	.15
81 Matt Clement	.15
82 Richard Hidalgo	.15
83 Jamie Moyer	.15
84 Brian Schneider	.15
85 John Franco	.15
86 Brian Buchanan	.15
87 Roy Oswalt	.25
88 Johnny Estrada	.15
89 Marcus Giles	.15
90 Carlos Valderrama	.15
91 Mark Mulder	.15
92 Mark Grace	.25
93 Andy Ashby	.15
94 Woody Williams	.15
95 Ben Petrick	.15
96 Roy Halladay	.30
97 Fred McGriff	.15
98 Shawn Green	.40
99 Todd Hundley	.15
100 Carlos Febles	.15
101 Jason Marquis	.15
102 Mike Redmond	.15
103 Shane Halter	.15
104 Trot Nixon	.15
105 Jeremy Giambi	.15
106 Carlos Delgado	.50
107 Richie Sexson	.15
108 Russ Ortiz	.15
109 David Ortiz	.25
110 Curtis Leskanic	.15
111 Jay Payton	.15
112 Travis Phelps	.15
113 J.T. Snow	.15
114 Edgar Renteria	.15
115 Freddy Garcia	.15
116 Cliff Floyd	.15
117 Charles Nagy	.15
118 Tony Batista	.15
119 Rafael Palmeiro	.65
120 Darren Dreifort	.15
121 Warren Morris	.15
122 Augie Ojeda	.15
123 Rusty Greer	.15
124 Esteban Yan	.15
125 Corey Patterson	.15
126 Matt Ginter	.15
127 Matt Lawton	.15
128 Miguel Batista	.15
129 Randy Winn	.15
130 Eric Milton	.15
131 Jack Wilson	.15
132 Sean Casey	.25
133 Mike Sweeney	.15
134 Jason Tyner	.15
135 Carlos Hernandez	.15
136 Shea Hillenbrand	.15
137 Shawn Wooten	.15
138 Peter Bergeron	.15
139 Travis Lee	.15
140 Craig Wilson	.15
141 Carlos Guillen	.15
142 Chipper Jones	1.00
143 Gabe Kapler	.15
144 Raul Ibanez	.15
145 Eric Chavez	.25
146 D'Angelo Jimenez	.15
147 Chad Hermansen	.15
148 Joe Kennedy	.15
149 Mariano Rivera	.25
150 Jeff Bagwell	.75
151 Joe McEwing	.15
152 Ronnie Belliard	.15
153 Desi Relaford	.15
154 Vinny Castilla	.15
155 Tim Hudson	.25
156 Wilton Guerrero	.15
157 Raul Casanova	.15
158 Edgardo Alfonzo	.15
159 Derrek Lee	.15
160 Phil Nevin	.15
161 Roger Clemens	1.25
162 Jason LaRue	.15
163 Brian Lawrence	.15
164 Adrian Beltre	.30
165 Troy Glaus	.75
166 Jeff Weaver	.15
167 B.J. Surhoff	.15
168 Eric Byrnes	.15
169 Mike Sirotka	.15
170 Bill Haselman	.15
171 Javier Vazquez	.15
172 Sidney Ponson	.15
173 Adam Everett	.15
174 Bubba Trammell	.15
175 Robb Nen	.15
176 Barry Larkin	.15
177 Tony Graffanino	.15
178 Rich Garces	.15
179 Juan Uribe	.15
180 Tom Glavine	.25
181 Eric Karros	.15
182 Michael Cuddyer	.15
183 Wade Miller	.15
184 Matt Williams	.15
185 Matt Morris	.15
186 Rickey Henderson	.75
187 Trevor Hoffman	.15
188 Wilson Betemit	.15
189 Steve Karsay	.15
190 Frank Catalanotto	.15
191 Jason Schmidt	.15
192 Roger Cedeno	.15
193 Magglio Ordonez	.15
194 Pat Hentgen	.15
195 Mike Lieberthal	.15
196 Andy Pettitte	.30
197 Jay Gibbons	.15
198 Rolando Arrojo	.15
199 Joe Mays	.15
200 Aubrey Huff	.15
201 Nelson Figueroa	.15
202 Paul Konerko	.25
203 Ken Griffey Jr.	1.50
204 Brandon Duckworth	.15
205 Sammy Sosa	1.50
206 Carl Everett	.15
207 Scott Rolen	.65
208 Orlando Hernandez	.15
209 Todd Helton	.75
210 Preston Wilson	.15
211 Gil Meche	.15
212 Bill Mueller	.15
213 Craig Biggio	.15
214 Dean Palmer	.15
215 Randy Wolf	.15
216 Jeff Suppan	.15
217 Jimmy Rollins	.25
218 Alexis Gomez	.15
219 Ellis Burks	.15
220 Ramon E. Martinez	.15
221 Ramiro Mendoza	.15
222 Einar Diaz	.15
223 Brent Abernathy	.15
224 Darin Erstad	.15
225 Reggie Taylor	.15
226 Jason Jennings	.15
227 Ray Durham	.15
228 John Parrish	.15
229 Kevin Young	.15
230 Xavier Nady	.15
231 Juan Cruz	.15
232 Greg Norton	.15
233 Barry Bonds	2.00
234 Kip Wells	.15
235 Paul LoDuca	.15
236 Javy Lopez	.25
237 Luis Castillo	.15
238 Tom Gordon	.15
239 Mike Mordecai	.15
240 Damian Rolls	.15
241 Julio Lugo	.15
242 Ichiro Suzuki	1.00
243 Tony Womack	.15
244 Matt Anderson	.15

245 Carlos Lee	.15
246 Alex Rodriguez	1.75
247 Bernie Williams	.30
248 Scott Sullivan	.15
249 Mike Hampton	.15
250 Orlando Cabrera	.15
251 Benito Santiago	.15
252 Steve Finley	.15
253 Dave Williams	.15
254 Adam Kennedy	.15
255 Omar Vizquel	.15
256 Garrett Stephenson	.15
257 Fernando Tatis	.15
258 Mike Piazza	1.50
259 Scott Spiezio	.15
260 Jacque Jones	.15
261 Russell Branyan	.15
262 Mark McLemore	.15
263 Mitch Meluskey	.15
264 Marlon Byrd	.15
265 Kyle Farnsworth	.15
266 Billy Sylvester	.15
267 C.C. Sabathia	.15
268 Mark Buehrle	.15
269 Geoff Blum	.15
270 Bret Prinz	.15
271 Placido Polanco	.15
272 John Olerud	.15
273 Pedro J. Martinez	.75
274 Doug Mientkiewicz	.15
275 Jason Bere	.15
276 Bud Smith	.15
277 Terrence Long	.15
278 Troy Percival	.15
279 Derek Jeter	2.00
280 Eric Owens	.15
281 Jay Bell	.15
282 Mike Cameron	.15
283 Joe Randa	.15
284 Brian Roberts	.15
285 Ryan Klesko	.15
286 Ryan Dempster	.15
287 Cristian Guzman	.15
288 Tim Salmon	.25
289 Mark Johnson	.15
290 Brian Giles	.15
291 Jon Lieber	.15
292 Fernando Vina	.15
293 Mike Mussina	.40
294 Juan Pierre	.40
295 Carlos Beltran	.40
296 Vladimir Guerrero	.75
297 Orlando Merced	.15
298 Jose Hernandez	.15
299 Mike Lamb	.15
300 David Eckstein	.15
301 Mark Loretta	.15
302 Greg Vaughn	.15
303 Jose Vidro	.15
304 Jose Ortiz	.15
305 Mark Grudzielanek	.15
306 Rob Bell	.15
307 Elmer Dessens	.15
308 Tomas Perez	.15
309 Jerry Hairston Jr.	.15
310 Mike Stanton	.15
311 Todd Walker	.15
312 Jason Varitek	.15
313 Masato Yoshii	.15
314 Ben Sheets	.15
315 Roberto Hernandez	.15
316 Eli Marrero	.15
317 Josh Beckett	.50
318 Robert Fick	.15
319 Aramis Ramirez	.15
320 Bartolo Colon	.15
321 Kenny Kelly	.15
322 Luis Gonzalez	.25
323 John Smoltz	.15
324 Homer Bush	.15
325 Kevin Millwood	.15
326 Manny Ramirez	.75
327 Armando Benitez	.15
328 Luis Alicea	.15
329 Mark Kotsay	.15
330 Felix Rodriguez	.15
331 Eddie Taubensee	.15
332 John Burkett	.15
333 Ramon Ortiz	.15
334 Daryle Ward	.15
335 Jarrod Washburn	.15
336 Benji Gil	.15
337 Mike Lowell	.15
338 Larry Walker	.15
339 Andruw Jones	.75
340 Scott Elarton	.15
341 Tony McKnight	.15
342 Frank Thomas	.50
343 Kevin Brown	.15
344 Jermaine Dye	.15
345 Luis Rivas	.15
346 Jeff Conine	.15
347 Bobby Kielty	.15
348 Jeffrey Hammonds	.15

349 Keith Foulke	.15
350 Dave Martinez	.15
351 Adam Eaton	.15
352 Brandon Inge	.15
353 Tyler Houston	.15
354 Bobby Abreu	.15
355 Ivan Rodriguez	.65
356 Doug Glanville	.15
357 Jorge Julio	.15
358 Kerry Wood	.50
359 Eric Munson	.15
360 Joe Crede	.15
361 Denny Neagle	.15
362 Vance Wilson	.15
363 Neifi Perez	.15
364 Darryl Kile	.15
365 Jose Macias	.15
366 Michael Coleman	.15
367 Erubiel Durazo	.15
368 Darrin Fletcher	.15
369 Matt White	.15
370 Marvin Benard	.15
371 Brad Penny	.15
372 Chuck Finley	.15
373 Delino DeShields	.15
374 Adrian Brown	.15
375 Corey Koskie	.15
376 Kazuhiro Sasaki	.15
377 Brent Butler	.15
378 Paul Wilson	.15
379 Scott Williamson	.15
380 Mike Young	.15
381 Toby Hall	.15
382 Shane Reynolds	.15
383 Tom Goodwin	.15
384 Seth Etherton	.15
385 Billy Wagner	.15
386 Josh Phelps	.15
387 Kyle Lohse	.15
388 Jeremy Fikac	.15
389 Jorge Posada	.30
390 Bret Boone	.15
391 Angel Berroa	.15
392 Matt Mantei	.15
393 Alex Gonzalez	.15
394 Scott Strickland	.15
395 Charles Johnson	.15
396 Ramon Hernandez	.15
397 Damian Jackson	.15
398 Albert Pujols	1.50
399 Gary Bennett	.15
400 Edgar Martinez	.15
401 Carl Pavano	.15
402 Chris Gomez	.15
403 Jaret Wright	.15
404 Lance Berkman	.15
405 Robert Person	.15
406 Brook Fordyce	.15
407 Adam Pettyjohn	.15
408 Chris Carpenter	.15
409 Rey Ordonez	.15
410 Eric Gagne	.25
411 Damion Easley	.15
412 A.J. Burnett	.15
413 Aaron Boone	.15
414 J.D. Drew	.25
415 Kelly Stinnett	.15
416 Mark Quinn	.15
417 Brad Radke	.15
418 Jose Cruz Jr.	.15
419 Greg Maddux	1.00
420 Steve Cox	.15
421 Torii Hunter	.15
422 Sandy Alomar	.15
423 Barry Zito	.40
424 Bill Hall	.15
425 Marquis Grissom	.15
426 Rich Aurilia	.15
427 Royce Clayton	.15
428 Travis Fryman	.15
429 Pablo Ozuna	.15
430 David Dellucci	.15
431 Vernon Wells	.15
432 Gregg Zaun	.15
433 Alex Gonzalez	.15
434 Hideo Nomo	.40
435 Jeromy Burnitz	.15
436 Gary Sheffield	.25
437 Tino Martinez	.15
438 Tsuyoshi Shinjo	.15
439 Chan Ho Park	.15
440 Tony Clark	.15
441 Brad Fullmer	.15
442 Jason Giambi	.50
443 Billy Koch	.15
444 Mo Vaughn	.15
445 Alex Ochoa	.15
446 Darren Lewis	.15
447 John Rocker	.15
448 Scott Hatteberg	.15
449 Brady Anderson	.15
450 Chuck Knoblauch	.15
451 Pokey Reese	.15
452 Brian Jordan	.15

453 Albie Lopez	.15
454 David Bell	.15
455 Juan Gonzalez	.75
456 Terry Adams	.15
457 Kenny Lofton	.25
458 Shawn Estes	.15
459 Josh Fogg	.15
460 Dmitri Young	.15
461 Johnny Damon	.25
462 Chris Singleton	.15
463 Ricky Ledee	.15
464 Dustin Hermanson	.15
465 Aaron Sele	.15
466 Chris Stynes	.15
467 Matt Stairs	.15
468 Kevin Appier	.15
469 Omar Daal	.15
470 Moises Alou	.15
471 Juan Encarnacion	.15
472 Robin Ventura	.15
473 Eric Hinske	.15
474 Rondell White	.15
475 Carlos Pena	.15
476 Craig Paquette	.15
477 Marty Cordova	.15
478 Brett Tomko	.15
479 Reggie Sanders	.15
480 Roberto Alomar	.15
481 Jeff Cirillo	.15
482 Todd Zeile	.15
483 John Vander Wal	.15
484 Rick Helling	.15
485 Jeff D'Amico	.15
486 David Justice	.15
487 Jason Isringhausen	.15
488 Shigetoshi Hasegawa	.15
489 Eric Young	.15
490 David Wells	.15
491 Ruben Sierra	.15
492 Aaron Cook RC	.50
493 Takahito Nomura RC	.15
494 Austin Kearns	.50
495 Kazuhisa Ishii RC	2.00
496 Mark Teixeira	.50
497 Rene Reyes RC	.50
498 Tim Spooneybarger	.15
499 Ben Broussard	.15
500 Eric Cyr RC	.25
501 Anastacio Martinez RC	.50
502 Morgan Ensberg	.15
503 Steve Kent RC	.25
504 Franklin Nunez RC	.25
505 Adam Walker RC	.25
506 Anderson Machado RC	.15
507 Ryan Drese	.15
508 Luis Ugueto RC	.25
509 Jorge Nunez RC	.25
510 Colby Lewis	.15
511 Ron Calloway RC	.25
512 Hansel Izquierdo RC	.50
513 Jason Lane	.15
514 Rafael Soriano	.15
515 Jackson Melian	.15
516 Edwin Almonte RC	.50
517 Satoru Komiyama RC	.50
518 Corey Thurman RC	.25
519 Jorge De La Rosa RC	.50
520 Victor Martinez	.15
521 Dewan Brazleton	.15
522 Marlon Byrd	.50
523 Jae Weong Seo	.15
524 Orlando Hudson	.15
525 Sean Burroughs	.15
526 Ryan Langerhans	.15
527 David Kelton	.15
528 So Taguchi RC	.50
529 Tyler Walker	.15
530 Hank Blalock	.50
531 Mark Prior	.75
532 Yankee Stadium	.50
533 Fenway Park	.50
534 Wrigley Field	.50
535 Dodger Stadium	.15
536 Camden Yards	.15
537 PacBell Park	.15
538 Jacobs Field	.15
539 SAFECO Field	.15
540 Miller Field	.15

Mini

Mini (1-540):	8-15X

Production 50 Sets
Retail Exclusive

Tiffany

Stars (1-540):	4-8X

Production 200 Sets

Barry Bonds Career Highlights

	NM/M
Complete Set (10):	40.00
Common Bonds 1-3:	3.00

Common 4-6 inserted	
1:125 H.	4.00
7-9 1:250 H	6.00
#10 1:383	6.00

Barry Bonds Career Highlights Autographs

No Pricing
25 Sets Produced

Barry Bonds 600 HR Supers

	NM/M
Barry Bonds (Facsimile signature.)	55.00
Barry Bonds (Autograph w/bat chip.)	250.00

2002 Fleer Barry Bonds Chasing History

	NM/M
Barry Bonds	125.00

2002 Fleer Barry Bonds 4X MVP Super

	NM/M
Barry Bonds	15.00

Classic Cuts Autographs

		NM/M
Inserted 1:432		
LA-A	Luis Aparicio	15.00
RC-A	Ron Cey	8.00
HK-A	Harmon Killebrew	35.00
TL-A	Tommy Lasorda/ SP/35	
JM-A	Juan Marichal	15.00
GP-A	Gaylord Perry/ SP/225	15.00
PR-A	Phil Rizzuto/ SP/125	50.00
BR-A	Brooks Robinson/ SP/200	40.00

Classic Cuts
Game-Used

		NM/M
Common Player:		5.00
Inserted 1:24		
SA-P	Sparky Anderson/ Pants	5.00
HB-B	Hank Bauer/Bat	5.00
JB-J	Johnny Bench/Jsy	15.00
PB-B	Paul Blair/Bat	5.00
WB-B	Wade Boggs/Bat/99	20.00
WB-J	Wade Boggs/Jsy	10.00
BB-B	Bobby Bonds/Bat	5.00
BB-J	Bobby Bonds/Jsy	5.00
GB-B	George Brett/ Bat/250	30.00
GB-J	George Brett/ Jsy/250	30.00
SC-P	Steve Carlton/Pants	6.00
OC-P	Orlando Cepeda/ Pants	5.00
AD-J	Andre Dawson/Jsy	8.00
BD-B	Bill Dickey/Bat/200	20.00
LD-B	Larry Doby/Bat/250	10.00
DE-B	Dwight Evans/ Bat/250	10.00
DE-J	Dwight Evans/Jsy	5.00
RF-J	Rollie Fingers/Jsy	5.00
CF-B	Carlton Fisk/Bat	10.00
CF-J	Carlton Fisk/ Jsy/150	20.00
NF-B	Nellie Fox/Bat/200	20.00
SG-B	Steve Garvey/Bat	5.00
KG-B	Kirk Gibson/Bat	5.00
GH-B	Gil Hodges/Bat/200	15.00
CH-J	Jim Hunter/Jsy	10.00
BJ-J	Bo Jackson/Jsy	15.00
RJ-P	Reggie Jackson/ Pants	10.00
GK-B	George Kell/Bat/150	15.00
TK-B	Ted Kluszewski/ Bat/200	15.00
TK-P	Ted Kluszewski/ Pants	10.00
RM-P	Roger Maris/ Pants/200	60.00
EM-B	Eddie Mathews/ Bat/200	20.00
DM-B	Don Mattingly/ Bat/200	50.00
DM-J	Don Mattingly/Jsy	40.00
WM-J	Willie McCovey/ Jsy/300	10.00
PM-B	Paul Molitor/ Bat/200	25.00
JM-B	Joe Morgan/Bat/250	8.00
TM-P	Thurman Munson/ Pants/10	
EM-B	Eddie Murray/Bat	10.00
EM-J	Eddie Murray/Jsy	10.00
JP-J	Jim Palmer/Jsy/273	8.00
DP-B	Dave Parker/Bat	5.00
TP-B	Tony Perez/Bat/250	10.00
TP-J	Tony Perez/Jsy	8.00
LP-P	Lou Piniella/Pants	5.00
KP-J	Kirby Puckett/Jsy	15.00
JR-B	Jim Rice/Bat/225	8.00
JR-J	Jim Rice/Jsy/90	5.00
CR-BG	Cal Ripken Jr./ Btg Glv/100	75.00
CR-FG	Cal Ripken Jr./ Fld Glv/50	125.00
CR-J	Cal Ripken Jr./Jsy	35.00
CR-P	Cal Ripken Jr./ Pants/200	40.00
BR-B	Brooks Robinson/ Bat/250	15.00
NR-J	Nolan Ryan/Jsy	50.00
NR-P	Nolan Ryan/ Pants/200	60.00
RS-B	Ryne Sandberg/Bat	25.00
OS-J	Ozzie Smith/ Jsy/250	15.00
WS-B	Willie Stargell/ Bat/250	15.00
JT-J	Joe Torre/Jsy/125	15.00
AT-B	Alan Trammell/Bat	10.00
EW-J	Earl Weaver/Jsy	5.00
HW-P	Hoyt Wilhelm/ Pants/150	15.00
TW-B	Ted Williams/Bat	85.00
TW-P	Ted Williams/Pants	120.00
DW-B	Dave Winfield/Bat	8.00
DW-J	Dave Winfield/ Jsy/231	10.00
DW-P	Dave Winfield/Pants	8.00
RY-B	Robin Yount/Bat	15.00

Classic Cuts Game
Used Autographs

	NM/M
Varying quantities produced	

LA-B	Luis Aparicio/Bat/45	25.00
BR-B	Brooks Robinson/ Bat/45	80.00

Diamond Standouts

		NM/M
Complete Set (10):		40.00
Common Player:		2.00
Production 1,200 Sets		
1DS	Mike Piazza	4.00
2DS	Derek Jeter	8.00
3DS	Ken Griffey Jr.	4.00
4DS	Barry Bonds	8.00
5DS	Sammy Sosa	4.00
6DS	Alex Rodriguez	4.00
7DS	Ichiro Suzuki	4.00
8DS	Greg Maddux	3.00
9DS	Jason Giambi	2.00
10DS	Nomar Garciaparra	4.00

Golden Memories

		NM/M
Complete Set (15):		20.00
Common Player:		1.00
Inserted 1:24		
1GM	Frank Thomas	1.50
2GM	Derek Jeter	4.00
3GM	Albert Pujols	3.00
4GM	Barry Bonds	4.00
5GM	Alex Rodriguez	3.00
6GM	Randy Johnson	1.50
7GM	Jeff Bagwell	1.50
8GM	Greg Maddux	2.00
9GM	Ivan Rodriguez	1.00
10GM	Ichiro Suzuki	2.50
11GM	Mike Piazza	2.50
12GM	Pat Burrell	1.00
13GM	Rickey Henderson	1.50
14GM	Vladimir Guerrero	1.50
15GM	Sammy Sosa	2.50

Headliners

		NM/M
Complete Set (20):		10.00
Common Player:		.25
Inserted 1:8		
1HL	Randy Johnson	.75
2HL	Alex Rodriguez	1.50
3HL	Todd Helton	.75
4HL	Pedro J. Martinez	.75
5HL	Ichiro Suzuki	1.50
6HL	Vladimir Guerrero	.75
7HL	Derek Jeter	2.00
8HL	Adam Dunn	.40
9HL	Luis Gonzalez	.25
10HL	Kazuhiro Sasaki	.25
11HL	Sammy Sosa	1.25
12HL	Jason Giambi	.60
13HL	Ken Griffey Jr.	1.25
14HL	Roger Clemens	1.00
15HL	Brandon Duckworth	.25
16HL	Nomar Garciaparra	1.25
17HL	Bud Smith	.25
18HL	Juan Gonzalez	.75
19HL	Chipper Jones	1.00
20HL	Barry Bonds	2.00

Rookie Flashback

		NM/M
Complete Set (20):		6.00
Common Player:		.25
Inserted 1:3 Retail		
1RF	Bret Prinz	.25
2RF	Albert Pujols	2.00
3RF	C.C. Sabathia	.25
4RF	Ichiro Suzuki	1.50
5RF	Juan Cruz	.25
6RF	Jay Gibbons	.50
7RF	Bud Smith	.25
8RF	Johnny Estrada	.25
9RF	Roy Oswalt	.50
10RF	Tsuyoshi Shinjo	.25
11RF	Brandon Duckworth	.25

12RF	Jackson Melian	.25
13RF	Josh Beckett	1.00
14RF	Morgan Ensberg	.25
15RF	Brian Lawrence	.25
16RF	Eric Hinske	.25
17RF	Juan Uribe	.25
18RF	Matt White	.25
19RF	Junior Spivey	.25
20RF	Wilson Betemit	.25

Rookie Sensations

		NM/M
Complete Set (20):		40.00
Common Player:		2.00
Production 1,500 Sets		
1RS	Bret Prinz	2.00
2RS	Albert Pujols	10.00
3RS	C.C. Sabathia	2.00
4RS	Ichiro Suzuki	8.00
5RS	Juan Cruz	2.00
6RS	Jay Gibbons	3.00
7RS	Bud Smith	2.00
8RS	Johnny Estrada	2.00
9RS	Roy Oswalt	4.00
10RS	Tsuyoshi Shinjo	2.00
11RS	Brandon Duckworth	2.00
12RS	Jackson Melian	2.00
13RS	Josh Beckett	4.00
14RS	Morgan Ensberg	2.00
15RS	Brian Lawrence	2.00
16RS	Eric Hinske	2.00
17RS	Juan Uribe	2.00
18RS	Matt White	2.00
19RS	Junior Spivey	2.00
20RS	Wilson Betemit	2.00

Then and Now

		NM/M
Common Card:		5.00
Production 275 Sets		
1TN	Eddie Mathews, Chipper Jones	5.00
2TN	Willie McCovey, Barry Bonds	15.00
3TN	Johnny Bench, Mike Piazza	5.00
4TN	Ernie Banks, Alex Rodriguez	8.00
5TN	Rickey Henderson, Ichiro Suzuki	10.00
6TN	Tom Seaver, Roger Clemens	10.00
7TN	Juan Marichal, Pedro J. Martinez	5.00
8TN	Reggie Jackson, Derek Jeter	15.00
9TN	Nolan Ryan, Kerry Wood	20.00
10TN	Joe Morgan, Ken Griffey Jr.	10.00

2002 Fleer Box Score

		NM/M
Complete Set (310):		
Common Player:		.25
Common (126-150):		3.00
Production 2,499		
Complete Rising Star Set (40):		30.00
Common (151-190):		1.00
Complete Intl. Set (40):		18.00
Common (191-230):		1.00
Complete All-Star Set (40):		20.00
Common (231-270):		1.00
Comp. Cooperstown Set (40):		30.00
Common Cooperstown (271-310):		1.00
Print run for all subsets is 2,950.		
Pack (7):		5.00
Box (18 Packs + Supp. Box):		80.00
1	Derek Jeter	2.00
2	Kevin Brown	.25
3	Nomar Garciaparra	1.25
4	Mark Buehrle	.25
5	Mike Piazza	1.25
6	David Justice	.25
7	Tino Martinez	.25
8	Paul Konerko	.25
9	Larry Walker	.25
10	Ben Sheets	.25
11	Mike Cameron	.25
12	David Wells	.25
13	Barry Zito	.35
14	Pat Burrell	.45
15	Mike Mussina	.50
16	Bud Smith	.25
17	Brian Jordan	.25
18	Chris Singleton	.25
19	Daryle Ward	.25
20	Russ Ortiz	.25
21	Jason Kendall	.25
22	Kerry Wood	.65
23	Jeff Weaver	.25
24	Tony Armas	.25
25	Toby Hall	.25
26	Brian Giles	.25
27	Juan Pierre	.25
28	Ken Griffey Jr.	1.25
29	Mike Sweeney	.25
30	John Smoltz	.25
31	Sean Casey	.35
32	Jeremy Giambi	.25
33	Mike Lieberthal	.25
34	Rich Aurilia	.25
35	Matt Lawton	.25
36	Dmitri Young	.25
37	Wade Miller	.25
38	Jason Giambi	.65
39	Jeff Cirillo	.25
40	Mark Grace	.35
41	Frank Thomas	.75
42	Preston Wilson	.25
43	Brad Radke	.25
44	Greg Maddux	1.00
45	Adam Dunn	.50
46	Roy Oswalt	.35
47	Troy Glaus	.75
48	Edgar Martinez	.25
49	Billy Koch	.25
50	Chipper Jones	1.00
51	Lance Berkman	.25
52	Shannon Stewart	.25
53	Eddie Guardado	.25
54	C.C. Sabathia	.25
55	Craig Biggio	.25
56	Roger Clemens	1.00
57	Jimmy Rollins	.25
58	Carlos Delgado	.50
59	Tony Clark	.25
60	Mike Hampton	.25
61	Jeromy Burnitz	.25
62	Jorge Posada	.35
63	Todd Helton	.75
64	Richie Sexson	.25
65	Ryan Klesko	.25
66	Cliff Floyd	.25
67	Eric Milton	.25
68	Scott Rolen	.65
69	Steve Finley	.25
70	Ray Durham	.25
71	Jeff Bagwell	.75
72	Geoff Jenkins	.25
73	Jamie Moyer	.25
74	David Eckstein	.25
75	Johnny Damon	.40
76	Pokey Reese	.25
77	Mo Vaughn	.25
78	Trevor Hoffman	.25
79	Albert Pujols	1.50
80	Ben Grieve	.25
81	Matt Morris	.25
82	Aubrey Huff	.25
83	Darin Erstad	.60
84	Garret Anderson	.25

85	Jacque Jones	.25
86	Matt Anderson	.25
87	Jose Vidro	.25
88	Carlos Lee	.25
89	Jeff Suppan	.25
90	Al Leiter	.25
91	Jeff Kent	.25
92	Randy Johnson	.75
93	Moises Alou	.25
94	Bobby Higginson	.25
95	Phil Nevin	.25
96	Alex Rodriguez	1.50
97	Luis Gonzalez	.40
98	A.J. Burnett	.25
99	Torii Hunter	.25
100	Ivan Rodriguez	.60
101	Pedro J. Martinez	.75
102	Brady Anderson	.25
103	Paul LoDuca	.25
104	Eric Chavez	.35
105	Tim Salmon	.35
106	Javier Vazquez	.25
107	Bret Boone	.25
108	Greg Vaughn	.25
109	J.D. Drew	.40
110	Jay Gibbons	.25
111	Jim Thome	.25
112	Shawn Green	.40
113	Tim Hudson	.35
114	John Olerud	.25
115	Raul Mondesi	.25
116	Curt Schilling	.50
117	Corey Patterson	.25
118	Robert Fick	.25
119	Corey Koskie	.25
120	Juan Gonzalez	.75
121	Jerry Hairston Jr.	.25
122	Gary Sheffield	.40
123	Mark Mulder	.25
124	Barry Bonds	2.00
125	Jim Edmonds	.25
126	Franklyn German RC	3.00
127	Rodrigo Rosario RC	3.00
128	Ryan Ludwick RC	3.00
129	Jorge de la Rosa RC	4.00
130	Jason Lane RC	3.00
131	Brian Mallette RC	3.00
132	Chris Baker RC	3.00
133	Kyle Kane RC	3.00
134	Doug DeVore RC	3.00
135	Raul Chavez RC	3.00
136	Miguel Asencio RC	3.00
137	Luis Garcia RC	3.00
138	Nick Johnson RC	3.00
139	Michael Crudale RC	3.00
140	P.J. Bevis RC	3.00
141	Josh Hancock RC	3.00
142	Jeremy Lambert RC	3.00
143	Ben Broussard RC	3.00
144	John Ennis RC	3.00
145	Wilson Valdez RC	3.00
146	Eric Good RC	3.00
147	Elio Serrano RC	3.00
148	Jaime Cerda RC	3.00
149	Hank Blalock	5.00
150	Brandon Duckworth	1.50
151	Drew Henson	1.50
152	Kazuhisa Ishii RC	3.00
153	Earl Snyder RC	1.00
154	J.M. Gold	1.00
155	Satoru Komiyama RC	1.00
156	Marlon Byrd RC	1.00
157	So Taguchi RC	2.00
158	Eric Hinske	1.00
159	Mark Prior	3.00
160	Jorge Padilla RC	1.50
161	Rene Reyes RC	1.00
162	Jorge Nunez RC	1.00
163	Nelson Castro RC	1.00
164	Anderson Machado RC	2.00
165	Mark Teixeira	2.00
166	Orlando Hudson	1.00
167	Edwin Almonte RC	1.00
168	Luis Ugueto RC	1.00
169	Felix Escalona RC	1.00
170	Ron Calloway RC	1.00
171	Kevin Mench	1.00
172	Takahito Nomura RC	1.00
173	Sean Burroughs	1.00
174	Steve Kent RC	1.00
175	Jorge Sosa RC	1.00
176	Mike Moriarty RC	1.00
177	Carlos Pena	1.00
178	Anastacio Martinez RC	1.00
179	Reed Johnson RC	1.00
180	Juan Brito RC	1.00
181	Wilson Betemit	1.00
182	Mike Rivera	1.00
183	David Espinosa	1.00
184	Todd Donovan RC	1.00
185	Morgan Ensberg	1.00
186	Dewon Brazelton	1.00
187	Ben Howard RC	1.00
188	Austin Kearns	2.00

189	Josh Beckett	2.00
190	Brandon Backe RC	1.50
191	Ichiro Suzuki	4.00
192	Tsuyoshi Shinjo	1.00
193	Hideo Nomo	2.00
194	Kazuhiro Sasaki	1.00
195	Edgardo Alfonzo	1.00
196	Chan Ho Park	1.00
197	Carlos Hernandez	1.00
198	Byung Kim	1.00
199	Omar Vizquel	1.00
200	Freddy Garcia	1.00
201	Richard Hidalgo	1.00
202	Magglio Ordonez	1.00
203	Bobby Abreu	1.00
204	Roger Cedeno	1.00
205	Andruw Jones	2.00
206	Mariano Rivera	1.50
207	Jose Macias	1.00
208	Orlando Hernandez	1.00
209	Rafael Palmeiro	2.00
210	Danys Baez	1.00
211	Bernie Williams	1.25
212	Carlos Beltran	3.00
213	Roberto Alomar	1.50
214	Jose Cruz Jr.	1.00
215	Ryan Dempster	1.00
216	Erubiel Durazo	1.00
217	Carlos Pena	1.00
218	Sammy Sosa	4.00
219	Adrian Beltre	1.50
220	Aramis Ramirez	1.00
221	Alfonso Soriano	2.00
222	Vladimir Guerrero	2.00
223	Juan Uribe	1.00
224	Cristian Guzman	1.00
225	Manny Ramirez	2.00
226	Juan Cruz	1.00
227	Ramon Ortiz	1.00
228	Juan Encarnacion	1.00
229	Bartolo Colon	1.00
230	Miguel Tejada	1.25
231	Cal Ripken Jr.	6.00
232	Derek Jeter	6.00
233	Pedro J. Martinez	2.00
234	Roberto Alomar	1.50
235	Sandy Alomar	1.00
236	Mike Piazza	4.00
237	Jeff Conine	1.00
238	Fred McGriff	1.00
239	Kirby Puckett	3.00
240	Ken Griffey Jr.	4.00
241	Roger Clemens	3.50
242	Joe Morgan	1.00
243	Willie McCovey	1.00
244	Brooks Robinson	1.00
245	Juan Marichal	1.00
246	Todd Helton	2.00
247	Alex Rodriguez	5.00
248	Barry Bonds	6.00
249	Nomar Garciaparra	4.00
250	Jeff Bagwell	2.00
251	Kenny Lofton	1.00
252	Barry Larkin	1.00
253	Tom Glavine	1.50
254	Magglio Ordonez	1.00
255	Randy Johnson	2.00
256	Chipper Jones	3.00
257	Kevin Brown	1.00
258	Rickey Henderson	2.00
259	Greg Maddux	3.00
260	Jim Thome	1.00
261	Rafael Palmeiro	1.50
262	Frank Thomas	2.00
263	Manny Ramirez	2.00
264	Travis Fryman	1.00
265	Gary Sheffield	1.25
266	Bernie Williams	1.25
267	Matt Williams	1.00
268	Ivan Rodriguez	1.50
269	Mike Mussina	1.25
270	Larry Walker	1.00
271	Jim Palmer	1.00
272	Cal Ripken Jr.	6.00
273	Brooks Robinson	1.00
274	Bobby Doerr	1.00
275	Ernie Banks	2.00
276	Fergie Jenkins	1.00
277	Luis Aparicio	1.00
278	Hoyt Wilhelm	1.00
279	Tom Seaver	1.50
280	Joe Morgan	1.00
281	Lou Boudreau	1.00
282	Larry Doby	1.00
283	Jim Bunning	1.00
284	George Kell	1.00
285	Pee Wee Reese	1.50
286	Eddie Mathews	1.00
287	Robin Yount	2.00
288	Rod Carew	1.00
289	Monte Irvin	1.00
290	Yogi Berra	2.00
291	Whitey Ford	2.00
292	Reggie Jackson	2.00

293	Rollie Fingers	1.00
294	Jim "Catfish" Hunter	1.00
295	Richie Ashburn	1.00
296	Willie Stargell	1.00
297	Ralph Kiner	1.00
298	Orlando Cepeda	1.00
299	Juan Marichal	1.00
300	Gaylord Perry	1.00
301	Willie McCovey	1.00
302	Red Schoendienst	1.00
303	Nolan Ryan	8.00
304	Bob Gibson	1.00
305	Al Kaline	1.00
306	Harmon Killebrew	1.00
307	Stan Musial	3.00
308	Phil Rizzuto	1.00
309	Mike Schmidt	4.00
310	Enos Slaughter	1.00

First Edition

Cards (1-125):	4-8X
Cards (126-150):	.5-1X
Cards (151-310):	1-2X
Production 100 Sets	

All-Star Lineup

	NM/M
Common Card:	15.00
1:All-Stars Box	
Derek Jeter, Nomar Garciaparra, Alex Rodriguez, Joe Morgan, Willie McCovey, Brooks Robinson, Alex Rodriguez, Ivan Rodriguez, Rafael Palmeiro	50.00
	15.00
	20.00
Derek Jeter, Mike Mussina, Bernie Williams, Barry Bonds, Cal Ripken Jr., Frank Thomas	35.00
	60.00
Cal Ripken Jr., Derek Jeter, Roberto Alomar, Pedro J. Martinez	60.00
Mike Piazza, Barry Bonds, Ken Griffey Jr., Jeff Bagwell, Roger Clemens, Greg Maddux, Randy Johnson, Pedro J. Martinez, Todd Helton, Roberto Alomar, Alex Rodriguez, Chipper Jones, Ken Griffey Jr., Barry Bonds, Larry Walker, Manny Ramirez	40.00
	35.00
	25.00
	35.00

Amazing Greats

	NM/M
Complete Set (20):	20.00
Common Player:	.50
Inserted 1:5	
1AG	Derek Jeter	4.00
2AG	Barry Bonds	4.00
3AG	Mike Piazza	2.50
4AG	Ivan Rodriguez	.75
5AG	Todd Helton	1.00
6AG	Nomar Garciaparra	2.50
7AG	Jim Thome	.50
8AG	Bernie Williams	.50
9AG	Kazuhiro Sasaki	.50
10AG	Torii Hunter	.50
11AG	Bret Boone	.50
12AG	Tim Hudson	.50
13AG	Randy Johnson	1.00
14AG	Rafael Palmeiro	.75
15AG	Scott Rolen	.75
16AG	Carlos Delgado	.75
17AG	Chipper Jones	2.00
18AG	Lance Berkman	.50
19AG	Frank Thomas	1.00
20AG	Greg Maddux	2.00

Amazing Greats Single Swatch

	NM/M
Common Player:	5.00

Inserted 1:13	
Dual Swatches:	1-2X
Inserted 1:90	
Derek Jeter	20.00
Barry Bonds	20.00
Mike Piazza	10.00
Ivan Rodriguez	8.00
Nomar Garciaparra	15.00
Jim Thome/bat	10.00
Bernie Williams	8.00
Kazuhiro Sasaki	5.00
Torii Hunter	6.00
Bret Boone	5.00
Rafael Palmeiro	8.00
Scott Rolen	8.00
Carlos Delgado	8.00
Lance Berkman	5.00
Frank Thomas	8.00
Greg Maddux	10.00

Amazing Greats Patch

	NM/M
Common Player:	15.00
Production 150 Sets	
Derek Jeter	50.00
Barry Bonds	50.00
Mike Piazza	25.00
Ivan Rodriguez	25.00
Nomar Garciaparra	40.00
Bernie Williams	25.00
Kazuhiro Sasaki	15.00
Torii Hunter	25.00
Bret Boone	15.00
Rafael Palmeiro	25.00
Scott Rolen	25.00
Carlos Delgado	20.00
Lance Berkman	15.00
Frank Thomas	25.00
Greg Maddux	30.00

Bat Rack

	NM/M
Common Card:	20.00
Production 300 Sets	
1BR	Derek Jeter, Alfonso Soriano, Bernie Williams	60.00
2BR	Mike Piazza, Roberto Alomar, Mo Vaughn	30.00
3BR	Jeff Bagwell, Lance Berkman, Craig Biggio	30.00
4BR	Eric Chavez, Miguel Tejada, Carlos Pena	15.00
5BR	Alex Rodriguez, Ivan Rodriguez, Rafael Palmeiro	30.00
6BR	Chipper Jones, Gary Sheffield, Andruw Jones	20.00
7BR	Carlos Delgado, Jim Thome, Frank Thomas	20.00
8BR	Derek Jeter, Nomar Garciaparra, Alex Rodriguez	60.00
9BR	Barry Bonds, Adam Dunn, Chipper Jones	35.00
10BR	Magglio Ordonez, Juan Gonzalez, Manny Ramirez	20.00

Bat Rack Quad

	NM/M
Common Card	25.00
Production 150 Sets	
Torii Hunter, Cristian Guzman, Frank Thomas, Magglio Ordonez	25.00
Alex Rodriguez, Ivan Rodriguez, Eric Chavez, Miguel Tejada	40.00
Mike Piazza, Roberto Alomar, Alfonso Soriano, Derek Jeter	80.00
Barry Bonds, Lance Berkman, Alex Rodriguez, Nomar Garciaparra	75.00
Barry Bonds, Chipper Jones, Mike Piazza, Ivan Rodriguez	75.00
Derek Jeter, Miguel Tejada, Nomar Garciaparra, Alex Rodriguez	75.00

Roberto Alomar,
Mo Vaughn, Jeff Bagwell,
Craig Biggio   25.00
Jim Palmer,
Carlos Delgado,
Jim Thome,
Frank Thomas   25.00
Magglio Ordonez,
Bernie Williams,
Juan Gonzalez,
Manny Ramirez   25.00
Chipper Jones,
Adam Dunn, Jeff Bagwell,
Mo Vaughn   25.00
Alex Rodriguez,
Jim Palmer,
Bernie Williams,
Alfonso Soriano   40.00
Carlos Pena, Eric Chavez,
Carlos Delgado,
Juan Gonzalez   20.00
Adam Dunn,
Lance Berkman,
Jim Thome,
Manny Ramirez   25.00

Box Score Debuts

	NM/M
Complete Set (15):	40.00
Common Player:	2.50
Production 2,002 Sets	
1 Hank Blalock	6.00
2 Eric Hinske	3.00
3 Kazuhisa Ishii	5.00
4 Sean Burroughs	3.00
5 Andres Torres	2.50
6 Satoru Komiyama	2.50
7 Mark Prior	10.00
8 Kevin Mench	2.50
9 Austin Kearns	3.00
10 Earl Snyder	2.50
11 Jon Rauch	2.50
12 Jason Lane	2.50
13 Ben Howard	2.50
14 Bobby Hill	2.50
15 Dennis Tankersley	2.50

Classic Miniatures

	NM/M
Complete Set (40):	25.00
Stars:	1.5-3X Base Card
Production 2,950 Sets	
One set per classic mini box.	
First Editions:	4-8X
Production 100 Sets	

Classic Miniatures Game-Used

	NM/M
Common Player:	6.00
One per Classic Mini box.	
Derek Jeter/Bat	20.00
Mike Piazza/Jsy	10.00
Adam Dunn/Jsy	6.00
Chipper Jones/Bat	10.00
Roger Clemens/Jsy	15.00
Alex Rodriguez/Jsy	10.00
Pedro Martinez/Jsy	10.00
Jim Thome/Bat	10.00
Curt Schilling/Jsy	8.00
Barry Bonds/Bat	20.00

Hall of Fame Material

	NM/M
Common Player:	8.00
1:Cooperstown Box	
Jim Palmer/Jsy	8.00
Cal Ripken Jr./Jsy	25.00
Brooks Robinson/Bat	10.00
Joe Morgan/Bat	8.00
Eddie Mathews/Bat	10.00
Robin Yount/Jsy	15.00
Reggie Jackson/Jsy	10.00
"Catfish" Hunter/Jsy	8.00
Willie McCovey/Jsy	8.00
Nolan Ryan/Jsy	30.00

Press Clippings

	NM/M
Complete Set (20):	90.00
Common Player:	4.00
Inserted 1:90	
1PC Mark Mulder	4.00
2PC Curt Schilling	6.00
3PC Alfonso Soriano	7.50
4PC Jeff Bagwell	7.50
5PC J.D. Drew	5.00
6PC Pedro J. Martinez	7.50
7PC Bobby Abreu	4.00
8PC Alex Rodriguez	12.00
9PC Mike Sweeney	4.00
10PC Carlos Pena	4.00

11PC Josh Beckett	6.00
12PC Roger Clemens	9.00
13PC Manny Ramirez	7.50
14PC Adam Dunn	6.00
15PC Kazuhisa Ishii	4.00
16PC Ken Griffey Jr.	10.00
17PC Sammy Sosa	10.00
18PC Ichiro Suzuki	9.00
19PC Albert Pujols	15.00
20PC Troy Glaus	7.50

Press Clippings Game-Used

	NM/M
Common Player:	5.00
Inserted 1:13	
Mark Mulder/Jsy	5.00
Curt Schilling/Jsy	8.00
Alfonso Soriano/Bat	10.00
Jeff Bagwell/Jsy	8.00
J.D. Drew/Jsy	5.00
Pedro Martinez/Jsy	10.00
Bobby Abreu/Jsy	5.00
Alex Rodriguez/Jsy	10.00
Mike Sweeney/Jsy	5.00
Carlos Pena/Jsy	5.00
Josh Beckett/Jsy	8.00
Manny Ramirez/Jsy	10.00
Adam Dunn/Jsy	6.00
Kazuhisa Ishii/Jsy	10.00
Ken Griffey Jr./Base	10.00
Sammy Sosa/Base	15.00
Ichiro Suzuki/Base	15.00
Albert Pujols/Base	10.00
Troy Glaus/Base	5.00
Roger Clemens/Jsy/40	

Wave of the Future

	NM/M
Common Player:	4.00
1:Rising Stars Box	
1WF Drew Henson/Bat	5.00
2WF Kazuhisa Ishii/Bat	5.00
3WF Marlon Byrd/Jsy	4.00
4WF So Taguchi/Bat	4.00
5WF Jorge Padilla/ Pants/75	10.00
6WF Rene Reyes/Jsy	8.00
7WF Mark Teixeira/100	10.00
8WF Carlos Pena/Bat	6.00
9WF Austin Kearns/Pants	6.00
10WF Josh Beckett/Jsy/50	15.00

World Piece

	NM/M
Common Player:	4.00
1:International Box	
1WP Ichiro Suzuki/Base	20.00
2WP Tsuyoshi Shinjo/Bat	4.00
3WP Hideo Nomo/Jsy	20.00
4WP Kazuhiro Sasaki/Jsy	4.00
5WP Chan Ho Park/Jsy	4.00
6WP Magglio Ordonez/ Jsy	6.00
7WP Andruw Jones/Jsy	8.00
8WP Rafael Palmeiro/Jsy	10.00
9WP Bernie Williams/Jsy	10.00
10WP Roberto Alomar/Bat	6.00

2002 Fleer E-X

	NM/M
Complete Set (140):	
Common Player:	.25
Common SP (101-125):	3.00
Common (126-140):	5.00
Inserted 1:24	
Pack (4):	2.50
Box (40):	40.00
1 Alex Rodriguez	1.50
2 Albert Pujols	1.50
3 Ken Griffey Jr.	1.25
4 Vladimir Guerrero	.75

5 Sammy Sosa	1.25
6 Ichiro Suzuki	1.25
7 Jorge Posada	.35
8 Matt Williams	.25
9 Adrian Beltre	.40
10 Pat Burrell	.40
11 Roger Cedeno	.25
12 Tony Clark	.25
13 Steve Finley	.25
14 Rafael Furcal	.25
15 Rickey Henderson	.75
16 Richard Hidalgo	.25
17 Jason Kendall	.25
18 Tino Martinez	.25
19 Scott Rolen	.65
20 Shannon Stewart	.25
21 Jose Vidro	.25
22 Preston Wilson	.25
23 Raul Mondesi	.25
24 Lance Berkman	.25
25 Rick Ankiel	.25
26 Kevin Brown	.25
27 Jeromy Burnitz	.25
28 Jeff Cirillo	.25
29 Carl Everett	.25
30 Eric Chavez	.35
31 Freddy Garcia	.25
32 Mark Grace	.35
33 David Justice	.25
34 Fred McGriff	.25
35 Mike Mussina	.50
36 John Olerud	.25
37 Magglio Ordonez	.25
38 Curt Schilling	.50
39 Aaron Sele	.25
40 Robin Ventura	.25
41 Adam Dunn	.50
42 Jeff Bagwell	.75
43 Barry Bonds	2.00
44 Roger Clemens	1.00
45 Cliff Floyd	.25
46 Jason Giambi	.50
47 Juan Gonzalez	.75
48 Luis Gonzalez	.35
49 Cristian Guzman	.25
50 Todd Helton	.75
51 Derek Jeter	2.00
52 Rafael Palmeiro	.65
53 Mike Sweeney	.25
54 Ben Grieve	.25
55 Phil Nevin	.25
56 Mike Piazza	1.25
57 Moises Alou	.25
58 Ivan Rodriguez	.65
59 Manny Ramirez	.75
60 Brian Giles	.25
61 Jim Thome	.25
62 Larry Walker	.25
63 Bobby Abreu	.25
64 Troy Glaus	.75
65 Garret Anderson	.25
66 Roberto Alomar	.40
67 Bret Boone	.25
68 Marty Cardova	.25
69 Craig Biggio	.25
70 Omar Vizquel	.25
71 Jermaine Dye	.25
72 Darin Erstad	.60
73 Carlos Delgado	.50
74 Nomar Garciaparra	1.25
75 Greg Maddux	1.00
76 Tom Glavine	.40
77 Frank Thomas	.75
78 Shawn Green	.40
79 Bobby Higginson	.25
80 Jeff Kent	.25
81 Chuck Knoblauch	.25
82 Paul Konerko	.25
83 Carlos Lee	.25
84 Jon Lieber	.25
85 Paul LoDuca	.25
86 Mike Lowell	.25
87 Edgar Martinez	.25
88 Doug Mientkiewicz	.25
89 Pedro J. Martinez	.75
90 Randy Johnson	.75
91 Aramis Ramirez	.25
92 J.D. Drew	.40
93 Chris Richard	.25
94 Jimmy Rollins	.50
95 Ryan Klesko	.25
96 Gary Sheffield	.40
97 Chipper Jones	1.00
98 Greg Vaughn	.25
99 Mo Vaughn	.25
100 Bernie Williams	.35
101 John Foster/2,999 RC	3.00
102 Jorge De La Rosa/ 2,999 RC	4.00
103 Edwin Almonte/ 2,999 RC	3.00
104 Chris Booker/2,999 RC	3.00
105 Victor Alvarez/ 2,999 RC	3.00
106 Clifford Bartosh/ 2,999 RC	3.00

107 Felix Escalona/ 2,999 RC	3.00
108 Corey Thurman/ 2,999 RC	3.00
109 Kazuhisa Ishii/ 2,999 RC	6.00
110 Miguel Ascencio/ 2,999 RC	3.00
111 P.J. Bevis/2,999 RC	3.00
112 Gustavo Chacin/ 2,499 RC	3.00
113 Steve Kent/2,499 RC	3.00
114 Takahito Nomura/ 2,499 RC	3.00
115 Adam Walker/2,499 RC	3.00
116 So Taguchi/2,499 RC	5.00
117 Reed Johnson/ 2,499 RC	5.00
118 Rodrigo Rosario/ 2,499 RC	3.00
119 Luis Martinez/2,499 RC	4.00
120 Satoru Komiyama/ 2,499 RC	3.00
121 Sean Burroughs/1,999	3.00
122 Hank Blalock/1,999	5.00
123 Marlon Byrd/1,999	3.00
124 Nick Johnson/1,999	3.00
125 Mark Teixeira/1,999	5.00
126 David Espinosa	3.00
127 Adrian Burnside RC	3.00
128 Mark Corey RC	3.00
129 Matt Thornton	3.00
130 Dane Sardinha	3.00
131 Juan Rivera	3.00
132 Austin Kearns	5.00
134 Ben Broussard	3.00
135 Orlando Hudson	3.00
136 Carlos Pena	3.00
137 Kenny Kelly	3.00
138 Bill Hall	3.00
139 Ron Chiavacci	3.00
140 Mark Prior	6.00

Quantity produced listed		
19	Scott Rolen/Bat/19	45.00
22	Preston Wilson/ Bat/22	15.00
24	Lance Berkman/ Bat/24	20.00
25	Rick Ankiel/Jsy/25	15.00
26	Kevin Brown/Jsy/26	20.00
27	Jeromy Burnitz/ Bat/27	20.00
28	Jeff Cirillo/Jsy/28	15.00
29	Carl Everett/Jsy/29	15.00
30	Eric Chavez/Bat/30	20.00
31	Freddy Garcia/Jsy/31	15.00
32	Mark Grace/Jsy/32	20.00
33	David Justice/Jsy/33	15.00
34	Fred McGriff/Jsy/34	15.00
35	Mike Mussina/Jsy/35	25.00
36	John Olerud/Jsy/36	10.00
37	Magglio Ordonez/ Jsy/37	15.00
38	Curt Schilling/Jsy/38	20.00
39	Aaron Sele/Jsy/39	10.00
40	Robin Ventura/Jsy/40	10.00
41	Adam Dunn/Bat/41	15.00
42	Jeff Bagwell/Jsy/42	20.00
43	Barry Bonds/ Pants/43	75.00
44	Roger Clemens/ Bat/44	50.00
45	Cliff Floyd/Bat/45	10.00
46	Jason Giambi/ Base/46	15.00
47	Juan Gonzalez/ Jsy/47	15.00
48	Luis Gonzalez/ Base/48	10.00
49	Cristian Guzman/ Bat/49	10.00
50	Todd Helton/Base/50	15.00
51	Derek Jeter/Bat/51	60.00
52	Rafael Palmeiro/ Bat/52	20.00
53	Mike Sweeney/ Bat/53	
54	Ben Grieve/Jsy/54	5.00
55	Phil Nevin/Bat/55	8.00
56	Mike Piazza/Base/56	20.00
57	Moises Alou/Bat/57	10.00
58	Ivan Rodriguez/ Jsy/58	15.00
59	Manny Ramirez/ Base/59	10.00
60	Brian Giles Bat/60	10.00
61	Jim Thome/61	15.00
62	Larry Walker/62	5.00
63	Bobby Abreu/63	5.00
64	Troy Glaus/64	8.00
65	Garret Anderson/65	8.00
66	Roberto Alomar/66	8.00
67	Bret Boone/67	5.00
68	Marty Cordova/68	5.00
69	Craig Biggio/69	5.00
70	Omar Vizquel/70	4.00

71	Jermaine Dye/71	4.00
72	Darin Erstad/72	5.00
73	Carlos Delgado/73	6.00
74	Nomar Garciaparra/74	15.00
75	Greg Maddux/75	15.00
76	Tom Glavine/76	5.00
77	Frank Thomas/77	8.00
78	Shawn Green/78	6.00
79	Bobby Higginson/79	4.00
80	Jeff Kent/80	5.00
81	Chuck Knoblauch/81	4.00
82	Paul Konerko/82	5.00
83	Carlos Lee/83	5.00
84	Jon Lieber/84	5.00
85	Paul LoDuca/85	5.00
86	Mike Lowell/86	6.00
87	Edgar Martinez/87	6.00
88	Doug Mientkiewicz/88	5.00
89	Pedro J. Martinez/89	10.00
90	Randy Johnson/90	10.00
91	Aramis Ramirez/91	6.00
92	J.D. Drew/92	6.00
93	Chris Richard/93	4.00
94	Jimmy Rollins/94	10.00
95	Ryan Klesko/95	6.00
96	Gary Sheffield/96	6.00
97	Chipper Jones/97	10.00
98	Gary Vaughn/98	4.00
99	Mo Vaughn/99	5.00
100	Bernie Williams/100	6.00
101	John Foster NT/101	4.00
102	Jorge De La Rosa NT/102	4.00
103	Edwin Almonte NT/103	4.00
104	Chris Booker NT/104	4.00
105	Victor Alvarez NT/105	4.00
106	Clifford Bartosh NT/106	4.00
107	Felix Escalona NT/107	4.00
108	Corey Thurman NT/108	4.00
109	Kazuhisa Ishii NT/109	10.00
110	Miguel Asencio NT/110	4.00
111	P.J. Bevis NT/111	4.00
112	Gustavo Chacin NT/112	4.00
113	Steve Kent NT/113	4.00
114	Takahito Nomura NT/114	4.00
115	Adam Walker NT/115	4.00
116	So Taguchi NT/116	6.00
117	Reed Johnson NT/117	6.00
118	Rodrigo Rosario NT/118	4.00
119	Luis Martinez NT/119	4.00
120	Satoru Komiyama NT/120	4.00
121	Sean Burroughs NT/121	5.00
122	Hank Blalock NT/122	6.00
123	Marlon Byrd NT/123	4.00
124	Nick Johnson NT/124	4.00
125	Mark Teixeira NT/125	6.00

Essential Credentials Future

NM/M

Quantity produced listed
1	Alex Rodriguez/Jsy/60	30.00
2	Albert Pujols/Base/59	25.00
3	Ken Griffey Jr./Base/58	20.00
4	Vladimir Guerrero/Base/57	15.00
5	Sammy Sosa/Base/56	25.00
6	Ichiro Suzuki/Base/55	40.00
7	Jorge Posada/Bat/54	12.00

8	Matt Williams/Bat/53	8.00
9	Adrian Beltre/Bat/52	8.00
10	Pat Burrell/Bat/51	10.00
11	Roger Cedeno/Bat/50	8.00
12	Tony Clark/Bat/49	8.00
13	Steve Finley/Bat/48	8.00
14	Rafael Furcal/Bat/47	12.00
15	Rickey Henderson/Bat/46	20.00
16	Richard Hidalgo/Bat/45	10.00
17	Jason Kendall/Bat/44	10.00
18	Tino Martinez/Bat/43	15.00
19	Scott Rolen/Bat/42	20.00
20	Shannon Stewart/Bat/41	10.00
21	Jose Vidro Bat/40	10.00
22	Preston Wilson/Bat/39	10.00
23	Raul Mondesi/Bat/38	10.00
24	Lance Berkman/Bat/37	10.00
25	Rick Ankiel/Jsy/36	8.00
26	Kevin Brown/Jsy/35	10.00
27	Jeromy Burnitz/Bat/34	8.00
28	Jeff Cirillo/Jsy/33	8.00
29	Carl Everett/Jsy/32	8.00
30	Eric Chavez/Bat/31	10.00
31	Freddy Garcia/Jsy/30	10.00
32	Mark Grace/Jsy/29	20.00
33	David Justice/Jsy/28	15.00
34	Fred McGriff/Jsy/27	15.00
35	Mike Mussina/Jsy/26	
36	John Olerud/Jsy/25	
37	Magglio Ordonez/Jsy/24	15.00
38	Curt Schilling Jsy/23	30.00
61	Jim Thome/125	8.00
62	Larry Walker/124	4.00
63	Bobby Abreu/123	4.00
64	Troy Glaus/122	6.00
65	Garret Anderson/121	6.00
66	Roberto Alomar/120	6.00
67	Bret Boone/119	6.00
68	Marty Cordova/118	4.00
69	Craig Biggio/117	4.00
70	Omar Vizquel/116	4.00
71	Jermaine Dye/115	4.00
72	Darin Erstad/114	4.00
73	Carlos Delgado/113	6.00
74	Nomar Garciaparra/112	10.00
75	Greg Maddux/111	10.00
76	Tom Glavine/110	6.00
77	Frank Thomas/109	6.00
78	Shawn Green/108	8.00
79	Bobby Higginson/107	3.00
80	Jeff Kent/106	4.00
81	Chuck Knoblauch/105	3.00
82	Paul Konerko/104	3.00
83	Carlos Lee/103	3.00
84	Jon Lieber/102	3.00
85	Paul LoDuca/101	3.00
86	Mike Lowell/100	3.00
87	Edgar Martinez/99	4.00
88	Doug Mientkiewicz/98	3.00
89	Pedro J. Martinez/97	8.00
90	Randy Johnson/96	8.00
91	Aramis Ramirez/95	4.00
92	J.D. Drew/94	4.00
93	Chris Richard/93	4.00
94	Jimmy Rollins/92	4.00
95	Ryan Klesko/91	4.00
96	Gary Sheffield/90	4.00
97	Chipper Jones/89	4.00
98	Greg Vaughn/88	3.00
99	Mo Vaughn/87	3.00
100	Bernie Williams/86	3.00
101	John Foster NT/85	3.00
102	Jorge De La Rosa NT/84	3.00
103	Edwin Almonte NT/83	3.00
104	Chris Booker NT/82	3.00
105	Victor Alvarez NT/81	3.00
106	Clifford Bartosh NT/80	3.00
107	Felix Escalona NT/79	3.00
108	Corey Thurman NT/78	3.00
109	Kazuhisa Ishii NT/77	12.00
110	Miguel Asencio NT/76	3.00
111	P.J. Bevis NT/75	3.00
112	Gustavo Chacin NT/74	3.00
113	Steve Kent NT/73	3.00
114	Takahito Nomura NT/72	3.00
115	Adam Walker NT/71	3.00
116	So Taguchi NT/70	6.00
117	Reed Johnson NT/69	6.00
118	Rodrigo Rosario NT/68	4.00
119	Luis Martinez NT/67	5.00
120	Satoru Komiyama NT/66	4.00

121	Sean Burroughs NT/65	5.00
122	Hank Blalock NT/64	6.00
123	Marlon Byrd NT/63	4.00
124	Nick Johnson NT/62	4.00
125	Mark Teixeira NT/61	6.00

Barry Bonds 4X MVP

No Pricing
Production 25 Sets

	NM/M
Complete Set (4):	20.00
Common Bonds:	6.00
1BB4X Barry Bonds/1990	6.00
2BB4X Barry Bonds/1,992	6.00
3BB4X Barry Bonds/1,993	6.00
4BB4X Barry Bonds/2,001	6.00

Behind the Numbers

	NM/M
Complete Set (35):	75.00
Common Player:	1.00
Inserted 1:8	
1BTN Ichiro Suzuki	5.00
2BTN Jason Giambi	2.50
3BTN Mike Piazza	5.00
4BTN Brian Giles	1.00
5BTN Barry Bonds	8.00
6BTN Pedro J. Martinez	3.00
7BTN Nomar Garciaparra	3.00
8BTN Randy Johnson	3.00
9BTN Craig Biggio	1.00
10BTN Manny Ramirez	3.00
11BTN Mike Mussina	1.50
12BTN Kerry Wood	2.50
13BTN Jim Edmonds	1.00
14BTN Ivan Rodriguez	2.50
15BTN Jeff Bagwell	3.00
16BTN Roger Clemens	4.50
17BTN Chipper Jones	4.00
18BTN Shawn Green	1.25
19BTN Albert Pujols	6.00
20BTN Andruw Jones	3.00
21BTN Luis Gonzalez	1.00
22BTN Todd Helton	3.00
23BTN Jorge Posada	1.25
24BTN Scott Rolen	2.50
25BTN Ben Sheets	1.00
26BTN Alfonso Soriano	2.50
27BTN Greg Maddux	4.00
28BTN Gary Sheffield	1.25
29BTN Barry Zito	1.25
30BTN Alex Rodriguez	6.00
31BTN Larry Walker	1.00
32BTN Derek Jeter	8.00
33BTN Ken Griffey Jr.	5.00
34BTN Vladimir Guerrero	5.00
35BTN Sammy Sosa	5.00

Behind the Numbers Game Jersey

	NM/M
Common Player:	5.00
Inserted 1:24	
1 Jeff Bagwell	10.00
2 Craig Biggio/Pants	5.00
4 Roger Clemens	20.00
5 Jim Edmonds	5.00
6 Brian Giles	5.00
7 Luis Gonzalez	5.00
8 Shawn Green	5.00

9	Todd Helton	8.00
10	Derek Jeter/SP	30.00
11	Randy Johnson/SP	10.00
12	Andruw Jones	8.00
13	Chipper Jones	10.00
14	Greg Maddux	10.00
15	Pedro J. Martinez	10.00
16	Mike Mussina	10.00
17	Mike Piazza/Pants	10.00
18	Jorge Posada	8.00
19	Manny Ramirez	10.00
20	Alex Rodriguez	10.00
21	Ivan Rodriguez	8.00
22	Scott Rolen	8.00
23	Alfonso Soriano/SP	10.00
24	Barry Zito	6.00

Behind the Numbers Game Jersey Dual

No Pricing
Production 25 Sets

Derek Jeter 4X Champ

	NM/M
Complete Set (4):	20.00
Common Jeter:	6.00
1DJFX Derek Jeter/1,996	6.00
2DJFX Derek Jeter/1,998	6.00
3DJFX Derek Jeter/1,999	6.00
4DJFX Derek Jeter/2,000	6.00

Game Essentials

	NM/M
Common Player:	5.00
Carlos Beltran	5.00
Kevin Brown	5.00
Jeromy Burnitz	5.00
Carlos Delgado	8.00
Jason Hart/SP	8.00
Rickey Henderson	20.00
Drew Henson/Shoe	5.00
Drew Henson/Glove	5.00
Derek Jeter/Shoe	40.00
Jason Kendall	5.00
Jeff Kent	10.00
Barry Larkin/Glove	20.00
Javy Lopez	8.00
Raul Mondesi/Batting Glove	8.00
Rafael Palmeiro	10.00
Adam Piatt	5.00
Brad Radke	5.00
Cal Ripken Jr.	30.00
Mariano Rivera	10.00
Alex Rodriguez/Batting Glove	15.00
Ivan Rodriguez/Shoe	10.00
Kazuhiro Sasaki	5.00
J.T. Snow	5.00
Mo Vaughn	5.00
Robin Ventura	8.00
Jose Vidro	5.00
Matt Williams	5.00

HardWear

	NM/M
Complete Set (10):	60.00
Common Player:	4.00
Inserted 1:72 Hobby	
1HW Ivan Rodriguez	4.00
2HW Mike Piazza	8.00
3HW Derek Jeter	15.00
4HW Barry Bonds	15.00
5HW Todd Helton	4.00
6HW Roberto Alomar	4.00
7HW Albert Pujols	10.00
8HW Ichiro Suzuki	8.00
9HW Ken Griffey Jr.	8.00
10HW Jason Giambi	5.00

Hit and Run

	NM/M
Complete Set (30):	50.00
Common Player:	1.00
Inserted 1:12	
1 Adam Dunn	1.00
2 Derek Jeter	6.00
3 Frank Thomas	2.00
4 Albert Pujols	5.00
5 J.D. Drew	1.00
6 Richard Hidalgo	1.00

7	John Olerud	1.00
8	Roberto Alomar	1.00
9	Pat Burrell	1.50
10	Darin Erstad	1.50
11	Mark Grace	1.00
12	Chipper Jones	3.00
13	Jose Vidro	1.00
14	Cliff Floyd	1.00
15	Mo Vaughn	1.00
16	Nomar Garciaparra	4.00
17	Ivan Rodriguez	1.50
18	Luis Gonzalez	1.00
19	Jason Giambi	1.50
20	Bernie Williams	1.00
21	Mike Piazza	4.00
22	Barry Bonds	6.00
23	Jose Ortiz	1.00
24	Magglio Ordonez	1.00
25	Troy Glaus	2.00
26	Alex Rodriguez	5.00
27	Ichiro Suzuki	4.00
28	Sammy Sosa	4.00
29	Ken Griffey Jr.	4.00
30	Vladimir Guerrero	2.00

Hit and Run Game Base

		NM/M
Inserted 1:120		
1	J.D. Drew	4.00
2	Adam Dunn	6.00
3	Jason Giambi	6.00
4	Troy Glaus	6.00
5	Ken Griffey Jr.	10.00
6	Vladimir Guerrero	8.00
7	Albert Pujols	15.00
8	Sammy Sosa	10.00
9	Ichiro Suzuki	15.00
10	Bernie Williams	6.00

Hit and Run Game Bat

		NM/M
Common Player:		4.00
Inserted 1:24		
1	Roberto Alomar	6.00
2	J.D. Drew	4.00
3	Darin Erstad	4.00
4	Cliff Floyd	4.00
5	Nomar Garciaparra	15.00
6	Luis Gonzalez	6.00
7	Richard Hidalgo	4.00
8	Derek Jeter	25.00
9	Chipper Jones	8.00
10	John Olerud	4.00
11	Magglio Ordonez	6.00
12	Jose Ortiz	4.00
13	Mike Piazza	10.00
14	Alex Rodriguez	15.00
15	Ivan Rodriguez	8.00
16	Frank Thomas	8.00
17	Mo Vaughn	4.00
18	Jose Vidro	4.00
19	Bernie Williams	8.00

Hit and Run Game Bat and Base

		NM/M
Common Player:		10.00
Inserted 1:240		
1	Roberto Alomar	15.00
2	Barry Bonds/SP	50.00
3	Nomar Garciaparra	30.00
4	Derek Jeter	40.00
5	Chipper Jones	15.00
6	Mike Piazza	20.00
7	Alex Rodriguez	25.00
8	Mo Vaughn	10.00

2002 Fleer Fall Classic

		NM/M
Complete Set (100):		30.00
Common Player:		.25
Common SP:		3.00
Inserted 1:18 Hobby		
Pack (5):		5.00
Box (24):		100.00
1	Rabbit Maranville	.25
2	Tris Speaker	.75
3	Harmon Killebrew	1.00
4	Lou Gehrig	2.00
5	Lou Boudreau	.25
6	Al Kaline	1.00
7	Paul Molitor	1.00
7	Paul Molitor/Brewers	4.00
8	Cal Ripken Jr.	3.00
9	Yogi Berra	1.00
10	Phil Rizzuto	.75
11	Luis Aparicio	.25
11	Luis Aparicio/Orioles	4.00
12	Stan Musial	1.00
13	Mel Ott	.75
14	Larry Doby	.25
15	Ozzie Smith	1.00
16	Babe Ruth	4.00
16	Babe Ruth/Red Sox	10.00
17	Red Schoendienst	.25
17	Red Schoendienst/Cards	3.00
18	Rollie Fingers	.25
19	Thurman Munson	1.50
20	Lou Brock	.50
21	Paul O'Neill	.25
21	Paul O'Neill/Reds	3.00
22	Jim Palmer	.50
23	Kirby Puckett	1.00
24	Tony Perez	.25
24	Tony Perez/Phila.	3.00
25	Don Larsen	.75
26	Steve Garvey	.25
26	Steve Garvey/Padres	3.00
27	Jim "Catfish" Hunter	.25
27	"Catfish" Hunter/Yanks	4.00
28	Juan Marichal	.50
29	Pee Wee Reese	.25
30	Orlando Cepeda	.25
31	Rich "Goose" Gossage	.25
32	Ray Knight	.25
33	Eddie Murray	.75
34	Nolan Ryan	3.00
35	Alan Trammell	.50
36	Grover Alexander	.75
37	Joe Carter	.25
38	Rogers Hornsby	1.00
39	Jimmie Foxx	1.00
40	Mike Schmidt	1.50
41	Eddie Mathews	1.00
42	Jackie Robinson	1.50
43	Eddie Collins	.25
43	Eddie Collins/White Sox	3.00
44	Willie McCovey	.25
45	Bob Gibson	1.00
46	Keith Hernandez	.50
46	Keith Hernandez/Cards	4.00
47	Brooks Robinson	1.00
48	Mordecai Brown	.25
49	Gary Carter	.50
50	Kirk Gibson	.25
50	Kirk Gibson/Tigers	3.00
51	Johnny Mize	.25
52	Johnny Podres	.25
53	Darrell Porter	.25
54	Willie Stargell	.75
55	Lenny Dykstra	.25
55	Lenny Dykstra/Phila.	3.00
56	Christy Mathewson	.75
57	Walter Johnson	1.00
58	Whitey Ford	.75
59	Lefty Grove	.50
60	Duke Snider	.75
61	Cy Young	1.00
62	Dave Winfield	.75
62	Dave Winfield/Yanks	5.00
63	Robin Yount	1.00
64	Fred Lynn	.25
65	Ty Cobb	2.00
66	Joe Morgan	.25
67	Bill Mazeroski	.25
68	Frank Baker	.25
69	Chief Bender	.25
70	Carlton Fisk	.50
71	Jerry Coleman	.25
72	Frankie Frisch	.25
73	Wade Boggs	1.00
73	Wade Boggs/Yanks	4.00
74	Johnny Bench	1.00
75	Roger Maris	2.00
75	Roger Maris/Cards	8.00
76	Dom DiMaggio	.25
77	George Brett	3.00
78	Dave Parker	.25
78	Dave Parker/A's	3.00
79	Hank Greenberg	.25
80	Pepper Martin	.25
81	Graig Nettles	.25
81	Graig Nettles/Padres	.50
82	Dennis Eckersley	.50
83	Donn Clendenon	.25
84	Tom Seaver	1.00
85	Honus Wagner	1.50
86	Reggie Jackson	.25
86	Reggie Jackson/A's	5.00
87	Goose Goslin	.25
87	Goose Goslin/Tigers	3.00
88	Tony Kubek	.25
89	Roy Campanella	1.00
90	Steve Carlton/Cards	4.00
91	Lou Gehrig, Mel Ott	2.00
92	Eddie Collins, Joe Morgan	.25
93	George Brett, Mike Schmidt	2.00
94	Cal Ripken Jr., Ozzie Smith	3.00
95	Thurman Munson, Johnny Bench	1.50
96	Willie Stargell, Stan Musial, Pepper Martin	1.00
97	Babe Ruth, Kirby Puckett, Reggie Jackson	3.00
98	Cy Young, Bob Gibson	1.00
99	Whitey Ford, Steve Carlton	1.00
100	Paul Molitor, Lou Brock	.50

Championship Gold

Golds:	5-10X
Gold SP's:	1-2X
Production 50 Sets	

HOF Plaque

	NM/M
Complete Set (30):	90.00
Common Player:	3.00

#'d to HOF induction year		
1HOF	Babe Ruth	8.00
2HOF	Christy Mathewson	3.00
3HOF	Honus Wagner	4.00
4HOF	Ty Cobb	5.00
5HOF	Walter Johnson	4.00
6HOF	Cy Young	4.00
7HOF	Tris Speaker	3.00
8HOF	Eddie Collins	3.00
9HOF	Lou Gehrig	6.00
10HOF	Jimmie Foxx	4.00
11HOF	Jackie Robinson	6.00
12HOF	Stan Musial	5.00
13HOF	Yogi Berra	4.00
14HOF	Duke Snider	4.00
15HOF	Juan Marichal	3.00
16HOF	Luis Aparicio	3.00
17HOF	Pee Wee Reese	3.00
18HOF	Willie McCovey	3.00
19HOF	Willie Stargell	3.00
20HOF	Johnny Bench	5.00
21HOF	Joe Morgan	3.00
22HOF	Jim Palmer	3.00
23HOF	Tom Seaver	5.00
24HOF	Reggie Jackson	4.00
25HOF	Steve Carlton	3.00
26HOF	George Brett	6.00
27HOF	Nolan Ryan	8.00
28HOF	Robin Yount	4.00
29HOF	Kirby Puckett	5.00
30HOF	Ozzie Smith	4.00

MVP Collection Game-Used

		NM/M
Common Player:		5.00
Inserted 1:100		
Golds:		.75-2X
Production 100 Sets		
JB	Johnny Bench/200	20.00
DC	Donn Clendenon	5.00
RF	Rollie Fingers/200	5.00
RJOK	Reggie Jackson/50	20.00
RJNY	Reggie Jackson	10.00
RK	Ray Knight	5.00
PM	Paul Molitor/250	15.00
DP	Darrell Porter/250	5.00
BR	Brooks Robinson/ 250	20.00
WS	Willie Stargell/200	10.00
AT	Alan Trammell	10.00

MVP Collection Patch

		NM/M
Numbered to MVP Year		
JB	Johnny Bench/76	45.00
RF	Rollie Fingers/74	20.00
RJNY	Reggie Jackson/77	40.00
BR	Brooks Robinson/70	40.00
AT	Alan Trammell/84	30.00

October Legends

		NM/M
Common Player:		5.00
Inserted 1:48		
Golds:		.75-1.5X
Production 100 Sets		
	Joe Morgan	5.00
	Wade Boggs/60	8.00
	Keith Hernandez/100	15.00
	Robin Yount	10.00
	Eddie Murray	10.00
	Lenny Dykstra/200	8.00
	Paul O'Neill	8.00
	Red Schoendienst/210	8.00
	Pepper Martin/50	5.00
	Keith Hernandez/150	20.00
	Willie Stargell/225	12.00
	George Brett	20.00
	Dave Parker/50	10.00
	Tony Perez	5.00
	Rollie Fingers	5.00
	Gary Carter/200	10.00
	Dennis Eckersley	5.00
	Juan Marichal	8.00
	Pee Wee Reese/200	15.00
	Roger Maris	60.00
	Duke Snider/200	15.00
	Darrell Porter/150	5.00
	Willie McCovey/150	10.00
	Paul Molitor/150	15.00

October Legends Dual

		NM/M
Common Card:		10.00
SP's Noted		
	Rollie Fingers, Dennis Eckersley, Keith Hernandez, Red Schoendienst	12.00
	Joe Morgan, Tony Perez	10.00

Wade Boggs, Keith Hernandez	20.00
Lenny Dykstra, Gary Carter	12.00
Robin Yount, Paul Molitor/150	35.00
Roger Maris, Paul O'Neill/200	50.00
Duke Snider, Pee Wee Reese/200	25.00
Juan Marichal, Willie McCovey	15.00
George Brett, Darrell Porter/150	35.00
Willie Stargell, Dave Parker	15.00
Gary Carter, Keith Hernandez	10.00
Cal Ripken Jr., Eddie Murray/200	40.00
Cal Ripken Jr., Eddie Murray/100	50.00
Pepper Martin, Frankie Frisch	15.00

Pennant Chase

	NM/M
Common Player:	10.00
Inserted 1:48 Hobby	
Yogi Berra/Pants/150	20.00
Carlton Fisk/Bat	10.00
Reggie Jackson/Jsy	10.00
Fred Lynn/Bat	10.00
Thurman Munson/ Bat	30.00
Wade Boggs/Jsy	10.00
Dave Winfield/Bat	10.00

Pennant Chase Dual

	NM/M
Production 50 Sets	
CFRJ Carlton Fisk/Bat, Reggie Jackson/ Jsy	30.00
FLTM Fred Lynn/Bat, Thurman Munson/ Bat	50.00
WBDW Wade Boggs/Jsy, Dave Winfield/Bat	30.00

Rival Factions

	NM/M
Common Card:	2.00
1-24 #'d to 1,000	
25-36 #'d to 500	
37-43 #'d to 50	
1RF Carlton Fisk, Thurman Munson	3.00
2RF Frank Baker, Babe Ruth	8.00
3RF Jimmie Foxx, Lou Gehrig	6.00
4RF Steve Carlton, Nolan Ryan	8.00
5RF Mordecai Brown, Honus Wagner	3.00
6RF Frankie Frisch, Duke Snider	3.00
7RF Ozzie Smith, Alan Trammell	3.00
8RF Larry Doby, Jackie Robinson	5.00
9RF Steve Garvey, Tony Perez	2.00
10RF Johnny Bench, Willie Stargell	4.00
11RF Ty Cobb, Eddie Collins	5.00
12RF Reggie Jackson, Brooks Robinson	4.00
13RF Yogi Berra, Roy Campanella	4.00
14RF Orlando Cepeda, Willie McCovey	2.00
15RF Al Kaline, Jim Palmer	4.00
16RF George Brett, Kirby Puckett	6.00
17RF Bob Gibson, Tom Seaver	4.00
18RF Cal Ripken Jr., Robin Yount	8.00
19RF Johnny Mize, Mel Ott	3.00
20RF Stan Musial, Pee Wee Reese	4.00
21RF Hank Greenburg, Lefty Grove	2.00
22RF Dave Parker, Mike Schmidt	4.00
23RF Bill Mazeroski, Joe Morgan	3.00
24RF Johnny Bench, Carlton Fisk	5.00

25RF George Brett, Mike Schmidt	8.00
26RF Pee Wee Reese, Phil Rizzuto	4.00
27RF Cal Ripken Jr., Alan Trammell	15.00
28RF Tom Seaver, Jim "Catfish" Hunter	4.00
29RF Ty Cobb, Honus Wagner	5.00
30RF Steve Carlton, Lefty Grove	3.00
31RF Ozzie Smith, Robin Yount	8.00
32RF Frankie Frisch, Joe Morgan	3.00
33RF Hank Greenberg, Jackie Robinson	5.00
34RF Jimmie Foxx, Pepper Martin	5.00
35RF Lou Gehrig, Cal Ripken Jr.	40.00
36RF Ozzie Smith, Honus Wagner	40.00
37RF Reggie Jackson, Dave Winfield	20.00
38RF Ty Cobb, Rogers Hornsby	35.00
39RF Babe Ruth, Roger Maris	50.00
40RF Yogi Berra, Thurman Munson	20.00
41RF Nolan Ryan, Tom Seaver	50.00
42RF Joe Morgan, Jackie Robinson	20.00
43RF Jimmie Foxx, Mel Ott	25.00

Rival Factions Game-Used Single

	NM/M
Common Card:	8.00
Inserted 1:32	
Carlton Fisk, Thurman Munson	25.00
Frank Baker, Babe Ruth	25.00
Jimmie Foxx, Lou Gehrig	35.00
Steve Carlton, Nolan Ryan	25.00
Frankie Frisch, Duke Snider	20.00
Ozzie Smith, Alan Trammell	15.00
Larry Doby, Jackie Robinson	15.00
Steve Garvey, Tony Perez	10.00
Johnny Bench, Willie Stargell	10.00
Reggie Jackson, Brooks Robinson	12.00
Orlando Cepeda, Willie McCovey	10.00
Al Kaline, Jim Palmer	10.00
George Brett, Kirby Puckett	25.00
Bob Gibson, Tom Seaver	20.00
Cal Ripken Jr., Robin Yount	30.00
Stan Musial, Pee Wee Reese	25.00
Hank Greenberg, Lefty Grove	20.00
Bill Mazeroski, Joe Morgan	8.00
Johnny Bench, Carlton Fisk	10.00
George Brett, Mike Schmidt	25.00
Pee Wee Reese, Phil Rizzuto	15.00
Cal Ripken Jr., Alan Trammell	35.00
Steve Carlton, Lefty Grove	15.00
Ozzie Smith, Robin Yount	15.00

Frankie Frisch, Joe Morgan	25.00
Hank Greenberg, Jackie Robinson	20.00
Jimmie Foxx, Pepper Martin	30.00
Lou Gehrig, Cal Ripken Jr.	40.00
Reggie Jackson, Dave Winfield	10.00
Babe Ruth, Roger Maris	60.00
Nolan Ryan, Tom Seaver	35.00

Rival Factions Game-Used Dual

	NM/M
Common Card:	12.00
Carlton Fisk, Thurman Munson	30.00
Steve Carlton, Nolan Ryan	40.00
Frankie Frisch, Duke Snider	15.00
Ozzie Smith, Alan Trammell	25.00
Larry Doby, Jackie Robinson/75	60.00
Steve Garvey, Tony Perez	10.00
Johnny Bench, Willie Stargell	20.00
Reggie Jackson, Brooks Robinson	20.00
Orlando Cepeda, Willie McCovey/200	15.00
George Brett, Kirby Puckett	40.00
Cal Ripken Jr., Robin Yount	30.00
Johnny Bench, Carlton Fisk	20.00
Cal Ripken Jr., Alan Trammell	30.00
Jim "Catfish" Hunter, Tom Seaver	15.00
Ozzie Smith, Robin Yount	25.00
Frankie Frisch, Joe Morgan	15.00
Hank Greenberg, Jackie Robinson/50	100.00
Jimmie Foxx, Pepper Martin/200	40.00
Reggie Jackson, Dave Winfield/150	20.00
Yogi Berra, Thurman Munson	40.00
Nolan Ryan, Tom Seaver	45.00
Joe Morgan, Jackie Robinson/50	50.00

Rival Factions Dual Patch

	NM/M
Production 50 Sets	12.00
Carlton Fisk, Thurman Munson	60.00
Steve Carlton, Nolan Ryan	100.00
Ozzie Smith, Alan Trammell	50.00
Steve Garvey, Tony Perez	30.00
Johnny Bench, Willie Stargell	50.00
Cal Ripken Jr., Robin Yount	125.00
Johnny Bench, Carlton Fisk	50.00
Cal Ripken Jr., Alan Trammell	100.00
Ozzie Smith, Robin Yount	60.00
Reggie Jackson, Dave Winfield	40.00

Series of Champions

	NM/M
Complete Set (20):	25.00

Common Player:	1.00
Inserted 1:6	
1 Yogi Berra	2.00
2 Wade Boggs	2.00
3 Dave Parker	1.00
4 Joe Carter	1.00
5 Kirk Gibson	1.00
6 Reggie Jackson	2.00
7 Tony Kubek	1.00
8 Don Larsen	1.00
9 Bill Mazeroski	1.00
10 Eddie Murray	1.50
11 Graig Nettles	1.00
12 Tony Perez	1.00
13 Phil Rizzuto	1.50
14 Mike Schmidt	2.50
15 Red Schoendienst	1.00
16 Duke Snider	2.00
17 Ty Cobb	2.50
18 Lou Gehrig	3.00
19 Babe Ruth	4.00

Series of Champions Game-Used

	NM/M
Common Player:	5.00
Inserted 1:36	
Golds:	.75-1.5X
Production 100 Sets	
Bat Knob numbered to 10 not priced.	
Yogi Berra/Bat	15.00
Wade Boggs/Jsy	10.00
Dave Parker/Bat	5.00
Joe Carter/Bat	5.00
Kirk Gibson/Bat	5.00
Reggie Jackson/Bat	10.00
Tony Kubek/Bat	10.00
Eddie Murray/Bat	10.00
Graig Nettles/Bat	5.00
Tony Perez/Bat	5.00
Red Schoendienst/Jsy	5.00
Duke Snider/Bat	10.00
Babe Ruth/Bat/25	180.00

2002 Fleer Flair

	NM/M
Complete Set (138):	
Common Player:	.25
Common (101-138):	3.00
Production 1,750	
Pack (5):	4.00
Hobby Box (20):	70.00
1 Scott Rolen	.75
2 Derek Jeter	3.00
3 Sean Casey	.40
4 Hideo Nomo	.75
5 Craig Biggio	.25

6	Randy Johnson	1.00
7	J.D. Drew	.50
8	Greg Maddux	1.50
9	Paul LoDuca	.25
10	John Olerud	.25
11	Barry Larkin	.25
12	Mark Grace	.35
13	Jimmy Rollins	.50
14	Todd Helton	1.00
15	Jim Edmonds	.25
16	Roy Oswalt	.35
17	Phil Nevin	.25
18	Tim Salmon	.35
19	Magglio Ordonez	.25
20	Roger Clemens	1.75
21	Raul Mondesi	.25
22	Edgar Martinez	.25
23	Pedro J. Martinez	1.00
24	Edgardo Alfonzo	.25
25	Bernie Williams	.35
26	Gary Sheffield	.40
27	D'Angelo Jimenez	.25
28	Toby Hall	.25
29	Joe Mays	.25
30	Alfonso Soriano	.75
31	Mike Piazza	2.00
32	Lance Berkman	.25
33	Jim Thome	.25
34	Ben Sheets	.25
35	Brandon Inge	.25
36	Luis Gonzalez	.35
37	Jeff Kent	.25
38	Ben Grieve	.25
39	Carlos Delgado	.50
40	Pat Burrell	.50
41	Mark Buehrle	.25
42	Cristian Guzman	.40
43	Shawn Green	.25
44	Nomar Garciaparra	2.00
45	Carlos Beltran	.60
46	Troy Glaus	.75
47	Paul Konerko	.25
48	Moises Alou	.25
49	Kerry Wood	.75
50	Jose Vidro	.25
51	Juan Encarnacion	.25
52	Bobby Abreu	.25
53	C.C. Sabathia	.25
54	Alex Rodriguez	2.50
55	Albert Pujols	2.50
56	Bret Boone	.25
57	Orlando Hernandez	.25
58	Jason Kendall	.25
59	Tim Hudson	.40
60	Darin Erstad	.60
61	Mike Mussina	.40
62	Ken Griffey Jr.	2.00
63	Adrian Beltre	.35
64	Jeff Bagwell	1.00
65	Vladimir Guerrero	1.00
66	Mike Sweeney	.25
67	Sammy Sosa	2.00
68	Andruw Jones	.75
69	Richie Sexson	.25
70	Matt Morris	.25
71	Ivan Rodriguez	.75
72	Shannon Stewart	.25
73	Barry Bonds	3.00
74	Matt Williams	.25
75	Jason Giambi	.60
76	Brian Giles	.25
77	Cliff Floyd	.25
78	Tino Martinez	.25
79	Juan Gonzalez	1.00
80	Frank Thomas	1.00
81	Ichiro Suzuki	2.00
82	Barry Zito	.35
83	Chipper Jones	1.50
84	Adam Dunn	.75
85	Kazuhiro Sasaki	.25
86	Mark Quinn	.25
87	Rafael Palmeiro	.60
88	Jeromy Burnitz	.25
89	Curt Schilling	.50
90	Chris Richards	.25
91	Jon Leiber	.25
92	Doug Mientkiewicz	.25
93	Roberto Alomar	.40
94	Rich Aurilia	.25
95	Eric Chavez	.35
96	Larry Walker	.25
97	Manny Ramirez	1.00
98	Tony Clark	.25
99	Tsuyoshi Shinjo	.25
100	Josh Beckett	.50
101	Dewon Brazelton	3.00
102	Jeremy Lambert RC	3.00
103	Andres Torres	3.00
104	Matt Childers RC	4.00
105	Wilson Betemit	3.00
106	Willie Harris	3.00
107	Drew Henson	4.00
108	Rafael Soriano	3.00
109	Carlos Valderrama	3.00
110	Victor Martinez	6.00
111	Juan Rivera	3.00
112	Felipe Lopez	3.00
113	Brandon Duckworth	3.00
114	Jeremy Owens	3.00
115	Aaron Cook RC	3.00
116	Derrick Lewis	3.00
117	Mark Teixeira	6.00
118	Ken Harvey	5.00
119	Tim Spooneybarger	3.00
120	Bill Hall	3.00
121	Adam Pettyjohn	3.00
122	Ramon Castro	3.00
123	Marlon Byrd	4.00
124	Matt White	3.00
125	Eric Cyr RC	3.00
126	Morgan Ensberg	3.00
127	Horacio Ramirez	4.00
128	Ron Calloway RC	3.00
129	Nick Punto	3.00
130	Joe Kennedy	3.00
131	So Taguchi RC	5.00
132	Austin Kearns	4.00
133	Mark Prior	6.00
134	Kazuhisa Ishii RC	8.00
135	Steve Torrealba	3.00
136	Adam Walker RC	3.00
137	Travis Hafner	4.00
138	Zach Day	3.00

Collection

Collection (1-100):	4-6X
Production 175	
Collection (101-138):	1-2X
Production 50	

Hot Numbers

	NM/M
Common Player:	15.00
Production 100 Sets	
Manny Ramirez	30.00
Randy Johnson	30.00
Curt Schilling	25.00
Pedro J. Martinez	30.00
Nomar Garciaparra	50.00
Barry Larkin	15.00
Todd Helton	30.00
Larry Walker	15.00
Sean Casey	20.00
Jeff Bagwell	30.00
Craig Biggio	15.00
Shawn Green	20.00
Edgardo Alfonzo	15.00
Mike Piazza	50.00
Derek Jeter	75.00
Chipper Jones	40.00
Jim Edmonds	15.00
J.D. Drew	20.00
Ivan Rodriguez	25.00
Rafael Palmeiro	25.00
Alex Rodriguez	60.00
Greg Maddux	40.00
Carlos Delgado	20.00

Jersey Heights

	NM/M
Common Player:	4.00
Inserted 1:18 Hobby	
1JH Edgardo Alfonzo	4.00
2JH Jeff Bagwell	8.00
3JH Craig Biggio	4.00
4JH Barry Bonds	20.00
5JH Sean Casey	4.00
6JH Roger Clemens	15.00
7JH Carlos Delgado	6.00
8JH J.D. Drew	6.00
9JH Jim Edmonds	6.00
10JH Nomar Garciaparra	15.00
11JH Shawn Green	5.00
12JH Todd Helton	8.00
13JH Derek Jeter	20.00
14JH Randy Johnson	8.00
15JH Chipper Jones	8.00
16JH Barry Larkin	6.00
17JH Greg Maddux	10.00
18JH Pedro J. Martinez	8.00
19JH Rafael Palmeiro	8.00
20JH Mike Piazza	10.00
21JH Manny Ramirez	8.00
22JH Alex Rodriguez	15.00
23JH Ivan Rodriguez	6.00
24JH Curt Schilling	6.00
25JH Larry Walker	4.00

Jersey Heights (Dual)

	NM/M
Common Card:	15.00
Production 100 Sets	
Randy Johnson, Curt Schilling	30.00
Pedro J. Martinez, Nomar Garciaparra	50.00
Edgardo Alfonzo, Mike Piazza	30.00
Derek Jeter, Roger Clemens	75.00
Greg Maddux, Chipper Jones	40.00
Jim Edmonds, Jeff Bagwell	20.00
Jeff Bagwell, Craig Biggio	25.00
Rafael Palmeiro, Ivan Rodriguez	25.00
Carlos Delgado, Shawn Green	15.00
Todd Helton, Larry Walker	20.00
Sean Casey, Barry Larkin	25.00
Alex Rodriguez, Manny Ramirez	40.00

Power Tools

	NM/M
Common Player:	4.00
Inserted 1:19	
Golds:	1-2.5X
Production 100	
1PT Roberto Alomar	6.00
2PT Jeff Bagwell/150	8.00
3PT Craig Biggio	4.00
4PT Barry Bonds	15.00
5PT Bret Boone	4.00
6PT Pat Burrell/225	6.00
8PT Eric Chavez	5.00
9PT J.D. Drew/150	8.00
10PT Jim Edmonds	6.00
11PT Juan Gonzalez	6.00
12PT Luis Gonzalez	4.00
13PT Shawn Green	5.00
15PT Derek Jeter	25.00
16PT Doug Mientkiewicz	4.00
17PT Magglio Ordonez	4.00
18PT Rafael Palmeiro/100	8.00
19PT Mike Piazza	10.00
20PT Alex Rodriguez	15.00
21PT Ivan Rodriguez	8.00
22PT Scott Rolen/42	15.00
23PT Reggie Sanders/120	5.00
24PT Gary Sheffield	6.00
25PT Tsuyoshi Shinjo	5.00
26PT Miguel Tejada	6.00
27PT Frank Thomas	8.00
28PT Jim Thome/225	15.00
29PT Larry Walker	4.00
30PT Bernie Williams	6.00

Power Tools Dual

	NM/M
Common Card:	10.00
Inserted 1:40	
Golds:	1-2.5X
Production 50 Sets	

1	Eric Chavez, Miguel Tejada	10.00
2	Barry Bonds, Tsuyoshi Shinjo	25.00
3	Jim Edmonds, J.D. Drew	15.00
4	Jeff Bagwell, Craig Biggio	15.00
5	Bernie Williams, Derek Jeter	35.00
6	Roberto Alomar, Mike Piazza	20.00
7	Sean Casey, Jim Thome/40	30.00
8	Pat Burrell, Scott Rolen	15.00
9	Gary Sheffield, Shawn Green	10.00
10	Ivan Rodriguez, Alex Rodriguez	15.00
11	Juan Gonzalez, Rafael Palmeiro	15.00
12	Magglio Ordonez, Frank Thomas	15.00
13	Larry Walker, Todd Helton/225	10.00
14	Luis Gonzalez, Reggie Sanders	10.00
15	Doug Mientkiewicz, Bret Boone	10.00

Sweet Swatch Autographs

	NM/M
Common Player:	15.00
Quantity produced listed	
Golds:	No Pricing
Production 15 Sets	
Derek Jeter/375	100.00
Barry Bonds/35	200.00
Drew Henson/785	40.00
Mark Teixeira/185	40.00
Dewon Brazelton/185	15.00
Mark Prior/285	40.00
Marlon Byrd/185	15.00
Ozzie Smith/185	65.00
Ron Cey/185	20.00
Paul Molitor/85	50.00
Maury Wills/285	20.00
Dale Murphy/285	60.00
David Espinosa/485	15.00
Dane Sardinha/485	15.00
Ben Sheets/85	50.00
Tony Perez/115	20.00
Brooks Robinson/185	50.00
So Taguchi/335	30.00
Al Kaline/285	50.00
Kazuhisa Ishii/335	30.00
Albert Pujols/50	125.00
Don Mattingly/85	150.00

Sweet Swatch Game-Used

	NM/M
Common Player:	8.00
1:Hobby Box	
Jeff Bagwell/490	10.00
Josh Beckett/500	10.00
Darin Erstad/525	8.00
Freddy Garcia/620	8.00
Brian Giles/445	8.00
Juan Gonzalez/505	10.00
Mark Grace/795	15.00
Derek Jeter/525	40.00
Jason Kendall/990	10.00
Paul LoDuca/440	10.00
Greg Maddux/475	15.00
Magglio Ordonez/495	10.00
Rafael Palmeiro/535	10.00
Mike Piazza/1,000	15.00
Alex Rodriguez/550	25.00
Ivan Rodriguez/475	10.00
Tim Salmon/465	8.00
Kazuhiro Sasaki/770	8.00
Alfonso Soriano/775	10.00
Larry Walker/430	8.00
Ted Williams/250	125.00

Sweet Swatch Patch

	NM/M
Common Player:	25.00
Random Box Topper	
Jeff Bagwell/45	75.00
Josh Beckett/60	55.00
Darin Erstad/50	45.00
Freddy Garcia/50	40.00
Juan Gonzalez/55	75.00
Mark Grace/75	60.00
Jason Kendall/120	25.00
Paul LoDuca/35	35.00
Greg Maddux/50	90.00
Magglio Ordonez/55	40.00

Rafael Palmeiro/60	40.00
Mike Piazza/95	100.00
Alex Rodriguez/50	90.00
Ivan Rodriguez/50	60.00
Tim Salmon/40	65.00
Kazuhiro Sasaki/80	50.00
Alfonso Soriano/35	65.00
Larry Walker/60	40.00

2002 Fleer Focus Jersey Edition

CHIPPER JONES

	NM/M
Complete Set (260):	60.00
Common Player:	.15
Common (226-260):	1.00
Inserted 1:4	
Pack (10):	2.00
Box (24):	40.00
1 Mike Piazza	1.50
2 Jason Giambi	.50
3 Jim Thome	.15
4 John Olerud	.15
5 J.D. Drew	.30
6 Richard Hidalgo	.15
7 Rusty Greer	.15
8 Tony Batista	.15
9 Omar Vizquel	.15
10 Randy Johnson	.75
11 Cristian Guzman	.15
12 Mark Grace	.25
13 Jeff Cirillo	.15
14 Mike Cameron	.15
15 Jeromy Burnitz	.15
16 Pokey Reese	.15
17 Richie Sexson	.15
18 Joe Randa	.15
19 Aramis Ramirez	.15
20 Pedro J. Martinez	.75
21 Todd Hollandsworth	.15
22 Rondell White	.15
23 Tsuyoshi Shinjo	.15
24 Melvin Mora	.15
25 Tim Hudson	.30
26 Darrin Fletcher	.15
27 Bill Mueller	.15
28 Jeff Weaver	.15
29 Tony Clark	.15
30 Tom Glavine	.40
31 Jarrod Washburn	.15
32 Greg Vaughn	.15
33 Lee Stevens	.15
34 Charles Johnson	.15
35 Lance Berkman	.15
36 Bud Smith	.15
37 Keith Foulke	.15
38 Ben Davis	.15
39 Daryle Ward	.15
40 Bernie Williams	.30
41 Dean Palmer	.15
42 Mark Mulder	.15
43 Jason LaRue	.15
44 Jay Gibbons	.15
45 Brandon Duckworth	.15
46 Carlos Delgado	.40
47 Barry Zito	.15
48 Matt Morris	.15
49 J.T. Snow	.15
50 Albert Pujols	1.50
51 Brad Fullmer	.15
52 Damion Easley	.15
53 Pat Burrell	.40
54 Kevin Brown	.15
55 Todd Walker	.15
56 Rich Garces	.15
57 Carlos Pena	.15
58 Paul LoDuca	.15
59 Mike Lieberthal	.15
60 Barry Larkin	.15
61 Jon Lieber	.15
62 Jose Cruz	.15
63 Mo Vaughn	.15

64 Ivan Rodriguez	.60
65 Jorge Posada	.25
66 Magglio Ordonez	.15
67 Juan Encarnacion	.15
68 Shawn Estes	.15
69 Kevin Appier	.15
70 Jeff Bagwell	.75
71 Tim Wakefield	.15
72 Shannon Stewart	.15
73 Scott Rolen	.65
74 Bobby Higginson	.15
75 Jim Edmonds	.15
76 Adam Dunn	.50
77 Eric Chavez	.30
78 Adrian Beltre	.30
79 Jason Varitek	.15
80 Barry Bonds	2.50
81 Edgar Renteria	.15
82 Raul Mondesi	.15
83 Eric Karros	.15
84 Ken Griffey Jr.	1.50
85 Jermaine Dye	.15
86 Carlos Beltran	.40
87 Mark Quinn	.15
88 Terrence Long	.15
89 Shawn Green	.40
90 Nomar Garciaparra	1.50
91 Sean Casey	.25
92 Homer Bush	.15
93 Bobby Abreu	.15
94 Jamey Wright	.15
95 Tony Womack	.15
96 Larry Walker	.15
97 Doug Mientkiewicz	.15
98 Jimmy Rollins	.40
99 Brady Anderson	.15
100 Derek Jeter	2.50
101 Kevin Young	.15
102 Juan Pierre	.15
103 Edgar Martinez	.15
104 Corey Koskie	.15
105 Jeffrey Hammonds	.15
106 Luis Gonzalez	.25
107 Travis Fryman	.15
108 Kerry Wood	.50
109 Rafael Palmeiro	.60
110 Ichiro Suzuki	1.00
111 Russ Ortiz	.15
112 Jeff Kent	.15
113 Scott Erickson	.15
114 Bruce Chen	.15
115 Craig Biggio	.15
116 Robin Ventura	.15
117 Alex Rodriguez	2.00
118 Roy Oswalt	.15
119 Fred McGriff	.15
120 Juan Gonzalez	.75
121 David Justice	.15
122 Pat Hentgen	.15
123 Hideo Nomo	.65
124 Ramon Ortiz	.15
125 David Ortiz	.25
126 Phil Nevin	.15
127 Ryan Dempster	.15
128 Toby Hall	.15
129 Vladimir Guerrero	.75
130 Chipper Jones	1.00
131 Russell Branyan	.15
132 Jose Vidro	.15
133 Bubba Trammell	.15
134 Tino Martinez	.15
135 Greg Maddux	1.00
136 Derrek Lee	.15
137 Troy Glaus	.75
138 Joe Crede	.15
139 Steve Cox	.15
140 Sammy Sosa	1.50
141 Corey Patterson	.15
142 Vernon Wells	.15
143 Matt Lawton	.15
144 Gabe Kapler	.15
145 Johnny Damon	.25
146 Marty Cordova	.15
147 Moises Alou	.15
148 Fernando Tatis	.15
149 Tanyon Sturtze	.15
150 Roger Clemens	1.25
151 Paul Konerko	.15
152 Chan Ho Park	.15
153 Marcus Giles	.15
154 David Eckstein	.15
155 Mike Lowell	.15
156 Preston Wilson	.15
157 John Vander Wal	.15
158 Tim Salmon	.25
159 Andy Pettitte	.35
160 Mike Mussina	.40
161 Doug Davis	.15
162 Peter Bergeron	.15
163 Rich Aurilia	.15
164 Eric Milton	.15
165 Geoff Jenkins	.15
166 Todd Helton	.75
167 Bret Boone	.15

168 Kris Benson	.15
169 Brian Anderson	.15
170 Roberto Alomar	.40
171 Javier Vazquez	.15
172 Scott Schoeneweis	.15
173 Ryan Klesko	.15
174 Jacque Jones	.15
175 Andruw Jones	.75
176 Aubrey Huff	.15
177 Mark Buehrle	.15
178 Josh Beckett	.40
179 Ben Sheets	.15
180 Curt Schilling	.40
181 C.C. Sabathia	.15
182 Denny Neagle	.15
183 Jamie Moyer	.15
184 Jason Kendall	.15
185 Dee Brown	.15
186 Frank Thomas	.75
187 Damian Rolls	.15
188 Carlos Lee	.15
189 Kevin Jarvis	.15
190 Manny Ramirez	.75
191 Cliff Floyd	.15
192 Freddy Garcia	.15
193 Orlando Cabrera	.15
194 Mike Sweeney	.15
195 Gary Sheffield	.35
196 Rafael Furcal	.15
197 Esteban Loaiza	.15
198 Mike Hampton	.15
199 Brian Giles	.15
200 Darin Erstad	.60
201 David Wells	.15
202 Kenny Lofton	.15
203 Aaron Sele	.15
204 Jason Schmidt	.15
205 Javy Lopez	.15
206 Dmitri Young	.15
207 Darryl Kile	.15
208 Matt Williams	.15
209 Joe Kennedy	.15
210 Chuck Knoblauch	.15
211 Brian Jordan	.15
212 Roberto Person	.15
213 Alex Ochoa	.15
214 Steve Finley	.15
215 Ben Petrick	.15
216 Al Leiter	.15
217 Mark Kotsay	.15
218 Miguel Tejada	.35
219 David Segui	.15
220 A.J. Burnett	.15
221 Marlon Anderson	.15
222 Wiki Gonzalez	.15
223 Jeff Suppan	.15
224 Dave Roberts	.15
225 Jose Hernandez	.15
226 Angel Berroa	1.00
227 Sean Burroughs	1.00
228 Luis Martinez RC	1.00
229 Adrian Burnside RC	1.00
230 John Ennis RC	1.00
231 Anastacio Martinez RC	1.00
232 Hank Blalock	2.00
233 Eric Hinske	1.00
234 Chris Booker RC	1.00
235 Colin Young RC	1.00
236 Mark Corey RC	1.00
237 Satoru Komiyama RC	1.00
238 So Taguchi RC	2.50
239 Elio Serrano RC	1.00
240 Reed Johnson RC	2.00
241 Jeremy Lambert RC	1.00
242 Chris Baker RC	1.00
243 Orlando Hudson RC	1.00
244 Travis Hughes RC	1.00
245 Kevin Frederick RC	1.00
246 Rodrigo Rosario RC	1.00
247 Jeremy Ward RC	1.00
248 Kazuhisa Ishii RC	4.00
249 Austin Kearns	1.00
250 Kyle Kane RC	1.00
251 Cam Esslinger RC	1.00
252 Jeff Austin RC	1.00
253 Brian Mallette RC	1.00
254 Mark Prior	4.00
255 Mark Teixeira	2.00
256 Carlos Valderrama	1.00
257 Jason Hart	1.00
258 Takahito Nomura RC	1.00
259 Matt Thornton	1.00
260 Marlon Byrd	1.00

Century

Cards (1-225):	6-10X
Cards (226-260):	.75-1.5X
Production 1:99	

Blue Chips

	NM/M
Complete Set (15):	10.00
Common Player:	.50
Inserted 1:6	

1BC Albert Pujols	3.00
2BC Sean Burroughs	.50
3BC Vernon Wells	.50
4BC Adam Dunn	1.50
5BC Pat Burrell	1.00
6BC Juan Pierre	.50
7BC Russell Branyan	.50
8BC Carlos Pena	.50
9BC Toby Hall	.50
10BC Mark Blalock	1.00
11BC Alfonso Soriano	1.50
12BC Jimmy Rollins	.75
13BC Jose Ortiz	.50
14BC Eric Hinske	.50
15BC Nick Johnson	.50

Blue Chips Game-Used

	NM/M
Inserted 1:96 Hobby	
Russell Branyan/Jsy	8.00
Nick Johnson/Jsy	10.00
Nick Johnson/	
Patch/100	20.00

International Diamond Company

	NM/M
Complete Set (25):	25.00
Common Player:	1.00
Inserted 1:8	
1 Bobby Abreu	1.00
2 Adrian Beltre	1.00
3 Jorge Posada	1.00
4 Vladimir Guerrero	3.00
5 Rafael Palmeiro	2.00
6 Sammy Sosa	4.00
7 Larry Walker	1.00
8 Manny Ramirez	3.00
9 Ichiro Suzuki	4.00
10 Jose Cruz	1.00
11 Juan Gonzalez	3.00
12 Bernie Williams	1.00
13 Ivan Rodriguez	2.00
14 Moises Alou	1.00
15 Cristian Guzman	1.00
16 Andruw Jones	3.00
17 Aramis Ramirez	1.00
18 Raul Mondesi	1.00
19 Edgar Martinez	1.00
20 Magglio Ordonez	1.00
21 Roberto Alomar	1.50
22 Chan Ho Park	1.00
23 Kazuhiro Sasaki	1.00
24 Tsuyoshi Shinjo	1.00
25 Hideo Nomo	3.00

International Diamond Company Game-Used

INTERNATIONAL DIAMOND COMPANY

EDGAR MARTINEZ

	NM/M
Common Player:	5.00
Inserted 1:144	
Jorge Posada/Jsy	15.00
Rafael Palmeiro/Jsy	8.00
Manny Ramirez/Jsy	10.00
Ivan Rodriguez/Jsy	6.00
Andruw Jones/Jsy	6.00
Aramis Ramirez/Jsy	5.00
Raul Mondesi/Jsy	5.00

Edgar Martinez/Jsy	6.00	
Chan Ho Park/Jsy	5.00	
Kazuhiro Sasaki/Jsy	6.00	
Hideo Nomo/Jsy	20.00	

International Diamond Company Patch

	NM/M
Common Player:	15.00
Production 100	
Manny Ramirez	25.00
Ivan Rodriguez	25.00
Raul Mondesi	15.00
Edgar Martinez	20.00
Chan Ho Park	20.00
Hideo Nomo	75.00

Jersey Number Parallel

(1-225) print run 26-50:	10-25X
(1-225) p/r 51-75:	8-15X
(1-225) p/r 76-99:	5-10X
Produced to player's jsy #.	

K Corps

		NM/M
Complete Set (15):		20.00
Common Player:		1.00
Inserted 1:12		
1KC	Roger Clemens	5.00
2KC	Randy Johnson	3.00
3KC	Tom Glavine	1.50
4KC	Josh Beckett	1.50
5KC	Matt Morris	1.00
6KC	Curt Schilling	1.50
7KC	Greg Maddux	4.00
8KC	Tim Hudson	1.00
9KC	Roy Oswalt	1.00
10KC	Kerry Wood	2.00
11KC	Barry Zito	1.00
12KC	Kevin Brown	1.00
13KC	Ryan Dempster	1.00
14KC	Ben Sheets	1.00
15KC	Pedro J. Martinez	3.00

K Corps Game-Used

		NM/M
Common Player:		5.00
Inserted 1:96		
2KC	Randy Johnson/Jsy	15.00
6KC	Curt Schilling/Jsy	10.00
7KC	Greg Maddux/Jsy	15.00
11KC	Barry Zito/Jsy	8.00
12KC	Kevin Brown/Jsy	5.00
15KC	Pedro Martinez/Jsy	10.00

K Corps Patch

	NM/M
Production 100	
Curt Schilling	20.00
Kevin Brown	20.00
Pedro Martinez	30.00

Kings of Swing

		NM/M
Complete Set (20):		80.00
Common Player:		2.00
Inserted 1:48		
1KS	Barry Bonds	10.00
2KS	Mike Piazza	6.00
3KS	Albert Pujols	8.00
4KS	Todd Helton	3.00
5KS	Ken Griffey Jr.	6.00
6KS	Alex Rodriguez	8.00
7KS	Sammy Sosa	6.00
8KS	Troy Glaus	3.00
9KS	Derek Jeter	10.00
10KS	Ichiro Suzuki	6.00
11KS	Manny Ramirez	3.00
12KS	Roberto Alomar	2.00
13KS	Juan Gonzalez	3.00
14KS	Shawn Green	2.00
15KS	Vladimir Guerrero	3.00
16KS	Nomar Garciaparra	6.00
17KS	Adam Dunn	2.00
18KS	Jason Giambi	2.50
19KS	Edgar Martinez	2.00
20KS	Chipper Jones	4.00

Kings of Swing Game-Used

		NM/M
Common Player:		5.00
Inserted 1:108		
	Mike Piazza	15.00
	Todd Helton	8.00
	Alex Rodriguez	15.00
	Derek Jeter	30.00
	Manny Ramirez	8.00
	Shawn Green	5.00
	Edgar Martinez	5.00
	Chipper Jones	10.00

Kings of Swing Patch

	NM/M
Production 100	
Todd Helton	25.00
Manny Ramirez	25.00
Shawn Green	20.00
Edgar Martinez	25.00
Mike Piazza	40.00

Larger Than Life

		NM/M
Common Player:		4.00
Inserted 1:240		
1LL	Jason Giambi	6.00
2LL	Carlos Delgado	5.00
3LL	Alex Rodriguez	20.00
4LL	Preston Wilson	4.00
5LL	Frank Thomas	9.00
6LL	Nomar Garciaparra	15.00
7LL	Jim Edmonds	4.00
8LL	Jim Thome	4.00
9LL	Barry Bonds	25.00
10LL	Mo Vaughn	4.00
11LL	Ichiro Suzuki	20.00
12LL	Ivan Rodriguez	5.00
13LL	Gary Sheffield	4.00
14LL	Derek Jeter	25.00
15LL	Jeff Bagwell	9.00
16LL	Mike Piazza	15.00
17LL	J.D. Drew	4.00
18LL	Sammy Sosa	15.00
19LL	Albert Pujols	20.00
20LL	Luis Gonzalez	4.00

Larger Than Life Game-Used

		NM/M
Common Player:		5.00
Inserted 1:144		
	Alex Rodriguez/Jsy	15.00
	Preston Wilson/Jsy	5.00
	Frank Thomas/Jsy	10.00
	Jim Edmonds/Jsy	6.00
	Mo Vaughn/Jsy	5.00
	Ivan Rodriguez/Jsy	8.00
	Derek Jeter/Jsy	25.00
	Jeff Bagwell/ Jsy/SP/20	25.00
	Mike Piazza/Jsy	15.00
	Luis Gonzalez/Jsy	5.00

Larger Than Life Patch

	NM/M
Common Player:	15.00
Production 100	
Preston Wilson	15.00
Frank Thomas	25.00

Jim Edmonds	15.00	
Ivan Rodriguez	25.00	
Mike Piazza	40.00	
Luis Gonzalez	15.00	

Lettermen

No Pricing
Production One Set

Materialistic Away

		NM/M
Complete Set (15):		75.00
Common Player:		4.00
Inserted 1:24		
Home:		1.5-3X
Production 50 Sets		
Away Oversized:		.5-1X
One per hobby box.		
Home Oversized:		2-4X
Production 50 Sets		
1MA	Derek Jeter	12.00
2MA	Alex Rodriguez	10.00
3MA	Mike Piazza	8.00
4MA	Ivan Rodriguez	4.00
5MA	Chipper Jones	6.00
6MA	Todd Helton	5.00
7MA	Nomar Garciaparra	8.00
8MA	Barry Bonds	12.00
9MA	Ichiro Suzuki	8.00
10MA	Ken Griffey Jr.	8.00
11MA	Jason Giambi	8.00
12MA	Sammy Sosa	8.00
13MA	Albert Pujols	10.00
14MA	Pedro J. Martinez	5.00
15MA	Vladimir Guerrero	5.00

2002 Fleer Genuine

	NM/M
Complete Set (140):	

Common Player:		.15
Common (101-140):		3.00
Production 2,002		
Pack (5):		3.00
Box (20):		50.00
1	Alex Rodriguez	2.50
2	Manny Ramirez	.75
3	Jim Thome	.15
4	Eric Milton	.15
5	Todd Helton	.75
6	Mike Mussina	.50
7	Ichiro Suzuki	1.50
8	Randy Johnson	1.00
9	Mark Mulder	.15
10	Johnny Damon	.25
11	Sean Casey	.25
12	Albert Pujols	2.50
13	Mark Grace	.25
14	Moises Alou, Mark Mulder	.15
15	Raul Mondesi, Roberto Alomar	.15
16	Cliff Floyd, Scott Rolen	.30
17	Vladimir Guerrero, Tom Glavine	.40
18	Pat Burrell, Bobby Abreu	.25
19	Ryan Klesko, Nomar Garciaparra	.50
20	Mike Hampton, Darin Erstad	.15
21	Shawn Green, Cliff Floyd	.15
22	Rich Aurilia, Tim Hudson	.15
23	Matt Morris, Jim Thome	.15
24	Curt Schilling, Nolan Ryan	1.00
25	Kevin Brown, Reggie Jackson	.25
26	Adrian Beltre, Rafael Palmeiro	.30
27	Joe Mays, Ken Griffey Jr.	.75
28	Luis Gonzalez, Sammy Sosa	.75
29	Barry Larkin, Vladimir Guerrero	.40
30	A.J. Burnett, Ichiro Suzuki	.75
31	Eric Munson	.15
32	Juan Gonzalez	.75
33	Lance Berkman	.15
34	Fred McGriff	.15
35	Paul Konerko	.15
36	Pedro J. Martinez	.75
37	Adam Dunn	.50
38	Jeromy Burnitz	.15
39	Mike Sweeney	.15
40	Bret Boone	.15
41	Ken Griffey Jr.	2.00
42	Eric Chavez	.25
43	Mark Quinn	.15
44	Roberto Alomar	.35
45	Bobby Abreu	.15
46	Bartolo Colon	.15
47	Jimmy Rollins	.25
48	Chipper Jones	1.00
49	Ben Sheets	.15
50	Freddy Garcia	.15
51	Sammy Sosa	2.00
52	Rafael Palmeiro	.65
53	Preston Wilson	.15
54	Troy Glaus	.75
55	Josh Beckett	.50
56	C.C. Sabathia	.15
57	Magglio Ordonez	.15
58	Brian Giles	.15
59	Darin Erstad	.60
60	Gary Sheffield	.35
61	Paul LoDuca	.15
62	Derek Jeter	3.00
63	Greg Maddux	1.50
64	Kerry Wood	.65
65	Toby Hall	.15
66	Barry Bonds	3.00
67	Jeff Bagwell	.75
68	Jason Kendall	.15
69	Richard Hidalgo	.15
70	J.D. Drew	.30
71	Tom Glavine	.30
72	Javier Vazquez	.15
73	Doug Mientkiewicz	.15
74	Jason Giambi	.50
75	Carlos Delgado	.40
76	Aramis Ramirez	.15
77	Torii Hunter	.15
78	Ivan Rodriguez	.65
79	Charles Johnson	.15
80	Jeff Kent	.15
81	Jacque Jones	.15
82	Larry Walker	.15
83	Cristian Guzman	.15
84	Jermaine Dye	.15

85	Roger Clemens	1.75
86	Mike Piazza	2.00
87	Craig Biggio	.15
88	Phil Nevin	.15
89	Jeff Cirillo	.15
90	Barry Zito	.25
91	Ryan Dempster	.15
92	Mark Buehrle	.15
93	Nomar Garciaparra	2.00
94	Frank Thomas	.75
95	Jim Edmonds	.15
96	Geoff Jenkins	.15
97	Scott Rolen	.65
98	Tim Hudson	.25
99	Shannon Stewart	.15
100	Richie Sexson	.15
101	Orlando Hudson	3.00
102	Doug DeVore RC	3.00
103	Rene Reyes RC	3.00
104	Steve Bechler RC	4.00
105	Jorge Nunez RC	3.00
106	Mitch Wylie RC	3.00
107	Jaime Cerda RC	3.00
108	Brandon Puffer RC	3.00
109	Tyler Yates RC	6.00
110	Bill Hall	3.00
111	Peter Zamora RC	3.00
112	Jeff Deardorff RC	3.00
113	J.J. Putz RC	3.00
114	Scotty Layfield RC	3.00
115	Brandon Backe RC	3.00
116	Andy Pratt RC	3.00
117	Mark Prior	8.00
118	Franklyn German RC	3.00
119	Todd Donovan RC	3.00
120	Franklin Nunez RC	3.00
121	Adam Walker RC	3.00
122	Ron Calloway RC	3.00
123	Tim Kalita RC	3.00
124	Kazuhisa Ishii RC	8.00
125	Mark Teixeira	5.00
126	Nate Field RC	3.00
127	Nelson Castro RC	3.00
128	So Taguchi RC	8.00
129	Marlon Byrd	3.00
130	Drew Henson	3.00
131	Kenny Kelly	3.00
132	John Ennis RC	3.00
133	Anastacio Martinez RC	3.00
134	Matt Guerrier	3.00
135	Tom Wilson RC	3.00
136	Ben Howard RC	4.00
137	Chris Baker RC	3.00
138	Kevin Frederick RC	3.00
159	Wilson Valdez RC	3.00
140	Austin Kearns	4.00

Bat's Incredible

		NM/M
Complete Set (25):		60.00
Common Player:		1.50
Inserted 1:10		
1BI	Todd Helton	2.00
2BI	Chipper Jones	3.00
3BI	Luis Gonzalez	1.50
4BI	Barry Bonds	8.00
5BI	Jason Giambi	2.00
6BI	Alex Rodriguez	6.00
7BI	Manny Ramirez	2.00
8BI	Jeff Bagwell	2.00
9BI	Shawn Green	1.50
10BI	Albert Pujols	6.00
11BI	Paul LoDuca	1.50
12BI	Mike Piazza	5.00
13BI	Derek Jeter	8.00
14BI	Edgar Martinez	1.50
15BI	Juan Gonzalez	2.00
16BI	Magglio Ordonez	1.50
17BI	Jermaine Dye	1.50
18BI	Larry Walker	1.50
19BI	Phil Nevin	1.50
20BI	Ivan Rodriguez	1.50
21BI	Ichiro Suzuki	5.00
22BI	J.D. Drew	1.50
23BI	Vladimir Guerrero	2.00
24BI	Sammy Sosa	5.00
25BI	Ken Griffey Jr.	5.00

Bat's Incredible Game-Used

	NM/M
Common Player:	5.00

Inserted 1:20	
Todd Helton	10.00
Chipper Jones	10.00
J.D. Drew	8.00
Alex Rodriguez	15.00
Manny Ramirez	10.00
Shawn Green	6.00
Derek Jeter	20.00
Edgar Martinez	8.00
Juan Gonzalez	8.00
Jermaine Dye	5.00
Phil Nevin	5.00
Ivan Rodriguez	10.00

Genuine Ink

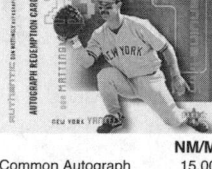

	NM/M
Common Autograph	15.00
Production varies	
Barry Bonds/150	150.00
Ron Cey/175	15.00
Derek Jeter/150	125.00
Al Kaline/300	60.00
Don Mattingly/50	100.00
Paul Molitor	50.00
Dale Murphy/700	40.00
Phil Rizzuto/700	30.00
Brooks Robinson/140	60.00
Maury Willis/975	15.00

Leaders

		NM/M
Complete Set (15):		25.00
Common Player:		1.00
Inserted 1:6		
1GL	Sammy Sosa	4.00
2GL	Todd Helton	2.00
3GL	Alex Rodriguez	4.00
4GL	Roger Clemens	3.00
5GL	Barry Bonds	5.00
6GL	Randy Johnson	2.00
7GL	Albert Pujols	4.00
8GL	Curt Schilling	1.00
9GL	Bernie Williams	1.00
10GL	Ken Griffey Jr.	4.00
11GL	Pedro J. Martinez	2.00
12GL	Juan Gonzalez	2.00
13GL	Hideo Nomo	2.00
14GL	Bret Boone	1.00
15GL	Ichiro Suzuki	5.00

Leaders Game-Used

	NM/M
Common Player:	8.00
Inserted 1:16	
Todd Helton	10.00
Alex Rodriguez	15.00
Roger Clemens	15.00
Barry Bonds	20.00
Randy Johnson	10.00
Curt Schilling	8.00
Bernie Williams	8.00
Pedro J. Martinez	10.00
Hideo Nomo	15.00

Tip of the Cap

	NM/M
Complete Set (25):	40.00
Common Player:	.50
Inserted 1:6	

1TC	Alex Rodriguez	6.00
2TC	Derek Jeter	8.00
3TC	Kazuhiro Sasaki	.50
4TC	Barry Bonds	8.00
5TC	J.D. Drew	.75
6TC	Tsuyoshi Shinjo	.50
7TC	Alfonso Soriano	1.50
8TC	Albert Pujols	6.00
9TC	Tom Seaver	1.50
10TC	Drew Henson	.75
11TC	Dave Winfield	1.50
12TC	Carlos Delgado	1.00
13TC	Lou Boudreau	.50
14TC	Shawn Green	.75
15TC	Roger Clemens	3.00
16TC	Randy Johnson	1.50
17TC	Sammy Sosa	4.00
18TC	Rafael Palmeiro	1.25
19TC	Ken Griffey Jr.	5.00
20TC	Ichiro Suzuki	5.00
21TC	Eric Chavez	.65
22TC	Andruw Jones	1.50
23TC	Miguel Tejada	.65
24TC	Pedro J. Martinez	1.50
25TC	Tim Salmon	.50

Tip of the Cap Game-Used

	NM/M
Common Player:	
Alex Rodriguez/670	20.00
Barry Bonds/32	75.00
Tom Seaver/224	25.00
Drew Henson/361	15.00
Dave Winfield/363	15.00
Carlos Delgado/219	15.00
Lou Boudreau/303	20.00
Randy Johnson/74	30.00
Rafael Palmeiro/300	20.00
Andruw Jones/19	40.00
Miguel Tejada/225	15.00

Touch 'Em All

		NM/M
Complete Set (25):		60.00
Common Player:		1.50
Inserted 1:10		
1	Derek Jeter	8.00
2	Sammy Sosa	5.00
3	Albert Pujols	6.00
4	Vladimir Guerrero	3.00
5	Ken Griffey Jr.	5.00
6	Nomar Garciaparra	5.00
7	Luis Gonzalez	1.50
8	Barry Bonds	8.00
9	Manny Ramirez	2.50
10	Jason Giambi	2.00
11	Chipper Jones	4.00
12	Ichiro Suzuki	5.00
13	Alex Rodriguez	6.00
14	Juan Gonzalez	2.50
15	Todd Helton	2.50
16	Roberto Alomar	1.50
17	Jeff Bagwell	2.50
18	Mike Piazza	5.00
19	Gary Sheffield	1.50
20	Ivan Rodriguez	2.00
21	Frank Thomas	2.50
22	Bobby Abreu	1.50
23	J.D. Drew	1.50
24	Scott Rolen	2.00
25	Darin Erstad	1.50

Touch 'Em All Base

	NM/M
Common Player:	4.00
Production 350 Sets	
Derek Jeter	15.00
Sammy Sosa	10.00
Albert Pujols	15.00

Vladimir Guerrero	10.00
Ken Griffey Jr.	10.00
Nomar Garciaparra	10.00
Luis Gonzalez	5.00
Barry Bonds	15.00
Manny Ramirez	8.00
Jason Giambi	8.00
Chipper Jones	8.00
Ichiro Suzuki	15.00
Alex Rodriguez	10.00
Juan Gonzalez	8.00
Todd Helton	8.00
Roberto Alomar	6.00
Jeff Bagwell	8.00
Mike Piazza	10.00
Gary Sheffield	6.00
Ivan Rodriguez	8.00
Frank Thomas	8.00
Bobby Abreu	4.00
J.D. Drew	4.00
Scott Rolen	8.00
Darin Erstad	4.00

Names of the Game

		NM/M
Complete Set (30):		60.00
Common Player:		1.00
Inserted 1:10 H, 1:20 R		
1	Mike Piazza	5.00
2	Chipper Jones	4.00
3	Jim Edmonds	1.00
4	Barry Larkin	1.00
5	Frank Thomas	3.00
6	Manny Ramirez	3.00
7	Carlos Delgado	1.50
8	Brian Giles	1.00
9	Kerry Wood	2.00
10	Derek Jeter	8.00
11	Adam Dunn	2.00
12	Gary Sheffield	1.50
13	Luis Gonzalez	1.00
14	Mark Mulder	1.00
15	Roberto Alomar	1.50
16	Scott Rolen	2.50
17	Tom Glavine	1.50
18	Bobby Abreu	1.00
19	Nomar Garciaparra	5.00
20	Darin Erstad	2.00
21	Cliff Floyd	1.00
22	Tim Hudson	1.00
23	Jim Thome	2.00
24	Nolan Ryan	8.00
25	Reggie Jackson	3.00
26	Rafael Palmeiro	2.00
27	Ken Griffey Jr.	5.00
28	Sammy Sosa	5.00
29	Vladimir Guerrero	3.00
30	Ichiro Suzuki	5.00

Names of the Game Memorabilia

		NM/M
Common Player:		5.00
1:24 H, 1:100 R		
1	Roberto Alomar	10.00
2	Carlos Delgado	8.00
3	Jim Edmonds	8.00
4	Darin Erstad	5.00
5	Cliff Floyd	5.00

6	Nomar Garciaparra/SP/90	60.00
7	Brian Giles	5.00
8	Luis Gonzalez	5.00
9	Tim Hudson	8.00
10	Derek Jeter	30.00
11	Chipper Jones	10.00
12	Barry Larkin	8.00
13	Mark Mulder	8.00
14	Rafael Palmeiro	10.00
15	Mike Piazza	15.00
16	Manny Ramirez	8.00
17	Scott Rolen	10.00
18	Nolan Ryan	40.00
19	Jim Thome	10.00

2002 Fleer Greats of the Game

Los Angeles Dodgers®

		NM/M
	Complete Set (100):	45.00
	Common Player:	.40
	Pack (5):	5.00
	Box (24):	100.00
1	Cal Ripken Jr.	6.00
2	Paul Molitor	1.50
3	Roberto Clemente	4.00
4	Cy Young	1.50
5	Tris Speaker	.75
6	Lou Brock	.50
7	Fred Lynn	.40
8	Harmon Killebrew	1.50
9	Ted Williams	6.00
10	Dave Winfield	1.00
11	Orlando Cepeda	.40
12	Johnny Mize	.40
13	Walter Johnson	1.50
14	Roy Campanella	1.50
15	George Sisler	.40
16	Bo Jackson	1.00
17	Rollie Fingers	.40
18	Brooks Robinson	1.50
19	Billy Williams	.40
20	Maury Wills	.40
21	Jimmie Foxx	1.50
22	Alan Trammell	.40
23	Rogers Hornsby	1.50
24	Don Drysdale	1.00
25	Bob Feller	.75
26	Jackie Robinson	5.00
27	Whitey Ford	1.50
28	Enos Slaughter	.40
29	Rod Carew	1.00
30	Eddie Mathews	1.50
31	Ron Cey	.40
32	Thurman Munson	2.00
33	Ty Cobb	3.00
34	Rocky Colavito	.75
35	Satchel Paige	1.50
36	Andre Dawson	.75
37	Phil Rizzuto	.75
38	Roger Maris	3.00
39	Earl Weaver	.40
40	Joe Carter	.40
41	Christy Mathewson	1.50
42	Tony Lazzeri	.40
43	Gil Hodges	.75
44	Gaylord Perry	.40
45	Steve Carlton	1.00
46	George Kell	.40
47	Mickey Cochrane	1.00
48	Joe Morgan	.60
49	Steve Garvey	.40
50	Bob Gibson	1.50
51	Lefty Grove	.40
52	Warren Spahn	1.50
53	Willie McCovey	.75
54	Frank Robinson	1.50
55	Rich "Goose" Gossage	.40
56	Hank Bauer	.40
57	Hoyt Wilhelm	.40
58	Mel Ott	1.00
59	Preacher Roe	.75

60	Yogi Berra	1.50
61	Nolan Ryan	6.00
62	Dizzy Dean	.75
63	Ryne Sandberg	2.00
64	Frank Howard	.40
65	Hack Wilson	.40
66	Robin Yount	1.50
67	Al Kaline	1.50
68	Mike Schmidt	2.00
69	Vida Blue	.40
70	George Brett	3.00
71	Sparky Anderson	.40
72	Tom Seaver	1.50
73	Bill "Moose" Skowron	.40
74	Don Mattingly	2.50
75	Carl Yastrzemski	1.50
76	Eddie Murray	1.00
77	Jim Palmer	1.00
78	Bill Dickey	.75
79	Ozzie Smith	1.50
80	Dale Murphy	.75
81	Nap Lajoie	1.00
82	Jim "Catfish" Hunter	1.00
83	Duke Snider	1.00
84	Luis Aparicio	.40
85	Reggie Jackson	1.50
86	Honus Wagner	1.50
87	Johnny Bench	2.00
88	Stan Musial	3.00
89	Carlton Fisk	.75
90	Tony Oliva	.75
91	Wade Boggs	2.00
92	Jim Rice	.40
93	Bill Mazeroski	.40
94	Ralph Kiner	.40
95	Tony Perez	.40
96	Kirby Puckett	2.00
97	Bobby Bonds	.75
98	Bill Terry	.40
99	Juan Marichal	.75
100	Hank Greenberg	1.00

Autographs

Brooklyn Dodgers®

		NM/M
	Common Autograph:	10.00
	Inserted 1:24	
SA	Sparky Anderson	15.00
LA	Luis Aparicio	15.00
HB	Hank Bauer	10.00
JB	Johnny Bench	50.00
YB	Yogi Berra	40.00
PB	Paul Blair	10.00
VB	Vida Blue	15.00
WB	Wade Boggs	20.00
BB	Bobby Bonds	15.00
GB	George Brett/150	125.00
LB	Lou Brock/250	25.00
RC	Rod Carew/250	40.00
SC	Steve Carlton	25.00
JC	Joe Carter	15.00
OC	Orlando Cepeda	15.00
CE	Ron Cey	10.00
CO	Rocky Colavito	35.00
AD	Andre Dawson	15.00
BF	Bob Feller	15.00
RF	Rollie Fingers	15.00
CF	Carlton Fisk/100	65.00
WF	Whitey Ford	40.00
SG	Steve Garvey	15.00
BG	Bob Gibson/200	30.00
RG	Rich "Goose" Gossage	10.00
FH	Frank Howard	15.00
RJ	Reggie Jackson/150	70.00
AK	Al Kaline	40.00
GK	George Kell	15.00
HK	Harmon Killebrew	30.00
RK	Ralph Kiner/250	25.00
FL	Fred Lynn	15.00
JM	Juan Marichal	15.00
DM	Don Mattingly/300	75.00
BM	Bill Mazeroski/200	20.00

WM	Willie McCovey	25.00
PM	Paul Molitor	25.00
JM	Joe Morgan	15.00
MU	Dale Murphy	40.00
EM	Eddie Murray/250	70.00
SM	Stan Musial/200	75.00
TO	Tony Oliva	15.00
JP	Jim Palmer	20.00
DP	Dave Parker	10.00
TP	Tony Perez	15.00
GP	Gaylord Perry/4	60.00
KP	Kirby Puckett/250	60.00
JR	Jim Rice	15.00
CR	Cal Ripken Jr./100	180.00
PR	Phil Rizzuto/300	50.00
BR	Brooks Robinson	30.00
FR	Frank Robinson/250	30.00
PR	Preacher Roe	15.00
NR	Nolan Ryan/150	100.00
RS	Ryne Sandberg/200	75.00
MS	Mike Schmidt/150	100.00
TS	Tom Seaver/150	50.00
BS	Bill "Moose" Skowron	10.00
ES	Enos Slaughter	15.00
OS	Ozzie Smith/300	65.00
DS	Duke Snider	25.00
WS	Warren Spahn	50.00
AT	Alan Trammell	20.00
HW	Hoyt Wilhelm	15.00
BW	Billy Williams	15.00
MW	Maury Wills	15.00
DW	Dave Winfield/250	25.00
CY	Carl Yastrzemski/200	75.00
RY	Robin Yount	70.00

Dueling Duos

JIM RICE BOSTON RED SOX® — EDDIE MURRAY BALTIMORE ORIOLES®

		NM/M
	Complete Set (29):	90.00
	Common Player:	2.00
	Inserted 1:6	
1DD	Johnny Bench, Carlton Fisk	4.00
2DD	Roy Campanella, Yogi Berra	5.00
3DD	Stan Musial, Ted Williams	8.00
4DD	Carl Yastrzemski, Reggie Jackson	3.00
5DD	Babe Ruth, Jimmie Foxx	8.00
6DD	Steve Carlton, Nolan Ryan	8.00
7DD	Wade Boggs, Don Mattingly	6.00
8DD	Brooks Robinson, Roger Maris	5.00
9DD	Paul Molitor, Don Mattingly	6.00
10DD	Sparky Anderson, Earl Weaver	2.00
11DD	Bob Gibson, Duke Snider	3.00
12DD	Yogi Berra, Gil Hodges	4.00
13DD	Joe Morgan, Ryne Sandberg	3.00
14DD	Tony Perez, Carl Yastrzemski	3.00
15DD	Jimmie Foxx, Bill Dickey	3.00
16DD	Ralph Kiner, Duke Snider	2.00
17DD	Nellie Fox, Rocky Colavito	2.00
18DD	Willie McCovey, Johnny Bench	3.00
19DD	Duke Snider, Eddie Mathews	4.00
20DD	Reggie Jackson, Jim Rice	3.00
21DD	Eddie Murray, Jim Rice	2.00
22DD	Paul Molitor, Dave Winfield	3.00
23DD	Robin Yount, Dave Winfield	3.00
24DD	Enos Slaughter, Ted Kluszewski	2.00
25DD	Wade Boggs, George Brett	4.00
26DD	George Brett, Eddie Murray	4.00
27DD	George Brett, Cal Ripken Jr.	8.00
28DD	Kirby Puckett, Don Mattingly	6.00
29DD	George Brett, Mike Schmidt	5.00

Dueling Duos Autograph

No Pricing
Production 25 Sets

Dueling Duos Game-Used Dual

No Pricing
Production 25 Sets

Dueling Duos Game-Used Single

RALPH KINER PITTSBURGH PIRATES® — DUKE SNIDER BROOKLYN DODGERS®

	NM/M
Common Card:	15.00
Inserted 1:24	
Johnny Bench, Carlton Fisk	20.00
Roy Campanella, Yogi Berra	25.00
Carl Yastrzemski, Reggie Jackson	25.00
Babe Ruth, Jimmie Foxx/75	50.00
Kirby Puckett, Don Mattingly	25.00
Steve Carlton, Nolan Ryan	80.00
Wade Boggs, Don Mattingly	25.00
Brooks Robinson, Roger Maris	25.00
Paul Molitor, Don Mattingly	25.00
Sparky Anderson, Earl Weaver	10.00
Bob Gibson, Duke Snider/200	20.00
Yogi Berra, Gil Hodges	25.00
Joe Morgan, Ryne Sandberg	25.00
Tony Perez, Carl Yastrzemski	25.00
Jimmie Foxx, Bill Dickey	20.00
Ralph Kiner, Duke Snider	20.00
Nellie Fox, Rocky Colavito	20.00
Willie McCovey, Johnny Bench	25.00
Duke Snider, Eddie Mathews	20.00
Reggie Jackson, Jim Rice	20.00
Eddie Murray, Jim Rice	15.00
Paul Molitor, Dave Winfield	15.00
Robin Yount, Dave Winfield	15.00
Enos Slaughter, Ted Kluszewski	10.00
Wade Boggs, George Brett	25.00
George Brett, Eddie Murray	20.00
George Brett, Cal Ripken Jr.	40.00

Through the Years Level 1

BLUE JAYS®

	NM/M
Common Player:	10.00

Inserted 1:24

George Brett	25.00
Reggie Jackson/A's	15.00
Reggie Jackson/Angels	15.00
Ted Williams/350	100.00
Robin Yount	20.00
Willie McCovey	10.00
Paul Molitor/Brewers	15.00
Paul Molitor/Blue Jays	15.00
Jim Palmer	10.00
Brooks Robinson	15.00
Carl Yastrzemski	15.00
Don Mattingly	25.00
Carlton Fisk/Hitting	15.00
Carlton Fisk/Fielding	15.00
Nolan Ryan	40.00
Eddie Murray	10.00
Wade Boggs	15.00
Tony Perez	10.00
Ted Kluszewski	10.00
Bo Jackson/Royals	15.00
Bo Jackson/White Sox	15.00
Johnny Bench	20.00
Jackie Robinson	65.00
Hoyt Wilhelm	10.00
Vida Blue	10.00
Dave Winfield	10.00
Frank Robinson	15.00
Jim Rice	10.00
Jim Rice	10.00
Cal Ripken/Hitting	40.00
Cal Ripken/Fielding	40.00

Through the Years Level 2

	NM/M
Common Player:	25.00
Production 100 Sets	
George Brett	80.00
Reggie Jackson	30.00
Ted Williams	120.00
Robin Yount	40.00
Willie McCovey	30.00
Paul Molitor	40.00
Jim Palmer	25.00
Carl Yastrzemski	65.00
Don Mattingly	60.00
Carlton Fisk	30.00
Nolan Ryan	75.00
Eddie Murray	25.00
Wade Boggs	30.00
Ted Kluszewski	30.00
Bo Jackson Royals	30.00
Bo Jackson/White Sox	30.00
Johnny Bench	40.00
Dave Winfield	25.00
Jim Rice	25.00
Jim Rice	25.00
Cal Ripken Jr.	60.00
Cal Ripken Jr.	60.00

Through the Years Level 3

No Pricing
Production 25 Sets

Through Years Patch Edition

	NM/M
Common Player:	25.00
Production 100 Sets	
George Brett	80.00
Reggie Jackson/A's	30.00
Reggie Jackson/Angels	30.00
Ted Williams	120.00
Robin Yount	50.00
Willie McCovey	30.00
Paul Molitor/Brewers	40.00
Paul Molitor/Blue Jays	40.00
Jim Palmer	25.00
Carl Yastrzemski	75.00
Don Mattingly	60.00
Carlton Fisk	30.00
Carlton Fisk	30.00
Nolan Ryan	75.00
Eddie Murray	25.00
Wade Boggs	30.00
Tony Perez	25.00
Ted Kluszewski	30.00
Bo Jackson/Royals	40.00
Bo Jackson/White Sox	40.00
Johnny Bench	40.00
Dave Winfield	30.00
Frank Robinson	30.00
Jim Rice	25.00
Jim Rice	25.00
Cal Ripken Jr.	80.00
Cal Ripken Jr.	80.00

2002 Fleer Hot Prospects

	NM/M
Complete Set (125):	
Common Player:	.25
Common (81-105):	8.00
Production 1,000	
Common (106-125):	3.00
Production 1,500	
Pack (5):	4.00
Box (18):	50.00
1 Derek Jeter	3.00
2 Garret Anderson	.25
3 Scott Rolen	.75
4 Bret Boone	.25
5 Lance Berkman	.25
6 Andruw Jones	1.00
7 Ivan Rodriguez	.75
8 Bernie Williams	.35
9 Cristian Guzman	.25
10 Mo Vaughn	.25
11 Troy Glaus	1.00
12 Tim Salmon	.35
13 Jason Giambi	.65
14 Cliff Floyd	.25
15 Tim Hudson	.35
16 Curt Schilling	.40
17 Sammy Sosa	2.00
18 Alex Rodriguez	2.50
19 Chuck Knoblauch	.25
20 Jason Kendall	.25
21 Ben Sheets	.25
22 Nomar Garciaparra	2.00
23 Ryan Klesko	.25
24 Greg Vaughn	.25
25 Rafael Palmeiro	.75
26 Miguel Tejada	.35
27 Shea Hillenbrand	.25
28 Jim Thome	.25
29 Randy Johnson	1.00
30 Barry Larkin	.25
31 Paul LoDuca	.25
32 Pedro J. Martinez	1.00
33 Luis Gonzalez	.35
34 Carlos Delgado	.50
35 Richie Sexson	.25
36 Albert Pujols	2.25
37 Bobby Abreu	.25
38 Gary Sheffield	.40
39 Magglio Ordonez	.25
40 Eric Chavez	.35
41 Jeff Bagwell	1.00
42 Doug Mientkiewicz	.25
43 Moises Alou	.25
44 Todd Helton	1.00
45 Ichiro Suzuki	2.00
46 Jose Cruz Jr.	.25
47 Freddy Garcia	.25
48 Tino Martinez	.25
49 Roger Clemens	1.75
50 Greg Maddux	1.50
51 Mike Piazza	2.00
52 Roberto Alomar	.50
53 Adam Dunn	.50
54 Kerry Wood	.75
55 Edgar Martinez	.25
56 Ken Griffey Jr.	2.00
57 Juan Gonzalez	1.00
58 Pat Burrell	.50
59 Corey Koskie	.25
60 Jose Vidro	.25
61 Ben Grieve	.25
62 Barry Bonds	3.00
63 Raul Mondesi	.25
64 Jimmy Rollins	.50
65 Mike Sweeney	.25
66 Josh Beckett	.50
67 Chipper Jones	1.50
68 Jeff Kent	.25
69 Tony Batista	.25
70 Phil Nevin	.25
71 Brian Jordan	.25
72 Rich Aurilia	.25
73 Brian Giles	.25
74 Frank Thomas	1.00
75 Larry Walker	.25
76 Shawn Green	.40
77 Manny Ramirez	1.00
78 Craig Biggio	.25
79 Vladimir Guerrero	1.00
80 Jeromy Burnitz	.25
81 Mark Teixeira	10.00
82 Corey Thurman RC	8.00
83 Mark Prior	15.00
84 Marlon Byrd	8.00
85 Austin Kearns	10.00
86 Satoru Komiyama RC	8.00
87 So Taguchi RC	12.00
88 Jorge Padilla RC	8.00
89 Rene Reyes RC	8.00
90 Jorge Nunez RC	8.00
91 Ron Calloway RC	8.00
92 Kazuhisa Ishii RC	10.00
93 Dewon Brazelton	8.00
94 Angel Berroa	8.00
95 Felix Escalona RC	8.00
96 Sean Burroughs	8.00
97 Brandon Duckworth	8.00
98 Hank Blalock	10.00
99 Eric Hinske	8.00
100 Carlos Pena	8.00
101 Morgan Ensberg	8.00
102 Ryan Ludwick	8.00
103 Chris Snelling RC	8.00
104 Jason Lane	8.00
105 Drew Henson	10.00
106 Bobby Kielty	3.00
107 Earl Snyder RC	3.00
108 Nate Field RC	3.00
109 Juan Diaz	3.00
110 Ryan Anderson	3.00
111 Esteban German	3.00
112 Takahito Nomura RC	3.00
113 David Kelton	3.00
114 Steve Kent RC	3.00
115 Colby Lewis	3.00
116 Jason Simontacchi RC	3.00
117 Rodrigo Rosario RC	3.00
118 Ben Howard RC	3.00
119 Hansel Izquierdo RC	3.00
120 John Ennis RC	3.00
121 Anderson Machado RC	3.00
122 Luis Ugueto RC	3.00
123 Anastacio Martinez RC	3.00
124 Reed Johnson RC	6.00
125 Juan Cruz	3.00

Co-Stars

	NM/M
Complete Set (15):	25.00
Common Card:	1.00
Inserted 1:6	
1CS Barry Bonds, Alex Rodriguez	6.00
2CS Derek Jeter, Nomar Garciaparra	5.00
3CS Andruw Jones, Chipper Jones	3.00
4CS Juan Gonzalez, Jim Thome	2.00
5CS Pedro J. Martinez, Randy Johnson	2.00
6CS Adam Dunn, Pat Burrell	1.50
7CS Frank Thomas, Manny Ramirez	2.00
8CS Jeff Bagwell, Lance Berkman	2.00
9CS So Taguchi, Kazuhisa Ishii	4.00
10CS Jimmy Rollins, Miguel Tejada	2.00
11CS Morgan Ensberg, Carlos Pena	1.00
12CS Adam Dunn, Austin Kearns	2.00
13CS Vladimir Guerrero, Scott Rolen	3.00
14CS Drew Henson, Xavier Nady	1.00
15CS Mike Piazza, Ivan Rodriguez	4.00

Future Swatch Autograph

	NM/M
Common Auto.	10.00
Production 100	
83 Mark Prior	40.00
87 So Taguchi	20.00
89 Rene Reyes	10.00
105 Drew Henson	20.00

Inside Barry Bonds

	NM/M
Common Bonds:	15.00
1BB Barry Bonds/Pants/1,000	20.00
2BB Barry Bonds/Pants/900	20.00
3BB Barry Bonds/Jsy/800	20.00
4BB Barry Bonds/Bat/700	20.00
5BB Barry Bonds/Base/600	15.00
6BB Barry Bonds/Cleat/500	25.00
7BB Barry Bonds/Glove/400	25.00
8BB Barry Bonds/Cap/300	30.00

Jerseygraphs

	NM/M
Common Player:	10.00
Inserted 1:186	
DJ Derek Jeter/108	150.00
BB Barry Bonds/65	250.00
CJ Chipper Jones/100	80.00
DH Drew Henson	30.00
ST So Taguchi/100	25.00
DE David Espinosa	10.00
DS Dane Sardinha	10.00
AB Adrian Beltre/169	35.00
GM Kazuhisa Ishii/40	

MLB Hot Materials

	NM/M
Common Player:	5.00
Inserted 1:9	
Red Hots:	1-2X
Production 50 Sets	
AD Adam Dunn	8.00
AR Alex Rodriguez	10.00
BB Bret Boone	5.00
BB2 Barry Bonds	20.00
BD Brandon Duckworth	5.00
BG Brian Giles	5.00
BW Bernie Williams	8.00
CD Carlos Delgado	6.00
CG Cristian Guzman	5.00
CP Carlos Pena	8.00
CP Corey Patterson	6.00
CS Curt Schilling	8.00
FT Frank Thomas	10.00
GK Gabe Kapler	5.00
GM Greg Maddux	15.00
GS Gary Sheffield	6.00
IR Ivan Rodriguez	10.00
JB Josh Beckett	8.00
JB2 Jeff Bagwell/108	20.00
JG Juan Gonzalez	8.00
JT Jim Thome	10.00
JU Juan Uribe	5.00
LB Lance Berkman	8.00
MM Mark Mulder	8.00
MA Moises Alou	6.00
MP Mike Piazza	15.00
MS Mike Sweeney	5.00
NJ Nick Johnson	5.00
PL Paul LoDuca	5.00
PM Pedro J. Martinez	10.00
RF Rafael Furcal	5.00
RO Roy Oswalt	5.00
RP Rafael Palmeiro	5.00
SB Sean Burroughs/350	10.00
SG Shawn Green	8.00
TA Tony Armas Jr.	5.00
TH Torii Hunter	5.00
TM Tino Martinez	8.00
VW Vernon Wells	5.00
TH Todd Helton	8.00
MO Magglio Ordonez	8.00
FG Freddy Garcia	5.00
ST So Taguchi	8.00

MLB Hot Tandems

	NM/M
Common Card:	10.00

Production 100 Sets
Red Hots 10 Sets. No Pricing

	NM/M
Adam Dunn, Lance Berkman	15.00
Alex Rodriguez, Ivan Rodriguez	30.00
Bret Boone, Freddy Garcia	10.00
Barry Bonds, Kazuhisa Ishii	40.00
Brandon Duckworth, Roy Oswalt	10.00
Bernie Williams, Jorge Posada	15.00
Carlos Delgado, Vernon Wells	10.00
Cristian Guzman, Torii Hunter	10.00
Carlos Pena, Corey Patterson	10.00
Curt Schilling, Greg Maddux	25.00
Frank Thomas, Magglio Ordonez	15.00
Gabe Kapler, Rafael Palmeiro	12.00
Gary Sheffield, Rafael Furcal	10.00
Josh Beckett, Roy Oswalt	10.00
Brandon Duckworth, Josh Beckett	15.00
Jeff Bagwell, Lance Berkman	15.00
Juan Gonzalez, Rafael Palmeiro	15.00
Jim Thome, Shawn Green	15.00
Paul LoDuca, Shawn Green	10.00
Juan Uribe, Miguel Tejada	15.00
Mark Mulder, Miguel Tejada	15.00
Moises Alou, Magglio Ordonez	10.00
Jorge Posada, Mike Piazza	25.00
Mike Sweeney, Todd Helton	15.00
Carlos Pena, Nick Johnson	10.00
Curt Schilling, Pedro J. Martinez	25.00
Tony Armas Jr., Freddy Garcia	10.00
Tino Martinez, Todd Helton	15.00
Barry Bonds, Derek Jeter	60.00
Kazuhisa Ishii, Derek Jeter	40.00
Juan Uribe, Cristian Guzman	10.00
Kazuhisa Ishii, So Taguchi	20.00
Adam Dunn, Corey Patterson	15.00
Bernie Williams, Nick Johnson	10.00
Bret Boone, Torii Hunter	10.00
Greg Maddux, Pedro J. Martinez	20.00
Sean Burroughs, Drew Henson	10.00
Kazuhisa Ishii, Satoru Komiyama	20.00
Kazuhisa Ishii, Mark Prior	20.00
Hank Blalock, Austin Kearns	15.00
Hank Blalock, Mark Teixeira	15.00
Marlon Byrd, Jorge Padilla	10.00
Marlon Byrd, Austin Kearns	10.00
Gabe Kapler, Juan Gonzalez	15.00
Jeff Bagwell, Mike Piazza	25.00

We're Number One

	NM/M
Complete Set (10):	35.00
Common Player:	1.50

Inserted 1:15

1WN	Derek Jeter	8.00
2WN	Barry Bonds	8.00
3WN	Ken Griffey Jr.	5.00
4WN	Roger Clemens	4.50
5WN	Alex Rodriguez	6.00
6WN	J.D. Drew	1.50
7WN	Chipper Jones	4.00
8WN	Manny Ramirez	3.00
9WN	Nomar Garciaparra	5.00
10WN	Todd Helton	3.00

We're Number One Memorabilia

	NM/M
Common Player:	5.00

Inserted 1:25

Derek Jeter/Jsy	25.00
Barry Bonds/Jsy	20.00
Ken Griffey Jr./Base	15.00
Alex Rodriguez/Jsy	15.00
J.D. Drew/Jsy	5.00
Chipper Jones/Jsy	10.00
Manny Ramirez/Jsy	10.00
Nomar Garciaparra/ Jsy	20.00
Todd Helton/Jsy	10.00

We're Number One Autograph

	NM/M
Common Player: Derek Jeter/92	
Barry Bonds/85	200.00

2002 Fleer Maximum

	NM/M
Complete Set (270):	
Common Player:	.15
Common (201-250):	5.00

Production 500

Common (251-270):	.50

Inserted 1:Hobby Pack

Pack (15):	2.50
Box (16):	35.00
1	Barry Bonds	2.00
2	Alex Rodriguez	1.50
3	Jim Edmonds	.15
4	Manny Ramirez	.75
5	Jeff Bagwell	.75
6	Kazuhiro Sasaki	.15
7	Jason Giambi	.50
8	J.D. Drew	.25
9	Barry Larkin	.15
10	Chipper Jones	1.00
11	Rafael Palmeiro	.65
12	Roberto Alomar	.35
13	Randy Johnson	.75
14	Juan Gonzalez	.75
15	Gary Sheffield	.25
16	Larry Walker	.15
17	Todd Helton	.75
18	Ivan Rodriguez	.65
19	Greg Maddux	1.00
20	Mike Piazza	1.25
21	Tsuyoshi Shinjo	.15
22	Luis Gonzalez	.25
23	Pedro Martinez	.75
24	Albert Pujols	1.50
25	Jose Canseco	.35
26	Edgar Martinez	.15
27	Moises Alou	.15
28	Vladimir Guerrero	.75
29	Shawn Green	.35
30	Miguel Tejada	.25
31	Bernie Williams	.30
32	Frank Thomas	.75
33	Jim Thome	.15
34	Derek Jeter	2.00
35	Julio Lugo	.15
36	Mo Vaughn	.15
37	Steve Cox	.15
38	Brad Radke	.15
39	Brian Jordan	.15
40	Garret Anderson	.15
41	Ichiro Suzuki	1.25
42	Mike Lieberthal	.15
43	Preston Wilson	.15
44	Bud Smith	.15
45	Curt Schilling	.40
46	Eric Chavez	.25
47	Javier Vazquez	.15
48	Jose Ortiz	.15
49	Mike Sweeney	.15
50	Travis Fryman	.15
51	Brady Anderson	.15
52	Chan Ho Park	.15
53	C.C. Sabathia	.15
54	Jack Wilson	.25
55	Joe Crede	.15
56	Mike Mussina	.40
57	Sean Casey	.30
58	Bobby Abreu	.15
59	Joe Randa	.15
60	Jose Vidro	.15
61	Juan Uribe	.15
62	Mark Grace	.25
63	Matt Morris	.15
64	Omar Vizquel	.15
65	Darryl Kile	.15
66	Dee Brown	.15
67	Fernando Tatis	.15
68	Jeff Cirillo	.15
69	Johnny Damon	.25
70	Milton Bradley	.15
71	Reggie Sanders	.15
72	Al Leiter	.15
73	Andres Galarraga	.15
74	Ellis Burks	.15
75	Jermaine Dye	.15
76	Juan Pierre	.15
77	Junior Spivey	.15
78	Mark Quinn	.15
79	Ben Sheets	.15
80	Brad Fullmer	.15
81	Bubba Trammell	.15
82	Dante Bichette	.15
83	Ken Griffey Jr.	1.25
84	Paul O'Neill	.15
85	Robert Fick	.15
86	Bret Boone	.15
87	Raul Mondesi	.15
88	Josh Beckett	.40
89	Geoff Jenkins	.15
90	Ramon Ortiz	.15
91	Robin Ventura	.15
92	Tom Glavine	.30
93	Jimmy Rollins	.15
94	Jamie Moyer	.15
95	Magglio Ordonez	.15
96	Mike Lowell	.15
97	Ryan Dempster	.15
98	Scott Schoeneweis	.15
99	Todd Zeile	.15
100	A.J. Burnett	.15
101	Aaron Sele	.15
102	Cal Ripken Jr.	2.00
103	Carlos Beltran	.45
104	David Eckstein	.15
105	Jason Marquis	.15
106	Matt Lawton	.15
107	Ben Grieve	.15
108	Brian Giles	.15
109	Josh Towers	.15
110	Lance Berkman	.15
111	Sammy Sosa	1.25
112	Torii Hunter	.15
113	Aubrey Huff	.15
114	Craig Biggio	.15
115	Doug Mientkiewicz	.15
116	Fred McGriff	.15
117	Jason Johnson	.15
118	Pat Burrell	.25
119	Aaron Boone	.15
120	Carlos Delgado	.50
121	Nomar Garciaparra	1.25
122	Richie Sexson	.15
123	Russ Ortiz	.15
124	Tim Hudson	.25
125	Tony Clark	.15
126	Jeromy Burnitz	.15
127	Jose Cruz	.15
128	Juan Encarnacion	.15
129	Mark Mulder	.15
130	Mike Hampton	.15
131	Rich Aurilia	.15
132	Trot Nixon	.15
133	Greg Vaughn	.15
134	Jacque Jones	.15
135	Jason Kendall	.15
136	Jay Gibbons	.15
137	Mark Buehrle	.15
138	Richard Hidalgo	.15
139	Rondell White	.15
140	Cristian Guzman	.15
141	Andy Pettitte	.30
142	Chris Richard	.15
143	Paul LoDuca	.15
144	Phil Nevin	.15
145	Ray Durham	.15
146	Todd Walker	.15
147	Bartolo Colon	.15
148	Ben Petrick	.15
149	Freddy Garcia	.15
150	Jon Lieber	.15
151	Jose Hernandez	.15
152	Matt Williams	.15
153	Shannon Stewart	.15
154	Adrian Beltre	.30
155	Carlos Lee	.15
156	Frank Catalanotto	.15
157	Jorge Posada	.30
158	Pokey Reese	.15
159	Ryan Klesko	.15
160	Ugueth Urbina	.15
161	Adam Dunn	.50
162	Alfonso Soriano	.50
163	Ben Davis	.15
164	Paul Konerko	.25
165	Eric Karros	.25
166	Jeff Weaver	.15
167	Ruben Sierra	.15
168	Bobby Higginson	.15
169	Eric Milton	.15
170	Kerry Wood	.65
171	Roy Oswalt	.30
172	Scott Rolen	.65
173	Tim Salmon	.25
174	Aramis Ramirez	.25
175	Jason Tyner	.15
176	Juan Cruz	.15
177	Keith Foulke	.15
178	Kevin Brown	.25
179	Roger Clemens	1.00
180	Tony Batista	.15
181	Andruw Jones	.75
182	Cliff Floyd	.15
183	Darin Erstad	.25
184	Joe Mays	.15
185	Mike Cameron	.15
186	Robert Person	.15
187	Jeff Kent	.25
188	Gabe Kapler	.25
189	Jason Jennings	.25
190	Jason Varitek	.15
191	Barry Zito	.25
192	Rickey Henderson	.75
193	Tino Martinez	.25
194	Brandon Duckworth	.15
195	Corey Koskie	.15
196	Derrek Lee	.25
197	Javy Lopez	.25
198	John Olerud	.25
199	Terrance Long	.15
200	Troy Glaus	.75
201	Scott MacRae	5.00
202	Scott Chiasson	5.00
203	Bart Miadich	5.00
204	Brian Bowles	5.00
205	David Williams	5.00
206	Victor Zambrano	5.00
207	Joe Beimel	5.00
208	Scott Stewart	5.00
209	Bob File	5.00
210	Ryan Jensen	5.00
211	Jason Karnuth	5.00
212	Brandon Knight	5.00
213	Andy Shibilo RC	5.00
214	Chad Ricketts RC	5.00
215	Mark Prior	8.00
216	Chad Paronto	5.00
217	Corky Miller	5.00
218	Luis Pineda	5.00
219	Ramon Vazquez	5.00
220	Tony Cogan	5.00
221	Roy Smith	5.00
222	Mark Lukasiewicz	5.00
223	Mike Rivera	5.00
224	Brad Voyles	5.00
225	Jamie Burke RC	5.00
226	Justin Duchscherer	5.00
227	Eric Cyr RC	5.00
228	Mark Lukasiewicz	5.00
229	Marlon Byrd	5.00
230	Chris Piersoll RC	5.00
231	Ramon Vazquez	5.00
232	Tony Cogan	5.00
233	Roy Smith	5.00
234	Franklin Nunez RC	5.00
235	Corky Miller	5.00
236	Jorge Nunez RC	5.00
237	Joe Beimel	5.00
238	Eric Knott	5.00
239	Victor Zambrano	5.00
240	Jason Karnuth	5.00
241	Jason Middlebrook	5.00
242	Scott Stewart	5.00
243	Tim Spooneybarger	5.00
244	David Williams	5.00
245	Bart Miadich	5.00
246	Mike Koplove	5.00
247	Ryan Jensen	5.00
248	Jeremy Fikac	5.00
249	Bob File	5.00

250	Craig Monroe	5.00
251	Albert Pujols	2.00
252	Ichiro Suzuki	2.00
253	Nomar Garciaparra	2.00
254	Barry Bonds	3.00
255	Jason Giambi	.75
256	Derek Jeter	3.00
257	Roberto Alomar	.75
258	Roger Clemens	2.00
259	Mike Piazza	1.50
260	Vladimir Guerrero	1.00
261	Todd Helton	.75
262	Shawn Green	.50
263	Chipper Jones	1.00
264	Pedro Martinez	1.00
265	Pat Burrell	.50
266	Sammy Sosa	2.00
267	Ken Griffey Jr.	1.50
268	Cal Ripken Jr.	3.00
269	Kerry Wood	1.00
270	Alex Rodriguez	2.50

Power

NM/M
Complete Set (25): 40.00
Inserted 1:20 Retail

1	Luis Gonzalez	1.00
2	Jimmy Rollins	1.00
3	Larry Walker	1.00
4	Frank Thomas	2.00
5	Manny Ramirez	2.00
6	Barry Bonds	8.00
7	Jim Thome	1.00
8	Tsuyoshi Shinjo	1.00
9	Bernie Williams	1.00
10	Chipper Jones	3.00
11	Shawn Green	1.50
12	Drew Henson	1.00
13	Juan Gonzalez	2.00
14	Jim Edmonds	1.00
15	Moises Alou	1.00
16	Roberto Alomar	1.50
17	Jose Canseco	1.50
18	Ivan Rodriguez	1.50
19	Barry Larkin	1.00
20	Mike Piazza	5.00
21	Gary Sheffield	1.00
22	J.D. Drew	1.00
23	Alex Rodriguez	6.00
24	Jason Giambi	1.50
25	Todd Helton	1.00

America's Game

NM/M
Complete Set (25): 25.00
Common Player: .50
Inserted 1:10 Retail

1	Pedro Martinez	1.50
2	Miguel Tejada	.75
3	Randy Johnson	1.50
4	Barry Bonds	5.00
5	Rafael Palmeiro	1.00
6	Mike Piazza	3.00
7	Greg Maddux	2.50
8	Jeff Bagwell	1.50
9	Edgar Martinez	.50
10	Albert Pujols	4.00
11	Todd Helton	1.50
12	Chipper Jones	2.50
13	Luis Gonzalez	.50
14	Jason Giambi	1.00
15	Kazuhiro Sasaki	.50
16	Dave Winfield	1.50
17	Reggie Jackson	1.50
18	Tom Glavine	.75
19	Carlos Delgado	.75
20	Bobby Abreu	.50
21	Larry Walker	.50
22	J.D. Drew	.75
23	Alex Rodriguez	4.00
24	Frank Thomas	1.50
25	C.C. Sabathia	.50

Americas Game
Jersey

NM/M
Common Player: 8.00
Inserted 1:24 H, 1:72 R

1	Jeff Bagwell	10.00
2	Craig Biggio	8.00
3	Barry Bonds	25.00
4	Carlos Delgado	8.00
5	J.D. Drew	5.00
6	Jason Giambi	10.00
7	Tom Glavine	10.00
8	Luis Gonzalez	5.00
9	Todd Helton	10.00
10	Reggie Jackson	10.00
11	Randy Johnson	10.00
12	Chipper Jones	10.00
13	Greg Maddux	10.00
14	Edgar Martinez	8.00
15	Pedro Martinez	10.00
16	Rafael Palmeiro	10.00
17	Chan Ho Park	5.00
18	Mike Piazza	10.00
19	Albert Pujols	20.00
20	Kazuhiro Sasaki	5.00
21	Miguel Tejada	5.00
22	Frank Thomas	10.00
23	Larry Walker	5.00
24	Dave Winfield	5.00

Americas Game
Stars and Stripes

No Pricing
Production 25 Sets

Coverage

NM/M
Common Player: 15.00
Production 100 Sets

1	Roberto Alomar/Bat	25.00
2	Jeff Bagwell/Jsy	20.00
3	Barry Bonds/Bat	50.00
4	Jose Canseco/Bat	25.00
5	J.D. Drew/Bat	25.00
6	Jim Edmonds/Bat	20.00
7	Jason Giambi/Bat	25.00
8	Juan Gonzalez/Bat	25.00
9	Luis Gonzalez/Jsy	15.00
10	Todd Helton/Jsy	20.00
11	Randy Johnson/Jsy	40.00
12	Chipper Jones/Bat	25.00
13	Greg Maddux/Jsy	40.00
14	Pedro Martinez/Jsy	30.00
15	Rafael Palmeiro/Pants	25.00
16	Albert Pujols/Jsy	50.00
17	Manny Ramirez/Bat	20.00
18	Alex Rodriguez/Bat	30.00
19	Ivan Rodriguez/Bat	25.00
20	Kazuhiro Sasaki/Jsy	20.00
21	Gary Sheffield/Bat	20.00
22	Tsuyoshi Shinjo/Bat	15.00

Coverage Autographs

NM/M
Quantity produced listed

1	Barry Bonds/Pants/50	200.00
2	J.D. Drew/Bat/100	25.00
3	Jim Edmonds/Bat/100	25.00
4	Drew Henson/Bat/100	25.00
5	Chipper Jones/Bat/50	60.00
6	Albert Pujols/Jsy/100	150.00
7	Gary Sheffield/Bat/100	30.00

Derek Jeter Legacy Collection

NM/M
Inserted 1:236

DJ	Derek Jeter/Bat	20.00
DJ	Derek Jeter/Bat/Auto./222	150.00
DJ	Derek Jeter/Jsy	20.00
DJ	Derek Jeter/Jsy/Auto.	200.00

Fencebusters
Autographed

NM/M
Numbered to 2001 HR Total.
Barry Bonds/73 275.00

Maximum Power Bat

NM/M
Common Player: 5.00
Inserted 1:24 H
Golds: 3-4X
Production 25 Sets

Luis Gonzalez	5.00
Larry Walker	5.00
Frank Thomas	10.00
Manny Ramirez	5.00
Barry Bonds	25.00
Jim Thome	10.00

Tsuyoshi Shinjo	5.00
Bernie Williams/175	25.00
Chipper Jones	10.00
Shawn Green	5.00
Juan Gonzalez	8.00
Jim Edmonds	10.00
Moises Alou	10.00
Roberto Alomar	10.00
Jose Canseco	10.00
Ivan Rodriguez	10.00
Barry Larkin/50	40.00
Mike Piazza	15.00
Gary Sheffield	8.00
J.D. Drew/200	25.00
Alex Rodriguez	15.00
Jason Giambi	10.00
Todd Helton	8.00

To The Max

Stars (1-200):	4-6X
Print Run 200-500	
Stars (1-200):	4-8X
Print Run 121-199	
Stars (1-200):	6-12X
Print Run 75-120	
Stars (1-200):	10-25X
Print Run 40-75	
Stars (1-200):	15-40X
Print Run 20-39	
Rookies (201-250):	.5-1X
Production 100	
Impact (251-270):	2-4X
Production 200-400	

2002 Fleer Platinum

NM/M
Complete Set (302): 125.00
Common Player: .15

	Common (251-260):	2.00
	Common (261-302):	1.50
	Inserted 1:3 H, 1:6 Retail	
	Hobby Pack (10):	2.00
	Hobby Box (24):	35.00
	Rack Box:	70.00
1	Garrett Anderson	.15
2	Randy Johnson	.65
3	Chipper Jones	.75
4	David Cone	.15
5	Corey Patterson	.15
6	Carlos Lee	.15
7	Barry Larkin	.15
8	Jim Thome	.15
9	Larry Walker	.15
10	Randall Simon	.15
11	Charles Johnson	.15
12	Richard Hidalgo	.15
13	Mark Quinn	.15
14	Paul LoDuca	.15
15	Cristian Guzman	.15
16	Orlando Cabrera	.15
17	Al Leiter	.15
18	Nick Johnson	.15
19	Eric Chavez	.25
20	Miguel Tejada	.25
21	Mike Lieberthal	.15
22	Robert Mackowiak	.15
23	Ryan Klesko	.15
24	Jeff Kent	.15
25	Edgar Martinez	.15
26	Steve Kline	.15
27	Toby Hall	.15
28	Rusty Greer	.15
29	Jose Cruz Jr.	.15
30	Darin Erstad	.50
31	Reggie Sanders	.15
32	Javy Lopez	.15
33	Carl Everett	.15
34	Sammy Sosa	1.00
35	Magglio Ordonez	.15
36	Todd Walker	.15
37	Omar Vizquel	.15
38	Matt Anderson	.15
39	Jeff Weaver	.15
40	Derek Lee	.15
41	Julio Lugo	.15
42	Joe Randa	.15
43	Chan Ho Park	.15
44	Torii Hunter	.15
45	Vladimir Guerrero	.65
46	Rey Ordonez	.15
47	Tino Martinez	.15
48	Johnny Damon	.25
49	Barry Zito	.25
50	Robert Person	.15
51	Aramis Ramirez	.15
52	Mark Kotsay	.15
53	Jason Schmidt	.15
54	Jamie Moyer	.15
55	David Justice	.15
56	Aubrey Huff	.15
57	Rick Helling	.15
58	Carlos Delgado	.40
59	Troy Glaus	.65
60	Curt Schilling	.40
61	Greg Maddux	.75
62	Nomar Garciaparra	1.00
63	Kerry Wood	.50
64	Frank Thomas	.65
65	Dmitri Young	.15
66	Alex Ochoa	.15
67	Jose Macias	.15
68	Antonio Alfonseca	.15
69	Mike Lowell	.15
70	Wade Miller	.15
71	Mike Sweeney	.15
72	Gary Sheffield	.25
73	Corey Koskie	.15
74	Lee Stevens	.15
75	Jay Payton	.15
76	Mike Mussina	.40
77	Jermaine Dye	.15
78	Bobby Abreu	.15
79	Scott Rolen	.50
80	Todd Ritchie	.15
81	D'Angelo Jimenez	.15
82	Rob Nenn	.15
83	John Olerud	.15
84	Matt Morris	.15
85	Joe Kennedy	.15
86	Gabe Kapler	.15
87	Chris Carpenter	.15
88	David Eckstein	.15
89	Matt Williams	.15
90	John Smoltz	.15
91	Pedro J. Martinez	.65
92	Eric Young	.15
93	Jose Valentin	.15
94	Erubiel Durazo	.15
95	Jeff Cirillo	.15
96	Brandon Inge	.15
97	Josh Beckett	.40
98	Preston Wilson	.15

99	Damian Jackson	.15
100	Adrian Beltre	.25
101	Jeromy Burnitz	.15
102	Joe Mays	.15
103	Michael Barrett	.15
104	Mike Piazza	1.00
105	Brady Anderson	.15
106	Jason Giambi	.40
107	Marlon Anderson	.15
108	Jimmy Rollins	.25
109	Jack Wilson	.15
110	Brian Lawrence	.15
111	Russ Ortiz	.15
112	Kazuhiro Sasaki	.15
113	Placido Polanco	.15
114	Damian Rolls	.15
115	Rafael Palmeiro	.50
116	Brad Fullmer	.15
117	Tim Salmon	.25
118	Tony Womack	.15
119	Tony Batista	.15
120	Trot Nixon	.15
121	Mark Buehrle	.15
122	Derek Jeter	1.50
123	Ellis Burks	.15
124	Mike Hampton	.15
125	Roger Cedeno	.15
126	A.J. Burnett	.15
127	Moises Alou	.15
128	Billy Wagner	.15
129	Kevin Brown	.15
130	Jose Hernandez	.15
131	Doug Mientkiewicz	.15
132	Javier Vazquez	.15
133	Tsuyoshi Shinjo	.15
134	Andy Pettitte	.30
135	Tim Hudson	.25
136	Pat Burrell	.40
137	Brian Giles	.15
138	Kevin Young	.15
139	Xavier Nady	.15
140	J.T. Snow	.15
141	Aaron Sele	.15
142	Albert Pujols	1.25
143	Jason Tyner	.15
144	Ivan Rodriguez	.50
145	Raul Mondesi	.15
146	Matt Lawton	.15
147	Rafael Furcal	.15
148	Jeff Conine	.15
149	Hideo Nomo	.60
150	Jose Canseco	.30
151	Aaron Boone	.15
152	Bartolo Colon	.15
153	Todd Helton	.65
154	Tony Clark	.15
155	Pablo Ozuna	.15
156	Jeff Bagwell	.65
157	Carlos Beltran	.50
158	Shawn Green	.25
159	Geoff Jenkins	.15
160	Eric Milton	.15
161	Jose Vidro	.15
162	Robin Ventura	.15
163	Jorge Posada	.25
164	Terrence Long	.15
165	Brandon Duckworth	.15
166	Chad Hermansen	.15
167	Ben Davis	.15
168	Phil Nevin	.15
169	Bret Boone	.15
170	J.D. Drew	.25
171	Edgar Renteria	.15
172	Randy Winn	.15
173	Alex Rodriguez	1.50
174	Shannon Stewart	.15
175	Steve Finley	.15
176	Marcus Giles	.15
177	Jay Gibbons	.15
178	Manny Ramirez	.65
179	Ray Durham	.15
180	Sean Casey	.25
181	Travis Fryman	.15
182	Denny Neagle	.15
183	Deivi Cruz	.15
184	Luis Castillo	.15
185	Lance Berkman	.15
186	Dee Brown	.15
187	Jeff Shaw	.15
188	Mark Loretta	.15
189	David Ortiz	.25
190	Edgardo Alfonzo	.15
191	Roger Clemens	.75
192	Mariano Rivera	.25
193	Jeremy Giambi	.15
194	Johnny Estrada	.15
195	Craig Wilson	.15
196	Adam Eaton	.15
197	Rich Aurilia	.15
198	Mike Cameron	.15
199	Jim Edmonds	.15
200	Fernando Vina	.15
201	Greg Vaughn	.15
202	Mike Young	.15

203	Vernon Wells	.15
204	Luis Gonzalez	.25
205	Tom Glavine	.30
206	Chris Richard	.15
207	Jon Lieber	.15
208	Keith Foulke	.15
209	Rondell White	.15
210	Bernie Williams	.30
211	Juan Pierre	.15
212	Juan Encarnacion	.15
213	Ryan Dempster	.15
214	Tim Redding	.15
215	Jeff Suppan	.15
216	Mark Grudzielanek	.15
217	Richie Sexson	.15
218	Brad Radke	.15
219	Armando Benitez	.15
220	Orlando Hernandez	.15
221	Alfonso Soriano	.40
222	Mark Mulder	.15
223	Travis Lee	.15
224	Jason Kendall	.15
225	Trevor Hoffman	.15
226	Barry Bonds	1.50
227	Freddy Garcia	.15
228	Darryl Kile	.15
229	Ben Grieve	.15
230	Frank Catalanotto	.15
231	Ruben Sierra	.15
232	Homer Bush	.15
233	Mark Grace	.25
234	Andruw Jones	.60
235	Brian Roberts	.15
236	Fred McGriff	.15
237	Paul Konerko	.15
238	Ken Griffey Jr.	1.00
239	John Burkett	.15
240	Juan Uribe	.15
241	Bobby Higginson	.15
242	Cliff Floyd	.15
243	Craig Biggio	.15
244	Neifi Perez	.15
245	Eric Karros	.15
246	Ben Sheets	.15
247	Tony Armas Jr.	.15
248	Mo Vaughn	.15
249	David Wells	.15
250	Juan Gonzalez	.60
251	Barry Bonds	5.00
252	Sammy Sosa	3.00
253	Ken Griffey Jr.	3.00
254	Roger Clemens	4.00
255	Greg Maddux	2.50
256	Chipper Jones	1.50
257	Alex Rodriguez, Derek Jeter, Nomar Garciaparra	5.00
258	Roberto Alomar	1.50
259	Jeff Bagwell	1.50
260	Mike Piazza	3.00
261	Mark Teixeira	2.00
262	Mark Prior	2.00
263	Alex Escobar	1.50
264	C.C. Sabathia	1.50
265	Drew Henson	1.50
266	Wilson Betemit	1.50
267	Roy Oswalt	1.50
268	Adam Dunn	2.00
269	Bud Smith	1.50
270	Dewon Brazelton	1.50
271	Brandon Backe, Jason Standridge	1.50
272	Wilfredo Rodriguez, Carlos Hernandez	1.50
273	Geronimo Gil, Luis Rivera	1.50
274	Carlos Pena, Jovanny Cedeno	1.50
275	Austin Kearns, Ben Broussard	1.50
276	Jorge De La Rosa, Kenny Kelly	1.50
277	Ryan Drese, Victor Martinez	1.50
278	Joel Pinero, Nate Cornejo	1.50
279	David Kelton, Carlos Zambrano	1.50
281	Donnie Bridges, Wilkin Ruan	1.50
282	Wily Mo Pena, Brandon Claussen	2.00
283	Jason Jennings, Rene Reyes RC	1.50
284	Steve Green, Alfredo Amezaga	1.50
285	Eric Hinske, Felipe Lopez	1.50
286	Anderson Machado, Brad Baisley	1.50
287	Carlos Garcia, Sean Douglass	1.50
288	Pat Strange, Jae Weong Seo	1.50
289	Marcus Thames, Alex Graman	1.50
290	Matt Childers, Hansel Izquierdo RC	1.50
291	Ron Calloway, Adam Walker RC	1.50
292	J.R. House, J.J. Davis	1.50
293	Ryan Anderson, Rafael Soriano	1.50
294	Mike Bynum, Dennis Tankersley	1.50
295	Kurt Ainsworth, Carlos Valderrama	1.50
296	Billy Hall, Cristian Guerrero	1.50
297	Miguel Olivo, Danny Wright	1.50
298	Marlon Byrd, Jorge Padilla RC	1.50
299	Juan Cruz, Ben Christensen	1.50
300	Adam Johnson, Michael Restovich	1.50
301	So Taguchi RC	2.00
302	Kazuhisa Ishii RC	3.00

Edition

Stars (1-250):	4-8X
Production 202	
Cards 251-302:	No Pricing
Production 22	

Barry Bonds RC Autograph

	NM/M
73 Cards Autographed	
Barry Bonds	400.00

Buy Back Autographs

No Pricing

Clubhouse Collection Memorabilia

	NM/M
Common Player:	5.00
Inserted 1:32	
Edgardo Alfonzo/Jsy	5.00
Rick Ankiel/Jsy	5.00
Craig Biggio/Bat	8.00
Adrian Beltre/Jsy	5.00
Sean Casey/Jsy	8.00
Barry Bonds/Jsy	25.00
Scott Rolen/Jsy	10.00
Eric Chavez/Jsy	8.00
Roger Clemens/Jsy	25.00
Carlos Delgado/Jsy	8.00
J.D. Drew/Jsy	5.00
Darin Erstad/Jsy	5.00
Jim Thome/Bat	10.00
Juan Gonzalez/Bat	8.00
Nomar Garciaparra/Jsy	15.00
Todd Helton/Jsy	8.00
Derek Jeter/Pants	25.00
Randy Johnson/Jsy	10.00
Andruw Jones/Jsy	8.00
Tim Hudson/Jsy	5.00
Jason Kendall/Jsy	5.00
Johnny Damon/Bat	5.00
Paul LoDuca/Jsy	5.00
Greg Maddux/Jsy	10.00
Pedro Martinez/Jsy	10.00
Raul Mondesi/Bat	5.00
Magglio Ordonez/Jsy	5.00
Mike Piazza/Jsy	10.00
Manny Ramirez/Jsy	8.00
Mariano Rivera/Jsy	8.00
Ivan Rodriguez/Jsy	10.00
Alex Rodriguez/Jsy	15.00
Kazuhiro Sasaki/Jsy	5.00
Frank Thomas/Jsy	10.00
Curt Schilling/Jsy	8.00
Gary Sheffield/Jsy	6.00
Omar Vizquel/Jsy	5.00

Clubhouse Collection - Dual

	NM/M
Common Card:	10.00
Inserted 1:96	

CLUBHOUSE COLLECTION

DARIN ERSTAD • Anaheim Angels

Edgardo Alfonzo	10.00
Rick Ankiel	8.00
Craig Biggio	
Adrian Beltre	10.00
Barry Bonds	40.00
Sean Casey	10.00
Eric Chavez	10.00
Roger Clemens	30.00
Carlos Delgado	10.00
J.D. Drew	10.00
Darin Erstad	10.00
Jim Thome	20.00
Juan Gonzalez	15.00
Nomar Garciaparra	30.00
Todd Helton	
Derek Jeter	40.00
Randy Johnson	20.00
Andruw Jones	10.00
Jason Kendall	
Johnny Damon	10.00
Paul LoDuca	10.00
Greg Maddux	20.00
Pedro J. Martinez	20.00
Raul Mondesi	
Magglio Ordonez	10.00
Mike Piazza	30.00
Manny Ramirez	15.00
Mariano Rivera	15.00
Ivan Rodriguez	20.00
Alex Rodriguez	25.00
Scott Rolen	20.00
Kazuhiro Sasaki	10.00
Curt Schilling	20.00
Gary Sheffield	10.00
Frank Thomas	20.00
Jim Thome	20.00
Omar Vizquel	10.00

Cornerstones

CORNERSTONES

		NM/M
Complete Set (40):		120.00
Inserted 1:12 Jumbo		
1	Bill Terry, Johnny Mize	1.50
2	Cal Ripken Jr., Eddie Murray	10.00
3	Eddie Mathews, Chipper Jones	3.00
4	Albert Pujols, George Sisler	6.00
5	Sean Casey, Tony Perez	1.50
6	Jimmie Foxx, Scott Rolen	4.00
7	Wade Boggs, George Brett	8.00
8	Rod Carew, Troy Glaus	1.50
9	Jeff Bagwell, Rafael Palmeiro	2.00
10	Willie Stargell, Pie Traynor	2.00
11	Cal Ripken Jr., Brooks Robinson	10.00
12	Tony Perez, Ted Kluszewski	1.50
13	Jason Giambi, Don Mattingly	8.00
14	Hank Greenberg, Jimmie Foxx	4.00
15	Ernie Banks, Willie McCovey	3.00
16	Jim Thome, Travis Fryman	3.00
17	Ted Kluszewski, Sean Casey	1.50
18	Gil Hodges, Johnny Mize	3.00
19	Brooks Robinson, Boog Powell	3.00
20	Bill Terry, George Sisler	2.00

21	Wade Boggs, Don Mattingly	8.00
22	Jason Giambi, Carlos Delgado	2.50
23	Willie Stargell, Bill Madlock	2.00
24	Mark Grace, Matt Williams	2.00
25	Paul Molitor, George Brett	8.00
26	Carlos Delgado, Mo Vaughn	1.50
27	Bill Terry, Willie McCovey	1.50
28	Mike Sweeney, George Brett	8.00
29	Eddie Mathews, Ernie Banks	4.00
30	Eric Karros, Gil Hodges	1.50
31	Paul Molitor, Don Mattingly	8.00
32	Brooks Robinson, Rod Carew	3.00
33	Chipper Jones, Albert Pujols	8.00
34	Harry Heilmann, Hank Greenberg	1.50
35	Frank Thomas, Carlos Delgado	2.50
36	Jeff Bagwell, Todd Helton	2.00
37	Rafael Palmeiro, Fred McGriff	2.00
38	Cal Ripken Jr., Wade Boggs	10.00
39	Orlando Cepeda, Willie McCovey	2.00
40	John Olerud, Mark Grace	2.00

Cornerstones Numbered

NM/M
Complete Set (40):
#1-10: Production 250
#11-20: Production 250
#21-30: Production 1,000
#31-40: Production 2,000

1	Bill Terry, Johnny Mize	10.00
2	Cal Ripken Jr., Eddie Murray	30.00
3	Eddie Mathews, Chipper Jones	10.00
4	Albert Pujols, George Sisler	20.00
5	Sean Casey, Tony Perez	8.00
6	Jimmie Foxx, Scott Rolen	10.00
7	Wade Boggs, George Brett	20.00
8	Rod Carew, Troy Glaus	10.00
9	Jeff Bagwell, Rafael Palmeiro	10.00
10	Willie Stargell, Pie Traynor	8.00
11	Cal Ripken Jr., Brooks Robinson	20.00
12	Tony Perez, Ted Kluszewski	5.00
13	Jason Giambi, Don Mattingly	15.00
14	Hank Greenberg, Jimmie Foxx	8.00
15	Ernie Banks, Willie McCovey	8.00
16	Jim Thome, Travis Fryman	6.00
17	Ted Kluszewski, Sean Casey	5.00
18	Gil Hodges, Johnny Mize	5.00
19	Brooks Robinson, Boog Powell	8.00
20	Bill Terry, George Sisler	5.00
21	Wade Boggs, Don Mattingly	10.00
22	Jason Giambi/Yanks, Carlos Delgado	3.00
23	Willie Stargell, Bill Madlock	4.00
24	Mark Grace, Matt Williams	4.00
25	Paul Molitor, George Brett	10.00
26	Carlos Delgado, Mo Vaughn	3.00
27	Bill Terry, Willie McCovey	4.00
28	Mike Sweeney, George Brett	10.00
29	Eddie Mathews, Ernie Banks	4.00
30	Eric Karros, Gil Hodges	3.00
31	Paul Molitor, Don Mattingly	8.00
32	Brooks Robinson, Rod Carew	3.00
33	Chipper Jones, Albert Pujols	6.00
34	Harry Heilmann, Hank Greenburg	3.00
35	Frank Thomas, Carlos Delgado	3.00
36	Jeff Bagwell, Todd Helton	3.00
37	Rafael Palmeiro, Fred McGriff	3.00
38	Cal Ripken Jr., Wade Boggs	8.00
39	Orlando Cepeda, Willie McCovey	3.00
40	John Olerud, Mark Grace	3.00

Cornerstones Memorabilia

No Pricing
Production 25 Sets

Fencebusters

NM/M
Common Player: 5.00
Rack Pack Exclusive

Derek Jeter	20.00
J.D. Drew	6.00
Brian Giles	5.00
Moises Alou	5.00
Rafael Palmeiro	6.00
Jeff Bagwell	8.00
Mike Piazza	15.00
Manny Ramirez	8.00
Tino Martinez	5.00
Jim Thome	5.00
Andruw Jones	8.00
Shawn Green	6.00
Frank Thomas	8.00
Miguel Tejada	6.00
Luis Gonzalez	5.00
Alex Rodriguez	12.50
Larry Walker	5.00
Barry Bonds	20.00
Todd Helton	8.00
Chipper Jones	10.00
Roberto Alomar	6.00
Jim Edmonds	5.00

National Patch Time

NM/M
Common Player: 20.00
Inserted 1:12 Jumbo

Barry Bonds/75	100.00
Todd Helton/110	40.00
Ivan Rodriguez/225	40.00
Kazuhiro Sasaki/310	20.00
Derek Jeter/65	100.00
Cal Ripken Jr/350	80.00
Darin Erstad/315	20.00
Jose Canseco/150	40.00
Miguel Tejada/55	35.00
Greg Maddux/775	30.00
Juan Gonzalez/50	50.00
J.D. Drew/210	40.00
Manny Ramirez/100	40.00
Pedro Martinez/45	50.00
Carlos Delgado/70	30.00
Magglio Ordonez/85	30.00
Pat Burrell/285	25.00
Adam Dunn/75	40.00
Alex Rodriguez/325	50.00

Wheelhouse

NM/M
Complete Set (20): 40.00
Common Player: 1.00
Inserted 1:12

1WH	Derek Jeter	6.00
2WH	Barry Bonds	6.00
3WH	Luis Gonzalez	1.00
4WH	Jason Giambi	1.00
5WH	Ivan Rodriguez	1.50
6WH	Mike Piazza	4.00
7WH	Troy Glaus	1.50
8WH	Nomar Garciaparra	4.00
9WH	Juan Gonzalez	1.50
10WH	Sammy Sosa	4.00
11WH	Albert Pujols	5.00
12WH	Ken Griffey Jr.	4.00
13WH	Scott Rolen	1.00
14WH	Jeff Bagwell	1.50
15WH	Ichiro Suzuki	4.00
16WH	Todd Helton	1.50
17WH	Chipper Jones	3.00
18WH	Alex Rodriguez	4.00
19WH	Vladimir Guerrero	2.00
20WH	Manny Ramirez	1.50

2002 Fleer Premium

NM/M
Complete Set (240): 50.00
Common Player: .15
Common SP (201-240): .50
Inserted 1:2
Pack (8): 2.00
Box (24): 35.00

1	Garret Anderson	.20
2	Derek Jeter	2.50
3	Ken Griffey Jr.	1.50
4	Luis Castillo	.15
5	Richie Sexson	.20
6	Mike Mussina	.40
7	Ricky Henderson	.75
8	Bud Smith	.15
9	David Eckstein	.15
10	Nomar Garciaparra	1.50
11	Barry Larkin	.20
12	Cliff Floyd	.15
13	Ben Sheets	.20
14	Jorge Posada	.30
15	Phil Nevin	.15
16	Fernando Vina	.15
17	Darin Erstad	.65
18	Shea Hillenbrand	.15
19	Todd Walker	.15
20	Charles Johnson	.15
21	Cristian Guzman	.15
22	Mariano Rivera	.30
23	Bubba Trammell	.15
24	Brent Abernathy	.15
25	Troy Glaus	.75
26	Pedro J. Martinez	.75
27	Dmitri Young	.15
28	Derrek Lee	.20
29	Torii Hunter	.20
30	Alfonso Soriano	.65
31	Rich Aurilia	.15
32	Ben Grieve	.15
33	Tim Salmon	.30
34	Trot Nixon	.15
35	Roberto Alomar	.40
36	Mike Lowell	.20
37	Jacque Jones	.15
38	Bernie Williams	.30
39	Barry Bonds	2.50
40	Toby Hall	.15
41	Mo Vaughn	.20
42	Hideo Nomo	.65
43	Travis Fryman	.15
44	Preston Wilson	.15
45	Corey Koskie	.15
46	Eric Chavez	.30
47	Andres Galarraga	.15
48	Greg Vaughn	.15
49	Shawn Wooten	.15
50	Manny Ramirez	.75
51	Juan Gonzalez	.75
52	Moises Alou	.20
53	Joe Mays	.15
54	Johnny Damon	.35
55	Jeff Kent	.20
56	Frank Catalanotto	.15
57	Steve Finley	.15
58	Jason Varitek	.15
59	Kenny Lofton	.20
60	Jeff Bagwell	.75
61	Doug Mientkiewicz	.15
62	Jermaine Dye	.15
63	John Vander Wal	.15
64	Gabe Kapler	.15
65	Luis Gonzalez	.30
66	Jon Lieber	.15
67	C.C. Sabathia	.15
68	Lance Berkman	.20
69	Eric Milton	.15
70	Jason Giambi	.50
71	Ichiro Suzuki	1.50
72	Rafael Palmeiro	.65
73	Mark Grace	.30
74	Fred McGriff	.20
75	Jim Thome	.20
76	Craig Biggio	.20
77	A.J. Pierzynski	.15
78	Ramon Hernandez	.15
79	Paul Abbott	.15
80	Alex Rodriguez	2.00
81	Randy Johnson	.75
82	Corey Patterson	.20
83	Omar Vizquel	.20
84	Richard Hidalgo	.15
85	Luis Rivas	.15
86	Tim Hudson	.30
87	Bret Boone	.20
88	Ivan Rodriguez	.60
89	Junior Spivey	.15
90	Sammy Sosa	1.50
91	Jeff Cirillo	.15
92	Roy Oswalt	.30
93	Orlando Cabrera	.15
94	Terrence Long	.15
95	Mike Cameron	.15
96	Homer Bush	.15
97	Reggie Sanders	.15
98	Rondell White	.20
99	Mike Hampton	.15
100	Carlos Beltran	.50
101	Vladimir Guerrero	.75
102	Miguel Tejada	.30
103	Freddy Garcia	.15
104	Jose Cruz Jr.	.15
105	Curt Schilling	.45
106	Kerry Wood	.65
107	Todd Helton	.75
108	Neifi Perez	.15
109	Javier Vazquez	.15
110	Barry Zito	.30
111	Edgar Martinez	.20
112	Carlos Delgado	.50
113	Matt Williams	.20
114	Eric Young	.15
115	Alex Ochoa	.15
116	Mark Quinn	.15
117	Jose Vidro	.20
118	Bobby Abreu	.20
119	David Bell	.15
120	Brad Fullmer	.15
121	Rafael Furcal	.15
122	Ray Durham	.15
123	Jose Ortiz	.15
124	Joe Randa	.15
125	Edgardo Alfonzo	.15
126	Marlon Anderson	.15
127	Jamie Moyer	.15
128	Alex Gonzalez	.15
129	Marcus Giles	.15
130	Keith Foulke	.15
131	Juan Pierre	.15
132	Mike Sweeney	.15
133	Matt Lawton	.15
134	Pat Burrell	.40
135	John Olerud	.20
136	Raul Mondesi	.20
137	Tom Glavine	.40
138	Paul Konerko	.20
139	Larry Walker	.20
140	Adrian Beltre	.35
141	Al Leiter	.20
142	Mike Lieberthal	.15
143	Kazuhiro Sasaki	.15
144	Shannon Stewart	.15
145	Andruw Jones	.75
146	Carlos Lee	.15
147	Roger Cedeno	.15
148	Kevin Brown	.20
149	Jay Payton	.15
150	Scott Rolen	.65
151	J.D. Drew	.35
152	Chipper Jones	1.00
153	Magglio Ordonez	.20

154	Tony Clark	.15
155	Shawn Green	.35
156	Mike Piazza	1.50
157	Jimmy Rollins	.25
158	Jim Edmonds	.20
159	Javy Lopez	.20
160	Chris Singleton	.15
161	Juan Encarnacion	.15
162	Eric Karros	.15
163	Tsuyoshi Shinjo	.20
164	Brian Giles	.20
165	Darryl Kile	.15
166	Greg Maddux	1.00
167	Frank Thomas	.75
168	Shane Halter	.15
169	Paul LoDuca	.15
170	Robin Ventura	.15
171	Jason Kendall	.15
172	Jason Hart	.15
173	Brady Anderson	.15
174	Jose Valentin	.15
175	Bobby Higginson	.15
176	Gary Sheffield	.40
177	Roger Clemens	1.25
178	Aramis Ramirez	.20
179	Matt Morris	.20
180	Jeff Conine	.15
181	Aaron Boone	.15
182	Jose Macias	.15
183	Jeromy Burnitz	.15
184	Carl Everett	.15
185	Trevor Hoffman	.15
186	Placido Polanco	.15
187	Jay Gibbons	.15
188	Sean Casey	.35
189	Josh Beckett	.40
190	Jeffrey Hammonds	.15
191	Chuck Knoblauch	.15
192	Ryan Klesko	.15
193	Albert Pujols	1.75
194	Chris Richard	.15
195	Adam Dunn	.50
196	A.J. Burnett	.15
197	Geoff Jenkins	.25
198	Tino Martinez	.15
199	Ray Lankford	.15
200	Edgar Renteria	.20
201	Eric Cyr RC	1.00
202	Travis Phelps	.50
203	Rick Bauer	.50
204	Mark Prior	2.00
205	Wilson Betemit	.50
206	Dewon Brazelton	.50
207	Cody Ransom	.50
208	Donnie Bridges	.50
209	Justin Duchscherer	.50
210	Nate Cornejo	.50
211	Jason Romano	.50
212	Juan Cruz	.50
213	Pedro Santana	.50
214	Ryan Drese	.50
215	Bert Snow	.50
216	Nate Frese	.50
217	Rafael Soriano	.50
218	Franklin Nunez RC	.50
219	Tim Spooneybarger	.50
220	Willie Harris	.50
221	Billy Sylvester	.50
222	Carlos Hernandez	.50
223	Mark Teixeira	3.00
224	Adrian Hernandez	.50
225	Andres Torres	.50
226	Marlon Byrd	.50
227	Juan Rivera	.50
228	Adam Johnson	.50
229	Justin Kaye	.50
230	Kyle Kessel	.50
231	Horacio Ramirez	.50
232	Brandon Larson	.50
233	Luis Lopez	.50
234	Robert Mackowiak	.50
235	Henry Mateo	.50
236	Corky Miller	.50
237	Greg Miller	.50
238	Dustan Mohr	.50
239	Bill Ortega	.50
240	Billy Hall	.50

Star Ruby

Stars (1-200):	4-8X
SP's (201-240):	1-2X
Production 125 Sets	

Diamond Stars

		NM/M
Complete Set (20):		100.00
Common Player:		2.00
Inserted 1:72		
1DS	Pedro J. Martinez	4.00
2DS	Derek Jeter	15.00
3DS	Sammy Sosa	8.00
4DS	Ken Griffey Jr.	8.00
5DS	Chipper Jones	5.00
6DS	Roger Clemens	10.00
7DS	Ichiro Suzuki	8.00
8DS	Jeff Bagwell	4.00
9DS	Luis Gonzalez	2.00
10DS	Manny Ramirez	4.00
11DS	Alex Rodriguez	12.50
12DS	Kazuhiro Sasaki	2.00
13DS	Mike Piazza	8.00
14DS	Vladimir Guerrero	4.00
15DS	Randy Johnson	4.00
16DS	Ivan Rodriguez	3.00
17DS	Nomar Garciaparra	8.00
18DS	Barry Bonds	15.00
19DS	Todd Helton	4.00
20DS	Greg Maddux	5.00

Diamond Stars Autograph

	NM/M
Numbered to 100	
Derek Jeter	125.00

Diamond Stars Game-Used

	NM/M
Common Player:	5.00
Inserted 1:105	
Barry Bonds/Jsy	20.00
Manny Ramirez/Jsy	8.00
Ivan Rodriguez/Jsy	8.00
Kazuhiro Sasaki/Jsy	5.00
Roger Clemens	20.00
Alex Rodriguez	15.00
Derek Jeter	25.00
Chipper Jones	10.00
Todd Helton	8.00
Luis Gonzalez	5.00
Mike Piazza	10.00
Nomar Garciaparra	25.00

Diamond Stars Game-Used Premium

	NM/M
Production 75 Sets	
Barry Bonds	60.00
Roger Clemens	60.00
Todd Helton	30.00
Chipper Jones	30.00
Manny Ramirez	25.00
Alex Rodriguez	50.00
Ivan Rodriguez	25.00
Luis Gonzalez	25.00
Mike Piazza	40.00
Kazuhiro Sasaki	20.00

Diamond Stars Dual Game-Used

	NM/M
Numbered to 100	
Barry Bonds	60.00
Todd Helton	20.00
Derek Jeter	60.00
Chipper Jones	30.00
Mike Piazza	35.00
Manny Ramirez	25.00
Alex Rodriguez	40.00

Diamond Stars Dual Game-Used Premium

Production 25 Sets

International Pride

		NM/M
Complete Set (15):		10.00
Common Player:		.50
Inserted 1:6		
1IP	Larry Walker	.50
2IP	Albert Pujols	3.00
3IP	Juan Gonzalez	.75
4IP	Ichiro Suzuki	2.00
5IP	Rafael Palmeiro	.65
6IP	Carlos Delgado	.50

7IP	Kazuhiro Sasaki	.50
8IP	Vladimir Guerrero	.75
9IP	Bobby Abreu	.50
10IP	Ivan Rodriguez	.60
11IP	Tsuyoshi Shinjo	.50
12IP	Pedro J. Martinez	.75
13IP	Andruw Jones	.75
14IP	Sammy Sosa	2.00
15IP	Chan Ho Park	.50

International Pride Game-Used

	NM/M
Common Player:	5.00
Inserted 1:90	
Carlos Delgado/Jsy	8.00
Juan Gonzalez/Jsy	8.00
Andruw Jones/Jsy	8.00
Pedro Martinez/Jsy	10.00
Rafael Palmeiro/Jsy	8.00
Chan Ho Park/Jsy	5.00
Albert Pujols/Jsy	20.00
Ivan Rodriguez/Bat	10.00
Kazuhiro Sasaki/Jsy	5.00
Tsuyoshi Shinjo/Jsy	5.00

International Pride Premium

	NM/M
Production 75 Sets	15.00
Carlos Delgado	25.00
Juan Gonzalez	40.00
Andruw Jones	40.00
Pedro J. Martinez	40.00
Chan Ho Park	15.00
Ivan Rodriguez	25.00
Tsuyoshi Shinjo	15.00
Rafael Palmeiro	25.00
Albert Pujols	75.00
Kazuhiro Sasaki	15.00

Legendary Dynasties

		NM/M
Complete Set (36):		125.00
Common Player:		1.50
Inserted 1:18		
Gold:		1X
Production 300 Sets		
1LD	Honus Wagner	4.00
2LD	Christy Mathewson	4.00
3LD	Lou Gehrig	8.00
4LD	Babe Ruth	12.00
5LD	Jimmie Foxx	4.00
6LD	Lefty Grove	2.00
7LD	Al Simmons	1.50
8LD	Bill Dickey	1.50
9LD	Stan Musial	5.00
10LD	Enos Slaughter	1.50
11LD	Johnny Mize	2.00
12LD	Yogi Berra	3.00
13LD	Whitey Ford	3.00
14LD	Jackie Robinson	8.00
15LD	Duke Snider	3.00
16LD	Roger Maris	5.00
17LD	Jim Palmer	2.00
18LD	Don Drysdale	2.00
19LD	Brooks Robinson	3.00
20LD	Rollie Fingers	1.50
21LD	Reggie Jackson	3.00
22LD	Joe Morgan	2.00
23LD	Johnny Bench	5.00
24LD	Thurman Munson	4.00
25LD	Jose Canseco	2.50
26LD	Tom Glavine	2.00
27LD	Chipper Jones	4.00
28LD	Greg Maddux	5.00
29LD	Roberto Alomar	3.00
30LD	David Cone	1.50
31LD	Jim Thome	3.00
32LD	Manny Ramirez	3.00
33LD	Roger Clemens	6.00
34LD	Derek Jeter	8.00
35LD	Bernie Williams	2.50
36LD	Alfonso Soriano	3.00

Legendary Dynasties Autographs

	NM/M
#'d to World Series Year	
Johnny Bench/76	80.00
Yogi Berra/51	60.00
Reggie Jackson/73	60.00
Derek Jeter/96	125.00

Legendary Dynasties Game-Used

	NM/M
Common Player:	8.00
Inserted 1:120	
Roberto Alomar/Jsy	8.00
Johnny Bench/Jsy	15.00
Yogi Berra/Bat/SP/75	50.00
Roger Clemens/Jsy	25.00
Bill Dickey/Bat	25.00
Rollie Fingers/Jsy	8.00
Reggie Jackson/Bat	25.00
Derek Jeter/Bat	30.00
Chipper Jones/Jsy	10.00
Roger Maris/Pants/SP	50.00
Johnny Mize/Bat	15.00
Joe Morgan/Bat	8.00
Thurman Munson/Bat	35.00
Jim Palmer/Jsy	10.00
Manny Ramirez/Jsy	10.00
Brooks Robinson/Bat	30.00
Jackie Robinson/SP/150	60.00
Babe Ruth/Bat	200.00
Duke Snider/Bat	30.00
Alfonso Soriano/Bat	10.00
Bernie Williams/Jsy	8.00

Legendary Dynasties Premium

	NM/M
Numbered to Highest win total.	
Rollie Fingers/93	15.00
Roger Clemens/114	50.00
Roger Maris/109	70.00
Roberto Alomar/96	25.00
Reggie Jackson/93	30.00
Manny Ramirez/99	25.00
Johnny Bench/108	35.00
Jim Palmer/109	20.00
Derek Jeter/114	80.00
Alfonso Soriano/99	30.00
Chipper Jones/106	30.00
Bernie Williams/114	20.00

On Base!

		NM/M
Complete Set (30):		125.00
Common Player:		2.00
#'d to 2001 OBP		
1OB	Frank Thomas/316	5.00
2OB	Ivan Rodriguez/347	5.00
3OB	Nomar Garciaparra/352	10.00
4OB	Ken Griffey Jr./365	8.00
5OB	Juan Gonzalez/370	4.00
6OB	Shawn Green/372	3.00
7OB	Vladimir Guerrero/377	5.00
8OB	Derek Jeter/377	15.00
9OB	Scott Rolen/378	5.00
10OB	Ichiro Suzuki/381	5.00
11OB	Mike Piazza/384	10.00
12OB	Bernie Williams/395	3.00
13OB	Moises Alou/396	3.00
14OB	Jeff Bagwell/397	4.00
15OB	Alex Rodriguez/399	10.00
16OB	Albert Pujols/403	10.00
17OB	Manny Ramirez/405	4.00
18OB	Carlos Delgado/408	4.00
19OB	Jim Edmonds/410	3.00
20OB	Roberto Alomar/415	3.00
21OB	Jim Thome/416	5.00
22OB	Gary Sheffield/417	3.00
23OB	Chipper Jones/427	5.00
24OB	Luis Gonzalez/429	2.00

25OB	Lance Berkman/430	3.00
26OB	Todd Helton/432	4.00
27OB	Sammy Sosa/437	10.00
28OB	Larry Walker/449	2.00
29OB	Jason Giambi/477	4.00
30OB	Barry Bonds/515	12.00

On Base! Game-Used

	NM/M
Common Player:	5.00
Production 100 Sets	
Roberto Alomar	8.00
Moises Alou	5.00
Jeff Bagwell	8.00
Lance Berkman	5.00
Barry Bonds	20.00
Carlos Delgado	8.00
Jim Edmonds	6.00
Nomar Garciaparra	15.00
Jason Giambi	8.00
Juan Gonzalez	8.00
Luis Gonzalez	5.00
Shawn Green	5.00
Ken Griffey Jr.	20.00
Vladimir Guerrero	8.00
Todd Helton	8.00
Derek Jeter	25.00
Chipper Jones	10.00
Mike Piazza	15.00
Albert Pujols	20.00
Manny Ramirez	10.00
Alex Rodriguez	15.00
Ivan Rodriguez	10.00
Scott Rolen	10.00
Gary Sheffield	6.00
Sammy Sosa	20.00
Ichiro Suzuki	25.00
Frank Thomas	10.00
Jim Thome	8.00
Larry Walker	5.00
Bernie Williams	6.00

2002 Fleer Showcase

	NM/M
Complete Set (166):	225.00
Common Player:	.25
Common (126-141):	5.00
Production 500	
Common (141-166)	4.00
Production 1,500	
Pack (5):	3.00
Box (24):	60.00

1	Albert Pujols	2.00
2	Pedro J. Martinez	.75
3	Frank Thomas	.75
4	Gary Sheffield	.40
5	Roberto Alomar	.40
6	Luis Gonzalez	.35
7	Bobby Abreu	.25
8	Carlos Lee	.25
9	Preston Wilson	.25
10	Todd Helton	.75
11	Juan Gonzalez	.75
12	Chuck Knoblauch	.25
13	Jason Kendall	.25
14	Aaron Sele	.25
15	Greg Vaughn	.25
16	Fred McGriff	.25
17	Doug Mientkiewicz	.25
18	Richard Hidalgo	.25
19	Alfonso Soriano	.50
20	Matt Williams	.25
21	Bobby Higginson	.25
22	Mo Vaughn	.25
23	Andruw Jones	.75
24	Omar Vizquel	.25
25	Bret Boone	.25
26	Bernie Williams	.35
27	Rafael Furcal	.25
28	Jeff Bagwell	.75
29	Marty Cordova	.25
30	Lance Berkman	.25
31	Vernon Wells	.25

32	Garret Anderson	.25
33	Larry Bigbie	.25
34	Steve Finley	.25
35	Barry Bonds	3.00
36	Eric Chavez	.35
37	Tony Clark	.25
38	Roger Clemens	1.50
39	Adam Dunn	.50
40	Roger Cedeno	.25
41	Carlos Delgado	.50
42	Jermaine Dye	.25
43	Brian Jordan	.25
44	Darin Erstad	.65
45	Paul LoDuca	.25
46	Jim Edmonds	.25
47	Tom Glavine	.50
48	Cliff Floyd	.25
49	Jon Lieber	.25
50	Adrian Beltre	.40
51	Joel Pineiro	.25
52	Jim Thome	.40
53	Jimmy Rollins	.40
54	Pat Burrell	.40
55	Jeromy Burnitz	.25
56	Larry Walker	.25
57	Damon Minor	.25
58	John Olerud	.25
59	Carlos Beltran	.50
60	Vladimir Guerrero	.75
61	David Justice	.25
62	Phil Nevin	.25
63	Tino Martinez	.25
64	Curt Schilling	.75
65	Corey Patterson	.25
66	Aubrey Huff	.25
67	Mark Grace	.35
68	Rafael Palmeiro	.65
69	Jorge Posada	.35
70	Craig Biggio	.25
71	Manny Ramirez	.75
72	Mark Quinn	.25
73	Raul Mondesi	.25
74	Shawn Green	.40
75	Brian Giles	.25
76	Paul Konerko	.25
77	Troy Glaus	.75
78	Mike Mussina	.40
79	Greg Maddux	1.00
80	Edgar Martinez	.25
81	Jose Vidro	.25
82	Scott Rolen	.65
83	Ben Grieve	.25
84	Jeff Kent	.25
85	Magglio Ordonez	.25
86	Freddy Garcia	.25
87	Ivan Rodriguez	.65
88	Pokey Reese	.25
89	Shannon Stewart	.25
90	Randy Johnson	.75
91	Cristian Guzman	.25
92	Tsuyoshi Shinjo	.25
93	Steve Cox	.25
94	Mike Sweeney	.25
95	Robert Fick	.25
96	Sean Casey	.40
97	Tim Hudson	.35
98	Bud Smith	.25
99	Corey Koskie	.25
100	Richie Sexson	.25
101	Aramis Ramirez	.25
102	Barry Larkin	.25
103	Rich Aurilia	.25
104	Charles Johnson	.25
105	Ryan Klesko	.25
106	Ben Sheets	.25
107	J.D. Drew	.40
108	Jay Gibbons	.25
109	Kerry Wood	.65
110	C.C. Sabathia	.25
111	Eric Munson	.25
112	Josh Beckett	.40
113	Javier Vasquez	.25
114	Barry Zito	.35
115	Kazuhiro Sasaki	.25
116	Bubba Trammell	.25
117	Russell Branyan	.25
118	Todd Walker	.25
119	Mike Hampton	.25
120	Jeff Weaver	.25
121	Geoff Jenkins	.25
122	Edgardo Alfonzo	.25
123	Mike Lieberthal	.25
124	Mike Lowell	.25
125	Kevin Brown	.25
126	Derek Jeter	8.00
127	Ichiro Suzuki	5.00
128	Nomar Garciaparra	5.00
129	Ken Griffey Jr.	5.00
130	Jason Giambi	5.00
131	Alex Rodriguez	6.00
132	Chipper Jones	5.00
133	Mike Piazza	5.00
134	Sammy Sosa	5.00
135	Hideo Nomo	5.00
136	Kazuhisa Ishii RC	8.00
137	Satoru Komiyama RC	5.00

138	So Taguchi RC	6.00
139	Jorge Padilla RC	5.00
140	Rene Reyes RC	5.00
141	Jorge Nunez RC	5.00
142	Nelson Castro RC	4.00
143	Anderson Machado RC	4.00
144	Edwin Almonte RC	4.00
145	Luis Ugueto RC	4.00
146	Felix Escalona RC	4.00
147	Ron Calloway RC	4.00
148	Hansel Izquierdo RC	4.00
149	Mark Teixeira	6.00
150	Orlando Hudson	4.00
151	Aaron Cook RC	4.00
152	Aaron Taylor RC	4.00
153	Takahito Nomura RC	4.00
154	Matt Thornton	4.00
155	Mark Prior	6.00
156	Reed Johnson RC	6.00
157	Doug DeVore	4.00
158	Ben Howard RC	4.00
159	Francis Beltran RC	4.00
160	Brian Mallette RC	4.00
161	Sean Burroughs	4.00
162	Michael Restovich	4.00
163	Austin Kearns	4.00
164	Marlon Byrd	4.00
165	Hank Blalock	6.00
166	Mike Rivera	4.00

Legacy

Stars (1-125):		3-5X
Legacy (126-166):		1X
Production 175 Sets		

Baseball's Best

	NM/M
Complete Set (20):	40.00
Common Player:	1.00
Inserted 1:8	

1	Derek Jeter	5.00
2	Barry Bonds	5.00
3	Mike Piazza	3.00
4	Alex Rodriguez	4.00
5	Pat Burrell	1.00
6	Rafael Palmeiro	1.00
7	Nomar Garciaparra	3.00
8	Todd Helton	1.50
9	Roger Clemens	2.50
10	Shawn Green	1.00
11	Chipper Jones	2.00
12	Pedro J. Martinez	1.50
13	Luis Gonzalez	1.00
14	Randy Johnson	1.50
15	Ichiro Suzuki	3.00
16	Ken Griffey Jr.	3.00
17	Vladimir Guerrero	1.50
18	Sammy Sosa	3.00
19	Jason Giambi	1.00
20	Albert Pujols	4.00

Baseball's Best Memorabilia

	NM/M
Common Player:	5.00
Inserted 1:24	
Golds:	1-2X
Production 100 Sets	
Derek Jeter/Jsy	20.00
Barry Bonds/Jsy	20.00
Mike Piazza/Jsy	10.00
Alex Rodriguez/Bat	15.00
Rafael Palmeiro/Jsy	8.00
Nomar Garciaparra/ Jsy	10.00
Todd Helton/Bat	8.00
Roger Clemens/Jsy	15.00
Shawn Green/Jsy	5.00
Chipper Jones/Jsy	10.00
Pedro Martinez/Jsy	8.00
Luis Gonzalez/Jsy	5.00
Randy Johnson/Jsy	10.00

Ichiro Suzuki/Base	15.00
Ken Griffey Jr./Base	10.00
Vladimir Guerrero/ Base	8.00
Sammy Sosa/Base	10.00
Jason Giambi/Base	8.00
Albert Pujols/Base	10.00

Baseball's Best Silver Autograph

	NM/M
Serial numbered to 400.	
Derek Jeter	125.00
Barry Bonds	200.00

Baseball's Best Gold Autograph

	NM/M
Serial numbered to 100.	
Derek Jeter	150.00
Barry Bonds	225.00

Derek Jeter's Legacy Collection

	NM/M
Complete Set (22):	80.00
Common Jeter (1-22):	5.00
Production 1,000 Sets	

Derek Jeter's Legacy Collection Memorabilia

	NM/M
Quantity produced listed	
Derek Jeter/Jsy/300	75.00
Derek Jeter/ Combo Jsy/175	90.00
Derek Jeter/ Glove/425	60.00

Sweet Signatures Wall

		NM/M
Common Player:		8.00
1	Bobby Abreu/70	20.00
2	Russell Branyan/200	8.00
5	Eric Chavez/108	15.00
6	Rafael Furcal/207	10.00
8	Brandon Inge/187	8.00
9	Jackson Melian/146	8.00
10	Xavier Nady/286	8.00
11	Jose Ortiz/116	8.00
12	Ben Sheets/150	20.00
13	Mike Sweeney/371	10.00

Sweet Signatures Lumber

		NM/M
Common Player:		5.00
1	Bobby Abreu/231	10.00
2	Russell Branyan/425	8.00
3	Pat Burrell/115	10.00
4	Sean Casey/64	20.00
6	Eric Chavez/256	15.00
7	Rafael Furcal/530	10.00
8	Brandon Inge/528	5.00
9	Jackson Melian/636	5.00
10	Xavier Nady/589	8.00
11	Jose Ortiz/515	8.00
12	Ben Sheets/458	15.00
13	Mike Sweeney/495	10.00

Sweet Sigs Leather

		NM/M
Common Player:		8.00
2	Russell Branyan/90	10.00
6	Rafael Furcal/92	15.00
8	Brandon Inge/122	8.00
10	Xavier Nady/301	8.00
11	Jose Ortiz/50	10.00

12	Ben Sheets/60	25.00
13	Mike Sweeney/103	15.00

2002 Fleer Tradition

MARK GRACE — Arizona Diamondbacks #77/13

	NM/M
Complete Set (500):	175.00
Common Player:	.15
Common SP (1-100):	1.50
Inserted 1:2	
Pack (10):	2.00
Box (36):	50.00

1	Barry Bonds	10.00
2	Cal Ripken Jr.	10.00
3	Tony Gwynn	5.00
4	Brad Radke	1.50
5	Jose Ortiz	1.50
6	Mark Mulder	1.50
7	Jon Lieber	1.50
8	John Olerud	1.50
9	Phil Nevin	1.50
10	Craig Biggio	1.50
11	Pedro Martinez	4.00
12	Fred McGriff	1.50
13	Vladimir Guerrero	4.00
14	Jason Giambi	3.00
15	Mark Kotsay	1.50
16	Bud Smith	1.50
17	Kevin Brown	1.50
18	Darin Erstad	3.00
19	Julio Franco	1.50
20	C.C. Sabathia	1.50
21	Larry Walker	1.50
22	Doug Mientkiewicz	1.50
23	Luis Gonzalez	2.00
24	Albert Pujols	8.00
25	Brian Lawrence	1.50
26	Al Leiter	1.50
27	Mike Sweeney	1.50
28	Jeff Weaver	1.50
29	Matt Morris	1.50
30	Hideo Nomo	4.00
31	Tom Glavine	2.50
32	Magglio Ordonez	1.50
33	Roberto Alomar	2.50
34	Roger Cedeno	1.50
35	Greg Vaughn	1.50
36	Chan Ho Park	1.50
37	Rich Aurilia	1.50
38	Tsuyoshi Shinjo	1.50
39	Eric Young	1.50
40	Bobby Higginson	1.50
41	Marlon Anderson	1.50
42	Mark Grace	2.00
43	Steve Cox	1.50
44	Cliff Floyd	1.50
45	Brian Roberts	1.50
46	Paul Konerko	1.50
47	Brandon Duckworth	1.50
48	Josh Beckett	2.50
49	David Ortiz	2.50
50	Geoff Jenkins	1.50
51	Ruben Sierra	1.50
52	John Franco	1.50
53	Einar Diaz	1.50
54	Luis Castillo	1.50
55	Mark Quinn	1.50
56	Shea Hillenbrand	1.50
57	Rafael Palmeiro	3.00
58	Paul O'Neill	1.50
59	Andruw Jones	4.00
60	Lance Berkman	1.50
61	Jimmy Rollins	2.00
62	Jose Hernandez	1.50
63	Rusty Greer	1.50
64	Wade Miller	1.50
65	David Eckstein	1.50
66	Jose Valentin	1.50
67	Javier Vazquez	1.50
68	Roger Clemens	6.00
69	Omar Vizquel	1.50
70	Roy Oswalt	1.50
71	Shannon Stewart	1.50
72	Byung-Hyun Kim	1.50
73	Jay Gibbons	1.50
74	Barry Larkin	1.50
75	Brian Giles	1.50
76	Andres Galarraga	1.50
77	Sammy Sosa	6.00
78	Manny Ramirez	4.00
79	Carlos Delgado	2.50
80	Jorge Posada	1.50
81	Todd Ritchie	1.50
82	Russ Ortiz	1.50
83	Brent Mayne	1.50
84	Mike Mussina	3.00
85	Raul Mondesi	1.50
86	Mark Loretta	1.50
87	Tim Raines	1.50
88	Ichiro Suzuki	6.00
89	Juan Pierre	1.50
90	Adam Dunn	2.50
91	Jason Tyner	1.50
92	Miguel Tejada	1.50
93	Elpidio Guzman	1.50
94	Freddy Garcia	1.50
95	Marcus Giles	1.50
96	Junior Spivey	1.50
97	Aramis Ramirez	1.50
98	Jose Rijo	1.50
99	Paul LoDuca	1.50
100	Mike Cameron	1.50
101	Alex Hernandez	.15
102	Benji Gil	.15
103	Benito Santiago	.15
104	Bobby Abreu	.15
105	Brad Penny	.15
106	Calvin Murray	.15
107	Chad Durbin	.15
108	Chris Singleton	.15
109	Chris Carpenter	.15
110	David Justice	.15
111	Eric Chavez	.25
112	Fernando Tatis	.15
113	Frank Castillo	.15
114	Jason LaRue	.15
115	Jim Edmonds	.15
116	Joe Kennedy	.15
117	Jose Jimenez	.15
118	Josh Towers	.15
119	Junior Herndon	.15
120	Luke Prokopec	.15
121	Mac Suzuki	.15
122	Mark DeRosa	.15
123	Marty Cordova	.15
124	Michael Tucker	.15
125	Michael Young	.15
126	Robin Ventura	.15
127	Shane Halter	.15
128	Shane Reynolds	.15
129	Tony Womack	.15
130	A.J. Pierzynski	.15
131	Aaron Rowand	.15
132	Antonio Alfonseca	.15
133	Arthur Rhodes	.15
134	Bob Wickman	.15
135	Brady Clark	.15
136	Chad Hermansen	.15
137	Marlon Byrd	.15
138	Dan Wilson	.15
139	David Cone	.15
140	Dean Palmer	.15
141	Denny Neagle	.15
142	Derek Jeter	2.50
143	Erubiel Durazo	.15
144	Felix Rodriguez	.15
145	Jason Hart	.15
146	Jay Bell	.15
147	Jeff Suppan	.15
148	Jeff Zimmerman	.15
149	Kerry Wood	.65
150	Kerry Robinson	.15
151	Kevin Appier	.15
152	Michael Barrett	.15
153	Mo Vaughn	.15
154	Rafael Furcal	.15
155	Sidney Ponson	.15
156	Terry Adams	.15
157	Tim Redding	.15
158	Toby Hall	.15
159	Aaron Sele	.15
160	Bartolo Colon	.15
161	Brad Ausmus	.15
162	Carlos Pena	.15
163	Jace Brewer	.15
164	David Wells	.15
165	David Segui	.15
166	Derek Lowe	.15
167	Derek Bell	.15
168	Jason Grabowski	.15
169	Johnny Damon	.25
170	Jose Mesa	.15
171	Juan Encarnacion	.15
172	Ken Caminiti	.15
173	Ken Griffey Jr.	1.50
174	Luis Rivas	.15
175	Mariano Rivera	.25
176	Mark Grudzielanek	.15
177	Mark McGwire	2.00
178	Mike Bordick	.15
179	Mike Hampton	.15
180	Nick Bierbrodt	.15
181	Paul Byrd	.15
182	Robb Nen	.15
183	Ryan Dempster	.15
184	Ryan Klesko	.15
185	Scott Spiezio	.15
186	Scott Strickland	.15
187	Todd Zeile	.15
188	Tom Gordon	.15
189	Troy Glaus	.75
190	Matt Williams	.15
191	Wes Helms	.15
192	Jerry Hairston Jr.	.15
193	Brook Fordyce	.15
194	Nomar Garciaparra	1.50
195	Kevin Tapani	.15
196	Mark Buehrle	.15
197	Dmitri Young	.15
198	John Rocker	.15
199	Juan Uribe	.15
200	Matt Anderson	.15
201	Alex Gonzalez	.15
202	Julio Lugo	.15
203	Roberto Hernandez	.15
204	Richie Sexson	.15
205	Corey Koskie	.15
206	Tony Armas Jr.	.15
207	Rey Ordonez	.15
208	Orlando Hernandez	.15
209	Pokey Reese	.15
210	Mike Lieberthal	.15
211	Kris Benson	.15
212	Jermaine Dye	.15
213	Livan Hernandez	.15
214	Bret Boone	.15
215	Dustin Hermanson	.15
216	Placido Polanco	.15
217	Jesus Colome	.15
218	Alex Gonzalez	.15
219	Adam Everett	.15
220	Adam Piatt	.15
221	Brad Fullmer	.15
222	Brian Buchanan	.15
223	Chipper Jones	1.00
224	Chuck Finley	.15
225	David Bell	.15
226	Jack Wilson	.25
227	Jason Bere	.15
228	Jeff Conine	.15
229	Jeff Bagwell	.75
230	Joe McEwing	.15
231	Kip Wells	.15
232	Mike Lansing	.15
233	Neifi Perez	.15
234	Omar Daal	.15
235	Reggie Sanders	.15
236	Shawn Wooten	.15
237	Shawn Chacon	.15
238	Shawn Estes	.15
239	Steve Sparks	.15
240	Steve Kline	.15
241	Tino Martinez	.15
242	Tyler Houston	.15
243	Xavier Nady	.15
244	Bengie Molina	.15
245	Ben Davis	.15
246	Casey Fossum	.15
247	Chris Stynes	.15
248	Danny Graves	.15
249	Pedro Feliz	.15
250	Darren Oliver	.15
251	Dave Veres	.15
252	Deivi Cruz	.15
253	Desi Relaford	.15
254	Devon White	.15
255	Edgar Martinez	.15
256	Eric Munson	.15
257	Eric Karros	.15
258	Homer Bush	.15
259	Jason Kendall	.15
260	Javy Lopez	.15
261	Keith Foulke	.15
262	Keith Ginter	.15
263	Nick Johnson	.15
264	Pat Burrell	.35
265	Ricky Gutierrez	.15
266	Russ Johnson	.15
267	Steve Finley	.15
268	Terrence Long	.15
269	Tony Batista	.15
270	Torii Hunter	.15
271	Vinny Castilla	.15
272	A.J. Burnett	.15
273	Adrian Beltre	.35
274	Alex Rodriguez	2.00
275	Armando Benitez	.15
276	Billy Koch	.15
277	Brady Anderson	.15
278	Brian Jordan	.15
279	Carlos Febles	.15
280	Daryle Ward	.15
281	Eli Marrero	.15
282	Garret Anderson	.15
283	Jack Cust	.15
284	Jacque Jones	.15
285	Jamie Moyer	.15
286	Jeffrey Hammonds	.15
287	Jim Thome	.15
288	Jon Garland	.15
289	Jose Offerman	.15
290	Matt Stairs	.15
291	Orlando Cabrera	.15
292	Ramiro Mendoza	.15
293	Ray Durham	.15
294	Rickey Henderson	.75
295	Rob Mackowiak	.15
296	Scott Rolen	.65
297	Tim Hudson	.25
298	Todd Helton	.75
299	Tony Clark	.15
300	B.J. Surhoff	.15
301	Bernie Williams	.30
302	Bill Mueller	.15
303	Chris Richard	.15
304	Craig Paquette	.15
305	Curt Schilling	.40
306	Damian Jackson	.15
307	Derrek Lee	.15
308	Eric Milton	.15
309	Frank Catalanotto	.15
310	J.T. Snow	.15
311	Jared Sandberg	.15
312	Jason Varitek	.15
313	Jeff Cirillo	.15
314	Jeromy Burnitz	.15
315	Joe Crede	.15
316	Joel Pineiro	.15
317	Jose Cruz Jr.	.15
318	Kevin Young	.15
319	Marquis Grissom	.15
320	Moises Alou	.15
321	Randall Simon	.15
322	Royce Clayton	.15
323	Tim Salmon	.25
324	Travis Fryman	.15
325	Travis Lee	.15
326	Vance Wilson	.15
327	Jarrod Washburn	.15
328	Ben Petrick	.15
329	Ben Grieve	.15
330	Carl Everett	.15
331	Eric Byrnes	.15
332	Doug Glanville	.15
333	Edgardo Alfonzo	.15
334	Ellis Burks	.15
335	Gabe Kapler	.15
336	Gary Sheffield	.25
337	Greg Maddux	1.00
338	J.D. Drew	.25
339	Jamey Wright	.15
340	Jeff Kent	.15
341	Jeremy Giambi	.15
342	Joe Randa	.15
343	Joe Mays	.15
344	Jose Macias	.15
345	Kazuhiro Sasaki	.15
346	Mike Kinkade	.15
347	Mike Lowell	.15
348	Randy Johnson	.75
349	Randy Wolf	.15
350	Richard Hidalgo	.15
351	Ron Coomer	.15
352	Sandy Alomar	.15
353	Sean Casey	.25
354	Trevor Hoffman	.15
355	Adam Eaton	.15
356	Alfonso Soriano	.50
357	Barry Zito	.25
358	Billy Wagner	.15
359	Brent Abernathy	.15
360	Bret Prinz	.15
361	Carlos Beltran	.40
362	Carlos Guillen	.15
363	Charles Johnson	.15
364	Cristian Guzman	.15
365	Damion Easley	.15
366	Darryl Kile	.15
367	Delino DeShields	.15
368	Eric Davis	.15
369	Frank Thomas	.75
370	Ivan Rodriguez	.65
371	Jay Payton	.15
372	Jeff D'Amico	.15
373	John Burkett	.15
374	Melvin Mora	.15
375	Ramon Ortiz	.15
376	Robert Person	.15
377	Russell Branyan	.15
378	Shawn Green	.25
379	Todd Hollandsworth	.15
380	Tony McKnight	.15
381	Trot Nixon	.15
382	Vernon Wells	.15
383	Troy Percival	.15
384	Albie Lopez	.15

385	Alex Ochoa	.15
386	Andy Pettitte	.25
387	Brandon Inge	.15
388	Bubba Trammell	.15
389	Corey Patterson	.15
390	Damian Rolls	.15
391	Dee Brown	.15
392	Edgar Renteria	.15
393	Eric Gagne	.35
394	Jason Johnson	.15
395	Jeff Nelson	.15
396	John Vander Wal	.15
397	Johnny Estrada	.15
398	Jose Canseco	.40
399	Juan Gonzalez	.75
400	Kevin Millwood	.15
401	Lee Stevens	.15
402	Matt Lawton	.15
403	Mike Lamb	.15
404	Octavio Dotel	.15
405	Ramon Hernandez	.15
406	Ruben Quevedo	.15
407	Todd Walker	.15
408	Troy O'Leary	.15
409	Wascar Serrano	.15
410	Aaron Boone	.15
411	Aubrey Huff	.15
412	Ben Sheets	.15
413	Carlos Lee	.15
414	Chuck Knoblauch	.15
415	Steve Karsay	.15
416	Dante Bichette	.15
417	David Dellucci	.15
418	Esteban Loaiza	.15
419	Fernando Vina	.15
420	Ismael Valdes	.15
421	Jason Isringhausen	.15
422	Jeff Shaw	.15
423	John Smoltz	.15
424	Jose Vidro	.15
425	Kenny Lofton	.15
426	Mark Little	.15
427	Mark McLemore	.15
428	Marvin Benard	.15
429	Mike Piazza	1.50
430	Pat Hentgen	.15
431	Preston Wilson	.15
432	Rick Helling	.15
433	Robert Fick	.15
434	Rondell White	.15
435	Adam Kennedy	.15
436	David Espinosa	.15
437	Dewon Brazelton	.15
438	Drew Henson	.25
439	Juan Cruz	.15
440	Jason Jennings	.15
441	Carlos Garcia	.15
442	Carlos Hernandez	.15
443	Wilkin Ruan	.15
444	Wilson Betemit	.15
445	Horacio Ramirez	.15
446	Danys Baez	.15
447	Abraham Nunez	.15
448	Josh Hamilton	.25
449	Chris George	.15
450	Rick Bauer	.15
451	Donnie Bridges	.15
452	Erick Almonte	.15
453	Cory Aldridge	.15
454	Ryan Drese	.15
455	Jason Romano	.15
456	Corky Miller	.15
457	Rafael Soriano	.15
458	Mark Prior	.75
459	Mark Teixeira	.50
460	Adrian Hernandez	.15
461	Tim Spooneybarger	.15
462	Bill Ortega	.15
463	D'Angelo Jimenez	.15
464	Andres Torres	.15
465	Alexis Gomez	.15
466	Angel Berroa	.15
467	Henry Mateo	.15
468	Endy Chavez	.15
469	Billy Sylvester	.15
470	Nate Frese	.15
471	Luis Gonzalez	.25
472	Barry Bonds	2.50
473	Rich Aurilia	.15
474	Albert Pujols	2.00
475	Todd Helton	.75
476	Moises Alou	.15
477	Lance Berkman	.15
478	Brian Giles	.15
479	Cliff Floyd	.15
480	Sammy Sosa	1.50
481	Shawn Green	.30
482	Jon Lieber	.15
483	Matt Morris	.15
484	Curt Schilling	.40
485	Randy Johnson	.75
486	Manny Ramirez	1.50
487	Ichiro Suzuki	1.50
488	Juan Gonzalez	.75
489	Derek Jeter	2.50
490	Alex Rodriguez	2.00
491	Bret Boone	.15
492	Roberto Alomar	.30
493	Jason Giambi	.50
494	Rafael Palmeiro	.65
495	Doug Mientkiewicz	.15
496	Jim Thome	.15
497	Freddy Garcia	.15
498	Mark Buehrle	.15
499	Mark Mulder	.15
500	Roger Clemens	1.25

Diamond Tributes

		NM/M
Complete Set (15):		15.00
Common Player:		.50
Inserted 1:6		
1DT	Cal Ripken Jr.	3.00
2DT	Tony Gwynn	1.00
3DT	Derek Jeter	3.00
4DT	Pedro Martinez	.75
5DT	Mark McGwire	2.50
6DT	Sammy Sosa	2.00
7DT	Barry Bonds	3.00
8DT	Roger Clemens	1.50
9DT	Mike Piazza	2.00
10DT	Alex Rodriguez	2.50
11DT	Randy Johnson	.75
12DT	Chipper Jones	1.00
13DT	Nomar Garciaparra	2.00
14DT	Ichiro Suzuki	2.00
15DT	Jason Giambi	.50

Grass Roots

		NM/M
Complete Set (10):		15.00
Common Player:		.75
Inserted 1:18		
1GR	Barry Bonds	5.00
2GR	Alex Rodriguez	4.00
3GR	Derek Jeter	5.00
4GR	Greg Maddux	2.50
5GR	Ivan Rodriguez	1.00
6GR	Cal Ripken Jr.	5.00
7GR	Bernie Williams	.75
8GR	Jeff Bagwell	1.50
9GR	Scott Rolen	1.00
10GR	Larry Walker	.75

Grass Roots Patch

	NM/M
Production 50 Sets	
Barry Bonds	100.00
Alex Rodriguez	75.00
Greg Maddux	50.00
Ivan Rodriguez	25.00
Cal Ripken Jr.	100.00
Bernie Williams	25.00
Jeff Bagwell	40.00
Scott Rolen	30.00
Larry Walker	20.00

Heads Up

		NM/M
Complete Set (10):		45.00
Common Player:		1.00
Inserted 1:36		
1HU	Derek Jeter	8.00
2HU	Ichiro Suzuki	5.00
3HU	Sammy Sosa	5.00

MARK McGWIRE / 1B

4HU	Mike Piazza	5.00
5HU	Ken Griffey Jr.	5.00
6HU	Alex Rodriguez	6.00
7HU	Barry Bonds	8.00
8HU	Nomar Garciaparra	5.00
9HU	Mark McGwire	6.00
10HU	Cal Ripken Jr.	8.00

Lumber Company

		NM/M
Complete Set (30):		40.00
Common Player:		1.00
Inserted 1:12		
1LC	Moises Alou	1.00
2LC	Luis Gonzalez	1.00
3LC	Todd Helton	2.50
4LC	Mike Piazza	4.00
5LC	J.D. Drew	1.50
6LC	Albert Pujols	5.00
7LC	Chipper Jones	3.00
8LC	Manny Ramirez	2.50
9LC	Miguel Tejada	1.00
10LC	Curt Schilling	1.50
11LC	Alex Rodriguez	5.00
12LC	Barry Larkin	2.00
13LC	Nomar Garciaparra	4.00
14LC	Cliff Floyd	1.00
15LC	Alfonso Soriano	1.50
16LC	Sean Casey	1.00
17LC	Scott Rolen	2.00
18LC	Jose Ortiz	1.00
19LC	Corey Patterson	1.00
20LC	Joe Crede	1.00
21LC	Jace Brewer	1.00
22LC	Derek Jeter	6.00
23LC	Jim Thome	1.00
24LC	Frank Thomas	2.50
25LC	Shawn Green	1.00
26LC	Drew Henson	1.00
27LC	Jimmy Rollins	1.50
28LC	Dave Justice	1.00
29LC	Roberto Alomar	1.50
30LC	Bernie Williams	1.00

Lumber Company Game Used

	NM/M
Common Player:	5.00
Inserted 1:72	
Moises Alou	5.00
Luis Gonzalez	5.00
Todd Helton	8.00
Mike Piazza	12.00
J.D. Drew	6.00
Albert Pujols	15.00
Chipper Jones	10.00
Manny Ramirez	8.00
Miguel Tejada	6.00
Curt Schilling	6.00
Alex Rodriguez	15.00
Barry Larkin	6.00
Nomar Garciaparra	12.00
Cliff Floyd	5.00
Alfonso Soriano	8.00
Sean Casey	6.00
Scott Rolen	8.00
Jose Ortiz	5.00
Corey Patterson	5.00
Joe Crede	5.00
Jace Brewer	5.00
Derek Jeter	25.00
Jim Thome	5.00
Frank Thomas	8.00
Shawn Green	5.00
Drew Henson	5.00
Jimmy Rollins	5.00
Dave Justice	5.00
Roberto Alomar	6.00
Bernie Williams	5.00

This Day in History

		NM/M
Complete Set (29):		120.00
Common Player:		1.50
Inserted 1:18		
1	Cal Ripken Jr.	10.00
2	Barry Bonds	10.00
3	George Brett	4.00
4	Tony Gwynn	3.00
5	Nolan Ryan	10.00
6	Reggie Jackson	3.00
7	Paul Molitor	2.00
8	Ichiro Suzuki	5.00
9	Alex Rodriguez	8.00
10	Don Mattingly	6.00
11	Sammy Sosa	5.00
12	Mark McGwire	8.00
13	Derek Jeter	10.00
14	Roger Clemens	4.00
15	Jim "Catfish" Hunter	1.50
16	Greg Maddux	3.00
17	Ken Griffey Jr.	5.00
18	Gil Hodges	1.50
19	Edgar Martinez	1.50
20	Mike Piazza	5.00
21	Jimmie Foxx	1.50
22	Albert Pujols	6.00
23	Chipper Jones	3.00
24	Not Issued	
25	Jeff Bagwell	2.00
26	Nomar Garciaparra	2.00
27	Randy Johnson	2.00
28	Todd Helton	2.00
29	Ted Kluszewski	1.50
30	Ivan Rodriguez	1.75

This Day in History Autographs

		NM/M
Common Player:		
3	Derek Jeter/100	100.00
4	Randy Johnson/75	50.00
5	Don Mattingly/75	90.00
7	Albert Pujols/50	200.00
8	Cal Ripken Jr./50	125.00

This Day in History Game Used

	NM/M
Common Player:	
Jeff Bagwell/Bat/100	15.00
Barry Bonds/Jsy/250	40.00
Roger Clemens/ Jsy/150	30.00
Jimmie Foxx/Bat/250	40.00
Todd Helton/Bat/150	15.00
Jim "Catfish" Hunter/ Jsy/100	15.00
Derek Jeter/Jsy/250	40.00
Greg Maddux/ Jsy/100	20.00
Mike Piazza/Bat/150	20.00
Alex Rodriguez/ Hat/250	30.00

2002 Fleer Tradition Update

	NM/M
Complete Set (400):	75.00
Common Player:	.15

TINO MARTINEZ

FLEER TRADITION

St. Louis Cardinals #21/1B

Common SP (1-100):		.50
Inserted 1:1		
Pack (10):		1.50
Box (36):		35.00

No.	Name	Price
1	P.J. Bevis RC	.50
2	Michael Crudale RC	.50
3	Ben Howard RC	.75
4	Travis Driskill RC	.50
5	Reed Johnson RC	.50
6	Kyle Kane RC	.50
7	Deivis Santos	.50
8	Tim Kalita RC	.50
9	Brandon Puffer RC	.50
10	Chris Snelling RC	1.00
11	Juan Brito RC	.50
12	Tyler Yates RC	.50
13	Victor Alvarez RC	.50
14	Takahito Nomura RC	.50
15	Ron Calloway RC	.50
16	Satoru Komiyama RC	.50
17	Julius Matos RC	.50
18	Jorge Nunez RC	.50
19	Anderson Machado RC	.50
20	Scotty Layfield RC	.50
21	Aaron Cook RC	.50
22	Alex Pelaez RC	.50
23	Corey Thurman RC	.50
24	Nelson Castro RC	.50
25	Jeff Austin RC	.50
26	Felix Escalona RC	.50
27	Luis Ugueto RC	.50
28	Jaime Cerda RC	.50
29	J.J. Trujillo RC	.50
30	Rodrigo Rosario RC	.50
31	Jorge Padilla RC	.50
32	Shawn Sedlacek RC	.50
33	Nate Field RC	.50
34	Earl Snyder RC	.75
35	Miguel Asencio RC	.50
36	Ken Huckaby RC	.50
37	Valentino Pascucci	.50
38	So Taguchi RC	1.00
39	Brian Mallette RC	.50
40	Kazuhisa Ishii RC	2.00
41	Matt Thornton	.50
42	Mark Corey	.50
43	Kirk Saarloos	.50
44	Brandon Bracke	.50
45	Hansel Izquierdo RC	.50
46	Rene Reyes RC	.50
47	Luis Garcia	.50
48	Jason Simontacchi RC	.50
49	John Ennis RC	.75
50	Franklyn German RC	.50
51	Aaron Guiel RC	.50
52	Howie Clark RC	.50
53	David Ross RC	.50
54	Walt McKeel	.50
55	Francis Beltran RC	.50
56	Barry Wesson RC	.50
57	Runelvys Hernandez RC	.50
58	Oliver Perez RC	2.00
59	Ryan Bukvich RC	.50
60	Steve Kent RC	.50
61	Julio Mateo RC	.50
62	Jason Jimenez	.50
63	Jayson Durocher RC	.75
64	Kevin Frederick RC	.50
65	Kevin Gryboski RC	.50
66	Edwin Almonte RC	.50
67	John Foster RC	.50
68	Doug DeVore RC	1.00
69	Tom Shearn RC	.50
70	Colin Young RC	.50
71	Jon Adkins RC	.50
72	Wilbert Nieves RC	.50
73	Matt Duff	.50
74	Carl Sadler RC	.50
75	Jason Kershner RC	.50
76	Brandon Backe RC	.50
77	Wilson Valdez RC	.50
78	Chris Baker RC	.50
79	Ryan Jamison RC	.50
80	Steve Bechler RC	.75
81	Allan Simpson RC	.50
82	Aaron Taylor RC	.50
83	Kevin Cash RC	.50
84	Chone Figgins RC	1.00
85	Clay Condrey RC	.50
86	Shane Nance RC	.50
87	Freddy Sanchez RC	.50
88	Jim Rushford RC	.50
89	Jeriome Robertson RC	.50
90	Trey Lunsford RC	.50
91	Cody McKay RC	.50
92	Trey Hodges RC	.50
93	Hee Seop Choi	1.00
94	Joe Borchard	.50
95	Orlando Hudson	.50
96	Carl Crawford	.50
97	Mark Prior	2.00
98	Brett Myers	.50
99	Kenny Lofton	.50
100	Cliff Floyd	.50
101	Randy Winn	.15
102	Ryan Dempster	.15
103	Josh Phelps	.15
104	Marcus Giles	.15
105	Rickey Henderson	.75
106	Jose Leon	.15
107	Tino Martinez	.15
108	Greg Norton	.15
109	Odalis Perez	.15
110	J.C. Romero	.15
111	Gary Sheffield	.35
112	Ismael Valdes	.15
113	Juan Acevedo	.15
114	Ben Broussard	.15
115	Deivi Cruz	.15
116	Geronimo Gil	.15
117	Eric Hinske	.15
118	Ted Lilly	.15
119	Quinton McCracken	.15
120	Antonio Alfonseca	.15
121	Brent Abernathy	.15
122	Johnny Damon	.25
123	Francisco Cordova	.15
124	Sterling Hitchcock	.15
125	Vladimir Nunez	.15
126	Andres Galarraga	.15
127	Timoniel Perez	.15
128	Tsuyoshi Shinjo	.15
129	Joe Girardi	.15
130	Roberto Alomar	.35
131	Ellis Burks	.15
132	Mike DeJean	.15
133	Alex Gonzalez	.15
134	Johan Santana	.35
135	Kenny Lofton	.15
136	Juan Encarnacion	.15
137	Dewon Brazelton	.15
138	Jeromy Burnitz	.15
139	Elmer Dessens	.15
140	Juan Gonzalez	.75
141	Todd Hundley	.15
142	Tomokazu Ohka	.15
143	Robin Ventura	.15
144	Rodrigo Lopez	.15
145	Ruben Sierra	.15
146	Jason Phillips	.15
147	Ryan Rupe	.15
148	Kevin Appier	.15
149	Sean Burroughs	.15
150	Masato Yoshii	.15
151	Juan Diaz	.15
152	Tony Graffanino	.15
153	Raul Ibanez	.15
154	Kevin Mench	.15
155	Pedro Astacio	.15
156	Brent Butler	.15
157	Kirk Rueter	.15
158	Eddie Guardado	.15
159	Hideki Irabu	.15
160	Wendell Magee	.15
161	Antonio Osuna	.15
162	Jose Vizcaino	.15
163	Danny Bautista	.15
164	Vinny Castilla	.15
165	Chris Singleton	.15
166	Mark Redman	.15
167	Olmedo Saenz	.15
168	Scott Erickson	.15
169	Ty Wigginton	.15
170	Jason Isringhausen	.15
171	Lou Merloni	.15
172	Chris Magruder	.15
173	Brandon Berger	.15
174	Roger Cedeno	.15
175	Kelvim Escobar	.15
176	Jose Guillen	.15
177	Damian Jackson	.15
178	Eric Owens	.15
179	Angel Berroa	.15
180	Alex Cintron	.15
181	Jeff Weaver	.15
182	Damon Minor	.15
183	Bobby Estalella	.15
184	David Justice	.15
185	Roy Halladay	.25
186	Brian Jordan	.15
187	Mike Maroth	.15
188	Pokey Reese	.15
189	Rey Sanchez	.15
190	Hank Blalock	.50
191	Jeff Cirillo	.15
192	Dmitri Young	.15
193	Carl Everett	.15
194	Joey Hamilton	.15
195	Jorge Julio	.15
196	Pablo Ozuna	.15
197	Jason Marquis	.15
198	Dustan Mohr	.15
199	Joe Borowski	.15
200	Tony Clark	.15
201	David Wells	.15
202	Josh Fogg	.15
203	Aaron Harang	.15
204	John McDonald	.15
205	John Stephens	.15
206	Chris Reitsma	.15
207	Alex Sanchez	.15
208	Milton Bradley	.15
209	Matt Clement	.15
210	Brad Fullmer	.15
211	Shigetoshi Hasegawa	.15
212	Austin Kearns	.50
213	Damaso Marte	.15
214	Vicente Padilla	.15
215	Raul Mondesi	.15
216	Russell Branyan	.15
217	Bartolo Colon	.15
218	Moises Alou	.15
219	Scott Hatteberg	.15
220	Bobby Kielty	.15
221	Kip Wells	.15
222	Scott Stewart	.15
223	Victor Martinez	.40
224	Marty Cordova	.15
225	Desi Relaford	.15
226	Reggie Sanders	.15
227	Jason Giambi	.50
228	Jimmy Haynes	.15
229	Billy Koch	.15
230	Damian Moss	.15
231	Chan Ho Park	.15
232	Cliff Floyd	.15
233	Todd Zeile	.15
234	Jeremy Giambi	.15
235	Rick Helling	.15
236	Matt Lawton	.15
237	Ramon Martinez	.15
238	Rondell White	.15
239	Scott Sullivan	.15
240	Hideo Nomo	.60
241	Todd Ritchie	.15
242	Ramon Santiago	.15
243	Jake Peavy	.15
244	Brad Wilkerson	.15
245	Reggie Taylor	.15
246	Carlos Pena	.15
247	Willis Roberts	.15
248	Jason Schmidt	.15
249	Mike Williams	.15
250	Alan Zinter	.15
251	Michael Tejera	.15
252	Dave Roberts	.15
253	Scott Schoeneweis	.15
254	Woody Williams	.15
255	John Thomson	.15
256	Ricardo Rodriguez	.15
257	Aaron Sele	.15
258	Paul Wilson	.15
259	Brett Tomko	.15
260	Kenny Rogers	.15
261	Mo Vaughn	.15
262	John Burkett	.15
263	Dennis Stark	.15
264	Ray Durham	.15
265	Scott Rolen	.65
266	Gabe Kapler	.15
267	Todd Hollandsworth	.15
268	Bud Smith	.15
269	Jay Payton	.15
270	Tyler Houston	.15
271	Brian Moehler	.15
272	David Espinosa	.15
273	Placido Polanco	.15
274	John Patterson	.15
275	Adam Hyzdu	.15
276	Albert Pujols	2.00
277	Larry Walker	.15
278	Magglio Ordonez	.15
279	Ryan Klesko	.15
280	Darin Erstad	.60
281	Jeff Kent	.15
282	Paul LoDuca	.15
283	Jim Edmonds	.15
284	Chipper Jones	1.00
285	Bernie Williams	.30
286	Pat Burrell	.40
287	Cliff Floyd	.15
288	Troy Glaus	.75
289	Brian Giles	.15
290	Jim Thome	.15
291	Greg Maddux	1.00
292	Roberto Alomar	.30
293	Jeff Bagwell	.75
294	Rafael Furcal	.15
295	Josh Beckett	.25
296	Carlos Delgado	.35
297	Ken Griffey Jr.	1.50
298	Jason Giambi	.50
299	Paul Konerko	.15
300	Mike Sweeney	.15
301	Alfonso Soriano	.50
302	Shea Hillenbrand	.15
303	Tony Batista	.15
304	Robin Ventura	.15
305	Alex Rodriguez	2.00
306	Nomar Garciaparra	1.50
307	Derek Jeter	2.50
308	Miguel Tejada	.30
309	Omar Vizquel	.15
310	Jorge Posada	.25
311	A.J. Pierzynski	.15
312	Ichiro Suzuki	1.50
313	Manny Ramirez	.75
314	Torii Hunter	.15
315	Garret Anderson	.15
316	Robert Fick	.15
317	Randy Winn	.15
318	Mark Buehrle	.15
319	Freddy Garcia	.15
320	Eddie Guardado	.15
321	Roy Halladay	.25
322	Derek Lowe	.15
323	Pedro J. Martinez	.75
324	Mariano Rivera	.25
325	Kazuhiro Sasaki	.15
326	Barry Zito	.25
327	Johnny Damon	.25
328	Ugueth Urbina	.15
329	Todd Helton	.75
330	Richie Sexson	.15
331	Jose Vidro	.15
332	Luis Castillo	.15
333	Junior Spivey	.15
334	Scott Rolen	.65
335	Mike Lowell	.15
336	Jimmy Rollins	.25
337	Jose Hernandez	.15
338	Mike Piazza	1.50
339	Benito Santiago	.15
340	Sammy Sosa	1.50
341	Barry Bonds	2.50
342	Vladimir Guerrero	.75
343	Lance Berkman	.15
344	Adam Dunn	.40
345	Shawn Green	.25
346	Luis Gonzalez	.25
347	Eric Gagne	.25
348	Tom Glavine	.30
349	Trevor Hoffman	.15
350	Randy Johnson	.75
351	Byung-Hyun Kim	.15
352	Matt Morris	.15
353	Odalis Perez	.15
354	Curt Schilling	.40
355	John Smoltz	.15
356	Mike Williams	.15
357	Andruw Jones	.75
358	Vicente Padilla	.15
359	Mike Remlinger	.15
360	Robb Nen	.15
361	Shawn Green	.25
362	Derek Jeter	2.50
363	Troy Glaus	.75
364	Ken Griffey Jr.	1.50
365	Mike Piazza	1.50
366	Jason Giambi	.50
367	Greg Maddux	1.00
368	Albert Pujols	2.00
369	Pedro J. Martinez	.75
370	Barry Zito	.25
371	Ichiro Suzuki	1.50
372	Nomar Garciaparra	1.50
373	Vladimir Guerrero	.75
374	Randy Johnson	.75
375	Barry Bonds	2.50
376	Sammy Sosa	1.50
377	Hideo Nomo	.75
378	Jeff Bagwell	.75
379	Curt Schilling	.35
380	Jim Thome	.15
381	Todd Helton	.75
382	Roger Clemens	1.25
383	Chipper Jones	1.00
384	Alex Rodriguez	2.00
385	Manny Ramirez	.40
386	Barry Bonds	2.50
387	Jim Thome	.15
388	Adam Dunn	.40
389	Alex Rodriguez	2.00
390	Shawn Green	.25
391	Jason Giambi	.50
392	Lance Berkman	.15
393	Pat Burrell	.40
394	Eric Chavez	.25
395	Mike Piazza	1.50
396	Vladimir Guerrero	.75
397	Paul Konerko	.15
398	Sammy Sosa	1.50

399	Richie Sexson	.15
400	Torii Hunter	.15

Glossy

Stars (1-100):		1-2X
Cards (101-400):		4-8X
Production 200 Sets		

Diamond Debuts

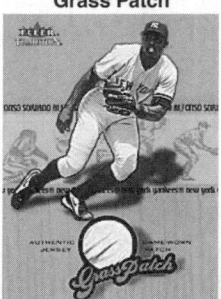

		NM/M
Complete Set (15):		10.00
Common Player:		.50
Inserted 1:6		
1DD	Mark Prior	1.50
2DD	Eric Hinske	.50
3DD	Kazuhisa Ishii	.50
4DD	Ben Broussard	.50
5DD	Sean Burroughs	.50
6DD	Austin Kearns	1.00
7DD	Hee Seop Choi	1.00
8DD	Kirk Saarloos	.50
9DD	Orlando Hudson	.50
10DD	So Taguchi	.50
11DD	Kevin Mench	.50
12DD	Carl Crawford	.50
13DD	John Patterson	.50
14DD	Hank Blalock	1.50
15DD	Brett Myers	.50

Grass Roots

		NM/M
Complete Set (10):		15.00
Common Player:		1.00
Inserted 1:24		
1GR	Alfonso Soriano	1.50
2GR	Torii Hunter	1.00
3GR	Andruw Jones	1.50
4GR	Jim Edmonds	1.00
5GR	Shawn Green	1.00
6GR	Todd Helton	1.50
7GR	Nomar Garciaparra	4.00
8GR	Roberto Alomar	1.00
9GR	Vladimir Guerrero	1.50
10GR	Ichiro Suzuki	4.00

Grass Patch

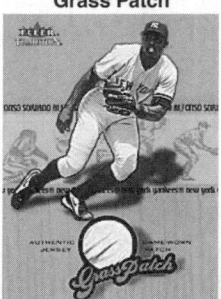

		NM/M
Common Player:		20.00
Production 50 Sets		
	Alfonso Soriano	30.00
	Torii Hunter	20.00
	Andruw Jones	30.00

	Jim Edmonds	20.00
	Shawn Green	20.00
	Nomar Garciaparra	50.00
	Roberto Alomar	25.00

Heads Up

		NM/M
Complete Set (10):		25.00
Common Player:		2.00
Inserted 1:48		
1HU	Roger Clemens	6.00
2HU	Adam Dunn	2.00
3HU	Kazuhisa Ishii	1.50
4HU	Barry Zito	1.50
5HU	Pedro J. Martinez	4.00
6HU	Alfonso Soriano	3.00
7HU	Mark Prior	2.00
8HU	Chipper Jones	5.00
9HU	Randy Johnson	4.00
10HU	Lance Berkman	1.50

Heads Up Game-Used

		NM/M
Common Player:		5.00
Production 150 Sets		
	Roger Clemens	25.00
	Adam Dunn	10.00
	Kazuhisa Ishii	5.00
	Barry Zito	5.00
	Alfonso Soriano	10.00
	Mark Prior	10.00
	Chipper Jones	15.00
	Randy Johnson	15.00
	Lance Berkman	5.00
	Mike Piazza	20.00
	Barry Bonds	50.00

Plays of the Week

		NM/M
Complete Set (30):		35.00
Common Player:		1.00
Inserted 1:12		
1PW	Troy Glaus	1.50
2PW	Andruw Jones	1.50
3PW	Curt Schilling	1.25
4PW	Manny Ramirez	1.50
5PW	Sammy Sosa	2.50
6PW	Magglio Ordonez	1.00
7PW	Ken Griffey Jr.	2.50
8PW	Jim Thome	1.00
9PW	Larry Walker	1.00
10PW	Robert Fick	1.00
11PW	Josh Beckett	1.00
12PW	Roy Oswalt	1.00
13PW	Mike Sweeney	1.00
14PW	Shawn Green	1.00
15PW	Torii Hunter	1.00
16PW	Vladimir Guerrero	1.50
17PW	Mike Piazza	2.50
18PW	Jason Giambi	1.25
19PW	Eric Chavez	1.00
20PW	Pat Burrell	1.25
21PW	Brian Giles	1.00
22PW	Ryan Klesko	1.00
23PW	Barry Bonds	5.00
24PW	Mike Cameron	1.00
25PW	Albert Pujols	4.00
26PW	Alex Rodriguez	4.00
27PW	Carlos Delgado	1.00
28PW	Richie Sexson	1.00
29PW	Jay Gibbons	1.00
30PW	Randy Winn	1.00

New York's Finest

		NM/M
Complete Set (15):		60.00
Common Player:		3.00
Inserted 1:83		
1	Edgardo Alfonzo	3.00
2	Roberto Alomar	4.00
3	Jeromy Burnitz	3.00
4	Satoru Komiyama	3.00
5	Rey Ordonez	3.00
6	Mike Piazza	10.00
7	Mo Vaughn	5.00
8	Roger Clemens	10.00
9	Jason Giambi	5.00
10	Derek Jeter	15.00
11	Mike Mussina	5.00
12	Jorge Posada	3.00
13	Alfonso Soriano	5.00
14	Robin Ventura	3.00
15	Bernie Williams	4.00

N.Y.'s Finest Single Swatch

	NM/M
Common Player:	5.00
Production 150 Sets	

		NM/M
Common Card:		5.00
Inserted 1:112		
	Derek Jeter/Jsy,	
	Rey Ordonez/Jsy	25.00
	Alfonso Soriano/Jsy,	
	Roberto Alomar	10.00
	Roger Clemens/Jsy,	
	Mike Piazza	15.00
	Mike Mussina/Jsy,	
	Mo Vaughn	8.00
	Bernie Williams/Jsy,	
	Jeromy Burnitz	8.00
	Derek Jeter/Jsy,	
	Satoru Komiyama	25.00
	Robin Ventura/Jsy,	
	Edgardo Alfonzo	8.00
	Jorge Posada/Jsy,	
	Mike Piazza	8.00
	Jason Giambi/Base,	
	Mo Vaughn	8.00
	Alfonso Soriano/Jsy,	
	Edgardo Alfonzo	10.00
	Derek Jeter,	
	Rey Ordonez/Jsy	5.00
	Alfonso Soriano,	
	Roberto Alomar/Jsy	8.00
	Roger Clemens,	
	Mike Piazza/Jsy	15.00
	Mike Mussina,	
	Mo Vaughn/Jsy	6.00
	Bernie Williams,	
	Jeromy Burnitz/Jsy	5.00
	Derek Jeter,	
	Satoru Komiyama/Bat	8.00
	Robin Ventura,	
	Edgardo Alfonzo/Jsy	5.00
	Jorge Posada,	
	Mike Piazza/Jsy	15.00
	Jason Giambi,	
	Mo Vaughn/Jsy	6.00
	Alfonso Soriano,	
	Edgardo Alfonzo/Jsy	5.00

N.Y.'s Finest Dual Swatch

New York's Finest

		NM/M
Common Card:		10.00
Production 100 Sets		
	Derek Jeter,	
	Rey Ordonez	75.00
	Alfonso Soriano,	
	Roberto Alomar	40.00
	Roger Clemens,	
	Mike Piazza	65.00
	Mike Mussina,	
	Mo Vaughn	30.00
	Bernie Williams,	
	Jeromy Burnitz	20.00
	Robin Ventura,	
	Edgardo Alfonzo	10.00

This Day in History

		NM/M
Complete Set (25):		40.00
Common Player:		1.00
1	Shawn Green	1.00
2	Ozzie Smith	2.50
3	Derek Lowe	1.00
4	Ken Griffey Jr.	3.00
5	Barry Bonds	5.00
6	Juan Gonzalez	1.50
7	Wade Boggs	2.00
8	Mark Prior	1.50
9	Thurman Munson	2.00
10	Curt Schilling	1.25
11	Jason Giambi	1.25
12	Cal Ripken Jr.	5.00
13	Craig Biggio	1.00
14	Drew Henson	1.00
15	Steve Carlton	1.00
16	Greg Maddux	2.50
17	Adam Dunn	1.00
18	Vladimir Guerrero	2.00
19	Alex Rodriguez	4.00
20	Carlton Fisk	1.50
21	Ichiro Suzuki	3.00
22	Johnny Bench	2.00
23	Kazuhisa Ishii	1.00
24	Derek Jeter	5.00
25	Jim Thome	1.00

This Day in History Memorabilia

		NM/M
Common Player:		5.00
Inserted 1:24		
	Shawn Green/Jsy	5.00
	Ozzie Smith/Jsy	10.00
	Barry Bonds/Jsy	15.00
	Barry Bonds/Bat	15.00
	Juan Gonzalez/Bat	6.00
	Wade Boggs/Jsy	6.00
	Wade Boggs/Pants	6.00
	Curt Schilling/Jsy	6.00
	Craig Biggio/Jsy	5.00
	Adam Dunn/Jsy	8.00
	Alex Rodriguez/Bat	10.00
	Alex Rodriguez/Jsy	10.00
	Carlton Fisk/Bat	8.00
	Kazuhisa Ishii/Bat	5.00
	Derek Jeter/Pants	20.00
	Jim Thome/Jsy	8.00
	Greg Maddux/Jsy	10.00

This Day in History Autograph

		NM/M
Inserted 1:582		
	Barry Bonds/150	200.00
	Mark Prior/64	40.00
	Drew Henson	20.00
	Greg Maddux/99	150.00
	Derek Jeter	100.00

2002 Fleer Triple Crown

	NM/M
Complete Set (270):	30.00
Common Player:	.15
Pack (10):	1.50
Box (24):	30.00
1 Mo Vaughn	.15
2 Derek Jeter	2.00
3 Ken Griffey Jr.	1.25
4 Charles Johnson	.15
5 Geoff Jenkins	.15
6 Chuck Knoblauch	.15
7 Jason Kendall	.15
8 Jim Edmonds	.15
9 David Eckstein	.15
10 Carl Everett	.15
11 Barry Larkin	.15
12 Cliff Floyd	.15
13 Ben Sheets	.15
14 Jeff Conine	.15
15 Brian Giles	.15
16 Darryl Kile	.15
17 Troy Glaus	.65
18 Trot Nixon	.15
19 Jim Thome	.15
20 Preston Wilson	.15
21 Roger Clemens	1.00
22 Chad Hermansen	.15
23 Matt Morris	.15
24 Shawn Wooten	.15
25 Manny Ramirez	.65
26 Roberto Alomar	.30
27 Josh Beckett	.25
28 Jose Hernandez	.15
29 Mike Mussina	.35
30 Jack Wilson	.15
31 Bud Smith	.15
32 Garret Anderson	.15
33 Pedro J. Martinez	.65
34 Travis Fryman	.15
35 Jeff Bagwell	.65
36 Doug Mientkiewicz	.15
37 Andy Pettitte	.25
38 Ryan Klesko	.15
39 Edgar Renteria	.15
40 Mariano Rivera	.25
41 Darin Erstad	.50
42 Hideo Nomo	.50
43 Ellis Burks	.15
44 Craig Biggio	.15
45 Corey Koskie	.15
46 Jason Varitek	.15
47 Xavier Nady	.15
48 Aubrey Huff	.15
49 Tim Salmon	.25
50 Nomar Garciaparra	1.25
51 Juan Gonzalez	.65
52 Moises Alou	.15
53 A.J. Pierzynski	.15
54 Bernie Williams	.30
55 Phil Nevin	.15
56 Ben Grieve	.15
57 Mark Grace	.25
58 Mike Lansing	.15
59 Kenny Lofton	.15
60 Lance Berkman	.15
61 David Ortiz	.25
62 Jason Giambi	.40
63 Mark Kotsay	.15
64 Greg Vaughn	.15
65 Junior Spivey	.15
66 Fred McGriff	.15
67 C.C. Sabathia	.15
68 Richard Hidalgo	.15
69 Torii Hunter	.15
70 Jason Hart	.15
71 Bubba Trammell	.15
72 Jace Brewer	.15
73 Matt Williams	.15
74 Matt Stairs	.15
75 Omar Vizquel	.15

76 Daryle Ward	.15
77 Joe Mays	.15
78 Eric Chavez	.15
79 Andres Galarraga	.15
80 Rafael Palmeiro	.50
81 Steve Finley	.15
82 Eric Young	.15
83 Todd Helton	.65
84 Roy Oswalt	.25
85 Eric Milton	.15
86 Ramon Hernandez	.15
87 Jeff Kent	.15
88 Ivan Rodriguez	.50
89 Luis Gonzalez	.25
90 Corey Patterson	.15
91 Jose Ortiz	.15
92 Mike Sweeney	.15
93 Cristian Guzman	.15
94 Johnny Damon	.15
95 Barry Bonds	2.00
96 Rusty Greer	.15
97 Reggie Sanders	.15
98 Sammy Sosa	1.25
99 Jeff Cirillo	.15
100 Carlos Febles	.15
101 Jose Vidro	.15
102 Jermaine Dye	.15
103 Rich Aurilia	.15
104 Gabe Kapler	.15
105 Randy Johnson	.65
106 Rondell White	.15
107 Ben Petrick	.15
108 Joe Randa	.15
109 Fernando Tatis	.15
110 Tim Hudson	.25
111 John Olerud	.15
112 Alex Rodriguez	1.50
113 Curt Schilling	.40
114 Kerry Wood	.40
115 Alex Ochoa	.15
116 Carlos Beltran	.40
117 Vladimir Guerrero	.65
118 Mark Mulder	.15
119 Bret Boone	.15
120 Carlos Delgado	.35
121 Marcus Giles	.15
122 Paul Konerko	.15
123 Juan Pierre	.15
124 Mark Quinn	.15
125 Edgardo Alfonzo	.15
126 Barry Zito	.25
127 Dan Wilson	.15
128 Jose Cruz Jr.	.15
129 Chipper Jones	.75
130 Ray Durham	.15
131 Larry Walker	.15
132 Neifi Perez	.15
133 Robin Ventura	.15
134 Miguel Tejada	.25
135 Edgar Martinez	.15
136 Raul Mondesi	.15
137 Javy Lopez	.15
138 Jose Canseco	.25
139 Mike Hampton	.15
140 Eric Karros	.15
141 Mike Piazza	1.25
142 Travis Lee	.15
143 Ichiro Suzuki	1.25
144 Shannon Stewart	.15
145 Andruw Jones	.65
146 Frank Thomas	.65
147 Tony Clark	.15
148 Adrian Beltre	.25
149 Matt Lawton	.15
150 Marlon Anderson	.15
151 Freddy Garcia	.15
152 Brian Jordan	.15
153 Carlos Lee	.15
154 Eric Munson	.15
155 Paul LoDuca	.15
156 Jay Payton	.15
157 Scott Rolen	.50
158 Jamie Moyer	.15
159 Tom Glavine	.30
160 Magglio Ordonez	.15
161 Brandon Inge	.15
162 Shawn Green	.25
163 Tsuyoshi Shinjo	.15
164 Mike Lieberthal	.15
165 Kazuhiro Sasaki	.15
166 Greg Maddux	.75
167 Chris Singleton	.15
168 Juan Encarnacion	.15
169 Gary Sheffield	.25
170 Nick Johnson	.15
171 Bobby Abreu	.15
172 Aaron Boone	.15
173 Rafael Furcal	.15
174 Mark Buehrle	.15
175 Bobby Higginson	.15
176 Kevin Brown	.15
177 Tino Martinez	.15
178 Pat Burrell	.30

179 Fernando Vina	.15
180 Jay Gibbons	.15
181 Jose Valentin	.15
182 Derek Lee	.15
183 Richie Sexson	.15
184 Alfonso Soriano	.50
185 Jimmy Rollins	.25
186 Albert Pujols	1.50
187 Brady Anderson	.15
188 Sean Casey	.25
189 Luis Castillo	.15
190 Jeromy Burnitz	.15
191 Jorge Posada	.25
192 Kevin Young	.15
193 Eli Marrero	.15
194 Shea Hillenbrand	.15
195 Adam Dunn	.40
196 Mike Lowell	.15
197 Jeffrey Hammonds	.15
198 David Justice	.15
199 Aramis Ramirez	.15
200 J.D. Drew	.25
201 Pedro Santana	.15
202 Endy Chavez	.15
203 Donnie Bridges	.15
204 Travis Phelps	.15
205 Drew Henson	.25
206 Angel Berroa	.15
207 George Perez	.15
208 Billy Sylvester	.15
209 Juan Cruz	.15
210 Horacio Ramirez	.15
211 J.J. Davis	.15
212 Cody Ransom	.15
213 Mark Teixeira	.50
214 Nate Frese	.15
215 Brian Rogers	.15
216 Dewon Brazelton	.15
217 Carlos Hernandez	.15
218 Juan Rivera	.15
219 Luis Lopez	.15
220 Benito Baez	.15
221 Bill Ortega	.15
222 Dustan Mohr	.15
223 Corky Miller	.15
224 Tyler Walker	.15
225 Rick Bauer	.15
226 Mark Prior	.50
227 Rafael Soriano	.15
228 Greg Miller	.15
229 Dave Williams	.15
230 Bert Snow	.15
231 Barry Bonds	1.50
232 Rickey Henderson	.50
233 Alex Rodriguez	1.25
234 Luis Gonzalez	.25
235 Derek Jeter	1.50
236 Bud Smith	.15
237 Sammy Sosa	.75
238 Jeff Bagwell	.50
239 Jim Thome	.15
240 Hideo Nomo	.50
241 Greg Maddux	.75
242 Ken Griffey Jr.	1.00
243 Curt Schilling	.15
244 Arizona Diamondbacks	.15
245 Ichiro Suzuki	.75
246 Albert Pujols	1.00
247 Ichiro Suzuki	.75
248 Barry Bonds	1.50
249 Roger Clemens	.65
250 Randy Johnson	.50
251 Todd Helton	.50
252 Rafael Palmeiro	.40
253 Mike Piazza	1.00
254 Alex Rodriguez	1.25
255 Manny Ramirez	.50
256 Ken Griffey Jr.	1.00
257 Jason Giambi	.40
258 Chipper Jones	.65
259 Larry Walker	.15
260 Sammy Sosa	.75
261 Vladimir Guerrero	.50
262 Nomar Garciaparra	.75
263 Randy Johnson	.50
264 Roger Clemens	.65
265 Ichiro Suzuki	1.00
266 Barry Bonds	1.50
267 Paul LoDuca	.15
268 Albert Pujols	1.00
269 Derek Jeter	1.50
270 Adam Dunn	.40

Values quoted in this guide reflect the retail price of a card, the price a collector can expect to pay when buying a card from a dealer.

Batting Average Parallel

Stars: 4-8X
Numbered to 2001 batting avg.
(See 2002 Fleer Triple Crown for checklist and base card values.)

Home Run Parallel

Stars Print Run 50-75:	10-20X
Stars P/R 31-50:	15-25X
Stars P/R 21-30:	20-40X

Numbered to 2001 HR total.

RBI Parallel

Stars Print Run 101-200:	4-8X
Stars P/R 76-100:	5-10X
Stars P/R 51-75:	6-12X
Stars P/R 25-50:	10-20X

Numbered to 2001 RBI total
(See 2002 Fleer Triple Crown for checklist and base card values.)

Diamond Immortality

	NM/M
Complete Set (10):	25.00
Common Player:	1.00
Inserted 1:12	
1DI Derek Jeter	5.00
2DI Barry Bonds	5.00
3DI Ricky Henderson	1.00
4DI Roger Clemens	2.50
5DI Alex Rodriguez	4.00
6DI Albert Pujols	4.00
7DI Nomar Garciaparra	3.00
8DI Ichiro Suzuki	3.00
9DI Chipper Jones	2.00
10DI Ken Griffey Jr.	3.00

Diamond Immortality Game-Used

	NM/M
Inserted 1:129	
Barry Bonds/Jsy	25.00
Roger Clemens/Jsy	20.00
Nomar Garciaparra/Jsy/SP	40.00
Ricky Henderson/Bat	10.00
Derek Jeter/Bat	25.00
Chipper Jones/Bat	10.00
Albert Pujols/Jsy	25.00
Alex Rodriguez/Jsy	20.00

Home Run Kings

	NM/M
Complete Set (25):	100.00
Common Player:	2.00
Inserted 1:24	

1	Ted Williams	10.00
2	Todd Helton	4.00
3	Eddie Murray	2.00
4	Jeff Bagwell	4.00
5	Babe Ruth	15.00
6	Eddie Mathews	5.00
7	Alex Rodriguez	10.00
8	Juan Gonzalez	4.00
9	Chipper Jones	5.00
10	Luis Gonzalez	2.00
11	Johnny Bench	5.00
12	Frank Thomas	4.00
13	Ernie Banks	3.00
14	Jimmie Foxx	4.00
15	Ken Griffey Jr.	8.00
16	Rafael Palmeiro	3.00
17	Sammy Sosa	8.00
18	Reggie Jackson	4.00
19	Barry Bonds	10.00
20	Willie McCovey	2.00
21	Manny Ramirez	4.00
22	Larry Walker	2.00
23	Jason Giambi	4.00
24	Mike Piazza	8.00
25	Jose Canseco	2.00

Home Run Kings Autograph

	NM/M
Common Player:	
Barry Bonds/73	300.00
Alex Rodriguez/52	100.00

Home Run Kings Game-Used

	NM/M
Common Player:	5.00
Inserted 1:155	
Jeff Bagwell/Jsy	10.00
Johnny Bench/ Bat/SP	50.00
Barry Bonds/Jsy	25.00
Jimmie Foxx/Bat	40.00
Jason Giambi/Jsy	10.00
Reggie Jackson/Bat	10.00
Eddie Mathews/Bat	15.00
Eddie Murray/Bat	10.00
Rafael Palmeiro/Bat	10.00
Mike Piazza/Jsy	15.00
Manny Ramirez/ Bat/SP	50.00
Todd Helton/Bat	10.00
Alex Rodriguez/Bat	15.00
Larry Walker/Bat	5.00
Ted Williams/Jsy	100.00

RBI Kings

	NM/M
Complete Set (15):	140.00
Common Player:	4.00
Inserted 1:144	
1 Sammy Sosa	15.00
2 Todd Helton	8.00
3 Albert Pujols	20.00
4 Manny Ramirez	8.00
5 Luis Gonzalez	4.00
6 Shawn Green	4.00
7 Barry Bonds	20.00
8 Ken Griffey Jr.	15.00
9 Alex Rodriguez	20.00
10 Jason Giambi	8.00
11 Jeff Bagwell	8.00
12 Vladimir Guerrero	8.00
13 Juan Gonzalez	8.00
14 Chipper Jones	8.00
15 Mike Piazza	8.00

RBI Kings Game-Used

	NM/M
Common Player:	

Inserted 1:70

Jeff Bagwell/Jsy	10.00
Barry Bonds/Jsy	25.00
Jason Giambi/Jsy	8.00
Luis Gonzalez/Bat	5.00
Juan Gonzalez/Bat	10.00
Shawn Green/Jsy	6.00
Todd Helton/Jsy	10.00
Mike Piazza/Jsy	15.00
Albert Pujols/Bat/SP	70.00
Manny Ramirez/Bat	10.00
Alex Rodriguez/ Shoe	25.00

Season Crowns

	NM/M
Complete Set (10):	25.00
Common Card:	2.00
Inserted 1:12	
1SC Barry Bonds, Sammy Sosa, Luis Gonzalez	4.00
2SC Larry Walker, Nomar Garciaparra, Todd Helton	4.00
3SC Sammy Sosa, Todd Helton, Manny Ramirez	4.00
4SC Pedro J. Martinez, Derek Jeter, Cal Ripken Jr.	6.00
5SC Jose Canseco, Barry Bonds, Alex Rodriguez	5.00
6SC Barry Bonds, Jeff Kent, Chipper Jones	4.00
7SC Ichiro Suzuki, Jason Giambi, Ivan Rodriguez	3.00
8SC Curt Schilling, Tom Glavine, Pedro J. Martinez	2.00
9SC Randy Johnson, Pedro J. Martinez, Greg Maddux	3.00
10SC Randy Johnson, Curt Schilling, John Smoltz	2.00

Season Crowns Autograph

	NM/M
Jeter #'d to 160.	
Derek Jeter/160	150.00
Barry Bonds/77	250.00

Season Crowns Game-Used

	NM/M
Common Player:	5.00
Inserted 1:90	
Barry Bonds/Jsy	25.00
Sammy Sosa/Base	15.00
Larry Walker/Bat	5.00
Nomar Garciaparra/ Jsy	20.00
Todd Helton/Jsy	10.00
Sammy Sosa/Base	15.00
Todd Helton/Jsy	10.00
Manny Ramirez/Jsy	10.00
Pedro Martinez/Jsy	10.00
Derek Jeter/Pants	25.00
Cal Ripken Jr/Bat	60.00
Jose Canseco/Jsy	8.00
Barry Bonds/Jsy	25.00
Alex Rodriguez/Jsy	20.00
Barry Bonds/Jsy	25.00
Jeff Kent/Jsy	5.00
Ichiro Suzuki/Base	25.00
Jason Giambi/Jsy	10.00

Ivan Rodriguez/Jsy	10.00
Curt Schilling/Jsy	10.00
Tom Glavine/Jsy	10.00
Pedro Martinez/Jsy	10.00
Randy Johnson/Jsy	10.00
Pedro Martinez/Jsy	10.00
Greg Maddux/Jsy	15.00
Randy Johnson/Jsy	10.00
Curt Schilling/Jsy	10.00
John Smoltz/Jsy	5.00

Season Crowns Triple Swatch

	NM/M
Production 100 Sets	
Barry Bonds, Sammy Sosa, Luis Gonzalez	100.00
Larry Walker, Nomar Garciaparra, Todd Helton	40.00
Sammy Sosa, Todd Helton, Manny Ramirez	50.00
Barry Bonds, Jeff Kent, Chipper Jones	80.00
Ichiro Suzuki, Jason Giambi, Ivan Rodriguez	80.00
Curt Schilling, Tom Glavine, Pedro J. Martinez	50.00
Randy Johnson, Pedro J. Martinez, Greg Maddux	50.00
Randy Johnson, Curt Schilling, John Smoltz	50.00

2003 Fleer Authentix

	NM/M
Complete Set (160):	
Common Player:	.25
Common (111-125):	3.00
Production 1,850	
Common (126-160):	1.50
Exclusive to Home Team boxes.	
Pack (5):	3.00
Box (24):	50.00
1 Derek Jeter	3.00
2 Tom Glavine	.40
3 Jason Jennings	.25
4 Craig Biggio	.40
5 Miguel Tejada	.40
6 Barry Bonds	3.00
7 Juan Gonzalez	1.00
8 Luis Gonzalez	.40
9 Johnny Damon	.40
10 Ellis Burks	.25
11 Frank Thomas	1.00
12 Richie Sexson	.25
13 Roger Clemens	1.50
14 Matt Morris	.25
15 Troy Glaus	1.00
16 Tony Batista	.25
17 Magglio Ordonez	.25
18 Jose Vidro	.25
19 Barry Zito	.40
20 Chipper Jones	1.50
21 Moises Alou	.25
22 Lance Berkman	.25
23 Jacque Jones	.25
24 Alfonso Soriano	.75
25 Sean Burroughs	.25
26 Scott Rolen	1.00
27 Mark Grace	.35
28 Manny Ramirez	1.00
29 Ken Griffey Jr.	2.00
30 Josh Beckett	.25
31 Kazuhisa Ishii	.25
32 Pat Burrell	1.00
33 Edgar Martinez	.25
34 Tim Salmon	.35
35 Raul Ibanez	.25

36	Vladimir Guerrero	1.00
37	Jermaine Dye	.25
38	Rich Aurilia	.25
39	Rafael Palmeiro	.75
40	Kerry Wood	.75
41	Omar Vizquel	.25
42	Fred McGriff	.25
43	Ben Sheets	.25
44	Bernie Williams	.40
45	Brian Giles	.25
46	Jim Edmonds	.25
47	Garret Anderson	.25
48	Pedro J. Martinez	1.00
49	Adam Dunn	.75
50	A.J. Burnett	.25
51	Eric Gagne	.25
52	Mo Vaughn	.25
53	Bobby Abreu	.25
54	Bret Boone	.25
55	Carlos Delgado	.40
56	Gary Sheffield	.40
57	Sammy Sosa	2.00
58	Jim Thome	.25
59	Jeff Bagwell	1.00
60	David Eckstein	.25
61	Jason Kendall	.25
62	Albert Pujols	2.50
63	Curt Schilling	.40
64	Nomar Garciaparra	2.00
65	Sean Casey	.35
66	Shawn Green	.40
67	Mike Piazza	2.00
68	Ichiro Suzuki	2.00
69	Eric Hinske	.25
70	Greg Maddux	1.50
71	Larry Walker	.25
72	Roy Oswalt	.40
73	Alex Rodriguez	2.50
74	Austin Kearns	.75
75	Cliff Floyd	.25
76	Kevin Brown	.25
77	Jason Giambi	.75
78	Jorge Julio	.25
79	Carlos Lee	.25
80	Mike Sweeney	.25
81	Edgardo Alfonzo	.25
82	Eric Chavez	.40
83	Andruw Jones	1.00
84	Mark Prior	.75
85	Todd Helton	1.00
86	Torii Hunter	.25
87	Ryan Klesko	.25
88	Aubrey Huff	.25
89	Randy Johnson	1.00
90	Barry Larkin	.25
91	Mike Lowell	.25
92	Jimmy Rollins	.40
93	Darin Erstad	.65
94	Jay Gibbons	.25
95	Paul Konerko	.40
96	Bobby Higginson	.25
97	Carlos Beltran	.60
98	Bartolo Colon	.25
99	Jeff Kent	.25
100	Ivan Rodriguez	.65
101	Joe Borchard	.25
102	Mark Teixeira	.50
103	Francisco Rodriguez	.25
104	Chris Snelling	.25
105	Hee Seop Choi	.25
106	Hank Blalock	.50
107	Marlon Byrd	.25
108	Michael Restovich	.25
109	Victor Martinez	.25
110	Lyle Overbay	.25
111	Brian Stokes RC	3.00
112	Josh Hall RC	4.00
113	Chris Waters RC	3.00
114	Lew Ford RC	5.00
115	Ian Ferguson RC	3.00
116	Josh Willingham RC	4.00
117	Josh Stewart RC	3.00
118	Pete LaForest RC	4.00
119	Jose Contreras RC	5.00
120	Terrmel Sledge RC	3.00
121	Guillermo Quiroz RC	4.00
122	Alejandro Machado RC	3.00
123	Nook Logan RC	3.00
124	Rontrez Johnson RC	4.00
125	Hideki Matsui RC	10.00
126	Phil Rizzuto	3.00
127	Robin Ventura	1.50
128	Andy Pettitte	4.00
129	Mike Mussina	3.00
130	Mariano Rivera	4.00
131	Jeff Weaver	1.50
132	David Wells	1.50
133	Tommy Lasorda	2.00
134	Pee Wee Reese	3.00
135	Hideo Nomo	4.00
136	Adrian Beltre	2.00
137	Chin-Feng Chen	4.00
138	Odalis Perez	1.50
139	Dave Roberts	1.50

140	Bobby Doerr	3.00
141	Jason Varitek	1.50
142	Trot Nixon	1.50
143	Tim Wakefield	1.50
144	John Burkett	1.50
145	Jeremy Giambi	1.50
146	Casey Fossum	1.50
147	Phil Niekro	1.50
148	Warren Spahn	4.00
149	Rafael Furcal	2.00
150	Vinny Castilla	1.50
151	Javy Lopez	1.50
152	Jason Marquis	1.50
153	Mike Hampton	1.50
154	Gaylord Perry	1.50
155	Ruben Sierra	1.50
156	Mike Cameron	1.50
157	Freddy Garcia	1.50
158	Joel Pineiro	1.50
159	Jamie Moyer	1.50
160	Carlos Guillen	1.50

Balcony

Stars (1-110):	3-6X
SP's (111-125):	.5-1.5X
Production 250 Sets	
Club Box (1-110):	5-10X
SP's (111-125):	.75-2X
Production 100 Sets	
Standing Room Only:	No Pricing
Production 25 Sets	

Autographed Authentix

		NM/M
Quantity produced listed		
DJ	Derek Jeter/50	150.00
DJ	Derek Jeter/150	125.00
DJ	Derek Jeter/250	125.00
BB	Barry Bonds/50	200.00
BB	Barry Bonds/150	200.00
BB	Barry Bonds/250	200.00

Autographed Jersey Authentix

		NM/M
Quantity produced listed		
DJ	Derek Jeter/100	150.00
DJ	Derek Jeter/200	150.00
DJ	Derek Jeter/300	125.00
NR	Nolan Ryan/100	185.00
NR	Nolan Ryan/200	150.00
NR	Nolan Ryan/300	125.00

Ballpark Classics

		NM/M
Complete Set (10):		25.00
Common Player:		1.50
Inserted 1:12		
1	Derek Jeter	6.00
2	Randy Johnson	2.00
3	Nomar Garciaparra	4.00
4	Barry Bonds	6.00
5	Alfonso Soriano	2.00
6	Alex Rodriguez	5.00
7	Jim Thome	1.50
8	Chipper Jones	3.00
9	Mike Piazza	4.00
10	Ichiro Suzuki	4.00

Bat Authentix

	NM/M
Common Player:	8.00
Inserted 1:78	
Unripped:	1.5-3X
Production 50 Sets	
AD	Adam Dunn	8.00
NG	Nomar Garciaparra	15.00
JG	Jason Giambi	15.00
VG	Vladimir Guerrero	10.00
DJ	Derek Jeter	30.00
CJ	Chipper Jones	10.00
MR	Manny Ramirez	10.00
SS	Sammy Sosa	15.00
JT	Jim Thome	15.00

Hometown Heroes Memorabilia

	NM/M
Common Player:	8.00

Home Team Box Exclusive

BB	Bret Boone/Jsy/200	8.00
KB	Kevin Brown/Jsy/150	10.00
CC	Chin-Feng Chen/ Jsy/150	35.00
RC	Roger Clemens	25.00
JD	Johnny Damon/ Jsy/100	8.00
FG	Freddy Garcia/Jsy/200	8.00
NG	Nomar Garciaparra	25.00
JG	Jason Giambi/ Bat/300	20.00
SG	Shawn Green/Jsy/100	8.00
KI	Kazuhisa Ishii/Jsy/100	8.00
DJ	Derek Jeter	40.00
AJ	Andruw Jones/ Jsy/150	10.00
CJ	Chipper Jones	15.00
GM	Greg Maddux/Jsy	15.00
EM	Edgar Martinez/ Jsy/200	10.00
PM	Pedro Martinez/ Jsy/100	15.00
MR	Manny Ramirez	10.00
GS	Gary Sheffield/Jsy/100	8.00
AS	Alfonso Soriano	15.00
I	Ichiro Suzuki/ Base/100	30.00

Jersey Authentix

		NM/M
Common Player:		5.00
Inserted 1:10		
Unripped:		1.5-3X
Production 50 Sets		
JB	Jeff Bagwell	8.00
JB2	Josh Beckett	5.00
LB	Lance Berkman	5.00
MB	Mark Buehrle	5.00
PB	Pat Burrell	10.00
SB	Sean Burroughs	5.00
RC	Roger Clemens	15.00
CD	Carlos Delgado	5.00
AD	Adam Dunn	8.00
NG	Nomar Garciaparra	15.00
VG	Vladimir Guerrero	8.00
EH	Eric Hinske	5.00
TH	Torii Hunter	6.00
DJ	Derek Jeter	25.00
RJ	Randy Johnson	8.00
CJ	Chipper Jones	8.00
GM	Greg Maddux	15.00
MP	Mike Piazza	12.00
MR	Manny Ramirez	8.00
AR	Alex Rodriguez	12.00
AS	Alfonso Soriano	10.00
SS	Sammy Sosa	12.00
MT	Miguel Tejada	5.00
KW	Kerry Wood	8.00

Jersey Authentix Game of the Week

	NM/M
Common Card:	10.00
Inserted 1:240	
Unripped:	1.5-3X
Production 50 Sets	
Derek Jeter, Nomar Garciaparra	45.00
Mike Piazza, Sammy Sosa	25.00
Chipper Jones, Pat Burrell	20.00
Greg Maddux, Randy Johnson	20.00
Alex Rodriguez, Miguel Tejada	20.00
Adam Dunn, Lance Berkman	10.00
Torii Hunter, Alfonso Soriano	15.00
Derek Jeter, Miguel Tejada	25.00

Eric Hinske, Torii Hunter		10.00
Alfonso Soriano, Sammy Sosa		15.00

Ticket Studs

	NM/M
Complete Set (15):	25.00
Common Player:	1.00
Inserted 1:6	
1TS	Curt Schilling	1.00
2TS	Greg Maddux	2.50
3TS	Torii Hunter	1.00
4TS	Mike Piazza	3.00
5TS	Pedro J. Martinez	2.00
6TS	Nomar Garciaparra	3.00
7TS	Derek Jeter	5.00
8TS	Alex Rodriguez	4.00
9TS	Alfonso Soriano	2.00
10TS	Pat Burrell	1.50
11TS	Barry Bonds	5.00
12TS	Jason Giambi	2.50
13TS	Sammy Sosa	2.50
14TS	Vladimir Guerrero	1.50
15TS	Ichiro Suzuki	3.00

2003 Fleer Avant

"Todd Helton / Rockies"

	NM/M
Complete Set (90):	240.00
Common Player:	.50
Common Retired SP (66-75):	5.00
Production 799	
Common Rk (76-90):	3.00
Production 699	
Pack (4):	4.00
Box (18):	60.00
1	Adam Dunn	.50
2	Barry Zito	.50
3	Preston Wilson	.50
4	Barry Bonds	4.00
5	Hank Blalock	1.00
6	Omar Vizquel	.50
7	Brian Giles	.50
8	Kerry Wood	.75
9	Miguel Tejada	.75
10	Magglio Ordonez	.50
11	Randy Johnson	1.00
12	Jeff Bagwell	1.00
13	Pat Burrell	.75
14	Jason Giambi	.75
15	Mark Prior	.75
16	Roger Clemens	2.00
17	Sammy Sosa	2.50
18	Jay Gibbons	.50
19	Torii Hunter	.75
20	Ichiro Suzuki	2.00
21	Derek Jeter	4.00
22	Tom Glavine	.50
23	Alfonso Soriano	1.00
24	Manny Ramirez	1.00
25	Frank Thomas	1.00
26	Carlos Pena	.50
27	Alex Rodriguez	3.00
28	Edgar Martinez	.50
29	Larry Walker	.50
30	Rafael Palmeiro	.75
31	Mike Piazza	2.00
32	Nomar Garciaparra	2.50
33	Lance Berkman	.50
34	Vladimir Guerrero	1.00
35	Troy Glaus	.75
36	Ivan Rodriguez	.75
37	Mark Mulder	.50
38	Curt Schilling	.75
39	Mike Sweeney	.50
40	Albert Pujols	3.00
41	Tim Hudson	.50
42	Greg Maddux	1.50
43	Shawn Green	.50
44	Scott Rolen	1.00
45	Gary Sheffield	.75

46	Richie Sexson	.75
47	Aubrey Huff	.50
48	Luis Gonzalez	.50
49	Todd Helton	1.00
50	Xavier Nady	.50
51	Juan Gonzalez	1.00
52	Pedro J. Martinez	1.00
53	Garret Anderson	.50
54	Craig Biggio	.50
55	Bret Boone	.50
56	Ken Griffey Jr.	2.00
57	Kevin Millwood	.50
58	Carlos Delgado	.75
59	Chipper Jones	1.50
60	Hideo Nomo	.50
61	Jim Edmonds	.50
62	Austin Kearns	.75
63	Jim Thome	.50
64	Vernon Wells	.50
65	Mike Lowell	.50
66	Whitey Ford	5.00
67	Bob Gibson	5.00
68	Reggie Jackson	5.00
69	Willie McCovey	5.00
70	Phil Rizzuto	6.00
71	Al Kaline	5.00
72	Brooks Robinson	5.00
73	Nolan Ryan	15.00
74	Mike Schmidt	10.00
75	Tom Seaver	6.00
76	Hideki Matsui RC	15.00
77	Rocco Baldelli	4.00
78	Jose Contreras RC	6.00
79	Hee Seop Choi	3.00
80	Jeremy Bonderman	6.00
81	Bo Hart RC	3.00
82	Brandon Webb RC	10.00
83	Ron Calloway	3.00
84	Jesse Foppert	3.00
85	Kyle Snyder	3.00
86	Mark Teixeira	5.00
87	Jose Reyes	5.00
88	Dontrelle Willis	4.00
89	Reed Johnson	3.00
90	Rickie Weeks RC	10.00

Black/White

Stars (1-65):	4-6X
SP's (66-90):	1-2X
Production 199 Sets	

Autographs

		NM/M
Common Autograph:		10.00
Varying quantities produced		
Parallel SP's:		1-1.5X
Production 75 or 150		
DJ	Derek Jeter/75	140.00
MR	Manny Ramirez/100	35.00
VW	Vernon Wells/200	10.00
HB	Hank Blalock/150	25.00
DW	Dontrelle Willis/300	30.00
AK	Al Kaline/200	35.00
BR	Brooks Robinson/300	20.00
BG	Bob Gibson/250	25.00
JR	Jose Reyes/300	30.00
BZ	Barry Zito/150	20.00
EM	Edgar Martinez/246	25.00
BH	Bo Hart/300	15.00
AH	Aubrey Huff/300	15.00
CP	Carlos Pena/150	15.00
MT	Miguel Tejada/150	20.00
ML	Mike Lowell/150	10.00
CB	Craig Biggio/250	15.00
BW	Brandon Webb/300	25.00
RB	Rocco Baldelli/250	30.00

Candid Collection

		NM/M
Complete Set (15):		50.00
Common Player:		2.00
Production 500 Sets		
1CC	Derek Jeter	6.00
2CC	Mike Piazza	4.00
3CC	Albert Pujols	6.00
4CC	Randy Johnson	3.00
5CC	Alex Rodriguez	6.00

ABBREVIATIONS
SP - Short Print

6CC	Vladimir Guerrero	3.00
7CC	Troy Glaus	2.00
8CC	Ichiro Suzuki	4.00
9CC	Barry Zito	2.00
10CC	Jim Thome	2.00
11CC	Sammy Sosa	5.00
12CC	Greg Maddux	4.00
13CC	Barry Bonds	8.00
14CC	Jason Giambi	3.00
15CC	Nomar Garciaparra	6.00

Candid Collection Memorabilia

NM/M

Common Player:
Production 150 Sets

Derek Jeter	30.00
Mike Piazza	12.00
Randy Johnson	8.00
Alex Rodriguez	15.00
Barry Zito	8.00
Jim Thome	15.00
Sammy Sosa	15.00
Greg Maddux	15.00
Jason Giambi	10.00
Nomar Garciaparra	15.00

Hall of Frame

NM/M

Complete Set (14): 80.00
Common Player: 6.00
Production 299 Sets

1	Richie Ashburn	6.00
2	Rod Carew	8.00
3	Whitey Ford	8.00
4	Bob Gibson	8.00
5	Reggie Jackson	8.00
6	Harmon Killebrew	8.00
7	Willie McCovey	6.00
8	Phil Rizzuto	8.00
9	Al Kaline	10.00
10	Brooks Robinson	8.00
11	Nolan Ryan	15.00
12	Mike Schmidt	10.00
13	Tom Seaver	8.00
14	Warren Spahn	8.00

Hall of Frame Memorabilia

NM/M

Production 99 Sets

Reggie Jackson	25.00
Willie McCovey	20.00
Al Kaline	35.00
Nolan Ryan	65.00
Mike Schmidt	40.00

Material

NM/M

Common Player:
Production 50 Sets

RB	Rocco Baldelli	25.00
AR	Alex Rodriguez	25.00
AS	Alfonso Soriano	20.00
SS	Sammy Sosa	20.00
NG	Nomar Garciaparra	20.00
MT	Miguel Tejada	10.00
CJ	Chipper Jones	20.00
RJ	Randy Johnson	15.00
JT	Jim Thome	15.00
GM	Greg Maddux	25.00
JG	Jason Giambi	15.00
VG	Vladimir Guerrero	15.00

On Display

NM/M

Complete Set (10): 50.00
Common Player: 3.00
Production 399 Sets

1OD	Derek Jeter	6.00

2OD	Barry Bonds	8.00
3OD	Rocco Baldelli	5.00
4OD	Alex Rodriguez	6.00
5OD	Alfonso Soriano	4.00
6OD	Sammy Sosa	6.00
7OD	Nomar Garciaparra	6.00
8OD	Hideki Matsui	20.00
9OD	Miguel Tejada	3.00
10OD	Chipper Jones	5.00

On Display Memorabilia

NM/M

Common Player: 5.00
Production 250 Sets

Derek Jeter	20.00
Barry Bonds	15.00
Rocco Baldelli	25.00
Alex Rodriguez	10.00
Alfonso Soriano	10.00
Sammy Sosa	12.00
Nomar Garciaparra	15.00
Hideki Matsui	40.00
Miguel Tejada	5.00
Chipper Jones	10.00

2003 Fleer Box Score

NM/M

Complete Set (245):
Common Player: .15
Common Box Score Debut (101-110): 4.00
Production 599
Common Rookie (111-125): 1.00
Inserted 1:6
Complete Rising Stars (30): 25.00
Common (126-155): 1.00
Complete All-Stars (30): 20.00
Common (156-185): .50
Comp. Intl. Road Trip (30): 20.00
Common (186-215): .50
Comp. Bronx Bombers (30): 30.00
Common (216-245): .50
Pack (7): 3.00
Box (18 + 1 Supplemental Box): 40.00

1	Troy Glaus	.75
2	Derek Jeter	3.00
3	Alex Rodriguez	2.50
4	Barry Zito	.40
5	Darin Erstad	.60
6	Tim Hudson	.40
7	Josh Beckett	.15
8	Adam Dunn	.60
9	Tim Salmon	.25
10	Ivan Rodriguez	.50
11	Mark Buehrle	.15
12	Sammy Sosa	2.00
13	Vicente Padilla	.15
14	Randy Johnson	1.00
15	Lance Berkman	.15
16	Jim Thome	.15
17	Luis Gonzalez	.25
18	Craig Biggio	.15
19	Cliff Floyd	.15
20	Pat Burrell	.50
21	Matt Morris	.15
22	Torii Hunter	.15
23	Curt Schilling	.40
24	Paul Konerko	.15
25	Jeff Bagwell	.75
26	Mike Piazza	2.00
27	A.J. Burnett	.15
28	Jimmy Rollins	.25
29	Greg Maddux	1.50
30	Jeff Kent	.15
31	Bobby Abreu	.15
32	Chipper Jones	1.50
33	Mike Sweeney	.15
34	Jason Kendall	.15
35	Gary Sheffield	.30
36	Carlos Beltran	.50
37	Brian Giles	.15
38	Jim Edmonds	.15
39	Roger Clemens	1.75
40	Andruw Jones	.75
41	Paul LoDuca	.15
42	Ryan Klesko	.15
43	Jay Gibbons	.15
44	Shawn Green	.40
45	Sean Burroughs	.15
46	Magglio Ordonez	.15
47	Tony Batista	.15
48	J.D. Drew	.45
49	Hideo Nomo	.50
50	Edgardo Alfonzo	.15
51	Nomar Garciaparra	2.00
52	Frank Thomas	.75
53	Kazuhisa Ishii	.15
54	Rich Aurilia	.15
55	Shea Hillenbrand	.15
56	Tom Glavine	.40
57	Richie Sexson	.15
58	Mo Vaughn	.15
59	Barry Bonds	3.00
60	Carlos Delgado	.50
61	Pedro J. Martinez	1.00
62	Jacque Jones	.15
63	Edgar Martinez	.15
64	Manny Ramirez	.75
65	Bret Boone	.15
66	Kerry Wood	.50
67	Roy Oswalt	.40
68	Cristian Guzman	.15
69	Moises Alou	.15
70	Bartolo Colon	.15
71	Ichiro Suzuki	1.50
72	Jose Vidro	.15
73	Scott Rolen	.75
74	Mark Prior	1.00
75	Vladimir Guerrero	.75
76	Albert Pujols	1.50
77	Aubrey Huff	.15
78	Ken Griffey Jr.	2.00
79	Roberto Alomar	.30
80	Ben Grieve	.15
81	Miguel Tejada	.40
82	Austin Kearns	.50
83	Jason Giambi	.75
84	John Olerud	.15
85	Omar Vizquel	.15
86	Juan Gonzalez	.75
87	Larry Walker	.15
88	Jorge Posada	.25
89	Rafael Palmeiro	.65
90	Todd Helton	.75
91	Bernie Williams	.30
92	Garret Anderson	.15
93	Eric Hinske	.15
94	Mike Lowell	.15
95	Jason Jennings	.15
96	Eric Chavez	.30
97	Alfonso Soriano	1.00
98	David Eckstein	.15
99	Bobby Higginson	.15
100	Roy Halladay	.15
101	Robby Hammock RC	4.00
102	Hideki Matsui RC	12.00
103	Chase Utley RC	4.00
104	Oscar Villarreal RC	4.00
105	Jose Contreras RC	8.00
106	Rocco Baldelli RC	4.00
107	Rontrez Johnson RC	4.00
108	Jeremy Bonderman RC	8.00
109	Shane Victorino RC	4.00
110	Ron Calloway RC	4.00
111	Brandon Webb RC	4.00
112	Guillermo Quiroz RC	2.00
113	Clint Barmes RC	2.00
114	Pete LaForest RC	1.00
115	Craig Brazell RC	2.00
116	Todd Wellemeyer RC	1.00
117	Bernie Castro RC	1.00
118	Alejandro Machado RC	1.50
119	Terrmel Sledge RC	1.00
120	Ian Ferguson RC	1.00
121	Lew Ford RC	3.00
122	Nook Logan RC	1.50
123	Mike Nicolas RC	1.00
124	Jeff Duncan RC	1.50
125	Tim Olson RC	1.00
126	Michael Hessman RC	1.00
127	Francisco Rosario RC	1.00
128	Felix Sanchez RC	1.00
129	Andrew Brown RC	1.50
130	Matt Bruback RC	2.00
131	Diegomar Markwell RC	2.00
132	Josh Willingham RC	1.00
133	Wes Obermueller	1.50
134	Phil Seibel RC	2.00
135	Arnie Munoz RC	1.00
136	Matt Kata RC	3.00
137	Joe Valentine RC	1.00
138	Ricardo Rodriguez RC	1.00
139	Lyle Overbay	2.00
140	Brian Stokes RC	1.50
141	Josh Hall RC	1.50
142	Kevin Hooper	1.00
143	Chien-Ming Wang RC	10.00
144	Prentice Redman RC	1.50
145	Chris Waters RC	1.00
146	Jon Leicester RC	1.50
147	Daniel Cabrera RC	3.00
148	Alfredo Gonzalez RC	1.50
149	Doug Waechter RC	1.00
150	Brandon Larson	1.00
151	Beau Kemp RC	1.50
152	Cory Stewart RC	1.00
153	Francisco Rodriguez	1.00
154	Hee Seop Choi	1.50
155	Mike Neu RC	1.00
156	Derek Jeter	3.00
157	Alex Rodriguez	2.50
158	Nomar Garciaparra	2.00
159	Barry Bonds	2.50
160	Sammy Sosa	1.50
161	Vladimir Guerrero	.75
162	Roger Clemens	2.00
163	Randy Johnson	1.00
164	Greg Maddux	1.50
165	Ken Griffey Jr.	1.50
166	Mike Piazza	2.00
167	Ichiro Suzuki	1.50
168	Barry Larkin	.50
169	Lance Berkman	.50
170	Jim Thome	.75
171	Jason Giambi	1.00
172	Gary Sheffield	.50
173	Ivan Rodriguez	.50
174	Miguel Tejada	.50
175	Manny Ramirez	.75
176	Mike Sweeney	.50
177	Larry Walker	.50
178	Jeff Bagwell	.75
179	Chipper Jones	1.50
180	Craig Biggio	.50
181	Curt Schilling	.50
182	Pedro J. Martinez	1.00
183	Roberto Alomar	.50
184	Bernie Williams	.50
185	Magglio Ordonez	.50
186	Jose Contreras	1.00
187	Rafael Palmeiro	1.00
188	Andruw Jones	.75
189	Bartolo Colon	.50
190	Vladimir Guerrero	.75
191	Pedro Martinez	1.00
192	Albert Pujols	1.50
193	Manny Ramirez	.75
194	Felix Rodriguez	.50
195	Alfonso Soriano	1.00
196	Sammy Sosa	1.50
197	Miguel Tejada	.50
198	Kazuhisa Ishii	.50
199	Hideki Matsui	5.00
200	Hideo Nomo	1.00
201	Tomokazu Ohka	.50
202	Kazuhiro Sasaki	.50
203	Tsuyoshi Shinjo	.50
204	Ichiro Suzuki	1.50
205	Vicente Padilla	.50
206	Carlos Beltran	.50
207	Jose Cruz Jr.	.50
208	Carlos Delgado	.50
209	Juan Gonzalez	.75
210	Jorge Posada	.50
211	Ivan Rodriguez	.50
212	Hee Seop Choi	.50
213	Bobby Abreu	.50
214	Magglio Ordonez	.50
215	Francisco Rodriguez	.50
216	Juan Acevedo	.50
217	Erick Almonte	.50
218	Yogi Berra	1.50
219	Brandon Claussen	1.00
220	Roger Clemens	2.00
221	Jose Contreras	1.00
222	Whitey Ford	1.00

223	Jason Giambi	1.00
225	Michel Hernandez RC	.50
226	Sterling Hitchcock	.50
227	Jim "Catfish" Hunter	.75
228	Reggie Jackson	1.00
229	Derek Jeter	3.00
230	Nick Johnson	.50
231	Hideki Matsui	5.00
232	Raul Mondesi	.50
233	Mike Mussina	.75
234	Andy Pettitte	.50
235	Jorge Posada	.50
236	Mariano Rivera	.50
237	Phil Rizzuto	1.00
238	Enos Slaughter	.50
239	Alfonso Soriano	1.00
240	Robin Ventura	.50
241	Chien-Ming Wang	2.00
242	Jeff Weaver	.50
243	David Wells	.50
244	Bernie Williams	.75
245	Todd Zeile	.50

First Edition

Stars (1-100): 4-8X
Rookies (101-125): 1.5-3X
Production 150 Sets

All-Star Lineup

NM/M

Common Card: 15.00
Inserted 1:All-Stars Set

Derek Jeter, Alex Rodriguez, Nomar Garciaparra	35.00
Barry Bonds, Sammy Sosa, Vladimir Guerrero	15.00
Roger Clemens, Randy Johnson, Greg Maddux	30.00
Jason Giambi, Alfonso Soriano, Derek Jeter	30.00
Craig Biggio, Jeff Bagwell, Lance Berkman	20.00
Chipper Jones, Gary Sheffield, Greg Maddux	30.00
Ivan Rodriguez, Mike Piazza, Randy Johnson, Roger Clemens	40.00
Roberto Alomar, Mike Piazza, Alfonso Soriano, Jason Giambi	45.00
Jim Thome, Roberto Alomar, Alex Rodriguez, Nomar Garciaparra	40.00

Bat Rack

NM/M

Common Card: 20.00
Production 250 Sets

Derek Jeter, Alfonso Soriano, Jason Giambi	35.00
Scott Rolen, Miguel Tejada, Troy Glaus	20.00
Jim Thome, Torii Hunter, Mike Piazza	25.00
Troy Glaus, Nomar Garciaparra, Alfonso Soriano	30.00
Lance Berkman, Vladimir Guerrero, Sammy Sosa	20.00
Chipper Jones, Lance Berkman, Vladimir Guerrero	20.00
Torii Hunter, Jason Giambi, Nomar Garciaparra	25.00
Derek Jeter, Miguel Tejada, Alex Rodriguez	25.00
Scott Rolen, Sammy Sosa, Alex Rodriguez	25.00

Bat Rack Quad

NM/M

Production 50 Sets

Derek Jeter, Torii Hunter, Troy Glaus, Miguel Tejada	40.00
Derek Jeter, Mike Piazza, Nomar Garciaparra, Chipper Jones	60.00
Alex Rodriguez, Jim Thome, Sammy Sosa, Barry Bonds	50.00

Bronx Bombers Jersey

NM/M

Common Player: 4.00
Inserted 1:Bronx Bombers Set

Roger Clemens	15.00
Jason Giambi	12.00
Derek Jeter	20.00
Nick Johnson	4.00
Mike Mussina	10.00
Jorge Posada	8.00
Alfonso Soriano	10.00
Robin Ventura	5.00
Bernie Williams	8.00

Classic Minatures

NM/M

Complete Set (30):		10.00
Common Player:		.25
1CM	Jim Thome	.40
2CM	Jason Giambi	.50
3CM	Miguel Tejada	.25
4CM	Alfonso Soriano	1.00
5CM	Ivan Rodriguez	.40
6CM	Troy Glaus	.40
7CM	Mike Piazza	1.00
8CM	Barry Bonds	1.50
9CM	Sammy Sosa	1.00
10CM	Lance Berkman	.25
11CM	Pat Burrell	.25
12CM	Chipper Jones	.75
13CM	Shawn Green	.25
14CM	Manny Ramirez	.50
15CM	Ichiro Suzuki	.75
16CM	Vladimir Guerrero	.50
17CM	Albert Pujols	.75
18CM	Ken Griffey Jr.	1.00
19CM	Bernie Williams	.40
20CM	Austin Kearns	.40
21CM	Randy Johnson	.50
22CM	Greg Maddux	.75
23CM	Roger Clemens	1.00
24CM	Hideo Nomo	.25
25CM	Pedro J. Martinez	.50
26CM	Kerry Wood	.40
27CM	Mark Prior	.50
28CM	Derek Jeter	1.50
29CM	Alex Rodriguez	1.00
30CM	Nomar Garciaparra	1.00

Classic Miniatures Mini Jersey

NM/M

Common Jersey:		4.00
1:Classic Miniatures Box		
NG	Nomar Garciaparra	10.00
JG	Jason Giambi	8.00
VG	Vladimir Guerrero	5.00
DJ	Derek Jeter	15.00
AK	Austin Kearns	8.00
GM	Greg Maddux	10.00
HN	Hideo Nomo	6.00

MP	Mark Prior	10.00
MT	Miguel Tejada	4.00
JT	Jim Thome	8.00

Jersey Rack

NM/M

Common Card: 15.00
Production 350 Sets

Derek Jeter, Alfonso Soriano, Jason Giambi	40.00
Curt Schilling, Randy Johnson, Greg Maddux	25.00
Roger Clemens, Pedro J. Martinez, Barry Zito	30.00
Alex Rodriguez, Vladimir Guerrero, Sammy Sosa	25.00
Derek Jeter, Nomar Garciaparra, Alex Rodriguez	30.00
Lance Berkman, Sammy Sosa, Torii Hunter	20.00
Vladimir Guerrero, Jim Thome, Alex Rodriguez	20.00
Derek Jeter, Miguel Tejada, Nomar Garciaparra	30.00
Alfonso Soriano, Eric Chavez, Jim Thome	20.00
Miguel Tejada, Eric Chavez, Barry Zito	15.00

Jersey Rack Quad

NM/M

Production 150 Sets

Derek Jeter, Alex Rodriguez, Nomar Garciaparra, Miguel Tejada	60.00
Jim Thome, Jason Giambi, Sammy Sosa, Vladimir Guerrero	50.00
Randy Johnson, Greg Maddux, Roger Clemens, Pedro J. Martinez	60.00
Curt Schilling, Vladimir Guerrero, Randy Johnson, Alex Rodriguez	40.00
Alfonso Soriano, Jim Thome, Sammy Sosa, Eric Chavez	40.00
Eric Chavez, Miguel Tejada, Barry Zito, Nomar Garciaparra	20.00

Press Clippings

NM/M

Complete Set (20):		40.00
Common Player:		1.00
Inserted 1:18		
1PC	Derek Jeter	6.00
2PC	Nomar Garciaparra	5.00
3PC	Miguel Tejada	1.00
4PC	Barry Bonds	5.00
5PC	Alex Rodriguez	5.00
6PC	Sammy Sosa	3.00
7PC	Lance Berkman	1.00
8PC	Torii Hunter	1.00
9PC	Troy Glaus	1.50
10PC	Eric Chavez	1.00
11PC	Tim Hudson	1.00
12PC	Randy Johnson	2.00
13PC	Mike Piazza	4.00
14PC	Roberto Alomar	1.50
15PC	Jim Thome	1.50
16PC	Alfonso Soriano	3.00
17PC	Roger Clemens	4.00
18PC	Pedro J. Martinez	2.00
19PC	Mark Prior	1.50
20PC	Curt Schilling	1.00

Press Clippings Dual

Complete Set (10): 35.00
Common Player: 2.00
Production 250 Sets

1	Derek Jeter, Nomar Garciaparra	8.00
2	Miguel Tejada, Barry Bonds	6.00
3	Alex Rodriguez, Sammy Sosa	6.00
4	Lance Berkman, Torii Hunter	2.00
5	Troy Glaus, Eric Chavez	2.00
6	Tim Hudson, Randy Johnson	3.00
7	Mike Piazza, Roberto Alomar	5.00
8	Jim Thome, Alfonso Soriano	4.00
9	Roger Clemens, Pedro J. Martinez	5.00
10	Mark Prior, Curt Schilling	2.00

Press Clippings Dual Patch

NM/M

Common Card: 25.00

Derek Jeter, Nomar Garciaparra/100	60.00
Miguel Tejada, Troy Glaus/150	25.00
Alex Rodriguez, Sammy Sosa/150	80.00
Lance Berkman, Torii Hunter/150	30.00
Troy Glaus, Eric Chavez/150	30.00
Tim Hudson, Randy Johnson/150	30.00
Mike Piazza, Roberto Alomar/150	40.00
Jim Thome, Alfonso Soriano/100	40.00
Roger Clemens, Pedro Martinez/100	50.00
Mark Prior, Curt Schilling/150	25.00

Press Clippings Game-Used

NM/M

Common Player: 4.00
Inserted 1:12

Derek Jeter	15.00
Nomar Garciaparra	15.00
Miguel Tejada	4.00
Alex Rodriguez	10.00
Sammy Sosa	12.00
Lance Berkman	4.00
Torii Hunter	6.00
Troy Glaus	5.00
Eric Chavez	4.00
Tim Hudson	4.00
Randy Johnson	8.00
Mike Piazza	12.00
Roberto Alomar	8.00
Jim Thome	10.00
Alfonso Soriano	10.00
Roger Clemens	12.00
Pedro J. Martinez	8.00

Mark Prior 6.00
Curt Schilling 4.00

Wave of the Future

NM/M
Common Player: 4.00
Inserted 1:Rising Stars Set
Jeremy Bonderman/Bat 12.00
Ron Calloway/Jsy 4.00
Hee Seop Choi/Jsy 10.00
Brandon Larson/Bat 8.00
Lyle Overbay/Bat 6.00
Francisco Rodriguez/Jsy 6.00
Chase Utley/Jsy 6.00

World Piece

NM/M
Common Player: 4.00
Inserted 1:Intl. Road Trip Set
Vladimir Guerrero 6.00
Pedro Martinez 10.00
Sammy Sosa 12.00
Miguel Tejada 4.00
Hideo Nomo 10.00
Jose Cruz Jr. 4.00
Ivan Rodriguez 6.00
Hee Seop Choi 10.00
Francisco Rodriguez 4.00
Kazuhiro Sasaki 4.00

2003 Fleer Double Header

ROBERTO ALOMAR
New York Mets®, 2b

NM/M
Complete Set (300): 60.00
Common Player: .20
Common (181-300): .40
Pack (8): 2.00
Box (20): 35.00
1 Ramon Vazquez .20
2 Derek Jeter 2.00
3 Orlando Hudson .20
4 Miguel Tejada .30
5 Steve Finley .20
6 Brad Wilkerson .20
7 Craig Biggio .20
8 Marlon Anderson .20
9 Phil Nevin .20
10 Hideo Nomo .50
11 Barry Larkin .20
12 Alfonso Soriano .75
13 Rodrigo Lopez .20
14 Paul Konerko .25
15 Carlos Beltran .50
16 Garret Anderson .20
17 Kazuhisa Ishii .20
18 Eddie Guardado .20
19 Juan Gonzalez .50
20 Mark Mulder .20
21 Sammy Sosa 1.25
22 Kazuhiro Sasaki .20
23 Jose Cruz Jr. .20
24 Tomokazu Ohka .20
25 Barry Bonds 2.00
26 Carlos Delgado .50
27 Scott Rolen .50
28 Steve Cox .20
29 Mike Sweeney .20
30 Ryan Klesko .20
31 Greg Maddux 1.00
32 Derek Lowe .20
33 David Wells .20
34 Kerry Wood .40
35 Randall Simon .20
36 Ben Howard .20
37 Jeff Suppan .20
38 Curt Schilling .40
39 Eric Gagne .20
40 Raul Mondesi .20
41 Jeffrey Hammonds .20
42 Mo Vaughn .20
43 Sidney Ponson .20
44 Adam Dunn .50
45 Pedro J. Martinez .75
46 Jason Simontacchi .20
47 Tom Glavine .40
48 Torii Hunter .20
49 Gabe Kapler .20
50 Andy Van Hekken .20
51 Ichiro Suzuki 1.25
52 Andruw Jones .50
53 Bobby Abreu .20
54 Junior Spivey .20
55 Ray Durham .20
56 Mark Buehrle .20
57 Drew Henson .20
58 Brandon Duckworth .20
59 Robert Mackowiak .20
60 Josh Beckett .20
61 Chan Ho Park .20
62 John Smoltz .20
63 Jimmy Rollins .40
64 Orlando Cabrera .20
65 Johnny Damon .20
66 Austin Kearns .40
67 Tsuyoshi Shinjo .20
68 Tim Hudson .30
69 Coco Crisp .20
70 Darin Erstad .60
71 Jacque Jones .20
72 Vicente Padilla .20
73 Hee Seop Choi .20
74 Shea Hillenbrand .20
75 Edgardo Alfonzo .20
76 Pat Burrell .50
77 Ben Sheets .20
78 Ivan Rodriguez .40
79 Josh Phelps .20
80 Adam Kennedy .20
81 Eric Chavez .30
82 Bobby Higginson .20
83 Nomar Garciaparra 1.50
84 J.D. Drew .30
85 Carl Crawford .20
86 Matt Morris .20
87 Chipper Jones 1.00
88 Luis Gonzalez .30
89 Richie Sexson .20
90 Eric Milton .20
91 Andres Galarraga .20
92 Paul LoDuca .20
93 Mark Grace .30
94 Ben Grieve .20
95 Mike Lowell .20
96 Roberto Alomar .35
97 Wade Miller .20
98 Sean Casey .20
99 Roger Clemens 1.25
100 Matt Williams .20
101 Brian Giles .20
102 Jim Thome .20
103 Troy Glaus .75
104 Joe Borchard .20
105 Vladimir Guerrero .75
106 Kevin Mench .20
107 Omar Vizquel .20
108 Magglio Ordonez .20
109 Ken Griffey Jr. 1.50
110 Mike Piazza 1.50
111 Mark Teixeira .40
112 Jason Jennings .20
113 Ellis Burks .20
114 Jason Varitek .20
115 Larry Walker .20
116 Frank Thomas .75
117 Ramon Ortiz .20
118 Mark Quinn .20
119 Preston Wilson .20
120 Carlos Lee .20
121 Brian Lawrence .20
122 Tim Salmon .20
123 Shawn Green .30
124 Randy Johnson .75
125 Jeff Bagwell .75
126 C.C. Sabathia .20
127 Bernie Williams .35
128 Roy Oswalt .30
129 Albert Pujols .75
130 Reggie Sanders .20
131 Jeff Conine .20
132 John Olerud .20
133 Lance Berkman .20
134 Geoff Jenkins .20
135 Jim Edmonds .20
136 Todd Helton .65
137 Jason Kendall .20
138 Robin Ventura .20
139 Randy Winn .20
140 Carl Everett .20
141 Jose Vidro .20
142 Pokey Reese .20
143 Edgar Renteria .20
144 Alex Rodriguez 1.75
145 Doug Mientkiewicz .20
146 Aramis Ramirez .20
147 Bobby Hill .20
148 Jorge Posada .35
149 Sean Burroughs .20
150 Jeff Kent .20
151 Tino Martinez .20
152 Mark Prior .50
153 Brad Radke .20
154 Al Leiter .20
155 Eric Karros .20
156 Manny Ramirez .50
157 Jason Lane .20
158 Mike Lieberthal .20
159 Shannon Stewart .20
160 Robert Fick .20
161 Derrek Lee .20
162 Jason Giambi .50
163 Rafael Palmeiro .65
164 Jay Payton .20
165 Adrian Beltre .20
166 Marlon Byrd .20
167 Bret Boone .20
168 Roy Halladay .20
169 Freddy Garcia .20
170 Rich Aurilia .20
171 Jared Sandberg .20
172 Paul Byrd .20
173 Gary Sheffield .30
174 Edgar Martinez .20
175 Eric Hinske .20
176 Milton Bradley .20
177 David Eckstein .20
178 Jay Gibbons .20
179 Corey Patterson .20
180 Barry Zito .20
181-182 Darin Erstad, Troy Glaus .50
183-184 Curt Schilling, Randy Johnson .75
185-186 Andruw Jones, Chipper Jones 1.00
187-188 Tony Batista, Jay Gibbons .40
189-190 Pedro Martinez, Nomar Garciaparra 1.25
191-192 Sammy Sosa, Kerry Wood 1.00
193-194 Paul Konerko, Joe Borchard .40
195-196 Austin Kearns, Adam Dunn .50
197-198 Omar Vizquel, Jim Thome .50
199-200 Larry Walker, Todd Helton .40
201-202 Josh Beckett, Luis Castillo .40
203-204 Craig Biggio, Jeff Bagwell .50
205-206 Paul Byrd, Mike Sweeney .40
207-208 Adrian Beltre, Shawn Green .40
209-210 Jose Hernandez, Richie Sexson .40
211-212 Jacque Jones, Torii Hunter .40
213-214 Vladimir Guerrero, Jose Vidro .75
215-216 Edgardo Alfonzo, Mike Piazza 1.50
217-218 Roger Clemens, Derek Jeter 2.00
219-220 Eric Chavez, Miguel Tejada .40
221-222 Marlon Byrd, Pat Burrell .50
223-224 Jason Kendall, Brian Giles .40
225-226 Phil Nevin, Sean Burroughs .40
227-228 Jeff Kent, Barry Bonds 2.00
229-230 Kazuhiro Sasaki, Ichiro Suzuki 1.25
231-232 Albert Pujols, J.D. Drew .75
233-234 Juan Gonzalez, Ivan Rodriguez .50
235-236 Eric Hinske, Orlando Hudson .40
237-238 Lance Berkman, Chipper Jones 1.00
239-240 Alex Rodriguez, Derek Jeter 2.00
241-242 Ichiro Suzuki, Hideo Nomo 1.25
243-244 Manny Ramirez, Bernie Williams .50
245-246 Tom Glavine, Roger Clemens 1.00
247-248 Ken Griffey Jr., Barry Larkin 1.25
249-250 Mark Teixeira, Mark Prior .40
251-252 Albert Pujols, Drew Henson .75
253-254 Jason Giambi, Todd Helton 1.00
255-256 Jose Vidro, Alfonso Soriano .75
257-258 Shea Hillenbrand, Scott Rolen .50
259-260 Jimmy Rollins, Alex Rodriguez 2.00
261-262 Torii Hunter, Vladimir Guerrero .75
263-264 Ichiro Suzuki, Sammy Sosa 1.25
265-266 Barry Bonds, Manny Ramirez 2.00
267-268 Mike Piazza, Jorge Posada 1.25
269-270 Robin Yount, Ozzie Smith 1.00
271-272 Josh Hancock, Freddy Sanchez .40
273-274 Ryan Bukvich, Shawn Sedlacek .40
275-276 Doug DeVore, Rene Reyes .40
277-278 Hank Blalock, Travis Hafner .50
279-280 Eric Junge, Brett Myers .40
281-282 Brad Lidge, Jeriome Robertson .40
283-284 Miguel Asencio, Runelvys Hernandez .40
285-286 Fernando Rodney, Barry Wesson .40
287-288 Victor Alvarez, David Ross .40
289-290 Tony Torcato, Chris Snelling .50
291-292 Kirk Saarloos, Morgan Ensberg .40
293-294 Josh Bard, Wilbert Nieves .40
295-296 Jung Bong, Trey Hodges .40
297-298 Kevin Cash, Reed Johnson .40
299-300 Chone Figgins, John Lackey .40

Flip Card Memorabilia

NM/M
Common Player: 4.00
Inserted 1:20
Golds: .75-2X
Production 100 Sets
1 Roberto Alomar/Bat/200 10.00
2 Jeff Bagwell/Jsy 8.00
3 Adrian Beltre/Jsy 4.00
4 Barry Bonds/Bat/200 15.00
5 Roger Clemens/Jsy/200 12.00
6 J.D. Drew/Jsy 6.00
7 Adam Dunn/Jsy/200 10.00
8 Nomar Garciaparra/Jsy/200 15.00
9 Mark Grace/Jsy 8.00
10 Todd Helton/Jsy/200 8.00
11 Derek Jeter/Jsy/200 20.00
12 Randy Johnson/Jsy/200 10.00
13 Chipper Jones/Jsy 8.00
14 Eric Karros/Jsy 4.00
15 Barry Larkin/Jsy/200 8.00
16 Greg Maddux/Jsy/200 10.00
17 Hideo Nomo/Jsy/200 8.00
18 Kazuhisa Ishii/Jsy 6.00
19 Mike Piazza/Jsy/200 10.00
20 Jorge Posada/Jsy/200 8.00
21 Mark Prior/Jsy/200 5.00
22 Alex Rodriguez/Jsy 10.00
23 Kazuhiro Sasaki/Jsy/200 6.00
24 Curt Schilling/Jsy/200 8.00
25 Alfonso Soriano/Jsy 8.00
26 Miguel Tejada/Jsy 8.00

27	Jim Thome/Jsy/200	10.00
28	Robin Ventura/Jsy	4.00
29	Bernie Williams/ Jsy/200	8.00
30	Kerry Wood/Jsy/200	10.00

Keystone Combination

		NM/M
Complete Set (10):		25.00
Common Card:		1.00
Inserted 1:10		
1KC	Derek Jeter, Bret Boone	6.00
2KC	Miguel Tejada, Jeff Kent	1.00
3KC	Nomar Garciaparra, Ray Durham	4.00
4KC	Omar Vizquel, Roberto Alomar	1.00
5KC	Pee Wee Reese, Joe Morgan	1.00
6KC	Alex Rodriguez, Craig Biggio	5.00
7KC	Orlando Hudson, Jose Vidro	1.00
8KC	Phil Rizzuto, Alfonso Soriano	3.00
9KC	Alex Rodriguez, Miguel Tejada	5.00
10KC	Nomar Garciaparra, Derek Jeter	6.00

Keystone Combination Memorabilia

	NM/M
Common Card:	4.00
Inserted 1:40	
Derek Jeter, Bret Boone/Jsy	8.00
Miguel Tejada, Jeff Kent/Jsy	4.00
N.Garciaparra/Jsy/175, Ray Durham	12.00
Omar Vizquel, Roberto Alomar/Jsy	6.00
Craig Biggio/Jsy	6.00
Orlando Hudson, Jose Vidro/Jsy	4.00
Phil Rizzuto, Alfonso Soriano/ Jsy/75	15.00
Alex Rodriguez/Bat, Miguel Tejada	10.00
N.Garciaparra/Jsy/175, Derek Jeter	12.00
Derek Jeter/Jsy/175, Bret Boone	20.00
Derek Jeter/Jsy/175, Nomar Garciaparra	20.00
Alex Rodriguez/Jsy/200, Craig Biggio	10.00
Miguel Tejada/Jsy, Jeff Kent	8.00
Miguel Tejada/Jsy, Alex Rodriguez	8.00

Let's Play, Too!

	NM/M
Complete Set (15):	8.00
Common Player:	.50

LET'S PLAY TOO! 20 03

REES REYES - COLORADO ROCKIES - OF

Inserted 1:5		
1LPT	Chris Snelling	1.00
2LPT	Kevin Mench	.50
3LPT	Brett Meyers	.50
4LPT	Julius Matos	.50
5LPT	Drew Henson	1.00
6LPT	Joe Borchard	.50
7LPT	Felix Escalona	.50
8LPT	Kirk Saarloos	.50
9LPT	Ben Howard	.50
10LPT	Hee Seop Choi	1.00
11LPT	Rene Reyes	.50
12LPT	Josh Bard	.50
13LPT	Marlon Byrd	.50
14LPT	Coco Crisp	.50
15LPT	Reed Johnson	.50

Matinee Idols

		NM/M
Complete Set (15):		50.00
Common Player:		2.00
Inserted 1:20		
1MI	Yogi Berra	3.00
2MI	Richie Ashburn	3.00
3MI	Whitey Ford	3.00
4MI	Eddie Mathews	3.00
5MI	Jim Palmer	2.00
6MI	Al Kaline	6.00
7MI	Brooks Robinson	3.00
8MI	Willie McCovey	3.00
9MI	Billy Williams	2.00
10MI	Willie Stargell	3.00
11MI	Nolan Ryan	15.00
12MI	Rod Carew	3.00
13MI	Reggie Jackson	3.00
14MI	Tom Seaver	4.00
15MI	Mike Schmidt	6.00

Twin Bill

TWIN BILL 51

		NM/M
Complete Set (20):		45.00
Common Player:		1.00
Inserted 1:10		
1a	Barry Bonds	5.00
1b	Lance Berkman	1.00
2a	Derek Jeter	6.00
2b	Alex Rodriguez	5.00
3a	Roger Clemens	3.00
3b	Pedro Martinez	2.00
4a	Roberto Alomar	1.25
4b	Chipper Jones	3.00
5a	Barry Zito	1.00
5b	Ichiro Suzuki.	4.00
6a	Sammy Sosa.	3.00
6b	Ken Griffey Jr.	4.00
7a	Bernie Williams.	1.00
7b	Manny Ramirez.	1.50
8a	Nomar Garciaparra.	6.00
8b	Derek Jeter.	2.00
9a	Randy Johnson.	2.00
9b	Greg Maddux.	3.00
10a	Albert Pujols.	2.00
10b	Adam Dunn.	1.50

Twin Bill Single Swatch

	NM/M
Common Player:	1.00
Barry Bonds/Cap/100	25.00
Alex Rodriguez/ Cap/100	15.00
Roger Clemens/ Cap/100	15.00
Pedro Martinez/ Cap/100	12.00
Roberto Alomar/Cap	10.00
Barry Zito/Cap/100	15.00
Bernie Williams/ Cap/100	10.00
Manny Ramirez/ Cap/75	12.00
Nomar Garciaparra/ Cap/100	25.00
Derek Jeter/Cap/100	30.00
Randy Johnson/ Cap/100	15.00
Adam Dunn/Cap/100	12.00

Twin Bill Dual Swatch

	NM/M
Common Card:	
Production 50 Sets	
Barry Bonds, Adam Dunn	40.00
Randy Johnson, Barry Zito	35.00

2003 Fleer E-X

HANK BLALOCK

		NM/M
Complete Set (102):		125.00
Common Player:		.50
Common SP (83-102):		3.00
Pack (3):		4.00
Box (20):		60.00
1	Troy Glaus	.75
2	Darin Erstad	.75
3	Garret Anderson	.50
4	Curt Schilling	.75
5	Randy Johnson	1.00
6	Luis Gonzalez	.50
7	Greg Maddux	1.50
8	Chipper Jones	1.50
9	Andruw Jones	1.00
10	Melvin Mora	.50
11	Jay Gibbons	.50
12	Nomar Garciaparra	2.00
13	Pedro J. Martinez	1.00
14	Manny Ramirez	1.00
15	Sammy Sosa	2.00
16	Kerry Wood	.75
17	Magglio Ordonez	.50
18	Frank Thomas	1.00
19	Roberto Alomar	.60
20	Barry Larkin	.50
21	Adam Dunn	1.00
22	Austin Kearns	.75
23	Omar Vizquel	.50
24	Larry Walker	.50
25	Todd Helton	1.00
26	Preston Wilson	.50
27	Dmitri Young	.50
28	Ivan Rodriguez	.75
29	Mike Lowell	.50
30	Jeff Kent	.50
31	Jeff Bagwell	1.00
32	Roy Oswalt	.75
33	Craig Biggio	.50
34	Mike Sweeney	.50
35	Carlos Beltran	.75
36	Shawn Green	.60
37	Kazuhisa Ishii	.50
38	Richie Sexson	.50
39	Torii Hunter	.50
40	Jacque Jones	.50
41	Jose Vidro	.50
42	Vladimir Guerrero	1.00
43	Mike Piazza	2.00
44	Tom Glavine	.60
45	Roger Clemens	1.75
46	Jason Giambi	.75
47	Bernie Williams	.60
48	Alfonso Soriano	1.00
49	Mike Mussina	.60
50	Barry Zito	.60
51	Miguel Tejada	.60
52	Eric Chavez	.50
53	Eric Byrnes	.50
54	Jim Thome	.50
55	Kevin Millwood	.50
56	Brian Giles	.50
57	Xavier Nady	.50
58	Barry Bonds	3.00
59	Bret Boone	.50
60	Edgar Martinez	.50
61	Kazuhiro Sasaki	.50
62	Edgar Renteria	.50
63	J.D. Drew	.50
64	Scott Rolen	1.00
65	Jim Edmonds	.50
66	Aubrey Huff	.50
67	Alex Rodriguez	2.50
68	Juan Gonzalez	1.00
69	Hank Blalock	.75
70	Mark Teixeira	.75
71	Carlos Delgado	.75
72	Vernon Wells	.50
73	Shea Hillenbrand	.50
74	Gary Sheffield	.60
75	Mark Prior	.75
76	Ken Griffey Jr.	2.00
77	Lance Berkman	.50
78	Hideo Nomo	.75
79	Derek Jeter	3.00
80	Ichiro Suzuki	2.00
81	Albert Pujols	2.50
82	Rafael Palmeiro	.75
83	Jose Reyes	4.00
84	Rocco Baldelli	4.00
85	Hee Seop Choi	3.00
86	Dontrelle Willis	4.00
87	Robby Hammock RC	3.00
88	Brandon Webb RC	8.00
89	Matt Kata RC	5.00
90	Todd Wellemeyer RC	3.00
91	Francisco Cruceta RC	3.00
92	Clint Barmes RC	6.00
93	Jeremy Bonderman	8.00
94	Dave Matranga RC	4.00
95	Ryan Wagner RC	5.00
96	Jeremy Griffiths	3.00
97	Hideki Matsui RC	15.00
98	Jose Contreras RC	6.00
99	Chien-Ming Wang RC	25.00
100	Bo Hart RC	4.00
101	Dan Haren	5.00
102	Rickie Weeks RC	10.00

Essential Credentials Now/Future

	NM/M
Cards serial numbered 26-50:	6-12X
Cards s/n 51-75:	4-8X
Cards s/n 76-102:	3-5X
SP's (83-102) s/n 83-102:	1-2X

Now is consecutively #'d from 1 to 102.
Future is consect. #'d from 102 to 1.

Behind the Numbers

		NM/M
Complete Set (15):		50.00
Common Player:		1.50
Inserted 1:80		
1	Derek Jeter	8.00
2	Alex Rodriguez	8.00
3	Randy Johnson	3.00
4	Chipper Jones	5.00
5	Jim Thome	3.00
6	Alfonso Soriano	4.00
7	Adam Dunn	2.00
8	Nomar Garciaparra	6.00
9	Roger Clemens	6.00

10	Gary Sheffield	1.50
11	Vladimir Guerrero	3.00
12	Greg Maddux	5.00
13	Sammy Sosa	6.00
14	Mike Piazza	5.00
15	Troy Glaus	2.00

Behind the Numbers Game-Used

		NM/M
Common Player:		5.00
Inserted 1:10		
Patch Version:		1.5-2.5X
DJ	Derek Jeter	15.00
AR	Alex Rodriguez	10.00
RJ	Randy Johnson	8.00
CJ	Chipper Jones	8.00
JT	Jim Thome	8.00
AS	Alfonso Soriano	8.00
AD	Adam Dunn	6.00
NG	Nomar Garciaparra	10.00
RC	Roger Clemens	10.00
GS	Gary Sheffield	5.00
VG	Vladimir Guerrero	8.00
GM	Greg Maddux	8.00
SS	Sammy Sosa	10.00
MP	Mike Piazza	8.00
TG	Troy Glaus	5.00
HB	Hank Blalock	6.00
TG	Tom Glavine	5.00
BM	Brett Myers	5.00
LB	Lance Berkman	5.00
RB	Rocco Baldelli	10.00
BZ	Barry Zito	6.00
DW	Dontrelle Willis	10.00
RP	Rafael Palmeiro	6.00
RA	Roberto Alomar	6.00
MB	Marlon Byrd	5.00

Behind the Numbers Autograph

No pricing due to scarcity.
Numbered to jersey number.

Emerald Essentials

		NM/M
Complete Set (10):		60.00
Common Player:		4.00
Inserted 1:240		
1	Austin Kearns	4.00
2	Alfonso Soriano	8.00
3	Miguel Tejada	4.00
4	Troy Glaus	4.00
5	Adam Dunn	4.00
6	Hideo Nomo	6.00
7	Kerry Wood	6.00
8	Nomar Garciaparra	15.00
9	Roger Clemens	15.00
10	Derek Jeter	15.00

Emerald Essentials Game-Used

		NM/M
Common Player:		4.00
Same price for levels #'d 175, 250 & 375.		
Patch Versions:		1.5-2.5X
Production 60		
AK	Austin Kearns	6.00
AS	Alfonso Soriano	8.00
MT	Miguel Tejada	4.00
TG	Troy Glaus	6.00
AD	Adam Dunn	6.00
HN	Hideo Nomo	15.00
KW	Kerry Wood	8.00
NG	Nomar Garciaparra	12.00
RC	Roger Clemens	12.00
AR	Alex Rodriguez	10.00

Emerald Essentials Autograph

		NM/M
Common Player:		
	Brandon Webb	40.00
	Hank Blalock	20.00

Diamond Essentials

	NM/M
Common Player:	5.00

Inserted 1:480		
1DE	Randy Johnson	15.00
2DE	Ichiro Suzuki	25.00
3DE	Albert Pujols	30.00
4DE	Barry Bonds	40.00
5DE	Hideki Matsui	30.00
6DE	Derek Jeter	40.00
7DE	Chipper Jones	20.00
8DE	Sammy Sosa	25.00
9DE	Jeff Bagwell	10.00
10DE	Mike Piazza	20.00
11DE	Pedro J. Martinez	15.00
12DE	Mark Prior	20.00
13DE	Jason Giambi	10.00
14DE	Jose Reyes	5.00
15DE	Alfonso Soriano	15.00

Diamond Essentials Game-Used

		NM/M
Common Player:		8.00
Same price for cards #'d 145, 245 & 345.		
Patch Versions:		1.5-2.5X
Production 55		
RJ	Randy Johnson	8.00
DJ	Derek Jeter	15.00
CJ	Chipper Jones	8.00
SS	Sammy Sosa	12.00
JB	Jeff Bagwell	8.00
MP	Mike Piazza	10.00
PM	Pedro J. Martinez	8.00
MP	Mark Prior	10.00
JG	Jason Giambi	8.00
JR	Jose Reyes	8.00

Diamond Essentials Autograph

		NM/M
Common Player:		
	Dontrelle Willis	30.00
	Ryan Wagner	20.00
	Rocco Baldelli	25.00
	Randy Johnson	
	Albert Pujols	150.00

X-tra Innings

		NM/M
Complete Set (10):		25.00
Common Player:		1.00
Inserted 1:32		
1XI	Ichiro Suzuki	3.00
2XI	Albert Pujols	4.00
3XI	Barry Bonds	5.00
4XI	Jason Giambi	1.50
5XI	Pedro J. Martinez	2.00
6XI	Mark Prior	3.00
7XI	Derek Jeter	5.00
8XI	Curt Schilling	1.00
9XI	Jeff Bagwell	1.50
10XI	Alex Rodriguez	5.00

2003 Fleer Fall Classic

		NM/M
Complete Set (87):		30.00
Common Player:		.25
Common SP:		
Hobby Pack (5):		4.00
Hobby Box (24):		75.00
1	Rod Carew	.50
2	Bobby Doerr	.25
3	Eddie Mathews	1.00
3	Eddie Mathews/ SP/Tigers	4.00
4	Tom Seaver	1.50
5	Lou Brock	.75
6	Nolan Ryan	3.00
6	Nolan Ryan/ SP/Astros	10.00
7	Pee Wee Reese	.25
8	Robin Yount	1.00
9	Bob Feller	.50
10	Harmon Killebrew	1.00
11	Hal Newhouser	.25
12	Al Kaline	1.00
13	Hoyt Wilhelm	.25
14	Early Wynn	.25
15	Yogi Berra	1.00
15	Yogi Berra/SP/Mets	4.00
16	Billy Williams	.25
17	Rollie Fingers	.25
18	Sparky Anderson	.25
18	Sparky Anderson/ SP/Reds	3.00
19	Lou Boudreau	.25
20	Warren Spahn	1.00
21	Enos Slaughter	.25
22	Luis Aparicio	.50
23	Phil Rizzuto	.75
24	Willie McCovey	.75
25	Joe Morgan	.50
26	Alan Trammell	.75
27	Eddie Plank	.25
28	Lefty Grove	.25
29	Walter Johnson	1.00
30	Roy Campanella	1.00
31	Carlton Fisk	.75
32	Bill Dickey	.25
33	Rogers Hornsby	1.00
33	Rogers Hornsby/ SP/Cubs	5.00
34	Wade Boggs	.75
35	Chick Stahl	.25
36	Don Drysdale	.75
36	Don Drysdale/ SP/Dodgers	4.00
37	Jose Canseco	.75
38	Roger Maris	2.00
38	Roger Maris/ SP/Yankees	8.00
39	Cal Ripken Jr.	3.00
40	Kiki Cuyler	.25
40	Kiki Cuyler/SP/Cubs	3.00
41	Hank Greenberg	.25
42	Don Larsen	.50
43	Eddie Murray	.75
43	Eddie Murray/ SP/Indians	4.00
44	Jimmy Sebring	.25
45	Ozzie Smith	1.50
46	Darryl Strawberry	.25
46	Darryl Strawberry/ SP/Yankees	3.00
47	Dave Parker	.25
48	Gil Hodges	.25
48	Gil Hodges/SP/Mets	3.00
49	Joe Carter	.50
50	Leo Durocher	.25
50	Leo Durocher/ SP/Giants	3.00
51	Christy Mathewson	.75
52	Elston Howard	.25
53	Hughie Jennings	.25
54	Nellie Fox	.50
55	Carl Yastrzemski	1.00
56	Frank Robinson	1.00
56	Frank Robinson/ SP/Reds	4.00
57	Dennis Eckersley	.50
58	Grover Alexander	.50
58	Grover Alexander/ SP/Cards	4.00
59	Carl Hubbell	.25
60	Dave Winfield	.75
61	Honus Wagner	1.50
62	Duke Snider	1.00
62	Duke Snider/ SP/Dodgers	5.00
63	Frankie Frisch	.25
63	Frankie Frisch/ SP/Cards	3.00
64	Dizzy Dean	.75
65	Bob Gibson	1.00
66	Johnny Bench	1.50
67	Ty Cobb	2.00
68	Lou Gehrig	2.50
69	Jim "Catfish" Hunter	.50
70	Willie Stargell	.75
71	Reggie Jackson	1.00
71	Reggie Jackson/ SP/Yankees	5.00
72	George Brett	2.50
73	Babe Ruth	3.00
73	Babe Ruth/ SP/Yankees	10.00
74	Cy Young	1.00
75	Jim Palmer	.50
76	Mickey Lolich	.25
77	Stan Musial	1.50
78	Steve Carlton	.75
79	Roberto Clemente	2.50
80	John McGraw	.25
81	Paul Molitor	.75
82	Red Ruffing	.25
83	Connie Mack	.25
84	Mike Schmidt	2.00
85	Mickey Cochrane	.50
85	Mickey Cochrane/ SP/Tigers	4.00
86	Brooks Robinson	1.00
87	Whitey Ford	1.00

Championship Gold

Cards 1-87:	3-6X
Production 50 Sets	

All-American Collection

		NM/M
Common Player:		8.00
OS	Ozzie Smith/100	20.00
TS	Tom Seaver/100	15.00
SM	Stan Musial/100	30.00
CR	Cal Ripken Jr./100	60.00
EM	Eddie Mathews/100	10.00
NR	Nolan Ryan	30.00
YB	Yogi Berra	15.00
EM	Eddie Murray/100	15.00
FR	Frank Robinson	8.00
DS	Duke Snider	8.00
RJ	Reggie Jackson	8.00
LA	Luis Aparicio/100	10.00
GH	Gil Hodges	8.00
AK	Al Kaline	10.00
BM	Bill Mazeroski/100	10.00
BR	Brooks Robinson/100	15.00
WB	Wade Boggs/100	12.00
AT	Alan Trammell/100	12.00

All American Collection Autograph

		NM/M
Common Autograph:		
Varying quantities produced		
SP version #'d to 100:		1-1.5X
SP version #'d to 50:		1-2X
LA	Luis Aparicio/150	10.00
VB	Vida Blue/450	8.00
RB	Rick Burleson/250	8.00
SC	Steve Carlton/100	20.00
BF	Bob Feller/300	15.00
CF	Carlton Fisk/75	30.00
AL	Al Kaline/325	20.00
HK	Harmon Killebrew/ 150	30.00
FL	Fred Lynn/275	8.00
BM	Bill Mazeroski/75	20.00
JP	Jim Palmer/100	15.00
BR	Brooks Robinson/325	20.00
PR	Preacher Roe/450	12.00
MS	Mike Schmidt/50	60.00
BS	"Moose" Skowron/ 150	10.00
OS	Ozzie Smith/50	65.00
DS	Duke Snider/100	25.00
WS	Warren Spahn/75	40.00
AT	Alan Trammell/150	15.00

All American Collection Jersey Autograph

		NM/M
Production 25 Sets		
GB	George Brett	160.00
SC	Steve Carlton	50.00

Legendary Collection

		NM/M
Common Player:		
Inserted 1:Legendary Star Pack		
EM	Eddie Mathews/SP	15.00
NR	Nolan Ryan	30.00
YB	Yogi Berra	15.00
EMY	Eddie Murray	8.00
FR	Frank Robinson	6.00

DS	Duke Snider/SP	10.00
DSy	Darryl Strawberry	5.00
RJ	Reggie Jackson	8.00
RM	Roger Maris/SP	30.00
GH	Gil Hodges/SP	10.00

Pennant Aggression

		NM/M
Complete Set (20):		50.00
Common Player:		3.00
Numbered to pennant year.		
1PA	Ty Cobb/1,908	4.00
2PA	Honus Wagner/1,909	3.00
3PA	Walter Johnson/1,924	3.00
4PA	Jimmie Foxx/1,930	4.00
5PA	Frankie Frisch/1,931	3.00
6PA	Pee Wee Reese/1,947	3.00
7PA	Yogi Berra/1,951	4.00
8PA	Roy Campanella/1,953	3.00
9PA	Whitey Ford/1,961	4.00
10PA	Frank Robinson/1,966	3.00
11PA	Carl Yastrzemski/1,967	3.00
12PA	Brooks Robinson/1,970	3.00
13PA	Johnny Bench/1,972	4.00
14PA	Reggie Jackson/1,973	3.00
15PA	Jim "Catfish" Hunter/1,974	3.00
16PA	Joe Morgan/1,975	3.00
17PA	Thurman Munson/1,976	4.00
18PA	Willie Stargell/1,979	3.00
19PA	Mike Schmidt/1,980	4.00
20PA	George Brett/1,985	4.00

Pennant Aggression Game-Used

		NM/M
Common Player:		8.00
Production 100		
Patches:		1.5-2X
Production 50		
YB	Yogi Berra	15.00
FB	Frank Robinson	10.00
CY	Carl Yastrzemski	20.00
BR	Brooks Robinson	15.00
JB	Johnny Bench	15.00
RJ	Reggie Jackson	12.00
CH	Jim "Catfish" Hunter	8.00
JM	Joe Morgan	8.00
TM	Thurman Munson	15.00
WS	Willie Stargell	10.00
MS	Mike Schmidt	25.00
GB	George Brett	35.00

Postseason Glory

		NM/M
Complete Set (30):		125.00
Common Player:		2.00
#1-15 Numbered to 1,500		
16-25 Numbered to 750		
26-30 Numbered to 100		
1	Carlton Fisk, Carl Yastrzemski	2.00
2	Enos Slaughter, Stan Musial	4.00
3	Reggie Jackson, Thurman Munson	4.00
4	Eddie Plank, Christy Mathewson	3.00
5	Cy Young, Jimmy Sebring	3.00
6	Yogi Berra, Whitey Ford	4.00
7	Mickey Lolich, Alan Trammell	2.00
8	Eddie Mathews, Al Schoendienst	3.00
9	Roy Campanella, Pee Wee Reese	3.00
10	Joe Carter, Bill Mazeroski	2.00
11	Brooks Robinson, Frank Robinson	3.00
12	Tom Seaver, Gil Hodges	3.00
13	Robin Yount, Paul Molitor	2.50
14	Dave Parker, Willie Stargell	2.00
15	Cal Ripken Jr., Jim Palmer	6.00
16	Babe Ruth, Whitey Ford	8.00
18	Lou Brock, Bob Gibson	4.00
19	Mike Schmidt, Brooks Robinson	5.00
20	Johnny Bench, Thurman Munson	5.00
21	Nolan Ryan, Walter Johnson	10.00
22	Don Drysdale, Duke Snider	4.00
23	Joe Carter, Paul Molitor	2.00
24	Hughie Jennings, Ty Cobb	4.00
25	Cal Ripken Jr., Eddie Murray	10.00
26	Mike Schmidt, Steve Carlton	5.00
27	Roberto Clemente, Willie Stargell	15.00
28	Jim Palmer, Nolan Ryan	25.00
29	Joe Morgan, Johnny Bench	10.00
30	Lou Gehrig, Babe Ruth	25.00

Postseason Glory Dual Game-Used

	NM/M
Production 100	
Single Jerseys:	.5X

Production 150		
Carlton Fisk, Carl Yastrzemski		25.00
Reggie Jackson, Thurman Munson		25.00
Yogi Berra, Whitey Ford		30.00
Brooks Robinson, Frank Robinson		20.00
Robin Yount, Paul Molitor		25.00
Dave Parker, Willie Stargell/Single/150		8.00
Lou Brock, Bob Gibson/Single/150		10.00
Joe Carter, Paul Molitor/Single/150		8.00
Don Drysdale, Duke Snider		25.00
Cal Ripken Jr., Eddie Murray		50.00
Mike Schmidt, Steve Carlton		25.00
Jim Palmer, Nolan Ryan		40.00
Joe Morgan, Johnny Bench		25.00
Babe Ruth/Single/150, Lou Gehrig		125.00

Postseason Glory Dual Patch

	NM/M
Production 50	
Single Patch:	.5-.75X
Production 75	
Carlton Fisk, Carl Yastrzemski	70.00
Robin Yount, Paul Molitor	50.00
Lou Brock, Bob Gibson	50.00
Cal Ripken Jr., Eddie Murray	120.00
Mike Schmidt, Steve Carlton	50.00
Jim Palmer, Nolan Ryan	80.00
Joe Morgan, Johnny Bench	50.00
Brooks Robinson, Frank Robinson	40.00

Series Contender

		NM/M
Common Player:		
Inserted 1:50 Retail		
Bat Knobs:		Not Priced
Production 9 or 10		
SK	Al Kaline	15.00
BD	Bill Dickey	10.00
DS	Darryl Strawberry	5.00
DM	Don Mattingly	30.00
PR	Phil Rizzuto/SP	10.00
WM	Willie McCovey/SP	10.00
HK	Harmon Killebrew	25.00
CF	Carlton Fisk	6.00
JC	Jose Canseco	10.00

Yankee Penstripes

		NM/M
Production 100		
World Series Edition:		No Pricing
Production 100		
RJ	Reggie Jackson	40.00
BSP	Bill "Moose" Skowron	15.00
WB	Wade Boggs	50.00
DM	Don Mattingly	75.00
DW	Dave Winfield	35.00

2003 Fleer Focus Jersey Edition

		NM/M
Complete Set (180):		45.00
Common Player:		.15
Common Prospect (161-180):		.75
Inserted 1:4		
Pack (7):		1.50
Box (24):		30.00
1	Derek Jeter	2.50
2	Preston Wilson	.15
3	Trevor Hoffman	.15
4	Moises Alou	.15
5	Roberto Alomar	.35
6	Tim Salmon	.25
7	Mike Lowell	.15
8	Barry Bonds	2.50
9	Fred McGriff	.15
10	Mo Vaughn	.15
11	Junior Spivey	.15
12	Roy Oswalt	.25
13	Ichiro Suzuki	1.50
14	Magglio Ordonez	.25
15	Adam Kennedy	.15
16	Randy Johnson	.75
17	Carlos Beltran	.50
18	John Olerud	.15
19	Joe Borchard	.15
20	Alfonso Soriano	.75
21	Curt Schilling	.50
22	Mike Sweeney	.15
23	Tino Martinez	.15
24	Barry Larkin	.15
25	Miguel Tejada	.40
26	Chipper Jones	1.00
27	Kevin Brown	.15
28	J.D. Drew	.15
29	Sean Casey	.15
30	Bernie Williams	.35
31	Troy Percival	.15
32	Jeff Bagwell	.75
33	Kenny Lofton	.15
34	Kerry Wood	.50
35	Armando Benitez	.15
36	David Eckstein	.15
37	Wade Miller	.15
38	Edgar Martinez	.15
39	Mark Prior	.75
40	Mike Piazza	1.50
41	Shea Hillenbrand	.15
42	Bartolo Colon	.15
43	Darin Erstad	.50
44	A.J. Burnett	.15
45	Jeff Kent	.15
46	Corey Patterson	.15
47	Derek Wigginton	.15
48	Troy Glaus	.75
49	Josh Beckett	.15
50	Brian Lawrence	.15
51	Frank Thomas	.75
52	Jason Giambi	.60
53	Luis Gonzalez	.25
54	Raul Ibanez	.15
55	Kazuhiro Sasaki	.15
56	Mark Buehrle	.15
57	Roger Clemens	1.25
58	Matt Williams	.15
59	Joe Randa	.15
60	Jamie Moyer	.15
61	Paul Konerko	.15
62	Mike Mussina	.50
63	Javy Lopez	.15
64	Brian Jordan	.15
65	Scott Rolen	.75
66	Aaron Boone	.15
67	Eric Chavez	.25
68	Mark Grace	.25
69	Shawn Green	.25
70	Albert Pujols	1.25
71	Sammy Sosa	1.50
72	Edgardo Alfonzo	.15
73	Garret Anderson	.15
74	Lance Berkman	.15
75	Bret Boone	.15
76	Joe Crede	.15
77	Al Leiter	.15
78	Jarrod Washburn	.15
79	Craig Biggio	.15
80	Rich Aurilia	.15
81	Adam Dunn	.60
82	Jermaine Dye	.15
83	Tom Glavine	.40
84	Eric Gagne	.15
85	Jared Sandberg	.15
86	Jim Thome	.15
87	Barry Zito	.35
88	Gary Sheffield	.25
89	Paul LoDuca	.15
90	Matt Morris	.15
91	Juan Pierre	.15
92	Randy Wolf	.15
93	Jay Gibbons	.15
94	Brad Radke	.15
95	Carlos Delgado	.35
96	Carlos Pena	.15
97	Brian Giles	.15
98	Rodrigo Lopez	.15
99	Jacque Jones	.15

100	Juan Gonzalez	.75
101	Randall Simon	.15
102	Mike Williams	.15
103	Derek Lowe	.15
104	Brad Wilkerson	.15
105	Eric Hinske	.15
106	Luis Castillo	.15
107	Phil Nevin	.15
108	Manny Ramirez	.75
109	Vladimir Guerrero	.75
110	Roy Halladay	.15
111	Ellis Burks	.15
112	Bobby Abreu	.15
113	Tony Batista	.15
114	Richie Sexson	.15
115	Rafael Palmeiro	.65
116	Todd Helton	.65
117	Pat Burrell	.60
118	John Smoltz	.15
119	Ben Sheets	.15
120	Aubrey Huff	.15
121	Andruw Jones	.75
122	Kazuhisa Ishii	.15
123	Jim Edmonds	.15
124	Austin Kearns	.60
125	Mark Mulder	.25
126	Greg Maddux	1.00
127	Jose Hernandez	.15
128	Ben Grieve	.15
129	Ken Griffey Jr.	1.50
130	Tim Hudson	.35
131	Jorge Julio	.15
132	Torii Hunter	.15
133	Ivan Rodriguez	.65
134	Jason Jennings	.15
135	Jason Kendall	.15
136	Nomar Garciaparra	1.50
137	Michael Cuddyer	.15
138	Shannon Stewart	.15
139	Larry Walker	.15
140	Aramis Ramirez	.15
141	Johnny Damon	.15
142	Orlando Cabrera	.15
143	Vernon Wells	.15
144	Bobby Higginson	.15
145	Sean Burroughs	.15
146	Pedro J. Martinez	.75
147	Jose Vidro	.15
148	Orlando Hudson	.15
149	Robert Fick	.15
150	Ryan Klesko	.15
151	Kevin Millwood	.15
152	Alex Sanchez	.15
153	Randy Winn	.15
154	Omar Vizquel	.15
155	Mike Lieberthal	.15
156	Marty Cordova	.15
157	Cristian Guzman	.15
158	Alex Rodriguez	2.00
159	C.C. Sabathia	.15
160	Jimmy Rollins	.25
161	Josh Willingham RC	2.00
162	Lance Niekro	.75
163	Nook Logan RC	.75
164	Chase Utley	.75
165	Pete LaForest RC	.75
166	Victor Martinez	.75
167	Adam LaRoche	.75
168	Ian Ferguson RC	.75
169	Mark Teixeira RC	.75
170	Chris Waters RC	.75
171	Hideki Matsui RC	5.00
172	Alejandro Machado RC	.75
173	Francisco Rosario RC	.75
174	Terrmel Sledge RC	.75
175	Guillermo Quiroz RC	.75
176	Lew Ford RC	3.00
177	Hank Blalock	.75
178	Lyle Overbay	.75
179	Matt Bruback RC	.75
180	Jose Contreras RC	3.00

Century Jersey Number

Stars (1-160): 5-10X
Prospects (161-180): 2-4X
Numbered to jsy number + 100.

Franchise Focus

		NM/M
Complete Set (20):		15.00
Common Player:		.50
Inserted 1:4		
1	Troy Glaus	.75
2	Randy Johnson	1.00
3	Chipper Jones	1.50
4	Nomar Garciaparra	2.00
5	Sammy Sosa	1.50
6	Ken Griffey Jr.	1.50
7	Jeff Bagwell	.75
8	Mike Sweeney	.50
9	Shawn Green	.50
10	Torii Hunter	.50
11	Vladimir Guerrero	1.00
12	Mike Piazza	2.00

13	Jason Giambi	1.00
14	Barry Zito	.50
15	Pat Burrell	.75
16	Barry Bonds	3.00
17	Ichiro Suzuki	1.50
18	Albert Pujols	1.00
19	Alex Rodriguez	2.50
20	Carlos Delgado	.50

Home and Aways

	NM/M
Common Player:	10.00
Inserted 1:288	
Lance Berkman	10.00
J.D. Drew	10.00
Nomar Garciaparra	20.00
Derek Jeter	40.00
Chipper Jones	20.00
Greg Maddux	20.00
Roy Oswalt	10.00
Alex Rodriguez	30.00
Alfonso Soriano	10.00

Materialistic

	NM/M
Common Player:	3.00
Inserted 1:192	
Action Home:	1.5-2.5X
Production 50 Sets	
Portrait Away:	.75-1.5X
Inserted 1:576	
Plus (Memorabilia):	1.5-2.5X
Production 250 Sets	
Portrait Home:	No Pricing
Production One Set	
1M	Greg Maddux	5.00
2M	Roger Clemens	5.00
3M	Nomar Garciaparra	6.00
4M	Derek Jeter	10.00
5M	Mike Piazza	6.00
6M	Pat Burrell	3.00
7M	Alfonso Soriano	5.00
8M	Chipper Jones	5.00
9M	Adam Dunn	3.00
10M	Alex Rodriguez	8.00
11M	Jason Giambi	4.00
12M	Sammy Sosa	5.00
13M	Albert Pujols	4.00
14M	Ken Griffey Jr.	5.00
15M	Ichiro Suzuki	5.00

Materialistic Oversize

	NM/M
Complete Set (16):	60.00
Common Player:	2.00
5-1/4" x 3-3/4" Box Topper	
(1)	Pat Burrell	2.00
(2)	Roger Clemens	6.00
(3)	Adam Dunn	2.00

(4)	Nomar Garciaparra	4.00
(5)	Jason Giambi	2.00
(6)	Ken Griffey Jr.	6.00
(7)	Reggie Jackson	5.00
(8)	Derek Jeter	12.50
(9)	Chipper Jones	5.00
(10)	Greg Maddux	5.00
(11)	Mike Piazza	6.00
(12)	Albert Pujols	10.00
(13)	Alex Rodriguez	10.00
(14)	Alfonso Soriano	2.00
(15)	Sammy Sosa	6.00
(16)	Ichiro Suzuki	7.50

Materialistic Oversize Autographs

	NM/M
Complete Set (3):	200.00
(1)	Reggie Jackson/360	50.00
(2)	Derek Jeter/360	100.00
(3)	Chipper Jones/80	75.00

Materialistic Flannels

No Pricing

Shirtified

	NM/M
Complete Set (15):	35.00
Common Player:	1.00
Inserted 1:24	
1	Manny Ramirez	2.00
2	Jarrod Washburn	1.00
3	Greg Maddux	4.00
4	Austin Kearns	2.00
5	Jim Thome	2.00
6	Kazuhisa Ishii	1.00
7	Mike Piazza	5.00
8	Alfonso Soriano	3.00
9	Pat Burrell	2.00
10	Derek Jeter	8.00
11	Miguel Tejada	1.50
12	Roger Clemens	4.00
13	Alex Rodriguez	6.00
14	Barry Bonds	8.00
15	Scott Rolen	2.00

Shirtified Game-Used

	NM/M
Common Player:	
Inserted 1:35	
Patches:	2-3X
Production 200	
Manny Ramirez	8.00
Greg Maddux	12.00
Mike Piazza	10.00
Alfonso Soriano	15.00
Derek Jeter	25.00
Miguel Tejada	6.00
Roger Clemens	12.00
Alex Rodriguez	12.00

Team Colors

	NM/M
Complete Sety Johnson	1.50

Team Colors Game-Used

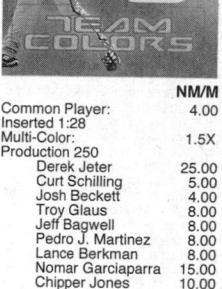

	NM/M
Common Player:	4.00
Inserted 1:28	
Multi-Color:	1.5X
Production 250	
Derek Jeter	25.00
Curt Schilling	5.00
Josh Beckett	4.00
Troy Glaus	8.00
Jeff Bagwell	8.00
Pedro J. Martinez	8.00
Lance Berkman	8.00
Nomar Garciaparra	15.00
Chipper Jones	10.00
Eric Chavez	6.00
Barry Bonds	
Adam Dunn	8.00
Randy Johnson	8.00

2003 Fleer Genuine

		NM/M
Complete Set (130):		150.00
Common Player:		.25
Common Gen. Upside		
(101-130):		3.00
Production 799		
Pack (5):		2.00
Box (24):		40.00
1	Derek Jeter	3.00
2	Mo Vaughn	.25
3	Adam Dunn	.75
4	Aubrey Huff	.25

5	Jacque Jones	.25
6	Kerry Wood	.60
7	Barry Bonds	3.00
8	Kevin Brown	.25
9	Sammy Sosa	2.00
10	Ray Durham	.25
11	Carlos Beltran	.50
12	Tony Batista	.25
13	Bobby Abreu	.25
14	Craig Biggio	.25
15	Gary Sheffield	.45
16	Jermaine Dye	.25
17	Carlos Pena	.25
18	Tim Salmon	.35
19	Mike Piazza	2.00
20	Moises Alou	.25
21	Edgardo Alfonzo	.25
22	Mike Sweeney	.25
23	Jay Gibbons	.25
24	Kevin Millwood	.25
25	A.J. Burnett	.25
26	Austin Kearns	.75
27	Rafael Palmeiro	.75
28	Vladimir Guerrero	1.00
29	Paul Konerko	.25
30	Scott Rolen	.75
31	Fred McGriff	.25
32	Frank Thomas	1.00
33	John Olerud	.25
34	Eric Gagne	.25
35	Nomar Garciaparra	2.00
36	Ryan Klesko	.25
37	Lance Berkman	.25
38	Andruw Jones	.75
39	Pat Burrell	.60
40	Juan Encarnacion	.25
41	Curt Schilling	.50
42	Jason Giambi	.65
43	Barry Larkin	.25
44	Alex Rodriguez	2.50
45	Kazuhisa Ishii	.25
46	Pedro J. Martinez	1.00
47	Sean Burroughs	.25
48	Roy Oswalt	.40
49	Chipper Jones	1.50
50	Barry Zito	.40
51	Jeff Kent	.25
52	Rodrigo Lopez	.25
53	Jim Thome	.25
54	Ivan Rodriguez	.60
55	Luis Gonzalez	.40
56	Alfonso Soriano	1.00
57	Josh Beckett	.25
58	Junior Spivey	.25
59	Bernie Williams	.40
60	Omar Vizquel	.25
61	Eric Hinske	.25
62	Jose Vidro	.25
63	Bartolo Colon	.25
64	Jim Edmonds	.25
65	Ben Sheets	.25
66	Mark Prior	1.00
67	Edgar Martinez	.25
68	Raul Ibanez	.25
69	Darin Erstad	.40
70	Roger Clemens	1.75
71	C.C. Sabathia	.25
72	Carlos Delgado	.50
73	Tom Glavine	.25
74	Magglio Ordonez	.40
75	Ichiro Suzuki	1.50
76	Johnny Damon	.40
77	Brian Giles	.25
78	Jeff Bagwell	1.00
79	Greg Maddux	1.50
80	Eric Chavez	.40
81	Larry Walker	.25
82	Randy Johnson	1.00
83	Miguel Tejada	.40
84	Todd Helton	.75
85	Jarrod Washburn	.25
86	Troy Glaus	.75
87	Ken Griffey Jr.	2.00
88	Albert Pujols	2.00
89	Torii Hunter	.25
90	Joe Crede	.25
91	Matt Morris	.25
92	Shawn Green	.40
93	Manny Ramirez	1.00
94	Jason Kendall	.25
95	Preston Wilson	.25
96	Garret Anderson	.25
97	Cliff Floyd	.25
98	Sean Casey	.25
99	Juan Gonzalez	.75
100	Richie Sexson	.25
101	Joe Borchard	3.00
102	Josh Stewart RC	3.00
103	Francisco Rodriguez	4.00
104	Jeremy Bonderman	8.00
105	Walter Young	3.00
106	Brandon Webb RC	6.00
107	Lyle Overbay	4.00
108	Jose Contreras RC	6.00
109	Victor Martinez	4.00

110	Hideki Matsui RC	10.00
111	Brian Stokes RC	3.00
112	Daniel Cabrera RC	6.00
113	Josh Willingham RC	3.00
114	Mark Teixeira RC	4.00
115	Pete LaForest RC	3.00
116	Chris Waters RC	3.00
117	Chien-Ming Wang RC	30.00
118	Ian Ferguson RC	3.00
119	Rocco Baldelli	4.00
120	Terrmel Sledge RC	4.00
121	Hank Blalock	4.00
122	Alejandro Machado RC	3.00
123	Hee Seop Choi	4.00
124	Guillermo Quiroz RC	4.00
125	Chase Utley	4.00
126	Nook Logan RC	3.00
127	Josh Hall RC	3.00
128	Ryan Church	3.00
129	Lew Ford RC	6.00
130	Francisco Rosario RC	3.00

Reflection

	NM/M
Cards 1-100 print run 25-50:8-15X	
Cards 101-130 p/r 101-130:.5-1.5X	
Cards 1-100 p/r 51-80:	4-8X
Cards 1-100 p/r 81-130:	3-5X
Ascending consecutively #'d from 1-130.	
Descending consecutively #'d from 130-1.	

Article Insider

	NM/M
Common Player:	4.00
Inserted 1:24	
Adam Dunn	5.00
Andruw Jones	6.00
Alex Rodriguez	10.00
Alfonso Soriano	8.00
Chipper Jones	8.00
Curt Schilling	5.00
Derek Jeter	15.00
Don Mattingly	25.00
Greg Maddux	10.00
Jeff Bagwell	6.00
Jason Giambi	10.00
Lance Berkman	4.00
Magglio Ordonez	4.00
Mike Piazza	10.00
Miguel Tejada	4.00
Nomar Garciaparra	15.00
Pat Burrell	4.00
Pedro J. Martinez	8.00
Randy Johnson	6.00
Shawn Green	4.00
Sammy Sosa	10.00
Troy Glaus	5.00
Torii Hunter	5.00
Todd Helton	6.00
Vladimir Guerrero	6.00

Article Insider Autograph

	NM/M
Quantity produced listed	
Lance Berkman/165	25.00
Lance Berkman/100	25.00
Lance Berkman/50	40.00
Derek Jeter/100	125.00
Don Mattingly/170	85.00
Don Mattingly/100	100.00

Long Ball Threats

	NM/M
Complete Set (15):	15.00
Common Card:	.50
Inserted 1:8	

1	Derek Jeter, Nomar Garciaparra	3.00
2	Jim Thome, Pat Burrell	1.00
3	Alex Rodriguez, Rafael Palmeiro	3.00
4	Alfonso Soriano, Hideki Matsui	3.00
5	Torii Hunter, Vladimir Guerrero	1.00
6	Mike Sweeney, Phil Nevin	.50
7	Mike Piazza, Sammy Sosa	2.00
8	Shawn Green, Jason Giambi	1.00
9	Magglio Ordonez, Andruw Jones	1.00
10	Eric Chavez, Carlos Delgado	.75
11	Manny Ramirez, Jeff Bagwell	1.00
12	Scott Rolen, Troy Glaus	1.00
13	Barry Bonds, Miguel Tejada	3.00
14	Albert Pujols, Lance Berkman	2.00
15	Chipper Jones, Todd Helton	1.50

Long Ball Threats Dual Jersey

	NM/M
Common Card:	5.00
Inserted 1:72	
Derek Jeter, Nomar Garciaparra	30.00
Jim Thome, Pat Burrell	15.00
Alex Rodriguez, Rafael Palmeiro	15.00
Torii Hunter, Vladimir Guerrero	10.00
Mike Sweeney, Phil Nevin	5.00
Mike Piazza, Sammy Sosa	20.00
Magglio Ordonez, Andruw Jones	10.00
Scott Rolen, Troy Glaus	10.00
Chipper Jones, Todd Helton	12.00

Long Ball Threats Single Jersey

	NM/M
Common Player:	3.00
Inserted 1:13	
Derek Jeter/Jsy, Nomar Garciaparra	15.00
Derek Jeter, Nomar Garciaparra/Jsy	10.00
Jim Thome/Jsy, Pat Burrell	6.00
Jim Thome, Pat Burrell/Jsy	6.00
Alfonso Soriano/Jsy, Hideki Matsui	8.00
Torii Hunter/Jsy, Vladimir Guerrero	6.00
Torii Hunter, Vladimir Guerrero/Jsy	6.00
Mike Sweeney/Jsy, Phil Nevin	3.00
Mike Sweeney, Phil Nevin/Jsy	3.00
Mike Piazza/Jsy, Sammy Sosa	8.00
Mike Piazza, Sammy Sosa/Jsy	10.00
Shawn Green/Jsy, Jason Giambi	4.00
Magglio Ordonez/Jsy, Andruw Jones	4.00
Eric Chavez, Carlos Delgado/Jsy	5.00
Manny Ramirez/Jsy, Jeff Bagwell	8.00
Manny Ramirez, Jeff Bagwell/Jsy	8.00
Scott Rolen/Jsy, Troy Glaus	6.00
Scott Rolen, Troy Glaus/Jsy	6.00
Barry Bonds, Miguel Tejada/Jsy	5.00
Albert Pujols, Lance Berkman/Jsy	4.00
Chipper Jones/Jsy, Todd Helton	8.00
Chipper Jones, Todd Helton/Jsy	6.00

Long Ball Threats Dual Patch

	NM/M
#'d to combined 2002 HR total	
Derek Jeter, Nomar Garciaparra/42	80.00
Jim Thome, Pat Burrell/89	30.00
Alex Rodriguez, Rafael Palmeiro/100	50.00
Mike Piazza, Sammy Sosa/82	75.00
Shawn Green, Jason Giambi/83	40.00
Magglio Ordonez, Andruw Jones/73	40.00
Manny Ramirez, Jeff Bagwell/64	40.00
Scott Rolen, Troy Glaus/61	50.00

Tools of the Game 1-Piece

	NM/M
Common Player:	
Inserted 1:42	
2-Piece:	1.5-3X
Production 250	
3-Piece:	3-6X
Production 100	
Adam Dunn	6.00
Mike Piazza	8.00
Derek Jeter	15.00
Alex Rodriguez	10.00
Alfonso Soriano	10.00
Jason Giambi	8.00
Sammy Sosa	10.00
Vladimir Guerrero	6.00

Tools of the Game

	NM/M
Complete Set (15):	20.00
Common Player:	.75
Inserted 1:20	
1	Adam Dunn	1.00
2	Chipper Jones	2.00
3	Torii Hunter	.75
4	Mike Piazza	1.50
5	Hideki Matsui	8.00
6	Nomar Garciaparra	3.00
7	Derek Jeter	4.00
8	Alex Rodriguez	3.00
9	Alfonso Soriano	2.00
10	Pat Burrell	.75
11	Barry Bonds	4.00
12	Jason Giambi	1.50
13	Sammy Sosa	2.00
14	Vladimir Guerrero	1.00
15	Ichiro Suzuki	2.00

2003 Fleer Hardball

	NM/M
Complete Set (280):	85.00
Common Player:	.15
Common (241-280):	.75
Inserted 1:2 Hobby	
Pack (7):	1.75
Box (24):	30.00
1	Barry Bonds	2.00
2	Derek Jeter	2.00
3	Jason Varitek	.15
4	Magglio Ordonez	.25
5	Ryan Dempster	.15
6	Adam Everett	.15
7	Paul LoDuca	.15

MARK GRACE

8	Brad Wilkerson	.15
9	Al Leiter	.15
10	Jermaine Dye	.15
11	Robert Mackowiak	.15
12	J.T. Snow	.15
13	Juan Gonzalez	.60
14	Eric Hinske	.15
15	Greg Maddux	1.00
16	Moises Alou	.15
17	Carlos Lee	.15
18	Richard Hidalgo	.15
19	Jorge Posada	.25
20	Mike Lieberthal	.15
21	Jeff Cirillo	.15
22	Corey Patterson	.15
23	C.C. Sabathia	.15
24	Brian Giles	.15
25	Edgar Martinez	.15
26	Trot Nixon	.15
27	Kerry Wood	.50
28	Austin Kearns	.40
29	Lance Berkman	.15
30	Hideo Nomo	.50
31	Brad Radke	.15
32	John Valentin	.15
33	Tim Hudson	.35
34	Aramis Ramirez	.15
35	Kevin Mench	.15
36	Kevin Appier	.15
37	Chris Richard	.15
38	Ruben Mateo	.15
39	Juan Pierre	.15
40	Nick Neugebauer	.15
41	Mike Mussina	.40
42	Rich Aurilia	.15
43	Albert Pujols	1.00
44	Carlos Delgado	.50
45	Junior Spivey	.15
46	Marcus Giles	.15
47	Johnny Damon	.25
48	Mark Prior	.50
49	Omar Vizquel	.15
50	Craig Biggio	.15
51	Chuck Knoblauch	.15
52	Eric Milton	.15
53	Jeromy Burnitz	.15
54	Jim Thome	.15
55	Steve Finley	.15
56	Kevin Millwood	.15
57	Alex Gonzalez	.15
58	Ben Broussard	.15
59	Derrek Lee	.15
60	Joe Randa	.15
61	Doug Mientkiewicz	.15
62	Jason L. Phillips	.15
63	Brett Myers	.15
64	Josh Fogg	.15
65	Reggie Sanders	.15
66	Chipper Jones	1.00
67	Roosevelt Brown	.15
68	Matt Lawton	.15
69	Charles Johnson	.15
70	Mark Quinn	.15
71	Jacque Jones	.15
72	Armando Benitez	.15
73	Bobby Abreu	.15
74	Jason Kendall	.15
75	Jeff Kent	.15
76	Mark Teixeira	.50
77	Garret Anderson	.15
78	Jerry Hairston Jr.	.15
79	Tony Graffanino	.15
80	Josh Beckett	.15
81	Eric Gagne	.15
82	Fernando Tatis	.15
83	Brett Tomko	.15
84	Fernando Vina	.15
85	Rafael Palmeiro	.65
86	Luis Gonzalez	.35
87	Javy Lopez	.15
88	Shea Hillenbrand	.15
89	Hee Seop Choi	.15
90	Preston Wilson	.15
91	Neifi Perez	.15
92	Ray Lankford	.15
93	Tsuyoshi Shinjo	.15
94	Ben Grieve	.15
95	Jarrod Washburn	.15

96	Gary Sheffield	.35
97	Derek Lowe	.15
98	Tony Womack	.15
99	Milton Bradley	.15
100	Brad Penny	.15
101	Mike Sweeney	.15
102	A.J. Pierzynski	.15
103	Edgardo Alfonzo	.15
104	Marlon Byrd	.15
105	Sean Burroughs	.15
106	Kazuhiro Sasaki	.15
107	Damian Rolls	.15
108	Troy Glaus	.60
109	Rafael Furcal	.15
110	Nomar Garciaparra	1.25
111	Josh Bard	.15
112	Alex Gonzalez	.15
113	Cristian Guzman	.15
114	Roger Cedeno	.15
115	Freddy Garcia	.15
116	Travis Phelps	.15
117	Juan Cruz	.15
118	Frank Thomas	.60
119	Jaret Wright	.15
120	Carlos Beltran	.45
121	Ronnie Belliard	.15
122	Roger Clemens	1.00
123	Vicente Padilla	.15
124	Joel Pineiro	.15
125	Jared Sandberg	.15
126	Tom Glavine	.35
127	Matt Clement	.15
128	Aaron Rowand	.15
129	Alex Escobar	.15
130	Randy Wolf	.15
131	Ichiro Suzuki	1.00
132	Toby Hall	.15
133	Scott Spiezio	.15
134	Bobby Higginson	.15
135	A.J. Burnett	.15
136	Cesar Izturis	.15
137	Roberto Alomar	.40
138	Trevor Hoffman	.15
139	Edgar Renteria	.15
140	Rusty Greer	.15
141	David Eckstein	.15
142	Pedro J. Martinez	.75
143	Joe Crede	.15
144	Robert Fick	.15
145	Mike Lowell	.15
146	Brian Jordan	.15
147	Mark Mulder	.25
148	Scott Rolen	.60
149	Ivan Rodriguez	.60
150	Adam Kennedy	.15
151	Ken Griffey Jr.	1.25
152	Larry Walker	.15
153	Carlos Pena	.15
154	Geoff Jenkins	.15
155	Bartolo Colon	.15
156	Mariano Rivera	.25
157	Robb Nen	.15
158	Bret Boone	.15
159	Shannon Stewart	.15
160	Chris Singleton	.15
161	Todd Walker	.15
162	Jay Payton	.15
163	Zach Day	.15
164	Bernie Williams	.40
165	Bubba Trammell	.15
166	Matt Morris	.15
167	Jose Cruz Jr.	.15
168	Mark Grace	.40
169	Andruw Jones	.75
170	Cliff Floyd	.15
171	Antonio Alfonseca	.15
172	Jeff Bagwell	.75
173	Shawn Green	.40
174	Joe Mays	.15
175	Mike Piazza	1.25
176	Adam Piatt	.15
177	Pokey Reese	.15
178	Carl Everett	.15
179	Tim Salmon	.35
180	Rodrigo Lopez	.15
181	Brandon Inge	.15
182	Kazuhisa Ishii	.15
183	Jose Vidro	.15
184	Barry Zito	.40
185	Phil Nevin	.15
186	J.D. Drew	.35
187	Vernon Wells	.15
188	Darin Erstad	.50
189	Barry Larkin	.15
190	Jason Jennings	.15
191	Luis Castillo	.15
192	Adrian Beltre	.15
193	Tony Armas	.15
194	Terrence Long	.15
195	Mark Kotsay	.15
196	Tino Martinez	.15
197	Jayson Werth	.15
198	Eric Chavez	.25
199	Matt Williams	.15

200	Jon Lieber	.15
201	Eddie Taubensee	.15
202	Shane Reynolds	.15
203	Alex Sanchez	.15
204	Jason Giambi	.60
205	Jimmy Rollins	.25
206	Jamie Moyer	.15
207	Francisco Rodriguez	.15
208	Marty Cordova	.15
209	Aaron Boone	.15
210	Mike Hampton	.15
211	Mark Redman	.15
212	Richie Sexson	.15
213	Andy Pettitte	.40
214	Livan Hernandez	.15
215	Jason Isringhausen	.15
216	Curt Schilling	.40
217	Manny Ramirez	.75
218	Jose Valentin	.15
219	Brent Butler	.15
220	Billy Wagner	.15
221	Ben Sheets	.15
222	Jeff Weaver	.15
223	Brent Abernathy	.15
224	Jay Gibbons	.15
225	Sean Casey	.15
226	Greg Norton	.15
227	Andy Van Hekken	.15
228	Kevin Brown	.15
229	Orlando Cabrera	.15
230	Scott Hatteberg	.15
231	Ryan Klesko	.15
232	Roy Halladay	.15
233	Randy Johnson	.75
234	Mark Buehrle	.15
235	Todd Helton	.60
236	Jeffrey Hammonds	.15
237	Sidney Ponson	.15
238	Kip Wells	.15
239	John Olerud	.15
240	Aubrey Huff	.15
241	Derek Jeter	4.00
242	Barry Bonds	4.00
243	Ichiro Suzuki	2.00
244	Troy Glaus	1.00
245	Alex Rodriguez	3.00
246	Sammy Sosa	2.00
247	Lance Berkman	.75
248	Jason Giambi	2.00
249	Nomar Garciaparra	2.50
250	Miguel Tejada	.75
251	Albert Pujols	1.50
252	Mike Piazza	2.50
253	Vladimir Guerrero	1.50
254	Shawn Green	.75
255	Todd Helton	.75
256	Ken Griffey Jr.	2.00
257	Torii Hunter	.75
258	Chipper Jones	2.00
259	Alfonso Soriano	1.50
260	Luis Gonzalez	.75
261	Pedro J. Martinez	1.50
262	Tim Hudson	.75
263	Roger Clemens	2.00
264	Greg Maddux	2.00
265	Randy Johnson	1.50
266	Vinnie Chulk	.50
267	Jose Castillo	1.50
268	Craig Brazell **RC**	1.50
269	Felix Sanchez **RC**	.50
270	John Webb	.50
271	Josh Hall **RC**	.50
272	Alexis Rios	.50
273	Phil Seibel **RC**	.50
274	Prentice Redman **RC**	1.50
275	Walter Young	1.00
276	Nic Jackson	.50
277	Adam Morrissey	.50
278	Bobby Jenks	.75
279	Rodrigo Rosario	.50
280	Chin-Feng Chen	1.00

Gold

Gold (1-240):	2-3X
Gold (241-280):	1-2X
Inserted 1:4 Hobby	

Platinum

Cards (1-240):	8-15X
Cards (241-280):	3-5X
Production 50 Sets	

Discs

	NM/M
Complete Set (20):	50.00
Common Player:	1.00
Inserted 1:24	
1D Derek Jeter	8.00
2D Barry Bonds	8.00
3D Ichiro Suzuki	4.00
4D Sammy Sosa	4.00
5D Nomar Garciaparra	5.00
6D Lance Berkman	1.50
7D Jason Giambi	4.00
8D Mike Piazza	5.00
9D Shawn Green	1.50

10D Barry Zito	1.50
11D Albert Pujols	3.00
12D Alex Rodriguez	6.00
13D Tim Salmon	1.00
14D Eric Chavez	1.00
15D Ken Griffey Jr.	4.00
16D Alfonso Soriano	3.00
17D Vladimir Guerrero	2.50
18D Francisco Rodriguez	1.00
19D Miguel Tejada	1.50
20D Randy Johnson	2.50

On the Ball

	NM/M
Complete Set (15):	20.00
Common Player:	1.00
Inserted 1:12	
1 Derek Jeter	4.00
2 Barry Bonds	4.00
3 Nomar Garciaparra	2.50
4 Alfonso Soriano	1.50
5 Mike Piazza	2.50
6 Alex Rodriguez	3.00
7 Chipper Jones	2.00
8 Randy Johnson	1.50
9 Pedro J. Martinez	1.50
10 Albert Pujols	1.50
11 Vladimir Guerrero	1.50
12 Sammy Sosa	2.00
13 Ichiro Suzuki	2.00
14 Troy Glaus	1.00
15 Jason Giambi	2.00

On the Ball Memorabilia

	NM/M
Common Player:	5.00
Inserted 1:18	
Derek Jeter/Bat	15.00
Barry Bonds/Jsy	15.00
Nomar Garciaparra/ Jsy	10.00
Alfonso Soriano/Jsy	10.00
Mike Piazza/Jsy	10.00
Alex Rodriguez/Jsy	10.00
Chipper Jones/Bat	8.00
Randy Johnson/Jsy	8.00
Pedro J. Martinez/Jsy	8.00
Troy Glaus/Jsy	5.00

Round Trippers

	NM/M
Complete Set (20):	15.00
Common Player:	.50
Inserted 1:8	

1	Alfonso Soriano	1.50
2	Alex Rodriguez	3.00
3	Lance Berkman	.75
4	Shawn Green	.75
5	Pat Burrell	1.00
6	Andruw Jones	.75
7	Garret Anderson	.50
8	Miguel Tejada	.75
9	Mike Piazza	2.50
10	Eric Chavez	.50
11	Rafael Palmeiro	.75
12	Chipper Jones	2.00
13	Manny Ramirez	1.00
14	Jeff Bagwell	1.00
15	Torii Hunter	.75
16	Nomar Garciaparra	2.50
17	Sammy Sosa	2.00
18	Vladimir Guerrero	1.50
19	Troy Glaus	1.00
20	Jason Giambi	2.00

Round Trippers
Rounding First

	NM/M
Common Player:	5.00

Quantity produced listed
Rounding Second: No Pricing
Production 10 Sets
Rounding Third: No Pricing
Production 3 Sets

Alfonso Soriano/ Jsy/228	10.00
Alex Rodriguez/ Jsy/536	12.00
Lance Berkman/ Jsy/557	5.00
Shawn Green/Bat/249	5.00
Pat Burrell/Bat/502	10.00
Andruw Jones/Jsy/569	5.00
Garret Anderson/ Bat/40	20.00
Miguel Tejada/Jsy/524	5.00
Mike Piazza/Bat/289	12.00
Eric Chavez/Jsy/572	5.00
Rafael Palmeiro/ Jsy/515	6.00
Chipper Jones/ Jsy/570	10.00
Manny Ramirez/ Jsy/530	8.00
Jeff Bagwell/Bat/344	6.00
Nomar Garciaparra/ Bat/529	12.00

Round Numbers

	NM/M
Complete Set (14):	50.00
Common Player:	3.00

Production 1,000 Sets

1	Nolan Ryan	10.00
2	Al Kaline	6.00
3	Mike Schmidt	6.00
4	Yogi Berra	4.00
5	Brooks Robinson	4.00
6	Tom Seaver	4.00
7	Willie McCovey	3.00
8	Harmon Killebrew	4.00
9	Richie Ashburn	3.00
10	Lou Brock	3.00
11	Jim Palmer	3.00
12	Willie Stargell	4.00

13	Whitey Ford	4.00
14	Robin Yount	5.00

Round Numbers
Memorabilia

	NM/M

Inserted 1:288

Al Kaline/Jsy	20.00
Mike Schmidt/Jsy	15.00
Harmon Killebrew/ Bat	30.00
Lou Brock/Jsy	30.00

Signatures

	NM/M

Bonds 600 HR Inscription:1-1.5X

Barry Bonds/255	200.00
Derek Jeter	110.00

2003 Fleer Hot Prospects

	NM/M
Complete Set (120):	
Common Player:	.25
Common SP (81-120):	5.00

Production 1,250 unless noted.

Pack (5):	4.00
Box (15):	50.00

1	Derek Jeter	3.00
2	Ryan Klesko	.25
3	Troy Glaus	.75
4	Jeff Kent	.40
5	Frank Thomas	.75
6	Gary Sheffield	.50
7	Jim Edmonds	.40
8	Pat Burrell	.50
9	Jacque Jones	.25
10	Jason Jennings	.25
11	Pedro J. Martinez	1.00
12	Rafael Palmeiro	.50
13	Jason Kendall	.25
14	Tom Glavine	.40
15	Josh Beckett	.25
16	Luis Gonzalez	.40
17	Edgar Martinez	.25
18	Miguel Tejada	.50
19	Fred McGriff	.40
20	Adam Dunn	.50
21	Lance Berkman	.50
22	Magglio Ordonez	.40
23	Darin Erstad	.40
24	Rich Aurilia	.25
25	Mike Piazza	1.50
26	Shawn Green	.50
27	Larry Walker	.40
28	Manny Ramirez	.75
29	Juan Gonzalez	.75
30	Eric Chavez	.50
31	Torii Hunter	.50
32	A.J. Burnett	.25
33	Sammy Sosa	1.50
34	Eric Hinske	.25
35	Brian Giles	.50
36	Mike Sweeney	.25
37	Sean Casey	.25

38	Chipper Jones	1.50
39	Scott Rolen	.75
40	Jason Giambi	1.00
41	Mo Vaughn	.25
42	Roy Oswalt	.25
43	Paul Konerko	.25
44	Tim Salmon	.40
45	Edgardo Alfonzo	.25
46	Jermaine Dye	.25
47	Ben Sheets	.25
48	Todd Helton	.75
49	Greg Maddux	1.50
50	Albert Pujols	2.00
51	Jim Thome	.75
52	Vladimir Guerrero	.75
53	Ivan Rodriguez	.50
54	Nomar Garciaparra	2.00
55	Alex Rodriguez	2.50
56	Alfonso Soriano	1.50
57	Kazuhisa Ishii	.25
58	Austin Kearns	.50
59	Curt Schilling	.50
60	Bret Boone	.40
61	Mark Prior	1.50
62	Garret Anderson	.40
63	Barry Bonds	2.50
64	Roger Clemens	2.00
65	Jeff Bagwell	.75
66	Omar Vizquel	.40
67	Jay Gibbons	.25
68	Aubrey Huff	.25
69	Bobby Abreu	.25
70	Richie Sexson	.50
71	Bobby Higginson	.25
72	Kerry Wood	.50
73	Carlos Delgado	.50
74	Sean Burroughs	.25
75	Jose Vidro	.25
76	Ken Griffey Jr.	1.50
77	Randy Johnson	1.00
78	Ichiro Suzuki	1.50
79	Barry Zito	.50
80	Carlos Beltran	.25
81	Joe Borchard	5.00
82	Mark Teixeira	5.00
83	Brandon Webb RC	8.00
84	Shane Victorino/ Auto./400 RC	8.00
85	Hee Seop Choi	5.00
86	Hank Blalock	6.00
87	Brett Myers	5.00
88	Mike Ryan RC	5.00
89	Jesse Foppert	8.00
90	Lyle Overbay	6.00
91	Brian Stokes/ Auto./400 RC	10.00
92	Josh Hall/ Auto./400 RC	10.00
93	Chris Waters/ Auto./400 RC	10.00
94	Lew Ford/Auto./ 400 RC	25.00
95	Ian Ferguson/ Auto./500 RC	8.00
96	Josh Willingham RC	5.00
97	Josh Stewart/ Auto./500 RC	8.00
98	Pete LaForest/ Auto./500 RC	8.00
99	J.Contreras/ Auto./Jsy/300 RC	40.00
100	Terrmel Sledge/ Auto./500 RC	8.00
101	Guillermo Quiroz/ Auto./500 RC	15.00
102	Alejandro Machado/ Auto./500 RC	8.00
103	Nook Logan/ Auto/Jsy/400 RC	10.00
104	Robby Hammock/ Auto./Jsy/400 RC	10.00
105	Hideki Matsui/ Base RC	15.00
106	Wilfredo Ledezma RC	5.00
107	Rocco Baldelli/Jsy	8.00
108	Oscar Villarreal RC	5.00
109	Todd Wellemeyer/ Auto./400 RC	8.00
110	Michael Hessman/ Auto./400 RC	8.00
111	Jeremy Bonderman/ Auto./Jsy/400	35.00
112	Craig Brazell/ Auto./Jsy/400 RC	10.00
113	Francisco Rosario/ Auto./Jsy/400 RC	10.00
114	Jeff Duncan/ Auto./Jsy/400 RC	10.00
115	Daniel Cabrera/ Auto./Jsy/400 RC	25.00
116	Dontrelle Willis/ Auto./Jsy/400	40.00
117	Cory Stewart/ Auto./500 RC	10.00

118	Tim Olson/Auto./ Jsy/400 RC	10.00
119	Chien-Ming Wang/Auto./ Jsy/500 RC	200.00

Class Of...

	NM/M
Common Duo:	10.00

Inserted 1:15

Barry Zito, Josh Beckett	10.00
Pat Burrell, J.D. Drew	12.00
Mark Prior, Mark Teixeira	15.00
Austin Kearns, Sean Burroughs	10.00
Troy Glaus, Lance Berkman	10.00
Darin Erstad, Todd Helton	10.00
Manny Ramirez, Shawn Green	10.00
Matt Morris, Kerry Wood	10.00
Nomar Garciaparra, Paul Konerko	15.00
Alex Rodriguez, Torii Hunter	20.00

Cream of the Crop

	NM/M
Complete Set (15):	35.00
Common Player:	1.50

Inserted 1:5

1	Barry Bonds	5.00
2	Derek Jeter	5.00
3	Ichiro Suzuki	3.00
4	Nomar Garciaparra	3.00
5	Roger Clemens	3.00
6	Alex Rodriguez	4.00
7	Greg Maddux	2.50
8	Mike Piazza	2.50
9	Sammy Sosa	2.50
10	Jason Giambi	2.00
11	Hideki Matsui	6.00
12	Albert Pujols	4.00
13	Vladimir Guerrero	1.50
14	Jim Thome	1.50
15	Pedro J. Martinez	1.50

Hot Materials

	NM/M
Common Player:	5.00

Production 499 Sets

Red-Hots:	1-2X

Production 50

1HM	Derek Jeter	20.00
2HM	Torii Hunter	8.00
3HM	Mark Prior	8.00
4HM	Nomar Garciaparra	15.00
5HM	Sammy Sosa	15.00
6HM	Rafael Palmeiro	6.00
7HM	Hee Seop Choi	10.00
8HM	Mark Teixeira	5.00
9HM	Mike Piazza	10.00
10HM	Pat Burrell	8.00
11HM	Jim Thome	8.00
12HM	Lance Berkman	5.00
13HM	Vladimir Guerrero	6.00
14HM	Troy Glaus	5.00

15HM	Chipper Jones	8.00
16HM	Lyle Overbay	5.00
17HM	Jason Giambi	8.00
18HM	Alex Rodriguez	10.00
19HM	Miguel Tejada	5.00
20HM	Adam Dunn	6.00
21HM	Randy Johnson	8.00
22HM	Josh Beckett	5.00
23HM	Alfonso Soriano	10.00
24HM	Greg Maddux	10.00
25HM	Shawn Green	5.00
26HM	Carlos Delgado	5.00
27HM	Todd Helton	6.00
28HM	Mike Sweeney	5.00
29HM	Manny Ramirez	6.00
30HM	Tom Glavine	5.00

Hot Tandems

NM/M

Common Duo: 8.00
Production 100 Sets
Red-Hots numbered to 10.

Derek Jeter, Chipper Jones	25.00
Derek Jeter, Mike Piazza	25.00
Derek Jeter, Miguel Tejada	25.00
Torii Hunter, Lance Berkman	10.00
Mark Prior, Sammy Sosa	25.00
Sammy Sosa, Pat Burrell	20.00
Rafael Palmeiro, Mark Teixeira	10.00
Hee Seop Choi, Lyle Overbay	15.00
Alex Rodriguez, Mark Teixeira	20.00
Mike Piazza, Chipper Jones	15.00
Pat Burrell, Jim Thome	10.00
Lance Berkman, Adam Dunn	8.00
Nomar Garciaparra, Miguel Tejada	15.00
Randy Johnson, Greg Maddux	12.00
Mark Prior, Josh Beckett	10.00
Miguel Tejada, Alex Rodriguez	15.00
Jason Giambi, Jim Thome	10.00

Hot Triple Patch

NM/M

Production 50 Sets
Some not priced yet.

Derek Jeter, Nomar Garciaparra, Alex Rodriguez	125.00
Mark Prior, Josh Beckett, Greg Maddux	80.00
Mike Piazza, Pat Burrell, Jim Thome	50.00
Lance Berkman, Troy Glaus, Chipper Jones	50.00
Randy Johnson, Alfonso Soriano, Shawn Green	50.00
Derek Jeter, Torii Hunter, Mark Prior	75.00
Nomar Garciaparra, Sammy Sosa, Mike Piazza	90.00
Pat Burrell, Jim Thome, Lance Berkman	40.00
Vladimir Guerrero, Troy Glaus, Chipper Jones	60.00
Alfonso Soriano, Greg Maddux, Shawn Green	60.00

Playergraphs

NM/M

Common Player: 10.00
Production 400 Sets

Red-Hots: 1-1.5X
Production 100

	Hank Blalock	20.00
	Brett Myers	10.00
	Mark Prior	35.00
	Carlos Zambrano	20.00
	Mark Teixeira	20.00
	Francisco Rodriguez	10.00
	Roy Oswalt	15.00
	Xavier Nady	10.00
	Jose Reyes	25.00
	Aubrey Huff	10.00

2003 Fleer Mystique

NM/M

Complete Set (130):		
Common Player:		.25
Common SP (81-130):		3.00
Production 699		
Pack (4):		3.00
Box (20):		40.00
1	Alex Rodriguez	2.50
2	Derek Jeter	3.00
3	Jose Vidro	.25
4	Miguel Tejada	.40
5	Albert Pujols	2.50
6	Rocco Baldelli	.25
7	Jose Reyes	.50
8	Hideo Nomo	.75
9	Hank Blalock	.75
10	Chipper Jones	1.50
11	Barry Larkin	.25
12	Alfonso Soriano	1.00
13	Aramis Ramirez	.25
14	Darin Erstad	.65
15	Jim Edmonds	.25
16	Garret Anderson	.25
17	Todd Helton	1.00
18	Jason Kendall	.25
19	Aubrey Huff	.25
20	Troy Glaus	.75
21	Sammy Sosa	2.00
22	Roger Clemens	1.75
23	Mark Teixeira	.50
24	Barry Bonds	3.00
25	Jim Thome	.25
26	Carlos Delgado	.50
27	Vladimir Guerrero	1.00
28	Austin Kearns	.50
29	Pat Burrell	.75
30	Ken Griffey Jr.	2.00
31	Greg Maddux	1.50
32	Corey Patterson	.25
33	Larry Walker	.25
34	Kerry Wood	.65
35	Frank Thomas	1.00
36	Dontrelle Willis	.25
37	Randy Johnson	1.00
38	Curt Schilling	.40
39	Jay Gibbons	.25
40	Dmitri Young	.25
41	Edgar Martinez	.25
42	Kevin Brown	.25
43	Scott Rolen	1.00
44	Adam Dunn	.75
45	Pedro J. Martinez	1.00
46	Corey Koskie	.25
47	Tom Glavine	.40
48	Torii Hunter	.25
49	Shawn Green	.40
50	Nomar Garciaparra	2.00
51	Bernie Williams	.40
52	Milton Bradley	.25
53	Jason Giambi	.75
54	Mike Lieberthal	.25
55	Jeff Bagwell	1.00
56	Carlos Pena	.25
57	Lance Berkman	.25
58	Jose Cruz Jr.	.25
59	Josh Beckett	.25
60	Mark Mulder	.40
61	Mike Piazza	2.00
62	Mark Prior	1.00

63	Sean Burroughs	.25
64	Angel Berroa	.25
65	Geoff Jenkins	.25
66	Magglio Ordonez	.25
67	Craig Biggio	.25
68	Roberto Alomar	.40
69	Hee Seop Choi	.25
70	J.D. Drew	.25
71	Richie Sexson	.25
72	Brian Giles	.25
73	Gary Sheffield	.50
74	Manny Ramirez	1.00
75	Barry Zito	.45
76	Andruw Jones	1.00
77	Ivan Rodriguez	.65
78	Ichiro Suzuki	2.00
79	Mike Sweeney	.25
80	Vernon Wells	.25
81	Craig Brazell **RC**	5.00
82	Wilfredo Ledezma **RC**	3.00
83	Josh Willingham **RC**	6.00
84	Chien-Ming Wang **RC**	35.00
85	Mike Ryan **RC**	3.00
86	Mike Gallo **RC**	3.00
87	Rickie Weeks **RC**	10.00
88	Brian Stokes **RC**	3.00
89	Humberto Quintero **RC**	3.00
90	Ramon Nivar **RC**	3.00
91	Jeremy Griffiths **RC**	3.00
92	Terrmel Sledge **RC**	4.00
93	Brandon Webb **RC**	10.00
94	David DeJesus **RC**	5.00
95	Doug Waechter **RC**	3.00
96	Jeremy Bonderman **RC**	10.00
97	Felix Sanchez **RC**	3.00
98	Colin Porter **RC**	3.00
99	Francisco Cruceta **RC**	3.00
100	Hideki Matsui **RC**	15.00
101	Chris Waters **RC**	5.00
102	Dan Haren **RC**	5.00
103	Lew Ford **RC**	5.00
104	Oscar Villarreal **RC**	3.00
105	Ryan Wagner **RC**	5.00
106	Prentice Redman **RC**	3.00
107	Josh Stewart **RC**	5.00
108	Carlos Mendez **RC**	3.00
109	Michael Hessman **RC**	5.00
110	Josh Hall **RC**	5.00
111	Daniel Garcia **RC**	5.00
112	Matt Kata **RC**	5.00
113	Michel Hernandez **RC**	3.00
114	Sergio Mitre **RC**	5.00
115	Pete LaForest **RC**	5.00
116	Edwin Jackson **RC**	5.00
117	Matt Diaz **RC**	5.00
118	Greg Aquino **RC**	3.00
119	Jose Contreras **RC**	8.00
120	Jeff Duncan **RC**	6.00
121	Richard Fischer **RC**	3.00
122	Todd Wellemeyer **RC**	5.00
123	Robby Hammock **RC**	5.00
124	Delmon Young **RC**	15.00
125	Clint Barmes **RC**	5.00
126	Phil Seibel **RC**	3.00
127	Bo Hart **RC**	5.00
128	Jon Leicester **RC**	5.00
129	Chad Gaudin **RC**	6.00
130	Guillermo Quiroz **RC**	5.00

Gold

Stars (1-80):	4-8X
Production 150	
SP's (81-130):	1-2X
Production 50	

Awe Pairs

NM/M

Complete Set (20):	60.00
Common Duo:	2.00
Production 250 Sets	
Golds:	1.5X

#'d to team win total for 2003.

1	Nomar Garciaparra, Pedro J. Martinez	8.00
2	Derek Jeter, Alfonso Soriano	8.00
3	Rocco Baldelli, Aubrey Huff	2.00
4	Carlos Delgado, Vernon Wells	2.00
5	Troy Glaus, Garret Anderson	2.00
6	Ichiro Suzuki, Bret Boone	5.00
7	Alex Rodriguez, Hank Blalock	8.00
8	Chipper Jones, Andruw Jones	5.00
9	Dontrelle Willis, Mike Lowell	3.00
10	Vladimir Guerrero, Orlando Cabrera	4.00
11	Tom Glavine, Mike Piazza	5.00
12	Jim Thome, Mike Lieberthal	3.00
13	Sammy Sosa, Corey Patterson	6.00
14	Jeff Bagwell, Lance Berkman	3.00
15	Geoff Jenkins, Richie Sexson	2.00
16	Albert Pujols, Jim Edmonds	6.00
17	Todd Helton, Larry Walker	3.00
18	Paul LoDuca, Shawn Green	2.00
19	Ryan Klesko, Sean Burroughs	2.00
20	Barry Bonds, Rich Aurilia	8.00

Awe Pairs Game-Used

NM/M

Common Duo: 10.00
Production 100 Sets
Golds: No Pricing
Production 10 Sets

Nomar Garciaparra, Pedro J. Martinez	25.00
Derek Jeter, Alfonso Soriano	30.00
Rocco Baldelli, Aubrey Huff	15.00
Carlos Delgado, Vernon Wells	10.00
Troy Glaus, Garret Anderson	10.00
Chipper Jones, Andruw Jones	15.00
Dontrelle Willis, Mike Lowell	25.00
Vladimir Guerrero, Orlando Cabrera	10.00
Tom Glavine, Mike Piazza	20.00
Jim Thome, Mike Lieberthal	15.00
Sammy Sosa, Corey Patterson	20.00
Jeff Bagwell, Lance Berkman	15.00
Geoff Jenkins, Richie Sexson	10.00
Albert Pujols, Jim Edmonds	20.00
Todd Helton, Larry Walker	10.00
Paul LoDuca, Shawn Green	10.00
Ryan Klesko, Sean Burroughs	10.00

Diamond Dominators

		NM/M
Complete Set (10):		50.00
Common Player:		3.00
Production 100 Sets		
1	Mike Piazza	8.00
2	Greg Maddux	8.00
3	Alfonso Soriano	5.00
4	Barry Zito	3.00
5	Alex Rodriguez	10.00
6	Roger Clemens	10.00
7	Sammy Sosa	10.00
8	Adam Dunn	3.00
9	Randy Johnson	5.00
10	Pedro J. Martinez	5.00

Diamond Dominators Gold

		NM/M
Some not priced due to scarcity.		
Numbered to jersey number.		
1DD	Mike Piazza/31	25.00
2DD	Greg Maddux/31	25.00
4DD	Barry Zito/75	5.00
8DD	Adam Dunn/44	6.00
9DD	Randy Johnson/51	8.00
10DD	Pedro Martinez/31	10.00

Diamond Dominators Game-Used

		NM/M
Common Player:		6.00
Production 75 Sets		
Golds:		No Pricing
Production 10 Sets		
RC	Roger Clemens	20.00
AD	Adam Dunn	6.00
RJ	Randy Johnson	10.00
GM	Greg Maddux	25.00
PM	Pedro Martinez	12.00
MP	Mike Piazza	15.00
AR	Alex Rodriguez	15.00
AS	Alfonso Soriano	12.00
SS	Sammy Sosa	20.00
BZ	Barry Zito	8.00

Ink Appeal Autographs

		NM/M
Common Player:		15.00
Production 50 Sets		
RB	Rocco Baldelli	40.00
HB	Hank Blalock	35.00
BH	Bo Hart	25.00
AH	Aubrey Huff	15.00
TH	Torii Hunter	20.00
CP	Corey Patterson	15.00
JR	Jose Reyes	30.00
MR	Mike Ryan	15.00
RW	Rickie Weeks	
JW	Josh Willingham	15.00
DW	Dontrelle Willis	

Ink Appeal Gold Autographs

		NM/M
Numbered to jersey number.		
Some not priced due to scarcity.		
BH	Bo Hart/31	50.00
TH	Torii Hunter/48	20.00
MR	Mike Ryan/54	15.00
JW	Josh Willingham/70	12.00

Ink Appeal Dual Autographs

No pricing due to scarcity.
Production 20 Sets
Golds: No Pricing
Production 5 Sets

Rare Finds

	NM/M
Complete Set (10):	40.00
Common Trio:	3.00
Production 250 Sets	

1	Jason Giambi, Roger Clemens, Derek Jeter	8.00
2	Randy Johnson, Curt Schilling, Brandon Webb	4.00
3	Nomar Garciaparra, Pedro J. Martinez, Manny Ramirez	8.00
4	Mark Prior, Kerry Wood, Sammy Sosa	5.00
5	Jeff Bagwell, Craig Biggio, Lance Berkman	
6	Austin Kearns, Adam Dunn, Barry Larkin	3.00
7	Jim Edmonds, Scott Rolen, J.D. Drew	3.00
8	Chipper Jones, Andruw Jones, Greg Maddux	3.00
9	Barry Zito, Miguel Tejada, Mark Mulder	3.00
10	Alex Rodriguez, Mark Teixeira, Rafael Palmeiro	8.00

Rare Finds Single Swatch

		NM/M
Common Player:		6.00
Production 150 Sets		
Golds:		No Pricing
Production 15 Sets		
JG	Jason Giambi, Roger Clemens, Derek Jeter	10.00
RC	Jason Giambi, Roger Clemens, Derek Jeter	15.00
DJ	Jason Giambi, Roger Clemens, Derek Jeter	20.00
RJ	Randy Johnson, Curt Schilling, Brandon Webb	8.00
BW	Randy Johnson, Curt Schilling, Brandon Webb	10.00
NG	Nomar Garciaparra, Pedro J. Martinez, Manny Ramirez	15.00
PM	Nomar Garciaparra, Pedro J. Martinez, Manny Ramirez	8.00
MP	Mark Prior, Kerry Wood, Sammy Sosa	10.00
SS	Mark Prior, Kerry Wood, Sammy Sosa	8.00
JB	Jeff Bagwell, Craig Biggio, Lance Berkman	6.00
AK	Austin Kearns, Adam Dunn, Barry Larkin	6.00
BL	Austin Kearns, Adam Dunn, Barry Larkin	6.00
SR	Jim Edmonds, Scott Rolen, J.D. Drew	10.00
JD	Jim Edmonds, Scott Rolen, J.D. Drew	6.00
CJ	Chipper Jones, Andruw Jones, Greg Maddux	10.00
GM	Chipper Jones, Andruw Jones, Greg Maddux	15.00
MT	Barry Zito, Miguel Tejada, Mark Mulder	6.00
MM	Barry Zito, Miguel Tejada, Mark Mulder	6.00
AR	Alex Rodriguez, Mark Teixeira, Rafael Palmeiro	15.00
MT	Alex Rodriguez, Mark Teixeira, Rafael Palmeiro	8.00

Rare Finds Autographs

No Pricing:
Production 15 Sets
Auto/Game-Used: No Pricing
Production 5 Sets

Rare Finds Dual Swatch

		NM/M
Common Dual:		10.00
Production 75 Sets		
Golds:		No Pricing
Production 10 Sets		
	Jason Giambi, Roger Clemens, Derek Jeter	35.00
	Jason Giambi, Roger Clemens, Derek Jeter	40.00
	Randy Johnson, Curt Schilling, Brandon Webb	15.00
	Randy Johnson, Curt Schilling, Brandon Webb	10.00
	Nomar Garciaparra, Pedro J. Martinez, Manny Ramirez	20.00
	Nomar Garciaparra, Pedro J. Martinez, Manny Ramirez	15.00
	Mark Prior, Kerry Wood, Sammy Sosa	15.00
	Mark Prior, Kerry Wood, Sammy Sosa	20.00
	Jeff Bagwell, Craig Biggio, Lance Berkman	10.00
	Austin Kearns, Adam Dunn, Barry Larkin	
	Jim Edmonds, Scott Rolen, J.D. Drew	15.00
	Chipper Jones, Andruw Jones, Greg Maddux	20.00
	Chipper Jones, Andruw Jones, Greg Maddux	20.00
	Barry Zito, Miguel Tejada, Mark Mulder	10.00
	Alex Rodriguez, Mark Teixeira, Rafael Palmeiro	20.00

Rare Finds Triple Swatch

		NM/M
Production 50 Sets		
Golds:		No Pricing
Production 5 Sets		
	Jason Giambi, Roger Clemens, Derek Jeter	50.00
	Randy Johnson, Curt Schilling, Brandon Webb	25.00
	Nomar Garciaparra, Pedro J. Martinez, Manny Ramirez	60.00
	Mark Prior, Kerry Wood, Sammy Sosa	40.00
	Jeff Bagwell, Craig Biggio, Lance Berkman	20.00
	Austin Kearns, Adam Dunn, Barry Larkin	20.00
	Jim Edmonds, Scott Rolen, J.D. Drew	25.00
	Chipper Jones, Andruw Jones, Greg Maddux	40.00
	Barry Zito, Miguel Tejada, Mark Mulder	15.00
	Alex Rodriguez, Mark Teixeira, Rafael Palmeiro	40.00

Secret Weapons

		NM/M
Complete Set (10):		25.00
Common Player:		2.00
Production 250 Sets		
Golds:		1X
#'d to career batting average		
1	Hank Blalock	3.00
2	Dontrelle Willis	3.00
3	Jose Reyes	4.00
4	Bo Hart	3.00
5	Corey Patterson	2.00
6	Hideki Matsui	8.00
7	Mark Teixeira	3.00
8	Brandon Webb	3.00
9	Rocco Baldelli	3.00
10	Mark Prior	5.00

Shining Stars

		NM/M
Complete Set (15):		50.00
Common Player:		2.00
Production 300 Sets		
1SS	Derek Jeter	8.00
2SS	Barry Bonds	8.00
3SS	Nomar Garciaparra	6.00

4SS	Austin Kearns	2.00
5SS	Vladimir Guerrero	3.00
6SS	Jim Thome	3.00
7SS	Ichiro Suzuki	5.00
8SS	Jason Giambi	3.00
9SS	Albert Pujols	6.00
10SS	Ken Griffey Jr.	5.00
11SS	Chipper Jones	5.00
12SS	Scott Rolen	3.00
13SS	Manny Ramirez	3.00
14SS	Jeff Bagwell	3.00
15SS	Torii Hunter	2.00

Shining Stars Game-Used

		NM/M
Common Player:		6.00
Production 100 Sets		
Patch:		1.5X
Production 50 Sets		
JB	Jeff Bagwell	8.00
CD	Carlos Delgado	6.00
NG	Nomar Garciaparra	15.00
JG	Jason Giambi	8.00
TH	Todd Helton	8.00
TH	Torii Hunter	8.00
DJ	Derek Jeter	20.00
AJ	Andruw Jones	6.00
CJ	Chipper Jones	10.00
AK	Austin Kearns	6.00
AP	Albert Pujols	15.00
MR	Manny Ramirez	8.00
SR	Scott Rolen	10.00
JT	Jim Thome	8.00

Shining Stars Gold

		NM/M
Numbered to career HR total.		
1SS	Derek Jeter/127	10.00
2SS	Barry Bonds/658	5.00
3SS	Nomar Garciaparra/173	10.00
4SS	Austin Kearns/28	10.00
5SS	Vladimir Guerrero/234	4.00
6SS	Jim Thome/381	3.00
7SS	Ichiro Suzuki/29	30.00
8SS	Jason Giambi/269	3.00
9SS	Albert Pujols/114	8.00
10SS	Ken Griffey Jr./481	4.00
11SS	Chipper Jones/280	5.00
12SS	Scott Rolen/192	4.00
13SS	Manny Ramirez/347	3.00
14SS	Jeff Bagwell/419	3.00
15SS	Torii Hunter/96	4.00

2003 Fleer Patchworks

	NM/M
Complete Set (115):	
Common Player:	.15

Common Prospect (91-115): 3.00
Production 1,500
Pack (5): 3.00
Box (24): 50.00

1	Luis Castillo	.15
2	Derek Jeter	2.00
3	Vladimir Guerrero	.75
4	Bobby Higginson	.15
5	Pat Burrell	.40
6	Ivan Rodriguez	.60
7	Craig Biggio	.15
8	Troy Glaus	.60
9	Barry Bonds	2.00
10	Hideo Nomo	.60
11	Barry Larkin	.15
12	Roberto Alomar	.35
13	Rodrigo Lopez	.15
14	Eric Chavez	.25
15	Shawn Green	.25
16	Joe Randa	.15
17	Mark Grace	.25
18	Jason Kendall	.15
19	Hee Seop Choi	.15
20	Luis Gonzalez	.25
21	Sammy Sosa	1.25
22	Larry Walker	.15
23	Phil Nevin	.15
24	Manny Ramirez	.75
25	Jim Thome	.15
26	Randy Johnson	.75
27	Jose Vidro	.15
28	Austin Kearns	.35
29	Mike Sweeney	.15
30	Magglio Ordonez	.15
31	Mike Piazza	1.25
32	Eric Hinske	.15
33	Alex Rodriguez	1.50
34	Kerry Wood	.60
35	Matt Morris	.15
36	Lance Berkman	.15
37	Michael Cuddyer	.15
38	Curt Schilling	.40
39	Sean Burroughs	.15
40	Ken Griffey Jr.	1.25
41	Edgardo Alfonzo	.15
42	Carlos Pena	.15
43	Adam Dunn	.50
44	Pedro J. Martinez	.75
45	Miguel Tejada	.35
46	Tom Glavine	.35
47	Torii Hunter	.15
48	Jason Giambi	.50
49	Tony Batista	.15
50	Ben Grieve	.15
51	Ichiro Suzuki	1.25
52	Bobby Abreu	.15
53	Todd Helton	.75
54	Kazuhiro Sasaki	.15
55	Nomar Garciaparra	1.25
56	Francisco Rodriguez	.15
57	Ellis Burks	.15
58	Frank Thomas	.75
59	Greg Maddux	1.00
60	Josh Beckett	.25
61	Brad Wilkerson	.15
62	Joe Borchard	.15
63	Carlos Delgado	.40
64	Alfonso Soriano	.75
65	Chipper Jones	1.00
66	J.D. Drew	.25
67	Mark Prior	.75
68	Rafael Palmeiro	.60
69	Jeff Kent	.15
70	Adrian Beltre	.25
71	Marlon Byrd	.15
72	Orlando Hudson	.15
73	Junior Spivey	.15
74	Jeff Bagwell	.75
75	Barry Zito	.35
76	Roger Clemens	1.00
77	Aubrey Huff	.15
78	Geoff Jenkins	.15
79	Andruw Jones	.75
80	Scott Rolen	.75
81	Omar Vizquel	.15
82	Darin Erstad	.50
83	Bernie Williams	.35
84	Freddy Garcia	.15
85	Richie Sexson	.15
86	Josh Phelps	.15
87	Albert Pujols	1.50
88	Aramis Ramirez	.15
89	Shea Hillenbrand	.15
90	Cristian Guzman	.15
91	Adam LaRoche RC	3.00
92	David Pember RC	3.00
93	Terrmel Sledge RC	3.00
94	Hideki Matsui RC	10.00
95	Nook Logan RC	4.00
96	Jose Contreras RC	4.00
97	Pete LaForest RC	3.00
98	Richard Fischer RC	3.00
99	Francisco Rosario RC	3.00
100	Josh Willingham RC	4.00

101	Alejandro Machado RC	3.00
102	Lew Ford RC	4.00
103	Joe Valentine RC	3.00
104	Guillermo Quiroz RC	4.00
105	Chien-Ming Wang RC	20.00
106	Jhonny Peralta	4.00
107	Shane Victorino RC	3.00
108	Prentice Redman RC	3.00
109	Matt Bruback RC	3.00
110	Lance Niekro	3.00
111	Travis Hughes	3.00
112	Nic Jackson	3.00
113	Hector Luna RC	4.00
114	Cliff Lee RC	3.00
115	Tim Olson RC	4.00

Star Ruby

Stars (1-90): 4-8X
Prospects (91-115): 1-3X
Production 100 Sets

Diamond Ink

NM/M

Quantity signed listed
Derek Jeter/210	90.00
Derek Jeter/101	125.00
Derek Jeter/50	175.00
Mark Prior/88	40.00
Troy Glaus/351	25.00
Mike Schmidt/194	75.00

Licensed Apparel - Jersey

NM/M

Common Player:	4.00

Production 500 Sets
J.D. Drew	8.00
Magglio Ordonez	6.00
Todd Helton	8.00
Paul Konerko	4.00
Shawn Green	6.00
Carlos Beltran	4.00
Kevin Brown	4.00
Shannon Stewart	4.00
Mike Mussina	8.00
Adam Dunn	10.00
Jimmy Rollins	4.00
Darin Erstad	6.00
Chipper Jones	10.00
Mike Piazza	10.00
Derek Jeter	20.00

Licensed Apparel - Patch

NM/M

Common Player:	10.00

Production 300 Sets
J.D. Drew	12.00
Magglio Ordonez	15.00
Todd Helton	20.00
Paul Konerko	10.00
Shawn Green	15.00
Carlos Beltran	10.00
Kevin Brown	10.00
Shannon Stewart	10.00
Mike Mussina	15.00
Adam Dunn	20.00
Jimmy Rollins	15.00
Darin Erstad	25.00
Chipper Jones	20.00
Mike Piazza	25.00
Derek Jeter	40.00

National Pastime

NM/M

Complete Set (25):		40.00
Common Player:		1.00

Inserted 1:12
1NP	Barry Bonds	6.00
2NP	Kazuhiro Sasaki	1.00
3NP	Mike Piazza	4.00
4NP	Barry Zito	1.50
5NP	Sammy Sosa	3.00
6NP	Pedro J. Martinez	2.00
7NP	Craig Biggio	1.00
8NP	Rafael Palmeiro	1.50
9NP	Greg Maddux	3.00
10NP	Manny Ramirez	2.00
11NP	Adam Dunn	1.50
12NP	Omar Vizquel	1.00
13NP	Hideo Nomo	1.00
14NP	Alex Rodriguez	5.00
15NP	Pat Burrell	1.00
16NP	Nomar Garciaparra	4.00
17NP	Randy Johnson	2.00
18NP	Juan Gonzalez	1.50
19NP	Chipper Jones	3.00
20NP	Frank Thomas	1.50
21NP	Vladimir Guerrero	2.00
22NP	Troy Glaus	2.00
23NP	Albert Pujols	3.00
24NP	Ichiro Suzuki	3.00
25NP	Ken Griffey Jr.	3.00

National Patchtime - Trim

NM/M

Common Player:	12.00

Production 200 Sets
Vladimir Guerrero	12.00
Manny Ramirez	15.00
Rafael Palmeiro	12.00
Nomar Garciaparra	25.00
Greg Maddux	20.00
Mike Piazza	20.00
Pedro J. Martinez	20.00
Hideo Nomo	20.00
Alex Rodriguez	25.00
Chipper Jones	20.00
Frank Thomas	20.00

National Patchtime - Number

NM/M

Common Player:	15.00

Production 75 Sets
Vladimir Guerrero	20.00
Manny Ramirez	25.00
Craig Biggio	15.00
Rafael Palmeiro	20.00
Nomar Garciaparra	40.00
Greg Maddux	25.00
Sammy Sosa	45.00
Mike Piazza	30.00
Pedro J. Martinez	25.00
Hideo Nomo	30.00
Alex Rodriguez	30.00
Pat Burrell	20.00
Randy Johnson	45.00
Chipper Jones	35.00
Frank Thomas	30.00

National Patchtime - Team Name

NM/M

Common Player:	15.00

Production 100 Sets
Vladimir Guerrero	15.00
Rafael Palmeiro	20.00
Nomar Garciaparra	35.00
Sammy Sosa	40.00
Mike Piazza	30.00
Barry Zito	20.00
Hideo Nomo	30.00
Alex Rodriguez	30.00
Pat Burrell	20.00
Randy Johnson	45.00
Chipper Jones	35.00
Troy Glaus	30.00
Omar Vizquel	20.00

National Patchtime - Nameplate

NM/M

Production 50 Sets
Vladimir Guerrero	40.00
Rafael Palmeiro	25.00
Nomar Garciaparra	40.00
Greg Maddux	30.00
Sammy Sosa	60.00
Mike Piazza	35.00
Barry Zito	40.00
Hideo Nomo	50.00
Alex Rodriguez	50.00
Pat Burrell	25.00
Randy Johnson	50.00
Chipper Jones	35.00
Frank Thomas	40.00
Troy Glaus	30.00

National Patchtime - Commemorative

Production 25 Sets: No Pricing

National Pastime - MLB Logo

Production One Set

Numbers Game

NM/M

Complete Set (15):		30.00
Common Player:		1.00

Inserted 1:24
1	Ichiro Suzuki	3.00
2	Derek Jeter	6.00
3	Alex Rodriguez	5.00
4	Miguel Tejada	1.00
5	Nomar Garciaparra	4.00
6	Jason Giambi	3.00
7	J.D. Drew	1.00
8	Barry Bonds	6.00
9	Alfonso Soriano	2.00
10	Jeff Bagwell	1.50
11	Barry Larkin	1.00
12	Roberto Alomar	1.00
13	Larry Walker	1.00
14	Roger Clemens	3.00
15	Ken Griffey Jr.	3.00

Numbers Game - Jersey

NM/M

Common Player:	4.00

Inserted 1:25
Barry Larkin	6.00
Roberto Alomar	4.00
Jeff Bagwell	8.00
Jason Giambi	8.00
Larry Walker	4.00
Derek Jeter	15.00
Alex Rodriguez	10.00
Alfonso Soriano	10.00
Roger Clemens	12.00
Miguel Tejada	4.00

Numbers Game - Patch

NM/M

Common Player:	10.00

Production 300 Sets
Barry Larkin	15.00
Roberto Alomar	15.00
Jeff Bagwell	25.00
Jason Giambi	15.00
Larry Walker	10.00
Derek Jeter	40.00
Alex Rodriguez	25.00
Alfonso Soriano	25.00
Roger Clemens	30.00
Miguel Tejada	10.00

Patchworks

NM/M

Common Player:		8.00

Production 250 Sets
2	Frank Thomas	12.00
8	Lance Berkman	15.00
9	Kazuhiro Sasaki	15.00
10	Roy Oswalt	15.00
11	Bernie Williams	15.00
12PW	Bob Abreu	15.00
14PW	Greg Maddux	20.00
15PW	Josh Beckett	8.00
16PW	Mark Grace	20.00
17PW	Eric Chavez	10.00
18PW	Andruw Jones	15.00
19PW	Adrian Beltre	8.00

Patchworks - Dual Color

	NM/M
Common Player:	10.00
Production 100 Sets	
Alex Rodriguez	35.00
Frank Thomas	20.00
Vladimir Guerrero	20.00
Roberto Alomar	20.00
Kerry Wood	35.00
Curt Schilling	15.00
Lance Berkman	20.00
Kazuhiro Sasaki	35.00
Roy Oswalt	20.00
Bernie Williams	25.00
Bob Abreu	10.00
Carlos Delgado	12.00
Greg Maddux	25.00
Josh Beckett	10.00
Mark Grace	15.00
Eric Chavez	15.00
Andruw Jones	15.00
Adrian Beltre	10.00

Patchworks - Multi-Color

	NM/M
Common Player:	20.00
Production 50 Sets	
Alex Rodriguez	60.00
Frank Thomas	30.00
Vladimir Guerrero	35.00
Roberto Alomar	35.00
Kerry Wood	40.00
Curt Schilling	20.00
Lance Berkman	25.00
Kazuhiro Sasaki	50.00
Roy Oswalt	40.00
Bernie Williams	35.00
Bob Abreu	25.00
Carlos Delgado	20.00
Greg Maddux	35.00
Josh Beckett	20.00
Mark Grace	30.00
Eric Chavez	30.00
Andruw Jones	30.00
Adrian Beltre	20.00

Past, Present, Future

	NM/M
Complete Set (10):	40.00
Common Card:	4.00
Inserted 1:72	
1 Eddie Mathews, Rafael Palmeiro, Alex Rodriguez	5.00
2 Phil Rizzuto, Derek Jeter, Alfonso Soriano	5.00
3 Reggie Jackson, Barry Bonds, Sammy Sosa	6.00
4 Billy Williams, Sammy Sosa, Hee Seop Choi	4.00
5 Joe Morgan, Roberto Alomar, Alfonso Soriano	3.00
6 Yogi Berra, Mike Piazza, Josh Phelps	4.00
7 Nolan Ryan, Roger Clemens, Kerry Wood	6.00
8 Mike Schmidt, Scott Rolen, Eric Hinske	4.00
9 Barry Bonds, Alex Rodriguez, Alfonso Soriano	5.00
10 Yogi Berra, Derek Jeter, Hideki Matsui	6.00

Patch, Present, Future Single

	NM/M
Common Player:	10.00
Production 200 Sets	
Rafael Palmeiro	15.00
Alex Rodriguez	20.00
Derek Jeter	50.00
Alfonso Soriano	50.00

Barry Bonds	50.00
Sammy Sosa	25.00
Sammy Sosa	25.00
Roberto Alomar	25.00
Alfonso Soriano	50.00
Mike Piazza	25.00
Roger Clemens	40.00
Kerry Wood	40.00
Eric Hinske	10.00
Alex Rodriguez	20.00
Alfonso Soriano	50.00
Derek Jeter	50.00

Patch, Present, Future Dual

Production 100 Sets

2003 Fleer Platinum

LANCE BERKMAN
OUTFIELD
ASTROS

	NM/M
Complete Set (250):	40.00
Common Player:	.15
Common SP (221-250):	.50
Hobby Pack (10):	1.50
Hobby Box (14 + 4 jumbo + 1 Rack):	35.00
Jumbo Pack:	3.00
Rack Pack:	5.00
1 Barry Bonds	2.50
2 Sean Casey	.25
3 Todd Walker	.15
4 Tony Batista	.15
5 Todd Zeile	.15
6 Ruben Sierra	.15
7 Jose Cruz Jr.	.15
8 Ben Grieve	.15
9 Robert Mackowiak	.15
10 Gary Sheffield	.25
11 Armando Benitez	.15
12 Tim Hudson	.25
13 Eric Milton	.15
14 Andy Pettitte	.40
15 Jeff Bagwell	.75
16 Jeff Kent	.15
17 Joe Randa	.15
18 Benito Santiago	.15
19 Russell Branyan	.15
20 Cliff Floyd	.15
21 Chris Richard	.15
22 Randy Winn	.15
23 Freddy Garcia	.15
24 Derek Lowe	.15
25 Ben Sheets	.15
26 Fred McGriff	.15
27 Bret Boone	.15
28 Jose Hernandez	.15
29 Phil Nevin	.15
30 Mike Piazza	1.50
31 Bobby Abreu	.15
32 Darin Erstad	.50
33 Andruw Jones	.75
34 Brad Wilkerson	.15
35 Brian Lawrence	.15
36 Vladimir Nunez	.15
37 Kazuhiro Sasaki	.15
38 Carlos Delgado	.45
39 Steve Cox	.15
40 Adrian Beltre	.25
41 Josh Bard	.15
42 Randall Simon	.15
43 Johnny Damon	.25
44 Ken Griffey Jr.	1.50
45 Sammy Sosa	1.50
46 Kevin Brown	.15
47 Kazuhisa Ishii	.15
48 Matt Morris	.15
49 Mark Prior	.75
50 Kip Wells	.15
51 Hee Seop Choi	.15
52 Craig Biggio	.15
53 Derek Jeter	2.50
54 Albert Pujols	1.25
55 Joe Borchard	.15

56 Robert Fick	.15
57 Jacque Jones	.15
58 Juan Pierre	.15
59 Bernie Williams	.35
60 Elmer Dessens	.15
61 Al Leiter	.15
62 Curt Schilling	.40
63 Carlos Pena	.15
64 Tino Martinez	.15
65 Fernando Vina	.15
66 Aaron Boone	.15
67 Michael Barrett	.15
68 Frank Thomas	.75
69 J.D. Drew	.25
70 Vladimir Guerrero	.75
71 Shannon Stewart	.15
72 Mark Buehrle	.15
73 Jamie Moyer	.15
74 Brad Radke	.15
75 Mike Williams	.15
76 Ryan Klesko	.15
77 Roberto Alomar	.35
78 Edgardo Alfonzo	.15
79 Matt Williams	.15
80 Edgar Martinez	.15
81 Shawn Green	.15
82 Kenny Lofton	.15
83 Josh Beckett	.15
84 Trevor Hoffman	.15
85 Kevin Millwood	.15
86 Odalis Perez	.15
87 Jarrod Washburn	.15
88 Jason Giambi	.60
89 Eric Young	.15
90 Barry Larkin	.15
91 Aramis Ramirez	.15
92 Ivan Rodriguez	.50
93 Steve Finley	.15
94 Brian Jordan	.15
95 Manny Ramirez	.75
96 Preston Wilson	.15
97 Rodrigo Lopez	.15
98 Ramon Ortiz	.15
99 Jim Thome	.15
100 Luis Castillo	.15
101 Alex Rodriguez	2.00
102 Jared Sandberg	.15
103 Ellis Burks	.15
104 Pat Burrell	.60
105 Brian Giles	.15
106 Mark Kotsay	.15
107 Dave Roberts	.15
108 Roy Halladay	.15
109 Chan Ho Park	.15
110 Erubiel Durazo	.15
111 Bobby Hill	.15
112 Cristian Guzman	.15
113 Troy Glaus	.60
114 Lance Berkman	.15
115 Juan Encarnacion	.15
116 Chipper Jones	1.00
117 Corey Patterson	.15
118 Vernon Wells	.15
119 Matt Clement	.15
120 Billy Koch	.15
121 Hideo Nomo	.50
122 Derrek Lee	.15
123 Todd Helton	.75
124 Sean Burroughs	.15
125 Jason Kendall	.15
126 Dmitri Young	.15
127 Adam Dunn	.60
128 Bobby Higginson	.15
129 Raul Mondesi	.15
130 Bubba Trammell	.15
131 A.J. Burnett	.15
132 Randy Johnson	.75
133 Mark Mulder	.15
134 Mariano Rivera	.25
135 Kerry Wood	.50
136 Mo Vaughn	.15
137 Jimmy Rollins	.25
138 Jose Valentin	.15
139 Brad Fullmer	.15
140 Mike Cameron	.15
141 Luis Gonzalez	.25
142 Kevin Appier	.15
143 Mike Hampton	.15
144 Pedro J. Martinez	.75
145 Javier Vazquez	.15
146 Doug Mientkiewicz	.15
147 Adam Kennedy	.15
148 Rafael Furcal	.15
149 Eric Chavez	.25
150 Mike Lieberthal	.15
151 Moises Alou	.15
152 Jermaine Dye	.15
153 Torii Hunter	.15
154 Trot Nixon	.15
155 Larry Walker	.15
156 Jorge Julio	.15
157 Mike Mussina	.40
158 Kirk Rueter	.15
159 Rafael Palmeiro	.65

160 Pokey Reese	.15
161 Miguel Tejada	.35
162 Robin Ventura	.15
163 Raul Ibanez	.15
164 Roger Cedeno	.15
165 Juan Gonzalez	.65
166 Carlos Lee	.15
167 Tim Salmon	.25
168 Orlando Hernandez	.15
169 Wade Miller	.15
170 Troy Percival	.15
171 Billy Wagner	.15
172 Jeff Conine	.15
173 Junior Spivey	.15
174 Edgar Renteria	.15
175 Scott Rolen	.65
176 Jason Varitek	.15
177 Ben Broussard	.15
178 Jeremy Giambi	.15
179 Gabe Kapler	.15
180 Armando Rios	.15
181 Ichiro Suzuki	2.00
182 Tom Glavine	.35
183 Greg Maddux	1.00
184 Roy Oswalt	.25
185 John Smoltz	.15
186 Eric Karros	.15
187 Alfonso Soriano	.75
188 Nomar Garciaparra	1.50
189 Joe Crede	.15
190 Javy Lopez	.15
191 Carlos Beltran	.50
192 Jim Edmonds	.15
193 Geoff Jenkins	.15
194 Magglio Ordonez	.25
195 Daryle Ward	.15
196 Roger Clemens	1.25
197 Byung-Hyun Kim	.15
198 Robb Nen	.15
199 C.C. Sabathia	.15
200 Barry Zito	.35
201 Mark Grace	.25
202 Paul Konerko	.25
203 Mike Sweeney	.15
204 John Olerud	.15
205 Jose Vidro	.15
206 Ray Durham	.15
207 Omar Vizquel	.15
208 Shea Hillenbrand	.15
209 Mike Lowell	.15
210 Aubrey Huff	.15
211 Eric Hinske	.15
212 Paul LoDuca	.15
213 Jay Gibbons	.15
214 Austin Kearns	.50
215 Richie Sexson	.15
216 Garret Anderson	.15
217 Eric Gagne	.15
218 Jason Jennings	.15
219 Damian Moss	.15
220 David Eckstein	.15
221 Mark Teixeira	1.00
222 Bill Hall	.50
223 Bobby Jenks	.75
224 Adam Morrisey	.50
225 Rodrigo Rosario	.50
226 Brett Myers	.75
227 Tony Alvarez	.50
228 Willie Bloomquist	2.00
229 Ben Howard	.50
230 Nic Jackson	.50
231 Carl Crawford	.50
232 Omar Infante	.50
233 Francisco Rodriguez	1.00
234 Andy Van Hekken	.50
235 Kirk Saarloos	.50
236 Dusty Wathan RC	.75
237 Jamey Carroll	1.50
238 Jason L. Phillips	1.50
239 Jose Castillo	4.00
240 Arnaldo Munoz RC	2.00
241 Orlando Hudson	.50
242 Drew Henson	.75
243 Jason Lane	.75
244 Vinnie Chulk	1.50
245 Prentice Redman RC	2.00
246 Marlon Byrd	1.00
247 Chin-Feng Chen	1.00
248 Craig Brazell RC	2.00
249 John Webb	1.50
250 Adam LaRoche	1.00

Platinum Finish

Stars (1-220):	5-10X
SP (221-250):	2-4X
Production 100 Sets	

Barry Bonds Chasing History

NM/M
Production 250 Sets
Five Player card #'d to 25.

Barry Bonds, Bobby Bonds, Barry Bonds, Roger Maris	35.00
	40.00
Barry Bonds, Willie McCovey	35.00
Barry Bonds, Babe Ruth	200.00
Barry Bonds	35.00
Barry Bonds, Babe Ruth, Roger Maris, Willie McCovey, Bobby Bonds	200.00

Guts and Glory

		NM/M
Complete Set (20):		12.00
Common Player:		.40
Inserted 1:4		
1GG	Jason Giambi	1.00
2GG	Alfonso Soriano	.75
3GG	Scott Rolen	.50
4GG	Ivan Rodriguez	.50
5GG	Barry Bonds	1.50
6GG	Jim Edmonds	.40
7GG	Darin Erstad	.40
8GG	Brian Giles	.40
9GG	Luis Gonzalez	.40
10GG	Adam Dunn	.50
11GG	Torii Hunter	.40
12GG	Andruw Jones	.40
13GG	Sammy Sosa	1.00
14GG	Ichiro Suzuki	1.50
15GG	Miguel Tejada	.40
16GG	Roger Clemens	1.00
17GG	Curt Schilling	.40
18GG	Nomar Garciaparra	1.50
19GG	Derek Jeter	2.00
20GG	Alex Rodriguez	1.50

Heart of the Order

		NM/M
Complete Set (20):		20.00
Common Card:		.75
Inserted 1:12		
1	Jason Giambi, Derek Jeter, Alfonso Soriano	3.00
2	Todd Helton, Preston Wilson, Larry Walker	.75
3	Rafael Palmeiro, Alex Rodriguez, Ivan Rodriguez	3.00

4	Adam Dunn, Ken Griffey Jr., Austin Kearns	3.00
5	Jeff Bagwell, Craig Biggio, Lance Berkman	1.00
6	Eric Chavez, Miguel Tejada, Jermaine Dye	.75
7	Troy Glaus, Garret Anderson, Darin Erstad	1.00
8	Mike Piazza, Mo Vaughn, Roberto Alomar	2.50
9	Torii Hunter, Jacque Jones, Corey Koskie	.75
10	Barry Bonds, Jeff Kent, Rich Aurilia	3.00
11	Pat Burrell, Bobby Abreu, Jimmy Rollins	1.50
12	Shawn Green, Adrian Beltre, Paul LoDuca	.75
13	Vladimir Guerrero, Brad Wilkerson, Jose Vidro	1.50
14	Chipper Jones, Andruw Jones, Gary Sheffield	2.00
15	Ichiro Suzuki, Bret Boone, Edgar Martinez	2.50
16	Albert Pujols, Scott Rolen, J.D. Drew	2.00
17	Sammy Sosa, Fred McGriff, Moises Alou	2.00
18	Nomar Garciaparra, Shea Hillenbrand, Manny Ramirez	2.50
19	Frank Thomas, Magglio Ordonez, Paul Konerko	1.00
20	Jason Kendall, Brian Giles, Aramis Ramirez	.75

Heart of the Order Memorabilia

	NM/M
Common Card:	5.00
Production 400 Sets	
Jason Giambi, Derek Jeter, Alfonso Soriano/Bat	15.00
Todd Helton/Jsy, Preston Wilson, Larry Walker	8.00
Rafael Palmeiro/Jsy, Alex Rodriguez, Ivan Rodriguez	6.00
Adam Dunn, Ken Griffey Jr., Austin Kearns/Pants	12.00
Troy Glaus, Garrett Anderson, Darin Erstad/Jsy	8.00
Mike Piazza/Jsy, Mo Vaughn, Roberto Alomar	10.00
Barry Bonds, Jeff Kent/Jsy, Rich Aurilia	6.00
Pat Burrell, Bobby Abreu, Jimmy Rollins/Jsy	6.00
Shawn Green, Adrian Beltre/Jsy, Paul LoDuca	5.00
Vladimir Guerrero, Brad Wilkerson, Jose Vidro/Jsy	5.00
Chipper Jones/Jsy, Andruw Jones, Gary Sheffield	10.00
Ichiro Suzuki, Bret Boone/Jsy, Edgar Martinez	5.00
Albert Pujols/Jsy, Scott Rolen, J.D. Drew/Jsy	8.00
Sammy Sosa/Jsy, Fred McGriff, Moises Alou	12.00
Nomar Garciaparra, Shea Hillenbrand, Manny Ramirez/Jsy	8.00
Frank Thomas, Magglio Ordonez/Jsy, Paul Konerko	5.00
Jason Kendall, Brian Giles/Bat, Aramis Ramirez	5.00

MLB Scouting Report

		NM/M
Complete Set (32):		55.00
Common Player:		1.00
Production 400 Sets		
1	Jason Giambi	3.00
2	Paul Konerko	1.00

3	Jim Thome	1.50
4	Alfonso Soriano	2.00
5	Troy Glaus	1.50
6	Eric Hinske	1.00
7	Paul LoDuca	1.00
8	Mike Piazza	4.00
9	Marlon Byrd	1.00
10	Garrett Anderson	1.00
11	Barry Bonds	5.00
12	Pat Burrell	1.50
13	Joe Crede	1.00
14	J.D. Drew	1.00
15	Ken Griffey Jr.	4.00
16	Vladimir Guerrero	2.00
17	Torii Hunter	1.00
18	Chipper Jones	3.00
19	Austin Kearns	1.00
20	Albert Pujols	2.00
21	Manny Ramirez	1.50
22	Gary Sheffield	1.00
23	Sammy Sosa	3.00
24	Ichiro Suzuki	4.00
25	Bernie Williams	1.25
26	Randy Johnson	2.00
27	Greg Maddux	3.00
28	Hideo Nomo	1.00
29	Nomar Garciaparra	4.00
30	Derek Jeter	6.00
31	Alex Rodriguez	5.00
32	Miguel Tejada	1.00

MLB Scouting Report Game-Used

		NM/M
Common Player:		6.00
Production 250 Sets		
3	Jim Thome/Jsy	10.00
4	Alfonso Soriano/Bat	10.00
8	Mike Piazza/Jsy	15.00
11	Barry Bonds/Jsy	20.00
13	J.D. Drew/Jsy	6.00
18	Chipper Jones/Jsy	10.00
19	Austin Kearns/Pants	10.00
21	Manny Ramirez/Jsy	8.00
23	Sammy Sosa/Jsy	15.00
26	Randy Johnson/Jsy	10.00
27	Greg Maddux/Jsy	10.00
28	Hideo Nomo/Jsy	20.00
30	Derek Jeter/Jsy	20.00

Nameplates

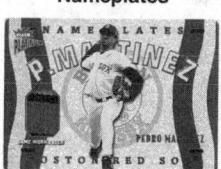

NM/M

Common Player:	
Jumbo Pack Exclusive	
Barry Larkin/97	30.00
Kazuhiro Sasaki/82	20.00
Greg Maddux/248	25.00
Craig Biggio/152	25.00
Pedro J. Martinez/244	35.00
Barry Zito/248	25.00
Nomar Garciaparra/258	40.00
Rickey Henderson	
John Olerud/180	25.00
Ivan Rodriguez/189	20.00
Jeff Bagwell/121	45.00
Chipper Jones/251	40.00
Adrian Beltre	
Johnny Damon	
Robin Ventura	
Frank Thomas/58	45.00
Roger Clemens/141	40.00
Mike Piazza/200	35.00
Mark Prior/123	25.00
Kazuhisa Ishii	
Manny Ramirez/94	30.00
Kerry Wood/49	45.00
Rafael Palmeiro/245	20.00
Jimmy Rollins/74	20.00
Barry Bonds/251	50.00
Adam Dunn/117	25.00
Alex Rodriguez/248	40.00
Miguel Tejada/225	20.00
Chin-Feng Chen/110	100.00

Portraits

	NM/M
Complete Set (20):	25.00
Common Player:	.75

		NM/M
Inserted 1:20		
1	Josh Beckett	.75
2	Roberto Alomar	1.00
3	Alfonso Soriano	2.00
4	Mike Piazza	3.00
5	Ivan Rodriguez	1.00
6	Edgar Martinez	.75
7	Barry Bonds	4.00
8	Adam Dunn	1.25
9	Juan Gonzalez	1.00
10	Chipper Jones	2.50
11	Albert Pujols	1.50
12	Magglio Ordonez	.75
13	Shea Hillenbrand	.75
14	Larry Walker	.75
15	Pedro J. Martinez	1.50
16	Kerry Wood	1.00
17	Barry Zito	1.00
18	Nomar Garciaparra	3.00
19	Derek Jeter	5.00
20	Alex Rodriguez	4.00

Portraits Game Jersey

		NM/M
Common Player:		5.00
Inserted 1:86		
4	Mike Piazza	10.00
5	Ivan Rodriguez	6.00
7	Barry Bonds	15.00
8	Adam Dunn	8.00
10	Chipper Jones	8.00
15	Pedro J. Martinez	8.00
16	Kerry Wood	8.00
17	Barry Zito	5.00
18	Nomar Garciaparra	10.00
19	Derek Jeter/SP/150	25.00

Portraits Game Patch

		NM/M
Common Player:		25.00
Production 100 Sets		
4	Mike Piazza	35.00
5	Ivan Rodriguez	25.00
7	Barry Bonds	40.00
8	Adam Dunn	25.00
10	Chipper Jones	25.00
15	Pedro J. Martinez	25.00
16	Kerry Wood	25.00
17	Barry Zito	25.00
18	Nomar Garciaparra	40.00
19	Derek Jeter	45.00

2003 Fleer Rookies and Greats

		NM/M
Complete Set (75):		30.00
Common Player:		.25
Pack (5):		6.00
Box (20):		100.00
1	Troy Glaus	.65
2	Gary Sheffield	.40

3	Sammy Sosa	2.00
4	Mark Prior	.75
5	Dontrelle Willis	.25
6	Shawn Green	.50
7	Vladimir Guerrero	.75
8	Jose Reyes	.50
9	Miguel Tejada	.40
10	Bret Boone	.25
11	Rocco Baldelli	.40
12	Rafael Palmeiro	.65
13	Ichiro Suzuki	1.50
14	Carlos Delgado	.50
15	Garret Anderson	.25
16	Richie Sexson	.25
17	Roger Clemens	1.75
18	Barry Zito	.40
19	Jim Thome	.25
20	Alex Rodriguez	2.50
21	Randy Johnson	.75
22	Chipper Jones	1.00
23	Kerry Wood	.60
24	Ken Griffey Jr.	1.50
25	Ivan Rodriguez	.60
26	Jeff Kent	.25
27	Todd Helton	.75
28	Jeff Bagwell	.75
29	Hideo Nomo	.60
30	Torii Hunter	.25
31	Brian Giles	.25
32	Albert Pujols	2.00
33	Vernon Wells	.25
34	Nomar Garciaparra	2.00
35	Magglio Ordonez	.25
36	C.C. Sabathia	.25
37	Preston Wilson	.25
38	Mike Sweeney	.25
39	Jose Vidro	.25
40	Jason Giambi	.60
41	Derek Jeter	3.00
42	Mike Piazza	1.50
43	Rich Harden	.25
44	Jason Kendall	.25
45	Barry Bonds	3.00
46	Barry Larkin	.25
47	Dmitri Young	.25
48	Craig Biggio	.25
49	Angel Berroa	.25
50	Alfonso Soriano	.75
51	Kevin Millwood	.25
52	Edgar Martinez	.25
53	Jim Edmonds	.25
54	Curt Schilling	.40
55	Jay Gibbons	.25
56	Pedro J. Martinez	.75
57	Greg Maddux	1.00
58	Manny Ramirez	.75
59	Frank Thomas	.75
60	Adam Dunn	.60
61	Babe Ruth	3.00
62	Bob Gibson	1.00
63	Willie Stargell	.75
64	Mike Schmidt	2.00
65	Nolan Ryan	3.00
66	Tom Seaver	1.00
67	Brooks Robinson	1.00
68	Willie McCovey	.50
69	Harmon Killebrew	1.00
70	Al Kaline	1.00
71	Reggie Jackson	1.00
72	Eddie Mathews	.75
73	Ralph Kiner	.25
74	Cal Ripken Jr.	3.00
75	Phil Rizzuto	.25

Ultra
Production 1,500

U-251	Chien-Ming Wang RC	8.00
U-252	Rickie Weeks RC	6.00
U-253	Brandon Webb RC	4.00
U-254	Hideki Matsui RC	8.00
U-255	Michael Hessman RC	2.00
U-256	Ryan Wagner RC	3.00
U-257	Matt Kata RC	3.00
U-258	Edwin Jackson RC	6.00
U-259	Jose Contreras RC	3.00
U-260	Delmon Young RC	8.00
U-261	Bo Hart RC	3.00
U-262	Jeff Duncan RC	3.00
U-263	Robby Hammock RC	2.00
U-264	Jeremy Bonderman	5.00
U-265	Clint Barmes RC	2.00

Showcase
Production 750

S-136	Chien-Ming Wang RC	12.00
S-137	Rickie Weeks RC	10.00
S-138	Brandon Webb RC	5.00
S-139	Hideki Matsui RC	10.00
S-140	Michael Hessman RC	4.00
S-141	Ryan Wagner RC	6.00
S-142	Bo Hart RC	5.00
S-143	Edwin Jackson RC	8.00
S-144	Jose Contreras RC	6.00
S-145	Delmon Young RC	10.00

Flair
Production 500

F-126	Jeff Duncan RC	6.00
F-127	Rickie Weeks RC	12.00
F-128	Brandon Webb RC	10.00
F-129	Robby Hammock RC	5.00
F-130	Jon Leicester RC	5.00
F-131	Ryan Wagner RC	8.00
F-132	Bo Hart RC	6.00
F-133	Edwin Jackson RC	10.00
F-134	Sergio Mitre RC	5.00
F-135	Delmon Young RC	15.00

Hot Prospects
Production 250

H-120	Josh Willingham RC	10.00
H-121	Rickie Weeks RC	15.00
H-122	Prentice Redman RC	8.00
H-123	Mike Ryan RC	8.00
H-124	Oscar Villarreal RC	8.00
H-125	Ryan Wagner RC	10.00
H-126	Bo Hart RC	10.00
H-127	Edwin Jackson RC	12.00

Authentix
Production 1,250

A-161	Chien-Ming Wang RC	10.00
A-162	Rickie Weeks RC	8.00
A-163	Brandon Webb RC	4.00
A-164	Craig Brazell RC	3.00
A-165	Michael Hessman RC	3.00
A-166	Ryan Wagner RC	5.00
A-167	Matt Kata RC	4.00
A-168	Edwin Jackson RC	4.00
A-169	Mike Ryan RC	3.00
A-170	Delmon Young RC	10.00
A-171	Bo Hart RC	4.00
A-172	Jeff Duncan RC	4.00
A-173	Robby Hammock RC	3.00
A-174	Jeremy Bonderman	5.00
A-175	Clint Barmes RC	3.00

Genuine
Production 1,000

G-131	Dan Haren	5.00
G-132	Rickie Weeks RC	8.00
G-133	Prentice Redman RC	4.00
G-134	Craig Brazell RC	4.00
G-135	Jon Leicester RC	4.00
G-136	Ryan Wagner RC	6.00
G-137	Matt Kata RC	4.00
G-138	Edwin Jackson RC	8.00
G-139	Mike Ryan RC	5.00
G-140	Delmon Young RC	10.00
G-141	Bo Hart RC	5.00
G-142	Jeff Duncan RC	5.00
G-143	Robby Hammock RC	4.00
G-144	Michael Hessman RC	4.00
G-145	Clint Barmes RC	4.00

Boyhood Idols

NM/M

Common Player: 5.00
Production 615 Sets

Carlton Fisk	8.00
Joe Carter	5.00
Cal Ripken Jr.	20.00
Mike Schmidt	15.00
Robin Yount	8.00
Joe Morgan	5.00
Jim Palmer	8.00
Harmon Killebrew	8.00
Brooks Robinson	8.00
Frank Howard	5.00
Bill "Moose" Skowron	5.00
Bucky Dent	5.00
Nolan Ryan	20.00
Don Mattingly	20.00

Boyhood Idols Autograph

NM/M

Production 50 unless noted.

Carlton Fisk	30.00
Brooks Robinson	35.00
Bucky Dent	20.00

Dynamic Debuts

NM/M

Complete Set (10): 10.00
Common Player: .50
Inserted 1:10

1DD	Rickie Weeks	4.00
2DD	Brandon Webb	1.00
3DD	Jose Reyes	1.00
4DD	Bo Hart	1.00
5DD	Dontrelle Willis	1.00
6DD	Rich Harden	.50
7DD	Ryan Wagner	.50
8DD	Rocco Baldelli	1.00
9DD	Mark Teixeira	1.00
10DD	Hideki Matsui	5.00

Dynamic Debuts Autograph

NM/M

Common Player: 10.00
Production 100

Rickie Weeks	25.00
Jose Reyes	35.00
Bo Hart	10.00
Dontrelle Willis	25.00
Ryan Wagner	10.00

Looming Large

NM/M

Complete Set (15): 30.00
Common Player: 1.50
Production 500 Sets
Uncommon: 1-2X
Production 150
Rare: No Pricing
Production 15

1LL	Chien-Ming Wang	4.00
2LL	Rickie Weeks	6.00
3LL	Brandon Webb	3.00
4LL	Hideki Matsui	6.00
5LL	Michael Hessman	1.50
6LL	Ryan Wagner	1.50
7LL	Matt Kata	1.50
8LL	Edwin Jackson	1.50
9LL	Jose Contreras	1.50
10LL	Delmon Young	6.00
11LL	Bo Hart	3.00
12LL	Jeff Duncan	1.50
13LL	Robby Hammock	1.50
14LL	Jeremy Bonderman	1.50
15LL	Clint Barmes	1.50

The Naturals

NM/M

Complete Set (25): 45.00
Common Player: .50
Inserted 1:5
Uncommons: 2-4X
Production 75 Sets

1	Cal Ripken Jr.	5.00
2	Mike Schmidt	3.00
3	Derek Jeter	5.00
4	Joe Carter	.50
5	Nomar Garciaparra	3.00
6	Frank Howard	.50
7	Al Kaline	2.00
8	Albert Pujols	4.00
9	Nolan Ryan	5.00
10	Duke Snider	1.50
11	Alex Rodriguez	4.00
12	Brooks Robinson	1.50
13	Roger Clemens	4.00
14	Sammy Sosa	3.00
15	Jim Palmer	1.00
16	Alfonso Soriano	2.00
17	Don Mattingly	3.00
18	Harmon Killebrew	1.50
19	Bob Feller	.50
20	Reggie Jackson	1.50
21	Ichiro Suzuki	2.50
22	Barry Bonds	5.00
23	Hideki Matsui	4.00
24	Willie Stargell	.50
25	Pee Wee Reese	.50

The Naturals Memorabilia

NM/M

Common Player: 5.00
Production 250 unless noted.

CR	Cal Ripken Jr.	30.00
MS	Mike Schmidt	15.00
DJ	Derek Jeter	20.00
JC	Joe Carter	5.00
NG	Nomar Garciaparra	15.00
FH	Frank Howard/400	5.00
AK	Al Kaline	15.00
AP	Albert Pujols	12.00
NR	Nolan Ryan/400	25.00
DS	Duke Snider	10.00
AR	Alex Rodriguez	10.00
BR	Brooks Robinson/400	10.00
RC	Roger Clemens/400	15.00
SS	Sammy Sosa	
JP	Jim Palmer	8.00
AS	Alfonso Soriano	8.00
DM	Don Mattingly	20.00
HK	Harmon Killebrew/400	10.00
BF	Bob Feller	
RJ	Reggie Jackson/400	10.00

The Naturals Autograph

NM/M

Common Player:
Production 50

Joe Carter	15.00
Bob Feller	25.00
Frank Howard	25.00
Al Kaline	40.00
Harmon Killebrew	35.00
Jim Palmer	15.00
Cal Ripken Jr.	140.00
Brooks Robinson	35.00
Nolan Ryan	100.00
Duke Snider	25.00

The Naturals Jersey Autograph

NM/M

Common Player:
Production 30

Joe Carter	25.00
Frank Howard	25.00
Al Kaline	60.00
Harmon Killebrew	50.00
Jim Palmer	25.00
Cal Ripken Jr.	150.00
Brooks Robinson	50.00
Nolan Ryan	120.00
Duke Snider	40.00

The Naturals Patch

No Pricing
Production 25
Patch Autos.: No Pricing
Production 5

Through the Years

NM/M

Common Duo: 10.00
Production 360
Patches: No Pricing
Production 25

Sammy Sosa, Mark Prior	20.00
Mark Prior, Jose Reyes	10.00
Nolan Ryan, Hank Blalock	25.00
Roger Clemens, Chien-Ming Wang	35.00
Jim Thome, Mike Schmidt	25.00
Alex Rodriguez, Mark Teixeira	25.00
Randy Johnson, Brandon Webb	15.00
Phil Rizzuto, Jose Reyes	15.00
Nomar Garciaparra, Bobby Doerr	20.00
Jason Giambi, Reggie Jackson	15.00
Derek Jeter, Phil Rizzuto	45.00
Barry Larkin, Joe Morgan	10.00
Harmon Killebrew, Torii Hunter	20.00
Willie McCovey, Barry Bonds	15.00
Bo Hart, Lou Brock	15.00
Jose Contreras, Mike Mussina	10.00
Michael Hessman, Chipper Jones	12.00
Steve Carlton, Kevin Millwood	12.00
Robin Yount, Scott Podsednik	20.00
Eddie Mathews, Chipper Jones	15.00

2003 Fleer Showcase

NM/M

Complete Set (135): 50.00
Common Player: .25
Common SP (106-135): 1.00

Inserted 1:4
Pack (5):		3.00
Box (24):		60.00
1	David Eckstein	.25
2	Curt Schilling	.75
3	Jay Gibbons	.25
4	Kerry Wood	.75
5	Jeff Bagwell	1.00
6	Hideo Nomo	.75
7	Tim Hudson	.40
8	J.D. Drew	.50
9	Josh Phelps	.25
10	Bartolo Colon	.25
11	Bobby Abreu	.25
12	Matt Morris	.25
13	Kazuhiro Sasaki	.25
14	Sean Burroughs	.25
15	Vicente Padilla	.25
16	Jorge Posada	.35
17	Torii Hunter	.25
18	Richie Sexson	.25
19	Lance Berkman	.25
20	Todd Helton	1.00
21	Paul Konerko	.25
22	Pedro J. Martinez	1.00
23	Rodrigo Lopez	.25
24	Gary Sheffield	.35
25	Darin Erstad	.50
26	Nomar Garciaparra	2.50
27	Adam Dunn	.75
28	Jason Giambi	.75
29	Miguel Tejada	.40
30	Chipper Jones	1.50
31	Alex Rodriguez	3.00
32	Barry Bonds	4.00
33	Roger Clemens	2.00
34	Sammy Sosa	2.50
35	Randy Johnson	1.00
36	Tim Salmon	.35
37	Shea Hillenbrand	.25
38	Larry Walker	.25
39	A.J. Burnett	.25
40	Shawn Green	.50
41	Cristian Guzman	.25
42	Bernie Williams	.35
43	Mark Mulder	.25
44	Brian Giles	.25
45	Bret Boone	.25
46	Juan Gonzalez	.75
47	Roy Halladay	.25
48	Wade Miller	.25
49	Jeff Kent	.25
50	Carlos Delgado	.50
51	Mike Lowell	.25
52	Jim Edmonds	.25
53	Ivan Rodriguez	.75
54	Aubrey Huff	.25
55	Ryan Klesko	.25
56	Paul LoDuca	.25
57	Roy Oswalt	.50
58	Omar Vizquel	.25
59	Manny Ramirez	1.00
60	Andruw Jones	1.00
61	Troy Glaus	1.00
62	Ichiro Suzuki	2.50
63	Albert Pujols	2.50
64	Derek Jeter	4.00
65	Mark Prior	1.00
66	Ken Griffey Jr.	2.50
67	Vladimir Guerrero	1.00
68	Mike Piazza	2.50
69	Alfonso Soriano	1.00
70	Greg Maddux	1.50
71	Adam Kennedy	.25
72	Junior Spivey	.25
73	Tom Glavine	.40
74	Derek Lowe	.25
75	Magglio Ordonez	.25
76	Jim Thome	.25
77	Robert Fick	.25
78	Josh Beckett	.25
79	Mike Sweeney	.25
80	Kazuhisa Ishii	.40
81	Roberto Alomar	.40
82	Barry Zito	.40
83	Pat Burrell	.65
84	Scott Rolen	1.00
85	John Olerud	.25
86	Eric Hinske	.25
87	Rafael Palmeiro	.75
88	Edgar Martinez	.40
89	Eric Chavez	.40
90	Jose Vidro	.25
91	Craig Biggio	.25
92	Rich Aurilia	.25
93	Austin Kearns	.75
94	Luis Gonzalez	.40
95	Garrett Anderson	.25
96	Yogi Berra	1.50
97	Al Kaline	1.50
98	Robin Yount	1.00
99	Reggie Jackson	1.00
100	Harmon Killebrew	1.50
101	Eddie Mathews	1.50
102	Willie McCovey	.50
103	Nolan Ryan	4.00
104	Mike Schmidt	2.50
105	Tom Seaver	1.00
106	Francisco Rodriguez	1.00
107	Carl Crawford	1.00
108	Ben Howard	1.00
109	Hank Blalock	2.00
110	Hee Seop Choi	2.00
111	Kirk Saarloos	1.00
112	Lew Ford RC	3.00
113	Andy Van Hekken	1.00
114	Drew Henson	1.50
115	Marlon Byrd	1.00
116	Jayson Werth	1.00
117	Willie Bloomquist	1.00
118	Joe Borchard	1.00
119	Mark Teixeira	2.00
120	Bobby Hill	1.00
121	Jason Lane	1.00
122	Omar Infante	1.00
123	Victor Martinez	1.50
124	Jorge Padilla	1.00
125	John Lackey	1.00
126	Anderson Machado	1.00
127	Rodrigo Rosario	1.00
128	Freddy Sanchez	1.00
129	Tony Alvarez	1.00
130	Matt Thornton	1.00
131	Joe Thurston	1.00
132	Brett Myers	1.00
133	Antonio Perez	1.00
134	Chris Snelling	1.00
135	Terrmel Sledge RC	2.00

Legacy

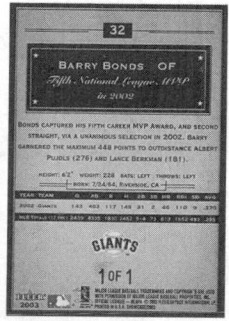

Legacy Stars (1-105): 3-6X
SP's (106-135): 1-3X
Production 150 Sets
Masterpiece 1 of 1 also exists.

Baseball's Best

		NM/M
Complete Set (15):		40.00
Common Player:		1.50
Inserted 1:24		
1	Curt Schilling	2.00
2	Barry Zito	2.00
3	Torii Hunter	2.00
4	Pedro J. Martinez	4.00
5	Bernie Williams	2.00
6	Magglio Ordonez	1.50
7	Alfonso Soriano	4.00
8	Hideo Nomo	2.00
9	Jason Giambi	5.00
10	Sammy Sosa	5.00
11	Vladimir Guerrero	4.00
12	Ken Griffey Jr.	5.00
13	Troy Glaus	3.00
14	Ichiro Suzuki	6.00
15	Albert Pujols	4.00

Baseball's Best
Memorabilia

		NM/M
Common Player:		5.00
Inserted 1:24		
CS	Curt Schilling	6.00
BZ	Barry Zito	6.00
TH	Torii Hunter	8.00
PM	Pedro J. Martinez	10.00

BW	Bernie Williams	8.00
MO	Magglio Ordonez	5.00
AS	Alfonso Soriano	15.00
HN	Hideo Nomo	8.00
JG	Jason Giambi	8.00
SS	Sammy Sosa	15.00

Hot Gloves

		NM/M
Complete Set (10):		15.00
Common Player:		1.00
Inserted 1:8		
1	Greg Maddux	2.00
2	Ivan Rodriguez	1.00
3	Derek Jeter	4.00
4	Mike Piazza	2.50
5	Nomar Garciaparra	2.50
6	Andruw Jones	1.00
7	Scott Rolen	1.00
8	Barry Bonds	3.00
9	Roger Clemens	2.00
10	Alex Rodriguez	3.00

Hot Gloves
Memorabilia

		NM/M
Common Player:		5.00
Production 350 Sets		
GM	Greg Maddux	12.00
IR	Ivan Rodriguez	5.00
DJ	Derek Jeter	25.00
MP	Mike Piazza	15.00
NG	Nomar Garciaparra	15.00
AJ	Andruw Jones	6.00
SR	Scott Rolen	15.00
BB	Barry Bonds	25.00
RC	Roger Clemens	15.00
AR	Alex Rodriguez	15.00

Sweet Signatures

		NM/M
Quantity produced listed		
DJ	Derek Jeter/250	130.00
DJ	Derek Jeter/50/Red	185.00
BB	Barry Bonds/ 90 MVP/150	200.00
BB	Barry Bonds/ 92 MVP/100	200.00
BB	Barry Bonds/ 93 MVP/75	200.00

Sweet Stitch

		NM/M
Complete Set (10):		12.00
Common Player:		.75
Inserted 1:8		
1SS	Derek Jeter	4.00
2SS	Randy Johnson	1.50
3SS	Jeff Bagwell	1.00
4SS	Nomar Garciaparra	2.50
5SS	Roger Clemens	2.00
6SS	Todd Helton	.75
7SS	Barry Bonds	3.00
8SS	Alfonso Soriano	1.50
9SS	Miguel Tejada	.75
10SS	Mark Prior	.75

Sweet Stitch
Memorabilia

		NM/M
Varying quantities produced		
DJ	Derek Jeter	25.00
RJ	Randy Johnson	8.00
JB	Jeff Bagwell	8.00
NG	Nomar Garciaparra	12.00
RC	Roger Clemens	12.00
TH	Todd Helton	5.00
BB	Barry Bonds	20.00
AS	Alfonso Soriano	12.00
MT	Miguel Tejada	5.00
MP	Mark Prior	10.00

Sweet Stitch Patch

		NM/M
Common Player:		20.00
DJ	Derek Jeter/50	60.00
RJ	Randy Johnson/150	40.00
JB	Jeff Bagwell/150	35.00
NG	Nomar Garciaparra/ 150	45.00
RC	Roger Clemens/50	45.00
TH	Todd Helton/50	30.00
BB	Barry Bonds/50	75.00
AS	Alfonso Soriano/50	40.00
MT	Miguel Tejada/150	20.00
MP	Mark Prior/150	25.00

Thundersticks

		NM/M
Complete Set (10):		12.00
Common Player:		.75
Inserted 1:8		
1TS	Adam Dunn	1.00
2TS	Alex Rodriguez	3.00
3TS	Barry Bonds	4.00
4TS	Jim Thome	1.00
5TS	Chipper Jones	2.00
6TS	Manny Ramirez	1.00
7TS	Carlos Delgado	.75
8TS	Mike Piazza	2.50
9TS	Shawn Green	.75
10TS	Pat Burrell	1.00

Thundersticks Bat

		NM/M
Common Player:		5.00
Golds:		1-2.5X
Production 99 Sets		
AD	Adam Dunn	10.00
AR	Alex Rodriguez	15.00
BB	Barry Bonds	20.00
JT	Jim Thome	8.00
CJS	Chipper Jones	8.00
MR	Manny Ramirez	8.00
SG	Shawn Green	5.00
PB	Pat Burrell	10.00

2003 Fleer Splendid
Splinters

		NM/M
Complete Set (150):		
Common Player:		.20
Common Wood (91-110):		6.00
Production 499		
Common SP (111-140):		1.50
Inserted 1:6		
Common (141-150):		3.00
Production 999		
Pack (5):		3.00
Box (24):		50.00
1	David Eckstein	.20
2	Barry Larkin	.40
3	Edgardo Alfonzo	.20
4	Darin Erstad	.50
5	Ellis Burks	.20
6	Omar Vizquel	.40
7	Bartolo Colon	.20

8	Roberto Alomar	.50
9	Garret Anderson	.40
10	Al Leiter	.20
11	Tim Salmon	.40
12	Larry Walker	.40
13	Jorge Posada	.50
14	Curt Schilling	.50
15	Jason Jennings	.20
16	Jason Giambi	1.00
17	Robert Fick	.20
18	Kazuhiro Sasaki	.20
19	Bernie Williams	.50
20	Junior Spivey	.20
21	Mike Lowell	.20
22	Luis Gonzalez	.40
23	Josh Beckett	.20
24	John Smoltz	.20
25	Mike Mussina	.50
26	Gary Sheffield	.40
27	Tom Glavine	.40
28	Tim Hudson	.40
29	Austin Kearns	.75
30	Andruw Jones	.50
31	Roger Clemens	1.50
32	Mark Mulder	.40
33	Jay Gibbons	.20
34	Jeff Kent	.40
35	Barry Zito	.40
36	Rodrigo Lopez	.20
37	Jeff Bagwell	.75
38	Eric Chavez	.40
39	Pedro J. Martinez	1.00
40	Lance Berkman	.50
41	Bobby Abreu	.40
42	Wade Miller	.20
43	Bret Boone	.20
44	Vicente Padilla	.20
45	Shea Hillenbrand	.20
46	Roy Oswalt	.40
47	Pat Burrell	.75
48	Manny Ramirez	.75
49	Craig Biggio	.40
50	Randy Wolf	.20
51	Kerry Wood	.50
52	Mike Sweeney	.40
53	Brian Giles	.40
54	Kazuhisa Ishii	.20
55	Jason Kendall	.20
56	Hideo Nomo	.40
57	Josh Phelps	.20
58	Sean Burroughs	.20
59	Paul Konerko	.20
60	Shawn Green	.40
61	Ryan Klesko	.40
62	Magglio Ordonez	.40
63	Paul LoDuca	.20
64	Edgar Martinez	.20
65	J.D. Drew	.30
66	Phil Nevin	.20
67	Jim Edmonds	.40
68	Matt Morris	.40
69	Aubrey Huff	.20
70	Adam Dunn	.75
71	John Olerud	.40
72	Juan Gonzalez	.50
73	Scott Rolen	.50
74	Rafael Palmeiro	.50
75	Roy Halladay	.20
76	Kevin Brown	.20
77	Ivan Rodriguez	.50
78	Eric Hinske	.20
79	Frank Thomas	.75
80	Carlos Delgado	.40
81	Bobby Higginson	.20
82	Trevor Hoffman	.20
83	Cliff Floyd	.20
84	Derek Lowe	.20
85	Richie Sexson	.50
86	Rich Aurilia	.20
87	Sean Casey	.20
88	Cristian Guzman	.20
89	Randy Winn	.20
90	Jose Vidro	.20

91	Mark Prior	6.00
92	Derek Jeter	15.00
93	Alex Rodriguez	12.00
94	Greg Maddux	9.00
95	Troy Glaus	7.50
96	Vladimir Guerrero	7.50
97	Todd Helton	7.50
98	Albert Pujols	10.00
99	Torii Hunter	6.00
100	Mike Piazza	10.00
101	Ichiro Suzuki	10.00
102	Sammy Sosa	10.00
103	Ken Griffey Jr.	10.00
104	Nomar Garciaparra	10.00
105	Barry Bonds	15.00
106	Chipper Jones	9.00
107	Jim Thome	6.00
108	Miguel Tejada	6.00
109	Randy Johnson	7.50
110	Alfonso Soriano	7.50
111	Guillermo Quiroz RC	3.00
112	Josh Willingham RC	3.00
113	Alejandro Machado RC	1.50
114	Chris Waters RC	2.00
115	Adam LaRoche RC	1.50
116	Prentice Redman RC	3.00
117	Jhonny Peralta RC	4.00
118	Francisco Rosario RC	1.50
119	Shane Victorino RC	2.00
120	Chien-Ming Wang RC	15.00
121	Matt Bruback RC	2.00
122	Rontrez Johnson RC	3.00
123	Josh Hall RC	2.00
124	Matt Kata RC	3.00
125	Hector Luna RC	2.00
126	Josh Stewart RC	2.00
127	Craig Brazell RC	2.00
128	Tim Olson RC	2.00
129	Michel Hernandez RC	1.50
130	Michael Hessman RC	2.00
131	Clint Barmes RC	5.00
132	Justin Morneau	1.50
133	Chris Snelling	1.50
134	Bobby Jenks	1.50
135	Tim Hummel RC	1.50
136	Adam Morrissey	1.50
137	Carl Crawford	1.50
138	Garrett Atkins	1.50
139	Jung Bong	1.50
140	Ken Harvey	1.50
141	Chin-Feng Chen	2.00
142	Hee Seop Choi	2.00
143	Lance Niekro	2.00
144	Mark Teixeira	2.00
145	Nook Logan RC	3.00
146	Terrmel Sledge RC	3.00
147	Lew Ford RC	6.00
148	Ian Ferguson RC	3.00
149	Hideki Matsui/499 RC	15.00
150	Jose Contreras RC	6.00

Bat Chips

		NM/M
Common Player:		4.00
Production 425 Sets		
1	Jason Giambi	8.00
2	Jeff Bagwell	8.00
3	Manny Ramirez	8.00
4	Adam Dunn	8.00
5	Derek Jeter	25.00
6	Alex Rodriguez	15.00
7	Troy Glaus	5.00
8	Mike Piazza	15.00
9	Sammy Sosa	12.00
10	Nomar Garciaparra	18.00
11	Barry Bonds	18.00
12	Jim Thome	10.00
13	Miguel Tejada	5.00
14	Alfonso Soriano	10.00
15	Ryan Klesko	4.00
16	Sean Casey	4.00
17	Bernie Williams	8.00
18	Vladimir Guerrero	8.00
19	Gary Sheffield	5.00

Family Tree

		NM/M
Complete Set (10):		10.00
Common Player:		.50
Inserted 1:8		
1	Lance Niekro, Phil Niekro	.50
2	Bob Boone, Bret Boone	.50
3	Sandy Alomar Jr., Roberto Alomar	.50
4	Ken Griffey Sr., Ken Griffey Jr.	2.00
5	Jason Giambi, Jeremy Giambi	1.50
6	Bobby Bonds, Barry Bonds	3.00
7	Tony Perez, Eduardo Perez	.50
8	Brian Giles, Marcus Giles	.75
9	Felipe Alou, Moises Alou	.75
10	Pedro J. Martinez, Ramon Martinez	1.50

Home Run Club

		NM/M
Complete Set (12):		50.00
Common Player:		2.00
Inserted 1:72		
1	Barry Bonds	10.00
2	Jason Giambi	5.00
3	Sammy Sosa	6.00
4	Jim Thome	4.00
5	Lance Berkman	2.00
6	Alfonso Soriano	5.00
7	Vladimir Guerrero	4.00
8	Shawn Green	2.00
9	Troy Glaus	3.00
10	Pat Burrell	3.00
11	Alex Rodriguez	10.00
12	Mike Piazza	8.00

Home Run Club Autographs

	NM/M
Quantity produced listed	
BB1 Barry Bonds/ Black ink/150	150.00
CR1 Cal Ripken Jr./ Black ink/300	100.00
CR2 Cal Ripken Jr./ Blue ink/150	125.00
CR3 Cal Ripken Jr./ Red ink/50	200.00
DJ1 Derek Jeter/ Black ink/400	80.00
DJ2 Derek Jeter/ Blue ink/250	100.00
DJ3 Derek Jeter/ Red ink/50	125.00

Home Run Club Memorabilia

	NM/M
Common Player:	5.00

Production 599 Sets

Barry Bonds/Jsy	20.00
Jason Giambi/Bat	8.00
Sammy Sosa/Jsy	12.00
Jim Thome/Bat	8.00
Lance Berkman/Bat	5.00
Alfonso Soriano/Jsy	15.00
Vladimir Guerrero/Jsy	8.00
Shawn Green/Jsy	5.00
Troy Glaus/Bat	6.00
Pat Burrell/Bat	10.00
Alex Rodriguez/Jsy	15.00
Mike Piazza/Jsy	12.00
Todd Helton/Jsy	8.00
Rafael Palmeiro/Jsy	6.00

Knot Hole Gang

		NM/M
Complete Set (15):		40.00
Common Player:		1.00
Inserted 1:24		
1	Derek Jeter	6.00
2	Barry Bonds	6.00
3	Sammy Sosa	3.00
4	Jason Giambi	3.00
5	Alfonso Soriano	2.00
6	Roger Clemens	3.00
7	Miguel Tejada	1.00
8	Greg Maddux	3.00
9	Randy Johnson	2.00
10	Chipper Jones	3.00
11	Nomar Garciaparra	4.00
12	Alex Rodriguez	5.00
13	Ichiro Suzuki	4.00
14	Vladimir Guerrero	2.00
15	Albert Pujols	2.00

Knot Hole Gang Game-Used

		NM/M
Common Player:		4.00
Inserted 1:40		
	Derek Jeter	20.00
	Barry Bonds	15.00
	Sammy Sosa	10.00
	Vladimir Guerrero	8.00
	Alfonso Soriano	8.00
	Roger Clemens	10.00
	Miguel Tejada	5.00
	Greg Maddux	10.00
	Randy Johnson	8.00
	Chipper Jones	8.00
	Nomar Garciaparra	12.00
	Alex Rodriguez	12.00
	Magglio Ordonez	4.00
	Lance Berkman	6.00

Knot Hole Gang Patch

		NM/M
Common Player:		15.00
Production 99 Sets		
	Derek Jeter	45.00
	Barry Bonds	45.00
	Sammy Sosa	35.00
	Vladimir Guerrero	25.00
	Alfonso Soriano	25.00
	Roger Clemens	25.00
	Miguel Tejada	15.00
	Greg Maddux	30.00
	Randy Johnson	20.00
	Chipper Jones	30.00
	Nomar Garciaparra	35.00
	Alex Rodriguez	35.00

Knot Hole Gang Triple

Common Player:	
Production 29 Sets:	No Pricing

Splendid Splinters

	NM/M
Complete Set (10):	15.00

Common Player: 1.00
Inserted 1:12
1	Derek Jeter	4.00
2	Barry Bonds	4.00
3	Scott Rolen	1.00
4	Nomar Garciaparra	2.50
5	Sammy Sosa	2.00
6	Alfonso Soriano	1.50
7	Alex Rodriguez	3.00
8	Mike Piazza	2.50
9	Manny Ramirez	1.00
10	Jeff Bagwell	1.00

Splendid Splinters G-U

NM/M
Common Player: 8.00
Production 349 Sets
Derek Jeter	20.00
Barry Bonds	20.00
Nomar Garciaparra	15.00
Sammy Sosa	10.00
Alfonso Soriano	10.00
Alex Rodriguez	12.00
Mike Piazza	12.00
Manny Ramirez	8.00
Jeff Bagwell	8.00

Splendid Splinters Dual

NM/M
Production 99 Sets
Derek Jeter, Alfonso Soriano	40.00
Barry Bonds, Sammy Sosa	50.00
Alex Rodriguez, Nomar Garciaparra	40.00
Mike Piazza, Jeff Bagwell	25.00

2003 Fleer Tradition

JASON GIAMBI
New York Yankees® - First Base

NM/M
Complete Set (485): 150.00
Common Player: .15
Common SP (1-100): 1.00
Inserted 1:1
Hobby Pack (10): 1.50
Hobby Box (40): 40.00
1	Jarrod Washburn, Troy Glaus, Garret Anderson, Ramon Ortiz	1.50
2	Luis Gonzalez, Randy Johnson, Andruw Jones	1.50
3	Andruw Jones, Chipper Jones, Tom Glavine, Kevin Millwood	2.00
4	Tony Batista, Rodrigo Lopez	1.00
5	Manny Ramirez, Nomar Garciaparra, Derek Lowe, Pedro J. Martinez	3.00
6	Sammy Sosa, Matt Clement, Kerry Wood	3.00
7	Mark Buehrle, Magglio Ordonez, Danny Wright	1.00
8	Adam Dunn, Aaron Boone, Jimmy Haynes	1.00
9	C.C. Sabathia, Jim Thome	1.50
10	Todd Helton, Jason Jennings	1.50
11	Randall Simon, Steve Sparks, Mark Redman	1.00
12	Derek Lee, Mike Lowell, A.J. Burnett	1.00
13	Lance Berkman, Roy Oswalt	1.50
14	Paul Byrd, Carlos Beltran	1.00
15	Shawn Green, Hideo Nomo	1.50
16	Richie Sexson, Ben Sheets	1.00
17	Torii Hunter, Kyle Lohse, Johan Santana	1.00
18	Vladimir Guerrero, Tomokazu Ohka, Javier Vazquez	2.00
19	Mike Piazza, Al Leiter	3.00
20	Jason Giambi, David Wells, Roger Clemens	4.00
21	Eric Chavez, Miguel Tejada, Barry Zito	1.50
22	Pat Burrell, Vicente Padilla, Randy Wolf	1.50
23	Brian Giles, Josh Fogg, Kip Wells	1.00
24	Ryan Klesko, Brian Lawrence	1.00
25	Barry Bonds, Russ Ortiz, Jason Schmidt	5.00
26	Mike Cameron, Bret Boone, Freddy Garcia	1.00
27	Albert Pujols, Matt Morris	3.00
28	Aubrey Huff, Randy Winn, Joe Kennedy, Tanyon Sturtze	1.00
29	Alex Rodriguez, Kenny Rogers, Chan Ho Park	5.00
30	Carlos Delgado, Roy Halladay	1.00
31	Greg Maddux	6.00
32	Nick Neugebauer	1.00
33	Larry Walker	1.50
34	Freddy Garcia	1.00
35	Rich Aurilia	1.00
36	Craig Wilson	1.00
37	Jeff Suppan	1.00
38	Joel Pineiro	1.00
39	Pedro Feliz	1.00
40	Bartolo Colon	1.50
41	Pete Walker	1.00
42	Mo Vaughn	1.50
43	Sidney Ponson	1.00
44	Jason Isringhausen	1.00
45	Hideki Irabu	1.00
46	Pedro J. Martinez	4.00
47	Tom Glavine	2.50
48	Matt Lawton	1.00
49	Kyle Lohse	1.00
50	Corey Patterson	1.00
51	Ichiro Suzuki	6.00
52	Wade Miller	1.00
53	Ben Diggins	1.00
54	Jayson Werth	1.00
55	Masato Yoshii	1.00
56	Mark Buehrle	1.00
57	Drew Henson	1.50
58	Dave Williams	1.00
59	Juan Rivera	1.00
60	Scott Schoeneweis	1.00
61	Josh Beckett	1.50
62	Vinny Castilla	1.00
63	Barry Zito	2.00
64	Jose Valentin	1.00
65	Jon Lieber	1.00
66	Jorge Padilla	1.00
67	Luis Aparicio	1.00
68	Boog Powell	1.00
69	Dick Radatz	1.00
70	Frank Malzone	1.00
71	Lou Brock	1.50
72	Billy Williams	1.00
73	Early Wynn	1.00
74	Jim Bunning	1.00
75	Al Kaline	5.00
76	Eddie Mathews	3.00
77	Harmon Killebrew	5.00
78	Gil Hodges	1.00
79	Duke Snider	3.00
80	Yogi Berra	4.00
81	Whitey Ford	3.00
82	Willie Stargell	1.50
83	Willie McCovey	1.50
84	Gaylord Perry	1.00
85	Red Schoendienst	1.00
86	Luis Castillo	1.00
87	Derek Jeter	8.00
88	Orlando Hudson	1.00
89	Bobby Higginson	1.00
90	Brent Butler	1.00
91	Brad Wilkerson	1.00
92	Craig Biggio	1.50
93	Marlon Anderson	1.00
94	Ty Wigginton	1.00
95	Hideo Nomo	3.00
96	Barry Larkin	2.00
97	Roberto Alomar	3.00
98	Omar Vizquel	1.50
99	Andres Galarraga	1.00
100	Shawn Green	1.50
101	Rafael Furcal	.15
102	Bill Selby	.15
103	Brent Abernathy	.15
104	Nomar Garciaparra	1.50
105	Michael Barrett	.15
106	Travis Hafner	.15
107	Carl Crawford	.15
108	Jeff Cirillo	.15
109	Mike Hampton	.15
110	Kip Wells	.15
111	Luis Alicea	.15
112	Ellis Burks	.15
113	Matt Anderson	.15
114	Carlos Beltran	.50
115	Paul LoDuca	.15
116	Lance Berkman	.15
117	Moises Alou	.15
118	Roger Cedeno	.15
119	Brad Fullmer	.15
120	Sean Burroughs	.15
121	Eric Byrnes	.15
122	Milton Bradley	.15
123	Jason Giambi	.75
124	Brook Fordyce	.15
125	Kevin Appier	.15
126	Steve Cox	.15
127	Danny Bautista	.15
128	Edgardo Alfonzo	.15
129	Matt Clement	.15
130	Robb Nen	.15
131	Roy Halladay	.15
132	Brian Jordan	.15
133	A.J. Burnett	.15
134	Aaron Cook	.15
135	Paul Byrd	.15
136	Ramon Ortiz	.15
137	Adam Hyzdu	.15
138	Rafael Soriano	.15
139	Marty Cordova	.15
140	Nelson Cruz	.15
141	Jamie Moyer	.15
142	Raul Mondesi	.15
143	Josh Bard	.15
144	Elmer Dessens	.15
145	Rickey Henderson	.75
146	Joe McEwing	.15
147	Luis Rivas	.15
148	Armando Benitez	.15
149	Keith Foulke	.15
150	Zach Day	.15
151	Troy Lunsford	.15
152	Bobby Abreu	.15
153	Juan Cruz	.15
154	Ramon Hernandez	.15
155	Brandon Duckworth	.15
156	Matt Ginter	.15
157	Robert Mackowiak	.15
158	Josh Pearce	.15
159	Marlon Byrd	.15
160	Todd Walker	.15
161	Chad Hermansen	.15
162	Felix Escalona	.15
163	Ruben Mateo	.15
164	Mark Johnson	.15
165	Juan Pierre	.15
166	Gary Sheffield	.30
167	Edgar Martinez	.15
168	Randy Winn	.15
169	Pokey Reese	.15
170	Kevin Mench	.15
171	Albert Pujols	1.50
172	J.T. Snow	.15
173	Dean Palmer	.15
174	Jay Payton	.15
175	Abraham Nunez	.15
176	Richie Sexson	.15
177	Jose Vidro	.15
178	Geoff Jenkins	.15
179	Dan Wilson	.15
180	John Olerud	.15
181	Javy Lopez	.15
182	Carl Everett	.15
183	Vernon Wells	.15
184	Juan Gonzalez	.75
185	Jorge Posada	.35
186	Mike Sweeney	.15
187	Cesar Izturis	.15
188	Jason Schmidt	.15
189	Chris Richard	.15
190	Jason Phillips	.15
191	Fred McGriff	.15
192	Shea Hillenbrand	.15
193	Ivan Rodriguez	.50
194	Mike Lowell	.15
195	Neifi Perez	.15
196	Kenny Lofton	.15
197	A.J. Pierzynski	.15
198	Larry Bigbie	.15
199	Juan Uribe	.15
200	Jeff Bagwell	.75
201	Timoniel Perez	.15
202	Jeremy Giambi	.15
203	Deivi Cruz	.15
204	Marquis Grissom	.15
205	Chipper Jones	1.00
206	Alex Gonzalez	.15
207	Steve Finley	.15
208	Ben Davis	.15
209	Mike Bordick	.15
210	Casey Fossum	.15
211	Aramis Ramirez	.15
212	Aaron Boone	.15
213	Orlando Cabrera	.15
214	Hee Seop Choi	.15
215	Jeromy Burnitz	.15
216	Todd Hollandsworth	.15
217	Rey Sanchez	.15
218	Jose Cruz Jr.	.15
219	Roosevelt Brown	.15
220	Odalis Perez	.15
221	Carlos Delgado	.40
222	Orlando Hernandez	.15
223	Adam Everett	.15
224	Adrian Beltre	.25
225	Ken Griffey Jr.	1.50
226	Brad Penny	.15
227	Carlos Lee	.15
228	J.C. Romero	.15
229	Ramon Martinez	.15
230	Matt Morris	.15
231	Ben Howard	.15
232	Damon Minor	.15
233	Jason Marquis	.15
234	Paul Wilson	.15
235	Ryan Dempster	.15
236	Jeffrey Hammonds	.15
237	Jaret Wright	.15
238	Carlos Pena	.15
239	Toby Hall	.15
240	Rick Helling	.15
241	Alex Escobar	.15
242	Trevor Hoffman	.15
243	Bernie Williams	.35
244	Jorge Julio	.15
245	Byung-Hyun Kim	.15
246	Mike Redmond	.15
247	Tony Armas	.15
248	Aaron Rowand	.15
249	Rusty Greer	.15
250	Aaron Harang	.15
251	Jeremy Fikac	.15
252	Jay Gibbons	.15
253	Brandon Puffer	.15
254	Dewayne Wise	.15
255	Chan Ho Park	.15
256	David Bell	.15
257	Kenny Rogers	.15
258	Mark Quinn	.15
259	Greg LaRocca	.15
260	Reggie Taylor	.15
261	Brett Tomko	.15
262	Jack Wilson	.15
263	Billy Wagner	.15
264	Greg Norton	.15
265	Tim Salmon	.25
266	Joe Randa	.15
267	Geronimo Gil	.15
268	Johnny Damon	.25
269	Robin Ventura	.15
270	Frank Thomas	.75
271	Terrence Long	.15
272	Mark Redman	.15
273	Mark Kotsay	.15
274	Ben Sheets	.15
275	Reggie Sanders	.15
276	Mark Grace	.25
277	Eddie Guardado	.15
278	Julio Mateo	.15
279	Bengie Molina	.15
280	Bill Hall	.15
281	Eric Chavez	.30
282	Joe Kennedy	.15
283	John Valentin	.15
284	Ray Durham	.15
285	Trot Nixon	.15
286	Rondell White	.15
287	Alex Gonzalez	.15
288	Tomas Perez	.15
289	Jared Sandberg	.15
290	Jacque Jones	.15
291	Cliff Floyd	.15
292	Ryan Klesko	.15
293	Morgan Ensberg	.15
294	Jerry Hairston Jr.	.15
295	Doug Mientkiewicz	.15
296	Darin Erstad	.50
297	Jeff Conine	.15
298	Johnny Estrada	.15
299	Mark Mulder	.15
300	Jeff Kent	.15
301	Roger Clemens	1.25

302	Endy Chavez	.15
303	Joe Crede	.15
304	J.D. Drew	.30
305	David Dellucci	.15
306	Eli Marrero	.15
307	Josh Fogg	.15
308	Mike Crudale	.15
309	Bret Boone	.15
310	Mariano Rivera	.30
311	Mike Piazza	1.50
312	Jason Jennings	.15
313	Jason Varitek	.15
314	Vicente Padilla	.15
315	Kevin Millwood	.15
316	Nick Johnson	.15
317	Shane Reynolds	.15
318	Joe Thurston	.15
319	Mike Lamb	.15
320	Aaron Sele	.15
321	Fernando Tatis	.15
322	Randy Wolf	.15
323	David Justice	.15
324	Andy Pettitte	.30
325	Freddy Sanchez	.15
326	Scott Spiezio	.15
327	Randy Johnson	.75
328	Karim Garcia	.15
329	Eric Milton	.15
330	Jermaine Dye	.15
331	Kevin Brown	.15
332	Adam Pettyjohn	.15
333	Jason Lane	.15
334	Mark Prior	.60
335	Mike Lieberthal	.15
336	Matt White	.15
337	John Patterson	.15
338	Marcus Giles	.15
339	Kazuhisa Ishii	.15
340	Willie Harris	.15
341	Travis Phelps	.15
342	Randall Simon	.15
343	Manny Ramirez	.75
344	Kerry Wood	.60
345	Shannon Stewart	.15
346	Mike Mays	.40
347	Joe Borchard	.15
348	Tyler Walker	.15
349	Preston Wilson	.15
350	Damian Moss	.15
351	Eric Karros	.15
352	Bobby Kielty	.15
353	Jason LaRue	.15
354	Phil Nevin	.15
355	Tony Graffanino	.15
356	Antonio Alfonseca	.15
357	Eddie Taubensee	.15
358	Luis Ugueto	.15
359	Greg Vaughn	.15
360	Corey Thurman	.15
361	Omar Infante	.15
362	Alex Cintron	.15
363	Esteban Loaiza	.15
364	Tino Martinez	.15
365	David Eckstein	.15
366	David Pember RC	.15
367	Damian Rolls	.15
368	Richard Hidalgo	.15
369	Brad Radke	.15
370	Alex Sanchez	.15
371	Ben Grieve	.15
372	Brandon Inge	.15
373	Adam Piatt	.15
374	Charles Johnson	.15
375	Rafael Palmeiro	.65
376	Joe Mays	.15
377	Derrek Lee	.15
378	Fernando Vina	.15
379	Andruw Jones	.75
380	Troy Glaus	.75
381	Bobby Hill	.15
382	C.C. Sabathia	.15
383	Jose Hernandez	.15
384	Al Leiter	.15
385	Jarrod Washburn	.15
386	Cody Ransom	.15
387	Matt Stairs	.15
388	Edgar Renteria	.15
389	Tsuyoshi Shinjo	.15
390	Matt Williams	.15
391	Bubba Trammell	.15
392	Jason Kendall	.15
393	Scott Rolen	.65
394	Chuck Knoblauch	.15
395	Jimmy Rollins	.25
396	Gary Bennett	.15
397	David Wells	.15
398	Ronnie Belliard	.15
399	Austin Kearns	.50
400	Tim Hudson	.30
401	Andy Van Hekken	.15
402	Ray Lankford	.15
403	Todd Helton	.75
404	Jeff Weaver	.15
405	Gabe Kapler	.15

406	Luis Gonzalez	.40
407	Sean Casey	.15
408	Kazuhiro Sasaki	.15
409	Mark Teixeira	.50
410	Brian Giles	.15
411	Robert Fick	.15
412	Wilkin Ruan	.15
413	Jose Rijo	.15
414	Ben Broussard	.15
415	Aubrey Huff	.15
416	Magglio Ordonez	.25
417	Barry Bonds	2.00
418	Miguel Tejada	.40
419	Randy Johnson	.75
420	Barry Zito	.30
421	Jason Jennings	.15
422	Eric Hinske	.15
423	Benito Santiago	.15
424	Adam Kennedy	.15
425	Troy Glaus	.65
426	Brandon Phillips	.15
427	Jake Peavy	.15
428	Jason Romano	.15
429	Jeriome Robertson	.15
430	Aaron Guiel	.15
431	Hank Blalock	.15
432	Brad Lidge	.15
433	Francisco Rodriguez	.15
434	Jaime Cerda	.15
435	Jung Bong	.15
436	Reed Johnson	.15
437	Rene Reyes	.15
438	Chris Snelling	.15
439	Miguel Olivo	.15
440	Brian Banks	.15
441	Eric Junge	.15
442	Kirk Saarloos	.15
443	Jamey Carroll	.15
444	Josh Hancock	.15
445	Michael Restovich	.15
446	William Bloomquist	.15
447	John Lackey	.15
448	Marcus Thames	.15
449	Victor Martinez	.15
450	Brett Myers	.15
451	Wes Obermueller	.15
452	Hansel Izquierdo	.15
453	Brian Tallet	.15
454	Craig Monroe	.15
455	Doug DeVore	.15
456	John Buck	.15
457	Tony Alvarez	.15
458	Wily Mo Pena	.15
459	John Stephens	.15
460	Tony Torcato	.15
461	Adam Kennedy	.15
462	Alex Rodriguez	.15
463	Derek Lowe	.15
464	Garret Anderson	.15
465	Pat Burrell	.50
466	Eric Gagne	.15
467	Tomokazu Ohka	.15
468	Josh Phelps	.15
469	Sammy Sosa	1.50
470	Jim Thome	.15
471	Vladimir Guerrero	.75
472	Jason Simontacchi	.15
473	Adam Dunn	.50
474	Jim Edmonds	.15
475	Barry Bonds	2.00
476	Paul Konerko	.25
477	Alfonso Soriano	.75
478	Curt Schilling	.40
479	John Smoltz	.15
480	Torii Hunter	.15
481	Rodrigo Lopez	.15
482	Miguel Tejada	.35
483	Eric Hinske	.15
484	Roy Oswalt	.25
485	Junior Spivey	.15

Glossy

SP's (1-100):	1-2X
Cards (101-485):	5-10X

Production 100 Sets
Randomly inserted in Update packs.

B/W Goudey

		NM/M
Complete Set (25):		80.00
Common Player:		1.50

Production 1,936 Sets

Golds:		4-8X

Production 36 Sets

1BWG	Jim Thome	2.50
2BWG	Derek Jeter	10.00
3BWG	Alex Rodriguez	8.00
4BWG	Mark Prior	1.00
5BWG	Nomar Garciaparra	6.00
6BWG	Curt Schilling	2.00
7BWG	Pat Burrell	2.00
8BWG	Frank Thomas	2.50
9BWG	Roger Clemens	5.00

Chicago Cubs™

10BWG	Chipper Jones	5.00
11BWG	Barry Larkin	1.50
12BWG	Hideo Nomo	2.00
13BWG	Pedro J. Martinez	3.00
14BWG	Jeff Bagwell	2.50
15BWG	Greg Maddux	5.00
16BWG	Vladimir Guerrero	3.00
17BWG	Ichiro Suzuki	6.00
18BWG	Mike Piazza	8.00
19BWG	Drew Henson	1.50
20BWG	Albert Pujols	3.00
21BWG	Sammy Sosa	5.00
22BWG	Jason Giambi	5.00
23BWG	Randy Johnson	3.00
24BWG	Ken Griffey Jr.	6.00
25BWG	Barry Bonds	8.00

Checklist

	NM/M
Complete Set (18):	6.00
Common Jeter Card (1-18):	.50

Inserted 1:4

Game-Used Parallel

FRANK THOMAS
Chicago White Sox® - Designated Hitter

	NM/M
Common Player:	5.00

Inserted 1:35

Golds:	1-2X

Production 100 Sets

Derek Jeter/Jsy/150	35.00
Craig Biggio/Bat	8.00
Hideo Nomo/Jsy/200	20.00
Barry Larkin/Jsy/200	10.00
Kazuhiro Sasaki/Jsy	10.00
Greg Maddux/Jsy	15.00
Mo Vaughn/Jsy/60	10.00
Pedro Martinez/Jsy/200	12.00
Barry Zito/Jsy	10.00
Luis Aparicio/Jsy/150	10.00
Willie Stargell/Pants/150	15.00
Nomar Garciaparra/Jsy/200	20.00
Edgardo Alfonzo/Jsy/200	8.00
John Olerud/Jsy	6.00
Juan Gonzalez/Bat/200	10.00
Jorge Posada/Bat	8.00
Shea Hillenbrand/Bat	10.00
Ivan Rodriguez/Jsy	8.00
Mike Lowell/Bat	5.00
Jeff Bagwell/Jsy/200	12.00
Chipper Jones/Jsy	15.00
Jeromy Burnitz/Jsy/200	6.00
Adrian Beltre/Jsy	6.00
Robin Ventura/Jsy	8.00
Frank Thomas/Jsy	10.00
Mark Grace/Jsy	10.00
Darin Erstad/Jsy	8.00
Roger Clemens/Jsy/150	20.00
J.D. Drew/Jsy	8.00
Mike Piazza/Jsy/150	20.00
Randy Johnson/Jsy/150	12.00
Mark Prior/Jsy/200	15.00
Kazuhisa Ishii/Jsy	10.00
Manny Ramirez/Jsy/150	10.00
Kerry Wood/Jsy/200	15.00
Mike Mussina/Jsy	10.00
Eric Karros/Jsy	5.00
Rafael Palmeiro/Jsy	8.00
Andruw Jones/Bat/150	10.00
Jason Kendall/Jsy	6.00
Jimmy Rollins/Jsy	8.00
Barry Bonds/Jsy/50	40.00
Miguel Tejada/Bat/150	8.00
Jason Jennings/Jsy	6.00

Hardball Preview

		NM/M
Complete Set (10):		125.00
Common Player:		5.00

Inserted 1:400

1	Miguel Tejada	5.00
2	Derek Jeter	25.00
3	Mike Piazza	20.00
4	Barry Bonds	20.00
5	Mark Prior	4.00
6	Ichiro Suzuki	20.00
7	Alex Rodriguez	20.00
8	Nomar Garciaparra	15.00
9	Alfonso Soriano	12.00
10	Ken Griffey Jr.	15.00

Milestones

		NM/M
Complete Set (25):		40.00
Common Player:		1.00

Inserted 1:5

1	Eddie Mathews	1.50
2	Rickey Henderson	1.50
3	Harmon Killebrew	1.50
4	Al Kaline	2.50
5	Willie McCovey	1.00
6	Tom Seaver	2.00
7	Reggie Jackson	2.00
8	Mike Schmidt	3.00
9	Nolan Ryan	5.00
10	Mike Piazza	4.00
11	Randy Johnson	2.00
12	Bernie Williams	1.50
13	Rafael Palmeiro	1.50
14	Juan Gonzalez	1.50
15	Ken Griffey Jr.	3.00
16	Derek Jeter	5.00
17	Roger Clemens	3.00
18	Roberto Alomar	1.50
19	Manny Ramirez	1.50
20	Luis Gonzalez	1.00
21	Barry Bonds	4.00
22	Nomar Garciaparra	3.00
23	Fred McGriff	1.00
24	Greg Maddux	2.50
25	Barry Bonds	4.00

Milestones Game-Used

PEDRO MARTINEZ

	NM/M
Common Player:	8.00

Inserted 1:143

Golds:	1-2X

Production 100 Sets

Roberto Alomar/Bat/200	8.00

	NM/M
Barry Bonds/ 600 HR/Bat/100	30.00
Barry Bonds/ 5 MVP/Jsy/200	25.00
Roger Clemens/ Jsy/150	20.00
Nomar Garciaparra/ Jsy/200	20.00
Juan Gonzalez/ Bat/250	10.00
Luis Gonzalez Derek Jeter/Jsy/150	35.00
Randy Johnson/ Jsy/100	15.00
Greg Maddux	20.00
Fred McGriff	5.00
Rafael Palmeiro/ Jsy/200	8.00
Mike Piazza/Jsy/100	20.00
Manny Ramirez/ Jsy/150	10.00
Bernie Williams/ Jsy/200	10.00

Lumber Company

	NM/M
Complete Set (30):	70.00
Common Player:	1.00
Inserted 1:10	
1 Mike Piazza	6.00
2 Derek Jeter	8.00
3 Alex Rodriguez	6.00
4 Miguel Tejada	1.00
5 Nomar Garciaparra	5.00
6 Andruw Jones	1.50
7 Pat Burrell	1.50
8 Albert Pujols	3.00
9 Jeff Bagwell	2.00
10 Chipper Jones	4.00
11 Ichiro Suzuki	6.00
12 Alfonso Soriano	3.00
13 Eric Chavez	1.50
14 Brian Giles	1.00
15 Shawn Green	1.50
16 Jim Thome	2.00
17 Lance Berkman	1.50
18 Bernie Williams	1.50
19 Manny Ramirez	2.00
20 Vladimir Guerrero	3.00
21 Carlos Delgado	1.25
22 Scott Rolen	1.50
23 Sammy Sosa	4.00
24 Ken Griffey Jr.	5.00
25 Barry Bonds	6.00
26 Todd Helton	1.50
27 Jason Giambi	4.00
28 Austin Kearns	1.50
29 Jeff Kent	1.00
30 Magglio Ordonez	1.00

Lumber Company Bat Gold

	NM/M
Numbered to 2002 HR total.	
Lance Berkman/42	25.00
Barry Bonds/46	70.00
Pat Burrell/37	50.00
Eric Chavez/34	20.00
Carlos Delgado/33	35.00
Nomar Garciaparra/ 24	60.00
Brian Giles/38	25.00
Shawn Green/42	35.00
Todd Helton/30	35.00
Derek Jeter/18	200.00
Andruw Jones/35	25.00
Chipper Jones/26	45.00
Austin Kearns/13	35.00
Jeff Kent/37	25.00
Magglio Ordonez/38	25.00
Mike Piazza/33	65.00
Alex Rodriguez/57	40.00
Miguel Tejada/34	35.00
Jim Thome/52	30.00

Lumber Company Bat

	NM/M
Common Player:	6.00
Inserted 1:108	
Jeff Bagwell/200	15.00
Lance Berkman/200	10.00
Barry Bonds/150	25.00

Pat Burrell/75	25.00
Eric Chavez/125	8.00
Carlos Delgado/200	6.00
Nomar Garciaparra/ 200	25.00
Brian Giles/200	8.00
Shawn Green/200	8.00
Todd Helton/200	8.00
Derek Jeter/96	35.00
Andruw Jones/200	8.00
Chipper Jones	15.00
Austin Kearns/75	18.00
Jeff Kent/200	6.00
Magglio Ordonez	6.00
Mike Piazza/200	20.00
Manny Ramirez	10.00
Alex Rodriguez	15.00
Scott Rolen/80	25.00
Alfonso Soriano/200	12.00
Miguel Tejada	10.00
Jim Thome/200	12.00
Bernie Williams	10.00

Standouts

ALEX RODRIGUEZ
SHORTSTOP   TEXAS RANGERS

	NM/M
Complete Set (15):	60.00
Common Player:	1.50
Inserted 1:40	
1SO Greg Maddux	5.00
2SO Derek Jeter	10.00
3SO Alex Rodriguez	8.00
4SO Miguel Tejada	2.00
5SO Nomar Garciaparra	6.00
6SO Barry Bonds	8.00
7SO Pat Burrell	2.00
8SO Ken Griffey Jr.	6.00
9SO Alfonso Soriano	4.00
10SO Mike Piazza	8.00
11SO Sammy Sosa	5.00
12SO Ichiro Suzuki	6.00
13SO Vladimir Guerrero	3.00
14SO Roger Clemens	5.00
15SO Adam Dunn	2.50

2003 Fleer Tradition Update

ROOKIE '03

DELMON YOUNG
Tampa Bay Devil Rays™ - Outfield

	NM/M
Complete Set (398):	175.00
Common Player:	.15
Common Rookie (286-398):	.50
Cards (286-299):	
Inserted 1:4	
Pack (10):	2.00
Box (32 + 25 Count Update Box):	50.00
1 Aaron Boone	.15
2 Carl Everett	.15
3 Eduardo Perez	.15
4 Jason Michaels	.15
5 Karim Garcia	.15
6 Rainier Olmedo	.15

7	Scott Williamson	.15
8	Adam Kennedy	.15
9	Carl Pavano	.15
10	Eli Marrero	.15
11	Jason Simontacchi	.15
12	Keith Foulke	.15
13	Preston Wilson	.15
14	Scott Hatteberg	.15
15	Adam Dunn	.50
16	Carlos Baerga	.15
17	Elmer Dessens	.15
18	Javier Vazquez	.15
19	Kenny Rogers	.15
20	Quinton McCracken	.15
21	Shane Reynolds	.15
22	Adam Eaton	.15
23	Carlos Zambrano	.15
24	Enrique Wilson	.15
25	Jeff DaVanon	.15
26	Kenny Lofton	.25
27	Ramon Castro	.15
28	Shannon Stewart	.15
29	Al Martin	.15
30	Carlos Guillen	.15
31	Eric Karros	.15
32	Tim Worrell	.15
33	Kevin Millwood	.25
34	Randall Simon	.15
35	Shawn Chacon	.15
36	Alex Rodriguez	1.50
37	Casey Blake	.15
38	Eric Munson	.15
39	Jeff Kent	.25
40	Kris Benson	.15
41	Randy Winn	.15
42	Shea Hillenbrand	.15
43	Alfonso Soriano	1.00
44	Chris George	.15
45	Eric Bruntlett	.15
46	Jeromy Burnitz	.15
47	Kyle Farnsworth	.15
48	Torii Hunter	.40
49	Sidney Ponson	.15
50	Andres Galarraga	.25
51	Chris Singleton	.15
52	Eric Gagne	.25
53	Jesse Foppert	.15
54	Lance Carter	.15
55	Ray Durham	.15
56	Tanyon Sturtze	.15
57	Andy Ashby	.15
58	Cliff Floyd	.15
59	Eric Young	.15
60	Jhonny Peralta	.50
61	Livan Hernandez	.15
62	Reggie Sanders	.15
63	Tim Spooneybarger	.15
64	Angel Berroa	.15
65	Coco Crisp	.15
66	Eric Hinske	.15
67	Jim Edmonds	.25
68	Luis Matos	.15
69	Rickey Henderson	.40
70	Todd Walker	.15
71	Antonio Alfonseca	.15
72	Corey Koskie	.15
73	Erubiel Durazo	.15
74	Jim Thome	.50
75	Lyle Overbay	.15
76	Robert Fick	.15
77	Todd Hollandsworth	.15
78	Aramis Ramirez	.15
79	Cristian Guzman	.15
80	Esteban Loaiza	.15
81	Jody Gerut	.15
82	Mark Grudzielanek	.15
83	Roberto Alomar	.40
84	Todd Hundley	.15
85	Mike Hampton	.15
86	Curt Schilling	.40
87	Francisco Rodriguez	.15
88	John Lackey	.15
89	Mark Redman	.15
90	Robin Ventura	.25
91	Todd Zeile	.15
92	B.J. Surhoff	.15
93	Raul Mondesi	.25
94	Frank Catalanotto	.15
95	John Smoltz	.25
96	Mark Ellis	.15
97	Rocco Baldelli	.50
98	Todd Pratt	.15
99	Barry Bonds	2.00
100	Danny Graves	.15
101	Fred McGriff	.25
102	John Burkett	.15
103	Marquis Grissom	.15
104	Rocky Biddle	.15
105	Tom Glavine	.25
106	Bartolo Colon	.25
107	Darren Bragg	.15
108	Gabe Kapler	.15
109	John Franco	.15
110	Matt Mantei	.15
111	Rod Beck	.15
112	Tomokazu Ohka	.15

113	Ben Petrick	.15
114	Darren Dreifort	.15
115	Garret Anderson	.25
116	John Vander Wal	.15
117	Melvin Mora	.15
118	Rodrigo Lopez	.15
119	Raul Ibanez	.15
120	Benito Santiago	.15
121	David Ortiz	.15
122	Gary Bennett	.15
123	Jon Garland	.15
124	Michael Young	.15
125	Rodrigo Rosario	.15
126	Travis Lee	.15
127	Bill Mueller	.15
128	Derek Lowe	.15
129	Gil Meche	.15
130	Jose Guillen	.15
131	Miguel Cabrera	.40
132	Ron Calloway	.15
133	Troy Percival	.15
134	Billy Koch	.15
135	Dmitri Young	.15
136	Glendon Rusch	.15
137	Jose Jimenez	.15
138	Miguel Tejada	.40
139	John Thomson	.15
140	Troy O'Leary	.15
141	Bobby Kielty	.15
142	Dontrelle Willis	.50
143	Greg Myers	.15
144	Jose Vizcaino	.15
145	Mike MacDougal	.15
146	Ronnie Belliard	.15
147	Tyler Houston	.15
148	Brady Clark	.15
149	Edgardo Alfonzo	.15
150	Guillermo Mota	.15
151	Jose Lima	.15
152	Mike Williams	.15
153	Roy Oswalt	.25
154	Scott Podsednik	.25
155	Brandon Lyon	.15
156	Henry Mateo	.15
157	Jose Macias	.15
158	Mike Bordick	.15
159	Royce Clayton	.15
160	Vance Wilson	.15
161	Brent Abernathy	.15
162	Horacio Ramirez	.15
163	Jose Reyes	.50
164	Nick Punto	.15
165	Ruben Sierra	.15
166	Victor Zambrano	.15
167	Brett Tomko	.15
168	Ivan Rodriguez	.75
169	Jose Mesa	.15
170	Octavio Dotel	.15
171	Russ Ortiz	.15
172	Vladimir Guerrero	.75
173	Brian Lawrence	.15
174	Jae Weong Seo	.15
175	Jose Cruz Jr.	.15
176	Pat Burrell	.40
177	Russell Branyan	.15
178	Warren Morris	.15
179	Brian Boehringer	.15
180	Jason Johnson	.15
181	Josh Phelps	.15
182	Paul Konerko	.15
183	Ryan Franklin	.15
184	Wes Helms	.15
185	Brooks Kieschnick	.15
186	Jason Davis	.15
187	Juan Pierre	.15
188	Paul Wilson	.15
189	Sammy Sosa	1.50
190	Wil Cordero	.15
191	Byung-Hyun Kim	.15
192	Juan Encarnacion	.15
193	Placido Polanco	.15
194	Sandy Alomar	.15
195	Julio Lugo	.15
196	Junior Spivey	.15
197	Woody Williams	.15
198	Xavier Nady	.15
199	Mark Loretta	.15
200	Deivi Cruz	.15
201	Jorge Posada	.25
202	Carlos Delgado	.25
203	Alfonso Soriano	.50
204	Alex Rodriguez	1.00
205	Troy Glaus	.25
206	Garret Anderson	.15
207	Hideki Matsui	2.00
208	Ichiro Suzuki	.75
209	Esteban Loaiza	.15
210	Manny Ramirez	.25
211	Roger Clemens	.75
212	Roy Halladay	.15
213	Jason Giambi	.25
214	Edgar Martinez	.15
215	Bret Boone	.15
216	Hank Blalock	.15
217	Nomar Garciaparra	.75
218	Vernon Wells	.15

219	Melvin Mora	.15
220	Magglio Ordonez	.15
221	Mike Sweeney	.15
222	Barry Zito	.25
223	Carl Everett	.15
224	Shigetoshi Hasegawa	.15
225	Jamie Moyer	.15
226	Mark Mulder	.15
227	Eddie Guardado	.15
228	Ramon Hernandez	.15
229	Keith Foulke	.15
230	Javy Lopez	.15
231	Todd Helton	.25
232	Marcus Giles	.15
233	Edgar Renteria	.15
234	Scott Rolen	.25
235	Barry Bonds	1.00
236	Albert Pujols	.75
237	Gary Sheffield	.25
238	Jim Edmonds	.25
239	Jason Schmidt	.15
240	Mark Prior	1.00
241	Dontrelle Willis	.25
242	Kerry Wood	.25
243	Kevin Brown	.15
244	Woody Williams	.15
245	Paul LoDuca	.15
246	Richie Sexson	.15
247	Jose Vidro	.15
248	Luis Castillo	.15
249	Aaron Boone	.15
250	Mike Lowell	.15
251	Rafael Furcal	.15
252	Andruw Jones	.25
253	Preston Wilson	.15
254	John Smoltz	.15
255	Eric Gagne	.15
256	Randy Wolf	.15
257	Billy Wagner	.15
258	Luis Gonzalez	.15
259	Russ Ortiz	.15
260	Jim Thome, Pedro J. Martinez	.40
261	Alfonso Soriano, Jeff Bagwell	.50
262	Dontrelle Willis, Rocco Baldelli	.15
263	Carlos Delgado, Vladimir Guerrero	.25
264	Sammy Sosa, Magglio Ordonez	.50
265	Jason Giambi, Adam Dunn	.25
266	Mike Sweeney, Albert Pujols	.50
267	Barry Bonds, Torii Hunter	.75
268	Ichiro Suzuki, Andruw Jones	.50
269	Chipper Jones, Hank Blalock	.50
270	Mark Prior, Vernon Wells	.75
271	Nomar Garciaparra, Scott Rolen	.75
272	Alex Rodriguez, Lance Berkman	.75
273	Roger Clemens, Kerry Wood	.75
274	Derek Jeter, Jose Reyes	.75
275	Greg Maddux, Barry Zito	.50
276	Carlos Delgado	.25
277	J.D. Drew	.15
278	Barry Bonds	1.00
279	Albert Pujols	.75
280	Jim Thome	.25
281	Sammy Sosa	.75
282	Alfonso Soriano	.50
283	Hideki Matsui	1.00
284	Mike Piazza	.50
285	Vladimir Guerrero	.40
286	Rich Harden	.50
287	Chin-Hui Tsao	.50
288	Edwin Jackson RC	4.00
289	Chien-Ming Wang RC	6.00
290	Josh Willingham RC	2.00
291	Matt Kata RC	2.00
292	Jose Contreras RC	2.00
293	Chris Bootcheck	.50
294	Javier Lopez	1.00
295	Delmon Young RC	8.00
296	Pedro Liriano	.50
297	Noah Lowry	.50
298	Khalil Greene	3.00
299	Rob Bowen	.50
300	Bo Hart RC	2.00
301	Beau Kemp RC	.25
302	Gerald Laird	.15
303	Miguel Ojeda RC	.40
304	Todd Wellemeyer RC	.75
305	Ryan Wagner RC	2.00
306	Jeff Duncan RC	1.50

307	Wilfredo Ledezma RC	1.50
308	Wes Obermueller	.15
309	Bernie Castro RC	.25
310	Tim Olson RC	.25
311	Colin Porter RC	.25
312	Francisco Cruceta RC	1.50
313	Guillermo Quiroz RC	1.50
314	Brian Stokes RC	.50
315	Robby Hammock RC	.50
316	Lew Ford RC	2.00
317	Todd Linden	.15
318	Mike Gallo RC	.50
319	Francisco Rosario RC	1.50
320	Rosman Garcia RC	.50
321	Felix Sanchez RC	.50
322	Chad Gaudin RC	1.00
323	Phil Seibel RC	.50
324	Jason Gilfillan RC	.50
325	Terrmel Sledge RC	.75
326	Alfredo Gonzalez RC	.50
327	Josh Stewart RC	1.00
328	Jeremy Griffiths	.15
329	Cory Stewart RC	.50
330	Josh Hall RC	1.00
331	Arnie Munoz RC	.50
332	Garrett Atkins	.15
333	Neal Cotts	.15
334	Dan Haren	2.00
335	Shane Victorino RC	.50
336	David Sanders RC	.50
337	Oscar Villarreal RC	.50
338	Michael Hessman RC	.50
339	Andrew Brown RC	.50
340	Kevin Hooper	.15
341	Prentice Redman RC	.50
342	Brandon Webb RC	3.00
343	Jimmy Gobble	.15
344	Pete LaForest RC	.50
345	Chris Waters RC	.75
346	Hideki Matsui RC	8.00
347	Chris Capuano RC	1.00
348	Jon Leicester RC	.50
349	Mike Nicolas RC	.50
350	Nook Logan RC	.50
351	Craig Brazell RC	1.00
352	Aaron Looper RC	.50
353	D.J. Carrasco RC	.50
354	Clint Barmes RC	1.00
355	Doug Waechter RC	.50
356	Julio Manon RC	.50
357	Jeremy Bonderman RC	3.00
358	Diegomar Markwell RC	.50
359	Dave Matranga RC	.75
360	Luis Ayala RC	.50
361	Jason Stanford RC	.15
362	Roger Deago RC	.50
363	Geoff Geary RC	1.00
364	Edgar Gonzalez RC	.50
365	Michel Hernandez RC	.50
366	Aquilino Lopez RC	.50
367	David Manning RC	1.00
368	Carlos Mendez RC	.50
369	Matt Miller RC	.15
370	Micheal Nakamura RC	1.00
371	Mike Neu RC	.50
372	Ramon Nivar RC	.50
373	Kevin Ohme RC	.50
374	Alex Prieto RC	1.00
375	Stephen Randolph RC	.50
376	Brian Sweeney RC	1.00
377	Matt Diaz RC	.50
378	Mike Gonzalez	.15
379	Daniel Cabrera RC	2.00
380	Fernando Cabrera RC	.50
381	David DeJesus RC	.50
382	Mike Ryan RC	1.00
383	Rick Roberts RC	.50
384	Seung Jun Song	.15
385	Rickie Weeks RC	6.00
386	Humberto Quintero RC	.50
387	Alexis Rios	.15
388	Aaron Miles RC	2.00
389	Tom Gregorio RC	.50
390	Anthony Ferrari RC	.75
391	Kevin Correia RC	.75
392	Rafael Betancourt RC	.75
393	Rett Johnson RC	.50
394	Richard Fischer RC	.50
395	Greg Aquino RC	.50
396	Daniel Garcia RC	1.00
397	Sergio Mitre RC	1.00
398	Edwin Almonte	.15

Glossy

Stars (1-285):		.5-10X
Rookies (286-398):		.5-1.5X

ELI MARRERO
Cardinals® • Outfield

Production 100 Sets

Diamond Debuts

		NM/M
Complete Set (25):		40.00
Common Player:		1.00
Inserted 1:10		
1	Dontrelle Willis	4.00
2	Bo Hart	1.00
3	Jose Reyes	4.00
4	Chin-Hui Tsao	1.00
5	Brandon Webb	3.00
6	Rich Harden	2.00
7	Jesse Foppert	1.00
8	Rocco Baldelli	2.00
9	Hideki Matsui	5.00
10	Ron Calloway	1.00
11	Jeremy Bonderman	1.50
12	Mark Teixeira	3.00
13	Ryan Wagner	2.00
14	Jose Contreras	2.00
15	Miguel Cabrera	4.00
16	Lew Ford	1.00
17	Jeff Duncan	1.50
18	Matt Kata	1.00
19	Jeremy Griffiths	1.00
20	Todd Wellemeyer	1.00
21	Robby Hammock	1.00
22	Dave Matranga	1.00
23	Laynce Nix	1.00
24	Jhonny Peralta	1.00
25	Oscar Villarreal	1.00

Long GONE!

		NM/M
Complete Set (20):		60.00
Common Player:		2.00
Quantity produced listed		
1	Barry Bonds/475	8.00

2	Jason Giambi/440	2.00
3	Albert Pujols/452	6.00
4	Chipper Jones/420	4.00
5	Manny Ramirez/430	2.00
6	Sammy Sosa/536	5.00
7	Alfonso Soriano/440	3.00
8	Alex Rodriguez/430	6.00
9	Jim Thome/445	3.00
10	Vladimir Guerrero/502	3.00
11	Austin Kearns/430	2.00
12	Jeff Bagwell/420	2.00
13	Andruw Jones/430	2.00
14	Carlos Delgado/451	2.00
15	Nomar Garciaparra/440	6.00
16	Adam Dunn/464	2.00
17	Mike Piazza/450	4.00
18	Derek Jeter/410	6.00
19	Ken Griffey Jr./420	4.00
20	Hank Blalock/424	2.00

Milestones

		NM/M
Complete Set (20):		25.00
Common Player:		1.00
Inserted 1:8		
1	Roger Clemens	3.00
2	Rafael Palmeiro	1.00
3	Jeff Bagwell	1.00
4	Barry Bonds	4.00
5	Sammy Sosa	2.50
6	Albert Pujols	3.00
7	Ichiro Suzuki	2.00
8	Alfonso Soriano	1.50
9	Alex Rodriguez	3.00
10	Randy Johnson	1.50
11	Manny Ramirez	1.00
12	Chipper Jones	2.00
13	Todd Helton	1.00
14	Ken Griffey Jr.	2.00
15	Jim Thome	1.00
16	Frank Thomas	1.00
17	Pedro J. Martinez	1.50
18	Hideo Nomo	1.00
19	Jason Schmidt	1.00
20	Carlos Delgado	1.00

Milestones Memorabilia

	NM/M
Common Player:	5.00
Inserted 1:20	
Golds:	1-2X
Production 100 Sets	
Roger Clemens	15.00
Rafael Palmeiro	5.00
Jeff Bagwell	8.00
Sammy Sosa	10.00
Alfonso Soriano	10.00
Alex Rodriguez	10.00
Randy Johnson	8.00
Manny Ramirez	5.00
Chipper Jones	8.00
Todd Helton	6.00
Jim Thome	8.00
Frank Thomas	8.00
Pedro J. Martinez	8.00
Hideo Nomo	8.00
Jason Schmidt	8.00
Carlos Delgado	5.00

Throwback Threads

	NM/M
Common Player:	4.00
Inserted 1:64	
Kevin Millwood	6.00
Vladimir Guerrero	8.00
Troy Glaus	6.00
Mike Piazza	10.00
Al Leiter	4.00

Throwback Threads Patch

	NM/M
Common Player:	10.00

Production 100 Sets

	Kevin Millwood	15.00
	Vladimir Guerrero	20.00
	Troy Glaus	15.00
	Mike Piazza	25.00
	Al Leiter	10.00

Throwback Threads Dual

	NM/M

Production 100

	Vladimir Guerrero, Troy Glaus	15.00
	Mike Piazza, Al Leiter	15.00

Turn Back the Clock

	NM/M
Complete Set (10):	75.00
Common Player:	4.00

Inserted 1:160

1	Yogi Berra	8.00
2	Mike Schmidt	15.00
3	Tom Seaver	6.00
4	Reggie Jackson	5.00
5	Pee Wee Reese	4.00
6	Phil Rizzuto	4.00
7	Jim Palmer	4.00
8	Robin Yount	15.00
9	Nolan Ryan	20.00
10	Al Kaline	10.00

2004 Fleer America's National Pastime

	NM/M
Common Player (1-60):	.25
Common Card (61-90):	3.00

Production 699 Sets

Pack (5):	10.00
Box (10):	100.00
1	Hideki Matsui	2.50
2	Khalil Greene	1.00
3	Pedro J. Martinez	1.00
4	Sammy Sosa	2.00
5	Mark Teixeira	.40
6	Orlando Cabrera	.25
7	Scott Podsednik	.25
8	Miguel Tejada	.60
9	Andruw Jones	.75
10	Manny Ramirez	.75
11	Jose Reyes	.25
12	Bobby Abreu	.40
13	Alex Rodriguez	2.50
14	Ivan Rodriguez	.60
15	Jason Schmidt	.40
16	Mike Piazza	1.50
17	Eric Chavez	.40
18	Mark Prior	1.50
19	Adam Dunn	.60
20	Richard Hidalgo	.25
21	Todd Helton	.75
22	Rocco Baldelli	.60
23	Roy Oswalt	.40
24	Angel Berroa	.25
25	Jason Giambi	1.00
26	Jim Thome	1.00
27	Javy Lopez	.40
28	Derek Jeter	3.00
29	Tom Glavine	.40
30	Magglio Ordonez	.40
31	Austin Kearns	.60
32	Scott Rolen	1.00
33	Miguel Cabrera	.75
34	Vernon Wells	.40
35	Frank Thomas	.75
36	Jeff Bagwell	.75
37	Shannon Stewart	.25
38	Richie Sexson	.60

39	Hideo Nomo	.40
40	Nomar Garciaparra	2.50
41	C.C. Sabathia	.25
42	Albert Pujols	2.50
43	Barry Zito	.60
44	Hank Blalock	.60
45	Carlos Delgado	.75
46	Greg Maddux	1.50
47	Randy Johnson	1.00
48	Josh Beckett	.75
49	Kerry Wood	.75
50	Roger Clemens	1.50
51	Garret Anderson	.40
52	Ichiro Suzuki	2.00
53	Kip Wells	.25
54	Vladimir Guerrero	1.00
55	Shawn Green	.40
56	Chipper Jones	1.50
57	Aubrey Huff	.25
58	Ken Griffey Jr.	1.50
59	Torii Hunter	.60
60	Alfonso Soriano	1.00
61	Chris Shelton RC	8.00
62	Graham Koonce	4.00
63	Kazuo Matsui RC	8.00
64	Alfredo Simon RC	4.00
65	Mike Gosling	3.00
66	Mike Rouse	4.00
67	Mariano Gomez RC	3.00
68	Justin Leone RC	3.00
69	Jose Capellan RC	3.00
70	Donald Kelly RC	4.00
71	Merkin Valdez RC	4.00
72	Greg Dobbs RC	4.00
73	Shingo Takatsu RC	4.00
74	Chris Aguila RC	3.00
75	Jerome Gamble RC	4.00
76	Onil Joseph RC	4.00
77	Ramon Ramirez RC	4.00
78	Angel Chavez RC	4.00
79	Hector Gimenez RC	3.00
80	Ivan Ochoa RC	4.00
81	Aarom Baldiris RC	4.00
82	Akinori Otsuka RC	4.00
83	Ruddy Yan RC	3.00
84	Jerry Gil RC	3.00
85	Shawn Hill RC	4.00
86	John Gall RC	4.00
87	Jason Bartlett RC	4.00
88	Jorge Sequea RC	4.00
89	Luis Gonzalez RC	4.00
90	Sean Henn	3.00

Red

(1-60):	1-4X
(61-90):	.75-1.25X

Production 150 Sets

White

(1-60):	2-6X
(61-90):	.75-2X

Production 50 Sets

Blue

No Pricing
Production One Set

American GAME

	NM/M
Common Player:	1.00

Inserted 1:10 (Hobby)
Inserted 1:12 (Retail)

1	Greg Maddux	2.50
2	Randy Johnson	2.00
3	Roger Clemens	4.00
4	Mark Prior	3.00
5	Mike Piazza	2.50
6	Alex Rodriguez	4.00
7	Adam Dunn	1.00
8	Jim Thome	2.00
9	Derek Jeter	5.00
10	Scott Rolen	2.00
11	Nomar Garciaparra	4.00
12	Kerry Wood	1.50
13	Chipper Jones	2.50
14	Frank Thomas	1.50
15	Jeff Bagwell	1.50

American Game - Jersey

	NM/M
Common Player:	8.00

Inserted 1:96
Patch #'d between 25 & 50: 2-6X
Patch #'d less than 25: No Pricing
Masterpiece: No Pricing
Production One Set

JB	Jeff Bagwell/50	8.00
RCL	Roger Clemens/47	10.00
AD	Adam Dunn/30	8.00
DJ	Derek Jeter/10	15.00
RJO	Randy Johnson/42	8.00
CJ	Chipper Jones/37	10.00
GM	Greg Maddux/46	12.00
MPR	Mark Prior/45	10.00
AR	Alex Rodriguez/13	15.00
SR	Scott Rolen/49	8.00
FT	Frank Thomas/35	8.00
JT	Jim Thome/47	8.00
KW	Kerry Wood/43	8.00

American Game - Dual

Numbered between 10 & 25.
No Pricing

American Game - Single

Numbered between 6 & 31.
No Pricing

American Flag Box Topper

No Pricing
Numbered to indicated quantity.

History in the Making

	NM/M
Common Player:	.75

Inserted 1:5 (Hobby)
Inserted 1:4 (Retail)

1	Pedro J. Martinez	1.50
2	Alex Rodriguez	3.00
3	Sammy Sosa	2.50
4	Mike Piazza	2.00
5	Jason Giambi	1.50
6	Jim Thome	1.50
7	Derek Jeter	4.00
8	Hideo Nomo	.75
9	Nomar Garciaparra	3.00
10	Albert Pujols	3.00
11	Greg Maddux	2.00
12	Randy Johnson	1.50
13	Roger Clemens	2.00
14	Ichiro Suzuki	2.50
15	Vladimir Guerrero	1.50
16	Chipper Jones	2.00
17	Ken Griffey Jr.	2.00
18	Manny Ramirez	1.00
19	Ivan Rodriguez	.75
20	Mark Prior	2.00
21	Austin Kearns	.75
22	Alfonso Soriano	1.50
23	Barry Zito	.75
24	Josh Beckett	1.00
25	Angel Berroa	.75
26	Jose Reyes	.75
27	Adam Dunn	.75
28	Todd Helton	1.00
29	Hank Blalock	.75
30	Kazuo Matsui	6.00

History in the Making - Jersey

	NM/M
Common Player:	5.00

Inserted 1:36
Patch: 2-6X
Numbered between 20 & 50.
Masterpiece: No Pricing
Production One Set

JB	Josh Beckett/45	8.00
AB	Angel Berroa/20	5.00
MB	Hank Blalock/48	8.00
RC	Roger Clemens/26	10.00
AD	Adam Dunn/49	8.00
JG	Jason Giambi/24	8.00
VG	Vladimir Guerrero/50	8.00
TH	Todd Helton/32	8.00
DJ	Derek Jeter/22	15.00
RJ	Randy Johnson/50	8.00
CJ	Chipper Jones/10	10.00
AK	Austin Kearns/41	8.00

GM	Greg Maddux/47	12.00
PM	Pedro J. Martinez/45	8.00
KM	Kazuo Matsui/20	20.00
HN	Hideo Nomo/50	5.00
MP	Mike Piazza/42	10.00
MPR	Mark Prior/49	10.00
AP	Albert Pujols/46	15.00
MR	Manny Ramirez/46	8.00
JR	Jose Reyes/37	5.00
AR	Alex Rodriguez/21	15.00
IR	Ivan Rodriguez/43	8.00
AS	Alfonso Soriano/48	8.00
SS	Sammy Sosa/39	12.00
JT	Jim Thome/49	8.00
BZ	Barry Zito/44	8.00

Dual Swatch

No Pricing
Production Five Sets
BRJF Babe Ruth, Jimmie Foxx

National Treasures

	NM/M
Common Card:	3.00

Production 500 Sets
Gold: Numbered to notable year.

#75-99:	1-3X
#25-74:	1-5X
Less than 25:	No Pricing
2NT	Kenesaw Landis	3.00
5NT	Leo Durocher	3.00
9NT	Peter Gammons	3.00
10NT	Ernie Harwell	3.00
11NT	Billy Martin	4.00
12NT	John McGraw	3.00
13NT	Red Barber	3.00
15NT	Casey Stengel	3.00
16NT	Sparky Anderson	3.00
17NT	Harry Caray	4.00
18NT	Ban Johnson	3.00
20NT	Ralph Kiner	3.00

National Treasures - Red

	NM/M
Peter Gammons/50	20.00
Ernie Harwell/50	20.00
Ralph Kiner/50	20.00

National Treasures - White

	NM/M
Ernie Harwell/30	15.00

National Treasures - Blue

No Pricing

National Treasures - Masterpiece

No Pricing

Signature Swing - Gold

	NM/M

Numbered to indicated quantity.

Carlos Beltran/176	25.00
Lance Berkman/173	15.00
Hank Blalock/265	15.00
Joe Carter/95	12.00

Sean Casey/169	12.00
Eric Chavez/138	15.00
David Eckstein/161	10.00
Carlton Fisk/36	40.00
Lew Ford/183	20.00
Luis Gonzalez/61	15.00
Frank Howard/60	20.00
Derek Jeter/35	125.00
Chipper Jones/116	40.00
Al Kaline/79	40.00
Javy Lopez/220	15.00
Edgar Martinez/85	20.00
Bill Mazeroski/61	25.00
Jim Palmer/33	25.00
Dave Parker/57	15.00
Mike Piazza/64	100.00
Albert Pujols/110	125.00
Gary Sheffield/25	60.00
Warren Spahn/188	30.00
Alan Trammell/138	10.00

Signature Swing - Red

Numbered to indicated quantity.

Carlos Beltran/109	25.00
Lance Berkman/98	20.00
Hank Blalock/109	20.00
George Brett/42	120.00
Sean Casey/108	15.00
Eric Chavez/85	20.00
Bucky Dent/35	20.00
David Eckstein/76	15.00
Carlton Fisk/51	40.00
Lew Ford/109	20.00
Jay Gibbons/33	20.00
Luis Gonzalez/109	10.00
Chipper Jones/88	40.00
Al Kaline/43	50.00
Javy Lopez/65	20.00
Don Mattingly/73	50.00
Bill Mazeroski/56	30.00
Stan Musial/36	60.00
Jim Palmer/25	25.00
Dave Parker/79	15.00
Mike Piazza/31	125.00
Albert Pujols/76	150.00
Gary Sheffield/26	60.00
Bill "Moose" Skowron/59	15.00
Warren Spahn/106	40.00
Alan Trammell/89	15.00

Signature Swing - White

NM/M

Numbered to indicated quantity.

Carlos Beltran/29	25.00
Lance Berkman/42	25.00
Hank Blalock/29	30.00
George Brett/30	120.00
Joe Carter/35	20.00
Sean Casey/25	20.00
Eric Chavez/34	25.00
Jim Edmonds/42	20.00
Carlton Fisk/37	40.00
Jay Gibbons/28	20.00
Luis Gonzalez/57	20.00
Vladimir Guerrero/44	30.00
Frank Howard/48	25.00
Aubrey Huff/34	15.00
Chipper Jones/45	50.00
Al Kaline/29	50.00
Javy Lopez/43	20.00
Edgar Martinez/37	30.00
Don Mattingly/35	80.00
Stan Musial/39	60.00
Rafael Palmeiro/47	50.00
Dave Parker/34	15.00
Mike Piazza/40	125.00
Albert Pujols/43	175.00
Cal Ripken Jr./25	200.00
Ivan Rodriguez/35	50.00
Scott Rolen/28	80.00
Gary Sheffield/43	60.00
Bill "Moose" Skowron/28	20.00
Frank Thomas/43	80.00
Alan Trammell/28	20.00

Signature Swing - Blue

NM/M

Numbered to indicated quantity.

Sean Casey/37	40.00
Adam Dunn/31	20.00
David Eckstein/44	15.00
Jim Edmonds/37	20.00
Lew Ford/44	40.00
Bill Mazeroski/49	50.00
Jim Palmer/44	25.00
Dave Parker/29	15.00
Scott Podsednik/38	20.00
Warren Spahn/26	50.00

Signature Swing - Masterpiece

No Pricing
Production One Set

Signs of the Future - Gold

NM/M

Numbered to indicated quantity.

Jeremy Bonderman/300	8.00
Miguel Cabrera/300	20.00
Bobby Crosby/299	20.00
Adam Everett/285	10.00
Luis Gonzalez/264	8.00
Mike Gosling/195	8.00
Khalil Greene/300	50.00
Rich Harden/304	10.00
Sean Henn/300	8.00
Koyie Hill/340	8.00
Ryan Howard/53	60.00
Tim Hudson/72	20.00
Adam LaRoche/78	8.00
Micheal Nakamura/231	8.00
Alexis Rios/45	15.00
Alfredo Simon/258	8.00
Javier Vazquez/21	20.00
Ryan Wagner/251	10.00
Dontrelle Willis/47	40.00
Kevin Youkilis/317	15.00

Signs of the Future - Red

NM/M

Numbered to indicated quantity.

Aarom Baldiris/64	10.00
Jeremy Bonderman/120	10.00
A.J. Burnett/58	20.00
Miguel Cabrera/133	25.00
Bobby Crosby/114	20.00
Adam Everett/106	12.00
Luis Gonzalez/132	10.00
Mike Gosling/132	10.00
Khalil Greene/121	50.00
Rich Harden/133	15.00
Sean Henn/128	10.00
Koyie Hill/58	12.00
Edwin Jackson/52	15.00
Graham Koonce/55	10.00
Josh Labandeira/55	8.00
Adam LaRoche/124	8.00
Justin Leone/68	20.00
Micheal Nakamura/133	10.00
Bubba Nelson/99	10.00
Jose Reyes/93	25.00
Mike Rouse/124	8.00
Alfredo Simon/112	10.00
Ryan Wagner/98	12.00
Kerry Wood/55	30.00
Kevin Youkilis/133	20.00

Signs of the Future - White

NM/M

Numbered to indicated quantity.

Garrett Atkins/25	15.00
Miguel Cabrera/34	40.00
Bobby Crosby/52	30.00
Adam Everett/36	15.00
Luis Gonzalez/50	15.00
Mike Gosling/41	12.00
Khalil Greene/52	80.00
Rich Harden/52	20.00
Sean Henn/48	12.00
Koyie Hill/27	15.00
Tim Hudson/28	40.00
Adam LaRoche/50	12.00
Micheal Nakamura/33	15.00
Jose Reyes/52	30.00
Alexis Rios/39	15.00
Mike Rouse/40	15.00
Alfredo Simon/28	15.00
Ryan Wagner/46	15.00
Kevin Youkilis/52	25.00

Signs of the Future - Blue

NM/M

Numbered to indicated quantity.

Javier Vazquez/98	15.00
Kerry Wood/98	25.00

Ted Williams Reprint Set

NM/M

Ted Williams Card (1-81):	6.00

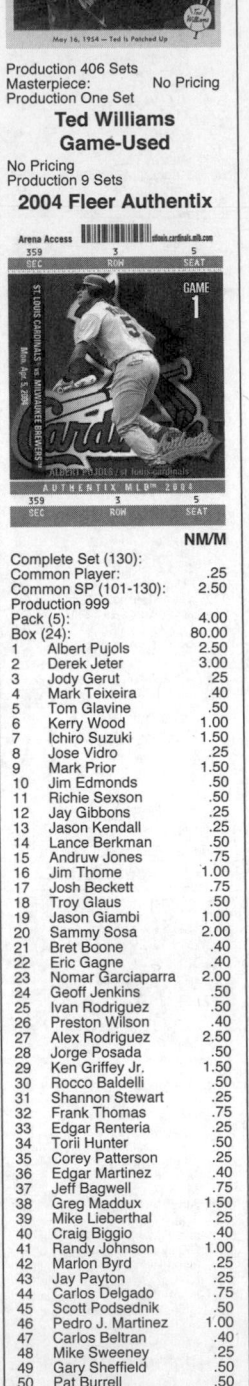

May 16, 1954 – Ted Is Patched Up

Production 406 Sets
Masterpiece: No Pricing
Production One Set

Ted Williams Game-Used

No Pricing
Production 9 Sets

2004 Fleer Authentix

NM/M

Complete Set (130):	
Common Player:	.25
Common SP (101-130):	2.50
Production 999	
Pack (5):	4.00
Box (24):	80.00
1	Albert Pujols	2.50
2	Derek Jeter	3.00
3	Jody Gerut	.25
4	Mark Teixeira	.40
5	Tom Glavine	.50
6	Kerry Wood	1.00
7	Ichiro Suzuki	1.50
8	Jose Vidro	.25
9	Mark Prior	1.50
10	Jim Edmonds	.50
11	Richie Sexson	.50
12	Jay Gibbons	.25
13	Jason Kendall	.25
14	Lance Berkman	.50
15	Andruw Jones	.75
16	Jim Thome	1.00
17	Josh Beckett	.75
18	Troy Glaus	.50
19	Jason Giambi	1.00
20	Sammy Sosa	2.00
21	Bret Boone	.40
22	Eric Gagne	.40
23	Nomar Garciaparra	2.00
24	Geoff Jenkins	.50
25	Ivan Rodriguez	.50
26	Preston Wilson	.40
27	Alex Rodriguez	2.50
28	Jorge Posada	.50
29	Ken Griffey Jr.	1.50
30	Rocco Baldelli	.50
31	Shannon Stewart	.25
32	Frank Thomas	.75
33	Edgar Renteria	.25
34	Torii Hunter	.50
35	Corey Patterson	.25
36	Edgar Martinez	.40
37	Jeff Bagwell	.75
38	Greg Maddux	1.50
39	Mike Lieberthal	.25
40	Craig Biggio	.40
41	Randy Johnson	1.00
42	Marlon Byrd	.25
43	Jay Payton	.25
44	Carlos Delgado	.75
45	Scott Podsednik	.50
46	Pedro J. Martinez	1.00
47	Carlos Beltran	.40
48	Mike Sweeney	.25
49	Gary Sheffield	.50
50	Pat Burrell	.50
51	Shawn Green	.40
52	Tony Batista	.25
53	Brian Giles	.40
54	Roy Oswalt	.40
55	Brandon Webb	.40
56	Miguel Tejada	.50
57	Miguel Cabrera	.75
58	Luis Gonzalez	.40
59	Billy Wagner	.25
60	Craig Monroe	.25
61	Vernon Wells	.40
62	Bernie Williams	.50
63	Austin Kearns	.50
64	Aubrey Huff	.25
65	Mike Piazza	1.50
66	Magglio Ordonez	.50
67	Bo Hart	.25
68	Hideo Nomo	.50
69	Curt Schilling	.50
70	Barry Zito	.50
71	Todd Helton	.75
72	Roy Halladay	.50
73	Alfonso Soriano	1.00
74	Roberto Alomar	.50
75	Scott Rolen	1.00
76	Manny Ramirez	.75
77	Sean Burroughs	.25
78	Angel Berroa	.25
79	Javy Lopez	.40
80	Reggie Sanders	.40
81	Juan Pierre	.25
82	Chipper Jones	1.50
83	Bobby Abreu	.40
84	Dontrelle Willis	.40
85	Tim Salmon	.40
86	Eric Chavez	.40
87	Adam Dunn	.50
88	Rafael Palmeiro	.75
89	Hideki Matsui	2.50
90	Esteban Loaiza	.25
91	Darin Erstad	.40
92	Vladimir Guerrero	1.00
93	David Ortiz	.25
94	Jason Schmidt	.40
95	Dmitri Young	.25
96	Garret Anderson	.50
97	Mark Mulder	.25
98	Omar Vizquel	.25
99	Hank Blalock	.50
100	Jose Reyes	.25
101	Rickie Weeks	8.00
102	Chad Gaudin	2.50
103	Ryan Wagner	3.00
104	Koyie Hill	2.50
105	Rich Harden	2.50
106	Edwin Jackson	4.00
107	Khalil Greene	3.00
108	Chien-Ming Wang	3.00
109	Matt Kata	2.50
110	Chin-Hui Tsao	2.50
111	Dan Haren	2.50
112	Delmon Young	8.00
113	Mike Hessman	2.50
114	Bobby Crosby	2.50
115	Cory Sullivan RC	2.50
116	Brandon Watson	2.50
117	Aaron Miles	2.50
118	Jonny Gomes	2.50
119	Graham Koonce	2.50
120	Shawn Hill RC	2.50
121	Garrett Atkins	2.50
122	John Gall RC	2.50
123	Chad Bentz RC	2.50
124	Alfredo Simon RC	2.50
125	Josh Labandeira RC	3.00
126	Ryan Howard	3.00
127	Jason Bartlett RC	2.50
128	Dallas McPherson	2.50
129	Greg Dobbs RC	2.50
130	Jerry Gil RC	2.50

Balcony

Stars (1-100):	4-8X
SP's (101-130):	1-2X
Production 100 Sets	

Club Box

Stars (1-100):	10-15X
SP's (101-130):	2-4X
Production 25 Sets	

Standing Room Only

No Pricing
Production 5 Sets

Autographed Authentix

NM/M

Common Autograph:	15.00
Production 75	
Championship:	No Pricing
Production 25	
Rocco Baldelli	40.00
Angel Berroa	15.00
Marlon Byrd	15.00
Miguel Cabrera	40.00

Eric Gagne	40.00
Roy Halladay	20.00
Trot Nixon	35.00
Juan Pierre	15.00
Albert Pujols	120.00
Vernon Wells	20.00

Ballpark Classics

	NM/M
Complete Set (10):	15.00
Common Player:	1.00
Inserted 1:12	
1BC Nomar Garciaparra	3.00
2BC Alfonso Soriano	1.50
3BC Chipper Jones	1.50
4BC Albert Pujols	3.00
5BC Jason Giambi	1.00
6BC Mark Prior	2.00
7BC Sammy Sosa	2.50
8BC Derek Jeter	4.00
9BC Greg Maddux	2.00
10BC Alex Rodriguez	3.00

Ballpar Classics Game-Used

	NM/M
Common Player:	8.00
Inserted 1:37	
Nomar Garciaparra	10.00
Jason Giambi	8.00
Derek Jeter	15.00
Chipper Jones	8.00
Greg Maddux	10.00
Mark Prior	10.00
Albert Pujols	15.00
Alex Rodriguez	10.00
Alfonso Soriano	8.00
Sammy Sosa	12.00

Jersey Authentix Ripped

	NM/M
Common Player:	4.00
Inserted 1:16	
Unripped:	2-3X
Production 50 Sets	
All-Star Unripped:	No Pricing
Production One Set	
Jeff Bagwell	8.00
Josh Beckett	6.00
Miguel Cabrera	8.00
Hee Seop Choi	4.00
Nomar Garciaparra	10.00
Jason Giambi	8.00
Torii Hunter	5.00
Derek Jeter	15.00
Randy Johnson	8.00
Chipper Jones	8.00
Austin Kearns	6.00
Greg Maddux	8.00
Juan Pierre	4.00
Mark Prior	10.00
Albert Pujols	15.00
Jose Reyes	8.00
Alex Rodriguez	10.00
Ivan Rodriguez	6.00
Alfonso Soriano	8.00
Sammy Sosa	12.00
Mark Teixeira	6.00
Jim Thome	8.00
Dontrelle Willis	6.00
Kerry Wood	8.00
Barry Zito	6.00

Jersey Authentix Autograph

	NM/M
Common Autograph:	15.00
Production 100	
All-Star Autographs:	1-1.25X
Production 50	
Championship Autos.:	No Pricing
Production 10	
Albert Pujols	125.00
Juan Pierre	15.00
Miguel Cabrera	40.00
Eric Gagne	40.00
Marlon Byrd	15.00
Rocco Baldelli	40.00
Roy Halladay	25.00

Vernon Wells	20.00
Trot Nixon	35.00

Jersey Authentix Game of the Week

	NM/M
Common Duo:	10.00
Inserted 1:120	
Unripped:	1-1.5X
Production 50	
1 Dontrelle Willis, Kerry Wood	20.00
2 Miguel Cabrera, Mark Teixeira	15.00
3 Nomar Garciaparra, Alfonso Soriano	15.00
4 Jim Thome, Ivan Rodriguez	10.00
5 Josh Beckett, Mark Prior	15.00
6 Alex Rodriguez, Derek Jeter	35.00
7 Jeff Bagwell, Austin Kearns	15.00
8 Jason Giambi, Barry Zito	10.00
9 Jose Reyes, Juan Pierre	10.00
10 Chipper Jones, Albert Pujols	20.00

Ticket for Four

	NM/M
Common Quad Jersey:	20.00
Production 100 Sets	
1 Dontrelle Willis, Josh Beckett, Mark Prior, Kerry Wood	20.00
2 Nomar Garciaparra, Alex Rodriguez, Derek Jeter, Jose Reyes	50.00
4 Jason Giambi, Jim Thome, Mark Teixeira, Jeff Bagwell	25.00
5 Chipper Jones, Albert Pujols, Sammy Sosa, Torii Hunter	40.00
6 Greg Maddux, Randy Johnson, Kerry Wood, Barry Zito	20.00
7 Nomar Garciaparra, Alfonso Soriano, Chipper Jones, Albert Pujols	40.00
8 Sammy Sosa, Derek Jeter, Alex Rodriguez, Jim Thome	50.00
9 Mark Prior, Greg Maddux, Austin Kearns, Ivan Rodriguez	15.00
10 Jason Giambi, Randy Johnson, Jeff Bagwell, Torii Hunter	20.00

Ticket Studs

	NM/M
Complete Set (15):	20.00
Common Player:	.75
Inserted 1:6	

1TS	Nomar Garciaparra	3.00
2TS	Josh Beckett	1.00
3TS	Derek Jeter	4.00
4TS	Mark Prior	2.00
5TS	Albert Pujols	3.00
6TS	Alfonso Soriano	1.50
7TS	Jim Thome	1.50
8TS	Ichiro Suzuki	2.00
9TS	Hideki Matsui	3.00
10TS	Dontrelle Willis	.75
11TS	Mike Schmidt	2.00
12TS	Nolan Ryan	4.00
13TS	Reggie Jackson	1.00
14TS	Tom Seaver	1.00
15TS	Brooks Robinson	1.00

2004 Fleer Classic Clippings

	NM/M
Common Player (1-75):	.25
Minor Stars (1-75):	.40
Unlisted Stars (1-75):	.60
Common Player (76-110):	5.00
Production 500 Sets	
Pack (5):	5.00
Box (18):	90.00
1 Juan Pierre	.25
2 Derek Jeter	3.00
3 Jose Reyes	.40
4 Eric Chavez	.40
5 Alex Rodriguez	2.50
6 Mark Prior	2.00
7 Carlos Beltran	.40
8 Ichiro Suzuki	2.00
9 Shawn Green	.40
10 Richie Sexson	.60
11 Andruw Jones	.75
12 Geoff Jenkins	.40
13 Luis Gonzalez	.40
14 Garret Anderson	.40
15 Adam Dunn	.60
16 Nomar Garciaparra	2.50
17 Albert Pujols	2.50
18 Jeff Bagwell	.75
19 Rocco Baldelli	.60
20 Preston Wilson	.25
21 Gary Sheffield	.60
22 Magglio Ordonez	.40
23 Kerry Wood	.75
24 Manny Ramirez	.75
25 Randy Johnson	1.00
26 Ken Griffey Jr.	1.50
27 Rafael Palmeiro	.40
28 Vernon Wells	.25
29 Mike Piazza	1.50
30 Hank Blalock	.60
31 Miguel Cabrera	.75
32 Jason Giambi	1.00
33 Troy Glaus	.60
34 Angel Berroa	.25
35 Greg Maddux	1.50
36 Lance Berkman	.40
37 Austin Kearns	.60
38 Hideo Nomo	.40
39 Sammy Sosa	2.00
40 Jose Vidro	.25
41 Curt Schilling	.60
42 Melvin Mora	.25
43 Scott Podsednik	.40
44 Dontrelle Willis	.40
45 Roy Halladay	.40
46 Hideki Matsui	2.50
47 Tom Glavine	.40
48 Torii Hunter	.60
49 Chipper Jones	1.50
50 Barry Zito	.60
51 Vladimir Guerrero	1.00
52 Jim Thome	1.00
53 Shannon Stewart	.25
54 Miguel Tejada	.60
55 Roy Oswalt	.40
56 Jason Kendall	.40
57 Brian Giles	.40
58 Jason Schmidt	.40
59 Pedro J. Martinez	1.00
60 Bret Boone	.40
61 Josh Beckett	.75
62 Scott Rolen	1.00
63 Aubrey Huff	.25
64 Pat Burrell	.40
65 Mark Teixeira	.40
66 Alfonso Soriano	1.00

67	Carlos Delgado	.75
68	Ivan Rodriguez	.60
69	Brandon Webb	.25
70	Eric Gagne	.40
71	Frank Thomas	.75
72	Jody Gerut	.25
73	Todd Helton	.75
74	Andy Pettitte	.60
75	Roger Clemens	1.50
76	Rickie Weeks	8.00
77	Chien-Ming Wang	8.00
78	Edwin Jackson	6.00
79	Dallas McPherson	8.00
80	John Gall RC	5.00
81	Ryan Wagner	6.00
82	Clint Barmes	8.00
83	Khalil Greene	6.00
84	Chin-Hui Tsao	6.00
85	Alexis Rios	6.00
86	Merkin Valdez RC	5.00
87	Aarom Baldiris RC	5.00
88	Onil Joseph RC	5.00
89	Ruddy Yan RC	5.00
90	Chad Bentz RC	5.00
91	Shawn Hill RC	5.00
92	Delmon Young	8.00
93	Hector Gimenez RC	5.00
94	William Bergolla RC	5.00
95	Ronny Cedeno RC	5.00
96	Angel Chavez RC	5.00
97	Justin Leone RC	5.00
98	Ivan Ochoa RC	5.00
99	Ian Snell RC	10.00
100	Rich Harden	6.00
101	Joe Mauer	10.00
102	Akinori Otsuka RC	10.00
103	Bobby Crosby	6.00
104	Garrett Atkins	5.00
105	Dan Haren	5.00
106	Koyie Hill	5.00
107	Kazuo Matsui RC	20.00
108	Adam LaRoche	5.00
109	Terrmel Sledge	5.00
110	Shingo Takatsu RC	5.00

First Edition

(1-75):	1-5X
(76-110):	.5-1.25X
Production 150 Sets	

Press Proof Cyan

(1-100):	No Pricing
Production One Set	

Press Proof Magenta

(1-100):	No Pricing
Production One Set	

Press Proof Yellow

(1-100):	No Pricing
Production One Set	

Press Proof Black

(1-100):	No Pricing
Production One Set	

Press Clippings

	NM/M
Common Player:	1.25
Inserted 1:6	
1PC Josh Beckett	1.75

2PC	Albert Pujols	4.00
3PC	Derek Jeter	5.00
4PC	Alex Rodriguez	5.00
5PC	Jim Thome	2.00
6PC	Angel Berroa	1.00
7PC	Dontrelle Willis	1.25
8PC	Roy Halladay	1.25
9PC	Kerry Wood	1.75
10PC	Mark Prior	3.00
11PC	Roger Clemens	3.00
12PC	Hideki Matsui	4.00
13PC	Ichiro Suzuki	3.50
14PC	Eric Gagne	1.25
15PC	Miguel Cabrera	1.75
16PC	Nomar Garciaparra	4.00
17PC	Hank Blalock	1.25
18PC	Chipper Jones	3.00
19PC	Sammy Sosa	3.50
20PC	Alfonso Soriano	2.00

Bat Rack (3 Bat) - Green

	NM/M
Common Card:	10.00
Production 175 Sets	
Red:	.5-1.5X
Production 50 Sets	
Gold:	1-2X
Production 25 Sets	
Derek Jeter,	
Alex Rodriguez,	
Gary Sheffield	40.00
Sammy Sosa, Derek Lee,	
Mark Prior	25.00
Miguel Cabrera,	
Juan Pierre,	
Josh Beckett	15.00
Nomar Garciaparra,	
Manny Ramirez,	
Curt Schilling	20.00
Alfonso Soriano,	
Hank Blalock,	
Mark Teixeira	15.00
Mike Piazza, Jose Reyes,	
Kazuo Matsui	20.00
Richie Sexson,	
Brandon Webb,	
Roberto Alomar,	
Mark Prior, Josh Beckett,	10.00
Curt Schilling	15.00
Carlos Delgado,	
Aubrey Huff,	
Jason Giambi	10.00
Albert Pujols, Scott Rolen,	
Jim Edmonds	30.00
Rocco Baldelli,	
Aubrey Huff,	
Carlos Delgado	10.00
Jeff Bagwell, Jim Thome,	
Todd Helton	15.00
Gary Sheffield,	
Manny Ramirez,	
Rocco Baldelli	10.00
Troy Glaus, Scott Rolen,	
Hank Blalock	15.00
Roberto Alomar,	
Jose Reyes,	
Alfonso Soriano	15.00
Alex Rodriguez,	
Miguel Tejada,	
Miguel Cabrera	15.00
Vladimir Guerrero,	
Juan Pierre,	
Chipper Jones	10.00
Jason Giambi, Jim Thome,	
Todd Helton	15.00
Vladimir Guerrero,	
Albert Pujols,	
Sammy Sosa	25.00
Derek Jeter, Hideki Matsui,	
Nomar Garciaparra	40.00

Bat Rack (4 Bat) - Green

	NM/M
Common Card:	15.00
Production 75 Sets.	
Red:	1-2X.
Production 25 Sets.	
Gold:	No Pricing.
Production 10 Sets.	
Derek Jeter,	
Alex Rodriguez,	
Gary Sheffield,	
Jason Giambi.	50.00
Sammy Sosa, Mark Prior,	
Miguel Cabrera,	
Josh Beckett.	30.00
Derek Jeter,	
Alex Rodriguez,	
Kazuo Matsui,	
Nomar Garciaparra.	60.00
Juan Pierre, Gary Sheffield,	
Miguel Cabrera,	
Rocco Baldelli.	15.00
Jim Thome, Jeff Bagwell,	
Mark Teixeira,	
Carlos Delgado.	20.00
Albert Pujols, Mark Prior,	
Alex Rodriguez,	
Curt Schilling.	40.00
Todd Helton, Jose Reyes,	
Kazuo Matsui,	
Scott Rolen.	40.00
Sammy Sosa,	
Vladimir Guerrero,	
Jim Edmonds,	
Chipper Jones.	25.00
Alfonso Soriano,	
Roberto Alomar,	
Hank Blalock,	
Troy Glaus.	15.00
Rocco Baldelli,	
Chipper Jones,	
Juan Pierre,	
Manny Ramirez.	20.00
Jim Thome, Jeff Bagwell,	
Todd Helton,	
Derek Lee.	20.00
Curt Schilling,	
Nomar Garciaparra,	
Brandon Webb,	
Richie Sexson.	25.00
Mike Piazza, Jose Reyes,	
Albert Pujols,	
Scott Rolen.	30.00
Vladimir Guerrero,	
Miguel Tejada,	
Jason Giambi,	
Mike Piazza.	25.00
Jeff Bagwell, Derrek Lee,	
Aubrey Huff,	
Carlos Delgado.	20.00

Bat Rack Autographs - Bronze

	NM/M
Common Player:	12.00
Production 75 Sets	
Roberto Alomar	40.00
Josh Beckett	40.00
Hank Blalock	30.00
Miguel Cabrera	40.00
Jim Edmonds	30.00
Aubrey Huff	12.00
Edgar Martinez	20.00
Jose Reyes	25.00
Gary Sheffield	30.00
Mark Teixeira	20.00

C.C. Signature Edition

	NM/M
Common Player:	15.00

Production 50 Sets		
Masterpiece:		No Pricing
Production One Set		
1	Nolan Ryan	125.00
2	Mike Schmidt	75.00
3	Cal Ripken Jr.	175.00
4	Don Mattingly	75.00
5	Albert Pujols	125.00
6	Randy Johnson	60.00
7	Khalil Greene	40.00
8	Rickie Weeks	30.00
9	Edwin Jackson	15.00
10	Rich Harden	15.00
16	Vladimir Guerrero	40.00
17	Mark Prior	40.00

Classic Clippings

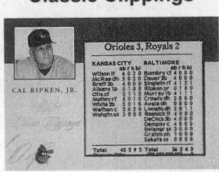

		NM/M
Common Player (1-20):		4.00
Production 750 Sets		
Common Player (21-25):		8.00
Production 100 Sets		
1CC	Nolan Ryan	15.00
2CC	Mike Schmidt	6.00
3CC	Cal Ripken Jr.	10.00
4CC	Don Mattingly	8.00
5CC	Roger Clemens	5.00
6CC	Randy Johnson	4.00
7CC	Mark Prior	3.00
8CC	Jim Thome	5.00
9CC	Sammy Sosa	5.00
10CC	Pedro J. Martinez	4.00
11CC	Chipper Jones	4.00
12CC	Vladimir Guerrero	4.00
13CC	Albert Pujols	6.00
14CC	Ichiro Suzuki	6.00
15CC	Derek Jeter	10.00
16CC	Alex Rodriguez	8.00
17CC	Greg Maddux	5.00
18CC	Nomar Garciaparra	8.00
19CC	Mike Piazza	6.00
20CC	Ken Griffey Jr.	8.00
21CC	Pie Traynor	8.00
22CC	Bill Dickey	8.00
23CC	George Sisler	10.00
24CC	Ted Williams	20.00
25CC	Enos Slaughter	8.00

Jersey Rack Autograph - Bronze

		NM/M
Common Player:		12.00
Production 149 Sets		
Silver Jersey:		.5-1.5X
Production 50 Sets		
Patch Rack Gold:		No Pricing
Production To Player's Jersey No.		
	Garret Anderson	15.00
	Garrett Atkins	12.00
	Rocco Baldelli	20.00
	Josh Beckett	20.00
	Angel Berroa	15.00
	Marlon Byrd	12.00
	Miguel Cabrera	40.00
	Carlos Delgado	20.00
	Jody Gerut	12.00
	Roy Halladay	15.00
	Dan Haren	12.00
	Torii Hunter	15.00
	Edwin Jackson	20.00
	Barry Larkin	40.00
	Mark Mulder	15.00
	Mike Mussina	30.00
	Andy Pettitte	40.00
	Albert Pujols	120.00
	Ivan Rodriguez	50.00
	Scott Rolen	50.00
	Ryan Wagner	12.00
	Brandon Webb	15.00
	Dontrelle Willis	20.00
	Kerry Wood	30.00

Phenom Lineup Autograph - Red

	NM/M
Common Card:	10.00
Production 150 Sets	
Silver:	.5-1.25X
Production 99 Sets	
Gold:	.5-1.5X
Production 50 Sets	

Cards contain autograph of the first player listed.

Ryan Howard, Jim Thome,	
Todd Helton	10.00
John Gall, Albert Pujols,	
Scott Rolen	10.00
Jose Reyes, Kazuo Matsui,	
Rickie Weeks	20.00
Hank Blalock, Troy Glaus,	
Alex Rodriguez	20.00
Rich Harden, Roy Halladay,	
Barry Zito	10.00
Alexis Rios,	
Carlos Delgado,	
Vernon Wells	10.00
Laynce Nix,	
Alex Rodriguez,	
Garret Anderson	10.00
Khalil Greene,	
Edgar Renteria,	
Mike Lowell	25.00
Dontrelle Willis, Mark Prior,	
Kerry Wood	15.00
Rickie Weeks, Luis Castillo,	
Jose Reyes	20.00
Dallas McPherson,	
Troy Glaus,	
Garret Anderson	15.00
Chien-Ming Wang,	
Hideki Matsui,	
Jason Giambi	20.00
Scott Podsednik,	
Albert Pujols,	
Andruw Jones	15.00
Bobby Crosby,	
Nomar Garciaparra,	
Alex Rodriguez	18.00
Ryan Wagner,	
Dontrelle Willis,	
Mark Prior	8.00
Delmon Young,	
Ichiro Suzuki,	
Hideki Matsui	30.00
Grady Sizemore,	
Manny Ramirez,	
Garret Anderson	20.00
Adam LaRoche,	
Albert Pujols,	
Jim Thome	10.00
Edwin Jackson, Mark Prior,	
Kerry Wood	10.00
Miguel Cabrera,	
Luis Castillo,	
Mike Lowell	40.00
Merkin Valdez,	
Edwin Jackson,	
Dontrelle Willis	10.00
Angel Berroa,	
Nomar Garciaparra,	
Alex Rodriguez	10.00

2004 Fleer EX

	NM/M
Common Player (1-40):	1.50
Minor Stars (1-40):	2.00
Unlisted Stars (1-40):	2.50
Common Player (41-65):	5.00
Production 500 Sets	
Die-Cuts (41-65):	.75-1.25X

First 150 seq. #'d cards are die-cut.

1	Vladimir Guerrero	3.50
2	Randy Johnson	3.50

3	Chipper Jones	4.00
4	Miguel Tejada	2.50
5	Pedro J. Martinez	3.50
6	Nomar Garciaparra	6.00
7	Sammy Sosa	5.00
8	Greg Maddux	4.00
9	Frank Thomas	3.00
10	Ken Griffey Jr.	4.00
11	Omar Vizquel	2.00
12	Todd Helton	3.00
13	Ivan Rodriguez	2.50
14	Miguel Cabrera	3.00
15	Dontrelle Willis	2.00
16	Jeff Bagwell	3.00
17	Roger Clemens	4.00
18	Carlos Beltran	2.00
19	Hideo Nomo	2.00
20	Scott Podsednik	1.50
21	Torii Hunter	2.50
22	Jose Vidro	1.50
23	Mike Piazza	4.00
24	Hideki Matsui	6.00
25	Alex Rodriguez	6.00
26	Derek Jeter	8.00
27	Tim Hudson	2.00
28	Jim Thome	3.50
29	Craig Wilson	1.50
30	Brian Giles	2.00
31	Jason Schmidt	2.00
32	Ichiro Suzuki	5.00
33	Scott Rolen	3.50
34	Albert Pujols	6.00
35	Rocco Baldelli	2.50
36	Alfonso Soriano	3.50
37	Carlos Delgado	3.00
38	Curt Schilling	2.50
39	Mark Prior	4.00
40	Josh Beckett	3.00
41	Merkin Valdez **RC**	5.00
42	Akinori Otsuka **RC**	8.00
43	Ian Snell **RC**	8.00
44	Kazuo Matsui **RC**	10.00
45	Jason Bartlett **RC**	8.00
46	Dennis Sarfate **RC**	5.00
47	Sean Henn	5.00
48	David Aardsma	5.00
49	Casey Kotchman	8.00
50	John Gall **RC**	5.00
51	William Bergolla **RC**	5.00
52	Angel Chavez **RC**	5.00
53	Hector Gimenez **RC**	5.00
54	Aarom Baldiris **RC**	5.00
55	Justin Leone **RC**	8.00
56	Onil Joseph **RC**	5.00
57	Freddy Guzman **RC**	5.00
58	Andres Blanco **RC**	5.00
59	Greg Dobbs **RC**	5.00
60	Joe Mauer	5.00
61	Luis Gonzalez **RC**	8.00
62	Chris Saenz **RC**	5.00
63	Zack Greinke	5.00
64	Jose Capellan **RC**	8.00
65	Brad Halsey **RC**	10.00

Essential Credentials Now

Cards 51-65:	1-2X
Cards 41-50:	1.25-2.25X
Cards 25-40:	3-5X
Cards 1-24:	No Pricing

Production 65 - 1 Sets

Essential Credentials Future

Cards 1-25:	.75-2X
Cards 26-40:	2-4X
Cards 41-65:	No Pricing

Production 65 - 1 Sets

ConnEXions

NM/M

Production 25 or 50 Sets

6	Casey Kotchman, Joe Mauer/50	100.00
7	Shannon Stewart, Torii Hunter/25	90.00
9	Johnny Damon, Trot Nixon/25	90.00
10	Carlos Lee, Magglio Ordonez/25	30.00
12	Scott Podsednik, Lyle Overbay/25	60.00
13	Barry Zito, Tim Hudson/25	125.00
14	Bucky Dent, Mike Torrez/50	40.00
15	Brian Giles, Marcus Giles/25	60.00
17	Dontrelle Willis, Miguel Cabrera/25	60.00
18	Michael Young, Khalil Greene/50	80.00
19	Mark Teixeira, Hank Blalock/25	100.00

Classic ConnEXions Doubles

No Pricing
Production 22 Sets

Emerald:	No Pricing

Production One Set

Classic ConnEXions Triples

No Pricing
Production 13 Sets

Emerald:	No Pricing

Production One Set

Clearly Authentics Black Patch

NM/M

Common Player:	10.00

Production 75 Sets

Jeff Bagwell	20.00
Rocco Baldelli	15.00
Josh Beckett	20.00
Lance Berkman	15.00
Hank Blalock	15.00
Pat Burrell	15.00
Miguel Cabrera	20.00
Rod Carew	30.00
Roger Clemens	30.00
Adam Dunn	15.00
Eric Gagne	15.00
Jason Giambi	25.00
Brian Giles	15.00
Troy Glaus	15.00
Shawn Green	15.00
Vladimir Guerrero	25.00
Tony Gwynn	30.00
Todd Helton	20.00
Rickey Henderson	30.00
Tim Hudson	15.00
Torii Hunter	15.00
Randy Johnson	25.00
Andruw Jones	20.00
Chipper Jones	30.00
Greg Maddux	30.00
Pedro J. Martinez	25.00
Hideki Matsui	40.00
Kazuo Matsui	40.00
Don Mattingly	40.00
Paul Molitor	30.00
Eddie Murray	50.00
Hideo Nomo	15.00
Magglio Ordonez	15.00
Rafael Palmeiro	20.00
Mike Piazza	30.00
Mark Prior	30.00
Albert Pujols	40.00
Manny Ramirez	20.00
Cal Ripken Jr.	75.00
Alex Rodriguez	40.00
Ivan Rodriguez	15.00
Scott Rolen	25.00
Curt Schilling	15.00
Ozzie Smith	25.00
Alfonso Soriano	25.00
Sammy Sosa	35.00
Mark Teixeira	15.00
Miguel Tejada	15.00
Frank Thomas	20.00
Jim Thome	25.00
Rickie Weeks	15.00
Dontrelle Willis	15.00
Kerry Wood	20.00
Barry Zito	15.00

Clearly Authentics Pewter Patch/Bat

.75-1.5X Black Patch Version
Production 44 Sets

Clearly Authentics Bronze Patch/Jersey

.75-1.5X Black Patch Version
Production 35 Sets

Clearly Authentics Turquoise Nameplate

No Pricing
Sequentially #'d to varying quantities.

Clearly Authentics Tan Double Patch

No Pricing
Production 22 Sets

Clearly Authentics Tan Double Patches

No Pricing
Production 22 Sets

Clearly Authentics Burgundy Triple Patch

No Pricing
Production 13 Sets

Clearly Authentics Royal Patch/ Bat/Jersey

No Pricing
Production 8 Sets

Clearly Authentics - Double MLB Logo

No Pricing
Production One Set

Clearly Authentics Signature Black Jersey

NM/M

Sequentially #'d to varying quantities.

Burgundy Buttons:	No Pricing

Production 6 Sets

Emerald MLB Logo:	No Pricing

Production 1 Set

Josh Beckett/50	30.00
Hank Blalock/50	50.00
Miguel Cabrera/50	30.00
Roger Clemens/50	150.00
J.D. Drew/50	30.00
Troy Glaus/50	50.00
Vladimir Guerrero/50	50.00
Todd Helton/50	40.00
Chipper Jones/50	40.00
Roy Oswalt/49	30.00
Rafael Palmeiro/43	60.00
Albert Pujols/50	225.00
Manny Ramirez/50	60.00
Mariano Rivera/50	80.00
Gary Sheffield/50	50.00
Frank Thomas/50	60.00
Bernie Williams/42	75.00

Dontrelle Willis/50	25.00
Kerry Wood/34	50.00

Clearly Authentics Signature Tan Patch

Sequentially #'d to varying quantities.

Clearly Authentics Pewter

Sequentially #'d to varying quantities.

Check Mates

NM/M

Production 1 or 25 Sets

1	Albert Pujols, Stan Musial/25	500.00
2	Eddie Murray, Rafael Palmeiro/25	200.00
4	Ernie Banks, Ryne Sandberg/25	300.00
9	Manny Ramirez, Pedro J. Martinez/25	300.00
10	Wade Boggs, Tony Gwynn/25	175.00
11	Reggie Jackson, Don Mattingly/25	200.00
14	Robin Yount, Kirby Puckett/25	150.00

Double Barrel

No Pricing
Production One Set

Signings of the Times Best Year

NM/M

Sequentially #'d to player's best year.

Emerald:	No Pricing

Production One Set

Ernie Banks/58/Bat	60.00
Johnny Bench/72/Jsy	60.00
Wade Boggs/87/Bat	40.00
George Brett/80/Jsy	80.00
Jose Canseco/88/Jsy	30.00
Will Clark/91/Jsy	40.00
Tony Gwynn/94/Jsy	50.00
Rickey Henderson/90/Jsy	75.00
Bo Jackson/89/Jsy	60.00
Don Mattingly/85/Jsy	80.00
Eddie Murray/83/Jsy	60.00
Stan Musial/48/Bat	75.00
Nolan Ryan/73/Jsy	150.00
Ryne Sandberg/90/Bat	60.00
Mike Schmidt/80/Jsy	80.00
Tom Seaver/69/Jsy	75.00
Ozzie Smith/87/Jsy	50.00
Duke Snider/55/Bat	50.00
Carl Yastrzemski/67/Bat	60.00

Signings of the Times HOF Year

NM/M

Sequentially #'d to player's HOF year.

Ernie Banks/77/Bat	60.00
Johnny Bench/89/Jsy	60.00
Yogi Berra/72/Bat	50.00
George Brett/99/Jsy	80.00
Reggie Jackson/93/Jsy	50.00
Stan Musial/69/Bat	75.00
Mike Schmidt/95/Jsy	75.00
Tom Seaver/92/Jsy	50.00
Duke Snider/80/Bat	30.00
Carl Yastrzemski/89/Bat	60.00

Signings of the Times Debut Year

NM/M

Sequentially #'d to player's debut year.

Ernie Banks/53/Bat	60.00
Johnny Bench/67/Jsy	60.00
Yogi Berra/46/Jsy	60.00
Wade Boggs/82/Bat	40.00
Jose Canseco/85/Jsy	30.00
Will Clark/86/Jsy	40.00
Tony Gwynn/82/Jsy	50.00
Rickey Henderson/79/Jsy	75.00
Bo Jackson/86/Jsy	60.00
Reggie Jackson/67/Jsy	50.00
Don Mattingly/82/Jsy	80.00
Eddie Murray/77/Jsy	60.00

Stan Musial/41/Bat	75.00
Kirby Puckett/84/Bat	50.00
Nolan Ryan/66/Jsy	150.00
Ryne Sandberg/81/Bat	60.00
Deion Sanders/89/Jsy	40.00
Mike Schmidt/72/Jsy	80.00
Ozzie Smith/78/Jsy	50.00
Duke Snider/47/Bat	50.00
Carl Yastrzemski/61/Bat	75.00
Robin Yount/74/Jsy	40.00

Signings of the Times Pewter

NM/M

Sequentially #'d to varying quantities.

Wade Boggs/32/Bat	50.00
Jose Canseco/27/Jsy	75.00
Rickey Henderson/32/Jsy	75.00
Bo Jackson/60/Jsy	50.00
Don Mattingly/33/Jsy	80.00
Eddie Murray/50/Jsy	80.00
Stan Musial/51/Bat	80.00
Kirby Puckett/31/Bat	50.00
Ryne Sandberg/28/Bat	60.00
Ozzie Smith/36/Jsy	80.00

2004 Fleer Flair

NM/M

Common Player (1-60):	1.00
Minor Star (1-60):	1.25
Unlisted Star (1-60):	1.75
Common Rookie (61-82):	5.00

Rookie Production 799 Sets

Collection Row (1-60):	1-3X
Collection Row (61-82):	.5-2X

Row 1 Production 125 Sets

Collection Row 2: No Pricing

Production One Set

Box (1):		100.00
1	Brandon Webb	1.00
2	Todd Helton	2.00
3	Jeff Bagwell	2.00
4	Shawn Green	1.25
5	Vladimir Guerrero	3.00
6	Tom Glavine	1.25
7	Jason Giambi	3.00
8	Barry Zito	1.75
9	Jason Kendall	1.25
10	Carlos Delgado	2.00
11	Curt Schilling	1.75
12	Ken Griffey Jr.	3.50
13	Mike Piazza	3.50
14	Alfonso Soriano	3.00
15	Albert Pujols	5.00
16	Chipper Jones	3.50
17	Alex Rodriguez	5.00
18	Miguel Tejada	1.75
19	Pedro J. Martinez	3.00
20	Mark Prior	4.00
21	Magglio Ordonez	1.25
22	Scott Podsednik	1.75
23	Shannon Stewart	1.00
24	Rocco Baldelli	1.75
25	Darin Erstad	1.25
26	Omar Vizquel	1.00
27	Angel Berroa	1.00
28	Jose Vidro	1.00
29	Rich Harden	1.00
30	Andruw Jones	2.00
31	Troy Glaus	1.75
32	Sammy Sosa	4.00
33	Dontrelle Willis	1.25
34	Ivan Rodriguez	1.75
35	Nomar Garciaparra	5.00
36	Josh Beckett	2.00
37	Jose Reyes	1.00
38	Scott Rolen	3.00
39	Greg Maddux	3.50
40	Andy Pettitte	1.75
41	Jason Schmidt	1.25
42	Edgar Martinez	1.25
43	Manny Ramirez	2.00
44	Torii Hunter	1.75
45	Mark Teixeira	1.25
46	Hideo Nomo	1.00
47	Brian Giles	1.25
48	Adam Dunn	1.75
49	Fernando Vina	1.00
50	Hideki Matsui	3.00
51	Jim Thome	3.00
52	Hank Blalock	1.75
53	Miguel Cabrera	2.00
54	Randy Johnson	3.00
55	Javy Lopez	1.25
56	Frank Thomas	2.00
57	Roger Clemens	3.50
58	Marlon Byrd	1.00
59	Derek Jeter	6.00
60	Ichiro Suzuki	4.00
61	Kazuo Matsui RC	25.00
62	Chad Bentz RC	8.00
63	Greg Dobbs RC	5.00
64	John Gall RC	5.00
65	Cory Sullivan RC	5.00
66	Hector Gimenez RC	5.00
67	Graham Koonce RC	5.00
68	Jason Bartlett RC	5.00
69	Angel Chavez RC	5.00
70	Ronny Cedeno RC	5.00
71	Donald Kelly RC	5.00
72	Ivan Ochoa RC	5.00
73	Ruddy Yan RC	5.00
74	Mike Gosling RC	5.00
75	Alfredo Simon RC	5.00
76	Jerome Gamble RC	5.00
77	Chris Aguila RC	5.00
78	Mike Rouse RC	5.00
79	Justin Leone RC	5.00
80	Merkin Valdez RC	5.00
81	Aarom Baldiris RC	5.00
82	Chris Shelton RC	10.00

Autograph Collection

NM/M

Common Player: 10.00

Production between 65-200 Sets

Crown: .5-1X

Production 100 Sets

Parchment: 1-1.75X

Production 25 Sets

Platinum: No Pricing

Production 10 Sets

Masterpiece: No Pricing

Production One Set

Garrett Atkins/195	10.00
Rocco Baldelli/180	25.00
Aarom Baldiris/180	10.00
Jason Bartlett/95	15.00
Josh Beckett/65	40.00
Angel Berroa/178	15.00
Miguel Cabrera/172	40.00
Bobby Crosby/87	30.00
Jim Edmonds/73	25.00
John Gall/94	30.00
Khalil Greene/40	195.00
Dan Haren/195	15.00
Ryan Howard/185	75.00
Edwin Jackson/183	15.00
Andruw Jones/163	25.00
Graham Koonce/175	10.00
Josh Labandeira/166	10.00
Adam LaRoche/280	15.00
Justin Leone/180	15.00
Ryan Meaux/180	10.00
Mike Mussina/69	50.00
Micheal Nakamura/180	10.00
Bubba Nelson/185	15.00
Corey Patterson/172	15.00
Juan Pierre/94	15.00
Scott Podsednik/96	25.00
Mark Prior/60	60.00
Alexis Rios/185	20.00
Michael Rouse/195	10.00
Chris Shelton/170	30.00
Grady Sizemore/197	30.00
Merkin Valdez/179	10.00
Javier Vazquez/187	30.00
Ryan Wagner/175	15.00
Chien-Ming Wang/178	50.00
Brandon Webb/122	15.00
Rickie Weeks/169	30.00
Dontrelle Willis/73	30.00
Kerry Wood/73	40.00
Delmon Young/177	25.00

Cuts and Glory

NM/M

Common Player: 25.00

Production 100 Sets

Silver: .75-1.25X

Production 50 Sets

Gold: No Pricing

Production 15 Sets

Platinum: No Pricing

Production 3 Sets

Masterpiece: No Pricing

Production One Set

Garret Anderson	30.00
Hank Blalock	25.00
Marlon Byrd	25.00
Carlos Delgado	30.00
Adam Dunn	40.00
Eric Gagne	40.00
Luis Gonzalez	25.00
Vladimir Guerrero	50.00
Ricky Henderson	100.00
Torii Hunter	25.00
Randy Johnson	60.00
Chipper Jones	60.00
Austin Kearns	25.00
Greg Maddux	75.00
Edgar Martinez	40.00
Magglio Ordonez	25.00
Albert Pujols	150.00
Jose Reyes	30.00
Scott Rolen	40.00
Mark Teixeira	25.00
Frank Thomas	75.00

Diamond Cuts Game-Used Blue

NM/M

Common Player: 5.00

Production 250 Sets

Blue Die-Cut: 1-3X

Production 25 Sets

Red: .5-1.25X

Production 175 Sets

Red Die-Cut: No Pricing

Production 18 Sets

Pewter: .5-1.5X

Production 125 Sets

Pewter Die-Cut: No Pricing

Production 13 Sets

Copper: .5-1.5X

Production 75 Sets

Die-Cut Copper: No Pricing

Production 8 Sets

Silver: .5-1.5X

Production 50 Sets

Silver Die-Cut: No Pricing

Production 5 Sets

Gold: 1-5X

Numbered to player's jersey No.

Gold Die-Cut: No Pricing

Production 3 Sets

Platinum: 2-5X

Numbered to 2003 HR/Win total.

Platinum Die-Cut: No Pricing

Production One Set

Purple: No Pricing

Production One Set

JB	Josh Beckett	8.00
HB	Hank Blalock	5.00
RC	Roger Clemens	10.00
NG	Nomar Garciaparra	12.00
DJ	Derek Jeter	15.00
AJ	Andruw Jones	8.00
CJ	Chipper Jones	8.00
PM	Pedro J. Martinez	8.00
HM	Hideki Matsui	12.00
ANP	Andy Pettitte	8.00
MIP	Mike Piazza	8.00
MAP	Mark Prior	8.00
ALP	Albert Pujols	12.00
JR	Jose Reyes	5.00
SR	Scott Rolen	8.00
SS	Curt Schilling	5.00
SS	Sammy Sosa	10.00
IS	Ichiro Suzuki	10.00
MT	Mark Teixeira	5.00
DW	Dontrelle Willis	5.00

Dual Patch

No Pricing

Production 10 Sets

Hot Numbers Game-Used Blue

NM/M

Common Player: 5.00

Production 250 Sets

Blue Die-Cut: 1-3X

Production 25 Sets

Red: .5-1.25X

Production 175 Sets

Red Die-Cut: No Pricing

Production 18 Sets

Pewter: .5-1.5X

Production 125 Sets

Pewter Die-Cut: No Pricing

Production 13 Sets

Copper: .5-1.5X

Production 75 Sets

Die-Cut Copper: No Pricing

Production 8 Sets

Silver: .5-1.5X

Production 50 Sets

Silver Die-Cut: No Pricing

Production 5 Sets

Gold: 1-5X

Numbered to player's jersey No.

Gold Die-Cut: No Pricing

Production 3 Sets

Platinum: 2-5X

Numbered to 2003 HR/Win total.

Platinum Die-Cut: No Pricing

Production One Set

Purple: No Pricing

Production One Set

Jeff Bagwell	8.00
Rocco Baldelli	5.00
Josh Beckett	8.00
Hank Blalock	5.00
Nomar Garciaparra	12.00
Jason Giambi	8.00
Troy Glaus	5.00
Tom Glavine	5.00
Vladimir Guerrero	8.00
Todd Helton	8.00
Derek Jeter	15.00
Randy Johnson	8.00
Chipper Jones	8.00
Barry Larkin	5.00
Greg Maddux	8.00
Pedro J. Martinez	8.00
Mike Mussina	5.00
Hideo Nomo	5.00
Mike Piazza	8.00
Mark Prior	8.00
Albert Pujols	12.00
Manny Ramirez	8.00
Alex Rodriguez	12.00
Curt Schilling	5.00
Sammy Sosa	10.00
Mark Teixeira	5.00
Frank Thomas	8.00
Jim Thome	8.00
Brandon Webb	5.00
Kerry Wood	8.00

Lettermen

No Pricing
Numbered to number of letters
in player's last name.

Power Tools
Game-Used Blue

	NM/M
Common Player:	5.00
Production 250 Sets	
Blue Die-Cut:	1-3X
Production 25 Sets	
Red:	.5-1.25X
Production 175 Sets	
Red Die-Cut:	No Pricing
Production 18 Sets	
Pewter:	.5-1.5X
Production 125 Sets	
Pewter Die-Cut:	No Pricing
Production 13 Sets	
Copper:	.5-1.5X
Production 75 Sets	
Die-Cut Copper:	No Pricing
Production 8 Sets	
Silver:	.5-1.5X
Production 50 Sets	
Silver Die-Cut:	No Pricing
Production 5 Sets	
Gold:	1-5X
Numbered to player's jersey No.	
Gold Die-Cut:	No Pricing
Production 3 Sets	
Platinum:	2-5X
Numbered to 2003 HR total.	
Platinum Die-Cut:	No Pricing
Production One Set	
Purple:	No Pricing
Production One Set	
Rocco Baldelli	5.00
Adam Dunn	5.00
Nomar Garciaparra	12.00
Jason Giambi	8.00
Vladimir Guerrero	8.00
Derek Jeter	15.00
Chipper Jones	8.00
Mike Piazza	10.00
Jorge Posada	8.00
Albert Pujols	12.00
Manny Ramirez	8.00
Alex Rodriguez	12.00
Alfonso Soriano	8.00
Sammy Sosa	10.00
Jim Thome	8.00

SIGnificant Cuts

	NM/M
Serially Numbered	
RA	Roberto Alomar/50	60.00
JB2	Johnny Bench/25	100.00
VC	Vince Carter/200	50.00
TC	Ty Cobb	2,650
DE	Dennis Eckersley/75	30.00
RH	Roy Halladay/50	40.00
BL	Barry Larkin/75	30.00
PM	Paul Molitor/75	50.00
AP1	Andy Pettitte/50	40.00
JR	Jose Reyes/25	40.00
MR	Mariano Rivera/50	75.00
IR	Ivan Rodriguez/50	40.00
NR	Nolan Ryan/25	200.00
MS	Mike Schmidt/25	125.00
GS	Gary Sheffield/50	50.00

2004 Fleer Genuine Insider

	NM/M
Common Player (1-90):	.25
Minor Stars:	.40
Unlisted Stars:	.60
Common Rookie Insider (91-100):	4.00
Production 499 Sets	
Common Upside (101-120):	4.00
Production 799 Sets	
Common Mini Rookie:	4.00
Production 350 Sets	
Pack (5):	4.00
Box (15):	75.00
1	Troy Glaus	.60
2	Eric Chavez	.40

3	Lance Berkman	.40
4	Pedro J. Martinez	1.00
5	Jim Edmonds	.40
6	Tom Glavine	.40
7	Ken Griffey Jr.	1.50
8	Vernon Wells	.40
9	Hideki Matsui	2.50
10	Jeff Bagwell	.75
11	Rafael Palmeiro	.40
12	Edgar Martinez	.40
13	Bernie Williams	.60
14	Josh Beckett	.75
15	Javy Lopez	.40
16	Ichiro Suzuki	2.00
17	Scott Podsednik	.40
18	Sammy Sosa	2.00
19	Mark Teixeira	.40
20	Jorge Posada	.60
21	Miguel Cabrera	.75
22	Chipper Jones	1.50
23	Sean Burroughs	.25
24	Dmitri Young	.25
25	Brandon Webb	.25
26	Bobby Abreu	.40
27	Hideo Nomo	.40
28	Frank Thomas	.75
29	Alex Rodriguez	2.50
30	Derek Jeter	3.00
31	Todd Helton	.75
32	Andruw Jones	.75
33	Jason Kendall	.40
34	Eric Gagne	.40
35	Omar Vizquel	.40
36	Vladimir Guerrero	1.00
37	Jim Thome	1.00
38	Mike Sweeney	.25
39	Manny Ramirez	.75
40	Scott Rolen	1.00
41	Jose Vidro	.25
42	Adam Dunn	.60
43	Garret Anderson	.40
44	Mike Lieberthal	.25
45	Roy Oswalt	.40
46	Geoff Jenkins	.40
47	Magglio Ordonez	.40
48	Hank Blalock	.60
49	Barry Zito	.60
50	Dontrelle Willis	.40
51	Greg Maddux	1.50
52	Brian Giles	.40
53	Shawn Green	.40
54	Carlos Lee	.25
55	Carlos Delgado	.75
56	Alfonso Soriano	1.00
57	Angel Berroa	.25
58	Kerry Wood	.75
59	Rocco Baldelli	.60
60	Gary Sheffield	.60
61	Ivan Rodriguez	.60
62	Richie Sexson	.60
63	Marlon Byrd	.25
64	Carlos Beltran	.40
65	Mark Prior	2.00
66	Aubrey Huff	.40
67	Jason Giambi	1.00
68	Curt Schilling	.60
69	Reggie Sanders	.25
70	Mike Piazza	1.50
71	Craig Monroe	.25
72	Randy Johnson	1.00
73	Pat Burrell	.40
74	Craig Biggio	.40
75	Nomar Garciaparra	2.50
76	Albert Pujols	2.50
77	Jose Reyes	.25
78	Preston Wilson	.25
79	Miguel Tejada	.60
80	Bret Boone	.40
81	Shannon Stewart	.25
82	Jody Gerut	.25
83	Tim Salmon	.25
84	Tim Hudson	.40
85	Juan Pierre	.25

86	Jay Gibbons	.40
87	Jason Schmidt	.40
88	Torii Hunter	.60
89	Austin Kearns	.25
90	Roy Halladay	.40
91	John Gall RC	8.00
92	Hideki Matsui RC	25.00
93	Merkin Valdez RC	4.00
94	William Bergolla RC	8.00
95	Angel Chavez RC	4.00
96	Hector Gimenez RC	4.00
97	Aarom Baldiris RC	4.00
98	Justin Leone RC	6.00
99	Onil Joseph RC	5.00
100	Freddy Guzman RC	5.00
101	Rickie Weeks	6.00
102	Chad Bentz RC	5.00
103	Bobby Crosby	6.00
104	Dallas McPherson	5.00
105	Brandon Watson RC	4.00
106	Garrett Atkins	6.00
107	Graham Koonce	4.00
108	Chien-Ming Wang	4.00
109	Jonny Gomes	4.00
110	Edwin Jackson	4.00
111	Alfredo Simon RC	5.00
112	Delmon Young	6.00
113	Angel Guzman	4.00
114	Ryan Howard	4.00
115	Scott Hairston	10.00
116	Edwin Encarnacion	5.00
117	Byron Gettis	4.00
118	Kevin Youkilis	8.00
119	Grady Sizemore	4.00
120	Corey Hart	4.00
121	Greg Dobbs RC	4.00
122	Jerry Gil RC	4.00
123	Shawn Hill RC	4.00
124	John Labandeira RC	4.00
125	Jason Bartlett RC	4.00
126	Ronny Cedeno RC	4.00
127	Donald Kelly RC	8.00
128	Ivan Ochoa RC	5.00
129	Mariano Gomez RC	5.00
130	Ruddy Yan RC	5.00

Genuine Reflection

(1-90):	.5-2X
(101-120):	.5-1.25X
Production 99 Sets	

Autograph Insider

	NM/M
Common Player:	10.00
Production as indicated.	
RA	Roberto Alomar/150	30.00
MB	Marlon Byrd/550	10.00
MC	Miguel Cabrera/250	40.00
DE	David Eckstein/350	10.00
JG	Jody Gerut/550	10.00
JG2	Jay Gibbons/350	10.00
OH	Orlando Hudson/550	15.00
AH	Aubrey Huff/550	10.00
AK	Austin Kearns/350	10.00
MO	Magglio Ordonez/250	10.00
RP	Rafael Palmeiro/150	50.00
SP	Scott Podsednik/550	10.00
JR	Jose Reyes/350	25.00
MR	Mariano Rivera/150	60.00
IR	Ivan Rodriguez/150	40.00
JR2	Jimmy Rollins/350	15.00
JS	Jason Schmidt/300	300.00
JS2	John Smoltz/150	30.00
MT	Mark Teixeira/350	20.00
BW	Brandon Webb/450	10.00

Autograph Insider - Bat

	NM/M
Common Card:	20.00
Production 50 Sets	
RA	Roberto Alomar	40.00
MB	Marlon Byrd	20.00
MC	Miguel Cabrera	60.00
DE	David Eckstein	30.00
JG	Jody Gerut	25.00
JG2	Jay Gibbons	20.00
OH	Orlando Hudson	20.00
AH	Aubrey Huff	25.00
AK	Austin Kearns	20.00
RP	Rafael Palmeiro	50.00
SP	Scott Podsednik	25.00
JR	Jose Reyes	35.00
IR	Ivan Rodriguez	50.00
JR2	Jimmy Rollins	30.00
MT	Mark Teixeira	25.00

Autograph Insider - Ball

No Pricing
Production 10 Sets

Autograph Insider - Jersey

	NM/M
Common Player:	10.00
Production 100 Sets	
RA	Roberto Alomar	30.00
MB	Marlon Byrd	10.00
MC	Miguel Cabrera	40.00
DE	David Eckstein	15.00
JG	Jody Gerut	25.00
JG2	Jay Gibbons	20.00
OH	Orlando Hudson	10.00
AH	Aubrey Huff	10.00
AK	Austin Kearns	20.00
MO	Magglio Ordonez	40.00
RP	Rafael Palmeiro	50.00
SP	Scott Podsednik	25.00
AP	Albert Pujols	100.00
JR	Jose Reyes	35.00
MR	Mariano Rivera	75.00
IR	Ivan Rodriguez	50.00
JR2	Jimmy Rollins	20.00
JS	Jason Schmidt	20.00
JS2	John Smoltz	50.00
MT	Mark Teixeira	25.00
BW	Brandon Webb	10.00

Autograph Insider-Cut Signatures

No Pricing

Classic Confrontations

	NM/M
Common Card:	3.00
Inserted 1:18	
1CC	Mike Piazza, Roger Clemens	4.00
2CC	Pedro J. Martinez, Derek Jeter	6.00
3CC	Randy Johnson, Jeff Bagwell	3.00
4CC	Mark Prior, Albert Pujols	4.00
5CC	Josh Beckett, Sammy Sosa	4.00
6CC	Eric Gagne, Hank Blalock	3.00
7CC	Mariano Rivera, Nomar Garciaparra	5.00
8CC	Curt Schilling, Chipper Jones	4.00
9CC	Kerry Wood, Jim Edmonds	3.00
10CC	Barry Zito, Alfonso Soriano	3.00
11CC	Randy Johnson, Ken Griffey Jr.	4.00
12CC	Derek Jeter, John Smoltz	6.00
13CC	Roy Oswalt, Ken Griffey Jr.	4.00
14CC	Dontrelle Willis, Hideki Matsui	4.00
15CC	Hideo Nomo, Ichiro Suzuki	4.00

Cl. Confrontations Jersey

	NM/M
Common Card:	5.00
Production 400 Sets	

JB	Jeff Bagwell with Randy Johnson	6.00
JB2	Josh Beckett with Sammy Sosa	6.00
HB	Hank Blalock with Eric Gagne	8.00
RC	Roger Clemens with Mike Piazza	15.00
JE	Jim Edmonds with Kerry Wood	5.00
EG	Eric Gagne with Hank Blalock	5.00
NG	Nomar Garciaparra with Mariano Rivera	8.00
DJ	Derek Jeter with Pedro J. Martinez	15.00
RJ1	Randy Johnson with Jeff Bagwell	8.00
RJ2	Randy Johnson with Ken Griffey Jr.	8.00
CJ	Chipper Jones with Curt Schilling	8.00
PM	Pedro J. Martinez with Derek Jeter	10.00
HN	Hideo Nomo with Ichiro Suzuki	12.00
RO	Roy Oswalt with Ken Griffey Jr.	5.00
MP	Mike Piazza with Roger Clemens	8.00
MP2	Mark Prior with Albert Pujols	8.00
AP	Albert Pujols with Mark Prior	12.00
MR	Mariano Rivera with Nomar Garciaparra	8.00
CS	Curt Schilling with Chipper Jones	5.00
JS	John Smoltz with Derek Jeter	5.00
AS	Alfonso Soriano with Barry Zito	8.00
SS	Sammy Sosa with Josh Beckett	8.00
DW	Dontrelle Willis with Matsui	5.00
KW	Kerry Wood with Jim Edmonds	8.00
BZ	Barry Zito with Alfonso Soriano	5.00

Classic Confrontations Dual Jersey

	NM/M
Common Card:	12.00
Production 100 Sets	
Dual Patch:	No Pricing
Production 10 Sets	
Barry Zito, Alfonso Soriano	12.00
Curt Schilling, Chipper Jones	12.00
Eric Gagne, Hank Blalock	12.00
Josh Beckett, Sammy Sosa	12.00
Kerry Wood, Jim Edmonds	15.00
Mark Prior, Albert Pujols	15.00
Roger Clemens, Mariano Rivera	15.00
Nomar Garciaparra, Pedro J. Martinez	20.00
Derek Jeter, Randy Johnson	20.00
Jeff Bagwell	12.00

Genuine Article Insider-Jersey

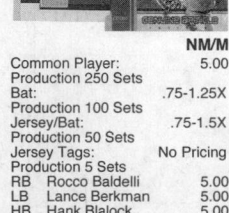

	NM/M
Common Player:	5.00
Production 250 Sets	
Bat:	.75-1.25X
Production 100 Sets	
Jersey/Bat:	.75-1.5X
Production 50 Sets	
Jersey Tags:	No Pricing
Production 5 Sets	
RB Rocco Baldelli	5.00
LB Lance Berkman	5.00
HB Hank Blalock	5.00
MC Miguel Cabrera	8.00
CD Carlos Delgado	6.00
AD Adam Dunn	5.00

NG	Nomar Garciaparra	12.00
JG	Jason Giambi	6.00
TG	Troy Glaus	5.00
VG	Vladimir Guerrero	8.00
TH	Todd Helton	8.00
DJ	Derek Jeter	18.00
CJ	Chipper Jones	8.00
MO	Magglio Ordonez	5.00
RP	Rafael Palmeiro	5.00
MP	Mike Piazza	8.00
AP	Albert Pujols	12.00
MR	Manny Ramirez	6.00
JR	Jose Reyes	6.00
AR	Alex Rodriguez	15.00
CS	Gary Sheffield	6.00
AS	Alfonso Soriano	8.00
SS	Sammy Sosa	10.00
MT	Mark Teixeira	5.00
JT	Jim Thome	6.00

Tools of the Game

	NM/M
Common Player:	1.00
Inserted 1:6	
1TG Jason Giambi	1.50
2TG Torii Hunter	1.00
3TG Derek Jeter	4.00
4TG Nomar Garciaparra	3.00
5TG Albert Pujols	3.00
6TG Jim Thome	1.50
7TG Alex Rodriguez	4.00
8TG Chipper Jones	2.00
9TG Sammy Sosa	2.50
10TG Jose Reyes	1.50
11TG Pedro J. Martinez	1.50
12TG Greg Maddux	2.00
13TG Randy Johnson	1.50
14TG Curt Schilling	1.00
15TG Mark Prior	2.00
16TG Ichiro Suzuki	2.50
17TG Hideki Matsui	3.00
18TG Kazuo Matsui	2.50
19TG Ken Griffey Jr.	2.00
20TG Josh Beckett	1.00

Tools of Game-Game Jersey

	NM/M
Common Player:	5.00
Production 250 Sets	
Jersey/Bat:	.75-2X
Production 125	
Jersey/Bat/Cap:	1-2.5X
Production 75	
NG Nomar Garciaparra	12.00
JG Jason Giambi	8.00
TH Torii Hunter	5.00
DJ Derek Jeter	15.00
RJ Randy Johnson	6.00
CJ Chipper Jones	8.00
GM Greg Maddux	6.00
PM Pedro J. Martinez	6.00
MP Mark Prior	10.00
AP Albert Pujols	12.00
JR Jose Reyes	8.00
AR Alex Rodriguez	15.00
CS Curt Schilling	5.00
SS Sammy Sosa	10.00
JT Jim Thome	6.00

2004 Fleer Greats of the Game

	NM/M
Common Player:	.40
Minor Stars:	.75
Pack (5):	10.00
Box (15):	130.00
1 Lou Gehrig	4.00
2 Ty Cobb	3.00
3 Dizzy Dean	1.50
4 Jimmie Foxx	1.50

5	Hank Greenberg	1.00
6	Babe Ruth	6.00
7	Honus Wagner	1.50
8	Mickey Cochrane	1.50
9	Pepper Martin	.40
10	Charlie Gehringer	.75
11	Carl Hubbell	.40
12	Bill Terry	.40
13	Mel Ott	.75
14	Bill Dickey	1.50
15	Ted Williams	6.00
16	Roger Maris	3.00
17	Thurman Munson	2.00
18	Phil Rizzuto	2.00
19	Stan Musial	3.00
20	Duke Snider	2.50
21	Reggie Jackson	1.50
22	Don Mattingly	1.50
23	Vida Blue	.75
24	Harmon Killebrew	1.50
25	Lou Brock	.75
26	Al Kaline	1.00
27	Dave Parker	.40
28	Nolan Ryan	6.00
29	Jim Rice	.40
30	Paul Molitor	2.00
31	Dwight Evans	.40
32	Brooks Robinson	1.50
33	Jose Canseco	.40
34	Alan Trammell	.40
35	Johnny Bench	2.00
36	Carlton Fisk	1.00
37	Jim Palmer	1.50
38	George Brett	2.00
39	Mike Schmidt	2.00
40	Tony Perez	.75
41	Paul Blair	.40
42	Fred Lynn	.40
43	Carl Yastrzemski	1.50
44	Steve Carlton	1.00
45	Dennis Eckersley	1.50
46	Tom Seaver	1.50
47	Juan Marichal	.75
48	Tony Gwynn	2.00
49	Bill "Moose" Skowron	.75
50	Bob Gibson	1.50
51	Luis Tiant	.75
52	Eddie Murray	1.00
53	Frank Robinson	2.00
54	Rocky Colavito	.75
55	Bobby Shantz	.40
56	Ernie Banks	2.00
57	Rod Carew	1.00
58	Gorman Thomas	.40
59	Bernie Carbo	.40
60	Joe Rudi	.40
61	Graig Nettles	.75
62	Ron Guidry	.75
63	Whitey Ford	1.50
64	George Kell	1.00
65	Cal Ripken Jr.	6.00
66	Willie McCovey	.75
67	Bo Jackson	1.00
68	Kirby Puckett	2.00
69	Ted Kluszewski	.75
70	Johnny Podres	.40
71	Davey Lopes	.40
72	Chris Short	.40
73	Jeff Torborg	.40
74	Bill Freehan	.40
75	Frank Tanana	.40
76	Jack Morris	.75
77	Rick Dempsey	.40
78	Yogi Berra	1.50
79	Tim McCarver	.40
80	Rusty Staub	.40
81	Tony Lazzeri	.40
82	Al Rosen	.40
83	Willie McGee	.75
84	Preacher Roe	.40
85	Dave Kingman	.40
86	Luis Aparicio	1.00
87	John Kruk	.40

88	Bing Miller	.40
89	Joe Charboneau	.40
90	Mark Fidrych	.40
91	Jim "Catfish" Hunter	2.00
92	Nap Lajoie	2.00
93	Eddie Murray	2.00
94	Johnny Pesky	1.00
95	Tom Seaver	2.00
96	Frank Robinson	2.00
97	Enos Slaughter	1.00
98	Cecil Travis	.40
99	Robin Yount	2.00
100	Don Zimmer	.75
101	Babe Herman	.40
102	Ron Santo	.40
103	Willie Stargell	2.00
104	Paul Molitor	
105	Jimmy Piersall	.75
106	Johnny Sain	.40
107	Joe Pepitone	.75
108	Ryne Sandberg	3.00
109	Jim Thorpe	3.00
110	Steve Garvey	1.50
111	Ray Knight	.75
112	Fernando Valenzuela	1.00
113	Will Clark	1.00
114	Tony Kubek	.75
115	Jim Bouton	.40
116	Jerry Koosman	.75
117	Steve Carlton	3.00
118	Richie Ashburn	.75
119	Roberto Clemente	6.00
120	Paul O'Neill	.40
121	Reggie Jackson	3.00
122	Andre Dawson	1.50
123	Hoyt Wilhelm	1.00
124	Dale Murphy	1.50
125	Dwight Gooden	1.50
126	Roger Maris	1.00
127	Bill Mazeroski	1.00
128	Don Newcombe	.75
129	Robin Roberts	.75
130	Duke Snider	2.00
131	Eddie Mathews	3.00
132	Wade Boggs	2.00
133	Rollie Fingers	1.50
134	Frankie Frisch	.40
135	Billy Williams	.75
136	Rod Carew	1.50
137	Dom DiMaggio	.75
138	Orel Hershiser	.40
139	Gary Carter	1.00
140	Keith Hernandez	.75
141	Bob Lemon	.75
142	Nolan Ryan	6.00
143	Ozzie Smith	1.50
144	Rick Sutcliffe	.40
145	Carlton Fisk	1.50

Blue

Cards 81-145	
Cards #'d to 51-96:	3-5X
Cards #'d to 26-50:	5-10X
Cards #'d to less than 25:	No Pricing

Gold Border Autographs

	NM/M
Common Player:	10.00
Randomly Inserted	
Ernie Banks	60.00
Johnny Bench	50.00
Yogi Berra	60.00
Paul Blair	10.00
Vida Blue	10.00
George Brett	125.00
Lou Brock	20.00
Jose Canseco	30.00
Bernie Carbo	10.00
Rod Carew	30.00
Steve Carlton	30.00

Rocky Colavito	100.00
Rick Dempsey	15.00
Dennis Eckersley	50.00
Dwight Evans	15.00
Carlton Fisk	40.00
Whitey Ford	40.00
Bill Freehan	10.00
Bob Gibson	25.00
Ron Guidry	20.00
Tony Gwynn	50.00
Bo Jackson	50.00
Reggie Jackson	100.00
Al Kaline	25.00
George Kell	15.00
Harmon Killebrew	30.00
Davey Lopes	10.00
Fred Lynn	10.00
Juan Marichal	20.00
Don Mattingly	80.00
Tim McCarver	15.00
Willie McCovey	40.00
Paul Molitor	40.00
Jack Morris	10.00
Eddie Murray	80.00
Stan Musial	100.00
Graig Nettles	15.00
Jim Palmer	20.00
Dave Parker	10.00
Tony Perez	30.00
Johnny Podres	10.00
Kirby Puckett	80.00
Jim Rice	20.00
Cal Ripken Jr.	150.00
Phil Rizzuto	40.00
Brooks Robinson	20.00
Frank Robinson	30.00
Joe Rudi	10.00
Nolan Ryan	150.00
Mike Schmidt	60.00
Tom Seaver	80.00
Bobby Shantz	10.00
Bill "Moose" Skowron	10.00
Duke Snider	30.00
Rusty Staub	10.00
Frank Tanana	10.00
Gorman Thomas	10.00
Luis Tiant	10.00
Jeff Torborg	10.00
Alan Trammell	10.00
Carl Yastrzemski	60.00

Gold Border Autograph Series 2

		NM/M
	Common Player:	15.00
	Inserted 1:75	
LA	Luis Aparicio	20.00
WB	Wade Boggs	40.00
JBO	Jim Bouton	15.00
RC2	Rod Carew/Twins	40.00
SC2	Steve Carlton Cards	30.00
GC	Gary Carter	25.00
JCH	Joe Charboneau	15.00
WC	Will Clark	40.00
DC	David Cone	40.00
AD	Andre Dawson	20.00
DD	Dom DiMaggio	50.00
RF	Rollie Fingers	15.00
CF2	Carlton Fisk/White Sox	40.00
SG	Steve Garvey	15.00
DG	Dwight Gooden	20.00
KH	Keith Hernandez	15.00
OH	Orel Hershiser	15.00
RJ2	Reggie Jackson/Angels	60.00
DK	Dave Kingman	15.00
RK	Ray Knight	15.00
JK	Jerry Koosman	20.00
JKR	John Kruk	15.00
TK	Tony Kubek	25.00
BM	Bill Mazeroski	30.00

WMG	Willie McGee	25.00
PM2	Paul Molitor/Jays	40.00
DMU	Dale Murphy	25.00
DN	Don Newcombe	15.00
PO	Paul O'Neill	30.00
JPP	Joe Pepitone	15.00
JPS	Johnny Pesky	25.00
JPI	Jimmy Piersall	20.00
RR	Robin Roberts	20.00
FR2	Frank Robinson/O's	30.00
PRO	Preacher Roe	25.00
AR	Al Rosen	15.00
NR2	Nolan Ryan/Angels	120.00
RS	Ryne Sandberg	75.00
DS	Deion Sanders	30.00
RST	Ron Santo	20.00
TS2	Tom Seaver/Reds	75.00
OS	Ozzie Smith	40.00
DS2	Duke Snider	40.00
BW	Billy Williams	20.00
RY	Robin Yount	40.00
DZ	Don Zimmer	25.00

Announcing Greats

		NM/M
	Common Card:	6.00
	Inserted 1:12 Retail	
1AG	Harry Kalas, Mike Schmidt	8.00
2AG	Vin Scully, Steve Garvey	12.00
3AG	Harry Caray, Ryne Sandberg	12.00
4AG	Ned Martin, Carlton Fisk	6.00
5AG	Ernie Harwell, Kirk Gibson	6.00
6AG	Ken Harrelson, Carl Yastrzemski	8.00
7AG	Don Mattingly, Phil Rizzuto	10.00
8AG	Yogi Berra, Mel Allen	10.00
9AG	Jonathan Miller, Cal Ripken Jr.	10.00
10AG	Marty Brennaman, Johnny Bench	8.00

Announcing Greats Autographs

NM/M
Sequentially #'d between 1 & 50.

Ken Harrelson, Carl Yastrzemski/50	75.00
Phil Rizzuto, Don Mattingly/26	225.00
Johnny Bench, Marty Brennaman/50	60.00

Battery Mates

		NM/M
	Common Card:	5.00
	Serially Numbered	
1BM	Steve Carlton, Tim McCarver/1972	5.00
2BM	Don Drysdale, Roy Campanella/1957	5.00
3BM	Tom Seaver, Johnny Bench/1979	8.00
4BM	Whitey Ford, Yogi Berra/1956	8.00
5BM	Ron Guidry, Thurman Munson/1978	8.00
6BM	Nolan Ryan, Jeff Torborg/1973	10.00
7BM	Denny McLain, Bill Freehan/1968	5.00
8BM	Lefty Gomez, Bill Dickey/1934	5.00
9BM	Jim Palmer, Rick Dempsey/1977	5.00
10BM	Luis Tiant, Carlton Fisk	5.00

Single Panel: Battery Mates

	NM/M
Common Card:	15.00

Serially Numbered

TM	Steve Carlton, Tim McCarver/72	30.00
TS-JB	Tom Seaver, Johnny Bench/79	60.00
WF-YB	Whitey Ford, Yogi Berra/56	40.00
RG-TM	Ron Guidry, Thurman Munson/78	25.00
NR-JT	Nolan Ryan, Jeff Torborg/73	15.00
DM-BF	Denny McLain, Bill Freehan/68	60.00
JP-RD	Jim Palmer, Rick Dempsey/77	25.00

Dual Panel: Battery Mates

No Pricing
Production 10 Sets

Comparison Cuts: Dual Cut

No Pricing
Production One Set

Single Cuts: Etched in Time

NM/M
No Pricing

ET-RC	Roberto Clemente/1 (7/04 Auction)	6,100

Etched In Time Series 2

NM/M
Sequentially #'d to indicated quantity.
Cards #'d 25 or less: No Pricing

EA	Ethan Allen/75	150.00
EAV	Earl Averill/50	125.00
DC	Dolph Camilli/40	250.00
BH	Babe Herman/35	250.00
HK	Harvey Kuenn/32	120.00
SM	Sal Maglie/40	100.00
ER	Edd Roush/95	100.00
PR	Pete Runnels/35	200.00
CS	Chris Short/30	120.00

Forever

NM/M
Common Player: 4.00
Sequentially #'d to player's rookie year.

1	Fernando Valenzuela/1980	4.00
2	Steve Garvey/1969	4.00
3	Zach Wheat/1909	4.00
4	Orel Hershiser/1983	4.00
5	Duke Snider/1947	6.00
6	Jim Rice/1974	5.00
7	Carlton Fisk/1969	6.00
8	Wade Boggs/1982	6.00
9	Ted Williams/1939	10.00
10	Carl Yastrzemski/1961	8.00
11	Dom DiMaggio/1940	5.00
12	Ron Santo/1960	5.00
13	Billy Williams/1959	5.00
14	Ryne Sandberg/1981	8.00
15	Ernie Banks/1953	8.00
16	Gabby Hartnett/1922	4.00
17	Hack Wilson/1923	6.00
18	Dwight Gooden/1984	5.00
19	Ray Knight/1974	4.00
20	Tom Seaver/1967	8.00
21	Nolan Ryan/1966	10.00
22	Keith Hernandez/1974	5.00
23	Darryl Strawberry/1983	5.00
24	Bob Gibson/1959	8.00
25	Pepper Martin/1928	4.00
26	Stan Musial/1941	8.00
27	Frankie Frisch/1919	4.00
28	Steve Carlton/1965	8.00
29	Ozzie Smith/1978	5.00

Forever Game-Used Jersey

NM/M
Common Player: 10.00
Production 149 Sets
Jersey: .75-1.5X
Production 99 Sets
Patch Number: 1-2X
Production 49 Sets
Patch Logo: No Pricing
Production 10 Sets

EB	Ernie Banks	20.00
WB	Wade Boggs	12.00
SC	Steve Carlton	12.00
DD	Dom DiMaggio	20.00
CF	Carlton Fisk	15.00
SG	Steve Garvey	10.00
BG	Bob Gibson	15.00
DG	Dwight Gooden	10.00
KH	Keith Hernandez	10.00
OH	Orel Hershiser	10.00
RK	Ray Knight	10.00
SM	Stan Musial	30.00
JR	Jim Rice	12.00
NR	Nolan Ryan	50.00
RS	Ryne Sandberg	25.00
RST	Ron Santo	10.00
TS	Tom Seaver	15.00
OS	Ozzie Smith	15.00
DS	Darryl Strawberry	12.00
FV	Fernando Valenzuela	10.00
BW	Billy Williams	10.00
TW	Ted Williams	75.00
CY	Carl Yastrzemski	20.00

Personality Cuts

No Pricing
Production One Set

Personality Cuts Series 2

No Pricing
Production 1 or 2 Sets

The Glory of Their Time

NM/M
Common Player: 4.00
Serially Numbered

1GOT	Harmon Killebrew/1961	4.00
2GOT	Johnny Bench/1974	5.00
3GOT	George Brett/1980	4.00
4GOT	Tony Gwynn/1987	4.00
5GOT	Paul Molitor/1987	5.00
6GOT	Don Mattingly/1986	8.00
7GOT	Reggie Jackson/1980	8.00
8GOT	Carlton Fisk/1985	5.00
9GOT	Cal Ripken Jr./1983	10.00
10GOT	Brooks Robinson/1964	4.00
11GOT	Eddie Murray/1980	5.00
12GOT	Bill "Moose" Skowron/1960	4.00
13GOT	Lou Brock/1974	5.00

14GOT	Don Drysdale/1962	5.00
15GOT	Tony Gwynn/1997	4.00
16GOT	Mike Schmidt/1980	8.00
17GOT	Carl Yastrzemski/	
	1967	8.00
18GOT	Babe Ruth/1927	10.00
19GOT	Nolan Ryan/1989	10.00
20GOT	Yogi Berra/1950	8.00
21GOT	Al Kaline/1955	5.00
22GOT	Ty Cobb/1911	5.00
23GOT	Duke Snider/1955	5.00
24GOT	Stan Musial/1948	8.00
25GOT	Jose Canseco/	
	1988	5.00
26GOT	Rocky Colavito/	
	1958	5.00
27GOT	Dave Winfield/	
	1979	4.00
28GOT	Nolan Ryan/1982	10.00
29GOT	Thurman Munson/	
	1977	8.00
30GOT	Jackie Robinson/	
	1949	8.00
31GOT	Kirby Puckett/1988	8.00
32GOT	Ted Kluszewski/	
	1954	5.00
33GOT	Warren Spahn/	
	1953	5.00
34GOT	Willie McCovey/	
	1969	4.00
35GOT	Phil Rizzuto/1950	5.00

The Glory/Time: Game-Used

		NM/M
Common Player:		10.00
Production 250 Sets		
Hobby Only		
Gold:		1.5-2X
Retail Not (Not Numbered)		
No Rizzuto Retail Version		
JB	Johnny Bench/Jsy	15.00
YB	Yogi Berra/Pants	15.00
GB	George Brett/Jsy	15.00
LB	Lou Brock/Jsy	15.00
JC1	Jose Canseco/Jsy	10.00
JC2	Jose Canseco/Bat	10.00
RC	Rocky Colavito/Bat	25.00
DD	Don Drysdale/Jsy	15.00
CF1	Carlton Fisk/Jsy	10.00
CF2	Carlton Fisk/Bat	10.00
TG1	Tony Gwynn/Jsy	10.00
TG2	Tony Gwynn/Jsy	10.00
RJ	Reggie Jackson/	
	Pants	20.00
AK	Al Kaline/Pants	15.00
HK	Harmon Killebrew/Bat	10.00
TK	Ted Kluszewski/	
	Pants	15.00
DM	Don Mattingly/Pants	20.00
WM	Willie McCovey/	
	Pants	10.00
PM	Paul Molitor/Jsy	15.00
TM	Thurman Munson/	
	Pants	15.00
EM	Eddie Murray/Jsy	10.00
KP	Kirby Puckett/Bat	20.00
CR	Cal Ripken Jr./Jsy	25.00
PR	Phil Rizzuto/Pants	15.00
BR	Brooks Robinson/Jsy	10.00
NR1	Nolan Ryan/Jsy	20.00
NR2	Nolan Ryan/Bat	20.00
MS	Mike Schmidt/Jsy	15.00
MS	Bill "Moose" Skowron/	
	Pants	10.00
WS	Warren Spahn/Jsy	20.00
DW	Dave Winfield/Jsy	10.00
CY	Carl Yastrzemski/Jsy	20.00

The Glory/Time: G-U Patch

No Pricing
Production 25 Sets

Yankee Clippings

		NM/M
Common Player:		25.00
Inserted 1:45		
YB	Yogi Berra	60.00
WB	Wade Boggs	40.00
RJ	Reggie Jackson	40.00
LG	Roger Maris	400.00
DM	Don Mattingly	100.00
PO	Paul O'Neill	30.00
PR	Phil Rizzuto	325.00
BS	Bill "Moose" Skowron	25.00

Yankee Clippings Autographs

No Pricing
Sequentially #'d between 3 & 26.

2004 Fleer Hot Prospects Draft Edition

		NM/M
Common Player (1-60):		.25
Minor Stars (1-60):		.40
Unlisted Stars (1-60):		.60
Common Rookie (61-70):		3.00
Common Rookie (71-120):		15.00
Production 1,000 Sets		
Cards 112 & 113 do not exist.		
Production 299 Sets		
Pack (5):		7.00
Box (15):		100.00
1	Miguel Tejada	.50
2	Jose Vidro	.25
3	Hideki Matsui	2.00
4	Roger Clemens	2.50
5	Craig Wilson	.25
6	Bobby Crosby	.25
7	Pat Burrell	.40
8	Mike Sweeney	.25
9	Craig Biggio	.40
10	Scott Rolen	1.00
11	Roy Halladay	.40
12	Lyle Overbay	.25
13	Rocco Baldelli	.50
14	Mike Piazza	1.50
15	Rafael Palmeiro	.75
16	Hank Blalock	.50
17	Sammy Sosa	1.50
18	Dontrelle Willis	.40
19	Alfonso Soriano	1.00
20	Gary Sheffield	.75
21	Jim Thome	1.00
22	Ivan Rodriguez	.75
23	Adam Dunn	.50
24	Kerry Wood	.50
25	Khalil Greene	.50
26	Richie Sexson	.50
27	Nomar Garciaparra	1.00
28	Andruw Jones	.75
29	Tom Glavine	.40
30	Carlos Beltran	.75
31	Chipper Jones	1.00
32	Jeff Bagwell	.75
33	Tim Hudson	.40
34	Alex Rodriguez	2.00
35	Omar Vizquel	.40
36	Albert Pujols	2.50
37	Frank Thomas	.75
38	Ben Sheets	.40
39	Jason Schmidt	.40
40	Miguel Cabrera	.75
41	Carlos Delgado	.75
42	Ichiro Suzuki	2.00
43	Curt Schilling	.75
44	Todd Helton	.75

45	Ken Griffey Jr.	1.50
46	Mark Prior	.75
47	Vladimir Guerrero	1.00
48	Pedro Martinez	1.00
49	Manny Ramirez	1.00
50	Joe Mauer	.50
51	Jorge Posada	.75
52	Troy Glaus	.50
53	Randy Johnson	1.00
54	Adrian Beltre	.40
55	Eric Gagne	.40
56	Josh Beckett	.50
57	Jason Giambi	.75
58	Barry Zito	.50
59	Lance Berkman	.50
60	Derek Jeter	3.00
61	Kazuo Matsui RC	5.00
62	Jason Bartlett RC	5.00
63	John Gall RC	3.00
64	Chris Saenz RC	3.00
65	Merkin Valdez RC	3.00
66	Akinori Otsuka RC	3.00
67	Joey Gathright RC	5.00
68	Brad Halsey RC	3.00
69	David Aardsma	3.00
70	Scott Kazmir	10.00
71	Matt Bush AU RC	30.00
72	John Bowker AU RC	25.00
73	Mike Ferris AU RC	15.00
74	Brian Bixler AU RC	15.00
75	Scott Elbert AU RC	40.00
76	Josh Fields AU RC	50.00
77	Bill Bray AU RC	15.00
78	Greg Golson AU RC	30.00
79	Neil Walker AU RC	30.00
80	Phillip Hughes	
	AU RC	150.00
81	Chris Nelson AU RC	40.00
82	Mark Rogers AU RC	30.00
83	Trevor Plouffe AU RC	25.00
84	Christian Garcia	
	AU RC	15.00
85	Thomas Diamond	
	AU RC	30.00
86	B.J. Szymanski	
	AU RC	25.00
87	Richie Robnett	
	AU RC	25.00
88	Seth Smith AU RC	25.00
89	Kyle Waldrop AU RC	25.00
90	Curtis Thigpen AU RC	15.00
91	J.P. Howell AU RC	15.00
92	Blake DeWitt AU RC	30.00
93	Taylor Tankersley	
	AU RC	15.00
94	Zach Jackson AU RC	15.00
95	Justin Orenduff	
	AU RC	15.00
96	Tyler Lumsden AU RC	15.00
97	Danny Putnam RC	20.00
98	Jon Poterson AU RC	20.00
99	Matt Fox AU RC	15.00
100	Gio Gonzalez AU RC	35.00
101	Huston Street AU RC	40.00
102	Jay Rainville AU RC	15.00
103	Matt Durkin AU RC	15.00
104	Brett Smith AU RC	15.00
105	Justin Hoyman	
	AU RC	20.00
106	Erick San Pedro	
	AU RC	15.00
107	Jeff Marquez AU RC	15.00
108	Hunter Pence	
	AU RC	160.00
109	Dustin Pedroia	
	AU RC	75.00
110	Kurt Suzuki AU RC	25.00
111	Billy Buckner AU RC	25.00
114	J.C. Holt AU RC	15.00
115	Homer Bailey AU RC	80.00
116	David Purcey AU RC	20.00
117	Jeremy Sowers	
	AU RC	25.00
118	Chris Lambert AU RC	15.00
119	Eric Hurley AU RC	40.00
120	Grant Johnson	
	AU RC	15.00

Red Hot

Veterans (1-60):		2-4X
Rookies (61-70):		1-2X
Production 150		
Rookies (71-120):		No Pricing
Production 25 Sets		

White Hot

Cards (1-120):		No Pricing
Production One Set		

Alumni Ink

No Pricing
Production 15 Sets
Red Hot: No Pricing
Production 5 Sets

White Hot:		No Pricing
Production One Set		

Double Team Jersey

		NM/M
Common Player:		10.00
Production 100 Sets		
Red Hot:		No Pricing
Production 25 Sets		
White Hot:		No Pricing
Production One Set		
Patch:		.75-1.5X
Production 50 Sets		
Patch Red Hot:		No Pricing
Production 10 Sets		
Patch White Hot:		No Pricing
Production One Set		
CB	Carlos Beltran	15.00
RCA	Rod Carew	20.00
RCL	Roger Clemens	20.00
JG	Jason Giambi	12.00
TG	Tom Glavine	10.00
VG	Vladimir Guerrero	15.00
RH	Rickey Henderson	20.00
RJ	Reggie Jackson	25.00
GM	Greg Maddux	15.00
PM	Pedro Martinez	15.00
EM	Eddie Murray	20.00
HN	Hideo Nomo	15.00
RP	Rafael Palmeiro	12.00
MP	Mike Piazza	20.00
MR	Manny Ramirez	15.00
IR	Ivan Rodriguez	10.00
SR	Scott Rolen	15.00
NR	Nolan Ryan	50.00
AS	Alfonso Soriano	12.00
MT	Miguel Tejada	10.00

Draft Rewind

		NM/M
Common Player:		2.00
Inserted 1:5		
1	Joe Mauer	2.00
2	Derek Jeter	6.00
3	Chipper Jones	3.50
4	Greg Maddux	3.50
5	Alex Rodriguez	5.00
6	Nomar Garciaparra	5.00
7	Curt Schilling	3.00
8	Kerry Wood	3.00
9	Troy Glaus	3.00
10	Pat Burrell	2.00
11	Mark Mulder	2.00
12	Josh Beckett	3.00
13	Barry Zito	3.00
14	Mark Prior	4.00
15	Rickie Weeks	2.00
16	Khalil Greene	2.00
17	Ken Griffey Jr.	3.50
18	Gary Sheffield	3.00
19	Todd Helton	3.00
20	Barry Larkin	2.00
21	Kevin Brown	2.00
22	Frank Thomas	3.00
23	Manny Ramirez	3.00
24	Roger Clemens	5.00
25	Lance Berkman	2.00
26	Randy Johnson	3.00
27	Jason Giambi	3.00
28	Ben Sheets	2.00
29	Scott Rolen	3.00
30	Tom Glavine	2.00

Draft Rewind Jersey

		NM/M
Common Player:		8.00
Sequentially #'d to indicated quantity.		
Red Hot:		No Pricing
Production 10 Sets		
White Hot:		No Pricing
Production One Set		
Patch		
Cards #'d 41-68:		.75-1.5X
Cards #'d 29 or less:		No Pricing
Patch Red Hot:		No Pricing
Production 5 Sets		
Patch White Hot:		No Pricing
Production One Set		
RB	Rocco Baldelli/119	8.00
JB	Josh Beckett/102	10.00
LB	Lance Berkman/116	8.00

KB	Kevin Brown/104	8.00
PB	Pat Burrell/101	8.00
EC	Eric Chavez/110	8.00
RC	Roger Clemens/119	15.00
JG	Jason Giambi/158	8.00
TG	Troy Glaus/103	8.00
TG	Tom Glavine/147	8.00
KG	Khalil Greene/113	15.00
ZG	Zack Greinke/106	15.00
TH	Todd Helton/108	10.00
RJ	Randy Johnson/136	10.00
CJ	Chipper Jones/101	12.00
CK	Casey Kotchman/113	8.00
BL	Barry Larkin/104	10.00
GM	Greg Maddux/123	12.00
JM	Joe Mauer/101	10.00
MM	Mark Mulder/102	8.00
MP	Mark Prior/102	8.00
MR	Manny Ramirez/113	10.00
SR	Scott Rolen/146	10.00
CS	Curt Schilling/139	10.00
BS	Ben Sheets/110	8.00
GS	Gary Sheffield/106	8.00
FT	Frank Thomas/107	15.00
RW	Rickie Weeks/102	8.00
KW	Kerry Wood/104	10.00
BZ	Barry Zito/109	8.00

Hot Tandems

		NM/M
Common Card:		3.00
Inserted 1:15		
1HT	Mark Prior, Greg Maddux	4.00
2HT	Jim Thome, Pat Burrell	3.50
3HT	Ken Griffey Jr., Adam Dunn	4.00
4HT	Mike Piazza, Tom Glavine	4.00
5HT	Alex Rodriguez, Derek Jeter	10.00
6HT	Roger Clemens, Andy Pettitte	6.00
7HT	Hideki Matsui, Jason Giambi	6.00
8HT	Hank Blalock, Alfonso Soriano	3.50
9HT	Manny Ramirez, David Ortiz	3.50
10HT	Miguel Cabrera, Dontrelle Willis	3.50
11HT	Hideki Matsui, Ichiro Suzuki	6.00
12HT	Albert Pujols, Scott Rolen	6.00
13HT	Curt Schilling, Pedro J. Martinez	3.50
14HT	Nomar Garciaparra, Sammy Sosa	5.00
15HT	Kazuo Matsui, Derek Jeter	8.00

Hot Materials

		NM/M
Common Player:		5.00
Production 325 Sets		
Red Hot:		1-2X
Production 50 Sets		
White Hot Patch:		No Pricing
Production One Set		
JB	Jeff Bagwell/Jsy	6.00
LB	Lance Berkman/Jsy	5.00
HB	Hank Blalock/Jsy	5.00
MC	Miguel Cabrera/Jsy	8.00
RC	Roger Clemens/Jsy	12.00
CD	Carlos Delgado/Jsy	6.00
JD	J.D. Drew/Jsy	6.00
AD	Adam Dunn/Jsy	6.00
JE	Jim Edmonds/Jsy	5.00
EG	Eric Gagne/Jsy	5.00
VG	Vladimir Guerrero/Jsy	8.00

THE	Todd Helton/Jsy	6.00
THU	Tim Hudson/Jsy	5.00
THN	Torii Hunter/Jsy	6.00
RJ	Randy Johnson/Jsy	6.00
AJ	Andruw Jones/Jsy	6.00
CJ	Chipper Jones/Jsy	8.00
HM	Hideki Matsui/Jsy	20.00
KM	Kazuo Matsui/Jsy	10.00
JM	Joe Mauer/Jsy	8.00
MM	Mike Mussina/Jsy	6.00
HN	Hideo Nomo/Jsy	8.00
LO	Lyle Overbay/Jsy	5.00
APE	Andy Pettitte/Jsy	6.00
MPI	Mike Piazza/Jsy	8.00
JP	Jorge Posada/Jsy	6.00
MPR	Mark Prior/Jsy	8.00
APU	Albert Pujols/Jsy	12.00
MR	Manny Ramirez/Jsy	8.00
IR	Ivan Rodriguez/Jsy	6.00
CS	Curt Schilling/Jsy	8.00
JS	Jason Schmidt/Jsy	5.00
AS	Alfonso Soriano/Jsy	6.00
SS	Sammy Sosa/Jsy	10.00
MTX	Mark Teixeira/Jsy	6.00
MTJ	Miguel Tejada/Jsy	5.00
FT	Frank Thomas/Jsy	8.00
JT	Jim Thome/Jsy	8.00
DW	Dontrelle Willis/Jsy	5.00
KW	Kerry Wood/Jsy	8.00

Past, Present, Future Triple Autograph

	NM/M
Production 33 Sets	
Red Hot:	No Pricing
Production 3 Sets	
White Hot:	No Pricing
Production One Set	
Matt Durkin, Mookie Wilson,	
Mike Piazza	150.00
Hideo Nomo, Scott Elbert, Kirk Gibson	250.00
Josh Fields, Carlton Fisk, Ryan Meaux	80.00
Greg Golson, Steve Carlton, Jim Thome	100.00
Jack Wilson, Neil Walker, Ralph Kiner	80.00
Ryne Sandberg, Mark Prior, Grant Johnson	250.00
Homer Bailey, Johnny Bench, Adam Dunn	150.00
Albert Pujols, Chris Lambert, Stan Musial	300.00
Richie Robnett, Reggie Jackson, Eric Chavez	80.00
Dustin Pedroia, Bill Buckner, Manny Ramirez	60.00

Double Team Autograph Patch Red Hot

No Pricing	
Production 22 Sets	
White Hot:	No Pricing
Production One Set	

2004 Fleer InScribed

ALBERT PUJOLS

	NM/M
Common Player (1-75):	.25
Minor Stars (1-75):	.40
Unlisted Stars (1-75):	.60
Common Player (76-85):	3.00

Production 1,000 Sets		
Numbered to 750		3.00
Not all 750 of each card not released.		
Pack (5):		10.00
Box (12):		85.00
1	Vladimir Guerrero	1.00
2	Bartolo Colon	.40
3	Troy Glaus	.60
4	Richie Sexson	.60
5	Randy Johnson	1.00
6	Luis Gonzalez	.40
7	J.D. Drew	.40
8	Chipper Jones	1.50
9	Andruw Jones	.75
10	Melvin Mora	.25
11	Miguel Tejada	.60
12	Curt Schilling	.60
13	Pedro J. Martinez	1.00
14	Nomar Garciaparra	2.50
15	Kerry Wood	.75
16	Mark Prior	2.00
17	Sammy Sosa	2.00
18	Frank Thomas	.75
19	Magglio Ordonez	.40
20	Sean Casey	.25
21	Ken Griffey Jr.	1.50
22	Adam Dunn	.60
23	Jody Gerut	.25
24	Omar Vizquel	.25
25	Todd Helton	.75
26	Vinny Castilla	.25
27	Alex Sanchez	.25
28	Ivan Rodriguez	.60
29	Dontrelle Willis	.40
30	Josh Beckett	.75
31	Miguel Cabrera	.75
32	Roger Clemens	1.50
33	Andy Pettitte	.60
34	Jeff Bagwell	.75
35	Ken Harvey	.25
36	Carlos Beltran	.60
37	Shawn Green	.40
38	Hideo Nomo	.40
39	Scott Podsednik	.25
40	Ben Sheets	.40
41	Torii Hunter	.60
42	Jacque Jones	.25
43	Jose Vidro	.25
44	Mike Piazza	1.50
45	Tom Glavine	.40
46	Derek Jeter	3.00
47	Alex Rodriguez	2.50
48	Jason Giambi	1.00
49	Hideki Matsui	2.50
50	Eric Chavez	.40
51	Barry Zito	.60
52	Tim Hudson	.40
53	Mark Mulder	.40
54	Jim Thome	1.00
55	Pat Burrell	.40
56	Chase Utley	.25
57	Jason Kendall	.40
58	Jack Wilson	.25
59	Khalil Greene	.75
60	Brian Giles	.40
61	Jason Schmidt	.40
62	Marquis Grissom	.25
63	Ichiro Suzuki	2.00
64	Bret Boone	.40
65	Albert Pujols	2.50
66	Scott Rolen	1.00
67	Jim Edmonds	.40
68	Tino Martinez	.25
69	Rocco Baldelli	.60
70	Alfonso Soriano	1.00
71	Michael Young	.25
72	Hank Blalock	.40
73	Roy Halladay	.40
74	Carlos Delgado	.75
75	Vernon Wells	.40
76	Johnny Bench	3.00
77	Reggie Jackson	5.00
78	Al Kaline	3.00
79	Nolan Ryan	10.00
80	Tom Seaver	3.00
81	Robin Yount	6.00
82	Mike Schmidt	5.00
83	Jim Palmer	3.00
84	Harmon Killebrew	5.00
85	Joe Morgan	3.00
86	Kazuo Matsui RC	5.00
87	Luis Gonzalez RC	3.00
88	Yadier Molina RC	4.00
89	Jon Knott RC	3.00
90	Kevin Youkilis	5.00
91	Chris Saenz RC	3.00
92	Andres Blanco RC	3.00
93	David Aardsma	3.00
94	Merkin Valdez RC	3.00
95	Jason Bartlett RC	3.00
96	John Gall RC	3.00
97	Zack Greinke	3.00
98	Scott Hairston	3.00

99	Matt Holliday	4.00
100	Casey Kotchman	5.00

Gold

Veterans (1-75):	2-5X
Rookies (76-100):	.75-2X
Production 199 Sets	

Red

No Pricing
Production 5 Sets

Autographs Silver

	NM/M
Common Player:	10.00
Numbered to indicated quantity.	
Red:	No Pricing
Production 25 Sets	
Purple:	.5-2X
Numbered to jersey number.	
RB	Rocco Baldelli/34	25.00
CB	Carlos Beltran/296	25.00
JB	Jeremy Bonderman/287	10.00
EC	Eric Chavez/322	15.00
EG	Eric Gagne/57	40.00
BG	Brian Giles/134	15.00
LG	Luis Gonzalez/55	15.00
RHL	Roy Halladay/139	15.00
RHR	Rich Harden/235	10.00
TH	Trevor Hoffman/174	15.00
BL	Barry Larkin/140	20.00
JL	Javy Lopez/257	15.00
WM	Wade Miller/195	10.00
TN	Trot Nixon/318	10.00
LO	Lyle Overbay/240	10.00
SP	Scott Podsednik/280	10.00
AP	Albert Pujols/5	
BR	Brad Radke/168	15.00

Award Winners

		NM/M
Common Player:		
Production 150 Sets		
1	Alex Rodriguez	10.00
2	Eric Gagne	3.00
3	Miguel Tejada	4.00
4	Roy Halladay	3.00
5	Randy Johnson	5.00
6	Barry Zito	3.00
7	Chipper Jones	3.00
8	Ivan Rodriguez	4.00
9	Pedro J. Martinez	5.00
10	Barry Larkin	3.00
11	Dontrelle Willis	3.00
12	Angel Berroa	3.00
13	Kerry Wood	5.00
14	Albert Pujols	8.00
15	Hideo Nomo	3.00

Award Winners Autographs

		NM/M
Common Player:		15.00
Numbered to Award Year.		
All cards not released for some cards.		
AB	Angel Berroa/103	15.00
RH	Roy Halladay/102	20.00
BL	Barry Larkin/103	30.00
DW	Dontrelle Willis/103	25.00

Award Winners Jersey Silver

		NM/M
Common Player:		
Production 175 Sets		
Copper:		.75-1.5X
Production 99 Sets		
Purple:		1-3X
Production 49 Sets		
AB	Angel Berroa	5.00
EG	Eric Gagne	8.00
RH	Roy Halladay	5.00
RJ	Randy Johnson	10.00
CJ	Chipper Jones	10.00
BL	Barry Larkin	5.00
PM	Pedro J. Martinez	10.00
HN	Hideo Nomo	5.00
AP	Albert Pujols	15.00
IR	Ivan Rodriguez	8.00
MT	Miguel Tejada	8.00
DW	Dontrelle Willis	5.00
KW	Kerry Wood	10.00
BZ	Barry Zito	8.00

Facsimile Signature Gold

Current (1-75):	3-5X

Retired (76-85): 1-2X
Rookies (86-100): .75-1.5X
Production 199 Sets

Induction Ceremony

		NM/M
Common Player:		6.00

Numbered to Year of Induction.
1	Carlton Fisk/100	8.00
2	Tony Perez/100	6.00
3	Nolan Ryan/99	20.00
4	Robin Yount/99	10.00
5	Orlando Cepeda/99	8.00
6	Bill Mazeroski/101	8.00
7	Larry Doby/98	6.00
8	Phil Niekro/97	6.00
9	Jim Bunning/96	6.00
10	Sparky Anderson/100	6.00
11	Phil Rizzuto/94	8.00
12	Rollie Fingers/92	6.00
13	Hal Newhouser/92	6.00
14	Rod Carew/91	8.00
15	Reggie Jackson/93	8.00
16	Tom Seaver/92	8.00
17	Bob Gibson/81	8.00
18	Jim Palmer/90	6.00
19	Joe Morgan/90	6.00
20	Al Kaline/80	10.00

Induction Ceremony Autograph Bronze

		NM/M
Common Player:		20.00

Numbered to 50
| Silver: | | No Pricing |

Production 15 Sets
| Gold: | | No Pricing |

Production 5 Sets
JB	Jim Bunning	20.00
OC	Orlando Cepeda/40	20.00
RF	Rollie Fingers	30.00
CF	Carlton Fisk	30.00
BG	Bob Gibson	40.00
AK	Al Kaline	50.00
TP	Tony Perez	30.00

Induction Ceremony Material Silver

		NM/M
Common Player:		10.00

Numbered (2-digit) to Induction Year.
| Masterpiece: | | No Pricing |

Production One Set
SA	Sparky Anderson/100	10.00
RC	Rod Carew/91	15.00
OC	Orlando Cepeda/99	10.00
LD	Larry Doby/98	20.00
RF	Rollie Fingers/92	10.00
CF	Carlton Fisk/100	15.00
RJ	Reggie Jackson/93	10.00
AK	Al Kaline/80	20.00
BM	Bill Mazeroski/101	10.00
JM	Joe Morgan/90	15.00
PN	Phil Niekro/97	10.00
JP	Jim Palmer/90	10.00
TP	Tony Perez/100	15.00
PR	Phil Rizzuto/94	20.00
NR	Nolan Ryan/92	25.00
TS	Tom Seaver/92	10.00
RY	Robin Yount/99	10.00

Names of the Game

		NM/M
Common Player:		2.00

Production 99 Sets
1	Nomar Garciaparra	8.00
2	Randy Johnson	3.00
3	Hideki Matsui	8.00
4	Frank Thomas	2.00
5	Ivan Rodriguez	2.00
6	Roger Clemens	5.00
7	Chipper Jones	5.00
8	Dontrelle Willis	2.00
9	Luis Gonzalez	2.00
10	Alex Rodriguez	8.00
11	Eric Gagne	2.00
12	Juan Gonzalez	2.00
13	Hideo Nomo	2.00
14	Sean Casey	2.00
15	Greg Maddux	5.00
16	Cal Ripken Jr.	15.00
17	Carl Yastrzemski	5.00
18	Tony Perez	3.00
19	Joe Morgan	3.00
20	Carlton Fisk	3.00
21	Willie McCovey	5.00
22	Al Kaline	5.00
23	Dennis Eckersley	3.00
24	Ted Williams	10.00
25	Willie Stargell	5.00
26	Rollie Fingers	3.00
27	Yogi Berra	2.00
28	Reggie Jackson	5.00
29	Harmon Killebrew	5.00
30	Nolan Ryan	10.00

Names of the Game Autograph Silver

		NM/M
Common Player:		15.00

Stated Production 99 Sets
All 99 not released for some cards.
| Gold: | | No Pricing |

Stated Production 25 Sets
All 25 not released for some cards.
SC	Sean Casey	20.00
DE	Dennis Eckersley/90	25.00
RF	Rollie Fingers/90	25.00
CF	Carlton Fisk/50	30.00
LG	Luis Gonzalez/75	15.00
CJ	Chipper Jones/40	40.00
AK	Al Kaline/90	40.00
DW	Dontrelle Willis	25.00

Names of the Game Material Copper

		NM/M
Common Player:		5.00

Production 250 Sets
| Gold: | | .5-1.25X |

Production 150 Sets
| Red: | | .75-1.5X |

Production 79 Sets
| Purple: | | 1-2X |

Production 33 Sets
YB	Yogi Berra	10.00
SC	Sean Casey	5.00
RC	Roger Clemens	10.00
DE	Dennis Eckersley	8.00
RF	Rollie Fingers	8.00
CF	Carlton Fisk	8.00
EG	Eric Gagne	10.00
JG	Juan Gonzalez	5.00
LG	Luis Gonzalez	5.00
RJA	Reggie Jackson	10.00
RJO	Randy Johnson	8.00
CJ	Chipper Jones	8.00
AK	Al Kaline	10.00
HK	Harmon Killebrew	10.00
GM	Greg Maddux	10.00
HM	Hideki Matsui	15.00
WM	Willie McCovey	10.00
JM	Joe Morgan	8.00
HN	Hideo Nomo	5.00
TP	Tony Perez	5.00
CR	Cal Ripken Jr.	30.00
IR	Ivan Rodriguez	5.00
NR	Nolan Ryan	20.00
WS	Willie Stargell	10.00

FT	Frank Thomas	5.00
TW	Ted Williams	25.00
DW	Dontrelle Willis	5.00
CY	Carl Yastrzemski	10.00

Rookie Autographs Notation

		NM/M
Common Player:		15.00

Stated Production 750 Sets
75 Notation Cards for each player
87	Luis A. Gonzalez	
	4/6/04	15.00
89	Jon Knott 5/30/04	15.00
90	Kevin Youkilis	
	5/15/04	20.00
91	Chris Saenz 4/24/04	15.00
92	Andres Blanco	
	4/17/04	15.00
94	Merkin Valdez	
	Go Giants	20.00
95	Jason Bartlett	
	Go Twins	20.00
96B	John Gall	
	Go Cards/50	20.00
98	Scott Hairston	
	5/17/04	15.00
100	Casey Kotchman	
	5/9/04	25.00

2004 Fleer Legacy

	NM/M
Common Player (1-60):	1.50
Minor Stars (1-60):	2.00
Unlisted Stars (1-60):	2.50
Common Rookie (61-75):	4.00

Production 599 Sets
Box (1 Pack, 1 Autographed	
Baseball):	150.00
1	Angel Berroa	1.50
2	Derek Jeter	8.00
3	Jody Gerut	1.50
4	Curt Schilling	2.50
5	Khalil Greene	3.00
6	Manny Ramirez	3.00
7	Rocco Baldelli	2.50
8	Sammy Sosa	5.00
9	Shawn Green	2.00
10	Austin Kearns	2.50
11	Frank Thomas	3.50
12	Alfonso Soriano	3.00
13	Alex Rodriguez	6.00
14	Carlos Delgado	3.00
15	Chipper Jones	4.00
16	Edgar Martinez	2.00
17	Ivan Rodriguez	2.50
18	Mark Prior	4.00
19	Mike Piazza	4.00
20	Orlando Cabrera	1.50
21	Adam Dunn	2.50
22	Andruw Jones	3.00
23	Eric Chavez	2.00
24	Mark Teixeira	2.00
25	Scott Podsednik	1.50
26	Torii Hunter	2.50
27	Miguel Cabrera	3.00
28	Hideki Matsui	6.00
29	Jose Reyes	1.50
30	Vladimir Guerrero	3.50
31	Albert Pujols	6.00
32	Greg Maddux	4.00
33	Jason Giambi	3.50
34	Randy Johnson	3.50
35	Roger Clemens	6.00
36	Casey Kotchman	2.00
37	Ken Griffey Jr.	4.00
38	Todd Helton	3.00
39	Javy Lopez	1.50
40	Jim Thome	3.50
41	Josh Beckett	3.00
42	Kerry Wood	3.00
43	Scott Rolen	3.50
44	Pat Burrell	2.00
45	Pedro J. Martinez	3.50
46	Barry Zito	2.50
47	Hank Blalock	2.50
48	Hideo Nomo	2.00
49	Jeff Bagwell	3.00
50	Magglio Ordonez	2.00
51	Ichiro Suzuki	5.00
52	Joe Mauer	2.00

53	Richie Sexson	2.50
54	Shannon Stewart	1.50
55	Craig Wilson	1.50
56	Miguel Tejada	2.50
57	Sean Casey	1.50
58	Tom Glavine	2.00
59	Jason Schmidt	2.00
60	Nomar Garciaparra	6.00
61	Kazuo Matsui RC	8.00
62	Justin Leone RC	4.00
63	Merkin Valdez RC	6.00
64	Shingo Takatsu RC	6.00
65	Andres Blanco RC	4.00
66	Angel Chavez RC	4.00
67	Hector Gimenez RC	4.00
68	Akinori Otsuka RC	4.00
69	Jason Bartlett RC	4.00
70	Luis Gonzalez RC	4.00
71	Sean Henn	4.00
72	Mike Rouse	4.00
73	Chris Aguila RC	4.00
74	Aarom Baldiris RC	4.00
75	Jerry Gil RC	4.00

Gold Legacy

| Veterans (1-60): | 2-4X |
| Rookies (61-75): | .75-1.5X |

Production 50 Sets

Ultimate Legacy

No Pricing
Production One Set

Franchise Legacy Patch

	NM/M
Common Player:	10.00

Production 99 Sets
| Patch 50: | .5-1.5X |

Production 50 Sets
| Patch 25: | No Pricing |

Production 25 Sets
| Masterpiece: | No Pricing |

Production One Set
JBA	Jeff Bagwell	15.00
JBE	Josh Beckett	15.00
JB	Johnny Bench	
RC	Roger Clemens	25.00
VG	Vladimir Guerrero	15.00
RJ	Randy Johnson	20.00
CJ	Chipper Jones	20.00
JL	Javy Lopez	10.00
GM	Greg Maddux	30.00
PM	Pedro Martinez	15.00
HM	Hideki Matsui	60.00
KM	Kazuo Matsui	20.00
DM	Don Mattingly	40.00
HN	Hideo Nomo	20.00
MP	Mike Piazza	20.00
MPR	Mark Prior	10.00
AP	Albert Pujols	50.00
CR	Cal Ripken Jr.	60.00
IR	Ivan Rodriguez	15.00
NR	Nolan Ryan	50.00
SS	Sammy Sosa	15.00
MT	Miguel Tejada	10.00
JT	Jim Thome	15.00
KW	Kerry Wood	15.00

Franchise Dual Patch

No Pricing
Sequentially #'d between 5 & 31.

Franchise Legacy Quad Patch

No Pricing
Sequentially #'d between 2 & 22.

Hit Kings Patch Silver

	NM/M
Common Player:	15.00

Production 99 Sets
Gold: .5-1.5X
Production 50 Sets
Masterpiece: No Pricing
Production One Set

JB	Jeff Bagwell	15.00
LB	Lance Berkman	15.00
HB	Hank Blalock	20.00
MC	Miguel Cabrera	20.00
CD	Carlos Delgado	20.00
AD	Adam Dunn	30.00
JG	Jason Giambi	15.00
VG	Vladimir Guerrero	20.00
CJ	Chipper Jones	20.00
AK	Austin Kearns	15.00
HM	Hideki Matsui	50.00
MP	Mike Piazza	25.00
AP	Albert Pujols	50.00
MR	Manny Ramirez	25.00
SR	Scott Rolen	20.00
MS	Mike Schmidt	40.00
RS	Richie Sexson	15.00
GS	Gary Sheffield	20.00
SS	Sammy Sosa	20.00
MT	Mark Teixeira	15.00
FT	Frank Thomas	15.00
JT	Jim Thome	25.00

Hit Kings Dual Patch

No Pricing
Sequentially numbered between 7 & 21.

2004 Fleer Patchworks

		NM/M
Common Player (1-90):		.15
Minor Stars:		.40
Unlisted Stars:		.60
Common Rookie (91-110):		2.00
Minor Rookies:		3.00
Unlisted Rookies:		5.00
Production 799 Sets		
Pack (5):		4.00
Box (18):		70.00
1	Kerry Wood	1.00
2	Brian Giles	.40
3	Tino Martinez	.15
4	Mark Mulder	.40
5	Andy Pettitte	.60
6	Gary Sheffield	.60
7	Mark Teixeira	.40
8	Garret Anderson	.40
9	Craig Biggio	.40
10	Alfonso Soriano	1.50
11	Bret Boone	.40
12	Mike Piazza	2.00
13	Todd Helton	1.00
14	Jay Gibbons	.40
15	Eric Chavez	.40
16	Andruw Jones	1.00
17	Adam Dunn	.60
18	Corey Koskie	.15
19	Rafael Palmeiro	1.00
20	Ivan Rodriguez	.60
21	Tom Glavine	.40
22	Luis Gonzalez	.40
23	Miguel Tejada	.60
24	Jose Vidro	.15
25	Richie Sexson	.60
26	Roy Halladay	.40
27	Vladimir Guerrero	1.50
28	Randy Johnson	1.50
29	Vernon Wells	.40
30	Pat Burrell	.40
31	Jason Schmidt	.40
32	Casey Blake	.15
33	Greg Maddux	2.00
34	Mike Lowell	.15
35	Hideo Nomo	.40
36	Carlos Delgado	1.00
37	Dontrelle Willis	.40
38	Shawn Green	.40
39	Pedro Martinez	1.50
40	Josh Beckett	1.00
41	Eric Gagne	.40
42	Manny Ramirez	1.00
43	Jim Edmonds	.40
44	Curt Schilling	.60
45	Mike Sweeney	.15
46	Albert Pujols	3.00
47	Nomar Garciaparra	3.00
48	Alex Rodriguez	3.00
49	Angel Berroa	.15
50	Jim Thome	1.50
51	Edgardo Alfonzo	.15
52	Jeremy Bonderman	.15
53	Miguel Cabrera	1.00
54	Bobby Higginson	.15
55	John Smoltz	.40
56	Jason Kendall	.40
57	Torii Hunter	.60
58	Troy Glaus	.60
59	Rafael Furcal	.40
60	Austin Kearns	.60
61	Esteban Loaiza	.15
62	Darin Erstad	.40
63	Jose Reyes	.15
64	Preston Wilson	.15
65	Rocco Baldelli	.60
66	Barry Zito	.60
67	Ken Griffey Jr.	2.00
68	Frank Thomas	1.00
69	Roger Clemens	2.00
70	Brett Myers	.15
71	Billy Wagner	.15
72	Scott Podsednik	.15
73	Jody Gerut	.15
74	Bartolo Colon	.40
75	Jeff Bagwell	1.00
76	Jason Giambi	1.50
77	Edgar Martinez	.40
78	Chipper Jones	2.00
79	Jason Bay	.15
80	Doug Mientkiewicz	.15
81	Hank Blalock	.60
82	Sammy Sosa	2.00
83	Derek Jeter	4.00
84	Ichiro Suzuki	2.00
85	Ben Sheets	.40
86	Magglio Ordonez	.40
87	Carlos Beltran	.40
88	Mark Prior	2.00
89	Sean Burroughs	.15
90	Tim Hudson	.40
91	Hector Gimenez RC	8.00
92	Khalil Greene RC	5.00
93	Rickie Weeks	8.00
94	Delmon Young	10.00
95	Donald Kelly RC	3.00
96	Chad Bentz RC	5.00
97	Greg Dobbs RC	3.00
98	John Gall RC	5.00
99	Cory Sullivan RC	3.00
100	Kazuo Matsui RC	25.00
101	Graham Koonce	3.00
102	Jason Bartlett RC	8.00
103	Angel Chavez RC	2.00
104	Ronny Cedeno RC	3.00
105	Jerry Gil RC	3.00
106	Ivan Ochoa RC	3.00
107	Ruddy Yan RC	8.00
108	Mike Gosling	2.00
109	Alfredo Simon RC	2.00
110	Koyie Hill RC	2.00

Ruby

Ruby (1-90):	3-10X
Ruby (91-110):	.5-2X
Production 50 Sets	

Autoworks

	NM/M
Common Player:	10.00
Inserted 1:54	
Parallel:	.5-1.25X
Production 100 Sets	
Patch	
Production 10 Sets	

1	Garret Anderson/145	15.00
2	Josh Beckett/145	30.00
3	Angel Berroa/145	10.00
4	Eric Gagne/193	20.00
5	Jody Gerut/376	10.00
6	Roy Halladay/286	10.00
7	Mark Mulder/190	15.00
8	Andy Pettitte/148	30.00
9	Scott Podsednik/146	25.00
10	Albert Pujols/193	120.00
11	Grady Sizemore/263	25.00
12	Miguel Tejada/164	25.00

By The Numbers

	NM/M
Common Player:	3.00
Inserted 1:24	

Patch:		3-8X
Production 100 Sets		
1	Albert Pujols	8.00
2	Derek Jeter	10.00
3	Mike Piazza	6.00
4	Nomar Garciaparra	8.00
5	Eric Gagne	4.00
6	Sammy Sosa	6.00
7	Josh Beckett	4.00
8	Vladimir Guerrero	6.00
9	Jose Reyes	3.00
10	Bret Boone	3.00
11	Alex Rodriguez	8.00
12	Randy Johnson	6.00
13	Chipper Jones	6.00
14	Tim Hudson	4.00
15	Rocco Baldelli	4.00

Game-Used Level 1

		NM/M
Common Player:		6.00
Production 200 Sets		
Level 2:		1-1.5X
Production 100 Sets		
Patch:		1-2X
Production 50 Sets		
1	Albert Pujols	15.00
2	Andy Pettitte	6.00
3	Dontrelle Willis	6.00
4	Mike Piazza	10.00
5	Barry Zito	6.00
6	Troy Glaus	6.00
7	Carlos Delgado	8.00
8	Torii Hunter	6.00
9	Roy Halladay	6.00
10	Andruw Jones	8.00
11	Garret Anderson	6.00
12	Larry Walker	6.00
13	Shawn Green	6.00
14	Bernie Williams	6.00
15	Alfonso Soriano	10.00
16	Bret Boone	6.00
17	Hank Blalock	6.00
18	Jose Reyes	6.00
19	Mark Prior	6.00

Licensed Apparel

		NM/M
Common Player:		5.00
Production 300 Sets		
Team Name:		1-2X
Production 150 Sets		
Number:		1-2X
Production 100 Sets		
Nameplate:		1-3X
Production 50 Sets		
Jersey Tags:		
Production 10 Sets		
MLB Logo		
Production One Set		
1	Albert Pujols	15.00
2	Derek Jeter	18.00
3	Alex Rodriguez	15.00
4	Jim Thome	8.00
5	Mike Piazza	10.00
6	Dontrelle Willis	5.00
7	Torii Hunter	5.00
8	Tim Hudson	5.00
9	Sammy Sosa	12.00
10	Troy Glaus	5.00
11	Andruw Jones	8.00
12	Austin Kearns	5.00
13	Jeff Bagwell	8.00
14	Mark Prior	10.00
15	Bret Boone	5.00

National Pastime

		NM/M
Common Player:		5.00
Production 250 Sets		
Jersey:		1-1.5X
Production 350 Sets		
Gold Jersey:		1-2X
Production 200 Sets		
Patch:		1-3X
Production 100 Sets		
1	Albert Pujols	15.00
2	Alex Rodriguez	15.00
3	Derek Jeter	18.00
4	Nomar Garciaparra	15.00
5	Jim Thome	8.00
6	Chipper Jones	10.00

7	Mark Prior	10.00
8	Ichiro Suzuki	12.00
9	Jeff Bagwell	6.00
10	Troy Glaus	5.00
11	Randy Johnson	8.00
12	Sammy Sosa	12.00
13	Austin Kearns	5.00
14	Miguel Cabrera	6.00
15	Vladimir Guerrero	8.00

Stitches In Time

		NM/M
Common Player:		2.00
Inserted 1:12		
Jersey:		
Production 350 Sets		
Patch:		
Production 150 Sets		
1	Albert Pujols	5.00
2	Alex Rodriguez	5.00
3	Derek Jeter	6.00
4	Nomar Garciaparra	5.00
5	Jim Thome	3.00
6	Chipper Jones	3.00
7	Mark Prior	4.00
8	Eric Gagne	2.00
9	Jeff Bagwell	3.00
10	Troy Glaus	2.00
11	Randy Johnson	3.00
12	Sammy Sosa	4.00
13	Austin Kearns	2.00
14	Miguel Cabrera	2.00
15	Vladimir Guerrero	3.00
16	Mike Piazza	3.00
17	Jason Giambi	3.00
18	Tim Hudson	2.00
19	Carlos Delgado	3.00
20	Rocco Baldelli	2.00
21	Ichiro Suzuki	4.00
22	Barry Zito	2.00
23	Pedro Martinez	3.00
24	Torii Hunter	2.00
25	Andruw Jones	3.00

2004 Fleer Platinum

	NM/M
Complete Set (200):	35.00
Common Player:	.15
Common SP (136-151):	.50
Inserted 1:3	
Pack (7):	2.00
Jumbo Pack (20):	5.00
Box (18 + 4 Jumbo):	55.00

1	Luis Castillo	.15
2	Preston Wilson	.15
3	Johan Santana	.15
4	Fred McGriff	.25
5	Albert Pujols	1.50
6	Reggie Sanders	.15
7	Ivan Rodriguez	.40
8	Roy Halladay	.25

Vladimir Guerrero
MONTREAL EXPOS™ • OUTFIELD

9	Brian Giles	.25
10	Bernie Williams	.40
11	Barry Larkin	.25
12	Marlon Anderson	.15
13	Ramon Ortiz	.15
14	Luis Matos	.15
15	Esteban Loaiza	.15
16	Orlando Cabrera	.15
17	Jamie Moyer	.15
18	Tino Martinez	.15
19	Josh Beckett	.50
20	Derek Jeter	2.00
21	Derek Lowe	.15
22	Jack Wilson	.15
23	Bret Boone	.25
24	Matt Morris	.15
25	Javier Vazquez	.15
27	Joe Crede	.15
27	Jose Vidro	.15
28	Mike Piazza	1.00
29	Curt Schilling	.40
30	Alex Rodriguez	1.50
31	John Olerud	.25
32	Dontrelle Willis	.25
33	Larry Walker	.25
34	Joe Randa	.15
35	Paul LoDuca	.15
36	Marlon Byrd	.15
37	Bo Hart	.15
38	Rafael Palmeiro	.50
39	Garret Anderson	.40
40	Tom Glavine	.25
41	Ichiro Suzuki	1.25
42	Derek Lee	.25
43	Lance Berkman	.25
44	Nomar Garciaparra	1.50
45	Mike Sweeney	.15
46	A.J. Burnett	.15
47	Sean Casey	.15
48	Eric Gagne	.25
49	Joel Pineiro	.15
50	Russ Ortiz	.15
51	Placido Polanco	.15
52	Sammy Sosa	1.25
53	Mark Teixeira	.25
54	Randy Wolf	.15
55	Vladimir Guerrero	.75
56	Tim Hudson	.25
57	Lew Ford	.15
58	Carlos Delgado	.50
59	Darin Erstad	.25
60	Mike Lieberthal	.15
61	Craig Biggio	.25
62	Ryan Klesko	.15
63	C.C. Sabathia	.15
64	Carlos Lee	.15
65	Al Leiter	.15
66	Brandon Webb	.15
67	Jacque Jones	.15
68	Kerry Wood	.50
69	Omar Vizquel	.25
70	Jeremy Bonderman	.15
71	Kevin Brown	.25
72	Richie Sexson	.40
73	Zach Day	.15
74	Mike Mussina	.40
75	Sidney Ponson	.15
76	Andruw Jones	.50
77	Woody Williams	.15
78	Kazuhiro Sasaki	.15
79	Matt Clement	.15
80	Shea Hillenbrand	.15
81	Bartolo Colon	.25
82	Ken Griffey Jr.	1.00
83	Todd Helton	.50
84	Dmitri Young	.15
85	Richard Hidalgo	.15
86	Carlos Beltran	.25
87	Brad Wilkerson	.15
88	Andy Pettitte	.40
89	Miguel Tejada	.40
90	Edgar Martinez	.25
91	Vernon Wells	.25
92	Magglio Ordonez	.25

93	Tony Batista	.15
94	Jose Reyes	.15
95	Matt Stairs	.15
96	Manny Ramirez	.50
97	Carlos Pena	.15
98	A.J. Pierzynski	.15
99	Jim Thome	.75
100	Aubrey Huff	.15
101	Roberto Alomar	.40
102	Luis Gonzalez	.25
103	Chipper Jones	1.00
104	Jay Gibbons	.25
105	Adam Dunn	.40
106	Jay Payton	.15
107	Scott Podsednik	.40
108	Roy Oswalt	.25
109	Milton Bradley	.15
110	Shawn Green	.25
111	Ryan Wagner	.15
112	Eric Chavez	.25
113	Pat Burrell	.25
114	Frank Thomas	.50
115	Jason Kendall	.25
116	Jake Peavy	.15
117	Mike Cameron	.15
118	Jim Edmonds	.25
119	Hank Blalock	.40
120	Troy Glaus	.40
121	Jeff Kent	.25
122	Jason Schmidt	.25
123	Corey Patterson	.15
124	Austin Kearns	.40
125	Edwin Jackson	.15
126	Alfonso Soriano	.75
127	Bobby Abreu	.25
128	Scott Rolen	.75
129	Jeff Bagwell	.50
130	Shannon Stewart	.15
131	Rich Aurilia	.15
132	Ty Wigginton	.15
133	Randy Johnson	.75
134	Rocco Baldelli	.40
135	Hideo Nomo	.25
136	Greg Maddux	2.00
137	Johnny Damon	1.50
138	Mark Prior	.75
139	Corey Koskie	.50
140	Miguel Cabrera	1.50
141	Hideki Matsui	2.00
142	Jose Cruz	.50
143	Barry Zito	1.00
144	Javy Lopez	.50
145	Jason Varitek	1.00
146	Moises Alou	1.00
147	Torii Hunter	1.00
148	Juan Encarnacion	.50
149	Jorge Posada	1.00
150	Marquis Grissom	.50
151	Rich Harden	1.00
152	Gary Sheffield	4.00
153	Pedro J. Martinez	5.00
154	Brad Radke	3.00
155	Mike Lowell	3.00
156	Jason Giambi	4.00
157	Mark Mulder	4.00
158	Ben Weber	.15
159	Mark DeRosa	.15
160	Melvin Mora	.15
161	Bill Mueller	.15
162	Jon Garland	.15
163	Jody Gerut	.15
164	Javier Lopez	.15
165	Craig Monroe	.15
166	Juan Pierre	.15
167	Morgan Ensberg	.15
168	Angel Berroa	.15
169	Geoff Jenkins	.25
170	Matt LeCroy	.15
171	Livan Hernandez	.15
172	Jason L. Phillips	.15
173	Mariano Rivera	.25
174	Erubiel Durazo	.15
175	Jason Michaels	.15
176	Kip Wells	.15
177	Ray Durham	.15
178	Randy Winn	.15
179	Edgar Renteria	.15
180	Carl Crawford	.15
181	Laynce Nix	.15
182	Greg Myers	.15
183	Delmon Young, Chad Gaudin	1.00
184	Humberto Quintero, Bernie Castro	.50
185	Craig Brazell, Daniel Garcia	.50
186	Ryan Wing, Francisco Cruceta	.50
187	William Bergolla, Josh Hall	.50
188	Clint Barmes, Garrett Atkins	.50
189	Chris Bootcheck, Richard Fischer	.50
190	Edgar Gonzalez, Matt Kata	.50

191	Andrew Brown, Koyie Hill	.50
192	John Gall, Dan Haren	.50
193	Chad Bentz, Luis Ayala	.50
194	Hector Gimenez, Eric Bruntlett	.50
195	Boof Bonser, Rob Bowen	.50
196	Chris Snelling, Rett Johnson	.50
197	Rickie Weeks, Adam Morrissey	1.00
198	Noah Lowry, Todd Linden	.50
199	Chris Waters, Brett Evert	.50
200	Jorge DePaula, Chien-Ming Wang	.50

Finish

Stars (1-200): 4-6X
Production 100 Sets

Big Signs

		NM/M
Complete Set (15):		25.00
Common Player:		.75
Inserted 1:9		
1	Albert Pujols	3.00
2	Derek Jeter	4.00
3	Mike Piazza	2.00
4	Jason Giambi	1.50
5	Ichiro Suzuki	2.50
6	Nomar Garciaparra	3.00
7	Mark Prior	2.00
8	Randy Johnson	1.50
9	Greg Maddux	2.00
10	Sammy Sosa	2.50
11	Ken Griffey Jr.	2.00
12	Dontrelle Willis	.75
13	Alex Rodriguez	3.00
14	Chipper Jones	2.00
15	Hank Blalock	.75

Big Signs Autographs

	NM/M
Production 100	
Hank Blalock	25.00
Mark Prior	
Albert Pujols	150.00
Dontrelle Willis	25.00

Classic Combinations

		NM/M
Complete Set (10):		50.00
Common Player:		3.00
Inserted 1:108		
1	Ivan Rodriguez, Mike Piazza	6.00
2	Alex Rodriguez, Sammy Sosa	8.00
3	Dontrelle Willis, Angel Berroa	3.00
4	Nomar Garciaparra, Derek Jeter	10.00
5	Ichiro Suzuki, Hideo Nomo	6.00
6	Josh Beckett, Kerry Wood	4.00
7	Albert Pujols, Carlos Delgado	8.00
8	Alfonso Soriano, Joe Morgan	4.00
9	Jason Giambi, Reggie Jackson	4.00
10	Nolan Ryan, Tom Seaver	5.00

Clubhouse Memorabilia

	NM/M
Common Player:	5.00
Inserted 1:24	
Rocco Baldelli	10.00
Josh Beckett	8.00
Hank Blalock	6.00
Nomar Garciaparra	12.00
Jason Giambi	8.00
Vladimir Guerrero	8.00
Todd Helton	6.00
Torii Hunter	6.00
Derek Jeter	15.00
Chipper Jones	8.00
Austin Kearns	6.00
Greg Maddux	10.00
Hideo Nomo	8.00
Mike Piazza	8.00
Mark Prior	10.00
Albert Pujols	12.00
Alex Rodriguez	10.00
Richie Sexson	5.00
Alfonso Soriano	8.00
Sammy Sosa	12.00
Miguel Tejada	5.00

Jim Thome	8.00
Dontrelle Willis	8.00

Clubhouse Memorabilia Dual

	NM/M
Common Player:	10.00
Production 50 Sets	
Hank Blalock	15.00
Nomar Garciaparra	30.00
Jason Giambi	15.00
Vladimir Guerrero	20.00
Todd Helton	20.00
Torii Hunter	15.00
Derek Jeter	35.00
Chipper Jones	15.00
Austin Kearns	10.00
Greg Maddux	30.00
Hideo Nomo	25.00
Mark Prior	20.00
Albert Pujols	30.00
Alex Rodriguez	25.00
Sammy Sosa	20.00
Jim Thome	20.00
Dontrelle Willis	

Nameplates

		NM/M
Common Player:		8.00
Inserted 1:4 Jumbo		
Varying quantities produced		
1	Austin Kearns	10.00
2	Juan Pierre	10.00
3	Albert Pujols	30.00
4	Manny Ramirez	15.00
5	Kerry Wood	20.00
6	Alex Rodriguez	20.00
8	Barry Zito	10.00
9	Hee Seop Choi	8.00
10	Kevin Brown	10.00
11	Jose Reyes	15.00
12	Marlon Byrd	10.00
13	Nomar Garciaparra	20.00
14	Josh Beckett	15.00
16	Hideo Nomo	15.00
19	Randy Johnson	15.00
20	Hank Blalock	12.00
21	Tom Glavine/25	25.00
22	Luis Castillo	8.00
23	Mark Teixeira	12.00
24	Gary Sheffield	10.00
25	Richie Sexson	10.00
26	Miguel Cabrera	20.00
27	Sammy Sosa	25.00
28	Curt Schilling	10.00
30	Chipper Jones	20.00

Portraits

	NM/M
Complete Set (10):	25.00

Common Player: 1.50
Inserted 1:18
1	Jason Giambi	1.50
2	Nomar Garciaparra	4.00
3	Vladimir Guerrero	1.50
4	Mark Prior	3.00
5	Jim Thome	1.50
6	Derek Jeter	5.00
7	Sammy Sosa	3.00
8	Alex Rodriguez	4.00
9	Greg Maddux	2.50
10	Albert Pujols	4.00

Portraits Jersey
NM/M
Common Player: 8.00
Inserted 1:48.
Nomar Garciaparra	15.00
Jason Giambi	8.00
Vladimir Guerrero	8.00
Derek Jeter	15.00
Greg Maddux	8.00
Mark Prior	6.00
Albert Pujols	15.00
Alex Rodriguez	10.00
Sammy Sosa	12.00
Jim Thome	8.00

Portraits Patch
NM/M
Common Player: 10.00
Production 100 Sets
Nomar Garciaparra	20.00
Jason Giambi	10.00
Vladimir Guerrero	10.00
Derek Jeter	25.00
Mark Prior	20.00
Albert Pujols	30.00
Alex Rodriguez	15.00
Sammy Sosa	20.00
Jim Thome	12.00

Scouting Report

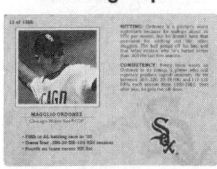

NM/M
Complete Set (15): 35.00
Common Player: 1.50
Production 400 Sets
1	Josh Beckett	2.00
2	Todd Helton	2.00
3	Rocco Baldelli	2.00
4	Pedro J. Martinez	3.00
5	Jeff Bagwell	2.00
6	Mark Prior	4.00
7	Ichiro Suzuki	4.00
8	Barry Zito	2.00
9	Manny Ramirez	2.00
10	Miguel Cabrera	2.00
11	Richie Sexson	1.50
12	Hideki Matsui	8.00
13	Magglio Ordonez	1.50
14	Brandon Webb	1.50
15	Kerry Wood	2.00

Scouting Report Memorabilia
NM/M
Common Player: 6.00
Production 250 Sets
Jeff Bagwell	8.00
Rocco Baldelli	8.00
Josh Beckett	8.00
Todd Helton	6.00
Pedro J. Martinez	8.00
Mark Prior	10.00
Manny Ramirez	6.00
Brandon Webb	6.00
Kerry Wood	8.00

2004 Fleer Showcase
NM/M
Complete Set (130):
Common Player: .25
Common SP (101-130): 1.00
Inserted 1:6
Pack (5): 4.50
Box (24): 90.00
1	Corey Patterson	.25
2	Ken Griffey Jr.	1.50
3	Preston Wilson	.40
4	Juan Pierre	.25
5	Jose Reyes	.50
6	Jason Schmidt	.40

7	Rocco Baldelli	.50
8	Carlos Delgado	.75
9	Hideki Matsui	2.50
10	Nomar Garciaparra	2.00
11	Brian Giles	.40
12	Darin Erstad	.40
13	Larry Walker	.40
14	Bernie Williams	.50
15	Laynce Nix	.25
16	Manny Ramirez	.75
17	Magglio Ordonez	.25
18	Khalil Greene	.25
19	Jim Edmonds	.50
20	Troy Glaus	.50
21	Curt Schilling	.50
22	Chipper Jones	1.50
23	Sammy Sosa	2.00
24	Frank Thomas	.75
25	Todd Helton	.75
26	Craig Biggio	.40
27	Shannon Stewart	.40
28	Mark Mulder	.40
29	Mike Lieberthal	.25
30	Reggie Sanders	.25
31	Edgar Martinez	.25
32	Bo Hart	.25
33	Mark Teixeira	.40
34	Jay Gibbons	.25
35	Roberto Alomar	.50
36	Kip Wells	.25
37	J.D. Drew	.25
38	Jason Varitek	.25
39	Craig Monroe	.25
40	Roy Oswalt	.40
41	Edgardo Alfonzo	.25
42	Roy Halladay	.50
43	Gary Sheffield	.50
44	Lance Berkman	.50
45	Torii Hunter	.50
46	Vladimir Guerrero	1.00
47	Marlon Byrd	.25
48	Austin Kearns	.25
49	Angel Berroa	.25
50	Geoff Jenkins	.50
51	Aubrey Huff	.25
52	Dontrelle Willis	.50
53	Tony Batista	.25
54	Shawn Green	.40
55	Jason Kendall	.25
56	Garret Anderson	.50
57	Andruw Jones	.75
58	Dmitri Young	.25
59	Richie Sexson	.50
60	Jorge Posada	.50
61	Bobby Abreu	.40
62	Vernon Wells	.40
63	Javy Lopez	.40
64	Josh Beckett	.75
65	Eric Chavez	.40
66	Tim Salmon	.40
67	Brandon Webb	.40
68	Pedro J. Martinez	1.00
69	Kerry Wood	1.00
70	Jose Vidro	.25
71	Alfonso Soriano	1.00
72	Barry Zito	.50
73	Sean Burroughs	.25
74	Jamie Moyer	.25
75	Luis Gonzalez	.40
76	Adam Dunn	.50
77	Mike Piazza	1.50
78	Pat Burrell	.50
79	Scott Rolen	1.00
80	Milton Bradley	.25
81	Mike Sweeney	.25
82	Hank Blalock	.25
83	Esteban Loaiza	.25
84	Hideo Nomo	.25
85	Derek Jeter	3.00
86	Albert Pujols	2.50
87	Greg Maddux	1.50
88	Mark Prior	1.50
89	Mike Lowell	.25
90	Jeff Bagwell	.75

91	Scott Podsednik	.50
92	Tom Glavine	.50
93	Jason Giambi	1.00
94	Jim Thome	1.00
95	Ichiro Suzuki	2.00
96	Randy Johnson	1.00
97	Omar Vizquel	.25
98	Ivan Rodriguez	.50
99	Miguel Tejada	.50
100	Alex Rodriguez	2.50
101	Rickie Weeks	3.00
102	Chad Gaudin	1.00
103	Rich Harden	1.00
104	Edwin Jackson	1.50
105	Chien-Ming Wang	1.00
106	Matt Kata	1.00
107	Delmon Young	3.00
108	Ryan Wagner	1.00
109	Jeff Duncan	1.00
110	Prentice Redman	1.00
111	Clint Barmes	1.00
112	Jeremy Guthrie	1.00
113	Brian Stokes	1.00
114	David DeJesus	1.00
115	Felix Sanchez	1.00
116	Josh Stewart	1.00
117	Daniel Garcia	1.00
118	Jon Leicester	1.00
119	Francisco Cruceta	1.00
120	Oscar Villarreal	1.00
121	Michael Hessman	1.00
122	Michel Hernandez	1.00
123	Richard Fischer	1.00
124	Robby Hammock	1.00
125	Guillermo Quiroz	1.00
126	Craig Brazell	1.00
127	Wilfredo Ledezma	1.00
128	Josh Willingham	1.00
129	Ramon Nivar	1.00
130	Matt Diaz	1.00

Legacy
Stars (1-100): 4-8X
SP's (101-130): 1-3X
Production 99 Sets

Masterpiece

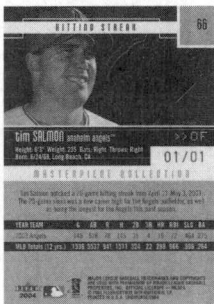

No Pricing
Production One Set

Albert Pujols Legacy Collectible Jersey
NM/M
Varying quantities produced
3	Albert Pujols/30	40.00
4	Albert Pujols/40	30.00
5	Albert Pujols/50	30.00
6	Albert Pujols/60	30.00
7	Albert Pujols/70	25.00
8	Albert Pujols/80	25.00
9	Albert Pujols/90	25.00
10	Albert Pujols/100	25.00

Albert Pujols Legacy Collectible Autograph
Varying quantities produced
No Pricing

Albert Pujols Legacy Collection

NM/M
Complete Set (10): 60.00
Common Pujols (1-10): 8.00
Production 1,000 Sets

Baseball's Best

NM/M
Complete Set (15): 20.00
Common Player: .75
Inserted 1:24
1	Derek Jeter	4.00
2	Mark Prior	2.00
3	Mike Piazza	2.50
4	Jeff Bagwell	1.00
5	Kerry Wood	1.00
6	Ivan Rodriguez	1.00
7	Albert Pujols	3.00
8	Jim Thome	1.50
9	Sammy Sosa	2.50
10	Vladimir Guerrero	1.50
11	Eric Gagne	.75
12	Randy Johnson	1.50
13	Todd Helton	1.00
14	Chipper Jones	2.00
15	Alex Rodriguez	4.00

Baseball's Best Memorabilia

NM/M
Common Player: 5.00
Inserted 1:72
Parallel 150: .75-1.5X
Production 150
Parallel 50: 1.5-2X
Patch versions: 2-4X
Production 50
Derek Jeter	15.00
Mark Prior	10.00
Mike Piazza	10.00
Jeff Bagwell	8.00
Kerry Wood	8.00
Ivan Rodriguez	5.00
Albert Pujols	15.00
Jim Thome	8.00
Sammy Sosa	10.00
Vladimir Guerrero	8.00
Eric Gagne	8.00
Randy Johnson	8.00
Todd Helton	8.00
Chipper Jones	8.00
Alex Rodriguez	10.00

Grace

NM/M
Complete Set (20): 20.00
Common Player: .75
Inserted 1:12
1	Kerry Wood	1.50
2	Derek Jeter	4.00
3	Nomar Garciaparra	3.00
4	Mike Piazza	2.50
5	Mark Prior	2.00
6	Jose Reyes	1.00
7	Dontrelle Willis	.75
8	Pedro J. Martinez	1.50
9	Tim Hudson	.75
10	Troy Glaus	.75
11	Hank Blalock	1.00
12	Albert Pujols	3.00
13	Juan Pierre	.75

14	Angel Berroa	.75
15	Rocco Baldelli	1.00
16	Carlos Delgado	1.00
17	Manny Ramirez	1.00
18	Alex Rodriguez	3.00
19	Andruw Jones	1.00
20	Luis Gonzalez	.75

Grace Memorabilia

NM/M

Common Player: 5.00
Inserted 1:48
Parallel 150: 1-1.5X
Production 150
Patch: 1.5-2.5X
Production 50

	Derek Jeter	15.00
	Nomar Garciaparra	10.00
	Mike Piazza	10.00
	Mark Prior	10.00
	Dontrelle Willis	5.00
	Pedro J. Martinez	8.00
	Albert Pujols	15.00
	Rocco Baldelli	8.00
	Manny Ramirez	8.00
	Alex Rodriguez	10.00

Hot Gloves

NM/M

Common Player: 8.00
Inserted 1:288

1	Derek Jeter	40.00
2	Nomar Garciaparra	30.00
3	Alex Rodriguez	30.00
4	Chipper Jones	15.00
5	Torii Hunter	8.00
6	Ichiro Suzuki	35.00
7	Mark Prior	20.00
8	Vladimir Guerrero	15.00
9	Albert Pujols	30.00
10	Ivan Rodriguez	10.00
11	Hideki Matsui	30.00
12	Sammy Sosa	25.00
13	Jim Thome	15.00
14	Rocco Baldelli	10.00
15	Jeff Bagwell	10.00

Hot Gloves Memorabilia

NM/M

Common Player: 20.00
All jerseys unless noted.
Production 50 Sets

	Derek Jeter	60.00
	Nomar Garciaparra	50.00
	Alex Rodriguez	40.00
	Chipper Jones	40.00
	Ichiro Suzuki/base	65.00
	Mark Prior	25.00
	Vladimir Guerrero	30.00
	Albert Pujols	50.00
	Ivan Rodriguez	20.00
	Hideki Matsui/base	60.00
	Sammy Sosa	40.00
	Jim Thome	20.00
	Rocco Baldelli	20.00
	Jeff Bagwell	20.00

Sweet Sigs

NM/M

Common Player: 6.00
Inserted 1:24
Sweet Sigs
Game-Used: No Pricing
Production 5

Hank Blalock/824	20.00
Taylor Bucholz/Redemp.	6.00
John Gall/Redemp.	8.00
Bo Hart/667	15.00
Torii Hunter/294	15.00
Austin Kearns/224	20.00
Wilfredo Ledezma/376	6.00
Mike Lowell/44	15.00
Chien-Ming Wang/35	
Corey Patterson/176	15.00
Carlos Pena/48	10.00
Albert Pujols/Redemp.	
Jose Reyes/115	120.00
Scott Rolen/200	40.00
Michael Ryan/288	25.00
Miguel Tejada/52	12.00
Ryan Wagner/Redemp.	20.00
Brandon Webb/1,000	10.00
Rickie Weeks/416	15.00
Josh Willingham/180	6.00
Dontrelle Willis/26	60.00
Delmon Young/1,000	25.00
Barry Zito/248	25.00

2004 Fleer Sweet Signatures

NM/M

Common Player (1-75): .20
Minor Stars (1-75): .40
Unlisted Star (1-75): .60
Common Future Sig-cess (76-100): 3.00
Future Sig-cess Production 999 Sets
Pack (6): 5.00
Box (12): 80.00

1	Manny Ramirez	1.00
2	Frank Thomas	1.00
3	Josh Beckett	1.00
4	Shawn Green	.40
5	Tom Glavine	.40
6	Marquis Grissom	.20
7	Nomar Garciaparra	3.00
8	Magglio Ordonez	.40
9	Alex Rodriguez	3.00
10	Chipper Jones	2.00
11	Jody Gerut	.40
12	Dontrelle Willis	.40
13	Lance Berkman	.40
14	Jose Vidro	.20
15	Barry Zito	.60
16	Jason Kendall	.40
17	Scott Rolen	1.50
18	Troy Glaus	.60
19	Brandon Webb	.20
20	Tim Hudson	.40
21	Shannon Stewart	.20
22	Darin Erstad	.40
23	Curt Schilling	.60
24	Bret Boone	.40
25	Richie Sexson	.60
26	Hideki Matsui	3.00
27	Albert Pujols	3.00
28	Greg Maddux	2.00
29	Austin Kearns	.60
30	Todd Helton	1.00
31	Miguel Cabrera	1.00
32	Jeff Bagwell	1.00
33	Marlon Byrd	.20
34	Ichiro Suzuki	2.50
35	Rocco Baldelli	.60
36	Garret Anderson	.40
37	Javy Lopez	.40
38	Kerry Wood	1.00
39	Adam Dunn	.60
40	Geoff Jenkins	.40
41	Derek Jeter	4.00
42	Rich Harden	.20
43	Alfonso Soriano	1.50
44	Ken Griffey Jr.	2.00
45	Ivan Rodriguez	.60
46	Pedro J. Martinez	1.50
47	Andy Pettitte	.60
48	Gary Sheffield	.60
49	Brian Giles	.40
50	Carlos Delgado	1.00
51	Mike Piazza	2.00
52	Hank Blalock	.60
53	Roger Clemens	2.00
54	Scott Podsednik	.20
55	Torii Hunter	.60
56	Jose Reyes	.20
57	Jim Thome	1.50
58	Jason Schmidt	.40
59	Jose Cruz	.20
60	Mark Teixeira	.40
61	Randy Johnson	1.50
62	Miguel Tejada	.60
63	Sammy Sosa	2.50
64	Larry Walker	.40
65	Carl Everett	.20
66	Luis Castillo	.20
67	Jason Giambi	1.50
68	Mike Sweeney	.20
69	Andruw Jones	1.00
70	Vladimir Guerrero	1.50
71	J.D. Drew	.40
72	Mark Prior	2.00
73	Angel Berroa	.20
74	Hideo Nomo	.40
75	Roy Halladay	.40
76	John Gall RC	3.00
77	Angel Chavez RC	3.00
78	Alfredo Simon RC	3.00
79	Merkin Valdez RC	3.00
80	Chad Bentz RC	3.00
81	Justin Leone RC	6.00
82	Mike Rouse	3.00
83	Aarom Baldiris RC	3.00
84	Chris Shelton RC	8.00
85	Akinori Otsuka RC	6.00
86	Ruddy Yan RC	3.00
87	Ramon Ramirez RC	3.00
88	Hector Gimenez RC	6.00
89	Mike Gosling	3.00
90	Greg Dobbs RC	3.00
91	Kazuo Matsui RC	8.00
92	Donald Kelly RC	6.00
93	Shingo Takatsu RC	6.00
94	Ivan Ochoa RC	5.00
95	Chris Aguila RC	5.00
96	Jason Bartlett RC	3.00
97	Graham Koonce RC	5.00
98	Ronny Cedeno RC	3.00
99	Jerome Gamble RC	3.00
100	Onil Joseph RC	3.00

Gold

(1-75): 1-5X
(76-100): .5-2X
Production 99 Sets

Black

(1-100): No Pricing
Production 5 Sets

Ballpark Heroes

NM/M

Common Player: 1.25
Inserted 1:6

1	Rocco Baldelli	1.75
2	Adam Dunn	1.75
3	Nomar Garciaparra	5.00
4	Ken Griffey Jr.	3.50
5	Vladimir Guerrero	3.00
6	Torii Hunter	1.75
7	Andruw Jones	2.00
8	Mike Piazza	3.50
9	Alfonso Soriano	3.00
10	Frank Thomas	2.00
11	Dontrelle Willis	1.25
12	Barry Zito	1.75
13	Javy Lopez	1.25
14	Miguel Cabrera	2.00
15	Kazuo Matsui	3.50
16	Josh Beckett	2.00
17	Derek Jeter	6.00
18	Greg Maddux	3.50
19	Pedro J. Martinez	3.00
20	Hideo Nomo	1.25
21	Mark Prior	4.00
22	Albert Pujols	5.00
23	Alex Rodriguez	5.00
24	Scott Rolen	3.00
25	Ichiro Suzuki	4.00

Ballpark Heroes Silver Jersey

NM/M

Common Player: 4.00

Ballpark Heroes Silver Jersey (Sequentially Numbered)

Sequentially Numbered

RB	Rocco Baldelli/250	4.00
JB	Josh Beckett/225	
MC	Miguel Cabrera/196	5.00
AD	Adam Dunn/215	4.00
VG	Vladimir Guerrero/200	6.00
GM	Greg Maddux/224	8.00
PM	Pedro J. Martinez/239	6.00
HN	Hideo Nomo/210	4.00
MP	Mike Piazza/163	8.00
AP	Albert Pujols/199	12.00
SR	Scott Rolen/221	6.00
AS	Alfonso Soriano/235	6.00
FT	Frank Thomas/242	5.00
DW	Dontrelle Willis/186	4.00
BZ	Barry Zito/195	4.00

Ballpark Heroes Copper Jersey

NM/M

Common Player: 5.00
Production 110 Sets
Gold Patch: 1-3X
Production 50 Sets
Masterpiece Patch: No Pricing
Production One Set

RB	Rocco Baldelli/110	5.00
MC	Miguel Cabrera/110	6.00
AD	Adam Dunn/110	5.00
VG	Vladimir Guerrero/110	8.00
GM	Greg Maddux/110	10.00
PM	Pedro J. Martinez/110	8.00
HN	Hideo Nomo/110	5.00
MP	Mike Piazza/110	10.00
AP	Albert Pujols/110	15.00
SR	Scott Rolen/110	8.00
AS	Alfonso Soriano/110	6.00
FT	Frank Thomas/110	6.00
DW	Dontrelle Willis/110	5.00
BZ	Barry Zito/110	5.00

Ballpark Heroes Black Patch

NM/M

Sequentially Numbered
MP Mike Piazza/31 50.00

Ballpark Heroes Duals

No Pricing
Sequentially Numbered

Ballpark Heroes Quad

NM/M

Sequentially Numbered

1	Josh Beckett, Greg Maddux, Pedro J. Martinez, Mark Prior/42	150.00
2	Dontrelle Willis, Kazuo Matsui, Miguel Cabrera, Rocco Baldelli/26	75.00
4	Dontrelle Willis, Josh Beckett, Derek Jeter, Alex Rodriguez/32	150.00
5	Albert Pujols, Vladimir Guerrero, Mike Piazza, Alex Rodriguez/37	150.00

Sweet Signatures Copper

NM/M

Common Player: 10.00
Sequentially Numbered
Gold: .75-1.5X
Production 30 Sets
Hideo Nomo #'d to 10.
No Roger Clemens or Ted Williams Gold card.
Masterpiece: No Pricing
Production One Set

GA	Garret Anderson/100	20.00
RB	Rocco Baldelli/75	25.00
JB	Josh Beckett/75	30.00
CB	Carlos Beltran/75	20.00
LB	Lance Berkman/150	20.00
AB	Angel Berroa/75	20.00
JB	Jeremy Bonderman/150	15.00
MC	Miguel Cabrera/150	30.00

MC	Mike Cameron/150	20.00
RC	Roger Clemens/52	400.00
CC	Carl Crawford/150	15.00
JD	Johnny Damon/150	30.00
JD	J.D. Drew/98	40.00
DE	Dennis Eckersley/75	40.00
AE	Adam Everett/150	10.00
JF	Julio Franco/150	30.00
LG	Luis Gonzalez/150	15.00
KG	Khalil Greene/150	40.00
VG	Vladimir Guerrero/75	75.00
TH	Torii Hunter/150	25.00
EJ	Edwin Jackson/75	15.00
RJ	Randy Johnson/28	150.00
CJ	Chipper Jones/50	100.00
MK	Matt Kata/150	10.00
BL	Barry Larkin/50	50.00
CL	Carlos Lee/150	15.00
AL	Al Leiter/75	25.00
KL	Kenny Lofton/50	50.00
JL	Javy Lopez/75	25.00
GM	Greg Maddux/50	75.00
PM	Pedro J. Martinez/75	125.00
JM	Joe Mauer/150	40.00
WM	Wade Miller/150	20.00
KM	Kevin Millwood/150	15.00
PM	Paul Molitor/75	40.00
SM	Stan Musial/25	80.00
MM	Mike Mussina/50	40.00
LN	Lance Niekro/150	10.00
JO	John Olerud/75	30.00
MO	Magglio Ordonez/150	20.00
RO	Russ Ortiz/150	15.00
RO	Roy Oswalt/150	20.00
AO	Akinori Otsuka/150	20.00
BP	Brad Penny/150	10.00
AP	Andy Pettitte/50	40.00
MP	Mike Piazza/150	120.00
AP	Albert Pujols/73	300.00
BR	Brad Radke/150	20.00
JR	Jose Reyes/163	30.00
AR	Alexis Rios/150	15.00
NR	Nolan Ryan/50	300.00
CS	C.C. Sabathia/150	20.00
TS	Tim Salmon/100	40.00
DS	Deion Sanders/50	50.00
JS	Johan Santana/150	80.00
MS	Mike Schmidt/50	60.00
SS	Shannon Stewart/75	20.00
FT	Frank Thomas/75	75.00
JV	Jason Varitek/75	40.00
TW	Tim Wakefield/150	30.00
VW	Vernon Wells/150	20.00
BW	Bernie Williams/50	80.00
DW	Dontrelle Willis/150	20.00
KW	Kerry Wood/75	60.00
CY	Carl Yastrzemski/50	100.00
BZ	Barry Zito/44	30.00

Sweet Sigs Jersey Number

		NM/M
No. 3-25:		1-3X Copper
No. 26-57:		.75-1.5X Copper

Numbered to player's jersey #.
No Hideo Nomo card.

MC	Mike Cameron/44	30.00

Sweet Stitches Silver Jersey

		NM/M
Common Player:		5.00

Sequentially Numbered

HB	Hank Blalock/166	5.00
MC	Miguel Cabrera/169	8.00
RC	Roger Clemens/165	8.00
JG	Jason Giambi/125	8.00
VG	Vladimir Guerrero/172	8.00
AJ	Andruw Jones/175	8.00
GM	Greg Maddux/156	8.00
MO	Magglio Ordonez/113	8.00
MP	Mike Piazza/174	8.00
MP	Mark Prior/172	8.00
AP	Albert Pujols/170	12.00
MR	Manny Ramirez/163	8.00
JR	Jose Reyes/171	8.00
SR	Scott Rolen/168	8.00
GS	Gary Sheffield/88	8.00
AS	Alfonso Soriano/162	8.00
SS	Sammy Sosa/158	10.00
MT	Mark Teixeira/158	5.00
MT	Miguel Tejada/162	5.00
FT	Frank Thomas/159	8.00
JT	Jim Thome/8	8.00
KW	Kerry Wood/134	8.00

Sweet Stitches Copper Jersey

		NM/M
Common Player:		5.00
Production 125 Sets		
Gold Patch:		1-3X
Production 50 Sets		
Masterpiece Patch:		No Pricing
Production One Set		
HB	Hank Blalock/125	5.00
MC	Miguel Cabrera/125	8.00
RC	Roger Clemens/125	8.00
JG	Jason Giambi/125	8.00
VG	Vladimir Guerrero/125	8.00
AJ	Andruw Jones/125	10.00
GM	Greg Maddux/125	8.00
MO	Magglio Ordonez/125	8.00
MP	Mike Piazza/125	8.00
MP;	Mark Prior/125	8.00
AP	Albert Pujols/125	15.00
MR	Manny Ramirez/125	8.00
JR	Jose Reyes/125	8.00
SR	Scott Rolen/125	8.00
GS	Gary Sheffield/125	8.00
AS	Alfonso Soriano/125	8.00
SS	Sammy Sosa/125	10.00
MT	Mark Teixeira/125	5.00
MT	Miguel Tejada/125	5.00
FT	Frank Thomas/125	8.00
JT	Jim Thome/125	8.00
KW	Kerry Wood/125	8.00

Sweet Stitches Black Patch

		NM/M

Sequentially Numbered

SS-GM	Greg Maddux/32	25.00

Sweet Stitches Quad Patches

	NM/M

Sequentially Numbered
No pricing for quantities less than 25.

4	Andruw Jones/31, Miguel Cabrera/31, Albert Pujols/31, Sammy Sosa/31	80.00
10	Greg Maddux/33, Sammy Sosa/33, Mark Prior/33, Kerry Wood/33	150.00

Sweet Swing

		NM/M
Common Player:		2.50

Inserted 1:12

1SS	Sammy Sosa	5.00
2SS	Vladimir Guerrero	3.50
3SS	Jason Giambi	3.50
4SS	Chipper Jones	4.00
5SS	Alfonso Soriano	3.50
6SS	Manny Ramirez	3.00
7SS	Todd Helton	3.00
8SS	Alex Rodriguez	6.00
9SS	Albert Pujols	6.00
10SS	Jeff Bagwell	3.00
11SS	Mike Piazza	4.00
12SS	Hank Blalock	2.50
13SS	Jim Thome	3.50
14SS	Carlos Delgado	3.00
15SS	Nomar Garciaparra	6.00

Sweet Swing Silver Bat

		NM/M
Common Player:		5.00

Sequentially Numbered

HB	Hank Blalock/15	
JG	Jason Giambi/247	6.00
VG	Vladimir Guerrero/250	6.00
CJ	Chipper Jones/235	8.00
MP	Mike Piazza/231	8.00
AP	Albert Pujols/237	12.00
MR	Manny Ramirez/224	5.00
AR	Alex Rodriguez/213	12.00
AS	Alfonso Soriano/216	6.00
SS	Sammy Sosa/221	10.00
JT	Jim Thome/245	6.00

Sweet Swing Copper Jersey

		NM/M
Common Player:		4.00
Production 200 Sets		
Gold Bat/Jersey:		1.5-4X
Production 50 Sets		
Masterpiece Bat/Patch		
Production One Set		
HB	Hank Blalock/200	4.00
JG	Jason Giambi/200	6.00
VG	Vladimir Guerrero/200	6.00
CJ	Chipper Jones/200	8.00
MP	Mike Piazza/200	8.00
AP	Albert Pujols/200	12.00
MR	Manny Ramirez/200	5.00
AR	Alex Rodriguez/200	12.00
AS	Alfonso Soriano/200	6.00
SS	Sammy Sosa/200	10.00
JT	Jim Thome/200	6.00

Sweet Swing Black Bat/Patch

	NM/M

Numbered to most home runs.

Sweet Swing Quad

		NM/M

Sequentially Numbered

1	Jason Giambi, Alex Rodriguez, Jeff Bagwell, Manny Ramirez/35	80.00
3	Mike Piazza, Alfonso Soriano, Todd Helton, Hank Blalock/32	125.00

2004 Fleer Tradition

Josh Beckett

	NM/M
Complete Set (500):	100.00
Common Player:	.15
Common SP (401-500):	.25
Pack (10):	1.75
Hobby Box (36):	50.00
1 Juan Pierre	.15
2 Josh Beckett	.50
3 Ivan Rodriguez	.50
4 Miguel Cabrera	.50
5 Dontrelle Willis	.25
6 Derek Jeter	2.00
7 Jason Giambi	.50
8 Bernie Williams	.40
9 Alfonso Soriano	.75
10 Hideki Matsui	2.00
11 Garret Anderson, Ramon Ortiz, John Lackey	.15
12 Luis Gonzalez, Brandon Webb, Curt Schilling	.25
13 Javy Lopez, Gary Sheffield, Russ Ortiz	.25
14 Tony Batista, Jay Gibbons, Sidney Ponson, Jason Johnson	.15
15 Manny Ramirez, Nomar Garciaparra, Derek Lowe, Pedro J. Martinez	.50
16 Sammy Sosa, Mark Prior, Kerry Wood	.75
17 Frank Thomas, Carlos Lee, Esteban Loaiza	.25
18 Adam Dunn, Sean Casey, Chris Reitsma, Paul Wilson	.25
19 Jody Gerut, C.C. Sabathia	.15
20 Preston Wilson, Darren Oliver, Jason Jennings	.15
21 Dmitri Young, Mike Maroth, Jeremy Bonderman	.15
22 Mike Lowell, Dontrelle Willis, Josh Beckett	.25
23 Jeff Bagwell, Jeriome Robertson, Wade Miller	.25
24 Carlos Beltran, Darrell May	.15
25 Adrian Beltre, Shawn Green, Hideo Nomo, Kevin Brown	.15
26 Richie Sexson, Ben Sheets	.15
27 Torii Hunter, Brad Radke, Johan Santana	.15
28 Vladimir Guerrero, Orlando Cabrera, Livan Hernandez, Javier Vazquez	.25
29 Cliff Floyd, Ty Wigginton, Steve Trachsel, Al Leiter	.15
30 Jason Giambi, Andy Pettitte, Mike Mussina	.40
31 Eric Chavez, Miguel Tejada, Tim Hudson	.25
32 Jim Thome, Randy Wolf	.25
33 Reggie Sanders, Josh Fogg, Kip Wells	.15
34 Ryan Klesko, Mark Loretta, Jake Peavy	.15
35 Jose Cruz, Edgardo Alfonzo, Jason Schmidt	.15
36 Bret Boone, Jamie Moyer, Joel Pineiro	.15
37 Albert Pujols, Woody Williams	.75
38 Aubrey Huff, Victor Zambrano	.15
39 Alex Rodriguez, John Thomson	.75
40 Carlos Delgado, Roy Halladay	.25
41 Greg Maddux	1.00
42 Ben Grieve	.15
43 Darin Erstad	.25
44 Ruben Sierra	.15
45 Byung-Hyun Kim	.15
46 Freddy Garcia	.15
47 Richard Hidalgo	.15
48 Tike Redman	.15
49 Kevin Millwood	.25
50 Marquis Grissom	.15
51 Jae Weong Seo	.15
52 Wil Cordero	.15
53 LaTroy Hawkins	.15
54 Jolbert Cabrera	.15
55 Kevin Appier	.15
56 John Lackey	.15
57 Garret Anderson	.25
58 R.A. Dickey	.15
59 David Segui	.15
60 Erubiel Durazo	.15
61 Bobby Abreu	.25
62 Travis Hafner	.15
63 Victor Zambrano	.15
64 Randy Johnson	.75
65 Bernie Williams	.40
66 J.T. Snow	.15
67 Sammy Sosa	1.50
68 Al Leiter	.15
69 Jason Jennings	.15
70 Matt Morris	.15
71 Mike Hampton	.15
72 Alex Encarnacion	.15
73 Alex Gonzalez	.15
74 Bartolo Colon	.25
75 Brett Myers	.15
76 Michael Young	.15

#	Player	Value	#	Player	Value	#	Player	Value	#	Player	Value
77	Ichiro Suzuki	1.50	181	John Smoltz	.25	285	Pat Burrell	.40	389	Danny Garcia	.15
78	Jason Johnson	.15	182	Toby Hall	.15	286	Luis Castillo	.15	390	Manny Ramirez	.50
79	Brad Ausmus	.15	183	Mark Buehrle	.15	287	Juan Uribe	.15	391	Dave McCarty	.15
80	Ted Lilly	.15	184	Howie Clark	.15	288	Raul Ibanez	.25	392	Mark Grudzielanek	.15
81	Ken Griffey Jr.	1.00	185	David Ortiz	.15	289	Sidney Ponson	.15	393	Mike Piazza	1.00
82	Chone Figgins	.15	186	Raul Mondesi	.15	290	Shane Hatteberg	.15	394	Jorge Posada	.40
83	Edgar Martinez	.25	187	Milton Bradley	.15	291	Jack Wilson	.15	395	Tim Hudson	.25
84	Adam Eaton	.15	188	Jorge Julio	.15	292	Reggie Sanders	.15	396	Placido Polanco	.15
85	Ken Harvey	.15	189	Victor Martinez	.15	293	Brian Giles	.25	397	Mark Loretta	.15
86	Francisco Rodriguez	.15	190	Gabe Kapler	.15	294	Craig Biggio	.25	398	Jesse Foppert	.15
87	Bill Mueller	.15	191	Julio Franco	.15	295	Kazuhisa Ishii	.15	399	Albert Pujols	1.50
88	Mike Maroth	.15	192	Ryan Freel	.15	296	Jim Edmonds	.25	400	Jeremi Gonzalez	.15
89	Charles Johnson	.15	193	Brad Fullmer	.15	297	Trevor Hoffman	.15	401	Paul Bako	.25
90	Jhonny Peralta	.15	194	Joe Borowski	.15	298	Ray Durham	.15	402	Luis Matos	.25
91	Kip Wells	.15	195	Darren Oliver	.15	299	Mike Lieberthal	.15	403	Johnny Damon	.50
92	Cesar Izturis	.15	196	Jason Varitek	.15	300	Todd Worrell	.15	404	Kerry Wood	1.00
93	Matt Clement	.15	197	Greg Myers	.15	301	Chris George	.15	405	Joe Crede	.25
94	Lyle Overbay	.15	198	Eric Munson	.15	302	Jamie Moyer	.15	406	Jason Davis	.25
95	Kirk Rueter	.15	199	Tim Wakefield	.15	303	Mike Cameron	.15	407	Larry Walker	.50
96	Cristian Guzman	.15	200	Kyle Farnsworth	.15	304	Matt Kinney	.15	408	Ivan Rodriguez	1.00
97	Garrett Stephenson	.15	201	John Vander Wal	.15	305	Aubrey Huff	.15	409	Nick Johnson	.25
98	Lance Berkman	.25	202	Alex Escobar	.15	306	Brian Lawrence	.15	410	Jose Lima	.25
99	Brett Tomko	.15	203	Sean Casey	.15	307	Carlos Guillen	.15	411	Brian Jordan	.25
100	Chris Stynes	.15	204	John Thomson	.15	308	J.D. Drew	.15	412	Eddie Guardado	.25
101	Nate Cornejo	.15	205	Carlos Zambrano	.15	309	Paul LoDuca	.15	413	Ron Calloway	.25
102	Aaron Rowand	.15	206	Kenny Lofton	.15	310	Tim Salmon	.25	414	Aaron Heilman	.25
103	Javier Vazquez	.15	207	Marcus Giles	.15	311	Jason Schmidt	.15	415	Eric Chavez	.50
104	Jason Kendall	.25	208	Wade Miller	.15	312	A.J. Pierzynski	.15	416	Randy Wolf	.25
105	Mark Redman	.15	209	Geoff Blum	.15	313	Lance Carter	.15	417	Jason Bay	.25
106	Benito Santiago	.15	210	Jason LaRue	.15	314	Julio Lugo	.15	418	Edgardo Alfonzo	.25
107	C.C. Sabathia	.15	211	Omar Vizquel	.25	315	Johan Santana	.15	419	Kazuhiro Sasaki	.25
108	David Wells	.15	212	Carlos Pena	.15	316	Laynce Nix	.15	420	Eduardo Perez	.25
109	Mark Ellis	.15	213	Adam Dunn	.40	317	John Olerud	.25	421	Carl Crawford	.25
110	Casey Blake	.15	214	Oscar Villarreal	.15	318	Robb Quinlan	.15	422	Troy Glaus	1.00
111	Sean Burroughs	.15	215	Paul Konerko	.15	319	Scott Spiezio	.15	423	Joaquin Benoit	.25
112	Carlos Beltran	.25	216	Hideo Nomo	.40	320	Tony Clark	.15	424	Russ Ortiz	.25
113	Ramon Hernandez	.15	217	Mike Sweeney	.15	321	Jose Vidro	.15	425	Larry Bigbie	.25
114	Eric Hinske	.15	218	Coco Crisp	.15	322	Shea Hillenbrand	.15	426	Todd Walker	.25
115	Luis Gonzalez	.25	219	Shawn Chacon	.15	323	Doug Glanville	.15	427	Kris Benson	.25
116	Jarrod Washburn	.15	220	Brook Fordyce	.15	324	Orlando Palmeiro	.15	428	Sandy Alomar	.25
117	Ronnie Belliard	.15	221	Josh Beckett	.50	325	Juan Gonzalez	.40	429	Jody Gerut	.25
118	Troy Percival	.15	222	Paul Wilson	.15	326	Jason Giambi	.75	430	Rene Reyes	.25
119	Jose Valentine	.15	223	Josh Towers	.15	327	Junior Spivey	.15	431	Mike Lowell	.25
120	Chase Utley	.15	224	Geoff Jenkins	.15	328	Tom Glavine	.25	432	Jeff Kent	.25
121	Odalis Perez	.15	225	Shawn Green	.25	329	Reed Johnson	.15	433	Mike MacDougal	.25
122	Steve Finley	.15	226	Derek Lee	.15	330	David Eckstein	.15	434	Dave Roberts	.25
123	Bret Boone	.25	227	Karim Garcia	.15	331	Damian Jackson	.15	435	Torii Hunter	.75
124	Jeff Conine	.15	228	Preston Wilson	.15	332	Orlando Hudson	.15	436	Tomokazu Ohka	.25
125	Jason Fogg	.15	229	Dane Sardinha	.15	333	Barry Zito	.40	437	Jeremy Griffiths	.25
126	Neifi Perez	.15	230	Aramis Ramirez	.15	334	Robert Fick	.15	438	Miguel Tejada	.75
127	Ben Sheets	.25	231	Doug Mientkiewicz	.15	335	Aaron Boone	.15	439	Vicente Padilla	.25
128	Randy Winn	.15	232	Jay Gibbons	.15	336	Rafael Palmeiro	.50	440	Bobby Hill	.25
129	Matt Stairs	.15	233	Adam Everett	.15	337	Bobby Kielty	.15	441	Rich Aurilia	.25
130	Carlos Delgado	.50	234	Brooks Kieschnick	.15	338	Tony Batista	.15	442	Shigetoshi Hasegawa	.25
131	Morgan Ensberg	.15	235	Dmitri Young	.15	339	Ryan Dempster	.15	443	So Taguchi	.25
132	Vinny Castilla	.15	236	Brad Penny	.15	340	Derek Lowe	.25	444	Damian Rolls	.25
133	Matt Mantei	.15	237	Todd Zeile	.15	341	Alex Cintron	.15	445	Roy Halladay	.75
134	Alex Rodriguez	1.50	238	Eric Gagne	.25	342	Jermaine Dye	.15	446	Rocco Baldelli	.75
135	Matthew LeCroy	.15	239	Esteban Loaiza	.15	343	John Burkett	.15	447	Dontrelle Willis	.75
136	Woody Williams	.15	240	Billy Wagner	.15	344	Javy Lopez	.25	448	Mark Prior	2.00
137	Frank Catalanotto	.15	241	Nomar Garciaparra	1.50	345	Eric Karros	.15	449	Jason Lane	.25
138	Rondell White	.15	242	Desi Relaford	.15	346	Corey Patterson	.25	450	Angel Berroa	.25
139	Scott Rolen	.75	243	Luis Rivas	.15	347	Josh Phelps	.15	451	Jose Reyes	.75
140	Cliff Floyd	.15	244	Andy Pettitte	.40	348	Ryan Klesko	.25	452	Ryan Wagner	.25
141	Chipper Jones	.75	245	Ty Wigginton	.15	349	Craig Wilson	.15	453	Marlon Byrd	.25
142	Robin Ventura	.15	246	Edgar Gonzalez	.15	350	Brian Roberts	.15	454	Hee Seop Choi	.25
143	Mariano Rivera	.25	247	Brian Anderson	.15	351	Roberto Alomar	.40	455	Brandon Webb	.50
144	Brady Clark	.15	248	Richie Sexson	.40	352	Frank Thomas	.50	456	Bo Hart	.75
145	Ramon Ortiz	.15	249	Russell Branyan	.15	353	Gary Sheffield	.40	457	Hank Blalock	1.00
146	Omar Infante	.15	250	Jose Guillen	.15	354	Alex Gonzalez	.15	458	Mark Teixeira	1.00
147	Mike Matheny	.15	251	Chin-Hui Tsao	.15	355	Jose Cruz	.15	459	Hideki Matsui	4.00
148	Pedro J. Martinez	.75	252	Jose Hernandez	.15	356	Jerome Williams	.15	460	Scott Podsednik	1.00
149	Carlos Baerga	.15	253	Kevin Brown	.25	357	Mark Kotsay	.15	461	Miguel Cabrera	1.00
150	Shannon Stewart	.15	254	Pete LaForest	.15	358	Chris Reitsma	.15	462	Josh Beckett	1.00
151	Travis Lee	.15	255	Adrian Beltre	.15	359	Carlos Lee	.15	463	Mariano Rivera	.50
152	Eric Byrnes	.15	256	Jacque Jones	.15	360	Todd Helton	.50	464	Ivan Rodriguez	1.00
153	Rafael Furcal	.25	257	Jimmy Rollins	.25	361	Gil Meche	.15	465	Alex Rodriguez	3.00
154	B.J. Surhoff	.15	258	Brandon Phillips	.15	362	Ryan Franklin	.15	466	Albert Pujols	3.00
155	Zach Day	.15	259	Derek Jeter	2.00	363	Josh Bard	.15	467	Roy Halladay	.75
156	Marlon Anderson	.15	260	Carl Everett	.15	364	Juan Pierre	.15	468	Eric Gagne	.50
157	Mark Hendrickson	.15	261	Wes Helms	.15	365	Barry Larkin	.25	469	Angel Berroa	.25
158	Mike Mussina	.50	262	Kyle Lohse	.15	366	Edgar Renteria	.15	470	Dontrelle Willis	.50
159	Randall Simon	.15	263	Jason L. Phillips	.15	367	Alex Sanchez	.15	471	Chris Bootcheck, Tom Gregorio, Richard Fischer	.25
160	Jeff DaVanon	.15	264	Jake Peavy	.15	368	Jeff Bagwell	.50	472	Matt Kata, Tim Olson, Robby Hammock	.25
161	Joel Pineiro	.15	265	Orlando Hernandez	.15	369	Ben Broussard	.15	473	Michael Hessman, Chris Waters, Humberto Quintero	.25
162	Vernon Wells	.25	266	Keith Foulke	.15	370	Chan Ho Park	.15	474	Carlos Mendez, Daniel Cabrera, Jeremy Guthrie	.25
163	Adam Kennedy	.15	267	Brad Wilkerson	.15	371	Darrell May	.15	475	Edwin Almonte, Phil Seibel, Felix Sanchez	.25
164	Trot Nixon	.15	268	Corey Koskie	.15	372	Roy Oswalt	.25	476	Todd Wellemeyer, Jon Leicester, Sergio Mitre	.25
165	Rodrigo Lopez	.15	269	Josh Hall	.15	373	Craig Monroe	.15	477	Josh Stewart, Neal Cotts, Aaron Miles	.25
166	Curt Schilling	.50	270	Bobby Higginson	.15	374	Fred McGriff	.25	478	Terrmel Sledge, Josh Hall, Brandon Claussen	.25
167	Horacio Ramirez	.15	271	Andres Galarraga	.15	375	Bengie Molina	.15			
168	Gerald Laird	.15	272	Alfonso Soriano	.75	376	Aaron Guiel	.15			
169	Magglio Ordonez	.25	273	Carlos Rivera	.15	377	Jeriome Robertson	.15			
170	Scott Schoeneweis	.15	274	Steve Trachsel	.15	378	Kenny Rogers	.15			
171	Andruw Jones	.50	275	David Bell	.15	379	Colby Lewis	.15			
172	Tino Martinez	.25	276	Endy Chavez	.15	380	Jeromy Burnitz	.15			
173	Moises Alou	.25	277	Jay Payton	.15	381	Orlando Cabrera	.15			
174	Kelvim Escobar	.15	278	Mark Mulder	.25	382	Joe Randa	.15			
175	Xavier Nady	.15	279	Terrence Long	.15	383	Miguel Batista	.15			
176	Ramon Martinez	.15	280	A.J. Burnett	.15	384	Brad Radke	.15			
177	Pat Hentgen	.15	281	Pokey Reese	.15	385	Jason Giambi	.75			
178	Austin Kearns	.40	282	Phil Nevin	.15	386	Vladimir Guerrero	.75			
179	D'Angelo Jimenez	.15	283	Jose Contreras	.25	387	Melvin Mora	.15			
180	Deivi Cruz	.15	284	Jim Thome	.75	388	Royce Clayton	.15			

479 Francisco Cruceta, Jason Stanford, Rafael Betancourt .25
480 Javier Lopez, Garrett Atkins, Clint Barmes .25
481 Wilfredo Ledezma, Nook Logan, Jeremy Bonderman .25
482 Josh Willingham, Kevin Hooper, Rick Roberts .25
483 Colin Porter, Mike Gallo, Dave Matranga .25
484 David DeJesus, Jason Gilfillan, Jimmy Gobble .25
485 Koyie Hill, Alfredo Gonzalez, Andrew Brown .25
486 Rickie Weeks, Pedro Liriano, Wes Obermueller 1.00
487 Alex Prieto, Mike Ryan, Lew Ford .25
488 Julio Manon, Luis Ayala, Seung Jun Song .25
489 Jeff Duncan, Prentice Redman, Craig Brazell .25
490 Chien-Ming Wang, Michel Hernandez, Mike Gonzalez .25
491 Rich Harden, Mike Neu, Geoff Geary .25
492 Diegomar Markwell, Chad Gaudin, David Sanders .25
493 Beau Kemp, Micheal Nakamura, D.J. Carrasco .25
494 Khalil Greene, Miguel Ojeda, Bernie Castro .25
495 Noah Lowry, Todd Linden, Kevin Correia .25
496 Aaron Looper, Brian Sweeney, Rett Johnson .25
497 Bo Hart, Dan Haren, Kevin Ohme .50
498 Delmon Young, Doug Waechter, Matt Diaz 1.00
499 Gerald Laird, Rosman Garcia, Ramon Nivar .25
500 Alexis Rios, Guillermo Quiroz, Francisco Rosario .25

Career Tributes

		NM/M
Complete Set (10):		30.00
Common Player:		3.00

Numbered to last season.
Die-Cuts: 2-3X
#'d to last two digits of last season

1CT	Mike Schmidt/1,989	5.00
2CT	Nolan Ryan/1,993	6.00
3CT	Tom Seaver/1,986	4.00
4CT	Reggie Jackson/1,987	3.00
5CT	Bob Gibson/1,975	4.00
6CT	Harmon Killebrew/1,975	4.00
7CT	Phil Rizzuto/1,956	3.00
8CT	Lou Brock/1,979	3.00
9CT	Eddie Mathews/1,968	3.00
10CT	Al Kaline/1,974	4.00

Diamond Tributes

		NM/M
Complete Set (20):		18.00
Common Player:		.50

Inserted 1:6

1DT	Derek Jeter	3.00
2DT	Chipper Jones	1.50
3DT	Vladimir Guerrero	1.00
4DT	Kerry Wood	.75
5DT	Jim Thome	1.00
6DT	Nomar Garciaparra	2.00
7DT	Alex Rodriguez	3.00
8DT	Mike Piazza	1.50
9DT	Jason Giambi	1.00
10DT	Barry Zito	.50
11DT	Dontrelle Willis	.50
12DT	Albert Pujols	2.50
13DT	Todd Helton	.75
14DT	Richie Sexson	.50

15DT	Randy Johnson	1.00
16DT	Pedro J. Martinez	1.00
17DT	Josh Beckett	.75
18DT	Manny Ramirez	.75
19DT	Roy Halladay	.50
20DT	Mark Prior	1.50

Diamond Tributes Game-Used

	NM/M
Common Player:	5.00

Inserted 1:36
Patch Versions: 2-3X
Production 50 Sets

Josh Beckett	8.00
Nomar Garciaparra	10.00
Jason Giambi	8.00
Vladimir Guerrero	8.00
Roy Halladay	5.00
Todd Helton	8.00
Derek Jeter	15.00
Randy Johnson	8.00
Chipper Jones	8.00
Pedro J. Martinez	10.00
Mike Piazza	8.00
Mark Prior	10.00
Albert Pujols	15.00
Manny Ramirez	8.00
Alex Rodriguez	10.00
Richie Sexson	6.00
Jim Thome	8.00
Dontrelle Willis	8.00
Kerry Wood	8.00
Barry Zito	8.00

Retrospection Collection

	NM/M
Complete Set (10):	60.00
Common Player:	4.00

Inserted 1:360

1RC	Rickie Weeks	10.00
2RC	Delmon Young	12.00
3RC	Torii Hunter	5.00
4RC	Aubrey Huff	4.00
5RC	Rocco Baldelli	6.00
6RC	Mike Lowell	4.00
7RC	Dontrelle Willis	6.00
8RC	Albert Pujols	10.00
9RC	Bo Hart	8.00
10RC	Brandon Webb	4.00

Retrospection Collection Autograph

	NM/M
Common Autograph:	10.00

Production 60

| Hank Blalock | 25.00 |

Bo Hart	25.00
Aubrey Huff	10.00
Torii Hunter	30.00
Austin Kearns	20.00
Corey Patterson	25.00
Albert Pujols	75.00
Jose Reyes	25.00
Scott Rolen	30.00
Mike Ryan	15.00
Ryan Wagner	15.00
Brandon Webb	20.00
Rickie Weeks	50.00
Josh Willingham	20.00
Dontrelle Willis	35.00
Delmon Young	50.00

Retrospection Collection Dual Autograph

No Pricing
Production 19 Sets

Standouts Game-Used

Marlon Byrd - PHILADELPHIA PHILLIES

	NM/M
Common Player:	4.00

Inserted 1:41

Rocco Baldelli	8.00
Angel Berroa	5.00
Hank Blalock	6.00
Marlon Byrd	5.00
Miguel Cabrera	8.00
Hee Seop Choi	4.00
Bo Hart	8.00
Jose Reyes	8.00
Mark Teixeira	6.00
Brandon Webb	5.00
Dontrelle Willis	6.00

Standouts Game-Used Gold

No Pricing
Numbered to player's age.

This Day in History

	NM/M
Complete Set (15):	12.00
Common Player:	.50

Inserted 1:18

1	Josh Beckett	1.00
2	Carlos Delgado	1.00
3	Javy Lopez	.50
4	Greg Maddux	2.00
5	Rafael Palmeiro	1.00
6	Sammy Sosa	2.50
7	Jeff Bagwell	1.00
8	Frank Thomas	1.00
9	Kevin Millwood	.50
10	Jose Reyes	.75
11	Rafael Furcal	.50
12	Alfonso Soriano	1.50
13	Eric Gagne	.50
14	Hideki Matsui	4.00
15	Hank Blalock	.75

This Day in History Memorabilia

	NM/M
Common Player:	5.00

Inserted 1:288

Jeff Bagwell	8.00
Carlos Delgado	5.00
Javy Lopez	5.00
Greg Maddux	15.00
Rafael Palmeiro	8.00
Jose Reyes	
Alfonso Soriano	8.00
Sammy Sosa	12.00
Frank Thomas	8.00

This Day/History Dual Memorabilia

	NM/M
Production 25 Sets	
Frank Thomas, Jeff Bagwell	25.00

2005 Fleer

	NM/M
Common Player (1-50):	1.00
Minor Stars (1-50):	1.25
Unlisted Stars (1-50):	1.75
Common Class '05 (51-80):	3.00
Minor Class '05 (51-80):	4.00
Production 699 Sets	
Common Veteran (81-90):	3.00
Production 699 Sets	
Box (1):	90.00

1	Curt Schilling	1.75
2	Jim Thome	3.00
3	Miguel Cabrera	2.00
4	Randy Johnson	3.50
5	David Ortiz	1.75
6	Vladimir Guerrero	3.00
7	Nomar Garciaparra	5.00
8	Ivan Rodriguez	1.75
9	Jason Schmidt	1.25
10	Khalil Greene	2.00
11	Jose Vidro	1.00
12	Lyle Overbay	1.00
13	Todd Helton	2.00
14	Vernon Wells	1.25
15	B.J. Upton	1.25
16	Hideki Matsui	5.00
17	Pedro Martinez	3.00
18	Victor Martinez	1.00
19	Adam Dunn	1.75
20	Andruw Jones	2.00
21	Jeff Bagwell	2.00
22	Mike Sweeney	1.00
23	Mike Piazza	3.50
24	Ben Sheets	1.25
25	Adrian Beltre	1.25
26	Chipper Jones	3.50
27	Greg Maddux	3.50
28	Manny Ramirez	2.00
29	Roger Clemens	5.00
30	Johan Santana	1.25
31	Derek Jeter	6.00
32	Jason Bay	1.00
33	Ken Griffey Jr.	3.50
34	Miguel Tejada	1.75
35	Richie Sexson	1.75
36	Scott Rolen	3.00
37	Alfonso Soriano	3.00
38	Ichiro Suzuki	4.00
39	Sammy Sosa	4.00
40	Barry Zito	1.75
41	Kazuo Matsui	3.00
42	Mark Teixeira	1.25
43	Carlos Beltran	1.75
44	Mark Prior	4.00
45	Travis Hafner	1.00
46	Alex Rodriguez	5.00
47	Lew Ford	1.00
48	Albert Pujols	5.00
49	Frank Thomas	2.00
50	Juan Pierre	1.00
51	David Aardsma	5.00
52	J.D. Durbin	3.00
53	Zack Greinke	4.00
54	Dioner Navarro	4.00
55	Edwin Encarnacion	4.00
56	Luis Hernandez RC	4.00
57	Jeff Baker	4.00
58	Victor Diaz	5.00
59	Joey Gathright	3.00
60	Casey Kotchman	4.00
61	David Wright	5.00
62	Jon Knott	3.00
63	Charlton Jimerson	4.00
64	Nick Swisher	5.00
65	Ryan Raburn	3.00
66	Josh Kroeger	3.00
67	Kelly Johnson	4.00
68	Justin Verlander RC	6.00
69	Taylor Buchholz	3.00
70	Ubaldo Jimenez RC	5.00
71	Russ Adams	4.00
72	Ronny Cedeno	4.00

73	Bobby Jenks	5.00
74	Dan Meyer	4.00
75	Jeff Francis	3.00
76	Scott Kazmir	5.00
77	Sean Burnett	3.00
78	Jose Lopez	4.00
79	Andres Blanco	3.00
80	Gavin Floyd	4.00
81	Tom Seaver	3.00
82	Steve Carlton	3.00
83	Al Kaline	4.00
84	Cal Ripken Jr.	10.00
85	Willie McCovey	5.00
86	Johnny Bench	5.00
87	Nolan Ryan	10.00
88	Mike Schmidt	4.00
89	Carlton Fisk	3.00
90	Don Mattingly	4.00

Row 1

Stars (1-50):	
Class of '05 (51-80):	.5-2X
Veterans:	.5-2X
Production 100 Sets	

Row 2

Cards 1-90:	No Pricing
Production One Set	

Cuts and Glory Jersey

	NM/M
Common Card:	15.00
Production 100 Sets	
Patch:	2-4X
Production 50 Sets	
Jersey and Patch:	No Pricing
Production 15 Sets	
Masterpiece Logo:	No Pricing
Production One Set	
HA	Hank Aaron	
JB	Johnny Bench	60.00
CC	Carl Crawford	20.00
JL	Javy Lopez	20.00
JP	Josh Phelps	15.00
BS	Ben Sheets	20.00
SS	Shannon Stewart	20.00

Cuts and Glory Dual Patch

Production 35 Sets	

Diamond Cuts Jersey

	NM/M
Common Player:	5.00
Production 150 Sets	
Die-Cut:	.75-1.5X
Production 75 Sets	
Patch:	1-3X
Production 50 Sets	
Super Patch:	No Pricing
Production 20 Sets	
Die-Cut Patch:	No Pricing
Production 10 Sets	
MLB Logo	
Masterpiece:	No Pricing
Production One Set	
JB	Jeff Bagwell	8.00
CB	Carlos Beltran	6.00
HB	Hank Blalock	6.00
MC	Miguel Cabrera	8.00
RC	Roger Clemens	12.00
AD	Adam Dunn	6.00
VG	Vladimir Guerrero	8.00
TH	Todd Helton	8.00
RJ	Randy Johnson	8.00
AJ	Andruw Jones	8.00
CJ	Chipper Jones	8.00
AK	Austin Kearns	6.00
PM	Pedro Martinez	8.00
VM	Victor Martinez	5.00
HM	Hideki Matsui	15.00
HN	Hideo Nomo	8.00
DO	David Ortiz	6.00
MP	Mike Piazza	8.00
MP2	Mark Prior	8.00
AP	Albert Pujols	12.00
MR	Manny Ramirez	8.00
SR	Scott Rolen	8.00
CS	Curt Schilling	6.00
GS	Gary Sheffield	6.00
AS	Alfonso Soriano	8.00
SS	Sammy Sosa	10.00
MT	Mark Teixeira	5.00
JT	Jim Thome	8.00
BU	B.J. Upton	5.00
KW	Kerry Wood	8.00

Diamond Cuts Dual Jersey

	NM/M
Common Card:	8.00
Production 99 Sets	

Die-Cut:		.5-1.5X
Production 50 Sets		
Patch:		No Pricing
Production 15 Sets		
Patch Die-Cut:		No Pricing
Production 5 Sets		
BC	Jeff Bagwell,	
	Roger Clemens	15.00
BM	Carlos Beltran,	
	Pedro Martinez	10.00
BS	Hank Blalock,	
	Alfonso Soriano	10.00
CH	Miguel Cabrera,	
	Todd Helton	10.00
DK	Adam Dunn,	
	Austin Kearns	8.00
JJ	Chipper Jones,	
	Andruw Jones	12.00
JS	Randy Johnson,	
	Curt Schilling	10.00
MS	Hideki Matsui,	
	Gary Sheffield	20.00
MT	Victor Martinez,	
	Mark Teixeira	8.00
NU	Hideo Nomo,	
	B.J. Upton	10.00
OR	David Ortiz,	
	Manny Ramirez	10.00
PR	Albert Pujols,	
	Scott Rolen	15.00
PT	Mike Piazza,	
	Jim Thome	12.00
PW	Mark Prior,	
	Kerry Wood	10.00
SG	Sammy Sosa,	
	Vladimir Guerrero	15.00

Dynasty Foundations

	NM/M
Common Card:	6.00
Production 500 Sets	
1DF	Rod Carew, Nolan Ryan,	
	Vladimir Guerrero,	
	Garret Anderson,	
	Darin Erstad	8.00
2DF	Cal Ripken Jr.,	
	Brooks Robinson,	
	Miguel Tejada,	
	Javy Lopez,	
	Jim Palmer	15.00
3DF	Ted Williams,	
	Manny Ramirez,	
	Johnny Damon,	
	Carl Yastrzemski,	
	David Ortiz	15.00
4DF	Ryne Sandberg,	
	Sammy Sosa,	
	Ernie Banks,	
	Greg Maddux,	
	Mark Prior	8.00
5DF	Adam Dunn,	
	Johnny Bench,	
	Tony Perez,	
	Austin Kearns,	
	Joe Morgan	8.00
6DF	Victor Martinez,	
	Travis Hafner, Bob Feller,	
	C.C. Sabathia,	
	Larry Doby	6.00
7DF	Aaron Miles,	
	Matt Holliday,	
	Todd Helton,	
	Garrett Atkins,	
	Preston Wilson	6.00
8DF	Miguel Cabrera,	
	Dontrelle Willis,	
	Juan Pierre, Al Leiter,	
	Josh Beckett	6.00
9DF	Lance Berkman,	
	Jeff Bagwell, Craig Biggio,	
	Roger Clemens,	
	Roy Oswalt	8.00
10DF	Ben Sheets,	
	Lyle Overbay,	
	Robin Yount,	
	Geoff Jenkins,	
	Paul Molitor	8.00
11DF	Johan Santana,	
	Shannon Stewart,	
	Harmon Killebrew, Torii	
	Hunter, Lee Ford	6.00
12DF	Tom Glavine,	
	Mike Piazza, Tom Seaver,	
	Nolan Ryan,	
	Pedro Martinez	8.00
13DF	Eric Chavez,	
	Reggie Jackson,	
	Bobby Crosby,	
	Dennis Eckersley,	
	Barry Zito	6.00
14DF	Jim Thome, Bobby Abreu,	
	Gavin Floyd,	
	Robin Roberts,	
	Mike Schmidt	6.00

15DF	Craig Wilson,	
	Willie Stargell,	
	Bill Mazeroski, Jason Bay,	
	Jack Wilson	6.00
16DF	Willie McCovey,	
	Jason Schmidt,	
	Juan Marichal,	
	Orlando Cepeda,	
	Ray Durham	6.00
17DF	Scott Rolen, Mark Mulder,	
	Albert Pujols,	
	Jim Edmonds,	
	Stan Musial	10.00
18DF	Rocco Baldelli,	
	Scott Kazmir, Aubrey Huff,	
	B.J. Upton,	
	Carl Crawford	6.00
19DF	Alfonso Soriano,	
	Mark Teixeira,	
	Hank Blalock,	
	Nolan Ryan,	
	Michael Young	10.00
20DF	Alexis Rios, Paul Molitor,	
	Roy Halladay,	
	Vernon Wells,	
	Orlando Hudson	6.00

Dynasty Foundations Dual Player Jersey

	NM/M
Common Card:	10.00
Production 150 Sets	
Patch:	1-3X
Production 50 Sets	
BO	Miguel Tejada,	
	Javy Lopez	15.00
BR	Manny Ramirez,	
	David Ortiz	10.00
CI	Victor Martinez,	
	Travis Hafner	10.00
CR1	Adam Dunn,	
	Austin Kearns	12.00
CR2	Todd Helton,	
	Preston Wilson	12.00
FM	Miguel Cabrera,	
	Juan Pierre	10.00
HA	Jeff Bagwell,	
	Lance Berkman	12.00
LA	Vladimir Guerrero,	
	Garret Anderson	12.00
MT	Johan Santana,	
	Torii Hunter	12.00
NM	Mike Piazza,	
	Tom Glavine	10.00
OA	Barry Zito,	
	Eric Chavez	10.00
PP	Jim Thome,	
	Bobby Abreu	10.00
SC	Scott Rolen,	
	Albert Pujols	25.00
TD	B.J. Upton,	
	Scott Kazmir	10.00
TR	Mark Teixeira,	
	Michael Young	10.00

Dynasty Foundations Three Player Jersey

	NM/M
Common Card:	15.00
Production 99 Sets	
Patch:	No Pricing
Production 25 Sets	
CR1	Adam Dunn, Austin Kearns,	
	Joe Morgan	15.00
FM	Miguel Cabrera,	
	Josh Beckett,	
	Juan Pierre	15.00
HA	Jeff Bagwell,	
	Lance Berkman,	
	Roger Clemens	40.00
LA	Vladimir Guerrero,	
	Garret Anderson,	
	Darin Erstad	20.00
MT	Johan Santana,	
	Torii Hunter,	
	Shannon Stewart	15.00
NM	Mike Piazza,	
	Pedro Martinez,	
	Tom Glavine	20.00
SC	Scott Rolen, Albert Pujols,	
	Jim Edmonds	40.00
TR	Alfonso Soriano,	
	Mark Teixeira,	
	Michael Young	15.00

Dynasty Foundations Four Player Jersey

	NM/M
Production 40 Sets	
Patch:	No Pricing
Production 15 Sets	

NM	Mike Piazza, Nolan Ryan,	
	Pedro Martinez,	
	Tom Glavine	100.00

Dynasty Foundations Five Player Jersey

	NM/M
No Pricing	
Production 25 Sets	
Patch:	No Pricing
Production 9 Sets	
MLB Logo	
Masterpiece:	No Pricing
Production One Set	

Dynasty Cornerstones Signatures

	NM/M
Sequentially Numbered	
JB	Jeremy	
	Bonderman/75	20.00
DG	Dwight Gooden/25	30.00
DO	David Ortiz/75	40.00

Dynasty Cornerstones Dual Signatures

Sequentially Numbered

Head of the Class Triple Player Jersey

	NM/M
Common Card:	15.00
Numbered to Debut Year.	
No pricing for quantities 3 or less.	
Patch:	1-3X
Production 33 Sets	
MLB Logo	
Masterpiece:	No Pricing
Production One Set	
AGJ	Bobby Abreu,	
	Vladimir Guerrero,	
	Andruw Jones/96	20.00
BGB	Carlos Beltran, Troy Glaus,	
	Adrian Beltre/98	15.00
BTR	Jeff Bagwell, Jim Thome,	
	Ivan Rodriguez/91	15.00
GBH	Eric Gagne, A.J. Burnett,	
	Tim Hudson/99	15.00
JDR	Chipper Jones,	
	Carlos Delgado,	
	Manny Ramirez/93	20.00
OHS	David Ortiz, Torii Hunter,	
	Richie Sexson/97	15.00
SNP	Jason Schmidt,	
	Hideo Nomo,	
	Andy Pettitte/95	20.00

Letterman

Sequentially numbered between 4-8.	
No Pricing	

Significant Dual

	NM/M
Common Player:	30.00
Production 40 Sets	
Dual Jersey:	No Pricing
Production 15 Sets	
Dual Patch:	No Pricing
Production 5 Sets	
BR	Adrian Beltre,	
	Jeremy Reed	60.00
CF	Steve Carlton,	
	Gavin Floyd	40.00
FM	Lew Ford,	
	Justin Morneau	40.00
MH	Victor Martinez,	
	Travis Hafner	30.00
SR	Mike Schmidt,	
	Cal Ripken Jr.	250.00

Significant Signings Blue

	NM/M
Common Player:	10.00
Sequentially #'d to indicated quantity.	
Silver Die-Cut:	1-3X
Cards #'d 50 or Less:	.25-1X
Production 50 Sets	
Gold Jersey:	No Pricing
Production 25 Sets	
Patch:	No Pricing
Production 15 Sets	
Masterpiece Jersey	
Tag:	No Pricing
Production One Set	
JB	Jason Bay/250	15.00
AB	Adrian Beltre/30	50.00
MC	Miguel Cabrera/250	20.00
SC	Steve Carlton/59	30.00
BC	Bobby Crosby/93	15.00

GF	Gavin Floyd/221	10.00
LF	Lew Ford/230	10.00
ZG	Zack Greinke/250	10.00
TH	Travis Hafner/250	10.00
SK	Scott Kazmir/250	10.00
CK	Casey Kotchman/250	10.00
PM	Pedro Martinez/101	40.00
VM	Victor Martinez/250	10.00
DM	Don Mattingly/103	40.00
JM	Justin Morneau/225	25.00
JR	Jeremy Reed/250	40.00
NR	Nolan Ryan/92	100.00
BU	B.J. Upton/250	10.00
KW	Kerry Wood/200	25.00
DW	David Wright/250	40.00

2005 Fleer America's National Pastime

	NM/M
Common Player (1-50):	.25
Minor Stars (1-50):	.40
Unlisted Stars (1-50):	.60
Common Player (51-70):	3.00
Production 699 Sets	
Common Player (71-80):	3.00
Production 699 Sets	
Pack (5):	7.00
Box (10):	60.00
1	Khalil Greene	.75
2	Pedro Martinez	1.00
3	Mark Teixeira	.40
4	Jim Thome	1.00
5	Jack Wilson	.25
6	Johan Santana	.40
7	Jason Bay	.25
8	Adam Dunn	.60
9	Lyle Overbay	.25
10	Jason Schmidt	.40
11	Bobby Crosby	.25
12	J.D. Drew	.40
13	Ken Griffey Jr.	1.50
14	Sammy Sosa	2.00
15	Hank Blalock	.60
16	Victor Martinez	.25
17	Randy Johnson	1.00
18	Vernon Wells	.40
19	Todd Helton	.75
20	Javy Lopez	.40
21	Kazuo Matsui	.60
22	Ben Sheets	.40
23	Brad Wilkerson	.25
24	Miguel Cabrera	.75
25	Mike Sweeney	.25
26	Roger Clemens	2.50
27	Chipper Jones	1.50
28	Hideki Matsui	2.50
29	Manny Ramirez	.75
30	Scott Rolen	1.00
31	Lance Berkman	.40
32	Jim Edmonds	.40
33	Derek Jeter	3.00
34	B.J. Upton	.40
35	Carlos Delgado	.75
36	Ichiro Suzuki	2.00
37	Nomar Garciaparra	2.50
38	Albert Pujols	2.50
39	Ivan Rodriguez	.60
40	Gary Sheffield	.60
41	Alfonso Soriano	1.00
42	Carlos Beltran	.60
43	Magglio Ordonez	.40
44	Alex Rodriguez	2.50
45	Curt Schilling	.60
46	Greg Maddux	1.50
47	Vladimir Guerrero	1.00
48	Mike Piazza	1.50
49	Miguel Tejada	.60
50	Adrian Beltre	.40
51	Scott Kazmir	5.00
52	Gavin Floyd	4.00
53	Zack Greinke	4.00
54	David Wright	5.00
55	David Aardsma	4.00
56	Ryan Raburn	3.00
57	Joey Gathright	3.00
58	J.D. Durbin	3.00
59	Sean Burnett	3.00
60	Jose Lopez	3.00
61	Nick Swisher	4.00
62	Bobby Jenks	3.00
63	Kelly A. Johnson	3.00
65	Ronny Cedeno	4.00
66	Edwin Encarnacion	3.00
67	Jeff Baker	3.00
68	Taylor Buchholz	3.00
69	Justin Verlander RC	5.00
70	Luis Hernandez RC	5.00
71	Mike Schmidt	5.00
72	Al Kaline	3.00
73	Yogi Berra	4.00
74	Robin Yount	4.00
75	Nolan Ryan	6.00
76	Johnny Bench	5.00
77	Eddie Murray	4.00
78	Tom Seaver	4.00
79	Willie McCovey	3.00
80	Cal Ripken Jr.	6.00

Red Foil

Cards 1-50:	1-3X
Cards 51-70:	.75-1.5X
Cards 71-80:	.75-1.5X
Production 150 Sets	

White Foil

Cards 1-50 #'d to 41-57:	2-6X
Cards 1-50 #'d to 26-40:	4-8X
Cards 1-50 #'d 25 or less:	No Pricing
Cards 71-80 #'d to 26-44:	1-3X
Cards 71-80 #'d 25 or less:	No Pricing
Numbered to player's jersey number.	

Blue Foil

No Pricing
Production One Set

Beltway Baseball

		NM/M
Common Card:		6.00
Production 202 Sets		
1	Ed Delahanty	8.00
2	Benjamin Harrison	8.00
3	William Howard Taft	6.00
4	Clark Griffith	6.00
5	Bobby Burke	8.00
6	Roy Seivers	8.00
7	Tom Cheney	8.00
8	Woodrow Wilson	8.00
9	Franklin D. Roosevelt	8.00
10	John F. Kennedy	10.00
11	Frank Howard	8.00
12	Griffith Stadium	10.00
13	RFK Stadium	8.00
14	All-Star Game	8.00
15	Ted Williams	15.00
16	Harmon Killebrew	12.00
17	Jeff Burroughs	8.00
18	All-Star Game	6.00
19	Unveiling the Nationals	10.00
20	New Logo	8.00

First Name Bases Autograph Silver

NM/M
Sequentially #'d to indicated quantity.

Blue:		No Pricing
Production One Set		
MCAM	Mike Cameron/375	10.00
SH	Shea Hillenbrand/316	10.00
JL	Javy Lopez/158	15.00
MT	Mark Teixeira/225	20.00
JV	Justin Verlander/401	15.00

First Name Bases Autograph White

NM/M
Cards #'d 25 or less: No Pricing
Sequentially #'d to indicated quantity.

AB	Adrian Beltre/48	25.00

First Name Bases Autograph Red

NM/M
Cards #'d 25 or less: No Pricing
Sequentially #'d to indicated quantity.

MCAM	Mike Cameron/90	15.00
BL	Barry Larkin/27	40.00
MT	Mark Teixeira/95	30.00
JV	Justin Verlander/99	20.00

First Name Bases Autograph Gold

NM/M
Cards #'d 25 or less: No Pricing
Sequentially #'d to indicated quantity.

AB	Adrian Beltre/96	25.00
MCAM	Mike Cameron/126	15.00
SH	Shea Hillenbrand/99	15.00
JL	Javy Lopez/73	15.00
AP	Albert Pujols/73	200.00

MT	Mark Teixeira/147	25.00
JV	Justin Verlander/149	20.00

Grand Old Gamers

		NM/M
Common Player:		.75
Inserted 1:5		
1	Pedro Martinez	1.50
2	Jim Thome	1.50
3	Ken Griffey Jr.	2.00
4	Sammy Sosa	2.50
5	Hank Blalock	1.00
6	Randy Johnson	1.50
7	Roger Clemens	3.00
8	Chipper Jones	2.00
9	Hideki Matsui	3.00
10	Manny Ramirez	1.25
11	Derek Jeter	4.00
12	Ichiro Suzuki	2.50
13	Nomar Garciaparra	3.00
14	Albert Pujols	3.00
15	Gary Sheffield	1.00
16	Alfonso Soriano	1.50
17	Alex Rodriguez	3.00
18	Curt Schilling	1.00
19	Vladimir Guerrero	1.50
20	Mike Piazza	2.00
21	Greg Maddux	2.00
22	Frank Thomas	1.25
23	Adrian Beltre	.75
24	Barry Larkin	.75
25	Todd Helton	1.25
26	Kerry Wood	1.25
27	Kazuo Matsui	1.00
28	Scott Rolen	1.50
29	Ivan Rodriguez	1.00
30	Miguel Tejada	1.00
31	Mark Teixeira	.75
32	Rafael Palmeiro	1.25
33	Andruw Jones	1.25
34	Carlos Beltran	1.00
35	Jeff Bagwell	1.25

Grand Old Gamers Jersey

		NM/M
Common Player:		6.00
Inserted 1:36 Retail		
JB	Jeff Bagwell	8.00
CB	Carlos Beltran	8.00
AB	Adrian Beltre	6.00
HB	Hank Blalock	8.00
RC	Roger Clemens/SP/50	15.00
VG	Vladimir Guerrero	8.00
TH	Todd Helton	8.00
RJ	Randy Johnson	8.00
AJ	Andruw Jones	8.00
CJ	Chipper Jones	8.00
BL	Barry Larkin	6.00
GM	Greg Maddux/SP/75	12.00
PM	Pedro Martinez	8.00
HM	Hideki Matsui/SP/50	15.00
KM	Kazuo Matsui	8.00
RP	Rafael Palmeiro	8.00
MP	Mike Piazza	8.00
AP	Albert Pujols	12.00
MR	Manny Ramirez	8.00
IR	Ivan Rodriguez	8.00
SR	Scott Rolen	8.00
CS	Curt Schilling	8.00
GS	Gary Sheffield	8.00
AS	Alfonso Soriano	8.00
SS	Sammy Sosa	12.00
MT	Mark Teixeira	6.00
FT	Frank Thomas	8.00
JT	Jim Thome	8.00
KW	Kerry Wood	8.00

Gamers Patch Blue

NM/M
Numbered to player's jersey number.

Cards numbered 25 or less:		No Pricing
Masterpiece:		No Pricing
Production One Set		
VG	Vladimir Guerrero/27	25.00
RJ	Randy Johnson/51	20.00
GM	Greg Maddux/31	25.00
PM	Pedro Martinez/45	20.00
HM	Hideki Matsui/55	50.00
MP	Mike Piazza/31	25.00
SR	Scott Rolen/27	25.00
CS	Curt Schilling/38	15.00
FT	Frank Thomas/35	15.00
KW	Kerry Wood/34	20.00

Gamers Dual Patch

Cards #'d to 25 or less: No Pricing
Production 5-33 Sets

	Ivan Rodriguez, Mike Piazza/31	75.00
	Hank Blalock, Mark Teixeira/33	30.00

Historical Record

		NM/M
Common Card:		2.00
Inserted 1:6		
1	Ichiro Suzuki/2004	2.50
2	Greg Maddux/2004	2.00
3	Alex Rodriguez/1998	3.00
4	Mike Piazza/2004	2.00
5	Nolan Ryan/1991	5.00
6	Albert Pujols/2001	3.00
7	Mike Schmidt/1987	4.00
8	Randy Johnson/2004	2.00
9	Sammy Sosa/2003	2.50
10	Cal Ripken Jr./1996	5.00
11	Roger Clemens/2004	3.00
12	Hideki Matsui/2003	3.00
13	Hideo Nomo/1994	2.00
14	Gene Autry/1961	2.00
15	Walter O'Malley/1944	2.00

Historical Record Jersey

		NM/M
Common Player:		6.00
Inserted 1:96 Retail		
RC	Roger Clemens	10.00
RJ	Randy Johnson	8.00
GM	Greg Maddux	8.00
HM	Hideki Matsui	12.00
HN	Hideo Nomo	8.00
MP	Mike Piazza	8.00
AP	Albert Pujols	10.00
CR	Cal Ripken Jr.	30.00
NR0	Nolan Ryan	20.00
MS	Mike Schmidt	25.00
SS	Sammy Sosa	10.00

Historical Record Patch Blue

No Pricing
Numbered to player's jersey number.

Masterpiece:	No Pricing
Production One Set	

Historical Record Dual Patch

No Pricing
Production 8-25 Sets

Signature Swings Silver

		NM/M
Common Player:		6.00
Gold:		.75-1.5X
Sequentially #'d between 50 & 199.		
BAY	Jason Bay	20.00
CC	Carl Craword	10.00
AE	Adam Everett	10.00
CF	Chone Figgins	10.00
LF	Lew Ford	10.00
JG	Joey Gathright	10.00
KG	Khalil Greene	30.00
TH	Travis Hafner	10.00
AH	Aubrey Huff	10.00
VAL	Val Majewski	10.00
JM	Joe Mauer	25.00
DM	Dallas McPherson	10.00
JMO	Justin Morneau	40.00
WMP	Wily Mo Pena	25.00
JP	Josh Phelps	10.00
RR	Ryan Raburn	10.00
SS	Shannon Stewart	10.00
NS	Nick Swisher	15.00
BJU	B.J. Upton	15.00
CU	Chase Utley	12.00
DW	David Wright	50.00
MY	Michael Young	10.00

Signature Swings Bat Red

		NM/M
Common Player:		20.00
Production 30-99 Sets		
BAY	Jason Bay/99	20.00
JB	Johnny Bench/42	80.00
LB	Lance Berkman/99	20.00
CC	Carl Crawford/99	20.00
LF	Lew Ford/76	20.00
CK	Casey Kotchman/99	20.00
BR	Brooks Robinson/64	40.00
MS	Mike Schmidt/30	100.00
SS	Shannon Stewart/99	20.00
DW	David Wright/99	60.00

Signature Swings Jersey White

		NM/M
Production 3-29 Sets		
Cards #'d less than 25:		No Pricing
LB	Lance Berkman/29	30.00
CC	Carl Crawford/29	30.00
JP	Josh Phelps/27	15.00

Signature Swings Patch Blue

		NM/M
Numbered to player's jersey number.		
Cards #'d less than 25:		No Pricing
Masterpiece:		No Pricing
Production One Set		
BAY	Jason Bay/38	60.00
JP	Josh Phelps/45	20.00

2005 Fleer Authentix

		NM/M
Common Player (1-100):		.25
Minor Stars (1-100):		.40
Unlisted Stars (1-100):		.60
Common Player Autograph (101-125):		10.00
Minor Stars Autograph (101-125):		15.00
Production 250 Sets		
Pack (5):		
Box ( ):		
1	Albert Pujols	2.50
2	Bernie Williams	.60
3	Vinny Castilla	.25
4	Rocco Baldelli	.60
5	Mike Piazza	1.50
6	Sean Casey	.25
7	Oliver Perez	.25
8	Tony Batista	.25
9	Paul Konerko	.25
10	Scott Rolen	1.00
11	Justin Morneau	.25
12	Nomar Garciaparra	2.50
13	Lance Berkman	.40
14	Mike Sweeney	.25
15	Miguel Tejada	.75
16	Craig Wilson	.25
17	Craig Biggio	.40
18	Shea Hillenbrand	.25
19	Mark Mulder	.40
20	Juan Pierre	.25
21	Troy Glaus	.60
22	Eric Chavez	.40
23	Jeromy Burnitz	.25
24	Carl Crawford	.25
25	Kazuo Matsui	.75
26	Ivan Rodriguez	.60
27	Aubrey Huff	.25
28	Derek Jeter	3.00
29	Casey Blake	.25
30	Mark Teixeira	.40
31	Brad Wilkerson	.25
32	Austin Kearns	.60
33	Jim Edmonds	.40
34	Johan Santana	.40
35	Kerry Wood	.75
36	Ichiro Suzuki	2.00
37	Lyle Overbay	.25
38	Melvin Mora	.25
39	Jason Bay	.25
40	Jake Westbrook	.25
41	Andruw Jones	.75
42	Chase Utley	.25
43	Carl Pavano	.25
44	Luis Gonzalez	.40
45	Bobby Crosby	.25
46	Carlos Guillen	.25
47	Carlos Delgado	.75
48	Alex Rodriguez	2.50
49	Todd Helton	.75
50	Michael Young	.25
51	Geoff Jenkins	.40
52	Pedro Martinez	1.00
53	Brian Giles	.40
54	Ken Harvey	.25
55	Johnny Estrada	.25
56	Billy Wagner	.25
57	Roger Clemens	2.50
58	Chipper Jones	1.50
59	Jim Thome	1.00
60	Miguel Cabrera	.75
61	Vladimir Guerrero	1.00
62	Gary Sheffield	.60
63	Travis Hafner	.25
64	Alfonso Soriano	1.00
65	Richard Hidalgo	.25
66	Adam Dunn	.60
67	Garret Anderson	.40
68	Lew Ford	.25
69	Mark Prior	1.50
70	Bret Boone	.40
71	Ben Sheets	.40
72	David Ortiz	.60
73	Mark Loretta	.25
74	Eric Gagne	.40
75	Curt Schilling	.60
76	Jason Schmidt	.40
77	Adrian Beltre	.40
78	Javy Lopez	.40
79	Jack Wilson	.25
80	Carlos Beltran	.60
81	J.D. Drew	.40
82	Bobby Abreu	.40
83	Jeff Bagwell	.75
84	Randy Johnson	1.00
85	Tim Hudson	.40
86	Carlos Pena	.25
87	Vernon Wells	.40
88	Tom Glavine	.40
89	Victor Martinez	.25
90	Hank Blalock	.60
91	Jose Vidro	.25
92	Magglio Ordonez	.40
93	Jake Peavy	.25
94	Torii Hunter	.60
95	Sammy Sosa	2.00
96	Hideki Matsui	2.50
97	Shawn Green	.40
98	Manny Ramirez	.75
99	Khalil Greene	.75
100	Jason Marquis	.25
101	B.J. Upton/Auto.	20.00
102	Scott Kazmir/Auto.	20.00
103	Gavin Floyd/Auto.	20.00
104	Jeff Francis/Auto.	20.00
105	Russ Adams/ Auto. Exch.	10.00
106	Zack Greinke/Auto.	15.00
107	David Wright/Auto.	60.00
108	David Aardsma/Auto.	20.00
109	Josh Kroeger/Auto.	10.00
110	Ryan Raburn/Auto.	30.00
111	Jason Kubel/Auto.	10.00
112	Casey Kotchman/ Auto.	20.00
113	Joey Gathright/Auto.	15.00
114	Jon Knott/Auto.	10.00
115	J.D. Durbin/Auto.	25.00
116	Andres Blanco/Auto.	10.00
117	Charlton Jimerson/ Auto.	10.00
118	Sean Burnett/Auto.	15.00
119	Joe Mauer/Auto.	30.00
120	Justin Verlander/ Auto. RC	30.00
121	Mike Gosling/Auto.	10.00
122	Jeff Keppinger/Auto.	10.00
123	David Krynzel/Auto.	10.00
124	Jose Lopez/Auto.	15.00
125	Ruben Gotay/Auto.	10.00

General Admission

	NM/M
Cards 1-100:	1-2.5X
Cards 101-125:	.75-1.5X
Production 100 Sets	

Mezzanine

	NM/M
Cards 1-100:	1-3X
Cards 101-125:	.75-2X
Production 75 Sets	

Club Box

	NM/M
Cards 1-100:	1-3.25X
Cards 101-125:	1-2X
Production 50 Sets	

Standing Room Only

	NM/M
Cards 1-125:	No Pricing
Production 10 Sets	

Autographed General Admission

		NM/M
Common Player:		15.00
Production 100 Sets		
Mezzanine:		1-2X
Production 40 Sets		
Club Box:		No Pricing
Production 5 Sets		
Standing Room Only:		No Pricing
Production One Set		
JB	Jason Bay	15.00
JE	Johnny Estrada	15.00
CF	Chone Figgins	20.00
LF	Lew Ford	15.00
KG	Khalil Greene	50.00
TH	Travis Hafner	15.00
JM	Justin Morneau	40.00
JS	Johan Santana	25.00
BS	Ben Sheets	20.00
CU	Chase Utley	15.00
JW	Jack Wilson	15.00

Autographed Jersey General Admission

		NM/M
Common Player:		20.00
Production 75 Sets		
Mezzanine:		No Pricing
Production 15 Sets		
Club Box:		No Pricing
Production 5 Sets		
Standing Room Only:		No Pricing
Production One Set		
JB	Jason Bay	20.00
MC	Miguel Cabrera	30.00
JE	Johnny Estrada	20.00
CF	Chone Figgins	25.00
LF	Lew Ford	20.00
KG	Khalil Greene	60.00
TH	Travis Hafner	20.00
JM	Justin Morneau	50.00
JS	Johan Santana	30.00
MS	Mike Schmidt	75.00
BS	Ben Sheets	25.00
CU	Chase Utley	20.00
JW	Jack Wilson	20.00

Autographed Patch General Admission

		NM/M
Production 40 Sets		
Mezzanine:		No Pricing
Production 10 Sets		
Club Box:		No Pricing
Production 5 Sets		
Standing Room Only		
Production One Set		
CF	Chone Figgins	25.00
MP	Mike Piazza	150.00
CR	Cal Ripken Jr.	400.00
MS	Mike Schmidt	150.00
JT	Jim Thome	80.00

Hot Ticket

		NM/M
Common Player:		2.00
Inserted 1:12		
1	Derek Jeter	6.00
2	Roger Clemens	5.00
3	Vladimir Guerrero	3.00
4	Manny Ramirez	2.00
5	Alex Rodriguez	5.00
6	Albert Pujols	5.00
7	Mike Piazza	3.50
8	Hideki Matsui	5.00
9	Sammy Sosa	4.00
10	Chipper Jones	3.50

Hot Ticket Jersey

		NM/M
Common Player:		8.00
Inserted 1:87		
Patch		
Cards #'d to 55:		1-3X
Cards #'d to 27:		2-4X
Cards #'d to 25 or less		No Pricing
Sequentially #'d to player's jersey #.		
MLB Logo:		No Pricing
Production One Set		
RC	Roger Clemens	15.00
VG	Vladimir Guerrero	8.00
CJ	Chipper Jones	10.00
HM	Hideki Matsui	25.00
MP	Mike Piazza	10.00
AP	Albert Pujols	20.00
MR	Manny Ramirez	8.00
SS	Sammy Sosa	12.00

Jersey General Admission

		NM/M
Common Player:		5.00
Inserted 1:16		
Jersey Mezzanine:		1-3X
Production 75 Sets		
Jersey Club Box:		No Pricing
Production 25 Sets		
Jersey Standing Room Only:		No Pricing
Production One Set		
Patch General Admission:		2-4X
Production 75 Sets		
Patch Mezzanine:		No Pricing
Production 15 Sets		
Patch Club Box:		No Pricing
Production 5 Sets		
Patch Standing Room Only:		No Pricing
Production One Set		
CB	Carlos Beltran	10.00
AB	Adrian Beltre	5.00
LB	Lance Berkman	5.00
HB	Hank Blalock	5.00
MC	Miguel Cabrera	8.00
RC	Roger Clemens	12.00
AD	Adam Dunn	5.00
EG	Eric Gagne	5.00
KG	Khalil Greene	10.00
VG	Vladimir Guerrero	8.00
TH	Todd Helton	5.00
RJ	Randy Johnson	8.00
CJ	Chipper Jones	8.00
PM	Pedro Martinez	8.00
HM	Hideki Matsui	20.00
KM	Kazuo Matsui	10.00
JM	Joe Mauer	8.00
HN	Hideo Nomo	8.00
DO	David Ortiz	10.00
MP	Mike Piazza	8.00
AP	Albert Pujols	15.00
MR	Manny Ramirez	8.00
MR2	Mariano Rivera	8.00
IR	Ivan Rodriguez	5.00
SR	Scott Rolen	8.00
JS	Johan Santana	5.00
CS	Curt Schilling	5.00
GS	Gary Sheffield	5.00
AS	Alfonso Soriano	5.00
SS	Sammy Sosa	10.00
JT	Jim Thome	8.00
BU	B.J. Upton	5.00
BW	Bernie Williams	5.00
KW	Kerry Wood	8.00
DW	David Wright	15.00

Jersey Game of the Week

		NM/M
Common Player:		10.00

Sequentially #'d between 10 & 200.
No pricing for cards #'d to 20 or less.

Patch:		No Pricing
Production 10 Sets		
BR	Carlos Beltran, Scott Rolen/120	15.00
BT	Tony Batista, Miguel Tejada/170	10.00
CG	Eric Chavez, Troy Glaus/150	12.00
CJ	Roger Clemens, Randy Johnson/70	15.00
CJ2	Miguel Cabrera, Chipper Jones/90	12.00
CP	Carl Crawford, Juan Pierre/190	10.00
DT	Adam Dunn, Jim Thome/110	20.00
GG	Shawn Green, Vladimir Guerrero/180	12.00
GS	Vladimir Guerrero, Alfonso Soriano/100	15.00
KG	Scott Kazmir, Zack Greinke/80	10.00
MM	Kazuo Matsui, Hideki Matsui/30	100.00
MM2	Joe Mauer, Victor Martinez/130	10.00
MR	Pedro Martinez, Mariano Rivera/60	12.00
OP	David Ortiz, Albert Pujols/200	15.00
OS	Magglio Ordonez, Sammy Sosa/160	15.00
RH	Manny Ramirez, Torii Hunter/140	10.00
SS	Johan Santana, Curt Schilling/40	30.00
WO	Kerry Wood, Roy Oswalt/50	30.00

Showstoppers

		NM/M
Common Player:		2.00
Inserted 1:8		
1	Nomar Garciaparra	4.00
2	Ichiro Suzuki	3.50
3	Ken Griffey Jr.	3.00
4	Alex Rodriguez	4.00
5	Albert Pujols	4.00
6	Derek Jeter	5.00
7	Roger Clemens	4.00
8	Randy Johnson	2.50
9	Hideo Nomo	2.00
10	Jim Thome	2.50
11	Mike Piazza	3.00
12	Hideki Matsui	4.00
13	Sammy Sosa	3.50
14	Kerry Wood	2.00
15	Eric Gagne	2.00

Teammate Trios

		NM/M
Common Card:		12.00
Production 75 Sets		
Hometown 1:		2-3X
Production 25 Sets		
Hometown 2:		No Pricing
Production 5 Sets		
BR	David Ortiz, Manny Ramirez, Pedro Martinez	25.00
NY	Hideki Matsui, Bernie Williams, Gary Sheffield	30.00
AB	J.D. Drew, Chipper Jones, Andruw Jones	15.00
CC	Sammy Sosa, Mark Prior, Nomar Garciaparra	15.00
CI	Victor Martinez, Travis Hafner, Casey Blake	12.00
HA	Lance Berkman, Roger Clemens, Carlos Beltran	25.00

MT	Johan Santana, Torii Hunter, Corey Koskie	12.00
WN	Tony Batista, Jose Vidro, Brad Wilkerson	12.00
NM	Mike Piazza, David Wright, Kazuo Matsui	40.00
OA	Barry Zito, Tim Hudson, Mark Mulder	12.00
PP	Bobby Abreu, Jim Thome, Pat Burrell	12.00
SC	Scott Rolen, Albert Pujols, Jim Edmonds	30.00
TD	Scott Kazmir, Rocco Baldelli, B.J. Upton	25.00
TR	Hank Blalock, Mark Teixeira, Alfonso Soriano	15.00
LD	Shawn Green, Adrian Beltre, Steve Finley	12.00

2005 Fleer Classic Clippings

		NM/M
Common Player (1-75):		.25
Minor Stars (1-75):		.40
Unlisted Stars (1-75):		.60
Common Legends (76-105): 2.00		
Production 999 Sets		
Common Player (106-125): 3.00		
Inserted 1:6		
1	Frank Thomas	.75
2	Vladimir Guerrero	1.00
3	Ken Griffey Jr.	1.50
4	Derek Jeter	3.00
5	Rafael Palmeiro	.75
6	Adrian Beltre	.40
7	Khalil Greene	.75
8	Richie Sexson	.60
9	Roger Clemens	2.50
10	Mike Piazza	1.50
11	Chipper Jones	1.50
12	Juan Pierre	.25
13	Todd Helton	.75
14	Ben Sheets	.40
15	John Smoltz	.40
16	Steve Finley	.25
17	Jim Thome	1.00
18	Vernon Wells	.40
19	Melvin Mora	.40
20	Dontrelle Willis	.40
21	Eric Gagne	.40
22	Craig Wilson	.25
23	Curt Schilling	.60
24	Justin Morneau	.25
25	Jason Schmidt	.40
26	Kerry Wood	.75
27	Ivan Rodriguez	.60
28	Rocco Baldelli	.60
29	Mark Prior	2.00
30	Josh Beckett	.75
31	Scott Rolen	1.00
32	Nomar Garciaparra	2.50
33	Carl Crawford	.25
34	Paul Konerko	.40
35	Miguel Cabrera	.75
36	Hank Blalock	.60
37	Sammy Sosa	2.00
38	Jim Edmonds	.40
39	David Ortiz	.60
40	Lance Berkman	.40
41	Ichiro Suzuki	2.00
42	Adam Dunn	.60
43	Carlos Guillen	.25
44	Alfonso Soriano	1.00
45	Victor Martinez	.25
46	Torii Hunter	.60
47	Kazuo Matsui	.60
48	Andruw Jones	.75
49	Matt Holliday	.50
50	Eric Chavez	.40
51	Randy Johnson	1.00
52	Lew Ford	.25
53	Hideki Matsui	2.50
54	Manny Ramirez	.75
55	Mark Teixeira	.40
56	Jose Vidro	.25
57	Mike Sweeney	.25
58	Jack Wilson	.25
59	Greg Maddux	1.50
60	Tony Batista	.25
61	Albert Pujols	2.50
62	Miguel Tejada	.60
63	Carlos Beltran	.60
64	Bobby Abreu	.40
65	Carlos Delgado	.75
66	Travis Hafner	.40
67	Scott Podsednik	.25
68	Gary Sheffield	.75
69	Johan Santana	.40
70	Barry Zito	.60

71	Pedro Martinez	1.00
72	Brian Giles	.40
73	Garret Anderson	.40
74	Jeff Bagwell	.75
75	Alex Rodriguez	2.50
76	Johnny Bench	4.00
77	Yogi Berra	3.00
78	Lou Brock	3.00
79	Rod Carew	3.00
80	Orlando Cepeda	2.00
81	Carlton Fisk	5.00
82	Bob Gibson	3.00
83	Reggie Jackson	5.00
84	Al Kaline	4.00
85	Harmon Killebrew	3.00
86	Ralph Kiner	4.00
87	Willie McCovey	2.00
88	Eddie Murray	4.00
89	Phil Rizzuto	4.00
90	Brooks Robinson	3.00
91	Nolan Ryan	5.00
92	Mike Schmidt	4.00
93	Tom Seaver	3.00
94	Willie Stargell	2.00
95	Rollie Fingers	2.00
96	Dennis Eckersley	2.00
97	Enos Slaughter	2.00
98	Jim Palmer	2.00
99	Warren Spahn	3.00
100	Joe Morgan	2.00
101	Richie Ashburn	3.00
102	Robin Yount	3.00
103	Bob Feller	3.00
104	Pee Wee Reese	2.00
105	Eddie Mathews	3.00
106	David Wright	6.00
107	David Aardsma	3.00
108	B.J. Upton	3.00
109	Scott Kazmir	4.00
110	Gavin Floyd	3.00
111	Jeff Francis	3.00
112	Dioner Navarro	3.00
113	Zack Greinke	3.00
114	Nick Swisher	5.00
115	Josh Kroeger	3.00
116	Ryan Raburn	3.00
117	Victor Diaz	4.00
118	Casey Kotchman	4.00
119	Joey Gathright	3.00
120	Jon Knott	3.00
121	J.D. Durbin	3.00
122	Andres Blanco	3.00
123	Charlton Jimerson	3.00
124	Russ Adams	3.00
125	Justin Verlander RC	5.00

First Edition

(1-75):		2-5X
(76-105):		1-1.5X
(106-125):		1-2X
Production 150 Sets		

Final Edition

No Pricing		
Production One Set		

Press Clippings

		NM/M
Common Player:		2.00
Inserted 1:6		
Gold:		No Pricing
Production 4 Sets		
1	Ichiro Suzuki	4.00
2	Manny Ramirez	2.00
3	Albert Pujols	5.00
4	David Ortiz	2.00
5	Greg Maddux	3.00
6	Ken Griffey Jr.	3.00
7	Vladimir Guerrero	3.00
8	Randy Johnson	3.00
9	Johan Santana	2.00
10	Roger Clemens	5.00
11	Bobby Crosby	2.00
12	Jason Bay	2.00

Bat Rack Quad Blue

		NM/M
Inserted 1:118		
Silver:		No Pricing
Production 10 Sets		
Purple:		No Pricing
Production One Set		
	Gary Sheffield, Vladimir Guerrero, Manny Ramirez, Sammy Sosa	20.00
	Manny Ramirez, Wade Boggs, Carl Yastrzemski, Bobby Doerr	40.00
	Kirby Puckett, Jacque Jones, Harmon Killebrew, Torii Hunter	40.00

	Brandon Webb, Randy Johnson, Curt Schilling, Roger Clemens	40.00
	Willie Stargell, Bill Madlock, Bill Mazeroski, Roberto Clemente	100.00
	Al Kaline, Tony Gwynn, Frank Howard, Rocky Colavito	50.00
	Jose Reyes, Gary Carter, Mike Piazza, Kazuo Matsui	25.00
	Bobby Abreu, Adam Dunn, Rocco Baldelli, Hideki Matsui	30.00
	Jim Thome, Albert Pujols, Jeff Bagwell, Todd Helton	40.00
	Hank Blalock, Miguel Tejada, Troy Glaus, Ivan Rodriguez	25.00
	Carlos Delgado, Jason Giambi, Rafael Palmeiro, Mark Teixeira	25.00

Classic Clippings

		NM/M
Common Player:		2.00
Gold:		2-5X
Production 51-95 Sets		
1	Nolan Ryan/1991	6.00
2	Cal Ripken Jr./1995	8.00
3	Joe Carter/1993	3.00
4	Bucky Dent/1978	3.00
5	Kirk Gibson/1988	3.00
6	Reggie Jackson/1977	5.00
7	Carlton Fisk/1975	4.00
8	Bobby Thomson/1951	3.00
9	Bill Mazeroski/1960	3.00
10	Don Larsen/1956	4.00

Cut of History Single Jersey Blue

		NM/M
Common Player:		6.00
Inserted 1:21		
Silver Patch:		No Pricing
Production 25 Sets		
Purple Patch:		No Pricing
Production One Set		
SA	Sparky Anderson	6.00
JB	Johnny Bench	15.00
OC	Orlando Cepeda	8.00
CF	Carlton Fisk	10.00
BG	Bob Gibson	8.00
DG	Dwight Gooden	6.00
RJ	Reggie Jackson	12.00
DM	Don Mattingly	15.00
WM	Willie McCovey	6.00
JM	Joe Morgan/SP/82	12.00
EM	Eddie Murray	10.00
CR	Cal Ripken Jr.	20.00
BR	Brooks Robinson	8.00
NR	Nolan Ryan/	20.00
MS	Mike Schmidt	12.00
TS	Tom Seaver	10.00
OS	Ozzie Smith	15.00
WS	Willie Stargell	10.00
DS	Darryl Strawberry	6.00
CY	Carl Yastrzemski	10.00

Cut of History Single Autograph Blue

		NM/M
Common Player:		20.00
Inserted 1:161		
Silver:		No Pricing
Production 25 Sets		
Purple:		No Pricing
Production One Set		
JB	Johnny Bench	50.00
BB	Bill Buckner	20.00
BF	Bob Feller	20.00
KG	Kirk Gibson	20.00
DG	Dwight Gooden	30.00
DL	Don Larsen	20.00
DM	Don Mattingly	50.00
JP	Jim Palmer	30.00
BR	Brooks Robinson	40.00
DS	Darryl Strawberry	25.00
MW	Mookie Wilson	20.00

Cut of History Dual Jersey Blue

		NM/M
Common Card:		15.00
Inserted 1:112		
Silver Patch:		No Pricing
Production 15 Sets		

Purple Patch: No Pricing
Production One Set

BF	Johnny Bench, Carlton Fisk	20.00
BS	Lou Brock, Mike Schmidt	25.00
CM	Orlando Cepeda, Willie McCovey	15.00
GS	Dwight Gooden, Darryl Strawberry	15.00
JY	Reggie Jackson, Carl Yastrzemski	20.00
RS	Cal Ripken Jr., Ozzie Smith	30.00
RS	Nolan Ryan, Tom Seaver	30.00
SJ	Willie Stargell, Reggie Jackson	20.00

Cut of History Triple Jersey Blue

NM/M

Inserted 1:67
Silver Patch: No Pricing
Production 25 Sets
Purple Patch: No Pricing
Production One Set

ACW	Hank Aaron, Roberto Clemente, Ted Williams	160.00
BSG	Lou Brock, Kirk Gibson, Ozzie Smith	50.00
JKM	Reggie Jackson, Harmon Killebrew, Willie McCovey	40.00
MMC	Eddie Murray, Orlando Cepeda, Willie McCovey	25.00
MRS	Don Mattingly, Cal Ripken Jr., Mike Schmidt	75.00
OJM	Paul O'Neill, Don Mattingly, Reggie Jackson	50.00
RCJ	Nolan Ryan, Roger Clemens, Randy Johnson	50.00

Cut of History Dual Autograph Blue

NM/M

Production 49 Sets
Silver: No Pricing
Production 22 Sets
Purple: No Pricing
Production One Set

GE	Kirk Gibson, Dennis Eckersley	50.00
GS	Dwight Gooden, Darryl Strawberry	40.00
WB	Mookie Wilson, Bill Buckner	40.00

Cut of History Triple Autograph Blue

No Pricing
Production 15 Sets
Silver: No Pricing
Production 5 Sets
Purple: No Pricing
Production One Set

Jersey Rack Dual Jersey Blue

NM/M

Common Card: 10.00
Inserted 1:100
Silver Patch: No Pricing
Production 25 Sets
Purple Patch: No Pricing
Production One Set

BW	Josh Beckett, Kerry Wood	10.00
CJ	Miguel Cabrera, Andruw Jones	12.00
DB	Adam Dunn, Lance Berkman	10.00
GS	Vladimir Guerrero, Sammy Sosa	15.00

GT	Khalil Greene, Miguel Tejada	10.00
HB	Todd Helton, Jeff Bagwell	10.00
HE	Torii Hunter, Jim Edmonds	10.00
JC	Randy Johnson, Roger Clemens	20.00
JW	Chipper Jones, David Wright	15.00
MM	Hideki Matsui, Kazuo Matsui	25.00
OG	David Ortiz, Jason Giambi	12.00
RB	Scott Rolen, Adrian Beltre	12.00
RS	Manny Ramirez, Gary Sheffield	12.00
SG	John Smoltz, Eric Gagne	10.00
SM	Jason Schmidt, Pedro Martinez	12.00
SM1	Alfonso Soriano, Kazuo Matsui	10.00
SP	Curt Schilling, Mark Prior	8.00
TP	Jim Thome, Mike Piazza	12.00
WS	Dontrelle Willis, Johan Santana	12.00

Triple Jersey Blue

NM/M

Common Card: 12.00
Inserted 1:54
Silver Patch: No Pricing
Production 25 Sets
Purple Patch: No Pricing

CJS	Roger Clemens, Randy Johnson, Jason Schmidt	20.00
CSJ	Roger Clemens, Curt Schilling, Randy Johnson	20.00
EHJ	Jim Edmonds, Torii Hunter, Andruw Jones	12.00
GRS	Vladimir Guerrero, Manny Ramirez, Gary Sheffield	15.00
GSR	Eric Gagne, John Smoltz, Mariano Rivera	15.00
HSB	Todd Helton, Alfonso Soriano, Adrian Beltre	12.00
MGT	Kazuo Matsui, Khalil Greene, Miguel Tejada	15.00
MRG	Hideki Matsui, Mariano Rivera, Jason Giambi	25.00
ORM	David Ortiz, Manny Ramirez, Pedro Martinez	15.00
PRE	Albert Pujols, Scott Rolen, Jim Edmonds	25.00
PTB	Albert Pujols, Jim Thome, Jeff Bagwell	20.00
RBJ	Scott Rolen, Adrian Beltre, Chipper Jones	15.00
SDC	Sammy Sosa, Adam Dunn, Miguel Cabrera	12.00
SJJ	John Smoltz, Chipper Jones, Andruw Jones	20.00
SPB	Jason Schmidt, Mark Prior, Josh Beckett	10.00
STB	Sammy Sosa, Miguel Tejada, Adrian Beltre	15.00
WPM	David Wright, Mike Piazza, Kazuo Matsui	20.00
WSW	Dontrelle Willis, Johan Santana, Kerry Wood	15.00

Diamond Signings Single Blue

NM/M

Inserted 1:29
Silver: No Pricing
Production 25 Sets
Purple: No Pricing
Production One Set

JB	Jason Bay	20.00
AB	Andres Blanco	15.00
CF	Chone Figgins	15.00
GF	Gavin Floyd	15.00
KG	Khalil Greene/150	25.00

ZG	Zack Greinke	15.00
TH	Travis Hafner	10.00
CJ	Charlton Jimerson	10.00
SK	Scott Kazmir	20.00
CK	Casey Kotchman	10.00
BL	Brad Lidge/97	40.00
JM	Justin Morneau/98	25.00
DN	Dioner Navarro	10.00
JP	Jake Peavy	20.00
NS	Nick Swisher	15.00
BU	B.J. Upton	15.00
JV	Justin Verlander/150	35.00
DW	David Wright/97	50.00

Diamond Signings Dual Blue

NM/M

Production 49 Sets
Silver: No Pricing
Production 22 Sets
Purple: No Pricing
Production One Set

BC	Jason Bay, B. Crosby Exch	30.00
FU	Gavin Floyd, Chase Utley	40.00

Diamond Signings Triple Blue

NM/M

Sequentially Numbered
Silver: No Pricing
Production 5 Sets
Purple: No Pricing
Production One Set

	Khalil Greene, B.J. Upton, Bobby Crosby/99	50.00
	Justin Verlander, Gavin Floyd, Scott Kazmir/99	75.00
	Nick Swisher, Charlton Jimerson, Chone Figgins/99	30.00
	Casey Kotchman, Justin Morneau, Jason Bay/86	40.00

2005 Fleer Patchworks

NM/M

Complete Set (100):
Common (1-70): .40
Common (71-90): 1.50
Production 499 Sets
Common (91-100): 2.00
Production 999 Sets
Pack (5): 4.00
Box (18): 60.00

1	Bobby Abreu	.50
2	Miguel Cabrera	1.00
3	J.D. Drew	.40
4	Justin Morneau	.40
5	David Ortiz	1.00
6	Ivan Rodriguez	.75
7	Jason Schmidt	.40
8	Frank Thomas	.75
9	Travis Hafner	.50
10	Curt Schilling	1.00
11	Jim Edmonds	.75
12	Randy Johnson	1.00
13	Jose Vidro	.40
14	Vernon Wells	.40
15	Lance Berkman	.50
16	Khalil Greene	.50
17	Andruw Jones	.75
18	Mark Prior	.75
19	Mark Teixeira	.75
20	Jack Wilson	.40
21	Adrian Beltre	.50
22	Lew Ford	.40
23	Shawn Green	.50
24	Juan Pierre	.40

25	Alfonso Soriano	.75
26	Mike Sweeney	.40
27	Chipper Jones	1.00
28	Javy Lopez	.40
29	Victor Martinez	.40
30	Kazuo Matsui	.40
31	Bernie Williams	.50
32	Kerry Wood	.50
33	Barry Zito	.50
34	Austin Kearns	.40
35	Todd Helton	.75
36	B.J. Upton	.40
37	Jeff Bagwell	.75
38	Pedro Martinez	1.00
39	Lyle Overbay	.40
40	Ichiro Suzuki	2.00
41	Jason Bay	.50
42	Bobby Crosby	.40
43	Vladimir Guerrero	1.00
44	Richie Sexson	.50
45	Johan Santana	1.00
46	Magglio Ordonez	.40
47	Derek Jeter	3.00
48	Eric Gagne	.40
49	Albert Pujols	3.00
50	Jim Thome	.75
51	Hideki Matsui	2.00
52	Torii Hunter	.40
53	Greg Maddux	2.00
54	Michael Young	.40
55	Carlos Beltran	.75
56	Carl Crawford	.40
57	Adam Dunn	.75
58	Nomar Garciaparra	1.00
59	Mike Piazza	1.00
60	Alex Rodriguez	3.00
61	Scott Rolen	.75
62	Ben Sheets	.50
63	Sammy Sosa	1.00
64	Hank Blalock	.50
65	Carlos Delgado	.50
66	Ken Griffey Jr.	2.00
67	Manny Ramirez	1.00
68	Miguel Tejada	.75
69	Roger Clemens	3.00
70	Gary Sheffield	.75
71	Jon Knott	1.50
72	Ryan Raburn	1.50
73	Zack Greinke	1.50
74	David Aardsma	1.50
75	Justin Verlander RC	4.00
76	Andres Blanco	1.50
77	David Wright	4.00
78	Jeff Baker	1.50
79	Charlton Jimerson	1.50
80	Sean Burnett	1.50
81	Joey Gathright	1.50
82	Victor Diaz	1.50
83	Scott Kazmir	1.50
84	Edwin Encarnacion	1.50
85	J.D. Durbin	1.50
86	Nick Swisher	1.50
87	Casey Kotchman	1.50
88	Gavin Floyd	1.50
89	Josh Kroeger	1.50
90	Taylor Buchholz	1.50
91	Reggie Jackson	2.00
92	Nolan Ryan	6.00
93	Eddie Murray	2.00
94	Carlton Fisk	2.00
95	Mike Schmidt	4.00
96	Joe Morgan	2.00
97	Rod Carew	2.00
98	Harmon Killebrew	3.00
99	Tom Seaver	3.00
100	Brooks Robinson	3.00

Gold

Gold (1-70): 3-6X
Gold (71-100): 1-2X
Production 99 Sets

Autoworks Copper

NM/M

Production 75-250
Masterpiece: No Pricing
Production One Set

RB	Rocco Baldelli/100	12.00
JB	Jason Bay/150	20.00
JBO	Jeremy Bonderman/100	15.00
SB	Sean Burnett/100	8.00
MC	Miguel Cabrera/75	25.00
CC	Carl Crawford/175	15.00
JD	J.D. Durbin/100	8.00
ZG	Zack Greinke/200	10.00
TH	Travis Hafner/150	15.00
BL	Brad Lidge/75	15.00
VM	Victor Martinez/100	15.00
JM	Justin Morneau/175	20.00
BU	B.J. Upton/150	15.00
JV	Justin Verlander/100	20.00
DW	David Wright/250	50.00

Autoworks Dual
Production 25 Sets

Autoworks Gold
		NM/M
Production 49 Sets

HA	Hank Aaron	200.00
RB	Rocco Baldelli	15.00
EB	Ernie Banks	50.00
JB	Jason Bay	20.00
LB	Lance Berkman	20.00
JBO	Jeremy Bonderman	20.00
SB	Sean Burnett	10.00
MC	Miguel Cabrera	30.00
MCA	Mike Cameron	12.00
CC	Carl Crawford	20.00
JD	J.D. Durbin	10.00
GF	Gavin Floyd	10.00
LF	Lew Ford	10.00
ZG	Zack Greinke	12.00
TH	Travis Hafner	20.00
BL	Brad Lidge	20.00
VM	Victor Martinez	20.00
JM	Justin Morneau	25.00
JP	Josh Phelps	10.00
BS	Ben Sheets	20.00
BU	B.J. Upton	20.00
DW	David Wright	60.00
MY	Michael Young	15.00

Autoworks Quad
Production 10 Sets

Autoworks Silver
		NM/M
Production 99 Sets

RB	Rocco Baldelli	12.00
JB	Jason Bay	20.00
JBO	Jeremy Bonderman	15.00
SB	Sean Burnett	8.00
MC	Miguel Cabrera	25.00
MCA	Mike Cameron	12.00
CC	Carl Crawford	15.00
JD	J.D. Durbin	8.00
LF	Lew Ford	10.00
ZG	Zack Greinke	10.00
TH	Travis Hafner	15.00
BL	Brad Lidge	15.00
VM	Victor Martinez	15.00
JM	Justin Morneau	20.00
JP	Josh Phelps	10.00
BS	Ben Sheets	15.00
BU	B.J. Upton	15.00
JV	Justin Verlander	20.00
DW	David Wright	60.00

By the Numbers

BY THE **NUMBERS**
ADRIAN BELTRE / SEATTLE MARINERS™

		NM/M
Common Player: | | 1.00
Inserted 1:18

1	Roy Oswalt	1.00
2	Hideki Matsui	3.00
3	Curt Schilling	1.50
4	Mike Piazza	2.00
5	Alex Rodriguez	4.00
6	Vladimir Guerrero	1.50
7	Victor Martinez	1.00
8	Adrian Beltre	1.00
9	Johnny Estrada	1.00
10	Ken Griffey Jr.	3.00
11	Sammy Sosa	2.00
12	Ichiro Suzuki	3.00
13	Roger Clemens	4.00
14	David Ortiz	1.50
15	Johan Santana	1.50
16	Pedro Martinez	1.50
17	Austin Kearns	1.00
18	Randy Johnson	1.50
19	Nomar Garciaparra	1.50
20	Albert Pujols	4.00

By the Numbers Jersey
		NM/M
Common Player: | | 4.00

AB	Adrian Beltre	4.00
RC	Roger Clemens/SP	10.00
JE	Johnny Estrada	4.00
VG	Vladimir Guerrero/SP	8.00
RJ	Randy Johnson	8.00
PM	Pedro Martinez	8.00
HM	Hideki Matsui	20.00
RO	Roy Oswalt	4.00
AP	Albert Pujols	15.00
JS	Johan Santana	6.00
CS	Curt Schilling	8.00
SS	Sammy Sosa	8.00

By the Numbers Jersey Die Cut
		NM/M
Production 199 Sets
Jersey Tag: | | No Pricing
Production One Set

AB	Adrian Beltre	4.00
RC	Roger Clemens	10.00
JE	Johnny Estrada	4.00
VG	Vladimir Guerrero	8.00
RJ	Randy Johnson	8.00
AK	Austin Kearns	4.00
PM	Pedro Martinez	8.00
HM	Hideki Matsui	20.00
DO	David Ortiz	8.00
RO	Roy Oswalt	4.00
MP	Mike Piazza/116	10.00
AP	Albert Pujols	15.00
JS	Johan Santana	6.00
CS	Curt Schilling	8.00
SS	Sammy Sosa	8.00

By the Numbers Patch
		NM/M
Production 99 Sets
Patch Die-Cut: | | No Pricing
Production 25 Sets

AB	Adrian Beltre	10.00
JE	Johnny Estrada	8.00
VG	Vladimir Guerrero	15.00
AK	Austin Kearns/78	10.00
HM	Hideki Matsui	30.00
DO	David Ortiz/46	15.00
RO	Roy Oswalt	8.00
MP	Mike Piazza	20.00
AP	Albert Pujols	30.00
JS	Johan Santana	15.00
CS	Curt Schilling	15.00
SS	Sammy Sosa	20.00

By the Numbers Patch Autographs
No Pricing
Production 25 Sets

Dual Jersey
		NM/M
Common Duo: | | 6.00
Die-Cut: | | 1-1.5X
Production 199 Sets
Dual MLB Logo: | | No Pricing
Production One Set
Dual Patch: | | No Pricing
Production 25 Sets
Dual Patch Die-Cut: | | No Pricing
Production 15 Sets

DWJB	Dontrelle Willis, Josh Beckett	6.00
DWMP	David Wright, Mike Piazza	15.00
GSBW	Gary Sheffield, Bernie Williams/SP	8.00
KWMP	Kerry Wood, Mark Prior/SP	8.00
MRDO	Manny Ramirez, David Ortiz	15.00
MYAS	Michael Young, Alfonso Soriano	8.00
SSTH	Shannon Stewart, Torii Hunter	6.00

Heart of the Team

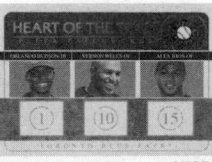
HEART OF THE

		NM/M
Inserted 1:108

1	Braves/Marlins	8.00
2	Red Sox/Yankees	15.00
3	Cardinals/Astros	10.00
4	Angels/A's	8.00
5	Phillies/Mets	8.00
6	Twins/White Sox	8.00
7	Reds/Cubs	10.00
8	Mariners/Rangers	10.00
9	Orioles/Nationals	8.00
10	Blue Jays/Devil Rays	6.00

Heart of the Team Jersey
Production 199 Sets
Patch: No Pricing
Production 15 Sets

Jersey
		NM/M
Common Player: | | 4.00

JB	Josh Beckett	4.00
TH	Torii Hunter	4.00
MARK	Mark Prior	4.00
MR	Manny Ramirez	8.00
GS	Gary Sheffield	6.00
AS	Alfonso Soriano	6.00
SS	Shannon Stewart	4.00
BW	Bernie Williams	6.00
DW	Dontrelle Willis	4.00
KW	Kerry Wood	4.00
DWR	David Wright	15.00
MY	Michael Young	4.00

Patch
		NM/M
Production 99 Sets
Die-Cut: | | 1-1.5X
Production 49 Sets

JB	Josh Beckett	8.00
TH	Torii Hunter	10.00
DO	David Ortiz/51	20.00
MIKE	Mike Piazza	20.00
MARK	Mark Prior	15.00
MR	Manny Ramirez	20.00
AS	Alfonso Soriano/73	12.00
SS	Shannon Stewart	10.00
BW	Bernie Williams	12.00
DW	Dontrelle Willis	15.00
KW	Kerry Wood	12.00
DWR	David Wright	35.00
MY	Michael Young	10.00

Property of
		NM/M
Common Player: | | 1.00
Inserted 1:6

1	Vladimir Guerrero	1.50
2	Luis Gonzalez	1.00
3	Chipper Jones	1.50
4	Miguel Tejada	1.50
5	David Ortiz	1.50
6	Kerry Wood	1.00
7	Frank Thomas	1.00
8	Adam Dunn	1.00
9	Victor Martinez	1.00
10	Todd Helton	1.50
11	Ivan Rodriguez	1.50
12	Miguel Cabrera	1.50
13	Jeff Bagwell	1.50
14	Mike Sweeney	1.00
15	Eric Gagne	1.00
16	Lyle Overbay	1.00
17	Johan Santana	1.50
18	Mike Piazza	2.00
19	Derek Jeter	5.00
20	Bobby Crosby	1.00
21	Jim Thome	1.50
22	Jason Bay	1.00
23	Khalil Greene	1.00
24	Jason Schmidt	1.00
25	Ichiro Suzuki	3.00
26	Albert Pujols	5.00
27	B.J. Upton	1.00
28	Hank Blalock	1.00
29	Vernon Wells	1.00
30	Jose Vidro	1.00

Property of Jersey
		NM/M
JB	Jeff Bagwell	6.00
JBA	Jason Bay	4.00
HB	Hank Blalock	4.00
MC	Miguel Cabrera	8.00
EG	Eric Gagne	4.00
LG	Luis Gonzalez	4.00
VG	Vladimir Guerrero/SP	8.00
CJ	Chipper Jones	8.00
AP	Albert Pujols	15.00
IR	Ivan Rodriguez	6.00
JS	Johan Santana/SP	8.00
JSC	Jason Schmidt	4.00
MT	Miguel Tejada	6.00
FT	Frank Thomas	6.00
JT	Jim Thome	6.00
BU	B.J. Upton	4.00
VW	Vernon Wells	4.00
KW	Kerry Wood	4.00

Property of Jersey Die Cut
		NM/M
Production 199 Sets
MLB Logo: | | No Pricing
Production One Set

JB	Jeff Bagwell	6.00
JBA	Jason Bay	4.00
HB	Hank Blalock	4.00
MC	Miguel Cabrera	8.00
EG	Eric Gagne	4.00
LG	Luis Gonzalez	4.00
KG	Khalil Greene	4.00
VG	Vladimir Guerrero	8.00
CJ	Chipper Jones	8.00
DO	David Ortiz	8.00
LO	Lyle Overbay/86 UER	4.00
MP	Mike Piazza	8.00
AP	Albert Pujols	15.00
IR	Ivan Rodriguez	6.00
JS	Johan Santana	6.00
JSC	Jason Schmidt	4.00
MT	Miguel Tejada	6.00
FT	Frank Thomas	6.00
JT	Jim Thome	6.00
BU	B.J. Upton	4.00
VW	Vernon Wells	4.00
KW	Kerry Wood	4.00

Property of Patch

		NM/M
Production 99 Sets
Die-Cut: | | No Pricing
Production 25 Sets
Nameplate: | | 1-2X
Production 49 Sets

JB	Jeff Bagwell	15.00
JBA	Jason Bay/84	10.00
HB	Hank Blalock	12.00
MC	Miguel Cabrera	15.00
AD	Adam Dunn/42	10.00
EG	Eric Gagne	10.00
LG	Luis Gonzalez	10.00
KG	Khalil Greene	10.00
VG	Vladimir Guerrero	15.00
CJ	Chipper Jones	15.00
DO	David Ortiz/45	20.00
MP	Mike Piazza	20.00
AP	Albert Pujols	30.00
IR	Ivan Rodriguez	15.00
JS	Johan Santana	15.00
JSC	Jason Schmidt	12.00
MS	Mike Sweeney/77	10.00
MT	Miguel Tejada	15.00
JT	Jim Thome	15.00
BU	B.J. Upton	10.00
VW	Vernon Wells/30	10.00
KW	Kerry Wood/89	15.00

(top right listing)
JT	Jim Thome	6.00
BU	B.J. Upton	4.00
VW	Vernon Wells	4.00
KW	Kerry Wood	4.00

2005 Fleer Platinum
		NM/M
Common Players (1-100):		.25
Minor Players (1-100):		.40
Unlisted Stars (1-100):		.50
Common Players (101-125):		3.00
Production 1,000 Sets		
Pack (5):		2.00
Box (24):		40.00
1	Nomar Garciaparra	1.50
2	Matt Holliday	.50
3	Rickie Weeks	.25
4	Jim Thome	.75
5	Roy Halladay	.40
6	Paul Konerko	.25
7	Lance Berkman	.40
8	Ichiro Suzuki	1.25

9	Kerry Wood	.60
10	Lew Ford	.25
11	Omar Vizquel	.40
12	Manny Ramirez	.60
13	Carlos Beltran	.50
14	Lyle Overbay	.25
15	Billy Wagner	.40
16	Jose Vidro	.25
17	Vladimir Guerrero	.75
18	Miguel Tejada	.50
19	Alex Rodriguez	1.50
20	Rocco Baldelli	.50
21	David Ortiz	.50
22	Victor Martinez	.25
23	Shawn Green	.40
24	Jason Bay	.25
25	Pedro Martinez	.75
26	Travis Hafner	.25
27	Eric Gagne	.40
28	Jack Wilson	.25
29	Ivan Rodriguez	.50
30	Jody Gerut	.25
31	Adrian Beltre	.40
32	Craig Wilson	.25
33	J.D. Drew	.40
34	Craig Biggio	.40
35	Mark Mulder	.40
36	Mark Teixeira	.50
37	Melvin Mora	.25
38	Ken Griffey Jr.	1.00
39	Mike Sweeney	.25
40	Khalil Greene	.60
41	Rafael Palmeiro	.60
42	Austin Kearns	.50
43	Garret Anderson	.40
44	Trevor Hoffman	.25
45	Andruw Jones	.60
46	Adam Dunn	.50
47	Angel Berroa	.25
48	Ryan Klesko	.40
49	Sean Casey	.25
50	Kazuo Matsui	.50
51	Jim Edmonds	.40
52	Magglio Ordonez	.40
53	Tom Glavine	.40
54	Larry Walker	.40
55	Johnny Estrada	.25
56	Brad Lidge	.25
57	Barry Zito	.50
58	Michael Young	.40
59	Chipper Jones	1.00
60	Andy Pettitte	.50
61	Eric Chavez	.40
62	Carlos Delgado	.60
63	David Eckstein	.25
64	Dmitri Young	.25
65	Mike Piazza	1.00
66	Albert Pujols	1.50
67	Luis Gonzalez	.40
68	Hideki Matsui	1.50
69	Gary Sheffield	.50
70	Carl Crawford	.25
71	Curt Schilling	.50
72	Todd Helton	.60
73	Ben Sheets	.40
74	Bobby Abreu	.25
75	Jose Guillen	.25
76	Richie Sexson	.50
77	Miguel Cabrera	.60
78	Bernie Williams	.50
79	Aubrey Huff	.40
80	John Smoltz	.40
81	Jeff Bagwell	.60
82	Tim Hudson	.40
83	Alfonso Soriano	.75
84	Freddy Garcia	.25
85	Johan Santana	.40
86	Bret Boone	.40
87	Troy Glaus	.50
88	Carlos Guillen	.25
89	Derek Jeter	2.00
90	Scott Rolen	.75
91	Sammy Sosa	1.25
92	Jacque Jones	.25
93	Jason Schmidt	.40
94	Randy Johnson	.75
95	Dontrelle Willis	.50
96	Mariano Rivera	.40
97	Hank Blalock	.50
98	Mark Prior	1.50
99	Torii Hunter	.50
100	Roger Clemens	1.50
101	David Wright	6.00
102	Justin Morneau	4.00
103	Scott Kazmir	4.00
104	Gavin Floyd	3.00
105	Justin Verlander RC	8.00
106	Zack Greinke	4.00
107	David Aardsma	3.00
108	Ryan Raburn	4.00
109	Joey Gathright	3.00
110	J.D. Durbin	3.00
111	Sean Burnett	3.00
112	Jose Lopez	5.00
113	Nick Swisher	4.00
114	Bobby Jenks	3.00
115	Kelly Johnson	8.00
116	B.J. Upton	5.00
117	Ronny Cedeno	3.00
118	Edwin Encarnacion	6.00
119	Jeff Baker	3.00
120	Taylor Buchholz	3.00
121	Livan Hernandez RC	4.00
122	Dioner Navarro	4.00
123	Victor Diaz	4.00
124	Jon Knott	4.00
125	Russ Adams	3.00

Finish

Cards 1-100:	3-6X
Cards 101-125:	.75-1.25X
Production 199 Sets	

Extreme

Cards 1-125:	No Pricing
Production 20 Sets	

Autograph Die Cuts

NM/M

Numbered to indicated quantities.

1	Lew Ford/99	10.00
3	Jason Bay/50	15.00
4	Travis Hafner/99	15.00
6	Brad Lidge/99	30.00
7	Michael Young/99	15.00
8	David Eckstein/99	20.00
9	Carl Crawford/50	15.00
10	Miguel Cabrera/50	25.00
11	David Wright/50	50.00
13	Scott Kazmir/99	15.00
14	Gavin Floyd/99	10.00
15	Justin Verlander/99	40.00
18	Joey Gathright/50	10.00

Decade of Excellence

NM/M

Common Player: 2.00
Inserted 1:199

1	Albert Pujols	6.00
2	Derek Jeter	8.00
3	Randy Johnson	4.00
4	Ichiro Suzuki	5.00
5	Alex Rodriguez	6.00
6	Mike Piazza	4.00
7	Greg Maddux	4.00
8	Curt Schilling	3.00
9	Frank Thomas	3.00
10	Torii Hunter	3.00
11	Al Kaline	6.00
12	Travis Hafner	2.00
13	Ivan Rodriguez	3.00
14	Rafael Palmeiro	3.00
15	Mike Schmidt	8.00
16	Johnny Bench	8.00
17	Jim Edmonds	2.00
18	Pedro Martinez	4.00
19	Robin Yount	6.00
20	Sammy Sosa	5.00

Decade of Excellence Jersey Silver

NM/M

Common Player: 5.00
Inserted 1:54
Gold: .75-1.25X
Production 99 Sets
Patch Platinum: No Pricing
Production 10 Sets

JB	Johnny Bench	15.00
JE	Jim Edmonds	5.00
TF	Travis Hafner	5.00
TH	Torii Hunter	5.00
RJ	Randy Johnson	8.00
AK	Al Kaline	10.00
GM	Greg Maddux	8.00
PM	Pedro Martinez	8.00
RP	Rafael Palmeiro	8.00
MP	Mike Piazza	8.00
AP	Albert Pujols	12.00
IR	Ivan Rodriguez	5.00
CS	Curt Schilling	5.00
MS	Mike Schmidt	15.00
SS	Sammy Sosa	10.00
FT	Frank Thomas	8.00
RY	Robin Yount	10.00

Decade of Excellence Autograph Jersey Platinum

No Pricing
Production 5 Sets

Diamond Dominators

NM/M

Common Player: 2.00
Inserted 1:12 Retail

1	Albert Pujols	6.00
2	Curt Schilling	3.00
3	Adrian Beltre	2.00
4	Randy Johnson	4.00
5	Ivan Rodriguez	3.00
6	Mike Piazza	4.00
7	Chipper Jones	4.00
8	Sammy Sosa	5.00
9	Tim Hudson	2.00
10	Rocco Baldelli	3.00
11	Alfonso Soriano	4.00
12	David Ortiz	3.00
13	Mariano Rivera	2.00
14	Kazuo Matsui	3.00
15	Khalil Greene	3.00
16	Eric Gagne	2.00
17	Vladimir Guerrero	4.00
18	Jason Giambi	4.00
19	Scott Rolen	4.00
20	Miguel Cabrera	3.00

Diamond Dominators Jersey Silver

NM/M

Common Player:
Inserted 1:45
Gold: .75-1.25X
Production 199 Sets (Hobby)
Red: .5-1X
Inserted 1:50 (Retail)

RB	Rocco Baldelli	5.00
AB	Adrian Beltre	5.00
MC	Miguel Cabrera	8.00
EG	Eric Gagne	5.00
JG	Jason Giambi	8.00
KG	Khalil Greene	8.00
VG	Vladimir Guerrero	8.00
TH	Tim Hudson	5.00
RJ	Randy Johnson	8.00
CJ	Chipper Jones	4.00
KM	Kazuo Matsui	5.00
DO	David Ortiz	5.00
MP	Mike Piazza	8.00
AP	Albert Pujols	12.00
IR	Ivan Rodriguez	5.00
SR	Scott Rolen	8.00
CS	Curt Schilling	5.00
AS	Alfonso Soriano	8.00
SS	Sammy Sosa	10.00

Diamond Dominators Metal

NM/M

Common Player: 2.00
Inserted 1:18 Hobby

1	Albert Pujols	6.00
2	Curt Schilling	3.00
3	Adrian Beltre	2.00
4	Randy Johnson	4.00
5	Ivan Rodriguez	3.00
6	Mike Piazza	4.00
7	Chipper Jones	4.00
8	Sammy Sosa	5.00
9	Tim Hudson	2.00
10	Rocco Baldelli	3.00
11	Alfonso Soriano	4.00
12	David Ortiz	3.00
13	Kazuo Matsui	3.00
14	Khalil Greene	3.00
15	Eric Gagne	2.00
16	Vladimir Guerrero	4.00
17	Jason Giambi	4.00
18	Scott Rolen	4.00
19	Miguel Cabrera	3.00

Diamond Dominators Metal Patch

NM/M

1-2X Diamond Dominators
  Jersey Silver
Sequentially #'d to 30.

HA	Hank Aaron	100.00

Diamond Dominators Metal Autograph

No Pricing
Production 10 Sets

Lumberjacks

NM/M

Common Player: .75
Inserted 1:6
Bat Silver: 2-3X
Inserted 1:9
Bat Gold: 2-4X
Production 250 Sets
Bat Patch: No Pricing
Production 20 Sets

1	Albert Pujols	2.50
2	Jim Thome	1.25
3	Andruw Jones	1.00
4	Kazuo Matsui	.75
5	Adam Dunn	.75
6	Bernie Williams	.75
7	Hank Blalock	.75
8	Bobby Abreu	.75
9	Rocco Baldelli	.75
10	Jacque Jones	.75
11	Mark Teixeira	.75
12	Ichiro Suzuki	2.00
13	Gary Sheffield	.75
14	Sean Casey	.75
15	Carl Crawford	.75

Lumberjacks Autograph Platinum

No Pricing
Production 20 Sets

Nameplates Patch Platinum

No Pricing
Production 25 Sets
Masterpiece: No Pricing
Production One Set

Nameplates Patch Autograph Platinum

No Pricing
Production 25 Sets

Nameplates Dual Patch Platinum

No Pricing
Production 25 Sets
Masterpiece: No Pricing
Production One Set

Nameplates Dual Patch Autograph Platinum

No Pricing
Production One Set

2005 Fleer Showcase

NM/M

Common Player (1-100):	.25
Minor Stars (1-100):	.40
Unlisted Stars (1-100):	.60
Common Showcasing Talent (101-110):	2.00
Inserted 1:5	
Common Showcasing History (111-135):	.40
Inserted 1:20	
Pack (5):	3.00
Box (20):	50.00

1	Albert Pujols	2.50
2	Rocco Baldelli	.60
3	Bernie Williams	.60
4	Shawn Green	.40
5	Garret Anderson	.40
6	Paul Konerko	.25
7	Mike Sweeney	.25
8	Jim Thome	1.00
9	Mark Teixeira	.40
10	Mark Prior	2.00
11	Angel Berroa	.25

12	Barry Zito	.60
13	Carlos Delgado	.75
14	Troy Glaus	.60
15	Travis Hafner	.25
16	Lyle Overbay	.25
17	David Ortiz	.60
18	Ivan Rodriguez	.60
19	Jack Wilson	.25
20	Jason Schmidt	.40
21	Mike Piazza	1.50
22	David Eckstein	.25
23	Ben Sheets	.40
24	Randy Johnson	1.00
25	Jacque Jones	.25
26	Jody Gerut	.25
27	Kris Benson	.25
28	Luis Gonzalez	.40
29	Victor Martinez	.25
30	Torii Hunter	.60
31	Gary Sheffield	.60
32	Miguel Tejada	.60
33	Dontrelle Willis	.60
34	Bret Boone	.40
35	Hideki Matsui	.60
36	Shea Hillenbrand	.25
37	Wily Mo Pena	.25
38	Johan Santana	.40
39	Derek Jeter	3.00
40	Chipper Jones	1.50
41	Sean Casey	.25
42	Corey Koskie	.25
43	Alex Rodriguez	2.50
44	Andruw Jones	.75
45	Austin Kearns	.60
46	Jose Vidro	.25
47	Adam Dunn	.60
48	Adrian Beltre	.40
49	Bobby Abreu	.40
50	Michael Young	.25
51	Freddy Garcia	.25
52	Eric Gagne	.40
53	Chase Utley	.25
54	Alfonso Soriano	1.00
55	Nick Johnson	.25
56	Johnny Estrada	.25
57	Jeff Bagwell	.75
58	Randy Winn	.25
59	Roy Halladay	.40
60	J.D. Drew	.40
61	Craig Biggio	.40
62	Scott Rolen	1.00
63	Nomar Garciaparra	2.50
64	Matt Holliday	.50
65	Billy Wagner	.25
66	Carl Crawford	.25
67	Pedro J. Martinez	1.00
68	Jeremy Bonderman	.25
69	Jason Bay	.25
70	A.J. Pierzynski	.25
71	Vladimir Guerrero	1.00
72	Rickie Weeks	.60
73	Mark Loretta	.25
74	Todd Helton	.75
75	Manny Ramirez	.75
76	Carlos Guillen	.25
77	Khalil Greene	.75
78	Javy Lopez	.40
79	Josh Beckett	.75
80	Ichiro Suzuki	2.00
81	Magglio Ordonez	.40
82	Ken Harvey	.25
83	Mark Mulder	.40
84	Hank Blalock	.60
85	Richard Hidalgo	.25
86	Curt Schilling	.60
87	Jeromy Burnitz	.25
88	Craig Wilson	.25
89	Aubrey Huff	.25
90	Kerry Wood	.75
91	Andy Pettitte	.60
92	Tim Hudson	.40
93	Jim Edmonds	.40
94	Melvin Mora	.25
95	Miguel Cabrera	.75
96	Trevor Hoffman	.25
97	J.T. Snow	.25
98	Sammy Sosa	2.00
99	Roger Clemens	2.50
100	Eric Chavez	4.00
101	B.J. Upton	5.00
102	Gavin Floyd	3.00
103	Casey Kotchman	3.00
104	David Wright	5.00
105	Dioner Navarro	3.00
106	Scott Kazmir	3.00
107	Andres Blanco	2.00
108	Joey Gathright	2.00
109	Jon Knott	2.00
110	Charlton Jimerson	3.00
111	Larry Doby	.75
112	Reggie Jackson	2.00
113	Enos Slaughter	.60
114	Bill "Moose" Skowron	.60
115	Duke Snider	.75
116	Harmon Killebrew	1.00
117	Willie McCovey	.75
118	Rollie Fingers	1.00
119	Preacher Roe	.40
120	Carlton Fisk	.60
121	Andre Dawson	.60
122	Orlando Cepeda	.60
123	Bucky Dent	.40
124	Cal Ripken Jr.	1.50
125	Nolan Ryan	3.00
126	Tony Perez	.60
127	Mike Schmidt	1.50
128	Johnny Bench	1.50
129	Sparky Anderson	.40
130	Ted Williams	2.50
131	Al Kaline	.75
132	Carl Yastrzemski	1.00
133	Eddie Murray	.75
134	Roberto Clemente	1.50
135	Yogi Berra	1.50

Showtime

Veterans (1-100):	3-6X
Showcasing Talent (101-110):	2-4X
Showcasing History (111-135):	1-3X
Production 99 Sets	
Masterpiece:	No Pricing
Production One Set	

Showdown

Cards (1-135):	No Pricing
Production 15 Sets	
Masterpiece:	No Pricing
Production One Set	

Masterpiece Legacy

Cards (1-135):	No Pricing
Production One Set	

Masterpiece Showpiece Patch

Cards (1-135):	No Pricing
Production One Set	
Autograph Patch:	No Pricing
Production One Set	
Patch Showdown:	No Pricing
Production One Set	
Patch Showtime:	No Pricing
Production One Set	

Autographed Legacy

		NM/M
Common Player:		15.00
Sequentially numbered		
8	Jim Thome/34	60.00
10	Mark Prior/43	30.00
12	Barry Zito/45	35.00
18	Ivan Rodriguez/217	40.00
19	Jack Wilson/298	15.00
20	Jason Schmidt/127	15.00
21	Mike Piazza/26	100.00
22	David Eckstein/40	35.00
23	Ben Sheets/427	15.00
40	Chipper Jones/41	60.00
45	Austin Kearns/460	10.00
47	Adam Dunn/52	35.00
48	Adrian Beltre/180	15.00
50	Michael Young/80	15.00
52	Eric Gagne/310	25.00
53	Chase Utley/446	25.00
59	Roy Halladay/99	15.00
68	Jeremy Bonderman/97	20.00
72	Rickie Weeks/453	20.00
75	Manny Ramirez/31	75.00
77	Khalil Greene/299	25.00
88	Craig Wilson/40	20.00
89	Aubrey Huff/453	15.00
90	Kerry Wood/28	25.00
92	Tim Hudson/183	25.00
95	Miguel Cabrera/32	35.00
99	Roger Clemens/64	100.00
100	Eric Chavez/204	15.00
103	Casey Kotchman/454	15.00
104	David Wright/298	40.00
106	Scott Kazmir/458	20.00
107	Andres Blanco/23	15.00
109	Jon Knott/402	10.00
114	Bill "Moose" Skowron/64	20.00
119	Preacher Roe/304	20.00
120	Carlton Fisk/86	30.00
123	Bucky Dent/99	15.00
135	Yogi Berra/25	75.00

Measures of Greatness

		NM/M
Common Player:		.75
Inserted 1:5		
Jersey Red:		2-4X
Production 340 Sets		
Patch:		No Pricing
Production 10 Sets		
Masterpiece:		No Pricing
Production One Set		
1	Albert Pujols	4.00
2	Mike Piazza	2.50
3	Vladimir Guerrero	2.00
4	Jim Thome	2.00
5	Pedro J. Martinez	2.00
6	Rafael Palmeiro	.75
7	Adrian Beltre	.75
8	Sammy Sosa	3.00
9	Todd Helton	1.50
10	Randy Johnson	2.00
11	Jeff Bagwell	1.50
12	Jason Giambi	1.50
13	Scott Rolen	2.00
14	Greg Maddux	2.50
15	Alfonso Soriano	2.00
16	Mariano Rivera	.75
17	Curt Schilling	1.00
18	Derek Jeter	5.00
19	Chipper Jones	2.50
20	Roger Clemens	4.00

Swing Time

		NM/M
Common Player:		2.50
Inserted 1:45		
Jersey Red:		1-3X
Production 610 Sets		
Patch:		2-5X
Production 50 Sets		
Masterpiece:		No Pricing
Production One Set		
1	Ivan Rodriguez	2.50
2	Gary Sheffield	2.50
3	Bernie Williams	2.50
4	Vladimir Guerrero	3.50
5	Jim Edmonds	2.50
6	Manny Ramirez	3.00
7	Todd Helton	3.00
8	Hank Blalock	2.50
9	Hideki Matsui	6.00
10	David Ortiz	2.50
11	Albert Pujols	6.00
12	Miguel Tejada	2.50
13	Miguel Cabrera	3.00
14	Alex Rodriguez	6.00
15	Ichiro Suzuki	5.00

Timepiece Extreme

No Pricing
Production One Set

Timepiece Ink

No Pricing
Production 10 Sets

Timepiece Teammates

No Pricing
Production One Set

Timepiece Unique

No Pricing
Production 5 Sets

Wave of the Future

		NM/M
Common Player:		1.00
Inserted 1:15		
Jersey Red:		1-3X
Production 610 Sets		
Patch:		2-5X
Production 50 Sets		
Masterpiece:		No Pricing
Production One Set		
1	Kazuo Matsui	5.00
2	Johan Santana	1.50
3	Khalil Greene	2.00
4	Dontrelle Willis	1.50
5	Mark Teixeira	1.50
6	Travis Hafner	1.00
7	Jason Bay	1.50
8	Angel Berroa	1.00
9	Miguel Cabrera	2.00
10	Joe Mauer	1.50
11	Adam Dunn	2.00
12	B.J. Upton	3.00
13	Victor Martinez	1.00
14	Michael Young	1.00
15	David Wright	3.00

2005 Fleer Tradition

	NM/M
Common Player (1-300):	.15
Minor Stars (1-300):	.25
Unlisted Stars (1-300):	.40
Common Card (301-330):	3.00
Unlisted Card (301-330):	4.00
Inserted 1:2	

Common Player (331-350): .15
Minor Stars (331-350): .25
Unlisted Stars (331-350): .40
Cards 1-12; 331-350 Inserted 1:2
Pack (10): 1.25
Box (36): 35.00

1 Johan Santana, Curt Schilling, Jake Westbrook, .40
2 Ben Sheets, Jake Peavy, Randy Johnson, .75
3 Johan Santana, Bartolo Colon, Curt Schilling, .40
4 Carl Pavano, Roy Oswalt, Roger Clemens, 1.50
5 Johan Santana, Pedro Martinez, Curt Schilling, .75
6 Jason Schmidt, Randy Johnson, Ben Sheets, .75
7 Melvin Mora, Vladimir Guerrero, Ichiro Suzuki, 1.25
8 Adrian Beltre, Todd Helton, Mark Loretta, .50
9 Manny Ramirez, Paul Konerko, David Ortiz, .50
10 Albert Pujols, Adrian Beltre, Adam Dunn, 1.50
11 David Ortiz, Manny Ramirez, Miguel Tejada, .50
12 Albert Pujols, Vinny Castilla, Scott Rolen, 1.50
13 Jason Bay .15
14 Greg Maddux 1.00
15 Melvin Mora .15
16 Matt Stairs .15
17 Scott Podsednik .25
18 Bartolo Colon .25
19 Roger Clemens 1.50
20 Eric Hinske .15
21 Johnny Estrada .15
22 Brett Tomko .15
23 John Buck .15
24 Nomar Garciaparra 1.50
25 Milton Bradley .15
26 Craig Biggio .25
27 Kyle Denney .50
28 Brad Penny .50
29 Todd Helton .50
30 Luis Gonzalez .25
31 Bill Hall .15
32 Ruben Sierra .15
33 Zack Greinke .15
34 Sandy Alomar Jr. .15
35 Jason Giambi .75
36 Ben Sheets .25
37 Edgardo Alfonzo .15
38 Kenny Rogers .15
39 Coco Crisp .15
40 Randy Choate .50
41 Braden Looper .15
42 Adam Dunn .40
43 Adam Eaton .15
44 Luis Castillo .25
45 Casey Fossum .15
46 Mike Piazza 1.00
47 Juan Pierre .15
48 Doug Davis .15
49 Manny Ramirez .50
50 Travis Hafner .15
51 Jack Wilson .15
52 Mike Maroth .15
53 Ken Harvey .15
54 Brooks Kieschnick .15
55 Brad Fullmer .15
56 Octavio Dotel .15
57 Mike Matheny .15
58 Andruw Jones .50
59 Alfonso Soriano .75
60 Royce Clayton .15
61 Jon Garland .15
62 John Mabry .15
63 Rafael Palmeiro .25
64 Garrett Atkins .15
65 Brian Meadows .15
66 Tony Armas Jr. .15
67 Toby Hall .15
68 Carlos Baerga .15
69 Barry Larkin .25
70 Jody Gerut .15
71 Brent Mayne .15
72 Shigetoshi Hasegawa .15
73 Jose Cruz Jr. .15
74 Dan Wilson .15
75 Sidney Ponson .15
76 Jason Jennings .15
77 A.J. Burnett .15
78 Tony Batista .15
79 Kris Benson .15
80 Sean Burroughs .15

81 Eric Young .15
82 Casey Kotchman .40
83 Derrek Lee .25
84 Mariano Rivera .25
85 Julio Franco .15
86 Corey Patterson .15
87 Carlos Beltran .40
88 Trevor Hoffman .15
89 Danny Garcia .15
90 Marco Scutaro .15
91 Marquis Grissom .15
92 Aubrey Huff .15
93 Tony Womack .15
94 Placido Polanco .15
95 Bengie Molina .15
96 Roger Cedeno .15
97 Geoff Jenkins .25
98 Kip Wells .15
99 Derek Jeter 2.00
100 Omar Infante .15
101 Phil Nevin .15
102 Edgar Renteria .15
103 B.J. Surhoff .15
104 David DeJesus .15
105 Raul Ibanez .15
106 Hank Blalock .40
107 Shawn Estes .15
108 Wily Mo Pena .15
109 Shawn Green .25
110 David Wright .50
111 Kenny Lofton .15
112 Matt Clement .15
113 Cesar Izturis .15
114 John Lackey .15
115 Torii Hunter .40
116 Charles Johnson .15
117 Ray Durham .15
118 Luke Hudson .15
119 Jeremy Bonderman .15
120 Sean Casey .15
121 Johnny Damon .25
122 Eric Milton .15
123 Shea Hillenbrand .15
124 Jim Edmonds .25
125 Jim Edmonds .25
126 Javier Vazquez .15
127 Jon Adkins .15
128 Mike Lowell .15
129 Khalil Greene .50
130 Quinton McCracken .15
131 Edgar Martinez .15
132 Matt Lawton .15
133 Jeff Weaver .15
134 Marlon Byrd .15
135 John Smoltz .25
136 Grady Sizemore .25
137 Brian Roberts .15
138 Dee Brown .15
139 Joel Pineiro .15
140 David Dellucci .15
141 Bobby Higginson .15
142 Ryan Madson .15
143 Scott Hatteberg .15
144 Gregg Zaun .15
145 Brian Jordan .15
146 Jason Isringhausen .15
147 Vinnie Chulk .15
148 Al Leiter .15
149 Pedro Martinez .15
150 Carlos Guillen .15
151 Randy Wolf .15
152 Vernon Wells .25
153 Barry Zito .40
154 Pedro Feliz .15
155 Omar Vizquel .15
156 Chone Figgins .15
157 David Ortiz .40
158 Sun-Woo Kim RC 1.00
159 Adam Kennedy .15
160 Carlos Lee .15
161 Rick Ankiel .15
162 Roy Oswalt .25
163 Armando Benitez .15
164 Erubiel Durazo .15
165 Adam Hyzdu .15
166 Esteban Yan .15
167 Victor Santos .15
168 Kevin Millwood .15
169 Andy Pettitte .60
170 Mike Cameron .15
171 Scott Rolen .75
172 Trot Nixon .15
173 Eric Munson .15
174 Roy Halladay .25
175 Juan Encarnacion .15
176 Eric Chavez .25
177 Terrmel Sledge .15
178 Jason Schmidt .25
179 Endy Chavez .15
180 Carlos Zambrano .15
181 Carlos Delgado .50
182 Dewon Brazelton .15
183 J.D. Drew .15
184 Orlando Cabrera .15
185 Craig Wilson .15
186 Chin-Hui Tsao .15

187 Jolbert Cabrera .15
188 Rod Barajas .15
189 Craig Monroe .15
190 Dave Berg .15
191 Carlos Silva .15
192 Eric Gagne .25
193 Marcus Giles .15
194 Nick Johnson .15
195 Kelvim Escobar .15
196 Wade Miller .15
197 David Bell .15
198 Rondell White .15
199 Brian Giles .25
200 Jeromy Burnitz .15
201 Carl Pavano .15
202 Alex Rios .15
203 Ryan Freel .15
204 R.A. Dickey .15
205 Miguel Cairo .15
206 Kerry Wood .50
207 C.C. Sabathia .15
208 Jaime Cerda .15
209 Jerome Williams .15
210 Ryan Wagner .15
211 Javy Lopez .15
212 Tike Redman .15
213 Richie Sexson .40
214 Shannon Stewart .15
215 Ben Davis .15
216 Jeff Bagwell .50
217 David Wells .15
218 Justin Leone .15
219 Brad Radke .15
220 Ramon Santiago .15
221 Richard Hidalgo .15
222 Aaron Miles .15
223 Mark Loretta .15
224 Aaron Boone .15
225 Steve Trachsel .15
226 Geoff Blum .15
227 Shingo Takatsu .15
228 Kevin Youkilis .15
229 Laynce Nix .15
230 Daniel Cabrera .15
231 Kyle Lohse .15
232 Todd Pratt .15
233 Reed Johnson .15
234 Lance Berkman .25
235 Hideki Matsui 1.50
236 Randy Winn .15
237 Joe Randa .15
238 Bob Howry .15
239 Jason LaRue .15
240 Jose Valentin .15
241 Livan Hernandez .15
242 Jamie Moyer .15
243 Garret Anderson .25
244 Brad Ausmus .15
245 Russell Branyan .15
246 Paul Wilson .15
247 Tim Wakefield .15
248 Roberto Alomar .40
249 Kazuhisa Ishii .15
250 Tino Martinez .15
251 Tomokazu Ohka .15
252 Mark Redman .15
253 Paul Byrd .15
254 Greg Aquino .15
255 Adrian Beltre .25
256 Ricky Ledee .15
257 Josh Fogg .15
258 Derek Lowe .15
259 Lew Ford .15
260 Bobby Crosby .15
261 Jim Thome .75
262 Jaret Wright .15
263 Chin-Feng Chen .15
264 Troy Glaus .40
265 Jorge Sosa .15
266 Mike Lamb .15
267 Russ Ortiz .15
268 Reggie Sanders .15
269 Orlando Hudson .15
270 Rodrigo Lopez .15
271 Jose Vidro .15
272 Akinori Otsuka .15
273 Victor Martinez .15
274 Carl Crawford .25
275 Roberto Novoa .25
276 Brian Lawrence .15
277 Angel Berroa .15
278 Josh Beckett .50
279 Lyle Overbay .15
280 Dustin Hermanson .15
281 Jeff Conine .15
282 Mark Prior 1.00
283 Kevin Brown .25
284 Magglio Ordonez .25
285 Dontrelle Willis .25
286 Dallas McPherson .25
287 Rafael Furcal .25
288 Ty Wigginton .15
289 Moises Alou .25
290 A.J. Pierzynski .15
291 Todd Walker .15
292 Hideo Nomo .15

293 Larry Walker .25
294 Choo Freeman .15
295 Eduardo Perez .15
296 Miguel Tejada .40
297 Corey Koskie .15
298 Jermaine Dye .15
299 John Riedling .15
300 John Olerud .25
301 Tim Bittner, Jake Woods, Bobby Jenks 5.00
302 Josh Kroeger, Casey Daigle, Brandon Medders 5.00
303 Kelly Johnson, Charles Thomas, Dan Meyer 4.00
304 Eddy Rodriguez, Ryan Hannaman, John Maine 6.00
305 Anastacio Martinez, Jerome Gamble, Lenny Dinardo 8.00
306 Ronny Cedeno, Carlos Vasquez, Renyel Pinto 6.00
307 Arnie Munoz, Ryan Wing, Felix Diaz 6.00
308 William Bergolla, Ray Olmedo, Edwin Encarnacion 4.00
309 Mariano Gomez, Ivan Ochoa, Kazuhito Tadano 3.00
310 Toby Miller, Jeff Baker, Matt Holliday 6.00
311 Preston Larrison, Curtis Granderson, Ryan Raburn 8.00
312 Josh Wilson, Logan Kensing, Kevin Cave 5.00
313 Hector Gimenez, Willy Taveras, Taylor Buchholz 3.00
314 Ruben Gotay, Brian Bass, Andres Blanco 4.00
315 Joel Hanrahan, Willy Aybar, Yhency Brazoban 3.00
316 David Krynzel, Ben Hendrickson, Corey Hart 3.00
317 Colby Miller, Jason Kubel, J.D. Durban 5.00
318 Maicer Izturis, Chad Cordero, Brandon Watson 3.00
319 Victor Diaz, Aarom Baldiris, Wayne Lydon 8.00
320 Edwardo Sierra, Dioner Navarro, Sean Henn 3.00
321 Nick Swisher, Joe Blanton, Dan Johnson 6.00
322 Ryan Howard, Gavin Floyd, Keith Bucktrot 6.00
323 Ryan Doumit, Sean Burnett, Bobby Bradley 6.00
324 Justin Germano, Rusty Tucker, Freddy Guzman 6.00
325 David Aardsma, Justin Knoedler, Alfredo Simon 4.00
326 Jose Lopez, Rene Rivera, Cha Sueng Baek 4.00
327 Yadier Molina, Evan Rust, Adam Wainwright 4.00
328 Jorge Cantu, Scott Kazmir, B.J. Upton 5.00
329 Adrian Gonzalez, Ramon Nivar, Jason Bourgeois 6.00
330 Russ Adams, Dustin McGowan, Gustavo Chacin 8.00
331 Alfonso Soriano .75
332 Albert Pujols 1.50
333 David Ortiz .40
334 Manny Ramirez .50
335 Jason Bay .15
336 Bobby Crosby .15
337 Roger Clemens 1.50
338 Johan Santana .25
339 Jim Thome .75
340 Vladimir Guerrero .75
341 David Ortiz .40
342 Alex Rodriguez 1.50
343 Albert Pujols 1.50
344 Carlos Beltran .40
345 Johnny Damon .25
346 Scott Rolen .75
347 Larry Walker .25
348 Curt Schilling .40
349 Pedro Martinez .75
350 David Ortiz .40

Gray Backs

Cards 13-300: .75-1.5X
Cards 1-10; 301-350: .5-1.25X
Inserted 1:2

Club 3,000/500/300

		NM/M
Inserted 1:360		
1	Ernie Banks/500	30.00
2	Stan Musial/3,000	40.00
3	Steve Carlton/3,000	15.00
4	Greg Maddux/300	25.00
5	Dave Winfield/3,000	15.00
6	Rafael Palmeiro/500	15.00
7	Rickey Henderson/ 3,000	15.00
8	Roger Clemens/ 3,000	30.00
9	Don Sutton/300	10.00
10	George Brett/3,000	25.00
11	Reggie Jackson/500	20.00
12	Wade Boggs/3,000	20.00
13	Bob Gibson/3,000	20.00
14	Eddie Murray/3,000	20.00
15	Tom Seaver/3,000	20.00
16	Willie McCovey/500	20.00
17	Rod Carew/3,000	20.00
18	Fergie Jenkins/300	15.00
19	Phil Niekro/300	10.00
20	Frank Robinson/500	20.00

Cooperstown Tribute

		NM/M
Common Player:		4.00

Sequentially #'d to HOF.
Induction Year.
Gold: .5-1X
Inserted 1:24
Jersey: 1-2X
Inserted 1:200
There are 20 total jersey cards for Joe Morgan & Yogi Berra.
No Pricing for Morgan & Berra jersey card.
Patch: No Pricing
Production 10 Sets

1	Mike Schmidt/1995	5.00
2	Al Kaline/1980	4.00
3	Yogi Berra/1972	6.00
4	Robin Yount/1999	4.00
5	Joe Morgan/1990	4.00
6	Willie Stargell/1988	4.00
7	Harmon Killebrew/ 1984	5.00
8	Nolan Ryan/1999	10.00
9	Carlton Fisk/2000	5.00
10	Johnny Bench/1989	6.00

Diamond Tributes

		NM/M
Common Player:		2.00
Inserted 1:6		
1	Albert Pujols	5.00
2	Alex Rodriguez	5.00
3	Ken Griffey Jr.	3.50
4	Sammy Sosa	4.00
5	Chipper Jones	3.50
6	Johan Santana	2.00
7	Roger Clemens	5.00
8	Pedro Martinez	3.00
9	Jim Thome	3.00
10	Greg Maddux	3.50
11	Alfonso Soriano	3.00
12	Derek Jeter	6.00
13	Randy Johnson	3.00
14	Miguel Cabrera	2.00
15	Adrian Beltre	2.00
16	Ivan Rodriguez	2.00
17	Manny Ramirez	2.00
18	Mark Teixeira	2.00
19	Adam Dunn	2.00
20	Scott Rolen	3.00

21	Mike Piazza	3.50
22	J.D. Drew	2.00
23	Hideki Matsui	5.00
24	Nomar Garciaparra	5.00
25	Kazuo Matsui	3.00

Diamond Tribute Jersey

		NM/M
Common Player:		6.00
Inserted 1:30		
Patch:		1-3X

Production 50 Sets

AB	Adrian Beltre/Bat	6.00
RC	Roger Clemens/Jsy	12.00
JD	J.D. Drew/Bat	6.00
NG	Nomar Garciaparra/ Bat	12.00
RJ	Randy Johnson/Jsy	8.00
CJ	Chipper Jones/Bat	10.00
GM	Greg Maddux/Jsy	10.00
PM	Pedro Martinez/Jsy	8.00
HM	Hideki Matsui/Bat	15.00
KM	Kazuo Matsui/Bat	8.00
MP	Mike Piazza/Bat	10.00
AP	Albert Pujols/Bat	15.00
MR	Manny Ramirez/Bat	8.00
JS	Johan Santana/Jsy	8.00
AS	Alfonso Soriano/Bat	8.00
SS	Sammy Sosa/Bat	10.00
MT	Mark Teixeira/Bat	6.00
JT	Jim Thome/Bat	8.00

Diamond Tributes Dual Patch

		NM/M
Common Player:		75.00

Production 50 Sets

APSR	Albert Pujols, Scott Rolen	100.00
ASMT	Alfonso Soriano, Mark Teixeira	75.00
CJJD	Chipper Jones, J.D. Drew	80.00
HMKM	Hideki Matsui, Kazuo Matsui	125.00
JTAB	Jim Thome, Adrian Beltre	75.00
MPIR	Mike Piazza, Ivan Rodriguez	75.00
PMMR	Pedro Martinez, Manny Ramirez	120.00
RCJS	Roger Clemens, Johan Santana	100.00
RJGM	Randy Johnson, Greg Maddux	75.00
SSMC	Miguel Cabrera, Sammy Sosa	80.00

Standouts

		NM/M
Common Player:		3.50
Inserted 1:18		
1	Albert Pujols	6.00
2	Ichiro Suzuki	5.00
3	Derek Jeter	8.00
4	Randy Johnson	3.50
5	Greg Maddux	4.00
6	Hideki Matsui	6.00
7	Mike Piazza	4.00
8	Vladimir Guerrero	3.50
9	Sammy Sosa	5.00
10	Jim Thome	3.50
11	Chipper Jones	4.00
12	Alex Rodriguez	6.00
13	Roger Clemens	6.00
14	Nomar Garciaparra	6.00
15	Lance Berkman	3.50

Standouts Jersey

	NM/M
Common Player:	10.00

Lance Berkman

		NM/M
Inserted 1:18		
Patch:		1-3X

Production 50 Sets

LB	Lance Berkman	6.00
RC	Roger Clemens	18.00
VG	Vladimir Guerrero	10.00
RJ	Randy Johnson	10.00
CJ	Chipper Jones	12.00
GM	Greg Maddux	12.00
HM	Hideki Matsui	20.00
MP	Mike Piazza	12.00
AP	Albert Pujols	18.00
SS	Sammy Sosa	15.00
JT	Jim Thome	10.00

2006 Fleer

DEREK Lee

	NM/M
Complete Set (400):	40.00
Complete Factory Set (430):	50.00

#'s 401-430 available in Factory Set

Common Player:	.15
Pack (10):	1.75
Box (36):	55.00
1	Adam Kennedy	.15
2	Bartolo Colon	.25
3	Bengie Molina	.15
4	Chone Figgins	.15
5	Dallas McPherson	.15
6	Darin Erstad	.15
7	Francisco Rodriguez	.15
8	Garret Anderson	.25
9	Jarrod Washburn	.15
10	John Lackey	.15
11	Orlando Cabrera	.15
12	Ryan Theriot (RC)	.50
13	Steve Finley	.15
14	Vladimir Guerrero	.75
15	Adam Everett	.15
16	Andy Pettitte	.40
17	Charlton Jimerson	.15
18	Brad Lidge	.15
19	Chris Burke	.15
20	Craig Biggio	.25
21	Jason Lane	.15
22	Jeff Bagwell	.40
23	Lance Berkman	.50
24	Morgan Ensberg	.15
25	Roger Clemens	2.00
26	Roy Oswalt	.25
27	Willy Taveras	.15
28	Barry Zito	.25
29	Bobby Crosby	.15
30	Bobby Kielty	.15
31	Dan Johnson	.15
32	Danny Haren	.15
33	Eric Chavez	.25
34	Huston Street	.15
35	Jason Kendall	.15
36	Jay Payton	.15

37	Joe Blanton	.15
38	Mark Kotsay	.15
39	Nick Swisher	.15
40	Rich Harden	.25
41	Ron Flores RC	.15
42	Alex Rios	.15
43	John-Ford Griffin (RC)	.15
44	David Bush	.15
45	Eric Hinske	.15
46	Frank Catalanotto	.15
47	Gustavo Chacin	.15
48	Josh Towers	.15
49	Miguel Batista	.15
50	Orlando Hudson	.15
51	Roy Halladay	.25
52	Shea Hillenbrand	.15
53	Shaun Marcum (RC)	.15
54	Vernon Wells	.25
55	Adam LaRoche	.15
56	Andruw Jones	.50
57	Chipper Jones	.75
58	Anthony Lerew (RC)	.15
59	Jeff Francoeur	.25
60	John Smoltz	.40
61	Johnny Estrada	.15
62	Julio Franco	.15
63	Joey Devine RC	1.00
64	Marcus Giles	.15
65	Mike Hampton	.15
66	Rafael Furcal	.25
67	Chuck James (RC)	.15
68	Tim Hudson	.25
69	Ben Sheets	.25
70	Bill Hall	.15
71	Brady Clark	.15
72	Carlos Lee	.25
73	Chris Capuano	.15
74	Nelson Cruz (RC)	.15
75	Derrick Turnbow	.15
76	Doug Davis	.15
77	Geoff Jenkins	.15
78	J.J. Hardy	.15
79	Lyle Overbay	.15
80	Prince Fielder (RC)	1.00
81	Rickie Weeks	.25
82	Albert Pujols	2.00
83	Chris Carpenter	.25
84	David Eckstein	.15
85	Jason Isringhausen	.15
86	Tyler Johnson (RC)	.15
87	Adam Wainwright (RC)	.15
88	Jim Edmonds	.25
89	Chris Duncan	.15
90	Mark Grudzielanek	.15
91	Mark Mulder	.25
92	Matt Morris	.15
93	Reggie Sanders	.15
94	Scott Rolen	.50
95	Yadier Molina	.15
96	Aramis Ramirez	.40
97	Carlos Zambrano	.25
98	Corey Patterson	.15
99	Derrek Lee	.50
100	Glendon Rusch	.15
101	Greg Maddux	1.00
102	Jeromy Burnitz	.15
103	Kerry Wood	.25
104	Mark Prior	.50
105	Michael Barrett	.15
106	Geovany Soto (RC)	.15
107	Nomar Garciaparra	.50
108	Ryan Dempster	.15
109	Todd Walker	.15
110	Alex Gonzalez	.15
111	Aubrey Huff	.15
112	Victor Diaz	.15
113	Carl Crawford	.25
114	Danys Baez	.15
115	Joey Gathright	.15
116	Jonny Gomes	.25
117	Jorge Cantu	.15
118	Julio Lugo	.15
119	Rocco Baldelli	.15
120	Scott Kazmir	.15
121	Toby Hall	.15
122	Tim Corcoran RC	.40
123	Alex Cintron	.15
124	Brandon Webb	.15
125	Chad Tracy	.15
126	Dustin Nippert (RC)	.15
127	Claudio Vargas	.15
128	Craig Counsell	.15
129	Javier Vazquez	.15
130	Jose Valverde	.15
131	Luis Gonzalez	.15
132	Royce Clayton	.15
133	Russ Ortiz	.15
134	Shawn Green	.15
135	Tony Clark	.15
136	Troy Glaus	.25
137	Brad Penny	.15
138	Cesar Izturis	.15
139	Derek Lowe	.15
140	Eric Gagne	.15

141	Hee Seop Choi	.15
142	J.D. Drew	.15
143	Jason Phillips	.15
144	Jayson Werth	.15
145	Jeff Kent	.25
146	Jeff Weaver	.15
147	Milton Bradley	.15
148	Odalis Perez	.15
149	Hong-Chih Kuo	.15
150	Brian Myrow RC	.25
151	Armando Benitez	.15
152	Edgardo Alfonzo	.15
153	J.T. Snow	.15
154	Jason Schmidt	.15
155	Lance Niekro	.15
156	Doug Clark	.15
157	Daniel Ortmeier (RC)	.15
158	Moises Alou	.25
159	Noah Lowry	.15
160	Omar Vizquel	.25
161	Pedro Feliz	.15
162	Randy Winn	.15
163	Jeremy Accardo RC	.15
164	Aaron Boone	.15
165	Ryan Garko (RC)	.15
166	C.C. Sabathia	.15
167	Casey Blake	.15
168	Cliff Lee	.15
169	Coco Crisp	.15
170	Grady Sizemore	.40
171	Jake Westbrook	.15
172	Jhonny Peralta	.15
173	Kevin Millwood	.15
174	Scott Elarton	.15
175	Travis Hafner	.50
176	Victor Martinez	.25
177	Adrian Beltre	.15
178	Eddie Guardado	.15
179	Felix Hernandez	.40
180	Gil Meche	.15
181	Ichiro Suzuki	1.50
182	Jamie Moyer	.15
183	Jeremy Reed	.15
184	Jaime Bubela (RC)	.15
185	Raul Ibanez	.15
186	Richie Sexson	.40
187	Ryan Franklin	.15
188	Jeff Harris RC	.25
189	A.J. Burnett	.15
190	Josh Wilson (RC)	.15
191	Josh Johnson (RC)	.15
192	Carlos Delgado	.40
193	Dontrelle Willis	.25
194	Bernie Castro	.15
195	Josh Beckett	.25
196	Juan Encarnacion	.15
197	Juan Pierre	.15
198	Robert Andino RC	.25
199	Miguel Cabrera	.75
200	Ryan Jorgensen RC	.25
201	Paul LoDuca	.15
202	Todd Jones	.15
203	Braden Looper	.15
204	Carlos Beltran	.50
205	Cliff Floyd	.15
206	David Wright	1.00
207	Doug Mientkiewicz	.15
208	Jae Weong Seo	.15
209	Jose Reyes	.50
210	Anderson Hernandez (RC)	.15
211	Miguel Cairo	.15
212	Mike Cameron	.15
213	Mike Piazza	.50
214	Pedro Martinez	.75
215	Tom Glavine	.25
216	Tim Hamulack	.15
217	Brad Wilkerson	.15
218	Darrell Rasner (RC)	.15
219	Chad Cordero	.15
220	Cristian Guzman	.15
221	Jason Bergmann RC	.50
222	John Patterson	.15
223	Jose Guillen	.15
224	Jose Vidro	.15
225	Livan Hernandez	.15
226	Nick Johnson	.15
227	Preston Wilson	.15
228	Ryan Zimmerman (RC)	.25
229	Vinny Castilla	.15
230	B.J. Ryan	.15
231	B.J. Surhoff	.15
232	Brian Roberts	.25
233	Walter Young	.15
234	Daniel Cabrera	.15
235	Erik Bedard	.15
236	Javy Lopez	.15
237	Jay Gibbons	.15
238	Luis Matos	.15
239	Melvin Mora	.25
240	Miguel Tejada	.50
241	Rafael Palmeiro	.25
242	Alejandro Freire RC	.15
243	Sammy Sosa	.75

244	Adam Eaton	.15
245	Brian Giles	.25
246	Brian Lawrence	.15
247	Dave Roberts	.15
248	Jake Peavy	.25
249	Khalil Greene	.15
250	Mark Loretta	.15
251	Ramon Hernandez	.15
252	Ryan Klesko	.15
253	Trevor Hoffman	.15
254	Woody Williams	.15
255	Craig Breslow RC	.25
256	Billy Wagner	.25
257	Bobby Abreu	.25
258	Brett Myers	.15
259	Chase Utley	.40
260	David Bell	.15
261	Jim Thome	.50
262	Jimmy Rollins	.40
263	Jon Lieber	.15
264	Danny Sandoval RC	.25
265	Mike Lieberthal	.15
266	Pat Burrell	.25
267	Randy Wolf	.15
268	Ryan Howard	1.00
269	J.J. Furmaniak (RC)	.15
270	Ronny Paulino (RC)	.15
271	Craig Wilson	.15
272	Bryan Bullington	.15
273	Jack Wilson	.15
274	Jason Bay	.25
275	Matt Capps (RC)	.15
276	Oliver Perez	.15
277	Robert Mackowiak	.15
278	Tom Gorzelanny (RC)	.15
279	Zachary Duke	.15
280	Alfonso Soriano	.50
281	Chris Young	.15
282	David Dellucci	.15
283	Francisco Cordero	.15
284	Jason Botts (RC)	.15
285	Hank Blalock	.25
286	Josh Rupe	.15
287	Kevin Mench	.15
288	Laynce Nix	.15
289	Mark Teixeira	.50
290	Michael Young	.25
291	Richard Hidalgo	.15
292	Scott Feldman RC	.25
293	Bill Mueller	.15
294	Hanley Ramirez (RC)	.40
295	Curt Schilling	.75
296	David Ortiz	.75
297	Alejandro Machado	.15
298	Edgar Renteria	.25
299	Jason Varitek	.40
300	Johnny Damon	.75
301	Keith Foulke	.15
302	Manny Ramirez	.75
303	Matt Clement	.15
304	Craig Hansen RC	2.00
305	Tim Wakefield	.15
306	Trot Nixon	.15
307	Aaron Harang	.15
308	Adam Dunn	.50
309	Austin Kearns	.25
310	Brandon Claussen	.15
311	Chris Booker	.15
312	Edwin Encarnacion	.15
313	Chris Denorfia (RC)	.15
314	Felipe Lopez	.15
315	Miguel Perez (RC)	.15
316	Ken Griffey Jr.	1.50
317	Ryan Freel	.15
318	Sean Casey	.15
319	Wily Mo Pena	.15
320	Mike Esposito	.15
321	Aaron Miles	.15
322	Brad Hawpe	.15
323	Brian Fuentes	.15
324	Clint Barmes	.15
325	Cory Sullivan	.15
326	Garrett Atkins	.15
327	J.D. Closser	.15
328	Jeff Francis	.15
329	Luis Gonzalez	.15
330	Matt Holliday	.25
331	Todd Helton	.50
332	Angel Berroa	.15
333	David DeJesus	.15
334	Emil Brown	.15
335	Jeremy Affeldt	.15
336	Chris Demaria RC	.50
337	Mark Teahen	.15
338	Matt Stairs	.15
339	Steve Stemle RC	.25
340	Mike Sweeney	.15
341	Runelvys Hernandez	.15
342	Jonah Bayliss RC	.25
343	Zack Greinke	.15
344	Brandon Inge	.15
345	Carlos Guillen	.15
346	Carlos Pena	.15
347	Chris Shelton	.25

348	Craig Monroe	.15
349	Dmitri Young	.15
350	Ivan Rodriguez	.40
351	Jeremy Bonderman	.15
352	Magglio Ordonez	.25
353	Mark Woodyard (RC)	.15
354	Omar Infante	.15
355	Placido Polanco	.15
356	Rondell White	.15
357	Brad Radke	.15
358	Carlos Silva	.15
359	Jacque Jones	.15
360	Joe Mauer	.25
361	Chris Heintz RC	.25
362	Joe Nathan	.15
363	Johan Santana	.50
364	Justin Morneau	.15
365	Francisco Liriano (RC)	.50
366	Travis Bowyer	.15
367	Michael Cuddyer	.15
368	Scott Baker	.15
369	Shannon Stewart	.15
370	Torii Hunter	.25
371	A.J. Pierzynski	.15
372	Aaron Rowand	.15
373	Carl Everett	.15
374	Dustin Hermanson	.15
375	Frank Thomas	.40
376	Freddy Garcia	.15
377	Jermaine Dye	.15
378	Joe Crede	.15
379	Jon Garland	.15
380	Jose Contreras	.15
381	Juan Uribe	.15
382	Mark Buehrle	.25
383	Orlando Hernandez	.15
384	Paul Konerko	.25
385	Scott Podsednik	.15
386	Tadahito Iguchi	.25
387	Alex Rodriguez	2.00
388	Bernie Williams	.25
389	Chien-Ming Wang	.40
390	Derek Jeter	2.00
391	Gary Sheffield	.40
392	Hideki Matsui	1.00
393	Jason Giambi	.40
394	Jorge Posada	.25
395	Michael Vento	.15
396	Mariano Rivera	.25
397	Mike Mussina	.25
398	Randy Johnson	.75
399	Robinson Cano	.25
400	Tino Martinez	.25
401	Alay Soler RC	.40
402	Boof Bonser (RC)	.40
403	Cole Hamels (RC)	1.50
404	Ian Kinsler (RC)	.40
405	Jason Kubel (RC)	.40
406	Joel Zumaya (RC)	1.00
407	Jonathan Papelbon (RC)	2.50
408	Jered Weaver (RC)	2.50
409	Kendry Morales (RC)	1.00
410	Lastings Milledge (RC)	1.00
411	Matthew Kemp (RC)	1.00
412	Taylor Buchholz (RC)	.40
413	Andre Ethier (RC)	2.50
414	Dan Uggla (RC)	1.00
415	Jeremy Sowers (RC)	.40
416	Chad Billingsley (RC)	.75
417	Josh Barfield (RC)	.40
418	Matt Cain (RC)	.75
419	Fausto Carmona (RC)	.40
420	Josh Willingham (RC)	.40
421	Jeremy Hermida (RC)	.75
422	Conor Jackson (RC)	.75
423	Dave Gassner (RC)	.40
424	Brian Bannister (RC)	.40
425	Fernando Nieve (RC)	.40
426	Justin Verlander (RC)	2.50
427	Scott Olsen (RC)	.40
428	Takashi Saito RC	.50
429	Willie Eyre (RC)	.40
430	Travis Ishikawa (RC)	.40

Glossy

Glossy:	2-3X

Inserted 1:12

Glossy Gold

Glossy Gold:	4-8X

Inserted 1:144

Autographics

		NM/M

Inserted 1:432

AN	Garret Anderson	15.00
GA	Garrett Atkins	10.00
JB	Joe Blanton	15.00
EC	Eric Chavez	20.00
KG	Ken Griffey Jr.	85.00
TI	Tadahito Iguchi	50.00
CS	Chris Shelton	30.00
NS	Nick Swisher	20.00
KY	Kevin Youkilis	15.00

Award Winners

		NM/M
Complete Set (6):		5.00
Common Player:		.50
1	Albert Pujols	3.00
2	Alex Rodriguez	3.00
3	Chris Carpenter	.50
4	Bartolo Colon	.50
5	Ryan Howard	1.00
6	Huston Street	.50

Fabrics

		NM/M

Inserted 1:36

BA	Bobby Abreu	6.00
CB	Carlos Beltran	8.00
MC	Miguel Cabrera	8.00
EC	Eric Chavez	4.00
RC	Roger Clemens	15.00
JD	Johnny Damon	8.00
JE	Jim Edmonds	6.00
EG	Eric Gagne	4.00
LG	Luis Gonzalez	4.00
GR	Khalil Greene	4.00
KG	Ken Griffey Jr.	15.00
VG	Vladimir Guerrero	8.00
RH	Roy Halladay	4.00
TH	Todd Helton	6.00
DJ	Derek Jeter	20.00
RJ	Randy Johnson	8.00
AJ	Andruw Jones	6.00
CJ	Chipper Jones	8.00
DL	Derrek Lee	8.00
GM	Greg Maddux	15.00
PM	Pedro Martinez	8.00
JM	Joe Mauer	4.00
DO	David Ortiz	8.00
JP	Jake Peavy	6.00
MP	Mark Prior	6.00
AP	Albert Pujols	20.00
AR	Aramis Ramirez	6.00
MR	Manny Ramirez	8.00
IR	Ivan Rodriguez	8.00
SR	Scott Rolen	8.00
JS	Johan Santana	8.00
CS	Curt Schilling	8.00
GS	Gary Sheffield/SP	10.00
SM	John Smoltz	8.00
AS	Alfonso Soriano	6.00
MT	Mark Teixeira	6.00
TE	Miguel Tejada	6.00
JT	Jim Thome	6.00
RW	Rickie Weeks	4.00
DW	Dontrelle Willis/SP	8.00
WR	David Wright	12.00
MY	Michael Young	4.00

Lumber Company

		NM/M
1	Adam Dunn	1.00
2	Albert Pujols	3.00
3	Alex Rodriguez	3.00
4	Alfonso Soriano	.75
5	Andruw Jones	.75
6	Aramis Ramirez	.75
7	Bobby Abreu	.75
8	Carlos Delgado	.75
9	Carlos Lee	.50
10	David Ortiz	1.00
11	David Wright	1.50

12	Derek Lee	1.00
13	Eric Chavez	.50
14	Gary Sheffield	.75
15	Jeff Kent	.50
16	Ken Griffey Jr.	2.00
17	Manny Ramirez	1.00
18	Mark Teixeira	1.00
19	Miguel Cabrera	1.00
20	Miguel Tejada	.75
21	Paul Konerko	.75
22	Richie Sexson	.50
23	Todd Helton	.75
24	Troy Glaus	.50
25	Vladimir Guerrero	1.00

Smoke 'n Heat

NM/M

1	Carlos Zambrano	.50
2	Chris Carpenter	.50
3	Curt Schilling	1.00
4	Dontrelle Willis	.50
5	Felix Hernandez	1.00
6	Jake Peavy	.75
7	Johan Santana	1.00
8	John Smoltz	.75
9	Mark Prior	.75
10	Pedro Martinez	1.00
11	Randy Johnson	1.00
12	Roger Clemens	3.00
13	Roy Halladay	.50
14	Roy Oswalt	.50
15	Scott Kazmir	.50

Smooth Leather

NM/M

Complete Set (14):	10.00
Common Player:	.50
1	Alex Rodriguez	3.00
2	Andruw Jones	1.00
3	Derek Jeter	3.00
4	Derek Lee	1.00
5	Eric Chavez	.50
6	Greg Maddux	2.00
7	Ichiro Suzuki	2.00
8	Ivan Rodriguez	.75
9	Jim Edmonds	.75
10	Mike Mussina	.75
11	Omar Vizquel	.50
12	Scott Rolen	1.00
13	Todd Helton	.75
14	Torii Hunter	.50

Stars of Tomorrow

NM/M

Complete Set (10):	5.00
Common Player:	.50
Inserted 1:10	
1	David Wright	1.50
2	Ryan Howard	1.00
3	Felix Hernandez	1.00
4	Jeff Francoeur	.50
5	Joe Mauer	.50
6	Mark Prior	.75
7	Mark Teixeira	1.00
8	Miguel Cabrera	1.00
9	Prince Fielder (RC)	1.00
10	Rickie Weeks	.50

Team Fleer

NM/M

Inserted 1:Case

1	Albert Pujols	40.00
2	Alex Rodriguez	30.00
3	Alfonso Soriano	10.00
4	Andruw Jones	10.00
5	Bobby Abreu	10.00
6	David Ortiz	15.00
7	David Wright	25.00
8	Eric Gagne	8.00
9	Ichiro Suzuki	30.00
10	Jason Varitek	15.00
11	Jeff Kent	8.00
12	Johan Santana	15.00
13	Jose Reyes	10.00
14	Manny Ramirez	15.00
15	Mariano Rivera	10.00
16	Miguel Cabrera	15.00
17	Miguel Tejada	10.00
18	Mike Piazza	15.00
19	Roger Clemens	30.00
20	Torii Hunter	8.00

Team Leaders

NM/M

Complete Set (30):	15.00
Common Player:	.50
1	Troy Glaus, Brandon Webb	.50
2	John Smoltz, Andruw Jones	.50
3	Miguel Tejada, Erik Bedard	.50
4	David Ortiz, Curt Schilling	.75
5	Derek Lee, Mark Prior	.75
6	Mark Buehrle, Paul Konerko	.50
7	Ken Griffey Jr., Aaron Harang	1.50
8	Cliff Lee, Travis Hafner	.50
9	Todd Helton, Jeff Francis	.50
10	Jeremy Bonderman, Ivan Rodriguez	.50
11	Miguel Cabrera, Dontrelle Willis	.75
12	Lance Berkman, Roger Clemens	2.00
13	Mike Sweeney, Zack Greinke	.50
14	Derek Lowe, Jeff Kent	.50
15	Carlos Lee, Ben Sheets	.50
16	Johan Santana, Torii Hunter	.50
17	Pedro Martinez, David Wright	1.00
18	Derek Jeter, Randy Johnson	2.00
19	Barry Zito, Eric Chavez	.50
20	Bobby Abreu, Brett Myers	.50
21	Jason Bay, Zachary Duke	.50
22	Jake Peavy, Brian Giles	.50
23	Moises Alou, Jason Schmidt	.50
24	Felix Hernandez, Ichiro Suzuki	1.00
25	Chris Carpenter, Albert Pujols	2.00
26	Scott Kazmir, Carl Crawford	.50
27	Mark Teixeira, Kenny Rogers	.50
28	Vernon Wells, Roy Halladay	.50
29	Livan Hernandez, Jose Guillen	.50
30	Bartolo Colon, Vladimir Guerrero	.50

Top 40

Common Player:	.50
Inserted 2:1 Fat Pack	
1	Ken Griffey Jr.	3.00
2	Derek Jeter	4.00
3	Albert Pujols	4.00
4	Alex Rodriguez	4.00
5	Vladimir Guerrero	1.50
6	Roger Clemens	3.00
7	Derek Lee	1.00
8	David Ortiz	1.50
9	Miguel Cabrera	1.50
10	Bobby Abreu	.50
11	Mark Teixeira	1.00
12	Johan Santana	1.00
13	Hideki Matsui	3.00
14	Ichiro Suzuki	3.00
15	Andruw Jones	1.00
16	Eric Chavez	.50
17	Roy Oswalt	.75
18	Curt Schilling	1.50
19	Randy Johnson	1.50
20	Ivan Rodriguez	1.00
21	Chipper Jones	1.50
22	Mark Prior	.50
23	Jason Bay	.75
24	Pedro Martinez	1.50
25	David Wright	2.00
26	Carlos Beltran	1.00
27	Jim Edmonds	.50
28	Chris Carpenter	.75
29	Roy Halladay	.75
30	Jake Peavy	.75
31	Paul Konerko	.75
32	Travis Hafner	.75
33	Barry Zito	.50
34	Miguel Tejada	.75
35	Josh Beckett	1.00
36	Todd Helton	1.00
37	Dontrelle Willis	.50
38	Manny Ramirez	1.50
39	Mariano Rivera	1.00
40	Jeff Kent	.75

2006 Fleer Greats of the Game

NM/M

Complete Set (100):	35.00
Common Player:	.40
Pack (5):	8.00
Box (15):	100.00
1	Al Kaline	1.50
2	Alan Trammell	.50
3	Andre Dawson	.75
4	Barry Larkin	.75
5	Bill Buckner	.40
6	Bill Freehan	.40
7	Bill Madlock	.40
8	Bill Mazeroski	.40
9	Billy Williams	.50
10	Bo Jackson	1.00
11	Bob Feller	1.00
12	Bob Gibson	.50
13	Bobby Doerr	.50
14	Bobby Murcer	.50
15	Boog Powell	.50
16	Brooks Robinson	1.50
17	Bruce Sutter	.40
18	Bucky Dent	.40
19	Cal Ripken Jr.	4.00
20	Rico Petrocelli	.40
21	Carlton Fisk	.75
22	Chris Chambliss	.40
23	Dave Concepcion	.40
24	Dave Parker	.50
25	Dave Winfield	1.00
26	David Cone	.50
27	Denny McLain	.50
28	Don Mattingly	3.00
29	Don Newcombe	.50
30	Don Sutton	.50
31	Dusty Baker	.50
32	Dwight Evans	.50
33	Eric Davis	.50
34	Ernie Banks	2.00
35	Fergie Jenkins	.75
36	Frank Robinson	1.00
37	Fred Lynn	.40
38	Fred McGriff	.50
39	Andre Thornton	.40
40	Garry Maddox	.40
41	Gary Matthews	.40
42	Gaylord Perry	.40
43	George Foster	.40
44	George Kell	.40
45	Graig Nettles	.40
46	Greg Luzinski	.40
47	Harmon Killebrew	1.50
48	Jack Clark	.50
49	Jack Morris	.50
50	Jim Palmer	.75
51	Jim Rice	.75
52	Joe Morgan	.75
53	John Kruk	.50
54	Johnny Bench	2.00
55	Jose Canseco	.75
56	Kirby Puckett	2.00
57	Kirk Gibson	.50
58	Lee Mazzilli	.40
59	Lou Brock	.75
60	Lou Piniella	.50
61	Luis Aparicio	.50
62	Luis Tiant	.50
63	Mark Fidrych	.50
64	Mark Grace	.75
65	Maury Wills	.50
66	Mike Schmidt	2.00
67	Nolan Ryan	3.00
68	Ozzie Smith	1.00
69	Paul Molitor	1.00
70	Paul O'Neill	.50
71	Phil Niekro	.50
72	Ralph Kiner	.50
73	Randy Hundley	.40
74	Red Schoendienst	.50
75	Reggie Jackson	1.00
76	Robin Yount	1.00
77	Rod Carew	.75
78	Rollie Fingers	.50
79	Ron Cey	.50
80	Ron Guidry	.50
81	Ron Santo	.75
82	Rusty Staub	.40
83	Ryne Sandberg	2.00
84	Sparky Lyle	.40
85	Stan Musial	2.00
86	Steve Carlton	.75
87	Steve Garvey	.50
88	Steve Sax	.40
89	Tommy Herr	.40
90	Tim McCarver	.50
91	Tim Raines	.50
92	Tom Seaver	1.00
93	Tony Gwynn	1.00
94	Tony Perez	.75
95	Wade Boggs	.75
96	Whitey Ford	1.00
97	Will Clark	.75
98	Willie Horton	.40
99	Willie McCovey	1.00
100	Yogi Berra	1.50

Copper

| Copper: | 2-4X |
| Production 299 Sets | |

Pewter

Pewter: 2X
Inserted 1:15

AUTOGRAPHics

NM/M

Inserted 1:180
Cards are not serial numbered.

LA	Luis Aparicio/25	20.00
LB	Lou Brock/25	25.00
RC	Rod Carew/25	30.00
SC	Steve Carlton/50	25.00
WC	Will Clark/25	40.00
AD	Andre Dawson	25.00
BF	Bob Feller/50	30.00
GF	George Foster/50	20.00
SG	Steve Garvey/50	25.00
BG	Bob Gibson/25	40.00
KG	Kirk Gibson/25	25.00
MG	Mark Grace/50	30.00
RG	Ron Guidry/99	50.00
BJ	Bo Jackson/25	75.00
FJ	Fergie Jenkins/25	30.00
AK	Al Kaline/99	35.00
HK	Harmon Killebrew/25	50.00
BL	Barry Larkin/50	40.00
BI	Bill Mazeroski/25	35.00
FM	Fred McGriff/99	30.00
PM	Paul Molitor/50	25.00
JM	Joe Morgan/25	35.00
BM	Bobby Murcer/99	30.00
DN	Don Newcombe/99	15.00
PN	Phil Niekro/50	20.00
JP	Jim Palmer/99	20.00
DP	Dave Parker/99	20.00
TP	Tony Perez/99	30.00
JR	Jim Rice/99	20.00
BR	Brooks Robinson/50	40.00
RS	Ron Santo/99	30.00
OS	Ozzie Smith/25	60.00
BS	Bruce Sutter/50	15.00
SU	Don Sutton/50	20.00
BW	Billy Williams/50	25.00
MW	Maury Wills/99	20.00

Autographs

NM/M

Common Autograph: 10.00

1	Al Kaline	25.00
2	Alan Trammell	15.00
3	Andre Dawson	20.00
4	Barry Larkin	35.00
5	Bill Buckner	12.00
6	Bill Freehan	12.00
7	Bill Madlock	15.00
8	Bill Mazeroski	35.00
9	Billy Williams	20.00
10	Bo Jackson	60.00
11	Bob Feller	25.00
12	Bob Gibson	40.00
13	Bobby Doerr	20.00
14	Bobby Murcer	15.00
15	Boog Powell	15.00
16	Brooks Robinson	25.00
17	Bruce Sutter	15.00
18	Bucky Dent	10.00
19	Cal Ripken Jr./SP	140.00
20	Rico Petrocelli	10.00
21	Carlton Fisk	30.00
22	Chris Chambliss	15.00
23	Dave Concepcion	15.00
24	Dave Parker	20.00
25	Dave Winfield	30.00
26	David Cone	15.00
27	Denny McLain	20.00
28	Don Mattingly	60.00
29	Don Newcombe	20.00
30	Don Sutton	15.00
31	Dusty Baker	25.00
32	Dwight Evans	20.00
33	Eric Davis	20.00
34	Ernie Banks	75.00
35	Fergie Jenkins	20.00
36	Frank Robinson	30.00
37	Fred Lynn	15.00
38	Fred McGriff	30.00
39	Andre Thornton	10.00
40	Garry Maddox	20.00
41	Gary Matthews	10.00
42	Gaylord Perry	15.00
43	George Foster	15.00
44	George Kell	15.00
45	Graig Nettles	20.00
46	Greg Luzinski	15.00
47	Harmon Killebrew	35.00
48	Jack Clark/SP/50	20.00
49	Jack Morris	15.00
50	Jim Palmer	20.00
51	Jim Rice	20.00
52	Joe Morgan	25.00
53	John Kruk	20.00
54	Johnny Bench	60.00
55	Kirby Puckett	100.00
56		

57	Kirk Gibson	20.00
58	Lee Mazzilli	15.00
59	Lou Brock	30.00
60	Lou Piniella	15.00
61	Luis Aparicio	15.00
62	Luis Tiant	15.00
63	Mark Fidrych	25.00
64	Mark Grace	25.00
65	Maury Wills	20.00
66	Mike Schmidt	50.00
67	Nolan Ryan/SP/50	100.00
68	Ozzie Smith	40.00
69	Paul Molitor	25.00
70	Paul O'Neill	25.00
71	Phil Niekro	20.00
72	Ralph Kiner	20.00
73	Randy Hundley	15.00
74	Red Schoendienst	25.00
75	Reggie Jackson	35.00
76	Robin Yount	50.00
77	Rod Carew	25.00
78	Rollie Fingers	20.00
79	Ron Cey	10.00
80	Ron Guidry/SP	50.00
81	Ron Santo	25.00
83	Ryne Sandberg/SP	50.00
84	Sparky Lyle	15.00
85	Stan Musial	65.00
86	Steve Carlton	25.00
87	Steve Garvey	25.00
88	Steve Sax	10.00
89	Tommy Herr	15.00
90	Tim McCarver	20.00
91	Tim Raines/SP	20.00
92	Tom Seaver	50.00
93	Tony Gwynn	40.00
94	Tony Perez	25.00
95	Wade Boggs	25.00
96	Whitey Ford	50.00
97	Will Clark SP	35.00
98	Willie Horton	15.00
99	Willie McCovey	35.00
100	Yogi Berra	60.00

Bat Barrel Autograph

No Pricing
Production 1-5

Cardinals Greats

NM/M

	Complete Set (10):	8.00
LB	Lou Brock	1.00
SC	Steve Carlton	.50
DD	Dizzy Dean	1.00
BG	Bob Gibson	1.00
TH	Tommy Herr	.25
RH	Rogers Hornsby	1.00
TM	Tim McCarver	.50
SM	Stan Musial	2.00
RS	Red Schoendienst	.50
OS	Ozzie Smith	1.00

Cardinals Greats Memorabilia Autograph

NM/M

Production 30 Sets

LB	Lou Brock	50.00
SC	Steve Carlton	35.00
BG	Bob Gibson	60.00
TH	Tommy Herr	20.00
TM	Tim McCarver	30.00
SM	Stan Musial	75.00
RS	Red Schoendienst	30.00
OS	Ozzie Smith	50.00

Cardinals Greats Autograph

NM/M

Production 30 Sets

LB	Lou Brock	40.00
SC	Steve Carlton	30.00
BG	Bob Gibson	50.00
TH	Tommy Herr	20.00
TM	Tim McCarver	30.00
SM	Stan Musial	75.00
RS	Red Schoendienst	25.00
OS	Ozzie Smith	50.00

Cardinals Greats Memorabilia

NM/M

	Common Player:	5.00
LB	Lou Brock	5.00
SC	Steve Carlton	5.00
DD	Dizzy Dean/SP	50.00
BG	Bob Gibson	15.00
TH	Tommy Herr	5.00
RH	Rogers Hornsby	40.00
TM	Tim McCarver	5.00
SM	Stan Musial	20.00
RS	Red Schoendienst	10.00
OS	Ozzie Smith	15.00

Cubs Greats

NM/M

	Complete Set (10):	8.00
EB	Ernie Banks	2.00
AD	Andre Dawson	1.00
MG	Mark Grace	1.00
RH	Randy Hundley	.50
FJ	Fergie Jenkins	.50
GM	Gary Mathews	.50
SA	Ryne Sandberg	2.00
RS	Ron Santo	1.00
BS	Bruce Sutter	.50
BW	Billy Williams	.50

Cubs Greats Memorabilia Autograph

NM/M

Production 30 Sets

EB	Ernie Banks	60.00
AD	Andre Dawson	30.00
FJ	Fergie Jenkins	25.00
GM	Gary Matthews	25.00
SA	Ryne Sandberg	60.00
RS	Ron Santo	40.00
BS	Bruce Sutter	20.00
BW	Billy Williams	30.00

Cubs Greats Autograph

NM/M

Production 30 Sets

EB	Ernie Banks	60.00
AD	Andre Dawson	30.00
MG	Mark Grace	30.00
FJ	Fergie Jenkins	25.00
GM	Gary Matthews	25.00
SA	Ryne Sandberg	60.00
RS	Ron Santo	40.00
BS	Bruce Sutter	20.00
BW	Billy Williams	30.00

Cubs Greats Memorabilia

NM/M

EB	Ernie Banks	20.00
AD	Andre Dawson	8.00
MG	Mark Grace	8.00
FJ	Fergie Jenkins	8.00
GM	Gary Matthews	15.00
SA	Ryne Sandberg	15.00
RS	Ron Santo	10.00
BS	Brian Sutter	5.00
BW	Billy Williams	8.00

Decade Greats

NM/M

	Complete Set (30):	20.00
EA	Earl Averill	.50
RO	Rod Carew	1.00
SC	Steve Carlton	.75
CC	Chris Chambliss	.50

JC	Jack Clark	.50
WC	Will Clark	1.00
RC	Roberto Clemente	3.00
MC	Mickey Cochrane	.50
BF	Bob Feller	1.00
TG	Tony Gwynn	1.00
BJ	Bo Jackson	1.00
JK	John Kruk	.50
BI	Bill Madlock	.50
EM	Eddie Mathews	1.00
BM	Bill Mazeroski	.50
WM	Willie McCovey	1.00
JM	Johnny Mize	.50
PM	Paul Molitor	1.00
MO	Mel Ott	1.00
DP	Dave Parker	.50
KP	Kirby Puckett	1.00
TR	Tim Raines	.50
CR	Cal Ripken Jr.	3.00
BR	Brooks Robinson	1.00
NR	Nolan Ryan	2.00
TS	Tom Seaver	1.00
MS	Mike Schmidt	1.00
WS	Willie Stargell	1.00
PT	Paul Traynor	.50
RY	Robin Yount	1.00

Decade Greats Memorablia Autograph

NM/M

Production 30 Sets

RO	Rod Carew	35.00
SC	Steve Carlton	35.00
CC	Chris Chambliss	25.00
JC	Jack Clark	25.00
WC	Will Clark	35.00
BF	Bob Feller	50.00
TG	Tony Gwynn	60.00
BJ	Bo Jackson	65.00
JK	John Kruk	25.00
BI	Bill Madlock	20.00
BM	Bill Mazeroski	35.00
WM	Willie McCovey	40.00
PM	Paul Molitor	35.00
DP	Dave Parker	20.00
KP	Kirby Puckett	100.00
TR	Tim Raines	20.00
CR	Cal Ripken Jr.	150.00
BR	Brooks Robinson	40.00
NR	Nolan Ryan	100.00
MS	Mike Schmidt	75.00
TS	Tom Seaver	50.00
RY	Robin Yount	50.00

Decade Greats Autograph

NM/M

Production 30 Sets

RO	Rod Carew	35.00
SC	Steve Carlton	35.00
CC	Chris Chambliss	25.00
JC	Jack Clark	25.00
WC	Will Clark	35.00
BF	Bob Feller	50.00
TG	Tony Gwynn	60.00
BJ	Bo Jackson	65.00
JK	John Kruk	25.00
BI	Bill Madlock	20.00
BM	Bill Mazeroski	35.00
WM	Willie McCovey	40.00
PM	Paul Molitor	35.00
DP	Dave Parker	20.00
KP	Kirby Puckett	100.00
TR	Tim Raines	20.00
CR	Cal Ripken Jr.	150.00
BR	Brooks Robinson	40.00
NR	Nolan Ryan	100.00
MS	Mike Schmidt	75.00
TS	Tom Seaver	50.00
RY	Robin Yount	50.00

Decade Greats Memorabilia

NM/M

	Common Player:	5.00
EA	Earl Averill	20.00
RO	Rod Carew	8.00
SC	Steve Carlton	5.00
CC	Chris Chambliss	5.00
JC	Jack Clark	5.00

WC	Will Clark	8.00
RC	Roberto Clemente	60.00
BF	Bob Feller	15.00
BJ	Bo Jackson	15.00
JK	John Kruk	8.00
BI	Bill Madlock	5.00
EM	Eddie Matthews	10.00
BM	Bill Mazeroski	8.00
WM	Willie McCovey	10.00
JM	Johnny Mize	15.00
PM	Paul Molitor	8.00
MO	Mel Ott/SP	50.00
DP	Dave Parker	5.00
KP	Kirby Puckett	15.00
TR	Tim Raines	5.00
CR	Cal Ripken Jr.	20.00
BR	Brooks Robinson	8.00
NR	Nolan Ryan	15.00
MS	Mike Schmidt	10.00
TS	Tom Seaver	10.00
WS	Willie Stargell	15.00
RY	Robin Yount	8.00

Dodgers Greats

		NM/M
Complete Set (10):		6.00
DB	Dusty Baker	.50
CA	Roy Campanella	1.00
RC	Ron Cey	.50
DD	Don Drysdale	1.00
SG	Steve Garvey	.50
PR	Pee Wee Reese	.50
JR	Jackie Robinson	2.00
SS	Steve Sax	.50
DS	Don Sutton	.50
MW	Maury Wills	.50

Dodgers Greats Autograph

		NM/M
Production 30 Sets		
DB	Dusty Baker	40.00
RC	Ron Cey	30.00
SG	Steve Garvey	35.00
SS	Steve Sax	25.00
DS	Don Sutton	35.00
MW	Maury Wills	35.00

Dodgers Greats Memorabilia Autograph

		NM/M
Production 30 Sets		
DB	Dusty Baker	40.00
RC	Ron Cey	30.00
SG	Steve Garvey	35.00
SS	Steve Sax	20.00
DS	Don Sutton	35.00
MW	Maury Wills	35.00

Dodgers Greats Memorabilia

		NM/M
Common Player:		5.00
DB	Dusty Baker	8.00
CA	Roy Campanella	35.00
RC	Ron Cey	5.00
DD	Don Drysdale	25.00
SG	Steve Garvey	8.00
PR	Pee Wee Reese	10.00
JR	Jackie Robinson	40.00
SS	Steve Sax	5.00
DS	Don Sutton	5.00
MW	Maury Wills	5.00

Nickname Greats

		NM/M
LA	Luis Aparicio	.50
SB	Steve Balboni	.50

DB	Don Baylor	.50
BE	Steve Bedrosian	.50
JB	Jim Bouton	.50
TB	Tom Brunansky	.50
RB	Rick Burleson	.50
RC	Ron Cey	.50
CH	Joe Charboneau	.50
JC	Jack Clark	.50
WC	Will Clark	1.00
DD	Darren Daulton	.50
DE	Dwight Evans	.50
BF	Bob Feller	1.00
SF	Sid Fernandez	.50
MF	Mark Fidrych	.50
CF	Carlton Fisk	.75
DF	Dan Ford	.50
GF	George Foster	.50
AG	Andres Galarraga	.50
RG	Ron Guidry	.50
MH	Mike Hargrove	.50
KH	Ken Harrelson	.50
TH	Tom Henke	.50
HE	Tommy Herr	.50
BH	Burt Hooton	.50
AH	Al Hrabosky	.50
GH	Glenn Hubbard	.50
HJ	Howard Johnson	.50
JJ	Jay Johnstone	.50
ML	Mike LaValliere	.50
BL	Bill Lee	.50
SL	Sparky Lyle	.50
GM	Garry Maddox	.50
BM	Bill Madlock	.50
MZ	Dennis Martinez	.50
MA	Gary Matthews	.50
DM	Don Mattingly	2.00
LM	Lee Mazzilli	.50
WM	Willie McCovey	1.00
SM	Sam McDowell	.50
JM	John Montefusco	.50
DP	Dave Parker	.50
JP	Joe Pepitone	.50
LP	Lou Piniella	.50
RA	Doug Rader	.50
TR	Tim Raines	.50
RR	Rick Reuschel	.50
DR	Dave Righetti	.50
MR	Mickey Rivers	.50
FR	Frank Robinson	1.00
GS	George Scott	.50
JS	John Shelby	.50
FS	Fred Stanley	.50
RS	Rusty Staub	.50
AT	Andre Thornton	.50
ST	Steve Trout	.50
EV	Ellis Valentine	.50
MW	Mitch Williams	.50
JW	Jimmy Wynn	.50

Nickname Greats Autograph

		NM/M
SB	Steve Balboni	15.00
BE	Steve Bedrosian	15.00
JB	Jim Bouton	35.00
TB	Tom Brunansky	15.00
RB	Rick Burleson	15.00
CH	Joe Charboneau	20.00
JC	Jack Clark	20.00
WC	Will Clark	30.00
DD	Darren Daulton	20.00
DE	Dwight Evans	20.00
BF	Bob Feller	50.00
SF	Sid Fernandez	15.00
MF	Mark Fidrych	35.00
CF	Carlton Fisk	50.00
DF	Dan Ford	15.00
GF	George Foster	20.00
RG	Ron Guidry	40.00
MH	Mike Hargrove	20.00
TH	Tom Henke	15.00

HE	Tommy Herr	15.00
BH	Burt Hooton	20.00
AH	Al Hrabosky	20.00
GH	Glenn Hubbard	15.00
HJ	Howard Johnson	25.00
JJ	Jay Johnstone	20.00
ML	Mike LaValliere	15.00
BL	Bill Lee	20.00
SL	Sparky Lyle	15.00
GM	Garry Maddox	20.00
BM	Bill Madlock	15.00
MZ	Dennis Martinez	20.00
MA	Gary Matthews	15.00
LM	Lee Mazzilli	15.00
WM	Willie McCovey	50.00
SM	Sam McDowell	20.00
JM	John Montefusco	20.00
DP	Dave Parker	20.00
JP	Joe Pepitone	20.00
LP	Lou Piniella	25.00
RA	Doug Rader	15.00
TR	Tim Raines	15.00
RR	Rick Reuschel	20.00
DR	Dave Righetti	20.00
MR	Mickey Rivers	20.00
FR	Frank Robinson	50.00
GS	George Scott	20.00
JS	John Shelby	15.00
FS	Fred Stanley	20.00
RS	Rusty Staub	20.00
AT	Andre Thornton	15.00
ST	Steve Trout	20.00
EV	Ellis Valentine	15.00
MW	Mitch Williams	15.00
JW	Jimmy Wynn	20.00

Red Sox Greats

		NM/M
Complete Set (10):		8.00
WB	Wade Boggs	1.00
BD	Bobby Doerr	.50
DE	Dwight Evans	.50
CF	Carlton Fisk	1.00
JF	Jimmie Foxx	2.00
FL	Fred Lynn	1.00
RP	Rico Petrocelli	.50
JR	Jim Rice	.75
LT	Luis Tiant	.50
TW	Ted Williams	2.00

Red Sox Greats Memorablia Autograph

		NM/M
Production 30 Sets		
WB	Wade Boggs	50.00
BD	Bobby Doerr	20.00
DE	Dwight Evans	25.00
CF	Carlton Fisk	35.00
FL	Fred Lynn	20.00
RP	Rico Petrocelli	20.00
JR	Jim Rice	25.00
LT	Luis Tiant	20.00

Red Sox Greats Autograph

		NM/M
Production 30 Sets		
WB	Wade Boggs	50.00
BD	Bobby Doerr	20.00
DE	Dwight Evans	25.00
CF	Carlton Fisk	35.00
FL	Fred Lynn	20.00
RP	Rico Petrocelli	20.00
JR	Jim Rice	25.00
LT	Luis Tiant	25.00

Red Sox Greats Memorabilia

		NM/M
Common Player:		10.00
WB	Wade Boggs	10.00
BD	Bobby Doerr	8.00
DE	Dwight Evans	8.00
CF	Carlton Fisk	8.00
JF	Jimmie Foxx	50.00
FL	Fred Lynn	5.00
RP	Rico Petrocelli	5.00
JR	Jim Rice	8.00
LT	Luis Tiant	5.00
TW	Ted Williams	50.00

Reds Greats

		NM/M
Complete Set (10):		8.00
JB	Johnny Bench	1.50
DC	Dave Concepcion	.50
ED	Eric Davis	.50
GF	George Foster	.50
KG	Ken Griffey Sr.	.50
BL	Barry Larkin	1.00
JM	Joe Morgan	1.00

TP	Tony Perez	1.00
FR	Frank Robinson	1.00
TS	Tom Seaver	1.00

Reds Greats Autograph

		NM/M
Production 30 Sets		
JB	Johnny Bench	65.00
DC	Dave Concepcion	25.00
ED	Eric Davis	30.00
GF	George Foster	25.00
KG	Ken Griffey Sr.	30.00
BL	Barry Larkin	40.00
JM	Joe Morgan	40.00
TP	Tony Perez	40.00
FR	Frank Robinson	50.00
TS	Tom Seaver	50.00

Reds Greats Memorabilia

		NM/M
Common Player:		5.00
JB	Johnny Bench	15.00
DC	Dave Concepcion	5.00
ED	Eric Davis	10.00
GF	George Foster	5.00
KG	Ken Griffey Sr.	5.00
BL	Barry Larkin	8.00
JM	Joe Morgan	8.00
TP	Tony Perez	8.00
FR	Frank Robinson	10.00
TS	Tom Seaver	10.00

Reds Greats Memorabilia Autograph

		NM/M
Production 30 Sets		
JB	Johnny Bench	65.00
DC	Dave Concepcion	25.00
ED	Eric Davis	30.00
GF	George Foster	25.00
KG	Ken Griffey Sr.	30.00
BL	Barry Larkin	40.00
JM	Joe Morgan	40.00
TP	Tony Perez	40.00
FR	Frank Robinson	50.00
TS	Tom Seaver	50.00

Tigers Greats

		NM/M
Complete Set (10):		6.00
TC	Ty Cobb	2.00
MF	Mark Fidrych	.50
BF	Bill Freehan	.50
KG	Kirk Gibson	1.00
WH	Willie Horton	.50
AK	Al Kaline	1.00
GK	George Kell	.50
DM	Denny McLain	1.00
JM	Jack Morris	.50
AT	Alan Trammell	.50

Tigers Greats Autograph

		NM/M
Production 30 Sets		
MF	Mark Fidrych	35.00
BF	Bill Freehan	30.00
KG	Kirk Gibson	35.00
WH	Willie Horton	20.00
AK	Al Kaline	50.00
GK	George Kell	40.00
DM	Denny McLain	35.00
JM	Jack Morris	25.00
AT	Alan Trammell	35.00

Tigers Greats
Memorabilia

		NM/M
	Common Player:	5.00
TC	Ty Cobb	85.00
MF	Mark Fidrych	10.00
BF	Bill Freehan	5.00
KG	Kirk Gibson	5.00
WH	Willie Horton	5.00
AK	Al Kaline	12.00
GK	George Kell	8.00
JM	Jack Morris	5.00
AT	Alan Trammell	5.00

Tigers Greats
Memorabilia Autograph

		NM/M
	Production 30 Sets	
MF	Mark Fidrych	35.00
BF	Bill Freehan	30.00
KG	Kirk Gibson	35.00
WH	Willie Horton	20.00
AK	Al Kaline	50.00
GK	George Kell	40.00
JM	Jack Morris	25.00
AT	Alan Trammell	35.00

Yankee Clippings

		NM/M
	Complete Set (10):	12.00
YB	Yogi Berra	1.50
JD	Joe DiMaggio	2.00
WF	Whitey Ford	1.00
RG	Ron Guidry	.50
RJ	Reggie Jackson	1.00
DM	Don Mattingly	2.00
TM	Thurman Munson	1.50
BM	Bobby Murcer	.50
GN	Graig Nettles	.50
BR	Babe Ruth	3.00

Yankee Clippings
Autograph

		NM/M
	Production 30 Sets	
YB	Yogi Berra	80.00
WF	Whitey Ford	60.00
RG	Ron Guidry	65.00
RJ	Reggie Jackson	50.00
DM	Don Mattingly	100.00
BM	Bobby Murcer	25.00
GN	Graig Nettles	40.00

Yankee Clippings
Memorabilia

		NM/M
	Common Player:	8.00
YB	Yogi Berra	25.00
JD	Joe DiMaggio	75.00
WF	Whitey Ford	15.00
RG	Ron Guidry	15.00
RJ	Reggie Jackson	12.00
DM	Don Mattingly	15.00
TM	Thurman Munson	20.00
BM	Bobby Murcer	10.00
GN	Graig Nettles	8.00
BR	Babe Ruth	200.00

Yankee Clippings
Memorabilia Autograph

		NM/M
	Production 30 Sets	
YB	Yogi Berra	80.00
WF	Whitey Ford	60.00
RG	Ron Guidry	65.00
RJ	Reggie Jackson	50.00
DM	Don Mattingly	100.00
BM	Bobby Murcer	25.00
GN	Graig Nettles	40.00

2006 Fleer Tradition

BONDERMAN
★ ★ ★ ★ Detroit Tigers® / P ★

		NM/M
Complete Set (200):		35.00
Common Player:		.15
Hobby Pack (10):		2.00
Hobby Box (36):		60.00
1	Andruw Jones	.50
2	Chipper Jones	.75
3	John Smoltz	.25
4	Tim Hudson	.25
5	Joey Devine (RC)	.25
6	Chuck James (RC)	.25
7	Alay Soler (RC)	.50
8	Conor Jackson (RC)	.25
9	Luis Gonzalez	.15
10	Brandon Webb	.15
11	Chad Tracy	.15
12	Orlando Hudson	.15
13	Shawn Green	.15
14	Vladimir Guerrero	.75
15	Bartolo Colon	.15
16	Chone Figgins	.15
17	Garret Anderson	.15
18	Francisco Rodriguez	.15
19	Casey Kotchman	.15
20	Lance Berkman	.25
21	Craig Biggio	.25
22	Andy Pettitte	.25
23	Morgan Ensberg	.15
24	Brad Lidge	.15
25	Jered Weaver (RC)	1.00
26	Roy Oswalt	.25
27	Eric Chavez	.25
28	Rich Harden	.15
29	Cole Hamels (RC)	.25
30	Huston Street	.15
31	Bobby Crosby	.15
32	Nick Swisher	.25
33	Vernon Wells	.25
34	Roy Halladay	.25
35	A.J. Burnett	.15
36	Troy Glaus	.25
37	B.J. Ryan	.15
38	Bengie Molina	.15
39	Alex Rios	.15
40	Prince Fielder (RC)	2.00
41	Jose Capellan (RC)	.25
42	Rickie Weeks	.15
43	Ben Sheets	.25
44	Carlos Lee	.25
45	J.J. Hardy	.15
46	Albert Pujols	2.00
47	Skip Schumaker (RC)	.25
48	Adam Wainwright (RC)	.25
49	Jim Edmonds	.25
50	Scott Rolen	.75
51	Chris Carpenter	.25
52	David Eckstein	.15
53	Derrek Lee	.50
54	Jon Lester (RC)	3.00
55	Mark Prior	.40
56	Aramis Ramirez	.15
57	Juan Pierre	.15
58	Greg Maddux	1.50
59	Michael Barrett	.15
60	Carl Crawford	.15
61	Scott Kazmir	.25
62	Jorge Cantu	.15
63	Jonny Gomes	.15
64	Julio Lugo	.15
65	Aubrey Huff	.15
66	Jeff Kent	.25
67	Nomar Garciaparra	.75
68	Rafael Furcal	.25
69	Tim Hamulack (RC)	.25
70	Chad Billingsley (RC)	.25
71	Hong-Chih Kuo (RC)	.25
72	J.D. Drew	.15
73	Moises Alou	.15
74	Randy Winn	.15
75	Jason Schmidt	.25
76	Jeremy Accardo RC	.25

77	Matt Cain (RC)	.50
78	Joel Zumaya (RC)	.50
79	Travis Hafner	.50
80	Victor Martinez	.25
81	Grady Sizemore	.40
82	C.C. Sabathia	.15
83	Jhonny Peralta	.15
84	Jason Michaels	.15
85	Jeremy Sowers (RC)	.25
86	Ichiro Suzuki	1.50
87	Richie Sexson	.25
88	Adrian Beltre	.25
89	Felix Hernandez	.25
90	Kenji Johjima RC	3.00
91	Jeff Harris RC	.25
92	Taylor Buchholz (RC)	.25
93	Miguel Cabrera	.75
94	Dontrelle Willis	.25
95	Jeremy Hermida (RC)	.25
96	Mike Jacobs (RC)	.25
97	Josh Johnson (RC)	.25
98	Hanley Ramirez (RC)	.40
99	Josh Willingham (RC)	.25
100	Dan Uggla (RC)	.25
101	David Wright	1.00
102	Jose Reyes	.50
103	Pedro Martinez	.75
104	Carlos Beltran	.50
105	Carlos Delgado	.40
106	Billy Wagner	.25
107	Lastings Milledge (RC)	.50
108	Alfonso Soriano	.75
109	Jose Vidro	.15
110	Livan Hernandez	.15
111	Matthew Kemp (RC)	.25
112	Brandon Watson (RC)	.25
113	Ryan Zimmerman (RC)	2.00
114	Miguel Tejada	.50
115	Ramon Hernandez	.15
116	Brian Roberts	.15
117	Melvin Mora	.15
118	Erik Bedard	.15
119	Jay Gibbons	.15
120	Aaron Rakers (RC)	.25
121	Jake Peavy	.25
122	Brian Giles	.25
123	Khalil Greene	.15
124	Trevor Hoffman	.25
125	Josh Barfield (RC)	.25
126	Ben Johnson (RC)	.25
127	Ryan Howard	1.50
128	Bobby Abreu	.25
129	Chase Utley	.50
130	Pat Burrell	.25
131	Jimmy Rollins	.50
132	Brett Myers	.15
133	Mike Thompson RC	.25
134	Jason Bay	.40
135	Oliver Perez	.15
136	Matt Capps (RC)	.25
137	Paul Maholm (RC)	.25
138	Nate McLouth (RC)	.25
139	John Van Benschoten (RC)	.25
140	Mark Teixeira	.50
141	Michael Young	.25
142	Hank Blalock	.25
143	Kevin Millwood	.25
144	Laynce Nix	.15
145	Francisco Cordero	.15
146	Ian Kinsler (RC)	.25
147	David Ortiz	.75
148	Manny Ramirez	.75
149	Jason Varitek	.75
150	Curt Schilling	.75
151	Josh Beckett	.25
152	Coco Crisp	.15
153	Jonathan Papelbon (RC)	2.00
154	Ken Griffey Jr.	1.50
155	Adam Dunn	.50
156	Felipe Lopez	.15
157	Bronson Arroyo	.15
158	Ryan Freel	.15
159	Chris Denorfia (RC)	.25
160	Todd Helton	.50
161	Garrett Atkins	.15
162	Matt Holliday	.25
163	Clint Barmes	.15
164	Kendry Morales (RC)	.25
165	Ryan Shealy (RC)	.25
166	Josh Wilson (RC)	.25
167	Reggie Sanders	.15
168	Angel Berroa	.15
169	Mike Sweeney	.15
170	Mark Grudzielanek	.15
171	Jeremy Affeldt	.15
172	Steve Stemle RC	.50
173	Justin Verlander (RC)	2.00
174	Ivan Rodriguez	.50
175	Chris Shelton	.15
176	Jeremy Bonderman	.25
177	Magglio Ordonez	.15
178	Carlos Guillen	.15
179	Placido Polanco	.15

180	Johan Santana	.75
181	Torii Hunter	.25
182	Joe Nathan	.15
183	Joe Mauer	.50
184	David Gassner (RC)	.25
185	Jason Kubel (RC)	.25
186	Francisco Liriano (RC)	2.00
187	Jim Thome	.50
188	Paul Konerko	.40
189	Scott Podsednik	.25
190	Tadahito Iguchi	.25
191	A.J. Pierzynski	.15
192	Jose Contreras	.15
193	Brian Anderson (RC)	.25
194	Hideki Matsui	1.50
195	Wilbert Nieves (RC)	.25
196	Alex Rodriguez	1.00
197	Gary Sheffield	.25
198	Randy Johnson	.25
199	Johnny Damon	.40
200	Derek Jeter	1.00

Black & White

B&W (1-200):		2-3X

Printing Plates

No Pricing
Production one set per color.

Sepia Tone

Sepia (1-200):		2-3X

Grass Roots

		NM/M
	Common Player:	.50
GR-1	Ken Griffey Jr.	2.50
GR-2	Albert Pujols	3.00
GR-3	Derek Jeter	3.00
GR-4	Derrek Lee	1.00
GR-5	Vladimir Guerrero	1.00
GR-6	Andruw Jones	1.00
GR-7	Manny Ramirez	1.00
GR-8	Johan Santana	1.00
GR-9	Victor Martinez	.75
GR-10	Todd Helton	1.00
GR-11	Ivan Rodriguez	1.00
GR-12	Miguel Cabrera	1.00
GR-13	Lance Berkman	.75
GR-14	Bartolo Colon	.50
GR-15	Jeff Kent	.50
GR-16	Carlos Lee	.75
GR-17	Torii Hunter	.50
GR-18	Carlos Beltran	1.00
GR-19	Alex Rodriguez	3.00
GR-20	Randy Johnson	1.00
GR-21	Eric Chavez	.50
GR-22	Ryan Howard	2.50
GR-23	Ichiro Suzuki	2.00
GR-24	Chris Carpenter	1.00
GR-25	Mark Teixeira	1.00

Signature Tradition

		NM/M
	Inserted 1:1,269 Hobby	
CH	Craig Hansen	35.00
JM	Joe Mauer/SP	30.00

Triple Crown
Contenders

		NM/M
Common Player:		.75

TC-1	Albert Pujols	3.00
TC-2	Derrek Lee	.75
TC-3	Manny Ramirez	1.00
TC-4	David Ortiz	1.00
TC-5	Mark Teixeira	.75
TC-6	Alex Rodriguez	3.00
TC-7	Andruw Jones	.75
TC-8	Todd Helton	.75
TC-9	Vladimir Guerrero	1.00
TC-10	Miguel Cabrera	1.00
TC-11	Hideki Matsui	2.00
TC-12	Travis Hafner	.75
TC-13	David Wright	2.00
TC-14	Ken Griffey Jr.	2.50
TC-15	Jason Bay	.75

Griffey Jr. 1989 Fleer Buyback Autograph

NM/M

Production 50
Ken Griffey Jr.	250.00

1934 Goudey Greats

NM/M

Common Player:		2.00
GG-1	Andruw Jones	5.00
GG-2	Chipper Jones	8.00
GG-3	John Smoltz	4.00
GG-4	Tim Hudson	3.00
GG-5	Conor Jackson	2.00
GG-6	Luis Gonzalez	2.00
GG-7	Brandon Webb	5.00
GG-8	Vladimir Guerrero	8.00
GG-9	Bartolo Colon	2.00
GG-10	Lance Berkman	3.00
GG-11	Craig Biggio	4.00
GG-12	Andy Pettitte	3.00
GG-13	Morgan Ensberg	2.00
GG-14	Roy Oswalt	3.00
GG-15	Eric Chavez	3.00
GG-16	Rich Harden	3.00
GG-17	Huston Street	3.00
GG-18	Vernon Wells	3.00
GG-19	Roy Halladay	5.00
GG-20	Troy Glaus	3.00
GG-21	Prince Fielder	10.00
GG-22	Rickie Weeks	3.00
GG-23	Ben Sheets	3.00
GG-24	Carlos Lee	3.00
GG-25	Albert Pujols	20.00
GG-26	Jim Edmonds	4.00
GG-27	Scott Rolen	8.00
GG-28	Chris Carpenter	5.00
GG-29	Derrek Lee	5.00
GG-30	Mark Prior	5.00
GG-31	Greg Maddux	15.00
GG-32	Carl Crawford	4.00
GG-33	Scott Kazmir	3.00
GG-34	Jorge Cantu	2.00
GG-35	Jeff Kent	3.00
GG-36	Nomar Garciaparra	8.00
GG-37	J.D. Drew	2.00
GG-38	Randy Winn	2.00
GG-39	Jason Schmidt	5.00
GG-40	Travis Hafner	5.00
GG-41	Victor Martinez	3.00
GG-42	Grady Sizemore	4.00
GG-43	Jhonny Peralta	2.00
GG-44	Ichiro Suzuki	15.00
GG-45	Richie Sexson	4.00
GG-46	Felix Hernandez	5.00
GG-47	Kenji Johjima	10.00
GG-48	Miguel Cabrera	8.00
GG-49	Dontrelle Willis	4.00
GG-50	Josh Willingham	2.00
GG-51	David Wright	15.00
GG-52	Jose Reyes	5.00
GG-53	Pedro Martinez	8.00
GG-54	Carlos Beltran	3.00
GG-55	Alfonso Soriano	8.00
GG-56	Ryan Zimmerman	8.00
GG-57	Miguel Tejada	4.00
GG-58	Brian Roberts	2.00
GG-59	Jake Peavy	3.00
GG-60	Brian Giles	2.00

GG-61	Khalil Greene	2.00
GG-62	Ryan Howard	15.00
GG-63	Bobby Abreu	4.00
GG-64	Chase Utley	5.00
GG-65	Jimmy Rollins	5.00
GG-66	Jason Bay	4.00
GG-67	Mark Teixeira	5.00
GG-68	Michael Young	3.00
GG-69	Hank Blalock	3.00
GG-70	David Ortiz	8.00
GG-71	Manny Ramirez	8.00
GG-72	Curt Schilling	8.00
GG-73	Josh Beckett	3.00
GG-74	Jonathan Papelbon	10.00
GG-75	Ken Griffey Jr.	15.00
GG-76	Adam Dunn	5.00
GG-77	Todd Helton	4.00
GG-78	Garrett Atkins	2.00
GG-79	Matt Holliday	2.00
GG-80	Reggie Sanders	2.00
GG-81	Justin Verlander	10.00
GG-82	Ivan Rodriguez	5.00
GG-83	Chris Shelton	2.00
GG-84	Jeremy Bonderman	3.00
GG-85	Magglio Ordonez	2.00
GG-86	Johan Santana	6.00
GG-87	Torii Hunter	3.00
GG-88	Joe Nathan	2.00
GG-89	Joe Mauer	5.00
GG-90	Francisco Liriano	8.00
GG-91	Jim Thome	5.00
GG-92	Paul Konerko	4.00
GG-93	Scott Podsednik	3.00
GG-94	Tadahito Iguchi	4.00
GG-95	A.J. Pierzynski	2.00
GG-96	Hideki Matsui	12.00
GG-97	Alex Rodriguez	20.00
GG-98	Gary Sheffield	4.00
GG-99	Derek Jeter	25.00
GG-100	Jason Giambi	6.00

Blue Chip Prospects

NM/M

Common Player:		.50
BC-1	Ryan Zimmerman	3.00
BC-2	Conor Jackson	.75
BC-3	Jonathan Papelbon	3.00
BC-4	Justin Verlander	3.00
BC-5	Jeremy Hermida	.75
BC-6	Josh Willingham	.50
BC-7	Hanley Ramirez	1.00
BC-8	Prince Fielder	3.00
BC-9	Francisco Liriano	2.00
BC-10	Lastings Milledge	2.00
BC-11	Jon Lester	2.00
BC-12	Matt Cain	1.50
BC-13	Adam Wainwright	.75
BC-14	Chuck James	1.00
BC-15	Kenji Johjima	3.00
BC-16	Josh Johnson	.75
BC-17	Jason Kubel	.50
BC-18	Brian Anderson	.50
BC-19	Cole Hamels	2.00
BC-20	Mike Jacobs	.50
BC-21	Jered Weaver	3.00
BC-22	Kendry Morales	.50
BC-23	Alay Soler	.50
BC-24	Chris Denorfia	.50
BC-25	Chad Billingsley	1.00

Diamond Tribute

NM/M

Common Player:		.50
DT-1	Derek Jeter	3.00

ABBREVIATIONS

SP - Short Print

DT-2	Ken Griffey Jr.	3.00
DT-3	Vladimir Guerrero	1.50
DT-4	Albert Pujols	3.00
DT-5	Derrek Lee	1.00
DT-6	David Ortiz	1.50
DT-7	Miguel Tejada	1.00
DT-8	Jim Thome	1.00
DT-9	Travis Hafner	1.00
DT-10	Grady Sizemore	1.00
DT-11	Chris Shelton	.50
DT-12	Dontrelle Willis	1.00
DT-13	Craig Biggio	1.00
DT-14	Roy Oswalt	1.00
DT-15	Prince Fielder	2.00
DT-16	David Wright	2.50
DT-17	Jose Reyes	1.00
DT-18	Hideki Matsui	2.00
DT-19	Rich Harden	.75
DT-20	Bobby Abreu	.75
DT-21	Jason Bay	1.00
DT-22	Jake Peavy	.75
DT-23	Felix Hernandez	.75
DT-24	Carl Crawford	.75
DT-25	Vernon Wells	.75

Traditional Threads

NM/M

Common Player:		4.00
JB	Josh Barfield	4.00
BA	Jason Bay	8.00
EB	Erik Bedard	4.00
HB	Hank Blalock	6.00
SC	Sean Casey	4.00
JD	Johnny Damon	10.00
ZD	Zachary Duke	4.00
PF	Prince Fielder	15.00
CF	Chone Figgins	4.00
BG	Brian Giles	4.00
MG	Marcus Giles	4.00
GR	Khalil Greene	4.00
KG	Ken Griffey Jr.	15.00
VG	Vladimir Guerrero	8.00
JH	Jeremy Hermida	6.00
FH	Felix Hernandez	6.00
LH	Livan Hernandez	4.00
GJ	Geoff Jenkins	4.00
DJ	Derek Jeter	20.00
CK	Casey Kotchman/SP	4.00
CL	Carlos Lee	6.00
DL	Derrek Lee	8.00
JL	Javy Lopez	4.00
GM	Greg Maddux	10.00
MM	Melvin Mora	4.00
DO	David Ortiz	10.00
RO	Roy Oswalt	6.00
JP	Jake Peavy	6.00
AP	Albert Pujols	20.00
AR	Aramis Ramirez	6.00
AS	Alfonso Soriano	8.00
BR	Brian Roberts	6.00
BS	Ben Sheets	6.00
TE	Mark Teixeira	8.00
MT	Miguel Tejada	6.00
JV	Jose Vidro	4.00
OV	Omar Vizquel	6.00
RW	Rickie Weeks	6.00
MY	Michael Young	6.00
CZ	Carlos Zambrano	4.00
RZ	Ryan Zimmerman	15.00

2007 Fleer

NM/M

Complete Set (400):	75.00
Common Player:	.15
Hobby Pack (10):	1.50
Hobby Box (36):	50.00
Rack Pack (52):	4.50
Rack Box (18):	75.00
1	Chad Cordero	.15
2	Alfonso Soriano	.50
3	Nick Johnson	.15
4	Austin Kearns	.15

5	Ramon Ortiz	.15
6	Brian Schneider	.15
7	Ryan Zimmerman	.40
8	Jose Vidro	.15
9	Felipe Lopez	.15
10	Cristian Guzman	.15
11	B.J. Ryan	.15
12	Alex Rios	.25
13	Vernon Wells	.25
14	Roy Halladay	.25
15	A.J. Burnett	.15
16	Lyle Overbay	.25
17	Troy Glaus	.25
18	Bengie Molina	.15
19	Gustavo Chacin	.15
20	Aaron Hill	.15
21	Vicente Padilla	.15
22	Kevin Millwood	.15
23	Akinori Otsuka	.15
24	Adam Eaton	.15
25	Hank Blalock	.25
26	Mark Teixeira	.40
27	Michael Young	.25
28	Mark DeRosa	.15
29	Gary Matthews	.15
30	Ian Kinsler	.15
31	Carlos Lee	.25
32	James Shields	.15
33	Scott Kazmir	.25
34	Carl Crawford	.25
35	Jonny Gomes	.15
36	Tim Corcoran	.15
37	B.J. Upton	.25
38	Rocco Baldelli	.25
39	Jae Weong Seo	.15
40	Jorge Cantu	.15
41	Ty Wigginton	.15
42	Chris Carpenter	.40
43	Albert Pujols	1.50
44	Scott Rolen	.50
45	Jim Edmonds	.40
46	Jason Isringhausen	.15
47	Yadier Molina	.15
48	Adam Wainwright	.25
49	Mark Mulder	.25
50	Jason Marquis	.15
51	Juan Encarnacion	.15
52	Aaron Miles	.15
53	Ichiro Suzuki	1.00
54	Felix Hernandez	.40
55	Kenji Johjima	.25
56	Richie Sexson	.40
57	Yuniesky Betancourt	.15
58	J.J. Putz	.15
59	Jarrod Washburn	.15
60	Ben Broussard	.15
61	Adrian Beltre	.25
62	Raul Ibanez	.15
63	Jose Lopez	.15
64	Matt Cain	.25
65	Noah Lowry	.15
66	Jason Schmidt	.25
67	Pedro Feliz	.15
68	Matt Morris	.15
69	Ray Durham	.15
70	Steve Finley	.15
71	Randy Winn	.15
72	Moises Alou	.25
73	Eliezer Alfonzo	.15
74	Armando Benitez	.15
75	Omar Vizquel	.25
76	Chris Young	.25
77	Adrian Gonzalez	.25
78	Khalil Greene	.15
79	Mike Piazza	.75
80	Josh Barfield	.25
81	Brian Giles	.25
82	Jake Peavy	.25
83	Trevor Hoffman	.25
84	Mike Cameron	.15
85	Dave Roberts	.15
86	David Wells	.15
87	Zachary Duke	.15

88 Ian Snell	.15	
89 Jason Bay	.40	
90 Freddy Sanchez	.15	
91 Jack Wilson	.15	
92 Tom Gorzelanny	.15	
93 Chris Duffy	.15	
94 Jose Castillo	.15	
95 Matt Capps	.15	
96 Mike Gonzalez	.15	
97 Chase Utley	.50	
98 Jimmy Rollins	.50	
99 Aaron Rowand	.15	
100 Ryan Howard	1.00	
101 Cole Hamels	.50	
102 Pat Burrell	.25	
103 Shane Victorino	.15	
104 Jamie Moyer	.15	
105 Mike Lieberthal	.15	
106 Tom Gordon	.15	
107 Brett Myers	.25	
108 Nick Swisher	.25	
109 Barry Zito	.25	
110 Jason Kendall	.15	
111 Milton Bradley	.25	
112 Bobby Crosby	.15	
113 Huston Street	.15	
114 Eric Chavez	.25	
115 Frank Thomas	.40	
116 Danny Haren	.25	
117 Jay Payton	.15	
118 Randy Johnson	.50	
119 Mike Mussina	.40	
120 Bobby Abreu	.40	
121 Jason Giambi	.40	
122 Derek Jeter	1.50	
123 Alex Rodriguez	1.50	
124 Jorge Posada	.40	
125 Robinson Cano	.40	
126 Mariano Rivera	.40	
127 Chien-Ming Wang	.40	
128 Hideki Matsui	1.00	
129 Gary Sheffield	.40	
130 Lastings Milledge	.25	
131 Tom Glavine	.25	
132 Billy Wagner	.25	
133 Pedro Martinez	.50	
134 Paul LoDuca	.15	
135 Carlos Delgado	.40	
136 Carlos Beltran	.40	
137 David Wright	.75	
138 Jose Reyes	.50	
139 Julio Franco	.15	
140 Michael Cuddyer	.15	
141 Justin Morneau	.40	
142 Johan Santana	.50	
143 Francisco Liriano	.25	
144 Joe Mauer	.25	
145 Torii Hunter	.25	
146 Luis Castillo	.15	
147 Joe Nathan	.15	
148 Carlos Silva	.15	
149 Boof Bonser	.15	
150 Ben Sheets	.25	
151 Prince Fielder	.50	
152 Bill Hall	.25	
153 Rickie Weeks	.25	
154 Geoff Jenkins	.15	
155 Kevin Mench	.15	
156 Francisco Cordero	.15	
157 Chris Capuano	.15	
158 Brady Clark	.15	
159 Tony Gwynn Jr.	.15	
160 Chad Billingsley	.25	
161 Russell Martin	.25	
162 Wilson Betemit	.15	
163 Nomar Garciaparra	.50	
164 Kenny Lofton	.15	
165 Rafael Furcal	.25	
166 Julio Lugo	.15	
167 Brad Penny	.15	
168 Jeff Kent	.25	
169 Greg Maddux	1.00	
170 Derek Lowe	.15	
171 Andre Ethier	.25	
172 Chone Figgins	.15	
173 Francisco Rodriguez	.25	
174 Garret Anderson	.15	
175 Orlando Cabrera	.25	
176 Adam Kennedy	.15	
177 John Lackey	.25	
178 Vladimir Guerrero	.50	
179 Bartolo Colon	.25	
180 Jered Weaver	.25	
181 Juan Rivera	.15	
182 Howie Kendrick	.25	
183 Ervin Santana	.25	
184 Mark Redman	.15	
185 David DeJesus	.15	
186 Joey Gathright	.15	
187 Mike Sweeney	.15	
188 Mark Teahen	.15	
189 Angel Berroa	.15	
190 Ambiorix Burgos	.15	
191 Luke Hudson	.15	
192 Mark Grudzielanek	.15	
193 Roger Clemens	1.50	
194 Willy Taveras	.15	
195 Craig Biggio	.25	
196 Andy Pettitte	.25	
197 Roy Oswalt	.40	
198 Lance Berkman	.40	
199 Morgan Ensberg	.15	
200 Brad Lidge	.15	
201 Chris Burke	.15	
202 Miguel Cabrera	.50	
203 Dontrelle Willis	.25	
204 Josh Johnson	.15	
205 Ricky Nolasco	.15	
206 Dan Uggla	.25	
207 Jeremy Hermida	.15	
208 Scott Olsen	.25	
209 Josh Willingham	.15	
210 Joe Borowski	.15	
211 Hanley Ramirez	.40	
212 Mike Jacobs	.15	
213 Kenny Rogers	.15	
214 Justin Verlander	.40	
215 Ivan Rodriguez	.40	
216 Magglio Ordonez	.15	
217 Todd Jones	.15	
218 Joel Zumaya	.25	
219 Jeremy Bonderman	.40	
220 Nate Robertson	.15	
221 Brandon Inge	.15	
222 Craig Monroe	.15	
223 Carlos Guillen	.25	
224 Jeff Francis	.15	
225 Brian Fuentes	.15	
226 Todd Helton	.40	
227 Matt Holliday	.25	
228 Garrett Atkins	.25	
229 Clint Barmes	.15	
230 Jason Jennings	.15	
231 Aaron Cook	.15	
232 Brad Hawpe	.25	
233 Cory Sullivan	.15	
234 Aaron Boone	.15	
235 C.C. Sabathia	.25	
236 Grady Sizemore	.50	
237 Travis Hafner	.40	
238 Jhonny Peralta	.15	
239 Jake Westbrook	.15	
240 Jeremy Sowers	.15	
241 Andy Marte	.15	
242 Victor Martinez	.25	
243 Jason Michaels	.15	
244 Cliff Lee	.15	
245 Bronson Arroyo	.15	
246 Aaron Harang	.15	
247 Ken Griffey Jr.	1.00	
248 Adam Dunn	.40	
249 Rich Aurilia	.15	
250 Eric Milton	.15	
251 David Ross	.15	
252 Brandon Phillips	.15	
253 Ryan Freel	.15	
254 Eddie Guardado	.15	
255 Jose Contreras	.15	
256 Freddy Garcia	.15	
257 Jon Garland	.15	
258 Mark Buehrle	.25	
259 Bobby Jenks	.15	
260 Paul Konerko	.25	
261 Jermaine Dye	.15	
262 Joe Crede	.25	
263 Jim Thome	.40	
264 Javier Vazquez	.15	
265 A.J. Pierzynski	.15	
266 Tadahito Iguchi	.15	
267 Carlos Zambrano	.40	
268 Derrek Lee	.40	
269 Aramis Ramirez	.40	
270 Ryan Theriot	.15	
271 Juan Pierre	.25	
272 Rich Hill	.25	
273 Ryan Dempster	.15	
274 Jacque Jones	.15	
275 Mark Prior	.25	
276 Kerry Wood	.25	
277 Josh Beckett	.25	
278 David Ortiz	.50	
279 Kevin Youkilis	.15	
280 Jason Varitek	.40	
281 Manny Ramirez	.50	
282 Curt Schilling	.50	
283 Jon Lester	.25	
284 Jonathan Papelbon	.50	
285 Alex Gonzalez	.15	
286 Mike Lowell	.25	
287 Kyle Snyder	.15	
288 Miguel Tejada	.40	
289 Erik Bedard	.25	
290 Ramon Hernandez	.15	
291 Melvin Mora	.15	
292 Nicholas Markakis	.25	
293 Brian Roberts	.25	
294 Corey Patterson	.15	
295 Kris Benson	.15	
296 Jay Gibbons	.15	
297 Rodrigo Lopez	.15	
298 Chris Ray	.15	
299 Andruw Jones	.50	
300 Brian McCann	.40	
301 Jeff Francoeur	.25	
302 Chuck James	.25	
303 John Smoltz	.40	
304 Bob Wickman	.15	
305 Edgar Renteria	.25	
306 Adam LaRoche	.25	
307 Marcus Giles	.15	
308 Tim Hudson	.25	
309 Chipper Jones	.50	
310 Miguel Batista	.15	
311 Claudio Vargas	.15	
312 Brandon Webb	.25	
313 Luis Gonzalez	.15	
314 Livan Hernandez	.15	
315 Stephen Drew	.25	
316 Johnny Estrada	.15	
317 Orlando Hudson	.15	
318 Conor Jackson	.15	
319 Chad Tracy	.15	
320 Carlos Quentin	.25	
321 Alvin Colina RC	.50	
322 Miguel Montero (RC)	.25	
323 Jeff Fiorentino (RC)	.25	
324 Jeff Baker (RC)	.25	
325 Brian Burres (RC)	.25	
326 David Murphy (RC)	.25	
327 Francisco Cruceta (RC)	.25	
328 Beltran Perez (RC)	.25	
329 Scott Moore (RC)	.25	
330 Sean Henn (RC)	.25	
331 Ryan Sweeney (RC)	.25	
332 Josh Fields (RC)	.25	
333 Jerry Owens (RC)	.25	
334 Vinny Rottino (RC)	.25	
335 Kevin Kouzmanoff (RC)	.50	
336 Alexi Casilla RC	.50	
337 Justin Hampson (RC)	.25	
338 Troy Tulowitzki (RC)	.50	
339 Jose Garcia RC	.50	
340 Andrew Miller RC	2.00	
341 Glen Perkins (RC)	.25	
342 Ubaldo Jimenez (RC)	.25	
343 Doug Slaten RC	.50	
344 Angel Sanchez RC	.50	
345 Mitch Maier RC	.50	
346 Ryan Braun (RC)	.50	
347 Joselo Diaz (RC)	.25	
348 Delwyn Young (RC)	.50	
349 Kevin Hooper (RC)	.25	
350 Dennis Sarfate (RC)	.50	
351 Andy Cannizaro RC	.50	
352 Devern Hansack RC	1.00	
353 Michael Bourn (RC)	.50	
354 Carlos Maldonado (RC)	.25	
355 Shane Youman RC	.50	
356 Philip Humber (RC)	.50	
357 Hector Gimenez (RC)	.25	
358 Fred Lewis (RC)	.25	
359 Ryan Feierabend (RC)	.25	
360 Juan Morillo (RC)	.25	
361 Travis Chick (RC)	.25	
362 Oswaldo Navarro RC	.50	
363 Cesar Jimenez RC	.25	
364 Brian Stokes (RC)	.25	
365 Delmon Young (RC)	.50	
366 Juan Salas (RC)	.25	
367 Shawn Riggans (RC)	.25	
368 Adam Lind (RC)	.50	
369 Joaquin Arias (RC)	.25	
370 Eric Stults RC	.50	
371 Brandon Webb	.25	
372 John Smoltz	.50	
373 Miguel Tejada	.50	
374 David Ortiz	1.00	
375 Carlos Zambrano	.50	
376 Jermaine Dye	.25	
377 Ken Griffey Jr.	1.50	
378 Victor Martinez	.25	
379 Todd Helton	.50	
380 Ivan Rodriguez	.50	
381 Miguel Cabrera	.50	
382 Lance Berkman	.50	
383 Mike Sweeney	.25	
384 Vladimir Guerrero	.50	
385 Derek Lowe	.25	
386 Bill Hall	.25	
387 Johan Santana	.75	
388 Carlos Beltran	.50	
389 Derek Jeter	2.00	
390 Nick Swisher	.25	
391 Ryan Howard	1.50	
392 Jason Bay	.50	
393 Trevor Hoffman	.25	
394 Omar Vizquel	.25	
395 Ichiro Suzuki	1.00	
396 Albert Pujols	2.00	
397 Carl Crawford	.50	
398 Mark Teixeira	.50	
399 Roy Halladay	.25	
400 Ryan Zimmerman	.50	

Printing Plates

No Pricing
Production one set per color.

Mini Die-Cuts

Mini:	1.5-2X
Inserted 1:2	
Mini Gold:	No Pricing
Inserted 1:576	

Autographics

Inserted 1:720

Crowning Achievement

	NM/M
Common Player:	.50
Inserted 1:5	
AP Albert Pujols	3.00
BZ Barry Zito	.50
CD Carlos Delgado	.75
CS Curt Schilling	.75
DJ Derek Jeter	3.00
DO David Ortiz	1.00
FT Frank Thomas	.75
GM Greg Maddux	2.00
IS Ichiro Suzuki	2.00
JS Johan Santana	.75
JT Jim Thome	.75
KG Ken Griffey Jr.	2.00
MC Miguel Cabrera	1.00
MP Mike Piazza	1.00
MR Manny Ramirez	1.00
PM Pedro Martinez	1.00
RC Roger Clemens	2.50
RH Ryan Howard	2.00
TG Tom Glavine	.75
TH Trevor Hoffman	.50

Fresh Ink

	NM/M
Inserted 1:720	
BB Brandon Backe	15.00
BW Brian Wilson	20.00
CB Clint Barmes	20.00
CC Craig Counsell	20.00
GQ Guillermo Quiroz	15.00
JB Joe Blanton	15.00
JV John Van Benschoten	10.00
LN Leo Nunez	10.00
MM Matt Murton	25.00
SR Saul Rivera	10.00

Genuine Coverage

	NM/M
Inserted 1:720	
AP Albert Pujols	25.00
AS Alfonso Soriano	20.00
BR Brian Roberts	15.00
DW Dontrelle Willis	8.00
ES Johnny Estrada	8.00
JB Josh Beckett	15.00
JE Jim Edmonds	15.00
JM Justin Morneau	15.00
JT Jim Thome	15.00
LB Lance Berkman	10.00
RC Robinson Cano	20.00
SM John Smoltz	15.00
VG Vladimir Guerrero	15.00

In the Zone

	NM/M
Common Player:	1.00

Inserted 1:10
AJ	Andruw Jones	1.00
AP	Albert Pujols	3.00
AR	Alex Rodriguez	2.50
DO	David Ortiz	1.50
DW	David Wright	1.50
KG	Ken Griffey Jr.	2.00
MC	Miguel Cabrera	1.00
MT	Mark Teixeira	1.00
RH	Ryan Howard	2.00
VG	Vladimir Guerrero	1.00

Perfect 10

NM/M
Common Player: .50
Inserted 1:5
CC	Carl Crawford	.75
DO	David Ortiz	1.50
DJ	Derek Jeter	3.00
IR	Ivan Rodriguez	.75
JD	Jermaine Dye	.50
JS	Johan Santana	1.00
MM	Mike Mussina	.75
MY	Michael Young	.75
RH	Roy Halladay	.50
VG	Vladimir Guerrero	1.00
AP	Albert Pujols	3.00
AS	Alfonso Soriano	1.00
BH	Bill Hall	.50
CB	Carlos Beltran	1.00
CJ	Chipper Jones	1.00
CU	Chase Utley	1.00
JB	Jason Bay	.75
MC	Miguel Cabrera	1.00
RC	Roger Clemens	2.50
RH	Ryan Howard	2.00

Rookie Sensations

NM/M
Common Player: .50
Inserted 1:1
BB	Boof Bonser	.50
CB	Chad Billingsley	1.00
CH	Cole Hamels	1.50
CJ	Conor Jackson	.75
DU	Dan Uggla	.50
FL	Francisco Liriano	.75
HR	Hanley Ramirez	1.00
IK	Ian Kinsler	.75
JB	Josh Barfield	.75
JH	Jeremy Hermida	.50
JJ	Josh Johnson	.50
JL	Jon Lester	1.00
JP	Jonathan Papelbon	2.00
JS	Jeremy Sowers	.50
JV	Justin Verlander	2.00
JW	Jered Weaver	1.00
KJ	Kenji Johjima	.75
LO	James Loney	.75
MK	Matthew Kemp	.75
NM	Nicholas Markakis	1.00
PF	Prince Fielder	1.50
RG	Matt Garza	1.00
RN	Ricky Nolasco	.50
RZ	Ryan Zimmerman	2.00
SO	Scott Olsen	.75

Soaring Stars

NM/M
Common Player: .50
Inserted 1:2 Rack Packs
AD	Adam Dunn	.75
AJ	Andruw Jones	1.00
AL	Alex Rodriguez	2.50
AP	Albert Pujols	3.00
AR	Alex Rios	.50
AS	Alfonso Soriano	1.00
BW	Brandon Webb	.50
BZ	Barry Zito	.50
CB	Carlos Beltran	1.00
CJ	Chipper Jones	1.00

CU	Chase Utley	1.00
DA	Johnny Damon	1.00
DJ	Derek Jeter	3.00
DL	Derrek Lee	1.00
DO	David Ortiz	1.00
DW	David Wright	1.50
HA	Roy Halladay	.50
IR	Ivan Rodriguez	.75
IS	Ichiro Suzuki	2.00
JB	Jason Bay	.75
JD	Jermaine Dye	.50
JG	Jon Garland	.50
JM	Joe Mauer	.75
JS	Johan Santana	1.00
JV	Justin Verlander	1.00
KG	Ken Griffey Jr.	2.00
LB	Lance Berkman	.75
MC	Miguel Cabrera	1.00
MP	Mike Piazza	1.50
MR	Manny Ramirez	1.00
MT	Mark Teixeira	.75
NG	Nomar Garciaparra	1.00
PF	Prince Fielder	1.00
PM	Pedro Martinez	1.00
RH	Ryan Howard	2.00
RI	Mariano Rivera	.75
RO	Roy Oswalt	.75
TE	Miguel Tejada	.75
TG	Tom Glavine	.75
TH	Travis Hafner	.75
VG	Vladimir Guerrero	1.00
WI	Dontrelle Willis	.75

Year in Review

NM/M
Common Player: .50
Inserted 1:5
AP	Albert Pujols	3.00
AR	Alex Rodriguez	2.50
AS	Alfonso Soriano	1.00
BA	Bobby Abreu	1.00
CU	Chase Utley	1.00
DJ	Derek Jeter	3.00
DO	David Ortiz	1.00
FL	Francisco Liriano	.75
FS	Freddy Sanchez	.50
HO	Ryan Howard	2.00
JD	Jermaine Dye	.50
JM	Joe Mauer	.75
JR	Jose Reyes	1.00
JV	Justin Verlander	1.00
JW	Jered Weaver	1.00
KG	Ken Griffey Jr.	2.00
MD	Mark DeRosa	.50
MO	Justin Morneau	1.00
RH	Roy Halladay	.50
TH	Travis Hafner	.75

L

1990 Leaf

NM/M
Complete Set (528):	75.00
Series 1 (264):	50.00
Series 2 (264):	25.00
Common Player:	.10
Series 1 Foil Pack (15):	4.00
Series 1 Foil Box (36):	80.00
Series 2 Foil Pack (15):	2.50
Series 2 Foil Box (36):	60.00
1	Introductory card	.10
2	Mike Henneman	.10
3	Steve Bedrosian	.10
4	Allan Anderson	.10
5	Mike Scott	.10
6	Rick Sutcliffe	.10
7	Gregg Olson	.10
8	Kevin Elster	.10

BOB TEWKSBURY P

9	Pete O'Brien	.10
10	Carlton Fisk	1.00
11	Joe Magrane	.10
12	Roger Clemens	2.50
13	Tom Glavine	.35
14	Tom Gordon	.10
15	Todd Benzinger	.10
16	Hubie Brooks	.10
17	Roberto Kelly	.10
18	Barry Larkin	.10
19	Mike Boddicker	.10
20	Roger McDowell	.10
21	Nolan Ryan	5.00
22	John Farrell	.10
23	Bruce Hurst	.10
24	Wally Joyner	.10
25	Greg Maddux	2.00
26	Chris Bosio	.10
27	John Cerutti	.10
28	Tim Burke	.10
29	Dennis Eckersley	.75
30	Glenn Davis	.10
31	Jim Abbott	.10
32	Mike LaValliere	.10
33	Andres Thomas	.10
34	Lou Whitaker	.10
35	Alvin Davis	.10
36	Melido Perez	.10
37	Craig Biggio	.10
38	Rick Aguilera	.10
39	Pete Harnisch	.10
40	David Cone	.10
41	Scott Garrelts	.10
42	Jay Howell	.10
43	Eric King	.10
44	Pedro Guerrero	.10
45	Mike Bielecki	.10
46	Bob Boone	.10
47	Kevin Brown	.10
48	Jerry Browne	.10
49	Mike Scioscia	.10
50	Chuck Cary	.10
51	Wade Boggs	2.00
52	Von Hayes	.10
53	Tony Fernandez	.10
54	Dennis Martinez	.10
55	Tom Candiotti	.10
56	Andy Benes	.10
57	Rob Dibble	.10
58	Chuck Crim	.10
59	John Smoltz	.10
60	Mike Heath	.10
61	Kevin Gross	.10
62	Mark McGwire	3.50
63	Bert Blyleven	.10
64	Bob Walk	.10
65	Mickey Tettleton	.10
66	Sid Fernandez	.10
67	Terry Kennedy	.10
68	Fernando Valenzuela	.10
69	Don Mattingly	2.50
70	Paul O'Neill	.10
71	Robin Yount	1.00
72	Bret Saberhagen	.10
73	Geno Petralli	.10
74	Brook Jacoby	.10
75	Roberto Alomar	.25
76	Devon White	.10
77	Jose Lind	.10
78	Pat Combs	.10
79	Dave Steib	.10
80	Tim Wallach	.10
81	Dave Stewart	.10
82	Eric Anthony RC	.10
83	Randy Bush	.10
84	Checklist	.10
85	Jaime Navarro	.10
86	Tommy Gregg	.10
87	Frank Tanana	.10
88	Omar Vizquel	.10
89	Ivan Calderon	.10
90	Vince Coleman	.10
91	Barry Bonds	5.00

92	Randy Milligan	.10
93	Frank Viola	.10
94	Matt Williams	.10
95	Alfredo Griffin	.10
96	Steve Sax	.10
97	Gary Gaetti	.10
98	Ryne Sandberg	2.00
99	Danny Tartabull	.10
100	Rafael Palmeiro	1.00
101	Jesse Orosco	.10
102	Garry Templeton	.10
103	Frank DiPino	.10
104	Tony Pena	.10
105	Dickie Thon	.10
106	Kelly Gruber	.10
107	Marquis Grissom RC	2.00
108	Jose Canseco	.60
109	Mike Blowers	.10
110	Tom Browning	.10
111	Greg Vaughn	.10
112	Oddibe McDowell	.10
113	Gary Ward	.10
114	Jay Buhner	.10
115	Eric Show	.10
116	Bryan Harvey	.10
117	Andy Van Slyke	.10
118	Jeff Ballard	.10
119	Barry Lyons	.10
120	Kevin Mitchell	.10
121	Mike Gallego	.10
122	Dave Smith	.10
123	Kirby Puckett	2.00
124	Jerome Walton	.10
125	Bo Jackson	.20
126	Harold Baines	.10
127	Scott Bankhead	.10
128	Ozzie Guillen	.10
129	Jose Oquendo	.10
130	John Dopson	.10
131	Charlie Hayes	.10
132	Fred McGriff	.10
133	Chet Lemon	.10
134	Gary Carter	1.00
135	Rafael Ramirez	.10
136	Shane Mack	.10
137	Mark Grace	.10
138	Phil Bradley	.10
139	Dwight Gooden	.10
140	Harold Reynolds	.10
141	Scott Fletcher	.10
142	Ozzie Smith	2.00
143	Mike Greenwell	.10
144	Pete Smith	.10
145	Mark Gubicza	.10
146	Chris Sabo	.10
147	Ramon Martinez	.10
148	Tim Leary	.10
149	Randy Myers	.10
150	Jody Reed	.10
151	Bruce Ruffin	.10
152	Jeff Russell	.10
153	Doug Jones	.10
154	Tony Gwynn	2.00
155	Mark Langston	.10
156	Mitch Williams	.10
157	Gary Sheffield	.60
158	Tom Henke	.10
159	Oil Can Boyd	.10
160	Rickey Henderson	1.00
161	Bill Doran	.10
162	Chuck Finley	.10
163	Jeff King	.10
164	Nick Esasky	.10
165	Cecil Fielder	.10
166	Dave Valle	.10
167	Robin Ventura	.10
168	Jim Deshaies	.10
169	Juan Berenguer	.10
170	Craig Worthington	.10
171	Gregg Jefferies	.10
172	Will Clark	.10
173	Kirk Gibson	.10
174	Checklist	.10
175	Bobby Thigpen	.10
176	John Tudor	.10
177	Andre Dawson	.35
178	George Brett	2.50
179	Steve Buechele	.10
180	Albert Belle	.10
181	Eddie Murray	1.00
182	Bob Geren	.10
183	Rob Murphy	.10
184	Tom Herr	.10
185	George Bell	.10
186	Spike Owen	.10
187	Cory Snyder	.10
188	Fred Lynn	.10
189	Eric Davis	.10
190	Dave Parker	.10
191	Jeff Blauser	.10
192	Matt Nokes	.10

193 Delino DeShields RC	.50	296 Doug Drabek	.10
194 Scott Sanderson	.10	297 Dave Justice RC	2.00
195 Lance Parrish	.10	298 Paul Gibson	.10
196 Bobby Bonilla	.10	299 Edgar Martinez	.10
197 Cal Ripken, Jr.	5.00	300 Frank Thomas RC	20.00
198 Kevin McReynolds	.10	301 Eric Yelding	.10
199 Robby Thompson	.10	302 Greg Gagne	.10
200 Tim Belcher	.10	303 Brad Komminsk	.10
201 Jesse Barfield	.10	304 Ron Darling	.10
202 Mariano Duncan	.10	305 Kevin Bass	.10
203 Bill Spiers	.10	306 Jeff Hamilton	.10
204 Frank White	.10	307 Ron Karkovice	.10
205 Julio Franco	.10	308 Milt Thompson	.10
206 Greg Swindell	.10	309 Mike Harkey	.10
207 Benito Santiago	.10	310 Mel Stottlemyre	.10
208 Johnny Ray	.10	311 Kenny Rogers	.10
209 Gary Redus	.10	312 Mitch Webster	.10
210 Jeff Parrett	.10	313 Kal Daniels	.10
211 Jimmy Key	.10	314 Matt Nokes	.10
212 Tim Raines	.10	315 Dennis Lamp	.10
213 Carney Lansford	.10	316 Ken Howell	.10
214 Gerald Young	.10	317 Glenallen Hill	.10
215 Gene Larkin	.10	318 Dave Martinez	.10
216 Dan Plesac	.10	319 Chris James	.10
217 Lonnie Smith	.10	320 Mike Pagliarulo	.10
218 Alan Trammell	.10	321 Hal Morris	.10
219 Jeffrey Leonard	.10	322 Rob Deer	.10
220 Sammy Sosa RC	20.00	323 Greg Olson	.10
221 Todd Zeile	.10	324 Tony Phillips	.10
222 Bill Landrum	.10	325 Larry Walker RC	8.00
223 Mike Devereaux	.10	326 Ron Hassey	.10
224 Mike Marshall	.10	327 Jack Howell	.10
225 Jose Uribe	.10	328 John Smiley	.10
226 Juan Samuel	.10	329 Steve Finley	.10
227 Mel Hall	.10	330 Dave Magadan	.10
228 Kent Hrbek	.10	331 Greg Litton	.10
229 Shawon Dunston	.10	332 Mickey Hatcher	.10
230 Kevin Seitzer	.10	333 Lee Guetterman	.10
231 Pete Incaviglia	.10	334 Norm Charlton	.10
232 Sandy Alomar	.10	335 Edgar Diaz	.10
233 Bip Roberts	.10	336 Willie Wilson	.10
234 Scott Terry	.10	337 Bobby Witt	.10
235 Dwight Evans	.10	338 Candy Maldonado	.10
236 Ricky Jordan	.10	339 Craig Lefferts	.10
237 John Olerud RC	5.00	340 Dante Bichette	.10
238 Zane Smith	.10	341 Wally Backman	.10
239 Walt Weiss	.10	342 Dennis Cook	.10
240 Alvaro Espinoza	.10	343 Pat Borders	.10
241 Billy Hatcher	.10	344 Wallace Johnson	.10
242 Paul Molitor	1.00	345 Willie Randolph	.10
243 Dale Murphy	.30	346 Danny Darwin	.10
244 Dave Bergman	.10	347 Al Newman	.10
245 Ken Griffey Jr.	3.00	348 Mark Knudson	.10
246 Ed Whitson	.10	349 Joe Boever	.10
247 Kirk McCaskill	.10	350 Larry Sheets	.10
248 Jay Bell	.10	351 Mike Jackson	.10
249 Ben McDonald RC	.50	352 Wayne Edwards	.10
250 Darryl Strawberry	.10	353 Bernard Gilkey RC	.50
251 Brett Butler	.10	354 Don Slaught	.10
252 Terry Steinbach	.10	355 Joe Orsulak	.10
253 Ken Caminiti	.10	356 John Franco	.10
254 Dan Gladden	.10	357 Jeff Brantley	.10
255 Dwight Smith	.10	358 Mike Morgan	.10
256 Kurt Stillwell	.10	359 Deion Sanders	.10
257 Ruben Sierra	.10	360 Terry Leach	.10
258 Mike Schooler	.10	361 Les Lancaster	.10
259 Lance Johnson	.10	362 Storm Davis	.10
260 Terry Pendleton	.10	363 Scott Coolbaugh	.10
261 Ellis Burks	.10	364 Checklist	.10
262 Len Dykstra	.10	365 Cecilio Guante	.10
263 Mookie Wilson	.10	366 Joey Cora	.10
264 Checklist (Nolan Ryan)	.10	367 Willie McGee	.10
265 Nolan Ryan (No-Hit King)	2.00	368 Jerry Reed	.10
266 Brian DuBois	.10	369 Darren Daulton	.10
267 Don Robinson	.10	370 Manny Lee	.10
268 Glenn Wilson	.10	371 Mark Gardner	.10
269 Kevin Tapani RC	.25	372 Rick Honeycutt	.10
270 Marvell Wynne	.10	373 Steve Balboni	.10
271 Billy Ripken	.10	374 Jack Armstrong	.10
272 Howard Johnson	.10	375 Charlie O'Brien	.10
273 Brian Holman	.10	376 Ron Gant	.10
274 Dan Pasqua	.10	377 Lloyd Moseby	.10
275 Ken Dayley	.10	378 Gene Harris	.10
276 Jeff Reardon	.10	379 Joe Carter	.10
277 Jim Presley	.10	380 Scott Bailes	.10
278 Jim Eisenreich	.10	381 R.J. Reynolds	.10
279 Danny Jackson	.10	382 Bob Melvin	.10
280 Orel Hershiser	.10	383 Tim Teufel	.10
281 Andy Hawkins	.10	384 John Burkett	.10
282 Jose Rijo	.10	385 Felix Jose	.10
283 Luis Rivera	.10	386 Larry Andersen	.10
284 John Kruk	.10	387 David West	.10
285 Jeff Huson	.10	388 Luis Salazar	.10
286 Joel Skinner	.10	389 Mike Macfarlane	.10
287 Jack Clark	.10	390 Charlie Hough	.10
288 Chili Davis	.10	391 Greg Briley	.10
289 Joe Girardi	.10	392 Donn Pall	.10
290 B.J. Surhoff	.10	393 Bryn Smith	.10
291 Luis Sojo	.10	394 Carlos Quintana	.10
292 Tom Foley	.10	395 Steve Lake	.10
293 Mike Moore	.10	396 Mark Whiten RC	.15
294 Ken Oberkfell	.10	397 Edwin Nunez	.10
295 Luis Polonia	.10	398 Rick Parker	.10
		399 Mark Portugal	.10

400 Roy Smith	.10	504 Eric Plunk	.10
401 Hector Villanueva	.10	505 Jeff Reed	.10
402 Bob Milacki	.10	506 Ted Higuera	.10
403 Alejandro Pena	.10	507 Joe Hesketh	.10
404 Scott Bradley	.10	508 Dan Petry	.10
405 Ron Kittle	.10	509 Matt Young	.10
406 Bob Tewksbury	.10	510 Jerald Clark	.10
407 Wes Gardner	.10	511 John Orton RC	.10
408 Ernie Whitt	.10	512 Scott Ruskin	.10
409 Terry Shumpert	.10	513 Chris Hoiles RC	.50
410 Tim Layana	.10	514 Daryl Boston	.10
411 Chris Gwynn	.10	515 Francisco Oliveras	.10
412 Jeff Robinson	.10	516 Ozzie Canseco	.10
413 Scott Scudder	.10	517 Xavier Hernandez RC	.10
414 Kevin Romine	.10	518 Fred Manrique	.10
415 Jose DeJesus	.10	519 Shawn Boskie	.10
416 Mike Jeffcoat	.10	520 Jeff Montgomery	.10
417 Rudy Seanez	.10	521 Jack Daugherty	.10
418 Mike Dunne	.10	522 Keith Comstock	.10
419 Dick Schofield	.10	523 Greg Hibbard RC	.10
420 Steve Wilson	.10	524 Lee Smith	.10
421 Bill Krueger	.10	525 Dana Kiecker	.10
422 Junior Felix	.10	526 Darrel Akerfelds	.10
423 Drew Hall	.10	527 Greg Myers	.10
424 Curt Young	.10	528 Checklist	.10
425 Franklin Stubbs	.10		
426 Dave Winfield	1.00		
427 Rick Reed	.10		
428 Charlie Leibrandt	.10		
429 Jeff Robinson	.10		
430 Erik Hanson	.10		
431 Barry Jones	.10		
432 Alex Trevino	.10		
433 John Moses	.10		
434 Dave Johnson	.10		
435 Mackey Sasser	.10		
436 Rick Leach	.10		
437 Lenny Harris	.10		
438 Carlos Martinez	.10		
439 Rex Hudler	.10		
440 Domingo Ramos	.10		
441 Gerald Perry	.10		
442 John Russell	.10		
443 Carlos Baerga RC	.50		
444 Checklist	.10		
445 Stan Javier	.10		
446 Kevin Maas RC	.10		
447 Tom Brunansky	.10		
448 Carmelo Martinez	.10		
449 Willie Blair RC	.10		
450 Andres Galarraga	.10		
451 Bud Black	.10		
452 Greg Harris	.10		
453 Joe Oliver	.10		
454 Greg Brock	.10		
455 Jeff Treadway	.10		
456 Lance McCullers	.10		
457 Dave Schmidt	.10		
458 Todd Burns	.10		
459 Max Venable	.10		
460 Neal Heaton	.10		
461 Mark Williamson	.10		
462 Keith Miller	.10		
463 Mike LaCoss	.10		
464 Jose Offerman RC	.25		
465 Jim Leyritz RC	.50		
466 Glenn Braggs	.10		
467 Ron Robinson	.10		
468 Mark Davis	.10		
469 Gary Pettis	.10		
470 Keith Hernandez	.10		
471 Dennis Rasmussen	.10		
472 Mark Eichhorn	.10		
473 Ted Power	.10		
474 Terry Mulholland	.10		
475 Todd Stottlemyre	.10		
476 Jerry Goff	.10		
477 Gene Nelson	.10		
478 Rich Gedman	.10		
479 Brian Harper	.10		
480 Mike Felder	.10		
481 Steve Avery	.10		
482 Jack Morris	.10		
483 Randy Johnson	1.00		
484 Scott Radinsky	.10		
485 Jose DeLeon	.10		
486 Stan Belinda RC	.10		
487 Brian Holton	.10		
488 Mark Carreon	.10		
489 Trevor Wilson	.10		
490 Mike Sharperson	.10		
491 Alan Mills RC	.10		
492 John Candelaria	.10		
493 Paul Assenmacher	.10		
494 Steve Crawford	.10		
495 Brad Arnsberg	.10		
496 Sergio Valdez	.10		
497 Mark Parent	.10		
498 Tom Pagnozzi	.10		
499 Greg Harris	.10		
500 Randy Ready	.10		
501 Duane Ward	.10		
502 Nelson Santovenia	.10		
503 Joe Klink	.10		

1990 Leaf Previews

JOE CARTER OF

	NM/M
Complete Set (12):	275.00
Common Player:	12.50
1 Steve Sax	12.50
2 Joe Carter	12.50
3 Dennis Eckersley	20.00
4 Ken Griffey Jr.	200.00
5 Barry Larkin	12.50
6 Mark Langston	12.50
7 Eric Anthony	12.50
8 Robin Ventura	12.50
9 Greg Vaughn	12.50
10 Bobby Bonilla	12.50
11 Gary Gaetti	12.50
12 Ozzie Smith	75.00

1991 Leaf

JOHN OLERUD 1B

	NM/M
Complete Set (528):	8.00
Common Player:	.05
Series 1 or 2 Pack (15):	.50
Series 1 or 2 Box (36):	12.50
1 The Leaf Card	.05
2 Kurt Stillwell	.05
3 Bobby Witt	.05
4 Tony Phillips	.05
5 Scott Garrelts	.05
6 Greg Swindell	.05
7 Billy Ripken	.05
8 Dave Martinez	.05
9 Kelly Gruber	.05
10 Juan Samuel	.05
11 Brian Holman	.05
12 Craig Biggio	.05

#	Player	Price	#	Player	Price	#	Player	Price	#	Player	Price
13	Lonnie Smith	.05	117	Ben McDonald	.05	220	Steve Sax	.05	324	John Candelaria	.05
14	Ron Robinson	.05	118	Bret Saberhagen	.05	221	Shawn Boskie	.05	325	David Howard	.05
15	Mike LaValliere	.05	119	Juan Gonzalez	.35	222	Rich DeLucia	.05	326	Jose Rijo	.05
16	Mark Davis	.05	120	Lou Whitaker	.05	223	Lloyd Moseby	.05	327	Todd Zeile	.05
17	Jack Daugherty	.05	121	Ellis Burks	.05	224	Mike Kingery	.05	328	Gene Nelson	.05
18	Mike Henneman	.05	122	Charlie O'Brien	.05	225	Carlos Baerga	.05	329	Dwayne Henry	.05
19	Mike Greenwell	.05	123	John Smiley	.05	226	Bryn Smith	.05	330	Mike Boddicker	.05
20	Dave Magadan	.05	124	Tim Burke	.05	227	Todd Stottlemyre	.05	331	Ozzie Guillen	.05
21	Mark Williamson	.05	125	John Olerud	.05	228	Julio Franco	.05	332	Sam Horn	.05
22	Marquis Grissom	.05	126	Eddie Murray	.45	229	Jim Gott	.05	333	Wally Whitehurst	.05
23	Pat Borders	.05	127	Greg Maddux	.60	230	Mike Schooler	.05	334	Dave Parker	.05
24	Mike Scioscia	.05	128	Kevin Tapani	.05	231	Steve Finley	.05	335	George Brett	.75
25	Shawon Dunston	.05	129	Ron Gant	.05	232	Dave Henderson	.05	336	Bobby Thigpen	.05
26	Randy Bush	.05	130	Jay Bell	.05	233	Luis Quinones	.05	337	Ed Whitson	.05
27	John Smoltz	.05	131	Chris Hoiles	.05	234	Mark Whiten	.05	338	Ivan Calderon	.05
28	Chuck Crim	.05	132	Tom Gordon	.05	235	Brian McRae	.05	339	Mike Pagliarulo	.05
29	Don Slaught	.05	133	Kevin Seitzer	.05	236	Rich Gossage	.05	340	Jack McDowell	.05
30	Mike Macfarlane	.05	134	Jeff Huson	.05	237	Rob Deer	.05	341	Dana Kiecker	.05
31	Wally Joyner	.05	135	Jerry Don Gleaton	.05	238	Will Clark	.10	342	Fred McGriff	.05
32	Pat Combs	.05	136	Jeff Brantley	.05	239	Albert Belle	.05	343	Mark Lee	.05
33	Tony Pena	.05	137	Felix Fermin	.05	240	Bob Melvin	.05	344	Alfredo Griffin	.05
34	Howard Johnson	.05	138	Mike Devereaux	.05	241	Larry Walker	.05	345	Scott Bankhead	.05
35	Leo Gomez	.05	139	Delino DeShields	.05	242	Dante Bichette	.05	346	Darrin Jackson	.05
36	Spike Owen	.05	140	David Wells	.05	243	Orel Hershiser	.05	347	Rafael Palmeiro	.35
37	Eric Davis	.05	141	Tim Crews	.05	244	Pete O'Brien	.05	348	Steve Farr	.05
38	Roberto Kelly	.05	142	Erik Hanson	.05	245	Pete Harnisch	.05	349	Hensley Meulens	.05
39	Jerome Walton	.05	143	Mark Davidson	.05	246	Jeff Treadway	.05	350	Danny Cox	.05
40	Shane Mack	.05	144	Tommy Gregg	.05	247	Julio Machado	.05	351	Alan Trammell	.05
41	Kent Mercker	.05	145	Jim Gantner	.05	248	Dave Johnson	.05	352	Edwin Nunez	.05
42	B.J. Surhoff	.05	146	Jose Lind	.05	249	Kirk Gibson	.05	353	Joe Carter	.05
43	Jerry Browne	.05	147	Danny Tartabull	.05	250	Kevin Brown	.05	354	Eric Show	.05
44	Lee Smith	.05	148	Geno Petralli	.05	251	Milt Cuyler	.05	355	Vance Law	.05
45	Chuck Finley	.05	149	Travis Fryman	.05	252	Jeff Reardon	.05	356	Jeff Gray	.05
46	Terry Mulholland	.05	150	Tim Naehring	.05	253	David Cone	.05	357	Bobby Bonilla	.05
47	Tom Bolton	.05	151	Kevin McReynolds	.05	254	Gary Redus	.05	358	Ernest Riles	.05
48	Tom Herr	.05	152	Joe Orsulak	.05	255	Junior Noboa	.05	359	Ron Hassey	.05
49	Jim Deshaies	.05	153	Steve Frey	.05	256	Greg Myers	.05	360	Willie McGee	.05
50	Walt Weiss	.05	154	Duane Ward	.05	257	Dennis Cook	.05	361	Mackey Sasser	.05
51	Hal Morris	.05	155	Stan Javier	.05	258	Joe Girardi	.05	362	Glenn Braggs	.05
52	Lee Guetterman	.05	156	Damon Berryhill	.05	259	Allan Anderson	.05	363	Mario Diaz	.05
53	Paul Assenmacher	.05	157	Gene Larkin	.05	260	Paul Marak	.05	364	Barry Bonds Checklist	.35
54	Brian Harper	.05	158	Greg Olson	.05	261	Barry Bonds	2.00	365	Kevin Bass	.05
55	Paul Gibson	.05	159	Mark Knudson	.05	262	Juan Bell	.05	366	Pete Incaviglia	.05
56	John Burkett	.05	160	Carmelo Martinez	.05	263	Russ Morman	.05	367	Luis Sojo	.05
57	Doug Jones	.05	161	Storm Davis	.05	264	George Brett Checklist	.25	368	Lance Parrish	.05
58	Jose Oquendo	.05	162	Jim Abbott	.05	265	Jerald Clark	.05	369	Mark Leonard	.05
59	Dick Schofield	.05	163	Len Dykstra	.05	266	Dwight Evans	.05	370	Heathcliff Slocumb	.05
60	Dickie Thon	.05	164	Tom Brunansky	.05	267	Roberto Alomar	.15	371	Jimmy Jones	.05
61	Ramon Martinez	.05	165	Dwight Gooden	.05	268	Danny Jackson	.05	372	Ken Griffey Jr.	1.00
62	Jay Buhner	.05	166	Jose Mesa	.05	269	Brian Downing	.05	373	Chris Hammond	.05
63	Mark Portugal	.05	167	Oil Can Boyd	.05	270	John Cerutti	.05	374	Chili Davis	.05
64	Bob Welch	.05	168	Barry Larkin	.05	271	Robin Ventura	.05	375	Joey Cora	.05
65	Chris Sabo	.05	169	Scott Sanderson	.05	272	Gerald Perry	.05	376	Ken Hill	.05
66	Chuck Cary	.05	170	Mark Grace	.05	273	Wade Boggs	.60	377	Darryl Strawberry	.05
67	Mark Langston	.05	171	Mark Guthrie	.05	274	Dennis Martinez	.05	378	Ron Darling	.05
68	Joe Boever	.05	172	Tom Glavine	.15	275	Andy Benes	.05	379	Sid Bream	.05
69	Jody Reed	.05	173	Gary Sheffield	.30	276	Tony Fossas	.05	380	Bill Swift	.05
70	Alejandro Pena	.05	174	Roger Clemens Checklist	.25	277	Franklin Stubbs	.05	381	Shawn Abner	.05
71	Jeff King	.05	175	Chris James	.05	278	John Kruk	.05	382	Eric King	.05
72	Tom Pagnozzi	.05	176	Milt Thompson	.05	279	Kevin Gross	.05	383	Mickey Morandini	.05
73	Joe Oliver	.05	177	Donnie Hill	.05	280	Von Hayes	.05	384	Carlton Fisk	.45
74	Mike Witt	.05	178	Wes Chamberlain	.05	281	Frank Thomas	.45	385	Steve Lake	.05
75	Hector Villanueva	.05	179	John Marzano	.05	282	Rob Dibble	.05	386	Mike Jeffcoat	.05
76	Dan Gladden	.05	180	Frank Viola	.05	283	Mel Hall	.05	387	Darren Holmes	.05
77	Dave Justice	.05	181	Eric Anthony	.05	284	Rick Mahler	.05	388	Tim Wallach	.05
78	Mike Gallego	.05	182	Jose Canseco	.30	285	Dennis Eckersley	.35	389	George Bell	.05
79	Tom Candiotti	.05	183	Scott Scudder	.05	286	Bernard Gilkey	.05	390	Craig Lefferts	.05
80	Ozzie Smith	.60	184	Dave Eiland	.05	287	Dan Plesac	.05	391	Ernie Whitt	.05
81	Luis Polonia	.05	185	Luis Salazar	.05	288	Jason Grimsley	.05	392	Felix Jose	.05
82	Randy Ready	.05	186	Pedro Munoz	.05	289	Mark Lewis	.05	393	Kevin Maas	.05
83	Greg Harris	.05	187	Steve Searcy	.05	290	Tony Gwynn	.60	394	Devon White	.05
84	Dave Justice Checklist	.05	188	Don Robinson	.05	291	Jeff Russell	.05	395	Otis Nixon	.05
85	Kevin Mitchell	.05	189	Sandy Alomar	.05	292	Curt Schilling	.25	396	Chuck Knoblauch	.05
86	Mark McLemore	.05	190	Jose DeLeon	.05	293	Pascual Perez	.05	397	Scott Coolbaugh	.05
87	Terry Steinbach	.05	191	John Orton	.05	294	Jack Morris	.05	398	Glenn Davis	.05
88	Tom Browning	.05	192	Darren Daulton	.05	295	Hubie Brooks	.05	399	Manny Lee	.05
89	Matt Nokes	.05	193	Mike Morgan	.05	296	Alex Fernandez	.05	400	Andre Dawson	.20
90	Mike Harkey	.05	194	Greg Briley	.05	297	Harold Reynolds	.05	401	Scott Chiamparino	.05
91	Omar Vizquel	.05	195	Karl Rhodes	.05	298	Craig Worthington	.05	402	Bill Gullickson	.05
92	Dave Bergman	.05	196	Harold Baines	.05	299	Willie Wilson	.05	403	Lance Johnson	.05
93	Matt Williams	.05	197	Bill Doran	.05	300	Mike Maddux	.05	404	Juan Agosto	.05
94	Steve Olin	.05	198	Alvaro Espinoza	.05	301	Dave Righetti	.05	405	Danny Darwin	.05
95	Craig Wilson	.05	199	Kirk McCaskill	.05	302	Paul Molitor	.45	406	Barry Jones	.05
96	Dave Stieb	.05	200	Jose DeJesus	.05	303	Gary Gaetti	.05	407	Larry Andersen	.05
97	Ruben Sierra	.05	201	Jack Clark	.05	304	Terry Pendleton	.05	408	Luis Rivera	.05
98	Jay Howell	.05	202	Daryl Boston	.05	305	Kevin Elster	.05	409	Jaime Navarro	.05
99	Scott Bradley	.05	203	Randy Tomlin	.05	306	Scott Fletcher	.05	410	Roger McDowell	.05
100	Eric Yelding	.05	204	Pedro Guerrero	.05	307	Jeff Robinson	.05	411	Brett Butler	.05
101	Rickey Henderson	.45	205	Billy Hatcher	.05	308	Jesse Barfield	.05	412	Dale Murphy	.15
102	Jeff Reed	.05	206	Tim Leary	.05	309	Mike LaCoss	.05	413	Tim Raines	.05
103	Jimmy Key	.05	207	Ryne Sandberg	.60	310	Andy Van Slyke	.05	414	Norm Charlton	.05
104	Terry Shumpert	.05	208	Kirby Puckett	.60	311	Glenallen Hill	.05	415	Greg Cadaret	.05
105	Kenny Rogers	.05	209	Charlie Leibrandt	.05	312	Bud Black	.05	416	Chris Nabholz	.05
106	Cecil Fielder	.05	210	Rick Honeycutt	.05	313	Kent Hrbek	.05	417	Dave Stewart	.05
107	Robby Thompson	.05	211	Joel Skinner	.05	314	Tim Teufel	.05	418	Rich Gedman	.05
108	Alex Cole	.05	212	Rex Hudler	.05	315	Tony Fernandez	.05	419	Willie Randolph	.05
109	Randy Milligan	.05	213	Bryan Harvey	.05	316	Beau Allred	.05	420	Mitch Williams	.05
110	Andres Galarraga	.05	214	Charlie Hayes	.05	317	Curtis Wilkerson	.05	421	Brook Jacoby	.05
111	Bill Spiers	.05	215	Matt Young	.05	318	Bill Sampen	.05	422	Greg Harris	.05
112	Kal Daniels	.05	216	Terry Kennedy	.05	319	Randy Johnson	.45	423	Nolan Ryan	2.00
113	Henry Cotto	.05	217	Carl Nichols	.05	320	Mike Heath	.05	424	Dave Rohde	.05
114	Casy Candaele	.05	218	Mike Moore	.05	321	Sammy Sosa	1.00	425	Don Mattingly	.75
115	Jeff Blauser	.05	219	Paul O'Neill	.05	322	Mickey Tettleton	.05	426	Greg Gagne	.05
116	Robin Yount	.45				323	Jose Vizcaino	.05	427	Vince Coleman	.05

428	Dan Pasqua	.05
429	Alvin Davis	.05
430	Cal Ripken, Jr.	2.00
431	Jamie Quirk	.05
432	Benito Santiago	.05
433	Jose Uribe	.05
434	Candy Maldonado	.05
435	Junior Felix	.05
436	Deion Sanders	.05
437	John Franco	.05
438	Greg Hibbard	.05
439	Floyd Bannister	.05
440	Steve Howe	.05
441	Steve Decker	.05
442	Vicente Palacios	.05
443	Pat Tabler	.05
444	Darryl Strawberry Checklist	.05
445	Mike Felder	.05
446	Al Newman	.05
447	Chris Donnels	.05
448	Rich Rodriguez	.05
449	Turner Ward	.05
450	Bob Walk	.05
451	Gilberto Reyes	.05
452	Mike Jackson	.05
453	Rafael Belliard	.05
454	Wayne Edwards	.05
455	Andy Allanson	.05
456	Dave Smith	.05
457	Gary Carter	.45
458	Warren Cromartie	.05
459	Jack Armstrong	.05
460	Bob Tewksbury	.05
461	Joe Klink	.05
462	Xavier Hernandez	.05
463	Scott Radinsky	.05
464	Jeff Robinson	.05
465	Gregg Jefferies	.05
466	Denny Neagle	.05
467	Carmelo Martinez	.05
468	Donn Pall	.05
469	Bruce Hurst	.05
470	Eric Bullock	.05
471	Rick Aguilera	.05
472	Charlie Hough	.05
473	Carlos Quintana	.05
474	Marty Barrett	.05
475	Kevin Brown	.05
476	Bobby Ojeda	.05
477	Edgar Martinez	.05
478	Bip Roberts	.05
479	Mike Flanagan	.05
480	John Habyan	.05
481	Larry Casian	.05
482	Wally Backman	.05
483	Doug Dascenzo	.05
484	Rick Dempsey	.05
485	Ed Sprague	.05
486	Steve Chitren	.05
487	Mark McGwire	1.50
488	Roger Clemens	.75
489	Orlando Merced	.05
490	Rene Gonzales	.05
491	Mike Stanton	.05
492	Al Osuna	.05
493	Rick Cerone	.05
494	Mariano Duncan	.05
495	Zane Smith	.05
496	John Morris	.05
497	Frank Tanana	.05
498	Junior Ortiz	.05
499	Dave Winfield	.45
500	Gary Varsho	.05
501	Chico Walker	.05
502	Ken Caminiti	.05
503	Ken Griffey Sr.	.05
504	Randy Myers	.05
505	Steve Bedrosian	.05
506	Cory Snyder	.05
507	Cris Carpenter	.05
508	Tim Belcher	.05
509	Jeff Hamilton	.05
510	Steve Avery	.05
511	Dave Valle	.05
512	Tom Lampkin	.05
513	Shawn Hillegas	.05
514	Reggie Jefferson	.05
515	Ron Karkovice	.05
516	Doug Drabek	.05
517	Tom Henke	.05
518	Chris Bosio	.05
519	Gregg Olson	.05
520	Bob Scanlan	.05
521	Alonzo Powell	.05
522	Jeff Ballard	.05
523	Ray Lankford	.05
524	Tommy Greene	.05
525	Mike Timlin	.05
526	Juan Berenguer	.05
527	Scott Erickson	.05
528	Sandy Alomar Jr. Checklist	.05

Gold Rookies

MO VAUGHN 1B

		NM/M
Complete Set (26):		10.00
Common Player:		.10
1	Scott Leius	.10
2	Luis Gonzalez	.40
3	Wil Cordero	.10
4	Gary Scott	.10
5	Willie Banks	.10
6	Arthur Rhodes	.10
7	Mo Vaughn	.25
8	Henry Rodriguez	.10
9	Todd Van Poppel	.10
10	Reggie Sanders	.10
11	Rico Brogna	.10
12	Mike Mussina	2.00
13	Kirk Dressendorfer	.10
14	Jeff Bagwell	6.00
15	Pete Schourek	.10
16	Wade Taylor	.10
17	Pat Kelly	.10
18	Tim Costo	.10
19	Roger Salkeld	.10
20	Andujar Cedeno	.10
21	Ryan Klesko	.10
22	Mike Huff	.10
23	Anthony Young	.10
24	Eddie Zosky	.10
25	Nolan Ryan (7th no-hitter)	.50
26	Rickey Henderson (Record Steal)	.25
265	Scott Leius	4.00
266	Luis Gonzalez	6.00
267	Wil Cordero	4.00
268	Gary Scott	4.00
269	Willie Banks	4.00
270	Arthur Rhodes	4.00
271	Mo Vaughn	10.00
272	Henry Rodriguez	4.00
273	Todd Van Poppel	4.00
274	Reggie Sanders	4.00
275	Rico Brogna	4.00
276	Mike Mussina	30.00

1992 Leaf

TRAVIS FRYMAN 3B

		NM/M
Complete Set (528):		7.50
Common Player:		.05
Series 1 or 2 Pack:		.40
Series 1 or 2 Wax Box:		7.50
1	Jim Abbott	.05
2	Cal Eldred	.05
3	Bud Black	.05
4	Dave Howard	.05
5	Luis Sojo	.05
6	Gary Scott	.05
7	Joe Oliver	.05
8	Chris Gardner	.05
9	Sandy Alomar	.05

10	Greg Harris	.05
11	Doug Drabek	.05
12	Darryl Hamilton	.05
13	Mike Mussina	.30
14	Kevin Tapani	.05
15	Ron Gant	.05
16	Mark McGwire	1.00
17	Robin Ventura	.05
18	Pedro Guerrero	.05
19	Roger Clemens	.65
20	Steve Farr	.05
21	Frank Tanana	.05
22	Joe Hesketh	.05
23	Erik Hanson	.05
24	Greg Cadaret	.05
25	Rex Hudler	.05
26	Mark Grace	.05
27	Kelly Gruber	.05
28	Jeff Bagwell	.45
29	Darryl Strawberry	.05
30	Dave Smith	.05
31	Kevin Appier	.05
32	Steve Chitren	.05
33	Kevin Gross	.05
34	Rick Aguilera	.05
35	Juan Guzman	.05
36	Joe Orsulak	.05
37	Tim Raines	.05
38	Harold Reynolds	.05
39	Charlie Hough	.05
40	Tony Phillips	.05
41	Nolan Ryan	1.50
42	Vince Coleman	.05
43	Andy Van Slyke	.05
44	Tim Burke	.05
45	Luis Polonia	.05
46	Tom Browning	.05
47	Willie McGee	.05
48	Gary DiSarcina	.05
49	Mark Lewis	.05
50	Phil Plantier	.05
51	Doug Dascenzo	.05
52	Cal Ripken, Jr.	1.50
53	Pedro Munoz	.05
54	Carlos Hernandez	.05
55	Jerald Clark	.05
56	Jeff Brantley	.05
57	Don Mattingly	.65
58	Roger McDowell	.05
59	Steve Avery	.05
60	John Olerud	.05
61	Bill Gullickson	.05
62	Juan Gonzalez	.30
63	Felix Jose	.05
64	Robin Yount	.45
65	Greg Briley	.05
66	Steve Finley	.05
67	Checklist	.05
68	Tom Gordon	.05
69	Rob Dibble	.05
70	Glenallen Hill	.05
71	Calvin Jones	.05
72	Joe Girardi	.05
73	Barry Larkin	.05
74	Andy Benes	.05
75	Milt Cuyler	.05
76	Kevin Bass	.05
77	Pete Harnisch	.05
78	Wilson Alvarez	.05
79	Mike Devereaux	.05
80	Doug Henry	.05
81	Orel Hershiser	.05
82	Shane Mack	.05
83	Mike Macfarlane	.05
84	Thomas Howard	.05
85	Alex Fernandez	.05
86	Reggie Jefferson	.05
87	Leo Gomez	.05
88	Mel Hall	.05
89	Mike Greenwell	.05
90	Jeff Russell	.05
91	Steve Buechele	.05
92	David Cone	.05
93	Kevin Reimer	.05
94	Mark Lemke	.05
95	Bob Tewksbury	.05
96	Zane Smith	.05
97	Mark Eichhorn	.05
98	Kirby Puckett	.60
99	Paul O'Neill	.05
100	Dennis Eckersley	.35
101	Duane Ward	.05
102	Matt Nokes	.05
103	Mo Vaughn	.05
104	Pat Kelly	.05
105	Ron Karkovice	.05
106	Bill Spiers	.05
107	Gary Gaetti	.05
108	Mackey Sasser	.05
109	Robby Thompson	.05
110	Marvin Freeman	.05
111	Jimmy Key	.05
112	Dwight Gooden	.05
113	Charlie Leibrandt	.05

114	Devon White	.05
115	Charles Nagy	.05
116	Rickey Henderson	.45
117	Paul Assenmacher	.05
118	Junior Felix	.05
119	Julio Franco	.05
120	Norm Charlton	.05
121	Scott Servais	.05
122	Gerald Perry	.05
123	Brian McRae	.05
124	Don Slaught	.05
125	Juan Samuel	.05
126	Harold Baines	.05
127	Scott Livingstone	.05
128	Jay Buhner	.05
129	Darrin Jackson	.05
130	Luis Mercedes	.05
131	Brian Harper	.05
132	Howard Johnson	.05
133	Checklist	.05
134	Dante Bichette	.05
135	Dave Righetti	.05
136	Jeff Montgomery	.05
137	Joe Grahe	.05
138	Delino DeShields	.05
139	Jose Rijo	.05
140	Ken Caminiti	.05
141	Steve Olin	.05
142	Kurt Stillwell	.05
143	Jay Bell	.05
144	Jaime Navarro	.05
145	Ben McDonald	.05
146	Greg Gagne	.05
147	Jeff Blauser	.05
148	Carney Lansford	.05
149	Ozzie Guillen	.05
150	Milt Thompson	.05
151	Jeff Reardon	.05
152	Scott Sanderson	.05
153	Cecil Fielder	.05
154	Greg Harris	.05
155	Rich DeLucia	.05
156	Roberto Kelly	.05
157	Bryn Smith	.05
158	Chuck McElroy	.05
159	Tom Henke	.05
160	Luis Gonzalez	.25
161	Steve Wilson	.05
162	Shawn Boskie	.05
163	Mark Davis	.05
164	Mike Moore	.05
165	Mike Scioscia	.05
166	Scott Erickson	.05
167	Todd Stottlemyre	.05
168	Alvin Davis	.05
169	Greg Hibbard	.05
170	David Valle	.05
171	Dave Winfield	.45
172	Alan Trammell	.05
173	Kenny Rogers	.05
174	John Franco	.05
175	Jose Lind	.05
176	Pete Schourek	.05
177	Von Hayes	.05
178	Chris Hammond	.05
179	John Burkett	.05
180	Dickie Thon	.05
181	Joel Skinner	.05
182	Scott Cooper	.05
183	Andre Dawson	.25
184	Billy Ripken	.05
185	Kevin Mitchell	.05
186	Brett Butler	.05
187	Tony Fernandez	.05
188	Cory Snyder	.05
189	John Habyan	.05
190	Dennis Martinez	.05
191	John Smoltz	.05
192	Greg Myers	.05
193	Rob Deer	.05
194	Ivan Rodriguez	.45
195	Ray Lankford	.05
196	Bill Wegman	.05
197	Edgar Martinez	.05
198	Darryl Kile	.05
199	Checklist	.05
200	Brent Mayne	.05
201	Larry Walker	.05
202	Carlos Baerga	.05
203	Russ Swan	.05
204	Mike Morgan	.05
205	Hal Morris	.05
206	Tony Gwynn	.60
207	Mark Leiter	.05
208	Kirt Manwaring	.05
209	Al Osuna	.05
210	Bobby Thigpen	.05
211	Chris Hoiles	.05
212	B.J. Surhoff	.05
213	Lenny Harris	.05
214	Scott Leius	.05
215	Gregg Jefferies	.05
216	Bruce Hurst	.05
217	Steve Sax	.05

218	Dave Otto	.05	322	Jose Offerman	.05	426	Moises Alou	.05
219	Sam Horn	.05	323	Tony Pena	.05	427	Mark McLemore	.05
220	Charlie Hayes	.05	324	Pat Borders	.05	428	Juan Guerrero	.05
221	Frank Viola	.05	325	Mike Henneman	.05	429	Scott Scudder	.05
222	Jose Guzman	.05	326	Kevin Brown	.05	430	Eric Davis	.05
223	Gary Redus	.05	327	Chris Nabholz	.05	431	Joe Slusarski	.05
224	Dave Gallagher	.05	328	Franklin Stubbs	.05	432	Todd Zeile	.05
225	Dean Palmer	.05	329	Tino Martinez	.05	433	Dwayne Henry	.05
226	Greg Olson	.05	330	Mickey Morandini	.05	434	Cliff Brantley	.05
227	Jose DeLeon	.05	331	Checklist	.05	435	Butch Henry	.05
228	Mike LaValliere	.05	332	Mark Gubicza	.05	436	Todd Worrell	.05
229	Mark Langston	.05	333	Bill Landrum	.05	437	Bob Scanlan	.05
230	Chuck Knoblauch	.05	334	Mark Whiten	.05	438	Wally Joyner	.05
231	Bill Doran	.05	335	Darren Daulton	.05	439	John Flaherty	.05
232	Dave Henderson	.05	336	Rick Wilkins	.05	440	Brian Downing	.05
233	Roberto Alomar	.20	337	Brian Jordan RC	.25	441	Darren Lewis	.05
234	Scott Fletcher	.05	338	Kevin Ward	.05	442	Gary Carter	.45
235	Tim Naehring	.05	339	Ruben Amaro	.05	443	Wally Ritchie	.05
236	Mike Gallego	.05	340	Trevor Wilson	.05	444	Chris Jones	.05
237	Lance Johnson	.05	341	Andujar Cedeno	.05	445	Jeff Kent	.05
238	Paul Molitor	.45	342	Michael Huff	.05	446	Gary Sheffield	.30
239	Dan Gladden	.05	343	Brady Anderson	.05	447	Ron Darling	.05
240	Willie Randolph	.05	344	Craig Grebeck	.05	448	Deion Sanders	.05
241	Will Clark	.10	345	Bobby Ojeda	.05	449	Andres Galarraga	.05
242	Sid Bream	.05	346	Mike Pagliarulo	.05	450	Chuck Finley	.05
243	Derek Bell	.05	347	Terry Shumpert	.05	451	Derek Lilliquist	.05
244	Bill Pecota	.05	348	Dann Bilardello	.05	452	Carl Willis	.05
245	Terry Pendleton	.05	349	Frank Thomas	.45	453	Wes Chamberlain	.05
246	Randy Ready	.05	350	Albert Belle	.05	454	Roger Mason	.05
247	Jack Armstrong	.05	351	Jose Mesa	.05	455	Spike Owen	.05
248	Todd Van Poppel	.05	352	Rich Monteleone	.05	456	Thomas Howard	.05
249	Shawon Dunston	.05	353	Bob Walk	.05	457	Dave Martinez	.05
250	Bobby Rose	.05	354	Monty Fariss	.05	458	Pete Incaviglia	.05
251	Jeff Huson	.05	355	Luis Rivera	.05	459	Keith Miller	.05
252	Bip Roberts	.05	356	Anthony Young	.05	460	Mike Fetters	.05
253	Doug Jones	.05	357	Geno Petralli	.05	461	Paul Gibson	.05
254	Lee Smith	.05	358	Otis Nixon	.05	462	George Bell	.05
255	George Brett	.65	359	Tom Pagnozzi	.05	463	Checklist	.05
256	Randy Tomlin	.05	360	Reggie Sanders	.05	464	Terry Mulholland	.05
257	Todd Benzinger	.05	361	Lee Stevens	.05	465	Storm Davis	.05
258	Dave Stewart	.05	362	Kent Hrbek	.05	466	Gary Pettis	.05
259	Mark Carreon	.05	363	Orlando Merced	.05	467	Randy Bush	.05
260	Pete O'Brien	.05	364	Mike Bordick	.05	468	Ken Hill	.05
261	Tim Teufel	.05	365	Dion James	.05	469	Rheal Cormier	.05
262	Bob Milacki	.05	366	Jack Clark	.05	470	Andy Stankiewicz	.05
263	Mark Guthrie	.05	367	Mike Stanley	.05	471	Dave Burba	.05
264	Darrin Fletcher	.05	368	Randy Velarde	.05	472	Henry Cotto	.05
265	Omar Vizquel	.05	369	Dan Pasqua	.05	473	Dale Sveum	.05
266	Chris Bosio	.05	370	Pat Listach	.05	474	Rich Gossage	.05
267	Jose Canseco	.30	371	Mike Fitzgerald	.05	475	William Suero	.05
268	Mike Boddicker	.05	372	Tom Foley	.05	476	Doug Strange	.05
269	Lance Parrish	.05	373	Matt Williams	.05	477	Bill Krueger	.05
270	Jose Vizcaino	.05	374	Brian Hunter	.05	478	John Wetteland	.05
271	Chris Sabo	.05	375	Joe Carter	.05	479	Melido Perez	.05
272	Royce Clayton	.05	376	Bret Saberhagen	.05	480	Lonnie Smith	.05
273	Marquis Grissom	.05	377	Mike Stanton	.05	481	Mike Jackson	.05
274	Fred McGriff	.05	378	Hubie Brooks	.05	482	Mike Gardiner	.05
275	Barry Bonds	1.50	379	Eric Bell	.05	483	David Wells	.05
276	Greg Vaughn	.05	380	Walt Weiss	.05	484	Barry Jones	.05
277	Gregg Olson	.05	381	Danny Jackson	.05	485	Scott Bankhead	.05
278	Dave Hollins	.05	382	Manuel Lee	.05	486	Terry Leach	.05
279	Tom Glavine	.25	383	Ruben Sierra	.05	487	Vince Horsman	.05
280	Bryan Hickerson	.05	384	Greg Swindell	.05	488	Dave Eiland	.05
281	Scott Radinsky	.05	385	Ryan Bowen	.05	489	Alejandro Pena	.05
282	Omar Olivares	.05	386	Kevin Ritz	.05	490	Julio Valera	.05
283	Ivan Calderon	.05	387	Curtis Wilkerson	.05	491	Joe Boever	.05
284	Kevin Maas	.05	388	Gary Varsho	.05	492	Paul Miller	.05
285	Mickey Tettleton	.05	389	Dave Hansen	.05	493	Arci Cianfrocco RC	.05
286	Wade Boggs	.60	390	Bob Welch	.05	494	Dave Fleming	.05
287	Stan Belinda	.05	391	Lou Whitaker	.05	495	Kyle Abbott	.05
288	Bret Barberie	.05	392	Ken Griffey Jr.	.75	496	Chad Kreuter	.05
289	Jose Oquendo	.05	393	Mike Maddux	.05	497	Chris James	.05
290	Frank Castillo	.05	394	Arthur Rhodes	.05	498	Donnie Hill	.05
291	Dave Stieb	.05	395	Chili Davis	.05	499	Jacob Brumfield	.05
292	Tommy Greene	.05	396	Eddie Murray	.45	500	Ricky Bones	.05
293	Eric Karros	.05	397	Checklist	.05	501	Terry Steinbach	.05
294	Greg Maddux	.60	398	Dave Cochrane	.05	502	Bernard Gilkey	.05
295	Jim Eisenreich	.05	399	Kevin Seitzer	.05	503	Dennis Cook	.05
296	Rafael Palmeiro	.35	400	Ozzie Smith	.60	504	Len Dykstra	.05
297	Ramon Martinez	.05	401	Paul Sorrento	.05	505	Mike Bielecki	.05
298	Tim Wallach	.05	402	Les Lancaster	.05	506	Bob Kipper	.05
299	Jim Thome	.45	403	Junior Noboa	.05	507	Jose Melendez	.05
300	Chito Martinez	.05	404	Dave Justice	.05	508	Rick Sutcliffe	.05
301	Mitch Williams	.05	405	Andy Ashby	.05	509	Ken Patterson	.05
302	Randy Johnson	.45	406	Danny Tartabull	.05	510	Andy Allanson	.05
303	Carlton Fisk	.45	407	Bill Swift	.05	511	Al Newman	.05
304	Travis Fryman	.05	408	Craig Lefferts	.05	512	Mark Gardner	.05
305	Bobby Witt	.05	409	Tom Candiotti	.05	513	Jeff Schaefer	.05
306	Dave Magadan	.05	410	Lance Blankenship	.05	514	Jim McNamara	.05
307	Alex Cole	.05	411	Jeff Tackett	.05	515	Peter Hoy	.05
308	Bobby Bonilla	.05	412	Sammy Sosa	.65	516	Curt Schilling	.30
309	Bryan Harvey	.05	413	Jody Reed	.05	517	Kirk McCaskill	.05
310	Rafael Belliard	.05	414	Bruce Ruffin	.05	518	Chris Gwynn	.05
311	Mariano Duncan	.05	415	Gene Larkin	.05	519	Sid Fernandez	.05
312	Chuck Crim	.05	416	John Vanderwal	.05	520	Jeff Parrett	.05
313	John Kruk	.05	417	Tim Belcher	.05	521	Scott Ruskin	.05
314	Ellis Burks	.05	418	Steve Frey	.05	522	Kevin McReynolds	.05
315	Craig Biggio	.05	419	Dick Schofield	.05	523	Rick Cerone	.05
316	Glenn Davis	.05	420	Jeff King	.05	524	Jesse Orosco	.05
317	Ryne Sandberg	.60	421	Kim Batiste	.05	525	Troy Afenir	.05
318	Mike Sharperson	.05	422	Jack McDowell	.05	526	John Smiley	.05
319	Rich Rodriguez	.05	423	Damon Berryhill	.05	527	Dale Murphy	.25
320	Lee Guetterman	.05	424	Gary Wayne	.05	528	Leaf Set Card	.05
321	Benito Santiago	.05	425	Jack Morris	.05			

1992 Leaf Gold Edition

JOSE VIZCAINO IF

	NM/M
Complete Set (528):	35.00
Common Player:	.10
Stars/Rookies:	3X

(See 1992 Leaf for checklist and base card values.)

1992 Leaf Gold Previews

CHRIS SABO 3B

		NM/M
Complete Set (33):		30.00
Common Player:		.50
1	Steve Avery	.50
2	Ryne Sandberg	2.00
3	Chris Sabo	.50
4	Jeff Bagwell	1.50
5	Darryl Strawberry	.50
6	Bret Barbarie	.50
7	Howard Johnson	.50
8	John Kruk	.50
9	Andy Van Slyke	.50
10	Felix Jose	.50
11	Fred McGriff	.50
12	Will Clark	.60
13	Cal Ripken, Jr.	4.00
14	Phil Plantier	.50
15	Lee Stevens	.50
16	Frank Thomas	1.50
17	Mark Whiten	.50
18	Cecil Fielder	.50
19	George Brett	2.50
20	Robin Yount	1.50
21	Scott Erickson	.50
22	Don Mattingly	2.50
23	Jose Canseco	1.00
24	Ken Griffey Jr.	3.00
25	Nolan Ryan	4.00
26	Joe Carter	.50
27	Deion Sanders	.50
28	Dean Palmer	.50
29	Andy Benes	.50
30	Gary DiSarcina	.50
31	Chris Hoiles	.50
32	Mark McGwire	3.00
33	Reggie Sanders	.50

Gold Rookies

		NM/M
Complete Set (24):		4.00
Common Player:		.25
Jumbo:		1.5X
1	Chad Curtis	.25
2	Brent Gates	.25
3	Pedro Martinez	3.00
4	Kenny Lofton	.35
5	Turk Wendell	.25
6	Mark Hutton	.25
7	Todd Hundley	.25

PAT MAHOMES RHP

8	Matt Stairs	.25
9	Ed Taubensee	.25
10	David Nied	.25
11	Salomon Torres	.25
12	Bret Boone	.50
13	John Ruffin	.25
14	Ed Martel	.25
15	Rick Trlicek	.25
16	Raul Mondesi	.25
17	Pat Mahomes	.25
18	Dan Wilson	.25
19	Donovan Osborne	.25
20	Dave Silvestri	.25
21	Gary DiSarcina	.25
22	Denny Neagle	.25
23	Steve Hosey	.25
24	John Doherty	.25

1993 Leaf

JUAN GONZALEZ RANGERS

		NM/M
Complete Set (550):		12.50
Common Player:		.05
Series 1 or 2 Pack (14):		.65
Series 1 or 2 Box (36):		12.50
Update Pack (14):		1.50
Update Box (36):		25.00
1	Ben McDonald	.05
2	Sid Fernandez	.05
3	Juan Guzman	.05
4	Curt Schilling	.40
5	Ivan Rodriguez	.65
6	Don Slaught	.05
7	Terry Steinbach	.05
8	Todd Zeile	.05
9	Andy Stankiewicz	.05
10	Tim Teufel	.05
11	Marvin Freeman	.05
12	Jim Austin	.05
13	Bob Scanlan	.05
14	Rusty Meacham	.05
15	Casey Candaele	.05
16	Travis Fryman	.05
17	Jose Offerman	.05
18	Albert Belle	.05
19	John Vander Wahl (Vander Wal)	.05
20	Dan Pasqua	.05
21	Frank Viola	.05
22	Terry Mulholland	.05
23	Gregg Olson	.05
24	Randy Tomlin	.05
25	Todd Stottlemyre	.05
26	Jose Oquendo	.05
27	Julio Franco	.05
28	Tony Gwynn	1.00
29	Ruben Sierra	.05
30	Bobby Thigpen	.05
31	Jim Bullinger	.05
32	Rick Aguilera	.05
33	Scott Servais	.05
34	Cal Eldred	.05
35	Mike Piazza	1.50
36	Brent Mayne	.05
37	Wil Cordero	.05
38	Milt Cuyler	.05
39	Howard Johnson	.05
40	Kenny Lofton	.05
41	Alex Fernandez	.05
42	Denny Neagle	.05
43	Tony Pena	.05
44	Bob Tewksbury	.05
45	Glenn Davis	.05
46	Fred McGriff	.05
47	John Olerud	.05
48	Steve Hosey	.05
49	Rafael Palmeiro	.65
50	Dave Justice	.05
51	Pete Harnisch	.05
52	Sam Militello	.05
53	Orel Hershiser	.05
54	Pat Mahomes	.05
55	Greg Colbrunn	.05
56	Greg Vaughn	.05
57	Vince Coleman	.05
58	Brian McRae	.05
59	Len Dykstra	.05
60	Dan Gladden	.05
61	Ted Power	.05
62	Donovan Osborne	.05
63	Ron Karkovice	.05
64	Frank Seminara	.05
65	Bob Zupcic	.05
66	Kirt Manwaring	.05
67	Mike Devereaux	.05
68	Mark Lemke	.05
69	Devon White	.05
70	Sammy Sosa	1.25
71	Pedro Astacio	.05
72	Dennis Eckersley	.60
73	Chris Nabholz	.05
74	Melido Perez	.05
75	Todd Hundley	.05
76	Kent Hrbek	.05
77	Mickey Morandini	.05
78	Tim McIntosh	.05
79	Andy Van Slyke	.05
80	Kevin McReynolds	.05
81	Mike Henneman	.05
82	Greg Harris	.05
83	Sandy Alomar Jr.	.05
84	Mike Jackson	.05
85	Ozzie Guillen	.05
86	Jeff Blauser	.05
87	John Valentin	.05
88	Rey Sanchez	.05
89	Rick Sutcliffe	.05
90	Luis Gonzalez	.25
91	Jeff Fassero	.05
92	Kenny Rogers	.05
93	Bret Saberhagen	.05
94	Bob Welch	.05
95	Darren Daulton	.05
96	Mike Gallego	.05
97	Orlando Merced	.05
98	Chuck Knoblauch	.05
99	Bernard Gilkey	.05
100	Billy Ashley	.05
101	Kevin Appier	.05
102	Jeff Brantley	.05
103	Bill Gullickson	.05
104	John Smoltz	.05
105	Paul Sorrento	.05
106	Steve Buechele	.05
107	Steve Sax	.05
108	Andujar Cedeno	.05
109	Billy Hatcher	.05
110	Checklist	.05
111	Alan Mills	.05
112	John Franco	.05
113	Jack Morris	.05
114	Mitch Williams	.05
115	Nolan Ryan	2.50
116	Jay Bell	.05
117	Mike Bordick	.05
118	Geronimo Pena	.05
119	Danny Tartabull	.05
120	Checklist	.05
121	Steve Avery	.05
122	Ricky Bones	.05
123	Mike Morgan	.05
124	Jeff Montgomery	.05
125	Jeff Bagwell	.75
126	Tony Phillips	.05
127	Lenny Harris	.05
128	Glenallen Hill	.05
129	Marquis Grissom	.05
130	Gerald Williams (Photo, stats actually Bernie Williams.)	.20
131	Greg Harris	.05
132	Tommy Greene	.05
133	Chris Hoiles	.05
134	Bob Walk	.05
135	Duane Ward	.05
136	Tom Pagnozzi	.05
137	Jeff Huson	.05
138	Kurt Stillwell	.05
139	Dave Henderson	.05
140	Darrin Jackson	.05
141	Frank Castillo	.05
142	Scott Erickson	.05
143	Darryl Kile	.05
144	Bill Wegman	.05
145	Steve Wilson	.05
146	George Brett	1.25
147	Moises Alou	.05
148	Lou Whitaker	.05
149	Chico Walker	.05
150	Jerry Browne	.05
151	Kirk McCaskill	.05
152	Zane Smith	.05
153	Matt Young	.05
154	Lee Smith	.05
155	Leo Gomez	.05
156	Dan Walters	.05
157	Pat Borders	.05
158	Matt Williams	.05
159	Dean Palmer	.05
160	John Patterson	.05
161	Doug Jones	.05
162	John Habyan	.05
163	Pedro Martinez	.75
164	Carl Willis	.05
165	Darrin Fletcher	.05
166	B.J. Surhoff	.05
167	Eddie Murray	.75
168	Keith Miller	.05
169	Ricky Jordan	.05
170	Juan Gonzalez	.65
171	Charles Nagy	.05
172	Mark Clark	.05
173	Bobby Thigpen	.05
174	Tim Scott	.05
175	Scott Cooper	.05
176	Royce Clayton	.05
177	Brady Anderson	.05
178	Sid Bream	.05
179	Derek Bell	.05
180	Otis Nixon	.05
181	Kevin Gross	.05
182	Ron Darling	.05
183	John Wetteland	.05
184	Mike Stanley	.05
185	Jeff Kent	.05
186	Brian Harper	.05
187	Mariano Duncan	.05
188	Robin Yount	.75
189	Al Martin	.05
190	Eddie Zosky	.05
191	Mike Munoz	.05
192	Andy Benes	.05
193	Dennis Cook	.05
194	Bill Swift	.05
195	Frank Thomas	.75
196	Damon Berryhill	.05
197	Mike Greenwell	.05
198	Mark Grace	.05
199	Darryl Hamilton	.05
200	Derrick May	.05
201	Ken Hill	.05
202	Kevin Brown	.05
203	Dwight Gooden	.05
204	Bobby Witt	.05
205	Juan Bell	.05
206	Kevin Maas	.05
207	Jeff King	.05
208	Scott Leius	.05
209	Rheal Cormier	.05
210	Darryl Strawberry	.05
211	Tom Gordon	.05
212	Bud Black	.05
213	Mickey Tettleton	.05
214	Pete Smith	.05
215	Felix Fermin	.05
216	Rick Wilkins	.05
217	George Bell	.05
218	Eric Anthony	.05
219	Pedro Munoz	.05
220	Checklist	.05
221	Lance Blankenship	.05
222	Deion Sanders	.10
223	Craig Biggio	.05
224	Ryne Sandberg	1.00
225	Ron Gant	.05
226	Tom Brunansky	.05
227	Chad Curtis	.05
228	Joe Carter	.05
229	Brian Jordan	.05
230	Brett Butler	.05
231	Frank Bolick	.05
232	Rod Beck	.05
233	Carlos Baerga	.05
234	Eric Karros	.05
235	Jack Armstrong	.05
236	Bobby Bonilla	.05
237	Don Mattingly	1.25
238	Jeff Gardner	.05
239	Dave Hollins	.05
240	Steve Cooke	.05
241	Jose Canseco	.35
242	Ivan Calderon	.05
243	Tim Belcher	.05
244	Freddie Benavides	.05
245	Roberto Alomar	.25
246	Rob Deer	.05
247	Will Clark	.10
248	Mike Felder	.05
249	Harold Baines	.05
250	David Cone	.05
251	Mark Guthrie	.05
252	Ellis Burks	.05
253	Jim Abbott	.05
254	Chili Davis	.05
255	Chris Bosio	.05
256	Bret Barberie	.05
257	Hal Morris	.05
258	Dante Bichette	.05
259	Storm Davis	.05
260	Gary DiSarcina	.05
261	Ken Caminiti	.05
262	Paul Molitor	.75
263	Joe Oliver	.05
264	Pat Listach	.05
265	Gregg Jefferies	.05
266	Jose Guzman	.05
267	Eric Davis	.05
268	Delino DeShields	.05
269	Barry Bonds	2.50
270	Mike Bielecki	.05
271	Jay Buhner	.05
272	Scott Pose RC	.05
273	Tony Fernandez	.05
274	Chito Martinez	.05
275	Phil Plantier	.05
276	Pete Incaviglia	.05
277	Carlos Garcia	.05
278	Tom Henke	.05
279	Roger Clemens	1.25
280	Rob Dibble	.05
281	Daryl Boston	.05
282	Greg Gagne	.05
283	Cecil Fielder	.05
284	Carlton Fisk	.75
285	Wade Boggs	1.00
286	Damion Easley	.05
287	Norm Charlton	.05
288	Jeff Conine	.05
289	Roberto Kelly	.05
290	Jerald Clark	.05
291	Rickey Henderson	.75
292	Chuck Finley	.05
293	Doug Drabek	.05
294	Dave Stewart	.05
295	Tom Glavine	.35
296	Jaime Navarro	.05
297	Ray Lankford	.05
298	Greg Hibbard	.05
299	Jody Reed	.05
300	Dennis Martinez	.05
301	Dave Martinez	.05
302	Reggie Jefferson	.05
303	John Cummings RC	.05
304	Orestes Destrade	.05
305	Mike Maddux	.05
306	David Segui	.05
307	Gary Sheffield	.35
308	Danny Jackson	.05
309	Criag Lefferts	.05
310	Andre Dawson	.20
311	Barry Larkin	.05
312	Alex Cole	.05
313	Mark Gardner	.05
314	Kirk Gibson	.05
315	Shane Mack	.05
316	Bo Jackson	.10
317	Jimmy Key	.05
318	Greg Myers	.05
319	Ken Griffey Jr.	1.50
320	Monty Fariss	.05
321	Kevin Mitchell	.05
322	Andres Galarraga	.05
323	Mark McGwire	2.00
324	Mark Langston	.05
325	Steve Finley	.05
326	Greg Maddux	1.00
327	Dave Nilsson	.05
328	Ozzie Smith	1.00
329	Candy Maldonado	.05
330	Checklist	.05
331	Tim Pugh RC	.05
332	Joe Girardi	.05
333	Junior Feliz	.05
334	Greg Swindell	.05
335	Ramon Martinez	.05
336	Sean Berry	.05
337	Joe Orsulak	.05
338	Wes Chamberlain	.05
339	Stan Belinda	.05
340	Checklist	.05
341	Bruce Hurst	.05
342	John Burkett	.05
343	Mike Mussina	.40
344	Scott Fletcher	.05

345	Rene Gonzales	.05
346	Roberto Hernandez	.05
347	Carlos Martinez	.05
348	Bill Krueger	.05
349	Felix Jose	.05
350	John Jaha	.05
351	Willie Banks	.05
352	Matt Nokes	.05
353	Kevin Seitzer	.05
354	Erik Hanson	.05
355	David Hulse RC	.05
356	Domingo Martinez RC	.05
357	Greg Olson	.05
358	Randy Myers	.05
359	Tom Browning	.05
360	Charlie Hayes	.05
361	Bryan Harvey	.05
362	Eddie Taubensee	.05
363	Tim Wallach	.05
364	Mel Rojas	.05
365	Frank Tanana	.05
366	John Kruk	.05
367	Tim Laker RC	.05
368	Rich Rodriguez	.05
369	Darren Lewis	.05
370	Harold Reynolds	.05
371	Jose Melendez	.05
372	Joe Grahe	.05
373	Lance Johnson	.05
374	Jose Mesa	.05
375	Scott Livingstone	.05
376	Wally Joyner	.05
377	Kevin Reimer	.05
378	Kirby Puckett	1.00
379	Paul O'Neill	.05
380	Randy Johnson	.75
381	Manuel Lee	.05
382	Dick Schofield	.05
383	Darren Holmes	.05
384	Charlie Hough	.05
385	John Orton	.05
386	Edgar Martinez	.05
387	Terry Pendleton	.05
388	Dan Plesac	.05
389	Jeff Reardon	.05
390	David Nied	.05
391	Dave Magadan	.05
392	Larry Walker	.05
393	Ben Rivera	.05
394	Lonnie Smith	.05
395	Craig Shipley	.05
396	Willie McGee	.05
397	Arthur Rhodes	.05
398	Mike Stanton	.05
399	Luis Polonia	.05
400	Jack McDowell	.05
401	Mike Moore	.05
402	Jose Lind	.05
403	Bill Spiers	.05
404	Kevin Tapani	.05
405	Spike Owen	.05
406	Tino Martinez	.05
407	Charlie Leibrandt	.05
408	Ed Sprague	.05
409	Bryn Smith	.05
410	Benito Santiago	.05
411	Jose Rijo	.05
412	Pete O'Brien	.05
413	Willie Wilson	.05
414	Bip Roberts	.05
415	Eric Young	.05
416	Walt Weiss	.05
417	Milt Thompson	.05
418	Chris Sabo	.05
419	Scott Sanderson	.05
420	Tim Raines	.05
421	Alan Trammell	.05
422	Mike Macfarlane	.05
423	Dave Winfield	.75
424	Bob Wickman	.05
425	David Valle	.05
426	Gary Redus	.05
427	Turner Ward	.05
428	Reggie Sanders	.05
429	Todd Worrell	.05
430	Julio Valera	.05
431	Cal Ripken, Jr.	2.50
432	Mo Vaughn	.05
433	John Smiley	.05
434	Omar Vizquel	.05
435	Billy Ripken	.05
436	Cory Snyder	.05
437	Carlos Quintana	.05
438	Omar Olivares	.05
439	Robin Ventura	.05
440	Checklist	.05
441	Kevin Higgins	.05
442	Carlos Hernandez	.05
443	Dan Peltier	.05
444	Derek Lilliquist	.05
445	Tim Salmon	.05
446	Sherman Obando RC	.05
447	Pat Kelly	.05
448	Todd Van Poppel	.05

449	Mark Whiten	.05
450	Checklist	.05
451	Pat Meares	.05
452	Tony Tarasco RC	.05
453	Chris Gwynn	.05
454	Armando Reynoso	.05
455	Danny Darwin	.05
456	Willie Greene	.05
457	Mike Blowers	.05
458	Kevin Roberson RC	.05
459	Graeme Lloyd RC	.05
460	David West	.05
461	Joey Cora	.05
462	Alex Arias	.05
463	Chad Kreuter	.05
464	Mike Lansing	.05
465	Mike Timlin	.05
466	Paul Wagner	.05
467	Mark Portugal	.05
468	Jim Leyritz	.05
469	Ryan Klesko	.05
470	Mario Diaz	.05
471	Guillermo Velasquez	.05
472	Fernando Valenzuela	.05
473	Raul Mondesi	.05
474	Mike Pagliarulo	.05
475	Chris Hammond	.05
476	Torey Lovullo	.05
477	Trevor Wilson	.05
478	Marcos Armas RC	.05
479	Dave Gallagher	.05
480	Jeff Treadway	.05
481	Jeff Branson	.05
482	Dickie Thon	.05
483	Eduardo Perez	.05
484	David Wells	.05
485	Brian Williams	.05
486	Domingo Cedeno	.05
487	Tom Candiotti	.05
488	Steve Frey	.05
489	Greg McMichael	.05
490	Marc Newfield	.05
491	Larry Andersen	.05
492	Damon Buford	.05
493	Ricky Gutierrez	.05
494	Jeff Russell	.05
495	Vinny Castilla	.05
496	Wilson Alvarez	.05
497	Scott Bullett	.05
498	Larry Casian	.05
499	Jose Vizcaino	.05
500	J.T. Snow RC	.75
501	Bryan Hickerson	.05
502	Jeremy Hernandez	.05
503	Jeromy Burnitz	.05
504	Steve Farr	.05
505	J. Owens	.05
506	Craig Paquette	.05
507	Jim Eisenreich	.05
508	Matt Whiteside	.05
509	Luis Aquino	.05
510	Mike LaValliere	.05
511	Jim Gott	.05
512	Mark McLemore	.05
513	Randy Milligan	.05
514	Gary Gaetti	.05
515	Lou Frazier	.05
516	Rich Amaral	.05
517	Gene Harris	.05
518	Aaron Sele	.05
519	Mark Wohlers	.05
520	Scott Kamieniecki	.05
521	Kent Mercker	.05
522	Jim Deshaies	.05
523	Kevin Stocker	.05
524	Jason Bere	.05
525	Tim Bogar	.05
526	Brad Pennington	.05
527	Curt Leskanic RC	.05
528	Wayne Kirby	.05
529	Tim Costo	.05
530	Doug Henry	.05
531	Trevor Hoffman	.05
532	Kelly Gruber	.05
533	Mike Harkey	.05
534	John Doherty	.05
535	Erik Pappas	.05
536	Brent Gates	.05
537	Roger McDowell	.05
538	Chris Haney	.05
539	Blas Minor	.05
540	Pat Hentgen	.05
541	Chuck Carr	.05
542	Doug Strange	.05
543	Xavier Hernandez	.05
544	Paul Quantrill	.05
545	Anthony Young	.05
546	Bret Boone	.05
547	Dwight Smith	.05
548	Bobby Munoz	.05
549	Russ Springer	.05
550	Roger Pavlik	.05
----	Dave Winfield (3,000 Hits)	2.00

Fasttrack

		NM/M
Complete Set (20):		15.00
Common Player:		.60
1	Frank Thomas	3.00
2	Tim Wakefield	.60
3	Kenny Lofton	.60
4	Mike Mussina	1.00
5	Juan Gonzalez	2.50
6	Chuck Knoblauch	.60
7	Eric Karros	.60
8	Ray Lankford	.60
9	Juan Guzman	.60
10	Pat Listach	.60
11	Carlos Baerga	.60
12	Felix Jose	.60
13	Steve Avery	.60
14	Robin Ventura	.60
15	Ivan Rodriguez	2.50
16	Cal Eldred	.60
17	Jeff Bagwell	3.00
18	Dave Justice	.60
19	Travis Fryman	.60
20	Marquis Grissom	.60

Gold All-Stars

		NM/M
Complete Set (20):		15.00
Common Player:		.25
1	Ivan Rodriguez, Darren Daulton	.75
2	Don Mattingly, Fred McGriff	1.50
3	Cecil Fielder, Jeff Bagwell	.75
4	Carlos Baerga, Ryne Sandberg	1.00
5	Chuck Knoblauch, Delino DeShields	.25
6	Robin Ventura, Terry Pendleton	.25
7	Ken Griffey Jr., Andy Van Slyke	2.00
8	Joe Carter, Dave Justice	.25
9	Jose Canseco, Tony Gwynn	1.00
10	Dennis Eckersley, Rob Dibble	.60
11	Mark McGwire, Will Clark	2.50
12	Frank Thomas, Mark Grace	.75
13	Roberto Alomar, Craig Biggio	.50
14	Barry Larkin, Cal Ripken, Jr.	3.00
15	Gary Sheffield, Edgar Martinez	.50

16	Juan Gonzalez, Barry Bonds	3.00
17	Kirby Puckett, Marquis Grissom	1.00
18	Jim Abbott, Tom Glavine	.40
19	Nolan Ryan, Greg Maddux	3.00
20	Roger Clemens, Doug Drabek	1.50

Gold Rookies

		NM/M
Complete Set (20):		5.00
Common Player:		.25
1	Kevin Young	.25
2	Wil Cordero	.25
3	Mark Kiefer	.25
4	Gerald Williams	.25
5	Brandon Wilson	.25
6	Greg Gohr	.25
7	Ryan Thompson	.25
8	Tim Wakefield	.25
9	Troy Neel	.25
10	Tim Salmon	.50
11	Kevin Rogers	.25
12	Rod Bolton	.25
13	Ken Ryan	.25
14	Phil Hiatt	.25
15	Rene Arocha	.25
16	Nigel Wilson	.25
17	J.T. Snow	.50
18	Benji Gil	.25
19	Chipper Jones	3.00
20	Darrell Sherman	.25

Heading for the Hall

		NM/M
Complete Set (10):		10.00
Common Player:		.75
1	Nolan Ryan	2.50
2	Tony Gwynn	1.00
3	Robin Yount	1.00
4	Eddie Murray	1.00
5	Cal Ripken, Jr.	2.50
6	Roger Clemens	2.00
7	George Brett	2.00
8	Ryne Sandberg	1.00
9	Kirby Puckett	1.00
10	Ozzie Smith	1.00

Frank Thomas

	NM/M
Complete Set (10):	4.50
Common Card:	.75
Autographed Card:	30.00
1 Frank Thomas/ Aggressive	.75
2 Frank Thomas/Serious	.75
3 Frank Thomas/Intense	.75

STRENGTH FRANK

		NM/M
4	Frank Thomas/ Confident	.75
5	Frank Thomas/ Assertive	.75
6	Frank Thomas/Power	.75
7	Frank Thomas/Control	.75
8	Frank Thomas/Strength	.75
9	Frank Thomas/ Concentration	.75
10	Frank Thomas/ Preparation	.75

Update Gold All-Stars

		NM/M
Complete Set (10):		7.50
Common Player:		.25
1	Mark Langston, Terry Mulholland	.25
2	Ivan Rodriguez, Darren Daulton	.50
3	John Olerud, John Kruk	.25
4	Roberto Alomar, Ryne Sandberg	1.00
5	Wade Boggs, Gary Sheffield	.75
6	Cal Ripken, Jr., Barry Larkin	3.00
7	Kirby Puckett, Barry Bonds	2.50
8	Marquis Grissom, Ken Griffey Jr.	2.00
9	Joe Carter, Dave Justice	.25
10	Mark Grace, Paul Molitor	.75

Update Gold Rookies

	NM/M
Complete Set (5):	3.50

Common Player:		.25
Jumbos:		1.5X
1	Allen Watson	.25
2	Jeffrey Hammonds	.25
3	David McCarty	.25
4	Mike Piazza	3.00
5	Roberto Meija	.25

1993 Leaf Update Frank Thomas Autograph

		NM/M
FT	Frank Thomas	35.00

Update Frank Thomas Super

	NM/M
Compleion	2.00

1994 Leaf

		NM/M
Complete Set (440):		10.00
Common Player:		.05
Series 1 or 2 Pack (12):		.75
Series 1 or 2 Box (36):		12.50
1	Cal Ripken, Jr.	2.50
2	Tony Tarasco	.05
3	Joe Girardi	.05
4	Bernie Williams	.20
5	Chad Kreuter	.05
6	Troy Neel	.05
7	Tom Pagnozzi	.05
8	Kirk Rueter	.05
9	Chris Bosio	.05
10	Dwight Gooden	.05
11	Mariano Duncan	.05
12	Jay Bell	.05
13	Lance Johnson	.05
14	Richie Lewis	.05
15	Dave Martinez	.05
16	Orel Hershiser	.05
17	Rob Butler	.05
18	Glenallen Hill	.05
19	Chad Curtis	.05
20	Mike Stanton	.05
21	Tim Wallach	.05
22	Milt Thompson	.05
23	Kevin Young	.05
24	John Smiley	.05
25	Jeff Montgomery	.05
26	Robin Ventura	.05
27	Scott Lydy	.05
28	Todd Stottlemyre	.05
29	Mark Whiten	.05
30	Robby Thompson	.05
31	Bobby Bonilla	.05
32	Andy Ashby	.05
33	Greg Myers	.05
34	Billy Hatcher	.05
35	Brad Holman	.05
36	Mark McLemore	.05
37	Scott Sanders	.05
38	Jim Abbott	.05
39	David Wells	.05
40	Roberto Kelly	.05
41	Jeff Conine	.05
42	Sean Berry	.05
43	Mark Grace	.05
44	Eric Young	.05
45	Rick Aguilera	.05
46	Chipper Jones	1.00
47	Mel Rojas	.05
48	Ryan Thompson	.05
49	Al Martin	.05
50	Cecil Fielder	.05
51	Pat Kelly	.05
52	Kevin Tapani	.05
53	Tim Costo	.05
54	Dave Hollins	.05
55	Kirt Manwaring	.05
56	Gregg Jefferies	.05
57	Ron Darling	.05
58	Bill Haselman	.05
59	Phil Plantier	.05
60	Frank Viola	.05
61	Todd Zeile	.05
62	Bret Barberie	.05
63	Roberto Mejia	.05
64	Chuck Knoblauch	.05
65	Jose Lind	.05
66	Brady Anderson	.05
67	Ruben Sierra	.05
68	Jose Vizcaino	.05
69	Joe Grahe	.05
70	Kevin Appier	.05
71	Wilson Alvarez	.05
72	Tom Candiotti	.05
73	John Burkett	.05
74	Anthony Young	.05
75	Scott Cooper	.05
76	Nigel Wilson	.05
77	John Valentin	.05
78	Dave McCarty	.05
79	Archi Cianfrocco	.05
80	Lou Whitaker	.05
81	Dante Bichette	.05
82	Mark Dewey	.05
83	Danny Jackson	.05
84	Harold Baines	.05
85	Todd Benzinger	.05
86	Damion Easley	.05
87	Danny Cox	.05
88	Jose Bautista	.05
89	Mike Lansing	.05
90	Phil Hiatt	.05
91	Tim Pugh	.05
92	Tino Martinez	.05
93	Raul Mondesi	.05
94	Greg Maddux	1.00
95	Al Leiter	.05
96	Benito Santiago	.05
97	Len Dykstra	.05
98	Sammy Sosa	1.25
99	Tim Bogar	.05
100	Checklist	.05
101	Deion Sanders	.10
102	Bobby Witt	.05
103	Wil Cordero	.05
104	Rich Amaral	.05
105	Mike Mussina	.50
106	Reggie Sanders	.05
107	Ozzie Guillen	.05
108	Paul O'Neill	.05
109	Tim Salmon	.05
110	Rheal Cormier	.05
111	Billy Ashley	.05
112	Jeff Kent	.05
113	Derek Bell	.05
114	Danny Darwin	.05
115	Chip Hale	.05
116	Tim Raines	.05
117	Ed Sprague	.05
118	Darrin Fletcher	.05
119	Darren Holmes	.05
120	Alan Trammell	.05
121	Don Mattingly	1.25
122	Greg Gagne	.05
123	Jose Offerman	.05
124	Joe Orsulak	.05
125	Jack McDowell	.05
126	Barry Larkin	.05
127	Ben McDonald	.05
128	Mike Bordick	.05
129	Devon White	.05
130	Mike Perez	.05
131	Jay Buhner	.05
132	Phil Leftwich	.05
133	Tommy Greene	.05
134	Charlie Hayes	.05
135	Don Slaught	.05
136	Mike Gallego	.05
137	Dave Winfield	.75
138	Steve Avery	.05
139	Derrick May	.05
140	Bryan Harvey	.05
141	Wally Joyner	.05
142	Andre Dawson	.20
143	Andy Benes	.05
144	John Franco	.05
145	Jeff King	.05
146	Joe Oliver	.05
147	Bill Gullickson	.05
148	Armando Reynoso	.05
149	Dave Fleming	.05
150	Checklist	.05
151	Todd Van Poppel	.05
152	Bernard Gilkey	.05
153	Kevin Gross	.05
154	Mike Devereaux	.05
155	Tim Wakefield	.05
156	Andres Galarraga	.05
157	Pat Meares	.05
158	Jim Leyritz	.05
159	Mike Macfarlane	.05
160	Tony Phillips	.05
161	Brent Gates	.05
162	Mark Langston	.05
163	Allen Watson	.05
164	Randy Johnson	.75
165	Doug Brocail	.05
166	Rob Dibble	.05
167	Roberto Hernandez	.05
168	Felix Jose	.05
169	Steve Cooke	.05
170	Darren Daulton	.05
171	Eric Karros	.05
172	Geronimo Pena	.05
173	Gary DiSarcina	.05
174	Marquis Grissom	.05
175	Joey Cora	.05
176	Jim Eisenreich	.05
177	Brad Pennington	.05
178	Terry Steinbach	.05
179	Pat Borders	.05
180	Steve Buechele	.05
181	Jeff Fassero	.05
182	Mike Greenwell	.05
183	Mike Henneman	.05
184	Ron Karkovice	.05
185	Pat Hentgen	.05
186	Jose Guzman	.05
187	Brett Butler	.05
188	Charlie Hough	.05
189	Terry Pendleton	.05
190	Melido Perez	.05
191	Orestes Destrade	.05
192	Mike Morgan	.05
193	Joe Carter	.05
194	Jeff Blauser	.05
195	Chris Hoiles	.05
196	Ricky Gutierrez	.05
197	Mike Moore	.05
198	Carl Willis	.05
199	Aaron Sele	.05
200	Checklist	.05
201	Tim Naehring	.05
202	Scott Livingstone	.05
203	Luis Alicea	.05
204	Torey Lovullo RC	.05
205	Jim Gott	.05
206	Bob Wickman	.05
207	Greg McMichael	.05
208	Scott Brosius	.05
209	Chris Gwynn	.05
210	Steve Sax	.05
211	Dick Schofield	.05
212	Robb Nen	.05
213	Ben Rivera	.05
214	Vinny Castilla	.05
215	Jamie Moyer	.05
216	Wally Whitehurst	.05
217	Frank Castillo	.05
218	Mike Blowers	.05
219	Tim Scott	.05
220	Paul Wagner	.05
221	Jeff Bagwell	.75

222	Ricky Bones	.05
223	Sandy Alomar Jr.	.05
224	Rod Beck	.05
225	Roberto Alomar	.20
226	Jack Armstrong	.05
227	Scott Erickson	.05
228	Rene Arocha	.05
229	Eric Anthony	.05
230	Jeromy Burnitz	.05
231	Kevin Brown	.05
232	Tim Belcher	.05
233	Bret Boone	.05
234	Dennis Eckersley	.60
235	Tom Glavine	.30
236	Craig Biggio	.05
237	Pedro Astacio	.05
238	Ryan Bowen	.05
239	Brad Ausmus	.05
240	Vince Coleman	.05
241	Jason Bere	.05
242	Ellis Burks	.05
243	Wes Chamberlain	.05
244	Ken Caminiti	.05
245	Willie Banks	.05
246	Sid Fernandez	.05
247	Carlos Baerga	.05
248	Carlos Garcia	.05
249	Jose Canseco	.50
250	Alex Diaz	.05
251	Albert Belle	.05
252	Moises Alou	.05
253	Bobby Ayala	.05
254	Tony Gwynn	1.00
255	Roger Clemens	1.25
256	Eric Davis	.05
257	Wade Boggs	1.00
258	Chili Davis	.05
259	Rickey Henderson	.75
260	Andujar Cedeno	.05
261	Cris Carpenter	.05
262	Juan Guzman	.05
263	Dave Justice	.05
264	Barry Bonds	2.50
265	Pete Incaviglia	.05
266	Tony Fernandez	.05
267	Cal Eldred	.05
268	Alex Fernandez	.05
269	Kent Hrbek	.05
270	Steve Farr	.05
271	Doug Drabek	.05
272	Brian Jordan	.05
273	Xavier Hernandez	.05
274	David Cone	.05
275	Brian Hunter	.05
276	Mike Harkey	.05
277	Delino DeShields	.05
278	David Hulse	.05
279	Mickey Tettleton	.05
280	Kevin McReynolds	.05
281	Darryl Hamilton	.05
282	Ken Hill	.05
283	Wayne Kirby	.05
284	Chris Hammond	.05
285	Mo Vaughn	.05
286	Ryan Klesko	.05
287	Rick Wilkins	.05
288	Bill Swift	.05
289	Rafael Palmeiro	.65
290	Brian Harper	.05
291	Chris Turner	.05
292	Luis Gonzalez	.25
293	Kenny Rogers	.05
294	Kirby Puckett	1.00
295	Mike Stanley	.05
296	Carlos Reyes	.05
297	Charles Nagy	.05
298	Reggie Jefferson	.05
299	Bip Roberts	.05
300	Darrin Jackson	.05
301	Mike Jackson	.05
302	Dave Nilsson	.05
303	Ramon Martinez	.05
304	Bobby Jones	.05
305	Johnny Ruffin	.05
306	Brian McRae	.05
307	Bo Jackson	.10
308	Dave Stewart	.05
309	John Smoltz	.05
310	Dennis Martinez	.05
311	Dean Palmer	.05
312	David Nied	.05
313	Eddie Murray	.75
314	Darryl Kile	.05
315	Rick Sutcliffe	.05
316	Shawon Dunston	.05
317	John Jaha	.05
318	Salomon Torres	.05
319	Gary Sheffield	.45
320	Curt Schilling	.30
321	Greg Vaughn	.05
322	Jay Howell	.05
323	Todd Hundley	.05
324	Chris Sabo	.05
325	Stan Javier	.05

326	Willie Greene	.05
327	Hipolito Pichardo	.05
328	Doug Strange	.05
329	Dan Wilson	.05
330	Checklist	.05
331	Omar Vizquel	.05
332	Scott Servais	.05
333	Bob Tewksbury	.05
334	Matt Williams	.05
335	Tom Foley	.05
336	Jeff Russell	.05
337	Scott Leius	.05
338	Ivan Rodriguez	.65
339	Kevin Seitzer	.05
340	Jose Rijo	.05
341	Eduardo Perez	.05
342	Kirk Gibson	.05
343	Randy Milligan	.05
344	Edgar Martinez	.05
345	Fred McGriff	.05
346	Kurt Abbott	.05
347	John Kruk	.05
348	Mike Felder	.05
349	Dave Staton	.05
350	Kenny Lofton	.05
351	Graeme Lloyd	.05
352	David Segui	.05
353	Danny Tartabull	.05
354	Bob Welch	.05
355	Duane Ward	.05
356	Tuffy Rhodes	.05
357	Lee Smith	.05
358	Chris James	.05
359	Walt Weiss	.05
360	Pedro Munoz	.05
361	Paul Sorrento	.05
362	Todd Worrell	.05
363	Bob Hamelin	.05
364	Julio Franco	.05
365	Roberto Petagine	.05
366	Willie McGee	.05
367	Pedro Martinez	.75
368	Ken Griffey Jr.	1.50
369	B.J. Surhoff	.05
370	Kevin Mitchell	.05
371	John Doherty	.05
372	Manuel Lee	.05
373	Terry Mulholland	.05
374	Zane Smith	.05
375	Otis Nixon	.05
376	Jody Reed	.05
377	Doug Jones	.05
378	John Olerud	.05
379	Greg Swindell	.05
380	Checklist	.05
381	Royce Clayton	.05
382	Jim Thome	.65
383	Steve Finley	.05
384	Ray Lankford	.05
385	Henry Rodriguez	.05
386	Dave Magadan	.05
387	Gary Redus	.05
388	Orlando Merced	.05
389	Tom Gordon	.05
390	Luis Polonia	.05
391	Mark McGwire	2.00
392	Mark Lemke	.05
393	Doug Henry	.05
394	Chuck Finley	.05
395	Paul Molitor	.75
396	Randy Myers	.05
397	Larry Walker	.05
398	Pete Harnisch	.05
399	Darren Lewis	.05
400	Frank Thomas	.75
401	Jack Morris	.05
402	Greg Hibbard	.05
403	Jeffrey Hammonds	.05
404	Will Clark	.10
405	Travis Fryman	.05
406	Scott Sanderson	.05
407	Gene Harris	.05
408	Chuck Carr	.05
409	Ozzie Smith	1.00
410	Kent Mercker	.05
411	Andy Van Slyke	.05
412	Jimmy Key	.05
413	Pat Mahomes	.05
414	John Wetteland	.05
415	Todd Jones	.05
416	Greg Harris	.05
417	Kevin Stocker	.05
418	Juan Gonzalez	.65
419	Pete Smith	.05
420	Pat Listach	.05
421	Trevor Hoffman	.05
422	Scott Fletcher	.05
423	Mark Lewis	.05
424	Mickey Morandini	.05
425	Ryne Sandberg	1.00
426	Erik Hanson	.05
427	Gary Gaetti	.05
428	Harold Reynolds	.05
429	Mark Portugal	.05

430	David Valle	.05
431	Mitch Williams	.05
432	Howard Johnson	.05
433	Hal Morris	.05
434	Tom Henke	.05
435	Shane Mack	.05
436	Mike Piazza	1.50
437	Bret Saberhagen	.05
438	Jose Mesa	.05
439	Jaime Navarro	.05
440	Checklist	.05

Clean-Up Crew

NM/M

Complete Set (12):		8.00
Common Player:		1.00
1	Larry Walker	1.00
2	Andres Galarraga	1.00
3	Dave Hollins	1.00
4	Bobby Bonilla	1.00
5	Cecil Fielder	1.00
6	Danny Tartabull	1.00
7	Juan Gonzalez	2.00
8	Joe Carter	1.00
9	Fred McGriff	1.00
10	Matt Williams	1.00
11	Albert Belle	1.00
12	Harold Baines	1.00

5th Anniversary

NM/M

300	Frank Thomas	2.50
400	Frank Thomas	5.00

1994 Leaf Frank Thomas Poster

NM/M

Frank Thomas	15.00

Gamers

NM/M

Complete Set (12):	30.00

Common Player:		1.00
1	Ken Griffey Jr.	6.00
2	Len Dykstra	1.00
3	Juan Gonzalez	3.00
4	Don Mattingly	6.00
5	Dave Justice	1.00
6	Mark Grace	1.00
7	Frank Thomas	4.00
8	Barry Bonds	7.50
9	Kirby Puckett	4.50
10	Will Clark	1.00
11	John Kruk	1.00
12	Mike Piazza	6.00

Gold Rookies

NM/M

Complete Set (20):		6.00
Common Player:		.25
1	Javier Lopez	.25
2	Rondell White	.25
3	Butch Huskey	.25
4	Midre Cummings	.25
5	Scott Ruffcorn	.25
6	Manny Ramirez	3.50
7	Danny Bautista	.25
8	Russ Davis	.25
9	Steve Karsay	.25
10	Carlos Delgado	2.50
11	Bob Hamelin	.25
12	Marcus Moore	.25
13	Miguel Jimenez	.25
14	Matt Walbeck	.25
15	James Mouton	.25
16	Rich Becker	.25
17	Brian Anderson	.25
18	Cliff Floyd	.25
19	Steve Trachsel	.25
20	Hector Carrasco	.25

Gold Stars

NM/M

Complete Set (15):	60.00

Common Player: 3.00
1 Roberto Alomar 4.00
2 Barry Bonds 12.00
3 Dave Justice 3.00
4 Ken Griffey Jr. 9.00
5 Len Dykstra 3.00
6 Don Mattingly 7.50
7 Andres Galarraga 3.00
8 Greg Maddux 6.00
9 Carlos Baerga 3.00
10 Paul Molitor 5.00
11 Frank Thomas 5.00
12 John Olerud 3.00
13 Juan Gonzalez 4.00
14 Fred McGriff 3.00
15 Jack McDowell 3.00

MVP Contenders

NM/M
Complete Set, Silver (30): 20.00
Complete Set, Gold (30): 40.00
Common Player, Silver: .25
Common Player, Gold: .50
AMERICAN LEAGUE 2.00
1a Albert Belle/Silver .25
1b Albert Belle/Gold .50
2a Jose Canseco/Silver 1.25
2b Jose Canseco/Gold 2.00
3a Joe Carter/Silver .25
3b Joe Carter/Gold .50
4a Will Clark/Silver .35
4b Will Clark/Gold .60
5a Cecil Fielder/Silver .25
5b Cecil Fielder/Gold .50
6a Juan Gonzalez/Silver 1.50
6b Juan Gonzalez/Gold 2.50
7a Ken Griffey Jr./Silver 4.00
7b Ken Griffey Jr./Gold 7.50
8a Paul Molitor/Silver 2.00
8b Paul Molitor/Gold 4.00
9a Rafael Palmeiro/Silver 1.50
9b Rafael Palmeiro/Gold 2.50
10a Kirby Puckett/Silver 2.50
10b Kirby Puckett/Gold 5.00
11a Cal Ripken, Jr./Silver 6.00
11b Cal Ripken, Jr./Gold 12.50
12a Frank Thomas/Silver 2.00
12b Frank Thomas/Gold 4.00
13a Mo Vaughn/Silver .25
13b Mo Vaughn/Gold .50
14a Carlos Baerga/Silver .25
14b Carlos Baerga/Gold .50
15 AL Bonus Card/Silver .25
NATIONAL LEAGUE .60
1a Gary Sheffield/Silver .35
1b Gary Sheffield/Gold .65
2a Jeff Bagwell/Silver 2.00
2b Jeff Bagwell/Gold 4.00
3a Dante Bichette/Silver .25
3b Dante Bichette/Gold .50
4a Barry Bonds/Silver 6.00
4b Barry Bonds/Gold 12.50
5a Darren Daulton/Silver .25
5b Darren Daulton/Gold .50
6a Andres Galarraga/Silver .25
6b Andres Galarraga/Gold .50
7a Gregg Jefferies/Silver .25
7b Gregg Jefferies/Gold .50
8a Dave Justice/Silver .25
8b Dave Justice/Gold .50
9a Ray Lankford/Silver .25
9b Ray Lankford/Gold .50
10a Fred McGriff/Silver .25
10b Fred McGriff/Gold .50
11a Barry Larkin/Silver .25
11b Barry Larkin/Gold .50
12a Mike Piazza/Silver 4.00
12b Mike Piazza/Gold 7.50
13a Deion Sanders/Silver .25
13b Deion Sanders/Gold .50
14a Matt Williams/Silver .25
14b Matt Williams/Gold .50
15 NL Bonus Card/Silver .25

Power Brokers

NM/M
Complete Set (10): 8.00
Common Player: .40
1 Frank Thomas .75
2 Dave Justice .40
3 Barry Bonds 3.00

4 Juan Gonzalez .65
5 Ken Griffey Jr. 2.00
6 Mike Piazza 2.00
7 Cecil Fielder .40
8 Fred McGriff .40
9 Joe Carter .40
10 Albert Belle .40

Slide Show

NM/M
Complete Set (10): 9.00
Common Player: .25
1 Frank Thomas 1.00
2 Mike Piazza 2.00
3 Darren Daulton .25
4 Ryne Sandberg 1.50
5 Roberto Alomar .50
6 Barry Bonds 3.00
7 Juan Gonzalez .75
8 Tim Salmon .25
9 Ken Griffey Jr. 2.00
10 Dave Justice .25

Statistical Standouts

NM/M
Complete Set (10): 10.00
Common Player: .40
1 Frank Thomas .75
2 Barry Bonds 2.50
3 Juan Gonzalez .65
4 Mike Piazza 2.00
5 Greg Maddux 1.00
6 Ken Griffey Jr. 2.00
7 Joe Carter .40
8 Dave Winfield .75
9 Tony Gwynn 1.00
10 Cal Ripken, Jr. 2.50

1994 Leaf/Limited

NM/M
Complete Set (160): 35.00
Common Player: .25
Pack (5): 2.50
Wax Box (20): 40.00
1 Jeffrey Hammonds .25
2 Ben McDonald .25
3 Mike Mussina .75
4 Rafael Palmeiro 1.50
5 Cal Ripken, Jr. 6.00

6 Lee Smith .25
7 Roger Clemens 3.00
8 Scott Cooper .25
9 Andre Dawson .40
10 Mike Greenwell .25
11 Aaron Sele .25
12 Mo Vaughn .25
13 Brian Anderson **RC** .25
14 Chad Curtis .25
15 Chili Davis .25
16 Gary DiSarcina .25
17 Mark Langston .25
18 Tim Salmon .25
19 Wilson Alvarez .25
20 Jason Bere .25
21 Julio Franco .25
22 Jack McDowell .25
23 Tim Raines .25
24 Frank Thomas 2.00
25 Robin Ventura .25
26 Carlos Baerga .25
27 Albert Belle .25
28 Kenny Lofton .25
29 Eddie Murray 2.00
30 Manny Ramirez 2.00
31 Cecil Fielder .25
32 Travis Fryman .25
33 Mickey Tettleton .25
34 Alan Trammell .25
35 Lou Whitaker .25
36 David Cone .25
37 Gary Gaetti .25
38 Greg Gagne .25
39 Bob Hamelin .25
40 Wally Joyner .25
41 Brian McRae .25
42 Ricky Bones .25
43 Brian Harper .25
44 John Jaha .25
45 Pat Listach .25
46 Dave Nilsson .25
47 Greg Vaughn .25
48 Kent Hrbek .25
49 Chuck Knoblauch .25
50 Shane Mack .25
51 Kirby Puckett 2.50
52 Dave Winfield 2.00
53 Jim Abbott .25
54 Wade Boggs 2.50
55 Jimmy Key .25
56 Don Mattingly 3.00
57 Paul O'Neill .25
58 Danny Tartabull .25
59 Dennis Eckersley 1.50
60 Rickey Henderson 2.00
61 Mark McGwire 5.00
62 Troy Neel .25
63 Ruben Sierra .25
64 Eric Anthony .25
65 Jay Buhner .25
66 Ken Griffey Jr. 4.00
67 Randy Johnson 2.00
68 Edgar Martinez .25
69 Tino Martinez .25
70 Jose Canseco .75
71 Will Clark .35
72 Juan Gonzalez 1.50
73 Dean Palmer .25
74 Ivan Rodriguez 1.50
75 Roberto Alomar .40
76 Joe Carter .25
77 Carlos Delgado 1.00
78 Paul Molitor 2.00
79 John Olerud .25
80 Devon White .25
81 Steve Avery .25
82 Tom Glavine .50
83 Dave Justice .25
84 Roberto Kelly .25
85 Ryan Klesko .25
86 Javier Lopez .25
87 Greg Maddux 2.50
88 Fred McGriff .25

89 Shawon Dunston .25
90 Mark Grace .25
91 Derrick May .25
92 Sammy Sosa 3.00
93 Rick Wilkins .25
94 Bret Boone .25
95 Barry Larkin .25
96 Kevin Mitchell .25
97 Hal Morris .25
98 Deion Sanders .25
99 Reggie Sanders .25
100 Dante Bichette .25
101 Ellis Burks .25
102 Andres Galarraga .25
103 Joe Girardi .25
104 Charlie Hayes .25
105 Chuck Carr .25
106 Jeff Conine .25
107 Bryan Harvey .25
108 Benito Santiago .25
109 Gary Sheffield .60
110 Jeff Bagwell 2.00
111 Craig Biggio .25
112 Ken Caminiti .25
113 Andujar Cedeno .25
114 Doug Drabek .25
115 Luis Gonzalez .40
116 Brett Butler .25
117 Delino DeShields .25
118 Eric Karros .25
119 Raul Mondesi .25
120 Mike Piazza 4.00
121 Henry Rodriguez .25
122 Tim Wallach .25
123 Moises Alou .25
124 Cliff Floyd .25
125 Marquis Grissom .25
126 Ken Hill .25
127 Larry Walker .25
128 John Wetteland .25
129 Bobby Bonilla .25
130 John Franco .25
131 Jeff Kent .25
132 Bret Saberhagen .25
133 Ryan Thompson .25
134 Darren Daulton .25
135 Mariano Duncan .25
136 Len Dykstra .25
137 Danny Jackson .25
138 John Kruk .25
139 Jay Bell .25
140 Jeff King .25
141 Al Martin .25
142 Orlando Merced .25
143 Andy Van Slyke .25
144 Bernard Gilkey .25
145 Gregg Jefferies .25
146 Ray Lankford .25
147 Ozzie Smith 2.50
148 Mark Whiten .25
149 Todd Zeile .25
150 Derek Bell .25
151 Andy Benes .25
152 Tony Gwynn 2.50
153 Phil Plantier .25
154 Bip Roberts .25
155 Rod Beck .25
156 Barry Bonds 6.00
157 John Burkett .25
158 Royce Clayton .25
159 Bill Swift .25
160 Matt Williams .25

Gold

NM/M
Complete Set (18): 20.00
Common Player: .25
1 Frank Thomas 1.50
2 Gregg Jefferies .25
3 Roberto Alomar .50
4 Mariano Duncan .25
5 Wade Boggs 2.00
6 Matt Williams .25

7	Cal Ripken, Jr.	4.00
8	Ozzie Smith	2.00
9	Kirby Puckett	2.00
10	Barry Bonds	4.00
11	Ken Griffey Jr.	3.00
12	Tony Gwynn	2.00
13	Joe Carter	.25
14	Dave Justice	.25
15	Ivan Rodriguez	1.25
16	Mike Piazza	3.00
17	Jimmy Key	.25
18	Greg Maddux	2.00

Rookies

		NM/M
Complete Set (80):		17.50
Common Player:		.25
Pack (5):		3.00
Box (20):		60.00
1	Charles Johnson	.25
2	Rico Brogna	.25
3	Melvin Nieves	.25
4	Rich Becker	.25
5	Russ Davis	.25
6	Matt Mieske	.25
7	Paul Shuey	.25
8	Hector Carrasco	.25
9	J.R. Phillips	.25
10	Scott Ruffcorn	.25
11	Kurt Abbott	.25
12	Danny Bautista	.25
13	Rick White	.25
14	Steve Dunn	.25
15	Joe Ausanio	.25
16	Salomon Torres	.25
17	Rick Bottalico	.25
18	Johnny Ruffin	.25
19	Kevin Foster	.25
20	W. Van Landingham RC	.25
21	Troy O'Leary	.25
22	Mark Acre	.25
23	Norberto Martin	.25
24	Jason Jacome RC	.25
25	Steve Trachsel	.25
26	Denny Hocking	.25
27	Mike Lieberthal	.25
28	Gerald Williams	.25
29	John Mabry	.25
30	Greg Blosser	.25
31	Carl Everett	.25
32	Steve Karsay	.25
33	Jose Valentin	.25
34	Jon Lieber	.25
35	Chris Gomez	.25
36	Jesus Tavarez	.25
37	Tony Longmire	.25
38	Luis Lopez	.25
39	Matt Walbeck	.25
40	Rikkert Faneyte	.25
41	Shane Reynolds	.25
42	Joey Hamilton	.25
43	Ismael Valdes	.25
44	Danny Miceli	.25
45	Darren Bragg	.25
46	Alex Gonzalez	.25
47	Rick Helling	.25
48	Jose Oliva	.25
49	Jim Edmonds	4.00
50	Miguel Jimenez	.25
51	Tony Eusebio	.25
52	Shawn Green	4.00
53	Billy Ashley	.25
54	Rondell White	.25
55	Cory Bailey	.25
56	Tim Davis	.25
57	John Hudek	.25
58	Darren Hall	.25
59	Darren Dreifort	.25
60	Mike Kelly	.25
61	Marcus Moore	.25
62	Garret Anderson	.25
63	Brian Hunter	.25

64	Mark Smith	.25
65	Garey Ingram	.25
66	Rusty Greer RC	.25
67	Marc Newfield	.25
68	Gar Finnvold	.25
69	Paul Spoljaric	.25
70	Ray McDavid	.25
71	Orlando Miller	.25
72	Jorge Fabregas	.25
73	Ray Holbert	.25
74	Armando Benitez	.25
75	Ernie Young	.25
76	James Mouton	.25
77	Robert Perez RC	.25
78	Chan Ho Park RC	1.00
79	Roger Salkeld	.25
80	Tony Tarasco	.25

Rookies Rookie Phenoms

		NM/M
Complete Set (10):		260.00
Common Player:		1.00
Production 5,000 Sets		
1	Raul Mondesi	1.00
2	Bob Hamelin	1.00
3	Midre Cummings	1.00
4	Carlos Delgado	8.00
5	Cliff Floyd	1.00
6	Jeffrey Hammonds	1.00
7	Ryan Klesko	1.00
8	Javier Lopez	1.00
9	Manny Ramirez	10.00
10	Alex Rodriguez	250.00

1995 Leaf

		NM/M
Complete Set (400):		12.50
Common Player:		.75
Series 1 or 2 Pack (12):		.75
Series 1 or 2 Wax		
Box (36):		15.00
1	Frank Thomas	.75
2	Carlos Garcia	.05
3	Todd Hundley	.05
4	Damion Easley	.05
5	Roberto Mejia	.05
6	John Mabry	.05
7	Aaron Sele	.05
8	Kenny Lofton	.05
9	John Doherty	.05
10	Joe Carter	.05
11	Mike Lansing	.05
12	John Valentin	.05
13	Ismael Valdes	.05
14	Dave McCarty	.05
15	Melvin Nieves	.05
16	Bobby Jones	.05
17	Trevor Hoffman	.05
18	John Smoltz	.05

19	Leo Gomez	.05
20	Roger Pavlik	.05
21	Dean Palmer	.05
22	Rickey Henderson	.75
23	Eddie Taubensee	.05
24	Damon Buford	.05
25	Mark Wohlers	.05
26	Jim Edmonds	.05
27	Wilson Alvarez	.05
28	Matt Williams	.05
29	Jeff Montgomery	.05
30	Shawon Dunston	.05
31	Tom Pagnozzi	.05
32	Jose Lind	.05
33	Royce Clayton	.05
34	Cal Eldred	.05
35	Chris Gomez	.05
36	Henry Rodriguez	.05
37	Dave Fleming	.05
38	Jon Lieber	.05
39	Scott Servais	.05
40	Wade Boggs	1.00
41	John Olerud	.05
42	Eddie Williams	.05
43	Paul Sorrento	.05
44	Ron Karkovice	.05
45	Kevin Foster	.05
46	Miguel Jimenez	.05
47	Reggie Sanders	.05
48	Rondell White	.05
49	Scott Leius	.05
50	Jose Valentin	.05
51	William Van Landingham	.05
52	Denny Hocking	.05
53	Jeff Fassero	.05
54	Chris Hoiles	.05
55	Walt Weiss	.05
56	Geronimo Berroa	.05
57	Rich Rowland	.05
58	Dave Weathers	.05
59	Sterling Hitchcock	.05
60	Raul Mondesi	.05
61	Rusty Greer	.05
62	Dave Justice	.05
63	Cecil Fielder	.05
64	Brian Jordan	.05
65	Mike Lieberthal	.05
66	Rick Aguilera	.05
67	Chuck Finley	.05
68	Andy Ashby	.05
69	Alex Fernandez	.05
70	Ed Sprague	.05
71	Steve Buechele	.05
72	Willie Greene	.05
73	Dave Nilsson	.05
74	Bret Saberhagen	.05
75	Jimmy Key	.05
76	Darren Lewis	.05
77	Steve Cooke	.05
78	Kirk Gibson	.05
79	Ray Lankford	.05
80	Paul O'Neill	.05
81	Mike Bordick	.05
82	Wes Chamberlain	.05
83	Rico Brogna	.05
84	Kevin Appier	.05
85	Juan Guzman	.05
86	Kevin Seitzer	.05
87	Mickey Morandini	.05
88	Pedro Martinez	.75
89	Matt Mieske	.05
90	Tino Martinez	.05
91	Paul Shuey	.05
92	Bip Roberts	.05
93	Chili Davis	.05
94	Deion Sanders	.05
95	Darrell Whitmore	.05
96	Joe Orsulak	.05
97	Bret Boone	.05
98	Kent Mercker	.05
99	Scott Livingstone	.05
100	Brady Anderson	.05
101	James Mouton	.05
102	Jose Rijo	.05
103	Bobby Munoz	.05
104	Ramon Martinez	.05
105	Bernie Williams	.10
106	Troy Neel	.05
107	Ivan Rodriguez	.65
108	Salomon Torres	.05
109	Johnny Ruffin	.05
110	Darryl Kile	.05
111	Bobby Ayala	.05
112	Ron Darling	.05
113	Jose Lima	.05
114	Joey Hamilton	.05
115	Greg Maddux	1.00
116	Greg Colbrunn	.05
117	Ozzie Guillen	.05
118	Brian Anderson	.05
119	Jeff Bagwell	.75
120	Pat Listach	.05
121	Sandy Alomar	.05

122	Jose Vizcaino	.05
123	Rick Helling	.05
124	Allen Watson	.05
125	Pedro Munoz	.05
126	Craig Biggio	.05
127	Kevin Stocker	.05
128	Wil Cordero	.05
129	Rafael Palmeiro	.65
130	Gar Finnvold	.05
131	Darren Hall	.05
132	Heath Slocumb	.05
133	Darrin Fletcher	.05
134	Cal Ripken Jr.	2.50
135	Dante Bichette	.05
136	Don Slaught	.05
137	Pedro Astacio	.05
138	Ryan Thompson	.05
139	Greg Gohr	.05
140	Javier Lopez	.05
141	Lenny Dykstra	.05
142	Pat Rapp	.05
143	Mark Kiefer	.05
144	Greg Gagne	.05
145	Eduardo Perez	.05
146	Felix Fermin	.05
147	Jeff Frye	.05
148	Terry Steinbach	.05
149	Jim Eisenreich	.05
150	Brad Ausmus	.05
151	Randy Myers	.05
152	Rick White	.05
153	Mark Portugal	.05
154	Delino DeShields	.05
155	Scott Cooper	.05
156	Pat Hentgen	.05
157	Mark Gubicza	.05
158	Carlos Baerga	.05
159	Joe Girardi	.05
160	Rey Sanchez	.05
161	Todd Jones	.05
162	Luis Polonia	.05
163	Steve Trachsel	.05
164	Roberto Hernandez	.05
165	John Patterson	.05
166	Rene Arocha	.05
167	Will Clark	.10
168	Jim Leyritz	.05
169	Todd Van Poppel	.05
170	Robb Nen	.05
171	Midre Cummings	.05
172	Jay Buhner	.05
173	Kevin Tapani	.05
174	Mark Lemke	.05
175	Marcus Moore	.05
176	Wayne Kirby	.05
177	Rich Amaral	.05
178	Lou Whitaker	.05
179	Jay Bell	.05
180	Rick Wilkins	.05
181	Paul Molitor	.75
182	Gary Sheffield	.35
183	Kirby Puckett	1.00
184	Cliff Floyd	.05
185	Darren Oliver	.05
186	Tim Naehring	.05
187	John Hudek	.05
188	Eric Young	.05
189	Roger Salkeld	.05
190	Kirt Manwaring	.05
191	Kurt Abbott	.05
192	David Nied	.05
193	Todd Zeile	.05
194	Wally Joyner	.05
195	Dennis Martinez	.05
196	Billy Ashley	.05
197	Ben McDonald	.05
198	Bob Hamelin	.05
199	Chris Turner	.05
200	Lance Johnson	.05
201	Willie Banks	.05
202	Juan Gonzalez	.50
203	Scott Sanders	.05
204	Scott Brosius	.05
205	Curt Schilling	.25
206	Alex Gonzalez	.05
207	Travis Fryman	.05
208	Tim Raines	.05
209	Steve Avery	.05
210	Hal Morris	.05
211	Ken Griffey Jr.	1.50
212	Ozzie Smith	1.00
213	Chuck Carr	.05
214	Ryan Klesko	.05
215	Robin Ventura	.05
216	Luis Gonzalez	.20
217	Ken Ryan	.05
218	Mike Piazza	1.50
219	Matt Walbeck	.05
220	Jeff Kent	.05
221	Orlando Miller	.05
222	Kenny Rogers	.05
223	J.T. Snow	.05
224	Alan Trammell	.05
225	John Franco	.05

226	Gerald Williams	.05
227	Andy Benes	.05
228	Dan Wilson	.05
229	Dave Hollins	.05
230	Vinny Castilla	.05
231	Devon White	.05
232	Fred McGriff	.05
233	Quilvio Veras	.05
234	Tom Candiotti	.05
235	Jason Bere	.05
236	Mark Langston	.05
237	Mel Rojas	.05
238	Chuck Knoblauch	.05
239	Bernard Gilkey	.05
240	Mark McGwire	2.00
241	Kirk Rueter	.05
242	Pat Kelly	.05
243	Ruben Sierra	.05
244	Randy Johnson	.75
245	Shane Reynolds	.05
246	Danny Tartabull	.05
247	Darryl Hamilton	.05
248	Danny Bautista	.05
249	Tom Gordon	.05
250	Tom Glavine	.25
251	Orlando Merced	.05
252	Eric Karros	.05
253	Benji Gil	.05
254	Sean Bergman	.05
255	Roger Clemens	1.25
256	Roberto Alomar	.20
257	Benito Santiago	.05
258	Robby Thompson	.05
259	Marvin Freeman	.05
260	Jose Offerman	.05
261	Greg Vaughn	.05
262	David Segui	.05
263	Geronimo Pena	.05
264	Tim Salmon	.75
265	Eddie Murray	.75
266	Mariano Duncan	.05
267	Hideo Nomo RC	2.50
268	Derek Bell	.05
269	Mo Vaughn	.05
270	Jeff King	.05
271	Edgar Martinez	.05
272	Sammy Sosa	1.25
273	Scott Ruffcorn	.05
274	Darren Daulton	.05
275	John Jaha	.05
276	Andres Galarraga	.05
277	Mark Grace	.05
278	Mike Moore	.05
279	Barry Bonds	2.50
280	Manny Ramirez	.75
281	Ellis Burks	.05
282	Greg Swindell	.05
283	Barry Larkin	.05
284	Albert Belle	.05
285	Shawn Green	.35
286	John Roper	.05
287	Scott Erickson	.05
288	Moises Alou	.05
289	Mike Blowers	.05
290	Brent Gates	.05
291	Sean Berry	.05
292	Mike Stanley	.05
293	Jeff Conine	.05
294	Tim Wallach	.05
295	Bobby Bonilla	.05
296	Bruce Ruffin	.05
297	Chad Curtis	.05
298	Mike Greenwell	.05
299	Tony Gwynn	1.00
300	Russ Davis	.05
301	Danny Jackson	.05
302	Pete Harnisch	.05
303	Don Mattingly	1.25
304	Rheal Cormier	.05
305	Larry Walker	.05
306	Hector Carrasco	.05
307	Jason Jacome	.05
308	Phil Plantier	.05
309	Harold Baines	.05
310	Mitch Williams	.05
311	Charles Nagy	.05
312	Ken Caminiti	.05
313	Alex Rodriguez	2.00
314	Chris Sabo	.05
315	Gary Gaetti	.05
316	Andre Dawson	.25
317	Mark Clark	.05
318	Vince Coleman	.05
319	Brad Clontz	.05
320	Steve Finley	.05
321	Doug Drabek	.05
322	Mark McLemore	.05
323	Stan Javier	.05
324	Ron Gant	.05
325	Charlie Hayes	.05
326	Carlos Delgado	.50
327	Ricky Bottalico	.05
328	Rod Beck	.05
329	Mark Acre	.05
330	Chris Bosio	.05
331	Tony Phillips	.05

332	Garret Anderson	.05
333	Pat Meares	.05
334	Todd Worrell	.05
335	Marquis Grissom	.05
336	Brent Mayne	.05
337	Lee Tinsley	.05
338	Terry Pendleton	.05
339	David Cone	.05
340	Tony Fernandez	.05
341	Jim Bullinger	.05
342	Armando Benitez	.05
343	John Smiley	.05
344	Dan Miceli	.05
345	Charles Johnson	.05
346	Lee Smith	.05
347	Brian McRae	.05
348	Jim Thome	.65
349	Jose Oliva	.05
350	Terry Mulholland	.05
351	Tom Henke	.05
352	Dennis Eckersley	.65
353	Sid Fernandez	.05
354	Paul Wagner	.05
355	John Dettmer	.05
356	John Wetteland	.05
357	John Burkett	.05
358	Marty Cordova	.05
359	Norm Charlton	.05
360	Mike Devereaux	.05
361	Alex Cole	.05
362	Brett Butler	.05
363	Mickey Tettleton	.05
364	Al Martin	.05
365	Tony Tarasco	.05
366	Pat Mahomes	.05
367	Gary DiSarcina	.05
368	Bill Swift	.05
369	Chipper Jones	1.00
370	Orel Hershiser	.05
371	Kevin Gross	.05
372	Dave Winfield	.75
373	Andujar Cedeno	.05
374	Jim Abbott	.05
375	Glenallen Hill	.05
376	Otis Nixon	.05
377	Roberto Kelly	.05
378	Chris Hammond	.05
379	Mike Macfarlane	.05
380	J.R. Phillips	.05
381	Luis Alicea	.05
382	Bret Barberie	.05
383	Tom Goodwin	.05
384	Mark Whiten	.05
385	Jeffrey Hammonds	.05
386	Omar Vizquel	.05
387	Mike Mussina	.35
388	Rickey Bones	.05
389	Steve Ontiveros	.05
390	Jeff Blauser	.05
391	Jose Canseco	.35
392	Bob Tewksbury	.05
393	Jacob Brumfield	.05
394	Doug Jones	.05
395	Ken Hill	.05
396	Pat Borders	.05
397	Carl Everett	.05
398	Gregg Jefferies	.05
399	Jack McDowell	.05
400	Denny Neagle	.05

Cornerstones

		NM/M
Complete Set (6):		3.50
Common Player:		.40
1	Frank Thomas, Robin Ventura	.75
2	Cecil Fielder, Travis Fryman	.40
3	Don Mattingly, Wade Boggs	2.00
4	Jeff Bagwell, Ken Caminiti	.75
5	Will Clark, Dean Palmer	.40
6	J.R. Phillips, Matt Williams	.40

Frank Thomas

		NM/M
Complete Set (6):		7.50
Common Card:		1.50
1	The Rookie	1.50
2	Sophomore Stardom	1.50
3	Super Star	1.50
4	AL MVP	1.50

5	Back-To-Back	1.50
6	The Big Hurt	1.50

Gold Rookies

		NM/M
Complete Set (16):		3.00
Common Player:		.10
1	Alex Rodriguez	2.50
2	Garret Anderson	.10
3	Shawn Green	.50
4	Armando Benitez	.10
5	Darren Dreifort	.10
6	Orlando Miller	.10
7	Jose Oliva	.10
8	Ricky Bottalico	.10
9	Charles Johnson	.10
10	Brian Hunter	.10
11	Ray McDavid	.10
12	Chan Ho Park	.10
13	Mike Kelly	.10
14	Cory Bailey	.10
15	Alex Gonzalez	.10
16	Andrew Lorraine	.10

Gold Stars

		NM/M
Complete Set (14):		35.00
Common Player:		1.00
1	Jeff Bagwell	2.50
2	Albert Belle	1.00
3	Tony Gwynn	3.50
4	Ken Griffey Jr.	4.50
5	Barry Bonds	6.00
6	Don Mattingly	4.00
7	Raul Mondesi	1.00
8	Joe Carter	1.00
9	Greg Maddux	3.50
10	Frank Thomas	2.50
11	Mike Piazza	4.50
12	Jose Canseco	1.50

13	Kirby Puckett	3.50
14	Matt Williams	1.00

Great Gloves

		NM/M
Complete Set (16):		3.00
Common Player:		.15
1	Jeff Bagwell	.35
2	Roberto Alomar	.20
3	Barry Bonds	1.00
4	Wade Boggs	.45
5	Andres Galarraga	.15
6	Ken Griffey Jr.	.60
7	Marquis Grissom	.15
8	Kenny Lofton	.15
9	Barry Larkin	.15
10	Don Mattingly	.50
11	Greg Maddux	.45
12	Kirby Puckett	.45
13	Ozzie Smith	.45
14	Cal Ripken Jr.	1.00
15	Matt Williams	.15
16	Ivan Rodriguez	.30

Heading For The Hall

		NM/M
Complete Set (8):		50.00
Common Player:		4.50
1	Frank Thomas	4.50
2	Ken Griffey Jr.	9.00
3	Jeff Bagwell	4.50
4	Barry Bonds	15.00
5	Kirby Puckett	6.00
6	Cal Ripken Jr.	15.00
7	Tony Gwynn	6.00
8	Paul Molitor	4.50

Opening Day

		NM/M
Complete Set (8):		6.00

	Common Player:	.25
1	Frank Thomas	.50
2	Jeff Bagwell	.50
3	Barry Bonds	2.00
4	Ken Griffey Jr.	1.00
5	Mike Piazza	1.00
6	Cal Ripken Jr.	2.00
7	Jose Canseco	.35
8	Larry Walker	.25

Slideshow

		NM/M
	Complete Set (16):	35.00
	Complete Series 1 (1a-8a):	20.00
	Complete Series 2 (1b-8b):	20.00
	Same CL and prices for both series.	
	Common Player:	1.50
1a	Raul Mondesi	1.50
1b	Raul Mondesi	1.50
2a	Frank Thomas	3.00
2b	Frank Thomas	3.00
3a	Fred McGriff	1.50
3b	Fred McGriff	1.50
4a	Cal Ripken Jr.	6.00
4b	Cal Ripken Jr.	6.00
5a	Jeff Bagwell	3.00
5b	Jeff Bagwell	3.00
6a	Will Clark	1.50
6b	Will Clark	1.50
7a	Matt Williams	1.50
7b	Matt Williams	1.50
8a	Ken Griffey Jr.	4.50
8b	Ken Griffey Jr.	4.50

Special Edition Jumbos

		NM/M
	Complete Set (2):	7.00
1	Frank Thomas	3.00
2	Barry Bonds	5.00

Statistical Standouts

		NM/M
	Complete Set (9):	95.00
	Common Player:	3.00
	Promos:	25-50%

1	Joe Carter	3.00
2	Ken Griffey Jr.	25.00
3	Don Mattingly	15.00
4	Fred McGriff	3.00
5	Paul Molitor	9.00
6	Kirby Puckett	12.50
7	Cal Ripken Jr.	30.00
8	Frank Thomas	9.00
9	Matt Williams	3.00

300 Club

		NM/M
	Complete Set (18):	12.50
	Common Player:	.25
1	Frank Thomas	1.00
2	Paul Molitor	1.00
3	Mike Piazza	3.00
4	Moises Alou	.25
5	Mike Greenwell	.25
6	Will Clark	.25
7	Hal Morris	.25
8	Edgar Martinez	.25
9	Carlos Baerga	.25
10	Ken Griffey Jr.	3.00
11	Wade Boggs	1.50
12	Jeff Bagwell	1.00
13	Tony Gwynn	1.50
14	John Kruk	.25
15	Don Mattingly	2.00
16	Mark Grace	.25
17	Kirby Puckett	1.50
18	Kenny Lofton	.25

1995 Leaf/Limited

		NM/M
	Complete Set (192):	20.00
	Common Player:	.10
	Series 1 or 2 Pack (5):	2.00
	Series 1 or 2 Wax Box (20):	30.00
1	Frank Thomas	.75
2	Geronimo Berroa	.10
3	Tony Phillips	.10
4	Roberto Alomar	.25
5	Steve Avery	.10
6	Darryl Hamilton	.10
7	Scott Cooper	.10
8	Mark Grace	.10
9	Billy Ashley	.10
10	Wil Cordero	.10
11	Barry Bonds	5.00
12	Kenny Lofton	.10
13	Jay Buhner	.10
14	Alex Rodriguez	3.00
15	Bobby Bonilla	.10
16	Brady Anderson	.10
17	Ken Caminiti	.10
18	Charlie Hayes	.10
19	Jay Bell	.10
20	Will Clark	.15
21	Jose Canseco	.35

22	Bret Boone	.10
23	Dante Bichette	.10
24	Kevin Appier	.10
25	Chad Curtis	.10
26	Marty Cordova	.10
27	Jason Bere	.10
28	Jimmy Key	.10
29	Rickey Henderson	.75
30	Tim Salmon	.10
31	Joe Carter	.10
32	Tom Glavine	.35
33	Pat Listach	.10
34	Brian Jordan	.10
35	Brian McRae	.10
36	Eric Karros	.10
37	Pedro Martinez	.75
38	Royce Clayton	.10
39	Eddie Murray	.75
40	Randy Johnson	.75
41	Jeff Conine	.10
42	Brett Butler	.10
43	Jeffrey Hammonds	.10
44	Andujar Cedeno	.10
45	Dave Hollins	.10
46	Jeff King	.10
47	Benji Gil	.10
48	Roger Clemens	2.00
49	Barry Larkin	.10
50	Joe Girardi	.10
51	Bob Hamelin	.10
52	Travis Fryman	.10
53	Chuck Knoblauch	.10
54	Ray Durham	.10
55	Don Mattingly	2.00
56	Ruben Sierra	.10
57	J.T. Snow	.10
58	Derek Bell	.10
59	David Cone	.10
60	Marquis Grissom	.10
61	Kevin Seitzer	.10
62	Ozzie Smith	1.50
63	Rick Wilkins	.10
64	Hideo Nomo RC	3.00
65	Tony Tarasco	.10
66	Manny Ramirez	.75
67	Charles Johnson	.10
68	Craig Biggio	.10
69	Bobby Jones	.10
70	Mike Mussina	.60
71	Alex Gonzalez	.10
72	Gregg Jefferies	.10
73	Rusty Greer	.10
74	Mike Greenwell	.10
75	Hal Morris	.10
76	Paul O'Neill	.10
77	Luis Gonzalez	.25
78	Chipper Jones	1.50
79	Mike Piazza	2.50
80	Rondell White	.10
81	Glenallen Hill	.10
82	Shawn Green	.50
83	Bernie Williams	.10
84	Jim Thome	.65
85	Terry Pendleton	.10
86	Rafael Palmeiro	.65
87	Tony Gwynn	1.50
88	Mickey Tettleton	.10
89	John Valentin	.10
90	Deion Sanders	.10
91	Larry Walker	.10
92	Michael Tucker	.10
93	Alan Trammell	.10
94	Tim Raines	.10
95	Dave Justice	.10
96	Tino Martinez	.10
97	Cal Ripken Jr.	5.00
98	Deion Sanders	.10
99	Darren Daulton	.10
100	Paul Molitor	.75
101	Randy Myers	.10
102	Wally Joyner	.10
103	Carlos Perez	.10
104	Brian Hunter	.10
105	Wade Boggs	1.50
106	Bobby Higginson RC	.50
107	Jeff Kent	.10
108	Jose Offerman	.10
109	Dennis Eckersley	.65
110	Dave Nilsson	.10
111	Chuck Finley	.10
112	Devon White	.10
113	Bip Roberts	.10
114	Ramon Martinez	.10
115	Greg Maddux	1.50
116	Curtis Goodwin	.10
117	John Jaha	.10
118	Ken Griffey Jr.	2.50
119	Geronimo Pena	.10
120	Shawon Dunston	.10
121	Ariel Prieto	.10
122	Kirby Puckett	1.50
123	Carlos Baerga	.10
124	Todd Hundley	.10
125	Tim Naehring	.10
126	Gary Sheffield	.45

127	Dean Palmer	.10
128	Rondell White	.10
129	Greg Gagne	.10
130	Jose Rijo	.10
131	Ivan Rodriguez	.65
132	Jeff Bagwell	.75
133	Greg Vaughn	.10
134	Chili Davis	.10
135	Al Martin	.10
136	Kenny Rogers	.10
137	Aaron Sele	.10
138	Raul Mondesi	.10
139	Cecil Fielder	.10
140	Tim Wallach	.10
141	Andres Galarraga	.10
142	Lou Whitaker	.10
143	Jack McDowell	.10
144	Matt Williams	.10
145	Ryan Klesko	.10
146	Carlos Garcia	.10
147	Albert Belle	.10
148	Ryan Thompson	.10
149	Roberto Kelly	.10
150	Edgar Martinez	.10
151	Robby Thompson	.10
152	Mo Vaughn	.10
153	Todd Zeile	.10
154	Harold Baines	.10
155	Phil Plantier	.10
156	Mike Stanley	.10
157	Ed Sprague	.10
158	Moises Alou	.10
159	Quilvio Veras	.10
160	Reggie Sanders	.10
161	Delino DeShields	.10
162	Rico Brogna	.10
163	Greg Colbrunn	.10
164	Steve Finley	.10
165	Orlando Merced	.10
166	Mark McGwire	3.00
167	Garret Anderson	.10
168	Paul Sorrento	.10
169	Mark Langston	.10
170	Danny Tartabull	.10
171	Vinny Castilla	.10
172	Javier Lopez	.10
173	Bret Saberhagen	.10
174	Eddie Williams	.10
175	Scott Leius	.10
176	Juan Gonzalez	.50
177	Gary Gaetti	.10
178	Jim Edmonds	.10
179	John Olerud	.10
180	Lenny Dykstra	.10
181	Ray Lankford	.10
182	Ron Gant	.10
183	Doug Drabek	.10
184	Fred McGriff	.10
185	Andy Benes	.10
186	Kurt Abbott	.10
187	Bernard Gilkey	.10
188	Sammy Sosa	2.00
189	Lee Smith	.10
190	Dennis Martinez	.10
191	Ozzie Guillen	.10
192	Robin Ventura	.10

Gold

		NM/M
	Complete Set (24):	10.00
	Common Player:	.25
1	Frank Thomas	.60
2	Jeff Bagwell	.60
3	Raul Mondesi	.25
4	Barry Bonds	1.50
5	Albert Belle	.25
6	Ken Griffey Jr.	1.00
7	Cal Ripkin (Ripken) Jr.	1.50
8	Will Clark	.25
9	Jose Canseco	.45
10	Larry Walker	.25
11	Kirby Puckett	.75
12	Don Mattingly	1.00
13	Tim Salmon	.25

14	Roberto Alomar	.35
15	Greg Maddux	.75
16	Mike Piazza	1.00
17	Matt Williams	.25
18	Kenny Lofton	.25
19	Alex Rodriquez (Rodriguez)	1.25
20	Tony Gwynn	.75
21	Mo Vaughn	.25
22	Chipper Jones	.75
23	Manny Ramirez	.60
24	Deion Sanders	.25

Lumberjacks

		NM/M
Complete Set (16):		55.00
Common Player:		2.00
1	Albert Belle	2.00
2	Barry Bonds	12.00
3	Juan Gonzalez	3.50
4	Ken Griffey Jr.	7.50
5	Fred McGriff	2.00
6	Mike Piazza	7.50
7	Kirby Puckett	6.00
8	Mo Vaughn	2.00
9	Frank Thomas	4.50
10	Jeff Bagwell	4.50
11	Matt Williams	2.00
12	Jose Canseco	3.00
13	Raul Mondesi	2.00
14	Manny Ramirez	4.50
15	Cecil Fielder	2.00
16	Cal Ripken Jr.	12.00

Bat Patrol

		NM/M
Complete Set (24):		7.50
Common Player:		.15
1	Frank Thomas	.75
2	Tony Gwynn	1.00
3	Wade Boggs	1.00
4	Larry Walker	.25
5	Ken Griffey Jr.	1.50
6	Jeff Bagwell	.75
7	Manny Ramirez	.75
8	Mark Grace	.25
9	Kenny Lofton	.15
10	Mike Piazza	1.50
11	Will Clark	.25
12	Mo Vaughn	.25
13	Carlos Baerga	.15
14	Rafael Palmeiro	.65
15	Barry Bonds	2.50
16	Kirby Puckett	1.00
17	Roberto Alomar	.35
18	Barry Larkin	.15
19	Eddie Murray	.75
20	Tim Salmon	.25
21	Don Mattingly	1.25
22	Fred McGriff	.15
23	Albert Belle	.25
24	Dante Bichette	.15

1996 Leaf

SAMMY SOSA

		NM/M
Complete Set (220):		10.00
Common Player:		.05
Pack (12):		1.00
Wax Box (30):		25.00
1	John Smoltz	.10
2	Dennis Eckersley	.60
3	Delino DeShields	.05
4	Cliff Floyd	.05
5	Chuck Finley	.05
6	Cecil Fielder	.05
7	Tim Naehring	.05
8	Carlos Perez	.05
9	Brad Ausmus	.05
10	Matt Lawton RC	.15
11	Alan Trammell	.05
12	Steve Finley	.05
13	Paul O'Neill	.05
14	Gary Sheffield	.40
15	Mark McGwire	1.50
16	Bernie Williams	.05
17	Jeff Montgomery	.05
18	Chan Ho Park	.05
19	Greg Vaughn	.05
20	Jeff Kent	.05
21	Cal Ripken Jr.	2.00
22	Charles Johnson	.05
23	Eric Karros	.05
24	Alex Rodriguez	1.50
25	Chris Snopek	.05
26	Jason Isringhausen	.05
27	Chili Davis	.05
28	Chipper Jones	.75
29	Bret Saberhagen	.05
30	Tony Clark	.05
31	Marty Cordova	.05
32	Dwayne Hosey	.05
33	Fred McGriff	.05
34	Deion Sanders	.05
35	Orlando Merced	.05
36	Brady Anderson	.05
37	Ray Lankford	.05
38	Manny Ramirez	.65
39	Alex Fernandez	.05
40	Greg Colbrunn	.05
41	Ken Griffey Jr.	1.00
42	Mickey Morandini	.05
43	Chuck Knoblauch	.05
44	Quinton McCracken	.05
45	Tim Salmon	.05
46	Jose Mesa	.05
47	Marquis Grissom	.05
48	Checklist	.05
49	Raul Mondesi	.05
50	Mark Grudzielanek	.05
51	Ray Durham	.05
52	Matt Williams	.05
53	Bob Hamelin	.05
54	Lenny Dykstra	.05
55	Jeff King	.05
56	LaTroy Hawkins	.05
57	Terry Pendleton	.05
58	Kevin Stocker	.05
59	Jose Timmons	.05
60	David Justice	.05
61	Ricky Bottalico	.05
62	Andy Ashby	.05
63	Larry Walker	.05
64	Jose Canseco	.40
65	Bret Boone	.05
66	Shawn Green	.35
67	Chad Curtis	.05
68	Travis Fryman	.05
69	Roger Clemens	1.00
70	David Bell	.05
71	Rusty Greer	.05
72	Bob Higginson	.05
73	Joey Hamilton	.05
74	Kevin Seitzer	.05
75	Julian Tavarez	.05
76	Troy Percival	.05
77	Kirby Puckett	.75
78	Barry Bonds	2.00
79	Michael Tucker	.05
80	Paul Molitor	.65
81	Carlos Garcia	.05
82	Johnny Damon	.35
83	Mike Hampton	.05
84	Ariel Prieto	.05
85	Tony Tarasco	.05
86	Pete Schourek	.05
87	Tom Glavine	.30
88	Rondell White	.05
89	Jim Edmonds	.05
90	Robby Thompson	.05
91	Wade Boggs	.75
92	Pedro Martinez	.65
93	Gregg Jefferies	.05
94	Albert Belle	.05
95	Benji Gil	.05
96	Denny Neagle	.05
97	Mark Langston	.05
98	Sandy Alomar	.05
99	Tony Gwynn	.75
100	Todd Hundley	.05
101	Dante Bichette	.05
102	Eddie Murray	.65
103	Lyle Mouton	.05
104	John Jaha	.05
105	Checklist	.05
106	Jon Nunnally	.05
107	Juan Gonzalez	.50
108	Kevin Appier	.05
109	Brian McRae	.05
110	Lee Smith	.05
111	Tim Wakefield	.05
112	Sammy Sosa	1.00
113	Jay Buhner	.05
114	Garret Anderson	.05
115	Edgar Martinez	.05
116	Edgardo Alfonzo	.05
117	Billy Ashley	.05
118	Joe Carter	.05
119	Javy Lopez	.05
120	Bobby Bonilla	.05
121	Ken Caminiti	.05
122	Barry Larkin	.05
123	Shannon Stewart	.05
124	Orel Hershiser	.05
125	Jeff Conine	.05
126	Mark Grace	.05
127	Kenny Lofton	.05
128	Luis Gonzalez	.25
129	Rico Brogna	.05
130	Mo Vaughn	.05
131	Brad Radke	.05
132	Jose Herrera	.05
133	Rick Aguilera	.05
134	Gary DiSarcina	.05
135	Andres Galarraga	.05
136	Carl Everett	.05
137	Steve Avery	.05
138	Vinny Castilla	.05
139	Dennis Martinez	.05
140	John Wetteland	.05
141	Alex Gonzalez	.05
142	Brian Jordan	.05
143	Todd Hollandsworth	.05
144	Terrell Wade	.05
145	Wilson Alvarez	.05
146	Reggie Sanders	.05
147	Will Clark	.10
148	Hideo Nomo	.50
149	J.T. Snow	.05
150	Frank Thomas	.65
151	Ivan Rodriguez	.60
152	Jay Bell	.05
153	Checklist	.05
154	David Cone	.05
155	Roberto Alomar	.20
156	Carlos Delgado	.40
157	Carlos Baerga	.05
158	Geronimo Berroa	.05
159	Joe Vitiello	.05
160	Terry Steinbach	.05
161	Doug Drabek	.05
162	David Segui	.05
163	Ozzie Smith	.75
164	Kurt Abbott	.05
165	Randy Johnson	.65
166	John Valentin	.05
167	Mickey Tettleton	.05
168	Ruben Sierra	.05
169	Jim Thome	.60
170	Mike Greenwell	.05
171	Quilvio Veras	.05
172	Robin Ventura	.05
173	Bill Pulsipher	.05
174	Rafael Palmeiro	.60
175	Hal Morris	.05
176	Ryan Klesko	.05
177	Eric Young	.05
178	Shane Andrews	.05
179	Brian Hunter	.05
180	Brett Butler	.05
181	John Olerud	.05
182	Moises Alou	.05
183	Glenallen Hill	.05
184	Ismael Valdes	.05
185	Andy Pettitte	.25
186	Yamil Benitez	.05
187	Jason Bere	.05
188	Dean Palmer	.05
189	Jimmy Haynes	.05
190	Trevor Hoffman	.05
191	Mike Mussina	.40
192	Greg Maddux	.75
193	Ozzie Guillen	.05
194	Pat Listach	.05
195	Derek Bell	.05
196	Darren Daulton	.05
197	John Mabry	.05
198	Ramon Martinez	.05
199	Jeff Bagwell	.65
200	Mike Piazza	1.00
201	Al Martin	.05
202	Aaron Sele	.05
203	Ed Sprague	.05
204	Rod Beck	.05
205	Checklist	.05
206	Mike Lansing	.05
207	Craig Biggio	.05
208	Jeffrey Hammonds	.05
209	Dave Nilsson	.05
210	Dante Bichette, Albert Belle Checklist, Inserts	.05
211	Derek Jeter	2.00
212	Alan Benes	.05
213	Jason Schmidt	.05
214	Alex Ochoa	.05
215	Ruben Rivera	.05
216	Roger Cedeno	.05
217	Jeff Suppan	.05
218	Billy Wagner	.05
219	Mark Loretta	.05
220	Karim Garcia	.10

1996 Leaf Press Proofs

BRIAN McRAE

	NM/M
Complete Set, Gold (220):	200.00
Complete Set, Silver (220):	100.00
Complete Set, Bronze (220):	75.00
Common Player, Gold:	1.00
Common Player, Silver:	.50
Common Player, Bronze:	.25

(Press Proof stars valued as follows in comparison to regular-issue '96 Leaf: Gold - 15X; Silver - 6X; Bronze - 4X.)

All-Star MVP Contenders

		NM/M
Complete Set (20):		12.50
Common Card:		.25
Golds:		1.5X
1	Frank Thomas	1.50
2	Mike Piazza	1.50
2c	Mike Piazza (Redeemed and punch-cancelled.)	1.00
3	Sammy Sosa	1.50

4	Cal Ripken Jr.	2.00
5	Jeff Bagwell	.75
6	Reggie Sanders	.25
7	Mo Vaughn	.25
8	Tony Gwynn	1.00
9	Dante Bichette	.25
10	Tim Salmon	.25
11	Chipper Jones	1.00
12	Kenny Lofton	.25
13	Manny Ramirez	.75
14	Barry Bonds	2.00
15	Raul Mondesi	.25
16	Kirby Puckett	1.00
17	Albert Belle	.25
18	Ken Griffey Jr.	1.50
19	Greg Maddux	1.00
20	Bonus Card	.10

Frank Thomas' Greatest Hits

		NM/M
Complete Set (8):		12.50
Common Card:		2.00
1	1990	2.00
2	1991	2.00
3	1992	2.00
4	1993	2.00
5	1994	2.00
6	1995	2.00
7	Career	2.00
8	MVP	2.00

Frank Thomas The Big Heart

		NM/M
Complete Set (4):		35.00
Common Card:		10.00
(1)	Frank Thomas (Bat on shoulder.)	10.00
(2)	Frank Thomas (Holding glove.)	10.00
(3)	Frank Thomas (Horizontal)	10.00
(4)	Frank Thomas/Seated	10.00

Gold Leaf Stars

		NM/M
Complete Set (15):		125.00
Common Player:		3.00
1	Frank Thomas	9.00
2	Dante Bichette	3.00
3	Sammy Sosa	15.00
4	Ken Griffey Jr.	15.00
5	Mike Piazza	15.00
6	Tim Salmon	3.00
7	Hideo Nomo	6.00
8	Cal Ripken Jr.	20.00
9	Chipper Jones	12.00
10	Albert Belle	3.00
11	Tony Gwynn	12.00
12	Mo Vaughn	3.00
13	Barry Larkin	3.00
14	Manny Ramirez	9.00
15	Greg Maddux	12.00

Hats Off

		NM/M
Complete Set (8):		30.00
Common Player:		3.00
1	Cal Ripken Jr.	12.00
2	Barry Larkin	3.00
3	Frank Thomas	4.50
4	Mo Vaughn	3.00
5	Ken Griffey Jr.	7.50
6	Hideo Nomo	4.00
7	Albert Belle	3.00
8	Greg Maddux	6.00

Picture Perfect

		NM/M
Complete Set (12):		22.50
Common Player:		1.00
Promos:		2X
1	Frank Thomas	2.00
2	Cal Ripken Jr.	5.00
3	Greg Maddux	2.50
4	Manny Ramirez	2.00
5	Chipper Jones	2.50
6	Tony Gwynn	2.50
7	Ken Griffey Jr.	3.00
8	Albert Belle	1.00
9	Jeff Bagwell	2.00
10	Mike Piazza	3.00
11	Mo Vaughn	1.00
12	Barry Bonds	5.00

Statistical Standouts

	NM/M
Complete Set (8):	60.00
Common Player:	3.00
1	Cal Ripken Jr.	20.00
2	Tony Gwynn	10.00
3	Frank Thomas	7.50
4	Ken Griffey Jr.	13.50
5	Hideo Nomo	6.00
6	Greg Maddux	10.00
7	Albert Belle	3.00
8	Chipper Jones	10.00

Total Bases

		NM/M
Complete Set (12):		25.00
Common Player:		1.00
Promos:		2X
1	Frank Thomas	2.50
2	Albert Belle	1.00
3	Rafael Palmeiro	2.00
4	Barry Bonds	6.00
5	Kirby Puckett	3.00
6	Joe Carter	1.00
7	Paul Molitor	2.50
8	Fred McGriff	1.00
9	Ken Griffey Jr.	4.00
10	Carlos Baerga	1.00
11	Juan Gonzalez	2.00
12	Cal Ripken Jr.	6.00

1996 Leaf/Limited

		NM/M
Complete Set (90):		15.00
Common Player:		.10
Gold Set (90):		50.00
Gold Stars/Rookies:		3X
Pack (5):		1.50
Wax Box (14):		20.00
1	Ivan Rodriguez	.60
2	Roger Clemens	1.50
3	Gary Sheffield	.40
4	Tino Martinez	.10
5	Sammy Sosa	1.50
6	Reggie Sanders	.10
7	Ray Lankford	.10
8	Manny Ramirez	.75
9	Jeff Bagwell	.75
10	Greg Maddux	1.00
11	Ken Griffey Jr.	1.50
12	Rondell White	.10
13	Mike Piazza	1.50
14	Marc Newfield	.10
15	Cal Ripken Jr.	3.00
16	Carlos Delgado	.40
17	Tim Salmon	.10
18	Andres Galarraga	.10
19	Chuck Knoblauch	.10
20	Matt Williams	.10
21	Mark McGwire	2.00
22	Ben McDonald	.10
23	Frank Thomas	.75
24	Johnny Damon	.35
25	Gregg Jefferies	.10
26	Travis Fryman	.10
27	Chipper Jones	1.00
28	David Cone	.10
29	Kenny Lofton	.10
30	Mike Mussina	.30
31	Alex Rodriguez	2.00
32	Carlos Baerga	.10
33	Brian Hunter	.10
34	Juan Gonzalez	.60
35	Bernie Williams	.10
36	Wally Joyner	.10
37	Fred McGriff	.10
38	Randy Johnson	.75
39	Marty Cordova	.10
40	Garret Anderson	.10
41	Albert Belle	.10
42	Edgar Martinez	.10
43	Barry Larkin	.10
44	Paul O'Neill	.10
45	Cecil Fielder	.10
46	Rusty Greer	.10
47	Mo Vaughn	.10
48	Dante Bichette	.10
49	Ryan Klesko	.10
50	Roberto Alomar	.25
51	Raul Mondesi	.10
52	Robin Ventura	.10
53	Tony Gwynn	1.00
54	Mark Grace	.10
55	Jim Thome	.60
56	Jason Giambi	.50
57	Tom Glavine	.25
58	Jim Edmonds	.10
59	Pedro Martinez	.75
60	Charles Johnson	.10
61	Wade Boggs	1.00
62	Orlando Merced	.10
63	Craig Biggio	.10
64	Brady Anderson	.10
65	Hideo Nomo	.60
66	Ozzie Smith	1.00
67	Eddie Murray	.75
68	Will Clark	.15
69	Jay Buhner	.10
70	Kirby Puckett	1.00
71	Barry Bonds	3.00
72	Ray Durham	.10
73	Sterling Hitchcock	.10
74	John Smoltz	.10
75	Andre Dawson	.35
76	Joe Carter	.10
77	Ryne Sandberg	1.00
78	Rickey Henderson	.75
79	Brian Jordan	.10
80	Greg Vaughn	.10
81	Andy Pettitte	.25
82	Dean Palmer	.10
83	Paul Molitor	.75
84	Rafael Palmeiro	.60
85	Henry Rodriguez	.10
86	Larry Walker	.10
87	Ismael Valdes	.10
88	Derek Bell	.10
89	J.T. Snow	.10
90	Jack McDowell	.10

Lumberjacks

		NM/M
Complete Set (10):		40.00
Common Player:		1.50
Lumberjack Blacks (500):		2X
Promos:		2X
1	Ken Griffey Jr.	5.00
2	Sammy Sosa	5.00
3	Cal Ripken Jr.	7.50
4	Frank Thomas	3.00
5	Alex Rodriguez	6.00
6	Mo Vaughn	1.50
7	Chipper Jones	4.00
8	Mike Piazza	5.00
9	Jeff Bagwell	3.00
10	Mark McGwire	6.00

Pennant Craze

	NM/M
Complete Set (10):	20.00

Common Player:	1.00
Promos:	2X
1 Juan Gonzalez	1.25
2 Cal Ripken Jr.	4.00
3 Frank Thomas	1.50
4 Ken Griffey Jr.	2.50
5 Albert Belle	1.00
6 Greg Maddux	2.00
7 Paul Molitor	1.50
8 Alex Rodriguez	3.00
9 Barry Bonds	4.00
10 Chipper Jones	2.00

Rookies

	NM/M
Complete Set (10):	7.50
Common Player:	.50
Limited Gold:	3X
1 Alex Ochoa	.50
2 Darin Erstad	1.00
3 Ruben Rivera	.50
4 Derek Jeter	5.00
5 Jermaine Dye	.50
6 Jason Kendall	.50
7 Mike Grace	.50
8 Andruw Jones	2.50
9 Rey Ordonez	.50
10 George Arias	.50

1996 Leaf/Preferred

	NM/M
Complete Set (150):	15.00
Common Player:	.05
Press Proofs:	12X
Pack (6):	1.00
Wax Box (24):	20.00
1 Ken Griffey Jr.	1.25
2 Rico Brogna	.05
3 Gregg Jefferies	.05
4 Reggie Sanders	.05
5 Manny Ramirez	.75
6 Shawn Green	.40
7 Tino Martinez	.05
8 Jeff Bagwell	.75
9 Marc Newfield	.05
10 Ray Lankford	.05
11 Jay Bell	.05
12 Greg Maddux	1.00
13 Frank Thomas	.75
14 Travis Fryman	.05
15 Mark McGwire	1.50
16 Chuck Knoblauch	.05
17 Sammy Sosa	1.25
18 Matt Williams	.05
19 Roger Clemens	1.25
20 Rondell White	.05
21 Ivan Rodriguez	.65
22 Cal Ripken Jr.	2.00
23 Ben McDonald	.05
24 Kenny Lofton	.05
25 Mike Piazza	1.25
26 David Cone	.05
27 Gary Sheffield	.40
28 Tim Salmon	.05
29 Andres Galarraga	.05
30 Johnny Damon	.35
31 Ozzie Smith	1.00
32 Carlos Baerga	.05
33 Raul Mondesi	.05
34 Moises Alou	.05
35 Alex Rodriguez	1.50
36 Mike Mussina	.40
37 Jason Isringhausen	.05
38 Barry Larkin	.05
39 Bernie Williams	.05
40 Chipper Jones	1.00
41 Joey Hamilton	.05
42 Charles Johnson	.05
43 Juan Gonzalez	.50
44 Greg Vaughn	.05
45 Robin Ventura	.05
46 Albert Belle	.05
47 Rafael Palmeiro	.65
48 Brian Hunter	.05
49 Mo Vaughn	.05
50 Paul O'Neill	.05
51 Mark Grace	.05
52 Randy Johnson	.75
53 Pedro Martinez	.75
54 Marty Cordova	.05
55 Garret Anderson	.05
56 Joe Carter	.05
57 Jim Thome	.60
58 Edgardo Alfonzo	.05
59 Dante Bichette	.05
60 Darryl Hamilton	.05
61 Roberto Alomar	.20
62 Fred McGriff	.05
63 Kirby Puckett	1.00
64 Hideo Nomo	.60
65 Alex Fernandez	.05
66 Ryan Klesko	.05
67 Wade Boggs	1.00
68 Eddie Murray	.75
69 Eric Karros	.05
70 Jim Edmonds	.05
71 Edgar Martinez	.05
72 Andy Pettitte	.30
73 Mark Grudzielanek	.05
74 Tom Glavine	.25
75 Ken Caminiti	.05
76 Will Clark	.10
77 Craig Biggio	.05
78 Brady Anderson	.05
79 Tony Gwynn	1.00
80 Larry Walker	.05
81 Brian Jordan	.05
82 Lenny Dykstra	.05
83 Butch Huskey	.05
84 Jack McDowell	.05
85 Cecil Fielder	.05
86 Jose Canseco	.40
87 Jason Giambi	.50
88 Rickey Henderson	.75
89 Kevin Seitzer	.05
90 Carlos Delgado	.40
91 Ryne Sandberg	1.00
92 Dwight Gooden	.05
93 Michael Tucker	.05
94 Barry Bonds	2.00
95 Eric Young	.05
96 Dean Palmer	.05
97 Henry Rodriguez	.05
98 John Mabry	.05
99 J.T. Snow	.05
100 Andre Dawson	.25
101 Ismael Valdes	.05
102 Charles Nagy	.05
103 Jay Buhner	.05
104 Derek Bell	.05
105 Paul Molitor	.75
106 Hal Morris	.05
107 Ray Durham	.05
108 Bernard Gilkey	.05
109 John Valentin	.05
110 Melvin Nieves	.05
111 John Smoltz	.05
112 Terrell Wade	.05
113 Chad Mottola	.05
114 Tony Clark	.05
115 John Wasdin	.05
116 Derek Jeter	2.00
117 Rey Ordonez	.05
118 Jason Thompson	.05
119 Robin Jennings RC	.05
120 Rocky Coppinger RC	.05
121 Billy Wagner	.05
122 Steve Gibralter	.05
123 Jermaine Dye	.05
124 Jason Kendall	.05
125 Mike Grace RC	.05
126 Jason Schmidt	.05
127 Paul Wilson	.05
128 Alan Benes	.05
129 Justin Thompson	.05
130 Brooks Kieschnick	.05
131 George Arias	.05
132 Osvaldo Fernandez RC	.20
133 Todd Hollandsworth	.05
134 Eric Owens	.05
135 Chan Ho Park	.05
136 Mark Loretta	.05
137 Ruben Rivera	.05
138 Jeff Suppan	.05
139 Ugueth Urbina	.05
140 LaTroy Hawkins	.05
141 Chris Snopek	.05
142 Edgar Renteria	.05
143 Raul Casanova	.05
144 Jose Herrera	.05
145 Matt Lawton RC	.05
146 Ralph Milliard RC	.05
147 Frank Thomas Checklist	.05
148 Jeff Bagwell Checklist	.05
149 Ken Griffey Jr. Checklist	.05
150 Mike Piazza Checklist	.05

Press Proofs

	NM/M
Complete Set (150):	100.00
Common Player:	.50
Stars/Rookies:	12X

(See 1996 Leaf Preferred for checklist and base card values.)

Leaf Steel

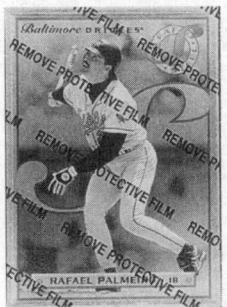

	NM/M
Complete Set (77):	25.00
Common Player:	.15
Gold:	2X
1 Frank Thomas	1.00
2 Paul Molitor	1.00
3 Kenny Lofton	.15
4 Travis Fryman	.15
5 Jeff Conine	.15
6 Barry Bonds	3.00
7 Gregg Jefferies	.15
8 Alex Rodriguez	2.50
9 Wade Boggs	1.50
10 David Justice	.15
11 Hideo Nomo	.75
12 Roberto Alomar	.30
13 Todd Hollandsworth	.15
14 Mark McGwire	2.50
15 Rafael Palmeiro	.75
16 Will Clark	.25
17 Cal Ripken Jr.	3.00
18 Derek Bell	.15
19 Gary Sheffield	.50
20 Juan Gonzalez	.65
21 Garret Anderson	.15
22 Mo Vaughn	.15
23 Robin Ventura	.15
24 Carlos Baerga	.15
25 Tim Salmon	.15
26 Matt Williams	.15
27 Fred McGriff	.15
28 Rondell White	.15
29 Ray Lankford	.15
30 Lenny Dykstra	.15
31 J.T. Snow	.15
32 Sammy Sosa	2.00
33 Chipper Jones	1.50
34 Bobby Bonilla	.15
35 Paul Wilson	.15
36 Darren Daulton	.15
37 Larry Walker	.15
38 Raul Mondesi	.15
39 Jeff Bagwell	1.00
40 Derek Jeter	3.00
41 Kirby Puckett	1.50
42 Jason Isringhausen	.15
43 Vinny Castilla	.15
44 Jim Edmonds	.15
45 Ron Gant	.15
46 Carlos Delgado	.50
47 Jose Canseco	.40
48 Tony Gwynn	1.50
49 Mike Mussina	.50
50 Charles Johnson	.15
51 Mike Piazza	2.00
52 Ken Griffey Jr.	2.00
53 Greg Maddux	1.50
54 Mark Grace	.15
55 Ryan Klesko	.15
56 Dennis Eckersley	.75
57 Rickey Henderson	1.00
58 Michael Tucker	.15
59 Joe Carter	.15
60 Randy Johnson	1.00
61 Brian Jordan	.15
62 Shawn Green	.50
63 Roger Clemens	2.00
64 Andres Galarraga	.15
65 Johnny Damon	.40
66 Ryne Sandberg	1.50
67 Alan Benes	.15
68 Albert Belle	.15
69 Barry Larkin	.15
70 Marty Cordova	.15
71 Dante Bichette	.15
72 Craig Biggio	.15
73 Reggie Sanders	.15
74 Moises Alou	.15
75 Chuck Knoblauch	.15
76 Cecil Fielder	.15
77 Manny Ramirez	1.00

Staremaster

	NM/M
Complete Set (12):	50.00
Common Player:	3.00
1 Chipper Jones	5.00
2 Alex Rodriguez	7.50
3 Derek Jeter	10.00
4 Tony Gwynn	5.00
5 Frank Thomas	4.00
6 Ken Griffey Jr.	6.00
7 Cal Ripken Jr.	10.00
8 Greg Maddux	5.00
9 Albert Belle	3.00
10 Barry Bonds	10.00
11 Jeff Bagwell	4.00
12 Mike Piazza	6.00

Steel Power

		NM/M
Complete Set (8):		17.50
Common Player:		1.00
1	Albert Belle	1.00
2	Mo Vaughn	1.00
3	Ken Griffey Jr.	3.50
4	Cal Ripken Jr.	5.00
5	Mike Piazza	3.50
6	Barry Bonds	5.00
7	Jeff Bagwell	2.50
8	Frank Thomas	2.50

1996 Leaf/Signature Series

		NM/M
Complete Set (150):		30.00
Complete 1st Series (100):		20.00
Complete Extended Series (50):		10.00
Common Player:		.05
Gold PP Stars/Rookies:		8X
Platinum PP Stars/Rookies:		20X
Pack (4):		3.50
Wax Box (12):		35.00
1	Mike Piazza	1.25
2	Juan Gonzalez	.65
3	Greg Maddux	1.00
4	Marc Newfield	.05
5	Wade Boggs	1.00
6	Ray Lankford	.05
7	Frank Thomas	.75
8	Rico Brogna	.05
9	Tim Salmon	.05
10	Ken Griffey Jr.	1.25
11	Manny Ramirez	.75
12	Cecil Fielder	.05
13	Gregg Jefferies	.05
14	Rondell White	.05
15	Cal Ripken Jr.	2.00
16	Alex Rodriguez	1.50
17	Bernie Williams	.05
18	Andres Galarraga	.50
19	Mike Mussina	.50
20	Chuck Knoblauch	.05
21	Joe Carter	.05
22	Jeff Bagwell	.75
23	Mark McGwire	1.50
24	Sammy Sosa	1.00
25	Reggie Sanders	.05
26	Chipper Jones	1.00
27	Jeff Cirillo	.05
28	Roger Clemens	1.25
29	Craig Biggio	.05
30	Gary Sheffield	.45
31	Paul O'Neill	.05
32	Johnny Damon	.35
33	Jason Isringhausen	.05
34	Jay Bell	.05

35	Henry Rodriguez	.05
36	Matt Williams	.05
37	Randy Johnson	.75
38	Fred McGriff	.05
39	Jason Giambi	.60
40	Ivan Rodriguez	.65
41	Raul Mondesi	.05
42	Barry Larkin	.05
43	Ryan Klesko	.05
44	Joey Hamilton	.05
45	Todd Hundley	.05
46	Jim Edmonds	.05
47	Dante Bichette	.05
48	Roberto Alomar	.20
49	Mark Grace	.05
50	Brady Anderson	.05
51	Hideo Nomo	.65
52	Ozzie Smith	1.00
53	Robin Ventura	.05
54	Andy Pettitte	.35
55	Kenny Lofton	.05
56	John Mabry	.05
57	Paul Molitor	.75
58	Rey Ordonez	.05
59	Albert Belle	.05
60	Charles Johnson	.05
61	Edgar Martinez	.05
62	Derek Bell	.05
63	Carlos Delgado	.50
64	Raul Casanova	.05
65	Ismael Valdes	.05
66	J.T. Snow	.05
67	Derek Jeter	2.00
68	Jason Kendall	.05
69	John Smoltz	.05
70	Chad Mottola	.05
71	Jim Thome	.60
72	Will Clark	.10
73	Mo Vaughn	.05
74	John Wasdin	.05
75	Rafael Palmeiro	.65
76	Mark Grudzielanek	.05
77	Larry Walker	.05
78	Alan Benes	.05
79	Michael Tucker	.05
80	Billy Wagner	.05
81	Paul Wilson	.05
82	Greg Vaughn	.05
83	Dean Palmer	.05
84	Ryne Sandberg	1.00
85	Eric Young	.05
86	Jay Buhner	.05
87	Tony Clark	.05
88	Jermaine Dye	.05
89	Barry Bonds	2.00
90	Ugueth Urbina	.05
91	Charles Nagy	.05
92	Ruben Rivera	.05
93	Todd Hollandsworth	.05
94	Darin Erstad RC	1.50
95	Brooks Kieschnick	.05
96	Edgar Renteria	.05
97	Lenny Dykstra	.05
98	Tony Gwynn	1.00
99	Kirby Puckett	1.00
100	Checklist	.05
101	Andruw Jones	.75
102	Alex Ochoa	.05
103	David Cone	.05
104	Rusty Greer	.05
105	Jose Canseco	.45
106	Ken Caminiti	.05
107	Mariano Rivera	.15
108	Ron Gant	.05
109	Darryl Strawberry	.05
110	Vladimir Guerrero	.75
111	George Arias	.05
112	Jeff Conine	.05
113	Bobby Higginson	.05
114	Eric Karros	.05
115	Brian Hunter	.05
116	Eddie Murray	.75
117	Todd Walker	.05
118	Chan Ho Park	.05
119	John Jaha	.05
120	David Justice	.05
121	Makoto Suzuki	.05
122	Scott Rolen	.65
123	Tino Martinez	.05
124	Kimera Bartee	.05
125	Garret Anderson	.05
126	Brian Jordan	.05
127	Andre Dawson	.30
128	Javier Lopez	.05
129	Bill Pulsipher	.05
130	Dwight Gooden	.05
131	Al Martin	.05
132	Terrell Wade	.05
133	Steve Gibralter	.05
134	Tom Glavine	.35
135	Kevin Appier	.05
136	Tim Raines	.05
137	Curtis Pride	.05
138	Todd Greene	.05

139	Bobby Bonilla	.05
140	Trey Beamon	.05
141	Marty Cordova	.05
142	Rickey Henderson	.75
143	Ellis Burks	.05
144	Dennis Eckersley	.65
145	Kevin Brown	.05
146	Carlos Baerga	.05
147	Brett Butler	.05
148	Marquis Grissom	.05
149	Karim Garcia	.05
150	Checklist	.05

Press Proofs

	NM/M
Common Gold:	2.00
Gold Stars:	8X
Common Platinum:	4.00
Platinum Stars:	20X
(See 1996 Leaf/Signature Series for checklist and base card values.)	

Series Autographs Promos

	NM/M
Frank Thomas (Facsimile signature.)	4.00
Frank Thomas (Genuine autograph.)	50.00

Autographs

	NM/M
Common Bronze Player:	4.00
Silver:	1.5X
Gold:	2X
SPs: 100 Gold, 200 Silver, 700 Bronze	

(1)	Kurt Abbott	4.00
(2)	Juan Acevedo	4.00
(3)	Terry Adams	4.00
(4)	Manny Alexander	4.00
(5)	Roberto Alomar/SP	35.00
(6)	Moises Alou	12.00
(7)	Wilson Alvarez	4.00
(8)	Garret Anderson	10.00
(9)	Shane Andrews	4.00
(10)	Andy Ashby	4.00
(11)	Pedro Astacio	4.00
(12)	Brad Ausmus	4.00
(13)	Bobby Ayala	4.00
(14)	Carlos Baerga	4.00
(15)	Harold Baines	10.00
(16)	Jason Bates	4.00
(17)	Allen Battle	4.00
(18)	Rich Becker	4.00
(19)	David Bell	4.00
(20)	Rafael Belliard	4.00
(21)	Andy Benes	4.00
(22)	Armando Benitez	4.00
(23)	Jason Bere	4.00
(24)	Geronimo Berroa	4.00
(25)	Willie Blair	4.00
(26)	Mike Blowers	4.00
(27)	Wade Boggs/SP	50.00
(28)	Ricky Bones	4.00
(29)	Mike Bordick	4.00
(30)	Toby Borland	4.00
(31)	Ricky Bottalico	4.00
(32)	Darren Bragg	4.00
(33)	Jeff Branson	4.00
(34)	Tilson Brito	4.00
(35)	Rico Brogna	4.00
(36)	Scott Brosius	7.50
(37)	Damon Buford	4.00
(38)	Mike Busby	4.00
(39)	Tom Candiotti	4.00
(40)	Frank Castillo	4.00
(41)	Andujar Cedeno	4.00
(42)	Domingo Cedeno	4.00
(43)	Roger Cedeno	4.00
(44)	Norm Charlton	4.00
(45)	Jeff Cirillo	4.00
(46)	Will Clark	10.00
(47)	Jeff Conine	4.00
(48)	Steve Cooke	4.00
(49)	Joey Cora	4.00
(50)	Marty Cordova	4.00
(51)	Rheal Cormier	4.00
(52)	Felipe Crespo	4.00
(53)	Chad Curtis	4.00
(54)	Johnny Damon	15.00
(55)	Russ Davis	4.00
(56)	Andre Dawson	10.00
(57a)	Carlos Delgado (Black autograph.)	15.00
(57b)	Carlos Delgado (Blue autograph.)	15.00
(58)	Doug Drabek	4.00
(59)	Darren Dreifort	4.00
(60)	Shawon Dunston	4.00
(61)	Ray Durham	4.00
(62)	Jim Edmonds	12.00
(63)	Joey Eischen	4.00
(64)	Jim Eisenreich	4.00
(65)	Sal Fasano	4.00
(66)	Jeff Fassero	4.00
(67)	Alex Fernandez	4.00
(68)	Darrin Fletcher	4.00
(69)	Chad Fonville	4.00
(70)	Kevin Foster	4.00
(71)	John Franco	4.00
(72)	Julio Franco	10.00
(73)	Marvin Freeman	4.00
(74)	Travis Fryman	4.00
(75)	Gary Gaetti	4.00
(76)	Carlos Garcia	4.00
(77)	Jason Giambi	10.00
(78)	Benji Gil	4.00
(79)	Greg Gohr	4.00
(80)	Chris Gomez	4.00
(81)	Leo Gomez	4.00
(82)	Tom Goodwin	4.00
(83)	Mike Grace	4.00
(84)	Mike Greenwell	6.00
(85)	Rusty Greer	4.00
(86)	Mark Grudzielanek	4.00
(87)	Mark Gubicza	4.00
(88)	Juan Guzman	4.00
(89)	Darryl Hamilton	4.00
(90)	Joey Hamilton	4.00
(91)	Chris Hammond	4.00
(92)	Mike Hampton	7.50
(93)	Chris Haney	4.00
(94)	Todd Haney	4.00
(95)	Erik Hanson	4.00
(96)	Pete Harnisch	4.00
(97)	LaTroy Hawkins	4.00
(98)	Charlie Hayes	4.00
(99)	Jimmy Haynes	4.00
(100)	Roberto Hernandez	4.00
(101)	Bobby Higginson	4.00

(102)	Glenallen Hill	4.00
(103)	Ken Hill	4.00
(104)	Sterling Hitchcock	4.00
(105)	Trevor Hoffman	10.00
(106)	Dave Hollins	4.00
(107)	Dwayne Hosey	4.00
(108)	Thomas Howard	4.00
(109)	Steve Howe	6.00
(110)	John Hudek	4.00
(111)	Rex Hudler	4.00
(112)	Brian Hunter	4.00
(113)	Butch Huskey	4.00
(114)	Mark Hutton	4.00
(115)	Jason Jacome	4.00
(116)	John Jaha	4.00
(117)	Reggie Jefferson	4.00
(118)	Derek Jeter/SP	150.00
(119)	Bobby Jones	4.00
(120)	Todd Jones	4.00
(121)	Brian Jordan	5.00
(122)	Kevin Jordan	4.00
(123)	Jeff Juden	4.00
(124)	Ron Karkovice	4.00
(125)	Roberto Kelly	4.00
(126)	Mark Kiefer	4.00
(127)	Brooks Kieschnick	4.00
(128)	Jeff King	4.00
(129)	Mike Lansing	4.00
(130)	Matt Lawton	7.50
(131)	Al Leiter	6.00
(132)	Mark Leiter	4.00
(133)	Curtis Leskanic	4.00
(134)	Darren Lewis	4.00
(135)	Mark Lewis	4.00
(136)	Felipe Lira	4.00
(137)	Pat Listach	4.00
(138)	Keith Lockhart	4.00
(139)	Kenny Lofton/SP	25.00
(140)	John Mabry	4.00
(141)	Mike Macfarlane	4.00
(142)	Kirt Manwaring	4.00
(143)	Al Martin	4.00
(144)	Norberto Martin	4.00
(145)	Dennis Martinez	5.00
(146)	Pedro Martinez	40.00
(147)	Sandy Martinez	4.00
(148)	Mike Matheny	4.00
(149)	T.J. Mathews	4.00
(150)	David McCarty	4.00
(151)	Ben McDonald	4.00
(152)	Pat Meares	4.00
(153)	Orlando Merced	4.00
(154)	Jose Mesa	4.00
(155)	Matt Mieske	4.00
(156)	Orlando Miller	4.00
(157)	Mike Mimbs	4.00
(158)	Paul Molitor/SP	40.00
(159)	Raul Mondesi/SP	20.00
(160)	Jeff Montgomery	4.00
(161)	Mickey Morandini	4.00
(162)	Lyle Mouton	4.00
(163)	James Mouton	4.00
(164)	Jamie Moyer	4.00
(165)	Rodney Myers	4.00
(166)	Denny Neagle	4.00
(167)	Robb Nen	4.00
(168)	Marc Newfield	4.00
(169)	Dave Nilsson	4.00
(170)	Jon Nunnally	4.00
(171)	Chad Ogea	4.00
(172)	Troy O'Leary	4.00
(173)	Rey Ordonez	4.00
(174)	Jayhawk Owens	4.00
(175)	Tom Pagnozzi	4.00
(176)	Dean Palmer	4.00
(177)	Roger Pavlik	4.00
(178)	Troy Percival	4.00
(179)	Carlos Perez	4.00
(180)	Robert Perez	4.00
(181)	Andy Pettitte	30.00
(182)	Phil Plantier	4.00
(183)	Mike Potts	4.00
(184)	Curtis Pride	4.00
(185)	Ariel Prieto	4.00
(186)	Bill Pulsipher	4.00
(187)	Brad Radke	4.00
(188)	Manny Ramirez/SP	35.00
(189)	Joe Randa	4.00
(190)	Pat Rapp	4.00
(191)	Bryan Rekar	4.00
(192)	Shane Reynolds	4.00
(193)	Arthur Rhodes	4.00
(194)	Mariano Rivera	45.00
(195a)	Alex Rodriguez/SP (Black autograph.)	120.00
(195b)	Alex Rodriguez/SP (Blue autograph.)	120.00
(196)	Frank Rodriguez	4.00
(197)	Mel Rojas	4.00
(198)	Ken Ryan	4.00
(199)	Bret Saberhagen	4.00
(200)	Tim Salmon	5.00
(201)	Rey Sanchez	4.00
(202)	Scott Sanders	4.00
(203)	Steve Scarsone	4.00
(204)	Curt Schilling	25.00
(205)	Jason Schmidt	20.00
(206)	David Segui	4.00
(207)	Kevin Seitzer	4.00
(208)	Scott Servais	4.00
(209)	Don Slaught	4.00
(210)	Zane Smith	4.00
(211)	Paul Sorrento	4.00
(212)	Scott Stahoviak	4.00
(213)	Mike Stanley	4.00
(214)	Terry Steinbach	4.00
(215)	Kevin Stocker	4.00
(216)	Jeff Suppan	4.00
(217)	Bill Swift	4.00
(218)	Greg Swindell	4.00
(219)	Kevin Tapani	4.00
(220)	Danny Tartabull	4.00
(221)	Julian Tavarez	4.00
(222a)	Frank Thomas/SP (Blue autograph.)	40.00
(222b)	Frank Thomas/SP (Black autograph.)	40.00
(223)	Jim Thome/SP/ Silver	40.00
(224)	Ozzie Timmons	4.00
(225a)	Michael Tucker (Black autograph.)	4.00
(225b)	Michael Tucker (Blue autograph.)	4.00
(226)	Ismael Valdez	4.00
(227)	Jose Valentin	4.00
(228)	Todd Van Poppel	4.00
(229)	Mo Vaughn/SP	15.00
(230)	Quilvio Veras	4.00
(231)	Fernando Vina	4.00
(232)	Joe Vitiello	4.00
(233)	Jose Vizcaino	4.00
(234)	Omar Vizquel	12.00
(235)	Terrell Wade	4.00
(236)	Paul Wagner	4.00
(237)	Matt Walbeck	4.00
(238)	Jerome Walton	4.00
(239)	Turner Ward	4.00
(240)	Allen Watson	4.00
(241)	David Weathers	4.00
(242)	Walt Weiss	4.00
(244)	Turk Wendell	4.00
(244)	Rondell White	5.00
(245)	Brian Williams	4.00
(246)	George Williams	4.00
(247)	Paul Wilson	4.00
(248)	Bobby Witt	4.00
(249)	Bob Wolcott	4.00
(250)	Eric Young	4.00
(251)	Ernie Young	4.00
(252)	Gregg Zaun	4.00
---	Frank Thomas (Autographed jumbo edition of 1,500.)	25.00

Extended Autographs

		NM/M
Common Player:		4.00
Extended Pack:		20.00
Extended Box:		150.00
(1)	Scott Aldred	4.00
(2)	Mike Aldrete	4.00
(3)	Rich Amaral	4.00
(4)	Alex Arias	4.00
(5)	Paul Assenmacher	4.00
(6)	Roger Bailey	4.00
(7)	Erik Bennett	4.00
(8)	Sean Bergman	4.00
(9)	Doug Bochtler	4.00
(10)	Tim Bogar	4.00
(11)	Pat Borders	4.00
(12)	Pedro Borbon	4.00
(13)	Shawn Boskie	4.00
(14)	Rafael Bournigal	4.00
(15)	Mark Brandenburg	4.00
(16)	John Briscoe	4.00
(17)	Jorge Brito	4.00
(18)	Doug Brocail	4.00
(19)	Jay Buhner/ SP/1,000	17.50
(20)	Scott Bullett	4.00
(21)	Dave Burba	4.00
(22)	Ken Caminiti/ SP/1,000	25.00
(23)	John Cangelosi	4.00
(24)	Cris Carpenter	4.00
(25)	Chuck Carr	4.00
(26)	Larry Casian	4.00
(27)	Tony Castillo	4.00
(28)	Jason Christiansen	4.00
(29)	Archi Cianfrocco	4.00
(30)	Mark Clark	4.00
(31)	Terry Clark	4.00
(32)	Roger Clemens/ SP/1,000	150.00
(33)	Jim Converse	4.00
(34)	Dennis Cook	4.00
(35)	Francisco Cordova	4.00
(36)	Jim Corsi	4.00
(37)	Tim Crabtree	4.00
(38)	Doug Creek/ SP/1,950	8.00
(39)	John Cummings	4.00
(40)	Omar Daal	4.00
(41)	Rich DeLucia	4.00
(42)	Mark Dewey	4.00
(43)	Alex Diaz	4.00
(44)	Jermaine Dye/ SP/2,500	12.00
(45)	Ken Edenfield	4.00
(46)	Mark Eichhorn	4.00
(47)	John Ericks	4.00
(48)	Darin Erstad	10.00
(49)	Alvaro Espinoza	4.00
(50)	Jorge Fabregas	4.00
(51)	Mike Fetters	4.00
(52)	John Flaherty	4.00
(53)	Bryce Florie	4.00
(54)	Tony Fossas	4.00
(55)	Lou Frazier	4.00
(56)	Mike Gallego	4.00
(57)	Karim Garcia/ SP/2,500	6.00
(58)	Jason Giambi	12.00
(59)	Ed Giovanola	4.00
(60)	Tom Glavine/ SP/1,250	40.00
(61)	Juan Gonzalez/ SP/1,000	30.00
(61)	Juan Gonzalez (Redemption card.)	5.00
(62)	Craig Grebeck	4.00
(63)	Buddy Groom	4.00
(64)	Kevin Gross	4.00
(65)	Eddie Guardado	4.00
(66)	Mark Guthrie	4.00
(67)	Tony Gwynn/ SP/1,000	60.00
(68)	Chip Hale	4.00
(69)	Darren Hall	4.00
(70)	Lee Hancock	4.00
(71)	Dave Hansen	4.00
(72)	Bryan Harvey	4.00
(73)	Bill Haselman	4.00
(74)	Mike Henneman	4.00
(75)	Doug Henry	4.00
(76)	Gil Heredia	4.00
(77)	Carlos Hernandez	4.00
(78)	Jose Hernandez	4.00
(79)	Darren Holmes	4.00
(80)	Mark Holzemer	4.00
(81)	Rick Honeycutt	4.00
(82)	Chris Hook	4.00
(83)	Chris Howard	4.00
(84)	Jack Howell	4.00
(85)	David Hulse	4.00
(86)	Edwin Hurtado	4.00
(87)	Jeff Huson	4.00
(88)	Mike James	4.00
(89)	Derek Jeter/ SP/1,000	160.00
(90)	Brian Johnson	4.00
(91)	Randy Johnson/ SP/1,000	125.00
(92)	Mark Johnson	4.00
(93)	Andruw Jones/ SP/2,000	30.00
(93)	Andruw Jones (Redemption card.)	5.00
(94)	Chris Jones	4.00
(95)	Ricky Jordan	4.00
(96)	Matt Karchner	4.00
(97)	Scott Karl	4.00
(98)	Jason Kendall/ SP/2,500	10.00
(99)	Brian Keyser	4.00
(100)	Mike Kingery	4.00
(101)	Wayne Kirby	4.00
(102)	Ryan Klesko/ SP/1,000	17.50
(103)	Chuck Knoblauch/ SP/1,000	15.00
(104)	Chad Kreuter	4.00
(105)	Tom Lampkin	4.00
(106)	Scott Leius	4.00
(107)	Jon Lieber	4.00
(108)	Nelson Liriano	4.00
(109)	Scott Livingstone	4.00
(110)	Graeme Lloyd	4.00
(111)	Kenny Lofton/ SP/1,000	10.00
(112)	Luis Lopez	4.00
(113)	Torey Lovullo	4.00
(114)	Greg Maddux/ SP/500	250.00
(115)	Mike Maddux	4.00
(116)	Dave Magadan	4.00
(117)	Mike Magnante	4.00
(118)	Joe Magrane	4.00
(119)	Pat Mahomes	4.00
(120)	Matt Mantei	4.00
(121)	John Marzano	4.00
(122)	Terry Matthews	4.00
(123)	Chuck McElroy	4.00
(124)	Fred McGriff/ SP/1,000	35.00
(125)	Mark McLemore	4.00
(126)	Greg McMichael	4.00
(127)	Blas Minor	4.00
(128)	Dave Mlicki	4.00
(129)	Mike Mohler	4.00
(130)	Paul Molitor/ SP/1,000	25.00
(131)	Steve Montgomery	4.00
(132)	Mike Mordecai	4.00
(133)	Mike Morgan	4.00
(134)	Mike Munoz	4.00
(135)	Greg Myers	4.00
(136)	Jimmy Myers	4.00
(137)	Mike Myers	4.00
(138)	Bob Natal	4.00
(139)	Dan Naulty	4.00
(140)	Jeff Nelson	4.00
(141)	Warren Newson	4.00
(142)	Chris Nichting	4.00
(143)	Melvin Nieves	4.00
(144)	Charlie O'Brien	4.00
(145)	Alex Ochoa	4.00
(146)	Omar Olivares	4.00
(147)	Joe Oliver	4.00
(148)	Lance Painter	4.00
(149)	Rafael Palmeiro/ SP/2,000	35.00
(150)	Mark Parent	4.00
(151)	Steve Parris/ SP/1,800	7.50
(152)	Bob Patterson	4.00
(153)	Tony Pena	7.50
(154)	Eddie Perez	4.00
(155)	Yorkis Perez	4.00
(156)	Robert Person	4.00
(157)	Mark Petkovsek	4.00
(158)	Andy Pettitte/ SP/1,000	60.00
(159)	J.R. Phillips	4.00
(160)	Hipolito Pichardo	4.00
(161)	Eric Plunk	4.00
(162)	Jimmy Poole	4.00
(163)	Kirby Puckett/ SP/1,000	80.00
(164)	Paul Quantrill	4.00
(165)	Tom Quinlan	4.00
(166)	Jeff Reboulet	4.00
(167)	Jeff Reed	4.00
(168)	Steve Reed	4.00
(169)	Carlos Reyes	4.00
(170)	Bill Risley	4.00
(171)	Kevin Ritz	4.00
(172)	Kevin Roberson	4.00
(173)	Rich Robertson	4.00
(174)	Alex Rodriguez/ SP/500	180.00
(174)	Alex Rodriguez (Redemption card.)	15.00
(175)	Ivan Rodriguez/ SP/1,250	40.00
(176)	Bruce Ruffin	4.00
(177)	Juan Samuel	4.00
(178)	Tim Scott	4.00
(179)	Kevin Sefcik	4.00
(180)	Jeff Shaw	4.00
(181)	Danny Sheaffer	4.00
(182)	Craig Shipley	4.00
(183)	Dave Silvestri	4.00
(184)	Aaron Small	4.00
(185)	John Smoltz/ SP/1,000	90.00
(186)	Luis Sojo	4.00
(187)	Sammy Sosa/ SP/1,000	160.00
(188)	Steve Sparks	4.00
(189)	Tim Spehr	4.00
(190)	Russ Springer	4.00
(191)	Matt Stairs	4.00

(192)	Andy Stankiewicz	4.00
(193)	Mike Stanton	4.00
(194)	Kelly Stinnett	4.00
(195)	Doug Strange	4.00
(196)	Mark Sweeney	4.00
(197)	Jeff Tabaka	4.00
(198)	Jesus Tavarez	4.00
(199)	Frank Thomas/ SP/1,000	45.00
(200)	Larry Thomas	4.00
(201)	Mark Thompson	4.00
(202)	Mike Timlin	4.00
(203)	Steve Trachsel	4.00
(204)	Tom Urbani	4.00
(205)	Julio Valera	4.00
(206)	Dave Valle	4.00
(207)	William Van Landingham	4.00
(208)	Mike Vaughn/ SP/1,000	10.00
(209)	Dave Veres	4.00
(210)	Ed Vosberg	4.00
(211)	Don Wengert	4.00
(212)	Matt Whiteside	4.00
(213)	Bob Wickman	4.00
(214)	Matt Williams/ SP/1,250	12.00
(215)	Mike Williams	4.00
(216)	Woody Williams	4.00
(217)	Craig Worthington	4.00
---	Frank Thomas (Autographed jumbo edition of 1,500).	30.00

Extended Autographs - Century Marks

		NM/M
Common Player:		15.00
(1)	Jay Buhner	30.00
(2)	Ken Caminiti	30.00
(3)	Roger Clemens	250.00
(4)	Jermaine Dye	30.00
(5)	Darin Erstad	45.00
(6)	Karim Garcia	30.00
(7)	Jason Giambi	75.00
(8)	Tom Glavine	90.00
(9)	Juan Gonzalez	90.00
(9)	Juan Gonzalez (Redemption card.)	7.50
(10)	Tony Gwynn	150.00
(11)	Derek Jeter	350.00
(11)	Derek Jeter (Redemption card.)	15.00
(12)	Randy Johnson	185.00
(13)	Andruw Jones	150.00
(13)	Andruw Jones (Redemption card.)	7.50
(14)	Jason Kendall	30.00
(15)	Ryan Klesko	30.00
(16)	Chuck Knoblauch	30.00
(17)	Kenny Lofton	30.00
(18)	Greg Maddux	200.00
(19)	Fred McGriff	30.00
(20)	Paul Molitor	110.00
(21)	Alex Ochoa	15.00
(22)	Rafael Palmeiro	110.00
(22)	Rafael Palmeiro (Redemption card.)	7.50
(23)	Andy Pettitte	75.00
(24)	Kirby Puckett	185.00
(25)	Alex Rodriguez	350.00
(25)	Alex Rodriguez (Redemption card.)	15.00
(26)	Ivan Rodriguez	100.00
(27)	John Smoltz	100.00
(28)	Sammy Sosa	350.00
(29)	Frank Thomas	135.00
(30)	Mo Vaughn	30.00
(31)	Matt Williams	30.00

1997 Leaf

		NM/M
Complete Set (400):		25.00
Common Player:		.05
Jackie Robinson 1948 Leaf Reprint:		10.00
Series 1 Pack (12):		2.00
Series 1 Wax Box (18):		30.00
Series 2 Pack (12):		1.50
Series 2 Wax Box (24):		30.00
1	Wade Boggs	1.50
2	Brian McRae	.05
3	Jeff D'Amico	.05
4	George Arias	.05
5	Billy Wagner	.05
6	Ray Lankford	.05
7	Will Clark	.10
8	Edgar Renteria	.05
9	Alex Ochoa	.05
10	Roberto Hernandez	.05
11	Joe Carter	.05
12	Gregg Jefferies	.05
13	Mark Grace	.05
14	Roberto Alomar	.10
15	Joe Randa	.05
16	Alex Rodriguez	2.50
17	Tony Gwynn	1.50
18	Steve Gibralter	.05
19	Scott Stahoviak	.05
20	Matt Williams	.05
21	Quinton McCracken	.05
22	Ugueth Urbina	.05
23	Jermaine Allensworth	.05
24	Paul Molitor	.75
25	Carlos Delgado	.50
26	Bob Abreu	.05
27	John Jaha	.05
28	Rusty Greer	.05
29	Kimera Bartee	.05
30	Ruben Rivera	.05
31	Jason Kendall	.05
32	Lance Johnson	.05
33	Robin Ventura	.05
34	Kevin Appier	.05
35	John Mabry	.05
36	Ricky Otero	.05
37	Mike Lansing	.05
38	Mark McGwire	2.50
39	Tim Naehring	.05
40	Tom Glavine	.30
41	Rey Ordonez	.05
42	Tony Clark	.05
43	Rafael Palmeiro	.65
44	Pedro Martinez	.75
45	Keith Lockhart	.05
46	Dan Wilson	.05
47	John Wetteland	.05
48	Chan Ho Park	.05
49	Gary Sheffield	.40
50	Shawn Estes	.05
51	Royce Clayton	.05
52	Jaime Navarro	.05
53	Raul Casanova	.05
54	Jeff Bagwell	1.00
55	Barry Larkin	.05
56	Charles Nagy	.05
57	Ken Caminiti	.05
58	Todd Hollandsworth	.05
59	Pat Hentgen	.05
60	Jose Valentin	.05
61	Frank Rodriguez	.05
62	Mickey Tettleton	.05
63	Marty Cordova	.05
64	Cecil Fielder	.05
65	Barry Bonds	3.00

ABBREVIATIONS

SP - Short Print

66	Scott Servais	.05
67	Ernie Young	.05
68	Wilson Alvarez	.05
69	Mike Grace	.05
70	Shane Reynolds	.05
71	Henry Rodriguez	.05
72	Eric Karros	.05
73	Mark Langston	.05
74	Scott Karl	.05
75	Trevor Hoffman	.05
76	Orel Hershiser	.05
77	John Smoltz	.05
78	Raul Mondesi	.05
79	Jeff Brantley	.05
80	Donne Wall	.05
81	Joey Cora	.05
82	Mel Rojas	.05
83	Chad Mottola	.05
84	Omar Vizquel	.05
85	Greg Maddux	1.50
86	Jamey Wright	.05
87	Chuck Finley	.05
88	Brady Anderson	.05
89	Alex Gonzalez	.05
90	Andy Benes	.05
91	Reggie Jefferson	.05
92	Paul O'Neill	.05
93	Javier Lopez	.05
94	Mark Grudzielanek	.05
95	Marc Newfield	.05
96	Kevin Ritz	.05
97	Fred McGriff	.05
98	Dwight Gooden	.05
99	Hideo Nomo	.65
100	Steve Finley	.05
101	Juan Gonzalez	.65
102	Jay Buhner	.05
103	Paul Wilson	.05
104	Alan Benes	.05
105	Manny Ramirez	1.00
106	Kevin Elster	.05
107	Frank Thomas	1.00
108	Orlando Miller	.05
109	Ramon Martinez	.05
110	Kenny Lofton	.05
111	Bernie Williams	.05
112	Robby Thompson	.05
113	Bernard Gilkey	.05
114	Ray Durham	.05
115	Jeff Cirillo	.05
116	Brian Jordan	.05
117	Rich Becker	.05
118	Al Leiter	.05
119	Mark Johnson	.05
120	Ellis Burks	.05
121	Sammy Sosa	2.00
122	Willie Greene	.05
123	Michael Tucker	.05
124	Eddie Murray	.75
125	Joey Hamilton	.05
126	Antonio Osuna	.05
127	Bobby Higginson	.05
128	Tomas Perez	.05
129	Tim Salmon	.05
130	Mark Wohlers	.05
131	Charles Johnson	.05
132	Randy Johnson	.75
133	Brooks Kieschnick	.05
134	Al Martin	.05
135	Dante Bichette	.05
136	Andy Pettitte	.30
137	Jason Giambi	.60
138	James Baldwin	.05
139	Ben McDonald	.05
140	Shawn Green	.35
141	Geronimo Berroa	.05
142	Jose Offerman	.05
143	Curtis Pride	.05
144	Terrell Wade	.05
145	Ismael Valdes	.05
146	Mike Mussina	.40
147	Mariano Rivera	.15
148	Ken Hill	.05
149	Darin Erstad	.25
150	Jay Bell	.05
151	Mo Vaughn	.05
152	Ozzie Smith	1.50
153	Jose Mesa	.05
154	Osvaldo Fernandez	.05
155	Vinny Castilla	.05
156	Jason Isringhausen	.05
157	B.J. Surhoff	.05
158	Robert Perez	.05
159	Ron Coomer	.05
160	Darren Oliver	.05
161	Mike Mohler	.05
162	Russ Davis	.05
163	Bret Boone	.05
164	Ricky Bottalico	.05
165	Derek Jeter	3.00
166	Orlando Merced	.05
167	John Valentin	.05
168	Andruw Jones	1.00
169	Angel Echevarria	.05

170	Todd Walker	.05
171	Desi Relaford	.05
172	Trey Beamon	.05
173	Brian Giles RC	.75
174	Scott Rolen	.60
175	Shannon Stewart	.05
176	Dmitri Young	.05
177	Justin Thompson	.05
178	Trot Nixon	.05
179	Josh Booty	.05
180	Robin Jennings	.05
181	Marvin Benard	.05
182	Luis Castillo	.05
183	Wendell Magee	.05
184	Vladimir Guerrero	1.00
185	Nomar Garciaparra	2.00
186	Ryan Hancock	.05
187	Mike Cameron	.05
188	Cal Ripken Jr.	1.50
189	Chipper Jones	.75
190	Albert Belle	.05
191	Mike Piazza	1.00
192	Chuck Knoblauch	.05
193	Ken Griffey Jr.	1.00
194	Ivan Rodriguez	.30
195	Jose Canseco	.25
196	Ryne Sandberg	.75
197	Jim Thome	.30
198	Andy Pettitte	.05
199	Andruw Jones	.50
200	Derek Jeter	1.50
201	Chipper Jones	1.50
202	Albert Belle	.05
203	Mike Piazza	2.00
204	Ken Griffey Jr.	2.00
205	Ryne Sandberg	1.50
206	Jose Canseco	.40
207	Chili Davis	.05
208	Roger Clemens	2.00
209	Deion Sanders	.05
210	Darryl Hamilton	.05
211	Jermaine Dye	.05
212	Matt Williams	.05
213	Kevin Elster	.05
214	John Wetteland	.05
215	Garret Anderson	.05
216	Kevin Brown	.05
217	Matt Lawton	.05
218	Cal Ripken Jr.	3.00
219	Moises Alou	.05
220	Chuck Knoblauch	.05
221	Ivan Rodriguez	.65
222	Travis Fryman	.05
223	Jim Thome	.65
224	Eddie Murray	.75
225	Eric Young	.05
226	Ron Gant	.05
227	Tony Phillips	.05
228	Reggie Sanders	.05
229	Johnny Damon	.35
230	Bill Pulsipher	.05
231	Jim Edmonds	.05
232	Melvin Nieves	.05
233	Ryan Klesko	.05
234	David Cone	.05
235	Derek Bell	.05
236	Julio Franco	.05
237	Juan Guzman	.05
238	Larry Walker	.05
239	Delino DeShields	.05
240	Troy Percival	.05
241	Andres Galarraga	.05
242	Rondell White	.05
243	John Burkett	.05
244	J.T. Snow	.05
245	Alex Fernandez	.05
246	Edgar Martinez	.05
247	Craig Biggio	.05
248	Todd Hundley	.05
249	Jimmy Key	.05
250	Cliff Floyd	.05
251	Jeff Conine	.05
252	Curt Schilling	.35
253	Jeff King	.05
254	Tino Martinez	.05
255	Carlos Baerga	.05
256	Jeff Fassero	.05
257	Dean Palmer	.05
258	Robb Nen	.05
259	Sandy Alomar Jr.	.05
260	Carlos Perez	.05
261	Rickey Henderson	.75
262	Bobby Bonilla	.05
263	Darren Daulton	.05
264	Jim Leyritz	.05
265	Dennis Martinez	.05
266	Butch Huskey	.05
267	Joe Vitiello	.05
268	Steve Trachsel	.05
269	Glenallen Hill	.05
270	Terry Steinbach	.05
271	Mark McLemore	.05
272	Devon White	.05
273	Jeff Kent	.05

No.	Player	Price
274	Tim Raines	.05
275	Carlos Garcia	.05
276	Hal Morris	.05
277	Gary Gaetti	.05
278	John Olerud	.05
279	Wally Joyner	.05
280	Brian Hunter	.05
281	Steve Karsay	.05
282	Denny Neagle	.05
283	Jose Herrera	.05
284	Todd Stottlemyre	.05
285	Bip Roberts	.05
286	Kevin Seitzer	.05
287	Benji Gil	.05
288	Dennis Eckersley	.65
289	Brad Ausmus	.05
290	Otis Nixon	.05
291	Darryl Strawberry	.05
292	Marquis Grissom	.05
293	Darryl Kile	.05
294	Quilvio Veras	.05
295	Tom Goodwin	.05
296	Benito Santiago	.05
297	Mike Bordick	.05
298	Roberto Kelly	.05
299	David Justice	.05
300	Carl Everett	.05
301	Mark Whiten	.05
302	Aaron Sele	.05
303	Darren Dreifort	.05
304	Bobby Jones	.05
305	Fernando Vina	.05
306	Ed Sprague	.05
307	Andy Ashby	.05
308	Tony Fernandez	.05
309	Roger Pavlik	.05
310	Mark Clark	.05
311	Mariano Duncan	.05
312	Tyler Houston	.05
313	Eric Davis	.05
314	Greg Vaughn	.05
315	David Segui	.05
316	Dave Nilsson	.05
317	F.P. Santangelo	.05
318	Wilton Guerrero	.05
319	Jose Guillen	.05
320	Kevin Orie	.05
321	Derek Lee	.05
322	Bubba Trammell RC	.50
323	Pokey Reese	.05
324	Hideki Irabu RC	.25
325	Scott Spiezio	.05
326	Bartolo Colon	.05
327	Damon Mashore	.05
328	Ryan McGuire	.05
329	Chris Carpenter	.05
330	Jose Cruz Jr. RC	.50
331	Todd Greene	.05
332	Brian Moehler	.05
333	Mike Sweeney	.05
334	Neifi Perez	.05
335	Matt Morris	.05
336	Marvin Benard	.05
337	Karim Garcia	.05
338	Jason Dickson	.05
339	Brant Brown	.05
340	Jeff Suppan	.05
341	Deivi Cruz RC	.25
342	Antone Williamson	.05
343	Curtis Goodwin	.05
344	Brooks Kieschnick	.05
345	Tony Womack RC	.25
346	Rudy Pemberton	.05
347	Todd Dunwoody	.05
348	Frank Thomas	.50
349	Andruw Jones	.50
350	Alex Rodriguez	1.25
351	Greg Maddux	.75
352	Jeff Bagwell	.50
353	Juan Gonzalez	.35
354	Barry Bonds	1.50
355	Mark McGwire	1.25
356	Tony Gwynn	.75
357	Gary Sheffield	.25
358	Derek Jeter	1.50
359	Manny Ramirez	.50
360	Hideo Nomo	.30
361	Sammy Sosa	1.00
362	Paul Molitor	.40
363	Kenny Lofton	.05
364	Eddie Murray	.40
365	Barry Larkin	.05
366	Roger Clemens	1.00
367	John Smoltz	.05
368	Alex Rodriguez	1.50
369	Frank Thomas	.40
370	Cal Ripken Jr.	1.50
371	Ken Griffey Jr.	1.50
372	Greg Maddux	1.00
373	Mike Piazza	1.25
374	Chipper Jones	1.00
375	Albert Belle	.05
376	Chuck Knoblauch	.05
377	Brady Anderson	.05
378	David Justice	.05
379	Randy Johnson	.40
380	Wade Boggs	.75
381	Kevin Brown	.05
382	Tom Glavine	.05
383	Raul Mondesi	.05
384	Ivan Rodriguez	.30
385	Larry Walker	.05
386	Bernie Williams	.05
387	Rusty Greer	.05
388	Rafael Palmeiro	.05
389	Matt Williams	.05
390	Eric Young	.05
391	Fred McGriff	.05
392	Ken Caminiti	.05
393	Roberto Alomar	.05
394	Brian Jordan	.05
395	Mark Grace	.05
396	Jim Edmonds	.05
397	Deion Sanders	.05
398	Vladimir Guerrero Checklist	.50
399	Darin Erstad Checklist	.10
400	Nomar Garciaparra Checklist	1.00

Banner Season

		NM/M
Complete Set (15):		30.00
Common Player:		.50
1	Jeff Bagwell	2.50
2	Ken Griffey Jr.	5.00
3	Juan Gonzalez	1.50
4	Frank Thomas	2.50
5	Alex Rodriguez	6.00
6	Kenny Lofton	.50
7	Chuck Knoblauch	.50
8	Mo Vaughn	.50
9	Chipper Jones	4.00
10	Ken Caminiti	.50
11	Craig Biggio	.50
12	John Smoltz	.50
13	Pat Hentgen	.50
14	Derek Jeter	7.50
15	Todd Hollandsworth	.50

Dress for Success

		NM/M
Complete Set (18):		17.50
Common Player:		.25
1	Greg Maddux	1.50
2	Cal Ripken Jr.	3.00
3	Albert Belle	.25
4	Frank Thomas	1.00
5	Dante Bichette	.25
6	Gary Sheffield	.50
7	Jeff Bagwell	1.00
8	Mike Piazza	2.00
9	Mark McGwire	2.25
10	Ken Caminiti	.25
11	Alex Rodriguez	2.50
12	Ken Griffey Jr.	2.00
13	Juan Gonzalez	.75
14	Brian Jordan	.25
15	Mo Vaughn	.25
16	Ivan Rodriguez	.75
17	Andruw Jones	1.00
18	Chipper Jones	1.50

Fractal Matrix

		NM/M
Common Bronze:		.35
Common Silver:		.50
Common Gold:		1.25
1	Wade Boggs G/Y	8.00
2	Brian McRae B/Y	.35
3	Jeff D'Amico B/Y	.35
4	George Arias S/Y	.50
5	Billy Wagner S/Y	.50
6	Ray Lankford B/Z	.35
7	Will Clark S/Y	.60
8	Edgar Renteria S/Y	.50
9	Alex Ochoa S/Y	.50
10	Roberto Hernandez B/X	.50
11	Joe Carter S/Y	.50
12	Gregg Jefferies B/Y	.35
13	Mark Grace S/Y	.75
14	Roberto Alomar G/Y	2.00
15	Joe Randa B/X	.35
16	Alex Rodriguez G/Z	10.00
17	Tony Gwynn G/Z	6.00
18	Steve Gibralter B/Y	.35
19	Scott Stahoviak B/X	.35
20	Matt Williams S/Z	.50
21	Quinton McCracken B/Y	.35
22	Ugueth Urbina B/X	.35
23	Jermaine Allensworth S/X	.50
24	Paul Molitor G/X	5.00
25	Carlos Delgado S/Y	1.00
26	Bob Abreu S/Y	.50
27	John Jaha S/Y	.50
28	Rusty Greer S/Z	.50
29	Kimera Bartee B/X	.35
30	Ruben Rivera S/Y	.50
31	Jason Kendall S/Y	.50
32	Lance Johnson B/X	.35
33	Robin Ventura B/Y	.35
34	Kevin Appier S/Y	.50
35	John Mabry S/Y	.50
36	Ricky Otero B/X	.35
37	Mike Lansing B/X	.35
38	Mark McGwire G/Z	10.00
39	Tim Naehring B/X	.35
40	Tom Glavine S/Z	1.00
41	Rey Ordonez S/Y	.50
42	Tony Clark S/Y	.75
43	Rafael Palmeiro S/Z	2.00
44	Pedro Martinez B/X	2.00
45	Keith Lockhart B/X	.35
46	Dan Wilson B/Y	.35
47	John Wetteland B/Y	.35
48	Chan Ho Park B/X	.35
49	Gary Sheffield G/Z	3.00
50	Shawn Estes B/X	.35
51	Royce Clayton B/X	.35
52	Jaime Navarro B/X	.35
53	Raul Casanova B/X	.35
54	Jeff Bagwell G/Z	5.00
55	Barry Larkin G/X	1.25
56	Charles Nagy B/Y	.35
57	Ken Caminiti G/X	1.25
58	Todd Hollandsworth S/Z	.50
59	Pat Hentgen S/X	.50
60	Jose Valentin B/X	.35
61	Frank Rodriguez B/X	.35
62	Mickey Tettleton B/X	.35
63	Marty Cordova G/X	1.25
64	Cecil Fielder S/X	.50
65	Barry Bonds G/Z	13.50
66	Scott Servais B/X	.35
67	Ernie Young B/X	.35
68	Wilson Alvarez B/X	.35
69	Mike Grace B/X	.35
70	Shane Reynolds S/X	.50
71	Henry Rodriguez S/Y	.50
72	Eric Karros B/X	.35
73	Mark Langston B/X	.35
74	Scott Karl B/X	.35
75	Trevor Hoffman B/X	.35
76	Orel Hershiser S/X	.50
77	John Smoltz G/Y	1.50
78	Raul Mondesi G/Z	1.25
79	Jeff Brantley B/X	.35
80	Donne Wall B/X	.35
81	Joey Cora B/X	.35
82	Mel Rojas B/X	.35
83	Chad Mottola B/X	.35
84	Omar Vizquel B/X	.35
85	Greg Maddux B/X	6.00
86	Jamey Wright S/Y	.50
87	Chuck Finley B/X	.35
88	Brady Anderson G/Y	1.25
89	Alex Gonzalez S/X	.50
90	Andy Benes B/X	.35
91	Reggie Jefferson B/X	.35
92	Paul O'Neill B/Y	.35
93	Javier Lopez S/X	.50
94	Mark Grudzielanek S/X	.50
95	Marc Newfield B/X	.35
96	Kevin Ritz B/X	.35
97	Fred McGriff G/Y	1.25
98	Dwight Gooden S/X	.50
99	Hideo Nomo S/X	1.50
100	Steve Finley B/X	.35
101	Juan Gonzalez G/Z	4.00
102	Jay Buhner S/Z	.50
103	Paul Wilson S/Y	.50
104	Alan Benes B/Y	.35
105	Manny Ramirez G/Z	5.00
106	Kevin Elster B/Y	.35
107	Frank Thomas G/Z	5.00
108	Orlando Miller B/X	.35
109	Ramon Martinez B/X	.35
110	Kenny Lofton G/Z	1.25
111	Bernie Williams G/Z	1.25
112	Robby Thompson B/X	.35
113	Bernard Gilkey B/Z	.35
114	Ray Durham B/X	.35
115	Jeff Cirillo S/Z	.50
116	Brian Jordan G/Z	1.25
117	Rich Becker S/Y	.50
118	Al Leiter B/X	.35
119	Mark Johnson B/X	.35
120	Ellis Burks B/Y	.35
121	Sammy Sosa G/Z	7.50
122	Willie Greene B/X	.35
123	Michael Tucker B/X	.35
124	Eddie Murray G/Y	6.00
125	Joey Hamilton S/Y	.50
126	Antonio Osuna B/X	.35
127	Bobby Higginson S/Y	.50
128	Tomas Perez B/X	.35
129	Tim Salmon G/Z	1.25
130	Mark Wohlers B/X	.35
131	Charles Johnson S/X	.50
132	Randy Johnson G/Z	2.00
133	Brooks Kieschnick S/X	.50
134	Al Martin S/Y	.50
135	Dante Bichette B/X	.35
136	Andy Pettitte G/Y	2.00
137	Jason Giambi G/Y	4.00
138	James Baldwin S/X	.50
139	Ben McDonald B/X	.35
140	Shawn Green B/Y	1.00
141	Geronimo Berroa B/Y	.35
142	Jose Offerman B/X	.35
143	Curtis Pride B/X	.35
144	Terrell Wade B/X	.35
145	Ismael Valdes S/X	.50
146	Mike Mussina S/Y	1.25
147	Mariano Rivera S/X	.75
148	Ken Hill B/Y	.35
149	Darin Erstad G/Z	4.00
150	Jay Bell B/X	.35
151	Mo Vaughn G/Z	1.25
152	Ozzie Smith G/Y	8.00
153	Jose Mesa B/X	.35
154	Osvaldo Fernandez B/X	.35
155	Vinny Castilla B/Y	.35
156	Jason Isringhausen S/Y	.50
157	B.J. Surhoff B/X	.35
158	Robert Perez B/X	.35
159	Ron Coomer B/X	.35
160	Darren Oliver B/X	.35
161	Mike Mohler B/X	.35
162	Russ Davis B/X	.35
163	Bret Boone B/X	.35
164	Ricky Bottalico B/X	.35
165	Derek Jeter G/Z	13.50
166	Orlando Merced B/X	.35
167	John Valentin B/X	.35
168	Andruw Jones G/Z	5.00
169	Angel Echevarria B/X	.35
170	Todd Walker G/X	1.25
171	Desi Relaford B/Y	.35
172	Trey Beamon S/X	.50

173	Brian Giles S/Y	.50
174	Scott Rolen G/Z	3.50
175	Shannon Stewart S/Z	.50
176	Dmitri Young G/Z	1.25
177	Justin Thompson B/X	.35
178	Trot Nixon S/Y	.50
179	Josh Booty S/Y	.50
180	Robin Jennings B/X	.35
181	Marvin Benard B/X	.35
182	Luis Castillo B/X	.35
183	Wendell Magee B/X	.35
184	Vladimir Guerrero G/X	5.00
185	Nomar Garciaparra G/X	12.50
186	Ryan Hancock B/X	.35
187	Mike Cameron S/X	.50
188	Cal Ripken Jr. B/Z	5.00
189	Chipper Jones S/Z	4.00
190	Albert Belle S/Z	1.00
191	Mike Piazza B/Y	4.00
192	Chuck Knoblauch S/Y	.50
193	Ken Griffey Jr. B/Z	3.50
194	Ivan Rodriguez G/Z	4.00
195	Jose Canseco S/X	1.25
196	Ryne Sandberg S/X	3.00
197	Jim Thome G/Y	1.50
198	Andy Pettitte B/Y Checklist	.75
199	Andruw Jones B/Y Checklist	2.00
200	Derek Jeter S/Y Checklist	2.00
201	Chipper Jones G/X	10.00
202	Albert Belle G/Y	1.25
203	Mike Piazza G/X	12.00
204	Ken Griffey Jr. G/X	15.00
205	Ryne Sandberg G/Z	6.00
206	Jose Canseco S/Y	.75
207	Chili Davis B/X	.35
208	Roger Clemens G/Z	6.50
209	Deion Sanders G/Z	1.50
210	Darryl Hamilton B/X	.35
211	Jermaine Dye S/X	.50
212	Matt Williams G/Y	1.25
213	Kevin Elster B/X	.35
214	John Wetteland S/X	.50
215	Garret Anderson G/Z	1.25
216	Kevin Brown G/Y	1.25
217	Matt Lawton S/Y	.50
218	Cal Ripken Jr. G/X	16.50
219	Moises Alou G/Y	1.25
220	Chuck Knoblauch G/Z	1.25
221	Ivan Rodriguez S/Y	5.50
222	Travis Fryman B/X	.35
223	Jim Thome B/Y	2.00
224	Eddie Murray S/Z	3.00
225	Eric Young G/Z	1.25
226	Ron Gant S/X	.50
227	Tony Phillips B/X	.35
228	Reggie Sanders B/Y	.35
229	Johnny Damon S/Z	1.00
230	Bill Pulsipher B/X	.35
231	Jim Edmonds G/Z	1.25
232	Melvin Nieves B/X	.35
233	Ryan Klesko B/X	1.25
234	David Cone S/X	.50
235	Derek Bell B/Y	.35
236	Julio Franco S/X	.50
237	Juan Guzman B/X	.35
238	Larry Walker G/Z	1.25
239	Delino DeShields B/X	.35
240	Troy Percival B/Y	.35
241	Andres Galarraga G/Z	1.25
242	Rondell White G/Z	1.25
243	John Burkett B/X	.35
244	J.T. Snow B/Y	.35
245	Alex Fernandez S/Y	.50
246	Edgar Martinez G/Z	1.25
247	Craig Biggio G/Z	1.25
248	Todd Hundley G/Y	1.25
249	Jimmy Key S/X	.50
250	Cliff Floyd B/Y	.35
251	Jeff Conine B/X	.35
252	Curt Schilling B/X	.65
253	Jeff King B/X	.35
254	Tino Martinez G/Z	1.25
255	Carlos Baerga S/Y	.50
256	Jeff Fassero B/Y	.35
257	Dean Palmer S/Y	.50
258	Robb Nen B/X	.35
259	Sandy Alomar Jr. S/Y	.50
260	Carlos Perez B/X	.35
261	Rickey Henderson S/Y	2.00
262	Bobby Bonilla S/Y	.50
263	Darren Daulton B/X	.35
264	Jim Leyritz B/X	.35
265	Dennis Martinez B/X	.35
266	Butch Huskey B/X	.35
267	Joe Vitiello B/X	.50
268	Steve Trachsel B/X	.35
269	Glenallen Hill B/X	.35
270	Terry Steinbach B/X	.35
271	Mark McLemore B/X	.35
272	Devon White B/X	.35
273	Jeff Kent B/X	.35
274	Tim Raines B/X	.35
275	Carlos Garcia B/X	.35
276	Hal Morris B/X	.35
277	Gary Gaetti B/X	.35
278	John Olerud S/Y	.50
279	Wally Joyner B/X	.35
280	Brian Hunter S/X	.50
281	Steve Karsay B/X	.35
282	Denny Neagle S/X	.50
283	Jose Herrera B/X	.35
284	Todd Stottlemyre B/X	.35
285	Bip Roberts S/X	.50
286	Kevin Seitzer B/X	.35
287	Benji Gil B/X	.35
288	Dennis Eckersley S/X	.50
289	Brad Ausmus B/X	.35
290	Otis Nixon B/X	.35
291	Darryl Strawberry B/X	.35
292	Marquis Grissom S/Y	.50
293	Darryl Kile B/X	.35
294	Quilvio Veras B/X	.35
295	Tom Goodwin B/X	.35
296	Benito Santiago B/X	.35
297	Mike Bordick B/X	.35
298	Roberto Kelly B/X	.35
299	David Justice G/X	1.25
300	Carl Everett B/X	.35
301	Mark Whiten B/X	.35
302	Aaron Sele B/X	.35
303	Darren Dreifort B/X	.35
304	Bobby Jones B/X	.35
305	Fernando Vina B/X	.35
306	Ed Sprague B/X	.35
307	Andy Ashby S/X	.50
308	Tony Fernandez B/X	.35
309	Roger Pavlik B/X	.35
310	Mark Clark B/X	.35
311	Mariano Duncan B/X	.35
312	Tyler Houston B/X	.35
313	Eric Davis S/Y	.50
314	Greg Vaughn B/Y	.35
315	David Segui S/Y	.50
316	Dave Nilsson B/X	.35
317	F.P. Santangelo S/X	.50
318	Wilton Guerrero G/Z	1.25
319	Jose Guillen G/Z	1.25
320	Kevin Orie S/Y	.50
321	Derrek Lee G/Z	2.50
322	Bubba Trammell S/Y	.50
323	Pokey Reese G/Z	1.25
324	Hideki Irabu G/X	1.25
325	Scott Spiezio S/Z	.50
326	Bartolo Colon G/Z	1.25
327	Damon Mashore S/Y	.50
328	Ryan McGuire S/Y	.50
329	Chris Carpenter B/X	.35
330	Jose Cruz, Jr. G/X	1.25
331	Todd Greene S/Z	.50
332	Brian Moehler B/X	.35
333	Mike Sweeney B/Y	.35
334	Neifi Perez G/Z	1.25
335	Matt Morris S/Y	.50
336	Marvin Benard B/Y	.35
337	Karim Garcia S/Z	.75
338	Jason Dickson S/Y	.50
339	Brant Brown S/Y	.50
340	Jeff Suppan S/Z	.50
341	Deivi Cruz B/X	.35
342	Antone Williamson G/Z	1.25
343	Curtis Goodwin B/X	.35
344	Brooks Kieschnick S/Y	.50
345	Tony Womack B/X	.35
346	Rudy Pemberton B/X	.35
347	Todd Dunwoody B/X	.35
348	Frank Thomas S/Y	2.25
349	Andruw Jones S/X	2.00
350	Alex Rodriguez B/Y	4.00
351	Greg Maddux S/Y	3.00
352	Jeff Bagwell S/Y	2.25
353	Juan Gonzalez S/Y	1.50
354	Barry Bonds S/Y	5.00
355	Mark McGwire S/X	4.00
356	Tony Gwynn B/Y	3.00
357	Gary Sheffield B/X	.75
358	Derek Jeter S/X	4.00
359	Manny Ramirez S/Y	2.00
360	Hideo Nomo B/X	4.00
361	Sammy Sosa B/X	3.50
362	Paul Molitor S/Z	3.00
363	Kenny Lofton B/Y	.35
364	Eddie Murray B/X	2.00
365	Barry Larkin S/Z	1.00
366	Roger Clemens S/Y	3.50
367	John Smoltz B/Z	.35
368	Alex Rodriguez S/X	3.25
369	Frank Thomas B/X	2.25
370	Cal Ripken Jr. S/Y	4.00
371	Ken Griffey Jr. S/Y	3.25
372	Greg Maddux S/X	3.00
373	Mike Piazza S/X	3.25
374	Chipper Jones B/Y	3.00
375	Albert Belle B/X	.50
376	Chuck Knoblauch B/X	.35
377	Brady Anderson B/X	.35
378	David Justice B/X	.35
379	Randy Johnson B/Z	2.00
380	Wade Boggs B/X	3.00
381	Kevin Brown B/X	.35
382	Tom Glavine G/Y	3.00
383	Raul Mondesi S/X	.50
384	Ivan Rodriguez B/X	1.25
385	Larry Walker B/Y	.35
386	Bernie Williams B/Z	.45
387	Rusty Greer G/Y	1.25
388	Rafael Palmeiro G/Y	4.50
389	Matt Williams B/X	.35
390	Eric Young B/X	.35
391	Fred McGriff B/X	.35
392	Ken Caminiti B/X	.35
393	Roberto Alomar B/X	.75
394	Brian Jordan B/X	.35
395	Mark Grace G/Z	1.25
396	Jim Edmonds B/Y	.35
397	Deion Sanders S/Y	.50
398	Vladimir Guerrero S/Z Checklist	1.25
399	Darin Erstad S/Y Checklist	1.00
400	Nomar Garciaparra S/Z Checklist	2.00

Get-A-Grip

		NM/M
Complete Set (16):		30.00
Common Card:		1.00
1	Ken Griffey Jr., Greg Maddux	3.00
2	John Smoltz, Frank Thomas	1.50
3	Mike Piazza, Andy Pettitte	3.00
4	Randy Johnson, Chipper Jones	2.50
5	Tom Glavine, Alex Rodriguez	4.00
6	Pat Hentgen, Jeff Bagwell	1.50
7	Kevin Brown, Juan Gonzalez	1.25
8	Barry Bonds, Mike Mussina	5.00
9	Hideo Nomo, Albert Belle	1.25
10	Troy Percival, Andruw Jones	1.50
11	Roger Clemens, Brian Jordan	3.00
12	Paul Wilson, Ivan Rodriguez	1.25
13	Andy Benes, Mo Vaughn	1.00
14	Al Leiter, Derek Jeter	5.00
15	Bill Pulsipher, Cal Ripken Jr.	5.00
16	Mariano Rivera, Ken Caminiti	1.00

Knot-Hole Gang

	NM/M
Complete Set (12):	18.00
Common Player:	.50
Promos:	2X

1	Chuck Knoblauch	.50
2	Ken Griffey Jr.	3.50
3	Frank Thomas	1.50
4	Tony Gwynn	2.50
5	Mike Piazza	3.50
6	Jeff Bagwell	1.50
7	Rusty Greer	.50
8	Cal Ripken Jr.	5.00
9	Chipper Jones	2.50
10	Ryan Klesko	.50
11	Barry Larkin	.50
12	Paul Molitor	1.50

Leagues of the Nation

		NM/M
Complete Set (15):		60.00
Common Card:		1.50
1	Juan Gonzalez, Barry Bonds	10.00
2	Cal Ripken Jr., Chipper Jones	10.00
3	Mark McGwire, Ken Caminiti	7.00
4	Derek Jeter, Kenny Lofton	10.00
5	Ivan Rodriguez, Mike Piazza	6.00
6	Ken Griffey Jr., Larry Walker	6.00
7	Frank Thomas, Sammy Sosa	5.00
8	Paul Molitor, Barry Larkin	3.00
9	Albert Belle, Deion Sanders	1.50
10	Matt Williams, Jeff Bagwell	3.00
11	Mo Vaughn, Gary Sheffield	1.50
12	Alex Rodriguez, Tony Gwynn	7.50
13	Tino Martinez, Scott Rolen	2.00
14	Darin Erstad, Wilton Guerrero	2.00
15	Tony Clark, Vladimir Guerrero	3.00

Statistical Standouts

		NM/M
Complete Set (15):		175.00
Common Player:		4.00
1	Albert Belle	4.00
2	Juan Gonzalez	9.00
3	Ken Griffey Jr.	20.00
4	Alex Rodriguez	25.00
5	Frank Thomas	12.00
6	Chipper Jones	15.00
7	Greg Maddux	15.00
8	Mike Piazza	20.00
9	Cal Ripken Jr.	30.00
10	Mark McGwire	25.00
11	Barry Bonds	30.00
12	Derek Jeter	30.00
13	Ken Caminiti	4.00
14	John Smoltz	4.00
15	Paul Molitor	12.00

Thomas Collection

		NM/M
Complete Set (6):		360.00
Common Card:		60.00
1	Frank Thomas/Hat	60.00
2	Frank Thomas/ Home Jersey	80.00
3	Frank Thomas/ Batting Glove	60.00
4	Frank Thomas/Bat	60.00
5	Frank Thomas/ Sweatband	60.00
6	Frank Thomas/ Away Jersey	80.00

Warning Track

		NM/M
Complete Set (18):		40.00
Common Player:		1.00
1	Ken Griffey Jr.	6.00
2	Albert Belle	1.00
3	Barry Bonds	7.50
4	Andruw Jones	4.00
5	Kenny Lofton	1.00
6	Tony Gwynn	5.00
7	Manny Ramirez	4.00
8	Rusty Greer	1.00
9	Bernie Williams	1.00
10	Gary Sheffield	2.00
11	Juan Gonzalez	2.50
12	Raul Mondesi	1.00
13	Brady Anderson	1.00
14	Rondell White	1.00
15	Sammy Sosa	6.00
16	Deion Sanders	1.00
17	David Justice	1.00
18	Jim Edmonds	1.00

22kt Gold Stars

		NM/M
Complete Set (36):		115.00
Common Player:		1.00
1	Frank Thomas	4.00
2	Alex Rodriguez	8.00
3	Ken Griffey Jr.	6.50
4	Andruw Jones	4.00
5	Chipper Jones	5.50
6	Jeff Bagwell	4.00
7	Derek Jeter	10.00

8	Deion Sanders	1.00
9	Ivan Rodriguez	3.50
10	Juan Gonzalez	3.00
11	Greg Maddux	5.50
12	Andy Pettitte	2.50
13	Roger Clemens	6.00
14	Hideo Nomo	3.00
15	Tony Gwynn	5.50
16	Barry Bonds	10.00
17	Kenny Lofton	1.00
18	Paul Molitor	4.00
19	Jim Thome	3.00
20	Albert Belle	1.00
21	Cal Ripken Jr.	10.00
22	Mark McGwire	8.00
23	Barry Larkin	1.00
24	Mike Piazza	6.50
25	Darin Erstad	2.00
26	Chuck Knoblauch	1.00
27	Vladimir Guerrero	4.00
28	Tony Clark	1.00
29	Scott Rolen	3.00
30	Nomar Garciaparra	6.50
31	Eric Young	1.00
32	Ryne Sandberg	5.50
33	Roberto Alomar	2.00
34	Eddie Murray	4.00
35	Rafael Palmeiro	3.50
36	Jose Guillen	1.00

1998 Leaf

		NM/M
Complete Set (200):		40.00
Common Player:		.05
Common SP (#148-197):		.40
Pack (10):		2.00
Wax Box (24):		40.00
1	Rusty Greer	.05
2	Tino Martinez	.05
3	Bobby Bonilla	.05
4	Jason Giambi	.50
5	Matt Morris	.05
6	Craig Counsell	.05
7	Reggie Jefferson	.05
8	Brian Rose	.05
9	Ruben Rivera	.05
10	Shawn Estes	.05
11	Tony Gwynn	1.00
12	Jeff Abbott	.05
13	Jose Cruz Jr.	.05
14	Francisco Cordova	.05
15	Ryan Klesko	.05
16	Tim Salmon	.05
17	Brett Tomko	.05
18	Matt Williams	.05
19	Joe Carter	.05
20	Harold Baines	.05
21	Gary Sheffield	.50
22	Charles Johnson	.05
23	Aaron Boone	.05
24	Eddie Murray	.75
25	Matt Stairs	.05
26	David Cone	.05
27	Jon Nunnally	.05
28	Chris Stynes	.05
29	Enrique Wilson	.05
30	Randy Johnson	.75
31	Garret Anderson	.05
32	Manny Ramirez	.75
33	Jeff Suppan	.05
34	Rickey Henderson	.75
35	Scott Spiezio	.05
36	Rondell White	.05
37	Todd Greene	.05
38	Delino DeShields	.05
39	Kevin Brown	.05
40	Chili Davis	.05
41	Jimmy Key	.05
42	Not Issued	
43	Mike Mussina	.40
44	Joe Randa	.05
45	Chan Ho Park	.05
46	Brad Radke	.05

47	Geronimo Berroa	.05
48	Wade Boggs	1.00
49	Kevin Appier	.05
50	Moises Alou	.05
51	David Justice	.05
52	Ivan Rodriguez	.65
53	J.T. Snow	.05
54	Brian Giles	.05
55	Will Clark	.10
56	Justin Thompson	.05
57	Javier Lopez	.05
58	Hideki Irabu	.05
59	Mark Grudzielanek	.05
60	Abraham Nunez	.05
61	Todd Hollandsworth	.05
62	Jay Bell	.05
63	Nomar Garciaparra	1.25
64	Vinny Castilla	.05
65	Lou Collier	.05
66	Kevin Orie	.05
67	John Valentin	.05
68	Robin Ventura	.05
69	Denny Neagle	.05
70	Tony Womack	.05
71	Dennis Reyes	.05
72	Wally Joyner	.05
73	Kevin Brown	.05
74	Ray Durham	.05
75	Mike Cameron	.05
76	Dante Bichette	.05
77	Jose Guillen	.05
78	Carlos Delgado	.50
79	Paul Molitor	.75
80	Jason Kendall	.05
81	Mark Belhorn	.05
82	Damian Jackson	.05
83	Bill Mueller	.05
84	Kevin Young	.05
85	Curt Schilling	.25
86	Jeffrey Hammonds	.05
87	Sandy Alomar Jr.	.05
88	Bartolo Colon	.05
89	Wilton Guerrero	.05
90	Bernie Williams	.05
91	Deion Sanders	.05
92	Mike Piazza	1.25
93	Butch Huskey	.05
94	Edgardo Alfonzo	.05
95	Alan Benes	.05
96	Craig Biggio	.05
97	Mark Grace	.05
98	Shawn Green	.25
99	Derrek Lee	.60
100	Ken Griffey Jr.	1.25
101	Tim Raines	.05
102	Pokey Reese	.05
103	Lee Stevens	.05
104	Shannon Stewart	.05
105	John Smoltz	.05
106	Frank Thomas	.75
107	Jeff Fassero	.05
108	Jay Buhner	.05
109	Jose Canseco	.50
110	Omar Vizquel	.05
111	Travis Fryman	.05
112	Dave Nilsson	.05
113	John Olerud	.05
114	Larry Walker	.05
115	Jim Edmonds	.05
116	Bobby Higginson	.05
117	Todd Hundley	.05
118	Paul O'Neill	.05
119	Bip Roberts	.05
120	Ismael Valdes	.05
121	Pedro Martinez	.75
122	Jeff Cirillo	.05
123	Andy Benes	.05
124	Bobby Jones	.05
125	Brian Hunter	.05
126	Darryl Kile	.05
127	Pat Hentgen	.05
128	Marquis Grissom	.05
129	Eric Davis	.05
130	Chipper Jones	1.00
131	Edgar Martinez	.05
132	Andy Pettitte	.20
133	Cal Ripken Jr.	2.00
134	Scott Rolen	.65
135	Ron Coomer	.05
136	Luis Castillo	.05
137	Fred McGriff	.05
138	Neifi Perez	.05
139	Eric Karros	.05
140	Alex Fernandez	.05
141	Jason Dickson	.05
142	Lance Johnson	.05
143	Ray Lankford	.05
144	Sammy Sosa	1.25
145	Eric Young	.05
146	Bubba Trammell	.05
147	Todd Walker	.05
148	Mo Vaughn/CC	.40
149	Jeff Bagwell/CC	1.00
150	Kenny Lofton/CC	.40

151	Raul Mondesi/CC	.40
152	Mike Piazza/CC	2.00
153	Chipper Jones/CC	1.50
154	Larry Walker/CC	.40
155	Greg Maddux/CC	1.50
156	Ken Griffey Jr./CC	1.00
157	Frank Thomas/CC	1.00
158	Darin Erstad/GLS	.75
159	Roberto Alomar/GLS	.60
160	Albert Belle/GLS	.40
161	Jim Thome/GLS	.75
162	Tony Clark/GLS	.40
163	Chuck Knoblauch/GLS	.40
164	Derek Jeter/GLS	3.00
165	Alex Rodriguez/GLS	2.50
166	Tony Gwynn/GLS	1.50
167	Roger Clemens/GLS	2.00
168	Barry Larkin/GLS	.40
169	Andres Galarraga/GLS	.40
170	Vladimir Guerrero/GLS	1.00
171	Mark McGwire/GLS	2.50
172	Barry Bonds/GLS	3.00
173	Juan Gonzalez/GLS	.75
174	Andruw Jones/GLS	1.00
175	Paul Molitor/GLS	1.00
176	Hideo Nomo/GLS	.75
177	Cal Ripken Jr./GLS	3.00
178	Brad Fullmer/GLR	.40
179	Jaret Wright/GLR	.40
180	Bobby Estalella/GLR	.40
181	Ben Grieve/GLR	.40
182	Paul Konerko/GLR	.60
183	David Ortiz/GLR	.75
184	Todd Helton/GLR	1.00
185	Juan Encarnacion/GLR	.40
186	Miguel Tejada/GLR	.60
187	Jacob Cruz/GLR	.40
188	Mark Kotsay/GLR	.40
189	Fernando Tatis/GLR	.40
190	Ricky Ledee/GLR	.40
191	Richard Hidalgo/GLR	.40
192	Richie Sexson/GLR	.40
193	Luis Ordaz/GLR	.40
194	Eli Marrero/GLR	.40
195	Livan Hernandez/GLR	.40
196	Homer Bush/GLR	.40
197	Raul Ibanez/GLR	.40
198	Nomar Garciaparra Checklist	.60
199	Scott Rolen Checklist	.30
200	Jose Cruz Jr. Checklist	.05
201	Al Martin	.05

Crusade

		NM/M
Complete Set (30):		400.00
Common Player:		6.00
Purples:		3X
Reds:		12X
3	Jim Edmonds	7.50
4	Darin Erstad	7.50
11	Mike Mussina	15.00
15	Albert Belle	6.00
18	Manny Ramirez	25.00
19	Jim Thome	20.00
24	Bubba Trammell	6.00
26	Bobby Higginson	6.00
28	Paul Molitor	25.00
30	Todd Walker	6.00
34	Andy Pettitte	10.00
35	Wade Boggs	30.00
40	Alex Rodriguez	60.00
41	Randy Johnson	25.00
46	Ivan Rodriguez	20.00
48	Roger Clemens	40.00
54	John Smoltz	6.00
56	Andruw Jones	25.00
58	Javier Lopez	6.00
59	Fred McGriff	6.00
64	Pokey Reese	6.00
66	Andres Galarraga	6.00
70	Eric Young	6.00

73	Moises Alou	6.00
76	Ben Grieve	6.00
79	Mike Piazza	50.00
91	Jason Kendall	6.00
95	Alan Benes	6.00
97	Tony Gwynn	30.00
98	Ken Caminiti	6.00

Heading for the Hall

HEADING FOR THE HALL

		NM/M
Complete Set (20):		35.00
Common Player:		.75
Samples:		1X
1	Roberto Alomar	1.00
2	Jeff Bagwell	1.50
3	Albert Belle	.75
4	Wade Boggs	2.00
5	Barry Bonds	5.00
6	Roger Clemens	2.50
7	Juan Gonzalez	1.50
8	Ken Griffey Jr.	3.00
9	Tony Gwynn	2.00
10	Barry Larkin	.75
11	Kenny Lofton	.75
12	Greg Maddux	2.00
13	Mark McGwire	4.00
14	Paul Molitor	1.50
15	Eddie Murray	1.50
16	Mike Piazza	3.00
17	Cal Ripken Jr.	5.00
18	Ivan Rodriguez	1.25
19	Ryne Sandberg	2.00
20	Frank Thomas	1.50

Statistical Standouts

		NM/M
Complete Set (24):		55.00
Common Player:		1.00
Die-Cuts:		2X
1	Frank Thomas	2.50
2	Ken Griffey Jr.	4.00
3	Alex Rodriguez	5.00
4	Mike Piazza	4.00
5	Greg Maddux	3.00
6	Cal Ripken Jr.	6.00
7	Chipper Jones	3.00
8	Juan Gonzalez	2.00
9	Jeff Bagwell	2.50
10	Mark McGwire	5.00
11	Tony Gwynn	3.00
12	Mo Vaughn	1.00
13	Nomar Garciaparra	4.00
14	Jose Cruz Jr.	1.00
15	Vladimir Guerrero	2.50
16	Scott Rolen	2.00
17	Andy Pettitte	1.50
18	Randy Johnson	2.50
19	Larry Walker	1.00
20	Kenny Lofton	1.00
21	Tony Clark	1.00
22	David Justice	1.00
23	Derek Jeter	6.00
24	Barry Bonds	6.00

Fractal Matrix

	NM/M
Complete Set (200):	250.00
Common Bronze:	.25
Common Silver:	.75
Common Gold:	2.00

BUTCH HUSKEY

1	Rusty Greer G/Z	2.00
2	Tino Martinez G/Z	2.00
3	Bobby Bonilla S/Y	.75
4	Jason Giambi S/Y	1.25
5	Matt Morris S/Y	.75
6	Craig Counsell B/X	.25
7	Reggie Jefferson B/X	.25
8	Brian Rose S/Y	.25
9	Ruben Rivera B/X	.25
10	Shawn Estes S/Y	.75
11	Tony Gwynn G/Z	10.00
12	Jeff Abbott B/X	.25
13	Jose Cruz Jr. G/Z	2.00
14	Francisco Cordova B/X	.25
15	Ryan Klesko B/X	.25
16	Tim Salmon G/Y	2.00
17	Brett Tomko B/X	.25
18	Matt Williams S/Y	.25
19	Joe Carter B/X	.25
20	Harold Baines B/X	.25
21	Gary Sheffield S/Z	1.25
22	Charles Johnson S/X	.75
23	Aaron Boone B/X	.25
24	Eddie Murray G/Y	7.50
25	Matt Stairs B/X	.25
26	David Cone B/X	.25
27	Jon Nunnally B/X	.25
28	Chris Stynes B/X	.25
29	Enrique Wilson B/Y	.25
30	Randy Johnson S/Z	2.00
31	Garret Anderson S/Y	.75
32	Manny Ramirez G/Z	7.50
33	Jeff Suppan S/X	.75
34	Rickey Henderson B/X	1.00
35	Scott Spiezio B/X	.75
36	Rondell White B/Y	.75
37	Todd Greene S/Z	.75
38	Delino DeShields B/X	.25
39	Kevin Brown B/X	.25
40	Chili Davis B/X	.25
41	Jimmy Key B/X	.25
42	NOT ISSUED	
43	Mike Mussina G/Y	5.00
44	Joe Randa B/X	.25
45	Chan Ho Park S/X	.75
46	Brad Radke B/X	.25
47	Geronimo Berroa B/X	.25
48	Wade Boggs S/Y	2.50
49	Kevin Appier B/X	.25
50	Moises Alou S/Y	.25
51	David Justice G/Y	2.00
52	Ivan Rodriguez G/Z	6.00
53	J.T. Snow B/X	.25
54	Brian Giles B/X	.25
55	Will Clark B/Y	.75
56	Justin Thompson S/Y	.75
57	Javier Lopez S/X	.75
58	Hideki Irabu B/Z	.25
59	Mark Grudzielanek B/X	.25
60	Abraham Nunez S/X	.75
61	Todd Hollandsworth B/X	.25
62	Jay Bell B/X	.25
63	Nomar Garciaparra G/Z	10.00
64	Vinny Castilla B/Y	.25
65	Lou Collier B/Y	.25
66	Kevin Orie S/Y	.75
67	John Valentin B/X	.25
68	Robin Ventura B/X	.25
69	Denny Neagle B/X	.25

ABBREVIATIONS

CC - Curtain Calls
GLR - Gold Leaf Rookies
GLS - Gold Leaf Stars
SP - Short Print

70	Tony Womack S/Y	.75
71	Dennis Reyes S/Y	.75
72	Wally Joyner B/X	.25
73	Kevin Brown B/Y	.25
74	Ray Durham B/X	.25
75	Mike Cameron S/Z	.75
76	Dante Bichette B/X	.25
77	Jose Guillen B/X	2.00
78	Carlos Delgado B/Y	.50
79	Paul Molitor G/Z	7.50
80	Jason Kendall B/X	.25
81	Mark Belhorn B/X	.25
82	Damian Jackson B/X	.25
83	Bill Mueller B/X	.25
84	Kevin Young B/X	.25
85	Curt Schilling B/X	.40
86	Jeffrey Hammonds B/X	.25
87	Sandy Alomar Jr. S/Y	.75
88	Bartolo Colon B/Y	.50
89	Wilton Guerrero B/Y	.25
90	Bernie Williams G/Y	2.00
91	Deion Sanders S/Y	.75
92	Mike Piazza G/X	12.50
93	Butch Huskey B/X	.25
94	Edgardo Alfonzo S/X	.75
95	Alan Benes S/Y	.75
96	Craig Biggio S/Y	.75
97	Mark Grace S/Y	.75
98	Shawn Green S/Y	1.50
99	Derrek Lee S/Y	.25
100	Ken Griffey Jr. G/Z	12.50
101	Tim Raines B/X	.25
102	Pokey Reese S/X	.25
103	Lee Stevens B/X	.25
104	Shannon Stewart S/Y	.75
105	John Smoltz S/Y	.75
106	Frank Thomas G/X	7.50
107	Jeff Fassero B/X	.25
108	Jay Buhner B/Y	.25
109	Jose Canseco B/X	.50
110	Omar Vizquel B/X	.25
111	Travis Fryman B/X	.25
112	Dave Nilsson B/X	.25
113	John Olerud B/X	.25
114	Larry Walker G/Z	2.00
115	Jim Edmonds S/Y	.75
116	Bobby Higginson S/X	.75
117	Todd Hundley S/Y	.75
118	Paul O'Neill B/X	.25
119	Bip Roberts B/X	.25
120	Ismael Valdes B/X	.25
121	Pedro Martinez S/Y	2.00
122	Jeff Cirillo B/X	.25
123	Andy Benes B/X	.25
124	Bobby Jones B/X	.25
125	Brian Hunter B/X	.25
126	Darryl Kile B/X	.25
127	Pat Hentgen B/X	.25
128	Marquis Grissom B/X	.25
129	Eric Davis B/X	.25
130	Chipper Jones G/Z	10.00
131	Edgar Martinez S/Z	.75
132	Andy Pettitte G/Z	3.00
133	Cal Ripken Jr. G/X	20.00
134	Scott Rolen G/Z	6.00
135	Ron Coomer B/X	.25
136	Luis Castillo B/Y	.25
137	Fred McGriff B/Y	.25
138	Neifi Perez S/Y	.75
139	Eric Karros B/X	.25
140	Alex Fernandez B/X	.25
141	Jason Dickson B/X	.25
142	Lance Johnson B/X	.25
143	Ray Lankford B/Y	.25
144	Sammy Sosa G/Y	10.00
145	Eric Young B/Y	.25
146	Bubba Trammell S/Y	.75
147	Todd Walker S/Y	.75
148	Mo Vaughn/CC S/X	.75
149	Jeff Bagwell/CC S/X	2.00
150	Kenny Lofton/CC S/X	.75
151	Raul Mondesi/CC S/X	.75
152	Mike Piazza/CC S/X	4.00
153	Chipper Jones/CC S/X	3.00
154	Larry Walker/CC S/X	.75
155	Greg Maddux/CC S/X	3.00
156	Ken Griffey Jr./CC S/X	4.00
157	Frank Thomas/CC S/X	2.00
158	Darin Erstad/GLS B/Z	.50
159	Roberto Alomar/GLS B/Y	.35
160	Albert Belle/GLS G/Y	2.00
161	Jim Thome/GLS G/Y	4.00
162	Tony Clark/GLS G/Y	2.00
163	Chuck Knoblauch/GLS B/Y	.25
164	Derek Jeter/GLS G/Z	20.00
165	Alex Rodriguez/GLS G/Z	15.00
166	Tony Gwynn/GLS B/X	1.25
167	Roger Clemens/GLS G/Z	12.00
168	Barry Larkin/GLS B/Y	.25

169	Andres Galarraga/GLS B/Y	.25
170	Vladimir Guerrero/GLS G/Z	7.50
171	Mark McGwire/GLS B/Z	2.00
172	Barry Bonds/GLS B/Z	3.00
173	Juan Gonzalez/GLS G/Z	4.00
174	Andruw Jones/GLS G/Z	7.50
175	Paul Molitor/GLS B/X	1.00
176	Hideo Nomo/GLS B/Z	.75
177	Cal Ripken Jr./GLS B/X	2.25
178	Brad Fullmer/GLR S/Z	.75
179	Jaret Wright/GLR G/Z	2.00
180	Bobby Estalella/GLR B/Y	.25
181	Ben Grieve/GLR G/X	2.00
182	Paul Konerko/GLR G/Z	3.00
183	David Ortiz/GLR G/Z	6.00
184	Todd Helton/GLR G/X	5.00
185	Juan Encarnacion/GLR G/Z	2.00
186	Miguel Tejada/GLR G/Z	4.00
187	Jacob Cruz/GLR B/Y	.25
188	Mark Kotsay/GLR G/Z	2.00
189	Fernando Tatis/GLR S/Z	.75
190	Ricky Ledee/GLR S/Y	.75
191	Richard Hidalgo/GLR S/Y	.75
192	Richie Sexson/GLR S/Y	.75
193	Luis Ordaz/GLR B/X	.25
194	Eli Marrero/GLR S/Z	.75
195	Livan Hernandez/GLR S/Z	.75
196	Homer Bush/GLR B/X	.25
197	Raul Ibanez/GLR B/X	.25
198	Nomar Garciaparra B/X Checklist	.75
199	Scott Rolen B/X Checklist	.35
200	Jose Cruz Jr. B/X Checklist	.25
201	Al Martin B/X	.25

Fractal Matrix Diamond Axis

WILTON GUERRERO

	NM/M
Common Player:	7.50
Stars/Rookies:	20X
SP (148-177):	12X

(See 1998 Leaf for checklist and base card values.)

1998 Leaf Fractal Foundation

	NM/M
Complete Set (200):	60.00
Common Player:	.20
Semistars:	.60
Unlisted Stars:	1.00
Pack (3):	2.00
Wax Box (18):	35.00
1 Rusty Greer	.20
2 Tino Martinez	.20
3 Bobby Bonilla	.20
4 Jason Giambi	.60
5 Matt Morris	.20
6 Craig Counsell	.20
7 Reggie Jefferson	.20
8 Brian Rose	.20
9 Ruben Rivera	.20
10 Shawn Estes	.20
11 Tony Gwynn	1.50
12 Jeff Abbott	.20

#	Player	Price
13	Jose Cruz Jr.	.20
14	Francisco Cordova	.20
15	Ryan Klesko	.20
16	Tim Salmon	.20
17	Brett Tomko	.20
18	Matt Williams	.20
19	Joe Carter	.20
20	Harold Baines	.20
21	Gary Sheffield	.50
22	Charles Johnson	.20
23	Aaron Boone	.20
24	Eddie Murray	1.00
25	Matt Stairs	.20
26	David Cone	.20
27	Jon Nunnally	.20
28	Chris Stynes	.20
29	Enrique Wilson	.20
30	Randy Johnson	1.00
31	Garret Anderson	.20
32	Manny Ramirez	1.00
33	Jeff Suppan	.20
34	Rickey Henderson	1.00
35	Scott Spiezio	.20
36	Rondell White	.20
37	Todd Greene	.20
38	Delino DeShields	.20
39	Kevin Brown	.20
40	Chili Davis	.20
41	Jimmy Key	.20
42	NOT ISSUED	
43	Mike Mussina	.40
44	Joe Randa	.20
45	Chan Ho Park	.20
46	Brad Radke	.20
47	Geronimo Berroa	.20
48	Wade Boggs	1.50
49	Kevin Appier	.20
50	Moises Alou	.20
51	David Justice	.20
52	Ivan Rodriguez	.75
53	J.T. Snow	.20
54	Brian Giles	.20
55	Will Clark	.20
56	Justin Thompson	.20
57	Javier Lopez	.20
58	Hideki Irabu	.20
59	Mark Grudzielanek	.20
60	Abraham Nunez	.20
61	Todd Hollandsworth	.20
62	Jay Bell	.20
63	Nomar Garciaparra	1.75
64	Vinny Castilla	.20
65	Lou Collier	.20
66	Kevin Orie	.20
67	John Valentin	.20
68	Robin Ventura	.20
69	Denny Neagle	.20
70	Tony Womack	.20
71	Dennis Reyes	.20
72	Wally Joyner	.20
73	Kevin Brown	.20
74	Ray Durham	.20
75	Mike Cameron	.20
76	Dante Bichette	.20
77	Jose Guillen	.20
78	Carlos Delgado	.50
79	Paul Molitor	1.00
80	Jason Kendall	.20
81	Mark Belhorn	.20
82	Damian Jackson	.20
83	Bill Mueller	.20
84	Kevin Young	.20
85	Curt Schilling	.40
86	Jeffrey Hammonds	.20
87	Sandy Alomar Jr.	.20
88	Bartolo Colon	.20
89	Wilton Guerrero	.20
90	Bernie Williams	.20
91	Deion Sanders	.20
92	Mike Piazza	2.00
93	Butch Huskey	.20
94	Edgardo Alfonzo	.20
95	Alan Benes	.20
96	Craig Biggio	.20
97	Mark Grace	.20
98	Shawn Green	.40
99	Derrek Lee	.50
100	Ken Griffey Jr.	2.00
101	Tim Raines	.20
102	Pokey Reese	.20
103	Lee Stevens	.20
104	Shannon Stewart	.20
105	John Smoltz	.20
106	Frank Thomas	1.00
107	Jeff Fassero	.20
108	Jay Buhner	.20
109	Jose Canseco	.40
110	Omar Vizquel	.20
111	Travis Fryman	.20
112	Dave Nilsson	.20
113	John Olerud	.20
114	Larry Walker	.20
115	Jim Edmonds	.20
116	Bobby Higginson	.20
117	Todd Hundley	.20
118	Paul O'Neill	.20
119	Bip Roberts	.20
120	Ismael Valdes	.20
121	Pedro Martinez	1.00
122	Jeff Cirillo	.20
123	Andy Benes	.20
124	Bobby Jones	.20
125	Brian Hunter	.20
126	Darryl Kile	.20
127	Pat Hentgen	.20
128	Marquis Grissom	.20
129	Eric Davis	.20
130	Chipper Jones	1.50
131	Edgar Martinez	.20
132	Andy Pettitte	.35
133	Cal Ripken Jr.	3.00
134	Scott Rolen	.75
135	Ron Coomer	.20
136	Luis Castillo	.20
137	Fred McGriff	.20
138	Neifi Perez	.20
139	Eric Karros	.20
140	Alex Fernandez	.20
141	Jason Dickson	.20
142	Lance Johnson	.20
143	Ray Lankford	.20
144	Sammy Sosa	1.75
145	Eric Young	.20
146	Bubba Trammell	.20
147	Todd Walker	.20
148	Mo Vaughn/CC	.20
149	Jeff Bagwell/CC	1.00
150	Kenny Lofton/CC	.20
151	Raul Mondesi/CC	.20
152	Mike Piazza/CC	2.00
153	Chipper Jones/CC	1.50
154	Larry Walker/CC	.20
155	Greg Maddux/CC	1.50
156	Ken Griffey Jr./CC	2.00
157	Frank Thomas/CC	1.00
158	Darin Erstad/GLS	.50
159	Roberto Alomar/GLS	.40
160	Albert Belle/GLS	.20
161	Jim Thome/GLS	.75
162	Tony Clark/GLS	.20
163	Chuck Knoblauch/GLS	.20
164	Derek Jeter/GLS	3.00
165	Alex Rodriguez/GLS	2.50
166	Tony Gwynn/GLS	1.50
167	Roger Clemens/GLS	1.75
168	Barry Larkin/GLS	.20
169	Andres Galarraga/GLS	.20
170	Vladimir Guerrero/GLS	1.00
171	Mark McGwire/GLS	2.50
172	Barry Bonds/GLS	3.00
173	Juan Gonzalez/GLS	.75
174	Andruw Jones/GLS	1.00
175	Paul Molitor/GLS	1.00
176	Hideo Nomo/GLS	.75
177	Cal Ripken Jr./GLS	3.00
178	Brad Fullmer/GLR	.20
179	Jaret Wright/GLR	.20
180	Bobby Estalella/GLR	.20
181	Ben Grieve/GLR	.20
182	Paul Konerko/GLR	.40
183	David Ortiz/GLR	.75
184	Todd Helton/GLR	1.00
185	Juan Encarnacion/GLR	.20
186	Miguel Tejada/GLR	.40
187	Jacob Cruz/GLR	.20
188	Mark Kotsay/GLR	.20
189	Fernando Tatis/GLR	.20
190	Ricky Ledee/GLR	.20
191	Richard Hidalgo/GLR	.20
192	Richie Sexson/GLR	.20
193	Luis Ordaz/GLR	.20
194	Eli Marrero/GLR	.20
195	Livan Hernandez/GLR	.20
196	Homer Bush/GLR	.20
197	Raul Ibanez/GLR	.20
198	Nomar Garciaparra Checklist	1.00
199	Scott Rolen Checklist	.30
200	Jose Cruz Jr. Checklist	.20

Leaf Fractal Materials

	NM/M
Complete Set (200):	375.00
Complete Plastic Set (100):	65.00
Common Plastic (3,250):	.35
Complete Leather Set (50):	55.00
Common Leather (1,000):	.75
Complete Nylon Set (30):	60.00
Common Nylon (500):	1.25
Complete Wood Set (20):	200.00
Common Wood (250):	5.00
Wax Box:	120.00

#	Player	Price
1	Rusty Greer/N	1.25
2	Tino Martinez/W	5.00
3	Bobby Bonilla/N	1.25
4	Jason Giambi/N	4.00
5	Matt Morris/L	.75
6	Craig Counsell/P	.35
7	Reggie Jefferson/P	.35
8	Brian Rose/P	.35
9	Ruben Rivera/L	.75
10	Shawn Estes/L	.75
11	Tony Gwynn/W	20.00
12	Jeff Abbott/P	.35
13	Jose Cruz Jr./W	5.00
14	Francisco Cordova/P	.35
15	Ryan Klesko/L	.75
16	Tim Salmon/W	5.00
17	Brett Tomko/L	.75
18	Matt Williams/N	1.25
19	Joe Carter/P	.35
20	Harold Baines/P	.35
21	Gary Sheffield/N	2.50
22	Charles Johnson/L	.75
23	Aaron Boone/P	.35
24	Eddie Murray/W	5.00
25	Matt Stairs/P	.35
26	David Cone/P	.35
27	Jon Nunnally/P	.35
28	Chris Stynes/P	.35
29	Enrique Wilson/P	.35
30	Randy Johnson/W	15.00
31	Garret Anderson/N	1.25
32	Manny Ramirez/W	15.00
33	Jeff Suppan/L	.75
34	Rickey Henderson/N	5.00
35	Scott Spiezio/L	.35
36	Rondell White/L	.75
37	Todd Greene/L	1.25
38	Delino DeShields/P	.35
39	Kevin Brown/L	.75
40	Chili Davis/P	.35
41	Jimmy Key/P	.35
42	NOT ISSUED	
43	Mike Mussina/L	4.00
44	Joe Randa/P	.35
45	Chan Ho Park/N	1.25
46	Brad Radke/P	.35
47	Geronimo Berroa/P	.35
48	Wade Boggs/N	6.00
49	Kevin Appier/P	.35
50	Moises Alou/L	1.25
51	David Justice/L	1.25
52	Ivan Rodriguez/W	12.50
53	J.T. Snow/L	.75
54	Brian Giles/P	.35
55	Will Clark/L	.75
56	Justin Thompson/P	1.25
57	Javier Lopez/P	.35
58	Hideki Irabu/L	.75
59	Mark Grudzielanek/P	.35
60	Abraham Nunez/P	.35
61	Todd Hollandsworth/P	.35
62	Jay Bell/P	.35
63	Nomar Garciaparra/W	20.00
64	Vinny Castilla/P	.35
65	Lou Collier/P	.35
66	Kevin Orie/L	.75
67	John Valentin/P	.35
68	Robin Ventura/P	.35
69	Denny Neagle/P	.35
70	Tony Womack/L	.75
71	Dennis Reyes/L	.75
72	Wally Joyner/P	.35
73	Kevin Brown/P	.35
74	Ray Durham/P	.35
75	Mike Cameron/N	1.25
76	Dante Bichette/L	.75
77	Jose Guillen/N	1.25
78	Carlos Delgado/L	1.50
79	Paul Molitor/W	15.00
80	Jason Kendall/P	.35
81	Mark Belhorn/L	.75
82	Damian Jackson/P	.35
83	Bill Mueller/P	.35
84	Kevin Young/P	.35
85	Curt Schilling/L	.60
86	Jeffrey Hammonds/P	.35
87	Sandy Alomar Jr./L	.75
88	Bartolo Colon/P	.35
89	Wilton Guerrero/L	.75
90	Bernie Williams/N	1.25
91	Deion Sanders/N	1.25
92	Mike Piazza/W	25.00
93	Butch Huskey/L	.75
94	Edgardo Alfonzo/L	.75
95	Alan Benes/L	.75
96	Craig Biggio/N	1.25
97	Mark Grace/L	.75
98	Shawn Green/L	1.25
99	Derrek Lee/L	2.00
100	Ken Griffey Jr./W	25.00
101	Tim Raines/P	.35
102	Pokey Reese/P	.35
103	Lee Stevens/P	.35
104	Shannon Stewart/N	1.25
105	John Smoltz/L	.75
106	Frank Thomas/W	15.00
107	Jeff Fassero/P	.35
108	Jay Buhner/L	.75
109	Jose Canseco/L	1.50
110	Omar Vizquel/P	.35
111	Travis Fryman/P	.35
112	Dave Nilsson/P	.35
113	John Olerud/P	.35
114	Larry Walker/W	5.00
115	Jim Edmonds/L	1.25
116	Bobby Higginson/L	.75
117	Todd Hundley/L	.75
118	Paul O'Neill/P	.35
119	Bip Roberts/P	.35
120	Ismael Valdes/P	.35
121	Pedro Martinez/L	5.00
122	Jeff Cirillo/P	.35
123	Andy Benes/P	.35
124	Bobby Jones/P	.35
125	Brian Hunter/P	.35
126	Darryl Kile/P	.35
127	Pat Hentgen/P	.35
128	Marquis Grissom/P	.35
129	Eric Davis/P	.35
130	Chipper Jones/W	20.00
131	Edgar Martinez/N	1.25
132	Andy Pettitte/W	10.00
133	Cal Ripken Jr./W	35.00
134	Scott Rolen/W	12.50
135	Ron Coomer/P	.35
136	Luis Castillo/P	.75
137	Fred McGriff/L	.75
138	Neifi Perez/P	.75
139	Eric Karros/P	.35
140	Alex Fernandez/P	.35
141	Jason Dickson/P	.35
142	Lance Johnson/P	.35
143	Ray Lankford/P	.35
144	Sammy Sosa/N	7.00
145	Eric Young/P	.35
146	Bubba Trammell/L	.75
147	Todd Walker/P	.75
148	Mo Vaughn/P/CC	.35
149	Jeff Bagwell/P/CC	3.00
150	Kenny Lofton/P/CC	.35
151	Raul Mondesi/P/CC	.35
152	Mike Piazza/P/CC	5.00
153	Chipper Jones/P/CC	4.00
154	Larry Walker/P/CC	.35
155	Greg Maddux/P/CC	4.00
156	Ken Griffey Jr./P/CC	5.00
157	Frank Thomas/P/CC	3.00
158	Darin Erstad/L/GLS	2.00
159	Roberto Alomar/L/GLS	.65
160	Albert Belle/L/GLS	.75
161	Jim Thome/L/GLS	2.00
162	Tony Clark/L/GLS	.75
163	Chuck Knoblauch/L/GLS	.75
164	Derek Jeter/P/GLS	7.50
165	Alex Rodriguez/P/GLS	6.00
166	Tony Gwynn/P/GLS	4.00
167	Roger Clemens/L/GLS	5.00
168	Barry Larkin/P/GLS	.35

#	Player	Value
169	Andres Galarraga/P/GLS	.35
170	Vladimir Guerrero/L/GLS	4.00
171	Mark McGwire/L/GLS	6.00
172	Barry Bonds/L/GLS	7.50
173	Juan Gonzalez/P/GLS	2.00
174	Andruw Jones/P/GLS	3.00
175	Paul Molitor/P/GLS	3.00
176	Hideo Nomo/L/GLS	2.00
177	Cal Ripken Jr./P/GLS	7.50
178	Brad Fullmer/P/GLR	.35
179	Jaret Wright/N/GLR	1.25
180	Bobby Estalella/P/GLR	.35
181	Ben Grieve/W/GLR	5.00
182	Paul Konerko/W/GLR	6.00
183	David Ortiz/N/GLR	2.50
184	Todd Helton/W/GLR	10.00
185	Juan Encarnacion/N/GLR	1.25
186	Miguel Tejada/N/GLR	1.50
187	Jacob Cruz/P/GLR	.35
188	Mark Kotsay/N/GLR	1.25
189	Fernando Tatis/L/GLR	.75
190	Ricky Ledee/P/GLR	.35
191	Richard Hidalgo/P/GLR	.35
192	Richie Sexson/P/GLR	.35
193	Luis Ordaz/P/GLR	.35
194	Eli Marrero/L/GLR	.75
195	Livan Hernandez/L/GLR	.75
196	Homer Bush/P/GLR	.35
197	Raul Ibanez/P/GLR	.35
198	Nomar Garciaparra/P Checklist	3.00
199	Scott Rolen/P Checklist	.40
200	Jose Cruz Jr./P Checklist	.35
201	Al Martin/L	.75

1998 Leaf Rookies & Stars

	NM/M
Complete Set (339):	200.00
Common Player:	.10
Common SP (131-230):	.20
Common SP (301-339):	.50
Inserted 1:2	
True Blues:	12X
SP True Blues:	2X
Production 500 Sets	
Longevitys:	50X
SP Longevitys:	15X
Production 50 Sets	
Pack (9):	7.50
Wax Box (24):	150.00

#	Player	Value
1	Andy Pettitte	.30
2	Roberto Alomar	.20
3	Randy Johnson	.75
4	Manny Ramirez	.75
5	Paul Molitor	.75
6	Mike Mussina	.50
7	Jim Thome	.65
8	Tino Martinez	.10
9	Gary Sheffield	.50
10	Chuck Knoblauch	.10
11	Bernie Williams	.10
12	Tim Salmon	.10
13	Sammy Sosa	1.25
14	Wade Boggs	1.00
15	Andres Galarraga	.10
16	Pedro Martinez	.75
17	David Justice	.10
18	Chan Ho Park	.10
19	Jay Buhner	.10
20	Ryan Klesko	.10
21	Barry Larkin	.10
22	Will Clark	.15
23	Raul Mondesi	.10
24	Rickey Henderson	.75
25	Jim Edmonds	.10
26	Ken Griffey Jr.	1.25

#	Player	Value
27	Frank Thomas	.75
28	Cal Ripken Jr.	2.00
29	Alex Rodriguez	1.50
30	Mike Piazza	1.25
31	Greg Maddux	1.00
32	Chipper Jones	1.00
33	Tony Gwynn	1.00
34	Derek Jeter	2.00
35	Jeff Bagwell	.75
36	Juan Gonzalez	.50
37	Nomar Garciaparra	1.00
38	Andruw Jones	.75
39	Hideo Nomo	.60
40	Roger Clemens	1.25
41	Mark McGwire	1.50
42	Scott Rolen	.60
43	Vladimir Guerrero	.75
44	Barry Bonds	2.00
45	Darin Erstad	.25
46	Albert Belle	.10
47	Kenny Lofton	.10
48	Mo Vaughn	.10
49	Ivan Rodriguez	.60
50	Jose Cruz Jr.	.10
51	Tony Clark	.10
52	Larry Walker	.10
53	Mark Grace	.10
54	Edgar Martinez	.10
55	Fred McGriff	.10
56	Rafael Palmeiro	.60
57	Matt Williams	.10
58	Craig Biggio	.10
59	Ken Caminiti	.10
60	Jose Canseco	.40
61	Brady Anderson	.10
62	Moises Alou	.10
63	Justin Thompson	.10
64	John Smoltz	.10
65	Carlos Delgado	.50
66	J.T. Snow	.10
67	Jason Giambi	.50
68	Garret Anderson	.10
69	Rondell White	.10
70	Eric Karros	.10
71	Javier Lopez	.10
72	Pat Hentgen	.10
73	Dante Bichette	.10
74	Charles Johnson	.10
75	Tom Glavine	.30
76	Rusty Greer	.10
77	Travis Fryman	.10
78	Todd Hundley	.10
79	Ray Lankford	.10
80	Denny Neagle	.10
81	Henry Rodriguez	.10
82	Sandy Alomar Jr.	.10
83	Robin Ventura	.10
84	John Olerud	.10
85	Omar Vizquel	.10
86	Darren Dreifort	.10
87	Kevin Brown	.10
88	Curt Schilling	.35
89	Francisco Cordova	.10
90	Brad Radke	.10
91	David Cone	.10
92	Paul O'Neill	.10
93	Vinny Castilla	.10
94	Marquis Grissom	.10
95	Brian Hunter	.10
96	Kevin Appier	.10
97	Bobby Bonilla	.10
98	Eric Young	.10
99	Jason Kendall	.10
100	Shawn Green	.40
101	Edgardo Alfonzo	.10
102	Alan Benes	.10
103	Bobby Higginson	.10
104	Todd Greene	.10
105	Jose Guillen	.15
106	Neifi Perez	.10
107	Edgar Renteria	.10
108	Chris Stynes	.10
109	Todd Walker	.10
110	Brian Jordan	.10
111	Joe Carter	.10
112	Ellis Burks	.10
113	Brett Tomko	.10
114	Mike Cameron	.10
115	Shannon Stewart	.10
116	Kevin Orie	.10
117	Brian Giles	.10
118	Hideki Irabu	.10
119	Delino DeShields	.10
120	David Segui	.10
121	Dustin Hermanson	.10
122	Kevin Young	.10
123	Jay Bell	.10
124	Doug Glanville	.10
125	John Roskos RC	.10
126	Damon Hollins RC	.10
127	Matt Stairs	.10
128	Cliff Floyd	.10
129	Derek Bell	.10
130	Darryl Strawberry	.10

#	Player	Value
131	Ken Griffey Jr.	1.25
132	Tim Salmon	.20
133	Manny Ramirez	.75
134	Paul Konerko	.30
135	Frank Thomas	.75
136	Todd Helton	.75
137	Larry Walker	.20
138	Mo Vaughn	.20
139	Travis Lee	.20
140	Ivan Rodriguez	.60
141	Ben Grieve	.20
142	Brad Fullmer	.20
143	Alex Rodriguez	1.50
144	Mike Piazza	1.25
145	Greg Maddux	1.00
146	Chipper Jones	1.00
147	Kenny Lofton	.20
148	Albert Belle	.20
149	Barry Bonds	2.00
150	Vladimir Guerrero	.75
151	Tony Gwynn	1.00
152	Derek Jeter	2.00
153	Jeff Bagwell	.75
154	Juan Gonzalez	.60
155	Nomar Garciaparra	1.00
156	Andruw Jones	.75
157	Hideo Nomo	.60
158	Roger Clemens	1.25
159	Mark McGwire	1.50
160	Scott Rolen	.60
161	Travis Lee	.20
162	Ben Grieve	.20
163	Jose Guillen	.20
164	John Olerud	.20
165	Kevin Appier	.20
166	Marquis Grissom	.20
167	Rusty Greer	.20
168	Ken Caminiti	.20
169	Craig Biggio	.20
170	Ken Griffey Jr.	1.25
171	Larry Walker	.20
172	Barry Larkin	.20
173	Andres Galarraga	.20
174	Wade Boggs	1.00
175	Sammy Sosa	1.25
176	Mike Piazza	1.50
177	Jim Thome	.60
178	Paul Molitor	.75
179	Tony Clark	.20
180	Jose Cruz Jr.	.20
181	Darin Erstad	.25
182	Barry Bonds	2.00
183	Vladimir Guerrero	.75
184	Scott Rolen	.60
185	Mark McGwire	1.50
186	Nomar Garciaparra	1.00
187	Gary Sheffield	.50
188	Cal Ripken Jr.	2.00
189	Frank Thomas	.75
190	Andy Petitte	.30
191	Paul Konerko	.35
192	Todd Helton	1.50
193	Mark Kotsay	.20
194	Brad Fullmer	.20
195	Kevin Millwood RC	8.00
196	David Ortiz	3.00
197	Kerry Wood	1.50
198	Miguel Tejada	.40
199	Fernando Tatis	.20
200	Jaret Wright	.20
201	Ben Grieve	.20
202	Travis Lee	.20
203	Wes Helms	.20
204	Geoff Jenkins	.20
205	Russell Branyan	.20
206	Esteban Yan RC	.20
207	Ben Ford RC	.20
208	Rich Butler RC	.75
209	Ryan Jackson RC	.50
210	A.J. Hinch	.20
211	Magglio Ordonez RC	25.00
212	David Dellucci RC	.50
213	Billy McMillon	.20
214	Mike Lowell RC	8.00
215	Todd Erdos RC	.20
216	Carlos Mendoza RC	.25
217	Frank Catalanotto RC	.75
218	Julio Ramirez RC	.20
219	John Halama RC	.50
220	Wilson Delgado	.20
221	Mike Judd RC	.20
222	Rolando Arrojo RC	1.00
223	Jason LaRue RC	.50
224	Manny Aybar RC	.50
225	Jorge Velandia	.20
226	Mike Kinkade RC	.75
227	Carlos Lee RC	20.00
228	Bobby Hughes	.20
229	Ryan Christenson RC	.50
230	Masato Yoshii RC	1.00
231	Richard Hidalgo	.10
232	Rafael Medina	.10
233	Damian Jackson	.10
234	Derek Lowe	.15

#	Player	Value
235	Mario Valdez	.10
236	Eli Marrero	.10
237	Juan Encarnacion	.10
238	Livan Hernandez	.10
239	Bruce Chen	.10
240	Eric Milton	.10
241	Jason Varitek	.10
242	Scott Elarton	.10
243	Manuel Barrios RC	.10
244	Mike Caruso	.10
245	Tom Evans	.10
246	Pat Cline	.10
247	Matt Clement	.15
248	Karim Garcia	.15
249	Richie Sexson	.10
250	Sidney Ponson	.10
251	Randall Simon	.10
252	Tony Saunders	.10
253	Javier Valentin	.10
254	Danny Clyburn	.10
255	Michael Coleman	.10
256	Hanley Frias RC	.10
257	Miguel Cairo	.10
258	Rob Stanifer RC	.10
259	Lou Collier	.10
260	Abraham Nunez	.10
261	Ricky Ledee	.10
262	Carl Pavano	.10
263	Derrek Lee	.50
264	Jeff Abbott	.10
265	Bob Abreu	.10
266	Bartolo Colon	.10
267	Mike Drumright	.10
268	Daryle Ward	.10
269	Gabe Alvarez	.10
270	Josh Booty	.10
271	Damian Moss	.10
272	Brian Rose	.10
273	Jarrod Washburn	.10
274	Bobby Estalella	.10
275	Enrique Wilson	.10
276	Derrick Gibson	.10
277	Ken Cloude	.10
278	Kevin Witt	.10
279	Donnie Sadler	.10
280	Sean Casey	.20
281	Jacob Cruz	.10
282	Ron Wright	.10
283	Jeremi Gonzalez	.10
284	Desi Relaford	.10
285	Bobby Smith	.10
286	Javier Vazquez	.10
287	Steve Woodard RC	.20
288	Greg Norton	.10
289	Cliff Politte	.10
290	Felix Heredia	.10
291	Braden Looper	.10
292	Felix Martinez	.10
293	Brian Meadows	.10
294	Edwin Diaz	.10
295	Pat Watkins	.10
296	Marc Pisciotta RC	.10
297	Rick Gorecki	.10
298	DaRond Stovall	.10
299	Andy Larkin	.10
300	Felix Rodriguez	.10
301	Blake Stein	.50
302	John Rocker RC	1.00
303	Justin Baughman RC	.50
304	Jesus Sanchez RC	.50
305	Randy Winn	.50
306	Lou Merloni	.50
307	Jim Parque RC	1.00
308	Dennis Reyes	.50
309	Orlando Hernandez RC	10.00
310	Jason Johnson	.50
311	Torii Hunter	1.00
312	Mike Piazza	2.50
313	Mike Frank RC	.50
314	Troy Glaus RC	60.00
315	Jin Cho RC	.75
316	Ruben Mateo RC	1.00
317	Ryan Minor RC	1.00
318	Aramis Ramirez	.75
319	Adrian Beltre	1.00
320	Matt Anderson RC	1.00
321	Gabe Kapler RC	2.00
322	Jeremy Giambi RC	1.00
323	Carlos Beltran	1.00
324	Dermal Brown	.50
325	Ben Davis	.50
326	Eric Chavez	1.50
327	Bob Howry RC	1.00
328	Roy Halladay	.50
329	George Lombard	.50
330	Michael Barrett	.50
331	Fernando Seguignol RC	1.00
332	J.D. Drew RC	20.00
333	Odalis Perez RC	4.00
334	Alex Cora RC	1.00
335	Placido Polanco RC	8.00
336	Armando Rios RC	.50

337	Sammy Sosa (HR Commemorative)	3.00
338	Mark McGwire (HR Commemorative)	4.00
339	Sammy Sosa, Mark McGwire (Checklist)	4.00

Longevity

		NM/M
Common Player:		3.00
Stars:		50X
SP Stars (131-230):		15X
SP Stars (301-339):		5X

(See 1998 Leaf Rookies & Stars for checklist and base card values.)

True Blue

		NM/M
Common Player:		1.00
Stars:		12X
SP Stars (131-230; 301-339):		2X

(See 1998 Leaf Rookies & Stars for checklist and base card values.)

Cross Training

		NM/M
Complete Set (10):		30.00
Common Player:		1.50
Production 1,000 Sets		
1	Kenny Lofton	1.50
2	Ken Griffey Jr.	5.00
3	Alex Rodriguez	6.00
4	Greg Maddux	4.00
5	Barry Bonds	7.50
6	Ivan Rodriguez	2.50

7	Chipper Jones	4.00
8	Jeff Bagwell	3.00
9	Nomar Garciaparra	4.00
10	Derek Jeter	7.50

Crusade

		NM/M
Complete Green Set (30):		225.00
Common Player:		7.50
Production 250 Sets		
Purples (100 Sets):		3X
Reds (25 Sets):		10X
101	Richard Hidalgo	7.50
102	Paul Konerko	15.00
103	Miguel Tejada	15.00
104	Fernando Tatis	7.50
105	Travis Lee	7.50
106	Wes Helms	7.50
107	Rich Butler	7.50
108	Mark Kotsay	7.50
109	Eli Marrero	7.50
110	David Ortiz	15.00
111	Juan Encarnacion	7.50
112	Jaret Wright	7.50
113	Livan Hernandez	7.50
114	Ron Wright	7.50
115	Ryan Christenson	7.50
116	Eric Milton	7.50
117	Brad Fullmer	7.50
118	Karim Garcia	10.00
119	Abraham Nunez	7.50
120	Ricky Ledee	7.50
121	Carl Pavano	7.50
122	Derrek Lee	15.00
123	A.J. Hinch	7.50
124	Brian Rose	7.50
125	Bobby Estalella	7.50
126	Kevin Millwood	10.00
127	Kerry Wood	30.00
128	Sean Casey	12.50
129	Russell Branyan	7.50
130	Magglio Ordonez	20.00

Extreme Measures

		NM/M
Complete Set (10):		50.00
Common Player:		3.00
1	Ken Griffey Jr./944	7.50
2	Frank Thomas/653	5.00
3	Tony Gwynn/628	6.00
4	Mark McGwire/942	9.00
5	Larry Walker/280	3.00
6	Mike Piazza/960	7.50
7	Roger Clemens/708	6.50
8	Greg Maddux/980	5.00
9	Jeff Bagwell/873	4.50
10	Nomar Garciaparra/989	6.50

Extreme Measures Die-Cuts

		NM/M
Complete Set (10):		375.00
Common Player:		2.50
1	Ken Griffey Jr./56	65.00
2	Frank Thomas/347	11.00
3	Tony Gwynn/372	13.50
4	Mark McGwire/58	80.00
5	Larry Walker/720	2.50
6	Mike Piazza/40	75.00

7	Roger Clemens/292	16.00
8	Greg Maddux/20	100.00
9	Jeff Bagwell/127	20.00
10	Nomar Garciaparra/11	125.00

Freshman Orientation

		NM/M
Complete Set (20):		20.00
Common Player:		.75
Production 5,000 Sets		
Samples:		1X
1	Todd Helton	4.00
2	Ben Grieve	.75
3	Travis Lee	.75
4	Paul Konerko	1.50
5	Jaret Wright	.75
6	Livan Hernandez	.75
7	Brad Fullmer	.75
8	Carl Pavano	.75
9	Richard Hidalgo	.75
10	Miguel Tejada	1.50
11	Mark Kotsay	.75
12	David Ortiz	1.50
13	Juan Encarnacion	.75
14	Fernando Tatis	.75
15	Kevin Millwood	1.50
16	Kerry Wood	2.50
17	Magglio Ordonez	1.50
18	Derrek Lee	1.50
19	Jose Cruz Jr.	.75
20	A.J. Hinch	.75

Great American Heroes

		NM/M
Complete Set (20):		35.00
Common Player:		.75
Production 2,500 Sets		
Samples:		1X
1	Frank Thomas	1.75
2	Cal Ripken Jr.	5.00
3	Ken Griffey Jr.	3.00
4	Alex Rodriguez	4.00
5	Greg Maddux	2.25
6	Mike Piazza	3.00
7	Chipper Jones	2.25
8	Tony Gwynn	2.25
9	Jeff Bagwell	1.75
10	Juan Gonzalez	1.25
11	Hideo Nomo	1.25
12	Roger Clemens	2.50
13	Mark McGwire	4.00
14	Barry Bonds	5.00
15	Kenny Lofton	.75
16	Larry Walker	.75
17	Paul Molitor	1.75
18	Wade Boggs	2.25
19	Barry Larkin	.75
20	Andres Galarraga	.75

Greatest Hits

		NM/M
Complete Set (20):		30.00
Common Player:		.50
Production 2,500 Sets		
1	Ken Griffey Jr.	2.50
2	Frank Thomas	1.50
3	Cal Ripken Jr.	4.00

4	Alex Rodriguez	3.00
5	Ben Grieve	.50
6	Mike Piazza	2.50
7	Chipper Jones	2.00
8	Tony Gwynn	2.00
9	Derek Jeter	4.00
10	Jeff Bagwell	1.50
11	Tino Martinez	.50
12	Juan Gonzalez	.75
13	Nomar Garciaparra	2.00
14	Mark McGwire	3.00
15	Scott Rolen	.75
16	David Justice	.50
17	Darin Erstad	.75
18	Mo Vaughn	.50
19	Ivan Rodriguez	1.00
20	Travis Lee	.50

Home Run Derby

		NM/M
Complete Set (20):		30.00
Common Player:		.75
Production 2,500 Sets		
1	Tino Martinez	.75
2	Jim Thome	1.25
3	Larry Walker	.75
4	Tony Clark	.75
5	Jose Cruz Jr.	.75
6	Barry Bonds	5.00
7	Scott Rolen	1.00
8	Paul Konerko	1.25
9	Travis Lee	.75
10	Todd Helton	1.25
11	Mark McGwire	4.00
12	Andruw Jones	1.50
13	Nomar Garciaparra	2.50
14	Juan Gonzalez	1.00
15	Jeff Bagwell	1.50
16	Chipper Jones	2.50
17	Mike Piazza	3.00
18	Frank Thomas	1.50
19	Ken Griffey Jr.	3.00
20	Albert Belle	.75

ML Hard Drives

		NM/M
Complete Set (20):		30.00
Common Player:		.70
Production 2,500 Sets		

Samples:		1X
1	Jeff Bagwell	1.50
2	Juan Gonzalez	1.00
3	Nomar Garciaparra	2.00
4	Ken Griffey Jr.	3.00
5	Frank Thomas	1.50
6	Cal Ripken Jr.	4.50
7	Alex Rodriguez	3.50
8	Mike Piazza	3.00
9	Chipper Jones	2.00
10	Tony Gwynn	2.00
11	Derek Jeter	4.50
12	Mo Vaughn	.75
13	Ben Grieve	.75
14	Manny Ramirez	1.50
15	Vladimir Guerrero	1.50
16	Scott Rolen	1.00
17	Darin Erstad	.75
18	Kenny Lofton	.75
19	Brad Fullmer	.75
20	David Justice	.75

MVPs

		NM/M
Complete Set (20):		35.00
Common Player:		.50
Production 4,500 Sets		
Pennant Editions:		2X
Production 500 Sets		
1	Frank Thomas	2.00
2	Chuck Knoblauch	.50
3	Cal Ripken Jr.	5.00
4	Alex Rodriguez	4.00
5	Ivan Rodriguez	1.50
6	Albert Belle	.50
7	Ken Griffey Jr.	3.00
8	Juan Gonzalez	1.50
9	Roger Clemens	2.75
10	Mo Vaughn	.50
11	Jeff Bagwell	2.00
12	Craig Biggio	.50
13	Chipper Jones	2.50
14	Barry Larkin	.50
15	Mike Piazza	3.00
16	Barry Bonds	5.00
17	Andruw Jones	2.00
18	Tony Gwynn	2.50
19	Greg Maddux	2.50
20	Mark McGwire	4.00

Standing Ovation

		NM/M
Complete Set (10):		12.50
Common Player:		.75
Production 5,000 Sets		
Samples:		1X
1	Barry Bonds	3.00
2	Mark McGwire	2.50
3	Ken Griffey Jr.	2.00
4	Frank Thomas	1.00

5	Tony Gwynn	1.50
6	Cal Ripken Jr.	3.00
7	Greg Maddux	1.50
8	Roger Clemens	1.75
9	Paul Molitor	1.00
10	Ivan Rodriguez	.75

Ticket Masters

		NM/M
Complete Set (20):		32.50
Common Card:		.50
Production 2,250 Sets		
Die-Cuts:		1.5X
Production 250 Sets		
1	Ken Griffey Jr., Alex Rodriguez	4.00
2	Frank Thomas, Albert Belle	1.50
3	Cal Ripken Jr., Roberto Alomar	5.00
4	Greg Maddux, Chipper Jones	2.00
5	Tony Gwynn, Ken Caminiti	2.00
6	Derek Jeter, Andy Pettitte	5.00
7	Jeff Bagwell, Craig Biggio	1.50
8	Juan Gonzalez, Ivan Rodriguez	1.25
9	Nomar Garciaparra, Mo Vaughn	2.00
10	Vladimir Guerrero, Brad Fullmer	1.50
11	Andruw Jones, Andres Galarraga	1.50
12	Tino Martinez, Chuck Knoblauch	.50
13	Raul Mondesi, Paul Konerko	.75
14	Roger Clemens, Jose Cruz Jr.	2.25
15	Mark McGwire, Brian Jordan	4.00
16	Kenny Lofton, Manny Ramirez	1.50
17	Larry Walker, Todd Helton	1.25
18	Darin Erstad, Tim Salmon	.75
19	Travis Lee, Matt Williams	.50
20	Ben Grieve, Jason Giambi	1.00

2001 Leaf Certified Materials

	NM/M
Complete Set (160):	
Common Player:	.40

Common SP (111-160):		10.00
Production 200		
Pack (5):		15.00
Box (12):		160.00
1	Alex Rodriguez	5.00
2	Barry Bonds	6.00
3	Cal Ripken Jr.	6.00
4	Chipper Jones	3.00
5	Derek Jeter	6.00
6	Troy Glaus	2.00
7	Frank Thomas	2.00
8	Greg Maddux	3.00
9	Ivan Rodriguez	2.00
10	Jeff Bagwell	2.00
11	Eric Karros	.40
12	Todd Helton	2.00
13	Ken Griffey Jr.	4.00
14	Manny Ramirez	2.00
15	Mark McGwire	5.00
16	Mike Piazza	4.00
17	Nomar Garciaparra	4.00
18	Pedro Martinez	2.00
19	Randy Johnson	2.00
20	Rick Ankiel	.75
21	Rickey Henderson	1.50
22	Roger Clemens	3.50
23	Sammy Sosa	4.00
24	Tony Gwynn	3.00
25	Vladimir Guerrero	2.00
26	Kazuhiro Sasaki	.40
27	Roberto Alomar	.75
28	Barry Zito	.60
29	Pat Burrell	1.00
30	Harold Baines	.40
31	Carlos Delgado	1.00
32	J.D. Drew	1.00
33	Jim Edmonds	.60
34	Darin Erstad	.50
35	Jason Giambi	1.00
36	Tom Glavine	.75
37	Juan Gonzalez	2.00
38	Mark Grace	.60
39	Shawn Green	1.00
40	Tim Hudson	.60
41	Andruw Jones	1.50
42	Jeff Kent	.40
43	Barry Larkin	.40
44	Rafael Furcal	.40
45	Mike Mussina	1.00
46	Hideo Nomo	1.50
47	Rafael Palmeiro	1.25
48	Scott Rolen	1.00
49	Gary Sheffield	.60
50	Bernie Williams	.60
51	Bobby Abreu	.40
52	Edgardo Alfonzo	.40
53	Edgar Martinez	.40
54	Magglio Ordonez	.60
55	Kerry Wood	1.25
56	Adrian Beltre	.75
57	Lance Berkman	.40
58	Kevin Brown	.40
59	Sean Casey	.60
60	Eric Chavez	.60
61	Bartolo Colon	.40
62	Johnny Damon	.60
63	Jermaine Dye	.40
64	Juan Encarnacion	.40
65	Carl Everett	.40
66	Brian Giles	.40
67	Mike Hampton	.40
68	Richard Hidalgo	.40
69	Geoff Jenkins	.40
70	Jacque Jones	.40
71	Jason Kendall	.40
72	Ryan Klesko	.40
73	Chan Ho Park	.40
74	Richie Sexson	.40
75	Mike Sweeney	.40
76	Fernando Tatis	.40
77	Miguel Tejada	.60
78	Jose Vidro	.40
79	Larry Walker	.40
80	Preston Wilson	.40
81	Craig Biggio	.40
82	Fred McGriff	.40
83	Jim Thome	1.50
84	Garret Anderson	.40
85	Russell Branyan	.40
86	Tony Batista	.40
87	Terrence Long	.40
88	Deion Sanders	.40
89	Rusty Greer	.40
90	Orlando Hernandez	.40
91	Gabe Kapler	.40
92	Paul Konerko	.40
93	Carlos Lee	.40
94	Kenny Lofton	.40
95	Raul Mondesi	.40
96	Jorge Posada	.60
97	Tim Salmon	.40
98	Greg Vaughn	.40
99	Mo Vaughn	.40
100	Omar Vizquel	.40

101	Ray Durham	.40
102	Jeff Cirillo	.40
103	Dean Palmer	.40
104	Ryan Dempster	.40
105	Carlos Beltran	.40
106	Timo Perez	.40
107	Robin Ventura	.40
108	Andy Pettitte	.60
109	Aramis Ramirez	.40
110	Phil Nevin	.40
111	Alex Escobar	10.00
112	Johnny Estrada RC	20.00
113	Pedro Feliz	10.00
114	Nate Frese RC	10.00
115	Joe Kennedy RC	10.00
116	Brandon Larson RC	10.00
117	Alexis Gomez RC	10.00
118	Jason Hart	10.00
119	Jason Michaels RC	10.00
120	Marcus Giles	10.00
121	Christian Parker RC	10.00
122	Jackson Melian RC	10.00
123	Donaldo Mendez RC	10.00
124	Adrian Hernandez RC	10.00
125	Bud Smith RC	10.00
126	Jose Mieses RC	10.00
127	Roy Oswalt	10.00
128	Eric Munson	10.00
129	Xavier Nady	10.00
130	Horacio Ramirez	20.00
131	Abraham Nunez	10.00
132	Jose Ortiz	10.00
133	Jeremy Owens RC	10.00
134	Claudio Vargas RC	10.00
135	Ricardo Rodriguez RC	10.00
136	Aubrey Huff	10.00
137	Ben Sheets	10.00
138	Adam Dunn	10.00
139	Andres Torres RC	10.00
140	Elpidio Guzman RC	20.00
141	Jay Gibbons RC	10.00
142	Wilkin Ruan RC	10.00
143	Tsuyoshi Shinjo RC	10.00
144	Alfonso Soriano	15.00
145	Josh Towers RC	10.00
146	Ichiro Suzuki RC	140.00
147	Juan Uribe RC	15.00
148	Joe Crede	10.00
149	Carlos Valderrama RC	10.00
150	Matt White RC	10.00
151	Dee Brown	10.00
152	Juan Cruz RC	10.00
153	Cory Aldridge RC	10.00
154	Wilmy Caceres	10.00
155	Josh Beckett	10.00
156	Wilson Betemit RC	10.00
157	Corey Patterson	10.00
158	Albert Pujols RC	220.00
159	Rafael Soriano RC	10.00
160	Jack Wilson RC	20.00

Mirror Red/Gold

	NM/M
Common Mirror Red (1-110):	2.00
Stars (1-110):	3-5X
Common Mirror Red (111-160):	6.00
Stars (111-160):	1-2X
Production 75	
Mirror Gold:	6-8X
Production 25	

(See 2001 Leaf Certified Materials for checklist and base card values.)

Fabric of the Game

		NM/M
Common Player:		5.00
1	Lou Gehrig/184	200.00
1	Lou Gehrig/23	375.00

FABRIC of the GAME CAREER
RAUL MONDESI
BLUE JAYS • OUTFIELD
STAR MATERIAL

2	Babe Ruth/136	250.00
2	Babe Ruth/60	400.00
3	Stan Musial/177	40.00
3	Stan Musial/39	100.00
4	Nolan Ryan	40.00
4	Nolan Ryan/61	60.00
4	Nolan Ryan/34	80.00
5	Roberto Clemente/166	100.00
5	Roberto Clemente/29	250.00
6	Al Kaline/137	25.00
7	Brooks Robinson	20.00
7	Brooks Robinson/68	30.00
8	Mel Ott	30.00
8	Mel Ott/72	50.00
9	Dave Winfield/88	15.00
10	Eddie Mathews/115	25.00
10	Eddie Mathews/72	40.00
11	Ernie Banks/50	40.00
11	Ernie Banks/47	40.00
12	Frank Robinson	15.00
13	George Brett/137	40.00
14	Hank Aaron	40.00
14	Hank Aaron/98	50.00
14	Hank Aaron/47	100.00
15	Harmon Killebrew	25.00
15	Harmon Killebrew/49	50.00
16	Joe Morgan	10.00
16	Joe Morgan/96	15.00
17	Johnny Bench	20.00
17	Johnny Bench/88	30.00
18	Kirby Puckett/134	40.00
19	Mike Schmidt	40.00
19	Mike Schmidt/59	60.00
20	Phil Rizzuto/149	15.00
21	Reggie Jackson	15.00
21	Reggie Jackson/44	30.00
22	Catfish Hunter	15.00
22	Catfish Hunter/42	25.00
23	Rod Carew/92	20.00
23	Rod Carew/100	20.00
24	Bob Feller	15.00
24	Bob Feller/44	30.00
25	Lou Brock	10.00
25	Lou Brock/141	15.00
26	Tom Seaver	15.00
26	Tom Seaver/61	30.00
27	Paul Molitor	15.00
27	Paul Molitor/114	25.00
27		40.00
28	Willie McCovey/126	15.00
29	Yogi Berra	20.00
29	Yogi Berra/49	40.00
30	Don Drysdale	15.00
30	Don Drysdale/49	30.00
31	Duke Snider	20.00
31	Duke Snider/99	30.00
33	Orlando Cepeda/46	20.00
34	Casey Stengel	10.00
34	Casey Stengel/103	15.00
35	Robin Yount	20.00
35	Robin Yount/126	40.00
36	Eddie Murray	15.00
36	Eddie Murray/35	40.00
37	Jim Palmer	10.00
38	Juan Marichal	10.00
38	Juan Marichal/52	20.00
39	Willie Stargell	15.00
39	Willie Stargell/55	20.00
40	Ted Williams	150.00
40	Ted Williams/71	100.00
40	Ted Williams/43	150.00
41	Cal Ripken Jr.	30.00
41	Cal Ripken/75	50.00
41	Cal Ripken/277	40.00
42	Vladimir Guerrero/322	15.00
42	Vladimir Guerrero/44	25.00
43	Greg Maddux	15.00
43	Greg Maddux/240	20.00
44	Barry Bonds	30.00
44	Barry Bonds/49	75.00

44	Barry Bonds/289	30.00
45	Pedro Martinez	15.00
45	Pedro Martinez/268	15.00
46	Ivan Rodriguez	10.00
46	Ivan Rodriguez/304	15.00
47	Roger Maris	50.00
47	Roger Maris/275	50.00
48	Randy Johnson	15.00
48	Randy Johnson/179	20.00
49	Roger Clemens	20.00
49	Roger Clemens/260	20.00
50	Todd Helton	10.00
50	Todd Helton/334	15.00
51	Tony Gwynn	15.00
51	Tony Gwynn/119	20.00
51	Tony Gwynn/134	20.00
52	Troy Glaus	8.00
52	Troy Glaus/47	15.00
52	Troy Glaus/256	8.00
53	Phil Niekro	8.00
53	Phil Niekro/245	10.00
54	Don Sutton	8.00
54	Don Sutton/178	10.00
55	Frank Thomas	10.00
55	Frank Thomas/321	15.00
56	Jeff Bagwell	10.00
56	Jeff Bagwell/305	15.00
57	Rickey Henderson	15.00
57	Rickey Henderson/282	15.00
58	Darin Erstad/301	8.00
59	Andruw Jones	10.00
59	Andruw Jones/272	10.00
60	Roberto Alomar	10.00
60	Roberto Alomar/120	15.00
60	Roberto Alomar/170	15.00
61	Mike Piazza	20.00
61	Mike Piazza/328	20.00
62	Chipper Jones	10.00
62	Chipper Jones/189	15.00
63	Shawn Green	8.00
63	Shawn Green/143	8.00
64	Don Mattingly	50.00
64	Don Mattingly/145	50.00
64	Don Mattingly/222	40.00
65	Rafael Palmeiro	10.00
66	Wade Boggs	10.00
66	Wade Boggs/116	15.00
66	Wade Boggs/89	20.00
67	Hoyt Wilhelm	8.00
67	Hoyt Wilhelm/143	10.00
68	Andre Dawson	8.00
68	Andre Dawson/49	15.00
68	Andre Dawson/314	10.00
69	Ryne Sandberg	30.00
69	Ryne Sandberg/282	35.00
70	Nomar Garciaparra/333	25.00
71	Tom Glavine	8.00
71	Tom Glavine/208	10.00
71	Tom Glavine/247	10.00
72	Magglio Ordonez	8.00
72	Magglio Ordonez/301	8.00
72	Magglio Ordonez/126	10.00
73	Bernie Williams	10.00
73	Bernie Williams/304	15.00
74	Jim Edmonds	8.00
74	Jim Edmonds/108	10.00
74	Jim Edmonds/291	10.00
75	Hideo Nomo	20.00
75	Hideo Nomo/69	30.00
76	Barry Larkin	10.00
76	Barry Larkin/300	10.00
77	Scott Rolen	10.00
77	Scott Rolen/284	10.00
78	Miguel Tejada	8.00
78	Miguel Tejada/253	8.00
79	Freddy Garcia	5.00
79	Freddy Garcia/170	5.00
79	Freddy Garcia/249	5.00
80	Edgar Martinez	10.00
80	Edgar Martinez/320	10.00
81	Edgardo Alfonzo	5.00
81	Edgardo Alfonzo/108	5.00
81	Edgardo Alfonzo/296	5.00
82	Steve Garvey	8.00
82	Steve Garvey/272	8.00
83	Larry Walker	5.00
83	Larry Walker/311	5.00
83	Larry Walker/49	10.00
84	A.J. Burnett	5.00
84	A.J. Burnett/90	8.00
85	Richie Sexson	8.00
85	Richie Sexson/242	8.00
85	Richie Sexson/116	8.00
86	Mark Mulder	8.00
86	Mark Mulder/88	10.00
87	Kerry Wood	10.00
87	Kerry Wood/233	10.00
88	Sean Casey	5.00
88	Sean Casey/312	5.00
89	Jermaine Dye	5.00
89	Jermaine Dye/118	5.00
89	Jermaine Dye/286	5.00

90	Kevin Brown	5.00
90	Kevin Brown/170	5.00
90	Kevin Brown/257	5.00
91	Craig Biggio	5.00
91	Craig Biggio/88	8.00
91	Craig Biggio/291	5.00
92	Mike Sweeney	5.00
92	Mike Sweeney/302	5.00
92	Mike Sweeney/144	5.00
93	Jim Thome	10.00
93	Jim Thome/233	10.00
93	Jim Thome/40	20.00
94	Al Leiter	5.00
94	Al Leiter/247	5.00
94	Al Leiter/106	5.00
95	Barry Zito	8.00
95	Barry Zito/272	8.00
95	Barry Zito/78	15.00
96	Rafael Furcal	5.00
96	Rafael Furcal/295	5.00
97	J.D. Drew	5.00
97	J.D. Drew/276	5.00
98	Andres Galarraga	5.00
98	Andres Galarraga/150	5.00
98	Andres Galarraga/291	5.00
99	Kazuhiro Sasaki	5.00
99	Kazuhiro Sasaki/266	5.00
100	Chan Ho Park	5.00
100	Chan Ho Park/65	5.00
100	Chan Ho Park/217	5.00
101	Eric Milton	5.00
101	Eric Milton/163	5.00
102	Carlos Lee	5.00
102	Carlos Lee/297	5.00
103	Preston Wilson	5.00
103	Preston Wilson/266	5.00
104	Adrian Beltre	5.00
104	Adrian Beltre/85	5.00
104	Adrian Beltre/272	5.00
105	Luis Gonzalez	5.00
105	Luis Gonzalez/281	5.00
105	Luis Gonzalez/114	5.00
106	Kenny Lofton	5.00
106	Kenny Lofton/306	5.00
107	Shannon Stewart	5.00
107	Shannon Stewart/297	5.00
108	Javy Lopez	5.00
108	Javy Lopez/290	5.00
108	Javy Lopez/106	5.00
109	Raul Mondesi	5.00
109	Raul Mondesi/286	5.00
110	Mark Grace	10.00
110	Mark Grace/51	20.00
110	Mark Grace/308	15.00
111	Curt Schilling	8.00
111	Curt Schilling/235	8.00
111	Curt Schilling/110	10.00
112	Cliff Floyd	5.00
112	Cliff Floyd/275	5.00
113	Moises Alou	5.00
113	Moises Alou/124	5.00
113	Moises Alou/303	5.00
114	Aaron Sele	5.00
114	Aaron Sele/92	5.00
115	Jose Cruz Jr.	5.00
115	Jose Cruz Jr/245	5.00
116	John Olerud	5.00
116	John Olerud/186	5.00
116	John Olerud/107	5.00
117	Jose Vidro	5.00
117	Jose Vidro/296	5.00
118	John Smoltz	5.00
118	John Smoltz/334	5.00

2001 Leaf Limited

ROOKIE
Brandon Berger • OF
KANSAS CITY ROYALS

NM/M

Complete Set (375):	
Common Player:	.75
Common Lumberjack (151-200):	5.00
#'d to 100, 250 or 500	
Common Rk (201-300):	5.00

Production 1,500		
Common Auto. (301-325):	10.00	
Production 1,000		
Pack (3):	10.00	
Box (18):	140.00	
1	Curt Schilling	1.00
2	Craig Biggio	.75
3	Brian Giles	.75
4	Scott Brosius	.75
5	Barry Larkin	.75
6	Bartolo Colon	.75
7	John Olerud	.75
8	Cal Ripken Jr.	6.00
9	Moises Alou	.75
10	Barry Zito	.75
11	Ken Griffey Jr.	4.00
12	Garret Anderson	.75
13	Andy Pettitte	1.00
14	Jim Edmonds	1.00
15	Tom Glavine	1.00
16	Jose Canseco	1.00
17	Fred McGriff	.75
18	Robin Ventura	.75
19	Tony Gwynn	3.00
20	Jeff Cirillo	.75
21	Brad Radke	.75
22	Ellis Burks	.75
23	Scott Rolen	1.50
24	Rickey Henderson	2.00
25	Edgar Martinez	.75
26	Kerry Wood	1.50
27	Al Leiter	.75
28	Jose Cruz Jr.	.75
29	Sean Casey	.75
30	Eric Chavez	.75
31	Jarrod Washburn	.75
32	Gary Sheffield	1.00
33	Jermaine Dye	.75
34	Bernie Williams	1.00
35	Tony Armas Jr.	.75
36	Carlos Beltran	1.50
37	Geoff Jenkins	.75
38	Shawn Green	1.50
39	Ryan Klesko	.75
40	Richie Sexson	.75
41	Pat Burrell	1.00
42	J.D. Drew	1.00
43	Larry Walker	.75
44	Andres Galarraga	.75
45	Tino Martinez	.75
46	Rafael Furcal	.75
47	Cristian Guzman	.75
48	Omar Vizquel	.75
49	Bret Boone	.75
50	Wade Miller	.75
51	Eric Milton	.75
52	Gabe Kapler	.75
53	Johnny Damon	.75
54	Shannon Stewart	.75
55	Kenny Lofton	.75
56	Raul Mondesi	.75
57	Jorge Posada	1.00
58	Mark Grace	1.00
59	Robert Fick	.75
60	Phil Nevin	.75
61	Mike Mussina	1.00
62	Joe Mays	.75
63	Todd Helton	2.00
64	Tim Hudson	1.00
65	Manny Ramirez	2.00
66	Sammy Sosa	4.00
67	Darin Erstad	1.00
68	Roberto Alomar	1.00
69	Jeff Bagwell	2.00
70	Mark McGwire	5.00
71	Jason Giambi	1.50
72	Cliff Floyd	.75
73	Barry Bonds	6.00
74	Juan Gonzalez	2.00
75	Jeremy Giambi	.75
76	Carlos Lee	.75
77	Randy Johnson	2.00
78	Frank Thomas	2.00
79	Carlos Delgado	1.00
80	Pedro Martinez	2.00
81	Rusty Greer	.75
82	Brian Jordan	.75
83	Vladimir Guerrero	2.00
84	Mike Sweeney	.75
85	Jose Vidro	.75
86	Paul LoDuca	.75
87	Matt Morris	.75
88	Adrian Beltre	.75
89	Aramis Ramirez	.75
90	Derek Jeter	6.00
91	Rich Aurilia	.75
92	Freddy Garcia	.75
93	Preston Wilson	.75
94	Greg Maddux	3.00
95	Miguel Tejada	1.00
96	Luis Gonzalez	.75
97	Torii Hunter	.75
98	Nomar Garciaparra	4.00
99	Jamie Moyer	.75

100	Javier Vazquez	.75
101	Ben Grieve	.75
102	Mike Piazza	4.00
103	Paul O'Neill	.75
104	Terrence Long	.75
105	Charles Johnson	.75
106	Rafael Palmeiro	1.50
107	David Cone	.75
108	Alex Rodriguez	5.00
109	John Burkett	.75
110	Chipper Jones	3.00
111	Ryan Dempster	.75
112	Bobby Abreu	.75
113	Brad Fullmer	.75
114	Kazuhiro Sasaki	.75
115	Mariano Rivera	1.00
116	Edgardo Alfonzo	.75
117	Ray Durham	.75
118	Richard Hidalgo	.75
119	Jeff Weaver	.75
120	Paul Konerko	.75
121	Jon Lieber	.75
122	Mike Hampton	.75
123	Mike Cameron	.75
124	Kevin Brown	.75
125	Doug Mientkiewicz	.75
126	Jim Thome	.75
127	Corey Koskie	.75
128	Trot Nixon	.75
129	Darryl Kile	.75
130	Ivan Rodriguez	1.50
131	Carl Everett	.75
132	Jeff Kent	.75
133	Rondell White	.75
134	Chan Ho Park	.75
135	Robert Person	.75
136	Troy Glaus	2.00
137	Aaron Sele	.75
138	Roger Clemens	3.50
139	Tony Clark	.75
140	Mark Buehrle	.75
141	David Justice	.75
142	Magglio Ordonez	.75
143	Bobby Higginson	.75
144	Hideo Nomo	2.00
145	Tim Salmon	.75
146	Mark Mulder	.75
147	Troy Percival	.75
148	Lance Berkman	.75
149	Russ Ortiz	.75
150	Andruw Jones	2.00
151	Mike Piazza	25.00
152	Manny Ramirez	8.00
153	Bernie Williams	6.00
154	Nomar Garciaparra	25.00
155	Andres Galarraga	5.00
156	Kenny Lofton	5.00
157	Scott Rolen	8.00
158	Jim Thome	6.00
159	Darin Erstad	5.00
160	Garret Anderson	5.00
161	Andruw Jones	8.00
162	Juan Gonzalez	8.00
163	Rafael Palmeiro	8.00
164	Magglio Ordonez	5.00
165	Jeff Bagwell	8.00
166	Eric Chavez	5.00
167	Brian Giles	5.00
168	Adrian Beltre	5.00
169	Tony Gwynn	15.00
170	Shawn Green	5.00
171	Todd Helton	8.00
172	Troy Glaus	8.00
173	Lance Berkman	5.00
174	Ivan Rodriguez	8.00
175	Sean Casey	5.00
176	Aramis Ramirez	5.00
177	J.D. Drew	5.00
178	Barry Bonds	40.00
179	Barry Larkin	5.00
180	Cal Ripken Jr.	40.00
181	Frank Thomas	8.00
182	Craig Biggio	5.00
183	Carlos Lee	5.00
184	Chipper Jones	10.00
185	Miguel Tejada	6.00
186	Jose Vidro	5.00
187	Terrence Long	5.00
188	Moises Alou	5.00
189	Trot Nixon	5.00
190	Shannon Stewart	5.00
191	Ryan Klesko	5.00
192	Carlos Beltran	7.00
193	Vladimir Guerrero	8.00
194	Edgar Martinez	5.00
195	Luis Gonzalez	5.00
196	Richard Hidalgo	5.00
197	Roberto Alomar	6.00
198	Mike Sweeney	5.00
199	Bobby Abreu	5.00
200	Cliff Floyd	5.00
201	Jackson Melian RC	5.00
202	Jason Jennings	5.00
203	Toby Hall	5.00
204	Jason Karnuth RC	5.00
205	Jason Smith RC	5.00
206	Mike Maroth RC	5.00
207	Sean Douglass RC	5.00
208	Adam Johnson	5.00
209	Luke Hudson RC	5.00
210	Nick Maness RC	5.00
211	Les Walrond RC	5.00
212	Travis Phelps RC	5.00
213	Carlos Garcia RC	5.00
214	Bill Ortega	5.00
215	Gene Altman RC	5.00
216	Nate Frese	5.00
217	Bob File RC	5.00
218	Steve Green RC	5.00
219	Kris Keller RC	5.00
220	Matt White RC	5.00
221	Nate Teut RC	5.00
222	Nick Johnson	5.00
223	Jeremy Fikac RC	5.00
224	Abraham Nunez	5.00
225	Mike Penney RC	5.00
226	Roy Smith RC	5.00
227	Tim Christman RC	5.00
228	Carlos Pena	5.00
229	Joe Beimel RC	5.00
230	Mike Koplove RC	5.00
231	Scott MacRae RC	5.00
232	Kyle Lohse RC	10.00
233	Jerrod Riggan RC	5.00
234	Scott Podsednik RC	12.00
235	Winston Abreu RC	5.00
236	Ryan Freel RC	5.00
237	Ken Vining RC	5.00
238	Bret Prinz RC	5.00
239	Paul Phillips RC	5.00
240	Josh Fogg RC	5.00
241	Saul Rivera RC	5.00
242	Esix Snead RC	5.00
243	John Grabow RC	5.00
244	Tony Cogan RC	5.00
245	Pedro Santana RC	5.00
246	Jack Cust	5.00
247	Joe Crede RC	5.00
248	Juan Moreno RC	5.00
249	Kevin Joseph RC	5.00
250	Scott Stewart RC	5.00
251	Rob Mackowiak RC	5.00
252	Luis Pineda RC	5.00
253	Bert Snow RC	5.00
254	Dustan Mohr RC	5.00
255	Justin Kaye RC	5.00
256	Chad Paronto RC	5.00
257	Nick Punto RC	5.00
258	Brian Roberts RC	15.00
259	Eric Hinske RC	8.00
260	Victor Zambrano RC	5.00
261	Juan Pena	5.00
262	Rick Bauer RC	5.00
263	Jorge Julio RC	5.00
264	Craig Monroe RC	5.00
265	Stubby Clapp RC	5.00
266	Martin Vargas RC	5.00
267	Josue Perez RC	5.00
268	Cody Ransom RC	5.00
269	Will Ohman RC	5.00
270	Juan Diaz RC	5.00
271	Ramon Vazquez RC	5.00
272	Grant Balfour RC	5.00
273	Ryan Jensen RC	5.00
274	Benito Baez RC	5.00
275	Angel Santos RC	5.00
276	Brian Reith RC	5.00
277	Brandon Lyon RC	5.00
278	Erik Hiljus RC	5.00
279	Brandon Knight RC	5.00
280	Jose Acevedo RC	5.00
281	Cesar Crespo RC	5.00
282	Kevin Olsen RC	5.00
283	Duaner Sanchez RC	5.00
284	Endy Chavez RC	5.00
285	Blaine Neal RC	5.00
286	Brett Jodie RC	5.00
287	Brad Voyles RC	5.00
288	Doug Nickle RC	5.00
289	Junior Spivey RC	8.00
290	Henry Mateo RC	5.00
291	Xavier Nady RC	5.00
292	Lance Davis RC	5.00
293	Willie Harris RC	5.00
294	Mark Lukasiewicz RC	5.00
295	Ryan Drese RC	5.00
296	Morgan Ensberg RC	10.00
297	Jose Mieses RC	5.00
298	Jason Michaels RC	5.00
299	Kris Foster RC	5.00
300	Justin Duchscherer RC	5.00
301	Elpidio Guzman RC	5.00
302	Cory Aldridge RC	8.00
303	Angel Berroa RC	15.00
304	Travis Hafner RC	125.00
305	Horacio Ramirez RC	15.00
306	Juan Uribe RC	10.00
307	Mark Prior RC	80.00
308	Brandon Larson RC	10.00
309	Nick Neugebauer RC	10.00
310	Zach Day RC	10.00
311	Jeremy Owens RC	10.00
312	Dewon Brazelton RC	10.00
313	Brandon Duckworth RC	10.00
314	Adrian Hernandez RC	10.00
315	Mark Teixeira RC	160.00
316	Brian Rogers RC	10.00
317	David Brous RC	10.00
318	Geronimo Gil RC	10.00
319	Erick Almonte RC	10.00
320	Claudio Vargas RC	10.00
321	Wilkin Ruan RC	10.00
322	David Williams RC	10.00
323	Alexis Gomez RC	10.00
324	Mike Rivera RC	10.00
325	Brandon Berger RC	10.00
326	Keith Ginter	10.00
327	Brandon Inge/700	10.00
328	Brent Abernathy/700	10.00
329	Billy Sylvester/700 RC	10.00
330	Bart Miadich/500 RC	10.00
331	Tsuyoshi Shinjo/500 RC	15.00
332	Eric Valent	10.00
333	Dee Brown/500	10.00
334	Andres Torres/125 RC	10.00
335	Timo Perez/700	10.00
336	Cesar Izturis/650	10.00
337	Pedro Feliz	10.00
338	Jason Hart/200	10.00
339	Greg Miller/700 RC	10.00
340	Eric Munson/700	10.00
341	Aubrey Huff/450	10.00
342	Wilmy Caceres/700 RC	10.00
343	Alex Escobar/650	10.00
344	Brian Lawrence/700 RC	10.00
345	Adam Pettyjohn/650 RC	10.00
346	Donaldo Mendez/700 RC	10.00
347	Carlos Valderrama RC	10.00
348	Christian Parker/650 RC	10.00
349	Corky Miller/500 RC	10.00
350	Michael Cuddyer/500	10.00
351	Adam Dunn/500	20.00
352	Josh Beckett/650	10.00
353	Juan Cruz/500 RC	10.00
354	Ben Sheets/400	10.00
355	Roy Oswalt/100	15.00
356	Rafael Soriano/650 RC	10.00
357	Ricardo Rodriguez/650 RC	10.00
358	Jimmy Rollins/300	10.00
359	C.C. Sabathia	10.00
360	Bud Smith/500 RC	10.00
361	Jose Ortiz	10.00
362	Marcus Giles/400	10.00
363	Jack Wilson RC	20.00
364	Wilson Betemit/100 RC	10.00
365	Corey Patterson/650	10.00
366	Jay Gibbons/Spikes/125 RC	35.00
367	Albert Pujols/250 RC	300.00
368	Joe Kennedy RC	10.00
369	Alfonso Soriano/Hat/100	40.00
370	Delvin James/650 RC	10.00
371	Josh Towers/500 RC	10.00
372	Jeremy Affeldt/650 RC	10.00
373	Tim Redding/500	10.00
374	Ichiro Suzuki/100 RC	400.00
375	Johnny Estrada/100 RC	30.00

	NM/M
Complete Set (300):	
Common Player:	.15
Common (101-200):	1.50
Inserted 1:4	
Common (201-300):	4.00
Inserted 1:24	
Pack (5):	6.00
Box (24):	125.00
1 Alex Rodriguez	2.50
2 Derek Jeter	3.00
3 Aramis Ramirez	.15
4 Cliff Floyd	.15
5 Nomar Garciaparra	2.00
6 Craig Biggio	.15
7 Ivan Rodriguez	.75
8 Cal Ripken Jr.	3.00
9 Fred McGriff	.15
10 Chipper Jones	1.50
11 Roberto Alomar	.50
12 Moises Alou	.15
13 Freddy Garcia	.15
14 Bobby Abreu	.15
15 Shawn Green	.50
16 Jason Giambi	.50
17 Todd Helton	1.00
18 Robert Fick	.15
19 Tony Gwynn	1.50
20 Luis Gonzalez	.35
21 Sean Casey	.25
22 Roger Clemens	1.75
23 Brian Giles	.15
24 Manny Ramirez	1.00
25 Barry Bonds	3.00
26 Richard Hidalgo	.15
27 Vladimir Guerrero	1.00
28 Kevin Brown	.15
29 Mike Sweeney	.15
30 Ken Griffey Jr.	2.00
31 Mike Piazza	2.00
32 Richie Sexson	.15
33 Matt Morris	.15
34 Jorge Posada	.25
35 Eric Chavez	.25
36 Mark Buehrle	.15
37 Jeff Bagwell	1.00
38 Curt Schilling	.35
39 Bartolo Colon	.15
40 Mark Quinn	.15
41 Tony Clark	.15
42 Brad Radke	.15
43 Gary Sheffield	.35
44 Doug Mientkiewicz	.15
45 Pedro Martinez	1.00
46 Carlos Lee	.15
47 Troy Glaus	1.00
48 Preston Wilson	.15
49 Phil Nevin	.15
50 Chan Ho Park	.15
51 Randy Johnson	1.00
52 Jermaine Dye	.15
53 Terrence Long	.15
54 Joe Mays	.15
55 Scott Rolen	.75
56 Miguel Tejada	.25
57 Jim Thome	.15
58 Jose Vidro	.15
59 Gabe Kapler	.15
60 Darin Erstad	.75
61 Jim Edmonds	.15
62 Jarrod Washburn	.15
63 Tom Glavine	.40
64 Adrian Beltre	.50
65 Sammy Sosa	2.00
66 Juan Gonzalez	1.00
67 Rafael Furcal	.15
68 Mike Mussina	.50
69 Mark McGwire	2.50
70 Ryan Klesko	.15
71 Raul Mondesi	.15
72 Trot Nixon	.15
73 Barry Larkin	.15
74 Rafael Palmeiro	.75
75 Mark Mulder	.25
76 Carlos Delgado	.60
77 Mike Hampton	.15
78 Carl Everett	.15
79 Paul Konerko	.15
80 Larry Walker	.15
81 Kerry Wood	.60
82 Frank Thomas	1.00
83 Andruw Jones	1.00
84 Eric Milton	.15
85 Ben Grieve	.15
86 Carlos Beltran	.50
87 Tim Hudson	.25
88 Hideo Nomo	1.00
89 Greg Maddux	1.50
90 Edgar Martinez	.15
91 Lance Berkman	.15
92 Pat Burrell	.45
93 Jeff Kent	.15
94 Magglio Ordonez	.15
95 Cristian Guzman	.15

2001 Leaf Rookies & Stars

96	Jose Canseco	.30
97	J.D. Drew	.60
98	Bernie Williams	.40
99	Kazuhiro Sasaki	.15
100	Rickey Henderson	1.00
101	Wilson Guzman RC	1.50
102	Nick Neugebauer RC	1.50
103	Lance Davis RC	1.50
104	Felipe Lopez	1.50
105	Toby Hall	1.50
106	Jack Cust	1.50
107	Jason Kamuth	1.50
108	Bart Miadich RC	1.50
109	Brian Roberts RC	10.00
110	Brandon Larson RC	2.00
111	Sean Douglass RC	1.50
112	Joe Crede	1.50
113	Tim Redding	1.50
114	Adam Johnson	1.50
115	Marcus Giles	1.50
116	Jose Ortiz	1.50
117	Jose Mieses RC	1.50
118	Nick Maness RC	1.50
119	Les Walrond RC	1.50
120	Travis Phelps RC	1.50
121	Troy Mattes RC	1.50
122	Carlos Garcia	1.50
123	Bill Ortega	1.50
124	Gene Altman RC	1.50
125	Nate Frese	1.50
126	Alfonso Soriano	1.00
127	Jose Nunez	1.50
128	Bob File RC	1.50
129	Dan Wright	1.50
130	Nick Johnson	1.50
131	Brent Abernathy	1.50
132	Steve Green RC	1.50
133	Billy Sylvester RC	1.50
134	Scott MacRae RC	1.50
135	Kris Keller RC	1.50
136	Scott Stewart RC	1.50
137	Henry Mateo RC	1.50
138	Timoniel Perez	1.50
139	Nate Teut RC	1.50
140	Jason Michaels RC	1.50
141	Junior Spivey RC	4.00
142	Carlos Pena	1.50
143	Wilmy Caceres RC	1.50
144	David Lundquist	1.50
145	Jack Wilson RC	6.00
146	Jeremy Fikac RC	1.50
147	Alex Escobar	1.50
148	Abraham Nunez	1.50
149	Xavier Nady	1.50
150	Michael Cuddyer	1.50
151	Greg Miller RC	1.50
152	Eric Munson	1.50
153	Aubrey Huff	1.50
154	Tim Christman RC	1.50
155	Erick Almonte RC	1.50
156	Mike Penny	1.50
157	Delvin James RC	1.50
158	Ben Sheets	1.50
159	Jason Hart	1.50
160	Jose Acevedo RC	1.50
161	Will Ohman RC	1.50
162	Erik Hiljus RC	1.50
163	Juan Moreno RC	1.50
164	Mike Koplove RC	1.50
165	Pedro Santana RC	1.50
166	Jimmy Rollins	1.50
167	Matt White RC	1.50
168	Cesar Crespo RC	1.50
169	Carlos Hernandez	1.50
170	Chris George	1.50
171	Brad Voyles RC	1.50
172	Luis Pineda RC	1.50
173	Carlos Zambrano	1.50
174	Nate Comejo	.60
175	Jason Smith RC	1.50
176	Craig Monroe RC	.15
177	Cody Ransom RC	1.50
178	John Grabow RC	1.50
179	Pedro Feliz	1.50
180	Jeremy Owens RC	1.50
181	Kurt Ainsworth	1.50
182	Luis Lopez	1.50
183	Stubby Clapp RC	1.50
184	Ryan Freel RC	1.50
185	Duaner Sanchez RC	1.50
186	Jason Jennings	1.50
187	Kyle Lohse RC	3.00
188	Jerrod Riggan RC	1.50
189	Joe Beimel RC	1.50
190	Nick Punto RC	1.50
191	Willie Harris RC	1.50
192	Ryan Jensen RC	1.50
193	Adam Pettyjohn RC	1.50
194	Donaldo Mendez RC	1.50
195	Bret Prinz RC	1.50
196	Paul Phillips RC	1.50
197	Brian Lawrence RC	2.00
198	Cesar Izturis	1.50
199	Blaine Neal RC	1.50

200	Josh Fogg RC	1.50
201	Josh Towers RC	4.00
202	Tim Spooneybarger RC	4.00
203	Mike Rivera RC	4.00
204	Juan Cruz RC	4.00
205	Albert Pujols RC	220.00
206	Josh Beckett RC	4.00
207	Roy Oswalt RC	4.00
208	Elpidio Guzman RC	4.00
209	Horacio Ramirez RC	8.00
210	Corey Patterson RC	4.00
211	Geronimo Gil RC	4.00
212	Jay Gibbons RC	10.00
213	Orlando Woodwards RC	4.00
214	David Espinosa RC	4.00
215	Angel Berroa RC	4.00
216	Brandon Duckworth RC	4.00
217	Brian Reith RC	4.00
218	David Brous RC	4.00
219	Bud Smith RC	4.00
220	Ramon Vazquez RC	4.00
221	Mark Teixeira RC	35.00
222	Justin Atchley RC	4.00
223	Tony Cogan RC	4.00
224	Grant Balfour RC	4.00
225	Ricardo Rodriguez RC	4.00
226	Brian Rogers RC	4.00
227	Adam Dunn RC	4.00
228	Wilson Betemit RC	4.00
229	Juan Diaz RC	4.00
230	Jackson Melian RC	4.00
231	Claudio Vargas RC	4.00
232	Wilkin Ruan RC	4.00
233	Justin Duchscherer RC	4.00
234	Kevin Olsen RC	4.00
235	Tony Fiore	4.00
236	Jeremy Affeldt RC	4.00
237	Mike Maroth RC	4.00
238	C.C. Sabathia	4.00
239	Cory Aldridge RC	4.00
240	Zach Day RC	6.00
241	Brett Jodie RC	4.00
242	Winston Abreu RC	4.00
243	Travis Hafner RC	20.00
244	Joe Kennedy RC	4.00
245	Rick Bauer RC	4.00
246	Mike Young	8.00
247	Ken Vining RC	4.00
248	Doug Nickle RC	4.00
249	Pablo Ozuno	4.00
250	Dustan Mohr RC	4.00
251	Ichiro Suzuki RC	50.00
252	Ryan Drese RC	4.00
253	Morgan Ensberg RC	10.00
254	George Perez RC	4.00
255	Roy Smith RC	4.00
256	Juan Uribe RC	6.00
257	Dewon Brazelton RC	4.00
258	Endy Chavez RC	4.00
259	Kris Foster RC	4.00
260	Eric Knott RC	4.00
261	Corky Miller RC	4.00
262	Larry Bigbie	4.00
263	Andres Torres RC	4.00
264	Adrian Hernandez RC	4.00
265	Johnny Estrada RC	6.00
266	David Williams RC	4.00
267	Steve Lomasney	4.00
268	Victor Zambrano RC	6.00
269	Keith Ginter	4.00
270	Casey Fossum RC	6.00
271	Josue Perez RC	4.00
272	Josh Phelps	4.00
273	Mark Prior RC	25.00
274	Brandon Berger RC	4.00
275	Scott Podsednik RC	10.00
276	Jorge Julio RC	6.00
277	Esix Snead RC	4.00
278	Brandon Knight RC	4.00
279	Saul Rivera RC	4.00
280	Benito Baez RC	4.00
281	Robert Mackowiak RC	4.00
282	Eric Hinske RC	8.00
283	Juan Rivera RC	4.00
284	Kevin Joseph RC	4.00
285	Juan Pena	4.00
286	Brandon Lyon RC	4.00
287	Adam Everett RC	4.00
288	Eric Valent RC	4.00
289	Ken Harvey RC	4.00
290	Bert Snow RC	4.00
291	Wily Mo Pena	4.00
292	Rafael Soriano RC	4.00
293	Carlos Valderrama RC	4.00
294	Christian Parker RC	4.00
295	Tsuyoshi Shinjo RC	4.00
296	Martin Vargas RC	4.00
297	Luke Hudson RC	4.00
298	Dee Brown	4.00
299	Alexis Gomez RC	4.00
300	Angel Santos RC	4.00

Longevity

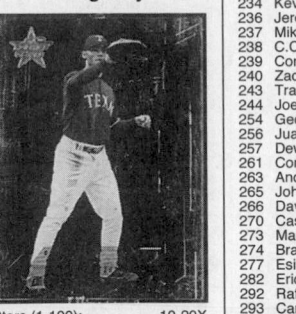

Stars (1-100): 10-20X
Production 50
#'s 101-300 Production 25

Autographs

		NM/M
	Common Player:	8.00
107	Jason Karnuth	8.00
110	Brandon Larson/100	10.00
117	Jose Mieses	8.00
118	Nick Maness	8.00
119	Les Walrond	8.00
122	Carlos Garcia	8.00
123	Bill Ortega	8.00
124	Gene Altman	8.00
125	Nate Frese	8.00
130	Nick Johnson/100	15.00
133	Billy Sylvester	8.00
135	Kris Keller	8.00
139	Nate Teut	8.00
140	Jason Michaels	8.00
143	Wilmy Caceres	8.00
145	Jack Wilson/100	25.00
151	Greg Miller	8.00
155	Erick Almonte	8.00
156	Mike Penney	8.00
157	Delvin James	8.00
161	Will Ohman	8.00
167	Matt White	8.00
180	Jeremy Owens	8.00
184	Ryan Freel	10.00
185	Duaner Sanchez	8.00
193	Adam Pettyjohn/100	8.00
194	Donaldo Mendez/100	10.00
196	Paul Phillips	8.00
197	Brian Lawrence/100	15.00
199	Blaine Neal	8.00
201	Josh Towers/100	15.00
203	Michael Rivera	8.00
204	Juan Cruz/100	10.00
205	Albert Pujols/50	
207	Roy Oswalt/50	50.00
208	Elpidio Guzman/100	8.00
209	Horacio Ramirez	15.00
210	Corey Patterson/SP	25.00
211	Geronimo Gil	8.00
212	Jay Gibbons/100	25.00
213	Orlando Woodwards	8.00
215	Angel Berroa/100	25.00
216	Brandon Duckworth/100	10.00
218	David Brous	8.00
219	Bud Smith/50	10.00
221	Mark Teixeira/100	250.00
223	Tony Cogan	8.00
225	Ricardo Rodriguez	8.00
226	Brian Rogers	8.00
227	Adam Dunn/50	50.00
228	Wilson Betemit/100	30.00
231	Claudio Vargas	8.00
232	Wilkin Ruan	8.00
234	Kevin Olsen	8.00
236	Jeremy Affeldt	10.00
237	Mike Maroth	8.00
238	C.C. Sabathia/50	25.00
239	Cory Aldridge	8.00
240	Zach Day	10.00
243	Travis Hafner	100.00
244	Joe Kennedy/100	15.00
254	George Perez	8.00
256	Juan Uribe	10.00
257	Dewon Brazelton/100	10.00
261	Corky Miller/100	8.00
263	Andres Torres/100	8.00
265	Johnny Estrada/100	15.00
266	David Williams	10.00
270	Casey Fossum	8.00
273	Mark Prior/100	150.00
274	Brandon Berger	8.00
277	Esix Snead	8.00
282	Eric Hinske	15.00
292	Rafael Soriano	10.00
293	Carlos Valderrama	8.00
299	Alexis Gomez	8.00

Dress For Success

		NM/M
	Common Player:	8.00
	Inserted 1:96	
	Prime Cuts:	2X
	Numbered to 50 each.	
1	Cal Ripken Jr.	40.00
2	Mike Piazza	35.00
3	Barry Bonds	40.00
4	Frank Thomas	20.00
5	Nomar Garciaparra	35.00
6	Richie Sexson	8.00
7	Brian Giles	8.00
8	Todd Helton	20.00
9	Ivan Rodriguez	15.00
10	Andruw Jones	20.00
11	Juan Gonzalez	20.00
12	Vladimir Guerrero	20.00
13	Greg Maddux	25.00
14	Tony Gwynn	25.00
15	Randy Johnson	20.00
16	Jeff Bagwell	20.00
17	Kerry Wood	15.00
18	Roberto Alomar	8.00
19	Chipper Jones	25.00
20	Pedro Martinez	20.00
21	Shawn Green	10.00
22	Magglio Ordonez	10.00
23	Darin Erstad	12.00
24	Rafael Palmeiro	15.00
25	Edgar Martinez	8.00

Dress For Success Autographs

Values Undetermined

Freshman Orientation

		NM/M
	Common Player:	8.00
	Inserted 1:96	
	Class Officers:	2X
	Numbered to 50 each.	
1	Adam Dunn	15.00
2	Josh Towers	8.00
3	Vernon Wells	10.00

4	Corey Patterson	10.00
5	Albert Pujols	
6	Ben Sheets	8.00
7	Pedro Feliz	8.00
8	Keith Ginter	8.00
9	Luis Rivas	8.00
10	Andres Torres	8.00
11	Carlos Valderrama	8.00
12	Brandon Inge	8.00
13	Jay Gibbons	15.00
14	Cesar Izturis	8.00
15	Marcus Giles	8.00
16	Tsuyoshi Shinjo	12.00
17	Eric Valent	8.00
18	David Espinosa	8.00
19	Aubrey Huff	8.00
20	Wilmy Caceres	8.00
21	Bud Smith	8.00
22	Ricardo Rodriguez	8.00
23	Wes Helms	8.00
24	Jason Hart	8.00
25	Dee Brown	8.00

Freshman Orientation Autograph

Values Undetermined

Great American Treasures

NM/M

Inserted 1:1,120

1	Barry Bonds/Jsy	100.00
2	Magglio Ordonez/Bat	40.00
3	Derek Jeter/Bat	150.00
4	Nolan Ryan/Ball	600.00
5	Sammy Sosa/Ball	125.00
6	Tom Glavine/Jsy	50.00
7	Ivan Rodriguez/Bat	30.00
8	Pedro Martinez/Ball	100.00
9	Mark McGwire/Ball	250.00
10	Ted Williams/Ball	350.00
11	Ryne Sandberg/Ball	60.00
12	Barry Bonds/Ball	300.00
13	Hideo Nomo/Ball	450.00
14	Roger Maris/Ball	300.00
15	Ty Cobb/Ball	750.00
16	Harmon Killebrew/Bat	150.00
17	Magglio Ordonez/Cap	30.00
18	Wade Boggs/Bat	100.00
19	Hank Aaron/Cap	400.00
20	David Cone/Ball	100.00

Great American Treasures Autograph

NM/M

GT-6	Tom Glavine 96 WS Jsy	125.00
GT-11	Ryne Sandberg 91 AS Bat	300.00
GT-16	Harmon Killebrew 570 HR Bat	200.00
GT-18	Wade Boggs WS Bat	150.00

Player's Collection

NM/M

Singles #'d to 100.

1	Tony Gwynn/Bat	30.00
2	Tony Gwynn/Jsy	30.00
3	Tony Gwynn/Pants	30.00
4	Tony Gwynn/Shoe	30.00
5	Tony Gwynn/Quad/25	
6	Cal Ripken/Jsy	75.00
7	Cal Ripken/Bat	75.00
8	Cal Ripken/Glove	75.00
9	Cal Ripken/Jsy	75.00
10	Cal Ripken/Quad/25	
11	Barry Bonds/Jsy	60.00
12	Barry Bonds/Shoe	60.00
13	Barry Bonds/Pants	60.00
14	Barry Bonds/Bat	60.00
15	Barry Bonds/Quad/25	

Player's Collection Autograph

No Pricing

Slideshow

NM/M

Common Player:		10.00
Production 100 Sets		
View Masters:		1.5X
Numbered to 25 each.		

1	Cal Ripken Jr.	40.00
2	Chipper Jones	20.00
3	Jeff Bagwell	15.00
4	Larry Walker	10.00
5	Greg Maddux	25.00
6	Ivan Rodriguez	15.00
7	Andruw Jones	15.00
8	Lance Berkman	10.00
9	Luis Gonzalez	10.00
10	Tony Gwynn	25.00
11	Troy Glaus	15.00
12	Todd Helton	20.00
13	Roberto Alomar	10.00
14	Barry Bonds	40.00
15	Vladimir Guerrero	20.00
16	Sean Casey	10.00
17	Curt Schilling	15.00
18	Frank Thomas	20.00
19	Pedro Martinez	20.00
20	Juan Gonzalez	15.00
21	Randy Johnson	20.00
22	Kerry Wood	10.00
23	Mike Sweeney	10.00
24	Magglio Ordonez	10.00
25	Kazuhiro Sasaki	10.00
26	Manny Ramirez	20.00
27	Roger Clemens	25.00
28	Albert Pujols	120.00
29	Hideo Nomo	25.00
30	Miguel Tejada	10.00

Slideshow Autographs

NM/M

No Pricing

Statistical Standouts

NM/M

Common Player:		5.00
Inserted 1:96		

1	Ichiro Suzuki	35.00
2	Barry Bonds	40.00
3	Ivan Rodriguez	10.00
4	Jeff Bagwell	10.00
5	Vladimir Guerrero	10.00
6	Mike Sweeney	5.00
7	Miguel Tejada	5.00
8	Mike Piazza	30.00
9	Darin Erstad	5.00
10	Alex Rodriguez	35.00
11	Jason Giambi	8.00
12	Cal Ripken Jr.	40.00
13	Albert Pujols	35.00
14	Carlos Delgado	8.00
15	Rafael Palmeiro	8.00
16	Lance Berkman	5.00

17	Luis Gonzalez	5.00
18	Sammy Sosa	30.00
19	Andruw Jones	10.00
20	Derek Jeter	40.00
21	Edgar Martinez	5.00
22	Troy Glaus	10.00
23	Magglio Ordonez	5.00
24	Mark McGwire	35.00
25	Manny Ramirez	10.00

Statistical Standouts Autograph

No Pricing

Triple Threads

NM/M

Common Card:		50.00
Numbered to 100.		
TT-1	Pedro Martinez, Manny Ramirez, Nomar Garciaparra	100.00
TT-2	Frank Robinson, Cal Ripken Jr., Brooks Robinson	200.00
TT-3	Yogi Berra, Lou Gehrig, Babe Ruth	500.00
TT-4	Andre Dawson, Ryne Sandberg, Ernie Banks	140.00
TT-5	Warren Spahn, Hank Aaron, Eddie Mathews	150.00
TT-6	Greg Maddux, Chipper Jones, Andruw Jones	75.00
TT-7	Nolan Ryan, Ivan Rodriguez, Juan Gonzalez	100.00
TT-8	Lance Berkman, Jeff Bagwell, Craig Biggio	50.00
TT-9	Rod Carew, Harmon Killebrew, Kirby Puckett	75.00
TT-10	Luis Gonzalez, Curt Schilling, Randy Johnson	60.00

2002 Leaf

NM/M

Complete Set (1-200):		80.00
Common Player:		.15
Common (151-200):		1.50
Inserted 1:6		
Pack (4):		1.50
Box (24):		30.00

1	Tim Salmon	.25
2	Troy Glaus	.65
3	Curt Schilling	.40
4	Luis Gonzalez	.25

5	Mark Grace	.25
6	Matt Williams	.15
7	Randy Johnson	.65
8	Tom Glavine	.40
9	Brady Anderson	.15
10	Hideo Nomo	.65
11	Pedro Martinez	.65
12	Corey Patterson	.15
13	Paul Konerko	.25
14	Jon Lieber	.15
15	Carlos Lee	.15
16	Magglio Ordonez	.15
17	Adam Dunn	.40
18	Ken Griffey Jr.	1.00
19	C.C. Sabathia	.15
20	Jim Thome	.50
21	Juan Gonzalez	.65
22	Kenny Lofton	.15
23	Juan Encarnacion	.15
24	Tony Clark	.15
25	A.J. Burnett	.15
26	Josh Beckett	.25
27	Lance Berkman	.15
28	Eric Karros	.15
29	Shawn Green	.30
30	Brad Radke	.15
31	Joe Mays	.15
32	Javier Vazquez	.15
33	Alfonso Soriano	.50
34	Jorge Posada	.25
35	Eric Chavez	.25
36	Mark Mulder	.15
37	Miguel Tejada	.25
38	Tim Hudson	.25
39	Bobby Abreu	.15
40	Pat Burrell	.40
41	Ryan Klesko	.15
42	Not Issued	
43	John Olerud	.15
44	Ellis Burks	.15
45	Mike Cameron	.15
46	Jim Edmonds	.15
47	Ben Grieve	.15
48	Carlos Pena	.15
49	Alex Rodriguez	1.50
50	Raul Mondesi	.15
51	Billy Koch	.15
52	Manny Ramirez	.65
53	Darin Erstad	.25
54	Troy Percival	.15
55	Andruw Jones	.65
56	Chipper Jones	.75
57	David Segui	.15
58	Chris Stynes	.15
59	Trot Nixon	.15
60	Sammy Sosa	1.00
61	Kerry Wood	.50
62	Frank Thomas	.65
63	Barry Larkin	.15
64	Bartolo Colon	.15
65	Kazuhiro Sasaki	.15
66	Roberto Alomar	.35
67	Mike Hampton	.15
68	Roger Cedeno	.15
69	Cliff Floyd	.15
70	Mike Lowell	.15
71	Billy Wagner	.15
72	Craig Biggio	.15
73	Jeff Bagwell	.65
74	Carlos Beltran	.50
75	Mark Quinn	.15
76	Mike Sweeney	.15
77	Gary Sheffield	.25
78	Kevin Brown	.15
79	Paul LoDuca	.15
80	Ben Sheets	.15
81	Jeromy Burnitz	.15
82	Richie Sexson	.15
83	Corey Koskie	.15
84	Eric Milton	.15
85	Jose Vidro	.15
86	Mike Piazza	1.00
87	Robin Ventura	.15

88	Andy Pettitte	.25
89	Mike Mussina	.40
90	Orlando Hernandez	.15
91	Roger Clemens	.85
92	Barry Zito	.25
93	Jermaine Dye	.15
94	Jimmy Rollins	.25
95	Jason Kendall	.15
96	Rickey Henderson	.65
97	Andres Galarraga	.15
98	Bret Boone	.15
99	Freddy Garcia	.15
100	J.D. Drew	.25
101	Jose Cruz Jr.	.15
102	Greg Maddux	.75
103	Javy Lopez	.15
104	Nomar Garciaparra	1.00
105	Fred McGriff	.15
106	Keith Foulke	.15
107	Ray Durham	.15
108	Sean Casey	.25
109	Todd Walker	.15
110	Omar Vizquel	.15
111	Travis Fryman	.15
112	Larry Walker	.15
113	Todd Helton	.65
114	Bobby Higginson	.15
115	Charles Johnson	.15
116	Moises Alou	.15
117	Richard Hidalgo	.15
118	Roy Oswalt	.25
119	Neifi Perez	.15
120	Adrian Beltre	.30
121	Chan Ho Park	.15
122	Geoff Jenkins	.15
123	Doug Mientkiewicz	.15
124	Torii Hunter	.15
125	Vladimir Guerrero	.65
126	Matt Lawton	.15
127	Tsuyoshi Shinjo	.15
128	Bernie Williams	.40
129	Derek Jeter	2.00
130	Mariano Rivera	.25
131	Tino Martinez	.15
132	Jason Giambi	.45
133	Scott Rolen	.50
134	Brian Giles	.15
135	Phil Nevin	.15
136	Trevor Hoffman	.15
137	Barry Bonds	2.00
138	Jeff Kent	.15
139	Shannon Stewart	.15
140	Shawn Estes	.15
141	Edgar Martinez	.15
142	Ichiro Suzuki	1.00
143	Albert Pujols	1.50
144	Bud Smith	.15
145	Matt Morris	.15
146	Frank Catalanotto	.15
147	Gabe Kapler	.15
148	Ivan Rodriguez	.45
149	Rafael Palmeiro	.45
150	Carlos Delgado	.40
151	Marlon Byrd	2.00
152	Alex Herrera	1.50
153	Brandon Backe RC	2.00
154	Jorge De La Rosa RC	2.00
155	Corky Miller	1.50
156	Dennis Tankersley	1.50
157	Kyle Kane RC	2.00
158	Justin Duchscherer	1.50
159	Brian Mallette RC	2.00
160	Eric Hinske	1.50
161	Jason Lane	1.50
162	Hee Seop Choi	3.00
163	Juan Cruz	1.50
164	Rodrigo Rosario RC	2.00
165	Matt Guerrier	1.50
166	Anderson Machado RC	2.00
167	Geronimo Gil	1.50
168	Dewon Brazelton	1.50
169	Mark Prior	4.00
170	Bill Hall	1.50
171	Jorge Padilla RC	2.00
172	Josh Pearce	1.50
173	Allan Simpson RC	2.00
174	Doug DeVore RC	2.00
175	Morgan Ensberg	1.50
176	Angel Berroa	1.50
177	Steve Bechler RC	2.00
178	Antonio Perez	1.50
179	Mark Teixeira	3.00
180	Mark Ellis	1.50
181	Michael Cuddyer	1.50
182	Mike Rivera	1.50
183	Raul Chavez RC	2.00
184	Juan Pena	1.50
185	Austin Kearns	2.00
186	Ryan Ludwick	1.50
187	Ed Rogers	1.50
188	Wilson Betemit	1.50
189	Nick Neugebauer	1.50
190	Tom Shearn RC	2.00
191	Eric Cyr RC	2.00
192	Victor Martinez	1.50
193	Brandon Berger	1.50
194	Erik Bedard	1.50
195	Franklin German RC	2.00
196	Joe Thurston	1.50
197	John Buck	1.50
198	Jeff Deardorff RC	2.00
199	Ryan Jamison RC	2.00
200	Alfredo Amezaga	1.50
201	So Taguchi/500 RC	6.00
202	Kazuhisa Ishii/250 RC	8.00

Press Proof Blue

Stars (1-150):		5-10X
Inserted 1:24 Retail		

Press Proof Red

Stars (1-150):		4-6X
Inserted 1:12 Retail		

Lineage

1999 Lineage (1-50):		2-5X
Inserted 1:12		
2000 Lineage (51-100):		2-5X
Inserted 1:12		
2001 Lineage (101-150):		2-5X
Inserted 1:12		
Silver Holofoils:		8-15X
Production 100		

Autograph

Quantity produced listed
201	So Taguchi/25	
202	Kazuhisa Ishii/25	

Burn n' Turn

		NM/M
Complete Set (10):		50.00
Common Player:		4.00
Inserted 1:96		
1	Fernando Vina, Edgar Renteria	4.00
2	Alex Rodriguez, Mike Young	10.00
3	Derek Jeter, Alfonso Soriano	15.00
4	Carlos Guillen, Bret Boone	4.00
5	Jose Vidro, Orlando Cabrera	4.00
6	Barry Larkin, Todd Walker	4.00
7	Carlos Febles, Neifi Perez	4.00
8	Jeff Kent, Rich Aurilia	4.00
9	Craig Biggio, Julio Lugo	4.00
10	Miguel Tejada, Mark Ellis	4.00

Clean Up Crew

		NM/M
Complete Set (15):		90.00
Common Player:		4.00
Inserted 1:192		
1	Barry Bonds	20.00
2	Sammy Sosa	12.00
3	Luis Gonzalez	4.00
4	Richie Sexson	4.00
5	Jim Thome	6.00
6	Chipper Jones	8.00
7	Alex Rodriguez	15.00
8	Troy Glaus	6.00
9	Rafael Palmeiro	5.00
10	Lance Berkman	4.00
11	Mike Piazza	12.00
12	Jason Giambi	5.00
13	Todd Helton	6.00
14	Shawn Green	5.00
15	Carlos Delgado	5.00

Clubhouse Signatures Bronze

		NM/M
Common Player:		5.00
(1)	Wilson Betemit/150	6.00
(2)	Marlon Byrd/200	6.00
(3)	Joe Crede/200	8.00
(4)	Andre Dawson/100	30.00
(5)	J.D. Drew/25	35.00
(6)	Adam Dunn/200	25.00
(7)	Jermaine Dye/125	10.00
(8)	Mark Ellis/300	8.00
(9)	Johnny Estrada/250	8.00
(10)	Bob Feller/250	15.00
(11)	Robert Fick/300	5.00
(12)	Steve Garvey/200	15.00
(13)	Austin Kearns/300	10.00
(14)	Jason Lane/250	5.00
(15)	Paul LoDuca/300	8.00
(16)	Terrence Long/250	5.00
(17)	Edgar Martinez/50	30.00
(18)	Don Mattingly/25	100.00
(19)	Joe Mays/200	6.00
(20)	Mark Mulder/50	25.00
(21)	Xavier Nady/200	8.00
(22)	Roy Oswalt/300	10.00
(23)	Aramis Ramirez/250	15.00
(24)	Tim Redding/300	5.00
(25)	Phil Rizzuto/25	45.00
(26)	Ryne Sandberg/25	100.00
(27)	Ron Santo/300	15.00
(28)	Bud Smith/200	5.00
(29)	Ozzie Smith/25	85.00
(30)	Alfonso Soriano/75	30.00
(31)	Alan Trammell/75	15.00
(32)	Billy Williams/150	10.00
(33)	Barry Zito/100	25.00

Clubhouse Signatures Silver

		NM/M
Common Player:		10.00
(1)	Rich Aurilia/100	15.00
(2)	Wilson Betemit/100	15.00
(3)	Marlon Byrd/100	15.00
(4)	Sean Casey/50	20.00
(5)	Eric Chavez/100	20.00
(6)	Roger Clemens/25	150.00
(7)	Joe Crede/50	20.00
(8)	Andre Dawson/100	30.00
(9)	Adam Dunn/100	40.00
(10)	Jermaine Dye/100	15.00
(11)	Mark Ellis/100	10.00
(12)	Johnny Estrada/100	15.00
(13)	Bob Feller/100	20.00
(14)	Robert Fick/100	15.00
(15)	Steve Garvey/100	20.00
(16)	Vladimir Guerrero/25	60.00
(17)	Todd Helton/25	50.00
(18)	Austin Kearns/100	20.00
(19)	Jason Lane/100	15.00
(20)	Paul LoDuca/100	15.00
(21)	Terrence Long/100	10.00
(22)	Edgar Martinez/100	25.00
(23)	Joe Mays/50	20.00
(24)	Mark Mulder/100	30.00
(25)	Xavier Nady/100	10.00
(26)	Roy Oswalt/100	20.00
(27)	Aramis Ramirez/100	20.00
(28)	Tim Redding/100	10.00
(29)	Cal Ripken Jr./25	225.00
(30)	Phil Rizzuto/25	50.00
(31)	Ron Santo/100	40.00
(32)	Mike Schmidt/75	75.00
(33)	Bud Smith/100	10.00
(34)	Miguel Tejada/100	30.00
(35)	Javier Vazquez/100	15.00
(36)	Billy Williams/100	20.00
(37)	Barry Zito/100	30.00

Clubhouse Signatures Gold

		NM/M
Common Player:		15.00
Numbered to 25		
(1)	Rich Aurilia	15.00
(2)	Josh Beckett	60.00
(3)	Wilson Betemit	15.00
(4)	Marlon Byrd	15.00
(5)	Sean Casey	25.00
(6)	Eric Chavez	30.00
(7)	Roger Clemens	150.00
(8)	Joe Crede	50.00
(9)	Andre Dawson	40.00
(10)	J.D. Drew	40.00
(11)	Adam Dunn	65.00
(12)	Jermaine Dye	20.00
(13)	Mark Ellis	15.00
(14)	Johnny Estrada	20.00
(15)	Bob Feller	45.00
(16)	Robert Fick	15.00
(17)	Steve Garvey	40.00
(18)	Luis Gonzalez	35.00
(19)	Vladimir Guerrero	75.00
(20)	Todd Helton	50.00
(21)	Orel Hershiser	35.00
(22)	Austin Kearns	50.00
(23)	Jason Lane	15.00
(24)	Paul LoDuca	25.00
(25)	Terrence Long	15.00
(26)	Edgar Martinez	30.00
(27)	Don Mattingly	125.00
(28)	Joe Mays	25.00
(29)	Mark Mulder	40.00
(30)	Xavier Nady	20.00
(31)	Roy Oswalt	30.00
(32)	Chan Ho Park	15.00
(33)	Kirby Puckett	125.00
(34)	Aramis Ramirez	40.00
(35)	Tim Redding	15.00
(36)	Cal Ripken Jr.	225.00
(37)	Phil Rizzuto	60.00
(38)	Ryne Sandberg	125.00
(39)	Ron Santo	65.00
(40)	Mike Schmidt	90.00
(41)	Bud Smith	20.00
(42)	Ozzie Smith	100.00
(43)	Alfonso Soriano	80.00
(44)	Miguel Tejada	30.00
(45)	Alan Trammell	25.00
(46)	Javier Vazquez	20.00
(47)	Billy Williams	35.00
(48)	Barry Zito	50.00

Cornerstones

		NM/M
Production 50 Sets		
Some not priced yet		
1	Andruw Jones, Chipper Jones	40.00
2	Craig Biggio, Jeff Bagwell	
3	Ivan Rodriguez, Rafael Palmeiro	
4	Curt Schilling, Randy Johnson	40.00
5	Gary Sheffield, Shawn Green	
6	Larry Walker, Todd Helton	25.00
7	Carlos Delgado, Shannon Stewart	25.00
8	Omar Vizquel, Jim Thome	
9	Vladimir Guerrero, Jose Vidro	
10	Bernie Williams, Roger Clemens	60.00

Future 500 Club

		NM/M
Complete Set (10):		40.00
Common Player:		2.00
Inserted 1:64		
1	Sammy Sosa	8.00
2	Mike Piazza	8.00
3	Alex Rodriguez	10.00
4	Chipper Jones	6.00
5	Jeff Bagwell	4.00
6	Carlos Delgado	2.00
7	Shawn Green	2.00
8	Ken Griffey Jr.	8.00

9 Rafael Palmeiro 3.00
10 Vladimir Guerrero 4.00

Game Collection

NM/M
Common Player: 5.00
Inserted 1:62 R
SP's Indicated
AB B   Adrian Beltre/Bat 5.00
AD BG Adam Dunn/
    Btg Glove/25 25.00
AG B   Andres Galarraga/
    Bat 5.00
AJ B   Andruw Jones/
    Bat/300 8.00
BG B   Brian Giles/Bat 5.00
BH B   Bobby Higginson/
    Bat 5.00
BS H   Ben Sheets/
    Hat/25 35.00
BW S   Bernie Williams/
    Shoe/25 30.00
BZ FG Barry Zito/
    Fielding Glove/25 25.00
CB B   Carlos Beltran/Bat 8.00
CBI B Craig Biggio/Bat 6.00
CF B   Carlton Fisk/Bat 10.00
CK B   Chuck Knoblauch/
    Bat 5.00
CP S   Corey Patterson/
    Shoe/25 25.00
EM B   Eddie Murray/
    Bat/250 15.00
GJ P   Geoff Jenkins/Pants 5.00
IR BG Ivan Rodriguez/
    Btg Glove/25 30.00
JB B   Jeff Bagwell/
    Bat/100 15.00
JD H   Johnny Damon/
    Hat/25 25.00
JE B   Juan Encarnacion/
    Bat 5.00
JG B   Juan Gonzalez/Bat 8.00
KL B   Kenny Lofton/Bat 5.00
KW S   Kerry Wood/
    Shoe/25 40.00
LB BG Lance Berkman/
    Btg Glove/25 25.00
LW B   Larry Walker/
    Bat/50 15.00
MB BG Marlon Byrd/
    Btg Glove/25 20.00
MG B   Mark Grace/Bat/200 8.00
MM FG Mike Mussina/
    Fielding Glove/25 55.00
MO B   Magglio Ordonez/
    Bat/150 6.00
MP B   Mike Piazza/
    Bat/100 15.00
PB B   Pat Burrell/Bat/100 15.00
RA B   Roberto Alomar/Bat 8.00
RD B   Ray Durham/Bat 5.00
RG B   Rusty Greer/Bat 5.00
RJ FG Randy Johnson/
    Fielding Glove 80.00
RP B   Rafael Palmeiro/
    Bat 10.00
RP BG Rafael Palmeiro/
    Batting Glove/25 30.00
RV B   Robin Ventura/Bat 5.00
SC B   Sean Casey/Bat 5.00
SR B   Scott Rolen/
    Bat/250 15.00
SS H   Shannon Stewart/
    Hat/25 20.00
TC B   Tony Clark/Bat 5.00
TG BG Tony Gwynn/
    Batting Glove/25 90.00
TH B   Todd Helton/Bat 10.00
TN B   Trot Nixon/Bat 5.00
WB B   Wade Boggs/Bat 5.00

Gold Leaf Rookies

NM/M
Complete Set (10): 20.00
Common Player: 2.00
Inserted 1:24
1 Josh Beckett 4.00
2 Marlon Byrd 2.00
3 Dennis Tankersley 2.00
4 Jason Lane 2.00
5 Dewon Brazelton 2.00

6 Mark Prior 4.00
7 Bill Hall 2.00
8 Angel Berroa 2.00
9 Mark Teixeira 4.00
10 John Buck 2.00

Heading for the Hall

NM/M
Complete Set (10): 40.00
Common Player: 2.00
Inserted 1:64
1 Greg Maddux 4.00
2 Ozzie Smith 4.00
3 Andre Dawson 2.00
4 Dennis Eckersley 2.00
5 Roberto Alomar 2.00
6 Cal Ripken Jr. 10.00
7 Roger Clemens 5.00
8 Tony Gwynn 4.00
9 Alex Rodriguez 8.00
10 Jeff Bagwell 3.00

Heading for the Hall Autographs

NM/M
Common Player: 25.00
Production 50 each.
1 Greg Maddux 125.00
2 Ozzie Smith 100.00
3 Andre Dawson 40.00
4 Dennis Eckersley 45.00
5 Roberto Alomar 25.00
6 Cal Ripken Jr. 200.00
7 Roger Clemens 150.00
8 Tony Gwynn 100.00
9 Alex Rodriguez 150.00
10 Jeff Bagwell 40.00

League of Nations

NM/M
Complete Set (10): 20.00
Common Player: 2.00
Inserted 1:60
1 Ichiro Suzuki 8.00
2 Tsuyoshi Shinjo 2.00
3 Chan Ho Park 2.00
4 Larry Walker 2.00
5 Andruw Jones 4.00
6 Hideo Nomo 4.00
7 Byung-Hyun Kim 2.00
8 Sun-Woo Kim 2.00
9 Orlando Hernandez 2.00
10 Luke Prokopec 2.00

Retired Numbers

#'d to jersey number
No Pricing

Rookie Reprints

FRANK THOMAS 1B

NM/M
Complete Set (6): 35.00
Common Player: 3.00
#'d to year of issue
1 Roger Clemens/
    1,985 10.00
2 Kirby Puckett/1,985 9.00
3 Andres Galarraga/
    1,986 3.00
4 Fred McGriff/1,986 3.00
5 Sammy Sosa/1,990 10.00
6 Frank Thomas/1,990 8.00

Shirt Off My Back

NM/M
Common Player: 5.00
Inserted 1:29
Patch Variations: 2-4X
RA   Roberto Alomar 8.00
JB   Jeff Bagwell/SP 20.00
MB   Michael Barrett 5.00
CB   Carlos Beltran 15.00
LB   Lance Berkman 5.00
GB   George Brett/SP 50.00
KB   Kevin Brown 5.00
MB   Mark Buehrle 5.00
AB   A.J. Burnett 5.00
JBU Jeromy Burnitz 5.00
CD   Carlos Delgado 8.00
RD   Ryan Dempster 5.00
DE   Darin Erstad/SP 15.00
CF   Cliff Floyd 5.00
FG   Freddy Garcia/SP 8.00
NG   Nomar
    Garciaparra/SP 40.00
TGL Troy Glaus/SP 20.00
TGL Tom Glavine 8.00
LG   Luis Gonzalez 5.00
TG   Tony Gwynn 25.00
MH   Mike Hampton 5.00
TH   Todd Helton 20.00
THU Tim Hudson 6.00
BJA Bo Jackson/SP 25.00
RJ   Randy Johnson 15.00
CJ   Chipper Jones/SP 30.00
AK   Al Kaline/SP 20.00
EK   Eric Karros 5.00
BL   Barry Larkin 5.00
CL   Carlos Lee 5.00
JL   Javy Lopez 5.00
GM   Greg Maddux/SP 30.00
EM   Edgar Martinez/SP 8.00
PM   Pedro Martinez/SP 5.00
DM   Don Mattingly/SP 50.00
KM   Kevin Millwood 5.00
HN   Hideo Nomo/SP 25.00
JO   John Olerud 5.00
MO   Magglio Ordonez 5.00
RP   Rafael Palmeiro 10.00
CHP Chan Ho Park/SP 8.00
TP   Troy Percival 5.00
AP   Andy Pettitte/SP 12.00
MP   Mike Piazza 30.00
KP   Kirby Puckett 25.00
BR   Brad Radke 5.00
MR   Manny Ramirez 20.00
CR   Cal Ripken Jr./
    SP/50 100.00
AR   Alex Rodriguez 35.00

SR   Scott Rolen/SP 15.00
KS   Kazuhiro Sasaki/SP 8.00
CS   Curt Schilling/SP 15.00
RS   Richie Sexson 5.00
TS   Tsuyoshi Shinjo/SP 8.00
JS   John Smoltz 5.00
MS   Mike Sweeney 5.00
MT   Miguel Tejada 6.00
LW   Larry Walker/SP 8.00
MW   Matt Williams 5.00
DW   Dave Winfield/SP 20.00

2002 Leaf Certified

NM/M
Complete Set (200): .50
Common Player: .50
Common (151-200): 5.00
Production 500
Pack (5): 6.00
Box (16): 75.00
1 Alex Rodriguez 4.00
2 Luis Gonzalez .65
3 Javier Vazquez .50
4 Juan Uribe .50
5 Ben Sheets .50
6 George Brett 4.00
7 Magglio Ordonez .50
8 Randy Johnson 1.00
9 Joe Kennedy .50
10 Richie Sexson .50
11 Larry Walker .50
12 Lance Berkman .50
13 Jose Cruz Jr. .50
14 Doug Davis .50
15 Cliff Floyd .50
16 Ryan Klesko .50
17 Troy Glaus 1.00
18 Robert Person .50
19 Bartolo Colon .50
20 Adam Dunn .75
21 Kevin Brown .50
22 John Smoltz .50
23 Edgar Martinez .50
24 Eric Karros .50
25 Tony Gwynn 2.00
26 Mark Mulder .50
27 Don Mattingly 4.00
28 Brandon Duckworth .50
29 C.C. Sabathia .50
30 Nomar Garciaparra 3.00
31 Adam Johnson .50
32 Miguel Tejada .65
33 Ryne Sandberg 2.00
34 Roger Clemens 2.50
35 Edgardo Alfonzo .50
36 Jason Jennings .50
37 Todd Helton 1.00
38 Nolan Ryan 5.00
39 Paul LoDuca .50
40 Cal Ripken Jr. 5.00
41 Terrence Long .50
42 Mike Sweeney .50
43 Carlos Lee .50
44 Ben Grieve .50
45 Tony Armas Jr. .50
46 Joe Mays .50
47 Jeff Kent .50
48 Andy Pettitte .65
49 Kirby Puckett 2.00
50 Aramis Ramirez .50
51 Tim Redding .50
52 Freddy Garcia .50
53 Javy Lopez .50
54 Mike Schmidt 4.00
55 Wade Miller .50
56 Ramon Ortiz .50
57 Ray Durham .50
58 J.D. Drew .75
59 Bret Boone .50
60 Mark Buehrle .50
61 Geoff Jenkins .50
62 Greg Maddux 2.00

63	Mark Grace	.65
64	Toby Hall	.50
65	A.J. Burnett	.50
66	Bernie Williams	.65
67	Roy Oswalt	.65
68	Shannon Stewart	.50
69	Barry Zito	.65
70	Juan Pierre	.50
71	Preston Wilson	.50
72	Rafael Furcal	.50
73	Sean Casey	.65
74	John Olerud	.50
75	Paul Konerko	.75
76	Vernon Wells	.50
77	Juan Gonzalez	1.00
78	Ellis Burks	.50
79	Jim Edmonds	.75
80	Robert Fick	.50
81	Michael Cuddyer	.50
82	Tim Hudson	.65
83	Phil Nevin	.50
84	Curt Schilling	.75
85	Juan Cruz	.50
86	Jeff Bagwell	1.00
87	Raul Mondesi	.50
88	Bud Smith	.50
89	Omar Vizquel	.50
90	Vladimir Guerrero	1.00
91	Garret Anderson	.50
92	Mike Piazza	3.00
93	Josh Beckett	.65
94	Carlos Delgado	1.00
95	Kazuhiro Sasaki	.50
96	Chipper Jones	2.00
97	Jacque Jones	.50
98	Pedro J. Martinez	1.00
99	Marcus Giles	.50
100	Craig Biggio	.50
101	Orlando Cabrera	.50
102	Al Leiter	.50
103	Michael Barrett	.50
104	Hideo Nomo	1.00
105	Mike Mussina	.75
106	Jeremy Giambi	.50
107	Cristian Guzman	.50
108	Frank Thomas	1.00
109	Carlos Beltran	1.00
110	Jorge Posada	.65
111	Roberto Alomar	.65
112	Bobby Abreu	.50
113	Robin Ventura	.50
114	Pat Burrell	.75
115	Kenny Lofton	.50
116	Adrian Beltre	.75
117	Gary Sheffield	.75
118	Jermaine Dye	.50
119	Manny Ramirez	1.00
120	Brian Giles	.50
121	Tsuyoshi Shinjo	.50
122	Rafael Palmeiro	.85
123	Mo Vaughn	.50
124	Kerry Wood	.75
125	Moises Alou	.50
126	Rickey Henderson	1.00
127	Corey Patterson	.50
128	Jim Thome	1.00
129	Richard Hidalgo	.50
130	Darin Erstad	.75
131	Johnny Damon	.75
132	Juan Encarnacion	.50
133	Scott Rolen	1.00
134	Tom Glavine	.75
135	Ivan Rodriguez	.85
136	Jay Gibbons	.50
137	Trot Nixon	.50
138	Nick Neugebauer	.50
139	Barry Larkin	.50
140	Andruw Jones	1.00
141	Shawn Green	.75
142	Jose Vidro	.50
143	Derek Jeter	5.00
144	Ichiro Suzuki	3.00
145	Ken Griffey Jr.	3.00
146	Barry Bonds	5.00
147	Albert Pujols	4.00
148	Sammy Sosa	3.00
149	Jason Giambi	.75
150	Alfonso Soriano	.75
151	Drew Henson/Bat	8.00
152	Luis Garcia/Bat	5.00
153	Geronimo Gil/Jsy	5.00
154	Corky Miller/Jsy	5.00
155	Mike Rivera/Bat	5.00
156	Mark Ellis/Jsy	5.00
157	Josh Pearce/Bat	5.00
158	Ryan Ludwick/Bat	5.00
159	So Taguchi/Bat RC	12.00
160	Cody Ransom/Jsy	5.00
161	Jeff Deardorff/Bat RC	5.00
162	Franklyn German/Bat RC	5.00
163	Ed Rogers/Jsy	5.00
164	Eric Cyr/Jsy RC	5.00
165	Victor Alvarez/Jsy RC	5.00
166	Victor Martinez/Jsy	15.00
167	Brandon Berger/Jsy	5.00
168	Juan Diaz/Jsy	5.00
169	Kevin Frederick/Jsy RC	5.00
170	Earl Snyder/Bat RC	5.00
171	Morgan Ensberg/Bat	8.00
172	Ryan Jamison/Jsy RC	5.00
173	Rodrigo Rosario/Jsy RC	5.00
174	Willie Harris/Bat	5.00
175	Ramon Vazquez/Bat	5.00
176	Kazuhisa Ishii/Bat RC	12.00
177	Hank Blalock/Jsy	10.00
178	Mark Prior/Bat	15.00
179	Dewon Brazelton/Jsy	5.00
180	Doug DeVore/Jsy RC	5.00
181	Jorge Padilla/Bat RC	5.00
182	Mark Teixeira/Jsy	10.00
183	Orlando Hudson/Jsy	5.00
184	John Buck/Jsy	5.00
185	Erik Bedard/Jsy	5.00
186	Allan Simpson/Jsy RC	5.00
187	Travis Hafner/Jsy	10.00
188	Jason Lane/Jsy	5.00
189	Marlon Byrd/Jsy	5.00
190	Joe Thurston/Jsy	5.00
191	Brandon Backe/Jsy RC	5.00
192	Josh Phelps/Jsy	5.00
193	Bill Hall/Bat	5.00
194	Chris Snelling/Bat RC	8.00
195	Austin Kearns/Bat	8.00
196	Antonio Perez/Bat	5.00
197	Angel Berroa/Bat	8.00
198	Anderson Machado/Jsy RC	5.00
199	Alfredo Amezaga/Jsy	5.00
200	Eric Hinske/Bat	8.00

Certified Skills

		NM/M
Complete Set (20):		65.00
Common Player:		2.00
Inserted 1:17		
Mirror Blues:		1.5-2.5X
Production 75 Sets		
Mirror Reds:		1-2X
Production 150 Sets		
Mirror Golds not priced 25 sets.		
1	Barry Bonds	8.00
2	Greg Maddux	4.00
3	Rickey Henderson	2.00
4	Ichiro Suzuki	5.00
5	Pedro J. Martinez	2.00
6	Kazuhisa Ishii	1.50
7	Alex Rodriguez	6.00
8	Mike Piazza	5.00
9	Sammy Sosa	5.00
10	Derek Jeter	8.00
11	Albert Pujols	6.00
12	Roger Clemens	4.50
13	Mark Prior	1.50
14	Chipper Jones	3.00
15	Ken Griffey Jr.	5.00
16	Frank Thomas	5.00
17	Randy Johnson	2.00
18	Vladimir Guerrero	2.00
19	Nomar Garciaparra	5.00
20	Jeff Bagwell	2.00

All Certified Team

		NM/M
Complete Set (25):		75.00
Common Player:		1.50
Inserted 1:17		
Mirror Blues:		2-4X
Production 50 Sets		
Mirror Reds:		1.5-3X
Production 75 Sets		
Golds not priced 25 sets produced.		
1	Ichiro Suzuki	5.00
2	Alex Rodriguez	6.00
3	Sammy Sosa	5.00
4	Jeff Bagwell	3.00
5	Greg Maddux	4.00
6	Todd Helton	3.00
7	Nomar Garciaparra	5.00
8	Ken Griffey Jr.	5.00
9	Roger Clemens	4.50
10	Adam Dunn	2.00
11	Chipper Jones	4.00
12	Hideo Nomo	3.00
13	Lance Berkman	1.50
14	Barry Bonds	8.00
15	Manny Ramirez	3.00
16	Jason Giambi	2.00
17	Rickey Henderson	3.00
18	Randy Johnson	3.00
19	Derek Jeter	8.00
20	Kazuhisa Ishii	1.50
21	Frank Thomas	3.00
22	Mike Piazza	5.00
23	Albert Pujols	6.00
24	Pedro J. Martinez	3.00
25	Vladimir Guerrero	3.00

Mirror Red

		NM/M
Common (1-200):		5.00
Cards (151-200):		.5-1X base
Production 150 Sets		
Mirror Blues (1-200):		.5-1.5X
Production 75 Sets		
Mirror Golds not priced.		
Production 25 Sets		
Mirror Emerald five sets produced.		
Mirror Black one set produced.		
1	Alex Rodriguez/Jsy	25.00
2	Luis Gonzalez/Jsy	5.00
3	Javier Vazquez/Bat	5.00
4	Juan Uribe/Jsy	5.00
5	Ben Sheets/Jsy	8.00
6	George Brett/Jsy	40.00
7	Magglio Ordonez/Jsy	8.00
8	Randy Johnson/Jsy	15.00
9	Joe Kennedy/Jsy	5.00
10	Richie Sexson/Jsy	10.00
11	Larry Walker/Jsy	8.00
12	Lance Berkman/Jsy	8.00
13	Jose Cruz Jr./Jsy	5.00
14	Doug Davis/Jsy	5.00
15	Cliff Floyd/Jsy	5.00
16	Ryan Klesko/Bat	5.00
17	Troy Glaus/Jsy	10.00
18	Robert Person/Jsy	5.00
19	Bartolo Colon/Jsy	5.00
20	Adam Dunn/Jsy	15.00
21	Kevin Brown/Jsy	8.00
22	John Smoltz/Jsy	8.00
23	Edgar Martinez/Jsy	8.00
24	Eric Karros/Jsy	5.00
25	Tony Gwynn/Jsy	20.00
26	Mark Mulder/Jsy	8.00
27	Don Mattingly/Jsy	40.00
28	Brandon Duckworth/Jsy	5.00
29	C.C. Sabathia/Jsy	5.00
30	Nomar Garciaparra/Jsy	20.00
31	Adam Johnson/Jsy	5.00
32	Miguel Tejada/Jsy	8.00
33	Ryne Sandberg/Jsy	40.00
34	Roger Clemens/Jsy	25.00
35	Edgardo Alfonzo/Jsy	5.00
36	Jason Jennings/Jsy	5.00
37	Todd Helton/Jsy	10.00
38	Nolan Ryan/Jsy	60.00
39	Paul LoDuca/Jsy	5.00
40	Cal Ripken Jr./Jsy	55.00
41	Terrence Long/Jsy	5.00
42	Mike Sweeney/Jsy	5.00
43	Carlos Lee/Jsy	5.00
44	Ben Grieve/Jsy	5.00
45	Tony Armas Jr./Jsy	5.00
46	Joe Mays/Jsy	5.00
47	Jeff Kent/Jsy	8.00
48	Andy Pettitte/Jsy	8.00
49	Kirby Puckett/Jsy	15.00
50	Aramis Ramirez/Jsy	8.00
51	Tim Redding/Jsy	5.00
52	Freddy Garcia/Jsy	5.00
53	Javy Lopez/Jsy	5.00
54	Mike Schmidt/Jsy	35.00
55	Wade Miller/Jsy	5.00
56	Ramon Ortiz/Jsy	5.00
57	Ray Durham/Jsy	5.00
58	J.D. Drew/Jsy	5.00
59	Bret Boone/Jsy	5.00
60	Mark Buehrle/Jsy	5.00
61	Geoff Jenkins/Jsy	5.00
62	Greg Maddux/Jsy	20.00
63	Mark Grace/Jsy	10.00
64	Toby Hall/Jsy	5.00
65	A.J. Burnett/Jsy	5.00
66	Bernie Williams/Jsy	8.00
67	Roy Oswalt/Jsy	8.00
68	Shannon Stewart/Jsy	5.00
69	Barry Zito/Jsy	8.00
70	Juan Pierre/Jsy	5.00
71	Preston Wilson/Jsy	5.00
72	Rafael Furcal/Jsy	5.00
73	Sean Casey/Jsy	5.00
74	John Olerud/Jsy	5.00
75	Paul Konerko/Jsy	5.00
76	Vernon Wells/Jsy	5.00
77	Juan Gonzalez/Jsy	8.00
78	Ellis Burks/Jsy	5.00
79	Jim Edmonds/Jsy	5.00
80	Robert Fick/Jsy	5.00
81	Michael Cuddyer/Jsy	5.00
82	Tim Hudson/Jsy	5.00
83	Phil Nevin/Jsy	5.00
84	Curt Schilling/Jsy	8.00
85	Juan Cruz/Jsy	5.00
86	Jeff Bagwell/Jsy	10.00
87	Raul Mondesi/Jsy	5.00
88	Bud Smith/Jsy	5.00
89	Omar Vizquel/Jsy	5.00
90	Vladimir Guerrero/Jsy	20.00
91	Garret Anderson/Jsy	8.00
92	Mike Piazza/Jsy	15.00
93	Josh Beckett/Jsy	8.00
94	Carlos Delgado/Jsy	8.00
95	Kazuhiro Sasaki/Jsy	5.00
96	Chipper Jones/Jsy	10.00
97	Jacque Jones/Jsy	5.00
98	Pedro Martinez/Jsy	15.00
99	Marcus Giles/Jsy	5.00
100	Craig Biggio/Jsy	6.00
101	Orlando Cabrera/Jsy	5.00
102	Al Leiter/Jsy	5.00
103	Michael Barrett/Jsy	5.00
104	Hideo Nomo/Jsy	15.00
105	Mike Mussina/Jsy	12.00
106	Jeremy Giambi/Jsy	5.00
107	Cristian Guzman/Jsy	5.00
108	Frank Thomas/Jsy	10.00
109	Carlos Beltran/Jsy	8.00
110	Jorge Posada/Bat	8.00
111	Roberto Alomar/Bat	12.00
112	Bobby Abreu/Bat	6.00
113	Robin Ventura/Bat	10.00
114	Pat Burrell/Bat	18.00
115	Kenny Lofton/Bat	8.00
116	Adrian Beltre/Bat	8.00
117	Gary Sheffield/Bat	6.00
118	Jermaine Dye/Bat	5.00
119	Manny Ramirez/Bat	8.00
120	Brian Giles/Bat	5.00
121	Tsuyoshi Shinjo/Bat	5.00
122	Rafael Palmeiro/Bat	10.00
123	Mo Vaughn/Bat	5.00
124	Kerry Wood/Bat	15.00
125	Moises Alou/Bat	8.00
126	Rickey Henderson/Bat	15.00
127	Corey Patterson/Bat	8.00
128	Jim Thome/Bat	15.00
129	Richard Hidalgo/Bat	5.00
130	Darin Erstad/Jsy	5.00
131	Johnny Damon/Bat	5.00
132	Juan Encarnacion/Bat	5.00
133	Scott Rolen/Bat	10.00
134	Tom Glavine/Bat	8.00
135	Ivan Rodriguez/Bat	8.00
136	Jay Gibbons/Bat	5.00

#	Player	Price
137	Trot Nixon/Bat	5.00
138	Nick Neugebauer/Bat	5.00
139	Barry Larkin/Jsy	10.00
140	Andruw Jones/Bat	8.00
141	Shawn Green/Bat	8.00
142	Jose Vidro/Jsy	5.00
143	Derek Jeter/Base	25.00
144	Ichiro Suzuki/Base	20.00
145	Ken Griffey Jr./Base	15.00
146	Barry Bonds/Base	20.00
147	Albert Pujols/Base	15.00
148	Sammy Sosa/Base	15.00
149	Jason Giambi/Base	8.00
150	Alfonso Soriano/Jsy	10.00
151	Drew Henson/Bat	5.00
152	Luis Garcia/Bat	5.00
153	Geronimo Gil/Jsy	5.00
154	Corky Miller/Jsy	5.00
155	Mike Rivera/Bat	5.00
156	Mark Ellis/Jsy	5.00
157	Josh Pearce/Bat	5.00
158	Ryan Ludwick/Bat	5.00
159	So Taguchi/Bat	12.00
160	Cody Ransom/Jsy	5.00
161	Jeff Deardorff/Bat	5.00
162	Franklyn German/Bat	5.00
163	Ed Rogers/Jsy	5.00
164	Eric Cyr/Jsy	5.00
165	Victor Alvarez/Jsy	5.00
166	Victor Martinez/Jsy	10.00
167	Brandon Berger/Jsy	5.00
168	Juan Diaz/Jsy	5.00
169	Kevin Frederick/Jsy	5.00
170	Earl Snyder/Bat	5.00
171	Morgan Ensberg/Bat	5.00
172	Ryan Jamison/Jsy	5.00
173	Rodrigo Rosario/Jsy	5.00
174	Willie Harris/Bat	5.00
175	Ramon Vazquez/Bat	5.00
176	Kazuhisa Ishii/Bat	15.00
177	Hank Blalock/Jsy	10.00
178	Mark Prior/Bat	10.00
179	Dewon Brazelton/Jsy	5.00
180	Doug DeVore/Jsy	5.00
181	Jorge Padilla/Bat	5.00
182	Mark Teixeira/Jsy	10.00
183	Orlando Hudson/Bat	5.00
184	John Buck/Jsy	5.00
185	Erik Bedard/Jsy	5.00
186	Allan Simpson/Jsy	5.00
187	Travis Hafner/Jsy	8.00
188	Jason Lane/Jsy	5.00
189	Marlon Byrd/Jsy	5.00
190	Joe Thurston/Jsy	5.00
191	Brandon Backe/Jsy	5.00
192	Josh Phelps/Jsy	5.00
193	Bill Hall/Bat	5.00
194	Chris Snelling/Bat	5.00
195	Austin Kearns/Bat	8.00
196	Antonio Perez/Bat	5.00
197	Angel Berroa/Bat	6.00
198	Anderson Machado/Jsy	5.00
199	Alfredo Amezaga/Jsy	5.00
200	Eric Hinske/Bat	6.00

Fabric of the Game

		NM/M
Common Player:		
1	Bobby Doerr/37	20.00
2	Ozzie Smith/78	40.00
3	Pee Wee Reese/40	35.00
4	Tommy Lasorda/80	8.00
4	Tommy Lasorda/73	15.00
4	Tommy Lasorda/50	15.00
5	Red Schoendienst/45	20.00
7	Harmon Killebrew/54	35.00
8	Roger Maris A's/57	75.00
10	Mel Ott/26	75.00
11	Paul Molitor/100	20.00
11	Paul Molitor/78	20.00
11	Paul Molitor/50	30.00
12	Duke Snider/47	40.00
13	Brooks Robinson/55	40.00
14	George Brett/40	75.00
14	George Brett/73	50.00
15	Johnny Bench/80	20.00
15	Johnny Bench/67	30.00
15	Johnny Bench/50	30.00
16	Lou Boudreau/38	20.00
17	Stan Musial/41	60.00
18	Al Kaline/53	30.00
19	Steve Garvey/100	8.00
19	Steve Garvey/69	15.00
19	Steve Garvey/45	15.00
20	Nomar Garciaparra/100	25.00
20	Nomar Garciaparra/96	25.00
20	Nomar Garciaparra/50	35.00
21	Joe Morgan/80	10.00
21	Joe Morgan/63	20.00
21	Joe Morgan/50	20.00
22	Willie Stargell/62	25.00
23	Andre Dawson/80	15.00
23	Andre Dawson/76	15.00
23	Andre Dawson/50	20.00
24	Gary Carter/100	10.00
24	Gary Carter/74	20.00
24	Gary Carter/50	20.00
25	Reggie Jackson A's/67	30.00
27	Phil Rizzuto/41	30.00
28	Luis Aparicio/56	20.00
29	Robin Yount/80	30.00
29	Robin Yount/74	30.00
29	Robin Yount/50	40.00
30	Tony Gwynn/100	20.00
30	Tony Gwynn/82	20.00
30	Tony Gwynn/50	30.00
31	Ernie Banks/53	40.00
32	Joe Torre/50	15.00
32	Joe Torre/60	15.00
33	Bo Jackson/100	20.00
33	Bo Jackson/86	20.00
33	Bo Jackson/35	50.00
34	Alfonso Soriano/80	20.00
34	Alfonso Soriano/99	20.00
34	Alfonso Soriano/50	25.00
35	Cal Ripken Jr./80	60.00
35	Cal Ripken Jr./81	60.00
35	Cal Ripken Jr./50	80.00
36	Miguel Tejada/100	10.00
36	Miguel Tejada/97	10.00
36	Miguel Tejada/50	20.00
37	Alex Rodriguez M's/100	20.00
37	Alex Rodriguez M's/94	20.00
37	Alex Rodriguez M's/50	35.00
38	Mike Schmidt/80	40.00
38	Mike Schmidt/72	40.00
38	Mike Schmidt/50	50.00
39	Lou Brock/61	25.00
40	Don Sutton/80	8.00
40	Don Sutton/66	10.00
40	Don Sutton/50	15.00
41	Roberto Clemente/55	125.00
42	Jim Palmer/65	20.00
43	Don Mattingly/40	75.00
43	Don Mattingly/82	50.00
44	Ryne Sandberg/40	60.00
44	Ryne Sandberg/81	40.00
45	Early Wynn/39	20.00
46	Mike Piazza Dodgers/100	20.00
46	Mike Piazza Dodgers/92	20.00
46	Mike Piazza Dodgers/31	40.00
46	Mike Piazza Dodgers/50	25.00
47	Wade Boggs/100	15.00
47	Wade Boggs/82	15.00
47	Wade Boggs/26	40.00
47	Wade Boggs/45	30.00
48	Jim "Catfish" Hunter/65	25.00
48	Jim "Catfish" Hunter/27	40.00
49	Juan Marichal/60	20.00
49	Juan Marichal/27	40.00
50	Carlton Fisk Red Sox/80	25.00
50	Carlton Fisk Red Sox/69	40.00
50	Carlton Fisk Red Sox/27	50.00
50	Carlton Fisk Red Sox/50	30.00
51	Curt Schilling/100	15.00
51	Curt Schilling/88	15.00
51	Curt Schilling/38	25.00
51	Curt Schilling/50	20.00
52	Rod Carew Angels/100	15.00
52	Rod Carew Angels/67	25.00
52	Rod Carew Angels/25	40.00
53	Rod Carew Twins/67	25.00
54	Joe Carter/100	8.00
54	Joe Carter/83	8.00
54	Joe Carter/29	15.00
54	Joe Carter/50	10.00
55	Nolan Ryan Angels/66	60.00
56	Orlando Cepeda/80	8.00
56	Orlando Cepeda/55	10.00
56	Orlando Cepeda/30	25.00
56	Orlando Cepeda/50	15.00
57	Dave Winfield/80	15.00
57	Dave Winfield/73	20.00
57	Dave Winfield/31	30.00
57	Dave Winfield/50	20.00
58	Hoyt Wilhelm/80	8.00
58	Hoyt Wilhelm/52	10.00
58	Hoyt Wilhelm/31	20.00
58	Hoyt Wilhelm/50	15.00
59	Steve Carlton/80	15.00
59	Steve Carlton/65	20.00
59	Steve Carlton/32	30.00
59	Steve Carlton/50	20.00
60	Eddie Murray/100	15.00
60	Eddie Murray/77	15.00
60	Eddie Murray/33	30.00
60	Eddie Murray/50	20.00
61	Nolan Ryan Rangers/40	75.00
61	Nolan Ryan Rangers/66	60.00
61	Nolan Ryan Rangers/34	75.00
62	Nolan Ryan Astros/40	75.00
62	Nolan Ryan Astros/66	60.00
62	Nolan Ryan Astros/34	75.00
63	Kirby Puckett/40	40.00
63	Kirby Puckett/84	20.00
63	Kirby Puckett/34	40.00
64	Yogi Berra/46	40.00
64	Yogi Berra/35	40.00
65	Phil Niekro/40	8.00
65	Phil Niekro/64	10.00
65	Phil Niekro/35	10.00
65	Phil Niekro/50	10.00
66	Gaylord Perry/80	8.00
66	Gaylord Perry/62	10.00
66	Gaylord Perry/36	15.00
66	Gaylord Perry/50	10.00
67	Pedro Martinez Expos/100	15.00
67	Pedro Martinez Expos/92	15.00
67	Pedro Martinez Expos/45	25.00
67	Pedro Martinez Expos/50	20.00
68	Alex Rodriguez Rgr/100	20.00
68	Alex Rodriguez Rgr/94	20.00
68	Alex Rodriguez Rgr/50	30.00
69	Dave Parker/100	8.00
69	Dave Parker/73	10.00
69	Dave Parker/39	15.00
69	Dave Parker/50	10.00
70	Darin Erstad/100	8.00
70	Darin Erstad/96	8.00
70	Darin Erstad/50	15.00
71	Eddie Matthews/52	30.00
71	Eddie Matthews HOF 78/5	
71	Eddie Matthews/41	35.00
72	Tom Seaver Mets/67	30.00
72	Tom Seaver Mets/41	40.00
73	Tom Seaver Reds/67	30.00
73	Tom Seaver Reds/41	40.00
74	Jackie Robinson/47	100.00
74	Jackie Robinson/42	100.00
75	Randy Johnson M's/80	15.00
75	Randy Johnson M's/88	15.00
75	Randy Johnson M's/51	25.00
75	Randy Johnson M's/50	25.00
76	Reggie Jackson Yanks/57	30.00
76	Reggie Jackson Yanks/44	40.00
77	Reggie Jackson Angels/80	20.00
77	Reggie Jackson Angels/67	30.00
77	Reggie Jackson Angels/44	40.00
77	Reggie Jackson Angels/50	40.00
78	Willie McCovey/80	10.00
78	Willie McCovey/59	15.00
78	Willie McCovey/44	20.00
78	Willie McCovey/50	20.00
79	Eric Davis/100	5.00
79	Eric Davis/84	5.00
79	Eric Davis/34	10.00
79	Eric Davis/50	8.00
80	Carlos Delgado/95	6.00
80	Carlos Delgado/93	6.00
81	Dale Murphy/100	20.00
81	Dale Murphy/76	20.00
81	Dale Murphy/50	30.00
82	Brian Giles/100	5.00
82	Brian Giles/95	5.00
82	Brian Giles/50	8.00
83	Kazuhiro Sasaki/100	8.00
83	Kazuhiro Sasaki/100	8.00
83	Kazuhiro Sasaki/50	10.00
84	Phil Nevin/100	5.00
84	Phil Nevin/95	5.00
84	Phil Nevin/50	5.00
85	Frank Thomas/80	15.00
85	Frank Thomas/90	15.00
85	Frank Thomas/35	25.00
85	Frank Thomas/50	15.00
86	Raul Mondesi/100	5.00
86	Raul Mondesi/93	5.00
86	Raul Mondesi/43	8.00
86	Raul Mondesi/50	8.00
87	Don Drysdale/56	25.00
87	Don Drysdale/53	25.00
88	Gary Sheffield/100	6.00
88	Gary Sheffield/88	6.00
88	Gary Sheffield/50	10.00
89	Andy Pettitte/100	15.00
89	Andy Pettitte/95	15.00
89	Andy Pettitte/46	30.00
89	Andy Pettitte/50	15.00
90	Lance Berkman/45	20.00
90	Lance Berkman/99	10.00
91	Paul LoDuca/100	5.00
91	Paul LoDuca/98	5.00
91	Paul LoDuca/50	8.00
92	Kevin Brown/86	5.00
92	Kevin Brown/27	15.00
93	Jim Thome/100	15.00
93	Jim Thome/91	15.00
93	Jim Thome/50	25.00
94	Mike Sweeney/100	5.00
94	Mike Sweeney/95	5.00
94	Mike Sweeney/29	15.00
94	Mike Sweeney/50	10.00
95	Pedro J. Martinez Red Sox/100	15.00
95	Pedro J. Martinez Red Sox/92	15.00
95	Pedro J. Martinez Red Sox/45	25.00
95	Pedro J. Martinez Red Sox/45	25.00
96	Cliff Floyd/100	5.00
96	Cliff Floyd/93	5.00
96	Cliff Floyd/30	15.00
96	Cliff Floyd/50	10.00
97	Larry Walker/100	8.00
97	Larry Walker/89	8.00
97	Larry Walker/33	30.00
97	Larry Walker/50	10.00
98	Ivan Rodriguez/80	10.00
98	Ivan Rodriguez/91	10.00
98	Ivan Rodriguez/50	20.00
99	Aramis Ramirez/100	8.00
99	Aramis Ramirez/98	8.00
99	Aramis Ramirez/50	12.00
100	Roberto Alomar/100	10.00
100	Roberto Alomar/88	10.00
100	Roberto Alomar/50	15.00
101	Ben Sheets/100	8.00
101	Ben Sheets/101	8.00
101	Ben Sheets/50	15.00
102	Adam Dunn/101	20.00
102	Adam Dunn/39	40.00
103	Hideo Nomo/95	30.00
104	C.C. Sabathia/50	10.00
104	C.C. Sabathia/101	5.00
104	C.C. Sabathia/52	10.00
104	C.C. Sabathia/50	10.00
105	Rickey Henderson A's/100	20.00
105	Rickey Henderson A's/79	20.00
105	Rickey Henderson A's/30	50.00
105	Rickey Henderson A's/50	30.00
106	Carlton Fisk White Sox/80	20.00
106	Carlton Fisk White Sox/69	30.00
106	Carlton Fisk White Sox/72	30.00
106	Carlton Fisk White Sox/50	30.00
107	Chan Ho Park/100	5.00
107	Chan Ho Park/94	5.00
107	Chan Ho Park/61	8.00
107	Chan Ho Park/50	8.00

108 Mike Mussina/100	20.00
108 Mike Mussina/91	20.00
108 Mike Mussina/35	50.00
108 Mike Mussina/50	30.00
109 Mark Mulder/100	8.00
109 Mark Mulder/100	8.00
109 Mark Mulder/20	20.00
109 Mark Mulder/35	20.00
110 Tsuyoshi Shinjo/100	5.00
110 Tsuyoshi Shinjo/101	5.00
110 Tsuyoshi Shinjo/30	20.00
111 Pat Burrell/100	10.00
111 Pat Burrell/100	10.00
111 Pat Burrell/50	15.00
112 Edgar Martinez/100	10.00
112 Edgar Martinez/87	10.00
112 Edgar Martinez/50	15.00
113 Barry Larkin/100	10.00
113 Barry Larkin/86	10.00
113 Barry Larkin/50	15.00
114 Jeff Kent/100	6.00
114 Jeff Kent/92	6.00
114 Jeff Kent/50	8.00
115 Chipper Jones/100	15.00
115 Chipper Jones/93	15.00
115 Chipper Jones/50	30.00
116 Magglio Ordonez/100	8.00
116 Magglio Ordonez/97	8.00
116 Magglio Ordonez/30	30.00
116 Magglio Ordonez/50	15.00
117 Jim Edmonds/100	8.00
117 Jim Edmonds/93	8.00
117 Jim Edmonds/50	15.00
118 Andruw Jones/100	10.00
118 Andruw Jones/96	10.00
118 Andruw Jones/45	20.00
119 Jose Canseco/100	15.00
119 Jose Canseco/85	15.00
119 Jose Canseco/50	30.00
120 Manny Ramirez/100	10.00
120 Manny Ramirez/93	10.00
120 Manny Ramirez/50	20.00
121 Sean Casey/100	10.00
121 Sean Casey/97	10.00
121 Sean Casey/50	15.00
122 Bret Boone/100	6.00
122 Bret Boone/92	6.00
122 Bret Boone/29	15.00
122 Bret Boone/50	10.00
123 Tim Hudson/100	8.00
123 Tim Hudson/99	8.00
123 Tim Hudson/50	15.00
124 Craig Biggio/100	10.00
124 Craig Biggio/88	10.00
124 Craig Biggio/50	15.00
125 Mike Piazza Mets/100	20.00
125 Mike Piazza Mets/92	40.00
125 Mike Piazza Mets/31	40.00
125 Mike Piazza Mets/51	25.00
126 Jack Morris/100	8.00
126 Jack Morris/77	5.00
126 Jack Morris/47	10.00
127 Roy Oswalt/100	8.00
127 Roy Oswalt/101	8.00
127 Roy Oswalt/39	15.00
127 Roy Oswalt/50	15.00
128 Shawn Green/100	8.00
128 Shawn Green/93	8.00
128 Shawn Green/50	15.00
129 Carlos Beltran/100	8.00
129 Carlos Beltran/98	8.00
129 Carlos Beltran/50	10.00
130 Todd Helton/100	10.00
130 Todd Helton/97	10.00
130 Todd Helton/50	20.00
131 Barry Zito/75	15.00
131 Barry Zito/100	10.00
131 Barry Zito/75	15.00
131 Barry Zito/30	30.00
132 J.D. Drew/100	15.00
132 J.D. Drew/98	15.00
132 J.D. Drew/50	20.00
133 Mark Grace/100	10.00
133 Mark Grace/88	10.00
133 Mark Grace/50	20.00
134 Rickey Henderson Mets/100	20.00
134 Rickey Henderson Mets/79	20.00
134 Rickey Henderson Mets/50	30.00
135 Greg Maddux/100	20.00
135 Greg Maddux/86	20.00
135 Greg Maddux/50	30.00
136 Garret Anderson/100	8.00
136 Garret Anderson/94	8.00
136 Garret Anderson/50	15.00
137 Rafael Palmeiro/100	15.00
137 Rafael Palmeiro/86	15.00
137 Rafael Palmeiro/50	20.00
138 Luis Gonzalez/100	10.00
138 Luis Gonzalez/90	8.00
138 Luis Gonzalez/45	15.00
139 Nick Johnson/100	5.00
139 Nick Johnson/101	5.00
139 Nick Johnson/26	20.00
139 Nick Johnson/50	10.00
140 Vladimir Guerrero/80	15.00
140 Vladimir Guerrero/96	15.00
140 Vladimir Guerrero/50	25.00
141 Mark Buehrle/100	5.00
141 Mark Buehrle/56	8.00
142 Troy Glaus/100	15.00
142 Troy Glaus/98	15.00
142 Troy Glaus/50	25.00
143 Juan Gonzalez/100	10.00
143 Juan Gonzalez/89	10.00
143 Juan Gonzalez/50	15.00
144 Kerry Wood/100	15.00
144 Kerry Wood/98	15.00
144 Kerry Wood/34	40.00
144 Kerry Wood/50	30.00
145 Roger Clemens/80	25.00
145 Roger Clemens/84	25.00
145 Roger Clemens/50	40.00
146 Bob Abreu/100	8.00
146 Bob Abreu/96	8.00
146 Bob Abreu/53	15.00
146 Bob Abreu/50	15.00
147 Bernie Williams/95	10.00
147 Bernie Williams/91	10.00
147 Bernie Williams/51	20.00
148 Tom Glavine/100	10.00
148 Tom Glavine/87	10.00
148 Tom Glavine/47	25.00
148 Tom Glavine/50	25.00
149 Jorge Posada/100	10.00
149 Jorge Posada/95	15.00
149 Jorge Posada/50	25.00
150 Randy Johnson D'Backs/80	15.00
150 Randy Johnson D'Backs/88	15.00
150 Randy Johnson D'Backs/51	30.00
150 Randy Johnson D'Backs/50	30.00

2002 Leaf Rookies & Stars

MIKE PIAZZA

	NM/M
Complete Set (400):	
Common Player:	.15
Common SP (1-300):	.75
Common (301-400):	.40
Inserted 1:2	
Pack (6):	1.50
Box (24):	30.00
1 Darin Erstad	.25
2 Garret Anderson	.15
3 Troy Glaus	.40
4 David Eckstein	.15
5 Adam Kennedy	.15
6 Kevin Appier	.15
6 Kevin Appier/SP/Mets	.75
6 Kevin Appier/SP/Royals	.75
7 Jarrod Washburn	.15
8 David Segui	.15
9 Jay Gibbons	.15
10 Tony Batista	.15
11 Scott Erickson	.15
12 Jeff Conine	.15
13 Melvin Mora	.15
14 Shea Hillenbrand	.15
15 Manny Ramirez	.65
15 Manny Ramirez/SP/Indians	2.00
16 Pedro J. Martinez	.65
16 Pedro J. Martinez/SP/Dodgers	2.50
16 Pedro J. Martinez/SP/Expos	2.50
17 Nomar Garciaparra	1.00
18 Rickey Henderson	.65
18 Rickey Henderson/SP/Angels	3.00
18 Rickey Henderson/SP/A's	3.00
18 Rickey Henderson/SP/Blue Jays	3.00
18 Rickey Henderson/SP/M's	3.00
18 Rickey Henderson/SP/Mets	3.00
18 Rickey Henderson/SP/Padres	3.00
18 Rickey Henderson/SP/Yankees	3.00
19 Johnny Damon	.25
19 Johnny Damon/SP/A's	1.00
19 Johnny Damon/SP/Royals	1.00
20 Trot Nixon	.15
21 Derek Lowe	.15
22 Jason Varitek	.15
23 Tim Wakefield	.15
24 Frank Thomas	.65
25 Kenny Lofton	.15
25 Kenny Lofton/SP/Indians	.75
26 Magglio Ordonez	.15
27 Ray Durham	.15
28 Mark Buehrle	.15
29 Paul Konerko	.15
29 Paul Konerko/SP/Dodgers	1.00
29 Paul Konerko/SP/Reds	1.00
30 Jose Valentin	.15
31 C.C. Sabathia	.15
32 Ellis Burks	.15
32 Ellis Burks/SP/Giants	.75
32 Ellis Burks/SP/Red Sox	.75
32 Ellis Burks/SP/Rockies	.75
33 Omar Vizquel	.15
33 Omar Vizquel/SP/Mariners	1.00
34 Jim Thome	.50
35 Matt Lawton	.15
36 Travis Fryman	.15
36 Travis Fryman/SP/Tigers	.75
37 Robert Fick	.15
38 Bobby Higginson	.15
39 Steve Sparks	.15
40 Mike Rivera	.15
41 Wendell Magee	.15
42 Randall Simon	.15
43 Carlos Pena	.15
43 Carlos Pena/SP/A's	.75
43 Carlos Pena/SP/Rangers	.75
44 Mike Sweeney	.15
45 Chuck Knoblauch	.15
46 Carlos Beltran	.50
47 Joe Randa	.15
48 Paul Byrd	.15
49 Mac Suzuki	.15
50 Torii Hunter	.15
51 Jacque Jones	.15
52 David Ortiz	.35
53 Corey Koskie	.15
54 Brad Radke	.15
55 Doug Mientkiewicz	.15
56 A.J. Pierzynski	.15
57 Dustan Mohr	.15
58 Derek Jeter	2.00
59 Bernie Williams	.30
60 Roger Clemens	.85
60 Roger Clemens/SP/Blue Jays	4.00
60 Roger Clemens/SP/Red Sox	4.00
61 Mike Mussina	.40
61 Mike Mussina/SP/Orioles	1.50
62 Jorge Posada	.25
63 Alfonso Soriano	.40
64 Jason Giambi	.40
64 Jason Giambi/SP/A's	2.50
65 Robin Ventura	.15
65 Robin Ventura/SP/Mets	.75
65 Robin Ventura/SP/White Sox	.75
66 Andy Pettitte	.25
67 David Wells	.15
67 David Wells/SP/Blue Jays	.75
67 David Wells/SP/Tigers	.75
68 Nick Johnson	.15
69 Jeff Weaver	.15
69 Jeff Weaver/SP/Tigers	.75
70 Raul Mondesi	.15
70 Raul Mondesi/SP/Blue Jays	.75
70 Raul Mondesi/SP/Dodgers	.75
71 Tim Hudson	.25
72 Barry Zito	.25
73 Mark Mulder	.25
74 Miguel Tejada	.25
75 Eric Chavez	.25
76 Billy Koch	.15
76 Billy Koch/SP/Blue Jays	.75
77 Jermaine Dye	.15
77 Jermaine Dye/SP/Royals	.75
78 Scott Hatteberg	.15
79 Ichiro Suzuki	1.00
80 Edgar Martinez	.15
81 Mike Cameron	.15
81 Mike Cameron/SP/White Sox	.75
82 John Olerud	.15
82 John Olerud/SP/Blue Jays	.75
82 John Olerud/SP/Mets	.75
83 Bret Boone	.15
84 Dan Wilson	.15
85 Freddy Garcia	.15
86 Jamie Moyer	.15
87 Carlos Guillen	.15
88 Ruben Sierra	.15
89 Kazuhiro Sasaki	.15
90 Mark McLemore	.15
91 Ben Grieve	.15
92 Aubrey Huff	.15
93 Steve Cox	.15
94 Toby Hall	.15
95 Randy Winn	.15
96 Brent Abernathy	.15
97 Chan Ho Park	.15
97 Chan Ho Park/SP/Dodgers	.75
98 Alex Rodriguez	1.50
98 Alex Rodriguez/SP/Mariners	4.00
99 Juan Gonzalez	.40
99 Juan Gonzalez/SP/Indians	1.50
99 Juan Gonzalez/SP/Tigers	1.50
100 Rafael Palmeiro	.60
100 Rafael Palmeiro/SP/Cubs	1.00
100 Rafael Palmeiro/SP/Orioles	1.00
101 Ivan Rodriguez	.50
102 Rusty Greer	.15
103 Kenny Rogers	.15
103 Kenny Rogers/SP/A's	.75
103 Kenny Rogers/SP/Yankees	.75
104 Hank Blalock	.40
105 Mark Teixeira	.25
106 Carlos Delgado	.40
107 Shannon Stewart	.15
108 Eric Hinske	.15
109 Roy Halladay	.25
110 Felipe Lopez	.15
111 Vernon Wells	.15
112 Curt Schilling	.40
112 Curt Schilling/SP/Phillies	1.50
113 Randy Johnson	.65
113 Randy Johnson/SP/Astros	3.00
113 Randy Johnson/SP/Expos	3.00
113 Randy Johnson/SP/Mariners	3.00
114 Luis Gonzalez	.25
114 Luis Gonzalez/SP/Astros	1.00
114 Luis Gonzalez/SP/Cubs	1.00
115 Mark Grace	.25
115 Mark Grace/SP/Cubs	1.50
116 Junior Spivey	.15
117 Tony Womack	.15
118 Matt Williams	.15
118 Matt Williams/SP/Giants	1.00
118 Matt Williams/SP/Indians	1.00
119 Danny Bautista	.15
120 Byung-Hyun Kim	.15
121 Craig Counsell	.15
122 Greg Maddux	.75
122 Greg Maddux/SP/Cubs	4.00
123 Tom Glavine	.25
124 John Smoltz	.15
124 John Smoltz/SP/Tigers	.75
125 Chipper Jones	.75
126 Gary Sheffield	.25
127 Andruw Jones	.65
128 Vinny Castilla	.15
129 Damian Moss	.15
130 Rafael Furcal	.15
131 Kerry Wood	.50
132 Fred McGriff	.15

132	Fred McGriff/ SP/Blue Jays	1.00
132	Fred McGriff/ SP/Braves	1.00
132	Fred McGriff/ SP/Devil Rays	1.00
132	Fred McGriff/ SP/Padres	1.00
133	Sammy Sosa	1.00
133	Sammy Sosa/ SP/Rangers	4.00
133	Sammy Sosa/ SP/White Sox	4.00
134	Alex Gonzalez	.15
135	Corey Patterson	.15
136	Moises Alou	.15
137	Mark Prior	.50
138	Jon Lieber	.15
139	Matt Clement	.15
140	Ken Griffey Jr.	1.00
140	Ken Griffey Jr./ SP/Mariners	4.00
141	Barry Larkin	.15
142	Adam Dunn	.40
143	Sean Casey	.15
143	Sean Casey/SP/Indians	.75
144	Jose Rijo	.15
145	Elmer Dessens	.15
146	Austin Kearns	.15
147	Corky Miller	.15
148	Todd Walker	.15
148	Todd Walker/ SP/Rockies	.75
148	Todd Walker/SP/Expos	.15
149	Chris Reitsma	.15
150	Ryan Dempster	.15
151	Larry Walker	.15
152	Todd Helton	.65
153	Juan Uribe	.15
154	Juan Pierre	.15
155	Mike Hampton	.15
156	Todd Zeile	.15
157	Josh Beckett	.25
158	Mike Lowell	.15
158	Mike Lowell/ SP/Yankees	.75
159	Derek Lee	.15
160	A.J. Burnett	.15
161	Luis Castillo	.15
162	Tim Raines	.15
163	Preston Wilson	.15
164	Juan Encarnacion	.15
165	Jeff Bagwell	.65
166	Craig Biggio	.15
167	Lance Berkman	.15
168	Wade Miller	.15
169	Roy Oswalt	.25
170	Richard Hidalgo	.15
171	Carlos Hernandez	.15
172	Daryle Ward	.15
173	Shawn Green	.30
173	Shawn Green/ SP/Blue Jays	1.00
174	Adrian Beltre	.35
175	Paul LoDuca	.15
176	Eric Karros	.15
177	Kevin Brown	.15
178	Hideo Nomo	.65
178	Hideo Nomo/ SP/Brewers	1.50
178	Hideo Nomo/SP/Mets	1.50
178	Hideo Nomo/ SP/Red Sox	1.50
178	Hideo Nomo/ SP/Tigers	1.50
179	Odalis Perez	.15
180	Eric Gagne	.35
181	Brian Jordan	.15
182	Cesar Izturis	.15
183	Geoff Jenkins	.15
184	Richie Sexson	.15
184	Richie Sexson/ SP/Indians	1.00
185	Jose Hernandez	.15
186	Ben Sheets	.15
187	Ruben Quevedo	.15
188	Jeffrey Hammonds	.15
189	Alex Sanchez	.15
190	Vladimir Guerrero	.65
191	Jose Vidro	.15
192	Orlando Cabrera	.15
193	Michael Barrett	.15
194	Javier Vazquez	.15
195	Tony Armas Jr.	.15
196	Andres Galarraga	.15
197	Tomokazu Ohka	.15
198	Bartolo Colon	.15
198	Bartolo Colon/ SP/Indians	.75
199	Cliff Floyd	.15
199	Cliff Floyd/SP/Marlins	.75
200	Mike Piazza	1.00
200	Mike Piazza/ SP/Dodgers	4.00

200	Mike Piazza/ SP/Marlins	4.00
201	Jeromy Burnitz	.15
202	Roberto Alomar	.35
202	Roberto Alomar/ SP/Blue Jays	1.50
202	Roberto Alomar/ SP/Indians	1.50
202	Roberto Alomar/ SP/Orioles	1.50
202	Roberto Alomar/ SP/Padres	1.50
203	Mo Vaughn	.15
203	Mo Vaughn/SP/Angels	1.00
203	Mo Vaughn/ SP/Red Sox	1.00
204	Al Leiter	.15
204	Al Leiter/SP/Blue Jays	.75
205	Pedro Astacio	.15
206	Edgardo Alfonzo	.15
207	Armando Benitez	.15
208	Scott Rolen	.50
209	Pat Burrell	.35
210	Bobby Abreu	.15
210	Bobby Abreu/ SP/Astros	1.00
211	Mike Lieberthal	.15
212	Brandon Duckworth	.15
213	Jimmy Rollins	.40
214	Jeremy Giambi	.15
215	Vicente Padilla	.15
216	Travis Lee	.15
217	Jason Kendall	.15
218	Brian Giles	.15
218	Brian Giles/SP/Indians	1.00
219	Aramis Ramirez	.15
220	Pokey Reese	.15
221	Kip Wells	.15
222	Josh Fogg	.15
222	Josh Fogg/ SP/White Sox	.75
223	Mike Williams	.15
224	Ryan Klesko	.15
224	Ryan Klesko/ SP/Braves	.75
225	Phil Nevin	.15
225	Phil Nevin/SP/Tigers	.75
226	Brian Lawrence	.15
227	Mark Kotsay	.15
228	Brett Tomko	.15
229	Trevor Hoffman	.15
229	Trevor Hoffman/ SP/Marlins	.75
230	Barry Bonds	2.00
230	Barry Bonds/ SP/Pirates	6.00
231	Jeff Kent	.15
231	Jeff Kent/ SP/Blue Jays	1.00
232	Rich Aurilia	.15
233	Tsuyoshi Shinjo	.15
233	Tsuyoshi Shinjo/ SP/Mets	1.00
234	Benito Santiago	.15
234	Benito Santiago/ SP/Padres	.75
235	Kirk Rueter	.15
236	Kurt Ainsworth	.15
237	Livan Hernandez	.15
238	Russ Ortiz	.15
239	David Bell	.15
240	Jason Schmidt	.15
241	Reggie Sanders	.15
242	Jim Edmonds	.25
242	Jim Edmonds/ SP/Angels	1.00
243	J.D. Drew	.25
244	Albert Pujols	1.50
245	Fernando Vina	.15
246	Tino Martinez	.15
246	Tino Martinez/ SP/Mariners	1.00
246	Tino Martinez/ SP/Yankees	1.00
247	Edgar Renteria	.15
248	Matt Morris	.15
249	Woody Williams	.15
250	Jason Isringhausen	.15
250	Jason Isringhausen/ SP/A's	.75
251	Cal Ripken Jr.	2.00
252	Cal Ripken Jr.	2.00
253	Cal Ripken Jr.	2.00
254	Cal Ripken Jr.	2.00
255	Ryne Sandberg	.75
256	Don Mattingly	1.00
257	Don Mattingly	1.00
258	Roger Clemens	.85
259	Roger Clemens	.85
260	Roger Clemens	.85
261	Roger Clemens	.85
262	Roger Clemens	.85
263	Roger Clemens	.85
264	Roger Clemens	.85

265	Rickey Henderson	.65
266	Rickey Henderson	.65
267	Jose Canseco	.40
268	Barry Bonds	2.00
269	Barry Bonds	2.00
270	Barry Bonds	2.00
271	Barry Bonds	2.00
272	Jeff Bagwell	.65
273	Kirby Puckett	.75
274	Kirby Puckett	.75
275	Greg Maddux	.75
276	Greg Maddux	.75
277	Greg Maddux	.75
278	Greg Maddux	.75
279	Ken Griffey Jr.	1.00
280	Mike Piazza	1.00
281	Kirby Puckett	.75
282	Mike Piazza	1.00
283	Frank Thomas	.65
284	Hideo Nomo	.65
285	Randy Johnson	.65
286	Juan Gonzalez	.65
287	Derek Jeter	2.00
288	Derek Jeter	2.00
289	Derek Jeter	2.00
290	Nomar Garciaparra	1.00
291	Pedro J. Martinez	.65
292	Kerry Wood	.50
293	Sammy Sosa	1.00
294	Chipper Jones	.75
295	Ivan Rodriguez	.50
296	Ivan Rodriguez	.50
297	Albert Pujols	1.50
298	Ichiro Suzuki	1.00
299	Ichiro Suzuki	1.00
300	Ichiro Suzuki	1.00
301	So Taguchi RC	1.00
302	Kazuhisa Ishii RC	2.00
303	Jeremy Lambert RC	.50
304	Sean Burroughs	.40
305	P.J. Bevis RC	.50
306	Jon Rauch	.40
307	Scotty Layfield RC	.50
308	Miguel Ascencio	.40
309	Franklyn German RC	.50
310	Luis Ugueto RC	.50
311	Jorge Sosa RC	.50
312	Felix Escalona RC	.50
313	Jose Valverde RC	.50
314	Jeremy Ward RC	.50
315	Kevin Gryboski RC	.50
316	Francis Beltran RC	.50
317	Joe Thurston	.40
318	Cliff Lee RC	1.00
319	Takahito Nomura RC	.50
320	Bill Hall	.40
321	Marlon Byrd	.50
322	Andy Shibilo RC	.50
323	Edwin Almonte RC	.50
324	Brandon Backe RC	.50
325	Chone Figgins RC	1.50
326	Brian Mallette RC	.50
327	Rodrigo Rosario RC	.50
328	Anderson Machado RC	.50
329	Jorge Padilla RC	.50
330	Allan Simpson RC	.50
331	Doug DeVore RC	.50
332	Drew Henson	.50
333	Raul Chavez RC	.50
334	Tom Shearn RC	.50
335	Ben Howard RC	.50
336	Chris Baker RC	.50
337	Travis Hughes RC	.50
338	Kevin Mench	.40
339	Brian Tallet	.40
340	Mike Moriarty RC	.50
341	Corey Thurman RC	.50
342	Terry Pearson RC	.50
343	Steve Kent RC	.50
344	Satoru Komiyama RC	.50
345	Jason Lane	.40
346	Freddy Sanchez RC	.50
347	Brandon Puffer RC	.50
348	Clay Condrey RC	.50
349	Rene Reyes RC	.50
350	Hee Seop Choi	.50
351	Rodrigo Lopez	.40
352	Colin Young RC	.50
353	Jason Simontacchi RC	.50
354	Oliver Perez RC	2.00
355	Kirk Saarloos RC	.50
356	Marcus Thames	.40
357	Jeff Austin RC	.50
358	Justin Kaye	.40
359	Julio Mateo RC	.50
360	Mike Smith RC	.50
361	Chris Snelling RC	.75
362	Dennis Tankersley	.50
363	Runelvys Hernandez RC	.50
364	Aaron Cook RC	.50
365	Joe Borchard	.40
366	Earl Snyder RC	.50
367	Shane Nance RC	.50
368	Aaron Guiel RC	.50

369	Steve Bechler RC	.50
370	Tim Kalita RC	.50
371	Shawn Sedlacek RC	.50
372	Eric Good RC	.50
373	Eric Junge RC	.40
374	Matt Thornton	.40
375	Travis Driskill RC	.50
376	Mitch Wylie RC	.50
377	John Ennis RC	.50
378	Reed Johnson RC	.75
379	Juan Brito RC	.50
380	Ron Calloway RC	.50
381	Adrian Burnside RC	.50
382	Josh Bard RC	.50
383	Matt Childers RC	.50
384	Gustavo Chacin RC	.50
385	Luis Martinez RC	.50
386	Trey Hodges RC	.50
387	Hansel Izquierdo RC	.50
388	Jeriome Robertson RC	.50
389	Victor Alvarez RC	.50
390	David Ross RC	.50
391	Ron Chiavacci	.40
392	Adam Walker RC	.50
393	Mike Gonzalez RC	.50
394	John Foster RC	.50
395	Kyle Kane RC	.50
396	Cam Esslinger RC	.50
397	Kevin Frederick RC	.50
398	Franklin Nunez RC	.50
399	Todd Donovan RC	.50
400	Kevin Cash RC	.50

Statistical Standouts

	NM/M
Complete Set (50):	120.00
Common Player:	1.50
Inserted 1:12	
1 Adam Dunn	2.50
2 Alex Rodriguez	8.00
3 Andruw Jones	4.00
4 Brian Giles	1.50
5 Chipper Jones	5.00
6 Cliff Floyd	1.50
7 Craig Biggio	1.50
8 Frank Thomas	4.00
9 Fred McGriff	1.50
10 Garret Anderson	1.50
11 Greg Maddux	5.00
12 Luis Gonzalez	1.50
13 Magglio Ordonez	1.50
14 Ivan Rodriguez	3.00
15 Ken Griffey Jr.	6.00
16 Ichiro Suzuki	6.00
17 Jason Giambi	2.50
18 Derek Jeter	10.00
19 Sammy Sosa	6.00
20 Albert Pujols	8.00
21 J.D. Drew	1.50
22 Jeff Bagwell	4.00
23 Jim Edmonds	1.50
24 Jose Vidro	1.50
25 Juan Encarnacion	1.50
26 Kerry Wood	3.00
27 Al Leiter	1.50
28 Curt Schilling	2.50
29 Manny Ramirez	4.00
30 Lance Berkman	1.50
31 Miguel Tejada	1.50
32 Mike Piazza	6.00
33 Nomar Garciaparra	6.00
34 Omar Vizquel	1.50
35 Pat Burrell	2.00
36 Paul Konerko	1.50
37 Rafael Palmeiro	3.00
38 Randy Johnson	4.00
39 Richie Sexson	1.50
40 Roger Clemens	5.50
41 Shawn Green	2.00
42 Todd Helton	4.00
43 Tom Glavine	1.50
44 Troy Glaus	1.50
45 Vladimir Guerrero	4.00
46 Mike Sweeney	1.50
47 Alfonso Soriano	3.00
48 Barry Zito	1.50
49 John Smoltz	1.50
50 Ellis Burks	1.50

Freshman Orientation

	NM/M
Common Player:	5.00

Inserted 1:142
Class Officer Parallel: 1.5X
Production 50 Sets

1	Andres Torres/Bat	8.00
2	Mark Ellis/Jsy	8.00
3	Erik Bedard/Bat	8.00
4	Delvin James/Jsy	5.00
5	Austin Kearns/Bat	10.00
6	Josh Pearce/Bat	5.00
7	Rafael Soriano/Jsy	8.00
8	Jason Lane/Bat	8.00
9	Mark Prior/Jsy	15.00
10	Alfredo Amezaga/Bat	5.00
11	Ryan Ludwick/Bat	5.00
12	So Taguchi/Bat	5.00
13	Duaner Sanchez/Bat	5.00
14	Kazuhisa Ishii/Jsy	15.00
15	Zach Day/Jsy	8.00
16	Eric Cyr/Bat	5.00
17	Francis Beltran/Jsy	5.00
18	Joe Borchard/Jsy	10.00
19	Jeremy Affeldt/Shoe	10.00
20	Alexis Gomez/Jsy	5.00

Dress For Success

		NM/M
Common Player:		5.00
Production 250 Sets		
Prime Cuts:		Not Priced
Production 25 Sets		
1	Mike Piazza	25.00
2	Cal Ripken Jr.	40.00
3	Carlos Delgado	8.00
4	Chipper Jones	20.00
5	Bernie Williams	8.00
6	Carlos Beltran	10.00
7	Curt Schilling	10.00
8	Greg Maddux	20.00
9	Ivan Rodriguez	12.00
10	Alex Rodriguez	20.00
11	Roger Clemens	20.00
12	Todd Helton	15.00
13	Jim Edmonds	8.00
14	Manny Ramirez	15.00
15	Mark Buehrle	8.00

BLC Homers

		NM/M
Common Player:		20.00
Production 25 Sets		
1	Luis Gonzalez	20.00
2	Luis Gonzalez	20.00
3	Luis Gonzalez	20.00
4	Todd Helton	35.00
5	Todd Helton	35.00
6	Todd Helton	35.00
7	Todd Helton	35.00
8	Todd Helton	35.00
9	Todd Helton	35.00
10	Todd Helton	35.00
11	Todd Helton	35.00
12	Jim Thome	35.00
13	Jim Thome	35.00
14	Jim Thome	35.00
15	Rafael Palmeiro	30.00
16	Rafael Palmeiro	30.00
17	Rafael Palmeiro	30.00
18	Rafael Palmeiro	30.00
19	Rafael Palmeiro	30.00
20	Troy Glaus	35.00
21	Troy Glaus	35.00

22	Troy Glaus	35.00
23	Gary Sheffield	20.00
24	Gary Sheffield	20.00
25	Gary Sheffield	20.00
26	Mike Piazza	50.00
27	Mike Piazza	50.00
28	Mike Piazza	50.00
29	Mike Piazza	50.00
30	Mike Piazza	50.00

Triple Threads

		NM/M
Common Card:		25.00
Production 100 Sets		
1	Reggie Jackson, Alfonso Soriano, Don Mattingly	80.00
2	Alex Rodriguez, Rafael Palmeiro, Ivan Rodriguez	30.00
3	Mike Piazza, Gary Carter, Rickey Henderson	40.00
4	Dale Murphy, Andruw Jones, Chipper Jones	40.00
5	Mike Schmidt, Steve Carlton, Scott Rolen	85.00
6	Rickey Henderson	40.00
7	Johnny Bench, Joe Morgan, Tom Seaver	50.00
8	Randy Johnson, Pedro J. Martinez, Vladimir Guerrero	35.00
9	Nolan Ryan, Rod Carew, Troy Glaus	75.00
10	Lou Brock, J.D. Drew, Stan Musial	65.00

View Masters

		NM/M
Common Player:		10.00
Production 100 Sets		
Slideshows:		Not Priced
Production 25 Sets		
1	Carlos Delgado	12.00
2	Todd Helton	20.00
3	Tony Gwynn	25.00
4	Bernie Williams	10.00
5	Luis Gonzalez	10.00
6	Larry Walker	10.00
7	Troy Glaus	20.00
8	Alfonso Soriano	15.00
9	Curt Schilling	12.00
10	Chipper Jones	25.00
11	Vladimir Guerrero	20.00
12	Adam Dunn	15.00
13	Rickey Henderson	20.00
14	Miguel Tejada	10.00
15	Kazuhisa Ishii	10.00
16	Greg Maddux	25.00
17	Pedro J. Martinez	20.00
18	Nomar Garciaparra	30.00
19	Mike Piazza	30.00
20	Lance Berkman	10.00

Great American Signings

	NM/M
Common Autograph:	5.00
Inserted 1:56	

Brent Abernathy/175	5.00
Brandon Backe/175	5.00
Chris Baker/175	5.00
Francis Beltran/175	5.00
Raul Chavez/175	5.00
Doug DeVore/175	5.00
Felix Escalona/100	8.00
Franklyn German/175	5.00
Jay Gibbons/150	10.00
Bill Hall/175	8.00
Drew Henson/50	35.00
Eric Hinske/175	8.00
Ben Howard/175	5.00
Aubrey Huff/175	8.00
Travis Hughes/175	5.00
Cesar Izturis/175	8.00
Nick Johnson/175	8.00
Austin Kearns/75	10.00
Satoru Komiyama/75	20.00
Jason Lane/150	8.00
Brian Lawrence/175	5.00
Anderson Machado/175	5.00
Don Mattingly/25	
Roy Oswalt/100	15.00
Jorge Padilla/175	5.00
Oliver Perez/175	25.00
Rene Reyes/175	5.00
Mike Rivera/175	5.00
Rodrigo Rosario/175	5.00
Tom Shearn/175	5.00
Chris Snelling/175	10.00
Mac Suzuki/100	30.00
So Taguchi/50	40.00
Dennis Tankersley/175	8.00
Corey Thurman/175	5.00
Luis Ugueto/175	5.00
Kip Wells/175	5.00

Stat. Standouts Materials

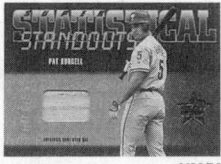

		NM/M
Common Player:		5.00
Inserted 1:69		
Super Materials:		2-3X
Production 25 Sets		
1	Adam Dunn/Bat/200	15.00
2	Alex Rodriguez/Bat/200	15.00
3	Andruw Jones/Bat/200	10.00
4	Brian Giles/Bat/200	8.00
5	Chipper Jones/Bat/200	15.00
6	Cliff Floyd/Jsy	5.00
7	Craig Biggio/Jsy	8.00
8	Frank Thomas/Jsy/125	12.00
9	Fred McGriff/Bat	10.00
10	Garret Anderson/Bat	8.00
11	Greg Maddux/Jsy/200	20.00
12	Luis Gonzalez/Jsy	8.00
13	Magglio Ordonez/Bat/150	10.00
14	Ivan Rodriguez/Jsy/100	15.00
15	Ken Griffey Jr./Base/100	15.00

16	Ichiro Suzuki/Base/100	30.00
17	Jason Giambi/Base	10.00
18	Derek Jeter/Base/100	25.00
19	Sammy Sosa/Base/100	15.00
20	Albert Pujols/Base/100	15.00
21	J.D. Drew/Bat/150	10.00
22	Jeff Bagwell/Jsy/150	15.00
23	Jim Edmonds/Bat	8.00
24	Jose Vidro/Bat	5.00
25	Juan Encarnacion/Bat	5.00
26	Kerry Wood/Jsy/200	15.00
27	Al Leiter/Jsy	8.00
28	Curt Schilling/Jsy/225	12.00
29	Manny Ramirez/Bat/100	15.00
30	Lance Berkman/Bat/150	10.00
31	Miguel Tejada/Jsy	10.00
32	Mike Piazza/Jsy/200	20.00
33	Nomar Garciaparra/Bat/200	20.00
34	Omar Vizquel/Jsy	8.00
35	Pat Burrell/Bat	10.00
36	Paul Konerko/Jsy	6.00
37	Rafael Palmeiro/Bat	10.00
38	Randy Johnson/Jsy/200	15.00
39	Richie Sexson/Jsy	10.00
40	Roger Clemens/Jsy/200	20.00
41	Shawn Green/Jsy	10.00
42	Todd Helton/Jsy/175	15.00
43	Tom Glavine/Jsy/125	10.00
44	Troy Glaus/Jsy	10.00
45	Vladimir Guerrero/Jsy	15.00
46	Mike Sweeney/Bat	5.00
47	Alfonso Soriano/Jsy/200	15.00
48	Barry Zito/Jsy/100	8.00
49	John Smoltz/Jsy	8.00
50	Ellis Burks/Jsy	5.00

Longevity

Stars (1-300):	5-10X
SP's (1-300):	1-3X
Production 100	
Rookies (301-400):	Not Priced
Production 25	

2003 Leaf

	NM/M
Complete Set (320):	40.00
Common Player:	.15
Pack (10):	1.50
Box (24):	30.00
1 Brad Fullmer	.15
2 Darin Erstad	.25

No.	Player	Price
3	David Eckstein	.15
4	Garret Anderson	.15
5	Jarrod Washburn	.15
6	Kevin Appier	.15
7	Tim Salmon	.25
8	Troy Glaus	.75
9	Troy Percival	.15
10	Buddy Groom	.15
11	Jay Gibbons	.15
12	Jeff Conine	.15
13	Marty Cordova	.15
14	Melvin Mora	.15
15	Rodrigo Lopez	.15
16	Tony Batista	.15
17	Jorge Julio	.15
18	Cliff Floyd	.15
19	Derek Lowe	.15
20	Jason Varitek	.15
21	Johnny Damon	.25
22	Manny Ramirez	.75
23	Nomar Garciaparra	1.25
24	Pedro J. Martinez	.75
25	Rickey Henderson	.75
26	Shea Hillenbrand	.15
27	Trot Nixon	.15
28	Carlos Lee	.15
29	Frank Thomas	.75
30	Jose Valentin	.15
31	Magglio Ordonez	.15
32	Mark Buehrle	.15
33	Paul Konerko	.25
34	C.C. Sabathia	.15
35	Danys Baez	.15
36	Ellis Burks	.15
37	Jim Thome	.75
38	Omar Vizquel	.15
39	Ricky Gutierrez	.15
40	Travis Fryman	.15
41	Bobby Higginson	.15
42	Carlos Pena	.15
43	Juan Acevedo	.15
44	Mark Redman	.15
45	Randall Simon	.15
46	Robert Fick	.15
47	Steve Sparks	.15
48	Carlos Beltran	.50
49	Joe Randa	.15
50	Michael Tucker	.15
51	Mike Sweeney	.15
52	Paul Byrd	.15
53	Raul Ibanez	.15
54	Runelvys Hernandez	.15
55	A.J. Pierzynski	.15
56	Brad Radke	.15
57	Corey Koskie	.15
58	Cristian Guzman	.15
59	David Ortiz	.50
60	Doug Mientkiewicz	.15
61	Dustan Mohr	.15
62	Eddie Guardado	.15
63	Jacque Jones	.15
64	Torii Hunter	.15
65	Alfonso Soriano	.50
66	Andy Pettitte	.35
67	Bernie Williams	.30
68	David Wells	.15
69	Derek Jeter	2.00
70	Jason Giambi	.40
71	Jeff Weaver	.15
72	Jorge Posada	.25
73	Mike Mussina	.30
74	Nick Johnson	.15
75	Raul Mondesi	.15
76	Robin Ventura	.15
77	Roger Clemens	1.00
78	Barry Zito	.25
79	Billy Koch	.15
80	David Justice	.25
81	Eric Chavez	.25
82	Jermaine Dye	.15
83	Mark Mulder	.15
84	Miguel Tejada	.30
85	Ray Durham	.15
86	Scott Hatteberg	.15
87	Ted Lilly	.15
88	Tim Hudson	.25
89	Bret Boone	.15
90	Carlos Guillen	.15
91	Chris Snelling	.15
92	Dan Wilson	.15
93	Edgar Martinez	.15
94	Freddy Garcia	.15
95	Ichiro Suzuki	1.25
96	Jamie Moyer	.15
97	Joel Pineiro	.15
98	John Olerud	.15
99	Mark McLemore	.15
100	Mike Cameron	.15
101	Kazuhiro Sasaki	.15
102	Aubrey Huff	.15
103	Ben Grieve	.15
104	Joe Kennedy	.15
105	Paul Wilson	.15
106	Randy Winn	.15
107	Steve Cox	.15
108	Alex Rodriguez	1.50
109	Chan Ho Park	.15
110	Hank Blalock	.50
111	Herbert Perry	.15
112	Ivan Rodriguez	.65
113	Juan Gonzalez	.75
114	Kenny Rogers	.15
115	Kevin Mench	.15
116	Rafael Palmeiro	.65
117	Carlos Delgado	.40
118	Eric Hinske	.15
119	Jose Cruz	.15
120	Josh Phelps	.15
121	Roy Halladay	.25
122	Shannon Stewart	.15
123	Vernon Wells	.15
124	Curt Schilling	.40
125	Junior Spivey	.15
126	Luis Gonzalez	.25
127	Mark Grace	.25
128	Randy Johnson	.75
129	Steve Finley	.15
130	Tony Womack	.15
131	Andruw Jones	.75
132	Chipper Jones	1.00
133	Gary Sheffield	.30
134	Greg Maddux	1.00
135	John Smoltz	.25
136	Kevin Millwood	.15
137	Rafael Furcal	.15
138	Tom Glavine	.40
139	Alex Gonzalez	.15
140	Corey Patterson	.15
141	Fred McGriff	.15
142	Jon Lieber	.15
143	Kerry Wood	.65
144	Mark Prior	.75
145	Matt Clement	.15
146	Moises Alou	.15
147	Sammy Sosa	1.25
148	Aaron Boone	.15
149	Adam Dunn	.50
150	Austin Kearns	.15
151	Barry Larkin	.15
152	Danny Graves	.15
153	Elmer Dessens	.15
154	Ken Griffey Jr.	1.25
155	Sean Casey	.25
156	Todd Walker	.15
157	Gabe Kapler	.15
158	Jason Jennings	.15
159	Jay Payton	.15
160	Larry Walker	.15
161	Mike Hampton	.15
162	Todd Helton	.75
163	Todd Zeile	.15
164	A.J. Burnett	.15
165	Derrek Lee	.15
166	Josh Beckett	.50
167	Juan Encarnacion	.15
168	Luis Castillo	.15
169	Mike Lowell	.15
170	Preston Wilson	.15
171	Billy Wagner	.15
172	Craig Biggio	.25
173	Daryle Ward	.15
174	Jeff Bagwell	.75
175	Lance Berkman	.15
176	Octavio Dotel	.15
177	Richard Hidalgo	.15
178	Roy Oswalt	.25
179	Adrian Beltre	.40
180	Eric Gagne	.40
181	Eric Karros	.15
182	Hideo Nomo	.65
183	Kazuhisa Ishii	.15
184	Kevin Brown	.15
185	Mark Grudzielanek	.15
186	Odalis Perez	.15
187	Paul LoDuca	.15
188	Shawn Green	.40
189	Alex Sanchez	.15
190	Ben Sheets	.15
191	Jeffrey Hammonds	.15
192	Jose Hernandez	.15
193	Takahito Nomura	.15
194	Richie Sexson	.15
195	Andres Galarraga	.15
196	Bartolo Colon	.15
197	Brad Wilkerson	.15
198	Javier Vazquez	.15
199	Jose Vidro	.15
200	Michael Barrett	.15
201	Tomokazu Ohka	.15
202	Vladimir Guerrero	.75
203	Al Leiter	.15
204	Armando Benitez	.15
205	Edgardo Alfonzo	.15
206	Mike Piazza	1.25
207	Mo Vaughn	.15
208	Pedro Astacio	.15
209	Roberto Alomar	.35
210	Roger Cedeno	.15
211	Timoniel Perez	.15
212	Bobby Abreu	.15
213	Jimmy Rollins	.25
214	Mike Lieberthal	.15
215	Pat Burrell	.25
216	Randy Wolf	.15
217	Travis Lee	.15
218	Vicente Padilla	.15
219	Aramis Ramirez	.15
220	Brian Giles	.15
221	Craig Wilson	.15
222	Jason Kendall	.15
223	Josh Fogg	.15
224	Kevin Young	.15
225	Kip Wells	.15
226	Mike Williams	.15
227	Brett Tomko	.15
228	Brian Lawrence	.15
229	Mark Kotsay	.15
230	Oliver Perez	.15
231	Phil Nevin	.15
232	Ryan Klesko	.15
233	Sean Burroughs	.15
234	Trevor Hoffman	.15
235	Barry Bonds	2.00
236	Benito Santiago	.15
237	Jeff Kent	.15
238	Kirk Rueter	.15
239	Livan Hernandez	.15
240	Kenny Lofton	.15
241	Rich Aurilia	.15
242	Russ Ortiz	.15
243	Albert Pujols	1.50
244	Edgar Renteria	.15
245	J.D. Drew	.40
246	Jason Isringhausen	.15
247	Jim Edmonds	.40
248	Matt Morris	.15
249	Tino Martinez	.15
250	Scott Rolen	.75
251	Curt Schilling	.25
252	Ivan Rodriguez	.35
253	Mike Piazza	.75
254	Sammy Sosa	.75
255	Matt Williams	.15
256	Frank Thomas	.25
257	Barry Bonds	1.00
258	Roger Clemens	.65
259	Rickey Henderson	.25
260	Ken Griffey Jr.	.60
261	Greg Maddux	.50
262	Randy Johnson	.40
263	Jeff Bagwell	.25
264	Roberto Alomar	.25
265	Tom Glavine	.25
266	Juan Gonzalez	.25
267	Mark Grace	.25
268	Mike Mussina	.25
269	Ryan Klesko	.15
270	Fred McGriff	.15
271	Joe Borchard	.15
272	Chris Snelling	.15
273	Brian Tallet	.15
274	Cliff Lee	.15
275	Freddy Sanchez	.15
276	Chone Figgins	.15
277	Kevin Cash	.15
278	Josh Bard	.15
279	Jeriome Robertson	.15
280	Jeremy Hill	.15
281	Shane Nance	.15
282	Jeff Baker	.15
283	Trey Hodges	.15
284	Eric Eckenstahler	.15
285	Jim Rushford	.15
286	Carlos Rivera	.15
287	Josh Bonifay	.15
288	Garrett Atkins	.15
289	Nic Jackson	.15
290	Corwin Malone	.15
291	Jimmy Gobble	.15
292	Josh Wilson	.15
293	Clint Barmes RC	.50
294	Jon Adkins	.15
295	Tim Kalita	.15
296	Nelson Castro	.15
297	Colin Young	.15
298	Adrian Burnside	.15
299	Luis Martinez	.15
300	Terrmel Sledge RC	.50
301	Todd Donovan	.15
302	Jeremy Ward	.15
303	Wilson Valdez	.15
304	Jose Contreras RC	.75
305	Marshall McDougall	.15
306	Mitch Wylie	.15
307	Ron Calloway	.15
308	Jose Valverde	.15
309	Jason Davis	.15
310	Scotty Layfield	.15
311	Matt Thornton	.15
312	Adam Walker	.15
313	Gustavo Chacin	.15
314	Ron Chiavacci	.15
315	Wilbert Nieves	.15
316	Clifford Bartosh	.15
317	Mike Gonzalez	.15
318	Jeremy Guthrie	.15
319	Eric Junge	.15
320	Ben Kozlowski	.15

Red Press Proofs

Stars:	3-5X

Inserted 1:12

Blue Press Proofs

Stars:	8-15X

Production 50 Sets

Green

No Pricing
Production 25 Sets

Clean Up Crew

NM/M

Complete Set (10):		30.00
Common Card:		1.50
Inserted 1:49		
1	Alex Rodriguez, Rafael Palmeiro, Ivan Rodriguez	6.00
2	Nomar Garciaparra, Manny Ramirez, Cliff Floyd	5.00
3	Jason Giambi, Bernie Williams, Jorge Posada	4.00
4	Rich Aurilia, Jeff Kent, Barry Bonds	6.00
5	Larry Walker, Todd Helton, Jay Payton	1.50
6	Lance Berkman, Jeff Bagwell, Daryle Ward	2.00
7	Scott Rolen, Albert Pujols, Jim Edmonds	5.00
8	Gary Sheffield, Chipper Jones, Andruw Jones	4.00
9	Miguel Tejada, Eric Chavez, Jermaine Dye	1.50
10	Sammy Sosa, Moises Alou, Fred McGriff	4.00

Clean Up Crew Memorabilia

NM/M

Production 50 Sets		
1	Alex Rodriguez, Rafael Palmeiro, Ivan Rodriguez	30.00
2	Nomar Garciaparra, Manny Ramirez, Cliff Floyd	25.00
3	Jason Giambi, Bernie Williams, Jorge Posada	25.00
4	Rich Aurilia, Jeff Kent, Barry Bonds	35.00
5	Larry Walker, Todd Helton, Jay Payton	20.00

		NM/M
6	Lance Berkman, Jeff Bagwell, Daryle Ward	25.00
7	Scott Rolen, Albert Pujols, Jim Edmonds	40.00
8	Gary Sheffield, Chipper Jones, Andruw Jones	30.00
9	Miguel Tejada, Eric Chavez, Jermaine Dye	20.00
10	Sammy Sosa, Moises Alou, Fred McGriff	30.00

Clubhouse Signatures Bronze

	NM/M
Common Bronze Auto.:	8.00
Inserted 1:300	
Silvers:	1-2X
Production 100 Sets	
Golds:	No Pricing
Production 25 Sets	

	Edwin Almonte	8.00
	Jeff Baker	10.00
	Josh Bard	10.00
	Angel Berroa	8.00
	Joe Crede/SP/25	15.00
	Andre Dawson/SP/50	25.00
	Bobby Doerr/SP/100	20.00
	Dwight "Doc" Gooden	25.00
	Drew Henson/SP/50	20.00
	Eric Hinske	10.00
	Torii Hunter/SP/75	35.00
	Omar Infante	8.00
	Brian Lawrence	8.00
	Kevin Mench	8.00
	Jack Morris/SP/100	15.00
	Franklin Nunez	8.00
	Magglio Ordonez/SP/50	25.00
	Corey Patterson/SP/100	15.00
	Jhonny Peralta	20.00
	J.C. Romero	10.00
	Chris Snelling/SP/10010.00	
	Alfonso Soriano/SP/25	40.00
	Brian Tallet/SP/100	8.00

Game Collection

		NM/M
Common Player:		8.00
Production 150 Sets		
1	Miguel Tejada/Cap	10.00
2	Shannon Stewart/Cap	6.00
3	Mike Schmidt/Jkt	40.00
4	Nolan Ryan/Jkt	75.00
5	Rafael Palmeiro/Glove	15.00
6	Andruw Jones/Shoe	10.00
7	Bernie Williams/Shoe	15.00
8	Ivan Rodriguez/Shoe	10.00
9	Lance Berkman/Shoe	10.00
10	Magglio Ordonez/Shoe	10.00
11	Roy Oswalt/Glove	10.00
12	Andy Pettitte/Shoe	10.00
13	Vladimir Guerrero/Glove	30.00
14	Jason Jennings/Glove	8.00
15	Mike Sweeney/Shoe	8.00
16	Joe Borchard/Shoe	10.00
17	Mark Prior/Shoe	10.00
18	Gary Carter/Jkt	10.00
19	Austin Kearns/Glove	10.00
20	Ryan Klesko/Glove	10.00

Gold Leaf Rookies

	NM/M
Complete Set (10):	10.00
Common Player:	1.00
Inserted 1:24	
Mirror Golds:	10-20X
Production 25 Sets	

1	Joe Borchard	1.00
2	Chone Figgins	1.00
3	Alexis Gomez	1.00
4	Chris Snelling	1.00
5	Cliff Lee	1.00
6	Victor Martinez	2.00
7	Hee Seop Choi	1.50
8	Michael Restovich	1.00
9	Anderson Machado	1.00
10	Drew Henson	2.00

Hard Hats

		NM/M
Complete Set (12):		15.00
Common Player:		1.00
Inserted 1:13		
1	Alex Rodriguez	4.00
2	Bernie Williams	1.00
3	Ivan Rodriguez	1.25
4	Jeff Bagwell	1.50
5	Rafael Furcal	1.00
6	Rafael Palmeiro	1.50
7	Tony Gwynn	2.00
8	Vladimir Guerrero	1.50
9	Adrian Beltre	1.00
10	Shawn Green	1.00
11	Andruw Jones	1.50
12	George Brett	4.00

Hard Hats Batting Helmets

		NM/M
Common Player:		15.00
Production 100 Sets		
1	Alex Rodriguez	50.00
2	Bernie Williams	35.00
3	Ivan Rodriguez	30.00
4	Jeff Bagwell	40.00
5	Rafael Furcal	15.00
6	Rafael Palmeiro	35.00
7	Tony Gwynn	35.00
8	Vladimir Guerrero	35.00
9	Adrian Beltre	20.00
10	Shawn Green	20.00
11	Andruw Jones	20.00
12	George Brett	100.00

Home / Away

	NM/M
Complete Set (20):	40.00
Common Player:	1.00
Home Inserted 1:34	

1	Andruw Jones/Home	1.50
2	Cal Ripken Jr./Home	6.00
3	Edgar Martinez/Home	1.00
4	Jim Thome/Home	1.50
5	Larry Walker/Home	1.00
6	Nomar Garciaparra/Home	4.00
7	Mark Prior/Home	1.00
8	Mike Piazza/Home	4.00
9	Vladimir Guerrero/Home	1.50
10	Chipper Jones/Home	3.00

Away Inserted 1:34		
1	Andruw Jones	1.50
2	Cal Ripken Jr.	6.00
3	Edgar Martinez	1.00
4	Jim Thome	2.00
5	Larry Walker	1.00
6	Nomar Garciaparra	4.00
7	Mark Prior	1.00
8	Mike Piazza	4.00
9	Vladimir Guerrero	2.00
10	Chipper Jones	3.00

Home / Away Memorabilia

	NM/M
Common Player:	6.00
Home Production 250	

1	Andruw Jones/Home	8.00
2	Cal Ripken Jr./Home	45.00
3	Edgar Martinez/Home	8.00
4	Jim Thome/Home	10.00
5	Larry Walker/Home	8.00
6	Nomar Garciaparra/Home	20.00
7	Mark Prior/Home	10.00
8	Mike Piazza/Home	15.00
9	Vladimir Guerrero/Home	12.00
10	Chipper Jones/Home	15.00

Away Production 250		
1	Andruw Jones	8.00
2	Cal Ripken Jr.	45.00
3	Edgar Martinez	8.00
4	Jim Thome	10.00
5	Larry Walker	6.00
6	Nomar Garciaparra	20.00
7	Mark Prior	10.00
8	Mike Piazza	15.00
9	Vladimir Guerrero	12.00
10	Chipper Jones	15.00

Maple & Ash

	NM/M
Common Player:	6.00
Production 400 Sets	

1	Jorge Posada	8.00
2	Mike Piazza	12.00
3	Alex Rodriguez	15.00
4	Jeff Bagwell	10.00
5	Joe Borchard	6.00
6	Miguel Tejada	6.00
7	Adam Dunn	8.00
8	Jim Thome	8.00
9	Lance Berkman	6.00
10	Torii Hunter	6.00
11	Carlos Delgado	6.00
12	Reggie Jackson	10.00
13	Juan Gonzalez	6.00
14	Vladimir Guerrero	10.00
15	Richie Sexson	6.00

Number Off My Back

	NM/M
Production 50 Sets	

1	Carlos Delgado	15.00
2	Don Mattingly	100.00
3	Todd Helton	30.00
4	Vernon Wells	10.00
5	Bernie Williams	20.00
6	Luis Gonzalez	20.00
7	Kerry Wood	30.00
8	Eric Chavez	10.00
9	Shawn Green	15.00
10	Roy Oswalt	15.00
11	Nomar Garciaparra	40.00
12	Robin Yount	60.00
13	Troy Glaus	20.00
14	C.C. Sabathia	10.00
15	Alex Rodriguez	50.00
16	Mark Mulder	10.00
17	Will Clark	60.00

18	Alfonso Soriano	30.00
19	Andy Pettitte	20.00
20	Curt Schilling	25.00

Shirt Off My Back

	NM/M
Common Player:	5.00
Production 500 Sets	
Number Off My Back:	2-4X
Production 50 Sets	

1	Carlos Delgado	6.00
2	Don Mattingly	25.00
3	Todd Helton	10.00
4	Vernon Wells	5.00
5	Bernie Williams	6.00
6	Luis Gonzalez	6.00
7	Kerry Wood	8.00
8	Eric Chavez	6.00
9	Shawn Green	6.00
10	Roy Oswalt	5.00
11	Nomar Garciaparra	12.00
12	Robin Yount	15.00
13	Troy Glaus	8.00
14	C.C. Sabathia	5.00
15	Alex Rodriguez	15.00
16	Mark Mulder	5.00
17	Will Clark	10.00
18	Alfonso Soriano	10.00
19	Andy Pettitte	8.00
20	Curt Schilling	8.00

Slick Leather

	NM/M
Complete Set (15):	20.00
Common Player:	1.00
Inserted 1:21	

1	Omar Vizquel	1.00
2	Roberto Alomar	1.50
3	Ivan Rodriguez	2.00
4	Greg Maddux	3.00
5	Scott Rolen	2.00
6	Todd Helton	2.00
7	Andruw Jones	2.00
8	Jim Edmonds	1.50
9	Barry Bonds	6.00
10	Eric Chavez	1.00
11	Ichiro Suzuki	5.00
12	Mike Mussina	1.50
13	John Olerud	1.00
14	Torii Hunter	1.00
15	Larry Walker	1.00

60

	NM/M
Complete Set (50):	80.00
Common Player:	.75
Inserted 1:8	
Foil Parallels:	3-5X
Production 60 Sets	

1	Troy Glaus	3.00
2	Curt Schilling	2.00
3	Randy Johnson	3.00
4	Andruw Jones	3.00
5	Chipper Jones	4.00
6	Greg Maddux	4.00
7	Tom Glavine	1.00
8	Manny Ramirez	3.00
9	Nomar Garciaparra	5.00
10	Pedro J. Martinez	3.00
11	Rickey Henderson	3.00

SHAWN GREEN
OUTFIELD—LOS ANGELES DODGERS*

#	Player	Price
12	Sammy Sosa	5.00
13	Frank Thomas	3.00
14	Magglio Ordonez	.75
15	Mark Buehrle	.75
16	Adam Dunn	1.50
17	Ken Griffey Jr.	5.00
18	Jim Thome	2.00
19	Omar Vizquel	.75
20	Larry Walker	.75
21	Todd Helton	3.00
22	Lance Berkman	.75
23	Roy Oswalt	.75
24	Mike Sweeney	.75
25	Hideo Nomo	3.00
26	Kazuhisa Ishii	1.00
27	Shawn Green	1.00
28	Torii Hunter	.75
29	Vladimir Guerrero	3.00
30	Mike Piazza	5.00
31	Alfonso Soriano	3.00
32	Bernie Williams	1.00
33	Derek Jeter	8.00
34	Jason Giambi	2.00
35	Roger Clemens	4.00
36	Barry Zito	.75
37	Miguel Tejada	.75
38	Pat Burrell	1.00
39	Ryan Klesko	.75
40	Barry Bonds	8.00
41	Jeff Kent	.75
42	Ichiro Suzuki	5.00
43	John Olerud	.75
44	Albert Pujols	5.00
45	Jim Edmonds	1.00
46	Scott Rolen	2.50
47	Alex Rodriguez	6.00
48	Ivan Rodriguez	2.50
49	Rafael Palmeiro	2.50
50	Roy Halladay	.75

2003 Leaf Certified Materials

	NM/M
Complete Set (250):	
Common Player:	.50
Common SP Auto.	
(206-250):	6.00
Production 400 unless noted.	
Mirror Red Auto. SP's	
(06-250):	1-1.5X
Production 100	
Mirror Blue Auto. SP's	
(206-250):	1-2X
Production 50	
Mirror Gold Autos.	
(206-250):	No Pricing
Production 25	
Pack (5):	20.00
Box (10):	150.00

#	Player	Price
1	Troy Glaus	1.00
2	Alfredo Amezaga	.50
3	Garret Anderson	1.00
4	Nolan Ryan	6.00
5	Darin Erstad	.75
6	Junior Spivey	.50
7	Randy Johnson	2.00
8	Curt Schilling	1.50
9	Luis Gonzalez	.75
10	Steve Finley	.50
11	Matt Williams	.75
12	Greg Maddux	3.00
13	Chipper Jones	2.00
14	Gary Sheffield	1.00
15	Adam LaRoche	.50
16	Andruw Jones	1.00
17	Robert Fick	.50
18	John Smoltz	1.00
19	Javy Lopez	.75
20	Jay Gibbons	.50
21	Geronimo Gil	.50
22	Cal Ripken Jr.	6.00
23	Nomar Garciaparra	4.00
24	Pedro J. Martinez	2.00
25	Freddy Sanchez	.50
26	Rickey Henderson	1.00
27	Manny Ramirez	1.50
28	Casey Fossum	.50
29	Sammy Sosa	3.00
30	Kerry Wood	2.00
31	Corey Patterson	1.00
32	Nic Jackson	.50
33	Mark Prior	1.50
34	Juan Cruz	.50
35	Steve Smyth	.50
36	Magglio Ordonez	.75
37	Joe Borchard	.50
38	Frank Thomas	1.50
39	Mark Buehrle	.50
40	Joe Crede	.50
41	Carlos Lee	.50
42	Paul Konerko	.50
43	Adam Dunn	1.50
44	Corky Miller	.50
45	Brandon Larson	.50
46	Ken Griffey Jr.	3.00
47	Barry Larkin	1.00
48	Sean Casey	.50
49	Wily Mo Pena	1.00
50	Austin Kearns	.75
51	Victor Martinez	1.00
52	Brian Tallet	.50
53	Cliff Lee	.50
54	Jeremy Guthrie	.50
55	C.C. Sabathia	.50
56	Ricardo Rodriguez	.50
57	Omar Vizquel	1.00
58	Travis Hafner	.50
59	Todd Helton	1.50
60	Jason Jennings	.50
61	Jeff Baker	.50
62	Larry Walker	1.00
63	Travis Chapman	.50
64	Mike Maroth	.50
65	Josh Beckett	1.00
66	Ivan Rodriguez	1.50
67	Brad Penny	.50
68	A.J. Burnett	.50
69	Craig Biggio	1.00
70	Roy Oswalt	1.00
71	Jason Lane	.50
72	Nolan Ryan	6.00
73	Wade Miller	.50
74	Richard Hidalgo	.50
75	Jeff Bagwell	1.50
76	Lance Berkman	1.00
77	Rodrigo Rosario	.50
78	Jeff Kent	1.00
79	John Buck	.50
80	Angel Berroa	.50
81	Mike Sweeney	.50
82	Mac Suzuki	.50
83	Alexis Gomez	.50
84	Carlos Beltran	1.50
85	Runelvys Hernandez	.50
86	Hideo Nomo	1.00
87	Paul LoDuca	.50
88	Cesar Izturis	.50
89	Kazuhisa Ishii	.50
90	Shawn Green	1.00
91	Joe Thurston	.50
92	Adrian Beltre	1.00
93	Kevin Brown	1.00
94	Richie Sexson	1.00
95	Ben Sheets	1.00
96	Takahito Nomura	.50
97	Geoff Jenkins	.50
98	Bill Hall	.50
99	Torii Hunter	1.00
100	A.J. Pierzynski	.50
101	Michael Cuddyer	.50
102	Jose Morban	.50
103	Brad Radke	.50
104	Jacque Jones	.50
105	Eric Milton	.50
106	Joe Mays	.50
107	Adam Johnson	.50
108	Javier Vazquez	.50
109	Vladimir Guerrero	2.00
110	Jose Vidro	.50
111	Michael Barrett	.50
112	Orlando Cabrera	.50
113	Tom Glavine	1.00
114	Roberto Alomar	1.00
115	Tsuyoshi Shinjo	.50
116	Cliff Floyd	.50
117	Mike Piazza	3.00
118	Al Leiter	.50
119	Don Mattingly	4.00
120	Roger Clemens	4.00
121	Derek Jeter	6.00
122	Alfonso Soriano	2.00
123	Drew Henson	.50
124	Brandon Claussen	.50
125	Christian Parker	.50
126	Jason Giambi	1.00
127	Mike Mussina	1.00
128	Bernie Williams	1.00
129	Jason Anderson	.50
130	Nick Johnson	.50
131	Jorge Posada	1.00
132	Andy Pettitte	1.00
133	Barry Zito	1.00
134	Miguel Tejada	1.00
135	Eric Chavez	1.00
136	Tim Hudson	1.00
137	Mark Mulder	.75
138	Terrence Long	.50
139	Mark Ellis	.50
140	Jim Thome	1.50
141	Pat Burrell	.75
142	Marlon Byrd	.50
143	Bobby Abreu	.75
144	Brandon Duckworth	.50
145	Robert Person	.50
146	Anderson Machado	.50
147	Aramis Ramirez	1.00
148	Jack Wilson	.50
149	Carlos Rivera	.50
150	Jose Castillo	.50
151	Walter Young	.50
152	Brian Giles	.75
153	Jason Kendall	.50
154	Ryan Klesko	.75
155	Mike Rivera	.50
156	Sean Burroughs	.50
157	Brian Lawrence	.50
158	Xavier Nady	.50
159	Dennis Tankersley	.50
160	Phil Nevin	.50
161	Barry Bonds	6.00
162	Kenny Lofton	.50
163	Rich Aurilia	.50
164	Ichiro Suzuki	4.00
165	Edgar Martinez	.75
166	Chris Snelling	.50
167	Rafael Soriano	.50
168	John Olerud	.75
169	Bret Boone	.75
170	Freddy Garcia	.50
171	Aaron Sele	.50
172	Kazuhiro Sasaki	.50
173	Albert Pujols	4.00
174	Scott Rolen	2.00
175	So Taguchi	.50
176	Jim Edmonds	1.00
177	Edgar Renteria	1.00
178	J.D. Drew	1.00
179	Antonio Perez	.50
180	Dewon Brazelton	.50
181	Aubrey Huff	.50
182	Toby Hall	.50
183	Ben Grieve	.50
184	Joe Kennedy	.50
185	Alex Rodriguez	5.00
186	Rafael Palmeiro	1.50
187	Hank Blalock	1.50
188	Mark Teixeira	1.00
189	Juan Gonzalez	1.50
190	Kevin Mench	.50
191	Nolan Ryan	6.00
192	Doug Davis	.50
193	Eric Hinske	.50
194	Vinnie Chulk	.50
195	Alexis Rios	.50
196	Carlos Delgado	1.00
197	Shannon Stewart	.50
198	Josh Phelps	.50
199	Vernon Wells	.75
200	Roy Halladay	.75
201	Babe Ruth	8.00
202	Lou Gehrig	6.00
203	Jackie Robinson	6.00
204	Ty Cobb	6.00
205	Thurman Munson	4.00
206	Prentice Redman RC	8.00
207	Craig Brazell RC	10.00
208	Nook Logan RC	15.00
209	Hong-Chih Kuo RC	75.00
210	Matt Kata RC	10.00
211	Chien-Ming Wang RC	225.00
212	Alejandro Machado RC	6.00
213	Michael Hessman RC	8.00
214	Francisco Rosario RC	8.00
215	Pedro Liriano	8.00
216	Jeremy Bonderman	35.00
217	Oscar Villarreal RC	10.00
218	Arnie Munoz RC	6.00
219	Tim Olson RC	10.00
220	Jose Contreras/100 RC	40.00
221	Francisco Cruceta RC	10.00
222	John Webb	10.00
223	Phil Seibel RC	6.00
224	Aaron Looper RC	10.00
225	Brian Stokes RC	10.00
226	Guillermo Quiroz RC	10.00
227	Fernando Cabrera RC	10.00
228	Josh Hall RC	10.00
229	Diegomar Markwell RC	8.00
230	Andrew Brown RC	10.00
231	Doug Waechter RC	10.00
232	Felix Sanchez RC	10.00
233	Gerardo Garcia	8.00
234	Matt Bruback RC	8.00
235	Michel Hernandez RC	10.00
236	Rett Johnson RC	10.00
237	Ryan Cameron RC	8.00
238	Rob Hammock RC	10.00
239	Clint Barmes RC	20.00
240	Brandon Webb RC	40.00
241	Jon Leicester RC	6.00
242	Shane Bazzell RC	10.00
243	Joe Valentine RC	10.00
244	Josh Stewart RC	10.00
245	Pete LaForest RC	8.00
246	Shane Victorino RC	8.00
247	Terrmel Sledge RC	10.00
248	Lew Ford RC	25.00
249	Todd Wellemeyer RC	10.00
250	Hideki Matsui/No Auto. RC	15.00

Mirror Red

Stars (1-205):	2-5X
SP's (206-250):	.2-.4X
Production 100 Sets	
Mirror Blues (1-205):	4-10X
SP's (206-250):	.3-.5X
Production 50 Sets	
Mirror Golds:	No Pricing
Production 25 Sets	
Mirror Emeralds:	No Pricing
Production 5 Sets	
Mirror Blacks: One Set Produced	

Fabric of the Game

	NM/M
Common Player:	4.00
Quantity produced listed	
1BA Bobby Doerr/5	15.00
1JY Bobby Doerr/39	15.00
1PS Bobby Doerr/50	15.00
2BA Ozzie Smith/100	25.00
2IN Ozzie Smith/50	30.00
2JY Ozzie Smith/88	20.00
2PS Ozzie Smith/50	30.00

Card	Player	Value
3DY	Pee Wee Reese/32	30.00
3JY	Pee Wee Reese/58	15.00
4BA	Jeff Bagwell/100	10.00
4DY	Jeff Bagwell/65	10.00
4IN	Jeff Bagwell/50	12.00
4JY	Jeff Bagwell/98	10.00
4PS	Jeff Bagwell/50	12.00
5BA	Tommy Lasorda/100	8.00
5DY	Tommy Lasorda/58	10.00
5JY	Tommy Lasorda/84	8.00
5PS	Tommy Lasorda/50	10.00
6JY	Red Schoendienst/55	10.00
7BA	Harmon Killebrew/50	15.00
7DY	Harmon Killebrew/61	15.00
7IN	Harmon Killebrew/50	15.00
7JY	Harmon Killebrew/71	15.00
7PS	Harmon Killebrew/50	15.00
8DY	Roger Maris/55	40.00
8JY	Roger Maris/58	40.00
8PS	Roger Maris/50	40.00
9BA	Alex Rodriguez/100	15.00
9DY	Alex Rodriguez/77	15.00
9IN	Alex Rodriguez/50	15.00
9JY	Alex Rodriguez/99	15.00
9PS	Alex Rodriguez/50	15.00
10BA	Alex Rodriguez/100	15.00
10DY	Alex Rodriguez/72	15.00
10IN	Alex Rodriguez/50	15.00
10JY	Alex Rodriguez/101	15.00
10PS	Alex Rodriguez/50	15.00
11BA	Dale Murphy/50	15.00
11DY	Dale Murphy/66	15.00
11IN	Dale Murphy/50	15.00
11JY	Dale Murphy/85	15.00
11PS	Dale Murphy/50	15.00
12BA	Alan Trammell/50	10.00
12IN	Alan Trammell/50	10.00
12JY	Alan Trammell/90	10.00
12PS	Alan Trammell/50	10.00
13BA	Babe Ruth/10	250.00
13DY	Babe Ruth/13	250.00
13IN	Babe Ruth/10	250.00
13JY	Babe Ruth/30	200.00
13PS	Babe Ruth/10	250.00
14JY	Lou Gehrig/38	200.00
15JY	Babe Ruth/30	250.00
16JY	Mel Ott/46	30.00
17BA	Paul Molitor/100	15.00
17DY	Paul Molitor/70	15.00
17IN	Paul Molitor/50	15.00
17JY	Paul Molitor/84	15.00
17PS	Paul Molitor/50	15.00
18DY	Duke Snider/58	15.00
18JY	Duke Snider/52	15.00
19BA	Miguel Tejada/50	10.00
19DY	Miguel Tejada/68	8.00
19IN	Miguel Tejada/50	10.00
19JY	Miguel Tejada/99	5.00
19PS	Miguel Tejada/50	10.00
20JY	Lou Gehrig/38	200.00
21DY	Brooks Robinson/54	15.00
21JY	Brooks Robinson/66	15.00
22BA	George Brett/50	30.00
22DY	George Brett/69	25.00
22IN	George Brett/50	30.00
22JY	George Brett/91	25.00
22PS	George Brett/50	30.00
23BA	Johnny Bench/50	15.00
23DY	Johnny Bench/59	15.00
23IN	Johnny Bench/50	15.00
23JY	Johnny Bench/81	15.00
23PS	Johnny Bench/50	15.00
24JY	Lou Boudreau/48	15.00
25BA	Nomar Garciaparra/100	20.00
25IN	Nomar Garciaparra/50	25.00
25JY	Nomar Garciaparra/100	20.00
25PS	Nomar Garciaparra/50	25.00
26BA	Tsuyoshi Shinjo/50	8.00
26DY	Tsuyoshi Shinjo/62	8.00
26JY	Tsuyoshi Shinjo/101	5.00
27BA	Pat Burrell/100	8.00
27DY	Pat Burrell/46	10.00
27JY	Pat Burrell/101	8.00
28BA	Albert Pujols/100	20.00
28IN	Albert Pujols/50	25.00
28JY	Albert Pujols/101	20.00
28PS	Albert Pujols/50	25.00
29JY	Stan Musial/43	30.00
30JY	Al Kaline/64	15.00
31BA	Ivan Rodriguez/100	8.00
31DY	Ivan Rodriguez/72	8.00
31IN	Ivan Rodriguez/50	10.00
31JY	Ivan Rodriguez/101	5.00
32BA	Craig Biggio/100	6.00
32DY	Craig Biggio/65	8.00
32JY	Craig Biggio/101	6.00
32PS	Craig Biggio/50	10.00
33DY	Joe Morgan/59	10.00
33JY	Joe Morgan/74	8.00
34BA	Willie Stargell/50	15.00
34JY	Willie Stargell/68	15.00
34PS	Willie Stargell/50	15.00
35BA	Andre Dawson/100	8.00
35IN	Andre Dawson/50	10.00
35JY	Andre Dawson/87	8.00
35PS	Andre Dawson/50	10.00
36BA	Gary Carter/100	10.00
36DY	Gary Carter/62	10.00
36IN	Gary Carter/50	10.00
36JY	Gary Carter/85	8.00
36PS	Gary Carter/50	10.00
37BA	Cal Ripken Jr./50	50.00
37DY	Cal Ripken Jr./54	50.00
37IN	Cal Ripken Jr./50	50.00
37JY	Cal Ripken Jr./101	40.00
37PS	Cal Ripken Jr./50	50.00
38JY	Enos Slaughter/53	20.00
39BA	Reggie Jackson/50	15.00
39DY	Reggie Jackson/68	15.00
39JY	Reggie Jackson/75	15.00
39PS	Reggie Jackson/50	15.00
40JY	Phil Rizzuto/47	15.00
41BA	Chipper Jones/100	10.00
41DY	Chipper Jones/66	10.00
41IN	Chipper Jones/50	10.00
41JY	Chipper Jones/101	10.00
41PS	Chipper Jones/50	15.00
42BA	Hideo Nomo/100	15.00
42DY	Hideo Nomo/58	15.00
42IN	Hideo Nomo/50	15.00
42JY	Hideo Nomo/95	10.00
42PS	Hideo Nomo/50	15.00
43JY	Luis Aparicio/69	10.00
44BA	Hideo Nomo/100	10.00
44IN	Hideo Nomo/50	15.00
44JY	Hideo Nomo/101	10.00
44PS	Hideo Nomo/50	15.00
45BA	Edgar Martinez/100	8.00
45DY	Edgar Martinez/77	8.00
45JY	Edgar Martinez/100	8.00
45PS	Edgar Martinez/50	10.00
46BA	Barry Larkin/100	6.00
46DY	Barry Larkin/59	10.00
46JY	Barry Larkin/100	6.00
46PS	Barry Larkin/50	10.00
47BA	Alfonso Soriano/100	10.00
47IN	Alfonso Soriano/50	15.00
47JY	Alfonso Soriano/102	10.00
47PS	Alfonso Soriano/50	15.00
48BA	Wade Boggs/100	8.00
48DY	Wade Boggs/98	8.00
48IN	Wade Boggs/50	10.00
48JY	Wade Boggs/99	8.00
48PS	Wade Boggs/50	10.00
49BA	Wade Boggs/50	10.00
49IN	Wade Boggs/50	10.00
49JY	Wade Boggs/94	8.00
49PS	Wade Boggs/50	10.00
50JY	Ernie Banks/50	15.00
51BA	Joe Torre/50	10.00
51DY	Joe Torre/66	10.00
51IN	Joe Torre/50	10.00
51JY	Joe Torre/66	10.00
51PS	Joe Torre/50	10.00
52BA	Tim Hudson/100	4.00
52DY	Tim Hudson/68	6.00
52JY	Tim Hudson/101	4.00
52PS	Tim Hudson/50	6.00
53BA	Shawn Green/100	4.00
53DY	Shawn Green/58	6.00
53JY	Shawn Green/102	4.00
53PS	Shawn Green/50	6.00
54BA	Carlos Beltran/100	6.00
54DY	Carlos Beltran/69	8.00
54JY	Carlos Beltran/101	6.00
54PS	Carlos Beltran/50	8.00
55BA	Bo Jackson/50	15.00
55DY	Bo Jackson/69	15.00
55JY	Bo Jackson/90	10.00
55PS	Bo Jackson/50	15.00
56BA	Hal Newhouser/50	8.00
56JY	Hal Newhouser/55	8.00
56PS	Hal Newhouser/50	8.00
57BA	Jason Giambi/100	6.00
57DY	Jason Giambi/68	8.00
57IN	Jason Giambi/50	8.00
57JY	Jason Giambi/101	6.00
57PS	Jason Giambi/50	8.00
58BA	Lance Berkman/100	6.00
58DY	Lance Berkman/65	8.00
58IN	Lance Berkman/50	8.00
58JY	Lance Berkman/102	6.00
58PS	Lance Berkman/50	8.00
59BA	Todd Helton/100	8.00
59DY	Todd Helton/93	6.00
59JY	Todd Helton/100	6.00
59PS	Todd Helton/50	8.00
60BA	Mark Grace/100	8.00
60DY	Mark Grace/95	8.00
60PS	Mark Grace/50	15.00
61BA	Fred Lynn/100	6.00
61JY	Fred Lynn/75	8.00
61PS	Fred Lynn/50	8.00
62JY	Bob Feller/52	15.00
63BA	Robin Yount/100	20.00
63DY	Robin Yount/70	20.00
63IN	Robin Yount/50	25.00
63JY	Robin Yount/88	20.00
63PS	Robin Yount/50	25.00
64BA	Tony Gwynn/100	15.00
64DY	Tony Gwynn/69	20.00
64IN	Tony Gwynn/50	20.00
64JY	Tony Gwynn/99	20.00
64PS	Tony Gwynn/50	20.00
65BA	Tony Gwynn/100	15.00
65DY	Tony Gwynn/69	15.00
65IN	Tony Gwynn/50	15.00
65JY	Tony Gwynn/99	15.00
65PS	Tony Gwynn/50	15.00
66DY	Frank Robinson/54	10.00
66JY	Frank Robinson/70	10.00
67BA	Mike Schmidt/50	20.00
67DY	Mike Schmidt/46	20.00
67IN	Mike Schmidt/50	20.00
67JY	Mike Schmidt/81	20.00
67PS	Mike Schmidt/50	20.00
68JY	Lou Brock/66	15.00
69BA	Don Sutton/50	8.00
69DY	Don Sutton/58	8.00
69JY	Don Sutton/72	8.00
70BA	Mark Mulder/100	4.00
70DY	Mark Mulder/68	4.00
70JY	Mark Mulder/101	4.00
70PS	Mark Mulder/50	6.00
71BA	Luis Gonzalez/100	4.00
71DY	Luis Gonzalez/98	4.00
71JY	Luis Gonzalez/101	4.00
71PS	Luis Gonzalez/50	6.00
72BA	Jorge Posada/100	6.00
72JY	Jorge Posada/101	6.00
72PS	Jorge Posada/50	8.00
73BA	Sammy Sosa/100	25.00
73IN	Sammy Sosa/50	25.00
73JY	Sammy Sosa/101	20.00
73PS	Sammy Sosa/50	25.00
74BA	Roberto Alomar/100	8.00
74DY	Roberto Alomar/62	10.00
74JY	Roberto Alomar/102	8.00
74PS	Roberto Alomar/50	10.00
75JY	Roberto Clemente/69	80.00
76BA	Jeff Kent/100	4.00
76DY	Jeff Kent/58	6.00
76JY	Jeff Kent/101	4.00
76PS	Jeff Kent/50	6.00
77DY	Sean Casey/59	8.00
77JY	Sean Casey/100	4.00
78BA	Roger Clemens/50	25.00
78IN	Roger Clemens/50	25.00
78JY	Roger Clemens/95	20.00
78PS	Roger Clemens/50	25.00
79DY	Warren Spahn/53	15.00
79JY	Warren Spahn/58	15.00
80BA	Roger Clemens/100	20.00
80IN	Roger Clemens/50	25.00
80JY	Roger Clemens/102	25.00
80PS	Roger Clemens/50	25.00
81BA	Jim Palmer/50	10.00
81DY	Jim Palmer/54	10.00
81JY	Jim Palmer/69	10.00
81PS	Jim Palmer/50	10.00
82BA	Juan Gonzalez/50	10.00
82JY	Juan Gonzalez/101	6.00
82PS	Juan Gonzalez/50	10.00
83BA	Will Clark/100	15.00
83DY	Will Clark/58	15.00
83JY	Will Clark/88	15.00
83PS	Will Clark/50	15.00
84BA	Don Mattingly/50	25.00
84IN	Don Mattingly/50	25.00
84JY	Don Mattingly/93	25.00
84PS	Don Mattingly/50	25.00
85BA	Ryne Sandberg/40	30.00
85IN	Ryne Sandberg/50	30.00
85JY	Ryne Sandberg/85	30.00
85PS	Ryne Sandberg/50	30.00
86JY	Early Wynn/55	8.00
87BA	Manny Ramirez/50	8.00
87JY	Manny Ramirez/102	8.00
87PS	Manny Ramirez/50	8.00
88BA	Rickey Henderson/100	10.00
88DY	Rickey Henderson/62	15.00
88IN	Rickey Henderson/50	15.00
88JY	Rickey Henderson/99	10.00
88PS	Rickey Henderson/50	15.00
89BA	Rickey Henderson/100	10.00
89DY	Rickey Henderson/69	15.00
89PS	Rickey Henderson/50	15.00
90BA	Jason Giambi/100	8.00
90IN	Jason Giambi/50	10.00
90JY	Jason Giambi/102	8.00
90PS	Jason Giambi/50	10.00
91BA	Carlos Delgado/100	4.00
91DY	Carlos Delgado/77	4.00
91JY	Carlos Delgado/100	4.00
91PS	Carlos Delgado/50	6.00
92BA	Jim Thome/100	8.00
92JY	Jim Thome/102	10.00
92PS	Jim Thome/50	10.00
93BA	Andruw Jones/100	6.00
93DY	Andruw Jones/66	8.00
93JY	Andruw Jones/101	6.00
93PS	Andruw Jones/50	8.00
94BA	Rafael Palmeiro/100	8.00
94DY	Rafael Palmeiro/72	8.00
94JY	Rafael Palmeiro/102	8.00
94PS	Rafael Palmeiro/50	8.00
95BA	Troy Glaus/100	6.00
95DY	Troy Glaus/97	6.00
95IN	Troy Glaus/100	6.00
95JY	Troy Glaus/100	6.00
95PS	Troy Glaus/50	6.00
96BA	Wade Boggs/100	8.00
96IN	Wade Boggs/50	10.00
96JY	Wade Boggs/26	25.00
96PS	Wade Boggs/86	8.00
96PS	Wade Boggs/50	10.00
97BA	Jim "Catfish" Hunter/50	10.00
97DY	Jim "Catfish" Hunter/68	10.00
97JN	Jim "Catfish" Hunter/27	15.00
97JY	Jim "Catfish" Hunter/68	10.00
97PS	Jim "Catfish" Hunter/50	10.00
98BA	Juan Marichal/50	10.00
98DY	Juan Marichal/58	10.00
98IN	Juan Marichal/27	20.00
98JY	Juan Marichal/67	10.00
98PS	Juan Marichal/50	10.00
99BA	Carlton Fisk/50	15.00
99IN	Carlton Fisk/25	
99JN	Carlton Fisk/27	25.00
99JY	Carlton Fisk/80	10.00
99PS	Carlton Fisk/50	15.00
100BA	Vladimir Guerrero/100	8.00
100DY	Vladimir Guerrero/69	15.00
100JN	Vladimir Guerrero/27	30.00
100JY	Vladimir Guerrero/101	8.00
100PS	Vladimir Guerrero/50	10.00
101BA	Rod Carew/100	10.00
101DY	Rod Carew/65	15.00
101JN	Rod Carew/29	20.00
101JY	Rod Carew/85	10.00
101PS	Rod Carew/50	15.00
102BA	Rod Carew/50	15.00
102DY	Rod Carew/61	15.00
102JN	Rod Carew/29	20.00
102JY	Rod Carew/71	10.00
102PS	Rod Carew/50	15.00
103BA	Joe Carter/50	6.00
103DY	Joe Carter/77	8.00
103JN	Joe Carter/29	15.00
103JY	Joe Carter/94	6.00
104BA	Mike Sweeney/100	4.00
104DY	Mike Sweeney/69	6.00
104JN	Mike Sweeney/29	15.00
104JY	Mike Sweeney/101	4.00
104PS	Mike Sweeney/50	6.00
105BA	Nolan Ryan/25	
105DY	Nolan Ryan/65	40.00
105IN	Nolan Ryan/25	
105JN	Nolan Ryan/30	50.00

105JY Nolan Ryan/70 40.00
105PS Nolan Ryan/50 40.00
106BA Orlando Cepeda/50 8.00
106DY Orlando Cepeda/58 8.00
106IN Orlando Cepeda/50 8.00
106JN Orlando Cepeda/30 15.00
106JY Orlando Cepeda/65 8.00
106PS Orlando Cepeda/50 8.00
107BA Magglio Ordonez/100 4.00
107JN Magglio Ordonez/30 15.00
107JY Magglio Ordonez/100 4.00
107PS Magglio Ordonez/50 6.00
108BA Hoyt Wilhelm/50 8.00
108JN Hoyt Wilhelm/31 15.00
108JY Hoyt Wilhelm/68 8.00
108PS Hoyt Wilhelm/50 8.00
109BA Mike Piazza/100 15.00
109DY Mike Piazza/62 20.00
109IN Mike Piazza/50 25.00
109JN Mike Piazza/31 30.00
109JY Mike Piazza/100 15.00
109PS Mike Piazza/50 20.00
110BA Greg Maddux/100 10.00
110DY Greg Maddux/66 15.00
110IN Greg Maddux/50 15.00
110JN Greg Maddux/31 30.00
110JY Greg Maddux/102 10.00
110PS Greg Maddux/50 15.00
111BA Mark Prior/100 8.00
111IN Mark Prior/50 10.00
111JY Mark Prior/102 8.00
111PS Mark Prior/50 10.00
112BA Torii Hunter/100 6.00
112DY Torii Hunter/61 8.00
112IN Torii Hunter/50 8.00
112JN Torii Hunter/48 10.00
112JY Torii Hunter/101 6.00
112PS Torii Hunter/50 8.00
113BA Steve Carlton/100 8.00
113DY Steve Carlton/46 15.00
113IN Steve Carlton/50 10.00
113JN Steve Carlton/32 15.00
113JY Steve Carlton/81 8.00
113PS Steve Carlton/50 10.00
114BA Jose Canseco/100 10.00
114DY Jose Canseco/68 15.00
114IN Jose Canseco/50 15.00
114JN Jose Canseco/33 15.00
114JY Jose Canseco/89 10.00
114PS Jose Canseco/50 15.00
115BA Nolan Ryan/50 30.00
115DY Nolan Ryan/72 30.00
115IN Nolan Ryan/50 30.00
115JN Nolan Ryan/34 40.00
115JY Nolan Ryan/90 30.00
115PS Nolan Ryan/50 30.00
116BA Nolan Ryan/50 30.00
116DY Nolan Ryan/65 30.00
116JN Nolan Ryan/34 40.00
116JY Nolan Ryan/84 30.00
116PS Nolan Ryan/50 30.00
118BA Kerry Wood/100 10.00
118JN Kerry Wood/34 25.00
118JY Kerry Wood/101 10.00
118PS Kerry Wood/50 15.00
119BA Mike Mussina/50 10.00
119JN Mike Mussina/35 25.00
119JY Mike Mussina/101 15.00
119PS Mike Mussina/50 15.00
120JN Yogi Berra/50 25.00
120JY Yogi Berra/47 25.00
121JY Thurman Munson/79 25.00
122BA Frank Thomas/100 8.00
122JN Frank Thomas/35 15.00
122JY Frank Thomas/94 6.00
122PS Frank Thomas/50 8.00
123BA Rickey Henderson/50 15.00
123DY Rickey Henderson/68 10.00
123JN Rickey Henderson/35 20.00
123JY Rickey Henderson/80 10.00
123PS Rickey Henderson/50 15.00
124BA Mike Mussina/100 6.00
124DY Mike Mussina/54 10.00
124JN Mike Mussina/35 20.00
124JY Mike Mussina/97 6.00
124PS Mike Mussina/50 8.00
125BA Gaylord Perry/100 6.00
125DY Gaylord Perry/77 6.00
125JN Gaylord Perry/36 10.00
125JY Gaylord Perry/82 6.00
125PS Gaylord Perry/50 8.00
126BA Nick Johnson/100 4.00
126JN Nick Johnson/36 6.00

126JY Nick Johnson/102 4.00
126PS Nick Johnson/50 8.00
127BA Curt Schilling/100 8.00
127DY Curt Schilling/98 8.00
127JN Curt Schilling/38 15.00
127JY Curt Schilling/102 8.00
127PS Curt Schilling/50 8.00
128BA Dave Parker/100 6.00
128JN Dave Parker/39 10.00
128JY Dave Parker/80 8.00
128PS Dave Parker/50 8.00
129DY Eddie Mathews/53 15.00
129JN Eddie Mathews/41 25.00
129JY Eddie Mathews/59 20.00
130DY Tom Seaver/62 15.00
130JN Tom Seaver/41 20.00
130JY Tom Seaver/59 15.00
131DY Tom Seaver/59 15.00
131JN Tom Seaver/41 25.00
131JY Tom Seaver/78 15.00
132JN Jackie Robinson/42 80.00
132JY Jackie Robinson/52 60.00
133BA Reggie Jackson/100 10.00
133DY Reggie Jackson/65 15.00
133IN Reggie Jackson/50 15.00
133JN Reggie Jackson/44 20.00
133JY Reggie Jackson/80 10.00
133PS Reggie Jackson/50 15.00
134BA Willie McCovey/100 8.00
134DY Willie McCovey/58 10.00
134JN Willie McCovey/44 10.00
134JY Willie McCovey/77 8.00
134PS Willie McCovey/50 10.00
135BA Eric Davis/100 6.00
135DY Eric Davis/59 8.00
135JN Eddie Davis/44 10.00
135JY Eric Davis/89 6.00
135PS Eric Davis/50 8.00
136BA Adam Dunn/100 8.00
136DY Adam Dunn/59 10.00
136JN Adam Dunn/44 15.00
136JY Adam Dunn/102 8.00
136PS Adam Dunn/50 10.00
137BA Roy Oswalt/100 4.00
137DY Roy Oswalt/65 6.00
137IN Roy Oswalt/50 6.00
137JN Roy Oswalt/44 8.00
137JY Roy Oswalt/102 4.00
137PS Roy Oswalt/50 6.00
138BA Pedro J. Martinez/50 15.00
138DY Pedro J. Martinez/69 15.00
138JN Pedro J. Martinez/45 20.00
138JY Pedro J. Martinez/95 6.00
138PS Pedro J. Martinez/50 10.00
139BA Pedro J. Martinez/100 8.00
139IN Pedro J. Martinez/50 10.00
139JN Pedro J. Martinez/45 15.00
139JY Pedro J. Martinez/102 8.00
139PS Pedro J. Martinez/50 10.00
140BA Andy Pettitte/100 6.00
140JN Andy Pettitte/46 10.00
140JY Andy Pettitte/97 6.00
140PS Andy Pettitte/50 8.00
141BA Jack Morris/100 6.00
141IN Jack Morris/50 8.00
141JN Jack Morris/47 10.00
141JY Jack Morris/85 6.00
141PS Jack Morris/50 8.00
142BA Tom Glavine/100 6.00
142DY Tom Glavine/66 10.00
142JN Tom Glavine/47 15.00
142JY Tom Glavine/100 6.00
142PS Tom Glavine/50 8.00
143BA Randy Johnson/100 10.00
143DY Randy Johnson/77 15.00
143IN Randy Johnson/50 15.00
143JN Randy Johnson/51 15.00
143JY Randy Johnson/98 10.00
143PS Randy Johnson/50 15.00
144BA Bernie Williams/100 8.00
144IN Bernie Williams/50 10.00
144JN Bernie Williams/50 10.00
144JY Bernie Williams/100 8.00
144PS Bernie Williams/50 10.00
145BA Randy Johnson/50 15.00
145DY Randy Johnson/98 10.00
145IN Randy Johnson/51 15.00
145JN Randy Johnson/51 15.00
145JY Randy Johnson/102 15.00

145PS Randy Johnson/50 15.00
146DY Don Drysdale/58 10.00
146JN Don Drysdale/53 10.00
146JY Don Drysdale/64 10.00
147BA Mark Buehrle/100 4.00
147JN Mark Buehrle/56 6.00
147JY Mark Buehrle/101 4.00
147PS Mark Buehrle/50 4.00
148BA Chan Ho Park/100 4.00
148DY Chan Ho Park/58 4.00
148JN Chan Ho Park/61 6.00
148JY Chan Ho Park/101 4.00
148PS Chan Ho Park/50 6.00
149BA Carlton Fisk/100 8.00
149IN Carlton Fisk/50 15.00
149JN Carlton Fisk/72 15.00
149JY Carlton Fisk/92 15.00
149PS Carlton Fisk/50 15.00
150BA Barry Zito/100 6.00
150DY Barry Zito/68 8.00
150JN Barry Zito/75 8.00
150JY Barry Zito/101 6.00
150PS Barry Zito/50 8.00

Mirror Red Materials

NM/M

Common Player: 4.00
Production 250 unless noted.
Mirror Red SP's (206-250): .5X
Mirror Blues: 1-1.5X
Production 100
Mirror Golds: No Pricing
Production 25 sets
Mirror Emeralds: No Pricing
Production 5 Sets
Mirror Blacks: One Set Produced
1 Troy Glaus 6.00
2 Alfredo Amezaga 4.00
3 Garret Anderson 6.00
4 Nolan Ryan/35 65.00
5 Darin Erstad 5.00
6 Junior Spivey 4.00
7 Randy Johnson 8.00
8 Curt Schilling 8.00
9 Luis Gonzalez 5.00
10 Steve Finley 4.00
11 Matt Williams 5.00
12 Greg Maddux 10.00
13 Chipper Jones 10.00
14 Gary Sheffield/125 6.00
15 Adam LaRoche 4.00
16 Andruw Jones 6.00
17 Robert Fick 4.00
18 John Smoltz 6.00
19 Javy Lopez 4.00
20 Jay Gibbons 4.00
21 Geronimo Gil 4.00
22 Cal Ripken Jr/35 75.00
23 Nomar Garciaparra 15.00
24 Pedro J. Martinez 10.00
25 Freddy Sanchez 4.00
26 Rickey Henderson 10.00
27 Manny Ramirez 8.00
28 Casey Fossum 4.00
29 Sammy Sosa 15.00
30 Kerry Wood 10.00
31 Corey Patterson 6.00
32 Nic Jackson 4.00
33 Mark Prior 8.00
34 Juan Cruz 4.00
35 Steve Smyth 4.00
36 Magglio Ordonez 6.00
37 Joe Borchard 4.00
38 Frank Thomas 10.00
39 Mark Buehrle 5.00
40 Joe Crede/100 4.00
41 Carlos Lee 4.00
42 Paul Konerko 6.00
43 Adam Dunn 8.00
44 Brandon Larson/150 4.00
45 Ken Griffey Jr. 12.00
46 Barry Larkin 8.00
47 Sean Casey 6.00

49 Wily Mo Pena 6.00
50 Austin Kearns 6.00
51 Victor Martinez/100 8.00
55 C.C. Sabathia 4.00
56 Ricardo Rodriguez 4.00
57 Omar Vizquel 6.00
58 Travis Hafner 6.00
59 Todd Helton 8.00
60 Jason Jennings 4.00
62 Larry Walker 6.00
63 Travis Chapman 6.00
64 Mike Maroth 4.00
65 Josh Beckett 6.00
66 Ivan Rodriguez 8.00
67 Brad Penny 4.00
68 A.J. Burnett 4.00
69 Craig Biggio 6.00
70 Roy Oswalt 4.00
71 Jason Lane 4.00
72 Nolan Ryan/35 65.00
73 Wade Miller 5.00
74 Richard Hidalgo 4.00
75 Jeff Bagwell 10.00
76 Lance Berkman 6.00
77 Rodrigo Rosario 4.00
78 Jeff Kent 6.00
79 John Buck 4.00
80 Angel Berroa 4.00
81 Mike Sweeney 4.00
84 Carlos Beltran 8.00
86 Hideo Nomo 15.00
87 Paul LoDuca 6.00
88 Cesar Izturis 4.00
89 Kazuhisa Ishii 5.00
90 Shawn Green 4.00
91 Joe Thurston 4.00
92 Adrian Beltre 6.00
93 Kevin Brown 6.00
94 Richie Sexson 6.00
95 Ben Sheets 4.00
97 Geoff Jenkins 5.00
98 Bill Hall 4.00
99 Torii Hunter 8.00
101 Michael Cuddyer 4.00
102 Jose Morban 4.00
103 Brad Radke 4.00
104 Jacque Jones 6.00
105 Eric Milton 4.00
106 Joe Mays 5.00
107 Adam Johnson 5.00
108 Javier Vazquez 5.00
109 Vladimir Guerrero 10.00
110 Jose Vidro 4.00
111 Michael Barrett/50 6.00
112 Orlando Cabrera 5.00
113 Tom Glavine 8.00
114 Roberto Alomar 10.00
115 Tsuyoshi Shinjo 4.00
116 Cliff Floyd 5.00
117 Mike Piazza 10.00
118 Al Leiter 5.00
119 Don Mattingly/35 60.00
120 Roger Clemens 25.00
121 Derek Jeter 20.00
122 Alfonso Soriano 8.00
123 Drew Henson 6.00
124 Brandon Claussen/50 10.00
125 Christian Parker 4.00
126 Jason Giambi 6.00
127 Mike Mussina 10.00
128 Bernie Williams 8.00
130 Nick Johnson 4.00
131 Jorge Posada 8.00
132 Andy Pettitte 10.00
133 Barry Zito 6.00
134 Miguel Tejada 6.00
135 Eric Chavez 6.00
136 Tim Hudson 6.00
137 Mark Mulder 4.00
138 Terrence Long 4.00
139 Mark Ellis 4.00
140 Jim Thome 8.00
141 Pat Burrell 6.00
142 Marlon Byrd 4.00
143 Bobby Abreu 6.00
144 Brandon Duckworth 4.00
145 Robert Person 4.00
146 Anderson Machado 4.00
147 Aramis Ramirez 6.00
148 Jack Wilson 4.00
150 Jose Castillo 4.00
151 Walter Young 4.00
152 Brian Giles 6.00
153 Jason Kendall 5.00
155 Mike Rivera 5.00
157 Brian Lawrence 4.00
158 Xavier Nady/60 8.00
159 Dennis Tankersley 4.00
160 Phil Nevin 4.00
161 Barry Bonds 20.00
162 Kenny Lofton 6.00
163 Rich Aurilia 5.00
164 Ichiro Suzuki 25.00

165	Edgar Martinez/100	8.00
166	Chris Snelling	4.00
167	Rafael Soriano	4.00
168	John Olerud	4.00
169	Bret Boone	5.00
170	Freddy Garcia	4.00
171	Aaron Sele	4.00
172	Kazuhiro Sasaki	4.00
173	Albert Pujols	25.00
174	Scott Rolen	10.00
175	So Taguchi	4.00
176	Jim Edmonds	6.00
177	Edgar Renteria	8.00
178	J.D. Drew	6.00
179	Antonio Perez	4.00
180	Dewon Brazelton	4.00
181	Aubrey Huff/50	8.00
182	Toby Hall	4.00
183	Ben Grieve	4.00
184	Joe Kennedy	4.00
185	Alex Rodriguez	15.00
186	Rafael Palmeiro	8.00
187	Hank Blalock	8.00
188	Mark Teixeira	8.00
189	Juan Gonzalez	8.00
190	Kevin Mench	4.00
191	Nolan Ryan/35	65.00
192	Doug Davis	4.00
193	Eric Hinske	8.00
196	Carlos Delgado	6.00
197	Shannon Stewart	5.00
198	Josh Phelps	4.00
199	Vernon Wells	5.00
200	Roy Halladay	8.00

Mirror Red Signatures

		NM/M
Common Player:		
Production 100 unless noted.		
Mirror Blues:		1-1.5X
Production 50		
Mirror Golds:		1.5-2X
Production 25 Sets		
Mirror Emeralds:		No Pricing
Production 5 Sets		
Mirror Blacks: One Set Produced		
2	Alfredo Amezaga	6.00
15	Adam LaRoche	10.00
17	Robert Fick/15	20.00
20	Jay Gibbons	15.00
21	Geronimo Gil/15	15.00
25	Freddy Sanchez	10.00
28	Casey Fossum/50	10.00
32	Nic Jackson	10.00
34	Juan Cruz/15	15.00
35	Steve Smyth/94	8.00
37	Joe Borchard/50	15.00
39	Mark Buehrle/50	20.00
40	Joe Crede/30	15.00
45	Brandon Larson	10.00
49	Wily Mo Pena	20.00
51	Victor Martinez/50	25.00
53	Cliff Lee/50	15.00
54	Jeremy Guthrie/50	15.00
56	Ricardo Rodriguez	10.00
60	Jason Jennings/50	12.00
61	Jeff Baker/50	8.00
63	Travis Chapman	10.00
64	Mike Maroth	10.00
70	Roy Oswalt/50	20.00
71	Jason Lane	10.00
73	Wade Miller/50	15.00
77	Rodrigo Rosario	10.00
80	Angel Berroa/50	15.00
85	Runelvys Hernandez	10.00
88	Cesar Izturis	6.00
91	Joe Thurston	8.00
98	Bill Hall	10.00
102	Jose Morban	8.00
107	Adam Johnson/50	10.00
117	Mike Piazza/20	150.00
124	Brandon Claussen/60	15.00
125	Christian Parker/50	10.00

129	Jason Anderson	10.00
138	Terrence Long/50	15.00
142	Marlon Byrd	10.00
144	Brandon Duckworth/50	10.00
145	Robert Person/50	10.00
146	Anderson Machado	8.00
149	Carlos Rivera	8.00
150	Jose Castillo	8.00
151	Walter Young	8.00
155	Mike Rivera	8.00
157	Brian Lawrence	8.00
166	Chris Snelling	10.00
167	Rafael Soriano/50	12.00
179	Antonio Perez/50	8.00
180	Dewon Brazelton/50	8.00
181	Aubrey Huff/50	15.00
182	Toby Hall/50	10.00
184	Joe Kennedy/50	12.00
187	Hank Blalock/50	40.00
188	Mark Teixeira/50	40.00
190	Kevin Mench	10.00
193	Eric Hinske	15.00
194	Vinnie Chulk	8.00
195	Alexis Rios	25.00

2003 Leaf Limited

		NM/M
Complete Set (170):		
Common Player (1-151):		1.50
Production 999		
Common (152-170):		4.00
Production 399		
Common Auto. Memor. (171-200):		15.00
Production 99		
Common Auto. (171-200):		8.00
Pack (4):		75.00
Box (4):		250.00
1	Derek Jeter	6.00
2	Eric Chavez	1.50
3	Alex Rodriguez	5.00
4	Miguel Tejada	1.50
5	Nomar Garciaparra	4.00
6	Jeff Bagwell	3.00
7	Jim Thome	2.00
8	Pat Burrell	1.50
9	Albert Pujols	5.00
10	Juan Gonzalez	3.00
11	Shawn Green	1.50
12	Craig Biggio	1.50
13	Chipper Jones	3.00
14	Hideo Nomo	2.00
15	Vernon Wells	1.50
16	Gary Sheffield	2.00
17	Barry Larkin	1.50
18	Josh Beckett	1.50
19	Edgar Martinez	1.50
20	Ivan Rodriguez	2.00
21	Jeff Kent	1.50
22	Roberto Alomar	1.50
23	Alfonso Soriano	3.00
24	Jim Thome	2.00
25	Juan Gonzalez	3.00
26	Carlos Beltran	2.00
27	Shawn Green	1.50
28	Tim Hudson	1.50
29	Deion Sanders	1.50
30	Rafael Palmeiro	2.00
31	Todd Helton	3.00
32	Lance Berkman	1.50
33	Mike Mussina	2.00
34	Kazuhisa Ishii	1.50
35	Bill Burrell	1.50
36	Miguel Tejada	1.50
37	Juan Gonzalez	2.00
38	Roberto Alomar	1.50
39	Roberto Alomar	1.50
40	Luis Gonzalez	1.50
41	Jorge Posada	1.50
42	Mark Mulder	1.50
43	Sammy Sosa	4.00
44	Mark Prior	2.00

45	Roger Clemens	4.00
46	Tom Glavine	1.50
47	Mark Teixeira	1.50
48	Manny Ramirez	2.00
49	Frank Thomas	2.00
50	Troy Glaus	3.00
51	Andruw Jones	3.00
52	Jason Giambi	2.00
53	Jim Thome	2.00
54	Barry Bonds	6.00
55	Rafael Palmeiro	2.00
56	Edgar Martinez	1.50
57	Vladimir Guerrero	3.00
58	Roberto Alomar	1.50
59	Mike Sweeney	1.50
60	Magglio Ordonez	1.50
61	Ken Griffey Jr.	4.00
62	Craig Biggio	1.50
63	Greg Maddux	4.00
64	Mike Piazza	4.00
65	Tom Glavine	1.50
66	Kerry Wood	2.00
67	Frank Thomas	3.00
68	Mike Mussina	2.00
69	Nick Johnson	1.50
70	Bernie Williams	1.50
71	Scott Rolen	2.00
72	Curt Schilling	2.00
73	Adam Dunn	2.00
74	Roy Oswalt	1.50
75	Pedro J. Martinez	3.00
76	Tom Glavine	1.50
77	Torii Hunter	1.50
78	Austin Kearns	1.50
79	Randy Johnson	3.00
80	Bernie Williams	1.50
81	Ichiro Suzuki	4.00
82	Kerry Wood	2.00
83	Kazuhisa Ishii	1.50
85	Randy Johnson	3.00
85	Nick Johnson	1.50
86	Josh Beckett	1.50
87	Curt Schilling	2.00
88	Mike Mussina	2.00
89	Pedro J. Martinez	3.00
90	Barry Zito	1.50
91	Jim Edmonds	1.50
92	Rickey Henderson	3.00
93	Rickey Henderson	3.00
94	Rickey Henderson	3.00
95	Rickey Henderson	3.00
96	Rickey Henderson	3.00
97	Randy Johnson	3.00
98	Mark Grace	1.50
99	Pedro J. Martinez	3.00
100	Hee Seop Choi	1.50
101	Ivan Rodriguez	2.00
102	Jeff Kent	1.50
103	Hideo Nomo	3.00
104	Hideo Nomo	3.00
105	Mike Piazza	4.00
106	Tom Glavine	1.50
107	Roberto Alomar	1.50
108	Roger Clemens	5.00
109	Jason Giambi	2.00
110	Jim Thome	2.00
111	Alex Rodriguez	5.00
112	Juan Gonzalez	2.00
113	Torii Hunter	1.50
114	Roy Oswalt	1.50
115	Curt Schilling	2.00
116	Magglio Ordonez	1.50
117	Rafael Palmeiro	2.00
118	Andruw Jones	3.00
119	Manny Ramirez	3.00
120	Mark Teixeira	1.50
121	Mark Mulder	1.50
122	Garret Anderson	1.50
123	Tim Hudson	1.50
124	Todd Helton	3.00
125	Troy Glaus	3.00
126	Derek Jeter	6.00
127	Barry Bonds	6.00
128	Greg Maddux	4.00
129	Roger Clemens	5.00
130	Nomar Garciaparra	4.00
131	Mike Piazza	4.00
132	Alex Rodriguez	5.00
133	Ichiro Suzuki	4.00
134	Randy Johnson	3.00
135	Sammy Sosa	4.00
136	Ken Griffey Jr.	4.00
137	Alfonso Soriano	3.00
138	Jason Giambi	2.00
139	Albert Pujols	5.00
140	Chipper Jones	3.00
141	Adam Dunn	2.00
142	Pedro J. Martinez	3.00
143	Vladimir Guerrero	3.00
144	Mark Prior	2.00
145	Barry Zito	1.50
146	Jeff Bagwell	3.00
147	Lance Berkman	1.50
148	Shawn Green	1.50

149	Jason Giambi	2.00
150	Randy Johnson	3.00
151	Alex Rodriguez	5.00
152	Babe Ruth	10.00
153	Ty Cobb	6.00
154	Jackie Robinson	6.00
155	Lou Gehrig	8.00
156	Thurman Munson	6.00
157	Roberto Clemente	8.00
158	Nolan Ryan	10.00
159	Nolan Ryan	10.00
160	Nolan Ryan	10.00
161	Cal Ripken Jr.	10.00
162	Don Mattingly	8.00
163	Stan Musial	6.00
164	Tony Gwynn	3.00
165	Yogi Berra	3.00
166	Johnny Bench	5.00
167	Mike Schmidt	8.00
168	George Brett	8.00
169	Ryne Sandberg	4.00
170	Ernie Banks	5.00
171	J. Bonderman/ Auto./Jsy	75.00
172	Jose Contreras/ Auto. RC	40.00
173	Chien-Ming Wang/ Auto. RC	350.00
174	Hideki Matsui/ Base RC	40.00
175	Hong-Chih Kuo/ Auto./Bat RC	120.00
176	Brandon Webb/ Auto./Bat RC	60.00
177	Richard Fischer/Auto.	8.00
178	Robby Hammock/ Auto./Bat	20.00
179	Todd Wellemeyer/ Auto./49 RC	15.00
180	Prentice Redman/ Auto./Bat RC	10.00
181	Nook Logan/Auto. RC	20.00
182	Craig Brazell/ Auto. RC	15.00
183	Tim Olson/ Auto./Bat RC	15.00
184	Matt Kata/ Auto./Bat RC	20.00
185	A. Machado/Auto.	8.00
186	Michael Hessman/ Auto. RC	10.00
187	Oscar Villarreal/ Auto. RC	8.00
188	Guillermo Quiroz/ Auto./Bat RC	20.00
189	Michel Hernandez/ Auto. RC	10.00
190	Clint Barmes/ Auto. RC	40.00
191	Pete LaForest/ Auto./Bat RC	20.00
192	Adam Loewen/ Auto. RC	25.00
193	Terrmel Sledge/ Auto./Bat RC	15.00
194	Lew Ford/ Auto./Bat RC	40.00
195	Todd Wellemeyer/ Auto./49 RC	15.00
196	Clint Barmes/ Auto./Bat RC	40.00
197	J. Bonderman/ Auto./Jsy	50.00
198	Brandon Webb/ Auto./Jsy RC	60.00
199	Hideki Matsui/ Base RC	30.00
200	Jose Contreras/ Auto. RC	40.00

Gold Spotlight

Golds (1-151):		2-4X
Golds (152-170):		1.5-3X

Production 50
Golds (171-200): No Pricing
Production 10 to 25

Silver Spotlight

Silvers (1-170):	1-2X

Production 100

Silver Auto. Memor. (171-200):	1X
Silver Memor. (171-200):	1X
Silver Auto.:	1X

Production 29 to 50

Jersey Numbers
NM/M

Common Player:
Production 5-100
Some not priced due to scarcity.

1	Rod Carew/50	20.00
2	Nolan Ryan/50	40.00
3	Reggie Jackson/50	20.00
4	Brooks Robinson/50	25.00
5	Frank Robinson/50	15.00
6	Cal Ripken Jr./100	40.00
7	Carlton Fisk/50	15.00
8	Roger Clemens/100	15.00
10	Lou Boudreau/50	10.00
11	Bob Feller/25	30.00
13	Alan Trammell/50	10.00
14	Harmon Killebrew/50	25.00
15	Rod Carew/50	20.00
16	Kirby Puckett/50	20.00
19	Yogi Berra/50	30.00
20	Thurman Munson/50	30.00
21	Don Mattingly/100	25.00
25	Alex Rodriguez/100	10.00
26	Randy Johnson/50	10.00
27	Nolan Ryan/100	30.00
28	Dale Murphy/50	20.00
29	Warren Spahn/50	20.00
30	Eddie Mathews/50	25.00
32	Ryne Sandberg/100	30.00
33	Johnny Bench/50	30.00
34	Joe Morgan/50	10.00
35	Randy Johnson/50	10.00
36	Nolan Ryan/100	30.00
37	Pee Wee Reese/50	15.00
38	Duke Snider/25	25.00
39	Jackie Robinson/50	65.00
40	Robin Yount/50	30.00
41	Paul Molitor/50	20.00
42	Pedro Martinez/50	10.00
43	Randy Johnson/50	10.00
44	Tom Seaver/25	25.00
45	Gary Carter/50	10.00
46	Mike Schmidt/50	30.00
47	Steve Carlton/50	10.00
48	Willie Stargell/50	20.00
50	Ozzie Smith/50	35.00
51	Stan Musial/100	30.00
52	Enos Slaughter/50	10.00
53	Orlando Cepeda/50	10.00
54	Willie McCovey/50	15.00
57	Harmon Killebrew, Rod Carew/25	50.00
58	Harmon Killebrew, Kirby Puckett/25	50.00
68	Thurman Munson, Yogi Berra/25	50.00
69	Don Mattingly, Yogi Berra/25	60.00
71	Dale Murphy, Warren Spahn/25	50.00
72	Dale Murphy, Eddie Mathews/25	45.00
73	Eddie Mathews, Warren Spahn/25	60.00
74	Joe Morgan, Johnny Bench/25	40.00
75	Duke Snider, Pee Wee Reese/25	40.00
78	Paul Molitor, Robin Yount/25	75.00
81	Ozzie Smith, Stan Musial/25	60.00
82	Enos Slaughter, Stan Musial/25	60.00
83	Orlando Cepeda, Willie McCovey/25	40.00
84	Nolan Ryan, Reggie Jackson/25	60.00
90	Alex Rodriguez, Randy Johnson/25	25.00
91	Pedro J. Martinez, Randy Johnson/25	35.00
94	Reggie Jackson/25	35.00
95	Nolan Ryan/25	60.00
96	Nolan Ryan/25	60.00
97	Nolan Ryan/25	60.00
98	Nolan Ryan/25	60.00
99	Cal Ripken Jr., Rafael Palmeiro/25	90.00
100	Dale Murphy, Deion Sanders/25	50.00

Jersey Numbers Retired
NM/M

Many not priced due to scarcity.

1	Rod Carew/29	30.00
2	Nolan Ryan/30	50.00
5	Frank Robinson/20	20.00
7	Carlton Fisk/27	30.00
9	Carlton Fisk/27	15.00
16	Kirby Puckett/34	35.00
21	Don Mattingly/23	50.00
27	Nolan Ryan/34	50.00
30	Eddie Mathews/41	20.00
36	Nolan Ryan/34	50.00
39	Jackie Robinson/42	50.00
44	Tom Seaver/41	20.00
46	Mike Schmidt/30	50.00
47	Steve Carlton/32	15.00
49	Roberto Clemente/21	100.00
53	Orlando Cepeda/30	15.00
54	Willie McCovey/44	10.00

Leather
NM/M

Common Player:
Production 10-25
Golds: No Pricing
Production 5-10
Leather & Lace: No Pricing
Production 10
Leather & Lace Gold: No Pricing
Production 5

1	Alex Rodriguez/25	40.00
2	Chipper Jones/25	30.00
3	Jimmie Foxx/25	65.00
4	Kirby Puckett/25	25.00
5	Mike Schmidt/25	65.00
6	Roger Clemens/25	45.00
8	Tony Gwynn/25	40.00
10	Vladimir Guerrero/25	25.00
11	Adam Dunn/25	20.00
12	Andruw Jones/25	25.00
13	Curt Schilling/25	20.00
14	Randy Johnson/25	25.00
15	Mark Prior/25	40.00

Lineups - Jerseys
NM/M

Production 5-50

1	Paul Molitor, Robin Yount/50	35.00
2	Bernie Williams, Don Mattingly/50	40.00
3	Hee Seop Choi, Sammy Sosa/50	30.00
4	Derek Jeter, Hideki Matsui/50/Base	30.00
5	Andre Dawson, Ryne Sandberg/50	35.00
6	Bo Jackson, George Brett/50	50.00
7	Jose Canseco, Reggie Jackson/50	25.00
8	Mark Grace, Ryne Sandberg/50	35.00
9	Jose Canseco, Rickey Henderson/50	25.00
10	Hideo Nomo, Mike Piazza/50	25.00

Lineups - Bats
NM/M

Common Player:
Production 25-50

1	Paul Molitor, Robin Yount/50	35.00
2	Bernie Williams, Don Mattingly/50	40.00
4	Derek Jeter, Hideki Matsui/25	60.00
5	Andre Dawson, Ryne Sandberg/50	40.00
6	Bo Jackson, George Brett/50	40.00
7	Jose Canseco, Reggie Jackson/50	25.00
8	Mark Grace, Ryne Sandberg/50	40.00
9	Jose Canseco, Rickey Henderson/50	30.00
10	Hideo Nomo, Mike Piazza/50	25.00

Lineups - Buttons

No Pricing
Production One Set

Lineups Tag Team

No Pricing
Production 5

Lumberjacks
NM/M

Some not priced due to scarcity.
Production 1-25
Black: No Pricing
Production 1-5
Silver: No Pricing
Production 1-10

1	Babe Ruth/25	200.00
2	Lou Gehrig/25	150.00
3	Roberto Clemente/25	120.00
4	Stan Musial/25	40.00
5	Rogers Hornsby/25	50.00
6	Don Mattingly/25	50.00
7	Rickey Henderson/25	20.00
8	Cal Ripken Jr./25	75.00
9	Yogi Berra/25	30.00
10	Reggie Jackson/25	35.00
11	George Brett/25	60.00
12	Mel Ott/25	40.00
13	Roger Maris/25	60.00
14	Ryne Sandberg/25	50.00
16	Richie Ashburn/25	40.00
17	Mike Schmidt/25	40.00
18	Tony Gwynn/25	25.00
19	Ty Cobb/25	110.00
20	Thurman Munson/25	35.00
21	Jimmie Foxx/25	60.00
22	Duke Snider/25	25.00
24	Alex Rodriguez/25	30.00
25	Nomar Garciaparra/25	30.00
26	Hideki Matsui/25/Base	50.00
27	Ichiro Suzuki/25/Base	35.00
28	Barry Bonds/25/Base	35.00
29	Mike Piazza/25	30.00
30	Alfonso Soriano/25	25.00
31	Al Kaline/25	30.00
33	Dale Murphy/25	25.00
34	Orlando Cepeda/25	30.00
35	Willie McCovey/25	30.00
37	Brooks Robinson/25	30.00

Lumberjacks - Barrel
NM/M

1/1 except where indicated
No pricing due to scarcity.

21	Jimmie Foxx (7/05 Auction)	1,525

Lumberjacks Combos
NM/M

Production 1-25
Black: No Pricing
Production 1-5
Silver: No Pricing
Production 1-10

38	Hideki Matsui, Ichiro Suzuki/25/Base	80.00
40	Don Mattingly, Lou Gehrig/25	240.00
41	Thurman Munson, Yogi Berra/25	50.00
42	Mike Schmidt, Richie Ashburn/25	60.00
43	Rogers Hornsby, Stan Musial/25	80.00
44	Don Mattingly, Roger Maris/25	100.00

Lumberjacks Combos - Jerseys
NM/M

Production 1-25
Some not priced due to scarcity.
Black: No Pricing
Production 1-5
Silver: No Pricing
Production 1-10

38	Hideki Matsui, Ichiro Suzuki/25/Ball	100.00
41	Thurman Munson, Yogi Berra/25	60.00

Lumberjacks Combos - Jerseys/Bats
NM/M

Production 1-25
Some not priced due to scarcity.
Black: No Pricing
Production 1-5
Silver: No Pricing
Production 1-10

38	Hideki Matsui, Ichiro Suzuki/25/Ball	100.00

41	Thurman Munson, Yogi Berra/25	50.00
42	Mike Schmidt, Richie Ashburn/25	60.00

Lumberjacks - Jerseys
NM/M

Production 1-25
Black: No Pricing
Production 1-5
Silver: No Pricing
Production 1-10

4	Stan Musial/25	40.00
6	Don Mattingly/25	50.00
8	Cal Ripken Jr./25	80.00
9	Yogi Berra/25	25.00
11	George Brett/25	60.00
12	Mel Ott/25	40.00
14	Ryne Sandberg/25	50.00
15	Eddie Mathews/25	25.00
17	Mike Schmidt/25	50.00
18	Tony Gwynn/25	25.00
20	Thurman Munson/25	25.00
22	Duke Snider/25	20.00
24	Alex Rodriguez/25	25.00
25	Nomar Garciaparra/25	30.00
26	Hideki Matsui/25/Ball	50.00
27	Ichiro Suzuki/25/Ball	30.00
28	Barry Bonds/25/Ball	40.00
29	Mike Piazza/25	25.00
30	Alfonso Soriano/25	25.00
32	Harmon Killebrew/25	25.00
33	Dale Murphy/25	25.00
34	Orlando Cepeda/25	15.00
35	Willie McCovey/25	20.00
36	Willie Stargell/25	30.00
37	Brooks Robinson/25	20.00

Lumberjacks - Jerseys/Bats
NM/M

Production 1-25
Some not priced due to scarcity.
Black: No Pricing
Production 1-5
Silver: No Pricing
Production 1-10

4	Stan Musial/25	60.00
6	Don Mattingly/25	75.00
8	Cal Ripken Jr./25	140.00
9	Yogi Berra/25	30.00
11	George Brett/25	80.00
13	Roger Maris/25	100.00
14	Ryne Sandberg/25	65.00
15	Eddie Mathews/25	40.00
17	Mike Schmidt/25	65.00
18	Tony Gwynn/25	40.00
20	Thurman Munson/25	40.00
24	Alex Rodriguez/25	40.00
25	Nomar Garciaparra/25	40.00
26	Hideki Matsui/25/Base/Ball	65.00
27	Ichiro Suzuki/25/Base/Ball	60.00
28	Barry Bonds/25/Base/Ball	60.00
29	Mike Piazza/25	40.00
30	Alfonso Soriano/25	25.00
33	Dale Murphy/25	40.00
35	Willie McCovey/25	35.00
36	Willie Stargell/25	30.00
37	Brooks Robinson/25	30.00

Material Monikers Jerseys
NM/M

Common Player:

2	Eric Chavez/25	25.00
4	Miguel Tejada/25	35.00
12	Craig Biggio/25	35.00
19	Vernon Wells/25	25.00
26	Edgar Martinez/25	40.00
28	Carlos Beltran/25	50.00
44	Tim Hudson/25	25.00
47	Mark Prior/25	40.00
69	Mark Teixeira/25	30.00
73	Nick Johnson/25	20.00
77	Adam Dunn/25	40.00
85	Roy Oswalt/25	25.00
113	Torii Hunter/25	25.00
114	Nick Johnson/25	20.00
120	Roy Oswalt/25	25.00
	Mark Teixeira/25	30.00

Material Monikers Bats
NM/M

Production 1-25
No pricing for many, due to scarcity.

2	Eric Chavez/25	35.00
12	Craig Biggio/25	40.00
15	Vernon Wells/25	30.00
19	Edgar Martinez/25	50.00
26	Carlos Beltran/25	40.00
28	Tim Hudson/25	40.00
44	Mark Prior/25	50.00
47	Mark Teixeira/25	40.00
69	Nick Johnson/25	25.00
73	Adam Dunn/25	40.00
74	Roy Oswalt/25	30.00
77	Torii Hunter/25	30.00
85	Nick Johnson/25	25.00
113	Torii Hunter/25	30.00
114	Roy Oswalt/25	30.00
120	Mark Teixeira/25	40.00

Material Monikers Jersey Numbers
NM/M

Production 1-25
Many not priced due to scarcity.

2	Eric Chavez/25	25.00
4	Miguel Tejada/25	30.00
12	Craig Biggio/25	35.00
15	Vernon Wells/25	20.00
19	Edgar Martinez/25	30.00
26	Carlos Beltran/25	50.00
28	Tim Hudson/25	25.00
44	Mark Prior/25	40.00
47	Mark Teixeira/25	40.00
69	Nick Johnson/25	15.00
73	Adam Dunn/25	40.00
74	Roy Oswalt/25	20.00
77	Torii Hunter/25	25.00
85	Nick Johnson/25	15.00
113	Torii Hunter/25	25.00
114	Roy Oswalt/25	20.00
120	Mark Teixeira/25	40.00

Material Monikers Jersey Position
NM/M

Production 1-25
Many not priced due to scarcity.

2	Eric Chavez/25	25.00
4	Miguel Tejada/25	30.00
12	Craig Biggio/25	35.00
15	Vernon Wells/25	20.00
19	Edgar Martinez/25	40.00
26	Carlos Beltran/25	50.00
28	Tim Hudson/25	25.00
29	Deion Sanders/25	50.00
44	Mark Prior/25	40.00
47	Mark Teixeira/25	40.00
69	Nick Johnson/25	20.00
73	Adam Dunn/25	40.00
74	Roy Oswalt/25	25.00
77	Torii Hunter/25	25.00
85	Nick Johnson/25	20.00
113	Torii Hunter/25	25.00
114	Roy Oswalt/25	25.00
120	Mark Teixeira/25	40.00

Player Threads
NM/M

Production 5-50
Some not priced due to scarcity.
Primes: No Pricing
Production 5-10

1	Roger Clemens/50	15.00
2	Alex Rodriguez/50	15.00
3	Pedro Martinez/50	10.00
4	Randy Johnson/50	8.00
5	Curt Schilling/50	8.00
7	Nolan Ryan/50	35.00
8	Hideo Nomo/50	12.00
9	Mike Piazza/50	15.00
11	Rickey Henderson/50	15.00
12	Ivan Rodriguez/50	10.00

13	Gary Sheffield/50	8.00
14	Jeff Kent/50	8.00
15	Roberto Alomar/50	10.00
16	Rafael Palmeiro/50	10.00
17	Juan Gonzalez/50	8.00
18	Shawn Green/50	8.00
19	Jason Giambi/50	8.00
20	Jim Thome/50	10.00
21	Scott Rolen/50	12.00
22	Mike Mussina/50	10.00
23	Tom Glavine/50	8.00
24	Sammy Sosa/50	15.00

Player Threads Double
NM/M

Production 5-50
Some not priced due to scarcity.
Double Primes: No Pricing
Production 5-10

1	Roger Clemens/50	25.00
2	Alex Rodriguez/50	25.00
3	Pedro Martinez/50	20.00
4	Randy Johnson/50	15.00
5	Curt Schilling/50	10.00
7	Nolan Ryan/50	50.00
8	Hideo Nomo/50	20.00
9	Mike Piazza/50	25.00
11	Rickey Henderson/50	20.00
12	Ivan Rodriguez/50	15.00
13	Gary Sheffield/50	10.00
14	Jeff Kent/50	10.00
15	Roberto Alomar/50	15.00
16	Rafael Palmeiro/50	15.00
17	Juan Gonzalez/50	15.00
18	Shawn Green/50	10.00
19	Jason Giambi/50	15.00
20	Jim Thome/50	15.00
21	Scott Rolen/50	20.00
22	Mike Mussina/50	15.00
23	Tom Glavine/50	10.00
24	Sammy Sosa/50	25.00

Player Threads Triple
NM/M

Production 50
Some not priced due to scarcity.
Triple Primes: No Pricing
Production 5-10

4	Randy Johnson/50	20.00
7	Nolan Ryan/50	75.00
8	Hideo Nomo/50	60.00
11	Rickey Henderson/50	30.00
13	Gary Sheffield/50	15.00
14	Jeff Kent/50	15.00
15	Roberto Alomar/50	25.00

Team Threads
NM/M

Production 10-50
Some not priced due to scarcity.
Primes: No Pricing
Production 5-10

26	Alex Rodriguez, Nolan Ryan/50	50.00
27	Hideo Nomo, Mike Piazza/50	20.00
28	Cal Ripken Jr., Mike Mussina/50	50.00
29	Hideo Nomo, Kazuhisa Ishii/50	15.00
30	Nolan Ryan, Randy Johnson/50	40.00

Team Trademarks Threads Jersey Number
NM/M

Some not priced due to scarcity.
Primes: 1-1.5X
Production 1-25
Some not priced due to scarcity.

3	Jim Palmer/22	20.00
12	Eric Davis/44	8.00
15	Jack Morris/47	8.00
17	Deion Sanders/24	25.00
19	Orlando Cepeda/30	10.00
23	Rod Carew/29	20.00
24	Will Clark/22	50.00
25	Willie McCovey/44	10.00
27	Nolan Ryan/34	50.00
31	Rod Carew/29	20.00
32	Nolan Ryan/34	50.00
34	Nolan Ryan/30	50.00
37	Greg Maddux/31	30.00

Team Trademarks Autographs
NM/M

Some not priced due to scarcity.

1	Alan Trammell/25	40.00
3	Jim Palmer/25	30.00

5	Gary Carter/25	40.00
6	Andre Dawson/25	30.00
8	Dale Murphy/25	50.00
10	Bobby Doerr/25	35.00
11	Brooks Robinson/25	50.00
12	Eric Davis/25	35.00
13	Fred Lynn/25	30.00
15	Jack Morris/25	25.00
16	Al Kaline/25	60.00
17	Deion Sanders/25	50.00
18	Luis Aparicio/25	35.00
20	Phil Rizzuto/25	40.00
24	Will Clark/25	70.00

Team Trademarks Jersey Autograph
NM/M

Some not priced due to scarcity.

12	Eric Davis/44	30.00
15	Jack Morris/47	25.00
23	Rod Carew/29	50.00
25	Willie McCovey/44	25.00
27	Nolan Ryan/34	140.00
31	Rod Carew/29	50.00
32	Nolan Ryan/34	140.00
34	Nolan Ryan/30	140.00
37	Greg Maddux/31	150.00

Threads

NM/M

Common Player: 8.00
Varying quantities produced

1	Derek Jeter/base/50	20.00
2	Eric Chavez/25	10.00
3	Alex Rodriguez/100	15.00
4	Miguel Tejada/50	8.00
5	Nomar Garciaparra/100	15.00
6	Jeff Bagwell/50	10.00
7	Jim Thome/50	10.00
8	Pat Burrell/25	10.00
9	Albert Pujols/25	20.00
10	Juan Gonzalez/25	20.00
11	Shawn Green/50	10.00
12	Craig Biggio/25	20.00
13	Chipper Jones/25	20.00
14	Hideo Nomo/100	12.00
15	Vernon Wells/25	10.00
16	Gary Sheffield/25	10.00
17	Barry Larkin/25	15.00
18	Josh Beckett/25	15.00
19	Edgar Martinez/25	20.00
20	Ivan Rodriguez/25	20.00
21	Jeff Kent/25	10.00
22	Roberto Alomar/25	15.00
23	Alfonso Soriano/100	8.00
24	Jim Thome/25	10.00
25	Juan Gonzalez/25	10.00
26	Carlos Beltran/25	20.00
27	Shawn Green/50	8.00
28	Tim Hudson/25	10.00
29	Deion Sanders/25	20.00
30	Rafael Palmeiro/25	20.00
31	Todd Helton/50	10.00
32	Lance Berkman/25	10.00
33	Mike Mussina/50	10.00
34	Kazuhisa Ishii/50	8.00
35	Pat Burrell/25	10.00
36	Miguel Tejada/50	8.00
37	Juan Gonzalez/25	10.00
38	Roberto Alomar/25	15.00
39	Roberto Alomar/25	15.00
40	Luis Gonzalez/25	10.00
41	Jorge Posada/25	15.00
42	Mark Mulder/25	10.00
43	Sammy Sosa/100	15.00
44	Mark Prior/25	15.00
45	Roger Clemens/100	10.00
46	Tom Glavine/25	15.00
47	Mark Teixeira/25	10.00
48	Manny Ramirez/25	12.00
49	Frank Thomas/25	15.00

50	Troy Glaus/50	8.00
51	Andruw Jones/50	8.00
52	Jason Giambi/100	8.00
53	Jim Thome/50	10.00
54	Barry Bonds/50/Base	25.00
55	Rafael Palmeiro/25	15.00
56	Edgar Martinez/25	10.00
57	Vladimir Guerrero/50	10.00
58	Roberto Alomar/25	10.00
59	Mike Sweeney/25	10.00
60	Magglio Ordonez/25	10.00
62	Craig Biggio/25	10.00
63	Greg Maddux/100	10.00
64	Mike Piazza/100	10.00
65	Tom Glavine/25	15.00
66	Kerry Wood/25	20.00
67	Frank Thomas/25	20.00
68	Mike Mussina/50	10.00
69	Nick Johnson/25	8.00
70	Bernie Williams/50	10.00
71	Scott Rolen/25	20.00
72	Curt Schilling/25	15.00
73	Adam Dunn/50	10.00
74	Roy Oswalt/25	10.00
75	Pedro Martinez/25	10.00
76	Tom Glavine/25	15.00
77	Torii Hunter/25	10.00
78	Austin Kearns/25	10.00
79	Randy Johnson/100	8.00
80	Bernie Williams/50	10.00
81	Ichiro Suzuki/50	25.00
82	Kerry Wood/25	20.00
83	Kazuhisa Ishii/50	8.00
84	Randy Johnson/50	8.00
85	Nick Johnson/25	8.00
86	Josh Beckett/25	10.00
87	Curt Schilling/25	15.00
88	Mike Mussina/50	10.00
89	Pedro Martinez/25	15.00
90	Barry Zito/75	8.00
91	Jim Edmonds/100	6.00
92	Rickey Henderson/100	8.00
93	Rickey Henderson/50	12.00
94	Rickey Henderson/50	12.00
95	Rickey Henderson/50	12.00
96	Rickey Henderson/50	12.00
97	Randy Johnson/50	8.00
98	Mark Grace/50	10.00
99	Pedro Martinez/25	15.00
100	Hee Seop Choi/25	8.00
101	Ivan Rodriguez/25	15.00
102	Jeff Kent/25	10.00
103	Hideo Nomo/5	
104	Hideo Nomo/50	10.00
105	Mike Piazza/100	10.00
106	Tom Glavine/50	15.00
107	Roberto Alomar/50	15.00
108	Roger Clemens/100	10.00
109	Jason Giambi/25	10.00
110	Jim Thome/25	15.00
111	Alex Rodriguez/100	10.00
112	Juan Gonzalez/25	10.00
113	Torii Hunter/25	10.00
114	Roy Oswalt/25	15.00
115	Curt Schilling/25	15.00
116	Magglio Ordonez/25	10.00
117	Rafael Palmeiro/25	15.00
118	Andruw Jones/50	8.00
119	Manny Ramirez/50	12.00
120	Mark Teixeira/25	10.00
121	Mark Mulder/25	10.00
123	Tim Hudson/25	10.00
124	Todd Helton/50	10.00
125	Troy Glaus/50	6.00
126	Derek Jeter/Base/50	20.00
127	Barry Bonds/Base/50	25.00
128	Greg Maddux/100	10.00
129	Roger Clemens/100	10.00
130	Nomar Garciaparra/100	10.00
131	Mike Piazza/100	10.00
132	Alex Rodriguez/100	10.00
133	Ichiro Suzuki/Base	25.00
134	Randy Johnson/100	8.00
135	Sammy Sosa/100	10.00
137	Alfonso Soriano/100	8.00
138	Jason Giambi/100	6.00
139	Albert Pujols/100	20.00
140	Chipper Jones/25	20.00
141	Adam Dunn/25	8.00
142	Pedro Martinez/25	10.00
143	Vladimir Guerrero/25	10.00
144	Mark Prior/25	15.00
145	Barry Zito/50	8.00
146	Jeff Bagwell/25	12.00
147	Lance Berkman/Socks/25	10.00
148	Shawn Green/25	10.00
149	Jason Giambi/25	10.00
150	Randy Johnson/25	20.00
151	Alex Rodriguez/100	10.00
153	Ty Cobb/100	100.00
154	Jackie Robinson/50	50.00

#	Player	Price
156	Thurman Munson/100	15.00
158	Nolan Ryan/100	30.00
159	Nolan Ryan/100	30.00
160	Nolan Ryan/100	30.00
161	Cal Ripken Jr./100	60.00
162	Don Mattingly/100	25.00
163	Stan Musial/100	25.00
164	Tony Gwynn/100	12.00
165	Yogi Berra/100	12.00
166	Johnny Bench/100	12.00
167	Mike Schmidt/100	25.00
168	George Brett/100	30.00
169	Ryne Sandberg/100	25.00
170	Ernie Banks/50	30.00

Threads Double

NM/M

Common Player:
Production 5 to 25
Some not priced due to scarcity.
Primes: No Pricing
Production 1 to 10

#	Player	Price
3	Alex Rodriguez/25	40.00
4	Miguel Tejada/25	25.00
10	Juan Gonzalez/25	20.00
12	Craig Biggio/25	25.00
14	Hideo Nomo/25	40.00
15	Vernon Wells/25	15.00
26	Carlos Beltran/25	25.00
28	Tim Hudson/25	20.00
31	Todd Helton/25	25.00
32	Lance Berkman/25	15.00
34	Kazuhisa Ishii/25	20.00
37	Juan Gonzalez/25	20.00
43	Sammy Sosa/25	50.00
44	Mark Prior/25	25.00
51	Andruw Jones/25	20.00
54	Barry Bonds/25	65.00
55	Rafael Palmeiro/25	30.00
60	Magglio Ordonez/25	20.00
73	Adam Dunn/25	20.00
75	Pedro Martinez/25	30.00
78	Austin Kearns/25	15.00
81	Ichiro Suzuki/25	60.00
90	Barry Zito/25	20.00
94	Rickey Henderson/25	25.00
101	Ivan Rodriguez/25	25.00
109	Jason Giambi/25	25.00
116	Magglio Ordonez/25	20.00
117	Rafael Palmeiro/25	30.00
118	Andruw Jones/25	20.00
123	Tim Hudson/25	20.00
124	Todd Helton/25	25.00
127	Barry Bonds/25	50.00
132	Alex Rodriguez/25	40.00
133	Ichiro Suzuki/25	60.00
135	Sammy Sosa/25	50.00
141	Adam Dunn/25	20.00
142	Pedro Martinez/25	35.00
144	Mark Prior/25	40.00
145	Barry Zito/25	20.00
146	Jeff Bagwell/25	30.00
147	Lance Berkman/25	15.00
149	Jason Giambi/25	20.00
158	Nolan Ryan/25	80.00
162	Don Mattingly/25	65.00
164	Tony Gwynn/25	40.00
165	Mike Schmidt/25	65.00
168	George Brett/25	75.00
169	Ryne Sandberg/25	65.00

Threads Position

NM/M

Common (2-151): 8.00
#'s 2-151
Production 25
#'s 152-170
Production 5-25
Primes: 1-1.5X
Production 25 for #'s 2-151.

#	Player	Price
2	Eric Chavez	8.00
3	Alex Rodriguez	25.00
4	Miguel Tejada	10.00
5	Nomar Garciaparra	30.00
6	Jeff Bagwell	15.00
7	Jim Thome	15.00
8	Pat Burrell	10.00
9	Albert Pujols	35.00
10	Juan Gonzalez	10.00
11	Shawn Green	10.00
12	Craig Biggio	8.00
13	Chipper Jones	25.00
14	Hideo Nomo	30.00
15	Vernon Wells	8.00
16	Gary Sheffield	10.00
17	Barry Larkin	15.00
18	Josh Beckett	15.00
19	Edgar Martinez	15.00
20	Ivan Rodriguez	15.00
21	Jeff Kent	8.00
22	Roberto Alomar	15.00
23	Alfonso Soriano	20.00
25	Juan Gonzalez	15.00
26	Carlos Beltran	8.00
27	Shawn Green	10.00
28	Tim Hudson	10.00
29	Deion Sanders	30.00
30	Rafael Palmeiro	15.00
31	Todd Helton	15.00
32	Lance Berkman	10.00
33	Mike Mussina	15.00
34	Kazuhisa Ishii	10.00
35	Pat Burrell	10.00
36	Miguel Tejada	10.00
37	Juan Gonzalez	15.00
38	Roberto Alomar	15.00
39	Roberto Alomar	15.00
40	Luis Gonzalez	10.00
41	Jorge Posada	15.00
42	Mark Mulder	10.00
43	Sammy Sosa	40.00
44	Mark Prior	25.00
45	Roger Clemens	40.00
46	Tom Glavine	15.00
47	Mark Teixeira	10.00
48	Manny Ramirez	15.00
49	Frank Thomas	15.00
50	Troy Glaus	10.00
51	Andruw Jones	15.00
52	Jason Giambi	15.00
53	Jim Thome	15.00
55	Rafael Palmeiro	15.00
56	Edgar Martinez	15.00
57	Vladimir Guerrero	15.00
58	Roberto Alomar	15.00
60	Magglio Ordonez	10.00
62	Craig Biggio	10.00
63	Greg Maddux	30.00
64	Mike Piazza	25.00
65	Tom Glavine	15.00
66	Kerry Wood	15.00
67	Frank Thomas	15.00
68	Mike Mussina	15.00
69	Nick Johnson	10.00
70	Bernie Williams	15.00
71	Scott Rolen	15.00
72	Curt Schilling	15.00
73	Adam Dunn	15.00
74	Roy Oswalt	8.00
75	Pedro J. Martinez	15.00
76	Tom Glavine	15.00
77	Torii Hunter	15.00
78	Austin Kearns	15.00
79	Randy Johnson	15.00
80	Bernie Williams	15.00
82	Kerry Wood	15.00
83	Kazuhisa Ishii	10.00
84	Randy Johnson	15.00
85	Nick Johnson	10.00
86	Josh Beckett	15.00
87	Curt Schilling	15.00
88	Mike Mussina	15.00
89	Pedro J. Martinez	15.00
90	Barry Zito	15.00
91	Jim Edmonds	15.00
93	Rickey Henderson	25.00
94	Rickey Henderson	25.00
95	Rickey Henderson	25.00
96	Rickey Henderson	25.00
97	Randy Johnson	15.00
98	Mark Grace	15.00
99	Pedro J. Martinez	15.00
100	Hee Seop Choi	10.00
101	Ivan Rodriguez	15.00
102	Jeff Kent	10.00
104	Hideo Nomo	30.00
105	Mike Piazza	25.00
106	Tom Glavine	15.00
107	Roberto Alomar	15.00
108	Roger Clemens	40.00
109	Jason Giambi	15.00
110	Jim Thome	15.00
111	Alex Rodriguez	25.00
112	Juan Gonzalez	15.00
113	Torii Hunter	15.00
114	Roy Oswalt	10.00
115	Curt Schilling	10.00
116	Magglio Ordonez	10.00
117	Rafael Palmeiro	15.00
118	Andruw Jones	15.00
119	Manny Ramirez	15.00
120	Mark Teixeira	15.00
121	Mark Mulder	10.00
123	Tim Hudson	15.00
124	Todd Helton	15.00
125	Troy Glaus	15.00
128	Greg Maddux	30.00
129	Roger Clemens	40.00
130	Nomar Garciaparra	30.00
131	Mike Piazza	25.00
132	Alex Rodriguez	25.00
134	Randy Johnson	15.00
135	Sammy Sosa	40.00
137	Alfonso Soriano	20.00
138	Jason Giambi	15.00
139	Albert Pujols	35.00
140	Chipper Jones	25.00
141	Adam Dunn	15.00
142	Pedro J. Martinez	15.00
143	Vladimir Guerrero	15.00
144	Mark Prior	25.00
146	Barry Zito	15.00
146	Jeff Bagwell	15.00
147	Lance Berkman	10.00
148	Shawn Green	10.00
149	Jason Giambi	15.00
150	Randy Johnson	15.00
151	Alex Rodriguez	25.00
153	Ty Cobb	125.00
155	Lou Gehrig/5	
156	Thurman Munson	30.00
158	Nolan Ryan	50.00
159	Nolan Ryan	50.00
160	Nolan Ryan	50.00
161	Cal Ripken Jr.	85.00
162	Don Mattingly	60.00
163	Stan Musial	60.00
164	Tony Gwynn	30.00
165	Yogi Berra	30.00
168	George Brett	60.00
169	Ryne Sandberg	60.00
170	Ernie Banks/5	

Threads Number

NM/M

Common Player:

#	Player	Price
7	Jim Thome/25	20.00
18	Josh Beckett/61	10.00
24	Jim Thome/25	20.00
29	Deion Sanders/21	35.00
30	Rafael Palmeiro/25	20.00
33	Mike Mussina/35	15.00
40	Luis Gonzalez/20	15.00
41	Jorge Posada/20	25.00
42	Mark Mulder/20	15.00
43	Sammy Sosa/21	50.00
44	Mark Prior/22	25.00
45	Roger Clemens/22	50.00
46	Tom Glavine/47	8.00
47	Mark Teixeira/23	15.00
48	Manny Ramirez/24	30.00
49	Frank Thomas/35	15.00
50	Troy Glaus/10	10.00
51	Andruw Jones/25	15.00
52	Jason Giambi/52	10.00
53	Jim Thome/25	20.00
55	Rafael Palmeiro/25	20.00
57	Vladimir Guerrero/27	20.00
59	Mike Sweeney/29	10.00
60	Magglio Ordonez/30	10.00
63	Greg Maddux/31	25.00
64	Mike Piazza/31	30.00
65	Tom Glavine/47	8.00
66	Kerry Wood/52	15.00
67	Frank Thomas/35	15.00
68	Mike Mussina/35	15.00
69	Nick Johnson/36	8.00
70	Bernie Williams/51	10.00
71	Scott Rolen/27	20.00
72	Curt Schilling/38	10.00
73	Adam Dunn/44	8.00
74	Roy Oswalt/44	6.00
75	Pedro Martinez/45	10.00
76	Tom Glavine/47	8.00
77	Torii Hunter/48	8.00
78	Austin Kearns/28	10.00
79	Randy Johnson/51	10.00
80	Bernie Williams/51	10.00
82	Kerry Wood/34	20.00
84	Randy Johnson/51	10.00
85	Nick Johnson/36	8.00
86	Josh Beckett/61	8.00
87	Curt Schilling/38	10.00
88	Mike Mussina/35	15.00
89	Pedro Martinez/45	10.00
90	Barry Zito/75	8.00
93	Rickey Henderson/24	25.00
94	Rickey Henderson/35	20.00
95	Rickey Henderson/24	25.00
96	Rickey Henderson/24	25.00
97	Randy Johnson/51	10.00
99	Pedro Martinez/45	10.00
105	Mike Piazza/31	30.00
106	Tom Glavine/47	8.00
108	Roger Clemens/21	50.00
110	Jim Thome/25	15.00
112	Juan Gonzalez/22	20.00
113	Torii Hunter/48	8.00
114	Roy Oswalt/44	6.00
115	Curt Schilling/38	10.00
116	Magglio Ordonez/30	8.00
117	Rafael Palmeiro/25	20.00
118	Andruw Jones/25	10.00
119	Manny Ramirez/24	25.00
120	Mark Teixeira/23	20.00
121	Mark Mulder/20	15.00
125	Troy Glaus/25	12.00
127	Greg Maddux/31	25.00
128	Roger Clemens/21	50.00
131	Mike Piazza/31	30.00
134	Randy Johnson/51	12.00
135	Sammy Sosa/21	50.00
138	Jason Giambi/25	10.00
141	Adam Dunn/44	8.00
142	Pedro Martinez/45	10.00
143	Vladimir Guerrero/27	20.00
144	Mark Prior/22	25.00
145	Barry Zito/75	8.00
150	Randy Johnson/51	10.00
154	Jackie Robinson/42	50.00
157	Roberto Clemente/21	140.00
158	Nolan Ryan/34	50.00
159	Nolan Ryan/30	50.00
160	Nolan Ryan/34	50.00
162	Don Mattingly/23	50.00
165	Yogi Berra/42	15.00
167	Mike Schmidt/20	60.00
169	Ryne Sandberg/23	60.00

Threads Button Up

Production 2-6
No Pricing

Timber

NM/M

Common Player: 10.00
Production 25 Sets

#	Player	Price
2	Eric Chavez	10.00
3	Alex Rodriguez	25.00
4	Miguel Tejada	10.00
5	Nomar Garciaparra	30.00
6	Jeff Bagwell	15.00
7	Jim Thome	15.00
8	Pat Burrell	15.00
9	Albert Pujols	35.00
10	Juan Gonzalez	15.00
11	Shawn Green	10.00
12	Craig Biggio	15.00
13	Chipper Jones	25.00
14	Hideo Nomo	30.00
15	Vernon Wells	10.00
16	Gary Sheffield	15.00
17	Barry Larkin	15.00
18	Josh Beckett	15.00
19	Edgar Martinez	15.00
20	Ivan Rodriguez	15.00
21	Jeff Kent	10.00
22	Roberto Alomar	20.00
23	Alfonso Soriano	20.00
24	Jim Thome	15.00
25	Juan Gonzalez	15.00
26	Carlos Beltran	10.00
27	Shawn Green	10.00
28	Tim Hudson	10.00
30	Rafael Palmeiro	10.00
31	Todd Helton	10.00
32	Lance Berkman	10.00
33	Mike Mussina	15.00
34	Kazuhisa Ishii	10.00
35	Pat Burrell	15.00
36	Miguel Tejada	15.00
37	Juan Gonzalez	15.00
38	Roberto Alomar	15.00
39	Roberto Alomar	15.00
40	Luis Gonzalez	15.00
41	Jorge Posada	15.00
42	Mark Mulder	15.00
43	Sammy Sosa	40.00
44	Mark Prior	25.00
45	Roger Clemens	40.00
46	Tom Glavine	15.00
47	Mark Teixeira	15.00
48	Manny Ramirez	15.00
49	Frank Thomas	15.00
50	Troy Glaus	10.00
51	Andruw Jones	15.00
52	Jason Giambi	15.00
53	Jim Thome	15.00
55	Rafael Palmeiro	15.00
56	Edgar Martinez	15.00
57	Vladimir Guerrero	15.00
58	Roberto Alomar	15.00
59	Mike Sweeney	10.00
60	Magglio Ordonez	10.00
62	Craig Biggio	10.00
63	Greg Maddux	30.00
64	Mike Piazza	25.00
65	Tom Glavine	15.00
66	Kerry Wood	15.00
67	Frank Thomas	15.00
68	Mike Mussina	15.00
69	Nick Johnson	10.00
70	Bernie Williams	10.00
71	Scott Rolen	15.00
72	Curt Schilling	15.00
73	Adam Dunn	15.00
74	Roy Oswalt	10.00
75	Pedro J. Martinez	15.00
77	Torii Hunter	15.00
78	Austin Kearns	15.00
79	Randy Johnson	15.00
80	Bernie Williams	15.00
82	Kerry Wood	15.00

#	Player	Price
83	Kazuhisa Ishii	10.00
84	Randy Johnson	15.00
85	Nick Johnson	10.00
86	Josh Beckett	15.00
87	Curt Schilling	15.00
88	Mike Mussina	15.00
89	Pedro J. Martinez	15.00
90	Barry Zito	15.00
91	Jim Edmonds	10.00
92	Rickey Henderson	15.00
93	Rickey Henderson	15.00
94	Rickey Henderson	15.00
95	Rickey Henderson	15.00
96	Rickey Henderson	15.00
97	Randy Johnson	15.00
98	Mark Grace	15.00
99	Pedro J. Martinez	15.00
101	Ivan Rodriguez	15.00
102	Jeff Kent	10.00
103	Hideo Nomo	30.00
104	Hideo Nomo	30.00
105	Mike Piazza	25.00
106	Tom Glavine	15.00
107	Roberto Alomar	15.00
108	Roger Clemens	40.00
109	Jason Giambi	15.00
110	Jim Thome	15.00
111	Alex Rodriguez	25.00
112	Juan Gonzalez	15.00
113	Torii Hunter	15.00
114	Roy Oswalt	10.00
115	Curt Schilling	15.00
116	Magglio Ordonez	10.00
117	Rafael Palmeiro	15.00
118	Andruw Jones	15.00
119	Manny Ramirez	15.00
120	Mark Teixeira	15.00
121	Mark Mulder	15.00
122	Garret Anderson	10.00
123	Tim Hudson	10.00
124	Todd Helton	15.00
125	Troy Glaus	10.00
128	Greg Maddux	30.00
129	Roger Clemens	40.00
130	Nomar Garciaparra	30.00
131	Mike Piazza	25.00
132	Alex Rodriguez	15.00
134	Randy Johnson	15.00
135	Sammy Sosa	40.00
137	Alfonso Soriano	20.00
138	Jason Giambi	15.00
139	Albert Pujols	35.00
140	Chipper Jones	25.00
141	Adam Dunn	15.00
142	Pedro J. Martinez	15.00
143	Vladimir Guerrero	15.00
144	Mark Prior	25.00
145	Barry Zito	15.00
146	Jeff Bagwell	15.00
147	Lance Berkman	10.00
148	Shawn Green	10.00
149	Jason Giambi	15.00
150	Randy Johnson	15.00
151	Alex Rodriguez	25.00
152	Babe Ruth	180.00
153	Ty Cobb	125.00
155	Lou Gehrig	150.00
156	Thurman Munson	30.00
157	Roberto Clemente	140.00
158	Nolan Ryan	50.00
159	Nolan Ryan	50.00
160	Nolan Ryan	50.00
161	Cal Ripken Jr.	85.00
162	Don Mattingly	60.00
163	Stan Musial	60.00
164	Tony Gwynn	30.00
165	Yogi Berra	30.00
166	Johnny Bench	35.00
167	Mike Schmidt	60.00
168	George Brett	60.00
169	Ryne Sandberg	60.00
170	Ernie Banks/1	10.00

TNT

NM/M
Production 25 unless noted.
Some not priced due to scarcity.
Primes: 1X
Production 1-25
No pricing production 15 or less.

#	Player	Price
2	Eric Chavez	15.00
3	Alex Rodriguez	45.00
4	Miguel Tejada	15.00
5	Nomar Garciaparra	45.00
6	Jeff Bagwell	25.00
7	Jim Thome	30.00
8	Pat Burrell	30.00
9	Albert Pujols	60.00
10	Juan Gonzalez	25.00
11	Shawn Green	15.00
12	Craig Biggio	15.00
13	Chipper Jones	40.00
14	Hideo Nomo	50.00
15	Vernon Wells	15.00
16	Gary Sheffield	25.00
17	Barry Larkin	20.00
18	Josh Beckett	25.00
19	Edgar Martinez	25.00
20	Ivan Rodriguez	25.00
21	Jeff Kent	10.00
22	Roberto Alomar	15.00
23	Alfonso Soriano	30.00
24	Jim Thome	30.00
25	Juan Gonzalez	25.00
26	Carlos Beltran	20.00
27	Shawn Green	15.00
28	Tim Hudson	20.00
30	Rafael Palmeiro	20.00
31	Todd Helton	20.00
32	Lance Berkman	20.00
33	Mike Mussina	25.00
34	Kazuhisa Ishii	10.00
35	Pat Burrell	30.00
36	Miguel Tejada	15.00
37	Juan Gonzalez	25.00
38	Roberto Alomar	20.00
39	Roberto Alomar	20.00
40	Luis Gonzalez	15.00
41	Jorge Posada	25.00
42	Mark Mulder	20.00
43	Sammy Sosa	40.00
44	Mark Prior	25.00
45	Roger Clemens	50.00
46	Tom Glavine	20.00
47	Mark Teixeira	20.00
48	Manny Ramirez	25.00
49	Frank Thomas	35.00
50	Troy Glaus	15.00
51	Andruw Jones	20.00
52	Jason Giambi	15.00
53	Jim Thome	30.00
55	Rafael Palmeiro	25.00
56	Edgar Martinez	25.00
57	Vladimir Guerrero	30.00
58	Mike Sweeney	10.00
60	Magglio Ordonez	15.00
62	Craig Biggio	20.00
63	Greg Maddux	40.00
64	Mike Piazza	40.00
65	Tom Glavine	20.00
66	Kerry Wood	30.00
67	Frank Thomas	35.00
68	Mike Mussina	25.00
69	Nick Johnson	15.00
70	Bernie Williams	15.00
71	Scott Rolen	30.00
72	Curt Schilling	20.00
73	Adam Dunn	25.00
74	Roy Oswalt	15.00
75	Pedro J. Martinez	35.00
76	Tom Glavine	20.00
77	Torii Hunter	15.00
78	Austin Kearns	15.00
79	Randy Johnson	30.00
80	Bernie Williams	20.00
82	Kerry Wood	30.00
83	Kazuhisa Ishii	10.00
84	Randy Johnson	30.00
85	Nick Johnson	15.00
86	Josh Beckett	20.00
87	Curt Schilling	25.00
88	Mike Mussina	25.00
89	Pedro J. Martinez	35.00
90	Barry Zito	20.00
91	Jim Edmonds	20.00
92	Rickey Henderson	35.00
93	Rickey Henderson	35.00
94	Rickey Henderson	35.00
95	Rickey Henderson	35.00
96	Rickey Henderson	35.00
97	Randy Johnson	30.00
98	Mark Grace	20.00
99	Pedro J. Martinez	35.00
101	Ivan Rodriguez	25.00
102	Jeff Kent	10.00
103	Hideo Nomo	40.00
104	Hideo Nomo	40.00
105	Mike Piazza	40.00
106	Tom Glavine	20.00
107	Roberto Alomar	25.00
108	Roger Clemens	50.00
109	Jason Giambi	20.00
110	Jim Thome	30.00
111	Alex Rodriguez	45.00
112	Juan Gonzalez	25.00
113	Torii Hunter	15.00
114	Roy Oswalt	15.00
115	Curt Schilling	25.00
116	Magglio Ordonez	15.00
117	Rafael Palmeiro	25.00
118	Andruw Jones	15.00
119	Manny Ramirez	30.00
120	Mark Teixeira	25.00
121	Mark Mulder	20.00
123	Tim Hudson	20.00
124	Todd Helton	20.00
125	Troy Glaus	15.00
128	Greg Maddux	40.00
129	Roger Clemens	40.00
130	Nomar Garciaparra	40.00
131	Mike Piazza	40.00
132	Alex Rodriguez	40.00
134	Randy Johnson	30.00
135	Sammy Sosa	40.00
137	Alfonso Soriano	30.00
138	Jason Giambi	20.00
139	Albert Pujols	60.00
140	Chipper Jones	30.00
141	Adam Dunn	25.00
142	Pedro J. Martinez	35.00
143	Vladimir Guerrero	30.00
144	Mark Prior	25.00
145	Barry Zito	15.00
146	Jeff Bagwell	25.00
147	Lance Berkman	20.00
148	Shawn Green	15.00
149	Jason Giambi	20.00
150	Randy Johnson	30.00
151	Alex Rodriguez	40.00
156	Thurman Munson	50.00
158	Nolan Ryan	65.00
159	Nolan Ryan	65.00
160	Nolan Ryan	65.00
161	Cal Ripken Jr.	100.00
162	Don Mattingly	65.00
163	Stan Musial	65.00
164	Tony Gwynn	40.00
165	Yogi Berra	40.00
166	Johnny Bench	40.00
167	Mike Schmidt	65.00
168	George Brett	75.00
169	Ryne Sandberg	65.00
170	Ernie Banks/1	

7th Inning Stretch

NM/M
Production 50 unless noted.

#	Player	Price
1	Alex Rodriguez	20.00
3	Sammy Sosa	25.00
4	Juan Gonzalez	10.00
5	Albert Pujols	30.00
6	Chipper Jones	15.00
7	Alfonso Soriano/40	15.00
8	Jim Thome	15.00
9	Mike Piazza	20.00
10	Rafael Palmeiro	15.00

2004 Leaf

Barry ZITO

NM/M
Complete Set (300): 50.00
Common Player: .15
Common (202-301): .25
Second Edition (1-301): 1X
Pack (8): 5.00
Box (24): 90.00

#	Player	Price
1	Darin Erstad	.25
2	Garret Anderson	.25
3	Jarrod Washburn	.15
4	Kevin Appier	.15
5	Tim Salmon	.25
6	Troy Glaus	.40
7	Troy Percival	.15
8	Jason Johnson	.15
9	Jay Gibbons	.25
10	Melvin Mora	.15
11	Sidney Ponson	.15
12	Tony Batista	.15
13	Derek Lowe	.25
14	Robert Person	.15
15	Manny Ramirez	.50
16	Nomar Garciaparra	1.50
17	Pedro J. Martinez	.75
18	Jorge de la Rosa	.15
19	Bartolo Colon	.25
20	Carlos Lee	.15
21	Esteban Loaiza	.15
22	Frank Thomas	.50
23	Joe Crede	.15
24	Magglio Ordonez	.25
25	Ryan Ludwick	.15
26	Luis Garcia	.15
27	Brandon Phillips	.15
28	C.C. Sabathia	.15
29	Jhonny Peralta	.15
30	Josh Bard	.15
31	Omar Vizquel	.25
32	Fernando Rodney	.15
33	Mike Maroth	.15
34	Bobby Higginson	.15
35	Omar Infante	.15
36	Dmitri Young	.15
37	Eric Munson	.15
38	Jeremy Bonderman	.15
39	Carlos Beltran	.25
40	Jeremy Affeldt	.15
41	Dee Brown	.15
42		.15
43	Mike Sweeney	.15
44	Brent Abernathy	.15
45	Runelvys Hernandez	.15
46	A.J. Pierzynski	.15
47	Corey Koskie	.15
48	Cristian Guzman	.15
49	Jacque Jones	.15
50	Kenny Rogers	.15
51	J.C. Romero	.15
52	Torii Hunter	.40
53	Alfonso Soriano	.75
54	Bernie Williams	.50
55	David Wells	.15
56	Derek Jeter	2.00
57	Hideki Matsui	1.50
58	Jason Giambi	.75
59	Jorge Posada	.40
60	Jose Contreras	.25
61	Mike Mussina	.50
62	Nick Johnson	.15
63	Roger Clemens	1.50
64	Barry Zito	.40
65	Justin Duchscherer	.15
66	Eric Chavez	.25
67	Erubiel Durazo	.15
68	Miguel Tejada	.40
69	Mark Mulder	.25
70	Terrence Long	.15
71	Tim Hudson	.25
72	Bret Boone	.25
73	Dan Wilson	.15
74	Edgar Martinez	.25
75	Freddy Garcia	.15
76	Rafael Soriano	.15
77	Ichiro Suzuki	1.25
78	Jamie Moyer	.15
79	John Olerud	.25
80	Kazuhiro Sasaki	.15
81	Aubrey Huff	.15
82	Carl Crawford	.15
83	Joe Kennedy	.15
84	Rocco Baldelli	.40
85	Toby Hall	.15
86	Alex Rodriguez	1.50
87	Kevin Mench	.15
88	Hank Blalock	.25
89	Juan Gonzalez	.50
90	Mark Teixeira	.25
91	Rafael Palmeiro	.50
92	Carlos Delgado	.50
93	Eric Hinske	.15
94	Josh Phelps	.15
95	Brian Bowles	.15
96	Roy Halladay	.40
97	Shannon Stewart	.15
98	Vernon Wells	.25
99	Curt Schilling	.40
100	Junior Spivey	.15
101	Luis Gonzalez	.25
102	Lyle Overbay	.15
103	Mark Grace	.40
104	Randy Johnson	.75
105	Shea Hillenbrand	.15
106	Andruw Jones	.50
107	Chipper Jones	.75
108	Gary Sheffield	.40
109	Greg Maddux	1.00
110	Javy Lopez	.25
111	John Smoltz	.25
112	Marcus Giles	.15
113	Rafael Furcal	.25
114	Corey Patterson	.15

115	Juan Cruz	.15
116	Kerry Wood	.50
117	Mark Prior	1.00
118	Moises Alou	.25
119	Sammy Sosa	1.00
120	Aaron Boone	.15
121	Adam Dunn	.50
122	Austin Kearns	.50
123	Barry Larkin	.40
124	Ken Griffey Jr.	1.00
125	Brian Reith	.15
126	Wily Mo Pena	.15
127	Jason Jennings	.15
128	Jay Payton	.15
129	Larry Walker	.25
130	Preston Wilson	.15
131	Todd Helton	.50
132	Dontrelle Willis	.40
133	Ivan Rodriguez	.50
134	Josh Beckett	.50
135	Juan Encarnacion	.15
136	Mike Lowell	.15
137	Craig Biggio	.25
138	Jeff Bagwell	.50
139	Jeff Kent	.25
140	Lance Berkman	.25
141	Richard Hidalgo	.15
142	Roy Oswalt	.25
143	Eric Gagne	.25
144	Fred McGriff	.25
145	Hideo Nomo	.40
146	Kazuhisa Ishii	.15
147	Kevin Brown	.25
148	Paul LoDuca	.15
149	Shawn Green	.25
150	Ben Sheets	.25
151	Geoff Jenkins	.25
152	Rey Sanchez	.15
153	Richie Sexson	.40
154	Wes Helms	.15
155	Shane Nance	.15
156	Fernando Tatis	.15
157	Javier Vazquez	.15
158	Jose Vidro	.15
159	Orlando Cabrera	.15
160	Henry Mateo	.15
161	Vladimir Guerrero	.75
162	Zach Day	.15
163	Edwin Almonte	.15
164	Al Leiter	.15
165	Cliff Floyd	.15
166	Jae Weong Seo	.15
167	Mike Piazza	1.00
168	Roberto Alomar	.50
169	Tom Glavine	.25
170	Bobby Abreu	.25
171	Brandon Duckworth	.15
172	Jim Thome	.75
173	Kevin Millwood	.25
174	Pat Burrell	.25
175	Aramis Ramirez	.15
176	Jack Wilson	.15
177	Brian Giles	.25
178	Jason Kendall	.25
179	Kenny Lofton	.15
180	Kip Wells	.15
181	Kris Benson	.15
182	Albert Pujols	1.50
183	J.D. Drew	.25
184	Jim Edmonds	.25
185	Matt Morris	.15
186	Scott Rolen	.75
187	Woody Williams	.15
188	Clifford Bartosh	.15
189	Brian Lawrence	.15
190	Ryan Klesko	.25
191	Sean Burroughs	.15
192	Xavier Nady	.15
193	Dennis Tankersley	.15
194	Donaldo Mendez	.15
195	Barry Bonds	2.00
196	Benito Santiago	.15
197	Edgardo Alfonzo	.15
198	Cody Ransom	.15
199	Jason Schmidt	.15
200	Rich Aurilia	.15
201	Ken Harvey	.15
202	Adam Loewen	.25
203	Alfredo Gonzalez	.25
204	Arnie Munoz	.25
205	Andrew Brown	.25
206	Josh Hall	.25
207	Josh Stewart	.25
208	Clint Barmes	.25
209	Brandon Webb	.25
210	Chien-Ming Wang	.40
211	Edgar Gonzalez	.25
212	Alejandro Machado	.25
213	Jeremy Griffiths	.25
214	Craig Brazell	.25
215	Daniel Cabrera	.25
216	Fernando Cabrera	.25
217	Terrmel Sledge	.25
218	Rob Hammock	.25
219	Francisco Rosario	.25
220	Francisco Cruceta	.25

221	Rett Johnson	.25
222	Guillermo Quiroz	.25
223	Hong-Chih Kuo	.25
224	Ian Ferguson	.25
225	Tim Olson	.25
226	Todd Wellemeyer	.25
227	Rich Fischer	.25
228	Phil Seibel	.25
229	Joe Valentine	.25
230	Matt Kata	.25
231	Michael Hessman	.25
232	Michel Hernandez	.25
233	Doug Waechter	.25
234	Prentice Redman	.25
235	Nook Logan	.25
236	Oscar Villarreal	.25
237	Pete LaForest	.25
238	Matt Bruback	.25
239	Josh Willingham	.25
240	Greg Aquino	.25
241	Lew Ford	.25
242	Jeff Duncan	.25
243	Chris Waters	.25
244	Miguel Ojeda	.25
245	Rosman Garcia	.25
246	Felix Sanchez	.25
247	Jon Leicester	.25
248	Roger Deago	.25
249	Mike Ryan	.25
250	Chris Capuano	.25
251	Matt White	.25
252	Bernie Williams	.50
253	Mark Grace	.50
254	Chipper Jones	1.00
255	Greg Maddux	1.50
256	Sammy Sosa	2.00
257	Mike Mussina	.75
258	Tim Salmon	.50
259	Barry Larkin	.50
260	Randy Johnson	1.00
261	Jeff Bagwell	.75
262	Roberto Alomar	.50
263	Tom Glavine	.50
264	Roger Clemens	2.50
265	Barry Bonds	3.00
266	Ivan Rodriguez	.75
267	Pedro J. Martinez	1.00
268	Ken Griffey Jr.	1.50
269	Jim Thome	1.00
270	Frank Thomas	.75
271	Mike Piazza	1.50
272	Troy Glaus	.40
273	Melvin Mora	.25
274	Nomar Garciaparra	2.00
275	Magglio Ordonez	.40
276	Omar Vizquel	.40
277	Dmitri Young	.25
278	Mike Sweeney	.25
279	Torii Hunter	.50
280	Derek Jeter	2.00
281	Barry Zito	.50
282	Ichiro Suzuki	1.50
283	Rocco Baldelli	.50
284	Alex Rodriguez	2.00
285	Carlos Delgado	.50
286	Randy Johnson	.75
287	Greg Maddux	1.00
288	Sammy Sosa	1.50
289	Ken Griffey Jr.	1.00
290	Todd Helton	.50
291	Ivan Rodriguez	.50
292	Jeff Bagwell	.50
293	Hideo Nomo	.50
294	Richie Sexson	.50
295	Vladimir Guerrero	.75
296	Mike Piazza	1.00
297	Jim Thome	.75
298	Jason Kendall	.40
299	Albert Pujols	1.50
300	Ryan Klesko	.40
301	Barry Bonds	2.00

Blue Press Proof

Josh BECKETT

Stars (1-301): 4-8X
Production 100 Sets

Black Press Proof

Stars (1-301): 5-10X
Production 50 Sets
Hot Pack Exclusive

Gold Press Proof

Cards (1-301): 12-25X
Production 25 Sets

Red Press Proof

Curt SCHILLING

Stars (1-301): 1-2X
Inserted 1:8

Autographs

Jorge DE LA ROSA

		NM/M
	Common Autograph	6.00
14	Robert Person	6.00
18	Jorge De La Rosa	6.00
25	Ryan Ludwick	8.00
26	Luis Garcia	6.00
29	Jhonny Peralta	6.00
30	Josh Bard	6.00
32	Fernando Rodney	6.00
33	Mike Maroth	6.00
35	Omar Infante	6.00
41	Dee Brown	6.00
44	Brent Abernathy/SP	10.00
51	J.C. Romero	6.00
65	Justin Duchscherer	10.00
70	Terrence Long/SP	15.00
76	Rafael Soriano	8.00
85	Toby Hall/SP	10.00
87	Kevin Mench	6.00
95	Brian Bowles	6.00
115	Juan Cruz	6.00
125	Brian Reith	6.00
126	Wily Mo Pena	8.00
127	Jason Jennings	6.00
150	Ben Sheets/17	
155	Shane Nance	6.00
160	Henry Mateo/SP	8.00
163	Edwin Almonte	6.00
171	Brandon Duckworth	6.00
176	Jack Wilson	6.00
180	Kip Wells	6.00
188	Clifford Bartosh	6.00
189	Brian Lawrence	6.00
193	Dennis Tankersley	6.00
194	Donaldo Mendez	6.00
198	Cody Ransom/SP	8.00
247	Jon Leicester/SP	8.00

Away

		NM/M
Complete Set (10):		20.00
Common Player:		1.00
Inserted 1:35		
1	Greg Maddux	2.50
2	Sammy Sosa	3.00
3	Alex Rodriguez	4.00
4	Albert Pujols	4.00
5	Jason Giambi	1.50
6	Chipper Jones	2.00
7	Vladimir Guerrero	1.50
8	Mike Piazza	2.50
9	Nomar Garciaparra	3.00
10	Austin Kearns	1.00

Away Jersey

SAMMY SOSA

		NM/M
Common Player:		5.00
Inserted 1:119		
Prime:		1.5-2X
Production 50		
1	Greg Maddux	8.00
2	Sammy Sosa	12.00
3	Alex Rodriguez	10.00
4	Albert Pujols	15.00
5	Jason Giambi	8.00
6	Chipper Jones	8.00
7	Vladimir Guerrero	8.00
8	Mike Piazza	10.00
9	Nomar Garciaparra	12.00
10	Austin Kearns	5.00

Clean Up Crew

		NM/M
Complete Set (10):		20.00
Common Player:		1.00
Inserted 1:49		
1	Sammy Sosa, Moises Alou, Hee Seop Choi	3.00
2	Jason Giambi, Alfonso Soriano, Hideki Matsui	5.00
3	Vernon Wells, Carlos Delgado, Josh Phelps	1.00
4	Alex Rodriguez, Juan Gonzalez, Hank Blalock	4.00
5	Gary Sheffield, Andruw Jones, Chipper Jones	2.50
6	Ken Griffey Jr., Austin Kearns, Aaron Boone	3.00
7	Albert Pujols, Jim Edmonds, Scott Rolen	4.00
8	Jeff Bagwell, Jeff Kent, Lance Berkman	1.50
9	Todd Helton, Preston Wilson, Larry Walker	1.50
10	Miguel Tejada, Erubiel Durazo, Eric Chavez	1.00

Clean Up Crew Materials

		NM/M
Common Card:		15.00
Production 50 Sets		
1	Sammy Sosa, Moises Alou, Hee Seop Choi	35.00
2	Jason Giambi, Alfonso Soriano, Hideki Matsui	60.00
3	Vernon Wells, Carlos Delgado, Josh Phelps	15.00
4	Alex Rodriguez, Juan Gonzalez, Hank Blalock	35.00
5	Gary Sheffield, Andruw Jones, Chipper Jones	20.00
6	Ken Griffey Jr., Austin Kearns, Aaron Boone	25.00

7	Albert Pujols, Jim Edmonds, Scott Rolen	40.00
8	Jeff Bagwell, Jeff Kent, Lance Berkman	25.00
9	Todd Helton, Preston Wilson, Larry Walker	20.00
10	Miguel Tejada, Erubiel Durazo, Eric Chavez	15.00

Cornerstones

		NM/M
Complete Set (10):		20.00
Common Player:		1.00
Inserted 1:78		
1	Alex Rodriguez, Hank Blalock	4.00
2	Kerry Wood, Mark Prior	3.00
3	Roger Clemens, Alfonso Soriano	4.00
4	Nomar Garciaparra, Manny Ramirez	4.00
5	Austin Kearns, Adam Dunn	1.00
6	Tom Glavine, Mike Piazza	2.50
7	Andruw Jones, Chipper Jones	2.50
8	Albert Pujols, Scott Rolen	4.00
9	Curt Schilling, Randy Johnson	2.00
10	Hideo Nomo, Kazuhisa Ishii	1.00

Cornerstones Materials

		NM/M
Common Duo:		15.00
Production 50 Sets		
1	Alex Rodriguez, Hank Blalock	25.00
2	Kerry Wood, Mark Prior	40.00
3	Roger Clemens, Alfonso Soriano	40.00
4	Nomar Garciaparra, Manny Ramirez	30.00
5	Austin Kearns, Adam Dunn	15.00
6	Tom Glavine, Mike Piazza	
7	Andruw Jones, Chipper Jones	20.00
8	Albert Pujols, Scott Rolen	40.00
9	Curt Schilling, Randy Johnson	20.00
10	Hideo Nomo, Kazuhisa Ishii	20.00

Exhibits

		NM/M
Common Player:		2.50
Production 66 Sets		
Variations #'d to 63:		1X
Variations #'d to 46:		1X
Variations #'d 21 to 27:		1.5X
1	Adam Dunn	2.50
2	Albert Pujols	8.00
3	Alex Rodriguez	8.00
4	Alfonso Soriano	4.00
5	Andruw Jones	3.00
6	Barry Bonds	10.00
7	Barry Larkin	2.50
8	Barry Zito	2.50
9	Cal Ripken Jr.	10.00
10	Chipper Jones	5.00
11	Dale Murphy	2.50
12	Derek Jeter	10.00
13	Don Mattingly	8.00
14	Ernie Banks	5.00
15	Frank Thomas	4.00
16	George Brett	6.00
17	Greg Maddux	5.00
18	Hank Blalock	2.50
19	Hideo Nomo	2.50
20	Ichiro Suzuki	6.00
21	Jason Giambi	3.00
22	Jim Thome	4.00
23	Juan Gonzalez	2.50
24	Ken Griffey Jr.	5.00
25	Kirby Puckett	4.00
26	Mark Prior	5.00
27	Mike Mussina	2.50
28	Mike Piazza	5.00
29	Mike Schmidt	6.00
30	Nolan Ryan	8.00
31	Nolan Ryan	8.00
32	Nolan Ryan	8.00
33	Nomar Garciaparra	8.00
34	Ozzie Smith	2.50
35	Pedro J. Martinez	4.00
36	Randy Johnson	3.00
37	Reggie Jackson	2.50
38	Reggie Jackson	2.50
39	Rickey Henderson	2.50
40	Roberto Alomar	2.50
41	Roberto Clemente	8.00
42	Rod Carew	3.00
43	Roger Clemens	8.00
44	Sammy Sosa	6.00
45	Stan Musial	6.00
46	Tom Glavine	2.50
47	Tom Seaver	4.00
48	Tony Gwynn	4.00
49	Vladimir Guerrero	4.00
50	Yogi Berra	4.00

Gamers

		NM/M
Complete Set (20):		40.00
Common Player:		1.00
Quantum:		2-4X
Production 100 Sets		
1	Albert Pujols	4.00
2	Alex Rodriguez	4.00
3	Alfonso Soriano	1.50
4	Barry Bonds	5.00
5	Barry Zito	1.00
6	Chipper Jones	2.00
7	Derek Jeter	5.00
8	Greg Maddux	2.50
9	Ichiro Suzuki	3.00
10	Jason Giambi	1.50
11	Jeff Bagwell	1.50
12	Ken Griffey Jr.	2.50
13	Manny Ramirez	1.50
14	Mark Prior	3.00
15	Mike Piazza	2.50
16	Nomar Garciaparra	3.00
17	Pedro J. Martinez	2.00
18	Randy Johnson	2.00
19	Roger Clemens	3.00
20	Sammy Sosa	3.00

Gold Leaf Rookies

		NM/M
Complete Set (10):		6.00
Common Player:		.50
Inserted 1:23		
Mirror Gold:		No Pricing
Production 25 Sets		
1	Adam Loewen	2.00
2	Rickie Weeks	5.00
3	Khalil Greene	.50
4	Chad Tracy	.50
5	Alexis Rios	.50
6	Craig Brazell	.50
7	Clint Barmes	.50
8	Pete LaForest	.50
9	Alfredo Gonzalez	.50
10	Arnie Munoz	.50

Home

VLADIMIR GUERRERO

		NM/M
Complete Set (10):		20.00
Common Player:		1.00
Inserted 1:35		
1	Greg Maddux	2.50
2	Sammy Sosa	3.00
3	Alex Rodriguez	4.00
4	Albert Pujols	4.00
5	Jason Giambi	1.50
6	Chipper Jones	2.00
7	Vladimir Guerrero	1.50
8	Mike Piazza	2.50
9	Nomar Garciaparra	3.00
10	Austin Kearns	1.00

Home Jersey

		NM/M
Common Player:		5.00
Inserted 1:119		
Primes:		1.5-2X
Production 50		
1	Greg Maddux	8.00
2	Sammy Sosa	12.00
3	Alex Rodriguez	10.00
4	Albert Pujols	15.00
5	Jason Giambi	8.00
6	Chipper Jones	8.00
7	Vladimir Guerrero	8.00
8	Mike Piazza	10.00
9	Nomar Garciaparra	12.00
10	Austin Kearns	5.00

Previews

		NM/M
Common Player:		2.00
Production 999 Sets		
Silver:		1-2X
Production 100 Sets		
Gold:		2-3X
Production 50 Sets		
1	Derek Jeter	8.00
2	Barry Zito	2.00
3	Ichiro Suzuki	6.00
4	Pedro J. Martinez	3.00
5	Alfonso Soriano	3.00
6	Alex Rodriguez	6.00
7	Greg Maddux	4.00
8	Mike Piazza	4.00
9	Mark Prior	2.00
10	Albert Pujols	8.00
11	Sammy Sosa	5.00
12	Ken Griffey Jr.	4.00
13	Nomar Garciaparra	4.00
14	Randy Johnson	3.00
15	Jason Giambi	2.00
16	Barry Bonds	8.00
17	Manny Ramirez	3.00
18	Chipper Jones	3.00
19	Jeff Bagwell	2.00
20	Roger Clemens	6.00

MVP Winners

		NM/M
Complete Set (20):		50.00
Common Player:		1.00
Gold:		1-2X
Production 500 Sets		
1	Stan Musial/1948 NL	3.00
2	Ernie Banks/1958 NL	2.00
3	Roberto Clemente/1966 NL	4.00
4	George Brett/1980 AL	4.00
5	Mike Schmidt/1980 NL	4.00
6	Cal Ripken Jr./1983 AL	5.00
7	Dale Murphy/1983 NL	1.50
8	Ryne Sandberg/1984 NL	3.00
9	Don Mattingly/1985 AL	3.00
10	Roger Clemens/1986 AL	4.00

11	Rickey Henderson/1990 AL	1.00
12	Cal Ripken Jr./1991 AL	5.00
13	Barry Bonds/1992 NL	5.00
14	Barry Bonds/1993 NL	5.00
15	Frank Thomas/1994 AL	1.50
16	Ken Griffey Jr./1997 AL	2.50
17	Sammy Sosa/1998 NL	3.00
18	Chipper Jones/1999 NL	2.00
19	Jason Giambi/2000 AL	1.50
20	Ichiro Suzuki/2001 AL	3.00

Picture Perfect

		NM/M
Complete Set (15):		25.00
Common Player:		1.00
Inserted 1:37		
1	Albert Pujols	5.00
2	Alex Rodriguez	5.00
3	Alfonso Soriano	2.00
4	Austin Kearns	1.00
5	Carlos Delgado	1.50
6	Chipper Jones	2.50
7	Hank Blalock	1.50
8	Jason Giambi	2.00
9	Jeff Bagwell	1.50
10	Jim Thome	2.00
11	Manny Ramirez	1.50
12	Mike Piazza	3.00
13	Nomar Garciaparra	4.00
14	Sammy Sosa	4.00
15	Todd Helton	1.50

Picture Perfect Materials

		NM/M
Common Player:		6.00
Inserted 1:437		
1	Albert Pujols	15.00
2	Alex Rodriguez	10.00
3	Alfonso Soriano	8.00
4	Austin Kearns	6.00
5	Carlos Delgado	6.00
6	Chipper Jones	6.00
7	Hank Blalock	6.00
8	Jason Giambi	8.00
9	Jeff Bagwell	8.00
10	Jim Thome	10.00
11	Manny Ramirez	6.00
12	Mike Piazza	10.00
13	Nomar Garciaparra	10.00
14	Sammy Sosa	10.00
15	Todd Helton	8.00

Recollection Autographs

All are 1990 Leaf cards.
No Pricing

Shirt Off My Back

		NM/M
Common Player:		4.00
Inserted 1:47		
1	Shawn Green	4.00
2	Andruw Jones	6.00
3	Ivan Rodriguez	6.00

4	Hideo Nomo	6.00
5	Don Mattingly	20.00
6	Mark Prior	10.00
7	Alfonso Soriano	6.00
8	Richie Sexson	5.00
9	Vernon Wells	4.00
10	Nomar Garciaparra	8.00
11	Jason Giambi	6.00
12	Austin Kearns	5.00
13	Chipper Jones	6.00
14	Rickey Henderson	6.00
15	Alex Rodriguez	12.00
16	Garret Anderson	4.00
17	Vladimir Guerrero	4.00
18	Sammy Sosa	10.00
19	Mike Piazza	8.00
20	David Wells	4.00
21	Scott Rolen	6.00
22	Adam Dunn	5.00
23	Carlos Delgado	5.00
24	Greg Maddux	8.00
25	Hank Blalock	5.00

Shirt Off My Back Team Logo Patch

NM/M

Common Player:		10.00
Autographs:		No Pricing
Production 5 Sets		
Jersey Number Patch:		.75-1X
Production 50 Sets		
Sosa #'d to 42.		
Jersey Number Patch		
Auto.:		No Pricing
Production 5 Sets		
1	Shawn Green/41	15.00
2	Andruw Jones/75	15.00
3	Ivan Rodriguez/75	15.00
4	Hideo Nomo/74	20.00
6	Mark Prior/46	20.00
7	Alfonso Soriano/28	25.00
8	Richie Sexson/38	15.00
9	Vernon Wells/74	10.00
10	Nomar Garciaparra/75	25.00
11	Jason Giambi/26	20.00
12	Austin Kearns/32	10.00
13	Chipper Jones/75	20.00
14	Rickey Henderson/40	20.00
15	Alex Rodriguez/75	30.00
16	Garret Anderson/71	10.00
17	Vladimir Guerrero/55	20.00
18	Sammy Sosa/39	25.00
19	Mike Piazza/75	20.00
20	David Wells/74	10.00
21	Scott Rolen/29	30.00
22	Adam Dunn/32	15.00
23	Carlos Delgado/56	15.00
24	Greg Maddux/75	20.00
25	Hank Blalock/62	15.00

Sunday Dress

NM/M

Complete Set (10):		10.00
Common Player:		.75
Inserted 1:17		
1	Frank Thomas	1.00
2	Barry Zito	.75
3	Mike Piazza	2.00
4	Mark Prior	2.00
5	Jeff Bagwell	1.00
6	Roy Oswalt	.75
7	Todd Helton	1.00
8	Magglio Ordonez	.75
9	Alex Rodriguez	3.00
10	Manny Ramirez	1.00

Sunday Dress Jersey

NM/M

Common Player:		5.00
Inserted 1:119		
Prime Jersey:		1-1.5X
Production 100		
1	Frank Thomas	8.00
2	Barry Zito	6.00
3	Mike Piazza	10.00
4	Mark Prior	10.00
5	Jeff Bagwell	8.00
6	Roy Oswalt	5.00
7	Todd Helton	8.00
8	Magglio Ordonez	6.00

9	Alex Rodriguez	10.00
10	Manny Ramirez	6.00

2004 Leaf Certified Cuts

NM/M

Complete Set (300):		
Common Player (1-200):		.75
Common (201-250):		2.00
Production 599		
Common (251-300):		5.00
Production 499		
Auto. Production 99-499		
Pack (5):		20.00
Box (10):		160.00
1	Vladimir Guerrero	1.50
2	Garret Anderson	.75
3	John Lackey	.75
4	Bartolo Colon	.75
5	Troy Glaus	.75
6	Tim Salmon	.75
7	Shea Hillenbrand	.75
8	Brandon Webb	.75
9	Roberto Alomar	.75
10	Randy Johnson	2.00
11	Alex Cintron	.75
12	Richie Sexson	.75
13	Luis Gonzalez	.75
14	Adam LaRoche	.75
15	Rafael Furcal	.75
16	Chipper Jones	2.00
17	Marcus Giles	.75
18	Andruw Jones	1.00
19	Russ Ortiz	.75
20	Rafael Palmeiro	1.00
21	Melvin Mora	.75
22	Luis Matos	.75
23	Jay Gibbons	.75
24	Adam Loewen	.75
25	Larry Bigbie	.75
26	Rodrigo Lopez	.75
27	Javy Lopez	.75
28	Miguel Tejada	1.00
29	Trot Nixon	.75
30	Curt Schilling	1.00
31	Jason Varitek	.75
32	Manny Ramirez	1.00
33	Keith Foulke	.75
34	Derek Lowe	.75
35	Pedro J. Martinez	1.50
36	Nomar Garciaparra	2.50
37	Bill Mueller	.75
38	Johnny Damon	.75
39	David Ortiz	1.50
40	Mark Prior	1.00
41	Kerry Wood	1.50
42	Sammy Sosa	2.50
43	Derrek Lee	.75
44	Greg Maddux	2.00
45	Aramis Ramirez	.75
46	Matt Clement	.75
47	Carlos Zambrano	.75
48	Todd Walker	.75
49	Moises Alou	.75
50	Corey Patterson	.75
51	Frank Thomas	1.00
52	Magglio Ordonez	.75
53	Carlos Lee	.75
54	Mark Buehrle	.75
55	Esteban Loaiza	.75
56	Joe Crede	.75
57	Paul Konerko	.75
58	Adam Dunn	1.00
59	Austin Kearns	.75
60	Barry Larkin	.75
61	Ryan Wagner	.75
62	Danny Graves	.75
63	Sean Casey	.75
64	Ken Griffey Jr.	2.00
65	Jody Gerut	.75
66	Cliff Lee	.75
67	Victor Martinez	.75
68	C.C. Sabathia	.75
69	Omar Vizquel	.75
70	Travis Hafner	.75
71	Todd Helton	1.00
72	Preston Wilson	.75
73	Jeromy Burnitz	.75
74	Larry Walker	.75
75	Ivan Rodriguez	1.00
76	Rondell White	.75
77	Miguel Cabrera	1.50

78	Luis Castillo	.75
79	Josh Beckett	.75
80	Mike Lowell	.75
81	Dontrelle Willis	.75
82	Brad Penny	.75
83	Hee Seop Choi	.75
84	Juan Pierre	.75
85	Andy Pettitte	.75
86	Jeff Bagwell	1.00
87	Roy Oswalt	.75
88	Lance Berkman	.75
89	Morgan Ensberg	.75
90	Craig Biggio	.75
91	Octavio Dotel	.75
92	Wade Miller	.75
93	Jeff Kent	.75
94	Richard Hidalgo	.75
95	Roger Clemens	3.00
96	Carlos Beltran	1.00
97	Angel Berroa	.75
98	Jeremy Affeldt	.75
99	Juan Gonzalez	.75
100	Mike Sweeney	.75
101	Kazuhisa Ishii	.75
102	Shawn Green	.75
103	Milton Bradley	.75
104	Paul LoDuca	.75
105	Hideo Nomo	.75
106	Eric Gagne	.75
107	Adrian Beltre	.75
108	Scott Podsednik	.75
109	Rickie Weeks	.75
110	Ben Sheets	.75
111	Geoff Jenkins	.75
112	Jacque Jones	.75
113	Johan Santana	1.00
114	Shannon Stewart	.75
115	Corey Koskie	.75
116	Lew Ford	.75
117	Torii Hunter	.75
118	Chad Cordero	.75
119	Orlando Cabrera	.75
120	Jose Vidro	.75
121	Nick Johnson	.75
122	Brad Wilkerson	.75
123	Mike Piazza	2.00
124	Jae Weong Seo	.75
125	Jose Reyes	.75
126	Tom Glavine	.75
127	Jorge Posada	.75
128	Gary Sheffield	1.00
129	Bernie Williams	.75
130	Mike Mussina	1.00
131	Mariano Rivera	.75
132	Bubba Crosby	.75
133	Kevin Brown	.75
134	Javier Vazquez	.75
135	Jason Giambi	.75
136	Derek Jeter	4.00
137	Alex Rodriguez	4.00
138	Hideki Matsui	3.00
139	Mark Mulder	.75
140	Jermaine Dye	.75
141	Tim Hudson	.75
142	Barry Zito	.75
143	Eric Chavez	.75
144	Bobby Crosby	.75
145	Eric Byrnes	.75
146	Marlon Byrd	.75
147	Billy Wagner	.75
148	Mike Lieberthal	.75
149	Jimmy Rollins	1.00
150	Jim Thome	1.50
151	Bobby Abreu	.75
152	Pat Burrell	.75
153	Jose Castillo	.75
154	Craig Wilson	.75
155	Jason Bay	.75
156	Jason Kendall	.75
157	Raul Mondesi	.75
158	Jay Payton	.75
159	Trevor Hoffman	.75
160	Jake Peavy	.75
161	Sean Burroughs	.75
162	Phil Nevin	.75
163	Brian Giles	.75
164	Ryan Klesko	.75
165	Todd Linden	.75
166	Jerome Williams	.75
167	Jason Schmidt	1.00
168	Ray Durham	.75
169	Marquis Grissom	.75
170	Shigetoshi Hasegawa	.75
171	Edgar Martinez	.75
172	Freddy Garcia	.75
173	Bret Boone	.75
174	Raul Ibanez	.75
175	Ichiro Suzuki	3.00
176	Randy Winn	.75
177	Scott Rolen	1.50
178	Jim Edmonds	.75
179	Albert Pujols	3.00
180	Matt Morris	.75
181	Edgar Renteria	.75

182	Aubrey Huff	.75
183	Delmon Young	.75
184	Dewon Brazelton	.75
185	Rocco Baldelli	.75
186	Carl Crawford	.75
187	Mark Teixeira	.75
188	Hank Blalock	1.00
189	Michael Young	.75
190	Laynce Nix	.75
191	Alfonso Soriano	1.50
192	Kevin Mench	.75
193	Adrian Gonzalez	.75
194	Alexis Rios	.75
195	Roy Halladay	.75
196	Vernon Wells	.75
197	Carlos Delgado	.75
198	Bill Hall	.75
199	Jose Guillen	.75
200	Jeremy Bonderman	.75
201	Roger Clemens/SP	6.00
202	Alex Rodriguez/SP	6.00
203	Greg Maddux/SP	4.00
204	Miguel Tejada/SP	2.00
205	Alfonso Soriano/SP	3.00
206	Andy Pettitte/SP	2.00
207	Curt Schilling/SP	2.00
208	Gary Sheffield/SP	2.00
209	Ivan Rodriguez/SP	2.00
210	Jim Thome/SP	2.00
211	Mike Mussina/SP	2.00
212	Mike Piazza/SP	4.00
213	Randy Johnson/SP	3.00
214	Roger Clemens/SP	6.00
215	Sammy Sosa/SP	4.00
216	Alex Rodriguez/SP	6.00
217	Randy Johnson/SP	3.00
218	Vladimir Guerrero/SP	3.00
219	Rafael Palmeiro/SP	2.00
220	Manny Ramirez/SP	2.00
221	Mike Piazza/SP	4.00
222	Cal Ripken Jr.	10.00
223	Ted Williams	8.00
224	Duke Snider	2.00
225	Ernie Banks	4.00
226	Ryne Sandberg	8.00
227	Mark Grace	2.00
228	Andre Dawson	2.00
229	Bob Feller	2.00
230	Bob Feller	6.00
231	George Brett	8.00
232	Bo Jackson	3.00
233	Robin Yount	4.00
234	Harmon Killebrew	4.00
235	Gary Carter	2.00
236	Don Mattingly	8.00
237	Phil Rizzuto	2.00
238	Babe Ruth	8.00
239	Lou Gehrig	8.00
240	Reggie Jackson	3.00
241	Rickey Henderson	3.00
242	Mike Schmidt	8.00
243	Roberto Clemente	8.00
244	Tony Gwynn	3.00
245	Will Clark	3.00
246	Lou Brock	2.00
247	Bob Gibson	3.00
248	Stan Musial	5.00
249	Nolan Ryan	10.00
250	Dale Murphy	2.00
251	Aarom Baldiris/ Auto./499 RC	8.00
252	Akinori Otsuka/ Auto./99 RC	40.00
253	Andres Blanco/ Auto./499 RC	8.00
254	Angel Chavez/ Auto./499 RC	5.00
255	Carlos Hines/ Auto./199 RC	8.00
256	Carlos Vasquez/ Auto./499 RC	10.00
257	Casey Daigle/499 RC	10.00
258	Chris Oxspring/ Auto./499 RC	8.00
259	Colby Miller/ Auto./499 RC	5.00
260	David Crouthers/ Auto./199	8.00
261	Donald Kelly/ Auto./499 RC	5.00
262	Eddy Rodriguez/ Auto./499 RC	10.00
263	Edwardo Sierra/ Auto./299 RC	8.00
264	Edwin Moreno/ Auto./499 RC	10.00
265	Fernando Nieve/ Auto./499 RC	5.00

ABBREVIATIONS

SP - Short Print

266 Freddy Guzman/
    Auto./499 **RC** 5.00
267 Greg Dobbs/
    Auto./499 **RC** 5.00
268 Brad Halsey/
    Auto./499 **RC** 5.00
269 Hector Gimenez/
    Auto./499 **RC** 8.00
270 Ivan Ochoa/
    Auto./499 **RC** 5.00
271 Jake Woods/Auto./499 8.00
272 Jamie Brown/
    Auto./499 **RC** 5.00
273 Jason Bartlett/
    Auto./499 **RC** 8.00
274 Jason Szuminski/
    Auto./499 **RC** 5.00
275 John Gall/499 **RC** 5.00
276 Jorge Vasquez/
    Auto./499 **RC** 5.00
277 Josh Labandeira/
    Auto./499 **RC** 8.00
278 Justin Hampson/
    Auto./499 **RC** 5.00
279 Kazuo Matsui/499 **RC** 15.00
280 Kevin Cave/
    Auto./499 **RC** 8.00
281 Lance Cormier/
    Auto./499 **RC** 5.00
282 Lincoln Holdzkom/
    Auto./199 **RC** 8.00
283 Merkin Valdez/
    Auto./199 **RC** 15.00
284 Mike Wuertz/
    Auto./499 **RC** 8.00
285 Mike Johnston/
    Auto./499 **RC** 5.00
286 Mike Rouse/Auto./329 8.00
287 Onil Joseph/
    Auto./499 **RC** 5.00
288 Phil Stockman/
    Auto./499 **RC** 5.00
289 Roberto Novoa/
    Auto./499 **RC** 8.00
290 Ronald Belisario/
    Auto./499 **RC** 5.00
291 Ronny Cedeno/
    Auto./499 **RC** 5.00
292 Ryan Meaux/
    Auto./499 **RC** 5.00
293 Scott Proctor/499 **RC** 5.00
294 Sean Henn/Auto./499 10.00
295 Shawn Camp/
    Auto./499 **RC** 5.00
296 Shawn Hill/
    Auto./499 **RC** 5.00
297 Shingo Takatsu/
    Auto./99 **RC** 40.00
298 Tim Bittner/
    Auto./199 **RC** 8.00
299 William Bergolla/
    499 **RC** 5.00
300 Yadier Molina/
    Auto./499 **RC** 15.00

Marble Black

No Pricing
Production One Set

Marble Blue

Blue 1-200: 3-5X
Blue 201-250: 2-3X
Blue 251-300: .5-1X
Production 50 Sets

Marble Emerald

No Pricing
Production 5 Sets

Marble Gold

Gold 1-200: 6-8X
Gold 201-250: 2-4X
Gold 251-300: No Pricing
Production 25 Sets

Marble Red

Red 1-200: 2-3X
Red 201-250: 1-2X
Red 251-300: .4-1X
Production 100 Sets

Marble Signature Black

No Pricing
Production One Set

Marble Material Red Position

                      NM/M
Quantity produced listed
1   Vladimir Guerrero/
    Jsy/100 10.00

2 Garret Anderson/
    Jsy/100 4.00
5 Troy Glaus/Jsy/75 4.00
6 Tim Salmon/Jsy/75 6.00
10 Randy Johnson/
    Jsy/100 8.00
13 Luis Gonzalez/Jsy/100 4.00
15 Rafael Furcal/Jsy/100 4.00
16 Chipper Jones/
    Jsy/100 8.00
17 Marcus Giles/Jsy/100 4.00
18 Andruw Jones/Jsy/100 6.00
20 Rafael Palmeiro/
    Jsy/100 8.00
21 Melvin Mora/Jsy/100 6.00
22 Luis Matos/Jsy/50 6.00
23 Jay Gibbons/Jsy/100 4.00
25 Larry Bigbie/Jsy/50 6.00
26 Rodrigo Lopez/Jsy/50 6.00
27 Javy Lopez/Jsy/25 10.00
28 Miguel Tejada/Jsy/100 6.00
30 Curt Schilling/Jsy/50 8.00
31 Jason Varitek/Jsy/100 4.00
32 Manny Ramirez/
    Jsy/100 8.00
35 Pedro J. Martinez/
    Jsy/100 10.00
39 David Ortiz/Jsy/100 8.00
40 Mark Prior/Jsy/100 8.00
41 Kerry Wood/
    Pants/100 10.00
42 Sammy Sosa/Jsy/100 8.00
44 Greg Maddux/Jsy/50 15.00
45 Aramis Ramirez/
    Jsy/100 6.00
51 Frank Thomas/
    Jsy/100 8.00
52 Magglio Ordonez/
    Jsy/100 4.00
53 Carlos Lee/Jsy/100 4.00
54 Mark Buehrle/Jsy/100 4.00
57 Paul Konerko/Jsy/50 6.00
58 Adam Dunn/Jsy/100 8.00
59 Austin Kearns/Jsy/100 4.00
60 Barry Larkin/Jsy/100 6.00
65 Jody Gerut/Jsy/100 4.00
66 Cliff Lee/Jsy/100 4.00
67 Victor Martinez/
    Jsy/100 6.00
68 C.C. Sabathia/Jsy/100 4.00
69 Omar Vizquel/Jsy/100 4.00
70 Travis Hafner/Jsy/100 4.00
71 Todd Helton/Jsy/100 8.00
72 Preston Wilson/
    Jsy/100 4.00
75 Ivan Rodriguez/
    Jsy/50 10.00
77 Miguel Cabrera/
    Jsy/100 8.00
79 Josh Beckett/Jsy/100 6.00
81 Dontrelle Willis/
    Jsy/100 4.00
82 Brad Penny/Jsy/100 4.00
86 Jeff Bagwell/Jsy/100 8.00
87 Roy Oswalt/Jsy/100 4.00
88 Lance Berkman/
    Jsy/100 4.00
89 Morgan Ensberg/
    Jsy/100 4.00
90 Craig Biggio/Jsy/100 6.00
93 Jeff Kent/Jsy/100 4.00
94 Richard Hidalgo/
    Pants/100 4.00
95 Roger Clemens/
    Jsy/25 30.00
96 Carlos Beltran/Jsy/100 6.00
97 Angel Berroa/
    Pants/100 4.00
100 Mike Sweeney/
    Jsy/100 4.00
101 Kazuhisa Ishii/Jsy/100 4.00
102 Shawn Green/Jsy/100 4.00
104 Paul LoDuca/Jsy/100 4.00
105 Hideo Nomo/Jsy/100 8.00
107 Adrian Beltre/Jsy/100 8.00
110 Ben Sheets/Jsy/100 6.00
111 Geoff Jenkins/Jsy/100 4.00
112 Jacque Jones/Jsy/100 4.00
113 Johan Santana/
    Jsy/100 4.00
114 Shannon Stewart/
    Jsy/100 4.00
117 Torii Hunter/Jsy/75 4.00
123 Mike Piazza/Jsy/100 10.00
125 Jose Reyes/Jsy/75 4.00
126 Tom Glavine/Jsy/75 6.00
127 Jorge Posada/Jsy/100 8.00
129 Bernie Williams/
    Jsy/100 6.00
130 Mike Mussina/Jsy/25 20.00
131 Mariano Rivera/
    Jsy/100 8.00
138 Hideki Matsui/
    Jsy/100 25.00

139 Mark Mulder/Jsy/100 4.00
141 Tim Hudson/Jsy/10
142 Barry Zito/Jsy/100 4.00
143 Eric Chavez/Jsy/100 4.00
146 Marlon Byrd/Jsy/100 4.00
150 Jim Thome/Jsy/100 8.00
151 Bobby Abreu/Jsy/100 4.00
152 Pat Burrell/Jsy/100 4.00
154 Craig Wilson/Jsy/100 4.00
156 Jason Kendall/Jsy/100 4.00
161 Sean Burroughs/
    Jsy/100 4.00
163 Brian Giles/Jsy/10
164 Ryan Klesko/Jsy/100 4.00
166 Jerome Williams/
    Jsy/25 10.00
171 Edgar Martinez/
    Jsy/100 6.00
172 Freddy Garcia/Jsy/100 4.00
177 Scott Rolen/Jsy/100 10.00
178 Jim Edmonds/Jsy/100 8.00
179 Albert Pujols/Jsy/100 20.00
180 Matt Morris/Jsy/75 4.00
181 Edgar Renteria/
    Jsy/25 8.00
182 Aubrey Huff/Jsy/100 4.00
185 Rocco Baldelli/Jsy/100 6.00
186 Carl Crawford/Jsy/100 4.00
187 Mark Teixeira/Jsy/25 8.00
188 Hank Blalock/Jsy/100 4.00
191 Alfonso Soriano/
    Jsy/100 8.00
192 Kevin Mench/Jsy/100 4.00
195 Roy Halladay/Jsy/100 4.00
196 Vernon Wells/Jsy/100 4.00
197 Carlos Delgado
    /Jsy/100 4.00
200 Jeremy Bonderman/
    Jsy/100 4.00
201 Roger Clemens/
    Jsy/100 10.00
202 Alex Rodriguez/
    Jsy/100 10.00
203 Greg Maddux/
    Jsy/100 10.00
204 Miguel Tejada/Jsy/100 4.00
205 Alfonso Soriano/
    Jsy/100 8.00
206 Andy Pettitte/Jsy/100 4.00
207 Curt Schilling/Jsy/100 8.00
208 Gary Sheffield/Jsy/50 8.00
209 Ivan Rodriguez/
    Jsy/100 8.00
210 Jim Thome/Jsy/25 20.00
211 Mike Mussina/Jsy/50 10.00
212 Mike Piazza/Jsy/100 10.00
213 Randy Johnson/
    Jsy/100 8.00
214 Roger Clemens/
    Jsy/100 10.00
215 Sammy Sosa/Jsy/100 15.00
216 Alex Rodriguez/
    Jsy/100 10.00
217 Randy Johnson/
    Jsy/100 8.00
218 Vladimir Guerrero/
    Jsy/100 8.00
219 Rafael Palmeiro/
    Jsy/100 8.00
221 Mike Piazza/Jsy/100 10.00
222 Cal Ripken Jr./
    Jsy/50 50.00
223 Ted Williams/Jsy/25 100.00
225 Ernie Banks/Jsy/50 15.00
226 Ryne Sandberg/
    Jsy/100 15.00
227 Mark Grace/Jsy/25 20.00
228 Andre Dawson/
    Jsy/100 6.00
229 Bob Feller/Jsy/25 20.00
231 George Brett/Jsy/100 15.00
232 Bo Jackson/Jsy/100 6.00
233 Robin Yount/Jsy/100 12.00
234 Harmon Killebrew/
    Jsy/25 25.00
235 Gary Carter/Jkt/100 6.00
236 Don Mattingly/Jsy/50 25.00
237 Phil Rizzuto/Pants/25 20.00
238 Babe Ruth/Pants/50 200.00
239 Lou Gehrig/
    Pants/50 150.00
240 Reggie Jackson/
    Jsy/100 8.00
241 Rickey Henderson/
    Jsy/100 10.00
242 Mike Schmidt/Jsy/50 25.00
243 Roberto Clemente/
    Jsy/50 75.00
244 Tony Gwynn/Jsy/100 10.00
245 Will Clark/Jsy/100 8.00
246 Lou Brock/Jsy/25 20.00
247 Bob Gibson/Jsy/25 20.00
248 Stan Musial/Jsy/25 60.00
249 Nolan Ryan/Jsy/50 40.00
250 Dale Murphy/Jsy/100 10.00

Marble Material Black

No Pricing
Production One Set

Marble Material Emerald Prime

No Pricing
Production 5 Sets

Marble Signature Blue

                      NM/M
Quantity produced listed
2 Garret Anderson/50 20.00
3 John Lackey/75 15.00
7 Shea Hillenbrand/75 15.00
8 Brandon Webb/75 10.00
11 Alex Cintron/75 10.00
14 Adam LaRoche/75 15.00
15 Rafael Furcal/50 20.00
17 Marcus Giles/50 15.00
19 Russ Ortiz/75 10.00
21 Melvin Mora/75 15.00
22 Luis Matos/75 10.00
23 Jay Gibbons/75 15.00
24 Adam Loewen/50 10.00
25 Larry Bigbie/75 15.00
26 Rodrigo Lopez/75 10.00
29 Trot Nixon/50 35.00
33 Keith Foulke/75 8.00
39 David Ortiz/50 40.00
40 Mark Prior/25 40.00
41 Kerry Wood/50 50.00
43 Derrek Lee/25 30.00
45 Aramis Ramirez/75 20.00
46 Matt Clement/25 15.00
47 Carlos Zambrano/75 35.00
48 Todd Walker/75 10.00
52 Magglio Ordonez/25 20.00
53 Carlos Lee/75 15.00
54 Mark Buehrle/50 15.00
55 Esteban Loaiza/25 15.00
58 Adam Dunn/25 40.00
59 Austin Kearns/25 15.00
63 Sean Casey/25 25.00
65 Jody Gerut/75 8.00
66 Cliff Lee/75 10.00
67 Victor Martinez/75 20.00
68 C.C. Sabathia/75 15.00
70 Travis Hafner/75 15.00
72 Preston Wilson/75 15.00
77 Miguel Cabrera/75 35.00
80 Mike Lowell/25 20.00
82 Brad Penny/75 10.00
87 Roy Oswalt/50 15.00
89 Morgan Ensberg/75 12.00
90 Craig Biggio/75 30.00
91 Octavio Dotel/75 10.00
92 Wade Miller/75 10.00
96 Carlos Beltran/50 50.00
97 Angel Berroa/75 10.00
98 Jeremy Affeldt/75 10.00
103 Milton Bradley/75 15.00
104 Paul LoDuca/50 15.00
108 Scott Podsednik/75 15.00
109 Rickie Weeks/25 25.00
112 Jacque Jones/75 10.00
113 Johan Santana/50 50.00
114 Shannon Stewart/50 15.00
116 Lew Ford/75 15.00
117 Torii Hunter/25 25.00
118 Chad Cordero/75 10.00
119 Orlando Cabrera/75 20.00
120 Jose Vidro/50 15.00
125 Jose Reyes/25 30.00
132 Bubba Crosby/75 10.00
139 Mark Mulder/25 25.00
140 Jermaine Dye/75 10.00
144 Bobby Crosby/75 40.00
145 Eric Byrnes/75 10.00
146 Marlon Byrd/75 15.00
148 Mike Lieberthal/75 15.00
153 Jose Castillo/75 10.00
154 Craig Wilson/75 15.00
155 Jason Bay/75 25.00
158 Jay Payton/75 10.00
161 Sean Burroughs/25 15.00
165 Todd Linden/75 8.00
170 Shigetoshi
    Hasegawa/75 40.00
171 Edgar Martinez/25 15.00
174 Raul Ibanez/75 10.00
177 Scott Rolen/75 35.00
182 Aubrey Huff/75 10.00
183 Delmon Young/25 25.00
184 Dewon Brazelton/75 10.00
186 Carl Crawford/75 40.00
187 Mark Teixeira/25 40.00
188 Hank Blalock/75 10.00
189 Michael Young/75 15.00
190 Laynce Nix/75 10.00
191 Alfonso Soriano/25 50.00
193 Adrian Gonzalez/75 10.00

194	Alexis Rios/75	20.00
196	Vernon Wells/50	15.00
198	Bill Hall/75	10.00
199	Jose Guillen/75	15.00
200	Jeremy Bonderman/75	10.00
222	Cal Ripken Jr./25	150.00
224	Duke Snider/35	35.00
228	Andre Dawson/50	20.00
229	Bob Feller/50	30.00
235	Gary Carter/25	20.00
237	Phil Rizzuto/25	40.00
245	Will Clark/25	50.00
246	Lou Brock/25	35.00
247	Bob Gibson/25	40.00
248	Stan Musial/25	75.00
249	Nolan Ryan/25	150.00
250	Dale Murphy/50	30.00
251	Aarom Baldiris/75	10.00
252	Akinori Otsuka/25	50.00
253	Andres Blanco/75	10.00
254	Angel Chavez/75	8.00
255	Carlos Hines/75	8.00
256	Carlos Vasquez/75	12.00
258	Chris Oxspring/75	10.00
259	Colby Miller/75	8.00
261	Donald Kelly/75	8.00
262	Eddy Rodriguez/75 .	
263	Edwardo Sierra/65	
264	Edwin Moreno/75	12.00
265	Fernando Nieve/75	8.00
266	Freddy Guzman/75	8.00
267	Greg Dobbs/75	8.00
268	Brad Halsey/75	8.00
269	Hector Gimenez/75	8.00
270	Ivan Ochoa/75	8.00
271	Jake Woods/75	10.00
272	Jamie Brown/75	8.00
273	Jason Bartlett/75	15.00
274	Jason Szuminski/75	8.00
275	John Gall/75	10.00
276	Jorge Vasquez/75	8.00
277	Josh Labandeira/75	8.00
278	Justin Hampson/75	8.00
280	Kevin Cave/75	10.00
281	Lance Cormier/75	8.00
283	Merkin Valdez/75	15.00
284	Mike Wuertz/75	10.00
285	Mike Johnston/75	8.00
287	Onil Joseph/75	8.00
288	Phil Stockman/75	8.00
289	Roberto Novoa/75	10.00
290	Ronald Belisario/75	8.00
291	Ronny Cedeno/75	8.00
292	Ryan Meaux/75	8.00
293	Scott Proctor/75	10.00
295	Shawn Camp/75	8.00
296	Shawn Hill/75	8.00
297	Shingo Takatsu/75	60.00
299	William Bergolla/75	8.00
300	Yadier Molina/75	25.00

Marble Signature Emerald

No Pricing
Production 1-5

Marble Signature Gold

No Pricing
Production 1-25

Marble Signature Red

NM/M
Quantity produced listed

2	Garret Anderson/50	20.00
3	John Lackey/100	15.00
7	Shea Hillenbrand/100	15.00
8	Brandon Webb/100	10.00
11	Alex Cintron/100	10.00
14	Adam LaRoche/100	15.00
15	Rafael Furcal/100	20.00
17	Marcus Giles/100	15.00
19	Russ Ortiz/100	10.00
21	Melvin Mora/100	15.00
22	Luis Matos/100	10.00
23	Jay Gibbons/100	15.00
25	Larry Bigbie/100	15.00
26	Rodrigo Lopez/100	10.00
29	Trot Nixon/50	35.00
33	Keith Foulke/100	8.00
39	David Ortiz/50	40.00
40	Mark Prior/50	40.00
43	Derrek Lee/50	25.00
45	Aramis Ramirez/100	20.00
46	Matt Clement/100	15.00
47	Carlos Zambrano/100	35.00
48	Todd Walker/100	10.00
53	Carlos Lee/100	15.00
54	Mark Buehrle/50	15.00
58	Esteban Loaiza/100	10.00
58	Adam Dunn/25	40.00
59	Austin Kearns/25	20.00

63	Sean Casey/25	25.00
65	Jody Gerut/100	8.00
66	Cliff Lee/100	10.00
67	Victor Martinez/100	8.00
68	C.C. Sabathia/100	15.00
70	Travis Hafner/100	15.00
72	Preston Wilson/100	15.00
77	Miguel Cabrera/50	35.00
80	Mike Lowell/25	20.00
82	Brad Penny/100	10.00
89	Morgan Ensberg/100	10.00
90	Craig Biggio/25	30.00
91	Octavio Dotel/100	15.00
92	Wade Miller/100	10.00
96	Carlos Beltran/50	50.00
97	Angel Berroa/50	10.00
98	Jeremy Affeldt/100	10.00
103	Milton Bradley/100	15.00
104	Paul LoDuca/50	15.00
108	Scott Podsednik/100	15.00
109	Rickie Weeks/25	25.00
112	Jacque Jones/100	10.00
113	Johan Santana/50	15.00
114	Shannon Stewart/50	15.00
116	Lew Ford/100	15.00
117	Torii Hunter/25	25.00
118	Chad Cordero/100	10.00
119	Orlando Cabrera/100	20.00
120	Jose Vidro/50	10.00
132	Bubba Crosby/100	10.00
139	Mark Mulder/25	25.00
140	Jermaine Dye/100	10.00
144	Bobby Crosby/100	40.00
145	Eric Byrnes/100	10.00
146	Marlon Byrd/100	10.00
148	Mike Lieberthal/100	15.00
153	Jose Castillo/100	10.00
154	Craig Wilson/100	10.00
155	Jason Bay/100	25.00
158	Jay Payton/100	10.00
161	Sean Burroughs/25	15.00
165	Todd Linden/100	8.00
170	Shigetoshi Hasegawa/50	40.00
171	Edgar Martinez/25	40.00
174	Raul Ibanez/100	10.00
177	Scott Rolen/25	35.00
182	Aubrey Huff/100	10.00
183	Delmon Young/25	25.00
184	Dewon Brazelton/100	10.00
186	Carl Crawford/100	20.00
187	Mark Teixeira/25	40.00
188	Hank Blalock/50	25.00
189	Michael Young/100	15.00
190	Laynce Nix/100	10.00
191	Alfonso Soriano/25	50.00
193	Adrian Gonzalez/100	10.00
194	Alexis Rios/100	20.00
196	Vernon Wells/50	15.00
198	Bill Hall/100	10.00
199	Jose Guillen/100	15.00
200	Jeremy Bonderman/100	10.00
222	Cal Ripken Jr./25	150.00
224	Duke Snider/25	40.00
228	Andre Dawson/100	20.00
229	Bob Feller/100	25.00
235	Gary Carter/25	20.00
237	Phil Rizzuto/25	40.00
245	Will Clark/25	50.00
247	Bob Gibson/25	40.00
249	Nolan Ryan/25	150.00
250	Dale Murphy/25	30.00
251	Aarom Baldiris/100	10.00
252	Akinori Otsuka/25	50.00
253	Andres Blanco/100	10.00
254	Angel Chavez/100	8.00
255	Carlos Hines/100	8.00
256	Carlos Vasquez/100	12.00
258	Chris Oxspring/100	10.00
259	Colby Miller/100	8.00
260	David Crouthers/100	8.00
261	Donald Kelly/100	8.00
262	Eddy Rodriguez/100	8.00
263	Edwardo Sierra/100	10.00
264	Edwin Moreno/100	10.00
266	Freddy Guzman/100	8.00
267	Greg Dobbs/100	8.00
268	Brad Halsey/100	8.00
269	Hector Gimenez/100	8.00
270	Ivan Ochoa/100	8.00
271	Jake Woods/100	10.00
272	Jamie Brown/100	8.00
273	Jason Bartlett/100	15.00
274	Jason Szuminski/100	8.00
275	John Gall/100	10.00
276	Jorge Vasquez/100	8.00
277	Josh Labandeira/100	8.00
280	Kevin Cave/100	10.00
281	Lance Cormier/100	8.00
283	Merkin Valdez/100	15.00
284	Mike Wuertz/100	10.00
285	Mike Johnston/100	8.00

287	Onil Joseph/100	8.00
288	Phil Stockman/100	8.00
289	Roberto Novoa/100	10.00
291	Ronny Cedeno/100	8.00
292	Ryan Meaux/100	8.00
293	Scott Proctor/100	10.00
295	Shawn Camp/100	8.00
297	Shingo Takatsu/25	60.00
299	William Bergolla/100	8.00
300	Yadier Molina/100	25.00

Marble Signature Material Gold Position

NM/M
Quantity produced listed

1	Vladimir Guerrero/Jsy/10	
2	Garret Anderson/Jsy/50	20.00
8	Brandon Webb/Jsy/50	15.00
15	Rafael Furcal/Jsy/50	20.00
17	Marcus Giles/Jsy/50	20.00
21	Melvin Mora/Jsy/50	20.00
22	Luis Matos/Jsy/50	15.00
23	Jay Gibbons/Jsy/50	15.00
25	Larry Bigbie/Jsy/50	15.00
26	Rodrigo Lopez/Jsy/50	10.00
45	Aramis Ramirez/Jsy/50	30.00
53	Carlos Lee/Jsy/50	20.00
54	Mark Buehrle/Jsy/50	20.00
59	Austin Kearns/Jsy/50	20.00
65	Jody Gerut/Jsy/50	10.00
66	Cliff Lee/Jsy/50	15.00
67	Victor Martinez/Jsy/50	25.00
68	C.C. Sabathia/Jsy/50	20.00
70	Travis Hafner/Jsy/50	20.00
72	Preston Wilson/Jsy/50	20.00
82	Brad Penny/Jsy/50	10.00
89	Morgan Ensberg/Jsy/50	10.00
96	Carlos Beltran/Jsy/50	50.00
97	Angel Berroa/Pants/50	10.00
104	Paul LoDuca/Jsy/50	25.00
112	Jacque Jones/Jsy/50	20.00
113	Johan Santana/Jsy/50	50.00
114	Shannon Stewart/Jsy/50	20.00
117	Torii Hunter/Jsy/25	25.00
119	Orlando Cabrera/Jsy/50	20.00
120	Jose Vidro/Jsy/50	10.00
139	Mark Mulder/Jsy/25	25.00
146	Marlon Byrd/Jsy/50	15.00
154	Craig Wilson/Jsy/50	15.00
161	Sean Burroughs/Jsy/50	15.00
171	Edgar Martinez/Jsy/25	50.00
182	Aubrey Huff/Jsy/50	20.00
186	Carl Crawford/Jsy/50	30.00
188	Hank Blalock/Jsy/50	50.00
200	Jeremy Bonderman/Jsy/50	10.00
228	Andre Dawson/Jsy/50	20.00
229	Bob Feller/Jsy/50	35.00
234	Harmon Killebrew/Jsy/25	65.00

Marble Signature Material Gold Number

NM/M
Quantity produced listed

1	Vladimir Guerrero/Jsy/27	60.00
8	Brandon Webb/Jsy/55	10.00
18	Andruw Jones/Jsy/25	40.00
22	Luis Matos/Jsy/32	15.00
23	Jay Gibbons/Jsy/31	25.00
32	Manny Ramirez/Jsy/24	75.00
39	David Ortiz/Jsy/34	50.00
40	Mark Prior/Jsy/22	50.00
41	Kerry Wood/Pants/34	50.00
42	Sammy Sosa/Jsy/21	150.00
44	Greg Maddux/Jsy/31	100.00
51	Frank Thomas/Jsy/35	50.00
52	Magglio Ordonez/Jsy/30	25.00
53	Carlos Lee/Jsy/45	20.00
54	Mark Buehrle/Jsy/56	20.00
58	Adam Dunn/Jsy/44	40.00
59	Austin Kearns/Jsy/28	25.00
66	Cliff Lee/Jsy/34	15.00

67	Victor Martinez/Jsy/41	25.00
68	C.C. Sabathia/Jsy/52	20.00
70	Travis Hafner/Jsy/48	20.00
71	Todd Helton/Jsy/17	60.00
72	Preston Wilson/Jsy/44	20.00
81	Dontrelle Willis/Jsy/35	30.00
82	Brad Penny/Jsy/31	15.00
85	Andy Pettitte/Jsy/27	50.00
104	Paul LoDuca/Jsy/16	35.00
113	Johan Santana/Jsy/57	50.00
114	Shannon Stewart/Jsy/23	25.00
117	Torii Hunter/Jsy/48	20.00
119	Orlando Cabrera/Jsy/18	15.00
123	Mike Piazza/Jsy/31	100.00
124	Jae Weong/Seo Jsy/26	20.00
127	Jorge Posada/Jsy/20	40.00
130	Mike Mussina/Jsy/35	40.00
139	Mark Mulder/Jsy/20	25.00
141	Tim Hudson/Jsy/15	30.00
146	Marlon Byrd/Jsy/29	15.00
177	Scott Rolen/Jsy/27	50.00
182	Aubrey Huff/Jsy/19	30.00
184	Dewon Brazelton/Jsy/45	15.00
187	Mark Teixeira/Jsy/23	50.00
195	Roy Halladay/Jsy/32	15.00
200	Jeremy Bonderman/Jsy/38	10.00
236	Don Mattingly/Jsy/23	85.00
240	Reggie Jackson/Jsy/44	50.00
241	Rickey Henderson/Jsy/35	50.00
242	Mike Schmidt/Pants/20	100.00
244	Tony Gwynn/Jsy/19	75.00
245	Will Clark/Jsy/22	50.00
246	Lou Brock/Jsy/20	40.00
247	Bob Gibson/Jsy/45	40.00
249	Nolan Ryan/Jsy/34	150.00

Marble Material Blue Number

NM/M
Quanity produced listed

1	Vladimir Guerrero/Jsy/27	25.00
2	Garret Anderson/Jsy/16	15.00
5	Troy Glaus/Jsy/25	10.00
8	Tim Salmon/Jsy/15	20.00
8	Brandon Webb/Jsy/55	5.00
10	Randy Johnson/Jsy/51	12.00
13	Luis Gonzalez/Jsy/20	10.00
17	Marcus Giles/Jsy/25	10.00
18	Andruw Jones/Jsy/25	10.00
20	Rafael Palmeiro/Jsy/15	15.00
22	Luis Matos/Jsy/32	5.00
23	Jay Gibbons/Jsy/31	5.00
26	Rodrigo Lopez/Jsy/19	10.00
27	Javy Lopez/Jsy/18	15.00
30	Curt Schilling/Jsy/38	12.00
31	Jason Varitek/Jsy/33	10.00
32	Manny Ramirez/Jsy/24	20.00
35	Pedro Martinez/Jsy/45	15.00
39	David Ortiz/Jsy/34	20.00
40	Mark Prior/Jsy/22	15.00
41	Kerry Wood/Pants/34	20.00
42	Sammy Sosa/Jsy/21	30.00
44	Greg Maddux/Jsy/31	25.00
45	Aramis Ramirez/Jsy/16	15.00
49	Moises Alou/Jsy/18	15.00
51	Frank Thomas/Jsy/35	20.00
52	Magglio Ordonez/Jsy/30	10.00
53	Carlos Lee/Jsy/45	5.00
54	Mark Buehrle/Jsy/56	5.00
58	Adam Dunn/Jsy/44	12.00
59	Austin Kearns/Jsy/28	10.00
63	Sean Casey/Jsy/21	10.00
66	Cliff Lee/Jsy/34	8.00
67	Victor Martinez/Jsy/41	8.00
68	C.C. Sabathia/Jsy/52	5.00
70	Travis Hafner/Jsy/48	5.00
71	Todd Helton/Jsy/17	20.00
72	Preston Wilson/Jsy/44	5.00
73	Jeromy Burnitz/Jsy/35	5.00
74	Larry Walker/Jsy/33	10.00
77	Miguel Cabrera/Jsy/24	20.00

79	Josh Beckett/Jsy/21	12.00
81	Dontrelle Willis/Jsy/35	10.00
82	Brad Penny/Jsy/31	8.00
85	Andy Pettitte/Jsy/21	15.00
87	Roy Oswalt/Jsy/44	5.00
88	Lance Berkman/Jsy/17	10.00
95	Roger Clemens/Jsy/22	25.00
100	Mike Sweeney/Jsy/29	10.00
101	Kazuhisa Ishii/Jsy/17	15.00
107	Adrian Beltre/Jsy/29	15.00
113	Johan Santana/Jsy/57	15.00
114	Shannon Stewart/Jsy/23	10.00
117	Torii Hunter/Jsy/48	5.00
119	Orlando Cabrera/Jsy/18	20.00
120	Jose Vidro/Jsy/3	
123	Mike Piazza/Jsy/31	30.00
124	Jae Weong/Seo/Jsy/26	10.00
125	Jose Reyes/Jsy/7	
126	Tom Glavine/Jsy/47	10.00
127	Jorge Posada/Jsy/20	15.00
129	Bernie Williams/Jsy/51	10.00
130	Mike Mussina/Jsy/35	15.00
131	Mariano Rivera/Jsy/42	
135	Jason Giambi/Jsy/25	10.00
138	Hideki Matsui/Jsy/45	40.00
139	Mark Mulder/Jsy/20	10.00
142	Barry Zito/Jsy/75	5.00
146	Marlon Byrd/Jsy/29	10.00
150	Jim Thome/Jsy/25	20.00
151	Bobby Abreu/Jsy/53	5.00
154	Craig Wilson/Jsy/36	5.00
161	Sean Burroughs/Jsy/32	10.00
163	Brian Giles/Jsy/24	8.00
164	Ryan Klesko/Jsy/30	10.00
166	Jerome Williams/Jsy/57	5.00
172	Freddy Garcia/Jsy/34	8.00
177	Scott Rolen/Jsy/27	20.00
178	Jim Edmonds/Jsy/15	10.00
180	Matt Morris/Jsy/35	10.00
181	Edgar Renteria/Jsy/15	15.00
182	Aubrey Huff/Jsy/19	10.00
184	Dewon Brazelton/Jsy/45	5.00
187	Mark Teixeira/Jsy/23	15.00
192	Kevin Mench/Jsy/28	8.00
195	Roy Halladay/Jsy/32	10.00
197	Carlos Delgado/Jsy/25	10.00
200	Jeremy Bonderman/Jsy/38	5.00
201	Roger Clemens/Jsy/22	30.00
203	Greg Maddux/Jsy/31	25.00
206	Andy Pettitte/Jsy/46	10.00
207	Curt Schilling/Jsy/38	12.00
210	Jim Thome/Jsy/25	20.00
211	Mike Mussina/Jsy/35	15.00
212	Mike Piazza/Jsy/31	30.00
213	Randy Johnson/Jsy/51	15.00
214	Roger Clemens/Jsy/21	30.00
215	Sammy Sosa/Jsy/21	30.00
217	Randy Johnson/Jsy/51	15.00
218	Vladimir Guerrero/Jsy/27	25.00
219	Rafael Palmeiro/Jsy/25	15.00
221	Mike Piazza/Jsy/25	30.00
226	Ryne Sandberg/Jsy/23	40.00
227	Mark Grace/Jsy/17	25.00
229	Bob Feller/Jsy/19	20.00
232	Bo Jackson/Jsy/16	40.00
233	Robin Yount/Jsy/19	40.00
236	Don Mattingly/Jsy/23	40.00
241	Rickey Henderson/Jsy/35	25.00
242	Mike Schmidt/Jsy/20	40.00
243	Roberto Clemente/Jsy/21	100.00
245	Will Clark/Jsy/22	30.00
246	Lou Brock/Jsy/20	20.00
247	Bob Gibson/Jsy/45	15.00
249	Nolan Ryan/Jsy/34	40.00

Check Signature Green

No Pricing
Production 1-15

Check Signature Red

No Pricing

Check Signature Material Red

		NM/M

Quantity produced listed

4	Bob Gibson/Hat/25	50.00
5	Bobby Doerr/Jsy/25	30.00
6	Brooks Robinson/Bat/25	65.00
13	Carlton Fisk/Jkt/25	50.00
14	Carlton Fisk/Jsy/25	50.00
16	Dale Murphy/Jsy/25	40.00
17	Dale Murphy/Jsy/25	40.00
22	Duke Snider/Pants/50	
26	Frank Robinson/Bat/25	40.00
27	George Brett/Jsy/15	100.00
28	George Brett/Jsy/15	100.00
29	George Brett/Bat/15	100.00
33	Harmon Killebrew/Shoe/25	65.00
34	Harmon Killebrew/Bat/25	65.00
41	Lou Brock/Jsy/25	40.00
43	Luis Aparicio/Pants/25	25.00
44	Mark Grace/Fld Glv/25	40.00
53	Paul Molitor/Bat/25	40.00
57	Red Schoendienst/Bat/25	25.00
65	Ryne Sandberg/Jsy/25	75.00
73	Tony Gwynn/Jsy/25	70.00
74	Tony Gwynn/Jsy/25	70.00
77	Whitey Ford/Pants/25	60.00
78	Will Clark/Jsy/25	40.00
79	Will Clark/Bat/25	40.00

Check Signature Material Green

		NM/M

Quantity produced listed

1	Al Kaline/Bat/33	65.00
2	Andre Dawson/Jsy/33	25.00
4	Bob Gibson/Hat/15	50.00
6	Brooks Robinson/Bat/15	80.00
22	Duke Snider/Pants/25	50.00
26	Frank Robinson/Bat/15	50.00
41	Lou Brock/Jsy/15	50.00
43	Luis Aparicio/Pants/15	30.00
44	Mark Grace/Fld Glv/15	40.00
53	Paul Molitor/Bat/15	40.00
77	Whitey Ford/Pants/15	75.00

Check Signature Blue

		NM/M

Quantity produced listed

1	Al Kaline/22	60.00
2	Andre Dawson/22	25.00
22	Duke Snider/20	40.00
31	George Kell/60	35.00

Check Signature Material Blue

		NM/M

Quantity produced listed

1	Al Kaline/Bat/50	50.00
2	Andre Dawson/Jsy/50	20.00
4	Bob Gibson/Hat/50	30.00
5	Bobby Doerr/Jsy/50	20.00
6	Brooks Robinson/Bat/50	50.00
7	Cal Ripken Jr./Jsy/25	200.00
8	Cal Ripken Jr./Jsy/25	200.00
9	Cal Ripken Jr./Bat/25	200.00
10	Cal Ripken Jr./Jkt/25	200.00
13	Carlton Fisk/Jkt/35	40.00
14	Carlton Fisk/Jsy/35	40.00
16	Dale Murphy/Jsy/50	30.00
17	Dale Murphy/Jsy/50	30.00
18	Don Mattingly/Jsy/25	80.00
19	Don Mattingly/Gray Jsy/25	80.00
20	Don Mattingly/Bat/25	80.00
21	Don Mattingly/Jkt/25	80.00
22	Duke Snider/Pants/100	40.00
23	Ozzie Smith/Jsy/40	60.00
24	Ozzie Smith/Jsy/40	60.00
25	Ozzie Smith/Bat/40	60.00
26	Frank Robinson/Bat/50	30.00
27	George Brett/White Jsy/30	80.00
28	George Brett/Blue Jsy/30	80.00
29	George Brett/Bat/30	80.00
32	Hal Newhouser/Jsy/15	30.00
33	Harmon Killebrew/Shoe/35	60.00
34	Harmon Killebrew/Bat/35	60.00
38	Kirby Puckett/Fld Glv/25	60.00
39	Kirby Puckett/Bat/25	60.00
40	Lou Boudreau/Jsy/15	100.00
41	Lou Brock/Jsy/50	30.00
43	Luis Aparicio/Pants/25	20.00
44	Mark Grace/Fld Glv/50	30.00
46	Mike Schmidt/Fld Glv/25	80.00
47	Mike Schmidt/Jsy/25	80.00
48	Mike Schmidt/Jkt/25	80.00
49	Mike Schmidt/Bat/25	80.00
50	Nolan Ryan/Astros Jkt/30	150.00
51	Nolan Ryan/Rgr Pants/25	150.00
52	Nolan Ryan/Angels Jkt/30	150.00
53	Paul Molitor/Bat/25	35.00
57	Red Schoendienst/Bat/50	20.00
63	Ron Santo/Bat/25	40.00
65	Ryne Sandberg/Jsy/50	65.00
67	Stan Musial/White Jsy/30	80.00
68	Stan Musial/Gray Jsy/30	80.00
69	Stan Musial/Bat/30	80.00
70	Steve Carlton/Pants/25	40.00
71	Steve Carlton/Jsy/25	40.00
73	Tony Gwynn/White Jsy/50	50.00
74	Tony Gwynn/Navy Jsy/50	50.00
77	Whitey Ford/Pants/50	50.00
78	Will Clark/Jsy/50	50.00
79	Will Clark/Jsy/50	50.00

Hall of Fame Souvenirs

		NM/M

Quantity produced listed

1	Ernie Banks/84	8.00
2	Stan Musial/93	15.00
3	Nolan Ryan/99	25.00
4	Duke Snider/87	8.00
5	Bob Feller/94	8.00
6	George Brett/98	20.00
7	Robin Yount/78	15.00
8	Harmon Killebrew/83	10.00
9	Gary Carter/78	4.00
10	Phil Rizzuto/75	8.00
11	Reggie Jackson/84	8.00
12	Mike Schmidt/97	20.00
13	Lou Brock/80	6.00
14	Bob Gibson/84	8.00
15	Bobby Doerr/77	6.00
16	Tony Perez/77	4.00
17	Whitey Ford/78	8.00
18	Juan Marichal/84	4.00
19	Monte Irvin/75	4.00
20	Fergie Jenkins/75	4.00
21	Ralph Kiner/75	8.00
22	Eddie Murray/85	10.00
23	George Kell/75	4.00
24	Hoyt Wilhelm/84	4.00
25	Carlton Fisk/80	6.00
26	Rod Carew/91	6.00
27	Frank Robinson/89	6.00
28	Gaylord Perry/77	4.00
29	Red Schoendienst/75	4.00
30	Brooks Robinson/92	6.00
31	Al Kaline/88	10.00
32	Orlando Cepeda/75	4.00
33	Steve Carlton/96	4.00
34	Luis Aparicio/85	4.00
35	Warren Spahn/83	8.00
36	Kirby Puckett/82	10.00
37	Phil Niekro/80	4.00
38	Jim Bunning/75	4.00
39	Tom Seaver/99	8.00
40	Paul Molitor/85	8.00
41	Johnny Bench/82	8.00
42	Don Sutton/82	4.00
43	Robin Roberts/87	6.00
44	Jim Palmer/93	6.00
45	Joe Morgan/82	4.00
46	Roberto Clemente/93	25.00
47	Lou Gehrig/100	10.00
48	Babe Ruth/95	20.00
49	Ty Cobb/98	10.00
50	Ted Williams/94	20.00

Hall of Fame Souvenirs Signature

		NM/M

Quantity produced listed

3	Nolan Ryan/34	150.00
4	Duke Snider/50	30.00
5	Bob Feller/50	30.00
8	Harmon Killebrew/25	50.00
9	Gary Carter/50	15.00
10	Phil Rizzuto/50	25.00
12	Mike Schmidt/20	60.00
13	Lou Brock/50	25.00
14	Bob Gibson/45	25.00
15	Bobby Doerr/50	15.00
16	Tony Perez/50	15.00
17	Whitey Ford/16	40.00
18	Juan Marichal/50	15.00
19	Monte Irvin/50	25.00
20	Fergie Jenkins/50	15.00
21	Ralph Kiner/50	25.00
22	Eddie Murray/50	60.00
23	George Kell/50	15.00
24	Hoyt Wilhelm/49	15.00
25	Carlton Fisk/27	30.00
26	Rod Carew/29	30.00
28	Gaylord Perry/50	15.00
29	Red Schoendienst/50	15.00
30	Brooks Robinson/50	40.00
31	Al Kaline/50	40.00
32	Orlando Cepeda/50	15.00
33	Steve Carlton/50	25.00
34	Luis Aparicio/50	15.00
35	Warren Spahn/21	50.00
36	Kirby Puckett/34	50.00
37	Phil Niekro/50	15.00
38	Jim Bunning/50	15.00
40	Paul Molitor/25	30.00
41	Johnny Bench/5	
42	Don Sutton/50	15.00
43	Robin Roberts/50	15.00
44	Jim Palmer/22	20.00
45	Joe Morgan/25	20.00

HOF Souvenirs Material

		NM/M

Production 25 Sets

1	Ernie Banks/Jsy	30.00
2	Stan Musial/Jsy	50.00
3	Nolan Ryan/Jsy	60.00
4	Duke Snider/Pants	20.00
5	Bob Feller/Jsy	20.00
6	George Brett/Jsy	50.00
7	Robin Yount/Jsy	40.00
8	Harmon Killebrew/Jsy	25.00
9	Gary Carter/Jkt	15.00
10	Phil Rizzuto/Pants	15.00
11	Reggie Jackson/Jsy	25.00
12	Mike Schmidt/Jsy	50.00
13	Lou Brock/Jsy	20.00
14	Bob Gibson/Jsy	20.00
15	Bobby Doerr/Jsy	15.00
16	Tony Perez/Bat	10.00

17	Whitey Ford/Pants	25.00
18	Juan Marichal/Jsy	15.00
20	Fergie Jenkins/Pants	10.00
21	Ralph Kiner/Bat	25.00
22	Eddie Murray/Jsy	25.00
24	Hoyt Wilhelm/Jsy	10.00
25	Carlton Fisk/Jsy	20.00
26	Rod Carew/Jsy	20.00
27	Frank Robinson/Jsy	15.00
29	Red Schoendienst/Jsy	15.00
30	Brooks Robinson/Bat	30.00
31	Al Kaline/Pants	30.00
32	Orlando Cepeda/Bat	10.00
33	Steve Carlton/Pants	15.00
34	Luis Aparicio/Pants	10.00
35	Warren Spahn/Pants	25.00
36	Kirby Puckett/Jsy	25.00
37	Phil Niekro/Jsy	10.00
39	Tom Seaver/Jsy	25.00
40	Paul Molitor/Bat	20.00
41	Johnny Bench/Jsy	25.00
42	Don Sutton/Jsy	10.00
43	Robin Roberts/Hat	15.00
44	Jim Palmer/Jsy	15.00
45	Joe Morgan/Jsy	15.00
46	Roberto Clemente/Jsy	80.00
47	Lou Gehrig/Pants	150.00
48	Babe Ruth/Pants	275.00
49	Ty Cobb/Pants	150.00
50	Ted Williams/Jsy	125.00

HOF Souvenirs Signature Material

NM/M
Quantity produced listed
3	Nolan Ryan/Jsy/34	180.00
5	Bob Feller/Jsy/19	50.00
12	Mike Schmidt/Jsy/20	80.00
13	Lou Brock/Jsy/24	40.00
14	Bob Gibson/Jsy/45	30.00
16	Tony Perez/Bat/24	25.00
17	Whitey Ford/Pants/16	50.00
18	Juan Marichal/Jsy/27	30.00
20	Fergie Jenkins/Pants/31	
22	Eddie Murray/Jsy/33	85.00
25	Carlton Fisk/Jsy/27	50.00
26	Rod Carew/Jsy/29	50.00
32	Orlando Cepeda/Bat/30	30.00
33	Steve Carlton/Pants/32	40.00
35	Warren Spahn/Pants/21	75.00
36	Kirby Puckett/Jsy/34	65.00
37	Phil Niekro/Jsy/35	25.00
42	Don Sutton/Jsy/40	20.00
43	Robin Roberts/Hat/36	25.00
44	Jim Palmer/Jsy/22	30.00
45	Joe Morgan/Jsy/16	35.00

K-Force

NM/M
Quantity produced listed
1	Nolan Ryan/500	8.00
2	Steve Carlton/500	2.00
3	Roger Clemens/500	6.00
4	Randy Johnson/500	3.00
5	Bert Blyleven/500	1.50
6	Tom Seaver/500	3.00
7	Don Sutton/500	1.50
8	Gaylord Perry/500	1.50
9	Phil Niekro/500	1.50
10	Fergie Jenkins/500	1.50
11	Bob Gibson/500	3.00
12	Nolan Ryan/383	8.00
13	Randy Johnson/308	3.00
14	Bob Feller/348	3.00
15	Curt Schilling/319	3.00
16	Pedro J. Martinez/313	3.00
17	Dwight Gooden/276	1.50
18	John Smoltz/276	2.00
19	Curt Schilling/316	3.00
20	Randy Johnson/319	3.00
21	Pedro Martinez/305	3.00
22	Roger Clemens/291	6.00
23	Roger Clemens/292	6.00
24	Tom Seaver/289	3.00
25	Hal Newhouser/275	2.00
26	Jim Bunning/201	2.00
27	Robin Roberts/198	3.00
28	Warren Spahn/191	4.00
29	Jack Morris/232	2.00
30	Nolan Ryan/270	8.00
31	Hideo Nomo/236	3.00
32	Barry Zito/205	2.00
33	Mike Mussina/214	3.00
34	Roy Oswalt/208	2.00
35	Mark Prior/245	3.00
36	Kerry Wood/266	4.00
37	Roy Halladay/204	2.00
38	Esteban Loaiza/207	1.50
39	Whitey Ford/94	6.00
40	Bob Gibson/17	12.00
41	Ben Sheets/18	8.00
42	Hoyt Wilhelm/139	3.00
43	Satchel Paige/91	10.00
44	Burleigh Grimes/136	3.00
45	Mark Prior, Kerry Wood/500	3.00
46	Nolan Ryan, Roger Clemens/500	10.00
47	Steve Carlton, Randy Johnson/500	3.00
48	Nolan Ryan, Roger Clemens/500	8.00
49	Nolan Ryan, Steve Carlton/500	8.00
50	Kerry Wood, Roger Clemens/20	30.00

K-Force Material

NM/M
Quantity produced listed
1	Nolan Ryan/Jsy/100	25.00
2	Steve Carlton/Jsy/32	12.00
3	Roger Clemens/Jsy/25	25.00
4	Randy Johnson/Jsy/51	15.00
5	Bert Blyleven/Jsy/28	10.00
6	Tom Seaver/Jsy/25	25.00
8	Gaylord Perry/Jsy/36	8.00
9	Phil Niekro/Jsy/35	10.00
10	Fergie Jenkins/Jsy/31	10.00
11	Bob Gibson/Jsy/45	15.00
12	Nolan Ryan/Jkt/100	25.00
13	Randy Johnson/Jsy/51	15.00
14	Bob Feller/Jsy/25	20.00
15	Curt Schilling/Jsy/25	12.00
16	Pedro J. Martinez/Jsy/45	15.00
17	Dwight Gooden/Jsy/25	10.00
18	John Smoltz/Jsy/25	15.00
19	Curt Schilling/Jsy/25	12.00
20	Randy Johnson/Jsy/51	15.00
21	Pedro Martinez/Jsy/45	15.00
22	Roger Clemens/Jsy/100	15.00
25	Hal Newhouser/Jsy/25	20.00
28	Warren Spahn/Jsy/50	15.00
29	Jack Morris/Jsy/47	8.00
30	Nolan Ryan/Jkt/100	25.00
31	Hideo Nomo/Jsy/25	20.00
32	Barry Zito/Jsy/25	10.00
33	Mike Mussina/Jsy/25	20.00
34	Roy Oswalt/Jsy/44	6.00
35	Mark Prior/Jsy/50	10.00
39	Whitey Ford/Jsy/50	15.00
40	Bob Gibson/Jsy/50	10.00
41	Ben Sheets/Jsy/25	10.00
43	Satchel Paige/Jsy/100	60.00
44	Burleigh Grimes/Pants/100	75.00
45	Mark Prior/Jsy, Kerry Wood/Pants/50	15.00
46	Nolan Ryan/Jsy, Roger Clemens/Jsy/50	40.00
47	Steve Carlton/Jsy, Randy Johnson/Jsy/50	25.00
48	Nolan Ryan/Pants, Roger Clemens/Jsy/50	40.00
49	Nolan Ryan/Jsy, Carlton Fisk/Pants/50	35.00
50	Kerry Wood/Jsy, Roger Clemens/Jsy/50	25.00

K-Force Signature

NM/M
Quantity produced listed
2	Steve Carlton/50	30.00
7	Don Sutton/50	15.00
8	Gaylord Perry/50	15.00
9	Phil Niekro/50	25.00
14	Fergie Jenkins/50	15.00
14	Bob Feller/50	30.00
17	Dwight Gooden/50	20.00
26	Jim Bunning/50	25.00
27	Robin Roberts/50	20.00
29	Jack Morris/50	15.00
34	Roy Oswalt/50	15.00
38	Esteban Loaiza/50	10.00

K-Force Signature Material

NM/M
Quantity produced listed
1	Nolan Ryan/Jsy/34	150.00
2	Steve Carlton/Jsy/32	50.00
5	Bert Blyleven/Jsy/28	25.00
8	Gaylord Perry/Jsy/36	25.00
9	Phil Niekro/Jsy/35	40.00
10	Fergie Jenkins/Pants/31	25.00
11	Bob Gibson/Jsy/45	40.00
12	Nolan Ryan/Jkt/100	150.00
14	Bob Feller/Jsy/19	50.00
17	Dwight Gooden/Jsy/16	30.00
28	Warren Spahn/Jsy/21	65.00
29	Jack Morris/Jsy/47	20.00
30	Nolan Ryan/Jkt/34	150.00
34	Roy Oswalt/Jsy/44	20.00
36	Kerry Wood/Jsy/34	50.00
37	Roy Halladay/Jsy/32	15.00
39	Whitey Ford/Jsy/16	50.00
40	Bob Gibson/Jsy/45	30.00

Stars

NM/M
Production 599 Sets
1	Ryne Sandberg	6.00
2	Mark Prior	2.00
3	Andre Dawson	2.00
4	Don Mattingly	6.00
5	Vladimir Guerrero	3.00
6	Garret Anderson	2.00
7	Dale Murphy	2.00
8	Cal Ripken Jr.	10.00
9	Mark Grace	3.00
10	Kerry Wood	3.00
11	Frank Thomas	3.00
12	Magglio Ordonez	2.00
13	Adam Dunn	3.00
14	Preston Wilson	3.00
15	Bo Jackson	3.00
16	Carlos Beltran	3.00
17	Tony Gwynn	4.00
18	Will Clark	3.00
19	Edgar Martinez	2.00
20	Scott Rolen	3.00
21	Alfonso Soriano	3.00
22	Randy Johnson	3.00
23	Chipper Jones	3.00
24	Andruw Jones	2.00
25	Javy Lopez	3.00
26	Curt Schilling	3.00
27	Manny Ramirez	5.00
28	Sammy Sosa	4.00
29	Greg Maddux	2.00
30	Todd Helton	3.00
31	Jeff Bagwell	3.00
32	Shawn Green	2.00
33	Mike Piazza	5.00
34	Jorge Posada	2.00
35	Gary Sheffield	3.00
36	Mike Mussina	3.00
37	Miguel Cabrera	3.00
38	Rickey Henderson	3.00
39	Albert Pujols	8.00
40	Vernon Wells	2.00
41	Fred Lynn	2.00
42	Alan Trammell	2.00
43	Lenny Dykstra	2.00
44	Dwight Gooden	2.00
45	Keith Hernandez	2.00
46	Luis Tiant	2.00
47	Orel Hershiser	2.00
48	George Foster	2.00
49	Darryl Strawberry	2.00
50	Marty Marion	2.00

Stars Signature

NM/M
Quantity produced listed
3	Andre Dawson/50	20.00
4	Don Mattingly/25	65.00
6	Garret Anderson/50	20.00
7	Dale Murphy/50	30.00
12	Magglio Ordonez/25	20.00
13	Adam Dunn/25	40.00
14	Preston Wilson/50	15.00
16	Carlos Beltran/50	40.00
18	Will Clark/25	40.00
19	Edgar Martinez/25	40.00
20	Scott Rolen/25	40.00
37	Miguel Cabrera/50	40.00
40	Vernon Wells/25	20.00
41	Fred Lynn/50	10.00
42	Alan Trammell/50	20.00
43	Lenny Dykstra/50	20.00
44	Dwight Gooden/50	20.00
45	Keith Hernandez/50	20.00
46	Luis Tiant/50	15.00
47	Orel Hershiser/50	25.00
48	George Foster/50	10.00
49	Darryl Strawberry/50	20.00

Stars Signature Jersey

NM/M
Quantity produced listed
1	Ryne Sandberg/23	75.00
2	Mark Prior/22	40.00
4	Don Mattingly/23	75.00
5	Vladimir Guerrero/27	60.00
6	Garret Anderson/16	35.00
9	Mark Grace/17	50.00
10	Kerry Wood/34	50.00
11	Frank Thomas/35	50.00
12	Magglio Ordonez/30	25.00
13	Adam Dunn/44	50.00
14	Preston Wilson/44	20.00
15	Bo Jackson/16	125.00
16	Carlos Beltran/15	75.00
17	Tony Gwynn/19	75.00
18	Will Clark/22	65.00
20	Scott Rolen/27	60.00
24	Andruw Jones/25	40.00
28	Sammy Sosa/21	150.00
29	Greg Maddux/31	100.00
30	Todd Helton/17	50.00
34	Jorge Posada/20	50.00
37	Miguel Cabrera/24	50.00
41	Fred Lynn/19	20.00
45	Keith Hernandez/37	20.00
46	Luis Tiant/25	50.00
48	George Foster/25	25.00
49	Darryl Strawberry/18	35.00
50	Marty Marion/25	25.00

2004 Leaf Certified Materials

NM/M
Complete Set (300):	
Common Player:	.50
Common (201-211):	4.00
Common (212-240):	4.00
Production 500 Sets	

Common Auto. (241-300):		8.00
Pack (5):		10.00
Box (10):		85.00

#	Player	Price
1	A.J. Burnett	.50
2	Adam Dunn	1.00
3	Adam LaRoche	.50
4	Adam Loewen	.50
5	Adrian Beltre	.75
6	Al Leiter	.50
7	Albert Pujols	3.00
8	Alex Rodriguez	3.00
9	Alexis Rios	.50
10	Alfonso Soriano	1.50
11	Andruw Jones	1.00
12	Andy Pettitte	.75
13	Angel Berroa	.50
14	Aramis Ramirez	.75
15	Aubrey Huff	.50
16	Austin Kearns	.50
17	Barry Larkin	.75
18	Barry Zito	.75
19	Ben Sheets	.75
20	Bernie Williams	.75
21	Bobby Abreu	.75
22	Brad Penny	.50
23	Brad Wilkerson	.50
24	Brandon Webb	.50
25	Brendan Harris	.50
26	Bret Boone	.50
27	Brett Myers	.50
28	Bubba Crosby	.50
29	Brian Giles	.50
30	Chad Cordero	.50
31	Bubba Nelson	.50
32	Byron Gettis	.50
33	C.C. Sabathia	.50
34	Carl Crawford	.50
35	Carl Everett	.50
36	Carlos Beltran	.75
37	Carlos Delgado	.75
38	Carlos Lee	.50
39	Chad Gaudin	.50
40	Cliff Lee	.50
41	Chipper Jones	1.50
42	Cliff Floyd	.50
43	Clint Barmes	.50
44	Corey Patterson	.75
45	Craig Biggio	.75
46	Curt Schilling	1.00
47	Dan Haren	.50
48	Darin Erstad	.50
49	David Ortiz	1.00
50	Delmon Young	.50
51	Derek Jeter	4.00
52	Dewon Brazelton	.50
53	Dontrelle Willis	.75
54	Edgar Martinez	.75
55	Edgar Renteria	.75
56	Edwin Almonte	.50
57	Edwin Jackson	.50
58	Eric Chavez	.75
59	Eric Hinske	.50
60	Eric Munson	.50
61	Erubiel Durazo	.50
62	Frank Thomas	1.00
63	Fred McGriff	.50
64	Freddy Garcia	.50
65	Garret Anderson	.75
66	Garrett Atkins	.50
67	Gary Sheffield	.75
68	Geoff Jenkins	.50
69	Greg Maddux	2.00
70	Hank Blalock	1.00
71	Hee Seop Choi	.50
72	Hideki Matsui	2.50
73	Hideo Nomo	.75
74	Craig Wilson	.50
75	Ichiro Suzuki	2.50
76	Ivan Rodriguez	1.00
77	J.D. Drew	.50
78	John Lackey	.50
79	Jacque Jones	.50
80	Jae Weong Seo	.50
81	Jamie Moyer	.50
82	Jason Giambi	1.00
83	Jason Jennings	.50
84	Jason Kendall	.50
85	Melvin Mora	.50
86	Jason Varitek	.75
87	Javier Vazquez	.75
88	Javy Lopez	.75
89	Jay Gibbons	.50
90	Jay Payton	.50
91	Jeff Bagwell	1.00
92	Jeff Baker	.50
93	Jeff Kent	.50
94	Jeremy Bonderman	.50
95	Milton Bradley	.50
96	Jerome Williams	.50
97	Jim Edmonds	.75
98	Jim Thome	1.50
99	Jody Gerut	.50
100	Joe Borchard	.50
101	Joe Crede	.50
102	Johan Santana	.50
103	John Olerud	.50
104	John Smoltz	.75
105	Johnny Damon	.75
106	Jorge Posada	.75
107	Jose Castillo	.50
108	Jose Reyes	.75
109	Jose Vidro	.50
110	Josh Beckett	1.00
111	Josh Phelps	.50
112	Juan Encarnacion	.50
113	Juan Gonzalez	1.00
114	Junior Spivey	.50
115	Kazuhisa Ishii	.50
116	Kenny Lofton	.50
117	Kerry Wood	1.50
118	Kevin Millwood	.50
119	Kevin Youkilis	.50
120	Lance Berkman	.50
121	Larry Bigbie	.50
122	Larry Walker	.75
123	Luis Castillo	.50
124	Luis Gonzalez	.50
125	Luis Matos	.50
126	Lyle Overbay	.50
127	Magglio Ordonez	.75
128	Manny Ramirez	1.00
129	Marcus Giles	.50
130	Mariano Rivera	.75
131	Mark Buehrle	.50
132	Mark Mulder	.75
133	Mark Prior	1.00
134	Mark Teixeira	.75
135	Marlon Byrd	.50
136	Matt Morris	.50
137	Miguel Cabrera	1.00
138	Mike Lowell	.50
139	Mike Mussina	.75
140	Mike Piazza	2.00
141	Mike Sweeney	.50
142	Morgan Ensberg	.50
143	Nick Johnson	.50
144	Nomar Garciaparra	2.00
145	Omar Vizquel	.50
146	Orlando Cabrera	.50
147	Orlando Hudson	.50
148	Pat Burrell	.50
149	Paul Konerko	.50
150	Paul LoDuca	.50
151	Pedro J. Martinez	1.50
152	Jermaine Dye	.50
153	Preston Wilson	.50
154	Rafael Furcal	.50
155	Rafael Palmeiro	1.00
156	Randy Johnson	1.50
157	Rich Aurilia	.50
158	Rich Harden	.50
159	Richard Hidalgo	.50
160	Richie Sexson	.75
161	Rickie Weeks	.75
162	Roberto Alomar	.75
163	Rocco Baldelli	.50
164	Roger Clemens	3.00
165	Roy Halladay	.50
166	Roy Oswalt	.75
167	Ryan Howard	1.50
168	Ryan Klesko	.50
169	Rodrigo Lopez	.50
170	Sammy Sosa	2.50
171	Scott Podsednik	.50
172	Scott Rolen	1.50
173	Sean Burroughs	.50
174	Sean Casey	.50
175	Shannon Stewart	.50
176	Shawn Green	.75
177	Shea Hillenbrand	.50
178	Shigetoshi Hasegawa	.50
179	Steve Finley	.50
180	Tim Hudson	.75
181	Todd Helton	1.00
182	Tom Glavine	.75
183	Torii Hunter	.75
184	Trot Nixon	.50
185	Troy Glaus	.75
186	Vernon Wells	.50
187	Victor Martinez	.75
188	Vladimir Guerrero	1.50
189	Wade Miller	.50
190	Brandon Larson	.50
191	Travis Hafner	.75
192	Tim Salmon	.75
193	Tim Redding	.50
194	Runelvys Hernandez	.50
195	Ramon Nivar	.50
196	Moises Alou	.75
197	Michael Young	.50
198	Laynce Nix	.50
199	Tino Martinez	.50
200	Randall Simon	.50
201	Roger Clemens/SP	8.00
202	Greg Maddux/SP	8.00
203	Vladimir Guerrero/SP	6.00
204	Miguel Tejada/SP	4.00
205	Kevin Brown/SP	4.00
206	Jason Giambi/SP	5.00
207	Curt Schilling/SP	5.00
208	Alex Rodriguez/SP	8.00
209	Alfonso Soriano/SP	6.00
210	Ivan Rodriguez/SP	6.00
211	Rafael Palmeiro/SP	6.00
212	Gary Carter	4.00
213	Duke Snider	5.00
214	Whitey Ford	4.00
215	Bob Feller	4.00
216	Reggie Jackson	5.00
217	Ryne Sandberg	10.00
218	Dale Murphy	4.00
219	Tony Gwynn	6.00
220	Don Mattingly	10.00
221	Mike Schmidt	10.00
222	Rickey Henderson	5.00
223	Cal Ripken Jr.	20.00
224	Nolan Ryan	15.00
225	George Brett	10.00
226	Bob Gibson	5.00
227	Lou Brock	4.00
228	Andre Dawson	4.00
229	Rod Carew	4.00
230	Wade Boggs	4.00
231	Roberto Clemente	12.00
232	Roy Campanella	5.00
233	Babe Ruth	15.00
234	Lou Gehrig	10.00
235	Ty Cobb	8.00
236	Roger Maris	6.00
237	Satchel Paige	6.00
238	Ernie Banks	6.00
239	Ted Williams	10.00
240	Stan Musial	6.00
241	Hector Gimenez/ Auto./500 RC	8.00
242	Justin Germano/ Auto./500 RC	8.00
243	Ian Snell/ Auto./500 RC	25.00
244	Graham Koonce/ Auto./500	8.00
245	Jose Capellan/ Auto./500 RC	25.00
246	Onil Joseph/ Auto./500 RC	8.00
247	Shingo Takatsu/ Auto./200 RC	40.00
248	Carlos Hines/ Auto./500 RC	8.00
249	Lincoln Holdzkom/ Auto./500 RC	8.00
250	Mike Gosling/ Auto./500	8.00
251	Edwardo Sierra/ Auto./500 RC	10.00
252	Renyel Pinto/ Auto./500 RC	10.00
253	Merkin Valdez/ Auto./500 RC	12.00
254	Angel Chavez/ Auto./500 RC	8.00
255	Ivan Ochoa/ Auto./1000 RC	8.00
256	Greg Dobbs/ Auto./300 RC	8.00
257	William Bergolla/ Auto./500 RC	8.00
258	Aarom Baldiris/ Auto./500 RC	10.00
259	Kazuo Matsui/500 RC	12.00
260	Carlos Vasquez/ Auto./500 RC	8.00
261	Freddy Guzman/ Auto./500 RC	8.00
262	Akinori Otsuka/ Auto./200 RC	40.00
263	Mariano Gomez/ Auto./200 RC	8.00
264	Nick Regilio/ Auto./500 RC	8.00
265	Jamie Brown/ Auto./500 RC	8.00
266	Shawn Hill/ Auto./500 RC	8.00
267	Roberto Novoa/ Auto./500 RC	8.00
268	Sean Henn/Auto./500	10.00
269	Ramon Ramirez/ Auto./500 RC	8.00
270	Ronny Cedeno/ Auto./1000 RC	8.00
271	Ryan Wing/Auto./400	8.00
272	Ruddy Yan/ Auto./500 RC	8.00
273	Fernando Nieve/ Auto./500 RC	8.00
274	Rusty Tucker/ Auto./500 RC	8.00
275	Jason Bartlett/ Auto./500 RC	8.00
276	Mike Rouse/Auto./500	8.00
277	Dennis Sarfate/ Auto./500 RC	8.00
278	Cory Sullivan/ Auto./500 RC	8.00
279	Casey Daigle/ Auto./250 RC	8.00
280	Chris Shelton/ Auto./400 RC	25.00
281	Jesse Harper/ Auto./400 RC	8.00
282	Mike Wuertz/ Auto./500 RC	12.00
283	Tim Bausher/ Auto./400 RC	8.00
284	Jorge Sequea/ Auto./500 RC	8.00
285	Josh Labandeira/ Auto./500 RC	12.00
286	Justin Leone/ Auto./500 RC	12.00
287	Tim Bittner/ Auto./500 RC	8.00
288	Andres Blanco/ Auto./500 RC	8.00
289	Kevin Cave/ Auto./1000 RC	8.00
290	Mike Johnston/ Auto./1000 RC	8.00
291	Jason Szuminski/ Auto./500 RC	8.00
292	Shawn Camp/500 RC	8.00
293	Colby Miller/ Auto./500 RC	8.00
294	Jake Woods/Auto./500	8.00
295	Ryan Meaux/ Auto./500 RC	8.00
296	Donald Kelly/ Auto./500 RC	8.00
297	Edwin Moreno/ Auto./500 RC	8.00
298	Phil Stockman/ Auto./500 RC	8.00
299	Jorge Vasquez/500 RC	8.00
300	Kazuhito Tadano/ Auto./500 RC	25.00

Mirror Black

No Pricing
Production One Set

Mirror Blue

Stars (1-200):	3-5X
Mirror Blue (201-240):	1-2X
Auto. (241-300):	.5X
No Auto. (241-300):	1X
Production 50 Sets	

Mirror Emerald

No Pricing
Production 5 Sets

Mirror Gold

Mirror Gold (1-200):	4-8X
Mirror Gold (201-240):	1.5-2X
Mirror Gold (241-300):No Pricing	
Production 25 Sets	

Mirror Red

Mirror Red (1-200):	2-4X
Mirror Red (201-240):	.5-1X
Mirror Red (241-300):	.5X
Production 100 Sets	

Mirror White

Mirror White (1-200):	2-4X
Mirror White (201-240):	.5-1X
Mirror White (241-300):	.5X
Production 100 Sets	

Fabric of the Game

	NM/M
Common Player:	6.00
Quantity produced listed	
AL/NL:	.75-1.5X
Production 1-100	
Jersey Number:	.75-2X
Production 1-72	
Position:	.75-2X
Production 1-100	
Prime:	No Pricing
Production One Set	
Game Reward:	.75-2X
Production 1-50	
Jersey Year:	.75-2X
Production 1-99	
Game Stats:	.75-2X
Production 1-66	
No Pricing production 20 or less.	

n	Ozzie Smith/Jsy/100	20.00
2	Al Kaline/Jsy/100	15.00
3	Alan Trammell/Jsy/100	10.00
4	Albert Pujols/Jsy/100	20.00
5	Alex Rodriguez/Jsy/100	12.00
6	Alex Rodriguez/Jsy/100	12.00
7	Andre Dawson/Jsy/100	8.00
8	Andre Dawson/Pants/100	8.00
11	Billy Williams/Jsy/100	10.00
12	Bo Jackson/Jsy/100	20.00
13	Bob Feller/Jsy/50	15.00
14	Bob Gibson/Jsy/100	15.00
15	Bobby Doerr/Jsy/100	8.00
16	Brooks Robinson/Jsy/25	25.00
17	Cal Ripken Jr./Jsy/100	30.00
18	Carl Yastrzemski/Jsy/100	20.00
19	Carlton Fisk/Jsy/100	10.00
20	Dale Murphy/Jsy/100	12.00
21	Darryl Strawberry/Pants/100	10.00
22	Darryl Strawberry/Jsy/100	10.00
23	Dave Parker/Jsy/100	10.00
24	Dave Parker/Jsy/100	10.00
25	Dave Winfield/Jsy/50	10.00
26	Dave Winfield/Jsy/100	10.00
27	Deion Sanders/Jsy/25	25.00
28	Derek Jeter/Jsy/100	20.00
29	Don Drysdale/Jsy/100	15.00
30	Don Mattingly/Jsy/100	20.00
31	Don Mattingly/Jkt/100	20.00
32	Don Sutton/Jsy/100	8.00
33	Duke Snider/Jsy/100	12.00
34	Dwight Gooden/Jsy/100	8.00
35	Early Wynn/Jsy/100	10.00
36	Eddie Mathews/Jsy/50	20.00
37	Eddie Murray/Jsy/100	15.00
38	Eddie Murray/Jsy/100	15.00
39	Enos Slaughter/Jsy/100	10.00
40	Eric Davis/Jsy/50	10.00

41	Ernie Banks/Jsy/100	15.00
42	Fergie Jenkins/Pants/100	10.00
43	Frank Robinson/Jsy/100	10.00
44	Fred Lynn/Jsy/10	
45	Gary Carter/Jsy/100	10.00
46	Gaylord Perry/Jsy/25	15.00
47	George Brett/White Jsy/100	20.00
48	George Foster/Jsy/100	8.00
49	Hal Newhouser/Jsy/100	8.00
50	Harmon Killebrew/Jsy/25	30.00
51	Harmon Killebrew/Pants/25	30.00
52	Harold Baines/Jsy/100	10.00
53	Hoyt Wilhelm/Jsy/50	10.00
54	Jack Morris/Jsy/100	8.00
55	Jackie Robinson/Jsy/10	
56	Jim "Catfish" Hunter/Jsy/100	10.00
57	Jim Palmer/Jsy/100	10.00
58	Jim Rice/Jsy/100	10.00
59	Joe Carter/Jsy/100	8.00
60	Joe Morgan/Jsy/100	10.00
61	Tommy Lasorda/Jsy/100	8.00
62	Johnny Mize/Pants/100	12.00
63	Johnny Bench/Jsy/100	15.00
64	Jose Canseco/Jsy/100	10.00
65	Juan Marichal/Jsy/100	10.00
66	Kirby Puckett/Jsy/100	15.00
67	Lou Boudreau/Jsy/100	10.00
68	Lou Brock/Jsy/100	10.00
71	Luis Aparicio/Jsy/100	10.00
72	Luis Aparicio/Pants/100	10.00
73	Mariano Rivera/Jsy/100	10.00
74	Mark Grace/Jsy/100	12.00
75	Mark Prior/Jsy/100	8.00
76	Mel Ott/Jsy/25	60.00
77	Mel Ott/Pants/25	60.00
78	Mike Schmidt/Jsy/100	20.00
79	Mike Schmidt/Pants/100	20.00
80	Mike Schmidt/Jkt/100	20.00
81	Nolan Ryan/Angels Jsy/100	25.00
82	Nolan Ryan/Angels Jkt/100	25.00
83	Nolan Ryan/Astros Jsy/100	25.00
84	Nolan Ryan/Astros Jkt/100	25.00
85	Nolan Ryan/Rgr Jsy/100	25.00
86	Nolan Ryan/Rgr Pants/100	25.00
87	Ty Cobb/Pants/10	
88	Ozzie Smith/Jsy/100	15.00
89	Paul Molitor/Jsy/100	12.00
90	Pee Wee Reese/Jsy/100	15.00
91	Phil Niekro/Jsy/100	8.00
92	Phil Rizzuto/Jsy/100	15.00
93	Phil Rizzuto/Pants/100	15.00
94	Red Schoendienst/Jsy/100	10.00
95	Reggie Jackson/Jkt/100	15.00
96	Reggie Jackson/Jsy/100	15.00
97	Richie Ashburn/Jsy/100	20.00
98	Rickey Henderson/Jsy/50	15.00
99	Roberto Clemente/Jsy/50	75.00
100	Robin Yount/Jsy/100	15.00
101	Rod Carew/Jsy/100	10.00
102	Rod Carew/Pants/100	10.00
103	Rod Carew/Jkt/100	10.00
104	Rod Carew/Jsy/100	10.00
105	Roger Clemens/Jsy/100	15.00
106	Roger Clemens/Jsy/100	15.00
107	Roger Maris/Jsy/100	30.00
108	Roger Maris/Pants/100	30.00
109	Roger Maris/Jsy/100	30.00

110	Roy Campanella/Pants/100	15.00
111	Ryne Sandberg/Jsy/100	10.00
112	Stan Musial/Jsy/50	30.00
113	Steve Carlton/Jsy/100	10.00
114	Ted Williams/Jsy/100	75.00
115	Ted Williams/Jkt/100	75.00
116	Thurman Munson/Jsy/100	25.00
117	Thurman Munson/Pants/100	25.00
118	Tony Gwynn/Jsy/100	15.00
119	Wade Boggs/Jsy/100	10.00
120	Wade Boggs/Jsy/100	10.00
121	Warren Spahn/Jsy/100	15.00
122	Warren Spahn/Pants/100	15.00
123	Whitey Ford/Jsy/100	15.00
124	Whitey Ford/Pants/100	15.00
125	Will Clark/Jsy/100	15.00
126	Willie McCovey/Jsy/100	10.00
127	Willie Stargell/Jsy/100	15.00
128	Yogi Berra/Jsy/25	35.00
129	Frankie Frisch/Jkt/100	15.00
130	Marty Marion/Jsy/100	10.00
131	Tommy John/Pants/100	8.00
132	Chipper Jones/Jsy/100	10.00
133	Sammy Sosa/Jsy/100	15.00
134	Rickey Henderson/Jsy/100	10.00
135	Mike Piazza/Jsy/100	12.00
136	Mike Piazza/Jsy/100	12.00
137	Nomar Garciaparra/Jsy/100	15.00
138	Hideo Nomo/Jsy/100	10.00
139	Hideo Nomo/Jsy/50	15.00
140	Randy Johnson/Jsy/100	10.00
141	Randy Johnson/Jsy/100	10.00
142	Randy Johnson/Jsy/100	10.00
143	Jason Giambi/Jsy/100	6.00
144	Jason Giambi/Jsy/100	6.00
145	Curt Schilling/Jsy/100	6.00
146	Dennis Eckersley/Jsy/100	10.00
147	Carlton Fisk/Jkt/100	10.00
148	Tom Seaver/Jsy/100	30.00
149	Joe Torre/Jsy/100	10.00
150	Pedro Martinez/Jsy/100	10.00
151	Albert Pujols/Jsy/100	20.00
152	Andre Dawson/Jsy/50	10.00
153	Bert Blyleven/Jsy/100	8.00
154	Bo Jackson/Jsy/100	15.00
155	Cal Ripken Jr./Pants/100	35.00
156	Carlton Fisk/Jsy/100	10.00
157	Curt Schilling/Jsy/100	6.00
158	Darryl Strawberry/Jsy/100	8.00
159	Dave Concepcion/Jsy/100	8.00
160	Dwight Evans/Jsy/100	8.00
161	Ernie Banks/Pants/100	15.00
162	Fred McGriff/Jsy/1	
163	Gary Carter/Pants/100	8.00
164	Gary Sheffield/Jsy/100	6.00
165	George Brett/Jsy/100	20.00
166	Greg Maddux/Jsy/100	10.00
167	Ivan Rodriguez/Jsy/100	10.00
168	Joe Morgan/Jsy/100	10.00
169	Jose Canseco/Jsy/100	10.00
170	Juan Gonzalez/Jsy/100	8.00
171	Juan Gonzalez/Jsy/100	8.00
172	Keith Hernandez/Jsy/100	10.00
173	Ken Boyer/Jsy/100	20.00
174	Kerry Wood/Jsy/100	8.00
175	Lee Smith/Jsy/100	8.00
176	Luis Tiant/Jsy/100	8.00
177	Manny Ramirez/Jsy/100	8.00
178	Mark Grace/Jsy/100	12.00
179	Matt Williams/Jsy/100	8.00
180	Miguel Tejada/Jsy/100	6.00

181	Mike Mussina/Jsy/100	10.00
182	Mike Piazza/Jsy/100	12.00
183	Nomar Garciaparra/Jsy/100	15.00
184	Pedro Martinez/Jsy/100	10.00
185	Rafael Palmeiro/Jsy/100	8.00
186	Reggie Jackson/Pants/100	12.00
187	Rickey Henderson/Jsy/100	10.00
188	Rickey Henderson/Pants/100	10.00
189	Rickey Henderson/Jsy/100	10.00
190	Sammy Sosa/Jsy/100	15.00
191	Satchel Paige/Jsy/100	60.00
192	Shawn Green/Jsy/100	6.00
193	Stan Musial/Jsy/50	35.00
194	Steve Carlton/Jsy/100	10.00
195	Steve Garvey/Jsy/100	8.00
196	Tom Seaver/Jsy/100	12.00
197	Tony Gwynn/Pants/100	12.00
198	Vladimir Guerrero/Jsy/100	10.00
199	Wade Boggs/Jsy/100	10.00
200	Willie Stargell/Jsy/100	10.00

Fabric of the Game Autograph

No Pricing	
Production 1-10	
AL/NL Auto:	No Pricing
Production 1-25	
Jersey Number Auto.:	No Pricing
Production 1-8	
Jersey Year Auto.:	No Pricing
Production 1-8	
Position Auto.:	No Pricing
Production 1-8	
Reward Auto.:	No Pricing
Production 1-8	
Stats Auto.:	No Pricing
Production 1-8	

Mirror Autograph Red

		NM/M
Quantity produced listed		
3	Adam LaRoche/250	8.00
4	Adam Loewen/250	8.00
9	Alexis Rios/250	15.00
10	Alfonso Soriano/250	50.00
11	Andruw Jones/25	25.00
12	Andy Pettitte/25	35.00
13	Angel Berroa/100	10.00
14	Aramis Ramirez/100	25.00
15	Aubrey Huff/250	8.00
16	Austin Kearns/200	12.00
17	Barry Larkin/25	40.00
22	Brad Penny/25	15.00
24	Brandon Webb/250	8.00
25	Brendan Harris/50	8.00
27	Brett Myers/100	8.00
28	Bubba Crosby/250	8.00
30	Chad Cordero/250	8.00
31	Bubba Nelson/250	8.00
32	Byron Gettis/250	8.00
36	Carlos Beltran/100	25.00
38	Carlos Lee/250	10.00
39	Chad Gaudin/100	8.00
40	Cliff Lee/250	10.00
43	Dan Haren/250	8.00
47	Dan Haren/250	8.00
49	David Ortiz/250	40.00
50	Delmon Young/50	30.00
52	Dewon Brazelton/250	8.00
55	Dontrelle Willis/100	20.00
56	Edwin Almonte/250	8.00
57	Edwin Jackson/250	8.00
58	Eric Chavez/25	30.00
62	Frank Thomas/50	50.00
65	Garret Anderson/250	15.00
67	Gary Sheffield/50	30.00
70	Hank Blalock/250	30.00
74	Craig Wilson/250	8.00
78	John Lackey/250	8.00
79	Jacque Jones/250	8.00
80	Jae Weong Seo/100	15.00
85	Melvin Mora/250	8.00
86	Jason Varitek/100	40.00
89	Jay Gibbons/250	8.00
90	Jay Payton/250	8.00
91	Jeff Bagwell/250	50.00
92	Jeff Baker/25	20.00
96	Jerome Williams/100	15.00
97	Jim Edmonds/25	35.00
99	Jody Gerut/250	10.00
100	Joe Borchard/250	8.00
101	Joe Crede/50	15.00

102	Johan Santana/250	25.00
106	Jorge Posada/25	50.00
107	Jose Castillo/250	8.00
109	Jose Vidro/250	10.00
110	Josh Beckett/25	50.00
113	Juan Gonzalez/25	40.00
114	Junior Spivey/25	15.00
117	Kerry Wood/50	50.00
119	Kevin Youkilis/250	10.00
120	Lance Berkman/25	30.00
121	Larry Bigbie/250	12.00
123	Luis Castillo/25	15.00
125	Luis Matos/250	8.00
127	Magglio Ordonez/250	15.00
129	Marcus Giles/250	12.00
131	Mark Buehrle/250	12.00
132	Mark Mulder/250	20.00
133	Mark Prior/100	40.00
134	Mark Teixeira/100	25.00
135	Marlon Byrd/250	8.00
137	Miguel Cabrera/250	30.00
140	Mike Piazza/250	125.00
142	Morgan Ensberg/250	8.00
146	Orlando Cabrera/25	20.00
150	Paul LoDuca/25	25.00
152	Jermaine Dye/250	10.00
153	Preston Wilson/250	10.00
154	Rafael Furcal/100	12.00
157	Rich Aurilia/25	15.00
158	Rich Harden/203	15.00
165	Roy Halladay/50	15.00
166	Roy Oswalt/50	15.00
167	Ryan Howard/100	80.00
169	Rodrigo Lopez/250	8.00
170	Sammy Sosa/50	100.00
171	Scott Podsednik/250	15.00
172	Scott Rolen/100	40.00
175	Shannon Stewart/100	8.00
176	Shawn Green/25	30.00
177	Shea Hillenbrand/250	10.00
178	Shigetoshi Hasegawa/250	40.00
179	Steve Finley/100	20.00
183	Torii Hunter/250	15.00
184	Trot Nixon/250	20.00
187	Victor Martinez/250	20.00
188	Vladimir Guerrero/50	75.00
190	Brandon Larson/200	10.00
191	Travis Hafner/250	15.00
197	Michael Young/250	15.00
212	Gary Carter/250	15.00
213	Duke Snider/250	25.00
214	Whitey Ford /50	40.00
215	Bob Feller /250	20.00
216	Reggie Jackson/50	50.00
217	Ryne Sandberg/50	60.00
218	Dale Murphy/50	30.00
219	Tony Gwynn/50	50.00
220	Don Mattingly/50	75.00
221	Mike Schmidt/50	75.00
222	Rickey Henderson/50	50.00
223	Cal Ripken Jr./50	180.00
224	Nolan Ryan/50	100.00
225	George Brett/50	75.00
226	Bob Gibson/100	25.00
227	Lou Brock/100	25.00
228	Andre Dawson/250	15.00
229	Rod Carew/50	25.00
230	Wade Boggs/50	25.00
238	Ernie Banks/50	60.00
240	Stan Musial/100	60.00
241	Hector Gimenez/200	8.00
242	Justin Germano/100	8.00
243	Ian Snell/100	25.00
244	Graham Koonce/200	8.00
245	Jose Capellan/100	40.00
246	Onil Joseph/200	8.00
247	Shingo Takatsu/50	50.00
248	Carlos Hines/200	8.00
249	Lincoln Holdzkom/100	8.00
250	Mike Gosling/100	10.00
251	Edwardo Sierra/200	10.00
252	Renyel Pinto/100	10.00
253	Merkin Valdez/200	12.00
254	Angel Chavez/200	8.00
255	Ivan Ochoa/200	8.00
257	William Bergolla/200	8.00
258	Aarom Baldiris/100	10.00
260	Carlos Vasquez/200	8.00
261	Freddy Guzman/200	8.00
262	Akinori Otsuka/50	50.00
264	Nick Regilio/200	8.00
266	Shawn Hill/200	8.00
268	Sean Henn/200	10.00
269	Ramon Ramirez/200	8.00
270	Ronny Cedeno/100	8.00
273	Fernando Nieve/200	8.00
274	Rusty Tucker/200	8.00
275	Jason Bartlett/200	8.00
276	Mike Rouse/200	8.00
277	Dennis Sarfate/200	8.00
278	Cory Sullivan/200	8.00

282	Mike Wuertz/200	8.00
284	Jorge Sequea/100	8.00
287	Tim Bittner/250	8.00
288	Andres Blanco/100	12.00
289	Kevin Cave/100	10.00
290	Mike Johnston/100	8.00
293	Colby Miller/100	8.00
294	Jake Woods/100	10.00
295	Ryan Meaux/200	8.00
296	Donald Kelly/100	8.00
297	Edwin Moreno/100	8.00
298	Phil Stockman/100	8.00

Mirror Autograph Black

No Pricing
Production One Set

Mirror Autograph Blue

Mirror Auto.
    Blue.   .5-1.5X Red Auto.
Production 1-100
No pricing 25 or less.

Mirror Autograph Emerald

No Pricing
Production 1-5

Mirror Autograph Gold

No Pricing
Production 1-25

Mirror Autograph White

White Auto. (1-240):   .75-1.5X Red Auto.
White Auto.
    (241-300): .5-1X Red Auto.
Production 1-100
No pricing 25 or less.

Mirror Bat Red

	NM/M
Common Player:	4.00

Quantity produced listed
Black: No Pricing
Production One Set
Emerald: No Pricing
Production 5 Sets

2	Adam Dunn/150	6.00
3	Adam LaRoche/250	4.00
5	Adrian Beltre/150	4.00
7	Albert Pujols/150	15.00
8	Alex Rodriguez/250	10.00
9	Alexis Rios/250	4.00
10	Alfonso Soriano/150	8.00
11	Andruw Jones/150	8.00
12	Andy Pettitte/250	6.00
13	Angel Berroa/150	4.00
15	Aubrey Huff/150	4.00
16	Austin Kearns/150	4.00
17	Barry Larkin/150	6.00
20	Bernie Williams/150	6.00
21	Bobby Abreu/150	4.00
24	Brandon Webb/150	4.00
25	Brendan Harris/250	4.00
26	Bret Boone/150	4.00
29	Brian Giles/250	4.00
35	Carl Everett/250	4.00
36	Carlos Beltran/150	6.00
37	Carlos Delgado/150	6.00
38	Carlos Lee/150	4.00
41	Chipper Jones/150	6.00
42	Cliff Floyd/250	4.00
43	Clint Barmes/250	4.00
44	Corey Patterson/250	6.00
45	Craig Biggio/150	6.00
47	Dan Haren/150	4.00
48	Darin Erstad/150	4.00
49	David Ortiz/250	8.00
50	Delmon Young/250	6.00
51	Derek Jeter/150	20.00
54	Edgar Martinez/150	6.00
55	Edgar Renteria/150	6.00
59	Eric Hinske/150	4.00
60	Eric Munson/250	4.00
61	Erubiel Durazo/250	4.00
62	Frank Thomas/150	8.00
63	Fred McGriff/150	4.00
65	Garret Anderson/150	6.00
67	Gary Sheffield/250	6.00
68	Geoff Jenkins/150	4.00
70	Hank Blalock/150	8.00
71	Hee Seop Choi/250	4.00
73	Hideo Nomo/150	8.00
76	Ivan Rodriguez /250	8.00
77	J.D. Drew/250	6.00
79	Jacque Jones/150	4.00
82	Jason Giambi/150	6.00
83	Jason Jennings/150	4.00
86	Jason Varitek/150	6.00

88	Javy Lopez/250	6.00
89	Jay Gibbons/150	4.00
91	Jeff Bagwell/150	8.00
92	Jeff Baker/250	4.00
93	Jeff Kent/150	4.00
97	Jim Edmonds/150	6.00
98	Jim Thome/150	8.00
100	Joe Borchard/150	4.00
101	Joe Crede/250	4.00
103	John Olerud/150	4.00
105	Johnny Damon/250	4.00
106	Jorge Posada/150	6.00
107	Jose Castillo/250	4.00
108	Jose Reyes/150	6.00
109	Jose Vidro/150	4.00
110	Josh Beckett/150	6.00
111	Josh Phelps/150	4.00
112	Juan Encarnacion/250	4.00
113	Juan Gonzalez/250	6.00
114	Junior Spivey/250	4.00
115	Kazuhisa Ishii/150	4.00
116	Kenny Lofton/250	4.00
117	Kerry Wood/150	8.00
119	Kevin Youkilis/250	4.00
120	Lance Berkman/150	4.00
122	Larry Walker/150	4.00
123	Luis Castillo/150	4.00
124	Luis Gonzalez/150	4.00
127	Lyle Overbay/250	4.00
127	Magglio Ordonez/150	4.00
128	Manny Ramirez/250	8.00
129	Marcus Giles/250	4.00
131	Mark Buehrle/150	4.00
132	Mark Mulder/150	6.00
133	Mark Prior/150	8.00
134	Mark Teixeira/150	6.00
135	Marlon Byrd/150	4.00
137	Miguel Cabrera/250	8.00
138	Mike Lowell/150	4.00
140	Mike Piazza/150	10.00
141	Mike Sweeney/150	4.00
143	Nick Johnson/250	4.00
144	Nomar Garciaparra/150	10.00
145	Omar Vizquel/150	4.00
146	Orlando Cabrera/250	4.00
147	Orlando Hudson/150	4.00
148	Pat Burrell/150	4.00
149	Paul Konerko/150	4.00
150	Paul LoDuca/150	4.00
152	Jermaine Dye/150	4.00
153	Preston Wilson/150	4.00
154	Rafael Furcal/150	4.00
155	Rafael Palmeiro/150	8.00
157	Rich Aurilia/250	4.00
159	Richard Hidalgo/150	4.00
160	Richie Sexson/250	4.00
161	Rickie Weeks/250	6.00
162	Roberto Alomar/250	4.00
163	Rocco Baldelli/150	4.00
164	Roger Clemens/250	12.00
168	Ryan Klesko/150	4.00
170	Sammy Sosa/150	12.00
174	Sean Casey/150	4.00
175	Shannon Stewart/150	4.00
176	Shawn Green/150	4.00
181	Todd Helton/150	6.00
183	Torii Hunter/150	6.00
184	Trot Nixon/150	4.00
185	Troy Glaus/150	6.00
186	Vernon Wells/150	4.00
187	Victor Martinez/250	4.00
188	Vladimir Guerrero/250	8.00
189	Wade Miller/250	4.00
190	Brandon Larson/175	4.00
191	Travis Hafner/250	4.00
192	Tim Salmon/150	4.00
195	Ramon Nivar/150	4.00
196	Moises Alou/250	6.00
197	Michael Young/250	4.00
198	Laynce Nix/150	4.00
199	Tino Martinez/250	4.00
200	Randall Simon/250	4.00
201	Roger Clemens/150	12.00
203	Vladimir Guerrero/150	8.00
204	Miguel Tejada/150	6.00
206	Jason Giambi/150	6.00
208	Alex Rodriguez/150	10.00
209	Alfonso Soriano/150	8.00
210	Ivan Rodriguez/150	8.00
211	Rafael Palmeiro/150	8.00
212	Gary Carter/150	8.00
216	Reggie Jackson/150	10.00
220	Don Mattingly/150	20.00
222	Rickey Henderson/150	8.00
227	Lou Brock/150	6.00
228	Andre Dawson/150	6.00
229	Rod Carew /150	8.00
230	Wade Boggs/150	8.00
240	Stan Musial/150	25.00

Mirror Bat Blue

	NM/M
Blue Bat:	1-1.5X Red Price

Production 25-100
Cards listed don't have a red version.

217	Ryne Sandberg/50	40.00
219	Tony Gwynn/50	20.00
221	Mike Schmidt/50	25.00
223	Cal Ripken Jr./50	50.00
224	Nolan Ryan/50	35.00
225	George Brett/50	30.00

Mirror Bat Gold

	NM/M
Gold Bat:	1.5-3X Red Price

Production 25 Sets
Cards listed don't have a red version.

69	Greg Maddux	25.00
217	Ryne Sandberg	50.00
219	Tony Gwynn	25.00
221	Mike Schmidt	40.00
223	Cal Ripken Jr.	90.00
224	Nolan Ryan	60.00
225	George Brett	40.00
231	Roberto Clemente	90.00
233	Babe Ruth	200.00
234	Lou Gehrig	150.00
235	Ty Cobb	125.00
236	Roger Maris	40.00
239	Ted Williams	80.00

Mirror Bat White

	NM/M
White Bat:	.75-1X Red Price

Production 25-200
Cards listed don't have a red version.

219	Tony Gwynn/100	15.00
221	Mike Schmidt/100	20.00
223	Cal Ripken Jr./100	40.00
224	Nolan Ryan/100	30.00
225	George Brett/100	20.00
231	Roberto Clemente/50	65.00
233	Babe Ruth/25	200.00
234	Lou Gehrig/25	150.00
235	Ty Cobb/25	125.00
236	Roger Maris/25	40.00
239	Ted Williams/25	80.00

Mirror Combo Red

	NM/M
Common (2-211):	6.00

Production 250
Common (212-239):   8.00
Production 50-250
Black Prime: No Pricing
Production One Set

2	Adam Dunn/Bat-Jsy	8.00
5	Adrian Beltre/Bat-Jsy	6.00
7	Albert Pujols/Bat-Jsy	25.00
11	Andruw Jones/Bat-Jsy	8.00
13	Angel Berroa/ Bat-Pants	6.00
15	Aubrey Huff/Bat-Jsy	6.00
16	Austin Kearns/Bat-Jsy	6.00
17	Barry Larkin/Bat-Jsy	8.00
18	Barry Zito/Bat-Jsy	6.00
19	Ben Sheets/Bat-Jsy	6.00
20	Bernie Williams/ Bat-Jsy	10.00
21	Bobby Abreu/Bat-Jsy	8.00
22	Brad Penny/Bat-Jsy	6.00
24	Brandon Webb/ Bat-Jsy	6.00
26	Bret Boone/Bat-Jsy	8.00
36	Carlos Beltran/Bat-Jsy	6.00
37	Carlos Delgado/ Bat-Jsy	8.00
38	Carlos Lee/Bat-Jsy	6.00
41	Chipper Jones/ Bat-Jsy	10.00

45 Craig Biggio/Bat-Pants 6.00
47 Dan Haren/Bat-Jsy 6.00
51 Derek Jeter/Bat-Jsy 30.00
52 Dewon Brazelton/Glv-Jsy 6.00
54 Edgar Martinez/Bat-Jsy 8.00
55 Edgar Renteria/Bat-Jsy 8.00
58 Eric Chavez/Bat-Jsy 8.00
59 Eric Hinske/Bat-Jsy 6.00
62 Frank Thomas/Bat-Jsy 10.00
63 Fred McGriff/Bat-Jsy 6.00
65 Garret Anderson/Bat-Jsy 8.00
68 Geoff Jenkins/Bat-Jsy 6.00
70 Hank Blalock/Bat-Jsy 10.00
73 Hideo Nomo/Bat-Jsy 10.00
79 Jacque Jones/Bat-Jsy 6.00
82 Jason Giambi/Bat-Jsy 10.00
83 Jason Jennings/Bat-Jsy 6.00
86 Jason Varitek/Bat-Jsy 10.00
89 Jay Gibbons/Bat-Jsy 6.00
91 Jeff Bagwell/Bat-Jsy 10.00
93 Jeff Kent/Bat-Jsy 6.00
97 Jim Edmonds/Bat-Jsy 8.00
98 Jim Thome/Bat-Jsy 10.00
100 Joe Borchard/Bat-Jsy 6.00
103 John Olerud/Bat-Jsy 6.00
106 Jorge Posada/Bat-Jsy 8.00
108 Jose Reyes/Bat-Jsy 8.00
109 Jose Vidro/Bat-Jsy 8.00
110 Josh Beckett/Bat-Jsy 8.00
111 Josh Phelps/Bat-Jsy 6.00
115 Kazuhisa Ishii/Bat-Jsy 6.00
117 Kerry Wood/Bat-Jsy 12.00
120 Lance Berkman/Bat-Jsy 6.00
122 Larry Walker/Bat-Jsy 6.00
123 Luis Castillo/Bat-Jsy 6.00
124 Luis Gonzalez/Bat-Jsy 6.00
127 Magglio Ordonez/Bat-Jsy 6.00
128 Manny Ramirez/Bat-Jsy 10.00
131 Mark Buehrle/Bat-Jsy 6.00
132 Mark Mulder/Bat-Jsy 8.00
133 Mark Prior/Bat-Jsy 8.00
134 Mark Teixeira/Bat-Jsy 8.00
135 Marlon Byrd/Bat-Jsy 6.00
138 Mike Lowell/Bat-Jsy 6.00
140 Mike Piazza/Bat-Jsy 12.00
141 Mike Sweeney/Bat-Jsy 6.00
142 Morgan Ensberg/Bat-Jsy 6.00
144 Nomar Garciaparra/Bat-Jsy 12.00
145 Omar Vizquel/Bat-Jsy 6.00
147 Orlando Hudson/Bat-Jsy 6.00
148 Pat Burrell/Bat-Jsy 6.00
149 Paul Konerko/Bat-Jsy 6.00
150 Paul LoDuca/Bat-Jsy 6.00
151 Pedro J. Martinez/Bat-Jsy 10.00
153 Preston Wilson/Bat-Jsy 6.00
154 Rafael Furcal/Bat-Jsy 6.00
155 Rafael Palmeiro/Bat-Jsy 10.00
156 Randy Johnson/Bat-Jsy 12.00
159 Richard Hidalgo/Bat-Pants 6.00
163 Rocco Baldelli/Bat-Jsy 6.00
166 Roy Oswalt/Bat-Jsy 6.00
168 Ryan Klesko/Bat-Jsy 6.00
170 Sammy Sosa/Bat-Jsy 15.00
172 Scott Rolen/Bat-Jsy 10.00
175 Shannon Stewart/Bat-Jsy 6.00
176 Shawn Green/Bat-Jsy 6.00
180 Tim Hudson/Bat-Jsy 8.00
181 Todd Helton/Bat-Jsy 10.00
182 Tom Glavine/Bat-Jsy 8.00
183 Torii Hunter/Bat-Jsy 8.00
184 Trot Nixon/Bat-Jsy 8.00
185 Troy Glaus/Bat-Jsy 6.00
186 Vernon Wells/Bat-Jsy 6.00
191 Travis Hafner/Bat-Jsy 8.00
192 Tim Salmon/Bat-Jsy 6.00
195 Ramon Nivar/Bat-Jsy 6.00
201 Roger Clemens/Bat-Jsy 15.00
203 Vladimir Guerrero/Bat-Jsy 12.00
204 Miguel Tejada/Bat-Jsy 8.00
206 Jason Giambi/Bat-Jsy 8.00

207 Curt Schilling/Bat-Jsy 8.00
208 Alex Rodriguez/Bat-Jsy 12.00
209 Alfonso Soriano/Bat-Jsy 10.00
210 Ivan Rodriguez/Bat-Jsy 10.00
211 Rafael Palmeiro/Bat-Jsy 10.00
212 Gary Carter/Bat-Pants/250 8.00
216 Reggie Jackson/Bat-Jsy/250 12.00
217 Ryne Sandberg/Bat-Jsy/250 25.00
218 Dale Murphy/Bat-Jsy/250 10.00
219 Tony Gwynn/Bat-Jsy/250 12.00
220 Don Mattingly/Bat-Jsy/250 25.00
221 Mike Schmidt/Bat-Pants/250 25.00
222 Rickey Henderson/Bat-Jsy/250 10.00
223 Cal Ripken Jr./Bat-Jsy/250 35.00
224 Nolan Ryan/Bat-Jsy/250 35.00
225 George Brett/Bat-Jsy/250 25.00
227 Lou Brock/Bat-Jsy/250 8.00
228 Andre Dawson/Bat-Jsy/250 8.00
229 Rod Carew/Bat-Jkt/250 10.00
230 Wade Boggs/Bat-Jsy/250 8.00
231 Roberto Clemente/Bat-Jsy/100 100.00
232 Roy Campanella/Bat-Pants/100 15.00
233 Babe Ruth/Bat-Pants/50 350.00
234 Lou Gehrig/Bat-Pants/50 200.00
235 Ty Cobb/Bat-Pants/50 200.00
236 Roger Maris/Bat-Pants/100 50.00
238 Ernie Banks/Bat-Pants/100 15.00
239 Ted Williams/Bat-Jkt/100 85.00

Mirror Fabric Red

NM/M
Common Player: 4.00
Quantity produced listed

1 A.J. Burnett/Jsy/250 4.00
2 Adam Dunn/Jsy/150 6.00
5 Adrian Beltre/Jsy/150 6.00
6 Al Leiter/Jsy/250 4.00
7 Albert Pujols/Jsy/150 15.00
11 Andruw Jones/Jsy/150 6.00
13 Angel Berroa/Pants/150 4.00
15 Aubrey Huff/Jsy/150 4.00
16 Austin Kearns/Jsy/150 4.00
17 Barry Larkin/Jsy/150 6.00
18 Barry Zito/Jsy/250 5.00
19 Ben Sheets/Jsy/150 4.00
20 Bernie Williams/Jsy/150 6.00
21 Bobby Abreu/Jsy/150 6.00
22 Brad Penny/Jsy/150 4.00
27 Brett Myers/Jsy/250 4.00
33 C.C. Sabathia/Jsy/250 4.00
34 Carl Crawford/Jsy/250 4.00
36 Carlos Beltran/Jsy/150 6.00
38 Carlos Lee/Jsy/250 4.00
39 Chad Gaudin/Jsy/250 4.00
41 Chipper Jones/Jsy/150 8.00
45 Craig Biggio/Pants/150 4.00
47 Dan Haren/Jsy/150 4.00
48 Darin Erstad/Jsy/150 4.00
51 Derek Jeter/Jsy/150 20.00
53 Dontrelle Willis/Jsy/250 6.00
54 Edgar Martinez/Jsy/250 6.00
55 Edgar Renteria/Jsy/150 6.00
58 Eric Chavez/Jsy/150 4.00
59 Eric Hinske/Jsy/150 4.00
62 Frank Thomas/Jsy/150 6.00
64 Freddy Garcia/Jsy/250 4.00
66 Garrett Atkins/Jsy/250 4.00
68 Geoff Jenkins/Jsy/150 4.00
70 Hank Blalock/Jsy/150 6.00

72 Hideki Matsui/Base/250 15.00
73 Hideo Nomo/Jsy/150 8.00
75 Ichiro Suzuki/Base/250 15.00
79 Jacque Jones/Jsy/250 4.00
81 Jamie Moyer/Jsy/250 4.00
82 Jason Giambi/Jsy/150 6.00
83 Jason Jennings/Jsy/150 4.00
84 Jason Kendall/Jsy/250 4.00
86 Jason Varitek/Jsy/150 6.00
89 Jay Gibbons/Jsy/150 4.00
91 Jeff Bagwell/Jsy/150 8.00
93 Jeff Kent/Jsy/150 4.00
96 Jerome Williams/Jsy/250 4.00
97 Jim Edmonds/Jsy/150 6.00
98 Jim Thome/Jsy/150 8.00
102 Jose Santana/Jsy/250 4.00
103 John Olerud/Jsy/250 4.00
104 John Smoltz/Jsy/250 4.00
108 Jose Reyes/Jsy/150 6.00
109 Jose Vidro/Jsy/150 4.00
110 Josh Beckett/Jsy/150 4.00
111 Josh Phelps/Jsy/150 4.00
115 Kazuhisa Ishii/Jsy/150 4.00
117 Kerry Wood/Jsy/150 8.00
118 Kevin Millwood/Jsy/250 4.00
120 Lance Berkman/Jsy/150 4.00
121 Larry Bigbie/Jsy/250 4.00
122 Larry Walker/Jsy/150 4.00
123 Luis Castillo/Jsy/150 4.00
124 Luis Gonzalez/Jsy/150 4.00
130 Mariano Rivera/Jsy/250 6.00
131 Mark Buehrle/Jsy/150 4.00
133 Mark Prior/Jsy/150 8.00
135 Marlon Byrd/Jsy/150 4.00
136 Matt Morris/Jsy/250 4.00
139 Mike Mussina/Jsy/250 6.00
140 Mike Piazza/Jsy/150 10.00
141 Mike Sweeney/Jsy/150 4.00
142 Morgan Ensberg/Jsy/150 4.00
144 Nomar Garciaparra/Jsy/150 10.00
145 Omar Vizquel/Jsy/150 4.00
147 Orlando Hudson/Jsy/150 4.00
148 Pat Burrell/Jsy/150 4.00
151 Pedro J. Martinez/Jsy/150 8.00
153 Preston Wilson/Jsy/150 4.00
154 Rafael Furcal/Jsy/150 4.00
156 Randy Johnson/Jsy/150 8.00
158 Rich Harden/Jsy/250 4.00
159 Richard Hidalgo/Pants/150 4.00
163 Rocco Baldelli/Jsy/150 4.00
165 Roy Halladay/Jsy/250 4.00
168 Ryan Klesko/Jsy/150 4.00
170 Sammy Sosa/Jsy/150 12.00
172 Scott Rolen/Jsy/150 4.00
173 Sean Burroughs/Jsy/250 4.00
175 Shannon Stewart/Jsy/150 4.00
176 Shawn Green/Jsy/150 4.00
179 Steve Finley/Jsy/250 4.00
180 Tim Hudson/Jsy/150 6.00
181 Todd Helton/Jsy/150 8.00
182 Tom Glavine/Jsy/150 6.00
185 Troy Glaus/Jsy/150 6.00
186 Vernon Wells/Jsy/150 4.00
191 Travis Hafner/Jsy/150 6.00
192 Tim Salmon/Jsy/150 6.00
193 Tim Redding/Jsy/250 4.00
194 Runelvys Hernandez/Jsy/250 4.00
195 Ramon Nivar/Jsy/150 4.00
201 Roger Clemens/Jsy/150 15.00
202 Greg Maddux/Jsy/250 10.00
203 Vladimir Guerrero/Jsy/150 8.00
204 Miguel Tejada/Jsy/150 6.00
205 Kevin Brown/Jsy/250 4.00
206 Jason Giambi/Jsy/150 6.00
207 Curt Schilling/Jsy/150 6.00
208 Alex Rodriguez/Jsy/150 10.00
209 Alfonso Soriano/Jsy/150 8.00
210 Ivan Rodriguez/Jsy/150 8.00
212 Gary Carter/Pants/150 6.00
226 Bob Gibson/Jsy/250 10.00
237 Satchel Paige/Jsy/100 50.00

Mirror Fabric Blue

NM/M
Blue: 1-1.5X Red Price
Production 25-100
Cards listed don't have red version.
217 Ryne Sandberg/100 25.00
219 Tony Gwynn/100 15.00
220 Don Mattingly/100 25.00
221 Mike Schmidt/100 20.00
223 Cal Ripken Jr./100 35.00
224 Nolan Ryan/100 25.00
225 George Brett/100 15.00
231 Roberto Clemente/25 90.00
233 Babe Ruth/25 240.00
234 Lou Gehrig/25 150.00
235 Ty Cobb/25 140.00
236 Roger Maris/25 50.00
237 Satchel Paige/25 90.00
239 Ted Williams/25 100.00

Mirror Fabric Gold

NM/M
Gold: 2-3X Red Price
Production 10-25
No pricing 20 or less.
Cards listed don't have red version.
217 Ryne Sandberg/25 45.00
219 Tony Gwynn/25 30.00
220 Don Mattingly/25 60.00
221 Mike Schmidt/25 40.00
223 Cal Ripken Jr./25 90.00
224 Nolan Ryan/25 60.00
225 George Brett/25 50.00

Mirror Fabric White

NM/M
White: .5-1.5X Red Price
Production 25-200
Cards listed don't have red version.
217 Ryne Sandberg/25 45.00
219 Tony Gwynn/25 25.00
220 Don Mattingly/25 50.00
221 Mike Schmidt/25 40.00
223 Cal Ripken Jr./25 90.00
224 Nolan Ryan/25 60.00
225 George Brett/25 50.00
231 Roberto Clemente/25 90.00
233 Babe Ruth/25 240.00
234 Lou Gehrig/25 150.00
235 Ty Cobb/25 140.00
236 Roger Maris/25 50.00
237 Satchel Paige/25 90.00
239 Ted Williams/25 100.00

2004 Leaf Limited

NM/M
Complete Set (275):

Common Player (1-200):	1.50
Common SP (201-229):	3.00
Production 499	
Common SP (251-275):	10.00
Production 99	
Pack (4):	60.00
Box (4):	200.00

1	Adam Dunn	2.00
2	Adrian Beltre	2.00
3	Albert Pujols	6.00
4	Alex Rodriguez	6.00
5	Alfonso Soriano	2.50
6	Andruw Jones	1.50
7	Andy Pettitte	1.50
8	Angel Berroa	1.50
9	Aramis Ramirez	1.50
10	Aubrey Huff	1.50
11	Aubrey Huff	1.50
12	Barry Larkin	1.50
13	Barry Zito	1.50
14	Bartolo Colon	1.50
15	Ben Sheets	1.50
16	Bernie Williams	1.50
17	Bobby Abreu	1.50
18	Brandon Webb	1.50
19	Brian Giles	1.50
20	C.C. Sabathia	1.50
21	Carlos Beltran	2.00
22	Carlos Delgado	1.50
23	Chipper Jones	3.00
24	Craig Biggio	1.50
25	Curt Schilling	3.00
26	Darin Erstad	1.50
27	Delmon Young	1.50
28	Derek Jeter	6.00
29	Derek Lee	1.50
30	Dontrelle Willis	1.50
31	Edgar Renteria	1.50
32	Eric Chavez	1.50
33	Esteban Loaiza	1.50
34	Frank Thomas	2.00
35	Fred McGriff	1.50
36	Garret Anderson	1.50
37	Gary Sheffield	1.50
38	Geoff Jenkins	1.50
39	Greg Maddux	3.00
40	Hank Blalock	2.00
41	Hideki Matsui	5.00
42	Hideo Nomo	1.50
43	Ichiro Suzuki	5.00
44	Ivan Rodriguez	2.00
45	J.D. Drew	1.50
46	Jacque Jones	1.50
47	Jae Weong Seo	1.50
48	Jake Peavy	1.50
49	Jamie Moyer	1.50
50	Jason Giambi	1.50
51	Jason Kendall	1.50
52	Jason Schmidt	1.50
53	Jason Varitek	1.50
54	Javier Vazquez	1.50
55	Javy Lopez	1.50
56	Jay Gibbons	1.50
57	Jay Payton	1.50
58	Jeff Bagwell	1.50
59	Jeff Kent	1.50
60	Jeremy Bonderman	1.50
61	Jermaine Dye	1.50
62	Jeromy Burnitz	1.50
63	Jim Edmonds	2.00
64	Jim Thome	1.50
65	Jimmy Rollins	1.50
66	Jody Gerut	1.50
67	Johan Santana	2.00
68	John Olerud	1.50
69	John Smoltz	1.50
70	Johnny Damon	2.00
71	Jorge Posada	1.50
72	Jose Contreras	1.50
73	Jose Reyes	1.50
74	Jose Vidro	1.50
75	Josh Beckett	1.50

76	Juan Gonzalez	1.50
77	Juan Pierre	1.50
78	Junior Spivey	1.50
79	Kazuhisa Ishii	1.50
80	Keith Foulke	1.50
81	Ken Griffey Jr.	3.00
82	Ken Harvey	1.50
83	Kenny Rogers	1.50
84	Kerry Wood	2.50
85	Kevin Brown	1.50
86	Kevin Millwood	1.50
87	Kip Wells	1.50
88	Lance Berkman	1.50
89	Larry Bigbie	1.50
90	Larry Walker	1.50
91	Laynce Nix	1.50
92	Luis Castillo	1.50
93	Luis Gonzalez	1.50
94	Luis Matos	1.50
95	Lyle Overbay	1.50
96	Magglio Ordonez	1.50
97	Manny Ramirez	2.00
98	Marcus Giles	1.50
99	Mark Buehrle	1.50
100	Mark Mulder	1.50
101	Mark Prior	2.00
102	Mark Teixeira	1.50
103	Marlon Byrd	1.50
104	Matt Morris	1.50
105	Melvin Mora	1.50
106	Michael Young	1.50
107	Miguel Cabrera	3.00
108	Miguel Tejada	2.00
109	Mike Lowell	1.50
110	Mike Mussina	2.00
111	Mike Piazza	4.00
112	Mike Sweeney	1.50
113	Milton Bradley	1.50
114	Moises Alou	1.50
115	Morgan Ensberg	1.50
116	Nick Johnson	1.50
117	Nomar Garciaparra	4.00
118	Omar Vizquel	1.50
119	Orlando Cabrera	1.50
120	Pat Burrell	1.50
121	Paul Konerko	1.50
122	Paul LoDuca	1.50
123	Pedro J. Martinez	3.00
124	Preston Wilson	1.50
125	Rafael Furcal	1.50
126	Rafael Palmeiro	2.00
127	Randy Johnson	3.00
128	Rich Harden	1.50
129	Richard Hidalgo	1.50
130	Richie Sexson	1.50
131	Rickie Weeks	1.50
132	Roberto Alomar	1.50
133	Robin Ventura	1.50
134	Rocco Baldelli	1.50
135	Roger Clemens	6.00
136	Roy Halladay	1.50
137	Roy Oswalt	1.50
138	Russ Ortiz	1.50
139	Ryan Klesko	1.50
140	Sammy Sosa	5.00
141	Scott Podsednik	1.50
142	Scott Rolen	3.00
143	Sean Burroughs	1.50
144	Sean Casey	1.50
145	Shannon Stewart	1.50
146	Shawn Green	1.50
147	Shigetoshi Hasegawa	1.50
148	Sidney Ponson	1.50
149	Steve Finley	1.50
150	Tim Hudson	1.50
151	Tim Salmon	1.50
152	Tino Martinez	1.50
153	Todd Helton	2.00
154	Tom Glavine	2.00
155	Torii Hunter	1.50
156	Trot Nixon	1.50
157	Troy Glaus	1.50
158	Vernon Wells	1.50
159	Victor Martinez	1.50
160	Vinny Castilla	1.50
161	Vladimir Guerrero	3.00
162	Alex Rodriguez	6.00
163	Alfonso Soriano	2.50
164	Andy Pettitte	1.50
165	Curt Schilling	3.00
166	Gary Sheffield	1.50
167	Greg Maddux	3.00
168	Hideo Nomo	1.50
169	Ivan Rodriguez	2.00
170	Jason Giambi	1.50
171	Jim Thome	2.00
172	Juan Gonzalez	1.50
173	Ken Griffey Jr.	3.00
174	Kevin Brown	1.50
175	Manny Ramirez	2.00
176	Miguel Tejada	2.00
177	Mike Mussina	1.50
178	Mike Piazza	4.00
179	Pedro Martinez	3.00

180	Rafael Palmeiro	2.00
181	Randy Johnson	3.00
182	Roger Clemens	6.00
183	Scott Rolen	3.00
184	Shawn Green	1.50
185	Tom Glavine	1.50
186	Vladimir Guerrero	3.00
187	Alex Rodriguez	6.00
188	Mike Piazza	4.00
189	Randy Johnson	3.00
190	Roger Clemens	6.00
191	Albert Pujols	6.00
192	Barry Zito	1.50
193	Chipper Jones	3.00
194	Garret Anderson	1.50
195	Jeff Bagwell	2.00
196	Josh Beckett	1.50
197	Magglio Ordonez	1.50
198	Mark Prior	2.00
199	Sammy Sosa	5.00
200	Todd Helton	2.00
201	Andre Dawson	3.00
202	Babe Ruth	8.00
203	Bob Feller	4.00
204	Bob Gibson	4.00
205	Bobby Doerr	3.00
206	Cal Ripken Jr.	10.00
207	Dale Murphy	4.00
208	Don Mattingly	8.00
209	Gary Carter	3.00
210	George Brett	8.00
211	Jackie Robinson	5.00
212	Lou Brock	4.00
213	Lou Gehrig	6.00
214	Mark Grace	4.00
215	Maury Wills	3.00
216	Mike Schmidt	8.00
217	Nolan Ryan	8.00
218	Orel Hershiser	3.00
219	Paul Molitor	4.00
220	Roberto Clemente	8.00
221	Rod Carew	4.00
222	Roy Campanella	4.00
223	Ryne Sandberg	8.00
224	Stan Musial	6.00
225	Ted Williams	8.00
226	Tony Gwynn	6.00
227	Ty Cobb	5.00
228	Whitey Ford	4.00
229	Yogi Berra	4.00
230	Carlos Beltran	3.00
231	David Ortiz	3.00
232	David Ortiz	3.00
233	Carlos Zambrano	1.50
234	Carlos Lee	1.50
235	Travis Hafner	1.50
236	Brad Penny	1.50
237	Wade Miller	1.50
238	Edgar Martinez	1.50
239	Carl Crawford	1.50
240	Roy Oswalt	1.50
241	Kazuo Matsui	8.00
242	Carlos Beltran	3.00
243	Carlos Beltran	3.00
244	Miguel Cabrera	2.00
245	Scott Rolen	3.00
246	Hank Blalock	2.00
247	Vernon Wells	1.50
248	Adam Dunn	2.00
249	Preston Wilson	1.50
250	Victor Martinez	1.50
251	Aarom Baldiris RC	10.00
252	Akinori Otsuka RC	35.00
253	Andres Blanco RC	10.00
254	Brad Halsey RC	10.00
255	Joey Gathright RC	25.00
256	Colby Miller RC	10.00
257	Fernando Nieve RC	10.00
258	Freddy Guzman RC	15.00
259	Hector Gimenez RC	10.00
260	Jake Woods RC	10.00
261	Jason Bartlett RC	10.00
262	John Gall RC	15.00
263	Jose Capellan RC	35.00
264	Josh Labandeira RC	10.00
265	Justin Germano RC	10.00
266	Kazuhito Tadano RC	40.00
267	Lance Cormier RC	10.00
268	Merkin Valdez RC	20.00
269	Mike Gosling RC	10.00
270	Ramon Ramirez RC	10.00
271	Rusty Tucker RC	10.00
272	Shawn Hill RC	10.00
273	Shingo Takatsu RC	40.00
274	William Bergolla RC	10.00
275	Yadier Molina RC	10.00

Bronze Spotlight

Bronze:	1-2X
Production 100 Sets	

Gold Spotlight

Golds (1-250):	3-5X
Production 25 Sets	

Platinum Spotlight

No Pricing
Production One Set

Silver Spotlight

Silver (1-250):	2-3X
Production 50 Sets	

Barrels

No Pricing
Production 1-5

Cuts

	NM/M

Quantity produced listed

1	Nolan Ryan/100	125.00
2	Bob Gibson/50	40.00
3	Harmon Killebrew/100	40.00
4	Duke Snider/100	30.00
5	George Brett/100	75.00
6	Stan Musial/100	80.00
7	Alan Trammell/100	20.00
8	Cal Ripken Jr./100	180.00
9	Steve Carlton/50	40.00
10	Phil Rizzuto/100	30.00
11	Mark Prior/50	40.00
12	Will Clark/100	40.00
13	Lou Brock/100	30.00
14	Ozzie Smith/100	60.00
15	Bob Feller/100	30.00
16	Gary Carter/50	25.00
17	Al Kaline/100	40.00
18	Brooks Robinson/100	40.00
19	Tony Gwynn/100	50.00
20	Mike Schmidt/100	75.00
21	Ralph Kiner/50	40.00
22	Jim Palmer/50	40.00
23	Don Mattingly/100	75.00
24	Paul Molitor/50	40.00
25	Dale Murphy/100	30.00

Cuts Gold

	NM/M

Quantity produced listed

1	Nolan Ryan/34	200.00
2	Bob Gibson/45	40.00
9	Steve Carlton/32	50.00
11	Mark Prior/22	60.00
12	Will Clark/22	65.00
13	Lou Brock/20	50.00
15	Bob Feller/28	50.00
19	Tony Gwynn/19	100.00
20	Mike Schmidt/20	100.00
22	Jim Palmer/20	50.00
23	Don Mattingly/23	100.00

Legends Material Autographs Number

	NM/M

Quanity produced listed

1	Al Kaline/Pants/50	50.00
3	Bob Feller/Jsy/50	30.00
4	Bob Gibson/Jsy/50	30.00
7	Carl Yastrzemski/Jsy/25	80.00
8	Harmon Killebrew/Jsy/25	65.00

9	Hoyt Wilhelm/Jsy/25	40.00
12	Lou Brock/Jsy/50	30.00
13	Luis Aparicio/	
	Pants/50	20.00
15	Reggie Jackson/	
	Jsy/50	50.00
16	Red Schoendienst/	
	Jsy/50	30.00
19	Stan Musial/Jsy/50	75.00
23	Whitey Ford/	
	Pants/25	50.00
24	Yogi Berra/Jsy/25	75.00

Legends Material Autographs Position

NM/M

Quantity produced listed
1	Al Kaline/Pants/50	50.00
3	Bob Feller/Jsy/50	30.00
4	Bob Gibson/Jsy/50	30.00
7	Carl Yastrzemski/	
	Jsy/25	80.00
8	Harmon Killebrew/	
	Jsy/25	65.00
9	Hoyt Wilhelm/Jsy/25	40.00
12	Lou Brock/Jsy/50	30.00
13	Luis Aparicio/	
	Pants/50	20.00
15	Reggie Jackson/	
	Jsy/50	50.00
16	Red Schoendienst/	
	Jsy/50	30.00
19	Stan Musial/Jsy/50	75.00
23	Whitey Ford/Pants/25	50.00
24	Yogi Berra/Jsy/25	75.00

Legends Material Number

NM/M

Quantity produced listed
1	Al Kaline/Pants/50	15.00
2	Babe Ruth/Pants/50	160.00
3	Bob Feller/Jsy/50	10.00
4	Bob Gibson/Jsy/50	10.00
6	Burleigh Grimes/	
	Pants/100	40.00
7	Carl Yastrzemski/	
	Jsy/100	15.00
8	Harmon Killebrew/	
	Jsy/25	25.00
9	Hoyt Wilhelm/Jsy/100	5.00
10	Johnny Mize/	
	Pants/100	10.00
11	Ernie Banks/Pants/50	15.00
12	Lou Brock/Jsy/50	10.00
13	Luis Aparicio/	
	Pants/100	5.00
14	Pee Wee Reese/	
	Jsy/50	10.00
15	Reggie Jackson/	
	Jsy/100	10.00
16	Red Schoendienst/	
	Jsy/50	8.00
17	Roberto Clemente/	
	Jsy/25	80.00
18	Roger Maris/	
	Pants/100	25.00
19	Stan Musial/Jsy/100	20.00
20	Ted Williams/Jsy/50	75.00
21	Ty Cobb/Pants/50	80.00
22	Warren Spahn/	
	Jsy/100	10.00
23	Whitey Ford/	
	Pants/100	10.00
24	Yogi Berra/Jsy/50	15.00
25	Satchel Paige/	
	CO Jsy/100	50.00

Legends Material Position

NM/M

Quantity produced listed
1	Al Kaline/Pants/50	15.00
2	Babe Ruth/Pants/50	160.00
3	Bob Feller/Jsy/50	10.00
4	Bob Gibson/Jsy/50	10.00
6	Burleigh Grimes/	
	Pants/100	40.00
7	Carl Yastrzemski/	
	Jsy/100	15.00
8	Harmon Killebrew/	
	Jsy/25	25.00
9	Hoyt Wilhelm/Jsy/100	5.00
10	Johnny Mize/	
	Pants/100	10.00
11	Ernie Banks/Pants/50	15.00
12	Lou Brock/Jsy/50	10.00
13	Luis Aparicio/	
	Pants/100	5.00
14	Pee Wee Reese/	
	Jsy/50	10.00

15	Reggie Jackson/	
	Jsy/100	10.00
16	Red Schoendienst/	
	Jsy/50	8.00
17	Roberto Clemente/	
	Jsy/25	80.00
18	Roger Maris/	
	Pants/100	25.00
19	Stan Musial/Jsy/100	20.00
20	Ted Williams/Jsy/50	75.00
21	Ty Cobb/Pants/50	80.00
22	Warren Spahn/	
	Jsy/100	10.00
23	Whitey Ford/	
	Pants/100	10.00
24	Yogi Berra/Jsy/50	15.00
25	Satchel Paige/	
	CO Jsy/100	50.00

Lumberjacks

NM/M

Common Player: 2.00
Quantity produced listed
Black: 1-3X
Production 16-100
1	Al Kaline/399	4.00
2	Albert Pujols/114	15.00
3	Andre Dawson/438	2.00
4	Babe Ruth/714	8.00
5	Bo Jackson/141	6.00
6	Bobby Doerr/223	3.00
7	Brooks Robinson/268	4.00
8	Cal Ripken Jr./431	10.00
9	Carlton Fisk/376	2.00
10	Dale Murphy/398	2.00
11	Darryl Strawberry/335	2.00
12	Don Mattingly/222	6.00
13	Duke Snider/407	3.00
14	Eddie Mathews/512	3.00
15	Eddie Murray/504	3.00
16	Frank Robinson/586	3.00
17	Frank Thomas/418	3.00
18	Gary Carter/324	2.00
19	George Brett/317	6.00
20	Harmon Killebrew/573	4.00
22	Lou Gehrig/493	5.00
23	Mark Grace/173	2.00
24	Mike Piazza/358	4.00
25	Mike Schmidt/548	5.00
26	Orlando Cepeda/379	2.00
27	Rafael Palmeiro/528	2.00
28	Ralph Kiner/369	2.00
29	Reggie Jackson/563	3.00
30	Rickey Henderson/297	3.00
31	Roger Maris/275	5.00
32	Ryne Sandberg/282	4.00
33	Sammy Sosa/539	4.00
34	Scott Rolen/192	4.00
35	Stan Musial/475	4.00
36	Ted Williams/521	6.00
37	Thurman Munson/113	5.00
38	Vladimir Guerrero/234	4.00
39	Willie McCovey/521	2.00
40	Willie Stargell/475	2.00
41	Roberto Clemente,	
	Stan Musial	6.00
42	Cal Ripken Jr.,	
	Ernie Banks	10.00
43	Babe Ruth,	
	Lou Gehrig	8.00
44	George Brett,	
	Mike Schmidt	8.00
45	Frank Robinson,	
	Jackie Robinson	4.00
46	Don Mattingly,	
	Roger Maris	8.00
47	Nomar Garciaparra,	
	Ted Williams	8.00
48	Johnny Bench,	
	Mike Piazza	4.00
49	Reggie Jackson,	
	Sammy Sosa	4.00
50	Mel Ott,	
	Willie McCovey	4.00

Lumberjacks Autographs

NM/M

Quantity produced listed
1	Al Kaline/100	30.00
2	Albert Pujols/10	
3	Andre Dawson/100	15.00

15	Reggie Jackson/	
	Jsy/100	10.00
16	Red Schoendienst/	
	Jsy/50	8.00
17	Roberto Clemente/	
	Jsy/25	80.00
18	Roger Maris/	
	Pants/100	25.00
19	Stan Musial/Jsy/100	20.00
20	Ted Williams/Jsy/50	75.00
21	Ty Cobb/Pants/50	80.00
22	Warren Spahn/	
	Jsy/100	10.00
23	Whitey Ford/	
	Pants/100	10.00
24	Yogi Berra/Jsy/50	15.00
25	Satchel Paige/	
	CO Jsy/100	50.00

5	Bo Jackson/25	60.00
6	Bobby Doerr/100	20.00
7	Brooks	
	Robinson/100	50.00
8	Cal Ripken Jr./25	180.00
9	Carlton Fisk/25	30.00
10	Dale Murphy/100	20.00
11	Darryl	
	Strawberry/100	15.00
12	Don Mattingly/25	70.00
13	Duke Snider/100	20.00
15	Eddie Murray/10	
16	Frank Robinson/100	20.00
17	Frank Thomas/50	50.00
18	Gary Carter/100	15.00
19	George Brett/25	70.00
20	Harmon	
	Killebrew/100	40.00
23	Mark Grace/25	40.00
24	Mike Piazza/10	
25	Mike Schmidt/50	65.00
26	Orlando Cepeda/1	
27	Rafael Palmeiro/1	
28	Ralph Kiner/100	20.00
29	Reggie Jackson/25	50.00
30	Rickey Henderson/25	50.00
32	Ryne Sandberg/25	90.00
33	Sammy Sosa/10	
34	Scott Rolen/25	40.00
35	Stan Musial/50	65.00
39	Willie McCovey/25	30.00

Lumberjacks Autographs Bat

NM/M

Quantity produced listed
1	Al Kaline/100	40.00
2	Albert Pujols/5	
3	Andre Dawson/25	20.00
5	Bo Jackson/25	70.00
6	Bobby Doerr/50	25.00
7	Brooks Robinson/25	60.00
8	Cal Ripken Jr./25	200.00
9	Carlton Fisk/25	40.00
10	Dale Murphy/100	25.00
11	Darryl Strawberry/25	25.00
12	Don Mattingly/25	80.00
17	Frank Thomas/25	70.00
18	Gary Carter/50	20.00
19	George Brett/25	80.00
20	Harmon Killebrew/50	50.00
23	Mark Grace/17	50.00
25	Mike Schmidt/25	80.00
28	Ralph Kiner/100	25.00
29	Reggie Jackson/25	60.00
32	Ryne Sandberg/25	90.00
34	Scott Rolen/25	50.00
35	Stan Musial/50	75.00
39	Willie McCovey/25	40.00

Lumberjacks Autographs Jersey

NM/M

Quantity produced listed
1	Al Kaline Pants/100	40.00
3	Andre Dawson/50	20.00
5	Bo Jackson/25	70.00
6	Bobby Doerr/100	15.00
7	Brooks Robinson/25	75.00
8	Cal Ripken Jr./25	200.00
9	Carlton Fisk/50	30.00
10	Dale Murphy/100	25.00
11	Darryl Strawberry/	
	Pants/25	25.00
12	Don Mattingly/25	80.00
15	Eddie Murray/25	70.00
16	Frank Robinson/50	30.00
17	Frank Thomas/25	70.00
18	Gary Carter/25	20.00
19	George Brett/25	80.00
20	Harmon Killebrew/25	60.00
23	Mark Grace/17	50.00
25	Mike Schmidt/25	80.00
26	Orlando Cepeda/	
	Pants/25	15.00
27	Rafael Palmeiro/5	
29	Reggie Jackson/25	60.00
30	Rickey Henderson/10	
32	Ryne Sandberg/25	90.00
33	Sammy Sosa/25	
34	Scott Rolen/25	50.00

35	Stan Musial/50	75.00
39	Willie McCovey/25	40.00

Lumberjacks Barrel

Quantity produced listed
No Pricing
Production 1-5

Lumberjacks Bat

NM/M

Quantity produced listed
1	Al Kaline/100	15.00
2	Albert Pujols/100	15.00
3	Andre Dawson/25	15.00
4	Babe Ruth/100	125.00
5	Bo Jackson/50	15.00
6	Bobby Doerr/25	12.00
7	Brooks Robinson/25	20.00
8	Cal Ripken Jr./100	40.00
9	Carlton Fisk/100	10.00
10	Dale Murphy/50	15.00
11	Darryl Strawberry/25	15.00
12	Don Mattingly/100	20.00
14	Eddie Mathews/100	10.00
15	Eddie Murray/100	15.00
16	Frank Robinson/100	8.00
17	Frank Thomas/25	20.00
18	Gary Carter/100	10.00
19	George Brett/100	20.00
20	Harmon	
	Killebrew/100	15.00
21	Hideki Matsui/100	25.00
22	Lou Gehrig/100	100.00
23	Mark Grace/25	15.00
24	Mike Piazza/50	15.00
25	Mike Schmidt/100	15.00
26	Orlando Cepeda/25	8.00
27	Rafael Palmeiro/50	10.00
28	Ralph Kiner/100	8.00
29	Reggie Jackson/100	10.00
30	Rickey	
	Henderson/100	10.00
31	Roger Maris/100	25.00
32	Ryne Sandberg/100	15.00
33	Sammy Sosa/100	10.00
34	Scott Rolen/25	15.00
35	Stan Musial/100	25.00
36	Ted Williams/100	50.00
37	Thurman	
	Munson/100	20.00
38	Vladimir Guerrero/25	15.00
39	Willie McCovey/100	10.00
40	Willie Stargell/100	10.00
41	Roberto Clemente,	
	Stan Musial/50	85.00
42	Cal Ripken Jr.,	
	Ernie Banks/50	100.00
43	Babe Ruth,	
	Lou Gehrig/25	250.00
44	George Brett,	
	Mike Schmidt/50	50.00
46	Don Mattingly,	
	Roger Maris/50	40.00
47	Nomar Garciaparra,	
	Ted Williams/100	75.00
48	Johnny Bench,	
	Mike Piazza/25	35.00
49	Reggie Jackson,	
	Sammy Sosa/50	20.00
50	Mel Ott,	
	Willie McCovey/100	40.00

Lumberjacks Combos

NM/M

Quantity produced listed
1	Al Kaline/	
	Bat-Pants/100	20.00
2	Albert Pujols/	
	Bat-Jsy/100	20.00
3	Andre Dawson/	
	Bat-Jsy/50	15.00

4	Babe Ruth/Bat-Jsy/25	400.00
5	Bo Jackson/Bat-Jsy/50	20.00
6	Bobby Doerr/Bat-Jsy/50	12.00
7	Brooks Robinson/Bat-Jsy/25	40.00
8	Cal Ripken Jr./Bat-Jsy/100	50.00
9	Carlton Fisk/Bat-Jsy/50	15.00
10	Dale Murphy/Bat-Jsy/100	15.00
11	Darryl Strawberry/Bat-Pants/25	15.00
12	Don Mattingly/Bat-Jsy/100	25.00
14	Eddie Mathews/Bat-Jsy/50	15.00
15	Eddie Murray/Bat-Jsy/50	20.00
16	Frank Robinson/Bat-Jsy/100	15.00
17	Frank Thomas/Bat-Jsy/50	20.00
18	Gary Carter/Bat-Jsy/50	10.00
19	George Brett/Bat-Jsy/100	25.00
20	Harmon Killebrew/Bat-Jsy/50	30.00
21	Hideki Matsui/Bat-Jsy/100	30.00
22	Lou Gehrig/Bat-Jsy/25	250.00
23	Mark Grace/Bat-Jsy/17	30.00
24	Mike Piazza/Bat-Jsy/100	15.00
25	Mike Schmidt/Bat-Jsy/100	20.00
26	Orlando Cepeda/Bat-Pants/50	10.00
27	Rafael Palmeiro/Bat-Jsy/50	15.00
29	Reggie Jackson/Bat-Jsy/100	15.00
30	Rickey Henderson/Bat-Jsy/100	15.00
31	Roger Maris/Bat-Jsy/50	40.00
32	Ryne Sandberg/Bat-Jsy/25	25.00
33	Sammy Sosa/Bat-Jsy/100	15.00
34	Scott Rolen/Bat-Jsy/25	20.00
35	Stan Musial/Bat-Jsy/100	30.00
36	Ted Williams/Bat-Jsy/50	75.00
37	Thurman Munson/Bat-Jsy/100	25.00
38	Vladimir Guerrero/Bat-Jsy/50	15.00
39	Willie McCovey/Bat-Jsy/100	15.00
40	Willie Stargell/Bat-Jsy/50	12.00

Lumberjacks Jersey

NM/M

Quantity produced listed

1	Al Kaline/Pants/50	20.00
2	Albert Pujols/100	15.00
3	Andre Dawson/25	15.00
4	Babe Ruth/25	300.00
5	Bo Jackson/100	10.00
6	Bobby Doerr/100	5.00
7	Brooks Robinson/25	30.00
8	Cal Ripken Jr./100	40.00
9	Carlton Fisk/100	10.00
10	Dale Murphy/100	10.00
11	Darryl Strawberry/Pants/50	8.00
12	Don Mattingly/100	20.00
14	Eddie Mathews/100	10.00
15	Eddie Murray/100	20.00
16	Frank Robinson/100	10.00
17	Frank Thomas/100	10.00
18	Gary Carter/100	10.00
19	George Brett/100	20.00
20	Harmon Killebrew/25	30.00
21	Hideki Matsui/100	25.00
22	Lou Gehrig/25	180.00
23	Mark Grace/100	8.00
24	Mike Piazza/100	10.00
25	Mike Schmidt/100	15.00
26	Orlando Cepeda/Pants/100	5.00
27	Rafael Palmeiro/50	10.00
29	Reggie Jackson/100	10.00
30	Rickey Henderson/100	10.00
31	Roger Maris/100	25.00
32	Ryne Sandberg/100	15.00
33	Sammy Sosa/100	10.00
34	Scott Rolen/50	10.00
35	Stan Musial/50	30.00
36	Ted Williams/100	50.00
37	Thurman Munson/100	20.00
38	Vladimir Guerrero/50	10.00
39	Willie McCovey/100	10.00
40	Willie Stargell/100	8.00
41	Roberto Clemente, Stan Musial/50	120.00
42	Cal Ripken Jr., Ernie Banks/Pants/100	65.00
43	Babe Ruth, Lou Gehrig/25	400.00
44	George Brett, Mike Schmidt/Jkt/100	30.00
45	Frank Robinson, Jackie Robinson/25	30.00
46	Don Mattingly, Roger Maris/Pants/100	25.00
47	Johnny Bench, Mike Piazza/100	10.00
49	Reggie Jackson, Sammy Sosa/100	15.00
50	Mel Ott Pants, Willie McCovey/25	80.00

Matching Numbers

NM/M

Quantity produced listed

Prime: No Pricing

Production One Set

1	Bobby Doerr/Jsy, Pee Wee Reese/100	10.00
2	Lou Gehrig/Pants, Mel Ott/Jsy/50	160.00
3	Albert Pujols/Pants, George Brett/Jsy/100	30.00
4	Cal Ripken Jr./Jsy, Carl Yastrzemski/Jsy/100	50.00
5	Dwight Gooden/Jsy, Whitey Ford/Pants/50	15.00
6	Mark Grace/Jsy, Todd Helton/Jsy/25	25.00
7	Robin Yount/Jsy, Tony Gwynn/Jsy/50	40.00
8	Frank Robinson/Jsy, Mike Schmidt/Jsy/100	25.00
9	Roberto Clemente/Jsy, Sammy Sosa/Jsy/100	75.00
10	Roger Clemens/Jsy, Warren Spahn/Pant/100	25.00
11	Mark Prior/Jsy, Roger Clemens/Jsy/100	15.00
12	Don Mattingly/Jkt, Ryne Sandberg/Jsy/100	30.00
13	Billy Williams/Jsy, Wade Boggs/Jsy/100	10.00
14	Jim "Catfish" Hunter/Jsy, Juan Marichal/Jsy/50	10.00
15	Fergie Jenkins/Pants, Greg Maddux/Jsy/50	20.00
16	Kerry Wood/Pants, Nolan Ryan/Jsy/100	35.00
17	Rickey Henderson/Jsy, Roger Maris/Pants/100	40.00
18	Dontrelle Willis/Jsy, Mike Mussina/Jsy/50	15.00
19	Reggie Jackson/Jsy, Willie McCovey/Jsy/100	15.00
20	Bob Gibson/Jsy, Pedro Martinez/Jsy/50	15.00
21	Duke Snider/Jsy, Paul Molitor/Jsy/100	10.00
22	Johnny Bench/Jsy, Lou Boudreau/Jsy/100	15.00
23	Andre Dawson/Jsy, Chipper Jones/Jsy/100	15.00
24	Ernie Banks/Jsy, Boyer/Jsy/100	15.00
25	Manny Ramirez/Jsy, Rickey Henderson/Jsy/100	15.00
26	Carlton Fisk/Jsy, Scott Rolen/Jsy/100	15.00
27	Nolan Ryan/Jsy, Orlando Cepeda/Pnt/100	25.00
28	Roy Halladay/Jsy, Steve Carlton/Jsy/100	8.00
29	Eddie Mathews/Jsy, Tom Seaver/Jsy/100	15.00
30	Brandon Webb/Jsy, Orel Hershiser/Jsy/100	10.00

Moniker Bat

NM/M

Quanity produced listed

1	Adam Dunn/50	30.00
3	Albert Pujols/5	
5	Alfonso Soriano/25	50.00
6	Andruw Jones/25	40.00
7	Andy Pettitte/10	
8	Angel Berroa/25	15.00
9	Aramis Ramirez/25	25.00
10	Aubrey Huff/25	25.00
15	Ben Sheets/25	25.00
21	Carlos Beltran/50	40.00
24	Craig Biggio/25	40.00
27	Delmon Young/50	30.00
30	Dontrelle Willis/25	25.00
31	Edgar Renteria/25	25.00
34	Frank Thomas/25	70.00
35	Fred McGriff/50	30.00
36	Garret Anderson/50	20.00
37	Gary Sheffield/25	20.00
40	Hank Blalock/50	35.00
61	Jermaine Dye/25	25.00
71	Jorge Posada/25	50.00
84	Kerry Wood/25	50.00
88	Lance Berkman/25	40.00
100	Mark Mulder/50	20.00
101	Mark Prior/50	40.00
102	Mark Teixeira/25	40.00
106	Michael Young/50	15.00
107	Miguel Cabrera/40	25.00
109	Mike Lowell/25	25.00
122	Paul LoDuca/25	25.00
124	Preston Wilson/25	20.00
131	Rickie Weeks/25	25.00
137	Roy Oswalt/25	20.00
144	Sean Casey/50	20.00
145	Shannon Stewart/25	25.00
155	Torii Hunter/25	25.00
156	Trot Nixon/25	20.00
159	Victor Martinez/50	25.00
163	Alfonso Soriano/25	50.00
166	Gary Sheffield/25	35.00
194	Garret Anderson/50	40.00
198	Mark Prior/50	40.00
201	Andre Dawson/50	25.00
205	Bobby Doerr/25	25.00
207	Dale Murphy/100	25.00
208	Don Mattingly/50	75.00
209	Gary Carter/100	15.00
212	Lou Brock/25	30.00
214	Mark Grace/25	30.00
216	Mike Schmidt/75	75.00
217	Nolan Ryan/50	150.00
219	Paul Molitor/50	25.00
221	Rod Carew/50	35.00
223	Ryne Sandberg/25	80.00
224	Stan Musial/50	75.00
226	Tony Gwynn/50	50.00
230	Carlos Beltran/50	40.00
231	David Ortiz/50	60.00
232	David Ortiz/50	60.00
234	Carlos Lee/50	20.00
235	Travis Hafner/25	25.00
238	Edgar Martinez/50	40.00
240	Roy Oswalt/25	30.00
242	Carlos Beltran/50	45.00
243	Carlos Beltran/50	45.00
244	Miguel Cabrera/50	40.00
245	Scott Rolen/15	
246	Hank Blalock/50	35.00
247	Vernon Wells/50	20.00
248	Adam Dunn/50	25.00
249	Preston Wilson/25	25.00
250	Victor Martinez/25	25.00

Moniker Bronze

NM/M

Quanity produced listed

Silver: .5-1.5X
Production 1-50
No pricing 15 or less.
Platinum: No Pricing
Production One Set

1	Adam Dunn/50	30.00
3	Albert Pujols/25	180.00
5	Alfonso Soriano/100	30.00
6	Andruw Jones/50	30.00
8	Angel Berroa/25	15.00
11	Austin Kearns/50	20.00
18	Brandon Webb/21	15.00
21	Carlos Beltran/50	40.00
23	Chipper Jones/25	65.00
24	Craig Biggio/5	40.00
30	Dontrelle Willis/50	30.00
31	Edgar Renteria/25	25.00
34	Frank Thomas/50	60.00
36	Garret Anderson/20	20.00
37	Gary Sheffield/50	25.00
39	Greg Maddux/25	85.00
40	Hank Blalock/50	35.00
46	Jacque Jones/25	25.00
58	Jeff Bagwell/25	75.00
76	Jorge Posada/25	50.00
79	Juan Gonzalez/25	30.00
84	Kerry Wood/25	50.00
88	Lance Berkman/30	30.00
98	Marcus Giles/25	25.00
100	Mark Mulder/100	15.00
101	Mark Prior/50	40.00
102	Mark Teixeira/50	30.00
106	Michael Young/50	15.00
107	Miguel Cabrera/50	40.00
109	Mike Lowell/25	25.00
122	Paul LoDuca/25	25.00
131	Rickie Weeks/25	25.00
137	Roy Oswalt/10	20.00
140	Sammy Sosa/25	85.00
142	Scott Rolen/25	60.00
144	Sean Casey/25	25.00
145	Shannon Stewart/25	25.00
153	Todd Helton/25	40.00
155	Torii Hunter/50	20.00
156	Trot Nixon/25	25.00
158	Vernon Wells/25	25.00
163	Alfonso Soriano/100	30.00
166	Gary Sheffield/10	30.00
167	Greg Maddux/5	80.00
172	Juan Gonzalez/25	40.00
183	Scott Rolen/25	50.00
191	Albert Pujols/5	180.00
193	Chipper Jones/5	65.00
194	Garret Anderson/10	20.00
195	Jeff Bagwell/25	75.00
198	Mark Prior/50	40.00
199	Sammy Sosa/25	80.00
200	Todd Helton/25	30.00
201	Andre Dawson/100	15.00
203	Bob Feller/100	20.00
204	Bob Gibson/100	20.00
205	Bobby Doerr/100	15.00
206	Cal Ripken Jr./25	180.00
207	Dale Murphy/100	25.00
208	Don Mattingly/100	60.00
209	Gary Carter/100	15.00
210	George Brett/100	75.00
212	Lou Brock/100	20.00
214	Mark Grace/100	20.00
215	Maury Wills/100	15.00
216	Mike Schmidt/100	60.00
217	Nolan Ryan/100	120.00
218	Orel Hershiser/100	40.00
219	Paul Molitor/100	25.00
221	Rod Carew/100	25.00
223	Ryne Sandberg/100	50.00
224	Stan Musial/100	60.00
226	Tony Gwynn/100	40.00
230	Carlos Beltran/50	45.00
231	David Ortiz/50	60.00
232	David Ortiz/50	60.00
233	Carlos Zambrano/25	15.00
234	Carlos Lee/50	20.00
238	Edgar Martinez/50	40.00
240	Roy Oswalt/50	20.00
242	Carlos Beltran/50	40.00
243	Carlos Beltran/50	40.00
244	Miguel Cabrera/50	40.00
245	Scott Rolen/50	50.00
246	Hank Blalock/50	35.00
247	Vernon Wells/25	25.00
248	Adam Dunn/50	35.00

Moniker Gold

NM/M

Quanity produced listed

5	Alfonso Soriano/25	40.00
21	Carlos Beltran/25	50.00
100	Mark Mulder/25	25.00
163	Alfonso Soriano/25	40.00
201	Andre Dawson/25	20.00
203	Bob Feller/25	35.00
204	Bob Gibson/25	40.00

205	Bobby Doerr/25	25.00
207	Dale Murphy/25	40.00
208	Don Mattingly/25	90.00
209	Gary Carter/25	25.00
212	Lou Brock/25	30.00
214	Mark Grace/25	30.00
215	Maury Wills/25	25.00
216	Mike Schmidt/25	85.00
217	Nolan Ryan/25	150.00
219	Paul Molitor/25	40.00
221	Rod Carew/25	35.00
223	Ryne Sandberg/25	75.00
224	Stan Musial/25	100.00
226	Tony Gwynn/25	50.00

Moniker Jersey Number

NM/M

Quanity produced listed
Prime: No Pricing
Production One Set

1	Adam Dunn/50	30.00
5	Alfonso Soriano/50	40.00
6	Andruw Jones/50	40.00
8	Angel Berroa/Pants/25	15.00
9	Aramis Ramirez/25	25.00
10	Aubrey Huff/25	25.00
11	Austin Kearns/25	25.00
15	Ben Sheets/25	25.00
18	Brandon Webb/25	25.00
20	C.C. Sabathia/25	25.00
21	Carlos Beltran/50	40.00
23	Chipper Jones/25	65.00
24	Craig Biggio/25	40.00
30	Dontrelle Willis/25	30.00
32	Eric Chavez/50	20.00
34	Frank Thomas/25	70.00
35	Fred McGriff/25	40.00
36	Garret Anderson/50	35.00
40	Hank Blalock/50	35.00
46	Jacque Jones/25	25.00
63	Jim Edmonds/25	40.00
66	Jody Gerut/25	15.00
67	Johan Santana/25	40.00
71	Jorge Posada/25	50.00
74	Jose Vidro/25	15.00
84	Kerry Wood/25	50.00
88	Lance Berkman/25	40.00
90	Larry Walker/25	20.00
98	Marcus Giles/25	25.00
99	Mark Buehrle/25	25.00
100	Mark Mulder/75	15.00
101	Mark Prior/50	40.00
102	Mark Teixeira/25	40.00
105	Melvin Mora/25	25.00
107	Miguel Cabrera/50	30.00
109	Mike Lowell/25	25.00
115	Morgan Ensberg/25	15.00
122	Paul LoDuca/25	25.00
124	Preston Wilson/25	25.00
137	Roy Oswalt/25	25.00
140	Sammy Sosa/25	120.00
142	Scott Rolen/25	50.00
143	Sean Burroughs/25	25.00
145	Shannon Stewart/25	25.00
149	Steve Finley/25	25.00
153	Todd Helton/25	40.00
154	Tom Glavine/25	40.00
155	Torii Hunter/25	25.00
156	Trot Nixon/25	25.00
158	Vernon Wells/50	20.00
159	Victor Martinez/25	20.00
165	Alfonso Soriano/50	40.00
166	Gary Sheffield/25	40.00
172	Juan Gonzalez/25	40.00
183	Scott Rolen/50	40.00
185	Tom Glavine/25	40.00
193	Chipper Jones/25	65.00
194	Garret Anderson/50	20.00
199	Sammy Sosa/25	120.00
200	Todd Helton/25	40.00

201	Andre Dawson/50	20.00
204	Bob Gibson/25	40.00
205	Bobby Doerr/50	20.00
207	Dale Murphy/100	25.00
208	Don Mattingly/50	70.00
209	Gary Carter/100	15.00
216	Mike Schmidt/50	75.00
217	Nolan Ryan/100	120.00
218	Orel Hershiser/50	30.00
219	Paul Molitor/25	30.00
221	Rod Carew/50	30.00
223	Ryne Sandberg/25	100.00
224	Stan Musial/25	100.00
226	Tony Gwynn/100	40.00
228	Whitey Ford/Pants/25	40.00
229	Yogi Berra/25	75.00
230	Carlos Beltran/50	40.00
231	David Ortiz/50	60.00
232	David Ortiz/50	60.00
234	Carlos Lee/25	20.00
235	Travis Hafner/25	25.00
236	Brad Penny/25	15.00
237	Wade Miller/25	15.00
238	Edgar Martinez/50	40.00
239	Carl Crawford/25	25.00
240	Roy Oswalt/25	25.00
242	Carlos Beltran/50	45.00
243	Carlos Beltran/50	45.00
244	Miguel Cabrera/50	40.00
245	Scott Rolen/50	40.00
246	Hank Blalock/50	35.00
247	Vernon Wells/50	20.00
248	Adam Dunn/50	35.00
249	Preston Wilson/25	25.00
250	Victor Martinez/25	20.00

Moniker Jersey

NM/M

Quanity produced listed
Prime: No Pricing
Production One Set

1	Adam Dunn/50	30.00
5	Alfonso Soriano/50	40.00
8	Andruw Jones/50	40.00
8	Angel Berroa/Pants/25	15.00
9	Aramis Ramirez/25	25.00
10	Aubrey Huff/25	25.00
11	Austin Kearns/25	25.00
15	Ben Sheets/25	25.00
18	Brandon Webb/25	15.00
20	C.C. Sabathia/25	25.00
21	Carlos Beltran/50	40.00
23	Chipper Jones/25	65.00
24	Craig Biggio/25	40.00
30	Dontrelle Willis/25	30.00
32	Eric Chavez/50	20.00
34	Frank Thomas/25	70.00
35	Fred McGriff/25	40.00
36	Garret Anderson/50	20.00
40	Hank Blalock/50	35.00
46	Jacque Jones/25	25.00
63	Jim Edmonds/25	40.00
66	Jody Gerut/25	15.00
67	Johan Santana/25	40.00
71	Jorge Posada/25	50.00
74	Jose Vidro/25	15.00
84	Kerry Wood/25	50.00
88	Lance Berkman/25	40.00
89	Larry Bigbie/25	20.00
98	Marcus Giles/25	25.00
99	Mark Buehrle/25	25.00
100	Mark Mulder/75	15.00
101	Mark Prior/50	40.00
102	Mark Teixeira/25	40.00
105	Melvin Mora/25	25.00
107	Miguel Cabrera/38	40.00
109	Mike Lowell/25	25.00
115	Morgan Ensberg/25	15.00
122	Paul LoDuca/25	25.00
124	Preston Wilson/25	25.00
137	Roy Oswalt/25	25.00
142	Scott Rolen/50	50.00
143	Sean Burroughs/25	25.00
144	Sean Casey/25	25.00
145	Shannon Stewart/25	25.00
149	Steve Finley/25	25.00
153	Todd Helton/25	40.00
154	Tom Glavine/25	25.00
155	Torii Hunter/25	25.00
156	Trot Nixon/25	20.00
158	Vernon Wells/50	20.00
159	Victor Martinez/25	20.00
163	Alfonso Soriano/50	40.00
166	Gary Sheffield/25	40.00
172	Juan Gonzalez/25	40.00
183	Scott Rolen/50	40.00
185	Tom Glavine/25	40.00
193	Chipper Jones/25	65.00
194	Garret Anderson/25	20.00
200	Todd Helton/25	40.00
201	Andre Dawson/50	20.00
204	Bob Gibson/50	30.00

205	Bobby Doerr/50	20.00
207	Dale Murphy/100	25.00
208	Don Mattingly/50	70.00
209	Gary Carter/100	15.00
216	Mike Schmidt/50	75.00
217	Nolan Ryan/100	120.00
218	Orel Hershiser/50	30.00
219	Paul Molitor/50	30.00
221	Rod Carew/50	30.00
223	Ryne Sandberg/25	100.00
224	Stan Musial/25	100.00
226	Tony Gwynn/100	40.00
228	Whitey Ford/Pants/25	40.00
229	Yogi Berra/25	75.00
230	Carlos Beltran/50	40.00
231	David Ortiz/50	60.00
232	David Ortiz/50	60.00
234	Carlos Lee/25	20.00
235	Travis Hafner/25	25.00
236	Brad Penny/25	15.00
237	Wade Miller/25	15.00
238	Edgar Martinez/50	40.00
239	Carl Crawford/25	25.00
240	Roy Oswalt/25	25.00
242	Carlos Beltran/50	45.00
243	Carlos Beltran/50	45.00
244	Miguel Cabrera/50	40.00
245	Scott Rolen/50	40.00
246	Hank Blalock/50	35.00
247	Vernon Wells/50	20.00
248	Adam Dunn/50	35.00
249	Preston Wilson/25	25.00

Player Threads Double

NM/M

Quantity produced listed

1	Mike Piazza/100	15.00
2	Roger Clemens/100	20.00
3	Nolan Ryan/100	30.00
4	Reggie Jackson/100	15.00
5	Wade Boggs/100	10.00
6	Steve Carlton/100	10.00
7	Ivan Rodriguez/100	10.00
8	Pedro Martinez/100	10.00
9	Rickey Henderson/50	25.00
10	Rickey Henderson/100	20.00
11	Randy Johnson/50	20.00
12	Curt Schilling/100	10.00
13	Roger Maris/100	40.00
14	Sammy Sosa/100	15.00
15	Gary Carter/100	8.00
16	Gary Sheffield/50	10.00
17	Eddie Murray/50	20.00
18	Hideo Nomo/50	15.00
19	Rafael Palmeiro/100	10.00
20	Andre Dawson/50	10.00

Player Threads Jersey Number

NM/M

Quantity produced listed
Prime: No Pricing
Production One Set

1	Mike Piazza/100	10.00
3	Nolan Ryan Jkt/100	20.00
4	Reggie Jackson/100	10.00
5	Wade Boggs/50	10.00
6	Steve Carlton/Pants/100	5.00
7	Ivan Rodriguez/25	15.00
8	Pedro Martinez/25	12.00
10	Rickey Henderson/Pants/100	10.00
11	Randy Johnson/50	10.00
12	Curt Schilling/25	20.00
13	Roger Maris/50	50.00
14	Sammy Sosa/100	10.00
15	Gary Carter Pants/50	8.00
16	Gary Sheffield/50	10.00
17	Eddie Murray/50	15.00
18	Hideo Nomo/50	10.00
19	Rafael Palmeiro/50	10.00
20	Andre Dawson/50	8.00

Player Threads Triple

NM/M

Quantity produced listed

1	Mike Piazza/50	30.00

2	Roger Clemens/25	50.00
3	Nolan Ryan/50	70.00
4	Reggie Jackson/25	40.00
5	Wade Boggs/25	30.00
6	Steve Carlton/25	25.00
7	Ivan Rodriguez/25	30.00
8	Pedro Martinez/25	30.00
9	Rickey Henderson/10	
10	Rickey Henderson/50	50.00
12	Curt Schilling/25	30.00
13	Roger Maris/25	120.00
14	Sammy Sosa/25	40.00
15	Gary Carter/25	20.00
17	Eddie Murray/25	40.00
18	Hideo Nomo/25	30.00
19	Rafael Palmeiro/25	20.00
20	Andre Dawson/25	20.00

Team Threads Jersey Number

NM/M

Common Card: 15.00
Production 100 Sets
Prime: No Pricing
Production One Set

1	Stan Musial, Albert Pujols	40.00
2	Cal Ripken Jr./Jkt, Mike Mussina	40.00
3	Carlton Fisk, Roger Clemens	25.00
4	Dale Murphy, Chipper Jones	15.00
5	Tony Gwynn, Dave Winfield	25.00
6	Don Mattingly, Hideki Matsui	50.00
7	Lou Boudreau, Early Wynn	15.00
8	Ernie Banks, Sammy Sosa	30.00
9	Nolan Ryan/Jkt, Jeff Bagwell	50.00
10	Mike Schmidt, Jim Thome	25.00

Team Trademarks

NM/M

Common Player: 5.00
Production 100 Sets
Gold: No Pricing
Production 10 Sets

1	Bob Gibson	8.00
2	Cal Ripken Jr.	30.00
3	Carl Yastrzemski	10.00
4	Dale Murphy	8.00
5	Gary Carter	5.00
6	George Brett	15.00
7	Tom Seaver	8.00
8	Kerry Wood	8.00
9	Lou Brock	5.00
10	Luis Aparicio	5.00
11	Mike Piazza	10.00
12	Nolan Ryan	15.00
13	Nolan Ryan	15.00
14	Randy Johnson	8.00
15	Reggie Jackson	10.00
16	Ricky Henderson	8.00
17	Robin Yount	10.00
18	Rod Carew	8.00
19	Ryne Sandberg	15.00
20	Steve Carlton	5.00
21	Steve Garvey	5.00
22	Johnny Bench	10.00
23	Tony Gwynn	10.00
24	Whitey Ford	8.00
25	Will Clark	8.00

Team Trademarks Autographs

NM/M

Quantity produced listed

1	Bob Gibson/100	20.00
2	Cal Ripken Jr./25	150.00
3	Carl Yastrzemski/25	60.00
4	Dale Murphy/100	20.00
5	Gary Carter/25	15.00
6	George Brett/25	65.00
7	Tom Seaver/25	50.00
8	Kerry Wood/25	40.00
9	Lou Brock/100	20.00
10	Luis Aparicio/100	15.00
12	Nolan Ryan/Astros/25	100.00
13	Nolan Ryan Rgr/25	100.00
15	Reggie Jackson/25	50.00
17	Robin Yount/50	50.00
18	Rod Carew/50	25.00
19	Ryne Sandberg/25	65.00
20	Steve Carlton/100	20.00
21	Steve Garvey/50	15.00

22	Johnny Bench/25	50.00
23	Tony Gwynn/100	30.00
24	Whitey Ford/25	30.00
25	Will Clark/34	50.00

Team Trademarks Autographs Jersey Numbers

NM/M
Quantity produced listed
Prime: No Pricing
Production One Set

1	Bob Gibson/100	25.00
2	Cal Ripken Jr./Pants/25	200.00
3	Carl Yastrzemski/25	75.00
4	Dale Murphy/100	25.00
5	Gary Carter/100	15.00
6	George Brett/25	80.00
7	Tom Seaver/25	65.00
8	Kerry Wood/Pants/25	50.00
9	Lou Brock/100	25.00
10	Luis Aparicio/Pants/25	15.00
12	Nolan Ryan/Astros/25	
13	Nolan Ryan Rgr/25	120.00
15	Reggie Jackson/Pants/25	60.00
17	Robin Yount/50	75.00
18	Rod Carew Jkt/50	30.00
19	Ryne Sandberg/50	65.00
20	Steve Carlton/25	40.00
22	Johnny Bench/50	50.00
23	Tony Gwynn/50	50.00
24	Whitey Ford/50	30.00
25	Will Clark/84	40.00

Team Trademarks Jersey Number

NM/M
Quantity produced listed
Prime: No Pricing
Production One Set

1	Bob Gibson/100	10.00
2	Cal Ripken Jr./Pants/100	40.00
3	Carl Yastrzemski/100	15.00
4	Dale Murphy/100	10.00
5	Gary Carter/100	5.00
6	George Brett/100	15.00
7	Tom Seaver/100	10.00
8	Kerry Wood/Pants/50	10.00
9	Lou Brock/100	10.00
10	Luis Aparicio/Pants/100	5.00
11	Mike Piazza/50	15.00
12	Nolan Ryan/Astros/100	20.00
13	Nolan Ryan/Rgr/100	20.00
14	Randy Johnson/100	10.00
15	Reggie Jackson/Pants/100	8.00
16	Ricky Henderson/100	10.00
17	Robin Yount/100	10.00
18	Rod Carew/Jkt/100	8.00
19	Ryne Sandberg/100	15.00
20	Steve Carlton/100	5.00
22	Johnny Bench/100	10.00
23	Tony Gwynn/100	10.00
24	Whitey Ford/100	10.00
25	Will Clark/50	15.00

Threads Jersey

NM/M
Quanity produced listed
Prime: No Pricing
Production One Set
Button: No Pricing
Production 1-6

1	Adam Dunn/25	15.00
3	Albert Pujols/50	
5	Alfonso Soriano/25	15.00
6	Andruw Jones/25	10.00
11	Austin Kearns/25	10.00
12	Barry Larkin/25	15.00
13	Barry Zito/25	8.00
16	Bernie Williams/50	8.00
21	Carlos Beltran/25	15.00
22	Carlos Delgado/25	8.00
23	Chipper Jones/50	10.00
24	Craig Biggio/25	15.00
25	Curt Schilling/25	
30	Dontrelle Willis/25	8.00
31	Edgar Renteria/25	10.00
32	Eric Chavez/25	8.00
34	Frank Thomas/25	20.00
36	Garret Anderson/25	10.00
39	Greg Maddux/50	15.00
40	Hank Blalock/25	10.00
41	Hideki Matsui/25	40.00
42	Hideo Nomo/50	10.00
44	Ivan Rodriguez/25	15.00
50	Jason Giambi/50	5.00
55	Javy Lopez/25	10.00
58	Jeff Bagwell/50	10.00
59	Jeff Kent/50	5.00
63	Jim Edmonds/50	10.00
64	Jim Thome/50	15.00
69	John Smoltz/25	15.00
71	Jorge Posada/25	15.00
75	Josh Beckett/25	10.00
76	Juan Gonzalez/25	15.00
84	Kerry Wood/50	12.00
88	Lance Berkman/50	5.00
90	Larry Walker/25	15.00
93	Luis Gonzalez/25	8.00
96	Magglio Ordonez/25	8.00
97	Manny Ramirez/50	15.00
100	Mark Mulder/25	10.00
101	Mark Prior/50	8.00
107	Miguel Cabrera/25	15.00
108	Miguel Tejada/25	10.00
110	Mike Mussina/50	10.00
111	Mike Piazza/50	15.00
112	Mike Sweeney/25	10.00
123	Pedro J. Martinez/50	12.00
126	Rafael Palmeiro/25	10.00
127	Randy Johnson/25	20.00
137	Roy Oswalt/25	10.00
140	Sammy Sosa/50	15.00
142	Scott Rolen/25	20.00
146	Shawn Green/25	8.00
150	Tim Hudson/25	10.00
153	Todd Helton/50	10.00
154	Tom Glavine/25	15.00
155	Torii Hunter/25	10.00
157	Troy Glaus/25	10.00
158	Vernon Wells/25	8.00
161	Vladimir Guerrero/25	10.00
162	Alex Rodriguez/100	10.00
163	Alfonso Soriano/25	10.00
164	Andy Pettitte/25	15.00
165	Curt Schilling/25	10.00
166	Gary Sheffield/25	15.00
167	Greg Maddux/25	15.00
168	Hideo Nomo/25	20.00
169	Ivan Rodriguez/50	12.00
170	Jason Giambi/25	8.00
172	Juan Gonzalez/25	15.00
174	Kevin Brown/25	10.00
176	Miguel Tejada/25	10.00
177	Mike Mussina/50	10.00
178	Mike Piazza/25	25.00
179	Pedro Martinez/25	20.00
180	Rafael Palmeiro/25	15.00
181	Randy Johnson/50	10.00
182	Roger Clemens/100	10.00
183	Scott Rolen/25	20.00
184	Shawn Green/25	15.00
185	Tom Glavine/25	15.00
186	Vladimir Guerrero/25	10.00
187	Alex Rodriguez/100	10.00
189	Randy Johnson/50	10.00
190	Roger Clemens/100	10.00
191	Albert Pujols/50	20.00
192	Barry Zito/50	10.00
193	Chipper Jones/50	10.00
194	Garret Anderson/25	10.00
195	Jeff Bagwell/50	10.00
196	Josh Beckett/50	10.00
197	Magglio Ordonez/50	8.00
198	Mark Prior/50	8.00
199	Sammy Sosa/50	15.00
200	Todd Helton/50	10.00
201	Andre Dawson/50	5.00
202	Babe Ruth/25	350.00
203	Bob Feller/25	20.00
205	Bobby Doerr/50	8.00
206	Cal Ripken Jr./100	40.00
207	Dale Murphy/100	10.00
208	Don Mattingly/75	25.00
209	Gary Carter/50	8.00
210	George Brett/100	15.00
211	Jackie Robinson/50	40.00
212	Lou Brock/25	20.00
213	Lou Gehrig/25	140.00
214	Mark Grace/25	15.00
215	Maury Wills/50	5.00
216	Mike Schmidt/100	15.00
217	Nolan Ryan/100	20.00
218	Orel Hershiser/25	15.00
219	Paul Molitor/50	10.00
220	Roberto Clemente/25	80.00
221	Rod Carew/100	10.00
222	Roy Campanella/Pants/50	15.00
223	Ryne Sandberg/50	25.00
224	Stan Musial/25	40.00
225	Ted Williams/25	75.00
226	Tony Gwynn/100	10.00
227	Ty Cobb Pants/100	75.00
228	Whitey Ford/Pants/25	20.00
229	Yogi Berra/25	25.00
230	Carlos Beltran/25	15.00
231	David Ortiz/25	20.00
232	David Ortiz/25	20.00
238	Edgar Martinez/25	10.00
240	Roy Oswalt/25	8.00
242	Carlos Beltran/25	15.00
243	Carlos Beltran/25	15.00
244	Miguel Cabrera/25	15.00
245	Scott Rolen/25	20.00
246	Hank Blalock/25	12.00
247	Vernon Wells/25	10.00
248	Adam Dunn/25	15.00

Threads Jersey Number

NM/M
Quanity produced listed
Prime: No Pricing
Production One Set
MLB Logo: No Pricing
Production One Set

1	Adam Dunn/25	15.00
3	Albert Pujols/50	20.00
5	Alfonso Soriano/25	15.00
6	Andruw Jones/25	10.00
11	Austin Kearns/25	8.00
12	Barry Larkin/25	15.00
13	Barry Zito/25	8.00
16	Bernie Williams/25	8.00
21	Carlos Beltran/25	15.00
22	Carlos Delgado/25	8.00
23	Chipper Jones/25	10.00
24	Craig Biggio/25	10.00
25	Curt Schilling/25	20.00
30	Dontrelle Willis/25	8.00
31	Edgar Renteria/25	10.00
32	Eric Chavez/25	8.00
34	Frank Thomas/25	15.00
36	Garret Anderson/25	10.00
39	Greg Maddux/25	15.00
40	Hank Blalock/25	12.00
41	Hideki Matsui/25	40.00
42	Hideo Nomo/50	10.00
44	Ivan Rodriguez/25	20.00
50	Jason Giambi/50	5.00
55	Javy Lopez/25	8.00
58	Jeff Bagwell/50	10.00
59	Jeff Kent/25	10.00
63	Jim Edmonds/25	10.00
64	Jim Thome/50	15.00
69	John Smoltz/25	15.00
71	Jorge Posada/25	15.00
75	Josh Beckett/25	10.00
76	Juan Gonzalez/25	15.00
84	Kerry Wood/50	12.00
88	Lance Berkman/50	5.00
90	Larry Walker/25	15.00
93	Luis Gonzalez/25	8.00
96	Magglio Ordonez/25	8.00
97	Manny Ramirez/50	12.00
100	Mark Mulder/25	10.00
107	Miguel Cabrera/25	15.00
108	Miguel Tejada/25	10.00
110	Mike Mussina/25	10.00
111	Mike Piazza/50	10.00
112	Mike Sweeney/25	10.00
123	Pedro J. Martinez/50	12.00
126	Rafael Palmeiro/25	10.00
127	Randy Johnson/25	20.00
137	Roy Oswalt/25	10.00
140	Sammy Sosa/25	15.00
142	Scott Rolen/25	20.00
146	Shawn Green/25	8.00
150	Tim Hudson/25	10.00
153	Todd Helton/25	10.00
154	Tom Glavine/25	15.00
155	Torii Hunter/25	10.00
157	Troy Glaus/25	8.00
158	Vernon Wells/25	10.00
161	Vladimir Guerrero/25	20.00
162	Alex Rodriguez/100	10.00
163	Alfonso Soriano/50	10.00
164	Andy Pettitte/25	15.00
165	Curt Schilling/25	10.00
166	Gary Sheffield/25	10.00
167	Greg Maddux/25	15.00
168	Hideo Nomo/25	20.00
169	Ivan Rodriguez/25	12.00
170	Jason Giambi/25	8.00
172	Juan Gonzalez/25	12.00
174	Kevin Brown/25	8.00
176	Miguel Tejada/25	10.00
177	Mike Mussina/50	10.00
178	Mike Piazza/25	25.00
179	Pedro Martinez/25	20.00
180	Rafael Palmeiro/25	15.00
181	Randy Johnson/50	10.00
182	Roger Clemens/100	10.00
183	Scott Rolen/25	20.00
184	Shawn Green/25	8.00
185	Tom Glavine/25	10.00
186	Vladimir Guerrero/25	20.00
187	Alex Rodriguez/100	10.00
189	Randy Johnson/25	10.00
190	Roger Clemens/100	10.00
191	Albert Pujols/50	20.00
192	Barry Zito/25	8.00
193	Chipper Jones/50	10.00
194	Garret Anderson/25	10.00
195	Jeff Bagwell/50	10.00
196	Josh Beckett/25	10.00
197	Magglio Ordonez/25	8.00
198	Mark Prior/25	8.00
199	Sammy Sosa/50	15.00
200	Todd Helton/50	10.00
201	Andre Dawson/50	8.00
202	Babe Ruth/25	300.00
203	Bob Feller/25	20.00
205	Bobby Doerr/50	8.00
206	Cal Ripken Jr./100	40.00
207	Dale Murphy/100	10.00
208	Don Mattingly/75	25.00
209	Gary Carter/50	8.00
210	George Brett/100	15.00
211	Jackie Robinson/100	40.00
212	Lou Brock/25	20.00
213	Lou Gehrig/25	150.00
214	Mark Grace/25	15.00
215	Maury Wills/50	8.00
216	Mike Schmidt/100	15.00
217	Nolan Ryan/100	20.00
218	Orel Hershiser/25	15.00
219	Paul Molitor/50	10.00
220	Roberto Clemente/25	80.00
221	Rod Carew/100	10.00
222	Roy Campanella/Pants/50	15.00
223	Ryne Sandberg/50	25.00
224	Stan Musial/25	40.00
225	Ted Williams/25	75.00
226	Tony Gwynn/100	10.00
227	Ty Cobb/Pants/100	60.00
228	Whitey Ford/Pants/25	20.00
229	Yogi Berra/25	25.00
230	Carlos Beltran/25	15.00
231	David Ortiz/25	20.00
232	David Ortiz/25	20.00
238	Edgar Martinez/25	10.00
240	Roy Oswalt H/25	15.00
242	Carlos Beltran/25	15.00
243	Carlos Beltran/25	15.00
244	Miguel Cabrera/25	15.00
245	Scott Rolen/25	20.00
246	Hank Blalock/25	10.00
247	Vernon Wells/25	10.00
248	Adam Dunn/25	15.00

Timber

NM/M
Quanity produced listed

1	Adam Dunn/25	15.00
4	Alex Rodriguez/100	15.00
5	Alfonso Soriano/25	15.00
6	Andruw Jones/25	10.00
7	Andy Pettitte/25	15.00
11	Austin Kearns/25	8.00
12	Barry Larkin/25	15.00
13	Barry Zito/25	8.00
16	Bernie Williams/25	12.00
21	Carlos Beltran/25	15.00
22	Carlos Delgado/25	10.00
23	Chipper Jones/25	20.00
24	Craig Biggio/25	12.00
25	Curt Schilling/25	20.00
30	Dontrelle Willis/25	8.00
32	Eric Chavez/25	8.00
34	Frank Thomas/25	20.00
35	Fred McGriff/25	12.00
36	Garret Anderson/25	8.00
37	Gary Sheffield/25	10.00
39	Greg Maddux/25	25.00
40	Hank Blalock/25	10.00
41	Hideki Matsui/25	60.00
42	Hideo Nomo/25	20.00
44	Ivan Rodriguez/25	20.00

50	Jason Giambi/25	8.00
55	Javy Lopez/25	8.00
58	Jeff Bagwell/25	15.00
59	Jeff Kent/25	8.00
63	Jim Edmonds/25	10.00
64	Jim Thome/25	20.00
71	Jorge Posada/25	15.00
75	Josh Beckett/25	10.00
76	Juan Gonzalez/25	15.00
84	Kerry Wood/25	20.00
85	Kevin Brown/25	8.00
88	Lance Berkman/25	8.00
90	Larry Walker/25	10.00
93	Luis Gonzalez/25	8.00
96	Magglio Ordonez/25	8.00
97	Manny Ramirez/25	15.00
100	Mark Mulder/25	8.00
101	Mark Prior/25	15.00
102	Mark Teixeira/25	10.00
106	Michael Young/25	8.00
107	Miguel Cabrera/25	15.00
108	Miguel Tejada/25	10.00
109	Mike Lowell/25	8.00
110	Mike Mussina/25	15.00
111	Mike Piazza/25	25.00
112	Mike Sweeney/25	8.00
116	Nick Johnson/25	8.00
117	Nomar Garciaparra/25	20.00
122	Paul LoDuca/25	8.00
123	Pedro J. Martinez/25	20.00
126	Rafael Palmeiro/25	15.00
127	Randy Johnson/25	20.00
130	Richie Sexson/25	10.00
134	Rocco Baldelli/25	8.00
135	Roger Clemens/25	25.00
137	Roy Oswalt/25	8.00
140	Sammy Sosa/50	15.00
142	Scott Rolen/25	20.00
146	Shawn Green/25	8.00
150	Tim Hudson/25	8.00
153	Todd Helton/25	15.00
154	Tom Glavine/25	15.00
155	Torii Hunter/25	8.00
156	Trot Nixon/25	10.00
157	Troy Glaus/25	8.00
158	Vernon Wells/25	8.00
161	Vladimir Guerrero/25	20.00
162	Alex Rodriguez/100	10.00
163	Alfonso Soriano/25	15.00
164	Andy Pettitte/25	15.00
165	Curt Schilling/25	8.00
166	Gary Sheffield/25	10.00
167	Greg Maddux/25	25.00
168	Hideo Nomo/25	15.00
169	Ivan Rodriguez/25	15.00
170	Jason Giambi/25	8.00
171	Jim Thome/25	15.00
172	Juan Gonzalez/25	10.00
174	Kevin Brown/25	8.00
175	Manny Ramirez/25	15.00
176	Miguel Tejada/25	15.00
177	Mike Mussina/25	15.00
178	Mike Piazza/25	25.00
179	Pedro Martinez/25	20.00
180	Rafael Palmeiro/25	15.00
181	Randy Johnson/25	25.00
182	Roger Clemens/25	25.00
183	Scott Rolen/25	20.00
184	Shawn Green/25	8.00
185	Tom Glavine/25	15.00
186	Vladimir Guerrero/25	20.00
187	Alex Rodriguez/100	10.00
188	Mike Piazza/25	25.00
189	Randy Johnson/25	20.00
190	Roger Clemens/25	25.00
191	Albert Pujols/25	20.00
192	Barry Zito/25	8.00
193	Chipper Jones/25	20.00
194	Garret Anderson/25	8.00
195	Jeff Bagwell/25	15.00
196	Josh Beckett/25	8.00
197	Magglio Ordonez/25	8.00
198	Mark Prior/25	15.00
199	Sammy Sosa/50	15.00
200	Todd Helton/25	15.00
201	Andre Dawson/50	8.00
202	Babe Ruth/100	120.00
206	Cal Ripken Jr./100	40.00
207	Dale Murphy/50	15.00
208	Don Mattingly/50	25.00
209	Gary Carter/25	10.00
210	George Brett/50	25.00
212	Lou Brock/25	15.00
213	Lou Gehrig/100	100.00
214	Mark Grace/25	15.00
216	Mike Schmidt/50	25.00
217	Nolan Ryan/50	30.00
219	Paul Molitor/50	10.00
220	Roberto Clemente/100	75.00
221	Rod Carew/25	25.00
222	Roy Campanella/100	10.00
223	Ryne Sandberg/25	25.00
224	Stan Musial/100	20.00
225	Ted Williams/100	50.00
226	Tony Gwynn/50	20.00
227	Ty Cobb/100	75.00
229	Yogi Berra/100	10.00
230	Carlos Beltran/25	15.00
231	David Ortiz/25	20.00
232	David Ortiz/25	20.00
238	Edgar Martinez/25	15.00
240	Roy Oswalt/25	10.00
242	Carlos Beltran/25	15.00
243	Carlos Beltran/25	15.00
244	Miguel Cabrera/25	15.00
245	Scott Rolen/25	20.00
246	Hank Blalock/25	10.00
248	Adam Dunn/25	15.00

TNT

NM/M

Quanity produced listed
Prime: No Pricing
Production One Set

1	Adam Dunn/ Bat-Jsy/50	10.00
3	Albert Pujols/ Bat-Jsy/100	15.00
5	Alfonso Soriano/ Bat-Jsy/50	10.00
6	Andruw Jones/ Bat-Jsy/50	8.00
11	Austin Kearns/ Bat-Jsy/50	5.00
12	Barry Larkin/ Bat-Jsy/50	20.00
13	Barry Zito/Bat-Jsy/50	5.00
16	Bernie Williams/ Bat-Jsy/50	10.00
21	Carlos Beltran/ Bat-Jsy/50	10.00
22	Carlos Delgado/ Bat-Jsy/50	5.00
23	Chipper Jones/ Bat-Jsy/50	15.00
24	Craig Biggio/ Bat-Jsy/50	8.00
25	Curt Schilling/ Bat-Jsy/50	25.00
32	Eric Chavez/ Bat-Jsy/50	10.00
34	Frank Thomas/ Bat-Jsy/50	20.00
36	Garret Anderson/ Bat-Jsy/50	10.00
39	Greg Maddux/ Bat-Jsy/50	20.00
40	Hank Blalock/ Bat-Jsy/50	8.00
41	Hideki Matsui/ Bat-Jsy/50	50.00
42	Hideo Nomo/ Bat-Jsy/50	20.00
44	Ivan Rodriguez/ Bat-Jsy/25	20.00
50	Jason Giambi/ Bat-Jsy/50	8.00
55	Javy Lopez/ Bat-Jsy/50	10.00
58	Jeff Bagwell/ Bat-Jsy/50	10.00
59	Jeff Kent/Bat-Jsy/25	10.00
63	Jim Edmonds/ Bat-Jsy/50	10.00
64	Jim Thome/ Bat-Jsy/50	15.00
71	Jorge Posada/ Bat-Jsy/50	20.00
75	Josh Beckett/ Bat-Jsy/50	10.00
76	Juan Gonzalez/ Bat-Jsy/50	20.00
84	Kerry Wood/ Bat-Jsy/50	15.00
88	Lance Berkman/ Bat-Jsy/50	5.00
90	Larry Walker/ Bat-Jsy/50	20.00
93	Luis Gonzalez/ Bat-Jsy/25	10.00
96	Magglio Ordonez/ Bat-Jsy/25	10.00
97	Manny Ramirez/ Bat-Jsy/50	15.00
100	Mark Mulder/ Bat-Jsy/50	10.00
101	Mark Prior/ Bat-Jsy/50	10.00
102	Mark Teixeira/ Bat-Jsy/50	10.00
107	Miguel Cabrera/ Bat-Jsy/50	20.00
108	Miguel Tejada/ Bat-Jsy/50	10.00
109	Mike Lowell/ Bat-Jsy/50	10.00
110	Mike Mussina/ Bat-Jsy/50	10.00
111	Mike Piazza/ Bat-Jsy/50	20.00
112	Mike Sweeney/ Bat-Jsy/25	10.00
123	Pedro J. Martinez/ Bat-Jsy/50	15.00
126	Rafael Palmeiro/ Bat-Jsy/25	20.00
127	Randy Johnson/ Bat-Jsy/50	15.00
137	Roy Oswalt/ Bat-Jsy/50	10.00
140	Sammy Sosa/ Bat-Jsy/50	20.00
142	Scott Rolen/ Bat-Jsy/25	25.00
146	Shawn Green/ Bat-Jsy/50	10.00
150	Tim Hudson/ Bat-Jsy/50	10.00
153	Todd Helton/ Bat-Jsy/50	10.00
154	Tom Glavine/ Bat-Jsy/50	20.00
155	Torii Hunter/ Bat-Jsy/50	10.00
157	Troy Glaus/ Bat-Jsy/50	10.00
158	Vernon Wells/ Bat-Jsy/50	10.00
161	Vladimir Guerrero/ Bat-Jsy/25	25.00
162	Alex Rodriguez/ Bat-Jsy/100	10.00
163	Alfonso Soriano/ Bat-Jsy/50	10.00
164	Andy Pettitte/ Bat-Jsy/50	20.00
165	Curt Schilling/ Bat-Jsy/50	10.00
166	Gary Sheffield/ Bat-Jsy/50	10.00
167	Greg Maddux/ Bat-Jsy/50	20.00
168	Hideo Nomo/ Bat-Jsy/50	20.00
169	Ivan Rodriguez/ Bat-Jsy/50	15.00
170	Jason Giambi/ Bat-Jsy/50	10.00
172	Juan Gonzalez/ Bat-Jsy/50	15.00
174	Kevin Brown/ Bat-Jsy/50	10.00
176	Miguel Tejada/ Bat-Jsy/50	10.00
177	Mike Mussina/ Bat-Jsy/50	10.00
178	Mike Piazza/ Bat-Jsy/50	20.00
179	Pedro Martinez/ Bat-Jsy/50	15.00
180	Rafael Palmeiro/ Bat-Jsy/50	10.00
181	Randy Johnson/ Bat-Jsy/50	15.00
182	Roger Clemens/ Bat-Jsy/100	10.00
183	Scott Rolen/ Bat-Jsy/25	25.00
184	Shawn Green/ Bat-Jsy/50	10.00
185	Tom Glavine/ Bat-Jsy/50	20.00
186	Vladimir Guerrero/ Bat-Jsy/25	25.00
187	Alex Rodriguez/ Bat-Jsy/100	10.00
189	Randy Johnson/ Bat-Jsy/50	15.00
190	Roger Clemens/ Bat-Jsy/100	10.00
191	Albert Pujols/ Bat-Jsy/25	25.00
192	Barry Zito/Bat-Jsy/25	10.00
193	Chipper Jones/ Bat-Jsy/25	15.00
194	Garret Anderson/ Bat-Jsy/25	10.00
195	Jeff Bagwell/ Bat-Jsy/25	10.00
196	Josh Beckett/ Bat-Jsy/25	10.00
197	Magglio Ordonez/ Bat-Jsy/25	10.00
198	Mark Prior/Bat-Jsy/50	10.00
199	Sammy Sosa/ Bat-Jsy/25	15.00
200	Todd Helton/ Bat-Jsy/25	10.00
201	Andre Dawson/ Bat-Jsy/50	8.00
202	Babe Ruth/ Bat-Jsy/25	425.00
206	Cal Ripken Jr./ Bat-Jsy/100	60.00
207	Dale Murphy/ Bat-Jsy/100	10.00
208	Don Mattingly/ Bat-Jsy/100	20.00
209	Gary Carter/ Bat-Jsy/50	10.00
210	George Brett/ Bat-Jsy/100	10.00
212	Lou Brock/Bat-Jsy/25	25.00
213	Lou Gehrig/ Bat-Jsy/25	250.00
214	Mark Grace/ Bat-Jsy/25	20.00
216	Mike Schmidt/ Bat-Jsy/50	30.00
217	Nolan Ryan/ Bat-Jsy/50	25.00
219	Paul Molitor/ Bat-Jsy/25	20.00
221	Rod Carew/ Bat-Jsy/50	15.00
222	Roy Campanella/ Bat-Pants/50	20.00
223	Ryne Sandberg/ Bat-Jsy/50	30.00
224	Stan Musial/ Bat-Jsy/50	50.00
225	Ted Williams/ Bat-Jsy/50	100.00
226	Tony Gwynn/ Bat-Jsy/100	15.00
227	Ty Cobb/ Bat-Pants/50	120.00
230	Carlos Beltran/ Bat-Jsy/25	20.00
231	David Ortiz/ Bat-Jsy/25	25.00
232	David Ortiz/ Bat-Jsy/25	25.00
238	Edgar Martinez/ Bat-Jsy/25	15.00
240	Roy Oswalt/ Bat-Jsy/25	10.00
242	Carlos Beltran/ Bat-Jsy/25	20.00
243	Carlos Beltran/ Bat-Jsy/25	20.00
244	Miguel Cabrera/ Bat-Jsy/25	20.00
245	Scott Rolen/ Bat-Jsy/25	20.00
246	Hank Blalock/ Bat-Jsy/25	10.00
247	Vernon Wells/ Bat-Jsy/25	10.00
248	Adam Dunn/ Bat-Jsy/25	20.00

2005 Leaf

MIGUEL TEJADA   SHORTSTOP
BALTIMORE ORIOLES

NM/M

Complete Set (300):	
Common Player (1-200):	.15
Common SP (201-250):	1.00
Inserted 1:3	
Common SP (251-300):	1.00
#251-270 inserted 1:6	
271-300 inserted 1:4	
Hobby pack (8):	4.00
Hobby box (24):	80.00
1 Bartolo Colon	.25
2 Casey Kotchman	.15
3 Chone Figgins	.15
4 Darin Erstad	.25
5 Francisco Rodriguez	.25
6 Garret Anderson	.15
7 Jarrod Washburn	.15
8 Troy Glaus	.25
9 Vladimir Guerrero	.50
10 Brandon Webb	.15
11 Casey Fossum	.15
12 Luis Gonzalez	.25
13 Randy Johnson	.50
14 Richie Sexson	.15
15 Andruw Jones	.25
16 Chipper Jones	.50
17 J.D. Drew	.25

18	John Smoltz	.25
19	Johnny Estrada	.15
20	Marcus Giles	.15
21	Rafael Furcal	.25
22	Russ Ortiz	.15
23	Javy Lopez	.25
24	Jay Gibbons	.15
25	Melvin Mora	.15
26	Miguel Tejada	.40
27	Rafael Palmeiro	.40
28	Sidney Ponson	.15
29	Bill Mueller	.15
30	Curt Schilling	.40
31	David Ortiz	.50
32	Doug Mientkiewicz	.15
33	Jason Varitek	.25
34	Johnny Damon	.40
35	Manny Ramirez	.50
36	Pedro J. Martinez	.50
37	Trot Nixon	.15
38	Aramis Ramirez	.25
39	Corey Patterson	.15
40	Derrek Lee	.25
41	Greg Maddux	.75
42	Kerry Wood	.50
43	Mark Prior	.50
44	Moises Alou	.25
45	Nomar Garciaparra	1.00
46	Sammy Sosa	1.00
47	Carlos Lee	.15
48	Kip Wells	.15
49	Magglio Ordonez	.25
50	Mark Buehrle	.15
51	Paul Konerko	.25
52	Roberto Alomar	.25
53	Adam Dunn	.40
54	Austin Kearns	.25
55	Barry Larkin	.25
56	Danny Graves	.15
57	Ken Griffey Jr.	1.00
58	Sean Casey	.15
59	C.C. Sabathia	.15
60	Cliff Lee	.15
61	Jody Gerut	.15
62	Omar Vizquel	.25
63	Travis Hafner	.15
64	Victor Martinez	.25
65	Charles Johnson	.15
66	Jason Jennings	.15
67	Jeromy Burnitz	.15
68	Preston Wilson	.15
69	Todd Helton	.40
70	Bobby Higginson	.15
71	Dmitri Young	.15
72	Eric Munson	.15
73	Ivan Rodriguez	.40
74	Jeremy Bonderman	.15
75	Rondell White	.15
76	A.J. Burnett	.15
77	Carl Pavano	.25
78	Dontrelle Willis	.25
79	Hee Seop Choi	.15
80	Josh Beckett	.25
81	Juan Pierre	.15
82	Miguel Cabrera	.50
83	Mike Lowell	.15
84	Paul LoDuca	.15
85	Andy Pettitte	.25
86	Carlos Beltran	.40
87	Craig Biggio	.25
88	Jeff Bagwell	.40
89	Jeff Kent	.25
90	Lance Berkman	.25
91	Roger Clemens	1.50
92	Roy Oswalt	.25
93	Andres Blanco	.15
94	Jeremy Affeldt	.15
95	Juan Gonzalez	.25
96	Ken Harvey	.15
97	Mike Sweeney	.15
98	Zack Greinke	.25
99	Adrian Beltre	.25
100	Brad Penny	.15
101	Eric Gagne	.25
102	Kazuhisa Ishii	.15
103	Milton Bradley	.15
104	Shawn Green	.25
105	Steve Finley	.15
106	Ben Sheets	.25
107	Bill Hall	.15
108	Danny Kolb	.15
109	Geoff Jenkins	.15
110	Junior Spivey	.15
111	Lyle Overbay	.15
112	Scott Podsednik	.15
113	A.J. Pierzynski	.15
114	Brad Radke	.15
115	Corey Koskie	.15
116	Jacque Jones	.15
117	Joe Mauer	.50
118	Joe Nathan	.15
119	Shannon Stewart	.15
120	Torii Hunter	.25
121	Brad Wilkerson	.15
122	Jeff Fassero	.15
123	Jose Vidro	.15

124	Livan Hernandez	.15
125	Nick Johnson	.15
126	Al Leiter	.25
127	Jose Reyes	.25
128	Kazuo Matsui	.25
129	Mike Cameron	.15
130	Mike Piazza	1.00
131	Richard Hidalgo	.15
132	Tom Glavine	.25
133	Alex Rodriguez	1.50
134	Bernie Williams	.25
135	Derek Jeter	1.50
136	Gary Sheffield	.40
137	Jason Giambi	.25
138	Javier Vazquez	.25
139	Jorge Posada	.25
140	Kevin Brown	.15
141	Mariano Rivera	.25
142	Mike Mussina	.25
143	Barry Zito	.25
144	Bobby Crosby	.25
145	Eric Chavez	.25
146	Erubiel Durazo	.15
147	Jermaine Dye	.25
148	Mark Mulder	.25
149	Tim Hudson	.25
150	Bobby Abreu	.25
151	Eric Milton	.15
152	Jim Thome	.50
153	Kevin Millwood	.15
154	Mike Lieberthal	.15
155	Pat Burrell	.25
156	Randy Wolf	.15
157	Craig Wilson	.15
158	Jack Wilson	.15
159	Jason Bay	.25
160	Jason Kendall	.15
161	Kris Benson	.15
162	Brian Giles	.15
163	Jake Peavy	.25
164	Jay Payton	.15
165	Khalil Greene	.25
166	Mark Loretta	.15
167	Ryan Klesko	.15
168	Sean Burroughs	.15
169	David Aardsma	.15
170	Edgardo Alfonzo	.15
171	Jason Schmidt	.25
172	Merkin Valdez	.15
173	Ray Durham	.15
174	Bret Boone	.15
175	Dan Wilson	.15
176	Ichiro Suzuki	1.25
177	Jamie Moyer	.15
178	Rich Aurilia	.15
179	Albert Pujols	1.50
180	Edgar Renteria	.25
181	Jason Isringhausen	.15
182	Jeff Suppan	.15
183	Jim Edmonds	.25
184	Scott Rolen	.50
185	Woody Williams	.15
186	Aubrey Huff	.15
187	Carl Crawford	.15
188	Dewon Brazelton	.15
189	Jose Cruz Jr.	.15
190	Rocco Baldelli	.25
191	Alfonso Soriano	.40
192	Hank Blalock	.40
193	Kenny Rogers	.15
194	Laynce Nix	.15
195	Mark Teixeira	.25
196	Michael Young	.15
197	Alexis Rios	.15
198	Carlos Delgado	.25
199	Roy Halladay	.25
200	Vernon Wells	.15
201	Josh Kroeger	1.00
202	Angel Guzman	1.00
203	Brad Halsey	1.00
204	Bucky Jacobsen	1.00
205	Carlos Hines	1.00
206	Carlos Vasquez	1.00
207	Billy Traber	1.00
208	Bubba Crosby	1.00
209	Chris Oxspring	1.00
210	Chris Shelton	1.00
211	Colby Miller	1.00
212	David Crouthers	1.00
213	Dennis Sarfate	1.00
214	Donald Kelly	1.00
215	Edwardo Sierra	1.00
216	Edwin Moreno	1.00
217	Fernando Nieve	1.00
218	Freddy Guzman	1.00
219	Greg Dobbs	1.00
220	Hector Gimenez	1.00
221	Andy Green	1.00
222	Jason Bartlett	1.00
223	Jerry Gil	1.00
224	Jesse Crain	2.00
225	Joey Gathright	1.00
226	John Gall	1.00
227	Jorge Sequea	1.00
228	Jorge Vasquez	1.00
229	Josh Labandeira	1.00

230	Justin Leone	1.00
231	Lance Cormier	1.00
232	Lincoln Holdzkom	1.00
233	Miguel Olivo	1.00
234	Mike Rouse	1.00
235	Onil Joseph	1.00
236	Phil Stockman	1.00
237	Ramon Ramirez	1.00
238	Robb Quinlan	1.00
239	Roberto Novoa	1.00
240	Ronald Belisario	1.00
241	Ronny Cedeno	1.00
242	Ruddy Yan	1.00
243	Ryan Meaux	1.00
244	Ryan Wing	1.00
245	Scott Proctor	1.00
246	Sean Henn	1.00
247	Tim Bausher	1.00
248	Tim Bittner	1.00
249	William Bergolla	1.00
250	Yadier Molina	1.00
251	Bernie Williams	1.00
252	Craig Biggio	1.00
253	Chipper Jones	2.00
254	Greg Maddux	3.00
255	Sammy Sosa	3.00
256	Mike Mussina	1.50
257	Tim Salmon	1.00
258	Barry Larkin	1.00
259	Randy Johnson	2.00
260	Jeff Bagwell	1.50
261	Roberto Alomar	1.50
262	Tom Glavine	1.00
263	Roger Clemens	4.00
264	Alex Rodriguez	4.00
265	Ivan Rodriguez	1.50
266	Pedro J. Martinez	2.00
267	Ken Griffey Jr.	3.00
268	Jim Thome	2.00
269	Frank Thomas	1.50
270	Mike Piazza	3.00
271	Garret Anderson	1.00
272	Luis Gonzalez	1.00
273	John Smoltz	1.00
274	Rafael Palmeiro	1.50
275	Curt Schilling	1.50
276	Mark Prior	1.50
277	Magglio Ordonez	1.50
278	Adam Dunn	1.50
279	Travis Hafner	1.00
280	Jeromy Burnitz	1.00
281	Carlos Guillen	1.00
282	Dontrelle Willis	1.00
283	Carlos Beltran	1.50
284	Zack Greinke	1.00
285	Adrian Beltre	1.00
286	Ben Sheets	1.00
287	Johan Santana	1.00
288	Livan Hernandez	1.00
289	Kazuo Matsui	1.00
290	Derek Jeter	4.00
291	Tim Hudson	1.00
292	Eric Milton	1.00
293	Jason Kendall	1.00
294	Jake Peavy	1.00
295	Ray Durham	1.00
296	Ichiro Suzuki	3.00
297	Scott Rolen	2.00
298	Carl Crawford	1.00
299	Hank Blalock	1.50
300	Roy Halladay	1.00

Press Proofs Blue

Blue (1-200):	5-10X
Blue (201-250):	1-2X
Blue (251-300):	2-4X
Production 75 Sets	

Press Proofs Gold

Gold (1-200):	10-20X
Gold (201-250):	2-4X
Blue (251-300):	4-8X
Production 25 Sets	

Press Proofs Red

Red (1-200):	2-4X
Red (201-300):	.5-1X
Red (251-300):	1-2X
Inserted 1:8	

4 Star Staffs

	NM/M
Common Card:	2.00
Inserted 1:48	
Die-cut:	1X
Production 250 Sets	

1	Greg Maddux, John Smoltz, Kevin Millwood, Tom Glavine	4.00
2	A.J. Burnett, Carl Pavano, Dontrelle Willis, Josh Beckett	2.00
3	Andy Pettitte, David Wells, Mike Mussina, Roger Clemens	6.00
4	Carlos Zambrano, Greg Maddux, Kerry Wood, Mark Prior	4.00
5	Andy Pettitte, Mariano Rivera, Mike Mussina, Roger Clemens	3.00
6	Curt Schilling, Derek Lowe, Pedro J. Martinez, Tim Wakefield	4.00
7	Barry Zito, Mark Mulder, Rich Harden, Tim Hudson	2.00
8	Brandon Webb, Byung-Hyun Kim, Curt Schilling, Randy Johnson	3.00
9	Jamie Moyer, Kenny Rogers, Kevin Brown, Nolan Ryan	8.00
10	Kelvim Escobar, Roger Clemens, Roy Halladay, Woody Williams	6.00
11	Andy Pettitte, Roger Clemens, Roy Oswalt, Wade Miller	6.00
12	Barry Zito, Billy Koch, Mark Mulder, Tim Hudson	2.00
13	Eric Gagne, Hideo Nomo, Kazuhisa Ishii, Kevin Brown	3.00
14	Greg Maddux, Jason Schmidt, John Smoltz, Tom Glavine	5.00
15	Derek Lowe, Hideo Nomo, Pedro Martinez, Tim Wakefield	4.00

Alternate Threads

	NM/M
Complete Set (25):	30.00
Common Player:	1.00
Inserted 1:18	
Holo:	1-2X
Production 150 Sets	
Holo Die-cut:	2-4X

Production 50 Sets

1	Adam Dunn	1.50
2	C.C. Sabathia	1.00
3	Curt Schilling	1.50
4	Dontrelle Willis	1.00
5	Greg Maddux	3.00
6	Hank Blalock	1.50
7	Ichiro Suzuki	4.00
8	Jeff Bagwell	1.50
9	Ken Griffey Jr.	3.00
10	Ken Harvey	1.00
11	Magglio Ordonez	1.00
12	Mark Mulder	1.00
13	Mark Teixeira	1.00
14	Michael Young	1.00
15	Miguel Tejada	1.50
16	Mike Piazza	4.00
17	Pedro Martinez	2.00
18	Randy Johnson	2.00
19	Roger Clemens	6.00
20	Sammy Sosa	4.00
21	Tim Hudson	1.00
22	Todd Helton	1.50
23	Torii Hunter	1.00
24	Travis Hafner	1.00
25	Vernon Wells	1.00

Autographs

NM/M

Common Autograph:		5.00
201	Josh Kroeger	5.00
202	Angel Guzman	15.00
203	Brad Halsey	5.00
204	Bucky Jacobsen	10.00
205	Carlos Hines	5.00
207	Bill Tucker	5.00
208	Bubba Crosby	10.00
210	Chris Shelton	8.00
211	Colby Miller	5.00
212	David Crouthers	5.00
217	Fernando Nieve	10.00
220	Hector Gimenez	5.00
221	Andy Green	5.00
222	Jason Bartlett	5.00
227	Jorge Sequea/84	10.00
228	Jorge Vasquez	8.00
232	Lincoln Holdzkom	8.00
233	Miguel Olivo	8.00
234	Mike Rouse	8.00
236	Phil Stockman	8.00
237	Ramon Ramirez	8.00
242	Ruddy Yan	5.00
245	Scott Proctor	8.00
247	Tim Bausher	8.00
249	William Bergolla	10.00

Autographs Blue

No Pricing
Production 15-25
Golds: No Pricing

Autographs Red

NM/M

Common Autograph:		
3	Chone Figgins/100	8.00
19	Johnny Estrada/100	15.00
24	Jay Gibbons/100	8.00
47	Carlos Lee/100	10.00
56	Danny Graves/100	8.00
60	Cliff Lee/100	10.00
63	Travis Hafner/100	15.00
74	Jeremy Bonderman/100	10.00
94	Jeremy Affeldt/100	8.00
96	Ken Harvey/100	10.00
103	Milton Bradley/100	10.00
111	Lyle Overbay/100	15.00
118	Joe Nathan/100	10.00
144	Bobby Crosby/100	25.00
154	Mike Lieberthal/50	15.00
157	Craig Wilson/100	15.00
158	Jack Wilson/100	12.00
163	Jake Peavy/50	25.00
172	Merkin Valdez/100	8.00
182	Jeff Suppan/100	10.00
187	Carl Crawford/50	15.00
188	Dewon Brazelton/50	10.00
194	Laynce Nix/100	10.00
201	Josh Kroeger/100	8.00
202	Angel Guzman/100	15.00
203	Brad Halsey/100	8.00
204	Bucky Jacobsen/100	8.00
205	Carlos Hines/100	8.00
207	Billy Traber/100	8.00
208	Bubba Crosby/100	10.00
210	Chris Shelton/100	8.00
211	Colby Miller/100	8.00
212	David Crouthers/100	8.00
217	Fernando Nieve/100	10.00
218	Freddy Guzman/100	8.00
220	Hector Gimenez/100	8.00
221	Andy Green/100	8.00
222	Jason Bartlett/100	8.00
224	Josh Crain/100	15.00
227	Jorge Sequea/84	10.00
228	Jorge Vasquez/100	8.00
233	Miguel Olivo/100	8.00
234	Mike Rouse/100	8.00
236	Phil Stockman/100	10.00
237	Ramon Ramirez/100	8.00
238	Robb Quinlan/100	8.00
241	Ronny Cedeno/65	10.00
242	Ruddy Yan/100	8.00
243	Ryan Meaux/93	8.00
247	Tim Bausher/100	8.00
249	William Bergolla/100	10.00
250	Yadier Molina/100	15.00

Clean Up Crew

NM/M

Complete Set (15):		45.00
Common Card:		
Inserted 1:49		
Die-cut:		1X
Production 250 Sets		
1	Albert Pujols, Jim Edmonds, Scott Rolen	6.00
2	Melvin Mora, Miguel Tejada, Rafael Palmeiro	3.00
3	Alfonso Soriano, Michael Young, Hank Blalock	3.00
4	Gary Sheffield, Alex Rodriguez, Hideki Matsui	5.00
5	Moises Alou, Sammy Sosa, Nomar Garciaparra	5.00
6	Paul LoDuca, Mike Lowell, Miguel Cabrera	3.00
7	Carlos Beltran, Lance Berkman, Jeff Bagwell	3.00
8	Paul Konerko, Magglio Ordonez, Frank Thomas	3.00
9	Sean Casey, Ken Griffey Jr., Adam Dunn	5.00
10	Vladimir Guerrero, Garret Anderson, Troy Glaus	3.00
11	Joe Morgan, Johnny Bench, Tony Perez	3.00
12	Keith Hernandez, Darryl Strawberry, Gary Carter	2.00
13	Jim Rice, Carl Yastrzemski, Dwight Evans	5.00
14	Ryne Sandberg, Andre Dawson, Mark Grace	6.00
15	Cal Ripken Jr., Eddie Murray, Rafael Palmeiro	10.00

Cornerstones

NM/M

Complete Set (20):		50.00
Common Card:		1.50
Inserted 1:37		
1	Albert Pujols, Scott Rolen	6.00
2	Hideki Matsui, Jorge Posada	5.00
3	Nomar Garciaparra, Sammy Sosa	4.00
4	David Ortiz, Manny Ramirez	3.00
5	Miguel Cabrera, Mike Lowell	3.00
6	Hank Blalock, Mark Teixeira	2.00
7	Chipper Jones, J.D. Drew	3.00
8	Craig Biggio, Jeff Bagwell	3.00
9	Kazuo Matsui, Mike Piazza	4.00
10	Shawn Green, Adrian Beltre	1.50
11	Bobby Abreu, Jim Thome	3.00
12	Mike Schmidt, Steve Carlton	6.00
13	Cal Ripken Jr., Eddie Murray	10.00
14	Carl Yastrzemski, Dwight Evans	5.00
15	Joe Morgan, Johnny Bench	3.00
16	Dale Murphy, Phil Niekro	2.00
17	Alan Trammell, Kirk Gibson	2.00
18	Jose Canseco, Rickey Henderson	3.00
19	Paul Molitor, Robin Yount	4.00
20	Bo Jackson, George Brett	6.00

Cornerstones Bats

NM/M

Common Dual Bat:		8.00
1	Albert Pujols, Scott Rolen	20.00
2	Hideki Matsui, Jorge Posada	35.00
3	Sammy Sosa, Nomar Garciaparra	15.00
4	Manny Ramirez, David Ortiz	20.00
5	Miguel Cabrera, Mike Lowell	10.00
6	Hank Blalock, Mark Teixeira	10.00
7	Chipper Jones, J.D. Drew	15.00
8	Craig Biggio, Jeff Bagwell	15.00
9	Mike Piazza, Kazuo Matsui	15.00
10	Shawn Green, Adrian Beltre	8.00

Cornerstones Jerseys

NM/M

Common Dual Jersey:		8.00
1	Albert Pujols, Scott Rolen	20.00
2	Hideki Matsui, Jorge Posada	35.00
4	Manny Ramirez, David Ortiz	20.00
5	Miguel Cabrera, Mike Lowell	10.00
6	Hank Blalock, Mark Teixeira	10.00
8	Craig Biggio, Jeff Bagwell	10.00
9	Mike Piazza, Kazuo Matsui	15.00
10	Shawn Green, Adrian Beltre	8.00

Cy Young Winners

NM/M

Complete Set (15):		30.00
Common Player:		1.50
Inserted 1:31		
Gold:		1X
Production 350 Sets		
Gold Die-cut:		1.5-2X
Production 100 Sets		
1	Warren Spahn	3.00
2	Whitey Ford	3.00
3	Bob Gibson	3.00
4	Tom Seaver	3.00
5	Steve Carlton	2.00
6	Jim Palmer	2.00
7	Rollie Fingers	1.50
8	Dwight Gooden	1.50
9	Roger Clemens	6.00
10	Orel Hershiser	1.50
11	Greg Maddux	4.00
12	Dennis Eckersley	2.00
13	Randy Johnson	3.00
14	Pedro Martinez	3.00
15	Eric Gagne	2.00

Fans of the Game

NM/M

Common Card:		1.50
Inserted 1:24		
1	Sean Astin	1.50
2	Tony Danza	1.50
3	Taye Diggs	1.50

Fans of the Game Autograph

NM/M

1	Sean Astin	30.00
3	Taye Diggs	30.00

Game Collection

NM/M

Inserted 1:118		
1	Cal Ripken Jr./Bat	30.00
2	Carl Crawford/Jsy	5.00
3	Dale Murphy/Bat	20.00
4	Don Mattingly/Bat	25.00
5	George Brett/Jsy	25.00
6	Victor Martinez/Bat	8.00
7	Sean Casey/Bat	5.00
8	Torii Hunter/Bat	5.00
9	Magglio Ordonez/Bat	5.00
10	Lance Berkman/Bat	5.00
11	Mike Schmidt/Bat	25.00
12	Nolan Ryan/Jkt	40.00
13	Paul LoDuca/Bat	5.00
14	Preston Wilson/Bat	5.00
15	Rod Carew/Jkt	10.00
16	Reggie Jackson/Bat	10.00
17	Ivan Rodriguez/Bat	8.00
18	Larry Walker/Cards Bat	10.00
19	Miguel Tejada/Bat	8.00
20	Vladimir Guerrero/Bat	10.00

Game Collection Autograph

NM/M

Production 5-200		
2	Carl Crawford/Jsy/200	15.00
6	Victor Martinez/Bat/200	20.00
7	Sean Casey/Bat/200	20.00
8	Torii Hunter/Bat/50	25.00
13	Paul LoDuca/Bat/100	20.00

Gamers

NM/M

Complete Set (15):	20.00

Common Player:		1.00
Inserted 1:13		
Quantum:		2-3X
Production 175 Sets		
Quantum Die-Cut:		3-5X
Production 50 Sets		
1	Albert Pujols	4.00
2	Alex Rodriguez	3.00
3	Alfonso Soriano	1.50
4	Chipper Jones	1.50
5	Derek Jeter	4.00
6	Greg Maddux	2.00
7	Ichiro Suzuki	3.00
8	Jim Thome	1.50
9	Ken Griffey Jr.	2.00
10	Lance Berkman	1.00
11	Miguel Tejada	1.00
12	Mike Piazza	2.50
13	Roger Clemens	4.00
14	Scott Rolen	1.50
15	Vladimir Guerrero	1.50

Gold Rookies

		NM/M
Complete Set (10):		15.00
Common Player:		2.00
Inserted 1:24		
Mirror:		3-5X
Production 25 Sets		
1	Dennis Sarfate	2.00
2	Donnie Kelly	2.00
3	Eddy Rodriguez	2.00
4	Edwin Moreno	2.00
5	Greg Dobbs	2.00
6	Josh Labandeira	2.00
7	Kevin Cave	2.00
8	Mariano Gomez	2.00
9	Ronald Belisario	2.00
10	Ruddy Yan	2.00

Gold Rookies Autograph

		NM/M
Common Autograph:		
Mirror:		No Pricing
Production 25 Sets		
1	Dennis Sarfate	10.00
2	Donnie Kelly	8.00
5	Greg Dobbs	8.00
7	Kevin Cave	10.00
9	Ronald Belisario	8.00
10	Ruddy Yan	8.00

Gold Stars

		NM/M
Complete Set (20):		40.00
Common Player:		.75
Inserted 1:27		
Mirror:		4-6X

Production 25 Sets		
1	Albert Pujols	4.00
2	Ichiro Suzuki	3.00
3	Derek Jeter	4.00
4	Alex Rodriguez	3.00
5	Scott Rolen	1.50
6	Randy Johnson	1.50
7	Roger Clemens	4.00
8	Greg Maddux	2.00
9	Alfonso Soriano	1.50
10	Mark Mulder	.75
11	Sammy Sosa	3.00
12	Mike Piazza	3.00
13	Rafael Palmeiro	.75
14	Ivan Rodriguez	.75
15	Miguel Cabrera	.75
16	Stan Musial	3.00
17	Nolan Ryan	6.00
18	Don Mattingly	4.00
19	George Brett	4.00
20	Cal Ripken Jr.	6.00

Home/Road

		NM/M
Common Player:		1.00
Inserted 1:22		
Home & Road price is identical.		
1H	Albert Pujols/H	4.00
1R	Albert Pujols/R	4.00
2H	Alfonso Soriano/H	1.50
2R	Alfonso Soriano/R	1.50
3H	Carlos Beltran/H	1.00
3R	Carlos Beltran/R	1.00
4H	Chipper Jones/H	1.50
4R	Chipper Jones/R	1.50
5H	Frank Thomas/H	1.50
5R	Frank Thomas/R	1.50
6H	Hank Blalock/H	1.00
6R	Hank Blalock/R	1.00
7H	Ivan Rodriguez/H	1.50
7R	Ivan Rodriguez/R	1.50
8H	Manny Ramirez/H	1.50
8R	Manny Ramirez/R	1.50
9H	Mark Prior/H	1.50
9R	Mark Prior/R	1.50
10H	Miguel Cabrera/H	1.50
10R	Miguel Cabrera/R	1.50
11H	Miguel Tejada/H	1.00
11R	Miguel Tejada/R	1.00
12H	Mike Piazza/H	2.50
12R	Mike Piazza/R	2.50
13H	Roger Clemens/H	4.00
13R	Roger Clemens/R	4.00
14H	Todd Helton/H	1.50
14R	Todd Helton/R	1.50
15H	Vladimir Guerrero/H	1.50
15R	Vladimir Guerrero/R	1.50

Home/Road Jersey

		NM/M
Common Player:		
1H	Albert Pujols/H	20.00
1R	Albert Pujols/R	20.00
2H	Alfonso Soriano/H	8.00
3H	Carlos Beltran/H	8.00
3R	Carlos Beltran/R	8.00
4R	Chipper Jones/R	8.00
5H	Frank Thomas/H	8.00
5R	Frank Thomas/R	8.00
6H	Hank Blalock/H	8.00
7H	Ivan Rodriguez/H	8.00
7R	Ivan Rodriguez/R	8.00
8R	Manny Ramirez/R	8.00
9H	Mark Prior/H	8.00
11H	Miguel Tejada/H	5.00
11R	Miguel Tejada/R	5.00
12H	Mike Piazza/H	12.00
13H	Roger Clemens/H	15.00
13R	Roger Clemens/R	15.00
14H	Todd Helton/H	8.00
14R	Todd Helton/R	8.00
15H	Vladimir Guerrero/H	8.00

Patch Off My Back

		NM/M
Common Patch:		15.00
Production 50 Sets		
1	Adam Dunn	25.00
2	Aubrey Huff	15.00
3	Austin Kearns	15.00
4	Bobby Crosby	25.00
5	C.C. Sabathia	15.00
7	David Ortiz	25.00
8	Dewon Brazelton	15.00
9	Edgar Martinez	20.00
10	Frankie Francisco	15.00
11	Garret Anderson	20.00
12	Hideki Matsui	50.00
13	Hideo Nomo	20.00
14	Jack Wilson	15.00
15	Javy Lopez	15.00
16	Jay Gibbons	15.00
17	Jim Edmonds	20.00
18	Jody Gerut	15.00
19	Joey Gathright	15.00
20	Johan Santana	20.00
21	Jose Reyes	15.00
22	Jose Vidro	15.00
23	Lance Berkman	15.00
24	Mariano Rivera	20.00
25	Mark Teixeira	20.00
26	Michael Young	15.00
27	Mike Cameron	15.00
28	Mike Sweeney	15.00
29	Omar Vizquel	15.00
30	Preston Wilson	15.00
31	Rocco Baldelli	15.00
32	Scott Rolen	25.00
33	Sean Burroughs	15.00
34	Sean Casey	15.00
35	Tim Hudson	20.00
36	Torii Hunter	20.00
37	Trevor Hoffman	20.00
38	Troy Glaus	20.00
39	Vernon Wells	15.00
40	Victor Martinez	20.00

Patch Off My Back Autograph

		NM/M
Production 10-75		
2	Aubrey Huff/50	35.00
4	Bobby Crosby/75	50.00
5	C.C. Sabathia/75	30.00
7	David Ortiz/50	100.00
8	Dewon Brazelton/75	25.00
14	Jack Wilson/75	30.00
16	Jay Gibbons/50	25.00
18	Jody Gerut/75	20.00
20	Johan Santana/50	60.00
22	Jose Vidro/75	25.00
26	Michael Young/75	35.00
33	Sean Burroughs/25	25.00
40	Victor Martinez/75	35.00

Picture Perfect

		NM/M
Complete Set (20):		30.00
Common Player:		1.00
Inserted 1:20		
Die-Cut:		2-3X
Production 100 Sets		

1	Albert Pujols	4.00
2	Alex Rodriguez	3.00
3	Alfonso Soriano	1.50
4	Derek Jeter	4.00
5	Greg Maddux	2.00
6	Hideki Matsui	3.00
7	Ichiro Suzuki	3.00
8	Ivan Rodriguez	1.00
9	Jim Thome	1.50
10	Mark Mulder	1.00
11	Mark Prior	1.50
12	Miguel Tejada	1.00
13	Mike Mussina	1.00
14	Mike Piazza	2.50
15	Nomar Garciaparra	2.50
16	Randy Johnson	1.50
17	Roger Clemens	4.00
18	Sammy Sosa	2.50
19	Scott Rolen	1.50
20	Vladimir Guerrero	1.50

Recollection Autographs

No Pricing
Production 1-29

Shirt Off My Back

		NM/M
Common Player:		5.00
Inserted 1:48		
1	Adam Dunn	15.00
4	Bobby Crosby	15.00
5	C.C. Sabathia	8.00
7	David Ortiz	15.00
8	Dewon Brazelton	5.00
9	Edgar Martinez	5.00
10	Frankie Francisco	5.00
11	Garret Anderson	5.00
12	Hideki Matsui	25.00
13	Hideo Nomo	8.00
14	Jack Wilson	5.00
15	Javy Lopez	8.00
16	Jay Gibbons	5.00
17	Jim Edmonds	15.00
18	Jody Gerut SP	5.00
19	Joey Gathright	5.00
20	Johan Santana	10.00
21	Jose Reyes	5.00
22	Jose Vidro	5.00
23	Lance Berkman	5.00
25	Mark Teixeira	5.00
26	Michael Young	5.00
27	Mike Cameron	5.00
28	Mike Sweeney	5.00
29	Omar Vizquel	8.00
30	Preston Wilson	5.00
31	Rocco Baldelli	8.00
32	Scott Rolen	10.00
33	Sean Burroughs	5.00
34	Sean Casey	5.00
35	Tim Hudson	5.00
36	Torii Hunter	5.00
37	Trevor Hoffman	5.00
38	Troy Glaus	5.00
39	Vernon Wells	5.00
40	Victor Martinez	8.00

Sportscasters 70 Green

Baseball

Steve Carlton

		NM/M
Common Player:		2.00
Production 70 Sets		
Variations #'d 35-65:		1X
Variations #'d 20-30:		1.5X
No pricing 15 or less.		
1	Adam Dunn	3.00
2	Al Kaline	5.00
3	Albert Pujols	8.00
4	Alex Rodriguez	8.00
5	Alfonso Soriano	3.00
6	Bob Gibson	3.00
7	Cal Ripken Jr.	25.00

8	Carl Yastrzemski	8.00
9	Dale Murphy	3.00
10	Derek Jeter	10.00
11	Don Mattingly	10.00
12	Duke Snider	4.00
13	Eric Gagne	3.00
14	Ernie Banks	6.00
15	Frank Robinson	3.00
16	George Brett	10.00
17	Greg Maddux	6.00
18	Harmon Killebrew	5.00
19	Ichiro Suzuki	8.00
20	Ivan Rodriguez	4.00
21	Jim Edmonds	2.00
22	Jim Palmer	2.00
23	Jim Thome	4.00
24	Johnny Bench	5.00
25	Ken Griffey Jr.	6.00
26	Larry Walker	3.00
27	Mark Mulder	2.00
28	Mark Prior	4.00
29	Miguel Tejada	3.00
30	Mike Mussina	3.00
31	Mike Piazza	6.00
32	Mike Schmidt	10.00
33	Nolan Ryan	15.00
34	Nomar Garciaparra	6.00
35	Pedro Martinez	4.00
36	Rafael Palmeiro	3.00
37	Randy Johnson	4.00
38	Reggie Jackson	3.00
39	Rickey Henderson	4.00
40	Roberto Clemente	15.00
41	Rod Carew	3.00
42	Roger Clemens	8.00
43	Ryne Sandberg	8.00
44	Sammy Sosa	6.00
45	Stan Musial	8.00
46	Steve Carlton	2.00
47	Tony Gwynn	5.00
48	Vladimir Guerrero	4.00
49	Warren Spahn	4.00
50	Willie McCovey	3.00

2005 Leaf Century

JOHAN SANTANA
minnesota twins

	NM/M
Complete Set (200):	40.00
Common Player:	.25
Pack (5):	12.00
Box (10):	100.00

1	Brian Roberts	.25
2	Derek Jeter	2.00
3	Harmon Killebrew	1.00
4	Angel Berroa	.25
5	George Brett	2.00
6	Stan Musial	1.50
7	Ivan Rodriguez	.25
8	Cal Ripken Jr.	3.00
9	Hank Blalock	.50
10	Miguel Tejada	.50
11	Barry Larkin	.40
12	Alfonso Soriano	.75
13	Alex Rodriguez	2.00
14	Paul Konerko	.25
15	Jim Edmonds	.40
16	Garret Anderson	.40
17	Todd Helton	.50
18	Moises Alou	.40
19	Tony Gwynn	.75
20	Mike Schmidt	2.00
21	Sammy Sosa	1.25
22	Roger Clemens	2.00
23	Tony Perez	.25
24	Manny Ramirez	.75
25	Jim Thome	.75
26	Chase Utley	.40
27	Scott Rolen	.75
28	Austin Kearns	.25
29	John Smoltz	.40
30	Ken Griffey Jr.	1.00
31	Mike Piazza	1.00
32	Steve Carlton	.50

33	Larry Walker	.40
34	Nolan Ryan	2.50
35	Mike Mussina	.40
36	Joe Nathan	.25
37	Kenny Rogers	.25
38	Eric Gagne	.40
39	Brett Myers	.25
40	Rich Harden	.25
41	Victor Martinez	.40
42	Mariano Rivera	.40
43	Dennis Eckersley	.50
44	Roy Oswalt	.40
45	Pedro Martinez	.75
46	Jason Bay	.40
47	Tom Glavine	.25
48	Torii Hunter	.25
49	Larry Bigbie	.25
50	Nomar Garciaparra	1.50
51	Ichiro Suzuki	1.50
52	C.C. Sabathia	.40
53	Bobby Abreu	.40
54	Doug Mientkiewicz	.25
55	Hideki Matsui	1.50
56	Mark Buehrle	.25
57	Johan Santana	.75
58	Johnny Damon	.50
59	Edgar Martinez	.40
60	Preston Wilson	.25
61	Livan Hernandez	.25
62	Eric Chavez	.40
63	Lyle Overbay	.40
64	Jason Schmidt	.50
65	Cliff Lee	.25
66	Shingo Takatsu	.25
67	Jeff Bagwell	.50
68	Danny Graves	.25
69	Kip Wells	.25
70	Steve Finley	.25
71	Lew Ford	.25
72	Chone Figgins	.25
73	Delmon Young	.40
74	Esteban Loaiza	.25
75	Barry Zito	.40
76	Carlos Delgado	.40
77	Joe Mauer	.50
78	Ryan Wagner	.25
79	John Lackey	.25
80	Adrian Beltre	.40
81	Vernon Wells	.25
82	Sean Burroughs	.25
83	Francisco Cordero	.25
84	Carlos Guillen	.25
85	Eric Byrnes	.25
86	Jose Reyes	.40
87	Rocco Baldelli	.40
88	Josh Beckett	.40
89	Casey Kotchman	.40
90	Scott Podsednik	.25
91	Mike Sweeney	.25
92	Khalil Greene	.50
93	Trot Nixon	.25
94	Chad Cordero	.25
95	Derek Lowe	.40
96	Jason Giambi	.40
97	Jose Guillen	.25
98	Craig Biggio	.40
99	Pat Burrell	.40
100	Kazuo Matsui	.25
101	Rafael Furcal	.25
102	Jack Wilson	.25
103	Edgar Renteria	.50
104	Carlos Beltran	.75
105	Albert Pujols	2.00
106	Melvin Mora	.25
107	J.D. Drew	.40
108	Andre Dawson	.50
109	Jody Gerut	.25
110	Michael Young	.25
111	Gary Sheffield	.50
112	Wade Boggs	.50
113	Carl Crawford	.50
114	Paul LoDuca	.25
115	Tim Hudson	.40
116	Aramis Ramirez	.40
117	Lance Berkman	.40
118	Javy Lopez	.40
119	Robin Yount	1.00
120	Mark Mulder	.25
121	Sean Casey	.25
122	Will Clark	.50
123	Don Mattingly	2.00
124	Miguel Cabrera	.75
125	Rafael Palmeiro	.50
126	David Ortiz	.75
127	Vladimir Guerrero	.75
128	Ken Harvey	.25
129	Rod Carew	.50
130	Magglio Ordonez	.25
131	Greg Maddux	1.00
132	Roy Halladay	.25
133	Javier Vazquez	.25
134	Kerry Wood	.75
135	Frank Thomas	.50
136	Tom Gordon	.25
137	Jake Peavy	.25

138	Curt Schilling	.75
139	Dewon Brazelton	.25
140	Jae Weong Seo	.25
141	Danny Kolb	.25
142	Jeff Kent	.40
143	Juan Encarnacion	.25
144	Adam Dunn	.50
145	Carlos Lee	.25
146	Matt Clement	.25
147	Guillermo Mota	.25
148	Travis Hafner	.40
149	Brad Wilkerson	.25
150	Eric Milton	.25
151	Randy Johnson	.75
152	Joe Crede	.25
153	Mark Kotsay	.25
154	Jason Varitek	.40
155	David Wright	.75
156	Brad Penny	.25
157	Francisco Rodriguez	.25
158	Gary Carter	.50
159	Adrian Gonzalez	.25
160	Derrek Lee	.40
161	Mark Prior	.50
162	Carlos Zambrano	.40
163	Bobby Crosby	.40
164	Jermaine Dye	.25
165	Kris Benson	.25
166	Dontrelle Willis	.40
167	Dallas McPherson	.40
168	Johnny Estrada	.25
169	Milton Bradley	.25
170	Shannon Stewart	.25
171	Ben Sheets	.40
172	Richard Hidalgo	.25
173	Laynce Nix	.25
174	B.J. Upton	.50
175	Craig Wilson	.25
176	Hideo Nomo	.40
177	Troy Glaus	.40
178	Akinori Otsuka	.25
179	Rickie Weeks	.40
180	Mike Lowell	.40
181	Marcus Giles	.25
182	Randy Wolf	.25
183	A.J. Burnett	.25
184	Aubrey Huff	.25
185	Billy Ripken	.25
186	Octavio Dotel	.25
187	Kazuhisa Ishii	.25
188	Mark Teixeira	.50
189	Todd Walker	.25
190	Dale Murphy	.50
191	Alexis Rios	.25
192	Reggie Sanders	.25
193	Orlando Cabrera	.25
194	Shawn Green	.40
195	Andy Pettitte	.40
196	Chipper Jones	.75
197	Jose Vidro	.25
198	Jacque Jones	.25
199	Brian Giles	.25
200	Andruw Jones	.40

Post Marks Gold

Golds:		4-8X
Production 50 Sets		

Post Marks Silver

	NM/M
Silvers:	3-6X
Production 100 Sets	

Post Marks Platinum

	NM/M
No Pricing	
Production One Set	

Air Mail Bat

	NM/M
Production 50-250	
1	Babe Ruth/50	150.00
2	Frank Robinson/250	12.00

3	Harmon Killebrew/100	20.00
4	Sammy Sosa/100	10.00
5	Reggie Jackson/250	15.00
6	Mike Schmidt/100	20.00
7	Rafael Palmeiro/100	8.00
8	Ted Williams/50	80.00
9	Willie McCovey/250	10.00
10	Ernie Banks/100	20.00

Air Mail Bat Signature

	NM/M
Production 1-25	
2	Frank Robinson/25	40.00
3	Harmon Killebrew/25	60.00
9	Willie McCovey/25	35.00

Material Bat

DERREK LEE
chicago cubs

	NM/M
Common Player:	5.00
3	Harmon Killebrew/250	12.00
4	Angel Berroa/50	5.00
5	George Brett/250	15.00
6	Stan Musial/250	15.00
7	Ivan Rodriguez/100	8.00
8	Cal Ripken Jr./250	25.00
9	Hank Blalock/100	8.00
10	Miguel Tejada/100	6.00
11	Barry Larkin/100	6.00
12	Alfonso Soriano/100	8.00
14	Paul Konerko/50	5.00
15	Jim Edmonds/100	5.00
16	Garret Anderson/100	5.00
17	Todd Helton/100	8.00
18	Moises Alou/50	5.00
19	Tony Gwynn/250	10.00
20	Mike Schmidt/100	15.00
21	Sammy Sosa/100	10.00
22	Roger Clemens/100	15.00
23	Tony Perez/100	8.00
24	Manny Ramirez/100	10.00
25	Jim Thome/100	12.00
27	Scott Rolen/100	10.00
28	Austin Kearns/50	5.00
31	Mike Piazza/100	12.00
32	Steve Carlton/250	8.00
33	Larry Walker/100	8.00
34	Nolan Ryan/250	20.00
35	Mike Mussina/100	8.00
41	Victor Martinez/50	8.00
44	Roy Oswalt/100	5.00
45	Pedro Martinez/100	8.00
47	Tom Glavine/100	6.00
48	Torii Hunter/100	6.00
50	Nomar Garciaparra/100	15.00
53	Bobby Abreu/25	10.00
54	Doug Mientkiewicz/50	5.00
55	Hideki Matsui/100	25.00
56	Mark Buehrle/50	5.00
58	Johnny Damon/100	12.00
59	Edgar Martinez/100	6.00
60	Preston Wilson/50	6.00
62	Eric Chavez/100	5.00
63	Lyle Overbay/50	8.00
67	Jeff Bagwell/100	8.00
73	Lew Ford/50	5.00
73	Delmon Young/100	8.00
75	Barry Zito/100	5.00
76	Carlos Delgado/100	5.00
80	Adrian Beltre/100	8.00
81	Vernon Wells/100	5.00
86	Jose Reyes/50	8.00
87	Rocco Baldelli/100	5.00
88	Josh Beckett/100	5.00
91	Mike Sweeney/50	5.00
93	Trot Nixon/50	6.00
96	Jason Giambi/100	5.00
98	Craig Biggio/100	6.00
99	Pat Burrell/50	8.00
100	Kazuo Matsui/100	8.00

101	Rafael Furcal/50	6.00
102	Jack Wilson/50	8.00
103	Edgar Renteria/100	6.00
104	Carlos Beltran/100	8.00
105	Albert Pujols/100	15.00
106	Melvin Mora/50	5.00
107	J.D. Drew/100	5.00
108	Andre Dawson/250	6.00
109	Jody Gerut/50	6.00
110	Michael Young/250	5.00
111	Gary Sheffield/100	6.00
112	Wade Boggs/250	8.00
114	Paul LoDuca/100	10.00
115	Tim Hudson/100	5.00
116	Aramis Ramirez/50	8.00
117	Lance Berkman/250	5.00
118	Javy Lopez/100	5.00
119	Robin Yount/250	10.00
120	Mark Mulder/50	5.00
121	Sean Casey/50	5.00
122	Will Clark/250	8.00
123	Don Mattingly/250	15.00
124	Miguel Cabrera/50	12.00
125	Rafael Palmeiro/250	8.00
126	David Ortiz/250	12.00
127	Vladimir Guerrero/250	8.00
128	Ken Harvey/50	5.00
129	Rod Carew/250	8.00
130	Magglio Ordonez/250	5.00
131	Greg Maddux/100	10.00
134	Kerry Wood/100	8.00
135	Frank Thomas/100	8.00
138	Curt Schilling/100	8.00
142	Jeff Kent/250	5.00
143	Juan Encarnacion/50	5.00
144	Adam Dunn/250	8.00
145	Carlos Lee/250	5.00
148	Travis Hafner/50	6.00
149	Brad Wilkerson/100	5.00
151	Randy Johnson/100	10.00
152	Joe Crede/50	6.00
154	Jason Varitek/250	10.00
156	Brad Penny/50	5.00
158	Gary Carter/250	8.00
160	Derrek Lee/250	5.00
161	Mark Prior/100	8.00
164	Jermaine Dye/50	5.00
166	Dontrelle Willis/100	6.00
168	Johnny Estrada/50	5.00
170	Shannon Stewart/100	5.00
171	Ben Sheets/50	8.00
172	Richard Hidalgo/50	5.00
173	Laynce Nix/50	5.00
174	B.J. Upton/50	8.00
175	Craig Wilson/100	8.00
176	Hideo Nomo/100	8.00
177	Troy Glaus/250	5.00
179	Rickie Weeks/25	8.00
180	Mike Lowell/100	5.00
183	A.J. Burnett/100	5.00
184	Aubrey Huff/50	5.00
187	Kazuhisa Ishii/100	5.00
188	Mark Teixeira/250	5.00
190	Dale Murphy/250	8.00
191	Alexis Rios/50	5.00
193	Orlando Cabrera/50	6.00
194	Shawn Green/250	5.00
195	Andy Pettitte/100	6.00
196	Chipper Jones/100	8.00
197	Jose Vidro/50	5.00
198	Jacque Jones/100	5.00
199	Brian Giles/250	5.00
200	Andruw Jones/250	6.00

Material Fabric Number

		NM/M
Common Player:		5.00
20	Mike Schmidt/Jsy/20	50.00
21	Sammy Sosa/Jsy/21	20.00
22	Roger Clemens/ Jsy/22	40.00
23	Tony Perez/Jsy/24	15.00
24	Manny Ramirez/ Jsy/24	20.00
25	Jim Thome/Jsy/25	20.00
27	Scott Rolen/Jsy/27	20.00
28	Austin Kearns/Jsy/28	15.00
29	John Smoltz/Jsy/29	20.00
31	Mike Piazza/Jsy/31	25.00
32	Steve Carlton/ Pants/32	15.00
34	Nolan Ryan/Jsy/34	50.00
35	Mike Mussina/Jsy/35	15.00
39	Brett Myers/Jsy/39	8.00
41	Victor Martinez/Jsy/41	8.00
42	Mariano Rivera/ Jsy/42	20.00
43	Dennis Eckersley/ Jsy/43	10.00
44	Roy Oswalt/Jsy/44	8.00
45	Pedro Martinez/ Jsy/45	10.00
47	Tom Glavine/Jsy/47	10.00

48	Torii Hunter/Jsy/48	8.00
52	C.C. Sabathia/Jsy/52	8.00
53	Bobby Abreu/Jsy/53	8.00
55	Hideki Matsui/Jsy/55	35.00
56	Mark Buehrle/Jsy/56	8.00
57	Johan Santana/ Jsy/57	15.00
60	Preston Wilson/Jsy/44	8.00
61	Livan Hernandez/ Jsy/61	5.00
65	Cliff Lee/Jsy/34	8.00
71	Lew Ford/Jsy/20	10.00
75	Barry Zito/Jsy/75	5.00
76	Carlos Delgado/ Jsy/25	10.00
78	Ryan Wagner/Jsy/38	5.00
80	Adrian Beltre/Jsy/29	15.00
82	Sean Burroughs/ Jsy/32	8.00
83	Francisco Cordero/ Jsy/31	8.00
85	Eric Byrnes/Jsy/22	8.00
91	Mike Sweeney/Jsy/29	8.00
96	Jason Giambi/Jsy/25	10.00
100	Kazuo Matsui/Jsy/25	12.00
118	Javy Lopez/Jsy/18	15.00
119	Robin Yount/Jsy/19	30.00
120	Mark Mulder/Jsy/20	12.00
121	Sean Casey/Jsy/21	10.00
122	Will Clark/Jsy/22	20.00
123	Don Mattingly/ Pants/23	40.00
124	Miguel Cabrera/ Jsy/24	20.00
125	Rafael Palmeiro/ Jsy/25	15.00
126	David Ortiz/Jsy/34	20.00
127	Vladimir Guerrero/ Jsy/27	20.00
128	Ken Harvey/Jsy/28	10.00
129	Rod Carew/Jsy/29	20.00
130	Magglio Ordonez/ Jsy/30	10.00
131	Greg Maddux/Jsy/31	25.00
132	Roy Halladay/Jsy/32	10.00
134	Kerry Wood/Jsy/34	20.00
135	Frank Thomas/ Jsy/35	20.00
138	Curt Schilling/Jsy/34	15.00
139	Dewon Brazelton/ Jsy/45	5.00
140	Jae Weong/Seo/ Jsy/40	5.00
141	Danny Kolb/Jsy/41	5.00
144	Adam Dunn/Jsy/44	15.00
145	Carlos Lee/Jsy/45	8.00
146	Matt Clement/Jsy/30	10.00
148	Travis Hafner/Jsy/48	8.00
151	Randy Johnson/ Pants/51	15.00
154	Jason Varitek/ Jsy/33	20.00
157	Francisco Rodriguez/ Jsy/57	5.00
162	Carlos Zambrano/ Jsy/38	8.00
164	Jermaine Dye/Jsy/24	10.00
166	Dontrelle Willis/ Jsy/35	12.00
168	Johnny Estrada/ Jsy/23	10.00
170	Shannon Stewart/ Jsy/23	10.00
175	Craig Wilson/Jsy/36	5.00
177	Troy Glaus/Jsy/25	15.00
180	Mike Lowell/Jsy/19	20.00
183	A.J. Burnett/Jsy/34	10.00
188	Mark Teixeira/Jsy/23	15.00
195	Andy Pettitte/Jsy/21	20.00
200	Andruw Jones/Jsy/5	15.00

Material Fabric Position

		NM/M
Common Player:		4.00
Prime:		No Pricing
Production One Set		
1	Brian Roberts/Jsy/250	4.00
3	Harmon Killebrew/ Jsy/250	12.00
4	Angel Berroa/Jsy/250	4.00
5	George Brett/Jsy/250	15.00
6	Stan Musial/ Pants/100	15.00
7	Ivan Rodriguez/ Jsy/250	6.00
8	Cal Ripken Jr./ Jkt/250	25.00
9	Hank Blalock/Jsy/250	4.00
10	Miguel Tejada/Jsy/250	6.00
11	Barry Larkin/Jsy/100	6.00
12	Alfonso Soriano/ Jsy/250	4.00
14	Paul Konerko/Jsy/250	4.00
15	Jim Edmonds/Jsy/250	6.00
16	Garret Anderson/ Jsy/250	4.00
17	Todd Helton/Jsy/250	6.00
19	Tony Gwynn/Jsy/250	10.00
20	Mike Schmidt/Jsy/250	15.00
21	Sammy Sosa/Jsy/250	10.00
22	Roger Clemens/ Jsy/250	12.00
23	Tony Perez/Jsy/250	6.00
24	Manny Ramirez/ Jsy/250	8.00
25	Jim Thome/Jsy/250	8.00
27	Scott Rolen/Jsy/250	8.00
28	Austin Kearns/Jsy/250	4.00
29	John Smoltz/Jsy/250	6.00
31	Mike Piazza/Jsy/250	10.00
32	Steve Carlton/ Pants/250	6.00
34	Nolan Ryan/Jsy/250	20.00
35	Mike Mussina/Jsy/250	6.00
39	Brett Myers/Jsy/250	4.00
41	Victor Martinez/ Jsy/250	4.00
42	Mariano Rivera/ Jsy/250	6.00
43	Dennis Eckersley/ Jsy/250	6.00
44	Roy Oswalt/Jsy/250	4.00
45	Pedro Martinez/ Jsy/250	8.00
46	Jason Bay/Jsy/250	4.00
47	Tom Glavine/Jsy/250	4.00
48	Torii Hunter/Jsy/250	4.00
49	Larry Bigbie/Jsy/250	4.00
52	C.C. Sabathia/Jsy/250	4.00
53	Bobby Abreu/Jsy/250	4.00
55	Hideki Matsui/ Jsy/250	20.00
56	Mark Buehrle/Jsy/250	4.00
57	Johan Santana/ Jsy/250	8.00
59	Edgar Martinez/ Jsy/250	6.00
60	Preston Wilson/ Jsy/250	4.00
61	Livan Hernandez/ Jsy/250	4.00
62	Eric Chavez/Jsy/250	6.00
63	Lyle Overbay/Jsy/250	4.00
65	Cliff Lee/Jsy/250	4.00
67	Jeff Bagwell/Jsy/250	8.00
71	Lew Ford/Jsy/250	4.00
72	Chone Figgins/ Jsy/250	4.00
75	Barry Zito/Jsy/250	4.00
76	Carlos Delgado/ Jsy/250	4.00
78	Ryan Wagner/Jsy/250	4.00
80	Adrian Beltre/Jsy/250	8.00
81	Vernon Wells/Jsy/250	4.00
82	Sean Burroughs/ Jsy/250	4.00
83	Francisco Cordero/ Jsy/250	4.00
85	Eric Byrnes/Jsy/250	10.00
86	Jose Reyes/Jsy/250	4.00
87	Rocco Baldelli/Jsy/ 250	4.00
88	Josh Beckett/Jsy/250	4.00
90	Scott Podsednik/ Jsy/250	4.00
91	Mike Sweeney/ Jsy/250	4.00
93	Trot Nixon/Jsy/250	4.00
96	Jason Giambi/Jsy/250	4.00
98	Craig Biggio/Jsy/250	6.00
99	Pat Burrell/Jsy/250	4.00
100	Kazuo Matsui/Jsy/250	4.00
101	Rafael Furcal/Jsy/250	4.00
102	Jack Wilson/Jsy/250	4.00
103	Edgar Renteria/ Jsy/250	6.00

104	Carlos Beltran/ Jsy/250	8.00
105	Albert Pujols/Jsy/250	15.00
106	Melvin Mora/Jsy/100	4.00
108	Andre Dawson/ Jsy/250	6.00
109	Jody Gerut/Jsy/250	4.00
110	Michael Young/ Jsy/250	4.00
111	Gary Sheffield/ Jsy/250	6.00
112	Wade Boggs/Jsy/100	8.00
113	Carl Crawford/Jsy/250	4.00
115	Tim Hudson/Jsy/250	4.00
116	Aramis Ramirez/ Jsy/250	6.00
117	Lance Berkman/ Jsy/250	4.00
118	Javy Lopez/Jsy/250	4.00
119	Robin Yount/Jsy/250	10.00
120	Mark Mulder/Jsy/250	4.00
121	Sean Casey/Jsy/250	4.00
122	Will Clark/Jsy/250	6.00
123	Don Mattingly/ Pants/250	15.00
124	Miguel Cabrera/ Jsy/250	8.00
125	Rafael Palmeiro/ Jsy/250	8.00
126	David Ortiz/Jsy/250	8.00
127	Vladimir Guerrero/ Jsy/250	8.00
128	Ken Harvey/Jsy/250	4.00
129	Rod Carew/Jsy/250	8.00
130	Magglio Ordonez/ Jsy/250	4.00
131	Greg Maddux/Jsy/250	10.00
132	Roy Halladay/Jsy/250	4.00
134	Kerry Wood/Jsy/250	8.00
135	Frank Thomas/Jsy/250	8.00
138	Curt Schilling/Jsy/250	8.00
139	Dewon Brazelton/ Jsy/100	4.00
140	Jae Weong/Seo/ Jsy/250	4.00
141	Danny Kolb/Jsy/250	4.00
142	Jeff Kent/Jsy/100	6.00
144	Adam Dunn/Jsy/250	6.00
145	Carlos Lee/Jsy/250	4.00
146	Matt Clement/Jsy/250	4.00
148	Travis Hafner/Jsy/250	4.00
151	Randy Johnson/ Pants/250	8.00
154	Jason Varitek/ Jsy/100	15.00
157	Francisco Rodriguez/ Jsy/100	4.00
158	Gary Carter/Jsy/250	6.00
161	Mark Prior/Jsy/250	8.00
162	Carlos Zambrano/ Jsy/250	6.00
163	Bobby Crosby/Jsy/250	4.00
164	Jermaine Dye/Jsy/100	4.00
166	Dontrelle Willis/ Jsy/250	4.00
168	Johnny Estrada/ Jsy/100	4.00
170	Shannon Stewart/ Jsy/250	4.00
171	Ben Sheets/Jsy/250	6.00
173	Laynce Nix/Jsy/100	4.00
175	Craig Wilson/Jsy/250	4.00
176	Hideo Nomo/Jsy/250	8.00
177	Troy Glaus/Jsy/250	4.00
180	Mike Lowell	4.00
183	A.J. Burnett/Jsy/100	4.00
184	Aubrey Huff/Jsy/250	4.00
187	Kazuhisa Ishii/Jsy/250	4.00
188	Mark Teixeira/Jsy/250	4.00
190	Dale Murphy/Jsy/250	8.00
194	Shawn Green/Jsy/250	4.00
195	Andy Pettitte/Jsy/250	6.00
196	Chipper Jones/Jsy/250	8.00
197	Jose Vidro/Jsy/100	4.00
198	Jacque Jones/Jsy/250	4.00
200	Andruw Jones/Jsy/250	6.00

Pennant Patches

		NM/M
Production 5-25		
1	Ozzie Smith/25	40.00
2	Keith Hernandez/25	20.00
3	Rickey Henderson/ 25	30.00
4	Paul Molitor/25	25.00
5	George Brett/25	50.00
6	Steve Garvey/25	20.00
7	Randy Johnson/25	25.00
8	Cal Ripken Jr./25	90.00
9	Darryl Strawberry/25	20.00
10	Chipper Jones/25	30.00
11	Steve Carlton/25	20.00
12	Orel Hershiser/25	20.00
13	Carlton Fisk/25	25.00

14	Dave Parker/25	20.00
15	Rollie Fingers/25	20.00
16	Dwight Gooden/25	20.00
17	Mark Grace/10	
18	Dontrelle Willis/25	15.00
19	Dave Righetti/25	15.00
20	Brooks Robinson/5	

Pennant Patches Signature
NM/M
Production 5-25

2	Keith Hernandez/25	40.00
6	Steve Garvey/25	35.00
9	Darryl Strawberry/25	40.00
11	Steve Carlton/25	40.00
15	Rollie Fingers/25	35.00
16	Dwight Gooden/25	40.00

Shirts
NM/M
Production 25-100

1	Rod Carew/100	10.00
2	Red Schoendienst/50	8.00
3	Harmon Killebrew/50	20.00
4	Joe Cronin/50	35.00
5	Early Wynn/50	8.00
6	Gaylord Perry/100	8.00
7	Willie McCovey/100	10.00
8	Carl Yastrzemski/100	20.00
9	Reggie Jackson/100	10.00
10	Duke Snider/50	15.00
11	Luis Aparicio/100	8.00
12	Bob Gibson/50	15.00
13	Maury Wills/50	8.00
14	Ernie Banks/50	20.00
15	Enos Slaughter/100	10.00
16	Whitey Ford/100	15.00
17	Warren Spahn/100	15.00
18	Roger Maris/100	35.00
19	Hal Newhouser/100	10.00
20	Marty Marion/25	12.00

Shirts Signature
NM/M
Production 5-50
Prime: No Pricing
Production One Set

2	Red Schoendienst/25	25.00
6	Gaylord Perry/50	20.00
7	Willie McCovey/50	30.00
11	Luis Aparicio/25	25.00
13	Maury Wills/50	20.00

Signature Post Marks Gold
Production 1-50

36	Joe Nathan/50	20.00
39	Brett Myers/50	12.00
40	Rich Harden/50	15.00
49	Larry Bigbie/50	15.00
61	Livan Hernandez/50	15.00
63	Lyle Overbay/50	15.00
65	Cliff Lee/50	12.00
68	Danny Graves/25	20.00
71	Lew Ford/50	15.00
72	Chone Figgins/50	20.00
74	Esteban Loaiza/50	20.00
78	Ryan Wagner/50	10.00
79	John Lackey/50	15.00
83	Francisco Cordero/25	15.00
85	Eric Byrnes/25	20.00
89	Casey Kotchman/25	15.00
90	Scott Podsednik/50	15.00
94	Chad Cordero/25	15.00
97	Jose Guillen/25	20.00
102	Jack Wilson/50	15.00
106	Melvin Mora/25	20.00
109	Jody Gerut/50	10.00
128	Ken Harvey/50	10.00
136	Tom Gordon/50	15.00
137	Jake Peavy/75	15.00
139	Dewon Brazelton/50	10.00
140	Jae Weong Seo/20	20.00
141	Danny Kolb/50	20.00
145	Carlos Lee/25	20.00
147	Guillermo Mota/50	10.00
148	Travis Hafner/50	15.00
156	Brad Penny/50	10.00
159	Adrian Gonzalez/50	15.00
163	Bobby Crosby/50	30.00
164	Jermaine Dye/25	20.00
169	Johnny Estrada/25	25.00
170	Shannon Stewart/25	15.00
173	Laynce Nix/25	20.00
175	Craig Wilson/50	15.00
182	Randy Wolf/50	15.00
185	Billy Ripken/25	10.00
186	Octavio Dotel/50	15.00
189	Todd Walker/25	20.00
191	Alexis Rios/50	15.00
198	Jacque Jones/25	15.00

Signature Post Marks Silver
NM/M
Production 1-250
Platinum: No Pricing
Production One Set

1	Brian Roberts/250	8.00
4	Angel Berroa/25	15.00
36	Joe Nathan/250	15.00
39	Brett Myers/250	8.00
40	Rich Harden/250	15.00
49	Larry Bigbie/250	10.00
52	C.C. Sabathia/25	20.00
56	Mark Buehrle/50	15.00
61	Livan Hernandez/100	10.00
63	Lyle Overbay/100	15.00
65	Cliff Lee/250	8.00
68	Danny Graves/100	10.00
71	Lew Ford/100	10.00
72	Chone Figgins/250	10.00
74	Esteban Loaiza/250	10.00
78	Ryan Wagner/250	10.00
79	John Lackey/250	10.00
82	Sean Burroughs/25	15.00
83	Francisco Cordero/100	8.00
85	Eric Byrnes/100	10.00
89	Casey Kotchman/250	20.00
90	Scott Podsednik/100	10.00
93	Trot Nixon/25	25.00
94	Chad Cordero/250	8.00
97	Jose Guillen/100	10.00
102	Jack Wilson/100	10.00
106	Melvin Mora/100	10.00
108	Andre Dawson/25	25.00
109	Jody Gerut/250	8.00
116	Aramis Ramirez/25	25.00
128	Ken Harvey/250	8.00
136	Tom Gordon/250	10.00
137	Jake Peavy/100	20.00
139	Dewon Brazelton/250	8.00
140	Jae Weong Seo/100	10.00
141	Danny Kolb/250	12.00
145	Carlos Lee/100	12.00
147	Guillermo Mota/250	8.00
148	Travis Hafner/100	15.00
155	David Wright/25	80.00
156	Brad Penny/250	8.00
157	Francisco Rodriguez/100	15.00
159	Adrian Gonzalez/250	10.00
160	Derrek Lee/25	30.00
162	Carlos Zambrano/25	25.00
163	Bobby Crosby/100	25.00
164	Jermaine Dye/250	10.00
168	Johnny Estrada/200	15.00
169	Milton Bradley/100	15.00
170	Shannon Stewart/50	15.00
173	Laynce Nix/250	10.00
175	Craig Wilson/100	15.00
181	Marcus Giles/25	20.00
182	Randy Wolf/250	12.00
184	Aubrey Huff/100	10.00
185	Billy Ripken/250	8.00
186	Octavio Dotel/250	15.00
189	Todd Walker/100	15.00
191	Alexis Rios/200	10.00
193	Orlando Cabrera/25	20.00
197	Jose Vidro/25	15.00
198	Jacque Jones/100	10.00

Stamps Masterpiece Signature Centennial
No Pricing
Production 1-2

Stamps Material Centennial
NM/M
Production 1-39

1	Pee Wee Reese/Bat/39	20.00
2	Red Schoendienst/Jsy/2	
3	Babe Ruth/Jsy/39	275.00
4	George Brett/Jsy/39	40.00
5	Stan Musial/Bat/39	40.00
6	Bob Feller/Pants/39	15.00
7	Cal Ripken Jr./Pants/39	
8	Ted Williams/Jsy/39	100.00
11	Dwight Evans/Jsy/39	25.00
12	Dave Concepcion/Jsy/39	
13	Ernie Banks/Jsy/39	25.00
14	Pedro J. Martinez/Jsy/39	20.00
16	Scott Rolen/Jsy/39	25.00
17	Tony Gwynn/Jsy/39	30.00
18	Mike Schmidt/Jsy/39	60.00
19	Roberto Clemente/Hat/21	200.00
20	Roger Clemens/Jsy/39	35.00
21	Don Mattingly/Jsy/39	50.00
22	Tony Perez/Bat/39	15.00
23	Roger Maris/Jsy/39	75.00
24	Billy Williams/Jsy/39	15.00
25	Juan Marichal/Pants/39	20.00
26	Hank Blalock/Jsy/39	20.00
27	Maury Wills/Jsy/39	15.00
28	Fergie Jenkins/Pants/39	20.00
29	Steve Carlton/Jsy/39	15.00
30	Dale Murphy/Jsy/39	15.00
31	Kerry Wood/Jsy/39	20.00
32	Gaylord Perry/Jsy/39	15.00
33	Fred Lynn/Jsy/39	20.00
34	Tom Seaver/Bat/39	20.00
36	Reggie Jackson/Pants/39	25.00
37	Bob Gibson/Jsy/39	20.00
38	Jack Morris/Jsy/39	20.00
39	Torii Hunter/Jsy/39	15.00
40	Andre Dawson/Jsy/39	20.00
41	Dave Righetti/Jsy/39	15.00
42	Hideki Matsui/Pants/39	65.00
43	Lou Brock/Jkt/39	25.00
44	Yogi Berra/Bat/39	30.00
45	Frankie Frisch/Jkt/39	25.00
46	Sean Casey/Jsy/39	15.00
47	Sammy Sosa/Jsy/39	30.00
48	Ralph Kiner/Bat/39	30.00
49	Hoyt Wilhelm/Jsy/39	15.00
50	Jim Rice/Jsy/39	20.00
51	Duke Snider/Pants/39	25.00
52	Harold Baines/Jsy/39	20.00
53	Willie Stargell/Jsy/39	20.00
54	Johnny Bench/Pants/39	25.00
55	Carlton Fisk/Jsy/39	25.00
56	Jim Palmer/Jsy/39	20.00
57	Bobby Doerr/Jsy/39	20.00
58	Mark Prior/Jsy/39	30.00
60	Lou Boudreau/Jsy/39	15.00
61	Alan Trammell/Bat/39	20.00
62	Al Kaline/Bat/39	25.00
63	Warren Spahn/Pants/39	30.00
64	Bert Blyleven/Jsy/39	20.00
65	Miguel Cabrera/Jsy/39	25.00
66	Luis Tiant/Jsy/39	15.00
67	Harmon Killebrew/Jsy/39	30.00
68	Richie Ashburn/Pants/39	25.00
69	Michael Young/Jsy/39	15.00
70	Tony Oliva/Jsy/39	20.00
71	Mark Mulder/Jsy/39	15.00
72	Nolan Ryan/Jsy/39	75.00
73	Willie McCovey/Jsy/39	25.00
74	Kirk Gibson/Jsy/39	20.00
75	Carl Yastrzemski/Pants/39	40.00

Stamps Material Legendary Fields
NM/M
Production 1-34

1	Pee Wee Reese/Bat/34	30.00
11	Dwight Evans/Jsy/34	25.00
12	Dave Concepcion/Jsy/34	20.00
13	Ernie Banks/Jsy/34	40.00
14	Pedro J. Martinez/Jsy/34	25.00
15	Whitey Ford/Jsy/34	35.00
19	Roberto Clemente/Hat/21	200.00
21	Don Mattingly/Jsy/34	50.00
22	Tony Perez/Bat/34	20.00
23	Roger Maris/Jsy/34	85.00
24	Billy Williams/Jsy/34	30.00
28	Fergie Jenkins/Pants/34	20.00
29	Steve Carlton/Jsy/34	25.00
31	Kerry Wood/Jsy/34	30.00
33	Fred Lynn/Jsy/34	20.00
36	Reggie Jackson/Pants/34	25.00
38	Jack Morris/Jsy/34	20.00
40	Andre Dawson/Jsy/34	20.00
41	Dave Righetti/Jsy/34	20.00
42	Hideki Matsui/Pants/34	80.00
44	Yogi Berra/Bat/34	40.00
47	Sammy Sosa/Jsy/34	40.00
48	Ralph Kiner/Bat/34	20.00
49	Hoyt Wilhelm/Jsy/34	15.00
50	Jim Rice/Jsy/34	20.00
51	Duke Snider/Pants/34	20.00
52	Harold Baines/Jsy/34	15.00
53	Willie Stargell/Jsy/34	30.00
54	Johnny Bench/Pants/34	40.00
55	Carlton Fisk/Jsy/34	25.00
57	Bobby Doerr/Jsy/34	25.00
58	Mark Prior/Jsy/34	40.00
61	Alan Trammell/Bat/34	30.00
62	Al Kaline/Bat/34	30.00
66	Luis Tiant/Jsy/34	25.00
74	Kirk Gibson/Jsy/34	30.00
75	Carl Yastrzemski/Pants/34	50.00

Stamps Material Legendary Players 20
NM/M
Complete Set (2):

3	Babe Ruth/Jsy/19	
19	Roberto Clemente/Hat/21	200.00

Stamps Material Legendary Players 33
NM/M
Complete Set (2):

19	Roberto Clemente/Hat/21	200.00

Stamps Material Olympic
NM/M
Production 1-92

1	Pee Wee Reese/Bat/92	15.00
4	George Brett/Jsy/92	30.00
5	Stan Musial/Bat/92	30.00
6	Bob Feller/Pants/92	15.00
7	Cal Ripken Jr./Pants/92	60.00
11	Dwight Evans/Jsy/92	20.00
13	Ernie Banks/Jsy/92	25.00
14	Pedro J. Martinez/Jsy/45	20.00
16	Scott Rolen/Jsy/27	20.00
17	Tony Gwynn/Jsy/92	30.00
18	Mike Schmidt/Jsy/92	40.00
19	Roberto Clemente/Hat/21	200.00
20	Roger Clemens/Jsy/92	30.00
21	Don Mattingly/Jsy/23	40.00
22	Tony Perez/Bat/24	30.00
24	Billy Williams/Jsy/26	20.00
25	Juan Marichal/Pants/92	15.00
26	Hank Blalock/Jsy/92	15.00
27	Maury Wills/Jsy/30	20.00
28	Fergie Jenkins/Pants/92	15.00
29	Steve Carlton/Jsy/92	15.00
30	Dale Murphy/Jsy/92	20.00
31	Kerry Wood/Jsy/92	15.00
32	Gaylord Perry/Jsy/92	15.00
33	Fred Lynn/Jsy/92	15.00
34	Tom Seaver/Bat/92	20.00
36	Reggie Jackson/Pants/44	20.00
37	Bob Gibson/Jsy/45	25.00
38	Jack Morris/Jsy/92	15.00
39	Torii Hunter/Jsy/48	15.00
41	Dave Righetti/Jsy/92	15.00
42	Hideki Matsui/Pants/92	40.00
43	Lou Brock/Jkt/92	15.00
44	Yogi Berra/Jsy/92	15.00
45	Frankie Frisch/Jkt/92	15.00
46	Sean Casey/Jsy/21	25.00
47	Sammy Sosa/Jsy/92	25.00
48	Ralph Kiner/Bat/92	20.00
49	Hoyt Wilhelm/Jsy/92	15.00
50	Jim Rice/Jsy/92	15.00
51	Duke Snider/Pants/92	20.00
52	Harold Baines/Jsy/92	15.00
53	Willie Stargell/Jsy/92	20.00
54	Johnny Bench/Pants/92	20.00
55	Carlton Fisk/Jsy/92	25.00
56	Jim Palmer/Jsy/92	20.00
57	Bobby Doerr/Jsy/92	15.00

58	Mark Prior/Jsy/92	20.00
60	Lou Boudreau/Jsy/92	20.00
61	Alan Trammell/Bat/92	15.00
62	Al Kaline Bat/92	20.00
63	Warren Spahn/ Pants/92	25.00
64	Bert Blyleven/Jsy/1	
65	Miguel Cabrera/ Jsy/92	20.00
66	Luis Tiant/Jsy/23	20.00
67	Harmon Killebrew/ Jsy/92	30.00
68	Richie Ashburn/ Pants/92	20.00
70	Tony Oliva/Jsy/92	15.00

Stamps Material Pro Ball
NM/M

Production 1-69

1	Pee Wee Reese/ Bat/69	20.00
4	George Brett/Jsy/69	40.00
5	Stan Musial/Bat/69	30.00
6	Bob Feller/Pants/69	20.00
7	Cal Ripken Jr./ Pants/69	60.00
11	Dwight Evans/Jsy/24	30.00
13	Ernie Banks/Jsy/69	30.00
14	Pedro J. Martinez/ Jsy/45	25.00
16	Scott Rolen/Jsy/27	40.00
17	Tony Gwynn/Jsy/69	35.00
18	Mike Schmidt/Jsy/69	60.00
19	Roberto Clemente/ Hat/21	200.00
20	Roger Clemens/ Jsy/69	30.00
21	Don Mattingly/Jsy/23	50.00
22	Tony Perez/Bat/24	20.00
23	Billy Williams/Jsy/69	15.00
25	Juan Marichal/ Pants/69	15.00
26	Hank Blalock/Jsy/69	15.00
27	Maury Wills/Jsy/69	15.00
28	Fergie Jenkins/ Pants/69	15.00
29	Steve Carlton/Jsy/69	15.00
30	Dale Murphy/Jsy/69	15.00
31	Kerry Wood/Jsy/69	20.00
32	Gaylord Perry/Jsy/69	15.00
33	Fred Lynn/Jsy/69	15.00
34	Tom Seaver/Bat/69	20.00
36	Reggie Jackson/ Pants/69	15.00
37	Bob Gibson/Jsy/45	25.00
38	Jack Morris/Jsy/69	15.00
39	Torii Hunter/Jsy/48	15.00
40	Andre Dawson/ Jsy/69	15.00
41	Dave Righetti/Jsy/69	15.00
42	Hideki Matsui/ Pants/69	40.00
43	Lou Brock/Jkt/69	15.00
44	Yogi Berra/Bat/69	25.00
45	Frankie Frisch/Jkt/69	20.00
46	Sean Casey/Jsy/69	20.00
47	Sammy Sosa/Jsy/69	20.00
48	Ralph Kiner/Bat/69	15.00
49	Hoyt Wilhelm/Jsy/69	15.00
50	Jim Rice/Jsy/69	15.00
51	Duke Snider/ Pants/69	20.00
52	Harold Baines/Jsy/69	15.00
53	Willie Stargell/Jsy/69	20.00
54	Johnny Bench/ Pants/69	20.00
55	Carlton Fisk/Jsy/69	15.00
56	Jim Palmer/Jsy/69	15.00
57	Bobby Doerr/Jsy/69	15.00
58	Mark Prior/Jsy/69	20.00
60	Lou Boudreau/Jsy/69	25.00
61	Alan Trammell/Bat/69	15.00
62	Al Kaline/Bat/69	20.00
63	Warren Spahn/ Pants/69	25.00
65	Miguel Cabrera/ Jsy/69	15.00
66	Luis Tiant/Jsy/69	15.00
67	Harmon Killebrew/ Jsy/69	35.00
68	Richie Ashburn/ Pants/69	20.00
69	Michael Young/ Jsy/69	15.00
70	Tony Oliva/Jsy/69	20.00
71	Mark Mulder/Jsy/20	25.00
72	Nolan Ryan/Jsy/69	60.00
73	Willie McCovey/ Jsy/69	25.00
74	Kirk Gibson/Jsy/69	15.00
75	Carl Yastrzemski/ Pants/69	30.00

Stamps Material USA Flag
NM/M

Production 1-100

1	Pee Wee Reese/ Bat/100	15.00
4	George Brett/Jsy/100	35.00
5	Stan Musial/Bat/100	25.00
6	Bob Feller/Pants/100	15.00
7	Cal Ripken Jr./ Pants/100	65.00
11	Dwight Evans/Jsy/24	30.00
13	Ernie Banks/Jsy/100	30.00
14	Pedro J. Martinez/ Jsy/45	25.00
16	Scott Rolen/Jsy/27	40.00
17	Tony Gwynn/Jsy/100	30.00
18	Mike Schmidt/ Jsy/100	50.00
19	Roberto Clemente/ Hat/21	200.00
20	Roger Clemens/ Jsy/100	25.00
21	Don Mattingly/ Jsy/100	30.00
22	Tony Perez/Bat/100	15.00
24	Billy Williams/ Jsy/100	10.00
25	Juan Marichal/ Pants/100	15.00
26	Hank Blalock/ Jsy/100	15.00
27	Maury Wills/Jsy/100	10.00
28	Fergie Jenkins/ Pants/100	15.00
29	Steve Carlton/ Jsy/100	15.00
30	Dale Murphy/Jsy/100	15.00
31	Kerry Wood/Jsy/100	20.00
32	Gaylord Perry/ Jsy/100	10.00
33	Fred Lynn/Jsy/100	10.00
34	Tom Seaver/Bat/100	15.00
36	Reggie Jackson/ Pants/44	20.00
37	Bob Gibson/Jsy/100	20.00
38	Jack Morris/Jsy/100	15.00
39	Torii Hunter/Jsy/48	15.00
40	Andre Dawson	15.00
41	Dave Righetti/Jsy/100	10.00
42	Hideki Matsui/ Pants/100	40.00
43	Lou Brock/Jkt/100	15.00
44	Yogi Berra/Bat/100	20.00
45	Frankie Frisch/ Jkt/100	15.00
46	Sean Casey/Jsy/100	10.00
47	Sammy Sosa/ Jsy/100	15.00
48	Ralph Kiner/Bat/100	15.00
49	Hoyt Wilhelm/ Jsy/100	10.00
50	Jim Rice/Jsy/100	12.00
51	Duke Snider/ Pants/100	15.00
52	Harold Baines/ Jsy/100	10.00
53	Willie Stargell/ Jsy/100	15.00
54	Johnny Bench/ Pants/100	20.00
55	Carlton Fisk/Jsy/72	15.00
56	Jim Palmer/Jsy/100	15.00
57	Bobby Doerr/Jsy/100	15.00
58	Mark Prior/Jsy/100	15.00
63	Al Kaline/Bat/100	15.00
63	Warren Spahn/ Pants/100	20.00
64	Bert Blyleven/Jsy/28	20.00
65	Miguel Cabrera/ Jsy/24	20.00
66	Luis Tiant/Jsy/23	20.00
67	Harmon Killebrew/ Jsy/100	30.00
68	Richie Ashburn/ Pants/100	15.00
70	Tony Oliva/Jsy/100	15.00
71	Mark Mulder/Jsy/20	25.00
72	Nolan Ryan/Jsy/50	50.00
73	Willie McCovey/ Jsy/44	25.00
74	Kirk Gibson/Jsy/100	10.00
75	Carl Yastrzemski/ Pants/100	25.00

Stamps Centennial Autograph
NM/M

Production 1-40

2	Red Schoendienst/39	40.00
6	Bob Feller/39	40.00
11	Dwight Evans/39	30.00
15	Whitey Ford/27	50.00
22	Tony Perez/24	40.00
24	Billy Williams/39	30.00
25	Juan Marichal/39	30.00
27	Maury Wills/39	25.00
28	Fergie Jenkins/39	30.00
29	Steve Carlton/39	30.00
30	Dale Murphy/39	50.00
32	Gaylord Perry/39	25.00
33	Fred Lynn/39	30.00
35	Ron Guidry/39	40.00
38	Jack Morris/39	25.00
39	Torii Hunter/39	30.00
40	Andre Dawson/39	30.00
41	Dave Righetti/39	20.00
43	Lou Brock/20	40.00
46	Sean Casey/21	40.00
48	Ralph Kiner/39	30.00
50	Jim Rice/39	35.00
52	Duke Snider/25	50.00
52	Harold Baines/39	25.00
56	Jim Palmer/45	40.00
57	Bobby Doerr/59	30.00
59	Monte Irvin/39	35.00
61	Alan Trammell/40	35.00
62	Al Kaline/39	50.00
64	Bert Blyleven/39	25.00
65	Miguel Cabrera/39	30.00
66	Luis Tiant/39	25.00
69	Michael Young/39	25.00
70	Tony Oliva/39	35.00
71	Mark Mulder/25	40.00

Stamps Legendary Fields Autograph
NM/M

Production 1-34

11	Dwight Evans/34	30.00
22	Tony Perez/34	35.00
24	Billy Williams/34	30.00
28	Fergie Jenkins/34	30.00
29	Steve Carlton/34	30.00
33	Fred Lynn/34	30.00
35	Ron Guidry/34	50.00
38	Jack Morris/34	25.00
40	Andre Dawson/34	30.00
41	Dave Righetti/34	20.00
48	Ralph Kiner/34	30.00
50	Jim Rice/34	35.00
52	Harold Baines/34	25.00
57	Bobby Doerr/34	35.00
59	Monte Irvin/34	35.00
66	Luis Tiant/23	30.00

Stamps Material Centennial Autograph
NM/M

Production 1-39

2	Red Schoendienst/ Jsy/39	40.00
6	Bob Feller/Pants/39	40.00
11	Dwight Evans/Jsy/39	30.00
22	Tony Perez/Bat/24	40.00
24	Billy Williams/Jsy/39	35.00
25	Juan Marichal/ Pants/39	30.00
27	Maury Wills/Jsy/39	30.00
28	Fergie Jenkins/ Pants/39	35.00
29	Steve Carlton/Jsy/39	30.00
30	Dale Murphy/Jsy/39	50.00
32	Gaylord Perry/Jsy/39	50.00
33	Fred Lynn/Jsy/39	30.00
37	Bob Gibson/Jsy/39	40.00
38	Jack Morris/Jsy/39	25.00
40	Andre Dawson/ Jsy/39	30.00
43	Lou Brock/Jkt/39	30.00
46	Sean Casey/Jsy/39	30.00
48	Ralph Kiner/Bat/39	30.00
50	Jim Rice/Jsy/39	35.00
51	Duke Snider/ Pants/39	50.00
52	Harold Baines/ Jsy/39	25.00
56	Jim Palmer/Jsy/22	50.00
57	Bobby Doerr/Jsy/39	35.00
61	Alan Trammell/ Bat/39	30.00
62	Al Kaline/Bat/39	50.00
64	Bert Blyleven/Jsy/39	25.00
65	Miguel Cabrera/ Jsy/39	50.00
66	Luis Tiant/Jsy/39	30.00
67	Harmon Killebrew/ Jsy/39	60.00
70	Tony Oliva/Jsy/39	35.00
71	Mark Mulder/Jsy/20	40.00
74	Kirk Gibson/Jsy/39	30.00

Stamps Material Legendary Fields Autograph
NM/M

Production 1-34

11	Dwight Evans/Jsy/34	30.00
22	Tony Perez/Bat/34	40.00
24	Billy Williams/Jsy/34	30.00
28	Fergie Jenkins/ Pants/34	35.00
29	Steve Carlton/Jsy/34	35.00
33	Fred Lynn/Jsy/34	30.00
38	Jack Morris/Jsy/34	30.00
40	Andre Dawson/ Jsy/34	30.00
41	Dave Righetti/Jsy/34	20.00
50	Jim Rice/Jsy/33	40.00
66	Luis Tiant/Jsy/23	35.00
74	Kirk Gibson/Jsy/23	30.00

Stamps Material Olympic Autograph
NM/M

Production 1-29

6	Bob Feller/Pants/29	45.00
11	Dwight Evans/Jsy/24	35.00
22	Tony Perez/Bat/29	40.00
24	Billy Williams/Jsy/29	35.00
25	Juan Marichal/ Pants/29	35.00
27	Maury Wills/Jsy/29	30.00
28	Fergie Jenkins/ Pants/29	35.00
29	Steve Carlton/Jsy/29	35.00
30	Dale Murphy/Jsy/29	50.00
32	Gaylord Perry/Jsy/29	30.00
33	Fred Lynn/Jsy/29	30.00
37	Bob Gibson/Jsy/29	40.00
38	Jack Morris/Jsy/29	30.00
40	Andre Dawson/ Jsy/25	35.00
43	Lou Brock/Jkt/20	40.00
46	Sean Casey/Jsy/21	40.00
56	Jim Palmer/Jsy/22	50.00
65	Bert Blyleven/Jsy/28	30.00
65	Miguel Cabrera/ Jsy/24	60.00
66	Luis Tiant/Jsy/23	30.00
71	Mark Mulder/Jsy/23	30.00
74	Kirk Gibson/Jsy/23	30.00

Stamps Material Pro Ball Autograph
NM/M

Production 1-69

6	Bob Feller/Pants/69	30.00
11	Dwight Evans/Jsy/69	30.00
22	Tony Perez/Bat/24	40.00
24	Billy Williams/Jsy/26	35.00
25	Juan Marichal/ Pants/27	35.00
27	Maury Wills/Jsy/69	20.00
28	Fergie Jenkins/ Pants/69	25.00
29	Steve Carlton/Jsy/69	35.00
30	Dale Murphy/Jsy/69	40.00
32	Gaylord Perry/Jsy/69	20.00
33	Fred Lynn/Jsy/69	25.00
37	Bob Gibson/Jsy/45	35.00
43	Lou Brock/Jsy/20	40.00
46	Sean Casey/Jsy/21	40.00
57	Bobby Doerr/Jsy/48	30.00
65	Miguel Cabrera/ Jsy/24	50.00
66	Luis Tiant/Jsy/23	30.00
71	Mark Mulder/Jsy/23	30.00
74	Kirk Gibson/Jsy/23	30.00

Stamps Material USA Flag Autograph
NM/M

Production 1-37

2	Red Schoendienst/ Jsy/37	40.00
6	Bob Feller/Pants/8	40.00
11	Dwight Evans/Jsy/37	35.00
22	Tony Perez/Bat/37	35.00
24	Billy Williams/Jsy/37	30.00
25	Juan Marichal/ Pants/37	30.00
27	Maury Wills/Jsy/37	25.00
28	Fergie Jenkins/ Pants/37	30.00
29	Steve Carlton/Jsy/37	30.00

30	Dale Murphy/Jsy/37	50.00
32	Gaylord Perry/Jsy/37	25.00
33	Fred Lynn/Jsy/37	30.00
37	Bob Gibson/Jsy/37	40.00
38	Jack Morris/Jsy/37	25.00
41	Dave Righetti/Jsy/37	20.00
43	Lou Brock/Jkt/37	30.00
46	Sean Casey/Jsy/37	30.00
48	Ralph Kiner/Bat/37	30.00
50	Jim Rice/Jsy/37	30.00
51	Duke Snider/Pants/37	40.00
52	Harold Baines/Jsy/37	25.00
56	Jim Palmer/Jsy/37	35.00
57	Bobby Doerr/Jsy/37	30.00
61	Alan Trammell/Bat/37	30.00
62	Al Kaline/Bat/37	50.00
64	Bert Blyleven/Jsy/37	25.00
65	Miguel Cabrera/Jsy/37	50.00
66	Luis Tiant/Jsy/37	25.00
67	Harmon Killebrew/Jsy/37	60.00
70	Tony Oliva/Jsy/37	30.00
71	Mark Mulder/Jsy/37	30.00
74	Kirk Gibson/Jsy/23	30.00
75	Carl Yastrzemski/Pants/8	

Stamps Olympic Autograph

NM/M

Production 1-92

2	Red Schoendienst/92	25.00
6	Bob Feller/92	25.00
11	Dwight Evans/92	20.00
22	Tony Perez/24	40.00
24	Billy Williams/26	35.00
25	Juan Marichal/27	35.00
27	Maury Wills/92	20.00
28	Fergie Jenkins/92	25.00
29	Steve Carlton/92	20.00
30	Dale Murphy/92	30.00
32	Gaylord Perry/92	20.00
33	Fred Lynn/92	20.00
35	Ron Guidry/48	35.00
38	Jack Morris/92	20.00
39	Torii Hunter/48	25.00
40	Andre Dawson/92	25.00
43	Lou Brock/20	40.00
46	Sean Casey/21	40.00
50	Jim Rice/92	25.00
52	Harold Baines/92	20.00
56	Jim Palmer/22	50.00
57	Bobby Doerr/92	25.00
59	Monte Irvin/92	40.00
61	Alan Trammell/92	25.00
62	Al Kaline/92	40.00
64	Bert Blyleven/92	20.00
65	Miguel Cabrera/24	60.00
66	Luis Tiant/92	20.00
70	Tony Oliva/91	20.00
71	Mark Mulder/20	40.00

Stamps Pro Ball Autograph

NM/M

Production 1-69

6	Bob Feller/69	30.00
11	Dwight Evans/69	25.00
22	Tony Perez/24	40.00
24	Billy Williams/26	35.00
25	Juan Marichal/27	35.00
27	Maury Wills/69	20.00
28	Fergie Jenkins/69	25.00
29	Steve Carlton/69	30.00
30	Dale Murphy/69	40.00
32	Gaylord Perry/69	20.00
33	Fred Lynn/69	25.00
35	Ron Guidry/49	40.00
38	Jack Morris/47	20.00
39	Torii Hunter/48	25.00
43	Lou Brock/69	40.00
46	Sean Casey/21	40.00
57	Bobby Doerr/69	30.00
59	Monte Irvin/20	40.00
64	Bert Blyleven/28	25.00
65	Miguel Cabrera/24	50.00
66	Luis Tiant/23	30.00
71	Mark Mulder/20	40.00

Stamps USA Flag Autograph

NM/M

Production 1-100

2	Red Schoendienst/100	25.00
6	Bob Feller/100	25.00
11	Dwight Evans/24	35.00
22	Tony Perez/24	40.00
24	Billy Williams/26	35.00
25	Juan Marichal/27	35.00
27	Maury Wills/100	20.00
28	Fergie Jenkins/100	25.00
29	Steve Carlton/100	20.00
30	Dale Murphy/100	30.00
32	Gaylord Perry/100	20.00
33	Fred Lynn/100	20.00
35	Ron Guidry/49	35.00
38	Jack Morris/100	20.00
39	Torii Hunter/48	25.00
40	Andre Dawson/100	25.00
43	Lou Brock/20	40.00
46	Sean Casey/21	40.00
48	Ralph Kiner/100	25.00
51	Duke Snider/25	45.00
52	Harold Baines/100	20.00
56	Jim Palmer/22	50.00
57	Bobby Doerr/100	25.00
59	Monte Irvin/100	40.00
61	Alan Trammell/100	25.00
62	Al Kaline/100	40.00
64	Bert Blyleven/100	20.00
65	Miguel Cabrera/24	60.00
66	Luis Tiant/100	20.00
70	Tony Oliva/100	20.00
71	Mark Mulder/20	40.00

Timeline Threads Jersey Number

NM/M

Production 1-43

6	Orlando Cepeda/Pants/30	10.00
9	Tony Perez/Jsy/24	15.00
11	Tommy John/Jsy/25	15.00
15	Carlton Fisk/Jsy/27	20.00
17	Bert Blyleven/Jsy/28	10.00
20	Lou Brock/Jsy/20	15.00
21	Sammy Sosa/Jsy/21	20.00
22	Roger Clemens/Jsy/22	40.00
23	Don Mattingly/Jsy/23	40.00
24	Rickey Henderson/Jsy/35	15.00
26	Wade Boggs/Jsy/26	20.00
29	Jim "Catfish" Hunter/Jsy/29	15.00
30	Maury Wills/Jsy/30	10.00
31	Hoyt Wilhelm/Jsy/31	10.00
33	Eddie Murray/Pants/33	30.00
34	Nolan Ryan/Pants/34	50.00
35	Phil Niekro/Jsy/35	10.00
38	Curt Schilling/Jsy/38	15.00
40	Sandy Koufax/Jsy/32	500.00
41	Don Sutton/Jsy/20	15.00
42	Randy Johnson/Jsy/51	15.00
43	Dennis Eckersley/Jsy/43	10.00
44	Frank Thomas/Jsy/35	15.00
45	Mike Mussina/Jsy/35	15.00
46	Greg Maddux/Jsy/31	25.00
47	Jim Palmer/Pants/22	15.00
49	Mike Piazza/Jsy/31	25.00

Timeline Threads Position

NM/M

Common Player:		4.00
1	Bobby Doerr/Jsy/39	10.00
2	Burleigh Grimes/Pants/26	50.00
3	Babe Ruth/Pants/30	200.00
4	Joe Cronin/Pants/38	20.00
5	Johnny Bench/Pants/14	15.00
6	Orlando Cepeda/Pants/62	8.00
7	Ivan Rodriguez/Jsy/103	8.00
8	Cal Ripken Jr./Jsy/78	40.00
9	Tony Perez/Jsy/78	8.00
10	Andre Dawson/Jsy/86	8.00
11	Tommy John/Jsy/86	4.00
12	Alfonso Soriano/Jsy/102	8.00
13	Ozzie Smith/Jsy/78	15.00
14	Ernie Banks/Jsy/70	15.00
15	Carlton Fisk/Jsy/80	8.00
16	Bo Jackson/Jsy/89	10.00
17	Bert Blyleven/Jsy/83	8.00
18	Darryl Strawberry/Jsy/88	6.00
19	Bob Feller/Pants/36	8.00
20	Lou Brock/Jsy/74	8.00
21	Sammy Sosa/Jsy/103	12.00
22	Roger Clemens/Jsy/101	15.00
23	Don Mattingly/Jsy/94	20.00
24	Rickey Henderson/Jsy/83	10.00
25	Albert Pujols/Jsy/103	15.00
26	Wade Boggs/Jsy/87	10.00
27	Joe Morgan/Jsy/82	8.00
28	Gary Carter/Jsy/86	8.00
29	Jim "Catfish" Hunter/Jsy/78	6.00
30	Maury Wills/Jsy/65	4.00
31	Hoyt Wilhelm/Jsy/68	4.00
32	Matt Williams/Jsy/95	4.00
33	Eddie Murray/Pants/88	8.00
34	Nolan Ryan/Pants/90	25.00
35	Phil Niekro/Jsy/80	6.00
36	Paul Molitor/Jsy/96	10.00
37	Dale Murphy/Jsy/83	8.00
38	Curt Schilling/Jsy/99	8.00
39	Fred Lynn/Jsy/75	4.00
40	Sandy Koufax/Jsy/64	260.00
41	Don Sutton/Jsy/76	4.00
42	Randy Johnson/Jsy/98	8.00
43	Dennis Eckersley/Jsy/97	6.00
44	Frank Thomas/Jsy/94	6.00
45	Mike Mussina/Jsy/100	6.00
46	Greg Maddux/Jsy/96	10.00
47	Jim Palmer/Pants/76	6.00
48	Harmon Killebrew/Jsy/62	20.00
49	Mike Piazza Jsy/99	10.00
50	Billy Martin Jsy/83	15.00

Timeline Threads Number Autograph

Production 1-19
Position Autograph: No Pricing
Production 1-19
Prime: No Pricing
Production One Set

2005 Leaf Certified Materials

NM/M

Complete Set (250):		
Common Player:		.50
Common Auto. (201-250):		6.00
Production 499 unless noted.		
Hobby Pack (5):		10.00
Hobby Box (10):		90.00
1	A.J. Burnett	.50
2	Adam Dunn	.75
3	Adrian Beltre	.75
4	Bret Boone	.50
5	Albert Pujols	2.50
6	Alex Rodriguez	2.50
7	Alfonso Soriano	1.00
8	Andruw Jones	1.00
9	Andy Pettitte	.75
10	Aramis Ramirez	.75
11	Aubrey Huff	.50
12	Austin Kearns	.50
13	B.J. Upton	.50
14	Brandon Webb	.50
15	Barry Zito	.50
16	Tim Salmon	.50
17	Bobby Abreu	.50
18	Bobby Crosby	.50
19	Brad Penny	.50
20	Preston Wilson	.50
21	C.C. Sabathia	.50
22	Carl Crawford	.50
23	Keith Foulke	.50
24	Carlos Beltran	.75
25	Casey Kotchman	.50
26	Chipper Jones	1.00
27	Chone Figgins	.50
28	Craig Biggio	.75
29	Craig Wilson	.50
30	Curt Schilling	1.00
31	Danny Kolb	.50
32	David Ortiz	1.00
33	Orlando Hudson	.50
34	David Wright	1.50
35	Derek Jeter	2.50
36	Jake Peavy	.50
37	Derrek Lee	.75
38	Dontrelle Willis	.75
39	Edgar Renteria	.50
40	Angel Berroa	.50
41	Eric Chavez	.50
42	Akinori Otsuka	.50
43	Francisco Rodriguez	.50
44	Garret Anderson	.50
45	Gary Sheffield	.75
46	Greg Maddux	1.50
47	Hideki Matsui	2.00
48	Hideo Nomo	.75
49	Ichiro Suzuki	2.00
50	Ivan Rodriguez	.75
51	J.D. Drew	.50
52	J.T. Snow	.50
53	Jack Wilson	.50
54	Jamie Moyer	.50
55	Jason Bay	.50
56	Jason Giambi	.75
57	Trot Nixon	.50
58	Jason Schmidt	.50
59	Jason Varitek	.50
60	Roy Oswalt	.50
61	Javy Lopez	.50
62	Eric Byrnes	.50
63	Jeff Bagwell	.75
64	Jeff Kent	.50
65	Jeff Suppan	.50
66	Jeremy Bonderman	.50
67	Jermaine Dye	.50
68	Kazuhito Tadano	.50
69	Jim Edmonds	.75
70	Jim Thome	.75
71	Johan Santana	1.00
72	John Smoltz	.75
73	Johnny Damon	1.00
74	Johnny Estrada	.50
75	Brett Myers	.50
76	Jose Guillen	.50
77	Jose Vidro	.50
78	Josh Beckett	.50
79	Edwin Jackson	.50
80	Raul Ibanez	.50
81	Rich Harden	.50
82	Justin Morneau	.75
83	Kazuhisa Ishii	.50
84	Kazuo Matsui	.50
85	Ken Griffey Jr.	1.50
86	Ken Harvey	.50
87	Frank Thomas	.75
88	Kerry Wood	.75
89	Wade Miller	.50
90	Kevin Millwood	.50
91	Jeremy Affeldt	.50
92	Francisco Cordero	.50
93	Lance Berkman	.50
94	Larry Walker	.50
95	Laynce Nix	.50
96	Luis Gonzalez	.50
97	Lyle Overbay	.50
98	Carlos Zambrano	.75
99	Manny Ramirez	1.00
100	Marcus Giles	.50
101	Mark Buehrle	.50
102	Mark Loretta	.50
103	Mark Mulder	.50
104	Mark Prior	1.00
105	Mark Teixeira	.75
106	Marlon Byrd	.50
107	Rafael Furcal	.50
108	Melvin Mora	.50
109	Michael Young	.50
110	Miguel Cabrera	1.00
111	Miguel Tejada	.75
112	Mike Lowell	.50
113	Mike Mussina	.75
114	Mike Piazza	1.50
115	Moises Alou	.50
116	Livan Hernandez	.50
117	Nomar Garciaparra	1.50
118	Omar Vizquel	.50
119	Orlando Cabrera	.50
120	Pat Burrell	.50
121	Paul Konerko	.50
122	Paul LoDuca	.50
123	Pedro Martinez	1.00
124	Rafael Palmeiro	.75
125	Randy Johnson	1.00
126	Richard Hidalgo	.50
127	Richie Sexson	.50
128	Magglio Ordonez	.50
129	Roger Clemens	2.50
130	Russ Ortiz	.50
131	Sammy Sosa	1.50
132	Scott Podsednik	.50
133	Scott Rolen	1.00
134	Sean Burroughs	.50
135	Sean Casey	.50

136	Shawn Green	.50
137	Jorge Posada	.75
138	Roy Halladay	.50
139	Steve Finley	.50
140	Tim Hudson	.75
141	Todd Helton	.75
142	Tom Glavine	.75
143	Torii Hunter	.50
144	Travis Hafner	.50
145	Trevor Hoffman	.50
146	Troy Glaus	.50
147	Vernon Wells	.50
148	Victor Martinez	.50
149	Vladimir Guerrero	1.00
150	Sammy Sosa	1.50
151	Hank Blalock	.75
152	Danny Graves	.50
153	Rocco Baldelli	.50
154	Carlos Delgado	.50
155	Bubba Nelson	.50
156	Kevin Youkilis	.50
157	Jacque Jones	.50
158	Mike Lieberthal	.50
159	Ben Sheets	.50
160	Lew Ford	.50
161	Ervin Santana	.50
162	Jody Gerut	.50
163	Nick Johnson	.50
164	Brian Roberts	.50
165	Joe Nathan	.50
166	Mike Sweeney	.50
167	Ryan Wagner	.50
168	David Dellucci	.50
169	Jae Weong Seo	.50
170	Tom Gordon	.50
171	Carlos Lee	.50
172	Octavio Dotel	.50
173	Jose Castillo	.50
174	Troy Percival	.50
175	Carlos Delgado	.50
176	Curt Schilling	1.00
177	David Ortiz	1.00
178	Greg Maddux	1.50
179	Ivan Rodriguez	.75
180	Jeff Kent	.50
181	Larry Walker	.50
182	Miguel Tejada	.75
183	Pedro J. Martinez	1.00
184	Rafael Palmeiro	.75
185	Roger Clemens	2.50
186	Shawn Green	.50
187	Tim Hudson	.75
188	Tom Glavine	.75
189	Troy Glaus	.50
190	Vladimir Guerrero	1.00
191	Cal Ripken Jr.	4.00
192	Don Mattingly	2.00
193	George Brett	2.00
194	Harmon Killebrew	1.50
195	Mike Schmidt	2.00
196	Nolan Ryan	3.00
197	Stan Musial	2.00
198	Tony Gwynn	1.00
199	Wade Boggs	1.00
200	Willie Mays	2.00
201	Ambiorix Concepcion/ Auto. RC	10.00
202	Agustin Montero/ Auto. RC	8.00
203	Carlos Ruiz/Auto. RC	15.00
204	Casey Rogowski/ Auto. RC	6.00
205	Chris Resop/Auto. RC	8.00
206	Chris Roberson/ Auto. RC	6.00
207	Colter Bean RC	2.00
208	Danny Rueckel/ Auto. RC	6.00
209	David Gassner/ Auto. RC	8.00
210	Devon Lowery/ Auto. RC	8.00
211	Norihiro Nakamura/ Auto./115 RC	40.00
212	Erick Threets/ Auto./299 RC	6.00
213	Garrett Jones/ Auto./299 RC	8.00
214	Geovany Soto/ Auto. RC	10.00
215	Jared Gothreaux/ Auto./299 RC	6.00
216	Jason Hammel/ Auto./299 RC	10.00
217	Jeff Miller/ Auto./299 RC	6.00
218	Jeff Niemann/ Auto./299 RC	20.00
219	Huston Street	2.00
220	John Hattig Jr./ Auto. RC	6.00
221	Justin Verlander/ Auto./299 RC	50.00

222	Justin Wechsler/ Auto. RC	6.00
223	Luke Scott/Auto. RC	30.00
224	Mark McLemore/ Auto. RC	8.00
225	Mark Woodyard/ Auto./299 RC	6.00
226	Matt Lindstrom/ Auto./299 RC	8.00
227	Miguel Negron/ Auto. RC	6.00
228	Mike Morse/Auto. RC	15.00
229	Nate McLouth/ Auto. RC	8.00
230	Paulino Reynoso/ Auto./299 RC	6.00
231	Philip Humber/ Auto./299 RC	15.00
232	Tony Pena/Auto. RC	6.00
233	Randy Messenger/ Auto. RC	6.00
234	Raul Tablado/Auto. RC	8.00
235	Russel Rohlicek/ Auto. RC	6.00
236	Ryan Speier/Auto. RC	8.00
237	Scott Munter/Auto. RC	8.00
238	Sean Thompson/ Auto. RC	6.00
239	Sean Tracey/ Auto./299 RC	6.00
240	Marcos Carvajal RC	1.50
241	Travis Bowyer/ Auto. RC	10.00
242	Ubaldo Jimenez/ Auto. RC	6.00
243	Wladimir Balentien/ Auto. RC	20.00
244	Eude Brito RC	8.00
245	Ambiorix Burgos RC	2.00
246	Tadahito Iguchi RC	5.00
247	Dae-Sung Koo RC	1.00
248	Chris Seddon RC	2.00
249	Keiichi Yabu/ Auto. RC	15.00
250	Yuniesky Betancourt/ Auto. RC	25.00

Mirror Black

No Pricing
Production One Set

Mirror Blue

Mirror Blue (1-200):	3-6X
Auto. (201-250):	.5X
No Auto. (201-250):	1-2X
Production 50 Sets	

Mirror Emerald

No Pricing
Production 5 Sets

Mirror Gold

Mirror Gold (1-200):	5-10X
Mirror Gol (201-250):	No Pricing
Production 25 Sets	

Mirror Red

Mirror Red (1-200):	2-4X
Auto. (201-250):	.4X
No Auto. (201-250):	1X
Production 100 Sets	

Mirror White

Mirror White (1-200):	2-4X
Auto. (201-250):	.4X
No Auto. (201-250):	1X
Production 100 Sets	

Cuts Blue

		NM/M
Production 1-80		
3	Willie Mays/26	150.00
7	Jim Palmer/50	25.00
12	Steve Carlton/50	25.00
15	Maury Wills/80	20.00
20	Dale Murphy/50	30.00

Cuts Green

		NM/M
Production 3-50		
7	Jim Palmer/50	25.00
12	Steve Carlton/50	25.00

15	Maury Wills/80	20.00
20	Dale Murphy/50	30.00

Cuts Red

		NM/M
Production 1-60		
7	Jim Palmer/50	25.00
12	Steve Carlton/50	25.00
15	Maury Wills/60	20.00
20	Dale Murphy/50	30.00

Cuts Materials Blue

		NM/M
Production 4-43		
2	Hank Aaron/Bat/43	275.00
3	Willie Mays/ Pants/24	175.00
4	Sandy Koufax/ Jsy/32	400.00
6	Nolan Ryan/Jsy/34	100.00
9	Rod Carew/Jsy/29	25.00
10	Ryne Sandberg/ Jsy/23	120.00
12	Steve Carlton/ Pants/32	25.00
14	Mike Schmidt/Jsy/20	65.00
19	Don Mattingly/Jsy/23	75.00

Cuts Materials Green

		NM/M
Production 4-32		
3	Willie Mays/ Pants/24	175.00
9	Rod Carew/Jsy/29	25.00
10	Ryne Sandberg/ Jsy/23	120.00
12	Steve Carlton/ Pants/32	25.00
14	Mike Schmidt/Jsy/20	65.00

Cuts Materials Red

		NM/M
Production 4-32		
3	Willie Mays/ Pants/24	175.00
9	Rod Carew/Jsy/29	25.00
10	Ryne Sandberg/ Jsy/23	120.00
12	Steve Carlton/ Pants/32	25.00
14	Mike Schmidt/Jsy/20	65.00

Fabric of the Game

		NM/M
Common Player:		
Production 5-100		
1	Al Oliver/Jsy/50	6.00
2	Alan Trammell/ Jsy/100	6.00
3	Andres Galarraga/ Jsy/100	4.00
4	Andres Galarraga/ Jsy/100	4.00
5	Babe Ruth/Jsy/10	
6	Babe Ruth/Pants/25	240.00
7	Billy Martin/ Pants/100	15.00
8	Billy Williams/Jsy/50	6.00
9	Bo Jackson/Jsy/100	10.00
10	Bo Jackson/Jsy/100	10.00
12	Bob Gibson/Jsy/25	12.00
13	Bobby Doerr/ Pants/50	10.00
14	Burleigh Grimes/ Pants/25	50.00
15	Cal Ripken Jr./Jsy/50	30.00
16	Cal Ripken Jr./Jsy/50	30.00
17	Carl Yastrzemski/ Pants/50	15.00
18	Carlton Fisk/Jkt/50	10.00
19	Jim "Catfish" Hunter/ Pants/50	8.00
20	Darryl Strawberry/ Jsy/25	
21	Darryl Strawberry/ Jsy/100	4.00
22	Dave Concepcion/ Jsy/50	6.00
23	Dave Righetti/Jsy/50	8.00
24	Dave Winfield/ Pants/100	8.00

25	David Cone/Jsy/100	4.00
26	David Justice/Jsy/100	4.00
27	Deion Sanders/Jsy/50	8.00
28	Deion Sanders/Jsy/50	8.00
29	Dennis Eckersley/ Jsy/50	8.00
30	Dennis Eckersley/ Pants/50	8.00
31	Don Mattingly/ Jsy/100	15.00
32	Don Sutton/Jsy/25	8.00
33	Don Sutton/Jsy/50	6.00
37	Dwight Gooden/ Jsy/100	6.00
38	Eddie Murray/Jsy/25	15.00
39	Eddie Murray/ Pants/50	8.00
40	Edgar Martinez/ Jsy/100	4.00
41	Ernie Banks/Jsy/25	15.00
42	Fergie Jenkins/Jsy/50	8.00
43	Frankie Frisch/Jkt/50	20.00
44	Fred Lynn/Jsy/50	4.00
45	Fred McGriff/Jsy/100	6.00
46	Gary Carter/Jsy/50	6.00
47	Gary Carter/Jsy/50	6.00
48	Gaylord Perry/Jsy/50	6.00
49	Gaylord Perry/Jsy/50	6.00
50	George Brett/Jsy/25	20.00
51	Hal Newhouser/Jsy/50	8.00
54	Harmon Killebrew/ Jsy/25	15.00
55	Harmon Killebrew/ Jsy/50	12.00
56	Harold Baines/Jsy/50	8.00
57	Hoyt Wilhelm/Jsy/100	6.00
58	Jack Morris/Jsy/100	4.00
59	Jim Thorpe/Jsy/25	300.00
60	Jose Cruz/Jsy/100	4.00
61	Jim Rice/Jsy/50	8.00
62	Joe Cronin/Jsy/50	15.00
63	Joe Cronin/Pants/100	15.00
64	Joe Morgan/Jsy/50	8.00
65	Joe Torre/Jsy/50	10.00
66	John Kruk/Jsy/100	10.00
67	Johnny Bench/Jsy/50	10.00
68	Juan Marichal/ Pants/100	6.00
71	Kirk Gibson/Jsy/100	4.00
72	Lee Smith/Jsy/100	4.00
73	Lenny Dykstra/ Jsy/100	6.00
74	Lou Boudreau/Jsy/25	15.00
75	Luis Aparicio/Jsy/50	8.00
76	Luis Tiant/Pants/100	4.00
77	Mark Grace/Jsy/100	8.00
78	Hoyt Wilhelm/Jsy/100	6.00
79	Matt Williams/Jsy/100	6.00
80	Matt Williams/Jsy/50	6.00
82	Nolan Ryan/Jsy/50	20.00
84	Nolan Ryan/Jsy/25	25.00
85	Nolan Ryan/Jsy/25	25.00
86	Orlando Cepeda/ Pants/50	8.00
87	Ozzie Smith/Pants/25	15.00
88	Paul Molitor/Jsy/50	8.00
89	Paul Molitor/Jsy/50	8.00
90	Paul Molitor/Pants/50	8.00
91	Phil Niekro/Jsy/50	8.00
92	Reggie Jackson/ Pants/100	8.00
93	Reggie Jackson/ Jkt/100	8.00
94	Reggie Jackson/ Jsy/50	8.00
95	Reggie Jackson/ Jsy/50	8.00
96	Rickey Henderson/ Jkt/100	10.00
97	Rickey Henderson/ Jsy/50	10.00
98	Rickey Henderson/ Jsy/50	10.00
99	Rickey Henderson/ Jsy/50	10.00
100	Rickey Henderson/ Jsy/50	10.00
101	Rickey Henderson/ Pants/50	10.00
102	Robin Ventura/ Jsy/100	6.00
103	Robin Ventura/ Jsy/100	6.00
104	Robin Yount/Jsy/50	12.00
106	Rod Carew/Jsy/100	8.00
107	Roger Maris/Pants/50	40.00
108	Ron Cey/Jsy/50	8.00
109	Ron Guidry/Pants/100	6.00
110	Ryne Sandberg/ Jsy/50	15.00
111	Sandy Koufax/ Jsy/25	180.00
112	Stan Musial/Jsy/25	25.00

113 Stan Musial/Pants/25 25.00
114 Steve Garvey/Jsy/100 6.00
115 Ted Williams/Jkt/50 50.00
116 Ted Williams/Jsy/25 50.00
117 Tom Seaver/Jsy/50 10.00
118 Tom Seaver/Pants/50 10.00
119 Tommy John/Jsy/100 4.00
120 Tommy John/Pants/100 4.00
121 Tommy Lasorda/Jsy/100 6.00
122 Tony Gwynn/Jsy/100 10.00
123 Tony Gwynn/Pants/100 10.00
124 Tony Perez/Jsy/50 8.00
125 Wade Boggs/Jsy/100 8.00
126 Warren Spahn/Jsy/25 15.00
127 Whitey Ford/Jsy/25 15.00
128 Will Clark/Jsy/50 8.00
129 Willie Mays/Pants/50 40.00
130 Willie McCovey/Pants/100 10.00
131 Roger Clemens/Jsy/50 15.00
132 Roger Clemens/Jsy/50 15.00
133 Roger Clemens/Jsy/50 15.00
134 Randy Johnson/Jsy/50 8.00
135 Randy Johnson/Jsy/50 8.00
136 Cal Ripken Jr./Jsy/50 30.00
137 Don Mattingly/Jsy/100 15.00
138 George Brett/Jsy/25 20.00
139 Harmon Killebrew/Jsy/25 15.00
140 Mike Schmidt/Jsy/50 20.00
141 Nolan Ryan/Jkt/25 25.00
143 Tony Gwynn/Jsy/100 10.00
144 Wade Boggs/Jsy/25 10.00
145 Willie Mays/Jsy/25 50.00
146 Hideo Nomo/Jsy/100 10.00
147 Dale Murphy/Jsy/100 10.00
148 Dale Murphy/Jsy/100 10.00
149 Bo Jackson/Jsy/50 12.00
150 Darryl Strawberry/Jsy/50 6.00
151 Deion Sanders/Jsy/50 8.00
152 Deion Sanders/Pants/50 8.00
153 Dennis Eckersley/Jsy/50 8.00
154 Dwight Gooden/Jsy/100 6.00
155 Edgar Martinez/Jsy/50 4.00
156 Lou Brock/Jsy/50 8.00
157 Steve Carlton/Pants/50 6.00
158 Albert Pujols/Jsy/50 20.00
159 Tom Glavine/Jsy/100 8.00
160 Hideki Matsui/Pants/50 20.00
161 Babe Ruth/Pants, Jim Thorpe/Jsy/25 500.00
162 Ted Williams/Jkt, Bob Gibson/Jsy/50 50.00
164 Whitey Ford/Jsy, Sandy Koufax/Jsy/25 150.00
165 Roger Maris/Pants, Don Mattingly/Jsy/25 50.00
166 Nolan Ryan/Jsy, Tom Seaver/Jsy/50 25.00
167 Cal Ripken Jr./Jsy, George Brett/Jsy/100 40.00
168 Ryne Sandberg/Jsy, Mike Schmidt/Jsy/50 30.00
169 Tony Gwynn/Jsy, Wade Boggs/Jsy/50 15.00
170 Carlton Fisk/Jsy, Johnny Bench/Pants/50 15.00
172 Reggie Jackson/Pants, Darryl Strawberry/Jsy/50 10.00
173 Robin Yount/Jsy, Paul Molitor/Jsy/25 20.00
174 Warren Spahn/Pants, Juan Marichal/Jsy/50 15.00
175 Bo Jackson/Jsy, Deion Sanders/Pants/100 15.00
176 Tony Gwynn/Jsy, Rickey Henderson/Jsy/100 15.00
177 Hideki Matsui/Jsy, Jim Edmonds/Jsy/100 20.00
178 Rickey Henderson/Pants, Lou Brock/Jsy/100 15.00
179 Roger Clemens/Jsy, Albert Pujols/Jsy/100 25.00
180 Hideo Nomo/Jsy, Kazuhisa Ishii/Jsy/100 12.00

Fabric of the Game Autograph

No Pricing
Production One Set

Fabric of the Game Reward

NM/M
Production 3-50
1 Al Oliver/Jsy/50 6.00
2 Alan Trammell/Jsy/50 8.00
3 Andres Galarraga/Jsy/50 6.00
4 Andres Galarraga/Jsy/50 6.00
7 Billy Martin/Pants/50 15.00
9 Bo Jackson/Jsy/50 12.00
10 Bo Jackson/Jsy/50 12.00
13 Bobby Doerr/Pants/25 12.00
17 Carl Yastrzemski/Pants/25 15.00
19 Jim "Catfish" Hunter/Pants/50 8.00
21 Darryl Strawberry/Jsy/50 6.00
23 Dave Righetti/Jsy/25 6.00
44 Fred Lynn/Jsy/50 4.00
46 Gary Carter/Jsy/50 6.00
47 Gary Carter/Jsy/50 8.00
48 Gaylord Perry/Jsy/50 6.00
49 Gaylord Perry/Jsy/50 8.00
51 Hal Newhouser/Jsy/50 8.00
58 Jack Morris/Jsy/50 6.00
61 Jim Rice/Jsy/50 8.00
62 Joe Cronin/Jsy/25 20.00
63 Joe Cronin/Pants/25 20.00
64 Joe Morgan/Jsy/25 10.00
66 John Kruk/Jsy/25 10.00
68 Juan Marichal/Pants/25 10.00
71 Kirk Gibson/Jsy/25 8.00
72 Lee Smith/Jsy/25 4.00
75 Luis Aparicio/Jsy/25 8.00
76 Luis Tiant/Pants/25 6.00
78 Hoyt Wilhelm/Jsy/25 10.00
79 Matt Williams/Jsy/25 8.00
82 Nolan Ryan/Jsy/25 25.00
85 Nolan Ryan/Jsy/25 25.00
86 Orlando Cepeda/Pants/25 10.00
87 Ozzie Smith/Pants/25 15.00
88 Paul Molitor/Jsy/50 8.00
89 Paul Molitor/Jsy/50 8.00
90 Paul Molitor/Pants/25 10.00
91 Phil Niekro/Jsy/25 8.00
92 Reggie Jackson/Pants/50 10.00
93 Reggie Jackson/Jkt/25 10.00
95 Reggie Jackson/Jsy/25 10.00
96 Rickey Henderson/Jkt/25 10.00
97 Rickey Henderson/Jsy/50 10.00
99 Rickey Henderson/Jsy/25 12.00
102 Robin Ventura/Jsy/50 6.00
103 Robin Ventura/Jsy/50 6.00
104 Robin Yount/Jsy/50 12.00
105 Rod Carew/Jsy/25 10.00
106 Rod Carew/Jsy/50 10.00
108 Ron Cey/Jsy/50 8.00
109 Ron Guidry/Pants/50 8.00
110 Ryne Sandberg/Jsy/50 10.00
111 Sandy Koufax/Jsy/25 180.00
113 Stan Musial/Pants/25 25.00
114 Steve Garvey/Jsy/25 8.00
115 Ted Williams/Jkt/25 50.00
118 Tom Seaver/Pants/50 10.00
119 Tommy John/Jsy/50 4.00
120 Tommy John/Pants/50 4.00
121 Tommy Lasorda/Jsy/50 6.00
122 Tony Gwynn/Jsy/50 10.00
123 Tony Gwynn/Pants/50 10.00
124 Tony Perez/Jsy/50 8.00
125 Wade Boggs/Jsy/50 10.00
126 Warren Spahn/Pants/50 12.00
128 Will Clark/Jsy/50 8.00
129 Willie Mays/Pants/25 50.00
130 Willie McCovey/Pants/50 10.00
131 Roger Clemens/Jsy/50 20.00
132 Roger Clemens/Jsy/50 15.00
133 Roger Clemens/Jsy/50 15.00
134 Randy Johnson/Jsy/50 10.00
135 Randy Johnson/Jsy/50 10.00
136 Cal Ripken Jr./Jsy/50 30.00
137 Don Mattingly/Jsy/50 15.00
138 George Brett/Jsy/50 20.00
139 Harmon Killebrew/Jsy/25 15.00
140 Mike Schmidt/Jsy/50 20.00
143 Tony Gwynn/Jsy/50 10.00
144 Wade Boggs/Jsy/50 10.00
145 Willie Mays/Jsy/50 50.00
146 Hideo Nomo/Jsy/50 10.00
147 Dale Murphy/Jsy/50 10.00
148 Dale Murphy/Jsy/50 10.00
150 Darryl Strawberry/Jsy/50 6.00
151 Deion Sanders/Jsy/50 8.00
152 Deion Sanders/Pants/50 8.00
153 Dennis Eckersley/Jsy/50 8.00
154 Dwight Gooden/Jsy/50 6.00
155 Edgar Martinez/Jsy/50 4.00
156 Lou Brock/Jsy/50 8.00
157 Steve Carlton/Pants/50 6.00
158 Albert Pujols/Jsy/50 20.00
159 Tom Glavine/Jsy/50 8.00
160 Hideki Matsui/Pants/50 20.00
161 Babe Ruth/Pants, Jim Thorpe/Jsy/25 500.00
162 Ted Williams/Jkt, Stan Musial/Jkt/25 50.00
163 Willie Mays/Jsy, Bob Gibson/Jsy/50 50.00
164 Whitey Ford/Jsy, Sandy Koufax/Jsy/25 150.00
165 Roger Maris/Pants, Don Mattingly/Jsy/50 50.00
166 Nolan Ryan/Jsy, Tom Seaver/Jsy/25 25.00
167 Cal Ripken Jr./Jsy, George Brett/Jsy/100 40.00
168 Ryne Sandberg/Jsy, Mike Schmidt/Jsy/50 30.00
169 Tony Gwynn/Jsy, Wade Boggs/Jsy/50 15.00
170 Carlton Fisk/Jsy, Johnny Bench/Pants/25 20.00
172 Reggie Jackson/Pants, Darryl Strawberry/Jsy/50 10.00
173 Robin Yount/Jsy, Paul Molitor/Jsy/25 20.00
174 Warren Spahn/Pants, Juan Marichal/Jsy/25 20.00
175 Bo Jackson/Jsy, Deion Sanders/Pants/50 15.00
176 Tony Gwynn/Jsy, Rickey Henderson/Jsy/50 20.00
177 Hideki Matsui/Jsy, Jim Edmonds/Jsy/50 20.00
178 Rickey Henderson/Pants, Lou Brock/Jsy/50 20.00
179 Roger Clemens/Jsy, Albert Pujols/Jsy/50 25.00
180 Hideo Nomo/Jsy, Kazuhisa Ishii/Jsy/50 15.00

Fabric of the Game Stats

NM/M
Production 3-75
1 Al Oliver/Jsy/75 6.00
3 Andres Galarraga/Jsy/75 6.00
4 Andres Galarraga/Jsy/75 6.00
7 Billy Martin/Pants/75 15.00
8 Billy Williams/Jsy/75 6.00
9 Bo Jackson/Jsy/75 10.00
10 Bo Jackson/Jsy/75 10.00
13 Bobby Doerr/Jsy/25 12.00
14 Burleigh Grimes/Pants/25 50.00
15 Cal Ripken Jr./Jsy/75 30.00
16 Cal Ripken Jr./Jsy/75 30.00
17 Carl Yastrzemski/Pants/25 15.00
18 Carlton Fisk/Jkt/75 10.00
19 Jim "Catfish" Hunter/Pants/75 8.00
21 Darryl Strawberry/Jsy/75 6.00
22 Dave Concepcion/Jsy/75 4.00
23 Dave Righetti/Jsy/75 8.00
24 Dave Winfield/Pants/75 4.00
25 David Cone/Jsy/75 4.00
26 David Justice/Jsy/75 4.00
27 Deion Sanders/Jsy/75 8.00
28 Deion Sanders/Jsy/75 8.00
29 Dennis Eckersley/Jsy/75 8.00
30 Dennis Eckersley/Pants/75 8.00
39 Eddie Murray/Jsy/75 12.00
40 Edgar Martinez/Jsy/75 4.00
43 Frankie Frisch/Jkt/75 15.00
44 Fred Lynn/Jsy/75 4.00
45 Fred McGriff/Jsy/75 6.00
46 Gary Carter/Jsy/50 6.00
47 Gary Carter/Jsy/75 6.00
48 Gaylord Perry/Jsy/50 6.00
49 Gaylord Perry/Jsy/75 8.00
51 Hal Newhouser/Jsy/75 10.00
54 Harmon Killebrew/Jsy/75 15.00
55 Harmon Killebrew/Jsy/50 12.00
56 Harold Baines/Jsy/50 8.00
57 Hoyt Wilhelm/Jsy/50 6.00
62 Joe Cronin/Jsy/25 20.00
63 Joe Cronin/Pants/25 20.00
64 Joe Morgan/Jsy/25 10.00
66 John Kruk/Jsy/75 10.00
71 Kirk Gibson/Jsy/75 8.00
72 Lee Smith/Jsy/75 4.00
73 Lenny Dykstra/Jsy/75 6.00
76 Luis Aparicio/Jsy/25 8.00
76 Luis Tiant/Pants/25 6.00
78 Hoyt Wilhelm/Jsy/75 10.00
79 Matt Williams/Jsy/75 8.00
82 Nolan Ryan/Jsy/25 25.00
85 Nolan Ryan/Jsy/25 25.00
86 Orlando Cepeda/Pants/25 10.00
87 Ozzie Smith/Pants/25 15.00
88 Paul Molitor/Jsy/50 8.00
89 Paul Molitor/Jsy/50 8.00
90 Paul Molitor/Pants/25 10.00
91 Phil Niekro/Jsy/25 8.00
92 Reggie Jackson/Pants/50 10.00
93 Reggie Jackson/Jkt/25 10.00
94 Reggie Jackson/Jsy/75 10.00
95 Reggie Jackson/Jsy/50 10.00
96 Rickey Henderson/Jkt/75 10.00
97 Rickey Henderson/Jsy/75 10.00
98 Rickey Henderson/Jsy/50 10.00
101 Rickey Henderson/Pants/75 10.00
102 Robin Ventura/Jsy/50 6.00
103 Robin Ventura/Jsy/50 6.00
104 Robin Yount/Jsy/50 12.00
105 Rod Carew/Jsy/25 10.00
106 Rod Carew/Jsy/75 8.00
107 Roger Maris/Pants/50 40.00
108 Ron Cey/Jsy/50 8.00
109 Ron Guidry/Pants/50 8.00
111 Sandy Koufax/Jsy/25 180.00
112 Stan Musial/Pants/5
113 Stan Musial/Pants/25 25.00
114 Steve Garvey/Jsy/75 8.00
115 Ted Williams/Jkt/25 50.00
117 Tom Seaver/Jsy/75 10.00
118 Tom Seaver/Pants/50 10.00
119 Tommy John/Jsy/25 6.00
120 Tommy John/Pants/25 6.00
121 Tommy Lasorda/Jsy/75 6.00
124 Tony Perez/Jsy/75 8.00
125 Wade Boggs/Jsy/50 10.00
126 Warren Spahn/Pants/75 12.00
128 Will Clark/Jsy/50 8.00
129 Willie Mays/Pants/25 50.00
130 Willie McCovey/Pants/75 10.00

131	Roger Clemens/Jsy/25	20.00
140	Mike Schmidt/Jsy/25	20.00
144	Wade Boggs/Jsy/25	10.00
145	Willie Mays/Jsy/25	25.00
146	Hideo Nomo/Jsy/75	10.00
147	Dale Murphy/Jsy/75	10.00
148	Dale Murphy/Jsy/75	10.00
153	Dennis Eckersley/Jsy/75	8.00
154	Dwight Gooden/Jsy/75	6.00
155	Edgar Martinez/Jsy/75	4.00
156	Lou Brock/Jsy/75	8.00
157	Steve Carlton/Pants/75	6.00
159	Tom Glavine/Jsy/75	8.00
160	Hideki Matsui/Pants/75	20.00
161	Babe Ruth/Pants, Jim Thorpe/Jsy/25	500.00
162	Ted Williams/Jkt, Stan Musial/Jsy/25	50.00
163	Willie Mays/Jsy, Bob Gibson/Jsy/25	50.00
164	Whitey Ford/Jsy, Sandy Koufax/Jsy/25	150.00
165	Roger Maris/Pants, Don Mattingly/Jsy/25	50.00
166	Nolan Ryan/Jsy, Tom Seaver/Jsy/50	25.00
167	Cal Ripken Jr./Jsy, George Brett/Jsy/50	40.00
168	Ryne Sandberg/Jsy, Mike Schmidt/Jsy/50	30.00
169	Tony Gwynn/Jsy, Wade Boggs/Jsy/50	15.00
170	Carlton Fisk/Jsy, Johnny Bench/Pants/25	20.00
172	Reggie Jackson/Pants, Darryl Strawberry/Jsy/50	10.00
173	Robin Yount/Jsy, Paul Molitor/Jsy/25	20.00
174	Warren Spahn/Pants, Juan Marichal/Jsy/25	20.00
175	Bo Jackson/Jsy, Deion Sanders/Pants/50	15.00
176	Tony Gwynn/Jsy, Rickey Henderson/Jsy/50	20.00
177	Hideki Matsui/Jsy, Jim Edmonds/Jsy/50	20.00
178	Rickey Henderson/Pants, Lou Brock/Jsy/50	20.00
179	Roger Clemens/Jsy, Albert Pujols/Jsy/50	25.00
180	Hideo Nomo/Jsy, Kazuhisa Ishii/Jsy/50	15.00

Gold Team

NM/M

Complete Set (25):
Common Player: 1.00
Inserted 1:7
Mirror: 2-3X

1	Albert Pujols	4.00
2	Alex Rodriguez	3.00
3	Carlos Beltran	1.00
4	Chipper Jones	1.50
5	Curt Schilling	1.50
6	Derek Jeter	4.00
7	Greg Maddux	2.50
8	Hank Blalock	1.00
9	Ichiro Suzuki	3.00
10	Ivan Rodriguez	1.00
11	Jim Thome	1.00
12	Ken Griffey Jr.	3.00
13	Lyle Overbay	1.00
14	Manny Ramirez	1.50
15	Mark Mulder	1.00
16	Mark Prior	1.50
17	Michael Young	1.00
18	Miguel Cabrera	1.50
19	Mike Piazza	2.00
20	Pedro Martinez	1.50
21	Randy Johnson	1.50
22	Roger Clemens	4.00
23	Sammy Sosa	2.00
24	Tim Hudson	1.00
25	Todd Helton	1.50

Gold Team Autograph

No Pricing
Production 5-10

Gold Team Jersey Number

NM/M

Production 100-250

1	Albert Pujols/100	20.00

3	Carlos Beltran/200	5.00
4	Chipper Jones/100	8.00
5	Curt Schilling/250	8.00
7	Greg Maddux/250	10.00
8	Hank Blalock/250	4.00
10	Ivan Rodriguez/120	6.00
11	Jim Thome/250	6.00
13	Lyle Overbay/250	4.00
14	Manny Ramirez/250	8.00
15	Mark Mulder/250	4.00
16	Mark Prior/100	4.00
17	Michael Young/250	4.00
18	Miguel Cabrera/100	8.00
19	Mike Piazza/250	10.00
20	Pedro Martinez/100	8.00
21	Randy Johnson/250	8.00
22	Roger Clemens/250	10.00
23	Sammy Sosa/250	8.00
24	Tim Hudson/100	4.00
25	Todd Helton/100	6.00

Mirror Autograph Blue

NM/M

Production 1-100
Black: No Pricing
Production One Set
Emerald: No Pricing
Production 1-5

18	Bobby Crosby/25	25.00
25	Casey Kotchman/25	15.00
33	Orlando Hudson/100	10.00
53	Jack Wilson/25	15.00
62	Eric Byrnes/25	12.00
66	Jeremy Bonderman/25	20.00
67	Jermaine Dye/25	15.00
68	Kazuhito Tadano/50	15.00
79	Edwin Jackson/100	8.00
80	Raul Ibanez/25	15.00
86	Ken Harvey/25	8.00
89	Wade Miller/100	10.00
91	Jeremy Affeldt/25	8.00
95	Laynce Nix/25	10.00
106	Marlon Byrd/100	8.00
155	Bubba Nelson/100	8.00
156	Kevin Youkilis/25	25.00
160	Lew Ford/25	15.00
161	Ervin Santana/100	10.00
165	Joe Nathan/25	20.00
167	Ryan Wagner/25	10.00
168	David Dellucci/25	20.00
169	Jae Weong Seo/25	15.00
173	Jose Castillo/100	10.00
223	Luke Scott/49	30.00
229	Nate McLouth/49	15.00
234	Raul Tablado/49	10.00
243	Wladimir Balentien/49	25.00

Mirror Autograph Gold

NM/M

Production 1-25

2	Adam Dunn/25	35.00
11	Aubrey Huff/25	15.00
12	Austin Kearns/25	10.00
13	B.J. Upton/25	15.00
14	Brandon Webb/25	15.00
16	Tim Salmon/25	30.00
18	Bobby Crosby/25	25.00
19	Brad Penny/25	15.00
21	C.C. Sabathia/25	15.00
23	Keith Foulke/25	15.00
25	Casey Kotchman/25	15.00
27	Chone Figgins/25	12.00
29	Craig Wilson/25	10.00
31	Danny Kolb/25	10.00
33	Orlando Hudson/25	10.00
34	David Wright/25	70.00
36	Jake Peavy/25	35.00
37	Derrek Lee/25	40.00
39	Edgar Renteria/25	20.00
40	Angel Berroa/25	10.00
41	Eric Chavez/25	20.00
42	Akinori Otsuka/25	25.00
43	Francisco Rodriguez/25	25.00
44	Garret Anderson/25	20.00
53	Jack Wilson/25	15.00
54	Jamie Moyer/25	15.00
55	Jason Bay/25	25.00
57	Trot Nixon/25	20.00
60	Roy Oswalt/25	25.00
62	Eric Byrnes/25	12.00
63	Jeff Bagwell/25	40.00
65	Jeff Suppan/25	15.00
66	Jeremy Bonderman/25	20.00
67	Jermaine Dye/25	15.00
68	Kazuhito Tadano/25	15.00
75	Brett Myers/25	20.00
76	Jose Guillen/25	15.00
77	Jose Vidro/25	15.00
79	Edwin Jackson/25	10.00
80	Raul Ibanez/25	15.00

81	Rich Harden/25	20.00
86	Ken Harvey/25	10.00
89	Wade Miller/25	15.00
91	Jeremy Affeldt/25	12.00
92	Francisco Cordero/25	15.00
95	Laynce Nix/25	12.00
97	Lyle Overbay/25	15.00
98	Carlos Zambrano/25	30.00
101	Mark Buehrle/25	25.00
102	Mark Loretta/25	15.00
106	Marlon Byrd/25	10.00
107	Rafael Furcal/25	25.00
109	Michael Young/25	25.00
110	Miguel Cabrera/25	40.00
128	Magglio Ordonez/25	15.00
134	Sean Burroughs/25	15.00
135	Sean Casey/25	15.00
139	Steve Finley/25	15.00
143	Torii Hunter/25	20.00
144	Travis Hafner/25	20.00
147	Vernon Wells/25	15.00
152	Danny Graves/25	12.00
155	Bubba Nelson/25	15.00
156	Kevin Youkilis/25	25.00
157	Jacque Jones/25	15.00
158	MikeLieberthal/25	15.00
160	Lew Ford/25	15.00
161	Ervin Santana/25	15.00
162	Jody Gerut/25	15.00
163	Nick Johnson/25	20.00
164	Brian Roberts/25	30.00
165	Joe Nathan/25	20.00
167	Ryan Wagner/25	10.00
168	David Dellucci/25	20.00
169	Jae Weong Seo/25	15.00
170	Tom Gordon/25	15.00
171	Carlos Lee/25	20.00
172	Octavio Dotel/25	12.00
173	Jose Castillo/25	15.00
174	Troy Percival/25	15.00
194	Harmon Killebrew/25	40.00

Mirror Autograph Red

NM/M

Production 1-250

16	Tim Salmon/25	30.00
18	Bobby Crosby/50	25.00
25	Casey Kotchman/50	12.00
33	Orlando Hudson/250	8.00
53	Jack Wilson/50	12.00
62	Eric Byrnes/50	10.00
66	Jeremy Bonderman/25	15.00
67	Jermaine Dye/50	15.00
68	Kazuhito Tadano/250	12.00
79	Edwin Jackson/250	8.00
80	Raul Ibanez/50	12.00
86	Ken Harvey/250	8.00
89	Wade Miller/250	10.00
91	Jeremy Affeldt/250	8.00
92	Francisco Cordero/25	15.00
95	Laynce Nix/100	8.00
106	Marlon Byrd/250	8.00
155	Bubba Nelson/250	6.00
156	Kevin Youkilis/50	20.00
160	Lew Ford/50	12.00
161	Ervin Santana/250	10.00
162	Jody Gerut/50	15.00
164	Brian Roberts/25	30.00
165	Joe Nathan/50	15.00
167	Ryan Wagner/50	15.00
168	David Dellucci/50	15.00
169	Jae Weong Seo/50	15.00
173	Jose Castillo/250	10.00
202	Agustin Montero/99	10.00
211	Norihiro Nakamura/99	50.00
212	Erick Threets/49	10.00
218	Jeff Niemann/49	25.00
221	Justin Verlander/49	40.00
223	Luke Scott/49	30.00
229	Nate McLouth/49	15.00
230	Paulino Reynoso/49	10.00
231	Philip Humber/49	25.00
234	Raul Tablado/99	12.00
239	Sean Tracey/49	10.00
243	Wladimir Balentien/99	15.00

Mirror Autograph White

NM/M

Production 1-50

18	Bobby Crosby/25	25.00
19	Brad Penny/25	15.00
25	Casey Kotchman/25	15.00
33	Orlando Hudson/50	8.00
53	Jack Wilson/50	15.00
62	Eric Byrnes/25	12.00
67	Jermaine Dye/25	15.00
68	Kazuhito Tadano/50	15.00
79	Edwin Jackson/25	15.00
80	Raul Ibanez/25	15.00

81	Rich Harden/50	15.00
86	Ken Harvey/50	8.00
89	Wade Miller/50	12.00
91	Jeremy Affeldt/50	10.00
95	Laynce Nix/50	10.00
106	Marlon Byrd/50	8.00
155	Bubba Nelson/50	8.00
156	Kevin Youkilis/25	25.00
160	Lew Ford/25	15.00
161	Ervin Santana/50	12.00
162	Jody Gerut/25	15.00
165	Joe Nathan/25	20.00
167	Ryan Wagner/25	20.00
168	David Dellucci/25	20.00
173	Jose Castillo/50	12.00
202	Agustin Montero/49	12.00
211	Norihiro Nakamura/49	60.00
212	Erick Threets/49	10.00
218	Jeff Niemann/49	25.00
221	Justin Verlander/49	40.00
223	Luke Scott/49	40.00
229	Nate McLouth/49	20.00
230	Paulino Reynoso/49	10.00
231	Philip Humber/49	25.00
234	Raul Tablado/49	15.00
239	Sean Tracey/49	10.00
243	Wladimir Balentien/49	20.00

Mirror Bat Blue

NM/M

Production 75-100
Black: No Pricing
Production One Set
Emerald: No Pricing
Production 5 Sets

2	Adam Dunn/100	6.00
5	Albert Pujols/100	20.00
8	Andruw Jones/100	8.00
11	Aubrey Huff/100	4.00
13	B.J. Upton/100	6.00
14	Brandon Webb/100	4.00
16	Tim Salmon/100	4.00
25	Casey Kotchman/100	4.00
26	Chipper Jones/100	8.00
32	David Ortiz/100	10.00
37	Derrek Lee/100	4.00
38	Dontrelle Willis/100	6.00
44	Garret Anderson/100	4.00
45	Gary Sheffield/100	6.00
59	Jason Varitek/100	4.00
61	Javy Lopez/100	4.00
63	Jeff Bagwell/100	4.00
77	Jose Vidro/100	4.00
93	Lance Berkman/100	4.00
99	Manny Ramirez/100	8.00
105	Mark Teixeira/100	4.00
109	Michael Young/100	4.00
110	Miguel Cabrera/5	8.00
111	Miguel Tejada/100	8.00
117	Nomar Garciaparra/100	8.00
121	Paul Konerko/100	6.00
124	Rafael Palmeiro/100	6.00
128	Magglio Ordonez/100	4.00
136	Shawn Green/100	4.00
141	Todd Helton/100	6.00
142	Tom Glavine/100	4.00
143	Torii Hunter/100	4.00
144	Travis Hafner/100	4.00
148	Victor Martinez/100	4.00
149	Vladimir Guerrero/100	8.00
150	Sammy Sosa/100	8.00
153	Rocco Baldelli/100	4.00
160	Lew Ford/100	4.00
166	Mike Sweeney/75	4.00
184	Rafael Palmeiro/100	6.00
188	Tom Glavine/100	4.00
190	Vladimir Guerrero/100	8.00

Mirror Bat Red

NM/M

Production 100-250
Gold: 1-2X
Production 25 Sets

2	Adam Dunn/250	6.00
5	Albert Pujols/250	15.00
8	Andruw Jones/250	6.00
11	Aubrey Huff/250	4.00
13	B.J. Upton/250	4.00
14	Brandon Webb/100	4.00
16	Tim Salmon/250	4.00
25	Casey Kotchman/250	4.00
26	Chipper Jones/250	6.00
28	Craig Biggio/250	6.00
29	Craig Wilson/250	4.00
34	David Wright/250	10.00
38	Dontrelle Willis/250	4.00
44	Garret Anderson/250	4.00
45	Gary Sheffield/250	6.00
59	Jason Varitek/250	6.00
61	Javy Lopez/250	4.00
63	Jeff Bagwell/250	6.00

77	Jose Vidro/250	4.00
93	Lance Berkman/250	4.00
99	Manny Ramirez/250	8.00
105	Mark Teixeira/250	6.00
109	Michael Young/250	4.00
110	Miguel Cabrera/250	8.00
111	Miguel Tejada/250	8.00
121	Paul Konerko/250	4.00
124	Rafael Palmeiro/250	6.00
128	Magglio Ordonez/250	4.00
136	Shawn Green/250	4.00
141	Todd Helton/250	6.00
142	Tom Glavine/250	4.00
143	Torii Hunter/200	4.00
148	Victor Martinez/250	4.00
149	Vladimir Guerrero/250	8.00
150	Sammy Sosa/250	8.00
153	Rocco Baldelli/250	4.00
160	Lew Ford/250	4.00
166	Mike Sweeney/100	4.00
184	Rafael Palmeiro/100	6.00
188	Tom Glavine/250	4.00
190	Vladimir Guerrero/250	8.00

Mirror Bat White
NM/M

Production 75-250

2	Adam Dunn/1	6.00
5	Albert Pujols/1	20.00
7	Alfonso Soriano/1	6.00
11	Aubrey Huff/10	4.00
12	Austin Kearns/5	4.00
13	B.J. Upton/5	6.00
14	Brandon Webb/50	4.00
25	Casey Kotchman/250	8.00
26	Chipper Jones/100	6.00
28	Craig Biggio/100	4.00
29	Craig Wilson/250	10.00
34	David Wright/100	8.00
37	Derrek Lee/250	6.00
38	Dontrelle Willis/100	4.00
44	Garret Anderson/100	6.00
45	Gary Sheffield/100	8.00
59	Jason Varitek/100	4.00
61	Javy Lopez/100	6.00
63	Jeff Bagwell/100	4.00
77	Jose Vidro/100	4.00
88	Kerry Wood/100	6.00
93	Lance Berkman/100	6.00
94	Larry Walker/100	6.00
99	Manny Ramirez/250	6.00
105	Mark Teixeira/250	8.00
109	Michael Young/250	8.00
110	Miguel Cabrera/250	4.00
111	Miguel Tejada/250	4.00
121	Paul Konerko/250	4.00
124	Rafael Palmeiro/75	6.00
128	Magglio Ordonez/100	4.00
136	Shawn Green/100	4.00
141	Todd Helton/100	6.00
142	Tom Glavine/100	4.00
143	Torii Hunter/100	4.00
148	Victor Martinez/100	4.00
149	Vladimir Guerrero/100	8.00
150	Sammy Sosa/100	4.00
153	Rocco Baldelli/100	4.00
160	Lew Ford/250	4.00
184	Rafael Palmeiro/250	6.00
188	Tom Glavine/100	4.00
190	Vladimir Guerrero/250	8.00

Mirror Fabric Blue
NM/M

Production 50-100

Black: No Pricing
Production One Set
Emerald: No Pricing
Production 5 Sets

2	Adam Dunn/Jsy/100	4.00
5	Albert Pujols/Jsy/100	15.00
7	Alfonso Soriano/Jsy/100	6.00
8	Andruw Jones/Jsy/100	6.00
10	Aramis Ramirez/Jsy/100	6.00
11	Aubrey Huff/Jsy/100	4.00
13	B.J. Upton/Jsy/100	4.00
14	Brandon Webb/Pants/100	4.00
15	Barry Zito/Jsy/100	4.00
17	Bobby Abreu/Jsy/100	4.00
18	Bobby Crosby/Jsy/50	6.00
25	Casey Kotchman/Jsy/100	4.00
26	Chipper Jones/Jsy/100	8.00
28	Craig Biggio/Jsy/100	8.00
30	Curt Schilling/Jsy/100	8.00
32	David Ortiz/Jsy/100	8.00
37	Derrek Lee/Jsy/100	8.00
38	Dontrelle Willis/Jsy/100	4.00
41	Eric Chavez/Jsy/100	4.00

43	Francisco Rodriguez/Jsy/100	4.00
44	Garret Anderson/Jsy/100	4.00
46	Greg Maddux/Jsy/100	10.00
47	Hideki Matsui/Pants/100	15.00
48	Hideo Nomo/Jsy/100	6.00
50	Ivan Rodriguez/Jsy/100	4.00
57	Trot Nixon/Jsy/100	4.00
60	Roy Oswalt/Jsy/50	4.00
61	Javy Lopez/Jsy/100	4.00
63	Jeff Bagwell/Jsy/100	4.00
69	Jim Edmonds/Jsy/100	6.00
70	Jim Thome/Jsy/100	6.00
71	Johan Santana/Jsy/100	6.00
73	Johnny Damon/Jsy/100	6.00
78	Josh Beckett/Jsy/100	4.00
82	Justin Morneau/Jsy/100	6.00
84	Kazuo Matsui/Jsy/100	4.00
87	Frank Thomas/Jsy/100	6.00
88	Kerry Wood/Jsy/100	6.00
92	Francisco Cordero/Jsy/100	4.00
93	Lance Berkman/Jsy/100	4.00
94	Larry Walker/Jsy/100	6.00
96	Luis Gonzalez/Jsy/100	4.00
97	Lyle Overbay/Jsy/100	4.00
98	Carlos Zambrano/Jsy/100	6.00
99	Manny Ramirez/Jsy/100	8.00
104	Mark Prior/Jsy/100	8.00
109	Michael Young/Jsy/100	4.00
110	Miguel Cabrera/Jsy/100	8.00
111	Miguel Tejada/Jsy/100	6.00
113	Mike Mussina/Jsy/50	6.00
114	Mike Piazza/Jsy/100	8.00
121	Paul Konerko/Jsy/100	4.00
124	Rafael Palmeiro/Jsy/100	6.00
129	Roger Clemens/Jsy/100	10.00
131	Sammy Sosa/Jsy/100	8.00
133	Scott Rolen/Jsy/100	4.00
135	Sean Casey/Jsy/100	4.00
138	Roy Halladay/Jsy/100	4.00
141	Todd Helton/Jsy/100	6.00
144	Travis Hafner/Jsy/100	4.00
147	Vernon Wells/Jsy/100	4.00
148	Victor Martinez/Jsy/100	4.00
149	Vladimir Guerrero/Jsy/100	8.00
151	Hank Blalock/Jsy/100	4.00
153	Rocco Baldelli/Jsy/100	4.00
159	Ben Sheets/Jsy/100	4.00
160	Lew Ford/Jsy/100	4.00
166	Mike Sweeney/Jsy/100	4.00
178	Greg Maddux/Jsy/100	10.00
179	Ivan Rodriguez/Jsy/100	4.00
183	Pedro J. Martinez/Jsy/100	8.00
184	Rafael Palmeiro/Pants/100	6.00
185	Roger Clemens/Jsy/100	10.00
188	Tom Glavine/Jsy/100	4.00
190	Vladimir Guerrero/Jsy/100	8.00

Mirror Fabric Red
NM/M

Production 100-250

Gold: 1-2X
Production 25 Sets

2	Adam Dunn/Jsy/250	6.00
5	Albert Pujols/Jsy/250	15.00
7	Alfonso Soriano/Jsy/250	6.00
8	Andruw Jones/Jsy/250	6.00
10	Aramis Ramirez/Jsy/250	6.00
11	Aubrey Huff/Jsy/250	4.00
13	B.J. Upton/Jsy/250	4.00
14	Brandon Webb/Pants/100	4.00
15	Barry Zito/Jsy/250	4.00
17	Bobby Abreu/Jsy/250	4.00
20	Preston Wilson/Jsy/250	4.00

25	Casey Kotchman/Jsy/250	4.00
26	Chipper Jones/Jsy/250	8.00
28	Craig Biggio/Jsy/250	4.00
30	Curt Schilling/Jsy/250	8.00
32	David Ortiz/Jsy/250	8.00
37	Derrek Lee/Jsy/250	8.00
38	Dontrelle Willis/Jsy/225	4.00
41	Eric Chavez/Jsy/250	4.00
43	Francisco Rodriguez/Jsy/250	4.00
44	Garret Anderson/Jsy/250	4.00
45	Gary Sheffield/Jsy/250	6.00
46	Greg Maddux/Jsy/250	10.00
47	Hideki Matsui/Jsy/250	15.00
48	Hideo Nomo/Jsy/100	6.00
50	Ivan Rodriguez/Jsy/250	4.00
57	Trot Nixon/Jsy/250	4.00
60	Roy Oswalt/Jsy/250	4.00
61	Javy Lopez/Jsy/250	4.00
63	Jeff Bagwell/Jsy/250	4.00
69	Jim Edmonds/Jsy/250	6.00
70	Jim Thome/Jsy/250	6.00
71	Johan Santana/Jsy/250	6.00
82	Justin Morneau/Jsy/250	6.00
84	Kazuo Matsui/Jsy/250	4.00
87	Frank Thomas/Jsy/250	6.00
88	Kerry Wood/Jsy/250	6.00
92	Francisco Cordero/Jsy/250	4.00
93	Lance Berkman/Jsy/250	4.00
94	Larry Walker/Jsy/250	6.00
96	Luis Gonzalez/Jsy/250	4.00
97	Lyle Overbay/Jsy/250	4.00
98	Carlos Zambrano/Jsy/250	4.00
99	Manny Ramirez/Jsy/250	8.00
104	Mark Prior/Jsy/250	8.00
109	Michael Young/Jsy/250	4.00
110	Miguel Cabrera/Jsy/250	8.00
111	Miguel Tejada/Jsy/250	6.00
114	Mike Piazza/Jsy/250	8.00
121	Paul Konerko/Jsy/250	4.00
124	Rafael Palmeiro/Jsy/250	6.00
129	Roger Clemens/Jsy/250	10.00
131	Sammy Sosa/Jsy/250	8.00
133	Scott Rolen/Jsy/250	4.00
135	Sean Casey/Jsy/250	4.00
138	Roy Halladay/Jsy/250	4.00
141	Todd Helton/Jsy/250	4.00
144	Travis Hafner/Jsy/250	4.00
147	Vernon Wells/Jsy/250	4.00
148	Victor Martinez/Jsy/250	4.00
149	Vladimir Guerrero/Jsy/250	8.00
153	Rocco Baldelli/Jsy/250	4.00
159	Ben Sheets/Jsy/250	4.00
160	Lew Ford/Jsy/250	4.00
166	Mike Sweeney/Jsy/250	4.00
178	Greg Maddux/Jsy/250	10.00
179	Ivan Rodriguez/Jsy/250	4.00
183	Pedro J. Martinez/Jsy/250	8.00
184	Rafael Palmeiro/Jsy/250	6
185	Roger Clemens/Jsy/250	
188	Tom Glavine/Jsy/25	
190	Vladimir Guerrero/Jsy/100	

Mirror Fabri...

Production 50-...

2	Adam D...	
5	Alber...	
7	Alfo...	
	Js...	
8		
10		

26	Chipper Jones/Jsy/250	8.00
28	Craig Biggio/Pants/250	4.00
30	Curt Schilling/Jsy/100	8.00
32	David Ortiz/Jsy/100	8.00
34	David Wright/Jsy/100	10.00
38	Dontrelle Willis/Jsy/50	4.00
41	Eric Chavez/Jsy/100	4.00
44	Garret Anderson/Jsy/100	4.00
45	Gary Sheffield/Jsy/50	6.00
46	Greg Maddux/Jsy/100	10.00
47	Hideki Matsui/Pants/100	15.00
48	Hideo Nomo/Jsy/100	6.00
57	Trot Nixon/Jsy/100	6.00
60	Roy Oswalt/Jsy/25	6.00
63	Jeff Bagwell/Jsy/100	6.00
69	Jim Edmonds/Jsy/100	6.00
70	Jim Thome/Jsy/100	6.00
71	Johan Santana/Jsy/100	6.00
78	Josh Beckett/Jsy/250	4.00
82	Justin Morneau/Jsy/100	6.00
84	Kazuo Matsui/Jsy/250	4.00
88	Kerry Wood/Jsy/50	6.00
93	Lance Berkman/Jsy/250	4.00
94	Larry Walker/Jsy/100	6.00
95	Laynce Nix/Jsy/100	6.00
96	Luis Gonzalez/Jsy/250	4.00
98	Carlos Zambrano/Jsy/100	6.00
99	Manny Ramirez/Jsy/100	8.00
104	Mark Prior/Jsy/100	8.00
109	Michael Young/Jsy/100	4.00
110	Miguel Cabrera/Jsy/150	8.00
111	Miguel Tejada/Jsy/100	8.00
113	Mike Mussina/Jsy/100	6.00
114	Mike Piazza/Jsy/100	8.00
121	Paul Konerko/Jsy/150	4.00
124	Rafael Palmeiro/Jsy/150	6.00
129	Roger Clemens/Jsy/100	10.00
131	Sammy Sosa/Jsy/150	4.00
133	Scott Rolen/Jsy/100	4.00
135	Sean Casey/Jsy/100	4.00
138	Roy Halladay/Jsy/100	4.00
141	Todd Helton/Jsy/100	6.00
144	Travis Hafner/Jsy/100	4.00
147	Vernon Wells/Jsy/250	4.00
148	Victor Martinez/Jsy/100	4.00
149	Vladimir Guerrero/Jsy/250	8.00
151	Hank Blalock/Jsy/100	4.00
159	Ben Sheets/Jsy/100	4.00
166	Mike Sweeney/Jsy/50	
178	Greg Maddux/Jsy/200	
179	Ivan Rodriguez/Jsy/250	
184	Rafael Palmeir/Jsy/250	
185	Roger Clem/Jsy/250	
188	Tom Gl	

Comp...
Inse...
M...

Skills Autographs

NM/M

Production 5-25

3	Bobby Crosby/25	25.00
11	Jason Bay/25	25.00

Skills Jersey Position

NM/M

Production 100-250
Prime: No Pricing
Production 5-25

1	Andy Pettitte/250	4.00
2	Barry Zito/250	4.00
3	Bobby Crosby/100	6.00
4	Brandon Webb/Pants/100	4.00
5	Craig Biggio/250	4.00
6	David Ortiz/250	8.00
7	Dontrelle Willis/100	4.00
8	Francisco Rodriguez/250	4.00
9	Gary Sheffield/50	6.00
10	Jack Wilson/50	4.00
11	Jason Bay/100	4.00
12	Jeff Bagwell/250	6.00
13	Jim Edmonds/250	6.00
14	Josh Beckett/250	4.00
15	Kerry Wood/50	6.00
16	Lance Berkman/250	4.00
17	Mark Buehrle/150	4.00
19	Miguel Tejada/250	8.00
20	Paul Konerko/100	4.00
21	Scott Rolen/100	6.00
22	Sean Burroughs/100	4.00
23	Vernon Wells/50	4.00
24	Victor Martinez/250	4.00
25	Vladimir Guerrero/250	8.00

2005 Leaf Limited

NM/M

Complete Set (205):
Common Player (1-150): 1.00
Production 699
Common (151-175, 197): 4.00
Production 99
Common Auto.
(176-196, 198-200): 12.00
Production 99
Pack (4): 70.00

1	Roger Clemens	5.00
2	Roger Clemens	5.00
3	Ichiro Suzuki	4.00
4	Ichiro Suzuki	4.00
	Todd Helton	1.50
		1.50
		2.00

55	Brad Radke	1.00
56	Brad Wilkerson	1.00
57	Sean Casey	1.00
58	Mike Lowell	1.00
59	Octavio Dotel	1.00
60	Francisco Rodriguez	1.00
61	Jose Guillen	1.00
62	Greg Maddux	3.00
63	A.J. Burnett	1.00
64	Chris Carpenter	1.50
65	Jose Reyes	1.50
66	Travis Hafner	1.50
67	Rich Harden	1.00
68	Bret Boone	1.00
69	Scott Podsednik	1.00
70	Andruw Jones	1.50
71	Milton Bradley	1.00
72	Zack Greinke	1.00
73	Torii Hunter	1.00
74	Paul Konerko	1.50
75	David Wells	1.00
76	Tim Hudson	1.50
77	Sammy Sosa	2.50
78	Jason Varitek	1.50
79	Lance Berkman	1.50
80	Justin Morneau	1.50
81	Troy Glaus	1.00
82	Jose Vidro	1.00
83	Joe Mauer	1.50
84	Josh Beckett	1.00
85	Craig Biggio	1.00
86	Luis Gonzalez	1.00
87	Larry Walker	1.00
88	Barry Zito	1.00
89	Jacque Jones	1.00
90	Lyle Overbay	1.00
91	Roy Halladay	1.50
92	Orlando Cabrera	1.00
93	Magglio Ordonez	1.00
94	Mike Sweeney	1.00
95	Rafael Palmeiro	1.50
96	Brandon Webb	1.00
97	Preston Wilson	1.00
98	Shannon Stewart	1.00
99	Trot Nixon	1.00
100	Mike Piazza	2.50
101	Dontrelle Willis	1.50
102	Ken Griffey Jr.	3.00
103	Andy Pettitte	1.00
104	Kazuo Matsui	1.00
105	Bobby Crosby	1.00
106	Shawn Green	1.00
107	Alfonso Soriano	2.00
108	Carlos Zambrano	1.00
109	Keith Foulke	1.00
110	Aubrey Huff	1.00
111	Adrian Beltre	1.00
112	Mark Teixeira	1.50
113	Randy Johnson	2.00
	Tejada	1.50
		4.00
		1.50

159	Don Mattingly	10.00
160	Bob Gibson	4.00
161	Hank Aaron	8.00
162	Al Kaline	6.00
163	Nolan Ryan	10.00
164	Stan Musial	6.00
165	George Kell	4.00
166	Harmon Killebrew	6.00
167	Cal Ripken Jr.	15.00
168	Babe Ruth	10.00
169	Roger Clemens/SP	8.00
170	Curt Schilling/SP	4.00
171	Rafael Palmeiro/SP	4.00
172	Randy Johnson/SP	5.00
173	Mike Piazza/SP	5.00
174	Greg Maddux/SP	5.00
175	Sammy Sosa/SP	5.00
176	Hayden Penn/Auto.	15.00
177	Ambiorix Concepcion/Auto. RC	15.00
178	Casey Rogowski/Auto. RC	25.00
179	Prince Fielder/Auto.	150.00
180	Geovany Soto/Auto. RC	30.00
181	Wladimir Balentien/Auto. RC	25.00
182	Jason Hammel/Auto. RC	15.00
183	Keiichi Yabu/Auto. RC	25.00
184	Brandon McCarthy/Auto. RC	40.00
185	Ubaldo Jimenez/Auto. RC	15.00
186	Keiichi Yabu/Auto. RC	25.00
187	Miguel Negron/Auto. RC	15.00
188	Mike Morse/Auto. RC	25.00
189	Nate McLouth/Auto. RC	15.00
190	Norihiro Nakamura/Auto. RC	40.00
191	Bill McCarthy/Auto. RC	50.00
192	Tony Pena/Auto. RC	12.00
193	Ambiorix Concepcion/Auto. RC	15.00
194	Raul Tablado/Auto. RC	15.00
195	Hayden Penn/Auto. RC	15.00
196	Sean Thompson/Auto. RC	15.00
197	Tadahito Iguchi RC	15.00
198	Ubaldo Jimenez/Auto. RC	15.00
199	Wladimir Balentien/Auto. RC	25.00
200	Prince Fielder/Auto.	150.00
201	Philip Humber/Auto./99 RC	60.00
	...nn/	40.00

6	Nolan Ryan/34	120.00
7	Jim Palmer/22	30.00
8	Tony Gwynn/19	60.00
9	Rod Carew/29	40.00
10	Ryne Sandberg/23	70.00
11	Stan Musial/28	70.00
12	Steve Carlton/32	30.00
14	Mike Schmidt/20	60.00
15	Harmon Killebrew/25	40.00
16	Duke Snider/53	30.00
18	Don Mattingly/25	50.00
19	Dale Murphy/25	35.00
20	Craig Biggio/7	
21	Juan Marichal/99	25.00
22	Greg Maddux/37	10.00
23	Lou Brock/20	
24	Paul Molitor/25	35.00
25	Wade Boggs/26	40.00
26	Mark Prior/27	40.00
28	Al Kaline/28	40.00
29	Minnie Minoso/25	

Cuts Gold

Production 3-30

Legends

NM/M

Common Player:
Production 50 Sets
Foil: No Pricing
Production 10 Sets

1	Billy Martin	4.00
2	Bobby Doerr	3.00
3	Carlton Fisk	4.00
4	Harmon Killebrew	5.00
5	Duke Snider	5.00
6	George Brett	6.00
7	Johnny Bench	5.00
8	Lou Boudreau	3.00
9	Brooks Robinson	4.00
10	Al Kaline	4.00
11	Stan Musial	5.00
12	Burleigh Grimes	3.00
13	Cal Ripken Jr.	10.00
14	Carl Yastrzemski	6.00
15	Willie Stargell	6.00
16	Yogi Berra	4.00
17	Enos Slaughter	3.00
18	Phil Rizzuto	3.00
19	Luis Aparicio	3.00
20	Ernie Banks	5.00
21	Hal Newhouser	3.00
22	Whitey Ford	4.00
23	Tony Gwynn	4.00
24	Bob Feller	4.00
25	Don Sutton	3.00
26	Lou Brock	3.00
27	Jim Palmer	3.00
28	Billy Williams	3.00
29	Juan Marichal	3.00
30	Rod Carew	3.00
31	Jim "Catfish" Hunter	2.00
32	Maury Wills	2.00
33	Joe Cronin	2.00
34	Fergie Jenkins	2.00
35	Sandy Koufax	5.00
36	Steve Carlton	3.00
37	Eddie Murray	3.00
38	Roger Maris	4.00
39	Gaylord Perry	2.00
40	Bob Gibson	3.00
41	Tom Seaver	3.00
42	Dennis Eckersley	2.00
43	Reggie Jackson	3.00
44	Willie McCovey	3.00
45	Willie Mays	3.00
46	Willie Mays	6.00
47	Rickey Henderson	3.00
48	Rickey Henderson	3.00
49	Nolan Ryan	6.00
50	Nolan Ryan	6.00

Legends Jersey Number Prime

NM/M

Production 1-25

3	Carlton Fisk/25	12.00
6	George Brett/25	20.00
13	Cal Ripken Jr./25	50.00
15	Willie Stargell/25	20.00
23	Tony Gwynn/25	25.00
26	Lou Brock/25	20.00
40	Bob Gibson/25	20.00
42	Dennis Eckersley/25	15.00
47	Rickey Henderson/25	20.00
48	Rickey Henderson/25	20.00

Legends Signature Jersey Number Prime

NM/M

42	Dennis Eckersley/25	30.00

Skills
White
Silver

No Pricing

	Cepeda/30	35.00
	Aaron/44	275.00
	Mays/24	175.00
	Koufax/32	400.00
	...pken Jr./25	150.00

Legends Jersey Number

NM/M

Production 1-45
3	Carlton Fisk/50	10.00
25	Don Sutton/20	8.00
26	Lou Brock/20	10.00
27	Jim Palmer/22	8.00
28	Billy Williams/26	8.00
29	Juan Marichal/27	8.00
30	Rod Carew/29	10.00
31	Jim "Catfish" Hunter/ Pants/29	8.00
34	Fergie Jenkins/31	6.00
35	Sandy Koufax/32	250.00
36	Steve Carlton/32	8.00
37	Eddie Murray/33	12.00
39	Gaylord Perry/36	6.00
40	Bob Gibson/45	10.00
41	Tom Seaver/41	10.00
42	Dennis Eckersley/45	5.00
43	Reggie Jackson/ Pants/44	8.00
44	Willie McCovey/44	10.00
45	Willie Mays/24	40.00
46	Willie Mays/24	40.00
49	Nolan Ryan/30	25.00
50	Nolan Ryan/30	25.00

Legends Signature

NM/M

Production 2-50
2	Bobby Doerr/50	15.00
4	Harmon Killebrew/50	30.00
5	Duke Snider/50	35.00
9	Brooks Robinson/50	25.00
10	Al Kaline/50	40.00
18	Phil Rizzuto/50	35.00
19	Luis Aparicio/50	20.00
24	Bob Feller/50	25.00
25	Don Sutton/50	15.00
26	Lou Brock/50	30.00
27	Jim Palmer/50	20.00
28	Billy Williams/25	20.00
29	Juan Marichal/50	35.00
30	Rod Carew/25	35.00
32	Maury Wills/50	15.00
34	Fergie Jenkins/50	15.00
36	Steve Carlton/50	25.00
39	Gaylord Perry/50	15.00
40	Bob Gibson/25	40.00
42	Dennis Eckersley/50	20.00

Legends Signature Jersey Number

NM/M

Production 5-30
2	Bobby Doerr/ Pants/25	25.00
4	Harmon Killebrew/25	40.00
11	Stan Musial/25	65.00
13	Cal Ripken Jr./25	150.00
18	Phil Rizzuto/ Pants/25	40.00
19	Luis Aparicio/25	25.00
23	Tony Gwynn/25	40.00
25	Don Sutton/20	20.00
27	Jim Palmer/22	25.00
34	Fergie Jenkins/25	20.00
36	Steve Carlton/25	30.00
39	Gaylord Perry/25	20.00
40	Bob Gibson/25	40.00
42	Dennis Eckersley/25	25.00
43	Reggie Jackson/ Pants/10	
44	Willie McCovey/25	40.00
45	Willie Mays/24	160.00
46	Willie Mays/24	160.00
49	Nolan Ryan/30	90.00
50	Nolan Ryan/30	90.00

Lettermen

Production 4-21
DU-H	Dale Murphy H/20	150.00
DU-M	Dale Murphy M/20	150.00
DU-P	Dale Murphy P/20	150.00
DU-R	Dale Murphy R/20	150.00
DU-U	Dale Murphy U/20	150.00
DU-Y	Dale Murphy Y/20	150.00
NR-A	Nolan Ryan A/21	200.00
NR-N	Nolan Ryan N/21	200.00
NR-R	Nolan Ryan R/21	200.00
NR-Y	Nolan Ryan Y/21	200.00

Lumberjacks

NM/M

Common Player:
Production 50 Sets
Foil:		No Pricing
1	Al Kaline	4.00
2	Albert Pujols	8.00
3	Andre Dawson	3.00
4	Babe Ruth	8.00
5	Cal Ripken Jr.	15.00
6	Chipper Jones	4.00
7	Dale Murphy	3.00
8	Dave Winfield	3.00
9	Don Mattingly	6.00
10	Duke Snider	4.00
11	Eddie Murray	3.00
12	Frank Robinson	4.00
13	Frank Thomas	4.00
14	Gary Carter	3.00
15	Hack Wilson	3.00
16	Hank Aaron	10.00
17	Harmon Killebrew	4.00
18	Joe Morgan	3.00
19	Johnny Bench	4.00
20	Kirby Puckett	4.00
21	Kirk Gibson	3.00
22	Manny Ramirez	4.00
23	Mark Grace	3.00
24	Mike Piazza	5.00
25	Mike Schmidt	6.00
26	Orlando Cepeda	3.00
27	Paul Molitor	4.00
28	Rafael Palmeiro	4.00
29	Ralph Kiner	3.00
30	Reggie Jackson	4.00
31	Richie Ashburn	3.00
32	Rickey Henderson	4.00
33	Robin Yount	5.00
34	Rod Carew	4.00
35	Ryne Sandberg	6.00
36	Stan Musial	5.00
37	Ted Williams	8.00
38	Tony Gwynn	4.00
39	Vladimir Guerrero	4.00
40	Willie Mays	8.00
41	Ernie Banks, Bernie Williams	6.00
42	Ted Williams, Joe Cronin	10.00
43	George Brett, Bo Jackson	8.00
44	John Kruk, Jim Thome	3.00
45	Willie Mays, Jim Thorpe	8.00
46	Wade Boggs, Johnny Damon	6.00
47	M. Williams, W. Clark	3.00
48	Willie Stargell, D. Parker	4.00
49	Ichiro Suzuki, Edgar Martinez	6.00
50	Carl Yastrzemski, Carlton Fisk	6.00

Lumberjacks Barrel

No Pricing
Production 1-5

Lumberjacks Bat

NM/M

Production 1-50
1	Al Kaline/50	10.00
4	Babe Ruth/25	180.00
8	Dave Winfield/50	15.00
11	Eddie Murray/50	15.00
12	Frank Robinson/50	15.00
14	Gary Carter/50	10.00
16	Hack Wilson/50	40.00
17	Hank Aaron/50	40.00
18	Joe Morgan/25	8.00
19	Johnny Bench/50	10.00
20	Kirby Puckett/50	10.00
25	Mike Schmidt/50	15.00
26	Orlando Cepeda/25	8.00
27	Paul Molitor/50	8.00
29	Ralph Kiner/25	15.00
31	Robin Yount/25	20.00
35	Ryne Sandberg/25	20.00
36	Stan Musial/50	20.00
37	Ted Williams/50	40.00
40	Willie Mays/50	30.00
43	George Brett, Bo Jackson/50	25.00
47	M. Williams, W. Clark/50	15.00
48	Willie Stargell, D. Parker/50	15.00
50	Carl Yastrzemski, Carlton Fisk/50	20.00

Lumberjacks Combos

NM/M

Production 1-50
2	Albert Pujols/ Bat-Jsy/50	30.00
5	Cal Ripken Jr./ Bat-Jsy/50	35.00
6	Chipper Jones/ Bat-Jsy/25	15.00
7	Dale Murphy/ Bat-Jsy/50	12.00
8	Dave Winfield/ Bat-Pants/50	8.00
11	Eddie Murray/ Bat-Jsy/25	20.00
13	Frank Thomas/ Bat-Jsy/25	15.00
16	Hank Aaron/ Bat-Jsy/25	60.00
19	Johnny Bench/ Bat-Jsy/25	15.00
20	Kirby Puckett/ Bat-Jsy/25	15.00
21	Kirk Gibson/ Bat-Jsy/50	8.00
22	Manny Ramirez/ Bat-Jsy/25	12.00
23	Mark Grace/ Bat-Jsy/25	12.00
24	Mike Piazza/ Bat-Jsy/25	15.00
25	Mike Schmidt/ Bat-Jsy/25	25.00
26	Orlando Cepeda/ Bat-Pants/50	8.00
27	Paul Molitor/ Bat-Jsy/50	12.00
31	Richie Ashburn/ Bat-Jsy/25	15.00
33	Robin Yount/ Bat-Jsy/25	15.00
36	Stan Musial/ Bat-Jsy/25	35.00
40	Willie Mays/ Bat-Jsy/25	50.00

Lumberjacks Combos Prime

NM/M

Production 1-50
2	Albert Pujols/ Bat-Jsy/50	35.00
3	Andre Dawson/ Bat-Jsy/50	8.00
5	Cal Ripken Jr./ Bat-Jsy/25	50.00
6	Chipper Jones/ Bat-Jsy/25	15.00
11	Eddie Murray/ Bat-Jsy/25	25.00
12	Frank Robinson/ Bat-Jsy/25	12.00
13	Frank Thomas/ Bat-Jsy/25	15.00
14	Gary Carter/ Bat-Jsy/25	10.00
18	Joe Morgan/ Bat-Jsy/25	15.00
21	Kirk Gibson/ Bat-Jsy/50	8.00
22	Manny Ramirez/ Bat-Jsy/25	20.00
24	Mike Piazza/ Bat-Jsy/25	15.00
28	Rafael Palmeiro/ Bat-Jsy/50	12.00
32	Rickey Henderson/ Bat-Jsy/25	15.00
33	Robin Yount/ Bat-Jsy/50	25.00
34	Rod Carew/ Bat-Jsy/50	12.00
39	Vladimir Guerrero/ Bat-Jsy/50	15.00

Lumberjacks Jersey

NM/M

Production 1-50
4	Babe Ruth/25	250.00
6	Dave Winfield/ Pants/50	6.00
10	Duke Snider/ Pants/50	10.00
11	Eddie Murray/25	15.00
14	Gary Carter/50	5.00
16	Hank Aaron/25	40.00
19	Johnny Bench/25	15.00
20	Kirby Puckett/25	15.00
27	Paul Molitor/50	8.00
30	Reggie Jackson/50	10.00
31	Richie Ashburn/50	10.00
33	Robin Yount/25	15.00
35	Ryne Sandberg/25	12.00
36	Stan Musial/25	25.00
37	Ted Williams/25	50.00
40	Willie Mays/25	35.00
41	Ernie Banks, Bernie Williams/25	30.00
42	Ted Williams, Joe Cronin/25	60.00
43	George Brett, Bo Jackson/50	30.00
44	John Kruk, Jim Thome/25	20.00
45	Willie Mays, Jim Thorpe/25	200.00
46	Wade Boggs, Johnny Damon/50	20.00
47	M. Williams, W. Clark/50	20.00
48	Willie Stargell, D. Parker/50	25.00

Lumberjacks Jersey Prime

NM/M
2	Albert Pujols/25	40.00
3	Andre Dawson/50	10.00
5	Cal Ripken Jr./25	50.00
6	Chipper Jones/25	20.00
11	Eddie Murray/25	25.00
12	Frank Robinson/25	10.00
13	Frank Thomas/25	15.00
14	Gary Carter/50	10.00
21	Kirk Gibson/50	10.00
24	Mike Piazza/50	15.00
25	Mike Schmidt/25	30.00
28	Rafael Palmeiro/25	15.00
32	Rickey Henderson/25	20.00
33	Robin Yount/50	15.00
34	Rod Carew/50	15.00
35	Ryne Sandberg/25	30.00
38	Tony Gwynn/50	20.00
39	Vladimir Guerrero/25	20.00

Lumberjacks Signature

NM/M

Production 1-50
1	Al Kaline/50	40.00
3	Andre Dawson/25	20.00
5	Cal Ripken Jr./21	120.00
7	Dale Murphy/50	25.00
9	Don Mattingly/50	50.00
10	Duke Snider/50	25.00
12	Frank Robinson/50	50.00
13	Frank Thomas/50	50.00
14	Gary Carter/50	20.00
17	Harmon Killebrew/50	35.00
18	Joe Morgan/25	25.00
19	Johnny Bench/50	40.00
20	Kirby Puckett/25	40.00
23	Mark Grace/50	35.00
25	Mike Schmidt/50	40.00
27	Paul Molitor/50	30.00
29	Ralph Kiner/50	30.00
34	Rod Carew/50	25.00
35	Ryne Sandberg/50	40.00
36	Stan Musial/50	50.00
38	Tony Gwynn/50	35.00
40	Willie Mays/25	140.00

Lumberjacks Signature Jersey Prime

NM/M

Production 1-25
3	Andre Dawson/25	30.00
5	Cal Ripken Jr./25	160.00
7	Dale Murphy/50	50.00
12	Frank Robinson/25	35.00
14	Gary Carter/25	30.00

Lumberjacks Signature Combos Prime

Production 1-25

Lumberjacks Signature Bat

NM/M

Production 1-100
1	Al Kaline/50	40.00
3	Andre Dawson/100	20.00
5	Cal Ripken Jr./100	140.00
7	Dale Murphy/100	25.00
9	Don Mattingly/50	50.00
12	Frank Robinson/100	35.00
13	Frank Thomas/50	50.00
14	Gary Carter/25	25.00
18	Joe Morgan/25	25.00
19	Johnny Bench/50	50.00
21	Kirk Gibson/25	25.00
23	Mark Grace/25	40.00
26	Orlando Cepeda/100	20.00

27	Paul Molitor/25	40.00
29	Ralph Kiner/100	30.00
33	Robin Yount/25	50.00
34	Rod Carew/25	30.00
36	Stan Musial/25	65.00
38	Tony Gwynn/25	40.00

Lumberjacks Signature Combos

		NM/M
Production 1-100		
3	Andre Dawson/Bat-Jsy/100	20.00
5	Cal Ripken Jr./Bat-Jsy/100	140.00
7	Dale Murphy/Bat-Jsy/100	25.00
9	Don Mattingly/Bat-Jsy/100	50.00
13	Frank Thomas/Bat-Jsy/25	50.00
14	Gary Carter/Bat-Jsy/25	25.00
23	Mark Grace/Bat-Jsy/50	40.00
38	Tony Gwynn/Bat-Jsy/25	45.00

Lumberjacks Signature Jersey

		NM/M
Production 1-100		
3	Andre Dawson/100	20.00
5	Cal Ripken Jr./25	140.00
7	Dale Murphy/100	25.00
9	Don Mattingly/50	50.00
10	Duke Snider/Pants/50	30.00
13	Frank Thomas/25	50.00
14	Gary Carter/25	40.00
17	Harmon Killebrew/25	40.00
19	Johnny Bench/25	50.00
23	Mark Grace/25	40.00
27	Paul Molitor/25	40.00
30	Reggie Jackson/25	40.00
33	Robin Yount/25	50.00
38	Tony Gwynn/50	40.00

Matching Numbers

		NM/M
Production 5-50		
Prime:		No Pricing
Production 1-5		
1	Ted Williams, Roger Maris/25	160.00
2	Nolan Ryan, Kerry Wood/50	35.00
3	Cal Ripken Jr., Gary Carter/50	40.00
5	Johnny Bench, Albert Pujols/50	40.00
6	Roger Clemens, W. Clark/50	35.00
7	Willie McCovey, Reggie Jackson/25	20.00
8	Ryne Sandberg, Don Mattingly/50	35.00
9	Duke Snider, Joe Cronin/25	25.00

Monikers Bronze

		NM/M
Production 1-100		
9	Miguel Cabrera/100	25.00
10	Miguel Cabrera/25	25.00
13	Mark Prior/50	35.00
14	Mark Prior/50	35.00
25	Ben Sheets/100	15.00
27	Melvin Mora/50	15.00
29	Rafael Furcal/25	20.00
32	Jake Peavy/25	25.00
33	Francisco Cordero/25	15.00
38	Michael Young/25	25.00
40	Joe Nathan/25	20.00
43	Eric Chavez/25	25.00
45	Roy Oswalt/25	25.00
49	Edgar Renteria/25	20.00
50	Mark Buehrle/25	30.00
57	Sean Casey/50	15.00
59	Octavio Dotel/25	12.00
60	Francisco Rodriguez/25	30.00
61	Jose Guillen/25	20.00
66	Travis Hafner/50	15.00
67	Rich Harden/50	15.00
71	Milton Bradley/25	15.00
73	Torii Hunter/25	25.00
74	Paul Konerko/50	30.00
76	Tim Hudson/25	25.00
80	Justin Morneau/100	25.00
82	Jose Vidro/25	15.00

84	Josh Beckett/25	30.00
85	Craig Biggio/25	30.00
89	Jacque Jones/50	15.00
91	Roy Halladay/25	15.00
93	Magglio Ordonez/100	15.00
96	Brandon Webb/50	15.00
97	Preston Wilson/50	15.00
98	Shannon Stewart/50	10.00
99	Trot Nixon/50	20.00
105	Bobby Crosby/40	15.00
107	Alfonso Soriano/25	30.00
108	Carlos Zambrano/50	25.00
109	Keith Foulke/25	30.00
110	Aubrey Huff/50	15.00
112	Mark Teixeira/100	25.00
116	Carlos Beltran/25	30.00
118	Johan Santana/100	30.00
121	Scott Rolen/25	45.00
123	Carlos Lee/50	20.00
124	Derrek Lee/50	25.00
130	Garret Anderson/100	15.00
131	Austin Kearns/100	15.00
133	Omar Vizquel/50	20.00
135	Mark Mulder/50	20.00
139	Mark Loretta/25	15.00
141	David Wright/50	60.00
144	Victor Martinez/25	15.00
151	Willie Mays/25	175.00
152	Ryne Sandberg/25	50.00
158	Duke Snider/50	25.00
159	Don Mattingly/25	50.00
160	Bob Gibson/50	50.00
162	Al Kaline/50	30.00
163	Nolan Ryan/25	80.00
164	Stan Musial/25	60.00
165	George Kell/50	15.00
166	Harmon Killebrew/50	30.00
167	Cal Ripken Jr./25	120.00
176	Hayden Penn/50	20.00
177	Ambiorix Concepcion/50	15.00
179	Prince Fielder/50	120.00
181	Wladimir Balentien/50	30.00
182	Jason Hammel/50	15.00
183	Keiichi Yabu/50	25.00
184	Brandon McCarthy/50	50.00
185	Ubaldo Jimenez/50	15.00
186	Keiichi Yabu/25	25.00
187	Miguel Negron/50	10.00
188	Mike Morse/50	30.00
189	Nate McLouth/50	15.00
190	Norihiro Nakamura/50	50.00
191	Brandon McCarthy/50	50.00
192	Tony Pena/50	10.00
193	Ambiorix Concepcion/50	15.00
194	Raul Tablado/50	15.00
195	Hayden Penn/50	20.00
196	Sean Thompson/50	12.00
198	Ubaldo Jimenez/50	15.00
199	Wladimir Balentien/50	30.00
200	Prince Fielder/50	120.00

Monikers Material Bat Bronze

		NM/M
Production 1-100		
Platinum:		No Pricing
Production One Set		
9	Miguel Cabrera/50	35.00
10	Miguel Cabrera/50	35.00
13	Mark Prior/50	40.00
14	Mark Prior/50	40.00
29	Rafael Furcal/75	15.00
34	Aramis Ramirez/100	20.00
37	Jason Bay/100	15.00
38	Michael Young/100	20.00
43	Eric Chavez/75	20.00
45	Roy Oswalt/50	25.00
50	Mark Buehrle/50	30.00
57	Sean Casey/25	15.00
66	Travis Hafner/100	15.00
73	Torii Hunter/50	20.00
74	Paul Konerko/50	25.00
80	Justin Morneau/100	25.00
82	Jose Vidro/50	10.00
85	Craig Biggio/25	30.00
93	Magglio Ordonez/50	20.00
97	Preston Wilson/50	15.00
98	Shannon Stewart/50	10.00
107	Alfonso Soriano/25	30.00
110	Aubrey Huff/25	12.00
111	Adrian Beltre/25	20.00
112	Mark Teixeira/50	30.00
116	Carlos Beltran/25	30.00
121	Scott Rolen/25	30.00
123	Carlos Lee/100	15.00
124	Derrek Lee/100	20.00

130	Garret Anderson/100	15.00
131	Austin Kearns/100	15.00
140	Vernon Wells/50	15.00
141	David Wright/50	70.00
143	David Ortiz/50	50.00
144	Victor Martinez/100	15.00
147	Angel Berroa/100	10.00

Monikers Material Button Gold

No Pricing		
Production 1-5		
Platinum:		No Pricing
Production One Set		

Monikers Material Jersey Number Silver

		NM/M
Production 1-75		
Prime Platinum:		No Pricing
Production One Set		
9	Miguel Cabrera/50	35.00
10	Miguel Cabrera/50	35.00
13	Mark Prior/25	40.00
25	Ben Sheets/Pants/50	20.00
33	Francisco Cordero/25	25.00
34	Aramis Ramirez/75	20.00
38	Michael Young/50	25.00
43	Eric Chavez/75	25.00
45	Roy Oswalt/75	25.00
57	Sean Casey/75	15.00
60	Francisco Rodriguez/75	25.00
66	Travis Hafner/50	20.00
70	Andruw Jones/25	40.00
85	Craig Biggio/50	30.00
89	Jacque Jones/25	15.00
90	Lyle Overbay/75	15.00
98	Shannon Stewart/75	10.00
99	Trot Nixon/50	35.00
101	Dontrelle Willis/24	30.00
107	Alfonso Soriano/50	30.00
112	Mark Teixeira/50	30.00
117	Bobby Abreu/75	20.00
121	Scott Rolen/75	25.00
124	Derrek Lee/25	25.00
128	Jim Edmonds/25	35.00
130	Garret Anderson/50	20.00
131	Austin Kearns/75	15.00
140	Vernon Wells/50	15.00
141	David Wright/75	70.00
143	David Ortiz/75	50.00
144	Victor Martinez/75	15.00
152	Ryne Sandberg/50	40.00
158	Duke Snider/25	25.00
159	Don Mattingly/50	60.00
160	Bob Gibson/50	30.00
163	Nolan Ryan/25	100.00
164	Stan Musial/25	80.00
166	Harmon Killebrew/50	35.00
167	Cal Ripken Jr./25	140.00

Monikers Material Jersey Prime Gold

		NM/M
Production 1-100		
Platinum:		No Pricing
Production One Set		
9	Miguel Cabrera/50	40.00
10	Miguel Cabrera/50	40.00
13	Mark Prior/25	50.00
14	Mark Prior/25	50.00
25	Ben Sheets/50	25.00
34	Aramis Ramirez/100	25.00
38	Michael Young/100	25.00
43	Eric Chavez/75	20.00
45	Roy Oswalt/100	30.00
57	Sean Casey/100	20.00
60	Francisco Rodriguez/75	30.00
66	Travis Hafner/100	25.00
70	Andruw Jones/40	40.00
84	Josh Beckett/25	40.00
88	Barry Zito/25	25.00
89	Jacque Jones/50	15.00
98	Shannon Stewart/75	15.00
107	Alfonso Soriano/50	40.00
112	Mark Teixeira/20	50.00
117	Bobby Abreu/100	25.00
121	Scott Rolen/50	35.00
128	Jim Edmonds/25	40.00
130	Garret Anderson/50	25.00
131	Austin Kearns/75	20.00
140	Vernon Wells/50	20.00
152	Ryne Sandberg/50	75.00
159	Don Mattingly/25	85.00
160	Bob Gibson/25	50.00
163	Nolan Ryan/25	120.00
167	Cal Ripken Jr./25	175.00

Monikers Silver

		NM/M
Production 1-50		
9	Miguel Cabrera/50	30.00
10	Miguel Cabrera/50	30.00
13	Mark Prior/25	40.00
14	Mark Prior/25	40.00
25	Ben Sheets/50	20.00
27	Melvin Mora/25	20.00
29	Rafael Furcal/25	20.00
32	Jake Peavy/50	25.00
33	Francisco Cordero/25	15.00
38	Michael Young/25	25.00
40	Joe Nathan/25	20.00
43	Eric Chavez/25	25.00
45	Roy Oswalt/25	30.00
49	Edgar Renteria/25	20.00
50	Mark Buehrle/25	30.00
57	Sean Casey/25	20.00
59	Octavio Dotel/25	12.00
60	Francisco Rodriguez/25	30.00
61	Jose Guillen/25	20.00
66	Travis Hafner/25	15.00
67	Rich Harden/50	15.00
71	Milton Bradley/25	15.00
80	Justin Morneau/50	25.00
89	Jacque Jones/25	15.00
93	Magglio Ordonez/50	15.00
96	Brandon Webb/25	15.00
97	Preston Wilson/25	20.00
98	Shannon Stewart/25	15.00
99	Trot Nixon/25	25.00
105	Bobby Crosby/29	20.00
108	Carlos Zambrano/50	25.00
109	Keith Foulke/25	30.00
110	Aubrey Huff/25	20.00
112	Mark Teixeira/25	30.00
118	Johan Santana/50	35.00
123	Carlos Lee/50	20.00
130	Garret Anderson/50	20.00
131	Austin Kearns/50	15.00
133	Omar Vizquel/25	20.00
135	Mark Mulder/50	20.00
139	Mark Loretta/25	20.00
141	David Wright/25	70.00
144	Victor Martinez/25	15.00
151	Willie Mays/25	175.00
152	Ryne Sandberg/25	50.00
158	Duke Snider/25	30.00
159	Don Mattingly/25	50.00
162	Al Kaline/25	35.00
163	Nolan Ryan/25	80.00
164	Stan Musial/25	60.00
165	George Kell/25	15.00
166	Harmon Killebrew/25	40.00
167	Cal Ripken Jr./25	120.00

Team Trademarks

		NM/M
Common Player:		3.00
Production 50 Sets		
Foil:		No Pricing
Production 10 Sets		
1	Ryne Sandberg	8.00
2	George Brett	8.00
3	Steve Carlton	3.00
4	Reggie Jackson	4.00
5	Edgar Martinez	3.00
6	Barry Larkin	4.00
7	Ozzie Smith	6.00
8	Carlton Fisk	5.00
9	Wade Boggs	5.00
10	Will Clark	4.00
11	Nolan Ryan	8.00
12	Gary Carter	3.00
13	Don Mattingly	4.00
14	Willie Stargell	4.00
15	Don Sutton	3.00
16	Kirk Gibson	4.00
17	Kirby Puckett	5.00
18	Dale Murphy	4.00
19	Rickey Henderson	4.00
20	Willie Mays	8.00
21	Cal Ripken Jr.	10.00
22	Paul Molitor	5.00
23	Tony Gwynn	5.00
24	Andre Dawson	4.00
25	Bob Feller	4.00
26	Alan Trammell	3.00
27	Dave Parker	3.00
28	Dave Righetti	3.00
29	Dwight Gooden	3.00
30	Harold Baines	3.00
31	Jack Morris	3.00
32	John Kruk	3.00
33	Lee Smith	3.00
34	Lenny Dykstra	3.00
35	Luis Tiant	3.00
36	Matt Williams	3.00
37	Ron Guidry	3.00
38	Tony Oliva	3.00

Team Trademarks
Jersey Number

		NM/M
Production 1-50		
1	Ryne Sandberg/23	20.00
3	Steve Carlton/ Pants/32	8.00
4	Reggie Jackson/44	10.00
8	Carlton Fisk/50	8.00
9	Wade Boggs/26	10.00
11	Nolan Ryan/Pants/34	25.00
20	Willie Mays/24	40.00

Team Trademarks
Jersey Number Prime

		NM/M
1	Ryne Sandberg/50	25.00
2	George Brett/50	25.00
3	Steve Carlton/50	10.00
4	Reggie Jackson/50	15.00
5	Edgar Martinez/50	15.00
6	Barry Larkin/50	15.00
7	Ozzie Smith/50	20.00
8	Carlton Fisk/50	15.00
9	Wade Boggs/50	15.00
10	Will Clark/50	15.00
11	Nolan Ryan/50	25.00
12	Gary Carter/50	12.00
13	Don Mattingly/40	25.00
14	Willie Stargell/50	15.00
15	Don Sutton/25	12.00
16	Kirk Gibson/50	12.00
18	Dale Murphy/50	12.00
19	Rickey Henderson/50	15.00
21	Cal Ripken Jr./25	50.00
23	Tony Gwynn/50	20.00
24	Andre Dawson/25	15.00
26	Alan Trammell/25	12.00
27	Dave Parker/50	10.00
29	Dwight Gooden/50	15.00
30	Harold Baines/25	15.00
31	Jack Morris/47	10.00
32	John Kruk/25	15.00
33	Lee Smith/47	10.00
34	Lenny Dykstra/25	15.00
38	Tony Oliva/25	15.00

Team Trademarks
Signature

		NM/M
Production 5-50		
1	Ryne Sandberg/25	50.00
3	Steve Carlton/25	25.00
4	Reggie Jackson/30	30.00
5	Edgar Martinez/50	20.00
6	Barry Larkin/50	25.00
7	Ozzie Smith/50	35.00
8	Carlton Fisk/25	25.00
9	Wade Boggs/25	35.00
10	Will Clark/50	25.00
11	Nolan Ryan/50	75.00
12	Gary Carter/50	15.00
13	Don Mattingly/25	50.00
15	Don Sutton/100	12.00
16	Kirk Gibson/50	20.00
17	Kirby Puckett/25	40.00
18	Dale Murphy/100	20.00
20	Willie Mays/25	160.00
21	Cal Ripken Jr./50	90.00
22	Paul Molitor/25	25.00
23	Tony Gwynn/50	40.00
24	Andre Dawson/100	15.00
25	Bob Feller/50	20.00
26	Alan Trammell/25	25.00
27	Dave Parker/50	15.00
28	Dave Righetti/25	20.00
29	Dwight Gooden/50	15.00
30	Harold Baines/50	15.00
31	Jack Morris/50	12.00
32	John Kruk/25	20.00
33	Lee Smith/50	15.00
34	Lenny Dykstra/25	20.00
35	Luis Tiant/50	15.00
36	Matt Williams/50	20.00
37	Ron Guidry/25	25.00
38	Tony Oliva/50	15.00

Team Trademarks
Signature Jersey
Number Prime

		NM/M
3	Steve Carlton/25	30.00
24	Andre Dawson/25	30.00
27	Dave Parker/39	20.00
31	Jack Morris/47	20.00
33	Lee Smith/47	25.00
38	Tony Oliva/26	35.00

Team Trademarks
Sign. Jersey Number

		NM/M
Production 1-72		
4	Reggie Jackson/44	50.00
8	Carlton Fisk/72	35.00
9	Wade Boggs/26	50.00
11	Nolan Ryan/Pants/34	90.00
17	Kirby Puckett/34	60.00
27	Dave Parker/39	25.00
31	Jack Morris/47	20.00
33	Lee Smith/47	25.00
37	Ron Guidry/Pants/49	20.00

Threads Button

No Pricing
Production 1-7

Threads Jersey
Number

		NM/M
Production 1-50		
Logo:		No Pricing
Production One Set		
152	Ryne Sandberg/50	15.00
154	Ted Williams/25	60.00
157	Whitey Ford/50	12.00
158	Duke Snider/25	15.00
164	Stan Musial/25	25.00
166	Harmon Killebrew/50	20.00

Threads Jersey Prime

		NM/M
Production 5-100		
1	Roger Clemens/25	25.00
5	Todd Helton/100	10.00
6	Todd Helton/100	10.00
7	Vladimir Guerrero/ 100	12.00
8	Vladimir Guerrero/ Jkt/30	20.00
9	Miguel Cabrera/100	10.00
10	Miguel Cabrera/100	10.00
12	Albert Pujols/50	30.00
13	Mark Prior/100	8.00
14	Mark Prior/25	10.00
15	Chipper Jones/100	10.00
16	Chipper Jones/100	8.00
17	Jeff Bagwell/100	8.00
18	Jeff Bagwell/100	8.00
19	Kerry Wood/100	8.00
22	Carl Crawford/100	5.00
23	Mariano Rivera/60	12.00
25	Ben Sheets/100	8.00
27	Melvin Mora/25	10.00
28	Corey Patterson/100	5.00
29	Rafael Furcal/100	5.00
30	Jim Thome/100	8.00
34	Aramis Ramirez/50	5.00
35	Javy Lopez/100	5.00
38	Michael Young/100	8.00
39	Ivan Rodriguez/100	8.00
42	Adam Dunn/100	8.00
43	Eric Chavez/100	5.00
45	Roy Oswalt/100	5.00
48	Johnny Damon/25	15.00
50	Mark Buehrle/50	8.00
53	Hank Blalock/100	5.00
55	Brad Radke/50	5.00
57	Sean Casey/50	5.00
58	Mike Lowell/50	5.00
60	Francisco Rodriguez/100	5.00
62	Greg Maddux/25	25.00
63	A.J. Burnett/75	5.00
66	Travis Hafner/100	5.00
68	Bret Boone/100	5.00
70	Andruw Jones/100	10.00
73	Torii Hunter/100	5.00
74	Paul Konerko/100	8.00
79	Lance Berkman/100	8.00
80	Justin Morneau/100	10.00
82	Jose Vidro/100	5.00
84	Josh Beckett/100	5.00
86	Luis Gonzalez/100	5.00
88	Barry Zito/100	5.00
91	Roy Halladay/100	5.00
94	Mike Sweeney/100	5.00
95	Rafael Palmeiro/100	8.00
97	Preston Wilson/100	5.00
98	Shannon Stewart/50	5.00
99	Trot Nixon/100	8.00
100	Mike Piazza/100	12.00
101	Dontrelle Willis/100	8.00
103	Andy Pettitte/100	10.00
104	Kazuo Matsui/100	5.00
107	Alfonso Soriano/100	8.00
110	Aubrey Huff/100	5.00
111	Adrian Beltre/50	5.00
112	Mark Teixeira/100	10.00
114	Miguel Tejada/100	8.00
117	Bobby Abreu/100	5.00

119	Manny Ramirez/60	15.00
121	Scott Rolen/100	10.00
124	Derrek Lee/50	10.00
127	John Smoltz/100	8.00
128	Jim Edmonds/100	8.00
130	Garret Anderson/60	8.00
131	Austin Kearns/100	5.00
138	Mike Mussina/50	10.00
140	Vernon Wells/100	5.00
141	David Wright/100	25.00
142	Marcus Giles/100	5.00
144	Victor Martinez/75	25.00
145	Hideki Matsui/100	40.00
146	C.C. Sabathia/100	5.00
150	Jorge Posada/100	10.00
152	Ryne Sandberg/50	25.00
153	Rickey Henderson/25	20.00
154	Ted Williams/5	
156	George Brett/50	25.00
159	Don Mattingly/50	25.00
160	Bob Gibson/25	20.00
161	Hank Aaron/25	75.00
163	Nolan Ryan/100	25.00
167	Cal Ripken Jr./100	30.00
169	Roger Clemens/50	20.00
170	Curt Schilling/100	8.00
171	Rafael Palmeiro/100	8.00
173	Mike Piazza/100	12.00
174	Greg Maddux/100	15.00
175	Sammy Sosa/100	15.00

Timber Barrel

No Pricing
Production 1-3

TNT

		NM/M
Production 1-50		
Prime:		.50-1.5X
Production 5-100		
7	Vladimir Guerrero/ Bat-Jsy/50	15.00
8	Miguel Cabrera/ Bat-Jsy/25	12.00
11	Albert Pujols/ Bat-Jsy/50	25.00
12	Albert Pujols/ Bat-Jsy/50	25.00
13	Mark Prior/Bat-Jsy/50	8.00
14	Mark Prior/Bat-Jsy/50	8.00
15	Chipper Jones/ Bat-Jsy/50	12.00
16	Chipper Jones/ Bat-Jsy/50	12.00
39	Ivan Rodriguez/ Bat-Jsy/50	12.00
42	Adam Dunn/ Bat-Jsy/50	5.00
62	Greg Maddux/ Bat-Jsy/25	20.00
100	Mike Piazza/ Bat-Jsy/50	12.00
107	Alfonso Soriano/ Bat-Jsy/50	12.00
112	Mark Teixeira/ Bat-Jsy/50	10.00
119	Manny Ramirez/ Bat-Jsy/50	12.00
121	Scott Rolen/ Bat-Jsy/50	10.00
124	Derrek Lee/ Bat-Jsy/50	8.00
143	David Ortiz/ Bat-Jsy/50	15.00
151	Willie Mays/ Bat-Jsy/25	50.00
153	Rickey Henderson/ Bat-Jsy/50	15.00
154	Ted Williams/ Bat-Jsy/25	85.00
159	Don Mattingly/ Bat-Jsy/50	20.00
161	Hank Aaron/ Bat-Jsy/25	50.00
163	Nolan Ryan/ Bat-Jsy/50	25.00
164	Stan Musial/ Bat-Jsy/50	30.00
166	Harmon Killebrew/ Bat-Jsy/50	20.00
167	Cal Ripken Jr./ Bat-Jsy/50	30.00
169	Roger Clemens/ Bat-Jsy/50	15.00
171	Rafael Palmeiro/ Bat-Jsy/50	10.00
172	Randy Johnson/ Bat-Jsy/50	15.00
174	Greg Maddux/ Bat-Jsy/50	15.00
175	Sammy Sosa/ Bat-Jsy/50	15.00

M

1996 Metal Universe

	NM/M
Complete Set (250):	17.50
Common Player:	.10
Platinum Set (250):	75.00
Common Platinum:	.25
Platinums:	5X
Pack (8):	1.50
Wax Box (24):	17.50
1 Roberto Alomar	.20
2 Brady Anderson	.10
3 Bobby Bonilla	.10
4 Chris Holles	.10
5 Ben McDonald	.10
6 Mike Mussina	.40
7 Randy Myers	.10
8 Rafael Palmeiro	.60
9 Cal Ripken Jr.	2.50
10 B.J. Surhoff	.10
11 Luis Alicea	.10
12 Jose Canseco	.50
13 Roger Clemens	1.25
14 Wil Cordero	.10
15 Tom Gordon	.10
16 Mike Greenwell	.10
17 Tim Naehring	.10
18 Troy O'Leary	.10
19 Mike Stanley	.10
20 John Valentin	.10
21 Mo Vaughn	.30
22 Tim Wakefield	.10
23 Garret Anderson	.10
24 Chili Davis	.10
25 Gary DiSarcina	.10
26 Jim Edmonds	.10
27 Chuck Finley	.10
28 Todd Greene	.10
29 Mark Langston	.10
30 Troy Percival	.10
31 Tony Phillips	.10
32 Tim Salmon	.30
33 Lee Smith	.10
34 J.T. Snow	.10
35 Ray Durham	.10
36 Alex Fernandez	.10
37 Ozzie Guillen	.10
38 Roberto Hernandez	.10
39 Lyle Mouton	.10
40 Frank Thomas	.75
41 Robin Ventura	.10
42 Sandy Alomar	.10
43 Carlos Baerga	.10
44 Albert Belle	.10
45 Orel Hershiser	.10
46 Kenny Lofton	.10
47 Dennis Martinez	.10
48 Jack McDowell	.10
49 Jose Mesa	.10
50 Eddie Murray	.75
51 Charles Nagy	.10
52 Manny Ramirez	.75
53 Julian Tavarez	.10
54 Jim Thome	.60
55 Omar Vizquel	.10
56 Chad Curtis	.10
57 Cecil Fielder	.10
58 John Flaherty	.10
59 Travis Fryman	.10
60 Chris Gomez	.10
61 Felipe Lira	.10
62 Kevin Appier	.10
63 Johnny Damon	.35
64 Tom Goodwin	.10
65 Mark Gubicza	.10
66 Jeff Montgomery	.10
67 Jon Nunnally	.10
68 Ricky Bones	.10

69	Jeff Cirillo	.10
70	John Jaha	.10
71	Dave Nilsson	.10
72	Joe Oliver	.10
73	Kevin Seitzer	.10
74	Greg Vaughn	.10
75	Marty Cordova	.10
76	Chuck Knoblauch	.10
77	Pat Meares	.10
78	Paul Molitor	.75
79	Pedro Munoz	.10
80	Kirby Puckett	1.00
81	Brad Radke	.10
82	Scott Stahoviak	.10
83	Matt Walbeck	.10
84	Wade Boggs	1.00
85	David Cone	.10
86	Joe Girardi	.10
87	Derek Jeter	2.50
88	Jim Leyritz	.10
89	Tino Martinez	.10
90	Don Mattingly	1.50
91	Paul O'Neill	.10
92	Andy Pettitte	.25
93	Tim Raines	.10
94	Kenny Rogers	.10
95	Ruben Sierra	.10
96	John Wetteland	.10
97	Bernie Williams	.10
98	Geronimo Berroa	.10
99	Dennis Eckersley	.65
100	Brent Gates	.10
101	Mark McGwire	2.00
102	Steve Ontiveros	.10
103	Terry Steinbach	.10
104	Jay Buhner	.10
105	Vince Coleman	.10
106	Joey Cora	.10
107	Ken Griffey Jr.	1.50
108	Randy Johnson	.75
109	Edgar Martinez	.10
110	Alex Rodriguez	2.00
111	Paul Sorrento	.10
112	Will Clark	.10
113	Juan Gonzalez	.50
114	Rusty Greer	.10
115	Dean Palmer	.10
116	Ivan Rodriguez	.65
117	Mickey Tettleton	.10
118	Joe Carter	.10
119	Alex Gonzalez	.10
120	Shawn Green	.30
121	Erik Hanson	.10
122	Pat Hentgen	.10
123	Sandy Martinez RC	.10
124	Otis Nixon	.10
125	John Olerud	.10
126	Steve Avery	.10
127	Tom Glavine	.40
128	Marquis Grissom	.10
129	Chipper Jones	1.00
130	David Justice	.10
131	Ryan Klesko	.10
132	Mark Lemke	.10
133	Javier Lopez	.10
134	Greg Maddux	1.00
135	Fred McGriff	.10
136	John Smoltz	.10
137	Mark Wohlers	.10
138	Frank Castillo	.10
139	Shawon Dunston	.10
140	Luis Gonzalez	.20
141	Mark Grace	.10
142	Brian McRae	.10
143	Jaime Navarro	.10
144	Rey Sanchez	.10
145	Ryne Sandberg	1.00
146	Sammy Sosa	1.25
147	Bret Boone	.10
148	Curtis Goodwin	.10
149	Barry Larkin	.10
150	Hal Morris	.10
151	Reggie Sanders	.10
152	Pete Schourek	.10
153	John Smiley	.10
154	Dante Bichette	.10
155	Vinny Castilla	.10
156	Andres Galarraga	.10
157	Bret Saberhagen	.10
158	Bill Swift	.10
159	Larry Walker	.10
160	Walt Weiss	.10
161	Kurt Abbott	.10
162	John Burkett	.10
163	Greg Colbrunn	.10
164	Jeff Conine	.10
165	Chris Hammond	.10
166	Charles Johnson	.10
167	Al Leiter	.10
168	Pat Rapp	.10
169	Gary Sheffield	.40
170	Quilvio Veras	.10
171	Devon White	.10
172	Jeff Bagwell	.75
173	Derek Bell	.10
174	Sean Berry	.10

175	Craig Biggio	.10
176	Doug Drabek	.10
177	Tony Eusebio	.10
178	Brian Hunter	.10
179	Orlando Miller	.10
180	Shane Reynolds	.10
181	Mike Blowers	.10
182	Roger Cedeno	.10
183	Eric Karros	.10
184	Ramon Martinez	.10
185	Raul Mondesi	.10
186	Hideo Nomo	.60
187	Mike Piazza	1.50
188	Moises Alou	.10
189	Yamil Benitez	.10
190	Darrin Fletcher	.10
191	Cliff Floyd	.10
192	Pedro Martinez	.75
193	Carlos Perez	.10
194	David Segui	.10
195	Tony Tarasco	.10
196	Rondell White	.10
197	Edgardo Alfonzo	.10
198	Rico Brogna	.10
199	Carl Everett	.10
200	Todd Hundley	.10
201	Jason Isringhausen	.10
202	Lance Johnson	.10
203	Bobby Jones	.10
204	Jeff Kent	.10
205	Bill Pulsipher	.10
206	Jose Vizcaino	.10
207	Ricky Bottalico	.10
208	Darren Daulton	.10
209	Lenny Dykstra	.10
210	Jim Eisenreich	.10
211	Gregg Jefferies	.10
212	Mickey Morandini	.10
213	Heathcliff Slocumb	.10
214	Jay Bell	.10
215	Carlos Garcia	.10
216	Jeff King	.10
217	Al Martin	.10
218	Orlando Merced	.10
219	Dan Miceli	.10
220	Denny Neagle	.10
221	Andy Benes	.10
222	Royce Clayton	.10
223	Gary Gaetti	.10
224	Ron Gant	.10
225	Bernard Gilkey	.10
226	Brian Jordan	.10
227	Ray Lankford	.10
228	John Mabry	.10
229	Ozzie Smith	1.00
230	Todd Stottlemyre	.10
231	Andy Ashby	.10
232	Brad Ausmus	.10
233	Ken Caminiti	.10
234	Steve Finley	.10
235	Tony Gwynn	1.00
236	Joey Hamilton	.10
237	Rickey Henderson	.75
238	Trevor Hoffman	.10
239	Wally Joyner	.10
240	Rod Beck	.10
241	Barry Bonds	2.50
242	Glenallen Hill	.10
243	Stan Javier	.10
244	Mark Leiter	.10
245	Deion Sanders	.10
246	William Van Landingham	.10
247	Matt Williams	.10
248	Checklist	.10
249	Checklist	.10
250	Checklist	.10

Platinum Edition

	NM/M
Complete Set (247):	75.00
Common Player:	.25
Stars:	5X

(See 1996 Metal Universe for checklist and base card values.)

Heavy Metal

		NM/M
Complete Set (10):		5.00
Common Player:		.35
1	Albert Belle	.35
2	Barry Bonds	1.50
3	Juan Gonzalez	.50
4	Ken Griffey Jr.	1.00
5	Mark McGwire	1.25
6	Mike Piazza	1.00
7	Sammy Sosa	.90
8	Frank Thomas	.60
9	Mo Vaughn	.35
10	Matt Williams	.35

Mining for Gold

		NM/M
Complete Set (12):		12.50
Common Player:		.75
1	Yamil Benitez	.75
2	Marty Cordova	.75
3	Shawn Green	2.00
4	Todd Greene	.75
5	Brian Hunter	.75
6	Derek Jeter	7.50
7	Charles Johnson	.75
8	Chipper Jones	3.50
9	Hideo Nomo	2.50
10	Alex Ochoa	.75
11	Andy Pettitte	1.00
12	Quilvio Veras	.75

Mother Lode

		NM/M
Complete Set (12):		15.00
Common Player:		.75
1	Barry Bonds	4.50
2	Jim Edmonds	.75
3	Ken Griffey Jr.	3.50

4	Kenny Lofton	.75
5	Raul Mondesi	.75
6	Rafael Palmeiro	1.50
7	Manny Ramirez	2.00
8	Cal Ripken Jr.	4.50
9	Tim Salmon	.75
10	Ryne Sandberg	3.00
11	Frank Thomas	2.00
12	Matt Williams	.75

Platinum Portraits

		NM/M
Complete Set (10):		4.00
Common Player:		.40
1	Garret Anderson	.40
2	Marty Cordova	.40
3	Jim Edmonds	.40
4	Jason Isringhausen	.40
5	Chipper Jones	2.25
6	Ryan Klesko	.40
7	Hideo Nomo	1.00
8	Carlos Perez	.40
9	Manny Ramirez	1.50
10	Rondell White	.40

Titanium

		NM/M
Complete Set (10):		15.00
Common Player:		.50
1	Albert Belle	.50
2	Barry Bonds	4.00
3	Ken Griffey Jr.	2.50
4	Tony Gwynn	1.50
5	Greg Maddux	1.50
6	Mike Piazza	2.50
7	Cal Ripken Jr.	4.00
8	Frank Thomas	1.00
9	Mo Vaughn	.50
10	Matt Williams	.50

1997 Metal Universe

		NM/M
Complete Set (250):		17.50
Common Player:		.10
Pack (8):		1.50
Wax Box (24):		18.00
1	Roberto Alomar	.20
2	Brady Anderson	.10
3	Rocky Coppinger	.10
4	Chris Hoiles	.10

5	Eddie Murray	.60
6	Mike Mussina	.40
7	Rafael Palmeiro	.50
8	Cal Ripken Jr.	2.00
9	B.J. Surhoff	.10
10	Brant Brown	.10
11	Mark Grace	.10
12	Brian McRae	.10
13	Jaime Navarro	.10
14	Ryne Sandberg	.75
15	Sammy Sosa	1.00
16	Amaury Telemaco	.10
17	Steve Trachsel	.10
18	Darren Bragg	.10
19	Jose Canseco	.40
20	Roger Clemens	1.00
21	Nomar Garciaparra	1.00
22	Tom Gordon	.10
23	Tim Naehring	.10
24	Mike Stanley	.10
25	John Valentin	.10
26	Mo Vaughn	.10
27	Jermaine Dye	.10
28	Tom Glavine	.30
29	Marquis Grissom	.10
30	Andruw Jones	.60
31	Chipper Jones	.75
32	Ryan Klesko	.10
33	Greg Maddux	.75
34	Fred McGriff	.10
35	John Smoltz	.10
36	Garret Anderson	.10
37	George Arias	.10
38	Gary DiSarcina	.10
39	Jim Edmonds	.10
40	Darin Erstad	.25
41	Chuck Finley	.10
42	Troy Percival	.10
43	Tim Salmon	.10
44	Bret Boone	.10
45	Jeff Brantley	.10
46	Eric Davis	.10
47	Barry Larkin	.10
48	Hal Morris	.10
49	Mark Portugal	.10
50	Reggie Sanders	.10
51	John Smiley	.10
52	Wilson Alvarez	.10
53	Harold Baines	.10
54	James Baldwin	.10
55	Albert Belle	.10
56	Mike Cameron	.10
57	Ray Durham	.10
58	Alex Fernandez	.10
59	Roberto Hernandez	.10
60	Tony Phillips	.10
61	Frank Thomas	.60
62	Robin Ventura	.10
63	Jeff Cirillo	.10
64	Jeff D'Amico	.10
65	John Jaha	.10
66	Scott Karl	.10
67	Ben McDonald	.10
68	Marc Newfield	.10
69	Dave Nilsson	.10
70	Jose Valentin	.10
71	Dante Bichette	.10
72	Ellis Burks	.10
73	Vinny Castilla	.10
74	Andres Galarraga	.10
75	Kevin Ritz	.10
76	Larry Walker	.10
77	Walt Weiss	.10
78	Jamey Wright	.10
79	Eric Young	.10
80	Julio Franco	.10
81	Orel Hershiser	.10
82	Kenny Lofton	.10
83	Jack McDowell	.10
84	Jose Mesa	.10
85	Charles Nagy	.10
86	Manny Ramirez	.60
87	Jim Thome	.50
88	Omar Vizquel	.10
89	Matt Williams	.10
90	Kevin Appier	.10
91	Johnny Damon	.35
92	Chili Davis	.10
93	Tom Goodwin	.10
94	Keith Lockhart	.10
95	Jeff Montgomery	.10
96	Craig Paquette	.10
97	Jose Rosado	.10
98	Michael Tucker	.10
99	Wilton Guerrero	.10
100	Todd Hollandsworth	.10
101	Eric Karros	.10
102	Ramon Martinez	.10
103	Raul Mondesi	.10
104	Hideo Nomo	.60
105	Mike Piazza	1.25
106	Ismael Valdes	.10
107	Todd Worrell	.10
108	Tony Clark	.10
109	Travis Fryman	.10
110	Bob Higginson	.10
111	Mark Lewis	.10
112	Melvin Nieves	.10
113	Justin Thompson	.10
114	Wade Boggs	.75
115	David Cone	.10
116	Cecil Fielder	.10
117	Dwight Gooden	.10
118	Derek Jeter	2.00
119	Tino Martinez	.10
120	Paul O'Neill	.10
121	Andy Pettitte	.20
122	Mariano Rivera	.20
123	Darryl Strawberry	.10
124	John Wetteland	.10
125	Bernie Williams	.10
126	Tony Batista	.10
127	Geronimo Berroa	.10
128	Scott Brosius	.10
129	Jason Giambi	.50
130	Jose Herrera	.10
131	Mark McGwire	1.50
132	John Wasdin	.10
133	Bob Abreu	.10
134	Jeff Bagwell	.60
135	Derek Bell	.10
136	Craig Biggio	.10
137	Brian Hunter	.10
138	Darryl Kile	.10
139	Orlando Miller	.10
140	Shane Reynolds	.10
141	Billy Wagner	.10
142	Donne Wall	.10
143	Jay Buhner	.10
144	Jeff Fassero	.10
145	Ken Griffey Jr.	1.25
146	Sterling Hitchcock	.10
147	Randy Johnson	.60
148	Edgar Martinez	.10
149	Alex Rodriguez	1.50
149p	Alex Rodriguez/OPS	1.50
150	Paul Sorrento	.10
151	Dan Wilson	.10
152	Moises Alou	.10
153	Darrin Fletcher	.10
154	Cliff Floyd	.10
155	Mark Grudzielanek	.10
156	Vladimir Guerrero	.60
157	Mike Lansing	.10
158	Pedro Martinez	.60
159	Henry Rodriguez	.10
160	Rondell White	.10
161	Will Clark	.10
162	Juan Gonzalez	.50
163	Rusty Greer	.10
164	Ken Hill	.10
165	Mark McLemore	.10
166	Dean Palmer	.10
167	Roger Pavlik	.10
168	Ivan Rodriguez	.50
169	Mickey Tettleton	.10
170	Bobby Bonilla	.10
171	Kevin Brown	.10
172	Greg Colbrunn	.10
173	Jeff Conine	.10
174	Jim Eisenreich	.10
175	Charles Johnson	.10
176	Al Leiter	.10
177	Robb Nen	.10
178	Edgar Renteria	.10
179	Gary Sheffield	.40
180	Devon White	.10
181	Joe Carter	.10
182	Carlos Delgado	.40
183	Alex Gonzalez	.10
184	Shawn Green	.35
185	Juan Guzman	.10
186	Pat Hentgen	.10
187	Orlando Merced	.10
188	John Olerud	.10
189	Robert Perez	.10
190	Ed Sprague	.10
191	Mark Clark	.10
192	John Franco	.10
193	Bernard Gilkey	.10
194	Todd Hundley	.10
195	Lance Johnson	.10
196	Bobby Jones	.10
197	Alex Ochoa	.10
198	Rey Ordonez	.10
199	Paul Wilson	.10
200	Ricky Bottalico	.10
201	Gregg Jefferies	.10
202	Wendell Magee Jr.	.10
203	Mickey Morandini	.10
204	Ricky Otero	.10
205	Scott Rolen	.50
206	Benito Santiago	.10
207	Curt Schilling	.25
208	Rich Becker	.10
209	Marty Cordova	.10
210	Chuck Knoblauch	.10
211	Pat Meares	.10
212	Paul Molitor	.60
213	Frank Rodriguez	.10
214	Terry Steinbach	.10
215	Todd Walker	.10
216	Andy Ashby	.10
217	Ken Caminiti	.10
218	Steve Finley	.10
219	Tony Gwynn	.75
220	Joey Hamilton	.10
221	Rickey Henderson	.60
222	Trevor Hoffman	.10
223	Wally Joyner	.10
224	Scott Sanders	.10
225	Fernando Valenzuela	.10
226	Greg Vaughn	.10
227	Alan Benes	.10
228	Andy Benes	.10
229	Dennis Eckersley	.50
230	Ron Gant	.10
231	Brian Jordan	.10
232	Ray Lankford	.10
233	John Mabry	.10
234	Tom Pagnozzi	.10
235	Todd Stottlemyre	.10
236	Jermaine Allensworth	.10
237	Francisco Cordova	.10
238	Jason Kendall	.10
239	Jeff King	.10
240	Al Martin	.10
241	Rod Beck	.10
242	Barry Bonds	2.00
243	Shawn Estes	.10
244	Mark Gardner	.10
245	Glenallen Hill	.10
246	Bill Mueller	.10
247	J.T. Snow	.10
248	Checklist	.10
249	Checklist	.10
250	Checklist	.10

Blast Furnace

		NM/M
Complete Set (12):		40.00
Common Player:		1.50
1	Jeff Bagwell	4.00
2	Albert Belle	1.50
3	Barry Bonds	7.50
4	Andres Galarraga	1.50
5	Juan Gonzalez	2.50
6	Ken Griffey Jr.	5.00
7	Todd Hundley	1.50
8	Mark McGwire	6.00
9	Mike Piazza	5.00
10	Alex Rodriguez	6.00
11	Frank Thomas	4.00
12	Mo Vaughn	1.50

Emerald Autographs

		NM/M
Complete Set (6):		75.00
Common Autograph:		4.00
1	Darin Erstad	6.00

2	Todd Hollandsworth	4.00
3	Alex Ochoa	4.00
4	Alex Rodriguez	60.00
5	Scott Rolen	10.00
6	Todd Walker	4.00

Magnetic Field

		NM/M
Complete Set (10):		15.00
Common Player:		.75
1	Roberto Alomar	.75
2	Jeff Bagwell	1.25
3	Barry Bonds	3.00
4	Ken Griffey Jr.	2.00
5	Derek Jeter	3.00
6	Kenny Lofton	.75
7	Edgar Renteria	.75
8	Cal Ripken Jr.	3.00
9	Alex Rodriguez	2.50
10	Matt Williams	.75

Mining for Gold

		NM/M
Complete Set (10):		12.00
Common Player:		.75
1	Bob Abreu	.75
2	Kevin Brown	.75
3	Nomar Garciaparra	3.50
4	Vladimir Guerrero	3.00
5	Wilton Guerrero	.75
6	Andruw Jones	3.00
7	Curt Lyons	.75
8	Neifi Perez	.75
9	Scott Rolen	2.00
10	Todd Walker	.75

Mother Lode

		NM/M
Complete Set (12):		80.00
Common Player:		2.00
1	Roberto Alomar	2.50
2	Jeff Bagwell	6.00
3	Barry Bonds	15.00
4	Ken Griffey Jr.	10.00
5	Andruw Jones	6.00
6	Chipper Jones	8.00
7	Kenny Lofton	2.00
8	Mike Piazza	10.00
9	Cal Ripken Jr.	15.00

10	Alex Rodriguez	12.50
11	Frank Thomas	6.00
12	Matt Williams	2.00

Platinum Portraits

		NM/M
Complete Set (10):		10.00
Common Player:		.60
1	James Baldwin	.60
2	Jermaine Dye	.60
3	Todd Hollandsworth	.60
4	Derek Jeter	5.00
5	Chipper Jones	2.00
6	Jason Kendall	.60
7	Rey Ordonez	.60
8	Andy Pettitte	1.00
9	Edgar Renteria	.60
10	Alex Rodriguez	3.25

Titanium

		NM/M
Complete Set (10):		24.00
Common Player:		1.50
1	Jeff Bagwell	2.00
2	Albert Belle	1.50
3	Ken Griffey Jr.	3.00
4	Chipper Jones	2.50
5	Greg Maddux	2.50
6	Mark McGwire	4.00
7	Mike Piazza	3.00
8	Cal Ripken Jr.	5.00
9	Alex Rodriguez	4.00
10	Frank Thomas	2.00

1998 Metal Universe

	NM/M
Complete Set (220):	15.00
Common Player:	.10
Pack (8):	1.50

Wax Box (24):		20.00
1	Jose Cruz Jr.	.10
2	Jeff Abbott	.10
3	Rafael Palmeiro	.65
4	Ivan Rodriguez	.65
5	Jaret Wright	.10
6	Derek Bell	.10
7	Chuck Finley	.10
8	Travis Fryman	.10
9	Randy Johnson	.75
10	Derrek Lee	.50
11	Bernie Williams	.10
12	Carlos Baerga	.10
13	Ricky Bottalico	.10
14	Ellis Burks	.10
15	Russ Davis	.10
16	Nomar Garciaparra	1.00
17	Joey Hamilton	.10
18	Jason Kendall	.10
19	Darryl Kile	.10
20	Edgardo Alfonzo	.10
21	Moises Alou	.10
22	Bobby Bonilla	.10
23	Jim Edmonds	.10
24	Jose Guillen	.10
25	Chuck Knoblauch	.10
26	Javy Lopez	.10
27	Billy Wagner	.10
28	Kevin Appier	.10
29	Joe Carter	.10
30	Todd Dunwoody	.10
31	Gary Gaetti	.10
32	Juan Gonzalez	.60
33	Jeffrey Hammonds	.10
34	Roberto Hernandez	.10
35	Dave Nilsson	.10
36	Manny Ramirez	.75
37	Robin Ventura	.10
38	Rondell White	.10
39	Vinny Castilla	.10
40	Will Clark	.10
41	Scott Hatteberg	.10
42	Russ Johnson	.10
43	Ricky Ledee	.10
44	Kenny Lofton	.10
45	Paul Molitor	.75
46	Justin Thompson	.10
47	Craig Biggio	.10
48	Damion Easley	.10
49	Brad Radke	.10
50	Ben Grieve	.10
51	Mark Bellhorn	.10
52	Henry Blanco RC	.10
53	Mariano Rivera	.20
54	Reggie Sanders	.10
55	Paul Sorrento	.10
56	Terry Steinbach	.10
57	Mo Vaughn	.10
58	Brady Anderson	.10
59	Tom Glavine	.40
60	Sammy Sosa	1.25
61	Larry Walker	.10
62	Rod Beck	.10
63	Jose Canseco	.45
64	Steve Finley	.10
65	Pedro Martinez	.75
66	John Olerud	.10
67	Scott Rolen	.60
68	Ismael Valdes	.10
69	Andrew Vessel	.10
70	Mark Grudzielanek	.10
71	Eric Karros	.10
72	Jeff Shaw	.10
73	Lou Collier	.10
74	Edgar Martinez	.10
75	Vladimir Guerrero	.75
76	Paul Konerko	.25
77	Kevin Orie	.10
78	Kevin Polcovich	.10
79	Brett Tomko	.10
80	Jeff Bagwell	.75
81	Barry Bonds	2.50
82	David Justice	.10
83	Hideo Nomo	.60
84	Ryne Sandberg	1.00
85	Shannon Stewart	.10
86	Derek Wallace	.10
87	Tony Womack	.10
88	Jason Giambi	.50
89	Mark Grace	.10
90	Pat Hentgen	.10
91	Raul Mondesi	.10
92	Matt Morris	.10
93	Matt Perisho	.10
94	Tim Salmon	.10
95	Jeremi Gonzalez	.10
96	Shawn Green	.25
97	Todd Greene	.10
98	Ruben Rivera	.10
99	Deion Sanders	.10
100	Alex Rodriguez	2.00
101	Will Cunnane	.10
102	Ray Lankford	.10
103	Ryan McGuire	.10
104	Charles Nagy	.10
105	Rey Ordonez	.10
106	Mike Piazza	1.50
107	Tony Saunders	.10
108	Curt Schilling	.25
109	Fernando Tatis	.10
110	Mark McGwire	2.00
111	David Dellucci RC	.10
112	Garret Anderson	.10
113	Shane Bowers	.10
114	David Cone	.10
115	Jeff King	.10
116	Matt Williams	.10
117	Aaron Boone	.10
118	Dennis Eckersley	.65
119	Livan Hernandez	.10
120	Richard Hidalgo	.10
121	Bobby Higginson	.10
122	Tino Martinez	.10
123	Tim Naehring	.10
124	Jose Vidro	.10
125	John Wetteland	.10
126	Jay Bell	.10
127	Albert Belle	.10
128	Marty Cordova	.10
129	Chili Davis	.10
130	Jason Dickson	.10
131	Rusty Greer	.10
132	Hideki Irabu	.10
133	Greg Maddux	1.00
134	Billy Taylor	.10
135	Jim Thome	.60
136	Gerald Williams	.10
137	Jeff Cirillo	.10
138	Delino DeShields	.10
139	Andres Galarraga	.10
140	Willie Greene	.10
141	John Jaha	.10
142	Charles Johnson	.10
143	Ryan Klesko	.10
144	Paul O'Neill	.10
145	Robinson Checo	.10
146	Roberto Alomar	.20
147	Wilson Alvarez	.10
148	Bobby Jones	.10
149	Raul Casanova	.10
150	Andruw Jones	.75
151	Mike Lansing	.10
152	Mickey Morandini	.10
153	Neifi Perez	.10
154	Pokey Reese	.10
155	Edgar Renteria	.10
156	Eric Young	.10
157	Darin Erstad	.20
158	Kelvim Escobar	.10
159	Carl Everett	.10
160	Tom Gordon	.10
161	Ken Griffey Jr.	1.50
162	Al Martin	.10
163	Bubba Trammell	.10
164	Carlos Delgado	.30
165	Kevin Brown	.10
166	Ken Caminiti	.10
167	Roger Clemens	1.25
168	Ron Gant	.10
169	Jeff Kent	.10
170	Mike Mussina	.40
171	Dean Palmer	.10
172	Henry Rodriguez	.10
173	Matt Stairs	.10
174	Jay Buhner	.10
175	Frank Thomas	.75
176	Mike Cameron	.10
177	Johnny Damon	.35
178	Tony Gwynn	1.00
179	John Smoltz	.10
180	B.J. Surhoff	.10
181	Antone Williamson	.10
182	Alan Benes	.10
183	Jeromy Burnitz	.10
184	Tony Clark	.10
185	Shawn Estes	.10
186	Todd Helton	.65
187	Todd Hundley	.10
188	Chipper Jones	1.00
189	Mark Kotsay	.10
190	Barry Larkin	.10
191	Mike Lieberthal	.10
192	Andy Pettitte	.25
193	Gary Sheffield	.35
194	Jeff Suppan	.10
195	Mark Wohlers	.10
196	Dante Bichette	.10
197	Trevor Hoffman	.10
198	J.T. Snow	.10
199	Derek Jeter	2.50
200	Cal Ripken Jr.	2.50
201	Steve Woodard RC	.25
202	Ray Durham	.10
203	Barry Bonds	1.50
204	Tony Clark	.10
205	Roger Clemens	.65
206	Ken Griffey Jr.	.75
207	Tony Gwynn	.50
208	Derek Jeter	1.50
209	Randy Johnson	.40
210	Mark McGwire	1.00
211	Hideo Nomo	.30
212	Mike Piazza	.75
213	Cal Ripken Jr.	1.50
214	Alex Rodriguez	1.00
215	Frank Thomas	.40
216	Mo Vaughn	.10
217	Larry Walker	.10
218	Ken Griffey Jr. Checklist	.50
219	Alex Rodriguez Checklist	.60
220	Frank Thomas Checklist	.30

Precious Metal Gems

CHARLES NAGY

	NM/M
Common Player:	3.00
Stars:	25X

Production 50 Sets
(See 1998 Metal Universe for checklist and base card values.)

All-Galactic Team

		NM/M
Complete Set (18):		140.00
Common Player:		3.00
Inserted 1:192		
1	Ken Griffey Jr.	12.50
2	Frank Thomas	7.50
3	Chipper Jones	10.00
4	Albert Belle	3.00
5	Juan Gonzalez	5.00
6	Jeff Bagwell	7.50
7	Andruw Jones	7.50
8	Cal Ripken Jr.	20.00
9	Derek Jeter	20.00
10	Nomar Garciaparra	10.00
11	Darin Erstad	4.00
12	Greg Maddux	10.00
13	Alex Rodriguez	15.00
14	Mike Piazza	12.50
15	Vladimir Guerrero	7.50
16	Jose Cruz Jr.	3.00
17	Mark McGwire	15.00
18	Scott Rolen	5.00

Diamond Heroes

		NM/M
Complete Set (6):		8.00
Common Player:		.50
Inserted 1:18		
1	Ken Griffey Jr.	2.00
2	Frank Thomas	1.50
3	Andruw Jones	1.50

4 Alex Rodriguez 2.50
5 Jose Cruz Jr. .50
6 Cal Ripken Jr. 3.00

Platinum Portraits

		NM/M
Complete Set (12):		90.00
Common Player:		4.00
Inserted 1:360		
1	Ken Griffey Jr.	12.00
2	Frank Thomas	7.50
3	Chipper Jones	9.00
4	Jose Cruz Jr.	4.00
5	Andruw Jones	7.50
6	Cal Ripken Jr.	17.50
7	Derek Jeter	17.50
8	Darin Erstad	4.00
9	Greg Maddux	9.00
10	Alex Rodriguez	15.00
11	Mike Piazza	12.00
12	Vladimir Guerrero	7.50

Titanium

		NM/M
Complete Set (15):		50.00
Common Player:		2.00
Inserted 1:96		
1	Ken Griffey Jr.	5.00
2	Frank Thomas	3.00
3	Chipper Jones	4.00
4	Jose Cruz Jr.	2.00
5	Juan Gonzalez	2.50
6	Scott Rolen	2.50
7	Andruw Jones	3.00
8	Derek Jeter	7.50
9	Nomar Garciaparra	4.00
10	Darin Erstad	2.50
11	Greg Maddux	4.00

13 Alex Rodriguez 6.00
14 Mike Piazza 5.00
15 Vladimir Guerrero 3.00

Universal Language

		NM/M
Complete Set (20):		16.00
Common Player:		.40
Inserted 1:6		
1	Ken Griffey Jr.	1.25
2	Frank Thomas	.75
3	Chipper Jones	1.00
4	Albert Belle	.40
5	Juan Gonzalez	.60
6	Jeff Bagwell	.75
7	Andruw Jones	.75
8	Cal Ripken Jr.	2.00
9	Derek Jeter	2.00
10	Nomar Garciaparra	1.00
11	Darin Erstad	.50
12	Greg Maddux	1.00
13	Alex Rodriguez	1.50
14	Mike Piazza	1.25
15	Vladimir Guerrero	.75
16	Jose Cruz Jr.	.40
17	Hideo Nomo	.60
18	Kenny Lofton	.40
19	Tony Gwynn	1.00
20	Scott Rolen	.60

1999 Metal Universe

		NM/M
Complete Set (300):		15.00
Common Player:		.10
Pack (8):		1.00
Wax Box (24):		20.00
1	Mark McGwire	1.50
2	Jim Edmonds	.10
3	Travis Fryman	.10
4	Tom Gordon	.10
5	Jeff Bagwell	.65
6	Rico Brogna	.10
7	Tom Evans	.10
8	John Franco	.10
9	Juan Gonzalez	.50
10	Paul Molitor	.65
11	Roberto Alomar	.20
12	Mike Hampton	.10
13	Orel Hershiser	.10
14	Todd Stottlemyre	.10
15	Robin Ventura	.10
16	Todd Walker	.10
17	Bernie Williams	.10
18	Shawn Estes	.10
19	Richie Sexson	.10
20	Kevin Millwood	.10
21	David Ortiz	.50
22	Mariano Rivera	.15
23	Ivan Rodriguez	.60
24	Mike Sirotka	.10
25	David Justice	.10
26	Carl Pavano	.10
27	Albert Belle	.10
28	Will Clark	.10
29	Jose Cruz Jr.	.10
30	Trevor Hoffman	.10
31	Dean Palmer	.10
32	Edgar Renteria	.10
33	David Segui	.10
34	B.J. Surhoff	.10
35	Miguel Tejada	.15
36	Bob Wickman	.10
37	Charles Johnson	.10
38	Andruw Jones	.65
39	Mike Lieberthal	.10
40	Eli Marrero	.10
41	Neifi Perez	.10
42	Jim Thome	.50
43	Barry Bonds	2.00
44	Carlos Delgado	.30
45	Chuck Finley	.10
46	Brian Meadows	.10
47	Tony Gwynn	.75
48	Jose Offerman	.10
49	Cal Ripken Jr.	2.00
50	Alex Rodriguez	1.50
51	Esteban Yan	.10
52	Matt Stairs	.10
53	Fernando Vina	.10
54	Rondell White	.10
55	Kerry Wood	.30
56	Dmitri Young	.10
57	Ken Caminiti	.10
58	Alex Gonzalez	.10
59	Matt Mantei	.10
60	Tino Martinez	.10
61	Hal Morris	.10
62	Rafael Palmeiro	.60
63	Troy Percival	.10
64	Bobby Smith	.10
65	Ed Sprague	.10
66	Brett Tomko	.10
67	Steve Trachsel	.10
68	Ugueth Urbina	.10
69	Jose Valentin	.10
70	Kevin Brown	.10
71	Shawn Green	.30
72	Dustin Hermanson	.10
73	Livan Hernandez	.10
74	Geoff Jenkins	.10
75	Jeff King	.10
76	Chuck Knoblauch	.10
77	Edgar Martinez	.10
78	Fred McGriff	.10
79	Mike Mussina	.40
80	Dave Nilsson	.10
81	Kenny Rogers	.10
82	Tim Salmon	.10
83	Reggie Sanders	.10
84	Wilson Alvarez	.10
85	Rod Beck	.10
86	Jose Guillen	.10
87	Bob Higginson	.10
88	Gregg Olson	.10
89	Jeff Shaw	.10
90	Masato Yoshii	.10
91	Todd Helton	.50
92	David Dellucci	.10
93	Johnny Damon	.35
94	Cliff Floyd	.10
95	Ken Griffey Jr.	1.00
96	Juan Guzman	.10
97	Derek Jeter	2.00
98	Barry Larkin	.10
99	Quinton McCracken	.10
100	Sammy Sosa	.85
101	Kevin Young	.10
102	Jay Bell	.10
103	Jay Buhner	.10
104	Jeff Conine	.10
105	Ryan Jackson	.10
106	Sidney Ponson	.10
107	Jeromy Burnitz	.10
108	Roberto Hernandez	.10
109	A.J. Hinch	.10
110	Hideki Irabu	.10
111	Paul Konerko	.20
112	Henry Rodriguez	.10
113	Shannon Stewart	.10
114	Tony Womack	.10
115	Wilton Guerrero	.10
116	Andy Benes	.10
117	Jeff Cirillo	.10
118	Chili Davis	.10
119	Eric Davis	.10
120	Vladimir Guerrero	.65
121	Dennis Reyes	.10
122	Rickey Henderson	.65
123	Mickey Morandini	.10
124	Jason Schmidt	.10
125	J.T. Snow	.10
126	Justin Thompson	.10
127	Billy Wagner	.10
128	Armando Benitez	.10
129	Sean Casey	.15
130	Brad Fullmer	.10
131	Ben Grieve	.10
132	Robb Nen	.10
133	Shane Reynolds	.10
134	Todd Zeile	.10
135	Brady Anderson	.10
136	Aaron Boone	.10
137	Orlando Cabrera	.10
138	Jason Giambi	.50
139	Randy Johnson	.65
140	Jeff Kent	.10
141	John Wetteland	.10
142	Rolando Arrojo	.10
143	Scott Brosius	.10
144	Mark Grace	.10
145	Jason Kendall	.10
146	Travis Lee	.10
147	Gary Sheffield	.40
148	David Cone	.10
149	Jose Hernandez	.10
150	Todd Jones	.10
151	Al Martin	.10
152	Ismael Valdes	.10
153	Wade Boggs	.75
154	Garret Anderson	.10
155	Bobby Bonilla	.10
156	Darryl Kile	.10
157	Ryan Klesko	.10
158	Tim Wakefield	.10
159	Kenny Lofton	.10
160	Jose Canseco	.40
161	Doug Glanville	.10
162	Todd Hundley	.10
163	Brian Jordan	.10
164	Steve Finley	.10
165	Tom Glavine	.25
166	Al Leiter	.10
167	Raul Mondesi	.10
168	Desi Relaford	.10
169	Bret Saberhagen	.10
170	Omar Vizquel	.10
171	Larry Walker	.10
172	Bobby Abreu	.10
173	Moises Alou	.10
174	Mike Caruso	.10
175	Royce Clayton	.10
176	Bartolo Colon	.10
177	Marty Cordova	.10
178	Darin Erstad	.30
179	Nomar Garciaparra	.75
180	Andy Ashby	.10
181	Dan Wilson	.10
182	Larry Sutton	.10
183	Tony Clark	.10
184	Andres Galarraga	.10
185	Ray Durham	.10
186	Hideo Nomo	.60
187	Steve Woodard	.10
188	Scott Rolen	.35
189	Mike Stanley	.10
190	Jaret Wright	.10
191	Vinny Castilla	.10
192	Jason Christiansen	.10
193	Paul Bako	.10
194	Carlos Perez	.10
195	Mike Piazza	1.00
196	Fernando Tatis	.10
197	Mo Vaughn	.10
198	Devon White	.10
199	Ricky Gutierrez	.10
200	Charlie Hayes	.10
201	Brad Radke	.10
202	Rick Helling	.10
203	John Smoltz	.10
204	Frank Thomas	.65
205	David Wells	.10
206	Roger Clemens	.85
207	Mark Grudzielanek	.10
208	Chipper Jones	.75
209	Ray Lankford	.10
210	Pedro Martinez	.65
211	Manny Ramirez	.65
212	Greg Vaughn	.10
213	Craig Biggio	.10
214	Rusty Greer	.10
215	Greg Maddux	.75
216	Rick Aguilera	.10
217	Andy Pettitte	.20
218	Dante Bichette	.10
219	Damion Easley	.10
220	Matt Morris	.10
221	John Olerud	.10
222	Chan Ho Park	.10
223	Curt Schilling	.25
224	John Valentin	.10
225	Matt Williams	.10
226	Ellis Burks	.10
227	Tom Goodwin	.10
228	Javy Lopez	.10
229	Eric Milton	.10
230	Paul O'Neill	.10
231	Magglio Ordonez	.15
232	Derek Lee	.45

233	Ken Griffey Jr.	.60
234	Randy Johnson	.30
235	Alex Rodriguez	.75
236	Darin Erstad	.15
237	Juan Gonzalez	.20
238	Derek Jeter	1.00
239	Tony Gwynn	.40
240	Kerry Wood	.20
241	Cal Ripken Jr.	1.00
242	Sammy Sosa	.50
243	Greg Maddux	.40
244	Mark McGwire	.75
245	Chipper Jones	.40
246	Barry Bonds	1.00
247	Ben Grieve	.10
248	Ben Davis	.10
249	Robert Fick	.10
250	Carlos Guillen	.10
251	Mike Frank	.10
252	Ryan Minor	.10
253	Troy Glaus	.65
254	Matt Anderson	.10
255	Josh Booty	.10
256	Gabe Alvarez	.10
257	Gabe Kapler	.10
258	Enrique Wilson	.10
259	Alex Gonzalez	.10
260	Preston Wilson	.10
261	Eric Chavez	.20
262	Adrian Beltre	.30
263	Corey Koskie	.10
264	Robert Machado RC	.10
265	Orlando Hernandez	.10
266	Matt Clement	.10
267	Luis Ordaz	.10
268	Jeremy Giambi	.10
269	J.D. Drew	.50
269a	J.D. Drew ("Sample" autographed edition of 35.)	30.00
270	Cliff Politte	.10
271	Carlton Loewer	.10
272	Aramis Ramirez	.10
273	Ken Griffey Jr.	.60
274	Randy Johnson	.30
275	Alex Rodriguez	.75
276	Darin Erstad	.20
277	Scott Rolen	.25
278	Juan Gonzalez	.20
279	Jeff Bagwell	.30
280	Mike Piazza	.65
281	Derek Jeter	1.00
282	Travis Lee	.10
283	Tony Gwynn	.40
284	Kerry Wood	.20
285	Albert Belle	.10
286	Sammy Sosa	.50
287	Mo Vaughn	.10
288	Nomar Garciaparra	.45
289	Frank Thomas	.30
290	Cal Ripken Jr.	1.00
291	Greg Maddux	.40
292	Chipper Jones	.40
293	Ben Grieve	.10
294	Andruw Jones	.30
295	Mark McGwire	.75
296	Roger Clemens	.50
297	Barry Bonds	1.00
298	Ken Griffey Jr.-Checklist	.60
299	Kerry Wood-Checklist	.20
300	Alex Rodriguez-Checklist	.75

Precious Metal Gems

	NM/M
Common Player:	3.00
Stars:	25X

Gem Master
1 of 1:(Value Undetermined)
(See 1999 Metal Universe for checklist and base card values.)

Boyz With The Wood

		NM/M
Complete Set (15):		17.50
Common Player:		.60
Inserted 1:18		
1	Ken Griffey Jr.	2.00
2	Frank Thomas	1.00
3	Jeff Bagwell	1.00
4	Juan Gonzalez	.75
5	Mark McGwire	2.50
6	Scott Rolen	.60
7	Travis Lee	.60
8	Tony Gwynn	2.00
9	Mike Piazza	2.00
10	Chipper Jones	2.00
11	Nomar Garciaparra	2.00
12	Derek Jeter	3.00
13	Cal Ripken Jr.	3.00
14	Andruw Jones	1.00
15	Alex Rodriguez	2.50

Diamond Soul

		NM/M
Complete Set (15):		60.00
Common Player:		1.50
Inserted 1:72		
1	Cal Ripken Jr.	12.00
2	Alex Rodriguez	9.00
3	Chipper Jones	6.00
4	Derek Jeter	12.00
5	Frank Thomas	4.00
6	Greg Maddux	6.00
7	Juan Gonzalez	3.00
8	Ken Griffey Jr.	7.50
9	Kerry Wood	3.00
10	Mark McGwire	9.00
11	Mike Piazza	7.50
12	Nomar Garciaparra	6.00
13	Scott Rolen	2.50
14	Tony Gwynn	6.00
15	Travis Lee	1.50

Linchpins

		NM/M
Complete Set (10):		75.00
Common Player:		5.00
Inserted 1:360		
1	Mike Piazza	10.00
2	Mark McGwire	12.50
3	Kerry Wood	5.00
4	Ken Griffey Jr.	10.00
5	Greg Maddux	7.50
6	Frank Thomas	6.00
7	Derek Jeter	15.00
8	Chipper Jones	7.50
9	Cal Ripken Jr.	15.00
10	Alex Rodriguez	12.50

Neophytes

		NM/M
Complete Set (15):		7.50
Common Player:		.35
Inserted 1:6		
1	Troy Glaus	3.00
2	Travis Lee	.75
3	Scott Elarton	.35
4	Ricky Ledee	.35
5	Richard Hidalgo	.35
6	J.D. Drew	1.50
7	Paul Konerko	.75
8	Orlando Hernandez	.75
9	Mike Caruso	.35
10	Mike Frank	.35
11	Miguel Tejada	.50
12	Matt Anderson	.35
13	Kerry Wood	1.00
14	Gabe Alvarez	.35
15	Adrian Beltre	.50

Planet Metal

		NM/M
Complete Set (15):		45.00
Common Player:		1.50
Inserted 1:36		
1	Alex Rodriguez	9.00
2	Andruw Jones	3.50
3	Cal Ripken Jr.	12.00
4	Chipper Jones	5.00
5	Darin Erstad	2.00
6	Derek Jeter	12.00
7	Frank Thomas	3.50
8	Travis Lee	1.50
9	Scott Rolen	2.50
10	Nomar Garciaparra	5.00
11	Mike Piazza	6.50
12	Mark McGwire	9.00
13	Ken Griffey Jr.	6.50
14	Juan Gonzalez	2.50
15	Jeff Bagwell	3.50

2000 Metal

		NM/M
Complete Set (250):		20.00
Common Player:		.10
Common Prospect (201-250):		.50
Inserted 1:2		
Pack (10):		1.50
Wax Box (28):		25.00
1	Tony Gwynn	1.00
2	Derek Jeter	2.50
3	Johnny Damon	.35
4	Javy Lopez	.10
5	Preston Wilson	.10

6	Derek Bell	.10
7	Richie Sexson	.10
8	Vinny Castilla	.10
9	Billy Wagner	.10
10	Carlos Beltran	.50
11	Chris Singleton	.10
12	Nomar Garciaparra	1.00
13	Carlos Febles	.10
14	Jason Varitek	.10
15	Luis Gonzalez	.20
16	Jon Lieber	.10
17	Mo Vaughn	.10
18	Dave Burba	.10
19	Brady Anderson	.10
20	Carlos Lee	.20
21	Chuck Finley	.10
22	Alex Gonzalez	.10
23	Matt Williams	.10
24	Chipper Jones	1.00
25	Pokey Reese	.10
26	Todd Helton	.65
27	Mike Mussina	.40
28	Butch Huskey	.10
29	Jeff Bagwell	.75
30	Juan Encarnacion	.10
31	A.J. Burnett	.10
32	Micah Bowie	.10
33	Brian Jordan	.10
34	Scott Erickson	.10
35	Sean Casey	.25
36	John Smoltz	.10
37	Edgard Clemente	.10
38	Mike Hampton	.10
39	Tom Glavine	.35
40	Albert Belle	.10
41	Jim Thome	.60
42	Jermaine Dye	.10
43	Sammy Sosa	1.25
44	Pedro Martinez	.75
45	Paul Konerko	.20
46	Damion Easley	.10
47	Cal Ripken Jr.	2.50
48	Jose Lima	.10
49	Mike Lowell	.10
50	Randy Johnson	.75
51	Dean Palmer	.10
52	Tim Salmon	.10
53	Kevin Millwood	.10
54	Mark Grace	.10
55	Aaron Boone	.10
56	Omar Vizquel	.10
57	Moises Alou	.10
58	Travis Fryman	.10
59	Erubiel Durazo	.10
60	Carl Everett	.10
61	Charles Johnson	.10
62	Trot Nixon	.10
63	Andres Galarraga	.10
64	Magglio Ordonez	.10
65	Pedro Astacio	.10
66	Roberto Alomar	.20
67	Pete Harnisch	.10
68	Scott Williamson	.10
69	Alex Fernandez	.10
70	Robin Ventura	.10
71	Chad Allen	.10
72	Darin Erstad	.20
73	Ron Coomer	.10
74	Ellis Burks	.10
75	Kent Bottenfield	.10
76	Ken Griffey Jr.	1.50
77	Mike Piazza	1.50
78	Jorge Posada	.20
79	Dante Bichette	.10
80	Adrian Beltre	.25
81	Andruw Jones	.75
82	Wilson Alvarez	.10
83	Edgardo Alfonzo	.10
84	Brian Giles	.10
85	Gary Sheffield	.25
86	Matt Stairs	.10
87	Bret Boone	.10
88	Kenny Rogers	.10

89	Barry Bonds	2.50
90	Scott Rolen	.60
91	Edgar Renteria	.10
92	Larry Walker	.10
93	Roger Cedeno	.10
94	Kevin Brown	.10
95	Lee Stevens	.10
96	Brad Radke	.10
97	Andy Pettitte	.25
98	Bobby Higginson	.10
99	Eric Chavez	.25
100	Alex Rodriguez	2.00
100s	Alex Rodriguez/OPS	2.00
101	Shannon Stewart	.10
102	Ryan Rupe	.10
103	Freddy Garcia	.10
104	John Jaha	.10
105	Greg Maddux	1.00
106	Hideki Irabu	.10
107	Rey Ordonez	.10
108	Troy O'Leary	.10
109	Frank Thomas	.75
110	Corey Koskie	.10
111	Bernie Williams	.10
112	Barry Larkin	.10
113	Kevin Appier	.10
114	Curt Schilling	.35
115	Bartolo Colon	.10
116	Edgar Martinez	.10
117	Ray Lankford	.10
118	Todd Walker	.10
119	John Wetteland	.10
120	David Nilsson	.10
121	Tino Martinez	.10
122	Phil Nevin	.10
123	Ben Grieve	.10
124	Ron Gant	.10
125	Jeff Kent	.10
126	Rick Helling	.10
127	Russ Ortiz	.10
128	Troy Glaus	.65
129	Chan Ho Park	.10
130	Jeromy Burnitz	.10
131	Aaron Sele	.10
132	Mike Sirotka	.10
133	Brad Ausmus	.10
134	Jose Rosado	.10
135	Mariano Rivera	.25
136	Jason Giambi	.50
137	Mike Lieberthal	.10
138	Chris Carpenter	.10
139	Henry Rodriguez	.10
140	Mike Sweeney	.10
141	Vladimir Guerrero	.75
142	Charles Nagy	.10
143	Jason Kendall	.10
144	Matt Lawton	.10
145	Michael Barrett	.10
146	David Cone	.10
147	Bobby Abreu	.10
148	Fernando Tatis	.10
149	Jose Canseco	.40
150	Craig Biggio	.10
151	Matt Mantei	.10
152	Jacque Jones	.10
153	John Halama	.10
154	Trevor Hoffman	.10
155	Rondell White	.10
156	Reggie Sanders	.10
157	Steve Finley	.10
158	Roberto Hernandez	.10
159	Geoff Jenkins	.10
160	Chris Widger	.10
161	Orel Hershiser	.10
162	Tim Hudson	.20
163	Kris Benson	.10
164	Kevin Young	.10
165	Rafael Palmeiro	.60
166	David Wells	.10
167	Ben Davis	.10
168	Jamie Moyer	.10
169	Randy Wolf	.10
170	Jeff Cirillo	.10
171	Warren Morris	.10
172	Billy Koch	.10
173	Marquis Grissom	.10
174	Geoff Blum	.10
175	Octavio Dotel	.10
176	Orlando Hernandez	.20
177	J.D. Drew	.25
178	Carlos Delgado	.40
179	Sterling Hitchcock	.10
180	Shawn Green	.25
181	Tony Clark	.10
182	Joe McEwing	.10
183	Fred McGriff	.10
184	Tony Batista	.10
185	Al Leiter	.10
186	Roger Clemens	1.25
187	Al Martin	.10
188	Eric Milton	.10
189	Bobby Smith	.10
190	Rusty Greer	.10
191	Shawn Estes	.10
192	Ken Caminiti	.10
193	Eric Karros	.10
194	Manny Ramirez	.75
195	Jim Edmonds	.10
196	Paul O'Neill	.10
197	Rico Brogna	.10
198	Ivan Rodriguez	.60
199	Doug Glanville	.10
200	Mark McGwire	2.00
201	Mark Quinn	.50
202	Norm Hutchins	.50
203	Ramon Ortiz	.50
204	Brett Laxton	.50
205	Jimmy Anderson	.50
206	Calvin Murray	.50
207	Wilton Veras	.50
208	Chad Hermansen	.50
209	Nick Johnson	.50
210	Kevin Barker	.50
211	Casey Blake	.50
212	Chad Meyers	.50
213	Kip Wells	.50
214	Eric Munson	.50
215	Lance Berkman	.50
216	Wily Pena	.50
217	Gary Matthews Jr.	.50
218	Travis Dawkins	.50
219	Josh Beckett	.75
220	Tony Armas Jr.	.50
221	Alfonso Soriano	1.00
222	Pat Burrell	1.00
223	Danys Baez RC	.50
224	Adam Kennedy	.50
225	Ruben Mateo	.50
226	Vernon Wells	.75
227	Brian Cooper	.50
228	Jeff DaVanon RC	.50
229	Glen Barker	.50
230	Robinson Cancel	.50
231	D'Angelo Jimenez	.50
232	Adam Piatt	.50
233	Buddy Carlyle	.50
234	Chad Hutchinson	.50
235	Matt Riley	.50
236	Cole Liniak	.50
237	Ben Petrick	.50
238	Peter Bergeron	.50
239	Cesar King	.50
241	Eric Gagne	.60
242	Joe Nathan	.50
243	Bruce Chen	.50
244	Rob Bell	.50
245	Juan Sosa RC	.60
246	Julio Ramirez	.50
247	Wade Miller	.50
248	Trace Coquillette RC	.50
249	Robert Ramsay	.50
250	Rick Ankiel	.60

Emerald

		NM/M
Complete Set (250):		100.00
Common Player:		.25
Stars:		2.5X
Inserted 1:4		
Prospects (201-250):		2.5X
Inserted 1:8		

Autographics

	NM/M
Common Player:	4.00
Bobby Abreu	8.00
Chad Allen	4.00
Marlon Anderson	4.00
Rick Ankiel	6.00
Glen Barker	4.00
Rob Bell	4.00
Mark Bellhorn	5.00
Peter Bergeron	4.00
Lance Berkman	8.00
Wade Boggs	25.00
Barry Bonds	150.00

Kent Bottenfield	4.00
Pat Burrell	10.00
Miguel Cairo	4.00
Mike Cameron	6.00
Chris Carpenter	6.00
Roger Cedeno	4.00
Mike Darr	6.00
Einar Diaz	4.00
J.D. Drew	15.00
Erubiel Durazo	6.00
Ray Durham	6.00
Damion Easley	4.00
Scott Elarton	4.00
Jeremy Giambi	4.00
Doug Glanville	4.00
Shawn Green	10.00
Jerry Hairston Jr.	4.00
Bob Howry	4.00
Norm Hutchins	4.00
Randy Johnson	40.00
Jacque Jones	4.00
Gabe Kapler	6.00
Cesar King	4.00
Mark Kotsay	4.00
Cole Liniak	4.00
Greg Maddux	50.00
Pedro Martinez	30.00
Ruben Mateo	4.00
Warren Morris	4.00
Heath Murray	4.00
Joe Nathan	4.00
Jim Parque	4.00
Angel Pena	4.00
Cal Ripken Jr.	100.00
Alex Rodriguez	60.00
Ryan Rupe	4.00
Randall Simon	4.00
Chris Singleton	4.00
Mike Sweeney	6.00
Wilton Veras	4.00
Scott Williamson	4.00
Randy Wolf	6.00
Tony Womack	6.00

Base Shredders

		NM/M
Complete Set (18):		160.00
Common Player:		5.00
Inserted 1:288		
(1)	Roberto Alomar	7.50
(2)	Michael Barrett	5.00
(3)	Tony Clark	5.00
(4)	Ben Davis	5.00
(5)	Erubiel Durazo	5.00
(6)	Troy Glaus	12.50
(7)	Ben Grieve	5.00
(8)	Vladimir Guerrero	15.00
(9)	Tony Gwynn	25.00
(10)	Todd Helton	12.50
(11)	Eric Munson	5.00
(12)	Rafael Palmeiro	10.00
(13)	Manny Ramirez	20.00
(14)	Ivan Rodriguez	10.00
(15)	Miguel Tejada	7.50
(16)	Mo Vaughn	5.00
(17)	Larry Walker	5.00
(18)	Matt Williams	5.00

Fusion

		NM/M
Complete Set (15):		12.50
Common Player:		.50
Inserted 1:4		
1	Ken Griffey Jr., Alex Rodriguez	2.00
2	Mark McGwire, Rick Ankiel	2.00
3	Scott Rolen, Curt Schilling	.50
4	Pedro Martinez, Nomar Garciaparra	1.25
5	Carlos Beltran, Carlos Febles	.60
6	Sammy Sosa, Mark Grace	1.50
7	Vladimir Guerrero, Ugueth Urbina	1.00
8	Roger Clemens, Derek Jeter	3.00
9	Jeff Bagwell, Craig Biggio	1.00
10	Chipper Jones, Andruw Jones	1.50
11	Cal Ripken Jr., Mike Mussina	2.50
12	Manny Ramirez, Roberto Alomar	1.00
13	Sean Casey, Barry Larkin	.50
14	Ivan Rodriguez, Rafael Palmeiro	.75
15	Mike Piazza, Robin Ventura	1.50

Heavy Metal

	NM/M
Complete Set (10):	15.00
Common Player:	1.50
Inserted 1:20	
1 Sammy Sosa	2.25
2 Mark McGwire	3.00
3 Ken Griffey Jr.	2.50
4 Mike Piazza	2.50
5 Nomar Garciaparra	2.00
6 Alex Rodriguez	3.00
7 Manny Ramirez	1.50
8 Jeff Bagwell	1.50
9 Chipper Jones	2.00
10 Vladimir Guerrero	1.50

Hit Machines

	NM/M
Complete Set (10):	20.00
Common Player:	1.00
Inserted 1:20	
1 Ken Griffey Jr.	3.00
2 Mark McGwire	4.00
3 Frank Thomas	1.50
4 Tony Gwynn	2.00
5 Rafael Palmeiro	1.25
6 Bernie Williams	1.00
7 Derek Jeter	6.00

8	Sammy Sosa	2.50
9	Mike Piazza	3.00
10	Chipper Jones	2.00

Platinum Portraits

		NM/M
Complete Set (10):		6.00
Common Player:		.25
Inserted 1:8		
1	Carlos Beltran	.50
2	Vladimir Guerrero	.75
3	Manny Ramirez	.75
4	Ivan Rodriguez	.65
5	Sean Casey	.40
6	Alex Rodriguez	1.50
7	Derek Jeter	2.00
8	Nomar Garciaparra	1.00
9	Vernon Wells	.25
10	Shawn Green	.50

Talent Show

		NM/M
Complete Set (15):		6.00
Common Player:		.30
Inserted 1:4		
1	Rick Ankiel	.45
2	Matt Riley	.30
3	Chad Hermansen	.30
4	Ruben Mateo	.30
5	Eric Munson	.30
6	Alfonso Soriano	1.50
7	Wilton Veras	.30
8	Vernon Wells	.75
9	Erubiel Durazo	.30
10	Pat Burrell	1.50
11	Ben Davis	.30
12	A.J. Burnett	.30
13	Peter Bergeron	.30
14	Mark Quinn	.30
15	Ben Petrick	.30

P

1993 Pacific

		NM/M
Complete Set (660):		20.00
Common Player:		.05
1	Rafael Belliard	.05
2	Sid Bream	.05
3	Francisco Cabrera	.05
4	Marvin Freeman	.05
5	Ron Gant	.05
6	Tom Glavine	.25
7	Brian Hunter	.05
8	Dave Justice	.05
9	Ryan Klesko	.05
10	Melvin Nieves	.05
11	Deion Sanders	.05
12	John Smoltz	.05
13	Mark Wohlers	.05
14	Brady Anderson	.05
15	Glenn Davis	.05
16	Mike Devereaux	.05
17	Leo Gomez	.05
18	Chris Hoiles	.05
19	Chito Martinez	.05
20	Ben McDonald	.05
21	Mike Mussina	.40
22	Gregg Olson	.05
23	Joe Orsulak	.05
24	Cal Ripken, Jr.	1.50
25	David Segui	.05
26	Rick Sutcliffe	.05
27	Wade Boggs	.65
28	Tom Brunansky	.05
29	Ellis Burks	.05
30	Roger Clemens	.75
31	John Dopson	.05
32	John Flaherty	.05
33	Mike Greenwell	.05
34	Tony Pena	.05
35	Carlos Quintana	.05
36	Luis Rivera	.05
37	Mo Vaughn	.05
38	Frank Viola	.05
39	Matt Young	.05
40	Scott Bailes	.05
41	Bert Blyleven	.05
42	Chad Curtis	.05
43	Gary DiSarcina	.05
44	Chuck Finley	.05
45	Mike Fitzgerald	.05
46	Gary Gaetti	.05
47	Rene Gonzales	.05
48	Mark Langston	.05
49	Scott Lewis	.05
50	Luis Polonia	.05
51	Tim Salmon	.05
52	Lee Stevens	.05
53	Steve Buechele	.05
54	Frank Castillo	.05
55	Doug Dascenzo	.05
56	Andre Dawson	.25
57	Shawon Dunston	.05
58	Mark Grace	.05
59	Mike Morgan	.05
60	Luis Salazar	.05
61	Rey Sanchez	.05
62	Ryne Sandberg	.65
63	Dwight Smith	.05
64	Jerome Walton	.05
65	Rick Wilkins	.05
66	Wilson Alvarez	.05
67	George Bell	.05
68	Joey Cora	.05
69	Alex Fernandez	.05
70	Carlton Fisk	.50
71	Craig Grebeck	.05
72	Ozzie Guillen	.05
73	Jack McDowell	.05
74	Scott Radinsky	.05
75	Tim Raines	.05
76	Bobby Thigpen	.05
77	Frank Thomas	.50
78	Robin Ventura	.05
79	Tom Browning	.05
80	Jacob Brumfield	.05
81	Rob Dibble	.05
82	Bill Doran	.05
83	Billy Hatcher	.05
84	Barry Larkin	.05
85	Hal Morris	.05
86	Joe Oliver	.05
87	Jeff Reed	.05
88	Jose Rijo	.05
89	Bip Roberts	.05
90	Chris Sabo	.05
91	Sandy Alomar, Jr.	.05
92	Brad Arnsberg	.05
93	Carlos Baerga	.05
94	Albert Belle	.05
95	Felix Fermin	.05
96	Mark Lewis	.05
97	Kenny Lofton	.05
98	Carlos Martinez	.05
99	Rod Nicholos	.05
100	Dave Rohde	.05
101	Scott Scudder	.05
102	Paul Sorrento	.05
103	Mark Whiten	.05
104	Mark Carreon	.05
105	Milt Cuyler	.05
106	Rob Deer	.05
107	Cecil Fielder	.05
108	Travis Fryman	.05
109	Dan Gladden	.05
110	Bill Gullickson	.05
111	Les Lancaster	.05
112	Mark Leiter	.05
113	Tony Phillips	.05
114	Mickey Tettleton	.05
115	Alan Trammell	.05
116	Lou Whitaker	.05
117	Jeff Bagwell	.50
118	Craig Biggio	.05
119	Joe Boever	.05
120	Casey Candaele	.05
121	Andujar Cedeno	.05
122	Steve Finley	.05
123	Luis Gonzalez	.05
124	Pete Harnisch	.05
125	Jimmy Jones	.05
126	Mark Portugal	.05
127	Rafael Ramirez	.05
128	Mike Simms	.05
129	Eric Yelding	.05
130	Luis Aquino	.05
131	Kevin Appier	.05
132	Mike Boddicker	.05
133	George Brett	.75
134	Tom Gordon	.05
135	Mark Gubicza	.05
136	David Howard	.05
137	Gregg Jefferies	.05
138	Wally Joyner	.05
139	Brian McRae	.05
140	Jeff Montgomery	.05
141	Terry Shumpert	.05
142	Curtis Wilkerson	.05
143	Brett Butler	.05
144	Eric Davis	.05
145	Kevin Gross	.05
146	Dave Hansen	.05
147	Lenny Harris	.05
148	Carlos Hernandez	.05
149	Orel Hershiser	.05
150	Jay Howell	.05
151	Eric Karros	.05
152	Ramon Martinez	.05
153	Jose Offerman	.05
154	Mike Sharperson	.05
155	Darryl Strawberry	.05
156	Jim Gantner	.05
157	Darryl Hamilton	.05
158	Doug Henry	.05
159	John Jaha	.05
160	Pat Listach	.05
161	Jaime Navarro	.05
162	Dave Nilsson	.05
163	Jesse Orosco	.05
164	Kevin Seitzer	.05
165	B.J. Surhoff	.05
166	Greg Vaughn	.05
167	Robin Yount	.50
168	Rick Aguilera	.05
169	Scott Erickson	.05
170	Mark Guthrie	.05
171	Kent Hrbek	.05
172	Chuck Knoblauch	.05
173	Gene Larkin	.05
174	Shane Mack	.05
175	Pedro Munoz	.05
176	Mike Pagliarulo	.05
177	Kirby Puckett	.65
178	Kevin Tapani	.05
179	Gary Wayne	.05
180	Moises Alou	.05
181	Brian Barnes	.05
182	Archie Cianfrocco	.05
183	Delino DeShields	.05
184	Darrin Fletcher	.05
185	Marquis Grissom	.05
186	Ken Hill	.05
187	Dennis Martinez	.05
188	Bill Sampen	.05
189	John VanderWal	.05
190	Larry Walker	.05
191	Tim Wallach	.05
192	Bobby Bonilla	.05
193	Daryl Boston	.05
194	Vince Coleman	.05
195	Kevin Elster	.05
196	Sid Fernandez	.05
197	John Franco	.05
198	Dwight Gooden	.05
199	Howard Johnson	.05
200	Willie Randolph	.05
201	Bret Saberhagen	.05
202	Dick Schofield	.05
203	Pete Schourek	.05
204	Greg Cadaret	.05
205	John Habyan	.05
206	Pat Kelly	.05
207	Kevin Maas	.05
208	Don Mattingly	.75
209	Matt Nokes	.05
210	Melido Perez	.05
211	Scott Sanderson	.05
212	Andy Stankiewicz	.05
213	Danny Tartabull	.05
214	Randy Velarde	.05
215	Bernie Williams	.05
216	Harold Baines	.05
217	Mike Bordick	.05
218	Scott Brosius	.05
219	Jerry Browne	.05
220	Ron Darling	.05
221	Dennis Eckersley	.40
222	Rickey Henderson	.50
223	Rick Honeycutt	.05
224	Mark McGwire	1.25
225	Ruben Sierra	.05
226	Terry Steinbach	.05
227	Bob Welch	.05
228	Willie Wilson	.05
229	Ruben Amaro	.05
230	Kim Batiste	.05
231	Juan Bell	.05
232	Wes Chamberlain	.05
233	Darren Daulton	.05
234	Mariano Duncan	.05
235	Len Dykstra	.05
236	Dave Hollins	.05
237	Stan Javier	.05
238	John Kruk	.05
239	Mickey Morandini	.05
240	Terry Mulholland	.05
241	Mitch Williams	.05
242	Stan Belinda	.05
243	Jay Bell	.05
244	Carlos Garcia	.05
245	Jeff King	.05
246	Mike LaValliere	.05
247	Lloyd McClendon	.05
248	Orlando Merced	.05
249	Paul Miller	.05
250	Gary Redus	.05
251	Don Slaught	.05
252	Zane Smith	.05
253	Andy Van Slyke	.05
254	Tim Wakefield	.05
255	Andy Benes	.05
256	Dann Bilardello	.05
257	Tony Gwynn	.65
258	Greg Harris	.05
259	Darrin Jackson	.05
260	Mike Maddux	.05
261	Fred McGriff	.05
262	Rich Rodriguez	.05
263	Benito Santiago	.05
264	Gary Sheffield	.35
265	Kurt Stillwell	.05
266	Tim Teufel	.05
267	Bud Black	.05
268	John Burkett	.05
269	Will Clark	.05
270	Royce Calyton	.05
271	Bryan Hickerson	.05
272	Chris James	.05
273	Darren Lewis	.05
274	Willie McGee	.05
275	Jim McNamara	.05
276	Francisco Oliveras	.05
277	Robby Thompson	.05
278	Matt Williams	.05
279	Trevor Wilson	.05
280	Bret Boone	.05

#	Player	Price
281	Greg Briley	.05
282	Jay Buhner	.05
283	Henry Cotto	.05
284	Rich DeLucia	.05
285	Dave Fleming	.05
286	Ken Griffey Jr.	1.00
287	Erik Hanson	.05
288	Randy Johnson	.50
289	Tino Martinez	.05
290	Edgar Martinez	.05
291	Dave Valle	.05
292	Omar Vizquel	.05
293	Luis Alicea	.05
294	Bernard Gilkey	.05
295	Felix Jose	.05
296	Ray Lankford	.05
297	Omar Olivares	.05
298	Jose Oquendo	.05
299	Tom Pagnozzi	.05
300	Geronimo Pena	.05
301	Gerald Perry	.05
302	Ozzie Smith	.65
303	Lee Smith	.05
304	Bob Tewksbury	.05
305	Todd Zeile	.05
306	Kevin Brown	.05
307	Todd Burns	.05
308	Jose Canseco	.35
309	Hector Fajardo	.05
310	Julio Franco	.05
311	Juan Gonzalez	.25
312	Jeff Huson	.05
313	Rob Maurer	.05
314	Rafael Palmeiro	.45
315	Dean Palmer	.05
316	Ivan Rodriguez	.45
317	Nolan Ryan	1.50
318	Dickie Thon	.05
319	Roberto Alomar	.20
320	Derek Bell	.05
321	Pat Borders	.05
322	Joe Carter	.05
323	Kelly Gruber	.05
324	Juan Guzman	.05
325	Manny Lee	.05
326	Jack Morris	.05
327	John Olerud	.05
328	Ed Sprague	.05
329	Todd Stottlemyre	.05
330	Duane Ward	.05
331	Steve Avery	.05
332	Damon Berryhill	.05
333	Jeff Blauser	.05
334	Mark Lemke	.05
335	Greg Maddux	.65
336	Kent Mercker	.05
337	Otis Nixon	.05
338	Greg Olson	.05
339	Bill Pecota	.05
340	Terry Pendleton	.05
341	Mike Stanton	.05
342	Todd Frohwirth	.05
343	Tim Hulett	.05
344	Mark McLemore	.05
345	Luis Mercedes	.05
346	Alan Mills	.05
347	Sherman Obando	.05
348	Jim Poole	.05
349	Harold Reynolds	.05
350	Arthur Rhodes	.05
351	Jeff Tackett	.05
352	Fernando Valenzuela	.05
353	Scott Bankhead	.05
354	Ivan Calderon	.05
355	Scott Cooper	.05
356	Danny Darwin	.05
357	Scott Fletcher	.05
358	Tony Fossas	.05
359	Greg Harris	.05
360	Joe Hesketh	.05
361	Jose Melendez	.05
362	Paul Quantrill	.05
363	John Valentin	.05
364	Mike Butcher	.05
365	Chuck Crim	.05
366	Chili Davis	.05
367	Damion Easley	.05
368	Steve Frey	.05
369	Joe Grahe	.05
370	Greg Myers	.05
371	John Orton	.05
372	J.T. Snow	.05
373	Ron Tingley	.05
374	Julio Valera	.05
375	Paul Assenmacher	.05
376	Jose Bautista	.05
377	Jose Guzman	.05
378	Greg Hibbard	.05
379	Candy Maldonado	.05
380	Derrick May	.05
381	Dan Plesac	.05
382	Tommy Shields	.05
383	Sammy Sosa	.75
384	Jose Vizcaino	.05
385	Greg Walbeck	.05
386	Ellis Burks	.05
387	Roberto Hernandez	.05
388	Mike Huff	.05
389	Bo Jackson	.10
390	Lance Johnson	.05
391	Ron Karkovice	.05
392	Kirk McCaskill	.05
393	Donn Pall	.05
394	Dan Pasqua	.05
395	Steve Sax	.05
396	Dave Stieb	.05
397	Bobby Ayala	.05
398	Tim Belcher	.05
399	Jeff Branson	.05
400	Cesar Hernandez	.05
401	Roberto Kelly	.05
402	Randy Milligan	.05
403	Kevin Mitchell	.05
404	Juan Samuel	.05
405	Reggie Sanders	.05
406	John Smiley	.05
407	Dan Wilson	.05
408	Mike Christopher	.05
409	Dennis Cook	.05
410	Alvaro Espinoza	.05
411	Glenallen Hill	.05
412	Reggie Jefferson	.05
413	Derek Lilliquist	.05
414	Jose Mesa	.05
415	Charles Nagy	.05
416	Junior Ortiz	.05
417	Eric Plunk	.05
418	Ted Power	.05
419	Scott Aldred	.05
420	Andy Ashby	.05
421	Freddie Benavides	.05
422	Dante Bichette	.05
423	Willie Blair	.05
424	Vinny Castilla	.05
425	Jerald Clark	.05
426	Alex Cole	.05
427	Andres Galarraga	.05
428	Joe Girardi	.05
429	Charlie Hayes	.05
430	Butch Henry	.05
431	Darren Holmes	.05
432	Dale Murphy	.20
433	David Nied	.05
434	Jeff Parrett	.05
435	Steve Reed **RC**	.05
436	Armando Reynoso	.05
437	Bruce Ruffin	.05
438	Bryn Smith	.05
439	Jim Tatum	.05
440	Eric Young	.05
441	Skeeter Barnes	.05
442	Tom Bolton	.05
443	Kirk Gibson	.05
444	Chad Krueger	.05
445	Bill Krueger	.05
446	Scott Livingstone	.05
447	Bob MacDonald	.05
448	Mike Moore	.05
449	Mike Munoz	.05
450	Gary Thurman	.05
451	David Wells	.05
452	Alex Arias	.05
453	Jack Armstrong	.05
454	Bret Barberie	.05
455	Ryan Bowen	.05
456	Cris Carpenter	.05
457	Chuck Carr	.05
458	Jeff Conine	.05
459	Steve Decker	.05
460	Orestes Destrade	.05
461	Monty Fariss	.05
462	Junior Felix	.05
463	Bryan Harvey	.05
464	Trevor Hoffman	.05
465	Charlie Hough	.05
466	Dave Magadan	.05
467	Bob McClure	.05
468	Rob Natal	.05
469	Scott Pose	.05
470	Rich Renteria	.05
471	Benito Santiago	.05
472	Matt Turner	.05
473	Walt Weiss	.05
474	Eric Anthony	.05
475	Chris Donnels	.05
476	Doug Drabek	.05
477	Xavier Hernandez	.05
478	Doug Jones	.05
479	Darryl Kile	.05
480	Scott Servais	.05
481	Greg Swindell	.05
482	Eddie Taubensee	.05
483	Jose Uribe	.05
484	Brian Williams	.05
485	Billy Brewer	.05
486	David Cone	.05
487	Greg Gagne	.05
488	Phil Hiatt	.05
489	Jose Lind	.05
490	Brent Mayne	.05
491	Kevin McReynolds	.05
492	Keith Miller	.05
493	Hipolito Pichardo	.05
494	Harvey Pulliam	.05
495	Rico Rossay	.05
496	Pedro Astacio	.05
497	Tom Candiotti	.05
498	Tom Goodwin	.05
499	Jim Gott	.05
500	Pedro Martinez	.50
501	Roger McDowell	.05
502	Mike Piazza	.75
503	Jody Reed	.05
504	Rick Trlicek	.05
505	Mitch Weber	.05
506	Steve Wilson	.05
507	James Austin	.05
508	Ricky Bones	.05
509	Alex Diaz	.05
510	Mike Fetters	.05
511	Teddy Higuera	.05
512	Graeme Lloyd	.05
513	Carlos Maldonado	.05
514	Josias Manzanillo	.05
515	Kevin Reimer	.05
516	Bill Spiers	.05
517	Bill Wegman	.05
518	Willie Banks	.05
519	J.T. Bruett	.05
520	Brian Harper	.05
521	Terry Jorgensen	.05
522	Scott Leius	.05
523	Pat Mahomes	.05
524	Dave McCarty	.05
525	Jeff Reboulet	.05
526	Mike Trombley	.05
527	Carl Willis	.05
528	Dave Winfield	.50
529	Sean Berry	.05
530	Frank Bolick	.05
531	Kent Bottenfield	.05
532	Wil Cordero	.05
533	Jeff Fassero	.05
534	Tim Laker	.05
535	Mike Lansing	.05
536	Chris Nabholz	.05
537	Mel Rojas	.05
538	John Wetteland	.05
539	Ted Wood (Front photo actually Frank Bollick.)	.05
540	Mike Draper	.05
541	Tony Fernandez	.05
542	Todd Hundley	.05
543	Jeff Innis	.05
544	Jeff McKnight	.05
545	Eddie Murray	.50
546	Charlie O'Brien	.05
547	Frank Tanana	.05
548	Ryan Thompson	.05
549	Chico Walker	.05
550	Anthony Young	.05
551	Jim Abbott	.05
552	Wade Boggs	.75
553	Steve Farr	.05
554	Neal Heaton	.05
555	Steve Howe	.05
556	Dion James	.05
557	Scott Kamieniecki	.05
558	Jimmy Key	.05
559	Jim Leyritz	.05
560	Paul O'Neill	.05
561	Spike Owen	.05
562	Lance Blankenship	.05
563	Joe Boever	.05
564	Storm Davis	.05
565	Kelly Downs	.05
566	Eric Fox	.05
567	Rich Gossage	.05
568	Dave Henderson	.05
569	Shawn Hillegas	.05
570	Mike Mohler **RC**	.05
571	Troy Neel	.05
572	Dale Sveum	.05
573	Larry Anderson	.05
574	Bob Ayrault	.05
575	Jose DeLeon	.05
576	Jim Eisenreich	.05
577	Pete Incaviglia	.05
578	Danny Jackson	.05
579	Ricky Jordan	.05
580	Ben Rivera	.05
581	Curt Schilling	.25
582	Milt Thompson	.05
583	David West	.05
584	John Candelaria	.05
585	Steve Cooke	.05
586	Tom Foley	.05
587	Al Martin	.05
588	Blas Minor	.05
589	Dennis Moeller	.05
590	Denny Neagle	.05
591	Tom Prince	.05
592	Randy Tomlin	.05
593	Bob Walk	.05
594	Kevin Young	.05
595	Pat Gomez	.05
596	Ricky Gutierrez	.05
597	Gene Harris	.05
598	Jeremy Hernandez	.05
599	Phil Plantier	.05
600	Tim Scott	.05
601	Frank Seminara	.05
602	Darrell Sherman	.05
603	Craig Shipley	.05
604	Guillermo Velasquez	.05
605	Dan Walters	.05
606	Mike Benjamin	.05
607	Barry Bonds	1.50
608	Jeff Brantley	.05
609	Dave Burba	.05
610	Craig Colbert	.05
611	Mike Jackson	.05
612	Kirt Manwaring	.05
613	Dave Martinez	.05
614	Dave Righetti	.05
615	Kevin Rogers	.05
616	Bill Swift	.05
617	Rich Amaral	.05
618	Mike Blowers	.05
619	Chris Bosio	.05
620	Norm Charlton	.05
621	John Cummings	.05
622	Mike Felder	.05
623	Bill Haselman	.05
624	Tim Leary	.05
625	Pete O'Brien	.05
626	Russ Swan	.05
627	Fernando Vina	.05
628	Rene Arocha	.05
629	Rod Brewer	.05
630	Ozzie Canseco	.05
631	Rheal Cormier	.05
632	Brian Jordan	.05
633	Joe Magrane	.05
634	Donovan Osborne	.05
635	Mike Perez	.05
636	Stan Royer	.05
637	Hector Villanueva	.05
638	Tracy Woodson	.05
639	Benji Gil	.05
640	Tom Henke	.05
641	David Hulse	.05
642	Charlie Leibrandt	.05
643	Robb Nen	.05
644	Dan Peltier	.05
645	Billy Ripken	.05
646	Kenny Rogers	.05
647	John Russell	.05
648	Dan Smith	.05
649	Matt Whiteside	.05
650	William Canate	.05
651	Darnell Coles	.05
652	Al Leiter	.05
653	Dominigo Martinez	.05
654	Paul Molitor	.50
655	Luis Sojo	.05
656	Dave Stewart	.05
657	Mike Timlin	.05
658	Turner Ward	.05
659	Devon White	.05
660	Eddie Zosky	.05

Beisbol Amigos

		NM/M
Complete Set (30):		7.50
Common Player:		.50
1	Edgar Martinez	.50
2	Luis Polonia,	
	Stan Javier	.50
3	George Bell,	
	Julio Franco	.50
4	Ozzie Guillen,	
	Ivan Rodriguez	.60
5	Carlos Baerga,	
	Sandy Alomar Jr.	.50
6	Sandy Alomar Jr.,	
	Alvaro Espinoza,	
	Paul Sorrento,	
	Carlos Baerga,	
	Felix Fermin, Junior Ortiz,	
	Jose Mesa,	
	Carlos Martinez	.50
7	Sandy Alomar Jr.,	
	Roberto Alomar	1.00
8	Jose Lind, Felix Jose	.50

#	Player	NM/M
9	Ricky Bones, Jaime Navarro	.50
10	Jaime Navarro, Jesse Orosco	.50
11	Tino Martinez, Edgar Martinez	.50
12	Juan Gonzalez, Ivan Rodriguez	.75
13	Juan Gonzalez, Julio Franco	.60
14	Julio Franco, Jose Canseco, Rafael Palmeiro	.60
15	Juan Gonzalez, Jose Canseco	.65
16	Ivan Rodriguez, Benji Gil	.60
17	Jose Guzman, Frank Castillo	.50
18	Rey Sanchez, Jose Vizcaino	.50
19	Derrick May, Sammy Sosa	2.00
20	Sammy Sosa, Candy Maldonado	2.00
21	Jose Rijo, Juan Samuel	
22	Freddie Benavides, Andres Galarraga	.50
23	Guillermo Velasquez, Benito Santiago	.50
24	Luis Gonzalez, Andujar Cedeno	.50
25	Wil Cordero, Dennis Martinez	.50
26	Moises Alou, Wil Cordero	.50
27	Ozzie Canseco, Jose Canseco	.75
28	Jose Oquendo, Luis Alicea	.50
29	Luis Alicea, Rene Arocha	.50
30	Geronimo Pena, Luis Alicea	.50

Estrellas de Beisbol

		NM/M
Complete Set (20):		6.00
Common Player:		.50
1	Moises Alou	.50
2	Bobby Bonilla	.50
3	Tony Fernandez	.50
4	Felix Jose	.50
5	Dennis Martinez	.50
6	Orlando Merced	.50
7	Jose Oquendo	.50
8	Geronimo Pena	.50
9	Jose Rijo	.50
10	Benito Santiago	.50
11	Sandy Alomar Jr.	.50
12	Carlos Baerga	.50
13	Jose Canseco	1.50
14	Juan "Igor" Gonzalez	2.00
15	Juan Guzman	.50
16	Edgar Martinez	.50
17	Rafael Palmeiro	2.00
18	Ruben Sierra	.50
19	Danny Tartabull	.50
20	Omar Vizquel	.50

Jugadores Calientes

		NM/M
Complete Set (36):		20.00
Common Player:		.50
1	Rich Amaral	.50
2	George Brett	1.75
3	Jay Buhner	.50
4	Roger Clemens	2.00
5	Kirk Gibson	.50
6	Juan Gonzalez	1.00
7	Ken Griffey Jr.	2.00

GEORGE BRETT

8	Bo Jackson	.75
9	Kenny Lofton	.50
10	Mark McGwire	2.25
11	Sherman Obando	.50
12	John Olerud	.50
13	Carlos Quintana	.50
14	Ivan Rodriguez	1.00
15	Nolan Ryan	2.50
16	J.T. Snow	.50
17	Fernando Valenzuela	1.25
18	Dave Winfield	1.25
19	Moises Alou	.50
20	Jeff Bagwell	1.25
21	Barry Bonds	2.50
22	Bobby Bonilla	.50
23	Vinny Castilla	.50
24	Andujar Cedeno	.50
25	Orestes Destrade	.50
26	Andres Galarraga	.50
27	Mark Grace	.50
28	Tony Gwynn	1.50
29	Roberto Kelly	.50
30	John Kruk	.50
31	Dave Magadan	.50
32	Derrick May	.50
33	Orlando Merced	.50
34	Mike Piazza	2.00
35	Armadno Reynoso	.50
36	Jose Vizcaino	.50

Prism Insert

ROBERTO ALOMAR

		NM/M
Complete Set (20):		60.00
Common Player:		3.00
1	Francisco Cabrera	3.00
2	Jose Lind	3.00
3	Dennis Martinez	3.00
4	Ramon Martinez	3.00
5	Jose Rijo	3.00
6	Benito Santiago	3.00
7	Roberto Alomar	9.00
8	Sandy Alomar Jr.	3.00
9	Carlos Baerga	3.00
10	George Bell	3.00
11	Jose Canseco	6.00
12	Alex Fernandez	3.00
13	Julio Franco	3.00
14	Igor (Juan) Gonzalez	12.00
15	Ozzie Guillen	3.00
16	Teddy Higuera	3.00
17	Edgar Martinez	3.00
18	Hipolito Pichardo	3.00
19	Luis Polonia	3.00
20	Ivan Rodriguez	7.50

1994 Pacific Crown

	NM/M
Complete Set (660):	20.00
Common Player:	.05
Pack (12):	1.00

THOMAS

#	Player	Value
	Wax Box (36):	20.00
1	Steve Avery	.05
2	Steve Bedrosian	.05
3	Damon Beryhill	.05
4	Jeff Blauser	.05
5	Sid Bream	.05
6	Francisco Cabrera	.05
7	Ramon Caraballo	.05
8	Ron Gant	.05
9	Tom Glavine	.25
10	Chipper Jones	.75
11	Dave Justice	.05
12	Ryan Klesko	.05
13	Mark Lemke	.05
14	Javier Lopez	.05
15	Greg Maddux	.75
16	Fred McGriff	.05
17	Greg McMichael	.05
18	Kent Mercker	.05
19	Otis Nixon	.05
20	Terry Pendleton	.05
21	Deion Sanders	.05
22	John Smoltz	.05
23	Tony Tarasco	.05
24	Manny Alexander	.05
25	Brady Anderson	.05
26	Harold Baines	.05
27	Damion Buford (Damon)	.05
28	Paul Carey	.05
29	Mike Devereaux	.05
30	Todd Frohwirth	.05
31	Leo Gomez	.05
32	Jeffrey Hammonds	.05
33	Chris Hoiles	.05
34	Tim Hullett	.05
35	Ben McDonald	.05
36	Mark McLemore	.05
37	Alan Mills	.05
38	Mike Mussina	.35
39	Sherman Obando	.05
40	Gregg Olson	.05
41	Mike Pagliarulo	.05
42	Jim Poole	.05
43	Harold Reynolds	.05
44	Cal Ripken, Jr.	2.00
45	David Segui	.05
46	Fernando Valenzuela	.05
47	Jack Voight	.05
48	Scott Bankhead	.05
49	Roger Clemens	1.00
50	Scott Cooper	.05
51	Danny Darwin	.05
52	Andre Dawson	.20
53	John Dopson	.05
54	Scott Fletcher	.05
55	Tony Fossas	.05
56	Mike Greenwell	.05
57	Billy Hatcher	.05
58	Jeff McNeely	.05
59	Jose Melendez	.05
60	Tim Naehring	.05
61	Tony Pena	.05
62	Carlos Quintana	.05
63	Paul Quantrill	.05
64	Luis Rivera	.05
65	Jeff Russell	.05
66	Aaron Sele	.05
67	John Valentin	.05
68	Mo Vaughn	.05
69	Frank Viola	.05
70	Bob Zupcic	.05
71	Mike Butcher	.05
72	Ron Correia	.05
73	Chad Curtis	.05
74	Chili Davis	.05
75	Gary DiSarcina	.05
76	Damion Easley	.05
77	John Farrell	.05
78	Chuck Finley	.05
79	Joe Grahe	.05
80	Stan Javier	.05
81	Mark Langston	.05
82	Phil Leftwich	.05
83	Torey Lovullo	.05
84	Joe Magrane	.05
85	Greg Myers	.05
86	Eduardo Perez	.05
87	Luis Polonia	.05
88	Tim Salmon	.05
89	J.T. Snow	.05
90	Kurt Stillwell	.05
91	Ron Tingley	.05
92	Chris Turner	.05
93	Julio Valera	.05
94	Jose Bautista	.05
95	Shawn Boskie	.05
96	Steve Buechele	.05
97	Frank Castillo	.05
98	Mark Grace	.05
99	Jose Guzman	.05
100	Mike Harkey	.05
101	Greg Hibbard	.05
102	Doug Jennings	.05
103	Derrick May	.05
104	Mike Morgan	.05
105	Randy Myers	.05
106	Karl Rhodes	.05
107	Kevin Robinson	.05
108	Rey Sanchez	.05
109	Ryne Sandberg	.75
110	Tommy Shields	.05
111	Dwight Smith	.05
112	Sammy Sosa	.75
113	Jose Vizcaino	.05
114	Turk Wendell	.05
115	Rick Wilkins	.05
116	Willie Wilson	.05
117	Eddie Zambrano	.05
118	Wilson Alvarez	.05
119	Tim Belcher	.05
120	Jason Bere	.05
121	Rodney Bolton	.05
122	Ellis Burks	.05
123	Joey Cora	.05
124	Alex Fernandez	.05
125	Ozzie Guillen	.05
126	Craig Grebeck	.05
127	Roberto Hernandez	.05
128	Bo Jackson	.10
129	Lance Johnson	.05
130	Ron Karkovice	.05
131	Mike Lavalliere	.05
132	Norberto Martin	.05
133	Kirk McCaskill	.05
134	Jack McDowell	.05
135	Scott Radinsky	.05
136	Tim Raines	.05
137	Steve Sax	.05
138	Frank Thomas	.60
139	Dan Pasqua	.05
140	Robin Ventura	.05
141	Jeff Branson	.05
142	Tom Browning	.05
143	Jacob Brumfield	.05
144	Tim Costo	.05
145	Rob Dibble	.05
146	Brian Dorsett	.05
147	Steve Foster	.05
148	Cesar Hernandez	.05
149	Roberto Kelly	.05
150	Barry Larkin	.05
151	Larry Luebbers	.05
152	Kevin Mitchell	.05
153	Joe Oliver	.05
154	Tim Pugh	.05
155	Jeff Reardon	.05
156	Jose Rijo	.05
157	Bip Roberts	.05
158	Chris Sabo	.05
159	Juan Samuel	.05
160	Reggie Sanders	.05
161	John Smiley	.05
162	Jerry Spradlin	.05
163	Gary Varsho	.05
164	Sandy Alomar Jr.	.05
165	Carlos Baerga	.05
166	Albert Belle	.05
167	Mark Clark	.05
168	Alvaro Espinoza	.05
169	Felix Fermin	.05
170	Reggie Jefferson	.05
171	Wayne Kirby	.05
172	Tom Kramer	.05
173	Jesse Levis	.05
174	Kenny Lofton	.05
175	Candy Maldonado	.05
176	Carlos Martinez	.05
177	Jose Mesa	.05
178	Jeff Mutis	.05
179	Charles Nagy	.05
180	Bob Ojeda	.05
181	Junior Ortiz	.05
182	Eric Plunk	.05
183	Manny Ramirez	.60
184	Paul Sorrento	.05
185	Jeff Treadway	.05

#	Player	Price	#	Player	Price	#	Player	Price	#	Player	Price
186	Bill Wertz	.05	290	Wally Joyner	.05	394	Rondell White	.05	498	Carlos Garcia	.05
187	Freddie Benavides	.05	291	Kevin Koslofski	.05	395	Tom Bogar	.05	499	Jeff King	.05
188	Dante Bichette	.05	292	Jose Lind	.05	396	Bobby Bonilla	.05	500	Al Martin	.05
189	Willie Blair	.05	293	Brent Mayne	.05	397	Jeromy Burnitz	.05	501	Lloyd McClendon	.05
190	Daryl Boston	.05	294	Mike Mcfarlane	.05	398	Mike Draper	.05	502	Orlando Merced	.05
191	Pedro Castellano	.05	295	Brian McRae	.05	399	Sid Fernandez	.05	503	Blas Minor	.05
192	Vinny Castilla	.05	296	Kevin McReynolds	.05	400	John Franco	.05	504	Denny Neagle	.05
193	Jerald Clark	.05	297	Keith Miller	.05	401	Dave Gallagher	.05	505	Tom Prince	.05
194	Alex Cole	.05	298	Jeff Montgomery	.05	402	Dwight Gooden	.05	506	Don Slaught	.05
195	Andres Galarraga	.05	299	Hipolito Pichardo	.05	403	Eric Hillman	.05	507	Zane Smith	.05
196	Joe Girardi	.05	300	Rico Rossy	.05	404	Todd Hundley	.05	508	Randy Tomlin	.05
197	Charlie Hayes	.05	301	Curtis Wilkerson	.05	405	Butch Huskey	.05	509	Andy Van Slyke	.05
198	Darren Holmes	.05	302	Pedro Astacio	.05	406	Jeff Innis	.05	510	Paul Wagner	.05
199	Chris Jones	.05	303	Rafael Bournigal	.05	407	Howard Johnson	.05	511	Tim Wakefield	.05
200	Curt Leskanic	.05	304	Brett Butler	.05	408	Jeff Kent	.05	512	Bob Walk	.05
201	Roberto Mejia	.05	305	Tom Candiotti	.05	409	Ced Landrum	.05	513	John Wehner	.05
202	David Nied	.05	306	Omar Daal	.05	410	Mike Maddux	.05	514	Kevin Young	.05
203	J. Owens	.05	307	Jim Gott	.05	411	Josias Manzanillo	.05	515	Billy Bean	.05
204	Steve Reed	.05	308	Kevin Gross	.05	412	Jeff McKnight	.05	516	Andy Benes	.05
205	Armando Reynoso	.05	309	Dave Hansen	.05	413	Eddie Murray	.60	517	Derek Bell	.05
206	Bruce Ruffin	.05	310	Carlos Hernandez	.05	414	Tito Navarro	.05	518	Doug Brocail	.05
207	Keith Shepherd	.05	311	Orel Hershiser	.05	415	Joe Orsulak	.05	519	Jarvis Brown	.05
208	Jim Tatum	.05	312	Eric Karros	.05	416	Bret Saberhagen	.05	520	Phil Clark	.05
209	Eric Young	.05	313	Pedro Martinez	.60	417	Dave Telgheder	.05	521	Mark Davis	.05
210	Skeeter Barnes	.05	314	Ramon Martinez	.05	418	Ryan Thompson	.05	522	Jeff Gardner	.05
211	Danny Bautista	.05	315	Roger McDowell	.05	419	Chico Walker	.05	523	Pat Gomez	.05
212	Tom Bolton	.05	316	Raul Mondesi	.05	420	Jim Abbott	.05	524	Ricky Gutierrez	.05
213	Eric Davis	.05	317	Jose Offerman	.05	421	Wade Boggs	.75	525	Tony Gwynn	.75
214	Storm Davis	.05	318	Mike Piazza	1.00	422	Mike Gallego	.05	526	Gene Harris	.05
215	Cecil Fielder	.05	319	Jody Reed	.05	423	Mark Hutton	.05	527	Kevin Higgins	.05
216	Travis Fryman	.05	320	Henry Rodriguez	.05	424	Dion James	.05	528	Trevor Hoffman	.05
217	Kirk Gibson	.05	321	Cory Snyder	.05	425	Domingo Jean	.05	529	Luis Lopez	.05
218	Dan Gladden	.05	322	Darryl Strawberry	.05	426	Pat Kelly	.05	530	Pedro A. Martinez	.05
219	John Doherty	.05	323	Tim Wallach	.05	427	Jimmy Key	.05	531	Melvin Nieves	.05
220	Chris Gomez	.05	324	Steve Wilson	.05	428	Jim Leyritz	.05	532	Phil Plantier	.05
221	David Haas	.05	325	Juan Bell	.05	429	Kevin Maas	.05	533	Frank Seminara	.05
222	Bill Krueger	.05	326	Ricky Bones	.05	430	Don Mattingly	1.00	534	Craig Shipley	.05
223	Chad Kreuter	.05	327	Alex Diaz	.05	431	Bobby Munoz	.05	535	Tim Tuefel	.05
224	Mark Leiter	.05	328	Cal Eldred	.05	432	Matt Nokes	.05	536	Guillermo Velasquez	.05
225	Bob MacDonald	.05	329	Darryl Hamilton	.05	433	Paul O'Neill	.05	537	Wally Whitehurst	.05
226	Mike Moore	.05	330	Doug Henry	.05	434	Spike Owen	.05	538	Rod Beck	.05
227	Tony Phillips	.05	331	John Jaha	.05	435	Melido Perez	.05	539	Todd Benzinger	.05
228	Rich Rowland	.05	332	Pat Listach	.05	436	Lee Smith	.05	540	Barry Bonds	2.00
229	Mickey Tettleton	.05	333	Graeme Lloyd	.05	437	Andy Stankiewicz	.05	541	Jeff Brantley	.05
230	Alan Trammell	.05	334	Carlos Maldonado	.05	438	Mike Stanley	.05	542	Dave Burba	.05
231	David Wells	.05	335	Angel Miranda	.05	439	Danny Tartabull	.05	543	John Burkett	.05
232	Lou Whitaker	.05	336	Jaime Navarro	.05	440	Randy Velarde	.05	544	Will Clark	.05
233	Luis Aquino	.05	337	Dave Nilsson	.05	441	Bernie Williams	.05	545	Royce Clayton	.05
234	Alex Arias	.05	338	Rafael Novoa	.05	442	Gerald Williams	.05	546	Brian Hickerson (Bryan)	.05
235	Jack Armstrong	.05	339	Troy O'Leary	.05	443	Mike Witt	.05	547	Mike Jackson	.05
236	Ryan Bowen	.05	340	Jesse Orosco	.05	444	Marcos Armas	.05	548	Darren Lewis	.05
237	Chuck Carr	.05	341	Kevin Seitzer	.05	445	Lance Blankenship	.05	549	Kirt Manwaring	.05
238	Matias Carrillo	.05	342	Bill Spiers	.05	446	Mike Bordick	.05	550	Dave Martinez	.05
239	Jeff Conine	.05	343	William Suero	.05	447	Ron Darling	.05	551	Willie McGee	.05
240	Henry Cotto	.05	344	B.J. Surhoff	.05	448	Dennis Eckersley	.45	552	Jeff Reed	.05
241	Orestes Destrade	.05	345	Dickie Thon	.05	449	Brent Gates	.05	553	Dave Righetti	.05
242	Chris Hammond	.05	346	Jose Valentin	.05	450	Goose Gossage	.05	554	Kevin Rogers	.05
243	Bryan Harvey	.05	347	Greg Vaughn	.05	451	Scott Hemond	.05	555	Steve Scarsone	.05
244	Charlie Hough	.05	348	Robin Yount	.60	452	Dave Henderson	.05	556	Bill Swift	.05
245	Richie Lewis	.05	349	Willie Banks	.05	453	Shawn Hillegas	.05	557	Robby Thompson	.05
246	Mitch Lyden	.05	350	Bernardo Brito	.05	454	Rick Honeycutt	.05	558	Salomon Torres	.05
247	Dave Magadan	.05	351	Scott Erickson	.05	455	Scott Lydy	.05	559	Matt Williams	.05
248	Bob Natal	.05	352	Mark Guthrie	.05	456	Mark McGwire	1.50	560	Trevor Wilson	.05
249	Benito Santiago	.05	353	Chip Hale	.05	457	Henry Mercedes	.05	561	Rich Amaral	.05
250	Gary Sheffield	.30	354	Brian Harper	.05	458	Mike Mohler	.05	562	Mike Blowers	.05
251	Matt Turner	.05	355	Kent Hrbek	.05	459	Troy Neel	.05	563	Chris Bosio	.05
252	David Weathers	.05	356	Terry Jorgenson	.05	460	Edwin Nunez	.05	564	Jay Buhner	.05
253	Walt Weiss	.05	357	Chuck Knoblauch	.05	461	Craig Paquette	.05	565	Norm Charlton	.05
254	Darrell Whitmore	.05	358	Gene Larkin	.05	462	Ruben Sierra	.05	566	Jim Converse	.05
255	Nigel Wilson	.05	359	Scott Leius	.05	463	Terry Steinbach	.05	567	Rich DeLucia	.05
256	Eric Anthony	.05	360	Shane Mack	.05	464	Todd Van Poppel	.05	568	Mike Felder	.05
257	Jeff Bagwell	.60	361	David McCarty	.05	465	Bob Welch	.05	569	Dave Fleming	.05
258	Kevin Bass	.05	362	Pat Meares	.05	466	Bobby Witt	.05	570	Ken Griffey Jr.	1.00
259	Craig Biggio	.05	363	Pedro Munoz	.05	467	Ruben Amaro	.05	571	Bill Haselman	.05
260	Ken Caminiti	.05	364	Derek Parks	.05	468	Larry Anderson	.05	572	Dwayne Henry	.05
261	Andujar Cedeno	.05	365	Kirby Puckett	.75	469	Kim Batiste	.05	573	Brad Holman	.05
262	Chris Donnels	.05	366	Jeff Reboulet	.05	470	Wes Chamberlain	.05	574	Randy Johnson	.60
263	Doug Drabek	.05	367	Kevin Tapani	.05	471	Darren Daulton	.05	575	Greg Litton	.05
264	Tom Edens	.05	368	Mike Trombley	.05	472	Mariano Duncan	.05	576	Edgar Martinez	.05
265	Steve Finley	.05	369	George Tsamis	.05	473	Len Dykstra	.05	577	Tino Martinez	.05
266	Luis Gonzalez	.05	370	Carl Willis	.05	474	Jim Eisenreich	.05	578	Jeff Nelson	.05
267	Pete Harnisch	.05	371	Dave Winfield	.60	475	Tommy Greene	.05	579	Mark Newfield	.05
268	Xavier Hernandez	.05	372	Moises Alou	.05	476	Dave Hollins	.05	580	Roger Salkeld	.05
269	Todd Jones	.05	373	Brian Barnes	.05	477	Pete Incaviglia	.05	581	Mackey Sasser	.05
270	Darryl Kile	.05	374	Sean Berry	.05	478	Danny Jackson	.05	582	Brian Turang	.05
271	Al Osuna	.05	375	Frank Bolick	.05	479	John Kruk	.05	583	Omar Vizquel	.05
272	Rick Parker	.05	376	Wil Cordero	.05	480	Tony Longmire	.05	584	Dave Valle	.05
273	Mark Portugal	.05	377	Delino DeShields	.05	481	Jeff Manto	.05	585	Luis Alicea	.05
274	Scott Servais	.05	378	Jeff Fassero	.05	482	Mike Morandini	.05	586	Rene Arocha	.05
275	Greg Swindell	.05	379	Darren Fletcher	.05	483	Terry Mulholland	.05	587	Rheal Cormier	.05
276	Eddie Taubensee	.05	380	Cliff Floyd	.05	484	Todd Pratt	.05	588	Tripp Cromer	.05
277	Jose Uribe	.05	381	Lou Frazier	.05	485	Ben Rivera	.05	589	Bernard Gilkey	.05
278	Brian Williams	.05	382	Marquis Grissom	.05	486	Curt Schilling	.25	590	Lee Guetterman	.05
279	Kevin Appier	.05	383	Gil Heredia	.05	487	Kevin Stocker	.05	591	Gregg Jefferies	.05
280	Billy Brewer	.05	384	Mike Lansing	.05	488	Milt Thompson	.05	592	Tim Jones	.05
281	David Cone	.05	385	Oreste Marrero	.05	489	David West	.05	593	Paul Kilgus	.05
282	Greg Gagne	.05	386	Dennis Martinez	.05	490	Mitch Williams	.05	594	Les Lancaster	.05
283	Tom Gordon	.05	387	Curtis Pride	.05	491	Jeff Ballard	.05	595	Omar Olivares	.05
284	Chris Gwynn	.05	388	Mel Rojas	.05	492	Jay Bell	.05	596	Jose Oquendo	.05
285	John Habyan	.05	389	Kirk Rueter	.05	493	Scott Bullett	.05	597	Donovan Osborne	.05
286	Chris Haney	.05	390	Joe Siddall	.05	494	Dave Clark	.05	598	Tom Pagnozzi	.05
287	Phil Hiatt	.05	391	John Vander Wal	.05	495	Steve Cooke	.05	599	Erik Pappas	.05
288	David Howard	.05	392	Larry Walker	.05	496	Midre Cummings	.05	600	Geronimo Pena	.05
289	Felix Jose	.05	393	John Wetteland	.05	497	Mark Dewey	.05	601	Mike Perez	.05

602	Gerald Perry	.05
603	Stan Royer	.05
604	Ozzie Smith	.75
605	Bob Tewksbury	.05
606	Allen Watson	.05
607	Mark Whiten	.05
608	Todd Zeile	.05
609	Jeff Bronkey	.05
610	Kevin Brown	.05
611	Jose Canseco	.35
612	Doug Dascenzo	.05
613	Butch Davis	.05
614	Mario Diaz	.05
615	Julio Franco	.05
616	Benji Gil	.05
617	Juan Gonzalez	.30
618	Tom Henke	.05
619	Jeff Huson	.05
620	David Hulse	.05
621	Craig Lefferts	.05
622	Rafael Palmeiro	.50
623	Dean Palmer	.05
624	Bob Patterson	.05
625	Roger Pavlik	.05
626	Gary Redus	.05
627	Ivan Rodriguez	.50
628	Kenny Rogers	.05
629	Jon Shave	.05
630	Doug Strange	.05
631	Matt Whiteside	.05
632	Roberto Alomar	.15
633	Pat Borders	.05
634	Scott Brow	.05
635	Rob Butler	.05
636	Joe Carter	.05
637	Tony Castillo	.05
638	Mark Eichhorn	.05
639	Tony Fernandez	.05
640	Huck Flener RC	.05
641	Alfredo Griffin	.05
642	Juan Guzman	.05
643	Rickey Henderson	.60
644	Pat Hentgen	.05
645	Randy Knorr	.05
646	Al Leiter	.05
647	Dominigo Martinez	.05
648	Paul Molitor	.60
649	Jack Morris	.05
650	John Olerud	.05
651	Ed Sprague	.05
652	Dave Stewart	.05
653	Devon White	.05
654	Woody Williams	.05
655	Barry Bonds (MVP)	1.00
656	Greg Maddux (CY)	.40
657	Jack McDowell (CY)	.05
658	Mike Piazza (ROY)	.65
659	Tim Salmon (ROY)	.05
660	Frank Thomas (MVP)	.25

All Latino All-Star Team

Omar Vizquel

		NM/M
Complete Set (20):		4.00
Common Player:		.25
1	Benito Santiago	.25
2	Dave Magadan	.25
3	Andres Galarraga	.25
4	Luis Gonzalez	.25
5	Jose Offerman	.25
6	Bobby Bonilla	.25
7	Dennis Martinez	.25
8	Mariano Duncan	.25
9	Orlando Merced	.25
10	Jose Rijo	.25
11	Danny Tartabull	.25
12	Ruben Sierra	.25
13	Ivan Rodriguez	1.00
14	Juan Gonzalez	1.00
15	Jose Canseco	.50
16	Rafael Palmeiro	1.00
17	Roberto Alomar	.50

18	Eduardo Perez	.25
19	Alex Fernandez	.25
20	Omar Vizquel	.25

Homerun Leaders

TIM SALMON

		NM/M
Complete Set (20):		25.00
Common Player:		1.00
1	Juan Gonzalez	1.50
2	Ken Griffey Jr.	3.00
3	Frank Thomas	2.50
4	Albert Belle	1.00
5	Rafael Palmeiro	1.50
6	Joe Carter	1.00
7	Dean Palmer	1.00
8	Mickey Tettleton	1.00
9	Tim Salmon	1.00
10	Danny Tartabull	1.00
11	Barry Bonds	5.00
12	Dave Justice	1.00
13	Matt Williams	1.00
14	Fred McGriff	1.00
15	Ron Gant	1.00
16	Mike Piazza	3.00
17	Bobby Bonilla	1.00
18	Phil Plantier	1.00
19	Sammy Sosa	3.00
20	Rick Wilkins	1.00

Jewels of the Crown

BARRY BONDS

		NM/M
Complete Set (36):		40.00
Common Player:		1.00
1	Robin Yount	2.50
2	Juan Gonzalez	1.25
3	Rafael Palmeiro	2.00
4	Paul Molitor	2.50
5	Roberto Alomar	1.25
6	John Olerud	1.00
7	Randy Johnson	2.50
8	Ken Griffey Jr.	4.00
9	Wade Boggs	3.00
10	Don Mattingly	3.50
11	Kirby Puckett	3.00
12	Tim Salmon	1.00
13	Frank Thomas	2.50
14	Fernando Valenzuela (Comeback Player)	1.00
15	Cal Ripken, Jr.	6.00
16	Carlos Baerga	1.00
17	Kenny Lofton	1.00
18	Cecil Fielder	1.00
19	John Burkett	1.00
20	Andres Galarraga (Comeback Player)	1.00
21	Charlie Hayes	1.00
22	Orestes Destrade	1.00
23	Jeff Conine	1.00
24	Jeff Bagwell	2.50
25	Mark Grace	1.00
26	Ryne Sandberg	3.00
27	Gregg Jefferies	1.00
28	Barry Bonds	6.00
29	Mike Piazza	3.50
30	Greg Maddux	3.00
31	Darren Daulton	1.00
32	John Kruk	1.00
33	Len Dykstra	1.00
34	Orlando Merced	1.00
35	Tony Gwynn	3.00
36	Robby Thompson	1.00

Jewels of the Crown - Retail

RANDY JOHNSON

		NM/M
Complete Set (36):		40.00
Common Player:		.75
1	Robin Yount	2.50
2	Juan Gonzalez	1.25
3	Rafael Palmeiro	1.25
4	Paul Molitor	1.00
5	Roberto Alomar	1.00
6	John Olerud	.75
7	Randy Johnson	2.50
8	Ken Griffey Jr.	4.00
9	Wade Boggs	3.00
10	Don Mattingly	3.50
11	Kirby Puckett	3.00
12	Tim Salmon	.75
13	Frank Thomas	2.50
14	Fernando Valenzuela (Comeback Player)	.75
15	Cal Ripken, Jr.	5.00
16	Carlos Baerga	.75
17	Kenny Lofton	.75
18	Cecil Fielder	.75
19	John Burkett	.75
20	Andres Galarraga (Comeback Player)	.75
21	Charlie Hayes	.75
22	Orestes Destrade	.75
23	Jeff Conine	.75
24	Jeff Bagwell	2.50
25	Mark Grace	.75
26	Ryne Sandberg	3.00
27	Gregg Jefferies	.75
28	Barry Bonds	5.00
29	Mike Piazza	3.50
30	Greg Maddux	3.00
31	Darren Daulton	.75
32	John Kruk	.75
33	Len Dykstra	.75
34	Orlando Merced	.75
35	Tony Gwynn	3.00
36	Robby Thompson	.75

1995 Pacific

	NM/M
Complete Set (450):	20.00
Common Player:	.05
Pack (12):	1.00

Wax Box (36):		20.00
1	Steve Avery	.05
2	Rafael Belliard	.05
3	Jeff Blauser	.05
4	Tom Glavine	.25
5	Dave Justice	.05
6	Mike Kelly	.05
7	Roberto Kelly	.05
8	Ryan Klesko	.05
9	Mark Lemke	.05
10	Javier Lopez	.05
11	Greg Maddux	.75
12	Fred McGriff	.05
13	Greg McMichael	.05
14	Jose Oliva	.05
15	John Smoltz	.05
16	Tony Tarasco	.05
17	Brady Anderson	.05
18	Harold Baines	.05
19	Armando Benitez	.05
20	Mike Devereaux	.05
21	Leo Gomez	.05
22	Jeffrey Hammonds	.05
23	Chris Hoiles	.05
24	Ben McDonald	.05
25	Mark McLemore	.05
26	Jamie Moyer	.05
27	Mike Mussina	.40
28	Rafael Palmeiro	.50
29	Jim Poole	.05
30	Cal Ripken Jr.	2.00
31	Lee Smith	.05
32	Mark Smith	.05
33	Jose Canseco	.35
34	Roger Clemens	1.00
35	Scott Cooper	.05
36	Andre Dawson	.25
37	Tony Fossas	.05
38	Mike Greenwell	.05
39	Chris Howard	.05
40	Jose Melendez	.05
41	Nate Minchey	.05
42	Tim Naehring	.05
43	Otis Nixon	.05
44	Carlos Rodriguez	.05
45	Aaron Sele	.05
46	Lee Tinsley	.05
47	Sergio Valdez	.05
48	John Valentin	.05
49	Mo Vaughn	.05
50	Brian Anderson	.05
51	Garret Anderson	.05
52	Rod Correia	.05
53	Chad Curtis	.05
54	Mark Dalesandro	.05
55	Chili Davis	.05
56	Gary DiSarcina	.05
57	Damion Easley	.05
58	Jim Edmonds	.05
59	Jorge Fabregas	.05
60	Chuck Finley	.05
61	Bo Jackson	.10
62	Mark Langston	.05
63	Eduardo Perez	.05
64	Tim Salmon	.05
65	J.T. Snow	.05
66	Willie Banks	.05
67	Jose Bautista	.05
68	Shawon Dunston	.05
69	Kevin Foster	.05
70	Mark Grace	.05
71	Jose Guzman	.05
72	Jose Hernandez	.05
73	Blaise Ilsley	.05
74	Derrick May	.05
75	Randy Myers	.05
76	Karl Rhodes	.05
77	Kevin Roberson	.05
78	Rey Sanchez	.05
79	Sammy Sosa	.75
80	Steve Trachsel	.05
81	Eddie Zambrano	.05
82	Wilson Alvarez	.05
83	Jason Bere	.05
84	Joey Cora	.05
85	Jose DeLeon	.05
86	Alex Fernandez	.05
87	Julio Franco	.05
88	Ozzie Guillen	.05
89	Joe Hall	.05
90	Roberto Hernandez	.05
91	Darrin Jackson	.05
92	Lance Johnson	.05
93	Norberto Martin	.05
94	Jack McDowell	.05
95	Tim Raines	.05
96	Olmedo Saenz	.05
97	Frank Thomas	.60
98	Robin Ventura	.05
99	Bret Boone	.05
100	Jeff Brantley	.05
101	Jacob Brumfield	.05
102	Hector Carrasco	.05
103	Brian Dorsett	.05

#	Player	Price		#	Player	Price		#	Player	Price		#	Player	Price
104	Tony Fernandez	.05		209	Brian McRae.	.05		314	Miguel Jimenez.	.05		419	Todd Zeile.	.05
105	Willie Greene	.05		210	Jeff Montgomery.	.05		315	Francisco Matos.	.05		420	Esteban Beltre.	.05
106	Erik Hanson	.05		211	Hipolito Pichardo.	.05		316	Mark McGwire.	1.50		421	Kevin Brown.	.05
107	Kevin Jarvis	.05		212	Pedro Astacio.	.05		317	Troy Neel.	.05		422	Cris Carpenter.	.05
108	Barry Larkin.	.05		213	Brett Butler.	.05		318	Steve Ontiveros.	.05		423	Will Clark.	.05
109	Kevin Mitchell.	.05		214	Omar Daal.	.05		319	Carlos Reyes.	.05		424	Hector Fajardo.	.05
110	Hal Morris.	.05		215	Delino DeShields.	.05		320	Ruben Sierra.	.05		425	Jeff Frye.	.05
111	Jose Rijo.	.05		216	Darren Dreifort.	.05		321	Terry Steinbach.	.05		426	Juan Gonzalez.	.30
112	Johnny Ruffin.	.05		217	Carlos Hernandez.	.05		322	Bob Welch.	.05		427	Rusty Greer.	.05
113	Deion Sanders.	.05		218	Orel Hershiser.	.05		323	Bobby Witt.	.05		428	Rick Honeycutt.	.05
114	Reggie Sanders.	.05		219	Garey Ingram.	.05		324	Larry Andersen.	.05		429	David Hulse.	.05
115	Sandy Alomar Jr.	.05		220	Eric Karros.	.05		325	Kim Batiste.	.05		430	Manny Lee.	.05
116	Ruben Amaro.	.05		221	Ramon Martinez.	.05		326	Darren Daulton.	.05		431	Junior Ortiz.	.05
117	Carlos Baerga.	.05		222	Raul Mondesi.	.05		327	Mariano Duncan.	.05		432	Dean Palmer.	.05
118	Albert Belle.	.05		223	Jose Offerman.	.05		328	Lenny Dykstra.	.05		433	Ivan Rodriguez.	.50
119	Alvaro Espinoza.	.05		224	Mike Piazza.	1.00		329	Jim Eisenreich.	.05		434	Dan Smith.	.05
120	Rene Gonzales.	.05		225	Henry Rodriguez.	.05		330	Danny Jackson.	.05		435	Roberto Alomar.	.15
121	Wayne Kirby.	.05		226	Ismael Valdes.	.05		331	John Kruk.	.05		436	Pat Borders.	.05
122	Kenny Lofton.	.05		227	Tim Wallach.	.05		332	Tony Longmire.	.05		437	Scott Brow.	.05
123	Candy Maldonado.	.05		228	Jeff Cirillo.	.05		333	Tom Marsh.	.05		438	Rob Butler.	.05
124	Dennis Martinez.	.05		229	Alex Diaz.	.05		334	Mickey Morandini.	.05		439	Joe Carter.	.05
125	Eddie Murray.	.60		230	Cal Eldred.	.05		335	Bobby Munoz.	.05		440	Tony Castillo.	.05
126	Charles Nagy.	.05		231	Mike Fetters.	.05		336	Todd Pratt.	.05		441	Domingo Cedeno.	.05
127	Tony Pena.	.05		232	Brian Harper.	.05		337	Tom Quinlan.	.05		442	Brad Cornett.	.05
128	Manny Ramirez.	.60		233	Ted Higuera.	.05		338	Kevin Stocker.	.05		443	Carlos Delgado.	.35
129	Paul Sorrento.	.05		234	John Jaha.	.05		339	Fernando Valenzuela.	.05		444	Alex Gonzalez	.05
130	Jim Thome.	.40		235	Graeme Lloyd.	.05		340	Jay Bell.	.05		445	Juan Guzman	.05
131	Omar Vizquel.	.05		236	Jose Mercedes.	.05		341	Dave Clark.	.05		446	Darren Hall	.05
132	Dante Bichette.	.05		237	Jaime Navarro.	.05		342	Steve Cooke.	.05		447	Paul Molitor	.60
133	Ellis Burks.	.05		238	Dave Nilsson.	.05		343	Carlos Garcia.	.05		448	John Olerud	.05
134	Vinny Castilla.	.05		239	Jesse Orosco.	.05		344	Jeff King.	.05		449	Robert Perez	.05
135	Marvin Freeman.	.05		240	Jody Reed.	.05		345	Jon Lieber.	.05		450	Devon White	.05
136	Andres Galarraga.	.05		241	Jose Valentin.	.05		346	Ravelo Manzanillo.	.05				
137	Joe Girardi.	.05		242	Greg Vaughn.	.05		347	Al Martin.	.05				
138	Charlie Hayes.	.05		243	Turner Ward.	.05		348	Orlando Merced.	.05				
139	Mike Kingery.	.05		244	Rick Aguilera.	.05		349	Denny Neagle.	.05				
140	Nelson Liriano.	.05		245	Rich Becker.	.05		350	Alejandro Pena.	.05				
141	Roberto Mejia.	.05		246	Jim Deshaies.	.05		351	Don Slaught.	.05				
142	David Nied.	.05		247	Steve Dunn.	.05		352	Zane Smith.	.05				
143	Steve Reed.	.05		248	Scott Erickson.	.05		353	Andy Van Slyke.	.05				
144	Armando Reynoso.	.05		249	Kent Hrbek.	.05		354	Rick White.	.05				
145	Bruce Ruffin.	.05		250	Chuck Knoblauch.	.05		355	Kevin Young.	.05				
146	John Vander Wal.	.05		251	Scott Leius.	.05		356	Andy Ashby.	.05				
147	Walt Weiss.	.05		252	David McCarty.	.05		357	Derek Bell.	.05				
148	Skeeter Barnes.	.05		253	Pat Meares.	.05		358	Andy Benes.	.05				
149	Tim Belcher.	.05		254	Pedro Munoz.	.05		359	Phil Clark.	.05				
150	Junior Felix.	.05		255	Kirby Puckett.	.75		360	Donnie Elliott.	.05				
151	Cecil Fielder.	.05		256	Carlos Pulido.	.05		361	Ricky Gutierrez.	.05				
152	Travis Fryman.	.05		257	Kevin Tapani.	.05		362	Tony Gwynn.	.75				
153	Kirk Gibson.	.05		258	Matt Walbeck.	.05		363	Trevor Hoffman.	.05				
154	Chris Gomez.	.05		259	Dave Winfield.	.60		364	Tim Hyers.	.05				
155	Buddy Groom.	.05		260	Moises Alou.	.05		365	Luis Lopez.	.05				
156	Chad Kreuter.	.05		261	Juan Bell.	.05		366	Jose Martinez.	.05				
157	Mike Moore.	.05		262	Freddie Benavides.	.05		367	Pedro A. Martinez.	.05				
158	Tony Phillips.	.05		263	Sean Berry.	.05		368	Phil Plantier.	.05				
159	Juan Samuel.	.05		264	Wil Cordero.	.05		369	Bip Roberts.	.05				
160	Mickey Tettleton.	.05		265	Jeff Fassero.	.05		370	A.J. Sager.	.05				
161	Alan Trammell.	.05		266	Darrin Fletcher.	.05		371	Jeff Tabaka.	.05				
162	David Wells.	.05		267	Cliff Floyd.	.05		372	Todd Benzinger.	.05				
163	Lou Whitaker.	.05		268	Marquis Grissom.	.05		373	Barry Bonds.	2.00				
164	Kurt Abbott.	.05		269	Gil Heredia.	.05		374	John Burkett.	.05				
165	Luis Aquino.	.05		270	Ken Hill.	.05		375	Mark Carreon.	.05				
166	Alex Arias.	.05		271	Pedro Martinez.	.60		376	Royce Clayton.	.05				
167	Bret Barberie.	.05		272	Mel Rojas.	.05		377	Pat Gomez.	.05				
168	Jerry Browne.	.05		273	Larry Walker.	.05		378	Erik Johnson.	.05				
169	Chuck Carr.	.05		274	John Wetteland.	.05		379	Darren Lewis.	.05				
170	Matias Carrillo.	.05		275	Rondell White.	.05		380	Kirt Manwaring.	.05				
171	Greg Colbrunn.	.05		276	Tim Bogar.	.05		381	Dave Martinez.	.05				
172	Jeff Conine.	.05		277	Bobby Bonilla.	.05		382	John Patterson.	.05				
173	Carl Everett.	.05		278	Rico Brogna.	.05		383	Mark Portugal.	.05				
174	Robb Nen.	.05		279	Jeromy Burnitz.	.05		384	Darryl Strawberry.	.05				
175	Yorkis Perez.	.05		280	John Franco.	.05		385	Salomon Torres.	.05				
176	Pat Rapp.	.05		281	Eric Hillman.	.05		386	Bill Van Landingham.	.05				
177	Benito Santiago.	.05		282	Todd Hundley.	.05		387	Matt Williams.	.05				
178	Gary Sheffield.	.35		283	Jeff Kent.	.05		388	Rich Amaral.	.05				
179	Darrell Whitmore.	.05		284	Mike Maddux.	.05		389	Bobby Ayala.	.05				
180	Jeff Bagwell.	.60		285	Joe Orsulak.	.05		390	Mike Blowers.	.05				
181	Kevin Bass.	.05		286	Luis Rivera.	.05		391	Chris Bosio.	.05				
182	Craig Biggio.	.05		287	Bret Saberhagen.	.05		392	Jay Buhner.	.05				
183	Andujar Cedeno.	.05		288	David Segui.	.05		393	Jim Converse.	.05				
184	Doug Drabek.	.05		289	Ryan Thompson.	.05		394	Tim Davis.	.05				
185	Tony Eusebio.	.05		290	Fernando Vina.	.05		395	Felix Fermin.	.05				
186	Steve Finley.	.05		291	Jose Vizcaino.	.05		396	Dave Fleming.	.05				
187	Luis Gonzalez.	.05		292	Jim Abbott.	.05		397	Goose Gossage.	.05				
188	Pete Harnisch.	.05		293	Wade Boggs.	.75		398	Ken Griffey Jr.	1.00				
189	John Hudek.	.05		294	Russ Davis.	.05		399	Randy Johnson.	.60				
190	Orlando Miller.	.05		295	Mike Gallego.	.05		400	Edgar Martinez.	.05				
191	James Mouton.	.05		296	Xavier Hernandez.	.05		401	Tino Martinez.	.05				
192	Roberto Petagine.	.05		297	Steve Howe.	.05		402	Alex Rodriguez.	1.50				
193	Shane Reynolds.	.05		298	Jimmy Key.	.05		403	Dan Wilson.	.05				
194	Greg Swindell.	.05		299	Don Mattingly.	1.00		404	Luis Alicea.	.05				
195	Dave Veres.	.05		300	Terry Mulholland.	.05		405	Rene Arocha.	.05				
196	Kevin Appier.	.05		301	Paul O'Neill.	.05		406	Bernard Gilkey.	.05				
197	Stan Belinda.	.05		302	Luis Polonia.	.05		407	Gregg Jefferies.	.05				
198	Vince Coleman.	.05		303	Mike Stanley.	.05		408	Ray Lankford.	.05				
199	David Cone.	.05		304	Danny Tartabull.	.05		409	Terry McGriff.	.05				
200	Gary Gaetti.	.05		305	Randy Velarde.	.05		410	Omar Olivares.	.05				
201	Greg Gagne.	.05		306	Bob Wickman.	.05		411	Jose Oquendo.	.05				
202	Mark Gubicza.	.05		307	Bernie Williams.	.05		412	Vicente Palacios.	.05				
203	Bob Hamelin.	.05		308	Mark Acre.	.05		413	Geronimo Pena.	.05				
204	Dave Henderson.	.05		309	Geronimo Berroa.	.05		414	Mike Perez.	.05				
205	Felix Jose.	.05		310	Mike Bordick.	.05		415	Gerald Perry.	.05				
206	Wally Joyner.	.05		311	Dennis Eckersley.	.50		416	Ozzie Smith.	.75				
207	Jose Lind.	.05		312	Rickey Henderson.	.60		417	Bob Tewksbury.	.05				
208	Mike Macfarlane.	.05		313	Stan Javier.	.05		418	Mark Whiten.	.05				

Gold Crown Die-Cut

		NM/M
Complete Set (20):		30.00
Common Player:		.45
1	Greg Maddux	2.50
2	Fred McGriff	.45
3	Rafael Palmeiro	1.50
4	Cal Ripken Jr.	4.50
5	Jose Canseco	1.00
6	Frank Thomas	2.00
7	Albert Belle	.45
8	Manny Ramirez	2.00
9	Andres Galarraga	.45
10	Jeff Bagwell	2.00
11	Chan Ho Park	.45
12	Raul Mondesi	.45
13	Mike Piazza	3.00
14	Kirby Puckett	2.50
15	Barry Bonds	4.50
16	Ken Griffey Jr.	3.00
17	Alex Rodriguez	3.50
18	Juan Gonzalez	1.00
19	Roberto Alomar	1.00
20	Carlos Delgado	1.25

Hot Hispanics

		NM/M
Complete Set (36):		20.00

Common Player:	.25
1 Roberto Alomar	1.25
2 Moises Alou	.25
3 Wilson Alvarez	.25
4 Carlos Baerga	.25
5 Geronimo Berroa	.25
6 Jose Canseco	1.00
7 Hector Carrasco	.25
8 Wil Cordero	.25
9 Carlos Delgado	1.50
10 Damion Easley	.25
11 Tony Eusebio	.25
12 Hector Fajardo	.25
13 Andres Galarraga	.25
14 Carlos Garcia	.25
15 Chris Gomez	.25
16 Alex Gonzalez	.25
17 Juan Gonzalez	1.25
18 Luis Gonzalez	.25
19 Felix Jose	.25
20 Javier Lopez	.25
21 Luis Lopez	.25
22 Dennis Martinez	.25
23 Orlando Miller	.25
24 Raul Mondesi	.25
25 Jose Oliva	.25
26 Rafael Palmeiro	2.00
27 Yorkis Perez	.25
28 Manny Ramirez	2.50
29 Jose Rijo	.25
30 Alex Rodriguez	4.00
31 Ivan Rodriguez	2.00
32 Carlos Rodriguez	.25
33 Sammy Sosa	3.00
34 Tony Tarasco	.25
35 Ismael Valdes	.25
36 Bernie Williams	.25

1995 Pacific Mariners Memories

	NM/M
Complete Set (50):	10.00
Common Player:	.10
1 Ken Griffey Jr. Griffey slams M's to brink	.50
2 Vince Coleman Mariners clinch tie in Texas	.10
3 Luis Sojo Mariners win the West	.10
4 Randy Johnson At last, something to celebrate	.25
5 Randy Johnson Johnson stands tall	.25
6 Ken Griffey Jr. Griffey has big debut	.50
7 Edgar Martinez, Tino Martinez Tino ignites Mariners	.10
8 Edgar Martinez Mariners tie Yankee series	.10
9 Ken Griffey Jr. Griffey scores winning run	.50
10 Thunder in the Kingdome	.10
11 Series win ends years of futility	.10
12 Bob Wolcott Bob who? beats Cleveland	.10
13 Jay Buhner Buhner rocks Cleveland	.10
14 Randy Johnson Johnson salutes Kingdome crowd	.25
15 Lou Piniella Fans give their all	.10
16 Joey Cora Cora eludes tag	.10
17 Dave Niehaus Voice of M's calls winner	.10
18 Rich Amaral	.10
19 Bobby Ayala	.10
20 Tim Belcher	.10

21 Andy Benes	.10
22 Mike Blowers	.10
23 Chris Bosio	.10
24 Darren Bragg	.10
25 Jay Buhner	.25
26 Rafael Carmona	.10
27 Norm Charlton	.10
28 Vince Coleman	.10
29 Joey Cora	.10
30 Alex Diaz	.10
31 Felix Fermin	.10
32 Ken Griffey Jr.	3.00
33 Lee Guetterman	.10
34 Randy Johnson	3.00
35 Edgar Martinez	.25
36 Tino Martinez	.25
37 Jeff Nelson	.10
38 Warren Newson	.10
39 Greg Pirkl	.10
40 Arquimedez Pozo	.10
41 Bill Risley	.10
42 Alex Rodriguez (Rodriguez)	5.00
43 Luis Sojo	.10
44 Doug Strange	.10
45 Salomon Torres	.10
46 Bob Wells	.10
47 Chris Widger	.10
48 Dan Wilson	.10
49 Bob Wolcott	.10
50 Lou Piniella	.25

Marquee Prism

	NM/M
Complete Set (36):	22.50
Common Player:	.35
1 Jose Canseco	.65
2 Gregg Jefferies	.35
3 Fred McGriff	.35
4 Joe Carter	.35
5 Tim Salmon	.35
6 Wade Boggs	1.25
7 Dave Winfield	1.00
8 Bob Hamelin	.35
9 Cal Ripken Jr.	3.00
10 Don Mattingly	1.50
11 Juan Gonzalez	.50
12 Carlos Delgado	.65
13 Barry Bonds	3.00
14 Albert Belle	.35
15 Raul Mondesi	.35
16 Jeff Bagwell	1.00
17 Mike Piazza	1.50
18 Rafael Palmeiro	.75
19 Frank Thomas	1.00
20 Matt Williams	.35
21 Ken Griffey Jr.	2.00
22 Will Clark	.35
23 Bobby Bonilla	.35
24 Kenny Lofton	.35
25 Paul Molitor	1.00
26 Kirby Puckett	1.25
27 Dave Justice	.35
28 Jeff Conine	.35
29 Bret Boone	.35
30 Larry Walker	.35
31 Cecil Fielder	.35
32 Manny Ramirez	1.00
33 Javier Lopez	.35
34 Jimmy Key	.35
35 Andres Galarraga	.35
36 Tony Gwynn	1.25

ABBREVIATIONS

OPS - Overprinted "Promotional Sample"

1995 Pacific Prism

	NM/M
Complete Set (144):	65.00
Common Player:	.25
Pack (2):	.60
Wax Box (36):	12.50
1 Dave Justice	.25
2 Ryan Klesko	.25
3 Javier Lopez	.25
4 Greg Maddux	2.00
5 Fred McGriff	.25
6 Tony Tarasco	.25
7 Jeffrey Hammonds	.25
8 Mike Mussina	.75
9 Rafael Palmeiro	1.25
10 Cal Ripken Jr.	5.00
11 Lee Smith	.25
12 Roger Clemens	2.50
13 Scott Cooper	.25
14 Mike Greenwell	.25
15 Carlos Rodriguez	.25
16 Mo Vaughn	.25
17 Chili Davis	.25
18 Jim Edmonds	.25
19 Jorge Fabregas	.25
20 Bo Jackson	.35
21 Tim Salmon	.25
22 Mark Grace	.25
23 Jose Guzman	.25
24 Randy Myers	.25
25 Rey Sanchez	.25
26 Sammy Sosa	2.50
27 Wilson Alvarez	.25
28 Julio Franco	.25
29 Ozzie Guillen	.25
30 Jack McDowell	.25
31 Frank Thomas	1.50
32 Bret Boone	.25
33 Barry Larkin	.25
34 Hal Morris	.25
35 Jose Rijo	.25
36 Deion Sanders	.25
37 Carlos Baerga	.25
38 Albert Belle	.25
39 Kenny Lofton	.25
40 Dennis Martinez	.25
41 Manny Ramirez	1.50
42 Omar Vizquel	.25
43 Dante Bichette	.25
44 Marvin Freeman	.25
45 Andres Galarraga	.25
46 Mike Kingery	.25
47 Danny Bautista	.25
48 Cecil Fielder	.25
49 Travis Fryman	.25
50 Tony Phillips	.25
51 Alan Trammell	.25
52 Lou Whitaker	.25
53 Alex Arias	.25
54 Bret Barberie	.25
55 Jeff Conine	.25
56 Charles Johnson	.25
57 Gary Sheffield	.65
58 Jeff Bagwell	1.50
59 Craig Biggio	.25
60 Doug Drabek	.25
61 Tony Eusebio	.25
62 Luis Gonzalez	.25
63 David Cone	.25
64 Bob Hamelin	.25
65 Felix Jose	.25
66 Wally Joyner	.25
67 Brian McRae	.25
68 Brett Butler	.25
69 Garey Ingram	.25
70 Ramon Martinez	.25
71 Raul Mondesi	.25
72 Mike Piazza	2.50
73 Henry Rodriguez	.25
74 Ricky Bones	.25
75 Pat Listach	.25
76 Dave Nilsson	.25

77 Jose Valentin	.25
78 Rick Aguilera	.25
79 Denny Hocking	.25
80 Shane Mack	.25
81 Pedro Munoz	.25
82 Kirby Puckett	2.00
83 Dave Winfield	1.50
84 Moises Alou	.25
85 Wil Cordero	.25
86 Cliff Floyd	.25
87 Marquis Grissom	.25
88 Pedro Martinez	1.50
89 Larry Walker	.25
90 Bobby Bonilla	.25
91 Jeromy Burnitz	.25
92 John Franco	.25
93 Jeff Kent	.25
94 Jose Vizcaino	.25
95 Wade Boggs	2.00
96 Jimmy Key	.25
97 Don Mattingly	2.50
98 Paul O'Neill	.25
99 Luis Polonia	.25
100 Danny Tartabull	.25
101 Geronimo Berroa	.25
102 Rickey Henderson	1.50
103 Ruben Sierra	.25
104 Terry Steinbach	.25
105 Darren Daulton	.25
106 Mariano Duncan	.25
107 Lenny Dykstra	.25
108 Mike Lieberthal	.25
109 Tony Longmire	.25
110 Tom Marsh	.25
111 Jay Bell	.25
112 Carlos Garcia	.25
113 Orlando Merced	.25
114 Andy Van Slyke	.25
115 Derek Bell	.25
116 Tony Gwynn	2.00
117 Luis Lopez	.25
118 Bip Roberts	.25
119 Rod Beck	.25
120 Barry Bonds	5.00
121 Darryl Strawberry	.25
122 Bill Van Landingham	.25
123 Matt Williams	.25
124 Jay Buhner	.25
125 Felix Fermin	.25
126 Ken Griffey Jr.	3.00
127 Randy Johnson	1.50
128 Edgar Martinez	.25
129 Alex Rodriguez	4.00
130 Rene Arocha	.25
131 Gregg Jefferies	.25
132 Mike Perez	.25
133 Ozzie Smith	2.00
134 Jose Canseco	.65
135 Will Clark	.25
136 Juan Gonzalez	1.00
137 Ivan Rodriguez	1.25
138 Roberto Alomar	.50
139 Joe Carter	.25
140 Carlos Delgado	.75
141 Alex Gonzalez	.25
142 Juan Guzman	.25
143 Paul Molitor	1.50
144 John Olerud	.25

1995 Pacific Prism Team Logos

	NM/M
Complete Set (31):	2.00
Common Player:	.10
1 Baltimore Orioles	.10
2 Boston Red Sox	.10
3 California Angels	.10
4 Chicago White Sox	.10
5 Cleveland Indians	.10
6 Detroit Tigers	.10
7 Kansas City Royals	.10
8 Milwaukee Brewers	.10
9 Minnesota Twins	.10
10 New York Yankees	.10
11 Oakland Athletics	.10
12 Seattle Mariners	.10
13 Texas Rangers	.10
14 Toronto Blue Jays	.10
15 Atlanta Braves	.10
16 Chicago Cubs	.10
17 Cincinnati Reds	.10
18 Colorado Rockies	.10

19	Florida Marlins	.10
20	Houston Astros	.10
21	Los Angeles Dodgers	.10
22	Montreal Expos	.10
23	New York Mets	.10
24	Philadelphia Phillies	.10
25	Pittsburgh Pirates	.10
26	St. Louis Cardinals	.10
27	San Diego Padres	.10
28	San Francisco Giants	.10
1	Checklist 1-72	.05
2	Checklist 73-144	.05
---	Pacific Logo Card	.05

1996 Pacific Crown

		NM/M
Complete Set (450):		17.50
Common Player:		.05
Pack (12):		1.00
Wax Box (36):		25.00
1	Steve Avery	.05
2	Ryan Klesko	.05
3	Pedro Borbon	.05
4	Chipper Jones	1.00
5	Kent Mercker	.05
6	Greg Maddux	1.00
7	Greg McMichael	.05
8	Mark Wohlers	.05
9	Fred McGriff	.05
10	John Smoltz	.05
11	Rafael Belliard	.05
12	Mark Lemke	.05
13	Tom Glavine	.30
14	Javier Lopez	.05
15	Jeff Blauser	.05
16	Dave Justice	.05
17	Marquis Grissom	.05
18	Greg Maddux (NL Cy Young)	.50
19	Randy Myers	.05
20	Scott Servais	.05
21	Sammy Sosa	1.00
22	Kevin Foster	.05
23	Jose Hernandez	.05
24	Jim Bullinger	.05
25	Mike Perez	.05
26	Shawon Dunston	.05
27	Rey Sanchez	.05
28	Frank Castillo	.05
29	Jaime Navarro	.05
30	Brian McRae	.05
31	Mark Grace	.05
32	Roberto Rivera	.05
33	Luis Gonzalez	.05
34	Hector Carrasco	.05
35	Bret Boone	.05
36	Thomas Howard	.05
37	Hal Morris	.05
38	John Smiley	.05
39	Jeff Brantley	.05
40	Barry Larkin	.05
41	Mariano Duncan	.05
42	Xavier Hernandez	.05
43	Pete Schourek	.05
44	Reggie Sanders	.05
45	Dave Burba	.05
46	Jeff Branson	.05
47	Mark Portugal	.05
48	Ron Gant	.05
49	Benito Santiago	.05
50	Barry Larkin (NL MVP)	.05
51	Steve Reed	.05
52	Kevin Ritz	.05
53	Dante Bichette	.05
54	Darren Holmes	.05
55	Ellis Burks	.05
56	Walt Weiss	.05
57	Armando Reynoso	.05
58	Vinny Castilla	.05
59	Jason Bates	.05
60	Mike Kingery	.05
61	Bryan Rekar	.05
62	Curtis Leskanic	.05
63	Bret Saberhagen	.05
64	Andres Galarraga	.05
65	Larry Walker	.05
66	Joe Girardi	.05
67	Quilvio Veras	.05
68	Robb Nen	.05
69	Mario Diaz	.05
70	Chuck Carr	.05
71	Alex Arias	.05
72	Pat Rapp	.05
73	Rich Garces	.05
74	Kurt Abbott	.05
75	Andre Dawson	.25
76	Greg Colbrunn	.05
77	John Burkett	.05
78	Terry Pendleton	.05
79	Jesus Tavarez	.05
80	Charles Johnson	.05
81	Yorkis Perez	.05
82	Jeff Conine	.05
83	Gary Sheffield	.45
84	Brian Hunter	.05
85	Derrick May	.05
86	Greg Swindell	.05
87	Derek Bell	.05
88	Dave Veres	.05
89	Jeff Bagwell	.75
90	Todd Jones	.05
91	Orlando Miller	.05
92	Pedro A. Martinez	.05
93	Tony Eusebio	.05
94	Craig Biggio	.05
95	Shane Reynolds	.05
96	James Mouton	.05
97	Doug Drabek	.05
98	Dave Magadan	.05
99	Ricky Gutierrez	.05
100	Hideo Nomo	.50
101	Delino DeShields	.05
102	Tom Candiotti	.05
103	Mike Piazza	1.50
104	Ramon Martinez	.05
105	Pedro Astacio	.05
106	Chad Fonville	.05
107	Raul Mondesi	.05
108	Ismael Valdes	.05
109	Jose Offerman	.05
110	Todd Worrell	.05
111	Eric Karros	.05
112	Brett Butler	.05
113	Juan Castro	.05
114	Roberto Kelly	.05
115	Omar Daal	.05
116	Antonio Osuna	.05
117	Hideo Nomo (NL Rookie of Year)	.50
118	Mike Lansing	.05
119	Mel Rojas	.05
120	Sean Berry	.05
121	David Segui	.05
122	Tavo Alvarez	.05
123	Pedro Martinez	.75
124	F.P. Santangelo RC	.05
125	Rondell White	.05
126	Cliff Floyd	.05
127	Henry Rodriguez	.05
128	Tony Tarasco	.05
129	Yamil Benitez	.05
130	Carlos Perez	.05
131	Wil Cordero	.05
132	Jeff Fassero	.05
133	Moises Alou	.05
134	John Franco	.05
135	Rico Brogna	.05
136	Dave Mlicki	.05
137	Bill Pulsipher	.05
138	Jose Vizcaino	.05
139	Carl Everett	.05
140	Edgardo Alfonzo	.05
141	Bobby Jones	.05
142	Alberto Castillo	.05
143	Joe Orsulak	.05
144	Jeff Kent	.05
145	Ryan Thompson	.05
146	Jason Isringhausen	.05
147	Todd Hundley	.05
148	Alex Ochoa	.05
149	Charlie Hayes	.05
150	Michael Mimbs	.05
151	Darren Daulton	.05
152	Toby Borland	.05
153	Andy Van Slyke	.05
154	Mickey Morandini	.05
155	Sid Fernandez	.05
156	Tom Marsh	.05
157	Kevin Stocker	.05
158	Paul Quantrill	.05
159	Gregg Jefferies	.05
160	Ricky Bottalico	.05
161	Lenny Dykstra	.05
162	Mark Whiten	.05
163	Tyler Green	.05
164	Jim Eisenreich	.05
165	Heathcliff Slocumb	.05
166	Esteban Loaiza	.05
167	Rich Aude	.05
168	Jason Christiansen	.05
169	Ramon Morel	.05
170	Orlando Merced	.05
171	Paul Wagner	.05
172	Jeff King	.05
173	Jay Bell	.05
174	Jacob Brumfield	.05
175	Nelson Liriano	.05
176	Dan Miceli	.05
177	Carlos Garcia	.05
178	Denny Neagle	.05
179	Angelo Encarnacion	.05
180	Al Martin	.05
181	Midre Cummings	.05
182	Eddie Williams	.05
183	Roberto Petagine	.05
184	Tony Gwynn	1.00
185	Andy Ashby	.05
186	Melvin Nieves	.05
187	Phil Clark	.05
188	Brad Ausmus	.05
189	Bip Roberts	.05
190	Fernando Valenzuela	.05
191	Marc Newfield	.05
192	Steve Finley	.05
193	Trevor Hoffman	.05
194	Andujar Cedeno	.05
195	Jody Reed	.05
196	Ken Caminiti	.05
197	Joey Hamilton	.05
198	Tony Gwynn (NL Batting Champ)	.50
199	Shawn Barton	.05
200	Deion Sanders	.05
201	Rikkert Faneyte	.05
202	Barry Bonds	2.50
203	Matt Williams	.05
204	Jose Bautista	.05
205	Mark Leiter	.05
206	Mark Carreon	.05
207	Robby Thompson	.05
208	Terry Mulholland	.05
209	Rod Beck	.05
210	Royce Clayton	.05
211	J.R. Phillips	.05
212	Kirt Manwaring	.05
213	Glenallen Hill	.05
214	William Van Landingham	.05
215	Scott Cooper	.05
216	Bernard Gilkey	.05
217	Allen Watson	.05
218	Donovan Osborne	.05
219	Ray Lankford	.05
220	Tony Fossas	.05
221	Tom Pagnozzi	.05
222	John Mabry	.05
223	Tripp Cromer	.05
224	Mark Petkovsek	.05
225	Mike Morgan	.05
226	Ozzie Smith	1.00
227	Tom Henke	.05
228	Jose Oquendo	.05
229	Brian Jordan	.05
230	Cal Ripken Jr.	2.50
231	Scott Erickson	.05
232	Harold Baines	.05
233	Jeff Manto	.05
234	Jesse Orosco	.05
235	Jeffrey Hammonds	.05
236	Brady Anderson	.05
237	Manny Alexander	.05
238	Chris Hoiles	.05
239	Rafael Palmeiro	.60
240	Ben McDonald	.05
241	Curtis Goodwin	.05
242	Bobby Bonilla	.05
243	Mike Mussina	.60
244	Kevin Brown	.05
245	Armando Benitez	.05
246	Jose Canseco	.50
247	Erik Hanson	.05
248	Mo Vaughn	.05
249	Tim Naehring	.05
250	Vaughn Eshelman	.05
251	Mike Greenwell	.05
252	Troy O'Leary	.05
253	Tim Wakefield	.05
254	Dwayne Hosey	.05
255	John Valentin	.05
256	Rick Aguilera	.05
257	Mike MacFarlane	.05
258	Roger Clemens	1.50
259	Luis Alicea	.05
260	Mo Vaughn (AL MVP)	.05
261	Mark Langston	.05
262	Jim Edmonds	.05
263	Rod Correia	.05
264	Tim Salmon	.05
265	J.T. Snow	.05
266	Orlando Palmeiro	.05
267	Jorge Fabregas	.05
268	Jim Abbott	.05
269	Eduardo Perez	.05
270	Lee Smith	.05
271	Gary DiSarcina	.05
272	Damion Easley	.05
273	Tony Phillips	.05
274	Garret Anderson	.05
275	Chuck Finley	.05
276	Chili Davis	.05
277	Lance Johnson	.05
278	Alex Fernandez	.05
279	Robin Ventura	.05
280	Chris Snopek	.05
281	Brian Keyser	.05
282	Lyle Mouton	.05
283	Luis Andujar RC	.05
284	Tim Raines	.05
285	Larry Thomas	.05
286	Ozzie Guillen	.05
287	Frank Thomas	.75
288	Roberto Hernandez	.05
289	Dave Martinez	.05
290	Ray Durham	.05
291	Ron Karkovice	.05
292	Wilson Alvarez	.05
293	Omar Vizquel	.05
294	Eddie Murray	.75
295	Sandy Alomar	.05
296	Orel Hershiser	.05
297	Jose Mesa	.05
298	Julian Tavarez	.05
299	Dennis Martinez	.05
300	Carlos Baerga	.05
301	Manny Ramirez	.75
302	Jim Thome	.60
303	Kenny Lofton	.05
304	Tony Pena	.05
305	Alvaro Espinoza	.05
306	Paul Sorrento	.05
307	Albert Belle	.05
308	Danny Bautista	.05
309	Chris Gomez	.05
310	Jose Lima	.05
311	Phil Nevin	.05
312	Alan Trammell	.05
313	Chad Curtis	.05
314	John Flaherty	.05
315	Travis Fryman	.05
316	Todd Steverson	.05
317	Brian Bohanon	.05
318	Lou Whitaker	.05
319	Bobby Higginson	.05
320	Steve Rodriguez	.05
321	Cecil Fielder	.05
322	Felipe Lira	.05
323	Juan Samuel	.05
324	Bob Hamelin	.05
325	Tom Goodwin	.05
326	Johnny Damon	.25
327	Hipolito Pichardo	.05
328	Dilson Torres	.05
329	Kevin Appier	.05
330	Mark Gubicza	.05
331	Jon Nunnally	.05
332	Gary Gaetti	.05
333	Brent Mayne	.05
334	Brent Cookson	.05
335	Tom Gordon	.05
336	Wally Joyner	.05
337	Greg Gagne	.05
338	Fernando Vina	.05
339	Joe Oliver	.05
340	John Jaha	.05
341	Jeff Cirillo	.05
342	Pat Listach	.05
343	Dave Nilsson	.05
344	Steve Sparks	.05
345	Ricky Bones	.05
346	David Hulse	.05
347	Scott Karl	.05
348	Darryl Hamilton	.05
349	B.J. Surhoff	.05
350	Angel Miranda	.05
351	Sid Roberson	.05
352	Matt Mieske	.05
353	Jose Valentin RC	.05
354	Matt Lawton RC	.25
355	Eddie Guardado	.05
356	Brad Radke	.05
357	Pedro Munoz	.05
358	Scott Stahoviak	.05
359	Erik Schullstrom	.05
360	Pat Meares	.05
361	Marty Cordova	.05
362	Scott Leius	.05
363	Matt Walbeck	.05
364	Rich Becker	.05
365	Kirby Puckett	1.00
366	Oscar Munoz	.05
367	Chuck Knoblauch	.05
368	Marty Cordova (AL Rookie of Year)	.05
369	Bernie Williams	.05
370	Mike Stanley	.05
371	Andy Pettitte	.25
372	Jack McDowell	.05
373	Sterling Hitchcock	.05
374	David Cone	.05
375	Randy Velarde	.05

376	Don Mattingly	1.50
377	Melido Perez	.05
378	Wade Boggs	1.00
379	Ruben Sierra	.05
380	Tony Fernandez	.05
381	John Wetteland	.05
382	Mariano Rivera	.15
383	Derek Jeter	2.50
384	Paul O'Neill	.05
385	Mark McGwire	2.00
386	Scott Brosius	.05
387	Don Wengert	.05
388	Terry Steinbach	.05
389	Brent Gates	.05
390	Craig Paquette	.05
391	Mike Bordick	.05
392	Ariel Prieto	.05
393	Dennis Eckersley	.65
394	Carlos Reyes	.05
395	Todd Stottlemyre	.05
396	Rickey Henderson	.75
397	Geronimo Berroa	.05
398	Steve Ontiveros	.05
399	Mike Gallego	.05
400	Stan Javier	.05
401	Randy Johnson	.75
402	Norm Charlton	.05
403	Mike Blowers	.05
404	Tino Martinez	.05
405	Dan Wilson	.05
406	Andy Benes	.05
407	Alex Diaz	.05
408	Edgar Martinez	.05
409	Chris Bosio	.05
410	Ken Griffey Jr.	1.50
411	Luis Sojo	.05
412	Bob Wolcott	.05
413	Vince Coleman	.05
414	Rich Amaral	.05
415	Jay Buhner	.05
416	Alex Rodriguez	2.00
417	Joey Cora	.05
418	Randy Johnson (AL Cy Young)	.25
419	Edgar Martinez (AL Batting Champ)	.05
420	Ivan Rodriguez	.65
421	Mark McLemore	.05
422	Mickey Tettleton	.05
423	Juan Gonzalez	.40
424	Will Clark	.05
425	Kevin Gross	.05
426	Dean Palmer	.05
427	Kenny Rogers	.05
428	Bob Tewksbury	.05
429	Benji Gil	.05
430	Jeff Russell	.05
431	Rusty Greer	.05
432	Roger Pavlik	.05
433	Esteban Beltre	.05
434	Otis Nixon	.05
435	Paul Molitor	.75
436	Carlos Delgado	.50
437	Ed Sprague	.05
438	Juan Guzman	.05
439	Domingo Cedeno	.05
440	Pat Hentgen	.05
441	Tomas Perez	.05
442	John Olerud	.05
443	Shawn Green	.25
444	Al Leiter	.05
445	Joe Carter	.05
446	Robert Perez	.05
447	Devon White	.05
448	Tony Castillo	.05
449	Alex Gonzalez	.05
450	Roberto Alomar	.20
450p	Roberto Alomar (Unmarked promo card, "Games: 128" on back.)	1.50

Cramer's Choice

		NM/M
Complete Set (10):		150.00
Common Player:		6.00
1	Roberto Alomar	7.50
2	Wade Boggs	15.00
3	Cal Ripken Jr.	30.00
4	Greg Maddux	15.00
5	Frank Thomas	12.50
6	Tony Gwynn	15.00
7	Mike Piazza	20.00
8	Ken Griffey Jr.	25.00
9	Manny Ramirez	12.50
10	Edgar Martinez	6.00

Gold Crown Die-Cuts

		NM/M
Complete Set (36):		45.00
Common Player:		.75
1	Roberto Alomar	1.00
2	Will Clark	.75
3	Johnny Damon	1.00
4	Don Mattingly	2.50
5	Edgar Martinez	.75
6	Manny Ramirez	1.50
7	Mike Piazza	2.50
8	Quilvio Veras	.75
9	Rickey Henderson	1.50
10	Jeff Bagwell	1.50
11	Andres Galarraga	.75
12	Tim Salmon	.75
13	Ken Griffey Jr.	2.50
14	Sammy Sosa	2.00
15	Cal Ripken Jr.	4.50
16	Raul Mondesi	.75
17	Jose Canseco	1.00
18	Frank Thomas	1.50
19	Hideo Nomo	1.00
20	Wade Boggs	2.00
21	Reggie Sanders	.75
22	Carlos Baerga	.75
23	Mo Vaughn	.75
24	Ivan Rodriguez	1.25
25	Kirby Puckett	2.00
26	Albert Belle	.75
27	Vinny Castilla	.75
28	Greg Maddux	2.00
29	Dante Bichette	.75
30	Deion Sanders	.75
31	Chipper Jones	2.00
32	Cecil Fielder	.75
33	Randy Johnson	1.50
34	Mark McGwire	3.50
35	Tony Gwynn	2.00
36	Barry Bonds	4.50

Estrellas Latinas

	NM/M
Complete Set (36):	16.00
Common Player:	.25

1	Roberto Alomar	.50
2	Moises Alou	.25
3	Carlos Baerga	.25
4	Geronimo Berroa	.25
5	Ricky Bones	.25
6	Bobby Bonilla	.25
7	Jose Canseco	.65
8	Vinny Castilla	.25
9	Pedro Martinez	1.50
10	John Valentin	.25
11	Andres Galarraga	.25
12	Juan Gonzalez	.75
13	Ozzie Guillen	.25
14	Esteban Loaiza	.25
15	Javier Lopez	.25
16	Dennis Martinez	.25
17	Edgar Martinez	.25
18	Tino Martinez	.25
19	Orlando Merced	.25
20	Jose Mesa	.25
21	Raul Mondesi	.25
22	Jaime Navarro	.25
23	Rafael Palmeiro	.75
24	Carlos Perez	.25
25	Manny Ramirez	1.50
26	Alex Rodriguez	3.50
27	Ivan Rodriguez	1.25
28	David Segui	.25
29	Ruben Sierra	.25
30	Sammy Sosa	2.00
31	Julian Tavarez	.25
32	Ismael Valdes	.25
33	Fernando Valenzuela	.25
34	Quilvio Veras	.25
35	Omar Vizquel	.25
36	Bernie Williams	.25

Hometown of the Players

		NM/M
Complete Set (20):		15.00
Common Player:		.50
1	Mike Piazza	1.50
2	Greg Maddux	1.00
3	Tony Gwynn	1.00
4	Carlos Baerga	.50
5	Don Mattingly	1.50
6	Cal Ripken Jr.	2.50
7	Chipper Jones	1.00
8	Andres Galarraga	.50
9	Manny Ramirez	.75
10	Roberto Alomar	.60
11	Ken Griffey Jr.	1.50
12	Jose Canseco	.60
13	Frank Thomas	.75
14	Vinny Castilla	.50
15	Roberto Kelly	.50
16	Dennis Martinez	.50
17	Kirby Puckett	1.00
18	Raul Mondesi	.50
19	Hideo Nomo	.60
20	Edgar Martinez	.50

Milestones

		NM/M
Complete Set (10):		12.50
Common Player:		.50
1	Albert Belle	.50
2	Don Mattingly	2.25
3	Tony Gwynn	2.00
4	Jose Canseco	1.00
5	Marty Cordova	.50
6	Wade Boggs	2.00
7	Greg Maddux	2.00
8	Eddie Murray	1.50

9	Ken Griffey Jr.	2.50
10	Cal Ripken Jr.	3.00

October Moments

		NM/M
Complete Set (20):		30.00
Common Player:		.60
1	Carlos Baerga	.60
2	Albert Belle	.75
3	Dante Bichette	.60
4	Jose Canseco	1.25
5	Tom Glavine	1.00
6	Ken Griffey Jr.	5.00
7	Randy Johnson	2.50
8	Chipper Jones	3.50
9	Dave Justice	.60
10	Ryan Klesko	.60
11	Kenny Lofton	.60
12	Javier Lopez	.60
13	Greg Maddux	3.50
14	Edgar Martinez	.60
15	Don Mattingly	4.00
16	Hideo Nomo	1.25
17	Mike Piazza	4.00
18	Manny Ramirez	2.50
19	Reggie Sanders	.60
20	Jim Thome	1.50

1996 Pacific Prism

		NM/M
Complete Set (144):		50.00
Common Player:		.35
Golds:		1.5X
Pack (2):		.65
Wax Box (36):		20.00
1	Tom Glavine	.75
2	Chipper Jones	2.00

#	Player	Price
3	David Justice	.35
4	Ryan Klesko	.35
5	Javier Lopez	.35
6	Greg Maddux	2.00
7	Fred McGriff	.35
8	Frank Castillo	.35
9	Luis Gonzalez	.35
10	Mark Grace	.35
11	Brian McRae	.35
12	Jaime Navarro	.35
13	Sammy Sosa	2.00
14	Bret Boone	.35
15	Ron Gant	.35
16	Barry Larkin	.35
17	Reggie Sanders	.35
18	Benito Santiago	.35
19	Dante Bichette	.35
20	Vinny Castilla	.35
21	Andres Galarraga	.35
22	Bryan Rekar	.35
23	Roberto Alomar	1.00
23p	Roberto Alomar ("Azulejos" rather than "Los Azulejos" on back, unmarked promo card.)	1.00
24	Jeff Conine	.35
25	Andre Dawson	.50
26	Charles Johnson	.35
27	Gary Sheffield	1.00
28	Quilvio Veras	.35
29	Jeff Bagwell	1.50
30	Derek Bell	.35
31	Craig Biggio	.35
32	Tony Eusebio	.35
33	Karim Garcia	.35
34	Eric Karros	.35
35	Ramon Martinez	.35
36	Raul Mondesi	.35
37	Hideo Nomo	1.00
38	Mike Piazza	3.00
39	Ismael Valdes	.35
40	Moises Alou	.35
41	Wil Cordero	.35
42	Pedro Martinez	1.50
43	Mel Rojas	.35
44	David Segui	.35
45	Edgardo Alfonzo	.35
46	Rico Brogna	.35
47	John Franco	.35
48	Jason Isringhausen	.35
49	Jose Vizcaino	.35
50	Ricky Bottalico	.35
51	Darren Daulton	.35
52	Lenny Dykstra	.35
53	Tyler Green	.35
54	Gregg Jefferies	.35
55	Jay Bell	.35
56	Jason Christiansen	.35
57	Carlos Garcia	.35
58	Esteban Loaiza	.35
59	Orlando Merced	.35
60	Andujar Cedeno	.35
61	Tony Gwynn	2.00
62	Melvin Nieves	.35
63	Phil Plantier	.35
64	Fernando Valenzuela	.35
65	Barry Bonds	4.50
66	J.R. Phillips	.35
67	Deion Sanders	.35
68	Matt Williams	.35
69	Bernard Gilkey	.35
70	Tom Henke	.35
71	Brian Jordan	.35
72	Ozzie Smith	2.00
73	Manny Alexander	.35
74	Bobby Bonilla	.35
75	Mike Mussina	1.00
76	Rafael Palmeiro	1.00
77	Cal Ripken Jr.	4.50
78	Jose Canseco	1.00
79	Roger Clemens	2.50
80	John Valentin	.35
81	Mo Vaughn	.35
82	Tim Wakefield	.35
83	Garret Anderson	.35
84	Damion Easley	.35
85	Jim Edmonds	.35
86	Tim Salmon	.35
87	Wilson Alvarez	.35
88	Alex Fernandez	.35
89	Ozzie Guillen	.35
90	Roberto Hernandez	.35
91	Frank Thomas	1.50
92	Robin Ventura	.35
93	Carlos Baerga	.35
94	Albert Belle	.35
95	Kenny Lofton	.35
96	Dennis Martinez	.35
97	Eddie Murray	1.50
98	Manny Ramirez	1.50
99	Omar Vizquel	.35
100	Chad Curtis	.35

#	Player	Price
101	Cecil Fielder	.35
102	Felipe Lira	.35
103	Alan Trammell	.35
104	Kevin Appier	.35
105	Johnny Damon	.35
106	Gary Gaetti	.35
107	Wally Joyner	.35
108	Ricky Bones	.35
109	John Jaha	.35
110	B.J. Surhoff	.35
111	Jose Valentin	.35
112	Fernando Vina	.35
113	Marty Cordova	.35
114	Chuck Knoblauch	.35
115	Scott Leius	.35
116	Pedro Munoz	.35
117	Kirby Puckett	2.00
118	Wade Boggs	2.00
119	Don Mattingly	2.50
120	Jack McDowell	.35
121	Paul O'Neill	.35
122	Ruben Rivera	.35
123	Bernie Williams	.35
124	Geronimo Berroa	.35
125	Rickey Henderson	1.50
126	Mark McGwire	3.50
127	Terry Steinbach	.35
128	Danny Tartabull	.35
129	Jay Buhner	.35
130	Joey Cora	.35
131	Ken Griffey Jr.	3.00
132	Randy Johnson	1.50
133	Edgar Martinez	.35
134	Tino Martinez	.35
135	Will Clark	.35
136	Juan Gonzalez	.75
137	Dean Palmer	.35
138	Ivan Rodriguez	1.25
139	Mickey Tettleton	.35
140	Larry Walker	.35
141	Joe Carter	.35
142	Carlos Delgado	1.00
143	Alex Gonzalez	.35
144	Paul Molitor	1.50

Gold

		NM/M
Complete Set (144):		100.00
Common Player:		1.50
Stars:		1.5X

(See 1996 Pacific Prism for checklist and base card values.)

Fence Busters

#		NM/M
Complete Set (19):		50.00
Common Player:		1.50
1	Albert Belle	1.50
2	Dante Bichette	1.50
3	Barry Bonds	7.50
4	Jay Buhner	1.50
5	Jose Canseco	2.25
6	Ken Griffey Jr.	5.00
7	Chipper Jones	4.00
8	David Justice	1.50
9	Eric Karros	1.50
10	Edgar Martinez	1.50
11	Mark McGwire	6.00
12	Eddie Murray	3.00
13	Mike Piazza	5.00

#	Player	Price
14	Kirby Puckett	4.00
15	Cal Ripken Jr.	7.50
16	Tim Salmon	1.50
17	Sammy Sosa	4.00
18	Frank Thomas	3.00
19	Mo Vaughn	1.50

Flame Throwers

#		NM/M
Complete Set (10):		25.00
Common Player:		1.50
1	Roger Clemens	6.50
2	David Cone	1.50
3	Tom Glavine	2.50
4	Randy Johnson	4.50
5	Greg Maddux	6.00
6	Ramon Martinez	1.50
7	Jose Mesa	1.50
8	Mike Mussina	2.50
9	Hideo Nomo	3.00
10	Jose Rijo	1.50

Red Hot Stars

#		NM/M
Complete Set (20):		25.00
Common Player:		.50
1	Roberto Alomar	.75
2	Jeff Bagwell	1.50
3	Albert Belle	.50
4	Wade Boggs	2.00
5	Barry Bonds	4.00
6	Jose Canseco	1.00
7	Ken Griffey Jr.	2.50
8	Tony Gwynn	2.00
9	Randy Johnson	1.50
10	Chipper Jones	2.00
11	Greg Maddux	2.00
12	Edgar Martinez	.50
13	Don Mattingly	2.50
14	Mike Piazza	2.50
15	Kirby Puckett	2.00
16	Manny Ramirez	1.50
17	Cal Ripken Jr.	4.00
18	Tim Salmon	.50
19	Frank Thomas	1.50
20	Mo Vaughn	.50

1997 Pacific Crown

		NM/M
Complete Set (450):		30.00
Common Player:		.05
Silver Stars/RC's:		15X
Light Blue:		1X
Pack (12):		1.25
Wax Box (36):		32.50
1	Garret Anderson	.05
2	George Arias	.05
3	Chili Davis	.05
4	Gary DiSarcina	.05
5	Jim Edmonds	.15
6	Darin Erstad	.15
7	Jorge Fabregas	.05
8	Chuck Finley	.05
9	Rex Hudler	.05
10	Mark Langston	.05
11	Orlando Palmeiro	.05
12	Troy Percival	.05
13	Tim Salmon	.05
14	J.T. Snow	.05
15	Randy Velarde	.05
16	Manny Alexander	.05
17	Roberto Alomar	.25
18	Brady Anderson	.05
19	Armando Benitez	.05
20	Bobby Bonilla	.05
21	Rocky Coppinger	.05
22	Scott Erickson	.05
23	Jeffrey Hammonds	.05
24	Chris Hoiles	.05
25	Eddie Murray	.75
26	Mike Mussina	.60
27	Randy Myers	.05
28	Rafael Palmeiro	.65
29	Cal Ripken Jr.	2.50
30	B.J. Surhoff	.05
31	Tony Tarasco	.05
32	Esteban Beltre	.05
33	Darren Bragg	.05
34	Jose Canseco	.60
35	Roger Clemens	1.50
36	Wil Cordero	.05
37	Alex Delgado	.05
38	Jeff Frye	.05
39	Nomar Garciaparra	1.00
40	Tom Gordon	.05
41	Mike Greenwell	.05
42	Reggie Jefferson	.05
43	Tim Naehring	.05
44	Troy O'Leary	.05
45	Heathcliff Slocumb	.05
46	Lee Tinsley	.05
47	John Valentin	.05
48	Mo Vaughn	.05
49	Wilson Alvarez	.05
50	Harold Baines	.05
51	Ray Durham	.05
52	Alex Fernandez	.05
53	Ozzie Guillen	.05
54	Roberto Hernandez	.05
55	Ron Karkovice	.05
56	Darren Lewis	.05
57	Norberto Martin	.05
58	Dave Martinez	.05
59	Lyle Mouton	.05
60	Jose Munoz	.05
61	Tony Phillips	.05
62	Rich Sauveur	.05
63	Danny Tartabull	.05
64	Frank Thomas	.75
65	Robin Ventura	.05
66	Sandy Alomar Jr.	.05
67	Albert Belle	.05
68	Julio Franco	.05
69	Brian Giles RC	.50
70	Danny Graves	.05
71	Orel Hershiser	.05
72	Jeff Kent	.05
73	Kenny Lofton	.05
74	Dennis Martinez	.05
75	Jack McDowell	.05
76	Jose Mesa	.05
77	Charles Nagy	.05
78	Manny Ramirez	.75
79	Julian Tavarez	.05
80	Jim Thome	.60
81	Jose Vizcaino	.05
82	Omar Vizquel	.05
83	Brad Ausmus	.05
84	Kimera Bartee	.05
85	Raul Casanova	.05
86	Tony Clark	.05
87	Travis Fryman	.05
88	Bobby Higginson	.05
89	Mark Lewis	.05
90	Jose Lima	.05
91	Felipe Lira	.05
92	Phil Nevin	.05
93	Melvin Nieves	.05
94	Curtis Pride	.05
95	Ruben Sierra	.05
96	Alan Trammell	.05
97	Kevin Appier	.05

98	Tim Belcher	.05
99	Johnny Damon	.35
100	Tom Goodwin	.05
101	Bob Hamelin	.05
102	David Howard	.05
103	Jason Jacome	.05
104	Keith Lockhart	.05
105	Mike Macfarlane	.05
106	Jeff Montgomery	.05
107	Jose Offerman	.05
108	Hipolito Pichardo	.05
109	Joe Randa	.05
110	Bip Roberts	.05
111	Chris Stynes	.05
112	Mike Sweeney	.05
113	Joe Vitiello	.05
114	Jeromy Burnitz	.05
115	Chuck Carr	.05
116	Jeff Cirillo	.05
117	Mike Fetters	.05
118	David Hulse	.05
119	John Jaha	.05
120	Scott Karl	.05
121	Jesse Levis	.05
122	Mark Loretta	.05
123	Mike Matheny	.05
124	Ben McDonald	.05
125	Matt Mieske	.05
126	Angel Miranda	.05
127	Dave Nilsson	.05
128	Jose Valentin	.05
129	Fernando Vina	.05
130	Ron Villone	.05
131	Gerald Williams	.05
132	Rick Aguilera	.05
133	Rich Becker	.05
134	Ron Coomer	.05
135	Marty Cordova	.05
136	Eddie Guardado	.05
137	Denny Hocking	.05
138	Roberto Kelly	.05
139	Chuck Knoblauch	.05
140	Matt Lawton	.05
141	Pat Meares	.05
142	Paul Molitor	.75
143	Greg Myers	.05
144	Jeff Reboulet	.05
145	Scott Stahoviak	.05
146	Todd Walker	.05
147	Wade Boggs	1.00
148	David Cone	.05
149	Mariano Duncan	.05
150	Cecil Fielder	.05
151	Dwight Gooden	.05
152	Derek Jeter	2.50
153	Jim Leyritz	.05
154	Tino Martinez	.05
155	Paul O'Neill	.25
156	Andy Pettitte	.25
157	Tim Raines	.05
158	Mariano Rivera	.15
159	Ruben Rivera	.05
160	Kenny Rogers	.05
161	Darryl Strawberry	.05
162	John Wetteland	.05
163	Bernie Williams	.05
164	Tony Batista	.05
165	Geronimo Berroa	.05
166	Mike Bordick	.05
167	Scott Brosius	.05
168	Brent Gates	.05
169	Jason Giambi	.65
170	Jose Herrera	.05
171	Brian Lesher	.05
172	Damon Mashore RC	.05
173	Mark McGwire	2.00
174	Ariel Prieto	.05
175	Carlos Reyes	.05
176	Matt Stairs	.05
177	Terry Steinbach	.05
178	John Wasdin	.05
179	Ernie Young	.05
180	Rich Amaral	.05
181	Bobby Ayala	.05
182	Jay Buhner	.05
183	Rafael Carmona	.05
184	Norm Charlton	.05
185	Joey Cora	.05
186	Ken Griffey Jr.	1.50
187	Sterling Hitchcock	.05
188	Dave Hollins	.05
189	Randy Johnson	.75
190	Edgar Martinez	.05
191	Jamie Moyer	.05
192	Alex Rodriguez	2.00
193	Paul Sorrento	.05
194	Salomon Torres	.05
195	Bob Wells	.05
196	Dan Wilson	.05
197	Will Clark	.05
198	Kevin Elster	.05
199	Rene Gonzales	.05
200	Juan Gonzalez	.40
201	Rusty Greer	.05
202	Darryl Hamilton	.05
203	Mike Henneman	.05
204	Ken Hill	.05
205	Mark McLemore	.05
206	Darren Oliver	.05
207	Dean Palmer	.05
208	Roger Pavlik	.05
209	Ivan Rodriguez	.65
210	Kurt Stillwell	.05
211	Mickey Tettleton	.05
212	Bobby Witt	.05
213	Tilson Brito	.05
214	Jacob Brumfield	.05
215	Miguel Cairo	.05
216	Joe Carter	.05
217	Felipe Crespo	.05
218	Carlos Delgado	.60
219	Alex Gonzalez	.05
220	Shawn Green	.15
221	Juan Guzman	.05
222	Pat Hentgen	.05
223	Charlie O'Brien	.05
224	John Olerud	.05
225	Robert Perez	.05
226	Tomas Perez	.05
227	Juan Samuel	.05
228	Ed Sprague	.05
229	Mike Timlin	.05
230	Rafael Belliard	.05
231	Jermaine Dye	.05
232	Tom Glavine	.25
233	Marquis Grissom	.05
234	Andruw Jones	.75
235	Chipper Jones	1.00
236	David Justice	.05
237	Ryan Klesko	.05
238	Mark Lemke	.05
239	Javier Lopez	.05
240	Greg Maddux	1.00
241	Fred McGriff	.05
242	Denny Neagle	.05
243	Eddie Perez	.05
244	John Smoltz	.05
245	Mark Wohlers	.05
246	Brant Brown	.05
247	Scott Bullett	.05
248	Leo Gomez	.05
249	Luis Gonzalez	.05
250	Mark Grace	.05
251	Jose Hernandez	.05
252	Brooks Kieschnick	.05
253	Brian McRae	.05
254	Jaime Navarro	.05
255	Mike Perez	.05
256	Rey Sanchez	.05
257	Ryne Sandberg	1.00
258	Scott Servais	.05
259	Sammy Sosa	1.00
260	Pedro Valdes RC	.05
261	Turk Wendell	.05
262	Bret Boone	.05
263	Jeff Branson	.05
264	Jeff Brantley	.05
265	Dave Burba	.05
266	Hector Carrasco	.05
267	Eric Davis	.05
268	Willie Greene	.05
269	Lenny Harris	.05
270	Thomas Howard	.05
271	Barry Larkin	.05
272	Hal Morris	.05
273	Joe Oliver	.05
274	Eric Owens	.05
275	Jose Rijo	.05
276	Reggie Sanders	.05
277	Eddie Taubensee	.05
278	Jason Bates	.05
279	Dante Bichette	.05
280	Ellis Burks	.05
281	Vinny Castilla	.05
282	Andres Galarraga	.05
283	Quinton McCracken	.05
284	Jayhawk Owens	.05
285	Jeff Reed	.05
286	Bryan Rekar	.05
287	Armando Reynoso	.05
288	Kevin Ritz	.05
289	Bruce Ruffin	.05
290	John Vander Wal	.05
291	Larry Walker	.05
292	Walt Weiss	.05
293	Eric Young	.05
294	Kurt Abbott	.05
295	Alex Arias	.05
296	Miguel Batista	.05
297	Kevin Brown	.05
298	Luis Castillo	.05
299	Greg Colbrunn	.05
300	Jeff Conine	.05
301	Charles Johnson	.05
302	Al Leiter	.05
303	Robb Nen	.05
304	Joe Orsulak	.05
305	Yorkis Perez	.05
306	Edgar Renteria	.05
307	Gary Sheffield	.30
308	Jesus Tavarez	.05
309	Quilvio Veras	.05
310	Devon White	.05
311	Jeff Bagwell	.75
312	Derek Bell	.05
313	Sean Berry	.05
314	Craig Biggio	.05
315	Doug Drabek	.05
316	Tony Eusebio	.05
317	Ricky Gutierrez	.05
318	Xavier Hernandez	.05
319	Brian L. Hunter	.05
320	Darryl Kile	.05
321	Derrick May	.05
322	Orlando Miller	.05
323	James Mouton	.05
324	Bill Spiers	.05
325	Pedro Astacio	.05
326	Brett Butler	.05
327	Juan Castro	.05
328	Roger Cedeno	.05
329	Delino DeShields	.05
330	Karim Garcia	.10
331	Todd Hollandsworth	.05
332	Eric Karros	.05
333	Oreste Marrero	.05
334	Ramon Martinez	.05
335	Raul Mondesi	.05
336	Hideo Nomo	.50
337	Antonio Osuna	.05
338	Chan Ho Park	.05
339	Mike Piazza	1.50
340	Ismael Valdes	.05
341	Moises Alou	.05
342	Omar Daal	.05
343	Jeff Fassero	.05
344	Cliff Floyd	.05
345	Mark Grudzielanek	.05
346	Mike Lansing	.05
347	Pedro Martinez	.75
348	Sherman Obando	.05
349	Jose Paniagua	.05
350	Henry Rodriguez	.05
351	Mel Rojas	.05
352	F.P. Santangelo	.05
353	Dave Segui	.05
354	Dave Silvestri	.05
355	Ugueth Urbina	.05
356	Rondell White	.05
357	Edgardo Alfonzo	.05
358	Carlos Baerga	.05
359	Tim Bogar	.05
360	Rico Brogna	.05
361	Alvaro Espinoza	.05
362	Carl Everett	.05
363	John Franco	.05
364	Bernard Gilkey	.05
365	Todd Hundley	.05
366	Butch Huskey	.05
367	Jason Isringhausen	.05
368	Bobby Jones	.05
369	Lance Johnson	.05
370	Brent Mayne	.05
371	Alex Ochoa	.05
372	Rey Ordonez	.05
373	Ron Blazier	.05
374	Ricky Bottalico	.05
375	David Doster	.05
376	Lenny Dykstra	.05
377	Jim Eisenreich	.05
378	Bobby Estalella	.05
379	Gregg Jefferies	.05
380	Kevin Jordan	.05
381	Ricardo Jordan	.05
382	Mickey Morandini	.05
383	Ricky Otero	.05
384	Benito Santiago	.05
385	Gene Schall	.05
386	Curt Schilling	.25
387	Kevin Sefcik	.05
388	Kevin Stocker	.05
389	Jermaine Allensworth	.05
390	Jay Bell	.05
391	Jason Christiansen	.05
392	Francisco Cordova	.05
393	Mark Johnson	.05
394	Jason Kendall	.05
395	Jeff King	.05
396	Jon Lieber	.05
397	Nelson Liriano	.05
398	Esteban Loaiza	.05
399	Al Martin	.05
400	Orlando Merced	.05
401	Ramon Morel	.05
402	Luis Alicea	.05
403	Alan Benes	.05
404	Andy Benes	.05
405	Terry Bradshaw	.05
406	Royce Clayton	.05
407	Dennis Eckersley	.65
408	Gary Gaetti	.05
409	Mike Gallego	.05
410	Ron Gant	.05
411	Brian Jordan	.05
412	Ray Lankford	.05
413	John Mabry	.05
414	Willie McGee	.05
415	Tom Pagnozzi	.05
416	Ozzie Smith	1.00
417	Todd Stottlemyre	.05
418	Mark Sweeney	.05
419	Andy Ashby	.05
420	Ken Caminiti	.05
421	Archi Cianfrocco	.05
422	Steve Finley	.05
423	Chris Gomez	.05
424	Tony Gwynn	1.00
425	Joey Hamilton	.05
426	Rickey Henderson	.75
427	Trevor Hoffman	.05
428	Brian Johnson	.05
429	Wally Joyner	.05
430	Scott Livingstone	.05
431	Jody Reed	.05
432	Craig Shipley	.05
433	Fernando Valenzuela	.05
434	Greg Vaughn	.05
435	Rich Aurilia	.05
436	Kim Batiste	.05
437	Jose Bautista	.05
438	Rod Beck	.05
439	Marvin Benard	.05
440	Barry Bonds	2.50
441	Shawon Dunston	.05
442	Shawn Estes	.05
443	Osvaldo Fernandez	.05
444	Stan Javier	.05
445	David McCarty	.05
446	Bill Mueller RC	.15
447	Steve Scarsone	.05
448	Robby Thompson	.05
449	Rick Wilkins	.05
450	Matt Williams	.05

Light Blue

	NM/M
Complete Set (450):	60.00
Common Player:	.25
Stars:	1X

(See 1997 Pacific Crown for checklist andbase card values.)

Silver

	NM/M
Common Player:	1.00
Stars/Rookies:	12X

(See 1997 Pacific Crown for checklist andbase card values.)

Card-Supials

	NM/M
Complete Set (72):	80.00
Complete Large Set (36):	60.00
Complete Small Set (36):	45.00
Common Large:	.75
Small Cards:	75%
1 Roberto Alomar	1.00
2 Brady Anderson	.75
3 Eddie Murray	2.00
4 Cal Ripken Jr.	5.00
5 Jose Canseco	1.00

6	Mo Vaughn	.75
7	Frank Thomas	2.00
8	Albert Belle	.75
9	Omar Vizquel	.75
10	Chuck Knoblauch	.75
11	Paul Molitor	2.00
12	Wade Boggs	2.50
13	Derek Jeter	5.00
14	Andy Pettitte	1.00
15	Mark McGwire	3.50
16	Jay Buhner	.75
17	Ken Griffey Jr.	3.00
18	Alex Rodriguez	3.50
19	Juan Gonzalez	1.00
20	Ivan Rodriguez	1.50
21	Andruw Jones	2.00
22	Chipper Jones	2.50
23	Ryan Klesko	.75
24	Greg Maddux	2.50
25	Ryne Sandberg	2.50
26	Andres Galarraga	.75
27	Gary Sheffield	1.00
28	Jeff Bagwell	2.00
29	Todd Hollandsworth	.75
30	Hideo Nomo	1.00
31	Mike Piazza	3.00
32	Todd Hundley	.75
33	Dennis Eckersley	1.50
34	Ken Caminiti	.75
35	Tony Gwynn	2.50
36	Barry Bonds	5.00

Cramer's Choice Awards

		NM/M
Complete Set (10):		75.00
Common Player:		4.50
1	Roberto Alomar	5.00
2	Frank Thomas	9.00
3	Albert Belle	4.50
4	Andy Pettitte	4.50
5	Ken Griffey Jr.	17.50
6	Alex Rodriguez	25.00
7	Chipper Jones	12.00
8	John Smoltz	4.50
9	Mike Piazza	15.00
10	Tony Gwynn	12.00

Fireworks Die-Cuts

		NM/M
Complete Set (20):		40.00
Common Player:		.75
1	Roberto Alomar	1.00
2	Brady Anderson	.75
3	Eddie Murray	2.50
4	Cal Ripken Jr.	7.50
5	Frank Thomas	2.50
6	Albert Belle	.75
7	Derek Jeter	7.50
8	Andy Pettitte	1.00

9	Bernie Williams	.75
10	Mark McGwire	6.50
11	Ken Griffey Jr.	5.00
12	Alex Rodriguez	6.50
13	Juan Gonzalez	1.25
14	Andruw Jones	2.50
15	Chipper Jones	3.50
16	Hideo Nomo	1.25
17	Mike Piazza	5.00
18	Henry Rodriguez	.75
19	Tony Gwynn	3.50
20	Barry Bonds	7.50

Gold Crown Die-Cuts

		NM/M
Complete Set (36):		65.00
Common Player:		1.00
1	Roberto Alomar	1.25
2	Brady Anderson	1.00
3	Mike Mussina	1.50
4	Eddie Murray	2.75
5	Cal Ripken Jr.	8.50
6	Jose Canseco	2.00
7	Frank Thomas	2.75
8	Albert Belle	1.00
9	Omar Vizquel	1.00
10	Wade Boggs	3.50
11	Derek Jeter	8.50
12	Andy Pettitte	1.25
13	Mariano Rivera	1.25
14	Bernie Williams	1.00
15	Mark McGwire	6.50
16	Ken Griffey Jr.	5.00
17	Edgar Martinez	1.00
18	Alex Rodriquez	6.50
19	Juan Gonzalez	1.50
20	Ivan Rodriguez	2.50
21	Andruw Jones	2.75
22	Chipper Jones	3.50
23	Ryan Klesko	1.00
24	John Smoltz	1.00
25	Ryne Sandberg	3.50
26	Andres Galarraga	1.00
27	Edgar Renteria	1.00
28	Jeff Bagwell	2.75
29	Todd Hollandsworth	1.00
30	Hideo Nomo	1.50
31	Mike Piazza	5.00
32	Todd Hundley	1.00
33	Brian Jordan	1.00
34	Ken Caminiti	1.00
35	Tony Gwynn	3.50
36	Barry Bonds	8.50

Latinos of the Major Leagues

		NM/M
Complete Set (36):		45.00
Common Player:		1.00
1	George Arias	1.00

2	Roberto Alomar	1.50
3	Rafael Palmeiro	2.50
4	Bobby Bonilla	1.00
5	Jose Canseco	2.00
6	Wilson Alvarez	1.00
7	Dave Martinez	1.00
8	Julio Franco	1.00
9	Manny Ramirez	3.00
10	Omar Vizquel	1.00
11	Marty Cordova	1.00
12	Roberto Kelly	1.00
13	Tino Martinez	1.00
14	Mariano Rivera	1.50
15	Ruben Rivera	1.00
16	Bernie Williams	1.00
17	Geronimo Berroa	1.00
18	Joey Cora	1.00
19	Edgar Martinez	1.00
20	Alex Rodriguez	6.00
21	Juan Gonzalez	2.00
22	Ivan Rodriguez	2.50
23	Andruw Jones	3.00
24	Javier Lopez	1.00
25	Sammy Sosa	4.50
26	Vinny Castilla	1.00
27	Andres Galarraga	1.00
28	Ramon Martinez	1.00
29	Raul Mondesi	1.00
30	Ismael Valdes	1.00
31	Pedro Martinez	3.00
32	Henry Rodriguez	1.00
33	Carlos Baerga	1.00
34	Rey Ordonez	1.00
35	Fernando Valenzuela	1.00
36	Osvaldo Fernandez	1.00

Triple Crown Die-Cuts

		NM/M
Complete Set (20):		75.00
Common Player:		2.00
1	Brady Anderson	2.00
2	Rafael Palmeiro	4.00
3	Mo Vaughn	2.00
4	Frank Thomas	5.00
5	Albert Belle	2.00
6	Jim Thome	4.00
7	Cecil Fielder	2.00
8	Mark McGwire	10.00
9	Ken Griffey Jr.	7.50
10	Alex Rodriguez	10.00
11	Juan Gonzalez	3.00
12	Andruw Jones	5.00
13	Chipper Jones	6.00
14	Dante Bichette	2.00
15	Ellis Burks	2.00
16	Andres Galarraga	2.00
17	Jeff Bagwell	5.00
18	Mike Piazza	7.50
19	Ken Caminiti	2.00
20	Barry Bonds	12.50

1997 Pacific Invincible

		NM/M
Complete Set (150):		30.00
Common Player:		.25
Light Blues:		1X
Platinums:		2X
Pack (3):		1.00
Wax Box (36):		25.00
1	Chili Davis	.25
2	Jim Edmonds	.25

3	Darin Erstad	.50
4	Orlando Palmeiro	.25
5	Tim Salmon	.25
6	J.T. Snow	.25
7	Roberto Alomar	.50
8	Brady Anderson	.25
9	Eddie Murray	1.50
10	Mike Mussina	1.00
11	Rafael Palmeiro	1.25
12	Cal Ripken Jr.	4.00
13	Jose Canseco	1.00
14	Roger Clemens	2.50
15	Nomar Garciaparra	2.00
16	Reggie Jefferson	.25
17	Mo Vaughn	.25
18	Wilson Alvarez	.25
19	Harold Baines	.25
20	Alex Fernandez	.25
21	Danny Tartabull	.25
22	Frank Thomas	1.50
23	Robin Ventura	.25
24	Sandy Alomar Jr.	.25
25	Albert Belle	.25
26	Kenny Lofton	.75
27	Jim Thome	.75
28	Omar Vizquel	.25
29	Raul Casanova	.25
30	Tony Clark	.25
31	Travis Fryman	.25
32	Bobby Higginson	.25
33	Melvin Nieves	.25
34	Justin Thompson	.25
35	Johnny Damon	.50
36	Tom Goodwin	.25
37	Jeff Montgomery	.25
38	Jose Offerman	.25
39	John Jaha	.25
40	Jeff Cirillo	.25
41	Dave Nilsson	.25
42	Jose Valentin	.25
43	Fernando Vina	.25
44	Marty Cordova	.25
45	Roberto Kelly	.25
46	Chuck Knoblauch	.25
47	Paul Molitor	1.50
48	Todd Walker	.25
49	Wade Boggs	2.00
50	Cecil Fielder	.25
51	Derek Jeter	4.00
52	Tino Martinez	.25
53	Andy Pettitte	.40
54	Mariano Rivera	.40
55	Bernie Williams	.25
56	Tony Batista	.25
57	Geronimo Berroa	.25
58	Jason Giambi	.75
59	Mark McGwire	3.00
60	Terry Steinbach	.25
61	Jay Buhner	.25
62	Joey Cora	.25
63	Ken Griffey Jr.	2.50
64	Edgar Martinez	.25
65	Alex Rodriguez	3.00
66	Paul Sorrento	.25
67	Will Clark	.25
68	Juan Gonzalez	.75
69	Rusty Greer	.25
70	Dean Palmer	.25
71	Ivan Rodriguez	1.25
72	Joe Carter	.25
73	Carlos Delgado	.75
74	Juan Guzman	.25
75	Pat Hentgen	.25
76	Ed Sprague	.25
77	Jermaine Dye	.25
78	Andruw Jones	1.50
79	Chipper Jones	2.00
80	Ryan Klesko	.25
81	Javier Lopez	.25
82	Greg Maddux	2.00
83	John Smoltz	.25
84	Mark Grace	.25
85	Luis Gonzalez	.25

86	Brooks Kieschnick	.25
87	Jaime Navarro	.25
88	Ryne Sandberg	2.00
89	Sammy Sosa	2.00
90	Bret Boone	.25
91	Jeff Brantley	.25
92	Eric Davis	.25
93	Barry Larkin	.25
94	Reggie Sanders	.25
95	Ellis Burks	.25
96	Dante Bichette	.25
97	Vinny Castilla	.25
98	Andres Galarraga	.25
99	Eric Young	.25
100	Kevin Brown	.25
101	Jeff Conine	.25
102	Charles Johnson	.25
103	Edgar Renteria	.25
104	Gary Sheffield	.75
105	Jeff Bagwell	1.50
106	Derek Bell	.25
107	Sean Berry	.25
108	Craig Biggio	.25
109	Shane Reynolds	.25
110	Karim Garcia	.25
111	Todd Hollandsworth	.25
112	Ramon Martinez	.25
113	Raul Mondesi	.25
114	Hideo Nomo	.75
115	Mike Piazza	2.50
116	Ismael Valdes	.25
117	Moises Alou	.25
118	Mark Grudzielanek	.25
119	Pedro Martinez	1.50
120	Henry Rodriguez	.25
121	F.P. Santangelo	.25
122	Carlos Baerga	.25
123	Bernard Gilkey	.25
124	Todd Hundley	.25
125	Lance Johnson	.25
126	Alex Ochoa	.25
127	Rey Ordonez	.25
128	Lenny Dykstra	.25
129	Gregg Jefferies	.25
130	Ricky Otero	.25
131	Benito Santiago	.25
132	Jermaine Allensworth	.25
133	Francisco Cordova	.25
134	Carlos Garcia	.25
135	Jason Kendall	.25
136	Al Martin	.25
137	Dennis Eckersley	1.25
138	Ron Gant	.25
139	Brian Jordan	.25
140	John Mabry	.25
141	Ozzie Smith	2.00
142	Ken Caminiti	.25
143	Steve Finley	.25
144	Tony Gwynn	2.00
145	Wally Joyner	.25
146	Fernando Valenzuela	.25
147	Barry Bonds	4.00
148	Jacob Cruz	.25
149	Osvaldo Fernandez	.25
150	Matt Williams	.25

Gate Attractions

		NM/M
Complete Set (32):		80.00
Common Player:		1.00
1	Roberto Alomar	1.00
2	Brady Anderson	1.00
3	Cal Ripken Jr.	8.00
4	Frank Thomas	2.50
5	Kenny Lofton	1.00
6	Omar Vizquel	1.00
7	Paul Molitor	2.50
8	Wade Boggs	3.00
9	Derek Jeter	8.00
10	Andy Pettitte	1.50
11	Bernie Williams	1.00

12	Geronimo Berroa	1.00
13	Mark McGwire	6.00
14	Ken Griffey Jr.	4.50
15	Alex Rodriguez	6.00
16	Juan Gonzalez	1.50
17	Andruw Jones	2.50
18	Chipper Jones	3.00
19	Greg Maddux	3.00
20	Ryne Sandberg	3.00
21	Sammy Sosa	3.00
22	Andres Galarraga	1.00
23	Jeff Bagwell	2.50
24	Todd Hollandsworth	1.00
25	Hideo Nomo	1.50
26	Mike Piazza	4.50
27	Todd Hundley	1.00
28	Lance Johnson	1.00
29	Ozzie Smith	3.00
30	Ken Caminiti	1.00
31	Tony Gwynn	3.00
32	Barry Bonds	8.00

Sizzling Lumber

		NM/M
Complete Set (36):		50.00
Common Player:		
1A	Cal Ripken Jr.	6.50
1B	Rafael Palmeiro	2.50
1C	Roberto Alomar	1.00
2A	Frank Thomas	3.00
2B	Robin Ventura	.50
2C	Harold Baines	.50
3A	Albert Belle	.50
3B	Manny Ramirez	3.00
3C	Kenny Lofton	.50
4A	Derek Jeter	6.50
4B	Bernie Williams	.50
4C	Wade Boggs	3.50
5A	Mark McGwire	5.00
5B	Jason Giambi	2.00
5C	Geronimo Berroa	.50
6A	Ken Griffey Jr.	4.00
6B	Alex Rodriguez	5.00
6C	Jay Buhner	.50
7A	Juan Gonzalez	1.50
7B	Dean Palmer	.50
7C	Ivan Rodriguez	2.50
8A	Ryan Klesko	.50
8B	Chipper Jones	3.50
8C	Andruw Jones	3.00
9A	Dante Bichette	.50
9B	Andres Galarraga	.50
9C	Vinny Castilla	.50
10A	Jeff Bagwell	3.00
10B	Craig Biggio	.50
10C	Derek Bell	.50
11A	Mike Piazza	4.00
11B	Raul Mondesi	.50
11C	Karim Garcia	.50
12A	Tony Gwynn	3.50
12B	Ken Caminiti	.50
12C	Greg Vaughn	.50

Sluggers & Hurlers

		NM/M
Complete Set (24):		80.00
Common Player:		2.00
SH-1a	Cal Ripken Jr.	10.00
SH-1b	Mike Mussina	2.50
SH-2a	Jose Canseco	2.50
SH-2b	Roger Clemens	6.00
SH-3a	Frank Thomas	3.50
SH-3b	Wilson Alvarez	2.00
SH-4a	Kenny Lofton	2.00
SH-4b	Orel Hershiser	2.00
SH-5a	Derek Jeter	10.00
SH-5b	Andy Pettitte	2.00
SH-6a	Ken Griffey Jr.	6.00
SH-6b	Randy Johnson	3.50
SH-7a	Alex Rodriguez	7.50

SH-7b	Jamie Moyer	2.00
SH-8a	Andruw Jones	3.50
SH-8b	Greg Maddux	4.50
SH-9a	Chipper Jones	4.50
SH-9b	John Smoltz	2.00
SH-10a	Jeff Bagwell	3.50
SH-10b	Shane Reynolds	2.00
SH-11a	Mike Piazza	6.00
SH-11b	Hideo Nomo	2.50
SH-12a	Tony Gwynn	4.50
SH-12b	Fernando Valenzuela	2.00

Gems of the Diamond

		NM/M
Complete Set (220):		20.00
Common Player:		.10
1	Jim Abbott	.10
2	Shawn Boskie	.10
3	Gary DiSarcina	.10
4	Jim Edmonds	.10
5	Todd Greene	.10
6	Jack Howell	.10
7	Jeff Schmidt	.10
8	Shad Williams	.10
9	Roberto Alomar	.35
10	Cesar Devarez	.10
11	Alan Mills	.10
12	Eddie Murray	.75
13	Jesse Orosco	.10
14	Arthur Rhodes	.10
15	Bill Ripken	.10
16	Cal Ripken Jr.	2.50
17	Mark Smith	.10
18	Roger Clemens	1.50
19	Vaughn Eshelman	.10
20	Rich Garces	.10
21	Bill Haselman	.10
22	Dwayne Hosey	.10
23	Mike Maddux	.10
24	Jose Malave	.10
25	Aaron Sele	.10
26	James Baldwin	.10
27	Pat Borders	.10
28	Mike Cameron	.10
29	Tony Castillo	.10
30	Domingo Cedeno	.10
31	Greg Norton	.10
32	Frank Thomas	.75
33	Albert Belle	.10
34	Einar Diaz	.10
35	Alan Embree	.10
36	Albie Lopez	.10
37	Chad Ogea	.10
38	Tony Pena	.10
39	Joe Roa	.10
40	Fausto Cruz	.10
41	Joey Eischen	.10
42	Travis Fryman	.10

43	Mike Myers	.10
44	A.J. Sager	.10
45	Duane Singleton	.10
46	Justin Thompson	.10
47	Jeff Granger	.10
48	Les Norman	.10
49	Jon Nunnally	.10
50	Craig Paquette	.10
51	Michael Tucker	.10
52	Julio Valera	.10
53	Kevin Young	.10
54	Cal Eldred	.10
55	Ramon Garcia	.10
56	Marc Newfield	.10
57	Al Reyes	.10
58	Tim Unroe	.10
59	Tim Vanegmond	.10
60	Turner Ward	.10
61	Bob Wickman	.10
62	Chuck Knoblauch	.10
63	Paul Molitor	.75
64	Kirby Puckett	1.00
65	Tom Quinlan	.10
66	Rich Robertson	.10
67	Dave Stevens	.10
68	Matt Walbeck	.10
69	Wade Boggs	1.00
70	Tony Fernandez	.10
71	Andy Fox	.10
72	Joe Girardi	.10
73	Charlie Hayes	.10
74	Pat Kelly	.10
75	Jeff Nelson	.10
76	Melido Perez	.10
77	Mark Acre	.10
78	Allen Battle	.10
79	Rafael Bournigal	.10
80	Mark McGwire	2.00
81	Pedro Munoz	.10
82	Scott Spiezio	.10
83	Don Wengert	.10
84	Steve Wojciechowski	.10
85	Alex Diaz	.10
86	Ken Griffey Jr.	1.50
87	Raul Ibanez	.10
88	Mike Jackson	.10
89	John Marzano	.10
90	Greg McCarthy	.10
91	Alex Rodriguez	2.00
92	Andy Sheets	.10
93	Makoto Suzuki	.10
94	Benji Gil	.10
95	Juan Gonzalez	.40
96	Kevin Gross	.10
97	Gil Heredia	.10
98	Luis Ortiz	.10
99	Jeff Russell	.10
100	Dave Valle	.10
101	Marty Janzen	.10
102	Sandy Martinez	.10
103	Julio Mosquera	.10
104	Otis Nixon	.10
105	Paul Spoljaric	.10
106	Shannon Stewart	.10
107	Woody Williams	.10
108	Steve Avery	.10
109	Mike Bielecki	.10
110	Pedro Borbon	.10
111	Ed Giovanola	.10
112	Chipper Jones	1.00
113	Greg Maddux	1.00
114	Mike Mordecai	.10
115	Terrell Wade	.10
116	Terry Adams	.10
117	Brian Dorsett	.10
118	Doug Glanville	.10
119	Tyler Houston	.10
120	Robin Jennings	.10
121	Ryne Sandberg	1.00
122	Terry Shumpert	.10
123	Amaury Telemaco	.10
124	Steve Trachsel	.10
125	Curtis Goodwin	.10
126	Mike Kelly	.10
127	Chad Mottola	.10
128	Mark Portugal	.10
129	Roger Salkeld	.10
130	John Smiley	.10
131	Lee Smith	.10
132	Roger Bailey	.10
133	Andres Galarraga	.10
134	Darren Holmes	.10
135	Curtis Leskanic	.10
136	Mike Munoz	.10
137	Jeff Reed	.10
138	Mark Thompson	.10
139	Jamey Wright	.10
140	Andre Dawson	.25
141	Craig Grebeck	.10
142	Matt Mantei	.10
143	Billy McMillon	.10
144	Kurt Miller	.10
145	Ralph Milliard	.10
146	Bob Natal	.10

147	Joe Siddall	.10
148	Bob Abreu	.25
149	Doug Brocail	.10
150	Danny Darwin	.10
151	Mike Hampton	.10
152	Todd Jones	.10
153	Kirt Manwaring	.10
154	Alvin Morman	.10
155	Billy Ashley	.10
156	Tom Candiotti	.10
157	Darren Dreifort	.10
158	Greg Gagne	.10
159	Wilton Guerrero	.10
160	Hideo Nomo	.40
161	Mike Piazza	1.50
162	Tom Prince	.10
163	Todd Worrell	.10
164	Moises Alou	.10
165	Shane Andrews	.10
166	Derek Aucoin	.10
167	Raul Chavez	.10
168	Darrin Fletcher	.10
169	Mark Leiter	.10
170	Henry Rodriguez	.10
171	Dave Veres	.10
172	Paul Byrd	.10
173	Alberto Castillo	.10
174	Mark Clark	.10
175	Rey Ordonez	.10
176	Roberto Petagine	.10
177	Andy Tomberlin	.10
178	Derek Wallace	.10
179	Paul Wilson	.10
180	Ruben Amaro Jr.	.10
181	Toby Borland	.10
182	Rich Hunter	.10
183	Tony Longmire	.10
184	Wendell Magee Jr.	.10
185	Bobby Munoz	.10
186	Scott Rolen	.60
187	Mike Williams	.10
188	Trey Beamon	.10
189	Jason Christiansen	.10
190	Elmer Dessens	.10
191	Angelo Encarnacion	.10
192	Carlos Garcia	.10
193	Mike Kingery	.10
194	Chris Peters	.10
195	Tony Womack	.10
196	Brian Barber	.10
197	David Bell	.10
198	Tony Fossas	.10
199	Rick Honeycutt	.10
200	T.J. Mathews	.10
201	Miguel Mejia	.10
202	Donovan Osborne	.10
203	Ozzie Smith	1.00
204	Andres Berumen	.10
205	Ken Caminiti	.10
206	Chris Gwynn	.10
207	Tony Gwynn	1.00
208	Rickey Henderson	.75
209	Scott Sanders	.10
210	Jason Thompson	.10
211	Fernando Valenzuela	.10
212	Tim Worrell	.10
213	Barry Bonds	2.50
214	Jay Canizaro	.10
215	Doug Creek	.10
216	Jacob Cruz	.10
217	Glenallen Hill	.10
218	Tom Lampkin	.10
219	Jim Poole	.10
220	Desi Wilson	.10

1998 Pacific

	NM/M
Complete Set (450):	40.00
Common Player:	.05
Silvers:	3X
Inserted 1:1 H	
Reds:	6X
Inserted 1:1 R	

Platinum Blues:		15X
Inserted 1:73		
Pack (12):		1.00
Wax Box (36):		20.00
1	Luis Alicea	.05
2	Garret Anderson	.05
3	Jason Dickson	.05
4	Gary DiSarcina	.05
5	Jim Edmonds	.05
6	Darin Erstad	.15
7	Chuck Finley	.05
8	Shigetosi Hasegawa	.05
9	Rickey Henderson	.75
10	Dave Hollins	.05
11	Mark Langston	.05
12	Orlando Palmeiro	.05
13	Troy Percival	.05
14	Tony Phillips	.05
15	Tim Salmon	.05
16	Allen Watson	.05
17	Roberto Alomar	.25
18	Brady Anderson	.05
19	Harold Baines	.05
20	Armando Benitez	.05
21	Geronimo Berroa	.05
22	Mike Bordick	.05
23	Eric Davis	.05
24	Scott Erickson	.05
25	Chris Hoiles	.05
26	Jimmy Key	.05
27	Aaron Ledesma	.05
28	Mike Mussina	.50
29	Randy Myers	.05
30	Jesse Orosco	.05
31	Rafael Palmeiro	.65
32	Jeff Reboulet	.05
33	Cal Ripken Jr.	2.00
34	B.J. Surhoff	.05
35	Steve Avery	.05
36	Darren Bragg	.05
37	Wil Cordero	.05
38	Jeff Frye	.05
39	Nomar Garciaparra	1.00
40	Tom Gordon	.05
41	Bill Haselman	.05
42	Scott Hatteberg	.05
43	Butch Henry	.05
44	Reggie Jefferson	.05
45	Tim Naehring	.05
46	Troy O'Leary	.05
47	Jeff Suppan	.05
48	John Valentin	.05
49	Mo Vaughn	.05
50	Tim Wakefield	.05
51	James Baldwin	.05
52	Albert Belle	.05
53	Tony Castillo	.05
54	Doug Drabek	.05
55	Ray Durham	.05
56	Jorge Fabregas	.05
57	Ozzie Guillen	.05
58	Matt Karchner	.05
59	Norberto Martin	.05
60	Dave Martinez	.05
61	Lyle Mouton	.05
62	Jaime Navarro	.05
63	Frank Thomas	.75
64	Mario Valdez	.05
65	Robin Ventura	.05
66	Sandy Alomar Jr.	.05
67	Paul Assenmacher	.05
68	Tony Fernandez	.05
69	Brian Giles	.05
70	Marquis Grissom	.05
71	Orel Hershiser	.05
72	Mike Jackson	.05
73	David Justice	.05
74	Albie Lopez	.05
75	Jose Mesa	.05
76	Charles Nagy	.05
77	Chad Ogea	.05
78	Manny Ramirez	.75
79	Jim Thome	.60
80	Omar Vizquel	.05
81	Matt Williams	.05
82	Jaret Wright	.05
83	Willie Blair	.05
84	Raul Casanova	.05
85	Tony Clark	.05
86	Deivi Cruz	.05
87	Damion Easley	.05
88	Travis Fryman	.05
89	Bobby Higginson	.05
90	Brian Hunter	.05
91	Todd Jones	.05
92	Dan Miceli	.05
93	Brian Moehler	.05
94	Melvin Nieves	.05
95	Jody Reed	.05
96	Justin Thompson	.05
97	Bubba Trammell	.05
98	Kevin Appier	.05
99	Jay Bell	.05
100	Yamil Benitez	.05

101	Johnny Damon	.35
102	Chili Davis	.05
103	Jermaine Dye	.05
104	Jed Hansen	.05
105	Jeff King	.05
106	Mike Macfarlane	.05
107	Felix Martinez	.05
108	Jeff Montgomery	.05
109	Jose Offerman	.05
110	Dean Palmer	.05
111	Hipolito Pichardo	.05
112	Jose Rosado	.05
113	Jeromy Burnitz	.05
114	Jeff Cirillo	.05
115	Cal Eldred	.05
116	John Jaha	.05
117	Doug Jones	.05
118	Scott Karl	.05
119	Jesse Levis	.05
120	Mark Loretta	.05
121	Ben McDonald	.05
122	Jose Mercedes	.05
123	Matt Mieske	.05
124	Dave Nilsson	.05
125	Jose Valentin	.05
126	Fernando Vina	.05
127	Gerald Williams	.05
128	Rick Aguilera	.05
129	Rich Becker	.05
130	Ron Coomer	.05
131	Marty Cordova	.05
132	Eddie Guardado	.05
133	LaTroy Hawkins	.05
134	Denny Hocking	.05
135	Chuck Knoblauch	.05
136	Matt Lawton	.05
137	Pat Meares	.05
138	Paul Molitor	.75
139	David Ortiz	.50
140	Brad Radke	.05
141	Terry Steinbach	.05
142	Bob Tewksbury	.05
143	Javier Valentin	.05
144	Wade Boggs	1.00
145	David Cone	.05
146	Chad Curtis	.05
147	Cecil Fielder	.05
148	Joe Girardi	.05
149	Dwight Gooden	.05
150	Hideki Irabu	.05
151	Derek Jeter	2.00
152	Tino Martinez	.05
153	Ramiro Mendoza	.05
154	Paul O'Neill	.05
155	Andy Pettitte	.20
156	Jorge Posada	.05
157	Mariano Rivera	.15
158	Rey Sanchez	.05
159	Luis Sojo	.05
160	David Wells	.05
161	Bernie Williams	.05
162	Rafael Bournigal	.05
163	Scott Brosius	.05
164	Jose Canseco	.50
165	Jason Giambi	.60
166	Ben Grieve	.05
167	Dave Magadan	.05
168	Brent Mayne	.05
169	Jason McDonald	.05
170	Izzy Molina	.05
171	Ariel Prieto	.05
172	Carlos Reyes	.05
173	Scott Spiezio	.05
174	Matt Stairs	.05
175	Bill Taylor	.05
176	Dave Telgheder	.05
177	Steve Wojciechowski	.05
178	Rich Amaral	.05
179	Bobby Ayala	.05
180	Jay Buhner	.05
181	Rafael Carmona	.05
182	Ken Cloude	.05
183	Joey Cora	.05
184	Russ Davis	.05
185	Jeff Fassero	.05
186	Ken Griffey Jr.	1.25
187	Raul Ibanez	.05
188	Randy Johnson	.75
189	Roberto Kelly	.05
190	Edgar Martinez	.05
191	Jamie Moyer	.05
192	Omar Olivares	.05
193	Alex Rodriguez	1.50
194	Heathcliff Slocumb	.05
195	Paul Sorrento	.05
196	Dan Wilson	.05
197	Scott Bailes	.05
198	John Burkett	.05
199	Domingo Cedeno	.05
200	Will Clark	.05
201	Hanley Frias RC	.05
202	Juan Gonzalez	.40
203	Tom Goodwin	.05
204	Rusty Greer	.05

205	Wilson Heredia	.05
206	Darren Oliver	.05
207	Billy Ripken	.05
208	Ivan Rodriguez	.65
209	Lee Stevens	.05
210	Fernando Tatis	.05
211	John Wetteland	.05
212	Bobby Witt	.05
213	Jacob Brumfield	.05
214	Joe Carter	.05
215	Roger Clemens	1.25
216	Felipe Crespo	.05
217	Jose Cruz Jr.	.05
218	Carlos Delgado	.50
219	Mariano Duncan	.05
220	Carlos Garcia	.05
221	Alex Gonzalez	.05
222	Juan Guzman	.05
223	Pat Hentgen	.05
224	Orlando Merced	.05
225	Tomas Perez	.05
226	Paul Quantrill	.05
227	Benito Santiago	.05
228	Woody Williams	.05
229	Rafael Belliard	.05
230	Jeff Blauser	.05
231	Pedro Borbon	.05
232	Tom Glavine	.25
233	Tony Graffanino	.05
234	Andruw Jones	.75
235	Chipper Jones	1.00
236	Ryan Klesko	.05
237	Mark Lemke	.05
238	Kenny Lofton	.05
239	Javier Lopez	.05
240	Fred McGriff	.05
241	Greg Maddux	1.00
242	Denny Neagle	.05
243	John Smoltz	.05
244	Michael Tucker	.05
245	Mark Wohlers	.05
246	Manny Alexander	.05
247	Miguel Batista	.05
248	Mark Clark	.05
249	Doug Glanville	.05
250	Jeremi Gonzalez	.05
251	Mark Grace	.05
252	Jose Hernandez	.05
253	Lance Johnson	.05
254	Brooks Kieschnick	.05
255	Kevin Orie	.05
256	Ryne Sandberg	1.00
257	Scott Servais	.05
258	Sammy Sosa	1.00
259	Kevin Tapani	.05
260	Ramon Tatis	.05
261	Bret Boone	.05
262	Dave Burba	.05
263	Brook Fordyce	.05
264	Willie Greene	.05
265	Barry Larkin	.05
266	Pedro A. Martinez	.05
267	Hal Morris	.05
268	Joe Oliver	.05
269	Eduardo Perez	.05
270	Pokey Reese	.05
271	Felix Rodriguez	.05
272	Deion Sanders	.05
273	Reggie Sanders	.05
274	Jeff Shaw	.05
275	Scott Sullivan	.05
276	Brett Tomko	.05
277	Roger Bailey	.05
278	Dante Bichette	.05
279	Ellis Burks	.05
280	Vinny Castilla	.05
281	Frank Castillo	.05
282	Mike DeJean RC	.05
283	Andres Galarraga	.05
284	Darren Holmes	.05
285	Kirt Manwaring	.05
286	Quinton McCracken	.05
287	Neifi Perez	.05
288	Steve Reed	.05
289	John Thomson	.05
290	Larry Walker	.05
291	Walt Weiss	.05
292	Kurt Abbott	.05
293	Antonio Alfonseca	.05
294	Moises Alou	.05
295	Alex Arias	.05
296	Bobby Bonilla	.05
297	Kevin Brown	.05
298	Craig Counsell	.05
299	Darren Daulton	.05
300	Jim Eisenreich	.05
301	Alex Fernandez	.05
302	Felix Heredia	.05
303	Livan Hernandez	.05
304	Charles Johnson	.05
305	Al Leiter	.05
306	Robb Nen	.05
307	Edgar Renteria	.05
308	Gary Sheffield	.45

309	Devon White	.05
310	Bob Abreu	.10
311	Brad Ausmus	.05
312	Jeff Bagwell	.75
313	Derek Bell	.05
314	Sean Berry	.05
315	Craig Biggio	.05
316	Ramon Garcia	.05
317	Luis Gonzalez	.05
318	Ricky Gutierrez	.05
319	Mike Hampton	.05
320	Richard Hidalgo	.05
321	Thomas Howard	.05
322	Darryl Kile	.05
323	Jose Lima	.05
324	Shane Reynolds	.05
325	Bill Spiers	.05
326	Tom Candiotti	.05
327	Roger Cedeno	.05
328	Greg Gagne	.05
329	Karim Garcia	.05
330	Wilton Guerrero	.05
331	Todd Hollandsworth	.05
332	Eric Karros	.05
333	Ramon Martinez	.05
334	Raul Mondesi	.05
335	Otis Nixon	.05
336	Hideo Nomo	.40
337	Antonio Osuna	.05
338	Chan Ho Park	.05
339	Mike Piazza	1.25
340	Dennis Reyes	.05
341	Ismael Valdes	.05
342	Todd Worrell	.05
343	Todd Zeile	.05
344	Darrin Fletcher	.05
345	Mark Grudzielanek	.05
346	Vladimir Guerrero	.75
347	Dustin Hermanson	.05
348	Mike Lansing	.05
349	Pedro Martinez	.75
350	Ryan McGuire	.05
351	Jose Paniagua	.05
352	Carlos Perez	.05
353	Henry Rodriguez	.05
354	F.P. Santangelo	.05
355	David Segui	.05
356	Ugueth Urbina	.05
357	Marc Valdes	.05
358	Jose Vidro	.05
359	Rondell White	.05
360	Juan Acevedo	.05
361	Edgardo Alfonzo	.05
362	Carlos Baerga	.05
363	Carl Everett	.05
364	John Franco	.05
365	Bernard Gilkey	.05
366	Todd Hundley	.05
367	Butch Huskey	.05
368	Bobby Jones	.05
369	Takashi Kashiwada	.05
370	Greg McMichael	.05
371	Brian McRae	.05
372	Alex Ochoa	.05
373	John Olerud	.05
374	Rey Ordonez	.05
375	Turk Wendell	.05
376	Ricky Bottalico	.05
377	Rico Brogna	.05
378	Lenny Dykstra	.05
379	Bobby Estalella	.05
380	Wayne Gomes	.05
381	Tyler Green	.05
382	Gregg Jefferies	.05
383	Mark Leiter	.05
384	Mike Lieberthal	.05
385	Mickey Morandini	.05
386	Scott Rolen	.60
387	Curt Schilling	.25
388	Kevin Stocker	.05
389	Danny Tartabull	.05
390	Jermaine Allensworth	.05
391	Adrian Brown	.05
392	Jason Christiansen	.05
393	Steve Cooke	.05
394	Francisco Cordova	.05
395	Jose Guillen	.05
396	Jason Kendall	.05
397	Jon Lieber	.05
398	Esteban Loaiza	.05
399	Al Martin	.05
400	Kevin Polcovich RC	.05
401	Joe Randa	.05
402	Ricardo Rincon	.05
403	Tony Womack	.05
404	Kevin Young	.05
405	Andy Benes	.05
406	Royce Clayton	.05
407	Delino DeShields	.05
408	Mike Difelice	.05
409	Dennis Eckersley	.60
410	John Frascatore	.05
411	Gary Gaetti	.05
412	Ron Gant	.05
413	Brian Jordan	.05
414	Ray Lankford	.05
415	Willie McGee	.05
416	Mark McGwire	1.50
417	Matt Morris	.05
418	Luis Ordaz	.05
419	Todd Stottlemyre	.05
420	Andy Ashby	.05
421	Jim Bruske	.05
422	Ken Caminiti	.05
423	Will Cunnane	.05
424	Steve Finley	.05
425	John Flaherty	.05
426	Chris Gomez	.05
427	Tony Gwynn	1.00
428	Joey Hamilton	.05
429	Carlos Hernandez	.05
430	Sterling Hitchcock	.05
431	Trevor Hoffman	.05
432	Wally Joyner	.05
433	Greg Vaughn	.05
434	Quilvio Veras	.05
435	Wilson Alvarez	.05
436	Rod Beck	.05
437	Barry Bonds	2.00
438	Jacob Cruz	.05
439	Shawn Estes	.05
440	Darryl Hamilton	.05
441	Roberto Hernandez	.05
442	Glenallen Hill	.05
443	Stan Javier	.05
444	Brian Johnson	.05
445	Jeff Kent	.05
446	Bill Mueller	.05
447	Kirk Rueter	.05
448	J.T. Snow	.05
449	Julian Tavarez	.05
450	Jose Vizcaino	.05

Red/Silver/Blue

	NM/M
Common Red:	1.50
Red Stars:	6X
Common Silver:	.75
Silver Stars:	3X
Common Platinum Blue:	3.00
Platinum Blue Stars:	15X

(See 1998 Pacific for checklist and base card values.)

Cramer's Choice

		NM/M
Complete Set (10):		150.00
Common Player:		7.50
Inserted 1:721		
1	Greg Maddux	15.00
2	Roberto Alomar	7.50
3	Cal Ripken Jr.	30.00
4	Nomar Garciaparra	15.00
5	Larry Walker	7.50
6	Mike Piazza	17.50
7	Mark McGwire	25.00
8	Tony Gwynn	15.00
9	Ken Griffey Jr.	20.00
10	Roger Clemens	17.50

Gold Crown Die-Cuts

		NM/M
Complete Set (36):		85.00
Common Player:		1.50
1	Chipper Jones	4.00
2	Greg Maddux	4.00
3	Denny Neagle	1.50
4	Roberto Alomar	2.00
5	Rafael Palmeiro	2.50
6	Cal Ripken Jr.	8.00
7	Nomar Garciaparra	4.00
8	Mo Vaughn	1.50
9	Frank Thomas	3.00
10	Sandy Alomar Jr.	1.50
11	David Justice	1.50
12	Manny Ramirez	3.00
13	Andres Galarraga	1.50
14	Larry Walker	1.50

ROBERTO ALOMAR

15	Moises Alou	1.50
16	Livan Hernandez	1.50
17	Gary Sheffield	2.00
18	Jeff Bagwell	3.00
19	Raul Mondesi	1.50
20	Hideo Nomo	2.00
21	Mike Piazza	4.50
22	Derek Jeter	8.00
23	Tino Martinez	1.50
24	Bernie Williams	1.50
25	Ben Grieve	1.50
26	Mark McGwire	6.50
27	Tony Gwynn	4.00
28	Barry Bonds	8.00
29	Ken Griffey Jr.	5.00
30	Randy Johnson	3.00
31	Edgar Martinez	1.50
32	Alex Rodriguez	6.50
33	Juan Gonzalez	2.00
34	Ivan Rodriguez	2.50
35	Roger Clemens	4.50
36	Jose Cruz Jr.	1.50

Home Run Hitters

		NM/M
Complete Set (20):		50.00
Common Player:		1.00
1	Rafael Palmeiro	3.00
2	Mo Vaughn	1.00
3	Sammy Sosa	4.00
4	Albert Belle	1.00
5	Frank Thomas	3.50
6	David Justice	1.00
7	Jim Thome	3.00
8	Matt Williams	1.00
9	Vinny Castilla	1.00
10	Andres Galarraga	1.00
11	Larry Walker	1.00
12	Jeff Bagwell	3.50
13	Mike Piazza	4.50
14	Tino Martinez	1.00
15	Mark McGwire	6.00
16	Barry Bonds	7.50
17	Jay Buhner	1.00
18	Ken Griffey Jr.	5.00
19	Alex Rodriguez	6.00
20	Juan Gonzalez	2.00

Home Run Heroes

SAMMY SOSA CHICAGO CUBS
FRIDAY SEPT. 25, 1998 HR #66 462 FT!!!
HOME RUN HEROES

		NM/M
Complete Set (6):		2.50
Common Player:		.25
1	Mark McGwire	1.00
2	Sammy Sosa	.65
3	Ken Griffey Jr.	.75
4	Greg Vaughn	.25
5	Albert Belle	.25
6	Jose Canseco	.50

In the Cage

TINO MARTINEZ

		NM/M
Complete Set (20):		175.00
Common Player:		4.00
1	Chipper Jones	12.00
2	Roberto Alomar	4.00
3	Cal Ripken Jr.	25.00
4	Nomar Garciaparra	12.00
5	Frank Thomas	10.00
6	Sandy Alomar Jr.	4.00
7	David Justice	4.00
8	Larry Walker	4.00
9	Bobby Bonilla	4.00
10	Mike Piazza	16.00
11	Tino Martinez	4.00
12	Bernie Williams	4.00
13	Mark McGwire	20.00
14	Tony Gwynn	12.00
15	Barry Bonds	25.00
16	Ken Griffey Jr.	16.00
17	Edgar Martinez	4.00
18	Alex Rodriguez	20.00
19	Juan Gonzalez	6.00
20	Ivan Rodriguez	7.50

Latinos of the Major Leagues

		NM/M
Complete Set (36):		30.00
Common Player:		.50
Inserted 2:37		
1	Andruw Jones	2.50
2	Javier Lopez	.50
3	Roberto Alomar	1.25
4	Geronimo Berroa	.50
5	Rafael Palmeiro	2.00
6	Nomar Garciaparra	3.00
7	Sammy Sosa	3.00
8	Ozzie Guillen	.50
9	Sandy Alomar Jr.	.50
10	Manny Ramirez	2.50
11	Omar Vizquel	.50
12	Vinny Castilla	.50
13	Andres Galarraga	.50
14	Moises Alou	.50
15	Bobby Bonilla	.50
16	Livan Hernandez	.50
17	Edgar Renteria	.50
18	Wilton Guerrero	.50
19	Raul Mondesi	.50
20	Ismael Valdes	.50
21	Fernando Vina	.50
22	Pedro Martinez	2.50
23	Edgardo Alfonzo	.50
24	Carlos Baerga	.50
25	Rey Ordonez	.50
26	Tino Martinez	.50
27	Mariano Rivera	1.00
28	Bernie Williams	.50

29	Jose Canseco	1.50
30	Joey Cora	.50
31	Roberto Kelly	.50
32	Edgar Martinez	.50
33	Alex Rodriguez	3.50
34	Juan Gonzalez	1.50
35	Ivan Rodriguez	2.00
36	Jose Cruz Jr.	.50

Team Checklists

	NM/M
Complete Set (30):	60.00
Common Player:	.50
1 Tim Salmon, Jim Edmonds	.50
2 Cal Ripken Jr., Roberto Alomar	6.00
3 Nomar Garciaparra, Mo Vaughn	3.50
4 Frank Thomas, Albert Belle	2.50
5 Sandy Alomar Jr., Manny Ramirez	2.50
6 Justin Thompson, Tony Clark	.50
7 Johnny Damon, Jermaine Dye	.75
8 Dave Nilsson, Jeff Cirillo	.50
9 Paul Molitor, Chuck Knoblauch	2.50
10 Tino Martinez, Derek Jeter	6.00
11 Ben Grieve, Jose Canseco	1.00
12 Ken Griffey Jr., Alex Rodriguez	5.00
13 Juan Gonzalez, Ivan Rodriguez	2.00
14 Jose Cruz Jr., Roger Clemens	4.00
15 Greg Maddux, Chipper Jones	3.50
16 Sammy Sosa, Mark Grace	3.50
17 Barry Larkin, Deion Sanders	.50
18 Larry Walker, Andres Galarraga	.50
19 Moises Alou, Bobby Bonilla	.50
20 Jeff Bagwell, Craig Biggio	2.50
21 Mike Piazza, Hideo Nomo	4.00
22 Pedro Martinez, Henry Rodriguez	2.50
23 Rey Ordonez, Carlos Baerga	.50
24 Curt Schilling, Scott Rolen	1.50
25 Al Martin, Tony Womack	.50
26 Mark McGwire, Dennis Eckersley	5.00
27 Tony Gwynn, Wally Joyner	3.50
28 Barry Bonds, J.T. Snow	6.00
29 Matt Williams, Jay Bell	.50
30 Fred McGriff, Roberto Hernandez	

1998 Pacific Aurora

	NM/M
Complete Set (200):	20.00
Common Player:	.05
Pack (6):	1.00
Wax Box (36):	20.00
1 Garret Anderson	.05
2 Jim Edmonds	.05
3 Darin Erstad	.15
4 Cecil Fielder	.05
5 Chuck Finley	.05
6 Todd Greene	.05
7 Ken Hill	.05
8 Tim Salmon	.05
9 Roberto Alomar	.20
10 Brady Anderson	.05
11 Joe Carter	.05
12 Mike Mussina	.35
13 Rafael Palmeiro	.65
14 Cal Ripken Jr.	2.50

15	B.J. Surhoff	.05
16	Steve Avery	.05
17	Nomar Garciaparra	1.00
18	Pedro Martinez	.75
19	John Valentin	.05
20	Jason Varitek	.05
21	Mo Vaughn	.05
22	Albert Belle	.05
23	Ray Durham	.05
24	Magglio Ordonez RC	1.50
25	Frank Thomas	.75
26	Robin Ventura	.05
27	Sandy Alomar Jr.	.05
28	Travis Fryman	.05
29	Dwight Gooden	.05
30	David Justice	.05
31	Kenny Lofton	.05
32	Manny Ramirez	.75
33	Jim Thome	.60
34	Omar Vizquel	.05
35	Enrique Wilson	.05
36	Jaret Wright	.05
37	Tony Clark	.05
38	Bobby Higginson	.05
39	Brian Hunter	.05
40	Bip Roberts	.05
41	Justin Thompson	.05
42	Jeff Conine	.05
43	Johnny Damon	.35
44	Jermaine Dye	.05
45	Jeff King	.05
46	Jeff Montgomery	.05
47	Hal Morris	.05
48	Dean Palmer	.05
49	Terry Pendleton	.05
50	Rick Aguilera	.05
51	Marty Cordova	.05
52	Paul Molitor	.75
53	Otis Nixon	.05
54	Brad Radke	.05
55	Terry Steinbach	.05
56	Todd Walker	.05
57	Chili Davis	.05
58	Derek Jeter	2.50
59	Chuck Knoblauch	.05
60	Tino Martinez	.05
61	Paul O'Neill	.05
62	Andy Pettitte	.20
63	Mariano Rivera	.15
64	Bernie Williams	.05
65	Jason Giambi	.50
66	Ben Grieve	.05
67	Rickey Henderson	.75
68	A.J. Hinch	.05
69	Kenny Rogers	.05
70	Jay Buhner	.05
71	Joey Cora	.05
72	Ken Griffey Jr.	1.50
73	Randy Johnson	.75
74	Edgar Martinez	.05
75	Jamie Moyer	.05
76	Alex Rodriguez	2.00
77	David Segui	.05
78	Rolando Arrojo RC	.35
79	Wade Boggs	1.00
80	Roberto Hernandez	.05
81	Dave Martinez	.05
82	Fred McGriff	.05
83	Paul Sorrento	.05
84	Kevin Stocker	.05
85	Will Clark	.05
86	Juan Gonzalez	.40
87	Tom Goodwin	.05
88	Rusty Greer	.05
89	Ivan Rodriguez	.65
90	John Wetteland	.05
91	Jose Canseco	.40
92	Roger Clemens	1.25
93	Jose Cruz Jr.	.05
94	Carlos Delgado	.50
95	Pat Hentgen	.05
96	Jay Bell	.05
97	Andy Benes	.05

98	Karim Garcia	.05
99	Travis Lee	.05
100	Devon White	.05
101	Matt Williams	.05
102	Andres Galarraga	.05
103	Tom Glavine	.30
104	Andruw Jones	.75
105	Chipper Jones	1.00
106	Ryan Klesko	.05
107	Javy Lopez	.05
108	Greg Maddux	1.00
109	Walt Weiss	.05
110	Rod Beck	.05
111	Jeff Blauser	.05
112	Mark Grace	.05
113	Lance Johnson	.05
114	Mickey Morandini	.05
115	Henry Rodriguez	.05
116	Sammy Sosa	1.00
117	Kerry Wood	.35
118	Lenny Harris	.05
119	Damian Jackson	.05
120	Barry Larkin	.05
121	Reggie Sanders	.05
122	Brett Tomko	.05
123	Dante Bichette	.05
124	Ellis Burks	.05
125	Vinny Castilla	.05
126	Todd Helton	.75
127	Darryl Kile	.05
128	Larry Walker	.05
129	Bobby Bonilla	.05
130	Livan Hernandez	.05
131	Charles Johnson	.05
132	Derrek Lee	.50
133	Edgar Renteria	.05
134	Gary Sheffield	.35
135	Moises Alou	.05
136	Jeff Bagwell	.75
137	Derek Bell	.05
138	Craig Biggio	.05
139	John Halama RC	.15
140	Mike Hampton	.05
141	Richard Hidalgo	.05
142	Wilton Guerrero	.05
143	Todd Hollandsworth	.05
144	Eric Karros	.05
145	Paul Konerko	.05
146	Raul Mondesi	.05
147	Hideo Nomo	.40
148	Chan Ho Park	.05
149	Mike Piazza	1.25
150	Jeromy Burnitz	.05
151	Todd Dunn	.05
152	Marquis Grissom	.05
153	John Jaha	.05
154	Dave Nilsson	.05
155	Fernando Vina	.05
156	Mark Grudzielanek	.05
157	Vladimir Guerrero	.75
158	F.P. Santangelo	.05
159	Jose Vidro	.05
160	Rondell White	.05
161	Edgardo Alfonzo	.05
162	Carlos Baerga	.05
163	John Franco	.05
164	Todd Hundley	.05
165	Brian McRae	.05
166	John Olerud	.05
167	Rey Ordonez	.05
168	Masato Yoshii RC	.25
169	Ricky Bottalico	.05
170	Doug Glanville	.05
171	Gregg Jefferies	.05
172	Desi Relaford	.05
173	Scott Rolen	.60
174	Curt Schilling	.30
175	Jose Guillen	.05
176	Jason Kendall	.05
177	Al Martin	.05
178	Abraham Nunez	.05
179	Kevin Young	.05
180	Royce Clayton	.05
181	Delino DeShields	.05
182	Gary Gaetti	.05
183	Ron Gant	.05
184	Brian Jordan	.05
185	Ray Lankford	.05
186	Willie McGee	.05
187	Mark McGwire	2.00
188	Kevin Brown	.05
189	Ken Caminiti	.05
190	Steve Finley	.05
191	Tony Gwynn	1.00
192	Wally Joyner	.05
193	Ruben Rivera	.05
194	Quilvio Veras	.05
195	Barry Bonds	2.50
196	Shawn Estes	.05
197	Orel Hershiser	.05
198	Jeff Kent	.05
199	Robb Nen	.05
200	J.T. Snow	.05

Cubes

	NM/M
Complete Set (20):	75.00
Common Player:	1.50
Inserted 1:Box	
1 Travis Lee	1.50
2 Chipper Jones	4.00
3 Greg Maddux	4.00
4 Cal Ripken Jr.	10.00
5 Nomar Garciaparra	4.00
6 Frank Thomas	3.00
7 Manny Ramirez	3.00
8 Larry Walker	1.50
9 Hideo Nomo	2.00
10 Mike Piazza	5.00
11 Derek Jeter	10.00
12 Ben Grieve	1.50
13 Mark McGwire	7.50
14 Tony Gwynn	4.00
15 Barry Bonds	10.00
16 Ken Griffey Jr.	6.00
17 Alex Rodriguez	7.50
18 Wade Boggs	4.00
19 Juan Gonzalez	2.00
20 Jose Cruz Jr.	1.50

Hardball Cel-Fusion

	NM/M
Complete Set (20):	60.00
Common Player:	2.00
Inserted 1:73	
1 Travis Lee	2.00
2 Chipper Jones	6.00
3 Greg Maddux	6.00
4 Cal Ripken Jr.	15.00
5 Nomar Garciaparra	6.00
6 Frank Thomas	4.50
7 David Justice	2.00
8 Jeff Bagwell	4.50
9 Hideo Nomo	3.00
10 Mike Piazza	7.50
11 Derek Jeter	15.00
12 Ben Grieve	2.00
13 Scott Rolen	3.00
14 Mark McGwire	12.00
15 Tony Gwynn	6.00
16 Ken Griffey Jr.	9.00
17 Alex Rodriguez	12.00
18 Ivan Rodriguez	3.50
19 Roger Clemens	7.50
20 Jose Cruz Jr.	2.00

Kings of the Major Leagues

	NM/M
Complete Set (10):	75.00
Common Player:	7.50
Inserted 1:361	
1 Chipper Jones	9.00
2 Greg Maddux	9.00

3	Cal Ripken Jr.	20.00
4	Nomar Garciaparra	9.00
5	Frank Thomas	7.50
6	Mike Piazza	10.00
7	Mark McGwire	15.00
8	Tony Gwynn	9.00
9	Ken Griffey Jr.	12.00
10	Alex Rodriguez	15.00

On Deck Laser-Cut

		NM/M
Complete Set (20):		30.00
Common Player:		.60
Inserted 1:9		
1	Travis Lee	.60
2	Chipper Jones	2.25
3	Greg Maddux	2.25
4	Cal Ripken Jr.	6.00
5	Nomar Garciaparra	2.25
6	Frank Thomas	1.50
7	Manny Ramirez	1.50
8	Larry Walker	.60
9	Hideo Nomo	1.00
10	Mike Piazza	2.50
11	Derek Jeter	6.00
12	Ben Grieve	.60
13	Mark McGwire	4.50
14	Tony Gwynn	2.25
15	Barry Bonds	6.00
16	Ken Griffey Jr.	3.00
17	Alex Rodriguez	4.50
18	Wade Boggs	2.25
19	Juan Gonzalez	1.00
20	Jose Cruz Jr.	.60

Pennant Fever

		NM/M
Complete Set (50):		25.00
Common Player:		.20
Inserted 1:1		
Reds (1:4 Retail):		2X
Silvers (250 Sets):		4X
Platinum Blues (100 Sets):		12X
Coppers (20 Sets):		40X
1	Tony Gwynn	1.00
2	Derek Jeter	2.00
3	Alex Rodriguez	1.50
4	Paul Molitor	.75
5	Nomar Garciaparra	1.00
6	Jeff Bagwell	.75

7	Ivan Rodriguez	.65
8	Cal Ripken Jr.	2.00
9	Matt Williams	.20
10	Chipper Jones	1.00
11	Edgar Martinez	.20
12	Wade Boggs	1.00
13	Paul Konerko	.30
14	Ben Grieve	.20
15	Sandy Alomar Jr.	.20
16	Travis Lee	.20
17	Scott Rolen	.65
18	Ryan Klesko	.20
19	Juan Gonzalez	.40
20	Albert Belle	.20
21	Roger Clemens	1.25
22	Javy Lopez	.20
23	Jose Cruz Jr.	.20
24	Ken Griffey Jr.	1.25
25	Mark McGwire	1.50
26	Brady Anderson	.20
27	Jaret Wright	.20
28	Roberto Alomar	.30
29	Joe Carter	.20
30	Hideo Nomo	.40
31	Mike Piazza	1.25
32	Andres Galarraga	.20
33	Larry Walker	.20
34	Tim Salmon	.20
35	Frank Thomas	.75
36	Moises Alou	.20
37	David Justice	.20
38	Manny Ramirez	.75
39	Jim Edmonds	.20
40	Barry Bonds	2.00
41	Jim Thome	.65
42	Mo Vaughn	.20
43	Rafael Palmeiro	.65
44	Darin Erstad	.30
45	Pedro Martinez	.75
46	Greg Maddux	1.00
47	Jose Canseco	.45
48	Vladimir Guerrero	.75
49	Bernie Williams	.20
50	Randy Johnson	.75

1998 Pacific Crown Royale

		NM/M
Complete Set (144):		60.00
Common Player:		.20
Pack (6):		1.00
Wax Box (24):		20.00
1	Garret Anderson	.20
2	Jim Edmonds	.20
3	Darin Erstad	.50
4	Tim Salmon	.20
5	Jarrod Washburn	.20
6	David Dellucci	.20
7	Travis Lee	.20
8	Devon White	.20
9	Matt Williams	.20
10	Andres Galarraga	.20
11	Tom Glavine	.35
12	Andruw Jones	2.00
13	Chipper Jones	3.00
14	Ryan Klesko	.20
15	Javy Lopez	.20
16	Greg Maddux	3.00
17	Walt Weiss	.20
18	Roberto Alomar	.75
19	Harold Baines	.20
20	Eric Davis	.20
21	Mike Mussina	1.00
22	Rafael Palmeiro	1.50
23	Cal Ripken Jr.	5.00
24	Nomar Garciaparra	3.00
25	Pedro Martinez	2.00
26	Troy O'Leary	.20
27	Mo Vaughn	.20
28	Tim Wakefield	.20
29	Mark Grace	.20
30	Mickey Morandini	.20
31	Sammy Sosa	3.00
32	Kerry Wood	.50
33	Albert Belle	.20
34	Mike Caruso	.20
35	Ray Durham	.20
36	Frank Thomas	2.00
37	Robin Ventura	.20
38	Bret Boone	.20
39	Sean Casey	.25
40	Barry Larkin	.20

41	Reggie Sanders	.20
42	Sandy Alomar Jr.	.20
43	David Justice	.20
44	Kenny Lofton	.20
45	Manny Ramirez	2.00
46	Jim Thome	1.00
47	Omar Vizquel	.20
48	Jaret Wright	.20
49	Dante Bichette	.20
50	Ellis Burks	.20
51	Vinny Castilla	.20
52	Todd Helton	2.00
53	Larry Walker	.20
54	Tony Clark	.20
55	Damion Easley	.20
56	Bobby Higginson	.20
57	Cliff Floyd	.20
58	Livan Hernandez	.20
59	Derrek Lee	.75
60	Edgar Renteria	.20
61	Moises Alou	.20
62	Jeff Bagwell	2.00
63	Derek Bell	.20
64	Craig Biggio	.20
65	Johnny Damon	.35
66	Jeff King	.20
67	Hal Morris	.20
68	Dean Palmer	.20
69	Bobby Bonilla	.20
70	Eric Karros	.20
71	Raul Mondesi	.20
72	Gary Sheffield	.75
73	Jeromy Burnitz	.20
74	Jeff Cirillo	.20
75	Marquis Grissom	.20
76	Fernando Vina	.20
77	Marty Cordova	.20
78	Pat Meares	.20
79	Paul Molitor	2.00
80	Terry Steinbach	.20
81	Todd Walker	.20
82	Brad Fullmer	.20
83	Vladimir Guerrero	2.00
84	Carl Pavano	.20
85	Rondell White	.20
86	Carlos Baerga	.20
87	Hideo Nomo	1.00
88	John Olerud	.20
89	Rey Ordonez	.20
90	Mike Piazza	3.00
91	Masato Yoshii RC	.75
92	Orlando Hernandez RC	.75
93	Hideki Irabu	.20
94	Derek Jeter	5.00
95	Chuck Knoblauch	.20
96	Ricky Ledee	.20
97	Tino Martinez	.20
98	Paul O'Neill	.20
99	Bernie Williams	.20
100	Jason Giambi	1.25
101	Ben Grieve	.20
102	Rickey Henderson	2.00
103	Matt Stairs	.20
104	Bob Abreu	.25
105	Doug Glanville	.20
106	Scott Rolen	1.50
107	Curt Schilling	.35
108	Jose Guillen	.20
109	Jason Kendall	.20
110	Jason Schmidt	.20
111	Kevin Young	.20
112	Delino DeShields	.20
113	Brian Jordan	.20
114	Ray Lankford	.20
115	Mark McGwire	4.00
116	Tony Gwynn	3.00
117	Wally Joyner	.20
118	Ruben Rivera	.20
119	Greg Vaughn	.20
120	Rich Aurilia	.20
121	Barry Bonds	5.00
122	Bill Mueller	.20
123	Robb Nen	.20
124	Jay Buhner	.20
125	Ken Griffey Jr.	3.50
126	Edgar Martinez	.20
127	Shane Monahan	.20
128	Alex Rodriguez	4.00
129	David Segui	.20
130	Rolando Arrojo RC	.75
131	Wade Boggs	3.00
132	Quinton McCracken	.20
133	Fred McGriff	.20
134	Bobby Smith	.20
135	Will Clark	.20
136	Juan Gonzalez	1.00
137	Rusty Greer	.20
138	Ivan Rodriguez	1.50
139	Aaron Sele	.20
140	John Wetteland	.20
141	Jose Canseco	1.00
142	Roger Clemens	3.50
143	Carlos Delgado	1.25
144	Shawn Green	.50

All-Stars

		NM/M
Complete Set (20):		110.00
Common Player:		1.50
Inserted 1:25		
1	Roberto Alomar	2.00
2	Cal Ripken Jr.	15.00
3	Kenny Lofton	1.50
4	Jim Thome	5.00
5	Derek Jeter	15.00
6	David Wells	1.50
7	Ken Griffey Jr.	10.00
8	Alex Rodriguez	12.00
9	Juan Gonzalez	4.00
10	Ivan Rodriguez	5.00
11	Gary Sheffield	2.50
12	Chipper Jones	7.50
13	Greg Maddux	7.50
14	Walt Weiss	1.50
15	Larry Walker	1.50
16	Craig Biggio	1.50
17	Mike Piazza	10.00
18	Mark McGwire	12.00
19	Tony Gwynn	7.50
20	Barry Bonds	15.00

Cramer's Choice Awards

		NM/M
Complete Set (10):		65.00
Common Player:		4.00
Inserted 1:box		
1	Cal Ripken Jr.	15.00
2	Ken Griffey Jr.	9.00
3	Alex Rodriguez	12.00
4	Juan Gonzalez	5.00
5	Travis Lee	4.00
6	Chipper Jones	7.50
7	Greg Maddux	7.50
8	Kerry Wood	5.00
9	Mark McGwire	12.00
10	Tony Gwynn	7.50

Diamond Knights

		NM/M
Complete Set (25):		20.00
Common Player:		.35
Inserted 1:1		
1	Andres Galarraga	.35
2	Chipper Jones	1.00
3	Greg Maddux	1.00
4	Cal Ripken Jr.	2.50
5	Nomar Garciaparra	1.50
6	Mo Vaughn	.35
7	Kerry Wood	.45
8	Frank Thomas	.75
9	Vinny Castilla	.35
10	Jeff Bagwell	.75

NM/M

Complete Set (10):		30.00
Common Player:		1.50
Inserted 1:73		
1	Andres Galarraga	1.50
2	Sammy Sosa	4.50
3	Albert Belle	1.50
4	Jim Thome	3.00
5	Mark McGwire	7.50
6	Greg Vaughn	1.50
7	Ken Griffey Jr.	6.00
8	Alex Rodriguez	7.50
9	Juan Gonzalez	2.50
10	Jose Canseco	2.50

11	Craig Biggio	.35
12	Paul Molitor	.75
13	Mike Piazza	1.50
14	Orlando Hernandez	.35
15	Derek Jeter	2.50
16	Ricky Ledee	.35
17	Mark McGwire	2.00
18	Tony Gwynn	1.00
19	Barry Bonds	2.50
20	Ken Griffey Jr.	1.75
21	Alex Rodriguez	2.00
22	Wade Boggs	1.00
23	Juan Gonzalez	.45
24	Ivan Rodriguez	.65
25	Jose Canseco	.50

Firestone on Baseball

NM/M

Complete Set (26):		50.00
Common Player:		.35
Firestone Auto. Card:		18.00
Inserted 1:12		
1	Travis Lee	.35
2	Chipper Jones	3.00
3	Greg Maddux	3.00
4	Cal Ripken Jr.	6.00
5	Nomar Garciaparra	3.00
6	Mo Vaughn	.35
7	Kerry Wood	1.00
8	Frank Thomas	2.25
9	Manny Ramirez	2.25
10	Larry Walker	.35
11	Gary Sheffield	1.00
12	Paul Molitor	2.25
13	Hideo Nomo	1.50
14	Mike Piazza	3.50
15	Ben Grieve	.35
16	Mark McGwire	5.00
17	Tony Gwynn	3.00
18	Barry Bonds	6.00
19	Ken Griffey Jr.	4.00
20	Randy Johnson	2.25
21	Alex Rodriquez	5.00
22	Wade Boggs	3.00
23	Juan Gonzalez	1.50
24	Ivan Rodriguez	1.75
25	Roger Clemens	3.50
26	Roy Firestone	.35

Home Run Fever

Pillars of the Game

NM/M

Complete Set (25):		20.00
Common Player:		.35
Inserted 1:1		
1	Jim Edmonds	.35
2	Travis Lee	.35
3	Chipper Jones	1.00
4	Tom Glavine, John Smoltz, Greg Maddux	1.00
5	Cal Ripken Jr.	2.50
6	Nomar Garciaparra	1.00
7	Mo Vaughn	.35
8	Sammy Sosa	1.00
9	Kerry Wood	.40
10	Frank Thomas	.75
11	Jim Thome	.65
12	Larry Walker	.35
13	Moises Alou	.35
14	Raul Mondesi	.35
15	Mike Piazza	1.25
16	Hideki Irabu	.35
17	Bernie Williams	.35
18	Ben Grieve	.35
19	Scott Rolen	.65
20	Mark McGwire	2.00
21	Tony Gwynn	1.00
22	Ken Griffey Jr.	1.50
23	Alex Rodriguez	2.00
24	Juan Gonzalez	.40
25	Roger Clemens	1.25

1998 Pacific Invincible

NM/M

Complete Set (150):		60.00
Common Player:		.20
Silvers:		4X
Inserted 2:37		
Platinum Blues:		6X
Inserted 1:73		
Pack (5):		1.25
Wax Box (36):		32.50
1	Garret Anderson	.20
2	Jim Edmonds	.20
3	Darin Erstad	.35
4	Chuck Finley	.20
5	Tim Salmon	.20
6	Roberto Alomar	.35
7	Brady Anderson	.20
8	Geronimo Berroa	.20
9	Eric Davis	.20
10	Mike Mussina	.50
11	Rafael Palmeiro	1.00
12	Cal Ripken Jr.	6.00
13	Steve Avery	.20
14	Nomar Garciaparra	2.50
15	John Valentin	.20
16	Mo Vaughn	.20
17	Albert Belle	.20
18	Ozzie Guillen	.20
19	Norberto Martin	.20
20	Frank Thomas	1.50
21	Robin Ventura	.20
22	Sandy Alomar Jr.	.20
23	David Justice	.20
24	Kenny Lofton	.20
25	Manny Ramirez	1.50
26	Jim Thome	1.00
27	Omar Vizquel	.20
28	Matt Williams	.20
29	Jaret Wright	.20
30	Raul Casanova	.20
31	Tony Clark	.20
32	Deivi Cruz	.20
33	Bobby Higginson	.20
34	Justin Thompson	.20
35	Yamil Benitez	.20
36	Johnny Damon	.35
37	Jermaine Dye	.20
38	Jed Hansen	.20
39	Larry Sutton	.20
40	Jeromy Burnitz	.20
41	Jeff Cirillo	.20
42	Dave Nilsson	.20
43	Jose Valentin	.20
44	Fernando Vina	.20
45	Marty Cordova	.20
46	Chuck Knoblauch	.20
47	Paul Molitor	1.50
48	Brad Radke	.20
49	Terry Steinbach	.20
50	Wade Boggs	2.50
51	Hideki Irabu	.20
52	Derek Jeter	6.00
53	Tino Martinez	.20
54	Andy Pettitte	.30
55	Mariano Rivera	.30
56	Bernie Williams	.20
57	Jose Canseco	.75
58	Jason Giambi	.75
59	Ben Grieve	.20
60	Aaron Small	.20
61	Jay Buhner	.20
62	Ken Cloude	.20
63	Joey Cora	.20
64	Ken Griffey Jr.	3.50
65	Randy Johnson	1.50
66	Edgar Martinez	.20
67	Alex Rodriguez	5.00
68	Will Clark	.20
69	Juan Gonzalez	.75
70	Rusty Greer	.20
71	Ivan Rodriguez	1.00
72	Joe Carter	.20
73	Roger Clemens	3.00
74	Jose Cruz Jr.	.20
75	Carlos Delgado	.75
76	Andruw Jones	1.50
77	Chipper Jones	2.50
78	Ryan Klesko	.20
79	Javier Lopez	.20
80	Greg Maddux	2.50
81	Miguel Batista	.20
82	Jeremi Gonzalez	.20
83	Mark Grace	.20
84	Kevin Orie	.20
85	Sammy Sosa	2.50
86	Barry Larkin	.20
87	Deion Sanders	.20
88	Reggie Sanders	.20
89	Chris Stynes	.20
90	Dante Bichette	.20
91	Vinny Castilla	.20
92	Andres Galarraga	.20
93	Neifi Perez	.20
94	Larry Walker	.20
95	Moises Alou	.20
96	Bobby Bonilla	.20
97	Kevin Brown	.20
98	Craig Counsell	.20
99	Livan Hernandez	.20
100	Edgar Renteria	.20
101	Gary Sheffield	.60
102	Jeff Bagwell	1.50
103	Craig Biggio	.20
104	Luis Gonzalez	.20
105	Darryl Kile	.20
106	Wilton Guerrero	.20
107	Eric Karros	.20
108	Ramon Martinez	.20
109	Raul Mondesi	.20
110	Hideo Nomo	.75
111	Chan Ho Park	.20
112	Mike Piazza	3.00
113	Mark Grudzielanek	.20
114	Vladimir Guerrero	1.50
115	Pedro Martinez	1.50
116	Henry Rodriguez	.20
117	David Segui	.20
118	Edgardo Alfonzo	.20
119	Carlos Baerga	.20
120	John Franco	.20
121	John Olerud	.20
122	Rey Ordonez	.20
123	Ricky Bottalico	.20
124	Gregg Jefferies	.20
125	Mickey Morandini	.20
126	Scott Rolen	1.00
127	Curt Schilling	.45
128	Jose Guillen	.20
129	Esteban Loaiza	.20
130	Al Martin	.20
131	Tony Womack	.20
132	Dennis Eckersley	1.00
133	Gary Gaetti	.20
134	Curtis King	.20
135	Ray Lankford	.20
136	Mark McGwire	5.00
137	Ken Caminiti	.20
138	Steve Finley	.20
139	Tony Gwynn	2.50
140	Carlos Hernandez	.20
141	Wally Joyner	.20
142	Barry Bonds	6.00
143	Jacob Cruz	.20
144	Shawn Estes	.20
145	Stan Javier	.20
146	J.T. Snow	.20
147	Nomar Garciaparra (ROY)	1.00
148	Scott Rolen (ROY)	.60
149	Ken Griffey Jr. (MVP)	1.75
150	Larry Walker (MVP)	.20

Cramer's Choice

NM/M

Complete Green Set (10):		200.00
Common Green (99 Sets):		10.00
Dark Blues (80 Sets):		1X
Light Blues (50 Sets):		1.5X
Reds (25 Sets):		2X
Golds (15 Sets):		3X
Purples (10 Sets):		5X
1	Greg Maddux	20.00
2	Roberto Alomar	10.00
3	Cal Ripken Jr.	40.00
4	Nomar Garciaparra	20.00
5	Larry Walker	10.00
6	Mike Piazza	22.50
7	Mark McGwire	30.00
8	Tony Gwynn	20.00
9	Ken Griffey Jr.	25.00
10	Roger Clemens	22.50

Gems of the Diamond

NM/M

Complete Set (220):		20.00
Common Player:		.10
1	Jim Edmonds	.10
2	Todd Greene	.10
3	Ken Hill	.10
4	Mike Holtz	.10
5	Mike James	.10
6	Chad Kreuter	.10
7	Tim Salmon	.10
8	Roberto Alomar	.20
9	Brady Anderson	.10
10	David Dellucci	.10
11	Jeffrey Hammonds	.10
12	Mike Mussina	.40
13	Rafael Palmeiro	.65
14	Arthur Rhodes	.10
15	Cal Ripken Jr.	2.50

16	Nerio Rodriguez	.10
17	Tony Tarasco	.10
18	Lenny Webster	.10
19	Mike Benjamin	.10
20	Rich Garces	.10
21	Nomar Garciaparra	1.00
22	Shane Mack	.10
23	Jose Malave	.10
24	Jesus Tavarez	.10
25	Mo Vaughn	.10
26	John Wasdin	.10
27	Jeff Abbott	.10
28	Albert Belle	.10
29	Mike Cameron	.10
30	Al Levine	.10
31	Robert Machado	.10
32	Greg Norton	.10
33	Magglio Ordonez	.20
34	Mike Sirotka	.10
35	Frank Thomas	.75
36	Mario Valdez	.10
37	Sandy Alomar Jr.	.10
38	David Justice	.10
39	Jack McDowell	.10
40	Eric Plunk	.10
41	Manny Ramirez	.75
42	Kevin Seitzer	.10
43	Paul Shuey	.10
44	Omar Vizquel	.10
45	Kimera Bartee	.10
46	Glenn Dishman	.10
47	Orlando Miller	.10
48	Mike Myers	.10
49	Phil Nevin	.10
50	A.J. Sager	.10
51	Ricky Bones	.10
52	Scott Cooper	.10
53	Shane Halter	.10
54	David Howard	.10
55	Glendon Rusch	.10
56	Joe Vitiello	.10
57	Jeff D'Amico	.10
58	Mike Fetters	.10
59	Mike Matheny	.10
60	Jose Mercedes	.10
61	Ron Villone	.10
62	Jack Voigt	.10
63	Brent Brede	.10
64	Chuck Knoblauch	.10
65	Paul Molitor	.75
66	Todd Ritchie	.10
67	Frankie Rodriguez	.10
68	Scott Stahoviak	.10
69	Greg Swindell	.10
70	Todd Walker	.10
71	Wade Boggs	1.00
72	Hideki Irabu	.10
73	Derek Jeter	2.50
74	Pat Kelly	.10
75	Graeme Lloyd	.10
76	Tino Martinez	.10
77	Jeff Nelson	.10
78	Scott Pose	.10
79	Mike Stanton	.10
80	Darryl Strawberry	.10
81	Bernie Williams	.10
82	Tony Batista	.10
83	Mark Bellhorn	.10
84	Ben Grieve	.10
85	Pat Lennon	.10
86	Brian Lesher	.10
87	Miguel Tejada	.20
88	George Williams	.10
89	Joey Cora	.10
90	Rob Ducey	.10
91	Ken Griffey Jr.	1.50
92	Randy Johnson	.75
93	Edgar Martinez	.10
94	John Marzano	.10
95	Greg McCarthy	.10
96	Alex Rodriguez	2.00
97	Andy Sheets	.10
98	Mike Timlin	.10
99	Lee Tinsley	.10
100	Damon Buford	.10
101	Alex Diaz	.10
102	Benji Gil	.10
103	Juan Gonzalez	.40
104	Eric Gunderson	.10
105	Danny Patterson	.10
106	Ivan Rodriguez	.65
107	Mike Simms	.10
108	Luis Andujar	.10
109	Joe Carter	.10
110	Roger Clemens	1.25
111	Jose Cruz Jr.	.10
112	Shawn Green	.30
113	Robert Perez	.10
114	Juan Samuel	.10
115	Ed Sprague	.10
116	Shannon Stewart	.10
117	Danny Bautista	.10
118	Chipper Jones	1.00
119	Ryan Klesko	.10

120	Keith Lockhart	.10
121	Javier Lopez	.10
122	Greg Maddux	1.00
123	Kevin Millwood	.10
124	Mike Mordecai	.10
125	Eddie Perez	.10
126	Randall Simon	.10
127	Miguel Cairo	.10
128	Dave Clark	.10
129	Kevin Foster	.10
130	Mark Grace	.10
131	Tyler Houston	.10
132	Mike Hubbard	.10
133	Kevin Orie	.10
134	Ryne Sandberg	1.00
135	Sammy Sosa	1.00
136	Lenny Harris	.10
137	Kent Mercker	.10
138	Mike Morgan	.10
139	Deion Sanders	.10
140	Chris Stynes	.10
141	Gabe White	.10
142	Jason Bates	.10
143	Vinny Castilla	.10
144	Andres Galarraga	.10
145	Curtis Leskanic	.10
146	Jeff McCurry	.10
147	Mike Munoz	.10
148	Larry Walker	.10
149	Jamey Wright	.10
150	Moises Alou	.10
151	Bobby Bonilla	.10
152	Kevin Brown	.10
153	John Cangelosi	.10
154	Jeff Conine	.10
155	Cliff Floyd	.10
156	Jay Powell	.10
157	Edgar Renteria	.10
158	Tony Saunders	.10
159	Gary Sheffield	.40
160	Jeff Bagwell	.75
161	Tim Bogar	.10
162	Tony Eusebio	.10
163	Chris Holt	.10
164	Ray Montgomery	.10
165	Luis Rivera	.10
166	Eric Anthony	.10
167	Brett Butler	.10
168	Juan Castro	.10
169	Tripp Cromer	.10
170	Raul Mondesi	.10
171	Hideo Nomo	.40
172	Mike Piazza	1.25
173	Tom Prince	.10
174	Adam Riggs	.10
175	Shane Andrews	.10
176	Shayne Bennett	.10
177	Raul Chavez	.10
178	Pedro Martinez	.75
179	Sherman Obando	.10
180	Andy Stankiewicz	.10
181	Alberto Castillo	.10
182	Shawn Gilbert	.10
183	Luis Lopez	.10
184	Roberto Petagine	.10
185	Armando Reynoso	.10
186	Midre Cummings	.10
187	Kevin Jordan	.10
188	Desi Relaford	.10
189	Scott Rolen	.65
190	Ken Ryan	.10
191	Kevin Sefcik	.10
192	Emil Brown	.10
193	Lou Collier	.10
194	Francisco Cordova	.10
195	Kevin Elster	.10
196	Mark Smith	.10
197	Marc Wilkins	.10
198	Manny Aybar	.10
199	Jose Bautista	.10
200	David Bell	.10
201	Rigo Beltran	.10
202	Delino DeShields	.10
203	Dennis Eckersley	.65
204	John Mabry	.10
205	Eli Marrero	.10
206	Willie McGee	.10
207	Mark McGwire	2.00
208	Ken Caminiti	.10
209	Tony Gwynn	1.00
210	Chris Jones	.10
211	Craig Shipley	.10
212	Pete Smith	.10
213	Jorge Velandia	.10
214	Dario Veras	.10
215	Rich Aurilia	.10
216	Damon Berryhill	.10
217	Barry Bonds	2.50
218	Osvaldo Fernandez	.10
219	Dante Powell	.10
220	Rich Rodriguez	.10

Interleague Players

	NM/M
Complete Set (30):	120.00

Common Player:		1.50
Inserted 1:73		
1A	Roberto Alomar	2.50
1N	Craig Biggio	1.50
2A	Cal Ripken Jr.	12.00
2N	Chipper Jones	6.00
3A	Nomar Garciaparra	4.00
3N	Scott Rolen	3.50
4A	Mo Vaughn	1.50
4N	Andres Galarraga	1.50
5A	Frank Thomas	4.50
5N	Tony Gwynn	6.00
6A	Albert Belle	1.50
6N	Barry Bonds	12.00
7A	Hideki Irabu	1.50
7N	Hideo Nomo	2.50
8A	Derek Jeter	12.00
8N	Rey Ordonez	1.50
9A	Tino Martinez	1.50
9N	Mark McGwire	10.00
10A	Alex Rodriguez	10.00
10N	Edgar Renteria	1.50
11A	Ken Griffey Jr.	7.50
11N	Larry Walker	1.50
12A	Randy Johnson	4.50
12N	Greg Maddux	6.00
13A	Ivan Rodriguez	3.50
13N	Mike Piazza	6.50
14A	Roger Clemens	6.50
14N	Pedro Martinez	4.50
15A	Jose Cruz Jr.	1.50
15N	Wilton Guerrero	1.50

8	Pedro Martinez	2.50
9	Derek Jeter	7.50
10	Tino Martinez	1.00
11	Mark McGwire	6.00
12	Tony Gwynn	3.50
13	Barry Bonds	7.50
14	Ken Griffey Jr.	5.00
15	Alex Rodriguez	6.00
16	Ivan Rodriguez	2.25
17	Roger Clemens	4.00
18	Jose Cruz Jr.	1.00

Team Checklists

Moments in Time

	NM/M
Complete Set (20):	100.00
Common Player:	3.00
Inserted 1:145	

1	Chipper Jones	10.00
2	Cal Ripken Jr.	17.50
3	Frank Thomas	7.50
4	David Justice	3.00
5	Andres Galarraga	3.00
6	Larry Walker	3.00
7	Livan Hernandez	3.00
8	Wilton Guerrero	3.00
9	Hideo Nomo	4.50
10	Mike Piazza	12.00
11	Pedro Martinez	7.50
12	Bernie Williams	3.00
13	Ben Grieve	3.00
14	Scott Rolen	6.00
15	Mark McGwire	15.00
16	Tony Gwynn	10.00
17	Ken Griffey Jr.	13.50
18	Alex Rodriguez	15.00
19	Juan Gonzalez	4.50
20	Jose Cruz Jr.	3.00

Photoengravings

	NM/M
Complete Set (18):	50.00
Common Player:	1.00
Inserted 1:37	

1	Greg Maddux	3.50
2	Cal Ripken Jr.	7.50
3	Nomar Garciaparra	3.50
4	Frank Thomas	2.50
5	Larry Walker	1.00
6	Mike Piazza	4.00
7	Hideo Nomo	2.00

	NM/M
Complete Set (30):	60.00
Common Player:	1.00
Inserted 2:37	

1	Jim Edmonds, Tim Salmon, Darin Erstad, Garret Anderson, Rickey Henderson Anaheim Angels	2.50
2	Greg Maddux, Chipper Jones, Javy Lopez, Ryan Klesko, Andruw Jones/ Atlanta Braves	3.00
3	Cal Ripken Jr., Roberto Alomar, Brady Anderson, Mike Mussina, Rafael Palmeiro/ Baltimore Orioles	6.00
4	Nomar Garciaparra, Mo Vaughn, Steve Avery, John Valentin/ Boston Red Sox	3.00
5	Sammy Sosa, Mark Grace, Ryne Sandberg, Jeremi Gonzalez/ Chicago Cubs	3.00
6	Frank Thomas, Albert Belle, Robin Ventura, Ozzie Guillen/ Chicago White Sox	2.50
7	Barry Larkin, Deion Sanders, Reggie Sanders, Brett Tomko/ Cincinnati Reds	1.00
8	Sandy Alomar Jr., Manny Ramirez, David Justice, Jim Thome, Omar Vizquel/ Cleveland Indians	2.50
9	Andres Galarraga, Larry Walker, Vinny Castilla, Dante Bichette, Ellis Burks Colorado Rockies	1.00
10	Jason Thompson, Tony Clark, Deivi Cruz, Bobby Higginson/ Detroit Tigers	1.00
11	Gary Sheffield, Edgar Renteria, Livan Hernandez, Charles Johnson, Bobby Bonilla Florida Marlins	1.00

12 Jeff Bagwell, Craig Biggio, Richard Hidalgo, Darryl Kile Houston Astros 2.50
13 Johnny Damon, Jermaine Dye, Chili Davis, Jose Rosado/ Kansas City Royals 1.00
14 Mike Piazza, Wilton Guerrero, Raul Mondesi, Hideo Nomo, Ramon Martinez Los Angeles Dodgers 4.00
15 David Nilsson, Fernando Vina, Jeromy Burnitz, Julio Franco, Jeff Cirillo Milwaukee Brewers 1.00
16 Paul Molitor, Chuck Knoblauch, Brad Radke, Terry Steinbach, Marty Cordova/ Minnesota Twins 2.50
17 Henry Rodriguez, Vladimir Guerrero, Pedro Martinez, David Segui, Mark Grudzielanek Montreal Expos 2.50
18 Carlos Baerga, Todd Hundley, Rey Ordonez, John Olerud, Edgardo Alfonzo/ New York Mets 1.00
19 Derek Jeter, Tino Martinez, Bernie Williams, Andy Pettitte, Mariano Rivera/ New York Yankees 6.00
20 Jose Canseco, Ben Grieve, Jason Giambi, Matt Stairs Oakland Athletics 1.75
21 Curt Schilling, Scott Rolen, Gregg Jefferies, Lenny Dykstra, Ricky Bottalico/ Philadelphia Phillies 1.75
22 Al Martin, Tony Womack, Jose Guillen, Esteban Loiaza/ Pittsburgh Pirates 1.00
23 Mark McGwire, Dennis Eckersley, Delino DeShields, Willie McGee, Ray Lankford/ St. Louis Cardinals 4.50
24 Tony Gwynn, Ken Caminiti, Wally Joyner, Steve Finley San Diego Padres 3.00
25 Barry Bonds, J.T. Snow, Stan Javier, Rod Beck, Jose Vizcaino/ San Francisco Giants 6.00
26 Ken Griffey Jr., Alex Rodriguez, Edgar Martinez, Randy Johnson, Jay Buhner/ Seattle Mariners 4.50
27 Juan Gonzalez, Ivan Rodriguez, Will Clark, John Wetteland, Rusty Greer/ Texas Rangers 2.00
28 Jose Cruz Jr., Roger Clemens, Pat Hentgen, Joe Carter Toronto Blue Jays 4.00
29 Yamil Benitez, Devon White, Matt Williams, Jay Bell Arizona Diamondbacks 1.00
30 Wade Boggs, Paul Sorrento, Fred McGriff, Roberto Hernandez/ Tampa Bay Devil Rays 3.00

1998 Pacific Omega

NM/M
Complete Set (250): 25.00
Common Player: .10
Reds: 4X

Pack (6): 1.00
Wax Box (36): 15.00
1 Garret Anderson .10
2 Gary DiSarcina .10
3 Jim Edmonds .10
4 Darin Erstad .20
5 Cecil Fielder .10
6 Chuck Finley .10
7 Shigetoshi Hasegawa .10
8 Tim Salmon .10
9 Brian Anderson .10
10 Jay Bell .10
11 Andy Benes .10
12 Yamil Benitez .10
13 Jorge Fabregas .10
14 Travis Lee .10
15 Devon White .10
16 Matt Williams .10
17 Andres Galarraga .10
18 Tom Glavine .35
19 Andruw Jones .10
20 Chipper Jones 1.00
21 Ryan Klesko .10
22 Javy Lopez .10
23 Greg Maddux 1.00
24 Kevin Millwood RC .50
25 Denny Neagle .10
26 John Smoltz .10
27 Roberto Alomar .20
28 Brady Anderson .10
29 Joe Carter .10
30 Eric Davis .10
31 Jimmy Key .10
32 Mike Mussina .40
33 Rafael Palmeiro .65
34 Cal Ripken Jr. 2.50
35 B.J. Surhoff .10
36 Dennis Eckersley .65
37 Nomar Garciaparra 1.00
38 Reggie Jefferson .10
39 Derek Lowe .10
40 Pedro Martinez .75
41 Brian Rose .10
42 John Valentin .10
43 Jason Varitek .10
44 Mo Vaughn .45
45 Jeff Blauser .10
46 Jeremi Gonzalez .10
47 Mark Grace .10
48 Lance Johnson .10
49 Kevin Orie .10
50 Henry Rodriguez .10
51 Sammy Sosa 1.00
52 Kerry Wood .35
53 Albert Belle .10
54 Mike Cameron .10
55 Mike Caruso .10
56 Ray Durham .10
57 Jaime Navarro .10
58 Greg Norton .10
59 Magglio Ordonez RC 1.50
60 Frank Thomas .75
61 Robin Ventura .10
62 Bret Boone .10
63 Willie Greene .10
64 Barry Larkin .10
65 Jon Nunnally .10
66 Eduardo Perez .10
67 Reggie Sanders .10
68 Brett Tomko .10
69 Sandy Alomar Jr. .10
70 Travis Fryman .10
71 David Justice .10
72 Kenny Lofton .10
73 Charles Nagy .10
74 Manny Ramirez .75
75 Jim Thome .65
76 Omar Vizquel .10
77 Enrique Wilson .10
78 Jaret Wright .10
79 Dante Bichette .10
80 Ellis Burks .10
81 Vinny Castilla .10
82 Todd Helton .75
83 Darryl Kile .10
84 Mike Lansing .10
85 Neifi Perez .10
86 Larry Walker .10
87 Raul Casanova .10
88 Tony Clark .10
89 Luis Gonzalez .10
90 Bobby Higginson .10
91 Brian Hunter .10
92 Bip Roberts .10
93 Justin Thompson .10
94 Josh Booty .10
95 Craig Counsell .10
96 Livan Hernandez .10
97 Ryan Jackson RC .10
98 Mark Kotsay .10
99 Derrek Lee .50
100 Mike Piazza 1.25
101 Edgar Renteria .10
102 Cliff Floyd .10

103 Moises Alou .10
104 Jeff Bagwell .75
105 Derrick Bell .10
106 Sean Berry .10
107 Craig Biggio .10
108 John Halama RC .15
109 Richard Hidalgo .10
110 Shane Reynolds .10
111 Tim Belcher .10
112 Brian Bevil .10
113 Jeff Conine .10
114 Johnny Damon .25
115 Jeff King .10
116 Jeff Montgomery .10
117 Dean Palmer .10
118 Terry Pendleton .10
119 Bobby Bonilla .10
120 Wilton Guerrero .10
121 Todd Hollandsworth .10
122 Charles Johnson .10
123 Eric Karros .10
124 Paul Konerko .20
125 Ramon Martinez .10
126 Raul Mondesi .10
127 Hideo Nomo .40
128 Gary Sheffield .45
129 Ismael Valdes .10
130 Jeromy Burnitz .10
131 Jeff Cirillo .10
132 Todd Dunn .10
133 Marquis Grissom .10
134 John Jaha .10
135 Scott Karl .10
136 Dave Nilsson .10
137 Jose Valentin .10
138 Fernando Vina .10
139 Rick Aguilera .10
140 Marty Cordova .10
141 Pat Meares .10
142 Paul Molitor .75
143 David Ortiz .50
144 Brad Radke .10
145 Terry Steinbach .10
146 Todd Walker .10
147 Shane Andrews .10
148 Brad Fullmer .10
149 Mark Grudzielanek .10
150 Vladimir Guerrero .75
151 F.P. Santangelo .10
152 Jose Vidro .10
153 Rondell White .10
154 Carlos Baerga .10
155 Bernard Gilkey .10
156 Todd Hundley .10
157 Butch Huskey .10
158 Bobby Jones .10
159 Brian McRae .10
160 John Olerud .10
161 Rey Ordonez .10
162 Masato Yoshii RC .25
163 David Cone .10
164 Hideki Irabu .10
165 Derek Jeter 2.50
166 Chuck Knoblauch .10
167 Tino Martinez .10
168 Paul O'Neill .10
169 Andy Pettitte .30
170 Mariano Rivera .15
171 Darryl Strawberry .10
172 David Wells .10
173 Bernie Williams .10
174 Ryan Christenson RC .15
175 Jason Giambi .60
176 Ben Grieve .10
177 Rickey Henderson .75
178 A.J. Hinch .10
179 Kenny Rogers .10
180 Ricky Bottalico .10
181 Rico Brogna .10
182 Doug Glanville .10
183 Gregg Jefferies .10
184 Mike Lieberthal .10
185 Scott Rolen .65
186 Curt Schilling .35
187 Jermaine Allensworth .10
188 Lou Collier .10
189 Jose Guillen .10
190 Jason Kendall .10
191 Al Martin .10
192 Tony Womack .10
193 Kevin Young .10
194 Royce Clayton .10
195 Delino DeShields .10
196 Gary Gaetti .10
197 Ron Gant .10
198 Brian Jordan .10
199 Ray Lankford .10
200 Mark McGwire 2.00
201 Todd Stottlemyre .10
202 Kevin Brown .10
203 Ken Caminiti .10
204 Steve Finley .10
205 Tony Gwynn 1.00
206 Carlos Hernandez .10

207 Wally Joyner .10
208 Greg Vaughn .10
209 Barry Bonds 2.50
210 Shawn Estes .10
211 Orel Hershiser .10
212 Stan Javier .10
213 Jeff Kent .10
214 Bill Mueller .10
215 Robb Nen .10
216 J.T. Snow .10
217 Jay Buhner .10
218 Ken Cloude .10
219 Joey Cora .10
220 Ken Griffey Jr. 1.50
221 Glenallen Hill .10
222 Randy Johnson .75
223 Edgar Martinez .10
224 Jamie Moyer .10
225 Alex Rodriguez 2.00
226 David Segui .10
227 Dan Wilson .10
228 Rolando Arrojo RC .25
229 Wade Boggs 1.00
230 Miguel Cairo .10
231 Roberto Hernandez .10
232 Quinton McCracken .10
233 Fred McGriff .10
234 Paul Sorrento .10
235 Kevin Stocker .10
236 Will Clark .10
237 Juan Gonzalez .40
238 Rusty Greer .10
239 Rick Helling .10
240 Roberto Kelly .10
241 Ivan Rodriguez .65
242 Aaron Sele .10
243 John Wetteland .10
244 Jose Canseco .50
245 Roger Clemens 1.25
246 Jose Cruz Jr. .10
247 Carlos Delgado .50
248 Alex Gonzalez .10
249 Ed Sprague .10
250 Shannon Stewart .10

Online

NM/M
Complete Set (36): 35.00
Common Player: .45
Inserted 1:9
1 Cal Ripken Jr. 5.00
2 Nomar Garciaparra 2.00
3 Pedro Martinez 1.50
4 Mo Vaughn .45
5 Frank Thomas 1.50
6 Sandy Alomar Jr. .45
7 Manny Ramirez 1.50
8 Jaret Wright .45
9 Paul Molitor 1.50
10 Derek Jeter 5.00
11 Bernie Williams .45
12 Ben Grieve .45
13 Ken Griffey Jr. 3.00
14 Edgar Martinez .45
15 Alex Rodriguez 4.00
16 Wade Boggs 2.00
17 Juan Gonzalez .75
18 Ivan Rodriguez 1.00
19 Roger Clemens 2.50
20 Travis Lee .45
21 Matt Williams .45
22 Andres Galarraga .45
23 Chipper Jones 2.00
24 Greg Maddux 2.00
25 Sammy Sosa 2.00
26 Kerry Wood .75
27 Barry Larkin .45
28 Larry Walker .45
29 Derrek Lee 1.00
30 Jeff Bagwell 1.50
31 Hideo Nomo .75
32 Mike Piazza 2.50
33 Scott Rolen 1.00

34	Mark McGwire	4.00
35	Tony Gwynn	2.00
36	Barry Bonds	5.00

Face to Face

		NM/M
Complete Set (10):		50.00
Common Player:		2.00
Inserted 1:145		
1	Alex Rodriguez, Nomar Garciaparra	9.00
2	Mark McGwire, Ken Griffey Jr.	9.00
3	Mike Piazza, Sandy Alomar Jr.	6.00
4	Kerry Wood, Roger Clemens	6.00
5	Cal Ripken Jr., Paul Molitor	10.00
6	Tony Gwynn, Wade Boggs	5.00
7	Frank Thomas, Chipper Jones	5.00
8	Travis Lee, Ben Grieve	2.00
9	Hideo Nomo, Hideki Irabu	3.50
10	Juan Gonzalez, Manny Ramirez	3.50

EO Portraits

MARK McGWIRE St. Louis

		NM/M
Complete Set (20):		70.00
Common Player:		1.25
Inserted 1:73		
1	Cal Ripken Jr.	10.00
2	Nomar Garciaparra	5.00
3	Mo Vaughn	1.25
4	Frank Thomas	4.00
5	Manny Ramirez	4.00
6	Ben Grieve	1.25
7	Ken Griffey Jr.	6.50
8	Alex Rodriguez	7.50
9	Juan Gonzalez	2.00
10	Ivan Rodriguez	3.50
11	Travis Lee	1.25
12	Greg Maddux	5.00
13	Chipper Jones	5.00
14	Kerry Wood	2.00
15	Larry Walker	1.25
16	Jeff Bagwell	4.00
17	Mike Piazza	6.00
18	Mark McGwire	7.50
19	Tony Gwynn	5.00
20	Barry Bonds	10.00

Prism

MIKE PIAZZA

	NM/M
Complete Set (20):	30.00

Common Player:		.75
Inserted 1:37		
1	Cal Ripken Jr.	4.50
2	Nomar Garciaparra	2.50
3	Pedro Martinez	1.50
4	Frank Thomas	1.50
5	Manny Ramirez	1.50
6	Brian Giles	.75
7	Derek Jeter	4.50
8	Ben Grieve	.75
9	Ken Griffey Jr.	3.00
10	Alex Rodriguez	3.50
11	Juan Gonzalez	1.00
12	Travis Lee	.75
13	Chipper Jones	2.50
14	Greg Maddux	2.50
15	Kerry Wood	1.00
16	Larry Walker	.75
17	Hideo Nomo	1.00
18	Mike Piazza	3.00
19	Mark McGwire	3.50
20	Tony Gwynn	2.50

Rising Stars

		NM/M
Complete Set (30):		15.00
Common Player:		.50
Inserted 1:9		
Tier 1 (# to 100):		3X
Tier 2 (# to 75):		4X
Tier 3 (# to 50):		5X
Tier 4 (# to 25):		10X
Tier 5 (1 of 1): Value Undetermined		
1	Nerio Rodriguez, Sidney Ponson	.50
2	Frank Catalanotto, Roberto Duran, Sean Runyan	.50
3	Kevin L. Brown, Carlos Almanzar	.50
4	Aaron Boone, Pat Watkins, Scott Winchester	.50
5	Brian Meadows, Andy Larkin, Antonio Alfonseca	.50
6	DaRond Stovall, Trey Moore, Shayne Bennett	.50
7	Felix Martinez, Larry Sutton, Brian Bevil	.50
8	Homer Bush, Mike Buddie	.50
9	Rich Butler, Esteban Yan	.50
10	Damon Hollins, Brian Edmondson	.50
11	Lou Collier, Jose Silva, Javier Martinez	.50
12	Steve Sinclair, Mark Dalesandro	.50
13	Jason Varitek, Brian Rose, Brian Shouse	.50
14	Mike Caruso, Jeff Abbott, Tom Fordham	.50
15	Jason Johnson, Bobby Smith	.50
16	Dave Berg, Mark Kotsay, Jesus Sanchez	.50
17	Richard Hidalgo, John Halama, Trever Miller	.50
18	Geoff Jenkins, Bobby Hughes, Steve Woodard	.50
19	Eli Marrero, Cliff Politte, Mike Busby	.50
20	Desi Relaford, Darrin Winston	.50
21	Todd Helton, Bobby Jones	1.50
22	Rolando Arrojo, Miguel Cairo, Dan Carlson	.50
23	David Ortiz, Javier Valentin, Eric Milton	1.25
24	Magglio Ordonez, Greg Norton	1.00
25	Brad Fullmer, Javier Vazquez, Rick DeHart	.50
26	Paul Konerko, Matt Luke	1.00

27	Derrek Lee, Ryan Jackson, John Roskos	1.25
28	Ben Grieve, A.J. Hinch, Ryan Christenson	.50
29	Travis Lee, Karim Garcia, David Dellucci	.65
30	Kerry Wood, Marc Pisciotta	1.00

1998 Pacific Online

		NM/M
Complete Set (800):		60.00
Common Player:		.05
Web Stars/RC's:		2X
Inserted 1:1		
Pack (9):		.75
Wax Box (36):		20.00
1	Garret Anderson	.05
2	Rich DeLucia RC	.05
3	Jason Dickson	.05
4	Gary DiSarcina	.05
5	Jim Edmonds	.05
6	Darin Erstad	.15
7	Cecil Fielder	.05
8	Chuck Finley	.05
9	Carlos Carcia	.05
10	Shigetosi Hasegawa	.05
11	Ken Hill	.05
12	Dave Hollins	.05
13	Mike Holtz	.05
14	Mike James	.05
15	Norberto Martin	.05
16	Damon Mashore	.05
17	Jack McDowell	.05
18	Phil Nevin	.05
19	Omar Olivares	.05
20	Troy Percival	.05
21	Rich Robertson	.05
22	Tim Salmon	.05
23	Craig Shipley	.05
24	Matt Walbeck	.05
25	Allen Watson	.05
26	Jim Edmonds (Angels Checklist)	.05
27	Brian Anderson	.05
28	Tony Batista	.05
29	Jay Bell	.05
30	Andy Benes	.05
31	Yamil Benitez	.05
32	Willie Blair	.05
33	Brent Brede	.05
34	Scott Brow	.05
35	Omar Daal	.05
36	David Dellucci	.05
37	Edwin Diaz	.05
38	Jorge Fabregas	.05
39	Andy Fox	.05
40	Karim Garcia	.05
41a	Travis Lee/Btg	.05
41b	Travis Lee/Fld	.05
42	Barry Manuel	.05
43	Gregg Olson	.05
44	Felix Rodriguez	.05
45	Clint Sodowsky	.05
46	Russ Springer	.05
47	Andy Stankiewicz	.05
48	Kelly Stinnett	.05
49	Jeff Suppan	.05
50	Devon White	.05
51	Matt Williams	.05
52	Travis Lee (Diamondbacks Checklist)	.05
53	Danny Bautista	.05
54	Rafael Belliard	.05
55	Adam Butler RC	.10
56	Mike Cather	.05
57	Brian Edmondson	.05
58	Alan Embree	.05
59	Andres Galarraga	.05
60	Tom Glavine	.35
61	Tony Graffanino	.05
62	Andruw Jones	.65
63a	Chipper Jones/Btg	.75

63b	Chipper Jones/Fld	.75
64	Ryan Klesko	.05
65	Keith Lockhart	.05
66	Javy Lopez	.05
67a	Greg Maddux/Btg	.75
67b	Greg Maddux/Pitching	.75
68	Dennis Martinez	.05
69	Kevin Millwood RC	.50
70	Denny Neagle	.05
71	Eddie Perez	.05
72	Curtis Pride	.05
73	John Smoltz	.05
74	Michael Tucker	.05
75	Walt Weiss	.05
76	Gerald Williams	.05
77	Mark Wohlers	.05
78	Chipper Jones (Braves Checklist)	.40
79	Roberto Alomar	.15
80	Brady Anderson	.05
81	Harold Baines	.05
82	Armando Benitez	.05
83	Mike Bordick	.05
84	Joe Carter	.05
85	Norm Charlton	.05
86	Eric Davis	.05
87	Doug Drabek	.05
88	Scott Erickson	.05
89	Jeffrey Hammonds	.05
90	Chris Hoiles	.05
91	Scott Kamieniecki	.05
92	Jimmy Key	.05
93	Terry Mathews	.05
94	Alan Mills	.05
95	Mike Mussina	.25
96	Jesse Orosco	.05
97	Rafael Palmeiro	.60
98	Sidney Ponson	.05
99	Jeff Reboulet	.05
100	Arthur Rhodes	.05
101a	Cal Ripken Jr./Btg	2.00
101b	Cal Ripken Jr./Btg (Close-up.)	2.00
102	Nerio Rodriguez	.05
103	B.J. Surhoff	.05
104	Lenny Webster	.05
105	Cal Ripken Jr. (Orioles Checklist)	1.00
106	Steve Avery	.05
107	Mike Benjamin	.05
108	Darren Bragg	.05
109	Damon Buford	.05
110	Jim Corsi	.05
111	Dennis Eckersley	.60
112	Rich Garces	.05
113a	Nomar Garciaparra/Btg	.75
113b	Nomar Garciaparra/Fld	.75
114	Tom Gordon	.05
115	Scott Hatteberg	.05
116	Butch Henry	.05
117	Reggie Jefferson	.05
118	Mark Lemke	.05
119	Darren Lewis	.05
120	Jim Leyritz	.05
121	Derek Lowe	.05
122	Pedro Martinez	.65
123	Troy O'Leary	.05
124	Brian Rose	.05
125	Bret Saberhagen	.05
126	Donnie Sadler	.05
127	Brian Shouse	.05
128	John Valentin	.05
129	Jason Varitek	.05
130	Mo Vaughn	.05
131	Tim Wakefield	.05
132	John Wasdin	.05
133	Nomar Garciaparra (Red Sox Checklist)	.45
134	Terry Adams	.05
135	Manny Alexander	.05
136	Rod Beck	.05
137	Jeff Blauser	.05
138	Brant Brown	.05
139	Mark Clark	.05
140	Jeremi Gonzalez	.05
141	Mark Grace	.05
142	Jose Hernandez	.05
143	Tyler Houston	.05
144	Lance Johnson	.05
145	Sandy Martinez	.05
146	Matt Mieske	.05
147	Mickey Morandini	.05
148	Terry Mulholland	.05
149	Kevin Orie	.05
150	Bob Patterson	.05
151	Marc Pisciotta	.05
152	Henry Rodriguez	.05
153	Scott Servais	.05
154	Sammy Sosa	.75
155	Kevin Tapani	.05
156	Steve Trachsel	.05
157a	Kerry Wood/Pitching	.30
157b	Kerry Wood/Pitching (Close-up.)	.30

No.	Name	Price
158	Kerry Wood (Cubs Checklist)	.20
159	Jeff Abbott	.05
160	James Baldwin	.05
161	Albert Belle	.05
162	Jason Bere	.05
163	Mike Cameron	.05
164	Mike Caruso	.05
165	Carlos Castillo	.05
166	Tony Castillo	.05
167	Ray Durham	.05
168	Scott Eyre	.05
169	Tom Fordham	.05
170	Keith Foulke	.05
171	Lou Frazier	.05
172	Matt Karchner	.05
173	Chad Kreuter	.05
174	Jaime Navarro	.05
175	Greg Norton	.05
176	Charlie O'Brien	.05
177	Magglio Ordonez	.15
178	Ruben Sierra	.05
179	Bill Simas	.05
180	Mike Sirotka	.05
181	Chris Snopek	.05
182a	Frank Thomas (In batter's box.)	.65
182b	Frank Thomas/Swinging	.65
183	Robin Ventura	.05
184	Frank Thomas (White Sox Checklist)	.40
185	Stan Belinda	.05
186	Aaron Boone	.05
187	Bret Boone	.05
188	Brook Fordyce	.05
189	Willie Greene	.05
190	Pete Harnisch	.05
191	Lenny Harris	.05
192	Mark Hutton	.05
193	Damian Jackson	.05
194	Ricardo Jordan	.05
195	Barry Larkin	.05
196	Eduardo Perez	.05
197	Pokey Reese	.05
198	Mike Remlinger	.05
199	Reggie Sanders	.05
200	Jeff Shaw	.05
201	Chris Stynes	.05
202	Scott Sullivan	.05
203	Eddie Taubensee	.05
204	Brett Tomko	.05
205	Pat Watkins	.05
206	David Weathers	.05
207	Gabe White	.05
208	Scott Winchester	.05
209	Barry Larkin (Reds Checklist)	.05
210	Sandy Alomar Jr.	.05
211	Paul Assenmacher	.05
212	Geronimo Berroa	.05
213	Pat Borders	.05
214	Jeff Branson	.05
215	Dave Burba	.05
216	Bartolo Colon	.05
217	Shawon Dunston	.05
218	Travis Fryman	.05
219	Brian Giles	.05
220	Dwight Gooden	.05
221	Mike Jackson	.05
222	David Justice	.05
223	Kenny Lofton	.05
224	Jose Mesa	.05
225	Alvin Morman	.05
226	Charles Nagy	.05
227	Chad Ogea	.05
228	Eric Plunk	.05
229	Manny Ramirez	.65
230	Paul Shuey	.05
231	Jim Thome	.65
232	Ron Villone	.05
233	Omar Vizquel	.05
234	Enrique Wilson	.05
235	Jaret Wright	.05
236	Manny Ramirez (Indians Checklist)	.40
237	Pedro Astacio	.05
238	Jason Bates	.05
239	Dante Bichette	.05
240	Ellis Burks	.05
241	Vinny Castilla	.05
242	Greg Colbrunn	.05
243	Mike DeJean	.05
244	Jerry Dipoto	.05
245	Curtis Goodwin	.05
246	Todd Helton	.05
247	Bobby Jones	.05
248	Darryl Kile	.05
249	Mike Lansing	.05
250	Curtis Leskanic	.05
251	Nelson Liriano	.05
252	Kirt Manwaring	.05
253	Mike McElroy	.05
254	Mike Munoz	.05
255	Neifi Perez	.05
256	Jeff Reed	.05
257	Mark Thompson	.05
258	John Vander Wal	.05
259	Dave Veres	.05
260a	Larry Walker/Btg	.05
260b	Larry Walker/Btg (Close-up.)	.05
261	Jamey Wright	.05
262	Larry Walker (Rockies Checklist)	.05
263	Kimera Bartee	.05
264	Doug Brocail	.05
265	Raul Casanova	.05
266	Frank Castillo	.05
267	Frank Catalanotto	.05
268	Tony Clark	.05
269	Deivi Cruz	.05
270	Roberto Duran	.05
271	Damion Easley	.05
272	Bryce Florie	.05
273	Luis Gonzalez	.05
274	Bob Higginson	.05
275	Brian Hunter	.05
276	Todd Jones	.05
277	Greg Keagle	.05
278	Jeff Manto	.05
279	Brian Moehler	.05
280	Joe Oliver	.05
281	Joe Randa	.05
282	Billy Ripken	.05
283	Bip Roberts	.05
284	Sean Runyan	.05
285	A.J. Sager	.05
286	Justin Thompson	.05
287	Tony Clark (Tigers Checklist)	.05
288	Antonio Alfonseca	.05
289	Dave Berg	.05
290	Josh Booty	.05
291	John Cangelosi	.05
292	Craig Counsell	.05
293	Vic Darensbourg	.05
294	Cliff Floyd	.05
295	Oscar Henriquez	.05
296	Felix Heredia	.05
297	Ryan Jackson RC	.05
298	Mark Kotsay	.05
299	Andy Larkin	.05
300	Derrek Lee	.60
301	Brian Meadows	.05
302	Rafael Medina	.05
303	Jay Powell	.05
304	Edgar Renteria	.05
305	Jesus Sanchez RC	.05
306	Rob Stanifer	.05
307	Gregg Zaun	.05
308	Derrek Lee (Marlins Checklist)	.30
309	Moises Alou	.05
310	Brad Ausmus	.05
311a	Jeff Bagwell/Btg	.65
311b	Jeff Bagwell/Fld	.65
312	Derek Bell	.05
313	Sean Bergman	.05
314	Sean Berry	.05
315	Craig Biggio	.05
316	Tim Bogar	.05
317	Jose Cabrera	.05
318	Dave Clark	.05
319	Tony Eusebio	.05
320	Carl Everett	.05
321	Ricky Gutierrez	.05
322	John Halama	.05
323	Mike Hampton	.05
324	Doug Henry	.05
325	Richard Hidalgo	.05
326	Jack Howell	.05
327	Jose Lima	.05
328	Mike Magnante	.05
329	Trever Miller	.05
330	C.J. Nitkowski	.05
331	Shane Reynolds	.05
332	Bill Spiers	.05
333	Billy Wagner	.05
334	Jeff Bagwell (Astros Checklist)	.40
335	Tim Belcher	.05
336	Brian Bevil	.05
337	Johnny Damon	.35
338	Jermaine Dye	.05
339	Sal Fasano	.05
340	Shane Halter	.05
341	Chris Haney	.05
342	Jed Hansen	.05
343	Jeff King	.05
344	Jeff Montgomery	.05
345	Hal Morris	.05
346	Jose Offerman	.05
347	Dean Palmer	.05
348	Terry Pendleton	.05
349	Hipolito Pichardo	.05
350	Jim Pittsley	.05
351	Pat Rapp	.05
352	Jose Rosado	.05
353	Glendon Rusch	.05
354	Scott Service	.05
355	Larry Sutton	.05
356	Mike Sweeney	.05
357	Joe Vitiello	.05
358	Matt Whisenant	.05
359	Ernie Young	.05
360	Jeff King (Royals Checklist)	.05
361	Bobby Bonilla	.05
362	Jim Bruske	.05
363	Juan Castro	.05
364	Roger Cedeno	.05
365	Mike Devereaux	.05
366	Darren Dreifort	.05
367	Jim Eisenreich	.05
368	Wilton Guerrero	.05
369	Mark Guthrie	.05
370	Darren Hall	.05
371	Todd Hollandsworth	.05
372	Thomas Howard	.05
373	Trenidad Hubbard	.05
374	Charles Johnson	.05
375	Eric Karros	.05
376	Paul Konerko	.20
377	Matt Luke	.05
378	Ramon Martinez	.05
379	Raul Mondesi	.05
380	Hideo Nomo	.35
381	Antonio Osuna	.05
382	Chan Ho Park	.05
383	Tom Prince	.05
384	Scott Radinsky	.05
385	Gary Sheffield	.40
386	Ismael Valdes	.05
387	Jose Vizcaino	.05
388	Eric Young	.05
389	Gary Sheffield (Dodgers Checklist)	.10
390	Jeromy Burnitz	.05
391	Jeff Cirillo	.05
392	Cal Eldred	.05
393	Chad Fox	.05
394	Marquis Grissom	.05
395	Bob Hamelin	.05
396	Bobby Hughes	.05
397	Darrin Jackson	.05
398	John Jaha	.05
399	Geoff Jenkins	.05
400	Doug Jones	.05
401	Jeff Juden	.05
402	Scott Karl	.05
403	Jesse Levis	.05
404	Mark Loretta	.05
405	Mike Matheny	.05
406	Jose Mercedes	.05
407	Mike Myers	.05
408	Marc Newfield	.05
409	Dave Nilsson	.05
410	Al Reyes	.05
411	Jose Valentin	.05
412	Fernando Vina	.05
413	Paul Wagner	.05
414	Bob Wickman	.05
415	Steve Woodard	.05
416	Marquis Grissom (Brewers Checklist)	.05
417	Rick Aguilera	.05
418	Ron Coomer	.05
419	Marty Cordova	.05
420	Brent Gates	.05
421	Eddie Guardado	.05
422	Denny Hocking	.05
423	Matt Lawton	.05
424	Pat Meares	.05
425	Orlando Merced	.05
426	Eric Milton	.05
427	Paul Molitor	.65
428	Mike Morgan	.05
429	Dan Naulty	.05
430	Otis Nixon	.05
431	Alex Ochoa	.05
432	David Ortiz	.40
433	Brad Radke	.05
434	Todd Ritchie	.05
435	Frank Rodriguez	.05
436	Terry Steinbach	.05
437	Greg Swindell	.05
438	Bob Tewksbury	.05
439	Mike Trombley	.05
440	Javier Valentin	.05
441	Todd Walker	.05
442	Paul Molitor (Twins Checklist)	.40
443	Shane Andrews	.05
444	Miguel Batista	.05
445	Shayne Bennett	.05
446	Rick DeHart	.05
447	Brad Fullmer	.05
448	Mark Grudzielanek	.05
449	Vladimir Guerrero	.65
450	Dustin Hermanson	.05
451	Steve Kline	.05
452	Scott Livingstone	.05
453	Mike Maddux	.05
454	Derrick May	.05
455	Ryan McGuire	.05
456	Trey Moore	.05
457	Mike Mordecai	.05
458	Carl Pavano	.05
459	Carlos Perez	.05
460	F.P. Santangelo	.05
461	DaRond Stovall	.05
462	Anthony Telford	.05
463	Ugueth Urbina	.05
464	Marc Valdes	.05
465	Jose Vidro	.05
466	Rondell White	.05
467	Chris Widger	.05
468	Vladimir Guerrero (Expos Checklist)	.40
469	Edgardo Alfonzo	.05
470	Carlos Baerga	.05
471	Rich Becker	.05
472	Brian Bohanon	.05
473	Alberto Castillo	.05
474	Dennis Cook	.05
475	John Franco	.05
476	Matt Franco	.05
477	Bernard Gilkey	.05
478	John Hudek	.05
479	Butch Huskey	.05
480	Bobby Jones	.05
481	Al Leiter	.05
482	Luis Lopez	.05
483	Brian McRae	.05
484	Dave Mlicki	.05
485	John Olerud	.05
486	Rey Ordonez	.05
487	Craig Paquette	.05
488a	Mike Piazza/Btg	1.00
488b	Mike Piazza/Btg (Close-up.)	1.00
489	Todd Pratt	.05
490	Mel Rojas	.05
491	Tim Spehr	.05
492	Turk Wendell	.05
493	Masato Yoshii RC	.25
494	Mike Piazza (Mets Checklist)	.45
495	Willie Banks	.05
496	Scott Brosius	.05
497	Mike Buddie	.05
498	Homer Bush	.05
499	David Cone	.05
500	Chad Curtis	.05
501	Chili Davis	.05
502	Joe Girardi	.05
503	Darren Holmes	.05
504	Hideki Irabu	.05
505a	Derek Jeter/Btg	2.00
505b	Derek Jeter/Fld	2.00
506	Chuck Knoblauch	.05
507	Graeme Lloyd	.05
508	Tino Martinez	.05
509	Ramiro Mendoza	.05
510	Jeff Nelson	.05
511	Paul O'Neill	.20
512	Andy Pettitte	.05
513	Jorge Posada	.05
514	Tim Raines	.05
515	Mariano Rivera	.15
516	Luis Sojo	.05
517	Mike Stanton	.05
518	Darryl Strawberry	.05
519	Dale Sveum	.05
520	David Wells	.05
521	Bernie Williams	.05
522	Bernie Williams (Yankees Checklist)	.05
523	Kurt Abbott	.05
524	Mike Blowers	.05
525	Rafael Bournigal	.05
526	Tom Candiotti	.05
527	Ryan Christenson	.05
528	Mike Fetters	.05
529	Jason Giambi	.50
530a	Ben Grieve/Btg	.05
530b	Ben Grieve/Running	.05
531	Buddy Groom	.05
532	Jimmy Haynes	.05
533	Rickey Henderson	.65
534	A.J. Hinch	.05
535	Mike Macfarlane	.05
536	Dave Magadan	.05
537	T.J. Mathews	.05
538	Jason McDonald	.05
539	Kevin Mitchell	.05
540	Mike Mohler	.05
541	Mike Oquist	.05
542	Ariel Prieto	.05
543	Kenny Rogers	.05
544	Aaron Small	.05
545	Scott Spiezio	.05
546	Matt Stairs	.05
547	Bill Taylor	.05
548	Dave Telgheder	.05
549	Jack Voigt	.05

550	Ben Grieve (A's Checklist)	.05
551	Bob Abreu	.10
552	Ruben Amaro	.05
553	Alex Arias	.05
554	Matt Beech	.05
555	Ricky Bottalico	.05
556	Billy Brewer	.05
557	Rico Brogna	.05
558	Doug Glanville	.05
559	Wayne Gomes	.05
560	Mike Grace	.05
561	Tyler Green	.05
562	Rex Hudler	.05
563	Gregg Jefferies	.05
564	Kevin Jordan	.05
565	Mark Leiter	.05
566	Mark Lewis	.05
567	Mike Lieberthal	.05
568	Mark Parent	.05
569	Yorkis Perez	.05
570	Desi Relaford	.05
571	Scott Rolen	.50
572	Curt Schilling	.35
573	Kevin Sefcik	.05
574	Jerry Spradlin	.05
575	Garrett Stephenson	.05
576	Darrin Winston	.05
577	Scott Rolen (Phillies Checklist)	.20
578	Jermaine Allensworth	.05
579	Jason Christiansen	.05
580	Lou Collier	.05
581	Francisco Cordova	.05
582	Elmer Dessens	.05
583	Freddy Garcia	.05
584	Jose Guillen	.05
585	Jason Kendall	.05
586	Jon Lieber	.05
587	Esteban Loaiza	.05
588	Al Martin	.05
589	Javier Martinez	.05
590	Chris Peters RC	.05
591	Kevin Polcovich	.05
592	Ricardo Rincon	.05
593	Jason Schmidt	.05
594	Jose Silva	.05
595	Mark Smith	.05
596	Doug Strange	.05
597	Turner Ward	.05
598	Marc Wilkins	.05
599	Mike Williams	.05
600	Tony Womack	.05
601	Kevin Young	.05
602	Tony Womack (Pirates Checklist)	.05
603	Manny Aybar	.05
604	Kent Bottenfield	.05
605	Jeff Brantley	.05
606	Mike Busby	.05
607	Royce Clayton	.05
608	Delino DeShields	.05
609	John Frascatore	.05
610	Gary Gaetti	.05
611	Ron Gant	.05
612	David Howard	.05
613	Brian Hunter	.05
614	Brian Jordan	.05
615	Tom Lampkin	.05
616	Ray Lankford	.05
617	Braden Looper	.05
618	John Mabry	.05
619	Eli Marrero	.05
620	Willie McGee	.05
621a	Mark McGwire/Btg	1.50
621b	Mark McGwire/Fld	1.50
622	Kent Mercker	.05
623	Matt Morris	.05
624	Donovan Osborne	.05
625	Tom Pagnozzi	.05
626	Lance Painter	.05
627	Mark Petkovsek	.05
628	Todd Stottlemyre	.05
629	Mark McGwire (Cardinals Checklist)	.75
630	Andy Ashby	.05
631	Brian Boehringer	.05
632	Kevin Brown	.05
633	Ken Caminiti	.05
634	Steve Finley	.05
635	Ed Giovanola	.05
636	Chris Gomez	.05
637a	Tony Gwynn (Blue jersey.)	.75
637b	Tony Gwynn (White jersey.)	.75
	SAMPLE Tony Gwynn (SAMPLE overprint on back.)	1.00
638	Joey Hamilton	.05
639	Carlos Hernandez	.05
640	Sterling Hitchcock	.05
641	Trevor Hoffman	.05
642	Wally Joyner	.05
643	Dan Miceli	.05

644	James Mouton	.05
645	Greg Myers	.05
646	Carlos Reyes	.05
647	Andy Sheets	.05
648	Pete Smith	.05
649	Mark Sweeney	.05
650	Greg Vaughn	.05
651	Quilvio Veras	.05
652	Tony Gwynn (Padres Checklist)	.40
653	Rich Aurilia	.05
654	Marvin Benard	.05
655a	Barry Bonds/Btg	2.00
655b	Barry Bonds/Btg (Close-up.)	2.00
656	Danny Darwin	.05
657	Shawn Estes	.05
658	Mark Gardner	.05
659	Darryl Hamilton	.05
660	Charlie Hayes	.05
661	Orel Hershiser	.05
662	Stan Javier	.05
663	Brian Johnson	.05
664	John Johnstone	.05
665	Jeff Kent	.05
666	Brent Mayne	.05
667	Bill Mueller	.05
668	Robb Nen	.05
669	Jim Poole	.05
670	Steve Reed	.05
671	Rich Rodriguez	.05
672	Kirk Rueter	.05
673	Rey Sanchez	.05
674	J.T. Snow	.05
675	Julian Tavarez	.05
676	Barry Bonds (Giants Checklist)	1.00
677	Rich Amaral	.05
678	Bobby Ayala	.05
679	Jay Buhner	.05
680	Ken Cloude	.05
681	Joey Cora	.05
682	Russ Davis	.05
683	Rob Ducey	.05
684	Jeff Fassero	.05
685	Tony Fossas	.05
686a	Ken Griffey Jr./Btg	1.25
686b	Ken Griffey Jr./Fld	1.25
687	Glenallen Hill	.05
688	Jeff Huson	.05
689	Randy Johnson	.65
690	Edgar Martinez	.05
691	John Marzano	.05
692	Jamie Moyer	.05
693a	Alex Rodriguez/Btg	1.50
693b	Alex Rodriguez/Fld	1.50
694	David Segui	.05
695	Heathcliff Slocumb	.05
696	Paul Spoljaric	.05
697	Bill Swift	.05
698	Mike Timlin	.05
699	Bob Wells	.05
700	Dan Wilson	.05
701	Ken Griffey Jr. (Mariners Checklist)	.50
702	Wilson Alvarez	.05
703	Rolando Arrojo RC	.30
704a	Wade Boggs/Btg	.75
704b	Wade Boggs/Fld	.75
705	Rich Butler	.05
706	Miguel Cairo	.05
707	Mike Difelice	.05
708	John Flaherty	.05
709	Roberto Hernandez	.05
710	Mike Kelly	.05
711	Aaron Ledesma	.05
712	Albie Lopez	.05
713	Dave Martinez	.05
714	Quinton McCracken	.05
715	Fred McGriff	.05
716	Jim Mecir	.05
717	Tony Saunders	.05
718	Bobby Smith	.05
719	Paul Sorrento	.05
720	Dennis Springer	.05
721	Kevin Stocker	.05
722	Ramon Tatis	.05
723	Bubba Trammell	.05
724	Esteban Yan	.05
725	Wade Boggs (Devil Rays Checklist)	.40
726	Luis Alicea	.05
727	Scott Bailes	.05
728	John Burkett	.05
729	Domingo Cedeno	.05
730	Will Clark	.05
731	Kevin Elster	.05
732a	Juan Gonzalez/Bat	.35
732b	Juan Gonzalez (No bat.)	.35
733	Tom Goodwin	.05
734	Rusty Greer	.05
735	Eric Gunderson	.05
736	Bill Haselman	.05
737	Rick Helling	.05

738	Roberto Kelly	.05
739	Mark McLemore	.05
740	Darren Oliver	.05
741	Danny Patterson	.05
742	Roger Pavlik	.05
743a	Ivan Rodriguez/Btg	.60
743b	Ivan Rodriguez/Fld	.60
744	Aaron Sele	.05
745	Mike Simms	.05
746	Lee Stevens	.05
747	Fernando Tatis	.05
748	John Wetteland	.05
749	Bobby Witt	.05
750	Juan Gonzalez (Rangers Checklist)	.20
751	Carlos Almanzar	.05
752	Kevin Brown	.05
753	Jose Canseco	.40
754	Chris Carpenter	.05
755	Roger Clemens	1.00
756	Felipe Crespo	.05
757	Jose Cruz Jr.	.05
758	Mark Dalesandro	.05
759	Carlos Delgado	.50
760	Kelvim Escobar	.05
761	Tony Fernandez	.05
762	Darrin Fletcher	.05
763	Alex Gonzalez	.05
764	Craig Grebeck	.05
765	Shawn Green	.35
766	Juan Guzman	.05
767	Erik Hanson	.05
768	Pat Hentgen	.05
769	Randy Myers	.05
770	Robert Person	.05
771	Dan Plesac	.05
772	Paul Quantrill	.05
773	Bill Risley	.05
774	Juan Samuel	.05
775	Steve Sinclair	.05
776	Ed Sprague	.05
777	Mike Stanley	.05
778	Shannon Stewart	.05
779	Woody Williams	.05
780	Roger Clemens (Blue Jays Checklist)	.45

Web Cards

Web Stars/RC's: 2X
Inserted 1:1
(See 1998 Pacific Online for checklist and base card values.)

1998 Pacific Paramount

	NM/M
Complete Set (250):	20.00
Common Player:	.10
Gold (1:1R):	1X
Copper (1:1H):	1X
Red (1:1 ANCO):	2X
Platinum Blue (1:73):	4X

Holographic Silver:		20X
Production 99 Sets		
Pack (6):		1.00
Wax Box (36):		15.00
1	Garret Anderson	.10
2	Gary DiSarcina	.10
3	Jim Edmonds	.10
4	Darin Erstad	.20
5	Cecil Fielder	.10
6	Chuck Finley	.10
7	Todd Greene	.10
8	Shigetosi Hasegawa	.10
9	Tim Salmon	.10
10	Roberto Alomar	.20
11	Brady Anderson	.10
12	Joe Carter	.10
13	Eric Davis	.10
14	Ozzie Guillen	.10
15	Mike Mussina	.40
16	Rafael Palmeiro	.65
17	Cal Ripken Jr.	2.50
18	B.J. Surhoff	.10
19	Steve Avery	.10
20	Nomar Garciaparra	1.00
21	Reggie Jefferson	.10
22	Pedro Martinez	.75
23	Tim Naehring	.10
24	John Valentin	.10
25	Mo Vaughn	.10
26	James Baldwin	.10
27	Albert Belle	.10
28	Ray Durham	.10
29	Benji Gil	.10
30	Jaime Navarro	.10
31	Magglio Ordonez RC	1.50
32	Frank Thomas	.75
33	Robin Ventura	.10
34	Sandy Alomar Jr.	.10
35	Geronimo Berroa	.10
36	Travis Fryman	.10
37	David Justice	.10
38	Kenny Lofton	.10
39	Charles Nagy	.10
40	Manny Ramirez	.75
41	Jim Thome	.65
42	Omar Vizquel	.10
43	Jaret Wright	.10
44	Raul Casanova	.10
45	Frank Catalanotto RC	.20
46	Tony Clark	.10
47	Bobby Higginson	.10
48	Brian Hunter	.10
49	Todd Jones	.10
50	Bip Roberts	.10
51	Justin Thompson	.10
52	Kevin Appier	.10
53	Johnny Damon	.35
54	Jermaine Dye	.10
55	Jeff King	.10
56	Jeff Montgomery	.10
57	Dean Palmer	.10
58	Jose Rosado	.10
59	Larry Sutton	.10
60	Rick Aguilera	.10
61	Marty Cordova	.10
62	Pat Meares	.10
63	Paul Molitor	.75
64	Otis Nixon	.10
65	Brad Radke	.10
66	Terry Steinbach	.10
67	Todd Walker	.10
68	Hideki Irabu	.10
69	Derek Jeter	2.50
70	Chuck Knoblauch	.10
71	Tino Martinez	.10
72	Paul O'Neill	.10
73	Andy Pettitte	.20
74	Mariano Rivera	.15
75	Bernie Williams	.10
76	Mark Bellhorn	.10
77	Tom Candiotti	.10
78	Jason Giambi	.50
79	Ben Grieve	.75
80	Rickey Henderson	.75
81	Jason McDonald	.10
82	Aaron Small	.10
83	Miguel Tejada	.20
84	Jay Buhner	.10
85	Joey Cora	.10
86	Jeff Fassero	.10
87	Ken Griffey Jr.	1.50
88	Randy Johnson	.75
89	Edgar Martinez	.10
90	Alex Rodriguez	2.00
91	David Segui	.10
92	Dan Wilson	.10
93	Wilson Alvarez	.10
94	Wade Boggs	1.00
95	Miguel Cairo	.10
96	John Flaherty	.10
97	Dave Martinez	.10
98	Quinton McCracken	.10
99	Fred McGriff	.10
100	Paul Sorrento	.10
101	Kevin Stocker	.10
102	John Burkett	.10

103	Will Clark	.10
104	Juan Gonzalez	.40
105	Rusty Greer	.10
106	Roberto Kelly	.10
107	Ivan Rodriguez	.65
108	Fernando Tatis	.10
109	John Wetteland	.10
110	Jose Canseco	.40
111	Roger Clemens	1.25
112	Jose Cruz Jr.	.10
113	Carlos Delgado	.50
114	Alex Gonzalez	.10
115	Pat Hentgen	.10
116	Ed Sprague	.10
117	Shannon Stewart	.10
118	Brian Anderson	.10
119	Jay Bell	.10
120	Andy Benes	.10
121	Yamil Benitez	.10
122	Jorge Fabregas	.10
123	Travis Lee	.10
124	Devon White	.10
125	Matt Williams	.10
126	Bob Wolcott	.10
127	Andres Galarraga	.10
128	Tom Glavine	.35
129	Andruw Jones	.75
130	Chipper Jones	1.00
131	Ryan Klesko	.10
132	Javy Lopez	.10
133	Greg Maddux	1.00
134	Denny Neagle	.10
135	John Smoltz	.10
136	Rod Beck	.10
137	Jeff Blauser	.10
138	Mark Grace	.10
139	Lance Johnson	.10
140	Mickey Morandini	.10
141	Kevin Orie	.10
142	Sammy Sosa	1.00
143	Aaron Boone	.10
144	Bret Boone	.10
145	Dave Burba	.10
146	Lenny Harris	.10
147	Barry Larkin	.10
148	Reggie Sanders	.10
149	Brett Tomko	.10
150	Pedro Astacio	.10
151	Dante Bichette	.10
152	Ellis Burks	.10
153	Vinny Castilla	.10
154	Todd Helton	.75
155	Darryl Kile	.10
156	Jeff Reed	.10
157	Larry Walker	.10
158	Bobby Bonilla	.10
159	Todd Dunwoody	.10
160	Livan Hernandez	.10
161	Charles Johnson	.10
162	Mark Kotsay	.10
163	Derrek Lee	.60
164	Edgar Renteria	.10
165	Gary Sheffield	.50
166	Moises Alou	.10
167	Jeff Bagwell	.75
168	Derek Bell	.10
169	Craig Biggio	.10
170	Mike Hampton	.10
171	Richard Hidalgo	.10
172	Chris Holt	.10
173	Shane Reynolds	.10
174	Wilton Guerrero	.10
175	Eric Karros	.10
176	Paul Konerko	.20
177	Ramon Martinez	.10
178	Raul Mondesi	.10
179	Hideo Nomo	.40
180	Chan Ho Park	.10
181	Mike Piazza	1.25
182	Ismael Valdes	.10
183	Jeromy Burnitz	.10
184	Jeff Cirillo	.10
185	Todd Dunn	.10
186	Marquis Grissom	.10
187	John Jaha	.10
188	Doug Jones	.10
189	Dave Nilsson	.10
190	Jose Valentin	.10
191	Fernando Vina	.10
192	Orlando Cabrera	.10
193	Steve Falteisek	.10
194	Mark Grudzielanek	.10
195	Vladimir Guerrero	.75
196	Carlos Perez	.10
197	F.P. Santangelo	.10
198	Jose Vidro	.10
199	Rondell White	.10
200	Edgardo Alfonzo	.10
201	Carlos Baerga	.10
202	John Franco	.10
203	Bernard Gilkey	.10
204	Todd Hundley	.10
205	Butch Huskey	.10
206	Bobby Jones	.10
207	Brian McRae	.10
208	John Olerud	.10
209	Rey Ordonez	.10
210	Ricky Bottalico	.10
211	Bobby Estalella	.10
212	Doug Glanville	.10
213	Gregg Jefferies	.10
214	Mike Lieberthal	.10
215	Desi Relaford	.10
216	Scott Rolen	.65
217	Curt Schilling	.35
218	Adrian Brown	.10
219	Emil Brown	.10
220	Francisco Cordova	.10
221	Jose Guillen	.10
222	Al Martin	.10
223	Abraham Nunez	.10
224	Tony Womack	.10
225	Kevin Young	.10
226	Alan Benes	.10
227	Royce Clayton	.10
228	Gary Gaetti	.10
229	Ron Gant	.10
230	Brian Jordan	.10
231	Ray Lankford	.10
232	Mark McGwire	2.00
233	Todd Stottlemyre	.10
234	Kevin Brown	.10
235	Ken Caminiti	.10
236	Steve Finley	.10
237	Tony Gwynn	1.00
238	Wally Joyner	.10
239	Ruben Rivera	.10
240	Greg Vaughn	.10
241	Quilvio Veras	.10
242	Barry Bonds	2.50
243	Jacob Cruz	.10
244	Shawn Estes	.10
245	Orel Hershiser	.10
246	Stan Javier	.10
247	Brian Johnson	.10
248	Jeff Kent	.10
249	Robb Nen	.10
250	J.T. Snow	.10

Gold/Copper/Red

	NM/M
Common Gold/Copper Player:	.25
Gold/Copper Stars:	1X
Inserted 1:1	
Common Red Player:	.30
Red Stars:	2X

(See 1998 Pacific Paramount for checklist and base card values.)

Holographic Silver

	NM/M
Common Player:	1.00
Holographic Silver Stars:	20X
Production 99 Sets	

(See 1998 Pacific Paramount for checklist and base card values.)

Platinum Blue

	NM/M
Common Platinum Blue Player:	1.00
Platinum Blue Stars:	4X
Inserted 1:73	

(See 1998 Pacific Paramount for checklist and base card values.)

Cooperstown Bound

		NM/M
Complete Set (10):		60.00
Common Player:		8.00
Inserted 1:361		
Pacific Proofs:		6X
Production 20 Sets		
1	Greg Maddux	10.00
2	Cal Ripken Jr.	15.00
3	Frank Thomas	8.00
4	Mike Piazza	8.00
5	Paul Molitor	8.00
6	Mark McGwire	12.00
7	Tony Gwynn	8.00
8	Barry Bonds	15.00
9	Ken Griffey Jr.	10.00
10	Wade Boggs	8.00

Fielder's Choice

		NM/M
Complete Set (20):		45.00
Common Player:		.75
Inserted 1:73		
1	Chipper Jones	3.00
2	Greg Maddux	3.00
3	Cal Ripken Jr.	6.00
4	Nomar Garciaparra	3.00
5	Frank Thomas	2.50
6	David Justice	.75
7	Larry Walker	.75
8	Jeff Bagwell	2.50
9	Hideo Nomo	1.25
10	Mike Piazza	3.50
11	Derek Jeter	6.00
12	Ben Grieve	.75
13	Mark McGwire	4.50
14	Tony Gwynn	3.00
15	Barry Bonds	6.00
16	Ken Griffey Jr.	4.00
17	Alex Rodriguez	4.50
18	Wade Boggs	3.00
19	Ivan Rodriguez	2.00
20	Jose Cruz Jr.	.75

Inaugural Issue

	NM/M
Common Player:	3.00

(Stars and rookies valued at 50-75X regular Paramount version.)

Special Delivery

		NM/M
Complete Set (20):		30.00
Common Player:		.50
Inserted 1:37		
1	Chipper Jones	2.50
2	Greg Maddux	2.50
3	Cal Ripken Jr.	5.00
4	Nomar Garciaparra	2.50
5	Pedro Martinez	2.00
6	Frank Thomas	2.00
7	David Justice	.50
8	Larry Walker	.50
9	Jeff Bagwell	2.00
10	Hideo Nomo	1.00
11	Mike Piazza	3.00
12	Vladimir Guerrero	2.00
13	Derek Jeter	5.00
14	Ben Grieve	.50
15	Mark McGwire	4.00
16	Tony Gwynn	2.50
17	Barry Bonds	5.00
18	Ken Griffey Jr.	3.50
19	Alex Rodriguez	4.00
20	Jose Cruz Jr.	.50

Team Checklists

		NM/M
Complete Set (30):		25.00
Common Player:		.25
Inserted 1:18		
1	Tim Salmon	.25
2	Cal Ripken Jr.	4.00
3	Nomar Garciaparra	1.50
4	Frank Thomas	1.00
5	Manny Ramirez	1.00
6	Tony Clark	.25
7	Dean Palmer	.25
8	Paul Molitor	1.00
9	Derek Jeter	4.00
10	Ben Grieve	.25
11	Ken Griffey Jr.	2.50
12	Wade Boggs	1.50
13	Ivan Rodriguez	.75
14	Roger Clemens	2.00
15	Matt Williams	.25

16	Chipper Jones	1.50
17	Sammy Sosa	1.50
18	Barry Larkin	.25
19	Larry Walker	.25
20	Livan Hernandez	.25
21	Jeff Bagwell	1.00
22	Mike Piazza	2.00
23	John Jaha	.25
24	Vladimir Guerrero	1.00
25	Todd Hundley	.25
26	Scott Rolen	.75
27	Kevin Young	.25
28	Mark McGwire	3.00
29	Tony Gwynn	1.50
30	Barry Bonds	4.00

1998 Pacific Revolution

		NM/M
Complete Set (150):		65.00
Common Player:		.25
Pack (3):		1.00
Wax Box (24):		20.00
1	Garret Anderson	.25
2	Jim Edmonds	.25
3	Darin Erstad	.40
4	Chuck Finley	.25
5	Tim Salmon	.25
6	Jay Bell	.25
7	Travis Lee	.25
8	Devon White	.25
9	Matt Williams	.25
10	Andres Galarraga	.25
11	Tom Glavine	.45
12	Andruw Jones	2.50
13	Chipper Jones	3.50
14	Ryan Klesko	.25
15	Javy Lopez	.25
16	Greg Maddux	3.50
17	Walt Weiss	.25
18	Roberto Alomar	.40
19	Joe Carter	.25
20	Mike Mussina	1.25
21	Rafael Palmeiro	2.00
22	Cal Ripken Jr.	6.00
23	B.J. Surhoff	.25
24	Nomar Garciaparra	3.00
25	Reggie Jefferson	.25
26	Pedro Martinez	2.50
27	Troy O'Leary	.25
28	Mo Vaughn	2.50
29	Mark Grace	.25
30	Mickey Morandini	.25
31	Henry Rodriguez	.25
32	Sammy Sosa	3.00
33	Kerry Wood	1.25
34	Albert Belle	.25
35	Ray Durham	.25
36	Magglio Ordonez RC	2.00
37	Frank Thomas	2.50
38	Robin Ventura	.25
39	Bret Boone	.25
40	Barry Larkin	.25
41	Reggie Sanders	.25
42	Brett Tomko	.25
43	Sandy Alomar	.25
44	David Justice	.25
45	Kenny Lofton	.25
46	Manny Ramirez	2.50
47	Jim Thome	2.00
48	Omar Vizquel	.25
49	Jaret Wright	.25
50	Dante Bichette	.25
51	Ellis Burks	.25
52	Vinny Castilla	.25
53	Todd Helton	2.50
54	Larry Walker	.25
55	Tony Clark	.25
56	Deivi Cruz	.25
57	Damion Easley	.25
58	Bobby Higginson	.25

59	Brian Hunter	.25
60	Cliff Floyd	.25
61	Livan Hernandez	.25
62	Derrek Lee	1.50
63	Edgar Renteria	.25
64	Moises Alou	.25
65	Jeff Bagwell	2.50
66	Derek Bell	.25
67	Craig Biggio	.25
68	Richard Hidalgo	.25
69	Johnny Damon	.40
70	Jeff King	.25
71	Hal Morris	.25
72	Dean Palmer	.25
73	Bobby Bonilla	.25
74	Charles Johnson	.25
75	Paul Konerko	.35
76	Raul Mondesi	.25
77	Gary Sheffield	.75
78	Jeromy Burnitz	.25
79	Marquis Grissom	.25
80	Dave Nilsson	.25
81	Fernando Vina	.25
82	Marty Cordova	.25
83	Pat Meares	.25
84	Paul Molitor	2.50
85	Brad Radke	.25
86	Terry Steinbach	.25
87	Todd Walker	.25
88	Brad Fullmer	.25
89	Vladimir Guerrero	2.50
90	Carl Pavano	.25
91	Rondell White	.25
92	Bernard Gilkey	.25
93	Hideo Nomo	1.25
94	John Olerud	.25
95	Rey Ordonez	.25
96	Mike Piazza	4.00
97	Masato Yoshii RC	.65
98	Hideki Irabu	.25
99	Derek Jeter	6.00
100	Chuck Knoblauch	.25
101	Tino Martinez	.25
102	Paul O'Neill	.25
103	Darryl Strawberry	.25
104	Bernie Williams	.25
105	Jason Giambi	1.50
106	Ben Grieve	.25
107	Rickey Henderson	2.50
108	Matt Stairs	.25
109	Doug Glanville	.25
110	Desi Relaford	.25
111	Scott Rolen	1.50
112	Curt Schilling	.45
113	Jason Kendall	.25
114	Al Martin	.25
115	Jason Schmidt	.25
116	Kevin Young	.25
117	Delino DeShields	.25
118	Gary Gaetti	.25
119	Brian Jordan	.25
120	Ray Lankford	.25
121	Mark McGwire	5.00
122	Kevin Brown	.25
123	Steve Finley	.25
124	Tony Gwynn	3.50
125	Wally Joyner	.25
126	Greg Vaughn	.25
127	Barry Bonds	6.00
128	Orel Hershiser	.25
129	Jeff Kent	.25
130	Bill Mueller	.25
131	Jay Buhner	.25
132	Ken Griffey Jr.	4.50
133	Randy Johnson	2.50
134	Edgar Martinez	.25
135	Alex Rodriguez	5.00
136	David Segui	.25
137	Rolando Arrojo RC	.75
138	Wade Boggs	3.50
139	Quinton McCracken	.25
140	Fred McGriff	.25
141	Will Clark	.25
142	Juan Gonzalez	1.25
143	Tom Goodwin	.25
144	Ivan Rodriguez	2.00
145	Aaron Sele	.25
146	John Wetteland	.25
147	Jose Canseco	.50
148	Roger Clemens	4.00
149	Jose Cruz Jr.	.25
150	Carlos Delgado	.65

Shadows

	NM/M
Common Player:	2.00
Stars/Rookies:	6X

(See 1998 Pacific Revolution for checklist and base card values.)

Foul Pole

		NM/M
Complete Set (20):		100.00
Common Player:		2.00
Inserted 1:49		
1	Cal Ripken Jr.	15.00
2	Nomar Garciaparra	7.50
3	Mo Vaughn	2.00
4	Frank Thomas	6.00
5	Manny Ramirez	6.00
6	Bernie Williams	2.00
7	Ben Grieve	2.00
8	Ken Griffey Jr.	10.00
9	Alex Rodriguez	12.00
10	Juan Gonzalez	3.00
11	Ivan Rodriguez	5.00
12	Travis Lee	2.00
13	Chipper Jones	7.50
14	Sammy Sosa	7.50
15	Vinny Castilla	2.00
16	Moises Alou	2.00
17	Gary Sheffield	3.00
18	Mike Piazza	9.00
19	Mark McGwire	12.00
20	Barry Bonds	15.00

Major League Icons

		NM/M
Complete Set (10):		50.00
Common Player:		4.50
Inserted 1:121		
1	Cal Ripken Jr.	15.00
2	Nomar Garciaparra	7.50
3	Frank Thomas	6.00
4	Ken Griffey Jr.	10.00

5	Alex Rodriguez	12.50
6	Chipper Jones	7.50
7	Kerry Wood	4.50
8	Mike Piazza	9.00
9	Mark McGwire	12.50
10	Tony Gwynn	7.50

Prime Time Performers

		NM/M
Complete Set (20):		25.00
Common Player:		.50
Inserted 1:25		
1	Cal Ripken Jr.	4.50
2	Nomar Garciaparra	2.00
3	Frank Thomas	1.50
4	Jim Thome	1.25
5	Hideki Irabu	.50
6	Derek Jeter	4.50
7	Ben Grieve	.50
8	Ken Griffey Jr.	3.00
9	Alex Rodriguez	3.50
10	Juan Gonzalez	.75
11	Ivan Rodriguez	1.25
12	Travis Lee	.50
13	Chipper Jones	2.00
14	Greg Maddux	2.00
15	Kerry Wood	.75
16	Larry Walker	.50
17	Jeff Bagwell	1.50
18	Mike Piazza	2.50
19	Mark McGwire	3.50
20	Tony Gwynn	2.00

Rookies and Hardball Heroes

		NM/M
Complete Set (30):		20.00
Common Player:		.25
Inserted 1:6		
Gold (1-20):		10X
Production 50 Sets		
1	Justin Baughman	.25
2	Jarrod Washburn	.25
3	Travis Lee	.25
4	Kerry Wood	.50
5	Magglio Ordonez	.50
6	Todd Helton	1.00
7	Derrek Lee	.25
8	Richard Hidalgo	.25
9	Mike Caruso	.25
10	David Ortiz	.75
11	Brad Fullmer	.25
12	Masato Yoshii	.25
13	Orlando Hernandez	.25
14	Ricky Ledee	.25
15	Ben Grieve	.25
16	Carlton Loewer	.25
17	Desi Relaford	.25
18	Ruben Rivera	.25
19	Rolando Arrojo	.25
20	Matt Perisho	.25
21	Chipper Jones	2.00
22	Greg Maddux	2.00
23	Cal Ripken Jr.	5.00
24	Nomar Garciaparra	2.00
25	Frank Thomas	1.00
26	Mark McGwire	4.00
27	Tony Gwynn	2.00
28	Ken Griffey Jr.	3.00
29	Alex Rodriguez	4.00
30	Juan Gonzalez	.50

Showstoppers

		NM/M
Complete Set (36):		30.00
Common Player:		.45
Inserted 1:12		
1	Cal Ripken Jr.	5.00

2 Nomar Garciaparra 2.50
3 Pedro Martinez 2.00
4 Mo Vaughn .45
5 Frank Thomas 2.00
6 Manny Ramirez 2.00
7 Jim Thome 1.75
8 Jaret Wright .45
9 Paul Molitor 2.00
10 Orlando Hernandez .60
11 Derek Jeter 5.00
12 Bernie Williams .45
13 Ben Grieve .45
14 Ken Griffey Jr. 3.50
15 Alex Rodriguez 4.00
16 Wade Boggs 2.50
17 Juan Gonzalez 1.00
18 Ivan Rodriguez 1.75
19 Jose Canseco .75
20 Roger Clemens 3.00
21 Travis Lee .45
22 Andres Galarraga .45
23 Chipper Jones 2.50
24 Greg Maddux 2.50
25 Sammy Sosa 2.50
26 Kerry Wood .75
27 Vinny Castilla .45
28 Larry Walker .45
30 Moises Alou .45
30 Raul Mondesi .45
31 Gary Sheffield .75
32 Hideo Nomo 1.00
33 Mike Piazza 3.00
34 Mark McGwire 4.00
35 Tony Gwynn 2.50
36 Barry Bonds 5.00

1999 Pacific

	NM/M
Complete Set (500):	30.00
Common Player:	.10
Platinum Blues (1:73):	15X
Reds (1:1R):	2.5X
Pack (10):	1.00
Wax Box (36):	35.00

1 Garret Anderson .10
2 Jason Dickson .10
3 Gary DiSarcina .10
4 Jim Edmonds .10
5 Darin Erstad .25
6 Chuck Finley .10
7 Shigetosi Hasegawa .10
8 Ken Hill .10
9 Dave Hollins .10
10 Phil Nevin .10
11 Troy Percival .10
12a Tim Salmon/Action .95
12b Tim Salmon/Portrait .95
13 Brian Anderson .10
14 Tony Batista .10
15 Jay Bell .10
16 Andy Benes .10

17 Yamil Benitez .10
18 Omar Daal .10
19 David Dellucci .10
20 Karim Garcia .10
21 Bernard Gilkey .10
22a Travis Lee/Action .10
22b Travis Lee/Portrait .10
23 Aaron Small .10
24 Kelly Stinnett .10
25 Devon White .10
26 Matt Williams .10
27a Bruce Chen/Action .10
27b Bruce Chen/Portrait .10
28a Andres Galarraga/Action .10
28b Andres Galarraga/Portrait .10
29 Tom Glavine .35
30 Ozzie Guillen .10
31 Andruw Jones 1.00
32a Chipper Jones/Action 1.50
32b Chipper Jones/Portrait 1.50
33 Ryan Klesko .10
34 George Lombard .10
35 Javy Lopez .10
36a Greg Maddux/Action 1.50
36b Greg Maddux/Portrait 1.50
37a Marty Malloy/Action .10
37b Marty Malloy/Portrait .10
38 Dennis Martinez .10
39 Kevin Millwood .10
40a Alex Rodriguez/Action 2.50
40b Alex Rodriguez/Portrait 2.50
41 Denny Neagle .10
42 John Smoltz .10
43 Michael Tucker .10
44 Walt Weiss .10
45a Roberto Alomar/Action .25
45b Roberto Alomar/Portrait .25
46 Brady Anderson .10
47 Harold Baines .10
48 Mike Bordick .10
49a Danny Clyburn/Action .10
49b Danny Clyburn/Portrait .10
50 Eric Davis .10
51 Scott Erickson .10
52 Chris Hoiles .10
53 Jimmy Key .10
54a Ryan Minor/Action .10
54b Ryan Minor/Portrait .10
55 Mike Mussina .40
56 Jesse Orosco .10
57a Rafael Palmeiro/Action .75
57b Rafael Palmeiro/Portrait .75
58 Sidney Ponson .10
59 Arthur Rhodes .10
60a Cal Ripken Jr./Action 3.00
60b Cal Ripken Jr./Portrait 3.00
61 B.J. Surhoff .10
62 Steve Avery .10
63 Darren Bragg .10
64 Dennis Eckersley .75
65a Nomar Garciaparra/Action 1.50
65b Nomar Garciaparra/Portrait 1.50
66a Sammy Sosa/Action 1.50
66b Sammy Sosa/Portrait 1.50
67 Tom Gordon .10
68 Reggie Jefferson .10
69 Darren Lewis .10
70a Mark McGwire/Action 2.50
70b Mark McGwire/Portrait 2.50
71 Pedro Martinez 1.00
72 Troy O'Leary .10
73 Bret Saberhagen .10
74 Mike Stanley .10
75 John Valentin .10
76 Jason Varitek .10
77 Mo Vaughn .10
78 Tim Wakefield .10
79 Manny Alexander .10
80 Rod Beck .10
81 Brant Brown .10
82 Mark Clark .10
83 Gary Gaetti .10
84 Mark Grace .10
85 Jose Hernandez .10
86 Lance Johnson .10
87a Jason Maxwell/Action .10
87b Jason Maxwell/Portrait .10
88 Mickey Morandini .10
89 Terry Mulholland .10
90 Henry Rodriguez .10
91 Scott Servais .10
92 Kevin Tapani .10
93 Pedro Valdes .10
94 Kerry Wood .40
95 Jeff Abbott .10
96 James Baldwin .10
97 Albert Belle .10
98 Mike Cameron .10
99 Mike Caruso .10
100 Wil Cordero .10

101 Ray Durham .10
102 Jaime Navarro .10
103 Greg Norton .10
104 Magglio Ordonez .25
105 Mike Sirotka .10
106a Frank Thomas/Action 1.00
106b Frank Thomas/Portrait 1.00
107 Robin Ventura .10
108 Craig Wilson .10
109 Aaron Boone .10
110 Bret Boone .10
111 Sean Casey .15
112 Pete Harnisch .10
113 John Hudek .10
114 Barry Larkin .10
115 Eduardo Perez .10
116 Mike Remlinger .10
117 Reggie Sanders .10
118 Chris Stynes .10
119 Eddie Taubensee .10
120 Brett Tomko .10
121 Pat Watkins .10
122 Dmitri Young .10
123 Sandy Alomar Jr. .10
124 Dave Burba .10
125 Bartolo Colon .10
126 Joey Cora .10
127 Brian Giles .10
128 Dwight Gooden .10
129 Mike Jackson .10
130 David Justice .10
131 Kenny Lofton .10
132 Charles Nagy .10
133 Chad Ogea .10
134a Manny Ramirez/Action 1.00
134b Manny Ramirez/Portrait 1.00
135 Richie Sexson .10
136a Jim Thome/Action .75
136b Jim Thome/Portrait .75
137 Omar Vizquel .10
138 Jaret Wright .10
139 Pedro Astacio .10
140 Jason Bates .10
141a Dante Bichette/Action .10
141b Dante Bichette/Portrait .10
142a Vinny Castilla/Action .10
142b Vinny Castilla/Portrait .10
143a Edgar Clemente/Action .10
143b Edgar Clemente/Portrait .10
144a Derrick Gibson/Action .10
144b Derrick Gibson/Portrait .10
145 Curtis Goodwin .10
146a Todd Helton/Action 1.00
146b Todd Helton/Portrait 1.00
147 Bobby Jones .10
148 Darryl Kile .10
149 Mike Lansing .10
150 Chuck McElroy .10
151 Neifi Perez .10
152 Jeff Reed .10
153 John Thomson .10
154a Larry Walker/Action 1.50
154b Larry Walker/Portrait .10
155 Jamey Wright .10
156 Kimera Bartee .10
157 Geronimo Berroa .10
158 Raul Casanova .10
159 Frank Catalanotto .10
160 Tony Clark .10
161 Deivi Cruz .10
162 Damion Easley .10
163 Juan Encarnacion .10
164 Luis Gonzalez .10
165 Seth Greisinger .10
166 Bob Higginson .10
167 Brian Hunter .10
168 Todd Jones .10
169 Justin Thompson .10
170 Antonio Alfonseca .10
171 Dave Berg .10
172 John Cangelosi .10
173 Craig Counsell .10
174 Todd Dunwoody .10
175 Cliff Floyd .10
176 Alex Gonzalez .10
177 Livan Hernandez .10
178 Ryan Jackson .10
179 Mark Kotsay .10
180 Derrek Lee .65
181 Matt Mantei .10
182 Brian Meadows .10
183 Edgar Renteria .10
184a Moises Alou/Action .10
184b Moises Alou/Portrait .10
185 Brad Ausmus .10
186a Jeff Bagwell/Action 1.00
186b Jeff Bagwell/Portrait 1.00
187 Derek Bell .10
188 Sean Berry .10
189 Craig Biggio .10
190 Carl Everett .10
191 Ricky Gutierrez .10

192 Mike Hampton .10
193 Doug Henry .10
194 Richard Hidalgo .10
195 Randy Johnson 1.00
196a Russ Johnson/Action .10
196b Russ Johnson/Portrait .10
197 Shane Reynolds .10
198 Bill Spiers .10
199 Kevin Appier .10
200 Tim Belcher .10
201 Jeff Conine .10
202 Johnny Damon .35
203 Jermaine Dye .10
204a Jeremy Giambi (Batting stance.) .10
204b Jeremy Giambi (Follow-through.) .10
205 Jeff King .10
206 Shane Mack .10
207 Jeff Montgomery .10
208 Hal Morris .10
209 Jose Offerman .10
210 Dean Palmer .10
211 Jose Rosado .10
212 Glendon Rusch .10
213 Larry Sutton .10
214 Mike Sweeney .10
215 Bobby Bonilla .10
216 Alex Cora .10
217 Darren Dreifort .10
218 Mark Grudzielanek .10
219 Todd Hollandsworth .10
220 Trenidad Hubbard .10
221 Charles Johnson .10
222 Eric Karros .10
223 Matt Luke .10
224 Ramon Martinez .10
225 Raul Mondesi .10
226 Chan Ho Park .10
227 Jeff Shaw .10
228 Gary Sheffield .40
229 Eric Young .10
230 Jeromy Burnitz .10
231 Jeff Cirillo .10
232 Marquis Grissom .10
233 Bobby Hughes .10
234 John Jaha .10
235 Geoff Jenkins .10
236 Scott Karl .10
237 Mark Loretta .10
238 Mike Matheny .10
239 Mike Myers .10
240 Dave Nilsson .10
241 Bob Wickman .10
242 Jose Valentin .10
243 Fernando Vina .10
244 Rick Aguilera .10
245 Ron Coomer .10
246 Marty Cordova .10
247 Denny Hocking .10
248 Matt Lawton .10
249 Pat Meares .10
250a Paul Molitor/Action 1.00
250b Paul Molitor/Portrait 1.00
251 Otis Nixon .10
252 Alex Ochoa .10
253 David Ortiz .65
254 A.J. Pierzynski .10
255 Brad Radke .10
256 Terry Steinbach .10
257 Bob Tewksbury .10
258 Todd Walker .10
259 Shane Andrews .10
260 Shayne Bennett .10
261 Orlando Cabrera .10
262 Brad Fullmer .10
263 Vladimir Guerrero 1.00
264 Wilton Guerrero .10
265 Dustin Hermanson .10
266 Terry Jones .10
267 Steve Kline .10
268 Carl Pavano .10
269 F.P. Santangelo .10
270a Fernando Seguignol/Action .10
270b Fernando Seguignol/Portrait .10
271 Ugueth Urbina .10
272 Jose Vidro .10
273 Chris Widger .10
274 Edgardo Alfonzo .10
275 Carlos Baerga .10
276 John Franco .10
277 Todd Hundley .10
278 Butch Huskey .10
279 Bobby Jones .10
280 Al Leiter .10
281 Greg McMichael .10
282 Brian McRae .10
283 Hideo Nomo .50
284 John Olerud .10
285 Rey Ordonez .10
286a Mike Piazza/Action 1.75
286b Mike Piazza/Portrait 1.75

287	Turk Wendell	.10
288	Masato Yoshii	.10
289	David Cone	.10
290	Chad Curtis	.10
291	Joe Girardi	.10
292	Orlando Hernandez	.10
293a	Hideki Irabu/Action	.10
293b	Hideki Irabu/Portrait	.10
294a	Derek Jeter/Action	3.00
294b	Derek Jeter/Portrait	3.00
295	Chuck Knoblauch	.10
296a	Mike Lowell/Action	.10
296b	Mike Lowell/Portrait	.10
297	Tino Martinez	.10
298	Ramiro Mendoza	.10
299	Paul O'Neill	.10
300	Andy Pettitte	.25
301	Jorge Posada	.10
302	Tim Raines	.10
303	Mariano Rivera	.15
304	David Wells	.10
305a	Bernie Williams/Action	.10
305b	Bernie Williams/Portrait	.10
306	Mike Blowers	.10
307	Tom Candiotti	.10
308a	Eric Chavez/Action	.15
308b	Eric Chavez/Portrait	.15
309	Ryan Christenson	.10
310	Jason Giambi	.65
311a	Ben Grieve/Action	.10
311b	Ben Grieve/Portrait	.10
312	Rickey Henderson	1.00
313	A.J. Hinch	.10
314	Jason McDonald	.10
315	Bip Roberts	.10
316	Kenny Rogers	.10
317	Scott Spiezio	.10
318	Matt Stairs	.10
319	Miguel Tejada	.20
320	Bob Abreu	.20
321	Alex Arias	.10
322a	Gary Bennett/Action RC	.10
322b	Gary Bennett/Portrait RC	.10
323	Ricky Bottalico	.10
324	Rico Brogna	.10
325	Bobby Estalella	.10
326	Doug Glanville	.10
327	Kevin Jordan	.10
328	Mark Leiter	.10
329	Wendell Magee	.10
330	Mark Portugal	.10
331	Desi Relaford	.10
332	Scott Rolen	.65
333	Curt Schilling	.35
334	Kevin Sefcik	.10
335	Adrian Brown	.10
336	Emil Brown	.10
337	Lou Collier	.10
338	Francisco Cordova	.10
339	Freddy Garcia	.10
340	Jose Guillen	.10
341	Jason Kendall	.10
342	Al Martin	.10
343	Abraham Nunez	.10
344	Aramis Ramirez	.10
345	Ricardo Rincon	.10
346	Jason Schmidt	.10
347	Turner Ward	.10
348	Tony Womack	.10
349	Kevin Young	.10
350	Juan Acevedo	.10
351	Delino DeShields	.10
352a	J.D. Drew/Action	.40
352b	J.D. Drew/Portrait	.40
353	Ron Gant	.10
354	Brian Jordan	.10
355	Ray Lankford	.10
356	Eli Marrero	.10
357	Kent Mercker	.10
358	Matt Morris	.10
359	Luis Ordaz	.10
360	Donovan Osborne	.10
361	Placido Polanco	.10
362	Fernando Tatis	.10
363	Andy Ashby	.10
364	Kevin Brown	.10
365	Ken Caminiti	.10
366	Steve Finley	.10
367	Chris Gomez	.10
368a	Tony Gwynn/Action	1.50
368b	Tony Gwynn/Portrait	1.50
369	Joey Hamilton	.10
370	Carlos Hernandez	.10
371	Trevor Hoffman	.10
372	Wally Joyner	.10
373	Jim Leyritz	.10
374	Ruben Rivera	.10
375	Greg Vaughn	.10
376	Quilvio Veras	.10
377	Rich Aurilia	.10
378a	Barry Bonds/Action	3.00
378b	Barry Bonds/Portrait	3.00
379	Ellis Burks	.10

380	Joe Carter	.10
381	Stan Javier	.10
382	Brian Johnson	.10
383	Jeff Kent	.10
384	Jose Mesa	.10
385	Bill Mueller	.10
386	Robb Nen	.10
387a	Armando Rios/Action	.10
387b	Armando Rios/Portrait	.10
388	Kirk Rueter	.10
389	Rey Sanchez	.10
390	J.T. Snow	.10
391	David Bell	.10
392	Jay Buhner	.10
393	Ken Cloude	.10
394	Russ Davis	.10
395	Jeff Fassero	.10
396a	Ken Griffey Jr./Action	2.00
396b	Ken Griffey Jr./Portrait	2.00
397	Giomar Guevara RC	.10
398	Carlos Guillen	.10
399	Edgar Martinez	.10
400	Shane Monahan	.10
401	Jamie Moyer	.10
402	David Segui	.10
403	Makoto Suzuki	.10
404	Mike Timlin	.10
405	Dan Wilson	.10
406	Wilson Alvarez	.10
407	Rolando Arrojo	.10
408	Wade Boggs	1.50
409	Miguel Cairo	.10
410	Roberto Hernandez	.10
411	Mike Kelly	.10
412	Aaron Ledesma	.10
413	Albie Lopez	.10
414	Dave Martinez	.10
415	Quinton McCracken	.10
416	Fred McGriff	.10
417	Bryan Rekar	.10
418	Paul Sorrento	.10
419	Randy Winn	.10
420	John Burkett	.10
421	Will Clark	.10
422	Royce Clayton	.10
423a	Juan Gonzalez/Action	.50
423b	Juan Gonzalez/Portrait	.50
424	Tom Goodwin	.10
425	Rusty Greer	.10
426	Rick Helling	.10
427	Roberto Kelly	.10
428	Mark McLemore	.10
429a	Ivan Rodriguez/Action	.75
429b	Ivan Rodriguez/Portrait	.75
430	Aaron Sele	.10
431	Lee Stevens	.10
432	Todd Stottlemyre	.10
433	John Wetteland	.10
434	Todd Zeile	.10
435	Jose Canseco	.50
436a	Roger Clemens/Action	1.75
436b	Roger Clemens/Portrait	1.75
437	Felipe Crespo	.10
438a	Jose Cruz Jr./Action	.10
438b	Jose Cruz Jr./Portrait	.10
439	Carlos Delgado	.50
440a	Tom Evans/Action	.10
440b	Tom Evans/Portrait	.10
441	Tony Fernandez	.10
442	Darrin Fletcher	.10
443	Alex Gonzalez	.10
444	Shawn Green	.30
445	Roy Halladay	.10
446	Pat Hentgen	.10
447	Juan Samuel	.10
448	Benito Santiago	.10
449	Shannon Stewart	.50
450	Woody Williams	.10

Cramer's Choice

		NM/M
Complete Set (10):		65.00

Common Player:		7.50
Inserted 1:721		
1	Cal Ripken Jr.	20.00
2	Nomar Garciaparra	12.50
3	Frank Thomas	10.00
4	Ken Griffey Jr.	15.00
5	Alex Rodriguez	17.50
6	Greg Maddux	12.50
7	Sammy Sosa	12.50
8	Kerry Wood	7.50
9	Mark McGwire	17.50
10	Tony Gwynn	12.50

Dynagon Diamond

		NM/M
Complete Set (20):		20.00
Common Player:		.40
Inserted 1:9		
Titanium (99 Sets):		8X
1	Cal Ripken Jr.	2.50
2	Nomar Garciaparra	1.00
3	Frank Thomas	.75
4	Derek Jeter	2.50
5	Ben Grieve	.40
6	Ken Griffey Jr.	1.50
7	Alex Rodriguez	2.00
8	Juan Gonzalez	.50
9	Travis Lee	.40
10	Chipper Jones	1.00
11	Greg Maddux	1.00
12	Sammy Sosa	1.00
13	Kerry Wood	.50
14	Jeff Bagwell	.75
15	Hideo Nomo	.50
16	Mike Piazza	12.50
17	J.D. Drew	.50
18	Mark McGwire	2.00
19	Tony Gwynn	1.00
20	Barry Bonds	2.50

Gold Crown Die-Cuts

		NM/M
Complete Set (36):		75.00
Common Player:		.75
Inserted 1:37		
1	Darin Erstad	1.00
2	Cal Ripken Jr.	7.50
3	Nomar Garciaparra	4.00
4	Pedro Martinez	3.00
5	Mo Vaughn	.75
6	Frank Thomas	3.00
7	Kenny Lofton	.75
8	Manny Ramirez	3.00
9	Paul Molitor	3.00
10	Derek Jeter	7.50
11	Bernie Williams	.75
12	Ben Grieve	.75
13	Ken Griffey Jr.	5.00
14	Alex Rodriguez	6.00

15	Wade Boggs	4.00
16	Juan Gonzalez	1.50
17	Ivan Rodriguez	2.50
18	Jose Canseco	1.50
19	Roger Clemens	4.50
20	Travis Lee	.75
21	Chipper Jones	4.00
22	Greg Maddux	4.00
23	Sammy Sosa	4.00
24	Kerry Wood	1.50
25	Todd Helton	3.00
26	Larry Walker	.75
27	Jeff Bagwell	3.00
28	Craig Biggio	.75
29	Raul Mondesi	.75
30	Vladimir Guerrero	3.00
31	Mike Piazza	4.50
32	Scott Rolen	2.00
33	J.D. Drew	1.50
34	Mark McGwire	6.00
35	Tony Gwynn	4.00
36	Barry Bonds	7.50

Hot Cards

		NM/M
Complete Set (10):		75.00
Common Player:		3.00
1	Alex Rodriguez	12.50
2	Tony Gwynn	7.50
3	Ken Griffey Jr.	10.00
4	Sammy Sosa	7.50
5	Ivan Rodriguez	6.00
6	Derek Jeter	15.00
7	Cal Ripken Jr.	15.00
8	Mark McGwire	12.50
9	J.D. Drew	4.50
10	Bernie Williams	3.00

Team Checklists

		NM/M
Complete Set (30):		30.00
Common Player:		.30
Inserted 1:18		
1	Darin Erstad	.50
2	Cal Ripken Jr.	3.00
3	Nomar Garciaparra	1.50
4	Frank Thomas	1.00
5	Manny Ramirez	1.00
6	Damion Easley	.30
7	Jeff King	.30
8	Paul Molitor	1.00
9	Derek Jeter	3.00
10	Ben Grieve	.30
11	Ken Griffey Jr.	2.00
12	Wade Boggs	1.50
13	Juan Gonzalez	.60
14	Roger Clemens	1.75
15	Travis Lee	.30
16	Chipper Jones	1.50
17	Sammy Sosa	1.50
18	Barry Larkin	.30
19	Todd Helton	1.00
20	Mark Kotsay	.30
21	Jeff Bagwell	1.00
22	Raul Mondesi	.30
23	Jeff Cirillo	.30
24	Vladimir Guerrero	1.00
25	Mike Piazza	1.75
26	Scott Rolen	.75
27	Jason Kendall	.30
28	Mark McGwire	2.50
29	Tony Gwynn	1.50
30	Barry Bonds	3.00

Timelines

		NM/M
Complete Set (20):		200.00
Common Player:		6.00
Inserted 1:181 H		
1	Cal Ripken Jr.	30.00
2	Frank Thomas	12.00

TIMELINES
RANDY JOHNSON

3	Jim Thome	10.00
4	Paul Molitor	12.00
5	Bernie Williams	6.00
6	Derek Jeter	30.00
7	Ken Griffey Jr.	20.00
8	Alex Rodriguez	25.00
9	Wade Boggs	15.00
10	Jose Canseco	9.00
11	Roger Clemens	17.50
12	Andres Galarraga	6.00
13	Chipper Jones	15.00
14	Greg Maddux	15.00
15	Sammy Sosa	15.00
16	Larry Walker	6.00
17	Randy Johnson	12.00
18	Mike Piazza	17.50
19	Mark McGwire	25.00
20	Tony Gwynn	15.00

1999 Pacific Aurora

		NM/M
Complete Set (200):		20.00
Common Player:		.10
Opening Days:		20X
Production 31 Sets		
Reds:		2X
Retail Only (1:6)		
Pack (6):		1.50
Wax Box (36):		22.50
1	Garret Anderson	.10
2	Jim Edmonds	.10
3	Darin Erstad	.30
4	Matt Luke	.10
5	Tim Salmon	.10
6	Mo Vaughn	.10
7	Jay Bell	.10
8	David Dellucci	.10
9	Steve Finley	.10
10	Bernard Gilkey	.10
11	Randy Johnson	1.00
12	Travis Lee	.10
13	Matt Williams	.10
14	Andres Galarraga	.35
15	Tom Glavine	.35
16	Andruw Jones	1.00
17	Chipper Jones	1.50
18	Brian Jordan	.10
19	Javy Lopez	.10
20	Greg Maddux	1.50
21	Albert Belle	.10
22	Will Clark	.10
23	Scott Erickson	.10
24	Mike Mussina	.40
25	Cal Ripken Jr.	3.00
26	B.J. Surhoff	.10
27	Nomar Garciaparra	1.50
28	Reggie Jefferson	.10
29	Darren Lewis	.10
30	Pedro Martinez	1.00
31	John Valentin	.10
32	Rod Beck	.10
33	Mark Grace	.10
34	Lance Johnson	.10
35	Mickey Morandini	.10
36	Sammy Sosa	1.50
37	Kerry Wood	.40
38	James Baldwin	.10
39	Mike Caruso	.10
40	Ray Durham	.10
41	Magglio Ordonez	.25
42	Frank Thomas	1.00

43	Aaron Boone	.10
44	Sean Casey	.20
45	Barry Larkin	.10
46	Hal Morris	.10
47	Denny Neagle	.10
48	Greg Vaughn	.10
49	Pat Watkins	.10
50	Roberto Alomar	.25
51	Sandy Alomar Jr.	.10
52	David Justice	.10
53	Kenny Lofton	.10
54	Manny Ramirez	1.00
55	Richie Sexson	.10
56	Jim Thome	.75
57	Omar Vizquel	.10
58	Dante Bichette	.10
59	Vinny Castilla	.10
60	Edgard Clemente RC	.10
61	Derrick Gibson	.10
62	Todd Helton	1.00
63	Darryl Kile	.10
64	Larry Walker	.10
65	Tony Clark	.10
66	Damion Easley	.10
67	Bob Higginson	.10
68	Brian Hunter	.10
69	Dean Palmer	.10
70	Justin Thompson	.10
71	Craig Counsell	.10
72	Todd Dunwoody	.10
73	Cliff Floyd	.10
74	Alex Gonzalez	.10
75	Livan Hernandez	.10
76	Mark Kotsay	.10
77	Derrek Lee	.65
78	Moises Alou	.10
79	Jeff Bagwell	1.00
80	Derek Bell	.10
81	Craig Biggio	.10
82	Ken Caminiti	.10
83	Richard Hidalgo	.10
84	Shane Reynolds	.10
85	Jeff Conine	.10
86	Johnny Damon	.35
87	Jermaine Dye	.10
88	Jeff King	.10
89	Jeff Montgomery	.10
90	Mike Sweeney	.10
91	Kevin Brown	.10
92	Mark Grudzielanek	.10
93	Eric Karros	.10
94	Raul Mondesi	.10
95	Chan Ho Park	.10
96	Gary Sheffield	.40
97	Jeromy Burnitz	.10
98	Jeff Cirillo	.10
99	Marquis Grissom	.10
100	Geoff Jenkins	.10
101	Dave Nilsson	.10
102	Jose Valentin	.10
103	Fernando Vina	.10
104	Marty Cordova	.10
105	Matt Lawton	.10
106	David Ortiz	.60
107	Brad Radke	.10
108	Todd Walker	.10
109	Shane Andrews	.10
110	Orlando Cabrera	.10
111	Brad Fullmer	.10
112	Vladimir Guerrero	1.00
113	Wilton Guerrero	.10
114	Carl Pavano	.10
115	Fernando Seguignol	.10
116	Ugueth Urbina	.10
117	Edgardo Alfonzo	.10
118	Bobby Bonilla	.10
119	Rickey Henderson	1.00
120	Hideo Nomo	.60
121	John Olerud	.10
122	Rey Ordonez	.10
123	Mike Piazza	2.00
124	Masato Yoshii	.10
125	Scott Brosius	.10
126	Orlando Hernandez	.10
127	Hideki Irabu	.10
128	Derek Jeter	3.00
129	Chuck Knoblauch	.10
130	Tino Martinez	.10
131	Jorge Posada	.10
132	Bernie Williams	.10
133	Eric Chavez	.20
134	Ryan Christenson	.10
135	Jason Giambi	.65
136	Ben Grieve	.10
137	A.J. Hinch	.10
138	Matt Stairs	.10
139	Miguel Tejada	.20
140	Bob Abreu	.20
141	Gary Bennett RC	.10
142	Desi Relaford	.10
143	Scott Rolen	.75
144	Curt Schilling	.35
145	Kevin Sefcik	.10
146	Brian Giles	.10

147	Jose Guillen	.10
148	Jason Kendall	.10
149	Aramis Ramirez	.10
150	Tony Womack	.10
151	Kevin Young	.10
152	Eric Davis	.10
153	J.D. Drew	.50
154	Ray Lankford	.10
155	Eli Marrero	.10
156	Mark McGwire	2.50
157	Luis Ordaz	.10
158	Edgar Renteria	.10
159	Andy Ashby	.10
160	Tony Gwynn	1.50
161	Trevor Hoffman	.10
162	Wally Joyner	.10
163	Jim Leyritz	.10
164	Ruben Rivera	.10
165	Reggie Sanders	.10
166	Quilvio Veras	.10
167	Rich Aurilia	.10
168	Marvin Benard	.10
169	Barry Bonds	3.00
170	Ellis Burks	.10
171	Jeff Kent	.10
172	Bill Mueller	.10
173	J.T. Snow	.10
174	Jay Buhner	.10
175	Jeff Fassero	.10
176	Ken Griffey Jr.	2.25
177	Carlos Guillen	.10
178	Edgar Martinez	.10
179	Alex Rodriguez	2.50
180	David Segui	.10
181	Dan Wilson	.10
182	Rolando Arrojo	.10
183	Wade Boggs	1.50
184	Jose Canseco	.40
185	Aaron Ledesma	.10
186	Dave Martinez	.10
187	Quinton McCracken	.10
188	Fred McGriff	.10
189	Juan Gonzalez	.60
190	Tom Goodwin	.10
191	Rusty Greer	.10
192	Roberto Kelly	.10
193	Rafael Palmeiro	.75
194	Ivan Rodriguez	.75
195	Roger Clemens	2.00
196	Jose Cruz Jr.	.10
197	Carlos Delgado	.60
198	Alex Gonzalez	.10
199	Roy Halladay	.10
200	Pat Hentgen	.10

Complete Players

		NM/M
Complete Set (10):		40.00
Common Player:		3.00
Production 299 Sets		
1	Cal Ripken Jr.	9.00
2	Nomar Garciaparra	4.50
3	Sammy Sosa	4.50
4	Kerry Wood	3.00
5	Frank Thomas	4.00
6	Mike Piazza	5.00
7	Mark McGwire	7.50
8	Tony Gwynn	4.50
9	Ken Griffey Jr.	6.00
10	Alex Rodriguez	7.50

Kings of the Major Leagues

		NM/M
Complete Set (10):		80.00
Common Player:		5.00
Inserted 1:361		
1	Cal Ripken Jr.	17.50
2	Nomar Garciaparra	9.00
3	Sammy Sosa	9.00
4	Kerry Wood	5.00
5	Frank Thomas	7.50

KINGS OF THE MAJOR LEAGUES

6	Mike Piazza	10.00
7	Mark McGwire	15.00
8	Tony Gwynn	9.00
9	Ken Griffey Jr.	12.50
10	Alex Rodriguez	15.00

On Deck

		NM/M
Complete Set (20):		17.50
Common Player:		.50
Inserted 1:9		
1	Chipper Jones	1.00
2	Cal Ripken Jr.	3.00
3	Nomar Garciaparra	1.00
4	Sammy Sosa	1.00
5	Frank Thomas	.75
6	Manny Ramirez	.75
7	Todd Helton	.75
8	Larry Walker	.50
9	Jeff Bagwell	.75
10	Vladimir Guerrero	.75
11	Mike Piazza	1.50
12	Derek Jeter	3.00
13	Bernie Williams	.50
14	J.D. Drew	.50
15	Mark McGwire	2.50
16	Tony Gwynn	1.00
17	Ken Griffey Jr.	2.00
18	Alex Rodriguez	2.50
19	Juan Gonzalez	.50
20	Ivan Rodriguez	.65

Pennant Fever

PENNANT FEVER

		NM/M
Complete Set (20):		30.00
Common Player:		.75
Silver (250 Sets):		2X
Platinum Blue (100):		6X
Copper (20):		20X

Tony Gwynn Autograph:		25.00
1	Chipper Jones	2.00
2	Greg Maddux	2.00
3	Cal Ripken Jr.	5.00
4	Nomar Garciaparra	2.00
5	Sammy Sosa	2.00
6	Kerry Wood	.75
7	Frank Thomas	1.50
8	Manny Ramirez	1.50
9	Todd Helton	1.50
10	Jeff Bagwell	1.50
11	Mike Piazza	2.50
12	Derek Jeter	5.00
13	Bernie Williams	.75
14	J.D. Drew	.75
15	Mark McGwire	4.00
16	Tony Gwynn	2.00
17	Ken Griffey Jr.	3.00
18	Alex Rodriguez	4.00
19	Juan Gonzalez	.75
20	Ivan Rodriguez	1.25

Styrotechs

		NM/M
Complete Set (20):		35.00
Common Player:		1.00
Inserted 1:37		
1	Chipper Jones	3.00
2	Greg Maddux	3.00
3	Cal Ripken Jr.	6.00
4	Nomar Garciaparra	3.00
5	Sammy Sosa	3.00
6	Kerry Wood	1.25
7	Frank Thomas	2.00
8	Manny Ramirez	2.00
9	Larry Walker	1.00
10	Jeff Bagwell	2.00
11	Mike Piazza	4.00
12	Derek Jeter	6.00
13	Bernie Williams	1.00
14	J.D. Drew	1.25
15	Mark McGwire	5.00
16	Tony Gwynn	3.00
17	Ken Griffey Jr.	4.50
18	Alex Rodriguez	5.00
19	Juan Gonzalez	1.25
20	Ivan Rodriguez	1.50

1999 Pacific Crown Collection

		NM/M
Complete Set (300):		20.00
Common Player:		.10
Red Stars:		6X
Inserted 1:9		
Platinum Blue Stars:		30X
Inserted 1:73		
Pack (12):		1.00
Wax Box (36):		22.50
1	Garret Anderson	.10

2	Gary DiSarcina	.10
3	Jim Edmonds	.10
4	Darin Erstad	.25
5	Shigetoshi Hasegawa	.10
6	Norberto Martin	.10
7	Omar Olivares	.10
8	Orlando Palmeiro	.10
9	Tim Salmon	.10
10	Randy Velarde	.10
11	Tony Batista	.10
12	Jay Bell	.10
13	Yamil Benitez	.10
14	Omar Daal	.10
15	David Dellucci	.10
16	Karim Garcia	.10
17	Travis Lee	.10
18	Felix Rodriguez	.10
19	Devon White	.10
20	Matt Williams	.10
21	Andres Galarraga	.10
22	Tom Glavine	.35
23	Ozzie Guillen	.10
24	Andruw Jones	1.00
25	Chipper Jones	1.50
26	Ryan Klesko	.10
27	Javy Lopez	.10
28	Greg Maddux	1.50
29	Dennis Martinez	.10
30	Odaliz Perez	.10
31	Rudy Seanez	.10
32	John Smoltz	.10
33	Roberto Alomar	.25
34	Armando Benitez	.10
35	Scott Erickson	.10
36	Juan Guzman	.10
37	Mike Mussina	.35
38	Jesse Orosco	.10
39	Rafael Palmeiro	.75
40	Sidney Ponson	.10
41	Cal Ripken Jr.	3.00
42	B.J. Surhoff	.10
43	Lenny Webster	.10
44	Dennis Eckersley	.75
45	Nomar Garciaparra	1.50
46	Darren Lewis	.10
47	Pedro Martinez	1.00
48	Troy O'Leary	.10
49	Bret Saberhagen	.10
50	John Valentin	.10
51	Mo Vaughn	.10
52	Tim Wakefield	.10
53	Manny Alexander	.10
54	Rod Beck	.10
55	Gary Gaetti	.10
56	Mark Grace	.10
57	Felix Heredia	.10
58	Jose Hernandez	.10
59	Henry Rodriguez	.10
60	Sammy Sosa	1.50
61	Kevin Tapani	.10
62	Kerry Wood	.45
63	James Baldwin	.10
64	Albert Belle	.10
65	Mike Caruso	.10
66	Carlos Castillo	.10
67	Wil Cordero	.10
68	Jaime Navarro	.10
69	Magglio Ordonez	.25
70	Frank Thomas	1.00
71	Robin Ventura	.10
72	Bret Boone	.10
73	Sean Casey	.20
74	Guillermo Garcia RC	.10
75	Barry Larkin	.10
76	Melvin Nieves	.10
77	Eduardo Perez	.10
78	Roberto Petagine	.10
79	Reggie Sanders	.10
80	Eddie Taubensee	.10
81	Brett Tomko	.10
82	Sandy Alomar Jr.	.10
83	Bartolo Colon	.10
84	Joey Cora	.10
85	Einar Diaz	.10
86	David Justice	.10
87	Kenny Lofton	.10
88	Manny Ramirez	1.00
89	Jim Thome	.75
90	Omar Vizquel	.10
91	Enrique Wilson	.10
92	Pedro Astacio	.10
93	Dante Bichette	.10
94	Vinny Castilla	.10
95	Edgard Clemente RC	.10
96	Todd Helton	1.00
97	Darryl Kile	.10
98	Mike Munoz	.10
99	Neifi Perez	.10
100	Jeff Reed	.10
101	Larry Walker	.10
102	Gabe Alvarez	.10
103	Kimera Bartee	.10
104	Frank Castillo	.10
105	Tony Clark	.10

106	Deivi Cruz	.10
107	Damion Easley	.10
108	Luis Gonzalez	.10
109	Marino Santana	.10
110	Justin Thompson	.10
111	Antonio Alfonseca	.10
112	Alex Fernandez	.10
113	Cliff Floyd	.10
114	Alex Gonzalez	.10
115	Livan Hernandez	.10
116	Mark Kotsay	.10
117	Derrek Lee	.65
118	Edgar Renteria	.10
119	Jesus Sanchez	.10
120	Moises Alou	.10
121	Jeff Bagwell	1.00
122	Derek Bell	.10
123	Craig Biggio	.10
124	Tony Eusebio	.10
125	Ricky Gutierrez	.10
126	Richard Hidalgo	.10
127	Randy Johnson	1.00
128	Jose Lima	.10
129	Shane Reynolds	.10
130	Johnny Damon	.40
131	Carlos Febles	.10
132	Jeff King	.10
133	Mendy Lopez	.10
134	Hal Morris	.10
135	Jose Offerman	.10
136	Jose Rosado	.10
137	Jose Santiago	.10
138	Bobby Bonilla	.10
139	Roger Cedeno	.10
140	Alex Cora	.10
141	Eric Karros	.10
142	Raul Mondesi	.10
143	Antonio Osuna	.10
144	Chan Ho Park	.10
145	Gary Sheffield	.30
146	Ismael Valdes	.10
147	Jeromy Burnitz	.10
148	Jeff Cirillo	.10
149	Valerio de los Santos	.10
150	Marquis Grissom	.10
151	Scott Karl	.10
152	Dave Nilsson	.10
153	Al Reyes	.10
154	Rafael Roque	.10
155	Jose Valentin	.10
156	Fernando Vina	.10
157	Rick Aguilera	.10
158	Hector Carrasco	.10
159	Marty Cordova	.10
160	Eddie Guardado	.10
161	Paul Molitor	1.00
162	Otis Nixon	.10
163	Alex Ochoa	.10
164	David Ortiz	.45
165	Frank Rodriguez	.10
166	Todd Walker	.10
167	Miguel Batista	.10
168	Orlando Cabrera	.10
169	Vladimir Guerrero	1.00
170	Wilton Guerrero	.10
171	Carl Pavano	.10
172	Robert Perez	.10
173	F.P. Santangelo	.25
174	Fernando Seguignol	.10
175	Ugueth Urbina	.10
176	Javier Vazquez	.10
177	Edgardo Alfonzo	.10
178	Carlos Baerga	.10
179	John Franco	.10
180	Luis Lopez	.10
181	Hideo Nomo	.50
182	John Olerud	.10
183	Rey Ordonez	.10
184	Mike Piazza	1.75
185	Armando Reynoso	.10
186	Masato Yoshii	.10
187	David Cone	.10
188	Orlando Hernandez	.10
189	Hideki Irabu	.10
190	Derek Jeter	3.00
191	Ricky Ledee	.10
192	Tino Martinez	.10
193	Ramiro Mendoza	.10
194	Paul O'Neill	.10
195	Jorge Posada	.10
196	Mariano Rivera	.15
197	Luis Sojo	.10
198	Bernie Williams	.10
199	Rafael Bournigal	.10
200	Eric Chavez	.20
201	Ryan Christenson	.10
202	Jason Giambi	.60
203	Ben Grieve	.10
204	Rickey Henderson	1.00
205	A.J. Hinch	.10
206	Kenny Rogers	.10
207	Miguel Tejada	.20
208	Jorge Velandia	.10
209	Bobby Abreu	.20

210	Marlon Anderson	.10
211	Alex Arias	.10
212	Bobby Estalella	.10
213	Doug Glanville	.10
214	Scott Rolen	.65
215	Curt Schilling	.35
216	Kevin Sefcik	.10
217	Adrian Brown	.10
218	Francisco Cordova	.10
219	Freddy Garcia	.10
220	Jose Guillen	.10
221	Jason Kendall	.10
222	Al Martin	.10
223	Abraham Nunez	.10
224	Aramis Ramirez	.10
225	Ricardo Rincon	.10
226	Kevin Young	.10
227	J.D. Drew	.40
228	Ron Gant	.10
229	Jose Jimenez	.10
230	Brian Jordan	.10
231	Ray Lankford	.10
232	Eli Marrero	.10
233	Mark McGwire	2.50
234	Luis Ordaz	.10
235	Placido Polanco	.10
236	Fernando Tatis	.10
237	Andy Ashby	.10
238	Kevin Brown	.10
239	Ken Caminiti	.10
240	Steve Finley	.10
241	Chris Gomez	.10
242	Tony Gwynn	1.50
243	Carlos Hernandez	.10
244	Trevor Hoffman	.10
245	Wally Joyner	.10
246	Ruben Rivera	.10
247	Greg Vaughn	.10
248	Quilvio Veras	.10
249	Rich Aurilia	.10
250	Barry Bonds	3.00
251	Stan Javier	.10
252	Jeff Kent	.10
253	Ramon Martinez	.10
254	Jose Mesa	.10
255	Armando Rios	.10
256	Rich Rodriguez	.10
257	Rey Sanchez	.10
258	J.T. Snow	.10
259	Julian Tavarez	.10
260	Jeff Fassero	.10
261	Ken Griffey Jr.	2.00
262	Giomar Guevara RC	.10
263	Carlos Guillen	.10
264	Raul Ibanez	.10
265	Edgar Martinez	.10
266	Jamie Moyer	.10
267	Alex Rodriguez	2.50
268	David Segui	.10
269	Makoto Suzuki	.10
270	Wilson Alvarez	.10
271	Rolando Arrojo	.10
272	Wade Boggs	1.50
273	Miguel Cairo	.10
274	Roberto Hernandez	.10
275	Aaron Ledesma	.10
276	Albie Lopez	.10
277	Quinton McCracken	.10
278	Fred McGriff	.10
279	Esteban Yan	.10
280	Luis Alicea	.10
281	Will Clark	.10
282	Juan Gonzalez	.50
283	Rusty Greer	.10
284	Rick Helling	.10
285	Xavier Hernandez	.10
286	Roberto Kelly	.10
287	Esteban Loaiza	.10
288	Ivan Rodriguez	.75
289	Aaron Sele	.10
290	John Wetteland	.10
291	Jose Canseco	.40
292	Roger Clemens	1.75
293	Felipe Crespo	.10
294	Jose Cruz Jr.	.10
295	Carlos Delgado	.60
296	Kelvim Escobar	.10
297	Tony Fernandez	.10
298	Alex Gonzalez	.10
299	Tomas Perez	.10
300	Juan Samuel	.10

In The Cage

		NM/M
Complete Set (20):		80.00
Common Player:		2.00
Inserted 1:145		
1	Chipper Jones	7.50
2	Cal Ripken Jr.	15.00
3	Nomar Garciaparra	7.50
4	Sammy Sosa	7.50
5	Frank Thomas	5.00
6	Manny Ramirez	5.00
7	Todd Helton	5.00

8	Moises Alou	2.00
9	Vladimir Guerrero	5.00
10	Mike Piazza	9.00
11	Derek Jeter	15.00
12	Ben Grieve	2.00
13	J.D. Drew	3.00
14	Mark McGwire	12.00
15	Tony Gwynn	7.50
16	Ken Griffey Jr.	10.00
17	Edgar Martinez	2.00
18	Alex Rodriguez	12.00
19	Juan Gonzalez	2.50
20	Ivan Rodriguez	4.00

Latinos/Major Leagues

		NM/M
Complete Set (36):		25.00
Common Player:		.30
Inserted 1:18		
1	Roberto Alomar	.60
2	Rafael Palmeiro	2.00
3	Nomar Garciaparra	3.50
4	Pedro Martinez	2.50
5	Magglio Ordonez	1.50
6	Sandy Alomar Jr.	.30
7	Bartolo Colon	.30
8	Manny Ramirez	2.50
9	Omar Vizquel	.30
10	Enrique Wilson	.30
11	David Ortiz	1.50
12	Orlando Hernandez	.30
13	Tino Martinez	.30
14	Mariano Rivera	.45
15	Bernie Williams	.30
16	Edgar Martinez	.30
17	Alex Rodriguez	5.00
18	David Segui	.30
19	Rolando Arrojo	.30
20	Juan Gonzalez	1.25
21	Ivan Rodriguez	2.00
22	Jose Canseco	1.00
23	Jose Cruz Jr.	.30
24	Andres Galarraga	.30
25	Andruw Jones	2.50
26	Javy Lopez	.30
27	Sammy Sosa	3.50
28	Vinny Castilla	.30
29	Alex Gonzalez	.30
30	Moises Alou	.30
31	Bobby Bonilla	.30
32	Raul Mondesi	.30
33	Fernando Vina	.30
34	Vladimir Guerrero	2.50
35	Carlos Baerga	.30
36	Rey Ordonez	.30

Pacific Cup

		NM/M
Complete Set (10):		80.00
Common Player:		5.00
Inserted 1:721		

1	Cal Ripken Jr.	20.00
2	Nomar Garciaparra	8.00
3	Frank Thomas	6.00
4	Ken Griffey Jr.	12.00
5	Alex Rodriguez	16.00
6	Greg Maddux	8.00
7	Sammy Sosa	8.00
8	Kerry Wood	5.00
9	Mark McGwire	16.00
10	Tony Gwynn	8.00

Players Choice

		NM/M
Complete Set (6):		55.00
Common Player:		5.00
10	Randy Velarde	5.00
41	Cal Ripken Jr.	30.00
47	Pedro Martinez	12.00
88	Manny Ramirez	12.00
112	Alex Fernandez	5.00
128	Jose Lima	5.00

Tape Measure

		NM/M
Complete Set (20):		20.00
Common Player:		.60
Inserted 1:73		
1	Andres Galarraga	.60
2	Chipper Jones	2.50
3	Nomar Garciaparra	2.50
4	Sammy Sosa	2.50
5	Frank Thomas	1.50
6	Manny Ramirez	1.50
7	Vinny Castilla	.60
8	Moises Alou	.60
9	Jeff Bagwell	1.50
10	Raul Mondesi	.60
11	Vladimir Guerrero	1.50
12	Mike Piazza	2.75
13	J.D. Drew	1.00
14	Mark McGwire	3.50
15	Greg Vaughn	.60
16	Ken Griffey Jr.	3.00
17	Alex Rodriguez	3.50
18	Juan Gonzalez	1.00
19	Ivan Rodriguez	1.25
20	Jose Canseco	1.00

Team Checklists

		NM/M
Complete Set (30):		25.00
Common Player:		.50
Inserted 1:37		
1	Darin Erstad	.60
2	Travis Lee	.50
3	Chipper Jones	1.75
4	Cal Ripken Jr.	4.00
5	Nomar Garciaparra	1.75
6	Sammy Sosa	1.75
7	Frank Thomas	1.25
8	Barry Larkin	.50
9	Manny Ramirez	1.25
10	Larry Walker	.50
11	Bob Higginson	.50
12	Livan Hernandez	.50
13	Moises Alou	.50
14	Jeff King	.50
15	Raul Mondesi	.50
16	Marquis Grissom	.50
17	David Ortiz	1.00
18	Vladimir Guerrero	1.25
19	Mike Piazza	2.00
20	Derek Jeter	4.00
21	Ben Grieve	.50
22	Scott Rolen	.75
23	Jason Kendall	.50
24	Mark McGwire	3.00
25	Tony Gwynn	1.75
26	Barry Bonds	4.00
27	Ken Griffey Jr.	2.50
28	Wade Boggs	1.75
29	Juan Gonzalez	.75
30	Jose Canseco	.60

1999 Pacific Crown Royale

		NM/M
Complete Set (144):		75.00
Common Player:		.25
Common SP:		.50
Limited Series (99 Sets):		6X
SP's:		2X
Opening Day (72 Sets):		12X
SP's:		2X
Pack (6):		2.00
Wax Box (24):		35.00
1	Jim Edmonds	.25
2	Darin Erstad	.50
3	Troy Glaus	2.00
4	Tim Salmon	.25
5	Mo Vaughn	.25
6	Jay Bell	.25
7	Steve Finley	.25
8	Randy Johnson	2.00
9	Travis Lee	.25
10	Matt Williams	.25
11	Andruw Jones	2.00
12	Chipper Jones	3.00
13	Brian Jordan	.25
14	Ryan Klesko	.25
15	Javy Lopez	.25
16	Greg Maddux	3.00
17	Randall Simon/SP	.50
18	Albert Belle	.25
19	Will Clark	.25
20	Delino DeShields	.25
21	Mike Mussina	.50
22	Cal Ripken Jr.	6.00
23	Nomar Garciaparra	3.00
24	Pedro Martinez	2.00
25	Jose Offerman	.25
26	John Valentin	.25
27	Mark Grace	.25
28	Lance Johnson	.25
29	Henry Rodriguez	.25
30	Sammy Sosa	3.00
31	Kerry Wood	1.00
32	Mike Caruso	.25
33	Ray Durham	.25
34	Magglio Ordonez	.40
35	Brian Simmons/SP	.50
36	Frank Thomas	2.00
37	Mike Cameron	.25
38	Barry Larkin	.25
39	Greg Vaughn	.25
40	Dmitri Young	.25
41	Roberto Alomar	.40
42	Sandy Alomar Jr.	.25
43	David Justice	.25
44	Kenny Lofton	.25
45	Manny Ramirez	2.00
46	Jim Thome	1.50
47	Dante Bichette	.25
48	Vinny Castilla	.25
49	Todd Helton	2.00
50	Larry Walker	.25
51	Tony Clark	.25
52	Damion Easley	.25
53	Bob Higginson	.25
54	Brian Hunter	.25
55	Gabe Kapler/SP	.50
56	Jeff Weaver/SP RC	2.50
57	Cliff Floyd	.25
58	Alex Gonzalez/SP	.50
59	Mark Kotsay	.25
60	Derrek Lee	1.00
61	Preston Wilson/SP	.75
62	Moises Alou	.25
63	Jeff Bagwell	2.00
64	Derek Bell	.25
65	Craig Biggio	.25
66	Ken Caminiti	.25
67	Carlos Beltran/SP	2.00
68	Johnny Damon	.45
69	Carlos Febles/SP	.65
70	Jeff King	.25
71	Kevin Brown	.25
72	Todd Hundley	.25
73	Eric Karros	.25
74	Raul Mondesi	.25
75	Gary Sheffield	.75
76	Jeromy Burnitz	.25
77	Jeff Cirillo	.25
78	Marquis Grissom	.25
79	Fernando Vina	.25
80	Chad Allen/SP RC	.50
81	Matt Lawton	.25
82	Doug Mientkiewicz/SP	.75
83	Brad Radke	.25
84	Todd Walker	.25
85	Michael Barrett/SP	.50
86	Brad Fullmer	.25
87	Vladimir Guerrero	2.00
88	Wilton Guerrero	.25
89	Ugueth Urbina	.25
90	Bobby Bonilla	.25
91	Rickey Henderson	2.00
92	Rey Ordonez	.25
93	Mike Piazza	3.50
94	Robin Ventura	.25
95	Roger Clemens	3.50
96	Orlando Hernandez	.25
97	Derek Jeter	6.00
98	Chuck Knoblauch	.25
99	Tino Martinez	.25
100	Bernie Williams	.25
101	Eric Chavez/SP	1.50
102	Jason Giambi	1.00
103	Ben Grieve	.25
104	Tim Raines	.25
105	Marlon Anderson/SP	.65
106	Doug Glanville	.25
107	Scott Rolen	1.25
108	Curt Schilling	.40
109	Brian Giles	.25
110	Jose Guillen	.25
111	Jason Kendall	.25
112	Kevin Young	.25
113	J.D. Drew/SP	2.00
114	Jose Jimenez/SP	.50
115	Ray Lankford	.25
116	Mark McGwire	5.00
117	Fernando Tatis	.25
118	Matt Clement/SP	.75
119	Tony Gwynn	3.00
120	Trevor Hoffman	.25
121	Wally Joyner	.25
122	Reggie Sanders	.25
123	Barry Bonds	6.00
124	Ellis Burks	.25
125	Jeff Kent	.25
126	J.T. Snow	.25
127	Freddy Garcia/SP RC	1.00
128	Ken Griffey Jr.	4.00
129	Edgar Martinez	.25
130	Alex Rodriguez	5.00
131	David Segui	.25
132	Rolando Arrojo	.25
133	Wade Boggs	3.00
134	Jose Canseco	.65
135	Quinton McCracken	.25
136	Fred McGriff	.25
137	Juan Gonzalez	1.00
138	Rusty Greer	.25
139	Rafael Palmeiro	1.50
140	Ivan Rodriguez	1.50
141	Jose Cruz Jr.	.25
142	Carlos Delgado	.75
143	Shawn Green	.75
144	Roy Halladay/SP	1.00

Pivotal Players

		NM/M
Complete Set (25):		20.00
Common Player:		.50
Inserted 1:1		
1	Mo Vaughn	.50
2	Chipper Jones	2.00
3	Greg Maddux	2.00
4	Albert Belle	.50
5	Cal Ripken Jr.	4.00
6	Nomar Garciaparra	2.00
7	Sammy Sosa	2.00
8	Frank Thomas	1.50
9	Manny Ramirez	1.50

		NM/M
Complete Set (20):		40.00
Common Player:		1.00
Inserted 2:25		
1	Chipper Jones	2.50
2	Greg Maddux	2.50
3	Cal Ripken Jr.	5.00
4	Nomar Garciaparra	2.50
5	Sammy Sosa	2.50
6	Frank Thomas	2.00
7	Raul Mondesi	1.00
8	Vladimir Guerrero	2.00
9	Mike Piazza	3.00
10	Roger Clemens	3.00
11	Derek Jeter	5.00
12	Scott Rolen	1.75
13	J.D. Drew	1.50
14	Mark McGwire	4.00
15	Tony Gwynn	2.50
16	Barry Bonds	5.00
17	Ken Griffey Jr.	3.50
18	Alex Rodriguez	4.00
19	Juan Gonzalez	1.50
20	Ivan Rodriguez	1.75

10	Craig Biggio	.50
11	Raul Mondesi	.50
12	Vladimir Guerrero	1.50
13	Mike Piazza	2.25
14	Roger Clemens	2.50
15	Derek Jeter	4.00
16	Bernie Williams	.50
17	Ben Grieve	.50
18	Scott Rolen	.60
19	J.D. Drew	.75
20	Mark McGwire	3.00
21	Tony Gwynn	2.00
22	Ken Griffey Jr.	2.50
23	Alex Rodriguez	3.00
24	Juan Gonzalez	.75
25	Ivan Rodriguez	1.00

Pillars of the Game

		NM/M
Complete Set (25):		30.00
Common Player:		.50
Inserted 1:1		
1	Mo Vaughn	.50
2	Chipper Jones	2.00
3	Greg Maddux	2.00
4	Albert Belle	.50
5	Cal Ripken Jr.	4.00
6	Nomar Garciaparra	2.00
7	Sammy Sosa	2.00
8	Frank Thomas	1.50
9	Manny Ramirez	1.50
10	Jeff Bagwell	1.50
11	Raul Mondesi	.50
12	Vladimir Guerrero	1.50
13	Mike Piazza	2.25
14	Roger Clemens	2.25
15	Derek Jeter	4.00
16	Bernie Williams	.50
17	Ben Grieve	.50
18	J.D. Drew	1.00
19	Mark McGwire	3.00
20	Tony Gwynn	2.00
21	Barry Bonds	4.00
22	Ken Griffey Jr.	2.50
23	Alex Rodriguez	3.00
24	Juan Gonzalez	1.00
25	Ivan Rodriguez	1.25

Master Performers

Century 21

		NM/M
Complete Set (10):		30.00
Common Player:		2.00
Inserted 1:25		
1	Cal Ripken Jr.	7.50
2	Nomar Garciaparra	4.00
3	Sammy Sosa	4.00
4	Frank Thomas	3.00
5	Mike Piazza	4.50
6	J.D. Drew	2.00
7	Mark McGwire	6.00
8	Tony Gwynn	4.00
9	Ken Griffey Jr.	5.00
10	Alex Rodriguez	6.00

Cramer's Choice Premiums

		NM/M
Complete Set (10):		20.00
Common Player:		2.00
Inserted 1:box		
Dark Blue (35 Sets):		5X
Green (30):		6X
Red (25):		8X
Light Blue (20):		10X
Gold (10):		15X
Purple (1):	Value Undetermined	
1	Cal Ripken Jr.	6.50
2	Nomar Garciaparra	3.00
3	Sammy Sosa	3.00
4	Frank Thomas	2.50
5	Mike Piazza	3.50
6	Derek Jeter	6.50

7	J.D. Drew	2.00
8	Mark McGwire	5.00
9	Tony Gwynn	3.00
10	Ken Griffey Jr.	4.00

Living Legends

		NM/M
Complete Set (10):		100.00
Common Player:		7.50
Production 375 Sets		
1	Greg Maddux	10.00
2	Cal Ripken Jr.	20.00
3	Nomar Garciaparra	10.00
4	Sammy Sosa	10.00
5	Frank Thomas	7.50
6	Mike Piazza	12.00
7	Mark McGwire	15.00
8	Tony Gwynn	10.00
9	Ken Griffey Jr.	13.50
10	Alex Rodriguez	15.00

Gold Crown Die-Cut Premiums

		NM/M
Complete Set (6):		15.00
Common Player:		2.50
Inserted 6:10 boxes.		
1	Cal Ripken Jr.	7.00
2	Mike Piazza	4.50
3	Ken Griffey Jr.	5.00
4	Tony Gwynn	3.00
5	Mark McGwire	6.00
6	J.D. Drew	2.50

Pivotal Players Show Cards

	NM/M
Common Card:	5.00
Stars:	6-8X
(See 1999 Pacific Crown Royale Pivotal Players for checklist and base values.)	

1999 Pacific Invincible

		NM/M
Complete Set (150):		60.00
Common Player:		.25
Opening Day (69 Sets):		6X
Platinum Blues (67):		6X
Pack (3):		1.50
Wax Box (24):		35.00
1	Jim Edmonds	.25
2	Darin Erstad	.50
3	Troy Glaus	2.50
4	Tim Salmon	.25
5	Mo Vaughn	.25
6	Steve Finley	.25
7	Randy Johnson	2.50
8	Travis Lee	.25

7	J.D. Drew	2.00
8	Mark McGwire	5.00
9	Tony Gwynn	3.00
10	Ken Griffey Jr.	4.00

9	Dante Powell	.25
10	Matt Williams	.25
11	Bret Boone	.25
12	Andruw Jones	2.50
13	Chipper Jones	3.00
14	Brian Jordan	.25
15	Ryan Klesko	.25
16	Javy Lopez	.25
17	Greg Maddux	3.00
18	Brady Anderson	.25
19	Albert Belle	.25
20	Will Clark	.25
21	Mike Mussina	.75
22	Cal Ripken Jr.	6.00
23	Nomar Garciaparra	3.00
24	Pedro Martinez	2.50
25	Trot Nixon	.25
26	Jose Offerman	.25
27	Donnie Sadler	.25
28	John Valentin	.25
29	Mark Grace	.25
30	Lance Johnson	.25
31	Henry Rodriguez	.25
32	Sammy Sosa	3.00
33	Kerry Wood	1.25
34	McKay Christensen	.25
35	Ray Durham	.25
36	Jeff Liefer	.25
37	Frank Thomas	2.50
38	Mike Cameron	.25
39	Barry Larkin	.25
40	Greg Vaughn	.25
41	Dmitri Young	.25
42	Roberto Alomar	.50
43	Sandy Alomar Jr.	.25
44	David Justice	.25
45	Kenny Lofton	.25
46	Manny Ramirez	2.50
47	Jim Thome	2.25
48	Dante Bichette	.25
49	Vinny Castilla	.25
50	Darryl Hamilton	.25
51	Todd Helton	2.50
52	Neifi Perez	.25
53	Larry Walker	.25
54	Tony Clark	.25
55	Damion Easley	.25
56	Bob Higginson	.25
57	Brian Hunter	.25
58	Gabe Kapler	.25
59	Cliff Floyd	.25
60	Alex Gonzalez	.25
61	Mark Kotsay	.25
62	Derrek Lee	2.00
63	Braden Looper	.25
64	Moises Alou	.25
65	Jeff Bagwell	2.50
66	Craig Biggio	.25
67	Ken Caminiti	.25
68	Scott Elarton	.25
69	Mitch Meluskey	.25
70	Carlos Beltran	.65
71	Johnny Damon	.50
72	Carlos Febles	.25
73	Jeremy Giambi	.25
74	Kevin Brown	.25
75	Todd Hundley	.25
76	Paul LoDuca	.25
77	Raul Mondesi	.25
78	Gary Sheffield	1.00
79	Geoff Jenkins	.25
80	Jeromy Burnitz	.25
81	Marquis Grissom	.25
82	Jose Valentin	.25
83	Fernando Vina	.25
84	Corey Koskie	.25
85	Matt Lawton	.25
86	Christian Guzman	.25
87	Torii Hunter	.25
88	Doug Mientkiewicz	.25
89	Michael Barrett	.25
90	Brad Fullmer	.25
91	Vladimir Guerrero	2.50

92	Fernando Seguignol	.25
93	Ugueth Urbina	.25
94	Bobby Bonilla	.25
95	Rickey Henderson	2.50
96	Rey Ordonez	.25
97	Mike Piazza	3.50
98	Robin Ventura	.25
99	Roger Clemens	3.50
100	Derek Jeter	6.00
101	Chuck Knoblauch	.25
102	Tino Martinez	.25
103	Paul O'Neill	.25
104	Bernie Williams	.25
105	Eric Chavez	.50
106	Ryan Christenson	.25
107	Jason Giambi	1.25
108	Ben Grieve	.25
109	Miguel Tejada	.50
110	Marlon Anderson	.25
111	Doug Glanville	.25
112	Scott Rolen	2.25
113	Curt Schilling	.50
114	Brian Giles	.25
115	Warren Morris	.25
116	Jason Kendall	.25
117	Kris Benson	.25
118	J.D. Drew	1.25
119	Ray Lankford	.25
120	Mark McGwire	5.00
121	Matt Clement	.25
122	Tony Gwynn	3.00
123	Trevor Hoffman	.25
124	Wally Joyner	.25
125	Reggie Sanders	.25
126	Barry Bonds	6.00
127	Ellis Burks	.25
128	Jeff Kent	.25
129	Stan Javier	.25
130	J.T. Snow	.25
131	Jay Buhner	.25
132	Freddy Garcia RC	2.00
133	Ken Griffey Jr.	4.00
134	Russ Davis	.25
135	Edgar Martinez	.25
136	Alex Rodriguez	5.00
137	David Segui	.25
138	Rolando Arrojo	.25
139	Wade Boggs	3.00
140	Jose Canseco	1.00
141	Quinton McCracken	.25
142	Fred McGriff	.25
143	Juan Gonzalez	1.25
144	Tom Goodwin	.25
145	Rusty Greer	.25
146	Ivan Rodriguez	2.25
147	Jose Cruz Jr.	.25
148	Carlos Delgado	1.00
149	Shawn Green	.75
150	Roy Halladay	.25

Diamond Magic

NM/M
Complete Set (10):		35.00
Common Player:		3.00
Inserted 1:49		
1	Cal Ripken Jr.	7.50
2	Nomar Garciaparra	4.00
3	Sammy Sosa	4.00
4	Frank Thomas	3.50
5	Mike Piazza	4.50
6	J.D. Drew	3.00
7	Mark McGwire	6.00
8	Tony Gwynn	4.00
9	Ken Griffey Jr.	5.00
10	Alex Rodriguez	6.00

Flash Point

NM/M
Complete Set (20):		50.00
Common Player:		1.25
Inserted 1:25		
1	Mo Vaughn	1.25
2	Chipper Jones	3.50
3	Greg Maddux	3.50
4	Cal Ripken Jr.	9.00
5	Nomar Garciaparra	3.50
6	Sammy Sosa	3.50
7	Frank Thomas	2.50
8	Manny Ramirez	2.50
9	Vladimir Guerrero	2.50
10	Mike Piazza	4.00
11	Roger Clemens	4.00

12	Derek Jeter	9.00
13	Ben Grieve	1.25
14	Scott Rolen	2.00
15	J.D. Drew	1.50
16	Mark McGwire	7.50
17	Tony Gwynn	3.50
18	Ken Griffey Jr.	5.00
19	Alex Rodriguez	7.50
20	Juan Gonzalez	1.50

Giants of the Game

NM/M
Complete Set (10):		300.00
Common Player:		25.00
Production 10 Sets		
1	Cal Ripken Jr.	75.00
2	Nomar Garciaparra	35.00
3	Sammy Sosa	35.00
4	Frank Thomas	30.00
5	Mike Piazza	40.00
6	J.D. Drew	25.00
7	Mark McGwire	60.00
8	Tony Gwynn	35.00
9	Ken Griffey Jr.	50.00
10	Alex Rodriguez	60.00

Sandlot Heroes

NM/M
Complete Set (20):		15.00
Common Player:		.50
Inserted 1:1		
SportsFest (10 Sets):		25X
1	Mo Vaughn	.50
2	Chipper Jones	1.00
3	Greg Maddux	1.00
4	Cal Ripken Jr.	3.00
5	Nomar Garciaparra	1.00
6	Sammy Sosa	1.00
7	Frank Thomas	.75
8	Manny Ramirez	.75
9	Vladimir Guerrero	.75
10	Mike Piazza	1.25
11	Roger Clemens	1.25
12	Derek Jeter	3.00
13	Eric Chavez	.50
14	Ben Grieve	.50
15	J.D. Drew	.60
16	Mark McGwire	2.00
17	Tony Gwynn	1.00
18	Ken Griffey Jr.	1.50
19	Alex Rodriguez	2.00
20	Juan Gonzalez	.60

Seismic Force

NM/M
Complete Set (20):		15.00
Common Player:		.50
Inserted 1:1		
SportsFest (20 Sets):		15X
1	Mo Vaughn	.50
2	Chipper Jones	1.00
3	Greg Maddux	1.00
4	Cal Ripken Jr.	3.00
5	Nomar Garciaparra	1.00
6	Sammy Sosa	1.00
7	Frank Thomas	.75
8	Manny Ramirez	.75
9	Vladimir Guerrero	.75
10	Mike Piazza	1.25
11	Bernie Williams	.50
12	Derek Jeter	3.00

13	Ben Grieve	.50
14	J.D. Drew	.60
15	Mark McGwire	2.00
16	Tony Gwynn	1.00
17	Ken Griffey Jr.	1.50
18	Alex Rodriguez	2.00
19	Juan Gonzalez	.50
20	Ivan Rodriguez	.65

Thunder Alley

NM/M
Complete Set (20):		75.00
Common Player:		2.50
Inserted 1:121		
1	Mo Vaughn	2.50
2	Chipper Jones	6.00
3	Cal Ripken Jr.	12.00
4	Nomar Garciaparra	6.00
5	Sammy Sosa	6.00
6	Frank Thomas	5.00
7	Manny Ramirez	5.00
8	Todd Helton	5.00
9	Vladimir Guerrero	5.00
10	Mike Piazza	7.50
11	Derek Jeter	12.00
12	Ben Grieve	2.50
13	Scott Rolen	4.50
14	J.D. Drew	3.00
15	Mark McGwire	10.00
16	Tony Gwynn	6.00
17	Ken Griffey Jr.	9.00
18	Alex Rodriguez	10.00
19	Juan Gonzalez	3.00
20	Ivan Rodriguez	4.50

1999 Pacific Omega

NM/M
Complete Set (250):		20.00
Common Player:		.10
Gold (299 Sets):		4X
Copper (99):		10X
Platinum Blue (75):		15X
Premire Date (50):		20X
Wax Pack (6):		1.50
Wax Box (36):		35.00
1	Garret Anderson	.10
2	Jim Edmonds	.10
3	Darin Erstad	.20
4	Chuck Finley	.10

5	Troy Glaus	.75
6	Troy Percival	.10
7	Chris Pritchett	.10
8	Tim Salmon	.10
9	Mo Vaughn	.10
10	Jay Bell	.10
11	Steve Finley	.10
12	Luis Gonzalez	.10
13	Randy Johnson	.75
14	Byung-Hyun Kim RC	.75
15	Travis Lee	.10
16	Matt Williams	.10
17	Tony Womack	.10
18	Bret Boone	.10
19	Mark DeRosa	.10
20	Tom Glavine	.35
21	Andruw Jones	.75
22	Chipper Jones	1.00
23	Brian Jordan	.10
24	Ryan Klesko	.10
25	Javy Lopez	.10
26	Greg Maddux	1.00
27	John Smoltz	.10
28	Bruce Chen, Odalis Perez	.10
29	Brady Anderson	.10
30	Harold Baines	.10
31	Albert Belle	.10
32	Will Clark	.10
33	Delino DeShields	.10
34	Jerry Hairston Jr.	.10
35	Charles Johnson	.10
36	Mike Mussina	.40
37	Cal Ripken Jr.	2.50
38	B.J. Surhoff	.10
39	Jin Ho Cho	.10
40	Nomar Garciaparra	1.00
41	Pedro Martinez	.75
42	Jose Offerman	.10
43	Troy O'Leary	.10
44	John Valentin	.10
45	Jason Varitek	.10
46	Juan Pena, Brian Rose	.10
47	Mark Grace	.10
48	Glenallen Hill	.10
49	Tyler Houston	.10
50	Mickey Morandini	.10
51	Henry Rodriguez	.10
52	Sammy Sosa	1.00
53	Kevin Tapani	.10
54	Mike Caruso	.10
55	Ray Durham	.10
56	Paul Konerko	.20
57	Carlos Lee	.10
58	Magglio Ordonez	.20
59	Mike Sirotka	.10
60	Frank Thomas	.75
61	Mark L. Johnson, Chris Singleton	.10
62	Mike Cameron	.10
63	Sean Casey	.20
64	Pete Harnisch	.10
65	Barry Larkin	.10
66	Pokey Reese	.10
67	Greg Vaughn	.10
68	Scott Williamson	.10
69	Dmitri Young	.10
70	Roberto Alomar	.25
71	Sandy Alomar Jr.	.10
72	Travis Fryman	.10
73	David Justice	.10
74	Kenny Lofton	.10
75	Manny Ramirez	.75
76	Richie Sexson	.10
77	Jim Thome	.65
78	Omar Vizquel	.10
79	Jaret Wright	.10
80	Dante Bichette	.10
81	Vinny Castilla	.10
82	Todd Helton	.75
83	Darryl Hamilton	.10
84	Darryl Kile	.10
85	Neifi Perez	.10
86	Larry Walker	.10
87	Tony Clark	.10
88	Damion Easley	.10
89	Juan Encarnacion	.10
90	Bobby Higginson	.10
91	Gabe Kapler	.10
92	Dean Palmer	.10
93	Justin Thompson	.10
94	Masao Kida, Jeff Weaver RC	1.00
95	Bruce Aven	.10
96	Luis Castillo	.10
97	Alex Fernandez	.10
98	Cliff Floyd	.10
99	Alex Gonzalez	.10
100	Mark Kotsay	.10
101	Preston Wilson	.10
102	Moises Alou	.10
103	Jeff Bagwell	.75
104	Derek Bell	.10
105	Craig Biggio	.10

106	Mike Hampton	.10
107	Richard Hidalgo	.10
108	Jose Lima	.10
109	Billy Wagner	.10
110	Russ Johnson, Daryle Ward	.10
111	Carlos Beltran	.50
112	Johnny Damon	.35
113	Jermaine Dye	.10
114	Carlos Febles	.10
115	Jeremy Giambi	.10
116	Joe Randa	.10
117	Mike Sweeney	.10
118	Orber Moreno, Jose Santiago	.10
119	Kevin Brown	.10
120	Todd Hundley	.10
121	Eric Karros	.10
122	Raul Mondesi	.10
123	Chan Ho Park	.10
124	Angel Pena	.10
125	Gary Sheffield	.45
126	Devon White	.10
127	Eric Young	.10
128	Ron Belliard	.10
129	Jeromy Burnitz	.10
130	Jeff Cirillo	.10
131	Marquis Grissom	.10
132	Geoff Jenkins	.10
133	David Nilsson	.10
134	Hideo Nomo	.40
135	Fernando Vina	.10
136	Ron Coomer	.10
137	Marty Cordova	.10
138	Corey Koskie	.10
139	Brad Radke	.10
140	Todd Walker	.10
141	Chad Allen, Torii Hunter	.10
142	Cristian Guzman, Jacque Jones	.10
143	Michael Barrett	.10
144	Orlando Cabrera	.10
145	Vladimir Guerrero	.75
146	Wilton Guerrero	.10
147	Ugueth Urbina	.10
148	Rondell White	.10
149	Chris Widger	.10
150	Edgardo Alfonzo	.10
151	Roger Cedeno	.10
152	Octavio Dotel	.10
153	Rickey Henderson	.75
154	John Olerud	.10
155	Rey Ordonez	.10
156	Mike Piazza	1.25
157	Robin Ventura	.10
158	Scott Brosius	.10
159	Roger Clemens	1.25
160	David Cone	.10
161	Chili Davis	.10
162	Orlando Hernandez	.10
163	Derek Jeter	2.50
164	Chuck Knoblauch	.10
165	Tino Martinez	.10
166	Paul O'Neill	.10
167	Bernie Williams	.10
168	Jason Giambi	.60
169	Ben Grieve	.10
170	Chad Harville RC	.10
171	Tim Hudson RC	2.00
172	Tony Phillips	.10
173	Kenny Rogers	.10
174	Matt Stairs	.10
175	Miguel Tejada	.25
176	Eric Chavez	.25
177	Bobby Abreu	.20
178	Ron Gant	.10
179	Doug Glanville	.10
180	Mike Lieberthal	.10
181	Desi Relaford	.10
182	Scott Rolen	.65
183	Curt Schilling	.35
184	Marlon Anderson, Randy Wolf	.10
185	Brant Brown	.10
186	Brian Giles	.10
187	Jason Kendall	.10
188	Al Martin	.10
189	Ed Sprague	.10
190	Kevin Young	.10
191	Kris Benson, Warren Morris	.10
192	Kent Bottenfield	.10
193	Eric Davis	.10
194	J.D. Drew	.45
195	Ray Lankford	.10
196	Joe McEwing RC	.25
197	Mark McGwire	2.00
198	Edgar Renteria	.10
199	Fernando Tatis	.10
200	Andy Ashby	.10
201	Ben Davis	.10
202	Tony Gwynn	1.00
203	Trevor Hoffman	.10
204	Wally Joyner	.10
205	Gary Matthews Jr.	.10
206	Ruben Rivera	.10
207	Reggie Sanders	.10
208	Rich Aurilia	.10
209	Marvin Benard	.10
210	Barry Bonds	2.50
211	Ellis Burks	.10
212	Stan Javier	.10
213	Jeff Kent	.10
214	Robb Nen	.10
215	J.T. Snow	.10
216	David Bell	.10
217	Jay Buhner	.10
218	Freddy Garcia RC	.50
219	Ken Griffey Jr.	1.50
220	Brian Hunter	.10
221	Butch Huskey	.10
222	Edgar Martinez	.10
223	Jamie Moyer	.10
224	Alex Rodriguez	2.00
225	David Segui	.10
226	Rolando Arrojo	.10
227	Wade Boggs	1.00
228	Miguel Cairo	.10
229	Jose Canseco	.60
230	Dave Martinez	.10
231	Fred McGriff	.10
232	Kevin Stocker	.10
233	Mike Duvall, David Lamb	.10
234	Royce Clayton	.10
235	Juan Gonzalez	.40
236	Rusty Greer	.10
237	Ruben Mateo	.10
238	Rafael Palmeiro	.65
239	Ivan Rodriguez	.65
240	John Wetteland	.10
241	Todd Zeile	.10
242	Jeff Zimmerman	.10
243	Homer Bush	.10
244	Jose Cruz Jr.	.10
245	Carlos Delgado	.60
246	Tony Fernandez	.10
247	Shawn Green	.35
248	Shannon Stewart	.10
249	David Wells	.10
250	Roy Halladay, Billy Koch	.10

Debut Duos

		NM/M
Complete Set (10):		45.00
Common Player:		2.50
Inserted 1:145		
1	Nomar Garciaparra, Vladimir Guerrero	6.00
2	Derek Jeter, Andy Pettitte	12.00
3	Garret Anderson, Alex Rodriguez	9.00
4	Chipper Jones, Raul Mondesi	6.00
5	Pedro Martinez, Mike Piazza	6.50
6	Mo Vaughn, Bernie Williams	2.50
7	Juan Gonzalez, Ken Griffey Jr.	7.50
8	Sammy Sosa, Larry Walker	6.00
9	Barry Bonds, Mark McGwire	12.00
10	Wade Boggs, Tony Gwynn	6.00

Diamond Masters

		NM/M
Complete Set (36):		27.50
Common Player:		.25
Inserted 1:9		
1	Darin Erstad	.35
2	Mo Vaughn	.25
3	Matt Williams	.25

4	Andruw Jones	.75
5	Chipper Jones	1.00
6	Greg Maddux	1.00
7	Cal Ripken Jr.	3.00
8	Nomar Garciaparra	1.00
9	Pedro Martinez	.75
10	Sammy Sosa	1.00
11	Frank Thomas	.75
12	Kenny Lofton	.25
13	Manny Ramirez	.75
14	Larry Walker	.25
15	Gabe Kapler	.25
16	Jeff Bagwell	.75
17	Craig Biggio	.25
18	Raul Mondesi	.25
19	Vladimir Guerrero	.75
20	Mike Piazza	1.25
21	Roger Clemens	1.25
22	Derek Jeter	3.00
23	Bernie Williams	.25
24	Scott Rolen	.65
25	J.D. Drew	.60
26	Mark McGwire	2.00
27	Fernando Tatis	.25
28	Tony Gwynn	1.00
29	Barry Bonds	3.00
30	Ken Griffey Jr.	1.50
31	Alex Rodriguez	2.00
32	Jose Canseco	.60
33	Juan Gonzalez	.40
34	Ruben Mateo	.25
35	Ivan Rodriguez	.65
36	Rusty Greer	.25

EO Portraits

		NM/M
Complete Set (20):		60.00
Common Player:		1.00
Inserted 1:73		
1-of-1 Numbered Parallels Exist		
1	Mo Vaughn	1.00
2	Chipper Jones	5.00
3	Greg Maddux	5.00
4	Cal Ripken Jr.	10.00
5	Nomar Garciaparra	5.00
6	Sammy Sosa	5.00
7	Frank Thomas	4.00
8	Manny Ramirez	4.00
9	Jeff Bagwell	4.00
10	Mike Piazza	5.50
11	Roger Clemens	5.50
12	Derek Jeter	10.00
13	Scott Rolen	3.00
14	Mark McGwire	8.00
15	Tony Gwynn	5.00
16	Barry Bonds	10.00
17	Ken Griffey Jr.	6.00
18	Alex Rodriguez	8.00
19	Jose Canseco	2.50
20	Juan Gonzalez	2.00

Hit Machine 3000

		NM/M
Complete Set (20):		24.00
Common Card:		1.50
1	The Hitting Machine	1.50
2	The Eyes Have It	1.50
3	The Art of Hitting	1.50
4	Solid as a Rock	1.50
5	Seeing Doubles	1.50
6	Pitcher's Worst Nightmare	1.50
7	Portrait of an All-Star	1.50
8	An American Hero	1.50
9	Fan Favorite	1.50
10	Mr. Batting Title	1.50
11	4-for-5!	1.50
12	Mission Accomplished	1.50
13	One Hit Away	1.50
14	A Tip of the Hat	1.50
15	It's a Base Hit!	1.50
16	2997th - Grand Slam!	1.50
17	2998th Hit	1.50
18	2999th Hit - 2-Run Double	1.50
19	3000th Hit!	1.50
20	3000 Hits, 8874 At-Bats, 18 Years	1.50

HR '99

		NM/M
Complete Set (20):		20.00
Common Player:		.25
Inserted 1:37		
1	Mo Vaughn	.25
2	Matt Williams	.25
3	Chipper Jones	2.00
4	Albert Belle	.25
5	Nomar Garciaparra	2.00
6	Sammy Sosa	2.00
7	Frank Thomas	1.25
8	Manny Ramirez	1.25
9	Jeff Bagwell	1.25
10	Raul Mondesi	.25
11	Vladimir Guerrero	1.25
12	Mike Piazza	2.25
13	Derek Jeter	4.00
14	Mark McGwire	3.00
15	Fernando Tatis	.25
16	Barry Bonds	4.00
17	Ken Griffey Jr.	2.50
18	Alex Rodriguez	3.00
19	Jose Canseco	.75
20	Juan Gonzalez	.65

5-Tool Talents

		NM/M
Complete Set (30):		40.00
Common Player:		.40
Inserted 4:37		
1	Randy Johnson	1.50
2	Greg Maddux	2.00
3	Pedro Martinez	1.50
4	Kevin Brown	.40
5	Roger Clemens	2.50
6	Carlos Lee	.40
7	Gabe Kapler	.40
8	Carlos Beltran	.75
9	J.D. Drew	.75
10	Ruben Mateo	.40
11	Chipper Jones	2.00
12	Sammy Sosa	2.00
13	Manny Ramirez	1.50

14	Vladimir Guerrero	1.50
15	Mark McGwire	4.00
16	Ken Griffey Jr.	3.00
17	Jose Canseco	.75
18	Nomar Garciaparra	2.00
19	Frank Thomas	1.50
20	Larry Walker	.40
21	Jeff Bagwell	1.50
22	Mike Piazza	2.50
23	Tony Gwynn	2.00
24	Juan Gonzalez	.75
25	Cal Ripken Jr.	5.00
26	Derek Jeter	5.00
27	Scott Rolen	1.25
28	Barry Bonds	5.00
29	Alex Rodriguez	4.00
30	Ivan Rodriguez	1.25

5-Tool Talents Tiered

		NM/M
TIER 1 (BLUE, 100 SETS)		
1	Randy Johnson	4.00
6	Carlos Lee	2.00
11	Chipper Jones	5.00
18	Nomar Garciaparra	5.00
21	Jeff Bagwell	4.00
28	Barry Bonds	7.50
TIER 2 (RED, 75 SETS)		
2	Greg Maddux	7.50
7	Gabe Kapler	2.00
13	Manny Ramirez	6.00
16	Ken Griffey Jr.	10.00
19	Frank Thomas	6.00
30	Ivan Rodriguez	5.00
TIER 3 (GREEN, 50 SETS)		
3	Pedro Martinez	12.50
8	Carlos Beltran	6.00
15	Mark McGwire	20.00
20	Larry Walker	2.00
25	Cal Ripken Jr.	30.00
26	Derek Jeter	30.00
TIER 4 (PURPLE, 25 SETS)		
4	Kevin Brown	7.50
9	J.D. Drew	15.00
12	Sammy Sosa	25.00
17	Jose Canseco	20.00
23	Tony Gwynn	25.00
29	Alex Rodriguez	35.00
TIER 5 (GOLD, 1 SET)		
5	Roger Clemens	
10	Ruben Mateo	
14	Vladimir Guerrero	
22	Mike Piazza	
24	Juan Gonzalez	
27	Scott Rolen	

1999 Pacific Paramount

		NM/M
Complete Set (250):		25.00
Common Player:		.10
Copper (1:1H):		2X
Red (1:1R):		2X
Gold (1:1R):		2X
Platinum Blue (1:73):		4X
Holographic Gold (199):		10X
Holographic Silver (99 Sets):		15X
Opening Day (74):		15X
Pack (6):		1.00
Wax Box (36):		25.00
1	Garret Anderson	.10
2	Gary DiSarcina	.10
3	Jim Edmonds	.10
4	Darin Erstad	.25
5	Chuck Finley	.10
6	Troy Glaus	.75
7	Troy Percival	.10
8	Tim Salmon	.10
9	Mo Vaughn	.10
10	Tony Batista	.10
11	Jay Bell	.10
12	Andy Benes	.10
13	Steve Finley	.10

14	Luis Gonzalez	.10
15	Randy Johnson	.75
16	Travis Lee	.10
17	Todd Stottlemyre	.10
18	Matt Williams	.10
19	David Dellucci	.10
20	Bret Boone	.10
21	Andres Galarraga	.10
22	Tom Glavine	.35
23	Andruw Jones	.75
24	Chipper Jones	1.50
25	Brian Jordan	.10
26	Ryan Klesko	.10
27	Javy Lopez	.10
28	Greg Maddux	1.50
29	John Smoltz	.10
30	Brady Anderson	.10
31	Albert Belle	.10
32	Will Clark	.10
33	Delino DeShields	.10
34	Charles Johnson	.10
35	Mike Mussina	.40
36	Cal Ripken Jr.	3.00
37	B.J. Surhoff	.10
38	Nomar Garciaparra	1.50
39	Reggie Jefferson	.10
40	Darren Lewis	.10
41	Pedro Martinez	.75
42	Troy O'Leary	.10
43	Jose Offerman	.10
44	Donnie Sadler	.10
45	John Valentin	.10
46	Rod Beck	.10
47	Gary Gaetti	.10
48	Mark Grace	.10
49	Lance Johnson	.10
50	Mickey Morandini	.10
51	Henry Rodriguez	.10
52	Sammy Sosa	1.50
53	Kerry Wood	.40
54	Mike Caruso	.10
55	Ray Durham	.10
56	Paul Konerko	.20
57	Jaime Navarro	.10
58	Greg Norton	.10
59	Magglio Ordonez	.30
60	Frank Thomas	.75
61	Aaron Boone	.10
62	Mike Cameron	.10
63	Barry Larkin	.10
64	Hal Morris	.10
65	Pokey Reese	.10
66	Brett Tomko	.10
67	Greg Vaughn	.10
68	Dmitri Young	.10
69	Roberto Alomar	.25
70	Sandy Alomar Jr.	.10
71	Bartolo Colon	.10
72	Travis Fryman	.10
73	David Justice	.10
74	Kenny Lofton	.10
75	Manny Ramirez	.75
76	Richie Sexson	.10
77	Jim Thome	.65
78	Omar Vizquel	.10
79	Dante Bichette	.10
80	Vinny Castilla	.10
81	Darryl Hamilton	.10
82	Todd Helton	.75
83	Darryl Kile	.10
84	Mike Lansing	.10
85	Neifi Perez	.10
86	Larry Walker	.10
87	Tony Clark	.10
88	Damion Easley	.10
89	Bob Higginson	.10
90	Brian Hunter	.10
91	Dean Palmer	.10
92	Justin Thompson	.10
93	Todd Dunwoody	.10
94	Cliff Floyd	.10
95	Alex Gonzalez	.10
96	Livan Hernandez	.10
97	Mark Kotsay	.10
98	Derek Lee	.60
99	Kevin Orie	.10
100	Moises Alou	.10
101	Jeff Bagwell	.75
102	Derek Bell	.10
103	Craig Biggio	.10
104	Ken Caminiti	.10
105	Ricky Gutierrez	.10
106	Richard Hidalgo	.10
107	Billy Wagner	.10
108	Jeff Conine	.10
109	Johnny Damon	.35
110	Carlos Febles	.10
111	Jeremy Giambi	.10
112	Jeff King	.10
113	Jeff Montgomery	.10
114	Joe Randa	.10
115	Kevin Brown	.10
116	Mark Grudzielanek	.10
117	Todd Hundley	.10

118	Eric Karros	.10
119	Raul Mondesi	.10
120	Chan Ho Park	.10
121	Gary Sheffield	.40
122	Devon White	.10
123	Eric Young	.10
124	Jeromy Burnitz	.10
125	Jeff Cirillo	.10
126	Marquis Grissom	.10
127	Geoff Jenkins	.10
128	Dave Nilsson	.10
129	Jose Valentin	.10
130	Fernando Vina	.10
131	Rick Aguilera	.10
132	Ron Coomer	.10
133	Marty Cordova	.10
134	Matt Lawton	.10
135	David Ortiz	.50
136	Brad Radke	.10
137	Terry Steinbach	.10
138	Javier Valentin	.10
139	Todd Walker	.10
140	Orlando Cabrera	.10
141	Brad Fullmer	.10
142	Vladimir Guerrero	.75
143	Wilton Guerrero	.10
144	Carl Pavano	.10
145	Ugueth Urbina	.10
146	Rondell White	.10
147	Chris Widger	.10
148	Edgardo Alfonzo	.10
149	Bobby Bonilla	.10
150	Rickey Henderson	.75
151	Brian McRae	.10
152	Hideo Nomo	.40
153	John Olerud	.10
154	Rey Ordonez	.10
155	Mike Piazza	1.75
156	Robin Ventura	.10
157	Masato Yoshii	.10
158	Roger Clemens	1.75
159	David Cone	.10
160	Orlando Hernandez	.10
161	Hideki Irabu	.10
162	Derek Jeter	3.00
163	Chuck Knoblauch	.10
164	Tino Martinez	.10
165	Paul O'Neill	.10
166	Darryl Strawberry	.10
167	Bernie Williams	.10
168	Eric Chavez	.20
169	Ryan Christenson	.10
170	Jason Giambi	.50
171	Ben Grieve	.10
172	Tony Phillips	.10
173	Tim Raines	.10
174	Scott Spiezio	.10
175	Miguel Tejada	.20
176	Bobby Abreu	.20
177	Rico Brogna	.10
178	Ron Gant	.10
179	Doug Glanville	.10
180	Desi Relaford	.10
181	Scott Rolen	.65
182	Curt Schilling	.35
183	Brant Brown	.10
184	Brian Giles	.10
185	Jose Guillen	.10
186	Jason Kendall	.10
187	Al Martin	.10
188	Ed Sprague	.10
189	Kevin Young	.10
190	Eric Davis	.10
191	J.D. Drew	.40
192	Ray Lankford	.10
193	Eli Marrero	.10
194	Mark McGwire	2.50
195	Edgar Renteria	.10
196	Fernando Tatis	.10
197	Andy Ashby	.10
198	Tony Gwynn	1.50
199	Carlos Hernandez	.10
200	Trevor Hoffman	.10
201	Wally Joyner	.10
202	Jim Leyritz	.10
203	Ruben Rivera	.10
204	Matt Clement	.10
205	Quilvio Veras	.10
206	Rich Aurilia	.10
207	Marvin Benard	.10
208	Barry Bonds	3.00
209	Ellis Burks	.10
210	Jeff Kent	.10
211	Bill Mueller	.10
212	Robb Nen	.10
213	J.T. Snow	.10
214	Jay Buhner	.10
215	Jeff Fassero	.10
216	Ken Griffey Jr.	2.00
217	Carlos Guillen	.10
218	Butch Huskey	.10
219	Edgar Martinez	.10
220	Alex Rodriguez	2.50
221	David Segui	.10

222	Dan Wilson	.10
223	Rolando Arrojo	.10
224	Wade Boggs	1.50
225	Jose Canseco	.50
226	Roberto Hernandez	.10
227	Dave Martinez	.10
228	Quinton McCracken	.10
229	Fred McGriff	.10
230	Kevin Stocker	.10
231	Randy Winn	.10
232	Royce Clayton	.10
233	Juan Gonzalez	.40
234	Tom Goodwin	.10
235	Rusty Greer	.10
236	Rick Helling	.10
237	Rafael Palmeiro	.65
238	Ivan Rodriguez	.65
239	Aaron Sele	.10
240	John Wetteland	.10
241	Todd Zeile	.10
242	Jose Cruz Jr.	.10
243	Carlos Delgado	.50
244	Tony Fernandez	.10
245	Cecil Fielder	.10
246	Alex Gonzalez	.10
247	Shawn Green	.35
248	Roy Halladay	.10
249	Shannon Stewart	.10
250	David Wells	.10

Cooperstown Bound

		NM/M
Complete Set (10):		35.00
Common Player:		3.00
Inserted 1:361		
1	Greg Maddux	4.00
2	Cal Ripken Jr.	10.00
3	Nomar Garciaparra	4.00
4	Sammy Sosa	4.00
5	Frank Thomas	3.00
6	Mike Piazza	5.00
7	Mark McGwire	10.00
8	Tony Gwynn	4.00
9	Ken Griffey Jr.	6.00
10	Alex Rodriguez	8.00

Fielder's Choice

		NM/M
Complete Set (20):		60.00
Common Player:		2.50
Inserted 1:73		
1	Chipper Jones	5.00
2	Greg Maddux	5.00
3	Cal Ripken Jr.	10.00
4	Nomar Garciaparra	5.00
5	Sammy Sosa	5.00
6	Kerry Wood	3.00
7	Frank Thomas	4.00
8	Manny Ramirez	4.00
9	Todd Helton	4.00
10	Jeff Bagwell	4.00
11	Mike Piazza	5.50
12	Derek Jeter	10.00
13	Bernie Williams	2.50
14	J.D. Drew	3.00
15	Mark McGwire	7.50
16	Tony Gwynn	5.00
17	Ken Griffey Jr.	6.00
18	Alex Rodriguez	7.50
19	Juan Gonzalez	2.50
20	Ivan Rodriguez	3.50

Personal Bests

		NM/M
Complete Set (36):		45.00
Common Player:		.50
Inserted 1:37		
1	Darin Erstad	.65
2	Mo Vaughn	.50
3	Travis Lee	.50
4	Chipper Jones	3.00
5	Greg Maddux	3.00
6	Albert Belle	.50
7	Cal Ripken Jr.	6.00
8	Nomar Garciaparra	3.00
9	Sammy Sosa	3.00
10	Kerry Wood	1.00
11	Frank Thomas	2.00
12	Greg Vaughn	.50
13	Manny Ramirez	2.00
14	Todd Helton	2.00
15	Larry Walker	.50
16	Jeff Bagwell	2.00
17	Craig Biggio	.50
18	Raul Mondesi	.50
19	Vladimir Guerrero	2.00
20	Hideo Nomo	1.00
21	Mike Piazza	3.50
22	Roger Clemens	3.50
23	Derek Jeter	6.00
24	Bernie Williams	.50
25	Eric Chavez	.75
26	Ben Grieve	.50
27	Scott Rolen	1.50
28	J.D. Drew	1.25
29	Mark McGwire	4.50
30	Tony Gwynn	3.00
31	Barry Bonds	6.00
32	Ken Griffey Jr.	4.00
33	Alex Rodriguez	4.50
34	Jose Canseco	1.25
35	Juan Gonzalez	1.00
36	Ivan Rodriguez	1.50

Team Checklists

		NM/M
Complete Set (30):		40.00
Common Player:		.50
Inserted 2:37		
1	Mo Vaughn	.50
2	Travis Lee	.50
3	Chipper Jones	3.00
4	Cal Ripken Jr.	6.00
5	Nomar Garciaparra	3.00
6	Sammy Sosa	3.00
7	Frank Thomas	2.50
8	Greg Vaughn	.50
9	Manny Ramirez	2.50
10	Larry Walker	.50
11	Damion Easley	.50
12	Mark Kotsay	.50
13	Jeff Bagwell	2.50

14	Jeremy Giambi	.50
15	Raul Mondesi	.50
16	Marquis Grissom	.50
17	Brad Radke	.50
18	Vladimir Guerrero	2.50
19	Mike Piazza	3.50
20	Roger Clemens	3.50
21	Ben Grieve	.50
22	Scott Rolen	2.00
23	Brian Giles	.50
24	Mark McGwire	5.00
25	Tony Gwynn	3.00
26	Barry Bonds	6.00
27	Ken Griffey Jr.	4.00
28	Jose Canseco	1.25
29	Juan Gonzalez	1.25
30	Jose Cruz Jr.	.50

1999 Pacific Prism

		NM/M
Complete Set (150):		50.00
Common Player:		.15
Red (2:25R):		3X
HoloGold (480 Sets):		3X
HoloPurple (320):		4X
HoloMirror (160):		8X
HoloBlue (80):		15X
Retail Pack (3):		1.00
Hobby Pack (5):		1.50
1	Garret Anderson	.15
2	Jim Edmonds	.15
3	Darin Erstad	.30
4	Chuck Finley	.15
5	Tim Salmon	.15
6	Jay Bell	.15
7	David Dellucci	.15
8	Travis Lee	.15
9	Matt Williams	.15
10	Andres Galarraga	.15
11	Tom Glavine	.40
12	Andruw Jones	1.50
13	Chipper Jones	2.00
14	Ryan Klesko	.15
15	Javy Lopez	.15
16	Greg Maddux	2.00
17	Roberto Alomar	.50
18	Ryan Minor	.15
19	Mike Mussina	.40
20	Rafael Palmeiro	1.25
21	Cal Ripken Jr.	4.00
22	Nomar Garciaparra	2.00
23	Pedro Martinez	1.50
24	John Valentin	.15
25	Mo Vaughn	.15
26	Tim Wakefield	.15
27	Rod Beck	.15
28	Mark Grace	.15
29	Lance Johnson	.15
30	Sammy Sosa	2.00
31	Kerry Wood	.50
32	Albert Belle	.15
33	Mike Caruso	.15
34	Magglio Ordonez	.30
35	Frank Thomas	1.50
36	Robin Ventura	.15
37	Aaron Boone	.15
38	Barry Larkin	.15
39	Reggie Sanders	.15
40	Brett Tomko	.15
41	Sandy Alomar Jr.	.15
42	Bartolo Colon	.15
43	David Justice	.15
44	Kenny Lofton	.15
45	Manny Ramirez	1.50
46	Richie Sexson	.15
47	Jim Thome	1.00
48	Omar Vizquel	.15
49	Dante Bichette	.15
50	Vinny Castilla	.15
51	Edgard Clemente RC	.15
52	Todd Helton	1.50
53	Quinton McCracken	.15

54	Larry Walker	.15
55	Tony Clark	.15
56	Damion Easley	.15
57	Luis Gonzalez	.15
58	Bob Higginson	.15
59	Brian Hunter	.15
60	Cliff Floyd	.15
61	Alex Gonzalez	.15
62	Livan Hernandez	.15
63	Derrek Lee	.65
64	Edgar Renteria	.15
65	Moises Alou	.15
66	Jeff Bagwell	1.50
67	Derek Bell	.15
68	Craig Biggio	.15
69	Randy Johnson	1.50
70	Johnny Damon	.35
71	Jeff King	.15
72	Hal Morris	.15
73	Dean Palmer	.15
74	Eric Karros	.15
75	Raul Mondesi	.15
76	Chan Ho Park	.15
77	Gary Sheffield	.50
78	Jeromy Burnitz	.15
79	Jeff Cirillo	.15
80	Marquis Grissom	.15
81	Jose Valentin	.15
82	Fernando Vina	.15
83	Paul Molitor	1.50
84	Otis Nixon	.15
85	David Ortiz	.65
86	Todd Walker	.15
87	Vladimir Guerrero	1.50
88	Carl Pavano	.15
89	Fernando Seguignol	.15
90	Ugueth Urbina	.15
91	Carlos Baerga	.15
92	Bobby Bonilla	.15
93	Hideo Nomo	.75
94	John Olerud	.15
95	Rey Ordonez	.15
96	Mike Piazza	2.25
97	David Cone	.15
98	Orlando Hernandez	.15
99	Hideki Irabu	.15
100	Derek Jeter	4.00
101	Tino Martinez	.15
102	Bernie Williams	.15
103	Eric Chavez	.25
104	Jason Giambi	1.00
105	Ben Grieve	.15
106	Rickey Henderson	1.50
107	Bob Abreu	.25
108	Doug Glanville	.15
109	Scott Rolen	1.00
110	Curt Schilling	.40
111	Emil Brown	.15
112	Jose Guillen	.15
113	Jason Kendall	.15
114	Al Martin	.15
115	Aramis Ramirez	.15
116	Kevin Young	.15
117	J.D. Drew	.75
118	Ron Gant	.15
119	Brian Jordan	.15
120	Eli Marrero	.15
121	Mark McGwire	3.00
122	Kevin Brown	.15
123	Tony Gwynn	2.00
124	Trevor Hoffman	.15
125	Wally Joyner	.15
126	Greg Vaughn	.15
127	Barry Bonds	4.00
128	Ellis Burks	.15
129	Jeff Kent	.15
130	Robb Nen	.15
131	J.T. Snow	.15
132	Jay Buhner	.15
133	Ken Griffey Jr.	2.50
134	Edgar Martinez	.15
135	Alex Rodriguez	3.00
136	David Segui	.15
137	Rolando Arrojo	.15
138	Wade Boggs	2.00
139	Aaron Ledesma	.15
140	Fred McGriff	.15
141	Will Clark	.15
142	Juan Gonzalez	.75
143	Rusty Greer	.15
144	Ivan Rodriguez	1.25
145	Aaron Sele	.15
146	Jose Canseco	.40
147	Roger Clemens	2.25
148	Jose Cruz Jr.	.15
149	Carlos Delgado	.50
150	Alex Gonzalez	.15

Ahead of the Game

		NM/M
Complete Set (20):		40.00
Common Player:		1.00
Inserted 1:49		
1	Darin Erstad	1.25

2	Travis Lee	1.00
3	Chipper Jones	3.00
4	Cal Ripken Jr.	6.00
5	Nomar Garciaparra	3.00
6	Sammy Sosa	3.00
7	Kerry Wood	1.25
8	Frank Thomas	2.00
9	Manny Ramirez	2.00
10	Todd Helton	2.00
11	Jeff Bagwell	2.00
12	Mike Piazza	3.50
13	Derek Jeter	6.00
14	Bernie Williams	1.00
15	J.D. Drew	1.25
16	Mark McGwire	5.00
17	Tony Gwynn	3.00
18	Ken Griffey Jr.	4.00
19	Alex Rodriguez	5.00
20	Ivan Rodriguez	1.50

Ballpark Legends

		NM/M
Complete Set (10):		40.00
Common Player:		2.50
Inserted 1:193		
1	Cal Ripken Jr.	10.00
2	Nomar Garciaparra	5.00
3	Frank Thomas	4.00
4	Ken Griffey Jr.	6.00
5	Alex Rodriguez	7.50
6	Greg Maddux	5.00
7	Sammy Sosa	5.00
8	Kerry Wood	2.50
9	Mark McGwire	7.50
10	Tony Gwynn	5.00

Diamond Glory

		NM/M
Complete Set (20):		25.00
Common Player:		.60
Inserted 2:25		
1	Darin Erstad	.60
2	Travis Lee	.60
3	Chipper Jones	2.00
4	Greg Maddux	2.00
5	Cal Ripken Jr.	3.50
6	Nomar Garciaparra	2.00
7	Sammy Sosa	2.00
8	Kerry Wood	.75
9	Frank Thomas	1.50

10	Todd Helton	1.50
11	Jeff Bagwell	1.50
12	Mike Piazza	2.25
13	Derek Jeter	3.50
14	Bernie Williams	.60
15	J.D. Drew	.75
16	Mark McGwire	3.00
17	Tony Gwynn	2.00
18	Ken Griffey Jr.	2.50
19	Alex Rodriguez	3.00
20	Juan Gonzalez	.75

Epic Performers

		NM/M
Complete Set (10):		60.00
Common Player:		4.00
Inserted 1:97 H		
1	Cal Ripken Jr.	15.00
2	Nomar Garciaparra	7.50
3	Frank Thomas	6.00
4	Ken Griffey Jr.	10.00
5	Alex Rodriguez	12.50
6	Greg Maddux	7.50
7	Sammy Sosa	7.50
8	Kerry Wood	4.00
9	Mark McGwire	12.50
10	Tony Gwynn	7.50

1999 Pacific Private Stock

		NM/M
Complete Set (150):		25.00
Common Player:		.10
Pack (6):		1.50
Wax Box (24):		20.00
Wax Box (36):		25.00
1	Jeff Bagwell	1.00
2	Roger Clemens	1.75
3	J.D. Drew	.60
4	Nomar Garciaparra	1.50
5	Juan Gonzalez	.50
6	Ken Griffey Jr.	2.00
7	Tony Gwynn	1.50
8	Derek Jeter	3.00
9	Chipper Jones	1.50
10	Travis Lee	.10
11	Greg Maddux	1.50
12	Mark McGwire	2.50
13	Mike Piazza	1.75
14	Manny Ramirez	1.00
15	Cal Ripken Jr.	3.00
16	Alex Rodriguez	2.50
17	Ivan Rodriguez	.75
18	Sammy Sosa	1.50
19	Frank Thomas	1.00
20	Kerry Wood	.40
21	Roberto Alomar	.25
22	Moises Alou	.10
23	Albert Belle	.10
24	Craig Biggio	.10
25	Wade Boggs	1.50
26	Barry Bonds	3.00
27	Jose Canseco	.50
28	Jim Edmonds	.10
29	Darin Erstad	.25
30	Andres Galarraga	.10
31	Tom Glavine	.35
32	Ben Grieve	.10
33	Vladimir Guerrero	1.00
34	Wilton Guerrero	.10
35	Todd Helton	1.00
36	Andruw Jones	1.00
37	Ryan Klesko	.10
38	Kenny Lofton	.10
39	Javy Lopez	.10
40	Pedro Martinez	1.00
41	Paul Molitor	1.00
42	Raul Mondesi	.10
43	Rafael Palmeiro	.75
44	Tim Salmon	.10
45	Jim Thome	.75
46	Mo Vaughn	.10
47	Larry Walker	.10
48	David Wells	.10
49	Bernie Williams	.10
50	Jaret Wright	.10
51	Bobby Abreu	.15
52	Garret Anderson	.10
53	Rolando Arrojo	.10
54	Tony Batista	.10
55	Rod Beck	.10
56	Derek Bell	.10
57	Marvin Benard	.10
58	Dave Berg	.10
59	Dante Bichette	.10
60	Aaron Boone	.10
61	Bret Boone	.10
62	Scott Brosius	.10
63	Brant Brown	.10
64	Kevin Brown	.10
65	Jeromy Burnitz	.10
66	Ken Caminiti	.10
67	Mike Caruso	.10
68	Sean Casey	.20
69	Vinny Castilla	.20
70	Eric Chavez	.20
71	Ryan Christenson	.10
72	Jeff Cirillo	.10
73	Tony Clark	.10
74	Will Clark	.10
75	Edgard Clemente RC	.10
76	David Cone	.10
77	Marty Cordova	.10
78	Jose Cruz Jr.	.10
79	Eric Davis	.10
80	Carlos Delgado	.50
81	David Dellucci	.10
82	Delino DeShields	.10
83	Gary DiSarcina	.10
84	Damion Easley	.10
85	Dennis Eckersley	.65
86	Cliff Floyd	.10
87	Jason Giambi	.65
88	Doug Glanville	.10
89	Alex Gonzalez	.10
90	Mark Grace	.10
91	Rusty Greer	.10
92	Jose Guillen	.10
93	Carlos Guillen	.10
94	Jeffrey Hammonds	.10
95	Rick Helling	.10
96	Bob Henley	.10
97	Livan Hernandez	.10
98	Orlando Hernandez	.10
99	Bob Higginson	.10
100	Trevor Hoffman	.10
101	Randy Johnson	1.00
102	Brian Jordan	.10
103	Wally Joyner	.10
104	Eric Karros	.10
105	Jason Kendall	.10
106	Jeff Kent	.10
107	Jeff King	.10
108	Mark Kotsay	.10
109	Ray Lankford	.10
110	Barry Larkin	.10
111	Mark Loretta	.10
112	Edgar Martinez	.10
113	Tino Martinez	.10
114	Quinton McCracken	.10
115	Fred McGriff	.10
116	Ryan Minor	.10
117	Hal Morris	.10
118	Bill Mueller	.10
119	Mike Mussina	.40
120	Dave Nilsson	.10
121	Otis Nixon	.10
122	Hideo Nomo	.50
123	Paul O'Neill	.10
124	Jose Offerman	.10
125	John Olerud	.10
126	Rey Ordonez	.10
127	David Ortiz	.50
128	Dean Palmer	.10
129	Chan Ho Park	.10
130	Aramis Rios	.10
131	Edgar Renteria	.10
132	Armando Rios	.10
133	Henry Rodriguez	.10
134	Scott Rolen	.75
135	Curt Schilling	.35
136	David Segui	.10
137	Richie Sexson	.10
138	Gary Sheffield	.45
139	John Smoltz	.10
140	Matt Stairs	.10
141	Justin Thompson	.10
142	Greg Vaughn	.10
143	Omar Vizquel	.10
144	Tim Wakefield	.10
145	Todd Walker	.10
146	Devon White	.10
147	Rondell White	.10
148	Matt Williams	.10
149	Enrique Wilson RC	.25
150	Kevin Young	.10

Exclusive Series

		NM/M
Complete Set (20):		50.00
Common Player:		1.00
Production:		299 Sets H
1	Jeff Bagwell	2.00
2	Roger Clemens	3.50
3	J.D. Drew	1.25
4	Nomar Garciaparra	3.00
5	Juan Gonzalez	1.25
6	Ken Griffey Jr.	4.00
7	Tony Gwynn	3.00
8	Derek Jeter	6.00
9	Chipper Jones	3.00
10	Travis Lee	1.00
11	Greg Maddux	3.00
12	Mark McGwire	5.00
13	Mike Piazza	3.50
14	Manny Ramirez	2.00
15	Cal Ripken Jr.	6.00
16	Alex Rodriguez	5.00
17	Ivan Rodriguez	1.50
18	Sammy Sosa	3.00
19	Frank Thomas	2.00
20	Kerry Wood	1.25

Platinum Series

		NM/M
Complete Set (50):		160.00
Common Player:		.75
Production 199 Sets		
1	Jeff Bagwell	5.00
2	Roger Clemens	6.50
3	J.D. Drew	3.00
4	Nomar Garciaparra	6.00
5	Juan Gonzalez	2.50
6	Ken Griffey Jr.	8.00
7	Tony Gwynn	6.00
8	Derek Jeter	12.00
9	Chipper Jones	6.00
10	Travis Lee	.75
11	Greg Maddux	6.00
12	Mark McGwire	10.00
13	Mike Piazza	6.50
14	Manny Ramirez	5.00
15	Cal Ripken Jr.	12.00
16	Alex Rodriguez	10.00
17	Ivan Rodriguez	4.00
18	Sammy Sosa	6.00
19	Frank Thomas	5.00
20	Kerry Wood	2.00
21	Roberto Alomar	1.50
22	Moises Alou	.75
23	Albert Belle	.75
24	Craig Biggio	.75
25	Wade Boggs	6.00
26	Barry Bonds	12.00
27	Jose Canseco	3.00
28	Jim Edmonds	.75
29	Darin Erstad	1.50
30	Andres Galarraga	.75
31	Tom Glavine	2.00
32	Ben Grieve	.75
33	Vladimir Guerrero	5.00
34	Wilton Guerrero	.75
35	Todd Helton	5.00
36	Andruw Jones	5.00
37	Ryan Klesko	.75
38	Kenny Lofton	.75
39	Javy Lopez	.75
40	Pedro Martinez	5.00
41	Paul Molitor	5.00
42	Raul Mondesi	.75
43	Rafael Palmeiro	4.00
44	Tim Salmon	.75
45	Jim Thome	3.50
46	Mo Vaughn	.75
47	Larry Walker	.75
48	David Wells	.75
49	Bernie Williams	.75
50	Jaret Wright	.75

Preferred Series

		NM/M
Complete Set (20):		37.50
Common Player:		.60
Production:		399 Sets
1	Jeff Bagwell	1.50
2	Roger Clemens	2.25
3	J.D. Drew	.75
4	Nomar Garciaparra	2.00
5	Juan Gonzalez	.75
6	Ken Griffey Jr.	2.50
7	Tony Gwynn	2.00
8	Derek Jeter	5.00
9	Chipper Jones	2.00
10	Travis Lee	.60
11	Greg Maddux	2.00
12	Mark McGwire	3.50
13	Mike Piazza	2.25
14	Manny Ramirez	1.50
15	Cal Ripken Jr.	5.00
16	Alex Rodriguez	3.50
17	Ivan Rodriguez	1.25
18	Sammy Sosa	2.00
19	Frank Thomas	1.50
20	Kerry Wood	.75

PS-206

		NM/M
Complete Set (150):		20.00
Common Player:		.15
Inserted 1:1		
Red Parallels:		4X
Inserted 1:25		
1	Jeff Bagwell	.75
2	Roger Clemens	1.25
3	J.D. Drew	.50
4	Nomar Garciaparra	1.00
5	Juan Gonzalez	.40

6	Ken Griffey Jr.	1.50
7	Tony Gwynn	1.00
8	Derek Jeter	3.00
9	Chipper Jones	1.00
10	Travis Lee	.15
11	Greg Maddux	1.00
12	Mark McGwire	2.00
13	Mike Piazza	1.25
14	Manny Ramirez	.75
15	Cal Ripken Jr.	3.00
16	Alex Rodriguez	2.00
17	Ivan Rodriguez	.65
18	Sammy Sosa	1.00
19	Frank Thomas	.75
20	Kerry Wood	.40
21	Roberto Alomar	.30
22	Moises Alou	.15
23	Albert Belle	.15
24	Craig Biggio	.15
25	Wade Boggs	1.00
26	Barry Bonds	3.00
27	Jose Canseco	.50
28	Jim Edmonds	.15
29	Darin Erstad	.30
30	Andres Galarraga	.15
31	Tom Glavine	.35
32	Ben Grieve	.15
33	Vladimir Guerrero	.75
34	Wilton Guerrero	.75
35	Todd Helton	.75
36	Andruw Jones	.75
37	Ryan Klesko	.15
38	Kenny Lofton	.15
39	Javy Lopez	.15
40	Pedro Martinez	.75
41	Paul Molitor	.75
42	Raul Mondesi	.15
43	Rafael Palmeiro	.65
44	Tim Salmon	.15
45	Jim Thome	.65
46	Mo Vaughn	.15
47	Larry Walker	.15
48	David Wells	.15
49	Bernie Williams	.15
50	Jaret Wright	.15
51	Bobby Abreu	.15
52	Garret Anderson	.15
53	Rolando Arrojo	.15
54	Tony Batista	.15
55	Rod Beck	.15
56	Derek Bell	.15
57	Marvin Benard	.15
58	Dave Berg	.15
59	Dante Bichette	.15
60	Aaron Boone	.15
61	Bret Boone	.15
62	Scott Brosius	.15
63	Brant Brown	.15
64	Kevin Brown	.15
65	Jeromy Burnitz	.15
66	Ken Caminiti	.15
67	Mike Caruso	.15
68	Sean Casey	.25
69	Vinny Castilla	.15
70	Eric Chavez	.25
71	Ryan Christenson	.15
72	Jeff Cirillo	.15
73	Tony Clark	.15
74	Will Clark	.15
75	Edgard Clemente	.15
76	David Cone	.15
77	Marty Cordova	.15
78	Jose Cruz Jr.	.15
79	Eric Davis	.15
80	Carlos Delgado	.60
81	David Dellucci	.15
82	Delino DeShields	.15
83	Gary DiSarcina	.15

84	Damion Easley	.15
85	Dennis Eckersley	.65
86	Cliff Floyd	.15
87	Jason Giambi	.60
88	Doug Glanville	.15
89	Alex Gonzalez	.15
90	Mark Grace	.15
91	Rusty Greer	.15
92	Jose Guillen	.15
93	Carlos Guillen	.15
94	Jeffrey Hammonds	.15
95	Rick Helling	.15
96	Bob Henley	.15
97	Livan Hernandez	.15
98	Orlando Hernandez	.15
99	Bob Higginson	.15
100	Trevor Hoffman	.15
101	Randy Johnson	.75
102	Brian Jordan	.15
103	Wally Joyner	.15
104	Eric Karros	.15
105	Jason Kendall	.15
106	Jeff Kent	.15
107	Jeff King	.15
108	Mark Kotsay	.15
109	Ray Lankford	.15
110	Barry Larkin	.15
111	Mark Loretta	.15
112	Edgar Martinez	.15
113	Tino Martinez	.15
114	Quinton McCracken	.15
115	Fred McGriff	.15
116	Ryan Minor	.15
117	Hal Morris	.15
118	Bill Mueller	.15
119	Mike Mussina	.40
120	Dave Nilsson	.15
121	Otis Nixon	.15
122	Hideo Nomo	.40
123	Paul O'Neill	.15
124	Jose Offerman	.15
125	John Olerud	.15
126	Rey Ordonez	.15
127	David Ortiz	.50
128	Dean Palmer	.15
129	Chan Ho Park	.15
130	Aramis Ramirez	.15
131	Edgar Renteria	.15
132	Armando Rios	.15
133	Henry Rodriguez	.15
134	Scott Rolen	.60
135	Curt Schilling	.35
136	David Segui	.15
137	Richie Sexson	.15
138	Gary Sheffield	.50
139	John Smoltz	.15
140	Matt Stairs	.15
141	Justin Thompson	.15
142	Greg Vaughn	.15
143	Omar Vizquel	.15
144	Tim Wakefield	.15
145	Todd Walker	.15
146	Devon White	.15
147	Rondell White	.15
148	Matt Williams	.15
149	Enrique Wilson	.15
150	Kevin Young	.15

Vintage Series

		NM/M
Complete Set (50):		375.00
Common Player:		2.50
Production:		99 Sets
1	Jeff Bagwell	12.50
2	Roger Clemens	17.50
3	J.D. Drew	7.50
4	Nomar Garciaparra	15.00
5	Juan Gonzalez	6.00
6	Ken Griffey Jr.	20.00
7	Tony Gwynn	15.00
8	Derek Jeter	30.00
9	Chipper Jones	15.00
10	Travis Lee	2.50
11	Greg Maddux	15.00
12	Mark McGwire	25.00
13	Mike Piazza	17.50
14	Manny Ramirez	12.50
15	Cal Ripken Jr.	30.00
16	Alex Rodriguez	25.00
17	Ivan Rodriguez	10.00
18	Sammy Sosa	15.00
19	Frank Thomas	12.50
20	Kerry Wood	6.00
21	Roberto Alomar	3.50
22	Moises Alou	2.50
23	Albert Belle	2.50
24	Craig Biggio	2.50
25	Wade Boggs	15.00
26	Barry Bonds	30.00
27	Jose Canseco	5.00
28	Jim Edmonds	2.50
29	Darin Erstad	3.50
30	Andres Galarraga	2.50
31	Tom Glavine	5.00

32	Ben Grieve	2.50
33	Vladimir Guerrero	12.50
34	Wilton Guerrero	2.50
35	Todd Helton	12.50
36	Andruw Jones	12.50
37	Ryan Klesko	2.50
38	Kenny Lofton	2.50
39	Javy Lopez	2.50
40	Pedro Martinez	12.50
41	Paul Molitor	12.50
42	Raul Mondesi	2.50
43	Rafael Palmeiro	10.00
44	Tim Salmon	2.50
45	Jim Thome	10.00
46	Mo Vaughn	2.50
47	Larry Walker	2.50
48	David Wells	2.50
49	Bernie Williams	2.50
50	Jaret Wright	2.50

1999 Pacific Revolution

		NM/M
Complete Set (150):		60.00
Common Player:		.15
Shadow (99 Sets H):		6X
SP:		3X
Red (299 R):		2X
SP:		1.5X
Premiere Date (49 H):		12X
SP:		6X
Wax Pack (3):		2.00
Wax Box (24):		35.00
1	Jim Edmonds	.15
2	Darin Erstad	.30
3	Troy Glaus	1.00
4	Tim Salmon	.15
5	Mo Vaughn	.15
6	Steve Finley	.15
7	Luis Gonzalez	.15
8	Randy Johnson	1.00
9	Travis Lee	.15
10	Matt Williams	.15
11	Andruw Jones	1.00
12	Chipper Jones	1.50
13	Brian Jordan	.15
14	Javy Lopez	.15
15	Greg Maddux	1.50
16	Kevin McGlinchy/ SP RC	1.00
17	John Smoltz	.15
18	Brady Anderson	.15
19	Albert Belle	.15
20	Will Clark	.15
21	Willis Otanez/SP RC	.25
22	Calvin Pickering/SP RC	.25
23	Cal Ripken Jr.	4.00
24	Nomar Garciaparra	1.50
25	Pedro Martinez	1.00
26	Troy O'Leary	.15
27	Jose Offerman	.15
28	Mark Grace	.15
29	Mickey Morandini	.15
30	Henry Rodriguez	.15
31	Sammy Sosa	1.50
32	Ray Durham	.15
33	Carlos Lee/SP	.50
34	Jeff Liefer/SP RC	.35
35	Magglio Ordonez	.30
36	Frank Thomas	1.00
37	Mike Cameron	.15
38	Sean Casey	.35
39	Barry Larkin	.15
40	Greg Vaughn	.15
41	Roberto Alomar	.35
42	Sandy Alomar Jr.	.15
43	David Justice	.15
44	Kenny Lofton	.15
45	Manny Ramirez	1.00
46	Richie Sexson	.15
47	Jim Thome	.65
48	Dante Bichette	.15

49	Vinny Castilla	.15
50	Darryl Hamilton	.15
51	Todd Helton	1.00
52	Larry Walker	.15
53	Tony Clark	.15
54	Damion Easley	.15
55	Bob Higginson	.15
56	Gabe Kapler/SP	.25
57	Alex Gonzalez/SP RC	.35
58	Mark Kotsay	.15
59	Kevin Orie	.15
60	Preston Wilson/SP	1.00
61	Jeff Bagwell	1.00
62	Derek Bell	.15
63	Craig Biggio	.15
64	Ken Caminiti	.15
65	Carlos Beltran/SP	.65
66	Johnny Damon	.35
67	Jermaine Dye	.15
68	Carlos Febles/SP	.35
69	Kevin Brown	.15
70	Todd Hundley	.15
71	Eric Karros	.15
72	Raul Mondesi	.15
73	Gary Sheffield	.45
74	Jeromy Burnitz	.15
75	Jeff Cirillo	.15
76	Marquis Grissom	.15
77	Fernando Vina	.15
78	Chad Allen/SP RC	.25
79	Corey Koskie/SP RC	1.50
80	Doug Mientkiewicz/ SP RC	1.00
81	Brad Radke	.15
82	Todd Walker	.15
83	Michael Barrett/SP RC	.35
84	Vladimir Guerrero	1.00
85	Wilton Guerrero	.15
86	Guillermo Mota/SP RC	.35
87	Rondell White	.15
88	Edgardo Alfonzo	.15
89	Rickey Henderson	1.00
90	John Olerud	.15
91	Mike Piazza	2.00
92	Robin Ventura	.15
93	Roger Clemens	2.00
94	Chili Davis	.15
95	Derek Jeter	4.00
96	Chuck Knoblauch	.15
97	Tino Martinez	.15
98	Paul O'Neill	.15
99	Bernie Williams	.15
100	Eric Chavez/SP	.35
101	Jason Giambi	.65
102	Ben Grieve	.15
103	John Jaha	.15
104	Olmedo Saenz/SP RC	.25
105	Bobby Abreu	.25
106	Doug Glanville	.15
107	Desi Relaford	.15
108	Scott Rolen	.75
109	Curt Schilling	.35
110	Brian Giles	.15
111	Jason Kendall	.15
112	Pat Meares	.15
113	Kevin Young	.15
114	J.D. Drew/SP	1.00
115	Ray Lankford	.15
116	Eli Marrero	.15
117	Joe McEwing/SP RC	.35
118	Mark McGwire	3.00
119	Fernando Tatis	.15
120	Tony Gwynn	1.50
121	Trevor Hoffman	.15
122	Wally Joyner	.15
123	Reggie Sanders	.15
124	Barry Bonds	4.00
125	Ellis Burks	.15
126	Jeff Kent	.15
127	Ramon Martinez/SP RC	.25
128	Joe Nathan/SP RC	.25
129	Freddy Garcia/SP RC	1.00
130	Ken Griffey Jr.	2.50
131	Brian Hunter	.15
132	Edgar Martinez	.15
133	Alex Rodriguez	3.00
134	David Segui	.15
135	Wade Boggs	1.50
136	Jose Canseco	.45
137	Quinton McCracken	.15
138	Fred McGriff	.15
139	Kelly Dransfeldt/SP RC	.25
140	Juan Gonzalez	.50
141	Rusty Greer	.15
142	Rafael Palmeiro	.75
143	Ivan Rodriguez	.75
144	Lee Stevens	.15
145	Jose Cruz Jr.	.15
146	Carlos Delgado	.60
147	Shawn Green	.50
148	Roy Halladay/SP RC	1.50
149	Shannon Stewart	.15
150	Kevin Witt/SP RC	.35

Shadow

		NM/M
Common Player:		4.00
Stars:		6X
SP's:		3X

(See 1999 Pacific Revolution for checklist and base card values.)

Diamond Legacy

		NM/M
Complete Set (36):		60.00
Common Player:		.50
Inserted 2:25		
1	Troy Glaus	2.00
2	Mo Vaughn	.50
3	Matt Williams	.50
4	Chipper Jones	3.00
5	Andruw Jones	2.00
6	Greg Maddux	3.00
7	Albert Belle	.50
8	Cal Ripken Jr.	6.00
9	Nomar Garciaparra	3.00
10	Sammy Sosa	3.00
11	Frank Thomas	2.00
12	Manny Ramirez	2.00
13	Todd Helton	2.00
14	Larry Walker	.50
15	Gabe Kapler	.50
16	Jeff Bagwell	2.00
17	Craig Biggio	.50
18	Raul Mondesi	.50
19	Vladimir Guerrero	2.00
20	Mike Piazza	3.50
21	Roger Clemens	3.50
22	Derek Jeter	6.00
23	Bernie Williams	.50
24	Ben Grieve	.50
25	Scott Rolen	1.75
26	J.D. Drew	1.50
27	Mark McGwire	5.00
28	Fernando Tatis	.50
29	Tony Gwynn	3.00
30	Barry Bonds	6.00
31	Ken Griffey Jr.	4.00
32	Alex Rodriguez	5.00
33	Jose Canseco	1.25
34	Juan Gonzalez	1.00
35	Ivan Rodriguez	1.75
36	Shawn Green	1.50

Foul Pole

		NM/M
Complete Set (20):		100.00
Common Player:		1.50
Inserted 1:49		
1	Chipper Jones	8.00
2	Andruw Jones	6.00
3	Cal Ripken Jr.	16.00

4	Nomar Garciaparra	8.00
5	Sammy Sosa	8.00
6	Frank Thomas	6.00
7	Manny Ramirez	6.00
8	Jeff Bagwell	6.00
9	Raul Mondesi	1.50
10	Vladimir Guerrero	6.00
11	Mike Piazza	9.00
12	Derek Jeter	16.00
13	Bernie Williams	1.50
14	Scott Rolen	5.00
15	J.D. Drew	3.00
16	Mark McGwire	12.00
17	Tony Gwynn	8.00
18	Ken Griffey Jr.	10.00
19	Alex Rodriguez	12.00
20	Juan Gonzalez	3.00

Icons

		NM/M
Complete Set (10):		50.00
Common Player:		4.00
Inserted 1:121		
1	Cal Ripken Jr.	10.00
2	Nomar Garciaparra	5.00
3	Sammy Sosa	5.00
4	Frank Thomas	4.00
5	Mike Piazza	6.50
6	Derek Jeter	10.00
7	Mark McGwire	8.00
8	Tony Gwynn	5.00
9	Ken Griffey Jr.	7.50
10	Alex Rodriguez	8.00

Thorn in the Side

		NM/M
Complete Set (20):		35.00
Common Player:		1.00
Inserted 1:25		

1	Mo Vaughn	1.00
2	Chipper Jones	3.00
3	Greg Maddux	3.00
4	Cal Ripken Jr.	6.00
5	Nomar Garciaparra	3.00
6	Sammy Sosa	3.00
7	Frank Thomas	2.25
8	Manny Ramirez	2.25
9	Jeff Bagwell	2.25
10	Mike Piazza	3.50
11	Derek Jeter	6.00
12	Bernie Williams	1.00
13	J.D. Drew	1.50
14	Mark McGwire	4.50
15	Tony Gwynn	3.00
16	Barry Bonds	6.00
17	Ken Griffey Jr.	4.00
18	Alex Rodriguez	4.50
19	Juan Gonzalez	1.50
20	Ivan Rodriguez	2.00

Tripleheader

		NM/M
Complete Set (30):		30.00
Common Player:		.25
Inserted 4:25 H		
Tier 1 (1-10)		
Production 99 Sets H		
Tier 2 (11-20)		
Production 199 Sets H		
Tier 3 (21-30)		
Production 299 Sets H		
1	Greg Maddux	1.50
2	Cal Ripken Jr.	3.00
3	Nomar Garciaparra	1.50
4	Sammy Sosa	1.50
5	Frank Thomas	1.00
6	Mike Piazza	1.75
7	Mark McGwire	2.50
8	Tony Gwynn	1.50
9	Ken Griffey Jr.	2.00
10	Alex Rodriguez	2.50
11	Mo Vaughn	.25
12	Chipper Jones	1.50
13	Manny Ramirez	1.00
14	Larry Walker	.25
15	Jeff Bagwell	1.00
16	Vladimir Guerrero	1.00
17	Derek Jeter	3.00
18	J.D. Drew	.60
19	Barry Bonds	3.00
20	Juan Gonzalez	.50
21	Troy Glaus	1.00
22	Andruw Jones	1.00
23	Matt Williams	.25
24	Craig Biggio	.25
25	Raul Mondesi	.25
26	Roger Clemens	1.75
27	Bernie Williams	.25
28	Scott Rolen	.75
29	Jose Canseco	.50
30	Ivan Rodriguez	.75

2000 Pacific

		NM/M
Complete Set (500):		60.00
Common Player:		.10
Pack (12):		1.50
Wax Box (24):		25.00
1	Garret Anderson	.15
2	Tim Belcher	.10
3	Gary DiSarcina	.10
4	Trent Durrington	.10
5	Jim Edmonds	.15
6a	Darin Erstad/Action	.35
6b	Darin Erstad/Portrait	.35
7	Chuck Finley	.10
8	Troy Glaus	.75
9	Todd Greene	.10
10	Bret Hemphill	.10
11	Ken Hill	.10
12	Ramon Ortiz	.10

HENRY RODRIGUEZ OF • CHICAGO CUBS

13	Troy Percival	.10
14	Mark Petkovsek	.10
15	Tim Salmon	.20
16a	Mo Vaughn	.15
16b	Mo Vaughn/Portrait	.15
17	Jay Bell	.10
18	Omar Daal	.10
19	Erubiel Durazo	.10
20	Steve Finley	.10
21	Bernard Gilkey	.10
22	Luis Gonzalez	.20
23	Randy Johnson	.75
24	Byung-Hyun Kim	.10
25	Travis Lee	.10
26	Matt Mantei	.10
27	Armando Reynoso	.10
28	Rob Ryan	.10
29	Kelly Stinnett	.10
30	Todd Stottlemyre	.10
31a	Matt Williams/Action	.15
31b	Matt Williams/Portrait	.15
32	Tony Womack	.10
33	Bret Boone	.10
34	Andres Galarraga	.15
35	Tom Glavine	.35
36	Ozzie Guillen	.10
37a	Andruw Jones/Action	.75
37b	Andruw Jones/Portrait	.75
38a	Chipper Jones/Action	1.00
38b	Chipper Jones/Portrait	1.00
39	Brian Jordan	.10
40	Ryan Klesko	.15
41	Javy Lopez	.15
42a	Greg Maddux/Action	1.00
42b	Greg Maddux/Portrait	1.00
43	Kevin Millwood	.15
44	John Rocker	.10
45	Randall Simon	.10
46	John Smoltz	.15
47	Gerald Williams	.10
48	Brady Anderson	.15
49a	Albert Belle/Action	.15
49b	Albert Belle/Portrait	.15
50	Mike Bordick	.10
51	Will Clark	.25
52	Jeff Conine	.10
53	Delino DeShields	.10
54	Jerry Hairston Jr.	.10
55	Charles Johnson	.10
56	Eugene Kingsale	.10
57	Ryan Minor	.10
58	Mike Mussina	.35
59	Sidney Ponson	.10
60a	Cal Ripken Jr./Action	2.50
60b	Cal Ripken Jr./Portrait	2.50
61	B.J. Surhoff	.10
62	Mike Timlin	.10
63	Rod Beck	.10
64a	Nomar Garciaparra/Action	1.50
64b	Nomar Garciaparra/Portrait	1.50
65	Tom Gordon	.10
66	Butch Huskey	.10
67	Derek Lowe	.10
68a	Pedro Martinez/Action	.75
68b	Pedro Martinez/Portrait	.75
69	Trot Nixon	.10
70	Jose Offerman	.10
71	Troy O'Leary	.10
72	Pat Rapp	.10
73	Donnie Sadler	.10
74	Mike Stanley	.10
75	John Valentin	.10
76	Jason Varitek	.10
77	Wilton Veras	.15
78	Tim Wakefield	.10
79	Rick Aguilera	.10
80	Manny Alexander	.10
81	Roosevelt Brown	.10
82	Mark Grace	.20
83	Glenallen Hill	.10
84	Lance Johnson	.10

No.	Player	Price
85	Jon Lieber	.10
86	Cole Liniak	.10
87	Chad Meyers	.10
88	Mickey Morandini	.10
89	Jose Nieves	.10
90	Henry Rodriguez	.10
91a	Sammy Sosa/Action	1.50
91b	Sammy Sosa/Portrait	1.50
92	Kevin Tapani	.10
93	Kerry Wood	.50
94	Mike Caruso	.10
95	Ray Durham	.10
96	Brook Fordyce	.10
97	Bobby Howry	.10
98	Paul Konerko	.25
99	Carlos Lee	.10
100	Aaron Myette	.10
101	Greg Norton	.10
102	Magglio Ordonez	.25
103	Jim Parque	.10
104	Liu Rodriguez	.10
105	Chris Singleton	.10
106	Mike Sirotka	.10
107a	Frank Thomas/Action	.75
107b	Frank Thomas/Portrait	.75
108	Kip Wells	.10
109	Aaron Boone	.10
110	Mike Cameron	.10
111a	Sean Casey/Action	.20
111b	Sean Casey/Portrait	.20
112	Jeffrey Hammonds	.10
113	Pete Harnisch	.10
114a	Barry Larkin/Portrait	.15
114b	Barry Larkin/Portrait	.15
115	Jason LaRue	.10
116	Denny Neagle	.10
117	Pokey Reese	.10
118	Scott Sullivan	.10
119	Eddie Taubensee	.10
120	Greg Vaughn	.10
121	Scott Williamson	.10
122	Dmitri Young	.10
123a	Roberto Alomar/Action	.35
123b	Roberto Alomar/Portrait	.35
124	Sandy Alomar Jr.	.10
125	Harold Baines	.10
126	Russell Branyan	.10
127	Dave Burba	.10
128	Bartolo Colon	.10
129	Travis Fryman	.15
130	Mike Jackson	.10
131	David Justice	.15
132a	Kenny Lofton/Action	.15
132b	Kenny Lofton/Portrait	.15
133	Charles Nagy	.10
134a	Manny Ramirez/Action	.75
134b	Manny Ramirez/Portrait	.75
135	Dave Roberts	.10
136	Richie Sexson	.10
137	Jim Thome	.60
138	Omar Vizquel	.15
139	Jaret Wright	.10
140	Pedro Astacio	.10
141	Dante Bichette	.10
142	Brian Bohanon	.10
143a	Vinny Castilla/Action	.10
143b	Vinny Castilla/Portrait	.10
144	Edgard Clemente	.10
145	Derrick Gibson	.10
146	Todd Helton	.75
147	Darryl Kile	.10
148	Mike Lansing	.10
149	Kirt Manwaring	.10
150	Neifi Perez	.10
151	Ben Petrick	.10
152	Juan Sosa RC	.20
153	Dave Veres	.10
154a	Larry Walker/Action	.15
154b	Larry Walker/Portrait	.15
155	Brad Ausmus	.10
156	Dave Borkowski	.10
157	Tony Clark	.10
158	Francisco Cordero	.10
159	Deivi Cruz	.10
160	Damion Easley	.10
161	Juan Encarnacion	.10
162	Robert Fick	.10
163	Bobby Higginson	.10
164	Gabe Kapler	.15
165	Brian Moehler	.10
166	Dean Palmer	.10
167	Luis Polonia	.10
168	Justin Thompson	.10
169	Jeff Weaver	.10
170	Antonio Alfonseca	.10
171	Bruce Aven	.10
172	A.J. Burnett	.15
173	Luis Castillo	.10
174	Ramon Castro	.10
175	Ryan Dempster	.10
176	Alex Fernandez	.10
177	Cliff Floyd	.10
178	Amaury Garcia	.10
179	Alex Gonzalez	.10
180	Mark Kotsay	.10
181	Mike Lowell	.15
182	Brian Meadows	.10
183	Kevin Orie	.10
184	Julio Ramirez	.10
185	Preston Wilson	.15
186	Moises Alou	.15
187a	Jeff Bagwell/Action	.75
187b	Jeff Bagwell/Portrait	.75
188	Glen Barker	.10
189	Derek Bell	.10
190a	Craig Biggio/Action	.15
190b	Craig Biggio/Portrait	.15
191	Ken Caminiti	.10
192	Scott Elarton	.10
193	Carl Everett	.10
194	Mike Hampton	.10
195	Carlos Hernandez	.10
196	Richard Hidalgo	.10
197	Jose Lima	.10
198	Shane Reynolds	.15
199	Bill Spiers	.10
200	Billy Wagner	.15
201a	Carlos Beltran/Action	.50
201b	Carlos Beltran/Portrait	.50
202	Dermal Brown	.10
203	Johnny Damon	.25
204	Jermaine Dye	.10
205	Carlos Febles	.10
206	Jeremy Giambi	.10
207	Mark Quinn	.10
208	Joe Randa	.10
209	Dan Reichert	.10
210	Jose Rosado	.10
211	Rey Sanchez	.10
212	Jeff Suppan	.10
213	Mike Sweeney	.10
214a	Kevin Brown/Action	.15
214b	Kevin Brown (Portrait)	.15
215	Darren Dreifort	.10
216	Eric Gagne	.10
217	Mark Grudzielanek	.10
218	Todd Hollandsworth	.10
219	Todd Hundley	.10
220	Eric Karros	.15
221	Raul Mondesi	.15
222	Chan Ho Park	.10
223	Jeff Shaw	.10
224a	Gary Sheffield/Action	.30
224b	Gary Sheffield/Portrait	.30
225	Ismael Valdes	.10
226	Devon White	.10
227	Eric Young	.10
228	Kevin Barker	.10
229	Ron Belliard	.10
230a	Jeromy Burnitz/Action	.10
230b	Jeromy Burnitz/Portrait	.10
231	Jeff Cirillo	.10
232	Marquis Grissom	.10
233	Geoff Jenkins	.10
234	Mark Loretta	.10
235	David Nilsson	.10
236	Hideo Nomo	.75
237	Alex Ochoa	.10
238	Kyle Peterson	.10
239	Fernando Vina	.10
240	Bob Wickman	.10
241	Steve Woodard	.10
242	Chad Allen	.10
243	Ron Coomer	.10
244	Marty Cordova	.10
245	Cristian Guzman	.10
246	Denny Hocking	.10
247	Jacque Jones	.10
248	Corey Koskie	.10
249	Matt Lawton	.10
250	Joe Mays	.10
251	Eric Milton	.10
252	Brad Radke	.10
253	Mark Redman	.10
254	Terry Steinbach	.10
255	Todd Walker	.10
256	Tony Armas Jr.	.10
257	Michael Barrett	.10
258	Peter Bergeron	.10
259	Geoff Blum	.10
260	Orlando Cabrera	.10
261	Trace Coquillette RC	.15
262	Brad Fullmer	.10
263a	Vladimir Guerrero/Action	.75
263b	Vladimir Guerrero/Portrait	.75
264	Wilton Guerrero	.10
265	Dustin Hermanson	.10
266	Manny Martinez	.10
267	Ryan McGuire	.10
268	Ugueth Urbina	.10
269	Jose Vidro	.10
270	Rondell White	.15
271	Chris Widger	.10
272	Edgardo Alfonzo	.10
273	Armando Benitez	.10
274	Roger Cedeno	.10
275	Dennis Cook	.10
276	Octavio Dotel	.10
277	John Franco	.10
278	Darryl Hamilton	.10
279	Rickey Henderson	.75
280	Orel Hershiser	.10
281	Al Leiter	.15
282a	John Olerud/Action	.15
282b	John Olerud/Portrait	.15
283	Rey Ordonez	.10
284a	Mike Piazza/Action	1.50
284b	Mike Piazza/Portrait	1.50
285	Kenny Rogers	.10
286	Jorge Toca	.10
287	Robin Ventura	.15
288	Scott Brosius	.10
289a	Roger Clemens/Action	1.25
289b	Roger Clemens/Portrait	1.25
290	David Cone	.15
291	Chili Davis	.10
292	Orlando Hernandez	.15
293	Hideki Irabu	.10
294a	Derek Jeter/Action	2.50
294b	Derek Jeter/Portrait	2.50
295	Chuck Knoblauch	.10
296	Ricky Ledee	.10
297	Jim Leyritz	.10
298	Tino Martinez	.15
299	Paul O'Neill	.15
300	Andy Pettitte	.25
301	Jorge Posada	.15
302	Mariano Rivera	.25
303	Alfonso Soriano	.75
304a	Bernie Williams/Action	.20
304b	Bernie Williams/Portrait	.20
305	Ed Yarnall	.10
306	Kevin Appier	.10
307	Rich Becker	.10
308	Eric Chavez	.25
309	Jason Giambi	.60
310	Ben Grieve	.10
311	Ramon Hernandez	.10
312	Tim Hudson	.25
313	John Jaha	.10
314	Doug Jones	.10
315	Omar Olivares	.10
316	Mike Oquist	.10
317	Matt Stairs	.10
318	Miguel Tejada	.25
319	Randy Velarde	.10
320	Bobby Abreu	.15
321	Marlon Anderson	.10
322	Alex Arias	.10
323	Rico Brogna	.10
324	Paul Byrd	.10
325	Ron Gant	.10
326	Doug Glanville	.10
327	Wayne Gomes	.10
328	Mike Lieberthal	.10
329	Robert Person	.10
330	Desi Relaford	.10
331a	Scott Rolen/Action	.60
331b	Scott Rolen/Portrait	.60
332a	Curt Schilling/Action	.35
332b	Curt Schilling/Portrait	.35
333	Kris Benson	.10
334	Adrian Brown	.10
335	Brant Brown	.10
336	Brian Giles	.15
337	Chad Hermansen	.10
338	Jason Kendall	.15
339	Al Martin	.10
340	Pat Meares	.10
341a	Warren Morris/Action	.10
341b	Warren Morris/Portrait	.10
342	Todd Ritchie	.10
343	Jason Schmidt	.10
344	Ed Sprague	.10
345	Mike Williams	.10
346	Kevin Young	.10
347	Rick Ankiel	.15
348	Ricky Bottalico	.10
349	Kent Bottenfield	.10
350	Darren Bragg	.10
351	Eric Davis	.15
352a	J.D. Drew/Action	.35
352b	J.D. Drew (Portrait)	.35
353	Adam Kennedy	.10
354	Ray Lankford	.10
355	Joe McEwing	.15
356a	Mark McGwire/Action	2.00
356b	Mark McGwire/Portrait	2.00
357	Matt Morris	.10
358	Darren Oliver	.10
359	Edgar Renteria	.10
360	Fernando Tatis	.10
361	Andy Ashby	.10
362	Ben Davis	.10
363a	Tony Gwynn/Action	1.00
363b	Tony Gwynn/Portrait	1.00
364	Sterling Hitchcock	.10
365	Trevor Hoffman	.10
366	Damian Jackson	.10
367	Wally Joyner	.10
368	Dave Magadan	.10
369	Gary Matthews Jr.	.10
370	Phil Nevin	.10
371	Eric Owens	.10
372	Ruben Rivera	.10
373a	Reggie Sanders/Action	.10
373b	Reggie Sanders/Portrait	.10
374	Quilvio Veras	.10
375	Rich Aurilia	.10
376	Marvin Benard	.10
377a	Barry Bonds/Action	2.50
377b	Barry Bonds/Portrait	2.50
378	Ellis Burks	.10
379	Shawn Estes	.10
380	Livan Hernandez	.10
381a	Jeff Kent/Action	.15
381b	Jeff Kent (Portrait)	.15
382	Brent Mayne	.10
383	Bill Mueller	.10
384	Calvin Murray	.10
385	Robb Nen	.10
386	Russ Ortiz	.10
387	Kirk Rueter	.10
388	J.T. Snow	.10
389	David Bell	.10
390	Jay Buhner	.15
391	Russ Davis	.10
392a	Freddy Garcia/Action	.10
392b	Freddy Garcia/Portrait	.10
393a	Ken Griffey Jr./Action	1.50
393b	Ken Griffey Jr./Portrait	1.50
394	Carlos Guillen	.10
395	John Halama	.10
396	Brian Hunter	.10
397	Ryan Jackson	.10
398	Edgar Martinez	.10
399	Gil Meche	.10
400	Jose Mesa	.10
401	Jamie Moyer	.10
402a	Alex Rodriguez/Action	2.00
402b	Alex Rodriguez/Portrait	2.00
403	Dan Wilson	.10
404	Wilson Alvarez	.10
405	Rolando Arrojo	.10
406a	Wade Boggs/Action	1.00
406b	Wade Boggs/Portrait	1.00
407	Miguel Cairo	.10
408a	Jose Canseco/Action	.40
408b	Jose Canseco/Portrait	.40
409	John Flaherty	.10
410	Jose Guillen	.10
411	Roberto Hernandez	.10
412	Terrell Lowery	.10
413	Dave Martinez	.10
414	Quinton McCracken	.10
415a	Fred McGriff/Action	.15
415b	Fred McGriff/Portrait	.15
416	Ryan Rupe	.10
417	Kevin Stocker	.10
418	Bubba Trammell	.10
419	Royce Clayton	.10
420a	Juan Gonzalez/Action	.75
420b	Juan Gonzalez/Portrait	.75
421	Tom Goodwin	.10
422	Rusty Greer	.10
423	Rick Helling	.10
424	Roberto Kelly	.10
425	Ruben Mateo	.10
426	Mark McLemore	.10
427	Mike Morgan	.10
428	Rafael Palmeiro	.65
429a	Ivan Rodriguez/Action	.65
429b	Ivan Rodriguez/Portrait	.65
430	Aaron Sele	.10
431	Lee Stevens	.10
432	John Wetteland	.10
433	Todd Zeile	.10
434	Jeff Zimmerman	.10
435	Tony Batista	.10
436	Casey Blake	.10
437	Homer Bush	.10
438	Chris Carpenter	.10
439	Jose Cruz Jr.	.10
440a	Carlos Delgado/Action	.50
440b	Carlos Delgado/Portrait	.50
441	Tony Fernandez	.10
442	Darrin Fletcher	.10
443	Alex Gonzalez	.10
444a	Shawn Green/Action	.35
444b	Shawn Green/Portrait	.35
445	Roy Halladay	.20
446	Billy Koch	.10
447	David Segui	.10
448	Shannon Stewart	.10
449	David Wells	.10
450	Vernon Wells	.15

Copper

	NM/M
Common Copper:	5.00
Stars:	4-8X
Production 99 Sets	

Platinum Blue

	NM/M
Common Player:	8.00
Stars:	6-10X
Production 75 Sets	

Premiere Date

	NM/M
Common Player:	15.00
Stars:	8-15X
Production 37 Sets	

Ruby Red (Seven-11)

	NM/M
Complete Set (500):	65.00
Common Player:	.15
Stars/Rookies 1.5X	

(See 2000 Pacific for checklist and base card values.)

Command Performers

		NM/M
Complete Set (20):		45.00
Common Player:		1.00
Inserted 1:24 Retail		
1	Chipper Jones	3.00
2	Greg Maddux	3.00
3	Cal Ripken Jr.	6.00
4	Nomar Garciaparra	4.00
5	Sammy Sosa	4.00
6	Sean Casey	1.00
7	Manny Ramirez	2.00
8	Larry Walker	1.00
9	Jeff Bagwell	2.00
10	Vladimir Guerrero	2.00
11	Mike Piazza	4.00
12	Roger Clemens	3.50
13	Derek Jeter	6.00
14	Mark McGwire	5.00
15	Tony Gwynn	3.00
16	Barry Bonds	6.00
17	Ken Griffey Jr.	4.00
18	Alex Rodriguez	5.00
19	Ivan Rodriguez	1.50
20	Shawn Green	1.25

Cramer's Choice Awards

		NM/M
Complete Set (10):		300.00
Common Player:		25.00
Inserted 1:721		
1	Chipper Jones	25.00
2	Cal Ripken Jr.	50.00
3	Nomar Garciaparra	30.00
4	Sammy Sosa	30.00
5	Mike Piazza	30.00
6	Derek Jeter	50.00
7	Mark McGwire	40.00
8	Tony Gwynn	25.00
9	Ken Griffey Jr.	30.00
10	Alex Rodriguez	40.00

Diamond Leaders

	NM/M
Complete Set (30):	25.00
Common Card:	.50

Inserted 2:25

1	Garret Anderson, Chuck Finley, Troy Percival, Mo Vaughn/ Anaheim Angels	.50
2	Albert Belle, Mike Mussina, B.J. Surhoff/ Baltimore Orioles	.50
3	Nomar Garciaparra, Pedro J. Martinez, Troy O'Leary/ Boston Red Sox	3.00
4	Ray Durham, Magglio Ordonez, Frank Thomas/ Chicago White Sox	1.50
5	Bartolo Colon, Manny Ramirez, Omar Vizquel/ Cleveland Indians	1.50
6	Deivi Cruz, Dave Mlicki, David Palmer/ Detroit Tigers	.50
7	Johnny Damon, Jermaine Dye, Jose Rosado, Mike Sweeney/ Kansas City Royals	.50
8	Corey Koskie, Eric Milton, Brad Radke/ Minnesota Twins	.50
9	Orlando Hernandez, Derek Jeter, Mariano Rivera, Bernie Williams/ New York Yankees	4.00
10	Jeremy Giambi, Tim Hudson, Matt Stairs/ Oakland Athletics	1.00
11	Freddy Garcia, Ken Griffey Jr., Edgar Martinez/ Seattle Mariners	3.00
12	Jose Canseco, Roberto Hernandez, Fred McGriff/ Tampa Bay Devil Rays	.75
13	Rafael Palmeiro, Ivan Rodriguez, John Wetteland/ Texas Rangers	1.00
14	Carlos Delgado, Shannon Stewart, David Wells/ Toronto Blue Jays	1.00
15	Luis Gonzalez, Randy Johnson, Matt Williams/Arizona Diamondbacks	1.50
16	Chipper Jones, Brian Jordan, Greg Maddux/ Atlanta Braves	2.00
17	Mark Grace, Jon Lieber, Sammy Sosa/ Chicago Cubs	3.00
18	Sean Casey, Pete Harnisch, Greg Vaughn/ Cincinnati Reds	.50
19	Pedro Astacio, Dante Bichette, Larry Walker/ Colorado Rockies	.50
20	Luis Castillo, Alex Fernandez, Preston Wilson/ Florida Marlins	.50
21	Jeff Bagwell, Mike Hampton, Billy Wagner/ Houston Astros	1.50
22	Kevin Brown, Mark Grudzielanek, Eric Karros/ Los Angeles Dodgers	.50
23	Jeromy Burnitz, Jeff Cirillo, Marquis Grissom, Hideo Nomo/ Milwaukee Brewers	1.00
24	Vladimir Guerrero, Dustin Hermanson, Ugueth Urbina/ Montreal Expos	1.50
25	Roger Cedeno, Rickey Henderson, Mike Piazza/ New York Mets	3.00
26	Bobby Abreu, Mike Lieberthal, Curt Schilling/ Philadelphia Phillies	.75
27	Brian Giles, Jason Kendall, Kevin Young/ Pittsburgh Pirates	.50
28	Kent Bottenfield, Ray Lankford, Mark McGwire/ St. Louis Cardinals	3.50
29	Tony Gwynn, Trevor Hoffman, Reggie Sanders/ San Diego Padres	2.00
30	Barry Bonds, Jeff Kent, Russ Ortiz/ San Francisco Giants	4.00

Gold Crown Die-Cuts

		NM/M
Complete Set (36):		150.00
Common Player:		1.50
Inserted 1:25		
1	Mo Vaughn	1.50
2	Matt Williams	1.50
3	Andruw Jones	6.00
4	Chipper Jones	8.00
5	Greg Maddux	8.00
6	Cal Ripken Jr.	15.00
7	Nomar Garciaparra	10.00
8	Pedro Martinez	6.00
9	Sammy Sosa	10.00
10	Magglio Ordonez	2.50
11	Frank Thomas	6.00
12	Sean Casey	1.50
13	Roberto Alomar	2.50
14	Manny Ramirez	6.00
15	Larry Walker	1.50
16	Jeff Bagwell	6.00
17	Craig Biggio	1.50
18	Carlos Beltran	4.00
19	Vladimir Guerrero	6.00
20	Mike Piazza	10.00
21	Roger Clemens	9.00
22	Derek Jeter	15.00
23	Bernie Williams	2.00
24	Scott Rolen	5.00
25	Warren Morris	1.50
26	J.D. Drew	2.00
27	Mark McGwire	12.00
28	Tony Gwynn	8.00
29	Barry Bonds	15.00
30	Ken Griffey Jr.	10.00
31	Alex Rodriguez	12.00
32	Jose Canseco	2.00
33	Juan Gonzalez	6.00
34	Rafael Palmeiro	5.00
35	Ivan Rodriguez	5.00
36	Shawn Green	3.00

Ornaments

		NM/M
Complete Set (20):		40.00
Common Player:		1.00
Inserted 2:25		
1	Mo Vaughn	1.00
2	Chipper Jones	3.00
3	Greg Maddux	3.00

4	Cal Ripken Jr.	6.00
5	Nomar Garciaparra	4.00
6	Sammy Sosa	4.00
7	Frank Thomas	2.00
8	Manny Ramirez	2.00
9	Larry Walker	1.00
10	Jeff Bagwell	2.00
11	Mike Piazza	4.00
12	Roger Clemens	3.50
13	Derek Jeter	6.00
14	Scott Rolen	1.50
15	J.D. Drew	1.25
16	Mark McGwire	5.00
17	Tony Gwynn	3.00
18	Ken Griffey Jr.	4.00
19	Alex Rodriguez	5.00
20	Ivan Rodriguez	1.50

Past & Present

		NM/M
Complete Set (20):		80.00
Common Player:		1.50
Inserted 1:49 H		
1	Chipper Jones	5.00
2	Greg Maddux	5.00
3	Cal Ripken Jr.	10.00
4	Nomar Garciaparra	6.00
5	Pedro Martinez	4.00
6	Sammy Sosa	6.00
7	Frank Thomas	4.00
8	Manny Ramirez	4.00
9	Larry Walker	1.50
10	Jeff Bagwell	4.00
11	Mike Piazza	6.00
12	Roger Clemens	5.50
13	Derek Jeter	10.00
14	Mark McGwire	8.00
15	Tony Gwynn	5.00
16	Barry Bonds	10.00
17	Ken Griffey Jr.	6.00
18	Alex Rodriguez	8.00
19	Wade Boggs	5.00
20	Ivan Rodriguez	3.00

Reflections

		NM/M
Common Player:		3.00
Inserted 1:97		
1	Andruw Jones	6.00
2	Chipper Jones	8.00
3	Cal Ripken Jr.	20.00
4	Nomar Garciaparra	12.00
5	Sammy Sosa	12.00
6	Frank Thomas	6.00
7	Manny Ramirez	6.00
8	Jeff Bagwell	6.00
9	Vladimir Guerrero	6.00
10	Mike Piazza	12.00
11	Derek Jeter	20.00
12	Bernie Williams	3.00
13	Scott Rolen	5.00
14	J.D. Drew	3.00
15	Mark McGwire	15.00
16	Tony Gwynn	8.00
17	Ken Griffey Jr.	12.00
18	Alex Rodriguez	15.00
19	Juan Gonzalez	6.00
20	Ivan Rodriguez	3.00

2000 Pacific Aurora

	NM/M
Complete Set (151):	25.00

Common Player:		.15
Pack (10):		2.00
Wax Box (24):		30.00
1	Darin Erstad	.25
2	Troy Glaus	.75
3	Tim Salmon	.25
4	Mo Vaughn	.15
5	Jay Bell	.15
6	Erubiel Durazo	.15
7	Luis Gonzalez	.25
8	Randy Johnson	.75
9	Matt Williams	.15
10	Tom Glavine	.35
11	Andruw Jones	.75
12	Chipper Jones	1.00
13	Brian Jordan	.15
14	Greg Maddux	1.00
15	Kevin Millwood	.15
16	Albert Belle	.15
17	Will Clark	.25
18	Mike Mussina	.35
19	Cal Ripken Jr.	2.50
20	B.J. Surhoff	.15
21	Nomar Garciaparra	1.50
22	Pedro Martinez	.75
23	Troy O'Leary	.15
24	Wilton Veras	.15
25	Mark Grace	.25
26	Henry Rodriguez	.15
27	Sammy Sosa	1.50
28	Kerry Wood	.50
29	Ray Durham	.15
30	Paul Konerko	.25
31	Carlos Lee	.15
32	Magglio Ordonez	.25
33	Chris Singleton	.15
34	Frank Thomas	.75
35	Mike Cameron	.15
36	Sean Casey	.25
37	Barry Larkin	.15
38	Pokey Reese	.15
39	Eddie Taubensee	.15
40	Roberto Alomar	.40
41	David Justice	.15
42	Kenny Lofton	.15
43	Manny Ramirez	.15
44	Richie Sexson	.15
45	Jim Thome	.60
46	Omar Vizquel	.15
47	Todd Helton	.75
48	Mike Lansing	.15
49	Neifi Perez	.15
50	Ben Petrick	.15
51	Larry Walker	.15
52	Tony Clark	.15
53	Damion Easley	.15
54	Juan Encarnacion	.15
55	Juan Gonzalez	.75
56	Dean Palmer	.15
57	Luis Castillo	.15
58	Cliff Floyd	.15
59	Alex Gonzalez	.15
60	Mike Lowell	.15
61	Preston Wilson	.15
62	Jeff Bagwell	.75
63	Craig Biggio	.15
64	Ken Caminiti	.15
65	Jose Lima	.15
66	Billy Wagner	.15
67	Carlos Beltran	.50
68	Johnny Damon	.25
69	Jermaine Dye	.15
70	Mark Quinn	.15
71	Mike Sweeney	.15
72	Kevin Brown	.15
73	Shawn Green	.35
74	Eric Karros	.15
75	Chan Ho Park	.15
76	Gary Sheffield	.40
77	Ron Belliard	.15
78	Jeromy Burnitz	.15
79	Marquis Grissom	.15
80	Geoff Jenkins	.15
81	David Nilsson	.15
82	Ron Coomer	.15
83	Jacque Jones	.15
84	Brad Radke	.15
85	Todd Walker	.15
86	Michael Barrett	.15
87	Peter Bergeron	.15
88	Vladimir Guerrero	.75
89	Jose Vidro	.15
90	Rondell White	.15
91	Edgardo Alfonzo	.15
92	Darryl Hamilton	.15
93	Rey Ordonez	.15
94	Mike Piazza	1.50
95	Robin Ventura	.15
96	Roger Clemens	1.25
97	Orlando Hernandez	.15
98	Derek Jeter	2.50
99	Tino Martinez	.15
100	Mariano Rivera	.25
101	Bernie Williams	.25
102	Eric Chavez	.25
103	Jason Giambi	.60
104	Ben Grieve	.15
105	Tim Hudson	.25
106	John Jaha	.15
107	Matt Stairs	.15
108	Bobby Abreu	.15
109	Doug Glanville	.15
110	Mike Lieberthal	.15
111	Scott Rolen	.60
112	Curt Schilling	.40
113	Brian Giles	.15
114	Chad Hermansen	.15
115	Jason Kendall	.15
116	Warren Morris	.15
117	Kevin Young	.15
118	Rick Ankiel	.25
119	J.D. Drew	.25
120	Ray Lankford	.15
121	Mark McGwire	2.00
122	Edgar Renteria	.15
123	Fernando Tatis	.15
124	Ben Davis	.15
125	Tony Gwynn	1.00
126	Trevor Hoffman	.15
127	Phil Nevin	.15
128	Barry Bonds	2.50
129	Ellis Burks	.15
130	Jeff Kent	.15
131	J.T. Snow	.15
132	Freddy Garcia	.15
133	Ken Griffey Jr.	1.50
133a	Ken Griffey Jr. Reds	2.00
134	Edgar Martinez	.15
135	Alex Rodriguez	2.00
136	Dan Wilson	.15
137	Jose Canseco	.40
138	Roberto Hernandez	.15
139	Dave Martinez	.15
140	Fred McGriff	.15
141	Rusty Greer	.15
142	Ruben Mateo	.15
143	Rafael Palmeiro	.65
144	Ivan Rodriguez	.65
145	Jeff Zimmerman	.15
146	Homer Bush	.15
147	Carlos Delgado	.50
148	Raul Mondesi	.15
149	Shannon Stewart	.15
150	Vernon Wells	.15

Copper

Stars:	2-4X
Production 399 Sets	

Silver

Stars:	3-6X
Production 199 Sets	

Platinum Blue

Stars:	5-10X
Production 67 Sets	

Pinstripes

		NM/M
Complete Set (50):		30.00
Common Player:		.25
Premiere Date:		3-6X
Production 51 Sets		
4	Mo Vaughn	.25
8	Randy Johnson	1.50
9	Matt Williams	.25
11	Andruw Jones	1.50
12	Chipper Jones	2.00
14	Greg Maddux	2.00
19	Cal Ripken Jr.	4.00
21	Nomar Garciaparra	2.50
22	Pedro Martinez	1.50
27	Sammy Sosa	2.50
32	Magglio Ordonez	.35
34	Frank Thomas	1.50
36	Sean Casey	.35
37	Barry Larkin	.25
42	Kenny Lofton	.25
43	Manny Ramirez	1.50
45	Jim Thome	1.50
47	Todd Helton	1.50
51	Larry Walker	.25
55	Juan Gonzalez	1.50
62	Jeff Bagwell	1.50
63	Craig Biggio	.25
67	Carlos Beltran	.50
73	Shawn Green	.40
76	Gary Sheffield	.40
78	Jeromy Burnitz	.25
88	Vladimir Guerrero	1.50
91	Edgardo Alfonzo	.25
94	Mike Piazza	2.50
96	Roger Clemens	2.25
97	Orlando Hernandez	.25
98	Derek Jeter	4.00
101	Bernie Williams	.35
102	Eric Chavez	.35
105	Tim Hudson	.35
111	Scott Rolen	1.25
112	Curt Schilling	.50
113	Brian Giles	.25
114	Rick Ankiel	.25
121	Mark McGwire	3.00
125	Tony Gwynn	2.00
128	Barry Bonds	4.00
130	Jeff Kent	.25
133	Ken Griffey Jr.	2.50
135	Alex Rodriguez	3.00
137	Jose Canseco	.50
140	Fred McGriff	.25
143	Rafael Palmeiro	.75
144	Ivan Rodriguez	.75
147	Carlos Delgado	1.00

At-Bat Styrotechs

		NM/M
Complete Set (20):		125.00
Common Player:		2.00
Production 299 Sets		
1	Chipper Jones	7.50
2	Cal Ripken Jr.	15.00
3	Nomar Garciaparra	10.00
4	Sammy Sosa	10.00
5	Frank Thomas	6.00
6	Manny Ramirez	6.00
7	Larry Walker	2.00
8	Jeff Bagwell	6.00
9	Carlos Beltran	2.00
10	Vladimir Guerrero	6.00
11	Mike Piazza	10.00
12	Derek Jeter	15.00
13	Bernie Williams	2.00
14	Mark McGwire	12.00
15	Tony Gwynn	7.50
16	Barry Bonds	15.00
17	Ken Griffey Jr.	10.00
18	Alex Rodriguez	12.00
19	Jose Canseco	3.00
20	Ivan Rodriguez	5.00

Dugout View Net-Fusions

	NM/M
Complete Set (20):	110.00
Common Player:	2.50

Inserted 1:37
1	Mo Vaughn	2.50
2	Chipper Jones	8.00
3	Cal Ripken Jr.	15.00
4	Nomar Garciaparra	10.00
5	Sammy Sosa	10.00
6	Manny Ramirez	6.00
7	Larry Walker	2.50
8	Juan Gonzalez	6.00
9	Jeff Bagwell	6.00
10	Craig Biggio	2.50
11	Shawn Green	3.00
12	Vladimir Guerrero	6.00
13	Mike Piazza	10.00
14	Derek Jeter	15.00
15	Scott Rolen	5.00
16	Mark McGwire	12.00
17	Tony Gwynn	8.00
18	Ken Griffey Jr.	10.00
19	Alex Rodriguez	12.00
20	Rafael Palmeiro	4.00

Pennant Fever

		NM/M
Complete Set (20):		25.00
Common Player:		1.00
T. Gwynn Auto./147		75.00
Inserted 4:37		
1	Andruw Jones	1.50
2	Chipper Jones	2.00
3	Greg Maddux	2.00
4	Cal Ripken Jr.	4.00
5	Nomar Garciaparra	2.50
6	Pedro Martinez	1.50
7	Sammy Sosa	2.50
8	Manny Ramirez	1.50
9	Jim Thome	1.50
10	Jeff Bagwell	1.50
11	Mike Piazza	2.50
12	Roger Clemens	2.25
13	Derek Jeter	4.00
14	Bernie Williams	1.00
15	Mark McGwire	3.00
16	Tony Gwynn	2.00
17	Ken Griffey Jr.	2.50
18	Alex Rodriguez	3.00
19	Rafael Palmeiro	1.00
20	Ivan Rodriguez	1.00

Star Factor

		NM/M
Complete Set (10):		200.00
Common Player:		20.00
Inserted 1:361		
1	Chipper Jones	20.00
2	Cal Ripken Jr.	40.00
3	Nomar Garciaparra	25.00
4	Sammy Sosa	25.00
5	Mike Piazza	25.00
6	Derek Jeter	40.00

7	Mark McGwire	30.00
8	Tony Gwynn	20.00
9	Ken Griffey Jr.	25.00
10	Alex Rodriguez	30.00

2000 Pacific Crown Collection

		NM/M
Complete Set (300):		25.00
Common Player:		.10
Pack (10):		1.50
Wax Box (36):		30.00
1	Garret Anderson	.10
2	Darin Erstad	.25
3	Ben Molina	.10
4	Ramon Ortiz	.10
5	Orlando Palmeiro	.10
6	Troy Percival	.10
7	Tim Salmon	.15
8	Mo Vaughn	.10
9	Mo Vaughn Checklist	.10
10	Jay Bell	.10
11	Omar Daal	.10
12	Erubiel Durazo	.10
13	Steve Finley	.10
14	Hanley Frias	.10
15	Luis Gonzalez	.25
16	Randy Johnson	.75
17	Matt Williams	.10
18	Matt Williams Checklist	.10
19	Andres Galarraga	.10
20	Tom Glavine	.35
21	Andruw Jones	.75
22	Chipper Jones	1.00
23	Brian Jordan	.10
24	Javy Lopez	.10
25	Greg Maddux	1.00
26	Kevin Millwood	.10
27	Eddie Perez	.10
28	John Smoltz	.10
29	Chipper Jones Checklist	.50
30	Albert Belle	.15
31	Jesse Garcia	.10
32	Jerry Hairston Jr.	.10
33	Charles Johnson	.10
34	Mike Mussina	.30
35	Sidney Ponson	.10
36	Cal Ripken Jr.	2.50
37	B.J. Surhoff	.10
38	Cal Ripken Jr. Checklist	1.00
39	Nomar Garciaparra	1.50
40	Pedro Martinez	.75
41	Ramon Martinez	.10
42	Trot Nixon	.10
43	Jose Offerman	.10
44	Troy O'Leary	.10
45	John Valentin	.10
46	Wilton Veras	.10
47	Nomar Garciaparra Checklist	.75
48	Mark Grace	.15
49	Felix Heredia	.10
50	Jose Molina	.10
51	Jose Nieves	.10
52	Henry Rodriguez	.10
53	Sammy Sosa	1.50
54	Kerry Wood	.65
55	Sammy Sosa Checklist	.60
56	Mike Caruso	.10
57	Carlos Castillo	.10
58	Jason Dellaero	.10
59	Carlos Lee	.10
60	Magglio Ordonez	.25
61	Jesus Pena	.10
62	Liu Rodriguez	.10
63	Frank Thomas	.75
64	Magglio Ordonez Checklist	.15
65	Aaron Boone	.10
66	Mike Cameron	.10
67	Sean Casey	.20

68	Juan Guzman	.10
69	Barry Larkin	.10
70	Pokey Reese	.10
71	Eddie Taubensee	.10
72	Greg Vaughn	.10
73	Sean Casey Checklist	.15
74	Roberto Alomar	.25
75	Sandy Alomar Jr.	.10
76	Bartolo Colon	.10
77	Jacob Cruz	.10
78	Einar Diaz	.10
79	David Justice	.10
80	Kenny Lofton	.10
81	Manny Ramirez	.75
82	Richie Sexson	.10
83	Jim Thome	.75
84	Omar Vizquel	.10
85	Enrique Wilson	.10
86	Manny Ramirez Checklist	.40
87	Pedro Astacio	.10
88	Henry Blanco	.10
89	Vinny Castilla	.10
90	Edgard Clemente	.10
91	Todd Helton	.75
92	Neifi Perez	.10
93	Terry Shumpert	.10
94	Juan Sosa RC	.20
95	Larry Walker	.25
96	Vinny Castilla Checklist	.10
97	Tony Clark	.10
98	Deivi Cruz	.10
99	Damion Easley	.10
100	Juan Encarnacion	.10
101	Karim Garcia	.10
102	Luis Garcia	.10
103	Juan Gonzalez	.75
104	Jose Macias	.10
105	Dean Palmer	.10
106	Juan Encarnacion Checklist	.10
107	Antonio Alfonseca	.10
108	Armando Almanza	.10
109	Bruce Aven	.10
110	Luis Castillo	.10
111	Ramon Castro	.10
112	Alex Fernandez	.10
113	Cliff Floyd	.10
114	Alex Gonzalez	.10
115	Michael Tejera RC	.10
116	Preston Wilson	.10
117	Luis Castillo Checklist	.10
118	Jeff Bagwell	.75
119	Craig Biggio	.25
120	Jose Cabrera	.10
121	Tony Eusebio	.10
122	Carl Everett	.10
123	Ricky Gutierrez	.10
124	Mike Hampton	.10
125	Richard Hidalgo	.10
126	Jose Lima	.10
127	Billy Wagner	.10
128	Jeff Bagwell Checklist	.40
129	Carlos Beltran	.50
130	Johnny Damon	.25
131	Jermaine Dye	.10
132	Carlos Febles	.10
133	Jeremy Giambi	.10
134	Jose Rosado	.10
135	Rey Sanchez	.10
136	Jose Santiago	.10
137	Carlos Beltran Checklist	.10
138	Kevin Brown	.10
139	Craig Counsell	.10
140	Shawn Green	.40
141	Eric Karros	.10
142	Angel Pena	.10
143	Gary Sheffield	.25
144	Ismael Valdes	.10
145	Jose Vizcaino	.10
146	Devon White	.10
147	Eric Karros Checklist	.10
148	Ron Belliard	.10
149	Jeromy Burnitz	.10
150	Jeff Cirillo	.10
151	Marquis Grissom	.10
152	Geoff Jenkins	.10
153	Dave Nilsson	.10
154	Rafael Roque	.10
155	Jose Valentin	.10
156	Fernando Vina	.10
157	Jeromy Burnitz	.10
158	Chad Allen	.10
159	Ron Coomer	.10
160	Eddie Guardado	.10
161	Cristian Guzman	.10
162	Jacque Jones	.10
163	Javier Valentin	.10
164	Todd Walker	.10
165	Ron Coomer Checklist	.10
166	Michael Barrett	.10
167	Miguel Batista	.10
168	Vladimir Guerrero	.75
169	Wilton Guerrero	.10

170	Fernando Seguignol	.10
171	Ugueth Urbina	.10
172	Javier Vazquez	.10
173	Jose Vidro	.10
174	Rondell White	.10
175	Vladimir Guerrero Checklist	.25
176	Edgardo Alfonzo	.10
177	Armando Benitez	.10
178	Roger Cedeno	.10
179	Octavio Dotel	.10
180	Melvin Mora	.10
181	Rey Ordonez	.10
182	Mike Piazza	1.50
183	Jorge Toca	.10
184	Robin Ventura	.10
185	Edgardo Alfonzo Checklist	.10
186	Roger Clemens	1.25
187	David Cone	.10
188	Orlando Hernandez	.10
189	Derek Jeter	2.50
190	Ricky Ledee	.10
191	Tino Martinez	.10
192	Ramiro Mendoza	.10
193	Jorge Posada	.10
194	Mariano Rivera	.15
195	Alfonso Soriano	.75
196	Bernie Williams	.30
197	Derek Jeter Checklist	1.00
198	Eric Chavez	.15
199	Jason Giambi	.60
200	Ben Grieve	.10
201	Ramon Hernandez	.10
202	Tim Hudson	.25
203	John Jaha	.10
204	Omar Olivares	.10
205	Olmedo Saenz	.10
206	Matt Stairs	.10
207	Miguel Tejada	.20
208	Tim Hudson Checklist	.20
209	Rico Brogna	.10
210	Bobby Abreu	.10
211	Marlon Anderson	.10
212	Alex Arias	.10
213	Doug Glanville	.10
214	Robert Person	.10
215	Scott Rolen	.60
216	Curt Schilling	.35
217	Scott Rolen Checklist	.25
218	Francisco Cordova	.10
219	Brian Giles	.10
220	Jason Kendall	.10
221	Warren Morris	.10
222	Abraham Nunez	.10
223	Aramis Ramirez	.10
224	Jose Silva	.10
225	Kevin Young	.10
226	Brian Giles Checklist	.10
227	Rick Ankiel	.15
228	Ricky Bottalico	.10
229	J.D. Drew	.25
230	Ray Lankford	.10
231	Mark McGwire	2.00
232	Eduardo Perez	.10
233	Placido Polanco	.10
234	Edgar Renteria	.10
235	Fernando Tatis	.10
236	Mark McGwire Checklist	.85
237	Carlos Almanzar	.10
238	Wiki Gonzalez	.10
239	Tony Gwynn	1.00
240	Trevor Hoffman	.10
241	Damian Jackson	.10
242	Wally Joyner	.10
243	Ruben Rivera	.10
244	Reggie Sanders	.10
245	Quilvio Veras	.10
246	Tony Gwynn Checklist	.50
247	Rich Aurilia	.10
248	Marvin Benard	.10
249	Barry Bonds	2.50
250	Ellis Burks	.10
251	Miguel Del Toro	.10
252	Edwards Guzman	.10
253	Livan Hernandez	.10
254	Jeff Kent	.10
255	Russ Ortiz	.10
256	Armando Rios	.10
257	Barry Bonds Checklist	1.00
258	Rafael Bournigal	.10
259	Freddy Garcia	.10
260	Ken Griffey Jr.	15.00
261	Carlos Guillen	.10
262	Raul Ibanez	.10
263	Edgar Martinez	.10
264	Jose Mesa	.10
265	Jamie Moyer	.10
266	John Olerud	.10
267	Jose Paniagua	.10
268	Alex Rodriguez	2.00
269	Alex Rodriguez Checklist	1.00

270	Wilson Alvarez	.10
271	Rolando Arrojo	.10
272	Wade Boggs	1.00
273	Miguel Cairo	.10
274	Jose Canseco	.40
275	Jose Guillen	.10
276	Roberto Hernandez	.10
277	Albie Lopez	.10
278	Fred McGriff	.10
279	Esteban Yan	.10
280	Jose Canseco Checklist	.20
281	Rusty Greer	.10
282	Roberto Kelly	.10
283	Esteban Loaiza	.10
284	Ruben Mateo	.10
285	Rafael Palmeiro	.65
286	Ivan Rodriguez	.65
287	Aaron Sele	.10
288	John Wetteland	.10
289	Ivan Rodriguez Checklist	.25
290	Tony Batista	.10
291	Jose Cruz Jr.	.10
292	Carlos Delgado	.50
293	Kelvim Escobar	.10
294	Tony Fernandez	.10
295	Billy Koch	.10
296	Raul Mondesi	.10
297	Willis Otanez	.10
298	David Segui	.10
299	David Wells	.10
300	Carlos Delgado Checklist	.20

Holographic Purple

Stars: 4-8X
Production 199 Sets

Platinum Blue

Stars: 8-15X
Production 67 Sets

In The Cage

		NM/M
Complete Set (20):		250.00
Common Player:		5.00
Inserted 1:145		
1	Mo Vaughn	5.00
2	Chipper Jones	15.00
3	Cal Ripken Jr.	30.00
4	Nomar Garciaparra	20.00
5	Sammy Sosa	20.00
6	Frank Thomas	10.00
7	Roberto Alomar	6.00
8	Manny Ramirez	10.00
9	Larry Walker	5.00
10	Jeff Bagwell	10.00
11	Vladimir Guerrero	10.00
12	Mike Piazza	20.00
13	Derek Jeter	30.00
14	Bernie Williams	5.00
15	Mark McGwire	25.00
16	Tony Gwynn	15.00
17	Ken Griffey Jr.	20.00
18	Alex Rodriguez	25.00
19	Rafael Palmeiro	8.00
20	Ivan Rodriguez	8.00

Catinos of the Major Leagues

	NM/M
Complete Set (36):	20.00

Common Player:		.25
Inserted 2:37		
Parallel:		2-4X
Production 99 Sets		
1	Erubiel Durazo	.25
2	Luis Gonzalez	.25
3	Andruw Jones	1.00
4	Nomar Garciaparra	2.00
5	Pedro Martinez	1.00
6	Sammy Sosa	2.00
7	Carlos Lee	.25
8	Magglio Ordonez	.25
9	Roberto Alomar	.65
10	Manny Ramirez	1.00
11	Omar Vizquel	.25
12	Vinny Castilla	.25
13	Juan Gonzalez	1.00
14	Luis Castillo	.25
15	Jose Lima	.25
16	Carlos Beltran	.75
17	Vladimir Guerrero	1.00
18	Edgardo Alfonzo	.25
19	Roger Cedeno	.25
20	Rey Ordonez	.25
21	Orlando Hernandez	.25
22	Tino Martinez	.25
23	Mariano Rivera	.35
24	Bernie Williams	.50
25	Miguel Tejada	.50
26	Bobby Abreu	.25
27	Fernando Tatis	.25
28	Freddy Garcia	.25
29	Edgar Martinez	.25
30	Alex Rodriguez	3.00
31	Jose Canseco	.65
32	Ruben Mateo	.25
33	Rafael Palmeiro	.75
34	Ivan Rodriguez	.75
35	Carlos Delgado	.65
36	Raul Mondesi	.25

Moment of Truth

		NM/M
Complete Set (30):		50.00
Common Player:		.50
Inserted 1:37		
1	Mo Vaughn	.50
2	Chipper Jones	3.00
3	Greg Maddux	3.00
4	Albert Belle	.50
5	Cal Ripken Jr.	6.00
6	Nomar Garciaparra	4.00
7	Pedro Martinez	2.00
8	Sammy Sosa	4.00
9	Frank Thomas	2.00
10	Barry Larkin	.50
11	Kenny Lofton	.50
12	Manny Ramirez	2.00
13	Larry Walker	.50
14	Juan Gonzalez	2.00
15	Jeff Bagwell	2.00
16	Craig Biggio	.50
17	Carlos Beltran	1.00
18	Vladimir Guerrero	2.00
19	Mike Piazza	4.00
20	Roger Clemens	3.50
21	Derek Jeter	6.00
22	Bernie Williams	.75
23	Mark McGwire	5.00
24	Tony Gwynn	3.00
25	Barry Bonds	6.00
26	Ken Griffey Jr.	4.00
27	Alex Rodriguez	5.00
28	Rafael Palmeiro	1.50
29	Ivan Rodriguez	1.50
30	Carlos Delgado	1.00

Pacific Cup

	NM/M
Complete Set (10):	220.00
Inserted 1:721	
1 Cal Ripken Jr.	40.00

2	Nomar Garciaparra	25.00
3	Pedro Martinez	15.00
4	Sammy Sosa	25.00
5	Vladimir Guerrero	15.00
6	Derek Jeter	40.00
7	Mark McGwire	35.00
8	Tony Gwynn	20.00
9	Ken Griffey Jr.	25.00
10	Alex Rodriguez	35.00

Timber 2000

		NM/M
Complete Set (20):		100.00
Common Player:		2.00
Inserted 1:73		
1	Chipper Jones	8.00
2	Nomar Garciaparra	10.00
3	Sammy Sosa	10.00
4	Magglio Ordonez	2.00
5	Manny Ramirez	6.00
6	Vinny Castilla	2.00
7	Juan Gonzalez	6.00
8	Jeff Bagwell	6.00
9	Shawn Green	3.00
10	Vladimir Guerrero	6.00
11	Mike Piazza	10.00
12	Derek Jeter	15.00
13	Bernie Williams	2.00
14	Mark McGwire	12.00
15	Ken Griffey Jr.	10.00
16	Alex Rodriguez	12.00
17	Jose Canseco	3.00
18	Rafael Palmeiro	5.00
19	Ivan Rodriguez	5.00
20	Carlos Delgado	4.00

2000 Pacific Crown Royale

		NM/M
Complete Set (144):		40.00
Common Player:		.25
Common SP:		1.00
Pack (6):		2.50
Box (24):		45.00
1	Darin Erstad	.40
2	Troy Glaus	1.00
3	Adam Kennedy/SP	1.00
4	Derrick Turnbow/SP RC	1.00
5	Mo Vaughn	.25
6	Erubiel Durazo	.25
7	Steve Finley	.25
8	Randy Johnson	1.00
9	Travis Lee	.25
10	Matt Williams	.25
11	Rafael Furcal/SP	1.00
12	Andres Galarraga	.25
13	Andruw Jones	1.00
14	Chipper Jones	1.50
15	Javy Lopez	.25
16	Greg Maddux	1.50
17	Albert Belle	.25
18	Will Clark	.35
19	Mike Mussina	.40
20	Cal Ripken Jr.	3.00
21	Carl Everett	.25
22	Nomar Garciaparra	2.00
23	Pedro Martinez	1.00
24	Jason Varitek	.25

25	Scott Downs/SP RC	1.00
26	Mark Grace	.35
27	Sammy Sosa	2.00
28	Kerry Wood	.65
29	Ray Durham	.25
30	Paul Konerko	.25
31	Carlos Lee	.25
32	Magglio Ordonez	.40
33	Frank Thomas	1.00
34	Rob Bell/SP	1.00
35	Sean Casey	.25
36	Ken Griffey Jr.	2.00
37	Barry Larkin	.25
38	Pokey Reese	.25
39	Roberto Alomar	.40
40	David Justice	.25
41	Kenny Lofton	.25
42	Manny Ramirez	1.00
43	Richie Sexson	.25
44	Jim Thome	.75
45	Rolando Arrojo	.25
46	Jeff Cirillo	.25
47	Tom Goodwin	.25
48	Todd Helton	1.00
49	Larry Walker	.25
50	Tony Clark	.25
51	Juan Encarnacion	.25
52	Juan Gonzalez	1.00
53	Hideo Nomo	1.00
54	Dean Palmer	.25
55	Cliff Floyd	.25
56	Alex Gonzalez	.25
57	Mike Lowell	.25
58	Brad Penny/SP	1.00
59	Preston Wilson	.25
60	Moises Alou	.25
61	Jeff Bagwell	1.00
62	Craig Biggio	.25
63	Roger Cedeno	.25
64	Julio Lugo/SP	1.00
65	Carlos Beltran	.60
66	Johnny Damon	.40
67	Jermaine Dye	.25
68	Carlos Febles	.25
69	Mark Quinn/SP	1.00
70	Kevin Brown	.25
71	Shawn Green	.50
72	Eric Karros	.25
73	Gary Sheffield	.50
74	Kevin Barker/SP	1.00
75	Ron Belliard	.25
76	Jeromy Burnitz	.25
77	Geoff Jenkins	.25
78	Jacque Jones	.25
79	Corey Koskie	.25
80	Matt LeCroy/SP	1.00
81	Brad Radke	.25
82	Peter Bergeron/SP	1.00
83	Matt Blank/SP	1.00
84	Vladimir Guerrero	1.00
85	Hideki Irabu	.25
86	Rondell White	.25
87	Edgardo Alfonzo	.25
88	Mike Hampton	.25
89	Rickey Henderson	1.00
90	Rey Ordonez	.25
91	Jay Payton/SP	1.00
92	Mike Piazza	2.00
93	Roger Clemens	1.75
94	Orlando Hernandez	.25
95	Derek Jeter	3.00
96	Tino Martinez	.25
97	Alfonso Soriano/SP	2.50
98	Bernie Williams	.40
99	Eric Chavez	.40
100	Jason Giambi	.75
101	Ben Grieve	.25
102	Tim Hudson	.50
103	Terrence Long/SP	1.00
104	Mark Mulder/SP	1.00
105	Adam Piatt/SP	1.00
106	Bobby Abreu	.25
107	Doug Glanville	.25
108	Mike Lieberthal	.25
109	Scott Rolen	.75
110	Brian Giles	.25
111	Chad Hermansen/SP	1.00
112	Jason Kendall	.25
113	Warren Morris	.25
114	Rick Ankiel/SP	1.00
115	Justin Brunette/SP RC	1.00
116	J.D. Drew	.25
117	Mark McGwire	2.50
118	Fernando Tatis	.25
119	Wiki Gonzalez/SP	1.00
120	Tony Gwynn	1.50
121	Trevor Hoffman	.25
122	Ryan Klesko	.25
123	Barry Bonds	3.00
124	Ellis Burks	.25
125	Jeff Kent	.25
126	Calvin Murray/SP	1.00
127	J.T. Snow	.25
128	Freddy Garcia	.25

129	John Olerud	.25
130	Alex Rodriguez	2.50
131	Kazuhiro Sasaki/SP RC	3.00
132	Jose Canseco	.50
133	Vinny Castilla	.25
134	Fred McGriff	.25
135	Greg Vaughn	.25
136	Gabe Kapler	.25
137	Mike Lamb/SP RC	1.00
138	Ruben Mateo SP	1.00
139	Rafael Palmeiro	.75
140	Ivan Rodriguez	.75
141	Tony Batista	.25
142	Carlos Delgado	.75
143	Raul Mondesi	.25
144	Shannon Stewart	.25

Platinum Blue
Stars: 3-6X
Production 75 Sets

Limited Series
Stars: 2-4X
Production 144 Sets

Premiere Date
Stars: 2-4X
Production 121 Sets

Red
All singles: 1X
Base cards in retail packs.

Card-Supials

		NM/M
Complete Set (20):		40.00
Common Card:		1.00
Inserted 2:25		
1	Randy Johnson, Erubiel Durazo	2.00
2	Chipper Jones, Andruw Jones	3.00
3	Cal Ripken Jr., Matt Riley	6.00
4	Nomar Garciaparra, Jason Varitek	4.00
5	Sammy Sosa, Kerry Wood	4.00
6	Frank Thomas, Magglio Ordonez	2.00
7	Ken Griffey Jr., Sean Casey	4.00
8	Manny Ramirez, Richie Sexson	2.00
9	Larry Walker, Ben Petrick	1.00
10	Juan Gonzalez, Juan Encarnacion	2.00
11	Jeff Bagwell, Lance Berkman	2.00
12	Shawn Green, Eric Gagne	1.00
13	Peter Bergeron, Vladimir Guerrero	2.00
14	Mike Piazza, Edgardo Alfonzo	4.00
15	Derek Jeter, Alfonso Soriano	5.00
16	Scott Rolen, Bobby Abreu	1.50
17	Mark McGwire, Rick Ankiel	5.00
18	Tony Gwynn, Ben Davis	3.00
19	Alex Rodriguez, Freddy Garcia	5.00
20	Ivan Rodriguez, Ruben Mateo	1.50

Cramer's Choice
Jumbo

	NM/M
Complete Set (10):	35.00
Common Player:	1.00
Inserted 1:Box H	
Aqua:	5-10X
Production 203 Sets	
Blue:	2-5X
Production 35 Sets	
Gold:	10-20X
Production 10 Sets	
Green:	3-6X
Production 30 Sets	

Red:		4-8X
Production 25 Sets		
1	Cal Ripken Jr.	6.00
2	Nomar Garciaparra	4.00
3	Ken Griffey Jr.	4.00
4	Sammy Sosa	4.00
5	Mike Piazza	4.00
6	Derek Jeter	6.00
7	Rick Ankiel	1.00
8	Mark McGwire	5.00
9	Tony Gwynn	2.00
10	Alex Rodriguez	5.00

Feature Attractions

		NM/M
Complete Set (25):		10.00
Common Player:		.25
Inserted 1:1		
Exclusive Showing:		30-50X
Production 20 Sets		
1	Erubiel Durazo	.25
2	Chipper Jones	1.00
3	Greg Maddux	1.00
4	Cal Ripken Jr.	2.50
5	Nomar Garciaparra	1.50
6	Pedro Martinez	.75
7	Sammy Sosa	1.50
8	Frank Thomas	.75
9	Ken Griffey Jr.	1.50
10	Manny Ramirez	.75
11	Larry Walker	.25
12	Juan Gonzalez	.75
13	Jeff Bagwell	.75
14	Carlos Beltran	.50
15	Shawn Green	.50
16	Vladimir Guerrero	.75
17	Mike Piazza	1.50
18	Roger Clemens	1.25
19	Derek Jeter	2.50
20	Ben Grieve	.25
21	Rick Ankiel	.35
22	Mark McGwire	2.00
23	Tony Gwynn	1.00
24	Alex Rodriguez	2.00
25	Ivan Rodriguez	.65

Final Numbers

	NM/M
Complete Set (25):	10.00

Common Player:		.25
Inserted 1:1		
1	Randy Johnson	.75
2	Andruw Jones	.75
3	Chipper Jones	1.00
4	Cal Ripken Jr.	2.50
5	Nomar Garciaparra	1.50
6	Pedro Martinez	.75
7	Sammy Sosa	1.50
8	Ken Griffey Jr.	1.50
9	Sean Casey	.35
10	Manny Ramirez	.75
11	Larry Walker	.25
12	Jeff Bagwell	.75
13	Craig Biggio	.25
14	Shawn Green	.50
15	Vladimir Guerrero	.75
16	Mike Piazza	1.50
17	Derek Jeter	2.50
18	Bernie Williams	.35
19	Scott Rolen	.65
20	Mark McGwire	2.00
21	Tony Gwynn	1.00
22	Barry Bonds	2.50
23	Alex Rodriguez	2.00
24	Jose Canseco	.40
25	Ivan Rodriguez	.65

Jumbo

		NM/M
Complete Set (6):		25.00
Inserted 6:10 Boxes H		
1	Cal Ripken Jr.	6.00
2	Nomar Garciaparra	4.00
3	Ken Griffey Jr.	4.00
4	Derek Jeter	6.00
5	Mark McGwire	5.00
6	Alex Rodriguez	5.00

Proofs

		NM/M
Complete Set (36):		90.00
Common Player:		1.00
Inserted 1:25		
Proofs:		2-3X
1	Erubiel Durazo	1.50
2	Randy Johnson	3.00
3	Chipper Jones	5.00
4	Greg Maddux	5.00
5	Cal Ripken Jr.	10.00
6	Nomar Garciaparra	8.00
7	Pedro Martinez	5.00
8	Sammy Sosa	5.00
9	Frank Thomas	2.50
10	Sean Casey	1.50
11	Ken Griffey Jr.	5.00
12	Manny Ramirez	2.50
13	Jim Thome	2.50
14	Larry Walker	1.50
15	Juan Gonzalez	2.50
16	Jeff Bagwell	2.50
17	Craig Biggio	1.50
18	Carlos Beltran	2.00
19	Shawn Green	2.00
20	Vladimir Guerrero	2.50
21	Edgardo Alfonzo	1.00
22	Mike Piazza	5.00
23	Roger Clemens	6.00
24	Derek Jeter	10.00
25	Alfonso Soriano	4.00
26	Bernie Williams	2.00
27	Ben Grieve	1.00
28	Rick Ankiel	1.00
29	Mark McGwire	8.00
30	Tony Gwynn	3.00
31	Barry Bonds	8.00
32	Alex Rodriguez	8.00
33	Jose Canseco	2.00
34	Vinny Castilla	1.00
35	Ivan Rodriguez	2.00
36	Rafael Palmeiro	2.00

Sweet Spot Signatures

		NM/M
Common Player:		5.00
1	Adam Kennedy	5.00
2	Trot Nixon	8.00
3	Magglio Ordonez	10.00
4	Sean Casey	8.00
5	Travis Dawkins	5.00
6	Todd Helton	25.00
7	Ben Petrick	5.00

8	Jeff Weaver	6.00
9	Preston Wilson	5.00
10	Lance Berkman	10.00
11	Roger Cedeno	5.00
12	Eric Gagne	10.00
13	Kevin Barker	5.00
14	Kyle Peterson	5.00
15	Tony Armas Jr.	5.00
16	Peter Bergeron	5.00
17	Alfonso Soriano	40.00
18	Ben Grieve	5.00
19	Ramon Hernandez	5.00
20	Brian Giles	8.00
21	Chad Hermansen	5.00
22	Warren Morris	5.00
23	Ben Davis	5.00
24	Rick Ankiel	5.00
25	Chad Hutchinson	5.00
26	Freddy Garcia	10.00
27	Gabe Kapler	5.00
28	Ruben Mateo	5.00
29	Billy Koch	5.00
30	Vernon Wells	5.00

2000 Pacific Invincible

		NM/M
Complete Set (150):		75.00
Common Player:		.25
Pack (3):		2.00
Box (36):		50.00
1	Darin Erstad	.50
2	Troy Glaus	1.50
3	Ramon Ortiz	.25
4	Tim Salmon	.35
5	Mo Vaughn	.25
6	Erubiel Durazo	.25
7	Luis Gonzalez	.35
8	Randy Johnson	1.50
9	Matt Williams	.25
10	Rafael Furcal	.25
11	Andres Galarraga	.25
12	Tom Glavine	.40
13	Andruw Jones	1.50
14	Chipper Jones	2.00
15	Greg Maddux	2.00
16	Kevin Millwood	.25
17	Albert Belle	.25
18	Will Clark	.35
19	Mike Mussina	.40
20	Matt Riley	.25
21	Cal Ripken Jr.	4.00
22	Carl Everett	.25
23	Nomar Garciaparra	2.50
24	Steve Lomasney	.25
25	Pedro Martinez	1.50
26	Tomo Ohka RC	.75
27	Wilton Veras	.25
28	Mark Grace	.35
29	Sammy Sosa	2.50
30	Kerry Wood	.75
31	Eric Young	.25
32	Julio Zuleta RC	.25
33	Paul Konerko	.35
34	Carlos Lee	.25
35	Magglio Ordonez	.35
36	Josh Paul	.25
37	Frank Thomas	1.50
38	Rob Bell	.25
39	Dante Bichette	.25
40	Sean Casey	.35
41	Ken Griffey Jr.	2.50

42	Barry Larkin	.25
43	Pokey Reese	.25
44	Roberto Alomar	.40
45	Manny Ramirez	1.50
46	Richie Sexson	.25
47	Jim Thome	1.50
48	Omar Vizquel	.25
49	Jeff Cirillo	.25
50	Todd Helton	1.50
51	Neifi Perez	.25
52	Larry Walker	.25
53	Tony Clark	.25
54	Juan Encarnacion	.25
55	Juan Gonzalez	1.50
56	Hideo Nomo	1.00
57	Luis Castillo	.25
58	Alex Gonzalez	.25
59	Brad Penny	.25
60	Preston Wilson	.25
61	Moises Alou	.25
62	Jeff Bagwell	1.50
63	Lance Berkman	.25
64	Craig Biggio	.25
65	Roger Cedeno	.25
66	Jose Lima	.25
67	Carlos Beltran	.50
68	Johnny Damon	.35
69	Chad Durbin RC	.50
70	Jermaine Dye	.25
71	Carlos Febles	.25
72	Mark Quinn	.25
73	Kevin Brown	.25
74	Eric Gagne	.25
75	Shawn Green	.50
76	Eric Karros	.25
77	Gary Sheffield	.40
78	Kevin Barker	.25
79	Ron Belliard	.25
80	Jeromy Burnitz	.25
81	Geoff Jenkins	.25
82	Jacque Jones	.25
83	Corey Koskie	.25
84	Matt LeCroy	.25
85	David Ortiz	.35
86	Johan Santana RC	20.00
87	Todd Walker	.25
88	Brad Bergeron	.25
89	Vladimir Guerrero	1.50
90	Jose Vidro	.25
91	Rondell White	.25
92	Edgardo Alfonzo	.25
93	Derek Bell	.25
94	Mike Hampton	.25
95	Rey Ordonez	.25
96	Mike Piazza	2.50
97	Robin Ventura	.25
98	Roger Clemens	2.25
99	Orlando Hernandez	.25
100	Derek Jeter	4.00
101	Alfonso Soriano	.75
102	Bernie Williams	.35
103	Eric Chavez	.40
104	Jason Giambi	.75
105	Ben Grieve	.25
106	Tim Hudson	.40
107	Miguel Tejada	.40
108	Bobby Abreu	.25
109	Doug Glanville	.25
110	Mike Lieberthal	.25
111	Scott Rolen	.75
112	Brian Giles	.25
113	Chad Hermansen	.25
114	Jason Kendall	.25
115	Warren Morris	.25
116	Aramis Ramirez	.25
117	Rick Ankiel	.25
118	J.D. Drew	.40
119	Mark McGwire	3.00
120	Fernando Tatis	.25
121	Fernando Vina	.25
122	Bret Boone	.25
123	Ben Davis	.25
124	Tony Gwynn	2.00
125	Trevor Hoffman	.25
126	Ryan Klesko	.25
127	Rich Aurilia	.25
128	Barry Bonds	4.00
129	Ellis Burks	.25
130	Jeff Kent	.25
131	Freddy Garcia	.25
132	Carlos Guillen	.25
133	Edgar Martinez	.25
134	John Olerud	.25
135	Robert Ramsay	.25
136	Alex Rodriguez	3.00
137	Kazuhiro Sasaki RC	3.00
138	Jose Canseco	.50
139	Vinny Castilla	.25
140	Fred McGriff	.25
141	Greg Vaughan (Front photo is Mo Vaughn.)	.25
142	Dan Wheeler	.25
143	Gabe Kapler	.25
144	Ruben Mateo	.25

145	Rafael Palmeiro	.75
146	Ivan Rodriguez	.75
147	Tony Batista	.25
148	Carlos Delgado	.65
149	Raul Mondesi	.25
150	Vernon Wells	.25

Holographic Purple

Stars:	2-3X
Production 299 Sets	

Platinum Blue

Stars:	4-8X
Production 67 Sets	

Diamond Aces

Complete Set (20):		5.00
Common Player:		.25
Inserted 1:1		
Edition of 399 Parallel:		2-3X
1	Randy Johnson	.75
2	Greg Maddux	1.00
3	Tom Glavine	.40
4	John Smoltz	.25
5	Mike Mussina	.50
6	Pedro Martinez	.75
7	Kerry Wood	.60
8	Bartolo Colon	.25
9	Brad Penny	.25
10	Billy Wagner	.25
11	Kevin Brown	.25
12	Mike Hampton	.25
13	Roger Clemens	1.50
14	David Cone	.25
15	Orlando Hernandez	.25
16	Mariano Rivera	.40
17	Tim Hudson	.40
18	Trevor Hoffman	.25
19	Rick Ankiel	.25
20	Freddy Garcia	.25

Game Gear

NM/M

Common Card:		4.00
1	Jeff Bagwell/Jsy/1000	8.00
2	Tom Glavine/Jsy/1000	6.00
3	Mark Grace/Jsy/1000	8.00
4	Eric Karros/Jsy/1000	4.00

5	Edgar Martinez/Jsy/800	6.00
6	Manny Ramirez/Jsy/975	8.00
7	Cal Ripken Jr./Jsy/1000	25.00
8	Alex Rodriguez/Jsy/900	15.00
9	Ivan Rodriguez/Jsy/675	6.00
10	Mo Vaughn Jsy/1000	4.00
11	Edgar Martinez/Bat-Jsy/200	8.00
12	Manny Ramirez/Jsy/145	15.00
13	Alex Rodriguez/Bat-Jsy/200	25.00
14	Ivan Rodriguez/Bat-Jsy/200	10.00
15	Edgar Martinez/Bat/200	10.00
16	Manny Ramirez/Bat/200	15.00
17	Ivan Rodriguez/Bat/200	8.00
18	Alex Rodriguez/Bat/200	20.00
19	Jeff Bagwell/Patch/125	30.00
20	Tom Glavine/Patch/110	25.00
21	Mark Grace/Patch/125	25.00
22	Tony Gwynn/Patch/65	40.00
23	Chipper Jones/Patch/80	40.00
24	Eric Karros/Patch/125	15.00
25	Greg Maddux/Patch/80	50.00
26	Edgar Martinez/Patch/125	20.00
27	Manny Ramirez/Patch/125	30.00
28	Cal Ripken Jr./Patch/125	65.00
29	Alex Rodriguez/Patch/125	50.00
30	Ivan Rodriguez/Patch/125	25.00
31	Frank Thomas/Patch/125	25.00
32	Mo Vaughn/Patch/125	15.00

Eyes of the World

NM/M

Complete Set (20):		30.00
Common Player:		.75
Inserted 1:25		
1	Erubiel Durazo	.75
2	Andruw Jones	2.00
3	Cal Ripken Jr.	6.00
4	Nomar Garciaparra	4.00
5	Pedro Martinez	2.00
6	Sammy Sosa	4.00
7	Ken Griffey Jr.	4.00
8	Manny Ramirez	2.00
9	Larry Walker	.75
10	Juan Gonzalez	2.00
11	Carlos Beltran	1.25
12	Vladimir Guerrero	2.00
13	Orlando Hernandez	.75
14	Derek Jeter	6.00
15	Mark McGwire	5.00
16	Tony Gwynn	3.00
17	Freddy Garcia	.75
18	Alex Rodriguez	5.00
19	Jose Canseco	1.25
20	Ivan Rodriguez	1.50

Kings of the Diamond

NM/M

Complete Set (30):		10.00
Common Player:		.20
Inserted 1:25		
1	Mo Vaughn	.20
2	Erubiel Durazo	.20
3	Andruw Jones	.65
4	Chipper Jones	.75
5	Cal Ripken Jr.	1.50
6	Nomar Garciaparra	1.00

7	Sammy Sosa	1.00
8	Frank Thomas	.65
9	Sean Casey	.25
10	Ken Griffey Jr.	1.00
11	Manny Ramirez	.65
12	Larry Walker	.20
13	Juan Gonzalez	.65
14	Jeff Bagwell	.65
15	Craig Biggio	.20
16	Carlos Beltran	.50
17	Shawn Green	.35
18	Vladimir Guerrero	.65
19	Mike Piazza	1.00
20	Derek Jeter	1.50
21	Bernie Williams	.40
22	Ben Grieve	.20
23	Scott Rolen	.40
24	Mark McGwire	1.25
25	Tony Gwynn	.75
26	Barry Bonds	1.50
27	Alex Rodriguez	1.25
28	Jose Canseco	.25
29	Rafael Palmeiro	.50
30	Ivan Rodriguez	.50

Lighting The Fire

NM/M

Complete Set (20):		120.00
Common Player:		3.00
Inserted 1:49		
1	Chipper Jones	8.00
2	Greg Maddux	8.00
3	Cal Ripken Jr.	15.00
4	Nomar Garciaparra	10.00
5	Pedro Martinez	6.00
6	Ken Griffey Jr.	10.00
7	Sammy Sosa	10.00
8	Manny Ramirez	6.00
9	Juan Gonzalez	6.00
10	Jeff Bagwell	6.00
11	Shawn Green	3.00
12	Vladimir Guerrero	6.00
13	Mike Piazza	10.00
14	Roger Clemens	9.00
15	Derek Jeter	15.00
16	Mark McGwire	12.00
17	Tony Gwynn	8.00
18	Alex Rodriguez	12.00
19	Jose Canseco	3.00
20	Ivan Rodriguez	5.00

Ticket To Stardom

NM/M

Complete Set (20):		250.00
Common Player:		5.00
Inserted 1:121		
1	Andruw Jones	10.00
2	Chipper Jones	15.00
3	Cal Ripken Jr.	30.00
4	Nomar Garciaparra	20.00
5	Pedro Martinez	10.00

6	Ken Griffey Jr.	20.00
7	Sammy Sosa	20.00
8	Manny Ramirez	10.00
9	Jeff Bagwell	10.00
10	Shawn Green	5.00
11	Vladimir Guerrero	10.00
12	Mike Piazza	20.00
13	Derek Jeter	30.00
14	Alfonso Soriano	8.00
15	Scott Rolen	6.00
16	Rick Ankiel	5.00
17	Mark McGwire	25.00
18	Tony Gwynn	15.00
19	Alex Rodriguez	25.00
20	Ivan Rodriguez	8.00

Wild Vinyl

No Pricing
Production 10 Sets

2000 Pacific Omega

		NM/M
Complete Set (255):		300.00
Common Player:		.10
Common (151-255):		4.00
Production 999 Sets		
1	Garret Anderson	.10
2	Darin Erstad	.25
3	Troy Glaus	.75
4	Tim Salmon	.20
5	Mo Vaughn	.10
6	Jay Bell	.10
7	Steve Finley	.10
8	Luis Gonzalez	.20
9	Randy Johnson	.75
10	Matt Williams	.10
11	Andres Galarraga	.10
12	Andruw Jones	.75
13	Chipper Jones	1.00
14	Brian Jordan	.10
15	Greg Maddux	1.00
16	B.J. Surhoff	.10
17	Brady Anderson	.10
18	Albert Belle	.10
19	Mike Mussina	.40
20	Cal Ripken Jr.	2.50
21	Carl Everett	.10
22	Nomar Garciaparra	1.50
23	Pedro Martinez	.75
24	Jason Varitek	.10
25	Mark Grace	.20
26	Sammy Sosa	1.50
27	Rondell White	.10
28	Kerry Wood	.35
29	Eric Young	.10
30	Ray Durham	.10
31	Carlos Lee	.10
32	Magglio Ordonez	.25
33	Frank Thomas	.75
34	Sean Casey	.20
35	Ken Griffey Jr.	1.50
36	Barry Larkin	.10
37	Pokey Reese	.10
38	Roberto Alomar	.40
39	Kenny Lofton	.10
40	Manny Ramirez	.75
41	David Segui	.10
42	Jim Thome	.60
43	Omar Vizquel	.10
44	Carl Cirillo	.10
45	Jeffrey Hammonds	.10
46	Todd Helton	.75
47	Todd Hollandsworth	.10
48	Larry Walker	.10
49	Tony Clark	.10
50	Juan Encarnacion	.10
51	Juan Gonzalez	.75
52	Bobby Higginson	.10
53	Hideo Nomo	.75
54	Dean Palmer	.10
55	Luis Castillo	.10
56	Cliff Floyd	.10
57	Derrek Lee	.10
58	Mike Lowell	.10
59	Henry Rodriguez	.10
60	Preston Wilson	.10
61	Moises Alou	.10
62	Jeff Bagwell	.75
63	Craig Biggio	.10
64	Ken Caminiti	.10
65	Richard Hidalgo	.10
66	Carlos Beltran	.40
67	Johnny Damon	.25
68	Jermaine Dye	.10
69	Joe Randa	.10
70	Mike Sweeney	.10
71	Adrian Beltre	.20
72	Kevin Brown	.10
73	Shawn Green	.35
74	Eric Karros	.10
75	Chan Ho Park	.10
76	Gary Sheffield	.30
77	Ron Belliard	.10
78	Jeromy Burnitz	.10
79	Geoff Jenkins	.10
80	Richie Sexson	.10
81	Ron Coomer	.10
82	Jacque Jones	.10
83	Corey Koskie	.10
84	Matt Lawton	.10
85	Vladimir Guerrero	.75
86	Lee Stevens	.10
87	Jose Vidro	.10
88	Edgardo Alfonzo	.10
89	Derek Bell	.10
90	Mike Bordick	.10
91	Mike Piazza	1.50
92	Robin Ventura	.10
93	Jose Canseco	.40
94	Roger Clemens	1.25
95	Orlando Hernandez	.10
96	Derek Jeter	2.50
97	David Justice	.10
98	Tino Martinez	.10
99	Jorge Posada	.10
100	Bernie Williams	.40
101	Eric Chavez	.20
102	Jason Giambi	.50
103	Ben Grieve	.10
104	Miguel Tejada	.25
105	Bobby Abreu	.10
106	Doug Glanville	.10
107	Travis Lee	.10
108	Mike Lieberthal	.10
109	Scott Rolen	.65
110	Brian S. Giles	.10
111	Jason Kendall	.10
112	Warren Morris	.10
113	Kevin Young	.10
114	Will Clark	.20
115	J.D. Drew	.20
116	Jim Edmonds	.10
117	Mark McGwire	2.00
118	Edgar Renteria	.10
119	Fernando Tatis	.10
120	Fernando Vina	.10
121	Bret Boone	.10
122	Tony Gwynn	1.00
123	Trevor Hoffman	.10
124	Phil Nevin	.10
125	Eric Owens	.10
126	Barry Bonds	2.50
127	Ellis Burks	.10
128	Jeff Kent	.10
129	J.T. Snow	.10
130	Jay Buhner	.10
131	Mike Cameron	.10
132	Rickey Henderson	.75
133	Edgar Martinez	.10
134	John Olerud	.10
135	Alex Rodriguez	2.00
136	Kazuhiro Sasaki RC	1.00
137	Fred McGriff	.10
138	Greg Vaughn	.10
139	Gerald Williams	.10
140	Rusty Greer	.10
141	Gabe Kapler	.10
142	Ricky Ledee	.10
143	Rafael Palmeiro	.65
144	Ivan Rodriguez	.65
145	Tony Batista	.10
146	Jose Cruz Jr.	.10
147	Carlos Delgado	.50
148	Brad Fullmer	.10
149	Shannon Stewart	.10
150	David Wells	.10
151	Juan Alvarez, Jeff DaVanon	6.00
152	Seth Etherton, Adam Kennedy	4.00
153	Ramon Ortiz, Lou Pote	4.00
154	Derrick Turnbow, Eric Weaver	4.00
155	Rod Barajas, Jason Conti	4.00
156	Byung-Hyun Kim, Rob Ryan	4.00
157	David Cortes, George Lombard	4.00
158	Ivanon Coffie, Melvin Mora	4.00
159	Ryan Kohlmeier, Luis Matos RC	6.00
160	Willie Morales, John Parrish RC	4.00
161	Chris Richard, Jay Spurgeon RC	5.00
162	Israel Alcantara, Tomokazu Ohka RC	5.00
163	Paxton Crawford, Sang-Hoon Lee RC	4.00
164	Mike Mahoney, Wilton Veras	4.00
165	Daniel Garibay, Ross Gload RC	4.00
166	Gary Matthews Jr., Phil Norton	4.00
167	Roosevelt Brown, Ruben Quevedo	4.00
168	Lorenzo Barcelo, Rocky Biddle RC	4.00
169	Mark Buehrle, John Garland	8.00
170	Aaron Myette, Josh Paul	4.00
171	Kip Wells, Kelly Wunsch	4.00
172	Rob Bell, Travis Dawkins	4.00
173	Hector Mercado, John Riedling RC	4.00
174	Russell Branyan, Sean DePaula	4.00
175	Tim Drew, Mark Watson	4.00
176	Craig House, Ben Petrick	5.00
177	Robert Fick, Jose Macias	4.00
178	Javier Cardona, Brandon Villafuerte	4.00
179	Armando Almanza, A.J. Burnett	4.00
180	Ramon Castro, Pablo Ozuna	4.00
181	Lance Berkman, Jason Green	4.00
182	Julio Lugo, Tony McKnight	4.00
183	Mitch Meluskey, Wade Miller	4.00
184	Chad Durbin, Hector Ortiz RC	5.00
185	Dermal Brown, Mark Quinn	4.00
186	Eric Gagne, Mike Judd	4.00
187	Kane Davis, Valerio de los Santos	4.00
188	Santiago Perez, Paul Rigdon RC	4.00
189	Matt Kinney, Matt LeCroy	4.00
190	Jason Maxwell, A.J. Pierzynski	4.00
191	J.C. Romero, Johan Santana RC	50.00
192	Tony Armas Jr., Peter Bergeron	4.00
193	Matt Blank, Milton Bradley	4.00
194	Tomas De La Rossa, Scott Forster	4.00
195	Yovanny Lara, Talmadge Nunnari RC	4.00
196	Brian Schneider, Andy Tracy	4.00
197	Scott Strickland, T.J. Tucker	4.00
198	Eric Cammack, Jim Mann RC	4.00
199	Grant Roberts, Jorge Toca	4.00
200	Alfonso Soriano, Jay Tessmer	8.00
201	Terrence Long, Mark Mulder	4.00
202	Pat Burrell, Cliff Politte	4.00
203	Jimmy Anderson, Bronson Arroyo	4.00
204	Mike Darr, Kory DeHaan	4.00
205	Adam Eaton, Wiki Gonzalez	4.00
206	Brandon Kolb, Kevin Walker	4.00
207	Damon Minor, Calvin Murray	4.00
208	Kevin Hodges, Joel Pineiro RC	40.00
209	Rob Ramsay, Kazuhiro Sasaki RC	8.00
210	Rick Ankiel, Mike Matthews	4.00
211	Steve Cox, Travis Harper	4.00
212	Kenny Kelly, Damian Rolls RC	4.00
213	Doug Davis, Scott Sheldon	4.00
214	Brian Sikorski, Pedro Valdes	4.00
215	Francisco Cordero, B.J. Waszgis	4.00
216	Matt DeWitt, Josh Phelps RC	8.00
217	Vernon Wells, Dewayne Wise	4.00
218	Geraldo Guzman, Jason Marquis	4.00
219	Rafael Furcal, Steve Sisco RC	4.00
220	B.J. Ryan, Kevin Beirne	4.00
221	Matt Ginter, Brad Penny	4.00
222	Julio Zuleta, Eric Munson	5.00
223	Dan Reichert, Jeff Williams	4.00
224	Jason LaRue, Danny Ardoin	4.00
225	Ray King, Mark Redman	4.00
226	Joe Crede, Mike Bell	4.00
227	Juan Pierre, Jay Payton	6.00
228	Wayne Franklin, Randy Choate RC	4.00
229	Chris Truby, Adam Piatt	4.00
230	Kevin Nicholson, Chris Woodward	4.00
231	Barry Zito, Jason Boyd	15.00
232	Brian O'Connor, Miguel Del Toro	4.00
233	Carlos Guillen, Aubrey Huff	4.00
234	Chad Hermansen, Jason Tyner	4.00
235	Aaron Fultz, Ryan Vogelsong	4.00
236	Shawn Wooten, Vance Wilson	4.00
237	Danny Klassen, Mike Lamb RC	4.00
238	Chad Bradford, Gene Stechschulte RC	4.00
239	Ismael Villegas, Hector Ramirez, Matt T. Williams, Luis Vizcaino	4.00

240	Mike Garcia,	
	Domingo Guzman,	
	Justin Brunette,	
	Pasqual Coco RC	4.00
241	Frank Charles,	
	Keith McDonald RC	4.00
242	Carlos Casimiro,	
	Morgan Burkhart RC	4.00
243	Raul Gonzalez,	
	Shawn Gilbert	4.00
244	Darrell Einertson,	
	Jeff Sparks RC	4.00
245	Augie Ojeda, Brady Clark,	
	Todd Belitz,	
	Eric Byrnes RC	6.00
246	Leo Estrella,	
	Charlie Greene	4.00
247	Trace Coquillette,	
	Pedro Feliz RC	6.00
248	Tike Redman,	
	David Newhan	4.00
249	Rodrigo Lopez,	
	John Bales	6.00
250	Corey Patterson,	
	Jose Ortiz RC	6.00
251	Britt Reames,	
	Oswaldo Mairena RC	4.00
252	Xavier Nady,	
	Timoniel Perez RC	6.00
253	Tom Jacquez,	
	Vicente Padilla	4.00
254	Elvis Pena,	
	Adam Melhuse RC	4.00
255	Ben Weber,	
	Alex Cabrera RC	6.00

Copper

Stars (1-150):	8-15X
Production 45 Sets	

Platinum Blue

Stars (1-150):	6-10X
Production 55 Sets	

Premiere Date

Stars (1-150):	4-8X
Production 77 Sets	

Gold

Stars (1-150):	4-8X
Production 120 Sets	
(Retail only, one per box.)	

AL Contenders

		NM/M
Complete Set (18):		20.00
Common Player:		.50
Inserted 2:37		
1	Darin Erstad	.75
2	Troy Glaus	1.50
3	Mo Vaughn	.50

4	Albert Belle	.50
5	Cal Ripken Jr.	4.00
6	Nomar Garciaparra	3.00
7	Pedro Martinez	1.50
8	Frank Thomas	1.50
9	Manny Ramirez	1.50
10	Jim Thome	1.25
11	Juan Gonzalez	1.50
12	Roger Clemens	2.50
13	Derek Jeter	4.00
14	Bernie Williams	.75
15	Jason Giambi	1.00
16	Alex Rodriguez	3.50
17	Edgar Martinez	.50
18	Carlos Delgado	1.00

NL Contenders

		NM/M
Complete Set (18):		20.00
Common Player:		.50
Inserted 2:37		
1	Randy Johnson	1.50
2	Chipper Jones	2.00
3	Greg Maddux	2.00
4	Sammy Sosa	2.50
5	Sean Casey	.50
6	Ken Griffey Jr.	2.50
7	Todd Helton	1.50
8	Jeff Bagwell	1.50
9	Shawn Green	.50
10	Gary Sheffield	.75
11	Vladimir Guerrero	1.50
12	Mike Piazza	2.50
13	Scott Rolen	1.00
14	Barry Bonds	4.00
15	Rick Ankiel	.50
16	J.D. Drew	.50
17	Jim Edmonds	.50
18	Mark McGwire	3.00

EO Portraits

		NM/M
Complete Set (20):		125.00
Common Player:		3.00
Inserted 1:73		
1-of-1 Die-Cut Parallels Exist		
1	Chipper Jones	8.00
2	Greg Maddux	8.00
3	Cal Ripken Jr.	15.00
4	Pedro Martinez	6.00
5	Nomar Garciaparra	10.00

6	Sammy Sosa	10.00
7	Frank Thomas	6.00
8	Ken Griffey Jr.	10.00
9	Gary Sheffield	4.00
10	Vladimir Guerrero	6.00
11	Mike Piazza	10.00
12	Roger Clemens	9.00
13	Derek Jeter	15.00
14	Pat Burrell	4.00
15	Tony Gwynn	8.00
16	Barry Bonds	15.00
17	Alex Rodriguez	12.00
18	Rick Ankiel	3.00
19	Mark McGwire	12.00
20	Ivan Rodriguez	5.00

Full Court

		NM/M
Complete Set (36):		30.00
Common Player:		.50
Inserted 4:37 H		
1	Magglio Ordonez	.50
2	Manny Ramirez	1.50
3	Todd Helton	1.50
4	David Justice	.50
5	Bernie Williams	.50
6	Jason Giambi	1.00
7	Scott Rolen	1.00
8	Jeff Kent	.50
9	Edgar Martinez	.50
10	Randy Johnson	1.50
11	Greg Maddux	2.00
12	Mike Mussina	.60
13	Pedro Martinez	1.50
14	Chuck Finley	.50
15	Kevin Brown	.50
16	Roger Clemens	2.25
17	Tim Hudson	.50
18	Rick Ankiel	.50
19	Troy Glaus	1.50
20	Chipper Jones	2.00
21	Nomar Garciaparra	2.50
22	Jeff Bagwell	1.50
23	Shawn Green	.60
24	Vladimir Guerrero	1.50
25	Mike Piazza	2.50
26	Jim Edmonds	.50
27	Rafael Palmeiro	.75
28	Cal Ripken Jr.	4.00
29	Sammy Sosa	2.50
30	Frank Thomas	1.50
31	Ken Griffey Jr.	2.50
32	Gary Sheffield	.50
33	Barry Bonds	4.00
34	Alex Rodriguez	3.00
35	Mark McGwire	3.00
36	Carlos Delgado	1.00

MLB Generations

		NM/M
Complete Set (20):		100.00
Common Card:		3.00
Inserted 1:145		
1	Mark McGwire,	
	Pat Burrell	12.00
2	Cal Ripken Jr.,	
	Alex Rodriguez	15.00
3	Randy Johnson,	
	Rick Ankiel	6.00
4	Tony Gwynn,	
	Darin Erstad	8.00
5	Barry Bonds,	
	Magglio Ordonez	15.00
6	Frank Thomas,	
	Jason Giambi	6.00
7	Roger Clemens,	
	Kerry Wood	10.00
8	Mike Piazza,	
	Mitch Meluskey	10.00
9	Ken Griffey Jr.,	
	Andruw Jones	10.00
10	Bernie Williams,	
	J.D. Drew	4.00
11	Chipper Jones,	
	Troy Glaus	8.00
12	Andres Galarraga,	
	Todd Helton	6.00
13	Juan Gonzalez,	
	Vladimir Guerrero	6.00
14	Craig Biggio,	
	Rafael Furcal	3.00
15	Sammy Sosa,	
	Jermaine Dye	10.00
16	Larry Walker,	
	Richard Hidalgo	3.00

17	Greg Maddux,	
	Adam Eaton	8.00
18	Barry Larkin,	
	Derek Jeter	15.00
19	Roberto Alomar,	
	Jose Vidro	4.00
20	Jeff Kent,	
	Edgardo Alfonzo	3.00

Signatures

		NM/M
Common Player:		5.00
1	Darin Erstad	10.00
2	Nomar Garciaparra	125.00
3	Cal Eldred	5.00
4	Magglio Ordonez	10.00
5	Frank Thomas	30.00
6	Brady Clark	5.00
7	Richard Hidalgo	5.00
8	Gary Sheffield	10.00
9	Pat Burrell	15.00
10	Jim Edmonds	10.00

Stellar Performers

		NM/M
Complete Set (20):		50.00
Common Player:		1.00
Inserted 1:37		
1	Darin Erstad	1.00
2	Chipper Jones	3.00
3	Greg Maddux	3.00
4	Cal Ripken Jr.	6.00
5	Pedro Martinez	2.00
6	Nomar Garciaparra	4.00
7	Sammy Sosa	4.00
8	Frank Thomas	2.00
9	Ken Griffey Jr.	4.00
10	Todd Helton	2.00
11	Jeff Bagwell	2.00
12	Vladimir Guerrero	2.00
13	Mike Piazza	4.00
14	Derek Jeter	6.00
15	Roger Clemens	3.50
16	Tony Gwynn	3.00
17	Barry Bonds	6.00
18	Alex Rodriguez	5.00
19	Mark McGwire	5.00
20	Ivan Rodriguez	1.50

2000 Pacific Paramount

		NM/M
Complete Set (250):		25.00
Common Player:		.10
Pack (6):		1.50
Wax Box (36):		40.00
1	Garret Anderson	.10
2	Jim Edmonds	.10
3	Darin Erstad	.25
4	Chuck Finley	.10
5	Troy Glaus	.75
6	Troy Percival	.10
7	Tim Salmon	.20
8	Mo Vaughn	.20
9	Jay Bell	.10
10	Erubiel Durazo	.10
11	Steve Finley	.10
12	Luis Gonzalez	.20
13	Randy Johnson	.75
14	Travis Lee	.10

15	Matt Mantei	.10
16	Matt Williams	.10
17	Tony Womack	.10
18	Bret Boone	.10
19	Tom Glavine	.35
20	Andruw Jones	.75
21	Chipper Jones	1.00
22	Brian Jordan	.10
23	Javy Lopez	.10
24	Greg Maddux	1.00
25	Kevin Millwood	.10
26	John Rocker	.10
27	John Smoltz	.10
28	Brady Anderson	.10
29	Albert Belle	.10
30	Will Clark	.20
31	Charles Johnson	.10
32	Mike Mussina	.35
33	Cal Ripken Jr.	2.00
34	B.J. Surhoff	.10
35	Nomar Garciaparra	1.25
36	Derek Lowe	.10
37	Pedro Martinez	.75
38	Trot Nixon	.10
39	Troy O'Leary	.10
40	Jose Offerman	.10
41	John Valentin	.10
42	Jason Varitek	.10
43	Mark Grace	.20
44	Glenallen Hill	.10
45	Jon Lieber	.10
46	Cole Liniak	.10
47	Jose Nieves	.10
48	Henry Rodriguez	.10
49	Sammy Sosa	1.25
50	Kerry Wood	.65
51	Jason Dellaero	.10
52	Ray Durham	.10
53	Paul Konerko	.10
54	Carlos Lee	.10
55	Greg Norton	.10
56	Magglio Ordonez	.10
57	Chris Singleton	.10
58	Frank Thomas	.75
59	Aaron Boone	.10
60	Mike Cameron	.10
61	Sean Casey	.20
62	Pete Harnisch	.10
63	Barry Larkin	.10
64	Pokey Reese	.10
65	Greg Vaughn	.10
66	Scott Williamson	.10
67	Roberto Alomar	.35
68	Sean DePaula RC	.20
69	Travis Fryman	.10
70	David Justice	.10
71	Kenny Lofton	.10
72	Manny Ramirez	.75
73	Richie Sexson	.10
74	Jim Thome	.65
75	Omar Vizquel	.10
76	Pedro Astacio	.10
77	Vinny Castilla	.10
78	Derrick Gibson	.10
79	Todd Helton	.75
80	Neifi Perez	.10
81	Ben Petrick	.10
82	Larry Walker	.10
83	Brad Ausmus	.10
84	Tony Clark	.10
85	Deivi Cruz	.10
86	Damion Easley	.10
87	Juan Encarnacion	.10
88	Juan Gonzalez	.75
89	Bobby Higginson	.10
90	Dave Mlicki	.10
91	Dean Palmer	.10
92	Bruce Aven	.10
93	Luis Castillo	.10
94	Ramon Castro	.10
95	Cliff Floyd	.10
96	Alex Gonzalez	.10
97	Mike Lowell	.10

98	Preston Wilson	.10
99	Jeff Bagwell	.75
100	Derek Bell	.10
101	Craig Biggio	.10
102	Ken Caminiti	.10
103	Carl Everett	.10
104	Mike Hampton	.10
105	Jose Lima	.10
106	Billy Wagner	.10
107	Daryle Ward	.10
108	Carlos Beltran	.40
109	Johnny Damon	.25
110	Jermaine Dye	.10
111	Carlos Febles	.10
112	Mark Quinn	.10
113	Joe Randa	.10
114	Jose Rosado	.10
115	Mike Sweeney	.10
116	Kevin Brown	.10
117	Shawn Green	.35
118	Mark Grudzielanek	.10
119	Todd Hollandsworth	.10
120	Eric Karros	.10
121	Chan Ho Park	.10
122	Gary Sheffield	.35
123	Devon White	.10
124	Eric Young	.10
125	Kevin Barker	.10
126	Ron Belliard	.10
127	Jeromy Burnitz	.10
128	Jeff Cirillo	.10
129	Marquis Grissom	.10
130	Geoff Jenkins	.10
131	David Nilsson	.10
132	Chad Allen	.10
133	Ron Coomer	.10
134	Jacque Jones	.10
135	Corey Koskie	.10
136	Matt Lawton	.10
137	Brad Radke	.10
138	Todd Walker	.10
139	Michael Barrett	.10
140	Peter Bergeron	.10
141	Brad Fullmer	.10
142	Vladimir Guerrero	.75
143	Ugueth Urbina	.10
144	Jose Vidro	.10
145	Rondell White	.10
146	Edgardo Alfonzo	.10
147	Armando Benitez	.10
148	Roger Cedeno	.10
149	Rickey Henderson	.75
150	Melvin Mora	.10
151	John Olerud	.10
152	Rey Ordonez	.10
153	Mike Piazza	1.25
154	Jorge Toca	.10
155	Robin Ventura	.10
156	Roger Clemens	1.00
157	David Cone	.10
158	Orlando Hernandez	.10
159	Derek Jeter	2.00
160	Chuck Knoblauch	.10
161	Ricky Ledee	.10
162	Tino Martinez	.10
163	Paul O'Neill	.10
164	Mariano Rivera	.20
165	Alfonso Soriano	.75
166	Bernie Williams	.25
167	Eric Chavez	.25
168	Jason Giambi	.50
169	Ben Grieve	.10
170	Tim Hudson	.25
171	John Jaha	.10
172	Matt Stairs	.10
173	Miguel Tejada	.25
174	Randy Velarde	.10
175	Bobby Abreu	.10
176	Marlon Anderson	.10
177	Rico Brogna	.10
178	Ron Gant	.10
179	Doug Glanville	.10
180	Mike Lieberthal	.10
181	Scott Rolen	.65
182	Curt Schilling	.35
183	Brian Giles	.10
184	Chad Hermansen	.10
185	Jason Kendall	.10
186	Al Martin	.10
187	Pat Meares	.10
188	Warren Morris	.10
189	Ed Sprague	.10
190	Kevin Young	.10
191	Rick Ankiel	.20
192	Kent Bottenfield	.10
193	Eric Davis	.10
194	J.D. Drew	.25
195	Adam Kennedy	.10
196	Ray Lankford	.10
197	Joe McEwing	.10
198	Mark McGwire	1.50
199	Edgar Renteria	.10
200	Fernando Tatis	.10
201	Mike Darr	.10

202	Ben Davis	.10
203	Tony Gwynn	1.00
204	Trevor Hoffman	.10
205	Damian Jackson	.10
206	Phil Nevin	.10
207	Reggie Sanders	.10
208	Quilvio Veras	.10
209	Rich Aurilia	.10
210	Marvin Benard	.10
211	Barry Bonds	2.00
212	Ellis Burks	.10
213	Livan Hernandez	.10
214	Jeff Kent	.10
215	Russ Ortiz	.10
216	J.T. Snow	.10
217	Paul Abbott	.10
218	David Bell	.10
219	Freddy Garcia	.10
220	Ken Griffey Jr.	1.50
221	Carlos Guillen	.10
222	Brian Hunter	.10
223	Edgar Martinez	.10
224	Jamie Moyer	.10
225	Alex Rodriguez	1.50
226	Wade Boggs	1.00
227	Miguel Cairo	.10
228	Jose Canseco	.40
229	Roberto Hernandez	.10
230	Dave Martinez	.10
231	Quinton McCracken	.10
232	Fred McGriff	.10
233	Kevin Stocker	.10
234	Royce Clayton	.10
235	Rusty Greer	.10
236	Ruben Mateo	.10
237	Rafael Palmeiro	.65
238	Ivan Rodriguez	.65
239	Aaron Sele	.10
240	John Wetteland	.10
241	Todd Zeile	.10
242	Tony Batista	.10
243	Homer Bush	.10
244	Carlos Delgado	.50
245	Tony Fernandez	.10
246	Billy Koch	.10
247	Raul Mondesi	.10
248	Shannon Stewart	.10
249	David Wells	.10
250	Vernon Wells	.10

Premiere Date

Stars: 8-15X
Production 50 Sets

Copper

Stars: 2X
Inserted 1:1 H

Holographic Silver

Stars: 5-10X
Production 99 Sets

Platinum Blue

Stars: 6-12X
Production 67 Sets

Ruby Red

Stars: 1-2X
RC's: 1X
Inserted 9 per 7-11 pack.

Holographic Gold

Stars: 3-6X
Production 199 Sets

Emerald

Stars: 1-2X
Yng Stars & RC's: 1X
Inserted 1:1 7-11 pack.
Inserted 1:1 R
Stars: 1-2X
Yng Stars & Rc's: 1X

Holographic Green

Stars: 6-10X
Production 99 Sets, 7-11 insert.

Cooperstown Bound

	NM/M
Complete Set (10):	220.00
Common Player:	20.00
Inserted 1:361	
Proofs:	2X
Production 20 Sets, hobby only.	
Canvas Proofs:	Values Undetermined

Production One Set

1	Greg Maddux	20.00
2	Cal Ripken Jr.	40.00
3	Nomar Garciaparra	25.00
4	Sammy Sosa	25.00
5	Roger Clemens	30.00
6	Derek Jeter	40.00
7	Mark McGwire	30.00
8	Tony Gwynn	20.00
9	Ken Griffey Jr.	25.00
10	Alex Rodriguez	30.00

Double Vision

	NM/M
Complete Set (36):	220.00
Common Player:	3.00
Inserted 1:37	

1	Chipper Jones	8.00
2	Cal Ripken Jr.	15.00
3	Nomar Garciaparra	10.00
4	Pedro Martinez	6.00
5	Sammy Sosa	10.00
6	Manny Ramirez	6.00
7	Jeff Bagwell	6.00
8	Craig Biggio	3.00
9	Vladimir Guerrero	6.00
10	Mike Piazza	10.00
11	Roger Clemens	9.00
12	Derek Jeter	15.00
13	Mark McGwire	12.00
14	Tony Gwynn	8.00
15	Ken Griffey Jr.	10.00
16	Alex Rodriguez	12.00
17	Rafael Palmeiro	5.00
18	Ivan Rodriguez	5.00
19	Chipper Jones	8.00
20	Cal Ripken Jr.	15.00
21	Nomar Garciaparra	10.00
22	Pedro Martinez	6.00
23	Sammy Sosa	10.00
24	Manny Ramirez	6.00
25	Jeff Bagwell	6.00
26	Craig Biggio	3.00
27	Vladimir Guerrero	6.00
28	Mike Piazza	10.00
29	Roger Clemens	9.00
30	Derek Jeter	15.00

31	Mark McGwire	12.00
32	Tony Gwynn	8.00
33	Ken Griffey Jr.	10.00
34	Alex Rodriguez	12.00
35	Rafael Palmeiro	5.00
36	Ivan Rodriguez	5.00

Fielder's Choice

		NM/M
Complete Set (20):		150.00
Common Player:		3.00
Inserted 1:73		
Gold Parallel		
(10 Sets Issued):		6-8X
1	Andruw Jones	5.00
2	Chipper Jones	8.00
3	Greg Maddux	8.00
4	Cal Ripken Jr.	8.00
5	Nomar Garciaparra	10.00
6	Sammy Sosa	10.00
7	Sean Casey	3.00
8	Manny Ramirez	5.00
9	Larry Walker	3.00
10	Jeff Bagwell	5.00
11	Mike Piazza	10.00
12	Derek Jeter	20.00
13	Bernie Williams	3.00
14	Scott Rolen	4.00
15	Mark McGwire	15.00
16	Tony Gwynn	8.00
17	Barry Bonds	20.00
18	Ken Griffey Jr.	10.00
19	Alex Rodriguez	15.00
20	Ivan Rodriguez	4.00

Maximum Impact

		NM/M
Complete Set (20):		25.00
Common Player:		.50
Inserted 2:25 7-11 packs.		
1	Chipper Jones	2.00
2	Cal Ripken Jr.	4.00
3	Nomar Garciaparra	2.00
4	Pedro Martinez	1.50
5	Sammy Sosa	2.50
6	Manny Ramirez	1.50
7	Larry Walker	.50
8	Jeff Bagwell	1.50
9	Carlos Beltran	.75
10	Vladimir Guerrero	1.50
11	Mike Piazza	2.50
12	Derek Jeter	4.00
13	Roger Clemens	2.25
14	Mark McGwire	3.00
15	Tony Gwynn	2.00
16	Barry Bonds	4.00
17	Ken Griffey Jr.	2.50
18	Alex Rodriguez	3.00
19	Ivan Rodriguez	1.00
20	Carlos Delgado	.75

Season in Review

		NM/M
Complete Set (30):		25.00
Common Player:		.50
Inserted 2:37		
1	Randy Johnson	1.50
2	Matt Williams	.50
3	Chipper Jones	2.00
4	Greg Maddux	2.00
5	Cal Ripken Jr.	4.00
6	Nomar Garciaparra	2.50
7	Pedro Martinez	1.50
8	Sammy Sosa	2.50
9	Manny Ramirez	1.50
10	Larry Walker	1.50
11	Jeff Bagwell	1.50
12	Craig Biggio	1.50
13	Carlos Beltran	.75
14	Mark Quinn	.50
15	Vladimir Guerrero	1.50
16	Mike Piazza	2.50
17	Robin Ventura	.50
18	Roger Clemens	2.25
19	David Cone	.50
20	Derek Jeter	4.00
21	Mark McGwire	3.00
22	Fernando Tatis	.50
23	Tony Gwynn	2.00
24	Barry Bonds	4.00
25	Ken Griffey Jr.	2.50
26	Alex Rodriguez	3.00
27	Wade Boggs	2.00
28	Jose Canseco	.65
29	Rafael Palmeiro	1.00
30	Ivan Rodriguez	1.00

2000 Pacific Paramount Update

		NM/M
Complete Set (100):		10.00
Common Player:		.10
Production 12,500 Sets; retail		
exclusive		
1-U	Adam Kennedy	.10
2-U	Bengie Molina	.10
3-U	Derrick Turnbow	.10
4-U	Randy Johnson	.75
5-U	Danny Klassen	.10
6-U	Vicente Padilla	.10
7-U	Rafael Furcal	.10
8-U	Andres Galarraga	.10
9-U	Chipper Jones	1.00
10-U	Fernando Lunar	.10
11-U	Willie Morales	.10
12-U	Cal Ripken Jr.	2.00
13-U	B.J. Ryan	.10
14-U	Carl Everett	.10
15-U	Nomar Garciaparra	1.25
16-U	Pedro Martinez	.75
17-U	Wilton Veras	.10
18-U	Scott Downs	.10
19-U	Daniel Garibay	.10
20-U	Sammy Sosa	1.25
21-U	Julio Zuleta	.10
22-U	Josh Paul	.10
23-U	Frank Thomas	.75
24-U	Rob Bell	.10
25-U	Dante Bichette	.10
26-U	Travis Dawkins	.10
27-U	Ken Griffey Jr.	1.25
28-U	Chuck Finley	.10
29-U	Manny Ramirez	.75
30-U	Paul Rigdon	.10
31-U	Jeff Cirillo	.10
32-U	Larry Walker	.10
33-U	Masato Yoshii	.10
34-U	Robert Fick	.10
35-U	Jose Macias	.10
36-U	Juan Gonzalez	.75
37-U	Hideo Nomo	.75
38-U	Jason Grilli	.10
39-U	Pablo Ozuna	.10
40-U	Brad Penny	.10
41-U	Jeff Bagwell	.75
42-U	Lance Berkman	.10
43-U	Roger Cedeno	.10
44-U	Octavio Dotel	.10
45-U	Chad Durbin	.10
46-U	Eric Gagne	.10
47-U	Shawn Green	.35
48-U	Jose Hernandez	.10
49-U	Matt LeCroy	.10
50-U	Johan Santana	.10
51-U	Vladimir Guerrero	.75
52-U	Hideki Irabu	.10
53-U	Andrew Tracy	.10
54-U	Derek Bell	.10
55-U	Eric Cammack	.10
56-U	Mike Hampton	.10
57-U	Jay Payton	.10
58-U	Mike Piazza	1.25
59-U	Todd Zeile	.10
60-U	Roger Clemens	1.00
61-U	Darrell Einertson	.10
62-U	Derek Jeter	2.00
63-U	Jason Giambi	.60
64-U	Terrence Long	.10
65-U	Mark Mulder	.10
66-U	Adam Piatt	.10
67-U	Luis Vizcaino	.10
68-U	Pat Burrell	.35
69-U	Scott Rolen	.65
70-U	Chad Hermansen	.10
71-U	Rick Ankiel	.15
72-U	Jim Edmonds	.10
73-U	Mark McGwire	1.50
74-U	Gene Stechschulte	.10
75-U	Fernando Vina	.10
76-U	Bret Boone	.10
77-U	Tony Gwynn	1.00
78-U	Ryan Klesko	.10
79-U	David Newhan	.10
80-U	Kevin Walker	.10
81-U	Barry Bonds	2.00
82-U	Aaron Fultz	.10
83-U	Ben Weber	.10
84-U	Rickey Henderson	.75
85-U	Kevin Hodges	.10
86-U	John Olerud	.10
87-U	Robert Ramsay	.10
88-U	Alex Rodriguez	1.50
89-U	Kazuhiro Sasaki	.15
90-U	Vinny Castilla	.10
91-U	Jeff Sparks	.10
92-U	Greg Vaughn	.10
93-U	Francisco Cordero	.10
94-U	Gabe Kapler	.10
95-U	Mike Lamb	.10
96-U	Ivan Rodriguez	.65
97-U	Clayton Andrews	.10
98-U	Brad Fullmer	.10
99-U	Raul Mondesi	.10
100-U	Dewayne Wise	.10

2000 Pacific Prism

		NM/M
Complete Set (150):		10.00
Common Player:		.10
Pack (5):		1.50
Wax Box (24):		15.00
1	Jeff DaVanon RC	.10
2	Troy Glaus	.50
3	Tim Salmon	.15
4	Mo Vaughn	.50
5	Jay Bell	.10
6	Erubiel Durazo	.10
7	Luis Gonzalez	.20
8	Randy Johnson	.50
9	Matt Williams	.10
10	Andres Galarraga	.10
11	Andruw Jones	.50
12	Chipper Jones	.65
13	Brian Jordan	.10
14	Greg Maddux	.65
15	Kevin Millwood	.10
16	John Smoltz	.10
17	Albert Belle	.15
18	Mike Mussina	.25
19	Calvin Pickering	.10
20	Cal Ripken Jr.	1.50
21	B.J. Surhoff	.10
22	Nomar Garciaparra	1.00
23	Pedro Martinez	.50
24	Troy O'Leary	.10
25	John Valentin	.10
26	Jason Varitek	.10
27	Mark Grace	.15
28	Henry Rodriguez	.10
29	Sammy Sosa	1.00
30	Kerry Wood	.25
31	Ray Durham	.10
32	Carlos Lee	.10
33	Magglio Ordonez	.10
34	Chris Singleton	.10
35	Frank Thomas	.50
36	Sean Casey	.15
37	Travis Dawkins	.10
38	Barry Larkin	.10
39	Pokey Reese	.10
40	Scott Williamson	.10
41	Roberto Alomar	.20
42	Bartolo Colon	.10
43	David Justice	.10
44	Manny Ramirez	.50
45	Richie Sexson	.10
46	Jim Thome	.50
47	Omar Vizquel	.10
48	Pedro Astacio	.10
49	Todd Helton	.50
50	Neifi Perez	.10
51	Ben Petrick	.10
52	Larry Walker	.10
53	Tony Clark	.10
54	Damion Easley	.10
55	Juan Gonzalez	.50
56	Dean Palmer	.10
57	A.J. Burnett	.10
58	Luis Castillo	.10
59	Cliff Floyd	.10
60	Alex Gonzalez	.10
61	Preston Wilson	.10
62	Jeff Bagwell	.50
63	Craig Biggio	.10
64	Ken Caminiti	.10
65	Jose Lima	.10
66	Billy Wagner	.10
67	Carlos Beltran	.30
68	Johnny Damon	.25
69	Jermaine Dye	.10
70	Carlos Febles	.10
71	Mike Sweeney	.10
72	Kevin Brown	.10
73	Shawn Green	.25
74	Eric Karros	.10
75	Chan Ho Park	.10
76	Gary Sheffield	.30
77	Ron Belliard	.10
78	Jeromy Burnitz	.10
79	Marquis Grissom	.10
80	Geoff Jenkins	.10
81	Mark Loretta	.10
82	Ron Coomer	.10
83	Jacque Jones	.10
84	Corey Koskie	.10
85	Brad Radke	.10
86	Todd Walker	.10
87	Michael Barrett	.10
88	Peter Bergeron	.10
89	Vladimir Guerrero	.50
90	Jose Vidro	.10
91	Rondell White	.10
92	Edgardo Alfonzo	.10

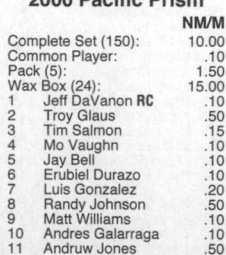

93	Rickey Henderson	.50
94	Rey Ordonez	.10
95	Mike Piazza	1.00
96	Robin Ventura	.10
97	Roger Clemens	.75
98	Orlando Hernandez	.10
99	Derek Jeter	1.50
100	Tino Martinez	.10
101	Mariano Rivera	.15
102	Alfonso Soriano	.50
103	Bernie Williams	.20
104	Eric Chavez	.15
105	Jason Giambi	.30
106	Ben Grieve	.10
107	Tim Hudson	.20
108	John Jaha	.10
109	Bobby Abreu	.10
110	Doug Glanville	.10
111	Mike Lieberthal	.10
112	Scott Rolen	.40
113	Curt Schilling	.25
114	Brian Giles	.10
115	Jason Kendall	.10
116	Warren Morris	.10
117	Kevin Young	.10
118	Rick Ankiel	.10
119	J.D. Drew	.15
120	Chad Hutchinson	.10
121	Ray Lankford	.10
122	Mark McGwire	1.25
123	Fernando Tatis	.10
124	Bret Boone	.10
125	Ben Davis	.10
126	Tony Gwynn	.65
127	Trevor Hoffman	.10
128	Barry Bonds	1.50
129	Ellis Burks	.10
130	Jeff Kent	.10
131	J.T. Snow	.10
132	Freddy Garcia	.10
133	Ken Griffey Jr.	1.00
134	Edgar Martinez	.10
135	John Olerud	.10
136	Alex Rodriguez	1.25
137	Jose Canseco	.20
138	Vinny Castilla	.10
139	Roberto Hernandez	.10
140	Fred McGriff	.10
141	Rusty Greer	.10
142	Ruben Mateo	.10
143	Rafael Palmeiro	.40
144	Ivan Rodriguez	.40
145	Lee Stevens	.10
146	Tony Batista	.10
147	Carlos Delgado	.35
148	Shannon Stewart	.10
149	David Wells	.10
150	Vernon Wells	.10

Texture Silver

	NM/M
Complete Set (150):	50.00
Common Player:	.50
Stars:	2-3X

(See 2000 Prism for checklist and base card values.)

Woodgrain Silver

	NM/M
Complete Set (150):	50.00
Common Player:	.50
Stars:	2-3X

(See 2000 Prism for checklist and base card values.)

Tinsel Silver

	NM/M
Complete Set (150):	50.00
Common Player:	.50
Stars:	2-3X

(See 2000 Prism for checklist and base card values.)

Rapture Gold

	NM/M
Complete Set (150):	50.00
Common Player:	.50
Stars:	2-3X

(See 2000 Prism for checklist and base card values.)

Holographic Purple

	NM/M
Common Player:	1.00
Stars:	6-8X

Production 99 Sets

Premiere Date

	NM/M
Common Player:	1.50
Stars:	8-10X

Production 61 Sets

Rapture Silver

	NM/M
Complete Set (150):	50.00
Common Player:	.50
Stars:	2-3X

(See 2000 Prism for checklist and base values.)

Holographic Blue

	NM/M
Common Player:	1.00
Stars:	4-6X

Production 80 Sets

Holographic Mirror

	NM/M
Common Player:	1.50
Stars:	4-6X

Production 160 Sets

Holographic Gold

	NM/M
Common Player:	.50
Stars:	2-4X

Production 480 Sets

Diamond Dial-A-Stats

	NM/M
Complete Set (10):	90.00
Common Player:	8.00

1	Chipper Jones	8.00
2	Greg Maddux	8.00
3	Cal Ripken Jr.	20.00
4	Sammy Sosa	10.00
5	Mike Piazza	10.00
6	Roger Clemens	9.00
7	Mark McGwire	15.00
8	Tony Gwynn	8.00
9	Ken Griffey Jr.	10.00
10	Alex Rodriguez	15.00

A.L. Legends

	NM/M
Complete Set (10):	15.00
Common Player:	.50
Inserted 1:25	

1	Mo Vaughn	.50
2	Cal Ripken Jr.	4.00
3	Nomar Garciaparra	2.50
4	Manny Ramirez	1.50
5	Roger Clemens	2.00
6	Derek Jeter	4.00
7	Ken Griffey Jr.	2.50
8	Alex Rodriguez	3.00
9	Jose Canseco	.75
10	Rafael Palmeiro	1.00

N.L. Legends

	NM/M
Complete Set (10):	15.00
Common Player:	.50
Inserted 1:25	

1	Chipper Jones	2.00
2	Greg Maddux	2.00
3	Sammy Sosa	2.50
4	Larry Walker	.50
5	Jeff Bagwell	1.00
6	Vladimir Guerrero	1.00
7	Mike Piazza	2.50
8	Mark McGwire	3.00
9	Tony Gwynn	2.00
10	Barry Bonds	4.00

Center Stage

	NM/M
Complete Set (20):	40.00
Common Player:	1.00
Inserted 1:25	

1	Chipper Jones	3.00
2	Cal Ripken Jr.	6.00
3	Nomar Garciaparra	4.00
4	Pedro Martinez	2.00
5	Sammy Sosa	4.00
6	Sean Casey	1.00
7	Manny Ramirez	2.00
8	Jim Thome	1.50
9	Jeff Bagwell	2.00
10	Carlos Beltran	1.50
11	Vladimir Guerrero	2.00
12	Mike Piazza	4.00
13	Derek Jeter	6.00
14	Bernie Williams	1.00
15	Scott Rolen	1.50
16	Mark McGwire	5.00
17	Tony Gwynn	3.00
18	Ken Griffey Jr.	4.00
19	Alex Rodriguez	5.00
20	Ivan Rodriguez	1.50

Prospects

	NM/M
Complete Set (10):	12.00
Common Player:	1.00
Inserted 1:97	

1	Erubiel Durazo	1.00
2	Wilton Veras	1.00
3	Ben Petrick	1.00
4	Mark Quinn	1.00
5	Peter Bergeron	1.00
6	Alfonso Soriano	5.00
7	Tim Hudson	2.00
8	Chad Hermansen	1.00
9	Rick Ankiel	1.50
10	Ruben Mateo	1.00

2000 Pacific Private Stock

	NM/M
Complete Set (150):	50.00
Common Player:	.15
Common SP Prospect:	1.00
Inserted 1:4	
Pack (7):	2.00
Wax Box (24):	35.00

1	Darin Erstad	.25
2	Troy Glaus	.75
3	Tim Salmon	.25
4	Mo Vaughn	.15
5	Jay Bell	.15
6	Luis Gonzalez	.25
7	Randy Johnson	.75
8	Matt Williams	.15
9	Andruw Jones	.75
10	Chipper Jones	1.00
11	Brian Jordan	.15
12	Greg Maddux	1.00
13	Kevin Millwood	.15
14	Albert Belle	.20
15	Mike Mussina	.35
16	Cal Ripken Jr.	2.00
17	B.J. Surhoff	.15
18	Nomar Garciaparra	1.25
19	Butch Huskey	.15
20	Pedro Martinez	.75
21	Troy O'Leary	.15
22	Mark Grace	.25
23	Bo Porter/SP	1.00
24	Henry Rodriguez	.15
25	Sammy Sosa	1.25
26	Kerry Wood	.40
27	Jason Dellaero/SP	1.00
28	Ray Durham	.15
29	Paul Konerko	.20
30	Carlos Lee	.15
31	Magglio Ordonez	.25
32	Frank Thomas	.75
33	Mike Cameron	.15
34	Sean Casey	.25
35	Barry Larkin	.25
36	Greg Vaughn	.15
37	Roberto Alomar	.40
38	Russell Branyan/SP	1.00
39	Kenny Lofton	.15
40	Manny Ramirez	.75
41	Richie Sexson	.15
42	Jim Thome	.75
43	Omar Vizquel	.15
44	Dante Bichette	.15
45	Vinny Castilla	.15
46	Todd Helton	.75
47	Ben Petrick/SP	1.00
48	Juan Sosa/SP	1.00
49	Larry Walker	.15
50	Tony Clark	.15
51	Damion Easley	.15
52	Juan Encarnacion	.15
53	Robert Fick/SP	1.00
54	Dean Palmer	.15
55	A.J. Burnett/SP	1.00
56	Luis Castillo	.15
57	Alex Gonzalez	.15
58	Julio Ramirez/SP	1.00
59	Preston Wilson	.15

60	Jeff Bagwell	.75
61	Craig Biggio	.15
62	Ken Caminiti	.15
63	Carl Everett	.15
64	Mike Hampton	.15
65	Billy Wagner	.15
66	Carlos Beltran	.50
67	Dermal Brown/SP	1.00
68	Jermaine Dye	.15
69	Carlos Febles	.15
70	Mark Quinn/SP	1.00
71	Mike Sweeney	.15
72	Kevin Brown	.15
73	Eric Gagne/SP	1.50
74	Eric Karros	.15
75	Raul Mondesi	.15
76	Gary Sheffield	.40
77	Jeromy Burnitz	.15
78	Jeff Cirillo	.15
79	Geoff Jenkins	.15
80	David Nilsson	.15
81	Ron Coomer	.15
82	Jacque Jones	.15
83	Corey Koskie	.15
84	Brad Radke	.15
85	Tony Armas Jr./SP	1.50
86	Peter Bergeron/SP	1.00
87	Vladimir Guerrero	.75
88	Jose Vidro	.15
89	Rondell White	.15
90	Edgardo Alfonzo	.15
91	Roger Cedeno	.15
92	Rickey Henderson	.75
93	Jay Payton/SP	1.00
94	Mike Piazza	1.25
95	Jorge Toca/SP	1.00
96	Robin Ventura	.15
97	Roger Clemens	1.00
98	David Cone	.15
99	Derek Jeter	2.00
100	D'Angelo Jimenez/SP	1.00
101	Tino Martinez	.15
102	Alfonso Soriano/SP	3.00
103	Bernie Williams	.25
104	Jason Giambi	.50
105	Ben Grieve	.15
106	Tim Hudson	.25
107	Matt Stairs	.15
108	Bobby Abreu	.15
109	Doug Glanville	.15
110	Scott Rolen	.65
111	Curt Schilling	.40
112	Brian Giles	.15
113	Chad Hermansen/SP	1.00
114	Jason Kendall	.15
115	Warren Morris	.15
116	Rick Ankiel/SP	1.00
117	J.D. Drew	.25
118	Adam Kennedy/SP	1.00
119	Ray Lankford	.15
120	Mark McGwire	1.50
121	Fernando Tatis	.15
122	Mike Darr/SP	1.00
123	Ben Davis	.15
124	Tony Gwynn	1.00
125	Trevor Hoffman	.15
126	Reggie Sanders	.15
127	Barry Bonds	2.00
128	Ellis Burks	.15
129	Jeff Kent	.15
130	J.T. Snow	.15
131	Freddy Garcia	.15
132	Ken Griffey Jr.	1.25
133	Carlos Guillen/SP	1.00
134	Edgar Martinez	.15
135	Alex Rodriguez	1.50
136	Miguel Cairo	.15
137	Jose Canseco	.40
138	Steve Cox/SP	1.00
139	Roberto Hernandez	.15
140	Fred McGriff	.15
141	Juan Gonzalez	.75
142	Rusty Greer	.15
143	Ruben Mateo/SP	1.00
144	Rafael Palmeiro	.65
145	Ivan Rodriguez	.65
146	Carlos Delgado	.50
147	Tony Fernandez	.15
148	Shawn Green	.35
149	Shannon Stewart	.15
150	Vernon Wells/SP	1.00

Premiere Date

Stars:	5-10X
Prospects:	1-2X
Inserted 1:24	

Gold Portraits

Stars:	5-10X
Prospects:	1-2X

Production 99 Sets

Silver Portraits

Stars:	3-6X
Prospects:	1-2X
Production 199 Sets	

Canvas

		NM/M
Complete Set (20):		120.00
Common Player:		2.00
Inserted 1:49		
1	Chipper Jones	8.00
2	Greg Maddux	8.00
3	Cal Ripken Jr.	15.00
4	Nomar Garciaparra	10.00
5	Sammy Sosa	10.00
6	Frank Thomas	6.00
7	Manny Ramirez	6.00
8	Larry Walker	2.00
9	Jeff Bagwell	6.00
10	Vladimir Guerrero	6.00
11	Mike Piazza	10.00
12	Roger Clemens	9.00
13	Derek Jeter	15.00
14	Mark McGwire	12.00
15	Tony Gwynn	8.00
16	Barry Bonds	15.00
17	Ken Griffey Jr.	10.00
18	Alex Rodriguez	12.00
19	Juan Gonzalez	6.00
20	Ivan Rodriguez	5.00

Extreme Action

		NM/M
Complete Set (20):		25.00
Common Player:		.50
Inserted 2:25		
1	Andruw Jones	1.50

2	Chipper Jones	2.00
3	Cal Ripken Jr.	4.00
4	Nomar Garciaparra	2.50
5	Sammy Sosa	2.50
6	Frank Thomas	1.50
7	Roberto Alomar	.60
8	Manny Ramirez	1.50
9	Larry Walker	.50
10	Jeff Bagwell	1.50
11	Vladimir Guerrero	1.50
12	Mike Piazza	2.50
13	Derek Jeter	4.00
14	Bernie Williams	.50
15	Scott Rolen	1.00
16	Mark McGwire	3.00
17	Tony Gwynn	2.00
18	Ken Griffey Jr.	2.50
19	Alex Rodriguez	3.00
20	Ivan Rodriguez	1.00

PS-2000

		NM/M
Complete Set (60):		15.00
Common Player:		.15
Inserted 2:Pack		
1	Mo Vaughn	.15
2	Greg Maddux	1.00
3	Andruw Jones	.75
4	Chipper Jones	1.00
5	Cal Ripken Jr.	2.50
6	Nomar Garciaparra	1.50
7	Pedro Martinez	.75
8	Sammy Sosa	1.50
9	Jason Dellaero	.15
10	Magglio Ordonez	.75
11	Frank Thomas	.75
12	Sean Casey	.25
13	Russell Branyan	.15
14	Manny Ramirez	.75
15	Richie Sexson	.15
16	Ben Petrick	.15
17	Juan Sosa	.15
18	Larry Walker	.15
19	Robert Fick	.15
20	Craig Biggio	.75
21	Jeff Bagwell	.75
22	Carlos Beltran	.50
23	Dermal Brown	.15
24	Mark Quinn	.15
25	Eric Gagne	.15
26	Jeromy Burnitz	.15
27	Tony Armas Jr.	.15
28	Peter Bergeron	.15
29	Vladimir Guerrero	.75
30	Edgardo Alfonzo	.15
31	Mike Piazza	1.50

32	Jorge Toca	.15
33	Roger Clemens	1.25
34	Alfonso Soriano	.65
35	Bernie Williams	.25
36	Derek Jeter	2.50
37	Tim Hudson	.25
38	Bobby Abreu	.15
39	Scott Rolen	.65
40	Brian Giles	.15
41	Chad Hermansen	.15
42	Warren Morris	.15
43	Rick Ankiel	.15
44	J.D. Drew	.25
45	Adam Kennedy	.15
46	Mark McGwire	2.00
47	Mike Darr	.15
48	Tony Gwynn	1.00
49	Barry Bonds	2.50
50	Ken Griffey Jr.	1.50
51	Carlos Guillen	.15
52	Alex Rodriguez	1.50
53	Juan Gonzalez	.75
54	Ruben Mateo	.15
55	Ivan Rodriguez	.65
56	Rafael Palmeiro	.65
57	Jose Canseco	.40
58	Steve Cox	.15
59	Shawn Green	.30
60	Vernon Wells	.15

PS-2000 Stars

		NM/M
Complete Set (20):		40.00
Common Player:		1.00
Production 299 Sets		
1	Mo Vaughn	1.00
2	Greg Maddux	4.00
3	Cal Ripken Jr.	8.00
4	Pedro Martinez	3.00
5	Sammy Sosa	5.00
6	Frank Thomas	3.00
7	Larry Walker	1.00
8	Craig Biggio	1.00
9	Jeff Bagwell	3.00
10	Mike Piazza	5.00
11	Roger Clemens	4.50
12	Bernie Williams	1.00
13	Mark McGwire	6.00
14	Tony Gwynn	4.00
15	Barry Bonds	8.00
16	Ken Griffey Jr.	5.00
17	Juan Gonzalez	3.00
18	Ivan Rodriguez	2.00
19	Rafael Palmeiro	2.00
20	Jose Canseco	1.50

PS-2000 New Wave

		NM/M
Complete Set (20):		40.00
Common Player:		1.00
Production 199 Sets		
1	Andruw Jones	3.50
2	Chipper Jones	5.00
3	Nomar Garciaparra	6.00
4	Magglio Ordonez	1.00
5	Sean Casey	1.00
6	Manny Ramirez	3.50
7	Richie Sexson	1.00
8	Carlos Beltran	2.00
9	Jeromy Burnitz	1.00
10	Vladimir Guerrero	3.50
11	Edgardo Alfonzo	1.00
12	Derek Jeter	10.00
13	Tim Hudson	1.00
14	Bobby Abreu	1.00
15	Scott Rolen	2.50
16	Brian Giles	1.00
17	Warren Morris	1.00

18	J.D. Drew	1.25
19	Alex Rodriguez	8.00
20	Shawn Green	1.25

PS-2000 Rookies

		NM/M
Complete Set (20):		20.00
Common Player:		1.00
Inserted 99 Sets		
1	Jason Dellaero	1.00
2	Russell Branyan	1.00
3	Ben Petrick	1.00
4	Juan Sosa	1.00
5	Robert Fick	1.00
6	Dermal Brown	1.00
7	Mark Quinn	1.00
8	Eric Gagne	1.50
9	Tony Armas Jr.	1.00
10	Peter Bergeron	1.00
11	Jorge Toca	1.00
12	Alfonso Soriano	6.00
13	Chad Hermansen	1.00
14	Rick Ankiel	1.00
15	Adam Kennedy	1.50
16	Mike Darr	1.00
17	Carlos Guillen	1.00
18	Steve Cox	1.00
19	Ruben Mateo	1.00
20	Vernon Wells	1.50

Reserve

		NM/M
Complete Set (20):		50.00
Common Player:		1.00
Inserted 1:25		
1	Chipper Jones	3.00
2	Greg Maddux	3.00
3	Cal Ripken Jr.	6.00
4	Nomar Garciaparra	4.00
5	Sammy Sosa	4.00
6	Frank Thomas	2.00
7	Manny Ramirez	2.00
8	Larry Walker	1.00
9	Jeff Bagwell	2.00
10	Vladimir Guerrero	2.00
11	Mike Piazza	4.00
12	Roger Clemens	3.50
13	Derek Jeter	6.00
14	Mark McGwire	5.00
15	Tony Gwynn	3.00
16	Barry Bonds	6.00
17	Ken Griffey Jr.	4.00
18	Alex Rodriguez	5.00
19	Ivan Rodriguez	1.50
20	Shawn Green	1.25

2000 Pacific Revolution

	NM/M
Complete Set (150):	60.00

Common Player:		.25
Common SP:		1.00
Pack (3):		2.00
Box:		35.00
1	Darin Erstad	.50
2	Troy Glaus	1.00
3	Adam Kennedy/SP	1.50
4	Mo Vaughn	.25
5	Erubiel Durazo	.25
6	Steve Finley	.25
7	Luis Gonzalez	.35
8	Randy Johnson	1.00
9	Travis Lee	.25
10	Vicente Padilla/SP	1.00
11	Matt Williams	.25
12	Rafael Furcal/SP	1.00
13	Andres Galarraga	.25
14	Andruw Jones	1.00
15	Chipper Jones	1.50
16	Greg Maddux	1.50
17	Luis Rivera/SP	1.00
18	Albert Belle	.25
19	Mike Bordick	.25
20	Will Clark	.35
21	Mike Mussina	.40
22	Cal Ripken Jr.	3.00
23	B.J. Surhoff	.25
24	Carl Everett	.25
25	Nomar Garciaparra	2.00
26	Pedro Martinez	1.00
27	Jason Varitek	.25
28	Wilton Veras/SP	1.00
29	Shane Andrews	.25
30	Scott Downs/SP RC	1.00
31	Mark Grace	.35
32	Sammy Sosa	2.00
33	Kerry Wood	.50
34	Ray Durham	.25
35	Paul Konerko	.35
36	Carlos Lee	.25
37	Magglio Ordonez	.25
38	Frank Thomas	1.00
39	Rob Bell/SP	1.00
40	Sean Casey	.40
41	Ken Griffey Jr.	2.00
42	Barry Larkin	.25
43	Pokey Reese	.25
44	Roberto Alomar	.40
45	David Justice	.25
46	Kenny Lofton	.25
47	Manny Ramirez	1.00
48	Richie Sexson	.25
49	Jim Thome	1.00
50	Jeff Cirillo	.25
51	Jeffrey Hammonds	.25
52	Todd Helton	1.00
53	Larry Walker	.25
54	Tony Clark	.25
55	Juan Gonzalez	1.00
56	Hideo Nomo	1.00
57	Dean Palmer	.25
58	Alex Gonzalez	.25
59	Mike Lowell	.25
60	Pablo Ozuna/SP	1.00
61	Brad Penny/SP	1.00
62	Preston Wilson	.25
63	Moises Alou	.25
64	Jeff Bagwell	1.00
65	Craig Biggio	.25
66	Ken Caminiti	.25
67	Julio Lugo/SP	1.00
68	Carlos Beltran	.60
69	Johnny Damon	.40
70	Jermaine Dye	.25
71	Carlos Febles	.25
72	Mark Quinn/SP	1.00
73	Kevin Brown	.25
74	Shawn Green	.65
75	Chan Ho Park	.25
76	Gary Sheffield	.50
77	Kevin Barker/SP	1.00
78	Ron Belliard	.25
79	Jeromy Burnitz	.25
80	Geoff Jenkins	.25
81	Cristian Guzman	.25
82	Jacque Jones	.25
83	Corey Koskie	.25
84	Matt Lawton	.25
85	Peter Bergeron/SP	1.00
86	Vladimir Guerrero	1.00
87	Andy Tracy/SP	1.00
88	Jose Vidro	.25
89	Rondell White	.25
90	Edgardo Alfonzo	.25
91	Derek Bell	.25
92	Eric Cammack/SP	1.00
93	Mike Piazza	2.00
94	Robin Ventura	.25
95	Roger Clemens	1.75
96	Orlando Hernandez	.25
97	Derek Jeter	3.00
98	Tino Martinez	.25
99	Alfonso Soriano/SP	3.00
100	Bernie Williams	.35

101	Eric Chavez	.35
102	Jason Giambi	.75
103	Ben Grieve	.25
104	Terrence Long/SP	1.00
105	Mark Mulder/SP	1.00
106	Adam Piatt/SP	1.00
107	Bobby Abreu	.25
108	Rico Brogna	.25
109	Doug Glanville	.25
110	Mike Lieberthal	.25
111	Scott Rolen	.75
112	Brian Giles	.25
113	Chad Hermansen/SP	1.00
114	Jason Kendall	.25
115	Warren Morris	.25
116	Rick Ankiel/SP	1.00
117	J.D. Drew	.40
118	Jim Edmonds	.25
119	Mark McGwire	2.50
120	Fernando Tatis	.25
121	Fernando Vina	.25
122	Tony Gwynn	1.50
123	Trevor Hoffman	.25
124	Ryan Klesko	.25
125	Eric Owens	.25
126	Barry Bonds	3.00
127	Ellis Burks	.25
128	Bobby Estalella	.25
129	Jeff Kent	.25
130	Scott Linebrink/SP RC	1.00
131	Jay Buhner	.25
132	Stan Javier	.25
133	Edgar Martinez	.25
134	John Olerud	.25
135	Alex Rodriguez	2.50
136	Kazuhiro Sasaki/SP RC	2.00
137	Jose Canseco	.40
138	Vinny Castilla	.25
139	Fred McGriff	.25
140	Greg Vaughn	.25
141	Gabe Kapler	.25
142	Mike Lamb/SP RC	1.00
143	Ruben Mateo	.25
144	Rafael Palmeiro	.75
145	Ivan Rodriguez	.75
146	Tony Batista	.25
147	Jose Cruz Jr.	.25
148	Carlos Delgado	.75
149	Brad Fullmer	.25
150	Raul Mondesi	.25

Red

Stars:	1-2X
SP's:	1X
Production 299 Sets	

Shadow

Stars:	3-6X
SP's:	1-2X
Production 99 Sets	

Foul Pole Net-Fusions

		NM/M
Complete Set (20):		110.00
Common Player:		2.00
Inserted 1:49		
1	Chipper Jones	8.00
2	Cal Ripken Jr.	15.00
3	Nomar Garciaparra	10.00
4	Pedro Martinez	6.00
5	Sammy Sosa	10.00

6	Frank Thomas	6.00
7	Ken Griffey Jr.	10.00
8	Manny Ramirez	6.00
9	Jeff Bagwell	6.00
10	Shawn Green	3.00
11	Vladimir Guerrero	6.00
12	Mike Piazza	10.00
13	Derek Jeter	15.00
14	Bernie Williams	2.00
15	Rick Ankiel	2.00
16	Mark McGwire	12.00
17	Tony Gwynn	8.00
18	Barry Bonds	15.00
19	Alex Rodriguez	12.00
20	Ivan Rodriguez	5.00

Game-Ball Signatures

		NM/M
Common Player:		5.00
1	Randy Johnson	40.00
2	Greg Maddux	90.00
3	Rafael Furcal	7.50
4	Shane Andrews	5.00
5	Sean Casey	10.00
6	Travis Dawkins	5.00
7	Alex Gonzalez	5.00
8	Shane Reynolds	5.00
9	Eric Gagne	10.00
10	Kevin Barker	5.00
11	Eric Milton	5.00
12	Mark Quinn	5.00
13	Alfonso Soriano	40.00
14	Brian Giles	6.00
15	Mark Mulder	10.00
16	Adam Piatt	5.00
17	Warren Morris	5.00
18	Rick Ankiel	6.00
19	Adam Kennedy	5.00
20	Fernando Tatis	5.00
21	Barry Bonds	100.00
22	Alex Rodriguez	75.00
23	Ruben Mateo	5.00
24	Billy Koch	5.00
25	Brad Penny	5.00

Icons

		NM/M
Complete Set (20):		250.00
Common Player:		8.00
Inserted 1:121		
1	Randy Johnson	10.00
2	Chipper Jones	15.00
3	Greg Maddux	15.00
4	Cal Ripken Jr.	30.00
5	Nomar Garciaparra	20.00
6	Pedro Martinez	10.00
7	Sammy Sosa	20.00
8	Frank Thomas	10.00
9	Ken Griffey Jr.	20.00
10	Juan Gonzalez	10.00
11	Jeff Bagwell	10.00

12	Vladimir Guerrero	10.00
13	Mike Piazza	20.00
14	Roger Clemens	17.50
15	Derek Jeter	30.00
16	Mark McGwire	25.00
17	Tony Gwynn	15.00
18	Barry Bonds	30.00
19	Alex Rodriguez	25.00
20	Ivan Rodriguez	8.00

On Deck

		NM/M
Complete Set (20):		40.00
Common Player:		1.00
Inserted 1:25		
1	Chipper Jones	3.00
2	Cal Ripken Jr.	6.00
3	Nomar Garciaparra	4.00
4	Sammy Sosa	4.00
5	Frank Thomas	2.00
6	Ken Griffey Jr.	4.00
7	Manny Ramirez	2.00
8	Larry Walker	1.00
9	Juan Gonzalez	2.00
10	Jeff Bagwell	2.00
11	Shawn Green	1.50
12	Vladimir Guerrero	2.00
13	Mike Piazza	4.00
14	Derek Jeter	6.00
15	Scott Rolen	1.50
16	Mark McGwire	5.00
17	Tony Gwynn	3.00
18	Alex Rodriguez	5.00
19	Jose Canseco	1.50
20	Ivan Rodriguez	1.75

Season Opener

		NM/M
Complete Set (36):		35.00
Common Player:		.50
Inserted 2:25		
1	Erubiel Durazo	.50
2	Randy Johnson	1.50
3	Andruw Jones	1.50
4	Chipper Jones	2.00
5	Greg Maddux	2.00
6	Cal Ripken Jr.	4.00
7	Nomar Garciaparra	3.00
8	Pedro Martinez	1.50
9	Sammy Sosa	2.50
10	Frank Thomas	1.50
11	Magglio Ordonez	.50
12	Ken Griffey Jr.	2.50
13	Barry Larkin	.50
14	Kenny Lofton	.50
15	Manny Ramirez	1.50
16	Jim Thome	1.50
17	Larry Walker	.50
18	Juan Gonzalez	1.50
19	Jeff Bagwell	1.50
20	Craig Biggio	.50
21	Carlos Beltran	.75
22	Shawn Green	.75
23	Vladimir Guerrero	1.50
24	Mike Piazza	2.50
25	Orlando Hernandez	.50
26	Derek Jeter	4.00
27	Bernie Williams	.50
28	Eric Chavez	.50
29	Scott Rolen	1.00
30	Jim Edmonds	.50

31	Tony Gwynn	2.00
32	Barry Bonds	4.00
33	Alex Rodriguez	3.00
34	Jose Canseco	.65
35	Ivan Rodriguez	1.00
36	Rafael Palmeiro	1.00

Triple Header

		NM/M
Complete Set (30):		25.00
Common Player:		.25
Inserted 4:25		
Parallel (1-10):		3-6X
99 Sets Produced		
Parallel (11-20):		3-6X
99 Sets Produced		
Parallel (21-30):		1-2X
599 Sets Produced		
1	Chipper Jones	1.50
2	Cal Ripken Jr.	3.00
3	Nomar Garciaparra	2.00
4	Frank Thomas	1.00
5	Larry Walker	.25
6	Vladimir Guerrero	1.00
7	Mike Piazza	2.00
8	Derek Jeter	3.00
9	Tony Gwynn	1.50
10	Ivan Rodriguez	.75
11	Sammy Sosa	2.00
12	Ken Griffey Jr.	2.00
13	Manny Ramirez	1.00
14	Jeff Bagwell	1.00
15	Shawn Green	.40
16	Mark McGwire	2.50
17	Barry Bonds	3.00
18	Alex Rodriguez	2.50
19	Jose Canseco	.50
20	Rafael Palmeiro	.75
21	Randy Johnson	1.00
22	Tom Glavine	.40
23	Greg Maddux	1.50
24	Mike Mussina	.40
25	Pedro Martinez	1.00
26	Kerry Wood	.60
27	Chuck Finley	.25
28	Kevin Brown	.25
29	Roger Clemens	1.75
30	Rick Ankiel	.25

2000 Pacific Vanguard

		NM/M
Complete Set (100):		30.00
Common Player:		.15
Pack (4):		2.00
Wax Box (24):		35.00
1	Troy Glaus	1.00
2	Tim Salmon	.25
3	Mo Vaughn	.15
4	Albert Belle	.15
5	Mike Mussina	.35
6	Cal Ripken Jr.	3.00

7	Nomar Garciaparra	2.00
8	Pedro Martinez	1.00
9	Troy O'Leary	.15
10	Wilton Veras	.15
11	Magglio Ordonez	.15
12	Chris Singleton	.15
13	Frank Thomas	1.00
14	Roberto Alomar	.40
15	Russell Branyan	.15
16	Manny Ramirez	1.00
17	Jim Thome	.75
18	Omar Vizquel	.15
19	Tony Clark	.15
20	Juan Gonzalez	1.00
21	Dean Palmer	.15
22	Carlos Beltran	.50
23	Johnny Damon	.30
24	Jermaine Dye	.15
25	Mark Quinn	.15
26	Jacque Jones	.15
27	Corey Koskie	.15
28	Brad Radke	.15
29	Roger Clemens	1.75
30	Derek Jeter	3.00
31	Alfonso Soriano	.75
32	Bernie Williams	.30
33	Eric Chavez	.30
34	Jason Giambi	.75
35	Ben Grieve	.15
36	Tim Hudson	.30
37	Mike Cameron	.15
38	Freddy Garcia	.15
39	Edgar Martinez	.15
40	Alex Rodriguez	2.50
41	Jose Canseco	.50
42	Vinny Castilla	.15
43	Fred McGriff	.15
44	Rusty Greer	.15
45	Ruben Mateo	.15
46	Rafael Palmeiro	.75
47	Ivan Rodriguez	.65
48	Carlos Delgado	.75
49	Shannon Stewart	.15
50	Vernon Wells	.15
51	Erubiel Durazo	.15
52	Randy Johnson	1.00
53	Matt Williams	.15
54	Andruw Jones	1.00
55	Chipper Jones	1.50
56	Greg Maddux	1.50
57	Mark Grace	.25
58	Sammy Sosa	2.00
59	Kerry Wood	.50
60	Sean Casey	.25
61	Ken Griffey Jr.	2.00
62	Barry Larkin	.15
63	Todd Helton	1.00
64	Ben Petrick	.15
65	Larry Walker	.15
66	Luis Castillo	.15
67	Alex Gonzalez	.15
68	Preston Wilson	.15
69	Jeff Bagwell	1.00
70	Craig Biggio	.15
71	Billy Wagner	.15
72	Kevin Brown	.15
73	Shawn Green	.40
74	Gary Sheffield	.40
75	Kevin Barker	.15
76	Ron Belliard	.15
77	Jeromy Burnitz	.15
78	Michael Barrett	.15
79	Peter Bergeron	.15
80	Vladimir Guerrero	1.00
81	Edgardo Alfonzo	.15
82	Rey Ordonez	.15
83	Mike Piazza	2.00
84	Robin Ventura	.15
85	Bobby Abreu	.15
86	Mike Lieberthal	.15
87	Scott Rolen	.75
88	Brian Giles	.15
89	Chad Hermansen	.15
90	Jason Kendall	.15
91	Rick Ankiel	.15
92	J.D. Drew	.25
93	Mark McGwire	2.50
94	Fernando Tatis	.15
95	Ben Davis	.15
96	Tony Gwynn	1.50
97	Trevor Hoffman	.15
98	Barry Bonds	3.00
99	Ellis Burks	.15
100	Jeff Kent	.15

Green

A.L. (1-50):	3-6X
Production 99 Sets	
N.L. (51-100):	2-4X
Production 199 Sets	

Gold

A.L. (1-50):	2-4X
Production 199 Sets R	

N.L. (51-100):	3-6X
Production 99 Sets R	

Premiere Date

Stars:	3-5X
Production 135 Sets H	

Purple

Production 10 Sets
Values Undetermined

A.L. Vanguard Press

		NM/M
Complete Set (10):		10.00
Common Player:		.65
Inserted 2:25		
1	Cal Ripken Jr.	3.00
2	Nomar Garciaparra	2.00
3	Pedro Martinez	1.00
4	Manny Ramirez	1.00
5	Carlos Beltran	.65
6	Roger Clemens	1.50
7	Derek Jeter	3.00
8	Alex Rodriguez	2.50
9	Rafael Palmeiro	.75
10	Ivan Rodriguez	.75

N.L. Vanguard Press

Guerrero sets Expos' homer record

Above: The Expos count on Vladimir to drive the Montreal offense.

		NM/M
Complete Set (10):		10.00
Common Player:		.50
Inserted 2:37		
1	Chipper Jones	1.50
2	Greg Maddux	1.50
3	Sammy Sosa	2.00
4	Ken Griffey Jr.	2.00
5	Larry Walker	.50
6	Jeff Bagwell	1.00
7	Vladimir Guerrero	1.00
8	Mike Piazza	2.00
9	Mark McGwire	2.50
10	Tony Gwynn	1.50

Cosmic Force

		NM/M
Complete Set (10):		30.00
Common Player:		3.00
Inserted 1:73		
1	Chipper Jones	3.00

2	Cal Ripken Jr.	6.00
3	Nomar Garciaparra	4.00
4	Sammy Sosa	4.00
5	Ken Griffey Jr.	4.00
6	Mike Piazza	4.00
7	Derek Jeter	6.00
8	Mark McGwire	5.00
9	Tony Gwynn	3.00
10	Alex Rodriguez	5.00

Diamond Architects

NM/M

Complete Set (20): 25.00
Common Player: .50
Inserted 1:25

1	Chipper Jones	2.00
2	Greg Maddux	2.00
3	Cal Ripken Jr.	4.00
4	Nomar Garciaparra	2.50
5	Sammy Sosa	2.50
6	Ken Griffey Jr.	2.50
7	Manny Ramirez	1.50
8	Larry Walker	.50
9	Jeff Bagwell	1.50
10	Vladimir Guerrero	1.50
11	Mike Piazza	2.50
12	Roger Clemens	2.25
13	Derek Jeter	4.00
14	Bernie Williams	.50
15	Scott Rolen	1.00
16	Mark McGwire	3.00
17	Tony Gwynn	2.00
18	Alex Rodriguez	3.00
19	Rafael Palmeiro	1.00
20	Ivan Rodriguez	.75

Game Worn Jersey

NM/M

Inserted 1:120

1	Greg Maddux	10.00
2	Tony Gwynn	10.00
3	Alex Rodriguez	20.00
4	Frank Thomas	8.00
5	Chipper Jones	10.00

High Voltage

NM/M

Complete Set (36): 10.00
Common Player: .15
Inserted 1:1

1	Mo Vaughn	.15
2	Erubiel Durazo	.15
3	Randy Johnson	.60
4	Andruw Jones	.60
5	Chipper Jones	.75
6	Greg Maddux	.75
7	Cal Ripken Jr.	2.00
8	Nomar Garciaparra	1.25
9	Pedro Martinez	.60

10	Sammy Sosa	1.25
11	Frank Thomas	.60
12	Sean Casey	.25
13	Ken Griffey Jr.	1.25
14	Barry Larkin	.15
15	Manny Ramirez	.60
16	Jim Thome	.50
17	Larry Walker	.15
18	Jeff Bagwell	.60
19	Craig Biggio	.15
20	Carlos Beltran	.40
21	Shawn Green	.25
22	Vladimir Guerrero	.60
23	Edgardo Alfonzo	.15
24	Mike Piazza	1.50
25	Roger Clemens	1.00
26	Derek Jeter	2.00
27	Bernie Williams	.25
28	Scott Rolen	.60
29	Brian Giles	.15
30	Rick Ankiel	.15
31	Mark McGwire	1.50
32	Tony Gwynn	.75
33	Barry Bonds	2.00
34	Alex Rodriguez	1.50
35	Rafael Palmeiro	.60
36	Ivan Rodriguez	.60

2001 Pacific

NM/M

Complete Set (500): 40.00
Common Player: .10
Pack (12): 1.00
Box (36): 25.00

1	Garret Anderson	.10
2	Gary DiSarcina	.10
3	Darin Erstad	.25
4	Seth Etherton	.10
5	Ron Gant	.10
6	Troy Glaus	.75
7	Shigetosi Hasegawa	.10
8	Adam Kennedy	.10
9	Ben Molina	.10
10	Ramon Ortiz	.10
11	Troy Percival	.10
12	Tim Salmon	.20
13	Scott Schoeneweis	.10
14	Mo Vaughn	.10
15	Jarrod Washburn	.10
16	Brian Anderson	.10
17	Danny Bautista	.10
18	Jay Bell	.10
19	Greg Colbrunn	.10
20	Erubiel Durazo	.10
21	Steve Finley	.10
22	Luis Gonzalez	.20
23	Randy Johnson	.75
24	Byung-Hyun Kim	.10
25	Matt Mantei	.10
26	Armando Reynoso	.10
27	Todd Stottlemyre	.10
28	Matt Williams	.10
29	Tony Womack	.10
30	Andy Ashby	.10
31	Bobby Bonilla	.10
32	Rafael Furcal	.10
33	Andres Galarraga	.10
34	Tom Glavine	.35
35	Andruw Jones	.75
36	Chipper Jones	1.00
37	Brian Jordan	.10
38	Wally Joyner	.10
39	Keith Lockhart	.10
40	Javy Lopez	.10
41	Greg Maddux	1.00
42	Kevin Millwood	.10
43	John Rocker	.10
44	Reggie Sanders	.10
45	John Smoltz	.10
46	B.J. Surhoff	.10
47	Quilvio Veras	.10
48	Walt Weiss	.10

49	Brady Anderson	.10
50	Albert Belle	.15
51	Jeff Conine	.10
52	Delino DeShields	.10
53	Brook Fordyce	.10
54	Jerry Hairston Jr.	.10
55	Mark Lewis	.10
56	Luis Matos	.10
57	Melvin Mora	.10
58	Mike Mussina	.35
59	Chris Richard	.10
60	Cal Ripken Jr.	2.00
61	Manny Alexander	.10
62	Rolando Arrojo	.10
63	Midre Cummings	.10
64	Carl Everett	.10
65	Nomar Garciaparra	1.25
66	Mike Lansing	.10
67	Darren Lewis	.10
68	Derek Lowe	.10
69	Pedro Martinez	.75
70	Ramon Martinez	.10
71	Trot Nixon	.10
72	Troy O'Leary	.10
73	Jose Offerman	.10
74	Tomo Ohka	.10
75	Jason Varitek	.10
76	Rick Aguilera	.10
77	Shane Andrews	.10
78	Brant Brown	.10
79	Damon Buford	.10
80	Joe Girardi	.10
81	Mark Grace	.20
82	Willie Greene	.10
83	Ricky Gutierrez	.10
84	Jon Lieber	.10
85	Sammy Sosa	1.25
86	Kevin Tapani	.10
87	Rondell White	.10
88	Kerry Wood	.50
89	Eric Young	.10
90	Harold Baines	.10
91	James Baldwin	.10
92	Ray Durham	.10
93	Cal Eldred	.10
94	Keith Foulke	.10
95	Charles Johnson	.10
96	Paul Konerko	.20
97	Carlos Lee	.10
98	Magglio Ordonez	.10
99	Jim Parque	.10
100	Herbert Perry	.10
101	Chris Singleton	.10
102	Mike Sirotka	.10
103	Frank Thomas	.75
104	Jose Valentin	.10
105	Rob Bell	.10
106	Aaron Boone	.10
107	Sean Casey	.20
108	Danny Graves	.10
109	Ken Griffey Jr.	1.25
110	Pete Harnisch	.10
111	Brian L. Hunter	.10
112	Barry Larkin	.10
113	Pokey Reese	.10
114	Benito Santiago	.10
115	Chris Stynes	.10
116	Michael Tucker	.10
117	Ron Villone	.10
118	Scott Williamson	.10
119	Dmitri Young	.10
120	Roberto Alomar	.35
121	Sandy Alomar Jr.	.10
122	Russell Branyan	.10
123	Dave Burba	.10
124	Bartolo Colon	.10
125	Wil Cordero	.10
126	Einar Diaz	.10
127	Chuck Finley	.10
128	Travis Fryman	.10
129	Kenny Lofton	.10
130	Charles Nagy	.10
131	Manny Ramirez	.75
132	David Segui	.10
133	Jim Thome	.65
134	Omar Vizquel	.10
135	Brian Bohanon	.10
136	Jeff Cirillo	.10
137	Jeff Frye	.10
138	Jeffrey Hammonds	.10
139	Todd Helton	.75
140	Todd Hollandsworth	.10
141	Jose Jimenez	.10
142	Brent Mayne	.10
143	Neifi Perez	.10
144	Ben Petrick	.10
145	Juan Pierre	.10
146	Larry Walker	.10
147	Todd Walker	.10
148	Masato Yoshii	.10
149	Brad Ausmus	.10
150	Rich Becker	.10
151	Tony Clark	.10
152	Deivi Cruz	.10

153	Damion Easley	.10
154	Juan Encarnacion	.10
155	Robert Fick	.10
156	Juan Gonzalez	.75
157	Bobby Higginson	.10
158	Todd Jones	.10
159	Wendell Magee Jr.	.10
160	Brian Moehler	.10
161	Hideo Nomo	.75
162	Dean Palmer	.10
163	Jeff Weaver	.10
164	Antonio Alfonseca	.10
165	David Berg	.10
166	A.J. Burnett	.10
167	Luis Castillo	.10
168	Ryan Dempster	.10
169	Cliff Floyd	.10
170	Alex Gonzalez	.10
171	Mark Kotsay	.10
172	Derrek Lee	.10
173	Mike Lowell	.10
174	Mike Redmond	.10
175	Henry Rodriguez	.10
176	Jesus Sanchez	.10
177	Preston Wilson	.10
178	Moises Alou	.10
179	Jeff Bagwell	.75
180	Glen Barker	.10
181	Lance Berkman	.10
182	Craig Biggio	.10
183	Tim Bogar	.10
184	Ken Caminiti	.10
185	Roger Cedeno	.10
186	Scott Elarton	.10
187	Tony Eusebio	.10
188	Richard Hidalgo	.10
189	Jose Lima	.10
190	Mitch Meluskey	.10
191	Shane Reynolds	.10
192	Bill Spiers	.10
193	Billy Wagner	.10
194	Daryle Ward	.10
195	Carlos Beltran	.40
196	Ricky Bottalico	.25
197	Johnny Damon	.10
198	Jermaine Dye	.10
199	Jorge Fabregas	.10
200	David McCarty	.10
201	Mark Quinn	.10
202	Joe Randa	.10
203	Jeff Reboulet	.10
204	Rey Sanchez	.10
205	Blake Stein	.10
206	Jeff Suppan	.10
207	Mac Suzuki	.10
208	Mike Sweeney	.10
209	Gregg Zaun	.10
210	Adrian Beltre	.25
211	Kevin Brown	.10
212	Alex Cora	.10
213	Darren Dreifort	.10
214	Tom Goodwin	.10
215	Shawn Green	.30
216	Mark Grudzielanek	.10
217	Todd Hundley	.10
218	Eric Karros	.10
219	Chad Kreuter	.10
220	Jim Leyritz	.10
221	Chan Ho Park	.10
222	Jeff Shaw	.10
223	Gary Sheffield	.25
224	Devon White	.10
225	Ron Belliard	.10
226	Henry Blanco	.10
227	Jeromy Burnitz	.10
228	Jeff D'Amico	.10
229	Marquis Grissom	.10
230	Charlie Hayes	.10
231	Jimmy Haynes	.10
232	Tyler Houston	.10
233	Geoff Jenkins	.10
234	Mark Loretta	.10
235	James Mouton	.10
236	Richie Sexson	.10
237	Jamey Wright	.10
238	Jay Canizaro	.10
239	Ron Coomer	.10
240	Cristian Guzman	.10
241	Denny Hocking	.10
242	Torii Hunter	.10
243	Jacque Jones	.10
244	Corey Koskie	.10
245	Matt Lawton	.10
246	Matt LeCroy	.10
247	Eric Milton	.10
248	David Ortiz	.25
249	Brad Radke	.10
250	Mark Redman	.10
251	Michael Barrett	.10
252	Peter Bergeron	.10
253	Milton Bradley	.10
254	Orlando Cabrera	.10
255	Vladimir Guerrero	.75
256	Wilton Guerrero	.10

257	Dustin Hermanson	.10
258	Hideki Irabu	.10
259	Fernando Seguignol	.10
260	Lee Stevens	.10
261	Andy Tracy	.10
262	Javier Vazquez	.10
263	Jose Vidro	.10
264	Edgardo Alfonzo	.10
265	Derek Bell	.10
266	Armando Benitez	.10
267	Mike Bordick	.10
268	John Franco	.10
269	Darryl Hamilton	.10
270	Mike Hampton	.10
271	Lenny Harris	.10
272	Al Leiter	.10
273	Joe McEwing	.10
274	Rey Ordonez	.10
275	Jay Payton	.10
276	Mike Piazza	1.25
277	Glendon Rusch	.10
278	Bubba Trammell	.10
279	Robin Ventura	.10
280	Todd Zeile	.10
281	Scott Brosius	.10
282	Jose Canseco	.25
283	Roger Clemens	1.00
284	David Cone	.10
285	Dwight Gooden	.10
286	Orlando Hernandez	.10
287	Glenallen Hill	.10
288	Derek Jeter	2.00
289	David Justice	.10
290	Chuck Knoblauch	.10
291	Tino Martinez	.10
292	Denny Neagle	.10
293	Paul O'Neill	.10
294	Andy Pettitte	.20
295	Jorge Posada	.10
296	Mariano Rivera	.20
297	Luis Sojo	.10
298	Jose Vizcaino	.10
299	Bernie Williams	.25
300	Kevin Appier	.10
301	Eric Chavez	.20
302	Ryan Christenson	.10
303	Jason Giambi	.50
304	Jeremy Giambi	.10
305	Ben Grieve	.10
306	Gil Heredia	.10
307	Ramon Hernandez	.10
308	Tim Hudson	.20
309	Jason Isringhausen	.10
310	Terrence Long	.10
311	Mark Mulder	.10
312	Adam Piatt	.10
313	Matt Stairs	.10
314	Miguel Tejada	.25
315	Randy Velarde	.10
316	Alex Arias	.10
317	Pat Burrell	.25
318	Omar Daal	.10
319	Travis Lee	.10
320	Mike Lieberthal	.10
321	Randy Wolf	.10
322	Bobby Abreu	.10
323	Jeff Brantley	.10
324	Bruce Chen	.10
325	Doug Glanville	.10
326	Kevin Jordan	.10
327	Robert Person	.10
328	Scott Rolen	.65
329	Jimmy Anderson	.10
330	Mike Benjamin	.10
331	Kris Benson	.10
332	Adam Brown	.10
333	Brian Giles	.10
334	Jason Kendall	.10
335	Pat Meares	.10
336	Warren Morris	.10
337	Aramis Ramirez	.10
338	Todd Ritchie	.10
339	Jason Schmidt	.10
340	John Vander Wal	.10
341	Mike Williams	.10
342	Enrique Wilson	.10
343	Kevin Young	.10
344	Rick Ankiel	.10
345	Andy Benes	.15
346	Will Clark	.10
347	Eric Davis	.10
348	J.D. Drew	.20
349	Shawon Dunston	.10
350	Jim Edmonds	.10
351	Pat Hentgen	.10
352	Darryl Kile	.10
353	Ray Lankford	.10
354	Mike Matheny	.10
355	Mark McGwire	1.50
356	Craig Paquette	.10
357	Edgar Renteria	.10
358	Garrett Stephenson	.10
359	Fernando Tatis	.10
360	Dave Veres	.10

361	Fernando Vina	.10
362	Bret Boone	.10
363	Matt Clement	.10
364	Ben Davis	.10
365	Adam Eaton	.10
366	Wiki Gonzalez	.10
367	Tony Gwynn	1.00
368	Damian Jackson	.10
369	Ryan Klesko	.10
370	John Mabry	.10
371	Dave Magadan	.10
372	Phil Nevin	.10
373	Eric Owens	.10
374	Desi Relaford	.10
375	Ruben Rivera	.10
376	Woody Williams	.10
377	Rich Aurilia	.10
378	Marvin Bernard	.10
379	Barry Bonds	2.00
380	Ellis Burks	.10
381	Bobby Estalella	.10
382	Shawn Estes	.10
383	Mark Gardner	.10
384	Livan Hernandez	.10
385	Jeff Kent	.10
386	Bill Mueller	.10
387	Robb Nen	.10
388	Russ Ortiz	.10
389	Armando Rios	.10
390	Kirk Rueter	.10
391	J.T. Snow	.10
392	David Bell	.10
393	Jay Buhner	.10
394	Mike Cameron	.10
395	Freddy Garcia	.10
396	Carlos Guillen	.10
397	John Halama	.10
398	Rickey Henderson	.75
399	Al Martin	.10
400	Edgar Martinez	.10
401	Mark McLemore	.10
402	Jamie Moyer	.10
403	John Olerud	.10
404	Joe Oliver	.10
405	Alex Rodriguez	1.50
406	Kazuhiro Sasaki	.15
407	Aaron Sele	.10
408	Dan Wilson	.10
409	Miguel Cairo	.10
410	Vinny Castilla	.10
411	Steve Cox	.10
412	John Flaherty	.10
413	Jose Guillen	.10
414	Roberto Hernandez	.10
415	Russ Johnson	.10
416	Felix Martinez	.10
417	Fred McGriff	.10
418	Greg Vaughn	.10
419	Gerald Williams	.10
420	Luis Alicea	.10
421	Frank Catalanotto	.10
422	Royce Clayton	.10
423	Chad Curtis	.10
424	Rusty Greer	.10
425	Bill Haselman	.10
426	Rick Helling	.10
427	Gabe Kapler	.10
428	Mike Lamb	.10
429	Ricky Ledee	.10
430	Ruben Mateo	.10
431	Rafael Palmeiro	.65
432	Ivan Rodriguez	.65
433	Kenny Rogers	.10
434	John Wetteland	.10
435	Jeff Zimmerman	.10
436	Tony Batista	.10
437	Homer Bush	.10
438	Chris Carpenter	.10
439	Marty Cordova	.10
440	Jose Cruz Jr.	.10
441	Carlos Delgado	.40
442	Darrin Fletcher	.10
443	Brad Fullmer	.10
444	Alex S. Gonzalez	.10
445	Billy Koch	.10
446	Raul Mondesi	.10
447	Mickey Morandini	.10
448	Shannon Stewart	.10
449	Steve Trachsel	.10
450	David Wells	.10
451	Juan Alvarez	.10
452	Shawn Wooten	.10
453	Ismael Villegas	.10
454	Carlos Casimiro	.10
455	Morgan Burkhart	.10
456	Paxton Crawford	.10
457	Dernell Stenson	.10
458	Ross Gload	.10
459	Raul Gonzalez	.10
460	Corey Patterson	.10
461	Julio Zuleta	.10
462	Rocky Biddle	.10
463	Joe Crede	.10
464	Matt Ginter	.10

465	Aaron Myette	.10
466	Mike Bell	.10
467	Travis Dawkins	.10
468	Mark Watson	.10
469	Elvis Pena	.10
470	Eric Munson	.10
471	Pablo Ozuna	.10
472	Frank Charles	.10
473	Mike Judd	.10
474	Hector Ramirez	.10
475	Jack Cressend	.10
476	Talmadge Nunnari	.10
477	Jorge Toca	.10
478	Alfonso Soriano	.65
479	Jay Tessmer	.10
480	Jake Westbrook	.10
481	Todd Belitz	.10
482	Eric Byrnes	.10
483	Jose Ortiz	.10
484	Tike Redman	.10
485	Domingo Guzman	.10
486	Rodrigo Lopez	.10
487	Pedro Feliz	.10
488	Damon Minor	.10
489	Ryan Vogelsong	.10
490	Joel Pineiro	.10
491	Justin Brunette	.10
492	Keith McDonald	.10
493	Aubrey Huff	.10
494	Kenny Kelly	.10
495	Damian Rolls	.10
496	John Bale	.10
497	Pasqual Coco	.10
498	Matt DeWitt	.10
499	Leo Estrella	.10
500	Josh Phelps	.10

Premiere Date

Stars:	20-30X
Production 35 Sets	

Extreme

Stars:	15-25X
Production 45 Sets	

Hobby Limited

Stars:	8-15X
Production 70 Sets	

AL Decade's Best

	NM/M
Complete Set (18):	20.00
Common Player:	.50
Inserted 2:37	
1 Rickey Henderson	1.50
2 Rafael Palmeiro	1.00
3 Cal Ripken Jr.	4.00
4 Jose Canseco	.75
5 Juan Gonzalez	1.50
6 Frank Thomas	1.50
7 Albert Belle	.50

8	Edgar Martinez	.50
9	Mo Vaughn	.50
10	Derek Jeter	4.00
11	Mark McGwire	3.00
12	Alex Rodriguez	3.00
13	Ken Griffey Jr.	2.50
14	Nomar Garciaparra	2.50
15	Roger Clemens	2.00
16	Bernie Williams	.50
17	Ivan Rodriguez	1.00
18	Pedro Martinez	1.50

NL Decade's Best

	NM/M
Complete Set (18):	15.00
Common Player:	.50
Inserted 2:37	
1 Barry Bonds	4.00
2 Jeff Bagwell	1.00
3 Tom Glavine	.65
4 Gary Sheffield	.65
5 Fred McGriff	.50
6 Greg Maddux	1.50
7 Mike Piazza	2.00
8 Tony Gwynn	1.50
9 Hideo Nomo	1.00
10 Andres Galarraga	.50
11 Larry Walker	.50
12 Scott Rolen	.75
13 Pedro Martinez	1.00
14 Sammy Sosa	2.00
15 Mark McGwire	3.00
16 Kerry Wood	.75
17 Chipper Jones	1.50
18 Mark Grace	.75

Cramer's Choice Awards

	NM/M
Complete Set (10):	275.00
Common Player:	15.00
Inserted 1:721	
Styrene & Canvas pricing unavailable.	
1 Cal Ripken Jr.	50.00
2 Nomar Garciaparra	30.00
3 Sammy Sosa	30.00
4 Frank Thomas	15.00
5 Ken Griffey Jr.	30.00
6 Mike Piazza	30.00
7 Derek Jeter	50.00
8 Mark McGwire	40.00
9 Barry Bonds	50.00
10 Alex Rodriguez	40.00

Gold Crown Die-Cuts

	NM/M
Complete Set (36):	100.00
Common Player:	1.50
Inserted 1:73	

1	Darin Erstad	1.50
2	Troy Glaus	4.00
3	Randy Johnson	4.00
4	Rafael Furcal	1.50
5	Andruw Jones	4.00
6	Chipper Jones	5.00
7	Greg Maddux	5.00
8	Cal Ripken Jr.	10.00
9	Nomar Garciaparra	8.00
10	Pedro Martinez	4.00
11	Sammy Sosa	8.00
12	Kerry Wood	2.50
13	Frank Thomas	4.00
14	Ken Griffey Jr.	8.00
15	Manny Ramirez	4.00
16	Todd Helton	4.00
17	Jeff Bagwell	4.00
18	Shawn Green	1.50
19	Gary Sheffield	1.50
20	Vladimir Guerrero	4.00
21	Mike Piazza	8.00
22	Jose Canseco	2.00
23	Roger Clemens	6.00
24	Derek Jeter	10.00
25	Jason Giambi	2.50
26	Pat Burrell	2.00
26	Rick Ankiel (Should be #27.)	1.50
28	Jim Edmonds	1.50
29	Mark McGwire	9.00
30	Tony Gwynn	5.00
31	Barry Bonds	10.00
32	Rickey Henderson	4.00
33	Edgar Martinez	1.50
34	Alex Rodriguez	9.00
35	Ivan Rodriguez	3.00
36	Carlos Delgado	2.00

On The Horizon

		NM/M
	Complete Set (10):	20.00
	Common Player:	2.00
	Inserted 1:145	
1	Rafael Furcal	2.00
2	Corey Patterson	2.50
3	Russell Branyan	2.00
4	Juan Pierre	2.50
5	Mark Quinn	2.00
6	Alfonso Soriano	6.00
7	Adam Piatt	2.00
8	Pat Burrell	4.50
9	Kazuhiro Sasaki	2.50
10	Aubrey Huff	2.00

Ornaments

		NM/M
	Complete Set (24):	25.00
	Common Player:	.50
	Inserted 2:37	
1	Rafael Furcal	.50
2	Chipper Jones	2.00
3	Greg Maddux	2.00
4	Cal Ripken Jr.	4.00
5	Nomar Garciaparra	2.50
6	Pedro Martinez	1.50
7	Sammy Sosa	2.50
8	Frank Thomas	1.50
9	Ken Griffey Jr.	2.50
10	Manny Ramirez	1.50
11	Todd Helton	1.50
12	Vladimir Guerrero	1.50
13	Mike Piazza	2.50
14	Roger Clemens	2.25
15	Derek Jeter	4.00
16	Pat Burrell	1.00
17	Rick Ankiel	.50
18	Mark McGwire	3.00
19	Barry Bonds	4.00
20	Alex Rodriguez	3.00
21	Troy Glaus	1.50
22	Tom Glavine	.50
23	Jim Edmonds	.50
24	Ivan Rodriguez	1.00

2001 Pacific Private Stock

		NM/M
	Complete Set (150):	50.00
	Common Player:	.25
	Common (126-150):	1.00
	Inserted 1:4	
	Hobby Pack (7):	10.00
	Hobby Box (10):	75.00
1	Darin Erstad	.50
2	Troy Glaus	1.00
3	Tim Salmon	.35
4	Mo Vaughn	.25
5	Steve Finley	.25
6	Luis Gonzalez	.35
7	Randy Johnson	1.00
8	Matt Williams	.25
9	Rafael Furcal	.25
10	Andres Galarraga	.25
11	Tom Glavine	.45
12	Andruw Jones	1.00
13	Chipper Jones	1.50
14	Greg Maddux	1.50
15	B.J. Surhoff	.25
16	Brady Anderson	.25
17	Albert Belle	.25
18	Mike Mussina	.45
19	Cal Ripken Jr.	3.00
20	Carl Everett	.25
21	Nomar Garciaparra	2.00
22	Pedro Martinez	1.00
23	Mark Grace	.35
24	Sammy Sosa	2.00
25	Kerry Wood	.50
26	Carlos Lee	.25
27	Magglio Ordonez	.25
28	Frank Thomas	1.00
29	Sean Casey	.35
30	Ken Griffey Jr.	2.00
31	Barry Larkin	.25
32	Pokey Reese	.25
33	Roberto Alomar	.40
34	Kenny Lofton	.25
35	Manny Ramirez	1.00
36	Jim Thome	.75
37	Omar Vizquel	.25
38	Jeff Cirillo	.25
39	Jeffrey Hammonds	.25
40	Todd Helton	1.00
41	Larry Walker	.25
42	Tony Clark	.25
43	Juan Encarnacion	.25
44	Juan Gonzalez	1.00
45	Hideo Nomo	1.00
46	Cliff Floyd	.25
47	Derek Lee	.25
48	Henry Rodriguez	.25
49	Preston Wilson	.25
50	Jeff Bagwell	1.00
51	Craig Biggio	.25
52	Richard Hidalgo	.25
53	Moises Alou	.25
54	Carlos Beltran	.50
55	Johnny Damon	.40
56	Jermaine Dye	.25
57	Mac Suzuki	.25
58	Mike Sweeney	.25
59	Adrian Beltre	.40
60	Kevin Brown	.25
61	Shawn Green	.50
62	Eric Karros	.25
63	Chan Ho Park	.25
64	Gary Sheffield	.40
65	Jeromy Burnitz	.25
66	Geoff Jenkins	.25
67	Richie Sexson	.25
68	Jacque Jones	.25
69	Matt Lawton	.25
70	Eric Milton	.25
71	Vladimir Guerrero	1.00
72	Jose Vidro	.25
73	Edgardo Alfonzo	.25
74	Mike Hampton	.25
75	Mike Piazza	2.00
76	Robin Ventura	.25
77	Jose Canseco	.50
78	Roger Clemens	1.75
79	Derek Jeter	3.00
80	David Justice	.25
81	Jorge Posada	.25
82	Bernie Williams	.35
83	Jason Giambi	.65
84	Ben Grieve	.25
85	Tim Hudson	.35
86	Terrence Long	.25
87	Miguel Tejada	.35
88	Bobby Abreu	.25
89	Pat Burrell	.50
90	Mike Lieberthal	.25
91	Scott Rolen	.75
92	Kris Benson	.25
93	Brian Giles	.25
94	Jason Kendall	.25
95	Aramis Ramirez	.25
96	Rick Ankiel	.25
97	Will Clark	.35
98	J.D. Drew	.25
99	Jim Edmonds	.25
100	Mark McGwire	2.50
101	Fernando Tatis	.25
102	Adam Eaton	.25
103	Tony Gwynn	1.50
104	Phil Nevin	.25
105	Eric Owens	.25
106	Barry Bonds	3.00
107	Jeff Kent	.25
108	J.T. Snow	.25
109	Rickey Henderson	1.00
110	Edgar Martinez	.25
111	John Olerud	.25
112	Alex Rodriguez	2.50
113	Kazuhiro Sasaki	.25
114	Vinny Castilla	.25
115	Fred McGriff	.25
116	Greg Vaughn	.25
117	Gabe Kapler	.25
118	Ruben Mateo	.25
119	Rafael Palmeiro	.75
120	Ivan Rodriguez	.75
121	Tony Batista	.25
122	Jose Cruz Jr.	.25
123	Carlos Delgado	.75
124	Shannon Stewart	.25
125	David Wells	.25
126	Shawn Wooten	1.00
127	George Lombard	1.00
128	Morgan Burkhart	1.00
129	Ross Gload	1.00
130	Corey Patterson	1.00
131	Julio Zuleta	1.00
132	Joe Crede	1.00
133	Matt Ginter	1.00
134	Travis Dawkins	1.00
135	Eric Munson	1.00
136	Dee Brown	1.00
137	Luke Prokopec	1.00
138	Timoniel Perez	1.00
139	Alfonso Soriano	2.00
140	Jake Westbrook	1.00
141	Eric Byrnes	1.00
142	Adam Hyzdu	1.50
143	Jimmy Rollins	1.00
144	Xavier Nady	1.00
145	Ryan Vogelsong	1.00
146	Joel Pineiro	2.00
147	Aubrey Huff	1.00
148	Kenny Kelly	1.00
149	Josh Phelps	1.00
150	Vernon Wells	1.00

Silver

Stars: .5-1.5X
SP's: .5-1X
Base cards in retail.

Silver Portraits

Stars: 2-5X
SP's: 1X
Production 290 Sets R

Gold Portraits

Stars: 6-10X
SP's (126-150): 1-2X
Production 75 Sets H

Artist's Canvas

		NM/M
	Complete Set (20):	50.00
	Common Player:	1.00
	Inserted 1:21	
1	Randy Johnson	2.50
2	Chipper Jones	4.00
3	Greg Maddux	4.00
4	Cal Ripken Jr.	8.00
5	Nomar Garciaparra	5.00
6	Pedro Martinez	2.50
7	Sammy Sosa	5.00
8	Frank Thomas	2.50
9	Ken Griffey Jr.	5.00
10	Manny Ramirez	2.50
11	Vladimir Guerrero	2.50
12	Mike Piazza	5.00
13	Roger Clemens	4.50
14	Derek Jeter	6.00
15	Jason Giambi	2.50
16	Rick Ankiel	1.00
17	Mark McGwire	6.00
18	Barry Bonds	8.00
19	Alex Rodriguez	6.00
20	Ivan Rodriguez	2.00

Premiere Date

Stars: 4-8X
SP's: 1-2X
Production 90 Sets

Game Gear

		NM/M
	Common Player:	4.00
	Inserted 1:1 H	
1	Garret Anderson/Bat	6.00
2	Darin Erstad/Jsy	5.00
3	Ron Gant/Bat	4.00

4	Troy Glaus/Jsy	8.00
5	Tim Salmon/Bat	5.00
6	Mo Vaughn/Jsy/Gray	4.00
7	Mo Vaughn/Jsy/White	4.00
8	Mo Vaughn/Bat	4.00
9	Jay Bell/Jsy	4.00
10	Jay Bell/Bat	4.00
11	Erubiel Durazo/Jsy/Black	4.00
12	Erubiel Durazo/Jsy/White	4.00
13	Erubiel Durazo/Bat	4.00
14	Steve Finley/Bat	4.00
15	Randy Johnson/Jsy	10.00
16	Byung-Hyun Kim/Jsy/White	4.00
17	Byung-Hyun Kim/Jsy/Gray	4.00
18	Matt Williams/Jsy/Gray	4.00
19	Matt Williams/Jsy/White	4.00
20	Matt Williams/Jsy/Purple	4.00
21	Bobby Bonilla/Jsy	4.00
22	Rafael Furcal/Bat	5.00
23	Andruw Jones/Bat	8.00
24	Chipper Jones/Jsy	10.00
25	Chipper Jones/Bat	10.00
26	Brian Jordan/Jsy	4.00
27	Javier Lopez/Bat	4.00
28	Greg Maddux/Jsy	15.00
29	Greg Maddux/Bat	15.00
30	Brady Anderson/Bat	4.00
31	Albert Belle/Bat	4.00
32	Nomar Garciaparra/Bat	15.00
33	Pedro Martinez/Bat	10.00
34	Jose Offerman/Bat	4.00
35	Damon Buford/Jsy	4.00
36	Jose Nieves/Bat	4.00
38	Kerry Wood/Bat	8.00
39	James Baldwin/Jsy	4.00
40	Ray Durham/Jsy	4.00
41	Ray Durham/Bat	4.00
42	Carlos Lee/Bat	4.00
43	Magglio Ordonez/Jsy	6.00
44	Magglio Ordonez/Bat	6.00
45	Chris Singleton/Jsy	4.00
46	Aaron Boone/Bat	4.00
47	Sean Casey/Bat	4.00
48	Barry Larkin/Jsy	6.00
49	Pokey Reese/Jsy	4.00
50	Pokey Reese/Bat	4.00
51	Dmitri Young/Bat	4.00
52	Roberto Alomar/Bat	8.00
53	Einar Diaz/Bat	4.00
54	Kenny Lofton/Jsy	4.00
55	David Segui/Bat	4.00
56	Omar Vizquel/Jsy	5.00
57	Luis Castillo/Jsy	4.00
58	Jeff Cirillo/Jsy	4.00
59	Jeff Frye/Bat	4.00
60	Todd Helton/Jsy	8.00
61	Todd Helton/Bat	8.00
62	Neifi Perez/Bat	4.00
63	Larry Walker/Jsy	4.00
64	Larry Walker/Bat	4.00
65	Masato Yoshii/Jsy	4.00
66	Brad Ausmus/Jsy	4.00
67	Rich Becker/Bat	4.00
68	Tony Clark/Bat	4.00
69	Deivi Cruz/Bat	4.00
70	Juan Gonzalez/Bat	6.00
71	Dean Palmer/Bat	4.00
72	Cliff Floyd/Jsy/White	4.00
73	Cliff Floyd/Jsy/Teal	4.00
74	Cliff Floyd/Bat	4.00
75	Alex Gonzalez/Jsy	4.00
76	Alex Gonzalez/Marlins Bat	4.00
77	Mark Kotsay/Bat	4.00
78	Derrek Lee/Bat	4.00
79	Pablo Ozuna/Bat	4.00
80	Craig Biggio/Bat	4.00
81	Ken Caminiti/Bat	4.00
82	Roger Cedeno/Bat	4.00
83	Ricky Bottalico/Bat	4.00
84	Dee Brown/Bat	4.00
85	Jermaine Dye/Bat	4.00
86	David McCarty/Bat	4.00
87	Hector Ortiz/Bat	4.00
88	Joe Randa/Bat	4.00
89	Adrian Beltre/Bat	4.00
90	Kevin Brown/Jsy	6.00
91	Alex Cora/Bat	4.00
92	Darren Dreifort/Bat	4.00
93	Shawn Green/Jsy/White	6.00
94	Shawn Green/Jsy/Gray	6.00
95	Shawn Green/Bat	6.00
96	Todd Hundley/Jsy	4.00
97	Eric Karros/Bat	4.00
98	Chan Ho Park/Jsy	4.00
99	Chan Ho Park/Bat	4.00
101	Gary Sheffield/Bat	6.00
102	Ismael Valdes/Bat	4.00
103	Jeromy Burnitz/Bat	4.00
104	Marquis Grissom/Bat	4.00
105	Matt Lawton/Bat	4.00
106	Fernando Seguignol/Bat	4.00
107	Edgardo Alfonzo/White Swing	4.00
108	Edgardo Alfonzo/Jsy/White Drop	4.00
109	Edgardo Alfonzo/Jsy/Black	4.00
110	Derek Bell/Jsy/White	4.00
111	Derek Bell/Jsy/Black	4.00
112	Armando Benitez/Bat	4.00
113	Al Leiter/Bat	4.00
114	Rey Ordonez/Jsy/Gray Field	4.00
115	Rey Ordonez/Jsy/White	4.00
116	Rey Ordonez/Jsy/Gray Bunt	4.00
117	Rey Ordonez/Bat	4.00
118	Jay Payton/Bat	4.00
119	Mike Piazza/Jsy	10.00
120	Robin Ventura/Jsy/Black Hit	4.00
121	Robin Ventura/Jsy/Black Field	4.00
122	Robin Ventura/Jsy White	4.00
123	Luis Polonia/Bat	4.00
124	Bernie Williams/Bat	6.00
125	Eric Chavez/Jsy	4.00
126	Jason Giambi/Jsy	8.00
127	Jason Giambi/Bat	8.00
128	Ben Grieve/Jsy	4.00
129	Ben Grieve/Bat	4.00
130	Ramon Hernandez/Bat	4.00
131	Tim Hudson/Jsy	6.00
132	Terrence Long/Bat	4.00
133	Mark Mulder/Jsy	6.00
134	Adam Piatt/Jsy	4.00
135	Olmedo Saenz/Bat	4.00
136	Matt Stairs/Bat	4.00
137	Mike Stanley/Bat	4.00
138	Miguel Tejada/Bat	6.00
139	Travis Lee/Bat	4.00
140	Brian Giles/Bat	5.00
141	Jason Kendall/Jsy	4.00
142	Will Clark/Bat	6.00
143	J.D. Drew/Bat	4.00
144	Jim Edmonds/Bat	6.00
145	Mark McGwire/Bat	50.00
146	Edgar Renteria/Bat	4.00
147	Garrett Stephenson/Jsy	4.00
148	Tony Gwynn/Jsy	10.00
149	Ruben Rivera/Bat	4.00
150	Barry Bonds/Jsy	40.00
151	Barry Bonds/Bat	40.00
152	Ellis Burks/Jsy	4.00
153	J.T. Snow/Bat	4.00
154	Jay Buhner/Jsy	4.00
155	Jay Buhner/Bat	4.00
156	Carlos Guillen/Jsy	4.00
157	Carlos Guillen/Bat	4.00
158	Rickey Henderson/Bat	15.00
159	Edgar Martinez/Bat	6.00
160	Gil Meche/Jsy	4.00
161	John Olerud/Bat	5.00
162	Joe Oliver/Bat	4.00
163	Alex Rodriguez/Jsy	30.00
164	Kazuhiro Sasaki/Jsy	4.00
165	Dan Wilson/Jsy	4.00
166	Dan Wilson/Bat	4.00
167	Vinny Castilla/Bat	4.00
168	Jose Guillen/Bat	4.00
169	Fred McGriff/Jsy	5.00
170	Rusty Greer/Bat	4.00
171	Mike Lamb/Bat	4.00
172	Ruben Mateo/Jsy	4.00
173	Ruben Mateo/Bat	4.00
174	Rafael Palmeiro/Jsy	8.00
175	Rafael Palmeiro/Bat	8.00
178	Tony Batista/Bat	4.00
179	Marty Cordova/Bat	4.00
180	Jose Cruz Jr./Bat	4.00
181	Alex Gonzalez/Blue Jays Bat	4.00
182	Raul Mondesi/Bat	4.00

Game Jersey Patch

		NM/M
	Common Player:	8.00
2	Darin Erstad	8.00
4	Troy Glaus	15.00
6	Mo Vaughn/Gray	8.00
7	Mo Vaughn/White	8.00

9	Jay Bell	8.00
11	Erubiel Durazo/Black	8.00
12	Erubiel Durazo/White	8.00
15	Randy Johnson	40.00
16	Byung-Hyun Kim/White	8.00
17	Byung-Hyun Kim/Gray	8.00
18	Matt Williams/Gray	8.00
19	Matt Williams/White	8.00
20	Matt Williams/Purple	8.00
21	Bobby Bonilla	8.00
24	Chipper Jones	25.00
26	Brian Jordan	8.00
28	Greg Maddux	80.00
35	Damon Buford	8.00
39	James Baldwin	8.00
40	Ray Durham	8.00
43	Magglio Ordonez	20.00
45	Chris Singleton	8.00
48	Barry Larkin	15.00
49	Pokey Reese	8.00
54	Kenny Lofton	10.00
56	Omar Vizquel	10.00
57	Luis Castillo	8.00
58	Jeff Cirillo	8.00
60	Todd Helton	20.00
63	Larry Walker	10.00
65	Masato Yoshii	8.00
66	Brad Ausmus	8.00
72	Cliff Floyd/White	8.00
73	Cliff Floyd Teal	8.00
75	Alex Gonzalez	8.00
79	Pablo Ozuna	8.00
89	Adrian Beltre	8.00
90	Kevin Brown	15.00
93	Shawn Green/White	15.00
94	Shawn Green/Gray	15.00
96	Todd Hundley	8.00
98	Chan Ho Park	8.00
107	Edgardo Alfonzo/White Swing	8.00
108	Edgardo Alfonzo/White Drop	8.00
109	Edgardo Alfonzo/Black	8.00
110	Derek Bell/White	8.00
111	Derek Bell/Black	8.00
114	Rey Ordonez/Gray Field	8.00
115	Rey Ordonez/White	8.00
116	Rey Ordonez/Gray Bunt	8.00
119	Mike Piazza	75.00
120	Robin Ventura/Black Hit	10.00
121	Robin Ventura/Black Field	10.00
122	Robin Ventura/White	10.00
125	Eric Chavez	15.00
126	Jason Giambi	15.00
128	Ben Grieve	8.00
131	Tim Hudson	15.00
133	Mark Mulder	15.00
134	Adam Piatt	8.00
141	Jason Kendall	10.00
147	Garrett Stephenson	8.00
148	Tony Gwynn	40.00
150	Barry Bonds	90.00
152	Ellis Burks	8.00
154	Jay Buhner	8.00
156	Carlos Guillen	8.00
160	Gil Meche	8.00
163	Alex Rodriguez	
164	Kazuhiro Sasaki	15.00
165	Dan Wilson	8.00
169	Fred McGriff	10.00
172	Ruben Mateo	8.00
174	Rafael Palmeiro	25.00

Extreme Action

		NM/M
	Complete Set (20):	20.00
	Common Player:	2.00
	Inserted 1:11	
1	Troy Glaus	1.00
2	Rafael Furcal	.50
3	Chipper Jones	1.50
4	Cal Ripken Jr.	3.00
5	Nomar Garciaparra	2.00
6	Sammy Sosa	2.00
7	Ken Griffey Jr.	2.00
8	Manny Ramirez	1.00
9	Todd Helton	1.00
10	Jeff Bagwell	1.00

11	Vladimir Guerrero	1.00
12	Derek Jeter	3.00
13	Mike Piazza	2.00
14	Pat Burrell	.75
15	Jim Edmonds	.50
16	Mark McGwire	2.50
17	Barry Bonds	3.00
18	Alex Rodriguez	2.50
19	Ivan Rodriguez	.75
20	Carlos Delgado	.75

PS-206 Stars

		NM/M
	Complete Set (20):	50.00
	Common Player:	1.00
	Inserted 3:Hobby Case	
1	Chipper Jones	3.00
2	Greg Maddux	3.00
3	Cal Ripken Jr.	6.00
4	Nomar Garciaparra	4.00
5	Pedro Martinez	2.00
6	Sammy Sosa	4.00
7	Frank Thomas	2.00
8	Ken Griffey Jr.	4.00
9	Manny Ramirez	2.00
10	Jeff Bagwell	2.00
11	Gary Sheffield	1.00
12	Mike Piazza	4.00
13	Roger Clemens	3.50
14	Derek Jeter	6.00
15	Rick Ankiel	1.00
16	Mark McGwire	5.00
17	Tony Gwynn	3.00
18	Barry Bonds	6.00
19	Alex Rodriguez	5.00
20	Ivan Rodriguez	1.50

PS-206 Action

		NM/M
	Complete Set (60):	20.00
	Common Player:	.15
	Inserted 2:Pack	
1	Darin Erstad	.25
2	Troy Glaus	.65
3	Randy Johnson	.65
4	Rafael Furcal	.15
5	Tom Glavine	.40
6	Andruw Jones	.65
7	Chipper Jones	.75
8	Greg Maddux	.75
9	Albert Belle	.15
10	Mike Mussina	.40
11	Cal Ripken Jr.	1.50
12	Nomar Garciaparra	1.00
13	Pedro Martinez	.65
14	Mark Grace	.25
15	Sammy Sosa	1.00
16	Kerry Wood	.35
17	Magglio Ordonez	.15
18	Frank Thomas	.65
19	Ken Griffey Jr.	1.00
20	Barry Larkin	.15
21	Roberto Alomar	.35
22	Manny Ramirez	.65
23	Jim Thome	.60
24	Jeff Cirillo	.15
25	Todd Helton	.65
26	Larry Walker	.65
27	Juan Gonzalez	.65
28	Hideo Nomo	.15
29	Preston Wilson	.15
30	Jeff Bagwell	.65
31	Craig Biggio	.15
32	Johnny Damon	.25
33	Jermaine Dye	.15

ABBREVIATIONS

SP - Short Print

34	Shawn Green	.30
35	Gary Sheffield	.25
36	Vladimir Guerrero	.65
37	Mike Piazza	1.00
38	Jose Canseco	.40
39	Roger Clemens	.85
40	Derek Jeter	1.50
41	Bernie Williams	.30
42	Jason Giambi	.50
43	Ben Grieve	.15
44	Pat Burrell	.40
45	Scott Rolen	.50
46	Rick Ankiel	.15
47	J.D. Drew	.25
48	Jim Edmonds	.15
49	Mark McGwire	1.25
50	Tony Gwynn	.75
51	Barry Bonds	1.50
52	Jeff Kent	.15
53	Edgar Martinez	.15
54	Alex Rodriguez	1.25
55	Kazuhiro Sasaki	.15
56	Fred McGriff	.15
57	Rafael Palmeiro	.50
58	Ivan Rodriguez	.50
59	Tony Batista	.15
60	Carlos Delgado	.45

PS-206 New Wave

NM/M

Complete Set (20): 30.00
Common Player: 1.00
Inserted 2:Hobby Case

1	Darin Erstad	1.50
2	Troy Glaus	5.00
3	Rafael Furcal	1.00
4	Andruw Jones	5.00
5	Magglio Ordonez	1.00
6	Carlos Lee	1.00
7	Todd Helton	5.00
8	Johnny Damon	1.50
9	Jermaine Dye	1.00
10	Vladimir Guerrero	5.00
11	Jason Giambi	4.00
12	Ben Grieve	1.00
13	Pat Burrell	3.00
14	Rick Ankiel	1.00
15	J.D. Drew	1.50
16	Adam Eaton	1.00
17	Kazuhiro Sasaki	1.00
18	Ruben Mateo	1.00
19	Tony Batista	1.00
20	Carlos Delgado	3.00

PS-206 Rookies

NM/M

Complete Set (20): 50.00
Common Player: 3.00
Inserted 1:Case

1	George Lombard	3.00
2	Morgan Burkhart	3.00
3	Corey Patterson	5.00
4	Julio Zuleta	3.00
5	Joe Crede	3.00
6	Matt Ginter	3.00
7	Aaron Myette	3.00
8	Travis Dawkins	3.00
9	Eric Munson	3.00
10	Dee Brown	3.00
11	Luke Prokopec	3.00
12	Jorge Toca	3.00
13	Alfonso Soriano	7.50
14	Eric Byrnes	3.00
15	Adam Hyzdu	3.00
16	Jimmy Rollins	4.00
17	Joel Pineiro	5.00
18	Aubrey Huff	4.00
19	Kenny Kelly	3.00
20	Vernon Wells	3.00

Reserve

NM/M

Complete Set (20): 25.00
Common Player: .50
Inserted 1:21 H

1	Randy Johnson	1.50
2	Chipper Jones	2.00
3	Greg Maddux	2.00
4	Cal Ripken Jr.	4.00
5	Nomar Garciaparra	2.50
6	Pedro Martinez	1.50
7	Sammy Sosa	2.50
8	Frank Thomas	1.50
9	Ken Griffey Jr.	2.50
10	Todd Helton	1.50
11	Vladimir Guerrero	1.50
12	Mike Piazza	2.50
13	Roger Clemens	2.25
14	Derek Jeter	4.00
15	Rick Ankiel	.50
16	Mark McGwire	3.00
17	Tony Gwynn	2.00
18	Barry Bonds	4.00
19	Alex Rodriguez	3.00
20	Ivan Rodriguez	1.00

1992 Pinnacle

NM/M

Complete Set (620): 15.00
Common Player: .05
Foil Pack (16): .75
Foil Box (36): 17.50
Jumbo Pack (24+3): 1.50
Jumbo Box (12): 22.50

1	Frank Thomas	.75
2	Benito Santiago	.05
3	Carlos Baerga	.05
4	Cecil Fielder	.05
5	Barry Larkin	.05
6	Ozzie Smith	1.00
7	Willie McGee	.05
8	Paul Molitor	.75
9	Andy Van Slyke	.05
10	Ryne Sandberg	1.00
11	Kevin Seitzer	.05
12	Len Dykstra	.05
13	Edgar Martinez	.05
14	Ruben Sierra	.05
15	Howard Johnson	.05
16	Dave Henderson	.05
17	Devon White	.05
18	Terry Pendleton	.05
19	Steve Finley	.05
20	Kirby Puckett	1.00
21	Orel Hershiser	.05
22	Hal Morris	.05
23	Don Mattingly	1.25
24	Delino DeShields	.05
25	Dennis Eckersley	.60
26	Ellis Burks	.05
27	Jay Buhner	.05
28	Matt Williams	.05
29	Lou Whitaker	.05
30	Alex Fernandez	.05
31	Albert Belle	.05
32	Todd Zeile	.05
33	Tony Pena	.05
34	Jay Bell	.05
35	Rafael Palmeiro	.65
36	Wes Chamberlain	.05
37	George Bell	.05
38	Robin Yount	.75
39	Vince Coleman	.05
40	Bruce Hurst	.05
41	Harold Baines	.05
42	Chuck Finley	.05
43	Ken Caminiti	.05
44	Ben McDonald	.05
45	Roberto Alomar	.15
46	Chili Davis	.05
47	Bill Doran	.05
48	Jerald Clark	.05
49	Jose Lind	.05
50	Nolan Ryan	2.00
51	Phil Plantier	.05
52	Gary DiSarcina	.05
53	Kevin Bass	.05
54	Pat Kelly	.05
55	Mark Wohlers	.05
56	Walt Weiss	.05
57	Lenny Harris	.05
58	Ivan Calderon	.05
59	Harold Reynolds	.05
60	George Brett	1.25
61	Gregg Olson	.05
62	Orlando Merced	.05
63	Steve Decker	.05
64	John Franco	.05
65	Greg Maddux	1.00
66	Alex Cole	.05
67	Dave Hollins	.05
68	Kent Hrbek	.05
69	Tom Pagnozzi	.05
70	Jeff Bagwell	.75
71	Jim Gantner	.05
72	Matt Nokes	.05
73	Brian Harper	.05
74	Andy Benes	.05
75	Tom Glavine	.35
76	Terry Steinbach	.05
77	Dennis Martinez	.05
78	John Olerud	.05
79	Ozzie Guillen	.05
80	Darryl Strawberry	.05
81	Gary Gaetti	.05
82	Dave Righetti	.05
83	Chris Hoiles	.05
84	Andujar Cedeno	.05
85	Jack Clark	.05
86	David Howard	.05
87	Bill Gullickson	.05
88	Bernard Gilkey	.05
89	Kevin Elster	.05
90	Kevin Maas	.05
91	Mark Lewis	.05
92	Greg Vaughn	.05
93	Bret Barberie	.05
94	Dave Smith	.05
95	Roger Clemens	1.25
96	Doug Drabek	.05
97	Omar Vizquel	.05
98	Jose Guzman	.05
99	Juan Samuel	.05
100	Dave Justice	.05
101	Tom Browning	.05
102	Mark Gubicza	.05
103	Mickey Morandini	.05
104	Ed Whitson	.05
105	Lance Parrish	.05
106	Scott Erickson	.05
107	Jack McDowell	.05
108	Dave Stieb	.05
109	Mike Moore	.05
110	Travis Fryman	.05
111	Dwight Gooden	.05
112	Fred McGriff	.05
113	Alan Trammell	.05
114	Roberto Kelly	.05
115	Andre Dawson	.25
116	Bill Landrum	.05
117	Brian McRae	.05
118	B.J. Surhoff	.05
119	Chuck Knoblauch	.05
120	Steve Olin	.05
121	Robin Ventura	.05
122	Will Clark	.05
123	Tino Martinez	.05
124	Dale Murphy	.25
125	Pete O'Brien	.05
126	Ray Lankford	.05
127	Juan Gonzalez	.40
128	Ron Gant	.05
129	Marquis Grissom	.05
130	Jose Canseco	.50
131	Mike Greenwell	.05
132	Mark Langston	.05
133	Brett Butler	.05
134	Kelly Gruber	.05
135	Chris Sabo	.05
136	Mark Grace	.05
137	Tony Fernandez	.05
138	Glenn Davis	.05
139	Pedro Munoz	.05
140	Craig Biggio	.05
141	Pete Schourek	.05
142	Mike Boddicker	.05
143	Robby Thompson	.05
144	Mel Hall	.05
145	Bryan Harvey	.05
146	Mike LaValliere	.05
147	John Kruk	.05
148	Joe Carter	.05
149	Greg Olson	.05
150	Julio Franco	.05
151	Darryl Hamilton	.05
152	Felix Fermin	.05
153	Jose Offerman	.05
154	Paul O'Neill	.05
155	Tommy Greene	.05
156	Ivan Rodriguez	.65
157	Dave Stewart	.05
158	Jeff Reardon	.05
159	Felix Jose	.05
160	Doug Dascenzo	.05
161	Tim Wallach	.05
162	Dan Plesac	.05
163	Luis Gonzalez	.05
164	Mike Henneman	.05
165	Mike Devereaux	.05
166	Luis Polonia	.05
167	Mike Sharperson	.05
168	Chris Donnels	.05
169	Greg Harris	.05
170	Deion Sanders	.05
171	Mike Schooler	.05
172	Jose DeJesus	.05
173	Jeff Montgomery	.05
174	Milt Cuyler	.05
175	Wade Boggs	1.00
176	Kevin Tapani	.05
177	Bill Spiers	.05
178	Tim Raines	.05
179	Randy Milligan	.05
180	Rob Dibble	.05
181	Kirt Manwaring	.05
182	Pascual Perez	.05
183	Juan Guzman	.05
184	John Smiley	.05
185	David Segui	.05
186	Omar Olivares	.05
187	Joe Slusarski	.05
188	Erik Hanson	.05
189	Mark Portugal	.05
190	Walt Terrell	.05
191	John Smoltz	.05
192	Wilson Alvarez	.05
193	Jimmy Key	.05
194	Larry Walker	.05
195	Lee Smith	.05
196	Pete Harnisch	.05
197	Mike Harkey	.05
198	Frank Tanana	.05
199	Terry Mulholland	.05
200	Cal Ripken, Jr.	2.00
201	Dave Magadan	.05
202	Bud Black	.05
203	Terry Shumpert	.05
204	Mike Mussina	.40
205	Mo Vaughn	.05
206	Steve Farr	.05
207	Darrin Jackson	.05
208	Jerry Browne	.05
209	Jeff Russell	.05
210	Mike Scioscia	.05
211	Rick Aguilera	.05
212	Jaime Navarro	.05
213	Randy Tomlin	.05
214	Bobby Thigpen	.05
215	Mark Gardner	.05
216	Norm Charlton	.05
217	Mark McGwire	1.75
218	Skeeter Barnes	.05
219	Bob Tewksbury	.05
220	Junior Felix	.05
221	Sam Horn	.05
222	Jody Reed	.05
223	Luis Sojo	.05
224	Jerome Walton	.05
225	Darryl Kile	.05
226	Mickey Tettleton	.05
227	Dan Pasqua	.05
228	Jim Gott	.05
229	Bernie Williams	.05
230	Shane Mack	.05
231	Steve Avery	.05
232	Dave Valle	.05
233	Mark Leonard	.05
234	Spike Owen	.05
235	Gary Sheffield	.20
236	Steve Chitren	.05
237	Zane Smith	.05
238	Tom Gordon	.05
239	Jose Oquendo	.05
240	Todd Stottlemyre	.05
241	Darren Daulton	.05
242	Tim Naehring	.05
243	Tony Phillips	.05
244	Shawon Dunston	.05
245	Manuel Lee	.05
246	Mike Pagliarulo	.05
247	Jim Thome	.65
248	Luis Mercedes	.05
249	Cal Eldred	.05
250	Derek Bell	.05
251	Arthur Rhodes	.05
252	Scott Cooper	.05
253	Roberto Hernandez	.05
254	Mo Sanford	.05
255	Scott Servais	.05
256	Eric Karros	.05
257	Andy Mota	.05
258	Keith Mitchell	.05
259	Joel Johnston	.05
260	John Wehner	.05
261	Gino Minutelli	.05
262	Greg Gagne	.05
263	Stan Royer	.05
264	Carlos Garcia	.05
265	Andy Ashby	.05
266	Kim Batiste	.05
267	Julio Valera	.05
268	Royce Clayton	.05
269	Gary Scott	.05
270	Kirk Dressendorfer	.05
271	Sean Berry	.05
272	Lance Dickson	.05
273	Rob Maurer	.05
274	Scott Brosius	.05
275	Dave Fleming	.05
276	Lenny Webster	.05
277	Mike Humphreys	.05
278	Freddie Benavides	.05
279	Harvey Pulliam	.05

#	Player	Price
280	Jeff Carter	.05
281	Jim Abbott, Nolan Ryan	.25
282	Wade Boggs, George Brett	.25
283	Ken Griffey Jr., Rickey Henderson	.50
284	Dale Murphy, Wally Joyner	.10
285	Chuck Knoblauch, Ozzie Smith	.20
286	Robin Ventura, Lou Gehrig	.20
287	Robin Yount	.30
288	Bob Tewksbury	.05
289	Kirby Puckett	.50
290	Kenny Lofton	.05
291	Jack McDowell	.05
292	John Burkett	.05
293	Dwight Smith	.05
294	Nolan Ryan	1.00
295	Manny Ramirez RC	2.50
296	Cliff Floyd RC	.50
297	Al Shirley RC	.05
298	Brian Barber RC	.05
299	Jon Farrell RC	.05
300	Scott Ruffcorn RC	.05
301	Tyrone Hill RC	.05
302	Benji Gil RC	.05
303	Tyler Green RC	.05
304	Allen Watson	.05
305	Jay Buhner	.05
306	Roberto Alomar	.05
307	Chuck Knoblauch	.05
308	Darryl Strawberry	.05
309	Danny Tartabull	.05
310	Bobby Bonilla	.05
311	Mike Felder	.05
312	Storm Davis	.05
313	Tim Teufel	.05
314	Tom Brunansky	.05
315	Rex Hudler	.05
316	Dave Otto	.05
317	Jeff King	.05
318	Dan Gladden	.05
319	Bill Pecota	.05
320	Franklin Stubbs	.05
321	Gary Carter	.75
322	Melido Perez	.05
323	Eric Davis	.05
324	Greg Myers	.05
325	Pete Incaviglia	.05
326	Von Hayes	.05
327	Greg Swindell	.05
328	Steve Sax	.05
329	Chuck McElroy	.05
330	Gregg Jefferies	.05
331	Joe Oliver	.05
332	Paul Faries	.05
333	David West	.05
334	Craig Grebeck	.05
335	Chris Hammond	.05
336	Billy Ripken	.05
337	Scott Sanderson	.05
338	Dick Schofield	.05
339	Bob Milacki	.05
340	Kevin Reimer	.05
341	Jose DeLeon	.05
342	Henry Cotto	.05
343	Daryl Boston	.05
344	Kevin Gross	.05
345	Milt Thompson	.05
346	Luis Rivera	.05
347	Al Osuna	.05
348	Rob Deer	.05
349	Tim Leary	.05
350	Mike Stanton	.05
351	Dean Palmer	.05
352	Trevor Wilson	.05
353	Mark Eichhorn	.05
354	Scott Aldred	.05
355	Mark Whiten	.05
356	Leo Gomez	.05
357	Rafael Belliard	.05
358	Carlos Quintana	.05
359	Mark Davis	.05
360	Chris Nabholz	.05
361	Carlton Fisk	.75
362	Joe Orsulak	.05
363	Eric Anthony	.05
364	Greg Hibbard	.05
365	Scott Leius	.05
366	Hensley Meulens	.05
367	Chris Bosio	.05
368	Brian Downing	.05
369	Sammy Sosa	1.00
370	Stan Belinda	.05
371	Joe Grahe	.05
372	Luis Salazar	.05
373	Lance Johnson	.05
374	Kal Daniels	.05
375	Dave Winfield	.75
376	Brook Jacoby	.05
377	Mariano Duncan	.05
378	Ron Darling	.05
379	Randy Johnson	.75
380	Chito Martinez	.05
381	Andres Galarraga	.05
382	Willie Randolph	.05
383	Charles Nagy	.05
384	Tim Belcher	.05
385	Duane Ward	.05
386	Vicente Palacios	.05
387	Mike Gallego	.05
388	Rich DeLucia	.05
389	Scott Radinsky	.05
390	Damon Berryhill	.05
391	Kirk McCaskill	.05
392	Pedro Guerrero	.05
393	Kevin Mitchell	.05
394	Dickie Thon	.05
395	Bobby Bonilla	.05
396	Bill Wegman	.05
397	Dave Martinez	.05
398	Rick Sutcliffe	.05
399	Larry Andersen	.05
400	Tony Gwynn	1.00
401	Rickey Henderson	.75
402	Greg Cadaret	.05
403	Keith Miller	.05
404	Bip Roberts	.05
405	Kevin Brown	.05
406	Mitch Williams	.05
407	Frank Viola	.05
408	Darren Lewis	.05
409	Bob Walk	.05
410	Bob Walk	.05
411	Todd Frohwirth	.05
412	Brian Hunter	.05
413	Ron Karkovice	.05
414	Mike Morgan	.05
415	Joe Hesketh	.05
416	Don Slaught	.05
417	Tom Henke	.05
418	Kurt Stillwell	.05
419	Hector Villanueva	.05
420	Glenallen Hill	.05
421	Pat Borders	.05
422	Charlie Hough	.05
423	Charlie Leibrandt	.05
424	Eddie Murray	.75
425	Jesse Barfield	.05
426	Mark Lemke	.05
427	Kevin McReynolds	.05
428	Gilberto Reyes	.05
429	Ramon Martinez	.05
430	Steve Buechele	.05
431	David Wells	.05
432	Kyle Abbott	.05
433	John Habyan	.05
434	Kevin Appier	.05
435	Gene Larkin	.05
436	Sandy Alomar, Jr.	.05
437	Mike Jackson	.05
438	Todd Benzinger	.05
439	Teddy Higuera	.05
440	Reggie Sanders	.05
441	Mark Carreon	.05
442	Bret Saberhagen	.05
443	Gene Nelson	.05
444	Jay Howell	.05
445	Roger McDowell	.05
446	Sid Bream	.05
447	Mackey Sasser	.05
448	Bill Swift	.05
449	Hubie Brooks	.05
450	David Cone	.05
451	Bobby Witt	.05
452	Brady Anderson	.05
453	Lee Stevens	.05
454	Luis Aquino	.05
455	Carney Lansford	.05
456	Carlos Hernandez	.05
457	Danny Jackson	.05
458	Gerald Young	.05
459	Tom Candiotti	.05
460	Billy Hatcher	.05
461	John Wetteland	.05
462	Mike Bordick	.05
463	Don Robinson	.05
464	Jeff Johnson	.05
465	Lonnie Smith	.05
466	Paul Assenmacher	.05
467	Alvin Davis	.05
468	Jim Eisenreich	.05
469	Brent Mayne	.05
470	Jeff Brantley	.05
471	Tim Burke	.05
472	Pat Mahomes RC	.05
473	Ryan Bowen	.05
474	Bryn Smith	.05
475	Mike Flanagan	.05
476	Reggie Jefferson	.05
477	Jeff Blauser	.05
478	Craig Lefferts	.05
479	Todd Worrell	.05
480	Scott Scudder	.05
481	Kirk Gibson	.05
482	Kenny Rogers	.05
483	Jack Morris	.05
484	Russ Swan	.05
485	Mike Huff	.05
486	Ken Hill	.05
487	Geronimo Pena	.05
488	Charlie O'Brien	.05
489	Mike Maddux	.05
490	Scott Livingstone	.05
491	Carl Willis	.05
492	Kelly Downs	.05
493	Dennis Cook	.05
494	Joe Magrane	.05
495	Bob Kipper	.05
496	Jose Mesa	.05
497	Charlie Hayes	.05
498	Joe Girardi	.05
499	Doug Jones	.05
500	Barry Bonds	2.00
501	Bill Krueger	.05
502	Glenn Braggs	.05
503	Eric King	.05
504	Frank Castillo	.05
505	Mike Gardiner	.05
506	Cory Snyder	.05
507	Steve Howe	.05
508	Jose Rijo	.05
509	Sid Fernandez	.05
510	Archi Cianfrocco RC	.05
511	Mark Guthrie	.05
512	Bob Ojeda	.05
513	John Doherty	.05
514	Dante Bichette	.05
515	Juan Berenguer	.05
516	Jeff Robinson	.05
517	Mike MacFarlane	.05
518	Matt Young	.05
519	Otis Nixon	.05
520	Brian Holman	.05
521	Chris Haney	.05
522	Jeff Kent RC	.75
523	Chad Curtis RC	.25
524	Vince Horsman	.05
525	Rod Nichols	.05
526	Peter Hoy RC	.05
527	Shawn Boskie	.05
528	Alejandro Pena	.05
529	Dave Burba	.05
530	Ricky Jordan	.05
531	David Silvestri	.05
532	John Patterson	.05
533	Jeff Branson	.05
534	Derrick May	.05
535	Esteban Beltre	.05
536	Jose Melendez	.05
537	Wally Joyner	.05
538	Eddie Taubensee	.05
539	Jim Abbott	.05
540	Brian Williams RC	.05
541	Donovan Osborne	.05
542	Patrick Lennon	.05
543	Mike Groppuso RC	.05
544	Jarvis Brown RC	.05
545	Shawn Livesy RC	.05
546	Jeff Ware	.05
547	Danny Tartabull	.05
548	Bobby Jones RC	.05
549	Ken Griffey Jr.	1.50
550	Rey Sanchez RC	.05
551	Pedro Astacio RC	.10
552	Juan Guerrero RC	.05
553	Jacob Brumfield RC	.05
554	Ben Rivera RC	.05
555	Brian Jordan RC	.40
556	Denny Neagle	.05
557	Cliff Brantley	.05
558	Anthony Young	.05
559	John VanderWal RC	.05
560	Monty Fariss RC	.05
561	Russ Springer RC	.05
562	Pat Listach RC	.05
563	Pat Hentgen	.05
564	Andy Stankiewicz	.05
565	Mike Perez	.05
566	Mike Bielecki	.05
567	Butch Henry	.05
568	Dave Nilsson RC	.05
569	Scott Hatteberg RC	.05
570	Ruben Amaro Jr.	.05
571	Todd Hundley	.05
572	Moises Alou	.05
573	Hector Fajardo	.05
574	Todd Van Poppel	.05
575	Willie Banks	.05
576	Bob Zupcic	.05
577	J.J. Johnson RC	.05
578	John Burkett	.05
579	Trever Miller	.05
580	Scott Bankhead	.05
581	Rich Amaral	.05
582	Kenny Lofton	.05
583	Matt Stairs	.05
584	Don Mattingly, Rod Carew	.25
585	Jack Morris, Steve Avery	.05
586	Roberto Alomar, Sandy Alomar	.10
587	Scott Sanderson, Catfish Hunter	.05
588	Dave Justice, Willie Stargell	.05
589	Rex Hudler, Roger Staubach	.05
590	David Cone, Jackie Gleason	.05
591	Willie Davis, Tony Gwynn	.15
592	Orel Hershiser	.05
593	John Wetteland	.05
594	Tom Glavine	.05
595	Randy Johnson	.25
596	Jim Gott	.05
597	Donald Harris	.05
598	Shawn Hare RC	.05
599	Chris Gardner	.05
600	Rusty Meacham	.05
601	Benito Santiago	.05
602	Eric Davis	.05
603	Jose Lind	.05
604	Dave Justice	.05
605	Tim Raines	.05
606	Randy Tomlin	.05
607	Jack McDowell	.05
608	Greg Maddux	.30
609	Charles Nagy	.05
610	Tom Candiotti	.05
611	David Cone	.05
612	Steve Avery	.05
613	Rod Beck RC	.10
614	Rickey Henderson	.25
615	Benito Santiago	.05
616	Ruben Sierra	.05
617	Ryne Sandberg	.50
618	Nolan Ryan	1.00
619	Brett Butler	.05
620	Dave Justice	.05

Mickey Mantle

#		NM/M
	Complete Set (30):	20.00
	Common Card:	1.00
1	Father and Son	1.00
2	High School	1.00
3	Commerce Comet	1.00
4	Spring Training	1.00
5	The Beginning	1.00
6	No. 6	1.00
7	The Rookie	1.00
8	Tape-Measure Shots	1.00
9	Shortstop	1.00
10	Outfield	1.00
11	Speed, Speed, Speed	1.00
12	Contracts	1.00
13	Three-time MVP	1.00
14	Triple Crown	1.00
15	Series Slam	1.00
16	Series Star	1.00
17	Switch Hitter	1.00
18	Fan Favorite	1.00
19	Milestones	1.00
20	Enthuiasm	1.00
21	Hitting	1.00
22	First Base	1.00
23	Courage	1.00
24	Mick & Stan (Musial)	1.00
25	Whitey & Yogi (Ford, Berra)	1.00
26	Mick & Billy (Martin)	1.00
27	Mick & Casey (Stengel)	1.00
28	Awards	1.00
29	Retirement	1.00
30	Cooperstown	1.00

Rookies

		NM/M
	Complete Set (30):	2.00
	Common Player:	.05
1	Luis Mercedes	.05
2	Scott Cooper	.05
3	Kenny Lofton	.25
4	John Doherty	.05
5	Pat Listach	.05
6	Andy Stankiewicz	.05
7	Derek Bell	.25
8	Gary DiSarcina	.05
9	Roberto Hernandez	.15
10	Joel Johnston	.05
11	Pat Mahomes	.05
12	Todd Van Poppel	.05
13	Dave Fleming	.05
14	Monty Fariss	.05
15	Gary Scott	.05
16	Moises Alou	.25
17	Todd Hundley	.25
18	Kim Batiste	.05
19	Denny Neagle	.05
20	Donovan Osborne	.05
21	Mark Wohlers	.05
22	Reggie Sanders	.10
23	Brian Williams	.05
24	Eric Karros	.25
25	Frank Seminara	.05
26	Royce Clayton	.05
27	Dave Nilsson	.05
28	Matt Stairs	.25
29	Chad Curtis	.25
30	Carlos Hernandez	.25

Rookie Idols

		NM/M
	Complete Set (18):	20.00
	Common Player:	.50
1	Reggie Sanders, Eric Davis	.50
2	Hector Fajardo, Jim Abbott	.50
3	Gary Cooper, George Brett	3.50
4	Mark Wohlers, Roger Clemens	3.50
5	Luis Mercedes, Julio Franco	.50
6	Willie Banks, Dwight Gooden	.50
7	Kenny Lofton, Rickey Henderson	1.50
8	Keith Mitchell, Dave Henderson	.50
9	Kim Batiste, Barry Larkin	.50
10	Thurman Munson, Todd Hundley	1.00
11	Eddie Zosky, Cal Ripken Jr.	4.50
12	Todd Van Poppel, Nolan Ryan	4.50
13	Ryne Sandberg, Jim Thome	2.50
14	Dave Fleming, Bobby Murcer	.50
15	Royce Clayton, Ozzie Smith	2.50

16	Don Harris, Darryl Strawberry	.50
17	Alan Trammell, Chad Curtis	.50
18	Derek Bell, Dave Winfield	1.50

Slugfest

		NM/M
	Complete Set (15):	15.00
	Common Player:	.30
1	Cecil Fielder	.30
2	Mark McGwire	2.50
3	Jose Canseco	.65
4	Barry Bonds	3.00
5	Dave Justice	.30
6	Bobby Bonilla	.30
7	Ken Griffey Jr.	2.00
8	Ron Gant	.30
9	Ryne Sandberg	1.50
10	Ruben Sierra	.30
11	Frank Thomas	1.00
12	Will Clark	.30
13	Kirby Puckett	1.50
14	Cal Ripken, Jr.	3.00
15	Jeff Bagwell	1.00

Team Pinnacle

		NM/M
	Complete Set (12):	40.00
	Common Player:	1.50
1	Roger Clemens, Ramon Martinez	8.00
2	Jim Abbott, Steve Avery	1.50
3	Benito Santiago, Ivan Rodriguez	3.00
4	Frank Thomas, Will Clark	3.00
5	Roberto Alomar, Ryne Sandberg	6.00
6	Robin Ventura, Matt Williams	1.50
7	Cal Ripken, Jr., Barry Larkin	10.00
8	Danny Tartabull, Barry Bonds	8.00
9	Brett Butler, Ken Griffey Jr.	8.00
10	Ruben Sierra, Dave Justice	1.50
11	Dennis Eckersley, Rob Dibble	1.50
12	Scott Radinsky, John Franco	1.50

Team 2000

		NM/M
	Complete Set (80):	3.00
	Common Player:	.05
1	Mike Mussina	.30
2	Phil Plantier	.05
3	Frank Thomas	.50
4	Travis Fryman	.05
5	Kevin Appier	.05
6	Chuck Knoblauch	.05
7	Pat Kelly	.05
8	Ivan Rodriguez	.40
9	Dave Justice	.05
10	Jeff Bagwell	.50
11	Marquis Grissom	.05
12	Andy Benes	.05
13	Gregg Olson	.05
14	Kevin Morton	.05
15	Tim Naehring	.05
16	Dave Hollins	.05
17	Sandy Alomar Jr.	.05
18	Albert Belle	.05
19	Charles Nagy	.05
20	Brian McRae	.05
21	Larry Walker	.05
22	Delino DeShields	.05
23	Jeff Johnson	.05
24	Bernie Williams	.05
25	Jose Offerman	.05
26	Juan Gonzalez	.25
27	Juan Guzman	.05
28	Eric Anthony	.05
29	Brian Hunter	.05
30	John Smoltz	.05
31	Deion Sanders	.05
32	Greg Maddux	.75
33	Andujar Cedeno	.05
34	Royce Clayton	.05
35	Kenny Lofton	.05
36	Cal Eldred	.05
37	Jim Thome	.50
38	Gary DiSarcina	.05
39	Brian Jordan	.05
40	Chad Curtis	.05
41	Ben McDonald	.05
42	Jim Abbott	.05
43	Robin Ventura	.05
44	Milt Cuyler	.05
45	Gregg Jefferies	.05
46	Scott Radinsky	.05
47	Ken Griffey Jr.	1.00
48	Roberto Alomar	.15
49	Ramon Martinez	.05
50	Bret Barberie	.05
51	Ray Lankford	.05
52	Leo Gomez	.05
53	Tommy Greene	.05
54	Mo Vaughn	.05
55	Sammy Sosa	.75
56	Carlos Baerga	.05
57	Mark Lewis	.05
58	Tom Gordon	.05
59	Gary Sheffield	.25
60	Scott Erickson	.05
61	Pedro Munoz	.05
62	Tino Martinez	.05
63	Darren Lewis	.05
64	Dean Palmer	.05
65	John Olerud	.05
66	Steve Avery	.05
67	Pete Harnisch	.05
68	Luis Gonzalez	.05
69	Kim Batiste	.05
70	Reggie Sanders	.05
71	Luis Mercedes	.05
72	Todd Van Poppel	.05
73	Gary Scott	.05
74	Monty Fariss	.05
75	Kyle Abbott	.05
76	Eric Karros	.05
77	Mo Sanford	.05
78	Todd Hundley	.05
79	Reggie Jefferson	.05
80	Pat Mahomes	.05

1993 Pinnacle

		NM/M
	Complete Set (620):	17.50
	Common Player:	.05
	Series 1 Pack (15):	.35
	Series 1 Box (36):	8.00
	Series 2 Pack (15):	.75
	Series 2 Box (36):	20.00
1	Gary Sheffield	.30
2	Cal Eldred	.05
3	Larry Walker	.05
4	Deion Sanders	.05
5	Dave Fleming	.05
6	Carlos Baerga	.05
7	Bernie Williams	.05
8	John Kruk	.05
9	Jimmy Key	.05
10	Jeff Bagwell	.60
11	Jim Abbott	.05
12	Terry Steinbach	.05
13	Bob Tewksbury	.05
14	Eric Karros	.05
15	Ryne Sandberg	.75
16	Will Clark	.05
17	Edgar Martinez	.05
18	Eddie Murray	.60
19	Andy Van Slyke	.05
20	Cal Ripken, Jr.	2.00
21	Ivan Rodriguez	.50
22	Barry Larkin	.05
23	Don Mattingly	.85
24	Gregg Jefferies	.05
25	Roger Clemens	.85
26	Cecil Fielder	.05
27	Kent Hrbek	.05
28	Robin Ventura	.05
29	Rickey Henderson	.60
30	Roberto Alomar	.15
31	Luis Polonia	.05
32	Andujar Cedeno	.05
33	Pat Listach	.05
34	Mark Grace	.05
35	Otis Nixon	.05
36	Felix Jose	.05
37	Mike Sharperson	.05
38	Dennis Martinez	.05
39	Willie McGee	.05
40	Kenny Lofton	.05
41	Randy Johnson	.60
42	Andy Benes	.05
43	Bobby Bonilla	.05
44	Mike Mussina	.50
45	Len Dykstra	.05
46	Ellis Burks	.05
47	Chris Sabo	.05
48	Jay Bell	.05
49	Jose Canseco	.40
50	Craig Biggio	.05
51	Wally Joyner	.05
52	Mickey Tettleton	.05
53	Tim Raines	.05
54	Brian Harper	.05
55	Rene Gonzales	.05
56	Mark Langston	.05
57	Jack Morris	.05
58	Mark McGwire	1.50
59	Ken Caminiti	.05
60	Terry Pendleton	.05
61	Dave Nilsson	.05
62	Tom Pagnozzi	.05
63	Mike Morgan	.05
64	Darryl Strawberry	.05
65	Charles Nagy	.05
66	Ken Hill	.05
67	Matt Williams	.05
68	Jay Buhner	.05
69	Vince Coleman	.05
70	Brady Anderson	.05
71	Fred McGriff	.05
72	Ben McDonald	.05
73	Terry Mulholland	.05
74	Randy Tomlin	.05
75	Nolan Ryan	2.00
76	Frank Viola	.05
77	Jose Rijo	.05
78	Shane Mack	.05
79	Travis Fryman	.05
80	Jack McDowell	.05
81	Mark Gubicza	.05
82	Matt Nokes	.05
83	Bert Blyleven	.05
84	Eric Anthony	.05
85	Mike Bordick	.05
86	John Olerud	.05
87	B.J. Surhoff	.05

#	Name	Value	#	Name	Value	#	Name	Value	#	Name	Value
88	Bernard Gilkey	.05	192	Scott Leius	.05	296	Bert Blyleven	.05	400	Mike Devereaux	.05
89	Shawon Dunston	.05	193	Milt Cuyler	.05	297	Jeff Bagwell	.30	401	Tim Wakefield	.05
90	Tom Glavine	.30	194	Chris Haney	.05	298	John Smoltz	.05	402	Curt Schilling	.30
91	Brett Butler	.05	195	Ron Karkovice	.05	299	Larry Walker	.05	403	Zane Smith	.05
92	Moises Alou	.05	196	Steve Farr	.05	300	Gary Sheffield	.15	404	Bob Zupcic	.05
93	Albert Belle	.05	197	John Orton	.05	301	Ivan Rodriguez	.30	405	Tom Browning	.05
94	Darren Lewis	.05	198	Kelly Gruber	.05	302	Delino DeShields	.05	406	Tony Phillips	.05
95	Omar Vizquel	.05	199	Ron Darling	.05	303	Tim Salmon	.05	407	John Doherty	.05
96	Dwight Gooden	.05	200	Ruben Sierra	.05	304	Bernard Gilkey	.05	408	Pat Mahomes	.05
97	Gregg Olson	.05	201	Chuck Finley	.05	305	Cal Ripken, Jr.	1.00	409	John Habyan	.05
98	Tony Gwynn	.75	202	Mike Moore	.05	306	Barry Larkin	.05	410	Steve Olin	.05
99	Darren Daulton	.05	203	Pat Borders	.05	307	Kent Hrbek	.05	411	Chad Curtis	.05
100	Dennis Eckersley	.50	204	Sid Bream	.05	308	Rickey Henderson	.30	412	Joe Grahe	.05
101	Rob Dibble	.05	205	Todd Zeile	.05	309	Darryl Strawberry	.05	413	John Patterson	.05
102	Mike Greenwell	.05	206	Rick Wilkins	.05	310	John Franco	.05	414	Brian Hunter	.05
103	Jose Lind	.05	207	Jim Gantner	.05	311	Todd Stottlemyre	.05	415	Doug Henry	.05
104	Julio Franco	.05	208	Frank Castillo	.05	312	Luis Gonzalez	.05	416	Lee Smith	.05
105	Tom Gordon	.05	209	Dave Hansen	.05	313	Tommy Greene	.05	417	Bob Scanlan	.05
106	Scott Livingstone	.05	210	Trevor Wilson	.05	314	Randy Velarde	.05	418	Kent Mercker	.05
107	Chuck Knoblauch	.05	211	Sandy Alomar, Jr.	.05	315	Steve Avery	.05	419	Mel Rojas	.05
108	Frank Thomas	.60	212	Sean Berry	.05	316	Jose Oquendo	.05	420	Mark Whiten	.05
109	Melido Perez	.05	213	Tino Martinez	.05	317	Rey Sanchez	.05	421	Carlton Fisk	.60
110	Ken Griffey Jr.	1.00	214	Chito Martinez	.05	318	Greg Vaughn	.05	422	Candy Maldonado	.05
111	Harold Baines	.05	215	Dan Walters	.05	319	Orel Hershiser	.05	423	Doug Drabek	.05
112	Gary Gaetti	.05	216	John Franco	.05	320	Paul Sorrento	.05	424	Wade Boggs	.75
113	Pete Harnisch	.05	217	Glenn Davis	.05	321	Royce Clayton	.05	425	Mark Davis	.05
114	David Wells	.05	218	Mariano Duncan	.05	322	John Vander Wal	.05	426	Kirby Puckett	.75
115	Charlie Leibrandt	.05	219	Mike LaValliere	.05	323	Henry Cotto	.05	427	Joe Carter	.05
116	Ray Lankford	.05	220	Rafael Palmeiro	.50	324	Pete Schourek	.05	428	Paul Molitor	.60
117	Kevin Seitzer	.05	221	Jack Clark	.05	325	David Segui	.05	429	Eric Davis	.05
118	Robin Yount	.60	222	Hal Morris	.05	326	Arthur Rhodes	.05	430	Darryl Kile	.05
119	Lenny Harris	.05	223	Ed Sprague	.05	327	Bruce Hurst	.05	431	Jeff Parrett/ED	.05
120	Chris James	.05	224	John Valentin	.05	328	Wes Chamberlain	.05	432	Jeff Blauser	.05
121	Delino DeShields	.05	225	Sam Militello	.05	329	Ozzie Smith	.75	433	Dan Plesac	.05
122	Kirt Manwaring	.05	226	Bob Wickman	.05	330	Scott Cooper	.05	434	Andres Galarraga/ED	.05
123	Glenallen Hill	.05	227	Damion Easley	.05	331	Felix Fermin	.05	435	Jim Gott	.05
124	Hensley Meulens	.05	228	John Jaha	.05	332	Mike Macfarlane	.05	436	Jose Mesa	.05
125	Darrin Jackson	.05	229	Bob Ayrault	.05	333	Dan Gladden	.05	437	Ben Rivera	.05
126	Todd Hundley	.05	230	Mo Sanford/ED	.05	334	Kevin Tapani	.05	438	Dave Winfield	.60
127	Dave Hollins	.05	231	Walt Weiss/ED	.05	335	Steve Sax	.05	439	Norm Charlton	.05
128	Sam Horn	.05	232	Dante Bichette/ED	.05	336	Jeff Montgomery	.05	440	Chris Bosio	.05
129	Roberto Hernandez	.05	233	Steve Decker/ED	.05	337	Gary DiSarcina	.05	441	Wilson Alvarez	.05
130	Vicente Palacios	.05	234	Jerald Clark/ED	.05	338	Lance Blankenship	.05	442	Dave Stewart	.05
131	George Brett	.85	235	Bryan Harvey/ED	.05	339	Brian Williams	.05	443	Doug Jones	.05
132	Dave Martinez	.05	236	Joe Girardi/ED	.05	340	Duane Ward	.05	444	Jeff Russell	.05
133	Kevin Appier	.05	237	Dave Magadan/ED	.05	341	Chuck McElroy	.05	445	Ron Gant	.05
134	Pat Kelly	.05	238	David Nied	.05	342	Joe Magrane	.05	446	Paul O'Neill	.05
135	Pedro Munoz	.05	239	Eric Wedge RC	.05	343	Jaime Navarro	.05	447	Charlie Hayes/ED	.05
136	Mark Carreon	.05	240	Rico Brogna	.05	344	Dave Justice	.05	448	Joe Hesketh	.05
137	Lance Johnson	.05	241	J.T. Bruett	.05	345	Jose Offerman	.05	449	Chris Hammond	.05
138	Devon White	.05	242	Jonathan Hurst	.05	346	Marquis Grissom	.05	450	Hipolito Pichardo	.05
139	Julio Valera	.05	243	Bret Boone	.05	347	Bill Swift	.05	451	Scott Radinsky	.05
140	Eddie Taubensee	.05	244	Manny Alexander	.05	348	Jim Thome	.50	452	Bobby Thigpen	.05
141	Willie Wilson	.05	245	Scooter Tucker	.05	349	Archi Cianfrocco	.05	453	Xavier Hernandez	.05
142	Stan Belinda	.05	246	Troy Neel	.05	350	Anthony Young	.05	454	Lonnie Smith	.05
143	John Smoltz	.05	247	Eddie Zosky	.05	351	Leo Gomez	.05	455	Jamie Arnold RC	.05
144	Darryl Hamilton	.05	248	Melvin Nieves	.05	352	Bill Gullickson	.05	456	B.J. Wallace	.05
145	Sammy Sosa	.75	249	Ryan Thompson	.05	353	Alan Trammell	.05	457	Derek Jeter RC	10.00
146	Carlos Hernandez	.05	250	Shawn Barton	.05	354	Dan Pasqua	.05	458	Jason Kendall RC	.75
147	Tom Candiotti	.05	251	Ryan Klesko	.05	355	Jeff King	.05	459	Rick Helling	.05
148	Mike Felder	.05	252	Mike Piazza	1.00	356	Kevin Brown	.05	460	Derek Wallace RC	.05
149	Rusty Meacham	.05	253	Steve Hosey	.05	357	Tim Belcher	.05	461	Sean Lowe RC	.05
150	Ivan Calderon	.05	254	Shane Reynolds	.05	358	Bip Roberts	.05	462	Shannon Stewart RC	.60
151	Pete O'Brien	.05	255	Dan Wilson	.05	359	Brent Mayne	.05	463	Benji Grigsby RC	.05
152	Erik Hanson	.05	256	Tom Marsh	.05	360	Rheal Cormier	.05	464	Todd Steverson RC	.05
153	Billy Ripken	.05	257	Barry Manuel	.05	361	Mark Guthrie	.05	465	Dan Serafini RC	.05
154	Kurt Stillwell	.05	258	Paul Miller	.05	362	Craig Grebeck	.05	466	Michael Tucker	.05
155	Jeff Kent	.05	259	Pedro Martinez	.60	363	Andy Stankiewicz	.05	467	Chris Roberts	.05
156	Mickey Morandini	.05	260	Steve Cooke	.05	364	Juan Guzman	.05	468	Pete Janicki RC	.05
157	Randy Milligan	.05	261	Johnny Guzman	.05	365	Bobby Witt	.05	469	Jeff Schmidt RC	.05
158	Reggie Sanders	.05	262	Mike Butcher	.05	366	Mark Portugal	.05	470	Don Mattingly	.45
159	Luis Rivera	.05	263	Bien Figueroa	.05	367	Brian McRae	.05	471	Cal Ripken, Jr.	1.00
160	Orlando Merced	.05	264	Rich Rowland	.05	368	Mark Lemke	.05	472	Jack Morris	.05
161	Dean Palmer	.05	265	Shawn Jeter	.05	369	Bill Wegman	.05	473	Terry Pendleton	.05
162	Mike Perez	.05	266	Gerald Williams	.05	370	Donovan Osborne	.05	474	Dennis Eckersley	.25
163	Scott Erikson	.05	267	Derek Parks	.05	371	Derrick May	.05	475	Carlton Fisk	.30
164	Kevin McReynolds	.05	268	Henry Mercedes	.05	372	Carl Willis	.05	476	Wade Boggs	.35
165	Kevin Maas	.05	269	David Hulse RC	.05	373	Chris Nabholz	.05	477	Len Dykstra	.05
166	Ozzie Guillen	.05	270	Tim Pugh RC	.05	374	Mark Lewis	.05	478	Danny Tartabull	.05
167	Rob Deer	.05	271	William Suero	.05	375	John Burkett	.05	479	Jeff Conine	.10
168	Danny Tartabull	.05	272	Ozzie Canseco	.05	376	Luis Mercedes	.05	480	Gregg Jefferies	.05
169	Lee Stevens	.05	273	Fernando Ramsey	.05	377	Ramon Martinez	.05	481	Paul Molitor	.30
170	Dave Henderson	.05	274	Bernardo Brito	.05	378	Kyle Abbott	.05	482	John Valentin	.05
171	Derek Bell	.05	275	Dave Mlicki	.05	379	Mark Wohlers	.05	483	Alex Arias	.10
172	Steve Finley	.05	276	Tim Salmon	.05	380	Bob Walk	.05	484	Barry Bonds	1.00
173	Greg Olson	.05	277	Mike Raczka	.05	381	Kenny Rogers	.05	485	Doug Drabek	.05
174	Geronimo Pena	.05	278	Ken Ryan RC	.05	382	Tim Naehring	.05	486	Dave Winfield	.30
175	Paul Quantrill	.05	279	Rafael Bournigal	.05	383	Alex Fernandez	.05	487	Brett Butler	.05
176	Steve Buechele	.05	280	Wil Cordero	.05	384	Keith Miller	.05	488	Harold Baines	.05
177	Kevin Gross	.05	281	Billy Ashley	.05	385	Mike Henneman	.05	489	David Cone	.05
178	Tim Wallach	.05	282	Paul Wagner	.05	386	Rick Aguilera	.05	490	Willie McGee	.05
179	Dave Valle	.05	283	Blas Minor	.05	387	George Bell	.05	491	Robby Thompson	.05
180	Dave Silvestri	.05	284	Rick Trlicek	.05	388	Mike Gallego	.05	492	Pete Incaviglia	.05
181	Bud Black	.05	285	Willie Greene	.05	389	Howard Johnson	.05	493	Manuel Lee	.05
182	Henry Rodriguez	.05	286	Ted Wood	.05	390	Kim Batiste	.05	494	Rafael Belliard	.05
183	Tim Teufel	.05	287	Phil Clark	.05	391	Jerry Browne	.05	495	Scott Fletcher	.05
184	Mark McLemore	.05	288	Jesse Levis	.05	392	Damon Berryhill	.05	496	Jeff Frye	.05
185	Bret Saberhagen	.05	289	Tony Gwynn	.40	393	Ricky Bones	.05	497	Andre Dawson	.25
186	Chris Hoiles	.05	290	Nolan Ryan	1.00	394	Omar Olivares	.05	498	Mike Scioscia	.05
187	Ricky Jordan	.05	291	Dennis Martinez	.05	395	Mike Harkey	.05	499	Spike Owen	.05
188	Don Slaught	.05	292	Eddie Murray	.30	396	Pedro Astacio	.05	500	Sid Fernandez	.05
189	Mo Vaughn	.05	293	Robin Yount	.30	397	John Wetteland	.05	501	Joe Orsulak	.05
190	Joe Oliver	.05	294	George Brett	.45	398	Rod Beck	.05	502	Benito Santiago/ED	.05
191	Juan Gonzalez	.30	295	Dave Winfield	.30	399	Thomas Howard	.05	503	Dale Murphy	.25

504	Barry Bonds	2.00
505	Jose Guzman	.05
506	Tony Pena	.05
507	Greg Swindell	.05
508	Mike Pagliarulo	.05
509	Lou Whitaker	.05
510	Greg Gagne	.05
511	Butch Henry/ED	.05
512	Jeff Brantley	.05
513	Jack Armstrong/ED	.05
514	Danny Jackson	.05
515	Junior Felix/ED	.05
516	Milt Thompson	.05
517	Greg Maddux	.75
518	Eric Young/ED	.05
519	Jody Reed	.05
520	Roberto Kelly	.05
521	Darren Holmes/ED	.05
522	Craig Lefferts	.05
523	Charlie Hough/ED	.05
524	Bo Jackson	.10
525	Bill Spiers	.05
526	Orestes Destrade/ED	.05
527	Greg Hibbard	.05
528	Roger McDowell	.05
529	Cory Snyder	.05
530	Harold Reynolds	.05
531	Kevin Reimer	.05
532	Rick Sutcliffe	.05
533	Tony Fernandez	.05
534	Tom Brunansky	.05
535	Jeff Reardon	.05
536	Chili Davis	.05
537	Bob Ojeda	.05
538	Greg Colbrunn	.05
539	Phil Plantier	.05
540	Brian Jordan	.05
541	Pete Smith	.05
542	Frank Tanana	.05
543	John Smiley	.05
544	David Cone	.05
545	Daryl Boston/ED	.05
546	Tom Henke	.05
547	Bill Krueger	.05
548	Freddie Benavides/ED	.05
549	Randy Myers	.05
550	Reggie Jefferson	.05
551	Kevin Mitchell	.05
552	Dave Stieb	.05
553	Bret Barberie/ED	.05
554	Tim Crews	.05
555	Doug Dascenzo	.05
556	Alex Cole/ED	.05
557	Jeff Innis	.05
558	Carlos Garcia	.05
559	Steve Howe	.05
560	Kirk McCaskill	.05
561	Frank Seminara	.05
562	Cris Carpenter/ED	.05
563	Mike Stanley	.05
564	Carlos Quintana	.05
565	Mitch Williams	.05
566	Juan Bell	.05
567	Eric Fox	.05
568	Al Leiter	.05
569	Mike Stanton	.05
570	Scott Kamieniecki	.05
571	Ryan Bowen/ED	.05
572	Andy Ashby/ED	.05
573	Bob Welch	.05
574	Scott Sanderson	.05
575	Joe Kmak	.05
576	Scott Pose/ED	.05
577	Ricky Gutierrez	.05
578	Mike Trombley	.05
579	Sterling Hitchcock RC	.10
580	Rodney Bolton	.05
581	Tyler Green	.05
582	Tim Costo	.05
583	Tim Laker RC	.05
584	Steve Reed/ED RC	.05
585	Tom Kramer RC	.05
586	Robb Nen	.05
587	Jim Tatum RC	.05
588	Frank Bolick	.05
589	Kevin Young	.05
590	Matt Whiteside RC	.05
591	Cesar Hernandez	.05
592	Mike Mohler RC	.05
593	Alan Embree	.05
594	Terry Jorgensen	.05
595	John Cummings RC	.05
596	Domingo Martinez	.05
597	Benji Gil	.05
598	Todd Pratt RC	.05
599	Rene Arocha RC	.05
600	Dennis Moeller	.05
601	Jeff Conine/ED	.05
602	Trevor Hoffman/ED	.05
603	Daniel Smith	.05
604	Lee Tinsley	.05
605	Dan Peltier	.05
606	Billy Brewer	.05
607	Matt Walbeck RC	.05
608	Richie Lewis/ED	.05
609	J.T. Snow RC	.40
610	Pat Gomez RC	.05
611	Phil Hiatt	.05
612	Alex Arias/ED	.05
613	Kevin Rogers	.05
614	Al Martin	.05
615	Greg Gohr	.05
616	Grame Lloyd RC	.05
617	Kent Bottenfield	.05
618	Chuck Carr/ED	.05
619	Darrell Sherman RC	.05
620	Mike Lansing RC	.15

Cooperstown

		NM/M
Complete Set (30):		7.50
Common Player:		.25
Dufex:		25X
Promo:		30X
1	Nolan Ryan	2.00
2	George Brett	.85
3	Robin Yount	.65
4	Carlton Fisk	.65
5	Dale Murphy	.35
6	Dennis Eckersley	.50
7	Rickey Henderson	.65
8	Ryne Sandberg	.75
9	Ozzie Smith	.75
10	Dave Winfield	.65
11	Andre Dawson	.35
12	Kirby Puckett	.75
13	Wade Boggs	.75
14	Don Mattingly	.85
15	Barry Bonds	2.00
16	Will Clark	.25
17	Cal Ripken, Jr.	2.00
18	Roger Clemens	.85
19	Dwight Gooden	.25
20	Tony Gwynn	.75
21	Joe Carter	.25
22	Ken Griffey Jr.	1.00
23	Paul Molitor	.60
24	Frank Thomas	.60
25	Juan Gonzalez	.35
26	Barry Larkin	.25
27	Eddie Murray	.60
28	Cecil Fielder	.25
29	Roberto Alomar	.35
30	Mark McGwire	1.50

Home Run Club

		NM/M
Complete Set (30):		6.00
Common Player:		.10
1	Juan Gonzalez	.40
2	Fred McGriff	.10
3	Cecil Fielder	.10
4	Barry Bonds	1.50
5	Albert Belle	.10
6	Gary Sheffield	.25
7	Joe Carter	.10
8	Mark McGwire	1.25
9	Darren Daulton	.10
10	Jose Canseco	.50
11	Dave Hollins	.10
12	Ryne Sandberg	.85
13	Ken Griffey Jr.	1.00
14	Larry Walker	.10
15	Rob Deer	.10
16	Andre Dawson	.25
17	Frank Thomas	.75
18	Mickey Tettleton	.10
19	Charlie Hayes	.10
20	Ron Gant	.10
21	Rickey Henderson	.75
22	Matt Williams	.10
23	Kevin Mitchell	.10
24	Robin Ventura	.10
25	Dean Palmer	.10
26	Mike Piazza	1.00
27	J.T. Snow	.10
28	Jeff Bagwell	.75
29	John Olerud	.10
30	Greg Vaughn	.10
31	Dave Justice	.10
32	Dave Winfield	.75
33	Danny Tartabull	.10
34	Eric Anthony	.10
35	Eddie Murray	.75
36	Jay Buhner	.10
37	Derek Bell	.10
38	Will Clark	.10
39	Carlos Baerga	.10
40	Mo Vaughn	.10
41	Bobby Bonilla	.10
42	Tim Salmon	.10
43	Bo Jackson	.10
44	Howard Johnson	.10
45	Kent Hrbek	.10
46	Ruben Sierra	.10
47	Cal Ripken, Jr.	1.50
48	Travis Fryman	.10

Rookie Team Pinnacle

		NM/M
Complete Set (10):		20.00
Common Player:		1.50
1	Pedro Martinez, Mike Trombley	6.00
2	Kevin Rogers, Sterling Hitchcock	1.50
3	Mike Piazza, Jesse Levis	10.00
4	Ryan Klesko, J.T. Snow	1.50
5	John Patterson, Bret Boone	1.50
6	Domingo Martinez, Kevin Young	1.50
7	Wil Cordero, Manny Alexander	1.50
8	Steve Hosey, Tim Salmon	1.50
9	Ryan Thompson, Gerald Williams	1.50
10	Melvin Nieves, David Hulse	1.50

Slugfest

		NM/M
Complete Set (30):		12.50
Common Player:		.25
1	Juan Gonzalez	.50
2	Mark McGwire	2.00
3	Cecil Fielder	.25
4	Joe Carter	.25
5	Fred McGriff	.25
6	Barry Bonds	2.50
7	Gary Sheffield	.50
8	Dave Hollins	.25
9	Frank Thomas	1.00
10	Danny Tartabull	.25
11	Albert Belle	.25
12	Ruben Sierra	.25
13	Larry Walker	.25
14	Jeff Bagwell	1.00
15	Dave Justice	.25
16	Kirby Puckett	1.25
17	John Kruk	.25
18	Howard Johnson	.25
19	Darryl Strawberry	.25
20	Will Clark	.25
21	Kevin Mitchell	.25
22	Mickey Tettleton	.25
23	Don Mattingly	1.50
24	Jose Canseco	.75
25	Sam Militello	.25
26	Andre Dawson	.50
27	Ryne Sandberg	1.25
28	Ken Griffey Jr.	1.75
29	Carlos Baerga	.25
30	Travis Fryman	.25

Team Pinnacle

		NM/M
Complete Set (11):		40.00
Common Player:		1.50
1	Greg Maddux, Mike Mussina	10.00
2	Tom Glavine, John Smiley	2.00
3	Darren Daulton, Ivan Rodriguez	3.00
4	Fred McGriff, Frank Thomas	4.00
5	Delino DeShields, Carlos Baerga	1.50
6	Gary Sheffield, Edgar Martinez	2.00
7	Ozzie Smith, Pat Listach	8.00
8	Barry Bonds, Juan Gonzalez	15.00
9	Kirby Puckett, Andy Van Slyke	8.00
10	Larry Walker, Joe Carter	1.50
11	Rick Aguilera, Rob Dibble	1.50

Team 2001

		NM/M
Complete Set (30):		5.00
Common Player:		.05
1	Wil Cordero	.05
2	Cal Eldred	.05
3	Mike Mussina	.60
4	Chuck Knoblauch	.05
5	Melvin Nieves	.05
6	Tim Wakefield	.05
7	Carlos Baerga	.05
8	Bret Boone	.05

9	Jeff Bagwell	1.00
10	Travis Fryman	.05
11	Royce Clayton	.05
12	Delino DeShields	.05
13	Juan Gonzalez	.50
14	Pedro Martinez	1.00
15	Bernie Williams	.05
16	Billy Ashley	.05
17	Marquis Grissom	.05
18	Kenny Lofton	.05
19	Ray Lankford	.05
20	Tim Salmon	.05
21	Steve Hosey	.05
22	Charles Nagy	.05
23	Dave Fleming	.05
24	Reggie Sanders	.05
25	Sam Militello	.05
26	Eric Karros	.05
27	Ryan Klesko	.05
28	Dean Palmer	.05
29	Ivan Rodriguez	.75
30	Sterling Hitchcock	.05

Tribute

George Brett

	NM/M
Complete Set (10):	10.00
George Brett Card (1-5):	1.00
Nolan Ryan Card (6-10):	1.50

1	George Brett/ Kansas City Royalty	1.00
2	George Brett The Chase for .400	1.00
3	Pine Tar Pandemonium - "The Bat"	1.00
4	George Brett MVP and a World Series, Too	1.00
5	George Brett 3,000 or Bust	1.00
6	Nolan Ryan The Rookie	1.50
7	Nolan Ryan Angel of No Mercy	1.50
8	Nolan Ryan Astronomical Success	1.50
9	Nolan Ryan 5,000 Ks	1.50
10	Nolan Ryan No-Hitter No. 7	1.50

1994 Pinnacle

	NM/M
Complete Set (540):	15.00
Common Player:	.05
Artist's Proofs:	20X
Museums:	6X
Series 1 or 2 Pack (14):	.75
Series 1 or 2 Box (24):	12.50

1	Frank Thomas	.65
2	Carlos Baerga	.05
3	Sammy Sosa	.75
4	Tony Gwynn	.75
5	John Olerud	.05
6	Ryne Sandberg	.75
7	Moises Alou	.05
8	Steve Avery	.05
9	Tim Salmon	.05
10	Cecil Fielder	.05
11	Greg Maddux	.75
12	Barry Larkin	.05
13	Mike Devereaux	.05
14	Charlie Hayes	.05
15	Albert Belle	.05
16	Andy Van Slyke	.05
17	Mo Vaughn	.05
18	Brian McRae	.05
19	Cal Eldred	.05
20	Craig Biggio	.05
21	Kirby Puckett	.75
22	Derek Bell	.05
23	Don Mattingly	.85
24	John Burkett	.05
25	Roger Clemens	.85
26	Barry Bonds	2.00
27	Paul Molitor	.65
28	Mike Piazza	1.00
29	Robin Ventura	.05
30	Jeff Conine	.05
31	Wade Boggs	.75
32	Dennis Eckersley	.50
33	Bobby Bonilla	.05
34	Len Dykstra	.05
35	Manny Alexander	.05
36	Ray Lankford	.05
37	Greg Vaughn	.05
38	Chuck Finley	.05
39	Todd Benzinger	.05
40	Dave Justice	.05
41	Rob Dibble	.05
42	Tom Henke	.05
43	David Nied	.05
44	Sandy Alomar Jr.	.05
45	Pete Harnisch	.05
46	Jeff Russell	.05
47	Terry Mulholland	.05
48	Kevin Appier	.05
49	Randy Tomlin	.05
50	Cal Ripken, Jr.	2.00
51	Andy Benes	.05
52	Jimmy Key	.05
53	Kirt Manwaring	.05
54	Kevin Tapani	.05
55	Jose Guzman	.05
56	Todd Stottlemyre	.05
57	Jack McDowell	.05
58	Orel Hershiser	.05
59	Chris Hammond	.05
60	Chris Nabholz	.05
61	Ruben Sierra	.05
62	Dwight Gooden	.05
63	John Kruk	.05
64	Omar Vizquel	.05
65	Tim Naehring	.05
66	Dwight Smith	.05
67	Mickey Tettleton	.05
68	J.T. Snow	.05
69	Greg McMichael	.05
70	Kevin Mitchell	.05
71	Kevin Brown	.05
72	Scott Cooper	.05
73	Jim Thome	.60
74	Joe Girardi	.05
75	Eric Anthony	.05
76	Orlando Merced	.05
77	Felix Jose	.05
78	Tommy Greene	.05
79	Bernard Gilkey	.05
80	Phil Plantier	.05
81	Danny Tartabull	.05
82	Trevor Wilson	.05
83	Chuck Knoblauch	.05
84	Rick Wilkins	.05
85	Devon White	.05
86	Lance Johnson	.05
87	Eric Karros	.05
88	Gary Sheffield	.35
89	Wil Cordero	.05
90	Ron Darling	.05
91	Darren Daulton	.05
92	Joe Orsulak	.05
93	Steve Cooke	.05
94	Darryl Hamilton	.05
95	Aaron Sele	.05
96	John Doherty	.05
97	Gary DiSarcina	.05
98	Jeff Blauser	.05
99	John Smiley	.05
100	Ken Griffey Jr.	1.00
101	Dean Palmer	.05
102	Felix Fermin	.05
103	Jerald Clark	.05
104	Doug Drabek	.05
105	Curt Schilling	.30
106	Jeff Montgomery	.05
107	Rene Arocha	.05
108	Carlos Garcia	.05
109	Wally Whitehurst	.05
110	Jim Abbott	.05
111	Royce Clayton	.05
112	Chris Hoiles	.05
113	Mike Morgan	.05
114	Joe Magrane	.05
115	Tom Candiotti	.05
116	Ron Karkovice	.05
117	Ryan Bowen	.05
118	Rod Beck	.05
119	John Wetteland	.05
120	Terry Steinbach	.05
121	Dave Hollins	.05
122	Jeff Kent	.05
123	Ricky Bones	.05
124	Brian Jordan	.05
125	Chad Kreuter	.05
126	John Valentin	.05
127	Billy Hathaway	.05
128	Wilson Alvarez	.05
129	Tino Martinez	.05
130	Rodney Bolton	.05
131	David Segui	.05
132	Wayne Kirby	.05
133	Eric Young	.05
134	Scott Servais	.05
135	Scott Radinsky	.05
136	Bret Barberie	.05
137	John Roper	.05
138	Ricky Gutierrez	.05
139	Bernie Williams	.05
140	Bud Black	.05
141	Jose Vizcaino	.05
142	Gerald Williams	.05
143	Duane Ward	.05
144	Danny Jackson	.05
145	Allen Watson	.05
146	Scott Fletcher	.05
147	Delino DeShields	.05
148	Shane Mack	.05
149	Jim Eisenreich	.05
150	Troy Neel	.05
151	Jay Bell	.05
152	B.J. Surhoff	.05
153	Mark Whiten	.05
154	Mike Henneman	.05
155	Todd Hundley	.05
156	Greg Myers	.05
157	Ryan Klesko	.05
158	Dave Fleming	.05
159	Mickey Morandini	.05
160	Blas Minor	.05
161	Reggie Jefferson	.05
162	David Hulse	.05
163	Greg Swindell	.05
164	Roberto Hernandez	.05
165	Brady Anderson	.05
166	Jack Armstrong	.05
167	Phil Clark	.05
168	Melido Perez	.05
169	Darren Lewis	.05
170	Sam Horn	.05
171	Mike Harkey	.05
172	Juan Guzman	.05
173	Bob Natal	.05
174	Deion Sanders	.05
175	Carlos Quintana	.05
176	Mel Rojas	.05
177	Willie Banks	.05
178	Ben Rivera	.05
179	Kenny Lofton	.05
180	Leo Gomez	.05
181	Roberto Mejia	.05
182	Mike Perez	.05
183	Travis Fryman	.05
184	Ben McDonald	.05
185	Steve Frey	.05
186	Kevin Young	.05
187	Dave Magadan	.05
188	Bobby Munoz	.05
189	Pat Rapp	.05
190	Jose Offerman	.05
191	Vinny Castilla	.05
192	Ivan Calderon	.05
193	Ken Caminiti	.05
194	Benji Gil	.05
195	Chuck Carr	.05
196	Derrick May	.05
197	Pat Kelly	.05
198	Jeff Brantley	.05
199	Jose Lind	.05
200	Steve Buechele	.05
201	Wes Chamberlain	.05
202	Eduardo Perez	.05
203	Bret Saberhagen	.05
204	Gregg Jefferies	.05
205	Darrin Fletcher	.05
206	Kent Hrbek	.05
207	Kim Batiste	.05
208	Jeff King	.05
209	Donovan Osborne	.05
210	Dave Nilsson	.05
211	Al Martin	.05
212	Mike Moore	.05
213	Sterling Hitchcock	.05
214	Geronimo Pena	.05
215	Kevin Higgins	.05
216	Norm Charlton	.05
217	Don Slaught	.05
218	Mitch Williams	.05
219	Derek Lilliquist	.05
220	Armando Reynoso	.05
221	Kenny Rogers	.05
222	Doug Jones	.05
223	Luis Aquino	.05
224	Mike Oquist	.05
225	Darryl Scott	.05
226	Kurt Abbott	.05
227	Andy Tomberlin	.05
228	Norberto Martin	.05
229	Pedro Castellano	.05
230	Curtis Pride RC	.05
231	Jeff McNeely	.05
232	Scott Lydy	.05
233	Darren Oliver	.05
234	Danny Bautista	.05
235	Butch Huskey	.05
236	Chipper Jones	.75
237	Eddie Zambrano	.05
238	Jean Domingo	.05
239	Javier Lopez	.05
240	Nigel Wilson	.05
241	Drew Denson RC	.05
242	Raul Mondesi	.05
243	Luis Ortiz	.05
244	Manny Ramirez	.65
245	Greg Blosser	.05
246	Rondell White	.05
247	Steve Karsay	.05
248	Scott Stahoviak	.05
249	Jose Valentin	.05
250	Marc Newfield	.05
251	Keith Kessinger	.05
252	Carl Everett	.05
253	John O'Donoghue	.05
254	Turk Wendell	.05
255	Scott Ruffcorn	.05
256	Tony Tarasco	.05
257	Andy Cook	.05
258	Matt Mieske	.05
259	Luis Lopez	.05
260	Ramon Caraballo	.05
261	Salomon Torres	.05
262	Brooks Kieschnick RC	.05
263	Daron Kirkreit RC	.05
264	Bill Wagner RC	.10
265	Matt Drews RC	.05
266	Scott Christman	.05
267	Torii Hunter RC	1.00
268	Jamey Wright RC	.05
269	Jeff Granger	.05
270	Trot Nixon RC	1.00
271	Randy Myers	.05
272	Trevor Hoffman	.05
273	Bob Wickman	.05
274	Willie McGee	.05
275	Hipolito Pichardo	.05
276	Bobby Witt	.05
277	Gregg Olson	.05
278	Randy Johnson	.65
279	Robb Nen	.05
280	Paul O'Neill	.05
281	Lou Whitaker	.05
282	Chad Curtis	.05
283	Doug Henry	.05
284	Tom Glavine	.30
285	Mike Greenwell	.05
286	Roberto Kelly	.05
287	Roberto Alomar	.15
288	Charlie Hough	.05
289	Alex Fernandez	.05
290	Jeff Bagwell	.65
291	Wally Joyner	.05
292	Andujar Cedeno	.05
293	Rick Aguilera	.05
294	Darryl Strawberry	.05
295	Mike Mussina	.35

No.	Player	Price
296	Jeff Gardner	.05
297	Chris Gwynn	.05
298	Matt Williams	.05
299	Brent Gates	.05
300	Mark McGwire	1.50
301	Jim Deshaies	.05
302	Edgar Martinez	.05
303	Danny Darwin	.05
304	Pat Meares	.05
305	Benito Santiago	.05
306	Jose Canseco	.40
307	Jim Gott	.05
308	Paul Sorrento	.05
309	Scott Kamieniecki	.05
310	Larry Walker	.05
311	Mark Langston	.05
312	John Jaha	.05
313	Stan Javier	.05
314	Hal Morris	.05
315	Robby Thompson	.05
316	Pat Hentgen	.05
317	Tom Gordon	.05
318	Joey Cora	.05
319	Luis Alicea	.05
320	Andre Dawson	.25
321	Darryl Kile	.05
322	Jose Rijo	.05
323	Luis Gonzalez	.05
324	Billy Ashley	.05
325	David Cone	.05
326	Bill Swift	.05
327	Phil Hiatt	.05
328	Craig Paquette	.05
329	Bob Welch	.05
330	Tony Phillips	.05
331	Archi Cianfrocco	.05
332	Dave Winfield	.65
333	David McCarty	.05
334	Al Leiter	.05
335	Tom Browning	.05
336	Mark Grace	.05
337	Jose Mesa	.05
338	Mike Stanley	.05
339	Roger McDowell	.05
340	Damion Easley	.05
341	Angel Miranda	.05
342	John Smoltz	.05
343	Jay Buhner	.05
344	Bryan Harvey	.05
345	Joe Carter	.05
346	Dante Bichette	.05
347	Jason Bere	.05
348	Frank Viola	.05
349	Ivan Rodriguez	.60
350	Juan Gonzalez	.35
351	Steve Finley	.05
352	Mike Felder	.05
353	Ramon Martinez	.05
354	Greg Gagne	.05
355	Ken Hill	.05
356	Pedro Munoz	.05
357	Todd Van Poppel	.05
358	Marquis Grissom	.05
359	Milt Cuyler	.05
360	Reggie Sanders	.05
361	Scott Erickson	.05
362	Billy Hatcher	.05
363	Gene Harris	.05
364	Rene Gonzales	.05
365	Kevin Rogers	.05
366	Eric Plunk	.05
367	Todd Zeile	.05
368	John Franco	.05
369	Brett Butler	.05
370	Bill Spiers	.05
371	Terry Pendleton	.05
372	Chris Bosio	.05
373	Orestes Destrade	.05
374	Dave Stewart	.05
375	Darren Holmes	.05
376	Doug Strange	.05
377	Brian Turang	.05
378	Carl Willis	.05
379	Mark McLemore	.05
380	Bobby Jones	.05
381	Scott Sanders	.05
382	Kirk Rueter	.05
383	Randy Velarde	.05
384	Fred McGriff	.05
385	Charles Nagy	.05
386	Rich Amaral	.05
387	Geronimo Berroa	.05
388	Eric Davis	.05
389	Ozzie Smith	.75
390	Alex Arias	.05
391	Brad Ausmus	.05
392	Cliff Floyd	.05
393	Roger Salkeld	.05
394	Jim Edmonds	.05
395	Jeromy Burnitz	.05
396	Dave Staton	.05
397	Rob Butler	.05
398	Marcos Armas	.05
399	Darrell Whitmore	.05
400	Ryan Thompson	.05
401	Ross Powell RC	.05
402	Joe Oliver	.05
403	Paul Carey	.05
404	Bob Hamelin	.05
405	Chris Turner	.05
406	Nate Minchey	.05
407	Lonnie Maclin RC	.05
408	Harold Baines	.05
409	Brian Williams	.05
410	Johnny Ruffin	.05
411	Julian Tavarez RC	.05
412	Mark Hutton	.05
413	Carlos Delgado	.50
414	Chris Gomez	.05
415	Mike Hampton	.05
416	Alex Diaz	.05
417	Jeffrey Hammonds	.05
418	Jayhawk Owens	.05
419	J.R. Phillips	.05
420	Cory Bailey RC	.05
421	Denny Hocking	.05
422	Jon Shave	.05
423	Damon Buford	.05
424	Troy O'Leary	.05
425	Tripp Cromer	.05
426	Albie Lopez	.05
427	Tony Fernandez	.05
428	Ozzie Guillen	.05
429	Alan Trammell	.05
430	John Wasdin RC	.05
431	Marc Valdes	.05
432	Brian Anderson RC	.20
433	Matt Brunson RC	.05
434	Wayne Gomes RC	.05
435	Jay Powell RC	.05
436	Kirk Presley RC	.05
437	Jon Ratliff RC	.05
438	Derrek Lee RC	2.00
439	Tom Pagnozzi	.05
440	Kent Mercker	.05
441	Phil Leftwich RC	.05
442	Jamie Moyer	.05
443	John Flaherty	.05
444	Mark Wohlers	.05
445	Jose Bautista	.05
446	Andres Galarraga	.05
447	Mark Lemke	.05
448	Tim Wakefield	.05
449	Pat Listach	.05
450	Rickey Henderson	.65
451	Mike Gallego	.05
452	Bob Tewksbury	.05
453	Kirk Gibson	.05
454	Pedro Astacio	.05
455	Mike Lansing	.05
456	Sean Berry	.05
457	Bob Walk	.05
458	Chili Davis	.05
459	Ed Sprague	.05
460	Kevin Stocker	.05
461	Mike Stanton	.05
462	Tim Raines	.05
463	Mike Bordick	.05
464	David Wells	.05
465	Tim Laker	.05
466	Cory Snyder	.05
467	Alex Cole	.05
468	Pete Incaviglia	.05
469	Roger Pavlik	.05
470	Greg W. Harris	.05
471	Xavier Hernandez	.05
472	Erik Hanson	.05
473	Jesse Orosco	.05
474	Greg Colbrunn	.05
475	Harold Reynolds	.05
476	Greg Harris	.05
477	Pat Borders	.05
478	Melvin Nieves	.05
479	Mariano Duncan	.05
480	Greg Hibbard	.05
481	Tim Pugh	.05
482	Bobby Ayala	.05
483	Sid Fernandez	.05
484	Tim Wallach	.05
485	Randy Milligan	.05
486	Walt Weiss	.05
487	Matt Walbeck	.05
488	Mike Macfarlane	.05
489	Jerry Browne	.05
490	Chris Sabo	.05
491	Tim Belcher	.05
492	Spike Owen	.05
493	Rafael Palmeiro	.60
494	Brian Harper	.05
495	Eddie Murray	.65
496	Ellis Burks	.05
497	Karl Rhodes	.05
498	Otis Nixon	.05
499	Lee Smith	.05
500	Bip Roberts	.05
501	Pedro Martinez	.65
502	Brian L. Hunter	.05
503	Tyler Green	.05
504	Bruce Hurst	.05
505	Alex Gonzalez	.05
506	Mark Portugal	.05
507	Bob Ojeda	.05
508	Dave Henderson	.05
509	Bo Jackson	.10
510	Bret Boone	.05
511	Mark Eichhorn	.05
512	Luis Polonia	.05
513	Will Clark	.05
514	Dave Valle	.05
515	Dan Wilson	.05
516	Dennis Martinez	.05
517	Jim Leyritz	.05
518	Howard Johnson	.05
519	Jody Reed	.05
520	Julio Franco	.05
521	Jeff Reardon	.05
522	Willie Greene	.05
523	Shawon Dunston	.05
524	Keith Mitchell	.05
525	Rick Helling	.05
526	Mark Kiefer	.05
527	Chan Ho Park RC	.75
528	Tony Longmire	.05
529	Rich Becker	.05
530	Tim Hyers	.05
531	Darrin Jackson	.05
532	Jack Morris	.05
533	Rick White	.05
534	Mike Kelly	.05
535	James Mouton	.05
536	Steve Trachsel	.05
537	Tony Eusebio	.05
538	Kelly Stinnett	.05
539	Paul Spoljaric	.05
540	Darren Dreifort	.05

No.	Player	Price
5	Aaron Sele	.25
6	Salomon Torres	.25
7	Wil Cordero	.25
8	Allen Watson	.25
9	J.T. Snow	.25
10	Cliff Floyd	.25
10a	Cliff Floyd/OPS	.50
11	Jeff McNeely	.25
12	Butch Huskey	.25
13	J.R. Phillips	.25
14	Bobby Jones	.25
15	Javier Lopez	.25
16	Scott Ruffcorn	.25
17	Manny Ramirez	1.25
18	Carlos Delgado	1.00
19	Rondell White	.25
20	Chipper Jones	1.50
21	Billy Ashley	.25
22	Nigel Wilson	.25
23	Jeromy Burnitz	.25
24	Danny Bautista	.25
25	Darrell Whitmore	.25

Artist's Proof

	NM/M
Complete Set (540):	250.00
Common Player:	1.50
Stars/Rookies:	20X

(See 1994 Pinnacle for checklist and base card values.)

Power Surge

	NM/M
Complete Set (25):	4.00
Common Player:	.25

No.	Player	Price
1	Dave Justice	.25
2	Chris Hoiles	.25
3	Mo Vaughn	.25
4	Tim Salmon	.25
5	J.T. Snow	.25
6	Frank Thomas	.65
7	Sammy Sosa	.75
8	Rick Wilkins	.25
9	Robin Ventura	.25
10	Reggie Sanders	.25
11	Albert Belle	.25
12	Carlos Baerga	.25
12a	Carlos Baerga/OPS	.50
13	Manny Ramirez	.65
14	Travis Fryman	.25
15	Gary Sheffield	.35
16	Jeff Bagwell	.65
17	Mike Piazza	1.00
18	Eric Karros	.25
19	Cliff Floyd	.25
20	Mark Whiten	.25
21	Phil Plantier	.25
22	Derek Bell	.25
23	Ken Griffey Jr.	1.00
24	Juan Gonzalez	.35
25	Dean Palmer	.25

Museum Collection

	NM/M
Complete Set (540):	225.00
Common Player:	1.00
Stars/Rookies:	6X

(See 1994 Pinnacle for checklist and base card values.)

New Generation

	NM/M
Complete Set (25):	5.00
Common Player:	.25
1 Tim Salmon	.25
2 Mike Piazza	2.00
3 Jason Bere	.25
4 Jeffrey Hammonds	.25

Rookie Team Pinnacle

	NM/M
Complete Set (9):	12.00
Common Player:	.75
1 Carlos Delgado, Javier Lopez	2.50
2 Bob Hamelin, J.R. Phillips	.75

3	Jon Shave,	
	Keith Kessinger	.75
4	Butch Huskey,	
	Luis Ortiz	.75
5	Chipper Jones,	
	Kurt Abbott	5.00
6	Rondell White,	
	Manny Ramirez	3.00
7	Cliff Floyd,	
	Jeffrey Hammonds	.75
8	Marc Newfield,	
	Nigel Wilson	.75
9	Salomon Torres,	
	Mark Hutton	.75

Run Creators

		NM/M
Complete Set (44):		17.50
Common Player:		.25
1	John Olerud	.25
2	Frank Thomas	1.00
3	Ken Griffey Jr.	3.00
4	Paul Molitor	1.00
5	Rafael Palmeiro	.75
6	Roberto Alomar	.35
7	Juan Gonzalez	.50
8	Albert Belle	.25
9	Travis Fryman	.25
10	Rickey Henderson	1.00
11	Tony Phillips	.25
12	Mo Vaughn	.25
13	Tim Salmon	.25
14	Kenny Lofton	.25
15	Carlos Baerga	.25
16	Greg Vaughn	.25
17	Jay Buhner	.25
18	Chris Hoiles	.25
19	Mickey Tettleton	.25
20	Kirby Puckett	1.50
21	Danny Tartabull	.25
22	Devon White	.25
23	Barry Bonds	4.00
24	Lenny Dykstra	.25
25	John Kruk	.25
26	Fred McGriff	.25
27	Gregg Jefferies	.25
28	Mike Piazza	3.00
29	Jeff Blauser	.25
30	Andres Galarraga	.25
31	Darren Daulton	.25
32	Dave Justice	.25
33	Craig Biggio	.25
34	Mark Grace	.25
35	Tony Gwynn	1.50
36	Jeff Bagwell	1.00
37	Jay Bell	.25
38	Marquis Grissom	.25
39	Matt Williams	.25
40	Charlie Hayes	.25
41	Dante Bichette	.25
42	Bernard Gilkey	.25

43	Brett Butler	.25
44	Rick Wilkins	.25

Team Pinnacle

		NM/M
Complete Set (9):		35.00
Common Player:		1.50
1	Jeff Bagwell,	
	Frank Thomas	4.00
2	Carlos Baerga,	
	Robby Thompson	1.50
3	Matt Williams,	
	Dean Palmer	1.50
4	Cal Ripken, Jr.,	
	Jay Bell	12.00
5	Ivan Rodriguez,	
	Mike Piazza	6.00
6	Len Dykstra,	
	Ken Griffey Jr.	8.00
7	Juan Gonzalez,	
	Barry Bonds	10.00
8	Tim Salmon,	
	Dave Justice	1.50
9	Greg Maddux,	
	Jack McDowell	8.00

The Naturals

		NM/M
Complete Set (25):		6.00
Common Player:		.15
1	Frank Thomas	.50
2	Barry Bonds	1.50
3	Ken Griffey Jr.	1.00
4	Juan Gonzalez	.25
5	Dave Justice	.15
6	Albert Belle	.15
7	Kenny Lofton	.15
8	Roberto Alomar	.35
9	Tim Salmon	.15
10	Randy Johnson	.50
11	Kirby Puckett	.65
12	Tony Gwynn	.65
13	Fred McGriff	.15
14	Ryne Sandberg	.65
15	Greg Maddux	.65
16	Matt Williams	.15
17	Lenny Dykstra	.15
18	Gary Sheffield	.35
18a	Gary Sheffield/OPS	.50
19	Mike Piazza	1.00
20	Dean Palmer	.15
21	Travis Fryman	.15
22	Carlos Baerga	.15
23	Cal Ripken, Jr.	1.50
24	John Olerud	.15
25	Roger Clemens	.75

Tribute

	NM/M
Complete Set (18):	15.00

		.25
Common Player:		.25
1	Paul Molitor	1.00
2	Jim Abbott	.25
3	Dave Winfield	1.00
4	Bo Jackson	.35
5	Dave Justice	.25
6	Len Dykstra	.25
7	Mike Piazza	2.50
8	Barry Bonds	4.50
9	Randy Johnson	1.00
10	Ozzie Smith	1.50
11	Mark Whiten	.25
12	Greg Maddux	1.50
13	Cal Ripken, Jr.	4.50
14	Frank Thomas	1.00
15	Juan Gonzalez	.45
16	Roberto Alomar	.25
17	Ken Griffey Jr.	3.00
18	Lee Smith	.25

1995 Pinnacle

		NM/M
Complete Set (450):		15.00
Common Player:		.10
Artist's Proofs:		10X
Museum Collection:		4X
Hobby Pack (12):		1.00
Hobby Wax Box (24):		15.00
Retail Pack (12):		1.00
Retail Wax Box (36):		20.00
1	Jeff Bagwell	.75
2	Roger Clemens	1.25
3	Mark Whiten	.10
4	Shawon Dunston	.10
5	Bobby Bonilla	.10
6	Kevin Tapani	.10
7	Eric Karros	.10
8	Cliff Floyd	.10
9	Pat Kelly	.10
10	Jeffrey Hammonds	.10
11	Jeff Conine	.10
12	Fred McGriff	.10
13	Chris Bosio	.10
14	Mike Mussina	.40
15	Danny Bautista	.10
16	Mickey Morandini	.10
17	Chuck Finley	.10
18	Jim Thome	.65
19	Luis Ortiz	.10
20	Walt Weiss	.10
21	Don Mattingly	1.25
22	Bob Hamelin	.10
23	Melido Perez	.10
24	Kevin Mitchell	.10
25	John Smoltz	.10
26	Hector Carrasco	.10
27	Pat Hentgen	.10
28	Derrick May	.10
29	Mike Kingery	.10
30	Chuck Carr	.10
31	Billy Ashley	.10

32	Todd Hundley	.10
33	Luis Gonzalez	.10
34	Marquis Grissom	.10
35	Jeff King	.10
36	Eddie Williams	.10
37	Tom Pagnozzi	.10
38	Chris Hoiles	.10
39	Sandy Alomar	.10
40	Mike Greenwell	.10
41	Lance Johnson	.10
42	Junior Felix	.10
43	Felix Jose	.10
44	Scott Leius	.10
45	Ruben Sierra	.10
46	Kevin Seitzer	.10
47	Wade Boggs	1.00
48	Reggie Jefferson	.10
49	Jose Canseco	.40
50	Dave Justice	.10
51	John Smiley	.10
52	Joe Carter	.10
53	Rick Wilkins	.10
54	Ellis Burks	.10
55	Dave Weathers	.10
56	Pedro Astacio	.10
57	Ryan Thompson	.10
58	James Mouton	.10
59	Mel Rojas	.10
60	Orlando Merced	.10
61	Matt Williams	.10
62	Bernard Gilkey	.10
63	J.R. Phillips	.10
64	Lee Smith	.10
65	Jim Edmonds	.10
66	Darrin Jackson	.10
67	Scott Cooper	.10
68	Ron Karkovice	.10
69	Chris Gomez	.10
70	Kevin Appier	.10
71	Bobby Jones	.10
72	Doug Drabek	.10
73	Matt Mieske	.10
74	Sterling Hitchcock	.10
75	John Valentin	.10
76	Reggie Sanders	.10
77	Wally Joyner	.10
78	Turk Wendell	.10
79	Wendell Hayes	.10
80	Bret Barberie	.10
81	Troy Neel	.10
82	Ken Caminiti	.10
83	Milt Thompson	.10
84	Paul Sorrento	.10
85	Trevor Hoffman	.10
86	Jay Bell	.10
87	Mark Portugal	.10
88	Sid Fernandez	.10
89	Charles Nagy	.10
90	Jeff Montgomery	.10
91	Chuck Knoblauch	.10
92	Jeff Frye	.10
93	Tony Gwynn	1.00
94	John Olerud	.10
95	David Nied	.10
96	Chris Hammond	.10
97	Edgar Martinez	.10
98	Kevin Stocker	.10
99	Jeff Fassero	.10
100	Curt Schilling	.30
101	Dave Clark	.10
102	Delino DeShields	.10
103	Leo Gomez	.10
104	Dave Hollins	.10
105	Tim Naehring	.10
106	Otis Nixon	.10
107	Ozzie Guillen	.10
108	Jose Lind	.10
109	Stan Javier	.10
110	Greg Vaughn	.10
111	Chipper Jones	1.00
112	Ed Sprague	.10
113	Mike Macfarlane	.10
114	Steve Finley	.10
115	Ken Hill	.10
116	Carlos Garcia	.10
117	Lou Whitaker	.10
118	Todd Zeile	.10
119	Gary Sheffield	.40
120	Ben McDonald	.10
121	Pete Harnisch	.10
122	Ivan Rodriguez	.65
123	Wilson Alvarez	.10
124	Travis Fryman	.10
125	Pedro Munoz	.10
126	Mark Lemke	.10
127	Jose Valentin	.10
128	Ken Griffey Jr.	1.50
129	Omar Vizquel	.10
130	Milt Cuyler	.10
131	Steve Traschel	.10
132	Alex Rodriguez	2.00
133	Garret Anderson	.10
134	Armando Benitez	.10
135	Shawn Green	.35
136	Jorge Fabregas	.10
137	Orlando Miller	.10

138	Rikkert Faneyte	.10
139	Ismael Valdes	.10
140	Jose Oliva	.10
141	Aaron Small	.10
142	Tim Davis	.10
143	Ricky Bottalacio	.10
144	Mike Matheny	.10
145	Roberto Petagine	.10
146	Fausto Cruz	.10
147	Bryce Florie	.10
148	Jose Lima	.10
149	John Hudek	.10
150	Duane Singleton	.10
151	John Mabry	.10
152	Robert Eenhoorn	.10
153	Jon Lieber	.10
154	Garey Ingram	.10
155	Paul Shuey	.10
156	Mike Lieberthal	.10
157	Steve Dunn	.10
158	Charles Johnson	.10
159	Ernie Young	.10
160	Jose Martinez	.10
161	Kurt Miller	.10
162	Joey Eischen	.10
163	Dave Stevens	.10
164	Brian Hunter	.10
165	Jeff Cirillo	.10
166	Mark Smith	.10
167	McKay Christensen RC	.10
168	C.J. Nitkowski	.10
169	Antone Williamson RC	.10
170	Paul Konerko	.15
171	Scott Elarton RC	.15
172	Jacob Shumate	.10
173	Terrence Long	.10
174	Mark Johnson RC	.10
175	Ben Grieve	.10
176	Jayson Peterson RC	.10
177	Checklist	.10
178	Checklist	.10
179	Checklist	.10
180	Checklist	.10
181	Brian Anderson	.10
182	Steve Buechele	.10
183	Mark Clark	.10
184	Cecil Fielder	.10
185	Steve Avery	.10
186	Devon White	.10
187	Craig Shipley	.10
188	Brady Anderson	.10
189	Kenny Lofton	.10
190	Alex Cole	.10
191	Brent Gates	.10
192	Dean Palmer	.10
193	Alex Gonzalez	.10
194	Steve Cooke	.10
195	Ray Lankford	.10
196	Mark McGwire	2.00
197	Marc Newfield	.10
198	Pat Rapp	.10
199	Darren Lewis	.10
200	Carlos Baerga	.10
201	Rickey Henderson	.75
202	Kurt Abbott	.10
203	Kirt Manwaring	.10
204	Cal Ripken Jr.	2.50
205	Darren Daulton	.10
206	Greg Colbrunn	.10
207	Darryl Hamilton	.10
208	Bo Jackson	.15
209	Tony Phillips	.10
210	Geronimo Berroa	.10
211	Rich Becker	.10
212	Tony Tarasco	.10
213	Karl Rhodes	.10
214	Phil Plantier	.10
215	J.T. Snow	.10
216	Mo Vaughn	.10
217	Greg Gagne	.10
218	Rickey Bones	.10
219	Mike Bordick	.10
220	Chad Curtis	.10
221	Royce Clayton	.10
222	Roberto Alomar	.15
223	Jose Rijo	.10
224	Ryan Klesko	.10
225	Mark Langston	.10
226	Frank Thomas	.75
227	Juan Gonzalez	.40
228	Ron Gant	.10
229	Javier Lopez	.10
230	Sammy Sosa	1.00
231	Kevin Brown	.10
232	Gary DiSarcina	.10
233	Albert Belle	.10
234	Jay Buhner	.10
235	Pedro Martinez	.75
236	Bob Tewksbury	.10
237	Mike Piazza	1.50
238	Darryl Kile	.10
239	Bryan Harvey	.10
240	Andres Galarraga	.10
241	Jeff Blauser	.10
242	Jeff Kent	.10
243	Bobby Munoz	.10

244	Greg Maddux	1.00
245	Paul O'Neill	.10
246	Lenny Dykstra	.10
247	Todd Van Poppel	.10
248	Bernie Williams	.05
249	Glenallen Hill	.10
250	Duane Ward	.10
251	Dennis Eckersley	.60
252	Pat Mahomes	.10
253	Rusty Greer (Photo actually Jeff Frye.)	.10
254	Roberto Kelly	.10
255	Randy Myers	.10
256	Scott Ruffcorn	.10
257	Robin Ventura	.10
258	Eduardo Perez	.10
259	Aaron Sele	.10
260	Paul Molitor	.75
261	Juan Guzman	.10
262	Darren Oliver	.10
263	Mike Stanley	.10
264	Tom Glavine	.30
265	Rico Brogna	.10
266	Craig Biggio	.10
267	Darrell Whitmore	.10
268	Jimmy Key	.10
269	Will Clark	.10
270	David Cone	.10
271	Brian Jordan	.10
272	Barry Bonds	2.50
273	Danny Tartabull	.10
274	Ramon Martinez	.10
275	Al Martin	.10
276	Fred McGriff	.10
277	Carlos Delgado	.25
278	Juan Gonzalez	.20
279	Shawn Green	.20
280	Carlos Baerga	.10
281	Cliff Floyd	.10
282	Ozzie Smith	.50
283	Alex Rodriguez	1.00
284	Kenny Lofton	.10
285	Dave Justice	.10
286	Tim Salmon	.10
287	Manny Ramirez	.40
288	Will Clark	.10
289	Garret Anderson	.10
290	Billy Ripken	.10
291	Tony Gwynn	.50
292	Raul Mondesi	.10
293	Rafael Palmeiro	.30
294	Matt Williams	.10
295	Don Mattingly	.60
296	Kirby Puckett	.50
297	Paul Molitor	.40
298	Albert Belle	.10
299	Barry Bonds	1.25
300	Mike Piazza	.85
301	Jeff Bagwell	.40
302	Frank Thomas	.40
303	Chipper Jones	.50
304	Ken Griffey Jr.	.75
305	Cal Ripken Jr.	1.25
306	Eric Anthony	.10
307	Todd Benzinger	.10
308	Jacob Brumfield	.10
309	Wes Chamberlain	.10
310	Tino Martinez	.10
311	Roberto Mejia	.10
312	Jose Offerman	.10
313	David Segui	.10
314	Eric Young	.10
315	Rey Sanchez	.10
316	Raul Mondesi	.10
317	Bret Boone	.10
318	Andre Dawson	.30
319	Brian McRae	.10
320	Dave Nilsson	.10
321	Moises Alou	.10
322	Don Slaught	.10
323	Dave McCarty	.10
324	Mike Huff	.10
325	Rick Aguilera	.10
326	Rod Beck	.10
327	Kenny Rogers	.10
328	Andy Benes	.10
329	Allen Watson	.10
330	Randy Johnson	.75
331	Willie Greene	.10
332	Hal Morris	.10
333	Ozzie Smith	1.00
334	Jason Bere	.10
335	Scott Erickson	.10
336	Dante Bichette	.10
337	Willie Banks	.10
338	Eric Davis	.10
339	Rondell White	.10
340	Kirby Puckett	1.00
341	Deion Sanders	.10
342	Eddie Murray	.75
343	Mike Harkey	.10
344	Joey Hamilton	.10
345	Roger Salkeld	.10
346	Wil Cordero	.10
347	John Wetteland	.10
348	Geronimo Pena	.10

349	Kirk Gibson	.10
350	Manny Ramirez	.75
351	William Van Landingham	.10
352	B.J. Surhoff	.10
353	Ken Ryan	.10
354	Terry Steinbach	.10
355	Bret Saberhagen	.10
356	John Jaha	.10
357	Joe Girardi	.10
358	Steve Karsay	.10
359	Alex Fernandez	.10
360	Salomon Torres	.10
361	John Burkett	.10
362	Derek Bell	.10
363	Tom Henke	.10
364	Gregg Jefferies	.10
365	Jack McDowell	.10
366	Andujar Cedeno	.10
367	Dave Winfield	.75
368	Carl Everett	.10
369	Danny Jackson	.10
370	Jeromy Burnitz	.10
371	Mark Grace	.10
372	Larry Walker	.10
373	Bill Swift	.10
374	Dennis Martinez	.10
375	Mickey Tettleton	.10
376	Mel Nieves	.10
377	Cal Eldred	.10
378	Orel Hershiser	.10
379	David Wells	.10
380	Gary Gaetti	.10
381	Tim Raines	.10
382	Barry Larkin	.10
383	Jason Jacome	.10
384	Tim Wallach	.10
385	Robby Thompson	.10
386	Frank Viola	.10
387	Dave Stewart	.10
388	Bip Roberts	.10
389	Ron Darling	.10
390	Carlos Delgado	.45
391	Tim Salmon	.10
392	Alan Trammell	.10
393	Kevin Foster	.10
394	Jim Abbott	.10
395	John Kruk	.10
396	Andy Van Slyke	.10
397	Dave Magadan	.10
398	Rafael Palmeiro	.65
399	Mike Devereaux	.10
400	Benito Santiago	.10
401	Brett Butler	.10
402	John Franco	.10
403	Matt Walbeck	.10
404	Terry Pendleton	.10
405	Chris Sabo	.10
406	Andrew Lorraine	.10
407	Dan Wilson	.10
408	Mike Lansing	.10
409	Ray McDavid	.10
410	Shane Andrews	.10
411	Tom Gordon	.10
412	Chad Ogea	.10
413	James Baldwin	.10
414	Russ Davis	.10
415	Ray Holbert	.10
416	Ray Durham	.10
417	Matt Nokes	.10
418	Rodney Henderson	.10
419	Gabe White	.10
420	Todd Hollandsworth	.10
421	Midre Cummings	.10
422	Harold Baines	.10
423	Troy Percival	.10
424	Joe Vitiello	.10
425	Andy Ashby	.10
426	Michael Tucker	.10
427	Mark Gubicza	.10
428	Jim Bullinger	.10
429	Jose Malave	.10
430	Pete Schourek	.10
431	Bobby Ayala	.10
432	Marvin Freeman	.10
433	Pat Listach	.10
434	Eddie Taubensee	.10
435	Steve Howe	.10
436	Kent Mercker	.10
437	Hector Fajardo	.10
438	Scott Kamieniecki	.10
439	Robb Nen	.10
440	Mike Kelly	.10
441	Tom Candiotti	.10
442	Albie Lopez	.10
443	Jeff Granger	.10
444	Rich Aude	.10
445	Luis Polonia	.10
446	Frank Thomas A.L. Checklist	.40
447	Ken Griffey Jr. A.L. Checklist	.65
448	Mike Piazza N.L. Checklist	.75
449	Jeff Bagwell N.L. Checklist	.40

450	Frank Thomas, Ken Griffey Jr., Mike Piazza, Jeff Bagwell Insert Checklist	.40

Artist's Proof

	NM/M
Complete Set (450):	300.00
Common Player:	1.00
Stars/Rookies:	10X

(See 1995 Pinnacle for checklist and base card values.)

Museum Collection

	NM/M
Complete Set (450):	200.00
Common Player:	.50
Stars/Rookies:	4X

(See 1995 Pinnacle for checklist and base card values.)

Redemption Card	.25

E.T.A. '95

		NM/M
	Complete Set (6):	5.00
	Common Player:	.70
1	Ben Grieve	.75
2	Alex Ochoa	.75
3	Joe Vitiello	.75
4	Johnny Damon	3.00
5	Trey Beamon	.75
6	Brooks Kieschnick	.75

FanFest

		NM/M
	Complete Set (30):	7.50
	Common Player:	.15
1	Cal Ripken Jr.	1.50
2	Roger Clemens	.75
3	Don Mattingly	.75
4	Albert Belle	.15
5	Kirby Puckett	.65
6	Cecil Fielder	.15
7	Kevin Appier	.15

8	Will Clark	.15
9	Juan Gonzalez	.25
10	Ivan Rodriguez	.45
11	Ken Griffey Jr.	1.00
12	Tim Salmon	.15
13	Frank Thomas	.50
14	Roberto Alomar	.20
15	Rickey Henderson	.50
16	Raul Mondesi	.15
17	Matt Williams	.15
18	Ozzie Smith	.65
19	Deion Sanders	.15
20	Tony Gwynn	.65
21	Greg Maddux	.65
22	Sammy Sosa	.65
23	Mike Piazza	1.00
24	Barry Bonds	1.50
25	Jeff Bagwell	.50
26	Len Dykstra	.15
27	Rico Brogna	.15
28	Larry Walker	.15
29	Gary Sheffield	.35
30	Wil Cordero	.15

Gate Attraction

		NM/M
Complete Set (18):		25.00
Common Player:		.50
1	Ken Griffey Jr.	3.50
2	Frank Thomas	1.50
3	Cal Ripken Jr.	5.00
4	Jeff Bagwell	1.50
5	Mike Piazza	3.50
6	Barry Bonds	5.00
7	Kirby Puckett	2.00
8	Albert Belle	.50
9	Tony Gwynn	2.00
10	Raul Mondesi	.50
11	Will Clark	.50
12	Don Mattingly	2.75
13	Roger Clemens	2.75
14	Paul Molitor	1.50
15	Matt Williams	.50
16	Greg Maddux	2.00
17	Kenny Lofton	.50
18	Cliff Floyd	.50

New Blood

		NM/M
Complete Set (9):		10.00
Common Player:		.70
1	Alex Rodriguez	5.00
2	Shawn Green	1.50
3	Brian Hunter	.75
4	Garret Anderson	.75
5	Charles Johnson	.75
6	Chipper Jones	3.00
7	Carlos Delgado	1.50

8	Billy Ashley	.75
9	J.R. Phillips	.75

Performers

		NM/M
Complete Set (18):		15.00
Common Player:		.35
1	Frank Thomas	2.00
2	Albert Belle	.35
3	Barry Bonds	3.50
4	Juan Gonzalez	1.00
5	Andres Galarraga	.35
6	Raul Mondesi	.35
7	Paul Molitor	2.00
8	Tim Salmon	.35
9	Mike Piazza	2.50
10	Gregg Jefferies	.35
11	Will Clark	.35
12	Greg Maddux	2.25
13	Manny Ramirez	2.00
14	Kirby Puckett	2.25
15	Shawn Green	1.25
16	Rafael Palmeiro	1.75
17	Paul O'Neill	.35
18	Jason Bere	.35

Team Pinnacle

		NM/M
Complete Set (9):		35.00
Common Player:		1.50
1	Mike Mussina, Greg Maddux	8.00
2	Carlos Delgado, Mike Piazza	6.00
3	Frank Thomas, Jeff Bagwell	4.00
4	Roberto Alomar, Craig Biggio	3.00
5	Cal Ripken Jr., Ozzie Smith	12.00
6	Travis Fryman, Matt Williams	1.50
7	Ken Griffey Jr., Barry Bonds	10.00
8	Albert Belle, Dave Justice	1.50
9	Kirby Puckett, Tony Gwynn	8.00

Upstarts

		NM/M
Complete Set (30):		10.00
Common Player:		.15
1	Frank Thomas	1.50
2	Roberto Alomar	.30
3	Mike Piazza	2.50
4	Javier Lopez	.15
5	Albert Belle	.15
6	Carlos Delgado	.75
7	Rusty Greer	.15
8	Tim Salmon	.15
9	Raul Mondesi	.15
10	Juan Gonzalez	.75
11	Manny Ramirez	1.50
12	Sammy Sosa	2.00
13	Jeff Kent	.15
14	Melvin Nieves	.15
15	Rondell White	.15
16	Shawn Green	.75
17	Bernie Williams	.15
18	Aaron Sele	.15
19	Jason Bere	.15
20	Joey Hamilton	.15
21	Mike Kelly	.15
22	Wil Cordero	.15
23	Moises Alou	.15
24	Roberto Kelly	.15
25	Deion Sanders	.15
26	Steve Karsay	.15
27	Bret Boone	.15
28	Willie Greene	.15
29	Billy Ashley	.15
30	Brian Anderson	.15

Red Hot

		NM/M
Complete Set (25):		35.00
Common Player:		.75
1	Cal Ripken Jr.	5.50
2	Ken Griffey Jr.	4.00
3	Frank Thomas	1.50
4	Jeff Bagwell	1.50
5	Barry Bonds	5.50
6	Albert Belle	.75
7	Tony Gwynn	2.00
8	Kirby Puckett	2.00
9	Don Mattingly	2.50
10	Matt Williams	.75

12	Greg Maddux	2.00
13	Raul Mondesi	.75
14	Paul Molitor	1.50
15	Manny Ramirez	1.50
16	Joe Carter	.75
17	Will Clark	.75
18	Roger Clemens	2.50
19	Tim Salmon	.75
20	Dave Justice	.75
21	Kenny Lofton	.75
22	Deion Sanders	.75
23	Roberto Alomar	1.00
24	Cliff Floyd	.75
25	Carlos Baerga	.75

White Hot

		NM/M
Complete Set (25):		140.00
Common Player:		2.50
1	Cal Ripken Jr.	16.00
2	Ken Griffey Jr.	13.50
3	Frank Thomas	8.00
4	Jeff Bagwell	8.00
5	Mike Piazza	13.50
6	Barry Bonds	16.00
7	Albert Belle	2.50
8	Tony Gwynn	10.00
9	Kirby Puckett	10.00
10	Don Mattingly	12.00
11	Matt Williams	2.50
12	Greg Maddux	10.00
13	Raul Mondesi	2.50
14	Paul Molitor	8.00
15	Manny Ramirez	8.00
16	Joe Carter	2.50
17	Will Clark	2.50
18	Roger Clemens	12.00
19	Tim Salmon	2.50
20	Dave Justice	2.50
21	Kenny Lofton	2.50
22	Deion Sanders	2.50
23	Roberto Alomar	3.50
24	Cliff Floyd	2.50
25	Carlos Baerga	2.50

1996 Pinnacle

		NM/M
Complete Set (400):		15.00
Common Player:		.10
Series 1 or 2 Pack (10):		.75
Series 1 or 2 Box (24):		15.00
1	Greg Maddux	1.00
2	Bill Pulsipher	.10
3	Dante Bichette	.10
4	Mike Piazza	1.50
5	Garret Anderson	.10
6	Steve Finley	.10
7	Andy Benes	.10
8	Chuck Knoblauch	.10
9	Tom Gordon	.10
10	Jeff Bagwell	.75

No.	Player	Price	No.	Player	Price	No.	Player	Price	No.	Player	Price
11	Wil Cordero	.10	115	Mark Gubicza	.10	212	David Cone	.10	315	John Smoltz	.10
12	John Mabry	.10	116	Ruben Sierra	.10	213	Will Clark	.10	316	Ariel Prieto	.10
13	Jeff Frye	.10	117	Eddie Murray	.75	214	Cal Ripken Jr.	2.00	317	Mark Carreon	.10
14	Travis Fryman	.10	118	Chad Curtis	.10	215	Wade Boggs	1.00	318	Kirby Puckett	.50
15	John Wetteland	.10	119	Hal Morris	.10	216	Pete Schourek	.10	319	Carlos Perez	.10
16	Jason Bates	.10	120	Ben McDonald	.10	217	Darren Daulton	.10	320	Gary DiSarcina	.10
17	Danny Tartabull	.10	121	Marty Cordova	.10	218	Carlos Baerga	.10	321	Trevor Hoffman	.10
18	Charles Nagy	.10	122	Ken Griffey Jr.	1.50	219	Larry Walker	.10	322	Mike Piazza	.65
19	Robin Ventura	.10	123	Gary Sheffield	.40	220	Denny Neagle	.10	323	Frank Thomas	.40
20	Reggie Sanders	.10	124	Charlie Hayes	.10	221	Jim Edmonds	.10	324	Juan Acevedo	.10
21	Dave Clark	.10	125	Shawn Green	.40	222	Lee Smith	.10	325	Bip Roberts	.10
22	Jaime Navarro	.10	126	Jason Giambi	.50	223	Jason Isringhausen	.10	326	Javier Lopez	.10
23	Joey Hamilton	.10	127	Mark Langston	.10	224	Jay Buhner	.10	327	Benito Santiago	.10
24	Al Leiter	.10	128	Mark Whiten	.10	225	John Olerud	.10	328	Mark Lewis	.10
25	Deion Sanders	.10	129	Greg Vaughn	.10	226	Jeff Conine	.10	329	Royce Clayton	.10
26	Tim Salmon	.10	130	Mark McGwire	1.75	227	Dean Palmer	.10	330	Tom Gordon	.10
27	Tino Martinez	.10	131	Hideo Nomo	.40	228	Jim Abbott	.10	331	Ben McDonald	.10
28	Mike Greenwell	.10	132	Eric Karros, Raul Mondesi, Hideo Nomo, Mike Piazza	.50	229	Raul Mondesi	.10	332	Dan Wilson	.10
29	Phil Plantier	.10				230	Tom Glavine	.35	333	Ron Gant	.10
30	Bobby Bonilla	.10	133	Jason Bere	.10	231	Kevin Seitzer	.10	334	Wade Boggs	.45
31	Kenny Rogers	.10	134	Ken Griffey Jr.	.65	232	Lenny Dykstra	.10	335	Paul Molitor	.75
32	Chili Davis	.10	135	Frank Thomas	.40	233	Brian Jordan	.10	336	Tony Gwynn	.50
33	Joe Carter	.10	136	Cal Ripken Jr.	1.00	234	Rondell White	.10	337	Sean Berry	.10
34	Mike Mussina	.40	137	Albert Belle	.10	235	Bret Boone	.10	338	Rickey Henderson	.75
35	Matt Mieske	.10	138	Mike Piazza	.65	236	Randy Johnson	.75	339	Wil Cordero	.10
36	Jose Canseco	.40	139	Dante Bichette	.10	237	Paul O'Neill	.10	340	Kent Mercker	.10
37	Brad Radke	.10	140	Sammy Sosa	.50	238	Jim Thome	.65	341	Kenny Rogers	.10
38	Juan Gonzalez	.40	141	Mo Vaughn	.10	239	Edgardo Alfonzo	.10	342	Ryne Sandberg	1.00
39	David Segui	.10	142	Tim Salmon	.10	240	Terry Pendleton	.10	343	Charlie Hayes	.10
40	Alex Fernandez	.10	143	Reggie Sanders	.10	241	Harold Baines	.10	344	Andy Benes	.10
41	Jeff Kent	.10	144	Cecil Fielder	.10	242	Roberto Alomar	.20	345	Sterling Hitchcock	.10
42	Todd Zeile	.10	145	Jim Edmonds	.10	243	Mark Grace	.10	346	Bernard Gilkey	.10
43	Darryl Strawberry	.10	146	Rafael Palmeiro	.10	244	Derek Bell	.10	347	Julio Franco	.10
44	Jose Rijo	.10	147	Edgar Martinez	.10	245	Vinny Castilla	.10	348	Ken Hill	.10
45	Ramon Martinez	.10	148	Barry Bonds	1.00	246	Cecil Fielder	.10	349	Russ Davis	.10
46	Manny Ramirez	.75	149	Manny Ramirez	.35	247	Roger Clemens	1.25	350	Mike Blowers	.10
47	Gregg Jefferies	.10	150	Larry Walker	.10	248	Orel Hershiser	.10	351	B.J. Surhoff	.10
48	Bryan Rekar	.10	151	Jeff Bagwell	.35	249	J.T. Snow	.10	352	Lance Johnson	.10
49	Jeff King	.10	152	Ron Gant	.10	250	Rafael Palmeiro	.65	353	Darryl Hamilton	.10
50	John Olerud	.10	153	Andres Galarraga	.10	251	Bret Saberhagen	.10	354	Shawon Dunston	.10
51	Marc Newfield	.10	154	Eddie Murray	.35	252	Todd Hollandsworth	.10	355	Rick Aguilera	.10
52	Charles Johnson	.10	155	Kirby Puckett	.50	253	Ryan Klesko	.10	356	Danny Tartabull	.10
53	Robby Thompson	.10	156	Will Clark	.10	254	Greg Maddux	.50	357	Todd Stottlemyre	.10
54	Brian Hunter	.10	157	Don Mattingly	.60	255	Ken Griffey Jr.	.65	358	Mike Bordick	.10
55	Mike Blowers	.10	158	Mark McGwire	.75	256	Hideo Nomo	.15	359	Jack McDowell	.10
56	Keith Lockhart	.10	159	Dean Palmer	.10	257	Frank Thomas	.40	360	Todd Zeile	.10
57	Ray Lankford	.10	160	Matt Williams	.10	258	Cal Ripken Jr.	1.00	361	Tino Martinez	.10
58	Tim Wallach	.10	161	Fred McGriff	.10	259	Jeff Bagwell	.35	362	Greg Gagne	.10
59	Ivan Rodriguez	.65	162	Joe Carter	.10	260	Barry Bonds	1.00	363	Mike Kelly	.10
60	Ed Sprague	.10	163	Juan Gonzalez	.15	261	Mo Vaughn	.10	364	Tim Raines	.10
61	Paul Molitor	.75	164	Alex Ochoa	.10	262	Albert Belle	.10	365	Ernie Young	.10
62	Eric Karros	.10	165	Ruben Rivera	.10	263	Sammy Sosa	.50	366	Mike Stanley	.10
63	Glenallen Hill	.10	166	Tony Clark	.10	264	Reggie Sanders	.10	367	Wally Joyner	.10
64	Jay Bell	.10	167	Brian Barber	.10	265	Mike Piazza	.65	368	Karim Garcia	.10
65	Tom Pagnozzi	.10	168	Matt Lawton	.10	266	Chipper Jones	.50	369	Paul Wilson	.10
66	Greg Colbrunn	.10	169	Terrell Wade	.10	267	Tony Gwynn	.50	370	Sal Fasano	.10
67	Edgar Martinez	.10	170	Johnny Damon	.30	268	Kirby Puckett	.50	371	Jason Schmidt	.10
68	Paul Sorrento	.10	171	Derek Jeter	2.00	269	Wade Boggs	.45	372	Livan Hernandez RC	.25
69	Kirt Manwaring	.10	172	Phil Nevin	.10	270	Will Clark	.10	373	George Arias	.10
70	Pete Schourek	.10	173	Robert Perez	.10	271	Gary Sheffield	.10	374	Steve Gibralter	.10
71	Orlando Merced	.10	174	C.J. Nitkowski	.10	272	Dante Bichette	.10	375	Jermaine Dye	.10
72	Shawon Dunston	.10	175	Joe Vitiello	.10	273	Randy Johnson	.35	376	Jason Kendall	.10
73	Ricky Bottalico	.10	176	Roger Cedeno	.10	274	Matt Williams	.10	377	Brooks Kieschnick	.10
74	Brady Anderson	.10	177	Ron Coomer	.10	275	Alex Rodriguez	.75	378	Jeff Ware	.10
75	Steve Ontiveros	.10	178	Chris Widger	.10	276	Tim Salmon	.10	379	Alan Benes	.10
76	Jim Abbott	.10	179	Jimmy Haynes	.10	277	Johnny Damon	.10	380	Rey Ordonez	.10
77	Carl Everett	.10	180	Mike Sweeney RC	.50	278	Manny Ramirez	.35	381	Jay Powell	.10
78	Mo Vaughn	.10	181	Howard Battle	.10	279	Derek Jeter	1.00	382	Osvaldo Fernandez RC	.15
79	Pedro Martinez	.75	182	John Wasdin	.10	280	Eddie Murray	.35	383	Wilton Guerrero RC	.10
80	Harold Baines	.10	183	Jim Pittsley	.10	281	Ozzie Smith	.50	384	Eric Owens	.10
81	Alan Trammell	.10	184	Bob Wolcott	.10	282	Garret Anderson	.10	385	George Williams	.10
82	Steve Avery	.10	185	LaTroy Hawkins	.10	283	Raul Mondesi	.10	386	Chan Ho Park	.10
83	Jeff Cirillo	.10	186	Nigel Wilson	.10	284	Terry Steinbach	.10	387	Jeff Suppan	.10
84	John Valentin	.10	187	Dustin Hermanson	.10	285	Carlos Garcia	.10	388	F.P. Santangelo RC	.10
85	Bernie Williams	.10	188	Chris Snopek	.10	286	Dave Justice	.10	389	Terry Adams	.10
86	Andre Dawson	.30	189	Mariano Rivera	.15	287	Eric Anthony	.10	390	Bob Abreu	.10
87	Dave Winfield	.75	190	Jose Herrera	.10	288	Benji Gil	.10	391	Quinton McCracken RC	.10
88	B.J. Surhoff	.10	191	Chris Stynes	.10	289	Bob Hamelin	.10	392	Mike Busby RC	.10
89	Jeff Blauser	.10	192	Larry Thomas	.10	290	Dwayne Hosey	.10	393	Cal Ripken Jr. (Checklist)	.75
90	Barry Larkin	.10	193	David Bell	.10	291	Andy Pettitte	.25	394	Ken Griffey Jr. (Checklist)	.60
91	Cliff Floyd	.10	194	Frank Thomas (Checklist)	.40	292	Rod Beck	.10	395	Frank Thomas (Checklist)	.40
92	Sammy Sosa	1.00	195	Ken Griffey Jr. (Checklist)	.65	293	Shane Andrews	.10	396	Chipper Jones (Checklist)	.50
93	Andres Galarraga	.10	196	Cal Ripken Jr. (Checklist)	.75	294	Julian Tavarez	.10	397	Greg Maddux (Checklist)	.50
94	Dave Nilsson	.10	197	Jeff Bagwell (Checklist)	.35	295	Willie Greene	.10	398	Mike Piazza (Checklist)	.65
95	James Mouton	.10	198	Mike Piazza (Checklist)	.60	296	Ismael Valdes	.10	399	Ken Griffey Jr., Frank Thomas, Cal Ripken Jr., Greg Maddux, Chipper Jones, Mike Piazza (Checklist)	.50
96	Marquis Grissom	.10	199	Barry Bonds (Checklist)	.75	297	Glenallen Hill	.10			
97	Matt Williams	.10	200	Garret Anderson, Chipper Jones (Checklist)	.25	298	Troy Percival	.10			
98	John Jaha	.10				299	Ray Durham	.10			
99	Don Mattingly	1.25	201	Frank Thomas	.75	300	Jeff Conine	.10			
100	Tim Naehring	.10	202	Michael Tucker	.10	301.8	Ken Griffey Jr.	.75			
101	Kevin Appier	.10	203	Kirby Puckett	1.00	302	Will Clark	.10			
102	Bobby Higginson	.10	204	Alex Gonzalez	.10	303	Mike Greenwell	.10			
103	Andy Pettitte	.25	205	Tony Gwynn	.10	304.9	Carlos Baerga	.10			
104	Ozzie Smith	1.00	206	Moises Alou	.10	305.3	Paul Molitor	.35			
105	Kenny Lofton	.10	207	Albert Belle	.10	305.6	Jeff Bagwell	.35			
106	Ken Caminiti	.10	208	Barry Bonds	2.00	306	Mark Grace	.10			
107	Walt Weiss	.10	209	Fred McGriff	.10	307	Don Mattingly	.60			
108	Jack McDowell	.10	210	Dennis Eckersley	.65	308	Hal Morris	.10			
109	Brian McRae	.10	211	Craig Biggio	.10	309	Butch Huskey	.10			
110	Gary Gaetti	.10				310	Ozzie Guillen	.10			
111	Curtis Goodwin	.10				311	Erik Hanson	.10			
112	Dennis Martinez	.10				312	Kenny Lofton	.10			
113	Omar Vizquel	.10				313	Edgar Martinez	.10			
114	Chipper Jones	1.00				314	Kurt Abbott	.10			

Starburst

	NM/M
Complete Set (200):	150.00
Common Player:	.40
Common Artist's Proof:	.75
Artist's Proofs:	2X
1 Greg Maddux	3.00
2 Bill Pulsipher	.40

PETE SCHOUREK

3	Dante Bichette	.40
4	Mike Piazza	4.00
5	Garret Anderson	.40
6	Chuck Knoblauch	.40
7	Jeff Bagwell	2.25
8	Wil Cordero	.40
9	Travis Fryman	.40
10	Reggie Sanders	.40
11	Deion Sanders	.40
12	Tim Salmon	.40
13	Tino Martinez	.40
14	Bobby Bonilla	.40
15	Joe Carter	.40
16	Mike Mussina	1.25
17	Jose Canseco	1.25
18	Manny Ramirez	2.25
19	Gregg Jefferies	.40
20	Charles Johnson	.40
21	Brian Hunter	.40
22	Ray Lankford	.40
23	Ivan Rodriguez	2.00
24	Paul Molitor	2.25
25	Eric Karros	.40
26	Edgar Martinez	.40
27	Shawon Dunston	.40
28	Mo Vaughn	.40
29	Pedro Martinez	2.25
30	Marty Cordova	.40
31	Ken Caminiti	.40
32	Gary Sheffield	.75
33	Shawn Green	.75
34	Cliff Floyd	.40
35	Andres Galarraga	.40
36	Matt Williams	.40
37	Don Mattingly	3.50
38	Kevin Appier	.40
39	Ozzie Smith	3.00
40	Kenny Lofton	.40
41	Ken Griffey Jr.	4.00
42	Jack McDowell	.40
43	Gary Gaetti	.40
44	Dennis Martinez	.40
45	Chipper Jones	3.00
46	Eddie Murray	2.25
47	Bernie Williams	.40
48	Andre Dawson	.60
49	Dave Winfield	2.25
50	B.J. Surhoff	.40
51	Barry Larkin	.40
52	Alan Trammell	.40
53	Sammy Sosa	3.00
54	Hideo Nomo	1.00
55	Mark McGwire	4.50
56	Jay Bell	.40
57	Juan Gonzalez	1.00
58	Chili Davis	.40
59	Robin Ventura	.40
60	John Mabry	.40
61	Ken Griffey Jr.	2.00
62	Frank Thomas	1.25
63	Cal Ripken Jr.	3.00
64	Albert Belle	.40
65	Mike Piazza	2.00
66	Dante Bichette	.40
67	Sammy Sosa	1.50
68	Mo Vaughn	.40
69	Tim Salmon	.40
70	Reggie Sanders	.40
71	Cecil Fielder	.40
72	Jim Edmonds	.40
73	Rafael Palmeiro	.75
74	Edgar Martinez	.40
75	Barry Bonds	3.00
76	Manny Ramirez	1.25
77	Larry Walker	.40
78	Jeff Bagwell	1.25
79	Ron Gant	.40
80	Andres Galarraga	.40
81	Eddie Murray	1.25
82	Kirby Puckett	1.50
83	Will Clark	.40
84	Don Mattingly	1.75
85	Mark McGwire	2.25

86	Dean Palmer	.40
87	Matt Williams	.40
88	Fred McGriff	.40
89	Joe Carter	.40
90	Juan Gonzalez	.65
91	Alex Ochoa	.40
92	Ruben Rivera	.40
93	Tony Clark	.40
94	Pete Schourek	.40
95	Terrell Wade	.40
96	Johnny Damon	.65
97	Derek Jeter	6.00
98	Phil Nevin	.40
99	Robert Perez	.40
100	Dustin Hermanson	.40
101	Frank Thomas	2.25
102	Michael Tucker	.40
103	Kirby Puckett	3.00
104	Alex Gonzalez	.40
105	Tony Gwynn	3.00
106	Moises Alou	.40
107	Albert Belle	.40
108	Barry Bonds	6.00
109	Fred McGriff	.40
110	Dennis Eckersley	1.50
111	Craig Biggio	.40
112	David Cone	.40
113	Will Clark	.40
114	Cal Ripken Jr.	6.00
115	Wade Boggs	3.00
116	Pete Schourek	.40
117	Darren Daulton	.40
118	Carlos Baerga	.40
119	Larry Walker	.40
120	Denny Neagle	.40
121	Jim Edmonds	.40
122	Lee Smith	.40
123	Jason Isringhausen	.40
124	Jay Buhner	.40
125	John Olerud	.40
126	Jeff Conine	.40
127	Dean Palmer	.40
128	Jim Abbott	.40
129	Raul Mondesi	.40
130	Tom Glavine	.60
131	Kevin Seitzer	.40
132	Lenny Dykstra	.40
133	Brian Jordan	.40
134	Rondell White	.40
135	Bret Boone	.40
136	Randy Johnson	2.25
137	Paul O'Neill	.40
138	Jim Thome	.75
139	Edgardo Alfonzo	.40
140	Terry Pendleton	.40
141	Harold Baines	.40
142	Roberto Alomar	.45
143	Mark Grace	.40
144	Derek Bell	.40
145	Vinny Castilla	.40
146	Cecil Fielder	.40
147	Roger Clemens	3.50
148	Orel Hershiser	.40
149	J.T. Snow	.40
150	Rafael Palmeiro	1.75
151	Bret Saberhagen	.40
152	Todd Hollandsworth	.40
153	Ryan Klesko	.40
154	Greg Maddux	1.50
155	Ken Griffey Jr.	2.00
156	Hideo Nomo	.65
157	Frank Thomas	1.25
158	Cal Ripken Jr.	3.00
159	Jeff Bagwell	1.25
160	Barry Bonds	3.00
161	Mo Vaughn	.40
162	Albert Belle	.40
163	Sammy Sosa	1.50
164	Reggie Sanders	.40
165	Mike Piazza	2.00
166	Chipper Jones	1.50
167	Tony Gwynn	1.50
168	Kirby Puckett	1.50
169	Wade Boggs	1.25
170	Will Clark	.40
171	Gary Sheffield	.45
172	Dante Bichette	.40
173	Randy Johnson	1.25
174	Matt Williams	.40
175	Alex Rodriguez	4.50
176	Tim Salmon	.40
177	Johnny Damon	.40
178	Manny Ramirez	1.25
179	Derek Jeter	3.00
180	Eddie Murray	1.25
181	Ozzie Smith	1.50
182	Garret Anderson	.40

183	Raul Mondesi	.40
184	Jeff Conine	.40
185	Ken Griffey Jr.	2.00
186	Will Clark	.40
187	Mike Greenwell	.40
188	Carlos Baerga	.40
189	Paul Molitor	1.25
190	Jeff Bagwell	1.25
191	Mark Grace	.40
192	Don Mattingly	1.75
193	Hal Morris	.40
194	Kenny Lofton	.40
195	Edgar Martinez	.40
196	Kirby Puckett	1.50
197	Mike Piazza	2.00
198	Frank Thomas	1.25
199	Wade Boggs	1.25
200	Tony Gwynn	1.50

Artist's Proof

PHIL NEVIN

	NM/M
Common Artist's Proof:	2.00
Stars:	3X

(See 1996 Pinnacle Starburst for checklist and base card values.)

Foil Series 2

	NM/M
Complete Set (200):	15.00
Common Player:	.20
Stars:	1.5X

(See 1996 Pinnacle #201-399 for checklist and base card values.)

Cal Ripken Tribute

	NM/M
1 of 1 Cal Ripken Jr.	5.00

Christie Brinkley Collection

		NM/M
Complete Set (16):		15.00
Common Player:		.80
1	Greg Maddux	3.50
2	Ryan Klesko	.75
3	Dave Justice	.75
4	Tom Glavine	1.50
5	Chipper Jones	3.50
6	Fred McGriff	.75
7	Javier Lopez	.75
8	Marquis Grissom	.75
9	Jason Schmidt	.75
10	Albert Belle	.75
11	Manny Ramirez	2.25
12	Carlos Baerga	.75
13	Sandy Alomar	.75
14	Jim Thome	2.25

Christie Brinkley Collection
ALBERT BELLE

15	Julio Franco	.75
16	Kenny Lofton	.75

Essence of the Game

Essence of the Game
ALBERT BELLE
CLEVELAND INDIANS

		NM/M
Complete Set (18):		35.00
Common Player:		.70
1	Cal Ripken Jr.	6.00
2	Greg Maddux	3.00
3	Frank Thomas	2.50
4	Matt Williams	.75
5	Chipper Jones	3.00
6	Reggie Sanders	.75
7	Ken Griffey Jr.	4.00
8	Kirby Puckett	3.00
9	Hideo Nomo	1.50
10	Mike Piazza	4.00
11	Jeff Bagwell	2.50
12	Mo Vaughn	.75
13	Albert Belle	.75
14	Tim Salmon	.75
15	Don Mattingly	3.50
16	Will Clark	.75
17	Eddie Murray	2.50
18	Barry Bonds	6.00

First Rate

1st RATE
ONES

		NM/M
Complete Set (18):		40.00
Common Player:		1.25
1	Ken Griffey Jr.	5.00
2	Frank Thomas	2.50
3	Mo Vaughn	1.25
4	Chipper Jones	3.50
5	Alex Rodriguez	6.50
6	Kirby Puckett	3.50
7	Gary Sheffield	1.75
8	Matt Williams	1.25
9	Barry Bonds	7.50

ABBREVIATIONS

ED - Expansion Draft

10	Craig Biggio	1.25
11	Robin Ventura	1.25
12	Michael Tucker	1.25
13	Derek Jeter	7.50
14	Manny Ramirez	2.50
15	Barry Larkin	1.25
16	Shawn Green	1.75
17	Will Clark	1.25
18	Mark McGwire	6.50

Pinnacle Power

REGGIE SANDERS

		NM/M
Complete Set (20):		40.00
Common Player:		1.25
1	Frank Thomas	2.50
2	Mo Vaughn	1.25
2p	Mo Vaughn (Promo)	1.50
3	Ken Griffey Jr.	4.50
4	Matt Williams	1.25
5	Barry Bonds	6.00
6	Reggie Sanders	1.25
7	Mike Piazza	4.50
8	Jim Edmonds	1.25
9	Dante Bichette	1.25
10	Sammy Sosa	3.50
11	Jeff Bagwell	2.50
12	Fred McGriff	1.25
13	Albert Belle	1.25
14	Tim Salmon	1.25
15	Joe Carter	1.25
16	Manny Ramirez	2.50
17	Eddie Murray	2.50
18	Cecil Fielder	1.25
19	Larry Walker	1.25
20	Juan Gonzalez	1.75

Project Stardom

		NM/M
Complete Set (18):		35.00
Common Player:		1.00
1	Paul Wilson	1.00
2	Derek Jeter	8.50
3	Karim Garcia	1.00
4	Johnny Damon	2.75
5	Alex Rodriguez	7.50
6	Chipper Jones	6.50
7	Charles Johnson	1.00
8	Bob Abreu	1.25
9	Alan Benes	1.00
10	Richard Hidalgo	1.00
11	Brooks Kieschnick	1.00
12	Garret Anderson	1.00
13	Livan Hernandez	1.00
14	Manny Ramirez	5.00
15	Jermaine Dye	1.00
16	Todd Hollandsworth	1.00
17	Raul Mondesi	1.00
18	Ryan Klesko	1.00

Skylines

		NM/M
Complete Set (18):		375.00
Common Player:		10.00
1	Ken Griffey Jr.	50.00
2	Frank Thomas	30.00
3	Greg Maddux	40.00
4	Cal Ripken Jr.	65.00
5	Albert Belle	10.00
6	Mo Vaughn	10.00
7	Mike Piazza	50.00
8	Wade Boggs	40.00
9	Will Clark	10.00
10	Barry Bonds	65.00
11	Gary Sheffield	10.00
12	Hideo Nomo	25.00
13	Tony Gwynn	40.00
14	Kirby Puckett	40.00
15	Chipper Jones	40.00
16	Jeff Bagwell	30.00
17	Manny Ramirez	30.00
18	Raul Mondesi	10.00

Slugfest

		NM/M
Complete Set (18):		40.00
Common Player:		1.25
1	Frank Thomas	2.75
2	Ken Griffey Jr.	4.00
3	Jeff Bagwell	2.75
4	Barry Bonds	5.00
5	Mo Vaughn	1.25
6	Albert Belle	1.25
7	Mike Piazza	4.00
8	Matt Williams	1.25
9	Dante Bichette	1.25
10	Sammy Sosa	3.00
11	Gary Sheffield	2.00
12	Reggie Sanders	1.25
13	Manny Ramirez	2.75
14	Eddie Murray	2.75
15	Juan Gonzalez	2.25
16	Dean Palmer	1.25
17	Rafael Palmeiro	2.75
18	Cecil Fielder	1.25

Team Pinnacle

		NM/M
Complete Set (9):		35.00
Common Player:		1.50
1	Frank Thomas, Jeff Bagwell	4.00
2	Chuck Knoblauch, Craig Biggio	1.50
3	Jim Thome, Matt Williams	3.00
4	Barry Larkin, Cal Ripken Jr.	12.00
5	Barry Bonds, Tim Salmon	10.00
6	Ken Griffey Jr., Reggie Sanders	8.00
7	Albert Belle, Sammy Sosa	6.00
8	Ivan Rodriguez, Mike Piazza	6.00
9	Greg Maddux, Randy Johnson	8.00

Team Spirit

Barry Bonds

		NM/M
Complete Set (12):		45.00
Common Player:		1.25
1	Greg Maddux	4.00
2	Ken Griffey Jr.	5.00
3	Derek Jeter	8.00
4	Mike Piazza	5.00
5	Cal Ripken Jr.	8.00
6	Frank Thomas	2.75
7	Jeff Bagwell	2.75
8	Mo Vaughn	1.25
9	Albert Belle	1.25
10	Chipper Jones	4.00
11	Johnny Damon	1.50
12	Barry Bonds	8.00

Team Tomorrow

		NM/M
Complete Set (10):		20.00
Common Player:		.50
1	Ruben Rivera	.50
2	Johnny Damon	1.00
3	Raul Mondesi	.50
4	Manny Ramirez	3.00
5	Hideo Nomo	1.50
6	Chipper Jones	4.00
7	Garret Anderson	.50
8	Alex Rodriguez	5.00
9	Derek Jeter	6.00
10	Karim Garcia	.50

1996 Pinnacle / Aficionado

		NM/M
Complete Set (200):		20.00
Common Player:		.10
Common Artist's Proof:		.10
Artist's Proof Stars:		8X
Pack (5):		1.50
Wax Box (16):		30.00
1	Jack McDowell	.10
2	Jay Bell	.10
3	Rafael Palmeiro	1.25
4	Wally Joyner	.10
5	Ozzie Smith	2.00
6	Mark McGwire	3.00
7	Kevin Seitzer	.10
8	Fred McGriff	.10
9	Roger Clemens	2.25
9s	Roger Clemens (Marked "SAMPLE.")	4.00
10	Randy Johnson	1.50
11	Cecil Fielder	.10
12	David Cone	.10
13	Chili Davis	.10
14	Andres Galarraga	.10
15	Joe Carter	.10
16	Ryne Sandberg	2.00
17	Paul O'Neill	.10
18	Cal Ripken Jr.	4.00
19	Wade Boggs	2.00
20	Greg Gagne	.10
21	Edgar Martinez	.10
22	Greg Maddux	2.00
23	Ken Caminiti	.10
24	Kirby Puckett	2.00
25	Craig Biggio	.10
26	Will Clark	.10
27	Ron Gant	.10
28	Eddie Murray	1.50
29	Lance Johnson	.10
30	Tony Gwynn	2.00
31	Dante Bichette	.10
32	Darren Daulton	.10
33	Danny Tartabull	.10
34	Jeff King	.10
35	Tom Glavine	.40
36	Rickey Henderson	1.50
37	Jose Canseco	1.00
38	Barry Larkin	.10
39	Dennis Martinez	.10
40	Ruben Sierra	.10
41	Bobby Bonilla	.10
42	Jeff Conine	.10
43	Lee Smith	.10
44	Charlie Hayes	.10
45	Walt Weiss	.10
46	Jay Buhner	.10
47	Kenny Rogers	.10
48	Paul Molitor	1.50
49	Hal Morris	.10
50	Todd Stottlemyre	.10
51	Mike Stanley	.10
52	Mark Grace	.10
53	Lenny Dykstra	.10
54	Andre Dawson	.25
55	Dennis Eckersley	1.25
56	Ben McDonald	.10
57	Ray Lankford	.10
58	Mo Vaughn	.10
59	Frank Thomas	1.50
60	Julio Franco	.10
61	Jim Abbott	.10
62	Greg Vaughn	.10
63	Marquis Grissom	.10
64	Tino Martinez	.10
65	Kevin Appier	.10
66	Matt Williams	.10
67	Sammy Sosa	2.00
68	Larry Walker	.10
69	Ivan Rodriguez	1.25
70	Eric Karros	.10
71	Bernie Williams	.10
72	Carlos Baerga	.10
73	Jeff Bagwell	1.50
74	Pete Schourek	.10
75	Ken Griffey Jr.	2.50
76	Bernard Gilkey	.10
77	Albert Belle	.10
78	Chuck Knoblauch	.10
79	John Smoltz	.10
80	Barry Bonds	4.00
81	Vinny Castilla	.10
82	John Olerud	.10
83	Mike Mussina	1.00
84	Alex Fernandez	.10
85	Shawon Dunston	.10
86	Travis Fryman	.10
87	Moises Alou	.10
88	Dean Palmer	.10
89	Gregg Jefferies	.10
90	Jim Thome	1.25
91	Dave Justice	.10
92	B.J. Surhoff	.10
93	Ramon Martinez	.10
94	Gary Sheffield	.40
95	Andy Benes	.10
96	Reggie Sanders	.10
97	Roberto Alomar	.35
98	Omar Vizquel	.10
99	Juan Gonzalez	.75
100	Robin Ventura	.10
101	Jason Isringhausen	.10
102	Greg Colbrunn	.10
103	Brian Jordan	.10
104	Shawn Green	.40
105	Brian Hunter	.10
106	Rondell White	.10
107	Ryan Klesko	.10
107s	Ryan Klesko (Marked "SAMPLE.")	1.00
108	Sterling Hitchcock	.10
109	Manny Ramirez	1.50

110	Bret Boone	.10
111	Michael Tucker	.10
112	Julian Tavarez	.10
113	Benji Gil	.10
114	Kenny Lofton	.10
115	Mike Kelly	.10
116	Ray Durham	.10
117	Trevor Hoffman	.10
118	Butch Huskey	.10
119	Phil Nevin	.10
120	Pedro Martinez	1.50
121	Wil Cordero	.10
122	Tim Salmon	.10
123	Jim Edmonds	.10
124	Mike Piazza	2.50
125	Rico Brogna	.10
126	John Mabry	.10
127	Chipper Jones	2.00
128	Johnny Damon	.35
129	Raul Mondesi	.10
130	Denny Neagle	.10
131	Marc Newfield	.10
132	Hideo Nomo	.75
133	Joe Vitiello	.10
134	Garret Anderson	.10
135	Dave Nilsson	.10
136	Alex Rodriguez	3.00
137	Russ Davis	.10
138	Frank Rodriguez	.10
139	Royce Clayton	.10
140	John Valentin	.10
141	Marty Cordova	.10
142	Alex Gonzalez	.10
143	Carlos Delgado	.75
144	Willie Greene	.10
145	Cliff Floyd	.10
146	Bobby Higginson	.10
147	J.T. Snow	.10
148	Derek Bell	.10
149	Edgardo Alfonzo	.10
150	Charles Johnson	.10
151	Hideo Nomo	.60
152	Larry Walker	.10
153	Bob Abreu	.10
154	Karim Garcia	.10
155	Dave Nilsson	.10
156	Chan Ho Park	.10
157	Dennis Martinez	.10
158	Sammy Sosa	1.25
159	Rey Ordonez	.10
160	Roberto Alomar	.10
161	George Arias	.10
162	Jason Schmidt	.10
163	Derek Jeter	4.00
164	Chris Snopek	.10
165	Todd Hollandsworth	.10
166	Sal Fasano	.10
167	Jay Powell	.10
168	Paul Wilson	.10
169	Jim Pittsley	.10
170	LaTroy Hawkins	.10
171	Bob Abreu	.10
172	Mike Grace RC	.10
173	Karim Garcia	.10
174	Richard Hidalgo	.10
175	Felipe Crespo	.10
176	Terrell Wade	.10
177	Steve Gibralter	.10
178	Jermaine Dye	.10
179	Alan Benes	.10
180	Wilton Guerrero RC	.10
181	Brooks Kieschnick	.10
182	Roger Cedeno	.10
183	Osvaldo Fernandez RC	.10
184	Matt Lawton RC	.50
185	George Williams	.10
186	Jimmy Haynes	.10
187	Mike Busby RC	.10
188	Chan Ho Park	.10
189	Marc Barcelo	.10
190	Jason Kendall	.10
191	Rey Ordonez	.10
192	Tyler Houston	.10
193	John Wasdin	.10
194	Jeff Suppan	.10
195	Jeff Ware	.10
196	Checklist	.10
197	Checklist	.10
198	Checklist	.10
199	Checklist	.10
200	Checklist	.10

First Pitch Previews

	NM/M
Complete Set (200):	250.00
Common Player:	2.00

(Star cards valued at 8-10X regular Aficionado edition.)

Magic Numbers

		NM/M
Complete Set (10):		15.50
Common Player:		.75
Samples:		1X
1	Ken Griffey Jr.	3.25
2	Greg Maddux	2.50
3	Frank Thomas	1.50
4	Mo Vaughn	.75
5	Jeff Bagwell	1.50
6	Chipper Jones	2.50
7	Albert Belle	.75
8	Cal Ripken Jr.	4.50
9	Matt Williams	.75
10	Sammy Sosa	2.50

Rivals

		NM/M
Complete Set (24):		65.00
Common Player:		2.00
1	Ken Griffey Jr., Frank Thomas	4.00
2	Frank Thomas, Cal Ripken Jr.	4.50
3	Cal Ripken Jr., Mo Vaughn	4.00
4	Mo Vaughn, Ken Griffey Jr.	2.50
5	Ken Griffey Jr., Cal Ripken Jr.	5.00
6	Frank Thomas, Mo Vaughn	2.00
7	Cal Ripken Jr., Ken Griffey Jr.	5.00
8	Mo Vaughn, Frank Thomas	2.00
9	Ken Griffey Jr., Mo Vaughn	2.50
10	Frank Thomas, Ken Griffey Jr.	4.00
11	Cal Ripken Jr., Frank Thomas	4.50
12	Mo Vaughn, Cal Ripken Jr.	4.00
13	Mike Piazza, Jeff Bagwell	2.50
14	Jeff Bagwell, Barry Bonds	4.50
15	Jeff Bagwell, Mike Piazza	2.50
16	Tony Gwynn, Mike Piazza	3.00
17	Mike Piazza, Barry Bonds	5.00
18	Jeff Bagwell, Tony Gwynn	2.00
19	Barry Bonds, Mike Piazza	5.00
20	Tony Gwynn, Jeff Bagwell	2.00
21	Mike Piazza, Tony Gwynn	3.00
22	Barry Bonds, Jeff Bagwell	4.50
23	Tony Gwynn, Barry Bonds	4.50
24	Barry Bonds, Tony Gwynn	4.50

Slick Picks

		NM/M
Complete Set (32):		40.00
Common Player:		.50
1	Mike Piazza	2.50
2	Cal Ripken Jr.	4.00
3	Ken Griffey Jr.	2.50
4	Paul Wilson	.50
5	Frank Thomas	1.50
6	Mo Vaughn	.50
7	Barry Bonds	4.00
8	Albert Belle	.50
9	Jeff Bagwell	1.50
10	Dante Bichette	.50
11	Hideo Nomo	.75
12	Raul Mondesi	.50
13	Manny Ramirez	1.50
14	Greg Maddux	2.00
15	Tony Gwynn	2.00
16	Ryne Sandberg	2.00
17	Reggie Sanders	.50
18	Derek Jeter	4.00
19	Johnny Damon	.75
20	Alex Rodriguez	3.00
21	Ryan Klesko	.50
22	Jim Thome	1.50
23	Kenny Lofton	.50
24	Tino Martinez	.50
25	Randy Johnson	1.50
26	Wade Boggs	2.00
27	Juan Gonzalez	.75
28	Kirby Puckett	2.00
29	Tim Salmon	.50
30	Chipper Jones	2.00
31	Garret Anderson	.50
32	Eddie Murray	1.50

1997 Pinnacle

		NM/M
Complete Set (200):		10.00
Common Player:		.05
Pack (10):		1.00
Wax Box (24):		12.50
Wax Retail Box (16):		10.00
1	Cecil Fielder	.05
2	Garret Anderson	.05
3	Charles Nagy	.05
4	Darryl Hamilton	.05
5	Greg Myers	.05
6	Eric Davis	.05
7	Jeff Frye	.05
8	Marquis Grissom	.05
9	Curt Schilling	.35
10	Jeff Fassero	.05
11	Alan Benes	.05
12	Orlando Miller	.05
13	Alex Fernandez	.05
14	Andy Pettitte	.25
15	Andre Dawson	.25
16	Mark Grudzielanek	.05
17	Joe Vitiello	.05
18	Juan Gonzalez	.40
19	Mark Whiten	.05
20	Lance Johnson	.05
21	Trevor Hoffman	.05
22	Marc Newfield	.05
23	Jim Eisenreich	.05
24	Joe Carter	.05
25	Jose Canseco	.30
26	Bill Swift	.05
27	Ellis Burks	.05
28	Ben McDonald	.05
29	Edgar Martinez	.05
30	Jamie Moyer	.05
31	Chan Ho Park	.05
32	Carlos Delgado	.50
33	Kevin Mitchell	.05
34	Carlos Garcia	.05
35	Darryl Strawberry	.05
36	Jim Thome	.60
37	Jose Offerman	.05
38	Ryan Klesko	.05
39	Ruben Sierra	.05
40	Devon White	.05
41	Brian Jordan	.05
42	Tony Gwynn	.75
43	Rafael Palmeiro	.50
44	Dante Bichette	.05
45	Scott Stahoviak	.05
46	Roger Cedeno	.05
47	Ivan Rodriguez	.50
48	Bob Abreu	.05
49	Darryl Kile	.05
50	Darren Dreifort	.05
51	Shawon Dunston	.05
52	Mark McGwire	1.50
53	Tim Salmon	.05
54	Gene Schall	.05
55	Roger Clemens	.85
56	Rondell White	.05
57	Ed Sprague	.05
58	Craig Paquette	.05
59	David Segui	.05
60	Jaime Navarro	.05
61	Tom Glavine	.35
62	Jeff Brantley	.05
63	Kimera Bartee	.05
64	Fernando Vina	.05
65	Eddie Murray	.65
66	Lenny Dykstra	.05
67	Kevin Elster	.05
68	Vinny Castilla	.05
69	Todd Greene	.05
70	Brett Butler	.05
71	Robby Thompson	.05
72	Reggie Jefferson	.05
73	Todd Hundley	.05
74	Jeff King	.05
75	Ernie Young	.05
76	Jeff Bagwell	.65
77	Dan Wilson	.05
78	Paul Molitor	.65
79	Kevin Seitzer	.05
80	Kevin Brown	.05
81	Ron Gant	.05
82	Dwight Gooden	.05
83	Todd Stottlemyre	.05
84	Ken Caminiti	.05
85	James Baldwin	.05
86	Jermaine Dye	.05
87	Harold Baines	.05
88	Pat Hentgen	.05
89	Frank Rodriguez	.05
90	Mark Johnson	.05
91	Jason Kendall	.05
92	Alex Rodriguez	1.50
93	Alan Trammell	.05
94	Scott Brosius	.05
95	Delino DeShields	.05
96	Chipper Jones	.75
97	Barry Bonds	2.00
98	Brady Anderson	.05
99	Ryne Sandberg	.75
100	Albert Belle	.05
101	Jeff Cirillo	.05
102	Frank Thomas	.65
103	Mike Piazza	1.00
104	Rickey Henderson	.65
105	Rey Ordonez	.05
106	Mark Grace	.05
107	Terry Steinbach	.05
108	Ray Durham	.05
109	Barry Larkin	.05
110	Tony Clark	.05
111	Bernie Williams	.05
112	John Smoltz	.05
113	Moises Alou	.05
114	Alex Gonzalez	.05
115	Rico Brogna	.05
116	Eric Karros	.05

117	Jeff Conine	.05
118	Todd Hollandsworth	.05
119	Troy Percival	.05
120	Paul Wilson	.05
121	Orel Hershiser	.05
122	Ozzie Smith	.75
123	Dave Hollins	.05
124	Ken Hill	.05
125	Rick Wilkins	.05
126	Scott Servais	.05
127	Fernando Valenzuela	.05
128	Mariano Rivera	.15
129	Mark Loretta	.05
130	Shane Reynolds	.05
131	Darren Oliver	.05
132	Steve Trachsel	.05
133	Darren Bragg	.05
134	Jason Dickson	.05
135	Darren Fletcher	.05
136	Gary Gaetti	.05
137	Joey Cora	.05
138	Terry Pendleton	.05
139	Derek Jeter	2.00
140	Danny Tartabull	.05
141	John Flaherty	.05
142	B.J. Surhoff	.05
143	Mark Sweeney	.05
144	Chad Mottola	.05
145	Andujar Cedeno	.05
146	Tim Belcher	.05
147	Mark Thompson	.05
148	Rafael Bournigal	.05
149	Marty Cordova	.05
150	Osvaldo Fernandez	.05
151	Mike Stanley	.05
152	Ricky Bottalico	.05
153	Donnie Wall	.05
154	Omar Vizquel	.05
155	Mike Mussina	.30
156	Brant Brown	.05
157	F.P. Santangelo	.05
158	Ryan Hancock	.05
159	Jeff D'Amico	.05
160	Luis Castillo	.05
161	Darin Erstad	.10
162	Ugueth Urbina	.05
163	Andruw Jones	.65
164	Steve Gibralter	.05
165	Robin Jennings	.05
166	Mike Cameron	.05
167	George Arias	.05
168	Chris Stynes	.05
169	Justin Thompson	.05
170	Jamey Wright	.05
171	Todd Walker	.05
172	Nomar Garciaparra	.75
173	Jose Paniagua	.05
174	Marvin Benard	.05
175	Rocky Coppinger	.05
176	Quinton McCracken	.05
177	Amaury Telemaco	.05
178	Neifi Perez	.05
179	Todd Greene	.05
180	Jason Thompson	.05
181	Wilton Guerrero	.05
182	Edgar Renteria	.05
183	Billy Wagner	.05
184	Alex Ochoa	.05
185	Billy McMillon	.05
186	Kenny Lofton	.05
187	Andres Galarraga	.05
188	Chuck Knoblauch	.05
189	Greg Maddux	.75
190	Mo Vaughn	.05
191	Cal Ripken Jr.	2.00
192	Hideo Nomo	.40
193	Ken Griffey Jr.	1.00
194	Sammy Sosa	.75
195	Jay Buhner	.05
196	Manny Ramirez	.65
197	Matt Williams	.05
198	Andruw Jones (Checklist)	.30
199	Darin Erstad (Checklist)	.05
200	Trey Beamon (Checklist)	.05

Museum Collection

	NM/M
Complete Set (200):	100.00
Common Player:	1.00
Stars/Rookies:	6X

ABBREVIATIONS

OPS - Overprint
"Promotional Sample"

(See 1997 Pinnacle for checklist and regular-issue card values.)

Artist's Proofs

	NM/M
Common Bronze (125):	1.00
Bronze Stars:	30X
Common Silver (50):	2.50
Silver Stars:	12X
Common Gold (25):	4.00
Gold Stars:	10X

(See 1997 Pinnacle for checklist and base card values.)

Cardfrontations

		NM/M
Complete Set (20):		35.00
Common Player:		.50
1	Greg Maddux, Mike Piazza	3.00
2	Tom Glavine, Ken Caminiti	.75
3	Randy Johnson, Cal Ripken Jr.	5.00
4	Kevin Appier, Mark McGwire	4.00
5	Andy Pettitte, Juan Gonzalez	1.00
6	Pat Hentgen, Albert Belle	.50
7	Hideo Nomo, Chipper Jones	2.00
8	Ismael Valdes, Sammy Sosa	2.50
9	Mike Mussina, Manny Ramirez	1.50
10	David Cone, Jay Buhner	.50

11	Mark Wohlers, Gary Sheffield	.75
12	Alan Benes, Barry Bonds	5.00
13	Roger Clemens, Ivan Rodriguez	2.50
14	Mariano Rivera, Ken Griffey Jr.	3.00
15	Dwight Gooden, Frank Thomas	1.50
16	John Wetteland, Darin Erstad	.50
17	John Smoltz, Brian Jordan	.50
18	Kevin Brown, Jeff Bagwell	1.50
19	Jack McDowell, Alex Rodriguez	4.00
20	Charles Nagy, Bernie Williams	.50

Home/Away

		NM/M
Complete Set (24):		65.00
Common Player:		2.00
1	Chipper Jones	5.00
2	Ken Griffey Jr.	6.00
3	Mike Piazza	6.00
4	Frank Thomas	4.00
5	Jeff Bagwell	4.00
6	Alex Rodriguez	8.00
7	Barry Bonds	10.00
8	Mo Vaughn	2.00
9	Derek Jeter	10.00
10	Mark McGwire	8.00
11	Cal Ripken Jr.	10.00
12	Albert Belle	2.00

Passport to the Majors

		NM/M
Complete Set (25):		55.00
Common Player:		1.00
1	Greg Maddux	4.00
1s	Greg Maddux/OPS	6.00
2	Ken Griffey Jr.	6.00
3	Frank Thomas	6.00
4	Cal Ripken Jr.	10.00
5	Mike Piazza	6.00
6	Alex Rodriguez	7.50
7	Mo Vaughn	1.00
8	Chipper Jones	4.00
9	Roberto Alomar	1.00
10	Edgar Martinez	1.00
11	Javier Lopez	1.00
12	Ivan Rodriguez	2.50
13	Juan Gonzalez	1.50
14	Carlos Baerga	1.00
15	Sammy Sosa	4.00
16	Manny Ramirez	3.00
17	Raul Mondesi	1.00
18	Henry Rodriguez	1.00
19	Rafael Palmeiro	2.50

20	Rey Ordonez	1.00
21	Hideo Nomo	1.50
22	Makoto Suzuki	1.00
23	Chan Ho Park	1.00
24	Larry Walker	1.00
25	Ruben Rivera	1.00

Shades

		NM/M
Complete Set (10):		15.00
Common Player:		.75
1	Ken Griffey Jr.	3.00
2	Juan Gonzalez	1.50
3	John Smoltz	.75
4	Gary Sheffield	1.00
5	Cal Ripken Jr.	5.00
6	Mo Vaughn	.75
7	Brian Jordan	.75
8	Mike Piazza	3.00
9	Frank Thomas	2.25
10	Alex Rodriguez	4.00

Team Pinnacle

		NM/M
Complete Set (10):		30.00
Common Player:		1.50
1	Frank Thomas, Jeff Bagwell	4.00
2	Chuck Knoblauch, Eric Young	1.50
3	Ken Caminiti, Jim Thome	3.00
4	Alex Rodriguez, Chipper Jones	6.00
5	Mike Piazza, Ivan Rodriguez	5.00
6	Albert Belle, Barry Bonds	8.00
7	Ken Griffey Jr., Ellis Burks	6.00
8	Juan Gonzalez, Gary Sheffield	3.00
9	John Smoltz, Andy Pettitte	2.00
10	All Players	2.00

1997 Pinnacle Certified

	NM/M
Complete Set (150):	30.00
Common Player:	.15
Common Certified Red:	1.00
Certified Red Stars:	5X
Common Mirror Red:	3.00
Mirror Red Stars:	12X
Common Mirror Blue:	4.00
Mirror Blue Stars:	15X
Common Mirror Gold:	7.50
Mirror Gold Stars:	35X
Jose Cruz Jr. Redemption:	2.00
Pack (6):	2.00

Wax Box (20):		35.00
1	Barry Bonds	3.00
2	Mo Vaughn	.15
3	Matt Williams	.15
4	Ryne Sandberg	1.25
5	Jeff Bagwell	1.00
6	Alan Benes	.15
7	John Wetteland	.15
8	Fred McGriff	.15
9	Craig Biggio	.15
10	Bernie Williams	.15
11	Brian L. Hunter	.15
12	Sandy Alomar Jr.	.15
13	Ray Lankford	.15
14	Ryan Klesko	.15
15	Jermaine Dye	.15
16	Andy Benes	.15
17	Albert Belle	.15
18	Tony Clark	.15
19	Dean Palmer	.15
20	Bernard Gilkey	.15
21	Ken Caminiti	.15
22	Alex Rodriguez	2.25
23	Tim Salmon	.15
24	Larry Walker	.15
25	Barry Larkin	.15
26	Mike Piazza	1.50
27	Brady Anderson	.15
28	Cal Ripken Jr.	3.00
29	Charles Nagy	.15
30	Paul Molitor	1.00
31	Darin Erstad	.25
32	Rey Ordonez	.15
33	Wally Joyner	.15
34	David Cone	.15
35	Sammy Sosa	1.25
36	Dante Bichette	.15
37	Eric Karros	.15
38	Omar Vizquel	.15
39	Roger Clemens	1.25
40	Joe Carter	.15
41	Frank Thomas	1.00
42	Javier Lopez	.15
43	Mike Mussina	.45
44	Gary Sheffield	.60
45	Tony Gwynn	1.25
46	Jason Kendall	.15
47	Jim Thome	.75
48	Andres Galarraga	.15
49	Mark McGwire	2.25
50	Troy Percival	.15
51	Derek Jeter	3.00
52	Todd Hollandsworth	.15
53	Ken Griffey Jr.	1.50
54	Randy Johnson	1.00
55	Pat Hentgen	.15
56	Rusty Greer	.15
57	John Jaha	.15
58	Kenny Lofton	.15
59	Chipper Jones	1.25
60	Robb Nen	.15
61	Rafael Palmeiro	.75
62	Mariano Rivera	.30
63	Hideo Nomo	.50
64	Greg Vaughn	.15
65	Ron Gant	.15
66	Eddie Murray	1.00
67	John Smoltz	.15
68	Manny Ramirez	1.00
69	Juan Gonzalez	.50
70	F.P. Santangelo	.15
71	Moises Alou	.15
72	Alex Ochoa	.15
73	Chuck Knoblauch	.15
74	Raul Mondesi	.15
75	J.T. Snow	.15
76	Rickey Henderson	1.00
77	Bobby Bonilla	.15
78	Wade Boggs	1.25
79	Ivan Rodriguez	.75
80	Brian Jordan	.15
81	Al Leiter	.15
82	Jay Buhner	.15
83	Greg Maddux	1.25
84	Edgar Martinez	.15
85	Kevin Brown	.15
86	Eric Young	.15
87	Todd Hundley	.15
88	Ellis Burks	.15
89	Marquis Grissom	.15
90	Jose Canseco	.60
91	Henry Rodriguez	.15
92	Andy Pettitte	.45
93	Mark Grudzielanek	.15
94	Dwight Gooden	.15
95	Roberto Alomar	.50
96	Paul Wilson	.15
97	Will Clark	.15
98	Rondell White	.15
99	Charles Johnson	.15
100	Jim Edmonds	.15
101	Jason Giambi	.60
102	Billy Wagner	.15
103	Edgar Renteria	.15

104	Johnny Damon	.45
105	Jason Isringhausen	.15
106	Andruw Jones	1.00
107	Jose Guillen	.15
108	Kevin Orie	.15
109	Brian Giles RC	1.25
110	Danny Patterson	.15
111	Vladimir Guerrero	1.00
112	Scott Rolen	.75
113	Damon Mashore	.15
114	Nomar Garciaparra	1.25
115	Todd Walker	.15
116	Wilton Guerrero	.15
117	Bob Abreu	.25
118	Brooks Kieschnick	.15
119	Pokey Reese	.15
120	Todd Greene	.15
121	Dmitri Young	.15
122	Raul Casanova	.15
123	Glendon Rusch	.15
124	Jason Dickson	.15
125	Jorge Posada	.15
126	Rod Myers RC	.15
127	Bubba Trammell RC	.40
128	Scott Spiezio	.15
129	Hideki Irabu RC	.40
130	Wendell Magee	.15
131	Bartolo Colon	.15
132	Chris Holt	.15
133	Calvin Maduro	.15
134	Ray Montgomery	.15
135	Shannon Stewart	.15
136	Ken Griffey Jr.	1.00
137	Vladimir Guerrero	.50
138	Roger Clemens	.75
139	Mark McGwire	1.25
140	Albert Belle	.15
141	Derek Jeter	1.50
142	Juan Gonzalez	.25
143	Greg Maddux	.60
144	Alex Rodriguez	1.25
145	Jeff Bagwell	.50
146	Cal Ripken Jr.	1.50
147	Tony Gwynn	.60
148	Frank Thomas	.50
149	Hideo Nomo	.25
150	Andruw Jones	.50

Red

		NM/M
Common Certified Red:		1.00
Certified Red Stars:		5X

(See 1997 Pinnacle Certified for checklist and base values.)

Mirror Red

		NM/M
Common Mirror Red:		3.00
Mirror Red Stars:		12X

(See 1997 Pinnacle Certified for checklist and base values.)

Mirror Blue

		NM/M
Common Mirror Blue:		4.00
Mirror Blue Stars:		15X

(See 1997 Pinnacle Certified for checklist and base values.)

Mirror Gold

		NM/M
Common Mirror Gold:		7.50
Mirror Gold Stars:		35X

(See 1997 Pinnacle Certified for checklist and base values.)

Mirror Black

	NM/M
Common Player:	100.00

(Star cards valued at 150-250X base value.)

Lasting Impression

		NM/M
Complete Set (20):		40.00
Common Player:		1.00
1	Cal Ripken Jr.	7.50
2	Ken Griffey Jr.	5.00
3	Mo Vaughn	1.00
4	Brian Jordan	1.00
5	Mark McGwire	6.00
6	Chuck Knoblauch	1.00
7	Sammy Sosa	3.00
8	Brady Anderson	1.00
9	Frank Thomas	2.00
10	Tony Gwynn	3.00
11	Roger Clemens	4.00
12	Alex Rodriguez	6.00
13	Paul Molitor	2.00
14	Kenny Lofton	1.00
15	John Smoltz	1.00
16	Roberto Alomar	1.50
17	Randy Johnson	2.00
18	Ryne Sandberg	3.00
19	Manny Ramirez	2.00
20	Mike Mussina	1.50

Team

		NM/M
Complete Set (20):		30.00
Common Player:		.50
Gold:		3X
Mirror Gold:		15X
Sample:		1X
1	Frank Thomas	1.50
2	Jeff Bagwell	1.50
3	Derek Jeter	4.00
4	Chipper Jones	2.00
5	Alex Rodriguez	3.00
6	Ken Caminiti	.50
7	Cal Ripken Jr.	4.00

8	Mo Vaughn	.50
9	Ivan Rodriguez	1.00
10	Mike Piazza	2.50
11	Juan Gonzalez	.75
12	Barry Bonds	4.00
13	Ken Griffey Jr.	2.50
14	Andruw Jones	1.50
15	Albert Belle	.50
16	Gary Sheffield	.75
17	Andy Pettitte	.65
18	Hideo Nomo	.75
19	Greg Maddux	2.00
20	John Smoltz	.50

1997 Pinnacle Inside

		NM/M
Complete Set (150):		15.00
Common Player:		.05
Common Club Edition:		.75
Club Edition Stars:		5X
Common Diamond Edition:		5.00
Diamond Edition Stars:		25X
Unopened Can (10):		2.00
Case Cans (48):		60.00
1	David Cone	.05
2	Sammy Sosa	1.00
3	Joe Carter	.05
4	Juan Gonzalez	.40
5	Hideo Nomo	.40
6	Moises Alou	.05
7	Marc Newfield	.05
8	Alex Rodriguez	2.00
9	Kimera Bartee	.05
10	Chuck Knoblauch	.05
11	Jason Isringhausen	.05
12	Jermaine Allensworth	.05
13	Frank Thomas	.75
14	Paul Molitor	.75
15	John Mabry	.05
16	Greg Maddux	1.00
17	Rafael Palmeiro	.65
18	Brian Jordan	.05
19	Ken Griffey Jr.	1.50
20	Brady Anderson	.05
21	Ruben Sierra	.05
22	Travis Fryman	.05
23	Cal Ripken Jr.	2.50
24	Will Clark	.05
25	Todd Hollandsworth	.05
26	Kevin Brown	.05
27	Mike Piazza	1.50
28	Craig Biggio	.05
29	Paul Wilson	.05
30	Andres Galarraga	.05
31	Chipper Jones	1.00
32	Jason Giambi	.65
33	Ernie Young	.05
34	Marty Cordova	.05
35	Albert Belle	.05
36	Roger Clemens	1.25
37	Ryne Sandberg	1.00

38	Henry Rodriguez	.05
39	Jay Buhner	.05
40	Raul Mondesi	.05
41	Jeff Fassero	.05
42	Edgar Martinez	.05
43	Trey Beamon	.05
44	Mo Vaughn	.05
45	Gary Sheffield	.40
46	Ray Durham	.05
47	Brett Butler	.05
48	Ivan Rodriguez	.65
49	Fred McGriff	.05
50	Dean Palmer	.05
51	Rickey Henderson	.75
52	Andy Pettitte	.30
53	Bobby Bonilla	.05
54	Shawn Green	.50
55	Tino Martinez	.05
56	Tony Gwynn	1.00
57	Tom Glavine	.35
58	Eric Young	.05
59	Kevin Appier	.05
60	Barry Bonds	2.50
61	Wade Boggs	1.00
62	Jason Kendall	.05
63	Jeff Bagwell	.75
64	Jeff Conine	.05
65	Greg Vaughn	.05
66	Eric Karros	.05
67	Manny Ramirez	.75
68	John Smoltz	.05
69	Terrell Wade	.05
70	John Wetteland	.05
71	Kenny Lofton	.05
72	Jim Thome	.65
73	Bill Pulsipher	.05
74	Darryl Strawberry	.05
75	Roberto Alomar	.25
76	Bobby Higginson	.05
77	James Baldwin	.05
78	Mark McGwire	2.00
79	Jose Canseco	.40
80	Mark Grudzielanek	.05
81	Ryan Klesko	.05
82	Javier Lopez	.05
83	Ken Caminiti	.05
84	Dave Nilsson	.05
85	Tim Salmon	.05
86	Cecil Fielder	.05
87	Derek Jeter	2.50
88	Garret Anderson	.05
89	Dwight Gooden	.05
90	Carlos Delgado	.50
91	Ugueth Urbina	.05
92	Chan Ho Park	.05
93	Eddie Murray	.75
94	Alex Ochoa	.05
95	Rusty Greer	.05
96	Mark Grace	.05
97	Pat Hentgen	.05
98	John Jaha	.05
99	Charles Johnson	.05
100	Jermaine Dye	.05
101	Quinton McCracken	.05
102	Troy Percival	.05
103	Shane Reynolds	.05
104	Rondell White	.05
105	Charles Nagy	.05
106	Alan Benes	.05
107	Tom Goodwin	.05
108	Ron Gant	.05
109	Dan Wilson	.05
110	Darin Erstad	.10
111	Matt Williams	.05
112	Barry Larkin	.05
113	Mariano Rivera	.15
114	Larry Walker	.05
115	Jim Edmonds	.05
116	Michael Tucker	.05
117	Todd Hundley	.05
118	Alex Fernandez	.05
119	J.T. Snow	.05
120	Ellis Burks	.05
121	Steve Finley	.05
122	Mike Mussina	.40
123	Curtis Pride	.05
124	Derek Bell	.05
125	Dante Bichette	.05
126	Terry Steinbach	.05
127	Randy Johnson	.75
128	Andruw Jones	.75
129	Vladimir Guerrero	.75
130	Ruben Rivera	.05
131	Billy Wagner	.05
132	Scott Rolen	.65
133	Rey Ordonez	.05
134	Karim Garcia	.05
135	George Arias	.05
136	Todd Greene	.05
137	Robin Jennings	.05
138	Raul Casanova	.05
139	Josh Booty	.05
140	Edgar Renteria	.05
141	Chad Mottola	.05
142	Dmitri Young	.05
143	Tony Clark	.05
144	Todd Walker	.05
145	Kevin Brown	.05
146	Nomar Garciaparra	1.00
147	Neifi Perez	.05
148	Derek Jeter, Todd Hollandsworth	.50
149	Pat Hentgen, John Smoltz	.05
150	Juan Gonzalez, Ken Caminiti	.05

Club Edition

NM/M

Complete Club Edition Set (150): 300.00
Common Club Edition: .75
Stars: 5X
(See 1997 Pinnacle Inside for checklist and base values.)

Diamond Edition

NM/M

Common Diamond Edition: 5.00
Stars: 25X
(See 1997 Pinnacle Inside for checklist and base values.)

Cans

NM/M

Complete Set (24): 10.00
Common Can: .25
Sealed Cans: 2X

1	Ken Griffey Jr.	.75
2	Juan Gonzalez	.30
3	Frank Thomas	.40
4	Cal Ripken Jr.	1.50
5	Derek Jeter	1.50
6	Andruw Jones	.40
7	Alex Rodriguez	1.00
8	Mike Piazza	.75
9	Mo Vaughn	.25
10	Jeff Bagwell	.40
11	Ken Caminiti	.25
12	Andy Pettitte	.30
13	Barry Bonds	1.50
14	Mark McGwire	1.00
15	Ryan Klesko	.25
16	Manny Ramirez	.40
17	Ivan Rodriguez	.35
18	Chipper Jones	.50
19	Albert Belle	.25
20	Tony Gwynn	.50
21	Kenny Lofton	.25
22	Greg Maddux	.50
23	Hideo Nomo	.40
24	John Smoltz	.25

Dueling Dugouts

NM/M

Complete Set (20): 65.00
Common Player: 1.25

1	Alex Rodriguez, Cal Ripken Jr.	10.00
2	Jeff Bagwell, Ken Caminiti	3.00
3	Barry Bonds, Albert Belle	10.00
4	Mike Piazza, Ivan Rodriguez	6.00
5	Chuck Knoblauch, Roberto Alomar	1.25
6	Ken Griffey Jr., Andruw Jones	6.00
7	Chipper Jones, Jim Thome	4.00
8	Frank Thomas, Mo Vaughn	3.00
9	Fred McGriff, Mark McGwire	7.50
10	Brian Jordan, Tony Gwynn	4.00
11	Barry Larkin, Derek Jeter	10.00
12	Kenny Lofton, Bernie Williams	1.25
13	Juan Gonzalez, Manny Ramirez	3.00
14	Will Clark, Rafael Palmeiro	2.50
15	Greg Maddux, Roger Clemens	4.50
16	John Smoltz, Andy Pettitte	1.25
17	Mariano Rivera, John Wetteland	1.25
18	Hideo Nomo, Mike Mussina	2.00
19	Todd Hollandsworth, Darin Erstad	1.25
20	Vladimir Guerrero, Karim Garcia	1.25

Fortysomething

NM/M

Complete Set (16): 50.00
Common Player: 1.00

1	Juan Gonzalez	3.00
2	Barry Bonds	12.00
3	Ken Caminiti	1.00
4	Mark McGwire	10.00
5	Todd Hundley	1.00
6	Albert Belle	1.00
7	Ellis Burks	1.00
8	Jay Buhner	1.00
9	Brady Anderson	1.00
10	Vinny Castilla	1.00
11	Mo Vaughn	1.00
12	Ken Griffey Jr.	7.50

13	Sammy Sosa	6.50
14	Andres Galarraga	1.00
15	Gary Sheffield	2.00
16	Frank Thomas	5.00

1997 Pinnacle Mint Collection

NM/M

Complete Set (30): 25.00
Common Player: .25
Silver Cards: 4X
Gold Cards: 6X
Die-Cuts: 50%
Wax Box (24): 25.00

1	Ken Griffey Jr.	2.00
2	Frank Thomas	1.25
3	Alex Rodriguez	2.50
4	Cal Ripken Jr.	3.00
5	Mo Vaughn	.25
6	Juan Gonzalez	.60
7	Mike Piazza	2.00
8	Albert Belle	.25
9	Chipper Jones	1.50
10	Andruw Jones	1.25
11	Greg Maddux	1.50
12	Hideo Nomo	.60
13	Jeff Bagwell	1.25
14	Manny Ramirez	1.25
15	Mark McGwire	2.50
16	Derek Jeter	3.00
17	Sammy Sosa	1.50
18	Barry Bonds	3.00
19	Chuck Knoblauch	.25
20	Dante Bichette	.25
21	Tony Gwynn	1.50
22	Ken Caminiti	.25
23	Gary Sheffield	.60
24	Tim Salmon	.25
25	Ivan Rodriguez	1.00
26	Henry Rodriguez	.25
27	Barry Larkin	.25
28	Ryan Klesko	.25
29	Brian Jordan	.25
30	Jay Buhner	.25

Coins

NM/M

Complete Set (30): 35.00
Common Brass Coin: .25
Nickel Coins: 2X
Gold Plated Coins: 6X
Silver Coins: 20X
24K Gold Coins: Value Undetermined

1	Ken Griffey Jr.	2.50
2	Frank Thomas	1.50
3	Alex Rodriguez	3.00
4	Cal Ripken Jr.	4.00
5	Mo Vaughn	.25
6	Juan Gonzalez	.75

7	Mike Piazza	2.50
8	Albert Belle	.25
9	Chipper Jones	2.00
10	Andruw Jones	1.50
11	Greg Maddux	2.00
12	Hideo Nomo	.75
13	Jeff Bagwell	1.50
14	Manny Ramirez	1.50
15	Mark McGwire	3.00
16	Derek Jeter	4.00
17	Sammy Sosa	2.00
18	Barry Bonds	4.00
19	Chuck Knoblauch	.25
20	Dante Bichette	.25
21	Tony Gwynn	2.00
22	Ken Caminiti	.25
23	Gary Sheffield	.65
24	Tim Salmon	.25
25	Ivan Rodriguez	1.00
26	Henry Rodriguez	.25
27	Barry Larkin	.25
28	Ryan Klesko	.25
29	Brian Jordan	.25
30	Jay Buhner	.25

1997 Pinnacle X-Press

		NM/M
Complete Set (150):		7.50
Common Player:		.05
Men of Summer:		4X
Pack (8):		.75
Wax Box (24):		10.00
1	Larry Walker	.05
2	Andy Pettitte	.30
3	Matt Williams	.05
4	Juan Gonzalez	.40
5	Frank Thomas	.75
6	Kenny Lofton	.05
7	Ken Griffey Jr.	1.25
8	Andres Galarraga	.05
9	Greg Maddux	1.00
10	Hideo Nomo	.40
11	Cecil Fielder	.05
12	Jose Canseco	.40
13	Tony Gwynn	1.00
14	Eddie Murray	.75
15	Alex Rodriguez	1.50
16	Mike Piazza	1.25
17	Ken Hill	.05
18	Chuck Knoblauch	.05
19	Ellis Burks	.05
20	Rafael Palmeiro	.65
21	Vinny Castilla	.05
22	Rusty Greer	.05
23	Chipper Jones	1.00
24	Rey Ordonez	.05
25	Mariano Rivera	.15
26	Garret Anderson	.05
27	Edgar Martinez	.05
28	Dante Bichette	.05
29	Todd Hundley	.05
30	Barry Bonds	2.00
31	Barry Larkin	.05
32	Derek Jeter	2.00
33	Marquis Grissom	.05
34	David Justice	.05
35	Ivan Rodriguez	.65
36	Jay Buhner	.05
37	Fred McGriff	.05
38	Brady Anderson	.05
39	Tony Clark	.05
40	Eric Young	.05
41	Charles Nagy	.05
42	Mark McGwire	1.50
43	Paul O'Neill	.05
44	Tino Martinez	.05
45	Ryne Sandberg	1.00

46	Bernie Williams	.05
47	Albert Belle	.05
48	Jeff Cirillo	.05
49	Tim Salmon	.05
50	Steve Finley	.05
51	Lance Johnson	.05
52	John Smoltz	.05
53	Javier Lopez	.05
54	Roger Clemens	1.00
55	Kevin Appier	.05
56	Ken Caminiti	.05
57	Cal Ripken Jr.	2.00
58	Moises Alou	.05
59	Marty Cordova	.05
60	David Cone	.05
61	Manny Ramirez	.75
62	Ray Durham	.05
63	Jermaine Dye	.05
64	Craig Biggio	.05
65	Will Clark	.05
66	Omar Vizquel	.05
67	Bernard Gilkey	.05
68	Greg Vaughn	.05
69	Wade Boggs	1.00
70	Dave Nilsson	.05
71	Mark Grace	.05
72	Dean Palmer	.05
73	Sammy Sosa	1.00
74	Mike Mussina	.30
75	Alex Fernandez	.05
76	Henry Rodriguez	.05
77	Travis Fryman	.05
78	Jeff Bagwell	.75
79	Pat Hentgen	.05
80	Gary Sheffield	.40
81	Jim Edmonds	.05
82	Darin Erstad	.10
83	Mark Grudzielanek	.05
84	Jim Thome	.65
85	Bobby Higginson	.05
86	Al Martin	.05
87	Jason Giambi	.50
88	Mo Vaughn	.05
89	Jeff Conine	.05
90	Edgar Renteria	.05
91	Andy Ashby	.05
92	Ryan Klesko	.05
93	John Jaha	.05
94	Paul Molitor	.75
95	Brian Hunter	.05
96	Randy Johnson	.75
97	Joey Hamilton	.05
98	Billy Wagner	.05
99	John Wetteland	.05
100	Jeff Fassero	.05
101	Rondell White	.05
102	Kevin Brown	.05
103	Andy Benes	.05
104	Raul Mondesi	.05
105	Todd Hollandsworth	.05
106	Alex Ochoa	.05
107	Bobby Bonilla	.05
108	Brian Jordan	.05
109	Tom Glavine	.35
110	Ron Gant	.05
111	Jason Kendall	.05
112	Roberto Alomar	.30
113	Troy Percival	.05
114	Michael Tucker	.05
115	Joe Carter	.05
116	Andruw Jones	.75
117	Nomar Garciaparra	1.00
118	Todd Walker	.05
119	Jose Guillen	.05
120	Bubba Trammell RC	.20
121	Wilton Guerrero	.05
122	Bob Abreu	.15
123	Vladimir Guerrero	.75
124	Dmitri Young	.05
125	Kevin Orie	.05
126	Glendon Rusch	.05
127	Brooks Kieschnick	.05
128	Scott Spiezio	.05
129	Brian Giles RC	.75
130	Jason Dickson	.05
131	Damon Mashore	.05
132	Wendell Magee	.05
133	Matt Morris	.05
134	Scott Rolen	.65
135	Shannon Stewart	.05
136	Deivi Cruz RC	.15
137	Hideki Irabu RC	.15
138	Larry Walker	.05
139	Ken Griffey Jr.	.65
140	Frank Thomas	.40
141	Ivan Rodriguez	.30
142	Randy Johnson	.40
143	Mark McGwire	.75
144	Tino Martinez	.05
145	Tony Clark	.05
146	Mike Piazza	.50
147	Alex Rodriguez	.75
148	Roger Clemens	
	Checklist	.50

149	Greg Maddux Checklist	.45
150	Hideo Nomo Checklist	.20

Men of Summer

		NM/M
Complete Set (150):		50.00
Common Player:		.25

(See 1997 Pinnacle X-Press for checklist and base card values.)

Stars:		3X

Far & Away

		NM/M
Complete Set (18):		25.00
Common Player:		.50
1	Albert Belle	.50
2	Mark McGwire	4.50
3	Frank Thomas	1.75
4	Mo Vaughn	.50
5	Jeff Bagwell	1.75
6	Juan Gonzalez	1.00
7	Mike Piazza	3.50
8	Andruw Jones	1.75
9	Chipper Jones	2.50
10	Gary Sheffield	1.00
11	Sammy Sosa	2.50
12	Darin Erstad	.75
13	Jay Buhner	.50
14	Ken Griffey Jr.	3.50
15	Ken Caminiti	.50
16	Brady Anderson	.50
17	Manny Ramirez	1.75
18	Alex Rodriguez	4.50

Melting Pot

		NM/M
Complete Set (20):		110.00
Common Player:		1.50
Samples:		1X
1	Jose Guillen	1.50
2	Vladimir Guerrero	8.00
3	Andruw Jones	8.00
4	Larry Walker	1.50
5	Manny Ramirez	8.00
6	Ken Griffey Jr.	10.00
7	Alex Rodriguez	12.00
8	Frank Thomas	8.00
9	Juan Gonzalez	4.00
10	Ivan Rodriguez	6.00

11	Hideo Nomo	4.00
12	Rafael Palmeiro	6.00
13	Dave Nilsson	1.50
14	Nomar Garciaparra	9.00
15	Wilton Guerrero	1.50
16	Sammy Sosa	9.00
17	Edgar Renteria	1.50
18	Cal Ripken Jr.	16.00
19	Derek Jeter	16.00
20	Rey Ordonez	1.50

Metal Works

		NM/M
Complete Set (20):		25.00
Common Player:		.50
Silver:		3X
Gold:		6X
1	Ken Griffey Jr.	2.00
2	Frank Thomas	1.00
3	Andruw Jones	1.00
4	Alex Rodriguez	2.50
5	Derek Jeter	3.00
6	Cal Ripken Jr.	3.00
7	Mike Piazza	2.00
8	Chipper Jones	1.50
9	Juan Gonzalez	.65
10	Greg Maddux	1.50
11	Tony Gwynn	1.50
12	Jeff Bagwell	1.00
13	Albert Belle	.50
14	Mark McGwire	2.50
15	Nomar Garciaparra	1.50
16	Mo Vaughn	.50
17	Andy Pettitte	.65
18	Manny Ramirez	1.00
19	Kenny Lofton	.50
20	Roger Clemens	1.75

Swing for the Fences

		NM/M
Complete Set (60):		20.00
Common Player:		.15
(1)	Sandy Alomar Jr.	.15
(2)	Moises Alou	.15
(3)	Brady Anderson	.15
(4)	Jeff Bagwell	1.00
(5)	Derek Bell	.15
(6)	Jay Bell	.15
(7)	Albert Belle	.15
(8)	Geronimo Berroa	.15
(9)	Dante Bichette	.15
(10)	Barry Bonds	2.50
(11)	Bobby Bonilla	.15
(12)	Jay Buhner	.15
(13)	Ellis Burks	.15
(14)	Ken Caminiti	.15
(15)	Jose Canseco	.40
(16)	Joe Carter	.15
(17)	Vinny Castilla	.15
(18)	Tony Clark	.15
(19)	Carlos Delgado	.50

(20) Jim Edmonds .15
(21) Cecil Fielder .15
(22) Andres Galarraga .15
(23) Ron Gant .15
(24) Bernard Gilkey .15
(25) Juan Gonzalez .50
(26) Ken Griffey Jr.
　　(AL Winner) 4.00
(27) Vladimir Guerrero 1.00
(28) Todd Hundley .15
(29) John Jaha .15
(30) Andruw Jones 1.00
(31) Chipper Jones 1.25
(32) David Justice .15
(33) Jeff Kent .15
(34) Ryan Klesko .15
(35) Barry Larkin .15
(36) Mike Lieberthal .15
(37) Javy Lopez .15
(38) Edgar Martinez .15
(39) Tino Martinez .15
(40) Fred McGriff .15
(41) Mark McGwire
　　(AL/NL Winner) 4.00
(42) Raul Mondesi .15
(43) Tim Naehring .15
(44) Dean Nillson .15
(45) Rafael Palmeiro .75
(46) Dean Palmer .15
(47) Mike Piazza 1.50
(48) Cal Ripken Jr. 2.50
(49) Henry Rodriguez .15
(50) Tim Salmon .15
(51) Gary Sheffield .40
(52) Sammy Sosa 1.25
(53) Terry Steinbach .15
(54) Frank Thomas 1.00
(55) Jim Thome .75
(56) Mo Vaughn .15
(57) Larry Walker
　　(NL Winner) 1.25
(58) Rondell White .15
(59) Matt Williams .15
(60) Todd Zeile .15

1998 Pinnacle

	NM/M
Complete Set (200):	12.50
Common Player:	.05
Pack (10):	1.00
Wax Box (18):	12.00

1 Tony Gwynn/AS 1.00
2 Pedro Martinez /AS .75
3 Kenny Lofton/AS .05
4 Curt Schilling/AS .35
5 Shawn Estes/AS .05
6 Tom Glavine/AS .35
7 Mike Piazza/AS 1.50
8 Ray Lankford/AS .05
9 Barry Larkin/AS .05
10 Tony Womack/AS .05
11 Jeff Blauser/AS .05
12 Rod Beck/AS .05
13 Larry Walker/AS .05
14 Greg Maddux/AS 1.00
15 Mark Grace/AS .05
16 Ken Caminiti/AS .05
17 Bobby Jones/AS .05
18 Chipper Jones/AS 1.00
19 Javier Lopez/AS .05
20 Moises Alou/AS .05
21 Royce Clayton/AS .05
22 Darryl Kile/AS .05
23 Barry Bonds/AS 2.50
24 Steve Finley/AS .05
25 Andres Galarraga/AS .05
26 Denny Neagle/AS .05
27 Todd Hundley/AS .05
28 Jeff Bagwell .75
29 Andy Pettitte .25
30 Darin Erstad .15
31 Carlos Delgado .50

32 Matt Williams .05
33 Will Clark .05
34 Vinny Castilla .05
35 Brad Radke .05
36 John Olerud .05
37 Andruw Jones .75
38 Jason Giambi .50
39 Scott Rolen .65
40 Gary Sheffield .40
41 Jimmy Key .05
42 Kevin Appier .05
43 Wade Boggs 1.00
44 Hideo Nomo .40
45 Manny Ramirez .75
46 Wilton Guerrero .05
47 Travis Fryman .05
48 Chili Davis .05
49 Jeromy Burnitz .05
50 Craig Biggio .05
51 Tim Salmon .05
52 Jose Cruz Jr. .05
53 Sammy Sosa 1.00
54 Hideki Irabu .05
55 Chan Ho Park .05
56 Robin Ventura .05
57 Jose Guillen .05
58 Deion Sanders .05
59 Jose Canseco .40
60 Jay Buhner .05
61 Rafael Palmeiro .65
62 Vladimir Guerrero .75
63 Mark McGwire 2.00
64 Derek Jeter 2.50
65 Bobby Bonilla .05
66 Raul Mondesi .05
67 Paul Molitor .75
68 Joe Carter .05
69 Marquis Grissom .05
70 Juan Gonzalez .40
71 Kevin Orie .05
72 Rusty Greer .05
73 Henry Rodriguez .05
74 Fernando Tatis .05
75 John Valentin .05
76 Matt Morris .05
77 Ray Durham .05
78 Geronimo Berroa .05
79 Scott Brosius .05
80 Willie Greene .05
81 Rondell White .05
82 Doug Drabek .05
83 Derek Bell .05
84 Butch Huskey .05
85 Doug Jones .05
86 Jeff Kent .05
87 Jim Edmonds .05
88 Mark McLemore .05
89 Todd Zeile .05
90 Edgardo Alfonzo .05
91 Carlos Baerga .05
92 Jorge Fabregas .05
93 Alan Benes .05
94 Troy Percival .05
95 Edgar Renteria .05
96 Jeff Fassero .05
97 Reggie Sanders .05
98 Dean Palmer .05
99 J.T. Snow .05
100 Dave Nilsson .05
101 Dan Wilson .05
102 Robb Nen .05
103 Damion Easley .05
104 Kevin Foster .05
105 Jose Offerman .05
106 Steve Cooke .05
107 Matt Stairs .05
108 Darryl Hamilton .05
109 Steve Karsay .05
110 Gary DiSarcina .05
111 Dante Bichette .05
112 Billy Wagner .05
113 David Segui .05
114 Bobby Higginson .05
115 Jeffrey Hammonds .05
116 Kevin Brown .05
117 Paul Sorrento .05
118 Mark Leiter .05
119 Charles Nagy .05
120 Danny Patterson .05
121 Brian McRae .05
122 Jay Bell .05
123 Jamie Moyer .05
124 Carl Everett .05
125 Greg Colbrunn .05
126 Jason Kendall .05
127 Luis Sojo .05
128 Mike Lieberthal .05
129 Reggie Jefferson .05
130 Cal Eldred .05
131 Orel Hershiser .05
132 Doug Glanville .05
133 Willie Blair .05
134 Neifi Perez .05
135 Sean Berry .05

136 Chuck Finley .05
137 Alex Gonzalez .05
138 Dennis Eckersley .65
139 Kenny Rogers .05
140 Troy O'Leary .05
141 Roger Bailey .05
142 Yamil Benitez .05
143 Wally Joyner .05
144 Bobby Witt .05
145 Pete Schourek .05
146 Terry Steinbach .05
147 B.J. Surhoff .05
148 Esteban Loaiza .05
149 Heathcliff Slocumb .05
150 Ed Sprague .05
151 Gregg Jefferies .05
152 Scott Erickson .05
153 Jaime Navarro .05
154 David Wells .05
155 Alex Fernandez .05
156 Tim Belcher .05
157 Mark Grudzielanek .05
158 Scott Hatteberg .05
159 Paul Konerko .15
160 Ben Grieve .05
161 Abraham Nunez .05
162 Shannon Stewart .05
163 Jaret Wright .05
164 Derrek Lee .50
165 Todd Dunwoody .05
166 Steve Woodard RC .10
167 Ryan McGuire .05
168 Jeremi Gonzalez .05
169 Mark Kotsay .05
170 Brett Tomko .05
171 Bobby Estalella .05
172 Livan Hernandez .05
173 Todd Helton .75
174 Garrett Stephenson .05
175 Pokey Reese .05
176 Tony Saunders .05
177 Antone Williamson .05
178 Bartolo Colon .05
179 Karim Garcia .05
180 Juan Encarnacion .05
181 Jacob Cruz .05
182 Alex Rodriguez 2.00
183 Cal Ripken Jr.,
　　Roberto Alomar 1.00
184 Roger Clemens 1.25
185 Derek Jeter 2.00
186 Frank Thomas .75
187 Ken Griffey Jr. 1.50
188 Mark McGwire 1.00
189 Tino Martinez .05
190 Larry Walker .05
191 Brady Anderson .05
192 Jeff Bagwell .75
193 Ken Griffey Jr. 1.50
194 Chipper Jones 1.00
195 Ray Lankford .05
196 Jim Thome .65
197 Nomar Garciaparra 1.00
198 Checklist
　　(1997 HR Contest) .05
199 Checklist (1997 HR
　　Contest Winner) .05
200 Checklist (Overall
　　View of the Park) .05
9 Ken Griffey Jr./
　　AS/OPS 2.00
24 Frank Thomas/
　　AS/OPS 1.50

Artist's Proofs

	NM/M
Complete Set (100):	375.00
Common Artist's Proof:	1.50

1 Tony Gwynn/AS 12.50
2 Pedro Martinez/AS 10.00
3 Kenny Lofton/AS 1.50
4 Curt Schilling/AS 3.00

5 Shawn Estes/AS 1.50
6 Tom Glavine/AS 3.00
7 Mike Piazza/AS 16.00
8 Ray Lankford/AS 1.50
9 Barry Larkin/AS 1.50
10 Tony Womack/AS 1.50
11 Jeff Blauser/AS 1.50
12 Rod Beck/AS 1.50
13 Larry Walker/AS 1.50
14 Greg Maddux/AS 12.50
15 Mark Grace/AS 1.50
16 Ken Caminiti/AS 1.50
17 Bobby Jones/AS 1.50
18 Chipper Jones/AS 12.50
19 Javier Lopez/AS 1.50
20 Moises Alou/AS 1.50
21 Royce Clayton/AS 1.50
22 Darryl Kile/AS 1.50
23 Barry Bonds/AS 25.00
24 Steve Finley/AS 1.50
25 Andres Galarraga/AS 1.50
26 Denny Neagle/AS 1.50
27 Todd Hundley/AS 1.50
28 Jeff Bagwell 10.00
29 Andy Pettitte 2.50
30 Darin Erstad 2.00
31 Carlos Delgado 4.00
32 Matt Williams 1.50
33 Will Clark 1.50
34 Brad Radke 1.50
35 John Olerud 1.50
36 Andruw Jones 10.00
37 Scott Rolen 7.50
38 Gary Sheffield 3.00
39 Jimmy Key 1.50
40 Wade Boggs 12.50
41 Hideo Nomo 5.00
42 Manny Ramirez 10.00
43 Wilton Guerrero 1.50
44 Travis Fryman 1.50
45 Craig Biggio 1.50
46 Tim Salmon 1.50
47 Jose Cruz Jr. 1.50
48 Sammy Sosa 12.50
49 Hideki Irabu 1.50
50 Jose Guillen 1.50
51 Deion Sanders 1.50
52 Jose Canseco 4.00
53 Jay Buhner 1.50
54 Rafael Palmeiro 7.50
55 Vladimir Guerrero 10.00
56 Mark McGwire 20.00
57 Derek Jeter 25.00
58 Bobby Bonilla 1.50
59 Raul Mondesi 1.50
60 Paul Molitor 10.00
61 Joe Carter 1.50
62 Marquis Grissom 1.50
63 Juan Gonzalez 5.00
64 Dante Bichette 1.50
65 Shannon Stewart 1.50
66 Jaret Wright 1.50
67 Derrek Lee 6.00
68 Todd Dunwoody 1.50
69 Steve Woodard 1.50
70 Ryan McGuire 1.50
71 Jeremi Gonzalez 1.50
72 Mark Kotsay 1.50
73 Brett Tomko 1.50
74 Bobby Estalella 1.50
75 Livan Hernandez 1.50
76 Todd Helton 10.00
77 Garrett Stephenson 1.50
78 Pokey Reese 1.50
79 Tony Saunders 1.50
80 Antone Williamson 1.50
81 Bartolo Colon 1.50
82 Karim Garcia 1.50
83 Juan Encarnacion 1.50
84 Jacob Cruz 1.50
85 Alex Rodriguez 20.00
86 Cal Ripken Jr.,
　　Roberto Alomar 15.00
87 Roger Clemens 13.50
88 Derek Jeter 25.00
89 Frank Thomas 10.00
90 Ken Griffey Jr. 16.00
91 Mark McGwire 20.00
92 Tino Martinez 1.50
93 Larry Walker 1.50
94 Brady Anderson 1.50
95 Jeff Bagwell 10.00
96 Ken Griffey Jr. 16.00
97 Chipper Jones 12.50
98 Ray Lankford 1.50
99 Jim Thome 7.50
100 Nomar Garciaparra 12.50

Museum Collection

	NM/M
Complete Museum Set (100):	110.00
Common Museum:	.50

1 Tony Gwynn/AS 3.00

85	Alex Rodriguez	5.00
86	Cal Ripken Jr., Roberto Alomar	3.50
87	Roger Clemens	2.50
88	Derek Jeter	6.00
89	Frank Thomas	2.50
90	Ken Griffey Jr.	4.00
91	Mark McGwire	5.00
92	Tino Martinez	.50
93	Larry Walker	.50
94	Brady Anderson	.50
95	Jeff Bagwell	2.50
96	Ken Griffey Jr.	4.00
97	Chipper Jones	3.00
98	Ray Lankford	.50
99	Jim Thome	2.00
100	Nomar Garciaparra	3.00

Press Plates

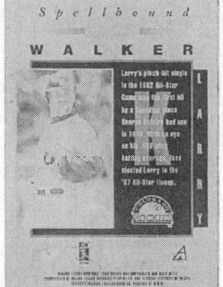

NM/M
Common Player: 50.00
(See 1998 Pinnacle and inserts for checklists.)

Epix

		NM/M
Complete Set (24):		45.00
Common Player:		1.00
Purples:		2X
Emeralds:		4X
1	Ken Griffey Jr./G	3.00
2	Juan Gonzalez/G	1.25
3	Jeff Bagwell/G	2.00
4	Ivan Rodriguez/G	1.50
5	Nomar Garciaparra/G	2.50
6	Ryne Sandberg/G	2.50
7	Frank Thomas/S	2.00
8	Derek Jeter/S	5.00
9	Tony Gwynn/S	2.50
10	Albert Belle/S	1.00
11	Scott Rolen/S	1.50
12	Barry Larkin/S	1.00
13	Alex Rodriguez/M	4.00
14	Cal Ripken Jr./M	5.00
15	Chipper Jones/M	2.50
16	Roger Clemens/M	2.75
17	Mo Vaughn/M	1.00
18	Mark McGwire/M	4.00
19	Mike Piazza/P	3.00
20	Andruw Jones/P	2.00
21	Greg Maddux/P	2.50
22	Barry Bonds/P	5.00
23	Paul Molitor/P	2.00
24	Eddie Murray/P	2.00

Hit It Here

		NM/M
Complete Set (10):		12.00
Common Player:		.50
Inserted 1:17		

2	Pedro Martinez/AS	2.50
3	Kenny Lofton/AS	.50
4	Curt Schilling/AS	1.50
5	Shawn Estes/AS	.50
6	Tom Glavine/AS	1.50
7	Mike Piazza/AS	4.00
8	Ray Lankford/AS	.50
9	Barry Larkin/AS	.50
10	Tony Womack/AS	.50
11	Jeff Blauser/AS	.50
12	Rod Beck/AS	.50
13	Larry Walker/AS	.50
14	Greg Maddux/AS	3.00
15	Mark Grace/AS	.50
16	Ken Caminiti/AS	.50
17	Bobby Jones/AS	.50
18	Chipper Jones/AS	3.00
19	Javier Lopez/AS	.50
20	Moises Alou/AS	.50
21	Royce Clayton/AS	.50
22	Darryl Kile/AS	.50
23	Barry Bonds/AS	6.00
24	Steve Finley/AS	.50
25	Andres Galarraga/AS	.50
26	Denny Neagle/AS	.50
27	Todd Hundley/AS	.50
28	Jeff Bagwell	2.50
29	Andy Pettitte	1.00
30	Darin Erstad	1.00
31	Carlos Delgado	1.50
32	Matt Williams	.50
33	Will Clark	.50
34	Brad Radke	.50
35	John Olerud	.50
36	Andruw Jones	2.50
37	Scott Rolen	2.00
38	Gary Sheffield	1.50
39	Jimmy Key	.50
40	Wade Boggs	3.00
41	Hideo Nomo	1.25
42	Manny Ramirez	2.50
43	Wilton Guerrero	.50
44	Travis Fryman	.50
45	Craig Biggio	.50
46	Tim Salmon	.50
47	Jose Cruz Jr.	.50
48	Sammy Sosa	3.00
49	Hideki Irabu	.50
50	Jose Guillen	.50
51	Deion Sanders	.50
52	Jose Canseco	1.50
53	Jay Buhner	.50
54	Rafael Palmeiro	2.00
55	Vladimir Guerrero	2.50
56	Mark McGwire	5.00
57	Derek Jeter	6.00
58	Bobby Bonilla	.50
59	Raul Mondesi	.50
60	Paul Molitor	2.50
61	Joe Carter	.50
62	Marquis Grissom	.50
63	Juan Gonzalez	1.25
64	Dante Bichette	.50
65	Shannon Stewart	.50
66	Jaret Wright	.50
67	Derrek Lee	2.00
68	Todd Dunwoody	.50
69	Steve Woodard	.50
70	Ryan McGuire	.50
71	Jeremi Gonzalez	.50
72	Mark Kotsay	.50
73	Brett Tomko	.50
74	Bobby Estalella	.50
75	Livan Hernandez	.50
76	Todd Helton	2.50
77	Garrett Stephenson	.50
78	Pokey Reese	.50
79	Tony Saunders	.50
80	Antone Williamson	.50
81	Bartolo Colon	.50
82	Karim Garcia	.50
83	Juan Encarnacion	.50
84	Jacob Cruz	.50

Samples:		1X
1	Larry Walker	.50
2	Ken Griffey Jr.	2.00
3	Mike Piazza	2.00
4	Frank Thomas	1.50
5	Barry Bonds	3.00
6	Albert Belle	.50
7	Tino Martinez	.50
8	Mark McGwire	2.50
9	Juan Gonzalez	.75
10	Jeff Bagwell	1.00

Spellbound

		NM/M
Complete Set (50):		90.00
Common Card:		.75
Inserted 1:17		
1	Mark McGwire/M	3.50
2	Mark McGwire/C	3.50
3	Mark McGwire/G	3.50
4	Mark McGwire/W	3.50
5	Mark McGwire/I	3.50
6	Mark McGwire/R	3.50
7	Mark McGwire/E	3.50
8	Roger Clemens/R	2.50
9	Roger Clemens/O	2.50
10	Roger Clemens/C	2.50
11	Roger Clemens/K	2.50
12	Roger Clemens/E	2.50
13	Roger Clemens/T	2.50
14	Frank Thomas/B	1.50
15	Frank Thomas/I	1.50
16	Frank Thomas/S	1.50
17	Frank Thomas/H	1.50
18	Frank Thomas/U	1.50
19	Frank Thomas/R	1.50
20	Frank Thomas/T	1.50
21	Scott Rolen/R	1.25
22	Scott Rolen/O	1.25
23	Scott Rolen/L	1.25
24	Scott Rolen/E	1.25
25	Scott Rolen/N	1.25
26	Ken Griffey Jr./G	3.00
27	Ken Griffey Jr./R	3.00
28	Ken Griffey Jr./I	3.00
29	Ken Griffey Jr./F	3.00
30	Ken Griffey Jr./F	3.00
31	Ken Griffey Jr./E	3.00
32	Ken Griffey Jr./Y	3.00
33	Larry Walker/W	.75
34	Larry Walker/A	.75
35	Larry Walker/L	.75
36	Larry Walker/K	.75
37	Larry Walker/E	.75
38	Larry Walker/R	.75
39	Nomar Garciaparra/N	2.25
40	Nomar Garciaparra/O	2.25
41	Nomar Garciaparra/M	2.25
42	Nomar Garciaparra/A	2.25
43	Nomar Garciaparra/R	2.25
44	Cal Ripken Jr./C	4.50

45	Cal Ripken Jr./A	4.50
46	Cal Ripken Jr./L	4.50
47	Tony Gwynn/T	2.25
48	Tony Gwynn/O	2.25
49	Tony Gwynn/N	2.25
50	Tony Gwynn/Y	2.25

1998 Pinnacle Inside

		NM/M
Complete Set (150):		12.00
Common Player:		.05
Club Edition (1:7):		4X
Diamond Edition (1:67):		10X
Can (10):		1.00
Box (48):		45.00
1	Darin Erstad	.15
2	Derek Jeter	2.50
3	Alex Rodriguez	2.00
4	Bobby Higginson	.05
5	Nomar Garciaparra	1.00
6	Kenny Lofton	.05
7	Ivan Rodriguez	.65
8	Cal Ripken Jr.	2.50
9	Todd Hundley	.05
10	Chipper Jones	1.00
11	Barry Larkin	.05
12	Roberto Alomar	.15
13	Mo Vaughn	.05
14	Sammy Sosa	1.00
15	Sandy Alomar Jr.	.05
16	Albert Belle	.05
17	Scott Rolen	.65
18	Pokey Reese	.05
19	Ryan Klesko	.05
20	Andres Galarraga	.05
21	Justin Thompson	.05
22	Gary Sheffield	.40
23	David Justice	.05
24	Ken Griffey Jr.	1.50
25	Andruw Jones	.75
26	Jeff Bagwell	.75
27	Vladimir Guerrero	.75
28	Mike Piazza	1.50
29	Chuck Knoblauch	.05
30	Rondell White	.05
31	Greg Maddux	1.00
32	Andy Pettitte	.20
33	Larry Walker	.05
34	Bobby Estalella	.05
35	Frank Thomas	.75
36	Tony Womack	.05
37	Tony Gwynn	1.00
38	Barry Bonds	2.50
39	Randy Johnson	.75
40	Mark McGwire	2.00
41	Juan Gonzalez	.40
42	Tim Salmon	.05
43	John Smoltz	.05
44	Rafael Palmeiro	.65
45	Mark Grace	.05
46	Mike Cameron	.05
47	Jim Thome	.65
48	Neifi Perez	.05
49	Kevin Brown	.05
50	Craig Biggio	.05
51	Bernie Williams	.05
52	Hideo Nomo	.40
53	Bob Abreu	.15
54	Edgardo Alfonzo	.05
55	Wade Boggs	1.00
56	Jose Guillen	.05
57	Ken Caminiti	.05
58	Paul Molitor	.75
59	Shawn Estes	.05
60	Edgar Martinez	.05
61	Livan Hernandez	.05
62	Ray Lankford	.05
63	Rusty Greer	.05
64	Jim Edmonds	.05
65	Tom Glavine	.35
66	Alan Benes	.05
67	Will Clark	.05
68	Garret Anderson	.05

69	Javier Lopez	.05
70	Mike Mussina	.35
71	Kevin Orie	.05
72	Matt Williams	.05
73	Bobby Bonilla	.05
74	Ruben Rivera	.05
75	Jason Giambi	.60
76	Todd Walker	.05
77	Tino Martinez	.05
78	Matt Morris	.05
79	Fernando Tatis	.05
80	Todd Greene	.05
81	Fred McGriff	.05
82	Brady Anderson	.05
83	Mark Kotsay	.05
84	Raul Mondesi	.05
85	Moises Alou	.05
86	Roger Clemens	1.25
87	Wilton Guerrero	.05
88	Shannon Stewart	.05
89	Chan Ho Park	.05
90	Carlos Delgado	.60
91	Jose Cruz Jr.	.75
92	Shawn Green	.35
93	Robin Ventura	.05
94	Reggie Sanders	.05
95	Orel Hershiser	.05
96	Dante Bichette	.05
97	Charles Johnson	.05
98	Pedro Martinez	.75
99	Mariano Rivera	.15
100	Joe Randa	.05
101	Jeff Kent	.05
102	Jay Buhner	.05
103	Brian Jordan	.05
104	Jason Kendall	.05
105	Scott Spiezio	.05
106	Desi Relaford	.05
107	Bernard Gilkey	.05
108	Manny Ramirez	.75
109	Tony Clark	.05
110	Eric Young	.05
111	Johnny Damon	.30
112	Glendon Rusch	.05
113	Ben Grieve	.05
114	Homer Bush	.05
115	Miguel Tejada	.25
116	Lou Collier	.05
117	Derrek Lee	.60
118	Jacob Cruz	.05
119	Raul Ibanez	.05
120	Ryan McGuire	.05
121	Antone Williamson	.05
122	Abraham Nunez	.05
123	Jeff Abbott	.05
124	Brett Tomko	.05
125	Richie Sexson	.05
126	Todd Helton	.75
127	Juan Encarnacion	.05
128	Richard Hidalgo	.05
129	Paul Konerko	.10
130	Brad Fullmer	.05
131	Jeremi Gonzalez	.05
132	Jaret Wright	.05
133	Derek Jeter	1.25
134	Frank Thomas	.40
135	Nomar Garciaparra	.50
136	Kenny Lofton	.50
137	Jeff Bagwell	.40
138	Todd Hundley	.05
139	Alex Rodriguez	1.00
140	Ken Griffey Jr.	.75
141	Sammy Sosa	.50
142	Greg Maddux	.50
143	Albert Belle	.05
144	Cal Ripken Jr.	1.25
145	Mark McGwire	1.00
146	Chipper Jones	.50
147	Charles Johnson	.05
148	Ken Griffey Jr. Checklist	.75
149	Jose Cruz Jr. Checklist	.05
150	Larry Walker Checklist	.05

Club Edition

	NM/M
Complete Set (150):	50.00
Common Player:	2.00
Stars:	4X
Inserted 1:7	

(See 1998 Pinnacle Inside for checklist and base card values.)

Diamond Edition

	NM/M
Common Card:	6.00
Stars:	10X
Inserted 1:67	

(See 1998 Pinnacle Inside for checklist and base card values.)

Behind the Numbers

		NM/M
Complete Set (20):		85.00
Common Player:		1.50
Inserted 1:23		
1	Ken Griffey Jr.	7.50
2	Cal Ripken Jr.	12.00
3	Alex Rodriguez	10.00
4	Jose Cruz Jr.	1.50
5	Mike Piazza	7.50
6	Nomar Garciaparra	5.50
7	Scott Rolen	2.50
8	Andruw Jones	4.00
9	Frank Thomas	4.00
10	Mark McGwire	10.00
11	Ivan Rodriguez	3.00
12	Greg Maddux	5.50
13	Roger Clemens	6.50
14	Derek Jeter	12.00
15	Tony Gwynn	5.50
16	Ben Grieve	1.50
17	Jeff Bagwell	4.00
18	Chipper Jones	5.50
19	Hideo Nomo	2.00
20	Sandy Alomar Jr.	1.50

Cans

		NM/M
Complete Set (23):		15.00
Common Can:		.40
Gold Cans:		2X
1	Ken Griffey Jr.	1.25
2	Frank Thomas	.65
3	Alex Rodriguez	1.50
4	Andruw Jones	.65
5	Mike Piazza	1.25
6	Ben Grieve	.40
7	Hideo Nomo	.50
8	Vladimir Guerrero	.65
9	Roger Clemens	1.00
10	Tony Gwynn	.75
11	Mark McGwire	1.50
12	Cal Ripken Jr.	2.00
13	Jose Cruz Jr.	.40
14	Greg Maddux	.75
15	Chipper Jones	.75

16	Derek Jeter	2.00
17	Juan Gonzalez	.50
18	Nomar Garciaparra (AL ROY)	1.00
19	Scott Rolen (NL ROY)	.65
20	Florida Marlins World Series Winner	.40
21	Larry Walker (NL MVP)	.40
22	Tampa Bay Devil Rays	.40
23	Arizona Diamondbacks	.40

Stand Up Guys

		NM/M
Complete Set (50):		35.00
Common Card:		.25
Sample:		3X
1-A/B	Ken Griffey Jr., Cal Ripken Jr.	2.00
1-C/D	Tony Gwynn, Mike Piazza	1.25
2-A/B	Andruw Jones, Alex Rodriguez	1.50
2-C/D	Scott Rolen, Nomar Garciaparra	1.00
3-A/B	Andruw Jones, Greg Maddux	1.00
3-C/D	Javy Lopez, Chipper Jones	1.00
4-A/B	Jay Buhner, Randy Johnson	.75
4-C/D	Ken Griffey Jr., Alex Rodriguez	1.50
5-A/B	Frank Thomas, Jeff Bagwell	.75
5-C/D	Mark McGwire, Mo Vaughn	1.50
6-A/B	Nomar Garciaparra, Derek Jeter	2.00
6-C/D	Alex Rodriguez, Barry Larkin	1.50
7-A/B	Mike Piazza, Ivan Rodriguez	1.25
7-C/D	Charles Johnson, Javy Lopez	.25
8-A/B	Cal Ripken Jr., Chipper Jones	2.00
8-C/D	Ken Caminiti, Scott Rolen	.65
9-A/B	Jose Cruz Jr., Vladimir Guerrero	.75
9-C/D	Andruw Jones, Jose Guillen	.75
10-A/B	Larry Walker, Dante Bichette	.25
10-C/D	Ellis Burks, Neifi Perez	.25
11-A/B	Juan Gonzalez, Sammy Sosa	1.00
11-C/D	Vladimir Guerrero, Manny Ramirez	.75
12-A/B	Greg Maddux, Roger Clemens	1.00
12-C/D	Hideo Nomo, Randy Johnson	.75
13-A/B	Ben Grieve, Paul Konerko	.40
13-C/D	Jose Cruz Jr., Fernando Tatis	.25
14-A/B	Ryne Sandberg, Chuck Knoblauch	1.00
14-C/D	Roberto Alomar, Craig Biggio	.35
15-A/B	Cal Ripken Jr., Brady Anderson	2.00
15-C/D	Rafael Palmeiro, Roberto Alomar	.65
16-A/B	Darin Erstad, Jim Edmonds	.35
16-C/D	Tim Salmon, Garret Anderson	.25
17-A/B	Mike Piazza, Hideo Nomo	1.25
17-C/D	Raul Mondesi, Eric Karros	.25
18-A/B	Ivan Rodriguez, Juan Gonzalez	.65
18-C/D	Will Clark, Rusty Greer	.25
19-A/B	Derek Jeter, Bernie Williams	2.00
19-C/D	Tino Martinez, Andy Pettitte	.25
20-A/B	Kenny Lofton, Ken Griffey Jr.	1.25
20-C/D	Brady Anderson, Bernie Williams	.25
21-A/B	Paul Molitor, Eddie Murray	.75
21-C/D	Ryne Sandberg, Rickey Henderson	1.00
22-A/B	Tony Clark, Frank Thomas	.75
22-C/D	Jeff Bagwell, Mark McGwire	1.50
23-A/B	Manny Ramirez, Jim Thome	.75
23-C/D	David Justice, Sandy Alomar Jr.	.25
24-A/B	Barry Bonds, Albert Belle	2.00
24-C/D	Jeff Bagwell, Dante Bichette	.60
25-A/B	Ken Griffey Jr., Frank Thomas	1.25
25-C/D	Alex Rodriguez, Andruw Jones	1.50

1998 Pinnacle Mint Collection

		NM/M
Complete Set (30):		10.00
Common Die-Cut:		.25
Bronze (1:1H):		2X
Silver (1:15H):		5X
Gold (1:47):		12X
Pack (3+2):		1.00
Wax Box (24):		12.00
1	Jeff Bagwell	.65
2	Albert Belle	.25
3	Barry Bonds	2.00
4	Tony Clark	.25
5	Roger Clemens	1.00
6	Juan Gonzalez	.35
7	Ken Griffey Jr.	1.25
8	Tony Gwynn	.75
9	Derek Jeter	2.00
10	Randy Johnson	.65
11	Chipper Jones	.75
12	Greg Maddux	.75
13	Tino Martinez	.25
14	Mark McGwire	1.50
15	Hideo Nomo	.35
16	Andy Pettitte	.25
17	Mike Piazza	1.25
18	Cal Ripken Jr.	2.00
19	Alex Rodriguez	1.50
20	Ivan Rodriguez	.50
21	Sammy Sosa	.75

22	Frank Thomas	.65
23	Mo Vaughn	.25
24	Larry Walker	.25
25	Jose Cruz Jr.	.25
26	Nomar Garciaparra	.75
27	Vladimir Guerrero	.65
28	Livan Hernandez	.25
29	Andruw Jones	.65
30	Scott Rolen	.50

Coins

		NM/M
Complete Set (30):		20.00
Common Brass Coin:		.25
Brass Proof (500):		5X
Nickel (1:41):		3X
Nickel Proof (250):		12X
Silver:		12X
Inserted 1:288 H, 1:960 R		
Gold Plated (1:199):		15X
Gold Proof (100):		20X
1	Jeff Bagwell	.75
2	Albert Belle	.25
3	Barry Bonds	2.00
4	Tony Clark	.25
5	Roger Clemens	1.00
6	Juan Gonzalez	.45
7	Ken Griffey Jr.	1.25
8	Tony Gwynn	1.00
9	Derek Jeter	2.00
10	Randy Johnson	.75
11	Chipper Jones	1.00
12	Greg Maddux	1.00
13	Tino Martinez	.25
14	Mark McGwire	1.50
15	Hideo Nomo	.45
16	Andy Pettitte	.35
17	Mike Piazza	1.25
18	Cal Ripken Jr.	2.00
19	Alex Rodriguez	1.50
20	Ivan Rodriguez	.65
21	Sammy Sosa	1.00
22	Frank Thomas	.75
23	Mo Vaughn	.25
24	Larry Walker	.25
25	Jose Cruz Jr.	.25
26	Nomar Garciaparra	1.00
27	Vladimir Guerrero	.75
28	Livan Hernandez	.25
29	Andruw Jones	.75
30	Scott Rolen	.65

Mint Gems

Scott Rolen

		NM/M
Complete Set (6):		20.00
Common Player:		2.00
Coins:		1X
1	Ken Griffey Jr.	6.00
2	Larry Walker	2.00
3	Roger Clemens	5.00
4	Pedro Martinez	4.00
5	Nomar Garciaparra	4.50
6	Scott Rolen	3.00

1998 Pinnacle Performers

		NM/M
Complete Set (150):		12.00
Common Player:		.05
Peak Performers (1:7):		2X
Pack (10):		1.00
Wax Box (24):		15.00
1	Ken Griffey Jr.	1.00
2	Frank Thomas	.65
3	Cal Ripken Jr.	1.50
4	Alex Rodriguez	1.25
5	Greg Maddux	.75
6	Mike Piazza	1.00
7	Chipper Jones	.75
8	Tony Gwynn	.75
9	Derek Jeter	1.50
10	Jeff Bagwell	.65
11	Juan Gonzalez	.35
12	Nomar Garciaparra	.75
13	Andruw Jones	.65
14	Hideo Nomo	.35
15	Roger Clemens	.85
16	Mark McGwire	1.25
17	Scott Rolen	.60
18	Vladimir Guerrero	.65
19	Barry Bonds	1.50
20	Darin Erstad	.15
21	Albert Belle	.05
22	Kenny Lofton	.05
23	Mo Vaughn	.05
24	Tony Clark	.05
25	Ivan Rodriguez	.60
26	Jose Cruz Jr.	.05
27	Larry Walker	.05
28	Jaret Wright	.05
29	Andy Pettitte	.25
30	Roberto Alomar	.20
31	Randy Johnson	.65
32	Manny Ramirez	.65
33	Paul Molitor	.65
34	Mike Mussina	.35
35	Jim Thome	.60
36	Tino Martinez	.05
37	Gary Sheffield	.45
38	Chuck Knoblauch	.05
39	Bernie Williams	.05
40	Tim Salmon	.05
41	Sammy Sosa	.75
42	Wade Boggs	.75
43	Will Clark	.05
44	Andres Galarraga	.05
45	Raul Mondesi	.05
46	Rickey Henderson	.65
47	Jose Canseco	.45
48	Pedro Martinez	.65
49	Jay Buhner	.05
50	Ryan Klesko	.05
51	Barry Larkin	.05
52	Charles Johnson	.05
53	Tom Glavine	.35
54	Edgar Martinez	.05
55	Fred McGriff	.05
56	Moises Alou	.05
57	Dante Bichette	.05
58	Jim Edmonds	.05
59	Mark Grace	.05
60	Chan Ho Park	.05
61	Justin Thompson	.05
62	John Smoltz	.05
63	Craig Biggio	.05
64	Ken Caminiti	.05
65	Richard Hidalgo	.05
66	Carlos Delgado	.50
67	David Justice	.05
68	J.T. Snow	.05
69	Jason Giambi	.50
70	Garret Anderson	.05
71	Rondell White	.05
72	Matt Williams	.05
73	Brady Anderson	.05
74	Eric Karros	.05
75	Javier Lopez	.05
76	Pat Hentgen	.05
77	Todd Hundley	.05
78	Ray Lankford	.05
79	Denny Neagle	.05
80	Sandy Alomar Jr.	.05
81	Jason Kendall	.05
82	Omar Vizquel	.05
83	Kevin Brown	.05
84	Kevin Appier	.05
85	Al Martin	.05
86	Rusty Greer	.05
87	Bobby Bonilla	.05
88	Shawn Estes	.05
89	Rafael Palmeiro	.60
90	Edgar Renteria	.05
91	Alan Benes	.05
92	Bobby Higginson	.05
93	Mark Grudzielanek	.05
94	Jose Guillen	.05
95	Neifi Perez	.05
96	Jeff Abbott	.05
97	Todd Walker	.05
98	Eric Young	.05
99	Brett Tomko	.05
100	Mike Cameron	.05
101	Karim Garcia	.05
102	Brian Jordan	.05
103	Jeff Suppan	.05
104	Robin Ventura	.05
105	Henry Rodriguez	.05
106	Shannon Stewart	.05
107	Kevin Orie	.05
108	Bartolo Colon	.05
109	Bob Abreu	.15
110	Vinny Castilla	.05
111	Livan Hernandez	.05
112	Derrek Lee	.50
113	Mark Kotsay	.05
114	Todd Greene	.05
115	Edgardo Alfonzo	.05
116	A.J. Hinch	.05
117	Paul Konerko	.15
118	Todd Helton	.65
119	Miguel Tejada	.20
120	Fernando Tatis	.05
121	Ben Grieve	.05
122	Travis Lee	.05
123	Kerry Wood	.25
124	Eli Marrero	.05
125	David Ortiz	.50
126	Juan Encarnacion	.05
127	Brad Fullmer	.05
128	Richie Sexson	.05
129	Aaron Boone	.05
130	Enrique Wilson	.05
131	Javier Valentin	.05
132	Abraham Nunez	.05
133	Ricky Ledee	.05
134	Carl Pavano	.05
135	Bobby Estalella	.05
136	Homer Bush	.05
137	Brian Rose	.05
138	Ken Griffey Jr.	.50
139	Frank Thomas	.35
140	Cal Ripken Jr.	.75
141	Alex Rodriguez	.65
142	Greg Maddux	.40
143	Chipper Jones	.40
144	Mike Piazza	.50
145	Tony Gwynn	.50
146	Derek Jeter	.75
147	Jeff Bagwell	.35
148	Hideo Nomo Checklist	.20
149	Roger Clemens Checklist	.45
150	Greg Maddux Checklist	.35

Big Bang

BIG BANG
MO VAUGHN

	NM/M
Complete Set (20):	27.50

Common Player:		.50
Production 2,500 Sets		
Sample:		1X
1	Ken Griffey Jr.	2.50
2	Frank Thomas	1.50
3	Mike Piazza	2.50
4	Chipper Jones	2.00
5	Alex Rodriguez	3.00
6	Nomar Garciaparra	2.00
7	Jeff Bagwell	1.50
8	Cal Ripken Jr.	3.50
9	Albert Belle	.50
10	Mark McGwire	3.00
11	Juan Gonzalez	.75
12	Larry Walker	.50
13	Tino Martinez	.50
14	Jim Thome	1.00
15	Manny Ramirez	1.50
16	Barry Bonds	3.50
17	Mo Vaughn	.50
18	Jose Cruz Jr.	.50
19	Tony Clark	.50
20	Andruw Jones	1.50

Big Bang Seasonal Outburst

		NM/M
Complete Set (20):		500.00
Common Player:		10.00
#'d to player's 1997 HR total		
Unnumbered:		25%
1	Ken Griffey Jr./56	40.00
2	Frank Thomas/35	20.00
3	Mike Piazza/40	40.00
4	Chipper Jones/21	65.00
5	Alex Rodriguez/23	75.00
6	Nomar Garciaparra/30	40.00
7	Jeff Bagwell/43	40.00
8	Cal Ripken Jr./17	80.00
9	Albert Belle/30	10.00
10	Mark McGwire/58	65.00
11	Juan Gonzalez/42	12.50
12	Larry Walker/49	10.00
13	Tino Martinez/44	10.00
14	Jim Thome/40	10.00
15	Manny Ramirez/26	25.00
16	Barry Bonds/40	75.00
17	Mo Vaughn/35	10.00
18	Jose Cruz Jr./26	10.00
19	Tony Clark/32	10.00
20	Andruw Jones/18	25.00

Launching Pad

Launching PAD

		NM/M
Complete Set (20):		25.00
Common Player:		.50
Inserted 1:9		
1	Ben Grieve	.50
2	Ken Griffey Jr.	2.50
3	Derek Jeter	3.50
4	Frank Thomas	1.00
5	Travis Lee	.50
6	Vladimir Guerrero	1.00
7	Tony Gwynn	2.00
8	Jose Cruz Jr.	.50
9	Cal Ripken Jr.	3.50
10	Chipper Jones	2.00
11	Scott Rolen	.75
12	Andruw Jones	1.00
13	Ivan Rodriguez	.75
14	Todd Helton	1.00
15	Nomar Garciaparra	2.00
16	Mark McGwire	3.00
17	Gary Sheffield	.60
18	Bernie Williams	.50
19	Alex Rodriguez	3.00
20	Mike Piazza	2.50

Peak Performers

		NM/M
Complete Set (150):		100.00
Common Player:		2.00
Stars:		6X
Inserted 1:7		

(See 1998 Pinnacle Performers for checklist and base card values.)

Power Trip

		NM/M
Complete Set (10):		16.00
Common Player:		1.00
Production 10,000 Sets		
1	Frank Thomas	1.00
2	Alex Rodriguez	3.00
3	Nomar Garciaparra	1.50
4	Jeff Bagwell	1.00
5	Cal Ripken Jr.	4.00
6	Mike Piazza	2.00
7	Chipper Jones	1.50
8	Ken Griffey Jr.	2.00
9	Mark McGwire	3.00
10	Juan Gonzalez	1.00

Swing for the Fences

		NM/M
Complete Set (50):		24.00
Common Player:		.25
Inserted 1:1		
1	Brady Anderson	.25
2	Albert Belle	.25
3	Jay Buhner	.25
4	Jose Canseco	.50
5	Tony Clark	.25
6	Jose Cruz Jr.	.25
7	Jim Edmonds	.25
8	Cecil Fielder	.25

9	Travis Fryman	.25
10	Nomar Garciaparra	1.00
11	Juan Gonzalez	.40
12	Ken Griffey Jr.	1.50
13	David Justice	.25
14	Travis Lee	.25
15	Edgar Martinez	.25
16	Tino Martinez	.25
17	Rafael Palmeiro	.65
18	Manny Ramirez	.75
19	Cal Ripken Jr.	2.50
20	Alex Rodriguez	2.00
21	Tim Salmon	.25
22	Frank Thomas	.75
23	Jim Thome	.65
24	Mo Vaughn	.25
25	Bernie Williams	.25
26	Fred McGriff	.25
27	Jeff Bagwell	.75
28	Dante Bichette	.25
29	Barry Bonds	2.50
30	Ellis Burks	.25
31	Ken Caminiti	.25
32	Vinny Castilla	.25
33	Andres Galarraga	.25
34	Vladimir Guerrero	.75
35	Todd Helton	.75
36	Todd Hundley	.25
37	Andruw Jones	.75
38	Chipper Jones	1.00
39	Eric Karros	.25
40	Ryan Klesko	.25
41	Ray Lankford	.25
42	Mark McGwire	2.00
43	Raul Mondesi	.25
44	Mike Piazza	1.50
45	Scott Rolen	.65
46	Gary Sheffield	.50
47	Sammy Sosa	1.00
48	Larry Walker	.25
49	Matt Williams	.25
50	WILDCARD	.25

1998 Pinnacle Plus

		NM/M
Complete Set (200):		12.00
Common Player:		.05
Pack (10):		1.00
Wax Box (20):		12.00
1	Roberto Alomar/AS	.20
2	Sandy Alomar Jr./AS	.05
3	Brady Anderson/AS	.05
4	Albert Belle/AS	.05
5	Jeff Cirillo/AS	.05
6	Roger Clemens/AS	1.25
7	David Cone/AS	.05
8	Nomar Garciaparra/AS	1.00
9	Ken Griffey Jr./AS	1.50
10	Jason Dickson/AS	.05
11	Edgar Martinez/AS	.05
12	Tino Martinez/AS	.05
13	Randy Johnson/AS	.75
14	Mark McGwire/AS	2.00
15	David Justice/AS	.05
16	Mike Mussina/AS	.40
17	Chuck Knoblauch/AS	.05
18	Joey Cora/AS	.05
19	Pat Hentgen/AS	.05
20	Randy Myers/AS	.05
21	Cal Ripken Jr./AS	2.50
22	Mariano Rivera/AS	.15
23	Jose Rosado/AS	.05
24	Frank Thomas/AS	.75
25	Alex Rodriguez/AS	2.00
26	Justin Thompson/AS	.05
27	Ivan Rodriguez/AS	.65
28	Bernie Williams/AS	.05
29	Pedro Martinez/AS	.75
30	Tony Clark	.05
31	Garret Anderson	.05
32	Travis Fryman	.05
33	Mike Piazza	1.50
34	Carl Pavano	.05

35	Kevin Millwood RC	1.00
36	Miguel Tejada	.20
37	Willie Blair	.05
38	Devon White	.05
39	Andres Galarraga	.05
40	Barry Larkin	.05
41	Al Leiter	.05
42	Moises Alou	.05
43	Eric Young	.05
44	John Jaha	.05
45	Bernard Gilkey	.05
46	Freddy Garcia	.05
47	Ruben Rivera	.05
48	Robb Nen	.05
49	Ray Lankford	.05
50	Kenny Lofton	.05
51	Joe Carter	.05
52	Jason McDonald	.05
53	Quinton McCracken	.05
54	Kerry Wood	.50
55	Mike Lansing	.05
56	Chipper Jones	1.00
57	Barry Bonds	2.50
58	Brad Fullmer	.05
59	Jeff Bagwell	.75
60	Rondell White	.05
61	Geronimo Berroa	.05
62	Magglio Ordonez RC	1.50
63	Dwight Gooden	.05
64	Brian Hunter	.05
65	Todd Walker	.05
66	Frank Catalanotto RC	.05
67	Tony Saunders	.05
68	Travis Lee	.05
69	Michael Tucker	.05
70	Reggie Sanders	.05
71	Derrek Lee	.50
72	Larry Walker	.05
73	Marquis Grissom	.05
74	Craig Biggio	.05
75	Kevin Brown	.05
76	J.T. Snow	.05
77	Eric Davis	.05
78	Jeff Abbott	.05
79	Jermaine Dye	.05
80	Otis Nixon	.05
81	Curt Schilling	.35
82	Enrique Wilson	.05
83	Tony Gwynn	1.00
84	Orlando Cabrera	.05
85	Ramon Martinez	.05
86	Greg Vaughn	.05
87	Alan Benes	.05
88	Dennis Eckersley	.65
89	Jim Thome	.65
90	Juan Encarnacion	.05
91	Jeff King	.05
92	Shannon Stewart	.05
93	Roberto Hernandez	.05
94	Raul Ibanez	.05
95	Darryl Kile	.05
96	Charles Johnson	.05
97	Rich Becker	.05
98	Hal Morris	.05
99	Ismael Valdes	.05
100	Orel Hershiser	.05
101	Mo Vaughn	.05
102	Aaron Boone	.05
103	Jeff Conine	.05
104	Paul O'Neill	.05
105	Tom Candiotti	.05
106	Wilson Alvarez	.05
107	Mike Stanley	.05
108	Carlos Delgado	.50
109	Tony Batista	.05
110	Dante Bichette	.05
111	Henry Rodriguez	.05
112	Karim Garcia	.05
113	Shane Reynolds	.05
114	Ken Caminiti	.05
115	Jose Silva	.05
116	Juan Gonzalez	.40
117	Brian Jordan	.05
118	Jim Leyritz	.05
119	Manny Ramirez	.75
120	Fred McGriff	.05
121	Brooks Kieschnick	.05
122	Sean Casey	.15
123	John Smoltz	.05
124	Rusty Greer	.05
125	Cecil Fielder	.05
126	Mike Cameron	.05
127	Reggie Jefferson	.05
128	Bobby Higginson	.05
129	Kevin Appier	.05
130	Robin Ventura	.05
131	Ben Grieve	.05
132	Wade Boggs	1.00
133	Jose Cruz Jr.	.05
134	Jeff Suppan	.05
135	Vinny Castilla	.05
136	Sammy Sosa	1.00
137	Mark Wohlers	.05
138	Jay Bell	.05

139	Brett Tomko	.05
140	Gary Sheffield	.40
141	Tim Salmon	.05
142	Jaret Wright	.05
143	Kenny Rogers	.05
144	Brian Anderson	.05
145	Darrin Fletcher	.05
146	John Flaherty	.05
147	Dmitri Young	.05
148	Andruw Jones	.75
149	Matt Williams	.05
150	Bobby Bonilla	.05
151	Mike Hampton	.05
152	Al Martin	.05
153	Mark Grudzielanek	.05
154	Dave Nilsson	.05
155	Roger Cedeno	.05
156	Greg Maddux	1.00
157	Mark Kotsay	.05
158	Steve Finley	.05
159	Wilson Delgado	.05
160	Ron Gant	.05
161	Jim Edmonds	.05
162	Jeff Blauser	.05
163	Dave Burba	.05
164	Pedro Astacio	.05
165	Livan Hernandez	.05
166	Neifi Perez	.05
167	Ryan Klesko	.05
168	Fernando Tatis	.05
169	Richard Hidalgo	.05
170	Carlos Perez	.05
171	Bob Abreu	.15
172	Francisco Cordova	.05
173	Todd Helton	.75
174	Doug Glanville	.05
175	Brian Rose	.05
176	Yamil Benitez	.05
177	Darin Erstad	.15
178	Scott Rolen	.60
179	John Wetteland	.05
180	Paul Sorrento	.05
181	Walt Weiss	.05
182	Vladimir Guerrero	.75
183	Ken Griffey Jr.	.75
184	Alex Rodriguez	1.00
185	Cal Ripken Jr.	1.25
186	Frank Thomas	.40
187	Chipper Jones	.50
188	Hideo Nomo	.20
189	Nomar Garciaparra	.60
190	Mike Piazza	1.00
191	Greg Maddux	.50
192	Tony Gwynn	.50
193	Mark McGwire	1.00
194	Roger Clemens	.65
195	Mike Piazza	.75
196	Mark McGwire	1.00
197	Chipper Jones	.50
198	Larry Walker	.05
199	Hideo Nomo	.20
200	Barry Bonds	1.25

Artist's Proofs

		NM/M
Complete Set (60):		150.00
Common Player:		.75
Inserted 1:35		
Golds:		10X
Production 100 Sets		
1	Roberto Alomar/AS	1.50
2	Albert Belle/AS	.75
3	Roger Clemens/AS	8.00
4	Nomar Garciaparra/AS	7.50
5	Ken Griffey Jr./AS	10.00
6	Tino Martinez/AS	.75
7	Randy Johnson/AS	6.00
8	Mark McGwire/AS	12.50
9	David Justice/AS	.75
10	Chuck Knoblauch/AS	.75
11	Cal Ripken Jr./AS	15.00
12	Frank Thomas/AS	6.00

13 Alex Rodriguez/AS 12.50
14 Ivan Rodriguez/AS 5.00
15 Bernie Williams/AS .75
16 Pedro Martinez 6.00
17 Tony Clark .75
18 Mike Piazza 10.00
19 Miguel Tejada 1.00
20 Andres Galarraga .75
21 Barry Larkin .75
22 Kenny Lofton .75
23 Chipper Jones 7.50
24 Barry Bonds 15.00
25 Brad Fullmer .75
26 Jeff Bagwell 6.00
27 Todd Walker .75
28 Travis Lee .75
29 Larry Walker .75
30 Craig Biggio .75
31 Tony Gwynn 7.50
32 Jim Thome 5.00
33 Juan Encarnacion .75
34 Mo Vaughn .75
35 Karim Garcia .75
36 Ken Caminiti .75
37 Juan Gonzalez 3.00
38 Manny Ramirez 6.00
39 Fred McGriff .75
40 Rusty Greer .75
41 Bobby Higginson .75
42 Ben Grieve .75
43 Wade Boggs 7.50
44 Jose Cruz Jr. .75
45 Sammy Sosa 7.50
46 Gary Sheffield 2.00
47 Tim Salmon .75
48 Jaret Wright .75
49 Andruw Jones 6.00
50 Matt Williams .75
51 Greg Maddux 7.50
52 Jim Edmonds .75
53 Livan Hernandez .75
54 Neifi Perez .75
55 Fernando Tatis .75
56 Richard Hidalgo .75
57 Todd Helton 6.00
58 Darin Erstad 1.50
59 Scott Rolen 5.00
60 Vladimir Guerrero 5.00

A Piece of the Game

NM/M
Complete Set (10): 8.00
Common Player: .50
Inserted 1:19
1 Ken Griffey Jr. 1.00
2 Frank Thomas .65
3 Alex Rodriguez 1.50
4 Chipper Jones .75
5 Cal Ripken Jr. 2.00
6 Mike Piazza 1.00
7 Greg Maddux .75
8 Juan Gonzalez .50
9 Nomar Garciaparra .75
10 Larry Walker .50

Epix All-Star Moment

NM/M
Complete Set (12): 25.00
Common Player: 1.00
Purples: 1.5X
Emeralds: 2.5X
Inserted 1:21
13 Alex Rodriguez 3.50
14 Cal Ripken Jr. 5.00
15 Chipper Jones 2.50
16 Roger Clemens 2.75
17 Mo Vaughn 1.00
18 Mark McGwire 3.50
19 Mike Piazza 3.00
20 Andruw Jones 2.00
21 Greg Maddux 2.50

22 Barry Bonds 5.00
23 Paul Molitor 2.00
24 Hideo Nomo 1.50

Lasting Memories

NM/M
Complete Set (30): 16.00
Common Player: .25
Inserted 1:5
1 Nomar Garciaparra .75
2 Ken Griffey Jr. 1.00
3 Livan Hernandez .25
4 Hideo Nomo .40
5 Ben Grieve .25
6 Scott Rolen .50
7 Roger Clemens .85
8 Cal Ripken Jr. 2.00
9 Mo Vaughn .25
10 Frank Thomas .65
11 Mark McGwire 1.50
12 Barry Larkin .25
13 Matt Williams .25
14 Jose Cruz Jr. .25
15 Andruw Jones .65
16 Mike Piazza 1.00
17 Jeff Bagwell .65
18 Chipper Jones .75
19 Juan Gonzalez .40
20 Kenny Lofton .25
21 Greg Maddux .75
22 Ivan Rodriguez .50
23 Alex Rodriguez 1.50
24 Derek Jeter 2.00
25 Albert Belle .25
26 Barry Bonds 2.00
27 Larry Walker .25
28 Sammy Sosa .75
29 Tony Gwynn .75
30 Randy Johnson .65

Team Pinnacle

NM/M
Complete Set (15): 50.00
Common Player: 1.50
Inserted 1:71
Golds: 2X
Inserted 1:199
1 Mike Piazza,
Ivan Rodriguez 6.00
2 Mark McGwire,
Mo Vaughn 5.00
3 Roberto Alomar,
Craig Biggio 2.00
4 Alex Rodriguez,
Barry Larkin 8.00
5 Cal Ripken Jr.,
Chipper Jones 10.00
6 Ken Griffey Jr.,
Larry Walker 6.00
7 Juan Gonzalez,
Tony Gwynn 4.00

8 Albert Belle,
Barry Bonds 8.00
9 Kenny Lofton,
Andruw Jones 3.00
10 Tino Martinez,
Jeff Bagwell 3.00
11 Frank Thomas,
Andres Galarraga 3.00
12 Roger Clemens,
Greg Maddux 8.00
13 Pedro Martinez,
Hideo Nomo 4.00
14 Nomar Garciaparra,
Scott Rolen 5.00
15 Ben Grieve,
Paul Konerko 1.50

Yardwork

NM/M
Complete Set (15): 12.50
Common Player: .35
Inserted 1:9
1 Mo Vaughn .35
2 Frank Thomas .75
3 Albert Belle .35
4 Nomar Garciaparra 1.00
5 Tony Clark .35
6 Tino Martinez .35
7 Ken Griffey Jr. 1.50
8 Juan Gonzalez .60
9 Sammy Sosa 1.00
10 Jose Cruz Jr. .35
11 Jeff Bagwell .75
12 Mike Piazza 1.50
13 Larry Walker .35
14 Mark McGwire 2.00
15 Barry Bonds 2.50

2001 Playoff Absolute Memorabilia

GEOFF JENKINS •OF

NM/M
Complete Set (200):
Common Player: .25
Common SP (151-200): 5.00
Production 700
Pack (6): 8.00
Box (18) w/baseball: 150.00
1 Alex Rodriguez 2.50
2 Barry Bonds 3.00
3 Cal Ripken Jr. 3.00
4 Chipper Jones 1.50
5 Derek Jeter 3.00
6 Troy Glaus 1.00
7 Frank Thomas 1.00
8 Greg Maddux 1.50
9 Ivan Rodriguez .75
10 Jeff Bagwell 1.00
11 Ryan Dempster .25
12 Todd Helton 1.00
13 Ken Griffey Jr. 2.00
14 Manny Ramirez 1.00
15 Mark McGwire 2.50
16 Mike Piazza 2.00
17 Nomar Garciaparra 2.00
18 Pedro Martinez 1.00
19 Randy Johnson 1.00
20 Rick Ankiel .25
21 Rickey Henderson 1.00
22 Roger Clemens 1.75
23 Sammy Sosa 2.00
24 Tony Gwynn 2.00
25 Vladimir Guerrero 1.00
26 Kazuhiro Sasaki .25
27 Roberto Alomar .50
28 Barry Zito .35
29 Pat Burrell .50
30 Harold Baines .25
31 Carlos Delgado .65
32 J.D. Drew .50
33 Jim Edmonds .25
34 Darin Erstad .50
35 Jason Giambi .75
36 Tom Glavine .50
37 Juan Gonzalez 1.00
38 Mark Grace .35
39 Shawn Green .50
40 Tim Hudson .50
41 Andruw Jones 1.00
42 David Justice .25
43 Jeff Kent .25
44 Barry Larkin .25
45 Rafael Furcal .25
46 Mike Mussina .50
47 Hideo Nomo 1.00
48 Rafael Palmeiro .75
49 Adam Piatt .25
50 Scott Rolen .75
51 Gary Sheffield .50
52 Bernie Williams .35
53 Bob Abreu .25
54 Edgardo Alfonzo .25
55 Edgar Renteria .25
56 Phil Nevin .25
57 Craig Biggio .25
58 Andres Galarraga .25
59 Edgar Martinez .25
60 Fred McGriff .25
61 Magglio Ordonez .25
62 Jim Thome .75
63 Matt Williams .25
64 Kerry Wood .65
65 Moises Alou .25
66 Brady Anderson .25
67 Garret Anderson .25
68 Russell Branyan .25
69 Tony Batista .25
70 Vernon Wells .25
71 Carlos Beltran .60
72 Adrian Beltre .25
73 Kris Benson .25
74 Lance Berkman .25
75 Kevin Brown .25
76 Dee Brown .25
77 Jeromy Burnitz .25
78 Timoniel Perez .25
79 Sean Casey .40
80 Luis Castillo .25
81 Eric Chavez .35
82 Jeff Cirillo .25
83 Bartolo Colon .25
84 David Cone .25
85 Freddy Garcia .25
86 Johnny Damon .40
87 Ray Durham .25
88 Jermaine Dye .25
89 Juan Encarnacion .25
90 Terrence Long .25
91 Carl Everett .25
92 Steve Finley .25
93 Cliff Floyd .25
94 Brad Fullmer .25
95 Brian Giles .25
96 Luis Gonzalez .35
97 Rusty Greer .25

98	Jeffrey Hammonds	.25
99	Mike Hampton	.25
100	Orlando Hernandez	.25
101	Richard Hidalgo	.25
102	Geoff Jenkins	.25
103	Jacque Jones	.25
104	Brian Jordan	.25
105	Gabe Kapler	.25
106	Eric Karros	.25
107	Jason Kendall	.25
108	Adam Kennedy	.25
109	Deion Sanders	.25
110	Ryan Klesko	.25
111	Chuck Knoblauch	.25
112	Paul Konerko	.25
113	Carlos Lee	.25
114	Kenny Lofton	.25
115	Javy Lopez	.25
116	Tino Martinez	.25
117	Ruben Mateo	.25
118	Kevin Millwood	.25
119	Jimmy Rollins	.25
120	Raul Mondesi	.25
121	Trot Nixon	.25
122	John Olerud	.25
123	Paul O'Neill	.25
124	Chan Ho Park	.25
125	Andy Pettitte	.35
126	Jorge Posada	.25
127	Mark Quinn	.25
128	Aramis Ramirez	.25
129	Mariano Rivera	.25
130	Tim Salmon	.35
131	Curt Schilling	.50
132	Richie Sexson	.25
133	John Smoltz	.25
134	J.T. Snow	.25
135	Jay Payton	.25
136	Shannon Stewart	.25
137	B.J. Surhoff	.25
138	Mike Sweeney	.25
139	Fernando Tatis	.25
140	Miguel Tejada	.35
141	Jason Varitek	.25
142	Greg Vaughn	.25
143	Mo Vaughn	.25
144	Robin Ventura	.25
145	Jose Vidro	.25
146	Omar Vizquel	.25
147	Larry Walker	.25
148	David Wells	.25
149	Rondell White	.25
150	Preston Wilson	.25
151	Bud Smith RC	5.00
152	Cory Aldridge RC	5.00
153	Wilmy Caceres RC	5.00
154	Josh Beckett	6.00
155	Wilson Betemit RC	10.00
156	Jason Michaels RC	5.00
157	Albert Pujols RC	125.00
158	Andres Torres RC	5.00
159	Jack Wilson RC	8.00
160	Alex Escobar RC	5.00
161	Ben Sheets	5.00
162	Rafael Soriano RC	10.00
163	Nate Frese RC	5.00
164	Carlos Garcia RC	5.00
165	Brandon Larson RC	5.00
166	Alexis Gomez RC	8.00
167	Jason Hart	5.00
168	Nick Johnson	5.00
169	Donaldo Mendez RC	5.00
170	Christian Parker RC	5.00
171	Jackson Melian RC	5.00
172	Jack Cust	5.00
173	Adrian Hernandez RC	5.00
174	Joe Crede	5.00
175	Jose Mieses RC	5.00
176	Roy Oswalt	5.00
177	Eric Munson	5.00
178	Xavier Nady	5.00
179	Horacio Ramirez RC	8.00
180	Abraham Nunez	5.00
181	Jose Ortiz	5.00
182	Jeremy Owens RC	5.00
183	Claudio Vargas RC	5.00
184	Marcus Giles	5.00
185	Aubrey Huff	5.00
186	C.C. Sabathia	5.00
187	Adam Dunn	5.00
188	Adam Pettyjohn RC	5.00
189	Elpidio Guzman RC	5.00
190	Jay Gibbons RC	10.00
191	Wilkin Ruan RC	5.00
192	Tsuyoshi Shinjo RC	5.00
193	Alfonso Soriano	8.00
194	Corey Patterson	5.00
195	Ichiro Suzuki RC	75.00
196	Billy Sylvester RC	5.00
197	Juan Uribe RC	5.00
198	Johnny Estrada RC	5.00
199	Carlos Valderrama RC	5.00
200	Matt White RC	5.00

Spectrum

Stars (1-150):	No Pricing
Production 10	
RK's (151-200):	2-4X
Production 25	

Ball Hoggs

			NM/M
Common Player:			8.00
Production 75 unless noted.			
1	Vladimir Guerrero		15.00
2	Troy Glaus		10.00
3	Tony Gwynn		20.00
4	Cal Ripken/125		50.00
5	Todd Helton		15.00
6	Jacque Jones/125		8.00
7	Shawn Green/100		8.00
8	Ichiro Suzuki		85.00
9	Scott Rolen		15.00
10	Roger Clemens		30.00
11	Ken Griffey/25		50.00
14	Sammy Sosa		25.00
15	J.D. Drew		10.00
16	Barry Bonds/100		40.00
17	Pat Burrell		15.00
18	Mark McGwire/100		65.00
19	Mike Piazza		25.00
20	Magglio Ordonez/150		10.00
21	Miguel Tejada		10.00
22	Albert Pujols/100		150.00
23	Derek Jeter		40.00
24	Johnny Damon		15.00
25	Mike Sweeney		8.00
26	Ben Grieve		8.00
27	Jeff Kent		8.00
28	Andres Galarraga		8.00
29	Richie Sexson		10.00
30	Juan Encarnacion		8.00
31	Ruben Mateo		8.00
33	Manny Ramirez		15.00
35	Ivan Rodriguez		15.00
36	Darin Erstad		15.00
37	Carlos Delgado		10.00
38	Jeff Bagwell		15.00
39	Jermaine Dye		8.00
40	Jose Ortiz		8.00
41	Gary Sheffield		10.00
42	Eric Chavez		8.00
43	Mark Grace		15.00
44	Rafael Palmeiro		15.00
45	Tsuyoshi Shinjo/100		15.00
46	Terrence Long		8.00
47	Carlos Delgado/25		20.00
48	Frank Thomas		15.00
49	Chipper Jones/25		40.00
50	Jason Giambi		15.00

Ballpark Souvenirs

	NM/M
Common Player:	4.00
Production 400 Sets	

Doubles:		1-1.5X
Production 200 Sets		
Triples:		1.5-2X
Production 75 Sets		
Home Runs:		2-4X
Production 25 Sets		
1	Barry Bonds	20.00
2	Cal Ripken Jr.	25.00
3	Pedro Martinez	10.00
4	Troy Glaus	6.00
5	Frank Thomas	8.00
6	Alex Rodriguez	10.00
7	Ivan Rodriguez	8.00
8	Jeff Bagwell	8.00
9	Mark McGwire	30.00
10	Todd Helton	8.00
11	Gary Sheffield	5.00
12	Manny Ramirez	8.00
13	Mike Piazza	10.00
14	Sammy Sosa	15.00
15	Preston Wilson	4.00
16	Tony Gwynn	8.00
17	Vladimir Guerrero	8.00
18	Carlos Delgado	6.00
19	Roberto Alomar	8.00
20	Todd Helton	8.00
21	Albert Pujols	50.00
22	Jason Giambi	8.00
23	Sammy Sosa	15.00
24	Ken Griffey Jr.	10.00
25	Darin Erstad	4.00
26	Mark McGwire	30.00
27	Carlos Delgado	6.00
28	Juan Gonzalez	8.00
29	Mike Sweeney	4.00
30	Alex Rodriguez	10.00
31	Roger Clemens	15.00
32	Tsuyoshi Shinjo	4.00
33	Ben Grieve	4.00
34	Jeff Kent	4.00
35	Vladimir Guerrero	8.00
36	Shawn Green	6.00
37	Rafael Palmeiro	6.00
38	Tony Gwynn	8.00
39	Scott Rolen	8.00
40	Ken Griffey Jr.	10.00
41	Albert Pujols	50.00
42	Barry Bonds	20.00
43	Mark Grace	8.00
44	Bernie Williams	6.00
45	Frank Thomas	8.00
46	Jermaine Dye	4.00
47	Mike Piazza	10.00
48	Chipper Jones	10.00
49	Richie Sexson	6.00
50	Magglio Ordonez	4.00

Boss Hoggs

		NM/M
Production 25 Sets		
4	Cal Ripken	80.00
6	Jacque Jones	15.00
7	Shawn Green	15.00
8	Ichiro Suzuki	100.00
9	Scott Rolen	20.00
11	Ken Griffey	50.00
14	Sammy Sosa	50.00
15	J.D. Drew	15.00
16	Barry Bonds	80.00
17	Pat Burrell	20.00
18	Mark McGwire	100.00
19	Mike Piazza	75.00
20	Magglio Ordonez	20.00
21	Miguel Tejada	15.00
23	Derek Jeter	85.00
24	Johnny Damon	15.00
25	Mike Sweeney	15.00
26	Ben Grieve	15.00
27	Jeff Kent	15.00
28	Andres Galarraga	15.00
29	Richie Sexson	20.00
30	Juan Encarnacion	15.00
31	Ruben Mateo	15.00

33	Manny Ramirez	20.00
35	Ivan Rodriguez	20.00
36	Darin Erstad	15.00
37	Carlos Delgado	20.00
38	Jeff Bagwell	20.00
39	Jermaine Dye	15.00
40	Jose Ortiz	15.00
42	Eric Chavez	15.00
43	Mark Grace	30.00
44	Rafael Palmeiro	30.00
45	Tsuyoshi Shinjo	20.00
46	Terrence Long	15.00
47	Carlos Delgado	20.00
48	Frank Thomas	25.00
50	Jason Giambi	25.00

Signing Bonus Baseballs

	NM/M
Common Auto. Baseball:	15.00
Inserted 1:Box	
Al Oliver/500	15.00
Andre Dawson/550	20.00
Barry Bonds/25	250.00
Bill Madlock/525	15.00
Bill Mazeroski/25	75.00
Billy Williams/325	20.00
Bob Feller/550	20.00
Bob Gibson/25	100.00
Bobby Doerr/300	25.00
Bobby Richardson/ 500	20.00
Boog Powell/500	20.00
Brian Jordan/25	40.00
Bucky Dent/500	15.00
Charles Johnson/25	40.00
Chipper Jones/25	100.00
Clete Boyer/500	20.00
Dale Murphy/500	80.00
Dave Concepcion/ 500	15.00
Dave Kingman/500	15.00
Don Larsen/200	40.00
Don Newcombe/500	15.00
Don Zimmer/500	15.00
Duke Snider/500	100.00
Earl Weaver/300	20.00
Enos Slaughter/525	20.00
Fergie Jenkins/1000	20.00
Frank Howard/500	20.00
Frank Robinson/25	100.00
Frank Thomas/25	85.00
Gary Carter/200	30.00
Gaylord Perry/1000	15.00
George Foster/500	15.00
George Kell/300	20.00
Goose Gossage/500	15.00
Greg Maddux/25	100.00
Hank Aaron/25	150.00
Hank Bauer/500	20.00
Harmon Killebrew/ 200	60.00
Henry Rodriguez/400	15.00
Herb Score/500	15.00
Hoyt Wilhelm/500	15.00
J.D. Drew/75	20.00
Javy Lopez/25	40.00
Jim Edmonds/25	50.00
Jim Palmer/500	20.00
Joe Pepitone/500	20.00
Johnny Bench/25	120.00
Johnny Podres/500	25.00
Juan Marichal/485	20.00
Kirby Puckett/25	100.00
Larry Doby/300	30.00
Lou Brock/25	75.00
Luis Tiant/400	15.00
Magglio Ordonez/200	25.00
Manny Ramirez/25	60.00
Maury Wills/500	20.00
Mike Schmidt/25	150.00
Minnie Minoso/1000	15.00
Monte Irvin/500	25.00
Moose Skowron/500	20.00
Nolan Ryan/25	200.00
Ozzie Smith/25	100.00
Phil Rizzuto/25	75.00
Ralph Kiner/100	40.00
Randy Johnson/25	100.00
Red Schoendienst/ 500	20.00
Reggie Jackson/25	80.00
Rickey Henderson/ 25	100.00
Robin Roberts/500	15.00
Roger Clemens/25	125.00
Rollie Fingers/575	20.00
Ryne Sandberg/25	100.00
Sean Casey/25	15.00
Stan Musial/25	100.00
Steve Carlton/25	75.00
Steve Garvey/1000	15.00
Todd Helton/25	50.00

Tom Glavine/25	50.00
Tom Seaver/25	75.00
Tommy John/1000	15.00
Tony Gwynn/25	75.00
Tony Perez/400	15.00
Wade Boggs/25	75.00
Warren Spahn/500	60.00
Whitey Ford/25	75.00
Willie Mays/25	150.00
Willie McCovey/25	60.00
Willie Stargell/25	75.00
Yogi Berra/25	75.00

Rookie Premiere Autographs

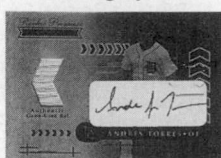

	NM/M
Production 25 Sets	
151 Bud Smith	15.00
152 Cory Aldridge	15.00
154 Josh Beckett	40.00
155 Wilson Betemit	15.00
157 Albert Pujols	500.00
158 Andres Torres	15.00
160 Alex Escobar	15.00
161 Ben Sheets	30.00
162 Rafael Soriano	30.00
164 Carlos Garcia	15.00
165 Brandon Larson	20.00
167 Jason Hart	15.00
168 Nick Johnson	25.00
169 Donaldo Mendez	15.00
170 Christian Parker	15.00
171 Jackson Melian	15.00
173 Adrian Hernandez	15.00
174 Joe Crede	15.00
175 Jose Mieses	15.00
176 Roy Oswalt	30.00
178 Xavier Nady	20.00
179 Horacio Ramirez	20.00
180 Abraham Nunez	15.00
181 Jose Ortiz	15.00
182 Jeremy Owens	15.00
183 Claudio Vargas	15.00
184 Marcus Giles	20.00
186 C.C. Sabathia	50.00
187 Adam Dunn	50.00
188 Adam Pettyjohn	15.00
190 Jay Gibbons	25.00
191 Wilkin Ruan	15.00
193 Alfonso Soriano	85.00
194 Corey Patterson	20.00
196 Billy Sylvester	15.00
197 Juan Uribe	15.00
198 Johnny Estrada	15.00
199 Carlos Valderrama	15.00
200 Matt White	15.00

Tools Of The Trade

	NM/M
Common Player:	5.00
Jerseys (1-20):	
Production 300	
Bats (21-40):	
Production 125	
Batting Glove (41-45):	
Production 50	
Hat (46-50):	
Production 100	
Autographs:	No Pricing
Production 25 Sets	
1 Vladimir Guerrero	10.00
2 Troy Glaus	6.00
3 Tony Gwynn	10.00
4 Todd Helton	8.00
5 Scott Rolen	8.00
6 Roger Clemens	20.00
7 Pedro Martinez	10.00
8 Richie Sexson	6.00
9 Magglio Ordonez	5.00
10 Ben Grieve	5.00
11 Jeff Bagwell	8.00
12 Edgar Martinez	5.00
13 Greg Maddux	25.00
15 Frank Thomas	10.00
16 Edgardo Alfonzo	5.00
17 Cal Ripken Jr.	40.00
18 Jose Vidro	5.00
19 Andruw Jones	8.00
20 Barry Bonds	50.00
21 Juan Gonzalez	8.00
22 Andruw Jones	8.00
23 Andruw Jones	8.00
24 Cal Ripken Jr.	60.00

25 Greg Maddux	30.00
26 Manny Ramirez	20.00
27 Roberto Alomar	8.00
28 Shawn Green	6.00
29 Edgardo Alfonzo	5.00
30 Rafael Palmeiro	10.00
31 Hideo Nomo	100.00
32 Andres Galarraga	6.00
33 Todd Helton	15.00
34 Darin Erstad	5.00
35 Ivan Rodriguez	15.00
36 Sean Casey	6.00
37 Vladimir Guerrero	20.00
39 Troy Glaus	8.00
40 Jeff Bagwell	10.00
41 Barry Bonds	100.00
42 Cal Ripken Jr.	125.00
43 Roberto Alomar	30.00
44 Sean Casey	20.00
45 Tony Gwynn	40.00
46 Bernie Williams	25.00
47 Barry Zito	25.00
48 Greg Maddux	
49 Tom Glavine	25.00
50 Troy Glaus	

2002 Playoff Absolute Memorabilia

	NM/M
Complete Set (200):	
Common Player:	.50
Common RK/Prospect (151-200):	3.00
Production 1,000	
Pack (6):	3.00
Box + 8 X 10:	140.00
1 David Eckstein	.50
2 Darin Erstad	.75
3 Troy Glaus	1.50
4 Garret Anderson	.50
5 Tim Salmon	.50
6 Curt Schilling	1.00
7 Randy Johnson	1.50
8 Luis Gonzalez	.50
9 Mark Grace	.60
10 Tom Glavine	.75
11 Greg Maddux	2.00
12 Chipper Jones	2.00
13 Gary Sheffield	.75
14 John Smoltz	.50
15 Andruw Jones	1.50
16 Wilson Betemit	.50
17 Tony Batista	.50
18 Javier Vazquez	.50
19 Scott Erickson	.50
20 Josh Towers	.50
21 Pedro J. Martinez	1.50
22 Johnny Damon	.60
23 Manny Ramirez	1.50
24 Rickey Henderson	1.50
25 Trot Nixon	.50
26 Nomar Garciaparra	2.50
27 Juan Cruz	.50
28 Kerry Wood	1.25
29 Fred McGriff	.50
30 Moises Alou	.50
31 Sammy Sosa	2.50
32 Corey Patterson	.50
33 Mark Buehrle	.50
34 Keith Foulke	.50
35 Frank Thomas	1.50
36 Kenny Lofton	.50
37 Magglio Ordonez	.50
38 Barry Larkin	.50
39 Ken Griffey Jr.	2.50
40 Adam Dunn	.75
41 Juan Encarnacion	.50
42 Sean Casey	.60
43 Bartolo Colon	.50
44 C.C. Sabathia	.50
45 Travis Fryman	.50
46 Jim Thome	1.50

47 Omar Vizquel	.50
48 Ellis Burks	.50
49 Russell Branyan	.50
50 Mike Hampton	.50
51 Todd Helton	1.50
52 Jose Ortiz	.50
53 Juan Uribe	.50
54 Juan Pierre	.50
55 Larry Walker	.50
56 Mike Rivera	.50
57 Robert Fick	.50
58 Bobby Higginson	.50
59 Josh Beckett	.50
60 Richard Hidalgo	.50
61 Cliff Floyd	.50
62 Mike Lowell	.50
63 Roy Oswalt	.50
64 Morgan Ensberg	.50
65 Jeff Bagwell	1.50
66 Craig Biggio	.50
67 Lance Berkman	.50
68 Carlos Beltran	.75
69 Mike Sweeney	.50
70 Neifi Perez	.50
71 Kevin Brown	.50
72 Hideo Nomo	1.50
73 Paul LoDuca	.50
74 Adrian Beltre	.60
75 Shawn Green	.75
76 Eric Karros	.50
77 Brad Radke	.50
78 Corey Koskie	.50
79 Doug Mientkiewicz	.50
80 Torii Hunter	.50
81 Jacque Jones	.50
82 Ben Sheets	.50
83 Richie Sexson	.50
84 Geoff Jenkins	.50
85 Tony Armas	.50
86 Michael Barrett	.50
87 Jose Vidro	.50
88 Vladimir Guerrero	1.50
89 Roger Clemens	2.25
90 Derek Jeter	4.00
91 Bernie Williams	.60
92 Jason Giambi	1.25
93 Jorge Posada	.50
94 Mike Mussina	.65
95 Andy Pettitte	.65
96 Nick Johnson	.50
97 Alfonso Soriano	1.25
98 Shawn Estes	.50
99 Al Leiter	.50
100 Mike Piazza	2.50
101 Roberto Alomar	.75
102 Mo Vaughn	.50
103 Jeromy Burnitz	.50
104 Tim Hudson	.65
105 Barry Zito	.50
106 Mark Mulder	.65
107 Eric Chavez	.65
108 Miguel Tejada	.65
109 Jeremy Giambi	.50
110 Jermaine Dye	.50
111 Mike Lieberthal	.50
112 Scott Rolen	1.25
113 Pat Burrell	.75
114 Brandon Duckworth	.50
115 Bobby Abreu	.50
116 Jason Kendall	.50
117 Aramis Ramirez	.50
118 Brian Giles	.50
119 Pokey Reese	.50
120 Phil Nevin	.50
121 Ryan Klesko	.50
122 Carlos Pena	.50
123 Trevor Hoffman	.50
124 Barry Bonds	4.00
125 Rich Aurilia	.50
126 Jeff Kent	.50
127 Tsuyoshi Shinjo	.50
128 Ichiro Suzuki	2.00
129 Edgar Martinez	.50
130 Freddy Garcia	.50
131 Bret Boone	.50
132 Matt Morris	.50
133 Tino Martinez	.50
134 Albert Pujols	3.00
135 J.D. Drew	.75
136 Jim Edmonds	.50
137 Gabe Kapler	.50
138 Paul Wilson	.50
139 Ben Grieve	.50
140 Wade Miller	.50
141 Chan Ho Park	.50
142 Alex Rodriguez	3.00
143 Rafael Palmeiro	1.25
144 Juan Gonzalez	1.50
145 Ivan Rodriguez	1.25
146 Carlos Delgado	.75
147 Jose Cruz Jr.	.50
148 Shannon Stewart	.50
149 Raul Mondesi	.50
150 Vernon Wells	.50

151 So Taguchi RC	8.00
152 Kazuhisa Ishii RC	8.00
153 Hank Blalock	6.00
154 Sean Burroughs	3.00
155 Geronimo Gil	3.00
156 Jon Rauch	3.00
157 Fernando Rodney	3.00
158 Miguel Asencio RC	3.00
159 Franklyn German RC	3.00
160 Luis Ugueto RC	3.00
161 Jorge Sosa RC	3.00
162 Felix Escalona RC	3.00
163 Colby Lewis	3.00
164 Mark Teixeira	5.00
165 Mark Prior	6.00
166 Francis Beltran RC	3.00
167 Joe Thurston	3.00
168 Earl Snyder RC	3.00
169 Takahito Nomura RC	3.00
170 Bill Hall	3.00
171 Marlon Byrd	3.00
172 Dave Williams	3.00
173 Yorvit Torrealba	3.00
174 Brandon Backe RC	3.00
175 Jorge de la Rosa RC	3.00
176 Brian Mallette RC	3.00
177 Rodrigo Rosario RC	3.00
178 Anderson Machado RC	3.00
179 Jorge Padilla	3.00
180 Allan Simpson RC	3.00
181 Doug DeVore RC	3.00
182 Steve Bechler RC	3.00
183 Raul Chavez	3.00
184 Tom Shearn RC	3.00
185 Ben Howard RC	3.00
186 Chris Baker RC	3.00
187 Travis Hughes RC	3.00
188 Kevin Mench	3.00
189 Drew Henson	3.00
190 Mike Moriarty RC	3.00
191 Corey Thurman RC	3.00
192 Bobby Hill	3.00
193 Steve Kent RC	3.00
194 Satoru Komiyama RC	3.00
195 Jason Lane	3.00
196 Angel Berroa	3.00
197 Brandon Puffer RC	3.00
198 Brian Fitzgerald RC	3.00
199 Rene Reyes RC	3.00
200 Hee Seop Choi	5.00

Spectrum

Stars (1-150):	3-5X
Production 100	
SP's:	1-1.5X
Production 50	

Absolutely Ink

	NM/M
Common Autograph:	5.00
Inserted 1:27	
Gold Parallel #'d to 25 not priced.	
Jsy Parallel #'d to Jsy # not priced.	
Adrian Beltre	20.00
Alex Rodriguez/50	100.00
Ben Sheets	20.00
Bobby Doerr	15.00
Blaine Neal	5.00
Carlos Beltran	25.00
Carlos Pena	5.00
Corey Patterson/150	15.00
Dave Parker	10.00
David Justice/65	25.00
Don Mattingly/75	65.00
Duaner Sanchez	5.00
Eric Chavez/100	15.00
Freddy Garcia	10.00
Gary Carter	25.00
Ivan Rodriguez/50	40.00
J.D. Drew/100	20.00
Jack Cust	5.00
Jason Michaels	5.00
Jermaine Dye/125	10.00
Jose Vidro	8.00
Josh Towers	6.00
Kerry Wood/50	40.00
Kirby Puckett/50	75.00
Luis Gonzalez/75	25.00
Luis Rivera	5.00
Manny Ramirez/50	40.00
Marcus Giles	10.00

Mark Prior/100 30.00
Mark Teixeira/100 25.00
Marlon Byrd/250 15.00
Matt Ginter 5.00
Moises Alou/150 15.00
Nate Frese 5.00
Nick Johnson 5.00
Pablo Ozuna 5.00
Paul LoDuca/200 20.00
Richie Sexson 15.00
Roberto Alomar/100 40.00
Roy Oswalt/300 15.00
Ryan Klesko/75 15.00
Sean Casey/125 10.00
Shannon Stewart 8.00
So Taguchi 15.00
Terrence Long 8.00
Timoniel Perez 5.00
Tony Gwynn/50 60.00
Troy Glaus/300 15.00
Vladimir
Guerrero/225 40.00
Wade Miller 15.00
Wilson Betemit 5.00

Signing Bonus

NM/M
Common Player:
Bobby Abreu/53 40.00
Roberto Alomar/100 50.00
Moises Alou/250 30.00
Carlos Beltran/50 50.00
Adrian Beltre/29 40.00
Adrian Beltre/18 30.00
Angel Berroa/50 20.00
Angel Berroa/100 20.00
Wilson Betemit/250 25.00
Hank Blalock/50 50.00
Hank Blalock/100 40.00
Lou Brock/100 60.00
Lou Brock/200 50.00
Kevin Brown/27 50.00
Kevin Brown/100 25.00
Kevin Brown/150 25.00
Mark Buehrle/56 60.00
Mark Buehrle/100 40.00
Marlon Byrd/61 25.00
Steve Carlton/100 50.00
Steve Carlton/150 40.00
Sean Casey/100 30.00
Eric Chavez/28 50.00
Juan Cruz/51 25.00
J.D. Drew/100 30.00
Brandon
Duckworth/56 25.00
Brandon
Duckworth/150 15.00
Adam Dunn/44 60.00
Jermaine Dye/100 40.00
Jermaine Dye/250 30.00
Morgan Ensberg/100 30.00
Cliff Floyd/200 25.00
Freddy Garcia/34 50.00
Freddy Garcia/125 25.00
Troy Glaus/50 65.00
Troy Glaus/100 40.00
Tom Glavine/200 60.00
Luis Gonzalez/125 30.00
Vladimir
Guerrero/27 120.00
Vladimir
Guerrero/150 80.00
Richard Hidalgo/100 20.00
Richard Hidalgo/135 20.00
Richard Hidalgo/150 20.00
Tim Hudson/50 60.00
Tim Hudson/100 40.00
Reggie Jackson/44 75.00
Nick Johnson/200 30.00
Andruw Jones/75 75.00
Al Kaline/250 60.00
Gabe Kapler/125 25.00
Gabe Kapler/175 25.00
Ryan Klesko/30 40.00
Jason Lane/100 30.00
Barry Larkin/50 60.00
Barry Larkin/150 50.00
Paul LoDuca/50 40.00
Fred Lynn/150 30.00
Fred Lynn/250 30.00
Greg Maddux/31 200.00

Edgar Martinez/150 50.00
Pedro J. Martinez/45 125.00
Don Mattingly/100 140.00
Willie McCovey/190 40.00
Willie McCovey/250 40.00
Wade Miller/52 25.00
Wade Miller/150 25.00
Wade Miller/250 20.00
Paul Molitor/75 50.00
Paul Molitor/100 40.00
Paul Molitor/125 40.00
Mark Mulder/40 35.00
Jose Ortiz/125 15.00
Roy Oswalt/44 40.00
Roy Oswalt/100 40.00
Jim Palmer/150 30.00
Jim Palmer/250 30.00
Dave Parker/150 25.00
Corey Patterson/250 25.00
Carlos Pena/150 15.00
Carlos Pena/250 15.00
Tony Perez/24 40.00
Tony Perez/250 25.00
Juan Pierre/75 25.00
Mark Prior/50 50.00
Mark Prior/75 40.00
Mark Prior/125 40.00
Kirby Puckett/34 125.00
Albert Pujols/100 250.00
Aramis Ramirez/50 50.00
Aramis Ramirez/125 40.00
Phil Rizzuto/10 265.00
Phil Rizzuto/250 70.00
Brooks Robinson/150 70.00
Brooks Robinson/250 60.00
Nolan Ryan/30 200.00
Nolan Ryan/34 200.00
Ryne Sandberg/50 150.00
Mike Schmidt/100 100.00
Richie Sexson/100 30.00
Ben Sheets/100 30.00
Ben Sheets/150 30.00
Alfonso Soriano/100 50.00
Shannon Stewart/100 25.00
Shannon Stewart/150 25.00
Mike Sweeney/100 30.00
So Taguchi/99 40.00
Mark Teixeira/23 65.00
Mark Teixeira/100 60.00
Miguel Tejada/40 60.00
Miguel Tejada/100 60.00
Frank Thomas/35 120.00
Javier Vazquez/125 25.00
Jose Vidro/150 20.00
Kerry Wood/34 75.00
Barry Zito/50 60.00

Team Quads

NM/M
Complete Set (20): 75.00
Common Card: 2.00
Inserted 1:18
Golds: 2X
Inserted 1:72
1 Troy Glaus, Darin Erstad, Garret Anderson, Troy Percival 2.00
2 Curt Schilling, Randy Johnson, Luis Gonzalez, Mark Grace 4.00
3 Chipper Jones, Andruw Jones, Greg Maddux, Tom Glavine 5.00
4 Nomar Garciaparra, Manny Ramirez, Trot Nixon, Pedro J. Martinez 6.00
5 Kerry Wood, Sammy Sosa, Fred McGriff, Moises Alou 6.00

6 Frank Thomas, Magglio Ordonez, Mark Buehrle, Kenny Lofton 3.00
7 Ken Griffey Jr., Barry Larkin, Juan Encarnacion, Sean Casey 6.00
8 C.C. Sabathia, Jim Thome, Bartolo Colon, Russell Branyan 4.00
9 Todd Helton, Larry Walker, Juan Pierre, Mike Hampton 2.50
10 Jeff Bagwell, Craig Biggio, Lance Berkman, Richard Hidalgo 3.00
11 Shawn Green, Adrian Beltre, Hideo Nomo, Paul LoDuca 2.00
12 Mike Piazza, Roberto Alomar, Mo Vaughn, Roger Cedeno 6.00
13 Roger Clemens, Derek Jeter, Jason Giambi, Mike Mussina 10.00
14 Barry Zito, Tim Hudson, Eric Chavez, Miguel Tejada 2.50
15 Pat Burrell, Scott Rolen, Bobby Abreu, Marlon Byrd 4.00
16 Bernie Williams, Jorge Posada, Alfonso Soriano, Andy Pettitte 3.00
17 Barry Bonds, Rich Aurilia, Tsuyoshi Shinjo, Jeff Kent 8.00
18 Ichiro Suzuki, Kazuhiro Sasaki, Bret Boone, Edgar Martinez 6.00
19 Albert Pujols, J.D. Drew, Jim Edmonds, Tino Martinez 8.00
20 Alex Rodriguez, Ivan Rodriguez, Juan Gonzalez, Rafael Palmeiro 8.00

Team Quads Game-Used

NM/M
Numbered to 100
Prime: No Pricing
Production 25
1 Troy Glaus, Darin Erstad, Garret Anderson, Troy Percival 25.00
2 Curt Schilling, Randy Johnson, Luis Gonzalez, Mark Grace 30.00
3 Chipper Jones, Andruw Jones, Greg Maddux, Tom Glavine 40.00
4 Nomar Garciaparra, Manny Ramirez, Trot Nixon, Pedro J. Martinez 50.00
5 Kerry Wood, Sammy Sosa, Fred McGriff, Moises Alou 35.00
6 Frank Thomas, Magglio Ordonez, Mark Buehrle, Kenny Lofton 25.00
8 C.C. Sabathia, Jim Thome, Bartolo Colon, Russell Branyan 40.00
9 Todd Helton, Larry Walker, Juan Pierre, Mike Hampton 30.00
10 Jeff Bagwell, Craig Biggio, Lance Berkman, Richard Hidalgo 30.00
11 Shawn Green, Adrian Beltre, Hideo Nomo, Paul LoDuca 40.00

ABBREVIATIONS

AS - All-Star
OPS - Overprint
"Promotional Sample"

12 Mike Piazza, Roberto Alomar, Mo Vaughn, Roger Cedeno 40.00
13 Roger Clemens, Derek Jeter, Jason Giambi, Mike Mussina 75.00
14 Barry Zito, Tim Hudson, Eric Chavez, Miguel Tejada 20.00
15 Pat Burrell, Scott Rolen, Bobby Abreu, Marlon Byrd 35.00
16 Bernie Williams, Jorge Posada, Alfonso Soriano, Andy Pettitte 30.00
17 Barry Bonds, Rich Aurilia, Tsuyoshi Shinjo, Jeff Kent 40.00
18 Ichiro Suzuki, Kazuhiro Sasaki, Bret Boone, Edgar Martinez 50.00
19 Albert Pujols, J.D. Drew, Jim Edmonds, Tino Martinez 40.00
20 Alex Rodriguez, Ivan Rodriguez, Juan Gonzalez, Rafael Palmeiro 40.00

Team Tandems

NM/M
Complete Set (40): 80.00
Common Card: 1.00
Golds: 2-3X
Inserted 1:72
1 Troy Glaus, Darin Erstad 1.50
2 Curt Schilling, Randy Johnson 3.00
3 Chipper Jones, Andruw Jones 3.00
4 Greg Maddux, Tom Glavine 4.00
5 Nomar Garciaparra, Manny Ramirez 6.00
6 Pedro J. Martinez, Trot Nixon 3.00
7 Kerry Wood, Sammy Sosa 5.00
8 Frank Thomas, Magglio Ordonez 2.00
9 Ken Griffey Jr., Barry Larkin 5.00
10 C.C. Sabathia, Jim Thome 2.50
11 Todd Helton, Larry Walker 2.00
12 Bobby Higginson, Shane Halter 1.00
13 Cliff Floyd, Brad Penny 1.00
14 Jeff Bagwell, Craig Biggio 2.00
15 Shawn Green, Adrian Beltre 1.50
16 Ben Sheets, Richie Sexson 1.50
17 Vladimir Guerrero, Jose Vidro 3.00
18 Mike Piazza, Roberto Alomar 5.00
19 Roger Clemens, Mike Mussina 6.00
20 Derek Jeter, Jason Giambi 8.00
21 Barry Zito, Tim Hudson 1.50
22 Eric Chavez, Miguel Tejada 1.50

23	Pat Burrell, Scott Rolen	3.00
24	Brian Giles, Aramis Ramirez	1.50
25	Ryan Klesko, Phil Nevin	1.50
26	Barry Bonds, Rich Aurilia	8.00
27	Ichiro Suzuki, Kazuhiro Sasaki	5.00
28	Albert Pujols, J.D. Drew	6.00
29	Alex Rodriguez, Ivan Rodriguez	6.00
30	Carlos Delgado, Shannon Stewart	1.50
31	Mo Vaughn, Roger Cedeno	1.00
32	Carlos Beltran, Mike Sweeney	1.50
33	Edgar Martinez, Bret Boone	1.50
34	Juan Gonzalez, Rafael Palmeiro	2.00
35	Johnny Damon, Rickey Henderson	1.50
36	Sean Casey, Adam Dunn	2.00
37	Jeff Kent, Tsuyoshi Shinjo	1.50
38	Lance Berkman, Richard Hidalgo	1.50
39	So Taguchi, Tino Martinez	1.50
40	Hideo Nomo, Kazuhisa Ishii	1.50

Team Tandems G-U

Craig Biggio

Jeff Bagwell

		NM/M
Common Card:		5.00
Inserted 1:33		
Golds:		2-3X
Production 50		
1	Troy Glaus, Darin Erstad	8.00
2	Curt Schilling, Randy Johnson	10.00
3	Chipper Jones, Andruw Jones	10.00
4	Greg Maddux, Tom Glavine	20.00
5	Nomar Garciaparra, Manny Ramirez	25.00
6	Pedro J. Martinez, Trot Nixon	15.00
7	Kerry Wood, Sammy Sosa	15.00
8	Frank Thomas, Magglio Ordonez	10.00
9	Ken Griffey Jr., Barry Larkin	15.00
10	C.C. Sabathia, Jim Thome	15.00
11	Todd Helton, Larry Walker	8.00
12	Bobby Higginson, Shane Halter	5.00
13	Cliff Floyd, Brad Penny	5.00
14	Jeff Bagwell, Craig Biggio	15.00
15	Shawn Green, Adrian Beltre	8.00
16	Ben Sheets, Richie Sexson	8.00
17	Vladimir Guerrero, Jose Vidro	12.00
18	Mike Piazza, Roberto Alomar	15.00
19	Roger Clemens, Mike Mussina	50.00
20	Derek Jeter, Jason Giambi	30.00

21	Barry Zito, Tim Hudson	15.00
22	Eric Chavez, Miguel Tejada	10.00
23	Pat Burrell, Scott Rolen	15.00
24	Brian Giles, Aramis Ramirez	10.00
25	Ryan Klesko, Phil Nevin	8.00
26	Barry Bonds, Rich Aurilia	15.00
27	Ichiro Suzuki, Kazuhiro Sasaki	
28	Albert Pujols, J.D. Drew	15.00
29	Alex Rodriguez, Ivan Rodriguez	15.00
30	Carlos Delgado, Shannon Stewart	8.00
31	Mo Vaughn, Roger Cedeno	5.00
32	Carlos Beltran, Mike Sweeney	8.00
33	Edgar Martinez, Bret Boone	8.00
34	Juan Gonzalez, Rafael Palmeiro	12.00
35	Johnny Damon, Rickey Henderson	10.00
36	Sean Casey, Adam Dunn	15.00
37	Jeff Kent, Tsuyoshi Shinjo	10.00
38	Lance Berkman, Richard Hidalgo	8.00
39	So Taguchi, Tino Martinez	15.00
40	Hideo Nomo, Kazuhisa Ishii	35.00

Tools of the Trade

	NM/M
Complete Set (95):	120.00
Common Player:	1.00
Inserted 1:9	
Golds:	2-3X
Inserted 1:45	
1 Mike Mussina	2.00
2 Rickey Henderson	2.00
3 Raul Mondesi	1.00
4 Nomar Garciaparra	6.00
5 Randy Johnson	3.00
6 Roger Clemens	6.00
7 Shawn Green	1.00
8 Todd Helton	2.00
9 Aramis Ramirez	1.50
10 Barry Larkin	1.50
11 Byung-Hyun Kim	1.00
12 C.C. Sabathia	1.00
13 Curt Schilling	2.50
14 Darin Erstad	1.50
15 Eric Karros	1.00
16 Freddy Garcia	1.00
17 Greg Maddux	4.00
18 Jason Kendall	1.00
19 Jim Thome	3.00
20 Juan Gonzalez	2.00
21 Kazuhiro Sasaki	1.00
22 Kerry Wood	3.00
23 Luis Gonzalez	1.50
24 Mark Mulder	1.00
25 Rich Aurilia	1.00
26 Ray Durham	1.00
27 Ben Grieve	1.00
28 Bret Boone	1.00
29 Edgar Martinez	1.00
30 Ivan Rodriguez	2.00
31 Jorge Posada	2.00
32 Mike Piazza	6.00
33 Pat Burrell	1.50
34 Robin Ventura	1.00
35 Trot Nixon	1.00
36 Adrian Beltre	1.00
37 Bernie Williams	1.50
38 Bobby Abreu	1.50
39 Carlos Delgado	1.50
40 Craig Biggio	1.50
41 Garret Anderson	1.50
42 Jermaine Dye	1.00
43 Johnny Damon	1.00
44 Tim Salmon	1.00

45 Tino Martinez	1.00
46 Fred McGriff	1.50
47 Gary Sheffield	1.00
48 Adam Dunn	2.00
49 Joe Mays	1.00
50 Kenny Lofton	1.00
51 Josh Beckett	1.50
52 Bud Smith	1.00
53 Johnny Estrada	1.00
54 Charles Johnson	1.00
55 Craig Wilson	1.00
56 Terrence Long	1.00
57 Andy Pettitte	1.50
58 Brian Giles	1.50
59 Juan Pierre	1.00
60 Cliff Floyd	1.00
61 Ivan Rodriguez	2.00
62 Andruw Jones	2.00
63 Lance Berkman	1.50
64 Mark Buehrle	1.00
65 Miguel Tejada	1.50
66 Wade Miller	1.00
67 Johnny Estrada	1.00
68 Tsuyoshi Shinjo	1.00
69 Scott Rolen	2.50
70 Roberto Alomar	2.00
71 Mark Grace	2.00
72 Larry Walker	1.50
73 Jim Edmonds	1.50
74 Jeff Kent	1.50
75 Frank Thomas	2.50
76 Carlos Beltran	1.50
77 Barry Zito	1.50
78 Alex Rodriguez	8.00
79 Troy Glaus	1.50
80 Ryan Klesko	1.00
81 Tom Glavine	1.50
82 Ben Sheets	1.50
83 Manny Ramirez	2.50
84 Shannon Stewart	1.00
85 Vladimir Guerrero	4.00
86 Chipper Jones	3.00
87 Jeff Bagwell	2.50
88 Richie Sexson	1.50
89 Sean Casey	1.50
90 Tim Hudson	1.50
91 J.D. Drew	1.50
92 Ivan Rodriguez	2.00
93 Magglio Ordonez	1.50
94 John Buck	1.00
95 Paul LoDuca	1.00

Tools of Trade G-U

	NM/M
Common Player:	5.00
Jerseys #'d to 300.	
Bats #'d to 250.	
Shoes #'d to 150.	
Shin Guard #'d to 150.	
Glove #'d to 125.	
Mask #'d to 100.	
Hat #'d to 50.	
Doubles #'d to 200.	
Triples #'d to 75.	
Quads #'d to 50.	
1 Mike Mussina/Jsy	10.00
2 Rickey Henderson/ Jsy	10.00
3 Raul Mondesi/Jsy	8.00
4 Nomar Garciaparra/Jsy	15.00
5 Randy Johnson/Jsy	10.00
6 Roger Clemens/Jsy	15.00
7 Shawn Green/Jsy	8.00
8 Todd Helton/Jsy	8.00
9 Aramis Ramirez/Jsy	8.00
10 Barry Larkin/Jsy	10.00
11 Byung-Hyun Kim/Jsy	5.00
12 C.C. Sabathia/Jsy	5.00
13 Curt Schilling/Jsy	10.00
14 Darin Erstad/Jsy	5.00
15 Eric Karros/Jsy	5.00
16 Freddy Garcia/Jsy	5.00
17 Greg Maddux/Jsy	15.00
18 Jason Kendall/Jsy	5.00
19 Jim Thome/Jsy	10.00
20 Juan Gonzalez/Jsy	8.00
21 Kazuhiro Sasaki/Jsy	5.00
22 Kerry Wood/Jsy	10.00
23 Luis Gonzalez/Jsy	8.00
24 Mark Mulder/Jsy	8.00
25 Rich Aurilia/Jsy	5.00
26 Ray Durham/Jsy	5.00

27 Ben Grieve/Jsy	5.00
28 Bret Boone/Jsy	5.00
29 Edgar Martinez/Jsy	8.00
30 Ivan Rodriguez/Jsy	10.00
31 Jorge Posada/Jsy	10.00
32 Mike Piazza/Jsy	15.00
33 Pat Burrell/Bat	8.00
34 Robin Ventura/Bat	5.00
35 Trot Nixon/Bat	8.00
36 Adrian Beltre/Bat	5.00
37 Bernie Williams/Bat	10.00
38 Bobby Abreu/Bat	8.00
39 Carlos Delgado/Bat	8.00
40 Craig Biggio/Bat	8.00
41 Garret Anderson/Bat	8.00
42 Jermaine Dye/Bat	5.00
43 Johnny Damon/Bat	8.00
44 Tim Salmon/Bat	8.00
45 Tino Martinez/Bat	10.00
46 Fred McGriff/Bat	8.00
47 Gary Sheffield/Bat	5.00
48 Adam Dunn/Shoe	15.00
49 Joe Mays/Shoe	8.00
50 Kenny Lofton/Shoe	10.00
51 Josh Beckett/Shoe	10.00
52 Bud Smith/Shoe	5.00
53 Johnny Estrada/Shin	10.00
54 Charles Johnson/Shin	8.00
55 Craig Wilson/Shin	15.00
56 Terrence Long/Shin	8.00
57 Andy Pettitte/Glove	15.00
58 Brian Giles/Glove	10.00
59 Juan Pierre/Glove	10.00
60 Cliff Floyd/Glove	10.00
61 Ivan Rodriguez/Glove	15.00
62 Andruw Jones/Hat	15.00
63 Lance Berkman/Hat	15.00
64 Mark Buehrle/Hat	15.00
65 Miguel Tejada/Hat	15.00
66 Wade Miller/Hat	10.00
67 Johnny Estrada/Shin	10.00
68 T. Shinjo/Bat/Shoe	15.00
69 S. Rolen/Bat/Jsy	20.00
70 R. Alomar/Bat/Shoe	20.00
71 M. Grace/Glv/Jsy	15.00
72 L. Walker/Jsy/Bat	10.00
73 J. Edmonds/Jsy/Bat	15.00
74 J. Kent/Jsy/Bat	10.00
75 F. Thomas/Jsy/Bat	15.00
76 C. Beltran/Jsy/Bat	15.00
77 B. Zito/Shoe/Jsy	15.00
78 A. Rodriguez/Jsy/Bat	25.00
79 T. Glaus/Dualjsy	15.00
80 R. Klesko/Bat/Glv	10.00
81 T. Glavine/Jsy/Shoe	20.00
82 B. Sheets/Bat/Jsy	10.00
83 M. Ramirez/ Shoe/Glv/Jsy	25.00
84 S. Stewart/Hat/ Jsy/Bat	15.00
85 V. Guerrero/Glv/ Bat/Jsy	45.00
86 C. Jones/Glv/Bat/Jsy	40.00
87 J. Bagwell/Jsy/ Hat/Bat	40.00
88 R. Sexson/Bat/ Jsy/Glv/Shoe	40.00
89 S. Casey/Jsy/Hat/ Shoe/Bat	30.00
90 T Hudson/Shoe/ Hat/Glv/Jsy	30.00
91 JD Drew/Shoe/ Jsy/Hat/Bat	40.00
92 I Rodriguez/Jsy/ Mask/Chst/Glv	60.00
93 M Ordonez/Hat/ Glv/Jsy/Shoe	40.00
94 J Buck/Glv/Chst/ Shin/Msk	20.00
95 P LoDuca/Jsy/ Chst/Shin/Msk	30.00

2002 Playoff Piece of the Game

	NM/M
Complete Set (100):	
Common Player:	.50
Common SP (51-100):	5.00
Production 500	
Pack (5):	15.00
Box (6):	75.00
1 Vladimir Guerrero	1.50

#	Player	Price
2	Troy Glaus	1.50
3	Ichiro Suzuki	2.50
4	Chipper Jones	2.00
5	Roberto Alomar	.75
6	Scott Rolen	1.25
7	Randy Johnson	1.50
8	Roger Clemens	2.25
9	Nomar Garciaparra	2.50
10	Greg Maddux	2.00
11	Barry Bonds	4.00
12	Derek Jeter	4.00
13	Albert Pujols	3.00
14	Kerry Wood	1.25
15	Jim Thome	1.50
16	Manny Ramirez	1.50
17	Carlos Delgado	.75
18	Magglio Ordonez	.50
19	Torii Hunter	.50
20	Garret Anderson	.50
21	Eric Chavez	.60
22	Rafael Palmeiro	1.25
23	Andruw Jones	1.50
24	Cliff Floyd	.50
25	Sammy Sosa	2.50
26	Mike Mussina	.60
27	Jeff Bagwell	1.50
28	Miguel Tejada	.60
29	Curt Schilling	1.00
30	Tom Glavine	.75
31	Frank Thomas	1.50
32	Jim Edmonds	.50
33	Juan Gonzalez	1.50
34	Todd Helton	1.50
35	Shawn Green	.75
36	Alfonso Soriano	1.25
37	Lance Berkman	.50
38	Barry Zito	.60
39	Ryan Klesko	.50
40	Larry Walker	.50
41	Craig Biggio	.50
42	Luis Gonzalez	.50
43	Ivan Rodriguez	1.25
44	J.D. Drew	.75
45	Roy Oswalt	.50
46	Jason Giambi	1.25
47	Brian Giles	.50
48	Richie Sexson	.50
49	Pat Burrell	.75
50	Alex Rodriguez	3.00
51	So Taguchi RC	8.00
52	Allan Simpson RC	5.00
53	Oliver Perez RC	10.00
54	Ben Howard RC	5.00
55	Kirk Saarloos RC	5.00
56	Francis Beltran RC	5.00
57	Jorge Padilla RC	5.00
58	Brandon Puffer RC	5.00
59	Brian Mallette RC	5.00
60	Kyle Kane RC	5.00
61	Travis Driskill RC	5.00
62	Jeremy Lambert RC	5.00
63	Steve Kent RC	5.00
64	Julius Matos RC	5.00
65	Julio Mateo RC	5.00
66	Kazuhisa Ishii RC	8.00
67	Franklyn German RC	5.00
68	John Foster RC	5.00
69	Luis Ugueto RC	5.00
70	Shawn Sedlacek RC	5.00
71	Earl Snyder RC	5.00
72	Alex Pelaez RC	5.00
73	Victor Alvarez RC	5.00
74	Tom Shearn RC	5.00
75	Corey Thurman RC	5.00
76	Eric Junge RC	5.00
77	Hansel Izquierdo RC	5.00
78	Elio Serrano RC	5.00
79	J.J. Trujillo RC	5.00
80	Chris Snelling RC	6.00
81	Satoru Komiyama RC	5.00
82	Brandon Backe RC	5.00
83	Anderson Machado RC	5.00
84	Doug DeVore RC	5.00
85	Steve Bechler RC	5.00
86	John Ennis RC	5.00
87	Rodrigo Rosario RC	5.00
88	Jorge Sosa RC	5.00
89	Ken Huckaby RC	5.00
90	Mike Moriarty RC	5.00
91	Michael Crudale RC	5.00
92	Kevin Frederick RC	5.00
93	Aaron Guiel RC	5.00
94	Jose Rodriguez RC	5.00
95	Andy Shibilo RC	5.00
96	Deivis Santos RC	5.00
97	Felix Escalona RC	5.00
98	Miguel Asencio RC	5.00
99	Takahito Nomura RC	5.00
100	Cam Esslinger RC	5.00

Materials

NM/M

Common Materials (1-90): 4.00
Team Connections (91-95):

Production 500
Superstar Combos (96-100):
Production 250
Bronze Materials (1-90): 1-2X
Production 250
Bronze Team Connect.
(91-95): 1.5-2X
Production 100
Bronze Combos (96-100): 2-3X
Production 50
Silver Materials (1-90): 1.5-2.5X
Production 150
Silver Tm. Connect.
(91-95): 1.5-3X
Production 50
Silver Combos
(96-100): No Pricing
Production 25
Gold Materials (1-90): 2-5X
Production 50
Gold Tm. Connect.
(91-95): No Pricing
Production 25
Gold Combos
(96-100): No Pricing
Production 10
Platinum Materials
(1-90): No Pricing
Production 25
Platinum Tm Connect.
(91-95): No Pricing
Production 10
Platinum Combos
(96-100): No Pricing
Production 5

#	Card	Price
1	Adam Dunn/Bat	8.00
2	Adrian Beltre/Bat	4.00
3	Albert Pujols/Base	10.00
4	Alex Rodriguez/Jsy	12.00
5	Alex Rodriguez/Bat	12.00
6	Andruw Jones/Jsy	5.00
7	Andruw Jones/Bat	5.00
8	Barry Bonds/Base	15.00
9	Barry Larkin/Bat	5.00
10	Juan Gonzalez/Jsy	5.00
11	Bernie Williams/Bat	6.00
12	Carlos Delgado/Jsy	5.00
13	Chipper Jones/Jsy	10.00
14	Chipper Jones/Bat	10.00
15	Craig Biggio/Jsy	5.00
16	Craig Biggio/Bat	5.00
17	Cristian Guzman/Jsy	5.00
18	Curt Schilling/Jsy	5.00
19	Derek Jeter/Base	15.00
20	Edgar Martinez/Jsy	5.00
21	Edgardo Alfonzo/Jsy	4.00
22	Ellis Burks/Jsy	4.00
23	Frank Thomas/Bat	6.00
24	Freddy Garcia/Jsy	4.00
25	Greg Maddux/Jsy	10.00
26	Harmon Killebrew/Pants	15.00
27	Hideo Nomo/Jsy	12.00
28	Ichiro Suzuki/bBase	15.00
29	Ivan Rodriguez/Jsy	8.00
30	Ivan Rodriguez/Bat	8.00
31	J.D. Drew/Bat	6.00
32	J.D. Drew/Jsy	6.00
33	Javy Lopez/Jsy	6.00
34	Jeff Bagwell/Jsy	6.00
35	Jim Edmonds/Jsy	6.00
36	Jim Edmonds/Bat	6.00
37	John Olerud/Bat	4.00
38	John Smoltz/Jsy	6.00
39	Jose Cruz Jr./Jsy	4.00
40	Jose Vidro/Jsy	4.00
41	Juan Gonzalez/Bat	6.00
42	Juan Pierre/Jsy	4.00
43	Ken Griffey Jr./Base	10.00
44	Kenny Lofton/Bat	4.00
45	Kerry Wood/Jsy	4.00
46	Kevin Brown/Jsy	4.00
47	Lance Berkman/Jsy	6.00
48	Lance Berkman/Bat	6.00
49	Larry Walker/Jsy	5.00
50	Luis Gonzalez/Jsy	5.00
51	Magglio Ordonez/Jsy	5.00
52	Magglio Ordonez/Bat	5.00
53	Manny Ramirez/Jsy	8.00
54	Manny Ramirez/Bat	5.00
55	Vladimir Guerrero/Jsy	8.00
56	Mark Grace/Bat	5.00
57	Michael Barrett/Jsy	4.00
58	Miguel Tejada/Jsy	8.00
59	Mike Piazza/Jsy	12.00
60	Mike Piazza/Bat	12.00
61	Mike Schmidt/Bat	15.00
62	Mike Sweeney/Jsy	4.00
63	Nolan Ryan/Jsy	30.00
64	Nomar Garciaparra/Jsy	15.00
65	Paul LoDuca/Jsy	4.00
66	Rafael Palmeiro/Jsy	8.00
67	Rafael Palmeiro/Bat	8.00
68	Jose Canseco/Bat	8.00
69	Raul Mondesi/Jsy	4.00
70	Reggie Jackson/Bat	8.00
71	Rickey Henderson/Bat	8.00
72	Roberto Alomar/Bat	6.00
73	Robin Ventura/Jsy	4.00
74	Rod Carew/Bat	10.00
75	Roger Clemens/Jsy	15.00
76	Sammy Sosa/Base	5.00
77	Sean Casey/Jsy	5.00
78	Shannon Stewart/Jsy	4.00
79	Shawn Green/Jsy	6.00
80	Shawn Green/Bat	6.00
81	Tim Hudson/Jsy	6.00
82	Todd Helton/Bat	6.00
83	Tom Glavine/Jsy	6.00
84	Tony Gwynn/Jsy	10.00
85	Tony Gwynn/Jsy	10.00
86	Tony Gwynn/Bat	10.00
87	Troy Glaus/Jsy	6.00
88	Tsuyoshi Shinjo/Bat	4.00
89	Vladimir Guerrero/Jsy	8.00
90	Vladimir Guerrero/Bat	8.00
91	Nomar Garciaparra, Pedro J. Martinez	30.00
92	Randy Johnson, Curt Schilling	15.00
93	Andruw Jones, Chipper Jones	15.00
94	Todd Helton, Larry Walker	15.00
95	Jeff Bagwell, Craig Biggio	15.00
96	Alex Rodriguez	25.00
97	Greg Maddux	25.00
98	Mike Piazza	25.00
99	Lance Berkman	15.00
100	Vladimir Guerrero	20.00

2003 Playoff Absolute Memorabilia

NM/M

Complete Set (200):
Common Player: .50
Common SP (151-200): 3.00
Production 1,500
Pack (6): 3.00
Box (18 + Glass Plaque): 85.00

#	Player	Price
1	Nomar Garciaparra	2.50
2	Barry Bonds	4.00
3	Greg Maddux	2.00
4	Roger Clemens	3.00
5	Derek Jeter	3.00
6	Alex Rodriguez	3.00
7	Chipper Jones	2.00
8	Sammy Sosa	2.50
9	Alfonso Soriano	1.00
10	Albert Pujols	3.00
11	Adam Dunn	1.00
12	Tom Glavine	.75
13	Pedro J. Martinez	1.50
14	Jim Thome	1.00
15	Hideo Nomo	1.50
16	Roberto Alomar	.75
17	Barry Zito	.65
18	Troy Glaus	1.50
19	Kerry Wood	1.00
20	Magglio Ordonez	.50
21	Todd Helton	1.50
22	Craig Biggio	.50
23	Roy Oswalt	.50
24	Torii Hunter	.50
25	Miguel Tejada	.65
26	Tsuyoshi Shinjo	.50
27	Scott Rolen	1.00
28	Rafael Palmeiro	1.00
29	Victor Martinez	.75
30	Hank Blalock	.75
31	Jason Lane	.50
32	Junior Spivey	.50
33	Gary Sheffield	.75
34	Corey Patterson	.50
35	Corky Miller	.50
36	Brian Tallet	.50
37	Cliff Lee	.50
38	Jason Jennings	.50
39	Kirk Saarloos	.50
40	Wade Miller	.50
41	Angel Berroa	.50
42	Mike Sweeney	.50
43	Paul LoDuca	.50
44	A.J. Pierzynski	.50
45	Drew Henson	.50
46	Eric Chavez	.65
47	Tim Hudson	.75
48	Aramis Ramirez	.50
49	Jack Wilson	.50
50	Ryan Klesko	.50
51	Antonio Perez	.50
52	Dewon Brazelton	.50
53	Mark Teixeira	.75
54	Eric Hinske	.50
55	Freddy Sanchez	.50
56	Mike Rivera	.50
57	Alfredo Amezaga	.50
58	Cliff Floyd	.50
59	Brandon Larson	.50
60	Richard Hidalgo	.50
61	Cesar Izturis	.50
62	Richie Sexson	.50
63	Michael Cuddyer	.50
64	Javier Vazquez	.50
65	Brandon Claussen	.50
66	Carlos Rivera	.50
67	Vernon Wells	.50
68	Kenny Lofton	.50
69	Aubrey Huff	.50
70	Adam LaRoche	.50
71	Jeff Baker	.50
72	Jose Castillo	.50
73	Joe Borchard	.50
74	Walter Young	.50
75	Jose Morban	.50
76	Vinnie Chulk	.50
77	Christian Parker	.50
78	Mike Piazza	2.50
79	Ichiro Suzuki	2.50
80	Kazuhisa Ishii	1.50
81	Rickey Henderson	1.50
82	Ken Griffey Jr.	2.50
83	Jason Giambi	.75
84	Randy Johnson	1.50
85	Curt Schilling	.75
86	Manny Ramirez	1.50
87	Barry Larkin	1.50
88	Jeff Bagwell	1.50
89	Vladimir Guerrero	1.50
90	Mike Mussina	.65
91	Juan Gonzalez	1.50
92	Andruw Jones	1.50
93	Frank Thomas	1.50
94	Sean Casey	.50
95	Josh Beckett	.50
96	Lance Berkman	.50
97	Shawn Green	.75
98	Bernie Williams	.65
99	Pat Burrell	.75
100	Edgar Martinez	.50
101	Ivan Rodriguez	1.00
102	Jeremy Guthrie	.50
103	Alexis Rios	.50
104	Nic Jackson	.50
105	Jason Anderson	.50
106	Travis Chapman	.50
107	Mac Suzuki	.50
108	Toby Hall	.50
109	Mark Prior	1.50
110	So Taguchi	.50
111	Marlon Byrd	.50
112	Garret Anderson	.50
113	Luis Gonzalez	.50
114	Jay Gibbons	.50
115	Mark Buehrle	.50
116	Wily Mo Pena	.50
117	C.C. Sabathia	.50
118	Ricardo Rodriguez	.50
119	Robert Fick	.50
120	Rodrigo Rosario	.50
121	Alexis Gomez	.50
122	Carlos Beltran	1.00
123	Joe Thurston	.50
124	Ben Sheets	.50
125	Jose Vidro	.50
126	Nick Johnson	.50
127	Mark Mulder	.50

128	Bobby Abreu	.50
129	Brian Giles	.50
130	Brian Lawrence	.50
131	Jeff Kent	.50
132	Chris Snelling	.50
133	Kevin Mench	.50
134	Carlos Delgado	.75
135	Orlando Hudson	.50
136	Juan Cruz	.50
137	Jim Edmonds	.50
138	Geronimo Gil	.50
139	Joe Crede	.50
140	Wilson Valdez	.50
141	Runelvys Hernandez	.50
142	Nick Neugebauer	.50
143	Takahito Nomura	.50
144	Andres Galarraga	.50
145	Mark Grace	.65
146	Brandon Duckworth	.50
147	Oliver Perez	.50
148	Xavier Nady	.50
149	Rafael Soriano	.50
150	Ben Kozlowski	.50
151	Prentice Redman RC	3.00
152	Craig Brazell RC	5.00
153	Nook Logan RC	4.00
154	Greg Aquino RC	3.00
155	Matt Kata RC	5.00
156	Ian Ferguson RC	3.00
157	Chien-Ming Wang RC	30.00
158	Beau Kemp RC	3.00
159	Alejandro Machado RC	3.00
160	Michael Hessman RC	3.00
161	Francisco Rosario RC	4.00
162	Pedro Liriano RC	3.00
163	Richard Fischer RC	3.00
164	Franklin Perez RC	3.00
165	Oscar Villarreal RC	3.00
166	Arnie Munoz RC	3.00
167	Tim Olson RC	4.00
168	Jose Contreras RC	5.00
169	Francisco Cruceta RC	4.00
170	Jeremy Bonderman	10.00
171	Jeremy Griffiths	3.00
172	John Webb	3.00
173	Phil Seibel RC	3.00
174	Aaron Looper RC	4.00
175	Brian Stokes RC	3.00
176	Guillermo Quiroz RC	4.00
177	Fernando Cabrera RC	3.00
178	Josh Hall RC	3.00
179	Diegomar Markwell RC	3.00
180	Andrew Brown RC	3.00
181	Doug Waechter RC	4.00
182	Felix Sanchez RC	3.00
183	Gerardo Garcia	3.00
184	Matt Bruback RC	3.00
185	Michel Hernandez RC	3.00
186	Rett Johnson RC	3.00
187	Ryan Cameron RC	3.00
188	Rob Hammock RC	4.00
189	Clint Barmes RC	10.00
190	Brandon Webb RC	10.00
191	Jon Leicester RC	3.00
192	Shane Bazzell RC	4.00
193	Joe Valentine RC	4.00
194	Josh Stewart RC	4.00
195	Pete LaForest RC	3.00
196	Shane Victorino RC	4.00
197	Terrmel Sledge RC	3.00
198	Lew Ford RC	5.00
199	Todd Wellemeyer RC	4.00
200	Hideki Matsui RC	10.00

Spectrum

Stars (1-150): 3-5X
Rookies (151-200): .75-2X
Production 100 Sets

Spectrum Signatures

NM/M
Common Autograph: 6.00
Varying quantities produced

10	Albert Pujols/10	275.00
16	Roberto Alomar/15	100.00
17	Barry Zito/25	50.00
20	Magglio Ordonez/25	50.00
23	Roy Oswalt/25	30.00
24	Torii Hunter/25	40.00
29	Victor Martinez/100	30.00
30	Hank Blalock/50	30.00
32	Junior Spivey/50	15.00
34	Corey Patterson/50	20.00
35	Corky Miller/100	6.00
36	Brian Tallet/100	6.00
37	Cliff Lee/100	8.00
38	Jason Jennings/100	8.00
39	Kirk Saarloos/100	6.00
40	Wade Miller/100	15.00
41	Angel Berroa/100	10.00
42	Mike Sweeney/50	15.00
43	Paul LoDuca/50	20.00
44	A.J. Pierzynski/100	15.00
45	Drew Henson/50	25.00
47	Tim Hudson/50	40.00
51	Antonio Perez/25	8.00
52	Dewon Brazelton/50	15.00
53	Mark Teixeira/50	40.00
54	Eric Hinske/100	15.00
55	Freddy Sanchez/100	15.00
57	Alfredo Amezaga/100	10.00
59	Brandon Larson/100	8.00
60	Richard Hidalgo/100	8.00
62	Richie Sexson/25	30.00
63	Michael Cuddyer/100	15.00
68	Kenny Lofton/50	30.00
69	Aubrey Huff/100	15.00
70	Adam LaRoche/100	15.00
71	Jeff Baker/100	10.00
72	Jose Castillo/100	10.00
73	Joe Borchard/100	10.00
74	Walter Young/100	8.00
76	Vinnie Chulk/100	8.00
80	Kazuhisa Ishii/25	60.00
87	Barry Larkin/50	50.00
89	Vladimir Guerrero/50	50.00
92	Andruw Jones/25	60.00
95	Josh Beckett/100	25.00
100	Edgar Martinez/50	25.00
102	Jeremy Guthrie/100	15.00
103	Alexis Rios/100	20.00
104	Nic Jackson/100	8.00
105	Jason Anderson/100	8.00
106	Travis Chapman/100	8.00
107	Mac Suzuki/304	15.00
109	Mark Prior/50	30.00
111	Marlon Byrd/100	10.00
114	Jay Gibbons/100	10.00
118	Ricardo Rodriguez/100	10.00
119	Robert Fick/100	10.00
120	Rodrigo Rosario/250	8.00
121	Alexis Gomez/100	10.00
124	Ben Sheets/50	20.00
126	Nick Johnson/50	10.00
127	Mark Mulder/50	40.00
132	Chris Snelling/100	8.00
133	Kevin Mench/100	10.00
135	Orlando Hudson/50	15.00
139	Joe Crede/100	10.00
140	Wilson Valdez/25	10.00
141	Runelvys Hernandez/100	10.00
143	Takahito Nomura/47	15.00
147	Oliver Perez/250	8.00
148	Xavier Nady/100	12.00
150	Ben Kozlowski/100	8.00
151	Prentice Redman/250	10.00
152	Craig Brazell/250	10.00
153	Nook Logan/250	6.00
154	Greg Aquino/250	8.00
155	Matt Kata/250	15.00
156	Ian Ferguson/250	6.00
157	Chien-Ming Wang/250	200.00
158	Beau Kemp/250	6.00
159	Alejandro Machado/250	6.00
160	Michael Hessman/160	6.00
161	Francisco Rosario/250	6.00
162	Pedro Liriano/250	6.00
163	Richard Fischer/250	6.00
164	Franklin Perez/250	6.00
165	Oscar Villarreal/250	10.00
166	Arnie Munoz/250	6.00
167	Tim Olson/250	8.00
168	Jose Contreras/250	25.00
169	Francisco Cruceta/250	8.00
170	Jeremy Bonderman/250	40.00
171	Jeremy Griffiths/250	8.00
172	John Webb/250	6.00
173	Phil Seibel/250	6.00
174	Aaron Looper/250	6.00
175	Brian Stokes/250	6.00
176	Guillermo Quiroz/250	8.00

177	Fernando Cabrera/250	10.00
178	Josh Hall/250	10.00
179	Diegomar Markwell/250	6.00
180	Andrew Brown/250	8.00
181	Doug Waechter/250	8.00
182	Felix Sanchez/250	8.00
183	Gerardo Garcia/250	8.00
184	Matt Bruback/250	6.00
185	Michel Hernandez/250	6.00
186	Rett Johnson/250	10.00
187	Ryan Cameron/250	6.00
188	Rob Hammock/250	15.00
189	Clint Barmes/250	15.00
190	Brandon Webb/250	25.00
191	Jon Leicester/250	6.00
192	Shane Bazzell/250	10.00
193	Joe Valentine/250	8.00
194	Josh Stewart/250	15.00
195	Pete LaForest/250	8.00
196	Shane Victorino/250	8.00
197	Terrmel Sledge/250	6.00
198	Lew Ford/250	15.00
199	Todd Wellemeyer/250	10.00

Absolutely Ink

NM/M
Inserted 1:552
Blues: No Pricing
Production 10-25
Golds: No Pricing
Production 5-10

1	Vladimir Guerrero	50.00
6	Eric Hinske	15.00
8	Jose Vidro	8.00
16	Rodrigo Rosario	8.00
17	Brandon Claussen	20.00
18	Jermaine Dye	8.00
22	Mark Prior	50.00
24	Brian Lawrence	8.00
29	Barry Larkin	50.00
30	Drew Henson	40.00
36	Mark Teixeira	30.00
38	Roberto Alomar	30.00
39	Barry Zito	35.00

Glass Plaques

NM/M
One Per Box:

Roberto Alomar/Bat/Jsy/100	40.00
Roberto Alomar/Jsy/150	30.00
Jeff Bagwell/Bat/Jsy/100	40.00
Jeff Bagwell/Jsy/150	30.00
Ernie Banks/Jsy/150	40.00
Lance Berkman/Bat/Jsy/100	35.00
Lance Berkman/Jsy/150	25.00
Barry Bonds/Ball/Base/50	85.00
Barry Bonds/Ball/Base/100	75.00
Barry Bonds/Base/200	50.00
George Brett/Bat/Jsy/50	125.00
George Brett/Jsy/200	50.00
Pat Burrell/Bat/Jsy/100	35.00
Pat Burrell/Jsy/150	30.00
Steve Carlton/Auto./50	60.00
Steve Carlton/Bat/Jsy/100	40.00
Steve Carlton/Jsy/150	30.00
Roger Clemens/Glv/Jsy/50	150.00
Roger Clemens/Jsy/150	60.00
Roger Clemens/Glv/Jsy/50	150.00
Roger Clemens/Jsy/200	60.00
Roberto Clemente/Bat/Jsy/150	80.00
Roberto Clemente/Jsy/200	60.00
Jose Contreras/Jsy/Jsy/100	30.00
Jose Contreras/Jsy/150	25.00
Adam Dunn/Bat/Jsy/100	40.00
Adam Dunn/Jsy/150	30.00
Bob Feller/Auto./50	65.00
Bob Feller/Jsy/50	50.00
Bob Feller/Jsy/100	30.00

Nomar Garciaparra/Bat/Jsy/100	65.00
Nomar Garciaparra/Jsy/200	55.00
Jason Giambi/Bat/Jsy/100	50.00
Jason Giambi/Jsy/150	40.00
Troy Glaus/Bat/Jsy/100	40.00
Troy Glaus/Jsy/150	35.00
Juan Gonzalez/Bat/Jsy/100	40.00
Juan Gonzalez/Jsy/150	30.00
Luis Gonzalez/Bat/Jsy/100	30.00
Luis Gonzalez/Jsy/150	25.00
Mark Grace/Auto./50	100.00
Mark Grace/Bat/Jsy/100	45.00
Mark Grace/Jsy/150	35.00
Shawn Green/Bat/Jsy/100	30.00
Shawn Green/Jsy/150	25.00
Ken Griffey Jr./Ball/Base/100	50.00
Ken Griffey Jr./Base/200	40.00
Vladimir Guerrero/Bat/Jsy/100	40.00
Vladimir Guerrero/Jsy/150	35.00
Tony Gwynn/Bat/Jsy/150	50.00
Tony Gwynn/Jsy/Jsy/200	40.00
Todd Helton/Bat/Jsy/100	40.00
Todd Helton/Jsy/Jsy/150	30.00
Rickey Henderson/Bat/Jsy/100	50.00
Rickey Henderson/Jsy/200	40.00
Tim Hudson/Auto./50	65.00
Tim Hudson/Hat/Jsy/100	40.00
Tim Hudson/Jsy/150	25.00
Torii Hunter/Auto./50	65.00
Torii Hunter/Hat/Jsy/100	40.00
Torii Hunter/Jsy/150	30.00
Kazuhisa Ishii/Bat/Jsy/100	30.00
Kazuhisa Ishii/Jsy/200	25.00
Derek Jeter/Ball/Base/150	60.00
Derek Jeter/Base/200	50.00
Randy Johnson/Bat/Jsy/100	50.00
Randy Johnson/Jsy/150	40.00
Andruw Jones/Bat/Jsy/100	35.00
Andruw Jones/Jsy/150	30.00
Chipper Jones/Bat/Jsy/100	40.00
Chipper Jones/Jsy/150	30.00
Al Kaline/Bat/Jsy/100	40.00
Al Kaline/Jsy/150	35.00
Barry Larkin/Auto./50	60.00
Barry Larkin/Bat/Jsy/100	40.00
Barry Larkin/Jsy/150	30.00
Greg Maddux/Bat/Jsy/100	50.00
Greg Maddux/Jsy/200	40.00
Pedro Martinez/Bat/Jsy/100	40.00
Pedro Martinez/Jsy/150	35.00
Hideki Matsui/Ball/Base/50	110.00
Hideki Matsui/Ball/Base/150	75.00
Hideki Matsui/Base/200	55.00
Don Mattingly/Bat/Jsy/100	65.00
Don Mattingly/Jsy/200	50.00
Mark Mulder/Auto./50	60.00
Mark Mulder/Auto./Jsy/25	
Mark Mulder/Jsy/150	25.00

Mark Mulder/ Jsy/Jsy/100	30.00
Stan Musial/ Bat/Jsy/150	65.00
Stan Musial/Jsy/200	60.00
Hideo Nomo/ Bat/Jsy/50	60.00
Hideo Nomo/ Bat/Jsy/100	40.00
Hideo Nomo/Jsy/200	30.00
Magglio Ordonez/ Auto./50	50.00
Magglio Ordonez/ Auto./Jsy/25	
Magglio Ordonez/ Bat/Jsy/100	30.00
Magglio Ordonez/ Jsy/150	25.00
Roy Oswalt/Auto./50	50.00
Roy Oswalt/Bat/ Jsy/100	
Roy Oswalt/Jsy/150	25.00
Rafael Palmeiro/ Bat/Jsy/100	40.00
Rafael Palmeiro/ Jsy/150	30.00
Mike Piazza/ Bat/Jsy/50	75.00
Mike Piazza/ Bat/Jsy/100	50.00
Mike Piazza/Jsy/200	40.00
Mark Prior/ Bat/Jsy/100	60.00
Mark Prior/Jsy/150	40.00
Albert Pujols/ Bat/Jsy/150	75.00
Albert Pujols/Jsy/150	60.00
Manny Ramirez/ Bat/Jsy/100	40.00
Manny Ramirez/ Jsy/150	30.00
Cal Ripken Jr./ Bat/Jsy/100	90.00
Cal Ripken Jr./ Jsy/200	70.00
Frank Robinson/ Auto./50	65.00
Frank Robinson/ Bat/Jsy/100	40.00
Frank Robinson/ Jsy/150	30.00
Alex Rodriguez/ Bat/Jsy/100	50.00
Alex Rodriguez/ Jsy/200	40.00
Nolan Ryan/ Jkt/Jsy/150	90.00
Nolan Ryan/Jsy/200	75.00
Nolan Ryan/ Jsy/Jsy/100	100.00
Ryne Sandberg/ Bat/Jsy/100	100.00
Ryne Sandberg/ Jsy/200	65.00
Curt Schilling/ Glv/Jsy/50	50.00
Curt Schilling/ Jsy/150	30.00
Mike Schmidt/ Bat/Jsy/100	70.00
Mike Schmidt/ Jsy/200	50.00
Ozzie Smith/ Bat/Jsy/150	65.00
Ozzie Smith/Jsy/150	50.00
Alfonso Soriano/ Bat/Jsy/150	60.00
Alfonso Soriano/ Jsy/150	50.00
Sammy Sosa/ Jsy/150	50.00
Sammy Sosa/ Jsy/200	40.00
Junior Spivey/ Auto./50	50.00
Junior Spivey/ Bat/Jsy/100	30.00
Junior Spivey/ Jsy/150	25.00
Ichiro Suzuki/ Ball/Base/50	80.00
Ichiro Suzuki/ Ball/Base/100	60.00
Ichiro Suzuki/ Base/200	40.00
Mark Teixeira/ Bat/Jsy/100	40.00
Mark Teixeira/ Jsy/150	30.00
Miguel Tejada/ Auto./50	60.00
Miguel Tejada/ Bat/Jsy/100	40.00

Miguel Tejada/ Jsy/150	30.00
Frank Thomas/ Bat/Jsy/100	40.00
Frank Thomas/ Jsy/150	30.00
Bernie Williams/ Bat/Jsy/100	40.00
Bernie Williams/ Jsy/150	35.00
Kerry Wood/Auto./50	80.00
Kerry Wood/ Bat/Jsy/100	45.00
Kerry Wood/Jsy/150	35.00
Barry Zito/Auto./50	75.00
Barry Zito/ Hat/Jsy/100	40.00
Barry Zito/Jsy/150	30.00

Player's Collection - Jersey

	NM/M
Common Player:	4.00
Production 75 Sets	
1 Adam Dunn	6.00
2 Adrian Beltre	4.00
3 Alex Rodriguez	15.00
4 Alfonso Soriano	12.00
5 Andruw Jones	8.00
6 Andy Pettitte	6.00
7 Barry Larkin	6.00
8 Barry Zito	6.00
9 Ben Grieve	4.00
10 Bernie Williams	8.00
11 Cal Ripken Jr.	40.00
12 Carlos Delgado	6.00
13 C.C. Sabathia	4.00
14 Chipper Jones	10.00
15 Craig Biggio	4.00
16 Curt Schilling	6.00
17 Alex Rodriguez	15.00
18 Frank Thomas	8.00
19 Freddy Garcia	4.00
20 Jay Bell	4.00
21 Roger Clemens	15.00
22 Tony Gwynn	10.00
23 Ivan Rodriguez	8.00
24 Jason Giambi	8.00
25 Jason Jennings	4.00
26 Jay Payton	4.00
27 J.D. Drew	5.00
28 Jeff Bagwell	8.00
29 Jeromy Burnitz	4.00
30 Jim Edmonds	6.00
31 Jim Thome	8.00
32 Joe Borchard	4.00
33 Joe Mays	4.00
34 John Olerud	5.00
35 David Wells	4.00
36 Juan Gonzalez	8.00
37 Kazuhiro Sasaki	4.00
38 Chan Ho Park	4.00
39 Kerry Wood	10.00
40 Kevin Brown	4.00
41 Lance Berkman	6.00
42 Larry Walker	4.00
43 Bret Boone	6.00
44 Magglio Ordonez	6.00
45 Manny Ramirez	8.00
46 Mark Mulder	6.00
47 Mark Prior	10.00
48 Matt Williams	4.00
49 Miguel Tejada	5.00
50 Mike Piazza	12.00
51 Nomar Garciaparra	15.00
52 Doug Davis	4.00
53 Paul Konerko	4.00
54 Paul LoDuca	4.00
55 Pedro J. Martinez	10.00
56 Preston Wilson	4.00
57	4.00
58 Marlon Byrd	4.00

59 Reggie Sanders	4.00
60 Richie Sexson	6.00
61	4.00
62 Rickey Henderson	8.00
63 Robert Person	4.00
64	4.00
65 Roger Clemens	15.00
66 Roy Oswalt	6.00
67 Ryan Klesko	4.00
68 Sammy Sosa	15.00
69 Shawn Green	6.00
70 Steve Finley	4.00
71 Terrence Long	4.00
72 Tim Hudson	6.00
73 Toby Hall	4.00
74 Todd Helton	8.00
75 Travis Lee	4.00
76 Troy Glaus	8.00
77 Tsuyoshi Shinjo	4.00
78 Vernon Wells	6.00
79 Vladimir Guerrero	8.00
80 Wes Helms	4.00

Player's Collection - Bat

	NM/M
Common Player:	4.00
Production 75 Sets	
81 Alex Rodriguez	15.00
82 Alfonso Soriano	12.00
83 Barry Larkin	8.00
84 Roberto Alomar	8.00
85 Ivan Rodriguez	8.00
86 Jason Giambi	8.00
87 Jeff Bagwell	8.00
88 Juan Gonzalez	8.00
89 Larry Walker	4.00
90 Luis Gonzalez	4.00
91 Magglio Ordonez	6.00
92 Manny Ramirez	8.00
93 Marlon Byrd	4.00
94 Mike Piazza	12.00
95 Pat Burrell	8.00
96 Todd Helton	8.00
97 Rickey Henderson	8.00
98 Andruw Jones	8.00
99 Craig Biggio	4.00
100 Mark Prior	10.00

Rookie Materials Jersey Number

	NM/M
Many not priced due to scarcity.	
1 Stan Musial/6	
2 Yogi Berra/35	40.00
3 Vladimir Guerrero/27	35.00
4 Randy Johnson/51	25.00
5 Andruw Jones/25	25.00
6 Jeff Kent/11	
7 Nomar Garciaparra/5	
8 Hideo Nomo/16	
9 Ivan Rodriguez/7	
10 Alfonso Soriano/33	35.00
11 Scott Rolen/17	
12 Juan Gonzalez/19	
13 Rafael Palmeiro/25	20.00
14 Mike Schmidt/20	
15 Cal Ripken Jr./8	

Materials Season

	NM/M
Common Player:	5.00
Quantity produced listed	
1 Stan Musial/42	75.00
2 Yogi Berra/47	40.00
3 Vladimir Guerrero/97	15.00
4 Randy Johnson/89	20.00
5 Andruw Jones/96	10.00
6 Jeff Kent/92	5.00
7 Hideo Nomo/95	20.00
9 Ivan Rodriguez/91	10.00
10 Alfonso Soriano/101	20.00
11 Scott Rolen/96	15.00
12 Juan Gonzalez/89	15.00
13 Rafael Palmeiro/86	15.00
14 Mike Schmidt/73	60.00
15 Cal Ripken Jr./82	75.00

Team Tandems

	NM/M
Common Duo:	2.00
Inserted 1:48	
Spectrums:	1-2X
Production 100 Sets	
1 Mark Prior, Sammy Sosa	5.00
2 Vladimir Guerrero, Jose Vidro	3.00
3 Bernie Williams, Alfonso Soriano	6.00
4 Mike Sweeney, Carlos Beltran	2.00
5 Magglio Ordonez, Paul Konerko	2.00

6 Adam Dunn, Austin Kearns	3.00
7 Randy Johnson, Curt Schilling	4.00
8 Hideo Nomo, Kazuhisa Ishii	2.00
9 Pat Burrell, Bobby Abreu	3.00
10 Todd Helton, Larry Walker	2.00

Team Tandems Material

	NM/M
Common Duo:	
Quantity produced listed	
Spectrums:	No Pricing
Production 25 or 10	
1 Mark Prior, Sammy Sosa/100	30.00
2 Vladimir Guerrero, Jose Vidro/100	10.00
3 Bernie Williams, Alfonso Soriano/100	20.00
4 Mike Sweeney, Carlos Beltran/100	6.00
5 Magglio Ordonez, Paul Konerko/100	6.00
6 Adam Dunn, Austin Kearns/100	15.00
7 Randy Johnson, Curt Schilling/100	15.00
8 Hideo Nomo, Kazuhisa Ishii/40	50.00
9 Pat Burrell, Bobby Abreu/40	20.00
10 Todd Helton, Larry Walker/100	8.00

Team Trios

	NM/M
Common Trio:	5.00
Inserted 1:88	
Spectrums:	1-2X
Production 50 Sets	
1 Greg Maddux, Chipper Jones, Andruw Jones	8.00
2 Sammy Sosa, Mark Prior, Kerry Wood	8.00
3 Pedro Martinez, Nomar Garciaparra, Manny Ramirez	8.00
4 Jason Giambi, Roger Clemens, Alfonso Soriano	8.00
5 Alex Rodriguez, Rafael Palmeiro, Mark Teixeira	8.00
6 Mike Piazza, Roberto Alomar, Tsuyoshi Shinjo	6.00
7 Jeff Bagwell, Craig Biggio, Lance Berkman	5.00
8 Troy Glaus, Garret Anderson, Troy Percival	5.00
9 Miguel Tejada, Eric Chavez, Barry Zito	5.00
10 Luis Gonzalez, Randy Johnson, Curt Schilling	6.00

Team Trios Materials

	NM/M
Quantity produced listed	5.00
Spectrums:	No Pricing
Production 10 or 25	
1 Greg Maddux, Chipper Jones, Andruw Jones/100	30.00

2	Sammy Sosa, Mark Prior, Kerry Wood/100	30.00
3	Pedro Martinez, Nomar Garciaparra, Manny Ramirez/50	50.00
4	Jason Giambi, Roger Clemens, Alfonso Soriano/100	40.00
5	Alex Rodriguez, Rafael Palmeiro, Mark Teixeira/100	25.00
6	Mike Piazza, Roberto Alomar, Tsuyoshi Shinjo/40	40.00
7	Jeff Bagwell, Craig Biggio, Lance Berkman/100	20.00
8	Troy Glaus, Garret Anderson, Troy Percival/40	25.00
9	Miguel Tejada, Eric Chavez, Barry Zito/100	20.00
10	Luis Gonzalez, Randy Johnson, Curt Schilling/100	25.00

Tools of the Trade

		NM/M
Complete Set (110):		125.00
Common Player:		1.00
Inserted 1:5		
1	Sammy Sosa	4.00
2	Nomar Garciaparra	5.00
3	Andruw Jones	1.50
4	Troy Glaus	1.00
5	Greg Maddux	4.00
6	Rickey Henderson	1.00
7	Alex Rodriguez	6.00
8	Manny Ramirez	1.50
9	Lance Berkman	1.00
10	Roger Clemens	5.00
11	Ivan Rodriguez	1.00
12	Kazuhisa Ishii	1.00
13	Alfonso Soriano	3.00
14	Austin Kearns	1.00
15	Mike Piazza	3.00
16	Curt Schilling	1.00
17	Jeff Bagwell	1.50
18	Todd Helton	1.50
19	Randy Johnson	2.00
20	Vladimir Guerrero	1.50
21	Kerry Wood	1.00
22	Rafael Palmeiro	1.00
23	Roy Oswalt	1.00
24	Chipper Jones	3.00
25	Pat Burrell	1.00
26	Jason Giambi	2.00
27	Pedro J. Martinez	2.00
28	Roberto Alomar	1.50
29	Shawn Green	1.00
30	Adam Dunn	1.00
31	Juan Gonzalez	1.50
32	Mark Prior	5.00
33	Hideo Nomo	1.00
34	Torii Hunter	1.00
35	Mark Teixeira	1.00
36	Craig Biggio	1.00
37	Rafael Palmeiro	1.00
38	Jeff Bagwell	1.50
39	Albert Pujols	6.00
40	Richie Sexson	1.00
41	Alex Rodriguez	6.00
42	Carlos Delgado	1.50
43	Frank Thomas	1.50
44	Sammy Sosa	4.00
45	Marlon Byrd	1.00
46	Mark Prior	5.00
47	Adrian Beltre	1.00
48	Tom Glavine	1.00
49	So Taguchi	1.00
50	Jeff Bagwell	1.50
51	Mike Sweeney	1.00
52	Luis Gonzalez	1.00
53	Chipper Jones	3.00
54	Jason Giambi	2.00
55	Miguel Tejada	1.00
56	Todd Helton	1.50
57	Andruw Jones	1.50
58	Mike Piazza	3.00
59	Manny Ramirez	1.50
60	Randy Johnson	2.00
61	Carlos Beltran	1.00
62	Victor Martinez	1.00

63	Orlando Hudson	1.00
64	Jeff Kent	1.00
65	Greg Maddux	4.00
66	Garret Anderson	1.00
67	Joe Thurston	1.00
68	Mark Teixeira	1.00
69	Kazuhisa Ishii	1.00
70	Austin Kearns	1.00
71	Pat Burrell	1.00
72	Joe Borchard	1.00
73	Josh Phelps	1.00
74	Travis Hafner	1.00
75	So Taguchi	1.00
76	Victor Martinez	1.00
77	Paul LoDuca	1.00
78	Bernie Williams	1.00
79	Josh Phelps	1.00
80	Marlon Byrd	1.00
81	Manny Ramirez	1.50
82	Jason Giambi	2.00
83	Jeff Bagwell	1.50
84	Sammy Sosa	4.00
85	Josh Phelps	1.00
86	Tim Hudson	1.00
87	Randy Johnson	2.00
88	Troy Glaus	1.00
89	Joe Thurston	1.00
90	Miguel Tejada	1.00
91	Adam Dunn	1.00
92	Magglio Ordonez	1.00
93	Mike Sweeney	1.00
94	Andruw Jones	1.50
95	Carlos Beltran	1.00
96	Joe Borchard	1.00
97	Austin Kearns	1.00
98	Richie Sexson	1.00
99	Mark Prior	5.00
100	Mark Teixeira	1.00
101	Ryan Klesko	1.00
102	Jason Jennings	1.00
103	Travis Hafner	1.00
104	Mark Buehrle	1.00
105	Eric Hinske	1.00
106	Rafael Palmeiro	1.00
107	Roy Oswalt	1.00
108	Kerry Wood	1.00
109	Brian Giles	1.00
110	Ivan Rodriguez	1.00

Tools of the Trade Materials

		NM/M
Common Player:		3.00
Quantity produced listed		
Spectrums:		1-2.5X
Production 10 to 50		
1	Sammy Sosa/250	10.00
2	Nomar Garciaparra/250	10.00
3	Andruw Jones/250	5.00
4	Troy Glaus/250	5.00
5	Greg Maddux/250	10.00
6	Rickey Henderson/40	25.00
7	Alex Rodriguez/250	10.00
8	Manny Ramirez/250	6.00
9	Lance Berkman/250	4.00
10	Roger Clemens/250	10.00
11	Ivan Rodriguez/250	6.00
12	Kazuhisa Ishii/40	5.00
13	Alfonso Soriano/250	10.00
14	Austin Kearns/250	5.00
15	Mike Piazza/250	10.00
16	Curt Schilling/250	5.00
17	Jeff Bagwell/250	6.00
18	Todd Helton/250	6.00
19	Randy Johnson/250	6.00
20	Vladimir Guerrero/250	6.00
21	Kerry Wood/250	6.00
22	Rafael Palmeiro/250	6.00
23	Roy Oswalt/250	3.00
24	Chipper Jones/250	8.00
25	Pat Burrell/40	15.00
26	Jason Giambi/250	8.00
27	Pedro J. Martinez/250	8.00
28	Roberto Alomar/40	15.00
29	Shawn Green/250	3.00
30	Adam Dunn/250	5.00
31	Juan Gonzalez/40	15.00
32	Mark Prior/250	8.00
33	Hideo Nomo/250	8.00
34	Torii Hunter/250	5.00
35	Mark Teixeira/250	5.00

36	Craig Biggio/250	4.00
37	Rafael Palmeiro/250	5.00
38	Jeff Bagwell/250	5.00
39	Albert Pujols/200	12.00
40	Richie Sexson/250	4.00
41	Alex Rodriguez/250	10.00
42	Carlos Delgado/250	3.00
43	Frank Thomas/75	8.00
44	Sammy Sosa/250	10.00
45	Marlon Byrd/250	3.00
46	Mark Prior/250	8.00
47	Adrian Beltre/250	3.00
48	Tom Glavine/250	3.00
49	So Taguchi/250	3.00
50	Jeff Bagwell/250	5.00
51	Mike Sweeney/250	3.00
52	Luis Gonzalez/250	3.00
53	Chipper Jones/100	8.00
54	Jason Giambi/250	6.00
55	Miguel Tejada/250	4.00
56	Todd Helton/250	5.00
57	Andruw Jones/250	5.00
58	Mike Piazza/250	8.00
59	Manny Ramirez/250	6.00
60	Randy Johnson/250	6.00
61	Carlos Beltran/250	3.00
62	Victor Martinez/250	3.00
63	Orlando Hudson/250	3.00
64	Jeff Kent/250	3.00
65	Greg Maddux/250	8.00
66	Garret Anderson/150	4.00
67	Joe Thurston/250	3.00
68	Mark Teixeira/250	4.00
69	Kazuhisa Ishii/250	3.00
70	Austin Kearns/250	4.00
71	Pat Burrell/100	8.00
72	Joe Borchard/250	3.00
73	Josh Phelps/250	3.00
74	Travis Hafner/250	3.00
75	So Taguchi/125	3.00
76	Victor Martinez/125	5.00
77	Paul LoDuca/125	3.00
78	Bernie Williams/125	8.00
79	Josh Phelps/125	5.00
80	Marlon Byrd/125	5.00
81	Manny Ramirez/100	10.00
82	Jason Giambi/125	10.00
83	Jeff Bagwell/50	15.00
84	Sammy Sosa/125	20.00
85	Josh Phelps/125	3.00
86	Tim Hudson/125	5.00
87	Randy Johnson/125	10.00
88	Troy Glaus/125	8.00
89	Joe Thurston/125	4.00
90	Miguel Tejada/125	5.00
91	Adam Dunn/100	15.00
92	Magglio Ordonez/100	10.00
93	Mike Sweeney/100	10.00
94	Andruw Jones/100	15.00
95	Carlos Beltran/100	8.00
96	Joe Borchard/100	8.00
97	Austin Kearns/100	15.00
98	Richie Sexson/50	15.00
99	Mark Prior/50	50.00
100	Mark Teixeira/50	20.00
101	Ryan Klesko/50	10.00
102	Jason Jennings/50	10.00
103	Travis Hafner/50	8.00
104	Mark Buehrle/50	15.00
105	Eric Hinske/50	20.00
106	Rafael Palmeiro/50	40.00
107	Roy Oswalt/50	20.00
108	Kerry Wood/50	40.00
109	Brian Giles/50	15.00
110	Ivan Rodriguez/50	25.00

Total Bases

		NM/M
Complete Set (30):		60.00
Common Player:		1.00
Inserted 1:16		
1	Albert Pujols	6.00
2	Nomar Garciaparra	6.00
3	Jason Giambi	3.00
4	Miguel Tejada	1.00
5	Rafael Palmeiro	1.50
6	Sammy Sosa	5.00
7	Pat Burrell	1.50
8	Lance Berkman	1.00
9	Bernie Williams	1.50
10	Jim Thome	2.00
11	Carlos Beltran	1.00
12	Eric Chavez	1.00

13	Alex Rodriguez	6.00
14	Magglio Ordonez	1.00
15	Brian Giles	1.00
16	Alfonso Soriano	3.00
17	Shawn Green	1.00
18	Vladimir Guerrero	2.00
19	Garret Anderson	1.00
20	Todd Helton	2.00
21	Barry Bonds	8.00
22	Jeff Kent	1.00
23	Torii Hunter	1.00
24	Ichiro Suzuki	4.00
25	Derek Jeter	8.00
26	Chipper Jones	4.00
27	Jeff Bagwell	2.00
28	Mike Piazza	4.00
29	Rickey Henderson	1.50
30	Ken Griffey Jr.	4.00

Total Bases Materials 1B

		NM/M
Common Player:		4.00
Quantity produced listed		
1	Albert Pujols/109	12.00
2	Nomar Garciaparra/112	12.00
3	Jason Giambi/100	8.00
4	Miguel Tejada/140	4.00
5	Rafael Palmeiro/58	5.00
6	Sammy Sosa/90	15.00
7	Pat Burrell/87	8.00
8	Lance Berkman/90	4.00
9	Bernie Williams/146	4.00
10	Jim Thome/73	4.00
11	Carlos Beltran/94	4.00
12	Eric Chavez/93	4.00
13	Alex Rodriguez/101	15.00
14	Magglio Ordonez/103	4.00
15	Brian Giles/68	4.00
16	Alfonso Soriano/117	10.00
17	Shawn Green/92	4.00
18	Vladimir Guerrero/128	6.00
19	Garret Anderson/107	4.00
20	Todd Helton/109	6.00
21	Barry Bonds/70	20.00
22	Jeff Kent/114	4.00
23	Torii Hunter/92	4.00
24	Ichiro Suzuki/165	25.00
25	Derek Jeter/147	25.00
26	Chipper Jones/117	8.00
27	Jeff Bagwell/100	5.00
28	Mike Piazza/76	10.00
29	Rickey Henderson/28	40.00
30	Ken Griffey Jr./36	40.00

Total Bases Materials 2B

		NM/M
Quantity produced listed		
1	Albert Pujols/40	40.00
2	Nomar Garciaparra/56	25.00
3	Jason Giambi/34	15.00
4	Miguel Tejada/30	10.00
5	Rafael Palmeiro/34	15.00
7	Pat Burrell/39	4.00
8	Lance Berkman/35	8.00
9	Bernie Williams/37	15.00
11	Carlos Beltran/44	8.00
12	Eric Chavez/31	10.00
13	Alex Rodriguez/27	50.00
14	Magglio Ordonez/47	8.00
15	Brian Giles/37	8.00
16	Alfonso Soriano/51	25.00
17	Shawn Green/31	10.00
18	Vladimir Guerrero/37	15.00
19	Garret Anderson/56	8.00
20	Todd Helton/39	15.00
21	Barry Bonds/31	50.00
22	Jeff Kent/42	8.00
23	Torii Hunter/37	15.00
25	Derek Jeter/26	50.00
26	Chipper Jones/35	25.00
27	Jeff Bagwell/33	25.00
28	Mike Piazza/23	35.00

Total Bases Materials 3B

No pricing due to scarcity.

Bases Materials HR

		NM/M
Quantity produced listed		
1	Albert Pujols/34	40.00
3	Jason Giambi/41	20.00
4	Miguel Tejada/41	10.00
5	Rafael Palmeiro/43	15.00
6	Sammy Sosa/49	30.00
7	Pat Burrell/37	5.00
8	Lance Berkman/42	10.00

10	Jim Thome/52	15.00
11	Carlos Beltran/29	10.00
12	Eric Chavez/34	12.00
13	Alex Rodriguez/57	25.00
14	Magglio Ordonez/58	8.00
15	Brian Giles/38	8.00
16	Alfonso Soriano/39	30.00
17	Shawn Green/42	8.00
18	Vladimir Guerrero/39	15.00
19	Garret Anderson/29	15.00
20	Todd Helton/30	15.00
21	Barry Bonds/46	40.00
22	Jeff Kent/37	8.00
23	Torii Hunter/29	25.00
26	Chipper Jones/26	35.00
27	Jeff Bagwell/31	20.00
28	Mike Piazza/33	30.00

2003 Playoff Piece of the Game

		NM/M
Common Player:		4.00
Pack (1):		12.00
Box (6):		60.00
1	Adam Dunn/Bat	8.00
2	Adam Dunn/Jsy	8.00
3	Adrian Beltre/Bat	6.00
4	Albert Pujols/Jsy	15.00
5	Albert Pujols/Bat	15.00
6	Alex Rodriguez/Bat	10.00
7	Alex Rodriguez/Blue Jsy	10.00
8	Alex Rodriguez/White Jsy	10.00
9	Alfonso Soriano/Bat	8.00
10	Alfonso Soriano/Gray Jsy	8.00
11	Alfonso Soriano/White Jsy	4.00
12	Brett Myers/Jsy	6.00
13	Andruw Jones/Jsy	6.00
14	Austin Kearns/Jsy	6.00
15	Barry Larkin/Jsy	6.00
16	Barry Zito/Jsy	6.00
17	Bernie Williams/Jsy	6.00
18	Brian Giles/Bat	4.00
19	Zach Day/Jsy	4.00
20	Carlos Beltran/Bat	8.00
21	Brandon Phillips/Bat	4.00
22	Carlos Lee/Bat	4.00
23	Casey Fossum/Jsy	4.00
24	Chipper Jones/Jsy	8.00
25	Marcus Giles/Jsy	4.00
26	Craig Biggio/Jsy	6.00
27	Curt Schilling/Jsy	8.00
28	Derek Jeter/Base	15.00
29	Edgar Martinez/Jsy	6.00
30	Eric Chavez/Jsy	6.00
31	Eric Hinske/Bat	4.00
32	Frank Thomas/190/Bat	8.00
33	Aubrey Huff/Jsy	4.00
34	Gary Carter/Jacket	8.00
35	Greg Maddux/Gray Jsy	8.00
36	Greg Maddux/White Jsy	8.00
37	Hideki Matsui/Base RC	15.00
38	Hideo Nomo/White Jsy	8.00
39	Rod Carew/Jacket	8.00
40	Ichiro Suzuki/Base	10.00
41	Ivan Rodriguez/Bat	8.00
42	Jason Giambi/Bat	6.00
43	Jason Giambi/Jsy	6.00
44	J.C. Romero/Jsy	4.00
45	Jason Giambi/White Jsy	6.00
46	Jeff Bagwell/Jsy	6.00
47	Josh Bard/Jsy	6.00
48	Jim Thome/Jsy	8.00
49	Jay Gibbons/Jsy	4.00
50	Jorge Posada/Jsy	6.00
51	Juan Gonzalez/Bat	6.00
52	Kazuhisa Ishii/Bat	4.00
53	George Brett/Bat	15.00
54	Kenny Lofton/Bat	4.00
55	Kerry Wood/Jsy	8.00
56	Kevin Brown/Jsy	4.00
57	Kirk Saarloos/Jsy	4.00
58	Lance Berkman/Jsy	5.00
59	Larry Walker/Jsy	4.00
60	Magglio Ordonez/Jsy	4.00
61	Manny Ramirez/Jsy	8.00
62	Mark Mulder/Jsy	4.00
63	Mark Prior/Jsy	8.00
64	Matt Williams/Jsy	4.00
65	Miguel Tejada/Jsy	6.00
66	Mike Mussina/Jsy	6.00
67	Mike Piazza/Bat	10.00
68	Mike Piazza/Black Jsy	10.00
69	Mike Piazza/White Jsy	10.00
70	Nomar Garciaparra/Bat	10.00
71	Nomar Garciaparra/Gray Jsy	10.00
72	Nomar Garciaparra/White Jsy	10.00
73	Paul LoDuca/Jsy	4.00
74	Pedro Martinez/Jsy	8.00
75	Rafael Palmeiro/Jsy	8.00
76	Randy Johnson/Gray Jsy	8.00
77	Randy Johnson/White Jsy	8.00
78	Rickey Henderson/Jsy	8.00
79	Roberto Alomar/Jsy	6.00
80	Rod Carew/Jacket	8.00
81	Roger Clemens/Gray Jsy	15.00
82	Roger Clemens/White Jsy	25.00
83	Cal Ripken Jr./Jsy	25.00
84	Roy Oswalt/Jsy	4.00
85	Jeremy Bonderman/Jsy	8.00
86	Ryne Sandberg/Bat	15.00
87	Sammy Sosa/Bat	12.00
88	Sammy Sosa/Grey Jsy	15.00
89	Sammy Sosa/White Jsy	15.00
90	Scott Rolen/Jsy	8.00
91	Frank Catalanotto/Jsy	4.00
92	Shawn Green/Jsy	5.00
93	Tim Hudson/Jsy	5.00
94	Todd Helton/Jsy	5.00
95	Tony Gwynn/Jsy	6.00
96	Torii Hunter/Jsy	6.00
97	Troy Glaus/Jsy	6.00
98	Runelvys Hernandez/Jsy	6.00
99	Vernon Wells/Jsy	4.00
100	Vladimir Guerrero/Jsy	8.00

Autographs

		NM/M
Common Player:		
Varying quantities produced		
Prime Autos:		No Pricing
Production 4-20		
12	Brett Myers	10.00
18	Brian Giles/30	30.00
19	Zach Day	8.00
21	Brandon Phillips	10.00
22	Carlos Lee	12.00
23	Casey Fossum	10.00
25	Marcus Giles	15.00
29	Edgar Martinez/100	40.00
30	Eric Chavez/75	25.00
31	Eric Hinske	10.00
33	Aubrey Huff	10.00
41	Ivan Rodriguez/50	50.00
41	Ivan Rodriguez/75	40.00
44	J.C. Romero	8.00
47	Josh Bard	8.00
49	Jay Gibbons	10.00
51	Juan Gonzalez/50	50.00
57	Kirk Saarloos	8.00
62	Mark Mulder/100	25.00
63	Mark Prior/25	75.00
64	Matt Williams	15.00
73	Paul LoDuca	15.00
84	Roy Oswalt/50	25.00
85	Jeremy Bonderman	15.00
86	Ryne Sandberg/40	100.00
90	Scott Rolen/50	40.00
96	Torii Hunter/140	20.00
98	Runelvys Hernandez	10.00
100	Vladimir Guerrero/150	40.00

Prime Materials

No Pricing
Production 25 Sets

Bronze Materials

Cards (1-100):	1-1.5X

Production 150 Sets

Silver Materials

Cards (1-100):	1-2X

Production 75 Sets

Gold Materials

Cards (1-100):	1.5-2.5X

Production 50 Sets

Platinum Materials

No pricing due to scarcity.
Production 25 Sets

2003 Playoff Portraits

Greg Maddux • Atlanta Braves

		NM/M
Complete Set (144):		40.00
Common Player:		.25
Pack (7):		4.00
Box (20):		60.00
1	Vladimir Guerrero	1.50
2	Luis Gonzalez	.35
3	Andruw Jones	1.50
4	Manny Ramirez	1.50
5	Derek Jeter	4.00
6	Eric Hinske	.25
7	Curt Schilling	.45
8	Adam Dunn	1.00
9	Jason Jennings	.25
10	Mike Piazza	2.50
11	Jason Giambi	.75
12	Jeff Bagwell	1.50
13	Rickey Henderson	1.50
14	Randy Johnson	1.50
15	Roger Clemens	3.00
16	Troy Glaus	1.50
17	Hideo Nomo	1.50
18	Joe Borchard	.25
19	Torii Hunter	.25
20	Lance Berkman	.25
21	Todd Helton	1.50
22	Mike Mussina	.40
23	Vernon Wells	.25
24	Pat Burrell	.50
25	Ichiro Suzuki	2.50
26	Shawn Green	.50
27	Frank Thomas	1.50
28	Barry Zito	.40
29	Barry Bonds	4.00
30	Ken Griffey Jr.	2.50
31	Albert Pujols	3.00
32	Roberto Alomar	.50
33	Barry Larkin	.25
34	Tony Gwynn	2.00
35	Chipper Jones	2.00
36	Pedro J. Martinez	1.50
37	Juan Gonzalez	1.50
38	Greg Maddux	2.00
39	Tim Hudson	.35
40	Sammy Sosa	2.50
41	Victor Martinez	.50
42	Mark Buehrle	.25
43	Austin Kearns	.25
44	Kerry Wood	1.00
45	Nomar Garciaparra	2.50
46	Alfonso Soriano	1.00
47	Mark Prior	1.50
48	Richie Sexson	.25
49	Mark Teixeira	.75
50	Craig Biggio	.25
51	Rafael Palmeiro	1.00
52	Carlos Beltran	.75
53	Bernie Williams	.35
54	Eric Chavez	.35
55	Paul Konerko	.35
56	Nolan Ryan	4.00
57	Mark Mulder	.25
58	Miguel Tejada	.35
59	Roy Oswalt	.25
60	Jim Edmonds	.25
61	Ryan Klesko	.25
62	Cal Ripken Jr.	4.00
63	Josh Beckett	.25
64	Kazuhisa Ishii	.25
65	Alex Rodriguez	3.00
66	Mike Sweeney	.25
67	C.C. Sabathia	.25
68	Jose Vidro	.25
69	Magglio Ordonez	.25
70	Carlos Delgado	.75
71	Jorge Posada	.25
72	Bobby Abreu	.25
73	Brian Giles	.25
74	Kirby Puckett	2.00
75	Yogi Berra	1.00
76	Ryne Sandberg	2.00
77	Tom Glavine	.45
78	Jim Thome	1.00
79	Chris Snelling	.25
80	Drew Henson	.25
81	Junior Spivey	.25
82	Mike Schmidt	3.00
83	Jeff Kent	.25
84	Stan Musial	2.00
85	Garret Anderson	.25
86	Jose Contreras RC	3.00
87	Ivan Rodriguez	1.00
88	Hideki Matsui RC	6.00
89	Don Mattingly	3.00
90	Angel Berroa	.25
91	George Brett	3.00
92	Jermaine Dye	.25
93	John Olerud	.25
94	Josh Phelps	.25
95	Sean Casey	.35
96	Larry Walker	.25
97	Jason Lane	.25
98	Travis Hafner	.25
99	Terrence Long	.25
100	Shannon Stewart	.25
101	Richard Hidalgo	.25
102	Joe Thurston	.25
103	Ben Sheets	.25
104	Orlando Cabrera	.25
105	Aramis Ramirez	.25
106	So Taguchi	.25
107	Frank Robinson	.75
108	Phil Nevin	.25
109	Dennis Tankersley	.25
110	J.D. Drew	.50
111	Paul LoDuca	.25
112	Ozzie Smith	2.00
113	Carlos Lee	.25
114	Nick Johnson	.25
115	Edgar Martinez	.25
116	Hank Blalock	.75
117	Orlando Hudson	.25
118	Corey Patterson	.25
119	Steve Carlton	.50
120	Wade Miller	.25
121	Adrian Beltre	.75
122	Scott Rolen	1.00
123	Brian Lawrence	.25
124	Rich Aurilia	.25
125	Tsuyoshi Shinjo	.25
126	John Buck	.25
127	Marlon Byrd	.25
128	Michael Cuddyer	.25
129	Marshall McDougall	.25
130	Travis Chapman	.25
131	Jose Morban	.25
132	Adam LaRoche	.25
133	Jose Castillo	.25
134	Walter Young	.25
135	Jeff Baker	.25
136	Jeremy Guthrie	.25
137	Pedro J. Martinez	.75
138	Randy Johnson	.75
139	Alex Rodriguez	1.50
140	Hideo Nomo	.50
141	Roger Clemens	1.00
142	Rickey Henderson	.50
143	Jason Giambi	.40
144	Mike Piazza	1.00

Gold

No Pricing
Production 10 Sets

Silver

Larry Walker • Colorado Rockies*

Silver: 4-8X
Production 50 Sets

Beige

Beige: 1-3X
Production 250 Sets

Bronze

Bronze: 2-4X
Production 100 Sets

Bronze Autographs

NM/M

Common Bronze Auto.:
Production 100 or less.
Silvers: 1-1.5X
Production 50 or less.
No Pricing for production 25 or less.
Golds: No Pricing
Production 25 or less.

1	Vladimir Guerrero/100	35.00
3	Andruw Jones/25	50.00
6	Eric Hinske/100	10.00
8	Adam Dunn/50	35.00
9	Jason Jennings/100	8.00
16	Troy Glaus/60	25.00
18	Joe Borchard/100	6.00
19	Torii Hunter/25	40.00
31	Albert Pujols/25	150.00
32	Roberto Alomar/100	35.00
33	Barry Larkin/95	25.00
34	Tony Gwynn/60	75.00
35	Chipper Jones/25	75.00
37	Juan Gonzalez/50	50.00
41	Victor Martinez/100	20.00
42	Mark Buehrle/100	10.00
44	Kerry Wood/40	40.00
47	Mark Prior/25	60.00
48	Richie Sexson/100	20.00
49	Mark Teixeira/25	40.00
50	Craig Biggio/50	40.00
56	Nolan Ryan/25	150.00
57	Mark Mulder/100	20.00
59	Roy Oswalt/40	25.00
61	Ryan Klesko/40	20.00
62	Cal Ripken Jr./25	150.00
67	C.C. Sabathia/50	15.00
72	Bobby Abreu/100	15.00
73	Brian Giles/50	15.00
74	Kirby Puckett/50	60.00
77	Tom Glavine/100	35.00
79	Chris Snelling/100	10.00
80	Drew Henson/100	40.00
81	Junior Spivey/100	10.00
82	Mike Schmidt/100	75.00
83	Jeff Kent/50	25.00
84	Stan Musial/50	65.00
85	Garret Anderson/25	30.00

86	Jose Contreras/50	40.00
89	Don Mattingly/50	90.00
90	Angel Berroa/100	10.00
92	Jermaine Dye/100	10.00
94	Josh Phelps/100	10.00
97	Jason Lane/100	8.00
98	Travis Hafner/100	12.00
99	Terrence Long/100	6.00
100	Shannon Stewart/100	8.00
101	Richard Hidalgo/25	20.00
102	Joe Thurston/100	8.00
103	Ben Sheets/100	15.00
105	Aramis Ramirez/40	15.00
106	So Taguchi/29	30.00
108	Phil Nevin/100	12.00
109	Dennis Tankersley/100	8.00
110	J.D. Drew/25	30.00
111	Paul LoDuca/100	15.00
112	Ozzie Smith/25	
113	Carlos Lee/100	10.00
114	Nick Johnson/100	10.00
115	Edgar Martinez/100	35.00
117	Orlando Hudson/100	8.00
118	Corey Patterson/100	15.00
119	Steve Carlton/25	40.00
120	Wade Miller/100	6.00
121	Adrian Beltre/25	30.00
122	Scott Rolen/100	30.00
123	Brian Lawrence/100	6.00
126	John Buck/100	6.00
127	Marlon Byrd/100	10.00
128	Michael Cuddyer/100	6.00
129	Marshall McDougall/100	6.00
130	Travis Chapman/100	6.00
131	Jose Morban/100	6.00
132	Adam LaRoche/100	12.00
133	Jose Castillo/100	6.00
134	Walter Young/100	6.00
135	Jeff Baker/100	6.00
136	Jeremy Guthrie/100	10.00

Silver Autographs

Production 50 or less.

Artifacts Bronze

NM/M

Common Player: 4.00
Production 100 or less.
Silvers: 1-1.5X
Production 50 or less.
Golds: No Pricing
Production 25 or less.
Bronze Combos: 1-1.5X
Production 50 or less.
Silver Combos: No Pricing
Production 25 or less.
Gold Combos: No Pricing
Production 10 or less.

1	Vladimir Guerrero/100	8.00
2	Luis Gonzalez/100	5.00
3	Andruw Jones/100	8.00
4	Manny Ramirez/50	10.00
5	Derek Jeter/100	20.00
6	Eric Hinske/100	4.00
7	Curt Schilling/100	8.00
8	Adam Dunn/50	
9	Jason Jennings/100	4.00
10	Mike Piazza/100	12.00
11	Jason Giambi/100	6.00
12	Jeff Bagwell/100	15.00
13	Rickey Henderson/50	20.00
14	Randy Johnson/100	10.00
15	Roger Clemens/100	20.00
16	Troy Glaus/100	6.00
17	Hideo Nomo/100	20.00
19	Torii Hunter/100	6.00
20	Lance Berkman/100	8.00
21	Todd Helton/100	15.00
22	Mike Mussina/100	8.00
23	Vernon Wells/100	4.00
24	Pat Burrell/100	8.00
25	Ichiro Suzuki/100	25.00
26	Shawn Green/100	6.00
27	Frank Thomas/100	10.00
28	Barry Zito/100	6.00
29	Barry Bonds/100	20.00
30	Ken Griffey Jr./100	15.00
31	Albert Pujols/100	20.00
32	Roberto Alomar/50	10.00
33	Barry Larkin/50	10.00
34	Tony Gwynn/100	15.00
35	Chipper Jones/100	10.00
36	Pedro Martinez/100	10.00
37	Juan Gonzalez/50	10.00
38	Greg Maddux/100	15.00
39	Tim Hudson/100	6.00
40	Sammy Sosa/100	20.00
41	Victor Martinez/100	8.00
42	Mark Buehrle/100	8.00
43	Austin Kearns/100	6.00
44	Kerry Wood/50	15.00

45	Nomar Garciaparra/100	15.00
46	Alfonso Soriano/100	10.00
47	Mark Prior/100	10.00
48	Richie Sexson/100	6.00
49	Mark Teixeira/50	8.00
50	Craig Biggio/50	8.00
51	Rafael Palmeiro/50	10.00
52	Carlos Beltran/50	10.00
53	Bernie Williams/50	10.00
54	Eric Chavez/100	6.00
55	Paul Konerko/100	4.00
56	Nolan Ryan/50	35.00
57	Mark Mulder/100	6.00
58	Miguel Tejada/100	6.00
59	Roy Oswalt/50	8.00
60	Jim Edmonds/50	8.00
61	Ryan Klesko/50	6.00
62	Cal Ripken Jr/100	40.00
63	Josh Beckett/100	6.00
64	Kazuhisa Ishii/50	6.00
65	Alex Rodriguez/100	15.00
66	Mike Sweeney/100	4.00
67	C.C. Sabathia/100	4.00
68	Jose Vidro/100	4.00
69	Magglio Ordonez/50	6.00
70	Carlos Delgado/50	8.00
71	Jorge Posada/100	8.00
72	Bobby Abreu/100	6.00
74	Kirby Puckett/50	30.00
75	Yogi Berra/50	25.00
76	Ryne Sandberg/50	40.00
77	Tom Glavine/50	8.00
78	Jim Thome/100	10.00
79	Chris Snelling/50	5.00
80	Drew Henson/50	10.00
81	Junior Spivey/50	8.00
82	Mike Schmidt/50	50.00
83	Jeff Kent/50	6.00
84	Stan Musial/100	30.00
85	Garret Anderson/50	8.00
87	Ivan Rodriguez/50	12.00
88	Hideki Matsui/50	25.00
89	Don Mattingly/50	30.00
90	Angel Berroa/100	4.00
91	George Brett/50	50.00
92	Jermaine Dye/50	4.00
93	John Olerud/100	4.00
94	Josh Phelps/50	4.00
95	Sean Casey/50	4.00
96	Larry Walker/50	8.00
97	Jason Lane/50	4.00
98	Travis Hafner/100	6.00
99	Terrence Long/100	4.00
100	Shannon Stewart/50	4.00
101	Richard Hidalgo/50	4.00
102	Joe Thurston/100	4.00
103	Ben Sheets/100	6.00
104	Orlando Cabrera/50	4.00
105	Aramis Ramirez/100	6.00
106	So Taguchi/50	4.00
107	Frank Robinson/50	12.00
109	Dennis Tankersley/100	4.00
110	J.D. Drew/100	6.00
111	Paul LoDuca/50	6.00
112	Ozzie Smith/50	40.00
113	Carlos Lee/100	4.00
114	Nick Johnson/100	4.00
115	Edgar Martinez/100	8.00
116	Hank Blalock/100	15.00
117	Orlando Hudson/100	6.00
118	Corey Patterson/100	6.00
119	Steve Carlton/100	10.00
120	Wade Miller/50	6.00
121	Adrian Beltre/50	8.00
122	Scott Rolen/50	20.00
123	Brian Lawrence/50	4.00
124	Rich Aurilia/50	4.00
125	Tsuyoshi Shinjo/50	8.00
126	John Buck/50	4.00
127	Marlon Byrd/100	4.00
128	Michael Cuddyer/50	4.00
130	Travis Chapman/100	4.00
131	Jose Morban/50	4.00
132	Adam LaRoche/100	4.00
133	Jose Castillo/100	4.00
134	Walter Young/100	4.00

2003 Playoff Prestige

NM/M

Complete Set (200):		35.00
Common Player:		.15
Pack (6):		2.00
Box (24):		45.00
1	Darin Erstad	.25
2	David Eckstein	.15
3	Garret Anderson	.15
4	Jarrod Washburn	.15
5	Tim Salmon	.25
6	Troy Glaus	.75
7	Jay Gibbons	.15
8	Marty Cordova	.15
9	Melvin Mora	.15

JUAN ENCARNACION
MARLINS OF

10	Rodrigo Lopez	.15
11	Tony Batista	.15
12	Cliff Floyd	.15
13	Derek Lowe	.15
14	Johnny Damon	.30
15	Manny Ramirez	.75
16	Nomar Garciaparra	1.50
17	Pedro J. Martinez	.75
18	Rickey Henderson	.15
19	Shea Hillenbrand	.15
20	Carlos Lee	.15
21	Frank Thomas	.75
22	Magglio Ordonez	.15
23	Mark Buehrle	.15
24	Paul Konerko	.15
25	C.C. Sabathia	.15
26	Danys Baez	.15
27	Ellis Burks	.15
28	Travis Hafner	.15
29	Omar Vizquel	.15
30	Bobby Higginson	.15
31	Carlos Pena	.15
32	Mark Redman	.15
33	Robert Fick	.15
34	Steve Sparks	.15
35	Carlos Beltran	.50
36	Joe Randa	.15
37	Mike Sweeney	.15
38	Paul Byrd	.15
39	Raul Ibanez	.15
40	Runelvys Hernandez	.15
41	Brad Radke	.15
42	Corey Koskie	.15
43	Cristian Guzman	.15
44	David Ortiz	.35
45	Doug Mientkiewicz	.15
46	Dustan Mohr	.15
47	Jacque Jones	.15
48	Torii Hunter	.15
49	Alfonso Soriano	.75
50	Andy Pettitte	.30
51	Bernie Williams	.30
52	David Wells	.15
53	Derek Jeter	2.00
54	Jason Giambi	.50
55	Jeff Weaver	.15
56	Jorge Posada	.15
57	Mike Mussina	.35
58	Roger Clemens	1.25
59	Barry Zito	.25
60	David Justice	.15
61	Eric Chavez	.30
62	Jermaine Dye	.15
63	Mark Mulder	.15
64	Miguel Tejada	.30
65	Ray Durham	.15
66	Tim Hudson	.30
67	Bret Boone	.15
68	Chris Snelling	.15
69	Edgar Martinez	.15
70	Freddy Garcia	.15
71	Ichiro Suzuki	1.50
72	Jamie Moyer	.15
73	John Olerud	.15
74	Kazuhiro Sasaki	.15
75	Aubrey Huff	.15
76	Joe Kennedy	.15
77	Paul Wilson	.15
78	Alex Rodriguez	1.75
79	Chan Ho Park	.15
80	Hank Blalock	.50
81	Ivan Rodriguez	.65
82	Juan Gonzalez	.75
83	Kevin Mench	.15
84	Rafael Palmeiro	.65
85	Carlos Delgado	.40
86	Eric Hinske	.15
87	Jose Cruz	.15
88	Josh Phelps	.15
89	Roy Halladay	.15
90	Shannon Stewart	.15
91	Vernon Wells	.15
92	Curt Schilling	.40

93	Junior Spivey	.15
94	Luis Gonzalez	.25
95	Mark Grace	.25
96	Randy Johnson	.75
97	Andruw Jones	.75
98	Chipper Jones	1.00
99	Gary Sheffield	.40
100	Greg Maddux	1.00
101	John Smoltz	.15
102	Kevin Millwood	.15
103	Mike Hampton	.15
104	Corey Patterson	.15
105	Fred McGriff	.15
106	Kerry Wood	.65
107	Mark Prior	.75
108	Moises Alou	.15
109	Sammy Sosa	1.50
110	Adam Dunn	.50
111	Austin Kearns	.15
112	Barry Larkin	.15
113	Ken Griffey Jr.	1.50
114	Sean Casey	.30
115	Jason Jennings	.15
116	Jay Payton	.15
117	Larry Walker	.15
118	Todd Helton	.75
119	A.J. Burnett	.15
120	Josh Beckett	.15
121	Juan Encarnacion	.15
122	Mike Lowell	.15
123	Craig Biggio	.15
124	Daryle Ward	.15
125	Jeff Bagwell	.75
126	Lance Berkman	.15
127	Roy Oswalt	.15
128	Adrian Beltre	.35
129	Hideo Nomo	.75
130	Kazuhisa Ishii	.15
131	Kevin Brown	.15
132	Odalis Perez	.15
133	Paul LoDuca	.15
134	Shawn Green	.35
135	Jeff Kent	.15
136	Ben Sheets	.15
137	Jeffrey Hammonds	.15
138	Jose Hernandez	.15
139	Richie Sexson	.15
140	Bartolo Colon	.15
141	Brad Wilkerson	.15
142	Javier Vazquez	.15
143	Jose Vidro	.15
144	Michael Barrett	.15
145	Vladimir Guerrero	.75
146	Al Leiter	.15
147	Mike Piazza	1.50
148	Mo Vaughn	.15
149	Pedro Astacio	.15
150	Roberto Alomar	.40
151	Roger Cedeno	.15
152	Tom Glavine	.40
153	Bobby Abreu	.15
154	Jimmy Rollins	.25
155	Mike Lieberthal	.15
156	Pat Burrell	.35
157	Vicente Padilla	.15
158	Jim Thome	.65
159	Aramis Ramirez	.15
160	Brian Giles	.15
161	Jason Kendall	.15
162	Josh Fogg	.15
163	Kip Wells	.15
164	Mark Kotsay	.15
165	Oliver Perez	.15
166	Phil Nevin	.15
167	Ryan Klesko	.15
168	Sean Burroughs	.15
169	Trevor Hoffman	.15
170	Barry Bonds	2.00
171	Benito Santiago	.15
172	Reggie Sanders	.15
173	Rich Aurilia	.15
174	Russ Ortiz	.15
175	Albert Pujols	1.75
176	J.D. Drew	.25
177	Jim Edmonds	.15
178	Matt Morris	.15
179	Tino Martinez	.15
180	Scott Rolen	.65
181	Joe Borchard	.15
182	Freddy Sanchez	.15
183	Jose Contreras RC	3.00
184	Jeff Baker	.15
185	Ryan Church	.15
186	Mario Ramos	.15
187	Corwin Malone	.15
188	Jimmy Gobble	.15
189	Jon Adkins	.15
190	Tim Kalita	.15
191	Nelson Castro	.15
192	Colin Young	.15
193	Luis Martinez	.15
194	Todd Donovan	.15
195	Jeremy Ward	.15
196	Wilson Valdez	.15

197	Hideki Matsui RC	6.00
198	Mitch Wylie	.15
199	Adam Walker	.15
200	Clifford Bartosh	.15

X-tra Points

Stars (1-180):	4-8X
Production 150	
Prospects (181-200):	4-8X
Production 50	

Award Winners

	NM/M
Complete Set (15):	25.00
Common Player:	1.00
#'d to year of award	
1 Barry Zito	1.00
2 Barry Bonds	5.00
3 Randy Johnson	1.50
4 Roger Clemens	2.50
5 Ichiro Suzuki	3.00
6 Chipper Jones	2.00
7 Ken Griffey Jr.	3.00
8 Miguel Tejada	1.00
9 Greg Maddux	2.00
10 Jeff Bagwell	1.50
11 Rickey Henderson	1.50
12 Tom Glavine	1.00
13 Albert Pujols	4.00
14 Nomar Garciaparra	3.00
15 Derek Jeter	5.00

Connections

	NM/M
Complete Set (70):	90.00
Common Duo:	1.00
Inserted 1:8	
Century Connections:	3-6X
Production 100 Sets	
1 Troy Glaus,	
Garret Anderson	1.50
2 Troy Glaus,	
Tim Salmon	1.50
3 Randy Johnson,	
Curt Schilling	1.50
4 Matt Williams,	
Luis Gonzalez	1.00
5 Greg Maddux,	
John Smoltz	2.00
6 Andruw Jones,	
Chipper Jones	2.00
7 Greg Maddux,	
Kevin Millwood	2.00
8 Tony Batista,	
Geronimo Gil	1.00
9 Pedro J. Martinez,	
Nomar Garciaparra	3.00
10 Manny Ramirez,	
Nomar Garciaparra	3.00
11 Nomar Garciaparra,	
Rickey Henderson	3.00
12 Trot Nixon,	
Manny Ramirez	1.50
13 Kerry Wood,	
Mark Prior	3.00
14 Sammy Sosa,	
Fred McGriff	3.00
15 Sammy Sosa,	
Corey Patterson	3.00

16	Frank Thomas,	
	Magglio Ordonez	1.50
17	Joe Borchard,	
	Magglio Ordonez	1.00
18	Adam Dunn,	
	Austin Kearns	1.00
19	Barry Larkin,	
	Ken Griffey Jr.	3.00
20	Adam Dunn,	
	Barry Larkin	1.00
21	Adam Dunn,	
	Ken Griffey Jr.	3.00
22	Victor Martinez,	
	Omar Vizquel	1.00
23	C.C. Sabathia,	
	Victor Martinez	1.00
24	Larry Walker,	
	Todd Helton	1.00
25	Carlos Pena,	
	Robert Fick	1.00
26	Josh Beckett,	
	Juan Encarnacion	1.00
27	Jeff Bagwell,	
	Craig Biggio	1.50
28	Lance Berkman,	
	Roy Oswalt	1.00
29	Lance Berkman,	
	Jeff Bagwell	1.50
30	Mike Sweeney,	
	Carlos Beltran	1.00
31	Mike Sweeney,	
	Angel Berroa	1.00
32	Kazuhisa Ishii,	
	Shawn Green	1.00
33	Adrian Beltre,	
	Shawn Green	1.00
34	Kazuhisa Ishii,	
	Hideo Nomo	1.50
35	Richie Sexson,	
	Ben Sheets	1.00
36	Jacque Jones,	
	Torii Hunter	1.00
37	Doug Mientkiewicz,	
	David Ortiz	1.00
38	Vladimir Guerrero,	
	Jose Vidro	1.50
39	Derek Jeter,	
	Jason Giambi	5.00
40	Derek Jeter,	
	Bernie Williams	5.00
41	Roger Clemens,	
	Mike Mussina	2.50
42	Alfonso Soriano,	
	Jorge Posada	1.50
43	Derek Jeter,	
	Alfonso Soriano	5.00
44	Mike Piazza,	
	Roberto Alomar	3.00
45	Mike Piazza,	
	Mo Vaughn	3.00
46	Eric Chavez,	
	Miguel Tejada	1.00
47	Mark Mulder,	
	Barry Zito	1.00
48	Tim Hudson, Barry Zito	1.00
49	Pat Burrell,	
	Bobby Abreu	1.00
50	Jim Thome, Pat Burrell	1.00
51	Jim Thome,	
	Marlon Byrd	1.00
52	Brian Giles,	
	Aramis Ramirez	1.00
53	Ryan Klesko,	
	Phil Nevin	1.00
54	Barry Bonds,	
	Benito Santiago	5.00
55	Jeff Kent, Rich Aurilia	1.00
56	Barry Bonds, Jeff Kent	5.00
57	Ichiro Suzuki,	
	Kazuhiro Sasaki	3.00
58	Edgar Martinez,	
	John Olerud	1.00
59	Albert Pujols,	
	Scott Rolen	4.00
60	Jim Edmonds,	
	J.D. Drew	1.00
61	Albert Pujols,	
	Jim Edmonds	4.00
62	Dewon Brazelton,	
	Joe Kennedy	1.00
63	Alex Rodriguez,	
	Ivan Rodriguez	4.00
64	Juan Gonzalez,	
	Rafael Palmeiro	1.50
65	Mark Teixeira,	
	Hank Blalock	1.00
66	Alex Rodriguez,	
	Juan Gonzalez	4.00
67	Alex Rodriguez,	
	Juan Gonzalez	4.00
68	Shannon Stewart,	
	Carlos Delgado	1.00
69	Josh Phelps,	
	Eric Hinske	1.00
70	Vernon Wells,	
	Roy Halladay	1.00

Diamond Heritage

	NM/M
Complete Set (30):	35.00
Common Player:	1.00
Inserted 1:21	
Golds:	5-10X
Production 50 Sets	
1 Larry Walker	1.00
2 Troy Glaus	1.50
3 Magglio Ordonez	1.00
4 Roy Oswalt	1.00
5 Barry Zito	1.00
6 Nomar Garciaparra	3.00
7 Kerry Wood	1.25
8 Roger Clemens	2.50
9 Pedro J. Martinez	1.50
10 Mark Prior	1.00
11 Sammy Sosa	3.00
12 Randy Johnson	1.50
13 Greg Maddux	2.00
14 Manny Ramirez	1.50
15 Torii Hunter	1.00
16 Alex Rodriguez	4.00
17 Mike Piazza	3.00
18 Vladimir Guerrero	1.50
19 Ivan Rodriguez	1.25
20 Lance Berkman	1.00
21 Miguel Tejada	1.00
22 Chipper Jones	2.00
23 Todd Helton	1.50
24 Shawn Green	1.00
25 Scott Rolen	1.25
26 Adam Dunn	1.25
27 Jim Thome	1.25
28 Rafael Palmeiro	1.25
29 Eric Chavez	1.00
30 Andruw Jones	1.50

Diamond Heritage Materials

	NM/M
Common Player:	5.00
Production 200 unless noted.	
Autographs:	Not Priced
Production 15 to 25	
1 Larry Walker	6.00
2 Troy Glaus	6.00
3 Magglio Ordonez	5.00
4 Roy Oswalt	5.00
5 Barry Zito	8.00
6 Nomar Garciaparra	15.00
7 Kerry Wood	8.00
8 Roger Clemens	15.00
9 Pedro J. Martinez	10.00
10 Mark Prior	6.00
11 Sammy Sosa	15.00
12 Randy Johnson	10.00
13 Greg Maddux	10.00
14 Manny Ramirez	8.00
15 Torii Hunter	10.00
16 Alex Rodriguez/	
Bat/100	15.00
17 Mike Piazza/Bat/100	15.00
18 V. Guerrero/Bat/100	8.00
19 Ivan Rodriguez/	
Bat/100	10.00
20 Lance Berkman/	
Bat/100	8.00
21 Miguel Tejada/Bat/100	8.00
22 Chipper Jones/	
Bat/100	15.00
23 Todd Helton/Bat/100	10.00
24 Shawn Green/Bat/100	8.00
25 Scott Rolen/Bat/100	15.00
26 Adam Dunn/Bat/100	12.00
27 Jim Thome/Bat/100	10.00
28 Rafael Palmeiro/	
Bat/100	10.00
29 Eric Chavez/Bat/100	8.00
30 Andruw Jones/Bat/100	8.00

Diamond Heritage Material Auto

Quantity produced listed
No Pricing

Draft Class Reunion

		NM/M
Complete Set (10):		20.00
Common Player:		1.00
Inserted 1:24		
1	Mike Piazza, John Olerud	3.00
2	Derek Jeter, Shannon Stewart	5.00
3	Alex Rodriguez, Torii Hunter	4.00
4	Nomar Garciaparra, Paul Konerko	3.00
5	Kerry Wood, Todd Helton	1.50
6	Eric Chavez, Billy Koch	1.00
7	Lance Berkman, Troy Glaus	1.50
8	Pat Burrell, Mark Mulder	1.50
9	Barry Zito, Jason Jennings	1.00
10	Mark Prior, Mark Teixeira	1.50

Inside The Numbers

		NM/M
Complete Set (25):		35.00
Common Player:		1.00
Production 2,002 Sets		
Die-Cuts:		10-25X
#'d to jersey number		
1	Roger Clemens	2.50
2	Greg Maddux	2.00
3	Miguel Tejada	1.00
4	Alex Rodriguez	4.00
5	Ichiro Suzuki	2.50
6	Sammy Sosa	3.00
7	Jim Thome	1.50
8	Derek Jeter	5.00
9	Randy Johnson	1.50
10	Barry Zito	1.00
11	Jason Giambi	1.50
12	Shawn Green	1.00
13	Curt Schilling	1.00
14	Albert Pujols	4.00
15	Vladimir Guerrero	1.50
16	Pedro J. Martinez	1.50
17	Alfonso Soriano	1.50
18	Barry Bonds	5.00
19	Magglio Ordonez	1.00
20	Chipper Jones	2.00
21	Pat Burrell	1.00
22	Luis Gonzalez	1.00
23	Jeff Bagwell	1.50
24	Garret Anderson	1.00
25	Larry Walker	1.00

Infield/Outfield Tandems Material

		NM/M
Common Duo:		8.00
Production 100 Sets		
1	Troy Glaus, Garret Anderson	10.00
2	Mark Grace, Luis Gonzalez	10.00
3	Nomar Garciaparra, Manny Ramirez	20.00
4	Alfonso Soriano, Bernie Williams	15.00
5	Jeff Bagwell, Lance Berkman	15.00

		NM/M
6	Alex Rodriguez, Juan Gonzalez	15.00
7	Barry Larkin, Adam Dunn	15.00
8	Scott Rolen, Jim Edmonds	20.00
9	Todd Helton, Larry Walker	10.00
10	Adam Beltre, Shawn Green	10.00
11	Jose Vidro, Vladimir Guerrero	12.00
12	Mike Sweeney, Carlos Beltran	10.00
13	Josh Phelps, Vernon Wells	8.00
14	Paul Konerko, Magglio Ordonez	10.00
15	Phil Nevin, Ryan Klesko	10.00

League Leaders

		NM/M
Complete Set (15):		25.00
Common Player:		1.00
Production 2,002 Sets		
1	Manny Ramirez	2.00
2	Sammy Sosa	3.00
3	Alex Rodriguez	4.00
4	Alfonso Soriano	2.00
5	Vladimir Guerrero	2.00
6	Nomar Garciaparra	3.00
7	Johnny Damon	1.00
8	Alfonso Soriano	2.00
9	Barry Bonds	5.00
10	Barry Zito	1.00
11	Pedro J. Martinez	2.00
12	John Smoltz	1.00
13	Randy Johnson	2.00
14	Lance Berkman	1.00
15	Randy Johnson	2.00

League Leaders Materials

		NM/M
Common Player:		4.00
Production 250 Sets		
1	Manny Ramirez/Jsy	8.00
2	Sammy Sosa/Base	4.00
3	Alex Rodriguez/Jsy	10.00
4	Alfonso Soriano/Jsy	10.00
5	Vladimir Guerrero/Jsy	8.00
6	Nomar Garciaparra/Jsy	10.00
7	Johnny Damon/Bat	4.00
8	Alfonso Soriano/Jsy	10.00
9	Barry Bonds/Base	12.00
10	Barry Zito/Jsy	6.00
11	Pedro J. Martinez/Jsy	8.00
12	John Smoltz	6.00
13	Randy Johnson/Jsy	10.00
14	Lance Berkman/Jsy	6.00
15	Randy Johnson/Jsy	10.00

Material Connections

		NM/M
Common Duo:		4.00
Production 400 Sets		
1	Troy Glaus, Garret Anderson	8.00
2	Troy Glaus, Tim Salmon	8.00
4	Matt Williams, Luis Gonzalez	6.00
5	Greg Maddux, John Smoltz	12.00
6	Andruw Jones, Chipper Jones	12.00
7	Greg Maddux, Kevin Millwood	12.00
8	Tony Batista, Geronimo Gil	4.00
9	Pedro J. Martinez, Nomar Garciaparra	15.00
10	Manny Ramirez, Nomar Garciaparra	15.00
11	Nomar Garciaparra, Rickey Henderson	15.00
12	Trot Nixon, Manny Ramirez	10.00

13	Kerry Wood, Mark Prior	10.00
14	Sammy Sosa, Fred McGriff	10.00
15	Sammy Sosa, Corey Patterson	10.00
16	Frank Thomas, Magglio Ordonez	8.00
17	Joe Borchard, Magglio Ordonez	6.00
18	Adam Dunn, Austin Kearns	20.00
20	Adam Dunn, Barry Larkin	15.00
22	Victor Martinez, Omar Vizquel	4.00
23	C.C. Sabathia, Victor Martinez	6.00
24	Larry Walker, Todd Helton	8.00
26	Josh Beckett, Juan Encarnacion	8.00
27	Jeff Bagwell, Craig Biggio	10.00
28	Lance Berkman, Roy Oswalt	8.00
29	Lance Berkman, Jeff Bagwell	10.00
30	Mike Sweeney, Carlos Beltran	8.00
31	Mike Sweeney, Angel Berroa	4.00
32	Kazuhisa Ishii, Shawn Green	10.00
33	Adrian Beltre, Shawn Green	6.00
34	Kazuhisa Ishii, Hideo Nomo	25.00
35	Richie Sexson, Ben Sheets	8.00
36	Jacque Jones, Torii Hunter	10.00
37	Doug Mientkiewicz, David Ortiz	6.00
38	Vladimir Guerrero, Jose Vidro	10.00
39	Derek Jeter, Jason Giambi	15.00
40	Derek Jeter, Bernie Williams	15.00
41	Roger Clemens, Mike Mussina	20.00
42	Alfonso Soriano, Jorge Posada	10.00
43	Derek Jeter, Alfonso Soriano	20.00
44	Mike Piazza, Roberto Alomar	15.00
45	Mike Piazza, Mo Vaughn	10.00
46	Eric Chavez, Miguel Tejada	8.00
47	Mark Mulder, Barry Zito	10.00
48	Tim Hudson, Barry Zito	10.00
49	Pat Burrell, Bobby Abreu	8.00
50	Jim Thome, Pat Burrell	10.00
51	Jim Thome, Marlon Byrd	10.00
52	Brian Giles, Aramis Ramirez	6.00
53	Ryan Klesko, Phil Nevin	6.00
54	Barry Bonds, Benito Santiago	12.00
55	Jeff Kent, Rich Aurilia	5.00
56	Barry Bonds, Jeff Kent	12.00
57	Ichiro Suzuki, Kazuhiro Sasaki	25.00
58	Edgar Martinez, John Olerud	8.00
59	Albert Pujols, Scott Rolen	15.00
60	Jim Edmonds, J.D. Drew	8.00
61	Albert Pujols, Jim Edmonds	12.00
62	Dewon Brazelton, Joe Kennedy	8.00
63	Alex Rodriguez, Ivan Rodriguez	12.00
64	Juan Gonzalez, Rafael Palmeiro	8.00
65	Mark Teixeira, Hank Blalock	10.00
66	Alex Rodriguez, Juan Gonzalez	15.00
67	Alex Rodriguez, Juan Gonzalez	12.00

68	Shannon Stewart, Carlos Delgado	6.00
69	Josh Phelps, Eric Hinske	4.00
70	Vernon Wells, Roy Halladay	4.00

Player Collection

		NM/M
Common Player:		4.00
Production 325 Sets		
1	Adam Dunn	8.00
2	Adrian Beltre	6.00
3	Alex Rodriguez	20.00
4	Alfonso Soriano	10.00
5	Andruw Jones	8.00
6	Andy Pettitte	6.00
7	Barry Larkin	4.00
8	Barry Zito	4.00
9	Ben Grieve	4.00
10	Bernie Williams	4.00
11	Cal Ripken Jr.	25.00
12	Carlos Delgado	5.00
13	C.C. Sabathia	4.00
14	Chipper Jones	12.00
15	Craig Biggio	4.00
16	Curt Schilling	5.00
17	Alex Rodriguez	20.00
18	Frank Thomas	8.00
19	Freddy Garcia	4.00
20	Jay Bell	4.00
21	Roger Clemens	15.00
22	Tony Gwynn	12.00
23	Ivan Rodriguez	8.00
24	Jason Giambi	8.00
25	Jason Jennings	4.00
26	Jay Payton	4.00
27	J.D. Drew	6.00
28	Jeff Bagwell	8.00
29	Jeromy Burnitz	4.00
30	Jim Edmonds	4.00
31	Jim Thome	8.00
32	Joe Borchard	4.00
33	Joe Mays	4.00
34	John Olerud	4.00
35	David Wells	4.00
36	Juan Gonzalez	8.00
37	Kazuhiro Sasaki	4.00
38	Chan Ho Park	4.00
39	Kerry Wood	8.00
40	Kevin Brown	4.00
41	Lance Berkman	4.00
42	Larry Walker	4.00
43	Bret Boone	4.00
44	Magglio Ordonez	4.00
45	Manny Ramirez	8.00
46	Mark Mulder	4.00
47	Mark Prior	6.00
48	Matt Williams	4.00
49	Miguel Tejada	4.00
50	Mike Piazza	15.00
51	Nomar Garciaparra	15.00
52	Doug Davis	4.00
53	Paul Konerko	4.00
54	Paul LoDuca	4.00
55	Pedro J. Martinez	8.00
56	Preston Wilson	4.00
57	Rafael Palmeiro	8.00
58	Marlon Byrd	4.00
59	Reggie Sanders	4.00
60	Richie Sexson	4.00
61	Rickey Henderson	10.00
62	Rickey Henderson	10.00
63	Robert Person	4.00
64	Jeff Bagwell	8.00
65	Roger Clemens	15.00
66	Roy Oswalt	4.00
67	Ryan Klesko	4.00
68	Sammy Sosa	15.00
69	Shawn Green	5.00
70	Steve Finley	4.00
71	Terrence Long	4.00
72	Tim Hudson	4.00

73	Toby Hall	4.00
74	Todd Helton	8.00
75	Travis Lee	4.00
76	Troy Glaus	8.00
77	Tsuyoshi Shinjo	4.00
78	Vernon Wells	4.00
79	Vladimir Guerrero	8.00
80	Wes Helms	4.00
81	Alex Rodriguez	20.00
82	Alfonso Soriano	10.00
83	Barry Larkin	4.00
84	Roberto Alomar	5.00
85	Ivan Rodriguez	8.00
86	Jason Giambi	6.00
87	Jeff Bagwell	8.00
88	Juan Gonzalez	8.00
89	Larry Walker	4.00
90	Luis Gonzalez	4.00
91	Magglio Ordonez	4.00
92	Manny Ramirez	8.00
93	Marlon Byrd	4.00
94	Mike Piazza	15.00
95	Pat Burrell	6.00
96	Todd Helton	8.00
97	Rickey Henderson	10.00
98	Andruw Jones	8.00
99	Craig Biggio	4.00
100	Mark Prior	6.00

Signature Impressions

NM/M

Varying quantities produced

1	A.J. Pierzynski/50	20.00
2	Adam Dunn/25	60.00
3	Barry Zito/25	50.00
4	Bobby Abreu/20	30.00
5	Brandon Phillips/25	25.00
7	Don Mattingly/15	250.00
9	Eric Hinske/25	25.00
12	John Candelaria/50	15.00
16	Lance Berkman/25	30.00
18	Miguel Tejada/25	40.00
22	Roy Oswalt/25	30.00
27	Yogi Berra/15	100.00
28	Joe Kennedy/50	10.00
30	Lenny Dykstra/50	25.00
39	Toby Hall/50	10.00
40	Victor Martinez/25	45.00
46	Brian Giles/15	40.00
50	Jeremy Bonderman/100	35.00

Stars of MLB

NM/M

Common Player:	5.00
Production 150 Sets	
Patches:	4-8X
Production 25 Sets	
Autographs:	No Pricing
Production 25	
Patch Autographs:	No Pricing
Production 5 to 10	

1	Roger Clemens	12.00
2	Randy Johnson	8.00
3	Sammy Sosa	12.00
4	Vladimir Guerrero	8.00
5	Lance Berkman	5.00
6	Alfonso Soriano	8.00
7	Alex Rodriguez	15.00
8	Roberto Alomar	6.00
9	Miguel Tejada	5.00
10	Pedro J. Martinez	8.00
11	Greg Maddux	10.00
12	Barry Zito	5.00
13	Magglio Ordonez	5.00
14	Chipper Jones	10.00
15	Manny Ramirez	8.00
16	Troy Glaus	8.00
17	Pat Burrell	6.00
18	Roy Oswalt	5.00
19	Mike Piazza	12.00
20	Nomar Garciaparra	12.00

2004 Playoff Absolute Memorabilia

NM/M

Complete Set (250):	
Common Player (1-200):	1.50
Production 1,349	
Common Non-Auto. (201-250):	2.00
Production 1,000	
Common Auto. (201-250):	8.00
Production 500-700	
Pack (4):	40.00
Box (6):	185.00

1	Troy Glaus	2.00
2	Garret Anderson	2.00
3	Tim Salmon	2.00
4	Bartolo Colon	1.50
5	Troy Percival	1.50
6	Nolan Ryan Angels	10.00
7	Vladimir Guerrero	4.00

8	Richie Sexson	2.00
9	Shea Hillenbrand	1.50
10	Luis Gonzalez	1.50
11	Brandon Webb	1.50
12	Randy Johnson	4.00
13	Robby Hammock	1.50
14	Edgar Gonzalez	1.50
15	Roberto Alomar	3.00
16	Andruw Jones	3.00
17	Chipper Jones	4.00
18	Dale Murphy	2.00
19	Rafael Furcal	1.50
20	J.D. Drew	2.00
21	Bubba Nelson	1.50
22	Julio Franco	1.50
23	Adam LaRoche	1.50
24	Michael Hessman	1.50
25	Warren Spahn	3.00
26	Jay Gibbons	1.50
27	Cal Ripken Jr.	10.00
28	Miguel Tejada	2.50
29	Adam Loewen	1.50
30	Rafael Palmeiro	3.00
31	Javy Lopez	2.00
32	Luis Matos	1.50
33	Jason Varitek	2.00
34	Carl Yastrzemski	3.00
35	Manny Ramirez	3.00
36	Trot Nixon	2.00
37	Curt Schilling	3.00
38	Pedro J. Martinez	4.00
39	Nomar Garciaparra	5.00
40	Luis Tiant	1.50
41	Kevin Youkilis	1.50
42	Michel Hernandez	1.50
43	Sammy Sosa	5.00
44	Greg Maddux	4.00
45	Kerry Wood	4.00
46	Mark Prior	4.00
47	Ernie Banks	4.00
48	Aramis Ramirez	2.00
49	Brendan Harris	1.50
50	Todd Wellemeyer	1.50
51	Frank Thomas	3.00
52	Magglio Ordonez	2.00
53	Carlos Lee	1.50
54	Joe Crede	1.50
55	Joe Borchard	1.50
56	Mark Buehrle	1.50
57	Sean Casey	2.00
58	Adam Dunn	2.50
59	Austin Kearns	2.00
60	Ken Griffey Jr.	5.00
61	Barry Larkin	2.00
62	Ryan Wagner	1.50
63	Jody Gerut	1.50
64	Jeremy Guthrie	1.50
65	Travis Hafner	2.00
66	Brian Tallet	1.50
67	Todd Helton	3.00
68	Preston Wilson	1.50
69	Jeff Baker	1.50
70	Clint Barmes	1.50
71	Joe Kennedy	1.50
72	Jack Morris	1.50
73	George Kell	1.50
74	Preston Larrison	1.50
75	Dmitri Young	1.50
76	Ivan Rodriguez	3.00
77	Dontrelle Willis	2.00
78	Josh Beckett	2.50
79	Miguel Cabrera	3.00
80	Mike Lowell	2.00
81	Luis Castillo	1.50
82	Juan Pierre	1.50
83	Jeff Bagwell	3.00
84	Jeff Kent	2.00
85	Craig Biggio	2.00
86	Lance Berkman	2.00
87	Andy Pettitte	2.00
88	Roy Oswalt	2.00
89	Chris Burke	1.50

90	Jason Lane	1.50
91	Roger Clemens	6.00
92	Mike Sweeney	1.50
93	Carlos Beltran	2.00
94	Angel Berroa	1.50
95	Juan Gonzalez	2.50
96	Ken Harvey	1.50
97	Byron Gettis	1.50
98	Alexis Gomez	1.50
99	Ian Ferguson	1.50
100	Duke Snider	3.00
101	Shawn Green	2.00
102	Hideo Nomo	2.00
103	Kazuhisa Ishii	1.50
104	Edwin Jackson	1.50
105	Fred McGriff	2.00
106	Hong-Chih Kou	1.50
107	Don Sutton RC	2.00
108	Rickey Henderson	2.00
109	Cesar Izturis	1.50
110	Robin Ventura	1.50
111	Paul LoDuca	1.50
112	Richie Weeks	2.00
113	Scott Podsednik	2.00
114	Junior Spivey	1.50
115	Lyle Overbay	2.00
116	Tony Oliva	1.50
117	Jacque Jones	1.50
118	Shannon Stewart	1.50
119	Torii Hunter	2.00
120	Johan Santana	1.50
121	J.D. Durbin	1.50
122	Jason Kubel	1.50
123	Michael Cuddyer	1.50
124	Nick Johnson	1.50
125	Jose Vidro	1.50
126	Orlando Cabrera	1.50
127	Zach Day	1.50
128	Mike Piazza	5.00
129	Tom Glavine	2.00
130	Jae Weong Seo	1.50
131	Gary Carter	2.00
132	Phil Seibel	1.50
133	Edwin Almonte	1.50
134	Aaron Boone	1.50
135	Kenny Lofton	2.00
136	Don Mattingly	6.00
137	Jason Giambi	3.00
138	Alex Rodriguez/Yanks	8.00
139	Jorge Posada	2.00
140	Bernie Williams	2.00
141	Hideki Matsui	5.00
142	Mike Mussina	2.00
143	Mariano Rivera	2.00
144	Gary Sheffield	2.00
145	Derek Jeter	8.00
146	Chien-Ming Wang	1.50
147	Javier Vazquez	1.50
148	Jose Contreras	1.50
149	Whitey Ford	2.00
150	Kevin Brown	2.00
151	Eric Chavez	2.00
152	Barry Zito	2.00
153	Mark Mulder	2.00
154	Tim Hudson	2.00
155	Rich Harden	1.50
156	Eric Byrnes	1.50
157	Jim Thome	4.00
158	Bobby Abreu	2.00
159	Marlon Byrd	1.50
160	Lenny Dykstra	1.50
161	Steve Carlton	2.00
162	Ryan Howard	2.00
163	Bobby Hill	1.50
164	Jose Castillo	1.50
165	Jay Payton	1.50
166	Ryan Klesko	1.50
167	Brian Giles	1.50
168	Henri Stanley	1.50
169	Jason Schmidt	1.50
170	Jerome Williams	1.50
171	J.T. Snow	1.50
172	Bret Boone	2.00
173	Edgar Martinez	2.00
174	Ichiro Suzuki	5.00
175	Jamie Moyer	1.50
176	Rich Aurilia	1.50
177	Chris Snelling	1.50
178	Scott Rolen	4.00
179	Albert Pujols	6.00
180	Jim Edmonds	2.00
181	Stan Musial	4.00
182	Dan Haren	1.50
183	Red Schoendienst	1.50
184	Aubrey Huff	1.50
185	Delmon Young	1.50
186	Rocco Baldelli	2.00
187	Dewon Brazelton	1.50
188	Mark Teixeira	2.50
189	Hank Blalock	2.00
190	Nolan Ryan/Ranger	10.00
191	Alfonso Soriano	4.00
192	Michael Young	1.50
193	Vernon Wells	1.50

194	Roy Halladay	2.00
195	Carlos Delgado	2.50
196	Dustin McGowan	1.50
197	Josh Phelps	1.50
198	Alexis Rios	1.50
199	Eric Hinske	1.50
200	Josh Towers	1.50
201	Kazuo Matsui/1000 RC	5.00
202	Fernando Nieve AU/500 RC	8.00
203	Mike Rouse/1000	3.00
204	Dennis Sarfate AU/500 RC	8.00
205	Josh Labandeira AU/500 RC	8.00
206	Chris Oxspring AU/500 RC	8.00
207	Alfredo Simon/1000 RC	2.00
208	Cory Sullivan AU/500 RC	8.00
209	Ruddy Yan AU/500 RC	8.00
210	Jason Bartlett AU/500 RC	8.00
211	Akinori Otsuka/1000 RC	5.00
212	Lincoln Holdzkom/1000 RC	2.00
213	Justin Leone/1000 RC	4.00
214	Jorge Sequea AU/500 RC	8.00
215	John Gall/1000 RC RC	3.00
216	Jerome Gamble/1000 RC RC	2.00
217	Tim Bittner AU/500 RC	8.00
218	Ronny Cedeno AU/500 RC	12.00
219	Justin Hampson/1000 RC	2.00
220	Ryan Wing AU/500	8.00
221	Mariano Gomez AU/500 RC	8.00
222	Carlos Vasquez/1000 RC	2.00
223	Casey Daigle AU/500 RC RC	8.00
224	Renyel Pinto AU/500 RC	8.00
225	Chris Shelton AU/500 RC	25.00
226	Mike Gosling AU/700	8.00
227	Aarom Baldiris AU/700 RC	8.00
228	Ramon Ramirez AU/700 RC	8.00
229	Roberto Novoa AU/500 RC	8.00
230	Sean Henn AU/500	10.00
231	Jamie Brown AU/500 RC	8.00
232	Nick Regilio AU/500 RC	8.00
233	David Crouthers AU/700	8.00
234	Greg Dobbs AU/500 RC	8.00
235	Angel Chavez AU/500 RC	8.00
236	Willy Taveras AU/500 RC	20.00
237	Justin Knoedler AU/500 RC	8.00
238	Ian Snell AU/700 RC	20.00
239	Jason Frasor AU/500 RC	8.00
240	Jerry Gil AU/500 RC	8.00
241	Carlos Hines AU/500 RC	8.00
242	Ivan Ochoa AU/500 RC	8.00
243	Jose Capellan AU/700 RC	10.00
244	Onil Joseph AU/700 RC	8.00
245	Hector Gimenez AU/700 RC	8.00
246	Shawn Hill AU/700 RC	8.00
247	Freddy Guzman AU/500 RC	8.00
248	Graham Koonce AU/500	8.00
249	Ronald Belisario AU/500 RC	8.00
250	Merkin Valdez AU/500 RC	8.00

Spectrum Silver

Stars (1-200):	1-2X
Gold. Auto. (201-250):	.25-.4X
Non-Auto. (201-250):	1X
Production 100 Sets	

Spectrum Platinum

No Pricing
Production One Set

Spectrum Gold

Stars (1-200):	2-4X
Gold Auto. (201-250):	.5X
Non-Auto. (201-250):	1-2X
Production 50 Sets	

Retail

Cards (1-200):	.15X
1-200 are not serial numbered	

Absolutely Ink

NM/M

Quantity produced listed
Spectrum: .75-1.5X
Production 1-25
No pricing 15 or less.

1	Adam Dunn/100	25.00
2	Al Kaline/100	25.00
3	Alan Trammell/100	15.00
6	Andre Dawson/Cubs/100	15.00
7	Andre Dawson/Expos/100	15.00
8	Andruw Jones/50	25.00
9	Angel Berroa/50	10.00
10	Aramis Ramirez/50	25.00
11	Aubrey Huff/100	12.00
12	Austin Kearns/100	15.00
13	Barry Larkin/50	30.00
16	Bert Blyleven/100	15.00
17	Billy Williams/100	15.00
19	Bob Feller/100	20.00
20	Bob Gibson/25	35.00
21	Bobby Doerr/100	15.00
22	Brandon Webb/100	10.00
23	Brett Myers/50	15.00
24	Brooks Robinson/100	40.00
27	Carlos Beltran/100	30.00
28	Carlos Lee/100	10.00
31	Craig Biggio/50	25.00
33	Dale Murphy/100	25.00
34	Darryl Strawberry/100	15.00
35	Dave Concepcion/100	20.00
36	Dave Parker/50	15.00
38	Don Mattingly/100	60.00
39	Dontrelle Willis/100	20.00
40	Duke Snider/100	30.00
41	Dwight Gooden/100	15.00
42	Edgar Martinez/100	30.00
43	Eric Chavez/50	25.00
44	Ernie Banks/100	50.00
45	Fergie Jenkins/100	15.00
46	Frank Robinson/100	20.00
47	Frank Thomas/25	50.00
48	Fred Lynn/50	15.00
49	Fred McGriff/25	50.00
50	Garret Anderson/100	15.00
51	Gary Carter/Expos/100	15.00
52	Gary Carter/Mets/100	15.00
53	Gary Sheffield/50	25.00
54	Gaylord Perry/100	15.00
57	Hank Blalock/100	25.00
58	Harold Baines/25	25.00
62	Jacque Jones/100	15.00
63	Jae Weong Seo/100	15.00
64	Jamie Moyer/25	25.00
65	Jason Varitek/25	35.00
66	Jay Gibbons/50	15.00
67	Jim Edmonds/25	35.00
68	Jim Palmer/100	20.00
69	Jim Rice/50	20.00
71	Johan Santana/50	40.00
72	Jorge Posada/50	40.00
73	Josh Beckett/25	40.00
74	Juan Gonzalez/25	40.00
75	Keith Hernandez/100	15.00
76	Kirby Puckett/25	60.00

77	Luis Tiant/100	15.00
78	Magglio Ordonez/100	15.00
81	Mark Grace/25	50.00
82	Mark Mulder/100	20.00
83	Mark Prior/100	40.00
84	Mark Teixeira/100	25.00
85	Marty Marion/100	15.00
86	Mike Lowell/25	25.00
90	Nolan Ryan/25	125.00
91	Orel Hershiser/100	30.00
92	Orlando Cepeda/100	15.00
97	Phil Niekro/100	15.00
98	Rafael Palmeiro/5	
99	Ralph Kiner/100	20.00
101	Red Schoendienst/100	15.00
103	Robin Roberts/50	25.00
104	Robin Ventura/100	15.00
106	Rocco Baldelli/25	30.00
109	Sammy Sosa/21	150.00
110	Sean Casey/23	25.00
111	Shannon Stewart/50	15.00
112	Shawn Green/10	
113	Stan Musial/100	60.00
114	Steve Carlton/50	40.00
115	Steve Garvey/100	15.00
116	Todd Helton/10	
117	Tommy John/100	15.00
118	Tony Gwynn/25	60.00
119	Tony Oliva/100	15.00
120	Torii Hunter/100	15.00
121	Trot Nixon/50	30.00
122	Troy Glaus/50	20.00
123	Vernon Wells/25	20.00
124	Vladimir Guerrero/100	35.00
125	Will Clark/100	35.00

Absolutely Ink Material

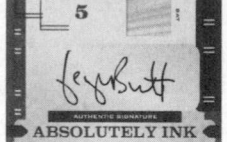

NM/M

Quantity produced listed
Prime: .5-1X
Production 1-25
No pricing 10 or less.

1	Adam Dunn/Jsy/100	30.00
2	Al Kaline/Pants/100	50.00
3	Alan Trammell/Jsy/100	20.00
6	Andre Dawson/Cubs Jsy/100	20.00
7	Andre Dawson/Expos Jsy/100	20.00
9	Angel Berroa/Jsy/100	10.00
11	Aubrey Huff/Jsy/100	15.00
12	Austin Kearns/Jsy/100	15.00
16	Bert Blyleven/Jsy/100	15.00
17	Billy Williams/Jsy/100	25.00
19	Bob Feller/Jsy/100	25.00
21	Bobby Doerr/Jsy/100	25.00
22	Brandon Webb/Jsy/50	15.00
23	Brett Myers/Jsy/100	15.00
24	Brooks Robinson/Jsy/100	40.00
27	Carlos Beltran/Jsy/100	40.00
28	Carlos Lee/Jsy/100	15.00
33	Dale Murphy/Jsy/100	30.00
34	Darryl Strawberry/Jsy/100	20.00
35	Dave Concepcion/Jsy/50	20.00
36	Dave Parker/Jsy/100	15.00
38	Don Mattingly/Jsy/100	75.00
39	Dontrelle Willis/Jsy/20	25.00
41	Dwight Gooden/Jsy/100	20.00
42	Edgar Martinez/Jsy/100	30.00
44	Ernie Banks/Jsy/50	50.00

45	Fergie Jenkins/Pants/100	15.00
46	Frank Robinson/Jsy/50	40.00
48	Fred Lynn/Jsy/100	15.00
49	Fred McGriff/Jsy/20	60.00
50	Garret Anderson/Jsy/100	15.00
51	Gary Carter/Expos Jsy/100	20.00
52	Gary Carter/Mets Jacket/100	20.00
53	Gary Sheffield/Jsy/100	20.00
54	Gaylord Perry/Jsy/100	15.00
57	Hank Blalock/Jsy/100	30.00
58	Harold Baines/Jsy/100	20.00
59	Hideo Nomo/Jsy/5	
63	Jae Weong Seo/Jsy/100	15.00
64	Jamie Moyer/Jsy/100	20.00
65	Jason Varitek/Jsy/100	30.00
66	Jay Gibbons/Jsy/100	15.00
68	Jim Palmer/Jsy/100	25.00
69	Jim Rice/Jsy/100	20.00
70	Joe Carter/Jsy/50	20.00
71	Johan Santana/Jsy/100	40.00
72	Jorge Posada/Jsy/15	75.00
75	Keith Hernandez/Jsy/100	15.00
77	Luis Tiant Jsy/100	20.00
82	Mark Mulder/Jsy/20	40.00
85	Marty Marion/Jsy/100	15.00
86	Mike Lowell/Jsy/60	20.00
92	Orlando Cepeda/Bat/65	20.00
97	Phil Niekro/Jsy/25	25.00
99	Ralph Kiner/Bat/100	25.00
101	Red Schoendienst/Jsy/60	20.00
103	Robin Roberts/Hat/50	25.00
104	Robin Ventura/Jsy/65	25.00
110	Sean Casey/Jsy/75	20.00
111	Shannon Stewart/Jsy/100	15.00
114	Steve Carlton/Jsy/50	40.00
115	Steve Garvey/Bat/100	20.00
117	Tommy John/Jsy/100	15.00
119	Tony Oliva/Jsy/100	20.00
120	Torii Hunter/Jsy/50	20.00
121	Trot Nixon/Jsy/100	30.00
124	Vladimir Guerrero/Jsy/55	50.00
125	Will Clark/Jsy/100	40.00

Absolutely Ink Triple

No Pricing
Production 1-10
Prime: No Pricing
Production 1-5

Fans of the Game

NM/M

251	Landon Donovan	1.50
252	Jennie Finch	4.00
253	Bonnie Blair	1.50
254	Dan Jansen	2.00
255	Kerri Strug	2.00

Fans of the Game Autograph

NM/M

251	Landon Donovan	25.00
252	Jennie Finch	100.00
253	Bonnie Blair	30.00
254	Dan Jansen	40.00
255	Kerri Strug	75.00

Marks of Fame

NM/M

Production 100 Sets
Spectrum: 1-2X
Production 25 Sets

1	Nolan Ryan	15.00
2	Ernie Banks	6.00
3	Bob Feller	4.00
4	Duke Snider	5.00
5	Sammy Sosa	10.00
6	Whitey Ford	6.00
7	Steve Carlton	4.00
8	Tony Gwynn	8.00
9	Jim Bunning	4.00
10	Stan Musial	8.00
11	Cal Ripken Jr.	20.00
12	George Brett	15.00

13	Gary Carter	4.00
14	Jim Palmer	4.00
15	Gaylord Perry	4.00

Marks of Fame Signature

NM/M

Quantity produced listed
Spectrum: .75-1.5X
Production 1-25
No pricing 15 or less.

1	Nolan Ryan/50	120.00
2	Ernie Banks/50	50.00
3	Bob Feller/100	25.00
4	Duke Snider/100	25.00
5	Sammy Sosa/21	125.00
6	Whitey Ford/25	50.00
7	Steve Carlton/100	25.00
8	Tony Gwynn/25	75.00
9	Jim Bunning/100	20.00
10	Stan Musial/50	60.00
12	George Brett/25	100.00
13	Gary Carter/100	20.00
14	Jim Palmer/50	25.00
15	Gaylord Perry/100	15.00

Signature Club

NM/M

Quantity produced listed

2	Gary Sheffield/Bat/100	20.00
4	Will Clark/Bat/50	40.00
5	Ernie Banks/Bat/50	50.00

Signature Material

NM/M

Quantity produced listed
Prime: No Pricing
Production 5 Sets
Combo: 1X
Production 25-50
Combo Prime: No Pricing
Production 5 Sets

2	Gary Carter/Jsy/50	25.00
3	Dale Murphy/Jsy/50	35.00
4	Don Mattingly/Jsy/25	100.00
5	Stan Musial/Jsy/25	100.00

Signature Spectrum Gold

NM/M

Quantity produced listed

1	Troy Glaus/15	35.00
2	Garret Anderson/100	15.00
7	Vladimir Guerrero/25	60.00
8	Richie Sexson/15	25.00
9	Shea Hillenbrand/100	10.00
11	Brandon Webb/100	10.00

#	Player	Price
15	Roberto Alomar/25	50.00
18	Dale Murphy/100	25.00
19	Rafael Furcal/100	12.00
22	Julio Franco/25	20.00
23	Adam LaRoche/100	10.00
26	Jay Gibbons/100	10.00
29	Adam Loewen/100	10.00
32	Luis Matos/50	15.00
33	Jason Varitek/25	40.00
36	Trot Nixon/100	20.00
40	Luis Tiant/50	20.00
41	Kevin Youkilis/25	40.00
45	Kerry Wood/25	50.00
46	Mark Prior/100	40.00
47	Ernie Banks/100	40.00
52	Magglio Ordonez/100	15.00
53	Carlos Lee/100	15.00
54	Joe Crede/50	10.00
59	Austin Kearns/100	15.00
61	Barry Larkin/25	40.00
62	Ryan Wagner/50	10.00
63	Jody Gerut/100	10.00
64	Jeremy Guthrie/25	15.00
65	Travis Hafner/25	15.00
68	Preston Wilson/100	10.00
69	Jeff Baker/25	15.00
73	George Kell/100	15.00
79	Miguel Cabrera/100	35.00
81	Luis Castillo/25	15.00
83	Jeff Bagwell/25	50.00
87	Andy Pettitte/25	50.00
93	Carlos Beltran/100	25.00
94	Angel Berroa/100	10.00
100	Duke Snider/100	25.00
104	Edwin Jackson/50	15.00
106	Hong-Chih Kuo/25	75.00
107	Don Sutton/25	25.00
112	Rickie Weeks/24	40.00
113	Scott Podsednik/100	15.00
116	Tony Oliva/25	25.00
117	Jacque Jones/100	15.00
119	Torii Hunter/50	15.00
130	Jae Weong Seo/100	10.00
131	Gary Carter/100	15.00
136	Don Mattingly/100	50.00
139	Jorge Posada/25	50.00
144	Gary Sheffield/100	25.00
146	Chien-Ming Wang/100	180.00
153	Mark Mulder/100	25.00
155	Rich Harden/50	15.00
159	Marlon Byrd/100	10.00
160	Lenny Dykstra/100	15.00
161	Steve Carlton/50	40.00
164	Jose Castillo/50	15.00
165	Jay Payton/100	10.00
170	Jerome Williams/50	25.00
178	Scott Rolen/50	40.00
181	Stan Musial/100	60.00
182	Dan Haren/25	15.00
183	Red Schoendienst/100	15.00
184	Aubrey Huff/100	10.00
185	Delmon Young/100	20.00
187	Dewon Brazelton/25	15.00
188	Mark Teixeira/25	30.00
189	Hank Blalock/25	25.00
192	Michael Young/100	25.00
194	Roy Halladay/25	25.00
198	Alexis Rios/50	25.00
202	Fernando Nieve/100	10.00
205	Josh Labandeira/100	10.00
206	Chris Oxspring/100	15.00
208	Cory Sullivan/100	10.00
209	Ruddy Yan/100	10.00
210	Jason Bartlett/100	15.00
212	Lincoln Holdzkom/100	10.00
213	Justin Leone/100	20.00
214	Jorge Sequea/100	10.00
217	Tim Bittner/100	10.00
219	Justin Hampson/100	10.00
220	Ryan Wing/100	10.00
221	Mariano Gomez/100	10.00
222	Carlos Vasquez/100	10.00
224	Renyel Pinto/100	10.00
225	Chris Shelton/100	35.00
230	Sean Henn/100	10.00
232	Nick Regilio/100	10.00
234	Greg Dobbs/50	15.00
235	Angel Chavez/100	10.00
242	Ivan Ochoa/100	10.00
248	Graham Koonce/100	10.00

Signature Spectrum Silver

NM/M

Quantity produced listed
1	Troy Glaus/34	25.00
2	Garret Anderson/100	15.00
6	Nolan Ryan/Angels/25	150.00

#	Player	Price
7	Vladimir Guerrero/100	40.00
8	Richie Sexson/34	20.00
9	Shea Hillenbrand/100	10.00
11	Brandon Webb/100	10.00
13	Robby Hammock/250	10.00
14	Edgar Gonzalez/104	10.00
15	Roberto Alomar/32	50.00
16	Andruw Jones/50	20.00
18	Dale Murphy/100	25.00
19	Rafael Furcal/100	12.00
21	Bubba Nelson/250	10.00
22	Julio Franco/100	10.00
23	Adam LaRoche/100	10.00
24	Michael Hessman/250	10.00
26	Jay Gibbons/100	10.00
29	Adam Loewen/100	10.00
32	Luis Matos/100	10.00
33	Jason Varitek/50	35.00
36	Trot Nixon/100	20.00
37	Curt Schilling/5	
40	Luis Tiant/100	15.00
41	Kevin Youkilis/25	40.00
42	Michel Hernandez/190	10.00
43	Sammy Sosa/21	150.00
45	Kerry Wood/50	40.00
46	Mark Prior/100	40.00
47	Ernie Banks/100	40.00
48	Aramis Ramirez/50	30.00
49	Brendan Harris/250	10.00
50	Todd Wellemeyer/250	10.00
51	Frank Thomas/50	40.00
52	Magglio Ordonez/100	24.00
53	Carlos Lee/100	15.00
54	Joe Crede/100	10.00
55	Joe Borchard/250	10.00
56	Mark Buehrle/10	
57	Sean Casey/100	20.00
58	Adam Dunn/100	25.00
59	Austin Kearns/100	15.00
61	Barry Larkin/50	30.00
62	Ryan Wagner/100	10.00
63	Jody Gerut/100	10.00
64	Jeremy Guthrie/50	10.00
65	Travis Hafner/50	20.00
66	Brian Tallet/25	
67	Todd Helton/10	
68	Preston Wilson/100	10.00
69	Jeff Baker/50	10.00
70	Clint Barmes/250	10.00
71	Joe Kennedy/250	10.00
72	Jack Morris/96	
73	George Kell/100	15.00
74	Preston Larrison/250	10.00
77	Dontrelle Willis/100	20.00
78	Josh Beckett/25	35.00
79	Miguel Cabrera/100	35.00
80	Mike Lowell/25	25.00
81	Luis Castillo/50	10.00
83	Jeff Bagwell/50	40.00
85	Craig Biggio/50	30.00
86	Lance Berkman/25	30.00
87	Andy Pettitte/50	50.00
88	Roy Oswalt/25	25.00
89	Chris Burke/250	10.00
90	Jason Lane/231	10.00
92	Carlos Beltran/100	25.00
94	Angel Berroa/100	10.00
95	Juan Gonzalez/25	40.00
96	Ken Harvey/200	15.00
97	Byron Gettis/250	10.00
98	Alexis Gomez/250	10.00
99	Ian Ferguson/104	10.00
100	Duke Snider/100	25.00
103	Kazuhisa Ishii/25	40.00
104	Edwin Jackson/100	10.00
105	Fred McGriff/50	15.00
106	Hong-Chih Kuo/50	50.00
107	Don Sutton/100	15.00
109	Cesar Izturis/101	10.00
110	Robin Ventura/25	20.00
111	Paul LoDuca/50	20.00
112	Rickie Weeks/21	40.00
113	Scott Podsednik/100	15.00
114	Junior Spivey/89	10.00
115	Lyle Overbay/89	15.00
116	Tony Oliva/72	15.00
117	Jacque Jones/100	15.00
118	Shannon Stewart/100	10.00
119	Torii Hunter/100	15.00
120	Johan Santana/30	30.00
121	J.D. Durbin/250	10.00
122	Jason Kubel/250	10.00
123	Michael Cuddyer/225	10.00
124	Nick Johnson/25	15.00
125	Jose Vidro/25	15.00
126	Orlando Cabrera/25	20.00
127	Zach Day/25	10.00
130	Jae Weong Seo/100	10.00
131	Gary Carter/100	15.00
132	Phil Seibel/177	10.00

#	Player	Price
133	Edwin Almonte/250	10.00
136	Don Mattingly/100	50.00
139	Jorge Posada/50	40.00
144	Gary Sheffield/100	15.00
146	Chien-Ming Wang/50	150.00
147	Javier Vazquez/25	40.00
148	Jose Contreras/25	35.00
149	Whitey Ford/50	40.00
151	Eric Chavez/50	25.00
153	Mark Mulder/100	25.00
154	Tim Hudson/50	25.00
155	Rich Harden/100	15.00
156	Eric Byrnes/250	10.00
159	Marlon Byrd/100	10.00
160	Lenny Dykstra/100	15.00
161	Steve Carlton/100	25.00
162	Ryan Howard/250	75.00
163	Bobby Hill/250	10.00
164	Jose Castillo/100	10.00
165	Jay Payton/100	10.00
168	Henri Stanley/112	10.00
170	Jerome Williams/100	15.00
171	J.T. Snow/89	15.00
173	Edgar Martinez/50	30.00
175	Jamie Moyer/19	25.00
176	Rich Aurilia/25	15.00
177	Chris Snelling/177	10.00
178	Scott Rolen/100	30.00
180	Jim Edmonds/50	30.00
181	Stan Musial/100	60.00
182	Dan Haren/200	10.00
183	Red Schoendienst/100	15.00
184	Aubrey Huff/100	10.00
185	Delmon Young/100	20.00
186	Rocco Baldelli/50	20.00
187	Dewon Brazelton/50	15.00
188	Mark Teixeira/100	20.00
189	Hank Blalock/50	30.00
190	Nolan Ryan/Rgr/25	125.00
192	Michael Young/100	25.00
194	Roy Halladay/50	20.00
196	Dustin McGowan/250	10.00
197	Josh Phelps/25	15.00
198	Alexis Rios/100	15.00
200	Josh Towers/158	10.00
202	Fernando Nieve/250	10.00
203	Mike Rouse/100	10.00
204	Dennis Sarfate/100	10.00
205	Josh Labandeira/250	10.00
206	Chris Oxspring/250	10.00
207	Alfredo Simon/100	10.00
208	Cory Sullivan/250	10.00
209	Ruddy Yan/250	10.00
210	Jason Bartlett/250	10.00
211	Akinori Otsuka/100	50.00
212	Lincoln Holdzkom/250	10.00
213	Justin Leone/250	20.00
214	Jorge Sequea/250	10.00
215	John Gall/50	25.00
217	Tim Bittner/250	10.00
219	Justin Hampson/250	10.00
220	Ryan Wing/250	10.00
221	Mariano Gomez/250	10.00
222	Carlos Vasquez/250	10.00
223	Casey Daigle/150	10.00
224	Renyel Pinto/250	15.00
229	Chris Shelton/250	35.00
229	Roberto Novoa/225	10.00
230	Sean Henn/250	10.00
231	Jamie Brown/200	10.00
232	Nick Regilio/250	10.00
234	Greg Dobbs/250	10.00
235	Angel Chavez/250	10.00
236	Willy Taveras/225	10.00
237	Justin Knoedler/250	10.00
239	Jason Frasor/225	10.00
240	Jerry Gil/225	10.00
241	Carlos Hines/250	10.00
242	Ivan Ochoa/250	10.00
248	Graham Koonce/250	10.00
249	Ronald Belisario/225	10.00

Team Quad

NM/M

Production 100 Sets
Spectrum: 1.5-2X
Production 25 Sets
1	Jeff Kent, Lance Berkman, Craig Biggio, Jeff Bagwell	6.00
2	Nomar Garciaparra, Manny Ramirez, Pedro Martinez, Trot Nixon	10.00
3	Paul Konerko, Carlos Lee, Magglio Ordonez, Frank Thomas	6.00
4	John Smoltz, Chipper Jones, Andruw Jones, Rafael Furcal	6.00

#	Player	Price
5	Garret Anderson, Troy Percival, Troy Glaus, Darin Erstad	4.00
6	Steve Finley, Brandon Webb, Randy Johnson, Luis Gonzalez	6.00
7	Paul LoDuca, Hideo Nomo, Shawn Green, Kazuhisa Ishii	6.00
8	Larry Walker, Todd Helton, Jason Jennings, Preston Wilson	6.00
9	Dontrelle Willis, Brad Penny, Josh Beckett	4.00
10	Jose Reyes, Jae Weong Seo, Tom Glavine, Mike Piazza	10.00
11	Bernie Williams, Derek Jeter, Jason Giambi, Alfonso Soriano	15.00
12	Rich Harden, Tim Hudson, Barry Zito, Mark Mulder	4.00
13	Kevin Millwood, Marlon Byrd, Jim Thome, Bobby Abreu	8.00
14	Edgar Renteria, Jim Edmonds, Albert Pujols, Scott Rolen	10.00
15	Roger Clemens, Andy Pettitte, Wade Miller, Roy Oswalt	10.00

Team Quad Material

NM/M

Production 100 Sets
Prime: No Pricing
Production 5 Sets
1	Jeff Kent, Lance Berkman, Craig Biggio, Jeff Bagwell	20.00
2	Nomar Garciaparra, Manny Ramirez, Pedro Martinez, Trot Nixon	35.00
3	Paul Konerko, Carlos Lee, Magglio Ordonez, Frank Thomas	20.00
4	John Smoltz, Chipper Jones, Andruw Jones, Rafael Furcal	20.00
5	Garret Anderson, Troy Percival, Troy Glaus, Darin Erstad	10.00
6	Steve Finley, Brandon Webb, Randy Johnson, Luis Gonzalez	20.00
7	Paul LoDuca, Hideo Nomo, Shawn Green, Kazuhisa Ishii	20.00
8	Larry Walker, Todd Helton, Jason Jennings, Preston Wilson	10.00
9	Dontrelle Willis, Brad Penny, Josh Beckett	20.00
10	Jose Reyes, Jae Weong Seo, Tom Glavine, Mike Piazza	20.00
11	Bernie Williams, Derek Jeter, Jason Giambi, Alfonso Soriano	40.00
12	Rich Harden, Tim Hudson, Barry Zito, Mark Mulder	10.00
13	Kevin Millwood, Marlon Byrd, Jim Thome, Bobby Abreu	20.00
14	Edgar Renteria, Jim Edmonds, Albert Pujols, Scott Rolen	40.00
15	Roger Clemens, Andy Pettitte, Wade Miller, Roy Oswalt	30.00

Team Tandem

NM/M

Production 250 Sets
Spectrum: 2-4X
Production 25 Sets
1	Vladimir Guerrero, Reggie Jackson	3.00
2	Dale Murphy, Chipper Jones	3.00
3	Gary Carter, Mike Piazza	4.00

4	Miguel Tejada,	
	Cal Ripken Jr.	8.00
5	Gary Sheffield,	
	Derek Jeter	6.00
6	Curt Schilling,	
	Pedro J. Martinez	3.00
7	Roger Clemens,	
	Andy Pettitte	5.00
8	Mike Sweeney,	
	George Brett	6.00
9	Kazuhisa Ishii,	
	Hideo Nomo	3.00
10	Austin Kearns,	
	Adam Dunn	3.00
11	Miguel Cabrera,	
	Dontrelle Willis	3.00
12	Don Mattingly,	
	Derek Jeter	8.00
13	Barry Zito,	
	Eric Chavez	2.00
14	Jim Thome,	
	Mike Schmidt	4.00
15	Albert Pujols,	
	Stan Musial	4.00
16	Nolan Ryan,	
	Alex Rodriguez	8.00
17	Kerry Wood,	
	Mark Prior	4.00
18	Rafael Palmeiro,	
	Jay Gibbons	3.00
19	Nomar Garciaparra,	
	Manny Ramirez	4.00
20	Ivan Rodriguez,	
	Mike Piazza	4.00

Team Tandem Material
NM/M

Production 250 Sets
Prime: No Pricing
Production 5 Sets

1	Reggie Jackson/Bat,	
	Vladimir Guerrero/Bat	10.00
2	Chipper Jones/Jsy,	
	Dale Murphy/Jsy	10.00
3	Gary Carter/Jsy,	
	Mike Piazza/Jsy	10.00
4	Miguel Tejada/Bat,	
	Cal Ripken Jr./Bat	25.00
5	Derek Jeter/Bat,	
	Gary Sheffield/Bat	25.00
6	Curt Schilling/Bat,	
	Pedro J. Martinez/Bat	10.00
7	Roger Clemens/Bat,	
	Andy Pettitte/Bat	15.00
8	Mike Sweeney/Jsy,	
	George Brett/Jsy	15.00
9	Kazuhisa Ishii/Jsy,	
	Hideo Nomo/Jsy	10.00
10	Austin Kearns/Jsy,	
	Adam Dunn/Jsy	10.00
11	Dontrelle Willis/Jsy,	
	Miguel Cabrera/Jsy	10.00
12	Don Mattingly/Jsy,	
	Derek Jeter/Jsy	35.00
13	Barry Zito/Jsy,	
	Eric Chavez/Jsy	8.00
14	Jim Thome/Jsy,	
	Mike Schmidt/Jsy	20.00
15	Albert Pujols/Jsy,	
	Stan Musial/Jsy	40.00
16	Nolan Ryan/Jsy,	
	Alex Rodriguez/Jsy	25.00
17	Mark Prior/Jsy,	
	Kerry Wood/Jsy	15.00
18	Rafael Palmeiro/Jsy,	
	Jay Gibbons/Jsy	10.00
19	Nomar Garciaparra/Jsy,	
	Manny Ramirez/Jsy	15.00
20	Ivan Rodriguez/Jsy,	
	Mike Piazza/Jsy	10.00

Team Trio

TEAM TRIOS

NM/M
Production 100 Sets

Spectrum:		1.5-2X
Production 25 Sets		
1	Sammy Sosa, Kerry Wood,	
	Mark Prior	10.00
2	Hank Blalock,	
	Mark Teixeira,	
	Alex Rodriguez	10.00
3	Vernon Wells,	
	Roy Halladay,	
	Carlos Delgado	4.00
4	Mike Mussina,	
	Jorge Posada,	
	Mariano Rivera	6.00
5	Shannon Stewart,	
	Torii Hunter,	
	Jacque Jones	4.00
6	Carlos Beltran,	
	Mike Sweeney,	
	Angel Berroa	4.00
7	Dontrelle Willis,	
	Miguel Cabrera,	
	Josh Beckett	6.00
8	Jeff Bagwell, Craig Biggio,	
	Lance Berkman	6.00
9	Nomar Garciaparra,	
	Pedro J. Martinez,	
	Manny Ramirez	10.00
10	Shawn Green,	
	Kazuhisa Ishii,	
	Hideo Nomo	4.00
11	Mark Mulder, Barry Zito,	
	Tim Hudson	4.00
12	Jim Edmonds, Scott Rolen,	
	Albert Pujols	15.00
13	Cal Ripken Jr.,	
	Jay Gibbons,	
	Rafael Palmeiro	20.00
14	Sammy Sosa, Mark Grace,	
	Ryne Sandberg	10.00
15	Nolan Ryan,	
	Roger Clemens,	
	Randy Johnson	20.00

Team Trio Material
NM/M

Production 100 Sets
Prime: No Pricing
Production 5 Sets

1	Sammy Sosa, Kerry Wood,	
	Mark Prior	25.00
2	Hank Blalock,	
	Mark Teixeira,	
	Alex Rodriguez	15.00
3	Vernon Wells,	
	Roy Halladay,	
	Carlos Delgado	8.00
4	Mike Mussina,	
	Jorge Posada,	
	Mariano Rivera	25.00
5	Shannon Stewart,	
	Torii Hunter,	
	Jacque Jones	8.00
6	Carlos Beltran,	
	Mike Sweeney,	
	Angel Berroa	8.00
7	Dontrelle Willis,	
	Miguel Cabrera,	
	Josh Beckett	15.00
8	Jeff Bagwell, Craig Biggio,	
	Lance Berkman	10.00
9	Nomar Garciaparra,	
	Pedro J. Martinez,	
	Manny Ramirez	20.00
10	Shawn Green,	
	Kazuhisa Ishii,	
	Hideo Nomo	10.00
11	Mark Mulder, Barry Zito,	
	Tim Hudson	8.00
12	Jim Edmonds, Scott Rolen,	
	Albert Pujols	25.00
13	Cal Ripken Jr.,	
	Jay Gibbons,	
	Rafael Palmeiro	40.00
14	Sammy Sosa, Mark Grace,	
	Ryne Sandberg	35.00
15	Nolan Ryan,	
	Roger Clemens,	
	Randy Johnson/25	80.00

Tools of Trade Blue

NM/M
Common Player: 1.50
Production 250 Sets

Black:		No Pricing
Production One Set		
Blue Spectrum:		1-1.5X
Production 125 Sets		
Green:		1-1.5X
Production 150 Sets		
Green Spectrum:		2-3X
Production 50 Sets		
Red:		1X
Production 200 Sets		
Red Spectrum:		1-2X
Production 100 Sets		
1	Adam Dunn/H	2.50
2	Adam Dunn/A	2.50
3	Alan Trammell	2.00
4	Albert Pujols/H	6.00
5	Albert Pujols/A	6.00
6	Alex Rodriguez	6.00
7	Alex Rodriguez	6.00
8	Alex Rodriguez	6.00
9	Alfonso Soriano	4.00
10	Andre Dawson	2.00
11	Andruw Jones/H	2.00
12	Andruw Jones/A	2.00
13	Andy Pettitte/H	2.00
14	Andy Pettitte/A	2.00
15	Angel Berroa	1.50
16	Aubrey Huff	1.50
17	Austin Kearns	2.00
18	Barry Zito	2.00
19	Barry Zito/A	2.00
20	Bernie Williams	2.00
21	Bobby Abreu	2.00
22	Brandon Webb	1.50
23	Cal Ripken Jr./H	8.00
24	Cal Ripken Jr./A	8.00
25	Cal Ripken Jr.	8.00
26	Carlos Beltran	2.00
27	Carlos Delgado/H	2.00
28	Carlos Delgado/A	2.00
29	Carlos Lee	1.50
30	Chipper Jones/H	3.00
31	Chipper Jones/A	3.00
32	Craig Biggio/H	2.00
33	Craig Biggio/A	2.00
34	Curt Schilling	2.00
35	Curt Schilling	2.00
36	Dale Murphy/H	2.00
37	Dale Murphy/A	2.00
38	Darryl Strawberry	1.50
39	Derek Jeter/H	8.00
40	Derek Jeter/A	8.00
41	Don Mattingly/H	8.00
42	Don Mattingly/A	8.00
43	Dontrelle Willis/H	2.00
44	Dontrelle Willis/A	2.00
45	Dwight Gooden	1.50
46	Edgar Martinez	1.50
47	Eric Chavez	2.00
48	Frank Thomas/A	2.00
49	Frank Thomas	2.00
50	Garret Anderson	2.00
51	Gary Carter	2.00
52	Gary Sheffield	2.00
53	George Brett/H	6.00
54	George Brett/A	6.00
55	Greg Maddux	4.00
56	Hank Blalock	2.00
57	Hideo Nomo	2.00
58	Ivan Rodriguez	2.00
59	Ivan Rodriguez	2.00
60	Jacque Jones	1.50
61	Jae Weong Seo	1.50
62	Jason Giambi	2.00
63	Jason Giambi	2.00
64	Javy Lopez	2.00
65	Jay Gibbons	1.50
66	Jeff Bagwell	2.00
67	Jeff Bagwell	2.00
68	Jeff Kent	1.50
69	Jim Edmonds	2.00
70	Jim Thome	3.00
71	Jorge Posada	2.00
72	Jose Canseco	2.00
73	Jose Reyes	2.00
74	Josh Beckett	2.00
75	Juan Gonzalez	2.00
76	Kazuhisa Ishii	1.50
77	Kerry Wood	3.00
78	Kerry Wood	3.00
79	Kirby Puckett	3.00
80	Lance Berkman	2.00
81	Lou Brock	2.00
82	Luis Castillo	1.50
83	Luis Gonzalez	1.50
84	Magglio Ordonez	1.50
85	Manny Ramirez	2.00
86	Manny Ramirez	2.00
87	Marcus Giles	1.50
88	Mark Grace	2.00
89	Mark Mulder	2.00
90	Mark Prior	4.00
91	Mark Prior	4.00
92	Mark Teixeira	2.00

93	Marlon Byrd	1.50
94	Miguel Cabrera	3.00
95	Miguel Tejada	2.00
96	Mike Lowell	2.00
97	Mike Mussina	2.00
98	Mike Mussina	2.00
99	Mike Piazza	4.00
100	Mike Piazza	4.00
101	Mike Piazza	4.00
102	Mike Schmidt	5.00
103	Mike Schmidt	5.00
104	Mike Sweeney	1.50
105	Nick Johnson	1.50
106	Nolan Ryan	8.00
107	Nolan Ryan	8.00
108	Nolan Ryan	8.00
109	Nomar Garciaparra	5.00
110	Nomar Garciaparra	5.00
111	Pat Burrell	2.00
112	Paul LoDuca	1.50
113	Pedro Martinez	3.00
114	Pedro Martinez	3.00
115	Preston Wilson	1.50
116	Rafael Palmeiro	2.00
117	Rafael Palmeiro	2.00
118	Randy Johnson	4.00
119	Randy Johnson	4.00
120	Richie Sexson	2.00
121	Rickey Henderson	2.00
122	Rickey Henderson	2.00
123	Rickey Henderson	2.00
124	Roberto Alomar	2.00
125	Rocco Baldelli	2.00
126	Rod Carew	2.00
127	Roger Clemens	6.00
128	Roger Clemens	6.00
129	Roy Halladay	2.00
130	Roy Oswalt	1.50
131	Ryne Sandberg	5.00
132	Sammy Sosa	5.00
133	Sammy Sosa	5.00
134	Sammy Sosa	5.00
135	Scott Rolen	4.00
136	Shawn Green	2.00
137	Steve Carlton	2.00
138	Tim Hudson	2.00
139	Todd Helton	2.00
140	Todd Helton	2.00
141	Tom Glavine	2.00
142	Tom Glavine	2.00
143	Tony Gwynn	4.00
144	Tony Gwynn	4.00
145	Torii Hunter	2.00
146	Trot Nixon	2.00
147	Troy Glaus	2.00
148	Vernon Wells	2.00
149	Vladimir Guerrero	4.00
150	Will Clark	3.00

Tools of Trade
Materrial Combo
NM/M

Production 25-250		
Single:		No Pricing
Production 1-5		
Combo Price Single:		2-4X
Production 1-25		
Trio:		1-3X
Production 5-100		
No pricing 15 or less.		
Quad:		2-4X
Production 1-50		
No pricing 15 or less.		
Five:		3-5X
Production 10-25		
Six:		3-6X
Production 5-25		
1	Adam Dunn/	
	Bat-Jsy/250	6.00
2	Adam Dunn/	
	Bat-Jsy/250	6.00
3	Alan Trammell/	
	Bat-Jsy/250	4.00
4	Albert Pujols/	
	Bat-Jsy/250	20.00
5	Albert Pujols/	
	Bat-Jsy/250	20.00
6	Alex Rodriguez/	
	Bat-Jsy/250	10.00
7	Alex Rodriguez/	
	Bat-Jsy/250	10.00
8	Alex Rodriguez/	
	Bat-Jsy/250	10.00
9	Alfonso Soriano/	
	Bat-Jsy/100	10.00
10	Andre Dawson/	
	Bat-Jsy/250	5.00
11	Andruw Jones/	
	Bat-Jsy/100	8.00
12	Andruw Jones/	
	Bat-Jsy/250	8.00
13	Andy Pettitte/	
	Bat-Jsy/100	10.00

14	Andy Pettitte/ Bat-Jsy/100	10.00
15	Angel Berroa/ Bat-Jsy/250	4.00
16	Aubrey Huff/ Bat-Jsy/250	4.00
17	Austin Kearns/ Bat-Jsy/250	6.00
18	Barry Zito/Bat-Jsy/250	6.00
19	Barry Zito/Bat-Jsy/250	6.00
20	Bernie Williams/ Bat-Jsy/250	8.00
21	Bobby Abreu/ Bat-Jsy/250	6.00
22	Brandon Webb/ Bat-Jsy/250	4.00
23	Cal Ripken Jr./ Bat-Jsy/250	30.00
24	Cal Ripken Jr./ Bat-Jsy/250	30.00
25	Cal Ripken Jr./ Bat-Jsy/250	30.00
26	Carlos Beltran/ Bat-Jsy/250	6.00
27	Carlos Delgado/ Bat-Jsy/250	6.00
28	Carlos Delgado/ Bat-Jsy/250	6.00
29	Carlos Lee/ Bat-Jsy/250	4.00
30	Chipper Jones/ Bat-Jsy/250	10.00
31	Chipper Jones/ Bat-Jsy/250	10.00
32	Craig Biggio/ Bat-Jsy/250	6.00
33	Craig Biggio/ Bat-Jsy/250	6.00
34	Curt Schilling/ Bat-Jsy/250	8.00
35	Curt Schilling/ Bat-Jsy/250	8.00
36	Dale Murphy/ Bat-Jsy/250	8.00
37	Dale Murphy/ Bat-Jsy/250	8.00
38	Darryl Strawberry/ Bat-Jsy/250	4.00
39	Derek Jeter/ Bat-Jsy/100	30.00
40	Derek Jeter/ Bat-Jsy/100	30.00
41	Don Mattingly/ Bat-Jsy/100	30.00
42	Don Mattingly/ Bat-Jsy/100	30.00
43	Dontrelle Willis/ Bat-Jsy/250	6.00
44	Dontrelle Willis/ Bat-Jsy/250	6.00
45	Dwight Gooden/ Bat-Jsy/250	6.00
46	Edgar Martinez/ Bat-Jsy/250	6.00
47	Eric Chavez/ Bat-Jsy/250	6.00
48	Frank Thomas/ Bat-Jsy/250	10.00
49	Frank Thomas/ Bat-Jsy/250	10.00
50	Garret Anderson/ Bat-Jsy/250	6.00
51	Gary Carter/ Bat-Jsy/250	6.00
52	Gary Sheffield/ Bat-Jsy/250	6.00
53	George Brett/ Bat-Jsy/250	20.00
54	George Brett/ Bat-Jsy/250	20.00
55	Greg Maddux/ Bat-Jsy/250	10.00
56	Hank Blalock/ Bat-Jsy/250	8.00
57	Hideo Nomo/ Bat-Jsy/250	10.00
58	Ivan Rodriguez/ Bat-Jsy/250	8.00
59	Ivan Rodriguez/ Bat-Jsy/250	8.00
60	Jacque Jones/ Bat-Jsy/250	4.00
62	Jason Giambi/ Bat-Jsy/250	8.00
63	Jason Giambi/ Bat-Jsy/250	8.00
64	Javy Lopez/ Bat-Jsy/250	6.00
65	Jay Gibbons/ Bat-Jsy/250	4.00
66	Jeff Bagwell/ Bat-Jsy/250	8.00
67	Jeff Bagwell/ Bat-Jsy/250	8.00
68	Jeff Kent/Bat-Jsy/250	5.00
69	Jim Edmonds/ Bat-Jsy/250	8.00
70	Jim Thome/ Bat-Jsy/250	12.00
71	Jorge Posada/ Bat-Jsy/250	8.00
72	Jose Canseco/ Bat-Jsy/250	8.00
73	Jose Reyes/ Bat-Jsy/250	8.00
74	Josh Beckett/ Bat-Jsy/250	8.00
75	Juan Gonzalez/ Bat-Jsy/250	8.00
76	Kazuhisa Ishii/ Bat-Jsy/250	4.00
77	Kerry Wood/ Bat-Jsy/250	10.00
78	Kerry Wood/ Bat-Jsy/250	10.00
79	Kirby Puckett/ Bat-Jsy/250	10.00
80	Lance Berkman/ Bat-Jsy/250	6.00
81	Lou Brock/Bat-Jsy/250	8.00
82	Luis Castillo/ Bat-Jsy/250	4.00
83	Luis Gonzalez/ Bat-Jsy/250	4.00
84	Magglio Ordonez/ Bat-Jsy/250	6.00
85	Manny Ramirez/ Bat-Jsy/250	8.00
86	Manny Ramirez/ Bat-Jsy/250	8.00
87	Marcus Giles/ Bat-Jsy/25	10.00
88	Mark Grace/ Bat-Jsy/250	8.00
89	Mark Mulder/ Bat-Jsy/250	8.00
90	Mark Prior/ Bat-Jsy/250	10.00
91	Mark Prior/ Bat-Jsy/250	10.00
92	Mark Teixeira/ Bat-Jsy/250	6.00
93	Marlon Byrd/ Bat-Jsy/250	4.00
94	Miguel Cabrera/ Bat-Jsy/250	10.00
95	Miguel Tejada/ Bat-Jsy/250	6.00
96	Mike Lowell/ Bat-Jsy/250	6.00
97	Mike Mussina/ Jsy-Pants/250	8.00
98	Mike Mussina/ Jsy-Jsy/250	8.00
99	Mike Piazza/ Bat-Jsy/250	12.00
100	Mike Piazza/ Bat-Jsy/250	12.00
101	Mike Piazza/B at-Jsy/250	12.00
102	Mike Schmidt/ Bat-Jsy/100	20.00
103	Mike Schmidt/ Bat-Jsy/100	20.00
104	Mike Sweeney/ Bat-Jsy/250	4.00
105	Nick Johnson/ Bat-Jsy/250	4.00
106	Nolan Ryan/ Jkt-Jsy/250	30.00
107	Nolan Ryan/ Jkt-Jsy/250	30.00
108	Nolan Ryan/ Jsy-Pants/250	30.00
109	Nomar Garciaparra/ Bat-Jsy/250	15.00
110	Nomar Garciaparra/ Bat-Jsy/250	15.00
111	Pat Burrell/ Bat-Jsy/250	6.00
112	Paul LoDuca/ Bat-Jsy/250	4.00
113	Pedro J. Martinez/ Bat-Jsy/250	10.00
114	Pedro Martinez/ Bat-Jsy/250	10.00
115	Preston Wilson/ Bat-Jsy/250	4.00
116	Rafael Palmeiro/ Bat-Jsy/250	8.00
117	Rafael Palmeiro/ Bat-Jsy/250	8.00
118	Randy Johnson/ Bat-Jsy/250	10.00
119	Randy Johnson/ Bat-Jsy/250	10.00
120	Richie Sexson/ Bat-Jsy/250	6.00
121	Rickey Henderson/ Bat-Jsy/250	8.00
122	Rickey Henderson/ Bat-Jsy/250	8.00
123	Rickey Henderson/ Bat-Jsy/250	8.00
124	Roberto Alomar/ Bat-Jsy/250	8.00
125	Rocco Baldelli/ Bat-Jsy/250	6.00
126	Rod Carew/ Bat-Jsy/250	8.00
127	Roger Clemens/ Bat-Jsy/250	15.00
128	Roger Clemens/ Bat-Jsy/250	15.00
129	Roy Halladay/ Jsy-Jsy/250	4.00
130	Roy Oswalt/ Bat-Jsy/250	6.00
131	Ryne Sandberg/ Bat-Jsy/250	15.00
132	Sammy Sosa/ Bat-Jsy/250	15.00
133	Sammy Sosa/ Bat-Jsy/250	15.00
134	Sammy Sosa/ Bat-Jsy/250	15.00
135	Scott Rolen/ Bat-Jsy/250	10.00
136	Shawn Green/ Bat-Jsy/250	6.00
137	Steve Carlton/ Bat-Jsy/250	6.00
138	Tim Hudson/ Bat-Jsy/250	6.00
139	Todd Helton/ Bat-Jsy/250	8.00
140	Todd Helton/ Bat-Jsy/250	8.00
141	Tom Glavine/ Bat-Jsy/250	8.00
142	Tom Glavine/ Bat-Jsy/250	8.00
143	Tony Gwynn/ Bat-Jsy/250	12.00
144	Tony Gwynn/ Bat-Jsy/250	12.00
145	Torii Hunter/ Bat-Jsy/250	6.00
146	Trot Nixon/Bat-Jsy/250	8.00
147	Troy Glaus/ Bat-Jsy/250	6.00
148	Vernon Wells/ Bat-Jsy/250	4.00
149	Vladimir Guerrero/ Bat-Jsy/250	10.00
150	Will Clark/Bat-Jsy/250	10.00

Tools of Trade Material Signature Sing

NM/M

Quantity produced listed
Combo: 1-2X
Production 1-25
Combo Prime: No Pricing
Production 1-5
Trio: No Pricing
Production 1-10
Quad: No Pricing
Production 1-10

1	Adam Dunn/H/Jsy/25	50.00
2	Adam Dunn/A/Jsy/25	50.00
3	Alan Trammell/Jsy/25	50.00
10	Andre Dawson/ Jsy/25	25.00
15	Angel Berroa/Jsy/50	15.00
17	Austin Kearns/Jsy/28	25.00
21	Bobby Abreu/Jsy/25	25.00
22	Brandon Webb/ Jsy/25	20.00
26	Carlos Beltran/ Jsy/15	20.00
29	Carlos Lee/Jsy/25	50.00
36	Dale Murphy/Jsy/25	40.00
37	Dale Murphy/Jsy/25	40.00
38	Darryl Strawberry/ Jsy/39	20.00
43	Dontrelle Willis/ Jsy/25	30.00
44	Dontrelle Willis/ Jsy/25	30.00
45	Dwight Gooden/ Jsy/16	35.00
50	Garret Anderson/ Jsy/16	30.00
61	Jae Weong/ Seo Jsy/25	20.00
71	Jorge Posada/Jsy/20	60.00
74	Josh Beckett/Jsy/21	40.00
82	Luis Castillo/Jsy/25	20.00
89	Mark Mulder/Jsy/20	40.00
93	Marlon Byrd/Jsy/29	20.00
94	Miguel Cabrera/ Jsy/20	50.00
96	Mike Lowell/Jsy/19	30.00
112	Paul LoDuca/Jsy/50	25.00
115	Preston Wilson/ Jsy/44	20.00
125	Rocco Baldelli/Jsy/25	30.00
129	Roy Halladay/Jsy/32	25.00
137	Steve Carlton/Jsy/25	50.00
145	Torii Hunter/Jsy/25	25.00
146	Trot Nixon/Jsy/25	50.00

Tools of Trade Signatre Blue Spectrum

NM/M

Quantity produced listed
Black: No Pricing
Production One Set
Green: No Pricing
Production 1-10
Red: .75-1.5X
Production 1-50
No pricing 15 or less.

3	Alan Trammell/100	15.00
10	Andre Dawson/100	15.00
15	Angel Berroa/100	8.00
16	Aubrey Huff/100	10.00
17	Austin Kearns/100	15.00
22	Brandon Webb/100	8.00
26	Carlos Beltran/100	20.00
29	Carlos Lee/100	15.00
36	Dale Murphy H/50	30.00
37	Dale Murphy A/50	30.00
38	Darryl Strawberry/50	20.00
41	Don Mattingly H/50	75.00
42	Don Mattingly A/50	75.00
43	Dontrelle Willis H/25	30.00
44	Dontrelle Willis A/25	30.00
45	Dwight Gooden/50	25.00
46	Edgar Martinez/25	50.00
48	Frank Thomas A/25	50.00
49	Frank Thomas/25	50.00
50	Garret Anderson/100	15.00
51	Gary Carter/100	15.00
60	Jacque Jones/50	20.00
61	Jae Weong Seo/25	25.00
65	Jay Gibbons/50	15.00
69	Jim Edmonds/25	35.00
71	Jorge Posada/25	40.00
73	Jose Reyes/25	25.00
75	Juan Gonzalez/20	40.00
77	Kerry Wood H/25	50.00
78	Kerry Wood/25	50.00
81	Lou Brock/100	25.00
84	Magglio Ordonez/50	20.00
87	Marcus Giles/50	20.00
88	Mark Grace/25	40.00
89	Mark Mulder/100	20.00
90	Mark Prior H/50	60.00
91	Mark Prior A/50	60.00
92	Mark Teixeira/50	30.00
93	Marlon Byrd/50	15.00
94	Miguel Cabrera/100	35.00
102	Mike Schmidt H/25	75.00
103	Mike Schmidt/25	75.00
106	Nolan Ryan/25	125.00
107	Nolan Ryan/25	125.00
108	Nolan Ryan/25	125.00
112	Paul LoDuca/25	15.00
115	Preston Wilson/100	15.00
129	Roy Halladay/25	30.00
135	Scott Rolen/50	40.00
137	Steve Carlton/50	50.00
143	Tony Gwynn A/25	60.00
144	Tony Gwynn/25	60.00
145	Torii Hunter/50	25.00
146	Trot Nixon/25	50.00
149	Vladimir Guerrero/25	65.00
150	Will Clark/50	50.00

2004 Playoff Honors

NM/M

Complete Set (250):
Common Player (1-200): .15
Common SP (201-250): 3.00
Production 1,999
Common SP Auto.
(226-250): 5.00
Pack (6): 5.00
Box (12): 55.00

1	Bartolo Colon	.15
2	Garret Anderson	.40
3	Tim Salmon	.25
4	Troy Glaus	.25
5	Vladimir Guerrero	.75
6	Brandon Webb	.15
7	Brian Bruney	.15
8	Luis Gonzalez	.25
9	Randy Johnson	.75
10	Richie Sexson	.40
11	Robby Hammock	.15
12	Roberto Alomar	.40
13	Shea Hillenbrand	.15

#	Player	Value
14	Steve Finley	.15
15	Adam LaRoche	.15
16	Andruw Jones	.50
17	Bubba Nelson	.15
18	Chipper Jones	.75
19	Dale Murphy	.50
20	J.D. Drew	.25
21	John Smoltz	.25
22	Marcus Giles	.15
23	Rafael Furcal	.15
24	Warren Spahn	.75
25	Greg Maddux	1.00
26	Adam Loewen	.15
27	Cal Ripken Jr.	3.00
28	Javy Lopez	.25
29	Jay Gibbons	.15
30	Luis Matos	.15
31	Miguel Tejada	.40
32	Rafael Palmeiro	.50
33	Bobby Doerr	.15
34	Curt Schilling	.50
35	Edwin Almonte	.15
36	Jason Varitek	.25
37	Kevin Youkilis	.15
38	Manny Ramirez	.50
39	Nomar Garciaparra	1.00
40	Pedro J. Martinez	.75
41	Trot Nixon	.25
42	Andre Dawson	.25
43	Aramis Ramirez	.40
44	Brendan Harris	.15
45	Derrek Lee	.25
46	Ernie Banks	.75
47	Kerry Wood	.75
48	Mark Prior	1.00
49	Ryne Sandberg	1.00
50	Sammy Sosa	1.50
51	Carlos Lee	.15
52	Frank Thomas	.50
53	Joe Borchard	.15
54	Joe Crede	.15
55	Magglio Ordonez	.25
56	Adam Dunn	.50
57	Austin Kearns	.25
58	Barry Larkin	.40
59	Brandon Larson	.15
60	Ken Griffey Jr.	1.00
61	Ryan Wagner	.15
62	Sean Casey	.25
63	Bob Feller	.25
64	Brian Tallet	.15
65	C.C. Sabathia	.15
66	Jeremy Guthrie	.15
67	Jody Gerut	.15
68	Clint Barmes	.15
69	Jeff Baker	.15
70	Joe Kennedy	.15
71	Larry Walker	.25
72	Preston Wilson	.25
73	Todd Helton	.50
74	Alan Trammell	.15
75	Dmitri Young	.15
76	Ivan Rodriguez	.50
77	Jeremy Bonderman	.15
78	Preston Larrison	.15
79	Dontrelle Willis	.25
80	Josh Beckett	.50
81	Juan Pierre	.15
82	Luis Castillo	.15
83	Miguel Cabrera	.75
84	Mike Lowell	.25
85	Andy Pettitte	.25
86	Chris Burke	.15
87	Craig Biggio	.25
88	Jeff Bagwell	.50
89	Jeff Kent	.25
90	Lance Berkman	.25
91	Morgan Ensberg	.15
92	Richard Hidalgo	.15
93	Roger Clemens	1.50
94	Roy Oswalt	.25
95	Angel Berroa	.15
96	Byron Gettis	.15
97	Carlos Beltran	.40
98	George Brett	2.00
99	Juan Gonzalez	.50
100	Mike Sweeney	.25
101	Duke Snider	.50
102	Edwin Jackson	.25
103	Eric Gagne	.50
104	Hideo Nomo	.40
105	Hong-Chih Kuo	.15
106	Kazuhisa Ishii	.15
107	Paul LoDuca	.15
108	Robin Ventura	.15
109	Shawn Green	.25
110	Junior Spivey	.15
111	Rickie Weeks	.25
112	Scott Podsednik	.25
113	J.D. Durbin	.15
114	Jacque Jones	.15
115	Jason Kubel	.25
116	Johan Santana	.15
117	Shannon Stewart	.15
118	Torii Hunter	.25
119	Brad Wilkerson	.15
120	Jose Vidro	.15
121	Nick Johnson	.15
122	Orlando Cabrera	.15
123	Gary Carter	.25
124	Jae Weong Seo	.15
125	Lenny Dykstra	.15
126	Mike Piazza	1.00
127	Tom Glavine	.25
128	Alex Rodriguez	1.50
129	Bernie Williams	.40
130	Chien-Ming Wang	1.00
131	Derek Jeter	2.00
132	Don Mattingly	1.50
133	Gary Sheffield	.40
134	Hideki Matsui	1.50
135	Jason Giambi	.50
136	Javier Vazquez	.25
137	Jorge Posada	.40
138	Jose Contreras	.15
139	Kevin Brown	.25
140	Mariano Rivera	.40
141	Mike Mussina	.40
142	Whitey Ford	.50
143	Barry Zito	.40
144	Eric Chavez	.25
145	Mark Mulder	.40
146	Rich Harden	.15
147	Tim Hudson	.25
148	Reggie Jackson	.50
149	Rickey Henderson	.50
150	Brett Myers	.15
151	Bobby Abreu	.25
152	Jim Thome	.75
153	Kevin Millwood	.25
154	Marlon Byrd	.15
155	Mike Schmidt	1.50
156	Ryan Howard	3.00
157	Jack Wilson	.15
158	Jason Kendall	.15
159	Brian Giles	.25
160	David Wells	.15
161	Jay Payton	.15
162	Phil Nevin	.15
163	Ryan Klesko	.15
164	Sean Burroughs	.15
165	A.J. Pierzynski	.15
166	J.T. Snow	.15
167	Jason Schmidt	.50
168	Jerome Williams	.15
169	Will Clark	.50
170	Bret Boone	.15
171	Chris Snelling	.15
172	Edgar Martinez	.25
173	Ichiro Suzuki	1.50
174	Randy Winn	.15
175	Rich Aurilia	.15
176	Shigetoshi Hasegawa	.15
177	Albert Pujols	.15
178	Dan Haren	.15
179	Edgar Renteria	.25
180	Jim Edmonds	.40
181	Matt Morris	.15
182	Scott Rolen	.75
183	Stan Musial	1.00
184	Aubrey Huff	.15
185	Chad Gaudin	.15
186	Delmon Young	.25
187	Fred McGriff	.25
188	Rocco Baldelli	.15
189	Alfonso Soriano	.75
190	Hank Blalock	.50
191	Mark Teixeira	.40
192	Nolan Ryan	2.00
193	Alexis Rios	.15
194	Carlos Delgado	.40
195	Dustin McGowan	.15
196	Guillermo Quiroz	.15
197	Josh Phelps	.15
198	Roy Halladay	.25
199	Vernon Wells	.15
200	Vinnie Chulk	.15
201	Jose Capellan/1999 RC	5.00
202	Kazuo Matsui/1999 RC	5.00
203	David Crouthers/1999	3.00
204	Akinori Otsuka/1999 RC	5.00
205	Nick Regilio/1999 RC	3.00
206	Justin Hampson/1999 RC	3.00
207	Lincoln Holdzkom/1999 RC	3.00
208	Jorge Sequea/1999 RC	3.00
209	Justin Leone/1999 RC	3.00
210	Renyel Pinto/1999 RC	3.00
211	Mariano Gomez/1999 RC	3.00
212	Onil Joseph/Auto./1000 RC	8.00
213	Josh Labandeira/AU/1000 RC	10.00
214	Cory Sullivan/1999 RC	3.00
215	Carlos Vasquez/Auto./675 RC	8.00
216	Chris Shelton/1999 RC	8.00
217	Willy Taveras/1999 RC	6.00
218	John Gall/1999 RC	5.00
219	Jerry Gil/1999 RC	3.00
220	Jason Frasor/1999 RC	3.00
221	Justin Knoedler/1999 RC	3.00
222	Ronald Belisario/1999 RC	3.00
223	Mike Rouse/1999 RC	3.00
224	Dennis Sarfate/1999 RC	3.00
225	Casey Daigle/1999 RC	3.00
226	Shingo Takatsu/Auto./800 RC	10.00
227	Jason Bartlett/Auto./800 RC	8.00
228	Alfredo Simon/Auto./1000 RC	8.00
229	Chris Oxspring/1999 RC	3.00
230	Fernando Nieve/Auto./1000 RC	8.00
231	Ruddy Yan/Auto./800 RC	8.00
232	Ryan Wing/1999	3.00
233	Tim Bittner/Auto./1000 RC	8.00
234	Ramon Ramirez/Auto./1000 RC	8.00
235	Sean Henn/Auto./1000	8.00
236	Roberto Novoa RC	4.00
237	Jerome Gamble/Auto./800 RC	8.00
238	Jamie Brown/Auto./800 RC	8.00
239	Ian Snell/Auto./800 RC	30.00
240	Freddy Guzman/Auto./800 RC	8.00
241	Aarom Baldiris./Auto./1000 RC	8.00
242	Greg Dobbs/1999 RC	3.00
243	Ivan Ochoa/1999 RC	3.00
244	Angel Chavez/Auto./800 RC	8.00
245	Merkin Valdez/Auto./800 RC	10.00
246	Mike Gosling/Auto./800	8.00
247	Carlos Hines/Auto./800 RC	8.00
248	Graham Koonce/Auto./1000	10.00
249	William Bergolla/Auto./1000 RC	8.00
250	Hector Gimenez/Auto./1000 RC	8.00

Credits Bronze

Bronze (1-200):	3-6X
Bronze (201-250):	.5-1X
Production 100 Sets	

Credits Gold

Gold (1-200):	8-15X
Gold (201-250):	No Pricing
Production 25 Sets	

Credits Silver

Silver (1-200):	4-8X
Silver (201-250):	No Pricing
Production 50 Sets	

Credits Platinum

No Pricing
Production One Set

Awards

	NM/M
Common Player:	2.00
Quantity produced listed	
1 Phil Rizzuto/1950	3.00
2 Fred Lynn/1975	2.00
3 George Brett/1980	8.00
4 Cal Ripken Jr./1983	10.00
5 Don Mattingly/1985	8.00
6 Rickey Henderson/1990	3.00
7 Stan Musial/1943	5.00
8 Marty Marion/1944	3.00
9 Ernie Banks/1958	5.00
10 Sammy Sosa/1998	6.00
11 Terry Pendleton/1991	2.00
12 Ryne Sandberg/1984	6.00
13 Andre Dawson/1987	3.00
14 George Foster/1977	2.00
15 Dave Parker/1978	2.00
16 Keith Hernandez/1979	3.00
17 Mike Schmidt/1980	6.00
18 Dale Murphy/1982	3.00
19 Whitey Ford/1961	3.00

#	Player	Value
20	Roy Halladay/2003	2.00
21	Orel Hershiser/1988	2.00
22	Bob Feller/1940	3.00
23	Dwight Gooden/1985	2.00
24	Steve Carlton/1972	3.00
25	Randy Johnson/2002	4.00

Awards Signature

	NM/M
Quantity produced listed	
1 Phil Rizzuto/50	25.00
5 Fred Lynn/100	15.00
7 Stan Musial/50	50.00
8 Marty Marion/50	10.00
10 Sammy Sosa/21	125.00
11 Terry Pendleton/100	10.00
13 Andre Dawson/100	15.00
14 George Foster/100	15.00
15 Dave Parker/88	5.00
16 Keith Hernandez/100	20.00
19 Whitey Ford/50	25.00
20 Roy Halladay/25	25.00
21 Orel Hershiser/25	40.00
22 Bob Feller/100	15.00
23 Dwight Gooden/100	10.00

Champions

	NM/M
Common Player:	2.00
Quantity produced listed	
1 Stan Musial/1951	5.00
2 Warren Spahn/1958	3.00
3 Bob Gibson/1968	3.00
4 Mike Schmidt/1980	6.00
5 Dale Murphy/1982	4.00
6 Steve Carlton/1983	4.00
7 Will Clark/1988	4.00
8 Nolan Ryan/1990	10.00
9 Ryne Sandberg/1990	6.00
10 Roger Clemens/1990	8.00
11 George Brett/1990	8.00
12 Tony Gwynn/1997	5.00
13 Todd Helton/2000	4.00
14 Troy Glaus/2000	2.00
15 Sammy Sosa/2000	6.00
16 Pedro J. Martinez/2000	4.00
17 Mark Mulder/2001	2.00
18 Manny Ramirez/2002	3.00
19 Lance Berkman/2002	2.00
20 Alex Rodriguez/Rgr/2002	6.00

Champions Jersey

	NM/M
Common Jersey:	5.00
Quantity produced listed	
1 Stan Musial/100	30.00
2 Warren Spahn/100	10.00
3 Bob Gibson/100	10.00
4 Mike Schmidt/100	20.00
5 Dale Murphy/82	10.00
6 Steve Carlton/100	8.00
7 Will Clark/100	8.00
8 Nolan Ryan/100	25.00
9 Ryne Sandberg/100	20.00
10 Roger Clemens/100	15.00
11 George Brett/100	25.00
12 Tony Gwynn/250	10.00
13 Todd Helton/250	8.00
14 Troy Glaus/250	5.00
15 Sammy Sosa/250	15.00
16 Pedro J. Martinez/250	8.00
17 Mark Mulder/250	5.00
18 Manny Ramirez/250	8.00
19 Lance Berkman/250	5.00
20 Alex Rodriguez/250	10.00

Champions Jersey Signature

No Pricing
Production 5 Sets

Champions Signature

NM/M

Quantity produced listed
1	Stan Musial/50	50.00
3	Bob Gibson/50	25.00
7	Will Clark/50	40.00
8	Nolan Ryan/34	100.00

Class Reunion

NM/M

Quantity produced listed
1	Eddie Murray, Gary Carter/2003	3.00
2	Carlton Fisk, Tony Perez/2000	3.00
3	Nolan Ryan, George Brett/1999	10.00
4	Rod Carew, Fergie Jenkins/1991	3.00
5	Joe Morgan, Jim Palmer/1990	3.00
6	Carl Yastrzemski, Johnny Bench/1989	5.00
7	Harmon Killebrew, Luis Aparicio/1984	3.00
8	Brooks Robinson, Juan Marichal/1983	3.00
9	Al Kaline, Duke Snider/1980	3.00
10	Roberto Clemente, Warren Spahn/1973	8.00
11	Mark Prior, Mark Teixeira/2001	3.00
12	Josh Beckett, Barry Zito/1999	3.00
13	Mark Mulder, Adam Dunn/1998	3.00
14	Vernon Wells, Lance Berkman/1997	3.00
15	Eric Chavez, Nick Johnson/1996	3.00
16	Kerry Wood, Roy Halladay/1995	4.00
17	Todd Helton, Carlos Beltran/1995	4.00
18	Derek Jeter, Jason Giambi/1992	8.00
19	Manny Ramirez, Shawn Green/1991	4.00
20	Chipper Jones, Mike Mussina/1990	4.00

Class Reunion Material

NM/M

Quantity produced listed
1	Eddie Murray/Jsy, Gary Carter/Jsy/100	15.00
2	Carlton Fisk/Jsy, Tony Perez/Bat/250	20.00
3	Nolan Ryan/Jsy, George Brett/Jsy/100	50.00
4	Rod Carew/Jsy, Fergie Jenkins/ Pants/250	15.00
5	Joe Morgan/Jsy, Jim Palmer/Jsy/100	10.00
6	Carl Yastrzemski/Jsy, Johnny Bench/ Jsy/250	30.00
7	Harmon Killebrew/Jsy, Luis Aparicio/Jsy/250	15.00
8	Brooks Robinson, Juan Marichal/ Jsy/100	15.00
9	Al Kaline/Jsy, Duke Snider/Jsy/25	35.00

10	Roger Clemens/Jsy, Warren Spahn/ Jsy/100	80.00
11	Mark Prior/Jsy, Mark Teixeira/ Jsy/250	10.00
12	Josh Beckett/Jsy, Barry Zito/Jsy/250	8.00
13	Mark Mulder/Jsy, Adam Dunn/Jsy/20	10.00
14	Vernon Wells/Jsy, Lance Berkman/ Jsy/250	8.00
15	Eric Chavez/Jsy, Nick Johnson/Jsy/250	8.00
16	Kerry Wood/Jsy, Roy Halladay/Jsy/250	12.00
17	Todd Helton/Jsy, Carlos Beltran/ Jsy/250	10.00
18	Derek Jeter/Jsy, Jason Giambi/ Jsy/250	20.00
19	Manny Ramirez/Jsy, Shawn Green/Jsy/50	10.00
20	Chipper Jones/Jsy, Mike Mussina/ Jsy/250	10.00

Fans of the Game

NM/M
251	Charlie Sheen	3.00
252	Corbin Bernsen	2.00
253	Peter Gammons	3.00
254	Jeff Garlin/SP	2.00
255	Larry King	2.00

Fans of the Game Signature

NM/M
251	Charlie Sheen	100.00
252	Corbin Bernsen	25.00
253	Peter Gammons	50.00
254	Jeff Garlin SP	80.00
255	Larry King	45.00

Game Day Souvenir

NM/M
2	Bob Gibson/Jsy/75	15.00
3	Frank Robinson/ Bat/61	10.00
4	Tony Gwynn/ Pants/99	20.00
5	Warren Spahn/Jsy/53	20.00
6	George Brett/Bat/77	25.00
7	Cal Ripken Jr./ Hat/19	100.00
8	Frank Thomas/Bat/93	10.00
9	Sammy Sosa/Jsy/100	15.00
10	Harmon Killebrew/ Bat/75	15.00

Game Day Souvenir Signature

No Pricing
Production Five Sets

Piece of the Game Bat

NM/M
1	Albert Pujols/250	15.00
2	Angel Berroa/250	4.00
3	Aubrey Huff/250	4.00
4	Barry Zito/250	6.00
5	Bobby Abreu/250	4.00
6	Carlos Beltran/250	4.00
7	Chipper Jones/250	8.00
8	Derek Jeter/250	20.00
9	Eric Chavez/150	6.00
10	Eric Hinske/50	6.00
11	Gary Sheffield/250	6.00
12	George Brett/250	15.00
13	Jay Gibbons/250	4.00
14	Jim Edmonds/250	6.00
15	Josh Beckett/250	6.00
16	Manny Ramirez/250	8.00
17	Mark Mulder/250	6.00
18	Marlon Byrd/250	4.00
19	Mike Lowell/250	4.00
20	Mike Schmidt/250	20.00
21	Nolan Ryan/250	20.00
22	Rafael Furcal/250	4.00

23	Randy Johnson/100	10.00
24	Rod Carew/250	8.00
25	Torii Hunter/250	4.00

Piece of the Game Bat Signature

No Pricing
Production 1-10

Piece of the Game Combo

NM/M
1	Albert Pujols/ Bat-Jsy/100	25.00
2	Angel Berroa/ Bat-Pants/100	6.00
3	Aubrey Huff/ Bat-Jsy/100	6.00
4	Barry Zito/Bat-Jsy/100	8.00
5	Bobby Abreu/ Bat-Jsy/100	6.00
6	Carlos Beltran/ Bat-Jsy/100	6.00
7	Chipper Jones/ Bat-Jsy/100	10.00
8	Derek Jeter/ Bat-Jsy/100	40.00
9	Eric Chavez/ Bat-Jsy/50	8.00
10	Eric Hinske/Bat-Jsy/25	8.00
12	George Brett/ Bat-Jsy/100	25.00
13	Jay Gibbons/ Bat-Jsy/100	6.00
14	Jim Edmonds/ Bat-Jsy/100	8.00
15	Josh Beckett/ Bat-Jsy/100	6.00
16	Manny Ramirez/ Bat-Jsy/100	10.00
17	Mark Mulder/ Bat-Jsy/25	15.00
18	Marlon Byrd/ Bat-Jsy/100	6.00
19	Mike Lowell/ Bat-Jsy/100	6.00
20	Mike Schmidt/ Bat-Jsy/50	50.00
21	Nolan Ryan/ Bat-Jsy/100	35.00
22	Rafael Furcal/ Bat-Jsy/100	6.00
23	Randy Johnson/ Bat-Jsy/100	15.00
24	Rod Carew/ Bat-Jsy/100	15.00
25	Torii Hunter/ Bat-Jsy/100	8.00

Piece of the Game Combo Signature

No Pricing
Production 1-10

Piece of the Game Jersey

NM/M

Quantity produced listed
1	Albert Pujols/250	15.00
2	Angel Berroa/250	4.00
3	Aubrey Huff/250	4.00
4	Barry Zito/250	6.00
5	Bobby Abreu/250	4.00
6	Carlos Beltran/250	4.00
7	Chipper Jones/250	8.00
8	Derek Jeter/250	40.00
9	Eric Chavez/250	5.00
10	Eric Hinske/100	4.00
12	George Brett/250	15.00
13	Jay Gibbons/250	4.00
14	Jim Edmonds/250	6.00
15	Josh Beckett/250	4.00
16	Manny Ramirez/250	6.00
17	Mark Mulder/100	6.00
18	Marlon Byrd/250	4.00
19	Mike Lowell/250	4.00
20	Mike Schmidt/50	35.00
21	Nolan Ryan/100	25.00
22	Rafael Furcal/250	4.00
23	Randy Johnson/250	8.00
24	Rod Carew/100	8.00
25	Torii Hunter/250	4.00

Piece of the Game Jersey Signature

Quantity produced listed

Prime Signature Autograph

NM/M
1	Garret Anderson/100	15.00

2	Rafael Palmeiro/50	40.00
3	Vladimir Guerrero/50	50.00
5	Dontrelle Willis/50	30.00
6	Miguel Cabrera/100	35.00
7	Shannon Stewart/100	10.00
9	Gary Sheffield/100	25.00
12	Tom Glavine/25	40.00
13	Brandon Webb/100	10.00
14	Carlos Lee/100	10.00
17	Magglio Ordonez/100	15.00
19	Andruw Jones/50	20.00
21	Sammy Sosa/50	100.00
22	Juan Gonzalez/50	25.00
23	Jeff Bagwell/25	50.00
24	Rickey Henderson/25	75.00
25	Mike Schmidt/50	60.00
26	Jim Rice/100	15.00
27	Billy Williams/100	15.00
28	Lou Brock/100	20.00
29	Robin Yount/25	75.00
30	Nolan Ryan/50	85.00
31	Darryl Strawberry/ 100	15.00
32	Cal Ripken Jr./25	200.00
33	Andre Dawson/100	15.00
34	Don Mattingly/50	75.00
35	Paul Molitor/50	50.00
36	Bo Jackson/50	75.00
37	Ernie Banks/50	50.00
38	Orel Hershiser/100	20.00
39	Mark Grace/50	40.00
40	Carlton Fisk/50	25.00

Prime Signature Autograph Bat

Quantity produced listed

Prime Signature Autograph Jersey

NM/M

Quantity produced listed
2	Rafael Palmeiro/25	75.00
6	Miguel Cabrera/20	75.00
7	Shannon Stewart/23	15.00
29	Robin Yount/19	75.00
31	Darryl Strawberry/25	25.00
34	Don Mattingly/23	100.00
39	Mark Grace/17	65.00

Prime Signature Insert

NM/M

Production 2,500 Sets
1	Garret Anderson	2.00
2	Rafael Palmeiro	3.00
3	Vladimir Guerrero	3.00
4	Alex Rodriguez	5.00
5	Dontrelle Willis	2.00
6	Miguel Cabrera	3.00
7	Shannon Stewart	2.00
8	Mike Piazza	4.00
9	Gary Sheffield	2.00
10	Ivan Rodriguez	3.00
11	Randy Johnson	3.00
12	Tom Glavine	2.00
13	Brandon Webb	2.00
14	Carlos Lee	2.00
15	Hideo Nomo	2.00
16	Mike Mussina	3.00
17	Magglio Ordonez	2.00
18	Austin Kearns	2.00
19	Andruw Jones	3.00
20	Mariano Rivera	3.00
21	Sammy Sosa	4.00
22	Juan Gonzalez	3.00
23	Jeff Bagwell	3.00
24	Rickey Henderson	2.00
25	Mike Schmidt	5.00
26	Jim Rice	2.00
27	Billy Williams	2.00
28	Lou Brock	2.00
29	Robin Yount	4.00
30	Nolan Ryan	8.00
31	Darryl Strawberry	2.00
32	Cal Ripken Jr.	10.00
33	Andre Dawson	2.00
34	Don Mattingly	8.00
35	Paul Molitor	3.00
36	Bo Jackson	3.00
37	Ernie Banks	4.00
38	Orel Hershiser	2.00
39	Mark Grace	3.00
40	Carlton Fisk	3.00

Quad Material

NM/M

Quantity produced listed
1	Matt Williams, Mark Grace, Will Clark, Keith Hernandez/100	60.00
2	Jason Giambi, Jim Thome, Carlos Delgado, Rafael Palmeiro/100	20.00

3 Albert Pujols, Ernie Banks, Jeff Bagwell, Jim Thome/100 — 50.00
4 Paul Molitor, Joe Morgan, Ryne Sandberg, Alfonso Soriano/50 — 50.00
5 Cal Ripken Jr., Derek Jeter, Alex Rodriguez, Nomar Garciaparra/100 — 75.00
6 Ozzie Smith, Robin Yount, Alan Trammell, Dave Concepcion/50 — 50.00
8 Johnny Bench, Carlton Fisk, Gary Carter, Mike Piazza/100 — 40.00
9 Todd Helton, Brian Giles, Edgar Renteria, Scott Rolen/25 — 40.00
10 Carlos Delgado, Alfonso Soriano, Alex Rodriguez, Troy Glaus/100 — 20.00
11 Harmon Killebrew, Reggie Jackson, Mike Schmidt, Sammy Sosa/100 — 65.00
12 Stan Musial, Rickey Henderson, Tony Gwynn, Lou Brock/25 — 80.00
13 Cal Ripken Jr., George Brett, Paul Molitor, Rod Carew/100 — 75.00
14 Sammy Sosa, Vladimir Guerrero, Manny Ramirez, Magglio Ordonez/100 — 40.00
15 Andruw Jones, Jim Edmonds, Torii Hunter, Vernon Wells/100 — 20.00
16 Chipper Jones, Shawn Green, Andruw Jones, Lance Berkman/100 — 20.00
17 Tony Gwynn, Dale Murphy, Kirby Puckett, Andre Dawson/100 — 40.00
19 Nolan Ryan, Roger Clemens, Kerry Wood, Josh Beckett/100 — 75.00
21 Dennis Eckersley, John Smoltz, Mariano Rivera, Lee Smith/100 — 40.00
22 Mike Mussina, Greg Maddux, Jack Morris, Bert Blyleven/100 — 40.00
23 Steve Carlton, Tom Glavine, Barry Zito, Andy Pettittte/100 — 20.00
24 Whitey Ford, Warren Spahn, Bob Feller, Juan Marichal/25 — 80.00
25 Nolan Ryan, Roger Clemens, Steve Carlton, Randy Johnson/100 — 80.00

Rookie Year Jersey Number

		NM/M
1	Gary Carter/50	10.00
2	Robin Yount/50	30.00
3	Roger Clemens/25	40.00
4	Gary Sheffield/50	8.00
5	Mike Piazza/25	30.00
6	Hideo Nomo/25	30.00
7	Alex Rodriguez/50	20.00
8	Mark Prior/25	15.00
9	Dontrelle Willis/100	10.00
10	Angel Berroa/100	8.00

Rookie Year Jersey Signature

No Pricing
Production 1-10

Signature Bronze

		NM/M
Quantity produced listed		
2	Garret Anderson/100	15.00
5	Vladimir Guerrero/50	50.00
6	Brandon Webb/100	8.00
7	Brian Bruney/96	8.00
11	Robby Hammock/100	8.00
13	Shea Hillenbrand/100	10.00
15	Adam LaRoche/100	10.00
16	Andruw Jones/25	25.00
17	Bubba Nelson/100	8.00
22	Marcus Giles/100	15.00
23	Rafael Furcal/50	15.00
26	Adam Loewen/100	8.00
27	Cal Ripken Jr./25	150.00
29	Jay Gibbons/100	8.00
30	Luis Matos/100	8.00
33	Bobby Doerr/100	15.00
35	Edwin Almonte/99	8.00
36	Jason Varitek/100	30.00
37	Kevin Youkilis/100	15.00
42	Andre Dawson/100	15.00
43	Aramis Ramirez/25	25.00
44	Brendan Harris/100	8.00
45	Derrek Lee/100	20.00
46	Ernie Banks/25	60.00
47	Kerry Wood/25	50.00
48	Mark Prior/50	40.00
50	Sammy Sosa/50	125.00
51	Carlos Lee/100	10.00
52	Frank Thomas/25	50.00
53	Joe Borchard/100	8.00
54	Joe Crede/50	10.00
55	Magglio Ordonez/50	15.00
58	Barry Larkin/25	40.00
59	Brandon Larson/100	8.00
61	Ryan Wagner/100	8.00
63	Bob Feller/100	20.00
64	Brian Tallet/100	8.00
66	Jeremy Guthrie/100	8.00
67	Jody Gerut/100	10.00
68	Clint Barmes/100	8.00
69	Jeff Baker/25	20.00
72	Preston Wilson/100	15.00
74	Alan Trammell/100	15.00
78	Preston Larrison/100	8.00
79	Dontrelle Willis/25	30.00
83	Miguel Cabrera/100	40.00
85	Andy Pettitte/25	50.00
86	Chris Burke/100	8.00
88	Jeff Bagwell/25	50.00
91	Morgan Ensberg/100	10.00
96	Byron Gettis/100	8.00
97	Carlos Beltran/100	30.00
98	George Brett/25	100.00
101	Duke Snider/100	25.00
102	Edwin Jackson/100	10.00
105	Hong-Chih Kuo/100	25.00
106	Kazuhisa Ishii/25	40.00
107	Paul LoDuca/100	15.00
108	Robin Ventura/50	15.00
110	Junior Spivey/50	10.00
112	Scott Podsednik/100	15.00
113	J.D. Durbin/100	8.00
114	Jacque Jones/100	15.00
116	Johan Santana/100	25.00
117	Shannon Stewart/100	10.00
123	Gary Carter/100	15.00
125	Lenny Dykstra/100	15.00
130	Chien-Ming Wang/100	100.00
132	Don Mattingly/25	80.00
133	Gary Sheffield/50	25.00
137	Jorge Posada/50	25.00
142	Whitey Ford/50	25.00
145	Mark Mulder/100	15.00
146	Rich Harden/100	15.00
147	Tim Hudson/25	40.00
148	Reggie Jackson/50	50.00
149	Rickey Henderson/25	80.00
150	Brett Myers/100	8.00
154	Marlon Byrd/100	8.00
155	Mike Schmidt/50	60.00
156	Ryan Howard/100	80.00
161	Jay Payton/100	10.00
168	Jerome Williams/50	20.00
169	Will Clark/50	50.00
171	Chris Snelling/100	8.00
176	Shigetoshi Hasegawa/100	50.00
178	Dan Haren/100	10.00
180	Jim Edmonds/25	30.00
182	Scott Rolen/50	30.00
183	Stan Musial/50	60.00
184	Aubrey Huff/100	15.00
185	Chad Gaudin/100	8.00
186	Delmon Young/50	30.00
188	Rocco Baldelli/10	
191	Mark Teixeira/25	25.00
192	Nolan Ryan/50	100.00
193	Alexis Rios/100	15.00
195	Dustin McGowan/100	10.00
196	Guillermo Quiroz/50	10.00
197	Josh Phelps/25	15.00
198	Roy Halladay/25	25.00
200	Vinnie Chulk/25	15.00
201	Jose Capellan/100	35.00
203	David Crouthers/100	8.00
204	Akinori Otsuka/100	35.00
205	Nick Regilio/100	8.00
206	Justin Hampson/100	8.00
207	Lincoln Holdzkom/100	8.00
208	Jorge Sequea/100	8.00
209	Justin Leone/100	15.00
210	Renyel Pinto/100	10.00
211	Mariano Gomez/100	8.00
214	Cory Sullivan/100	8.00
216	Chris Shelton/100	40.00
217	Willy Taveras/25	8.00
218	John Gall/100	15.00
222	Ronald Belisario/100	8.00
223	Mike Rouse/100	8.00
224	Dennis Sarfate/100	8.00

Signature Gold

Gold: .75-1.5X Bronze
Production 1-50
No pricing 25 or less.

Signature Silver

Silver: .75-1.5X Bronze
Production 1-100
No pricing 25 or less.

Signature Platinum

No Pricing
Production One Set

Signs of Greatness

		NM/M
Quantity produced listed		
1	Mark Prior/25	50.00
2	Scott Podsednik/25	25.00
3	Dontrelle Willis/25	30.00
5	Rocco Baldelli/20	40.00
6	Brandon Webb/25	20.00
7	Rich Harden/25	25.00
8	Miguel Cabrera/25	50.00
9	Josh Beckett/25	40.00
10	Mark Teixeira/25	40.00

Tandem Material

		NM/M
Common Duo:		10.00
Quantity produced listed		
1	Bo Jackson, Deion Sanders/100	30.00
2	Eddie Murray, Rafael Palmeiro/250	15.00
3	Alex Rodriguez, Dale Murphy/250	15.00
4	Carlton Fisk, Ivan Rodriguez/250	15.00
5	Rickey Henderson, Lou Brock/50	30.00
6	Sammy Sosa, Ernie Banks/250	25.00
7	Warren Spahn, Steve Carlton/100	15.00
8	Carl Yastrzemski, Darrell Evans/250	25.00
9	Keith Hernandez, Lenny Dykstra/250	10.00
10	Pee Wee Reese, Marty Marion/100	15.00
11	Hideo Nomo, Chipper Jones/250	15.00
12	Willie McCovey, Reggie Jackson/100	20.00
13	Mark Prior, Barry Zito/100	10.00
14	Cal Ripken Jr., Miguel Tejada/Bat/100	50.00
15	Roberto Clemente, Vladimir Guerrero/Bat/100	75.00
16	Gary Carter, Mike Piazza/250	15.00
17	Jim Rice, Fred Lynn/50	20.00
18	Willie Stargell, Keith Hernandez/250	15.00
19	Nomar Garciaparra, Mark Teixeira/100	20.00
20	Derek Jeter, Phil Rizzuto/50	50.00
21	Eric Chavez, Hank Blalock/100	10.00
22	Eric Davis, Darryl Strawberry/100	15.00
23	Rickey Henderson, Deion Sanders/100	30.00
24	Dave Parker, Austin Kearns/250	10.00
25	Luis Aparicio, Dave Concepcion/100	15.00
26	Rafael Palmeiro, Will Clark/100	25.00
27	Ryne Sandberg, Ozzie Smith/250	50.00
28	Alex Rodriguez M's, Jose Canseco/250	15.00
29	Sammy Sosa, Juan Gonzalez/250	15.00
30	Pedro J. Martinez, Juan Marichal/50	20.00
31	Stan Musial, Duke Snider/5	
32	Dwight Gooden, Gary Sheffield/250	10.00
33	Lou Boudreau, Omar Vizquel/100	15.00
34	Mark Prior, Ron Santo Bat/100	30.00
35	Albert Pujols, Ken Boyer/250	25.00
36	Tom Seaver, Curt Schilling/250	15.00
37	Joe Morgan, Jeff Kent/250	10.00
38	Steve Garvey, Ozzie Smith/250	25.00
39	Mike Piazza, Ivan Rodriguez/250	15.00
40	Mike Schmidt, Jim Thome/100	25.00

2004 Playoff Prestige

		NM/M
Complete Set (200):		35.00
Common Player:		.15
Pack (6):		3.50
Box (24):		75.00
1	Bengie Molina	.15
2	Garret Anderson	.25
3	Jarrod Washburn	.15
4	Scott Spiezio	.15
5	Tim Salmon	.25
6	Troy Glaus	.40
7	Alex Cintron	.15
8	Brandon Webb	.25
9	Curt Schilling	.50
10	Edgar Gonzalez	.50
11	Luis Gonzalez	.25
12	Randy Johnson	.75
13	Steve Finley	.15
14	Andruw Jones	.50
15	Bubba Nelson	.50
16	Chipper Jones	1.00
17	Gary Sheffield	.40
18	Greg Maddux	1.00
19	Javy Lopez	.40
20	John Smoltz	.25
21	Marcus Giles	.25
22	Rafael Furcal	.25
23	Brian Roberts	.15
24	Jason Johnson	.15
25	Jay Gibbons	.25
26	Luis Matos	.15
27	Melvin Mora	.15
28	Tony Batista	.15
29	Bill Mueller	.25
30	David Ortiz	.40
31	Johnny Damon	.25
32	Kevin Youkilis	1.00
33	Manny Ramirez	.50
34	Nomar Garciaparra	1.50
35	Pedro Martinez	.75
36	Trot Nixon	.25
37	Aramis Ramirez	.25
38	Brendan Harris	.50
39	Carlos Zambrano	.15
40	Corey Patterson	.25
41	Kenny Lofton	.25
42	Kerry Wood	.75
43	Mark Prior	1.50
44	Sammy Sosa	1.50
45	Bartolo Colon	.25
46	Carlos Lee	.25
47	Esteban Loaiza	.15
48	Frank Thomas	.50
49	Joe Crede	.15

50	Magglio Ordonez	.40
51	Roberto Alomar	.40
52	Adam Dunn	.40
53	Austin Kearns	.40
54	Josh Hall	.15
55	Ken Griffey Jr.	1.00
56	Sean Casey	.15
57	Micheal Nakamura	.15
58	C.C. Sabathia	.15
59	Casey Blake	.15
60	Jody Gerut	.15
61	Matt Lawton	.15
62	Milton Bradley	.15
63	Omar Vizquel	.25
64	Jason Jennings	.15
65	Jay Payton	.25
66	Larry Walker	.25
67	Preston Wilson	.25
68	Todd Helton	.50
69	Bobby Higginson	.15
70	Carlos Pena	.15
71	Dmitri Young	.15
72	Jeremy Bonderman	.15
73	Preston Larrison	.50
74	Derrek Lee	.25
75	Dontrelle Willis	.40
76	Ivan Rodriguez	.50
77	Josh Beckett	.50
78	Juan Pierre	.15
79	Miguel Cabrera	.75
80	Mike Lowell	.25
81	Chris Burke	.15
82	Craig Biggio	.25
83	Jeff Bagwell	.50
84	Jeff Kent	.25
85	Lance Berkman	.40
86	Richard Hidalgo	.25
87	Roy Oswalt	.25
88	Aaron Guiel	.15
89	Angel Berroa	.15
90	Carlos Beltran	.40
91	Jeremy Affeldt	.15
92	Michael Sweeney	.15
93	Runelvys Hernandez	.15
94	Dave Roberts	.15
95	Eric Gagne	.40
96	Hideo Nomo	.40
97	Kevin Brown	.25
98	Paul Lo Duca	.15
99	Shawn Green	.40
100	Ben Sheets	.40
101	Geoff Jenkins	.40
102	Richie Sexson	.40
103	Rickie Weeks	1.00
104	Scott Podsednik	.50
105	J.D. Durbin	.50
106	Jacque Jones	.15
107	Jason Kubel	.50
108	Shannon Stewart	.15
109	Torii Hunter	.40
110	Chad Cordero	.50
111	Javier Vazquez	.25
112	Jose Vidro	.15
113	Livan Hernandez	.15
114	Orlando Cabrera	.15
115	Tony Armas Jr.	.15
116	Vladimir Guerrero	.75
117	Al Leiter	.15
118	Cliff Floyd	.15
119	Jae Weong So	.15
120	Jose Reyes	.50
121	Mike Piazza	1.00
122	Tom Glavine	.25
123	Aaron Boone	.15
124	Alfonso Soriano	.75
125	Andy Pettitte	.15
126	Derek Jeter	.15
127	Hideki Matsui	.15
128	Jason Giambi	.15
129	Jorge Posada	.50
130	Jose Contreras	.25
131	Mike Mussina	.50
132	Barry Zito	.40
133	Eric Byrnes	.15
134	Eric Chavez	.40
135	Jose Guillen	.15
136	Mark Mulder	.40
137	Miguel Tejada	.40
138	Ramon Hernandez	.15
139	Rich Harden	.15
140	Tim Hudson	.40
141	Bobby Abreu	.25
142	Brett Myers	.15
143	Jim Thome	.75
144	Kevin Millwood	.40
145	Mike Lieberthal	.15
146	Ryan Howard	1.50
147	Craig Wilson	.15
148	Jack Wilson	.15
149	Jason Kendall	.15
150	Kip Wells	.15
151	Reggie Sanders	.15
152	Albert Pujols	1.50
153	Edgar Renteria	.25

154	Jim Edmonds	.40
155	Matt Morris	.25
156	Scott Rolen	.75
157	Tino Martinez	.15
158	Woody Williams	.15
159	Brian Giles	.25
160	Freddy Guzman RC	.50
161	Jake Peavy	.25
162	Khalil Greene	.50
163	Phil Nevin	.15
164	Ryan Klesko	.25
165	Ray Durham	.15
166	Jason Schmidt	.25
167	Jerome Williams	.50
168	Jesse Foppert	.15
169	Jose Cruz	.15
170	Marquis Grissom	.15
171	Merkin Valdez RC	1.50
172	Rich Aurilia	.15
173	Bret Boone	.25
174	Freddy Garcia	.15
175	Ichiro Suzuki	1.50
176	Jamie Moyer	.15
177	John Olerud	.25
178	Mike Cameron	.15
179	Randy Winn	.15
180	Aubrey Huff	.25
181	Carl Crawford	.25
182	Chad Gaudin	.50
183	Rocco Baldelli	.50
184	Toby Hall	.15
185	Travis Lee	.15
186	Alex Rodriguez	1.50
187	Hank Blalock	.40
188	John Thomson	.15
189	Juan Gonzalez	.50
190	Mark Teixeira	.40
191	Michael Young	.15
192	Rafael Palmeiro	.50
193	Ramon Nivar	.50
194	Carlos Delgado	.50
195	Dustin McGowan	.50
196	Frank Catalanotto	.15
197	Vinnie Chulk	.15
198	Orlando Hudson	.15
199	Roy Halladay	.40
200	Vernon Wells	.25

Xtra Bases Black

Black (1-200):	4-8X
Production 75 Sets	

Xtra Bases Purple

Purple (1-200):	2-5X
Production 150 Sets	

Xtra Bases Black Autographs

No Pricing
Production 25 Sets

Xtra Bases Green Autographs

No Pricing

Xtra Bases Purple Autographs

	NM/M
Production 100 Sets	
10 Edgar Gonzalez	6.00
15 Bubba Nelson	8.00
32 Kevin Youkilis	15.00
38 Brendan Harris	8.00
57 Micheal Nakamura	6.00
73 Preston Larrison	6.00
79 Miguel Cabrera	35.00
81 Chris Burke	15.00
105 J.D. Durbin	10.00
107 Jason Kubel	8.00
146 Ryan Howard	75.00

193	Ramon Nivar	8.00
195	Dustin McGowan	10.00
198	Orlando Hudson	8.00

Xtra Bases Red Autographs

No Pricing

Achievements

		NM/M
1	Hideo Nomo/95 ROY	1.50
2	Don Mattingly/ 85 MVP	6.00
3	Roger Clemens/ 86 CY/MVP	6.00
4	Greg Maddux/95 CY	4.00
5	Stan Musial/43 MVP	4.00
6	Roberto Clemente/ 66 MVP	6.00
7	Derek Jeter/96 ROY	6.00
8	Albert Pujols/01 ROY	6.00
9	Cal Ripken Jr./91 MVP	8.00
10	George Brett/80 MVP	8.00
11	Carl Yastrzemski/ 67 MVP	4.00
12	Rickey Henderson/ 90 MVP	2.00
13	Sammy Sosa/98 MVP	5.00
14	Randy Johnson/02 CY	3.00
15	Bob Gibson/ 68 CY/MVP	3.00

Autographs

		NM/M
Quantity produced listed		
8	Brandon Webb/100	20.00
10	Edgar Gonzalez PROS/150	8.00
15	Bubba Nelson PROS/250	10.00
25	Jay Gibbons/50	20.00
32	Kevin Youkilis PROS/100	20.00
36	Trot Nixon/25	40.00
37	Aramis Ramirez/25	25.00
38	Brendan Harris PROS/400	8.00
49	Joe Crede/25	15.00
54	Josh Hall/25	15.00
57	Mike Nakamura/250	8.00
60	Jody Gerut/50	15.00
73	Preston Larrison PROS/250	8.00
75	Dontrelle Willis/25	40.00
79	Miguel Cabrera/100	30.00
81	Chris Burke PROS/250	10.00
93	Runelvys Hernandez/50	7.00
96	Hideo Nomo/5	
98	Paul Lo Duca/25	15.00
102	Richie Sexson/25	25.00
105	J.D. Durbin P ROS/500	10.00
106	Jacque Jones/50	12.00
107	Jason Kubel PROS/400	8.00
108	Shannon Stewart/50	15.00
112	Jose Vidro/50	15.00
114	Orlando Cabrera/25	20.00
119	Jae Weong Seo/25	20.00
133	Eric Byrnes/50	15.00
136	Mark Mulder/25	20.00
139	Rich Harden/50	25.00
146	Ryan Howard PROS/400	75.00
193	Ramon Nivar PROS/250	8.00
195	Dustin McGowan PROS/100	10.00
197	Vinnie Chulk/112	8.00
198	Orlando Hudson/100	10.00

Changing Stripes

		NM/M
Inserted 1:11		
Foil:		1-2X
Production 150 Sets		
Holofoil:		2-3X
Production 50 Sets		
1	Rickey Henderson/ A's-Yanks	4.00
2	Mike Mussina/ O's-Yanks	2.00
3	Jim Thome/ Indians-Phils	3.00
4	Hideo Nomo/ Sox-Dodgers	1.50
5	Scott Rolen/ Phils-Cards	3.00
6	Jason Giambi/ A's-Yanks	3.00
7	Randy Johnson/ Astros-D'backs	3.00
8	Shawn Green/ Jays-Dodgers	1.50
9	Curt Schilling/ Phils-D'backs	2.00
10	Alex Rodriguez/ M's-Rangers	5.00
11	Greg Maddux/ Cubs-Braves	4.00
12	Randy Johnson/ M's-Astros	3.00
13	Hideo Nomo/ Dodgers-Mets	1.50
14	Juan Rodriguez/ Rgr-Marlins	2.00
15	Juan Gonzalez/ Indians-Rangers	2.00
16	Manny Ramirez/ Indians-Sox	2.00
17	Mike Piazza/ Dodgers-Mets	4.00
18	Nolan Ryan/ Angels-Astros	8.00
19	Nolan Ryan/ Astros-Rangers	8.00
20	Pedro Martinez/ Expos-Sox	3.00
21	Reggie Jackson/ Yanks-Angels	2.00
22	Roberto Alomar/ Mets-Sox	1.50
23	Rod Carew/ Twins-Angels	2.00
24	Roger Clemens/ Sox-Yanks	6.00
25	Sammy Sosa/ Sox-Cubs	5.00

Changing Stripes Dual Jersey

		NM/M
Prodcution 150 Sets		
Primes:		No Pricing
Production 25 Sets		
1	Rickey Henderson/ A's-Yanks	10.00
2	Mike Mussina/ O's-Yanks	8.00
3	Jim Thome/ Indians-Phils	10.00
4	Hideo Nomo/ Sox-Dodgers	15.00
5	Scott Rolen/ Phils-Cards	10.00
6	Jason Giambi/ A's-Yanks	12.00
7	Randy Johnson/ Astros-D'backs	10.00

8	Shawn Green/Jays-Dodgers	6.00
9	Curt Schilling/Phils-D'backs	8.00
10	Alex Rodriguez/M's-Rangers	15.00
12	Randy Johnson/M's-Astros	10.00
13	Hideo Nomo/Dodgers-Mets	15.00
14	Ivan Rodriguez/Rgr-Marlins	10.00
15	Juan Gonzalez/Indians-Rangers	8.00
16	Manny Ramirez/Indians-Sox	8.00
17	Mike Piazza/Dodgers-Mets	10.00
18	Nolan Ryan/Angels-Astros	30.00
19	Nolan Ryan/Astrs-Rangers	30.00
20	Pedro Martinez/Expos-Sox	10.00
22	Roberto Alomar/Mets-Sox	8.00
23	Rod Carew/Twins-Angels	12.00
24	Roger Clemens/Sox-Yanks	15.00
25	Sammy Sosa/Sox-Cubs	15.00

Connections

NM/M

Inserted 1:9
Foil: 1.5-2X
Production 100 Sets
Holofoil: No Pricing
Production 21 Sets

1	Derek Jeter, Alfonso Soriano	4.00
2	Greg Maddux, Chipper Jones	2.00
3	Albert Pujols, Scott Rolen	3.00
4	Randy Johnson, Curt Schilling	1.50
5	Nomar Garciaparra, Manny Ramirez	3.00
6	Alex Rodriguez, Mark Teixeira	3.00
7	Barry Zito, Tim Hudson	.75
8	Sammy Sosa, Mark Prior	2.00
9	Derek Jeter, Jason Giambi	4.00
10	Roger Clemens, Mike Mussina	3.00
11	Mark Prior, Kerry Wood	2.00
12	Alex Rodriguez, Hank Blalock	3.00
13	Frank Thomas, Magglio Ordonez	1.00
14	Nomar Garciaparra, Pedro Martinez	3.00
15	Carlos Delgado, Vernon Wells	1.00
16	Miguel Tejada, Eric Chavez	.75
17	Jeff Bagwell, Lance Berkman	1.00
18	Jim Thome, Bobby Abreu	1.50
19	Todd Helton, Preston Wilson	1.00
20	Vladimir Guerrero, Javier Vazquez	1.50

Connections Material

NM/M

Production 250 Sets

1	Derek Jeter/Bat, Alfonso Soriano/Bat	20.00
2	Greg Maddux/Bat, Chipper Jones/Jsy	12.00
3	Albert Pujols/Bat, Scott Rolen/Bat	15.00
4	Randy Johnson/Bat, Curt Schilling/Bat	10.00
5	Nomar Garciaparra/Bat, Manny Ramirez/Bat	10.00
6	Alex Rodriguez/Bat, Mark Teixeira/Bat	10.00
7	Barry Zito/Bat, Tim Hudson/Bat	10.00
8	Sammy Sosa/Bat, Mark Prior/Bat	15.00
9	Derek Jeter/Bat, Jason Giambi/Bat	20.00
10	Pedro Clemens/Jsy, Mike Mussina/Bat	15.00
11	Mark Prior/Bat, Kerry Wood/Bat	10.00
12	Alex Rodriguez/Bat, Hank Blalock/Bat	10.00
13	Frank Thomas/Bat, Magglio Ordonez/Bat	8.00
14	Nomar Garciaparra/Bat, Pedro Martinez/Bat	15.00
15	Carlos Delgado/Bat, Vernon Wells/Bat	8.00
16	Miguel Tejada/Bat, Eric Chavez/Bat	8.00
17	Jeff Bagwell/Bat, Lance Berkman/Bat	10.00
18	Jim Thome/Jsy, Bobby Abreu/Bat	10.00
19	Todd Helton/Bat, Preston Wilson	8.00
20	Vladimir Guerrero/Bat, Javier Vazquez/Jsy	10.00

Diamond Heritage

NM/M

Inserted 1:13

1	Mike Piazza	3.00
2	Greg Maddux	2.50
3	Nomar Garciaparra	3.00
4	Chipper Jones	2.00
5	Albert Pujols	4.00
6	Derek Jeter	5.00
7	Shawn Green	.75
8	Alex Rodriguez	4.00
9	Jim Thome	2.00
10	Jason Giambi	1.50
11	Sammy Sosa	3.00
12	Hank Blalock	1.00
13	Garret Anderson	.75
14	Manny Ramirez	1.50
15	Scott Rolen	1.50
16	Jeff Bagwell	1.50
17	Randy Johnson	2.00
18	Ichiro Rodriguez	3.00
19	Ivan Rodriguez	1.50
20	Alfonso Soriano	1.50

Diamond Heritage Material

NM/M

Inserted 1:92

1	Mike Piazza/Bat	10.00
2	Greg Maddux/Bat	8.00
3	Nomar Garciaparra/Bat	10.00
4	Chipper Jones/Jsy	8.00
5	Albert Pujols/Bat	15.00
6	Derek Jeter/Bat	15.00
7	Shawn Green/Bat	5.00
8	Alex Rodriguez/Bat	10.00
9	Jim Thome/Jsy	8.00
10	Jason Giambi/Bat	8.00
11	Sammy Sosa/Bat	12.00
12	Hank Blalock/Bat	6.00

13	Garret Anderson/Bat	5.00
14	Manny Ramirez/Bat	6.00
15	Scott Rolen/Bat	6.00
16	Jeff Bagwell/Bat	6.00
17	Randy Johnson/Bat	8.00
19	Ivan Rodriguez/Bat	6.00
20	Alfonso Soriano/Bat	6.00

League Leaders Double

NM/M

Production 500 Sets
Foil: 1-2X
Production 75 Sets
Holofoil: No Pricing
Production 10 Sets

1	Alex Rodriguez, Jim Thome HR	5.00
2	Mark Prior, Pedro Martinez ERA	4.00
3	Roger Clemens, Kerry Wood SO	5.00
4	Nomar Garciaparra, Albert Pujols Hit	5.00
5	Derek Jeter, Albert Pujols Avg	5.00

League Leaders Double Material

NM/M

Production 100 Sets

1	Alex Rodriguez/Bat, Jim Thome/Bat	20.00
2	Mark Prior/Jsy, Pedro Martinez/Jsy	15.00
3	Roger Clemens/Jsy, Kerry Wood/Jsy	20.00
4	Nomar Garciaparra/Bat, Albert Pujols/Bat	25.00
5	Derek Jeter/Jsy, Albert Pujols/Bat	25.00

League Leaders Quad

NM/M

Production 250 Sets
Foil: 1-2X
Production 50 Sets
Holofoil: No Pricing
Production 5 Sets

1	Albert Pujols, Todd Helton, Edgar Renteria, Gary Sheffield	10.00
2	Derek Jeter, Manny Ramirez, Nomar Garciaparra, Ichiro Suzuki	10.00
3	Mark Prior, Curt Schilling, Nomar Garciaparra, Kevin Brown	8.00
4	Richie Sexson, Sammy Sosa, Albert Pujols, Jim Thome	10.00
5	Alex Rodriguez, Frank Thomas, Jason Giambi, Carlos Delgado	8.00

League Leaders Quad Material

NM/M

Production 50 Sets

1	Albert Pujols, Todd Helton, Edgar Renteria, Gary Sheffield	30.00
3	Mark Prior, Curt Schilling, Hideo Nomo, Kevin Brown	30.00
4	Richie Sexson, Sammy Sosa, Albert Pujols, Jim Thome	40.00
5	Alex Rodriguez, Frank Thomas, Jason Giambi, Carlos Delgado	35.00

League Leaders Single

NM/M

Foil: 2-3X
Production 100 Sets

Holofoil: No Pricing
Production 25 Sets

1	Alex Rodriguez/AL HR	3.00
2	Albert Pujols/NL Hit	3.00
3	Albert Pujols/NL Avg	3.00
4	Nomar Garciaparra/AL Hit	2.00
5	Mark Prior/NL ERA	2.00
6	Pedro Martinez/AL ERA	1.00
7	Kerry Wood/NL SO	1.00
8	Derek Jeter/AL Avg	1.00
9	Jason Giambi/AL BB	1.00
10	Roger Clemens/AL SO	2.00

League Leaders Single Material

NM/M

Production 250 Sets

1	Alex Rodriguez/Bat	10.00
2	Albert Pujols/Bat	15.00
3	Albert Pujols/Bat	15.00
4	Nomar Garciaparra/Bat	10.00
5	Mark Prior/Jsy	10.00
6	Pedro Martinez/Jsy	8.00
7	Kerry Wood/Jsy	8.00
8	Derek Jeter/Jsy	15.00
9	Jason Giambi/Jsy	6.00
10	Roger Clemens/Jsy	12.00

Players Collection Jersey

NM/M

Inserted 1:79
Platinum: 1-2X
Production 50

1	Adam Dunn	5.00
2	Adam Dunn	5.00
3	Adam Dunn	5.00
4	Alex Rodriguez	10.00
5	Alex Rodriguez	10.00
6	Alex Rodriguez	10.00
7	Alex Rodriguez	10.00
8	Andruw Jones	6.00
9	Andruw Jones	6.00
10	Austin Kearns	6.00
11	Brandon Webb	4.00
12	C.C. Sabathia	4.00
13	Cal Ripken Jr.	25.00
14	Carlos Beltran	5.00
15	Carlos Delgado	6.00
16	Carlos Lee	6.00
17	Chipper Jones	8.00
18	Chipper Jones	8.00
19	Craig Biggio	4.00
20	Curt Schilling	4.00
21	David Wells	4.00
22	Don Mattingly	15.00
23	Dontrelle Willis	6.00
24	Frank Thomas	8.00
25	Frank Thomas	8.00
26	Fred McGriff	6.00
27	Garret Anderson	6.00
28	Gary Sheffield	6.00
29	Gary Sheffield	6.00
30	Greg Maddux	10.00
31	Hank Blalock	6.00
32	Hank Blalock	6.00

33	Hee Seop Choi	4.00
34	Hideo Nomo	8.00
35	Hideo Nomo	8.00
36	Hideo Nomo	8.00
37	Ivan Rodriguez	6.00
38	Ivan Rodriguez	6.00
39	Jason Giambi	6.00
40	Jim Edmonds	6.00
41	Jim Thome	8.00
42	John Olerud	4.00
43	John Smoltz	6.00
44	Josh Beckett	6.00
45	Josh Phelps	4.00
46	Juan Gonzalez	6.00
47	Juan Gonzalez	6.00
48	Kazuhisa Ishii	4.00
49	Lance Berkman	5.00
50	Larry Walker	5.00
51	Larry Walker	5.00
52	Luis Gonzalez	5.00
53	Magglio Ordonez	6.00
54	Magglio Ordonez	6.00
55	Manny Ramirez	6.00
56	Manny Ramirez	6.00
57	Mark Prior	8.00
58	Mark Prior	8.00
59	Mark Teixeira	6.00
60	Mike Mussina	6.00
61	Mike Piazza	8.00
62	Mike Piazza	8.00
63	Mike Piazza	8.00
64	Nomar Garciaparra	8.00
65	Nomar Garciaparra	8.00
66	Pat Burrell	6.00
67	Paul Konerko	5.00
68	Paul Lo Duca	5.00
69	Pedro Martinez	8.00
70	Rafael Furcal	5.00
71	Rafael Palmeiro	8.00
72	Rafael Palmeiro	8.00
73	Ramon Hernandez	4.00
74	Rickey Henderson	8.00
75	Rickey Henderson	8.00
76	Rickey Henderson	8.00
77	Roberto Alomar	6.00
78	Roberto Alomar	6.00
79	Robin Ventura	5.00
80	Roger Clemens	10.00
81	Roger Clemens	10.00
82	Roy Halladay	6.00
83	Sammy Sosa	12.00
84	Sammy Sosa	12.00
85	Sammy Sosa	12.00
86	Scott Rolen	8.00
87	Shannon Stewart	4.00
88	Shawn Green	5.00
89	Shawn Green	5.00
90	Shawn Green	5.00
91	Terrence Long	4.00
92	Tim Hudson	6.00
93	Todd Helton	8.00
94	Todd Helton	8.00
95	Tom Glavine	6.00
96	Tom Glavine	6.00
97	Torii Hunter	6.00
98	Vernon Wells	4.00
99	Vladimir Guerrero	8.00
100	Vladimir Guerrero	8.00

Prestigious Pros

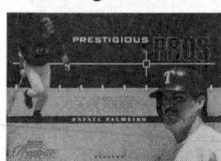

		NM/M
Inserted 1:23		
1	Mark Prior	3.00
2	Derek Jeter	5.00
3	Mike Mussina	1.50
4	Nomar Garciaparra	3.00
5	Roger Clemens	4.00
6	Jason Giambi	1.50
7	Randy Johnson	2.00
8	Rafael Palmeiro	1.50
9	Barry Zito	1.00
10	Pat Burrell	1.00

Stars of MLB

		NM/M
Foil:		1-2X
Production 100 Sets		
Holofoil:		No Pricing
Prod. 25 Sets		
1	Albert Pujols	6.00
2	Derek Jeter	8.00
3	Mike Piazza	4.00
4	Greg Maddux	4.00

5	Ichiro Suzuki	5.00
6	Nomar Garciaparra	5.00
7	Ivan Rodriguez	2.00
8	Randy Johnson	3.00
9	Alex Rodriguez	6.00
10	Sammy Sosa	5.00
11	Alfonso Soriano	3.00
12	Vladimir Guerrero	3.00
13	Jason Giambi	3.00
14	Mark Prior	4.00
15	Chipper Jones	3.00

Stars of MLB Jersey

		NM/M
Production 250 Sets		
Prime:		1-2X
Production 50		
1	Albert Pujols	15.00
2	Derek Jeter	15.00
3	Mike Piazza	8.00
4	Greg Maddux	10.00
6	Nomar Garciaparra	8.00
7	Ivan Rodriguez	6.00
8	Randy Johnson	8.00
9	Alex Rodriguez	10.00
10	Sammy Sosa	12.00
11	Alfonso Soriano	8.00
12	Vladimir Guerrero	8.00
13	Jason Giambi	6.00
14	Mark Prior	10.00
15	Chipper Jones	8.00

Stars of MLB Jersey Autographs

		NM/M
Quantity produced listed		
14	Mark Prior/50	75.00

2004 Playoff Prime Cuts

		NM/M
Complete Set (50):		150.00
Common Player:		1.50
Production 949 Sets		
Box (1):		185.00
1	Roger Clemens	6.00
2	Nomar Garciaparra	6.00
3	Albert Pujols	6.00
4	Sammy Sosa	6.00
5	Greg Maddux	4.00

6	Jason Giambi	3.00
7	Hideo Nomo	1.50
8	Mike Piazza	4.00
9	Ichiro Suzuki	5.00
10	Jeff Bagwell	2.00
11	Derek Jeter	8.00
12	Manny Ramirez	2.00
13	Rickey Henderson	1.50
14	Alex Rodriguez	6.00
15	Troy Glaus	1.50
16	Mike Mussina	1.50
17	Kerry Wood	2.00
18	Kazuhisa Ishii	1.00
19	Hideki Matsui	8.00
20	Frank Thomas	2.00
21	Barry Bonds	8.00
22	Adam Dunn	1.50
23	Randy Johnson	3.00
24	Alfonso Soriano	3.00
25	Pedro J. Martinez	3.00
26	Andruw Jones	2.00
27	Mark Prior	4.00
28	Vladimir Guerrero	3.00
29	Chipper Jones	4.00
30	Todd Helton	2.00
31	Rafael Palmeiro	2.00
32	Mark Grace	2.00
33	Pedro J. Martinez	3.00
34	Randy Johnson	3.00
35	Randy Johnson	3.00
36	Roger Clemens	6.00
37	Roger Clemens	6.00
38	Alex Rodriguez	6.00
39	Greg Maddux	4.00
40	Mike Piazza	4.00
41	Mike Piazza	4.00
42	Hideo Nomo	1.50
43	Rickey Henderson	1.50
44	Rickey Henderson	1.50
45	Barry Bonds	8.00
46	Ivan Rodriguez	2.00
47	George Brett	6.00
48	Cal Ripken Jr.	8.00
49	Nolan Ryan	10.00
50	Don Mattingly	6.00

Century

		NM/M
Cards (1-50):		1-2X
Production 100 Sets		
Century Gold:		No Pricing
Production 10 Sets		
Century Proof:		No Pricing
Production One Set		

Icons Material

		NM/M
Varying quantities produced		
4	Johnny Bench/50	35.00
5	Lefty Grove/25	75.00
6	Carlton Fisk/50	25.00
7	Mel Ott/25	75.00
8	Bob Feller/25	30.00
9	Jackie Robinson/25	75.00
10	Ted Williams/50	135.00
11	Roy Campanella/50	40.00
12	Stan Musial/50	40.00
13	Yogi Berra/50	40.00
14	Babe Ruth/25	750.00
15	Roberto Clemente/50	100.00
16	Warren Spahn/50	40.00
17	Ernie Banks/50	40.00
18	Eddie Mathews/50	35.00
19	Ryne Sandberg/50	40.00
20	Rod Carew/50	25.00
21	Duke Snider/50	25.00
22	Jim Palmer/50	20.00
24	Frank Robinson/50	25.00
25	Brooks Robinson/50	40.00
26	Harmon Killebrew/50	40.00
27	Carl Yastrzemski/50	40.00
28	Reggie Jackson/50	25.00
29	Mike Schmidt/50	40.00
30	Robin Yount/50	30.00
31	George Brett/50	40.00
32	Nolan Ryan/50	40.00
33	Kirby Puckett/50	40.00
34	Cal Ripken Jr./50	60.00
35	Don Mattingly/50	35.00
36	Tony Gwynn/19	65.00
37	Deion Sanders/19	45.00
38	Dave Winfield/19	50.00
39	Eddie Murray/19	60.00

40	Tom Seaver/19	50.00
41	Willie Stargell/19	50.00
42	Wade Boggs/19	50.00
43	Ozzie Smith/19	60.00
44	Willie McCovey/19	40.00
45	Reggie Jackson/19	40.00
46	Whitey Ford/19	40.00
47	Lou Brock/19	40.00
48	Lou Boudreau/19	30.00
49	Steve Carlton/19	45.00
50	Rod Carew/19	40.00
51	Bob Gibson/19	35.00
52	Thurman Munson/19	60.00
53	Roger Maris/19	80.00
54	Nolan Ryan/50	80.00
55	Nolan Ryan/50	40.00
56	Bo Jackson/19	50.00
57	Joe Morgan/19	30.00
58	Phil Rizzuto/19	35.00
60	Gary Carter/19	40.00
61	Paul Molitor/19	50.00
62	Don Drysdale/19	50.00
62	Jim "Catfish" Hunter/19	30.00
63	Fergie Jenkins/19	40.00
64	Pee Wee Reese/19	40.00
65	Dave Winfield/19	40.00
66	Wade Boggs/19	40.00
67	Lefty Grove/19	80.00
68	Rickey Henderson/19	45.00
69	Roger Clemens/19	50.00
70	Roger Clemens/19	50.00

Icons Material Combo Prime

		NM/M
Varying quantities produced		
6	Carlton Fisk/25	50.00
7	Mel Ott/25	85.00
11	Roy Campanella/25	70.00
15	Roberto Clemente/25	200.00
17	Ernie Banks/25	85.00
18	Eddie Mathews/25	50.00
19	Ryne Sandberg/25	50.00
20	Rod Carew/25	50.00
24	Frank Robinson/25	40.00
25	Brooks Robinson/25	50.00
27	Carl Yastrzemski/25	80.00
28	Reggie Jackson/25	50.00
29	Mike Schmidt/25	75.00
30	Robin Yount/25	60.00
31	George Brett/25	75.00
32	Nolan Ryan/25	75.00
33	Kirby Puckett/25	60.00
34	Cal Ripken Jr./25	120.00
35	Don Mattingly/25	70.00
36	Tony Gwynn/19	80.00
37	Deion Sanders/19	60.00
38	Dave Winfield/19	60.00
39	Eddie Murray/19	70.00
41	Willie Stargell/19	60.00
42	Wade Boggs/19	60.00
43	Ozzie Smith/19	70.00
44	Willie McCovey/19	50.00
45	Reggie Jackson/19	50.00
46	Whitey Ford/19	50.00
47	Lou Brock/19	50.00
48	Lou Boudreau/19	40.00
49	Steve Carlton/19	60.00
50	Rod Carew/19	50.00
52	Thurman Munson/19	70.00
53	Roger Maris/19	110.00
54	Nolan Ryan/19	75.00
55	Nolan Ryan/19	75.00
56	Bo Jackson/19	60.00
57	Joe Morgan/19	40.00
58	Phil Rizzuto/19	45.00
59	Gary Carter/19	50.00
60	Paul Molitor/19	60.00
63	Fergie Jenkins/19	40.00
64	Pee Wee Reese/19	50.00
65	Dave Winfield/19	50.00
66	Wade Boggs/19	50.00
69	Roger Clemens/19	50.00
70	Roger Clemens/19	60.00

Icons Material Signature Prime

		NM/M
Many not priced due to scarcity.		
6	Carlton Fisk/50	60.00
11	Roy Campanella/1 (8/05 Auction)	2,020
12	Stan Musial/20	120.00
16	Warren Spahn/50	90.00
17	Ernie Banks/50	70.00
19	Ryne Sandberg/50	100.00
20	Rod Carew/50	50.00
21	Duke Snider/15	
22	Jim Palmer/50	40.00
24	Frank Robinson/50	40.00

25	Brooks Robinson/50	60.00
26	Harmon Killebrew/20	100.00
27	Carl Yastrzemski/50	90.00
28	Reggie Jackson/50	60.00
29	Mike Schmidt/20	125.00
30	Robin Yount/50	75.00
31	George Brett/50	100.00
32	Nolan Ryan/50	120.00
33	Kirby Puckett/34	70.00
34	Cal Ripken Jr./50	150.00
35	Don Mattingly/50	100.00
36	Tony Gwynn/50	70.00
37	Deion Sanders/50	50.00
38	Dave Winfield/50	45.00
39	Eddie Murray/50	75.00
42	Wade Boggs/50	60.00
43	Ozzie Smith/50	75.00
44	Willie McCovey/50	50.00
45	Reggie Jackson/50	50.00
46	Whitey Ford/50	50.00
47	Lou Brock/25	50.00
48	Lou Boudreau/50	75.00
49	Steve Carlton/50	50.00
50	Rod Carew/50	70.00
51	Bob Gibson/50	40.00
54	Nolan Ryan/50	125.00
55	Nolan Ryan/50	125.00
56	Bo Jackson/50	60.00
57	Joe Morgan/50	35.00
58	Phil Rizzuto/50	45.00
59	Gary Carter/50	50.00
60	Paul Molitor/50	55.00
63	Fergie Jenkins/50	40.00
65	Dave Winfield/50	45.00
66	Wade Boggs/50	60.00
68	Rickey Henderson/50	85.00
69	Roger Clemens/25	150.00
70	Roger Clemens/50	120.00

Icons Material Signature

NM/M
Varying quantities produced

4	Johnny Bench/18	75.00
8	Bob Feller/45	50.00
12	Stan Musial/30	100.00
13	Yogi Berra/42	65.00
21	Duke Snider/35	50.00
26	Harmon Killebrew/30	100.00
33	Kirby Puckett/16	80.00
69	Roger Clemens/25	150.00

Icons Signature

NM/M
Varying quantities produced

4	Johnny Bench/50	60.00
6	Carlton Fisk/50	40.00
8	Bob Feller/50	40.00
12	Stan Musial/50	65.00
13	Yogi Berra/50	50.00
16	Warren Spahn/25	100.00
17	Ernie Banks/50	60.00
18	Eddie Mathews/12	
19	Ryne Sandberg/25	70.00
20	Rod Carew/5	
21	Duke Snider/25	50.00
22	Jim Palmer/25	40.00
24	Frank Robinson/50	40.00
25	Brooks Robinson/50	50.00
26	Harmon Killebrew/25	75.00
27	Carl Yastrzemski/50	60.00
28	Reggie Jackson/50	50.00
29	Mike Schmidt/20	75.00
30	Robin Yount/50	65.00
31	George Brett/25	120.00
32	Nolan Ryan/50	110.00
33	Kirby Puckett/25	60.00
34	Cal Ripken Jr./25	200.00
35	Don Mattingly/50	85.00
36	Tony Gwynn/25	70.00
38	Dave Winfield/25	50.00
39	Eddie Murray/25	70.00
42	Wade Boggs/25	60.00
43	Ozzie Smith/25	75.00
44	Willie McCovey/25	50.00
45	Reggie Jackson/25	50.00
47	Lou Brock/25	50.00
48	Lou Boudreau/25	90.00
51	Bob Gibson/25	40.00
56	Bo Jackson/25	65.00
57	Joe Morgan/25	35.00
59	Gary Carter/25	45.00
60	Paul Molitor/25	55.00
65	Dave Winfield/25	50.00
66	Wade Boggs/25	50.00

Material Combos

NM/M
Production 25 Sets

1	Roger Clemens	60.00
2	Nomar Garciaparra	50.00
3	Albert Pujols	80.00
4	Sammy Sosa	50.00
5	Greg Maddux	50.00
6	Jason Giambi	40.00
7	Hideo Nomo	30.00
8	Mike Piazza	40.00
9	Ichiro Suzuki	70.00
10	Jeff Bagwell	40.00
11	Derek Jeter	60.00
12	Manny Ramirez	30.00
13	Rickey Henderson	40.00
14	Alex Rodriguez	70.00
15	Troy Glaus	35.00
16	Mike Mussina	40.00
17	Kerry Wood	50.00
18	Kazuhisa Ishii	35.00
19	Hideki Matsui	75.00
20	Frank Thomas	45.00
21	Barry Bonds	60.00
22	Adam Dunn	35.00
23	Randy Johnson	50.00
24	Alfonso Soriano	45.00
25	Pedro J. Martinez	45.00
26	Andruw Jones	45.00
27	Mark Prior	40.00
28	Vladimir Guerrero	45.00
29	Chipper Jones	45.00
30	Todd Helton	40.00
31	Rafael Palmeiro	45.00
32	Mark Grace	40.00
33	Pedro J. Martinez	45.00
34	Randy Johnson	50.00
35	Randy Johnson	50.00
36	Roger Clemens	60.00
38	Alex Rodriguez	70.00
40	Mike Piazza	40.00
42	Hideo Nomo	25.00
43	Rickey Henderson	40.00
44	Rickey Henderson	40.00
46	Ivan Rodriguez	35.00
47	George Brett	85.00
48	Cal Ripken Jr.	140.00
49	Nolan Ryan	75.00
50	Don Mattingly	75.00

Prime Cut Material Signature

NM/M
Varying quantities produced

1	Roger Clemens/25	185.00
3	Albert Pujols/25	180.00
5	Greg Maddux/25	175.00
10	Jeff Bagwell/25	70.00
12	Manny Ramirez/25	60.00
13	Rickey Henderson/25	100.00
14	Alex Rodriguez/25	180.00
15	Troy Glaus/50	40.00
16	Mike Mussina/25	70.00
17	Kerry Wood/25	90.00
18	Kazuhisa Ishii/50	50.00
20	Frank Thomas/25	80.00
22	Adam Dunn/25	60.00
24	Alfonso Soriano/25	85.00
26	Andruw Jones/25	60.00
27	Mark Prior/50	75.00
28	Vladimir Guerrero/50	75.00
29	Chipper Jones/25	85.00
30	Todd Helton/50	60.00
31	Rafael Palmeiro/25	75.00
32	Mark Grace/50	70.00
36	Roger Clemens/25	185.00
38	Alex Rodriguez/25	180.00
44	Rickey Henderson/25	100.00
46	Ivan Rodriguez/25	60.00
47	George Brett/50	120.00
48	Cal Ripken Jr./50	200.00
49	Nolan Ryan/25	140.00
50	Don Mattingly/50	120.00

Prime Cut Materials

NM/M
Varying quantities produced

1	Roger Clemens/150	40.00
2	Nomar Garciaparra/150	45.00
3	Albert Pujols/150	40.00
4	Sammy Sosa/150	40.00
5	Greg Maddux/150	40.00
6	Jason Giambi/125	40.00
7	Hideo Nomo/150	30.00
8	Mike Piazza/150	30.00
9	Ichiro Suzuki/25	60.00
10	Jeff Bagwell/25	35.00
11	Derek Jeter/25	50.00
12	Manny Ramirez/25	25.00
13	Rickey Henderson/50	30.00
14	Alex Rodriguez/25	60.00
15	Troy Glaus/25	30.00
17	Kerry Wood/25	40.00
18	Kazuhisa Ishii/25	30.00
19	Hideki Matsui/25	65.00
20	Frank Thomas/25	40.00
21	Barry Bonds/25	50.00
22	Adam Dunn/25	30.00
23	Randy Johnson/25	40.00
24	Alfonso Soriano/35	35.00
25	Pedro J. Martinez/25	40.00
26	Andruw Jones/25	30.00
27	Mark Prior/50	30.00
28	Vladimir Guerrero/25	40.00
29	Chipper Jones/25	35.00
30	Todd Helton/25	35.00
31	Rafael Palmeiro/25	30.00
32	Mark Grace/25	35.00
33	Pedro J. Martinez/25	40.00
34	Randy Johnson/25	40.00
35	Randy Johnson/25	40.00
36	Roger Clemens/50	45.00
38	Alex Rodriguez/25	60.00
40	Mike Piazza/50	30.00
42	Hideo Nomo/50	25.00
43	Rickey Henderson/50	30.00
44	Rickey Henderson/50	30.00
46	Ivan Rodriguez/25	30.00
47	George Brett/50	50.00
48	Cal Ripken Jr./50	65.00
49	Nolan Ryan/50	50.00
50	Don Mattingly/50	40.00

Signature

NM/M
Varying quantities produced

1	Roger Clemens/25	150.00
3	Albert Pujols/25	150.00
10	Jeff Bagwell/25	60.00
13	Rickey Henderson/25	80.00
14	Alex Rodriguez/25	150.00
15	Troy Glaus/25	35.00
16	Mike Mussina/25	60.00
17	Kerry Wood/25	80.00
18	Kazuhisa Ishii/25	40.00
20	Frank Thomas/25	70.00
22	Adam Dunn/25	50.00
24	Alfonso Soriano/25	75.00
26	Andruw Jones/25	50.00
27	Mark Prior/25	80.00
28	Vladimir Guerrero/25	60.00
29	Chipper Jones/25	75.00
31	Rafael Palmeiro/25	65.00
32	Mark Grace/25	60.00
36	Roger Clemens/25	150.00
37	Roger Clemens/25	150.00
38	Alex Rodriguez/25	150.00
43	Rickey Henderson/25	80.00
44	Rickey Henderson/25	80.00
46	Ivan Rodriguez/25	50.00
47	George Brett/25	120.00
48	Cal Ripken Jr./25	200.00
49	Nolan Ryan/25	125.00
50	Don Mattingly/25	100.00

Timeline - Material

NM/M
Varying quantities produced

4	Ted Williams/50	140.00
5	Roy Campanella/50	30.00
6	Stan Musial/50	35.00
7	Yogi Berra/50	35.00
9	Roberto Clemente/50	85.00
12	Carl Yastrzemski/50	35.00
13	Mike Schmidt/50	30.00
14	George Brett/50	30.00
15	Nolan Ryan/50	35.00
16	Stan Musial/50	35.00
17	Ted Williams/50	140.00
18	Roberto Clemente/50	90.00
19	Greg Maddux/50	25.00
21	Robin Yount/50	20.00
22	Nolan Ryan/50	35.00
23	Ted Williams/50	140.00
24	George Brett/50	30.00
25	Yogi Berra/50	25.00
26	Rod Carew/50	20.00
27	Dale Murphy/25	40.00

Timeline Dual Achievement Material Combo

No Pricing

Timeline Dual Achievement Material Prime

NM/M
Varying quantities produced

4	George Brett, Mike Schmidt/19	120.00
5	Cal Ripken Jr., Dale Murphy/19	120.00
6	Mike Schmidt, Roger Clemens/19	90.00
10	George Brett, Nolan Ryan/19	140.00

Timeline Dual Achievement Material Signature

NM/M
Varying quantities produced

4	George Brett, Mike Schmidt/24	150.00
5	Cal Ripken Jr., Dale Murphy/19	200.00
6	Mike Schmidt, Roger Clemens/24	220.00
7	Babe Ruth, Ty Cobb/1 (4/04 auction)	18,000
10	George Brett, Nolan Ryan/25	220.00

Timeline Dual Achievement Material

NM/M
Varying quantities produced

3	Stan Musial, Ted Williams/19	175.00
4	George Brett, Mike Schmidt/19	75.00
5	Cal Ripken Jr., Dale Murphy/19	90.00
6	Mike Schmidt, Roger Clemens/19	65.00
10	George Brett, Nolan Ryan/19	100.00
12	Al Kaline, Duke Snider/19	50.00

Timeline Dual Achievement Signature

NM/M
Production 24 or 25

4	George Brett, Mike Schmidt/24	160.00
5	Cal Ripken Jr., Dale Murphy/25	180.00
6	Mike Schmidt, Roger Clemens/24	220.00
10	George Brett, Nolan Ryan/25	220.00
12	Al Kaline, Duke Snider/25	100.00

Timeline Material Combo

NM/M
Varying quantities produced

10	Will Clark/19	60.00
12	Carl Yastrzemski/19	80.00
13	Mike Schmidt/19	60.00
14	George Brett/19	65.00
15	Nolan Ryan/19	100.00
19	Greg Maddux/19	50.00
21	Robin Yount/19	50.00
22	Nolan Ryan/19	100.00
24	George Brett/19	65.00
26	Rod Carew/19	40.00
27	Dale Murphy/19	50.00

Timeline Material Signature

NM/M
Varying quantities produced

6	Stan Musial/33	100.00
7	Yogi Berra/42	75.00
8	Stan Musial/38	100.00
25	Yogi Berra/42	75.00

Timeline Material
Signature Prime
NM/M

Varying quantities produced
10	Will Clark/50	75.00
12	Carl Yastrzemski/50	80.00
13	Mike Schmidt/20	120.00
14	George Brett/25	100.00
15	Nolan Ryan/50	125.00
19	Greg Maddux/50	125.00
21	Robin Yount/50	75.00
22	Nolan Ryan/50	125.00
24	George Brett/25	100.00

Timeline Material Prime
NM/M

Varying quantities produced
5	Roy Campanella/25	40.00
10	Will Clark/25	50.00
12	Carl Yastrzemski/25	75.00
13	Mike Schmidt/25	50.00
14	George Brett/25	50.00
15	Nolan Ryan/25	50.00
19	Greg Maddux/25	40.00
21	Robin Yount/25	40.00
22	Nolan Ryan/25	50.00
24	George Brett/25	50.00
26	Rod Carew/25	40.00
27	Dale Murphy/25	40.00

Timeline Signature
NM/M

Varying quantities produced
6	Stan Musial/50	70.00
7	Yogi Berra/50	50.00
10	Will Clark/25	100.00
12	Carl Yastrzemski/50	80.00
13	Mike Schmidt/20	85.00
14	George Brett/50	90.00
15	Nolan Ryan/50	110.00
16	Stan Musial/50	70.00
19	Greg Maddux/31	120.00
21	Robin Yount/25	75.00
22	Nolan Ryan/50	110.00
24	George Brett/25	90.00
25	Yogi Berra/50	50.00
26	Rod Carew/10	
27	Dale Murphy/25	50.00

Timeline Dual League
Leader Material
NM/M

Production 9 or 19
4	Jim Palmer, Steve Carlton/19	40.00
7	Nolan Ryan, Steve Carlton/19	70.00
8	Don Mattingly, Tony Gwynn/19	70.00
9	Nolan Ryan, Roger Clemens/19	80.00

Timeline Dual League
Leader Material Prime
NM/M

Production 9 or 19
7	Nolan Ryan, Steve Carlton/19	80.00
8	Don Mattingly, Tony Gwynn/19	80.00
9	Nolan Ryan, Roger Clemens/19	100.00

Timeline Dual League
Leader Material Signature
NM/M

Varying quantities produced
4	Jim Palmer, Steve Carlton/50	60.00
7	Nolan Ryan, Steve Carlton/25	200.00
8	Don Mattingly, Tony Gwynn/25	150.00
9	Nolan Ryan, Roger Clemens/25	350.00

Timeline Dual League
Leader Signature
NM/M

Production 25 or 50
4	Jim Palmer, Steve Carlton/50	60.00
7	Nolan Ryan, Steve Carlton/25	180.00
8	Don Mattingly, Tony Gwynn/25	140.00
9	Nolan Ryan, Roger Clemens/25	300.00

Timeline Dual League
Leader Material
Combo
NM/M

Production 9 or 19
8	Don Mattingly, Tony Gwynn/19	80.00
9	Nolan Ryan, Roger Clemens/19	100.00

2004 Playoff Prime Cuts II

NM/M

Complete Set (100):
Common (1-91):	1.50
Common (92-100):	3.00

Production 699
Wood Box (One Pack): 150.00
1	Mark Prior	2.00
2	Derek Jeter	8.00
3	Eric Chavez	1.50
4	Carlos Delgado	1.50
5	Albert Pujols	8.00
6	Miguel Cabrera	2.00
7	Ivan Rodriguez	2.00
8	Javy Lopez	1.50
9	Hank Blalock	2.00
10	Chipper Jones	3.00
11	Gary Sheffield	2.00
12	Alfonso Soriano	3.00
13	Alex Rodriguez/Yanks	6.00
14	Edgar Renteria	1.50
15	Jim Edmonds	1.50
16	Garret Anderson	1.50
17	Lance Berkman	1.50
18	Brandon Webb	1.50
19	Mike Lowell	1.50
20	Mark Mulder	1.50
21	Sammy Sosa	5.00
22	Roger Clemens/Astros	8.00
23	Mark Teixeira	1.50
24	Manny Ramirez	3.00
25	Rafael Palmeiro	2.00
26	Ichiro Suzuki	6.00
27	Vladimir Guerrero	3.00
28	Austin Kearns	1.50
29	Troy Glaus	1.50
30	Ken Griffey Jr.	4.00
31	Greg Maddux	4.00
32	Roy Halladay	1.50
33	Roy Oswalt	1.50
34	Kerry Wood	3.00
35	Mike Mussina/Yanks	2.00
36	Michael Young	1.50
37	Juan Gonzalez	1.50
38	Curt Schilling	2.00
39	Shannon Stewart	1.50
40	Todd Helton	2.00
41	Larry Walker Cards	1.50
42	Mariano Rivera	1.50
43	Nomar Garciaparra	4.00
44	Adam Dunn	2.00
45	Pedro J. Martinez/Sox	3.00
46	Bernie Williams	1.50
47	Tom Glavine	2.00
48	Torii Hunter	1.50
49	David Ortiz	3.00
50	Frank Thomas	4.00
51	Randy Johnson/ D'backs	3.00
52	Jason Giambi	1.50
53	Carlos Lee	1.50
54	Mike Sweeney	1.50
55	Hideki Matsui	6.00
56	Dontrelle Willis	1.50
57	Tim Hudson	1.50
58	Jose Vidro	1.50
59	Jeff Bagwell	2.00
60	Rocco Baldelli	1.50
61	Craig Biggio	1.50
62	Mike Piazza Mets	4.00
63	Magglio Ordonez	1.50
64	Hideo Nomo	1.50
65	Miguel Tejada	2.00
66	Vernon Wells	1.50
67	Barry Larkin	1.50
68	Jacque Jones	1.50
69	Scott Rolen	3.00
70	Jeff Kent	1.50
71	Steve Finley	1.50
72	Kazuo Matsui	6.00
73	Carlos Beltran	2.00
74	Shawn Green	1.50
75	Barry Zito	1.50
76	Aramis Ramirez	1.50
77	Paul LoDuca	1.50
78	Kazuhisa Ishii	1.50
79	Aubrey Huff	1.50
80	Jim Thome	3.00
81	Andy Pettitte Astros	1.50
82	Andruw Jones	1.50
83	Josh Beckett	1.50
84	Sean Casey	1.50
85	Alex Rodriguez/M's	6.00
86	Roger Clemens/Yanks	8.00
87	Mike Mussina/O's	2.00
88	Pedro Martinez/Dgr	3.00
89	Randy Johnson/Astros	3.00
90	Mike Piazza/Dgr	4.00
91	Andy Pettitte/Yanks	1.50
92	Cal Ripken Jr.	15.00
93	Dale Murphy	3.00
94	Don Mattingly	8.00
95	Gary Carter	3.00
96	George Brett	8.00
97	Nolan Ryan	10.00
98	Ozzie Smith	8.00
99	Steve Carlton	3.00
100	Tony Gwynn	6.00

Gold
Gold (1-91):	2-4X
Gold (92-100):	1.5-2X

Production 25 Sets

Silver
Silver (1-91):	1-2X
Silver (92-100):	1-1.5X

Production 50 Sets

Platinum
No Pricing
Production One Set

Material Combo
NM/M

Many not priced due to scarcity.
Prime: No Pricing
Production 1-9
1	Mark Prior/ Hat-Jsy/22	20.00
12	Alfonso Soriano/ Bat-Jsy/25	25.00
15	Jim Edmonds/ Bat-Jsy/15	20.00
16	Garret Anderson/ Bat-Jsy/16	15.00
21	Sammy Sosa/ Bat-Jsy/21	40.00
22	Roger Clemens/ Bat-Jsy/22	50.00
24	Manny Ramirez/ Bat-Jsy/24	25.00
25	Rafael Palmeiro/ Bat-Jsy/25	20.00
27	Vladimir Guerrero/ Bat-Jsy/27	25.00
31	Greg Maddux/ Bat-Jsy/31	40.00
35	Mike Mussina/ Bat-Jsy/35	25.00
40	Roger Clemens/ Bat-Jsy/17	25.00
86	Roger Clemens/ Fld Glv-Jsy/22	50.00
92	Cal Ripken Jr./ Bat-Jsy/25	75.00
93	Dale Murphy/ Bat-Jsy/25	20.00
94	Don Mattingly/ Bat-Jsy/25	50.00
96	George Brett/ Bat-Jsy/25	50.00
97	Nolan Ryan/ Bat-Jkt/25	60.00
98	Ozzie Smith/ Bat-Jsy/25	40.00

Material Number
NM/M

Most not priced.
Prime: No Pricing
Production 1-10
86	Roger Clemens/ Jsy/25	40.00
92	Cal Ripken Jr./ Jsy/25	60.00
93	Dale Murphy/Jsy/25	20.00
94	Don Mattingly/Jsy/25	40.00
96	George Brett/Jsy/25	40.00
97	Nolan Ryan/Jkt/25	50.00
98	Ozzie Smith/Jsy/25	30.00

Icons
NM/M

Common Player:		4.00
Production 50 Sets		
Gold:		No Pricing
Production 10 Sets		
Platinum:		No Pricing
Production One Set		
Silver:		1-1.5X

Production 25 Sets
1	Dale Murphy	6.00
2	Eddie Mathews	8.00
3	Brooks Robinson	6.00
4	Cal Ripken Jr.	25.00
5	Cal Ripken Jr.	25.00
6	Eddie Murray	8.00
7	Frank Robinson	4.00
8	Jim Palmer	4.00
9	Bobby Doerr	4.00
10	Carl Yastrzemski	10.00
11	Carlton Fisk	6.00
12	Dennis Eckersley	6.00
13	Luis Aparicio	4.00
14	Luis Tiant	4.00
15	Ted Williams	12.00
16	Wade Boggs	4.00
17	Duke Snider	6.00
18	Jackie Robinson	8.00
19	Pee Wee Reese	4.00
20	Burleigh Grimes	4.00
21	Nolan Ryan	20.00
22	Reggie Jackson	6.00
23	Rod Carew	6.00
24	Rod Carew	6.00
25	Billy Williams	4.00
26	Ernie Banks	8.00
27	Mark Grace	6.00
28	Ron Santo	6.00
29	Paul Molitor	6.00
30	Bo Jackson	8.00
31	Carlton Fisk	6.00
32	Johnny Bench	8.00
33	Tom Seaver	6.00
34	Tony Perez	4.00
35	Bob Feller	4.00
36	Lou Boudreau	4.00
37	Al Kaline	8.00
38	Alan Trammell	4.00
39	Ty Cobb	8.00
40	Don Sutton	4.00
41	Nolan Ryan	20.00
42	Roger Maris	8.00
43	Bo Jackson	8.00
44	George Brett	12.00
45	George Brett	12.00
46	Maury Wills	4.00
47	Warren Spahn	6.00
48	Robin Yount	10.00
49	Harmon Killebrew	8.00
50	Kirby Puckett	8.00
51	Paul Molitor	6.00
52	Andre Dawson	4.00
53	Mel Ott	6.00
54	Mel Ott	6.00
55	Duke Snider	6.00
56	Rickey Henderson	8.00
57	Tom Seaver	6.00
58	Babe Ruth	15.00
59	Babe Ruth	15.00
60	Jim "Catfish" Hunter	4.00
61	Dave Righetti	4.00
62	Dave Winfield	4.00
63	Don Mattingly	15.00
64	Don Mattingly	15.00
65	Lou Gehrig	10.00
66	Lou Gehrig	10.00
67	Phil Niekro	4.00
68	Phil Rizzuto	4.00
69	Reggie Jackson	6.00
70	Rickey Henderson	6.00
71	Roger Maris	8.00
72	Thurman Munson	8.00
73	Thurman Munson	8.00
74	Wade Boggs	4.00
75	Whitey Ford	6.00
76	Yogi Berra	8.00
77	Lefty Grove	4.00
78	Mike Schmidt	10.00
79	Mike Schmidt	10.00
80	Steve Carlton	4.00
81	Ralph Kiner	4.00
82	Roberto Clemente	15.00
83	Roberto Clemente	15.00
84	Dave Winfield	4.00
85	Rickey Henderson	6.00
86	Steve Garvey	4.00
87	Tony Gwynn	8.00
88	Tony Gwynn	8.00
89	Gaylord Perry	4.00
90	Joe Morgan	4.00
91	Juan Marichal	4.00
92	Steve Carlton	4.00
93	Will Clark	6.00

94	Willie McCovey	4.00
95	Bob Gibson	6.00
96	Lou Brock	6.00
97	Stan Musial	10.00
98	Fergie Jenkins	4.00
99	Nolan Ryan	20.00
100	Harmon Killebrew	8.00

Icons Material Combo

NM/M
Many not priced.
Prime: No Pricing
Production 1-10

4	Cal Ripken Jr./Bat-Jsy/25	75.00
5	Cal Ripken Jr./Jkt-Pants/25	75.00
6	Eddie Murray/Bat-Jsy/25	30.00
7	Frank Robinson/Bat-Jsy/20	20.00
10	Carl Yastrzemski/Bat-Jsy/25	40.00
11	Carlton Fisk/Bat-Jsy/25	25.00
15	Ted Williams/Bat-Jsy/25	100.00
17	Duke Snider/Jsy-Pants/25	25.00
18	Jackie Robinson/Jkt-Jsy/25	80.00
21	Nolan Ryan/Jkt-Jsy/25	50.00
22	Reggie Jackson/Hat-Jsy/25	25.00
23	Rod Carew/Bat-Jsy/25	25.00
24	Rod Carew/Jkt-Jsy/25	25.00
29	Paul Molitor/Jsy-Pants/25	25.00
31	Carlton Fisk/Bat-Jsy/25	25.00
33	Tom Seaver/Bat-Jsy/25	25.00
39	Ty Cobb/Bat-Pants/25	150.00
41	Nolan Ryan/Bat-Jsy/25	50.00
42	Roger Maris/Jsy-Pants/25	75.00
44	George Brett/Bat-Jsy/25	50.00
45	George Brett/Hat-Jsy/25	50.00
47	Warren Spahn/Jsy-Pants/25	30.00
48	Robin Yount/Bat-Jsy/19	50.00
49	Harmon Killebrew/Jsy-Jsy/25	40.00
53	Mel Ott/Bat-Jsy/25	50.00
54	Mel Ott/Bat-Pants/25	50.00
55	Duke Snider/Jsy-Pants/25	25.00
58	Babe Ruth/Bat-Jsy/25	300.00
59	Babe Ruth/Bat-Pants/25	300.00
65	Lou Gehrig/Bat-Jsy/25	200.00
66	Lou Gehrig/Bat-Pants/25	200.00
69	Reggie Jackson/Bat-Jsy/25	25.00
71	Roger Maris/Bat-Pants/25	60.00
72	Thurman Munson/Bat-Jsy/25	50.00
73	Thurman Munson/Bat-Pants/25	50.00
75	Whitey Ford/Jsy-Pants/16	40.00
78	Mike Schmidt/Bat-Jsy/20	50.00
79	Mike Schmidt/Hat-Jkt/20	50.00
80	Steve Carlton/Fld Glv-Pants/10	
82	Roberto Clemente/Bat-Jsy/21	150.00
83	Roberto Clemente/Bat-Hat/21	150.00
93	Will Clark/Bat-Jsy/22	30.00
94	Willie McCovey/Jsy-Jsy/25	25.00
99	Nolan Ryan/Jsy-Pants/25	50.00
100	Harmon Killebrew/Bat-Jsy/25	40.00

Icons Material Number

NM/M
Many not priced.

1	Dale Murphy/Jsy/25	20.00
3	Brooks Robinson/Jsy/25	20.00
4	Cal Ripken Jr./Jsy/25	60.00
5	Cal Ripken Jr./Jkt/25	60.00
6	Eddie Murray/Jsy/25	30.00
7	Frank Robinson/Jsy/25	10.00
8	Jim Palmer/Jsy/25	15.00
9	Bobby Doerr/Jsy/25	10.00
10	Carl Yastrzemski/Jsy/25	40.00
11	Carlton Fisk/Jsy/25	20.00
15	Ted Williams/Jsy/50	100.00
17	Duke Snider Jsy/25	20.00
18	Jackie Robinson/Jkt/50	65.00
19	Pee Wee Reese/Jsy/25	20.00
20	Burleigh Grimes/Pants/25	50.00
21	Nolan Ryan Jsy/25	40.00
22	Reggie Jackson/Jsy/25	2.00
23	Rod Carew/Jsy/25	20.00
24	Rod Carew/Jkt/25	20.00
25	Billy Williams/Jsy/25	10.00
26	Ernie Banks/Jsy/25	25.00
29	Paul Molitor/Pants/25	25.00
31	Carlton Fisk/Jsy/25	20.00
32	Johnny Bench/Jsy/25	30.00
33	Tom Seaver/Jsy/25	25.00
35	Bob Feller/Jsy/25	15.00
36	Lou Boudreau/Jsy/25	25.00
39	Ty Cobb/Pants/50	100.00
41	Nolan Ryan/Jsy/25	40.00
42	Roger Maris/Jsy/25	50.00
44	George Brett/Jsy/25	40.00
45	George Brett/Jsy/25	40.00
47	Warren Spahn/Jsy/25	25.00
48	Robin Yount/Jsy/25	30.00
49	Harmon Killebrew/Jsy/25	30.00
50	Kirby Puckett/Jsy/25	25.00
51	Paul Molitor/Jsy/25	20.00
53	Mel Ott/Jsy/25	40.00
54	Mel Ott/Pants/25	40.00
55	Duke Snider/Jsy/25	20.00
58	Babe Ruth/Jsy/25	300.00
59	Babe Ruth/Pants/50	180.00
60	Jim "Catfish" Hunter/Jsy/25	20.00
63	Don Mattingly/Jsy/25	40.00
64	Don Mattingly/Jkt/25	40.00
65	Lou Gehrig/Jsy/25	150.00
66	Lou Gehrig/Pants/50	100.00
68	Phil Rizzuto/Pants/25	20.00
69	Reggie Jackson/Jsy/25	20.00
71	Roger Maris/Pants/25	40.00
72	Thurman Munson/Jsy/50	35.00
73	Thurman Munson/Pants/50	35.00
77	Lefty Grove/Hat/25	120.00
78	Mike Schmidt/Jsy/20	40.00
79	Mike Schmidt/Jkt/20	40.00
82	Roberto Clemente/Jsy/21	100.00
83	Roberto Clemente/Hat/21	100.00
91	Juan Marichal/Jsy/25	15.00
93	Will Clark/Jsy/22	25.00
94	Willie McCovey/Jsy/25	20.00
95	Bob Gibson/Jsy/25	25.00
96	Lou Brock/Jkt/20	20.00
99	Nolan Ryan/Pants/25	40.00
100	Harmon Killebrew/Jsy/25	35.00

Icons Material Prime

No Pricing
Production 1-10

Icons Signature Century Gold

NM/M
Many not priced.

1	Dale Murphy/25	40.00
3	Brooks Robinson/25	40.00
7	Frank Robinson/20	35.00
8	Jim Palmer/22	35.00
9	Bobby Doerr/25	30.00
17	Duke Snider/25	35.00
32	Johnny Bench/25	50.00
34	Tony Perez/24	40.00
35	Bob Feller/19	40.00
37	Al Kaline/25	50.00

43	Bo Jackson/16	75.00
49	Harmon Killebrew/25	50.00
51	Paul Molitor/25	35.00
55	Duke Snider/25	40.00
63	Don Mattingly/23	75.00
64	Don Mattingly/23	75.00
80	Steve Carlton/25	35.00
81	Ralph Kiner/25	45.00
87	Tony Gwynn/19	50.00
88	Tony Gwynn/19	50.00
92	Steve Carlton/25	35.00
95	Bob Gibson/25	40.00
96	Lou Brock/20	40.00
97	Stan Musial/25	90.00
100	Harmon Killebrew/25	50.00

Icons Signature Century Platinum

No Pricing
Production One Set

Icons Signature Century Silver

NM/M

1	Dale Murphy/25	40.00
3	Brooks Robinson/50	30.00
4	Cal Ripken Jr./25	180.00
5	Cal Ripken Jr./25	180.00
6	Eddie Murray/25	50.00
7	Frank Robinson/50	30.00
8	Jim Palmer/50	30.00
9	Bobby Doerr/25	30.00
10	Carl Yastrzemski/25	75.00
11	Carlton Fisk/27	40.00
12	Dennis Eckersley/43	30.00
13	Luis Aparicio/25	25.00
16	Wade Boggs/26	40.00
17	Duke Snider/50	30.00
21	Nolan Ryan/30	100.00
22	Reggie Jackson/25	50.00
23	Rod Carew/29	35.00
24	Rod Carew/29	35.00
25	Billy Williams/26	20.00
29	Paul Molitor/25	35.00
30	Bo Jackson/25	50.00
31	Carlton Fisk/25	40.00
32	Johnny Bench/50	30.00
33	Tom Seaver/25	40.00
34	Tony Perez/25	40.00
35	Bob Feller/25	30.00
37	Al Kaline/50	40.00
40	Don Sutton/20	20.00
41	Nolan Ryan/34	100.00
43	Bo Jackson/25	50.00
44	George Brett/25	100.00
45	George Brett/25	100.00
48	Robin Yount/19	65.00
49	Harmon Killebrew/50	40.00
51	Paul Molitor/50	30.00
55	Duke Snider/50	30.00
56	Rickey Henderson/24	60.00
57	Tom Seaver/25	40.00
62	Dave Winfield/31	35.00
63	Don Mattingly/50	60.00
64	Don Mattingly/50	60.00
67	Phil Niekro/35	20.00
68	Phil Rizzuto/25	40.00
69	Reggie Jackson/25	50.00
70	Rickey Henderson/24	60.00
75	Whitey Ford/25	50.00
76	Yogi Berra/25	50.00
78	Mike Schmidt/20	80.00
79	Mike Schmidt/20	80.00
80	Steve Carlton/32	30.00
81	Ralph Kiner/25	45.00
84	Dave Winfield/31	35.00
85	Rickey Henderson/24	60.00
87	Tony Gwynn/50	40.00
88	Tony Gwynn/50	50.00
89	Gaylord Perry/36	20.00
90	Joe Morgan/24	25.00
91	Juan Marichal/27	25.00
92	Steve Carlton/32	30.00
93	Will Clark/22	30.00
94	Willie McCovey/25	30.00
95	Bob Gibson/45	30.00
96	Lou Brock/50	30.00
97	Stan Musial/50	65.00
98	Fergie Jenkins/31	25.00
99	Nolan Ryan/34	100.00
100	Harmon Killebrew/50	40.00

Icons Signature Material Combo

NM/M
Many not priced.
Prime: No Pricing
Production 1-10

1	Dale Murphy/Bat-Jsy/25	50.00
7	Frank Robinson/Bat-Jsy/20	45.00
8	Jim Palmer/Hat-Jsy/22	50.00
9	Bobby Doerr/Bat-Jsy/25	40.00
17	Duke Snider/Jsy-Pants/25	50.00
25	Billy Williams/Bat-Jsy/26	30.00
29	Paul Molitor/Jsy-Pants/25	50.00
34	Tony Perez/Bat-Fld Glv/24	50.00
48	Robin Yount/Bat-Jsy/19	100.00
49	Harmon Killebrew/Jsy-Jsy/25	80.00
51	Paul Molitor/Bat-Jsy/25	50.00
63	Don Mattingly/Bat-Jsy/23	100.00
64	Don Mattingly/Hat-Jkt/23	100.00
78	Mike Schmidt/Bat-Jsy/20	100.00
79	Mike Schmidt/Hat-Jkt/20	100.00
80	Steve Carlton/Fld Glv-Pants/32	50.00
87	Tony Gwynn/Fld Glv-Jsy/19	80.00
88	Tony Gwynn/Jsy-Pants/19	80.00
92	Steve Carlton/Bat-Jsy/32	50.00
93	Will Clark/Bat-Jsy/22	75.00
98	Fergie Jenkins/Fld Glv-Hat/31	40.00

Icons Signature Material Number

NM/M
Many not priced.
Prime: No Pricing
Production 1-10

7	Frank Robinson/Jsy/20	40.00
8	Jim Palmer/Jsy/22	40.00
9	Bobby Doerr/Jsy/25	30.00
11	Carlton Fisk/Jsy/27	40.00
12	Dennis Eckersley/Jsy/43	30.00
16	Wade Boggs/Jsy/26	40.00
21	Nolan Ryan/Jsy/30	100.00
22	Reggie Jackson/Jsy/44	50.00
25	Billy Williams/Jsy/26	25.00
27	Mark Grace/Jsy/17	45.00
35	Bob Feller/Jsy/19	30.00
40	Don Sutton/Jsy/20	25.00
41	Nolan Ryan/Jsy/34	100.00
43	Bo Jackson/Jsy/16	75.00
48	Robin Yount/Jsy/19	65.00
62	Dave Winfield/Pants/31	40.00
63	Don Mattingly/Jsy/23	80.00
64	Don Mattingly/Jkt/23	80.00
69	Reggie Jackson/Jsy/44	50.00
78	Mike Schmidt/Jsy/20	80.00
79	Mike Schmidt/Jkt/20	80.00
80	Steve Carlton/Pants/32	40.00
84	Dave Winfield/Jsy/31	40.00
87	Tony Gwynn/Jsy/23	75.00
88	Tony Gwynn/Jsy/19	75.00
89	Gaylord Perry/Jsy/36	20.00
91	Juan Marichal/Jsy/27	25.00
92	Steve Carlton/Jsy/32	40.00
93	Will Clark/Jsy/22	65.00
95	Bob Gibson/Jsy/45	35.00
96	Lou Brock/Jkt/20	40.00
98	Fergie Jenkins/Hat/31	25.00
99	Nolan Ryan/Pants/34	100.00

Signature Century Gold

No Pricing
Production 1-17

Signature Century Platinum

No Pricing
Production One Set

Signature Century Silver

Many not priced.

		NM/M
1	Mark Prior/22	30.00
6	Miguel Cabrera/24	40.00
9	Hank Blalock/25	40.00
11	Gary Sheffield/25	40.00
15	Jim Edmonds/25	40.00
16	Garret Anderson/25	25.00
17	Lance Berkman/25	30.00
20	Mark Mulder/20	25.00
21	Sammy Sosa/21	125.00
23	Mark Teixeira/40	40.00
24	Manny Ramirez/24	75.00
25	Rafael Palmeiro/25	50.00
31	Greg Maddux/31	100.00
34	Kerry Wood/34	50.00
35	Mike Mussina/35	40.00
37	Juan Gonzalez/22	40.00
44	Adam Dunn/44	30.00
49	David Ortiz/34	50.00
50	Frank Thomas/35	40.00
61	Craig Biggio/25	35.00
63	Magglio Ordonez/30	25.00
66	Vernon Wells/25	20.00
69	Scott Rolen/27	50.00
82	Andruw Jones/25	35.00
83	Josh Beckett/21	25.00
87	Mike Mussina/35	40.00
92	Cal Ripken Jr./25	175.00
93	Dale Murphy/25	40.00
94	Don Mattingly/23	75.00
95	Gary Carter/25	25.00
97	Nolan Ryan/25	100.00
99	Steve Carlton/32	30.00
100	Tony Gwynn/25	50.00

Signature Material Combo

		NM/M
Most not priced.
Prime: No Pricing
Production 1-9

1	Mark Prior/ Hat/22	50.00
20	Mark Mulder/ Jsy/20	35.00
40	Todd Helton/ Bat-Jsy/17	75.00
83	Josh Beckett/ Bat-Jsy/21	35.00
93	Dale Murphy/ Bat-Jsy/25	50.00
94	Don Mattingly/ Bat-Jsy/25	100.00

Signature Material Number

		NM/M
Most not priced.
Prime: No Pricing
Production 1-9

1	Mark Prior/Jsy/22	40.00
17	Lance Berkman/ Jsy/17	50.00
19	Mike Lowell/Jsy/1	
20	Mark Mulder/Jsy/20	25.00
40	Todd Helton/Jsy/17	60.00
57	Tim Hudson/Jsy/15	35.00
83	Josh Beckett/Jsy/21	25.00
94	Don Mattingly/ Jsy/23	100.00
97	Nolan Ryan/Jkt/34	125.00
99	Steve Carlton/Jsy/32	40.00
100	Tony Gwynn/Jsy/19	80.00

Timeline

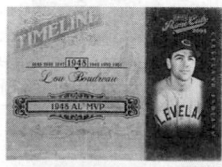

		NM/M
Common Player: 4.00
Production 50 Sets
Century Gold: No Pricing
Production 10 Sets
Century Platinum: No Pricing

Production One Set
Century Silver: 1-1.5X
Production 25 Sets

1	Al Kaline	8.00
2	Alex Rodriguez	10.00
3	Andre Dawson	4.00
4	Babe Ruth	15.00
5	Barry Zito	4.00
6	Bob Feller	4.00
7	Bob Gibson	6.00
8	Bobby Doerr	4.00
9	Brooks Robinson	6.00
10	Cal Ripken Jr.	25.00
11	Carl Hubbell	4.00
12	Carl Yastrzemski	10.00
13	Carlton Fisk	6.00
14	Jim "Catfish" Hunter	4.00
15	Chipper Jones	8.00
16	Cy Young	6.00
17	Dale Murphy	6.00
18	Dave Parker	4.00
19	Dennis Eckersley	6.00
20	Don Drysdale	6.00
21	Don Mattingly	15.00
22	Duke Snider	6.00
23	Dwight Gooden	4.00
24	Early Wynn	4.00
25	Eddie Mathews	8.00
26	Eddie Murray	6.00
27	Enos Slaughter	4.00
28	Ernie Banks	8.00
29	Fergie Jenkins	4.00
30	Frank Robinson	6.00
31	Frank Thomas	8.00
32	Frankie Frisch	4.00
33	Fred Lynn	4.00
34	Gary Carter	4.00
35	Gaylord Perry	4.00
36	George Brett	15.00
37	Greg Maddux	10.00
38	Hal Newhouser	4.00
39	Harmon Killebrew	8.00
40	Honus Wagner	6.00
41	Hoyt Wilhelm	4.00
42	Ivan Rodriguez	8.00
43	Jackie Robinson	6.00
44	Jason Giambi	6.00
45	Jeff Bagwell	6.00
46	Jim Palmer	4.00
47	Jimmie Foxx	8.00
48	Joe Morgan	4.00
49	Johnny Bench	8.00
50	Johnny Mize	4.00
51	Jose Canseco	6.00
52	Juan Gonzalez	6.00
53	Juan Marichal	4.00
54	Keith Hernandez	4.00
55	Kirby Puckett	8.00
56	Lefty Grove	4.00
57	Lou Boudreau	4.00
58	Lou Brock	6.00
59	Lou Gehrig	10.00
60	Luis Aparicio	4.00
61	Marty Marion	4.00
62	Mel Ott	6.00
63	Miguel Tejada	6.00
64	Mike Schmidt	10.00
65	Nellie Fox	4.00
66	Nolan Ryan	15.00
67	Orel Hershiser	4.00
68	Orlando Cepeda	4.00
69	Paul Molitor	6.00
70	Pedro Martinez	8.00
71	Pee Wee Reese	6.00
72	Phil Niekro	4.00
73	Phil Rizzuto	6.00
74	Ralph Kiner	4.00
75	Randy Johnson	8.00
76	Red Schoendienst	4.00
77	Reggie Jackson	6.00
78	Rickey Henderson	6.00
79	Roberto Clemente	15.00
80	Robin Yount	10.00
81	Rod Carew	6.00
82	Roger Clemens	10.00
83	Roger Maris	10.00
84	Rogers Hornsby	6.00
85	Roy Campanella	8.00
86	Ozzie Smith	10.00
87	Sammy Sosa	10.00
88	Satchel Paige	6.00
89	Stan Musial	10.00
90	Steve Carlton	4.00
91	Ted Williams	10.00
92	Thurman Munson	8.00
93	Tom Seaver	6.00
94	Ty Cobb	10.00
95	Walter Johnson	6.00
96	Warren Spahn	8.00
97	Whitey Ford	6.00
98	Willie McCovey	6.00
99	Willie Stargell	6.00
100	Yogi Berra	8.00

Timeline Material Combo

		NM/M
Quantity produced listed

4	Babe Ruth/ Jsy-Jsy/25	350.00
7	Bob Gibson/ Hat-Jsy/25	35.00
10	Cal Ripken Jr./ Jkt-Jsy/25	75.00
13	Carlton Fisk/ Bat-Jsy/25	25.00
14	Jim "Catfish" Hunter/Jsy-Jsy/27	25.00
17	Dale Murphy/ Bat-Jsy/25	25.00
21	Don Mattingly/ Btg Glv-Pants/25	50.00
25	Eddie Mathews/ Bat-Jsy/41	40.00
26	Eddie Murray/ Bat-Jsy/33	40.00
36	George Brett/ Hat-Jsy/25	60.00
39	Harmon Killebrew/ Bat-Jsy/25	50.00
43	Jackie Robinson/ Jkt-Jsy/42	100.00
46	Jim Palmer/ Hat-Jsy/22	20.00
47	Jimmie Foxx/ Bat-Fld Glv/25	125.00
49	Johnny Bench/ Bat-Jsy/25	40.00
58	Lou Brock/ Bat-Jsy/20	25.00
59	Lou Gehrig/ Jsy-Pants/25	250.00
62	Mel Ott/Jsy-Pants/25	50.00
64	Mike Schmidt/ Bat-Jsy/20	60.00
66	Nolan Ryan/ Jsy-Pants/25	60.00
68	Orlando Cepeda/ Bat-Pants/25	20.00
71	Pee Wee Reese/ Bat-Jsy/25	30.00
77	Reggie Jackson/ Jsy-Jsy/25	30.00
79	Roberto Clemente/ Hat-Jsy/21	150.00
80	Robin Yount/ Bat-Jsy/19	50.00
81	Rod Carew/ Bat-Jsy/29	30.00
82	Roger Clemens/ Jsy-Jsy/21	40.00
83	Roger Maris/ Jsy-Pants/25	75.00
85	Roy Campanella/ Bat-Pants/39	35.00
86	Ozzie Smith/ Bat-Jsy/21	40.00
87	Sammy Sosa/ Bat-Jsy/21	40.00
90	Steve Carlton/ Hat-Jsy/32	20.00
91	Ted Williams/ Jsy-Jsy/25	140.00
92	Thurman Munson/ Jsy-Pants/10	50.00
94	Ty Cobb/ Bat-Pants/25	160.00
96	Warren Spahn/ Jsy/21	40.00
98	Willie McCovey/ Bat-Jsy/25	25.00

Timeline Material Combo CY

Quantity produced listed
No Pricing

Timeline Material Number

		NM/M
Quantity produced listed

4	Babe Ruth/Jsy/25	350.00
6	Bob Feller/Pants/19	25.00
7	Bob Gibson/Jsy/25	30.00
10	Cal Ripken Jr./Jsy/25	60.00
12	Carl Yastrzemski/ Jsy/25	40.00
13	Carlton Fisk/Jsy/27	25.00
14	Jim "Catfish" Hunter/27	20.00
20	Don Drysdale/Jsy/25	40.00
22	Duke Snider/ Pants/25	25.00
24	Early Wynn/Jsy/24	15.00

25	Eddie Mathews/ Jsy/25	30.00
26	Eddie Murray/Jsy/25	25.00
28	Ernie Banks/Jsy/25	35.00
32	Frankie Frisch/Jkt/25	40.00
36	George Brett/Jsy/25	40.00
39	Harmon Killebrew/ Jsy/25	35.00
43	Jackie Robinson/ Jkt/42	60.00
46	Jim Palmer/Jsy/22	15.00
47	Jimmie Foxx/ Fld Glv/25	85.00
49	Johnny Bench/Jsy/25	25.00
53	Juan Marichal/Jsy/25	15.00
55	Kirby Puckett/Jsy/25	30.00
58	Lou Brock/Jsy/20	25.00
59	Lou Gehrig/Jsy/25	180.00
62	Mel Ott/Pants/25	40.00
64	Mike Schmidt/Jsy/20	50.00
66	Nolan Ryan/Jsy/25	50.00
67	Orlando Cepeda/ Pants/25	15.00
71	Pee Wee Reese/ Jsy/25	25.00
74	Ralph Kiner/Bat/25	25.00
77	Reggie Jackson/ Jsy/25	25.00
80	Robin Yount/Jsy/19	40.00
81	Rod Carew/Jsy/25	25.00
82	Roger Clemens/ Jsy/21	30.00
83	Roger Maris/Jsy/25	60.00
84	Rogers Hornsby/ Bat/25	75.00
85	Roy Campanella/ Pants/25	30.00
86	Ozzie Smith/Jsy/25	35.00
87	Sammy Sosa/Jsy/21	30.00
88	Satchel Paige/Jsy/25	75.00
90	Steve Carlton/Jsy/25	15.00
91	Ted Williams/Jsy/25	100.00
92	Thurman Munson/ Jsy/25	40.00
93	Tom Seaver/ Pants/25	25.00
94	Ty Cobb/Pants/25	140.00
96	Warren Spahn/ Jsy/21	35.00
98	Willie McCovey/Jsy/8	25.00

Timeline Material Position

		NM/M
Quantity produced listed

4	Babe Ruth/Jsy/25	350.00
6	Bob Feller/Pants/19	25.00
7	Bob Gibson/Jsy/25	30.00
10	Cal Ripken Jr./ Jsy/25	60.00
12	Carl Yastrzemski/ Jsy/25	40.00
13	Carlton Fisk/Jsy/27	25.00
14	Jim "Catfish" Hunter/Jsy/27	20.00
20	Don Drysdale/Jsy/25	40.00
22	Duke Snider/ Pants/25	15.00
24	Early Wynn/Jsy/24	15.00
25	Eddie Mathews/ Jsy/25	30.00
26	Eddie Murray/Jsy/25	25.00
28	Ernie Banks/Jsy/25	35.00
32	Frankie Frisch/Jkt/25	40.00
36	George Brett/Jsy/25	40.00
39	Harmon Killebrew/ Jsy/25	35.00
43	Jackie Robinson/ Jkt/42	60.00
46	Jim Palmer/Jsy/22	15.00
47	Jimmie Foxx/ Fld Glv/25	85.00
49	Johnny Bench/Jsy/25	25.00
53	Juan Marichal/Jsy/27	15.00
55	Kirby Puckett/Jsy/25	30.00
58	Lou Brock/Jsy/20	25.00
59	Lou Gehrig/Jsy/25	180.00
62	Mel Ott/Pants/25	40.00
64	Mike Schmidt/Jsy/20	50.00
66	Nolan Ryan/Jsy/25	50.00
68	Orlando Cepeda/ Pants/25	15.00
71	Pee Wee Reese/ Jsy/25	25.00
74	Ralph Kiner/Bat/25	25.00
77	Reggie Jackson/ Jsy/25	25.00
80	Robin Yount/Jsy/19	40.00
81	Rod Carew/Jsy/25	25.00
82	Roger Clemens/ Jsy/21	30.00
83	Roger Maris/Jsy/9	
84	Rogers Hornsby/ Bat/25	75.00

86	Ozzie Smith/Jsy/25	35.00
87	Sammy Sosa/Jsy/21	30.00
88	Satchel Paige/CO Jsy/25	75.00
89	Stan Musial/Jsy/6	
90	Steve Carlton/Jsy/25	15.00
92	Thurman Munson/Jsy/15	50.00
93	Tom Seaver/Pants/25	25.00
96	Warren Spahn/Jsy/21	35.00
98	Willie McCovey/Jsy/25	25.00

Timeline Material Prime
No Pricing
Production 1-10

Timeline Material Quad
No Pricing
Production 1-25

Timeline Material Trio
NM/M
Most not priced.

Trio HOF:		No Pricing
Production 1-9		
Trio MVP:		No Pricing
Production 1-10		
Trio Stats:		No Pricing
Production 1-15		
10	Cal Ripken Jr./Jkt-Jsy-Pants/25	100.00
17	Dale Murphy/Bat-Jsy/25	40.00
21	Don Mattingly/Bat-Jkt-Pants/25	75.00
26	Eddie Murray/Bat-Jsy-Shoe/25	85.00
80	Robin Yount/Bat-Jsy/19	70.00
82	Roger Clemens/Bat-Jsy/21	50.00

Timeline Signature Material Combo
NM/M
Most not priced.

7	Bob Gibson/Hat-Jsy/25	50.00
8	Bobby Doerr/Bat-Jsy/25	50.00

Timeline Signature Material Combo CY
NM/M
Most not priced.

7	Bob Gibson/Hat-Jsy/25	50.00
46	Jim Palmer/Hat-Jsy/22	50.00
90	Steve Carlton/Hat-Jsy/32	50.00

Timeline Signature Material Number
NM/M
Most not priced.

6	Bob Feller/Pants/19	40.00
7	Bob Gibson/Jsy/25	50.00
8	Bobby Doerr/Jsy/25	40.00
21	Don Mattingly/Pants/23	80.00
46	Jim Palmer/Jsy/22	40.00
53	Juan Marichal/Jsy/27	40.00
58	Lou Brock/Jsy/20	50.00
66	Nolan Ryan/Jsy/34	150.00
90	Steve Carlton/Jsy/32	40.00

Timeline Signature Material Position
NM/M
Most not priced.

6	Bob Feller/Pants/19	40.00
8	Bobby Doerr/Jsy/25	40.00
21	Don Mattingly/Pants/23	80.00
46	Jim Palmer/Jsy/22	40.00
53	Juan Marichal/Jsy/27	40.00
58	Lou Brock/Jsy/20	50.00
66	Nolan Ryan/Jsy/34	150.00
67	Orel Hershiser/Jsy/25	30.00

Timeline Signature Material Prime
No Pricing
Production 1-9

Timeline Signature Material Quad
NM/M
Most not priced.

21	Don Mattingly/25	180.00

Timeline Signature Material Trio

NM/M
No Pricing
Production 1-9

Trio HOF:		No Pricing
Production 1-9		
Trio MVP:		No Pricing
Production 1-8		
Trio Stats:		No Pricing
Production 1-9		
91	Ted Williams/Bat-Jkt-Jsy/1 (2/06 Auction)	1,483

2005 Playoff Absolute Memorabilia
NM/M

Complete Set (100):		
Common Player:		.50
Retail:		.3X
Retail doesn't have foil front.		
Pack (4):		40.00
Box (4):		150.00
1	Andruw Jones	.75
2	B.J. Upton	.75
3	Jim Edmonds	.75
4	Johan Santana	1.00
5	Jeff Bagwell	.75
6	Derek Jeter	3.00
7	Eric Chavez	.75
8	Albert Pujols	3.00
9	Craig Biggio	.75
10	Hank Blalock	.75
11	Chipper Jones	1.00
12	Jacque Jones	.50
13	Alfonso Soriano	1.00
14	Carl Crawford	.50
15	Ben Sheets	.50
16	Garret Anderson	.75
17	Luis Gonzalez	.50
18	Andy Pettitte	.75
19	Miguel Tejada	.75
20	Carlos Delgado	.75
21	Austin Kearns	.50
22	Adrian Beltre	.50
23	Rafael Palmeiro	.75
24	Greg Maddux	2.00
25	Jason Bay	.50
26	Jason Varitek	.75
27	David Ortiz	1.00
28	Dontrelle Willis	.75
29	Adam Dunn	1.00
30	Carlos Lee	.50
31	Manny Ramirez	1.00
32	Rocco Baldelli	.50
33	Jeff Kent	.50
34	Jake Peavy	.75
35	Vernon Wells	.50
36	Ichiro Suzuki	2.00
37	C.C. Sabathia	.50
38	Hideki Matsui	2.00
39	Gary Sheffield	.75
40	Paul LoDuca	.50
41	Vladimir Guerrero	1.00
42	Omar Vizquel	.50
43	Lance Berkman	.50
44	Shawn Green	.50
45	Josh Beckett	.50
46	Barry Zito	.50
47	Roger Clemens	3.00
48	Sean Casey	.50
49	Edgar Renteria	.50
50	Mark Teixeira	.75
51	Frank Thomas	.75
52	Khalil Greene	.75
53	Bobby Abreu	.75
54	Rafael Furcal	.50
55	Jose Vidro	.50
56	Nomar Garciaparra	1.00
57	Melvin Mora	.50
58	Trot Nixon	.50
59	Magglio Ordonez	.50
60	Michael Young	.50
61	Richie Sexson	.50
62	Alex Rodriguez	3.00
63	Tim Hudson	.50
64	Todd Helton	.75
65	Mike Lowell	.50
66	Mark Mulder	.50
67	Sammy Sosa	1.50
68	Mark Prior	1.00
69	Shannon Stewart	.50
70	Miguel Cabrera	1.00
71	Troy Glaus	.50
72	Scott Rolen	1.00
73	Ken Griffey Jr.	2.00
74	Mike Piazza	1.00
75	Roy Halladay	.50
76	Larry Walker	.75
77	Kerry Wood	.75
78	Mike Mussina	.75
79	Curt Schilling	1.00
80	Rich Harden	.50
81	Victor Martinez	.50
82	Roy Oswalt	.50
83	Pedro Martinez	1.00
84	Tom Glavine	.50
85	Randy Johnson	1.00
86	Ivan Rodriguez	1.00
87	Carlos Beltran	.75
88	Torii Hunter	.50
89	Hideo Nomo	.50
90	Jim Thome	1.00
91	Aramis Ramirez	.50
92	J.D. Drew	.50
93	Javy Lopez	.50
94	David Wright	2.00
95	Bobby Crosby	.75
96	Jeff Niemann RC	3.00
97	Yuniesky Betancourt RC	3.00
98	Tadahito Iguchi RC	5.00
99	Philip Humber RC	3.00
100	Justin Verlander RC	5.00

Black
Black: 2-4X
Inserted 1:18 Retail

Blue
Blue: 1-2X
Inserted 1:3 Retail

Red
Red: 2-3X
Inserted 1:8 Retail

Spectrum Gold
No Pricing
Production 10 Sets

Spectrum Platinum
No Pricing
Production One Set

Spectrum Silver
Silver: 2-3X
Production 100 Sets

Absolutely Ink Swatch Double
NM/M
Production 1-50

1	Rafael Furcal B-J/50	20.00
2	Dale Murphy B-J/50	30.00
7	Bobby Crosby J-J/50	20.00
8	Cal Ripken Jr. J-P/25	150.00
10	Vernon Wells J-J/25	20.00
11	Omar Vizquel J-J/50	15.00
13	Omar Vizquel J-J/50	25.00
16	Aramis Ramirez J-J/25	30.00
18	Travis Hafner BG-J/50	25.00
22	Juan Gonzalez B-J/25	25.00
23	Mark Teixeira FG-J/50	35.00
27	Darryl Strawberry J-J/50	20.00
30	Magglio Ordonez B-J/25	20.00
31	Jay Gibbons B-J/50	15.00
32	Steve Carlton FG-J/25	40.00
37	Keith Hernandez B-J/50	20.00
38	Carlos Zambrano J-J/25	25.00
39	Brett Myers J-J/50	15.00
41	Danny Kolb J-J/25	15.00
42	Mark Prior FG-J/25	40.00
43	Joey Gathright B-J/25	15.00
44	David Cone J-J/50	15.00
45	Carlos Lee FG-J/50	20.00
49	Garret Anderson J-J/25	25.00
51	Dave Parker B-J/25	25.00
52	C.C. Sabathia J-J/50	20.00
55	Brandon Webb B-P/50	15.00
56	Sean Casey B-J/50	20.00
57	Johan Santana J-J/25	60.00
58	Miguel Cabrera J-J/50	40.00
59	Bert Blyleven J-J/50	15.00
60	Casey Kotchman B-J/50	20.00
62	Milton Bradley J-J/25	15.00
63	John Kruk J-J/25	25.00
64	Michael Young B-J/50	20.00
69	Lew Ford B-J/50	15.00
70	Jody Gerut B-J/50	15.00
71	Don Sutton J-J/50	15.00
73	Austin Kearns B-J/50	15.00
77	Ryan Wagner J-J/50	15.00
78	Jermaine Dye J-J/50	15.00
80	Al Oliver B-J/50	15.00
81	Angel Berroa B-P/50	15.00
82	Edgar Renteria J-J/25	20.00
84	Roy Oswalt FG-J/25	25.00
86	Dave Righetti J-J/50	15.00
87	Aubrey Huff H-J/25	20.00
89	Jose Vidro B-J/50	15.00
90	Harold Baines J-J/50	15.00
93	Ken Harvey J-J/50	15.00
95	Jason Bay B-J/50	20.00
96	Dwight Evans B-J/50	40.00
99	Brian Roberts J-J/50	40.00

Absolutely Ink Swatch Double Spectrum
NM/M

Production 1-25		
Prime:		No Pricing
Production One Set		
1	Rafael Furcal B-J/25	20.00
3	Dale Murphy B-J/25	40.00
7	Bobby Crosby B-J/25	25.00
10	Vernon Wells J-J/25	20.00
11	Lyle Overbay J-J/25	15.00
18	Travis Hafner BG-J/25	30.00
27	Darryl Strawberry J-J/25	25.00
31	Jay Gibbons B-J/25	20.00
37	Keith Hernandez B-J/25	25.00
38	Carlos Zambrano J-J/25	30.00
39	Brett Myers J-J/25	15.00
41	Danny Kolb J-J/25	15.00
45	Carlos Lee FG-J/25	20.00
55	Brandon Webb B-P/25	25.00
59	Bert Blyleven J-J/25	15.00
60	Casey Kotchman B-J/25	25.00
62	Milton Bradley J-J/25	25.00
63	John Kruk J-J/25	25.00
64	Michael Young B-J/25	25.00
69	Lew Ford B-J/25	15.00
70	Jody Gerut B-J/25	15.00
71	Don Sutton J-J/25	20.00
73	Austin Kearns B-J/25	
77	Ryan Wagner J-J/25	15.00
78	Jermaine Dye J-J/25	15.00
81	Angel Berroa B-P/25	15.00
89	Jose Vidro B-J/25	15.00
90	Harold Baines J-J/25	20.00
93	Ken Harvey J-J/25	15.00
95	Jason Bay B-J/25	25.00
96	Dwight Evans B-J/25	40.00
99	Brian Roberts J-J/25	40.00

Absolutely Ink Swatch Single
NM/M

Production 5-50		
1	Rafael Furcal/Jsy/50	15.00
3	Dale Murphy/Jsy/50	25.00
4	Duke Snider/Pants/25	40.00
5	Bill Madlock/Bat/50	20.00
7	Bobby Crosby/Jsy/50	15.00
8	Cal Ripken Jr./Jsy/25	140.00
9	Hank Blalock/Jsy/25	25.00
10	Vernon Wells/Jsy/50	15.00
11	Lyle Overbay/Jsy/50	15.00
13	Omar Vizquel/Jsy/50	25.00

15	Ben Sheets/Jsy/25	20.00
16	Aramis Ramirez/	
	Jsy/25	30.00
18	Travis Hafner/Jsy/25	20.00
19	Mike Lowell/Jsy/25	15.00
20	Frank Robinson/	
	Bat/50	30.00
22	Juan Gonzalez/	
	Jsy/50	25.00
27	Darryl Strawberry/	
	Jsy/50	20.00
28	Alexis Rios/Bat/50	15.00
30	Magglio Ordonez/	
	Jsy/50	15.00
31	Jay Gibbons/Jsy/50	15.00
32	Steve Carlton/Jsy/25	35.00
34	Kerry Wood/Jsy/25	35.00
36	Eric Chavez/Jsy/25	25.00
37	Keith Hernandez/	
	Jsy/50	15.00
38	Carlos Zambrano/	
	Jsy/50	25.00
39	Brett Myers/Jsy/50	15.00
40	Rich Harden/Jsy/50	20.00
41	Danny Kolb/Jsy/50	15.00
42	Mark Prior/Jsy/50	40.00
43	Joey Gathright/Jsy/25	15.00
44	David Cone/Jsy/50	15.00
45	Carlos Lee/Jsy/50	20.00
47	Jack Morris/Jsy/50	20.00
48	Torii Hunter/Jsy/50	20.00
49	Garret Anderson/	
	Jsy/50	25.00
51	Dave Parker/Bat/50	20.00
52	C.C. Sabathia/Jsy/50	15.00
53	Dennis Eckersley/	
	Jsy/50	15.00
54	Barry Larkin/Jsy/25	40.00
55	Brandon Webb/	
	Pants/50	15.00
56	Sean Casey/Jsy/50	20.00
57	Johan Santana/	
	Jsy/50	40.00
58	Miguel Cabrera/	
	Jsy/50	40.00
59	Bert Blyleven/Jsy/50	15.00
60	Casey Kotchman/	
	Jsy/50	15.00
61	Dwight Gooden/	
	Jsy/50	20.00
62	Milton Bradley/Jsy/50	15.00
63	John Kruk/Jsy/50	25.00
64	Michael Young/	
	Jsy/50	20.00
66	Robin Ventura/Jsy/50	20.00
67	Tim Hudson/Jsy/25	30.00
68	Will Clark/Bat/50	40.00
69	Lew Ford/Jsy/50	15.00
70	Jody Gerut/Jsy/50	15.00
71	Don Sutton/Jsy/50	15.00
72	B.J. Upton/Bat/25	20.00
73	Austin Kearns/Jsy/50	15.00
77	Ryan Wagner/Jsy/50	15.00
78	Jermaine Dye/Jsy/50	15.00
80	Al Oliver/Jsy/50	15.00
81	Angel Berroa/	
	Pants/50	15.00
82	Edgar Renteria/	
	Jsy/50	20.00
83	Dennis Eckersley/	
	Jsy/50	25.00
84	Roy Oswalt/Jsy/50	20.00
86	Dave Righetti/Jsy/50	20.00
87	Aubrey Huff/Jsy/25	20.00
89	Jose Vidro/Jsy/50	15.00
90	Harold Baines/Jsy/50	15.00
93	Ken Harvey/Jsy/50	15.00
95	Jason Bay/Jsy/50	20.00
96	Dwight Evans/Jsy/50	30.00
97	Luis Tiant/Pants/50	15.00
98	Ron Santo/Bat/50	30.00
99	Brian Roberts/Jsy/50	40.00
100	Marty Marion/Jsy/50	15.00

Absolutely Ink Swatch Single Spectrum

NM/M

Production 1-25
Prime: No Pricing
Production One Set

1	Rafael Furcal/Jsy/25	20.00
3	Dale Murphy/Jsy/25	35.00
5	Bill Madlock/Bat/25	25.00
7	Bobby Crosby/Jsy/25	20.00
11	Lyle Overbay/Jsy/25	15.00
13	Omar Vizquel/Jsy/25	25.00
18	Travis Hafner/Jsy/25	25.00
23	Mark Teixeira/Jsy/25	50.00
27	Darryl Strawberry/	
	Jsy/25	20.00
28	Alexis Rios/Bat/25	15.00
30	Magglio Ordonez/	
	Jsy/25	15.00

31	Jay Gibbons/Jsy/25	15.00
37	Keith Hernandez/	
	Jsy/25	20.00
38	Carlos Zambrano/	
	Jsy/25	30.00
39	Brett Myers/Jsy/25	15.00
40	Rich Harden/Jsy/25	25.00
41	Danny Kolb/Jsy/25	15.00
45	Carlos Lee/Jsy/25	20.00
47	Jack Morris/Jsy/25	20.00
51	Dave Parker/Bat/25	20.00
52	C.C. Sabathia/Jsy/25	20.00
55	Brandon Webb/	
	Pants/25	25.00
56	Sean Casey/Jsy/25	20.00
57	Johan Santana/	
	Jsy/25	50.00
58	Miguel Cabrera/	
	Jsy/25	50.00
59	Bert Blyleven/Jsy/25	20.00
60	Casey Kotchman/	
	Jsy/25	25.00
61	Dwight Gooden/	
	Jsy/25	25.00
62	Milton Bradley/Jsy/25	20.00
63	John Kruk/Jsy/25	25.00
64	Michael Young/	
	Jsy/25	25.00
69	Lew Ford/Jsy/25	15.00
70	Jody Gerut/Jsy/25	15.00
71	Don Sutton/Jsy/25	20.00
73	Austin Kearns/Jsy/25	20.00
77	Ryan Wagner/Jsy/25	15.00
78	Jermaine Dye/Jsy/25	15.00
80	Al Oliver/Jsy/25	15.00
81	Angel Berroa/	
	Pants/25	15.00
89	Jose Vidro/Jsy/25	15.00
90	Harold Baines/Jsy/25	20.00
92	Mark Mulder/Jsy/25	25.00
93	Ken Harvey/Jsy/25	15.00
95	Jason Bay/Jsy/25	25.00
96	Dwight Evans/Jsy/25	40.00
97	Luis Tiant/Pants/25	15.00
98	Ron Santo/Bat/25	30.00
99	Brian Roberts/Jsy/25	25.00
100	Marty Marion/Jsy/25	25.00

Absolutely Ink Swatch Triple

NM/M

Production 1-75

1	Rafael Furcal/50	20.00
3	Dale Murphy/50	30.00
8	Cal Ripken Jr./25	160.00
9	Hank Blalock/25	30.00
13	Omar Vizquel/25	30.00
16	Aramis Ramirez/25	35.00
18	Travis Hafner/50	25.00
22	Juan Gonzalez/25	30.00
23	Mark Teixeira/75	40.00
27	Darryl Strawberry/25	20.00
31	Jay Gibbons/25	20.00
37	Keith Hernandez/25	25.00
45	Carlos Lee/50	20.00
49	Garret Anderson/25	30.00
52	C.C. Sabathia/25	20.00
53	Dennis Eckersley/25	25.00
55	Brandon Webb/50	20.00
56	Sean Casey/25	25.00
58	Miguel Cabrera/25	50.00
60	Casey Kotchman/25	25.00
64	Michael Young/75	25.00
69	Lew Ford/50	15.00
70	Jody Gerut/50	15.00
73	Austin Kearns/50	20.00
77	Ryan Wagner/50	15.00
78	Jermaine Dye/50	15.00
81	Angel Berroa/50	15.00
86	Dave Righetti/50	20.00
89	Jose Vidro/50	15.00
90	Harold Baines/50	20.00
95	Jason Bay/50	20.00
96	Dwight Evans/25	40.00

Absolutely Ink Swatch Triple Spectrum

NM/M

Production 1-25
Prime: No Pricing
Production One Set

1	Rafael Furcal/25	20.00
3	Dale Murphy/25	40.00
18	Travis Hafner/25	25.00
23	Mark Teixeira/50	50.00
27	Darryl Strawberry/25	20.00
45	Carlos Lee/25	20.00
60	Casey Kotchman/25	25.00
64	Michael Young/25	30.00
69	Lew Ford/25	15.00
70	Jody Gerut/25	15.00
73	Austin Kearns/25	20.00
77	Ryan Wagner/25	15.00

78	Jermaine Dye/25	15.00
81	Angel Berroa/25	15.00
89	Jose Vidro/25	15.00
90	Harold Baines/25	20.00

Absolute Memorabilia Heroes

NM/M

Common Player: 1.50
Production 250 Sets
Spectrum: 1-2X
Production 50 Sets
Reverse Spectrum: 2-4X
Production 25 Sets

1	Billy Martin	3.00
2	Rickey Henderson	2.00
3	Alan Trammell	2.00
4	Lenny Dykstra	1.50
5	Jeff Bagwell	2.00
6	Steve Garvey	1.50
7	Jim "Catfish" Hunter	2.00
8	Cal Ripken Jr.	10.00
9	Reggie Jackson	3.00
10	Gary Sheffield	2.00
11	Edgar Martinez	1.50
12	Roberto Alomar	2.00
13	Luis Tiant	1.50
14	Jim Rice	2.00
15	Carlos Beltran	2.00
16	Hideo Nomo	2.00
17	Mark Grace	2.00
18	Joe Cronin	2.00
19	Tony Gwynn	3.00
20	Bo Jackson	2.00
21	Roger Clemens	5.00
22	Roger Clemens	5.00
23	Don Mattingly	2.00
24	Willie Mays	5.00
25	Andruw Jones	2.00
26	Andre Dawson	2.00
27	Carlton Fisk	2.00
28	Robin Yount	3.00
29	Joe Carter	1.50
30	Dale Murphy	2.00
31	Greg Maddux	3.00
32	Ichiro Suzuki	4.00
33	Jose Canseco	2.00
34	Nolan Ryan	8.00
35	Frank Thomas	2.00
36	Fred Lynn	1.50
37	Curt Schilling	2.00
38	Curt Schilling	2.00
39	Dave Parker	1.50
40	Randy Johnson	2.50
41	Randy Johnson	2.50
42	Vladimir Guerrero	2.50
43	Bernie Williams	1.50
44	Wade Boggs	2.00
45	Pedro Martinez	2.00
46	Andy Pettitte	1.50
47	Fergie Jenkins	2.00
48	Darryl Strawberry	1.50
49	Rafael Palmeiro	2.00
50	Albert Pujols	5.00

Heroes Autograph Swatch Double Spectrum Prime

NM/M

No Pricing
Production 1-15
Triple: No Pricing
Production One Set

Heroes Swatch Double

NM/M

Production 25-50
Spectrum Prime: No Pricing
Production 1-25

1	Billy Martin J-P/50	25.00
2	Rickey Henderson	
	B-J/50	10.00
3	Alan Trammell B-J/50	10.00
4	Lenny Dykstra B-J/50	8.00
5	Jeff Bagwell B-J/50	10.00
6	Steve Garvey B-J/50	8.00
7	Jim "Catfish" Hunter	
	J-J/25	10.00
8	Cal Ripken Jr. J-P/50	40.00

9	Reggie Jackson	
	JK-J/50	10.00
10	Gary Sheffield	
	FG-J/50	8.00
11	Edgar Martinez J-J/50	8.00
12	Roberto Alomar	
	J-J/50	8.00
13	Luis Tiant H-J/25	10.00
14	Jim Rice J-P/50	8.00
15	Carlos Beltran B-J/50	8.00
16	Hideo Nomo B-J/50	10.00
17	Mark Grace FG-J/50	10.00
18	Joe Cronin J-P/50	30.00
19	Tony Gwynn B-J/50	15.00
20	Bo Jackson B-J/50	10.00
21	Roger Clemens	
	J-J/50	25.00
22	Roger Clemens	
	J-J/50	25.00
23	Don Mattingly B-J/50	20.00
24	Willie Mays B-J/50	50.00
25	Andruw Jones B-J/50	8.00
26	Andre Dawson J-P/50	8.00
28	Robin Yount H-J/50	15.00
29	Joe Carter B-J/50	8.00
30	Dale Murphy B-J/50	8.00
31	Greg Maddux J-J/50	15.00
33	Jose Canseco H-J/50	10.00
34	Nolan Ryan B-J/50	30.00
35	Frank Thomas J-P/50	10.00
36	Fred Lynn B-J/50	8.00
37	Curt Schilling J-J/50	10.00
38	Curt Schilling J-J/50	10.00
39	Dave Parker B-J/50	8.00
40	Randy Johnson	
	J-J/50	10.00
41	Randy Johnson	
	B-J/50	10.00
42	Vladimir Guerrero	
	J-J/50	10.00
43	Bernie Williams J-J/50	8.00
44	Wade Boggs B-J/50	10.00
45	Pedro Martinez	
	J-J/50	10.00
46	Andy Pettitte J-J/50	8.00
47	Fergie Jenkins H-J/50	8.00
48	Darryl Strawberry	
	J-P/50	8.00
49	Rafael Palmeiro	
	B-J/50	10.00
50	Albert Pujols J-J/50	30.00

Heroes Swatch Triple

NM/M

Production 1-50
Spectrum Prime: No Pricing
Production 1-15

1	Billy Martin/25	35.00
2	Rickey Henderson/25	15.00
3	Alan Trammell/25	10.00
4	Lenny Dykstra/25	10.00
5	Jeff Bagwell/25	10.00
6	Steve Garvey/25	8.00
8	Cal Ripken Jr./25	50.00
9	Reggie Jackson/25	15.00
11	Edgar Martinez/25	10.00
12	Roberto Alomar/50	10.00
14	Jim Rice/25	10.00
15	Carlos Beltran/25	10.00
16	Hideo Nomo/25	20.00
17	Mark Grace/25	15.00
18	Joe Cronin/25	40.00
19	Tony Gwynn/25	25.00
20	Bo Jackson/25	20.00
21	Roger Clemens/25	25.00
22	Roger Clemens/50	25.00
23	Don Mattingly/50	30.00
25	Andruw Jones/50	10.00
26	Andre Dawson/25	10.00
28	Robin Yount/25	60.00
31	Greg Maddux/50	40.00
34	Nolan Ryan/25	40.00
35	Frank Thomas/50	15.00
36	Fred Lynn/25	10.00
37	Curt Schilling/50	15.00
38	Curt Schilling/50	15.00
39	Dave Parker/25	15.00
42	Vladimir Guerrero/50	15.00
43	Bernie Williams/25	10.00
44	Wade Boggs/25	15.00
45	Pedro Martinez/50	10.00
46	Andy Pettitte/50	10.00
47	Fergie Jenkins/25	10.00
48	Darryl Strawberry/50	10.00
49	Rafael Palmeiro/25	10.00
50	Albert Pujols/50	40.00

Marks of Fame

NM/M

Common Player: 2.00
Production 150 Sets
Spectrum: 2-3X
Production 25 Sets

#	Player	Price
1	Bobby Doerr	2.00
2	Reggie Jackson	3.00
3	Harmon Killebrew	4.00
4	Duke Snider	3.00
5	Brooks Robinson	3.00
6	Al Kaline	4.00
7	Carlton Fisk	3.00
8	Willie Stargell	3.00
9	Enos Slaughter	2.00
10	Nolan Ryan	10.00
11	Luis Aparicio	2.00
12	Hoyt Wilhelm	2.00
13	Orlando Cepeda	2.00
14	Mike Schmidt	6.00
15	Frank Robinson	3.00
16	Whitey Ford	3.00
17	Don Sutton	2.00
18	Joe Morgan	2.00
19	Bob Feller	3.00
20	Lou Brock	3.00
21	Warren Spahn	4.00
22	Jim Palmer	2.00
23	Reggie Jackson	3.00
24	Willie Mays	8.00
25	George Brett	8.00
26	Billy Williams	2.00
27	Juan Marichal	2.00
28	Early Wynn	2.00
29	Rod Carew	3.00
30	Maury Wills	2.00
31	Fergie Jenkins	2.00
32	Steve Carlton	3.00
33	Eddie Murray	3.00
34	Kirby Puckett	3.00
35	Johnny Bench	4.00
36	Gaylord Perry	2.00
37	Gary Carter	2.00
38	Tony Perez	2.00
39	Tony Oliva	2.00
40	Luis Aparicio	2.00
41	Tom Seaver	3.00
42	Paul Molitor	3.00
43	Dennis Eckersley	2.00
44	Willie McCovey	3.00
45	Bob Gibson	3.00
46	Robin Roberts	2.00
47	Carl Yastrzemski	4.00
48	Ozzie Smith	4.00
49	Nolan Ryan	10.00
50	Stan Musial	6.00

Marks of Fame Autograph Swatch Double

NM/M

Production 1-75
Prime: No Pricing
Production 1-10

#	Player	Price
1	Bobby Doerr B-P/50	25.00
3	Harmon Killebrew B-J/50	40.00
4	Duke Snider J-P/25	40.00
5	Brooks Robinson B-J/25	40.00
7	Carlton Fisk B-JK/25	40.00
10	Nolan Ryan J-P/25	100.00
11	Luis Aparicio B-J/75	20.00
12	Hoyt Wilhelm J-J/25	25.00
13	Orlando Cepeda B-P/25	25.00
14	Mike Schmidt B-J/25	75.00
15	Frank Robinson B-S/25	50.00
16	Whitey Ford J-J/25	50.00
17	Don Sutton J-J/25	20.00
20	Lou Brock B-JK/25	50.00
22	Jim Palmer H-P/25	30.00
27	Juan Marichal J-P/25	25.00
29	Rod Carew B-J/25	40.00
31	Fergie Jenkins FG-P/25	20.00
32	Steve Carlton B-P/25	40.00
35	Johnny Bench B-J/25	50.00
36	Gaylord Perry J-J/25	20.00
37	Gary Carter B-J/25	25.00
38	Tony Perez FG-J/25	25.00
39	Tony Oliva B-J/75	20.00
41	Tom Seaver J-P/25	40.00
42	Paul Molitor B-J/25	35.00
43	Dennis Eckersley J-J/25	25.00
44	Willie McCovey J-P/25	40.00
48	Ozzie Smith H-P/25	50.00
49	Nolan Ryan JK-J/25	100.00
50	Stan Musial B-P/25	80.00

Marks of Fame Autograph Swatch Single

NM/M

Production 5-125

#	Player	Price
1	Bobby Doerr/Pants/125	20.00
3	Harmon Killebrew/Jsy/50	40.00
4	Duke Snider/Jsy/25	40.00
5	Brooks Robinson/Jsy/125	30.00
6	Al Kaline/Bat/125	35.00
7	Carlton Fisk/Jkt/50	40.00
10	Nolan Ryan/Pants/50	80.00
11	Luis Aparicio/Jsy/125	20.00
13	Orlando Cepeda/Pants/50	25.00
14	Mike Schmidt/Jsy/50	60.00
15	Frank Robinson/Bat/125	25.00
16	Whitey Ford/Jsy/50	50.00
17	Don Sutton/Jsy/125	20.00
19	Bob Feller/Pants/125	30.00
20	Lou Brock/Jkt/125	30.00
22	Jim Palmer/Pants/50	25.00
26	Billy Williams/Jsy/50	25.00
27	Juan Marichal/Pants/125	25.00
29	Rod Carew/Jsy/50	35.00
31	Fergie Jenkins/Pants/125	20.00
32	Steve Carlton/Pants/125	25.00
35	Johnny Bench/Pants/50	50.00
36	Gaylord Perry/Jsy/125	15.00
37	Gary Carter/Pants/50	20.00
38	Tony Perez/Jsy/50	20.00
39	Tony Oliva/Jsy/125	25.00
40	Luis Aparicio/Bat/125	20.00
41	Tom Seaver/Pants/50	35.00
42	Paul Molitor/Pants/50	35.00
43	Dennis Eckersley/Jsy/125	25.00
44	Willie McCovey/Pants/50	35.00
46	Robin Roberts/Hat/50	35.00
48	Ozzie Smith/Pants/50	50.00
49	Nolan Ryan/Jkt/50	80.00
50	Stan Musial/Pants/50	60.00

Marks of Fame Autograph Swatch Triple

No Pricing
Production 1-10
Prime: No Pricing
Production One Set

Marks of Fame Swatch Double

NM/M

Production 1-50
Spectrum Prime: No Pricing
Production 1-25

#	Player	Price
1	Bobby Doerr/50	10.00
2	Reggie Jackson B-P/50	10.00
3	Harmon Killebrew B-J/50	15.00
4	Duke Snider J-P/25	15.00
5	Brooks Robinson B-J/50	10.00
7	Carlton Fisk B-JK/50	10.00
8	Willie Stargell B-J/50	10.00
9	Enos Slaughter J-J/50	10.00
10	Nolan Ryan J-P/50	25.00
11	Luis Aparicio B-J/50	8.00
12	Hoyt Wilhelm J-J/50	8.00
13	Orlando Cepeda B-P/50	10.00
14	Mike Schmidt B-J/50	20.00
15	Frank Robinson B-S/50	15.00
16	Whitey Ford J-J/50	15.00
17	Don Sutton J-J/50	8.00
18	Joe Morgan B-J/50	8.00
20	Lou Brock B-JK/50	10.00
21	Warren Spahn J-P/50	12.00
22	Jim Palmer H-P/50	10.00
23	Reggie Jackson B-J/50	10.00
24	Willie Mays B-J/50	50.00
26	Billy Williams J-J/50	8.00
27	Juan Marichal J-J/50	8.00
28	Early Wynn J-J/50	10.00
29	Rod Carew B-J/50	10.00
31	Fergie Jenkins FG-P/50	8.00
32	Steve Carlton B-P/50	8.00
33	Eddie Murray B-J/50	15.00
34	Kirby Puckett B-J/50	15.00
35	Johnny Bench B-J/50	15.00
36	Gaylord Perry J-J/50	8.00
37	Gary Carter B-J/50	8.00
39	Tony Oliva B-J/50	8.00
41	Tom Seaver J-P/50	15.00
42	Paul Molitor B-J/50	15.00
43	Dennis Eckersley J-J/50	10.00
44	Willie McCovey J-P/50	10.00
47	Carl Yastrzemski B-J/50	20.00
48	Ozzie Smith H-P/50	20.00
49	Nolan Ryan JK-J/50	25.00
50	Stan Musial B-P/50	30.00

Marks of Fame Swatch Triple

NM/M

Production 1-25
Spectrum Prime: No Pricing
Production 1-15

#	Player	Price
7	Carlton Fisk/25	15.00
8	Willie Stargell/25	15.00
10	Nolan Ryan/25	40.00
11	Luis Aparicio/25	12.00
12	Hoyt Wilhelm/25	10.00
14	Mike Schmidt/25	30.00
18	Joe Morgan/25	12.00
20	Lou Brock/25	15.00
21	Warren Spahn/25	50.00
23	Reggie Jackson/25	15.00
24	Willie Mays/25	60.00
27	Juan Marichal/25	12.00
29	Rod Carew/25	15.00
32	Steve Carlton/25	12.00
33	Eddie Murray/25	20.00
34	Kirby Puckett/25	20.00
35	Johnny Bench/25	20.00
37	Gary Carter/25	12.00
39	Tony Oliva/25	12.00
41	Tom Seaver/25	15.00
42	Paul Molitor/25	15.00
43	Dennis Eckersley/25	12.00
44	Willie McCovey/25	15.00
47	Carl Yastrzemski/25	25.00
48	Ozzie Smith/25	25.00
49	Nolan Ryan/25	40.00
50	Stan Musial/25	40.00

Team Quads

NM/M

Common Quad:
Production 150 Sets
Spectrum: 1X
Production 100 Sets

#	Team	Price
1	St. Louis Card Active	6.00
2	Cleveland Indians	2.00
3	California Angels	2.00
4	Boston Red Sox	5.00
5	New York Yanks Active	6.00
6	Atlanta Braves	3.00
7	Oakland A's	3.00
8	Anaheim Angels	3.00
9	Texas Rangers Active	2.00
10	Minnesota Twins Active	3.00
11	New York Mets	4.00
12	Houston Astros	5.00
13	San Diego Padres	4.00
14	Cincinnati Reds	2.00
15	Texas Rangers Retro	8.00
16	New York Yanks Retro	8.00
17	St. Louis Cards Retro	6.00
18	Pittsburgh Pirates	2.00
19	Chicago Cubs	4.00
20	Minnesota Twins Retro	3.00

Team Quads Swatch Double

NM/M

Production 25-75

#	Team	Price
1	St. Louis Card Active/75	25.00
3	California Angels/75	30.00
4	Boston Red Sox/75	30.00
5	New York Yanks Active/25	75.00
6	Atlanta Braves/25	60.00
7	Oakland A's/75	20.00
8	Anaheim Angels/25	40.00
9	Texas Rangers Active/25	20.00
10	Minnesota Twins Active/25	40.00
11	New York Mets/75	30.00
12	Houston Astros/25	75.00
13	San Diego Padres/75	40.00
14	Cincinnati Reds/75	20.00
15	Texas Rangers Retro/75	50.00
18	Pittsburgh Pirates/75	20.00
20	Minnesota Twins Retro/75	30.00

Team Quads Swatch Double Spectrum

NM/M

Production 1-25
Prime Black: No Pricing
Production 1-5

#	Team	Price
1	St. Louis Card Active/25	40.00
3	California Angels/25	50.00
4	Boston Red Sox/25	60.00
9	Texas Rangers Active/25	30.00
11	New York Mets/25	50.00
12	Houston Astros/10	
13	San Diego Padres/25	60.00
14	Cincinnati Reds/25	30.00
15	Texas Rangers Retro/25	70.00

Team Quads Swatch Single

NM/M

Production 25-100

#	Team	Price
1	St. Louis Card Active/100	25.00
2	Cleveland Indians/100	30.00
3	California Angels/100	15.00
4	Boston Red Sox/100	20.00
5	New York Yanks Active/100	10.00
6	Atlanta Braves/100	25.00
7	Oakland A's/100	10.00
8	Anaheim Angels/100	15.00
9	Texas Rangers Active/100	10.00
10	Minnesota Twins Active/25	25.00
11	New York Mets/100	20.00
12	Houston Astros/100	30.00
13	San Diego Padres/100	10.00
14	Cincinnati Reds/100	10.00
15	Texas Rangers Retro/100	30.00
16	New York Yanks Retro/100	50.00
17	St. Louis Cards Retro/25	50.00
18	Pittsburgh Pirates/100	15.00
19	Chicago Cubs/100	25.00
20	Minnesota Twins Retro/100	20.00

Team Quads Swatch Single Spectrum

NM/M

Production 10-35
Prime Black: No Pricing
Production 10 Sets

#	Team	Price
1	St. Louis Card Active/35	40.00
2	Cleveland Indians/35	50.00
3	California Angels/35	25.00
4	Boston Red Sox/35	30.00
5	New York Yanks Active/35	40.00
6	Atlanta Braves/35	40.00
7	Oakland A's/35	20.00
8	Anaheim Angels/35	25.00
9	Texas Rangers Active/35	40.00
11	New York Mets/35	30.00
12	Houston Astros/35	50.00
13	San Diego Padres/35	40.00
14	Cincinnati Reds/35	20.00
15	Texas Rangers Retro/35	40.00
16	New York Yanks Retro/35	75.00
18	Pittsburgh Pirates/35	20.00
19	Chicago Cubs/35	40.00
20	Minnesota Twins Retro/35	30.00

Team Six

NM/M

Common Card: 1.50
Production 100 Sets
Spectrum: 1-1.5X
Production 50 Sets

#	Team	Price
1	San Francisco Giants	8.00
2	Houston Astros	6.00
3	Cincinnati Reds	5.00

4	St. Louis Cardinals	8.00
5	New York Yankees	10.00
6	Chicago Cubs	6.00
7	Arizona Diamondbacks	1.50
8	Los Angeles Dodgers	6.00
9	Anaheim Angels	4.00
10	Boston Red Sox	8.00
11	Seattle Mariners	8.00
12	Chicago White Sox	4.00
13	Philadelphia Phillies	10.00
14	New York Mets	10.00
15	Atlanta Braves	4.00

Team Six Swatch Single

Production 15-50

1	San Francisco Giants/50	80.00
2	Houston Astros/50	40.00
5	New York Yankees/50	60.00
6	Chicago Cubs/50	40.00
7	Arizona Diamondbacks/50	20.00
8	Los Angeles Dodgers/50	40.00
9	Anaheim Angels/50	30.00
10	Boston Red Sox/50	50.00
12	Chicago White Sox/50	30.00
13	Philadelphia Phillies/50	40.00
14	New York Mets/50	40.00
15	Atlanta Braves/50	40.00

Team Six Swatch Single Spectrum

NM/M

Production 5-25
Prime Black: No Pricing
Production 5 Sets

1	San Francisco Giants/25	100.00
2	Houston Astros/25	50.00
5	New York Yankees/25	75.00
6	Chicago Cubs/25	50.00
7	Arizona Diamondbacks/25	25.00
8	Los Angeles Dodgers/25	50.00
9	Anaheim Angels/10	50.00
10	Boston Red Sox/25	65.00
12	Chicago White Sox/25	40.00
13	Philadelphia Phillies/25	50.00
14	New York Mets/25	50.00
15	Atlanta Braves/25	50.00

Team Tandems

NM/M

Common Card: 1.50
Production 250 Sets
Spectrum: .75-1.5X
Production 150 Sets

1	Mark Prior, Kerry Wood	2.00
2	Barry Zito, Tim Hudson	1.50
3	Curt Schilling, Pedro Martinez	2.50
4	Will Clark, Matt Williams	2.00
5	Bernie Williams, Jason Giambi	2.00
6	Vernon Wells, Roy Halladay	1.50
7	Josh Beckett, A.J. Burnett	1.50
8	Dale Murphy, Phil Niekro	2.00
9	Mike Schmidt, Steve Carlton	5.00
10	Tony Oliva, Harmon Killebrew	2.00
11	Robin Yount, Paul Molitor	2.50
12	Francisco Rodriguez, Troy Percival	1.50
13	Ben Sheets, Danny Kolb	1.50
14	Andruw Jones, Rafael Furcal	1.50
15	Todd Helton, Preston Wilson	1.50
16	Wade Boggs, Fred McGriff	2.00
17	Manny Ramirez, David Ortiz	2.50
18	Miguel Cabrera, Dontrelle Willis	2.00
19	Edgar Renteria, Scott Rolen	2.00
20	Carlos Beltran, Jeff Kent	2.00
21	Eric Davis, Deion Sanders	2.00
22	Frank Thomas, Paul Konerko	2.00
23	Mike Piazza, Al Leiter	3.00
24	Sean Burroughs, Ryan Klesko	1.50
25	Ken Harvey, Mike Sweeney	1.50
26	David Sanders, Hideki Matsui	4.00
27	Steve Carlton, Mark Buehrle	2.00
28	Gaylord Perry, Randy Johnson	2.00
29	Joe Morgan, Steve Carlton	2.00
30	Vladimir Guerrero, Orlando Cabrera	2.00
31	Scott Rolen, John Kruk	2.00
32	Aaron Boone, Dmitri Young	1.50
33	Rickey Henderson, Vladimir Guerrero	2.00
34	Charles Johnson, Cliff Floyd	1.50
35	Cal Ripken Jr., Rafael Palmeiro	8.00

Team Tandems Swatch Double

NM/M

Production 1-125
Spectrum: 1-2X
Production 1-50
No pricing 20 or less.

1	Mark Prior, Kerry Wood/125	8.00
2	Barry Zito, Tim Hudson/125	8.00
3	Curt Schilling, Pedro Martinez/125	15.00
5	Bernie Williams, Jason Giambi/125	10.00
7	Josh Beckett, A.J. Burnett/125	8.00
8	Dale Murphy, Phil Niekro/125	20.00
10	Tony Oliva, Harmon Killebrew/50	30.00
11	Robin Yount, Paul Molitor/125	20.00
14	Andruw Jones, Rafael Furcal/125	8.00
15	Todd Helton, Preston Wilson/125	10.00
16	Wade Boggs, Fred McGriff/125	15.00
17	Manny Ramirez, David Ortiz/125	15.00
18	Miguel Cabrera, Dontrelle Willis/125	12.00
20	Carlos Beltran, Jeff Kent/50	12.00
21	Eric Davis, Deion Sanders/25	15.00
22	Frank Thomas, Paul Konerko/50	15.00
23	Mike Piazza, Al Leiter/50	20.00
24	Sean Burroughs, Ryan Klesko/50	10.00
26	Deion Sanders, Hideki Matsui/125	35.00
27	Steve Carlton, Mark Buehrle/50	12.00
29	Joe Morgan, Steve Carlton/25	15.00
30	Vladimir Guerrero, Orlando Cabrera/10	
33	Rickey Henderson, Vladimir Guerrero/50	15.00
34	Charles Johnson, Cliff Floyd/125	8.00
35	Cal Ripken Jr., Rafael Palmeiro/125	40.00

Team Tandems Swatch Single

NM/M

Production 10-125

1	Mark Prior, Kerry Wood/125	6.00
2	Barry Zito, Tim Hudson/125	5.00
3	Curt Schilling, Pedro Martinez/125	8.00
4	Will Clark, Matt Williams/125	8.00
5	Bernie Williams, Jason Giambi/125	8.00
6	Vernon Wells, Roy Halladay/125	5.00
7	Josh Beckett, A.J. Burnett/125	5.00
8	Dale Murphy, Phil Niekro/125	15.00
9	Mike Schmidt, Steve Carlton/125	15.00
10	Tony Oliva, Harmon Killebrew/50	15.00
11	Robin Yount, Paul Molitor/125	15.00
12	Felix Rodriguez, Troy Percival/25	10.00
13	Ben Sheets, Danny Kolb/125	5.00
14	Andruw Jones, Rafael Furcal/125	5.00
15	Todd Helton, Preston Wilson/125	5.00
16	Wade Boggs, Fred McGriff/50	10.00
17	Manny Ramirez, David Ortiz/125	12.00
18	Miguel Cabrera, Dontrelle Willis/125	10.00
19	Edgar Renteria, Scott Rolen/125	10.00
20	Carlos Beltran, Jeff Kent Bat/125	8.00
21	Eric Davis Bat, Deion Sanders/125	8.00
22	Frank Thomas, Paul Konerko/50	10.00
23	Mike Piazza, Al Leiter/125	12.00
24	Sean Burroughs, Ryan Klesko/125	5.00
25	Ken Harvey, Mike Sweeney/125	5.00
26	Deion Sanders, Hideki Matsui/125	25.00
27	Steve Carlton, Mark Buehrle/50	8.00
28	Gaylord Perry, Randy Johnson/125	10.00
29	Joe Morgan, Steve Carlton/125	10.00
31	Scott Rolen, John Kruk/125	10.00
32	Aaron Boone, Dmitri Young/125	5.00
33	Rickey Henderson Hat, Vladimir Guerrero/25	15.00
34	Charles Johnson, Cliff Floyd/125	5.00
35	Cal Ripken Jr., Rafael Palmeiro/125	25.00

Team Tandems Swatch Single Spectrum

NM/M

Production 1-75

1	Mark Prior, Kerry Wood/75	6.00
2	Barry Zito, Tim Hudson/75	5.00
3	Curt Schilling, Pedro Martinez/75	10.00
4	Will Clark, M. Williams/75	8.00
5	Bernie Williams, Jason Giambi/75	5.00
6	Vernon Wells, Roy Halladay/75	5.00
7	Josh Beckett, A.J. Burnett/75	5.00
8	Dale Murphy, Phil Niekro/75	10.00
11	Robin Yount, Paul Molitor/75	15.00
13	Ben Sheets, Danny Kolb/75	5.00
14	Andruw Jones, Rafael Furcal/75	5.00
15	Todd Helton, Preston Wilson/75	5.00
17	Manny Ramirez, David Ortiz/75	10.00
18	Miguel Cabrera, Dontrelle Willis/75	8.00
19	Edgar Renteria, Scott Rolen/75	8.00
20	Carlos Beltran, Jeff Kent Bat/75	8.00
21	Eric Davis Bat, Deion Sanders/75	
23	Mike Piazza, Al Leiter/75	10.00
24	Sean Burroughs, Ryan Klesko/75	5.00
25	Ken Harvey, Mike Sweeney/75	5.00
26	Deion Sanders, Hideki Matsui/75	25.00
28	Gaylord Perry, Randy Johnson/75	8.00
31	Scott Rolen, John Kruk/75	8.00
32	Aaron Boone, D. Young/75	5.00
34	Charles Johnson, Cliff Floyd/75	5.00
35	Cal Ripken Jr., Rafael Palmeiro/75	25.00

Team Trios

NM/M

Common Card:
Production 200 Sets
Spectrum: 1X
Production 125 Sets

1	Cal Ripken Jr., Jim Palmer, Eddie Murray	10.00
2	Roger Clemens, Wade Boggs, Evans	5.00
3	Rafael Palmeiro, Miguel Tejada, Javy Lopez	2.00
4	Carl Crawford, Rocco Baldelli, B.J. Upton	1.50
5	Mark Buehrle, Magglio Ordonez, Carlos Lee	1.50
6	Victor Martinez, Travis Hafner, Jody Gerut	1.50
7	Bobby Abreu, Brett Myers, Kevin Millwood	1.50
8	Sammy Sosa, Aramis Ramirez, Carlos Zambrano	3.00
9	Bo, George Brett, Carlos Beltran	5.00
10	Hideo Nomo, Adrian Beltre, Shawn Green	2.00
11	Wilson, Wilson, Jason Bay	1.50
12	Tom Seaver, Nolan Ryan, Dwight Gooden	8.00
13	David Dellucci, Laynce Nix, Kevin Mench	1.50
14	Alan Trammell, Morris, Gibson	2.00
15	M. Will, Grace, Randy Johnson	2.00
16	Dawson, Gary Carter, Tony Perez	2.00
17	Dale Murphy, John Kruk, Lenny Dykstra	2.00
18	B. Roberts, Ian Gibb, Larry Bigbie	1.50
19	Mike Lowell, Ivan Rodriguez, Brad Penny	2.00
20	Murray, Darryl Strawberry, Oliver	2.00
21	Darryl Strawberry, Rickey Henderson, Gary Sheffield	2.00
22	Roberto Alomar, Joe Crede, Durham	2.00
23	Jason Kendall, Giles, Aramis Ramirez	1.50
24	Delmon, Aubrey Huff, Tino	2.00
25	Jeff Bagwell, Cruz, Joe Morgan	2.00
26	Snow, Rich Aurilia, Jeff Kent	1.50
27	Jenkins, Nolan Ryan, Cordero	8.00
28	Lofton, Jim Thome, Roberto Alomar	3.00
29	Atkins, Todd Helton, Jennings	2.00
30	Gary Carter, Pedro, Randy Johnson	2.50

Team Trios Swatch Double

NM/M

Production 25-100
Spectrum: .75-1.5X
Production 5-35
No pricing production 20 or less.
Prime Black: No Pricing
Production 5-10

1	Cal Ripken Jr., Jim Palmer, Murray/100	75.00

2	Roger Clemens, Wade Boggs, Evans/100	50.00
3	Rafael Palmeiro, Miguel Tejada, Javy Lopez/50	25.00
5	Mark Buehrle, Magglio Ordonez, Carlos Lee/100	15.00
6	Victor Martinez, Travis Hafner, Jody Gerut/50	20.00
9	Bo, George Brett, Carlos Beltran/100	40.00
10	Hideo Nomo, Adrian Beltre, Shawn Green/100	25.00
11	Wilson, Wilson, Jason Bay/100	15.00
12	Tom Seaver, Nolan Ryan, Dwight Gooden/100	50.00
14	Alan Trammell, Morris, Gibson/50	30.00
15	M. Will, Mark Grace, Randy Johnson/50	30.00
16	Dawson, Gary Carter, Tony Perez/100	20.00
19	Mike Lowell, Ivan Rodriguez, Brad Penny/50	25.00
20	Murray, Darryl Strawberry, Oliver/100	30.00
21	Darryl Strawberry, Rickey Henderson, Gary Sheffield/100	25.00
22	Roberto Alomar, Joe Crede, Durham/100	20.00
28	Lofton, Jim Thome, Roberto Alomar/25	40.00
29	Atkins, Todd Helton, Jennings/100	20.00
30	Gary Carter, Pedro, Randy Johnson/50	30.00

Team Trios Swatch Single

NM/M

Production 50 unless noted.

1	Cal Ripken Jr., Jim Palmer, Murray	40.00
2	Roger Clemens, Wade Boggs, Evans	25.00
3	Rafael Palmeiro, Miguel Tejada, Javy Lopez	12.00
4	Carl Crawford, Rocco Baldelli, B.J. Upton	10.00
5	Mark Buehrle, Magglio Ordonez, Carlos Lee	10.00
6	Victor Martinez, Travis Hafner, Jody Gerut	10.00
7	Bobby Abreu, Brett Myers, Kevin Millwood	10.00
8	Sammy Sosa, Aramis Ramirez, Carlos Zambrano	15.00
9	Bo, George Brett, Carlos Beltran	30.00
10	Hideo Nomo, Adrian Beltre, Shawn Green	15.00
11	Wilson, Wilson, Jason Bay	10.00
12	Tom Seaver, Nolan Ryan, Dwight Gooden	35.00
13	David Dellucci, Laynce Nix, Kevin Mench	8.00
14	Alan Trammell, Morris, Gibson	
15	M. Will, Grace, Randy Johnson	15.00
16	Dawson, Gary Carter, Tony Perez	10.00
17	Dale Murphy, Tomas Kurka, Lenny Dykstra	20.00
18	Roberts, Ian Gibb, Larry Bigbie	15.00
19	Mike Lowell, Ivan Rodriguez, Brad Penny	
20	Murray, Darryl Strawberry, Oliver	20.00
21	Darryl Strawberry, Rickey Henderson, Gary Sheffield	15.00
22	Roberto Alomar, Joe Crede, Durham	10.00
23	Jason Kendall, Giles, Aramis Ramirez	10.00
24	Delmon, Aubrey Huff, Tino	10.00
25	Jeff Bagwell, Cruz, Joe Morgan	12.00
26	Snow, Rich Aurilia, Jeff Kent	8.00
27	Jenkins, Nolan Ryan, Cordero	25.00
28	Lofton, Jim Thome, Roberto Alomar	20.00
29	Atkins, Todd Helton, Jennings	15.00
30	Gary Carter, Pedro, Randy Johnson	15.00

Team Trios Swatch Single Spectrum

NM/M

Production 10-50

Prime Black: No Pricing

Production 10 Sets

1	Cal Ripken Jr., Jim Palmer, Murray/50	40.00
2	Roger Clemens, Wade Boggs, Evans/50	30.00
4	Carl Crawford, Rocco Baldelli, B.J. Upton/50	10.00
5	Mark Buehrle, Magglio Ordonez, Carlos Lee/50	10.00
7	Bobby Abreu, Brett Myers, Kevin Millwood/50	10.00
8	Sammy Sosa, Aramis Ramirez, Carlos Zambrano/50	15.00
9	Bo, George Brett, Carlos Beltran/50	25.00
10	Hideo Nomo, Adrian Beltre, Shawn Green/50	15.00
11	Wilson, Wilson, Jason Bay/50	8.00
12	Tom Seaver, Nolan Ryan, Dwight Gooden/50	30.00
13	David Dellucci, Laynce Nix, Kevin Mench/50	10.00
14	Alan Trammell, Morris, Gibson/50	15.00
16	Dawson, Gary Carter, Tony Perez/50	10.00
17	Dale Murphy, Tomas Kurka, Lenny Dykstra/50	15.00
18	Roberts, Ian Gibb, Larry Bigbie/50	10.00
19	Mike Lowell, Ivan Rodriguez, Brad Penny/25	
20	Murray, Darryl Strawberry, Oliver/50	20.00
21	Darryl Strawberry, Rickey Henderson, Gary Sheffield/50	15.00
22	Roberto Alomar, Joe Crede, Durham/50	10.00
23	Jason Kendall, Giles, Aramis Ramirez/10	
24	Delmon, Aubrey Huff, Tino/50	10.00
25	Jeff Bagwell, Cruz, Joe Morgan/50	10.00
26	Snow, Rich Aurilia, Jeff Kent/50	8.00
27	Jenkins, Nolan Ryan, Cordero/50	25.00
28	Lofton, Jim Thome, Roberto Alomar/50	10.00
29	Atkins, Todd Helton, Jennings/50	15.00
30	Gary Carter, Pedro, Randy Johnson/50	15.00

Tools of Trade Autograph Swatch Double

NM/M

Production 1-75

Prime Red: .75-1.5X

Production 1-50

No pricing production 20 or less.

Prime Black: No Pricing

Production One Set

1	Ozzie Smith B-P/25	50.00
3	Dale Murphy J-J/50	30.00
4	Paul Molitor J-P/25	40.00
20	Lou Brock B-JK/50	40.00
22	Paul LoDuca B-J/25	25.00
36	Sean Casey J-P/50	20.00
37	Juan Gonzalez J-P/25	30.00
39	Darryl Strawberry B-J/50	25.00
41	Tom Seaver J-P/25	40.00
48	Torii Hunter B-J/40	25.00
56	Brad Penny FG-J/75	10.00
57	Gary Carter J-P/25	30.00
62	Andre Dawson B-J/50	25.00
64	Adrian Beltre B-J/50	25.00
66	Juan Gonzalez B-J/25	30.00
70	Andre Dawson J-P/50	25.00
73	Cal Ripken Jr. J-P/25	160.00
88	Magglio Ordonez B-S/25	20.00
91	Gary Carter B-J/25	30.00
95	Curt Schilling J-J/5	
96	Bobby Doerr B-P/50	25.00
98	Eric Chavez B-J/25	25.00
100	Harmon Killebrew H-J/25	50.00

Tools of Trade Autograph Swatch Double Reverse

NM/M

Production 1-75

20	Lou Brock B-JK/50	40.00
36	Sean Casey J-P/50	25.00
39	Darryl Strawberry B-J/75	20.00
48	Torii Hunter B-J/50	25.00
56	Brad Penny FG-J/50	12.00
62	Andre Dawson B-J/25	30.00
64	Adrian Beltre B-J/50	20.00
66	Juan Gonzalez B-J/25	30.00
70	Andre Dawson J-P/25	30.00

Tools of Trade Autograph Swatch Quad

NM/M

Production 1-25

Prime Red: No Pricing

Production 1-5

20	Lou Brock/25	80.00
23	Don Mattingly/25	120.00
36	Sean Casey/25	40.00
39	Darryl Strawberry/25	40.00
41	Tom Seaver/25	75.00
42	Mike Schmidt/25	100.00
56	Brad Penny/25	20.00
57	Gary Carter/25	40.00
73	Cal Ripken Jr./25	200.00
78	Tony Gwynn/25	75.00
88	Magglio Ordonez/25	30.00
91	Gary Carter/25	40.00
100	Harmon Killebrew/25	80.00

Tools of Trade Autograph Swatch Quad Reverse

No Pricing

Production 1-15

Tools of Trade Autograph Swatch Triple

NM/M

Production 1-75

Prime Red: No Pricing

Production 1-25

Prime Black: No Pricing

Production One Set

2	Carlos Beltran/25	40.00
3	Dale Murphy/25	50.00
18	Darryl Strawberry/75	20.00
20	Lou Brock/50	40.00
36	Sean Casey/75	20.00
39	Juan Gonzalez/75	25.00
39	Darryl Strawberry/75	20.00
56	Brad Penny/25	20.00
57	Gary Carter/25	30.00
64	Adrian Beltre/25	20.00
66	Juan Gonzalez/50	25.00
70	Andre Dawson/75	25.00
73	Cal Ripken Jr./25	200.00
82	Carlos Beltran/25	40.00
91	Gary Carter/25	30.00
96	Bobby Doerr/25	30.00
100	Harmon Killebrew/25	60.00

Tools of Trade Autograph Swatch Triple Reverse

NM/M

Production 1-50

18	Darryl Strawberry/50	25.00
20	Lou Brock/50	50.00
36	Sean Casey/25	25.00
37	Juan Gonzalez/25	30.00
39	Darryl Strawberry/50	25.00
70	Andre Dawson/50	25.00

Laundry Tag Prime Red

No Pricing

Production One Set

Tools of the Trade Red

NM/M

Common Player:	
Production 250 Sets	
Black:	1-1.5X
Production 100 Sets	
Blue:	1-1.5X
Production 150 Sets	
Rev. Spectrum Red:	1-2X
Production 50 Sets	
Rev. Spectrum Blue:	No Pricing
Production 10 Sets	
1	Ozzie Smith	5.00
---	---	---
2	Carlos Beltran	2.00
3	Dale Murphy	2.00
4	Paul Molitor	2.00
5	George Brett	6.00
6	Stan Musial	5.00
7	Ivan Rodriguez	2.00
8	Carl Yastrzemski	4.00
9	Reggie Jackson	2.00
10	Hideo Nomo	2.00
11	Gary Sheffield	2.00
12	Roberto Alomar	2.00
13	Pedro Martinez	3.00
14	Ernie Banks	3.00
15	Tim Hudson	1.50
16	Dwight Gooden	1.50
17	Lance Berkman	1.50
18	Darryl Strawberry	1.50
19	Larry Walker	1.50
20	Lou Brock	2.00
21	Roger Clemens	6.00
22	Paul LoDuca	1.50
23	Don Mattingly	6.00
24	Willie Mays	6.00
25	Rafael Palmeiro	2.00
26	Roy Oswalt	1.50
27	Vladimir Guerrero	3.00
28	Austin Kearns	1.50
29	Rod Carew	2.00
30	Nolan Ryan	8.00
31	Richie Sexson	2.00
32	Steve Carlton	2.00
33	Eddie Murray	3.00
34	Nolan Ryan	8.00
35	Mike Mussina	2.00
36	Sean Casey	1.50
37	Juan Gonzalez	1.50
38	Curt Schilling	2.00
39	Darryl Strawberry	1.50
40	Alfonso Soriano	3.00
41	Tom Seaver	3.00
42	Mike Schmidt	5.00
43	Todd Helton	2.00
44	Reggie Jackson	2.00
45	Shawn Green	1.50
46	Mike Mussina	2.00
47	Tom Glavine	1.50
48	Torii Hunter	1.50
49	Kerry Wood	2.00
50	Carlos Delgado	2.00
51	Randy Johnson	3.00
52	David Ortiz	3.00
53	Troy Glaus	2.00
54	Rickey Henderson	2.00
55	Craig Biggio	2.00
56	Brad Penny	1.50
57	Gary Carter	2.00
58	Andy Pettitte	1.50
59	Mark Prior	2.00
60	Kirby Puckett	3.00
61	Willie McCovey	3.00
62	Andre Dawson	2.00
63	Greg Maddux	4.00
64	Adrian Beltre	1.50
65	Andruw Jones	2.00
66	Juan Gonzalez	1.50
67	Frank Thomas	2.00
68	Victor Martinez	1.50
69	Randy Johnson	3.00
70	Andre Dawson	2.00
71	Adam Dunn	2.00
72	Carlton Fisk	2.00

#	Player	Price
73	Cal Ripken Jr.	8.00
74	Kenny Lofton	1.50
75	Barry Zito	1.50
76	Sammy Sosa	4.00
77	Deion Sanders	2.00
78	Tony Gwynn	3.00
79	Mike Piazza	4.00
80	Jeff Bagwell	2.00
81	Manny Ramirez	3.00
82	Carlos Beltran	2.00
83	Mark Grace	2.00
84	Robin Yount	4.00
85	Albert Pujols	6.00
86	Dontrelle Willis	2.00
87	Jim Thome	2.00
88	Magglio Ordonez	1.50
89	Miguel Tejada	2.00
90	Mark Teixeira	2.00
91	Gary Carter	2.00
92	Ivan Rodriguez	2.00
93	Jason Giambi	1.50
94	Rickey Henderson	2.00
95	Curt Schilling	2.00
96	Bobby Doerr	2.00
97	Chipper Jones	3.00
98	Eric Chavez	1.50
99	Johnny Bench	4.00
100	Harmon Killebrew	3.00

Tools of the Trade Swatch Double

NM/M

Production 1-150
Prime Red: No Pricing
Production 1-25
Prime Black: No Pricing
Production 1-25

#	Player	Price
1	Ozzie Smith B-P/150	15.00
2	Carlos Beltran J-S/50	8.00
3	Dale Murphy J-J/50	8.00
4	Paul Molitor B-J/50	8.00
5	George Brett B-H/25	25.00
6	Stan Musial B-P/25	30.00
7	Ivan Rodriguez J-J/150	8.00
8	Carl Yastrzemski B-J/25	30.00
9	Reggie Jackson J-J/50	8.00
10	Hideo Nomo J-P/150	10.00
11	Gary Sheffield H-J/25	8.00
12	Roberto Alomar B-J/150	8.00
13	Pedro Martinez J-P/150	8.00
15	Tim Hudson H-J/100	5.00
17	Lance Berkman B-J/150	5.00
19	Larry Walker J-J/150	5.00
20	Lou Brock B-JK/150	10.00
21	Roger Clemens B-J/150	15.00
22	Paul LoDuca B-J/50	5.00
23	Don Mattingly BG-P/50	20.00
24	Willie Mays B-P/25	50.00
25	Rafael Palmeiro B-J/150	8.00
27	Vladimir Guerrero B-J/150	8.00
29	Rod Carew JK-JK/150	8.00
30	Nolan Ryan B-JK/150	25.00
31	Richie Sexson H-J/150	8.00
32	Steve Carlton B-H/150	8.00
33	Eddie Murray B-J/150	10.00
34	Nolan Ryan B-J/150	25.00
35	Mike Mussina J-P/125	8.00
36	Sean Casey J-P/150	5.00
38	Curt Schilling J-J/150	8.00
39	Darryl Strawberry B-J/150	5.00
41	Tom Seaver J-P/150	10.00
42	Mike Schmidt B-J/150	15.00
43	Todd Helton B-J/150	5.00
45	Shawn Green B-J/150	5.00
47	Tom Glavine N-J/150	8.00
49	Kerry Wood FG-J/150	8.00
50	Carlos Delgado B-J/100	5.00
51	R. John J-P/150	8.00
52	David Ortiz B-J/150	8.00
53	Troy Glaus J-J/150	5.00
54	Rickey Henderson B-J/150	8.00
55	Craig Biggio B-J/150	8.00
56	Brad Penny FG-J/150	5.00
57	Gary Carter J-P/150	8.00
58	Andy Pettitte J-J/150	5.00
59	Mark Prior FG-J/150	5.00

#	Player	Price
60	Kirby Puckett B-FG/100	10.00
61	Willie McCovey J-P/150	10.00
63	Greg Maddux B-J/50	15.00
64	Adrian Beltre B-J/150	5.00
65	Andruw Jones B-J/150	8.00
67	Frank Thomas J-J/150	8.00
68	Victor Martinez CP-J/150	5.00
69	R. John J-P/150	8.00
71	Adam Dunn B-J/95	8.00
72	Carlton Fisk B-J/150	8.00
73	Cal Ripken Jr. J-P/150	25.00
74	Kenny Lofton B-H/150	5.00
75	Barry Zito J-J/150	5.00
76	Sammy Sosa B-J/150	10.00
77	Deion Sanders J-P/150	10.00
78	Tony Gwynn J-P/150	10.00
79	Mike Piazza J-P/150	10.00
80	Jeff Bagwell J-P/150	8.00
81	Manny Ramirez B-J/150	8.00
83	Mark Grace B-J/150	8.00
84	Robin Yount B-J/150	12.00
85	Albert Pujols B-J/150	20.00
86	Dontrelle Willis B-J/150	8.00
88	Magglio Ordonez B-S/150	5.00
89	Miguel Tejada FG-J/150	8.00
90	Mark Teixeira FG-J/150	8.00
91	Gary Carter B-J/25	10.00
92	Ivan Rodriguez CP-J/150	8.00
93	Jason Giambi H-J/150	5.00
94	Rickey Henderson B-P/150	5.00
95	Curt Schilling J-J/150	8.00
96	Bobby Doerr B-P/150	8.00
97	Chipper Jones B-J/150	8.00
99	Johnny Bench B-P/150	10.00
100	Harmon Killebrew H-J/50	10.00

Tools of the Trade Swatch Five

NM/M

Production 1-50
Prime Red: No Pricing
Production 1-10
Prime Black: No Pricing
Production One Set
Reverse: No Pricing
Production 1-15

#	Player	Price
1	Ozzie Smith/1	
4	Paul Molitor/25	35.00
7	Ivan Rodriguez/25	25.00
12	Roberto Alomar/25	20.00
13	Pedro Martinez/25	30.00
15	Tim Hudson/25	25.00
17	Lance Berkman/25	20.00
22	Paul LoDuca/25	15.00
23	Don Mattingly/25	65.00
25	Rafael Palmeiro/25	25.00
26	Roy Oswalt/25	20.00
28	Austin Kearns/25	20.00
29	Rod Carew/25	40.00
31	Richie Sexson/25	15.00
33	Eddie Murray/25	50.00
36	Sean Casey/25	20.00
42	Mike Schmidt/25	70.00
43	Todd Helton/25	25.00
52	David Ortiz/50	35.00
53	Troy Glaus/25	20.00
54	Rickey Henderson/50	25.00
55	Craig Biggio/50	25.00
56	Brad Penny/45	15.00
57	Gary Carter/40	25.00
58	Andy Pettitte/25	25.00
59	Mark Prior/25	25.00
60	Kirby Puckett/25	50.00
64	Adrian Beltre/25	20.00
65	Andruw Jones/25	20.00
67	Frank Thomas/25	25.00
68	Victor Martinez/25	20.00
69	R. John/1	
73	Cal Ripken Jr./50	75.00
76	Sammy Sosa/25	35.00
78	Tony Gwynn/25	40.00
79	Mike Piazza/25	50.00
80	Jeff Bagwell/25	25.00
82	Carlos Beltran/20	25.00
84	Robin Yount/25	40.00
88	Magglio Ordonez/25	20.00
89	Miguel Tejada/25	25.00
90	Mark Teixeira/50	20.00
91	Gary Carter/25	25.00

#	Player	Price
92	Ivan Rodriguez/25	25.00
94	Rickey Henderson/50	25.00
95	Curt Schilling/50	25.00

Tools of the Trade Swatch Quad

NM/M

Production 1-100
Prime Red: No Pricing
Production 1-10
Prime Black: No Pricing
Production One Set

#	Player	Price
3	Dale Murphy/50	20.00
4	Paul Molitor/50	30.00
7	Ivan Rodriguez/50	15.00
8	Carl Yastrzemski/25	50.00
9	Reggie Jackson/100	25.00
10	Hideo Nomo/75	15.00
11	Gary Sheffield/30	15.00
12	Roberto Alomar/50	15.00
13	Pedro Martinez/100	20.00
14	Ernie Banks/25	40.00
15	Tim Hudson/100	10.00
17	Lance Berkman/65	10.00
19	Larry Walker/100	10.00
20	Lou Brock/50	20.00
21	Roger Clemens/25	40.00
22	Paul LoDuca/100	10.00
23	Don Mattingly/50	40.00
24	Willie Mays/25	80.00
25	Rafael Palmeiro/100	10.00
26	Roy Oswalt/30	15.00
27	Vladimir Guerrero/20	20.00
29	Rod Carew/25	15.00
31	Richie Sexson/100	10.00
33	Eddie Murray/100	15.00
36	Sean Casey/75	10.00
39	Darryl Strawberry/50	15.00
41	Tom Seaver/35	25.00
42	Mike Schmidt/25	40.00
43	Todd Helton/100	12.00
45	Shawn Green/100	10.00
46	Mike Mussina/25	20.00
50	Carlos Delgado/50	10.00
52	David Ortiz/90	30.00
53	Troy Glaus/50	12.00
54	Rickey Henderson/50	25.00
55	Craig Biggio/100	10.00
56	Brad Penny/25	10.00
57	Gary Carter/50	15.00
58	Andy Pettitte/50	15.00
59	Mark Prior/50	15.00
60	Kirby Puckett/50	25.00
64	Adrian Beltre/50	10.00
65	Andruw Jones/100	10.00
66	Juan Gonzalez/30	20.00
67	Frank Thomas/50	25.00
68	Victor Martinez/25	10.00
70	Andre Dawson/25	15.00
72	Carlton Fisk/25	25.00
73	Cal Ripken Jr./100	50.00
74	Kenny Lofton/100	10.00
75	Barry Zito/50	10.00
76	Sammy Sosa/100	15.00
78	Tony Gwynn/100	20.00
79	Mike Piazza/100	20.00
80	Jeff Bagwell/100	10.00
83	Mark Grace/50	20.00
85	Albert Pujols/50	60.00
86	Dontrelle Willis/50	15.00
88	Magglio Ordonez/50	10.00
89	Miguel Tejada/100	15.00
90	Mark Teixeira/50	15.00
91	Gary Carter/90	15.00
92	Ivan Rodriguez/50	15.00
93	Jason Giambi/25	15.00
94	Rickey Henderson/100	15.00
95	Curt Schilling/100	15.00
100	Harmon Killebrew/25	40.00

Swatch Single Jumbo

NM/M

Production 1-100
Prime Red: No Pricing
Production 1-25
Reverse: 1-2X
Production 1-10
Prime Black: No Pricing
Production One Set

#	Player	Price
1	Ozzie Smith/25	30.00
2	Carlos Beltran/Jsy/100	10.00
3	Dale Murphy/Jsy/25	20.00
4	Paul Molitor/Jsy/25	25.00
6	Stan Musial/Pants/50	50.00
7	Ivan Rodriguez/ Jsy/100	10.00
10	Hideo Nomo/Jsy/100	15.00
11	Gary Sheffield/Jsy/25	15.00
12	Roberto Alomar/ Jsy/100	10.00
13	Pedro Martinez/ Jsy/50	12.00

#	Player	Price
15	Tim Hudson/Jsy/100	10.00
17	Lance Berkman/ Jsy/75	8.00
19	Larry Walker/Jsy/100	10.00
20	Lou Brock/Jkt/50	20.00
21	Roger Clemens/ Jsy/50	30.00
23	Don Mattingly/Jsy/25	40.00
25	Rafael Palmeiro/ Jsy/100	10.00
27	Vladimir Guerrero/ Jsy/50	15.00
29	Rod Carew/Jsy/50	15.00
30	Nolan Ryan/Jsy/25	50.00
31	Richie Sexson/ Jsy/100	10.00
33	Eddie Murray/Jsy/100	20.00
35	Mike Mussina/Jsy/50	12.00
36	Sean Casey/Jsy/100	8.00
37	Juan Gonzalez/ Jsy/25	15.00
38	Curt Schilling/ Jsy/100	15.00
39	Darryl Strawberry/ Jsy/100	10.00
40	Alfonso Soriano/Jsy/1	
41	Tom Seaver/Jsy/50	15.00
42	Mike Schmidt/Jsy/25	40.00
43	Todd Helton/Jsy/100	10.00
45	Shawn Green/Jsy/100	8.00
47	Tom Glavine/Jsy/100	10.00
49	Kerry Wood/Jsy/50	10.00
51	R. John/Jsy/25	20.00
52	David Ortiz/Jsy/75	15.00
53	Troy Glaus/Jsy/100	10.00
54	Rickey Henderson/ Jsy/25	15.00
55	Craig Biggio/Jsy/75	10.00
56	Brad Penny/Jsy/100	8.00
57	Gary Carter/Jsy/25	15.00
58	Andy Pettitte/Jsy/100	10.00
59	Mark Prior/Jsy/50	10.00
60	Kirby Puckett/Jsy/50	20.00
61	Willie McCovey/ Jsy/50	15.00
63	Greg Maddux/ Jsy/100	20.00
65	Andruw Jones/ Jsy/100	10.00
68	Victor Martinez/Jsy/100	8.00
70	Andre Dawson/ Jsy/50	10.00
71	Adam Dunn/Jsy/5	
72	Carlton Fisk/Jsy/100	10.00
73	Cal Ripken Jr./ Jsy/100	35.00
74	Kenny Lofton/Hat/25	10.00
75	Barry Zito/Jsy/100	8.00
76	Sammy Sosa/ Jsy/100	15.00
77	Deion Sanders/ Jsy/25	20.00
78	Tony Gwynn/Jsy/100	20.00
79	Mike Piazza/Jsy/100	20.00
80	Jeff Bagwell/Jsy/100	10.00
83	Mark Grace/Jsy/50	15.00
84	Robin Yount/Jsy/100	20.00
85	Albert Pujols/Jsy/100	30.00
86	Dontrelle Willis/ Jsy/50	10.00
89	Miguel Tejada/ Jsy/100	12.00
90	Mark Teixeira/Jsy/25	15.00
92	Ivan Rodriguez/ Jsy/100	10.00
93	Jason Giambi/Jsy/25	10.00
94	Rickey Henderson/ Jsy/25	15.00
95	Curt Schilling/Jsy/50	10.00
96	Bobby Doerr/ Pants/25	20.00
97	Chipper Jones/ Jsy/25	20.00
98	Eric Chavez/Jsy/100	8.00
99	Johnny Bench/Jsy/25	25.00
100	Harmon Killebrew/ Jsy/25	20.00

Tools of the Trade Swatch Six

NM/M

Production 1-50
Reverse: No Pricing
Production 1-10
Prime Red: No Pricing
Production 1-5
Prime Black: No Pricing
Production One Set

#	Player	Price
22	Paul LoDuca/50	20.00
31	Richie Sexson/50	20.00
52	David Ortiz/50	40.00
53	Troy Glaus/50	25.00
57	Gary Carter/25	35.00
73	Cal Ripken Jr./50	85.00
76	Sammy Sosa/25	40.00

78	Tony Gwynn/50	40.00
79	Mike Piazza/50	40.00
80	Jeff Bagwell/50	25.00
90	Mark Teixeira/50	25.00
92	Ivan Rodriguez/25	30.00
94	Rickey Henderson/50	30.00

Tools of the Trade Swatch Triple

NM/M

Production 1-25
Prime Red: No Pricing
Production 1-25
Prime Black: No Pricing
Production 1-15

1	Ozzie Smith/10	
2	Carlos Beltran/25	15.00
3	Dale Murphy/25	15.00
4	Paul Molitor/25	20.00
5	George Brett/25	35.00
6	Stan Musial/25	40.00
7	Ivan Rodriguez/25	10.00
9	Reggie Jackson/25	15.00
10	Hideo Nomo/25	20.00
12	Roberto Alomar/25	10.00
13	Pedro Martinez/25	15.00
15	Tim Hudson/25	10.00
17	Lance Berkman/25	10.00
19	Larry Walker/25	10.00
21	Roger Clemens/25	30.00
22	Paul LoDuca/25	10.00
23	Don Mattingly/25	30.00
25	Rafael Palmeiro/25	15.00
27	Vladimir Guerrero/25	15.00
29	Rod Carew/25	15.00
30	Nolan Ryan/25	40.00
31	Richie Sexson/25	10.00
33	Eddie Murray/25	20.00
34	Nolan Ryan/25	40.00
36	Sean Casey/25	10.00
37	Juan Gonzalez/25	10.00
38	Curt Schilling/25	15.00
42	Mike Schmidt/25	30.00
43	Todd Helton/25	12.00
45	Shawn Green/25	10.00
47	Tom Glavine/25	10.00
49	Kerry Wood/25	15.00
50	Carlos Delgado/25	10.00
51	R. John/25	15.00
52	David Ortiz/25	15.00
53	Troy Glaus/25	10.00
54	Rickey Henderson/25	15.00
55	Craig Biggio/25	12.00
56	Brad Penny/25	10.00
57	Gary Carter/25	15.00
58	Andy Pettitte/25	10.00
59	Mark Prior/25	10.00
60	Kirby Puckett/25	20.00
63	Greg Maddux/25	25.00
64	Adrian Beltre/25	10.00
65	Andruw Jones/25	12.00
67	Frank Thomas/25	15.00
68	Victor Martinez/25	10.00
70	Andre Dawson/25	12.00
72	Carlton Fisk/25	15.00
73	Cal Ripken Jr./25	40.00
74	Kenny Lofton/25	10.00
75	Barry Zito/25	10.00
76	Sammy Sosa/25	15.00
77	Deion Sanders/25	20.00
78	Tony Gwynn/25	20.00
79	Mike Piazza/25	20.00
80	Jeff Bagwell/25	15.00
81	Manny Ramirez/25	15.00
83	Mark Grace/25	15.00
84	Robin Yount/25	20.00
85	Albert Pujols/25	40.00
86	Dontrelle Willis/25	15.00
88	Magglio Ordonez/25	10.00
89	Miguel Tejada/25	15.00
90	Mark Teixeira/25	12.00
91	Gary Carter/25	15.00
92	Ivan Rodriguez/25	10.00
93	Jason Giambi/25	10.00
94	Rickey Henderson/25	15.00
95	Curt Schilling/25	15.00
96	Bobby Doerr/25	15.00
97	Chipper Jones/25	15.00
98	Eric Chavez/25	10.00
99	Johnny Bench/25	20.00
100	Harmon Killebrew/25	30.00

2005 Playoff Prestige

NM/M

Complete Set (200):		35.00
Common Player:		.25
Hobby pack (8):		3.00
Hobby box (24):		65.00
1	Rafael Furcal	.25
2	Derek Jeter	2.00
3	Edgar Renteria	.40
4	Jeff Bagwell	.50
5	Nomar Garciaparra	1.25
6	Melvin Mora	.25

7	Craig Biggio	.40
8	Brad Penny	.25
9	Hank Blalock	.50
10	Vernon Wells	.25
11	Gary Sheffield	.50
12	Jeff Kent	.25
13	Carl Crawford	.25
14	Paul Konerko	.25
15	Carlos Beltran	.50
16	Garret Anderson	.40
17	Todd Helton	.50
18	Javy Lopez	.40
19	Mike Lowell	.25
20	Robb Quinlan	.25
21	Andy Pettitte	.40
22	Roger Clemens	2.00
23	Mark Teixeira	.50
24	Miguel Cabrera	.75
25	Andruw Jones	.40
26	Josh Beckett	.40
27	Scott Rolen	.75
28	J.J. Putz	.25
29	Adrian Beltre	.50
30	Magglio Ordonez	.25
31	Mike Piazza	1.00
32	Danny Graves	.25
33	Larry Walker	.40
34	Kerry Wood	.75
35	Mike Mussina	.50
36	Joe Nathan	.25
37	Chone Figgins	.25
38	Curt Schilling	.75
39	Brett Myers	.25
40	Jae Weong Seo	.25
41	Danny Kolb	.25
42	Mariano Rivera	.50
43	Francisco Cordero	.25
44	Adam Dunn	.50
45	Pedro Martinez	.75
46	Frank Thomas	.50
47	Tom Glavine	.40
48	Torii Hunter	.40
49	Ben Sheets	.40
50	Shawn Green	.25
51	Randy Johnson	.75
52	C.C. Sabathia	.25
53	Bobby Abreu	.40
54	Octavio Dotel	.25
55	Hideki Matsui	1.50
56	Mark Buehrle	.25
57	Johan Santana	.50
58	Brandon Inge	.25
59	Dewon Brazelton	.25
60	Ryan Wagner	.25
61	Kevin Brown	.25
62	Laynce Nix	.25
63	Jason Bay	.40
64	J.D. Drew	.40
65	Jacque Jones	.25
66	Jason Schmidt	.40
67	Joe Kennedy	.25
68	Miguel Tejada	.50
69	Hideo Nomo	.40
70	Michael Young	.25
71	Lyle Overbay	.25
72	Omar Vizquel	.25
73	Johnny Estrada	.25
74	Khalil Greene	.40
75	Barry Zito	.25
76	Wilson Valdez	.25
77	Nick Green	.25
78	Bucky Jacobsen	.25
79	Keith Foulke	.25
80	Sean Burroughs	.25
81	Carlos Zambrano	.40
82	Orlando Cabrera	.25
83	Shigetoshi Hasegawa	.25
84	Troy Glaus	.40
85	Mike Sweeney	.25
86	Jason Giambi	.40
87	Derrek Lee	.40
88	Carlos Delgado	.40
89	Kazuo Matsui	.25
90	Lew Ford	.25
91	Akinori Otsuka	.25

92	Bobby Crosby	.25
93	Jose Reyes	.40
94	Jose Vidro	.25
95	Shingo Takatsu	.25
96	Sean Casey	.25
97	Tim Olson	.25
98	Jeff Suppan	.25
99	Rafael Palmeiro	.50
100	Esteban Loaiza	.25
101	Brian Roberts	.25
102	Jack Wilson	.25
103	Eric Chavez	.40
104	Eric Milton	.25
105	Albert Pujols	2.00
106	Jake Peavy	.25
107	Ivan Rodriguez	.50
108	Chad Cordero	.25
109	Jody Gerut	.25
110	Chipper Jones	.75
111	Barry Larkin	.40
112	Alfonso Soriano	.75
113	Alex Rodriguez	1.50
114	Paul LoDuca	.25
115	Jim Edmonds	.40
116	Aramis Ramirez	.40
117	Lance Berkman	.40
118	Johnny Damon	.75
119	Aubrey Huff	.25
120	Mark Mulder	.40
121	Sammy Sosa	1.50
122	Mark Prior	.75
123	Shannon Stewart	.25
124	Manny Ramirez	.75
125	Jim Thome	.75
126	Doug DeVore	.25
127	Vladimir Guerrero	.75
128	Ken Harvey	.25
129	Jacob Cruz	.25
130	Ken Griffey Jr.	1.00
131	Greg Maddux	1.00
132	Derek Lowe	.25
133	Craig Monroe	.25
134	David Ortiz	.75
135	Dontrelle Willis	.40
136	Tom Gordon	.25
137	David Dellucci	.25
138	Vance Wilson	.25
139	Milton Bradley	.25
140	Ichiro Suzuki	1.50
141	Victor Martinez	.40
142	Wade Miller	.25
143	Francisco Rodriguez	.25
144	Roy Oswalt	.40
145	Carlos Lee	.25
146	Kazuhisa Ishii	.25
147	Tim Hudson	.40
148	Travis Hafner	.25
149	Jermaine Dye	.25
150	Steve Finley	.25
151	Justin Verlander RC	1.50
152	Yadier Molina	.25
153	Andy Green	.25
154	Nick Swisher	.25
155	Clint Nageotte	.25
156	Grady Sizemore	.50
157	Gavin Floyd	.25
158	Josh Kroeger	.25
159	Russ Adams	.25
160	Jeff Baker	.25
161	Dioner Navarro	.25
162	Shawn Hill	.25
163	Ryan Howard	1.00
164	Scott Proctor	.25
165	Jason Kubel	.25
166	Jose Lopez	.25
167	Ryan Church	.25
168	Yhency Brazoban	.25
169	Jeff Francis	.25
170	Angel Guzman	.25
171	John Van Benschoten	.25
172	Adrian Gonzalez	.25
173	Casey Kotchman	.25
174	David Wright	.75
175	B.J. Upton	.50
176	Dallas McPherson	.50
177	Rene Rivera	.25
178	Denny Bautista	.25
179	Logan Kensing	.25
180	Matt Peterson	.25
181	Jeremy Reed	.25
182	Jairo Garcia	.25
183	Val Majewski	.25
184	Victor Diaz	.25
185	David Krynzel	.25
186	Ron Cey	.25
187	Bill Madlock	.25
188	Dave Stewart	.25
189	Billy Ripken	.25
190	Gary Carter	.50
191	Darryl Strawberry	.50
192	Dave Parker	.25
193	Ron Guidry	.25
194	Gaylord Perry	.25
195	Fred Lynn	.25
196	Jack Morris	.25
197	Steve Garvey	.25
198	Andre Dawson	.50
199	Nolan Ryan	2.50
200	Paul Molitor	.75

Red Foil

Red Foil:	8-15X
Production 25 Sets	

Xtra Bases Black

Black:	8-15X
Production 25 Sets	

Xtra Bases Green

Green:	5-10X
Production 50 Sets	

Xtra Bases Purple

Purple:	4-8X
Production 100 Sets	

Xtra Bases Red

Red:	3-6X
Production 150 Sets	

Autographs

NM/M

Common Autograph:		8.00
20	Robb Quinlan	8.00
28	J.J. Putz	8.00
58	Brandon Inge/SP	15.00
67	Joe Kennedy	8.00
76	Wilson Valdez	8.00
77	Nick Green	8.00
78	Bucky Jacobsen	10.00
97	Tim Olson	10.00
98	Jeff Suppan/SP	15.00
126	Doug DeVore	8.00
129	Jacob Cruz	8.00
133	Craig Monroe	10.00
138	Vance Wilson	8.00
153	Andy Green	8.00
164	Scott Proctor	8.00

Signature Xtra Bases Purple

NM/M

Production 5-50

6	Melvin Mora/25	25.00
8	Brad Penny/50	10.00
13	Carl Crawford/25	25.00
20	Robb Quinlan/50	8.00
28	J.J. Putz/50	8.00
32	Danny Graves/50	10.00
36	Joe Nathan/50	25.00
37	Chone Figgins/50	10.00
39	Brett Myers/50	10.00
41	Danny Kolb/50	10.00
43	Francisco Cordero/50	10.00
52	C.C. Sabathia/25	25.00
54	Octavio Dotel/50	15.00
56	Mark Buehrle/50	20.00
58	Brandon Inge/50	15.00
59	Dewon Brazelton/50	10.00
60	Ryan Wagner/50	8.00
62	Laynce Nix/50	15.00
63	Jason Bay/50	15.00
65	Jacque Jones/25	20.00
67	Joe Kennedy/50	8.00
71	Lyle Overbay/25	20.00
73	Johnny Estrada/50	15.00
76	Wilson Valdez/50	8.00
77	Nick Green/50	8.00
78	Bucky Jacobsen/50	10.00
79	Keith Foulke/50	10.00
81	Carlos Zambrano/25	35.00
82	Orlando Cabrera/25	10.00
90	Lew Ford/50	15.00
92	Bobby Crosby/50	20.00
97	Tim Olson/50	10.00
98	Jeff Suppan/50	15.00
100	Esteban Loaiza/50	10.00
101	Brian Roberts/25	35.00
102	Jack Wilson/50	15.00

106	Jake Peavy/25	30.00
108	Chad Cordero/50	10.00
109	Jody Gerut/25	10.00
126	Doug DeVore/50	8.00
128	Ken Harvey/50	10.00
129	Jacob Cruz/50	8.00
133	Craig Monroe/50	10.00
134	David Ortiz/5	
136	Tom Gordon/50	15.00
137	David Dellucci/50	20.00
138	Vance Wilson/50	8.00
139	Milton Bradley/50	15.00
141	Victor Martinez/25	30.00
142	Wade Miller/50	15.00
145	Carlos Lee/25	20.00
148	Travis Hafner/50	15.00
149	Jermaine Dye/25	15.00
152	Yadier Molina/25	20.00
153	Andy Green/50	8.00
161	Dioner Navarro/50	12.00
162	Shawn Hill/50	8.00
164	Scott Proctor/50	15.00
165	Jason Kubel/50	15.00
168	Yhency Brazoban/50	10.00
170	Angel Guzman/50	15.00
172	Adrian Gonzalez/50	12.00
173	Casey Kotchman	15.00
187	Bill Madlock/25	20.00
189	Billy Ripken/25	10.00
190	Gary Carter/25	25.00
191	Darryl Strawberry/25	20.00
192	Dave Parker/25	25.00
195	Fred Lynn/25	20.00
196	Jack Morris/25	25.00
198	Andre Dawson/25	25.00

Signature Xtra Bases Black

No Pricing
Production 3-10

Changing Stripes

		NM/M
Complete Set (25):		25.00
Common Player:		.75
Inserted 1:8		
Foil:		2-3X
Production 100 Sets		
Holo-Foil:		3-6X
Production 25 Sets		
1	Ivan Rodriguez	1.00
2	Roger Clemens	4.00
3	Curt Schilling	1.50
4	Alex Rodriguez	4.00
5	Greg Maddux	2.00
6	Juan Gonzalez	.75
7	Pedro Martinez	1.50
8	Roberto Alomar	.75
9	Randy Johnson	1.50
10	Ken Griffey Jr.	2.00
11	Carlos Beltran	1.00
12	Andy Pettitte	1.00
13	Tom Glavine	.75
14	Miguel Tejada	1.50
15	Alfonso Soriano	1.50
16	Shannon Stewart	.75
17	Nomar Garciaparra	2.00
18	Jeff Kent	.75
19	David Ortiz	1.50
20	Sean Casey	.75
21	Rickey Henderson	1.00
22	Carlton Fisk	1.00
23	Phil Niekro	.75
24	Dale Murphy	1.00
25	Reggie Jackson	1.50

Changing Stripes Material Dual Jersey

		NM/M
Production 12-250		
1	Ivan Rodriguez/250	10.00

2	Roger Clemens/50	20.00
3	Curt Schilling/250	12.00
6	Juan Gonzalez/250	8.00
7	Pedro Martinez/100	15.00
8	Roberto Alomar/250	10.00
9	Randy Johnson/100	15.00
11	Carlos Beltran/100	15.00
12	Andy Pettitte/250	10.00
13	Tom Glavine/50	15.00
14	Miguel Tejada/250	10.00
15	Alfonso Soriano/100	10.00
16	Shannon Stewart/100	8.00
19	David Ortiz/100	15.00
20	Sean Casey/50	10.00
21	Rickey Henderson/250	15.00
22	Carlton Fisk/250	15.00
23	Phil Niekro/250	8.00
24	Dale Murphy/250	15.00
25	Reggie Jackson/100	15.00

Connections

		NM/M
Complete Set (25):		40.00
Common Duo:		1.50
Inserted 1:8		
Foil:		2-3X
Production 100 Sets		
Holo-Foil:		3-6X
Production 25 Sets		
1	Josh Beckett, Dontrelle Willis	1.50
2	Andruw Jones, Chipper Jones	2.00
3	Kazuo Matsui, Jose Reyes	1.50
4	Bobby Abreu, Jim Thome	2.00
5	Jeff Bagwell, Lance Berkman	2.00
6	Roger Clemens, Roy Oswalt	4.00
7	Scott Rolen, Larry Walker	2.00
8	Albert Pujols, Jim Edmonds	4.00
9	Greg Maddux, Sammy Sosa	2.50
10	Mark Prior, Nomar Garciaparra	2.00
11	Barry Larkin, Sean Casey	1.50
12	Adrian Beltre, Shawn Green	1.50
13	Alex Rodriguez, Derek Jeter	6.00
14	Manny Ramirez, Jason Varitek	3.00
15	Miguel Tejada, Javy Lopez	2.00
16	B.J. Upton, Carl Crawford	1.50
17	Frank Thomas, Paul Konerko	2.00
18	Joe Mauer, Justin Morneau	2.00
19	Victor Martinez, Jody Gerut	1.50
20	Bobby Crosby, Barry Zito	1.50
21	Mark Teixeira, Hank Blalock	2.00
22	Reggie Jackson, Rod Carew	2.00
23	Rickey Henderson, Tony Gwynn	2.50
24	Tom Seaver, Johnny Bench	3.00
25	Don Mattingly, Dave Righetti	4.00

Connections Material Dual Bat

		NM/M
Production 25-250		
2	Andruw Jones, Chipper Jones/250	10.00
3	Kazuo Matsui, Jose Reyes/100	10.00
4	Bobby Abreu, Jim Thome/100	12.00
5	Jeff Bagwell, Lance Berkman/250	10.00
6	Roger Clemens, Roy Oswalt/250	15.00
10	Mark Prior, Nomar Garciaparra/100	10.00
11	Barry Larkin, Sean Casey/100	10.00
12	Shawn Green, Adrian Beltre/250	5.00
14	Jason Varitek, Manny Ramirez/100	15.00
15	Miguel Tejada, Javy Lopez/100	10.00
17	Frank Thomas, Paul Konerko/100	10.00
19	Victor Martinez, Jody Gerut/25	12.00
21	Mark Teixeira, Hank Blalock/100	10.00
22	Reggie Jackson, Rod Carew/250	10.00
23	Tony Gwynn, Rickey Henderson/250	15.00
24	Tom Seaver, Johnny Bench/250	15.00

Connections Material Dual Jersey

		NM/M
Production 10-250		
Prime:		1-2X
Production 10-25		
No pricing 20 or less.		
1	Josh Beckett, Dontrelle Willis/250	8.00
2	Andruw Jones, Chipper Jones/250	10.00
3	Kazuo Matsui, Jose Reyes/100	10.00
4	Bobby Abreu, Jim Thome/250	10.00
5	Jeff Bagwell, Lance Berkman/250	10.00
6	Roger Clemens, Roy Oswalt/250	15.00
8	Albert Pujols, Jim Edmonds/250	25.00
11	Barry Larkin, Sean Casey/50	15.00
12	Shawn Green, Adrian Beltre/250	8.00
14	Jason Varitek, Manny Ramirez/50	20.00
15	Miguel Tejada, Javy Lopez/50	12.00
17	Frank Thomas/Pants, Paul Konerko/250	10.00
20	Bobby Crosby, Barry Zito/250	10.00
21	Mark Teixeira, Hank Blalock/100	10.00
22	Reggie Jackson, Rod Carew Jkt/250	12.00
23	Rickey Henderson, Tony Gwynn/250	15.00
24	Tom Seaver, Johnny Bench/Pants/100	15.00
25	Don Mattingly, Dave Righetti/250	20.00

Diamond Heritage

		NM/M
Complete Set (15):		20.00
Common Player:		.75
Inserted 1:12		
1	Pedro Martinez	1.50

2	Mark Teixeira	1.00
3	Lance Berkman	.75
4	Vladimir Guerrero	1.50
5	Albert Pujols	4.00
6	Roger Clemens	4.00
7	Manny Ramirez	1.50
8	Mike Piazza	2.00
9	Jim Thome	1.50
10	Mark Prior	1.00
11	Gary Sheffield	.75
12	Sammy Sosa	2.50
13	Tim Hudson	.75
14	Hideki Matsui	3.00
15	Jim Edmonds	.75

Diamond Heritage Matierial Bat

		NM/M
Production 100 Sets		
1	Pedro Martinez	10.00
2	Mark Teixeira	10.00
3	Lance Berkman	5.00
4	Vladimir Guerrero	10.00
6	Roger Clemens	15.00
7	Manny Ramirez	10.00
8	Mike Piazza	10.00
9	Jim Thome	10.00
10	Mark Prior	8.00
11	Gary Sheffield	8.00
12	Sammy Sosa	10.00
13	Tim Hudson	5.00
14	Hideki Matsui	25.00
15	Jim Edmonds	8.00

Diamond Heritage Material Jersey

		NM/M
Production 100 Sets		
1	Pedro Martinez	10.00
2	Mark Teixeira	10.00
3	Lance Berkman	5.00
4	Vladimir Guerrero	10.00
5	Albert Pujols	25.00
6	Roger Clemens	15.00
7	Manny Ramirez	10.00
8	Mike Piazza	10.00
9	Jim Thome	10.00
10	Mark Prior	8.00
11	Gary Sheffield	8.00
12	Sammy Sosa	10.00
13	Tim Hudson	5.00
14	Hideki Matsui Pants	25.00
15	Jim Edmonds	8.00

Fans of the Game

		NM/M
Inserted 1:24		
1	Tony Hawk	3.00
2	Tia Carrere	2.00
3	Mathew Modine	2.00

Fans of the Game Signature Gold

		NM/M
Production 100 Sets		
Platinum:		1X
Production 50 Sets		
1	Tony Hawk	75.00
2	Tia Carrere	85.00
3	Mathew Modine	40.00

Fans of the Game Signature Silver

		NM/M
Common Autograph:		40.00
1	Tony Hawk	75.00
2	Tia Carrere	85.00
3	Mathew Modine	40.00

League Leaders Double

		NM/M
Complete Set (5):		15.00
Inserted 1:39		
Foil:		2-3X
Production 100 Sets		
Holo-Foil:		3-6X
Production 25 Sets		

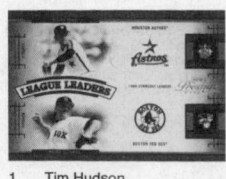

1	Tim Hudson, Roy Oswalt	2.00
2	Ivan Rodriguez, Todd Helton	3.00
3	Mark Teixeira, Jim Edmonds	2.00
4	Nolan Ryan, Roger Clemens	8.00
5	Sammy Sosa, Troy Glaus	3.00

League Leader Double Material Bat

		NM/M
Production 250 Sets		
1	Tim Hudson, Roy Oswalt	8.00
2	Ivan Rodriguez, Todd Helton	15.00
3	Mark Teixeira, Jim Edmonds	10.00
4	Nolan Ryan, Roger Clemens	25.00
5	Sammy Sosa, Troy Glaus	15.00

League Leaders Double Material Jersey

		NM/M
Production 50-250		
1	Tim Hudson, Roy Oswalt/100	10.00
2	Ivan Rodriguez, Todd Helton/50	15.00
3	Mark Teixeira, Jim Edmonds/250	15.00
4	Nolan Ryan, Roger Clemens/250	25.00
5	Sammy Sosa, Troy Glaus/250	15.00

League Leaders Quad

		NM/M
Inserted 1:39		
Foil:		1-2X
Production 100 Sets		
Holo-Foil:		3-5X
Production 25 Sets		
1	Wade Boggs, Paul Molitor, Alan Trammell, Kirby Puckett	4.00
2	Dale Murphy, Mike Schmidt, Gary Carter, Darryl Strawberry	6.00
3	Jose Canseco, Kirby Puckett, Will Clark, Darryl Strawberry	4.00
4	Pedro Martinez, Kevin Brown, Randy Johnson, Roger Clemens	6.00
5	Don Mattingly, Dave Parker, Eddie Murray, Dale Murphy	4.00

League Leaders Quad Material Bat

		NM/M
Production 100 Sets		
2	Dale Murphy, Mike Schmidt, Gary Carter, Darryl Strawberry	40.00
4	Pedro Martinez, Kevin Brown, Randy Johnson, Roger Clemens	50.00
5	Don Mattingly, Dave Parker, Eddie Murray, Dale Murphy	50.00

League Leaders Quad Material Jersey

		NM/M
Production 100 Sets		
1	Wade Boggs, Paul Molitor, Alan Trammell, Kirby Puckett	40.00

2	Dale Murphy, Mike Schmidt, Gary Carter, Darryl Strawberry	40.00
3	Jose Canseco, Kirby Puckett, Will Clark, Darryl Strawberry	40.00
4	Pedro Martinez, Kevin Brown, Randy Johnson, Roger Clemens	50.00
5	Don Mattingly, Dave Parker, Eddie Murray, Dale Murphy	50.00

League Leaders Single

		NM/M
Complete Set (10):		25.00
Inserted 1:21		
Foil:		2-4X
Production 100 Sets		
Holo-Foil:		4-8X
Production 25 Sets		
1	Gary Sheffield	2.00
2	Ben Sheets	2.00
3	Adrian Beltre	2.00
4	Scott Rolen	3.00
5	George Brett	4.00
6	Johan Santana	3.00
7	Manny Ramirez	3.00
8	Cal Ripken Jr.	8.00
9	Carlos Zambrano	2.00
10	Tony Gwynn	4.00

League Leader Single Material Bat

		NM/M
Production 250 Sets		
1	Gary Sheffield	8.00
2	Ben Sheets	5.00
3	Adrian Beltre	5.00
5	George Brett	12.00
7	Manny Ramirez	10.00
8	Cal Ripken Jr.	25.00
10	Tony Gwynn	8.00

League Leaders Single Material Jersey

		NM/M
Production 25-250		
1	Gary Sheffield/250	8.00
2	Ben Sheets/250	5.00
3	Adrian Beltre/50	8.00
4	Scott Rolen/250	8.00
5	George Brett/250	15.00
6	Johan Santana/25	20.00
7	Manny Ramirez/250	8.00
8	Cal Ripken Jr./250	25.00
9	Carlos Zambrano/250	5.00
10	Tony Gwynn/250	8.00

Playoff Champions Combo Wild Card

		NM/M
Inserted 1:391		
Division Combo:		.75-1X
League Combo:		.75-1X
World Series Combo:		.75-1X
Redemption Deadline 4-15-06.		
1	Andruw Jones, Johnny Estrada, Chipper Jones	10.00
2	Miguel Cabrera, Josh Beckett, Dontrelle Willis	10.00
3	Chad Cordero, Nick Johnson, Brad Wilkerson	5.00
4	Jim Thome, Bobby Abreu, Chase Utley	10.00
5	Mike Piazza, Kazuo Matsui, David Wright	10.00
6	Albert Pujols, Scott Rolen, Jim Edmonds	15.00
7	Kerry Wood, Mark Prior, Carlos Zambrano	8.00
8	Ben Sheets, Geoff Jenkins, Lyle Overbay	5.00

2	Dale Murphy, Mike Schmidt, Gary Carter, Darryl Strawberry	40.00
3	Jose Canseco, Kirby Puckett, Will Clark, Darryl Strawberry	40.00
4	Pedro Martinez, Kevin Brown, Randy Johnson, Roger Clemens	50.00
5	Don Mattingly, Dave Parker, Eddie Murray, Dale Murphy	50.00

9	Kip Wells, Jack Wilson, Jason Bay	5.00
10	Austin Kearns, Adam Dunn, Ken Griffey Jr.	10.00
11	Roy Oswalt, Lance Berkman, Jeff Bagwell	10.00
12	Jason Jennings, Matt Holliday, Todd Helton	10.00
13	Eric Gagne, Jayson Werth, Milton Bradley	10.00
14	Alex Cintron, Brandon Webb, Luis Gonzalez	5.00
15	Jason Schmidt, Edgardo Alfonzo, Kirk Rueter	5.00
16	Khalil Greene, Jake Peavy, Trevor Hoffman	10.00
17	Manny Ramirez, Curt Schilling, David Ortiz	15.00
18	Miguel Tejada, Melvin Mora, Javy Lopez	8.00
19	Roy Halladay, Alexis Rios, Gabe Gross	5.00
20	Alex Rodriguez, Derek Jeter, Hideki Matsui	20.00
21	B.J. Upton, Scott Kazmir, Carl Crawford	10.00
22	Frank Thomas, Shingo Takatsu, Aaron Rowand	8.00
23	Victor Martinez, C.C. Sabathia, Travis Hafner	5.00
24	Torii Hunter, Johan Santana, Justin Morneau	10.00
25	Zack Greinke, Mike Sweeney, Ken Harvey	5.00
26	Ivan Rodriguez, Jeremy Bonderman, Carlos Guillen	8.00
27	Rich Harden, Bobby Crosby, Barry Zito	5.00
28	Bret Boone, Ichiro Suzuki, Jeremy Reed	12.00
29	Michael Young, Mark Teixeira, Hank Blalock	10.00
30	Vladimir Guerrero, Darin Erstad, Garret Anderson	10.00

Playoff Game Jersey Collection

Inserted 1:8 Retail

Prestigious Pros Blue

		NM/M
Common Player:		1.00
Production 900 Sets		
Black:		No Pricing
Production 10 Sets		
Bronze:		2-3X
Production 100 Sets		
Gold:		2-4X
Production 50 Sets		
Green:		1-2X
Production 350 Sets		
Orange:		1-1.5X
Production 500 Sets		
Platinum:		3-5X
Production 25 Sets		
Purple:		1-2X
Production 200 Sets		
Red:		1X
Production 70 Sets		
Silver:		2-3X
Production 75 Sets		
1	Ozzie Smith	3.00
2	Derek Jeter	6.00
3	Eric Chavez	1.00
4	Paul Molitor	2.00
5	Jeff Bagwell	1.50
6	Melvin Mora	1.00

7	Craig Biggio	1.00
8	Cal Ripken Jr.	8.00
9	Hank Blalock	1.50
10	Miguel Tejada	2.00
11	Jacque Jones	1.00
12	Alfonso Soriano	2.00
13	Omar Vizquel	1.00
14	Paul Konerko	1.00
15	Tim Hudson	1.00
16	Garret Anderson	1.00
17	Lance Berkman	1.00
18	Randy Johnson	2.00
19	Robin Yount	3.00
20	Mark Mulder	1.00
21	Sean Casey	1.00
22	Jim Palmer	1.50
23	Don Mattingly	5.00
24	Manny Ramirez	2.00
25	Rafael Palmeiro	1.50
26	Vernon Wells	1.00
27	Vladimir Guerrero	2.00
28	Ken Harvey	1.00
29	Rod Carew	1.50
30	Nolan Ryan	8.00
31	Mike Piazza	3.00
32	Steve Carlton	1.50
33	Miguel Cabrera	2.00
34	Kerry Wood	2.00
35	Mike Mussina	1.00
36	Gaylord Perry	1.00
37	Gary Sheffield	1.50
38	Curt Schilling	2.00
39	Don Sutton	1.00
40	Roger Clemens	6.00
41	Victor Martinez	1.00
42	Jason Giambi	1.00
43	Dennis Eckersley	1.00
44	Adam Dunn	1.50
45	Pedro Martinez	2.00
46	Tony Perez	1.00
47	Tom Glavine	1.00
48	Torii Hunter	1.00
49	Hideo Nomo	1.00
50	Scott Rolen	2.00
51	Ichiro Suzuki	5.00
52	C.C. Sabathia	1.00
53	George Brett	5.00
54	David Ortiz	2.00
55	Hideki Matsui	4.00
56	Nomar Garciaparra	4.00
57	Johan Santana	2.00
58	Phil Niekro	1.00
59	Dontrelle Willis	1.00
60	Magglio Ordonez	1.00
61	Livan Hernandez	1.00
62	Edgar Renteria	1.00
63	Todd Helton	1.50
64	Carlos Beltran	1.50
65	Sammy Sosa	4.00
66	Albert Pujols	6.00
67	Mike Lowell	1.00
68	Mark Prior	1.50
69	Ivan Rodriguez	1.50
70	Jake Peavy	1.00
71	Jim Thome	2.00
72	Mark Teixeira	1.50
73	Shawn Green	1.00
74	Rollie Fingers	1.00
75	Barry Zito	1.00
76	Jose Vidro	1.00
77	Ben Sheets	1.00
78	Roy Halladay	1.00
79	Frank Thomas	1.50
80	Chipper Jones	2.00
81	Jason Bay	1.00
82	Tony Gwynn	2.00
83	Shannon Stewart	1.00
84	Carl Crawford	1.00
85	Andruw Jones	1.00
86	Greg Maddux	3.00
87	Barry Larkin	1.00
88	Alex Rodriguez	5.00
89	Rickey Henderson	1.50
90	Troy Glaus	1.00
91	Roy Oswalt	1.00
92	Michael Young	1.00
93	Carlos Lee	1.00
94	Jim Edmonds	1.00
95	Fergie Jenkins	1.00
96	Paul LoDuca	1.00
97	Aubrey Huff	1.00
98	Ken Griffey Jr.	3.00
99	Carlos Delgado	1.50
100	Mike Schmidt	5.00

Prestigious Pros Material Jersey Gold

		NM/M
Production 5-50		
No pricing 20 or less.		
Platinum Patch:		No Pricing
Production 5-10		
1	Ozzie Smith/50	25.00

3	Eric Chavez/25	10.00
4	Paul Molitor/50	12.00
5	Jeff Bagwell/25	10.00
6	Melvin Mora/25	10.00
7	Craig Biggio/25	15.00
8	Cal Ripken Jr./50	40.00
10	Miguel Tejada/25	12.00
13	Omar Vizquel/25	15.00
14	Paul Konerko/25	8.00
15	Tim Hudson/25	10.00
17	Lance Berkman/50	8.00
18	Randy Johnson/25	20.00
19	Robin Yount/50	15.00
20	Mark Mulder/20	10.00
21	Sean Casey/25	10.00
22	Jim Palmer/50	8.00
23	Don Mattingly/50	25.00
26	Vernon Wells/25	8.00
27	Vladimir Guerrero/25	20.00
28	Ken Harvey/25	8.00
29	Rod Carew/50	10.00
30	Nolan Ryan/50	35.00
31	Mike Piazza/50	20.00
32	Steve Carlton/50	8.00
34	Kerry Wood/25	15.00
35	Mike Mussina/25	15.00
36	Gaylord Perry/50	8.00
37	Gary Sheffield/25	10.00
38	Curt Schilling/25	15.00
39	Don Sutton/50	8.00
40	Roger Clemens/25	25.00
41	Victor Martinez/25	10.00
42	Jason Giambi/25	10.00
43	Dennis Eckersley/50	10.00
45	Pedro Martinez/25	15.00
46	Tony Perez/25	8.00
49	Hideo Nomo/25	25.00
50	Scott Rolen/25	20.00
52	C.C. Sabathia/25	10.00
53	George Brett/25	25.00
54	David Ortiz/10	
55	Hideki Matsui/25	40.00
57	Johan Santana/5	
58	Phil Niekro/50	8.00
59	Dontrelle Willis/25	10.00
60	Magglio Ordonez/25	8.00
61	Livan Hernandez/25	8.00
62	Edgar Renteria/25	10.00
63	Todd Helton/25	15.00
65	Sammy Sosa/25	20.00
66	Albert Pujols/25	35.00
67	Mike Lowell/10	
68	Mark Prior/25	10.00
71	Jim Thome/25	15.00
72	Mark Teixeira/25	12.00
73	Shawn Green/25	10.00
74	Rollie Fingers/25	8.00
77	Ben Sheets/25	10.00
78	Roy Halladay/25	10.00
79	Frank Thomas/25	15.00
80	Chipper Jones/25	15.00
81	Jason Bay/25	10.00
82	Tony Gwynn/25	15.00
83	Shannon Stewart/5	
84	Carl Crawford/25	10.00
85	Andruw Jones/25	10.00
86	Greg Maddux/25	20.00
87	Barry Larkin/25	12.00
89	Rickey Henderson/50	15.00
90	Troy Glaus/25	10.00
91	Roy Oswalt/10	
92	Michael Young/25	10.00
93	Carlos Lee/25	10.00
94	Jim Edmonds/25	12.00
95	Fergie Jenkins/25	10.00
97	Aubrey Huff/25	10.00
99	Carlos Delgado/25	10.00
100	Mike Schmidt/50	25.00

Prestigious Pros Material Bat Silver

NM/M

Production 5-50
No pricing 20 or less.

1	Ozzie Smith/50	25.00
3	Eric Chavez/25	10.00
4	Paul Molitor/50	12.00
5	Jeff Bagwell/50	10.00
7	Craig Biggio/25	15.00
8	Cal Ripken Jr./50	40.00
9	Hank Blalock/25	12.00
10	Miguel Tejada/25	12.00
14	Paul Konerko/25	8.00
15	Tim Hudson/25	10.00
16	Garret Anderson/25	10.00
17	Lance Berkman/50	8.00
18	Randy Johnson/25	20.00
19	Robin Yount/50	15.00
21	Sean Casey/25	10.00
23	Don Mattingly/50	25.00

25	Rafael Palmeiro/25	15.00
27	Vladimir Guerrero/25	20.00
28	Ken Harvey/25	8.00
29	Rod Carew/50	10.00
30	Nolan Ryan/50	35.00
31	Mike Piazza/25	20.00
32	Steve Carlton/50	8.00
33	Miguel Cabrera/10	
34	Kerry Wood/25	15.00
35	Mike Mussina/25	15.00
37	Gary Sheffield/25	10.00
38	Curt Schilling/25	15.00
40	Roger Clemens/25	25.00
41	Victor Martinez/25	10.00
42	Jason Giambi/25	10.00
44	Adam Dunn/25	12.00
45	Pedro Martinez/25	15.00
46	Tony Perez/50	8.00
47	Tom Glavine/25	12.00
48	Torii Hunter/25	8.00
49	Hideo Nomo/25	25.00
50	Scott Rolen/25	20.00
53	George Brett/50	25.00
54	David Ortiz/50	12.00
55	Hideki Matsui/50	40.00
56	Nomar Garciaparra/25	20.00
58	Phil Niekro/50	8.00
60	Magglio Ordonez/25	8.00
62	Edgar Renteria/25	10.00
63	Todd Helton/25	15.00
64	Carlos Beltran/25	15.00
65	Sammy Sosa/50	15.00
67	Mike Lowell/25	10.00
68	Mark Prior/25	15.00
69	Ivan Rodriguez/50	10.00
71	Jim Thome/25	10.00
72	Mark Teixeira/25	10.00
73	Shawn Green/25	10.00
76	Jose Vidro/25	8.00
78	Ben Sheets/25	10.00
79	Frank Thomas/25	15.00
81	Jason Bay/25	10.00
82	Tony Gwynn/50	15.00
83	Shannon Stewart/25	8.00
85	Andruw Jones/25	10.00
87	Barry Larkin/50	10.00
89	Rickey Henderson/50	15.00
90	Troy Glaus/25	10.00
91	Roy Oswalt/25	10.00
92	Michael Young/25	10.00
93	Carlos Lee/25	10.00
94	Jim Edmonds/50	10.00
96	Paul LoDuca/25	10.00
99	Carlos Delgado/25	10.00
100	Mike Schmidt/25	25.00

Prestigious Pros Signature Black

No Pricing
Production 5 Sets

Stars of MLB

NM/M

Complete Set (15): 20.00
Common Player: 1.00
Inserted 1:12
Foil: 2-4X
Production 100 Sets
Holo-Foil: 4-8X
Production 25 Sets

1	Randy Johnson	3.00
2	Adrian Beltre	1.00
3	Eric Chavez	1.00
4	Mike Mussina	1.50
5	Todd Helton	2.00
6	Curt Schilling	2.00
7	Miguel Cabrera	3.00
8	Kerry Wood	2.50
9	David Ortiz	3.00
10	Michael Young	1.00
11	Mark Mulder	1.00
12	Victor Martinez	1.00
13	Johan Santana	2.00
14	Scott Rolen	3.00
15	Carlos Beltran	2.00

Stars of MLB Material Bat

NM/M

Production 50-100

1	Randy Johnson/100	10.00
2	Adrian Beltre/100	5.00
3	Eric Chavez/100	5.00
4	Mike Mussina/100	8.00
5	Todd Helton/100	8.00
6	Curt Schilling/100	10.00
7	Miguel Cabrera/100	8.00
8	Kerry Wood/100	10.00
9	David Ortiz/100	10.00
10	Michael Young/100	5.00
11	Mark Mulder/100	8.00
14	Scott Rolen/100	10.00
15	Carlos Beltran/100	8.00

Stars of MLB Material Jersey

NM/M

Production 100 Sets
Prime: 1-2X
Production 25 Sets

1	Randy Johnson/Pants	10.00
2	Adrian Beltre	5.00
3	Eric Chavez	5.00
4	Mike Mussina	8.00
5	Todd Helton	8.00
6	Curt Schilling	10.00
7	Miguel Cabrera	10.00
8	Kerry Wood	10.00
9	David Ortiz	12.00
10	Michael Young	5.00
11	Mark Mulder	5.00
12	Victor Martinez	5.00
13	Johan Santana	10.00
14	Scott Rolen	10.00
15	Carlos Beltran	8.00

Stars of MLB Signature Material Bat

NM/M

Production 10-50

2	Adrian Beltre/50	25.00
3	Eric Chavez/50	20.00
8	Kerry Wood/25	50.00
9	David Ortiz/50	40.00
10	Michael Young/50	25.00
15	Carlos Beltran/25	50.00

Stars of MLB Signature Material Jersey

NM/M

Production 10-50
Prime: No Pricing
Production 5 Sets

1	Randy Johnson/Pants/10	
2	Adrian Beltre/50	25.00
3	Eric Chavez/50	20.00
8	Kerry Wood/25	50.00
9	David Ortiz/50	40.00
10	Michael Young/25	25.00
12	Victor Martinez/50	20.00
13	Johan Santana/50	50.00
15	Carlos Beltran/25	50.00

1988 Score

NM/M

Unopened Fact. Set (660): 9.00

(Mark McGwire card)

Complete Set (660): 6.00
Common Player: .05
Pack: .35
Wax Box: 9.00
Rack Pack (54): .75
Rack Box (24): 12.00

1	Don Mattingly	.65
2	Wade Boggs	.50
3	Tim Raines	.05
4	Andre Dawson	.25
5	Mark McGwire	.75
6	Kevin Seitzer	.05
7	Wally Joyner	.05
8	Jesse Barfield	.05
9	Pedro Guerrero	.05
10	Eric Davis	.05
11	George Brett	.65
12	Ozzie Smith	.50
13	Rickey Henderson	.40
14	Jim Rice	.15
15	Matt Nokes RC	.05
16	Mike Schmidt	.65
17	Dave Parker	.05
18	Eddie Murray	.40
19	Andres Galarraga	.05
20	Tony Fernandez	.05
21	Kevin McReynolds	.05
22	B.J. Surhoff	.05
23	Pat Tabler	.05
24	Kirby Puckett	.50
25	Benny Santiago	.05
26	Ryne Sandberg	.50
27	Kelly Downs	.05
28	Jose Cruz	.05
29	Pete O'Brien	.05
30	Mark Langston	.05
31	Lee Smith	.05
32	Juan Samuel	.05
33	Kevin Bass	.05
34	R.J. Reynolds	.05
35	Steve Sax	.05
36	John Kruk	.05
37	Alan Trammell	.05
38	Chris Bosio	.05
39	Brook Jacoby	.05
40	Willie McGee	.05
41	Dave Magadan	.05
42	Fred Lynn	.05
43	Kent Hrbek	.05
44	Brian Downing	.05
45	Jose Canseco	.30
46	Jim Presley	.05
47	Mike Stanley	.05
48	Tony Pena	.05
49	David Cone	.05
50	Rick Sutcliffe	.05
51	Doug Drabek	.05
52	Bill Doran	.05
53	Mike Scioscia	.05
54	Candy Maldonado	.05
55	Dave Winfield	.40
56	Lou Whitaker	.05
57	Tom Henke	.05
58	Ken Gerhart	.05
59	Glenn Braggs	.05
60	Julio Franco	.05
61	Charlie Leibrandt	.05
62	Gary Gaetti	.05
63	Bob Boone	.05
64	Luis Polonia RC	.05
65	Dwight Evans	.05
66	Phil Bradley	.05
67	Mike Boddicker	.05
68	Vince Coleman	.05
69	Howard Johnson	.05
70	Tim Wallach	.05
71	Keith Moreland	.05
72	Barry Larkin	.05
73	Alan Ashby	.05
74	Rick Rhoden	.05
75	Darrell Evans	.05

No.	Player	Value
76	Dave Stieb	.05
77	Dan Plesac	.05
78	Will Clark	.05
79	Frank White	.05
80	Joe Carter	.05
81	Mike Witt	.05
82	Terry Steinbach	.05
83	Alvin Davis	.05
84	Tom Herr	.05
85	Vance Law	.05
86	Kal Daniels	.05
87	Rick Honeycutt	.05
88	Alfredo Griffin	.05
89	Bret Saberhagen	.05
90	Bert Blyleven	.05
91	Jeff Reardon	.05
92	Cory Snyder	.05
93	Greg Walker	.05
94	Joe Magrane RC	.10
95	Rob Deer	.05
96	Ray Knight	.05
97	Casey Candaele	.05
98	John Cerutti	.05
99	Buddy Bell	.05
100	Jack Clark	.05
101	Eric Bell	.05
102	Willie Wilson	.05
103	Dave Schmidt	.05
104	Dennis Eckersley	.35
105	Don Sutton	.35
106	Danny Tartabull	.05
107	Fred McGriff	.05
108	Les Straker RC	.05
109	Lloyd Moseby	.05
110	Roger Clemens	.65
111	Glenn Hubbard	.05
112	Ken Williams RC	.05
113	Ruben Sierra	.05
114	Stan Jefferson	.05
115	Milt Thompson	.05
116	Bobby Bonilla	.05
117	Wayne Tolleson	.05
118	Matt Williams	.05
119	Chet Lemon	.05
120	Dale Sveum	.05
121	Dennis Boyd	.05
122	Brett Butler	.05
123	Terry Kennedy	.05
124	Jack Howell	.05
125	Curt Young	.05
126a	Dale Valle (First name incorrect.)	.25
126b	Dave Valle (Correct spelling.)	.05
127	Curt Wilkerson	.05
128	Tim Teufel	.05
129	Ozzie Virgil	.05
130	Brian Fisher	.05
131	Lance Parrish	.05
132	Tom Browning	.05
133a	Larry Anderson (Incorrect spelling.)	.25
133b	Larry Andersen (Correct spelling.)	.05
134a	Bob Brenley (Incorrect spelling.)	.25
134b	Bob Brenly (Correct spelling.)	.05
135	Mike Marshall	.05
136	Gerald Perry	.05
137	Bobby Meacham	.05
138	Larry Herndon	.05
139	Fred Manrique RC	.05
140	Charlie Hough	.05
141	Ron Darling	.05
142	Herm Winningham	.05
143	Mike Diaz	.05
144	Mike Jackson RC	.05
145	Denny Walling	.05
146	Rob Thompson	.05
147	Franklin Stubbs	.05
148	Albert Hall	.05
149	Bobby Witt	.05
150	Lance McCullers	.05
151	Scott Bradley	.05
152	Mark McLemore	.05
153	Tim Laudner	.05
154	Greg Swindell	.05
155	Marty Barrett	.05
156	Mike Heath	.05
157	Gary Ward	.05
158a	Lee Mazilli (Incorrect spelling.)	.25
158b	Lee Mazzilli (Correct spelling.)	.05
159	Tom Foley	.05
160	Robin Yount	.40
161	Steve Bedrosian	.05
162	Bob Walk	.05
163	Nick Esasky	.05
164	Ken Caminiti RC	.15
165	Jose Uribe	.05
166	Dave Anderson	.05
167	Ed Whitson	.05
168	Ernie Whitt	.05
169	Cecil Cooper	.05
170	Mike Pagliarulo	.05
171	Pat Sheridan	.05
172	Chris Bando	.05
173	Lee Lacy	.05
174	Steve Lombardozzi	.05
175	Mike Greenwell	.05
176	Greg Minton	.05
177	Moose Haas	.05
178	Mike Kingery	.05
179	Greg Harris	.05
180	Bo Jackson	.10
181	Carmelo Martinez	.05
182	Alex Trevino	.05
183	Ron Oester	.05
184	Danny Darwin	.05
185	Mike Krukow	.05
186	Rafael Palmeiro	.40
187	Tim Burke	.05
188	Roger McDowell	.05
189	Garry Templeton	.05
190	Terry Pendleton	.05
191	Larry Parrish	.05
192	Rey Quinones	.05
193	Joaquin Andujar	.05
194	Tom Brunansky	.05
195	Donnie Moore	.05
196	Dan Pasqua	.05
197	Jim Gantner	.05
198	Mark Eichhorn	.05
199	John Grubb	.05
200	Bill Ripken RC	.05
201	Sam Horn RC	.05
202	Todd Worrell	.05
203	Terry Leach	.05
204	Garth Iorg	.05
205	Brian Dayett	.05
206	Bo Diaz	.05
207	Craig Reynolds	.05
208	Brian Holton	.05
209	Marvelle Wynne (Marvell)	.05
210	Dave Concepcion	.05
211	Mike Davis	.05
212	Devon White	.05
213	Mickey Brantley	.05
214	Greg Gagne	.05
215	Oddibe McDowell	.05
216	Jimmy Key	.05
217	Dave Bergman	.05
218	Calvin Schiraldi	.05
219	Larry Sheets	.05
220	Mike Easler	.05
221	Kurt Stillwell	.05
222	Chuck Jackson RC	.05
223	Dave Martinez	.05
224	Tim Leary	.05
225	Steve Garvey	.20
226	Greg Mathews	.05
227	Doug Sisk	.05
228	Dave Henderson	.05
229	Jimmy Dwyer	.05
230	Larry Owen	.05
231	Andre Thornton	.05
232	Mark Salas	.05
233	Tom Brookens	.05
234	Greg Brock	.05
235	Rance Mulliniks	.05
236	Bob Brower	.05
237	Joe Niekro	.05
238	Scott Bankhead	.05
239	Doug DeCinces	.05
240	Tommy John	.05
241	Rich Gedman	.05
242	Ted Power	.05
243	Dave Meads RC	.05
244	Jim Sundberg	.05
245	Ken Oberkfell	.05
246	Jimmy Jones	.05
247	Ken Landreaux	.05
248	Jose Oquendo	.05
249	John Mitchell RC	.05
250	Don Baylor	.05
251	Scott Fletcher	.05
252	Al Newman	.05
253	Carney Lansford	.05
254	Johnny Ray	.05
255	Gary Pettis	.05
256	Ken Phelps	.05
257	Rick Leach	.05
258	Tim Stoddard	.05
259	Ed Romero	.05
260	Sid Bream	.05
261a	Tom Neidenfuer (Incorrect spelling.)	.25
261b	Tom Niedenfuer (Correct spelling.)	.05
262	Rick Dempsey	.05
263	Lonnie Smith	.05
264	Bob Forsch	.05
265	Barry Bonds	1.00
266	Willie Randolph	.05
267	Mike Ramsey	.05
268	Don Slaught	.05
269	Mickey Tettleton	.05
270	Jerry Reuss	.05
271	Marc Sullivan	.05
272	Jim Morrison	.05
273	Steve Balboni	.05
274	Dick Schofield	.05
275	John Tudor	.05
276	Gene Larkin RC	.05
277	Harold Reynolds	.05
278	Jerry Browne	.05
279	Willie Upshaw	.05
280	Ted Higuera	.05
281	Terry McGriff	.05
282	Terry Puhl	.05
283	Mark Wasinger RC	.05
284	Luis Salazar	.05
285	Ted Simmons	.05
286	John Shelby	.05
287	John Smiley RC	.05
288	Curt Ford	.05
289	Steve Crawford	.05
290	Dan Quisenberry	.05
291	Alan Wiggins	.05
292	Randy Bush	.05
293	John Candelaria	.05
294	Tony Phillips	.05
295	Mike Morgan	.05
296	Bill Wegman	.05
297a	Terry Franconia (Incorrect spelling.)	.25
297b	Terry Francona (Correct spelling.)	.05
298	Mickey Hatcher	.05
299	Andres Thomas	.05
300	Bob Stanley	.05
301	Alfredo Pedrique RC	.05
302	Jim Lindeman	.05
303	Wally Backman	.05
304	Paul O'Neill	.05
305	Hubie Brooks	.05
306	Steve Buechele	.05
307	Bobby Thigpen	.05
308	George Hendrick	.05
309	John Moses	.05
310	Ron Guidry	.05
311	Bill Schroeder	.05
312	Jose Nunez RC	.05
313	Bud Black	.05
314	Joe Sambito	.05
315	Scott McGregor	.05
316	Rafael Santana	.05
317	Frank Williams	.05
318	Mike Fitzgerald	.05
319	Rick Mahler	.05
320	Jim Gott	.05
321	Mariano Duncan	.05
322	Jose Guzman	.05
323	Lee Guetterman	.05
324	Dan Gladden	.05
325	Gary Carter	.40
326	Tracy Jones	.05
327	Floyd Youmans	.05
328	Bill Dawley	.05
329	Paul Noce RC	.05
330	Angel Salazar	.05
331	Goose Gossage	.10
332	George Frazier	.05
333	Ruppert Jones	.05
334	Billy Jo Robidoux	.05
335	Mike Scott	.05
336	Randy Myers	.05
337	Bob Sebra	.05
338	Eric Show	.05
339	Mitch Williams	.05
340	Paul Molitor	.40
341	Gus Polidor	.05
342	Steve Trout	.05
343	Jerry Don Gleaton	.05
344	Bob Knepper	.05
345	Mitch Webster	.05
346	John Morris	.05
347	Andy Hawkins	.05
348	Dave Leiper	.05
349	Ernest Riles	.05
350	Dwight Gooden	.05
351	Dave Righetti	.05
352	Pat Dodson	.05
353	John Habyan	.05
354	Jim Deshaies	.05
355	Butch Wynegar	.05
356	Bryn Smith	.05
357	Matt Young	.05
358	Tom Pagnozzi RC	.05
359	Floyd Rayford	.05
360	Darryl Strawberry	.05
361	Sal Butera	.05
362	Domingo Ramos	.05
363	Chris Brown	.05
364	Jose Gonzalez	.05
365	Dave Smith	.05
366	Andy McGaffigan	.05
367	Stan Javier	.05
368	Henry Cotto	.05
369	Mike Birkbeck	.05
370	Len Dykstra	.05
371	Dave Collins	.05
372	Spike Owen	.05
373	Geno Petralli	.05
374	Ron Karkovice	.05
375	Shane Rawley	.05
376	DeWayne Buice RC	.05
377	Bill Pecota RC	.05
378	Leon Durham	.05
379	Ed Olwine	.05
380	Bruce Hurst	.05
381	Bob McClure	.05
382	Mark Thurmond	.05
383	Buddy Biancalana	.05
384	Tim Conroy	.05
385	Tony Gwynn	.50
386	Greg Gross	.05
387	Barry Lyons RC	.05
388	Mike Felder	.05
389	Pat Clements	.05
390	Ken Griffey	.05
391	Mark Davis	.05
392	Jose Rijo	.05
393	Mike Young	.05
394	Willie Fraser	.05
395	Dion James	.05
396	Steve Shields RC	.05
397	Randy St. Claire	.05
398	Danny Jackson	.05
399	Cecil Fielder	.05
400	Keith Hernandez	.05
401	Don Carman	.05
402	Chuck Crim RC	.05
403	Rob Woodward	.05
404	Junior Ortiz	.05
405	Glenn Wilson	.05
406	Ken Howell	.05
407	Jeff Kunkel	.05
408	Jeff Reed	.05
409	Chris James	.05
410	Zane Smith	.05
411	Ken Dixon	.05
412	Ricky Horton	.05
413	Frank DiPino	.05
414	Shane Mack RC	.05
415	Danny Cox	.05
416	Andy Van Slyke	.05
417	Danny Heep	.05
418	John Cangelosi	.05
419a	John Christiansen (Incorrect spelling.)	.25
419b	John Christensen (Correct spelling.)	.05
420	Joey Cora RC	.05
421	Mike LaValliere	.05
422	Kelly Gruber	.05
423	Bruce Benedict	.05
424	Len Matuszek	.05
425	Kent Tekulve	.05
426	Rafael Ramirez	.05
427	Mike Flanagan	.05
428	Mike Gallego	.05
429	Juan Castillo	.05
430	Neal Heaton	.05
431	Phil Garner	.05
432	Mike Dunne RC	.05
433	Wallace Johnson	.05
434	Jack O'Connor	.05
435	Steve Jeltz	.05
436	Donnell Nixon RC	.05
437	Jack Lazorko	.05
438	Keith Comstock RC	.05
439	Jeff Robinson	.05
440	Graig Nettles	.05
441	Mel Hall	.05
442	Gerald Young RC	.05
443	Gary Redus	.05
444	Charlie Moore	.05
445	Bill Madlock	.05
446	Mark Clear	.05
447	Greg Booker	.05
448	Rick Schu	.05
449	Ron Kittle	.05
450	Dale Murphy	.25
451	Bob Dernier	.05
452	Dale Mohorcic	.05
453	Rafael Belliard	.05
454	Charlie Puleo	.05
455	Dwayne Murphy	.05
456	Jim Eisenreich	.05
457	David Palmer	.05
458	Dave Stewart	.05
459	Pascual Perez	.05
460	Glenn Davis	.05
461	Dan Petry	.05
462	Jim Winn	.05
463	Darrell Miller	.05
464	Mike Moore	.05
465	Mike LaCoss	.05
466	Steve Farr	.05
467	Jerry Mumphrey	.05
468	Kevin Gross	.05
469	Bruce Bochy	.05

470	Orel Hershiser	.05
471	Eric King	.05
472	Ellis Burks **RC**	.25
473	Darren Daulton	.05
474	Mookie Wilson	.05
475	Frank Viola	.05
476	Ron Robinson	.05
477	Bob Melvin	.05
478	Jeff Musselman	.05
479	Charlie Kerfeld	.05
480	Richard Dotson	.05
481	Kevin Mitchell	.05
482	Gary Roenicke	.05
483	Tim Flannery	.05
484	Rich Yett	.05
485	Pete Incaviglia	.05
486	Rick Cerone	.05
487	Tony Armas	.05
488	Jerry Reed	.05
489	Davey Lopes	.05
490	Frank Tanana	.05
491	Mike Loynd	.05
492	Bruce Ruffin	.05
493	Chris Speier	.05
494	Tom Hume	.05
495	Jesse Orosco	.05
496	Robby Wine, Jr. **RC**	.05
497	Jeff Montgomery **RC**	.15
498	Jeff Dedmon	.05
499	Luis Aguayo	.05
500	Reggie Jackson/ 1968-75	.15
501	Reggie Jackson/1976	.15
502	Reggie Jackson/ 1977-81	.15
503	Reggie Jackson/ 1982-86	.15
504	Reggie Jackson/1987	.15
505	Billy Hatcher	.05
506	Ed Lynch	.05
507	Willie Hernandez	.05
508	Jose DeLeon	.05
509	Joel Youngblood	.05
510	Bob Welch	.05
511	Steve Ontiveros	.05
512	Randy Ready	.05
513	Juan Nieves	.05
514	Jeff Russell	.05
515	Von Hayes	.05
516	Mark Gubicza	.05
517	Ken Dayley	.05
518	Don Aase	.05
519	Rick Reuschel	.05
520	Mike Henneman **RC**	.10
521	Rick Aguilera	.05
522	Jay Howell	.05
523	Ed Correa	.05
524	Manny Trillo	.05
525	Kirk Gibson	.05
526	Wally Ritchie **RC**	.05
527	Al Nipper	.05
528	Atlee Hammaker	.05
529	Shawon Dunston	.05
530	Jim Clancy	.05
531	Tom Paciorek	.05
532	Joel Skinner	.05
533	Scott Garrelts	.05
534	Tom O'Malley	.05
535	John Franco	.05
536	Paul Kilgus **RC**	.05
537	Darrell Porter	.05
538	Walt Terrell	.05
539	Bill Long **RC**	.05
540	George Bell	.05
541	Jeff Sellers	.05
542	Joe Boever **RC**	.05
543	Steve Howe	.05
544	Scott Sanderson	.05
545	Jack Morris	.05
546	Todd Benzinger **RC**	.05
547	Steve Henderson	.05
548	Eddie Milner	.05
549	Jeff Robinson **RC**	.05
550	Cal Ripken, Jr.	1.00
551	Jody Davis	.05
552	Kirk McCaskill	.05
553	Craig Lefferts	.05
554	Darnell Coles	.05
555	Phil Niekro	.35
556	Mike Aldrete	.05
557	Pat Perry	.05
558	Juan Agosto	.05
559	Rob Murphy	.05
560	Dennis Rasmussen	.05
561	Manny Lee	.05
562	Jeff Blauser **RC**	.10
563	Bob Ojeda	.05
564	Dave Dravecky	.05
565	Gene Garber	.05
566	Ron Roenicke	.05
567	Tommy Hinzo **RC**	.05
568	Eric Nolte **RC**	.05
569	Ed Hearn	.05
570	Mark Davidson	.05

571	Jim Walewander **RC**	.05
572	Donnie Hill	.05
573	Jamie Moyer	.05
574	Ken Schrom	.05
575	Nolan Ryan	1.00
576	Jim Acker	.05
577	Jamie Quirk	.05
578	Jay Aldrich **RC**	.05
579	Claudell Washington	.05
580	Jeff Leonard	.05
581	Carmen Castillo	.05
582	Daryl Boston	.05
583	Jeff DeWillis **RC**	.05
584	John Marzano **RC**	.05
585	Bill Gullickson	.05
586	Andy Allanson	.05
587	Lee Tunnell	.05
588	Gene Nelson	.05
589	Dave LaPoint	.05
590	Harold Baines	.05
591	Bill Buckner	.05
592	Carlton Fisk	.40
593	Rick Manning	.05
594	Doug Jones **RC**	.10
595	Tom Candiotti	.05
596	Steve Lake	.05
597	Jose Lind **RC**	.05
598	Ross Jones **RC**	.05
599	Gary Matthews	.05
600	Fernando Valenzuela	.05
601	Dennis Martinez	.05
602	Les Lancaster **RC**	.05
603	Ozzie Guillen	.05
604	Tony Bernazard	.05
605	Chili Davis	.05
606	Roy Smalley	.05
607	Ivan Calderon	.05
608	Jay Tibbs	.05
609	Guy Hoffman	.05
610	Doyle Alexander	.05
611	Mike Bielecki	.05
612	Shawn Hillegas **RC**	.05
613	Keith Atherton	.05
614	Eric Plunk	.05
615	Sid Fernandez	.05
616	Dennis Lamp	.05
617	Dave Engle	.05
618	Harry Spilman	.05
619	Don Robinson	.05
620	John Farrell **RC**	.05
621	Nelson Liriano **RC**	.05
622	Floyd Bannister	.05
623	Randy Milligan **RC**	.05
624	Kevin Elster **RC**	.10
625	Jody Reed **RC**	.05
626	Shawn Abner **RC**	.05
627	Kirt Manwaring **RC**	.10
628	Pete Stanicek **RC**	.05
629	Rob Ducey **RC**	.05
630	Steve Kiefer	.05
631	Gary Thurman **RC**	.05
632	Darrel Akerfelds **RC**	.05
633	Dave Clark	.05
634	Roberto Kelly **RC**	.05
635	Keith Hughes **RC**	.05
636	John Davis **RC**	.05
637	Mike Devereaux **RC**	.10
638	Tom Glavine **RC**	1.00
639	Keith Miller **RC**	.05
640	Chris Gwynn **RC**	.05
641	Tim Crews **RC**	.05
642	Mackey Sasser **RC**	.05
643	Vicente Palacios **RC**	.05
644	Kevin Romine	.05
645	Gregg Jefferies **RC**	.25
646	Jeff Treadway **RC**	.05
647	Ron Gant **RC**	.25
648	Mark McGwire, Matt Nokes Rookie Sluggers	.35
649	Tim Raines, Eric Davis Speed and Power	.05
650	Jack Clark, Don Mattingly Game Breakers	.25
651	Tony Fernandez, Cal Ripken, Jr., Alan Trammell Super Shortstops	.25
652	Vince Coleman	.05
653	Kirby Puckett	.05
654	Benito Santiago	.05
655	Juan Nieves	.05
656	Steve Bedrosian	.05
657	Mike Schmidt	.30
658	Don Mattingly	.30
659	Mark McGwire	.35
660	Paul Molitor	.20

Glossy

	NM/M
Complete Set (660):	65.00
Common Player:	.25
Stars:	15X

(See 1988 Score for checklist and base card values.)

Traded/Rookie

		NM/M
Complete Set (110):		12.00
Common Player:		.05
1	Jack Clark	.05
2	Danny Jackson	.05
3	Brett Butler	.05
4	Kurt Stillwell	.05
5	Tom Brunansky	.05
6	Dennis Lamp	.05
7	Jose DeLeon	.05
8	Tom Herr	.05
9	Keith Moreland	.05
10	Kirk Gibson	.05
11	Bud Black	.05
12	Rafael Ramirez	.05
13	Luis Salazar	.05
14	Goose Gossage	.05
15	Bob Welch	.05
16	Vance Law	.05
17	Ray Knight	.05
18	Dan Quisenberry	.05
19	Don Slaught	.05
20	Lee Smith	.25
21	Rick Cerone	.05
22	Pat Tabler	.05
23	Larry McWilliams	.05
24	Rick Horton	.05
25	Graig Nettles	.05
26	Dan Petry	.05
27	Jose Rijo	.05
28	Chili Davis	.05
29	Dickie Thon	.05
30	Mackey Sasser	.05
31	Mickey Tettleton	.05
32	Rick Dempsey	.05
33	Ron Hassey	.05
34	Phil Bradley	.05
35	Jay Howell	.05
36	Bill Buckner	.05
37	Alfredo Griffin	.05
38	Gary Pettis	.05
39	Calvin Schiraldi	.05
40	John Candelaria	.05
41	Joe Orsulak	.05
42	Willie Upshaw	.05
43	Herm Winningham	.05
44	Ron Kittle	.05
45	Bob Dernier	.05
46	Steve Balboni	.05
47	Steve Shields	.05
48	Henry Cotto	.05
49	Dave Henderson	.05
50	Dave Parker	.05
51	Mike Young	.05
52	Mark Salas	.05
53	Mike Davis	.05
54	Rafael Santana	.05
55	Don Baylor	.05
56	Dan Pasqua	.05
57	Ernest Riles	.05
58	Glenn Hubbard	.05
59	Mike Smithson	.05
60	Richard Dotson	.05
61	Jerry Reuss	.05
62	Mike Jackson	.05
63	Floyd Bannister	.05
64	Jesse Orosco	.05
65	Larry Parrish	.05
66	Jeff Bittiger	.05
67	Ray Hayward	.05
68	Ricky Jordan **RC**	.05
69	Tommy Gregg	.05
70	Brady Anderson **RC**	.50
71	Jeff Montgomery	.05
72	Darryl Hamilton	.05
73	Cecil Espy	.05
74	Greg Briley	.05
75	Joey Meyer	.05
76	Mike Macfarlane **RC**	.05
77	Oswald Peraza	.05
78	Jack Armstrong	.05

79	Don Heinkel	.05
80	Mark Grace **RC**	1.50
81	Steve Curry	.05
82	Damon Berryhill	.05
83	Steve Ellsworth	.05
84	Pete Smith	.05
85	Jack McDowell **RC**	.25
86	Rob Dibble	.05
87	Bryan Harvey	.05
88	John Dopson	.05
89	Dave Gallagher	.05
90	Todd Stottlemyre **RC**	.25
91	Mike Schooler	.05
92	Don Gordon	.05
93	Sil Campusano	.05
94	Jeff Pico	.05
95	Jay Buhner **RC**	.75
96	Nelson Santovenia	.05
97	Al Leiter	.05
98	Luis Alicea	.05
99	Pat Borders	.05
100	Chris Sabo **RC**	.25
101	Tim Belcher	.05
102	Walt Weiss	.05
103	Craig Biggio **RC**	6.00
104	Don August	.05
105	Roberto Alomar **RC**	4.00
106	Todd Burns	.05
107	John Costello	.05
108	Melido Perez	.05
109	Darrin Jackson	.05
110	Orestes Destrade	.05

Traded/ Rookie Glossy

	NM/M
Complete Set (110):	60.00
Common Player:	.25
Stars:	3X

(See 1988 Score Traded/ Rookie for checklist and base card values.)

1989 Score

		NM/M
Unopened Fact. Set (660):		12.00
Complete Set (660):		9.00
Common Player:		.05
Pack (16):		.50
Wax Box (36):		10.00
1	Jose Canseco	.25
2	Andre Dawson	.25
3	Mark McGwire	.65
4	Benny Santiago	.05
5	Rick Reuschel	.05
6	Fred McGriff	.05
7	Kal Daniels	.05
8	Gary Gaetti	.05
9	Ellis Burks	.05
10	Darryl Strawberry	.05
11	Julio Franco	.05
12	Lloyd Moseby	.05
13	Jeff Pico **RC**	.05
14	Johnny Ray	.05
15	Cal Ripken, Jr.	.75
16	Dick Schofield	.05
17	Mel Hall	.05
18	Bill Ripken	.05
19	Brook Jacoby	.05
20	Kirby Puckett	.50
21	Bill Doran	.05
22	Pete O'Brien	.05
23	Matt Nokes	.05
24	Brian Fisher	.05
25	Jack Clark	.05
26	Gary Pettis	.05
27	Dave Valle	.05
28	Willie Wilson	.05
29	Curt Young	.05
30	Dale Murphy	.20
31	Barry Larkin	.05
32	Dave Stewart	.05
33	Mike LaValliere	.05

No.	Player	Price
34	Glenn Hubbard	.05
35	Ryne Sandberg	.50
36	Tony Pena	.05
37	Greg Walker	.05
38	Von Hayes	.05
39	Kevin Mitchell	.05
40	Tim Raines	.05
41	Keith Hernandez	.05
42	Keith Moreland	.05
43	Ruben Sierra	.05
44	Chet Lemon	.05
45	Willie Randolph	.05
46	Andy Allanson	.05
47	Candy Maldonado	.05
48	Sid Bream	.05
49	Denny Walling	.05
50	Dave Winfield	.40
51	Alvin Davis	.05
52	Cory Snyder	.05
53	Hubie Brooks	.05
54	Chili Davis	.05
55	Kevin Seitzer	.05
56	Jose Uribe	.05
57	Tony Fernandez	.05
58	Tim Teufel	.05
59	Oddibe McDowell	.05
60	Les Lancaster	.05
61	Billy Hatcher	.05
62	Dan Gladden	.05
63	Marty Barrett	.05
64	Nick Esasky	.05
65	Wally Joyner	.05
66	Mike Greenwell	.05
67	Ken Williams	.05
68	Bob Horner	.05
69	Steve Sax	.05
70	Rickey Henderson	.40
71	Mitch Webster	.05
72	Rob Deer	.05
73	Jim Presley	.05
74	Albert Hall	.05
75a	George Brett ("At age 33 ...")	1.00
75b	George Brett ("At age 35 ...")	.50
76	Brian Downing	.05
77	Dave Martinez	.05
78	Scott Fletcher	.05
79	Phil Bradley	.05
80	Ozzie Smith	.50
81	Larry Sheets	.05
82	Mike Aldrete	.05
83	Darnell Coles	.05
84	Len Dykstra	.05
85	Jim Rice	.15
86	Jeff Treadway	.05
87	Jose Lind	.05
88	Willie McGee	.05
89	Mickey Brantley	.05
90	Tony Gwynn	.50
91	R.J. Reynolds	.05
92	Milt Thompson	.05
93	Kevin McReynolds	.05
94	Eddie Murray	.40
95	Lance Parrish	.05
96	Ron Kittle	.05
97	Gerald Young	.05
98	Ernie Whitt	.05
99	Jeff Reed	.05
100	Don Mattingly	.60
101	Gerald Perry	.05
102	Vance Law	.05
103	John Shelby	.05
104	Chris Sabo	.05
105	Danny Tartabull	.05
106	Glenn Wilson	.05
107	Mark Davidson	.05
108	Dave Parker	.05
109	Eric Davis	.05
110	Alan Trammell	.05
111	Ozzie Virgil	.05
112	Frank Tanana	.05
113	Rafael Ramirez	.05
114	Dennis Martinez	.05
115	Jose DeLeon	.05
116	Bob Ojeda	.05
117	Doug Drabek	.05
118	Andy Hawkins	.05
119	Greg Maddux	.50
120	Cecil Fielder (Reversed negative.)	.05
121	Mike Scioscia	.05
122	Dan Petry	.05
123	Terry Kennedy	.05
124	Kelly Downs	.05
125	Greg Gross	.05
126	Fred Lynn	.05
127	Barry Bonds	.75
128	Harold Baines	.05
129	Doyle Alexander	.05
130	Kevin Elster	.05
131	Mike Heath	.05
132	Teddy Higuera	.05
133	Charlie Leibrandt	.05
134	Tim Laudner	.05
135a	Ray Knight (Photo reversed.)	.40
135b	Ray Knight (Correct photo.)	.05
136	Howard Johnson	.05
137	Terry Pendleton	.05
138	Andy McGaffigan	.05
139	Ken Oberkfell	.05
140	Butch Wynegar	.05
141	Rob Murphy	.05
142	Rich Renteria RC	.05
143	Jose Guzman	.05
144	Andres Galarraga	.05
145	Rick Horton	.05
146	Frank DiPino	.05
147	Glenn Braggs	.05
148	John Kruk	.05
149	Mike Schmidt	.60
150	Lee Smith	.05
151	Robin Yount	.40
152	Mark Eichhorn	.05
153	DeWayne Buice	.05
154	B.J. Surhoff	.05
155	Vince Coleman	.05
156	Tony Phillips	.05
157	Willie Fraser	.05
158	Lance McCullers	.05
159	Greg Gagne	.05
160	Jesse Barfield	.05
161	Mark Langston	.05
162	Kurt Stillwell	.05
163	Dion James	.05
164	Glenn Davis	.05
165	Walt Weiss	.05
166	Dave Concepcion	.05
167	Alfredo Griffin	.05
168	Don Heinkel RC	.05
169	Luis Rivera	.05
170	Shane Rawley	.05
171	Darrell Evans	.05
172	Robby Thompson	.05
173	Jody Davis	.05
174	Andy Van Slyke	.05
175	Wade Boggs	.50
176	Garry Templeton	.05
177	Gary Redus	.05
178	Craig Lefferts	.05
179	Carney Lansford	.05
180	Ron Darling	.05
181	Kirk McCaskill	.05
182	Tony Armas	.05
183	Steve Farr	.05
184	Tom Brunansky	.05
185	Bryan Harvey RC	.05
186	Mike Marshall	.05
187	Bo Diaz	.05
188	Willie Upshaw	.05
189	Mike Pagliarulo	.05
190	Mike Krukow	.05
191	Tommy Herr	.05
192	Jim Pankovits	.05
193	Dwight Evans	.05
194	Kelly Gruber	.05
195	Bobby Bonilla	.05
196	Wallace Johnson	.05
197	Dave Stieb	.05
198	Pat Borders RC	.05
199	Rafael Palmeiro	.35
200	Dwight Gooden	.05
201	Pete Incaviglia	.05
202	Chris James	.05
203	Marvell Wynne	.05
204	Pat Sheridan	.05
205	Don Baylor	.05
206	Paul O'Neill	.05
207	Pete Smith	.05
208	Mark McLemore	.05
209	Henry Cotto	.05
210	Kirk Gibson	.05
211	Claudell Washington	.05
212	Randy Bush	.05
213	Joe Carter	.05
214	Bill Buckner	.05
215	Bert Blyleven	.05
216	Brett Butler	.05
217	Lee Mazzilli	.05
218	Spike Owen	.05
219	Bill Swift	.05
220	Tim Wallach	.05
221	David Cone	.05
222	Don Carman	.05
223	Rich Gossage	.05
224	Bob Walk	.05
225	Dave Righetti	.05
226	Kevin Bass	.05
227	Kevin Gross	.05
228	Tim Burke	.05
229	Rick Mahler	.05
230	Lou Whitaker	.05
231	Luis Alicea RC	.05
232	Roberto Alomar	.25
233	Bob Boone	.05
234	Dickie Thon	.05
235	Shawon Dunston	.05
236	Pete Stanicek	.05
237	Craig Biggio	.05
238	Dennis Boyd	.05
239	Tom Candiotti	.05
240	Gary Carter	.40
241	Mike Stanley	.05
242	Ken Phelps	.05
243	Chris Bosio	.05
244	Les Straker	.05
245	Dave Smith	.05
246	John Candelaria	.05
247	Joe Orsulak	.05
248	Storm Davis	.05
249	Floyd Bannister	.05
250	Jack Morris	.05
251	Bret Saberhagen	.05
252	Tom Niedenfuer	.05
253	Neal Heaton	.05
254	Eric Show	.05
255	Juan Samuel	.05
256	Dale Sveum	.05
257	Jim Gott	.05
258	Scott Garrelts	.05
259	Larry McWilliams	.05
260	Steve Bedrosian	.05
261	Jack Howell	.05
262	Jay Tibbs	.05
263	Jamie Moyer	.05
264	Doug Sisk	.05
265	Todd Worrell	.05
266	John Farrell	.05
267	Dave Collins	.05
268	Sid Fernandez	.05
269	Tom Brookens	.05
270	Shane Mack	.05
271	Paul Kilgus	.05
272	Chuck Crim	.05
273	Bob Knepper	.05
274	Mike Moore	.05
275	Guillermo Hernandez	.05
276	Dennis Eckersley	.35
277	Graig Nettles	.05
278	Rich Dotson	.05
279	Larry Herndon	.05
280	Gene Larkin	.05
281	Roger McDowell	.05
282	Greg Swindell	.05
283	Juan Agosto	.05
284	Jeff Robinson	.05
285	Mike Dunne	.05
286	Greg Mathews	.05
287	Kent Tekulve	.05
288	Jerry Mumphrey	.05
289	Jack McDowell	.05
290	Frank Viola	.05
291	Mark Gubicza	.05
292	Dave Schmidt	.05
293	Mike Henneman	.05
294	Jimmy Jones	.05
295	Charlie Hough	.05
296	Rafael Santana	.05
297	Chris Speier	.05
298	Mike Witt	.05
299	Pascual Perez	.05
300	Nolan Ryan	.75
301	Mitch Williams	.05
302	Mookie Wilson	.05
303	Mackey Sasser	.05
304	John Cerutti	.05
305	Jeff Reardon	.05
306	Randy Myers	.05
307	Greg Brock	.05
308	Bob Welch	.05
309	Jeff Robinson	.05
310	Harold Reynolds	.05
311	Jim Walewander	.05
312	Dave Magadan	.05
313	Jim Gantner	.05
314	Walt Terrell	.05
315	Wally Backman	.05
316	Luis Salazar	.05
317	Rick Rhoden	.05
318	Tom Henke	.05
319	Mike Macfarlane	.05
320	Dan Plesac	.05
321	Carlton Schiraldi	.05
322	Stan Javier	.05
323	Devon White	.05
324	Scott Bradley	.05
325	Bruce Hurst	.05
326	Manny Lee	.05
327	Rick Aguilera	.05
328	Bruce Ruffin	.05
329	Ed Whitson	.05
330	Bo Jackson	.10
331	Ivan Calderon	.05
332	Mickey Hatcher	.05
333	Barry Jones	.05
334	Ron Hassey	.05
335	Bill Wegman	.05
336	Damon Berryhill	.05
337	Steve Ontiveros	.05
338	Dan Pasqua	.05
339	Bill Pecota	.05
340	Greg Cadaret	.05
341	Scott Bankhead	.05
342	Ron Guidry	.10
343	Danny Heep	.05
344	Bob Brower	.05
345	Rich Gedman	.05
346	Nelson Santovenia RC	.05
347	George Bell	.05
348	Ted Power	.05
349	Mark Grant	.05
350a	Roger Clemens (778 Wins)	2.00
350b	Roger Clemens (78 Wins)	.60
351	Bill Long	.05
352	Jay Bell	.05
353	Steve Balboni	.05
354	Bob Kipper	.05
355	Steve Jeltz	.05
356	Jesse Orosco	.05
357	Bob Dernier	.05
358	Mickey Tettleton	.05
359	Duane Ward	.05
360	Darrin Jackson	.05
361	Rey Quinones	.05
362	Mark Grace	.05
363	Steve Lake	.05
364	Pat Perry	.05
365	Terry Steinbach	.05
366	Alan Ashby	.05
367	Jeff Montgomery	.05
368	Steve Buechele	.05
369	Chris Brown	.05
370	Orel Hershiser	.05
371	Todd Benzinger	.05
372	Ron Gant	.05
373	Paul Assenmacher	.05
374	Joey Meyer	.05
375	Neil Allen	.05
376	Mike Davis	.05
377	Jeff Parrett	.05
378	Jay Howell	.05
379	Rafael Belliard	.05
380	Luis Polonia	.05
381	Keith Atherton	.05
382	Kent Hrbek	.05
383	Bob Stanley	.05
384	Dave LaPoint	.05
385	Rance Mulliniks	.05
386	Melido Perez	.05
387	Doug Jones	.05
388	Steve Lyons	.05
389	Alejandro Pena	.05
390	Frank White	.05
391	Pat Tabler	.05
392	Eric Plunk	.05
393	Mike Maddux	.05
394	Allan Anderson	.05
395	Bob Brenly	.05
396	Rick Cerone	.05
397	Scott Terry	.05
398	Mike Jackson	.05
399	Bobby Thigpen	.05
400	Don Sutton	.35
401	Cecil Espy	.05
402	Junior Ortiz	.05
403	Mike Smithson	.05
404	Bud Black	.05
405	Tom Foley	.05
406	Andres Thomas	.05
407	Rick Sutcliffe	.05
408	Brian Harper	.05
409	John Smiley	.05
410	Juan Nieves	.05
411	Shawn Abner	.05
412	Wes Gardner	.05
413	Darren Daulton	.05
414	Juan Berenguer	.05
415	Charles Hudson	.05
416	Rick Honeycutt	.05
417	Greg Booker	.05
418	Tim Belcher	.05
419	Don August	.05
420	Dale Mohorcic	.05
421	Steve Lombardozzi	.05
422	Atlee Hammaker	.05
423	Jerry Don Gleaton	.05
424	Scott Bailes	.05
425	Bruce Sutter	.40
426	Randy Ready	.05
427	Jerry Reed	.05
428	Bryn Smith	.05
429	Tim Leary	.05
430	Mark Clear	.05
431	Terry Leach	.05
432	John Moses	.05
433	Ozzie Guillen	.05
434	Gene Nelson	.05
435	Gary Ward	.05
436	Luis Aguayo	.05
437	Fernando Valenzuela	.05
438	Jeff Russell	.05
439	Cecilio Guante	.05

No.	Player	Price
440	Don Robinson	.05
441	Rick Anderson	.05
442	Tom Glavine	.35
443	Daryl Boston	.05
444	Joe Price	.05
445	Stewart Cliburn	.05
446	Manny Trillo	.05
447	Joel Skinner	.05
448	Charlie Puleo	.05
449	Carlton Fisk	.40
450	Will Clark	.05
451	Otis Nixon	.05
452	Rick Schu	.05
453	Todd Stottlemyre	.05
454	Tim Birtsas	.05
455	Dave Gallagher RC	.05
456	Barry Lyons	.05
457	Fred Manrique	.05
458	Ernest Riles	.05
459	Doug Jennings RC	.05
460	Joe Magrane	.05
461	Jamie Quirk	.05
462	Jack Armstrong RC	.05
463	Bobby Witt	.05
464	Keith Miller	.05
465	Todd Burns RC	.05
466	John Dopson RC	.05
467	Rich Yett	.05
468	Craig Reynolds	.05
469	Dave Bergman	.05
470	Rex Hudler	.05
471	Eric King	.05
472	Joaquin Andujar	.05
473	Sil Campusano RC	.05
474	Terry Mulholland	.05
475	Mike Flanagan	.05
476	Greg Harris	.05
477	Tommy John	.10
478	Dave Anderson	.05
479	Fred Toliver	.05
480	Jimmy Key	.05
481	Donell Nixon	.05
482	Mark Portugal	.05
483	Tom Pagnozzi	.05
484	Jeff Kunkel	.05
485	Frank Williams	.05
486	Jody Reed	.05
487	Roberto Kelly	.05
488	Shawn Hillegas	.05
489	Jerry Reuss	.05
490	Mark Davis	.05
491	Jeff Sellers	.05
492	Zane Smith	.05
493	Al Newman	.05
494	Mike Young	.05
495	Larry Parrish	.05
496	Herm Winningham	.05
497	Carmen Castillo	.05
498	Joe Hesketh	.05
499	Darrell Miller	.05
500	Mike LaCoss	.05
501	Charlie Lea	.05
502	Bruce Benedict	.05
503	Chuck Finley	.05
504	Brad Wellman	.05
505	Tim Crews	.05
506	Ken Gerhart	.05
507a	Brian Holton (Born: 1/25/65, Denver.)	.15
507b	Brian Holton (Born: 11/29/59, McKeesport.)	.05
508	Dennis Lamp	.05
509	Bobby Meacham	.05
510	Tracy Jones	.05
511	Mike Fitzgerald	.05
512	Jeff Bittiger RC	.05
513	Tim Flannery	.05
514	Ray Hayward	.05
515	Dave Leiper	.05
516	Rod Scurry	.05
517	Carmelo Martinez	.05
518	Curtis Wilkerson	.05
519	Stan Jefferson	.05
520	Dan Quisenberry	.05
521	Lloyd McClendon	.05
522	Steve Trout	.05
523	Larry Andersen	.05
524	Don Aase	.05
525	Bob Forsch	.05
526	Geno Petralli	.05
527	Angel Salazar	.05
528	Mike Schooler RC	.05
529	Jose Oquendo	.05
530	Jay Buhner	.05
531	Tom Bolton	.05
532	Al Nipper	.05
533	Dave Henderson	.05
534	John Costello RC	.05
535	Donnie Moore	.05
536	Mike Laga	.05
537	Mike Gallego	.05
538	Jim Clancy	.05
539	Joel Youngblood	.05
540	Rick Leach	.05
541	Kevin Romine	.05
542	Mark Salas	.05
543	Greg Minton	.05
544	Dave Palmer	.05
545	Dwayne Murphy	.05
546	Jim Deshaies	.05
547	Don Gordon	.05
548	Ricky Jordan	.05
549	Mike Boddicker	.05
550	Mike Scott	.05
551	Jeff Ballard	.05
552a	Jose Rijo (Uniform number #24 on card back.)	.15
552b	Jose Rijo (Uniform number #27 on card back.)	.10
553	Danny Darwin	.05
554	Tom Browning	.05
555	Danny Jackson	.05
556	Rick Dempsey	.05
557	Jeffrey Leonard	.05
558	Jeff Musselman	.05
559	Ron Robinson	.05
560	John Tudor	.05
561	Don Slaught	.05
562	Dennis Rasmussen	.05
563	Brady Anderson	.05
564	Pedro Guerrero	.05
565	Paul Molitor	.40
566	Terry Clark RC	.05
567	Terry Puhl	.05
568	Mike Campbell	.05
569	Paul Mirabella	.05
570	Jeff Hamilton	.05
571	Oswald Peraza RC	.05
572	Bob McClure	.05
573	Jose Bautista RC	.05
574	Alex Trevino	.05
575	John Franco	.05
576	Mark Parent RC	.05
577	Nelson Liriano	.05
578	Steve Shields	.05
579	Odell Jones	.05
580	Al Leiter	.05
581	Dave Stapleton	.05
582	Jose Canseco, Kirk Gibson, Orel Hershiser, Dave Stewart 1988 World Series	.10
583	Donnie Hill	.05
584	Chuck Jackson	.05
585	Rene Gonzales	.05
586	Tracy Woodson	.05
587	Jim Adduci	.05
588	Mario Soto	.05
589	Jeff Blauser	.05
590	Jim Traber	.05
591	Jon Perlman	.05
592	Mark Williamson	.05
593	Dave Meads	.05
594	Jim Eisenreich	.05
595a	Paul Gibson RC (Player in background adjusting cup.)	.25
595b	Paul Gibson RC (Hand airbrushed away.)	.05
596	Mike Birkbeck	.05
597	Terry Francona	.05
598	Paul Zuvella (RC)	.05
599	Franklin Stubbs	.05
600	Gregg Jefferies	.05
601	John Cangelosi	.05
602	Mike Sharperson	.05
603	Mike Diaz	.05
604	Gary Varsho RC	.05
605	Terry Blocker RC	.05
606	Charlie O'Brien	.05
607	Jim Eppard	.05
608	John Davis	.05
609	Ken Griffey Sr.	.05
610	Buddy Bell	.05
611	Ted Simmons	.05
612	Matt Williams	.05
613	Danny Cox	.05
614	Al Pedrique	.05
615	Ron Oester	.05
616	John Smoltz	.05
617	Bob Melvin	.05
618	Rob Dibble RC	.10
619	Kirt Manwaring	.05
620	Felix Fermin	.05
621	Doug Dascenzo RC	.05
622	Bill Brennan RC	.05
623	Carlos Quintana RC	.05
624	Mike Harkey RC	.05
625	Gary Sheffield RC	1.25
626	Tom Prince RC	.05
627	Steve Searcy RC	.05
628	Charlie Hayes RC	.05
629	Felix Jose RC	.05
630	Sandy Alomar RC	.50
631	Derek Lilliquist RC	.05
632	Geronimo Berroa RC	.05
633	Luis Medina RC	.05
634	Tom Gordon RC	.10
635	Ramon Martinez RC	.25
636	Craig Worthington RC	.05
637	Edgar Martinez	.05
638	Chad Krueter RC	.05
639	Ron Jones RC	.05
640	Van Snider RC	.05
641	Lance Blankenship RC	.05
642	Dwight Smith RC	.05
643	Cameron Drew RC	.05
644	Jerald Clark RC	.05
645	Randy Johnson RC	2.00
646	Norm Charlton RC	.05
647	Todd Frohwirth	.05
648	Luis de los Santos RC	.05
649	Tim Jones RC	.05
650	Dave West RC	.05
651	Bob Milacki RC	.05
652	1988 Highlight (Wrigley Field)	.05
653	Orel Hershiser 1988 Highlight	.05
654a	Wade Boggs 1988 Highlight ("...sixth consecutive seaason..." on back)	2.00
654b	Wade Boggs 1988 Highlight ("Season" corrected.)	.10
655	Jose Canseco 1988 Highlight	.15
656	Doug Jones 1988 Highlight	.05
657	Rickey Henderson 1988 Highlight	.10
658	Tom Browning 1988 Highlight	.05
659	Mike Greenwell 1988 Highlight	.05
660	Joe Morgan 1988 Highlight (A.L. Win Streak)	.05

Rookie/Traded

	NM/M
Complete Set (110):	10.00
Common Player:	.05

No.	Player	Price
1	Rafael Palmeiro	.35
2	Nolan Ryan	1.00
3	Jack Clark	.05
4	Dave LaPoint	.05
5	Mike Moore	.05
6	Pete O'Brien	.05
7	Jeffrey Leonard	.05
8	Rob Murphy	.05
9	Tom Herr	.05
10	Claudell Washington	.05
11	Mike Pagliarulo	.05
12	Steve Lake	.05
13	Spike Owen	.05
14	Andy Hawkins	.05
15	Todd Benzinger	.05
16	Mookie Wilson	.05
17	Bert Blyleven	.05
18	Jeff Treadway	.05
19	Bruce Hurst	.05
20	Steve Sax	.05
21	Juan Samuel	.05
22	Jesse Barfield	.05
23	Carmelo Castillo	.05
24	Terry Leach	.05
25	Mark Langston	.05
26	Eric King	.05
27	Steve Balboni	.05
28	Len Dykstra	.05
29	Keith Moreland	.05
30	Terry Kennedy	.05
31	Eddie Murray	.45
32	Mitch Williams	.05
33	Jeff Parrett	.05
34	Wally Backman	.05
35	Julio Franco	.05
36	Lance Parrish	.05
37	Nick Esasky	.05
38	Luis Polonia	.05
39	Kevin Gross	.05
40	John Dopson	.05
41	Willie Randolph	.05
42	Jim Clancy	.05
43	Tracy Jones	.05
44	Phil Bradley	.05
45	Milt Thompson	.05
46	Chris James	.05
47	Scott Fletcher	.05
48	Kal Daniels	.05
49	Steve Bedrosian	.05
50	Rickey Henderson	.45
51	Dion James	.05
52	Tim Leary	.05
53	Roger McDowell	.05
54	Mel Hall	.05
55	Dickie Thon	.05
56	Zane Smith	.05
57	Danny Heep	.05
58	Bob McClure	.05
59	Brian Holton	.05
60	Randy Ready	.05
61	Bob Melvin	.05
62	Harold Baines	.05
63	Lance McCullers	.05
64	Jody Davis	.05
65	Darrell Evans	.05
66	Joel Youngblood	.05
67	Frank Viola	.05
68	Mike Aldrete	.05
69	Greg Cadaret	.05
70	John Kruk	.05
71	Pat Sheridan	.05
72	Oddibe McDowell	.05
73	Tom Brookens	.05
74	Bob Boone	.05
75	Walt Terrell	.05
76	Joel Skinner	.05
77	Randy Johnson	1.50
78	Felix Fermin	.05
79	Rick Mahler	.05
80	Rich Dotson	.05
81	Cris Carpenter	.05
82	Bill Spiers	.05
83	Junior Felix	.05
84	Joe Girardi	.05
85	Jerome Walton	.05
86	Greg Litton	.05
87	Greg Harris	.05
88	Jim Abbott	.05
89	Kevin Brown	.05
90	John Wetteland RC	.10
91	Gary Wayne	.05
92	Rich Monteleone	.05
93	Bob Geren	.05
94	Clay Parker	.05
95	Steve Finley	.05
96	Gregg Olson	.05
97	Ken Patterson	.05
98	Ken Hill	.05
99	Scott Scudder	.05
100	Ken Griffey Jr. RC	6.00
101	Jeff Brantley	.05
102	Donn Pall	.05
103	Carlos Martinez	.05
104	Joe Oliver	.05
105	Omar Vizquel	.25
106	Albert Belle RC	1.00
107	Kenny Rogers RC	.10
108	Mark Carreon	.05
109	Rolando Roomes	.05
110	Pete Harnisch	.05

1990 Score

	NM/M
Hobby Factory Set (714):	8.00
Retail Factory Set (704):	7.00
Complete Set (704):	6.00
Common Player:	.05
Plastic Pack (16):	.40
Plastic Wax Box (36):	9.00
1 Don Mattingly	.50
2 Cal Ripken, Jr.	1.00

No.	Player	Value
3	Dwight Evans	.05
4	Barry Bonds	1.00
5	Kevin McReynolds	.05
6	Ozzie Guillen	.05
7	Terry Kennedy	.05
8	Bryan Harvey	.05
9	Alan Trammell	.05
10	Cory Snyder	.05
11	Jody Reed	.05
12	Roberto Alomar	.20
13	Pedro Guerrero	.05
14	Gary Redus	.05
15	Marty Barrett	.05
16	Ricky Jordan	.05
17	Joe Magrane	.05
18	Sid Fernandez	.05
19	Rich Dotson	.05
20	Jack Clark	.05
21	Bob Walk	.05
22	Ron Karkovice	.05
23	Lenny Harris	.05
24	Phil Bradley	.05
25	Andres Galarraga	.05
26	Brian Downing	.05
27	Dave Martinez	.05
28	Eric King	.05
29	Barry Lyons	.05
30	Dave Schmidt	.05
31	Mike Boddicker	.05
32	Tom Foley	.05
33	Brady Anderson	.05
34	Jim Presley	.05
35	Lance Parrish	.05
36	Von Hayes	.05
37	Lee Smith	.05
38	Herm Winningham	.05
39	Alejandro Pena	.05
40	Mike Scott	.05
41	Joe Orsulak	.05
42	Rafael Ramirez	.05
43	Gerald Young	.05
44	Dick Schofield	.05
45	Dave Smith	.05
46	Dave Magadan	.05
47	Dennis Martinez	.05
48	Greg Minton	.05
49	Milt Thompson	.05
50	Orel Hershiser	.05
51	Bip Roberts	.05
52	Jerry Browne	.05
53	Bob Ojeda	.05
54	Fernando Valenzuela	.05
55	Matt Nokes	.05
56	Brook Jacoby	.05
57	Frank Tanana	.05
58	Scott Fletcher	.05
59	Ron Oester	.05
60	Bob Boone	.05
61	Dan Gladden	.05
62	Darnell Coles	.05
63	Gregg Olson	.05
64	Todd Burns	.05
65	Todd Benzinger	.05
66	Dale Murphy	.25
67	Mike Flanagan	.05
68	Jose Oquendo	.05
69	Cecil Espy	.05
70	Chris Sabo	.05
71	Shane Rawley	.05
72	Tom Brunansky	.05
73	Vance Law	.05
74	B.J. Surhoff	.05
75	Lou Whitaker	.05
76	Ken Caminiti	.05
77	Nelson Liriano	.05
78	Tommy Gregg	.05
79	Don Slaught	.05
80	Eddie Murray	.40
81	Joe Boever	.05
82	Charlie Leibrandt	.05
83	Jose Lind	.05
84	Tony Phillips	.05
85	Mitch Webster	.05
86	Dan Plesac	.05
87	Rick Mahler	.05
88	Steve Lyons	.05
89	Tony Fernandez	.05
90	Ryne Sandberg	.45
91	Nick Esasky	.05
92	Luis Salazar	.05
93	Pete Incaviglia	.05
94	Ivan Calderon	.05
95	Jeff Treadway	.05
96	Kurt Stillwell	.05
97	Gary Sheffield	.30
98	Jeffrey Leonard	.05
99	Andres Thomas	.05
100	Roberto Kelly	.05
101	Alvaro Espinoza	.05
102	Greg Gagne	.05
103	John Farrell	.05
104	Willie Wilson	.05
105	Glenn Braggs	.05
106	Chet Lemon	.05
107	Jamie Moyer	.05
108	Chuck Crim	.05
109	Dave Valle	.05
110	Walt Weiss	.05
111	Larry Sheets	.05
112	Don Robinson	.05
113	Danny Heep	.05
114	Carmelo Martinez	.05
115	Dave Gallagher	.05
116	Mike LaValliere	.05
117	Bob McClure	.05
118	Rene Gonzales	.05
119	Mark Parent	.05
120	Wally Joyner	.05
121	Mark Gubicza	.05
122	Tony Pena	.05
123	Carmen Castillo	.05
124	Howard Johnson	.05
125	Steve Sax	.05
126	Tim Belcher	.05
127	Tim Burke	.05
128	Al Newman	.05
129	Dennis Rasmussen	.05
130	Doug Jones	.05
131	Fred Lynn	.05
132	Jeff Hamilton	.05
133	German Gonzalez	.05
134	John Morris	.05
135	Dave Parker	.05
136	Gary Pettis	.05
137	Dennis Boyd	.05
138	Candy Maldonado	.05
139	Rick Cerone	.05
140	George Brett	.50
141	Dave Clark	.05
142	Dickie Thon	.05
143	Junior Ortiz	.05
144	Don August	.05
145	Gary Gaetti	.05
146	Kirt Manwaring	.05
147	Jeff Reed	.05
148	Jose Alvarez	.05
149	Mike Schooler	.05
150	Mark Grace	.05
151	Geronimo Berroa	.05
152	Barry Jones	.05
153	Geno Petralli	.05
154	Jim Deshaies	.05
155	Barry Larkin	.05
156	Alfredo Griffin	.05
157	Tom Henke	.05
158	Mike Jeffcoat	.05
159	Bob Welch	.05
160	Julio Franco	.05
161	Henry Cotto	.05
162	Terry Steinbach	.05
163	Damon Berryhill	.05
164	Tim Crews	.05
165	Tom Browning	.05
166	Frd Manrique	.05
167	Harold Reynolds	.05
168a	Ron Hassey (Uniform #27 on back.)	.05
168b	Ron Hassey (Uniform #24 on back.)	.50
169	Shawon Dunston	.05
170	Bobby Bonilla	.05
171	Tom Herr	.05
172	Mike Heath	.05
173	Rich Gedman	.05
174	Bill Ripken	.05
175	Pete O'Brien	.05
176a	Lloyd McClendon (Uniform number 1 on back.)	.50
176b	Lloyd McClendon (Uniform number 10 on back.)	.05
177	Brian Holton	.05
178	Jeff Blauser	.05
179	Jim Eisenreich	.05
180	Bert Blyleven	.05
181	Rob Murphy	.05
182	Bill Doran	.05
183	Curt Ford	.05
184	Mike Henneman	.05
185	Eric Davis	.05
186	Lance McCullers	.05
187	Steve Davis RC	.05
188	Bill Wegman	.05
189	Brian Harper	.05
190	Mike Moore	.05
191	Dale Mohorcic	.05
192	Tim Wallach	.05
193	Keith Hernandez	.05
194	Dave Righetti	.05
195a	Bret Saberhagen ("Joke" on card back.)	.10
195b	Bret Saberhagen ("Joker" on card back.)	.30
196	Paul Kilgus	.05
197	Bud Black	.05
198	Juan Samuel	.05
199	Ken Seitzer	.05
200	Darryl Strawberry	.05
201	Dave Steib	.05
202	Charlie Hough	.05
203	Jack Morris	.05
204	Rance Mulliniks	.05
205	Alvin Davis	.05
206	Jack Howell	.05
207	Ken Patterson	.05
208	Terry Pendleton	.05
209	Craig Lefferts	.05
210	Kevin Brown	.05
211	Dan Petry	.05
212	Dave Leiper	.05
213	Daryl Boston	.05
214	Kevin Hickey	.05
215	Mike Krukow	.05
216	Terry Francona	.05
217	Kirk McCaskill	.05
218	Scott Bailes	.05
219	Bob Forsch	.05
220	Mike Aldrete	.05
221	Steve Buechele	.05
222	Jesse Barfield	.05
223	Juan Berenguer	.05
224	Andy McGaffigan	.05
225	Pete Smith	.05
226	Mike Witt	.05
227	Jay Howell	.05
228	Scott Bradley	.05
229	Jerome Walton RC	.05
230	Greg Swindell	.05
231	Atlee Hammaker	.05
232a	Mike Devereaux (RF)	.05
232b	Mike Devereaux (CF)	2.00
233	Ken Hill	.05
234	Craig Worthington	.05
235	Scott Terry	.05
236	Brett Butler	.05
237	Doyle Alexander	.05
238	Dave Anderson	.05
239	Bob Milacki	.05
240	Dwight Smith	.05
241	Otis Nixon	.05
242	Pat Tabler	.05
243	Derek Lilliquist	.05
244	Danny Tartabull	.05
245	Wade Boggs	.45
246	Scott Garrelts	.05
247	Spike Owen	.05
248	Norm Charlton	.05
249	Gerald Perry	.05
250	Nolan Ryan	1.00
251	Kevin Gross	.05
252	Randy Milligan	.05
253	Mike LaCoss	.05
254	Dave Bergman	.05
255	Tony Gwynn	.45
256	Felix Fermin	.05
257	Greg Harris	.05
258	Junior Felix RC	.05
259	Mark Davis	.05
260	Vince Coleman	.05
261	Paul Gibson	.05
262	Mitch Williams	.05
263	Jeff Russell	.05
264	Omar Vizquel	.05
265	Andre Dawson	.25
266	Storm Davis	.05
267	Guillermo Hernandez	.05
268	Mike Felder	.05
269	Tom Candiotti	.05
270	Bruce Hurst	.05
271	Fred McGriff	.05
272	Glenn Davis	.05
273	John Franco	.05
274	Rich Yett	.05
275	Craig Biggio	.05
276	Gene Larkin	.05
277	Rob Dibble	.05
278	Randy Bush	.05
279	Kevin Bass	.05
280a	Jackson ("Watham" on back.)	.15
280b	Jackson ("Wathan" on back.)	.50
281	Wally Backman	.05
282	Larry Andersen	.05
283	Chris Bosio	.05
284	Juan Agosto	.05
285	Ozzie Smith	.45
286	George Bell	.05
287	Rex Hudler	.05
288	Pat Borders	.05
289	Danny Jackson	.05
290	Carlton Fisk	.40
291	Tracy Jones	.05
292	Allan Anderson	.05
293	Johnny Ray	.05
294	Lee Guetterman	.05
295	Paul O'Neill	.05
296	Carney Lansford	.05
297	Tom Brookens	.05
298	Claudell Washington	.05
299	Hubie Brooks	.05
300	Will Clark	.05
301	Kenny Rogers	.05
302	Darrell Evans	.05
303	Greg Briley	.05
304	Donn Pall	.05
305	Teddy Higuera	.05
306	Dan Pasqua	.05
307	Dave Winfield	.40
308	Dennis Powell	.05
309	Jose DeLeon	.05
310	Roger Clemens	.50
311	Melido Perez	.05
312	Devon White	.05
313	Dwight Gooden	.05
314	Carlos Martinez RC	.05
315	Dennis Eckersley	.35
316	Clay Parker	.05
317	Rick Honeycutt	.05
318	Tim Laudner	.05
319	Joe Carter	.05
320	Robin Yount	.40
321	Felix Jose	.05
322	Mickey Tettleton	.05
323	Mike Gallego	.05
324	Edgar Martinez	.05
325	Dave Henderson	.05
326	Chili Davis	.05
327	Steve Balboni	.05
328	Jody Davis	.05
329	Shawn Hillegas	.05
330	Jim Abbott	.05
331	John Dopson	.05
332	Mark Williamson	.05
333	Jeff Robinson	.05
334	John Smiley	.05
335	Bobby Thigpen	.05
336	Garry Templeton	.05
337	Marvell Wynne	.05
338a	Ken Griffey Sr. (Uniform #25 on card back.)	.05
338b	Ken Griffey Sr. (Uniform #30 on card back.)	1.00
339	Steve Finley	.05
340	Ellis Burks	.05
341	Frank Williams	.05
342	Mike Morgan	.05
343	Kevin Mitchell	.05
344	Joel Youngblood	.05
345	Mike Greenwell	.05
346	Glenn Wilson	.05
347	John Costello	.05
348	Wes Gardner	.05
349	Jeff Ballard	.05
350	Mark Thurmond	.05
351	Randy Myers	.05
352	Shawn Abner	.05
353	Jesse Orosco	.05
354	Greg Walker	.05
355	Pete Harnisch	.05
356	Steve Farr	.05
357	Dave LaPoint	.05
358	Willie Fraser	.05
359	Mickey Hatcher	.05
360	Rickey Henderson	.40
361	Mike Fitzgerald	.05
362	Bill Schroeder	.05
363	Mark Carreon	.05
364	Ron Jones	.05
365	Jeff Montgomery	.05
366	Bill Krueger	.05
367	John Cangelosi	.05
368	Jose Gonzalez	.05
369	Greg Hibbard RC	.05
370	John Smoltz	.05
371	Jeff Brantley RC	.05
372	Frank White	.05
373	Ed Whitson	.05
374	Willie McGee	.05
375	Jose Canseco	.30
376	Randy Ready	.05
377	Don Aase	.05
378	Tony Armas	.05
379	Steve Bedrosian	.05
380	Chuck Finley	.05
381	Kent Hrbek	.05
382	Jim Gantner	.05
383	Mel Hall	.05
384	Mike Marshall	.05
385	Mark McGwire	.75
386	Wayne Tolleson	.05
387	Brian Holton	.05
388	John Wetteland	.05
389	Darren Daulton	.05
390	Rob Deer	.05
391	John Moses	.05
392	Todd Worrell	.05
393	Chuck Cary	.05
394	Stan Javier	.05
395	Willie Randolph	.05
396	Bill Buckner	.05
397	Robby Thompson	.05
398	Mike Scioscia	.05
399	Lonnie Smith	.05
400	Kirby Puckett	.45
401	Mark Langston	.05
402	Danny Darwin	.05

403	Greg Maddux	.45
404	Lloyd Moseby	.05
405	Rafael Palmeiro	.35
406	Chad Kreuter	.05
407	Jimmy Key	.05
408	Tim Birtsas	.05
409	Tim Raines	.05
410	Dave Stewart	.05
411	Eric Yelding RC	.05
412	Kent Anderson RC	.05
413	Les Lancaster	.05
414	Rick Dempsey	.05
415	Randy Johnson	.40
416	Gary Carter	.40
417	Rolando Roomes	.05
418	Dan Schatzeder	.05
419	Bryn Smith	.05
420	Ruben Sierra	.05
421	Steve Jeltz	.05
422	Ken Oberkfell	.05
423	Sid Bream	.05
424	Jim Clancy	.05
425	Kelly Gruber	.05
426	Rick Leach	.05
427	Len Dykstra	.05
428	Jeff Pico	.05
429	John Cerutti	.05
430	David Cone	.05
431	Jeff Kunkel	.05
432	Luis Aquino	.05
433	Ernie Whitt	.05
434	Bo Diaz	.05
435	Steve Lake	.05
436	Pat Perry	.05
437	Mike Davis	.05
438	Cecilio Guante	.05
439	Duane Ward	.05
440	Andy Van Slyke	.05
441	Gene Nelson	.05
442	Luis Polonia	.05
443	Kevin Elster	.05
444	Keith Moreland	.05
445	Roger McDowell	.05
446	Ron Darling	.05
447	Ernest Riles	.05
448	Mookie Wilson	.05
449a	Bill Spiers RC (66 missing for year of birth)	.50
449b	Bill Spiers RC (1966 for birth year)	.05
450	Rick Sutcliffe	.05
451	Nelson Santovenia	.05
452	Andy Allanson	.05
453	Bob Melvin	.05
454	Benny Santiago	.05
455	Jose Uribe	.05
456	Bill Landrum	.05
457	Bobby Witt	.05
458	Kevin Romine	.05
459	Lee Mazzilli	.05
460	Paul Molitor	.40
461	Ramon Martinez	.05
462	Frank DiPino	.05
463	Walt Terrell	.05
464	Bob Geren RC	.05
465	Rick Reuchel	.05
466	Mark Grant	.05
467	John Kruk	.05
468	Gregg Jefferies	.05
469	R.J. Reynolds	.05
470	Harold Baines	.05
471	Dennis Lamp	.05
472	Tom Gordon	.05
473	Terry Puhl	.05
474	Curtis Wilkerson	.05
475	Dan Quisenberry	.05
476	Oddibe McDowell	.05
477a	Zane Smith (Career ERA 3.93.)	.50
477b	Zane Smith	.05
478	Franklin Stubbs	.05
479	Wallace Johnson	.05
480	Jay Tibbs	.05
481	Tom Glavine	.35
482	Manny Lee	.05
483	Joe Hesketh	.05
484	Mike Bielecki	.05
485	Greg Brock	.05
486	Pascual Perez	.05
487	Kirk Gibson	.05
488	Scott Sanderson	.05
489	Domingo Ramos	.05
490	Kal Daniels	.05
491a	David Wells (Reversed negative on back photo.)	1.50
491b	David Wells (Corrected)	.05
492	Jerry Reed	.05
493	Eric Show	.05
494	Mike Pagliarulo	.05
495	Ron Robinson	.05
496	Brad Komminsk	.05
497	Greg Litton RC	.05
498	Chris James	.05
499	Luis Quinones	.05
500	Frank Viola	.05
501	Tim Teufel	.05
502	Terry Leach	.05
503	Matt Williams	.05
504	Tim Leary	.05
505	Doug Drabek	.05
506	Mariano Duncan	.05
507	Charlie Hayes	.05
508	Albert Belle	.05
509	Pat Sheridan	.05
510	Mackey Sasser	.05
511	Jose Rijo	.05
512	Mike Smithson	.05
513	Gary Ward	.05
514	Dion James	.05
515	Jim Gott	.05
516	Drew Hall	.05
517	Doug Bair	.05
518	Scott Scudder RC	.05
519	Rick Aguilera	.05
520	Rafael Belliard	.05
521	Jay Buhner	.05
522	Jeff Reardon	.05
523	Steve Rosenberg	.05
524	Randy Velarde	.05
525	Jeff Musselman	.05
526	Bill Long	.05
527	Gary Wayne RC	.05
528	Dave Johnson RC	.05
529	Ron Kittle	.05
530	Erik Hanson	.05
531	Steve Wilson	.05
532	Joey Meyer	.05
533	Curt Young	.05
534	Kelly Downs	.05
535	Joe Girardi	.05
536	Lance Blankenship	.05
537	Greg Mathews	.05
538	Donell Nixon	.05
539	Mark Knudson	.05
540	Jeff Wetherby RC	.05
541	Darrin Jackson	.05
542	Terry Mulholland	.05
543	Eric Hetzel	.05
544	Rick Reed RC	.05
545	Dennis Cook	.05
546	Mike Jackson	.05
547	Brian Fisher	.05
548	Gene Harris RC	.05
549	Jeff King	.05
550	Dave Dravecky (Salute)	.05
551	Randy Kutcher	.05
552	Mark Portugal	.05
553	Jim Corsi RC	.05
554	Todd Stottlemyre	.05
555	Scott Bankhead	.05
556	Ken Dayley	.05
557	Rick Wrona RC	.10
558	Sammy Sosa RC	3.00
559	Keith Miller	.05
560	Ken Griffey Jr.	.65
561a	Ryne Sandberg (3B on front.)	2.00
561b	Ryne Sandberg (No position.)	.25
562	Billy Hatcher	.05
563	Jay Bell	.05
564	Jack Daugherty RC	.05
565	Rich Monteleone RC	.05
566	Bo Jackson (All-Star MVP)	.10
567	Tony Fossas RC	.05
568	Roy Smith RC	.05
569	Jaime Navarro RC	.05
570	Lance Johnson	.05
571	Mike Dyer RC	.05
572	Kevin Ritz RC	.05
573	Dave West	.05
574	Gary Mielke RC	.05
575	Scott Lusader	.05
576	Joe Oliver	.05
577	Sandy Alomar, Jr.	.05
578	Andy Benes	.05
579	Tim Jones	.05
580	Randy McCament RC	.05
581	Curt Schilling	.35
582	John Orton RC	.05
583a	Milt Cuyler RC (998 games)	1.00
583b	Milt Cuyler RC (98 games)	.05
584	Eric Anthony RC	.05
585	Greg Vaughn RC	.15
586	Deion Sanders RC	.50
587	Jose DeJesus	.05
588	Chip Hale RC	.05
589	John Olerud RC	.50
590	Steve Olin RC	.05
591	Marquis Grissom RC	.40
592	Moises Alou RC	.40
593	Mark Lemke	.05
594	Dean Palmer RC	.15
595	Robin Ventura	.05
596	Tino Martinez	.05
597	Mike Huff RC	.05
598	Scott Hemond RC	.05
599	Wally Whitehurst RC	.05
600	Todd Zeile RC	.15
601	Glenallen Hill	.05
602	Hal Morris	.05
603	Juan Bell	.05
604	Bobby Rose RC	.05
605	Matt Merullo RC	.05
606	Kevin Maas RC	.05
607	Randy Nosek RC	.05
608a	Billy Bates RC ("12 triples" mentioned in second-last line)	.05
608b	Billy Bates (Triples not mentioned.)	.75
609	Mike Stanton RC	.05
610	Goose Gozzo RC	.05
611	Charles Nagy RC	.40
612	Scott Coolbaugh RC	.10
613	Jose Vizcaino RC	.10
614	Greg Smith RC	.05
615	Jeff Huson RC	.05
616	Mickey Weston RC	.05
617	John Pawlowski RC	.05
618a	Joe Skalski RC (Uniform #27 on card back.)	.15
618b	Joe Skalski RC (Uniform #67 on card back.)	1.00
619	Bernie Williams RC	1.00
620	Shawn Holman RC	.05
621	Gary Eave RC	.05
622	Darrin Fletcher RC	.10
623	Pat Combs RC	.05
624	Mike Blowers RC	.05
625	Kevin Appier	.05
626	Pat Austin RC	.05
627	Kelly Mann RC	.05
628	Matt Kinzer RC	.05
629	Chris Hammond RC	.10
630	Dean Wilkins RC	.05
631	Larry Walker RC	.50
632	Blaine Beatty RC	.05
633a	Tom Barrett (Uniform #29 on card back.)	.05
633b	Tom Barrett (Uniform #14 on card back.)	1.00
634	Stan Belinda RC	.05
635	Tex Smith RC	.05
636	Hensley Meulens RC	.10
637	Juan Gonzalez RC	1.50
638	Lenny Webster RC	.10
639	Mark Gardner RC	.05
640	Tommy Greene RC	.05
641	Mike Hartley RC	.05
642	Phil Stephenson RC	.05
643	Kevin Mmahat RC	.05
644	Ed Whited RC	.05
645	Delino DeShields RC	.15
646	Kevin Blankenship	.05
647	Paul Sorrento RC	.05
648	Mike Roesler RC	.05
649	Jason Grimsley RC	.05
650	Dave Justice RC	1.00
651	Scott Cooper RC	.05
652	Dave Eiland	.05
653	Mike Munoz RC	.05
654	Jeff Fischer RC	.05
655	Terry Jorgenson RC	.05
656	George Canale RC	.05
657	Brian DuBois RC	.05
658	Carlos Quintana	.05
659	Luis de los Santos	.05
660	Jerald Clark	.05
661	Donald Harris RC	.05
662	Paul Coleman RC	.05
663	Frank Thomas RC	2.00
664	Brent Mayne RC	.10
665	Eddie Zosky RC	.05
666	Steve Hosey RC	.05
667	Scott Bryant RC	.05
668	Tom Goodwin RC	.10
669	Cal Eldred RC	.10
670	Earl Cunningham RC	.05
671	Alan Zinter RC	.05
672	Chuck Knoblauch RC	.40
672(a)	Chuck Knoblauch (3,000 autographed cards with a special hologram on back were inserted into 1992 rack packs)	10.00
673	Kyle Abbott RC	.10
674	Roger Salkeld RC	.05
675	Mo Vaughn RC	.50
676	Kiki Jones RC	.05
677	Tyler Houston RC	.10
678	Jeff Jackson RC	.05
679	Greg Gohr RC	.05
680	Ben McDonald RC	.15
681	Greg Blosser RC	.05
682	Willie Green RC (Greene)	.05
683	Wade Boggs	.25

684	Will Clark	.05
685	Tony Gwynn	.25
686	Rickey Henderson	.20
687	Bo Jackson	.15
688	Mark Langston	.05
689	Barry Larkin	.05
690	Kirby Puckett	.25
691	Ryne Sandberg	.25
692	Mike Scott	.05
693	Terry Steinbach	.05
694	Bobby Thigpen	.05
695	Mitch Williams	.05
696	Nolan Ryan	.40
697	Bo Jackson (FB/BB)	.25
698	Rickey Henderson (ALCS MVP)	.20
699	Will Clark (NLCS MVP)	.05
700	World Series Games 1-2	.05
701	Lights Out: Candlestick	.15
702	World Series Game 3	.05
703	World Series Wrap-up	.05
704	Wade Boggs	.25

Traded

		NM/M
Complete Set (110):		4.00
Common Player:		.05
1	Dave Winfield	.75
2	Kevin Bass	.05
3	Nick Esasky	.05
4	Mitch Webster	.05
5	Pascual Perez	.05
6	Gary Pettis	.05
7	Tony Pena	.05
8	Candy Maldonado	.05
9	Cecil Fielder	.05
10	Carmelo Martinez	.05
11	Mark Langston	.05
12	Dave Parker	.05
13	Don Slaught	.05
14	Tony Phillips	.05
15	John Franco	.05
16	Randy Myers	.05
17	Jeff Reardon	.05
18	Sandy Alomar, Jr.	.05
19	Joe Carter	.05
20	Fred Lynn	.05
21	Storm Davis	.05
22	Craig Lefferts	.05
23	Pete O'Brien	.05
24	Dennis Boyd	.05
25	Lloyd Moseby	.05
26	Mark Davis	.05
27	Tim Leary	.05
28	Gerald Perry	.05
29	Don Aase	.05
30	Ernie Whitt	.05
31	Dale Murphy	.35
32	Alejandro Pena	.05
33	Juan Samuel	.05
34	Hubie Brooks	.05
35	Gary Carter	.75
36	Jim Presley	.05
37	Wally Backman	.05
38	Matt Nokes	.05
39	Dan Petry	.05
40	Franklin Stubbs	.05
41	Jeff Huson	.05
42	Billy Hatcher	.05
43	Terry Leach	.05
44	Phil Bradley	.05
45	Claudell Washington	.05
46	Luis Polonia	.05
47	Daryl Boston	.05
48	Lee Smith	.05
49	Tom Brunansky	.05
50	Mike Witt	.05
51	Willie Randolph	.05
52	Stan Javier	.05
53	Brad Komminsk	.05
54	John Candelaria	.05
55	Bryn Smith	.05

56	Glenn Braggs	.05
57	Keith Hernandez	.05
58	Ken Oberkfell	.05
59	Steve Jeltz	.05
60	Chris James	.05
61	Scott Sanderson	.05
62	Bill Long	.05
63	Rick Cerone	.05
64	Scott Bailes	.05
65	Larry Sheets	.05
66	Junior Ortiz	.05
67	Francisco Cabrera	.05
68	Gary DiSarcina	.05
69	Greg Olson	.05
70	Beau Allred	.05
71	Oscar Azocar	.05
72	Kent Mercker	.05
73	John Burkett	.05
74	Carlos Baerga	.05
75	Dave Hollins	.05
76	Todd Hundley RC	.25
77	Rick Parker	.05
78	Steve Cummings	.05
79	Bill Sampen	.05
80	Jerry Kutzler	.05
81	Derek Bell	.05
82	Kevin Tapani	.05
83	Jim Leyritz RC	.25
84	Ray Lankford RC	.25
85	Wayne Edwards	.05
86	Frank Thomas	2.00
87	Tim Naehring	.05
88	Willie Blair	.05
89	Alan Mills RC	.05
90	Scott Radinsky	.05
91	Howard Farmer	.05
92	Julio Machado	.05
93	Rafael Valdez	.05
94	Shawn Boskie RC	.05
95	David Segui	.05
96	Chris Hoiles	.05
97	D.J. Dozier	.05
98	Hector Villanueva	.05
99	Eric Gunderson	.05
100	Eric Lindros RC	1.00
101	Dave Otto	.05
102	Dana Kiecker	.05
103	Tim Drummond	.05
104	Mickey Pina	.05
105	Craig Grebeck	.05
106	Bernard Gilkey RC	.25
107	Tim Layana	.05
108	Scott Chiamparino	.05
109	Steve Avery	.05
110	Terry Shumpert	.05

1991 Score

	NM/M
Unopened Fact. Set (900):	10.00
Complete Set (893):	6.00
Common Player:	.05
Series 1 or 2 Pack (16):	.25
Series 1 or 2 Box (36):	6.00

1	Jose Canseco	.25
2	Ken Griffey Jr.	.60
3	Ryne Sandberg	.50
4	Nolan Ryan	.75
5	Bo Jackson	.10
6	Bret Saberhagen	.05
7	Will Clark	.05
8	Ellis Burks	.05
9	Joe Carter	.05
10	Rickey Henderson	.40
11	Ozzie Guillen	.05
12	Wade Boggs	.50
13	Jerome Walton	.05
14	John Franco	.05
15	Ricky Jordan	.05
16	Wally Backman	.05
17	Rob Dibble	.05
18	Glenn Braggs	.05
19	Cory Snyder	.05
20	Kal Daniels	.05

21	Mark Langston	.05
22	Kevin Gross	.05
23	Don Mattingly	.55
24	Dave Righetti	.05
25	Roberto Alomar	.15
26	Robby Thompson	.05
27	Jack McDowell	.05
28	Bip Roberts	.05
29	Jay Howell	.05
30	Dave Steib	.05
31	Johnny Ray	.05
32	Steve Sax	.05
33	Terry Mulholland	.05
34	Lee Guetterman	.05
35	Tim Raines	.05
36	Scott Fletcher	.05
37	Lance Parrish	.05
38	Tony Phillips	.05
39	Todd Stottlemyre	.05
40	Alan Trammell	.05
41	Todd Burns	.05
42	Mookie Wilson	.05
43	Chris Bosio	.05
44	Jeffrey Leonard	.05
45	Doug Jones	.05
46	Mike Scott	.05
47	Andy Hawkins	.05
48	Harold Reynolds	.05
49	Paul Molitor	.40
50	John Farrell	.05
51	Danny Darwin	.05
52	Jeff Blauser	.05
53	John Tudor	.05
54	Milt Thompson	.05
55	Dave Justice	.05
56	Greg Olson RC	.05
57	Willie Blair RC	.05
58	Rick Parker RC	.05
59	Shawn Boskie	.05
60	Kevin Tapani	.05
61	Dave Hollins	.05
62	Scott Radinsky RC	.05
63	Francisco Cabrera	.05
64	Tim Layana RC	.05
65	Jim Leyritz	.05
66	Wayne Edwards	.05
67	Lee Stevens	.05
68	Bill Sampen RC	.05
69	Craig Grebeck RC	.05
70	John Burkett	.05
71	Hector Villanueva RC	.05
72	Oscar Azocar RC	.05
73	Alan Mills	.05
74	Carlos Baerga	.05
75	Charles Nagy	.05
76	Tim Drummond	.05
77	Dana Kiecker RC	.05
78	Tom Edens RC	.05
79	Kent Mercker	.05
80	Steve Avery	.05
81	Lee Smith	.05
82	Dave Martinez	.05
83	Dave Winfield	.40
84	Bill Spiers	.05
85	Dan Pasqua	.05
86	Randy Milligan	.05
87	Tracy Jones	.05
88	Greg Myers	.05
89	Keith Hernandez	.05
90	Todd Benzinger	.05
91	Mike Jackson	.05
92	Mike Stanley	.05
93	Candy Maldonado	.05
94	John Kruk	.05
95	Cal Ripken, Jr.	.75
96	Willie Fraser	.05
97	Mike Felder	.05
98	Bill Landrum	.05
99	Chuck Crim	.05
100	Chuck Finley	.05
101	Kirt Manwaring	.05
102	Jaime Navarro	.05
103	Dickie Thon	.05
104	Brian Downing	.05
105	Jim Abbott	.05
106	Tom Brookens	.05
107	Darryl Hamilton	.05
108	Bryan Harvey	.05
109	Greg Harris	.05
110	Greg Swindell	.05
111	Juan Berenguer	.05
112	Mike Heath	.05
113	Scott Bradley	.05
114	Jack Morris	.05
115	Barry Jones	.05
116	Kevin Romine	.05
117	Garry Templeton	.05
118	Scott Sanderson	.05
119	Roberto Kelly	.05
120	George Brett	.50
121	Oddibe McDowell	.05
122	Jim Acker	.05
123	Bill Swift	.05
124	Eric King	.05

125	Jay Buhner	.05
126	Matt Young	.05
127	Alvaro Espinoza	.05
128	Greg Hibbard	.05
129	Jeff Robinson	.05
130	Mike Greenwell	.05
131	Dion James	.05
132	Donn Pall	.05
133	Lloyd Moseby	.05
134	Randy Velarde	.05
135	Allan Anderson	.05
136	Mark Davis	.05
137	Eric Davis	.05
138	Phil Stephenson	.05
139	Felix Fermin	.05
140	Pedro Guerrero	.05
141	Charlie Hough	.05
142	Mike Henneman	.05
143	Jeff Montgomery	.05
144	Lenny Harris	.05
145	Bruce Hurst	.05
146	Eric Anthony	.05
147	Paul Assenmacher	.05
148	Jesse Barfield	.05
149	Carlos Quintana	.05
150	Dave Stewart	.05
151	Roy Smith	.05
152	Paul Gibson	.05
153	Mickey Hatcher	.05
154	Jim Eisenreich	.05
155	Kenny Rogers	.05
156	Dave Schmidt	.05
157	Lance Johnson	.05
158	Dave West	.05
159	Steve Balboni	.05
160	Jeff Brantley	.05
161	Craig Biggio	.05
162	Brook Jacoby	.05
163	Dan Gladden	.05
164	Jeff Reardon	.05
165	Mark Carreon	.05
166	Mel Hall	.05
167	Gary Mielke	.05
168	Cecil Fielder	.05
169	Darrin Jackson	.05
170	Rick Aguilera	.05
171	Walt Weiss	.05
172	Steve Farr	.05
173	Jody Reed	.05
174	Mike Jeffcoat	.05
175	Mark Grace	.05
176	Larry Sheets	.05
177	Bill Gullickson	.05
178	Chris Gwynn	.05
179	Melido Perez	.05
180	Sid Fernandez	.05
181	Tim Burke	.05
182	Gary Pettis	.05
183	Rob Murphy	.05
184	Craig Lefferts	.05
185	Howard Johnson	.05
186	Ken Caminiti	.05
187	Tim Belcher	.05
188	Greg Cadaret	.05
189	Matt Williams	.05
190	Dave Magadan	.05
191	Geno Petralli	.05
192	Jeff Robinson	.05
193	Jim Deshaies	.05
194	Willie Randolph	.05
195	George Bell	.05
196	Hubie Brooks	.05
197	Tom Gordon	.05
198	Mike Fitzgerald	.05
199	Mike Pagliarulo	.05
200	Kirby Puckett	.50
201	Shawon Dunston	.05
202	Dennis Boyd	.05
203	Junior Felix	.05
204	Alejandro Pena	.05
205	Pete Smith	.05
206	Tom Glavine	.35
207	Luis Salazar	.05
208	John Smoltz	.05
209	Doug Dascenzo	.05
210	Tim Wallach	.05
211	Greg Gagne	.05
212	Mark Gubicza	.05
213	Mark Parent	.05
214	Ken Oberkfell	.05
215	Gary Carter	.40
216	Rafael Palmeiro	.35
217	Tom Niedenfuer	.05
218	Dave LaPoint	.05
219	Jeff Treadway	.05
220	Mitch Williams	.05
221	Jose DeLeon	.05
222	Mike LaValliere	.05
223	Darrel Akerfelds	.05
224a	Kent Anderson ("Flachy" in first line.)	.05
224b	Kent Anderson ("Flashy" in first line.)	.05
225	Dwight Evans	.05

226	Gary Redus	.05
227	Paul O'Neill	.05
228	Marty Barrett	.05
229	Tom Browning	.05
230	Terry Pendleton	.05
231	Jack Armstrong	.05
232	Mike Boddicker	.05
233	Neal Heaton	.05
234	Marquis Grissom	.05
235	Bert Blyleven	.05
236	Curt Young	.05
237	Don Carman	.05
238	Charlie Hayes	.05
239	Mark Knudson	.05
240	Todd Zeile	.05
241	Larry Walker	.05
242	Jerald Clark	.05
243	Jeff Ballard	.05
244	Jeff King	.05
245	Tom Brunansky	.05
246	Darren Daulton	.05
247	Scott Terry	.05
248	Rob Deer	.05
249	Brady Anderson	.05
250	Len Dykstra	.05
251	Greg Harris	.05
252	Mike Hartley	.05
253	Joey Cora	.05
254	Ivan Calderon	.05
255	Ted Power	.05
256	Sammy Sosa	.50
257	Steve Buechele	.05
258	Mike Devereaux	.05
259	Brad Komminsk	.05
260	Teddy Higuera	.05
261	Shawn Abner	.05
262	Dave Valle	.05
263	Jeff Huson	.05
264	Edgar Martinez	.05
265	Carlton Fisk	.40
266	Steve Finley	.05
267	John Wetteland	.05
268	Kevin Appier	.05
269	Steve Lyons	.05
270	Mickey Tettleton	.05
271	Luis Rivera	.05
272	Steve Jeltz	.05
273	R.J. Reynolds	.05
274	Carlos Martinez	.05
275	Dan Plesac	.05
276	Mike Morgan	.05
277	Jeff Russell	.05
278	Pete Incaviglia	.05
279	Kevin Seitzer	.05
280	Bobby Thigpen	.05
281	Stan Javier	.05
282	Henry Cotto	.05
283	Gary Wayne	.05
284	Shane Mack	.05
285	Brian Holman	.05
286	Gerald Perry	.05
287	Steve Crawford	.05
288	Nelson Liriano	.05
289	Don Aase	.05
290	Randy Johnson	.40
291	Harold Baines	.05
292	Kent Hrbek	.05
293a	Les Lancaster ("Dallas Texas")	.05
293b	Les Lancaster ("Dallas, Texas")	.05
294	Jeff Musselman	.05
295	Kurt Stillwell	.05
296	Stan Belinda	.05
297	Lou Whitaker	.05
298	Glenn Wilson	.05
299	Omar Vizquel	.05
300	Ramon Martinez	.05
301	Dwight Smith	.05
302	Tim Crews	.05
303	Lance Blankenship	.05
304	Sid Bream	.05
305	Rafael Ramirez	.05
306	Steve Wilson	.05
307	Mackey Sasser	.05
308	Franklin Stubbs	.05
309	Jack Daugherty	.05
310	Eddie Murray	.40
311	Bob Welch	.05
312	Brian Harper	.05
313	Lance McCullers	.05
314	Dave Smith	.05
315	Bobby Bonilla	.05
316	Jerry Don Gleaton	.05
317	Greg Maddux	.50
318	Keith Miller	.05
319	Mark Portugal	.05
320	Robin Ventura	.05
321	Bob Ojeda	.05
322	Mike Harkey	.05
323	Jay Bell	.05
324	Mark McGwire	.65
325	Gary Gaetti	.05
326	Jeff Pico	.05

No.	Name	Value
327	Kevin McReynolds	.05
328	Frank Tanana	.05
329	Eric Yelding	.05
330	Barry Bonds	.75
331	Brian McRae RC	.05
332	Pedro Munoz RC	.05
333	Daryl Irvine RC	.05
334	Chris Hoiles	.05
335	Thomas Howard RC	.05
336	Jeff Schulz RC	.05
337	Jeff Manto	.05
338	Beau Allred	.05
339	Mike Bordick RC	.10
340	Todd Hundley	.05
341	Jim Vatcher RC	.05
342	Luis Sojo	.05
343	Jose Offerman RC	.05
344	Pete Coachman RC	.05
345	Mike Benjamin	.05
346	Ozzie Canseco RC	.05
347	Tim McIntosh	.05
348	Phil Plantier RC	.05
349	Terry Shumpert RC	.05
350	Darren Lewis	.05
351	David Walsh RC	.05
352a	Scott Chiamparino RC (Bats: Left)	.05
352b	Scott Chiamparino RC (Bats: Right)	.05
353	Julio Valera RC	.05
354	Anthony Telford RC	.05
355	Kevin Wickander RC	.05
356	Tim Naehring RC	.05
357	Jim Poole RC	.05
358	Mark Whiten RC	.05
359	Terry Wells RC	.05
360	Rafael Valdez RC	.05
361	Mel Stottlemyre RC	.05
362	David Segui RC	.10
363	Paul Abbott	.05
364	Steve Howard RC	.05
365	Karl Rhodes RC	.10
366	Rafael Novoa RC	.05
367	Joe Grahe RC	.05
368	Darren Reed RC	.05
369	Jeff McKnight	.05
370	Scott Leius	.05
371	Mark Dewey RC	.05
372	Mark Lee RC	.05
373	Rosario Rodriguez RC	.05
374	Chuck McElroy	.05
375	Mike Bell RC	.05
376	Mickey Morandini	.05
377	Bill Haselman RC	.05
378	Dave Pavlas RC	.05
379	Derrick May	.05
380	Jeromy Burnitz RC	.25
381	Donald Peters RC	.05
382	Alex Fernandez RC	.05
383	Mike Mussina RC	1.00
384	Daniel Smith RC	.05
385	Lance Dickson RC	.10
386	Carl Everett RC	.40
387	Thomas Nevers RC	.05
388	Adam Hyzdu RC	.05
389	Todd Van Poppel RC	.10
390	Rondell White RC	.30
391	Marc Newfield RC (1st Draft Pick)	.05
392	Julio Franco/AS	.05
393	Wade Boggs/AS	.25
394	Ozzie Guillen/AS	.05
395	Cecil Fielder/AS	.05
396	Ken Griffey Jr./AS	.30
397	Rickey Henderson/AS	.20
398	Jose Canseco/AS	.15
399	Roger Clemens/AS	.30
400	Sandy Alomar,Jr./AS	.05
401	Bobby Thigpen/AS	.05
402	Bobby Bonilla	.05
403	Eric Davis	.05
404	Fred McGriff	.05
405	Glenn Davis	.05
406	Kevin Mitchell	.05
407	Rob Dibble	.05
408	Ramon Martinez	.05
409	David Cone	.05
410	Bobby Witt	.05
411	Mark Langston	.05
412	Bo Jackson	.10
413	Shawon Dunston	.05
414	Jesse Barfield	.05
415	Ken Caminiti	.05
416	Benito Santiago	.05
417	Nolan Ryan	.40
418	Bobby Thigpen (HL)	.05
419	Ramon Martinez (HL)	.05
420	Bo Jackson (HL)	.10
421	Carlton Fisk (HL)	.20
422	Jimmy Key	.05
423	Junior Noboa	.05
424	Al Newman	.05
425	Pat Borders	.05
426	Von Hayes	.05
427	Tim Teufel	.05
428	Eric Plunk	.05
429	John Moses	.05
430	Mike Witt	.05
431	Otis Nixon	.05
432	Tony Fernandez	.05
433	Rance Mulliniks	.05
434	Dan Petry	.05
435	Bob Geren	.05
436	Steve Frey	.05
437	Jamie Moyer	.05
438	Junior Ortiz	.05
439	Tom O'Malley	.05
440	Pat Combs	.05
441	Jose Canseco/DT	.15
442	Alfredo Griffin	.05
443	Andres Galarraga	.05
444	Bryn Smith	.05
445	Andre Dawson	.25
446	Juan Samuel	.05
447	Mike Aldrete	.05
448	Ron Gant	.05
449	Fernando Valenzuela	.05
450	Vince Coleman	.05
451	Kevin Mitchell	.05
452	Spike Owen	.05
453	Mike Bielecki	.05
454	Dennis Martinez	.05
455	Brett Butler	.05
456	Ron Darling	.05
457	Dennis Rasmussen	.05
458	Ken Howell	.05
459	Steve Bedrosian	.05
460	Frank Viola	.05
461	Jose Lind	.05
462	Chris Sabo	.05
463	Dante Bichette	.05
464	Rick Mahler	.05
465	John Smiley	.05
466	Devon White	.05
467	John Orton	.05
468	Mike Stanton	.05
469	Billy Hatcher	.05
470	Wally Joyner	.05
471	Gene Larkin	.05
472	Doug Drabek	.05
473	Gary Sheffield	.30
474	David Wells	.05
475	Andy Van Slyke	.05
476	Mike Gallego	.05
477	B.J. Surhoff	.05
478	Gene Nelson	.05
479	Mariano Duncan	.05
480	Fred McGriff	.05
481	Jerry Browne	.05
482	Alvin Davis	.05
483	Bill Wegman	.05
484	Dave Parker	.05
485	Dennis Eckersley	.35
486	Erik Hanson	.05
487	Bill Ripken	.05
488	Tom Candiotti	.05
489	Mike Schooler	.05
490	Gregg Olson	.05
491	Chris James	.05
492	Pete Harnisch	.05
493	Julio Franco	.05
494	Greg Briley	.05
495	Ruben Sierra	.05
496	Steve Olin	.05
497	Mike Fetters	.05
498	Mark Williamson	.05
499	Bob Tewksbury	.05
500	Tony Gwynn	.50
501	Randy Myers	.05
502	Keith Comstock	.05
503	Craig Worthington	.05
504	Mark Eichhorn	.05
505	Barry Larkin	.05
506	Dave Johnson	.05
507	Bobby Witt	.05
508	Joe Orsulak	.05
509	Pete O'Brien	.05
510	Brad Arnsberg	.05
511	Storm Davis	.05
512	Bob Milacki	.05
513	Bill Pecota	.05
514	Glenallen Hill	.05
515	Danny Tartabull	.05
516	Mike Moore	.05
517	Ron Robinson	.05
518	Mark Gardner	.05
519	Rick Wrona	.05
520	Mike Scioscia	.05
521	Frank Wills	.05
522	Greg Brock	.05
523	Jack Clark	.05
524	Bruce Ruffin	.05
525	Robin Yount	.40
526	Tom Foley	.05
527	Pat Perry	.05
528	Greg Vaughn	.05
529	Wally Whitehurst	.05
530	Norm Charlton	.05
531	Marvell Wynne	.05
532	Jim Gantner	.05
533	Greg Litton	.05
534	Manny Lee	.05
535	Scott Bailes	.05
536	Charlie Leibrandt	.05
537	Roger McDowell	.05
538	Andy Benes	.05
539	Rick Honeycutt	.05
540	Dwight Gooden	.05
541	Scott Garrelts	.05
542	Dave Clark	.05
543	Lonnie Smith	.05
544	Rick Rueschel	.05
545	Delino DeShields	.05
546	Mike Sharperson	.05
547	Mike Kingery	.05
548	Terry Kennedy	.05
549	David Cone	.05
550	Orel Hershiser	.05
551	Matt Nokes	.05
552	Eddie Williams	.05
553	Frank DiPino	.05
554	Fred Lynn	.05
555	Alex Cole	.05
556	Terry Leach	.05
557	Chet Lemon	.05
558	Paul Mirabella	.05
559	Bill Long	.05
560	Phil Bradley	.05
561	Duane Ward	.05
562	Dave Bergman	.05
563	Eric Show	.05
564	Xavier Hernandez	.05
565	Jeff Parrett	.05
566	Chuck Cary	.05
567	Ken Hill	.05
568	Bob Welch	.05
569	John Mitchell	.05
570	Travis Fryman	.05
571	Derek Lilliquist	.05
572	Steve Lake	.05
573	John Barfield RC	.05
574	Randy Bush	.05
575	Joe Magrane	.05
576	Edgar Diaz	.05
577	Casy Candaele	.05
578	Jesse Orosco	.05
579	Tom Henke	.05
580	Rick Cerone	.05
581	Drew Hall	.05
582	Tony Castillo	.05
583	Jimmy Jones	.05
584	Rick Reed	.05
585	Joe Girardi	.05
586	Jeff Gray RC	.05
587	Luis Polonia	.05
588	Joe Klink	.05
589	Rex Hudler	.05
590	Kirk McCaskill	.05
591	Juan Agosto	.05
592	Wes Gardner	.05
593	Rich Rodriguez RC	.05
594	Mitch Webster	.05
595	Kelly Gruber	.05
596	Dale Mohorcic	.05
597	Willie McGee	.05
598	Bill Krueger	.05
599	Bob Walk	.05
600	Kevin Maas	.05
601	Danny Jackson	.05
602	Craig McMurtry	.05
603	Curtis Wilkerson	.05
604	Adam Peterson	.05
605	Sam Horn	.05
606	Tommy Gregg	.05
607	Ken Dayley	.05
608	Carmelo Castillo	.05
609	John Shelby	.05
610	Don Slaught	.05
611	Calvin Schiraldi	.05
612	Dennis Lamp	.05
613	Andres Thomas	.05
614	Jose Gonzales	.05
615	Randy Ready	.05
616	Kevin Bass	.05
617	Mike Marshall	.05
618	Daryl Boston	.05
619	Andy McGaffigan	.05
620	Joe Oliver	.05
621	Jim Gott	.05
622	Jose Oquendo	.05
623	Jose DeJesus	.05
624	Mike Brumley	.05
625	John Olerud	.05
626	Ernest Riles	.05
627	Gene Harris	.05
628	Jose Uribe	.05
629	Darnell Coles	.05
630	Carney Lansford	.05
631	Tim Leary	.05
632	Tim Hulett	.05
633	Kevin Elster	.05
634	Tony Fossas	.05
635	Francisco Oliveras	.05
636	Bob Patterson	.05
637	Gary Ward	.05
638	Rene Gonzales	.05
639	Don Robinson	.05
640	Darryl Strawberry	.05
641	Dave Anderson	.05
642	Scott Scudder	.05
643	Reggie Harris RC	.05
644	Dave Henderson	.05
645	Ben McDonald	.05
646	Bob Kipper	.05
647	Hal Morris	.05
648	Tim Birtsas	.05
649	Steve Searcy	.05
650	Dale Murphy	.20
651	Ron Oester	.05
652	Mike LaCoss	.05
653	Ron Jones	.05
654	Kelly Downs	.05
655	Roger Clemens	.55
656	Herm Winningham	.05
657	Trevor Wilson	.05
658	Jose Rijo	.05
659	Dann Bilardello	.05
660	Gregg Jefferies	.05
661	Doug Drabek/AS	.05
662	Randy Myers/AS	.05
663	Benito Santiago/AS	.05
664	Will Clark/AS	.05
665	Ryne Sandberg/AS	.25
666	Barry Larkin/AS	.05
667	Matt Williams/AS	.05
668	Barry Bonds/AS	.35
669	Eric Davis	.05
670	Bobby Bonilla/AS	.05
671	Chipper Jones RC	1.50
672	Eric Christopherson RC	.05
673	Robbie Beckett RC	.05
674	Shane Andrews RC	.15
675	Steve Karsay RC	.10
676	Aaron Holbert RC	.05
677	Donovan Osborne RC	.05
678	Todd Ritchie RC	.05
679	Ron Walden RC	.05
680	Tim Costo RC	.05
681	Dan Wilson RC	.10
682	Kurt Miller RC	.05
683	Mike Lieberthal RC	.25
684	Roger Clemens	.25
686	Nolan Ryan	.35
687	Frank Viola	.05
688	Erik Hanson	.05
689	Matt Williams	.05
690	Jose Canseco	.10
691	Darryl Strawberry	.05
692	Bo Jackson	.10
693	Cecil Fielder	.05
694	Sandy Alomar, Jr.	.05
695	Cory Snyder	.05
696	Eric Davis	.05
697	Ken Griffey Jr.	.30
698	Andy Van Slyke	.05
699	Mark Langston, Mike Witt	.05
700	Randy Johnson	.20
701a	Nolan Ryan (White background on stat box.)	2.00
701b	Nolan Ryan (Blue background on stat box.)	.35
702	Dave Stewart	.05
703	Fernando Valenzuela	.05
704	Andy Hawkins	.05
705	Melido Perez	.05
706	Terry Mulholland	.05
707	Dave Stieb	.05
708	Brian Barnes RC	.05
709	Bernard Gilkey	.05
710	Steve Decker RC	.05
711	Paul Faries RC	.05
712	Paul Marak RC	.05
713	Wes Chamberlain RC	.05
714	Kevin Belcher RC	.05
715	Dan Boone	.05
716	Steve Adkins RC	.05
717	Geronimo Pena RC	.05
718	Howard Farmer RC	.05
719	Mark Leonard RC	.05
720	Tom Lampkin	.05
721	Mike Gardiner RC	.05
722	Jeff Conine RC	.25
723	Efrain Valdez RC	.05
724	Chuck Malone	.05
725	Leo Gomez RC	.05
726	Paul McClellan RC	.05
727	Mark Leiter RC	.05

ABBREVIATIONS

AS - All-Star
DT - Double Team

728	Rich DeLucia RC	.05
729	Mel Rojas	.05
730	Hector Wagner RC	.05
731	Ray Lankford	.05
732	Turner Ward RC	.05
733	Gerald Alexander RC	.05
734	Scott Anderson RC	.05
735	Tony Perezchica	.05
736	Jimmy Kremers	.05
737a	American Flag (SCORE 1991 copyright, unmarked promo.)	.25
737b	American Flag (1991 SCORE in copyright)	.25
738	Mike York RC	.05
739	Mike Rochford	.05
740	Scott Aldred	.05
741	Rico Brogna RC	.05
742	Dave Burba RC	.05
743	Ray Stephens RC	.05
744	Eric Gunderson RC	.05
745	Troy Afenir RC	.05
746	Jeff Shaw	.05
747	Orlando Merced RC	.10
748	Omar Oliveras RC	.05
749	Jerry Kutzler	.05
750	Mo Vaughn	.05
751	Matt Stark RC	.05
752	Randy Hennis RC	.05
753	Andujar Cedeno RC	.05
754	Kelvin Torve	.05
755	Joe Kraemer	.05
756	Phil Clark RC	.05
757	Ed Vosberg RC	.05
758	Mike Perez RC	.05
759	Scott Lewis RC	.05
760	Steve Chitren RC	.05
761	Ray Young RC	.05
762	Andres Santana RC	.05
763	Rodney McCray RC	.05
764	Sean Berry	.05
765	Brent Mayne	.05
766	Mike Simms RC	.05
767	Glenn Sutko RC	.05
768	Gary Disarcina	.05
769	George Brett (HL)	.25
770	Cecil Fielder (HL)	.05
771	Jim Presley	.05
772	John Dopson	.05
773	Bo Jackson (Breaker)	.10
774	Brent Knackert	.05
775	Bill Doran	.05
776	Dick Schofield	.05
777	Nelson Santovenia	.05
778	Mark Guthrie	.05
779	Mark Lemke	.05
780	Terry Steinbach	.05
781	Tom Bolton	.05
782	Randy Tomlin RC	.05
783	Jeff Kunkel	.05
784	Felix Jose	.05
785	Rick Sutcliffe	.05
786	John Cerutti	.05
787	Jose Vizcaino	.05
788	Curt Schilling	.35
789	Ed Whitson	.05
790	Tony Pena	.05
791	Jim Candelaria	.05
792	Carmelo Martinez	.05
793	Sandy Alomar, Jr.	.05
794	Jim Neidlinger RC	.05
795	Barry Larkin, Chris Sabo Red's October	.10
796	Paul Sorrento	.05
797	Tom Pagnozzi	.05
798	Tino Martinez	.05
799	Scott Ruskin	.05
800	Kirk Gibson	.05
801	Walt Terrell	.05
802	John Russell	.05
803	Chili Davis	.05
804	Chris Nabholz	.05
805	Juan Gonzalez	.20
806	Ron Hassey	.05
807	Todd Worrell	.05
808	Tommy Greene	.05
809	Joel Skinner	.05
810	Benito Santiago	.05
811	Pat Tabler	.05
812	Scott Erickson RC	.05
813	Moises Alou	.05
814	Dale Sveum	.05
815	Ryne Sandberg (Man of the Year)	.25
816	Rick Dempsey	.05
817	Scott Bankhead	.05
818	Jason Grimsley	.05
819	Doug Jennings	.05
820	Tom Herr	.05
821	Rob Ducey	.05
822	Luis Quinones	.05
823	Greg Minton	.05
824	Mark Grant	.05
825	Ozzie Smith	.50
826	Dave Eiland	.05
827	Danny Heep	.05
828	Hensley Meulens	.05
829	Charlie O'Brien	.05
830	Glenn Davis	.05
831	John Marzano	.05
832	Steve Ontiveros	.05
833	Ron Karkovice	.05
834	Jerry Goff	.05
835	Ken Griffey Sr.	.05
836	Kevin Reimer	.05
837	Randy Kutcher	.05
838	Mike Blowers	.05
839	Mike Macfarlane	.05
840	Frank Thomas	.40
841	Ken Griffey Sr., Ken Griffey Jr.	.20
842	Jack Howell	.05
843	Mauro Gozzo	.05
844	Gerald Young	.05
845	Zane Smith	.05
846	Kevin Brown	.05
847	Sil Campusano	.05
848	Larry Andersen	.05
849	Cal Ripken, Jr.	.35
850	Roger Clemens	.30
851	Sandy Alomar, Jr.	.05
852	Alan Trammell	.05
853	George Brett	.25
854	Robin Yount	.25
855	Kirby Puckett	.25
856	Don Mattingly	.30
857	Rickey Henderson	.20
858	Ken Griffey Jr.	.30
859	Ruben Sierra	.05
860	John Olerud	.05
861	Dave Justice	.05
862	Ryne Sandberg	.25
863	Eric Davis	.05
864	Darryl Strawberry	.05
865	Tim Wallach	.05
866	Dwight Gooden	.05
867	Len Dykstra	.05
868	Barry Bonds	.35
869	Todd Zeile	.05
870	Benito Santiago	.05
871	Will Clark	.05
872	Craig Biggio	.05
873	Wally Joyner	.05
874	Frank Thomas	.20
875	Rickey Henderson	.20
876	Barry Bonds	.35
877	Bob Welch (Cy Young)	.05
878	Doug Drabek (Cy Young)	.05
879	Sandy Alomar, Jr. (ROY)	.05
880	Dave Justice (ROY)	.05
881	Damon Berryhill	.05
882	Frank Viola	.05
883	Dave Stewart	.05
884	Doug Jones	.05
885	Randy Myers	.05
886	Will Clark	.05
887	Roberto Alomar	.10
888	Barry Larkin	.05
889	Wade Boggs	.25
890	Rickey Henderson	.20
891	Kirby Puckett	.25
892	Ken Griffey Jr.	.30
893	Benito Santiago	.05

Hot Rookies

HAL MORRIS

		NM/M
Complete Set (10):		2.50
Common Player:		.10
1	Dave Justice	.25
2	Kevin Maas	.10
3	Hal Morris	.10
4	Frank Thomas	1.50
5	Jeff Conine	.10
6	Sandy Alomar Jr.	.10
7	Ray Lankford	.10
8	Steve Decker	.10
9	Juan Gonzalez	.50
10	Jose Offerman	.10

Mickey Mantle

		NM/M
Complete Set (7):		35.00
Common Card:		6.00
Autographed Card:		575.00
1	The Rookie	9.00
2	Triple Crown	7.50
3	World Series	7.50
4	Going, Going, Gone	7.50
5	Speed and Grace	7.50
6	A True Yankee	7.50
7	Twilight	7.50

Cooperstown

COOPERSTOWN CARD

NOLAN RYAN

		NM/M
Complete Set (7):		3.50
Common Player:		.25
B1	Wade Boggs	.50
B2	Barry Larkin	.25
B3	Ken Griffey Jr.	1.00
B4	Rickey Henderson	.35
B5	George Brett	.75
B6	Will Clark	.25
B7	Nolan Ryan	1.50

Traded

GEORGE BELL LF CUBS

		NM/M
Complete Set (110):		4.00
Common Player:		.05
1	Bo Jackson	.10
2	Mike Flanagan	.05
3	Pete Incaviglia	.05
4	Jack Clark	.05
5	Hubie Brooks	.05
6	Ivan Calderon	.05
7	Glenn Davis	.05
8	Wally Backman	.05
9	Dave Smith	.05
10	Tim Raines	.05
11	Joe Carter	.05
12	Sid Bream	.05
13	George Bell	.05
14	Steve Bedrosian	.05
15	Willie Wilson	.05
16	Darryl Strawberry	.05
17	Danny Jackson	.05
18	Kirk Gibson	.05
19	Willie McGee	.05
20	Junior Felix	.05
21	Steve Farr	.05
22	Pat Tabler	.05
23	Brett Butler	.05
24	Danny Darwin	.05
25	Mickey Tettleton	.05
26	Gary Carter	.50
27	Mitch Williams	.05
28	Candy Maldonado	.05
29	Otis Nixon	.05
30	Brian Downing	.05
31	Tom Candiotti	.05
32	John Candelaria	.05
33	Rob Murphy	.05
34	Deion Sanders	.05
35	Willie Randolph	.05
36	Pete Harnisch	.05
37	Dante Bichette	.05
38	Garry Templeton	.05
39	Gary Gaetti	.05
40	John Cerutti	.05
41	Rick Cerone	.05
42	Mike Pagliarulo	.05
43	Ron Hassey	.05
44	Roberto Alomar	.20
45	Mike Boddicker	.05
46	Bud Black	.05
47	Rob Deer	.05
48	Devon White	.05
49	Luis Sojo	.05
50	Terry Pendleton	.05
51	Kevin Gross	.05
52	Mike Huff	.05
53	Dave Righetti	.05
54	Matt Young	.05
55	Ernest Riles	.05
56	Bill Gullickson	.05
57	Vince Coleman	.05
58	Fred McGriff	.05
59	Franklin Stubbs	.05
60	Eric King	.05
61	Cory Snyder	.05
62	Dwight Evans	.05
63	Gerald Perry	.05
64	Eric Show	.05
65	Shawn Hillegas	.05
66	Tony Fernandez	.05
67	Tim Teufel	.05
68	Mitch Webster	.05
69	Mike Heath	.05
70	Chili Davis	.05
71	Larry Andersen	.05
72	Gary Varsho	.05
73	Juan Berenguer	.05
74	Jack Morris	.05
75	Barry Jones	.05
76	Rafael Belliard	.05
77	Steve Buechele	.05
78	Scott Sanderson	.05
79	Bob Ojeda	.05
80	Curt Schilling	.35
81	Brian Drahman	.05
82	Ivan Rodriguez RC	1.00
83	David Howard	.05
84	Heath Slocumb	.05
85	Mike Timlin	.05
86	Darryl Kile	.05
87	Pete Schourek	.05
88	Bruce Walton	.05
89	Al Osuna	.05
90	Gary Scott	.05
91	Doug Simons	.05
92	Chris Jones	.05
93	Chuck Knoblauch	.05
94	Dana Allison	.05
95	Erik Pappas	.05
96	Jeff Bagwell RC	2.50
97	Kirk Dressendorfer	.05
98	Freddie Benavides	.05
99	Luis Gonzalez RC	.50
100	Wade Taylor	.05
101	Ed Sprague	.05
102	Bob Scanlan	.05
103	Rick Wilkins	.05
104	Chris Donnels	.05
105	Joe Slusarski	.05
106	Mark Lewis	.05
107	Pat Kelly	.05
108	John Briscoe	.05
109	Luis Lopez	.05
110	Jeff Johnson	.05

1992 Score

NOLAN RYAN

SCORE 92 PITCHER

		NM/M
Unopened Fact. Set (910):		7.50
Complete Set (893):		5.00
Common Player:		.05
Wax Pack (16):		.40
Wax Box (36):		7.50

#	Player	Price
1	Ken Griffey Jr.	.65
2	Nolan Ryan	1.00
3	Will Clark	.05
4	Dave Justice	.05
5	Dave Henderson	.05
6	Bret Saberhagen	.05
7	Fred McGriff	.05
8	Erik Hanson	.05
9	Darryl Strawberry	.05
10	Dwight Gooden	.05
11	Juan Gonzalez	.20
12	Mark Langston	.05
13	Lonnie Smith	.05
14	Jeff Montgomery	.05
15	Roberto Alomar	.20
16	Delino DeShields	.05
17	Steve Bedrosian	.05
18	Terry Pendleton	.05
19	Mark Carreon	.05
20	Mark McGwire	.75
21	Roger Clemens	.60
22	Chuck Crim	.05
23	Don Mattingly	.60
24	Dickie Thon	.05
25	Ron Gant	.05
26	Milt Cuyler	.05
27	Mike Macfarlane	.05
28	Dan Gladden	.05
29	Melido Perez	.05
30	Willie Randolph	.05
31	Albert Belle	.05
32	Dave Winfield	.40
33	Jimmy Jones	.05
34	Kevin Gross	.05
35	Andres Galarraga	.05
36	Mike Devereaux	.05
37	Chris Bosio	.05
38	Mike LaValliere	.05
39	Gary Gaetti	.05
40	Felix Jose	.05
41	Alvaro Espinoza	.05
42	Rick Aguilera	.05
43	Mike Gallego	.05
44	Eric Davis	.05
45	George Bell	.05
46	Tom Brunansky	.05
47	Steve Farr	.05
48	Duane Ward	.05
49	David Wells	.05
50	Cecil Fielder	.05
51	Walt Weiss	.05
52	Todd Zeile	.05
53	Doug Jones	.05
54	Bob Walk	.05
55	Rafael Palmeiro	.35
56	Rob Deer	.05
57	Paul O'Neill	.05
58	Jeff Reardon	.05
59	Randy Ready	.05
60	Scott Erickson	.05
61	Paul Molitor	.40
62	Jack McDowell	.05
63	Jim Acker	.05
64	Jay Buhner	.05
65	Travis Fryman	.05
66	Marquis Grissom	.05
67	Mike Harkey	.05
68	Luis Polonia	.05
69	Ken Caminiti	.05
70	Chris Sabo	.05
71	Gregg Olson	.05
72	Carlton Fisk	.40
73	Juan Samuel	.05
74	Todd Stottlemyre	.05
75	Andre Dawson	.25
76	Alvin Davis	.05
77	Bill Doran	.05
78	B.J. Surhoff	.05
79	Kirk McCaskill	.05
80	Dale Murphy	.25
81	Jose DeLeon	.05
82	Alex Fernandez	.05
83	Ivan Calderon	.05
84	Brent Mayne	.05
85	Jody Reed	.05
86	Randy Tomlin	.05
87	Randy Milligan	.05
88	Pascual Perez	.05
89	Hensley Meulens	.05
90	Joe Carter	.05
91	Mike Moore	.05
92	Ozzie Guillen	.05
93	Shawn Hillegas	.05
94	Chili Davis	.05
95	Vince Coleman	.05
96	Jimmy Key	.05
97	Billy Ripken	.05
98	Dave Smith	.05
99	Tom Bolton	.05
100	Barry Larkin	.05
101	Kenny Rogers	.05
102	Mike Boddicker	.05
103	Kevin Elster	.05
104	Ken Hill	.05
105	Charlie Leibrandt	.05
106	Pat Combs	.05
107	Hubie Brooks	.05
108	Julio Franco	.05
109	Vicente Palacios	.05
110	Kal Daniels	.05
111	Bruce Hurst	.05
112	Willie McGee	.05
113	Ted Power	.05
114	Milt Thompson	.05
115	Doug Drabek	.05
116	Rafael Belliard	.05
117	Scott Garrelts	.05
118	Terry Mulholland	.05
119	Jay Howell	.05
120	Danny Jackson	.05
121	Scott Ruskin	.05
122	Robin Ventura	.05
123	Bip Roberts	.05
124	Jeff Russell	.05
125	Hal Morris	.05
126	Teddy Higuera	.05
127	Luis Sojo	.05
128	Carlos Baerga	.05
129	Jeff Ballard	.05
130	Tom Gordon	.05
131	Sid Bream	.05
132	Rance Mulliniks	.05
133	Andy Benes	.05
134	Mickey Tettleton	.05
135	Rich DeLucia	.05
136	Tom Pagnozzi	.05
137	Harold Baines	.05
138	Danny Darwin	.05
139	Kevin Bass	.05
140	Chris Nabholz	.05
141	Pete O'Brien	.05
142	Jeff Treadway	.05
143	Mickey Morandini	.05
144	Eric King	.05
145	Danny Tartabull	.05
146	Lance Johnson	.05
147	Casey Candaele	.05
148	Felix Fermin	.05
149	Rich Rodriguez	.05
150	Dwight Evans	.05
151	Joe Klink	.05
152	Kevin Reimer	.05
153	Orlando Merced	.05
154	Mel Hall	.05
155	Randy Myers	.05
156	Greg Harris	.05
157	Jeff Brantley	.05
158	Jim Eisenreich	.05
159	Luis Rivera	.05
160	Cris Carpenter	.05
161	Bruce Ruffin	.05
162	Omar Vizquel	.05
163	Gerald Alexander	.05
164	Mark Guthrie	.05
165	Scott Lewis	.05
166	Bill Sampen	.05
167	Dave Anderson	.05
168	Kevin McReynolds	.05
169	Jose Vizcaino	.05
170	Bob Geren	.05
171	Mike Morgan	.05
172	Jim Gott	.05
173	Mike Pagliarulo	.05
174	Mike Jeffcoat	.05
175	Craig Lefferts	.05
176	Steve Finley	.05
177	Wally Backman	.05
178	Kent Mercker	.05
179	John Cerutti	.05
180	Jay Bell	.05
181	Dale Sveum	.05
182	Greg Gagne	.05
183	Donnie Hill	.05
184	Rex Hudler	.05
185	Pat Kelly	.05
186	Jeff Robinson	.05
187	Jeff Gray	.05
188	Jerry Willard	.05
189	Carlos Quintana	.05
190	Dennis Eckersley	.35
191	Kelly Downs	.05
192	Gregg Jefferies	.05
193	Darrin Fletcher	.05
194	Mike Jackson	.05
195	Eddie Murray	.40
196	Billy Landrum	.05
197	Eric Yelding	.05
198	Devon White	.05
199	Larry Walker	.05
200	Ryne Sandberg	.50
201	Dave Magadan	.05
202	Steve Chitren	.05
203	Scott Fletcher	.05
204	Dwayne Henry	.05
205	Scott Coolbaugh	.05
206	Tracy Jones	.05
207	Von Hayes	.05
208	Bob Melvin	.05
209	Scott Scudder	.05
210	Luis Gonzalez	.25
211	Scott Sanderson	.05
212	Chris Donnels	.05
213	Heath Slocumb	.05
214	Mike Timlin	.05
215	Brian Harper	.05
216	Juan Berenguer	.05
217	Mike Henneman	.05
218	Bill Spiers	.05
219	Scott Terry	.05
220	Frank Viola	.05
221	Mark Eichhorn	.05
222	Ernest Riles	.05
223	Ray Lankford	.05
224	Pete Harnisch	.05
225	Bobby Bonilla	.05
226	Mike Scioscia	.05
227	Joel Skinner	.05
228	Brian Holman	.05
229	Gilberto Reyes	.05
230	Matt Williams	.05
231	Jaime Navarro	.05
232	Jose Rijo	.05
233	Atlee Hammaker	.05
234	Tim Teufel	.05
235	John Kruk	.05
236	Kurt Stillwell	.05
237	Dan Pasqua	.05
238	Tim Crews	.05
239	Dave Gallagher	.05
240	Leo Gomez	.05
241	Steve Avery	.05
242	Bill Gullickson	.05
243	Mark Portugal	.05
244	Lee Guetterman	.05
245	Benny Santiago	.05
246	Jim Gantner	.05
247	Robby Thompson	.05
248	Terry Shumpert	.05
249	Mike Bell RC	.05
250	Harold Reynolds	.05
251	Mike Felder	.05
252	Bill Pecota	.05
253	Bill Krueger	.05
254	Alfredo Griffin	.05
255	Lou Whitaker	.05
256	Roy Smith	.05
257	Jerald Clark	.05
258	Sammy Sosa	.50
259	Tim Naehring	.05
260	Dave Righetti	.05
261	Paul Gibson	.05
262	Chris James	.05
263	Larry Andersen	.05
264	Storm Davis	.05
265	Jose Lind	.05
266	Greg Hibbard	.05
267	Norm Charlton	.05
268	Paul Kilgus	.05
269	Greg Maddux	.50
270	Ellis Burks	.05
271	Frank Tanana	.05
272	Gene Larkin	.05
273	Ron Hassey	.05
274	Jeff Robinson	.05
275	Steve Howe	.05
276	Daryl Boston	.05
277	Mark Lee	.05
278	Jose Segura RC	.05
279	Lance Blankenship	.05
280	Don Slaught	.05
281	Russ Swan	.05
282	Bob Tewksbury	.05
283	Geno Petralli	.05
284	Shane Mack	.05
285	Bob Scanlan	.05
286	Tim Leary	.05
287	John Smoltz	.05
288	Pat Borders	.05
289	Mark Davidson	.05
290	Sam Horn	.05
291	Lenny Harris	.05
292	Franklin Stubbs	.05
293	Thomas Howard	.05
294	Steve Lyons	.05
295	Francisco Oliveras	.05
296	Terry Leach	.05
297	Barry Jones	.05
298	Lance Parrish	.05
299	Wally Whitehurst	.05
300	Bob Welch	.05
301	Charlie Hayes	.05
302	Charlie Hough	.05
303	Gary Redus	.05
304	Scott Bradley	.05
305	Jose Oquendo	.05
306	Pete Incaviglia	.05
307	Marvin Freeman	.05
308	Gary Pettis	.05
309	Joe Slusarski	.05
310	Kevin Seitzer	.05
311	Jeff Reed	.05
312	Pat Tabler	.05
313	Mike Maddux	.05
314	Bob Milacki	.05
315	Eric Anthony	.05
316	Dante Bichette	.05
317	Steve Decker	.05
318	Jack Clark	.05
319	Doug Dascenzo	.05
320	Scott Leius	.05
321	Jim Lindeman	.05
322	Bryan Harvey	.05
323	Spike Owen	.05
324	Roberto Kelly	.05
325	Stan Belinda	.05
326	Joey Cora	.05
327	Jeff Innis	.05
328	Willie Wilson	.05
329	Juan Agosto	.05
330	Charles Nagy	.05
331	Scott Bailes	.05
332	Pete Schourek	.05
333	Mike Flanagan	.05
334	Omar Olivares	.05
335	Dennis Lamp	.05
336	Tommy Greene	.05
337	Randy Velarde	.05
338	Tom Lampkin	.05
339	John Russell	.05
340	Bob Kipper	.05
341	Todd Burns	.05
342	Ron Jones	.05
343	Dave Valle	.05
344	Mike Heath	.05
345	John Olerud	.05
346	Gerald Young	.05
347	Ken Patterson	.05
348	Les Lancaster	.05
349	Steve Crawford	.05
350	John Candelaria	.05
351	Mike Aldrete	.05
352	Mariano Duncan	.05
353	Julio Machado	.05
354	Ken Williams	.05
355	Walt Terrell	.05
356	Mitch Williams	.05
357	Al Newman	.05
358	Bud Black	.05
359	Joe Hesketh	.05
360	Paul Assenmacher	.05
361	Bo Jackson	.05
362	Jeff Blauser	.05
363	Mike Brumley	.05
364	Jim Deshaies	.05
365	Brady Anderson	.05
366	Chuck McElroy	.05
367	Matt Merullo	.05
368	Tim Belcher	.05
369	Luis Aquino	.05
370	Joe Oliver	.05
371	Greg Swindell	.05
372	Lee Stevens	.05
373	Mark Knudson	.05
374	Bill Wegman	.05
375	Jerry Don Gleaton	.05
376	Pedro Guerrero	.05
377	Randy Bush	.05
378	Greg Harris	.05
379	Eric Plunk	.05
380	Jose DeJesus	.05
381	Bobby Witt	.05
382	Curtis Wilkerson	.05
383	Gene Nelson	.05
384	Wes Chamberlain	.05
385	Tom Henke	.05
386	Mark Lemke	.05
387	Greg Briley	.05

No.	Player	Val.	No.	Player	Val.	No.	Player	Val.	No.	Player	Val.
388	Rafael Ramirez	.05	489	Gary Carter	.40	593	Carlos Martinez	.05	697	Paul Abbott	.05
389	Tony Fossas	.05	490	Ruben Sierra	.05	594	Scott Bankhead	.05	698	Steve Searcy	.05
390	Henry Cotto	.05	491	Gerald Perry	.05	595	Tim Wallach	.05	699	Jose Offerman	.05
391	Tim Hulett	.05	492	Rob Murphy	.05	596	Tino Martinez	.05	700	Ivan Rodriguez	.35
392	Dean Palmer	.05	493	Zane Smith	.05	597	Roger McDowell	.05	701	Joe Girardi	.05
393	Glenn Braggs	.05	494	Darryl Kile	.05	598	Cory Snyder	.05	702	Tony Perezchica	.05
394	Mark Salas	.05	495	Kelly Gruber	.05	599	Andujar Cedeno	.05	703	Paul McClellan	.05
395	Rusty Meacham RC	.05	496	Jerry Browne	.05	600	Kirby Puckett	.50	704	David Howard RC	.05
396	Andy Ashby RC	.10	497	Darryl Hamilton	.05	601	Rick Parker	.05	705	Dan Petry	.05
397	Jose Melendez RC	.05	498	Mike Stanton	.05	602	Todd Hundley	.05	706	Jack Howell	.05
398	Warren Newson RC	.05	499	Mark Leonard	.05	603	Greg Litton	.05	707	Jose Mesa	.05
399	Frank Castillo RC	.05	500	Jose Canseco	.30	604	Dave Johnson	.05	708	Randy St. Claire	.05
400	Chito Martinez RC	.05	501	Dave Martinez	.05	605	John Franco	.05	709	Kevin Brown	.05
401	Bernie Williams	.05	502	Jose Guzman	.05	606	Mike Fetters	.05	710	Ron Darling	.05
402	Derek Bell	.05	503	Terry Kennedy	.05	607	Luis Alicea	.05	711	Jason Grimsley	.05
403	Javier Ortiz RC	.05	504	Ed Sprague	.05	608	Trevor Wilson	.05	712	John Orton	.05
404	Tim Sherrill RC	.05	505	Frank Thomas	.40	609	Rob Ducey	.05	713	Shawn Boskie	.05
405	Rob MacDonald RC	.05	506	Darren Daulton	.05	610	Ramon Martinez	.05	714	Pat Clements	.05
406	Phil Plantier	.05	507	Kevin Tapani	.05	611	Dave Burba	.05	715	Brian Barnes	.05
407	Troy Afenir	.05	508	Luis Salazar	.05	612	Dwight Smith	.05	716	Luis Lopez RC	.05
408	Gino Minutelli RC	.05	509	Paul Faries	.05	613	Kevin Maas	.05	717	Bob McClure	.05
409	Reggie Jefferson RC	.05	510	Sandy Alomar, Jr.	.05	614	John Costello	.05	718	Mark Davis	.05
410	Mike Remlinger RC	.05	511	Jeff King	.05	615	Glenn Davis	.05	719	Dann Bilardello	.05
411	Carlos Rodriguez RC	.05	512	Gary Thurman	.05	616	Shawn Abner	.05	720	Tom Edens	.05
412	Joe Redfield RC	.05	513	Chris Hammond	.05	617	Scott Hemond	.05	721	Willie Fraser	.05
413	Alonzo Powell	.05	514	Pedro Munoz RC	.05	618	Tom Prince	.05	722	Curt Young	.05
414	Scott Livingstone RC	.05	515	Alan Trammell	.05	619	Wally Ritchie	.05	723	Neal Heaton	.05
415	Scott Kamieniecki RC	.05	516	Geronimo Pena	.05	620	Jim Abbott	.05	724	Craig Worthington	.05
416	Tim Spehr RC	.05	517	Rodney McCray	.05	621	Charlie O'Brien	.05	725	Mel Rojas	.05
417	Brian Hunter RC	.05	518	Manny Lee	.05	622	Jack Daugherty	.05	726	Daryl Irvine	.05
418	Ced Landrum RC	.05	519	Felix Jose	.05	623	Tommy Gregg	.05	727	Roger Mason	.05
419	Bret Barberie RC	.05	520	Kirk Gibson	.05	624	Jeff Shaw	.05	728	Kirk Dressendorfer	.05
420	Kevin Morton	.05	521	Darrin Jackson	.05	625	Tony Gwynn	.50	729	Scott Aldred	.05
421	Doug Henry RC	.05	522	John Burkett	.05	626	Mark Leiter	.05	730	Willie Blair	.05
422	Doug Piatt RC	.05	523	Jeff Johnson	.05	627	Jim Clancy	.05	731	Allan Anderson	.05
423	Pat Rice RC	.05	524	Jim Corsi	.05	628	Tim Layana	.05	732	Dana Kiecker	.05
424	Juan Guzman	.05	525	Robin Yount	.40	629	Jeff Schaefer	.05	733	Jose Gonzalez	.05
425	Nolan Ryan	.50	526	Jamie Quirk	.05	630	Lee Smith	.05	734	Brian Drahman	.05
426	Tommy Greene	.05	527	Bob Ojeda	.05	631	Wade Taylor	.05	735	Brad Komminsk	.05
427	Bob Milacki, Mike Flanagan, Mark Williamson, Gregg Olson	.05	528	Mark Lewis	.05	632	Mike Simms	.05	736	Arthur Rhodes RC	.10
			529	Bryn Smith	.05	633	Terry Steinbach	.05	737	Terry Mathews RC	.05
428	Wilson Alvarez	.05	530	Kent Hrbek	.05	634	Shawon Dunston	.05	738	Jeff Fassero RC	.05
429	Otis Nixon	.05	531	Dennis Boyd	.05	635	Tim Raines	.05	739	Mike Magnante RC	.05
430	Rickey Henderson	.20	532	Ron Karkovice	.05	636	Kirt Manwaring	.05	740	Kip Gross RC	.05
431	Cecil Fielder/AS	.05	533	Don August	.05	637	Warren Cromartie	.05	741	Jim Hunter RC	.05
432	Julio Franco/AS	.05	534	Todd Frohwirth	.05	638	Luis Quinones	.05	742	Jose Mota RC	.05
433	Cal Ripken, Jr./AS	.50	535	Wally Joyner	.05	639	Greg Vaughn	.05	743	Joe Bitker	.05
434	Wade Boggs/AS	.25	536	Dennis Rasmussen	.05	640	Kevin Mitchell	.05	744	Tim Mauser RC	.05
435	Joe Carter/AS	.05	537	Andy Allanson	.05	641	Chris Hoiles	.05	745	Ramon Garcia RC	.05
436	Ken Griffey Jr./AS	.35	538	Rich Gossage	.05	642	Tom Browning	.05	746	Rod Beck RC	.10
437	Ruben Sierra/AS	.05	539	John Marzano	.05	643	Mitch Webster	.05	747	Jim Austin RC	.05
438	Scott Erickson/AS	.05	540	Cal Ripken, Jr.	1.00	644	Steve Olin	.05	748	Keith Mitchell RC	.05
439	Tom Henke/AS	.05	541	Bill Swift	.05	645	Tony Fernandez	.05	749	Wayne Rosenthal RC	.05
440	Terry Steinbach/AS	.05	542	Kevin Appier	.05	646	Juan Bell	.05	750	Bryan Hickerson RC	.05
441	Rickey Henderson	.20	543	Dave Bergman	.05	647	Joe Boever	.05	751	Bruce Egloff RC	.05
442	Ryne Sandberg	.30	544	Bernard Gilkey	.05	648	Carney Lansford	.05	752	John Wehner RC	.05
443	Otis Nixon	.05	545	Mike Greenwell	.05	649	Mike Benjamin	.05	753	Darren Holmes	.05
444	Scott Radinsky	.05	546	Jose Uribe	.05	650	George Brett	.60	754	Dave Hansen	.05
445	Mark Grace	.05	547	Jesse Orosco	.05	651	Tim Burke	.05	755	Mike Mussina	.30
446	Tony Pena	.05	548	Bob Patterson	.05	652	Jack Morris	.05	756	Anthony Young RC	.05
447	Billy Hatcher	.05	549	Mike Stanley	.05	653	Orel Hershiser	.05	757	Ron Tingley	.05
448	Glenallen Hill	.05	550	Howard Johnson	.05	654	Mike Schooler	.05	758	Ricky Bones RC	.05
449	Chris Gwynn	.05	551	Joe Orsulak	.05	655	Andy Van Slyke	.05	759	Mark Wohlers RC	.05
450	Tom Glavine	.35	552	Dick Schofield	.05	656	Dave Stieb	.05	760	Wilson Alvarez	.05
451	John Habyan	.05	553	Dave Hollins	.05	657	Dave Clark	.05	761	Harvey Pulliam RC	.05
452	Al Osuna	.05	554	David Segui	.05	658	Ben McDonald	.05	762	Ryan Bowen RC	.05
453	Tony Phillips	.05	555	Barry Bonds	1.00	659	John Smiley	.05	763	Terry Bross	.05
454	Greg Cadaret	.05	556	Mo Vaughn	.05	660	Wade Boggs	.50	764	Joel Johnston RC	.05
455	Rob Dibble	.05	557	Craig Wilson	.05	661	Eric Bullock	.05	765	Terry McDaniel RC	.05
456	Rick Honeycutt	.05	558	Bobby Rose	.05	662	Eric Show	.05	766	Esteban Beltre RC	.05
457	Jerome Walton	.05	559	Rod Nichols	.05	663	Lenny Webster	.05	767	Rob Maurer RC	.05
458	Mookie Wilson	.05	560	Len Dykstra	.05	664	Mike Huff	.05	768	Ted Wood	.05
459	Mark Gubicza	.05	561	Craig Grebeck	.05	665	Rick Sutcliffe	.05	769	Mo Sanford RC	.05
460	Craig Biggio	.05	562	Darren Lewis	.05	666	Jeff Manto	.05	770	Jeff Carter RC	.05
461	Dave Cochrane	.05	563	Todd Benzinger	.05	667	Mike Fitzgerald	.05	771	Gil Heredia RC	.05
462	Keith Miller	.05	564	Ed Whitson	.05	668	Matt Young	.05	772	Monty Fariss	.05
463	Alex Cole	.05	565	Jesse Barfield	.05	669	Dave West	.05	773	Will Clark/AS	.05
464	Pete Smith	.05	566	Lloyd McClendon	.05	670	Mike Hartley	.05	774	Ryne Sandberg/AS	.25
465	Brett Butler	.05	567	Dan Plesac	.05	671	Curt Schilling	.35	775	Barry Larkin/AS	.05
466	Jeff Huson	.05	568	Danny Cox	.05	672	Brian Bohanon	.05	776	Howard Johnson/AS	.05
467	Steve Lake	.05	569	Skeeter Barnes	.05	673	Cecil Espy	.05	777	Barry Bonds/AS	.50
468	Lloyd Moseby	.05	570	Bobby Thigpen	.05	674	Joe Grahe	.05	778	Brett Butler/AS	.05
469	Tim McIntosh	.05	571	Deion Sanders	.05	675	Sid Fernandez	.05	779	Tony Gwynn/AS	.25
470	Dennis Martinez	.05	572	Chuck Knoblauch	.05	676	Edwin Nunez	.05	780	Ramon Martinez/AS	.05
471	Greg Myers	.05	573	Matt Nokes	.05	677	Hector Villanueva	.05	781	Lee Smith/AS	.05
472	Mackey Sasser	.05	574	Herm Winningham	.05	678	Sean Berry	.05	782	Mike Scioscia/AS	.05
473	Junior Ortiz	.05	575	Tom Candiotti	.05	679	Dave Eiland	.05	783	Dennis Martinez	.05
474	Greg Olson	.05	576	Jeff Bagwell	.40	680	David Cone	.05	784	Dennis Martinez	.05
475	Steve Sax	.05	577	Brook Jacoby	.05	681	Mike Bordick	.05	785	Mark Gardner	.05
476	Ricky Jordan	.05	578	Chico Walker	.05	682	Tony Castillo	.05	786	Bret Saberhagen	.05
477	Max Venable	.05	579	Brian Downing	.05	683	John Barfield	.05	787	Kent Mercker, Mark Wohlers, Alejandro Pena	.05
478	Brian McRae	.05	580	Dave Stewart	.05	684	Jeff Hamilton	.05			
479	Doug Simons	.05	581	Francisco Cabrera	.05	685	Ken Dayley	.05	788	Cal Ripken (MVP)	.50
480	Rickey Henderson	.40	582	Rene Gonzales	.05	686	Carmelo Martinez	.05	789	Terry Pendleton (MVP)	.50
481	Gary Varsho	.05	583	Stan Javier	.05	687	Mike Capel	.05	790	Roger Clemens (CY)	.35
482	Carl Willis	.05	584	Randy Johnson	.40	688	Scott Chiamparino	.05	791	Tom Glavine (CY)	.05
483	Rick Wilkins	.05	585	Chuck Finley	.05	689	Rich Gedman	.05	792	Chuck Knoblauch (ROY)	.05
484	Donn Pall	.05	586	Mark Gardner	.05	690	Rich Monteleone	.05	793	Jeff Bagwell (ROY)	.20
485	Edgar Martinez	.05	587	Mark Whiten	.05	691	Alejandro Pena	.05	794	Cal Ripken, Jr. (Man of the Year)	.50
486	Tom Foley	.05	588	Garry Templeton	.05	692	Oscar Azocar	.05	795	David Cone	.05
487	Mark Williamson	.05	589	Gary Sheffield	.30	693	Jim Poole	.05	796	Kirby Puckett	.25
488	Jack Armstrong	.05	590	Ozzie Smith	.50	694	Mike Gardiner	.05			
			591	Candy Maldonado	.05	695	Steve Buechele	.05			
			592	Mike Sharperson	.05	696	Rudy Seanez	.05			

797	Steve Avery	.05
798	Jack Morris	.05
799	Allen Watson RC	.05
800	Manny Ramirez RC	2.00
801	Cliff Floyd RC	.50
802	Al Shirley RC	.05
803	Brian Barber RC	.05
804	Jon Farrell RC	.05
805	Brent Gates RC	.05
806	Scott Ruffcorn RC	.05
807	Tyrone Hill RC	.05
808	Benji Gil RC	.05
809	Aaron Sele RC	.25
810	Tyler Green RC	.05
811	Chris Jones	.05
812	Steve Wilson	.05
813	Cliff Young RC	.05
814	Don Wakamatsu RC	.05
815	Mike Humphreys RC	.05
816	Scott Servais RC	.05
817	Rico Rossy RC	.05
818	John Ramos RC	.05
819	Rob Mallicoat	.05
820	Milt Hill RC	.05
821	Carlos Carcia	.05
822	Stan Royer	.05
823	Jeff Plympton RC	.05
824	Braulio Castillo RC	.05
825	David Haas RC	.05
826	Luis Mercedes RC	.05
827	Eric Karros RC	.05
828	Shawn Hare RC	.05
829	Reggie Sanders RC	.05
830	Tom Goodwin	.05
831	Dan Gakeler RC	.05
832	Stacy Jones RC	.05
833	Kim Batiste RC	.05
834	Cal Eldred RC	.05
835	Chris George RC	.05
836	Wayne Housie RC	.05
837	Mike Ignasiak RC	.05
838	Josias Manzanillo RC	.05
839	Jim Olander RC	.05
840	Gary Cooper RC	.05
841	Royce Clayton	.05
842	Hector Fajardo	.05
843	Blaine Beatty	.05
844	Jorge Pedre RC	.05
845	Kenny Lofton	.05
846	Scott Brosius	.05
847	Chris Cron RC	.05
848	Denis Boucher	.05
849	Kyle Abbott	.05
850	Bob Zupcic	.05
851	Rheal Cormier RC	.05
852	Jim Lewis RC	.05
853	Anthony Telford	.05
854	Cliff Brantley RC	.05
855	Kevin Campbell RC	.05
856	Craig Shipley RC	.05
857	Chuck Carr	.05
858	Tony Eusebio RC	.10
859	Jim Thome	.35
860	Vinny Castilla RC	.30
861	Dann Howitt	.05
862	Kevin Ward RC	.05
863	Steve Wapnick RC	.05
864	Rod Brewer	.05
865	Todd Van Poppel	.05
866	Jose Hernandez RC	.05
867	Amalio Carreno RC	.05
868	Calvin Jones RC	.05
869	Jeff Gardner RC	.05
870	Jarvis Brown RC	.05
871	Eddie Taubensee RC	.10
872	Andy Mota RC	.05
873	Chris Haney (Front photo actually Scott Ruskin.)	.05
874	Roberto Hernandez	.05
875	Laddie Renfroe RC	.05
876	Scott Cooper	.05
877	Armando Reynoso RC	.05
878	Ty Cobb	.30
879	Babe Ruth	.40
880	Honus Wagner	.30
881	Lou Gehrig	.30
882	Satchel Paige	.35
883	Will Clark	.50
884	Cal Ripken, Jr.	.50
885	Wade Boggs	.25
886	Kirby Puckett	.30
887	Tony Gwynn	.30
888	Craig Biggio	.05
889	Scott Erickson	.05
890	Tom Glavine	.10
891	Rob Dibble	.05
892	Mitch Williams	.05
893	Frank Thomas	.25

1992 Score Factory Set Inserts - World Series

Game 6

	NM/M
Complete Set (7):	1.00
Common Card:	.15
1 Greg Gagne World Series Game 1	.15
2 Scott Leius World Series Game 2	.15
3 David Justice, Brian Harper World Series Game 3	.15
4 Lonnie Smith, Brian Harper World Series Game 4	.15
5 David Justice World Series Game 5	.15
6 Kirby Puckett World Series Game 6	1.00
7 Gene Larkin World Series Game 7	.15

Factory Set Inserts - Cooperstown

CARLTON FISK

	NM/M
Complete Set (4):	1.50
Common Player:	.50
B8 Carlton Fisk	.50
B9 Ozzie Smith	.75
B10 Dave Winfield	.50
B11 Robin Yount	.50

Factory Set Inserts - DiMaggio

JOE DiMAGGIO
The Stylish Fielder

	NM/M
Complete Set (3):	4.00

	Common Card:	1.25
B12	Joe DiMaggio (The Hard Hitter)	1.50
B13	Joe DiMaggio (The Stylish Fielder)	1.50
B14	Joe DiMaggio (The Championship Player)	1.50

Factory Set Inserts - Yastrzemski

CARL YASTRZEMSKI
"25 YEARS" The Impossible Dream

	NM/M
Complete Set (3):	2.00
Common Card:	1.00
B15 Carl Yastrzemski (The Impossible Dream)	1.00
B16 Carl Yastrzemski (The Triple Crown)	1.00
B17 Carl Yastrzemski (The World Series)	1.00

Hot Rookies

HOT ROOKIE
TINO MARTINEZ

	NM/M
Complete Set (10):	4.00
Common Player:	.50
1 Cal Eldred	.50
2 Royce Clayton	.50
3 Kenny Lofton	.75
4 Todd Van Poppel	.50
5 Scott Cooper	.50
6 Todd Hundley	.50
7 Tino Martinez	.75
8 Anthony Telford	.50
9 Derek Bell	.50
10 Reggie Jefferson	.50

Joe DiMaggio

JOE DiMAGGIO
THE BEST

	NM/M
Complete DiMaggio Set (5):	25.00

Common Card:		8.00
Autographed Card:		365.00

The Franchise

CARL YASTRZEMSKI

	NM/M
Complete Set (4):	5.00
Common Player:	1.25
Musial Autograph:	80.00
Mantle Autograph:	450.00
Yastrzemski Autograph:	80.00
Triple Autograph:	1,100
1 Stan Musial	1.50
2 Mickey Mantle	2.50
3 Carl Yastrzemski	1.25
4 Stan Musial, Mickey Mantle, Carl Yastrzemski	1.50

Rookie & Traded

SAMMY SOSA
CENTER FIELD

	NM/M
Complete Set (110):	5.00
Common Player:	.05
1 Gary Sheffield	.20
2 Kevin Seitzer	.05
3 Danny Tartabull	.05
4 Steve Sax	.05
5 Bobby Bonilla	.05
6 Frank Viola	.05
7 Dave Winfield	.60
8 Rick Sutcliffe	.05
9 Jose Canseco	.45
10 Greg Swindell	.05
11 Eddie Murray	.60
12 Randy Myers	.05
13 Wally Joyner	.05
14 Kenny Lofton	.05
15 Jack Morris	.05
16 Charlie Hayes	.05
17 Pete Incaviglia	.05
18 Kevin Mitchell	.05
19 Kurt Stillwell	.05
20 Bret Saberhagen	.05
21 Steve Buechele	.05
22 John Smiley	.05
23 Sammy Sosa	3.00
24 George Bell	.05
25 Curt Schilling	.30
26 Dick Schofield	.05
27 David Cone	.05
28 Dan Gladden	.05
29 Kirk McCaskill	.05
30 Mike Gallego	.05
31 Kevin McReynolds	.05
32 Bill Swift	.05
33 Dave Martinez	.05
34 Storm Davis	.05
35 Willie Randolph	.05
36 Melido Perez	.05
37 Mark Carreon	.05
38 Doug Jones	.05
39 Gregg Jefferies	.05

#	Player	Price
40	Mike Jackson	.05
41	Dickie Thon	.05
42	Eric King	.05
43	Herm Winningham	.05
44	Derek Lilliquist	.05
45	Dave Anderson	.05
46	Jeff Reardon	.05
47	Scott Bankhead	.05
48	Cory Snyder	.05
49	Al Newman	.05
50	Keith Miller	.05
51	Dave Burba	.05
52	Bill Pecota	.05
53	Chuck Crim	.05
54	Mariano Duncan	.05
55	Dave Gallagher	.05
56	Chris Gwynn	.05
57	Scott Ruskin	.05
58	Jack Armstrong	.05
59	Gary Carter	.60
60	Andres Galarraga	.05
61	Ken Hill	.05
62	Eric Davis	.05
63	Ruben Sierra	.05
64	Darrin Fletcher	.05
65	Tim Belcher	.05
66	Mike Morgan	.05
67	Scott Scudder	.05
68	Tom Candiotti	.05
69	Hubie Brooks	.05
70	Kal Daniels	.05
71	Bruce Ruffin	.05
72	Billy Hatcher	.05
73	Bob Melvin	.05
74	Lee Guetterman	.05
75	Rene Gonzales	.05
76	Kevin Bass	.05
77	Tom Bolton	.05
78	John Wetteland	.05
79	Bip Roberts	.05
80	Pat Listach	.05
81	John Doherty	.05
82	Sam Militello	.05
83	Brian Jordan	.05
84	Jeff Kent	.10
85	Dave Fleming	.05
86	Jeff Tackett	.05
87	Chad Curtis	.05
88	Eric Fox	.05
89	Denny Neagle	.05
90	Donovan Osborne	.05
91	Carlos Hernandez	.05
92	Tim Wakefield	.05
93	Tim Salmon	.05
94	Dave Nilsson	.05
95	Mike Perez	.05
96	Pat Hentgen	.05
97	Frank Seminara	.05
98	Ruben Amaro Jr.	.05
99	Archi Cianfrocco	.05
100	Andy Stankiewicz	.05
101	Jim Bullinger	.05
102	Pat Mahomes	.05
103	Hipolito Pichardo	.05
104	Bret Boone	.05
105	John Vander Wal	.05
106	Vince Horsman	.05
107	James Austin	.05
108	Brian Williams	.05
109	Dan Walters	.05
110	Wil Cordero	.05

1993 Score

CHUCK KNOBLAUCH

	NM/M
Complete Set (660):	15.00
Common Player:	.05
Pack (16):	.75
Wax Box (36):	17.50
1 Ken Griffey Jr.	.65
2 Gary Sheffield	.30
3 Frank Thomas	.40
4 Ryne Sandberg	.45
5 Larry Walker	.05

#	Player	Price
6	Cal Ripken, Jr.	1.00
7	Roger Clemens	.50
8	Bobby Bonilla	.05
9	Carlos Baerga	.05
10	Darren Daulton	.05
11	Travis Fryman	.05
12	Andy Van Slyke	.05
13	Jose Canseco	.30
14	Roberto Alomar	.15
15	Tom Glavine	.30
16	Barry Larkin	.05
17	Gregg Jefferies	.05
18	Craig Biggio	.05
19	Shane Mack	.05
20	Brett Butler	.05
21	Dennis Eckersley	.35
22	Will Clark	.05
23	Don Mattingly	.50
24	Tony Gwynn	.45
25	Ivan Rodriguez	.35
26	Shawon Dunston	.05
27	Mike Mussina	.30
28	Marquis Grissom	.05
29	Charles Nagy	.05
30	Len Dykstra	.05
31	Cecil Fielder	.05
32	Jay Bell	.05
33	B.J. Surhoff	.05
34	Bob Tewksbury	.05
35	Danny Tartabull	.05
36	Terry Pendleton	.05
37	Jack Morris	.05
38	Hal Morris	.05
39	Luis Polonia	.05
40	Ken Caminiti	.05
41	Robin Ventura	.05
42	Darryl Strawberry	.05
43	Wally Joyner	.05
44	Fred McGriff	.05
45	Kevin Tapani	.05
46	Matt Williams	.05
47	Robin Yount	.40
48	Ken Hill	.05
49	Edgar Martinez	.05
50	Mark Grace	.05
51	Juan Gonzalez	.20
52	Curt Schilling	.30
53	Dwight Gooden	.05
54	Chris Hoiles	.05
55	Frank Viola	.05
56	Ray Lankford	.05
57	George Brett	.50
58	Kenny Lofton	.05
59	Nolan Ryan	1.00
60	Mickey Tettleton	.05
61	John Smoltz	.05
62	Howard Johnson	.05
63	Eric Karros	.05
64	Rick Aguilera	.05
65	Steve Finley	.05
66	Mark Langston	.05
67	Bill Swift	.05
68	John Olerud	.05
69	Kevin McReynolds	.05
70	Jack McDowell	.05
71	Rickey Henderson	.40
72	Brian Harper	.05
73	Mike Morgan	.05
74	Rafael Palmeiro	.40
75	Dennis Martinez	.05
76	Tino Martinez	.05
77	Eddie Murray	.40
78	Ellis Burks	.05
79	John Kruk	.05
80	Gregg Olson	.05
81	Bernard Gilkey	.05
82	Milt Cuyler	.05
83	Mike LaValliere	.05
84	Albert Belle	.05
85	Bip Roberts	.05
86	Melido Perez	.05
87	Otis Nixon	.05
88	Bill Spiers	.05
89	Jeff Bagwell	.40
90	Orel Hershiser	.05
91	Andy Benes	.05
92	Devon White	.05
93	Willie McGee	.05
94	Ozzie Guillen	.05
95	Ivan Calderon	.05
96	Keith Miller	.05
97	Steve Buechele	.05
98	Kent Hrbek	.05
99	Dave Hollins	.05
100	Mike Bordick	.05
101	Randy Tomlin	.05
102	Omar Vizquel	.05
103	Lee Smith	.05
104	Leo Gomez	.05
105	Jose Rijo	.05
106	Mark Whiten	.05
107	Dave Justice	.05
108	Eddie Taubensee	.05
109	Lance Johnson	.05

#	Player	Price
110	Felix Jose	.05
111	Mike Harkey	.05
112	Randy Milligan	.05
113	Anthony Young	.05
114	Rico Brogna	.05
115	Bret Saberhagen	.05
116	Sandy Alomar, Jr.	.05
117	Terry Mulholland	.05
118	Darryl Hamilton	.05
119	Todd Zeile	.05
120	Bernie Williams	.05
121	Zane Smith	.05
122	Derek Bell	.05
123	Deion Sanders	.05
124	Luis Sojo	.05
125	Joe Oliver	.05
126	Craig Grebeck	.05
127	Andujar Cedeno	.05
128	Brian McRae	.05
129	Jose Offerman	.05
130	Pedro Munoz	.05
131	Bud Black	.05
132	Mo Vaughn	.05
133	Bruce Hurst	.05
134	Dave Henderson	.05
135	Tom Pagnozzi	.05
136	Erik Hanson	.05
137	Orlando Merced	.05
138	Dean Palmer	.05
139	John Franco	.05
140	Brady Anderson	.05
141	Ricky Jordan	.05
142	Jeff Blauser	.05
143	Sammy Sosa	.45
144	Bob Walk	.05
145	Delino DeShields	.05
146	Kevin Brown	.05
147	Mark Lemke	.05
148	Chuck Knoblauch	.05
149	Chris Sabo	.05
150	Bobby Witt	.05
151	Luis Gonzalez	.05
152	Ron Karkovice	.05
153	Jeff Brantley	.05
154	Kevin Appier	.05
155	Darrin Jackson	.05
156	Kelly Gruber	.05
157	Royce Clayton	.05
158	Chuck Finley	.05
159	Jeff King	.05
160	Greg Vaughn	.05
161	Geronimo Pena	.05
162	Steve Farr	.05
163	Jose Oquendo	.05
164	Mark Lewis	.05
165	John Wetteland	.05
166	Mike Henneman	.05
167	Todd Hundley	.05
168	Wes Chamberlain	.05
169	Steve Avery	.05
170	Mike Devereaux	.05
171	Reggie Sanders	.05
172	Jay Buhner	.05
173	Eric Anthony	.05
174	John Burkett	.05
175	Tom Candiotti	.05
176	Phil Plantier	.05
177	Doug Henry	.05
178	Scott Leius	.05
179	Kirt Manwaring	.05
180	Jeff Parrett	.05
181	Don Slaught	.05
182	Scott Radinsky	.05
183	Luis Alicea	.05
184	Tom Gordon	.05
185	Rick Wilkins	.05
186	Todd Stottlemyre	.05
187	Moises Alou	.05
188	Joe Grahe	.05
189	Jeff Kent	.05
190	Bill Wegman	.05
191	Kim Batiste	.05
192	Matt Nokes	.05
193	Mark Wohlers	.05
194	Paul Sorrento	.05
195	Chris Hammond	.05
196	Scott Livingstone	.05
197	Doug Jones	.05
198	Scott Cooper	.05
199	Ramon Martinez	.05
200	Dave Valle	.05
201	Mariano Duncan	.05
202	Ben McDonald	.05
203	Darren Lewis	.05
204	Kenny Rogers	.05
205	Manuel Lee	.05
206	Scott Erickson	.05
207	Dan Gladden	.05
208	Bob Welch	.05
209	Greg Olson	.05
210	Dan Pasqua	.05
211	Tim Wallach	.05
212	Jeff Montgomery	.05
213	Derrick May	.05

#	Player	Price
214	Ed Sprague	.05
215	David Haas	.05
216	Darrin Fletcher	.05
217	Brian Jordan	.05
218	Jaime Navarro	.05
219	Randy Velarde	.05
220	Ron Gant	.05
221	Paul Quantrill	.05
222	Damion Easley	.05
223	Charlie Hough	.05
224	Brad Brink RC	.05
225	Barry Manual RC	.05
226	Kevin Koslofski RC	.05
227	Ryan Thompson RC	.05
228	Mike Munoz RC	.05
229	Dan Wilson RC	.10
230	Peter Hoy RC	.05
231	Pedro Astacio RC	.10
232	Matt Stairs RC	.10
233	Jeff Reboulet RC	.05
234	Manny Alexander RC	.05
235	Willie Banks RC	.05
236	John Jaha RC	.05
237	Scooter Tucker RC	.05
238	Russ Springer RC	.05
239	Paul Miller RC	.05
240	Dan Peltier RC	.05
241	Ozzie Canseco RC	.05
242	Ben Rivera RC	.05
243	John Valentin RC	.05
244	Henry Rodriguez RC	.05
245	Derek Parks RC	.05
246	Carlos Garcia RC	.10
247	Tim Pugh RC	.05
248	Melvin Nieves RC	.05
249	Rich Amaral RC	.05
250	Willie Greene RC	.05
251	Tim Scott RC	.05
252	Dave Silvestri RC	.05
253	Rob Mallicoat RC	.05
254	Donald Harris RC	.05
255	Craig Colbert RC	.05
256	Jose Guzman	.05
257	Domingo Martinez RC	.05
258	William Suero RC	.05
259	Juan Guerrero RC	.05
260	J.T. Snow RC	.45
261	Tony Pena	.05
262	Tim Fortugno RC	.05
263	Tom Marsh RC	.05
264	Kurt Knudsen RC	.05
265	Tim Costo RC	.05
266	Steve Shifflett RC	.05
267	Billy Ashley RC	.05
268	Jerry Nielsen RC	.05
269	Pete Young RC	.05
270	Johnny Guzman RC	.05
271	Greg Colbrunn RC	.05
272	Jeff Nelson RC	.05
273	Kevin Young RC	.05
274	Jeff Frye RC	.05
275	J.T. Bruett RC	.05
276	Todd Pratt RC	.05
277	Mike Butcher RC	.05
278	John Flaherty RC	.05
279	John Patterson RC	.05
280	Eric Hillman RC	.05
281	Bien Figueros RC	.05
282	Shane Reynolds RC	.05
283	Rich Rowland RC	.05
284	Steve Foster RC	.05
285	Dave Mlicki RC	.05
286	Mike Piazza RC	.65
287	Mike Trombley RC	.05
288	Jim Pena RC	.05
289	Bob Ayrault RC	.05
290	Henry Mercedes RC	.05
291	Bob Wickman	.05
292	Jacob Brumfield RC	.05
293	David Hulse RC	.05
294	Ryan Klesko	.05
295	Doug Linton	.05
296	Steve Cooke	.05
297	Eddie Zosky	.05
298	Gerald Williams RC	.05
299	Jonathan Hurst RC	.05
300	Larry Carter RC	.05
301	William Pennyfeather RC	.05
302	Cesar Hernandez RC	.05
303	Steve Hosey RC	.05
304	Blas Minor RC	.05
305	Jeff Grotewold RC	.05
306	Bernardo Brito RC	.05
307	Rafael Bournigal RC	.05
308	Jeff Branson RC	.05
309	Tom Quinlan RC	.05
310	Pat Gomez RC	.05
311	Sterling Hitchcock RC	.10
312	Kent Bottenfield	.05
313	Alan Trammell	.05
314	Cris Colon RC	.05
315	Paul Wagner RC	.05
316	Matt Maysey RC	.05
317	Mike Stanton	.05

#	Player	Price
318	Rick Trlicek **RC**	.05
319	Kevin Rogers **RC**	.05
320	Mark Clark **RC**	.05
321	Pedro Martinez	.40
322	Al Martin **RC**	.05
323	Mike Macfarlane	.05
324	Rey Sanchez **RC**	.10
325	Roger Pavlik **RC**	.05
326	Troy Neel	.05
327	Kerry Woodson **RC**	.05
328	Wayne Kirby **RC**	.05
329	Ken Ryan **RC**	.05
330	Jesse Levis **RC**	.05
331	James Austin	.05
332	Dan Walters	.05
333	Brian Williams	.05
334	Wil Cordero	.05
335	Bret Boone	.05
336	Hipolito Pichardo	.05
337	Pat Mahomes	.05
338	Andy Stankiewicz	.05
339	Jim Bullinger	.05
340	Archi Cianfrocco	.05
341	Ruben Amaro Jr.	.05
342	Frank Seminara	.05
343	Pat Hentgen	.05
344	Dave Nilsson	.05
345	Mike Perez	.05
346	Tim Salmon	.05
347	Tim Wakefield **RC**	.10
348	Carlos Hernandez	.05
349	Donovan Osborne	.05
350	Denny Naegle	.05
351	Sam Militello	.05
352	Eric Fox	.05
353	John Doherty	.05
354	Chad Curtis	.05
355	Jeff Tackett	.05
356	Dave Fleming	.05
357	Pat Listach	.05
358	Kevin Wickander	.05
359	John VanderWal	.05
360	Arthur Rhodes	.05
361	Bob Scanlan	.05
362	Bob Zupcic	.05
363	Mel Rojas	.05
364	Jim Thome	.35
365	Bill Pecota	.05
366	Mark Carreon	.05
367	Mitch Williams	.05
368	Cal Eldred	.05
369	Stan Belinda	.05
370	Pat Kelly	.05
371	Pheal Cormier	.05
372	Juan Guzman	.05
373	Damon Berryhill	.05
374	Gary DiSarcina	.05
375	Norm Charlton	.05
376	Roberto Hernandez	.05
377	Scott Kamieniecki	.05
378	Rusty Meacham	.05
379	Kurt Stillwell	.05
380	Lloyd McClendon	.05
381	Mark Leonard	.05
382	Jerry Browne	.05
383	Glenn Davis	.05
384	Randy Johnson	.40
385	Mike Greenwell	.05
386	Scott Chiamparino	.05
387	George Bell	.05
388	Steve Olin	.05
389	Chuck McElroy	.05
390	Mark Gardner	.05
391	Rod Beck	.05
392	Dennis Rasmussen	.05
393	Charlie Leibrandt	.05
394	Julio Franco	.05
395	Pete Harnisch	.05
396	Sid Bream	.05
397	Milt Thompson	.05
398	Glenallen Hill	.05
399	Chico Walker	.05
400	Alex Cole	.05
401	Trevor Wilson	.05
402	Jeff Conine	.05
403	Kyle Abbott	.05
404	Tom Browning	.05
405	Jerald Clark	.05
406	Vince Horsman	.05
407	Kevin Mitchell	.05
408	Pete Smith	.05
409	Jeff Innis	.05
410	Mike Timlin	.05
411	Charlie Hayes	.05
412	Alex Fernandez	.05
413	Jeff Russell	.05
414	Jody Reed	.05
415	Mickey Morandini	.05
416	Darnell Coles	.05
417	Xavier Hernandez	.05
418	Steve Sax	.05
419	Joe Girardi	.05
420	Mike Fetters	.05
421	Danny Jackson	.05
422	Jim Gott	.05
423	Tim Belcher	.05
424	Jose Mesa	.05
425	Junior Felix	.05
426	Thomas Howard	.05
427	Julio Valera	.05
428	Dante Bichette	.05
429	Mike Sharperson	.05
430	Darryl Kile	.05
431	Lonnie Smith	.05
432	Monty Fariss	.05
433	Reggie Jefferson	.05
434	Bob McClure	.05
435	Craig Lefferts	.05
436	Duane Ward	.05
437	Shawn Abner	.05
438	Roberto Kelly	.05
439	Paul O'Neill	.05
440	Alan Mills	.05
441	Roger Mason	.05
442	Gary Pettis	.05
443	Steve Lake	.05
444	Gene Larkin	.05
445	Larry Anderson	.05
446	Doug Dascenzo	.05
447	Daryl Boston	.05
448	John Candelaria	.05
449	Storm Davis	.05
450	Tom Edens	.05
451	Mike Maddux	.05
452	Tim Naehring	.05
453	John Orton	.05
454	Joey Cora	.05
455	Chuck Crim	.05
456	Dan Plesac	.05
457	Mike Bielecki	.05
458	Terry Jorgensen **RC**	.05
459	John Habyan	.05
460	Pete O'Brien	.05
461	Jeff Treadway	.05
462	Frank Castillo	.05
463	Jimmy Jones	.05
464	Tommy Greene	.05
465	Tracy Woodson	.05
466	Rich Rodriguez	.05
467	Joe Hesketh	.05
468	Greg Myers	.05
469	Kirk McCaskill	.05
470	Ricky Bones	.05
471	Lenny Webster	.05
472	Francisco Cabrera	.05
473	Turner Ward	.05
474	Dwayne Henry	.05
475	Al Osuna	.05
476	Craig Wilson	.05
477	Chris Nabholz	.05
478	Rafael Belliard	.05
479	Terry Leach	.05
480	Tim Teufel	.05
481	Dennis Eckersley	.15
482	Barry Bonds	.50
483	Dennis Eckersley	.15
484	Greg Maddux (Award Winner)	.25
485	Pat Listach (ROY)	.05
486	Eric Karros (ROY)	.05
487	Jamie Arnold **RC**	.05
488	B.J. Wallace	.05
489	Derek Jeter **RC**	8.00
490	Jason Kendall **RC**	.45
491	Rick Helling	.05
492	Derek Wallace **RC**	.05
493	Sean Lowe **RC**	.05
494	Shannon Stewart **RC**	.65
495	Benji Grigsby **RC**	.05
496	Todd Steverson **RC**	.05
497	Dan Serafini **RC**	.05
498	Michael Tucker	.05
499	Chris Roberts	.05
500	Pete Janicki **RC**	.05
501	Jeff Schmidt **RC**	.05
502	Edgar Martinez/AS	.05
503	Omar Vizquel/AS	.05
504	Ken Griffey Jr./AS	.35
505	Kirby Puckett/AS	.25
506	Joe Carter/AS	.05
507	Ivan Rodriguez/AS	.15
508	Jack Morris/AS	.05
509	Dennis Eckersley/AS	.15
510	Frank Thomas/AS	.20
511	Roberto Alomar/AS	.10
512	Mickey Morandini	.05
513	Dennis Eckersley	.15
514	Jeff Reardon	.05
515	Danny Tartabull	.05
516	Bip Roberts	.05
517	George Brett	.30
518	Robin Yount	.20
519	Kevin Gross	.05
520	Ed Sprague	.05
521	Dave Winfield	.20
522	Ozzie Smith/AS	.25
523	Barry Bonds/AS	.50
524	Andy Van Slyke/AS	.05
525	Tony Gwynn/AS	.25
526	Darren Daulton/AS	.05
527	Greg Maddux/AS	.25
528	Fred McGriff/AS	.05
529	Lee Smith/AS	.05
530	Ryne Sandberg/AS	.25
531	Gary Sheffield/AS	.10
532	Ozzie Smith	.25
533	Kirby Puckett	.25
534	Gary Sheffield	.10
535	Andy Van Slyke	.05
536	Ken Griffey Jr.	.35
537	Ivan Rodriguez	.15
538	Charles Nagy	.05
539	Tom Glavine	.10
540	Dennis Eckersley	.15
541	Frank Thomas	.20
542	Roberto Alomar	.10
543	Sean Barry	.05
544	Mike Schooler	.05
545	Chuck Carr	.05
546	Lenny Harris	.05
547	Gary Scott	.05
548	Derek Lilliquist	.05
549	Brian Hunter	.05
550	Kirby Puckett (MOY)	.25
551	Jim Eisenreich	.05
552	Andre Dawson	.25
553	David Nied	.05
554	Spike Owen	.05
555	Greg Gagne	.05
556	Sid Fernandez	.05
557	Mark McGwire	.75
558	Bryan Harvey	.05
559	Harold Reynolds	.05
560	Barry Bonds	1.00
561	Eric Wedge **RC**	.05
562	Ozzie Smith	.45
563	Rick Sutcliffe	.05
564	Jeff Reardon	.05
565	Alex Arias **RC**	.05
566	Greg Swindell	.05
567	Brook Jacoby	.05
568	Pete Incaviglia	.05
569	Butch Henry **RC**	.05
570	Eric Davis	.05
571	Kevin Seitzer	.05
572	Tony Fernandez	.05
573	Steve Reed **RC**	.05
574	Cory Snyder	.05
575	Joe Carter	.05
576	Greg Maddux	.45
577	Bert Blyleven	.05
578	Kevin Bass	.05
579	Carlton Fisk	.40
580	Doug Drabek	.05
581	Mark Gubicza	.05
582	Bobby Thigpen	.05
583	Chili Davis	.05
584	Scott Bankhead	.05
585	Harold Baines	.05
586	Eric Young **RC**	.15
587	Lance Parrish	.05
588	Juan Bell	.05
589	Bob Ojeda	.05
590	Joe Orsulak	.05
591	Benito Santiago	.05
592	Wade Boggs	.45
593	Robby Thompson	.05
594	Erik Plunk	.05
595	Hensley Meulens	.05
596	Lou Whitaker	.05
597	Dale Murphy	.25
598	Paul Molitor	.40
599	Greg W. Harris	.05
600	Darren Holmes	.05
601	Dave Martinez	.05
602	Tom Henke	.05
603	Mike Benjamin	.05
604	Rene Gonzales	.05
605	Roger McDowell	.05
606	Kirby Puckett	.45
607	Randy Myers	.05
608	Ruben Sierra	.05
609	Wilson Alvarez	.05
610	Dave Segui	.05
611	Juan Samuel	.05
612	Tom Brunansky	.05
613	Willie Randolph	.05
614	Tony Phillips	.05
615	Candy Maldonado	.05
616	Chris Bosio	.05
617	Bret Barberie	.05
618	Scott Sanderson	.05
619	Ron Darling	.05
620	Dave Winfield	.40
621	Mike Felder	.05
622	Greg Hibbard	.05
623	Mike Scioscia	.05
624	John Smiley	.05
625	Alejandro Pena	.05
626	Terry Steinbach	.05
627	Freddie Benavides	.05
628	Kevin Reimer	.05
629	Braulio Castillo	.05
630	Dave Stieb	.05
631	Dave Magadan	.05
632	Scott Fletcher	.05
633	Cris Carpenter	.05
634	Kevin Maas	.05
635	Todd Worrell	.05
636	Rob Deer	.05
637	Dwight Smith	.05
638	Chito Martinez	.05
639	Jimmy Key	.05
640	Greg Harris	.05
641	Mike Moore	.05
642	Pat Borders	.05
643	Bill Gullickson	.05
644	Gary Gaetti	.05
645	David Howard	.05
646	Jim Abbott	.05
647	Willie Wilson	.05
648	David Wells	.05
649	Andres Galarraga	.05
650	Vince Coleman	.05
651	Rob Dibble	.05
652	Frank Tanana	.05
653	Steve Decker	.05
654	David Cone	.05
655	Jack Armstrong	.05
656	Dave Stewart	.05
657	Billy Hatcher	.05
658	Tim Raines	.05
659	Walt Weiss	.05
660	Jose Lind	.05

Boys of Summer

		NM/M
Complete Set (30):		12.50
Common Player:		.25
1	Billy Ashley	.25
2	Tim Salmon	.50
3	Pedro Martinez	4.00
4	Luis Mercedes	.25
5	Mike Piazza	8.00
6	Troy Neel	.25
7	Melvin Nieves	.25
8	Ryan Klesko	.25
9	Ryan Thompson	.25
10	Kevin Young	.25
11	Gerald Williams	.25
12	Willie Greene	.25
13	John Patterson	.25
14	Carlos Garcia	.25
15	Eddie Zosky	.25
16	Sean Berry	.25
17	Rico Brogna	.25
18	Larry Carter	.25
19	Bobby Ayala	.25
20	Alan Embree	.25
21	Donald Harris	.25
22	Sterling Hitchcock	.25
23	David Nied	.25
24	Henry Mercedes	.25
25	Ozzie Canseco	.25
26	David Hulse	.25
27	Al Martin	.25
28	Dan Wilson	.25
29	Paul Miller	.25
30	Rich Rowland	.25

The Franchise

		NM/M
Complete Set (28):		50.00
Common Player:		.60
1	Cal Ripken, Jr.	12.00
2	Roger Clemens	6.00
3	Mark Langston	.60
4	Frank Thomas	3.50
5	Carlos Baerga	.60
6	Cecil Fielder	.60
7	Gregg Jefferies	.60
8	Robin Yount	3.50
9	Kirby Puckett	5.00
10	Don Mattingly	6.00

11	Dennis Eckersley	3.00
12	Ken Griffey Jr.	9.00
13	Juan Gonzalez	3.50
14	Roberto Alomar	1.50
15	Terry Pendleton	.60
16	Ryne Sandberg	5.00
17	Barry Larkin	.60
18	Jeff Bagwell	3.50
19	Brett Butler	.60
20	Larry Walker	.60
21	Bobby Bonilla	.60
22	Darren Daulton	.60
23	Andy Van Slyke	.60
24	Ray Lankford	.60
25	Gary Sheffield	1.50
26	Will Clark	.60
27	Bryan Harvey	.60
28	David Nied	.60

Dream Team

		NM/M
Complete Set (12):		5.00
Common Player:		.25
1	Ozzie Smith	1.00
2	Kirby Puckett	1.00
3	Gary Sheffield	.35
4	Andy Van Slyke	.25
5	Ken Griffey Jr.	2.00
6	Ivan Rodriguez	.60
7	Charles Nagy	.25
8	Tom Glavine	.35
9	Dennis Eckersley	.60
10	Frank Thomas	.75
11	Roberto Alomar	.30
---	Header Card	.05

1994 Score

	NM/M
Complete Set (660):	15.00

Common Player:		.05
Gold Rush:		2X
Pack (14):		.75
Wax Box (36):		15.00
1	Barry Bonds	1.00
2	John Olerud	.05
3	Ken Griffey Jr.	.65
4	Jeff Bagwell	.40
5	John Burkett	.05
6	Jack McDowell	.05
7	Albert Belle	.05
8	Andres Galarraga	.05
9	Mike Mussina	.30
10	Will Clark	.05
11	Travis Fryman	.05
12	Tony Gwynn	.50
13	Robin Yount	.40
14	Dave Magadan	.05
15	Paul O'Neill	.05
16	Ray Lankford	.05
17	Damion Easley	.05
18	Andy Van Slyke	.05
19	Brian McRae	.05
20	Ryne Sandberg	.50
21	Kirby Puckett	.50
22	Dwight Gooden	.05
23	Don Mattingly	.60
24	Kevin Mitchell	.05
25	Roger Clemens	.60
26	Eric Karros	.05
27	Juan Gonzalez	.20
28	John Kruk	.05
29	Gregg Jefferies	.05
30	Tom Glavine	.30
31	Ivan Rodriguez	.35
32	Jay Bell	.05
33	Randy Johnson	.40
34	Darren Daulton	.05
35	Rickey Henderson	.40
36	Eddie Murray	.40
37	Brian Harper	.05
38	Delino DeShields	.05
39	Jose Lind	.05
40	Benito Santiago	.05
41	Frank Thomas	.40
42	Mark Grace	.05
43	Roberto Alomar	.20
44	Andy Benes	.05
45	Luis Polonia	.05
46	Brett Butler	.05
47	Terry Steinbach	.05
48	Craig Biggio	.05
49	Greg Vaughn	.05
50	Charlie Hayes	.05
51	Mickey Tettleton	.05
52	Jose Rijo	.05
53	Carlos Baerga	.05
54	Jeff Blauser	.05
55	Leo Gomez	.05
56	Bob Tewksbury	.05
57	Mo Vaughn	.05
58	Orlando Merced	.05
59	Tino Martinez	.05
60	Len Dykstra	.05
61	Jose Canseco	.25
62	Tony Fernandez	.05
63	Donovan Osborne	.05
64	Ken Hill	.05
65	Kent Hrbek	.05
66	Bryan Harvey	.05
67	Wally Joyner	.05
68	Derrick May	.05
69	Lance Johnson	.05
70	Willie McGee	.05
71	Mark Langston	.05
72	Terry Pendleton	.05
73	Joe Carter	.05
74	Barry Larkin	.05
75	Jimmy Key	.05
76	Joe Girardi	.05
77	B.J. Surhoff	.05
78	Pete Harnisch	.05
79	Lou Whitaker	.05
80	Cory Snyder	.05
81	Brent Mayne	.05
82	Fred McGriff	.05
83	Mike Greenwell	.05
84	Mike Perez	.05
85	Cal Ripken, Jr.	1.00
86	Don Slaught	.05
87	Omar Vizquel	.05
88	Curt Schilling	.30
89	Chuck Knoblauch	.05
90	Moises Alou	.05
91	Greg Gagne	.05
92	Bret Saberhagen	.05
93	Ozzie Guillen	.05
94	Matt Williams	.05
95	Chad Curtis	.05
96	Mike Harkey	.05
97	Devon White	.05
98	Walt Weiss	.05
99	Kevin Brown	.05
100	Gary Sheffield	.25

101	Wade Boggs	.50
102	Orel Hershiser	.05
103	Tony Phillips	.05
104	Andujar Cedeno	.05
105	Bill Spiers	.05
106	Otis Nixon	.05
107	Felix Fermin	.05
108	Bip Roberts	.05
109	Dennis Eckersley	.35
110	Dante Bichette	.05
111	Ben McDonald	.05
112	Jim Poole	.05
113	John Dopson	.05
114	Rob Dibble	.05
115	Jeff Treadway	.05
116	Ricky Jordan	.05
117	Mike Henneman	.05
118	Willie Blair	.05
119	Doug Henry	.05
120	Gerald Perry	.05
121	Greg Myers	.05
122	John Franco	.05
123	Roger Mason	.05
124	Chris Hammond	.05
125	Hubie Brooks	.05
126	Kent Mercker	.05
127	Jim Abbott	.05
128	Kevin Bass	.05
129	Rick Aguilera	.05
130	Mitch Webster	.05
131	Eric Plunk	.05
132	Mark Carreon	.05
133	Dave Stewart	.05
134	Willie Wilson	.05
135	Dave Fleming	.05
136	Jeff Tackett	.05
137	Geno Petralli	.05
138	Gene Harris	.05
139	Scott Bankhead	.05
140	Trevor Wilson	.05
141	Alvaro Espinoza	.05
142	Ryan Bowen	.05
143	Mike Moore	.05
144	Bill Pecota	.05
145	Jaime Navarro	.05
146	Jack Daugherty	.05
147	Bob Wickman	.05
148	Chris Jones	.05
149	Todd Stottlemyre	.05
150	Brian Williams	.05
151	Chuck Finley	.05
152	Lenny Harris	.05
153	Alex Fernandez	.05
154	Candy Maldonado	.05
155	Jeff Montgomery	.05
156	David West	.05
157	Mark Williamson	.05
158	Milt Thompson	.05
159	Ron Darling	.05
160	Stan Belinda	.05
161	Henry Cotto	.05
162	Mel Rojas	.05
163	Doug Strange	.05
164	Rene Arocha (1993 Rookie)	.05
165	Tim Hulett	.05
166	Steve Avery	.05
167	Jim Thome	.35
168	Tom Browning	.05
169	Mario Diaz	.05
170	Steve Reed (1993 Rookie)	.05
171	Scott Livingstone	.05
172	Chris Donnels	.05
173	John Jaha	.05
174	Carlos Hernandez	.05
175	Dion James	.05
176	Bud Black	.05
177	Tony Castillo	.05
178	Jose Guzman	.05
179	Torey Lovullo	.05
180	John Vander Wal	.05
181	Mike LaValliere	.05
182	Sid Fernandez	.05
183	Brent Mayne	.05
184	Terry Mulholland	.05
185	Willie Banks	.05
186	Steve Cooke (1993 Rookie)	.05
187	Brent Gates (1993 Rookie)	.05
188	Erik Pappas (1993 Rookie)	.05
189	Bill Haseman (1993 Rookie)	.05
190	Fernando Valenzuela	.05
191	Gary Redus	.05
192	Danny Darwin	.05
193	Mark Portugal	.05
194	Derek Lilliquist	.05
195	Charlie O'Brien	.05
196	Matt Nokes	.05
197	Danny Sheaffer	.05
198	Bill Gullickson	.05

199	Alex Arias (1993 Rookie)	.05
200	Mike Fetters	.05
201	Brian Jordan	.05
202	Joe Grahe	.05
203	Tom Candiotti	.05
204	Jeremy Stanton	.05
205	Mike Stanton	.05
206	David Howard	.05
207	Darren Holmes	.05
208	Rick Honeycutt	.05
209	Danny Jackson	.05
210	Rich Amaral (1993 Rookie)	.05
211	Blas Minor (1993 Rookie)	.05
212	Kenny Rogers	.05
213	Jim Leyritz	.05
214	Mike Morgan	.05
215	Dan Gladden	.05
216	Randy Velarde	.05
217	Mitch Williams	.05
218	Hipolito Pichardo	.05
219	Dave Burba	.05
220	Wilson Alvarez	.05
221	Bob Zupcic	.05
222	Francisco Cabrera	.05
223	Julio Valera	.05
224	Paul Assenmacher	.05
225	Jeff Branson	.05
226	Todd Frohwirth	.05
227	Armando Reynoso	.05
228	Rich Rowland (1993 Rookie)	.05
229	Freddie Benavides	.05
230	Wayne Kirby (1993 Rookie)	.05
231	Darryl Kile	.05
232	Skeeter Barnes	.05
233	Ramon Martinez	.05
234	Tom Gordon	.05
235	Dave Gallagher	.05
236	Ricky Bones	.05
237	Larry Andersen	.05
238	Pat Meares (1993 Rookie)	.05
239	Zane Smith	.05
240	Tim Leary	.05
241	Phil Clark	.05
242	Danny Cox	.05
243	Mike Jackson	.05
244	Mike Gallego	.05
245	Lee Smith	.05
246	Todd Jones (1993 Rookie)	.05
247	Steve Bedrosian	.05
248	Troy Neel	.05
249	Jose Bautista	.05
250	Steve Frey	.05
251	Jeff Reardon	.05
252	Stan Javier	.05
253	Mo Sanford (1993 Rookie)	.05
254	Steve Sax	.05
255	Luis Aquino	.05
256	Domingo Jean (1993 Rookie)	.05
257	Scott Servais	.05
258	Brad Pennington (1993 Rookie)	.05
259	Dave Hansen	.05
260	Goose Gossage	.05
261	Jeff Fassero	.05
262	Junior Ortiz	.05
263	Anthony Young	.05
264	Chris Bosio	.05
265	Ruben Amaro Jr.	.05
266	Mark Eichhorn	.05
267	Dave Clark	.05
268	Gary Thurman	.05
269	Les Lancaster	.05
270	Jamie Moyer	.05
271	Ricky Gutierrez (1993 Rookie)	.05
272	Greg Harris	.05
273	Mike Benjamin	.05
274	Gene Nelson	.05
275	Damon Berryhill	.05
276	Scott Radinsky	.05
277	Mike Aldrete	.05
278	Jerry DiPoto (1993 Rookie)	.05
279	Chris Haney	.05
280	Richie Lewis (1993 Rookie)	.05
281	Jarvis Brown	.05
282	Juan Bell	.05
283	Joe Klink	.05
284	Graeme Lloyd (1993 Rookie)	.05
285	Casey Candaele	.05
286	Bob MacDonald	.05
287	Mike Sharperson	.05
288	Gene Larkin	.05

#	Player	Price
289	Brian Barnes	.05
290	David McCarty (1993 Rookie)	.05
291	Jeff Innis	.05
292	Bob Patterson	.05
293	Ben Rivera	.05
294	John Habyan	.05
295	Rich Rodriguez	.05
296	Edwin Nunez	.05
297	Rod Brewer	.05
298	Mike Timlin	.05
299	Jesse Orosco	.05
300	Gary Gaetti	.05
301	Todd Benzinger	.05
302	Jeff Nelson	.05
303	Rafael Belliard	.05
304	Matt Whiteside	.05
305	Vinny Castilla	.05
306	Matt Turner	.05
307	Eduardo Perez	.05
308	Joel Johnston	.05
309	Chris Gomez	.05
310	Pat Rapp	.05
311	Jim Tatum	.05
312	Kirk Rueter	.05
313	John Flaherty	.05
314	Tom Kramer	.05
315	Mark Whiten (Highlights)	.05
316	Chris Bosio (Highlights)	.05
317	Orioles Checklist	.05
318	Red Sox Checklist	.05
319	Angels Checklist	.05
320	White Sox Checklist	.05
321	Indians Checklist	.05
322	Tigers Checklist	.05
323	Royals Checklist	.05
324	Brewers Checklist	.05
325	Twins Checklist	.05
326	Yankees Checklist	.05
327	Athletics Checklist	.05
328	Mariners Checklist	.05
329	Rangers Checklist	.05
330	Blue Jays Checklist	.05
331	Frank Viola	.05
332	Ron Gant	.05
333	Charles Nagy	.05
334	Roberto Kelly	.05
335	Brady Anderson	.05
336	Alex Cole	.05
337	Alan Trammell	.05
338	Derek Bell	.05
339	Bernie Williams	.05
340	Jose Offerman	.05
341	Bill Wegman	.05
342	Ken Caminiti	.05
343	Pat Borders	.05
344	Kirt Manwaring	.05
345	Chili Davis	.05
346	Steve Buechele	.05
347	Robin Ventura	.05
348	Teddy Higuera	.05
349	Jerry Browne	.05
350	Scott Kamieniecki	.05
351	Kevin Tapani	.05
352	Marquis Grissom	.05
353	Jay Buhner	.05
354	Dave Hollins	.05
355	Dan Wilson	.05
356	Bob Walk	.05
357	Chris Hoiles	.05
358	Todd Zeile	.05
359	Kevin Appier	.05
360	Chris Sabo	.05
361	David Segui	.05
362	Jerald Clark	.05
363	Tony Pena	.05
364	Steve Finley	.05
365	Roger Pavlik	.05
366	John Smoltz	.05
367	Scott Fletcher	.05
368	Jody Reed	.05
369	David Wells	.05
370	Jose Vizcaino	.05
371	Pat Listach	.05
372	Orestes Destrade	.05
373	Danny Tartabull	.05
374	Greg W. Harris	.05
375	Juan Guzman	.05
376	Larry Walker	.05
377	Gary DiSarcina	.05
378	Bobby Bonilla	.05
379	Tim Raines	.05
380	Tommy Greene	.05
381	Chris Gwynn	.05
382	Jeff King	.05
383	Shane Mack	.05
384	Ozzie Smith	.50
385	Eddie Zambrano RC	.05
386	Mike Devereaux	.05
387	Erik Hanson	.05
388	Scott Cooper	.05
389	Dean Palmer	.05
390	John Wetteland	.05
391	Reggie Jefferson	.05
392	Mark Lemke	.05
393	Cecil Fielder	.05
394	Reggie Sanders	.05
395	Darryl Hamilton	.05
396	Daryl Boston	.05
397	Pat Kelly	.05
398	Joe Orsulak	.05
399	Ed Sprague	.05
400	Eric Anthony	.05
401	Scott Sanderson	.05
402	Jim Gott	.05
403	Ron Karkovice	.05
404	Phil Plantier	.05
405	David Cone	.05
406	Robby Thompson	.05
407	Dave Winfield	.40
408	Dwight Smith	.05
409	Ruben Sierra	.05
410	Jack Armstrong	.05
411	Mike Felder	.05
412	Wil Cordero	.05
413	Julio Franco	.05
414	Howard Johnson	.05
415	Mark McLemore	.05
416	Pete Incaviglia	.05
417	John Valentin	.05
418	Tim Wakefield	.05
419	Jose Mesa	.05
420	Bernard Gilkey	.05
421	Kirk Gibson	.05
422	Dave Justice	.05
423	Tom Brunansky	.05
424	John Smiley	.05
425	Kevin Maas	.05
426	Doug Drabek	.05
427	Paul Molitor	.40
428	Darryl Strawberry	.05
429	Tim Naehring	.05
430	Bill Swift	.05
431	Ellis Burks	.05
432	Greg Hibbard	.05
433	Felix Jose	.05
434	Bret Barberie	.05
435	Pedro Munoz	.05
436	Darrin Fletcher	.05
437	Bobby Witt	.05
438	Wes Chamberlain	.05
439	Mackey Sasser	.05
440	Mark Whiten	.05
441	Harold Reynolds	.05
442	Greg Olson	.05
443	Billy Hatcher	.05
444	Joe Oliver	.05
445	Sandy Alomar Jr.	.05
446	Tim Wallach	.05
447	Karl Rhodes	.05
448	Royce Clayton	.05
449	Cal Eldred	.05
450	Rick Wilkins	.05
451	Mike Stanley	.05
452	Charlie Hough	.05
453	Jack Morris	.05
454	Jon Ratliff RC	.05
455	Rene Gonzales	.05
456	Eddie Taubensee	.05
457	Roberto Hernandez	.05
458	Todd Hundley	.05
459	Mike MacFarlane	.05
460	Mickey Morandini	.05
461	Scott Erickson	.05
462	Lonnie Smith	.05
463	Dave Henderson	.05
464	Ryan Klesko	.05
465	Edgar Martinez	.05
466	Tim Pagnozzi	.05
467	Charlie Leibrandt	.05
468	Brian Anderson RC	.10
469	Harold Baines	.05
470	Tim Belcher	.05
471	Andre Dawson	.25
472	Eric Young	.05
473	Paul Sorrento	.05
474	Luis Gonzalez	.05
475	Rob Deer	.05
476	Mike Piazza	.65
477	Kevin Reimer	.05
478	Jeff Gardner	.05
479	Melido Perez	.05
480	Darren Lewis	.05
481	Duane Ward	.05
482	Rey Sanchez	.05
483	Mark Lewis	.05
484	Jeff Conine	.05
485	Joey Cora	.05
486	Trot Nixon RC	.50
487	Kevin McReynolds	.05
488	Mike Lansing	.05
489	Mike Pagliarulo	.05
490	Mariano Duncan	.05
491	Mike Bordick	.05
492	Kevin Young	.05
493	Dave Valle	.05
494	Wayne Gomes RC	.05
495	Rafael Palmeiro	.35
496	Deion Sanders	.05
497	Rick Sutcliffe	.05
498	Randy Milligan	.05
499	Carlos Quintana	.05
500	Chris Turner	.05
501	Thomas Howard	.05
502	Greg Swindell	.05
503	Chad Kreuter	.05
504	Eric Davis	.05
505	Dickie Thon	.05
506	Matt Drews RC	.05
507	Spike Owen	.05
508	Rod Beck	.05
509	Pat Hentgen	.05
510	Sammy Sosa	.50
511	J.T. Snow	.05
512	Chuck Carr	.05
513	Bo Jackson	.10
514	Dennis Martinez	.05
515	Phil Hiatt	.05
516	Jeff Kent	.05
517	Brooks Kieschnick RC	.05
518	Kirk Presley RC	.05
519	Kevin Seitzer	.05
520	Carlos Garcia	.05
521	Mike Blowers	.05
522	Luis Alicea	.05
523	David Hulse	.05
524	Greg Maddux	.50
525	Gregg Olson	.05
526	Hal Morris	.05
527	Daron Kirkreit	.05
528	David Nied	.05
529	Jeff Russell	.05
530	Kevin Gross	.05
531	John Doherty	.05
532	Matt Brunson RC	.05
533	Dave Nilsson	.05
534	Randy Myers	.05
535	Steve Farr	.05
536	Billy Wagner RC	.10
537	Darnell Coles	.05
538	Frank Tanana	.05
539	Tim Salmon	.05
540	Kim Batiste	.05
541	George Bell	.05
542	Tom Henke	.05
543	Sam Horn	.05
544	Doug Jones	.05
545	Scott Leius	.05
546	Al Martin	.05
547	Bob Welch	.05
548	Scott Christman RC	.05
549	Norm Charlton	.05
550	Mark McGwire	.75
551	Greg McMichael	.05
552	Tim Costo	.05
553	Rodney Bolton	.05
554	Pedro Martinez	.40
555	Marc Valdes	.05
556	Darrell Whitmore	.05
557	Tim Bogar	.05
558	Steve Karsay	.05
559	Danny Bautista	.05
560	Jeffrey Hammonds	.05
561	Aaron Sele	.05
562	Russ Springer	.05
563	Jason Bere	.05
564	Billy Brewer	.05
565	Sterling Hitchcock	.05
566	Pedro Munoz	.05
567	Craig Paquette	.05
568	Bret Boone	.05
569	Dan Peltier	.05
570	Jeromy Burnitz	.05
571	John Wasdin RC	.05
572	Chipper Jones	.50
573	Jamey Wright RC	.05
574	Jeff Granger	.05
575	Jay Powell RC	.05
576	Ryan Thompson	.05
577	Lou Frazier	.05
578	Paul Wagner	.05
579	Brad Ausmus	.05
580	Jack Voigt	.05
581	Kevin Rogers	.05
582	Damon Buford	.05
583	Paul Quantrill	.05
584	Marc Newfield	.05
585	Derrek Lee RC	1.00
586	Shane Reynolds	.05
587	Cliff Floyd	.05
588	Jeff Schwarz	.05
589	Ross Powell RC	.05
590	Gerald Williams	.05
591	Mike Trombley	.05
592	Ken Ryan	.05
593	John O'Donoghue	.05
594	Rod Correia	.05
595	Darrell Sherman	.05
596	Steve Scarsone	.05
597	Sherman Obando	.05
598	Kurt Abbott	.05
599	Dave Telgheder	.05
600	Rick Trlicek	.05
601	Carl Everett	.05
602	Luis Ortiz	.05
603	Larry Luebbers RC	.05
604	Kevin Roberson	.05
605	Butch Huskey	.05
606	Benji Gil	.05
607	Todd Van Poppel	.05
608	Mark Hutton	.05
609	Chip Hale	.05
610	Matt Maysey	.05
611	Scott Ruffcorn	.05
612	Hilly Hathaway	.05
613	Allen Watson	.05
614	Carlos Delgado	.30
615	Roberto Mejia	.05
616	Turk Wendell	.05
617	Tony Tarasco	.05
618	Raul Mondesi	.05
619	Kevin Stocker	.05
620	Javier Lopez	.05
621	Keith Kessinger RC	.05
622	Bob Hamelin	.05
623	John Roper	.05
624	Len Dykstra	.05
625	Joe Carter	.05
626	Jim Abbott (Highlight)	.05
627	Lee Smith (Highlight)	.05
628	Ken Griffey Jr. (HL)	.35
629	Dave Winfield (Highlight)	.05
630	Darryl Kile (Highlight)	.05
631	Frank Thomas (MVP)	.25
632	Barry Bonds (MVP)	.50
633	Jack McDowell (Cy Young)	.05
634	Greg Maddux (Cy Young)	.25
635	Tim Salmon (ROY)	.05
636	Mike Piazza (ROY)	.40
637	Brian Turang RC	.05
638	Rondell White	.05
639	Nigel Wilson	.05
640	Torii Hunter RC	.75
641	Salomon Torres	.05
642	Kevin Higgins	.05
643	Eric Wedge	.05
644	Roger Salkeld	.05
645	Manny Ramirez	.40
646	Jeff McNeely	.05
647	Braves Checklist	.05
648	Cubs Checklist	.05
649	Reds Checklist	.05
650	Rockies Checklist	.05
651	Marlins Checklist	.05
652	Astros Checklist	.05
653	Dodgers Checklist	.05
654	Expos Checklist	.05
655	Mets Checklist	.05
656	Phillies Checklist	.05
657	Pirates Checklist	.05
658	Cardinals Checklist	.05
659	Padres Checklist	.05
660	Giants Checklist	.05

Gold Rush

Cal Ripken, Jr. — BALTIMORE ORIOLES

	NM/M
Complete Set (660):	40.00
Common Player:	.15
Stars:	2X

(See 1994 Score for checklist and base card values.)

Boys of Summer

		NM/M
Complete Set (60):		25.00
Common Player:		.25
1	Jeff Conine	.25
2	Aaron Sele	.25
3	Kevin Stocker	.25
4	Pat Meares	.25
5	Jeromy Burnitz	.25

6	Mike Piazza	6.00
7	Allen Watson	.25
8	Jeffrey Hammonds	.25
9	Kevin Roberson	.25
10	Hilly Hathaway	.25
11	Kirk Reuter	.25
12	Eduardo Perez	.25
13	Ricky Gutierrez	.25
14	Domingo Jean	.25
15	David Nied	.25
16	Wayne Kirby	.25
17	Mike Lansing	.25
18	Jason Bere	.25
19	Brent Gates	.25
20	Javier Lopez	.25
21	Greg McMichael	.25
22	David Hulse	.25
23	Roberto Mejia	.25
24	Tim Salmon	.50
25	Rene Arocha	.25
26	Bret Boone	.25
27	David McCarty	.25
28	Todd Van Poppel	.25
29	Lance Painter	.25
30	Erik Pappas	.25
31	Chuck Carr	.25
32	Mark Hutton	.25
33	Jeff McNeely	.25
34	Willie Greene	.25
35	Nigel Wilson	.25
36	Rondell White	.25
37	Brian Turang	.25
38	Manny Ramirez	3.00
39	Salomon Torres	.25
40	Melvin Nieves	.25
41	Ryan Klesko	.25
42	Keith Kessinger	.25
43	Eric Wedge	.25
44	Bob Hamelin	.25
45	Carlos Delgado	2.50
46	Marc Newfield	.25
47	Raul Mondesi	.25
48	Tim Costo	.25
49	Pedro Martinez	3.00
50	Steve Karsay	.25
51	Danny Bautista	.25
52	Butch Huskey	.25
53	Kurt Abbott	.25
54	Darrell Sherman	.25
55	Damon Buford	.25
56	Ross Powell	.25
57	Darrell Whitmore	.25
58	Chipper Jones	5.00
59	Jeff Granger	.25
60	Cliff Floyd	.25

The Cycle

		NM/M
Complete Set (20):		12.00
Common Player:		.50
1	Brett Butler	.50

2	Kenny Lofton	.50
3	Paul Molitor	2.00
4	Carlos Baerga	.50
5	Gregg Jefferies, Tony Phillips	.50
6	John Olerud	.50
7	Charlie Hayes	.50
8	Len Dykstra	.50
9	Dante Bichette	.50
10	Devon White	.50
11	Lance Johnson	.50
12	Joey Cora, Steve Finley	.50
13	Tony Fernandez	.50
14	David Hulse, Brett Butler	.50
15	Jay Bell, Brian McRae, Mickey Morandini	.50
16	Juan Gonzalez, Barry Bonds	4.00
17	Ken Griffey Jr.	4.00
18	Frank Thomas	2.50
19	Dave Justice	.50
20	Matt Williams, Albert Belle	.50

Dream Team

		NM/M
Complete Set (10):		15.00
Common Player:		1.00
1	Mike Mussina	2.00
2	Tom Glavine	2.00
3	Don Mattingly	10.00
4	Carlos Baerga	1.00
5	Barry Larkin	1.00
6	Matt Williams	1.00
7	Juan Gonzalez	4.00
8	Andy Van Slyke	1.00
9	Larry Walker	1.00
10	Mike Stanley	1.00

Gold Stars

		NM/M
Complete Set (60):		40.00
Common Player:		.25
1	Barry Bonds	6.00
2	Orlando Merced	.25
3	Mark Grace	.25
4	Darren Daulton	.25
5	Jeff Blauser	.25
6	Deion Sanders	.25
7	John Kruk	.25
8	Jeff Bagwell	2.50
9	Gregg Jefferies	.25
10	Matt Williams	.25
11	Andres Galarraga	.25
12	Jay Bell	.25
13	Mike Piazza	4.50
14	Ron Gant	.25
15	Barry Larkin	.25
16	Tom Glavine	.50

17	Len Dykstra	.25
18	Fred McGriff	.25
19	Andy Van Slyke	.25
20	Gary Sheffield	.75
21	John Burkett	.25
22	Dante Bichette	.25
23	Tony Gwynn	3.50
24	Dave Justice	.25
25	Marquis Grissom	.25
26	Bobby Bonilla	.25
27	Larry Walker	.25
28	Brett Butler	.25
29	Robby Thompson	.25
30	Jeff Conine	.25
31	Joe Carter	.25
32	Ken Griffey Jr.	4.50
33	Juan Gonzalez	1.25
34	Rickey Henderson	2.50
35	Bo Jackson	.35
36	Cal Ripken, Jr.	6.00
37	John Olerud	.25
38	Carlos Baerga	.25
39	Jack McDowell	.25
40	Cecil Fielder	.25
41	Kenny Lofton	.25
42	Roberto Alomar	1.00
43	Randy Johnson	2.50
44	Tim Salmon	.25
45	Frank Thomas	2.50
46	Albert Belle	.25
47	Greg Vaughn	.25
48	Travis Fryman	.25
49	Don Mattingly	4.00
50	Wade Boggs	3.50
51	Mo Vaughn	.25
52	Kirby Puckett	3.50
53	Devon White	.25
54	Tony Phillips	.25
55	Brian Harper	.25
56	Chad Curtis	.25
57	Paul Molitor	2.50
58	Ivan Rodriguez	2.00
59	Rafael Palmeiro	2.00
60	Brian McRae	.25

Cal Ripken, Jr.

		NM/M
Complete Set (9):		3.00
Complete Set, Gold (9):		6.00
Common Player:		.50
Common Card, Gold:		1.00
Autographed Card:		200.00
1	Double Honors	.50
1a	Double Honors/Gold	1.00
2	Perennial All-Star	.50
2a	Perennial All-Star/Gold	1.00
3	Peerless Power	.50
3a	Peerless Power/Gold	1.00
4	Fitness Fan	.50
4a	Fitness Fan/Gold	1.00
5	Prime Concerns	.50
5a	Prime Concerns/Gold	1.00
6	Home Run Club	.50
6a	Home Run Club/Gold	1.00
7	The Iron Man	.50
7a	The Iron Man/Gold	1.00
8	Heavy Hitter	.50
8a	Heavy Hitter/Gold	1.00
9	Gold Glover	.50
9a	Gold Glover/Gold	1.00

1994 Score Rookie/Traded

		NM/M
Complete Set (165):		5.00
Common Player:		.05
Gold Rush:		2X
Pack (10):		.40
Wax Box (36):		9.00
1	Will Clark	.05
2	Lee Smith	.05

3	Bo Jackson	.10
4	Ellis Burks	.05
5	Eddie Murray	1.00
6	Delino DeShields	.05
7	Erik Hanson	.05
8	Rafael Palmeiro	.75
9	Luis Polonia	.05
10	Omar Vizquel	.05
11	Kurt Abbott	.05
12	Vince Coleman	.05
13	Rickey Henderson	1.00
14	Terry Mulholland	.05
15	Greg Hibbard	.05
16	Walt Weiss	.05
17	Chris Sabo	.05
18	Dave Henderson	.05
19	Rick Sutcliffe	.05
20	Harold Reynolds	.05
21	Jack Morris	.05
22	Dan Wilson	.05
23	Dave Magadan	.05
24	Dennis Martinez	.05
25	Wes Chamberlain	.05
26	Otis Nixon	.05
27	Eric Anthony	.05
28	Randy Milligan	.05
29	Julio Franco	.05
30	Kevin McReynolds	.05
31	Anthony Young	.05
32	Brian Harper	.05
33	Lenny Harris	.05
34	Eddie Taubensee	.05
35	David Segui	.05
36	Stan Javier	.05
37	Felix Fermin	.05
38	Darrin Jackson	.05
39	Tony Fernandez	.05
40	Jose Vizcaino	.05
41	Willie Banks	.05
42	Brian Hunter	.05
43	Reggie Jefferson	.05
44	Junior Felix	.05
45	Jack Armstrong	.05
46	Bip Roberts	.05
47	Jerry Browne	.05
48	Marvin Freeman	.05
49	Jody Reed	.05
50	Alex Cole	.05
51	Sid Fernandez	.05
52	Pete Smith	.05
53	Xavier Hernandez	.05
54	Scott Sanderson	.05
55	Turner Ward	.05
56	Rex Hudler	.05
57	Deion Sanders	.05
58	Sid Bream	.05
59	Tony Pena	.05
60	Bret Boone	.05
61	Bobby Ayala	.05
62	Pedro Martinez	1.00
63	Howard Johnson	.05
64	Mark Portugal	.05
65	Roberto Kelly	.05
66	Spike Owen	.05
67	Jeff Treadway	.05
68	Mike Harkey	.05
69	Doug Jones	.05
70	Steve Farr	.05
71	Billy Taylor	.05
72	Manny Ramirez	1.00
73	Bob Hamelin	.05
74	Steve Karsay	.05
75	Ryan Klesko	.05
76	Cliff Floyd	.05
77	Jeffrey Hammonds	.05
78	Javier Lopez	.05
79	Roger Salkeld	.05
80	Hector Carrasco	.05
81	Gerald Williams	.05
82	Raul Mondesi	.05
83	Sterling Hitchcock	.05
84	Danny Bautista	.05

85	Chris Turner	.05
86	Shane Reynolds	.05
87	Rondell White	.05
88	Salomon Torres	.05
89	Turk Wendell	.05
90	Tony Tarasco	.05
91	Shawn Green	.65
92	Greg Colbrunn	.05
93	Eddie Zambrano	.05
94	Rich Becker	.05
95	Chris Gomez	.05
96	John Patterson	.05
97	Derek Parks	.05
98	Rich Rowland	.05
99	James Mouton	.05
100	Tim Hyers	.05
101	Jose Valentin	.05
102	Carlos Delgado	.65
103	Robert Esenhoorn	.05
104	John Hudek	.05
105	Domingo Cedeno	.05
106	Denny Hocking	.05
107	Greg Pirkl	.05
108	Mark Smith	.05
109	Paul Shuey	.05
110	Jorge Fabregas	.05
111	Rikkert Faneyte	.05
112	Rob Butler	.05
113	Darren Oliver	.05
114	Troy O'Leary	.05
115	Scott Brow	.05
116	Tony Eusebio	.05
117	Carlos Reyes	.05
118	J.R. Phillips	.05
119	Alex Diaz	.05
120	Charles Johnson	.05
121	Nate Minchey	.05
122	Scott Sanders	.05
123	Daryl Boston	.05
124	Joey Hamilton	.05
125	Brian Anderson	.05
126	Dan Miceli	.05
127	Tom Brunansky	.05
128	Dave Staton	.05
129	Mike Oquist	.05
130	John Mabry	.05
131	Norberto Martin	.05
132	Hector Fajardo	.05
133	Mark Hutton	.05
134	Fernando Vina	.05
135	Lee Tinsley	.05
136	Chan Ho Park RC	1.50
137	Paul Spoljaric	.05
138	Matias Carrillo	.05
139	Mark Kiefer	.05
140	Stan Royer	.05
141	Bryan Eversgerd	.05
143	Joe Hall	.05
144	Johnny Ruffin	.05
145	Alex Gonzalez	.05
146	Keith Lockhart	.05
147	Tom Marsh	.05
148	Tony Longmire	.05
149	Keith Mitchell	.05
150	Melvin Nieves	.05
151	Kelly Stinnett	.05
152	Miguel Jimenez	.05
153	Jeff Juden	.05
154	Matt Walbeck	.05
155	Marc Newfield	.05
156	Matt Mieske	.05
157	Marcus Moore	.05
158	Jose Lima RC	.25
159	Mike Kelly	.05
160	Jim Edmonds	.05
161	Steve Trachsel	.05
162	Greg Blosser	.05
163	Mark Acre	.05
164	AL Checklist	.05
165	NL Checklist	.05

Changing Places

	NM/M
Complete Set (10):	15.00

Common Player:		1.00
1	Will Clark	1.00
2	Rafael Palmeiro	4.00
3	Roberto Kelly	1.00
4	Bo Jackson	1.25
5	Otis Nixon	1.00
6	Rickey Henderson	5.00
7	Ellis Burks	1.00
8	Lee Smith	1.00
9	Delino DeShields	1.00
10	Deion Sanders	1.00

Rookie/Traded Super Rookies

	NM/M
Complete Set (18):	15.00

Common Player:		1.00
1	Carlos Delgado	5.00
2	Manny Ramirez	5.00
3	Ryan Klesko	1.00
4	Raul Mondesi	1.00
5	Bob Hamelin	1.00
6	Steve Karsay	1.00
7	Jeffrey Hammonds	1.00
8	Cliff Floyd	1.00
9	Kurt Abbott	1.00
10	Marc Newfield	1.00
11	Javier Lopez	1.00
12	Rich Becker	1.00
13	Greg Pirkl	1.00
14	Rondell White	1.00
15	James Mouton	1.00
16	Tony Tarasco	1.00
17	Brian Anderson	1.00
18	Jim Edmonds	1.00

1995 Score

	NM/M
Complete Set (605):	13.50
Common Player:	.05
Gold Rush:	2X
Platinums:	3X
Series 1 or 2 Pack (12):	.75
Series 1 or 2 Box (36):	12.50
1	Frank Thomas	.50
2	Roberto Alomar	.15
3	Cal Ripken, Jr.	1.50
4	Jose Canseco	.30
5	Matt Williams	.05
6	Esteban Beltre	.05
7	Domingo Cedeno	.05
8	John Valentin	.05
9	Glenallen Hill	.05
10	Rafael Belliard	.05
11	Randy Myers	.05
12	Mo Vaughn	.05
13	Hector Carrasco	.05
14	Chili Davis	.05
15	Dante Bichette	.05
16	Darren Jackson	.05

17	Mike Piazza	.75
18	Junior Felix	.05
19	Moises Alou	.05
20	Mark Gubicza	.05
21	Bret Saberhagen	.05
22	Len Dykstra	.05
23	Steve Howe	.05
24	Mark Dewey	.05
25	Brian Harper	.05
26	Ozzie Smith	.60
27	Scott Erickson	.05
28	Tony Gwynn	.60
29	Bob Welch	.05
30	Barry Bonds	1.50
31	Leo Gomez	.05
32	Greg Maddux	.60
33	Mike Greenwell	.05
34	Sammy Sosa	.60
35	Darnell Coles	.05
36	Tommy Greene	.05
37	Will Clark	.05
38	Steve Ontiveros	.05
39	Stan Javier	.05
40	Bip Roberts	.05
41	Paul O'Neill	.05
42	Bill Haselman	.05
43	Shane Mack	.05
44	Orlando Merced	.05
45	Kevin Seitzer	.05
46	Trevor Hoffman	.05
47	Greg Gagne	.05
48	Jeff Kent	.05
49	Tony Phillips	.05
50	Ken Hill	.05
51	Carlos Baerga	.05
52	Henry Rodriguez	.05
53	Scott Sanderson	.05
54	Jeff Conine	.05
55	Chris Turner	.05
56	Ken Caminiti	.05
57	Harold Baines	.05
58	Charlie Hayes	.05
59	Roberto Kelly	.05
60	John Olerud	.05
61	Tim Davis	.05
62	Rich Rowland	.05
63	Rey Sanchez	.05
64	Junior Ortiz	.05
65	Ricky Gutierrez	.05
66	Rex Hudler	.05
67	Johnny Ruffin	.05
68	Jay Buhner	.05
69	Tom Pagnozzi	.05
70	Julio Franco	.05
71	Eric Young	.05
72	Mike Bordick	.05
73	Don Slaught	.05
74	Goose Gossage	.05
75	Lonnie Smith	.05
76	Jimmy Key	.05
77	Dave Hollins	.05
78	Mickey Tettleton	.05
79	Luis Gonzalez	.05
80	Dave Winfield	.50
81	Ryan Thompson	.05
82	Felix Jose	.05
83	Rusty Meacham	.05
84	Darryl Hamilton	.05
85	John Wetteland	.05
86	Tom Brunansky	.05
87	Mark Lemke	.05
88	Spike Owen	.05
89	Shawon Dunston	.05
90	Wilson Alvarez	.05
91	Lee Smith	.05
92	Scott Kamieniecki	.05
93	Jacob Brumfield	.05
94	Kirk Gibson	.05
95	Joe Girardi	.05
96	Mike Macfarlane	.05
97	Greg Colbrunn	.05
98	Ricky Bones	.05
99	Delino DeShields	.05
100	Pat Meares	.05
101	Jeff Fassero	.05
102	Jim Leyritz	.05
103	Gary Redus	.05
104	Terry Steinbach	.05
105	Kevin McReynolds	.05
106	Felix Fermin	.05
107	Danny Jackson	.05
108	Chris James	.05
109	Jeff King	.05
110	Pat Hentgen	.05
111	Gerald Perry	.05
112	Tim Raines	.05
113	Eddie Williams	.05
114	Jamie Moyer	.05
115	Bud Black	.05
116	Chris Gomez	.05
117	Luis Lopez	.05
118	Roger Clemens	.65
119	Javier Lopez	.05
120	Dave Nilsson	.05

121	Karl Rhodes	.05
122	Rick Aguilera	.05
123	Tony Fernandez	.05
124	Bernie Williams	.05
125	James Mouton	.05
126	Mark Langston	.05
127	Mike Lansing	.05
128	Tino Martinez	.05
129	Joe Orsulak	.05
130	David Hulse	.05
131	Pete Incaviglia	.05
132	Mark Clark	.05
133	Tony Eusebio	.05
134	Chuck Finley	.05
135	Lou Frazier	.05
136	Craig Grebeck	.05
137	Kelly Stinnett	.05
138	Paul Shuey	.05
139	David Nied	.05
140	Billy Brewer	.05
141	Dave Weathers	.05
142	Scott Leius	.05
143	Brian Jordan	.05
144	Melido Perez	.05
145	Tony Tarasco	.05
146	Dan Wilson	.05
147	Rondell White	.05
148	Mike Henneman	.05
149	Brian Johnson	.05
150	Tom Henke	.05
151	John Patterson	.05
152	Bobby Witt	.05
153	Eddie Taubensee	.05
154	Pat Borders	.05
155	Ramon Martinez	.05
156	Mike Kingery	.05
157	Zane Smith	.05
158	Benito Santiago	.05
159	Matias Carrillo	.05
160	Scott Brosius	.05
161	Dave Clark	.05
162	Mark McLemore	.05
163	Curt Schilling	.30
164	J.T. Snow	.05
165	Rod Beck	.05
166	Scott Fletcher	.05
167	Bob Tewksbury	.05
168	Mike LaValliere	.05
169	Dave Hansen	.05
170	Pedro Martinez	.50
171	Kirk Rueter	.05
172	Jose Lind	.05
173	Luis Alicea	.05
174	Mike Moore	.05
175	Andy Ashby	.05
176	Jody Reed	.05
177	Darryl Kile	.05
178	Carl Willis	.05
179	Jeromy Burnitz	.05
180	Mike Gallego	.05
181	W. Van Landingham RC	.05
182	Sid Fernandez	.05
183	Kim Batiste	.05
184	Greg Myers	.05
185	Steve Avery	.05
186	Steve Farr	.05
187	Robb Nen	.05
188	Dan Pasqua	.05
189	Bruce Ruffin	.05
190	Jose Valentin	.05
191	Willie Banks	.05
192	Mike Aldrete	.05
193	Randy Milligan	.05
194	Steve Karsay	.05
195	Mike Stanley	.05
196	Jose Mesa	.05
197	Tom Browning	.05
198	John Vander Wal	.05
199	Kevin Brown	.05
200	Mike Oquist	.05
201	Greg Swindell	.05
202	Eddie Zambrano	.05
203	Joe Boever	.05
204	Gary Varsho	.05
205	Chris Gwynn	.05
206	David Howard	.05
207	Jerome Walton	.05
208	Danny Darwin	.05
209	Darryl Strawberry	.05
210	Todd Van Poppel	.05
211	Scott Livingstone	.05
212	Dave Fleming	.05
213	Todd Worrell	.05
214	Carlos Delgado	.40
215	Bill Pecota	.05
216	Jim Lindeman	.05
217	Rick White	.05
218	Jose Oquendo	.05
219	Tony Castillo	.05
220	Fernando Vina	.05
221	Jeff Bagwell	.50
222	Randy Johnson	.50
223	Albert Belle	.05
224	Chuck Carr	.05

No.	Player	Price
225	Mark Leiter	.05
226	Hal Morris	.05
227	Robin Ventura	.05
228	Mike Munoz	.05
229	Jim Thome	.40
230	Mario Diaz	.05
231	John Doherty	.05
232	Bobby Jones	.05
233	Raul Mondesi	.05
234	Ricky Jordan	.05
235	John Jaha	.05
236	Carlos Garcia	.05
237	Kirby Puckett	.60
238	Orel Hershiser	.05
239	Don Mattingly	.65
240	Sid Bream	.05
241	Brent Gates	.05
242	Tony Longmire	.05
243	Robby Thompson	.05
244	Rick Sutcliffe	.05
245	Dean Palmer	.05
246	Marquis Grissom	.05
247	Paul Molitor	.50
248	Mark Carreon	.05
249	Jack Voight	.05
250	Greg McMichael (Photo on front is Mike Stanton.)	.05
251	Damon Berryhill	.05
252	Brian Dorsett	.05
253	Jim Edmonds	.05
254	Barry Larkin	.05
255	Jack McDowell	.05
256	Wally Joyner	.05
257	Eddie Murray	.50
258	Lenny Webster	.05
259	Milt Cuyler	.05
260	Todd Benzinger	.05
261	Vince Coleman	.05
262	Todd Stottlemyre	.05
263	Turner Ward	.05
264	Ray Lankford	.05
265	Matt Walbeck	.05
266	Deion Sanders	.05
267	Gerald Williams	.05
268	Jim Gott	.05
269	Jeff Frye	.05
270	Jose Rijo	.05
271	Dave Justice	.05
272	Ismael Valdes	.05
273	Ben McDonald	.05
274	Darren Lewis	.05
275	Graeme Lloyd	.05
276	Luis Ortiz	.05
277	Julian Tavarez	.05
278	Mark Dalesandro	.05
279	Brett Merriman	.05
280	Ricky Bottalico	.05
281	Robert Eenhoorn	.05
282	Rikkert Faneyte	.05
283	Mike Kelly	.05
284	Mark Smith	.05
285	Turk Wendell	.05
286	Greg Blosser	.05
287	Garey Ingram	.05
288	Jorge Fabregas	.05
289	Blaise Ilsley	.05
290	Joe Hall	.05
291	Orlando Miller	.05
292	Jose Lima	.05
293	Greg O'Halloran	.05
294	Mark Kiefer	.05
295	Jose Oliva	.05
296	Rich Becker	.05
297	Brian Hunter	.05
298	Dave Silvestri	.05
299	Armando Benitez RC	.10
300	Darren Dreifort	.05
301	John Mabry	.05
302	Greg Pirkl	.05
303	J.R. Phillips	.05
304	Shawn Green	.30
305	Roberto Petagine	.05
306	Keith Lockhart	.05
307	Jonathon Hurst	.05
308	Paul Spoljaric	.05
309	Mike Lieberthal	.05
310	Garret Anderson	.05
311	John Johnston	.05
312	Alex Rodriguez	1.50
313	Kent Mercker	.05
314	John Valentin	.05
315	Kenny Rogers	.05
316	Fred McGriff	.05
317	Atlanta Braves, Baltimore Orioles	.05
318	Chicago Cubs, Boston Red Sox	.05
319	Cincinnati Reds, California Angels	.05
320	Colorado Rockies, Chicago White Sox	.05
321	Cleveland Indians, Florida Marlins	.05
322	Houston Astros, Detroit Tigers	.05
323	Los Angels Dodgers, Kansas City Royals	.05
324	Montreal Expos, Milwaukee Brewers	.05
325	New York Mets, Minnesota Twins	.05
326	Philadelphia Phillies, New York Yankees	.05
327	Pittsburgh Pirates, Oakland Athletics	.05
328	San Diego Padres, Seattle Mariners	.05
329	San Francisco Giants, Texas Rangers	.05
330	St. Louis Cardinals, Toronto Blue Jays	.05
331	Pedro Munoz	.05
332	Ryan Klesko	.05
333a	Andre Dawson/Red Sox	.25
333b	Andre Dawson/Marlins	.35
334	Derrick May	.05
335	Aaron Sele	.05
336	Kevin Mitchell	.05
337	Steve Traschel	.05
338	Andres Galarraga	.05
339a	Terry Pendleton/Braves	.05
339b	Terry Pendleton/Marlins	.10
340	Gary Sheffield	.30
341	Travis Fryman	.05
342	Bo Jackson	.10
343	Gary Gaetti	.05
344a	Brett Butler/Dodgers	.05
344b	Brett Butler/Mets	.10
345	B. J. Surhoff	.05
346a	Larry Walker/Expos	.05
346b	Larry Walker/Rockies	.10
347	Kevin Tapani	.05
348	Rick Wilkins	.05
349	Wade Boggs	.60
350	Mariano Duncan	.05
351	Ruben Sierra	.05
352a	Andy Van Slyke/Pirates	.05
352b	Andy Van Slyke/Orioles	.10
353	Reggie Jefferson	.05
354	Gregg Jefferies	.05
355	Tim Naehring	.05
356	John Roper	.05
357	Joe Carter	.05
358	Kurt Abbott	.05
359	Lenny Harris	.05
360	Lance Johnson	.05
361	Brian Anderson	.05
362	Jim Eisenreich	.05
363	Jerry Browne	.05
364	Mark Grace	.05
365	Devon White	.05
366	Reggie Sanders	.05
367	Ivan Rodriguez	.40
368	Kirt Manwaring	.05
369	Pat Kelly	.05
370	Ellis Burks	.05
371	Charles Nagy	.05
372	Kevin Bass	.05
373	Lou Whitaker	.05
374	Rene Arocha	.05
375	Derrick Parks	.05
376	Mark Whiten	.05
377	Mark McGwire	1.00
378	Doug Drabek	.05
379	Greg Vaughn	.05
380	Al Martin	.05
381	Ron Darling	.05
382	Tim Wallach	.05
383	Alan Trammell	.05
384	Randy Velarde	.05
385	Chris Sabo	.05
386	Wil Cordero	.05
387	Darrin Fletcher	.05
388	David Segui	.05
389	Steve Buechele	.05
390	Otis Nixon	.05
391	Jeff Brantley	.05
392a	Chad Curtis/Angels	.05
392b	Chad Curtis/Tigers	.10
393	Cal Eldred	.05
394	Jason Bere	.05
395	Bret Barberie	.05
396	Paul Sorrento	.05
397	Steve Finley	.05
398	Cecil Fielder	.05
399	Eric Karros	.05
400	Jeff Montgomery	.05
401	Cliff Floyd	.05
402	Matt Mieske	.05
403	Brian Hunter	.05
404	Alex Cole	.05
405	Kevin Stocker	.05
406	Eric Davis	.05
407	Marvin Freeman	.05
408	Dennis Eckersley	.40
409	Todd Zeile	.05
410	Keith Mitchell	.05
411	Andy Benes	.05
412	Juan Bell	.05
413	Royce Clayton	.05
414	Ed Sprague	.05
415	Mike Mussina	.30
416	Todd Hundley	.05
417	Pat Listach	.05
418	Joe Oliver	.05
419	Rafael Palmeiro	.40
420	Tim Salmon	.05
421	Brady Anderson	.05
422	Kenny Lofton	.05
423	Craig Biggio	.05
424	Bobby Bonilla	.05
425	Kenny Rogers	.05
426	Derek Bell	.05
427a	Scott Cooper/Red Sox	.05
427b	Scott Cooper/Cardinals	.10
428	Ozzie Guillen	.05
429	Omar Vizquel	.05
430	Phil Plantier	.05
431	Chuck Knoblauch	.05
432	Darren Daulton	.05
433	Bob Hamelin	.05
434	Tom Glavine	.30
435	Walt Weiss	.05
436	Jose Vizcaino	.05
437	Ken Griffey Jr.	.75
438	Jay Bell	.05
439	Juan Gonzalez	.25
440	Jeff Blauser	.05
441	Rickey Henderson	.50
442	Bobby Ayala	.05
443a	David Cone/Royals	.05
443b	David Cone/Blue Jays	.10
444	Pedro Martinez	.05
445	Manny Ramirez	.50
446	Mark Portugal	.05
447	Damion Easley	.05
448	Gary DiSarcina	.05
449	Roberto Hernandez	.05
450	Jeffrey Hammonds	.05
451	Jeff Treadway	.05
452a	Jim Abbott/Yankees	.05
452b	Jim Abbott/White Sox	.10
453	Carlos Rodriguez	.05
454	Joey Cora	.05
455	Bret Boone	.05
456	Danny Tartabull	.05
457	John Franco	.05
458	Roger Salkeld	.05
459	Fred McGriff	.05
460	Pedro Astacio	.05
461	Jon Lieber	.05
462	Luis Polonia	.05
463	Geronimo Pena	.05
464	Tom Gordon	.05
465	Brad Ausmus	.05
466	Willie McGee	.05
467	Doug Jones	.05
468	John Smoltz	.05
469	Troy Neel	.05
470	Luis Sojo	.05
471	John Smiley	.05
472	Rafael Bournigal	.05
473	Billy Taylor	.05
474	Juan Guzman	.05
475	Dave Magadan	.05
476	Mike Devereaux	.05
477	Andujar Cedeno	.05
478	Edgar Martinez	.05
479	Troy Neel	.05
480	Allen Watson	.05
481	Ron Karkovice	.05
482	Joey Hamilton	.05
483	Vinny Castilla	.05
484	Kevin Gross	.05
485	Bernard Gilkey	.05
486	John Burkett	.05
487	Matt Nokes	.05
488	Mel Rojas	.05
489	Craig Shipley	.05
490	Chip Hale	.05
491	Bill Swift	.05
492	Pat Rapp	.05
493a	Brian McRae/Royals	.05
493b	Brian McRae/Cubs	.10
494	Mickey Morandini	.05
495	Tony Pena	.05
496	Danny Bautista	.05
497	Armando Reynoso	.05
498	Ken Ryan	.05
499	Billy Ripken	.05
500	Pat Mahomes	.05
501	Mark Acre	.05
502	Geronimo Berroa	.05
503	Norberto Martin	.05
504	Chad Kreuter	.05
505	Howard Johnson	.05
506	Eric Anthony	.05
507	Mark Wohlers	.05
508	Scott Sanders	.05
509	Pete Harnisch	.05
510	Wes Chamberlain	.05
511	Tom Candiotti	.05
512	Albie Lopez	.05
513	Denny Neagle	.05
514	Sean Berry	.05
515	Billy Hatcher	.05
516	Todd Jones	.05
517	Wayne Kirby	.05
518	Butch Henry	.05
519	Sandy Alomar Jr.	.05
520	Kevin Appier	.05
521	Robert Mejia	.05
522	Steve Cooke	.05
523	Terry Shumpert	.05
524	Mike Jackson	.05
525	Kent Mercker	.05
526	David Wells	.05
527	Juan Samuel	.05
528	Salomon Torres	.05
529	Duane Ward	.05
530a	Rob Dibble/Reds	.05
530b	Rob Dibble/White Sox	.10
531	Mike Blowers	.05
532	Mark Eichhorn	.05
533	Alex Diaz	.05
534	Dan Miceli	.05
535	Jeff Branson	.05
536	Dave Stevens	.05
537	Charlie O'Brien	.05
538	Shane Reynolds	.05
539	Rich Amaral	.05
540	Rusty Greer	.05
541	Alex Arias	.05
542	Eric Plunk	.05
543	John Hudek	.05
544	Kirk McCaskill	.05
545	Jeff Reboulet	.05
546	Sterling Hitchcock	.05
547	Warren Newson	.05
548	Bryan Harvey	.05
549	Mike Huff	.05
550	Lance Parrish	.05
551	Ken Griffey Jr.	.65
552	Matt Williams	.05
553	Roberto Alomar	.10
554	Jeff Bagwell	.25
555	Dave Justice	.05
556	Cal Ripken Jr.	.75
557	Albert Belle	.05
558	Mike Piazza	.45
559	Kirby Puckett	.35
560	Wade Boggs	.30
561	Tony Gwynn	.35
562	Barry Bonds	.75
563	Mo Vaughn	.05
564	Don Mattingly	.40
565	Carlos Baerga	.05
566	Paul Molitor	.25
567	Raul Mondesi	.05
568	Manny Ramirez	.25
569	Alex Rodriguez	.75
570	Will Clark	.05
571	Frank Thomas	.30
572	Moises Alou	.05
573	Jeff Conine	.05
574	Joe Ausanio	.05
575	Charles Johnson	.05
576	Ernie Young	.05
577	Jeff Granger	.05
578	Robert Perez	.05
579	Melvin Nieves	.05
580	Gar Finnvold	.05
581	Duane Singleton	.05
582	Chan Ho Park	.05
583	Fausto Cruz	.05
584	Dave Staton	.05
585	Denny Hocking	.05
586	Nate Minchey	.05
587	Marc Newfield	.05
588	Jayhawk Owens	.05
589	Darren Bragg	.05
590	Kevin King	.05
591	Kurt Miller	.05
592	Aaron Small	.05
593	Troy O'Leary	.05
594	Phil Stidham	.05
595	Steve Dunn	.05
596	Cory Bailey	.05
597	Alex Gonzalez	.05
598	Jim Bowie	.05
599	Jeff Cirillo	.05
600	Mark Hutton	.05
601	Russ Davis	.05
602	Checklist #331-400	.05
603	Checklist #401-469	.05
604	Checklist #470-537	.05
605	Checklist #538-605	.05
----	"You Trade 'em" Redemption Card (Expired Dec. 31, 1995.)	.10

Gold Rush

	NM/M
Complete Set (605):	35.00
Common Player:	.10

Gold Rush Stars: 2X
(See 1995 Score for checklist and base card values.)

Airmail

		NM/M
Complete Set (18):		8.00
Common Player:		.25
1	Bob Hamelin	.25
2	John Mabry	.25
3	Marc Newfield	.25
4	Jose Oliva	.25
5	Charles Johnson	.25
6	Russ Davis	.25
7	Ernie Young	.25
8	Billy Ashley	.25
9	Ryan Klesko	.25
10	J.R. Phillips	.25
11	Cliff Floyd	.25
12	Carlos Delgado	1.50
13	Melvin Nieves	.25
14	Raul Mondesi	.25
15	Manny Ramirez	2.00
16	Mike Kelly	.25
17	Alex Rodriguez	5.00
18	Rusty Greer	.25

Double Gold Champions

		NM/M
Complete Set (12):		25.00
Common Player:		.40
1	Frank Thomas	2.00
2	Ken Griffey Jr.	3.50
3	Barry Bonds	5.00
4	Tony Gwynn	2.50
5	Don Mattingly	3.00
6	Greg Maddux	2.50
7	Roger Clemens	3.00
8	Kenny Lofton	.40
9	Jeff Bagwell	2.00
10	Matt Williams	.40
11	Kirby Puckett	2.50
12	Cal Ripken Jr.	5.00

Draft Picks

	NM/M
Complete Set (18):	4.00
Common Player:	.50

1	McKay Christensen	.50
2	Brett Wagner	.50
3	Paul Wilson	.50
4	C.J. Nitkowski	.50
5	Josh Booty	.50
6	Antone Williamson	.50
7	Paul Konerko	1.50
8	Scott Elarton	.50
9	Jacob Shumate	.50
10	Terrence Long	.50
11	Mark Johnson	.50
12	Ben Grieve	.50
13	Doug Million	.50
14	Jayson Peterson	.50
15	Dustin Hermanson	.50
16	Matt Smith	.50
17	Kevin Witt	.50
18	Brian Buchanan	.50

Dream Team Gold

		NM/M
Complete Set (12):		12.00
Common Player:		.30
1	Frank Thomas	1.25
2	Roberto Alomar	.50
3	Cal Ripken Jr.	4.00
4	Matt Williams	.30
5	Mike Piazza	2.50
6	Albert Belle	.30
7	Ken Griffey Jr.	2.50
8	Tony Gwynn	1.50
9	Paul Molitor	1.25
10	Jimmy Key	.30
11	Greg Maddux	1.50
12	Lee Smith	.30

Hall of Gold

		NM/M
Complete Set (110):		25.00
Common Player:		.10
1	Ken Griffey Jr.	1.25
2	Matt Williams	.10
3	Roberto Alomar	.25
4	Jeff Bagwell	.75
5	Dave Justice	.10
6	Cal Ripken Jr.	2.00
7	Randy Johnson	.75
8	Barry Larkin	.10
9	Albert Belle	.10
10	Mike Piazza	1.25
11	Kirby Puckett	1.00
12	Moises Alou	.10
13	Jose Canseco	.45
14	Tony Gwynn	1.00
15	Roger Clemens	1.00
16	Barry Bonds	2.00
17	Mo Vaughn	.10
18	Greg Maddux	1.00
19	Dante Bichette	.10
20	Will Clark	.10
21	Len Dykstra	.10
22	Don Mattingly	1.00
23	Carlos Baerga	.10
24	Ozzie Smith	1.00
25	Paul Molitor	.75
26	Paul O'Neill	.10
27	Deion Sanders	.10
28	Jeff Conine	.10
29	John Olerud	.10
30	Jose Rijo	.10
31	Sammy Sosa	1.00
32	Robin Ventura	.10
33	Raul Mondesi	.10
34	Eddie Murray	.75
35	Marquis Grissom	.10
36	Darryl Strawberry	.10
37	Dave Nilsson	.10
38	Manny Ramirez	.75
39	Delino DeShields	.10
40	Lee Smith	.10
41	Alex Rodriguez	1.50
42	Julio Franco	.10
43	Bret Saberhagen	.10
44	Ken Hill	.10
45	Roberto Kelly	.10
46	Hal Morris	.10
47	Jimmy Key	.10
48	Terry Steinbach	.10
49	Mickey Tettleton	.10
50	Tony Phillips	.10
51	Carlos Garcia	.10
52	Jim Edmonds	.10
53	Rod Beck	.10
54	Shane Mack	.10
55	Ken Caminiti	.10
56	Frank Thomas	.75
57	Kenny Lofton	.10
58	Jack McDowell	.10
59	Jason Bere	.10
60	Joe Carter	.10
61	Gary Sheffield	.45
62	Andres Galarraga	.10
63	Gregg Jefferies	.10
64	Bobby Bonilla	.10
65	Tom Glavine	.35
66	John Smoltz	.10
67	Fred McGriff	.10
68	Craig Biggio	.10
69	Reggie Sanders	.10
70	Kevin Mitchell	.10
71a	Larry Walker/Expos	.10
71b	Larry Walker/Rockies	.10
72	Carlos Delgado	.50
73	Andujar Cedeno	.10
74	Ivan Rodriguez	.65
75	Ryan Klesko	.10
76a	John Kruk/Phillies	.10
76b	John Kruk/White Sox	.10
77a	Brian McRae/Royals	.10
77b	Brian McRae/Cubs	.10
78	Tim Salmon	.10
79	Travis Fryman	.10
80	Chuck Knoblauch	.10
81	Jay Bell	.10
82	Cecil Fielder	.10
83	Cliff Floyd	.10
84	Ruben Sierra	.10
85	Mike Mussina	.45
86	Mark Grace	.10
87	Dennis Eckersley	.65
88	Dennis Martinez	.10
89	Rafael Palmeiro	.65
90	Ben McDonald	.10
91	Dave Hollins	.10
92	Steve Avery	.10
93a	David Cone/Royals	.10
93b	David Cone/Blue Jays	.10
94	Darren Daulton	.10
95	Bret Boone	.10
96	Wade Boggs	1.00
97	Doug Drabek	.10
98	Derek Bell	.10
99	Jim Thome	.65
100	Chili Davis	.10
101	Jeffrey Hammonds	.10
102	Rickey Henderson	.75
103	Brett Butler	.10
104	Tim Wallach	.10
105	Wil Cordero	.10
106	Mark Whiten	.10
107	Bob Hamelin	.10
108	Rondell White	.10
109	Devon White	.10
110a	Tony Tarasco/Braves	.10
110b	Tony Tarasco/Expos	.10
----	Redemption Trade Card (Expired Dec. 31, 1995.)	.10

Rookie Dream Team

		NM/M
Complete Set (12):		9.00
Common Player:		.50
1	J.R. Phillips	.50
2	Alex Gonzalez	.50
3	Alex Rodriguez	6.00
4	Jose Oliva	.50
5	Charles Johnson	.50
6	Shawn Green	1.50
7	Brian Hunter	.50
8	Garret Anderson	.50
9	Julian Tavarez	.50
10	Jose Lima	.50
11	Armando Benitez	.50
12	Ricky Bottalico	.50

Rookie Greatness

		NM/M
RG1	Ryan Klesko	1.00
SG1	Ryan Klesko/Auto.	7.50

Score Rules

		NM/M
Complete Set (30):		30.00
Common Player:		.30
1	Ken Griffey Jr.	3.50
2	Frank Thomas	1.50
3	Mike Piazza	3.50
4	Jeff Bagwell	1.50
5	Alex Rodriguez	4.50
6	Albert Belle	.30
7	Matt Williams	.30
8	Roberto Alomar	.45

#	Player	Price
9	Barry Bonds	5.00
10	Raul Mondesi	.30
11	Jose Canseco	.60
12	Kirby Puckett	2.50
13	Fred McGriff	.30
14	Kenny Lofton	.30
15	Greg Maddux	2.50
16	Juan Gonzalez	.75
17	Cliff Floyd	.30
18	Cal Ripken, Jr.	5.00
19	Will Clark	.30
20	Tim Salmon	.30
21	Paul O'Neill	.30
22	Jason Bere	.30
23	Tony Gwynn	2.50
24	Manny Ramirez	1.50
25	Don Mattingly	3.00
26	Dave Justice	.30
27	Javier Lopez	.30
28	Ryan Klesko	.30
29	Carlos Delgado	.90
30	Mike Mussina	.60

1996 Score

	NM/M
Complete Set (510):	15.00
Common Player:	.05
Wax Pack (10):	.45
Wax Box (36):	10.00

#	Player	Price
1	Will Clark	.05
2	Rich Becker	.05
3	Ryan Klesko	.05
4	Jim Edmonds	.05
5	Barry Larkin	.05
6	Jim Thome	.40
7	Raul Mondesi	.05
8	Don Mattingly	.65
9	Jeff Conine	.05
10	Rickey Henderson	.50
11	Chad Curtis	.05
12	Darren Daulton	.05
13	Larry Walker	.05
14	Carlos Garcia	.05
15	Carlos Baerga	.05
16	Tony Gwynn	.60
17	Jon Nunally	.05
18	Deion Sanders	.05
19	Mark Grace	.05
20	Alex Rodriguez	1.00
21	Frank Thomas	.50
22	Brian Jordan	.05
23	J.T. Snow	.05
24	Shawn Green	.30
25	Tim Wakefield	.05
26	Curtis Goodwin	.05
27	John Smoltz	.05
28	Devon White	.05
29	Brian Hunter	.05
30	Rusty Greer	.05
31	Rafael Palmeiro	.40
32	Bernard Gilkey	.05
33	John Valentin	.05
34	Randy Johnson	.50
35	Garret Anderson	.05
36	Rikkert Faneyte	.05
37	Ray Durham	.05
38	Bip Roberts	.05
39	Jaime Navarro	.05
40	Mark Johnson	.05
41	Darren Lewis	.05
42	Tyler Green	.05
43	Bill Pulsipher	.05
44	Jason Giambi	.40
45	Kevin Ritz	.05
46	Jack McDowell	.05
47	Felipe Lira	.05
48	Rico Brogna	.05
49	Terry Pendleton	.05
50	Rondell White	.05
51	Andre Dawson	.25
52	Kirby Puckett	.60
53	Wally Joyner	.05
54	B.J. Surhoff	.05
55	Chan Ho Park	.05
56	Greg Vaughn	.05
57	Roberto Alomar	.20
58	Dave Justice	.05
59	Kevin Seitzer	.05
60	Cal Ripken Jr.	1.50
61	Ozzie Smith	.60
62	Mo Vaughn	.05
63	Ricky Bones	.05
64	Gary DiSarcina	.05
65	Matt Williams	.05
66	Wilson Alvarez	.05
67	Lenny Dykstra	.05
68	Brian McRae	.05
69	Todd Stottlemyre	.05
70	Bret Boone	.05
71	Sterling Hitchcock	.05
72	Albert Belle	.05
73	Todd Hundley	.05
74	Vinny Castilla	.05
75	Moises Alou	.05
76	Cecil Fielder	.05
77	Brad Radke	.05
78	Quilvio Veras	.05
79	Eddie Murray	.50
80	James Mouton	.05
81	Pat Listach	.05
82	Mark Gubicza	.05
83	Dave Winfield	.50
84	Fred McGriff	.05
85	Darryl Hamilton	.05
86	Jeffrey Hammonds	.05
87	Pedro Munoz	.05
88	Craig Biggio	.05
89	Cliff Floyd	.05
90	Tim Naehring	.05
91	Brett Butler	.05
92	Kevin Foster	.05
93	Patrick Kelly	.05
94	John Smiley	.05
95	Terry Steinbach	.05
96	Orel Hershiser	.05
97	Darrin Fletcher	.05
98	Walt Weiss	.05
99	John Wetteland	.05
100	Alan Trammell	.05
101	Steve Avery	.05
102	Tony Eusebio	.05
103	Sandy Alomar	.05
104	Joe Girardi	.05
105	Rick Aguilera	.05
106	Tony Tarasco	.05
107	Chris Hammond	.05
108	Mike McFarlane	.05
109	Doug Drabek	.05
110	Derek Bell	.05
111	Ed Sprague	.05
112	Todd Hollandsworth	.05
113	Otis Nixon	.05
114	Keith Lockhart	.05
115	Donovan Osborne	.05
116	Dave Magadan	.05
117	Edgar Martinez	.05
118	Chuck Carr	.05
119	J.R. Phillips	.05
120	Sean Bergman	.05
121	Andujar Cedeno	.05
122	Eric Young	.05
123	Al Martin	.05
124	Ken Hill	.05
125	Jim Eisenreich	.05
126	Benito Santiago	.05
127	Ariel Prieto	.05
128	Jim Bullinger	.05
129	Russ Davis	.05
130	Jim Abbott	.05
131	Jason Isringhausen	.05
132	Carlos Perez	.05
133	David Segui	.05
134	Troy O'Leary	.05
135	Pat Meares	.05
136	Chris Hoiles	.05
137	Ismael Valdes	.05
138	Jose Oliva	.05
139	Carlos Delgado	.35
140	Tom Goodwin	.05
141	Bob Tewksbury	.05
142	Chris Gomez	.05
143	Jose Oquendo	.05
144	Mark Lewis	.05
145	Salomon Torres	.05
146	Luis Gonzalez	.05
147	Mark Carreon	.05
148	Lance Johnson	.05
149	Melvin Nieves	.05
150	Lee Smith	.05
151	Jacob Brumfield	.05
152	Armando Benitez	.05
153	Curt Schilling	.30
154	Javier Lopez	.05
155	Frank Rodriguez	.05
156	Alex Gonzalez	.05
157	Todd Worrell	.05
158	Benji Gil	.05
159	Greg Gagne	.05
160	Tom Henke	.05
161	Randy Myers	.05
162	Joey Cora	.05
163	Scott Ruffcorn	.05
164	William Van Landingham	.05
165	Tony Phillips	.05
166	Eddie Williams	.05
167	Bobby Bonilla	.05
168	Denny Neagle	.05
169	Troy Percival	.05
170	Billy Ashley	.05
171	Andy Van Slyke	.05
172	Jose Offerman	.05
173	Mark Parent	.05
174	Edgardo Alfonzo	.05
175	Trevor Hoffman	.05
176	David Cone	.05
177	Dan Wilson	.05
178	Steve Ontiveros	.05
179	Dean Palmer	.05
180	Mike Kelly	.05
181	Jim Leyritz	.05
182	Ron Karkovice	.05
183	Kevin Brown	.05
184	Jose Valentin RC	.05
185	Jorge Fabregas	.05
186	Jose Mesa	.05
187	Brent Mayne	.05
188	Carl Everett	.05
189	Paul Sorrento	.05
190	Pete Shourek	.05
191	Scott Kamieniecki	.05
192	Roberto Hernandez	.05
193	Randy Johnson	.25
194	Greg Maddux	.35
195	Hideo Nomo	.15
196	David Cone	.05
197	Mike Mussina	.15
198	Andy Benes	.05
199	Kevin Appier	.05
200	John Smoltz	.05
201	John Wetteland	.05
202	Mark Wohlers	.05
203	Stan Belinda	.05
204	Brian Anderson	.05
205	Mike Devereaux	.05
206	Mark Wohlers	.05
207	Omar Vizquel	.05
208	Jose Rijo	.05
209	Willie Blair	.05
210	Jamie Moyer	.05
211	Craig Shipley	.05
212	Shane Reynolds	.05
213	Chad Fonville	.05
214	Jose Vizcaino	.05
215	Sid Fernandez	.05
216	Andy Ashby	.05
217	Frank Castillo	.05
218	Kevin Tapani	.05
219	Kent Mercker	.05
220	Karim Garcia	.05
221	Chris Snopek	.05
222	Tim Unroe	.05
223	Johnny Damon	.25
224	LaTroy Hawkins	.05
225	Mariano Rivera	.10
226	Jose Alberro	.05
227	Angel Martinez	.05
228	Jason Schmidt	.05
229	Tony Clark	.05
230	Kevin Jordan	.05
231	Mark Thompson	.05
232	Jim Dougherty	.05
333	Roger Cedeno	.05
234	Ugueth Urbina	.05
235	Ricky Otero	.05
236	Mark Smith	.05
237	Brian Barber	.05
238	Marc Kroon	.05
239	Joe Rosselli	.05
240	Derek Jeter	1.50
241	Michael Tucker	.05
242	Joe Borowski RC	.05
243	Joe Vitiello	.05
244	Orlando Palmeiro	.05
245	James Baldwin	.05
246	Alan Embree	.05
247	Shannon Penn	.05
248	Chris Stynes	.05
249	Oscar Munoz	.05
250	Jose Herrera	.05
251	Scott Sullivan	.05
252	Reggie Williams	.05
253	Mark Grudzielanek	.05
254	Kevin Jordan	.05
255	Terry Bradshaw	.05
256	F.P. Santangelo RC	.05
257	Doug Johns	.05
258	George Williams	.05
259	Larry Thomas	.05
260	Rudy Pemberton	.05
261	Jim Pittsley	.05
262	Les Norman	.05
263	Ruben Rivera	.05
264	Cesar Devarez RC	.05
265	Gregg Zaun	.05
266	Eric Owens	.05
267	John Frascatore	.05
268	Shannon Stewart	.05
269	Checklist	.05
270	Checklist	.05
271	Checklist	.05
272	Checklist	.05
273	Checklist	.05
274	Checklist	.05
275	Checklist	.05
276	Greg Maddux	.60
277	Pedro Martinez	.50
278	Bobby Higginson	.05
279	Ray Lankford	.05
280	Shawon Dunston	.05
281	Gary Sheffield	.35
282	Ken Griffey Jr.	.75
283	Paul Molitor	.50
284	Kevin Appier	.05
285	Chuck Knoblauch	.05
286	Alex Fernandez	.05
287	Steve Finley	.05
288	Jeff Blauser	.05
289	Charles Johnson	.05
290	John Franco	.05
291	Mark Langston	.05
292	Bret Saberhagen	.05
293	John Mabry	.05
294	Ramon Martinez	.05
295	Mike Blowers	.05
296	Paul O'Neill	.05
297	Dave Nilsson	.05
298	Dante Bichette	.05
299	Marty Cordova	.05
300	Jay Bell	.05
301	Mike Mussina	.30
302	Ivan Rodriguez	.40
303	Jose Canseco	.30
304	Jeff Bagwell	.50
305	Manny Ramirez	.50
306	Dennis Martinez	.05
307	Charlie Hayes	.05
308	Joe Carter	.05
309	Travis Fryman	.05
310	Mark McGwire	1.00
311	Reggie Sanders	.05
312	Julian Tavarez	.05
313	Jeff Montgomery	.05
314	Andy Benes	.05
315	John Jaha	.05
316	Jeff Kent	.05
317	Mike Piazza	.75
318	Erik Hanson	.05
319	Kenny Rogers	.05
320	Hideo Nomo	.25
321	Gregg Jefferies	.05
322	Chipper Jones	.60
323	Jay Buhner	.05
324	Dennis Eckersley	.40
325	Kenny Lofton	.05
326	Robin Ventura	.05
327	Tom Glavine	.35
328	Tim Salmon	.05
329	Andres Galarraga	.05
330	Hal Morris	.05
331	Brady Anderson	.05
332	Chili Davis	.05
333	Roger Clemens	.65
334	Marquis Grissom	.05
335	Jeff (Mike) Greenwell	.05
336	Sammy Sosa	.60
337	Ron Gant	.05
338	Ken Caminiti	.05
339	Danny Tartabull	.05
340	Barry Bonds	1.50
341	Ben McDonald	.05
342	Ruben Sierra	.05
343	Bernie Williams	.05
344	Wil Cordero	.05
345	Wade Boggs	.60
346	Gary Gaetti	.05
347	Greg Colbrunn	.05
348	Juan Gonzalez	.25
349	Marc Newfield	.05
350	Charles Nagy	.05
351	Robby Thompson	.05
352	Roberto Petagine	.05
353	Darryl Strawberry	.05
354	Tino Martinez	.05
355	Eric Karros	.05
356	Cal Ripken Jr.	.75
357	Cecil Fielder	.05
358	Kirby Puckett	.35
359	Jim Edmonds	.05
360	Matt Williams	.05
361	Alex Rodriguez	.50
362	Barry Larkin	.05
363	Rafael Palmeiro	.20
364	David Cone	.05
365	Roberto Alomar	.10
366	Eddie Murray	.25
367	Randy Johnson	.20
368	Ryan Klesko	.05
369	Raul Mondesi	.05
370	Mo Vaughn	.05

Card	Player	Price
371	Will Clark	.05
372	Carlos Baerga	.05
373	Frank Thomas	.30
374	Larry Walker	.05
375	Garret Anderson	.05
376	Edgar Martinez	.05
377	Don Mattingly	.40
378	Tony Gwynn	.35
379	Albert Belle	.05
380	Jason Isringhausen	.05
381	Ruben Rivera	.05
382	Johnny Damon	.05
383	Karim Garcia	.05
384	Derek Jeter	.75
385	David Justice	.05
386	Royce Clayton	.05
387	Mark Whiten	.05
388	Mickey Tettleton	.05
389	Steve Trachsel	.05
390	Danny Bautista	.05
391	Midre Cummings	.05
392	Scott Leius	.05
393	Manny Alexander	.05
394	Brent Gates	.05
395	Rey Sanchez	.05
396	Andy Pettitte	.20
397	Jeff Cirillo	.05
398	Kurt Abbott	.05
399	Lee Tinsley	.05
400	Paul Assenmacher	.05
401	Scott Erickson	.05
402	Todd Zeile	.05
403	Tom Pagnozzi	.05
404	Ozzie Guillen	.05
405	Jeff Frye	.05
406	Kirt Manwaring	.05
407	Chad Ogea	.05
408	Harold Baines	.05
409	Jason Bere	.05
410	Chuck Finley	.05
411	Jeff Fassero	.05
412	Joey Hamilton	.05
413	John Olerud	.05
414	Kevin Stocker	.05
415	Eric Anthony	.05
416	Aaron Sele	.05
417	Chris Bosio	.05
418	Michael Mimbs	.05
419	Orlando Miller	.05
420	Stan Javier	.05
421	Matt Mieske	.05
422	Jason Bates	.05
423	Orlando Merced	.05
424	John Flaherty	.05
425	Reggie Jefferson	.05
426	Scott Stahoviak	.05
427	John Burkett	.05
428	Rod Beck	.05
429	Bill Swift	.05
430	Scott Cooper	.05
431	Mel Rojas	.05
432	Todd Van Poppel	.05
433	Bobby Jones	.05
434	Mike Harkey	.05
435	Sean Berry	.05
436	Glenallen Hill	.05
437	Ryan Thompson	.05
438	Luis Alicea	.05
439	Esteban Loaiza	.05
440	Jeff Reboulet	.05
441	Vince Coleman	.05
442	Ellis Burks	.05
443	Allen Battle	.05
444	Jimmy Key	.05
445	Ricky Bottalico	.05
446	Delino DeShields	.05
447	Albie Lopez	.05
448	Mark Petkovsek	.05
449	Tim Raines	.05
450	Bryan Harvey	.05
451	Pat Hentgen	.05
452	Tim Laker	.05
453	Tom Gordon	.05
454	Phil Plantier	.05
455	Ernie Young	.05
456	Pete Harnisch	.05
457	Roberto Kelly	.05
458	Mark Portugal	.05
459	Mark Leiter	.05
460	Tony Pena	.05
461	Roger Pavlik	.05
462	Jeff King	.05
463	Bryan Rekar	.05
464	Al Leiter	.05
465	Phil Nevin	.05
466	Jose Lima	.05
467	Mike Stanley	.05
468	David McCarty	.05
469	Herb Perry	.05
470	Geronimo Berroa	.05
471	David Wells	.05
472	Vaughn Eshelman	.05
473	Greg Swindell	.05
474	Steve Sparks	.05
475	Luis Sojo	.05
476	Derrick May	.05
477	Joe Oliver	.05
478	Alex Arias	.05
479	Brad Ausmus	.05
480	Gabe White	.05
481	Pat Rapp	.05
482	Damon Buford	.05
483	Turk Wendell	.05
484	Jeff Brantley	.05
485	Curtis Leskanic	.05
486	Robb Nen	.05
487	Lou Whitaker	.05
488	Melido Perez	.05
489	Luis Polonia	.05
490	Scott Brosius	.05
491	Robert Perez	.05
492	Mike Sweeney RC	.50
493	Mark Loretta	.05
494	Alex Ochoa	.05
495	Matt Lawton RC	.10
496	Shawn Estes	.05
497	John Wasdin	.05
498	Marc Kroon	.05
499	Chris Snopek	.05
500	Jeff Suppan	.05
501	Terrell Wade	.05
502	Marvin Benard RC	.10
503	Chris Widger	.05
504	Quinton McCracken	.05
505	Bob Wolcott	.05
506	C.J. Nitkowski	.05
507	Aaron Ledesma	.05
508	Scott Hatteberg	.05
509	Jimmy Haynes	.05
510	Howard Battle	.05

Dugout Collection

	NM/M
Complete Set (220):	60.00
Complete Series 1 (1-110):	30.00
Complete Series 2 (1-110):	30.00
Common Player:	.20
Artist's Proofs:	4X

SERIES 1

Card	Player	Price
1	Will Clark	.20
2	Rich Becker	.20
3	Ryan Klesko	.20
4	Jim Edmonds	.20
5	Barry Larkin	.20
6	Jim Thome	.65
7	Raul Mondesi	.20
8	Don Mattingly	1.25
9	Jeff Conine	.20
10	Rickey Henderson	.75
11	Chad Curtis	.20
12	Darren Daulton	.20
13	Larry Walker	.20
14	Carlos Baerga	.20
15	Tony Gwynn	1.00
16	Jon Nunnally	.20
17	Deion Sanders	.20
18	Mark Grace	.20
19	Alex Rodriguez	2.00
20	Frank Thomas	.75
21	Brian Jordan	.20
22	J.T. Snow	.20
23	Shawn Green	.50
24	Tim Wakefield	.20
25	Curtis Goodwin	.20
26	John Smoltz	.20
27	Devon White	.20
28	Brian Hunter	.20
29	Rusty Greer	.20
30	Rafael Palmeiro	.65
31	Bernard Gilkey	.20
32	John Valentin	.20
33	Randy Johnson	.75
34	Garret Anderson	.20
35	Ray Durham	.20
36	Bip Roberts	.20
37	Tyler Green	.20
38	Bill Pulsipher	.20
39	Jason Giambi	.50
40	Jack McDowell	.20
41	Rico Brogna	.20
42	Terry Pendleton	.20
43	Rondell White	.20
44	Andre Dawson	.35
45	Kirby Puckett	1.00
46	Wally Joyner	.20
47	B.J. Surhoff	.20
48	Randy Velarde	.20
49	Greg Vaughn	.20
50	Roberto Alomar	.30
51	David Justice	.20
52	Cal Ripken Jr.	3.00
53	Ozzie Smith	1.00
54	Mo Vaughn	.20
55	Gary DiSarcina	.20
56	Matt Williams	.20
57	Lenny Dykstra	.20
58	Bret Boone	.20
59	Albert Belle	.20
60	Vinny Castilla	.20
61	Moises Alou	.20
62	Cecil Fielder	.20
63	Brad Radke	.20
64	Quilvio Veras	.20
65	Eddie Murray	.75
66	Dave Winfield	.75
67	Fred McGriff	.20
68	Craig Biggio	.20
69	Cliff Floyd	.20
70	Tim Naehring	.20
71	John Wetteland	.20
72	Alan Trammell	.20
73	Steve Avery	.20
74	Rick Aguilera	.20
75	Derek Bell	.20
76	Todd Hollandsworth	.20
77	Edgar Martinez	.20
78	Mark Lemke	.20
79	Ariel Prieto	.20
80	Russ Davis	.20
81	Jim Abbott	.20
82	Jason Isringhausen	.20
83	Carlos Perez	.20
84	David Segui	.20
85	Troy O'Leary	.20
86	Ismael Valdes	.20
87	Carlos Delgado	.50
88	Lee Smith	.20
89	Javy Lopez	.20
90	Frank Rodriguez	.20
91	Alex Gonzalez	.20
92	Benji Gil	.20
93	Greg Gagne	.20
94	Randy Myers	.20
95	Bobby Bonilla	.20
96	Billy Ashley	.20
97	Andy Van Slyke	.20
98	Edgardo Alfonzo	.20
99	David Cone	.20
100	Dean Palmer	.20
101	Jose Mesa	.20
102	Karim Garcia	.20
103	Johnny Damon	.40
104	LaTroy Hawkins	.20
105	Mark Smith	.20
106	Derek Jeter	3.00
107	Michael Tucker	.20
108	Joe Vitiello	.20
109	Ruben Rivera	.20
110	Gregg Zaun	.20

SERIES 2

Card	Player	Price
1	Greg Maddux	1.00
2	Pedro Martinez	.75
3	Bobby Higginson	.20
4	Ray Lankford	.20
5	Shawon Dunston	.20
6	Gary Sheffield	.45
7	Ken Griffey Jr.	1.50
8	Paul Molitor	.75
9	Kevin Appier	.20
10	Chuck Knoblauch	.20
11	Alex Fernandez	.20
12	Steve Finley	.20
13	Mark Blauser	.20
14	Charles Johnson	.20
15	John Franco	.20
16	Mark Langston	.20
17	Bret Saberhagen	.20
18	John Mabry	.20
19	Ramon Martinez	.20
20	Mike Blowers	.20
21	Paul O'Neill	.20
22	Dave Nilsson	.20
23	Dante Bichette	.20
24	Marty Cordova	.20
25	Jay Bell	.20
26	Mike Mussina	.40
27	Ivan Rodriguez	.65
28	Jose Canseco	.50
29	Jeff Bagwell	.75
30	Manny Ramirez	.75
31	Dennis Martinez	.20
32	Charlie Hayes	.20
33	Joe Carter	.20
34	Travis Fryman	.50
35	Mark McGwire	2.00
36	Reggie Sanders	.20
37	Julian Tavarez	.20
38	Jeff Montgomery	.20
39	Andy Benes	.20
40	John Jaha	.20
41	Jeff Kent	.20
42	Mike Piazza	1.50
43	Erik Hanson	.20
44	Kenny Rogers	.20
45	Hideo Nomo	.50
46	Gregg Jefferies	.20
47	Chipper Jones	1.00
48	Jay Buhner	.20
49	Dennis Eckersley	.65
50	Kenny Lofton	.20
51	Robin Ventura	.20
52	Tom Glavine	.30
53	Tim Salmon	.20
54	Andres Galarraga	.20
55	Hal Morris	.20
56	Brady Anderson	.20
57	Chili Davis	.20
58	Roger Clemens	1.25
59	Marquis Grissom	.20
60	Mike Greenwell	.20
61	Sammy Sosa	1.00
62	Ron Gant	.20
63	Ken Caminiti	.20
64	Danny Tartabull	.20
65	Barry Bonds	3.00
66	Ben McDonald	.20
67	Ruben Sierra	.20
68	Bernie Williams	.20
69	Wil Cordero	.20
70	Wade Boggs	1.00
71	Gary Gaetti	.20
72	Greg Colbrunn	.20
73	Juan Gonzalez	.50
74	Marc Newfield	.20
75	Charles Nagy	.20
76	Robby Thompson	.20
77	Roberto Petagine	.20
78	Darryl Strawberry	.20
79	Tino Martinez	.20
80	Eric Karros	.20
81	Cal Ripken Jr.	1.50
82	Cecil Fielder	.20
83	Kirby Puckett	.50
84	Jim Edmonds	.20
85	Matt Williams	.20
86	Alex Rodriguez	1.00
87	Barry Larkin	.20
88	Rafael Palmeiro	.40
89	David Cone	.20
90	Roberto Alomar	.25
91	Eddie Murray	.40
92	Randy Johnson	.40
93	Ryan Klesko	.20
94	Raul Mondesi	.20
95	Mo Vaughn	.20
96	Will Clark	.20
97	Carlos Baerga	.20
98	Frank Thomas	.45
99	Larry Walker	.20
100	Garret Anderson	.20
101	Edgar Martinez	.20
102	Don Mattingly	.60
103	Tony Gwynn	.50
104	Albert Belle	.20
105	Jason Isringhausen	.20
106	Ruben Rivera	.20
107	Johnny Damon	.35
108	Karim Garcia	.20
109	Derek Jeter	1.50
110	David Justice	.20

Dugout Collection Artist's Proofs

	NM/M
Complete Set (220):	300.00
Common Player:	1.00
Artist's Proof Stars:	4X

(See 1996 Score Dugout Collection for checklist and base card values.)

All-Stars

		NM/M
Complete Set (20):		13.50
Common Player:		.25
1	Frank Thomas	1.25
2	Albert Belle	.25
3	Ken Griffey Jr.	2.00
4	Cal Ripken Jr.	3.00
5	Mo Vaughn	.25
6	Matt Williams	.25
7	Barry Bonds	3.00
8	Dante Bichette	.25
9	Tony Gy	1.25
10	Greg Maddux	1.50
11	Randy Johnson	1.25
12	Hideo Nomo	.75
13	Tim Salmon	.25
14	Jeff Bagwell	1.25
15	Edgar Martinez	.25
16	Reggie Sanders	.25
17	Larry Walker	.25
18	Chipper Jones	1.50
19	Manny Ramirez	1.25
20	Eddie Murray	1.25

Big Bats

		NM/M
Complete Set (20):		12.50
Common Player:		.45
1	Cal Ripken Jr.	3.00
2	Ken Griffey Jr.	2.00
3	Frank Thomas	.75
4	Jeff Bagwell	.75
5	Mike Piazza	2.00
6	Barry Bonds	3.00
7	Matt Williams	.45
8	Raul Mondesi	.45
9	Tony Gwynn	1.25
10	Albert Belle	.45
11	Manny Ramirez	.75
12	Carlos Baerga	.45
13	Mo Vaughn	.45
14	Derek Bell	.45
15	Larry Walker	.45
16	Kenny Lofton	.45
17	Edgar Martinez	.45
18	Reggie Sanders	.45
19	Eddie Murray	.75
20	Chipper Jones	1.25

Diamond Aces

		NM/M
Complete Set (30):		25.00
Common Player:		.35
1	Hideo Nomo	.60
2	Brian Hunter	.35
3	Ray Durham	.35
4	Frank Thomas	1.00
5	Cal Ripken Jr.	3.50
6	Barry Bonds	3.50
7	Greg Maddux	1.25
8	Chipper Jones	1.25
9	Raul Mondesi	.35
10	Mike Piazza	2.00
11	Derek Jeter	3.50
12	Bill Pulsipher	.35
13	Larry Walker	.35
14	Ken Griffey Jr.	2.00
15	Alex Rodriguez	3.00
16	Manny Ramirez	1.00
17	Mo Vaughn	.35
18	Reggie Sanders	.35
19	Derek Bell	.35
20	Jim Edmonds	.35
21	Albert Belle	.35
22	Eddie Murray	1.00
23	Tony Gwynn	1.25
24	Jeff Bagwell	1.00
25	Carlos Baerga	.35
26	Matt Williams	.35
27	Garret Anderson	.35
28	Todd Hollandsworth	.35
29	Johnny Damon	.75
30	Tim Salmon	.35

Dream Team

		NM/M
Complete Set (9):		15.00
Common Player:		.75
1	Cal Ripken Jr.	4.00
2	Frank Thomas	1.50
3	Carlos Baerga	.75
4	Matt Williams	.75
5	Mike Piazza	3.00
6	Barry Bonds	4.00
7	Ken Griffey Jr.	3.00
8	Manny Ramirez	1.50
9	Greg Maddux	2.00

Reserve Collection

		NM/M
Complete Set (221):		250.00
Common Player:		1.00
Reserve Collection Stars:		8X

(See 1997 Score #331-551 for checklist and base card values.)

Gold Stars

		NM/M
Complete Set (30):		20.00
Common Player:		.20
1	Ken Griffey Jr.	2.00
2	Frank Thomas	1.00
3	Reggie Sanders	.20
4	Tim Salmon	.20
5	Mike Piazza	2.00
6	Tony Gwynn	1.50

BARRY LARKIN

7	Gary Sheffield	.45
8	Matt Williams	.20
9	Bernie Williams	.20
10	Jason Isringhausen	.20
11	Albert Belle	.20
12	Chipper Jones	1.50
13	Edgar Martinez	.20
14	Barry Larkin	.20
15	Barry Bonds	3.00
16	Jeff Bagwell	1.00
17	Greg Maddux	1.50
18	Mo Vaughn	.20
19	Ryan Klesko	.20
20	Sammy Sosa	1.50
21	Darren Daulton	.20
22	Ivan Rodriguez	.75
23	Dante Bichette	.20
24	Hideo Nomo	.50
25	Cal Ripken Jr.	3.00
26	Rafael Palmeiro	.75
27	Larry Walker	.20
28	Carlos Baerga	.20
29	Randy Johnson	1.00
30	Manny Ramirez	1.00

Future Franchise

Marc Newfield

		NM/M
Complete Set (16):		20.00
Common Player:		.75
1	Jason Isringhausen	.75
2	Chipper Jones	2.50
3	Derek Jeter	5.00
4	Alex Rodriguez	4.00
5	Alex Ochoa	.75
6	Manny Ramirez	1.50
7	Johnny Damon	1.00
8	Ruben Rivera	.75
9	Karim Garcia	.75
10	Garret Anderson	.75
11	Marty Cordova	.75
12	Bill Pulsipher	.75
13	Hideo Nomo	1.00
14	Marc Newfield	.75
15	Charles Johnson	.75
16	Raul Mondesi	.75

Power Pace

	NM/M
Complete Set (18):	24.00

Common Player:		.50
1	Mark McGwire	4.00
2	Albert Belle	.50
3	Jay Buhner	.50
4	Frank Thomas	1.50
5	Matt Williams	.50
6	Gary Sheffield	.75
7	Mike Piazza	3.00
8	Larry Walker	.50
9	Mo Vaughn	.50
10	Rafael Palmeiro	1.25
11	Dante Bichette	.50
12	Ken Griffey Jr.	3.00
13	Barry Bonds	5.00
14	Manny Ramirez	1.50
15	Sammy Sosa	2.00
16	Tim Salmon	.50
17	Dave Justice	.50
18	Eric Karros	.50

Numbers Game

		NM/M
Complete Set (30):		17.50
Common Player:		.15
1	Cal Ripken Jr.	2.50
2	Frank Thomas	.75
3	Ken Griffey Jr.	1.50
4	Mike Piazza	1.50
5	Barry Bonds	2.50
6	Greg Maddux	1.00
7	Jeff Bagwell	.75
8	Derek Bell	.15
9	Tony Gwynn	1.00
10	Hideo Nomo	.50
11	Raul Mondesi	.15
12	Manny Ramirez	.75
13	Albert Belle	.15
14	Matt Williams	.15
15	Jim Edmonds	.15
16	Edgar Martinez	.15
17	Mo Vaughn	.15
18	Reggie Sanders	.15
19	Chipper Jones	1.00
20	Larry Walker	.15
21	Juan Gonzalez	.50
22	Kenny Lofton	.15
23	Don Mattingly	1.25
24	Ivan Rodriguez	.65
25	Randy Johnson	.75
26	Derek Jeter	2.50
27	J.T. Snow	.15
28	Will Clark	.15
29	Rafael Palmeiro	.65
30	Alex Rodriguez	2.00

Reflexions

		NM/M
Complete Set (20):		35.00
Common Player:		.45
1	Cal Ripken Jr., Chipper Jones	5.00
2	Ken Griffey Jr., Alex Rodriguez	4.50
3	Frank Thomas, Mo Vaughn	2.50
4	Kenny Lofton, Brian Hunter	.45
5	Don Mattingly, J.T. Snow	3.75
6	Manny Ramirez, Raul Mondesi	2.50

7	Tony Gwynn,	
	Garret Anderson	3.75
8	Roberto Alomar,	
	Carlos Baerga	.50
9	Andre Dawson,	
	Larry Walker	.50
10	Barry Larkin,	
	Derek Jeter	5.00
11	Barry Bonds,	
	Reggie Sanders	5.00
12	Mike Piazza,	
	Albert Belle	4.00
13	Wade Boggs,	
	Edgar Martinez	3.75
14	David Cone,	
	John Smoltz	.45
15	Will Clark,	
	Jeff Walker	2.50
16	Mark McGwire,	
	Cecil Fielder	4.50
17	Greg Maddux,	
	Mike Mussina	3.75
18	Randy Johnson,	
	Hideo Nomo	2.50
19	Jim Thome,	
	Dean Palmer	2.00
20	Chuck Knoblauch,	
	Craig Biggio	.45

Titantic Taters

		NM/M
Complete Set (18):		25.00
Common Player:		.60
1	Albert Belle	.60
2	Frank Thomas	2.00
3	Mo Vaughn	.60
4	Ken Griffey Jr.	3.00
5	Matt Williams	.60
6	Mark McGwire	3.50
7	Dante Bichette	.60
8	Tim Salmon	.60
9	Jeff Bagwell	2.00
10	Rafael Palmeiro	1.50
11	Mike Piazza	3.00
12	Cecil Fielder	.60
13	Larry Walker	.60
14	Sammy Sosa	2.50
15	Manny Ramirez	2.00
16	Gary Sheffield	.90
17	Barry Bonds	5.00
18	Jay Buhner	.60

1997 Score

		NM/M
Complete Set (551):		16.00
Factory Tin-Box Set (551):		17.50
Common Player:		.05
Wax Pack (10):		.50
Wax Box (36):		12.00
1	Jeff Bagwell	.50
2	Mickey Tettleton	.05
3	Johnny Damon	.25
4	Jeff Conine	.05
5	Bernie Williams	.05
6	Will Clark	.05
7	Ryan Klesko	.05
8	Cecil Fielder	.05
9	Paul Wilson	.05
10	Gregg Jefferies	.05
11	Chili Davis	.05
12	Albert Belle	.05
13	Ken Hill	.05
14	Cliff Floyd	.05
15	Jaime Navarro	.05
16	Ismael Valdes	.05
17	Jeff King	.05
18	Chris Bosio	.05
19	Reggie Sanders	.05
20	Darren Daulton	.05
21	Ken Caminiti	.05
22	Mike Piazza	.75
23	Chad Mottola	.05
24	Darin Erstad	.15
25	Dante Bichette	.05
26	Frank Thomas	.50
27	Ben McDonald	.05
28	Raul Casanova	.05
29	Kevin Ritz	.05
30	Garret Anderson	.05
31	Jason Kendall	.05
32	Billy Wagner	.05
33	David Justice	.05
34	Marty Cordova	.05
35	Derek Jeter	1.50
36	Trevor Hoffman	.05
37	Geronimo Berroa	.05
38	Walt Weiss	.05
39	Kirt Manwaring	.05
40	Alex Gonzalez	.05
41	Sean Berry	.05
42	Kevin Appier	.05
43	Rusty Greer	.05
44	Pete Incaviglia	.05
45	Rafael Palmeiro	.45
46	Eddie Murray	.50
47	Moises Alou	.05
48	Mark Lewis	.05
49	Hal Morris	.05
50	Edgar Renteria	.05
51	Rickey Henderson	.50
52	Pat Listach	.05
53	John Wasdin	.05
54	James Baldwin	.05
55	Brian Jordan	.05
56	Edgar Martinez	.05
57	Wil Cordero	.05
58	Danny Tartabull	.05
59	Keith Lockhart	.05
60	Rico Brogna	.05
61	Ricky Bottalico	.05
62	Terry Pendleton	.05
63	Bret Boone	.05
64	Charlie Hayes	.05
65	Marc Newfield	.05
66	Sterling Hitchcock	.05
67	Roberto Alomar	.15
68	John Jaha	.05
69	Greg Colbrunn	.05
70	Sal Fasano	.05
71	Brooks Kieschnick	.05
72	Pedro Martinez	.50
73	Kevin Elster	.05
74	Ellis Burks	.05
75	Chuck Finley	.05
76	John Olerud	.05
77	Jay Bell	.05
78	Allen Watson	.05
79	Darryl Strawberry	.05
80	Orlando Miller	.05
81	Jose Herrera	.05
82	Andy Pettitte	.20
83	Juan Guzman	.05
84	Alan Benes	.05
85	Jack McDowell	.05
86	Ugueth Urbina	.05
87	Rocky Coppinger	.05
88	Jeff Cirillo	.05
89	Tom Glavine	.35
90	Robby Thompson	.05
91	Barry Bonds	1.50
92	Carlos Delgado	.40
93	Mo Vaughn	.05
94	Ryne Sandberg	.65
95	Alex Rodriguez	1.00
96	Brady Anderson	.05
97	Scott Brosius	.05
98	Dennis Eckersley	.45
99	Brian McRae	.05
100	Rey Ordonez	.05
101	John Valentin	.05
102	Brett Butler	.05
103	Eric Karros	.05
104	Harold Baines	.05
105	Javier Lopez	.05
106	Alan Trammell	.05
107	Jim Thome	.45
108	Frank Rodriguez	.05
109	Bernard Gilkey	.05
110	Reggie Jefferson	.05
111	Scott Stahoviak	.05
112	Steve Gibralter	.05
113	Todd Hollandsworth	.05
114	Ruben Rivera	.05
115	Dennis Martinez	.05
116	Mariano Rivera	.10
117	John Smoltz	.05
118	John Mabry	.05
119	Tom Gordon	.05
120	Alex Ochoa	.05
121	Jamey Wright	.05
122	Dave Nilsson	.05
123	Bobby Bonilla	.05
124	Al Leiter	.05
125	Rick Aguilera	.05
126	Jeff Brantley	.05
127	Kevin Brown	.05
128	George Arias	.05
129	Darren Oliver	.05
130	Bill Pulsipher	.05
131	Roberto Hernandez	.05
132	Delino DeShields	.05
133	Mark Grudzielanek	.05
134	John Wetteland	.05
135	Carlos Baerga	.05
136	Paul Sorrento	.05
137	Leo Gomez	.05
138	Andy Ashby	.05
139	Julio Franco	.05
140	Brian Hunter	.05
141	Jermaine Dye	.05
142	Tony Clark	.05
143	Ruben Sierra	.05
144	Donovan Osborne	.05
145	Mark McLemore	.05
146	Terry Steinbach	.05
147	Bob Wells	.05
148	Chan Ho Park	.05
149	Tim Salmon	.05
150	Paul O'Neill	.05
151	Cal Ripken Jr.	1.50
152	Wally Joyner	.05
153	Omar Vizquel	.05
154	Mike Mussina	.30
155	Andres Galarraga	.05
156	Ken Griffey Jr.	.75
157	Kenny Lofton	.05
158	Ray Durham	.05
159	Hideo Nomo	.25
160	Ozzie Guillen	.05
161	Roger Pavlik	.05
162	Manny Ramirez	.50
163	Mark Lemke	.05
164	Mike Stanley	.05
165	Chuck Knoblauch	.05
166	Kimera Bartee	.05
167	Wade Boggs	.65
168	Jay Buhner	.05
169	Eric Young	.05
170	Jose Canseco	.30
171	Dwight Gooden	.05
172	Fred McGriff	.05
173	Sandy Alomar Jr.	.05
174	Andy Benes	.05
175	Dean Palmer	.05
176	Larry Walker	.05
177	Charles Nagy	.05
178	David Cone	.05
179	Mark Grace	.05
180	Robin Ventura	.05
181	Roger Clemens	.70
182	Bobby Witt	.05
183	Vinny Castilla	.05
184	Gary Sheffield	.35
185	Dan Wilson	.05
186	Roger Cedeno	.05
187	Mark McGwire	1.00
188	Darren Bragg	.05
189	Quinton McCracken	.05
190	Randy Myers	.05
191	Jeromy Burnitz	.05
192	Randy Johnson	.50
193	Chipper Jones	.65
194	Greg Vaughn	.05
195	Travis Fryman	.05
196	Tim Naehring	.05
197	B.J. Surhoff	.05
198	Juan Gonzalez	.25
199	Terrell Wade	.05
200	Jeff Frye	.05
201	Joey Cora	.05
202	Raul Mondesi	.05
203	Ivan Rodriguez	.45
204	Armando Reynoso	.05
205	Jeffrey Hammonds	.05
206	Darren Dreifort	.05
207	Kevin Seitzer	.05
208	Tino Martinez	.05
209	Jim Bruske	.05
210	Jeff Suppan	.05
211	Mark Carreon	.05
212	Wilson Alvarez	.05
213	John Burkett	.05
214	Tony Phillips	.05
215	Greg Maddux	.65
216	Mark Whiten	.05
217	Curtis Pride	.05
218	Lyle Mouton	.05
219	Todd Hundley	.05
220	Greg Gagne	.05
221	Rich Amaral	.05
222	Tom Goodwin	.05
223	Chris Hoiles	.05
224	Jayhawk Owens	.05
225	Kenny Rogers	.05
226	Mike Greenwell	.05
227	Mark Wohlers	.05
228	Henry Rodriguez	.05
229	Robert Perez	.05
230	Jeff Kent	.05
231	Darryl Hamilton	.05
232	Alex Fernandez	.05
233	Ron Karkovice	.05
234	Jimmy Haynes	.05
235	Craig Biggio	.05
236	Ray Lankford	.05
237	Lance Johnson	.05
238	Matt Williams	.05
239	Chad Curtis	.05
240	Mark Thompson	.05
241	Jason Giambi	.40
242	Barry Larkin	.05
243	Paul Molitor	.50
244	Sammy Sosa	.65
245	Kevin Tapani	.05
246	Marquis Grissom	.05
247	Joe Carter	.05
248	Ramon Martinez	.05
249	Tony Gwynn	.65
250	Andy Fox	.05
251	Troy O'Leary	.05
252	Warren Newson	.05
253	Troy Percival	.05
254	Jamie Moyer	.05
255	Danny Graves	.05
256	David Wells	.05
257	Todd Zeile	.05
258	Raul Ibanez	.05
259	Tyler Houston	.05
260	LaTroy Hawkins	.05
261	Joey Hamilton	.05
262	Mike Sweeney	.05
263	Brant Brown	.05
264	Pat Hentgen	.05
265	Mark Johnson	.05
266	Robb Nen	.05
267	Justin Thompson	.05
268	Ron Gant	.05
269	Jeff D'Amico	.05
270	Shawn Estes	.05
271	Derek Bell	.05
272	Fernando Valenzuela	.05
273	Luis Castillo	.05
274	Ray Montgomery	.05
275	Ed Sprague	.05
276	F.P. Santangelo	.05
277	Todd Greene	.05
278	Butch Huskey	.05
279	Steve Finley	.05
280	Eric Davis	.05
281	Shawn Green	.30
282	Al Martin	.05
283	Michael Tucker	.05
284	Shane Reynolds	.05
285	Matt Mieske	.05
286	Jose Rosado	.05
287	Mark Langston	.05
288	Ralph Milliard	.05
289	Mike Lansing	.05
290	Scott Servais	.05
291	Royce Clayton	.05
292	Mike Grace	.05
293	James Mouton	.05
294	Charles Johnson	.05
295	Gary Gaetti	.05
296	Kevin Mitchell	.05
297	Carlos Garcia	.05
298	Desi Relaford	.05
299	Jason Thompson	.05
300	Osvaldo Fernandez	.05
301	Fernando Vina	.05
302	Jose Offerman	.05
303	Yamil Benitez	.05
304	J.T. Snow	.05
305	Rafael Bournigal	.05
306	Jason Isringhausen	.05
307	Bob Higginson	.05
308	Nerio Rodriguez **RC**	.05
309	Brian Giles **RC**	.50
310	Andruw Jones	.50
311	Billy McMillon	.05
312	Arquimedez Pozo	.05
313	Jermaine Allensworth	.05
314	Luis Andujar	.05
315	Angel Echevarria	.05
316	Karim Garcia	.05
317	Trey Beamon	.05
318	Makoto Suzuki	.05
319	Robin Jennings	.05

320	Dmitri Young	.05
321	Damon Mashore RC	.05
322	Wendell Magee	.05
323	Dax Jones RC	.05
324	Todd Walker	.05
325	Marvin Benard	.05
326	Brian Raabe RC	.05
327	Marcus Jensen	.05
328	Checklist	.05
329	Checklist	.05
330	Checklist	.05
331	Norm Charlton	.05
332	Bruce Ruffin	.05
333	John Wetteland	.05
334	Marquis Grissom	.05
335	Sterling Hitchcock	.05
336	John Olerud	.05
337	David Wells	.05
338	Chili Davis	.05
339	Mark Lewis	.05
340	Kenny Lofton	.05
341	Alex Fernandez	.05
342	Ruben Sierra	.05
343	Delino DeShields	.05
344	John Wasdin	.05
345	Dennis Martinez	.05
346	Kevin Elster	.05
347	Bobby Bonilla	.05
348	Jaime Navarro	.05
349	Chad Curtis	.05
350	Terry Steinbach	.05
351	Ariel Prieto	.05
352	Jeff Kent	.05
353	Carlos Garcia	.05
354	Mark Whiten	.05
355	Todd Zelle	.05
356	Eric Davis	.05
357	Greg Colbrunn	.05
358	Moises Alou	.05
359	Allen Watson	.05
360	Jose Canseco	.30
361	Matt Williams	.05
362	Jeff King	.05
363	Darryl Hamilton	.05
364	Mark Clark	.05
365	J.T. Snow	.05
366	Kevin Mitchell	.05
367	Orlando Miller	.05
368	Rico Brogna	.05
369	Mike James	.05
370	Brad Ausmus	.05
371	Darryl Kile	.05
372	Edgardo Alfonzo	.05
373	Julian Tavarez	.05
374	Darren Lewis	.05
375	Steve Karsay	.05
376	Lee Stevens	.05
377	Albie Lopez	.05
378	Orel Hershiser	.05
379	Lee Smith	.05
380	Rick Helling	.05
381	Carlos Perez	.05
382	Tony Tarasco	.05
383	Melvin Nieves	.05
384	Benji Gil	.05
385	Devon White	.05
386	Armando Benitez	.05
387	Bill Swift	.05
388	John Smiley	.05
389	Midre Cummings	.05
390	Tim Belcher	.05
391	Tim Raines	.05
392	Todd Worrell	.05
393	Quilvio Veras	.05
394	Matt Lawton	.05
395	Aaron Sele	.05
396	Bip Roberts	.05
397	Denny Neagle	.05
398	Tyler Green	.05
399	Hipolito Pichardo	.05
400	Scott Erickson	.05
401	Bobby Jones	.05
402	Jim Edmonds	.05
403	Chad Ogea	.05
404	Cal Eldred	.05
405	Pat Listach	.05
406	Todd Stottlemyre	.05
407	Phil Nevin	.05
408	Otis Nixon	.05
409	Billy Ashley	.05
410	Jimmy Key	.05
411	Mike Timlin	.05
412	Joe Vitiello	.05
413	Rondell White	.05
414	Jeff Fassero	.05
415	Rex Hudler	.05
416	Curt Schilling	.35
417	Rich Becker	.05
418	William Van Landingham	.05
419	Chris Snopek	.05
420	David Segui	.05
421	Eddie Murray	.50
422	Shane Andrews	.05
423	Gary DiSarcina	.05
424	Brian Hunter	.05
425	Willie Greene	.05
426	Felipe Crespo	.05
427	Jason Bates	.05
428	Albert Belle	.05
429	Rey Sanchez	.05
430	Roger Clemens	.70
431	Deion Sanders	.05
432	Ernie Young	.05
433	Jay Bell	.05
434	Jeff Blauser	.05
435	Lenny Dykstra	.05
436	Chuck Carr	.05
437	Russ Davis	.05
438	Carl Everett	.05
439	Damion Easley	.05
440	Pat Kelly	.05
441	Pat Rapp	.05
442	David Justice	.05
443	Graeme Lloyd	.05
444	Damon Buford	.05
445	Jose Valentin	.05
446	Jason Schmidt	.05
447	Dave Martinez	.05
448	Danny Tartabull	.05
449	Jose Vizcaino	.05
450	Steve Avery	.05
451	Mike Devereaux	.05
452	Jim Eisenreich	.05
453	Mark Leiter	.05
454	Roberto Kelly	.05
455	Benito Santiago	.05
456	Steve Trachsel	.05
457	Gerald Williams	.05
458	Pete Schourek	.05
459	Esteban Loaiza	.05
460	Mel Rojas	.05
461	Tim Wakefield	.05
462	Tony Fernandez	.05
463	Doug Drabek	.05
464	Joe Girardi	.05
465	Mike Bordick	.05
466	Jim Leyritz	.05
467	Erik Hanson	.05
468	Michael Tucker	.05
469	Tony Womack RC	.10
470	Doug Glanville	.05
471	Rudy Pemberton	.05
472	Keith Lockhart	.05
473	Nomar Garciaparra	.65
474	Scott Rolen	.40
475	Jason Dickson	.05
476	Glendon Rusch	.05
477	Todd Walker	.05
478	Dmitri Young	.05
479	Rod Myers RC	.05
480	Wilton Guerrero	.05
481	Jorge Posada	.05
482	Brant Brown	.05
483	Bubba Trammell RC	.10
484	Jose Guillen	.05
485	Scott Spiezio	.05
486	Bob Abreu	.10
487	Chris Holt	.05
488	Deivi Cruz RC	.15
489	Vladimir Guerrero	.50
490	Julio Santana	.05
491	Ray Montgomery	.05
492	Kevin Orie	.05
493	Todd Hundley	.05
494	Tim Salmon	.05
495	Albert Belle	.05
496	Manny Ramirez	.25
497	Rafael Palmeiro	.20
498	Juan Gonzalez	.15
499	Ken Griffey Jr.	.40
500	Andruw Jones	.25
501	Mike Piazza	.40
502	Jeff Bagwell	.25
503	Bernie Williams	.05
504	Barry Bonds	.65
505	Ken Caminiti	.05
506	Darin Erstad	.10
507	Alex Rodriguez	.50
508	Frank Thomas	.30
509	Chipper Jones	.35
510	Mo Vaughn	.05
511	Mark McGwire	.50
512	Fred McGriff	.05
513	Jay Buhner	.05
514	Jim Thome	.20
515	Gary Sheffield	.20
516	Dean Palmer	.05
517	Henry Rodriguez	.05
518	Andy Pettitte	.10
519	Mike Mussina	.10
520	Greg Maddux	.35
521	John Smoltz	.05
522	Hideo Nomo	.15
523	Troy Percival	.05
524	John Wetteland	.05
525	Roger Clemens	.40
526	Charles Nagy	.05
527	Mariano Rivera	.10
528	Tom Glavine	.15
529	Randy Johnson	.25
530	Jason Isringhausen	.05
531	Alex Fernandez	.05
532	Kevin Brown	.05
533	Chuck Knoblauch	.05
534	Rusty Greer	.05
535	Tony Gwynn	.35
536	Ryan Klesko	.05
537	Ryne Sandberg	.35
538	Barry Larkin	.05
539	Will Clark	.05
540	Kenny Lofton	.05
541	Paul Molitor	.30
542	Roberto Alomar	.10
543	Rey Ordonez	.05
544	Jason Giambi	.25
545	Derek Jeter	.75
546	Cal Ripken Jr.	.75
547	Ivan Rodriguez	.25
548	Ken Griffey Jr. Checklist	.35
549	Frank Thomas Checklist	.25
550	Mike Piazza Checklist	.40
551a	Hideki Irabu/SP RC (English on back; factory sets/retailpacks.)	.25
551b	Hideki Irabu/SP RC (Japanese back; Hobby Reserve packs.)	.35

Showcase

	NM/M
Complete Set (551):	200.00
Common Player:	.50
Showcase Stars:	3X

(See 1997 Score for checklist and base card values.)

Showcase Artist's Proofs

	NM/M
Common Player:	1.00
Showcase AP Stars:	10X

(See 1997 Score for checklist and base card values.)

Premium Stock

	NM/M
Complete Set (330):	17.50

Common Player:	.10
Premium Stock Stars:	3X

(See 1997 Score #1-330 for checklist and base card values.)

White Border Artist's Proofs

	NM/M
Complete Set (330):	150.00
Common Player:	.50
Artist's Proof Stars:	10X

(See 1997 Score for checklist and base card values.)

Hobby Reserve

	NM/M
Complete Set (221):	35.00
Common Player:	.10
Hobby Reserve Stars:	3X

(See 1997 Score #331-551 for checklist and base card values.)

Blast Masters

		NM/M
Complete Set (18):		17.50
Common Player:		.25
1	Mo Vaughn	.25
2	Mark McGwire	2.25
3	Juan Gonzalez	.75
4	Albert Belle	.25
5	Barry Bonds	3.00
6	Ken Griffey Jr.	2.00
7	Andruw Jones	1.25
8	Chipper Jones	1.50
9	Mike Piazza	2.00
10	Jeff Bagwell	1.25
11	Dante Bichette	.25
12	Alex Rodriguez	2.25

13	Gary Sheffield	.60
14	Ken Caminiti	.25
15	Sammy Sosa	1.50
16	Vladimir Guerrero	1.25
17	Brian Jordan	.25
18	Tim Salmon	.25

Heart of the Order

		NM/M
Complete Set (36):		35.00
Complete Retail Set (1-18):		20.00
Complete Hobby Set (19-36):		15.00
Common Player:		.50
1	Ivan Rodriguez	1.00
2	Will Clark	.50
3	Juan Gonzalez	.75
4	Frank Thomas	1.25
5	Albert Belle	.50
6	Robin Ventura	.50
7	Alex Rodriguez	3.00
8	Ken Griffey Jr.	2.50
9	Jay Buhner	.50
10	Roberto Alomar	.65
11	Rafael Palmeiro	1.00
12	Cal Ripken Jr.	4.00
13	Manny Ramirez	1.25
14	Matt Williams	.50
15	Jim Thome	.50
16	Derek Jeter	4.00
17	Wade Boggs	2.00
18	Bernie Williams	.50
19	Chipper Jones	2.00
20	Andruw Jones	1.25
21	Ryan Klesko	.50
22	Wilton Guerrero	.50
23	Mike Piazza	2.50
24	Raul Mondesi	.50
25	Tony Gwynn	2.00
26	Ken Caminiti	.50
27	Greg Vaughn	.50
28	Brian Jordan	.50
29	Ron Gant	.50
30	Dmitri Young	.50
31	Darin Erstad	.50
32	Jim Edmonds	.50
33	Tim Salmon	.50
34	Chuck Knoblauch	.50
35	Paul Molitor	1.25
36	Todd Walker	.50

Highlight Zone

		NM/M
Complete Set (18):		30.00
Common Player:		.60
1	Frank Thomas	1.50
2	Ken Griffey Jr.	3.00
3	Mo Vaughn	.60
4	Albert Belle	.60
5	Mike Piazza	3.00
6	Barry Bonds	4.50
7	Greg Maddux	2.25
8	Sammy Sosa	2.25
9	Jeff Bagwell	1.50
10	Alex Rodriguez	3.50
11	Chipper Jones	2.25
12	Brady Anderson	.60
13	Ozzie Smith	2.25
14	Edgar Martinez	.60
15	Cal Ripken Jr.	4.50

16	Ryan Klesko	.60
17	Randy Johnson	1.50
18	Eddie Murray	1.50

Pitcher Perfect

PITCHER PERFECT CAL RIPKEN JR and ALEX RODRIGUEZ

		NM/M
Complete Set (15):		6.50
Common Player:		.15
1	Cal Ripken Jr.	2.00
2	Alex Rodriguez	1.25
3	Cal Ripken Jr., Alex Rodriguez	1.25
4	Edgar Martinez	.15
5	Ivan Rodriguez	.50
6	Mark McGwire	1.25
7	Tim Salmon	.15
8	Chili Davis	.15
9	Joe Carter	.15
10	Frank Thomas	.60
11	Will Clark	.15
12	Mo Vaughn	.15
13	Wade Boggs	.75
14	Ken Griffey Jr.	1.00
15	Randy Johnson	.60

Stand & Deliver

		NM/M
Complete Set (24):		50.00
Common Player:		.50
Gold:		4X
1	Andruw Jones	3.00
2	Greg Maddux	4.00
3	Chipper Jones	4.00
4	John Smoltz	.50
5	Ken Griffey Jr.	5.00
6	Alex Rodriguez	6.00
7	Jay Buhner	.50
8	Randy Johnson	3.00
9	Derek Jeter	7.50
10	Andy Pettitte	.75
11	Bernie Williams	.50
12	Mariano Rivera	.50
13	Mike Piazza	5.00
14	Hideo Nomo	1.50
15	Raul Mondesi	.50
16	Todd Hollandsworth	.50
17	Manny Ramirez	3.00
18	Jim Thome	2.00
19	David Justice	.50
20	Matt Williams	.50
21	Juan Gonzalez	1.50
22	Jeff Bagwell	3.00
23	Cal Ripken Jr.	7.50
24	Frank Thomas	3.00

Stellar Season

		NM/M
Complete Set (18):		15.00
Common Player:		.50
1	Juan Gonzalez	.75
2	Chuck Knoblauch	.50
3	Jeff Bagwell	1.50
4	John Smoltz	.50
5	Mark McGwire	3.00
6	Ken Griffey Jr.	2.50
7	Frank Thomas	1.50
8	Alex Rodriguez	3.00
9	Mike Piazza	2.50
10	Albert Belle	.50
11	Roberto Alomar	.60

12	Sammy Sosa	2.00
13	Mo Vaughn	.50
14	Brady Anderson	.50
15	Henry Rodriguez	.50
16	Eric Young	.50
17	Gary Sheffield	.75
18	Ryan Klesko	.50

The Franchise

		NM/M
Complete Set (9):		5.00
Common Player:		.15
Glowing:		2.5X
Samples:		2.5X
1	Ken Griffey Jr.	1.00
2	John Smoltz	.15
3	Cal Ripken Jr.	2.00
4	Chipper Jones	.75
5	Mike Piazza	1.00
6	Albert Belle	.15
7	Frank Thomas	.60
8	Sammy Sosa	.75
9	Roberto Alomar	.30

Titanic Taters

		NM/M
Complete Set (18):		25.00
Common Player:		.35
1	Mark McGwire	4.00
2	Mike Piazza	3.50
3	Ken Griffey Jr.	3.50
4	Juan Gonzalez	1.00
5	Frank Thomas	1.50
6	Albert Belle	.35
7	Sammy Sosa	2.50
8	Jeff Bagwell	1.50
9	Todd Hundley	.35
10	Ryan Klesko	.35
11	Brady Anderson	.35
12	Mo Vaughn	.35
13	Jay Buhner	.35
14	Chipper Jones	2.75
15	Barry Bonds	6.00
16	Gary Sheffield	.75
17	Alex Rodriguez	4.00
18	Cecil Fielder	.35

1998 Score

		NM/M
Complete Set (270):		12.00
Common Player:		.05
Pack (10):		.75
Wax Box (36):		15.00
All-Star Edition Box (36/10):		10.00
Jumbo Pack (20):		1.00
Jumbo Box (24):		15.00
1	Andruw Jones	.50
2	Dan Wilson	.05

3	Hideo Nomo	.30
4	Chuck Carr	.05
5	Barry Bonds	1.50
6	Jack McDowell	.05
7	Albert Belle	.05
8	Francisco Cordova	.05
9	Greg Maddux	.65
10	Alex Rodriguez	1.00
11	Steve Avery	.05
12	Chuck McElroy	.05
13	Larry Walker	.05
14	Hideki Irabu	.05
15	Roberto Alomar	.20
16	Neifi Perez	.05
17	Jim Thome	.40
18	Rickey Henderson	.50
19	Andres Galarraga	.05
20	Jeff Fassero	.05
21	Kevin Young	.05
22	Derek Jeter	1.50
23	Andy Benes	.05
24	Mike Piazza	.75
25	Todd Stottlemyre	.05
26	Michael Tucker	.05
27	Denny Neagle	.05
28	Javier Lopez	.05
29	Aaron Sele	.05
30	Ryan Klesko	.05
31	Dennis Eckersley	.40
32	Quinton McCracken	.05
33	Brian Anderson	.05
34	Ken Griffey Jr.	.75
35	Shawn Estes	.05
36	Tim Wakefield	.05
37	Jimmy Key	.05
38	Jeff Bagwell	.50
39	Edgardo Alfonzo	.05
40	Mike Cameron	.05
41	Mark McGwire	1.00
42	Tino Martinez	.05
43	Cal Ripken Jr.	1.50
44	Curtis Goodwin	.05
45	Bobby Ayala	.05
46	Sandy Alomar Jr.	.05
47	Bobby Jones	.05
48	Omar Vizquel	.05
49	Roger Clemens	.70
50	Tony Gwynn	.65
51	Chipper Jones	.65
52	Ron Coomer	.05
53	Dmitri Young	.05
54	Brian Giles	.05
55	Steve Finley	.05
56	David Cone	.05
57	Andy Pettitte	.20
58	Wilton Guerrero	.05
59	Deion Sanders	.05
60	Carlos Delgado	.30
61	Jason Giambi	.30
62	Ozzie Guillen	.05
63	Jay Bell	.05
64	Barry Larkin	.05
65	Sammy Sosa	.65
66	Bernie Williams	.05
67	Terry Steinbach	.05
68	Scott Rolen	.40
69	Melvin Nieves	.05
70	Craig Biggio	.05
71	Todd Greene	.05
72	Greg Gagne	.05
73	Shigetosi Hasegawa	.05
74	Mark McLemore	.05
75	Darren Bragg	.05
76	Brett Butler	.05
77	Ron Gant	.05
78	Mike Difelice	.05
79	Charles Nagy	.05
80	Scott Hatteberg	.05
81	Brady Anderson	.05
82	Jay Buhner	.05
83	Todd Hollandsworth	.05
84	Geronimo Berroa	.05
85	Jeff Suppan	.05

#	Player	
86	Pedro Martinez	.50
87	Roger Cedeno	.05
88	Ivan Rodriguez	.40
89	Jaime Navarro	.05
90	Chris Hoiles	.05
91	Nomar Garciaparra	.65
92	Rafael Palmeiro	.40
93	Darin Erstad	.15
94	Kenny Lofton	.05
95	Mike Timlin	.05
96	Chris Clemons	.05
97	Vinny Castilla	.05
98	Charlie Hayes	.05
99	Lyle Mouton	.05
100	Jason Dickson	.05
101	Justin Thompson	.05
102	Pat Kelly	.05
103	Chan Ho Park	.05
104	Ray Lankford	.05
105	Frank Thomas	.50
106	Jermaine Allensworth	.05
107	Doug Drabek	.05
108	Todd Hundley	.05
109	Carl Everett	.05
110	Edgar Martinez	.05
111	Robin Ventura	.05
112	John Wetteland	.05
113	Mariano Rivera	.10
114	Jose Rosado	.05
115	Ken Caminiti	.05
116	Paul O'Neill	.05
117	Tim Salmon	.05
118	Eduardo Perez	.05
119	Mike Jackson	.05
120	John Smoltz	.05
121	Brant Brown	.05
122	John Mabry	.05
123	Chuck Knoblauch	.05
124	Reggie Sanders	.05
125	Ken Hill	.05
126	Mike Mussina	.25
127	Chad Curtis	.05
128	Todd Worrell	.05
129	Chris Widger	.05
130	Damon Mashore	.05
131	Kevin Brown	.05
132	Bip Roberts	.05
133	Tim Naehring	.05
134	Dave Martinez	.05
135	Jeff Blauser	.05
136	David Justice	.05
137	Dave Hollins	.05
138	Pat Hentgen	.05
139	Darren Daulton	.05
140	Ramon Martinez	.05
141	Raul Casanova	.05
142	Tom Glavine	.30
143	J.T. Snow	.05
144	Tony Graffanino	.05
145	Randy Johnson	.50
146	Orlando Merced	.05
147	Jeff Juden	.05
148	Darryl Kile	.05
149	Ray Durham	.05
150	Alex Fernandez	.05
151	Joey Cora	.05
152	Royce Clayton	.05
153	Randy Myers	.05
154	Charles Johnson	.05
155	Alan Benes	.05
156	Mike Bordick	.05
157	Heathcliff Slocumb	.05
158	Roger Bailey	.05
159	Reggie Jefferson	.05
160	Ricky Bottalico	.05
161	Scott Erickson	.05
162	Matt Williams	.05
163	Robb Nen	.05
164	Matt Stairs	.05
165	Ismael Valdes	.05
166	Lee Stevens	.05
167	Gary DiSarcina	.05
168	Brad Radke	.05
169	Mike Lansing	.05
170	Armando Benitez	.05
171	Mike James	.05
172	Russ Davis	.05
173	Lance Johnson	.05
174	Joey Hamilton	.05
175	John Valentin	.05
176	David Segui	.05
177	David Wells	.05
178	Delino DeShields	.05
179	Eric Karros	.05
180	Jim Leyritz	.05
181	Raul Mondesi	.05
182	Travis Fryman	.05
183	Todd Zeile	.05
184	Brian Jordan	.05
185	Rey Ordonez	.05
186	Jim Edmonds	.05
187	Terrell Wade	.05
188	Marquis Grissom	.05
189	Chris Snopek	.05
190	Shane Reynolds	.05
191	Jeff Frye	.05
192	Paul Sorrento	.05
193	James Baldwin	.05
194	Brian McRae	.05
195	Fred McGriff	.65
196	Troy Percival	.05
197	Rich Amaral	.05
198	Juan Guzman	.05
199	Cecil Fielder	.05
200	Willie Blair	.05
201	Chili Davis	.05
202	Gary Gaetti	.05
203	B.J. Surhoff	.05
204	Steve Cooke	.05
205	Chuck Finley	.05
206	Jeff Kent	.05
207	Ben McDonald	.05
208	Jeffrey Hammonds	.05
209	Tom Goodwin	.05
210	Billy Ashley	.05
211	Wil Cordero	.05
212	Shawon Dunston	.05
213	Tony Phillips	.05
214	Jamie Moyer	.05
215	John Jaha	.05
216	Troy O'Leary	.05
217	Brad Ausmus	.05
218	Garret Anderson	.05
219	Wilson Alvarez	.05
220	Kent Mercker	.05
221	Wade Boggs	.65
222	Mark Wohlers	.05
223	Kevin Appier	.05
224	Tony Fernandez	.05
225	Ugueth Urbina	.05
226	Gregg Jefferies	.05
227	Mo Vaughn	.05
228	Arthur Rhodes	.05
229	Jorge Fabregas	.05
230	Mark Gardner	.05
231	Shane Mack	.05
232	Jorge Posada	.05
233	Jose Cruz Jr.	.05
234	Paul Konerko	.15
235	Derek Lee	.30
236	Steve Woodard **RC**	.15
237	Todd Dunwoody	.05
238	Fernando Tatis	.05
239	Jacob Cruz	.05
240	Pokey Reese **RC**	.25
241	Mark Kotsay	.05
242	Matt Morris	.05
243	Antone Williamson **RC**	.05
244	Ben Grieve	.05
245	Ryan McGuire	.05
246	Lou Collier **RC**	.05
247	Shannon Stewart	.05
248	Brett Tomko **RC**	.10
249	Bobby Estalella	.05
250	Livan Hernandez **RC**	.15
251	Todd Helton	.40
252	Jaret Wright	.05
253	Darryl Hamilton	.05
254	Stan Javier	.05
255	Glenallen Hill	.05
256	Mark Gardner	.05
257	Cal Ripken Jr.	.75
258	Mike Mussina	.15
259	Mike Piazza	.45
260	Sammy Sosa	.35
261	Todd Hundley	.05
262	Eric Karros	.05
263	Denny Neagle	.05
264	Jeromy Burnitz	.05
265	Greg Maddux	.35
266	Tony Clark	.05
267	Vladimir Guerrero	.25
268	Checklist	.05
269	Checklist	.05
270	Checklist	.05

Artist's Proofs

		NM/M
Complete Set (160):		125.00
Common Player:		.50
Inserted 1:35		
1	Andruw Jones	1.25
2	Dan Wilson	.50
3	Hideo Nomo	.75
4	Neifi Perez	.50
5	Jim Thome	1.00
6	Jeff Fassero	.50
7	Derek Jeter	4.00
8	Andy Benes	.50
9	Michael Tucker	.50
10	Ryan Klesko	.50
11	Dennis Eckersley	1.00
12	Jimmy Key	.50
13	Edgardo Alfonzo	.50
14	Mike Cameron	.50
15	Omar Vizquel	.50
16	Ron Coomer	.50
17	Dmitri Young	.50
18	Brian Giles	.50
19	Steve Finley	.50
20	Andy Pettitte	.75
21	Wilton Guerrero	.50
22	Deion Sanders	.50
23	Carlos Delgado	.75
24	Jason Giambi	.75
25	David Cone	.50
26	Jay Bell	.50
27	Sammy Sosa	2.00
28	Barry Larkin	.50
29	Scott Rolen	1.00
30	Todd Greene	.50
31	Bernie Williams	.50
32	Brett Butler	.50
33	Ron Gant	.50
34	Brady Anderson	.50
35	Craig Biggio	.50
36	Charles Nagy	.50
37	Jay Buhner	.50
38	Geronimo Berroa	.50
39	Jeff Suppan	.50
40	Rafael Palmeiro	1.00
41	Darin Erstad	.65
42	Mike Timlin	.50
43	Vinny Castilla	.50
44	Carl Everett	.50
45	Robin Ventura	.50
46	John Wetteland	.50
47	Paul O'Neill	.50
48	Tim Salmon	.50
49	Mike Jackson	.50
50	John Smoltz	.50
51	Brant Brown	.50
52	Reggie Sanders	.50
53	Ken Hill	.50
54	Todd Worrell	.50
55	Bip Roberts	.50
56	Tim Naehring	.50
57	Darren Daulton	.50
58	Ramon Martinez	.50
59	Raul Casanova	.50
60	J.T. Snow	.50
61	Jeff Juden	.50
62	Royce Clayton	.50
63	Charles Johnson	.50
64	Alan Benes	.50
65	Reggie Jefferson	.50
66	Ricky Bottalico	.50
67	Scott Erickson	.50
68	Matt Williams	.50
69	Robb Nen	.50
70	Matt Stairs	.50
71	Ismael Valdes	.50
72	Brad Radke	.50
73	Armando Benitez	.50
74	Russ Davis	.50
75	Lance Johnson	.50
76	Joey Hamilton	.50
77	John Valentin	.50
78	David Segui	.50
79	David Wells	.50
80	Eric Karros	.50
81	Raul Mondesi	.50
82	Travis Fryman	.50
83	Todd Zeile	.50
84	Brian Jordan	.50
85	Rey Ordonez	.50
86	Jim Edmonds	.50
87	Marquis Grissom	.50
88	Shane Reynolds	.50
89	Paul Sorrento	.50
90	Brian McRae	.50
91	Fred McGriff	.50
92	Troy Percival	.50
93	Juan Guzman	.50
94	Cecil Fielder	.50
95	Chili Davis	.50
96	B.J. Surhoff	.50
97	Chuck Finley	.50
98	Jeff Kent	.50
99	Ben McDonald	.50
100	Jeffrey Hammonds	.50
101	Tom Goodwin	.50
102	Wil Cordero	.50
103	Tony Phillips	.50
104	John Jaha	.50
105	Garret Anderson	.50
106	Wilson Alvarez	.50
107	Wade Boggs	2.00
108	Mark Wohlers	.50
109	Kevin Appier	.50
110	Mo Vaughn	.50
111	Ray Durham	.50
112	Alex Fernandez	.50
113	Barry Bonds	4.00
114	Albert Belle	.50
115	Greg Maddux	2.00
116	Alex Rodriguez	3.00
117	Larry Walker	.50
118	Roberto Alomar	.60
119	Andres Galarraga	.50
120	Mike Piazza	2.50
121	Denny Neagle	.50
122	Javier Lopez	.50
123	Ken Griffey Jr.	2.50
124	Shawn Estes	.50
125	Jeff Bagwell	1.25
126	Mark McGwire	3.00
127	Tino Martinez	.50
128	Cal Ripken Jr.	4.00
129	Sandy Alomar Jr.	.50
130	Bobby Jones	.50
131	Roger Clemens	2.25
132	Tony Gwynn	2.00
133	Chipper Jones	2.00
134	Orlando Merced	.50
135	Todd Stottlemyre	.50
136	Delino DeShields	.50
137	Pedro Martinez	1.25
138	Ivan Rodriguez	1.00
139	Nomar Garciaparra	2.00
140	Kenny Lofton	.50
141	Jason Dickson	.50
142	Justin Thompson	.50
143	Ray Lankford	.50
144	Frank Thomas	1.25
145	Todd Hundley	.50
146	Edgar Martinez	.50
147	Mariano Rivera	.50
148	Jose Rosado	.50
149	Ken Caminiti	.50
150	Chuck Knoblauch	.50
151	Mike Mussina	.65
152	Kevin Brown	.50
153	Jeff Blauser	.50
154	David Justice	.50
155	Pat Hentgen	.50
156	Tom Glavine	.65
157	Randy Johnson	1.25
158	Darryl Kile	.50
159	Joey Cora	.50
160	Randy Myers	.50

Showcase Series

		NM/M
Complete Set (160):		40.00
Common Player:		.25
Inserted 1:7		
1	Andruw Jones	.75
2	Dan Wilson	.25
3	Hideo Nomo	.40
4	Neifi Perez	.25
5	Jim Thome	.60
6	Jeff Fassero	.25
7	Derek Jeter	2.00
8	Andy Benes	.25
9	Michael Tucker	.25
10	Ryan Klesko	.25
11	Dennis Eckersley	.65
12	Jimmy Key	.25
13	Edgardo Alfonzo	.25
14	Mike Cameron	.25
15	Omar Vizquel	.25
16	Ron Coomer	.25

17	Dmitri Young	.25
18	Brian Giles	.25
19	Steve Finley	.25
20	Andy Pettitte	.40
21	Wilton Guerrero	.25
22	Deion Sanders	.25
23	Carlos Delgado	.50
24	Jason Giambi	.50
25	David Cone	.25
26	Jay Bell	.25
27	Sammy Sosa	1.00
28	Barry Larkin	.25
29	Scott Rolen	.60
30	Todd Greene	.25
31	Bernie Williams	.25
32	Brett Butler	.25
33	Ron Gant	.25
34	Brady Anderson	.25
35	Craig Biggio	.25
36	Charles Nagy	.25
37	Jay Buhner	.25
38	Geronimo Berroa	.25
39	Jeff Suppan	.25
40	Rafael Palmeiro	.65
41	Darin Erstad	.35
42	Mike Timlin	.25
43	Vinny Castilla	.25
44	Carl Everett	.25
45	Robin Ventura	.25
46	John Wetteland	.25
47	Paul O'Neill	.25
48	Tim Salmon	.25
49	Mike Jackson	.25
50	John Smoltz	.25
51	Brant Brown	.25
52	Reggie Sanders	.25
53	Ken Hill	.25
54	Todd Worrell	.25
55	Bip Roberts	.25
56	Tim Naehring	.25
57	Darren Daulton	.25
58	Ramon Martinez	.25
59	Raul Casanova	.25
60	J.T. Snow	.25
61	Jeff Juden	.25
62	Royce Clayton	.25
63	Charles Johnson	.25
64	Alan Benes	.25
65	Reggie Jefferson	.25
66	Ricky Bottalico	.25
67	Scott Erickson	.25
68	Matt Williams	.25
69	Robb Nen	.25
70	Matt Stairs	.25
71	Ismael Valdes	.25
72	Brad Radke	.25
73	Armando Benitez	.25
74	Russ Davis	.25
75	Lance Johnson	.25
76	Joey Hamilton	.25
77	John Valentin	.25
78	David Segui	.25
79	David Wells	.25
80	Eric Karros	.25
81	Raul Mondesi	.25
82	Travis Fryman	.25
83	Todd Zeile	.25
84	Brian Jordan	.25
85	Rey Ordonez	.25
86	Jim Edmonds	.25
87	Marquis Grissom	.25
88	Shane Reynolds	.25
89	Paul Sorrento	.25
90	Brian McRae	.25
91	Fred McGriff	.25
92	Troy Percival	.25
93	Juan Guzman	.25
94	Cecil Fielder	.25
95	Chili Davis	.25
96	B.J. Surhoff	.25
97	Chuck Finley	.25
98	Jeff Kent	.25
99	Ben McDonald	.25
100	Jeffrey Hammonds	.25
101	Tom Goodwin	.25
102	Wil Cordero	.25
103	Tony Phillips	.25
104	John Jaha	.25
105	Garret Anderson	.25
106	Wilson Alvarez	.25
107	Wade Boggs	1.00
108	Mark Wohlers	.25
109	Kevin Appier	.25
110	Mo Vaughn	.25
111	Ray Durham	.25
112	Alex Fernandez	.25
113	Barry Bonds	2.00
114	Albert Belle	.25
115	Greg Maddux	1.00
116	Alex Rodriguez	1.50
117	Larry Walker	.25
118	Roberto Alomar	.35
119	Andres Galarraga	.25
120	Mike Piazza	1.25

121	Denny Neagle	.25
122	Javier Lopez	.25
123	Ken Griffey Jr.	1.25
124	Shawn Estes	.25
125	Jeff Bagwell	.75
126	Mark McGwire	1.50
127	Tino Martinez	.25
128	Cal Ripken Jr.	2.00
129	Sandy Alomar Jr.	.25
130	Bobby Jones	.25
131	Roger Clemens	1.00
132	Tony Gwynn	1.00
133	Chipper Jones	1.00
134	Orlando Merced	.25
135	Todd Stottlemyre	.25
136	Delino DeShields	.25
137	Pedro Martinez	.75
138	Ivan Rodriguez	.65
139	Nomar Garciaparra	1.00
140	Kenny Lofton	.25
141	Jason Dickson	.25
142	Justin Thompson	.25
143	Ray Lankford	.25
144	Frank Thomas	.75
145	Todd Hundley	.25
146	Edgar Martinez	.25
147	Mariano Rivera	.25
148	Jose Rosado	.25
149	Ken Caminiti	.25
150	Chuck Knoblauch	.25
151	Mike Mussina	.40
152	Kevin Brown	.25
153	Jeff Blauser	.25
154	David Justice	.25
155	Pat Hentgen	.25
156	Tom Glavine	.40
157	Randy Johnson	.75
158	Darryl Kile	.25
159	Joey Cora	.25
160	Randy Myers	.25

All Score Team

Roger Clemens   Blue Jays' P

		NM/M
Complete Set (20):		15.00
Common Player:		.25
Inserted 1:35		
1	Mike Piazza	1.50
2	Ivan Rodriguez	.65
3	Frank Thomas	.75
4	Mark McGwire	2.00
5	Ryne Sandberg	1.00
6	Roberto Alomar	.35
7	Cal Ripken Jr.	2.50
8	Barry Larkin	.25
9	Paul Molitor	.75
10	Travis Fryman	.25
11	Kirby Puckett	1.00
12	Tony Gwynn	1.00
13	Ken Griffey Jr.	1.50
14	Juan Gonzalez	.45
15	Barry Bonds	2.50
16	Andruw Jones	.75
17	Roger Clemens	1.25
18	Randy Johnson	.75
19	Greg Maddux	1.00
20	Dennis Eckersley	.65

Values quoted in this guide reflect the retail price of a card, the price a collector can expect to pay when buying a card from a dealer.

All Score Team Andruw Jones Autograph

Andruw Jones   Braves' RF

		NM/M
16	Andruw Jones	25.00

Complete Players

		NM/M
Complete Set (30):		75.00
Common Player:		1.00
Inserted 1:23		
Golds:		75%
1A	Ken Griffey Jr.	3.25
1B	Ken Griffey Jr.	3.25
1C	Ken Griffey Jr.	3.25
2A	Mark McGwire	3.75
2B	Mark McGwire	3.75
2C	Mark McGwire	3.75
3A	Derek Jeter	5.00
3B	Derek Jeter	5.00
3C	Derek Jeter	5.00
4A	Cal Ripken Jr.	5.00
4B	Cal Ripken Jr.	5.00
4C	Cal Ripken Jr.	5.00
5A	Mike Piazza	3.25
5B	Mike Piazza	3.25
5C	Mike Piazza	3.25
6A	Darin Erstad	1.00
6B	Darin Erstad	1.00
6C	Darin Erstad	1.00
7A	Frank Thomas	2.00
7B	Frank Thomas	2.00
7C	Frank Thomas	2.00
8A	Andruw Jones	2.00
8B	Andruw Jones	2.00
8C	Andruw Jones	2.00
9A	Nomar Garciaparra	3.00
9B	Nomar Garciaparra	3.00
9C	Nomar Garciaparra	3.00
10A	Manny Ramirez	2.00
10B	Manny Ramirez	2.00
10C	Manny Ramirez	2.00

Epix

		NM/M
Common Card:		.50
Purple:		2X
Emeralds:		3X
1	Ken Griffey Jr./P	2.50
2	Juan Gonzalez/P	.75
3	Jeff Bagwell/P	1.25
4	Ivan Rodriguez/P	1.25
5	Nomar Garciaparra/P	2.00
6	Ryne Sandberg/P	1.50
7	Frank Thomas/G	1.25
8	Derek Jeter/G	3.50
9	Tony Gwynn/G	2.00
10	Albert Belle/G	.50

11	Scott Rolen/G	1.00
12	Barry Larkin/G	.50
13	Alex Rodriguez/S	6.00
14	Cal Ripken Jr./S	7.50
15	Chipper Jones/S	4.00
16	Roger Clemens/S	4.50
17	Mo Vaughn/S	1.50
18	Mark McGwire/S	6.00
19	Mike Piazza/M	8.00
20	Andruw Jones/M	4.00
21	Greg Maddux/M	6.00
22	Barry Bonds/M	12.00
23	Paul Molitor/M	4.00
24	Eddie Murray/M	4.00

First Pitch

		NM/M
Complete Set (20):		25.00
Common Player:		.50
Inserted 1:11 All-Star Edition.		
1	Ken Griffey Jr.	2.00
2	Frank Thomas	1.25
3	Alex Rodriguez	2.50
4	Cal Ripken Jr.	3.25
5	Chipper Jones	1.50
6	Juan Gonzalez	.75
7	Derek Jeter	3.25
8	Mike Piazza	2.00
9	Andruw Jones	1.25
10	Nomar Garciaparra	1.50
11	Barry Bonds	3.25
12	Jeff Bagwell	1.25
13	Scott Rolen	1.00
14	Hideo Nomo	.75
15	Roger Clemens	1.75
16	Mark McGwire	2.50
17	Greg Maddux	1.50
18	Albert Belle	.50
19	Ivan Rodriguez	1.00
20	Mo Vaughn	.50

Loaded Lineup

		NM/M
Complete Set (10):		20.00
Common Player:		.50
Inserted 1:45 All-Star Edition.		
LL1	Chuck Knoblauch	.50
LL2	Tony Gwynn	2.25
LL3	Frank Thomas	1.50
LL4	Ken Griffey Jr.	3.00
LL5	Mike Piazza	3.00
LL6	Barry Bonds	4.50
LL7	Cal Ripken Jr.	4.50

LL8	Paul Molitor	1.50
LL9	Nomar Garciaparra	2.25
LL10	Greg Maddux	2.25

New Season

		NM/M
Complete Set (15):		18.00
Common Player:		.50
Inserted 1:23 All-Star Edition.		
NS1	Kenny Lofton	.50
NS2	Nomar Garciaparra	2.00
NS3	Todd Helton	1.00
NS4	Miguel Tejada	.75
NS5	Jaret Wright	.50
NS6	Alex Rodriguez	3.00
NS7	Vladimir Guerrero	1.25
NS8	Ken Griffey Jr.	2.50
NS9	Ben Grieve	.50
NS10	Travis Lee	.50
NS11	Jose Cruz Jr.	.50
NS12	Paul Konerko	.75
NS13	Frank Thomas	1.25
NS14	Chipper Jones	2.00
NS15	Cal Ripken Jr.	4.00

1998 Score Rookie & Traded

		NM/M
Complete Set (270):		10.00
Common SP (1-50):		.10
Common Player (51-270):		.05
Paul Molitor Auto. (500):		15.00
Pack (10):		.65
Wax Box (36):		15.00
Jumbo Pack (20):		1.50
Jumbo Box (24):		25.00
1	Tony Clark	.10
2	Juan Gonzalez	.35
3	Frank Thomas	.60
4	Greg Maddux	.75
5	Barry Larkin	.10
6	Derek Jeter	1.50
7	Randy Johnson	.60
8	Roger Clemens	.85
9	Tony Gwynn	.75
10	Barry Bonds	1.50
11	Jim Edmonds	.10
12	Bernie Williams	.10
13	Ken Griffey Jr.	1.00
14	Tim Salmon	.10
15	Mo Vaughn	.10
16	David Justice	.10
17	Jose Cruz Jr.	.10
18	Andruw Jones	.60
19	Sammy Sosa	.75
20	Jeff Bagwell	.60
21	Scott Rolen	.50
22	Darin Erstad	.30
23	Andy Pettitte	.35
24	Mike Mussina	.40
25	Mark McGwire	1.25
26	Hideo Nomo	.35
27	Chipper Jones	.75
28	Cal Ripken Jr.	1.50
29	Chuck Knoblauch	.10
30	Alex Rodriguez	1.25
31	Jim Thome	.50
32	Mike Piazza	1.00
33	Ivan Rodriguez	.50
34	Roberto Alomar	.40
35	Nomar Garciaparra	.75
36	Albert Belle	.10
37	Vladimir Guerrero	.60
38	Raul Mondesi	.10
39	Larry Walker	.10
40	Manny Ramirez	.60
41	Tino Martinez	.10
42	Craig Biggio	.10
43	Jay Buhner	.10
44	Kenny Lofton	.10
45	Pedro Martinez	.60
46	Edgar Martinez	.10
47	Gary Sheffield	.45
48	Jose Guillen	.10
49	Ken Caminiti	.10
50	Bobby Higginson	.05
51	Alan Benes	.05
52	Shawn Green	.05
53	Ron Coomer	.05
54	Charles Nagy	.05
55	Steve Karsay	.05
56	Matt Morris	.05
57	Bobby Jones	.05
58	Jason Kendall	.05
59	Jeff Conine	.05
60	Joe Girardi	.05
61	Mark Kotsay	.05
62	Eric Karros	.05
63	Bartolo Colon	.05
64	Mariano Rivera	.10
65	Alex Gonzalez	.05
66	Scott Spiezio	.05
67	Luis Castillo	.05
68	Joey Cora	.05
69	Mark McLemore	.05
70	Reggie Jefferson	.05
71	Lance Johnson	.05
72	Damian Jackson	.05
73	Jeff D'Amico	.05
74	David Ortiz	.30
75	J.T. Snow	.05
76	Todd Hundley	.05
77	Billy Wagner	.05
78	Vinny Castilla	.05
79	Ismael Valdes	.05
80	Neifi Perez	.05
81	Derek Bell	.05
82	Ryan Klesko	.05
83	Rey Ordonez	.05
84	Carlos Garcia	.05
85	Curt Schilling	.30
86	Robin Ventura	.05
87	Pat Hentgen	.05
88	Glendon Rusch	.05
89	Hideki Irabu	.05
90	Antone Williamson	.05
91	Denny Neagle	.05
92	Kevin Orie	.05
93	Reggie Sanders	.05
94	Brady Anderson	.05
95	Andy Benes	.05
96	John Valentin	.05
97	Bobby Bonilla	.05
98	Walt Weiss	.05
99	Robin Jennings	.05
100	Marty Cordova	.05
101	Brad Ausmus	.05
102	Brian Rose	.05
103	Calvin Maduro	.05
104	Raul Casanova	.05
105	Jeff King	.05
106	Sandy Alomar	.05
107	Tim Naehring	.05
108	Mike Cameron	.05
109	Omar Vizquel	.05
110	Brad Radke	.05
111	Jeff Fassero	.05
112	Deivi Cruz	.05
113	Dave Hollins	.05
114	Dean Palmer	.05
115	Esteban Loaiza	.05
116	Brian Giles	.05
117	Steve Finley	.05
118	Jose Canseco	.30
119	Al Martin	.05
120	Eric Young	.05
121	Curtis Goodwin	.05
122	Ellis Burks	.05
123	Mike Hampton	.05
124	Lou Collier	.05
125	John Olerud	.05
126	Ramon Martinez	.05
127	Todd Dunwoody	.05
128	Jermaine Allensworth	.05
129	Eduardo Perez	.05
130	Dante Bichette	.05
131	Edgar Renteria	.05
132	Bob Abreu	.10
133	Rondell White	.05
134	Michael Coleman	.05
135	Jason Giambi	.30
136	Brant Brown	.05
137	Michael Tucker	.05
138	Dave Nilsson	.05
139	Benito Santiago	.05
140	Ray Durham	.05
141	Jeff Kent	.05
142	Matt Stairs	.05
143	Kevin Young	.05
144	Eric Davis	.05
145	John Wetteland	.05
146	Esteban Yan	.05
147	Wilton Guerrero	.05
148	Moises Alou	.05
149	Edgardo Alfonzo	.05
150	Andy Ashby	.05
151	Todd Walker	.05
152	Jermaine Dye	.05
153	Brian Hunter	.05
154	Shawn Estes	.05
155	Bernard Gilkey	.05
156	Tony Womack	.05
157	John Smoltz	.05
158	Delino DeShields	.05
159	Jacob Cruz	.05
160	Javier Valentin	.05
161	Chris Hoiles	.05
162	Garret Anderson	.05
163	Dan Wilson	.05
164	Paul O'Neill	.05
165	Matt Williams	.05
166	Travis Fryman	.05
167	Javier Lopez	.05
168	Ray Lankford	.05
169	Bobby Estalella	.05
170	Henry Rodriguez	.05
171	Quinton McCracken	.05
172	Jaret Wright	.05
173	Darryl Kile	.05
174	Wade Boggs	.65
175	Orel Hershiser	.05
176	B.J. Surhoff	.05
177	Fernando Tatis	.05
178	Carlos Delgado	.30
179	Jorge Fabregas	.05
180	Tony Saunders	.05
181	Devon White	.05
182	Dmitri Young	.05
183	Ryan McGuire	.05
184	Mark Bellhorn	.05
185	Joe Carter	.05
186	Kevin Stocker	.05
187	Mike Lansing	.05
188	Jason Dickson	.05
189	Charles Johnson	.05
190	Will Clark	.05
191	Shannon Stewart	.05
192	Johnny Damon	.20
193	Todd Greene	.05
194	Carlos Baerga	.05
195	David Cone	.05
196	Pokey Reese	.05
197	Livan Hernandez	.05
198	Tom Glavine	.25
199	Geronimo Berroa	.05
200	Darryl Hamilton	.05
201	Terry Steinbach	.05
202	Robb Nen	.05
203	Ron Gant	.05
204	Rafael Palmeiro	.40
205	Rickey Henderson	.40
206	Justin Thompson	.05
207	Jeff Suppan	.05
208	Kevin Brown	.05
209	Jimmy Key	.05
210	Brian Jordan	.05
211	Aaron Sele	.05
212	Fred McGriff	.05
213	Jay Bell	.05
214	Andres Galarraga	.05
215	Mark Grace	.05
216	Brett Tomko	.05
217	Francisco Cordova	.05
218	Rusty Greer	.05
219	Bubba Trammell	.05
220	Derek Lee	.35
221	Brian Anderson	.05
222	Mark Grudzielanek	.05
223	Marquis Grissom	.05
224	Gary DiSarcina	.05
225	Jim Leyritz	.05
226	Jeffrey Hammonds	.05
227	Karim Garcia	.05
228	Chan Ho Park	.05
229	Brooks Kieschnick	.05
230	Trey Beamon	.05
231	Kevin Appier	.05
232	Wally Joyner	.05
233	Richie Sexson	.05
234	Frank Catalanotto RC	.15
235	Rafael Medina	.05
236	Travis Lee	.05
237	Eli Marrero	.05
238	Carl Pavano	.05
239	Enrique Wilson	.05
240	Richard Hidalgo	.05
241	Todd Helton	.40
242	Ben Grieve	.05
243	Mario Valdez	.05
244	Magglio Ordonez RC	.75
245	Juan Encarnacion	.05
246	Russell Branyan	.05
247	Sean Casey	.10
248	Abraham Nunez	.05
249	Brad Fullmer	.05
250	Paul Konerko	.20
251	Miguel Tejada	.15
252	Mike Lowell RC	.50
253	Ken Griffey Jr.	.35
254	Frank Thomas	.25
255	Alex Rodriguez	.45
256	Jose Cruz Jr.	.05
257	Jeff Bagwell	.20
258	Chipper Jones	.30
259	Mo Vaughn	.05
260	Nomar Garciaparra	.30
261	Jim Thome	.05
262	Derek Jeter	.50
263	Mike Piazza	.45
264	Tony Gwynn	.30
265	Scott Rolen	.15
266	Andruw Jones	.20
267	Cal Ripken Jr.	.50
268	Ken Griffey Jr. Checklist	.30
269	Cal Ripken Jr. Checklist	.45
270	Jose Cruz Jr. Checklist	.05

Showcase Series

		NM/M
Complete Set (160):		10.00
Common Player:		.15
1	Tony Clark	.15
2	Juan Gonzalez	.30
3	Frank Thomas	.60
4	Greg Maddux	.75
5	Barry Larkin	.15
6	Derek Jeter	1.50
7	Randy Johnson	.60
8	Roger Clemens	.85
9	Tony Gwynn	.75
10	Barry Bonds	1.50
11	Jim Edmonds	.15
12	Bernie Williams	.15
13	Ken Griffey Jr.	1.00
14	Tim Salmon	.15
15	Mo Vaughn	.15
16	David Justice	.15
17	Jose Cruz Jr.	.15
18	Andruw Jones	.60
19	Sammy Sosa	.75
20	Jeff Bagwell	.60
21	Scott Rolen	.50
22	Darin Erstad	.25

23	Andy Pettitte	.30
24	Mike Mussina	.30
25	Mark McGwire	1.25
26	Hideo Nomo	.30
27	Chipper Jones	.75
28	Cal Ripken Jr.	1.50
29	Chuck Knoblauch	.15
30	Alex Rodriguez	1.25
31	Jim Thome	.50
32	Mike Piazza	1.00
33	Ivan Rodriguez	.50
34	Roberto Alomar	.25
35	Nomar Garciaparra	1.00
36	Albert Belle	.15
37	Vladimir Guerrero	.60
38	Raul Mondesi	.15
39	Larry Walker	.15
40	Manny Ramirez	.60
41	Tino Martinez	.15
42	Craig Biggio	.15
43	Jay Buhner	.15
44	Kenny Lofton	.15
45	Pedro Martinez	.60
46	Edgar Martinez	.15
47	Gary Sheffield	.40
48	Jose Guillen	.15
49	Ken Caminiti	.15
50	Bobby Higginson	.15
51	Alan Benes	.15
52	Shawn Green	.35
53	Matt Morris	.15
54	Jason Kendall	.15
55	Mark Kotsay	.15
56	Bartolo Colon	.15
57	Damian Jackson	.15
58	David Ortiz	.35
59	J.T. Snow	.15
60	Todd Hundley	.15
61	Neifi Perez	.15
62	Ryan Klesko	.15
63	Robin Ventura	.15
64	Pat Hentgen	.15
65	Antone Williamson	.15
66	Kevin Orie	.15
67	Brady Anderson	.15
68	Bobby Bonilla	.15
69	Brian Rose	.15
70	Sandy Alomar Jr.	.15
71	Mike Cameron	.15
72	Omar Vizquel	.15
73	Steve Finley	.15
74	Jose Canseco	.40
75	Al Martin	.15
76	Eric Young	.15
77	Ellis Burks	.15
78	Todd Dunwoody	.15
79	Dante Bichette	.15
80	Edgar Renteria	.15
81	Bobby Abreu	.15
82	Rondell White	.15
83	Michael Coleman	.15
84	Jason Giambi	.50
85	Wilton Guerrero	.15
86	Moises Alou	.15
87	Todd Walker	.15
88	Shawn Estes	.15
89	John Smoltz	.15
90	Jacob Cruz	.15
91	Javier Valentin	.15
92	Garret Anderson	.15
93	Paul O'Neill	.15
94	Matt Williams	.15
95	Travis Fryman	.15
96	Javier Lopez	.15
97	Ray Lankford	.15
98	Bobby Estalella	.15
99	Jaret Wright	.15
100	Wade Boggs	.75
101	Fernando Tatis	.15
102	Carlos Delgado	.50
103	Joe Carter	.15
104	Jason Dickson	.15
105	Charles Johnson	.15
106	Will Clark	.15
107	Shannon Stewart	.15
108	Todd Greene	.15
109	Pokey Reese	.15
110	Livan Hernandez	.15
111	Tom Glavine	.35
112	Rafael Palmeiro	.50
113	Justin Thompson	.15
114	Jeff Suppan	.15
115	Kevin Brown	.15
116	Brian Jordan	.15
117	Fred McGriff	.15
118	Andres Galarraga	.15
119	Mark Grace	.15
120	Rusty Greer	.15
121	Bubba Trammell	.15
122	Derrek Lee	.40
123	Brian Anderson	.15
124	Karim Garcia	.15
125	Chan Ho Park	.15
126	Richie Sexson	.15
127	Frank Catalanotto	.15

128	Rafael Medina	.15
129	Travis Lee	.15
130	Eli Marrero	.15
131	Carl Pavano	.15
132	Enrique Wilson	.15
133	Richard Hidalgo	.15
134	Todd Helton	.40
135	Ben Grieve	.15
136	Mario Valdez	.15
137	Magglio Ordonez	.25
138	Juan Encarnacion	.15
139	Russell Branyan	.15
140	Sean Casey	.25
141	Abraham Nunez	.15
142	Brad Fullmer	.15
143	Paul Konerko	.25
144	Miguel Tejada	.30
145	Mike Lowell	.15
146	Ken Griffey Jr.	.50
147	Frank Thomas	.35
148	Alex Rodriguez	.65
149	Jose Cruz Jr.	.15
150	Jeff Bagwell	.35
151	Chipper Jones	.40
152	Mo Vaughn	.15
153	Nomar Garciaparra	.40
154	Jim Thome	.30
155	Derek Jeter	.75
156	Mike Piazza	.50
157	Tony Gwynn	.40
158	Scott Rolen	.25
159	Andruw Jones	.35
160	Cal Ripken Jr.	.75

Artist's Proofs

		NM/M
Common Player:		1.00
AP Stars:		4X

(See 1998 Score Rookie & Traded Showcase for checklist and base card values.)

Complete Players

		NM/M
Complete Set (30):		65.00
Common Player:		1.00
Inserted 1:11		
Samples:		1X
1A	Ken Griffey Jr.	3.50
1B	Ken Griffey Jr.	3.50
1C	Ken Griffey Jr.	3.50
2A	Larry Walker	1.00
2B	Larry Walker	1.00
2C	Larry Walker	1.00
3A	Alex Rodriguez	4.00
3B	Alex Rodriguez	4.00
3C	Alex Rodriguez	4.00
4A	Jose Cruz Jr.	1.00
4B	Jose Cruz Jr.	1.00
4C	Jose Cruz Jr.	1.00
5A	Jeff Bagwell	2.00

5B	Jeff Bagwell	2.00
5C	Jeff Bagwell	2.00
6A	Greg Maddux	2.75
6B	Greg Maddux	2.75
6C	Greg Maddux	2.75
7A	Ivan Rodriguez	1.75
7B	Ivan Rodriguez	1.75
7C	Ivan Rodriguez	1.75
8A	Roger Clemens	3.00
8B	Roger Clemens	3.00
8C	Roger Clemens	3.00
9A	Chipper Jones	2.75
9B	Chipper Jones	2.75
9C	Chipper Jones	2.75
10A	Hideo Nomo	1.50
10B	Hideo Nomo	1.50
10C	Hideo Nomo	1.50

Epix All-Star Moment

		NM/M
Complete Set (12):		25.00
Common Player:		1.00
Purples:		1.5X
Emeralds:		2.5X
1	Ken Griffey Jr.	4.00
2	Juan Gonzalez	1.50
3	Jeff Bagwell	2.50
4	Ivan Rodriguez	2.00
5	Nomar Garciaparra	3.00
6	Ryne Sandberg	3.00
7	Frank Thomas	2.50
8	Derek Jeter	5.00
9	Tony Gwynn	3.00
10	Albert Belle	1.00
11	Scott Rolen	2.00
12	Barry Larkin	1.00

Star Gazing

		NM/M
Complete Set (20):		12.00
Common Player:		.25
Inserted 1:35		
1	Ken Griffey Jr.	1.00
2	Frank Thomas	.60
3	Chipper Jones	.75
4	Mark McGwire	1.25
5	Cal Ripken Jr.	1.50
6	Mike Piazza	1.00
7	Nomar Garciaparra	.75
8	Derek Jeter	1.50
9	Juan Gonzalez	.35
10	Vladimir Guerrero	.60
11	Alex Rodriguez	1.25
12	Tony Gwynn	.75
13	Andruw Jones	.60
14	Scott Rolen	.40
15	Jose Cruz Jr.	.25
16	Mo Vaughn	.25
17	Bernie Williams	.25
18	Greg Maddux	.75

19	Tony Clark	.25
20	Ben Grieve	.25

1993 Select

Tim Raines

		NM/M
Complete Set (405):		15.00
Common Player:		.05
Pack (15):		.75
Wax Box (36):		22.50
1	Barry Bonds	1.50
2	Ken Griffey Jr.	1.00
3	Will Clark	.05
4	Kirby Puckett	.75
5	Tony Gwynn	.75
6	Frank Thomas	.65
7	Tom Glavine	.35
8	Roberto Alomar	.25
9	Andre Dawson	.25
10	Ron Darling	.05
11	Bobby Bonilla	.05
12	Danny Tartabull	.05
13	Darren Daulton	.05
14	Roger Clemens	.85
15	Ozzie Smith	.75
16	Mark McGwire	1.25
17	Terry Pendleton	.05
18	Cal Ripken, Jr.	1.50
19	Fred McGriff	.05
20	Cecil Fielder	.05
21	Darryl Strawberry	.05
22	Robin Yount	.65
23	Barry Larkin	.05
24	Don Mattingly	.85
25	Craig Biggio	.05
26	Sandy Alomar Jr.	.05
27	Larry Walker	.05
28	Junior Felix	.05
29	Eddie Murray	.65
30	Robin Ventura	.05
31	Greg Maddux	.75
32	Dave Winfield	.65
33	John Kruk	.05
34	Wally Joyner	.05
35	Andy Van Slyke	.05
36	Chuck Knoblauch	.05
37	Tom Pagnozzi	.05
38	Dennis Eckersley	.60
39	Dave Justice	.05
40	Juan Gonzalez	.35
41	Gary Sheffield	.40
42	Paul Molitor	.65
43	Delino DeShields	.05
44	Travis Fryman	.05
45	Hal Morris	.05
46	Gregg Olson	.05
47	Ken Caminiti	.05
48	Wade Boggs	.75
49	Orel Hershiser	.05
50	Albert Belle	.05
51	Bill Swift	.05
52	Mark Langston	.05
53	Joe Girardi	.05
54	Keith Miller	.05
55	Gary Carter	.65
56	Brady Anderson	.05
57	Dwight Gooden	.05
58	Julio Franco	.05
59	Len Dykstra	.05
60	Mickey Tettleton	.05
61	Randy Tomlin	.05
62	B.J. Surhoff	.05
63	Todd Zeile	.05
64	Roberto Kelly	.05
65	Rob Dibble	.05
66	Leo Gomez	.05
67	Doug Jones	.05
68	Ellis Burks	.05
69	Mike Scioscia	.05
70	Charles Nagy	.05
71	Cory Snyder	.05
72	Devon White	.05
73	Mark Grace	.05

#	Name	Price
74	Luis Polonia	.05
75	John Smiley	.05
76	Carlton Fisk	.65
77	Luis Sojo	.05
78	George Brett	.85
79	Mitch Williams	.05
80	Kent Hrbek	.05
81	Jay Bell	.05
82	Edgar Martinez	.05
83	Lee Smith	.05
84	Deion Sanders	.05
85	Bill Gullickson	.05
86	Paul O'Neill	.05
87	Kevin Seitzer	.05
88	Steve Finley	.05
89	Mel Hall	.05
90	Nolan Ryan	1.50
91	Eric Davis	.05
92	Mike Mussina	.35
93	Tony Fernandez	.05
94	Frank Viola	.05
95	Matt Williams	.05
96	Joe Carter	.05
97	Ryne Sandberg	.75
98	Jim Abbott	.05
99	Marquis Grissom	.05
100	George Bell	.05
101	Howard Johnson	.05
102	Kevin Appier	.05
103	Dale Murphy	.20
104	Shane Mack	.05
105	Jose Lind	.05
106	Rickey Henderson	.65
107	Bob Tewksbury	.05
108	Kevin Mitchell	.05
109	Steve Avery	.05
110	Candy Maldonado	.05
111	Bip Roberts	.05
112	Lou Whitaker	.05
113	Jeff Bagwell	.65
114	Dante Bichette	.05
115	Brett Butler	.05
116	Melido Perez	.05
117	Andy Benes	.05
118	Randy Johnson	.65
119	Willie McGee	.05
120	Jody Reed	.05
121	Shawon Dunston	.05
122	Carlos Baerga	.05
123	Bret Saberhagen	.05
124	John Olerud	.05
125	Ivan Calderon	.05
126	Bryan Harvey	.05
127	Terry Mulholland	.05
128	Ozzie Guillen	.05
129	Steve Buechele	.05
130	Kevin Tapani	.05
131	Felix Jose	.05
132	Terry Steinbach	.05
133	Ron Gant	.05
134	Harold Reynolds	.05
135	Chris Sabo	.05
136	Ivan Rodriguez	.60
137	Eric Anthony	.05
138	Mike Henneman	.05
139	Robby Thompson	.05
140	Scott Fletcher	.05
141	Bruce Hurst	.05
142	Kevin Maas	.05
143	Tom Candiotti	.05
144	Chris Hoiles	.05
145	Mike Morgan	.05
146	Mark Whiten	.05
147	Dennis Martinez	.05
148	Tony Pena	.05
149	Dave Magadan	.05
150	Mark Lewis	.05
151	Mariano Duncan	.05
152	Gregg Jefferies	.05
153	Doug Drabek	.05
154	Brian Harper	.05
155	Ray Lankford	.05
156	Carney Lansford	.05
157	Mike Sharperson	.05
158	Jack Morris	.05
159	Otis Nixon	.05
160	Steve Sax	.05
161	Mark Lemke	.05
162	Rafael Palmeiro	.60
163	Jose Rijo	.05
164	Omar Vizquel	.05
165	Sammy Sosa	.75
166	Milt Cuyler	.05
167	John Franco	.05
168	Darryl Hamilton	.05
169	Ken Hill	.05
170	Mike Devereaux	.05
171	Don Slaught	.05
172	Steve Farr	.05
173	Bernard Gilkey	.05
174	Mike Fetters	.05
175	Vince Coleman	.05
176	Kevin McReynolds	.05
177	John Smoltz	.05
178	Greg Gagne	.05
179	Greg Swindell	.05
180	Juan Guzman	.05
181	Kal Daniels	.05
182	Rick Sutcliffe	.05
183	Orlando Merced	.05
184	Bill Wegman	.05
185	Mark Gardner	.05
186	Rob Deer	.05
187	Dave Hollins	.05
188	Jack Clark	.05
189	Brian Hunter	.05
190	Tim Wallach	.05
191	Tim Belcher	.05
192	Walt Weiss	.05
193	Kurt Stillwell	.05
194	Charlie Hayes	.05
195	Willie Randolph	.05
196	Jack McDowell	.05
197	Jose Offerman	.05
198	Chuck Finley	.05
199	Darrin Jackson	.05
200	Kelly Gruber	.05
201	John Wetteland	.05
202	Jay Buhner	.05
203	Mike LaValliere	.05
204	Kevin Brown	.05
205	Luis Gonzalez	.05
206	Rick Aguilera	.05
207	Norm Charlton	.05
208	Mike Bordick	.05
209	Charlie Leibrandt	.05
210	Tom Brunansky	.05
211	Tom Henke	.05
212	Randy Milligan	.05
213	Ramon Martinez	.05
214	Mo Vaughn	.05
215	Randy Myers	.05
216	Greg Hibbard	.05
217	Wes Chamberlain	.05
218	Tony Phillips	.05
219	Pete Harnisch	.05
220	Mike Gallego	.05
221	Bud Black	.05
222	Greg Vaughn	.05
223	Milt Thompson	.05
224	Ben McDonald	.05
225	Billy Hatcher	.05
226	Paul Sorrento	.05
227	Mark Gubicza	.05
228	Mike Greenwell	.05
229	Curt Schilling	.35
230	Alan Trammell	.05
231	Zane Smith	.05
232	Bobby Thigpen	.05
233	Greg Olson	.05
234	Joe Orsulak	.05
235	Joe Oliver	.05
236	Tim Raines	.05
237	Juan Samuel	.05
238	Chili Davis	.05
239	Spike Owen	.05
240	Dave Stewart	.05
241	Jim Eisenreich	.05
242	Phil Plantier	.05
243	Sid Fernandez	.05
244	Dan Gladden	.05
245	Mickey Morandini	.05
246	Tino Martinez	.05
247	Kirt Manwaring	.05
248	Dean Palmer	.05
249	Tom Browning	.05
250	Brian McRae	.05
251	Scott Leius	.05
252	Bert Blyleven	.05
253	Scott Erickson	.05
254	Bob Welch	.05
255	Pat Kelly	.05
256	Felix Fermin	.05
257	Harold Baines	.05
258	Duane Ward	.05
259	Bill Spiers	.05
260	Jaime Navarro	.05
261	Scott Sanderson	.05
262	Gary Gaetti	.05
263	Bob Ojeda	.05
264	Jeff Montgomery	.05
265	Scott Bankhead	.05
266	Lance Johnson	.05
267	Rafael Belliard	.05
268	Kevin Reimer	.05
269	Benito Santiago	.05
270	Mike Moore	.05
271	Dave Fleming	.05
272	Moises Alou	.05
273	Pat Listach	.05
274	Reggie Sanders	.05
275	Kenny Lofton	.05
276	Donovan Osborne	.05
277	Rusty Meacham	.05
278	Eric Karros	.05
279	Andy Stankiewicz	.05
280	Brian Jordan	.05
281	Gary DiSarcina	.05
282	Mark Wohlers	.05
283	Dave Nilsson	.05
284	Anthony Young	.05
285	Jim Bullinger	.05
286	Derek Bell	.05
287	Brian Williams	.05
288	Julio Valera	.05
289	Dan Walters	.05
290	Chad Curtis	.05
291	Michael Tucker	.05
292	Bob Zupcic	.05
293	Todd Hundley	.05
294	Jeff Tackett	.05
295	Greg Colbrunn	.05
296	Cal Eldred	.05
297	Chris Roberts	.05
298	John Doherty	.05
299	Denny Neagle	.05
300	Arthur Rhodes	.05
301	Mark Clark	.05
302	Scott Cooper	.05
303	Jamie Arnold RC	.05
304	Jim Thome	.60
305	Frank Seminara	.05
306	Kurt Knudsen	.05
307	Tim Wakefield	.05
308	John Jaha	.05
309	Pat Hentgen	.05
310	B.J. Wallace	.05
311	Roberto Hernandez	.05
312	Hipolito Pichardo	.05
313	Eric Fox	.05
314	Willie Banks	.05
315	Sam Militello	.05
316	Vince Horsman	.05
317	Carlos Hernandez	.05
318	Jeff Kent	.05
319	Mike Perez	.05
320	Scott Livingstone	.05
321	Jeff Conine	.05
322	James Austin	.05
323	John Vander Wal	.05
324	Pat Mahomes	.05
325	Pedro Astacio	.05
326	Bret Boone	.05
327	Matt Stairs	.05
328	Damion Easley	.05
329	Ben Rivera	.05
330	Reggie Jefferson	.05
331	Luis Mercedes	.05
332	Kyle Abbott	.05
333	Eddie Taubensee	.05
334	Tim McIntosh	.05
335	Phil Clark	.05
336	Wil Cordero	.05
337	Russ Springer	.05
338	Craig Colbert	.05
339	Tim Salmon	.05
340	Braulio Castillo	.05
341	Donald Harris	.05
342	Eric Young	.05
343	Bob Wickman	.05
344	John Valentin	.05
345	Dan Wilson	.05
346	Steve Hosey	.05
347	Mike Piazza	1.00
348	Willie Greene	.05
349	Tom Goodwin	.05
350	Eric Hillman	.05
351	Steve Reed RC	.05
352	Dan Serafini RC	.05
353	Todd Steverson RC	.05
354	Benji Grigsby	.05
355	Shannon Stewart RC	1.00
356	Sean Lowe	.05
357	Derek Wallace	.05
358	Rick Helling	.05
359	Jason Kendall RC	1.00
360	Derek Jeter RC	10.00
361	David Cone	.05
362	Jeff Reardon	.05
363	Bobby Witt	.05
364	Jose Canseco	.40
365	Jeff Russell	.05
366	Ruben Sierra	.05
367	Alan Mills	.05
368	Matt Nokes	.05
369	Pat Borders	.05
370	Pedro Munoz	.05
371	Danny Jackson	.05
372	Geronimo Pena	.05
373	Craig Lefferts	.05
374	Joe Grahe	.05
375	Roger McDowell	.05
376	Jimmy Key	.05
377	Steve Olin	.05
378	Glenn Davis	.05
379	Rene Gonzales	.05
380	Manuel Lee	.05
381	Ron Karkovice	.05
382	Sid Bream	.05
383	Gerald Williams	.05
384	Lenny Harris	.05
385	J.T. Snow RC	.75
386	Dave Stieb	.05
387	Kirk McCaskill	.05
388	Lance Parrish	.05
389	Craig Greback	.05
390	Rick Wilkins	.05
391	Manny Alexander	.05
392	Mike Schooler	.05
393	Bernie Williams	.05
394	Kevin Koslofski	.05
395	Willie Wilson	.05
396	Jeff Parrett	.05
397	Mike Harkey	.05
398	Frank Tanana	.05
399	Doug Henry	.05
400	Royce Clayton	.05
401	Eric Wedge	.05
402	Derrick May	.05
403	Carlos Garcia	.05
404	Henry Rodriguez	.05
405	Ryan Klesko	.05

Dufex Proofs

DAVE FLEMING P

Select Rookies:	15X
Select Stars:	20X
Select Triple Crown:	20X

(See 1993 Select Rookies, Stars and Triple Crown for checklist and base card values.)

Aces

		NM/M
Complete Set (24):		20.00
Common Player:		1.00
1	Roger Clemens	6.00
2	Tom Glavine	3.00
3	Jack McDowell	1.00
4	Greg Maddux	4.50
5	Jack Morris	1.00
6	Dennis Martinez	1.00
7	Kevin Brown	1.00
8	Dwight Gooden	1.00
9	Kevin Appier	1.00
10	Mike Morgan	1.00
11	Juan Guzman	1.00
12	Charles Nagy	1.00
13	John Smiley	1.00
14	Ken Hill	1.00
15	Bob Tewksbury	1.00
16	Doug Drabek	1.00
17	John Smoltz	1.00
18	Greg Swindell	1.00
19	Bruce Hurst	1.00
20	Mike Mussina	2.00
21	Cal Eldred	1.00
22	Melido Perez	1.00
23	Dave Fleming	1.00
24	Kevin Tapani	1.00

Rookies

	NM/M
Complete Set (21):	4.00

	Common Player:	.50
1	Pat Listach	.50
2	Moises Alou	.50
3	Reggie Sanders	.50
4	Kenny Lofton	.50
5	Eric Karros	.50
6	Brian Williams	.50
7	Donovan Osborne	.50
8	Sam Militello	.50
9	Chad Curtis	.50
10	Bob Zupcic	.50
11	Tim Salmon	1.50
12	Jeff Conine	.50
13	Pedro Astacio	.50
14	Arthur Rhodes	.50
15	Cal Eldred	.50
16	Tim Wakefield	.50
17	Andy Stankiewicz	.50
18	Wil Cordero	.50
19	Todd Hundley	.50
20	Dave Fleming	.50
21	Bret Boone	1.00

Stars

		NM/M
	Complete Set (24):	40.00
	Common Player:	.60
1	Fred McGriff	.60
2	Ryne Sandberg	4.00
3	Ozzie Smith	4.00
4	Gary Sheffield	1.25
5	Darren Daulton	.60
6	Andy Van Slyke	.60
7	Barry Bonds	7.50
8	Tony Gwynn	4.00
9	Greg Maddux	4.00
10	Tom Glavine	1.00
11	John Franco	.60
12	Lee Smith	.60
13	Cecil Fielder	.60
14	Roberto Alomar	1.00
15	Cal Ripken, Jr.	7.50
16	Edgar Martinez	.60
17	Ivan Rodriguez	2.50
18	Kirby Puckett	4.00
19	Ken Griffey Jr.	6.00
20	Joe Carter	4.00
21	Roger Clemens	4.50
22	Dave Fleming	.60
(22)	Dave Fleming (Blank-back sample card.)	1.00
23	Paul Molitor	3.00
(23)	Paul Molitor (Blank-back sample card.)	2.75
24	Dennis Eckersley	2.50

Stat Leaders

		NM/M
	Complete Set (90):	8.00
	Common Player:	.05
1	Edgar Martinez	.05
2	Kirby Puckett	.30
3	Frank Thomas	.25
4	Gary Sheffield	.15
5	Andy Van Slyke	.05
6	John Kruk	.05
7	Kirby Puckett	.30
8	Carlos Baerga	.05
9	Paul Molitor	.25
10	Andy Van Slyke, Terry Pendleton	.05
11	Ryne Sandberg	.30
12	Mark Grace	.05
13	Frank Thomas	.25
14	Don Mattingly	.35
15	Ken Griffey Jr.	.45
16	Andy Van Slyke	.05
17	Mariano Duncan, Jerald Clark, Ray Lankford	.05
18	Marquis Grissom, Terry Pendleton	.05
19	Lance Johnson	.05
20	Mike Devereaux	.05
21	Brady Anderson	.05
22	Deion Sanders	.05
23	Steve Finley	.05
24	Andy Van Slyke	.05
25	Juan Gonzalez	.15
26	Mark McGwire	.50
27	Cecil Fielder	.05
28	Fred McGriff	.60
29	Barry Bonds	.60
30	Gary Sheffield	.15
31	Cecil Fielder	.05
32	Joe Carter	.05
33	Frank Thomas	.25
34	Darren Daulton	.05
35	Terry Pendleton	.05
36	Fred McGriff	.05
37	Tony Phillips	.05
38	Frank Thomas	.25
39	Roberto Alomar	.15
40	Barry Bonds	.60
41	Dave Hollins	.05
42	Andy Van Slyke	.05
43	Mark McGwire	.50
44	Edgar Martinez	.05
45	Frank Thomas	.25
46	Barry Bonds	.60
47	Gary Sheffield	.15
48	Fred McGriff	.05
49	Frank Thomas	.25
50	Danny Tartabull	.05
51	Roberto Alomar	.15
52	Barry Bonds	.60
53	John Kruk	.05
54	Brett Butler	.05
55	Kenny Lofton	.05
56	Pat Listach	.05
57	Brady Anderson	.05
58	Marquis Grissom	.05
59	Delino DeShields	.05
60	Steve Finley, Bip Roberts	.05
61	Jack McDowell	.05
62	Kevin Brown	.05
63	Melido Perez	.05
64	Terry Mulholland	.05
65	Curt Schilling	.20
66	John Smoltz, Doug Drabek, Greg Maddux	.05
67	Dennis Eckersley	.20
68	Rick Aguilera	.05
69	Jeff Montgomery	.05
70	Lee Smith	.05
71	Randy Myers	.05
72	John Wetteland	.05
73	Randy Johnson	.25
74	Melido Perez	.05
75	Roger Clemens	.35
76	John Smoltz	.05
77	David Cone	.05
78	Greg Maddux	.30
79	Roger Clemens	.35
80	Kevin Appier	.05
81	Mike Mussina	.15
82	Bill Swift	.05
83	Bob Tewksbury	.05
84	Greg Maddux	.30
85	Kevin Brown	.05
86	Jack McDowell	.05
87	Roger Clemens	.35
88	Tom Glavine	.10
89	Ken Hill, Bob Tewksbury	.05
90	Dennis Martinez, Mike Morgan	.05

Triple Crown

		NM/M
	Complete Set (3):	35.00
	Common Player:	10.00
1	Mickey Mantle	22.50
2	Frank Robinson	10.00
3	Carl Yastrzemski	12.50

Rookie/Traded

		NM/M
	Complete Set (150):	11.00
	Common Player:	.05
	Pack (12):	1.25
	Wax Box (24):	20.00
1	Rickey Henderson	.75
2	Rob Deer	.05
3	Tim Belcher	.05
4	Gary Sheffield	.35
5	Fred McGriff	.05
6	Mark Whiten	.05
7	Jeff Russell	.05
8	Harold Baines	.05
9	Dave Winfield	.75
10	Ellis Burks	.05
11	Andre Dawson	.25
12	Gregg Jefferies	.05
13	Jimmy Key	.05
14	Harold Reynolds	.05
15	Tom Henke	.05
16	Paul Molitor	.75
17	Wade Boggs	1.00
18	David Cone	.05
19	Tony Fernandez	.05
20	Roberto Kelly	.05
21	Paul O'Neill	.05
22	Jose Lind	.05
23	Barry Bonds	2.00
24	Dave Stewart	.05
25	Randy Myers	.05
26	Benito Santiago	.05
27	Tim Wallach	.05
28	Greg Gagne	.05
29	Kevin Mitchell	.05
30	Jim Abbott	.05
31	Lee Smith	.05
32	Bobby Munoz RC	.05
33	Mo Sanford RC	.05
34	John Roper	.05
35	David Hulse RC	.05
36	Pedro Martinez	.75
37	Chuck Carr RC	.05
38	Armando Reynoso RC	.10
39	Ryan Thompson	.05
40	Carlos Garcia RC	.05
41	Matt Whiteside	.05
42	Benji Gil	.05
43	Rodney Bolton RC	.05
44	J.T. Snow	.05
45	David McCarty	.05
46	Paul Quantrill RC	.05
47	Al Martin	.05
48	Lance Painter	.05
49	Lou Frazier RC	.05
50	Eduardo Perez	.05
51	Kevin Young	.05
52	Mike Trombley	.05
53	Sterling Hitchcock RC	.10
54	Tim Bogar RC	.05
55	Hilly Hathaway RC	.05
56	Wayne Kirby RC	.05
57	Craig Paquette RC	.05
58	Bret Boone	.05
59	Greg McMichael RC	.05
60	Mike Lansing RC	.35
61	Brent Gates	.05
62	Rene Arocha	.05
63	Ricky Gutierrez	.05
64	Kevin Rogers RC	.05
65	Ken Ryan RC	.05
66	Phil Hiatt	.05
67	Pat Meares RC	.05
68	Troy Neel	.05
69	Steve Cooke	.05
70	Sherman Obando RC	.05
71	Blas Minor RC	.05
72	Angel Miranda RC	.05
73	Tom Kramer RC	.05
74	Chip Hale RC	.05
75	Brad Pennington RC	.05
76	Graeme Lloyd RC	.05
77	Darrell Whitmore RC	.05
78	David Nied	.05
79	Todd Van Poppel	.05
80	Chris Gomez RC	.10
81	Jason Bere	.05
82	Jeffrey Hammonds	.05
83	Brad Ausmus RC	.10
84	Kevin Stocker	.05
85	Jeromy Burnitz	.05
86	Aaron Sele	.05
87	Roberto Mejia RC	.05
88	Kirk Rueter RC	.10
89	Kevin Roberson RC	.05
90	Allen Watson RC	.05
91	Charlie Leibrandt	.05
92	Eric Davis	.05
93	Jody Reed	.05
94	Danny Jackson	.05
95	Gary Gaetti	.05
96	Norm Charlton	.05
97	Doug Drabek	.05
98	Scott Fletcher	.05
99	Greg Swindell	.05
100	John Smiley	.05
101	Kevin Reimer	.05
102	Andres Galarraga	.05
103	Greg Hibbard	.05
104	Chris Hammond	.05
105	Darnell Coles	.05
106	Mike Felder	.05
107	Jose Guzman	.05
108	Chris Bosio	.05
109	Spike Owen	.05
110	Felix Jose	.05
111	Cory Snyder	.05
112	Craig Lefferts	.05
113	David Wells	.05
114	Pete Incaviglia	.05
115	Mike Pagliarulo	.05
116	Dave Magadan	.05
117	Charlie Hough	.05
118	Ivan Calderon	.05
119	Manuel Lee	.05
120	Bob Patterson	.05
121	Bob Ojeda	.05
122	Scott Bankhead	.05
123	Greg Maddux	1.00
124	Chili Davis	.05
125	Milt Thompson	.05
126	Dave Martinez	.05
127	Frank Tanana	.05
128	Phil Plantier	.05
129	Juan Samuel	.05
130	Eric Young	.05
131	Joe Orsulak	.05
132	Derek Bell	.05
133	Darrin Jackson	.05

134	Tom Brunansky	.05
135	Jeff Reardon	.05
136	Kevin Higgins RC	.05
137	Joel Johnston RC	.05
138	Rick Trlicek RC	.05
139	Richie Lewis RC	.05
140	Jeff Gardner RC	.05
141	Jack Voigt RC	.05
142	Rod Correia RC	.05
143	Billy Brewer RC	.05
144	Terry Jorgensen RC	.05
145	Rich Amaral RC	.05
146	Sean Berry RC	.05
147	Dan Peltier RC	.05
148	Paul Wagner RC	.05
149	Damon Buford RC	.05
150	Wil Cordero	.05

Rookie/Traded Inserts

	NM/M
Complete Set (3):	60.00
Common Player:	6.00
1NR	Nolan Ryan	40.00
1ROY	Tim Salmon	6.00
2ROY	Mike Piazza	20.00

Rookie/Traded All-Star Rookies

	NM/M
Complete Set (10):	30.00
Common Player:	1.00
1	Jeff Conine	1.00
2	Brent Gates	1.00
3	Mike Lansing	1.00
4	Kevin Stocker	1.00
5	Mike Piazza	25.00
6	Jeffrey Hammonds	1.00
7	David Hulse	1.00
8	Tim Salmon	2.00
9	Rene Arocha	1.00
10	Greg McMichael	1.00

1994 Select

	NM/M
Complete Set (420):	12.50
Common Player:	.05
Pack (12):	1.25
Wax Box (24):	16.00

1	Ken Griffey Jr.	1.50
2	Greg Maddux	1.00
3	Paul Molitor	.75
4	Mike Piazza	1.50
5	Jay Bell	.05
6	Frank Thomas	.75
7	Barry Larkin	.05
8	Paul O'Neill	.05
9	Darren Daulton	.05
10	Mike Greenwell	.05
11	Chuck Carr	.05
12	Joe Carter	.05
13	Lance Johnson	.05
14	Jeff Blauser	.05
15	Chris Hoiles	.05
16	Rick Wilkins	.05
17	Kirby Puckett	1.00
18	Larry Walker	.05
19	Randy Johnson	.75
20	Bernard Gilkey	.05
21	Devon White	.05
22	Randy Myers	.05
23	Don Mattingly	1.25
24	John Kruk	.05
25	Ozzie Guillen	.05
26	Jeff Conine	.05
27	Mike Macfarlane	.05
28	Dave Hollins	.05
29	Chuck Knoblauch	.05
30	Ozzie Smith	1.00
31	Harold Baines	.05
32	Ryne Sandberg	1.00
33	Ron Karkovice	.05
34	Terry Pendleton	.05
35	Wally Joyner	.05
36	Mike Mussina	.35
37	Felix Jose	.05
38	Derrick May	.05
39	Scott Cooper	.05
40	Jose Rijo	.05
41	Robin Ventura	.05
42	Charlie Hayes	.05
43	Jimmy Key	.05
44	Eric Karros	.05
45	Ruben Sierra	.05
46	Ryan Thompson	.05
47	Brian McRae	.05
48	Pat Hentgen	.05
49	John Valentin	.05
50	Al Martin	.05
51	Jose Lind	.05
52	Kevin Stocker	.05
53	Mike Gallego	.05
54	Dwight Gooden	.05
55	Brady Anderson	.05
56	Jeff King	.05
57	Mark McGwire	1.75
58	Sammy Sosa	1.00
59	Ryan Bowen	.05
60	Mark Lemke	.05
61	Roger Clemens	1.25
62	Brian Jordan	.05
63	Andres Galarraga	.05
64	Kevin Appier	.05
65	Don Slaught	.05
66	Mike Bowers	.05
67	Wes Chamberlain	.05
68	Troy Neel	.05
69	John Wetteland	.05
70	Joe Girardi	.05
71	Reggie Sanders	.05
72	Edgar Martinez	.05
73	Todd Hundley	.05
74	Pat Borders	.05
75	Roberto Mejia	.05
76	David Cone	.05
77	Tony Gwynn	1.00
78	Jim Abbott	.05
79	Jay Buhner	.05
80	Mark McLemore	.05
81	Wil Cordero	.05
82	Pedro Astacio	.05
83	Bob Tewksbury	.05
84	Dave Winfield	.75
85	Jeff Kent	.05
86	Todd Van Poppel	.05
87	Steve Avery	.05
88	Mike Lansing	.05
89	Len Dykstra	.05
90	Jose Guzman	.05
91	Brian Hunter	.05
92	Tim Raines	.05
93	Andre Dawson	.25
94	Joe Orsulak	.05
95	Ricky Jordan	.05
96	Billy Hatcher	.05
97	Jack McDowell	.05
98	Tom Pagnozzi	.05
99	Darryl Strawberry	.05
100	Mike Stanley	.05
101	Bret Saberhagen	.05
102	Willie Greene	.05
103	Bryan Harvey	.05
104	Tim Bogar	.05

105	Jack Voight	.05
106	Brad Ausmus	.05
107	Ramon Martinez	.05
108	Mike Perez	.05
109	Jeff Montgomery	.05
110	Danny Darwin	.05
111	Wilson Alvarez	.05
112	Kevin Mitchell	.05
113	David Nied	.05
114	Rich Amaral	.05
115	Stan Javier	.05
116	Mo Vaughn	.05
117	Ben McDonald	.05
118	Tom Gordon	.05
119	Carlos Garcia	.05
120	Phil Plantier	.05
121	Mike Morgan	.05
122	Pat Meares	.05
123	Kevin Young	.05
124	Jeff Fassero	.05
125	Gene Harris	.05
126	Bob Welch	.05
127	Walt Weiss	.05
128	Bobby Witt	.05
129	Andy Van Slyke	.05
130	Steve Cooke	.05
131	Mike Devereaux	.05
132	Joey Cora	.05
133	Bret Barberie	.05
134	Orel Hershiser	.05
135	Ed Sprague	.05
136	Shawon Dunston	.05
137	Alex Arias	.05
138	Archi Cianfrocco	.05
139	Tim Wallach	.05
140	Bernie Williams	.05
141	Karl Rhodes	.05
142	Pat Kelly	.05
143	Dave Magadan	.05
144	Kevin Tapani	.05
145	Eric Young	.05
146	Derek Bell	.05
147	Dante Bichette	.05
148	Geronimo Pena	.05
149	Joe Oliver	.05
150	Orestes Destrade	.05
151	Tim Naehring	.05
152	Ray Lankford	.05
153	Phil Clark	.05
154	David McCarty	.05
155	Tommy Greene	.05
156	Wade Boggs	1.00
157	Kevin Gross	.05
158	Hal Morris	.05
159	Moises Alou	.05
160	Rick Aguilera	.05
161	Curt Schilling	.35
162	Chip Hale	.05
163	Tino Martinez	.05
164	Mark Whiten	.05
165	Dave Stewart	.05
166	Steve Buechele	.05
167	Bobby Jones	.05
168	Darrin Fletcher	.05
169	John Smiley	.05
170	Cory Snyder	.05
171	Scott Erickson	.05
172	Kirk Rueter	.05
173	Dave Fleming	.05
174	John Smoltz	.05
175	Ricky Gutierrez	.05
176	Mike Bordick	.05
177	Chan Ho Park RC	1.00
178	Alex Gonzalez	.05
179	Steve Karsay	.05
180	Jeffrey Hammonds	.05
181	Manny Ramirez	.75
182	Salomon Torres	.05
183	Raul Mondesi	.05
184	James Mouton	.05
185	Cliff Floyd	.05
186	Danny Bautista	.05
187	Kurt Abbott RC	.05
188	Javier Lopez	.05
189	John Patterson	.05
190	Greg Blosser	.05
191	Bob Hamelin	.05
192	Tony Eusebio	.05
193	Carlos Delgado	.50
194	Chris Gomez	.05
195	Kelly Stinnett	.05
196	Shane Reynolds	.05
197	Ryan Klesko	.05
198	Jim Edmonds	.05
199	James Hurst	.05
200	Dave Staton	.05
201	Rondell White	.05
202	Keith Mitchell	.05
203	Darren Oliver	.05
204	Mike Matheny	.05
205	Chris Turner	.05
206	Matt Mieske	.05
207	N.L. Team Checklist	.05
208	N.L. Team Checklist	.05

209	A.L. Team Checklist	.05
210	A.L. Team Checklist	.05
211	Barry Bonds	2.00
212	Juan Gonzalez	.40
213	Jim Eisenreich	.05
214	Ivan Rodriguez	.65
215	Tony Phillips	.05
216	John Jaha	.05
217	Lee Smith	.05
218	Bip Roberts	.05
219	Dave Hansen	.05
220	Pat Listach	.05
221	Willie McGee	.05
222	Damion Easley	.05
223	Dean Palmer	.05
224	Mike Moore	.05
225	Brian Harper	.05
226	Gary DiSarcina	.05
227	Delino DeShields	.05
228	Otis Nixon	.05
229	Roberto Alomar	.30
230	Mark Grace	.05
231	Kenny Lofton	.05
232	Gregg Jefferies	.05
233	Cecil Fielder	.05
234	Jeff Bagwell	.75
235	Albert Belle	.05
236	Dave Justice	.05
237	Tom Henke	.05
238	Bobby Bonilla	.05
239	John Olerud	.05
240	Robby Thompson	.05
241	Dave Valle	.05
242	Marquis Grissom	.05
243	Greg Swindell	.05
244	Todd Zeile	.05
245	Dennis Eckersley	.65
246	Jose Offerman	.05
247	Greg McMichael	.05
248	Tim Belcher	.05
249	Cal Ripken, Jr.	2.00
250	Tom Glavine	.05
251	Luis Polonia	.05
252	Bill Swift	.05
253	Juan Guzman	.05
254	Rickey Henderson	.75
255	Terry Mulholland	.05
256	Gary Sheffield	.40
257	Terry Steinbach	.05
258	Brett Butler	.05
259	Jason Bere	.05
260	Doug Strange	.05
261	Kent Hrbek	.05
262	Graeme Lloyd	.05
263	Lou Frazier	.05
264	Charles Nagy	.05
265	Bret Boone	.05
266	Kirk Gibson	.05
267	Kevin Brown	.05
268	Matt Williams	.05
270	Greg Gagne	.05
271	Mariano Duncan	.05
272	Jeff Russell	.05
273	Eric Davis	.05
274	Shane Mack	.05
275	Jose Vizcaino	.05
276	Jose Canseco	.45
277	Roberto Hernandez	.05
278	Royce Clayton	.05
279	Carlos Baerga	.05
280	Pete Incaviglia	.05
281	Brent Gates	.05
282	Jeromy Burnitz	.05
283	Chili Davis	.05
284	Pete Harnisch	.05
285	Alan Trammell	.05
286	Eric Anthony	.05
287	Ellis Burks	.05
288	Julio Franco	.05
289	Jack Morris	.05
290	Erik Hanson	.05
291	Chuck Finley	.05
292	Reggie Jefferson	.05
293	Kevin McReynolds	.05
294	Greg Hibbard	.05
295	Travis Fryman	.05
296	Craig Biggio	.05
297	Kenny Rogers	.05
298	Dave Henderson	.05
299	Jim Thome	.50
300	Rene Arocha	.05
301	Pedro Munoz	.05
302	David Hulse	.05
303	Greg Vaughn	.05
304	Darren Lewis	.05
305	Deion Sanders	.05
306	Danny Tartabull	.05
307	Darryl Hamilton	.05
308	Andujar Cedeno	.05
309	Tim Salmon	.05
310	Tony Fernandez	.05
311	Alex Fernandez	.05
312	Roberto Kelly	.05
313	Harold Reynolds	.05

314	Chris Sabo	.05
315	Howard Johnson	.05
316	Mark Portugal	.05
317	Rafael Palmeiro	.65
318	Pete Smith	.05
319	Will Clark	.05
320	Henry Rodriguez	.05
321	Omar Vizquel	.05
322	David Segui	.05
323	Lou Whitaker	.05
324	Felix Fermin	.05
325	Spike Owen	.05
326	Darryl Kile	.05
327	Chad Kreuter	.05
328	Rod Beck	.05
329	Eddie Murray	.75
330	B.J. Surhoff	.05
331	Mickey Tettleton	.05
332	Pedro Martinez	.75
333	Roger Pavlik	.05
334	Eddie Taubensee	.05
335	John Doherty	.05
336	Jody Reed	.05
337	Aaron Sele	.05
338	Leo Gomez	.05
339	Dave Nilsson	.05
340	Rob Dibble	.05
341	John Burkett	.05
342	Wayne Kirby	.05
343	Dan Wilson	.05
344	Armando Reynoso	.05
345	Chad Curtis	.05
346	Dennis Martinez	.05
347	Cal Eldred	.05
348	Luis Gonzalez	.05
349	Doug Drabek	.05
350	Jim Leyritz	.05
351	Mark Langston	.05
352	Darrin Jackson	.05
353	Sid Fernandez	.05
354	Benito Santiago	.05
355	Kevin Seitzer	.05
356	Bo Jackson	.10
357	David Wells	.05
358	Paul Sorrento	.05
359	Ken Caminiti	.05
360	Eduardo Perez	.05
361	Orlando Merced	.05
362	Steve Finley	.05
363	Andy Benes	.05
364	Manuel Lee	.05
365	Todd Benzinger	.05
366	Sandy Alomar Jr.	.05
367	Rex Hudler	.05
368	Mike Henneman	.05
369	Vince Coleman	.05
370	Kirt Manwaring	.05
371	Ken Hill	.05
372	Glenallen Hill	.05
373	Sean Berry	.05
374	Geronimo Berroa	.05
375	Duane Ward	.05
376	Allen Watson	.05
377	Marc Newfield	.05
378	Dan Miceli	.05
379	Denny Hocking	.05
380	Mark Kiefer	.05
381	Tony Tarasco	.05
382	Tony Longmire	.05
383	Brian Anderson RC	.05
384	Fernando Vina	.05
385	Hector Carrasco	.05
386	Mike Kelly	.05
387	Greg Colbrunn	.05
388	Roger Salkeld	.05
389	Steve Trachsel	.05
390	Rich Becker	.05
391	Billy Taylor RC	.05
392	Rich Rowland	.05
393	Carl Everett	.05
394	Johnny Ruffin	.05
395	Keith Lockhart RC	.05
396	J.R. Phillips	.05
397	Sterling Hitchcock	.05
398	Jorge Fabregas	.05
399	Jeff Granger	.05
400	Eddie Zambrano RC	.05
401	Rikkert Faneyte RC	.05
402	Gerald Williams	.05
403	Joey Hamilton	.05
404	Joe Hall RC	.05
405	John Hudek RC	.05
406	Roberto Petagine	.05
407	Charles Johnson	.05
408	Mark Smith	.05
409	Jeff Juden	.05
410	Carlos Pulido RC	.05
411	Paul Shuey	.05
412	Rob Butler	.05
413	Mark Acre	.05
414	Greg Pirkl	.05
415	Melvin Nieves	.05
416	Tim Hyers RC	.05
417	N.L. Checklist	.05

418	N.L. Checklist	.05
419	A.L. Checklist	.05
420	A.L. Checklist	.05

MVP

NM/M

MVP1	Paul Molitor	5.00

Rookie of the Year

NM/M

RY1	Carlos Delgado	7.50

Rookie Surge

NM/M

	Complete Set (18):		10.00
	Common Player:		.75
1	Cliff Floyd		.75
2	Bob Hamelin		.75
3	Ryan Klesko		.75
4	Carlos Delgado		3.00
5	Jeffrey Hammonds		.75
6	Rondell White		.75
7	Salomon Torres		.75
8	Steve Karsay		.75
9	Javier Lopez		.75
10	Manny Ramirez		3.00
11	Tony Tarasco		.75
12	Kurt Abbott		.75
13	Chan Ho Park		.75
14	Rich Becker		.75
15	James Mouton		.75
16	Alex Gonzalez		.75
17	Raul Mondesi		.75
18	Steve Trachsel		.75

Salute

NM/M

	Complete Set (2):	15.00

1	Cal Ripken, Jr.	12.50
2	Dave Winfield	5.00

Skills

NM/M

	Complete Set (10):	15.00
	Common Player:	.75
1	Randy Johnson	3.00
2	Barry Larkin	.75
3	Len Dykstra	.75
4	Kenny Lofton	.75
5	Juan Gonzalez	1.50
6	Barry Bonds	6.00
7	Marquis Grissom	.75
8	Ivan Rodriguez	2.50
9	Larry Walker	.75
10	Travis Fryman	.75

1995 Select

NM/M

	Complete Set (251):	9.00
	Common Player:	.05
	Pack (12):	1.50
	Wax Box (24):	17.50
1	Cal Ripken Jr.	1.50
2	Robin Ventura	.05
3	Al Martin	.05
4	Jeff Frye	.05
5	Darryl Strawberry	.05
6	Chan Ho Park	.05
7	Steve Avery	.05
8	Bret Boone	.05
9	Danny Tartabull	.05
10	Dante Bichette	.05
11	Rondell White	.05
12	Dave McCarty	.05
13	Bernard Gilkey	.05
14	Mark McGwire	1.25
15	Ruben Sierra	.05
16	Wade Boggs	.75
17	Mike Piazza	1.00
18	Jeffrey Hammonds	.05
19	Mike Mussina	.35
20	Darryl Kile	.05
21	Greg Maddux	.75
22	Frank Thomas	.65
23	Kevin Appier	.05
24	Jay Bell	.05
25	Kirk Gibson	.05

26	Pat Hentgen	.05
27	Joey Hamilton	.05
28	Bernie Williams	.05
29	Aaron Sele	.05
30	Delino DeShields	.05
31	Danny Bautista	.05
32	Jim Thome	.45
33	Rikkert Faneyte	.05
34	Roberto Alomar	.20
35	Paul Molitor	.65
36	Allen Watson	.05
37	Jeff Bagwell	.65
38	Jay Buhner	.05
39	Marquis Grissom	.05
40	Jim Edmonds	.05
41	Ryan Klesko	.05
42	Fred McGriff	.05
43	Tony Tarasco	.05
44	Darren Daulton	.05
45	Marc Newfield	.05
46	Barry Bonds	1.50
47	Bobby Bonilla	.05
48	Greg Pirkl	.05
49	Steve Karsay	.05
50	Bob Hamelin	.05
51	Javier Lopez	.05
52	Barry Larkin	.05
53	Kevin Young	.05
54	Sterling Hitchcock	.05
55	Tom Glavine	.05
56	Carlos Delgado	.40
57	Darren Oliver	.05
58	Cliff Floyd	.05
59	Tim Salmon	.05
60	Albert Belle	.05
61	Salomon Torres	.05
62	Gary Sheffield	.35
63	Ivan Rodriguez	.50
64	Charles Nagy	.05
65	Eduardo Perez	.05
66	Terry Steinbach	.05
67	Dave Justice	.05
68	Jason Bere	.05
69	Dave Nilsson	.05
70	Brian Anderson	.05
71	Billy Ashley	.05
72	Roger Clemens	.85
73	Jimmy Key	.05
74	Wally Joyner	.05
75	Andy Benes	.05
76	Ray Lankford	.05
77	Jeff Kent	.05
78	Moises Alou	.05
79	Kirby Puckett	.75
80	Joe Carter	.05
81	Manny Ramirez	.65
82	J.R. Phillips	.05
83	Matt Mieske	.05
84	John Olerud	.05
85	Andres Galarraga	.05
86	Juan Gonzalez	.35
87	Pedro Martinez	.65
88	Dean Palmer	.05
89	Ken Griffey Jr.	1.00
90	Brian Jordan	.05
91	Hal Morris	.05
92	Lenny Dykstra	.05
93	Wil Cordero	.05
94	Tony Gwynn	.75
95	Alex Gonzalez	.05
96	Cecil Fielder	.05
97	Mo Vaughn	.05
98	John Valentin	.05
99	Will Clark	.05
100	Geronimo Pena	.05
101	Don Mattingly	.85
102	Charles Johnson	.05
103	Raul Mondesi	.05
104	Reggie Sanders	.05
105	Royce Clayton	.05
106	Reggie Jefferson	.05
107	Craig Biggio	.05
108	Jack McDowell	.05
109	James Mouton	.05
110	Mike Greenwell	.05
111	David Cone	.05
112	Matt Williams	.05
113	Garret Anderson	.05
114	Carlos Garcia	.05
115	Alex Fernandez	.05
116	Deion Sanders	.05
117	Chili Davis	.05
118	Mike Kelly	.05
119	Jeff Conine	.05
120	Kenny Lofton	.05
121	Rafael Palmeiro	.50
122	Chuck Knoblauch	.05
123	Ozzie Smith	.75
124	Carlos Baerga	.05
125	Brett Butler	.05
126	Sammy Sosa	.75
127	Ellis Burks	.05
128	Bret Saberhagen	.05
129	Doug Drabek	.05

130	Dennis Martinez	.05
131	Paul O'Neill	.05
132	Travis Fryman	.05
133	Brent Gates	.05
134	Rickey Henderson	.65
135	Randy Johnson	.65
136	Mark Langston	.05
137	Greg Colbrunn	.05
138	Jose Rijo	.05
139	Bryan Harvey	.05
140	Dennis Eckersley	.50
141	Ron Gant	.05
142	Carl Everett	.05
143	Jeff Granger	.05
144	Ben McDonald	.05
145	Kurt Abbott	.05
146	Jim Abbott	.05
147	Jason Jacome	.05
148	Rico Brogna	.05
149	Cal Eldred	.05
150	Rich Becker	.05
151	Pete Harnisch	.05
152	Roberto Petagine	.05
153	Jacob Brumfield	.05
154	Todd Hundley	.05
155	Roger Cedeno	.05
156	Harold Baines	.05
157	Steve Dunn	.05
158	Tim Belk	.05
159	Marty Cordova	.05
160	Russ Davis	.05
161	Jose Malave	.05
162	Brian Hunter	.05
163	Andy Pettitte	.20
164	Brooks Kieschnick	.05
165	Midre Cummings	.05
166	Frank Rodriguez	.05
167	Chad Mottola	.05
168	Brian Barber	.05
169	Tim Unroe	.05
170	Shane Andrews	.05
171	Kevin Flora	.05
172	Ray Durham	.05
173	Chipper Jones	.75
174	Butch Huskey	.05
175	Ray McDavid	.05
176	Jeff Cirillo	.05
177	Terry Pendleton	.05
178	Scott Ruffcorn	.05
179	Ray Holbert	.05
180	Joe Randa	.05
181	Jose Oliva	.05
182	Andy Van Slyke	.05
183	Albie Lopez	.05
184	Chad Curtis	.05
185	Ozzie Guillen	.05
186	Chad Ogea	.05
187	Dan Wilson	.05
188	Tony Fernandez	.05
189	John Smoltz	.05
190	Willie Greene	.05
191	Darren Lewis	.05
192	Orlando Miller	.05
193	Kurt Miller	.05
194	Andrew Lorraine	.05
195	Ernie Young	.05
196	Jimmy Haynes	.05
197	Raul Casanova RC	.05
198	Joe Vitiello	.05
199	Brad Woodall	.05
200	Juan Acevedo	.05
201	Michael Tucker	.05
202	Shawn Green	.35
203	Alex Rodriguez	1.25
204	Julian Tavarez	.05
205	Jose Lima	.05
206	Wilson Alvarez	.05
207	Rich Aude	.05
208	Armando Benitez	.05
209	Dwayne Hosey	.05
210	Gabe White	.05
211	Joey Eischen	.05
212	Bill Pulsipher	.05
213	Robby Thompson	.05
214	Toby Borland	.05
215	Rusty Greer	.05
216	Fausto Cruz	.05
217	Luis Ortiz	.05
218	Duane Singleton	.05
219	Troy Percival	.05
220	Gregg Jefferies	.05
221	Mark Grace	.05
222	Mickey Tettleton	.05
223	Phil Plantier	.05
224	Larry Walker	.05
225	Ken Caminiti	.05
226	Dave Winfield	.65
227	Brady Anderson	.05
228	Kevin Brown	.05
229	Andujar Cedeno	.05
230	Roberto Kelly	.05
231	Jose Canseco	.35
231	Scott Ruffcorn	.05
232	Billy Ashley	.05

234	J.R. Phillips	.05
235	Chipper Jones	.40
236	Charles Johnson	.05
237	Midre Cummings	.05
238	Brian Hunter	.05
239	Garret Anderson	.05
240	Shawn Green	.10
241	Alex Rodriguez	.65
242	Frank Thomas Checklist #1	.35
243	Ken Griffey Jr. Checklist #2	.50
244	Albert Belle Checklist #3	.05
245	Cal Ripken Jr. Checklist #4	.65
246	Barry Bonds Checklist #5	.75
247	Raul Mondesi Checklist #6	.05
248	Mike Piazza Checklist #7	.65
249	Jeff Bagwell Checklist #8	.30
250	Jeff Bagwell, Frank Thomas, Ken Griffey Jr., Mike Piazza Checklist #9	.25
251	Hideo Nomo	.35

Artist's Proofs

	NM/M
Complete Set (250):	100.00
Common Player:	1.00
AP Stars:	10X

(See 1995 Select for checklist and base card values.)

Big Sticks

		NM/M
Complete Set (12):		40.00
Common Player:		1.50
1	Frank Thomas	4.00
2	Ken Griffey Jr.	7.50
3	Cal Ripken Jr.	10.00
4	Mike Piazza	7.50
5	Don Mattingly	6.00
6	Will Clark	1.50
7	Tony Gwynn	5.00
8	Jeff Bagwell	4.00
9	Barry Bonds	10.00
10	Paul Molitor	4.00
11	Matt Williams	1.50
12	Albert Belle	1.50

Can't Miss

		NM/M
Complete Set (12):		10.00
Common Player:		.35
1	Cliff Floyd	.35
2	Ryan Klesko	.35
3	Charles Johnson	.35
4	Raul Mondesi	.35
5	Manny Ramirez	2.00
6	Billy Ashley	.35
7	Alex Gonzalez	.35
8	Carlos Delgado	.75
9	Garret Anderson	.35

10	Alex Rodriguez	5.00
11	Chipper Jones	3.00
12	Shawn Green	.75

Sure Shots

		NM/M
Complete Set (10):		10.00
Common Player:		1.00
1	Ben Grieve	1.00
2	Kevin Witt	1.00
3	Mark Farris	1.00
4	Paul Konerko	3.00
5	Dustin Hermanson	1.00
6	Ramon Castro	1.00
7	McKay Christensen	1.00
8	Brian Buchanan	1.00
9	Paul Wilson	1.00
10	Terrence Long	1.00

1995 Select Certified

		NM/M
Complete Set (135):		10.00
Common Player:		.05
Pack (6):		2.00
Wax Box (20):		25.00
1	Barry Bonds	2.50
2	Reggie Sanders	.05
3	Terry Steinbach	.05
4	Eduardo Perez	.05
5	Frank Thomas	.75
6	Wil Cordero	.05
7	John Olerud	.05
8	Deion Sanders	.05
9	Mike Mussina	.40
10	Mo Vaughn	.05
11	Will Clark	.05
12	Chili Davis	.05
13	Jimmy Key	.05
14	Eddie Murray	.75

15	Bernard Gilkey	.05
16	David Cone	.05
17	Tim Salmon	.05
18	(Not issued, see #2131.)	
19	Steve Ontiveros	.05
20	Andres Galarraga	.05
21	Don Mattingly	1.25
22	Kevin Appier	.05
23	Paul Molitor	.75
24	Edgar Martinez	.05
25	Andy Benes	.05
26	Rafael Palmeiro	.65
27	Barry Larkin	.05
28	Gary Sheffield	.25
29	Wally Joyner	.05
30	Wade Boggs	1.00
31	Rico Brogna	.05
32	Eddie Murray (Murray Tribute)	.40
33	Kirby Puckett	1.00
34	Bobby Bonilla	.05
35	Hal Morris	.05
36	Moises Alou	.05
37	Javier Lopez	.05
38	Chuck Knoblauch	.05
39	Mike Piazza	1.50
40	Travis Fryman	.05
41	Rickey Henderson	.75
42	Jim Thome	.60
43	Carlos Baerga	.05
44	Dean Palmer	.05
45	Kirk Gibson	.05
46	Bret Saberhagen	.05
47	Cecil Fielder	.05
48	Manny Ramirez	.75
49	Derek Bell	.05
50	Mark McGwire	2.00
51	Jim Edmonds	.05
52	Robin Ventura	.05
53	Ryan Klesko	.05
54	Jeff Bagwell	.75
55	Ozzie Smith	1.00
56	Albert Belle	.05
57	Darren Daulton	.05
58	Jeff Conine	.05
59	Greg Maddux	1.00
60	Lenny Dykstra	.05
61	Randy Johnson	.75
62	Fred McGriff	.05
63	Ray Lankford	.05
64	Dave Justice	.05
65	Paul O'Neill	.05
66	Tony Gwynn	1.00
67	Matt Williams	.05
68	Dante Bichette	.05
69	Craig Biggio	.05
70	Ken Griffey Jr.	1.50
71	J.T. Snow	.05
72	Cal Ripken Jr.	2.50
73	Jay Bell	.05
74	Joe Carter	.05
75	Roberto Alomar	.30
76	Benji Gil	.05
77	Ivan Rodriguez	.65
78	Raul Mondesi	.05
79	Cliff Floyd	.05
80	Eric Karros, Mike Piazza, Raul Mondesi (Dodger Dynasty)	.30
81	Royce Clayton	.05
82	Billy Ashley	.05
83	Joey Hamilton	.05
84	Sammy Sosa	1.00
85	Jason Bere	.05
86	Dennis Martinez	.05
87	Greg Vaughn	.05
88	Roger Clemens	1.25
89	Larry Walker	.05
90	Mark Grace	.05
91	Kenny Lofton	.05
92	Carlos Perez RC	.05
93	Roger Cedeno	.05
94	Scott Ruffcorn	.05
95	Jim Pittsley	.05
96	Andy Pettitte	.20
97	James Baldwin	.05
98	Hideo Nomo RC	1.50
99	Ismael Valdes	.05
100	Armando Benitez	.05
101	Jose Malave	.05
102	Bobby Higginson RC	.25
103	LaTroy Hawkins	.05
104	Russ Davis	.05
105	Shawn Green	.40
106	Joe Vitiello	.05
107	Chipper Jones	1.00
108	Shane Andrews	.05
109	Jose Oliva	.05
110	Ray Durham	.05
111	Jon Nunnally	.05
112	Alex Gonzalez	.05
113	Vaughn Eshelman	.05
114	Marty Cordova	.05
115	Mark Grudzielanek RC	.25

116	Brian Hunter	.05
117	Charles Johnson	.05
118	Alex Rodriguez	2.00
119	David Bell	.05
120	Todd Hollandsworth	.05
121	Joe Randa	.05
122	Derek Jeter	2.50
123	Frank Rodriguez	.05
124	Curtis Goodwin	.05
125	Bill Pulsipher	.05
126	John Mabry	.05
127	Julian Tavarez	.05
128	Edgardo Alfonzo	.05
129	Orlando Miller	.05
130	Juan Acevedo	.05
131	Jeff Cirillo	.05
132	Roberto Petagine	.05
133	Antonio Osuna	.05
134	Michael Tucker	.05
135	Garret Anderson	.05
2131	Cal Ripken Jr. (Consecutive Game Record)	1.00

Mirror Gold

	NM/M
Complete Set (135):	150.00
Common Player:	1.00
Mirror Gold Stars:	5X

(See 1995 Select for checklist and base card values.)

Future

		NM/M
Complete Set (10):		10.00
Common Player:		.50
1	Chipper Jones	2.00
2	Curtis Goodwin	.50
3	Hideo Nomo	1.00
4	Shawn Green	1.00
5	Ray Durham	.50
6	Todd Hollandsworth	.50
7	Brian Hunter	.50
8	Carlos Delgado	1.00
9	Michael Tucker	.50
10	Alex Rodriguez	4.00

Gold Team

		NM/M
Complete Set (12):		40.00
Common Player:		2.00
1	Ken Griffey Jr.	7.50
2	Frank Thomas	4.00
3	Cal Ripken Jr.	10.00
4	Jeff Bagwell	4.00
5	Mike Piazza	7.50
6	Barry Bonds	10.00
7	Matt Williams	2.00
8	Don Mattingly	6.00
9	Will Clark	2.00

10	Tony Gwynn	5.00
11	Kirby Puckett	5.00
12	Jose Canseco	2.50

Potential Unlimited

		NM/M
Complete Set (20):		35.00
Common Player:		1.00
903's:		2.5X
1	Cliff Floyd	1.00
2	Manny Ramirez	4.50
3	Raul Mondesi	1.00
4	Scott Ruffcorn	1.00
5	Billy Ashley	1.00
6	Alex Gonzalez	1.00
7	Midre Cummings	1.00
8	Charles Johnson	1.00
9	Garret Anderson	1.00
10	Hideo Nomo	2.00
11	Chipper Jones	7.00
12	Curtis Goodwin	1.00
13	Frank Rodriguez	1.00
14	Shawn Green	2.00
15	Ray Durham	1.00
16	Todd Hollandsworth	1.00
17	Brian Hunter	1.00
18	Carlos Delgado	2.00
19	Michael Tucker	1.00
20	Alex Rodriguez	9.00

1996 Select

		NM/M
Complete Set (200):		9.00
Common Player:		.05
Pack (10):		1.00
Wax Box (24):		16.00
1	Wade Boggs	1.00
2	Shawn Green	.35
3	Andres Galarraga	.05
4	Bill Pulsipher	.05
5	Chuck Knoblauch	.05
6	Ken Griffey Jr.	1.25
7	Greg Maddux	1.00
8	Manny Ramirez	.75
9	Ivan Rodriguez	.65
10	Tim Salmon	.05
11	Frank Thomas	.75
12	Jeff Bagwell	.75
13	Travis Fryman	.05
14	Kenny Lofton	.05
15	Matt Williams	.05
16	Jay Bell	.05
17	Ken Caminiti	.05
18	Ray Lankford	.05
19	Cal Ripken Jr.	2.00
20	Roger Clemens	1.00
21	Carlos Baerga	.05
22	Mike Piazza	1.25
23	Gregg Jefferies	.05
24	Reggie Sanders	.05
25	Rondell White	.05
26	Sammy Sosa	1.00
27	Kevin Appier	.05
28	Kevin Seitzer	.05
29	Gary Sheffield	.40
30	Mike Mussina	.35
31	Mark McGwire	1.50
32	Barry Larkin	.05
33	Marc Newfield	.05
34	Ismael Valdes	.05
35	Marty Cordova	.05
36	Albert Belle	.05
37	Johnny Damon	.35
38	Garret Anderson	.05
39	Cecil Fielder	.05
40	John Mabry	.05
41	Chipper Jones	1.00
42	Omar Vizquel	.05
43	Jose Rijo	.05
44	Charles Johnson	.05
45	Alex Rodriguez	1.50
46	Rico Brogna	.05
47	Joe Carter	.05
48	Mo Vaughn	.05
49	Moises Alou	.05
50	Raul Mondesi	.05
51	Robin Ventura	.05
52	Jim Thome	.60
53	Dave Justice	.05
54	Jeff King	.05
55	Brian Hunter	.05
56	Juan Gonzalez	.40
57	John Olerud	.05
58	Rafael Palmeiro	.65
59	Tony Gwynn	1.00
60	Eddie Murray	.75
61	Jason Isringhausen	.05
62	Dante Bichette	.05
63	Randy Johnson	.75
64	Kirby Puckett	1.00
65	Jim Edmonds	.05
66	David Cone	.05
67	Ozzie Smith	1.00
68	Fred McGriff	.05
69	Darren Daulton	.05
70	Edgar Martinez	.05
71	J.T. Snow	.05
72	Butch Huskey	.05
73	Hideo Nomo	.40
74	Pedro Martinez	.75
75	Bobby Bonilla	.05
76	Jeff Conine	.05
77	Ryan Klesko	.05
78	Bernie Williams	.05
79	Andre Dawson	.25
80	Trevor Hoffman	.05
81	Mark Grace	.05
82	Benji Gil	.05
83	Eric Karros	.05
84	Pete Schourek	.05
85	Edgardo Alfonzo	.05
86	Jay Buhner	.05
87	Vinny Castilla	.05
88	Bret Boone	.05
89	Ray Durham	.05
90	Brian Jordan	.05
91	Jose Canseco	.40
92	Paul O'Neill	.05
93	Chili Davis	.05
94	Tom Glavine	.30
95	Julian Tavarez	.05
96	Derek Bell	.05
97	Will Clark	.05
98	Larry Walker	.05
99	Denny Neagle	.05
100	Alex Fernandez	.05
101	Barry Bonds	2.00
102	Ben McDonald	.05
103	Andy Pettitte	.25
104	Tino Martinez	.05
105	Sterling Hitchcock	.05
106	Royce Clayton	.05
107	Jim Abbott	.05
108	Rickey Henderson	.75
109	Ramon Martinez	.05
110	Paul Molitor	.75
111	Dennis Eckersley	.65
112	Alex Gonzalez	.05
113	Marquis Grissom	.05
114	Greg Vaughn	.05
115	Lance Johnson	.05
116	Todd Stottlemyre	.05
117	Jack McDowell	.05
118	Ruben Sierra	.05
119	Brady Anderson	.05
120	Julio Franco	.05
121	Brooks Kieshnick	.05
122	Roberto Alomar	.20
123	Greg Gagne	.05
124	Wally Joyner	.05
125	John Smoltz	.05
126	John Valentin	.05
127	Russ Davis	.05
128	Joe Vitiello	.05
129	Shawon Dunston	.05
130	Frank Rodriguez	.05
131	Charlie Hayes	.05
132	Andy Benes	.05
133	B.J. Surhoff	.05
134	Dave Nilsson	.05
135	Carlos Delgado	.50
136	Walt Weiss	.05
137	Mike Stanley	.05
138	Greg Colbrunn	.05
139	Mike Kelly	.05
140	Ryne Sandberg	1.00
141	Lee Smith	.05
142	Dennis Martinez	.05
143	Bernard Gilkey	.05
144	Lenny Dykstra	.05
145	Danny Tartabull	.05
146	Dean Palmer	.05
147	Craig Biggio	.05
148	Juan Acevedo	.05
149	Michael Tucker	.05
150	Bobby Higginson	.05
151	Ken Griffey Jr.	.65
152	Frank Thomas	.45
153	Cal Ripken Jr.	1.00
154	Albert Belle	.05
155	Mike Piazza	.65
156	Barry Bonds	1.00
157	Sammy Sosa	.60
158	Mo Vaughn	.05
159	Greg Maddux	.50
160	Jeff Bagwell	.40
161	Derek Jeter	2.00
162	Paul Wilson	.05
163	Chris Snopek	.05
164	Jason Schmidt	.05
165	Jimmy Haynes	.05
166	George Arias	.05
167	Steve Gibralter	.05
168	Bob Wolcott	.05
169	Jason Kendall	.05
170	Gregg Zaun	.05
171	Quinton McCracken	.05
172	Alan Benes	.05
173	Rey Ordonez	.05
174	Ugueth Urbina	.05
175	Osvaldo Fernandez RC	.10
176	Marc Barcelo	.05
177	Sal Fasano	.05
178	Mike Grace RC	.05
179	Chan Ho Park	.05
180	Robert Perez	.05
181	Todd Hollandsworth	.05
182	Wilton Guerrero RC	.05
183	John Wasdin	.05
184	Jim Pittsley	.05
185	LaTroy Hawkins	.05
186	Jay Powell	.05
187	Felipe Crespo	.05
188	Jermaine Dye	.05
189	Bob Abreu	.05
190	Matt Luke RC	.05
191	Richard Hidalgo	.05
192	Karim Garcia	.05
193	Tavo Alvarez	.05
194	Andy Fox RC	.05
195	Terrell Wade	.05
196	Frank Thomas (Checklist)	.40
197	Ken Griffey Jr. (Checklist)	.65
198	Greg Maddux (Checklist)	.50
199	Mike Piazza (Checklist)	.65
200	Cal Ripken Jr. (Checklist)	.75

Artist's Proofs

	NM/M
Complete Set (200):	200.00
Common Player:	1.00
AP Stars:	7X

(See 1996 Select for checklist and base card values.)

Claim to Fame

		NM/M
Complete Set (20):		45.00
Common Player:		.75
1	Cal Ripken Jr.	7.50
2	Greg Maddux	4.50
3	Ken Griffey Jr.	6.00
4	Frank Thomas	3.50
5	Mo Vaughn	.75
6	Albert Belle	.75
7	Jeff Bagwell	3.50
8	Sammy Sosa	4.50
8s	Sammy Sosa/OPS	2.50
9	Reggie Sanders	.75
10	Hideo Nomo	2.00
11	Chipper Jones	4.50
12	Mike Piazza	6.00
13	Matt Williams	.75
14	Tony Gwynn	4.50
15	Johnny Damon	1.50
16	Dante Bichette	.75
17	Kirby Puckett	4.50
18	Barry Bonds	7.50
19	Randy Johnson	3.50
20	Eddie Murray	3.50

En Fuego

		NM/M
Complete Set (25):		35.00
Common Player:		.75
1	Ken Griffey Jr.	3.50
2	Frank Thomas	2.00
3	Cal Ripken Jr.	5.00
4	Greg Maddux	3.00
5	Jeff Bagwell	2.00
6	Barry Bonds	5.00
7	Mo Vaughn	.75
8	Albert Belle	.75
9	Sammy Sosa	3.00
10	Reggie Sanders	.75
11	Mike Piazza	3.50
12	Chipper Jones	3.00
13	Tony Gwynn	3.00
14	Kirby Puckett	3.00
15	Wade Boggs	3.00
16	Dan Patrick	.75
17	Gary Sheffield	1.25
18	Dante Bichette	.75
19	Randy Johnson	2.00
20	Matt Williams	.75
21	Alex Rodriguez	4.00
22	Tim Salmon	.75
23	Johnny Damon	1.25
24	Manny Ramirez	2.00
25	Hideo Nomo	1.25

Team Nucleus

	NM/M
Complete Set (28):	20.00
Common Player:	.50

1	Albert Belle, Manny Ramirez, Carlos Baerga	1.00
2	Ray Lankford, Brian Jordan, Ozzie Smith	1.25
3	Jay Bell, Jeff King, Denny Neagle	.50
4	Dante Bichette, Andres Galarraga, Larry Walker	.50
5	Mark McGwire, Mike Bordick, Terry Steinbach	1.75
6	Bernie Williams, Wade Boggs, David Cone	1.25
7	Joe Carter, Alex Gonzalez, Shawn Green	.50
8	Roger Clemens, Mo Vaughn, Jose Canseco	1.25
9	Ken Griffey Jr., Edgar Martinez, Randy Johnson	1.50
10	Gregg Jefferies, Darren Daulton, Lenny Dykstra	.50
11	Mike Piazza, Raul Mondesi, Hideo Nomo	1.50
12	Greg Maddux, Chipper Jones, Ryan Klesko	1.25
13	Cecil Fielder, Travis Fryman, Phil Nevin	.50
14	Ivan Rodriguez, Will Clark, Juan Gonzalez	1.00
15	Ryne Sandberg, Sammy Sosa, Mark Grace	1.50
16	Gary Sheffield, Charles Johnson, Andre Dawson	.60
17	Johnny Damon, Michael Tucker, Kevin Appier	.65
18	Barry Bonds, Matt Williams, Rod Beck	2.00
19	Kirby Puckett, Chuck Knoblauch, Marty Cordova	1.25
20	Cal Ripken Jr., Bobby Bonilla, Mike Mussina	2.00
21	Jason Isringhausen, Bill Pulsipher, Rico Brogna	.50
22	Tony Gwynn, Ken Caminiti, Marc Newfield	1.25
23	Tim Salmon, Garret Anderson, Jim Edmonds	.50
24	Moises Alou, Rondell White, Cliff Floyd	.50
25	Barry Larkin, Reggie Sanders, Bret Boone	.50
26	Jeff Bagwell, Craig Biggio, Derek Bell	1.00
27	Frank Thomas, Robin Ventura, Alex Fernandez	1.00
28	John Jaha, Greg Vaughn, Kevin Seitzer	.50

1996 Select Certified

		NM/M
Complete Set (144):		20.00
Common Player:		.15
Pack (6):		2.50
Wax Box (20):		40.00
1	Frank Thomas	1.25
2	Tino Martinez	.15
3	Gary Sheffield	.50
4	Kenny Lofton	.15

5	Joe Carter	.15
6	Alex Rodriguez	2.50
7	Chipper Jones	1.50
8	Roger Clemens	1.75
9	Jay Bell	.15
10	Eddie Murray	1.00
11	Will Clark	.15
12	Mike Mussina	.35
13	Hideo Nomo	.50
14	Andres Galarraga	.15
15	Marc Newfield	.15
16	Jason Isringhausen	.15
17	Randy Johnson	1.00
18	Chuck Knoblauch	.15
19	J.T. Snow	.15
20	Mark McGwire	2.50
21	Tony Gwynn	1.50
22	Albert Belle	.15
23	Gregg Jefferies	.15
24	Reggie Sanders	.15
25	Bernie Williams	.15
26	Ray Lankford	.15
27	Johnny Damon	.40
28	Ryne Sandberg	1.50
29	Rondell White	.15
30	Mike Piazza	2.00
31	Barry Bonds	3.00
32	Greg Maddux	1.50
33	Craig Biggio	.15
34	John Valentin	.15
35	Ivan Rodriguez	.75
36	Rico Brogna	.15
37	Tim Salmon	.15
38	Sterling Hitchcock	.15
39	Charles Johnson	.15
40	Travis Fryman	.15
41	Barry Larkin	.15
42	Tom Glavine	.35
43	Marty Cordova	.15
44	Shawn Green	.40
45	Ben McDonald	.15
46	Robin Ventura	.15
47	Ken Griffey Jr.	2.00
48	Orlando Merced	.15
49	Paul O'Neill	.15
50	Ozzie Smith	1.50
51	Manny Ramirez	1.00
52	Ismael Valdes	.15
53	Cal Ripken Jr.	3.00
54	Jeff Bagwell	1.00
55	Greg Vaughn	.15
56	Juan Gonzalez	.50
57	Raul Mondesi	.15
58	Carlos Baerga	.15
59	Sammy Sosa	1.50
60	Mike Kelly	.15
61	Edgar Martinez	.15
62	Kirby Puckett	1.50
63	Cecil Fielder	.15
64	David Cone	.15
65	Moises Alou	.15
66	Fred McGriff	.15
67	Mo Vaughn	.15
68	Edgardo Alfonzo	.15
69	Jim Thome	.75
70	Rickey Henderson	1.00
71	Dante Bichette	.15
72	Lenny Dykstra	.15
73	Benji Gil	.15
74	Wade Boggs	1.50
75	Jim Edmonds	.15
76	Michael Tucker	.15
77	Carlos Delgado	.65
78	Butch Huskey	.15
79	Billy Ashley	.15
80	Dean Palmer	.15
81	Paul Molitor	1.00
82	Ryan Klesko	.15
83	Brian Hunter	.15
84	Jay Buhner	.15
85	Larry Walker	.15
86	Mike Bordick	.15
87	Matt Williams	.15
88	Jack McDowell	.15
89	Hal Morris	.15
90	Brian Jordan	.15
91	Andy Pettitte	.35
92	Melvin Nieves	.15
93	Pedro Martinez	1.00
94	Mark Grace	.15
95	Garret Anderson	.15
96	Andre Dawson	.30
97	Ray Durham	.15
98	Jose Canseco	.50
99	Roberto Alomar	.30
100	Derek Jeter	3.00
101	Alan Benes	.15
102	Karim Garcia	.15
103	Robin Jennings RC	.15
104	Bob Abreu	.15
105	Sal Fasano (Livan Hernandez' name on front.)	.15
106	Steve Gibralter	.15
107	Jermaine Dye	.15
108	Jason Kendall	.15
109	Mike Grace RC	.15
110	Jason Schmidt	.15
111	Paul Wilson	.15
112	Rey Ordonez	.15
113	Wilton Guerrero RC	.15
114	Brooks Kieschnick	.15
115	George Arias	.15
116	Osvaldo Fernandez RC	.15
117	Todd Hollandsworth RC	.15
118	John Wasdin	.15
119	Eric Owens	.15
120	Chan Ho Park	.15
121	Mark Loretta	.15
122	Richard Hidalgo	.15
123	Jeff Suppan	.15
124	Jim Pittsley	.15
125	LaTroy Hawkins	.15
126	Chris Snopek	.15
127	Justin Thompson	.15
128	Jay Powell	.15
129	Alex Ochoa	.15
130	Felipe Crespo	.15
131	Matt Lawton RC	.15
132	Jimmy Haynes	.15
133	Terrell Wade	.15
134	Ruben Rivera	.15
135	Frank Thomas	.55
136	Ken Griffey Jr.	1.00
137	Greg Maddux	.65
138	Mike Piazza	.75
139	Cal Ripken Jr.	1.50
140	Albert Belle	.15
141	Mo Vaughn	.15
142	Chipper Jones	.65
143	Hideo Nomo	.25
144	Ryan Klesko	.15

Artist's Proofs

	NM/M
Complete Set (144):	200.00
Common Player:	1.00
AP Stars:	7X
(See 1996 Select Certified for checklist and base card values.)	

ABBREVIATIONS

OPS - Overprint
"Promotional Sample"

Red, Blue

	NM/M
Common Red:	.50
Red Stars:	3X
Common Blue:	2.50
Blue Stars:	10X

(See 1996 Select Certified for checklist and base card values.)

Mirror Red, Blue, Gold

	NM/M
Common Mirror Red:	6.00
Mirror Red Stars:	20X
Common Mirror Blue:	12.00
Mirror Blue Stars:	30X
Common Mirror Gold:	20.00
Mirror Gold Stars:	100X

(See 1996 Select Certified for checklist and base card values.)

Interleague Preview

		NM/M
Complete Set (25):		45.00
Common Card:		.75
Promos:		1X
1	Ken Griffey Jr., Hideo Nomo	3.50
2	Greg Maddux, Mo Vaughn	3.00
3	Frank Thomas, Sammy Sosa	3.00
4	Mike Piazza, Jim Edmonds	3.50
5	Ryan Klesko, Roger Clemens	3.25
6	Derek Jeter, Rey Ordonez	4.50
7	Johnny Damon, Ray Lankford	1.00
8	Manny Ramirez, Reggie Sanders	2.50
9	Barry Bonds, Jason Isringhausen,	4.50
10	Jason Isringhausen, Wade Boggs	3.00
11	David Cone, Chipper Jones	3.00
12	Jeff Bagwell, Will Clark	2.50
13	Tony Gwynn, Randy Johnson	3.00
14	Cal Ripken Jr., Tom Glavine	4.50
15	Kirby Puckett, Alan Benes	3.00
16	Gary Sheffield, Mike Mussina	1.00
17	Raul Mondesi, Tim Salmon	.75
18	Rondell White, Carlos Delgado	1.00
19	Cecil Fielder, Ryne Sandberg	3.00
20	Kenny Lofton, Brian Hunter	.75
21	Paul Wilson, Paul O'Neill	.75
22	Ismael Valdes, Edgar Martinez	.75
23	Matt Williams, Mark McGwire	4.00
24	Albert Belle, Barry Larkin	.75
25	Brady Anderson, Marquis Grissom	.75

Select Few

		NM/M
Complete Set (18):		40.00
Common Player:		1.00
1	Sammy Sosa	3.00
2	Derek Jeter	5.00
3	Ken Griffey Jr.	3.50
4	Albert Belle	1.00
5	Cal Ripken Jr.	5.00
6	Greg Maddux	3.00
7	Frank Thomas	2.50
8	Mo Vaughn	1.00
9	Chipper Jones	3.00
10	Mike Piazza	3.50
11	Ryan Klesko	1.00
12	Hideo Nomo	1.50
13	Alan Benes	1.00
14	Manny Ramirez	2.50
15	Gary Sheffield	2.00
16	Barry Bonds	5.00
17	Matt Williams	1.00
18	Johnny Damon	2.00

1997 Select

		NM/M
Complete Set (200):		30.00
Series 1 (#1-150):		20.00
Common Red Player:		.10
Common Blue Player:		.25
High Series (#151-200):		10.00
Common High Series:		.25
Pack (6):		1.50
Wax Box (24):		25.00
1	Juan Gonzalez/B	2.00
2	Mo Vaughn/B	.25
3	Tony Gwynn	1.50
4	Manny Ramirez/B	2.00
5	Jose Canseco	.50
6	David Cone	.10
7	Chan Ho Park	.10
8	Frank Thomas/B	2.50
9	Todd Hollandsworth	.10
10	Marty Cordova	.10
11	Gary Sheffield/B	.75
12	John Smoltz/B	.25
13	Mark Grudzielanek	.10
14	Sammy Sosa/B	3.00
15	Paul Molitor	1.00
16	Kevin Brown	.10
17	Albert Belle/B	.25
18	Eric Young	.10
19	John Wetteland	.10
20	Ryan Klesko/B	.25
21	Joe Carter	.10
22	Alex Ochoa	.10
23	Greg Maddux/B	3.00
24	Roger Clemens/B	3.25
25	Ivan Rodriguez/B	1.50
26	Barry Bonds/B	5.00
27	Kenny Lofton/B	.25
28	Javy Lopez	.10
29	Hideo Nomo/B	1.00
30	Rusty Greer	.10
31	Rafael Palmeiro	.10
32	Mike Piazza/B	3.50
33	Ryne Sandberg	1.50
34	Wade Boggs	1.50
35	Jim Thome/B	1.50
36	Ken Caminiti/B	.25
37	Mark Grace	.10
38	Brian Jordan/B	.25
39	Craig Biggio	.10
40	Henry Rodriguez	.10
41	Dean Palmer	.10
42	Jason Kendall	.10
43	Bill Pulsipher	.10
44	Tim Salmon/B	.25
45	Marc Newfield	.10
46	Pat Hentgen	.10
47	Ken Griffey Jr./B	3.50
48	Paul Wilson	.10
49	Jay Buhner/B	.25
50	Rickey Henderson	1.00
51	Jeff Bagwell/B	2.00
52	Cecil Fielder	.10
53	Alex Rodriguez/B	4.00
54	John Jaha	.10
55	Brady Anderson/B	.25
56	Andres Galarraga	.10
57	Raul Mondesi	.10
58	Andy Pettitte	.30
59	Roberto Alomar/B	1.00
60	Derek Jeter/B	5.00
61	Charles Johnson	.10
62	Travis Fryman	.10
63	Chipper Jones/B	3.00
64	Edgar Martinez	.10
65	Bobby Bonilla	.10
66	Greg Vaughn	.10
67	Bobby Higginson	.10
68	Garret Anderson	.10
69	Chuck Knoblauch/B	.25
70	Jermaine Dye	.10
71	Cal Ripken Jr./B	5.00
72	Jason Giambi	.60
73	Trey Beamon	.10
74	Shawn Green	.35
75	Mark McGwire/B	4.00
76	Carlos Delgado	.60
77	Jason Isringhausen	.10
78	Randy Johnson/B	2.00
79	Troy Percival/B	.25
80	Ron Gant	.10
81	Ellis Burks	.10
82	Mike Mussina/B	1.00
83	Todd Hundley	.10
84	Jim Edmonds	.10
85	Charles Nagy	.10
86	Dante Bichette	.25
87	Mariano Rivera	.20
88	Matt Williams/B	.25
89	Rondell White	.10
90	Steve Finley	.10
91	Alex Fernandez	.10
92	Barry Larkin	.25
93	Tom Goodwin	.10
94	Will Clark	.10
95	Michael Tucker	.10
96	Derek Bell	.10
97	Larry Walker	.10
98	Alan Benes	.10
99	Tom Glavine	.35
100	Darin Erstad/B	.35
101	Andruw Jones/B	2.00
102	Scott Rolen	.65
103	Todd Walker/B	.25
104	Dmitri Young	.10
105	Vladimir Guerrero/B	2.00
106	Nomar Garciaparra	1.50
107	Danny Patterson RC	.10
108	Karim Garcia	.10
109	Todd Greene	.10
110	Ruben Rivera	.10
111	Raul Casanova	.10
112	Mike Cameron	.10
113	Bartolo Colon	.10
114	Rod Myers RC	.10
115	Todd Dunn	.10
116	Torii Hunter	.10
117	Jason Dickson	.10
118	Gene Kingsale RC	.10
119	Rafael Medina	.10
120	Raul Ibanez	.10
121	Bobby Henley RC	.10
122	Scott Spiezio	.10
123	Bobby Smith RC	.10
124	J.J. Johnson	.10
125	Bubba Trammell RC	.50
126	Jeff Abbott	.10
127	Neifi Perez	.10
128	Derrek Lee	.65
129	Kevin Brown RC	.10
130	Mendy Lopez	.10
131	Kevin Orie	.10
132	Ryan Jones	.10
133	Juan Encarnacion	.10
134	Jose Guillen/B	.25
135	Greg Norton	.10
136	Richie Sexson	.10
137	Jay Payton	.10
138	Bob Abreu	.15
139	Ronnie Belliard RC	.10
140	Wilton Guerrero/B	.25
141	Alex Rodriguez/B	2.00
142	Juan Gonzalez/B	.50
143	Ken Caminiti/B	.25
144	Frank Thomas/B	1.25
145	Ken Griffey Jr./B	1.75
146	John Smoltz /B	.25
147	Mike Piazza/B	1.75
148	Derek Jeter/B	3.00
149	Frank Thomas (Checklist)	.75
150	Ken Griffey Jr. (Checklist)	1.00
151	Jose Cruz Jr. RC	1.00
152	Moises Alou	.25
153	Hideki Irabu RC	.50
154	Glendon Rusch	.25
155	Ron Coomer	.25
156	Jeremi Gonzalez RC	.25
157	Fernando Tatis RC	.40
158	John Olerud	.25
159	Rickey Henderson	1.00
160	Shannon Stewart	.25
161	Kevin Polcovich	.25
162	Jose Rosado	.25
163	Ray Lankford	.25
164	David Justice	.25
165	Mark Kotsay RC	.50
166	Deivi Cruz RC	.50
167	Billy Wagner	.25
168	Jacob Cruz	.25
169	Matt Morris	.25
170	Brian Banks	.25
171	Brett Tomko	.25
172	Todd Helton	.75
173	Eric Young	.25
174	Bernie Williams	.25
175	Jeff Fassero	.25
176	Ryan McGuire	.25
177	Darryl Kile	.25
178	Kelvim Escobar RC	.50
179	Dave Nilsson	.25
180	Geronimo Berroa	.25
181	Livan Hernandez	.25
182	Tony Womack RC	.50
183	Deion Sanders	.25
184	Jeff Kent	.25
185	Brian Hunter	.25
186	Jose Malave	.25
187	Steve Woodard RC	.50
188	Brad Radke	.25
189	Todd Dunwoody	.25
190	Joey Hamilton	.25
191	Denny Naegle	.25
192	Bobby Jones	.25
193	Tony Clark	.25
194	Jaret Wright RC	.50
195	Matt Stairs	.25
196	Francisco Cordova	.25
197	Justin Thompson	.25
198	Pokey Reese	.25
199	Garrett Stephenson	.25
200	Carl Everett	.25

Artist's Proofs

	NM/M
Complete Set (150):	450.00
Common Red:	1.25
Red Stars:	5X
Common Blue:	2.50
Blue Stars:	1.5X

(See 1997 Select #1-150 for checklist and base card values.)

Registered Gold

	NM/M
Complete Set (150):	300.00
Common Red Gold:	.75
Common Blue Gold:	1.50

(See 1997 Select #1-150 for checklist and base card values.)

Registered Gold Stars:	2X

Autographs

	NM/M
Complete Set (4):	15.00
Common Autograph:	3.00
AU1 Wilton Guerrero	3.00
AU2 Jose Guillen	3.00
AU3 Andruw Jones	10.00
AU4 Todd Walker	3.00

Company

	NM/M
Complete Set (200):	150.00
Common Player:	.50
Red Stars:	3X
Blue Stars:	1.5X
High-Series Stars:	1.5X
Samples:	10X

(See 1997 Select for checklist and base card values.)

Rookie Revolution

	NM/M
Complete Set (20):	21.00
Common Player:	.50
1 Andruw Jones	2.50
2 Derek Jeter	6.00
3 Todd Hollandsworth	.50
4 Edgar Renteria	.50
5 Jason Kendall	.50

6 Rey Ordonez	.50
7 F.P. Santangelo	.50
8 Jermaine Dye	.50
9 Alex Ochoa	.50
10 Vladimir Guerrero	2.50
11 Dmitri Young	.50
12 Todd Walker	.50
13 Scott Rolen	1.50
14 Nomar Garciaparra	3.50
15 Ruben Rivera	.50
16 Darin Erstad	1.00
17 Todd Greene	.50
18 Mariano Rivera	1.00
19 Trey Beamon	.50
20 Karim Garcia	.50

Tools of the Trade

	NM/M
Complete Set (25):	25.00
Common Player:	.40
Mirror Blues:	2.5X
1 Ken Griffey Jr., Andruw Jones	2.00
2 Greg Maddux, Andy Pettitte	1.50
3 Cal Ripken Jr., Chipper Jones	2.50
4 Mike Piazza, Jason Kendall	2.00
5 Albert Belle, Karim Garcia	.40
6 Mo Vaughn, Dmitri Young	.40
7 Juan Gonzalez, Vladimir Guerrero	1.00
8 Tony Gwynn, Jermaine Dye	1.50
9 Barry Bonds, Alex Ochoa	2.50
10 Jeff Bagwell, Jason Giambi	1.00
11 Kenny Lofton, Darin Erstad	.50
12 Gary Sheffield, Manny Ramirez	1.00
13 Tim Salmon, Todd Hollandsworth	.40
14 Sammy Sosa, Ruben Rivera	1.50
15 Paul Molitor, George Arias	1.00
16 Jim Thome, Todd Walker	.75
17 Wade Boggs, Scott Rolen	1.50
18 Ryne Sandberg, Chuck Knoblauch	1.50
19 Mark McGwire, Frank Thomas	2.25
20 Ivan Rodriguez, Charles Johnson	.75
21 Brian Jordan, Trey Beamon	.40
22 Roger Clemens, Troy Percival	1.75
23 John Smoltz, Mike Mussina	.65
24 Alex Rodriguez, Rey Ordonez	2.25
25 Derek Jeter, Nomar Garciaparra	2.50

1995 SkyBox E-Motion

	NM/M
Complete Set (200):	15.00
Common Player:	.05
Pack (8):	1.00
Wax Box (36):	20.00
1 Brady Anderson	.05
2 Kevin Brown	.05
3 Curtis Goodwin	.05
4 Jeffrey Hammonds	.05
5 Ben McDonald	.05
6 Mike Mussina	.35
7 Rafael Palmeiro	.65
8 Cal Ripken Jr.	2.00
9 Jose Canseco	.45
10 Roger Clemens	1.00
11 Vaughn Eshelman	.05
12 Mike Greenwell	.05
13 Erik Hanson	.05
14 Tim Naehring	.05
15 Aaron Sele	.05
16 John Valentin	.05
17 Mo Vaughn	.05
18 Chili Davis	.05
19 Gary DiSarcina	.05
20 Chuck Finley	.05
21 Tim Salmon	.05
22 Lee Smith	.05
23 J.T. Snow	.05
24 Jim Abbott	.05
25 Jason Bere	.05
26 Ray Durham	.05
27 Ozzie Guillen	.05
28 Tim Raines	.05
29 Frank Thomas	.75
30 Robin Ventura	.05
31 Carlos Baerga	.05
32 Albert Belle	.05
33 Orel Hershiser	.05
34 Kenny Lofton	.05
35 Dennis Martinez	.05
36 Eddie Murray	.75
37 Manny Ramirez	.75
38 Julian Tavarez	.05
39 Jim Thome	.60
40 Dave Winfield	.75
41 Chad Curtis	.05
42 Cecil Fielder	.05
43 Travis Fryman	.05
44 Kirk Gibson	.05
45 Bob Higginson RC	.25
46 Alan Trammell	.05
47 Lou Whitaker	.05
48 Kevin Appier	.05
49 Gary Gaetti	.05
50 Jeff Montgomery	.05
51 Jon Nunnally	.05
52 Ricky Bones	.05
53 Cal Eldred	.05
54 Joe Oliver	.05
55 Kevin Seitzer	.05
56 Marty Cordova	.05
57 Chuck Knoblauch	.05
58 Kirby Puckett	1.00
59 Wade Boggs	1.00
60 Derek Jeter	2.00
61 Jimmy Key	.05
62 Don Mattingly	1.00
63 Jack McDowell	.05
64 Paul O'Neill	.05
65 Andy Pettitte	.30
66 Ruben Rivera	.05
67 Mike Stanley	.05
68 John Wetteland	.05
69 Geronimo Berroa	.05
70 Dennis Eckersley	.65
71 Rickey Henderson	.75
72 Mark McGwire *	1.50
73 Steve Ontiveros	.05
74 Ruben Sierra	.05
75 Terry Steinbach	.05
76 Jay Buhner	.05
77 Ken Griffey Jr.	1.25
78 Randy Johnson	.75
79 Edgar Martinez	.05
80 Tino Martinez	.05
81 Marc Newfield	.05
82 Alex Rodriguez	1.50
83 Will Clark	.05
84 Benji Gil	.05
85 Juan Gonzalez	.40
86 Rusty Greer	.05
87 Dean Palmer	.05
88 Ivan Rodriguez	.65
89 Kenny Rogers	.05
90 Roberto Alomar	.30
91 Joe Carter	.05
92 David Cone	.05
93 Alex Gonzalez	.05
94 Shawn Green	.40
95 Pat Hentgen	.05
96 Paul Molitor	.75
97 John Olerud	.05
98 Devon White	.05
99 Steve Avery	.05
100 Tom Glavine	.35
101 Marquis Grissom	.05
102 Chipper Jones	1.00
103 Dave Justice	.05
104 Ryan Klesko	.05
105 Javier Lopez	.05
106 Greg Maddux	1.00
107 Fred McGriff	.05
108 John Smoltz	.05
109 Shawon Dunston	.05
110 Mark Grace	.05
111 Brian McRae	.05
112 Randy Myers	.05
113 Sammy Sosa	1.00
114 Steve Trachsel	.05
115 Bret Boone	.05
116 Ron Gant	.05
117 Barry Larkin	.05
118 Deion Sanders	.05
119 Reggie Sanders	.05
120 Pete Schourek	.05
121 John Smiley	.05
122 Jason Bates	.05
123 Dante Bichette	.05
124 Vinny Castilla	.05
125 Andres Galarraga	.05
126 Larry Walker	.05
127 Greg Colbrunn	.05
128 Jeff Conine	.05
129 Andre Dawson	.30
130 Chris Hammond	.05
131 Charles Johnson	.05
132 Gary Sheffield	.45
133 Quilvio Veras	.05
134 Jeff Bagwell	.75
135 Derek Bell	.05
136 Craig Biggio	.05
137 Jim Dougherty	.05
138 John Hudek	.05
139 Orlando Miller	.05
140 Phil Plantier	.05
141 Eric Karros	.05
142 Ramon Martinez	.05
143 Raul Mondesi	.05
144 Hideo Nomo RC	2.00
145 Mike Piazza	1.25
146 Ismael Valdes	.05
147 Todd Worrell	.05
148 Moises Alou	.05
149 Yamil Benitez RC	.05
150 Wil Cordero	.05
151 Jeff Fassero	.05
152 Cliff Floyd	.05
153 Pedro Martinez	.75
154 Carlos Perez RC	.05
155 Tony Tarasco	.05
156 Rondell White	.05
157 Edgardo Alfonzo	.05
158 Bobby Bonilla	.05
159 Rico Brogna	.05
160 Bobby Jones	.05
161 Bill Pulsipher	.05
162 Bret Saberhagen	.05
163 Ricky Bottalico	.05
164 Darren Daulton	.05
165 Lenny Dykstra	.05
166 Charlie Hayes	.05
167 Dave Hollins	.05
168 Gregg Jefferies	.05
169 Michael Mimbs RC	.05

170	Curt Schilling	.35
171	Heathcliff Slocumb	.05
172	Jay Bell	.05
173	Micah Franklin RC	.05
174	Mark Johnson RC	.05
175	Jeff King	.05
176	Al Martin	.05
177	Dan Miceli	.05
178	Denny Neagle	.05
179	Bernard Gilkey	.05
180	Ken Hill	.05
181	Brian Jordan	.05
182	Ray Lankford	.05
183	Ozzie Smith	1.00
184	Andy Benes	.05
185	Ken Caminiti	.05
186	Steve Finley	.05
187	Tony Gwynn	1.00
188	Joey Hamilton	.05
189	Melvin Nieves	.05
190	Scott Sanders	.05
191	Rod Beck	.05
192	Barry Bonds	2.00
193	Royce Clayton	.05
194	Glenallen Hill	.05
195	Darren Lewis	.05
196	Mark Portugal	.05
197	Matt Williams	.05
198	Checklist	.05
199	Checklist	.05
200	Checklist	.05

Cal Ripken Jr. Timeless

		NM/M
Complete Set (15):		20.00
Common Card:		1.50
1	High School Pitcher	1.50
2	Role Model	1.50
3	Rookie of the Year	1.50
4	1st MVP Season	1.50
5	95 Consecutive Errorless Games	1.50
6	All-Star MVP	1.50
7	Conditioning	1.50
8	Shortstop HR Record	1.50
9	Literacy Work	1.50
10	2000th Consecutive Game	1.50
11	All-Star Selection	2.25
12	Record-tying Game	2.25
13	Record-breaking Game	2.25
14	2,153 and Counting	2.25
15	Birthday	2.25

Masters

		NM/M
Complete Set (10):		12.00
Common Player:		.50
1	Barry Bonds	2.50
2	Juan Gonzalez	.65
3	Ken Griffey Jr.	2.00
4	Tony Gwynn	1.50
5	Kenny Lofton	.50
6	Greg Maddux	1.50
7	Raul Mondesi	.50
8	Cal Ripken Jr.	2.50
9	Frank Thomas	1.00
10	Matt Williams	.50

N-Tense

		NM/M
Complete Set (12):		16.00
Common Player:		.50
1	Jeff Bagwell	2.00
2	Albert Belle	.50
3	Barry Bonds	4.00
4	Cecil Fielder	.50
5	Ron Gant	.50
6	Ken Griffey Jr.	2.50
7	Mark McGwire	3.00
8	Mike Piazza	2.50
9	Manny Ramirez	2.00
10	Frank Thomas	2.00
11	Mo Vaughn	.50
12	Matt Williams	.50

Rookies

		NM/M
Complete Set (10):		6.50
Common Player:		.25
1	Edgardo Alfonzo	.25
2	Jason Bates	.25
3	Marty Cordova	.25
4	Ray Durham	.25
5	Alex Gonzalez	.25
6	Shawn Green	.75
7	Charles Johnson	.25
8	Chipper Jones	1.50
9	Hideo Nomo	1.00
10	Alex Rodriguez	3.00

1996 SkyBox E-Motion XL

		NM/M
Complete Set (300):		10.00
Common Player:		.05
Pack (7):		1.00
Wax Box (24):		20.00
1	Roberto Alomar	.15
2	Brady Anderson	.05
3	Bobby Bonilla	.05
4	Jeffrey Hammonds	.05
5	Chris Hoiles	.05
6	Mike Mussina	.30
7	Randy Myers	.05
8	Rafael Palmeiro	.50
9	Cal Ripken Jr.	2.00
10	B.J. Surhoff	.05
11	Jose Canseco	.25
12	Roger Clemens	1.00

13	Wil Cordero	.05
14	Mike Greenwell	.05
15	Dwayne Hosey	.05
16	Tim Naehring	.05
17	Troy O'Leary	.05
18	Mike Stanley	.05
19	John Valentin	.05
20	Mo Vaughn	.05
21	Jim Abbott	.05
22	Garret Anderson	.05
23	George Arias	.05
24	Chili Davis	.05
25	Jim Edmonds	.05
26	Chuck Finley	.05
27	Todd Greene	.05
28	Mark Langston	.05
29	Troy Percival	.05
30	Tim Salmon	.05
31	Lee Smith	.05
32	J.T. Snow	.05
33	Harold Baines	.05
34	Jason Bere	.05
35	Ray Durham	.05
36	Alex Fernandez	.05
37	Ozzie Guillen	.05
38	Darren Lewis	.05
39	Lyle Mouton	.05
40	Tony Phillips	.05
41	Danny Tartabull	.05
42	Frank Thomas	.60
43	Robin Ventura	.05
44	Sandy Alomar	.05
45	Carlos Baerga	.05
46	Albert Belle	.05
47	Julio Franco	.05
48	Orel Hershiser	.05
49	Kenny Lofton	.05
50	Dennis Martinez	.05
51	Jack McDowell	.05
52	Jose Mesa	.05
53	Eddie Murray	.60
54	Charles Nagy	.05
55	Manny Ramirez	.05
55p	Manny Ramirez/OPS	.60
56	Jim Thome	.45
57	Omar Vizquel	.05
58	Chad Curtis	.05
59	Cecil Fielder	.05
60	Travis Fryman	.05
61	Chris Gomez	.05
62	Felipe Lira	.05
63	Alan Trammell	.05
64	Kevin Appier	.05
65	Johnny Damon	.35
66	Tom Goodwin	.05
67	Mark Gubicza	.05
68	Jeff Montgomery	.05
69	Jon Nunnally	.05
70	Bip Roberts	.05
71	Ricky Bones	.05
72	Chuck Carr	.05
73	John Jaha	.05
74	Ben McDonald	.05
75	Matt Mieske	.05
76	Dave Nilsson	.05
77	Kevin Seitzer	.05
78	Greg Vaughn	.05
79	Rick Aguilera	.05
80	Marty Cordova	.05
81	Roberto Kelly	.05
82	Chuck Knoblauch	.05
83	Pat Meares	.05
84	Paul Molitor	.60
85	Kirby Puckett	.75
86	Brad Radke	.05
87	Wade Boggs	.75
88	David Cone	.05
89	Dwight Gooden	.05
90	Derek Jeter	2.00
91	Tino Martinez	.05
92	Paul O'Neill	.05
93	Andy Pettitte	.15
94	Tim Raines	.05
95	Ruben Rivera	.05
96	Kenny Rogers	.05
97	Ruben Sierra	.05
98	John Wetteland	.05
99	Bernie Williams	.05
100	Allen Battle	.05
101	Geronimo Berroa	.05
102	Brent Gates	.05
103	Doug Johns	.05
104	Mark McGwire	1.50
105	Pedro Munoz	.05
106	Ariel Prieto	.05
107	Terry Steinbach	.05
108	Todd Van Poppel	.05
109	Chris Bosio	.05
110	Jay Buhner	.05
111	Joey Cora	.05
112	Russ Davis	.05
113	Ken Griffey Jr.	1.25
114	Sterling Hitchcock	.05
115	Randy Johnson	.60
116	Edgar Martinez	.05
117	Alex Rodriguez	1.50
118	Paul Sorrento	.05
119	Dan Wilson	.05
120	Will Clark	.05
121	Juan Gonzalez	.30
122	Rusty Greer	.05
123	Kevin Gross	.05
124	Ken Hill	.05
125	Dean Palmer	.05
126	Roger Pavlik	.05
127	Ivan Rodriguez	.50
128	Mickey Tettleton	.05
129	Joe Carter	.05
130	Carlos Delgado	.40
131	Alex Gonzalez	.05
132	Shawn Green	.25
133	Erik Hanson	.05
134	Pat Hentgen	.05
135	Otis Nixon	.05
136	John Olerud	.05
137	Ed Sprague	.05
138	Steve Avery	.05
139	Jermaine Dye	.05
140	Tom Glavine	.35
141	Marquis Grissom	.05
142	Chipper Jones	.75
143	David Justice	.05
144	Ryan Klesko	.05
145	Javier Lopez	.05
146	Greg Maddux	.75
147	Fred McGriff	.05
148	Jason Schmidt	.05
149	John Smoltz	.05
150	Mark Wohlers	.05
151	Jim Bullinger	.05
152	Frank Castillo	.05
153	Kevin Foster	.05
154	Luis Gonzalez	.05
155	Mark Grace	.05
156	Brian McRae	.05
157	Jaime Navarro	.05
158	Rey Sanchez	.05
159	Ryne Sandberg	.75
160	Sammy Sosa	.75
161	Bret Boone	.05
162	Jeff Brantley	.05
163	Vince Coleman	.05
164	Steve Gibralter	.05
165	Barry Larkin	.05
166	Hal Morris	.05
167	Mark Portugal	.05
168	Reggie Sanders	.05
169	Pete Schourek	.05
170	John Smiley	.05
171	Jason Bates	.05
172	Dante Bichette	.05
173	Ellis Burks	.05
174	Vinny Castilla	.05
175	Andres Galarraga	.05
176	Kevin Ritz	.05
177	Bill Swift	.05
178	Larry Walker	.05
179	Walt Weiss	.05
180	Eric Young	.05
181	Kurt Abbott	.05
182	Kevin Brown	.05
183	John Burkett	.05
184	Greg Colbrunn	.05
185	Jeff Conine	.05
186	Chris Hammond	.05
187	Charles Johnson	.05
188	Terry Pendleton	.05
189	Pat Rapp	.05
190	Gary Sheffield	.25
191	Quilvio Veras	.05
192	Devon White	.05
193	Jeff Bagwell	.60
194	Derek Bell	.05
195	Sean Berry	.05
196	Craig Biggio	.05
197	Doug Drabek	.05

198	Tony Eusebio	.05
199	Mike Hampton	.05
200	Brian Hunter	.05
201	Derrick May	.05
202	Orlando Miller	.05
203	Shane Reynolds	.05
204	Mike Blowers	.05
205	Tom Candiotti	.05
206	Delino DeShields	.05
207	Greg Gagne	.05
208	Karim Garcia	.05
209	Todd Hollandsworth	.05
210	Eric Karros	.05
211	Ramon Martinez	.05
212	Raul Mondesi	.05
213	Hideo Nomo	.30
214	Chan Ho Park	.05
215	Mike Piazza	1.25
216	Ismael Valdes	.05
217	Todd Worrell	.05
218	Moises Alou	.05
219	Yamil Benitez	.05
220	Jeff Fassero	.05
221	Darrin Fletcher	.05
222	Cliff Floyd	.05
223	Pedro Martinez	.60
224	Carlos Perez	.05
225	Mel Rojas	.05
226	David Segui	.05
227	Rondell White	.05
228	Rico Brogna	.05
229	Carl Everett	.05
230	John Franco	.05
231	Bernard Gilkey	.05
232	Todd Hundley	.05
233	Jason Isringhausen	.05
234	Lance Johnson	.05
235	Bobby Jones	.05
236	Jeff Kent	.05
237	Rey Ordonez	.05
238	Bill Pulsipher	.05
239	Jose Vizcaino	.05
240	Paul Wilson	.05
241	Ricky Bottalico	.05
242	Darren Daulton	.05
243	Lenny Dykstra	.05
244	Jim Eisenreich	.05
245	Sid Fernandez	.05
246	Gregg Jefferies	.05
247	Mickey Morandini	.05
248	Benito Santiago	.05
249	Curt Schilling	.35
250	Mark Whiten	.05
251	Todd Zeile	.05
252	Jay Bell	.05
253	Carlos Garcia	.05
254	Charlie Hayes	.05
255	Jason Kendall	.05
256	Jeff King	.05
257	Al Martin	.05
258	Orlando Merced	.05
259	Dan Miceli	.05
260	Denny Neagle	.05
261	Alan Benes	.05
262	Andy Benes	.05
263	Royce Clayton	.05
264	Dennis Eckersley	.50
265	Gary Gaetti	.05
266	Ron Gant	.05
267	Brian Jordan	.05
268	Ray Lankford	.05
269	John Mabry	.05
270	Tom Pagnozzi	.05
271	Ozzie Smith	.75
272	Todd Stottlemyre	.05
273	Andy Ashby	.05
274	Brad Ausmus	.05
275	Ken Caminiti	.05
276	Steve Finley	.05
277	Tony Gwynn	.75
278	Joey Hamilton	.05
279	Rickey Henderson	.60
280	Trevor Hoffman	.05
281	Wally Joyner	.05
282	Jody Reed	.05
283	Bob Tewksbury	.05
284	Fernando Valenzuela	.05
285	Rod Beck	.05
286	Barry Bonds	2.00
287	Mark Carreon	.05
288	Shawon Dunston	.05
289	Osvaldo Fernandez RC	.10
290	Glenallen Hill	.05
291	Stan Javier	.05
292	Mark Leiter	.05
293	Kirt Manwaring	.05
294	Robby Thompson	.05
295	William Van Landingham	.05
296	Allen Watson	.05
297	Matt Williams	.05
298	Checklist	.05
299	Checklist	.05
300	Checklist	.05

D-Fense

		NM/M
Complete Set (10):		9.00
Common Player:		.50
1	Roberto Alomar	.65
2	Barry Bonds	3.50
3	Mark Grace	.50
4	Ken Griffey Jr.	2.50
5	Kenny Lofton	.50
6	Greg Maddux	1.50
7	Raul Mondesi	.50
8	Cal Ripken Jr.	3.50
9	Ivan Rodriguez	1.00
10	Matt Williams	.50

Legion of Boom

		NM/M
Complete Set (12):		27.50
Common Player:		2.00
1	Albert Belle	2.00
2	Barry Bonds	6.00
3	Juan Gonzalez	2.50
4	Ken Griffey Jr.	4.00
5	Mark McGwire	5.00
6	Mike Piazza	4.00
7	Manny Ramirez	3.00
8	Tim Salmon	2.00
9	Sammy Sosa	3.50
10	Frank Thomas	3.00
11	Mo Vaughn	2.00
12	Matt Williams	2.00

N-Tense

		NM/M
Complete Set (10):		17.50
Common Player:		.50
1	Albert Belle	.50
2	Barry Bonds	3.50
3	Jose Canseco	1.00
4	Ken Griffey Jr.	3.00

5	Tony Gwynn	2.50
6	Randy Johnson	2.00
7	Greg Maddux	2.50
8	Cal Ripken Jr.	3.50
9	Frank Thomas	2.00
10	Matt Williams	.50

Rare Breed

		NM/M
Complete Set (10):		50.00
Common Player:		3.00
1	Garret Anderson	3.00
2	Marty Cordova	3.00
3	Brian Hunter	3.00
4	Jason Isringhausen	3.00
5	Charles Johnson	3.00
6	Chipper Jones	16.00
7	Raul Mondesi	3.00
8	Hideo Nomo	6.00
9	Manny Ramirez	12.00
10	Rondell White	3.00

1997 SkyBox E-X2000

		NM/M
Complete Set (100):		20.00
Common Player:		.15
Pack (2):		1.25
Wax Box (24):		20.00
1	Jim Edmonds	.15
2	Darin Erstad	.25
3	Eddie Murray	1.00
4	Roberto Alomar	.25
5	Brady Anderson	.15
6	Mike Mussina	.45
7	Rafael Palmeiro	.75
8	Cal Ripken Jr.	3.00
9	Steve Avery	.15
10	Nomar Garciaparra	1.50
11	Mo Vaughn	.15
12	Albert Belle	.15
13	Mike Cameron	.15
14	Ray Durham	.15
15	Frank Thomas	1.00
16	Robin Ventura	.15
17	Manny Ramirez	1.00
18	Jim Thome	.65
19	Matt Williams	.15
20	Tony Clark	.15
21	Travis Fryman	.15
22	Bob Higginson	.15
23	Kevin Appier	.15
24	Johnny Damon	.45
25	Jermaine Dye	.15
26	Jeff Cirillo	.15
27	Ben McDonald	.15
28	Chuck Knoblauch	.15
29	Paul Molitor	1.00
30	Todd Walker	.15
31	Wade Boggs	1.50
32	Cecil Fielder	.15
33	Derek Jeter	3.00

34	Andy Pettitte	.25
35	Ruben Rivera	.15
36	Bernie Williams	.15
37	Jose Canseco	.50
38	Mark McGwire	2.50
39	Jay Buhner	.15
40	Ken Griffey Jr.	2.00
41	Randy Johnson	1.00
42	Edgar Martinez	.15
43	Alex Rodriguez	2.50
44	Dan Wilson	.15
45	Will Clark	.40
46	Juan Gonzalez	.50
47	Ivan Rodriguez	.75
48	Joe Carter	.15
49	Roger Clemens	1.75
50	Juan Guzman	.15
51	Pat Hentgen	.15
52	Tom Glavine	.35
53	Andruw Jones	1.00
54	Chipper Jones	1.50
55	Ryan Klesko	.15
56	Kenny Lofton	.15
57	Greg Maddux	1.50
58	Fred McGriff	.15
59	John Smoltz	.15
60	Mark Wohlers	.15
61	Mark Grace	.15
62	Ryne Sandberg	1.50
63	Sammy Sosa	1.50
64	Barry Larkin	.15
65	Deion Sanders	.15
66	Reggie Sanders	.15
67	Dante Bichette	.15
68	Ellis Burks	.15
69	Andres Galarraga	.15
70	Moises Alou	.15
71	Kevin Brown	.15
72	Cliff Floyd	.15
73	Edgar Renteria	.15
74	Gary Sheffield	.50
75	Bob Abreu	.15
76	Jeff Bagwell	1.00
77	Craig Biggio	.15
78	Todd Hollandsworth	.15
79	Eric Karros	.15
80	Raul Mondesi	.15
81	Hideo Nomo	.50
82	Mike Piazza	2.00
83	Vladimir Guerrero	1.00
84	Henry Rodriguez	.15
85	Todd Hundley	.15
86	Rey Ordonez	.15
87	Alex Ochoa	.15
88	Gregg Jefferies	.15
89	Scott Rolen	.65
90	Jermaine Allensworth	.15
91	Jason Kendall	.15
92	Ken Caminiti	.15
93	Tony Gwynn	1.50
94	Rickey Henderson	1.00
95	Barry Bonds	3.00
96	J.T. Snow	.15
97	Dennis Eckersley	.75
98	Ron Gant	.15
99	Brian Jordan	.15
100	Ray Lankford	.15

Credentials

		NM/M
Common Player:		1.00
Credentials Stars:		6X
(See E-X2000 for checklist, base card values)		

Essential Credentials

		NM/M
Common Player:		3.00

Essential Credentials Stars: 10X
(See 1997 SkyBox E-X2000 for checklist and base card values.)

A Cut Above

		NM/M
Complete Set (10):		55.00
Common Player:		2.00
1	Frank Thomas	7.50
2	Ken Griffey Jr.	9.00
3	Alex Rodriguez	12.00
4	Albert Belle	2.00
5	Juan Gonzalez	4.00
6	Mark McGwire	10.00
7	Mo Vaughn	2.00
8	Manny Ramirez	7.50
9	Barry Bonds	12.00
10	Fred McGriff	2.00

Alex Rodriguez Jumbo

		NM/M
Alex Rodriguez		12.00

Emerald Autographs

		NM/M
Complete Set (6):		75.00
Common Player:		3.00
2	Darin Erstad	12.00
30	Todd Walker	5.00
43	Alex Rodriguez	60.00
78	Todd Hollandsworth	3.00
86	Alex Ochoa	3.00
89	Scott Rolen	25.00

Hall or Nothing

		NM/M
Complete Set (20):		55.00
Common Player:		1.00
1	Frank Thomas	2.50
2	Ken Griffey Jr.	5.00
3	Eddie Murray	2.50
4	Cal Ripken Jr.	7.00
5	Ryne Sandberg	4.00
6	Wade Boggs	4.00
7	Roger Clemens	4.50
8	Tony Gwynn	4.00
9	Alex Rodriguez	6.00
10	Mark McGwire	6.00
11	Barry Bonds	7.00
12	Greg Maddux	4.00
13	Juan Gonzalez	1.25
14	Albert Belle	1.00
15	Mike Piazza	5.00
16	Jeff Bagwell	2.50
17	Dennis Eckersley	1.50
18	Mo Vaughn	1.00
19	Roberto Alomar	1.00
20	Kenny Lofton	1.00

Star Date 2000

		NM/M
Complete Set (15):		10.00
Common Player:		.40
1	Alex Rodriguez	2.00
2	Andruw Jones	1.25
3	Andy Pettitte	.60
4	Brooks Kieschnick	.40
5	Chipper Jones	1.50
6	Darin Erstad	.60
7	Derek Jeter	2.50
8	Jason Kendall	.40
9	Jermaine Dye	.40
10	Neifi Perez	.40
11	Scott Rolen	.90
12	Todd Hollandsworth	.40
13	Todd Walker	.40
14	Tony Clark	.40
15	Vladimir Guerrero	1.25

1998 SkyBox Dugout Axcess

		NM/M
Complete Set (150):		12.00
Common Player:		.05
Pack (12):		1.00
Wax Box (36):		20.00
1	Travis Lee	.05
2	Matt Williams	.05
3	Andy Benes	.05
4	Chipper Jones	.75
5	Ryan Klesko	.05
6	Greg Maddux	.75
7	Sammy Sosa	.75
8	Henry Rodriguez	.05
9	Mark Grace	.05
10	Barry Larkin	.05
11	Bret Boone	.05
12	Reggie Sanders	.05
13	Vinny Castilla	.05
14	Larry Walker	.05
15	Darryl Kile	.05
16	Charles Johnson	.05
17	Edgar Renteria	.05
18	Gary Sheffield	.40
19	Jeff Bagwell	.65
20	Craig Biggio	.05
21	Moises Alou	.05
22	Mike Piazza	1.00
23	Hideo Nomo	.35
24	Raul Mondesi	.05
25	John Jaha	.05
26	Jeff Cirillo	.05
27	Jeromy Burnitz	.05
28	Mark Grudzielanek	.05
29	Vladimir Guerrero	.65
30	Rondell White	.05
31	Edgardo Alfonzo	.05
32	Rey Ordonez	.05
33	Bernard Gilkey	.05
34	Scott Rolen	.50
35	Curt Schilling	.35
36	Ricky Bottalico	.05
37	Tony Womack	.05
38	Al Martin	.05
39	Jason Kendall	.05
40	Ron Gant	.05
41	Mark McGwire	1.25
42	Ray Lankford	.05
43	Tony Gwynn	.75
44	Ken Caminiti	.05
45	Kevin Brown	.05
46	Barry Bonds	1.50
47	J.T. Snow	.05
48	Shawn Estes	.05
49	Jim Edmonds	.05
50	Tim Salmon	.05
51	Jason Dickson	.05
52	Cal Ripken Jr.	1.50
53	Mike Mussina	.35
54	Roberto Alomar	.20
55	Mo Vaughn	.05
56	Pedro Martinez	.65
57	Nomar Garciaparra	.75
58	Albert Belle	.05
59	Frank Thomas	.65
60	Robin Ventura	.05
61	Jim Thome	.60
62	Sandy Alomar Jr.	.05
63	Jaret Wright	.05
64	Bobby Higginson	.05
65	Tony Clark	.05
66	Justin Thompson	.05
67	Dean Palmer	.05
68	Kevin Appier	.05
69	Johnny Damon	.35
70	Paul Molitor	.65
71	Marty Cordova	.05
72	Brad Radke	.05
73	Derek Jeter	1.50
74	Bernie Williams	.05
75	Andy Pettitte	.25
76	Matt Stairs	.05
77	Ben Grieve	.05
78	Jason Giambi	.50
79	Randy Johnson	.65
80	Ken Griffey Jr.	1.00
81	Alex Rodriguez	1.25
82	Fred McGriff	.05
83	Wade Boggs	.75
84	Wilson Alvarez	.05
85	Juan Gonzalez	.35
86	Ivan Rodriguez	.50
87	Fernando Tatis	.05
88	Roger Clemens	.85
89	Jose Cruz Jr.	.05
90	Shawn Green	.30
91	Jeff Suppan	.05
92	Eli Marrero	.05
93	Mike Lowell RC	.50
94	Ben Grieve	.05
95	Cliff Politte	.05
96	Rolando Arrojo RC	.25
97	Mike Caruso	.05
98	Miguel Tejada	.15
99	Rod Myers	.05
100	Juan Encarnacion	.05
101	Enrique Wilson	.05
102	Brian Giles	.05
103	Magglio Ordonez RC	1.00
104	Brian Rose	.05
105	Ryan Jackson RC	.05
106	Mark Kotsay	.05
107	Desi Relaford	.05
108	A.J. Hinch	.05
109	Eric Milton	.05
110	Ricky Ledee	.05
111	Karim Garcia	.05
112	Derrek Lee	.60
113	Brad Fullmer	.05
114	Travis Lee	.05
115	Greg Norton	.05
116	Rich Butler	.05
117	Masato Yoshii RC	.25
118	Paul Konerko	.20
119	Richard Hidalgo	.05
120	Todd Helton	.60
121	Nomar Garciaparra	.40
122	Scott Rolen	.20
123	Cal Ripken Jr.	.75
124	Derek Jeter	.75
125	Mike Piazza	.45
126	Tony Gwynn	.40
127	Mark McGwire	.65
128	Kenny Lofton	.05
129	Greg Maddux	.40
130	Jeff Bagwell	.30
131	Randy Johnson	.30
132	Alex Rodriguez	.65
133	Mo Vaughn	.05
134	Chipper Jones	.40
135	Juan Gonzalez	.15
136	Tony Clark	.05
137	Fred McGriff	.05
138	Roger Clemens	.45
139	Ken Griffey Jr.	.65
140	Ivan Rodriguez	.25
141	Vinny Castilla	.05
142	Livan Hernandez	.05
143	Jose Cruz Jr.	.05
144	Andruw Jones	.30
145	Rafael Palmeiro	.50
146	Chuck Knoblauch	.05
147	Jay Buhner	.05
148	Andres Galarraga	.05
149	Frank Thomas	.35
150	Todd Hundley	.05

Inside Axcess

		NM/M
Common Player:		4.00
Inside Axcess Stars:		25X

(See 1998 SkyBox Dugout Axcess for checklist and base card values.)

Dishwashers

		NM/M
Complete Set (10):		7.00
Common Player:		.50

Inserted 1:8

D1	Greg Maddux	2.00
D2	Kevin Brown	.50
D3	Pedro Martinez	1.00
D4	Randy Johnson	1.00
D5	Curt Schilling	.75
D6	John Smoltz	.50
D7	Darryl Kile	.50

D8	Roger Clemens	2.25
D9	Andy Pettitte	.60
D10	Mike Mussina	.65

Double Header

		NM/M
Complete Set (20):		2.00
Common Player:		.05
Inserted 2:1		
DH1	Jeff Bagwell	.15
DH2	Albert Belle	.05
DH3	Barry Bonds	.40
DH4	Derek Jeter	.40
DH5	Tony Clark	.05
DH6	Nomar Garciaparra	.20
DH7	Juan Gonzalez	.10
DH8	Ken Griffey Jr.	.25
DH9	Chipper Jones	.20
DH10	Kenny Lofton	.05
DH11	Mark McGwire	.30
DH12	Mo Vaughn	.05
DH13	Mike Piazza	.25
DH14	Cal Ripken Jr.	.40
DH15	Ivan Rodriguez	.10
DH16	Scott Rolen	.10
DH17	Frank Thomas	.15
DH18	Tony Gwynn	.20
DH19	Travis Lee	.05
DH20	Jose Cruz Jr.	.05

Frequent Flyers

		NM/M
Complete Set (10):		2.50
Common Player:		.25
Inserted 1:4		
FF1	Brian Hunter	.25
FF2	Kenny Lofton	.25
FF3	Chuck Knoblauch	.25
FF4	Tony Womack	.25
FF5	Marquis Grissom	.25
FF6	Craig Biggio	.25
FF7	Barry Bonds	2.00
FF8	Tom Goodwin	.25
FF9	Delino DeShields	.25
FF10	Eric Young	.25

Gronks

		NM/M
Complete Set (10):		30.00
Common Player:		1.50
Inserted 1:72		
G1	Jeff Bagwell	3.50
G2	Albert Belle	1.50
G3	Juan Gonzalez	2.00
G4	Ken Griffey Jr.	6.00
G5	Mark McGwire	7.50
G6	Mike Piazza	6.00
G7	Frank Thomas	3.50
G8	Mo Vaughn	1.50
G9	Ken Caminiti	1.50
G10	Tony Clark	1.50

SuperHeroes

		NM/M
Complete Set (10):		10.00
Common Player:		.50
Inserted 1:20		
SH1	Barry Bonds	3.00
SH2	Andres Galarraga	1.00
SH3	Ken Griffey Jr.	1.50
SH4	Chipper Jones	1.00
SH5	Andruw Jones	.75
SH6	Hideo Nomo	.60
SH7	Cal Ripken Jr.	3.00
SH8	Alex Rodriguez	2.00
SH9	Frank Thomas	.75
SH10	Mo Vaughn	.50

Todd Helton Autograph

		NM/M
120	Todd Helton	15.00

1998 SkyBox E-X2001

		NM/M
Complete Set (100):		25.00
Common Player:		.15
Pack (2):		1.50
Wax Box (24):		25.00
1	Alex Rodriguez	2.50
2	Barry Bonds	3.00
3	Greg Maddux	1.50
4	Roger Clemens	1.75
5	Juan Gonzalez	.50
6	Chipper Jones	1.50
7	Derek Jeter	3.00
8	Frank Thomas	1.00
9	Cal Ripken Jr.	3.00
10	Ken Griffey Jr.	2.00
11	Mark McGwire	2.50
12	Hideo Nomo	.50
13	Tony Gwynn	1.50
14	Ivan Rodriguez	.75
15	Mike Piazza	2.00
16	Roberto Alomar	.30
17	Jeff Bagwell	1.00
18	Andruw Jones	1.00
19	Albert Belle	.15
20	Mo Vaughn	.15
21	Kenny Lofton	.15
22	Gary Sheffield	.40
23	Tony Clark	.15
24	Mike Mussina	.30
25	Barry Larkin	.15
26	Moises Alou	.15
27	Brady Anderson	.15
28	Andy Pettitte	.25
29	Sammy Sosa	1.50
30	Raul Mondesi	.15
31	Andres Galarraga	.15
32	Chuck Knoblauch	.15
33	Jim Thome	.65
34	Craig Biggio	.15
35	Jay Buhner	.15
36	Rafael Palmeiro	.75
37	Curt Schilling	.35
38	Tino Martinez	.15
39	Pedro Martinez	1.00
40	Jose Canseco	.50
41	Jeff Cirillo	.15
42	Dean Palmer	.15
43	Tim Salmon	.15
44	Jason Giambi	.50
45	Bobby Higginson	.15
46	Jim Edmonds	.15
47	David Justice	.15
48	John Olerud	.15
49	Ray Lankford	.15
50	Al Martin	.15
51	Mike Lieberthal	.15
52	Henry Rodriguez	.15
53	Edgar Renteria	.15
54	Eric Karros	.15
55	Marquis Grissom	.15
56	Wilson Alvarez	.15
57	Darryl Kile	.15
58	Jeff King	.15
59	Shawn Estes	.15
60	Tony Womack	.15
61	Willie Greene	.15
62	Ken Caminiti	.15
63	Vinny Castilla	.15
64	Mark Grace	.15
65	Ryan Klesko	.15
66	Robin Ventura	.15
67	Todd Hundley	.15
68	Travis Fryman	.15
69	Edgar Martinez	.15
70	Matt Williams	.15
71	Paul Molitor	1.00
72	Kevin Brown	.15
73	Randy Johnson	1.00
74	Bernie Williams	.15
75	Manny Ramirez	1.00
76	Fred McGriff	.15
77	Tom Glavine	.35
78	Carlos Delgado	.60
79	Larry Walker	.15
80	Hideki Irabu	.15
81	Ryan McGuire	.15
82	Justin Thompson	.15
83	Kevin Orie	.15
84	Jon Nunnally	.15
85	Mark Kotsay	.15
86	Todd Walker	.15
87	Jason Dickson	.15
88	Fernando Tatis	.15
89	Karim Garcia	.15
90	Ricky Ledee	.15
91	Paul Konerko	.25
92	Jaret Wright	.15
93	Darin Erstad	.30
94	Livan Hernandez	.15
95	Nomar Garciaparra	1.50
96	Jose Cruz Jr.	.15
97	Scott Rolen	.65
98	Ben Grieve	.15
99	Vladimir Guerrero	1.00
100	Travis Lee	.15

Essential Credentials Now

	NM/M
Common Player:	5.00
Kenny Lofton/21	10.00
Gary Sheffield/22	20.00
Tony Clark/23	10.00
Mike Mussina/24	30.00
Barry Larkin/25	10.00
Moises Alou/26	10.00
Brady Anderson/27	10.00
Andy Pettitte/28	15.00
Sammy Sosa/29	30.00
Raul Mondesi/30	10.00
Andres Galarraga/31	10.00
Chuck Knoblauch/32	10.00
Jim Thome/33	25.00
Craig Biggio/34	10.00
Jay Buhner/35	10.00
Rafael Palmeiro/36	25.00
Curt Schilling/37	20.00
Tino Martinez/38	10.00
Pedro Martinez/39	30.00
Jose Canseco/40	20.00
Jeff Cirillo/41	5.00
Dean Palmer/42	5.00
Tim Salmon/43	5.00
Jason Giambi/44	15.00
Bobby Higginson/45	5.00
Jim Edmonds/46	5.00
David Justice/47	5.00
John Olerud/48	5.00
Ray Lankford/49	5.00
Al Martin/50	5.00
Mike Lieberthal/51	5.00
Henry Rodriguez/52	5.00
Edgar Renteria/53	5.00
Eric Karros/54	5.00
Marquis Grissom/55	5.00
Wilson Alvarez/56	5.00
Darryl Kile/57	5.00
Jeff King/58	5.00
Shawn Estes/59	5.00
Tony Womack/60	5.00
Willie Greene/61	5.00
Ken Caminiti/62	5.00
Vinny Castilla/63	5.00
Mark Grace/64	5.00
Ryan Klesko/65	5.00
Robin Ventura/66	5.00
Todd Hundley/67	5.00
Travis Fryman/68	5.00
Edgar Martinez/69	5.00
Matt Williams/70	5.00
Paul Molitor/71	15.00
Kevin Brown/72	5.00
Randy Johnson/73	20.00
Bernie Williams/74	20.00
Manny Ramirez/75	20.00
Fred McGriff/76	5.00
Tom Glavine/77	12.00
Carlos Delgado/78	10.00
Larry Walker/79	5.00
Hideki Irabu/80	5.00
Ryan McGuire/81	5.00
Justin Thompson/82	5.00
Kevin Orie/83	5.00
Jon Nunnally/84	5.00
Mark Kotsay/85	5.00
Todd Walker/86	5.00
Jason Dickson/87	5.00
Fernando Tatis/88	5.00
Karim Garcia/89	5.00
Ricky Ledee/90	5.00
Paul Konerko/91	7.50
Jaret Wright/92	5.00
Darin Erstad/93	5.00
Livan Hernandez/94	5.00

95	Nomar Garciaparra/95	20.00
96	Jose Cruz Jr./96	5.00
97	Scott Rolen/97	10.00
98	Ben Grieve/98	5.00
99	Vladimir Guerrero/99	12.00
100	Travis Lee/100	5.00

Essential Credentials Future

		NM/M
Common Player:		5.00
1	Alex Rodriguez/100	55.00
2	Barry Bonds/99	60.00
3	Greg Maddux/98	40.00
4	Roger Clemens/97	45.00
5	Juan Gonzalez/96	15.00
6	Chipper Jones/95	40.00
7	Derek Jeter/94	55.00
8	Frank Thomas/93	35.00
9	Cal Ripken Jr./92	65.00
10	Ken Griffey Jr./91	45.00
11	Mark McGwire/90	55.00
12	Hideo Nomo/89	15.00
13	Tony Gwynn/88	25.00
14	Ivan Rodriguez/87	25.00
15	Mike Piazza/86	40.00
16	Roberto Alomar/85	15.00
17	Jeff Bagwell/84	25.00
18	Andruw Jones/83	25.00
19	Albert Belle/82	5.00
20	Mo Vaughn/81	5.00
21	Kenny Lofton/80	5.00
22	Gary Sheffield/79	12.00
23	Tony Clark/78	5.00
24	Mike Mussina/77	25.00
25	Barry Larkin/76	5.00
26	Moises Alou/75	5.00
27	Brady Anderson/74	5.00
28	Andy Pettitte/73	7.50
29	Sammy Sosa/72	40.00
30	Raul Mondesi/71	5.00
31	Andres Galarraga/70	6.00
32	Chuck Knoblauch/69	6.00
33	Jim Thome/68	20.00
34	Craig Biggio/67	6.00
35	Jay Buhner/66	6.00
36	Rafael Palmeiro/65	30.00
37	Curt Schilling/64	20.00
38	Tino Martinez/63	6.00
39	Pedro Martinez/62	32.50
40	Jose Canseco/61	30.00
41	Jeff Cirillo/60	6.00
42	Dean Palmer/59	6.00
43	Tim Salmon/58	7.50
44	Jason Giambi/57	25.00
45	Bobby Higginson/56	6.00
46	Jim Edmonds/55	6.00
47	David Justice/54	6.00
48	John Olerud/53	6.00
49	Ray Lankford/52	6.00
50	Al Martin/51	6.00
51	Mike Lieberthal/50	6.00
52	Henry Rodriguez/49	6.00
53	Edgar Renteria/48	6.00
54	Eric Karros/47	6.00
55	Marquis Grissom/46	6.00
56	Wilson Alvarez/45	6.00
57	Darryl Kile/44	6.00
58	Jeff King/43	6.00
59	Shawn Estes/42	6.00
60	Tony Womack/41	6.00
61	Willie Greene/40	6.00
62	Ken Caminiti/39	6.00
63	Vinny Castilla/38	6.00
64	Mark Grace/37	6.00
65	Ryan Klesko/36	6.00
66	Robin Ventura/35	6.00
67	Todd Hundley/34	6.00
68	Travis Fryman/33	6.00
69	Edgar Martinez/32	7.50
70	Matt Williams/31	7.50

71	Paul Molitor/30	45.00
72	Kevin Brown/29	7.50
73	Randy Johnson/28	40.00
74	Bernie Williams/27	20.00
75	Manny Ramirez/26	45.00
76	Fred McGriff/25	20.00
77	Tom Glavine/24	35.00
78	Carlos Delgado/23	35.00
79	Larry Walker/22	9.00
80	Hideki Irabu/21	9.00
81	Ryan McGuire/20	9.00
82	Justin Thompson/19	9.00
83	Kevin Orie/18	9.00
84	Jon Nunnally/17	9.00
85	Mark Kotsay/16	9.00

Cheap Seat Treats

		NM/M
Complete Set (20):		30.00
Common Player:		1.00
Inserted 1:24		
1	Frank Thomas	2.00
2	Ken Griffey Jr.	3.00
3	Mark McGwire	4.00
4	Tino Martinez	1.00
5	Larry Walker	1.00
6	Juan Gonzalez	1.50
7	Mike Piazza	3.00
8	Jeff Bagwell	2.00
9	Tony Clark	1.00
10	Albert Belle	1.00
11	Andres Galarraga	1.00
12	Jim Thome	1.50
13	Mo Vaughn	1.00
14	Barry Bonds	5.00
15	Vladimir Guerrero	2.00
16	Scott Rolen	1.25
17	Travis Lee	1.00
18	David Justice	1.00
19	Jose Cruz Jr.	1.00
20	Andruw Jones	2.00

Destination: Cooperstown

		NM/M
Complete Set (15):		375.00
Common Player:		8.00
Inserted 1:720		
1	Alex Rodriguez	40.00
2	Frank Thomas	20.00
3	Cal Ripken Jr.	50.00
4	Roger Clemens	30.00
5	Greg Maddux	25.00
6	Chipper Jones	25.00
7	Ken Griffey Jr.	35.00
8	Mark McGwire	40.00
9	Tony Gwynn	25.00
10	Mike Piazza	35.00
11	Jeff Bagwell	20.00

12	Jose Cruz Jr.	8.00
13	Derek Jeter	50.00
14	Hideo Nomo	10.00
15	Ivan Rodriguez	15.00

Kerry Wood

		NM/M
Complete Set (2):		2.00
---	Kerry Wood (Cardboard trade card.)	1.00
101	Kerry Wood (Plastic redemption card.)	4.00

Signature 2001

		NM/M
Complete Set (17):		100.00
Common Player:		3.00
Inserted 1:60		
1	Ricky Ledee	3.00
2	Derrick Gibson	3.00
3	Mark Kotsay	3.00
4	Kevin Millwood	10.00
5	Brad Fullmer	3.00
6	Todd Walker	4.00
7	Ben Grieve	3.00
8	Tony Clark	3.00
9	Jaret Wright	4.00
10	Randall Simon	3.00
11	Paul Konerko	15.00
12	Todd Helton	15.00
13	David Ortiz	30.00
14	Alex Gonzalez	4.00
15	Bobby Estalella	3.00
16	Alex Rodriguez	50.00
17	Mike Lowell	10.00

Star Date 2001

		NM/M
Complete Set (15):		5.00
Common Player:		.25
Inserted 1:12		
1	Travis Lee	.25
2	Jose Cruz Jr.	.25
3	Paul Konerko	1.00
4	Bobby Estalella	.25
5	Magglio Ordonez	1.00
6	Juan Encarnacion	.25
7	Richard Hidalgo	.25

8	Abraham Nunez	.25
9	Sean Casey	.50
10	Todd Helton	1.50
11	Brad Fullmer	.25
12	Ben Grieve	.25
13	Livan Hernandez	.25
14	Jaret Wright	.25
15	Todd Dunwoody	.25

1999 SkyBox E-X Century

		NM/M
Complete Set (120):		35.00
Common Player:		.15
Common SP (91-120):		.60
Inserted 1:2		
Pack (3):		3.00
Wax Box (18):		40.00
1	Scott Rolen	.75
2	Nomar Garciaparra	1.50
3	Mike Piazza	2.00
4	Tony Gwynn	1.50
5	Sammy Sosa	1.50
6	Alex Rodriguez	2.50
7	Vladimir Guerrero	1.00
8	Chipper Jones	1.50
9	Derek Jeter	3.00
10	Kerry Wood	.50
11	Juan Gonzalez	.50
12	Frank Thomas	1.00
13	Mo Vaughn	.15
14	Greg Maddux	1.50
15	Jeff Bagwell	1.00
16	Mark McGwire	2.50
17	Ken Griffey Jr.	2.00
18	Roger Clemens	1.75
19	Cal Ripken Jr.	3.00
20	Travis Lee	.15
21	Todd Helton	.75
22	Darin Erstad	.30
23	Pedro Martinez	1.00
24	Barry Bonds	3.00
25	Andruw Jones	1.00
26	Larry Walker	.15
27	Albert Belle	.15
28	Ivan Rodriguez	.75
29	Magglio Ordonez	.25
30	Andres Galarraga	.15
31	Mike Mussina	.35
32	Randy Johnson	1.00
33	Tom Glavine	.35
34	Barry Larkin	.15
35	Jim Thome	.75
36	Gary Sheffield	.45
37	Bernie Williams	.15
38	Carlos Delgado	.60
39	Rafael Palmeiro	.75
40	Edgar Renteria	.15
41	Brad Fullmer	.15
42	David Wells	.15
43	Dante Bichette	.15
44	Jaret Wright	.15
45	Ricky Ledee	.15
46	Ray Lankford	.15
47	Mark Grace	.15
48	Jeff Cirillo	.15
49	Rondell White	.15
50	Jeromy Burnitz	.15
51	Sean Casey	.25
52	Rolando Arrojo	.15
53	Jason Giambi	.65
54	John Olerud	.15
55	Will Clark	.15
56	Raul Mondesi	.15
57	Scott Brosius	.15
58	Bartolo Colon	.15
59	Steve Finley	.15
60	Javy Lopez	.15
61	Tim Salmon	.15
62	Roberto Alomar	.30
63	Vinny Castilla	.15
64	Craig Biggio	.15

65	Jose Guillen	.15
66	Greg Vaughn	.15
67	Jose Canseco	.40
68	Shawn Green	.50
69	Curt Schilling	.35
70	Orlando Hernandez	.15
71	Jose Cruz Jr.	.15
72	Alex Gonzalez	.15
73	Tino Martinez	.15
74	Todd Hundley	.15
75	Brian Giles	.15
76	Cliff Floyd	.15
77	Paul O'Neill	.15
78	Ken Caminiti	.15
79	Ron Gant	.15
80	Juan Encarnacion	.15
81	Ben Grieve	.15
82	Brian Jordan	.15
83	Rickey Henderson	1.00
84	Tony Clark	.15
85	Shannon Stewart	.15
86	Robin Ventura	.15
87	Todd Walker	.15
88	Kevin Brown	.15
89	Moises Alou	.15
90	Manny Ramirez	1.00
91	Gabe Alvarez	.60
92	Jeremy Giambi	.60
93	Adrian Beltre	.75
94	George Lombard	.60
95	Ryan Minor	.60
96	Kevin Witt	.60
97	Scott Hunter RC	.60
98	Carlos Guillen	.60
99	Derrick Gibson	.60
100	Trot Nixon	.75
101	Troy Glaus	3.00
102	Armando Rios	.60
103	Preston Wilson	.60
104	Pat Burrell RC	3.00
105	J.D. Drew	1.50
106	Bruce Chen	.60
107	Matt Clement	.60
108	Carlos Beltran	1.50
109	Carlos Febles	.60
110	Rob Fick	.60
111	Russell Branyan	.60
112	Roosevelt Brown RC	.60
113	Corey Koskie	.60
114	Mario Encarnacion	.60
115	Peter Tucci RC	.60
116	Eric Chavez	.75
117	Gabe Kapler	.60
118	Marlon Anderson	.60
119	A.J. Burnett RC	.75
120	Ryan Bradley	.60
---	Checklist 1-96	.05
---	Checklist 97-120/Inserts	.05

Essential Credentials Future

		NM/M
	Common Player:	7.50
1	Scott Rolen/120	10.00
2	Nomar Garciaparra/119	15.00
3	Mike Piazza/118	25.00
4	Tony Gwynn/117	20.00
5	Sammy Sosa/116	15.00
6	Alex Rodriguez/115	40.00
7	Vladimir Guerrero/114	15.00
8	Chipper Jones/113	20.00
9	Derek Jeter/112	50.00
10	Kerry Wood/111	10.00
11	Juan Gonzalez/110	10.00
12	Frank Thomas/109	25.00
13	Mo Vaughn/108	5.00
14	Greg Maddux/107	25.00
15	Jeff Bagwell/106	15.00
16	Mark McGwire/105	20.00
17	Ken Griffey Jr./104	25.00

18	Roger Clemens/103	25.00
19	Cal Ripken Jr./102	40.00
20	Travis Lee/101	5.00
21	Todd Helton/100	15.00
22	Darin Erstad/99	5.00
23	Pedro Martinez/98	15.00
24	Barry Bonds/97	40.00
25	Andruw Jones/96	10.00
26	Larry Walker/95	5.00
27	Albert Belle/94	5.00
28	Ivan Rodriguez/93	15.00
29	Magglio Ordonez/92	5.00
30	Andres Galarraga/91	5.00
31	Mike Mussina/90	10.00
32	Randy Johnson/89	20.00
33	Tom Glavine/88	15.00
34	Barry Larkin/87	8.00
35	Jim Thome/86	15.00
36	Gary Sheffield/85	15.00
37	Bernie Williams/84	5.00
38	Carlos Delgado/83	15.00
39	Rafael Palmeiro/82	10.00
40	Edgar Renteria/81	5.00
41	Brad Fullmer/80	5.00
42	David Wells/79	5.00
43	Dante Bichette/78	5.00
44	Jaret Wright/77	5.00
45	Ricky Ledee/76	5.00
46	Ray Lankford/75	5.00
47	Mark Grace/74	8.00
48	Jeff Cirillo/73	5.00
49	Rondell White/72	5.00
50	Jeromy Burnitz/71	5.00
51	Sean Casey/70	5.00
52	Rolando Arrojo/69	5.00
53	Jason Giambi/68	10.00
54	John Olerud/67	5.00
55	Will Clark/66	8.00
56	Raul Mondesi/65	5.00
57	Scott Brosius/64	5.00
58	Bartolo Colon/63	5.00
59	Steve Finley/62	5.00
60	Javy Lopez/61	5.00
61	Tim Salmon/60	5.00
62	Roberto Alomar/59	10.00
63	Vinny Castilla/58	5.00
64	Craig Biggio/57	8.00
65	Jose Guillen/56	5.00
66	Greg Vaughn/55	5.00
67	Jose Canseco/54	10.00
68	Shawn Green/53	5.00
69	Curt Schilling/52	15.00
70	Orlando Hernandez/51	5.00
71	Jose Cruz Jr./50	5.00
72	Alex Gonzalez/49	5.00
73	Tino Martinez/48	8.00
74	Todd Hundley/47	5.00
75	Brian Giles/46	5.00
76	Cliff Floyd/45	5.00
77	Paul O'Neill/44	10.00
78	Ken Caminiti/43	5.00
79	Ron Gant/42	5.00
80	Juan Encarnacion/41	8.00
81	Ben Grieve/40	5.00
82	Brian Jordan/39	5.00
83	Rickey Henderson/38	15.00
84	Tony Clark/37	5.00
85	Shannon Stewart/36	5.00
86	Robin Ventura/35	5.00
87	Todd Walker/34	5.00
88	Kevin Brown/33	5.00
89	Moises Alou/32	10.00
90	Manny Ramirez/31	25.00
91	Gabe Alvarez/30	5.00
92	Jeremy Giambi/29	5.00
93	Adrian Beltre/28	5.00
94	George Lombard/27	5.00
95	Ryan Minor/26	5.00
96	Kevin Witt/25	5.00
97	Scott Hunter/24	5.00
98	Carlos Guillen/23	10.00
99	Derrick Gibson/22	5.00
100	Trot Nixon/21	5.00

Essential Credentials Now

		NM/M
	Common Player:	7.50
21	Todd Helton/21	15.00
22	Darin Erstad/22	5.00
23	Pedro Martinez/23	20.00
24	Barry Bonds/24	50.00
25	Andruw Jones/25	10.00
26	Larry Walker/26	8.00
27	Albert Belle/27	5.00
28	Ivan Rodriguez/28	10.00
29	Magglio Ordonez/29	10.00
30	Andres Galarraga/30	5.00
31	Mike Mussina/31	10.00
32	Randy Johnson/32	15.00
33	Tom Glavine/33	10.00
34	Barry Larkin/34	5.00
35	Jim Thome/35	10.00

36	Gary Sheffield/36	10.00
37	Bernie Williams/37	10.00
38	Carlos Delgado/38	10.00
39	Rafael Palmeiro/39	10.00
40	Edgar Renteria/40	10.00
41	Brad Fullmer/41	5.00
42	David Wells/42	5.00
43	Dante Bichette/43	5.00
44	Jaret Wright/44	5.00
45	Ricky Ledee/45	5.00
46	Ray Lankford/46	5.00
47	Mark Grace/47	8.00
48	Jeff Cirillo/48	5.00
49	Rondell White/49	5.00
50	Jeromy Burnitz/50	5.00
51	Sean Casey/51	5.00
52	Rolando Arrojo/52	5.00
53	Jason Giambi/53	10.00
54	John Olerud/54	5.00
55	Will Clark/55	8.00
56	Raul Mondesi/56	5.00
57	Scott Brosius/57	5.00
58	Bartolo Colon/58	5.00
59	Steve Finley/59	5.00
60	Javy Lopez/60	5.00
61	Tim Salmon/61	5.00
62	Roberto Alomar/62	8.00
63	Vinny Castilla/63	5.00
64	Craig Biggio/64	8.00
65	Jose Guillen/65	5.00
66	Greg Vaughn/66	5.00
67	Jose Canseco/67	10.00
68	Shawn Green/68	5.00
69	Curt Schilling/69	15.00
70	Orlando Hernandez/70	5.00
71	Jose Cruz Jr./71	5.00
72	Alex Gonzalez/72	5.00
73	Tino Martinez/73	8.00
74	Todd Hundley/74	5.00
75	Brian Giles/75	5.00
76	Cliff Floyd/76	5.00
77	Paul O'Neill/77	5.00
78	Ken Caminiti/78	5.00
79	Ron Gant/79	5.00
80	Juan Encarnacion/80	5.00
81	Ben Grieve/81	5.00
82	Brian Jordan/82	5.00
83	Rickey Henderson/83	10.00
84	Tony Clark/84	5.00
85	Shannon Stewart/85	5.00
86	Robin Ventura/86	5.00
87	Todd Walker/87	5.00
88	Kevin Brown/88	5.00
89	Moises Alou/89	5.00
90	Manny Ramirez/90	15.00
91	Gabe Alvarez/91	5.00
92	Jeremy Giambi/92	5.00
93	Adrian Beltre/93	5.00
94	George Lombard/94	5.00
95	Ryan Minor/95	5.00
96	Kevin Witt/96	5.00
97	Scott Hunter/97	5.00
98	Carlos Guillen/98	8.00
99	Derrick Gibson/99	5.00
100	Trot Nixon/100	5.00
101	Troy Glaus/101	8.00
102	Armando Rios/102	5.00
103	Preston Wilson/103	5.00
104	Pat Burrell/104	5.00
105	J.D. Drew/105	5.00
106	Bruce Chen/106	5.00
107	Matt Clement/107	5.00
108	Carlos Beltran/108	10.00
109	Carlos Febles/109	5.00
110	Rob Fick/110	5.00
111	Russell Branyan/111	5.00
112	Roosevelt Brown/112	5.00
113	Corey Koskie/113	5.00
114	Mario Encarnacion/114	5.00
115	Peter Tucci/115	5.00
116	Eric Chavez/116	8.00
117	Gabe Kapler/117	5.00
118	Marlon Anderson/118	5.00

119	A.J. Burnett/119	5.00
120	Ryan Bradley/120	5.00

Authen-Kicks

Travis Lee

		NM/M
	Common Player:	2.50
(1)	J.D. Drew/160	8.00
(1ab)	J.D. Drew/8 (Autographed black.)	75.00
(1ar)	J.D. Drew/8 (Autographed red.)	75.00
(2)	Travis Lee/175	4.00
(3)	Kevin Millwood/160	6.00
(4)	Bruce Chen/205	4.00
(5)	Troy Glaus/205	10.00
(6)	Todd Helton/205	15.00
(7)	Ricky Ledee/180	4.00
(8)	Scott Rolen/205	15.00
(9)	Jeremy Giambi/205	4.00

E-X Quisite

		NM/M
	Complete Set (15):	15.00
	Common Player:	.50
	Inserted 1:18	
1	Troy Glaus	3.00
2	J.D. Drew	2.00
3	Pat Burrell	2.00
4	Russell Branyan	.50
5	Kerry Wood	1.50
6	Eric Chavez	1.00
7	Ben Grieve	.50
8	Gabe Kapler	.50
9	Adrian Beltre	1.00
10	Todd Helton	4.00
11	Roosevelt Brown	.50
12	Marlon Anderson	.50
13	Jeremy Giambi	.50
14	Magglio Ordonez	1.50
15	Travis Lee	.50

Favorites for Fenway

		NM/M
	Complete Set (20):	45.00
	Common Player:	1.00
	Inserted 1:36	
1	Mo Vaughn	1.00
2	Nomar Garciaparra	2.00
3	Frank Thomas	2.00
4	Ken Griffey Jr.	3.00
5	Roger Clemens	2.50
6	Alex Rodriguez	4.00
7	Derek Jeter	5.00
8	Juan Gonzalez	1.50
9	Cal Ripken Jr.	5.00
10	Ivan Rodriguez	1.50
11	J.D. Drew	1.50
12	Barry Bonds	5.00
13	Tony Gwynn	2.00

14	Vladimir Guerrero	2.00
15	Chipper Jones	2.00
16	Kerry Wood	1.50
17	Mike Piazza	3.00
18	Sammy Sosa	2.00
19	Scott Rolen	1.50
20	Mark McGwire	4.00

Milestones of the Century

Roger Clemens

		NM/M
Common Player:		5.00

Numbered to featured milestone.

1	Kerry Wood/20	15.00
2	Mark McGwire/70	20.00
3	Sammy Sosa/66	15.00
4	Ken Griffey Jr./350	15.00
5	Roger Clemens/98	25.00
6	Cal Ripken Jr./17	100.00
7	Alex Rodriguez/40	40.00
8	Barry Bonds/400	25.00
9	N.Y. Yankees/114	15.00
10	Travis Lee/98	5.00

1999 SkyBox Molten Metal

Carlos Beltran No. 36

		NM/M
Complete Set (150):		35.00
Common Metalsmiths (1-100):		.15
Inserted 4:1		
Common Heavy Metal (101-130):		.25
Inserted 1:1		
Common Supernatural (131-150):		.50
Inserted 1:2		
Pack (6):		1.00
Wax Box (24):		20.00
1	Larry Walker	.15
2	Jose Canseco	.50
3	Brian Jordan	.15
4	Rafael Palmeiro	.65
5	Edgar Renteria	.15
6	Dante Bichette	.15
7	Mark Kotsay	.15
8	Denny Neagle	.15
9	Ellis Burks	.15
10	Paul O'Neill	.15
11	Miguel Tejada	.30
12	Ken Caminiti	.15
13	David Cone	.15
14	Jason Kendall	.15
15	Ruben Rivera	.15
16	Todd Walker	.15
17	Bobby Higginson	.15
18	Derrek Lee	.60
19	Rondell White	.15
20	Pedro J. Martinez	.75

21	Jeff Kent	.15
22	Randy Johnson	.75
23	Matt Williams	.15
24	Sean Casey	.25
25	Eric Davis	.15
26	Ryan Klesko	.15
27	Curt Schilling	.35
28	Geoff Jenkins	.15
29	Armand Abreu	.15
30	Vinny Castilla	.15
31	Will Clark	.15
32	Ray Durham	.15
33	Ray Lankford	.15
34	Richie Sexson	.15
35	Derrick Gibson	.15
36	Mark Grace	.15
37	Greg Vaughn	.15
38	Bartolo Colon	.15
39	Steve Finley	.15
40	Chuck Knoblauch	.15
41	Ricky Ledee	.15
42	John Smoltz	.15
43	Moises Alou	.15
44	Jim Edmonds	.15
45	Cliff Floyd	.15
46	Javy Lopez	.15
47	Jim Thome	.65
48	J.T. Snow	.15
49	Sandy Alomar Jr.	.15
50	Andy Pettitte	.25
51	Juan Encarnacion	.15
52	Travis Fryman	.15
53	Eli Marrero	.15
54	Jeff Cirillo	.15
55	Brady Anderson	.15
56	Jose Cruz Jr.	.15
57	Edgar Martinez	.15
58	Garret Anderson	.15
59	Paul Konerko	.30
60	Eric Milton	.15
61	Jason Giambi	.45
62	Tom Glavine	.35
63	Justin Thompson	.15
64	Brad Fullmer	.15
65	Marquis Grissom	.15
66	Fernando Tatis	.15
67	Carlos Beltran	.45
68	Charles Johnson	.15
69	Raul Mondesi	.15
70	Richard Hildalgo	.15
71	Barry Larkin	.15
72	David Wells	.15
73	Jay Buhner	.15
74	Matt Clement	.15
75	Eric Karros	.15
76	Carl Pavano	.15
77	Mariano Rivera	.25
78	Livan Hernandez	.15
79	A.J. Hinch	.15
80	Tino Martinez	.15
81	Rusty Greer	.15
82	Jose Guillen	.15
83	Robin Ventura	.15
84	Kevin Brown	.15
85	Chan Ho Park	.15
86	John Olerud	.15
87	Johnny Damon	.35
88	Todd Hundley	.15
89	Fred McGriff	.15
90	Wade Boggs	1.00
91	Mike Cameron	.15
92	Gary Sheffield	.50
93	Rickey Henderson	.75
94	Pat Hentgen	.15
95	Omar Vizquel	.15
96	Craig Biggio	.15
97	Mike Caruso	.15
98	Neifi Perez	.15
99	Mike Mussina	.50
100	Carlos Delgado	.45
101	Andruw Jones	1.00
102	Pat Burrell RC	3.00
103	Orlando Hernandez	.25
104	Darin Erstad	.40
105	Roberto Alomar	.35
106	Tim Salmon	.25
107	Albert Belle	.25
108	Chad Allen RC	.25
109	Travis Lee	.25
110	Jesse Garcia RC	.25
111	Tony Clark	.25
112	Ivan Rodriguez	.75
113	Troy Glaus	1.00
114	A.J. Burnett RC	1.50
115	David Justice	.25
116	Adrian Beltre	.50
117	Eric Chavez	.35
118	Kenny Lofton	.25
119	Michael Barrett	.25
120	Jeff Weaver RC	1.50
121	Manny Ramirez	1.00
122	Barry Bonds	2.00
123	Bernie Williams	.25
124	Freddy Garcia RC	1.50

125	Scott Hunter RC	.25
126	Jeremy Giambi	.25
127	Masao Kida RC	.25
128	Todd Helton	1.00
129	Mike Figga	.25
130	Mo Vaughn	.25
131	J.D. Drew	.65
132	Cal Ripken Jr.	3.00
133	Ken Griffey Jr.	1.50
134	Mark McGwire	2.00
135	Nomar Garciaparra	1.00
136	Greg Maddux	1.00
137	Mike Piazza	1.50
138	Alex Rodriguez	2.00
139	Frank Thomas	.85
140	Juan Gonzalez	.65
141	Tony Gwynn	1.00
142	Derek Jeter	3.00
143	Chipper Jones	1.00
144	Scott Rolen	.65
145	Sammy Sosa	1.00
146	Kerry Wood	.50
147	Roger Clemens	1.25
148	Jeff Bagwell	.75
149	Vladimir Guerrero	.75
150	Ben Grieve	.50

Xplosion

MIKE FIGGA

		NM/M
Complete Set (150):		300.00
Common Player:		1.00
Stars:		3X

Inserted 1:2
(See 1999 SkyBox Molten Metal for checklist and base card values.)

Fusion

MANNY Ramirez cleveland indians

		NM/M
Complete Set (50):		100.00
Common Heavy Metal (1-30):		1.00
Inserted 1:12		
Common Supernatural (31-50):		2.50
Inserted 1:24		
Sterling (31-50):		1.5X
Production 500 Sets		
Titanium (31-50):		6X
Production 50 Sets		
1	Andruw Jones	4.00
2	Pat Burrell	2.00
3	Orlando Hernandez	1.00
4	Darin Erstad	1.50
5	Roberto Alomar	1.50
6	Tim Salmon	1.00
7	Albert Belle	1.00
8	Chad Allen	1.00
9	Travis Lee	1.00
10	Jesse Garcia	1.00
11	Tony Clark	1.00
12	Ivan Rodriguez	3.00
13	Troy Glaus	3.00

14	A.J. Burnett	1.00
15	David Justice	1.00
16	Adrian Beltre	1.50
17	Eric Chavez	1.50
18	Kenny Lofton	1.00
19	Michael Barrett	1.00
20	Jeff Weaver	1.00
21	Manny Ramirez	4.00
22	Barry Bonds	10.00
23	Bernie Williams	1.00
24	Freddy Garcia	1.00
25	Scott Hunter	1.00
26	Jeremy Giambi	1.00
27	Masao Kida	1.00
28	Todd Helton	3.00
29	Mike Figga	1.00
30	Mo Vaughn	1.00
31	J.D. Drew	2.00
32	Cal Ripken Jr.	10.00
33	Ken Griffey Jr.	6.00
34	Mark McGwire	7.50
35	Nomar Garciaparra	5.00
36	Greg Maddux	5.00
37	Mike Piazza	6.00
38	Alex Rodriguez	7.50
39	Frank Thomas	4.00
40	Juan Gonzalez	1.50
41	Tony Gwynn	5.00
42	Derek Jeter	10.00
43	Chipper Jones	5.00
44	Scott Rolen	3.00
45	Sammy Sosa	5.00
46	Kerry Wood	2.00
47	Roger Clemens	5.50
48	Jeff Bagwell	4.00
49	Vladimir Guerrero	4.00
50	Ben Grieve	1.00

Fusion - Sterling

Beltre

		NM/M
Common Player:		1.50
Sterling Stars:		1.5X

(See 1999 Molten Metal Fusion for checklist and base card values.)

Fusion - Titanium

TONY Gwynn san diego - padres

		NM/M
Common Player:		4.00
Titanium Stars:		6X

(See 1999 SkyBox Molten Metal Fusion for checklist and base card values.)

Oh Atlanta!

		NM/M
Complete Set (30):		30.00
Common Player:		.60
Inserted 1:1		
1	Kenny Lofton	.60
2	Kevin Millwood	.60
3	Bret Boone	.60
4	Otis Nixon	.60

5	Vinny Castilla	.60
6	Brian Jordan	.60
7	Chipper Jones	8.00
8	Dave Justice	.60
9	Micah Bowie	.60
10	Fred McGriff	.60
11	Ron Gant	.60
12	Andruw Jones	4.00
13	Kent Mercker	.60
14	Greg McMichael	.60
15	Steve Avery	.60
16	Marquis Grissom	.60
17	Jason Schmidt	.60
18	Ryan Klesko	.60
19	Charlie O'Brien	.60
20	Terry Pendleton	.60
21	Denny Neagle	.60
22	Greg Maddux	8.00
23	Tom Glavine	1.50
24	Javy Lopez	.60
25	John Rocker	.60
26	Walt Weiss	.60
27	John Smoltz	.60
28	Michael Tucker	.60
29	Odalis Perez	.60
30	Andres Galarraga	.60

1999 SkyBox Premium

		NM/M
Complete Set (300):		20.00
Complete Set w/SP's (350):		40.00
Common Player:		.10
Common SP (223-272):		.60
SP's inserted 1:8		
Pack (8):		1.50
Wax Box (24):		25.00
1	Alex Rodriguez	2.00
2	Sidney Ponson	.10
3	Shawn Green	.35
4	Dan Wilson	.10
5	Rolando Arrojo	.10
6	Roberto Alomar	.30
7	Matt Anderson	.10
8	David Segui	.10
9	Alex Gonzalez	.10
10	Edgar Renteria	.10
11	Benito Santiago	.10
12	Todd Stottlemyre	.10
13	Rico Brogna	.10
14	Troy Glaus	.65
15	Al Leiter	.10
16	Pedro J. Martinez	.75
17	Paul O'Neill	.10
18	Manny Ramirez	.75
19	Scott Rolen	.65
20	Curt Schilling	.35
21	Bobby Abreu	.15
22	Robb Nen	.10
23	Andy Pettitte	.25
24	John Wetteland	.10

25	Bobby Bonilla	.10
26	Darin Erstad	.20
27	Shawn Estes	.10
28	John Franco	.10
29	Nomar Garciaparra	1.00
30	Rick Helling	.10
31	David Justice	.10
32	Chuck Knoblauch	.10
33	Quinton McCracken	.10
34	Kenny Rogers	.10
35	Brian Giles	.10
36	Armando Benitez	.10
37	Trevor Hoffman	.10
38	Charles Johnson	.10
39	Travis Lee	.10
40	Tom Glavine	.35
41	Rondell White	.10
42	Orlando Hernandez	.10
43	Mickey Morandini	.10
44	Darryl Kile	.10
45	Greg Vaughn	.10
46	Gregg Jefferies	.10
47	Mark McGwire	2.00
48	Kerry Wood	.40
49	Jeromy Burnitz	.10
50	Ron Gant	.10
51	Vinny Castilla	.10
52	Doug Glanville	.10
53	Juan Guzman	.10
54	Dustin Hermanson	.10
55	Jose Hernandez	.10
56	Bob Higginson	.10
57	A.J. Hinch	.10
58	Randy Johnson	.75
59	Eli Marrero	.10
60	Rafael Palmeiro	.65
61	Carl Pavano	.10
62	Brett Tomko	.10
63	Jose Guillen	.10
64	Mike Lieberthal	.10
65	Jim Abbott	.10
66	Dante Bichette	.10
67	Jeff Cirillo	.10
68	Eric Davis	.10
69	Delino DeShields	.10
70	Steve Finley	.10
71	Mark Grace	.10
72	Jason Kendall	.10
73	Jeff Kent	.10
74	Desi Relaford	.10
75	Ivan Rodriguez	.65
76	Shannon Stewart	.10
77	Geoff Jenkins	.10
78	Ben Grieve	.10
79	Cliff Floyd	.10
80	Jason Giambi	.50
81	Rod Beck	.10
82	Derek Bell	.10
83	Will Clark	.10
84	David Dellucci	.10
85	Joey Hamilton	.10
86	Livan Hernandez	.10
87	Barry Larkin	.10
88	Matt Mantei	.10
89	Dean Palmer	.10
90	Chan Ho Park	.10
91	Jim Thome	.65
92	Miguel Tejada	.20
93	Justin Thompson	.10
94	David Wells	.10
95	Bernie Williams	.10
96	Jeff Bagwell	.75
97	Derrek Lee	.50
98	Devon White	.10
99	Jeff Shaw	.10
100	Brad Radke	.10
101	Mark Grudzielanek	.10
102	Javy Lopez	.10
103	Mike Sirotka	.10
104	Robin Ventura	.10
105	Andy Ashby	.10
106	Juan Gonzalez	.40
107	Albert Belle	.10
108	Andy Benes	.10
109	Jay Buhner	.10
110	Ken Caminiti	.10
111	Roger Clemens	1.25
112	Mike Hampton	.10
113	Pete Harnisch	.10
114	Mike Piazza	1.50
115	J.T. Snow	.10
116	John Olerud	.10
117	Tony Womack	.10
118	Todd Zeile	.10
119	Tony Gwynn	1.00
120	Brady Anderson	.10
121	Sean Casey	.20
122	Jose Cruz Jr.	.10
123	Carlos Delgado	.50
124	Edgar Martinez	.10
125	Jose Mesa	.10
126	Shane Reynolds	.10
127	John Valentin	.10
128	Mo Vaughn	.10

129	Kevin Young	.10
130	Jay Bell	.10
131	Aaron Boone	.10
132	John Smoltz	.10
133	Mike Stanley	.10
134	Bret Saberhagen	.10
135	Tim Salmon	.10
136	Mariano Rivera	.15
137	Ken Griffey Jr.	1.50
138	Jose Offerman	.10
139	Troy Percival	.10
140	Greg Maddux	1.00
141	Frank Thomas	.75
142	Steve Avery	.10
143	Kevin Millwood	.10
144	Sammy Sosa	1.00
145	Larry Walker	.10
146	Matt Williams	.10
147	Mike Caruso	.10
148	Todd Helton	.65
149	Andruw Jones	.75
150	Ray Lankford	.10
151	Craig Biggio	.10
152	Ugueth Urbina	.10
153	Wade Boggs	1.00
154	Derek Jeter	2.50
155	Wally Joyner	.10
156	Mike Mussina	.30
157	Gregg Olson	.10
158	Henry Rodriguez	.10
159	Reggie Sanders	.10
160	Fernando Tatis	.10
161	Dmitri Young	.10
162	Rick Aguilera	.10
163	Marty Cordova	.10
164	Johnny Damon	.30
165	Ray Durham	.10
166	Brad Fullmer	.10
167	Chipper Jones	1.00
168	Bobby Smith	.10
169	Omar Vizquel	.10
170	Todd Hundley	.10
171	David Cone	.10
172	Royce Clayton	.10
173	Ryan Klesko	.10
174	Jeff Montgomery	.10
175	Magglio Ordonez	.10
176	Billy Wagner	.10
177	Masato Yoshii	.10
178	Jason Christiansen	.10
179	Chuck Finley	.10
180	Tom Gordon	.10
181	Wilton Guerrero	.10
182	Rickey Henderson	.75
183	Sterling Hitchcock	.10
184	Kenny Lofton	.10
185	Tino Martinez	.10
186	Fred McGriff	.10
187	Matt Stairs	.10
188	Neifi Perez	.10
189	Bob Wickman	.10
190	Barry Bonds	2.50
191	Jose Canseco	.40
192	Damion Easley	.10
193	Jim Edmonds	.10
194	Juan Encarnacion	.10
195	Travis Fryman	.10
196	Tom Goodwin	.10
197	Rusty Greer	.10
198	Roberto Hernandez	.10
199	B.J. Surhoff	.10
200	Scott Brosius	.10
201	Brian Jordan	.10
202	Paul Konerko	.20
203	Ismael Valdes	.10
204	Eric Milton	.10
205	Adrian Beltre	.25
206	Tony Clark	.10
207	Bartolo Colon	.10
208	Cal Ripken Jr.	2.50
209	Moises Alou	.10
210	Wilson Alvarez	.10
211	Kevin Brown	.10
212	Orlando Cabrera	.10
213	Vladimir Guerrero	.75
214	Jose Rosado	.10
215	Raul Mondesi	.10
216	Dave Nilsson	.10
217	Carlos Perez	.10
218	Jason Schmidt	.10
219	Richie Sexson	.10
220	Gary Sheffield	.40
221	Fernando Vina	.10
222	Todd Walker	.10
223	Scott Sauerbeck RC	.10
223	Scott Sauerbeck/SP RC	.60
224	Pascual Matos RC	.10
224	Pascual Matos/SP RC	.60
225	Kyle Farnsworth RC	.15
225	Kyle Farnsworth/SP RC	.60
226	Freddy Garcia RC	.75
226	Freddy Garcia/SP RC	1.50
227	David Lundquist RC	.10
227	David Lundquist/SP RC	.60

228	Jolbert Cabrera RC	.10
228	Jolbert Cabrera/SP RC	.60
229	Dan Perkins RC	.10
229	Dan Perkins/SP RC	.60
230	Warren Morris	.10
230	Warren Morris/SP	.60
231	Carlos Febles	.10
231	Carlos Febles/SP	.60
232	Brett Hinchliffe RC	.10
232	Brett Hinchliffe/SP RC	.60
233	Jason Phillips RC	.10
233	Jason Phillips/SP RC	.60
234	Glen Barker RC	.10
234	Glen Barker/SP RC	.60
235	Jose Macias RC	.25
235	Jose Macias/SP RC	1.00
236	Joe Mays RC	.10
236	Joe Mays/SP RC	.60
237	Chad Allen RC	.10
237	Chad Allen/SP RC	.60
238	Miguel Del Toro RC	.10
238	Miguel Del Toro/SP RC	.60
239	Chris Singleton	.10
239	Chris Singleton/SP	.60
240	Jesse Garcia RC	.10
240	Jesse Garcia/SP	.60
241	Kris Benson	.10
241	Kris Benson/SP	.60
242	Clay Bellinger RC	.10
242	Clay Bellinger/SP RC	.60
243	Scott Williamson	.10
243	Scott Williamson/SP	.60
244	Masao Kida RC	.10
244	Masao Kida/SP RC	.60
245	Guillermo Garcia RC	.10
245	Guillermo Garcia/SP RC	.60
246	A.J. Burnett RC	.25
246	A.J. Burnett/SP RC	1.50
247	Bo Porter RC	.10
247	Bo Porter/SP RC	.60
248	Pat Burrell RC	1.50
248	Pat Burrell/SP RC	4.00
249	Carlos Lee	.50
249	Carlos Lee/SP	1.50
250	Jeff Weaver RC	.50
250	Jeff Weaver/SP RC	1.50
251	Ruben Mateo	.10
251	Ruben Mateo/SP	.60
252	J.D. Drew	.40
252	J.D. Drew/SP	2.00
253	Jeremy Giambi	.10
253	Jeremy Giambi/SP	.60
254	Gary Bennett RC	.10
254	Gary Bennett/SP RC	.60
255	Edwards Guzman RC	.10
255	Edwards Guzman/ SP RC	.60
256	Ramon Martinez	.10
256	Ramon Martinez/SP	.60
257	Giomar Guevara RC	.10
257	Giomar Guevara/ SP RC	.60
258	Joe McEwing RC	.10
258	Joe McEwing/SP RC	.60
259	Tom Davey RC	.10
259	Tom Davey/SP RC	.60
260	Gabe Kapler	.10
260	Gabe Kapler/SP	.60
261	Ryan Rupe RC	.10
261	Ryan Rupe/SP RC	.60
262	Kelly Dransfeldt RC	.10
262	Kelly Dransfeldt/ SP RC	.60
263	Michael Barrett	.10
263	Michael Barrett/SP	.60
264	Eric Chavez	.25
264	Eric Chavez/SP	1.00
265	Orber Moreno RC	.10
265	Orber Moreno/SP RC	.60
266	Marlon Anderson	.10
266	Marlon Anderson/SP	.60
267	Carlos Beltran	.50
267	Carlos Beltran/SP	1.50
268	Doug Mientkiewicz	.10
268	Doug Mientkiewicz/SP	.60
269	Roy Halladay	.10
269	Roy Halladay/SP	.60
270	Torii Hunter	.10
270	Torii Hunter/SP	.60
271	Stan Spencer	.10
271	Stan Spencer/SP	.60
272	Alex Gonzalez	.10
272	Alex Gonzalez/SP	.60
273	Mark McGwire	1.00
274	Scott Rolen	.30
275	Jeff Bagwell	.40
276	Derek Jeter	1.50
277	Tony Gwynn	.50
278	Frank Thomas	.40
279	Sammy Sosa	.50
280	Nomar Garciaparra	.50
281	Cal Ripken Jr.	1.50
282	Albert Belle	.10

283	Kerry Wood	.20
284	Greg Maddux	.50
285	Barry Bonds	1.50
286	Juan Gonzalez	.25
287	Ken Griffey Jr.	.75
288	Alex Rodriguez	1.00
289	Ben Grieve	.10
290	Travis Lee	.10
291	Mo Vaughn	.10
292	Mike Piazza	.85
293	Roger Clemens	.60
294	J.D. Drew	.20
295	Randy Johnson	.40
296	Chipper Jones	.50
297	Vladimir Guerrero	.40
298	Nomar Garciaparra Checklist	.40
299	Ken Griffey Jr. Checklist	.50
300	Mark McGwire Checklist	.60

Star Rubies

Star Rubies:	50X
Production 50 Sets	
SP Star Rubies:	15X
Production 15 Sets	

(See 1999 SkyBox Premium for checklist and base card values.)

Autographics

	NM/M
Common Player:	3.00
Inserted 1:68	
Blue Ink:	1.5X
Production 50 Sets	
Roberto Alomar	15.00
Paul Bako	3.00
Michael Barrett	8.00
Kris Benson	8.00
Micah Bowie	3.00
Roosevelt Brown	3.00
A.J. Burnett	8.00
Pat Burrell	15.00
Ken Caminiti	15.00
Royce Clayton	3.00
Edgard Clemente	3.00
Bartolo Colon	10.00
J.D. Drew	15.00
Damion Easley	5.00
Derrin Ebert	3.00
Mario Encarnacion	3.00
Juan Encarnacion	5.00
Troy Glaus	15.00
Tom Glavine	20.00
Juan Gonzalez/SP	50.00
Shawn Green	10.00
Wilton Guerrero	3.00
Jose Guillen	8.00
Tony Gwynn	30.00
Mark Harriger	3.00
Bobby Higginson	3.00

	Todd Hollandsworth	3.00
	Scott Hunter	3.00
	Gabe Kapler	3.00
	Scott Karl	3.00
	Mike Kinkade	3.00
	Ray Lankford	3.00
	Barry Larkin	15.00
	Matt Lawton	5.00
	Ricky Ledee	3.00
	Travis Lee	3.00
	Eli Marrero	5.00
	Ruben Mateo	3.00
	Joe McEwing	5.00
	Doug Mientkiewicz	4.00
	Russ Ortiz	5.00
	Jim Parque	3.00
	Robert Person	3.00
	Alex Rodriguez	80.00
	Scott Rolen	20.00
	Benj Sampson	3.00
	Luis Saturria	3.00
	Curt Schilling	35.00
	David Segui	3.00
	Fernando Tatis	3.00
	Peter Tucci	3.00
	Javier Vasquez	6.00
	Robin Ventura	10.00

Diamond Debuts

	NM/M
Complete Set (15):	17.50
Common Player:	2.00
Inserted 1:49	
1 Eric Chavez	3.00
2 Kyle Farnsworth	2.00
3 Ryan Rupe	2.00
4 Jeremy Giambi	2.00
5 Marlon Anderson	2.00
6 J.D. Drew	4.00
7 Carlos Febles	2.00
8 Joe McEwing	2.00
9 Jeff Weaver	2.00
10 Alex Gonzalez	2.00
11 Chad Allen	2.00
12 Michael Barrett	2.00
13 Gabe Kapler	2.00
14 Carlos Lee	2.00
15 Edwards Guzman	2.00

Intimidation Nation

	NM/M
Complete Set (15):	280.00
Common Player:	12.00
Production 99 Sets	
1 Cal Ripken Jr.	40.00
2 Tony Gwynn	20.00
3 Nomar Garciaparra	20.00
4 Frank Thomas	15.00
5 Mike Piazza	25.00
6 Mark McGwire	30.00
7 Scott Rolen	12.00
8 Chipper Jones	20.00
9 Greg Maddux	20.00
10 Ken Griffey Jr.	25.00
11 Juan Gonzalez	12.00
12 Derek Jeter	40.00
13 J.D. Drew	12.00
14 Roger Clemens	22.50
15 Alex Rodriguez	30.00

Live Bats

	NM/M
Complete Set (15):	10.00
Common Player:	.25
Inserted 1:7	
1 Juan Gonzalez	.35
2 Mark McGwire	1.50
3 Jeff Bagwell	.50
4 Frank Thomas	.50
5 Mike Piazza	1.00
6 Nomar Garciaparra	.75
7 Alex Rodriguez	1.50
8 Scott Rolen	.40

9	Travis Lee	.25
10	Tony Gwynn	.75
11	Derek Jeter	2.00
12	Ben Grieve	.25
13	Chipper Jones	.75
14	Ken Griffey Jr.	1.00
15	Cal Ripken Jr.	2.00

Show Business

	NM/M
Complete Set (15):	60.00
Common Player:	2.00
Inserted 1:70	
1 Mark McGwire	7.50
2 Tony Gwynn	5.00
3 Nomar Garciaparra	5.00
4 Juan Gonzalez	2.50
5 Roger Clemens	5.00
6 Chipper Jones	5.00
7 Cal Ripken Jr.	10.00
8 Alex Rodriguez	7.50
9 Orlando Hernandez	2.00
10 Greg Maddux	5.00
11 Mike Piazza	6.00
12 Frank Thomas	4.00
13 Ken Griffey Jr.	6.00
14 Scott Rolen	3.00
15 Derek Jeter	10.00

Soul of The Game

	NM/M
Complete Set (15):	15.00
Common Player:	.60
Inserted 1:14	
1 Alex Rodriguez	2.00
2 Vladimir Guerrero	.90
3 Chipper Jones	1.25
4 Derek Jeter	2.50
5 Tony Gwynn	1.25
6 Scott Rolen	.60

7	Juan Gonzalez	.60
8	Mark McGwire	2.00
9	Ken Griffey Jr.	1.50
10	Jeff Bagwell	.90
11	Cal Ripken Jr.	2.50
12	Frank Thomas	.90
13	Mike Piazza	1.50
14	Nomar Garciaparra	1.25
15	Sammy Sosa	1.25

1999 SkyBox Thunder

	NM/M
Complete Set (300):	15.00
Common Player (1-240):	.05
Common Player (241-300):	.15
Raves:	15X
Production 150 Sets	
SuperRaves:	45X
Production 25 Sets	
Pack (8):	1.50
Wax Box (36):	25.00

1	John Smoltz	.05
2	Garret Anderson	.05
3	Matt Williams	.05
4	Daryle Ward	.05
5	Andy Ashby	.05
6	Miguel Tejada	.15
7	Dmitri Young	.05
8	Roberto Alomar	.25
9	Kevin Brown	.05
10	Eric Young	.05
11	Odalis Perez	.05
12	Preston Wilson	.05
13	Jeff Abbott	.05
14	Bret Boone	.05
15	Mendy Lopez	.05
16	B.J. Surhoff	.05
17	Steve Woodard	.05
18	Ron Coomer	.05
19	Rondell White	.05
20	Edgardo Alfonzo	.05
21	Kevin Millwood	.05
22	Jose Canseco	.45
23	Blake Stein	.05
24	Quivilo Veras	.05
25	Chuck Knoblauch	.05
26	David Segui	.05
27	Eric Davis	.05
28	Francisco Cordova	.05
29	Randy Winn	.05
30	Will Clark	.05
31	Billy Wagner	.05
32	Kevin Witt	.05
33	Jim Edmonds	.05
34	Todd Stottlemyre	.05
35	Shane Andrews	.05
36	Michael Tucker	.05
37	Sandy Alomar Jr.	.05
38	Neifi Perez	.05
39	Jaret Wright	.05
40	Devon White	.05
41	Edgar Renteria	.05
42	Shane Reynolds	.05
43	Jeff King	.05
44	Darren Dreifort	.05
45	Fernando Vina	.05
46	Marty Cordova	.05
47	Ugueth Urbina	.05
48	Bobby Bonilla	.05
49	Omar Vizquel	.05
50	Tom Gordon	.05
51	Ryan Christenson	.05
52	Aaron Boone	.05
53	Jamie Moyer	.05
54	Brian Giles	.05
55	Kevin Tapani	.05
56	Scott Brosius	.05
57	Ellis Burks	.05
58	Al Leiter	.05
59	Royce Clayton	.05
60	Chris Carpenter	.05
61	Bubba Trammell	.05
62	Tom Glavine	.35
63	Shannon Stewart	.05

64	Todd Zeile	.05
65	J.T. Snow	.05
66	Matt Clement	.05
67	Matt Stairs	.05
68	Ismael Valdes	.05
69	Todd Walker	.05
70	Jose Lima	.05
71	Mike Caruso	.05
72	Brett Tomko	.05
73	Mike Lansing	.05
74	Justin Thompson	.05
75	Damion Easley	.05
76	Derek Lee	.50
77	Derek Bell	.05
78	Brady Anderson	.05
79	Charles Johnson	.05
80	Rafael Roque RC	.05
81	Corey Koskie	.05
82	Fernando Seguignol	.05
83	Jay Tessmer	.05
84	Jason Giambi	.50
85	Mike Lieberthal	.05
86	Jose Guillen	.05
87	Jim Leyritz	.05
88	Shawn Estes	.05
89	Ray Lankford	.05
90	Paul Sorrento	.05
91	Javy Lopez	.05
92	John Wetteland	.05
93	Sean Casey	.15
94	Chuck Finley	.05
95	Trot Nixon	.05
96	Ray Durham	.05
97	Reggie Sanders	.05
98	Bartolo Colon	.05
99	Henry Rodriguez	.05
100	Rolando Arrojo	.05
101	Geoff Jenkins	.05
102	Darryl Kile	.05
103	Mark Kotsay	.05
104	Craig Biggio	.05
105	Omar Daal	.05
106	Carlos Febles	.05
107	Eric Karros	.05
108	Matt Lawton	.05
109	Carl Pavano	.05
110	Brian McRae	.05
111	Mariano Rivera	.15
112	Jay Buhner	.05
113	Doug Glanville	.05
114	Jason Kendall	.05
115	Wally Joyner	.05
116	Jeff Kent	.05
117	Shane Monahan	.05
118	Eli Marrero	.05
119	Bobby Smith	.05
120	Shawn Green	.20
121	Kirk Rueter	.05
122	Tom Goodwin	.05
123	Andy Benes	.05
124	Ed Sprague	.05
125	Mike Mussina	.25
126	Jose Offerman	.05
127	Mickey Morandini	.05
128	Paul Konerko	.20
129	Denny Neagle	.05
130	Travis Fryman	.05
131	John Rocker	.05
132	Rob Fick RC	.05
133	Livan Hernandez	.05
134	Ken Caminiti	.05
135	Johnny Damon	.30
136	Jeff Kubenka	.05
137	Marquis Grissom	.05
138	Doug Mientkiewicz	.05
139	Dustin Hermanson	.05
140	Carl Everett	.05
141	Hideo Nomo	.40
142	Jorge Posada	.05
143	Rickey Henderson	.75
144	Robb Nen	.05
145	Ron Gant	.05
146	Aramis Ramirez	.05
147	Trevor Hoffman	.05
148	Bill Mueller	.05
149	Edgar Martinez	.05
150	Fred McGriff	.05
151	Rusty Greer	.05
152	Tom Evans	.05
153	Todd Greene	.05
154	Jay Bell	.05
155	Mike Lowell	.05
156	Orlando Cabrera	.05
157	Troy O'Leary	.05
158	Jose Hernandez	.05
159	Magglio Ordonez	.05
160	Barry Larkin	.05
161	David Justice	.05
162	Derrick Gibson	.05

163	Luis Gonzalez	.05
164	Alex Gonzalez	.05
165	Scott Elarton	.05
166	Dermal Brown	.05
167	Eric Milton	.05
168	Raul Mondesi	.05
169	Jeff Cirillo	.05
170	Benj Sampson	.05
171	John Olerud	.05
172	Andy Pettitte	.20
173	A.J. Hinch	.05
174	Rico Brogna	.05
175	Jason Schmidt	.05
176	Dean Palmer	.05
177	Matt Morris	.05
178	Quinton McCracken	.05
179	Rick Helling	.05
180	Walt Weiss	.05
181	Troy Percival	.05
182	Tony Batista	.05
183	Brian Jordan	.05
184	Jerry Hairston Jr.	.05
185	Bret Saberhagen	.05
186	Mark Grace	.05
187	Brian Simmons	.05
188	Pete Harnisch	.05
189	Kenny Lofton	.05
190	Vinny Castilla	.05
191	Bobby Higginson	.05
192	Joey Hamilton	.05
193	Cliff Floyd	.05
194	Andres Galarraga	.05
195	Chan Ho Park	.05
196	Jeromy Burnitz	.05
197	David Ortiz	.35
198	Wilton Guerrero	.05
199	Rey Ordonez	.05
200	Paul O'Neill	.05
201	Kenny Rogers	.05
202	Marlon Anderson	.05
203	Tony Womack	.05
204	Robin Ventura	.05
205	Russ Ortiz	.05
206	Mike Frank	.05
207	Fernando Tatis	.05
208	Miguel Cairo	.05
209	Ivan Rodriguez	.65
210	Carlos Delgado	.50
211	Tim Salmon	.15
212	Brian Anderson	.05
213	Ryan Klesko	.05
214	Scott Erickson	.05
215	Mike Stanley	.05
216	Brant Brown	.05
217	Rod Beck	.05
218	Guillermo Garcia RC	.05
219	David Wells	.05
220	Dante Bichette	.05
221	Armando Benitez	.05
222	Todd Dunwoody	.05
223	Kelvim Escobar	.05
224	Richard Hidalgo	.05
225	Angel Pena	.05
226	Ronnie Belliard	.05
227	Brad Radke	.05
228	Brad Fullmer	.05
229	Jay Payton	.05
230	Tino Martinez	.05
231	Scott Spiezio	.05
232	Bobby Abreu	.05
233	John Valentin	.05
234	Kevin Young	.05
235	Steve Finley	.05
236	David Cone	.05
237	Armando Rios	.05
238	Russ Davis	.05
239	Wade Boggs	1.00
240	Aaron Sele	.05
241	Jose Cruz Jr.	.15
242	George Lombard	.15
243	Todd Helton	.65
244	Andruw Jones	.75
245	Troy Glaus	.65
246	Manny Ramirez	.75
247	Ben Grieve	.15
247p	Ben Grieve/OPS	1.00
248	Richie Sexson	.15
249	Juan Encarnacion	.15
250	Randy Johnson	.75
251	Gary Sheffield	.45
252	Rafael Palmeiro	.65
253	Roy Halladay	.15
254	Mike Piazza	1.50
255	Tony Gwynn	1.00
256	Juan Gonzalez	.40
257	Jeremy Giambi	.15
258	Ben Davis	.15
259	Russ Branyan	.15
260	Pedro Martinez	.75
261	Frank Thomas	.75
262	Calvin Pickering	.15
263	Chipper Jones	1.00
264	Ryan Minor	.15
265	Roger Clemens	1.25
266	Sammy Sosa	1.00
267	Mo Vaughn	.15

268	Carlos Beltran	.50
269	Jim Thome	.65
270	Mark McGwire	2.00
271	Travis Lee	.15
272	Darin Erstad	.30
273	Derek Jeter	2.50
274	Greg Maddux	1.00
275	Ricky Ledee	.15
276	Alex Rodriguez	2.00
277	Vladimir Guerrero	.75
278	Greg Vaughn	.15
279	Scott Rolen	.60
280	Carlos Guillen	.15
281	Jeff Bagwell	.75
282	Bruce Chen	.15
283	Tony Clark	.15
284	Albert Belle	.05
285	Cal Ripken Jr.	2.50
286	Barry Bonds	2.50
287	Curt Schilling	.35
288	Eric Chavez	.30
289	Larry Walker	.15
290	Orlando Hernandez	.15
291	Moises Alou	.15
292	Ken Griffey Jr.	1.50
293	Kerry Wood	.50
294	Nomar Garciaparra	1.00
295	Gabe Kapler	.15
296	Bernie Williams	.05
297	Matt Anderson	.15
298	Adrian Beltre	.35
299	J.D. Drew	.40
300	Ryan Bradley	.15
---	Checklist 1-230	.05
---	Checklist 231-300 and Inserts	.05
---	Derek Jeter Video Game Sweepstakes Form	.05

Rant

Common Player:	.50
Rant Stars:	8X

(See 1999 SkyBox Thunder for checklist and base card values.)

Dial 1

		NM/M
Complete Set (10):		70.00
Common Player:		2.50
Inserted 1:300		
1D	Nomar Garciaparra	7.50
2D	Juan Gonzalez	3.40
3D	Ken Griffey Jr.	10.00
4D	Chipper Jones	7.50
5D	Mark McGwire	12.50
6D	Mike Piazza	10.00
7D	Manny Ramirez	6.00
8D	Alex Rodriguez	12.50
9D	Sammy Sosa	7.50
10D	Mo Vaughn	2.50

Hip-No-Tized

		NM/M
Complete Set (15):		20.00
Common Player:		1.25
Inserted 1:36		
1H	J.D. Drew	1.25
2H	Nomar Garciaparra	2.00
3H	Juan Gonzalez	1.25
4H	Ken Griffey Jr.	2.50
5H	Derek Jeter	4.00
6H	Randy Johnson	1.50
7H	Chipper Jones	2.00
8H	Mark McGwire	3.00
9H	Mike Piazza	2.50
10H	Cal Ripken Jr.	4.00
11H	Alex Rodriguez	3.00
12H	Sammy Sosa	2.00
13H	Frank Thomas	1.50
14H	Jim Thome	1.25
15H	Kerry Wood	1.25

In Depth

		NM/M
Complete Set (10):		17.50
Common Player:		1.00
Inserted 1:24		
1ID	Albert Belle	1.00
2ID	Barry Bonds	5.00
3ID	Roger Clemens	1.50
4ID	Juan Gonzalez	1.25
5ID	Ken Griffey Jr.	3.00
6ID	Mark McGwire	4.00
7ID	Mike Piazza	3.00
8ID	Sammy Sosa	2.50
9ID	Mo Vaughn	1.00
10ID	Kerry Wood	1.25

Todd Helton Autograph

		NM/M
243	Todd Helton	15.00

Turbo Charged

		NM/M
Complete Set (10):		35.00
Common Player:		2.00
Inserted 1:72		
1TC	Jose Canseco	2.50
2TC	Juan Gonzalez	2.00
3TC	Ken Griffey Jr.	5.00
4TC	Vladimir Guerrero	3.00
5TC	Mark McGwire	6.00
6TC	Mike Piazza	5.00
7TC	Manny Ramirez	3.00
8TC	Alex Rodriguez	6.00
9TC	Sammy Sosa	4.00
10TC	Mo Vaughn	2.00

Unleashed

		NM/M
Complete Set (15):		10.00
Common Player:		.50
Inserted 1:6		
1U	Carlos Beltran	1.50
2U	Adrian Beltre	1.00
3U	Eric Chavez	.75
4U	J.D. Drew	1.00
5U	Juan Encarnacion	.50
6U	Jeremy Giambi	.50
7U	Troy Glaus	2.00
8U	Ben Grieve	.50
9U	Todd Helton	2.00
10U	Orlando Hernandez	.50
11U	Gabe Kapler	.50
12U	Travis Lee	.50
13U	Calvin Pickering	.50
14U	Richie Sexson	.50
15U	Kerry Wood	1.00

www.Batterz.com

		NM/M
Complete Set (10):		12.00
Common Player:		.50
Inserted 1:18		
1WB	J.D. Drew	.60
2WB	Nomar Garciaparra	1.00
3WB	Ken Griffey Jr.	1.50
4WB	Tony Gwynn	1.00
5WB	Derek Jeter	3.00
6WB	Mark McGwire	2.00
7WB	Alex Rodriguez	2.00
8WB	Scott Rolen	.65
9WB	Sammy Sosa	1.00
10WB	Bernie Williams	.50

2000 SkyBox

		NM/M
Complete Set (250):		25.00
Comp. Set w/SP's (300):		60.00
Common Player:		.10
Common SP (201-240):		1.00
Inserted 1:8		
Common SP (241-250):		.50
Inserted 1:12		
Pack (10):		1.50
Wax Box (24):		30.00
1	Cal Ripken Jr.	2.00
2	Ivan Rodriguez	.65
3	Chipper Jones	1.00
4	Dean Palmer	.10
5	Devon White	.10
6	Ugueth Urbina	.10
7	Doug Glanville	.10
8	Damian Jackson	.10
9	Jose Canseco	.40
10	Billy Koch	.10
11	Brady Anderson	.10
12	Vladimir Guerrero	.75
13	Dan Wilson	.10
14	Kevin Brown	.10
15	Eddie Taubensee	.10
16	Jose Lima	.10
17	Greg Maddux	1.00
18	Manny Ramirez	.75
19	Brad Fullmer	.10
20	Ron Gant	.10
21	Edgar Martinez	.10
22	Pokey Reese	.10
23	Jason Varitek	.10
24	Neifi Perez	.10
25	Shane Reynolds	.10
26	Robin Ventura	.10
27	Scott Rolen	.65
28	Trevor Hoffman	.10
29	John Valentin	.10
30	Shannon Stewart	.10
31	Troy Glaus	.75
32	Kerry Wood	.65
33	Jim Thome	.65
34	Rafael Roque	.10
35	Tino Martinez	.10
36	Jeffrey Hammonds	.10
37	Orlando Hernandez	.10
38	Kris Benson	.10
39	Fred McGriff	.10
40	Brian Jordan	.10
41	Trot Nixon	.10
42	Matt Clement	.10
43	Ray Durham	.10
44	Johnny Damon	.30
45	Todd Hollandsworth	.10
46	Edgardo Alfonzo	.10
47	Tim Hudson	.25
48	Tony Gwynn	1.00
49	Barry Bonds	2.00
50	Andruw Jones	.75
51	Pedro Martinez	.75
52	Mike Hampton	.10
53	Miguel Tejada	.25
54	Kevin Young	.10
55	J.T. Snow	.10
56	Carlos Delgado	.50
57	Bobby Howry	.10
58	Andres Galarraga	.10
59	Paul Konerko	.20
60	Mike Cameron	.10
61	Jeremy Giambi	.10
62	Todd Hundley	.10
63	Al Leiter	.10
64	Matt Stairs	.10
65	Edgar Renteria	.10
66	Jeff Kent	.10
67	John Wetteland	.10
68	Nomar Garciaparra	1.25
69	Jeff Weaver	.10
70	Matt Williams	.10
71	Kyle Farnsworth	.10
72	Brad Radke	.10
73	Eric Chavez	.25
74	J.D. Drew	.25
75	Steve Finley	.10
76	Pete Harnisch	.10
77	Chad Kreuter	.10
78	Todd Pratt	.10
79	John Jaha	.10
80	Armando Rios	.10
81	Luis Gonzalez	.25
82	Ryan Minor	.10
83	Juan Gonzalez	.75
84	Rickey Henderson	.75
85	Jason Giambi	.50
86	Shawn Estes	.10
87	Chad Curtis	.10
88	Jeff Cirillo	.10
89	Juan Encarnacion	.10
90	Tony Womack	.10
91	Mike Mussina	.35
92	Jeff Bagwell	.75
93	Rey Ordonez	.10
94	Joe McEwing	.10
95	Robb Nen	.10
96	Will Clark	.10
97	Chris Singleton	.10
98	Jason Kendall	.10
99	Ken Griffey Jr.	1.25
100	Rusty Greer	.10
101	Charles Johnson	.10
102	Carlos Lee	.10
103	Brad Ausmus	.10
104	Preston Wilson	.10
105	Ronnie Belliard	.10
106	Mike Lieberthal	.10
107	Alex Rodriguez	1.50
108	Jay Bell	.10
109	Frank Thomas	.75
110	Adrian Beltre	.30
111	Ron Coomer	.10
112	Ben Grieve	.10
113	Darryl Kile	.10
114	Erubiel Durazo	.10
115	Magglio Ordonez	.10
116	Gary Sheffield	.40
117	Joe Mays	.10
118	Fernando Tatis	.10
119	David Wells	.10
120	Tim Salmon	.20
121	Troy O'Leary	.10
122	Roberto Alomar	.40
123	Damion Easley	.10
124	Brant Brown	.10
125	Carlos Beltran	.45
126	Eric Karros	.10
127	Geoff Jenkins	.10
128	Roger Clemens	1.00
129	Warren Morris	.10
130	Eric Owens	.10
131	Jose Cruz Jr.	.10
132	Mo Vaughn	.10
133	Eric Young	.10
134	Kenny Lofton	.10
135	Marquis Grissom	.10
136	A.J. Burnett	.10
137	Bernie Williams	.25
138	Javy Lopez	.10
139	Jose Offerman	.10
140	Sean Casey	.25
141	Alex Gonzalez	.10
142	Carlos Febles	.10
143	Mike Piazza	1.25
144	Curt Schilling	.35
145	Ben Davis	.10
146	Rafael Palmeiro	.65
147	Scott Williamson	.10
148	Darin Erstad	.25
149	Joe Girardi	.10
150	Gerald Williams	.10
151	Richie Sexson	.10
152	Corey Koskie	.10
153	Paul O'Neill	.10
154	Chad Hermansen	.10
155	Randy Johnson	.75
156	Henry Rodriguez	.10
157	Bartolo Colon	.10
158	Tony Clark	.10
159	Mike Lowell	.10
160	Moises Alou	.10
161	Todd Walker	.10
162	Mariano Rivera	.20
163	Mark McGwire	1.50
164	Roberto Hernandez	.10
165	Larry Walker	.10
166	Albert Belle	.15
167	Barry Larkin	.10
168	Rolando Arrojo	.10
169	Mark Kotsay	.10
170	Ken Caminiti	.10
171	Dermal Brown	.10
172	Michael Barrett	.10
173	Jay Buhner	.10
174	Ruben Mateo	.10
175	Jim Edmonds	.10
176	Sammy Sosa	1.25
177	Omar Vizquel	.10
178	Todd Helton	.75
179	Kevin Barker	.10
180	Derek Jeter	2.00
181	Brian Giles	.10
182	Greg Vaughn	.10
183	Roy Halladay	.10
184	Tom Glavine	.35
185	Craig Biggio	.10
186	Jose Vidro	.10
187	Andy Ashby	.10
188	Freddy Garcia	.10
189	Garret Anderson	.10
190	Mark Grace	.20
191	Travis Fryman	.10
192	Jeromy Burnitz	.10
193	Jacque Jones	.10
194	David Cone	.10
195	Ryan Rupe	.10
196	John Smoltz	.10
197	Daryle Ward	.10
198	Rondell White	.10
199	Bobby Abreu	.10
200	Justin Thompson	.10
201	Norm Hutchins	.10
201	Norm Hutchins/SP	1.00
202	Ramon Ortiz	.10
202	Ramon Ortiz/SP	1.00
203	Dan Wheeler	.10
203	Dan Wheeler/SP	1.00
204	Matt Riley	.10
204	Matt Riley/SP	1.00
205	Steve Lomasney	.10
205	Steve Lomasney/SP	1.00
206	Chad Meyers	.10
206	Chad Meyers/SP	1.00
207	Gary Glover RC	.20
207	Gary Glover/SP	1.00
208	Joe Crede	.10
208	Joe Crede/SP	1.00
209	Kip Wells	.10
209	Kip Wells/SP	1.00
210	Travis Dawkins	.10
210	Travis Dawkins/SP	1.00
211	Denny Stark RC	.20
211	Denny Stark/SP	1.00
212	Ben Petrick	.10
212	Ben Petrick/SP	1.00
213	Eric Munson	.10
213	Eric Munson/SP	1.00
214	Josh Beckett	.25
214	Josh Beckett/SP	1.50
215	Pablo Ozuna	.10
215	Pablo Ozuna/SP	1.00
216	Brad Penny	.10
216	Brad Penny/SP	1.00
217	Julio Ramirez	.10
217	Julio Ramirez/SP	1.00
218	Danny Peoples	.10
218	Danny Peoples/SP	1.00
219	Wilfredo Rodriguez RC	.10
219	Wilfredo Rodriguez/SP RC	1.00
220	Julio Lugo	.10
220	Julio Lugo/SP	1.00
221	Mark Quinn	.10
221	Mark Quinn/SP	1.00
222	Eric Gagne	.10
222	Eric Gagne/SP	1.00
223	Chad Green	.10
223	Chad Green/SP	1.00
224	Tony Armas Jr.	.10
224	Tony Armas Jr./SP	1.00
225	Milton Bradley	.10
225	Milton Bradley/SP	1.00
226	Rob Bell	.10
226	Rob Bell/SP	1.00
227	Alfonso Soriano	1.00
227	Alfonso Soriano/SP	4.00
228	Wily Pena	.10
228	Wily Pena/SP	1.00
229	Nick Johnson	.10
229	Nick Johnson/SP	1.50
230	Ed Yarnall	.10
230	Ed Yarnall/SP	1.00
231	Ryan Bradley	.10
231	Ryan Bradley/SP	1.00
232	Adam Piatt	.10

232	Adam Piatt/SP	1.00
233	Chad Harville	.10
233	Chad Harville/SP	1.00
234	Alex Sanchez	.10
234	Alex Sanchez/SP	1.00
235	Michael Coleman	.10
235	Michael Coleman/SP	1.00
236	Pat Burrell	.25
236	Pat Burrell/SP	1.50
237	Wascar Serrano RC	.10
237	Wascar Serrano/SP RC	1.00
238	Rick Ankiel	.10
238	Rick Ankiel/SP	1.00
239	Mike Lamb RC	.10
239	Mike Lamb/SP RC	1.00
240	Vernon Wells	.10
240	Vernon Wells/SP	1.00
241	Jorge Toca, Goefrey Tomlinson	.10
241	Jorge Toca, Goefrey Tomlinson/SP	.50
242	Shea Hillenbrand, Josh Phelps RC	2.00
242	Shea Hillenbrand, Josh Phelps/SP RC	4.00
243	Aaron Myette, Doug Davis	.10
243	Aaron Myette, Doug Davis/SP	.50
244	Brett Laxton, Robert Ramsay	.10
244	Brett Laxton, Robert Ramsay/SP	.50
245	B.J. Ryan, Corey Lee	.10
245	B.J. Ryan, Corey Lee/SP	.50
246	Chris Haas, Wilton Veras	.10
246	Chris Haas, Wilton Veras/SP	.50
247	Jimmy Anderson, Kyle Peterson	.10
247	Jimmy Anderson, Kyle Peterson/SP	.50
248	Jason Dewey, Giuseppe Chiaramonte	.10
248	Jason Dewey, Giuseppe Chiaramonte/SP	.50
249	Guillermo Mota, Orber Moreno	.10
249	Guillermo Mota, Orber Moreno/SP	.50
250	Steve Cox, Julio Zuleta RC	.15
250	Steve Cox, Julio Zuleta/SP RC	.50

Star Rubies

	NM/M
Complete Set (250):	200.00
Common Player (1-200):	.50
Common SP Prospect (201-250):	3.00
Stars:	6X
Star SP's:	3X

(See 2000 SkyBox for checklist and base card values.)

Speed Merchants

	NM/M
Complete Set (10):	12.00
Common Player:	.50
Inserted 1:8	
Star Ruby:	3-6X
Production 100 Sets	
1	Derek Jeter	3.00
2	Sammy Sosa	1.25
3	Nomar Garciaparra	1.25
4	Alex Rodriguez	2.50
5	Randy Johnson	1.00
6	Ken Griffey Jr.	1.50
7	Pedro Martinez	1.00
8	Pat Burrell	.50
9	Barry Bonds	3.00
10	Mark McGwire	2.50

Autographics

	NM/M
Common Player:	5.00
Rick Ankiel	6.00
Michael Barrett	5.00
Josh Beckett	25.00
Rob Bell	5.00
Adrian Beltre	15.00
Peter Bergeron	5.00
Lance Berkman	15.00
Rico Brogna	5.00
Pat Burrell	20.00
Orlando Cabrera	15.00
Mike Cameron	8.00
Roger Cedeno	5.00
Eric Chavez	15.00
Bruce Chen	5.00
Johnny Damon	20.00
Ben Davis	5.00
Jason Dewey	5.00
Octavio Dotel	6.00
J.D. Drew	15.00
Erubiel Durazo	8.00
Jason Giambi	20.00
Doug Glanville	5.00
Troy Glaus	20.00
Alex Gonzalez	8.00
Shawn Green	15.00
Jason Grilli	5.00
Tony Gwynn	40.00
Mike Hampton	8.00
Tim Hudson	15.00
Norm Hutchins	5.00
John Jaha	5.00
Derek Jeter	100.00
D'Angelo Jimenez	5.00
Randy Johnson	60.00
Andruw Jones	20.00
Gabe Kapler	8.00
Jason Kendall	10.00
Adam Kennedy	8.00
Cesar King	5.00
Paul Konerko	8.00
Mark Kotsay	6.00
Carlos Lee	8.00
Mike Lieberthal	8.00
Steve Lomasney	5.00
Greg Maddux	60.00
Edgar Martinez	15.00
Aaron McNeal	5.00
Kevin Millwood	10.00
Raul Mondesi	8.00
Joe Nathan	5.00
Magglio Ordonez	15.00
Eric Owens	5.00
Rafael Palmeiro	25.00
Angel Pena	5.00
Wily Pena	15.00
Cal Ripken Jr.	85.00
Scott Rolen	20.00
Jimmy Rollins	15.00
B.J. Ryan	5.00
Tim Salmon	10.00
Chris Singleton	5.00
J.T. Snow	6.00
Mike Sweeney	8.00
Jose Vidro	8.00
Rondell White	8.00
Jaret Wright	5.00

E-Ticket

	NM/M
Complete Set (14):	15.00
Common Player:	.50
Inserted 1:4	
Star Ruby:	4-8X
Production 100 Sets	
1	Alex Rodriguez	2.50
2	Derek Jeter	3.00
3	Nomar Garciaparra	1.50
4	Cal Ripken Jr.	3.00

5	Sean Casey	.50
6	Mark McGwire	2.50
7	Sammy Sosa	1.50
8	Ken Griffey Jr.	2.00
9	Tony Gwynn	1.50
10	Pedro Martinez	1.00
11	Chipper Jones	1.50
12	Vladimir Guerrero	1.00
13	Roger Clemens	1.75
14	Mike Piazza	2.00

Genuine Coverage

	NM/M
Common Player:	8.00
Inserted 1:399	
1	Troy Glaus	15.00
2	Cal Ripken Jr.	40.00
3	Alex Rodriguez	25.00
4	Mike Mussina	10.00
5	J.D. Drew	8.00
6	Robin Ventura	8.00
7	Matt Williams	8.00

Genuine Coverage HOBBY

	NM/M
Common Player:	10.00
Inserted 1:144	
1	Ivan Rodriguez	12.00
2	Jose Canseco	10.00
3	Frank Thomas	15.00
4	Manny Ramirez	15.00

Higher Level

	NM/M
Complete Set (10):	20.00
Common Player:	1.00
Inserted 1:24	
Star Ruby:	5-10X
Production 50 Sets	
1	Cal Ripken Jr.	4.00
2	Derek Jeter	4.00
3	Nomar Garciaparra	2.00
4	Chipper Jones	2.00
5	Mike Piazza	2.50
6	Ivan Rodriguez	1.00
7	Ken Griffey Jr.	2.50
8	Sammy Sosa	2.00
9	Alex Rodriguez	3.00
10	Mark McGwire	3.00

Hobby Bullpen Embossed

	NM/M
49	Barry Bonds	6.00

Preeminence

	NM/M
Complete Set (10):	15.00
Common Player:	.50
Inserted 1:24	
Star Ruby:	5-10X
Production 50 Sets	
1	Pedro Martinez	1.25
2	Derek Jeter	4.00
3	Nomar Garciaparra	1.50
4	Alex Rodriguez	3.00
5	Mark McGwire	3.00
6	Sammy Sosa	1.50
7	Sean Casey	.50
8	Mike Piazza	2.00
9	Chipper Jones	1.50
10	Ivan Rodriguez	1.00

SkyLines

	NM/M
Complete Set (10):	10.00
Common Player:	.50
Inserted 1:11	
Star Ruby:	10-20X
Production 50 Sets	
1	Cal Ripken Jr.	2.00
2	Mark McGwire	1.50
3	Alex Rodriguez	1.50
4	Sammy Sosa	.75
5	Derek Jeter	2.00
6	Mike Piazza	1.00
7	Nomar Garciaparra	.75
8	Chipper Jones	.75
9	Ken Griffey Jr.	1.00
10	Manny Ramirez	.50

The Technique

	NM/M
Complete Set (15):	20.00
Common Player:	.50
Inserted 1:11	
Star Ruby:	3-6X

Production 50 Sets
1	Alex Rodriguez	3.00
2	Tony Gwynn	1.50
3	Sean Casey	.50
4	Mark McGwire	3.00
5	Sammy Sosa	1.50
6	Ken Griffey Jr.	2.00
7	Mike Piazza	2.00
8	Nomar Garciaparra	1.50
9	Derek Jeter	4.00
10	Vladimir Guerrero	1.00
11	Cal Ripken Jr.	4.00
12	Chipper Jones	1.50
13	Frank Thomas	1.00
14	Manny Ramirez	1.00
15	Jeff Bagwell	1.00

2000 SkyBox Dominion

		NM/M
Complete Set (300):		20.00
Common Player:		.10
Pack (10):		1.50
Wax Box (36):		30.00
1	Mark McGwire, Ken Griffey Jr.	.40
2	Mark McGwire, Manny Ramirez	.40
3	Larry Walker, Nomar Garciaparra	.25
4	Tony Womack, Brian Hunter	.10
5	Mike Hampton, Pedro Martinez	.20
6	Randy Johnson, Pedro Martinez	.20
7	Randy Johnson, Pedro Martinez	.20
8	Ugueth Urbina, Mariano Rivera	.10
9	Vinny Castilla	.10
10	Orioles Host Cuban National Team	.10
11	Jose Canseco	.10
12	Fernando Tatis	.10
13	Robin Ventura	.10
14	Roger Clemens	.50
15	Jose Jimenez	.10
16	David Cone	.10
17	Mark McGwire	.65
18	Cal Ripken Jr.	.75
19	Tony Gwynn	.30
20	Wade Boggs	.25
21	Ivan Rodriguez	.20
22	Chuck Finley	.10
23	Eric Milton	.10
24	Adrian Beltre	.10
25	Brad Radke	.10
26	Derek Bell	.10
27	Garret Anderson	.10
28	Ivan Rodriguez	.40
29	Jeff Kent	.10
30	Jeremy Giambi	.10
31	John Franco	.10
32	Jose Hernandez	.10
33	Jose Offerman	.10
34	Jose Rosado	.10
35	Kevin Appier	.10
36	Kris Benson	.10
37	Mark McGwire	1.00
38	Matt Williams	.10
39	Paul O'Neill	.10
40	Rickey Henderson	.50
41	Todd Greene	.10
42	Russ Ortiz	.10
43	Sean Casey	.20
44	Tony Womack	.10
45	Troy O'Leary	.10
46	Ugueth Urbina	.10
47	Tom Glavine	.25
48	Mike Mussina	.30
49	Carlos Febles	.10
50	Jon Lieber	.10
51	Juan Gonzalez	.30
52	Matt Clement	.10
53	Moises Alou	.10
54	Ray Durham	.10
55	Robb Nen	.10
56	Tino Martinez	.10
57	Troy Glaus	.40
58	Curt Schilling	.30
59	Mike Sweeney	.10
60	Steve Finley	.10
61	Roger Cedeno	.10
62	Bobby Jones	.10
63	John Smoltz	.10
64	Darin Erstad	.20
65	Carlos Delgado	.35
66	Ray Lankford	.10
67	Todd Stottlemyre	.10
68	Andy Ashby	.10
69	Bobby Abreu	.15
70	Chuck Finley	.10
71	Damion Easley	.10
72	Dustin Hermanson	.10
73	Frank Thomas	.50
74	Kevin Brown	.10
75	Kevin Millwood	.10
76	Mark Grace	.10
77	Matt Stairs	.10
78	Mike Hampton	.10
79	Omar Vizquel	.10
80	Preston Wilson	.10
81	Robin Ventura	.10
82	Todd Helton	.40
83	Tony Clark	.10
84	Al Leiter	.10
85	Alex Fernandez	.10
86	Bernie Williams	.10
87	Edgar Martinez	.10
88	Edgar Renteria	.10
89	Fred McGriff	.10
90	Jermaine Dye	.10
91	Joe McEwing	.10
92	John Halama	.10
93	Lee Stevens	.10
94	Matt Lawton	.10
95	Mike Piazza	.75
96	Pete Harnisch	.10
97	Scott Karl	.10
98	Tony Fernandez	.10
99	Sammy Sosa	.60
100	Bobby Higginson	.10
101	Tony Gwynn	.60
102	J.D. Drew	.20
103	Roberto Hernandez	.10
104	Rondell White	.10
105	David Nilsson	.10
106	Shane Reynolds	.10
107	Jaret Wright	.10
108	Jeff Bagwell	.50
109	Jay Bell	.10
110	Kevin Tapani	.10
111	Michael Barrett	.10
112	Neifi Perez	.10
113	Pat Hentgen	.10
114	Roger Clemens	.65
115	Travis Fryman	.10
116	Aaron Sele	.10
117	Eric Davis	.10
118	Trevor Hoffman	.10
119	Chris Singleton	.10
120	Ryan Klesko	.10
121	Scott Rolen	.40
122	Jorge Posada	.10
123	Abraham Nunez	.10
124	Alex Gonzalez	.10
125	B.J. Surhoff	.10
126	Barry Bonds	1.50
127	Billy Koch	.10
128	Billy Wagner	.10
129	Brad Ausmus	.10
130	Bret Boone	.10
131	Cal Ripken Jr.	1.50
132	Chad Allen	.10
133	Chris Carpenter	.10
134	Craig Biggio	.10
135	Dante Bichette	.10
136	Dean Palmer	.10
137	Derek Jeter	1.50
138	Ellis Burks	.10
139	Freddy Garcia	.10
140	Gabe Kapler	.10
141	Greg Maddux	.60
142	Greg Vaughn	.10
143	Jason Kendall	.10
144	Jim Parque	.10
145	John Valentin	.10
146	Jose Vidro	.10
147	Ken Griffey Jr.	.75
148	Kenny Lofton	.10
149	Kenny Rogers	.10
150	Kent Bottenfield	.10
151	Chuck Knoblauch	.10
152	Larry Walker	.10
153	Manny Ramirez	.50
154	Mickey Morandini	.10
155	Mike Cameron	.10
156	Mike Lieberthal	.10
157	Mo Vaughn	.10
158	Randy Johnson	.50
159	Rey Ordonez	.10
160	Roberto Alomar	.20
161	Scott Williamson	.10
162	Shawn Estes	.10
163	Tim Wakefield	.10
164	Tony Batista	.10
165	Will Clark	.10
166	Wade Boggs	.60
167	David Cone	.10
168	Doug Glanville	.10
169	Jeff Cirillo	.10
170	John Jaha	.10
171	Mariano Rivera	.20
172	Tom Gordon	.10
173	Wally Joyner	.10
174	Alex Gonzalez	.10
175	Andruw Jones	.50
176	Barry Larkin	.10
177	Bartolo Colon	.10
178	Brian Giles	.10
179	Carlos Lee	.10
180	Darren Dreifort	.10
181	Eric Chavez	.20
182	Henry Rodriguez	.10
183	Ismael Valdes	.10
184	Jason Giambi	.40
185	John Wetteland	.10
186	Juan Encarnacion	.10
187	Luis Gonzalez	.10
188	Reggie Sanders	.10
189	Richard Hidalgo	.10
190	Ryan Rupe	.10
191	Sean Berry	.10
192	Rick Helling	.10
193	Randy Wolf	.10
194	Cliff Floyd	.10
195	Jose Lima	.10
196	Chipper Jones	.60
197	Charles Johnson	.10
198	Nomar Garciaparra	.60
199	Magglio Ordonez	.10
200	Shawn Green	.25
201	Travis Lee	.10
202	Jose Canseco	.35
203	Fernando Tatis	.10
204	Bruce Aven	.10
205	Johnny Damon	.35
206	Gary Sheffield	.25
207	Ken Caminiti	.10
208	Ben Grieve	.10
209	Sidney Ponson	.10
210	Vinny Castilla	.10
211	Alex Rodriguez	1.00
212	Chris Widger	.10
213	Carl Pavano	.10
214	J.T. Snow	.10
215	Jim Thome	.40
216	Kevin Young	.10
217	Mike Sirotka	.10
218	Rafael Palmeiro	.40
219	Rico Brogna	.10
220	Todd Walker	.10
221	Todd Zelle	.10
222	Brian Rose	.10
223	Chris Fussell	.10
224	Corey Koskie	.10
225	Rich Aurilia	.10
226	Geoff Jenkins	.10
227	Pedro Martinez	.50
228	Todd Hundley	.10
229	Brian Jordan	.10
230	Cristian Guzman	.10
231	Raul Mondesi	.10
232	Tim Hudson	.20
233	Albert Belle	.10
234	Andy Pettitte	.25
235	Brady Anderson	.10
236	Brian Bohannon	.10
237	Carlos Beltran	.35
238	Doug Mientkiewicz	.10
239	Jason Schmidt	.10
240	Jeff Zimmerman	.10
241	John Olerud	.10
242	Paul Byrd	.10
243	Vladimir Guerrero	.50
244	Warren Morris	.10
245	Eric Karros	.10
246	Jeff Weaver	.10
247	Jeromy Burnitz	.10
248	David Bell	.10
249	Rusty Greer	.10
250	Kevin Stocker	.10
251	Shea Hillenbrand	.15
252	Alfonso Soriano	.50
253	Micah Bowie	.10
254	Gary Matthews Jr.	.10
255	Lance Berkman	.10
256	Pat Burrell	.25
257	Ruben Mateo	.10
258	Kip Wells	.10
259	Wilton Veras	.10
260	Ben Davis	.10
261	Eric Munson	.10
262	Ramon Hernandez	.10
263	Tony Armas Jr.	.10
264	Erubiel Durazo	.10
265	Chad Meyers	.10
266	Rick Ankiel	.10
267	Ramon Ortiz	.10
268	Adam Kennedy	.10
269	Vernon Wells	.10
270	Chad Hermansen	.10
271	Norm Hutchins, Trent Durrington	.10
272	Gabe Molina, B.J. Ryan	.10
273	Juan Pena, Tomokazu Ohka RC	.25
274	Pat Daneker, Aaron Myette	.15
275	Jason Rakers, Russell Branyan	.10
276	Beiker Graterol, Dave Borkowski	.10
277	Mark Quinn, Dan Reichert	.10
278	Mark Redman, Jacque Jones	.15
279	Ed Yarnall, Wily Pena	.10
280	Chad Harville, Brett Laxton	.10
281	Aaron Scheffer, Gil Meche	.10
282	Jim Morris, Dan Wheeler	.10
283	Danny Kolb, Kelly Dransfeldt	.10
284	Peter Munro, Casey Blake	.10
285	Rob Ryan, Byung-Hyun Kim	.10
286	Derrin Ebert, Pascual Matos	.10
287	Richard Barker, Kyle Farnsworth	.10
288	Jason LaRue, Travis Dawkins	.10
289	Chris Sexton, Edgard Clemente	.10
290	Amaury Garcia, A.J. Burnett	.10
291	Carlos Hernandez, Daryle Ward	.10
292	Eric Gagne, Jeff Williams	.10
293	Kyle Peterson, Kevin Barker	.10
294	Fernando Seguignol, Guillermo Mota	.10
295	Melvin Mora, Octavio Dotel	.10
296	Anthony Shumaker, Cliff Politte	.10
297	Yamid Haad, Jimmy Anderson	.10
298	Rick Heiserman, Chad Hutchinson	.10
299	Mike Darr, Wiki Gonzalez	.10
300	Joe Nathan, Calvin Murray	.10

Autographics

		NM/M
Common Player:		5.00
Inserted 1:144		
1	Rick Ankiel	6.00
2	Peter Bergeron	5.00
3	Wade Boggs	25.00
4	Barry Bonds	200.00
5	Pat Burrell	20.00
6	Miguel Cairo	5.00
7	Mike Cameron	8.00
8	Ben Davis	5.00
9	Russ Davis	5.00
10	Einar Diaz	5.00
11	Scott Elarton	5.00

12	Jeremy Giambi	5.00
13	Todd Greene	5.00
14	Vladimir Guerrero	25.00
15	Tony Gwynn	30.00
16	Bobby Howry	5.00
17	Tim Hudson	15.00
18	Randy Johnson	50.00
19	Andruw Jones	20.00
20	Jacque Jones	8.00
21	Jason LaRue	5.00
22	Matt Lawton	6.00
23	Greg Maddux	50.00
24	Pedro Martinez	50.00
25	Pokey Reese	5.00
26	Alex Rodriguez	75.00
27	Ryan Rupe	5.00
28	J.T. Snow	6.00
29	Jose Vidro	6.00
30	Tony Womack	6.00
31	Ed Yarnall	5.00
32	Kevin Young	5.00

Eye on October

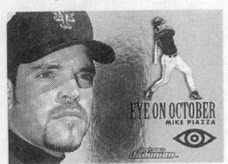

		NM/M
Complete Set (15):		25.00
Common Player:		.50
Inserted 1:24		
Plus:		2-4X
Inserted 1:240		
1	Ken Griffey Jr.	2.50
2	Mark McGwire	3.00
3	Derek Jeter	4.00
4	Juan Gonzalez	1.00
5	Chipper Jones	2.00
6	Sammy Sosa	2.00
7	Greg Maddux	2.00
8	Frank Thomas	1.50
9	Nomar Garciaparra	2.00
10	Shawn Green	1.00
11	Cal Ripken Jr.	4.00
12	Manny Ramirez	1.50
13	Scott Rolen	1.25
14	Mike Piazza	2.50
15	Alex Rodriguez	3.00

Double Play

		NM/M
Complete Set (10):		10.00
Common Player:		1.00
Inserted 1:9		
Plus:		2-4X
Inserted 1:90		
WarpTek:		10-20X
Inserted 1:900		
1	Nomar Garciaparra	1.50
2	Pedro Martinez	1.25
3	Chipper Jones	1.50
4	Mark McGwire	2.50
5	Cal Ripken Jr.	3.00
6	Roger Clemens	1.75
7	Juan Gonzalez	1.00
8	Tony Gwynn	1.50
9	Sammy Sosa	1.50
10	Mike Piazza	2.00

ABBREVIATIONS

SP - Short Print

Hats Off

		NM/M
Common Player:		15.00
Inserted 1:468 H		
1	Wade Boggs	25.00
2	Barry Bonds	75.00
3	J.D. Drew	15.00
4	Shawn Green	15.00
5	Vladimir Guerrero	25.00
6	Randy Johnson	30.00
7	Andruw Jones	20.00
8	Greg Maddux	40.00
9	Pedro Martinez	25.00
10	Mike Mussina	15.00
11	Rafael Palmeiro	20.00
12	Alex Rodriguez	50.00
13	Scott Rolen	15.00
14	Tim Salmon	15.00
15	Robin Ventura	15.00

Milestones

		NM/M
Common Player:		15.00
Inserted 1:1,999		
1	Mark McGwire	60.00
2	Roger Clemens	40.00
3	Tony Gwynn	25.00
4	Wade Boggs	25.00
5	Cal Ripken Jr.	75.00
6	Jose Canseco	15.00

New Era

		NM/M
Complete Set (20):		5.00
Common Player:		.25
Inserted 1:3		
Plus:		2-4X
Inserted 1:30		
WarpTek:		5-10X
Inserted 1:300		
1	Pat Burrell	.75
2	Ruben Mateo	.25
3	Wilton Veras	.25
4	Eric Munson	.25
5	Jeff Weaver	.25
6	Tim Hudson	.50
7	Carlos Beltran	1.00
8	Chris Singleton	.25
9	Lance Berkman	.25
10	Freddy Garcia	.25
11	Erubiel Durazo	.25
12	Randy Wolf	.25
13	Shea Hillenbrand	.25
14	Kip Wells	.25
15	Alfonso Soriano	1.50
16	Rick Ankiel	.25
17	Ramon Ortiz	.25
18	Adam Kennedy	.25
19	Vernon Wells	.25
20	Chad Hermansen	.25

2004 SkyBox Autographics

		NM/M
Complete Set (100):		
Common Player:		.40
Hobby Box (4):		75.00
1	Albert Pujols	2.50
2	Richie Sexson	.75
3	Scott Rolen	1.00
4	Rafael Palmeiro	.75
5	Ichiro Suzuki	2.00
6	Craig Biggio	.50
7	Todd Helton	.75
8	Miguel Cabrera	.75
9	Ken Griffey Jr.	1.50
10	Pat Burrell	.50
11	Jose Reyes	.50
12	Hideki Matsui	2.50

13	Geoff Jenkins	.50
14	Mark Prior	2.00
15	Gary Sheffield	.50
16	Nomar Garciaparra	2.00
17	Luis Gonzalez	.50
18	Troy Glaus	.50
19	Rocco Baldelli	.75
20	Hank Blalock	.50
21	Bret Boone	.50
22	Mike Sweeney	.40
23	Dmitri Young	.40
24	Dontrelle Willis	.50
25	Austin Kearns	.50
26	Jason Kendall	.40
27	Derek Jeter	3.00
28	Miguel Tejada	.50
29	Torii Hunter	.50
30	Sammy Sosa	2.00
31	Chipper Jones	1.50
32	Pedro J. Martinez	1.00
33	Curt Schilling	.75
34	Roy Halladay	.50
35	Jim Edmonds	.50
36	Alex Rodriguez	2.50
37	Jason Schmidt	.50
38	Jeff Bagwell	.75
39	Omar Vizquel	.40
40	Ivan Rodriguez	.75
41	Magglio Ordonez	.50
42	Jim Thome	1.00
43	Mike Piazza	2.00
44	Alfonso Soriano	1.00
45	Hideo Nomo	.50
46	Kerry Wood	1.00
47	Greg Maddux	1.50
48	Tony Batista	.40
49	Randy Johnson	1.00
50	Garret Anderson	.50
51	Mark Teixeira	.50
52	Carlos Delgado	.75
53	Darin Erstad	.50
54	Shawn Green	.50
55	Josh Beckett	.75
56	Lance Berkman	.50
57	Adam Dunn	.50
58	Brian Giles	.50
59	Jason Giambi	1.00
60	Barry Zito	.50
61	Vladimir Guerrero	1.00
62	Frank Thomas	.75
63	Jay Gibbons	.40
64	Manny Ramirez	.75
65	Andruw Jones	.75
66	Rickie Weeks RC	5.00
67	Chad Bentz RC	4.00
68	Bobby Crosby	4.00
69	Greg Dobbs RC	5.00
70	John Gall RC	3.00
71	Kazuo Matsui RC	20.00
72	Dallas McPherson RC	3.00
73	Brandon Watson	3.00
74	Jerry Gil RC	3.00
75	Garrett Atkins	3.00
76	Cory Sullivan RC	3.00
77	Khalil Greene	5.00
78	Shawn Hill RC	3.00
79	Graham Koonce	3.00
80	Chien-Ming Wang RC	3.00
81	Josh Labandeira RC	3.00
82	Jonny Gomes	3.00
83	Edwin Jackson	3.00
84	Alfredo Simon RC	4.00
85	Delmon Young	6.00
86	Jason Bartlett RC	5.00
87	Angel Chavez RC	3.00
88	Angel Guzman	3.00
89	Ryan Howard	5.00
90	Scott Hairston	3.00
91	Ronny Cedeno RC	3.00
92	Donald Kelly RC	3.00
93	Ivan Ochoa RC	3.00
94	Edwin Encarnacion	3.00
95	Byron Gettis	3.00
96	Kevin Youkilis	4.00
97	Grady Sizemore	3.00
98	Mariano Gomez RC	3.00
99	Hector Gimenez RC	3.00
100	Ruddy Yan RC	3.00

Insignia

Cards (1-65):	3-5X
Rookies (66-100):	1-2X
Production 150 Sets	

Royal Insignia

No Pricing
Production 25 Sets

Autoclassics

	NM/M
Complete Set (15):	25.00
Common Player:	1.50
Johnny Bench	4.00
Wade Boggs	2.00
Steve Carlton	2.00
Albert Chandler	1.50
Ty Cobb	4.00
Carlton Fisk	1.50
George Kelly	1.50
Sal Maglie	2.00
Bill Mazeroski	1.50
Jim Palmer	2.00
Nolan Ryan	6.00
Mike Schmidt	3.00
Joe Sewell	2.00
Duke Snider	3.00
Warren Spahn	4.00

Autoclassics Memorabilia

	NM/M
Common Player:	8.00
Johnny Bench	15.00
Wade Boggs	12.00
Steve Carlton	8.00
Carlton Fisk	15.00
Bill Mazeroski	15.00
Jim Palmer	8.00
Nolan Ryan	25.00
Mike Schmidt	15.00
Duke Snider	15.00
Warren Spahn	15.00

Autoclassics Signature

	NM/M
Production 3-50	
Johnny Bench/50	50.00
Wade Boggs/50	40.00
Steve Carlton/50	20.00
Albert Chandler/25	120.00
Carlton Fisk/50	40.00
George Kelly/25	150.00
Sal Maglie/25	150.00
Bill Mazeroski/50	35.00
Jim Palmer/50	20.00
Nolan Ryan/38	150.00
Mike Schmidt/25	100.00
Joe Sewell/25	120.00
Duke Snider/50	40.00
Warren Spahn/50	50.00

Autographics Blue

	NM/M
Common Player:	5.00
Silver:	.75-1.5X
Production 100 Sets	
Gold:	1.5-2X
Production 25 Sets	
Purple:	No Pricing
Production One Set	
Garrett Atkins/175	5.00
Rocco Baldelli/255	15.00
Josh Beckett/100	25.00
Angel Berroa/182	10.00
Hank Blalock/205	15.00
A.J. Burnett/485	10.00
Marlon Byrd/240	8.00
Edwin Encarnacion/188	10.00
Eric Gagne/225	25.00
Jonny Gomes/265	15.00
Khalil Greene/190	25.00
Rich Harden/185	10.00
Dan Haren/176	10.00
Koyie Hill/240	5.00
Shea Hillenbrand/213	10.00
Ryan Howard/170	75.00
Tim Hudson/169	15.00
Aubrey Huff/296	10.00
Torii Hunter/215	10.00
Edwin Jackson/224	10.00
Bobby Jenks/307	10.00
Matt Kata/197	10.00
Austin Kearns/275	8.00
Graham Koonce/190	10.00
Barry Larkin/195	25.00
Dallas McPherson/179	8.00
Aaron Miles/140	10.00
Mark Mulder/186	15.00
Laynce Nix/185	8.00
Trot Nixon/210	15.00
Corey Patterson/220	12.00
Juan Pierre/220	15.00
Scott Podsednik/210	25.00
Albert Pujols/103	160.00
Jose Reyes/195	30.00
Juan Richardson/345	5.00
Gary Sheffield/210	20.00
Chris Snelling/200	5.00
Shannon Stewart/340	10.00
Cory Sullivan/170	5.00
Javier Vazquez/210	15.00
Billy Wagner/180	25.00
Chien-Ming Wang/195	100.00
Brandon Webb/310	12.00
Rickie Weeks/187	20.00
Dontrelle Willis/225	25.00
Kerry Wood/191	25.00
Delmon Young/205	25.00

Autographics Memorabilia

	NM/M
Production 125 Sets	
Patch:	1-2X
Production 25 Sets	
Rocco Baldelli	25.00
Josh Beckett	40.00
Hank Blalock	25.00
Torii Hunter	20.00
Corey Patterson	15.00
Albert Pujols	175.00
Billy Wagner	40.00
Brandon Webb	15.00
Dontrelle Willis	30.00

Jerseygraphics Blue

	NM/M
Common Player:	5.00
Silver:	1-2X
Production 100 Sets	
Gold:	No Pricing
Production 25 Sets	
Bobby Abreu	5.00
Rocco Baldelli	5.00
Josh Beckett	10.00
Lance Berkman	5.00
Craig Biggio	5.00

Hank Blalock	8.00
Pat Burrell	8.00
Miguel Cabrera	10.00
Carlos Delgado	5.00
Adam Dunn	8.00
Jim Edmonds	5.00
Darin Erstad	5.00
Nomar Garciaparra	8.00
Jason Giambi	8.00
Jay Gibbons	8.00
Troy Glaus	8.00
Shawn Green	8.00
Vladimir Guerrero	8.00
Roy Halladay	8.00
Todd Helton	5.00
Torii Hunter	5.00
Derek Jeter	15.00
Andruw Jones	5.00
Chipper Jones	10.00
Austin Kearns	5.00
Greg Maddux	15.00
Pedro J. Martinez	10.00
Kevin Millwood	5.00
Hideo Nomo	8.00
Magglio Ordonez	
David Ortiz	10.00
Rafael Palmeiro	5.00
Mike Piazza	10.00
Mark Prior	10.00
Albert Pujols	15.00
Manny Ramirez	10.00
Jose Reyes	10.00
Alex Rodriguez	15.00
Ivan Rodriguez	5.00
Scott Rolen	10.00
Curt Schilling	10.00
Alfonso Soriano	8.00
Sammy Sosa	15.00
Mark Teixeira	8.00
Miguel Tejada	8.00
Frank Thomas	10.00
Jim Thome	10.00
Dontrelle Willis	5.00
Kerry Wood	4.00
Barry Zito	5.00

Jeter Legacy Collection

Production 25

Prospects Endorsed

	NM/M
Complete Set (15):	10.00
Common Duo:	.50
1 Albert Pujols, Delmon Young	3.00
2 Eric Gagne, Bobby Jenks	.50
3 Barry Larkin, Kazuo Matsui	2.00
4 Andruw Jones, Jonny Gomes	1.00
5 Hideo Nomo, Chien-Ming Wang	.50
6 Gary Sheffield, Cory Sullivan	.75
7 Billy Wagner, Ryan Howard	1.00
8 Jorge Posada, Koyie Hill	.75
9 Curt Schilling, Ryan Wagner	.75
10 Jose Reyes, Rickie Weeks	1.50
11 Alfonso Soriano, Matt Kata	1.50
12 Barry Zito, Rich Harden	.75
13 Randy Johnson, Brandon Webb	1.50
14 Alex Rodriguez, Angel Berroa	3.00
15 Dontrelle Willis, Edwin Jackson	.50

Prospects Endorsed Dual Autograph

	NM/M
Production 50 Sets	.50
APDY Albert Pujols, Delmon Young	275.00

EGBJ Eric Gagne, Bobby Jenks	30.00
BLEE Barry Larkin, Edwin Encarnacion	30.00
AJJG Andruw Jones, Jonny Gomes	35.00
GSCS Gary Sheffield, Cory Sullivan	25.00
BWRY Billy Wagner, Ryan Howard	100.00
JRRW Jose Reyes, Rickie Weeks	40.00

Prospects Endorsed Dual Jersey

	NM/M
Common Duo:	5.00
APDY Albert Pujols, Delmon Young	15.00
BLKZ Barry Larkin, Kazuo Matsui	8.00
HNCW Hideo Nomo, Chien-Ming Wang	50.00
CSRW Curt Schilling, Ryan Wagner	8.00
JRRW Jose Reyes, Rickie Weeks	10.00
ASMK Alfonso Soriano, Matt Kata	8.00
BZRH Barry Zito, Rich Harden	5.00
RJBW Randy Johnson, Brandon Webb	8.00
ARAB Alex Rodriguez, Angel Berroa	10.00
DWEJ Dontrelle Willis, Edwin Jackson	8.00

Prospects Endorsed Dual Patch

	NM/M
Common Duo:	25.00
APDY Albert Pujols, Delmon Young	50.00
HNCW Hideo Nomo, Chien-Ming Wang	180.00
CSRW Curt Schilling, Ryan Wagner	25.00
JRRW Jose Reyes, Rickie Weeks	25.00
ASMK Alfonso Soriano, Matt Kata	25.00
BZRH Barry Zito, Rich Harden	25.00
RJBW Randy Johnson, Brandon Webb	25.00
ARAB Alex Rodriguez, Angel Berroa	35.00
DWEJ Dontrelle Willis, Edwin Jackson	25.00

2004 SkyBox LE

	NM/M
Complete Set (160):	
Common Player (1-110):	.25
Common SP (111-160):	4.00
Production 299 unless noted.	
Pack (3):	5.00
Box (18):	80.00

1	Juan Pierre	.25
2	Derek Jeter	3.00
3	Brandon Webb	.25
4	Jeff Bagwell	.75
5	Jason Schmidt	.40
6	Marlon Byrd	.25
7	Garret Anderson	.50
8	Miguel Cabrera	.75
9	Jose Reyes	.50
10	Rocco Baldelli	.50
11	Tony Batista	.25
12	Carlos Beltran	.50
13	Nomar Garciaparra	2.00
14	Shawn Green	.50
15	Albert Pujols	2.50
16	Magglio Ordonez	.50
17	Kip Wells	.25
18	Andruw Jones	.75
19	Ryan Wagner	.25
20	Alex Rodriguez	3.00
21	Vernon Wells	.50
22	Todd Helton	.75
23	David Ortiz	.25
24	Troy Glaus	.50
25	Jim Thome	1.00
26	Greg Maddux	1.50
27	Roberto Alomar	.50
28	Edgardo Alfonzo	.25
29	Hee Seop Choi	.25
30	Ken Griffey Jr.	1.50
31	Tim Hudson	.50
32	Shannon Stewart	.25
33	Ichiro Suzuki	2.00
34	Luis Gonzalez	.50
35	Darin Erstad	.50
36	Dmitri Young	.25
37	Ivan Rodriguez	.75
38	Scott Podsednik	.50
39	Jose Vidro	.25
40	Mark Prior	2.00
41	Mike Mussina	.75
42	Gary Sheffield	.50
43	Manny Ramirez	.75
44	C.C. Sabathia	.40
45	Curt Schilling	.75
46	Scott Rolen	1.00
47	Hideo Nomo	.50
48	Torii Hunter	.50
49	Aubrey Huff	.25
50	Javy Lopez	.50
51	Austin Kearns	.50
52	Mike Piazza	1.50
53	Sean Burroughs	.25
54	Kerry Wood	.75
55	Marquis Grissom	.25
56	Preston Wilson	.25
57	Angel Berroa	.25
58	Jason Kendall	.25
59	Rafael Palmeiro	.75
60	Mike Lowell	.40
61	Eric Chavez	.50
62	Bartolo Colon	.50
63	Adam Dunn	.50
64	Pedro J. Martinez	1.00
65	Lance Berkman	.50
66	Bret Boone	.40
67	Eric Gagne	.40
68	Vladimir Guerrero	1.00
69	Jay Gibbons	.25
70	Larry Walker	.40
71	Orlando Cabrera	.40
72	Jorge Posada	.50
73	Jamie Moyer	.25
74	Carl Crawford	.25
75	Hank Blalock	.50
76	Josh Beckett	.75
77	Jody Gerut	.25
78	Kevin Brown	.50
79	Sammy Sosa	2.00
80	Chipper Jones	1.00
81	Tom Glavine	.50
82	Barry Zito	.50
83	Edgar Renteria	.50
84	Esteban Loaiza	.25
85	Jason Giambi	1.00
86	Miguel Tejada	.50
87	Randy Johnson	1.00
88	A.J. Burnett	.25
89	Richie Sexson	.75
90	Reggie Sanders	.25
91	Carlos Delgado	.75
92	Pat Burrell	.50
93	Jacque Jones	.25
94	Roy Oswalt	.50
95	Frank Thomas	.75
96	Melvin Mora	.25
97	Jeremy Bonderman	.25
98	Mike Sweeney	.25
99	Brian Giles	.50
100	Edgar Martinez	.40
101	Mark Teixeira	.50
102	Sean Casey	.25
103	Javier Vazquez	.50
104	Hideki Matsui	2.50

105	Jim Edmonds	.40
106	Roy Halladay	.50
107	Craig Biggio	.40
108	Geoff Jenkins	.50
109	Alfonso Soriano	1.00
110	Barry Larkin	.50
111	Chris Bootcheck	4.00
112	Dallas McPherson/99	6.00
113	Matt Kata/99	6.00
114	Scott Hairston	4.00
115	Bobby Crosby	8.00
116	Adam Wainright/99	6.00
117	Daniel Cabrera	4.00
118	Kevin Youkilis	8.00
119	Ronny Cedeno RC	6.00
120	Ruddy Yan RC	4.00
121	Ryan Wing	4.00
122	William Bergolla RC	5.00
123	Edwin Encarnacion	4.00
124	Jonny Gomes	4.00
125	Garrett Atkins	4.00
126	Clint Barmes	4.00
127	Wilfredo Ledezma	4.00
128	Cody Ross	6.00
129	Josh Willingham/99	6.00
130	Chin-Hui Tsao	4.00
131	Hector Gimenez RC	6.00
132	David DeJesus	4.00
133	Jimmy Gobble	4.00
134	Edwin Jackson/99	6.00
135	Koyie Hill	4.00
136	Rickie Weeks/99	8.00
137	Graham Koonce	4.00
138	Rob Bowen	6.00
139	Shawn Hill RC	4.00
140	Craig Brazell	4.00
141	Mike Hessman	4.00
142	Jorge DePaula	4.00
143	Chien-Ming Wang/99	6.00
144	Rich Harden	4.00
145	Ryan Howard/99	6.00
146	Alfredo Simon RC	4.00
147	Ian Snell RC	6.00
148	Ryan Doumit	4.00
149	Khalil Greene/99	4.00
150	Angel Chavez RC	4.00
151	Dan Haren	6.00
152	Chris Snelling	4.00
153	Aaron Miles	4.00
154	John Gall RC	8.00
155	Chris Narveson	4.00
156	Delmon Young/99	8.00
157	Chad Gaudin	4.00
158	Gerald Laird	4.00
159	Alexis Rios	8.00
160	Jason Arnold	4.00

Gold Proof

Cards (1-110):	3-5X
SP's (111-160):	1X
Production 150 Sets	

Artist's Proof

Cards (1-110):	3-6X
SP's (110-160):	1-1.5X
Production 50 Sets	

Photographer Proof

Cards (1-110):	6-12X
SP's (110-160):	2-3X
Production 25 Sets	

Executive Proof

No Pricing
Production One Set

History of the Draft Game-Used

	NM/M
Common Player:	5.00
Numbered to last 2 digits of draft yr.	
Silver Proof:	1-1.5X
Production 50 Sets	
Gold Proof:	No Pricing
Production 10 Sets	
Garret Anderson	6.00
Josh Beckett	10.00
Carlos Beltran	5.00
Lance Berkman	5.00
Hank Blalock	10.00
Bret Boone	5.00
A.J. Burnett	5.00
Pat Burrell	8.00
Marlon Byrd	5.00
Eric Chavez	6.00
Adam Dunn	8.00
Darin Erstad	6.00
Nomar Garciaparra	10.00
Jason Giambi	5.00
Shawn Green	5.00
Roy Halladay	6.00
Todd Helton	10.00
Tim Hudson	6.00

Aubrey Huff	8.00
Torii Hunter	8.00
Derek Jeter	15.00
Chipper Jones	10.00
Austin Kearns	8.00
Mike Lowell	5.00
Mike Mussina	10.00
Corey Patterson	6.00
Juan Pierre	5.00
Scott Podsednik	10.00
Jorge Posada	10.00
Albert Pujols	20.00
Manny Ramirez	8.00
Alex Rodriguez	15.00
Scott Rolen	10.00
Jason Schmidt	6.00
Richie Sexson	8.00
Shannon Stewart	5.00
Javier Vazquez	5.00
Vernon Wells	6.00
Kerry Wood	5.00
Barry Zito	8.00

History of the Draft Autographs

	NM/M
Common Autograph:	10.00
Production 199 Sets	
Draft Year:	1-1.25X
#'d to last 2 digits of draft year	
Silver Proof:	1-1.5X
Production 50 Sets	
Gold Proof:	No Pricing
Production 10 Sets	
Hank Blalock	20.00
A.J. Burnett	10.00
Marlon Byrd	10.00
Roy Halladay	20.00
Tim Hudson	15.00
Aubrey Huff	15.00
Torii Hunter	15.00
Austin Kearns	20.00
Mike Lowell	10.00
Corey Patterson	20.00
Juan Pierre	15.00
Scott Podsednik	20.00
Albert Pujols	120.00
Scott Rolen	30.00
Shannon Stewart	10.00
Javier Vazquez	10.00
Vernon Wells	15.00

Jersey Proof

		NM/M
Common Player:		5.00
Production 299 Sets		
Silver Proof:		1.5-2X
Production 50 Sets		
Gold Proof:		No Pricing
Production 10 Sets		
1	Troy Glaus	5.00
2	Curt Schilling	6.00
3	Randy Johnson	8.00
4	Brandon Webb	5.00
5	Gary Sheffield	5.00
6	Greg Maddux	15.00
7	Chipper Jones	10.00
8	David Ortiz	10.00
9	Nomar Garciaparra	15.00
10	Pedro J. Martinez	8.00
11	Manny Ramirez	8.00
12	Kerry Wood	8.00
13	Mark Prior	10.00
14	Sammy Sosa	12.00
15	Frank Thomas	8.00
16	Austin Kearns	6.00
17	Todd Helton	8.00
18	Preston Wilson	5.00
19	Juan Pierre	5.00
20	Josh Beckett	6.00
21	Ivan Rodriguez	6.00
22	Miguel Cabrera	8.00
23	Mike Lowell	6.00
24	Lance Berkman	6.00
25	Jeff Bagwell	8.00
26	Angel Berroa	5.00
27	Hideo Nomo	10.00
28	Eric Gagne	8.00
29	Scott Podsednik	6.00
30	Richie Sexson	6.00
31	Torii Hunter	6.00
32	Mike Piazza	10.00
33	Jose Reyes	8.00
34	Tom Glavine	8.00
35	Derek Jeter	30.00
36	Jorge Posada	6.00
37	Jason Giambi	6.00
38	Alfonso Soriano	8.00
39	Eric Chavez	6.00
40	Miguel Tejada	5.00
41	Jim Thome	10.00
42	Albert Pujols	15.00
43	Scott Rolen	8.00

44	Rocco Baldelli	10.00
45	Alex Rodriguez	10.00
46	Hank Blalock	8.00
47	Mark Teixeira	6.00
48	Rafael Palmeiro	10.00
49	Carlos Delgado	6.00
50	Roy Halladay	6.00

L.E.ague L.E.aders

ALEX RODRIGUEZ/SS

		NM/M
Complete Set (10):		10.00
Common Player:		.50
Inserted 1:18		
1LL	Alex Rodriguez	3.00
2LL	Jim Thome	1.50
3LL	Albert Pujols	3.00
4LL	Pedro J. Martinez	1.50
5LL	Roy Halladay	.75
6LL	Jason Schmidt	.50
7LL	Kerry Wood	1.00
8LL	Juan Pierre	.50
9LL	Preston Wilson	.50
10LL	Carlos Delgado	.50

L.E.ague L.E.aders Game-Used

JUAN PIERRE/OF

	NM/M
Common Player:	6.00
Production 75 Sets	
Silver Proof:	1-1.5X
Production 50 Sets	
Gold Proof:	No Pricing
Production 10 Sets	
Alex Rodriguez	12.00
Jim Thome	10.00
Albert Pujols	20.00
Pedro J. Martinez	10.00
Roy Halladay	8.00
Jason Schmidt	8.00
Kerry Wood	8.00
Juan Pierre	6.00
Preston Wilson	6.00
Carlos Delgado	8.00

Rare Form

		NM/M
Common Player:		5.00
Inserted 1:288		
1	Albert Pujols	20.00
2	Miguel Cabrera	5.00
3	Jim Thome	10.00
4	Derek Jeter	30.00
5	Nomar Garciaparra	15.00
6	Mike Piazza	15.00
7	Alex Rodriguez	20.00
8	Delmon Young	15.00
9	Chipper Jones	12.00
10	Rickie Weeks	10.00

Rare Form Autographs

	NM/M
Common Autograph:	10.00
Production 299 Sets	
Level 2:	1-1.5X
Production 99 Sets	
Silver Proof:	1.5X
Production 50 Sets	
Gold Proof:	No Pricing
Production 10 Sets	
Rocco Baldelli	25.00
Angel Berroa	15.00
Miguel Cabrera	
Rich Harden	20.00
Edwin Jackson	20.00
Matt Kata	10.00
Dallas McPherson	15.00
Brandon Webb	15.00
Rickie Weeks	30.00
Delmon Young	30.00

Rare Form Game-Used Silver Proof

	NM/M
Common Player:	8.00
Production 50 Sets	
Gold Proof:	No Pricing
Production 10 Sets	
Rocco Baldelli	15.00
Miguel Cabrera	8.00
Nomar Garciaparra	15.00
Derek Jeter	30.00
Chipper Jones	12.00
Mike Piazza	25.00
Albert Pujols	25.00
Alex Rodriguez	15.00
Jim Thome	12.00

Rare Form Memorabilia Jersey Number

	NM/M
Numbered to jersey number.	
Most not priced due to scarcity.	
Mike Piazza/31	30.00
Jim Thome/25	25.00

Sky's the Limit

		NM/M
Complete Set (20):		20.00
Common Player:		.50
Inserted 1:6		
1SL	Dontrelle Willis	1.00
2SL	Rocco Baldelli	1.00
3SL	Miguel Cabrera	1.00
4SL	Mark Prior	3.00
5SL	Hideki Matsui	4.00
6SL	Kerry Wood	1.50
7SL	Alfonso Soriano	1.50
8SL	Ichiro Suzuki	2.50
9SL	Brandon Webb	.50
10SL	Alex Rodriguez	3.00
11SL	Barry Zito	1.00
12SL	Hank Blalock	1.00
13SL	Jose Reyes	.75
14SL	Torii Hunter	.75
15SL	Josh Beckett	1.00
16SL	Manny Ramirez	1.00
17SL	Andruw Jones	1.00
18SL	Vladimir Guerrero	1.50
19SL	Miguel Tejada	.75
20SL	Carlos Delgado	1.00

Sky's the Limit Game-Used

	NM/M
Common Player:	5.00
Production 99 Sets	
Silver Proof:	1X
Production 50 Sets	
Gold Proof:	No Pricing
Production 10 Sets	
Rocco Baldelli	15.00
Josh Beckett	8.00
Hank Blalock	6.00
Miguel Cabrera	8.00
Vladimir Guerrero	8.00
Torii Hunter	8.00
Andruw Jones	6.00
Mark Prior	10.00
Manny Ramirez	8.00
Jose Reyes	6.00
Alex Rodriguez	10.00
Alfonso Soriano	8.00
Miguel Tejada	6.00
Brandon Webb	5.00
Dontrelle Willis	5.00
Kerry Wood	10.00
Barry Zito	6.00

2005 SkyBox Autographics

	NM/M
Complete Set (115):	
Common Player (1-60):	.15
Common (61-115):	1.50
Production 750	
Pack (5):	8.00
Box (12):	85.00
1 Vladimir Guerrero	.75
2 Garret Anderson	.25
3 Troy Glaus	.25
4 Shawn Green	.25
5 Chipper Jones	.75
6 Andruw Jones	.40
7 Miguel Tejada	.50
8 Melvin Mora	.15
9 Manny Ramirez	.75
10 Curt Schilling	.75
11 Nomar Garciaparra	.75
12 Mark Prior	.50
13 Sammy Sosa	1.00
14 Frank Thomas	.40
15 Paul Konerko	.25
16 Adam Dunn	.50
17 Ken Griffey Jr.	1.50
18 Victor Martinez	.25
19 Travis Hafner	.50
20 Todd Helton	.50
21 Ivan Rodriguez	.50
22 Carlos Guillen	.15
23 Miguel Cabrera	.75
24 Juan Pierre	.15
25 Roger Clemens	2.00
26 Jeff Bagwell	.50
27 Lance Berkman	.25
28 Mike Sweeney	.15
29 Eric Gagne	.15
30 J.D. Drew	.15
31 Ben Sheets	.25
32 Lyle Overbay	.15
33 Johan Santana	.50
34 Torii Hunter	.15
35 Mike Piazza	1.00
36 Pedro Martinez	.75
37 Carlos Beltran	.50
38 Derek Jeter	2.00
39 Alex Rodriguez	2.00
40 Hideki Matsui	1.50
41 Randy Johnson	.75
42 Eric Chavez	.25
43 Jim Thome	.50
44 Craig Wilson	.15
45 Khalil Greene	.25
46 Jake Peavy	.25
47 Jason Schmidt	.15
48 Ichiro Suzuki	1.50
49 Adrian Beltre	.25
50 Albert Pujols	2.00
51 Scott Rolen	.50
52 Carl Crawford	.15
53 Rocco Baldelli	.15
54 Alfonso Soriano	.50
55 Hank Blalock	.25
56 Vernon Wells	.15
57 Jose Vidro	.15
58 David Ortiz	.75
59 Bobby Abreu	.25
60 Gary Sheffield	.40
61 Nolan Ryan	15.00
62 Mike Schmidt	10.00
63 Johnny Bench	8.00
64 Lou Brock	3.00
65 Dennis Eckersley	2.00
66 Carlton Fisk	3.00
67 Bob Gibson	4.00
68 Reggie Jackson	4.00
69 Al Kaline	3.00
70 Bill Mazeroski	2.00
71 Willie McCovey	3.00
72 Jim Palmer	2.00
73 Phil Rizzuto	2.00
74 Warren Spahn	4.00
75 Brooks Robinson	3.00
76 Willie Stargell	3.00
77 Jim "Catfish" Hunter	2.00
78 Tony Perez	2.00
79 George Kell	2.00
80 Robin Yount	4.00
81 Fergie Jenkins	2.00
82 Tom Seaver	3.00
83 Eddie Mathews	3.00
84 Enos Slaughter	2.00
85 Pee Wee Reese	2.00
86 Harmon Killebrew	3.00
87 Eddie Murray	3.00
88 Orlando Cepeda	2.00
89 Billy Williams	2.00
90 Ralph Kiner	2.00
91 Ryan Raburn	1.50
92 Justin Morneau	2.00
93 Zack Greinke	1.50
94 David Aardsma	1.50
95 B.J. Upton	2.00
96 Gavin Floyd	1.50
97 David Wright	8.00
98 Russ Adams	1.50
99 Jose Lopez	2.00
100 Scott Kazmir	2.00
101 Mike Gosling	1.50
102 Jeff Keppinger	1.50
103 David Krynzel	1.50
104 Jeff Niemann RC	6.00
105 Ruben Gotay	1.50
106 Dioner Navarro	1.50
107 Nick Swisher	1.50
108 Yadier Molina	1.50
109 Joey Gathright	1.50
110 Jon Knott	1.50
111 J.D. Durbin	1.50
112 Andres Blanco	1.50
113 Charlton Jimerson	1.50
114 Sean Barnett	1.50
115 Justin Verlander RC	6.00

Insignia

Insignia (1-60):	2-3X
Insignia (61-115):	1X
Production 150 Sets	

Royal Insignia

Royal Insignia (1-60):	4-6X
Royal Insignia (61-115):	1.5-2X
Production 25 Sets	

Future Signs

	NM/M
Common Player:	.50
Inserted 1:6	
1 Bobby Crosby	.50
2 David Aardsma	.50
3 Russ Adams	.50
4 J.D. Durbin	.50
5 Johnny Estrada	.50
6 Chone Figgins	.50
7 Jason Bay	.75
8 Gavin Floyd	.50
9 Lew Ford	.50
10 Victor Martinez	.50
11 Joe Mauer	.75
12 Justin Morneau	.50
13 Laynce Nix	.50
14 Sean Burnett	.50
15 B.J. Upton	.75
16 Justin Verlander	1.50
17 David Wright	3.00
18 Delmon Young	1.00
19 Michael Young	.50
20 Zack Greinke	.50

Future Signs Autograph Blue

	NM/M
Production 8-505	
Cards not serial numbered.	
JB Jason Bay/264	15.00
ZG Zack Greinke/264	10.00
VM Victor Martinez/500	12.00
JM Justin Morneau/224	20.00
AO Akinori Otsuka/639	10.00
JV Justin Verlander/505	25.00

Future Signs Autograph Gold

	NM/M
Production 65 Sets	
JB Jason Bay	15.00
SB Sean Burnett	10.00
JD J.D. Durbin	5.00
EE Edwin Encarnacion	10.00
ZG Zack Greinke	8.00
SH Scott Hairston	8.00
VMJ Val Majewski	15.00
VM Victor Martinez	15.00
JM Justin Morneau	20.00
AO Akinori Otsuka	10.00
AS Alfredo Simon	5.00
BU B.J. Upton	15.00
JV Justin Verlander	30.00
RW Rickie Weeks	25.00
DW David Wright	50.00

Future Signs Autograph Gold Embossed

	NM/M
Production 45 Sets	
JB Jason Bay	15.00
SB Sean Burnett	10.00
JD J.D. Durbin	5.00
EE Edwin Encarnacion	10.00
ZG Zack Greinke	8.00
SH Scott Hairston	8.00
VMJ Val Majewski	15.00
VM Victor Martinez	15.00
JM Justin Morneau	20.00
AO Akinori Otsuka	10.00
AS Alfredo Simon	5.00
BU B.J. Upton	15.00
JV Justin Verlander	30.00
RW Rickie Weeks	25.00
DW David Wright	50.00
DY Delmon Young	25.00

Future Signs Autograph Platinum

	NM/M
Production 25 Sets	
Gold Embossed:	No Pricing
Production 5 Sets	
JB Jason Bay	20.00
SB Sean Burnett	10.00
JD J.D. Durbin	8.00
EE Edwin Encarnacion	10.00
ZG Zack Greinke	10.00
SH Scott Hairston	10.00
VMJ Val Majewski	15.00
VM Victor Martinez	20.00
JM Justin Morneau	25.00
AO Akinori Otsuka	15.00
AS Alfredo Simon	8.00
BU B.J. Upton	15.00
JV Justin Verlander	35.00
RW Rickie Weeks	30.00
DW David Wright	60.00
DY Delmon Young	30.00

Future Signs Autograph Silver

	NM/M
Production 100 Sets	
Silver Embossed:	1X
Production 85 Sets	
JB Jason Bay	15.00
SB Sean Burnett	10.00
JD J.D. Durbin	5.00
EE Edwin Encarnacion	10.00
ZG Zack Greinke	8.00
VMJ Val Majewski	15.00
VM Victor Martinez	15.00
JM Justin Morneau	20.00
AO Akinori Otsuka	10.00
AS Alfredo Simon	5.00
BU B.J. Upton	15.00
JV Justin Verlander	30.00
RW Rickie Weeks	25.00
DW David Wright	50.00

Jerseygraphics Blue

	NM/M
Common Player:	4.00
Inserted 1:40 Retail	
Gold:	1-2X
Inserted 1:240 Retail	
Silver:	1X
Inserted 1:80 Retail	
GA Garret Anderson	4.00
JB Jeff Bagwell	6.00
RB Rocco Baldelli	4.00
JBE Josh Beckett	4.00
AB Adrian Beltre	4.00
HB Hank Blalock	4.00
MB Marlon Byrd	4.00
MC Miguel Cabrera	8.00
CD Carlos Delgado	4.00
AD Adam Dunn	6.00
EG Eric Gagne	4.00
BG Brian Giles	4.00
TG Troy Glaus	4.00
TGL Tom Glavine	4.00
TH Torii Hunter	4.00
AK Austin Kearns	4.00
MO Magglio Ordonez	4.00
JR Jose Reyes	6.00
BS Ben Sheets	4.00
MT Mark Teixeira	6.00

Master Collection

Production 25 Sets
All are Jsy/Jsy/Patch combos.

One of a Kind:	No Pricing
Production One Set	

Signature Blue

	NM/M
Print run info provided by UD.	
Cards are not serial #'d.	
Jsy Gold:	1-1.5X
Production 45 Sets	
Jsy Gold Embossed:	1-2X
Production 30 Sets	
Jsy Silver:	1X
Production 100 Sets	
Jsy Silver Embossed:	1X
Production 75 Sets	
EP Jeremy Bonderman/369	12.00
MC Miguel Cabrera/250	30.00
MCA Mike Cameron/200	10.00
CC Carl Crawford/150	15.00
DE David Eckstein/546	20.00
AE Adam Everett/590	6.00
LG Luis Gonzalez/187	6.00
THA Travis Hafner/246	15.00
TH Trevor Hoffman/590	12.00

OH	Orlando Hudson/231	8.00
CK	Casey Kotchman/227	10.00
JK	Jason Kubel/137	8.00
BL	Brad Lidge/164	20.00
JO	John Olerud/446	15.00
CP	Corey Patterson/329	8.00
EP	Eduardo Perez/584	6.00
JR	Jose Reyes	
JS	Johan Santana/200	30.00

Signatures Game Patch Gold

No Pricing
Production 5 Sets
Gold Embossed
Production 15 Sets
Masterpiece Embossed:
No Pricing
Production One Set

Signatures Game Patch Silver

		NM/M
	Production 25 Sets	
RB	Rocco Baldelli	40.00
JB	Jeremy Bonderman	40.00
SS	Shannon Stewart	20.00

Signature Moments

		NM/M
Complete Set (10):		15.00
Common Player:		1.00
Inserted 1:12		
1	Manny Ramirez	1.50
2	Derek Jeter	4.00
3	Ichiro Suzuki	3.00
4	Roger Clemens	4.00
5	Albert Pujols	4.00
6	Nolan Ryan	4.00
7	Reggie Jackson	1.50
8	Carlton Fisk	1.00
9	Mike Schmidt	1.50
10	Johnny Bench	1.50

1993 SP

		NM/M
Complete Set (290):		75.00
Common Player:		.10
Pack (12):		10.00
Wax Box (24):		220.00
1	Roberto Alomar	.30
2	Wade Boggs	2.00
3	Joe Carter	.10
4	Ken Griffey Jr.	2.50
5	Mark Langston	.10
6	John Olerud	.10
7	Kirby Puckett	2.00
8	Cal Ripken, Jr.	4.00

9	Ivan Rodriguez	1.25
10	Barry Bonds	4.00
11	Darren Daulton	.10
12	Marquis Grissom	.10
13	Dave Justice	.10
14	John Kruk	.10
15	Barry Larkin	.10
16	Terry Mulholland	.10
17	Ryne Sandberg	2.00
18	Gary Sheffield	.10
19	Chad Curtis	.10
20	Chili Davis	.10
21	Gary DiSarcina	.10
22	Damion Easley	.10
23	Chuck Finley	.10
24	Luis Polonia	.10
25	Tim Salmon	.10
26	J.T. Snow RC	1.00
27	Russ Springer	.10
28	Jeff Bagwell	1.50
29	Craig Biggio	.10
30	Ken Caminiti	.10
31	Andujar Cedeno	.10
32	Doug Drabek	.10
33	Steve Finley	.10
34	Luis Gonzalez	.10
35	Pete Harnisch	.10
36	Darryl Kile	.10
37	Mike Bordick	.10
38	Dennis Eckersley	1.25
39	Brent Gates	.10
40	Rickey Henderson	1.50
41	Mark McGwire	3.00
42	Craig Paquette	.10
43	Ruben Sierra	.10
44	Terry Steinbach	.10
45	Todd Van Poppel	.10
46	Pat Borders	.10
47	Tony Fernandez	.10
48	Juan Guzman	.10
49	Pat Hentgen	.10
50	Paul Molitor	1.50
51	Jack Morris	.10
52	Ed Sprague	.10
53	Duane Ward	.10
54	Devon White	.10
55	Steve Avery	.10
56	Jeff Blauser	.10
57	Ron Gant	.10
58	Tom Glavine	.40
59	Greg Maddux	2.00
60	Fred McGriff	.10
61	Terry Pendleton	.10
62	Deion Sanders	.10
63	John Smoltz	.10
64	Cal Eldred	.10
65	Darryl Hamilton	.10
66	John Jaha	.10
67	Pat Listach	.10
68	Jaime Navarro	.10
69	Kevin Reimer	.10
70	B.J. Surhoff	.10
71	Greg Vaughn	.10
72	Robin Yount	1.50
73	Rene Arocha RC	.10
74	Bernard Gilkey	.10
75	Gregg Jefferies	.10
76	Ray Lankford	.10
77	Tom Pagnozzi	.10
78	Lee Smith	.10
79	Ozzie Smith	2.00
80	Bob Tewksbury	.10
81	Mark Whiten	.10
82	Steve Buechele	.10
83	Mark Grace	.10
84	Jose Guzman	.10
85	Derrick May	.10
86	Mike Morgan	.10
87	Randy Myers	.10
88	Kevin Roberson RC	.10
89	Sammy Sosa	2.00
90	Rick Wilkins	.10
91	Brett Butler	.10
92	Eric Davis	.10
93	Orel Hershiser	.10
94	Eric Karros	.10
95	Ramon Martinez	.10
96	Raul Mondesi	.10
97	Jose Offerman	.10
98	Mike Piazza	2.50
99	Darryl Strawberry	.10
100	Moises Alou	.10
101	Wil Cordero	.10
102	Delino DeShields	.10
103	Darrin Fletcher	.10
104	Ken Hill	.10
105	Mike Lansing RC	.40
106	Dennis Martinez	.10
107	Larry Walker	.10
108	John Wetteland	.10
109	Rod Beck	.10
110	John Burkett	.10
111	Will Clark	.10
112	Royce Clayton	.10
113	Darren Lewis	.10
114	Willie McGee	.10

115	Bill Swift	.10
116	Robby Thompson	.10
117	Matt Williams	.10
118	Sandy Alomar Jr.	.10
119	Carlos Baerga	.10
120	Albert Belle	.10
121	Reggie Jefferson	.10
122	Kenny Lofton	.10
123	Wayne Kirby	.10
124	Carlos Martinez	.10
125	Charles Nagy	.10
126	Paul Sorrento	.10
127	Rich Amaral	.10
128	Jay Buhner	.10
129	Norm Charlton	.10
130	Dave Fleming	.10
131	Erik Hanson	.10
132	Randy Johnson	1.50
133	Edgar Martinez	.10
134	Tino Martinez	.10
135	Omar Vizquel	.10
136	Bret Barberie	.10
137	Chuck Carr	.10
138	Jeff Conine	.10
139	Orestes Destrade	.10
140	Chris Hammond	.10
141	Bryan Harvey	.10
142	Benito Santiago	.10
143	Walt Weiss	.10
144	Darrell Whitmore RC	.10
145	Tim Bolger RC	.10
146	Bobby Bonilla	.10
147	Jeromy Burnitz	.10
148	Vince Coleman	.10
149	Dwight Gooden	.10
150	Todd Hundley	.10
151	Howard Johnson	.10
152	Eddie Murray	1.50
153	Bret Saberhagen	.10
154	Brady Anderson	.10
155	Mike Devereaux	.10
156	Jeffrey Hammonds	.10
157	Chris Hoiles	.10
158	Ben McDonald	.10
159	Mark McLemore	.10
160	Mike Mussina	.50
161	Gregg Olson	.10
162	David Segui	.10
163	Derek Bell	.10
164	Andy Benes	.10
165	Archi Cianfrocco	.10
166	Ricky Gutierrez	.10
167	Tony Gwynn	2.00
168	Gene Harris	.10
169	Trevor Hoffman	.10
170	Ray McDavid RC	.10
171	Phil Plantier	.10
172	Mariano Duncan	.10
173	Len Dykstra	.10
174	Tommy Greene	.10
175	Dave Hollins	.10
176	Pete Incaviglia	.10
177	Mickey Morandini	.10
178	Curt Schilling	.40
179	Kevin Stocker	.10
180	Mitch Williams	.10
181	Stan Belinda	.10
182	Jay Bell	.10
183	Steve Cooke	.10
184	Carlos Garcia	.10
185	Jeff King	.10
186	Orlando Merced	.10
187	Don Slaught	.10
188	Andy Van Slyke	.10
189	Kevin Young	.10
190	Kevin Brown	.10
191	Jose Canseco	.60
192	Julio Franco	.10
193	Benji Gil	.10
194	Juan Gonzalez	.75
195	Tom Henke	.10
196	Rafael Palmeiro	1.25
197	Dean Palmer	.10
198	Nolan Ryan	4.00
199	Roger Clemens	2.25
200	Scott Cooper	.10
201	Andre Dawson	.35
202	Mike Greenwell	.10
203	Carlos Quintana	.10
204	Jeff Russell	.10
205	Aaron Sele	.10
206	Mo Vaughn	.10
207	Frank Viola	.10
208	Rob Dibble	.10
209	Roberto Kelly	.10
210	Kevin Mitchell	.10
211	Hal Morris	.10
212	Joe Oliver	.10
213	Jose Rijo	.10
214	Bip Roberts	.10
215	Chris Sabo	.10
216	Reggie Sanders	.10
217	Dante Bichette	.10
218	Jerald Clark	.10
219	Alex Cole	.10
220	Andres Galarraga	.10

221	Joe Girardi	.10
222	Charlie Hayes	.10
223	Robert Mejia RC	.10
224	Armando Reynoso	.10
225	Eric Young	.10
226	Kevin Appier	.10
227	George Brett	2.25
228	David Cone	.10
229	Phil Hiatt	.10
230	Felix Jose	.10
231	Wally Joyner	.10
232	Mike Macfarlane	.10
233	Brian McRae	.10
234	Jeff Montgomery	.10
235	Rob Deer	.10
236	Cecil Fielder	.10
237	Travis Fryman	.10
238	Mike Henneman	.10
239	Tony Phillips	.10
240	Mickey Tettleton	.10
241	Alan Trammell	.10
242	David Wells	.10
243	Lou Whitaker	.10
244	Rick Aguilera	.10
245	Scott Erickson	.10
246	Brian Harper	.10
247	Kent Hrbek	.10
248	Chuck Knoblauch	.10
249	Shane Mack	.10
250	David McCarty	.10
251	Pedro Munoz	.10
252	Dave Winfield	1.50
253	Alex Fernandez	.10
254	Ozzie Guillen	.10
255	Bo Jackson	.20
256	Lance Johnson	.10
257	Ron Karkovice	.10
258	Jack McDowell	.10
259	Tim Raines	.10
260	Frank Thomas	1.50
261	Robin Ventura	.10
262	Jim Abbott	.10
263	Steve Farr	.10
264	Jimmy Key	.10
265	Don Mattingly	2.25
266	Paul O'Neill	.10
267	Mike Stanley	.10
268	Danny Tartabull	.10
269	Bob Wickman	.10
270	Bernie Williams	.10
271	Jason Bere	.10
272	Roger Cedeno RC	.50
273	Johnny Damon RC	12.00
274	Russ Davis RC	.25
275	Carlos Delgado	.75
276	Carl Everett	.10
277	Cliff Floyd	.10
278	Alex Gonzalez	.10
279	Derek Jeter RC	75.00
280	Chipper Jones	2.00
281	Javier Lopez	.10
282	Chad Mottola RC	.10
283	Marc Newfield	.10
284	Eduardo Perez	.10
285	Manny Ramirez	1.50
286	Todd Steverson RC	.10
287	Michael Tucker	.10
288	Allen Watson	.10
289	Rondell White	.10
290	Dmitri Young	.10

Platinum Power

		NM/M
Complete Set (20):		27.50
Common Player:		.50
1	Albert Belle	.50
2	Barry Bonds	5.00
3	Joe Carter	.50
4	Will Clark	.50
5	Darren Daulton	.50
6	Cecil Fielder	.50
7	Ron Gant	.50
8	Juan Gonzalez	1.00
9	Ken Griffey Jr.	3.00
10	Dave Hollins	.50

11	Dave Justice	.50
12	Fred McGriff	.50
13	Mark McGwire	5.00
14	Dean Palmer	.50
15	Mike Piazza	3.00
16	Tim Salmon	.50
17	Ryne Sandberg	2.50
18	Gary Sheffield	.75
19	Frank Thomas	2.00
20	Matt Williams	.50

1994 SP

	NM/M
Complete Set (200):	100.00
Common Player:	.10
Die-Cut:	1-2X
Pack (8):	15.00
Wax Box (32):	450.00

1	Mike Bell RC	.10
2	D.J. Boston	.10
3	Johnny Damon	.45
4	Brad Fullmer RC	.75
5	Joey Hamilton	.10
6	Todd Hollandsworth	.10
7	Brian Hunter	.10
8	LaTroy Hawkins RC	.25
9	Brooks Kieschnick RC	.10
10	Derrek Lee RC	15.00
11	Trot Nixon RC	3.00
12	Alex Ochoa	.10
13	Chan Ho Park RC	1.50
14	Kirk Presley RC	.10
15	Alex Rodriguez RC	140.00
16	Jose Silva RC	.10
17	Terrell Wade RC	.10
18	Billy Wagner RC	1.00
19	Glenn Williams RC	.10
20	Preston Wilson	.10
21	Brian Anderson	.10
22	Chad Curtis	.10
23	Chili Davis	.10
24	Bo Jackson	.25
25	Mark Langston	.10
26	Tim Salmon	.10
27	Jeff Bagwell	1.00
28	Craig Biggio	.10
29	Ken Caminiti	.10
30	Doug Drabek	.10
31	John Hudek	.10
32	Greg Swindell	.10
33	Brent Gates	.10
34	Rickey Henderson	1.00
35	Steve Karsay	.10
36	Mark McGwire	2.50
37	Ruben Sierra	.10
38	Terry Steinbach	.10
39	Roberto Alomar	.30
40	Joe Carter	.10
41	Carlos Delgado	.50
42	Alex Gonzalez	.10
43	Juan Guzman	.10
44	Paul Molitor	1.00
45	John Olerud	.10
46	Devon White	.10
47	Steve Avery	.10
48	Jeff Blauser	.10
49	Tom Glavine	.35
50	Dave Justice	.10
51	Roberto Kelly	.10
52	Ryan Klesko	.10
53	Javier Lopez	.10
54	Greg Maddux	1.25
55	Fred McGriff	.10
56	Ricky Bones	.10
57	Cal Eldred	.10
58	Brian Harper	.10
59	Pat Listach	.10
60	B.J. Surhoff	.10
61	Greg Vaughn	.10
62	Bernard Gilkey	.10
63	Gregg Jefferies	.10
64	Ray Lankford	.10
65	Ozzie Smith	1.25
66	Bob Tewksbury	.10

67	Mark Whiten	.10
68	Todd Zeile	.10
69	Mark Grace	.10
70	Randy Myers	.10
71	Ryne Sandberg	1.25
72	Sammy Sosa	1.25
73	Steve Trachsel	.10
74	Rick Wilkins	.10
75	Brett Butler	.10
76	Delino DeShields	.10
77	Orel Hershiser	.10
78	Eric Karros	.10
79	Raul Mondesi	.10
80	Mike Piazza	2.00
81	Tim Wallach	.10
82	Moises Alou	.10
83	Cliff Floyd	.10
84	Marquis Grissom	.10
85	Pedro Martinez	1.00
86	Larry Walker	.10
87	John Wetteland	.10
88	Rondell White	.10
89	Rod Beck	.10
90	Barry Bonds	3.00
91	John Burkett	.10
92	Royce Clayton	.10
93	Billy Swift	.10
94	Robby Thompson	.10
95	Matt Williams	.10
96	Carlos Baerga	.10
97	Albert Belle	.10
98	Kenny Lofton	.10
99	Dennis Martinez	.10
100	Eddie Murray	1.00
101	Manny Ramirez	1.00
102	Eric Anthony	.10
103	Chris Bosio	.10
104	Jay Buhner	.10
105	Ken Griffey Jr.	2.00
106	Randy Johnson	1.00
107	Edgar Martinez	.10
108	Chuck Carr	.10
109	Jeff Conine	.10
110	Carl Everett	.10
111	Chris Hammond	.10
112	Bryan Harvey	.10
113	Charles Johnson	.10
114	Gary Sheffield	.45
115	Bobby Bonilla	.10
116	Dwight Gooden	.10
117	Todd Hundley	.10
118	Bobby Jones	.10
119	Jeff Kent	.10
120	Bret Saberhagen	.10
121	Jeffrey Hammonds	.10
122	Chris Hoiles	.10
123	Ben McDonald	.10
124	Mike Mussina	.40
125	Rafael Palmeiro	.75
126	Cal Ripken, Jr.	3.00
127	Lee Smith	.10
128	Derek Bell	.10
129	Andy Benes	.10
130	Tony Gwynn	1.25
131	Trevor Hoffman	.10
132	Phil Plantier	.10
133	Bip Roberts	.10
134	Darren Daulton	.10
135	Len Dykstra	.10
136	Dave Hollins	.10
137	Danny Jackson	.10
138	John Kruk	.10
139	Kevin Stocker	.10
140	Jay Bell	.10
141	Carlos Garcia	.10
142	Jeff King	.10
143	Orlando Merced	.10
144	Andy Van Slyke	.10
145	Paul Wagner	.10
146	Jose Canseco	.50
147	Will Clark	.10
148	Juan Gonzalez	.50
149	Rick Helling	.10
150	Dean Palmer	.10
151	Ivan Rodriguez	.75
152	Roger Clemens	1.50
153	Scott Cooper	.10
154	Andre Dawson	.30
155	Mike Greenwell	.10
156	Aaron Sele	.10
157	Mo Vaughn	.50
158	Bret Boone	.10
159	Barry Larkin	.10
160	Kevin Mitchell	.10
161	Jose Rijo	.10
162	Deion Sanders	.10
163	Reggie Sanders	.10
164	Dante Bichette	.10
165	Ellis Burks	.10
166	Andres Galarraga	.10
167	Charlie Hayes	.10
168	David Nied	.10
169	Walt Weiss	.10
170	Kevin Appier	.10
171	David Cone	.10
172	Jeff Granger	.10

173	Felix Jose	.10
174	Wally Joyner	.10
175	Brian McRae	.10
176	Cecil Fielder	.10
177	Travis Fryman	.10
178	Mike Henneman	.10
179	Tony Phillips	.10
180	Mickey Tettleton	.10
181	Alan Trammell	.10
182	Rick Aguilera	.10
183	Rich Becker	.10
184	Scott Erickson	.10
185	Chuck Knoblauch	.10
186	Kirby Puckett	1.25
187	Dave Winfield	1.00
188	Wilson Alvarez	.10
189	Jason Bere	.10
190	Alex Fernandez	.10
191	Julio Franco	.10
192	Jack McDowell	.10
193	Frank Thomas	1.00
194	Robin Ventura	.10
195	Jim Abbott	.10
196	Wade Boggs	1.25
197	Jimmy Key	.10
198	Don Mattingly	1.50
199	Paul O'Neill	.10
200	Danny Tartabull	.10

Die-Cut

(Star cards valued at 1-2X corresponding cards in regular SP issue.)

Holoview Blue

	NM/M
Common Player:	1.50
1 Roberto Alomar	2.00
2 Kevin Appier	1.50
3 Jeff Bagwell	3.00
4 Jose Canseco	3.00
5 Roger Clemens	6.00
6 Carlos Delgado	2.00
7 Cecil Fielder	1.50
8 Cliff Floyd	1.50
9 Travis Fryman	1.50
10 Andres Galarraga	1.50
11 Juan Gonzalez	2.00
12 Ken Griffey Jr.	6.00
13 Tony Gwynn	4.00
14 Jeffrey Hammonds	1.50
15 Bo Jackson	3.00
16 Michael Jordan	15.00
17 Dave Justice	1.50
18 Steve Karsay	1.50
19 Jeff Kent	2.00
20 Brooks Kieschnick	1.50
21 Ryan Klesko	1.50
22 John Kruk	1.50
23 Barry Larkin	2.00
24 Pat Listach	1.50
25 Don Mattingly	5.00

26	Mark McGwire	8.00
27	Raul Mondesi	1.50
28	Trot Nixon	1.50
29	Mike Piazza	6.00
30	Kirby Puckett	4.00
31	Manny Ramirez	3.00
32	Cal Ripken, Jr.	10.00
33	Alex Rodriguez	75.00
34	Tim Salmon	1.50
35	Gary Sheffield	2.00
36	Ozzie Smith	4.00
37	Sammy Sosa	4.00
38	Andy Van Slyke	1.50

Holoview Red

	NM/M
Common Player:	12.00
1 Roberto Alomar	15.00
2 Kevin Appier	12.00
3 Jeff Bagwell	30.00
4 Jose Canseco	20.00
5 Roger Clemens	50.00
6 Carlos Delgado	20.00
7 Cecil Fielder	12.00
8 Cliff Floyd	12.00
9 Travis Fryman	12.00
10 Andres Galarraga	12.00
11 Juan Gonzalez	20.00
12 Ken Griffey Jr.	50.00
13 Tony Gwynn	40.00
14 Jeffrey Hammonds	12.00
15 Bo Jackson	20.00
16 Michael Jordan	120.00
17 Dave Justice	12.00
18 Steve Karsay	12.00
19 Jeff Kent	12.00
20 Brooks Kieschnick	12.00
21 Ryan Klesko	12.00
22 John Kruk	12.00
23 Barry Larkin	12.00
24 Pat Listach	12.00
25 Don Mattingly	45.00
26 Mark McGwire	60.00
27 Raul Mondesi	12.00
28 Trot Nixon	20.00
29 Mike Piazza	50.00
30 Kirby Puckett	40.00
31 Manny Ramirez	30.00
32 Cal Ripken, Jr.	80.00
33 Alex Rodriguez	1,200.00
34 Tim Salmon	12.00
35 Gary Sheffield	15.00
36 Ozzie Smith	40.00
37 Sammy Sosa	40.00
38 Andy Van Slyke	12.00

Alex Rodriguez Autographed Jumbo

	NM/M
15 Alex Rodriguez	250.00

1995 SP

	NM/M
Complete Set (207):	12.50
Common Player:	.05
Pack (8):	1.25
Wax Box (32):	25.00
1 Cal Ripken Jr.	2.00
2 Nolan Ryan	2.00
3 George Brett	1.25
4 Mike Schmidt	1.25
5 Dustin Hermanson	.05
6 Antonio Osuna	.05
7 Mark Grudzielanek RC	.35
8 Ray Durham	.05
9 Ugueth Urbina	.05
10 Ruben Rivera	.05
11 Curtis Goodwin	.05
12 Jimmy Hurst	.05
13 Jose Malave	.05
14 Hideo Nomo RC	1.50
15 Juan Acevedo	.05
16 Tony Clark	.05
17 Jim Pittsley	.05
18 Freddy Garcia RC	.50
19 Carlos Perez RC	.05
20 Raul Casanova RC	.05
21 Quilvio Veras	.05
22 Edgardo Alfonzo	.05
23 Marty Cordova	.05
24 C.J. Nitkowski	.05
25 Wade Boggs Checklist 1-69	.30
26 Dave Winfield Checklist 70-138	.25
27 Eddie Murray Checklist 139-207	.25
28 Dave Justice	.05
29 Marquis Grissom	.05
30 Fred McGriff	.05
31 Greg Maddux	1.00
32 Tom Glavine	.35
33 Steve Avery	.05
34 Chipper Jones	1.00
35 Sammy Sosa	1.00
36 Jaime Navarro	.05
37 Randy Myers	.05
38 Mark Grace	.05
39 Todd Zeile	.05
40 Brian McRae	.05
41 Reggie Sanders	.05
42 Ron Gant	.05
43 Deion Sanders	.05
44 Barry Larkin	.05
45 Bret Boone	.05
46 Jose Rijo	.05
47 Jason Bates	.05
48 Andres Galarraga	.05
49 Bill Swift	.05
50 Larry Walker	.05
51 Vinny Castilla	.05
52 Dante Bichette	.05
53 Jeff Conine	.05
54 John Burkett	.05
55 Gary Sheffield	.40
56 Andre Dawson	.30
57 Terry Pendleton	.05
58 Charles Johnson	.05
59 Brian L. Hunter	.05
60 Jeff Bagwell	.75
61 Craig Biggio	.05
62 Phil Nevin	.05
63 Doug Drabek	.05
64 Derek Bell	.05
65 Raul Mondesi	.05
66 Eric Karros	.05
67 Roger Cedeno	.05
68 Delino DeShields	.05
69 Ramon Martinez	.05
70 Mike Piazza	1.50
71 Billy Ashley	.05
72 Jeff Fassero	.05
73 Shane Andrews	.05

74 Wil Cordero	.05
75 Tony Tarasco	.05
76 Rondell White	.05
77 Pedro Martinez	.75
78 Moises Alou	.05
79 Rico Brogna	.05
80 Bobby Bonilla	.05
81 Jeff Kent	.05
82 Brett Butler	.05
83 Bobby Jones	.05
84 Bill Pulsipher	.05
85 Bret Saberhagen	.05
86 Gregg Jefferies	.05
87 Lenny Dykstra	.05
88 Dave Hollins	.05
89 Charlie Hayes	.05
90 Darren Daulton	.05
91 Curt Schilling	.35
92 Heathcliff Slocumb	.05
93 Carlos Garcia	.05
94 Denny Neagle	.05
95 Jay Bell	.05
96 Orlando Merced	.05
97 Dave Clark	.05
98 Bernard Gilkey	.05
99 Scott Cooper	.05
100 Ozzie Smith	1.00
100 Ken Griffey Jr./PC	2.00
101 Tom Henke	.05
102 Ken Hill	.05
103 Brian Jordan	.05
104 Ray Lankford	.05
105 Tony Gwynn	1.00
106 Andy Benes	.05
107 Ken Caminiti	.05
108 Steve Finley	.05
109 Joey Hamilton	.05
110 Bip Roberts	.05
111 Eddie Williams	.05
112 Rod Beck	.05
113 Matt Williams	.05
114 Glenallen Hill	.05
115 Barry Bonds	2.50
116 Robby Thompson	.05
117 Mark Portugal	.05
118 Brady Anderson	.05
119 Mike Mussina	.35
120 Rafael Palmeiro	.65
121 Chris Hoiles	.05
122 Harold Baines	.05
123 Jeffrey Hammonds	.05
124 Tim Naehring	.05
125 Mo Vaughn	.05
126 Mike Macfarlane	.05
127 Roger Clemens	1.25
128 John Valentin	.05
129 Aaron Sele	.05
130 Jose Canseco	.50
131 J.T. Snow	.05
132 Mark Langston	.05
133 Chili Davis	.05
134 Chuck Finley	.05
135 Tim Salmon	.05
136 Tony Phillips	.05
137 Jason Bere	.05
138 Robin Ventura	.05
139 Tim Raines	.05
140a Frank Thomas (5-yr. BA .326)	.75
140b Frank Thomas (5-yr. BA .303)	.75
141 Alex Fernandez	.05
142 Jim Abbott	.05
143 Wilson Alvarez	.05
144 Carlos Baerga	.05
145 Albert Belle	.05
146 Jim Thome	.65
147 Dennis Martinez	.05
148 Eddie Murray	.75
149 Dave Winfield	.75
150 Kenny Lofton	.05
151 Manny Ramirez	.75
152 Chad Curtis	.05
153 Lou Whitaker	.05
154 Alan Trammell	.05
155 Cecil Fielder	.05
156 Kirk Gibson	.05
157 Michael Tucker	.05
158 Jon Nunnally	.05
159 Wally Joyner	.05
160 Kevin Appier	.05
161 Jeff Montgomery	.05
162 Greg Gagne	.05
163 Ricky Bones	.05
164 Cal Eldred	.05
165 Greg Vaughn	.05
166 Kevin Seitzer	.05
167 Jose Valentin	.05
168 Joe Oliver	.05
169 Rick Aguilera	.05
170 Kirby Puckett	1.00
171 Scott Stahoviak	.05
172 Kevin Tapani	.05
173 Chuck Knoblauch	.05

174 Rich Becker	.05
175 Don Mattingly	1.25
176 Jack McDowell	.05
177 Jimmy Key	.05
178 Paul O'Neill	.05
179 John Wetteland	.05
180 Wade Boggs	1.00
181 Derek Jeter	2.50
182 Rickey Henderson	.75
183 Terry Steinbach	.05
184 Ruben Sierra	.05
185 Mark McGwire	2.00
186 Todd Stottlemyre	.05
187 Dennis Eckersley	.65
188 Alex Rodriguez	2.00
189 Randy Johnson	.75
190 Ken Griffey Jr.	1.50
191 Tino Martinez	.05
192 Jay Buhner	.05
193 Edgar Martinez	.05
194 Mickey Tettleton	.05
195 Juan Gonzalez	.40
196 Benji Gil	.05
197 Dean Palmer	.05
198 Ivan Rodriguez	.65
199 Kenny Rogers	.05
200 Will Clark	.05
201 Roberto Alomar	.05
202 David Cone	.05
203 Paul Molitor	.75
204 Shawn Green	.40
205 Joe Carter	.05
206 Alex Gonzalez	.05
207 Pat Hentgen	.05

SuperbaFoil

Frank Thomas
Chicago White Sox

	NM/M
Complete Set (207):	30.00
Common Player:	.10
SuperbaFoil Stars:	1.5X
(See 1995 SP for checklist and base values.)	

Griffey Gold Signature

	NM/M
190 Ken Griffey Jr.	65.00

Platinum Power

	NM/M
Complete Set (20):	10.00
Common Player:	.20
1 Jeff Bagwell	.75
2 Barry Bonds	2.00
3 Ron Gant	.20
4 Fred McGriff	.20
5 Raul Mondesi	.20
6 Mike Piazza	1.25
7 Larry Walker	.20
8 Matt Williams	.20
9 Albert Belle	.20
10 Cecil Fielder	.20

11 Juan Gonzalez	.40
12 Ken Griffey Jr.	1.25
13 Mark McGwire	1.50
14 Eddie Murray	.75
15 Manny Ramirez	.75
16 Cal Ripken Jr.	2.00
17 Tim Salmon	.20
18 Frank Thomas	.75
19 Jim Thome	.65
20 Mo Vaughn	.20

Special F/X

	NM/M
Complete Set (48):	200.00
Common Player:	2.00
1 Jose Canseco	6.00
2 Roger Clemens	20.00
3 Mo Vaughn	2.00
4 Tim Salmon	2.00
5 Chuck Finley	2.00
6 Robin Ventura	2.00
7 Jason Bere	2.00
8 Carlos Baerga	2.00
9 Albert Belle	2.00
10 Kenny Lofton	3.00
11 Manny Ramirez	8.00
12 Jeff Montgomery	2.00
13 Kirby Puckett	15.00
14 Wade Boggs	5.00
15 Don Mattingly	15.00
16 Cal Ripken Jr.	25.00
17 Ruben Sierra	2.00
18 Ken Griffey Jr.	20.00
19 Randy Johnson	8.00
20 Alex Rodriguez	25.00
21 Will Clark	5.00
22 Juan Gonzalez	4.00
23 Roberto Alomar	4.00
24 Joe Carter	3.00
25 Alex Gonzalez	2.00
26 Paul Molitor	6.00
27 Ryan Klesko	2.00
28 Fred McGriff	3.00
29 Greg Maddux	15.00
30 Sammy Sosa	10.00
31 Bret Boone	2.00
32 Barry Larkin	5.00
33 Reggie Sanders	2.00
34 Dante Bichette	2.00
35 Andres Galarraga	2.00
36 Charles Johnson	2.00
37 Gary Sheffield	5.00
38 Jeff Bagwell	6.00
39 Craig Biggio	4.00
40 Eric Karros	2.00
41 Billy Ashley	2.00
42 Raul Mondesi	2.00
43 Mike Piazza	10.00
44 Rondell White	2.00
45 Bret Saberhagen	2.00
46 Tony Gwynn	8.00

47	Melvin Nieves	2.00
48	Matt Williams	2.00

1995 SP/Championship

		NM/M
Complete Set (200):		25.00
Common Player:		.05
Die-Cuts:		1.5X
Wax Pack (6):		1.00
Wax Box (44):		30.00
1	Hideo Nomo RC	1.50
2	Roger Cedeno	.05
3	Curtis Goodwin	.05
4	Jon Nunnally	.05
5	Bill Pulsipher	.05
6	C.J. Nitkowski	.05
7	Dustin Hermanson	.05
8	Marty Cordova	.05
9	Ruben Rivera	.05
10	Ariel Prieto RC	.05
11	Edgardo Alfonzo	.05
12	Ray Durham	.05
13	Quilvio Veras	.05
14	Ugueth Urbina	.05
15	Carlos Perez RC	.05
16	Glenn Dishman RC	.05
17	Jeff Suppan	.05
18	Jason Bates	.05
19	Jason Isringhausen	.05
20	Derek Jeter	2.00
21	Fred McGriff	.05
22	Marquis Grissom	.05
23	Fred McGriff	.05
24	Tom Glavine	.35
25	Greg Maddux	1.00
26	Chipper Jones	1.00
27	Sammy Sosa	.50
28	Randy Myers	.05
29	Mark Grace	.05
30	Sammy Sosa	1.00
31	Todd Zeile	.05
32	Brian McRae	.05
33	Ron Gant	.05
34	Reggie Sanders	.05
35	Ron Gant	.05
36	Barry Larkin	.05
37	Bret Boone	.05
38	John Smiley	.05
39	Larry Walker	.05
40	Andres Galarraga	.05
41	Bill Swift	.05
42	Larry Walker	.05
43	Vinny Castilla	.05
44	Dante Bichette	.05
45	Jeff Conine	.05
46	Charles Johnson	.05
47	Gary Sheffield	.45
48	Andre Dawson	.25
49	Jeff Conine	.05
50	Jeff Bagwell	.40
51	Phil Nevin	.05
52	Craig Biggio	.05
53	Brian L. Hunter	.05
54	Doug Drabek	.05
55	Jeff Bagwell	.75
56	Derek Bell	.05
57	Mike Piazza	.65
58	Raul Mondesi	.05
59	Eric Karros	.05
60	Mike Piazza	1.25
61	Ramon Martinez	.05
62	Billy Ashley	.05
63	Rondell White	.05
64	Jeff Fassero	.05
65	Moises Alou	.05
66	Tony Tarasco	.05
67	Rondell White	.05
68	Pedro Martinez	.75
69	Bobby Jones	.05
70	Bobby Bonilla	.05
71	Bobby Jones	.05
72	Bret Saberhagen	.05
73	Darren Daulton	.05
74	Darren Daulton	.05
75	Gregg Jefferies	.05
76	Tyler Green	.05
77	Heathcliff Slocumb	.05
78	Lenny Dykstra	.05
79	Jay Bell	.05
80	Denny Neagle	.05
81	Orlando Merced	.05
82	Jay Bell	.05
83	Ozzie Smith	.50
84	Ken Hill	.05
85	Ozzie Smith	1.00
86	Bernard Gilkey	.05
87	Ray Lankford	.05
88	Tony Gwynn	.50
89	Ken Caminiti	.05
90	Tony Gwynn	1.00
91	Joey Hamilton	.05
92	Bip Roberts	.05
93	Deion Sanders	.05
94	Glenallen Hill	.05
95	Matt Williams	.05
96	Barry Bonds	2.00
97	Rod Beck	.05
98	Eddie Murray (Checklist)	.35
99	Cal Ripken Jr. (Checklist)	1.00
100	Roberto Alomar	.10
101	George Brett	.60
102	Joe Carter	.05
103	Will Clark	.05
104	Dennis Eckersley	.40
105	Whitey Ford	.40
106	Steve Garvey	.05
107	Kirk Gibson	.05
108	Orel Hershiser	.05
109	Reggie Jackson	.50
110	Paul Molitor	.40
111	Kirby Puckett	.50
112	Mike Schmidt	.60
113	Dave Stewart	.05
114	Alan Trammell	.05
115	Cal Ripken Jr.	1.00
116	Brady Anderson	.05
117	Mike Mussina	.30
118	Rafael Palmeiro	.65
119	Chris Hoiles	.05
120	Cal Ripken Jr.	2.00
121	Mo Vaughn	.05
122	Roger Clemens	1.25
123	Tim Naehring	.05
124	John Valentin	.05
125	Mo Vaughn	.05
126	Tim Wakefield	.05
127	Jose Canseco	.40
128	Rick Aguilera	.05
129	Chili Davis	.05
130	Lee Smith	.05
131	Jim Edmonds	.05
132	Chuck Finley	.05
133	Chili Davis	.05
134	J.T. Snow	.05
135	Tim Salmon	.05
136	Frank Thomas	.45
137	Jason Bere	.05
138	Robin Ventura	.05
139	Tim Raines	.05
140	Frank Thomas	.75
141	Alex Fernandez	.05
142	Eddie Murray	.40
143	Carlos Baerga	.05
144	Eddie Murray	.75
145	Albert Belle	.65
146	Jim Thome	.65
147	Dennis Martinez	.05
148	Dave Winfield	.75
149	Kenny Lofton	.05
150	Manny Ramirez	.75
151	Cecil Fielder (Major League ProFiles)	.05
152	Lou Whitaker	.05
153	Alan Trammell	.05
154	Kirk Gibson	.05
155	Cecil Fielder	.05
156	Bobby Higginson RC	.25
157	Kevin Appier	.05
158	Wally Joyner	.05
159	Jeff Montgomery	.05
160	Kevin Appier	.05
161	Gary Gaetti	.05
162	Greg Gagne	.05
163	Ricky Bones	.05
164	Greg Vaughn	.05
165	Kevin Seitzer	.05
166	Ricky Bones	.05
167	Kirby Puckett	.50
168	Pedro Munoz	.05
169	Chuck Knoblauch	.05
170	Kirby Puckett	1.00
171	Don Mattingly	.60
172	Wade Boggs	1.00
173	Paul O'Neill	.05
174	John Wetteland	.05
175	Don Mattingly	1.25
176	Jack McDowell	.05
177	Mark McGwire	.75
178	Rickey Henderson	.75
179	Terry Steinbach	.05
180	Ruben Sierra	.05
181	Mark McGwire	1.50
182	Dennis Eckersley	.05
183	Ken Griffey Jr.	.65
184	Alex Rodriguez	1.50
185	Ken Griffey Jr.	1.25
186	Randy Johnson	.75
187	Jay Buhner	.05
188	Edgar Martinez	.05
189	Will Clark	.05
190	Juan Gonzalez	.40
191	Benji Gil	.05
192	Ivan Rodriguez	.65
193	Kenny Rogers	.05
194	Will Clark	.05
195	Paul Molitor	.40
196	Roberto Alomar	.20
197	David Cone	.05
198	Paul Molitor	.75
199	Shawn Green	.30
200	Joe Carter	.05
CR1	Cal Ripken Jr. (2,131 games tribute)	5.00
CR1	Cal Ripken Jr. Die-Cut	7.50

Die-Cuts

	NM/M
Complete Set (200):	50.00
Common Player:	.25
Die-Cut Stars:	1.5X

(See 1995 SP/Championship for checklist and base values.)

Classic Performances

		NM/M
Complete Set (10):		8.00
Common Player:		.50
Complete Die-Cut Set (10):		16.00
Common Die-Cuts:		1.00
CP1	Reggie Jackson (Game 6 of '77 WS)	.60
CP1	Reggie Jackson	2.00
CP2	Nolan Ryan (Game 3 of '69 WS)	4.00
CP2	Nolan Ryan	8.00
CP3	Kirk Gibson (Game 1 of '88 WS)	.50
CP3	Kirk Gibson	1.00
CP4	Joe Carter (Game 6 of '93 WS)	.50
CP4	Joe Carter	1.00
CP5	George Brett (Game 3 of '80 ALCS)	1.25
CP5	George Brett	2.50
CP6	Roberto Alomar (Game 4 of '92 ALCS)	.50
CP6	Roberto Alomar	1.00
CP7	Ozzie Smith (Game 5 of '85 NLCS)	.75
CP7	Ozzie Smith	2.00
CP8	Kirby Puckett (Game 6 of '91 WS)	1.25
CP8	Kirby Puckett	2.00
CP9	Bret Saberhagen (Game 7 of '85 WS)	.50
CP9	Bret Saberhagen	1.00
CP10	Steve Garvey (Game 4 of '84 NLCS)	.50
CP10	Steve Garvey	1.00

Destination: Fall Classic

	NM/M
Complete Set (9):	18.00
Common Player:	1.00
Complete Die-Cut Set (9):	36.00
Common Die-Cut:	2.00
1 Ken Griffey Jr.	3.00
1 Ken Griffey Jr.	6.00
2 Frank Thomas	2.00
2 Frank Thomas	4.00
3 Albert Belle	1.00
3 Albert Belle	2.00
4 Mike Piazza	3.00
4 Mike Piazza	6.00
5 Don Mattingly	2.75
5 Don Mattingly	5.50
6 Hideo Nomo	1.50
6 Hideo Nomo	2.00
7 Greg Maddux	2.50
7 Greg Maddux	5.00
8 Fred McGriff	1.00
8 Fred McGriff	2.00
9 Barry Bonds	5.00
9 Barry Bonds	8.00

Ripken Tribute Jumbo

	NM/M
CR1 Cal Ripken Jr.	12.00

1996 SP

	NM/M
Complete Set (188):	12.50
Common Player:	.05
Pack (8):	1.25
Wax Box (30):	25.00
1 Rey Ordonez	.05
2 George Arias	.05
3 Osvaldo Fernandez RC	.25
4 Darin Erstad RC	2.00
5 Paul Wilson	.05
6 Richard Hidalgo	.05

Raul Mondesi
Los Angeles DODGERS - of

#	Player	Price
7	Bob Wolcott	.05
8	Jimmy Haynes	.05
9	Edgar Renteria	.05
10	Alan Benes	.05
11	Chris Snopek	.05
12	Billy Wagner	.05
13	Mike Grace RC	.05
14	Todd Greene	.05
15	Karim Garcia	.05
16	John Wasdin	.05
17	Jason Kendall	.05
18	Bob Abreu	.15
19	Jermaine Dye	.05
20	Jason Schmidt	.05
21	Javy Lopez	.05
22	Ryan Klesko	.05
23	Tom Glavine	.35
24	John Smoltz	.05
25	Greg Maddux	1.00
26	Chipper Jones	1.00
27	Fred McGriff	.05
28	David Justice	.05
29	Roberto Alomar	.20
30	Cal Ripken Jr.	2.00
31	Jeffrey Hammonds	.05
32	Bobby Bonilla	.05
33	Mike Mussina	.30
34	Randy Myers	.05
35	Rafael Palmeiro	.65
36	Brady Anderson	.05
37	Tim Naehring	.05
38	Jose Canseco	.40
39	Roger Clemens	1.00
40	Mo Vaughn	.05
41	Jose Valentin RC	.05
42	Kevin Mitchell	.05
43	Chili Davis	.05
44	Garret Anderson	.05
45	Tim Salmon	.05
46	Chuck Finley	.05
47	Mark Langston	.05
48	Jim Abbott	.05
49	J.T. Snow	.05
50	Jim Edmonds	.05
51	Sammy Sosa	1.00
52	Brian McRae	.05
53	Ryne Sandberg	1.00
54	Mark Grace	.05
55	Jaime Navarro	.05
56	Harold Baines	.05
57	Robin Ventura	.05
58	Tony Phillips	.05
59	Alex Fernandez	.05
60	Frank Thomas	.75
61	Ray Durham	.05
62	Bret Boone	.05
63	Barry Larkin	.05
64	Pete Schourek	.05
65	Reggie Sanders	.05
66	John Smiley	.05
67	Carlos Baerga	.05
68	Jim Thome	.65
69	Eddie Murray	.75
70	Albert Belle	.75
71	Dennis Martinez	.05
72	Jack McDowell	.05
73	Kenny Lofton	.05
74	Manny Ramirez	.75
75	Dante Bichette	.05
76	Vinny Castilla	.05
77	Andres Galarraga	.05
78	Walt Weiss	.05
79	Ellis Burks	.05
80	Larry Walker	.05
81	Cecil Fielder	.05
82	Melvin Nieves	.05
83	Travis Fryman	.05
84	Chad Curtis	.05
85	Alan Trammell	.05
86	Gary Sheffield	.45
87	Charles Johnson	.05
88	Andre Dawson	.30
89	Jeff Conine	.05
90	Greg Colbrunn	.05
91	Derek Bell	.05
92	Brian Hunter	.05
93	Doug Drabek	.05
94	Craig Biggio	.05
95	Jeff Bagwell	.75
96	Kevin Appier	.05
97	Jeff Montgomery	.05
98	Michael Tucker	.05
99	Bip Roberts	.05
100	Johnny Damon	.35
101	Eric Karros	.05
102	Raul Mondesi	.05
103	Ramon Martinez	.05
104	Ismael Valdes	.05
105	Mike Piazza	1.25
106	Hideo Nomo	.40
107	Chan Ho Park	.05
108	Ben McDonald	.05
109	Kevin Seitzer	.05
110	Greg Vaughn	.05
111	Jose Valentin	.05
112	Rick Aguilera	.05
113	Marty Cordova	.05
114	Brad Radke	.05
115	Kirby Puckett	1.00
116	Chuck Knoblauch	.05
117	Paul Molitor	.75
118	Pedro Martinez	.75
119	Mike Lansing	.05
120	Rondell White	.05
121	Moises Alou	.05
122	Mark Grudzielanek	.05
123	Jeff Fassero	.05
124	Rico Brogna	.05
125	Jason Isringhausen	.05
126	Jeff Kent	.05
127	Bernard Gilkey	.05
128	Todd Hundley	.05
129	David Cone	.05
130	Andy Pettitte	.25
131	Wade Boggs	1.00
132	Paul O'Neill	.05
133	Ruben Sierra	.05
134	John Wetteland	.05
135	Derek Jeter	2.00
136	Geronimo Pena	.05
137	Terry Steinbach	.05
138	Ariel Prieto	.05
139	Scott Brosius	.05
140	Mark McGwire	1.50
141	Lenny Dykstra	.05
142	Todd Zeile	.05
143	Benito Santiago	.05
144	Mickey Morandini	.05
145	Gregg Jefferies	.05
146	Denny Neagle	.05
147	Orlando Merced	.05
148	Charlie Hayes	.05
149	Carlos Garcia	.05
150	Jay Bell	.05
151	Ray Lankford	.05
152	Alan Benes	.05
153	Dennis Eckersley	.65
154	Gary Gaetti	.05
155	Ozzie Smith	1.00
156	Ron Gant	.05
157	Brian Jordan	.05
158	Ken Caminiti	.05
159	Rickey Henderson	.75
160	Tony Gwynn	1.00
161	Wally Joyner	.05
162	Andy Ashby	.05
163	Steve Finley	.05
164	Glenallen Hill	.05
165	Matt Williams	.05
166	Barry Bonds	2.00
167	William Van Landingham	.05
168	Rod Beck	.05
169	Randy Johnson	.75
170	Ken Griffey Jr.	1.25
170p	Ken Griffey Jr. (Unmarked promo; bio on back says, ". . .against Cleveland" as opposed to ". . . against the Indians.")	4.00
171	Alex Rodriguez	1.50
172	Edgar Martinez	.05
173	Jay Buhner	.05
174	Russ Davis	.05
175	Juan Gonzalez	.40
176	Mickey Tettleton	.05
177	Will Clark	.05
178	Ken Hill	.05
179	Dean Palmer	.05
180	Ivan Rodriguez	.65
181	Carlos Delgado	.50
182	Alex Gonzalez	.05
183	Shawn Green	.30
184	Erik Hanson	.05
185	Joe Carter	.05
186	Hideo Nomo Checklist	.20
187	Cal Ripken Jr. Checklist	1.00
188	Ken Griffey Jr. Checklist	.65

Baseball Heroes

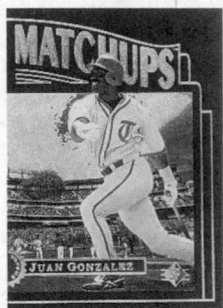

FRANK THOMAS

	NM/M
Complete Set (10):	65.00
Common Player:	4.00
81 Ken Griffey Jr. Header	8.00
82 Frank Thomas	6.50
83 Albert Belle	4.00
84 Barry Bonds	12.00
85 Chipper Jones	8.00
86 Hideo Nomo	5.00
87 Mike Piazza	10.00
88 Manny Ramirez	6.50
89 Greg Maddux	8.00
90 Ken Griffey Jr.	10.00

Marquee Matchups Blue

JUAN GONZALEZ

	NM/M
Complete Set (20):	15.00
Common Player:	.35
1 Ken Griffey Jr.	2.00
2 Hideo Nomo	.50
3 Derek Jeter	3.00
4 Rey Ordonez	.50
5 Tim Salmon	.50
6 Mike Piazza	1.50
7 Mark McGwire	1.50
8 Barry Bonds	2.00
9 Cal Ripken Jr.	3.00
10 Greg Maddux	1.50
11 Albert Belle	.50
12 Barry Larkin	1.00
13 Jeff Bagwell	.75
14 Juan Gonzalez	.75
15 Frank Thomas	1.00
16 Sammy Sosa	1.00
17 Mike Mussina	.75
18 Chipper Jones	1.00
19 Roger Clemens	2.00
20 Fred McGriff	.50

Marquee Matchups Red

	NM/M
Common Player:	1.50
1 Ken Griffey Jr.	10.00
2 Hideo Nomo	2.00
3 Derek Jeter	15.00
4 Rey Ordonez	1.50
5 Tim Salmon	1.50
6 Mike Piazza	8.00
7 Mark McGwire	8.00
8 Barry Bonds	15.00
9 Cal Ripken Jr.	15.00

MARQUEE

ROGER CLEMENS

10	Greg Maddux	10.00
11	Albert Belle	1.50
12	Barry Larkin	4.00
13	Jeff Bagwell	4.00
14	Juan Gonzalez	3.00
15	Frank Thomas	5.00
16	Sammy Sosa	5.00
17	Mike Mussina	4.00
18	Chipper Jones	5.00
19	Roger Clemens	10.00
20	Fred McGriff	3.00

Ripken Collection

CAL RIPKEN JR.
Baltimore Orioles

	NM/M
Complete Set (5):	25.00
Common Ripken:	5.00

SpecialFX

SPECIALFX

	NM/M
Complete Set (48):	50.00
Common Player:	.60
1 Greg Maddux	2.50
2 Eric Karros	.60
3 Mike Piazza	3.00
4 Raul Mondesi	.60
5 Hideo Nomo	1.00
6 Jim Edmonds	.60
7 Jason Isringhausen	.60
8 Jay Buhner	.60
9 Barry Larkin	.60
10 Ken Griffey Jr.	3.00
11 Gary Sheffield	1.25
12 Craig Biggio	.60
13 Paul Wilson	.60
14 Rondell White	.60
15 Chipper Jones	2.50
16 Kirby Puckett	2.50
17 Ron Gant	.60
18 Wade Boggs	2.50

19	Fred McGriff	.60
20	Cal Ripken Jr.	5.00
21	Jason Kendall	.60
22	Johnny Damon	.90
23	Kenny Lofton	.60
24	Roberto Alomar	1.00
25	Barry Bonds	5.00
26	Dante Bichette	.60
27	Mark McGwire	4.00
28	Rafael Palmeiro	1.50
29	Juan Gonzalez	1.00
30	Albert Belle	.60
31	Randy Johnson	1.75
32	Jose Canseco	1.25
33	Sammy Sosa	2.50
34	Eddie Murray	1.75
35	Frank Thomas	1.75
36	Tom Glavine	.90
37	Matt Williams	.60
38	Roger Clemens	2.75
39	Paul Molitor	1.75
40	Tony Gwynn	2.50
41	Mo Vaughn	.60
42	Tim Salmon	.60
43	Manny Ramirez	1.75
44	Jeff Bagwell	1.75
45	Edgar Martinez	.60
46	Rey Ordonez	.60
47	Osvaldo Fernandez	.60
48	Derek Jeter	5.00

SpecialFX Red

		NM/M
Common Player:		3.00
Inserted 1:75		
1	Greg Maddux	20.00
2	Eric Karros	3.00
3	Mike Piazza	10.00
4	Raul Mondesi	3.00
5	Hideo Nomo	4.00
6	Jim Edmonds	4.00
7	Jason Isringhausen	4.00
8	Jay Buhner	3.00
9	Barry Larkin	5.00
10	Ken Griffey Jr.	20.00
11	Gary Sheffield	8.00
12	Craig Biggio	5.00
13	Paul Wilson	3.00
14	Rondell White	3.00
15	Chipper Jones	15.00
16	Kirby Puckett	20.00
17	Ron Gant	3.00
18	Wade Boggs	6.00
19	Fred McGriff	4.00
20	Cal Ripken Jr.	25.00
21	Jason Kendall	3.00
22	Johnny Damon	8.00
23	Kenny Lofton	4.00
24	Roberto Alomar	5.00
25	Barry Bonds	25.00
26	Dante Bichette	3.00
27	Mark McGwire	15.00
28	Rafael Palmeiro	6.00
29	Juan Gonzalez	5.00
30	Albert Belle	3.00
31	Randy Johnson	10.00
32	Jose Canseco	5.00
33	Sammy Sosa	10.00
34	Eddie Murray	8.00
35	Frank Thomas	10.00
36	Tom Glavine	10.00
37	Matt Williams	4.00
38	Roger Clemens	20.00
39	Paul Molitor	8.00
40	Tony Gwynn	10.00
41	Mo Vaughn	5.00
42	Tim Salmon	4.00
43	Manny Ramirez	10.00
44	Jeff Bagwell	8.00
45	Edgar Martinez	3.00
46	Rey Ordonez	3.00
47	Osvaldo Fernandez	3.00
48	Derek Jeter	25.00

1996 SPx

		NM/M
Complete Set (60):		17.50
Common Player:		.15
Golds:		1.5X
Pack (1):		1.25
Wax Box (36):		25.00
1	Greg Maddux	1.50
2	Chipper Jones	1.50
3	Fred McGriff	.15
4	Tom Glavine	.50
5	Cal Ripken Jr.	3.00
6	Roberto Alomar	.50
7	Rafael Palmeiro	1.00
8	Jose Canseco	.65
9	Roger Clemens	1.75
10	Mo Vaughn	.15
11	Jim Edmonds	.15
12	Tim Salmon	.15
13	Sammy Sosa	1.50
14	Ryne Sandberg	1.50
15	Mark Grace	.15
16	Frank Thomas	1.25
17	Barry Larkin	.15
18	Kenny Lofton	.15
19	Albert Belle	.15
20	Eddie Murray	1.25
21	Manny Ramirez	1.25
22	Dante Bichette	.15
23	Larry Walker	.15
24	Vinny Castilla	.15
25	Andres Galarraga	.15
26	Cecil Fielder	.15
27	Gary Sheffield	.75
28	Craig Biggio	.15
29	Jeff Bagwell	1.25
30	Derek Bell	.15
31	Johnny Damon	.60
32	Eric Karros	.15
33	Mike Piazza	2.00
34	Raul Mondesi	.15
35	Hideo Nomo	.65
36	Kirby Puckett	1.50
37	Paul Molitor	1.25
38	Marty Cordova	.15
39	Rondell White	.15
40	Jason Isringhausen	.15
41	Paul Wilson	.15
42	Rey Ordonez	.15
43	Derek Jeter	3.00
44	Wade Boggs	1.50
45	Mark McGwire	2.50
46	Jason Kendall	.15
47	Ron Gant	.15
48	Ozzie Smith	1.50
49	Tony Gwynn	1.50
50	Ken Caminiti	.15
51	Barry Bonds	3.00
52	Matt Williams	.15
53	Osvaldo Fernandez RC	.25
54	Jay Buhner	.15
55	Ken Griffey Jr.	2.00
55p	Ken Griffey Jr./OPS	2.00
56	Randy Johnson	1.25
57	Alex Rodriguez	2.50
58	Juan Gonzalez	.65
59	Joe Carter	.15
60	Carlos Delgado	.75

Bound for Glory

		NM/M
Complete Set (10):		18.00
Common Player:		1.00
1	Ken Griffey Jr.	3.00
2	Frank Thomas	1.50
3	Barry Bonds	4.00
4	Cal Ripken Jr.	4.00
5	Greg Maddux	2.00
6	Chipper Jones	2.00
7	Roberto Alomar	1.00

8	Manny Ramirez	1.50
9	Tony Gwynn	2.00
10	Mike Piazza	3.00

Ken Griffey Jr. Commemorative

		NM/M
KG1	Ken Griffey Jr.	2.50
KGA1	Ken Griffey Jr./ Auto.	100.00

Mike Piazza Tribute

		NM/M
MP1	Mike Piazza	2.00
MP1	Mike Piazza/Auto.	125.00

1997 SP

		NM/M
Complete Set (184):		12.00
Common Player:		.05
Pack (8):		2.00
Wax Box (30):		45.00
1	Andruw Jones	.75
2	Kevin Orie	.75
3	Nomar Garciaparra	1.00
4	Jose Guillen	.05
5	Todd Walker	.05
6	Derrick Gibson	.05
7	Aaron Boone	.05
8	Bartolo Colon	.05
9	Derek Lee	.50
10	Vladimir Guerrero	.75
11	Wilton Guerrero	.05
12	Luis Castillo	.05
13	Jason Dickson	.05
14	Bubba Trammell RC	.25
15	Jose Cruz Jr. RC	.50
16	Eddie Murray	.75
17	Darin Erstad	.20
18	Garret Anderson	.05
19	Jim Edmonds	.05
20	Tim Salmon	.05
21	Chuck Finley	.05
22	John Smoltz	.05
23	Greg Maddux	1.00
24	Kenny Lofton	.05
25	Chipper Jones	1.00
26	Ryan Klesko	.05
27	Javier Lopez	.05
28	Fred McGriff	.05
29	Roberto Alomar	.20
30	Rafael Palmeiro	.65
31	Mike Mussina	.30
32	Brady Anderson	.05
33	Rocky Coppinger	.05
34	Cal Ripken Jr.	2.00
35	Mo Vaughn	.05
36	Steve Avery	.05

37	Tom Gordon	.05
38	Tim Naehring	.05
39	Troy O'Leary	.05
40	Sammy Sosa	1.00
41	Brian McRae	.05
42	Mel Rojas	.05
43	Ryne Sandberg	1.00
44	Mark Grace	.05
45	Albert Belle	.05
46	Robin Ventura	.05
47	Roberto Hernandez	.05
48	Ray Durham	.05
49	Harold Baines	.05
50	Frank Thomas	.75
51	Bret Boone	.05
52	Reggie Sanders	.05
53	Deion Sanders	.05
54	Hal Morris	.05
55	Barry Larkin	.05
56	Jim Thome	.65
57	Marquis Grissom	.05
58	David Justice	.05
59	Charles Nagy	.05
60	Manny Ramirez	.75
61	Matt Williams	.05
62	Jack McDowell	.05
63	Vinny Castilla	.05
64	Dante Bichette	.05
65	Andres Galarraga	.05
66	Ellis Burks	.05
67	Larry Walker	.05
68	Eric Young	.05
69	Brian L. Hunter	.05
70	Travis Fryman	.05
71	Tony Clark	.05
72	Bobby Higginson	.05
73	Melvin Nieves	.05
74	Jeff Conine	.05
75	Gary Sheffield	.40
76	Moises Alou	.05
77	Edgar Renteria	.05
78	Alex Fernandez	.05
79	Charles Johnson	.05
80	Bobby Bonilla	.05
81	Darryl Kile	.05
82	Derek Bell	.05
83	Shane Reynolds	.05
84	Craig Biggio	.05
85	Jeff Bagwell	.75
86	Billy Wagner	.05
87	Chili Davis	.05
88	Kevin Appier	.05
89	Jay Bell	.05
90	Johnny Damon	.35
91	Jeff King	.05
92	Hideo Nomo	.40
93	Todd Hollandsworth	.05
94	Eric Karros	.05
95	Mike Piazza	1.25
96	Ramon Martinez	.05
97	Todd Worrell	.05
98	Raul Mondesi	.05
99	Dave Nilsson	.05
100	John Jaha	.05
101	Jose Valentin	.05
102	Jeff Cirillo	.05
103	Jeff D'Amico	.05
104	Ben McDonald	.05
105	Paul Molitor	.75
106	Rich Becker	.05
107	Frank Rodriguez	.05
108	Marty Cordova	.05
109	Terry Steinbach	.05
110	Chuck Knoblauch	.05
111	Mark Grudzielanek	.05
112	Mike Lansing	.05
113	Pedro Martinez	.75
114	Henry Rodriguez	.05
115	Rondell White	.05
116	Rey Ordonez	.05
117	Carlos Baerga	.05
118	Lance Johnson	.05
119	Bernard Gilkey	.05
120	Todd Hundley	.05
121	John Franco	.05
122	Bernie Williams	.05
123	David Cone	.05
124	Cecil Fielder	.05
125	Derek Jeter	2.00
126	Tino Martinez	.05
127	Mariano Rivera	.15
128	Andy Pettitte	.15
129	Wade Boggs	1.00
130	Mark McGwire	1.50
131	Jose Canseco	.50
132	Geronimo Berroa	.05
133	Jason Giambi	.45
134	Ernie Young	.05
135	Scott Rolen	.65
136	Ricky Bottalico	.05
137	Curt Schilling	.35
138	Gregg Jefferies	.05
139	Mickey Morandini	.05
140	Jason Kendall	.05
141	Kevin Elster	.05

142	Al Martin	.05
143	Joe Randa	.05
144	Jason Schmidt	.05
145	Ray Lankford	.05
146	Brian Jordan	.05
147	Andy Benes	.05
148	Alan Benes	.05
149	Gary Gaetti	.05
150	Ron Gant	.05
151	Dennis Eckersley	.65
152	Rickey Henderson	.75
153	Joey Hamilton	.05
154	Ken Caminiti	.05
155	Tony Gwynn	1.00
156	Steve Finley	.05
157	Trevor Hoffman	.05
158	Greg Vaughn	.05
159	J.T. Snow	.05
160	Barry Bonds	2.00
161	Glenallen Hill	.05
162	William Van Landingham	.05
163	Jeff Kent	.05
164	Jay Buhner	.05
165	Ken Griffey Jr.	1.25
166	Alex Rodriguez	1.50
167	Randy Johnson	.75
168	Edgar Martinez	.05
169	Dan Wilson	.05
170	Ivan Rodriguez	.65
171	Roger Pavlik	.05
172	Will Clark	.05
173	Dean Palmer	.05
174	Rusty Greer	.05
175	Juan Gonzalez	.40
176	John Wetteland	.05
177	Joe Carter	.05
178	Ed Sprague	.05
179	Carlos Delgado	.45
180	Roger Clemens	1.00
181	Juan Guzman	.05
182	Pat Hentgen	.05
183	Ken Griffey Jr. (Checklist)	.65
184	Hideki Irabu RC	.25

Buy-Back Autographed Inserts

Common Autograph:		7.50
1993 SP		
4	Ken Griffey Jr./16	600.00
28	Jeff Bagwell/7	100.00
167	Tony Gwynn/17	250.00
280	Chipper Jones/34	110.00
1993 SP Platinum Power		
PP9	Ken Griffey Jr./5	800.00
1994 SP		
6	Todd Hollandsworth/167	7.50
15	Alex Rodriguez/94	1,200
105	Ken Griffey Jr./103	125.00
114	Gary Sheffield/130	25.00
130	Tony Gwynn/367	25.00
1994 SP Holoview Blue		
13	Tony Gwynn/31	150.00
1994 SP Holoview Red		
35	Gary Sheffield/4	60.00
1995 SP		
34	Chipper Jones/60	125.00
60	Jeff Bagwell/173	40.00
75	Gary Sheffield/221	20.00
105	Tony Gwynn/64	60.00
188	Alex Rodriguez/63	200.00
190	Ken Griffey/57	15.00
1996 SP		
1	Rey Ordonez/111	7.50
18	Gary Sheffield/58	30.00
26	Chipper Jones/102	50.00
40	Mo Vaughn/250	15.00

95	Jeff Bagwell/292	20.00
160	Tony Gwynn/20	200.00
170	Ken Griffey Jr./312	65.00
171	Alex Rodriguez/73	125.00
173	Jay Buhner/79	30.00
1996 SP Marquee Matchups		
MM13	Jeff Bagwell/23	65.00
MM4	Rey Ordonez/40	15.00
1996 SP Special F/X		
8	Jay Buhner/27	30.00

Game Film

		NM/M
Complete Set (10):		175.00
Common Player:		12.00
1	Alex Rodriguez	25.00
2	Frank Thomas	12.00
3	Andruw Jones	10.00
4	Cal Ripken Jr.	30.00
5	Mike Piazza	15.00
6	Derek Jeter	30.00
7	Mark McGwire	20.00
8	Chipper Jones	15.00
9	Barry Bonds	30.00
10	Ken Griffey Jr.	20.00

Griffey Baseball Heroes

	NM/M
Complete Set (10):	75.00
Common Griffey Jr.:	10.00

Inside Info

		NM/M
Complete Set (25):		75.00
Common Player:		1.00
1	Ken Griffey Jr.	5.00
2	Mark McGwire	6.00
3	Kenny Lofton	1.00
4	Paul Molitor	3.00
5	Frank Thomas	3.00
6	Greg Maddux	3.50
7	Mo Vaughn	1.00
8	Cal Ripken Jr.	7.50
9	Jeff Bagwell	3.00
10	Alex Rodriguez	6.00
11	John Smoltz	1.00
12	Manny Ramirez	3.00
13	Sammy Sosa	3.50

14	Vladimir Guerrero	3.00
15	Albert Belle	1.00
16	Mike Piazza	5.00
17	Derek Jeter	7.50
18	Scott Rolen	2.00
19	Tony Gwynn	3.50
20	Barry Bonds	7.50
21	Ken Caminiti	1.00
22	Chipper Jones	3.50
23	Juan Gonzalez	1.50
24	Roger Clemens	4.00
25	Andruw Jones	3.00

Marquee Matchups

		NM/M
Complete Set (20):		20.00
Common Player:		.25
1	Ken Griffey Jr.	1.50
2	Andres Galarraga	.25
3	Barry Bonds	3.00
4	Mark McGwire	2.00
5	Mike Piazza	1.50
6	Tim Salmon	.25
7	Tony Gwynn	1.00
8	Alex Rodriguez	2.00
9	Chipper Jones	1.00
10	Derek Jeter	3.00
11	Manny Ramirez	.75
12	Jeff Bagwell	.75
13	Greg Maddux	1.00
14	Cal Ripken Jr.	3.00
15	Mo Vaughn	.25
16	Gary Sheffield	.45
17	Jim Thome	.65
18	Barry Larkin	.25
19	Frank Thomas	.75
20	Sammy Sosa	1.00

Special FX

		NM/M
Common Player:		.75
1	Ken Griffey Jr.	6.00
2	Frank Thomas	3.00
3	Barry Bonds	8.00
4	Albert Belle	.75
5	Mike Piazza	4.00
6	Greg Maddux	5.00
7	Chipper Jones	4.00
8	Cal Ripken Jr.	8.00
9	Jeff Bagwell	2.00
10	Alex Rodriguez	8.00
11	Mark McGwire	5.00
12	Kenny Lofton	.75
13	Juan Gonzalez	1.50
14	Mo Vaughn	.75
15	John Smoltz	1.00
16	Derek Jeter	8.00
17	Tony Gwynn	3.00
18	Ivan Rodriguez	2.00
19	Barry Larkin	1.00
20	Sammy Sosa	3.00

21	Mike Mussina	1.50
22	Gary Sheffield	2.00
23	Brady Anderson	.75
24	Roger Clemens	6.00
25	Ken Caminiti	.75
26	Roberto Alomar	1.50
27	Hideo Nomo	1.00
28	Bernie Williams	1.00
29	Todd Hundley	.75
30	Manny Ramirez	3.00
31	Eric Karros	.75
32	Tim Salmon	.75
33	Jay Buhner	.75
34	Andy Pettitte	1.50
35	Jim Thome	2.00
36	Ryne Sandberg	3.00
37	Matt Williams	1.00
38	Ryan Klesko	.75
39	Jose Canseco	1.50
40	Paul Molitor	2.00
41	Eddie Murray	2.00
42	Darin Erstad	.75
43	Todd Walker	.75
44	Wade Boggs	2.50
45	Andruw Jones	2.00
46	Scott Rolen	2.00
47	Vladimir Guerrero	3.00
48	Not Issued	
49	Alex Rodriguez (1996 Design)	8.00

SPx Force

		NM/M
Complete Set (10):		60.00
Common Player:		6.00
1	Ken Griffey Jr., Jay Buhner, Andres Galarraga, Dante Bichette	7.50
2	Albert Belle, Brady Anderson, Mark McGwire, Cecil Fielder	9.00
3	Mo Vaughn, Ken Caminiti, Frank Thomas, Jeff Bagwell	6.00
4	Gary Sheffield, Sammy Sosa, Barry Bonds, Jose Canseco	12.00
5	Greg Maddux, Roger Clemens, John Smoltz, Randy Johnson	6.00
6	Alex Rodriguez, Derek Jeter, Chipper Jones, Rey Ordonez	12.00
7	Todd Hollandsworth, Mike Piazza, Raul Mondesi, Hideo Nomo	7.50
8	Juan Gonzalez, Manny Ramirez, Roberto Alomar, Ivan Rodriguez	6.00
9	Tony Gwynn, Wade Boggs, Eddie Murray, Paul Molitor	6.00
10	Andruw Jones, Vladimir Guerrero, Todd Walker, Scott Rolen	6.00

SPx Force Autographs

		NM/M
Common Player:		20.00
1	Ken Griffey Jr.	125.00
2	Albert Belle	25.00
3	Mo Vaughn	20.00
4	Gary Sheffield	25.00
5	Greg Maddux	100.00
6	Alex Rodriguez	160.00
7	Todd Hollandsworth	20.00

8	Roberto Alomar	30.00
9	Tony Gwynn	75.00
10	Andruw Jones	40.00

1997 SPx

		NM/M
Complete Set (50):		20.00
Common Player:		.15
Steel:		1.5X
Bronze:		1.5X
Silver:		1.5X
Gold:		3X
Grand Finale:		4X
Pack (3):		2.00
Wax Box (18):		30.00
1	Eddie Murray	1.00
2	Darin Erstad	.35
3	Tim Salmon	.15
4	Andruw Jones	1.00
5	Chipper Jones	1.50
6	John Smoltz	.15
7	Greg Maddux	1.50
8	Kenny Lofton	.15
9	Roberto Alomar	.30
10	Rafael Palmeiro	.75
11	Brady Anderson	.15
12	Cal Ripken Jr.	3.00
13	Nomar Garciaparra	1.50
14	Mo Vaughn	.15
15	Ryne Sandberg	1.50
16	Sammy Sosa	1.50
17	Frank Thomas	1.00
18	Albert Belle	.15
19	Barry Larkin	.15
20	Deion Sanders	.15
21	Manny Ramirez	1.00
22	Jim Thome	.65
23	Dante Bichette	.15
24	Andres Galarraga	.15
25	Larry Walker	.15
26	Gary Sheffield	.50
27	Jeff Bagwell	1.00
28	Raul Mondesi	.15
29	Hideo Nomo	.50
30	Mike Piazza	2.00
31	Paul Molitor	1.00
32	Todd Walker	.15
33	Vladimir Guerrero	1.00
34	Todd Hundley	.15
35	Andy Pettitte	.25
36	Derek Jeter	3.00
37	Jose Canseco	.50
38	Mark McGwire	2.50
39	Scott Rolen	.65
40	Ron Gant	.15
41	Ken Caminiti	.15
42	Tony Gwynn	1.50
43	Barry Bonds	3.00
44	Jay Buhner	.15
45	Ken Griffey Jr.	2.00
45s	Ken Griffey Jr. (Overprinted "SAMPLE" on back.)	2.00
46	Alex Rodriguez	2.50
47	Jose Cruz Jr. RC	1.00
48	Juan Gonzalez	.50
49	Ivan Rodriguez	.75
50	Roger Clemens	1.75

Bound for Glory

		NM/M
Complete Set (20):		60.00
Common Player:		1.00
1	Andruw Jones	3.00
2	Chipper Jones	4.00
3	Greg Maddux	4.00
4	Kenny Lofton	1.00
5	Cal Ripken Jr.	7.50
6	Mo Vaughn	1.00
7	Frank Thomas	3.00
8	Albert Belle	1.00
9	Manny Ramirez	3.00
10	Gary Sheffield	1.50
11	Jeff Bagwell	3.00
12	Mike Piazza	5.00
13	Derek Jeter	7.50
14	Mark McGwire	6.00
15	Tony Gwynn	4.00
16	Ken Caminiti	1.00
17	Barry Bonds	7.50
18	Alex Rodriguez	6.00
19	Ken Griffey Jr.	5.00
20	Juan Gonzalez	1.50

Bound for Glory Supreme Signatures

		NM/M
Complete Set (5):		250.00
Common Player:		25.00
1	Jeff Bagwell	40.00
2	Ken Griffey Jr.	120.00
3	Andruw Jones	40.00
4	Alex Rodriguez	160.00
5	Gary Sheffield	30.00

Cornerstones of the Game

		NM/M
Complete Set (10):		150.00
Common Player:		12.00
1	Ken Griffey Jr., Barry Bonds	25.00
2	Frank Thomas, Albert Belle	12.00
3	Chipper Jones, Greg Maddux	15.00
4	Tony Gwynn, Paul Molitor	15.00
5	Andruw Jones, Vladimir Guerrero	12.00
6	Jeff Bagwell, Ryne Sandberg	15.00
7	Mike Piazza, Ivan Rodriguez	20.00
8	Cal Ripken Jr., Eddie Murray	25.00
9	Mo Vaughn, Mark McGwire	20.00
10	Alex Rodriguez, Derek Jeter	25.00

1998 SP Authentic

PEDRO MARTINEZ

		NM/M
Complete Set (198):		15.00
Common Player:		.05
Pack (5):		2.00
Wax Box (24):		35.00
1	Travis Lee	.10
2	Mike Caruso	.05
3	Kerry Wood	.65
4	Mark Kotsay	.05
5	Magglio Ordonez RC	5.00
6	Scott Elarton	.05
7	Carl Pavano	.10
8	A.J. Hinch	.05
9	Rolando Arrojo RC	.40
10	Ben Grieve	.05
11	Gabe Alvarez	.05
12	Mike Kinkade RC	.40
13	Bruce Chen	.05
14	Juan Encarnacion	.05
15	Todd Helton	.75
16	Aaron Boone	.05
17	Sean Casey	.15
18	Ramon Hernandez	.05
19	Daryle Ward	.05
20	Paul Konerko	.15
21	David Ortiz	.50
22	Derrek Lee	.50
23	Brad Fullmer	.05
24	Javier Vazquez	.05
25	Miguel Tejada	.15
26	David Dellucci	.05
27	Alex Gonzalez	.05
28	Matt Clement	.05
29	Eric Milton	.05
30	Russell Branyan	.05
31	Chuck Finley	.05
32	Jim Edmonds	.05
33	Darin Erstad	.20
34	Jason Dickson	.05
35	Tim Salmon	.05
36	Cecil Fielder	.05
37	Todd Greene	.05
38	Andy Benes	.05
39	Jay Bell	.05
40	Matt Williams	.05
41	Brian Anderson	.05
42	Karim Garcia	.05
43	Javy Lopez	.05
44	Tom Glavine	.35
45	Greg Maddux	1.50
46	Andruw Jones	1.00
47	Chipper Jones	1.50
48	Ryan Klesko	.05
49	John Smoltz	.05
50	Andres Galarraga	.05
51	Rafael Palmeiro	.75
52	Mike Mussina	.30
53	Roberto Alomar	.20
54	Joe Carter	.05
55	Cal Ripken Jr.	3.00
56	Brady Anderson	.05
57	Mo Vaughn	.05
58	John Valentin	.05
59	Dennis Eckersley	.75
60	Nomar Garciaparra	1.50
61	Pedro J. Martinez	1.00
62	Jeff Blauser	.05
63	Kevin Orie	.05
64	Henry Rodriguez	.05
65	Mark Grace	.05
66	Albert Belle	.05
67	Mike Cameron	.05
68	Robin Ventura	.05
69	Frank Thomas	1.00
70	Barry Larkin	.05
71	Brett Tomko	.05
72	Willie Greene	.05
73	Reggie Sanders	.05
74	Sandy Alomar Jr.	.05
75	Kenny Lofton	.05
76	Jaret Wright	.05
77	David Justice	.05
78	Omar Vizquel	.05
79	Manny Ramirez	1.00
80	Jim Thome	.75
81	Travis Fryman	.05
82	Neifi Perez	.05
83	Mike Lansing	.05
84	Vinny Castilla	.05
85	Larry Walker	.05
86	Dante Bichette	.05
87	Darryl Kile	.05
88	Justin Thompson	.05
89	Damion Easley	.05
90	Tony Clark	.05
91	Bobby Higginson	.05
92	Brian L. Hunter	.05
93	Edgar Renteria	.05
94	Craig Counsell	.05
95	Mike Piazza	2.00
96	Livan Hernandez	.05
97	Todd Zeile	.05
98	Richard Hidalgo	.05
99	Moises Alou	.05
100	Jeff Bagwell	1.00
101	Mike Hampton	.05
102	Craig Biggio	.05
103	Dean Palmer	.05
104	Tim Belcher	.05
105	Jeff King	.05
106	Jeff Conine	.05
107	Johnny Damon	.30
108	Hideo Nomo	.50
109	Raul Mondesi	.05
110	Gary Sheffield	.45
111	Ramon Martinez	.05
112	Chan Ho Park	.05
113	Eric Young	.05
114	Charles Johnson	.05
115	Eric Karros	.05
116	Bobby Bonilla	.05
117	Jeromy Burnitz	.05
118	Carl Eldred	.05
119	Jeff D'Amico	.05
120	Marquis Grissom	.05
121	Dave Nilsson	.05
122	Brad Radke	.05
123	Marty Cordova	.05
124	Ron Coomer	.05
125	Paul Molitor	1.00
126	Todd Walker	.05
127	Rondell White	.05
128	Mark Grudzielanek	.05
129	Carlos Perez	.05
130	Vladimir Guerrero	1.00
131	Dustin Hermanson	.05
132	Butch Huskey	.05
133	John Franco	.05
134	Rey Ordonez	.05
135	Todd Hundley	.05
136	Edgardo Alfonzo	.05
137	Bobby Jones	.05
138	John Olerud	.05
139	Chili Davis	.05
140	Tino Martinez	.05
141	Andy Pettitte	.15
142	Chuck Knoblauch	.05
143	Bernie Williams	.05
144	David Cone	.05
145	Derek Jeter	3.00
146	Paul O'Neill	.05
147	Rickey Henderson	1.00
148	Jason Giambi	.50
149	Kenny Rogers	.05
150	Scott Rolen	.75
151	Curt Schilling	.35
152	Ricky Bottalico	.05
153	Mike Lieberthal	.05
154	Francisco Cordova	.05
155	Jose Guillen	.05
156	Jason Schmidt	.05
157	Jason Kendall	.05
158	Kevin Young	.05
159	Delino DeShields	.05
160	Mark McGwire	2.50
161	Ray Lankford	.05
162	Brian Jordan	.05
163	Ron Gant	.05
164	Todd Stottlemyre	.05
165	Ken Caminiti	.05
166	Kevin Brown	.05
167	Trevor Hoffman	.05
168	Steve Finley	.05
169	Wally Joyner	.05
170	Tony Gwynn	1.50
171	Shawn Estes	.05
172	J.T. Snow	.05
173	Jeff Kent	.05
174	Robb Nen	.05
175	Barry Bonds	3.00
176	Randy Johnson	1.00
177	Edgar Martinez	.05
178	Jay Buhner	.05
179	Alex Rodriguez	2.50
180	Ken Griffey Jr.	2.00
181	Ken Cloude	.05
182	Wade Boggs	1.50
183	Tony Saunders	.05
184	Wilson Alvarez	.05
185	Fred McGriff	.05
186	Roberto Hernandez	.05
187	Kevin Stocker	.05
188	Fernando Tatis	.05
189	Will Clark	.05
190	Juan Gonzalez	.50
191	Rusty Greer	.05
192	Ivan Rodriguez	.75
193	Jose Canseco	.45
194	Carlos Delgado	.50
195	Roger Clemens	1.75
196	Pat Hentgen	.05
197	Randy Myers	.05
198	Ken Griffey Jr. Checklist	.85

Chirography

		NM/M
Common Card:		4.00
Inserted 1:25		
RA	Roberto Alomar	15.00
RB	Russell Branyan	4.00
SC	Sean Casey	10.00
TC	Tony Clark	4.00
RC	Roger Clemens/ SP/400	80.00
JC	Jose Cruz Jr.	4.00

DE	Darin Erstad	7.50
NG	Nomar Garciaparra/ SP/400	60.00
BG	Ben Grieve	4.00
KG	Ken Griffey Jr./ SP/400	60.00
VG	Vladimir Guerrero	30.00
TG	Tony Gwynn/SP/850	30.00
TH	Todd Helton	15.00
LH	Livan Hernandez	6.00
CJ	Charles Johnson	6.00
AJ	Andruw Jones	17.50
CHIP	Chipper Jones/ SP/800	30.00
PK	Paul Konerko	15.00
MK	Mark Kotsay	6.00
RL	Ray Lankford	6.00
TL	Travis Lee	6.00
PM	Paul Molitor/SP/800	20.00
MM	Mike Mussina	20.00
AR	Alex Rodriguez/ SP/800	80.00
IR	Ivan Rodriguez	30.00
SR	Scott Rolen	20.00
GS	Gary Sheffield	15.00
MT	Miguel Tejada	20.00
JW	Jaret Wright	6.00
MV	Mo Vaughn/SP/800	12.50

Jersey Swatch

		NM/M
Complete Set (6):		130.00
Common Player:		7.50
(1)	Jay Buhner/125	7.50
(2)	Ken Griffey Jr./125	50.00
(3)	Tony Gwynn/415	10.00
(4)	Greg Maddux/125	30.00
(5)	Alex Rodriguez/125	60.00
(6)	Gary Sheffield/125	12.00

Ken Griffey Jr. 300th HR Redemption

		NM/M
KG300	Ken Griffey Jr.	30.00

Sheer Dominance

		NM/M
Complete Set (42):		32.50
Common Player:		.25
Inserted 1:3		
Gold (2,000 Sets):		2X
Titanium (100 Sets):		12X
SD1	Ken Griffey Jr.	1.75
SD2	Rickey Henderson	1.00
SD3	Jaret Wright	.25
SD4	Craig Biggio	.25
SD5	Travis Lee	.25
SD6	Kenny Lofton	.25
SD7	Raul Mondesi	.25
SD8	Cal Ripken Jr.	2.50

SD9	Matt Williams	.25
SD10	Mark McGwire	2.00
SD11	Alex Rodriguez	2.00
SD12	Fred McGriff	.25
SD13	Scott Rolen	.75
SD14	Paul Molitor	1.00
SD15	Nomar Garciaparra	1.50
SD16	Vladimir Guerrero	1.00
SD17	Andruw Jones	1.00
SD18	Manny Ramirez	1.00
SD19	Tony Gwynn	1.50
SD20	Barry Bonds	2.50
SD21	Ben Grieve	.25
SD22	Ivan Rodriguez	.75
SD23	Jose Cruz Jr.	.25
SD24	Pedro J. Martinez	1.00
SD25	Chipper Jones	1.50
SD26	Albert Belle	.25
SD27	Todd Helton	.75
SD28	Paul Konerko	.35
SD29	Sammy Sosa	1.50
SD30	Frank Thomas	1.00
SD31	Greg Maddux	1.50
SD32	Randy Johnson	1.00
SD33	Larry Walker	.25
SD34	Roberto Alomar	.45
SD35	Roger Clemens	1.50
SD36	Mo Vaughn	.25
SD37	Jim Thome	.75
SD38	Jeff Bagwell	1.00
SD39	Tino Martinez	.25
SD40	Mike Piazza	1.75
SD41	Derek Jeter	2.50
SD42	Juan Gonzalez	.50

Trade Cards

		NM/M
Common Card:		5.00
(1)	Roberto Alomar/ Auto. Ball/100	15.00
(2)	Albert Belle/ Auto. Ball/100	7.50
(3)	Jay Buhner/ Jersey Card 125	5.00
(4)	Ken Griffey Jr./ Auto. Glove/30	200.00
(5)	Ken Griffey Jr./ Auto. Jsy/30	200.00
(6)	Ken Griffey Jr. Jersey Card/125	25.00
(7)	Ken Griffey Jr./ Standee/200	15.00
(8)	Ken Griffey Jr. 300th HR Card/1000	5.00
(9)	Tony Gwynn/ Jersey Card/415	15.00
(10)	Brian Jordan/ Auto. Ball/50	10.00
(11)	Greg Maddux/ Jersey Card/125	20.00
(12)	Raul Mondesi/ Auto. Ball/100	5.00
(13)	Alex Rodriguez/ Jersey Card/125	40.00
(14)	Gary Sheffield/ Jersey Card/125	5.00
(15)	Robin Ventura/ Auto. Ball/50	10.00

1998 SPx Finite

		NM/M
Complete Set (360):		200.00

Common Youth Movement: (#1-30, 181-210):		.50
Radiance YM (2,500):		1.5X
Spectrum YM (1,250):		2X
Common Power Explosion: (#31-50):		.50
Radiance PE (1,000):		2X
Spectrum PE (50):		25X
Common Base Card (#51-140, 241-330):		.15
Radiance Base Card (4,500):		1X
Spectrum Base Card (2,250):		2X
Common Star Focus: (#141-170):		.35
Radiance SF (3,500):		1X
Spectrum SF (1,750):		2X
Common Heroes of the Game (#171-180):		2.50
Radiance HG (100):		15X
Common Power Passion: (#211-240):		.50
Radiance PP (3,500):		1X
Spectrum PP (1,750):		2X
Common Tradewinds: (#331-350):		.75
Radiance TW (1,000):		2X
Spectrum TW (50):		25X
Common Cornerstones/ Game (#351-360):		1.50
Radiance CG (100):		15X
Pack (3):		2.00
Wax Box:		25.00
1	Nomar Garciaparra	3.00
2	Miguel Tejada	.75
3	Mike Cameron	.50
4	Ken Cloude	.50
5	Jaret Wright	.50
6	Mark Kotsay	.50
7	Craig Counsell	.50
8	Jose Guillen	.50
9	Neifi Perez	.50
10	Jose Cruz Jr.	.50
11	Brett Tomko	.50
12	Matt Morris	.50
13	Justin Thompson	.50
14	Jeremi Gonzalez	.50
15	Scott Rolen	1.50
16	Vladimir Guerrero	2.00
17	Brad Fullmer	.50
18	Brian Giles	.50
19	Todd Dunwoody	.50
20	Ben Grieve	.50
21	Juan Encarnacion	.50
22	Aaron Boone	.50
23	Richie Sexson	.50
24	Richard Hidalgo	.50
25	Andruw Jones	2.00
26	Todd Helton	1.50
27	Paul Konerko	.75
28	Dante Powell	.50
29	Elieser Marrero	.50
30	Derek Jeter	5.00
31	Mike Piazza	3.00
32	Tony Clark	.50
33	Larry Walker	.50
34	Jim Thome	1.50
35	Juan Gonzalez	1.00
36	Jeff Bagwell	2.00
37	Jay Buhner	.50
38	Tim Salmon	.50
39	Albert Belle	.50
40	Mark McGwire	4.00
41	Sammy Sosa	2.50
42	Manny Ramirez	2.00
43	Tino Martinez	.50
44	Frank Thomas	2.00
45	Nomar Garciaparra	2.50
46	Alex Rodriguez	4.00
47	Chipper Jones	2.50
48	Barry Bonds	5.00
49	Ken Griffey Jr.	3.00
50	Jason Dickson	.15
51	Jim Edmonds	.15
52	Darin Erstad	.35
53	Tim Salmon	.15
54	Chipper Jones	2.00
55	Ryan Klesko	.15
56	Tom Glavine	.35
57	Denny Neagle	.15
58	John Smoltz	.15
59	Javy Lopez	.15
60	Roberto Alomar	.30
61	Rafael Palmeiro	1.25
62	Mike Mussina	.35
63	Cal Ripken Jr.	4.00
64	Mo Vaughn	.15
65	Tim Naehring	.15
66	John Valentin	.15
67	Mark Grace	.15
68	Kevin Orie	.15
69	Sammy Sosa	2.50
70	Albert Belle	.15
71	Frank Thomas	1.50
72	Robin Ventura	.15
73	David Justice	.15
74	Kenny Lofton	.15
75	Omar Vizquel	.15
76	Manny Ramirez	1.50
77	Jim Thome	.65
78	Dante Bichette	.15
79	Larry Walker	.15
80	Vinny Castilla	.15
81	Ellis Burks	.15
82	Bobby Higginson	.15
83	Brian L. Hunter	.15
84	Tony Clark	.15
85	Mike Hampton	.15
86	Jeff Bagwell	1.50
87	Craig Biggio	.15
88	Derek Bell	.15
89	Mike Piazza	3.00
90	Ramon Martinez	.15
91	Raul Mondesi	.15
92	Hideo Nomo	.75
93	Eric Karros	.15
94	Paul Molitor	1.50
95	Marty Cordova	.15
96	Brad Radke	.15
97	Mark Grudzielanek	.15
98	Carlos Perez	.15
99	Rondell White	.15
100	Todd Hundley	.15
101	Edgardo Alfonzo	.15
102	John Franco	.15
103	John Olerud	.15
104	Tino Martinez	.15
105	David Cone	.15
106	Paul O'Neill	.15
107	Andy Pettitte	.25
108	Bernie Williams	.15
109	Rickey Henderson	1.50
110	Jason Giambi	.75
111	Matt Stairs	.15
112	Gregg Jefferies	.15
113	Rico Brogna	.15
114	Curt Schilling	.35
115	Jason Schmidt	.15
116	Jose Guillen	.15
117	Kevin Young	.15
118	Ray Lankford	.15
119	Mark McGwire	3.00
120	Delino DeShields	.15
121	Ken Caminiti	.15
122	Tony Gwynn	2.00
123	Trevor Hoffman	.15
124	Barry Bonds	4.00
125	Jeff Kent	.15
126	Shawn Estes	.15
127	J.T. Snow	.15
128	Jay Buhner	.15
129	Ken Griffey Jr.	2.50
130	Dan Wilson	.15
131	Edgar Martinez	.15
132	Alex Rodriguez	3.00
133	Rusty Greer	.15
134	Juan Gonzalez	.75
135	Fernando Tatis	.15
136	Ivan Rodriguez	1.00
137	Carlos Delgado	.75
138	Pat Hentgen	.15
139	Roger Clemens	2.25
140	Chipper Jones	2.00
141	Greg Maddux	2.00
142	Rafael Palmeiro	1.25
143	Mike Mussina	.65
144	Cal Ripken Jr.	4.00
145	Nomar Garciaparra	2.00
146	Mo Vaughn	.35
147	Sammy Sosa	2.00
148	Albert Belle	.35
149	Frank Thomas	1.50
150	Jim Thome	1.25
151	Kenny Lofton	.35
152	Manny Ramirez	1.50
153	Larry Walker	.35
154	Jeff Bagwell	1.50
155	Craig Biggio	.35
156	Mike Piazza	2.50
157	Paul Molitor	1.50
158	Derek Jeter	4.00
159	Tino Martinez	.35
160	Curt Schilling	.50
161	Mark McGwire	3.00
162	Tony Gwynn	2.00
163	Barry Bonds	4.00
164	Ken Griffey Jr.	2.50
165	Randy Johnson	1.50
166	Alex Rodriguez	3.00
167	Juan Gonzalez	.75
168	Ivan Rodriguez	1.25
169	Roger Clemens	2.25
170	Greg Maddux	3.00
171	Cal Ripken Jr.	6.50
172	Frank Thomas	2.00
173	Jeff Bagwell	3.00
174	Mike Piazza	4.00
175	Mark McGwire	5.00

177	Barry Bonds	6.50
178	Ken Griffey Jr.	4.00
179	Alex Rodriguez	5.00
180	Roger Clemens	3.25
181	Mike Caruso	.50
182	David Ortiz	1.00
183	Gabe Alvarez	.50
184	Gary Matthews Jr.	.50
185	Kerry Wood	1.25
186	Carl Pavano	.50
187	Alex Gonzalez	.50
188	Masato Yoshii	.50
189	Larry Sutton	.50
190	Russell Branyan	.50
191	Bruce Chen	.50
192	Rolando Arrojo	.50
193	Ryan Christenson	.50
194	Cliff Politte	.50
195	A.J. Hinch	.50
196	Kevin Witt	.50
197	Daryle Ward	.50
198	Corey Koskie	.50
199	Mike Lowell	.50
200	Travis Lee	.50
201	Kevin Millwood RC	1.00
202	Robert Smith	.50
203	Magglio Ordonez RC	10.00
204	Eric Milton	.50
205	Geoff Jenkins	.50
206	Rich Butler	.50
207	Mike Kinkade RC	.75
208	Braden Looper	.50
209	Matt Clement	.50
210	Derrek Lee	1.50
211	Randy Johnson	1.50
212	John Smoltz	.50
213	Roger Clemens	2.25
214	Curt Schilling	.75
215	Pedro J. Martinez	1.50
216	Vinny Castilla	.50
217	Jose Cruz Jr.	.50
218	Jim Thome	1.20
219	Alex Rodriguez	3.00
220	Frank Thomas	1.50
221	Tim Salmon	.50
222	Larry Walker	.50
223	Albert Belle	.50
224	Manny Ramirez	1.50
225	Mark McGwire	3.00
226	Mo Vaughn	.50
227	Andres Galarraga	.50
228	Scott Rolen	1.25
229	Travis Lee	.50
230	Mike Piazza	2.50
231	Nomar Garciaparra	2.00
232	Andruw Jones	1.50
233	Barry Bonds	4.00
234	Jeff Bagwell	1.50
235	Juan Gonzalez	.75
236	Tino Martinez	.50
237	Vladimir Guerrero	1.50
238	Rafael Palmeiro	1.25
239	Russell Branyan	.50
240	Ken Griffey Jr.	2.50
241	Cecil Fielder	.15
242	Chuck Finley	.15
243	Jay Bell	.15
244	Andy Benes	.15
245	Matt Williams	.15
246	Brian Anderson	.15
247	David Dellucci	.15
248	Andres Galarraga	.15
249	Andruw Jones	1.50
250	Greg Maddux	2.00
251	Brady Anderson	.15
252	Joe Carter	.15
253	Eric Davis	.15
254	Pedro J. Martinez	1.50
255	Nomar Garciaparra	2.00
256	Dennis Eckersley	1.25
257	Henry Rodriguez	.15
258	Jeff Blauser	.15
259	Jaime Navarro	.15
260	Ray Durham	.15
261	Chris Stynes	.15
262	Willie Greene	.15
263	Reggie Sanders	.15
264	Bret Boone	.15
265	Barry Larkin	.15
266	Travis Fryman	.15
267	Charles Nagy	.15
268	Sandy Alomar Jr.	.15
269	Darryl Kile	.15
270	Mike Lansing	.15
271	Pedro Astacio	.15
272	Damion Easley	.15
273	Joe Randa	.15
274	Luis Gonzalez	.15
275	Mike Piazza	2.50
276	Todd Zeile	.15
277	Edgar Renteria	.15
278	Livan Hernandez	.15
279	Cliff Floyd	.15
280	Moises Alou	.15

281	Billy Wagner	.15
282	Jeff King	.15
283	Hal Morris	.15
284	Johnny Damon	.35
285	Dean Palmer	.15
286	Tim Belcher	.15
287	Eric Young	.15
288	Bobby Bonilla	.15
289	Gary Sheffield	.60
290	Chan Ho Park	.15
291	Charles Johnson	.15
292	Jeff Cirillo	.15
293	Jeromy Burnitz	.15
294	Jose Valentin	.15
295	Marquis Grissom	.15
296	Todd Walker	.15
297	Terry Steinbach	.15
298	Rick Aguilera	.15
299	Vladimir Guerrero	1.50
300	Rey Ordonez	.15
301	Butch Huskey	.15
302	Bernard Gilkey	.15
303	Mariano Rivera	.25
304	Chuck Knoblauch	.15
305	Derek Jeter	4.00
306	Ricky Bottalico	.15
307	Bob Abreu	.15
308	Scott Rolen	1.25
309	Al Martin	.15
310	Jason Kendall	.15
311	Brian Jordan	.15
312	Ron Gant	.15
313	Todd Stottlemyre	.15
314	Greg Vaughn	.15
315	J. Kevin Brown	.15
316	Wally Joyner	.15
317	Robb Nen	.15
318	Orel Hershiser	.15
319	Russ Davis	.15
320	Randy Johnson	1.50
321	Quinton McCracken	.15
322	Tony Saunders	.15
323	Wilson Alvarez	.15
324	Wade Boggs	2.00
325	Fred McGriff	.15
326	Lee Stevens	.15
327	John Wetteland	.15
328	Jose Canseco	.60
329	Randy Myers	.15
330	Jose Cruz Jr.	.15
331	Matt Williams	.50
332	Andres Galarraga	.50
333	Walt Weiss	.50
334	Joe Carter	.50
335	Pedro J. Martinez	2.00
336	Henry Rodriguez	.50
337	Travis Fryman	.50
338	Darryl Kile	.50
339	Mike Lansing	.50
340	Mike Piazza	4.00
341	Moises Alou	.50
342	Charles Johnson	.50
343	Chuck Knoblauch	.50
344	Rickey Henderson	2.00
345	J. Kevin Brown	.50
346	Orel Hershiser	.50
347	Wade Boggs	3.00
348	Fred McGriff	.50
349	Jose Canseco	1.00
350	Gary Sheffield	1.00
351	Travis Lee	2.50
352	Nomar Garciaparra	5.00
353	Frank Thomas	4.00
354	Cal Ripken Jr.	10.00
355	Mark McGwire	8.00
356	Mike Piazza	6.00
357	Alex Rodriguez	8.00
358	Barry Bonds	10.00
359	Tony Gwynn	5.00
360	Ken Griffey Jr.	6.00

1999 SP Authentic

	NM/M
Complete Set (135):	100.00

Common Player (1-90):		.10
Common Future Watch (91-120):		2.00
Production:		(2,700)
Common Season to Remember (121-135):		2.00
Production:		(2,700)
Pack (5):		3.50
Wax Box (24):		75.00
1	Mo Vaughn	.10
2	Jim Edmonds	.10
3	Darin Erstad	.25
4	Travis Lee	.10
5	Matt Williams	.10
6	Randy Johnson	1.50
7	Chipper Jones	1.75
8	Greg Maddux	1.75
9	Andruw Jones	1.50
10	Andres Galarraga	.10
11	Tom Glavine	.35
12	Cal Ripken Jr.	3.00
13	Brady Anderson	.10
14	Albert Belle	.10
15	Nomar Garciaparra	1.75
16	Donnie Sadler	.10
17	Pedro Martinez	1.50
18	Sammy Sosa	1.75
19	Kerry Wood	.60
20	Mark Grace	.10
21	Mike Caruso	.10
22	Frank Thomas	1.50
23	Paul Konerko	.20
24	Sean Casey	.20
25	Barry Larkin	.10
26	Kenny Lofton	.10
27	Manny Ramirez	1.50
28	Jim Thome	1.25
29	Bartolo Colon	.10
30	Jaret Wright	.10
31	Larry Walker	.10
32	Todd Helton	1.25
33	Tony Clark	.10
34	Dean Palmer	.10
35	Mark Kotsay	.10
36	Cliff Floyd	.10
37	Ken Caminiti	.10
38	Craig Biggio	.10
39	Jeff Bagwell	1.50
40	Moises Alou	.10
41	Johnny Damon	.35
42	Larry Sutton	.10
43	Kevin Brown	.10
44	Gary Sheffield	.40
45	Raul Mondesi	.10
46	Jeromy Burnitz	.10
47	Jeff Cirillo	.10
48	Todd Walker	.10
49	David Ortiz	.50
50	Brad Radtke	.10
51	Vladimir Guerrero	1.50
52	Rondell White	.10
53	Brad Fullmer	.10
54	Mike Piazza	2.00
55	Robin Ventura	.10
56	John Olerud	.10
57	Derek Jeter	3.00
58	Tino Martinez	.10
59	Bernie Williams	.10
60	Roger Clemens	1.75
61	Ben Grieve	.10
62	Miguel Tejada	.20
63	A.J. Hinch	.10
64	Scott Rolen	1.00
65	Curt Schilling	.35
66	Doug Glanville	.10
67	Aramis Ramirez	.10
68	Tony Womack	.10
69	Jason Kendall	.10
70	Tony Gwynn	1.75
71	Wally Joyner	.10
72	Greg Vaughn	.10
73	Barry Bonds	3.00
74	Ellis Burks	.10
75	Jeff Kent	.10
76	Ken Griffey Jr.	2.00
77	Alex Rodriguez	2.50
78	Edgar Martinez	.10
79	Mark McGwire	2.50
80	Eli Marrero	.10
81	Matt Morris	.10
82	Rolando Arrojo	.10
83	Quinton McCracken	.10
84	Jose Canseco	.50
85	Ivan Rodriguez	1.25
86	Juan Gonzalez	.75
87	Royce Clayton	.10
88	Shawn Green	.30
89	Jose Cruz Jr.	.10
90	Carlos Delgado	.60
91	Troy Glaus	6.00
92	George Lombard	2.00
93	Ryan Minor	2.00
94	Calvin Pickering	2.00
95	Jin Ho Cho	2.00

96	Russ Branyon	2.00
97	Derrick Gibson	2.00
98	Gabe Kapler	2.00
99	Matt Anderson	2.00
100	Preston Wilson	2.00
101	Alex Gonzalez	2.00
102	Carlos Beltran	6.00
103	Dee Brown	2.00
104	Jeremy Giambi	2.00
105	Angel Pena	2.00
106	Geoff Jenkins	2.00
107	Corey Koskie	2.00
108	A.J. Pierzynski	2.00
109	Michael Barrett	2.00
110	Fernando Seguignol	2.00
111	Mike Kinkade	2.00
112	Ricky Ledee	2.00
113	Mike Lowell	2.00
114	Eric Chavez	2.50
115	Matt Clement	2.00
116	Shane Monahan	2.00
117	J.D. Drew	4.00
118	Bubba Trammell	2.00
119	Kevin Witt	2.00
120	Roy Halladay	2.50
121	Mark McGwire	5.00
122	Mark McGwire, Sammy Sosa	4.00
123	Sammy Sosa	2.50
124	Ken Griffey Jr.	3.00
125	Cal Ripken Jr.	6.00
126	Juan Gonzalez	2.50
127	Kerry Wood	2.50
128	Trevor Hoffman	2.00
129	Barry Bonds	5.00
130	Alex Rodriguez	4.00
131	Ben Grieve	2.00
132	Tom Glavine	2.00
133	David Wells	2.00
134	Mike Piazza	3.00
135	Scott Brosius	2.00

Chirography

		NM/M
Common Player:		4.00
Inserted 1:24		
EC	Eric Chavez	8.00
GK	Gabe Kapler	4.00
GMj	Gary Matthews Jr.	4.00
CP	Calvin Pickering	4.00
CK	Corey Koskie	6.00
SM	Shane Monahan	4.00
RH	Richard Hidalgo	4.00
MK	Mike Kinkade	4.00
CB	Carlos Beltran	35.00
AG	Alex Gonzalez	4.00
BC	Bruce Chen	4.00
MA	Matt Anderson	4.00
RM	Ryan Minor	4.00
RL	Ricky Ledee	4.00
RR	Ruben Rivera	4.00
BF	Brad Fullmer	4.00
RB	Russ Branyan	4.00
ML	Mike Lowell	6.00
JG	Jeremy Giambi	4.00
GL	George Lombard	4.00
KW	Kevin Witt	4.00
TW	Todd Walker	4.00
SR	Scott Rolen	20.00
KW	Kerry Wood	25.00
BG	Ben Grieve	4.00
JR	Ken Griffey Jr.	75.00
CJ	Chipper Jones	30.00
IR	Ivan Rodriguez	25.00
TGl	Troy Glaus	15.00
TL	Travis Lee	4.00
VG	Vladimir Guerrero	30.00
GV	Greg Vaughn	4.00
JT	Jim Thome	25.00
JD	J.D. Drew	15.00
TH	Todd Helton	15.00
GM	Greg Maddux	75.00

		NM/M
NG	Nomar Garciaparra	75.00
TG	Tony Gwynn	30.00
CR	Cal Ripken Jr.	125.00

Chirography Gold

		NM/M
Common Player:		5.00
Inserted 1:24		
EC	Eric Chavez/30	40.00
GK	Gabe Kapler/51	10.00
GMj	Gary Matthews Jr./68	5.00
CP	Calvin Pickering/6	40.00
CK	Corey Koskie/47	15.00
SM	Shane Monahan/12	20.00
RH	Richard Hidalgo/15	30.00
MK	Mike Kinkade/33	10.00
CB	Carlos Beltran/36	75.00
AG	Alex Gonzalez/22	20.00
BC	Bruce Chen/48	10.00
MA	Matt Anderson/14	20.00
RM	Ryan Minor/10	35.00
RL	Ricky Ledee/38	10.00
RR	Ruben Rivera/28	10.00
BF	Brad Fullmer/20	10.00
RB	Russ Branyon/66	10.00
ML	Mike Lowell/60	15.00
JG	Jeremy Giambi/15	20.00
GL	George Lombard/26	10.00
KW	Kevin Witt/6	20.00
TW	Todd Walker/34	40.00
SR	Scott Rolen/17	75.00
KW	Kerry Wood/34	60.00
BG	Ben Grieve/14	35.00
JR	Ken Griffey Jr./24	250.00
CJ	Chipper Jones/10	200.00
IR	Ivan Rodriguez/7	125.00
TGI	Troy Glaus/14	90.00
TL	Travis Lee/16	35.00
VG	Vladimir Guerrero/27	75.00
GV	Greg Vaughn/23	10.00
JT	Jim Thome/25	40.00
JD	J.D. Drew/8	125.00
TH	Todd Helton/17	75.00
GM	Greg Maddux/31	150.00
NG	Nomar Garciaparra/5	375.00
TG	Tony Gwynn/19	125.00
CR	Cal Ripken Jr./8	650.00

Home Run Chronicles

		NM/M
Complete Set (70):		50.00
Common Player:		.15
Inserted 1:1		
Die-Cuts:		10X
Production 70 Sets		
HR01	Mark McGwire	1.50
HR02	Sammy Sosa	1.25
HR03	Ken Griffey Jr.	1.00
HR04	Mark McGwire	1.50
HR05	Mark McGwire	1.50
HR06	Albert Belle	.15
HR07	Jose Canseco	.30
HR08	Juan Gonzalez	.45
HR09	Manny Ramirez	.65
HR10	Rafael Palmeiro	.50
HR11	Mo Vaughn	.15
HR12	Carlos Delgado	.45
HR13	Nomar Garciaparra	.75
HR14	Barry Bonds	1.50
HR15	Alex Rodriguez	1.25
HR16	Tony Clark	.15
HR17	Jim Thome	.50
HR18	Edgar Martinez	.15
HR19	Frank Thomas	.65
HR20	Greg Vaughn	.15
HR21	Vinny Castilla	.15
HR22	Andres Galarraga	.15
HR23	Moises Alou	.15
HR24	Jeromy Burnitz	.15
HR25	Vladimir Guerrero	.65
HR26	Jeff Bagwell	.65
HR27	Chipper Jones	.75
HR28	Javier Lopez	.15
HR29	Mike Piazza	1.00
HR30	Andruw Jones	.65
HR31	Henry Rodriguez	.15
HR32	Jeff Kent	.15
HR33	Ray Lankford	.15
HR34	Scott Rolen	.50
HR35	Raul Mondesi	.15
HR36	Ken Caminiti	.15
HR37	J.D. Drew	.40
HR38	Troy Glaus	.50
HR39	Gabe Kapler	.15
HR40	Alex Rodriguez	1.25
HR41	Ken Griffey Jr.	1.00
HR42	Sammy Sosa	1.25
HR43	Mark McGwire	1.50
HR44	Sammy Sosa	1.25
HR45	Mark McGwire	1.50
HR46	Vinny Castilla	.15
HR47	Sammy Sosa	1.25
HR48	Mark McGwire	1.50
HR49	Sammy Sosa	1.25
HR50	Greg Vaughn	.15
HR51	Sammy Sosa	1.25
HR52	Mark McGwire	1.50
HR53	Sammy Sosa	1.25
HR54	Mark McGwire	1.50
HR55	Sammy Sosa	1.25
HR56	Ken Griffey Jr.	1.00
HR57	Sammy Sosa	1.25
HR58	Mark McGwire	1.50
HR59	Sammy Sosa	1.25
HR60	Mark McGwire	1.50
HR61	Mark McGwire	2.50
HR62	Mark McGwire	2.50
HR63	Mark McGwire	1.50
HR64	Mark McGwire	1.50
HR65	Mark McGwire	1.50
HR66	Sammy Sosa	2.50
HR67	Mark McGwire	1.50
HR68	Mark McGwire	1.50
HR69	Mark McGwire	1.50
HR70	Mark McGwire	4.00

Epic Figures

		NM/M
Complete Set (30):		30.00
Common Player:		.50
Inserted 1:7		
E01	Mo Vaughn	.50
E02	Travis Lee	.50
E03	Andres Galarraga	.50
E04	Andruw Jones	1.00
E05	Chipper Jones	1.25
E06	Greg Maddux	1.25
E07	Cal Ripken Jr.	3.00
E08	Nomar Garciaparra	1.25
E09	Sammy Sosa	1.25
E10	Frank Thomas	1.00
E11	Kerry Wood	.60
E12	Kenny Lofton	.50
E13	Manny Ramirez	1.00
E14	Larry Walker	.50
E15	Jeff Bagwell	1.00
E16	Paul Molitor	1.00
E17	Vladimir Guerrero	1.00
E18	Derek Jeter	3.00
E19	Tino Martinez	.50
E20	Mike Piazza	1.50
E21	Ben Grieve	.50
E22	Scott Rolen	.75
E23	Mark McGwire	2.00
E24	Tony Gwynn	1.25
E25	Barry Bonds	3.00
E26	Ken Griffey Jr.	1.50
E27	Alex Rodriguez	2.00
E28	J.D. Drew	.65
E29	Juan Gonzalez	.60
E30	Kevin Brown	.50

Reflections

		NM/M
Complete Set (30):		60.00
Common Player:		.75
Inserted 1:23		
R01	Mo Vaughn	.75
R02	Travis Lee	.75
R03	Andres Galarraga	.75
R04	Andruw Jones	2.50
R05	Chipper Jones	3.00
R06	Greg Maddux	3.00
R07	Cal Ripken Jr.	6.00
R08	Nomar Garciaparra	3.00
R09	Sammy Sosa	3.00
R10	Frank Thomas	2.50
R11	Kerry Wood	1.50
R12	Kenny Lofton	.75
R13	Manny Ramirez	2.50
R14	Larry Walker	.75
R15	Jeff Bagwell	2.50
R16	Paul Molitor	2.50
R17	Vladimir Guerrero	2.50
R18	Derek Jeter	6.00
R19	Tino Martinez	.75
R20	Mike Piazza	3.50
R21	Ben Grieve	.75
R22	Scott Rolen	2.00
R23	Mark McGwire	4.50
R24	Tony Gwynn	3.00
R25	Barry Bonds	6.00
R26	Ken Griffey Jr.	3.50
R27	Alex Rodriguez	4.50
R28	J.D. Drew	1.25
R29	Juan Gonzalez	1.25
R30	Roger Clemens	3.25

SP Authentics

	NM/M
Common Card:	10.00
(1) K.Griffey Jr./75/ Auto. Ball	60.00
(2) Ken Griffey Jr./200/ Glove	20.00
(3) K. Griffey Jr./346 HR Cel Card	10.00
(4) Ken Griffey Jr./25/ Auto. Jsy	125.00
(5) K. Griffey Jr./75 Auto. Mini Helmet	80.00
(6) Ken Griffey Jr./200/ SI Cover	15.00
(7) K. Griffey Jr./75 SI Cover Auto.	75.00
(8) Ken Griffey Jr./300/ Standee	10.00
(9) Mark McGwire/1/ Auto. 62 HR Ticket/1 (Autographed 62HR ticket.)	
(10) Mark McGwire/3/ Auto. 70 HR Ticket	

500 Club Piece of History

		NM/M
EB	Ernie Banks	120.00
EB	Ernie Banks/ Auto./14	325.00

1999 SP Signature Edition

		NM/M
Complete Set (180):		60.00
Common Player:		.15
Pack (3):		20.00
Wax Box (12):		250.00
1	Nomar Garciaparra	2.00
2	Ken Griffey Jr.	2.50
3	J.D. Drew	.50
4	Alex Rodriguez	3.00
5	Juan Gonzalez	.60
6	Mo Vaughn	.15
7	Greg Maddux	2.00
8	Chipper Jones	2.00
9	Frank Thomas	1.50
10	Vladimir Guerrero	1.50
11	Mike Piazza	2.50
12	Eric Chavez	.25
13	Tony Gwynn	2.00
14	Orlando Hernandez	.15
15	Pat Burrell RC	6.00
16	Darin Erstad	.30
17	Greg Vaughn	.15
18	Russ Branyan	.15
19	Gabe Kapler	.15
20	Craig Biggio	.15
21	Troy Glaus	1.25
22	Pedro J. Martinez	1.50
23	Carlos Beltran	.50
24	Derrek Lee	.50
25	Manny Ramirez	1.50
26	Shea Hillenbrand RC	1.00
27	Carlos Lee	.15
28	Angel Pena	.15
29	Rafael Roque	.15
30	Octavio Dotel	.15
31	Jeromy Burnitz	.15
32	Jeremy Giambi	.15
33	Andruw Jones	1.50
34	Todd Helton	1.25
35	Scott Rolen	1.25
36	Jason Kendall	.15
37	Trevor Hoffman	.15
38	Barry Bonds	4.00
39	Ivan Rodriguez	1.25
40	Roy Halladay	.15
41	Rickey Henderson	1.50
42	Ryan Minor	.15
43	Brian Jordan	.15
44	Alex Gonzalez	.15
45	Raul Mondesi	.15
46	Corey Koskie	.15
47	Paul O'Neill	.15
48	Todd Walker	.15
49	Carlos Febles	.15
50	Travis Fryman	.15
51	Albert Belle	.15
52	Travis Lee	.15
53	Bruce Chen	.15
54	Reggie Taylor	.15
55	Jerry Hairston Jr.	.15
56	Carlos Guillen	.15
57	Michael Barrett	.15
58	Jason Conti	.15
59	Joe Lawrence	.15
60	Jeff Cirillo	.15
61	Juan Melo	.15
62	Chad Hermansen	.15
63	Ruben Mateo	.15
64	Ben Davis	.15
65	Mike Caruso	.15
66	Jason Giambi	.50
67	Jose Canseco	.50
68	Chad Hutchinson RC	.15
69	Mitch Meluskey	.15
70	Adrian Beltre	.25
71	Mark Kotsay	.15
72	Juan Encarnacion	.15
73	Dermal Brown	.15
74	Kevin Witt	.15
75	Vinny Castilla	.15
76	Aramis Ramirez	.15
77	Marlon Anderson	.15
78	Mike Kinkade	.15
79	Kevin Barker	.15
80	Ron Belliard	.15

81	Chris Haas	.15
82	Bob Henley	.15
83	Fernando Seguignol	.15
84	Damon Minor	.15
85	A.J. Burnett RC	1.00
86	Calvin Pickering	.15
87	Mike Darr	.15
88	Cesar King	.15
89	Rob Bell	.15
90	Derrick Gibson	.15
91	Ober Moreno RC	.15
92	Robert Fick	.15
93	Doug Mientkiewicz RC	.75
94	A.J. Pierzynski	.15
95	Orlando Palmeiro	.15
96	Sidney Ponson	.15
97	Ivanon Coffie	.15
98	Juan Pena RC	1.00
99	Mark Karchner	.15
100	Carlos Castillo	.15
101	Bryan Ward	.15
102	Mario Valdez	.15
103	Billy Wagner	.15
104	Miguel Tejada	.25
105	Jose Cruz Jr.	.15
106	George Lombard	.15
107	Geoff Jenkins	.15
108	Ray Lankford	.15
109	Todd Stottlemyre	.15
110	Mike Lowell	.15
111	Matt Clement	.15
112	Scott Brosius	.15
113	Preston Wilson	.15
114	Bartolo Colon	.15
115	Rolando Arrojo	.15
116	Jose Guillen	.15
117	Ron Gant	.15
118	Ricky Ledee	.15
119	Carlos Delgado	.50
120	Abraham Nunez	.15
121	John Olerud	.15
122	Chan Ho Park	.15
123	Brad Radke	.15
124	Al Leiter	.15
125	Gary Matthews Jr.	.15
126	F.P. Santangelo	.15
127	Brad Fullmer	.15
128	Matt Anderson	.15
129	A.J. Hinch	.15
130	Sterling Hitchcock	.15
131	Edgar Martinez	.15
132	Fernando Tatis	.15
133	Bobby Smith	.15
134	Paul Konerko	.25
135	Sean Casey	.25
136	Donnie Sadler	.15
137	Denny Neagle	.15
138	Sandy Alomar	.15
139	Mariano Rivera	.25
140	Emil Brown	.15
141	J.T. Snow	.15
142	Eli Marrero	.15
143	Rusty Greer	.15
144	Johnny Damon	.35
145	Damion Easley	.15
146	Eric Milton	.15
147	Rico Brogna	.15
148	Ray Durham	.15
149	Wally Joyner	.15
150	Royce Clayton	.15
151	David Ortiz	.50
152	Wade Boggs	2.00
153	Ugueth Urbina	.15
154	Richard Hidalgo	.15
155	Bobby Abreu	.15
156	Robb Nen	.15
157	David Segui	.15
158	Sean Berry	.15
159	Kevin Tapani	.15
160	Jason Varitek	.15
161	Fernando Vina	.15
162	Jim Leyritz	.15
163	Enrique Wilson	.15
164	Jim Parque	.15
165	Doug Glanville	.15
166	Jesus Sanchez	.15
167	Nolan Ryan	4.00
168	Robin Yount	.50
169	Stan Musial	1.00
170	Tom Seaver	.50
171	Mike Schmidt	1.00
172	Willie Stargell	.50
173	Rollie Fingers	.45
174	Willie McCovey	.50
175	Harmon Killebrew	.50
176	Eddie Mathews	.50
177	Reggie Jackson	1.00
178	Frank Robinson	.50
179	Ken Griffey Sr.	.15
180	Eddie Murray	1.50

Autographs

NM/M

Common Player: 3.00

Inserted 1:1

BA	Bobby Abreu	10.00
SA	Sandy Alomar	5.00
MA	Marlon Anderson	4.00
KB	Kevin Barker	3.00
MB	Michael Barrett	4.00
RoB	Rob Bell	3.00
AB	Albert Belle	15.00
RBe	Ron Belliard	3.00
CBe	Carlos Beltran	50.00
ABe	Adrian Beltre	25.00
BB	Barry Bonds	180.00
RB	Russ Branyan	3.00
SB	Scott Brosius/SP	30.00
DB	Dermal Brown	3.00
EB	Emil Brown	3.00
AJB	A.J. Burnett (Exchange Card)	3.00
AJB	A.J. Burnett/Auto.	15.00
PB	Pat Burrell	12.50
JoC	Jose Canseco	30.00
MC	Mike Caruso	3.00
SC	Sean Casey (Exchange Card)	3.00
SC	Sean Casey/Auto.	15.00
VC	Vinny Castilla (Exchange Card)	3.00
VC	Vinny Castilla/Auto.	8.00
CC	Carlos Castillo	3.00
EC	Eric Chavez	10.00
BC	Bruce Chen	3.00
JCi	Jeff Cirillo	3.00
RC	Royce Clayton	3.00
MCl	Matt Clement	6.00
IC	Ivanon Coffie	3.00
BCo	Bartolo Colon (Exchange Card)	3.00
BCo	Bartolo Colon/Auto.	8.00
JC	Jason Conti	3.00
JDa	Johnny Damon	25.00
BD	Ben Davis	3.00
CD	Carlos Delgado	15.00
OD	Octavio Dotel	3.00
JD	J.D. Drew	15.00
RD	Ray Durham	3.00
DEa	Damion Easley	3.00
JE	Juan Encarnacion	3.00
DE	Darin Erstad	8.00
CF	Carlos Febles	3.00
Rob	Robert Fick	3.00
Rol	Rollie Fingers	8.00
BF	Brad Fullmer	3.00
RGa	Ron Gant	3.00
NG	Nomar Garciaparra	75.00
JaG	Jason Giambi	20.00
DG	Derrick Gibson	3.00
DGI	Doug Glanville	3.00
TGI	Troy Glaus	15.00
AG	Alex Gonzalez	5.00
RGr	Rusty Greer	3.00
Jr.	Ken Griffey Jr.	80.00
1	Ken Griffey Jr. (Facsimile autographed "SAMPLE.")	15.00
Sr.	Ken Griffey Sr.	8.00
VG	Vladimir Guerrero	30.00
JG	Jose Guillen	8.00
TG	Tony Gwynn	35.00
CHa	Chris Haas	3.00
JHj	Jerry Hairston Jr.	3.00
RH	Roy Halladay	10.00
THe	Todd Helton	20.00
BH	Bob Henley	3.00
ED	Orlando Hernandez	40.00
CH	Chad Hermansen	3.00
ShH	Shea Hillenbrand	8.00
StH	Sterling Hitchcock	3.00
THo	Trevor Hoffman	5.00
CHu	Chad Hutchinson	3.00
RJ	Reggie Jackson/SP	40.00
GJ	Geoff Jenkins	5.00
AJ	Andruw Jones	20.00
CJ	Chipper Jones	40.00
WJ	Wally Joyner	8.00
GK	Gabe Kapler	3.00
MKa	Mark Karchner	3.00
JK	Jason Kendall	6.00
HK	Harmon Killebrew	40.00
CKi	Cesar King	3.00
MKi	Mike Kinkade	3.00
PK	Paul Konerko	10.00
CK	Corey Koskie	6.00
MK	Mark Kotsay	4.00

RL	Ray Lankford	5.00
JLa	Joe Lawrence	3.00
CL	Carlos Lee	10.00
DL	Derrek Lee	25.00
AL	Al Leiter	6.00
JLe	Jim Leyritz	6.00
GL	George Lombard	3.00
GM	Greg Maddux	80.00
Eli	Eli Marrero	3.00
EM	Edgar Martinez	20.00
PM	Pedro J. Martinez (Exchange Card)	5.00
PM	Pedro J. Martinez/ Auto.	100.00
RMa	Ruben Mateo (Exchange Card)	3.00
RMa	Ruben Mateo/Auto.	8.00
EMa	Eddie Mathews	60.00
GMj	Gary Matthews Jr.	3.00
WMc	Willie McCovey	35.00
JM	Juan Melo	3.00
MMe	Mitch Meluskey	3.00
DoM	Doug Mientkiewicz	6.00
EMi	Eric Milton	3.00
DaM	Damon Minor	3.00
RM	Ryan Minor	3.00
EMu	Eddie Murray	20.00
SM	Stan Musial	50.00
RN	Robb Nen	3.00
AN	Abraham Nunez	3.00
JO	John Olerud	10.00
PO	Paul O'Neill	17.50
DO	David Ortiz	35.00
OP	Orlando Palmeiro	3.00
JP	Jim Parque	3.00
AP	Angel Pena	3.00
MP	Mike Piazza (Exchange Card)	6.00
MP	Mike Piazza/Auto.	175.00
CP	Calvin Pickering	3.00
AJP	A.J. Pierzynski	5.00
SP	Sidney Ponson	8.00
BR	Brad Radke	4.00
ARa	Aramis Ramirez	10.00
MR	Manny Ramirez	50.00
MRi	Mariano Rivera	25.00
FR	Frank Robinson	25.00
AR	Alex Rodriguez	120.00
PG	Ivan Rodriguez	25.00
SR	Scott Rolen (Exchange Card)	3.00
SR	Scott Rolen/Auto.	25.00
RR	Rafael Roque	3.00
NR	Nolan Ryan	120.00
DS	Donnie Sadler	3.00
JS	Jesus Sanchez	3.00
MS	Mike Schmidt	60.00
TSe	Tom Seaver	35.00
DSe	David Segui	3.00
FS	Fernando Seguignol	3.00
BS	Bobby Smith	3.00
JT	J.T. Snow (Exchange Card)	3.00
JT	J.T. Snow/Auto.	6.00
POP	Willie Stargell (Exchange Card)	3.00
POP	Willie Stargell/Auto.	40.00
TSt	Todd Stottlemyre	3.00
FTa	Fernando Tatis	3.00
RT	Reggie Taylor	3.00
MT	Miguel Tejada	20.00
FT	Frank Thomas	50.00
MV	Mario Valdez	3.00
JV	Jason Varitek	30.00
GV	Greg Vaughn	3.00
MO	Mo Vaughn	8.00
FV	Fernando Vina	3.00
BWa	Billy Wagner	10.00
TW	Todd Walker	3.00
BW	Bryan Ward	3.00
EW	Enrique Wilson	3.00
KW	Kevin Witt	3.00
RY	Robin Yount	40.00

Autographs Gold

NM/M

Common Player: 12.00

Production 50 Sets

MA	Marlon Anderson	12.00
KB	Kevin Barker	12.00
MB	Michael Barrett	12.00
RoB	Rob Bell	12.00
AB	Albert Belle	20.00

RBe	Ron Belliard	12.00
CBe	Carlos Beltran	75.00
ABe	Adrian Beltre	40.00
CB	Craig Biggio (Unsigned)	3.00
BB	Barry Bonds	250.00
RB	Russ Branyan	12.00
DB	Dermal Brown	12.00
AJB	A.J. Burnett (Exchange Card)	4.00
AJB	A.J. Burnett (Autographed edition of 20.)	40.00
JB	Jeromy Burnitz (Unsigned)	3.00
PB	Pat Burrell	40.00
JoC	Jose Canseco	50.00
MC	Mike Caruso	12.00
VC	Vinny Castilla (Exchange Card)	3.00
VC	Vinny Castilla (Autographed)	20.00
CC	Carlos Castillo	12.00
EC	Eric Chavez	20.00
BC	Bruce Chen	12.00
JCi	Jeff Cirillo	12.00
JC	Jason Conti	12.00
MD	Mike Darr (Unsigned)	3.00
BD	Ben Davis	12.00
OD	Octavio Dotel	12.00
JD	J.D. Drew	30.00
JE	Juan Encarnacion	12.00
DE	Darin Erstad	20.00
CF	Carlos Febles	12.00
TF	Travis Fryman (Unsigned)	3.00
BF	Brad Fullmer	12.00
NG	Nomar Garciaparra	100.00
JaG	Jason Giambi	40.00
JeG	Jeremy Giambi (Unsigned)	3.00
DG	Derrick Gibson	12.00
DGI	Doug Glanville	12.00
TGI	Troy Glaus	30.00
AG	Alex Gonzalez	12.00
JG	Juan Gonzalez (Unsigned)	6.00
Jr.	Ken Griffey Jr.	150.00
Sr.	Ken Griffey Sr.	12.00
VG	Vladimir Guerrero	75.00
JG	Jose Guillen (Unsigned)	3.00
TG	Tony Gwynn	60.00
CHa	Chris Haas	12.00
JHj	Jerry Hairston Jr.	12.00
RH	Roy Halladay	25.00
THe	Todd Helton	30.00
RH	Rickey Henderson (Unsigned)	6.00
BH	Bob Henley	12.00
ED	Orlando Hernandez	25.00
CH	Chad Hermansen	12.00
ShH	Shea Hillenbrand	20.00
StH	Sterling Hitchcock	12.00
THo	Trevor Hoffman	30.00
CHu	Chad Hutchinson	12.00
GJ	Geoff Jenkins	12.00
AJ	Andruw Jones	40.00
CJ	Chipper Jones	80.00
BJ	Brian Jordan (Unsigned)	3.00
WJ	Wally Joyner	25.00
GK	Gabe Kapler	12.00
MKa	Mark Karchner	12.00
JK	Jason Kendall	20.00
CKi	Cesar King	12.00
MKi	Mike Kinkade	12.00
PK	Paul Konerko	15.00
CK	Corey Koskie	20.00
MK	Mark Kotsay	12.00
RL	Ray Lankford	12.00
JLa	Joe Lawrence	12.00
CL	Carlos Lee	25.00
DL	Derrek Lee	50.00
TL	Travis Lee (Unsigned)	4.00
AL	Al Leiter	12.00
JLe	Jim Leyritz	12.00
GL	George Lombard	12.00
GM	Greg Maddux	150.00
PM	Pedro Martinez (Exchange Card)	6.00
PM	Pedro Martinez (Autographed)	200.00
RMa	Ruben Mateo (Exchange Card)	3.00
RMa	Ruben Mateo (Autographed)	15.00
GMj	Gary Matthews Jr.	12.00
JM	Juan Melo	12.00
MMe	Mitch Meluskey	12.00
DoM	Doug Mientkiewicz	12.00
EMi	Eric Milton	12.00
DaM	Damon Minor	12.00
RM	Ryan Minor	12.00
PO	Paul O'Neill	30.00

DO	David Ortiz	75.00
OP	Orlando Palmeiro	12.00
AP	Angel Pena	12.00
MP	Mike Piazza (Exchange Card)	10.00
MP	Mike Piazza/Auto.	250.00
CP	Calvin Pickering	12.00
ARa	Aramis Ramirez	30.00
MR	Manny Ramirez	80.00
AR	Alex Rodriguez	185.00
PG	Ivan Rodriguez	45.00
SR	Scott Rolen (Exchange Card)	4.00
SR	Scott Rolen/Auto.	75.00
RR	Rafael Roque	12.00
DSe	David Segui	12.00
FS	Fernando Seguignol	12.00
BS	Bobby Smith	12.00
RT	Reggie Taylor	12.00
FT	Frank Thomas	70.00
MV	Mario Valdez	12.00
GV	Greg Vaughn	12.00
MO	Mo Vaughn	20.00
TW	Todd Walker	12.00
KW	Kevin Witt	12.00

Legendary Cuts

No Pricing
Production One Set

500 Club Piece of History

		NM/M
MO	Mel Ott/350	100.00

1999 SPx

	NM/M
Complete Set (120):	100.00
Common Player:	.50
Common SPx Rookie (81-120):	2.00
Production 1,999 Sets	
Radiance (1-80):	7X
Radiance SP (81-120):	1.5X
Spectrum (1-of-1):	Values Undetermined
Pack (3):	3.00
Wax Box (18):	40.00

1	Mark McGwire #61	2.50
2	Mark McGwire #62	1.00
3	Mark McGwire #63	1.00
4	Mark McGwire #64	1.00
5	Mark McGwire #65	1.00
6	Mark McGwire #66	1.00
7	Mark McGwire #67	1.00
8	Mark McGwire #68	1.00
9	Mark McGwire #69	1.00
10	Mark McGwire #70	2.50
11	Mo Vaughn	.50
12	Darin Erstad	.75
13	Travis Lee	.50
14	Randy Johnson	1.50
15	Matt Williams	.50
16	Chipper Jones	2.00
17	Greg Maddux	2.00
18	Andruw Jones	1.50
19	Andres Galarraga	.50
20	Cal Ripken Jr.	4.00
21	Albert Belle	.50
22	Mike Mussina	.75
23	Nomar Garciaparra	2.00
24	Pedro Martinez	1.50
25	John Valentin	.50
26	Kerry Wood	1.00
27	Sammy Sosa	2.00
28	Mark Grace	.50
29	Frank Thomas	1.50
30	Mike Caruso	.50
31	Barry Larkin	.50
32	Sean Casey	.50
33	Jim Thome	1.25
34	Kenny Lofton	.50
35	Manny Ramirez	1.50
36	Larry Walker	.50
37	Todd Helton	1.25
38	Vinny Castilla	.50
39	Tony Clark	.50
40	Derrek Lee	1.00
41	Mark Kotsay	.50
42	Jeff Bagwell	1.50
43	Craig Biggio	.50
44	Moises Alou	.50
45	Larry Sutton	.50
46	Johnny Damon	1.00
47	Gary Sheffield	1.00
48	Raul Mondesi	.50
49	Jeromy Burnitz	.50
50	Todd Walker	.50
51	David Ortiz	1.00
52	Vladimir Guerrero	1.50
53	Rondell White	.50
54	Mike Piazza	2.50
55	Derek Jeter	4.00
56	Tino Martinez	.50
57	David Wells	.50
58	Ben Grieve	.50
59	A.J. Hinch	.50
60	Scott Rolen	1.25
61	Doug Glanville	.50
62	Aramis Ramirez	.50
63	Jose Guillen	.50
64	Tony Gwynn	2.00
65	Greg Vaughn	.50
66	Ruben Rivera	.50
67	Barry Bonds	4.00
68	J.T. Snow	.50
69	Alex Rodriguez	3.00
70	Ken Griffey Jr.	2.50
71	Jay Buhner	.50
72	Mark McGwire	3.00
73	Fernando Tatis	.50
74	Quinton McCracken	.50
75	Wade Boggs	2.00
76	Ivan Rodriguez	1.25
77	Juan Gonzalez	1.00
78	Rafael Palmeiro	1.25
79	Jose Cruz Jr.	.50
80	Carlos Delgado	1.00
81	Troy Glaus	5.00
82	Vladimir Nunez	2.00
83	George Lombard	2.00
84	Bruce Chen	2.00
85	Ryan Minor	2.00
86	Calvin Pickering	2.00
87	Jin Ho Cho	2.00
88	Russ Branyan	2.00
89	Derrick Gibson	2.00
90	Gabe Kapler/Auto.	6.00
91	Matt Anderson	2.00
92	Robert Fick	2.00
93	Juan Encarnacion	2.00
94	Preston Wilson	2.00
95	Alex Gonzalez	2.00
96	Carlos Beltran	5.00
97	Jeremy Giambi	2.00
98	Dee Brown	2.00
99	Adrian Beltre	4.00
100	Alex Cora	2.00
101	Angel Pena	2.00
102	Geoff Jenkins	2.00
103	Ronnie Belliard	2.00
104	Corey Koskie	2.00
105	A.J. Pierzynski	2.00
106	Michael Barrett	2.00
107	Fernando Seguignol	2.00
108	Mike Kinkade	2.00
109	Mike Lowell	2.00
110	Ricky Ledee	2.00
111	Eric Chavez	3.00
112	Abraham Nunez	2.00
113	Matt Clement	2.00
114	Ben Davis	2.00
115	Mike Darr	2.00
116	Ramon Martinez	2.00
117	Carlos Guillen	2.00
118	Shane Monahan	2.00
119	J.D. Drew/Auto.	15.00
120	Kevin Witt	2.00

Dominance

	NM/M
Complete Set (20):	35.00
Common Player:	1.00
Inserted 1:17	

1	Chipper Jones	2.00

TONY GWYNN • PADRES™

2	Greg Maddux	2.00
3	Cal Ripken Jr.	4.00
4	Nomar Garciaparra	2.00
5	Mo Vaughn	1.00
6	Sammy Sosa	2.00
7	Albert Belle	1.00
8	Frank Thomas	1.50
9	Jim Thome	1.25
10	Jeff Bagwell	1.50
11	Vladimir Guerrero	1.50
12	Mike Piazza	2.50
13	Derek Jeter	4.00
14	Tony Gwynn	2.00
15	Barry Bonds	4.00
16	Ken Griffey Jr.	2.50
17	Alex Rodriguez	3.00
18	Mark McGwire	3.00
19	J.D. Drew	1.25
20	Juan Gonzalez	1.25

Power Explosion

	NM/M
Complete Set (30):	15.00
Common Player:	.20
Inserted 1:3	

1	Troy Glaus	.65
2	Mo Vaughn	.20
3	Travis Lee	.20
4	Chipper Jones	1.00
5	Andres Galarraga	.20
6	Brady Anderson	.20
7	Albert Belle	.20
8	Nomar Garciaparra	1.00
9	Sammy Sosa	1.00
10	Frank Thomas	.75
11	Jim Thome	.65
12	Manny Ramirez	.75
13	Larry Walker	.20
14	Tony Clark	.20
15	Jeff Bagwell	.75
16	Moises Alou	.20
17	Ken Caminiti	.20
18	Vladimir Guerrero	.75
19	Mike Piazza	1.25
20	Tino Martinez	.20
21	Ben Grieve	.20
22	Scott Rolen	.60
23	Greg Vaughn	.20
24	Barry Bonds	2.00
25	Ken Griffey Jr.	1.25
26	Alex Rodriguez	1.50
27	Mark McGwire	1.50
28	J.D. Drew	.35
29	Juan Gonzalez	.45
30	Ivan Rodriguez	.60

Premier Stars

	NM/M
Complete Set (30):	45.00
Common Player:	1.00
Inserted 1:17	

1	Mark McGwire	3.00

2	Sammy Sosa	2.00
3	Frank Thomas	1.50
4	J.D. Drew	1.25
5	Kerry Wood	1.25
6	Moises Alou	1.00
7	Kenny Lofton	1.00
8	Jeff Bagwell	1.50
9	Tony Clark	1.00
10	Roberto Alomar	1.00
11	Cal Ripken Jr.	4.00
12	Derek Jeter	4.00
13	Mike Piazza	2.50
14	Jose Cruz Jr.	1.00
15	Chipper Jones	2.00
16	Nomar Garciaparra	2.00
17	Greg Maddux	2.00
18	Scott Rolen	1.25
19	Vladimir Guerrero	1.50
20	Albert Belle	1.00
21	Ken Griffey Jr.	2.50
22	Alex Rodriguez	3.00
23	Ben Grieve	1.00
24	Juan Gonzalez	1.25
25	Barry Bonds	4.00
26	Larry Walker	1.00
27	Tony Gwynn	2.00
28	Randy Johnson	1.50
29	Travis Lee	1.00
30	Mo Vaughn	1.00

Star Focus

	NM/M
Complete Set (30):	50.00
Common Player:	.75
Inserted 1:8	

1	Chipper Jones	2.25
2	Greg Maddux	2.25
3	Cal Ripken Jr.	4.50
4	Nomar Garciaparra	2.25
5	Mo Vaughn	.75
6	Sammy Sosa	2.25
7	Albert Belle	.75
8	Frank Thomas	1.50
9	Jim Thome	1.25
10	Kenny Lofton	.75
11	Manny Ramirez	1.50
12	Larry Walker	.75
13	Jeff Bagwell	1.50
14	Craig Biggio	.75
15	Randy Johnson	1.50
16	Vladimir Guerrero	1.50
17	Mike Piazza	3.00
18	Derek Jeter	4.50
19	Tino Martinez	.75
20	Bernie Williams	.75
21	Curt Schilling	1.00
22	Tony Gwynn	2.25
23	Barry Bonds	4.50
24	Ken Griffey Jr.	3.00
25	Alex Rodriguez	4.00
26	Mark McGwire	4.00
27	J.D. Drew	1.00
28	Juan Gonzalez	1.00
29	Ivan Rodriguez	1.25
30	Ben Grieve	.75

Winning Materials

	NM/M
Complete Set (8):	90.00
Common Player:	5.00
Inserted 1:251	

VC	Vinny Castilla	5.00
JD	J.D. Drew	7.50
JR	Ken Griffey Jr.	20.00
VG	Vladimir Guerrero	12.00
TG	Tony Gwynn	15.00
TH	Todd Helton	10.00
TL	Travis Lee	5.00
IR	Ivan Rodriguez	10.00

500 Club Piece of History

		NM/M
WM	Willie Mays/350	275.00
WM	Willie Mays/Auto./24	1,700

2000 SP Authentic

		NM/M
Complete Set (135):		150.00
Common Player:		.15
Common (91-105):		2.00
Production 2,500 Sets		
Common (106-135):		2.00
Production 2,500 Sets		
Pack (5):		3.00
Box (24):		60.00
1	Mo Vaughn	.15
2	Troy Glaus	.50
3	Jason Giambi	.75
4	Tim Hudson	.40
5	Eric Chavez	.25
6	Shannon Stewart	.15
7	Raul Mondesi	.15
8	Carlos Delgado	.50
9	Jose Canseco	.50
10	Vinny Castilla	.15
11	Greg Vaughn	.15
12	Manny Ramirez	1.00
13	Roberto Alomar	.40
14	Jim Thome	.75
15	Richie Sexson	.40
16	Alex Rodriguez	2.50
17	Fred Garcia	.15
18	John Olerud	.15
19	Albert Belle	.25
20	Cal Ripken Jr.	3.00
21	Mike Mussina	.50
22	Ivan Rodriguez	.75
23	Gabe Kapler	.15
24	Rafael Palmeiro	.75
25	Nomar Garciaparra	1.00
26	Pedro Martinez	1.00
27	Carl Everett	.15
28	Carlos Beltran	.50
29	Jermaine Dye	.15
30	Juan Gonzalez	.50
31	Dean Palmer	.15
32	Corey Koskie	.15
33	Jacque Jones	.15
34	Frank Thomas	.75
35	Paul Konerko	.40
36	Magglio Ordonez	.25
37	Bernie Williams	.40
38	Derek Jeter	2.50
39	Roger Clemens	2.00
40	Mariano Rivera	.40
41	Jeff Bagwell	.50
42	Craig Biggio	.40
43	Jose Lima	.15
44	Moises Alou	.25
45	Chipper Jones	1.00
46	Greg Maddux	1.50
47	Andruw Jones	1.00
48	Kevin Millwood	.15
49	Jeromy Burnitz	.15
50	Geoff Jenkins	.15
51	Mark McGwire	1.50
52	Fernando Tatis	.15
53	J.D. Drew	.25
54	Sammy Sosa	1.00
55	Kerry Wood	.50
56	Mark Grace	.25
57	Matt Williams	.15
58	Randy Johnson	1.00
59	Erubiel Durazo	.15
60	Gary Sheffield	.50
61	Kevin Brown	.15
62	Shawn Green	.40
63	Vladimir Guerrero	1.00
64	Michael Barrett	.15
65	Barry Bonds	2.50
66	Jeff Kent	.25
67	Russ Ortiz	.15
68	Preston Wilson	.15
69	Mike Lowell	.15
70	Mike Piazza	1.00
71	Mike Hampton	.15
72	Robin Ventura	.15
73	Edgardo Alfonzo	.15
74	Tony Gwynn	1.50
75	Ryan Klesko	.15
76	Trevor Hoffman	.15
77	Scott Rolen	1.00
78	Bob Abreu	.40
79	Mike Lieberthal	.15
80	Curt Schilling	.75
81	Jason Kendall	.15
82	Brian Giles	.15
83	Kris Benson	.15
84	Ken Griffey Jr.	2.00
85	Sean Casey	.25
86	Pokey Reese	.15
87	Barry Larkin	.40
88	Larry Walker	.25
89	Todd Helton	.75
90	Jeff Cirillo	.15
91	Ken Griffey Jr.	4.00
92	Mark McGwire	4.00
93	Chipper Jones	3.00
94	Derek Jeter	6.00
95	Shawn Green	2.00
96	Pedro Martinez	4.00
97	Mike Piazza	4.00
98	Alex Rodriguez	5.00
99	Jeff Bagwell	2.50
100	Cal Ripken Jr.	6.00
101	Sammy Sosa	3.00
102	Barry Bonds	5.00
103	Jose Canseco	2.00
104	Nomar Garciaparra	4.00
105	Ivan Rodriguez	2.50
106	Rick Ankiel	2.00
107	Pat Burrell	2.50
108	Vernon Wells	2.50
109	Nick Johnson	2.00
110	Kip Wells	2.00
111	Matt Riley	2.00
112	Alfonso Soriano	8.00
113	Josh Beckett	4.00
114	Danys Baez RC	6.00
115	Travis Dawkins	2.50
116	Eric Gagne	4.00
117	Mike Lamb RC	4.00
118	Eric Munson	2.50
119	Wilfredo Rodriguez RC	2.00
120	Kazuhiro Sasaki RC	3.00
121	Chad Hutchinson	2.00
122	Peter Bergeron	2.00
123	Wascar Serrano RC	2.00
124	Tony Armas Jr.	2.00
125	Ramon Ortiz	2.00
126	Adam Kennedy	2.00
127	Joe Crede	5.00
128	Roosevelt Brown	2.00
129	Mark Mulder	2.50
130	Brad Penny	2.00
131	Terrence Long	2.00
132	Ruben Mateo	2.00
133	Wily Mo Pena	2.00
134	Rafael Furcal	2.00
135	Mario Encarnacion	2.00

Limited

Cards (1-90):	4-8X
Cards (91-105):	2-3X
Cards (106-135):	1-2X

Production 100 Sets

Chirography

		NM/M
Common Player:		5.00
Inserted 1:23		
RA	Rick Ankiel	8.00
CBe	Carlos Beltran	30.00
BB	Barry Bonds	200.00
PB	Pat Burrell	15.00
JC	Jose Canseco	25.00
SC	Sean Casey	8.00
RC	Roger Clemens	100.00
ED	Erubiel Durazo	10.00
TGl	Troy Glaus	20.00
VG	Vladimir Guerrero	30.00
TG	Tony Gwynn	40.00
DJ	Derek Jeter	120.00
NJ	Nick Johnson	10.00
CJ	Chipper Jones	35.00
AJ	Andruw Jones	25.00
SK	Sandy Koufax	250.00
BP	Ben Petrick	5.00
MQ	Mark Quinn	5.00
MR	Manny Ramirez	40.00
CR	Cal Ripken Jr.	100.00
AR	Alex Rodriguez	85.00
IR	Ivan Rodriguez	30.00
SR	Scott Rolen	30.00
AS	Alfonso Soriano	30.00
MV	Mo Vaughn	8.00
EY	Ed Yarnall	5.00

Chirography Gold

		NM/M
Common Player:		
RA	Rick Ankiel/66 EXCH	50.00
CBe	Carlos Beltran/15	65.00
BB	Barry Bonds/25	300.00
PB	Pat Burrell/33 EXCH	50.00
JC	Jose Canseco/33	75.00
SC	Sean Casey/21	65.00
RC	Roger Clemens/22	300.00
ED	Erubiel Durazo/44	25.00
VG	Vladimir Guerrero/27	100.00
TG	Tony Gwynn/19	200.00
NJ	Nick Johnson/63	15.00
BP	Ben Petrick/15	30.00
MR	Manny Ramirez/24 EXCH	100.00
AS	Alfonso Soriano/53	60.00
MV	Mo Vaughn/42	25.00
EY	Ed Yarnall/41	15.00

Joe DiMaggio Game Jersey

		NM/M
DiMaggio Jersey Card		
JD	Joe DiMaggio/Jsy/500	120.00
JD	Joe DiMaggio/Jsy Gold/56	200.00

Midsummer Classics

		NM/M
Complete Set (10):		10.00
Common Player:		.50
Inserted 1:12		
1	Cal Ripken Jr.	3.00
2	Roger Clemens	1.75
3	Jeff Bagwell	.75
4	Barry Bonds	3.00
5	Jose Canseco	.50
6	Frank Thomas	.75
7	Mike Piazza	2.00
8	Tony Gwynn	1.50
9	Juan Gonzalez	.75
10	Greg Maddux	1.50

Premier Performers

		NM/M
Complete Set (10):		10.00
Common Player:		.75
Inserted 1:12		
1	Mark McGwire	2.00
2	Alex Rodriguez	2.50
3	Cal Ripken Jr.	3.00
4	Nomar Garciaparra	1.50
5	Ken Griffey Jr.	2.00
6	Chipper Jones	1.50
7	Derek Jeter	3.00
8	Ivan Rodriguez	.75
9	Vladimir Guerrero	.75
10	Sammy Sosa	1.50

SP Buyback

		NM/M
Common Player:		
1	Jeff Bagwell Exch.	50.00
2	Craig Biggio '93/59	50.00
3	Craig Biggio '94/69	50.00

4 Craig Biggio '95/171 40.00
5 Craig Biggio '96/71 50.00
6 Craig Biggio '97/46 50.00
7 Craig Biggio '98/40 50.00
8 Craig Biggio '99/125 40.00
15 Barry Bonds '99/520 150.00
16 Jose Canseco '93/29 60.00
17 Jose Canseco '94/20 60.00
19 Jose Canseco '96/23 60.00
20 Jose Canseco '97/23 60.00
21 Jose Canseco '98/24 60.00
22 Jose Canseco '99/502 30.00
24 Sean Casey '99/139 20.00
25 Roger Clemens '93/68 85.00
26 Roger Clemens '94/60 85.00
27 Roger Clemens '95/68 85.00
28 Roger Clemens '96/68 85.00
30 Roger Clemens '98/25 200.00
31 Roger Clemens '99/134 75.00
32 Jason Giambi '97/34 50.00
33 Jason Giambi '98/25 50.00
34 Tom Glavine '93/99 40.00
35 Tom Glavine '94/107 40.00
36 Tom Glavine '95/97 40.00
37 Tom Glavine '96/42 50.00
38 Tom Glavine '98/40 50.00
39 Tom Glavine '99/138 40.00
40 Shawn Green '96/55 30.00
41 Shawn Green '99/530 20.00
42 Ken Griffey Jr. '96/12 275.00
47 Tony Gwynn '97/24 150.00
49 Tony Gwynn '99/129 50.00
50 Tony Gwynn '99/369 40.00
56 Derek Jeter '99/119 200.00
57 Randy Johnson '93/60 75.00
58 Randy Johnson '94/45 80.00
59 Randy Johnson '95/70 75.00
60 Randy Johnson '96/60 75.00
63 Randy Johnson '99/113 75.00
64 Andruw Jones Exch. 40.00
65 Chipper Jones Exch. 75.00
66 Kenny Lofton '94/100 25.00
67 Kenny Lofton '95/84 25.00
68 Kenny Lofton '96/34 40.00
69 Kenny Lofton '97/82 25.00
70 Kenny Lofton '98/21 40.00
71 Kenny Lofton '99/99 20.00
72 Javy Lopez '93/106 15.00
73 Javy Lopez '94/160 20.00
74 Javy Lopez '96/99 15.00
75 Javy Lopez '97/61 20.00
77 Greg Maddux '93/22 275.00
78 Greg Maddux '94/19 275.00
83 Greg Maddux '99/504 275.00
84 Paul O'Neill '93/110 25.00
85 Paul O'Neill '94/97 30.00
86 Paul O'Neill '95/142 25.00
87 Paul O'Neill '96/70 30.00
88 Paul O'Neill '98/23 40.00
89 Manny Ramirez/Redemp. 50.00
91 Cal Ripken Jr. '94/22 300.00
96 Cal Ripken Jr. '99/510 125.00
97 Alex Rodriguez Exch. 150.00

98 Ivan Rodriguez '93/29 100.00
100 Ivan Rodriguez '95/18 125.00
101 Ivan Rodriguez '96/22 125.00
103 Ivan Rodriguez '98/27 125.00
109 Frank Thomas '97/20 75.00
111 Frank Thomas '99/100 50.00
112 Greg Vaughn '93/79 20.00
113 Greg Vaughn '94/75 20.00
114 Greg Vaughn '95/155 15.00
115 Greg Vaughn '96/113 15.00
117 Greg Vaughn '99/527 10.00
118 Mo Vaughn '93/119 20.00
119 Mo Vaughn '94/96 20.00
120 Mo Vaughn '95/121 20.00
121 Mo Vaughn '96/114 20.00
122 Mo Vaughn '97/61 25.00
124 Mo Vaughn '99/537 15.00
125 Robin Ventura '93/59 25.00
126 Robin Ventura '94/49 25.00
127 Robin Ventura '95/125 20.00
128 Robin Ventura '96/55 25.00
129 Robin Ventura '97/44 30.00
130 Robin Ventura '98/28 35.00
131 Robin Ventura '99/370 15.00
133 Matt Williams '94/50 40.00
134 Matt Williams '95/137 40.00
135 Matt Williams '96/77 40.00
136 Matt Williams '97/54 40.00
137 Matt Williams '98/29 60.00
138 Matt Williams '99/529 15.00
139 Preston Wilson '94/249 15.00
140 Preston Wilson '99/195 15.00

SP Cornerstones

NM/M
Complete Set (7): 15.00
Common Player: 2.00
Inserted 1:23
1 Ken Griffey Jr. 2.00
2 Cal Ripken Jr. 4.00
3 Mike Piazza 2.00
4 Derek Jeter 4.00
5 Mark McGwire 3.00
6 Nomar Garciaparra 2.00
7 Sammy Sosa 2.00

SP Supremacy

NM/M
Complete Set (7): 8.00
Common Player: .75
Inserted 1:23
1 Alex Rodriguez 3.00

2 Shawn Green .75
3 Pedro Martinez 1.00
4 Chipper Jones 2.00
5 Tony Gwynn 2.00
6 Ivan Rodriguez 1.00
7 Jeff Bagwell 1.00

United Nations

NM/M
Complete Set (10): 5.00
Common Player: .50
Inserted 1:4
1 Sammy Sosa (Dominican Rep.) 1.50
2 Ken Griffey Jr. (USA) 2.00
3 Orlando Hernandez (Cuba) .50
4 Andres Galarraga (Venezuela) .50
5 Kazuhiro Sasaki (Japan) .50
6 Larry Walker (Canada) .50
7 Vinny Castilla (Mexico) .50
8 Andruw Jones (Neth. Antilles) .75
9 Ivan Rodriguez (Puerto Rico) .75
10 Chan Ho Park (So. Korea) .50

3,000 Hit Club

NM/M
PW Paul Waner/Bat/350 50.00
TS Tris Speaker/Bat/350 100.00

2000 SPx

NM/M
Complete Set (120): 400.00
Common Player: .15
Common Rookie (91-120): 10.00
Pack (4): 6.00
Box (18): 80.00
1 Troy Glaus .50
2 Mo Vaughn .15
3 Ramon Ortiz .15
4 Jeff Bagwell .75
5 Moises Alou .25
6 Craig Biggio .40
7 Jose Lima .15
8 Jason Giambi .75
9 John Jaha .15
10 Matt Stairs .15
11 Chipper Jones 1.00
12 Greg Maddux 1.50
13 Andres Galarraga .15
14 Andruw Jones 1.00
15 Jeromy Burnitz .15
16 Ron Belliard .15

17 Carlos Delgado .75
18 David Wells .15
19 Tony Batista .15
20 Shannon Stewart .15
21 Sammy Sosa 1.00
22 Mark Grace .50
23 Henry Rodriguez .15
24 Mark McGwire 2.00
25 J.D. Drew .25
26 Luis Gonzalez .25
27 Randy Johnson 1.00
28 Matt Williams .15
29 Steve Finley .15
30 Shawn Green .25
31 Kevin Brown .15
32 Gary Sheffield .50
33 Jose Canseco .50
34 Greg Vaughn .15
35 Vladimir Guerrero 1.00
36 Michael Barrett .15
37 Russ Ortiz .15
38 Barry Bonds 3.00
39 Jeff Kent .25
40 Richie Sexson .40
41 Manny Ramirez 1.00
42 Jim Thome 1.00
43 Roberto Alomar .50
44 Edgar Martinez .15
45 Alex Rodriguez 2.50
46 John Olerud .15
47 Alex Gonzalez .15
48 Cliff Floyd .15
49 Mike Piazza 1.50
50 Al Leiter .15
51 Robin Ventura .15
52 Edgardo Alfonzo .15
53 Albert Belle .15
54 Cal Ripken Jr. 3.00
55 B.J. Surhoff .15
56 Tony Gwynn 1.50
57 Trevor Hoffman .15
58 Brian Giles .15
59 Jason Kendall .15
60 Kris Benson .15
61 Bob Abreu .15
62 Scott Rolen 1.00
63 Curt Schilling .75
64 Mike Lieberthal .15
65 Sean Casey .25
66 Dante Bichette .15
67 Ken Griffey Jr. 2.00
68 Pokey Reese .15
69 Mike Sweeney .15
70 Carlos Febles .15
71 Ivan Rodriguez 1.00
72 Ruben Mateo .15
73 Rafael Palmeiro 1.00
74 Larry Walker .40
75 Todd Helton .75
76 Nomar Garciaparra 1.00
77 Pedro Martinez 1.00
78 Troy O'Leary .15
79 Jacque Jones .15
80 Corey Koskie .15
81 Juan Gonzalez .50
82 Dean Palmer .15
83 Juan Encarnacion .15
84 Frank Thomas 1.00
85 Magglio Ordonez .25
86 Paul Konerko .50
87 Bernie Williams .50
88 Derek Jeter 3.00
89 Roger Clemens 2.50
90 Orlando Hernandez .15
91 Vernon Wells AU-1,000 25.00
92 Rick Ankiel AU-1,000 35.00
93 Eric Chavez AU-1,000 20.00
94 Alfonso Soriano AU-1,000 50.00
95 Eric Gagne AU-1,000 25.00
96 Rob Bell AU-1,500 10.00
97 Matt Riley AU-1,500 10.00
98 Josh Beckett AU-1,000 90.00
99 Ben Petrick AU-1,500 10.00
100 Rob Ramsay AU-1,500 RC 10.00
101 Scott Williamson AU-1,500 10.00
102 Doug Davis AU-1,500 15.00
103 Eric Munson AU-1,500 10.00
104 Pat Burrell AU-500 30.00
105 Jim Morris AU-1,500 20.00
106 Gabe Kapler AU-500 15.00
107 Lance Berkman 1,500 20.00
108 Erubiel Durazo AU-1,500 15.00

109	Tim Hudson AU-1,500	30.00
110	Ben Davis AU-1,500	10.00
111	Nick Johnson AU-1,500	20.00
112	Octavio Dotel AU-1,500	10.00
113	Jerry Hairston Jr. 1,500	10.00
114	Ruben Mateo 1,500	10.00
115	Chris Singleton 1,500	10.00
116	Bruce Chen AU-1,500	10.00
117	Derrick Gibson AU-1,500	10.00
118	Carlos Beltran AU-500	100.00
119	Fred Garcia AU-500	10.00
120	Preston Wilson AU-500	15.00

Radiance

	NM/M
Stars (1-90):	4-8X
Common Young Star (91-120):	10.00
Production 100 Sets	

Foundations

		NM/M
Complete Set (10):		15.00
Common Player:		.50
Inserted 1:32		
1	Ken Griffey Jr.	3.00
2	Nomar Garciaparra	3.00
3	Cal Ripken Jr.	4.00
4	Chipper Jones	2.00
5	Mike Piazza	3.00
6	Derek Jeter	4.00
7	Manny Ramirez	1.00
8	Jeff Bagwell	1.00
9	Tony Gwynn	2.00
10	Larry Walker	.50

Heart of the Order

		NM/M
Complete Set (20):		10.00
Common Player:		.40
Inserted 1:8		
1	Bernie Williams	.50
2	Mike Piazza	2.00
3	Ivan Rodriguez	.75
4	Mark McGwire	2.50
5	Manny Ramirez	1.00
6	Ken Griffey Jr.	2.00
7	Matt Williams	.40
8	Sammy Sosa	2.00
9	Mo Vaughn	.40
10	Carlos Delgado	.75
11	Brian Giles	.40
12	Chipper Jones	1.50

13	Sean Casey	.40
14	Tony Gwynn	1.50
15	Barry Bonds	3.00
16	Carlos Beltran	.65
17	Scott Rolen	.75
18	Juan Gonzalez	1.00
19	Larry Walker	.40
20	Vladimir Guerrero	1.00

Highlight Heroes

		NM/M
Complete Set (10):		10.00
Common Player:		.50
Inserted 1:16		
1	Pedro Martinez	1.00
2	Ivan Rodriguez	.75
3	Carlos Beltran	.65
4	Nomar Garciaparra	2.00
5	Ken Griffey Jr.	2.00
6	Randy Johnson	1.00
7	Chipper Jones	1.50
8	Scott Williamson	.50
9	Larry Walker	.50
10	Mark McGwire	2.50

Power Brokers

		NM/M
Complete Set (20):		10.00
Common Player:		.25
Inserted 1:8		
1	Rafael Palmeiro	.75
2	Carlos Delgado	.65
3	Ken Griffey Jr.	2.00
4	Matt Stairs	.25
5	Mike Piazza	2.00
6	Vladimir Guerrero	1.00
7	Chipper Jones	1.50
8	Mark McGwire	2.50
9	Matt Williams	.25
10	Juan Gonzalez	1.00
11	Shawn Green	.50
12	Sammy Sosa	2.00
13	Brian Giles	.25
14	Jeff Bagwell	1.00
15	Alex Rodriguez	2.50
16	Frank Thomas	1.00
17	Larry Walker	.25
18	Albert Belle	.25
19	Dean Palmer	.25
20	Mo Vaughn	.25

SPxcitement

		NM/M
Complete Set (20):		15.00
Common Player:		.25
Inserted 1:4		
1	Nomar Garciaparra	1.25
2	Mark McGwire	1.50
3	Derek Jeter	2.00

4	Cal Ripken Jr.	2.00
5	Barry Bonds	2.00
6	Alex Rodriguez	1.50
7	Scott Rolen	.75
8	Pedro Martinez	.75
9	Sean Casey	.25
10	Sammy Sosa	1.25
11	Randy Johnson	.75
12	Ivan Rodriguez	.75
13	Frank Thomas	.75
14	Greg Maddux	1.00
15	Tony Gwynn	1.00
16	Ken Griffey Jr.	1.25
17	Carlos Beltran	.50
18	Mike Piazza	1.25
19	Chipper Jones	1.00
20	Craig Biggio	.25

SPx Signatures

		NM/M
Common Player:		10.00
Inserted 1:179		
JB	Jeff Bagwell	30.00
BB	Barry Bonds	150.00
JC	Jose Canseco	25.00
SC	Sean Casey	15.00
RC	Roger Clemens	125.00
KG	Ken Griffey Jr.	100.00
VG	Vladimir Guerrero	35.00
TG	Tony Gwynn	40.00
OH	Orlando Hernandez	40.00
DJ	Derek Jeter	125.00
CJ	Chipper Jones	40.00
MR	Manny Ramirez	40.00
CR	Cal Ripken Jr.	125.00
IR	Ivan Rodriguez	30.00
SR	Scott Rolen	30.00

Untouchable Talents

	NM/M
Complete Set (10):	30.00

Common Player:		1.50
Inserted 1:96		
1	Mark McGwire	8.00
2	Ken Griffey Jr.	6.00
3	Shawn Green	2.00
4	Ivan Rodriguez	2.50
5	Sammy Sosa	6.00
6	Derek Jeter	10.00
7	Sean Casey	1.50
8	Chipper Jones	4.50
9	Pedro Martinez	3.00
10	Vladimir Guerrero	3.00

Winning Materials

		NM/M
Common Bat/Jsy:		6.00
AR	Alex Rodriguez Bat/Jsy	25.00
AR	Alex Rodriguez/ Cap/Jsy/100	40.00
AR	Alex Rodriguez/ Ball/Jsy/50	50.00
DJ	Derek Jeter/Bat/Jsy	40.00
DJ	Derek Jeter/ Ball/Jsy/50	75.00
BB	Barry Bonds/Bat/Jsy	30.00
BB	Barry Bonds/ Cap/Jsy/100	50.00
BB	Barry Bonds/ Ball/Jsy/Auto./25	350.00
JB	Jeff Bagwell/Bat/Jsy	8.00
JB	Jeff Bagwell/ Cap/Jsy/100	15.00
JB	Jeff Bagwell/ Ball/Jsy/50	25.00
KG	Ken Griffey Jr./ Bat/Jsy	20.00
KG	Ken Griffey Jr./ Ball/Jsy/50	50.00
KG	Ken Griffey Jr./ Jsy/Bat/Auto./24	225.00
TG	Tony Gwynn/Bat/Jsy	10.00
TG	Tony Gwynn/ Ball/Jsy/50	40.00
TG	Tony Gwynn/ Cap/Jsy/100	30.00
BW	Bernie Williams/ Bat/Jsy	8.00
EC	Eric Chavez/Bat/Jsy	8.00
EC	Eric Chavez/ Cap/Jsy/100	15.00
GM	Greg Maddux/Bat/Jsy	25.00
IR	Ivan Rodriguez/ Bat/Jsy	8.00
JC	Jose Canseco/Bat/Jsy	8.00
JL	Javy Lopez/Bat/Jsy	6.00
JL	Javy Lopez/ Cap/Jsy/100	8.00
MM	Mark McGwire/ Base/Ball/500	50.00
MR	Manny Ramirez/ Bat/Jsy	10.00
MW	Matt Williams/Bat/Jsy	6.00
PM	Pedro Martinez/ Cap/Jsy/100	25.00
PO	Paul O'Neill/Bat/Jsy	6.00
VG	Vladimir Guerrero/ Bat/Jsy	10.00
VG	Vladimir Guerrero/ Cap/Jsy/100	20.00
VG	Vladimir Guerrero/ Ball/Jsy/50	30.00
TG	Troy Glaus Bat/Jsy	8.00

3,000 Hit Club

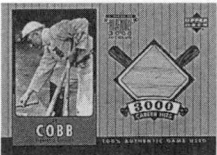

	M/M
TC-B Ty Cobb/Bat/350	130.00

2001 SP Authentic

	NM/M
Common Player:	.25
Common SP (91-135):	4.00
Production 1,250	
Common SP (136-180):	2.00
Production 1,250	
Pack (5):	15.00
Box (24):	340.00
1 Troy Glaus	.50
2 Darin Erstad	.40
3 Jason Giambi	.75
4 Tim Hudson	.50
5 Eric Chavez	.40

#	Player	Price
6	Miguel Tejada	.50
7	Jose Ortiz	.25
8	Carlos Delgado	.75
9	Tony Batista	.25
10	Raul Mondesi	.25
11	Aubrey Huff	.25
12	Greg Vaughn	.25
13	Roberto Alomar	.50
14	Juan Gonzalez	.50
15	Jim Thome	.75
16	Omar Vizquel	.25
17	Edgar Martinez	.25
18	Fred Garcia	.25
19	Cal Ripken Jr.	3.00
20	Ivan Rodriguez	.75
21	Rafael Palmeiro	.75
22	Alex Rodriguez	2.00
23	Manny Ramirez	1.00
24	Pedro Martinez	1.00
25	Nomar Garciaparra	1.00
26	Mike Sweeney	.25
27	Jermaine Dye	.25
28	Bobby Higginson	.25
29	Dean Palmer	.25
30	Matt Lawton	.25
31	Eric Milton	.25
32	Frank Thomas	1.00
33	Magglio Ordonez	.25
34	David Wells	.25
35	Paul Konerko	.50
36	Derek Jeter	3.00
37	Bernie Williams	.50
38	Roger Clemens	2.00
39	Mike Mussina	.50
40	Jorge Posada	.50
41	Jeff Bagwell	.75
42	Richard Hidalgo	.25
43	Craig Biggio	.50
44	Greg Maddux	2.00
45	Chipper Jones	1.00
46	Andruw Jones	1.00
47	Rafael Furcal	.40
48	Tom Glavine	.50
49	Jeromy Burnitz	.25
50	Jeffrey Hammonds	.25
51	Mark McGwire	2.00
52	Jim Edmonds	.50
53	Rick Ankiel	.25
54	J.D. Drew	.40
55	Sammy Sosa	1.50
56	Corey Patterson	.50
57	Kerry Wood	.50
58	Randy Johnson	1.00
59	Luis Gonzalez	.40
60	Curt Schilling	.75
61	Gary Sheffield	.50
62	Shawn Green	.25
63	Kevin Brown	.25
64	Vladimir Guerrero	1.00
65	Jose Vidro	.25
66	Barry Bonds	3.00
67	Jeff Kent	.50
68	Livan Hernandez	.25
69	Preston Wilson	.25
70	Charles Johnson	.25
71	Ryan Dempster	.25
72	Mike Piazza	1.50
73	Al Leiter	.25
74	Edgardo Alfonzo	.25
75	Robin Ventura	.25
76	Tony Gwynn	1.50
77	Phil Nevin	.25
78	Trevor Hoffman	.25
79	Scott Rolen	1.00
80	Pat Burrell	.50
81	Bob Abreu	.40
82	Jason Kendall	.25
83	Brian Giles	.25
84	Kris Benson	.25
85	Ken Griffey Jr.	2.00
86	Barry Larkin	.50
87	Sean Casey	.40
88	Todd Helton	.75
89	Mike Hampton	.25
90	Larry Walker	.25
91	Ichiro Suzuki RC	180.00
92	Wilson Betemit RC	4.00
93	Adrian Hernandez RC	4.00
94	Juan Uribe RC	6.00
95	Travis Hafner RC	50.00
96	Morgan Ensberg RC	15.00
97	Sean Douglass RC	4.00
98	Juan Diaz RC	4.00
99	Erick Almonte RC	4.00
100	Ryan Freel RC	8.00
101	Elpidio Guzman RC	4.00
102	Christian Parker RC	4.00
103	Josh Fogg RC	6.00
104	Bert Snow RC	4.00
105	Horacio Ramirez RC	8.00
106	Ricardo Rodriguez RC	4.00
107	Tyler Walker RC	4.00
108	Jose Mieses RC	6.00
109	Billy Sylvester RC	4.00
110	Martin Vargas RC	4.00
111	Andres Torres RC	4.00
112	Greg Miller RC	4.00
113	Alexis Gomez RC	4.00
114	Grant Balfour RC	4.00
115	Henry Mateo RC	4.00
116	Esix Snead RC	4.00
117	Jackson Melian RC	4.00
118	Nate Teut RC	4.00
119	Tsuyoshi Shinjo RC	4.00
120	Carlos Valderrama RC	6.00
121	Johnny Estrada RC	10.00
122	Jason Michaels RC	4.00
123	William Ortega RC	4.00
124	Jason Smith RC	4.00
125	Brian Lawrence RC	4.00
126	Albert Pujols RC	450.00
127	Wilken Ruan RC	4.00
128	Josh Towers RC	6.00
129	Kris Keller RC	4.00
130	Nick Maness RC	4.00
131	Jack Wilson RC	10.00
132	Brandon Duckworth RC	4.00
133	Mike Penney RC	4.00
134	Jay Gibbons RC	10.00
135	Cesar Crespo RC	4.00
136	Ken Griffey Jr.	8.00
137	Mark McGwire	8.00
138	Derek Jeter	10.00
139	Alex Rodriguez	10.00
140	Sammy Sosa	4.00
141	Carlos Delgado	3.00
142	Cal Ripken Jr.	12.00
143	Pedro Martinez	5.00
144	Frank Thomas	5.00
145	Juan Gonzalez	3.00
146	Troy Glaus	4.00
147	Jason Giambi	4.00
148	Ivan Rodriguez	4.00
149	Chipper Jones	5.00
150	Vladimir Guerrero	5.00
151	Mike Piazza	5.00
152	Jeff Bagwell	4.00
153	Randy Johnson	5.00
154	Todd Helton	4.00
155	Gary Sheffield	3.00
156	Tony Gwynn	5.00
157	Barry Bonds	10.00
158	Nomar Garciaparra	5.00
159	Bernie Williams	3.00
160	Greg Vaughn	2.00
161	David Wells	2.00
162	Roberto Alomar	3.00
163	Jermaine Dye	2.00
164	Rafael Palmeiro	4.00
165	Andruw Jones	4.00
166	Preston Wilson	2.00
167	Edgardo Alfonzo	2.00
168	Pat Burrell	3.00
169	Jim Edmonds	3.00
170	Mike Hampton	2.00
171	Jeff Kent	2.00
172	Kevin Brown	2.00
173	Manny Ramirez	5.00
174	Magglio Ordonez	2.00
175	Roger Clemens	8.00
176	Jim Thome	4.00
177	Barry Zito	2.00
178	Brian Giles	2.00
179	Rick Ankiel	2.00
180	Corey Patterson	2.00

Limited

Stars (1-90):	8-15X	
SP (91-135):	1-2X	
SP (136-180):	1-3X	
Production 50 Sets		

Buyback Autographs

NM/M

Inserted 1:144
Some not priced due to scarcity.

#	Player	Price
4	Ken Griffey '93 SP/34	125.00
105	Ken Griffey '94 SP/182	80.00
190	Ken Griffey '95 SP/116	80.00
170	Ken Griffey '96 SP/53	100.00
84	Ken Griffey '00 SP/333	70.00
188	Alex Rodriguez '95 SP Red/117	80.00
171	Alex Rodriguez '96 SP/72	100.00
16	Alex Rodriguez '00 SP/332	75.00
260	Frank Thomas '93 SP/79	40.00
193	Frank Thomas '94 SP/165	35.00
50	Frank Thomas '97 SP/34	75.00
34	Frank Thomas '00 SP/302	35.00
34	Chipper Jones '95 SP/118	40.00
26	Chipper Jones '96 SP/72	45.00
45	Chipper Jones '00 SP/303	30.00
132	Randy Johnson '93 SP/97	60.00
106	Randy Johnson '94 SP/146	40.00
189	Randy Johnson '95 SP/121	40.00
169	Randy Johnson '96 SP/78	50.00
58	Randy Johnson '00 SP/213	40.00
41	Carlos Delgado '94 SP/279	15.00
181	Carlos Delgado '96 SP/83	20.00
8	Carlos Delgado '00 SP/174	15.00
50	Jim Edmonds '96 SP/74	20.00
167	Tony Gwynn '93 SP/101	40.00
130	Tony Gwynn '94 SP/88	40.00
105	Tony Gwynn '95 SP/179	30.00
160	Tony Gwynn '96 SP/92	40.00
74	Tony Gwynn '00 SP/95	40.00
3	Jason Giambi '00 SP/290	30.00
9	Ivan Rodriguez '93 SP/89	40.00
180	Ivan Rodriguez '96 SP/64	40.00
22	Ivan Rodriguez '00 SP/163	30.00
47	Andruw Jones '00 SP/336	25.00
10	Barry Bonds '93 SP/75	180.00
90	Barry Bonds '94 SP/103	180.00
166	Barry Bonds '96 SP/49	180.00
65	Barry Bonds '00 SP/146	180.00
18	Gary Sheffield '93 SP/83	20.00
114	Gary Sheffield '94 SP/70	20.00
86	Gary Sheffield '96 SP/69	20.00
60	Gary Sheffield '00 SP/133	15.00
89	Sammy Sosa '93 SP/73	100.00
126	Cal Ripken '94 SP/99	100.00
1	Cal Ripken '95 SP/37	150.00
20	Cal Ripken '00 SP/266	100.00
89	Todd Helton '00 SP/194	25.00
4	Tim Hudson '00 SP/291	20.00
62	Shawn Green '00 SP/340	20.00
52	Fernando Tatis '00 SP/267	8.00
57	Matt Williams '00 SP/340	10.00
72	Robin Ventura '00 SP/340	10.00
2	Troy Glaus '00 SP/340	15.00
39	Roger Clemens '00 SP/145	100.00

Combo Game Jersey

NM/M

Overall jersey odds 1:24.

SD	Sammy Sosa, Andre Dawson	25.00
RS	Alex Rodriguez, Ozzie Smith	35.00
GD	Ken Griffey Jr., Joe DiMaggio/98	120.00
SW	Gary Sheffield, Dave Winfield	15.00
MD	Mickey Mantle, Joe DiMaggio/98	300.00
MG	Mickey Mantle, Ken Griffey /98	160.00

Cooperstown Calling Game Jersey

NM/M

Common Player:		5.00

Overall jersey odds 1:24.

JB	Jeff Bagwell	8.00
WB	Wade Boggs	8.00
GC	Gary Carter	5.00
RC	Roger Clemens	30.00
AD	Andre Dawson	5.00
SG	Steve Garvey	5.00
GG	Goose Gossage	5.00
TG	Tony Gwynn	10.00
RM	Roger Maris/243	75.00
PM	Pedro Martinez/SP	15.00
DM	Don Mattingly	30.00
BM	Bill Mazeroski	5.00
PM	Paul Molitor	8.00
EM	Eddie Murray	5.00
MP	Mike Piazza/SP	25.00
KP	Kirby Puckett	10.00
MR	Manny Ramirez/SP	15.00
CR	Cal Ripken Jr.	30.00
RS	Ryne Sandberg	20.00
OS	Ozzie Smith	10.00
DW	Dave Winfield	5.00

Chirography

NM/M

Common Player:		5.00

Inserted 1:72

EA	Edgardo Alfonzo	5.00
AB	Albert Belle	15.00
CB	Carlos Beltran	35.00
MB	Milton Bradley	12.00
PB	Pat Burrell	10.00
JC	Jose Canseco	30.00

CD	Carlos Delgado	12.00
DD	Darren Dreifort/206	5.00
JD	J.D. Drew	15.00
JE	Jim Edmonds	20.00
DEr	Darin Erstad	10.00
DEs	David Espinosa	5.00
CF	Cliff Floyd	10.00
RF	Rafael Furcal/222	15.00
JG	Jason Giambi	15.00
TrG	Troy Glaus	15.00
LG	Luis Gonzalez/271	15.00
SG	Shawn Green/82	25.00
KG	Ken Griffey Jr/126	80.00
ToG	Tony Gwynn/76	40.00
RH	Rick Helling/211	5.00
ToH	Todd Helton/152	30.00
TiH	Tim Hudson	15.00
RJ	Randy Johnson/143	50.00
AJ	Andruw Jones	20.00
CJ	Chipper Jones/184	40.00
DJ	David Justice	8.00
MK	Mark Kotsay/228	5.00
TL	Travis Lee/226	5.00
AlP	Albert Pujols	550.00
CR	Cal Ripken/109	125.00
AR	Alex Rodriguez/229	100.00
DS	Dane Sardinha	5.00
BS	Ben Sheets	20.00
SS	Sammy Sosa/76	100.00
MS	Mike Sweeney	8.00
MV	Mo Vaughn/103	8.00
RV	Robin Ventura/92	10.00
DW	David Wells	8.00
RW	Rondell White	8.00
MW	Matt Williams	8.00

Chirography Gold

NM/M

Common Player:
AB	Albert Belle/88	15.00
CD	Carlos Delgado/25	50.00
DD	Darren Dreifort/37	25.00
DES	David Espinosa/79	15.00
KG	Ken Griffey Jr./30	150.00
RH	Rick Helling/32	15.00
RJ	Randy Johnson/50	65.00
DJ	David Justice/28	30.00
DS	Dane Sardinha/50	15.00
MS	Mike Sweeney/29	25.00
MV	Mo Vaughn/42	15.00
DW	David Wells/33	20.00

Game Jersey

NM/M

Common Player: 5.00
Overall jersey odds 1:24.
JD	Joe DiMaggio/243	100.00
KG	Ken Griffey Jr.	15.00
MM	Mickey Mantle/243	150.00
AR	Alex Rodriguez	15.00
GS	Gary Sheffield	5.00
SS	Sammy Sosa	10.00

Sultan of Swatch Jersey/Cut

No Pricing
Production One Set

Sultan of Swatch Jersey or Pants

NM/M

Quantity produced listed
Common Ruth Card
(1-21): 350.00

Stars of Japan

Tsuyoshi Shinjo

NM/M

Complete Set (30): 50.00
Common Player: 1.00
One Pack/Hobby Box
RS1	Ichiro Suzuki, Tsuyoshi Shinjo	5.00
RS2	Shigetosi Hasegawa, Hideki Irabu	1.00
RS3	Tomokazu Ohka, Mac Suzuki	1.00
RS4	Tsuyoshi Shinjo, Hideki Irabu	1.00
RS5	Ichiro Suzuki, Hideo Nomo	5.00
RS6	Tsuyoshi Shinjo, Mac Suzuki	1.00
RS7	Tsuyoshi Shinjo, Kazuhiro Sasaki	1.00
RS8	Hideo Nomo, Tomokazu Ohka	1.50
RS9	Ichiro Suzuki, Mac Suzuki	5.00
RS10	Hideo Nomo, Shigetosi Hasegawa	1.50
RS11	Hideo Nomo, Masato Yoshii	1.50
RS12	Hideo Nomo, Hideki Irabu	1.50
RS13	Shigetosi Hasegawa, Kazuhiro Sasaki	1.00
RS14	Shigetosi Hasegawa, Mac Suzuki	1.00
RS15	Tsuyoshi Shinjo, Hideo Nomo	1.50
RS16	Tsuyoshi Shinjo, Tomokazu Ohka	1.00
RS17	Ichiro Suzuki, Kazuhiro Sasaki	5.00
RS18	Masato Yoshii, Hideki Irabu	1.00
RS19	Ichiro Suzuki, Tomokazu Ohka	5.00
RS20	Hideki Irabu, Kazuhiro Sasaki	1.00
RS21	Tsuyoshi Shinjo, Masato Yoshii	1.00
RS22	Ichiro Suzuki, Shigetosi Hasegawa	5.00
RS23	Mac Suzuki, Kazuhiro Sasaki	1.00
RS24	Ichiro Suzuki, Hideki Irabu	5.00
RS25	Tomokazu Ohka, Kazuhiro Sasaki	1.00
RS26	Tsuyoshi Shinjo, Shigetosi Hasegawa	1.00
RS27	Masato Yoshii, Kazuhiro Sasaki	1.00
RS28	Hideo Nomo, Kazuhiro Sasaki	1.50
RS29	Ichiro Suzuki, Masato Yoshii	5.00
RS30	Hideo Nomo, Ichiro Suzuki	5.00

Stars of Japan Game Ball

NM/M

Common Player: 8.00
SH	Shigetosi Hasegawa/ SP/30	15.00
HI	Hideki Irabu	8.00
KS	Kazuhiro Sasaki	10.00
TS	Tsuyoshi Shinjo/ SP/50	20.00
IS	Ichiro Suzuki	75.00
MY	Masato Yoshii	10.00

Stars of Japan Game Ball Gold

NM/M

Production 25 Sets
SH	Shigetosi Hasegawa	40.00
HI	Hideki Irabu	20.00
KS	Kazuhiro Sasaki	40.00

Stars of Japan Game Ball-Base Combos

NM/M

Inserted 1:576
HI-KS	Hideki Irabu, Kazuhiro Sasaki/ SP/30	25.00
HN-KS	Hideo Nomo, Kazuhiro Sasaki/ SP/50	75.00
HN-SH	Hideo Nomo, Shigetosi Hasegawa	20.00
IS-KS	Ichiro Suzuki, Kazuhiro Sasaki/ SP/30	120.00
IS-MY	Ichiro Suzuki, Masato Yoshii	50.00
IS-SH	Ichiro Suzuki, Shigetosi Hasegawa/ SP/72	75.00
IS-TS	Ichiro Suzuki, Tsuyoshi Shinjo/ SP/40	125.00
MS-KS	Mac Suzuki, Kazuhiro Sasaki/ SP/30	20.00
MY-KS	Masato Yoshii, Kazuhiro Sasaki/ SP/30	25.00
SH-KS	Shigetosi Hasegawa, Kazuhiro Sasaki/ SP/30	25.00
TO-KS	Tomokazu Ohka, Kazuhiro Sasaki	20.00
TS-HI	Tsuyoshi Shinjo, Hideki Irabu/SP/30	25.00
TS-KS	Tsuyoshi Shinjo, Kazuhiro Sasaki/ SP/30	25.00
TS-SH	Tsuyoshi Shinjo, Shigetosi Hasegawa/ SP/30	25.00

Stars of Japan Game Ball-Base Combos Gold

NM/M

Common Card: 20.00
Production 25 Sets
HI-KS	Hideki Irabu, Kazuhiro Sasaki	25.00
HN-KS	Hideo Nomo, Kazuhiro Sasaki	65.00
HN-SH	Hideo Nomo, Shigetosi Hasegawa	65.00
IS-KS	Ichiro Suzuki, Kazuhiro Sasaki	150.00
IS-MY	Ichiro Suzuki, Masato Yoshii	150.00
IS-SH	Ichiro Suzuki, Shigetosi Hasegawa	150.00
IS-TS	Ichiro Suzuki, Tsuyoshi Shinjo	150.00
MS-KS	Mac Suzuki, Kazuhiro Sasaki	20.00
MY-KS	Masato Yoshii, Kazuhiro Sasaki	20.00
SH-KS	Shigetosi Hasegawa, Kazuhiro Sasaki	20.00
TO-KS	Tomokazu Ohka, Kazuhiro Sasaki	20.00
TS-HI	Tsuyoshi Shinjo, Hideki Irabu	25.00
TS-KS	Tsuyoshi Shinjo, Kazuhiro Sasaki	25.00
TS-SH	Tsuyoshi Shinjo, Shigetosi Hasegawa	25.00

Stars of Japan Game Ball-Base Trio

NM/M

Complete Set (1):
RS	Kazuhiro Sasaki, Ichiro Suzuki, Hideo Nomo	175.00

Stars of Japan Game Ball-Base Trio Gold

Production 25
No Pricing

Stars of Japan Game Base

NM/M

Common Player: 15.00
SH	Shigetosi Hasegawa/ SP/33	20.00
HI	Hideki Irabu/SP/33	15.00
TO	Tomokazu Ohka/ SP/33	15.00
KS	Kazuhiro Sasaki/ SP/33	25.00
TS	Tsuyoshi Shinjo/ SP/33	25.00
MS	Mac Suzuki/SP/23	20.00
MY	Masato Yoshii/SP/33	20.00

Stars of Japan Game Base Gold

NM/M

Common Player: 25.00
Production 25 Sets
SH	Shigetosi Hasegawa	25.00
HI	Hideki Irabu	25.00
TO	Tomokazu Ohka	25.00
KS	Kazuhiro Sasaki	30.00
TS	Tsuyoshi Shinjo	35.00
MS	Mac Suzuki	25.00
MY	Masato Yoshii	25.00

Stars of Japan Game Bat

NM/M

Inserted 1:12
HN	Hideo Nomo/SP/30	60.00
TS	Tsuyoshi Shinjo/ SP/30	20.00
MY	Masato Yoshii	5.00

Stars of Japan Game Bat Gold

		NM/M
Common Player:		10.00
Production 25 Sets		
HN	Hideo Nomo	80.00
TS	Tsuyoshi Shinjo	30.00
MY	Masato Yoshii	10.00

Stars of Japan Game Jersey-Bat Combos

		NM/M
Common Player:		15.00
HS	Shigetosi Hasegawa, Tsuyoshi Shinjo	15.00
NN	Hideo Nomo	60.00
SN	Kazuhiro Sasaki, Hideo Nomo	40.00
SH	Kazuhiro Sasaki, Shigetoshi Hasegawa	15.00

Stars of Japan Game Bat-Jersey Combo Gold

		NM/M
Production 25 Sets		
BB-HS	Shigetoshi Hasegawa, Tsuyoshi Shinjo	40.00

Stars of Japan Game Jersey

		NM/M
Common Player:		5.00
Inserted 1:12		
SH	Shigetosi Hasegawa	5.00
HN	Hideo Nomo	40.00
KS	Kazuhiro Sasaki	8.00
TS	Tsuyoshi Shinjo	8.00
IS	Ichiro Suzuki/ SP/260 EXCH	100.00
MY	Masato Yoshii	5.00

Stars of Japan Game Jersey Gold

		NM/M
Common Player:		10.00
Production 25 Sets		
SH	Shigetoshi Hasegawa	10.00
HN	Hideo Nomo	60.00
KS	Kazuhiro Sasaki	15.00
TS	Tsuyoshi Shinjo	15.00
MY	Masato Yoshii	10.00

2001 SP Game Bat

		NM/M
Complete Set (90):		40.00
Common Player:		.25
Pack (4):		10.00
Box (16):		150.00
1	Troy Glaus	.50
2	Darin Erstad	.50
3	Mo Vaughn	.25
4	Jason Giambi	.75
5	Ben Grieve	.25

6	Eric Chavez	.50
7	Carlos Delgado	.75
8	Tony Batista	.25
9	Shannon Stewart	.25
10	Jose Cruz Jr.	.25
11	Fred McGriff	.25
12	Greg Vaughn	.25
13	Roberto Alomar	.50
14	Manny Ramirez	1.00
15	Jim Thome	.75
16	Russ Branyan	.25
17	Alex Rodriguez	2.00
18	John Olerud	.25
19	Edgar Martinez	.25
20	Cal Ripken Jr.	3.00
21	Albert Belle	.25
22	Ivan Rodriguez	.75
23	Rafael Palmeiro	.50
24	Nomar Garciaparra	1.00
25	Carl Everett	.25
26	Dante Bichette	.25
27	Mike Sweeney	.25
28	Jermaine Dye	.25
29	Carlos Beltran	.75
30	Juan Gonzalez	.50
31	Dean Palmer	.25
32	Bobby Higginson	.25
33	Matt Lawton	.25
34	Jacque Jones	.25
35	Frank Thomas	1.00
36	Magglio Ordonez	.25
37	Paul Konerko	.25
38	Carlos Lee	.40
39	Bernie Williams	.50
40	Derek Jeter	3.00
41	Paul O'Neill	.40
42	Jose Canseco	.50
43	Ken Caminiti	.25
44	Jeff Bagwell	.75
45	Craig Biggio	.40
46	Richard Hidalgo	.25
47	Andruw Jones	1.00
48	Chipper Jones	1.00
49	Andres Galarraga	.25
50	B.J. Surhoff	.25
51	Jeromy Burnitz	.25
52	Geoff Jenkins	.25
53	Richie Sexson	.40
54	Mark McGwire	2.50
55	Jim Edmonds	.50
56	J.D. Drew	.40
57	Fernando Tatis	.25
58	Sammy Sosa	1.50
59	Mark Grace	.50
60	Eric Young	.25
61	Matt Williams	.25
62	Luis Gonzalez	.40
63	Steve Finley	.25
64	Shawn Green	.40
65	Gary Sheffield	.50
66	Eric Karros	.25
67	Vladimir Guerrero	1.00
68	Jose Vidro	.25
69	Barry Bonds	3.00
70	Jeff Kent	.40
71	Preston Wilson	.25
72	Mike Lowell	.25
73	Luis Castillo	.25
74	Mike Piazza	1.50
75	Robin Ventura	.25
76	Edgardo Alfonzo	.25
77	Tony Gwynn	1.00
78	Eric Owens	.25
79	Ryan Klesko	.25
80	Scott Rolen	.75
81	Bobby Abreu	.50
82	Pat Burrell	.50
83	Brian Giles	.25
84	Jason Kendall	.25
85	Aaron Boone	.25
86	Ken Griffey Jr.	2.00
87	Barry Larkin	.50
88	Todd Helton	1.00
89	Larry Walker	.25
90	Jeffrey Hammonds	.25

Big League Hit Parade

		NM/M
Complete Set (6):		15.00
Common Player:		1.50
Inserted 1:15		
1	Nomar Garciaparra	1.50
2	Ken Griffey Jr.	3.00
3	Sammy Sosa	2.00
4	Alex Rodriguez	4.00
5	Mark McGwire	4.00
6	Ivan Rodriguez	1.50

In the Swing

		NM/M
Complete Set (15):		25.00
Common Player:		1.00
Inserted 1:7		
1	Ken Griffey Jr.	2.50
2	Jim Edmonds	1.00
3	Carlos Delgado	1.00
4	Frank Thomas	1.50
5	Barry Bonds	4.00
6	Nomar Garciaparra	2.00
7	Gary Sheffield	1.00
8	Vladimir Guerrero	1.50
9	Alex Rodriguez	3.00
10	Todd Helton	1.50
11	Darin Erstad	1.00
12	Derek Jeter	4.00
13	Sammy Sosa	2.50
14	Mark McGwire	3.00
15	Jason Giambi	1.00

Lineup Time

		NM/M
Complete Set (11):		20.00
Common Player:		1.00
Inserted 1:8		
1	Mark McGwire	3.00
2	Roberto Alomar	1.00
3	Alex Rodriguez	3.00
4	Chipper Jones	2.00
5	Ivan Rodriguez	1.00
6	Ken Griffey Jr.	2.50
7	Sammy Sosa	2.50
8	Barry Bonds	4.00
9	Frank Thomas	1.50
10	Pedro Martinez	1.50
11	Derek Jeter	4.00

Piece of the Game

		NM/M
Common Player:		4.00
Inserted 1:1		
SP production 1,500 or fewer.		
Golds:		2-5X
Production 25 Sets		
EA	Edgardo Alfonzo/SP	10.00
RA	Roberto Alomar	8.00
SA	Sandy Alomar	4.00
RA	Rick Ankiel	4.00
JB	Jeff Bagwell/SP	15.00
TB	Tony Batista	5.00
CB	Carlos Beltran	5.00
JB	Johnny Bench/SP	25.00
BB	Barry Bonds	25.00
KB	Kevin Brown/SP	10.00
PB	Pat Burrell	8.00
JC	Jose Canseco	6.00
WC	Will Clark	8.00
CD	Carlos Delgado	6.00
JoD	Joe DiMaggio/SP	100.00
JD	J.D. Drew	6.00
JE	Jim Edmonds	6.00
DE	Darin Erstad/SP	10.00
RF	Rafael Furcal	6.00
BG	Bob Gibson/SP	20.00
TGl	Tom Glavine/SP	15.00
MG	Mark Grace	8.00
SG	Shawn Green	6.00
KG	Ken Griffey Jr.	15.00
TGw	Tony Gwynn	10.00
TH	Todd Helton	8.00
TH	Todd Hundley/SP	10.00
RJ	Reggie Jackson/SP	20.00
RJ	Randy Johnson	10.00
AJ	Andruw Jones	8.00
CJ	Chipper Jones	10.00
DJ	David Justice	5.00
KL	Kenny Lofton	4.00
GM	Greg Maddux	15.00
EM	Edgar Martinez	6.00
TM	Tino Martinez	6.00
FM	Fred McGriff/SP	10.00
PN	Phil Nevin/SP	6.00
JO	John Olerud	6.00
PO	Paul O'Neill	6.00
MO	Magglio Ordonez/SP	10.00
MQ	Mark Quinn/SP	10.00
MR	Manny Ramirez	8.00
CR	Cal Ripken Jr./SP	40.00
AR	Alex Rodriguez	10.00
IR	Ivan Rodriguez	8.00
SR	Scott Rolen	8.00
NR	Nolan Ryan/SP	35.00
TS	Tim Salmon/SP	10.00
GS	Gary Sheffield	5.00
SS	Sammy Sosa/SP	25.00
SS	Shannon Stewart	4.00
FT	Frank Thomas	8.00
GV	Greg Vaughn	4.00
MV	Mo Vaughn	4.00
RV	Robin Ventura	4.00
BW	Bernie Williams	6.00
MW	Matt Williams	4.00
PW	Preston Wilson	4.00

Piece of the Game Autograph

		NM/M
Common Autograph:		30.00
Inserted 1:96		
BB	Barry Bonds	180.00
JC	Jose Canseco	40.00
KG	Ken Griffey Jr.	100.00
TGw	Tony Gwynn	50.00
AJ	Andruw Jones	30.00
AR	Alex Rodriguez	120.00
NR	Nolan Ryan	125.00
FT	Frank Thomas	50.00

The Lumber Yard

		NM/M
Complete Set (10):		15.00
Common Player:		.50
Inserted 1:10		
1	Jason Giambi	1.00
2	Chipper Jones	1.50
3	Carl Everett	.50
4	Alex Rodriguez	3.00
5	Frank Thomas	1.50
6	Barry Bonds	4.00
7	Jeff Bagwell	1.50
8	Sammy Sosa	2.50
9	Carlos Delgado	1.00
10	Mike Piazza	2.50

2001 SP Game Bat - Milestone

Gwynn went 3-for-5 with a triple and single vs Colorado on 4/17/01.

		NM/M
Complete Set (96):		
Common Player:		.40
Common Rookie (91-96):		5.00
Production 500		
Pack (4):		16.00
Box (10):		140.00
1	Troy Glaus	.50
2	Darin Erstad	.50

3	Jason Giambi	.75
4	Jermaine Dye	.40
5	Eric Chavez	.50
6	Carlos Delgado	.75
7	Raul Mondesi	.40
8	Shannon Stewart	.40
9	Greg Vaughn	.40
10	Aubrey Huff	.40
11	Juan Gonzalez	.50
12	Roberto Alomar	.50
13	Jim Thome	.75
14	Omar Vizquel	.40
15	Mike Cameron	.40
16	Edgar Martinez	.40
17	John Olerud	.40
18	Bret Boone	.40
19	Cal Ripken Jr.	3.00
20	Tony Batista	.40
21	Alex Rodriguez	2.50
22	Ivan Rodriguez	.75
23	Rafael Palmeiro	.75
24	Manny Ramirez	1.00
25	Pedro Martinez	1.00
26	Nomar Garciaparra	1.00
27	Carl Everett	.40
28	Mike Sweeney	.40
29	Neifi Perez	.40
30	Mark Quinn	.40
31	Bobby Higginson	.40
32	Tony Clark	.40
33	Doug Mientkiewicz	.40
34	Cristian Guzman	.40
35	Joe Mays	.40
36	David Ortiz	1.00
37	Frank Thomas	1.00
38	Magglio Ordonez	.40
39	Carlos Lee	.50
40	Alfonso Soriano	1.00
41	Bernie Williams	.50
42	Derek Jeter	3.00
43	Roger Clemens	2.50
44	Jeff Bagwell	1.00
45	Richard Hidalgo	.40
46	Moises Alou	.40
47	Chipper Jones	1.00
48	Greg Maddux	2.00
49	Rafael Furcal	.50
50	Andruw Jones	1.00
51	Jeromy Burnitz	.40
52	Geoff Jenkins	.40
53	Richie Sexson	.40
54	Edgar Renteria	.40
55	Mark McGwire	2.50
56	Jim Edmonds	.50
57	J.D. Drew	.50
58	Sammy Sosa	1.50
59	Bill Mueller	.40
60	Luis Gonzalez	.50
61	Randy Johnson	1.00
62	Gary Sheffield	.50
63	Shawn Green	.40
64	Kevin Brown	.40
65	Vladimir Guerrero	1.00
66	Jose Vidro	.40
67	Fernando Tatis	.40
68	Barry Bonds	3.00
69	Jeff Kent	.50
70	Rich Aurilia	.40
71	Preston Wilson	.40
72	Charles Johnson	.40
73	Cliff Floyd	.40
74	Mike Piazza	1.00
75	Matt Lawton	.40
76	Edgardo Alfonzo	.40
77	Tony Gwynn	1.50
78	Phil Nevin	.40
79	Scott Rolen	1.00
80	Pat Burrell	.50
81	Bobby Abreu	.50
82	Brian Giles	.40
83	Jason Kendall	.40
84	Aramis Ramirez	.40
85	Sean Casey	.50
86	Ken Griffey Jr.	2.50
87	Barry Larkin	.50
88	Todd Helton	.75
89	Mike Hampton	.40
90	Larry Walker	.50
91	Ichiro Suzuki RC	70.00
92	Albert Pujols RC	180.00
93	Tsuyoshi Shinjo RC	8.00
94	Jack Wilson RC	8.00
95	Donaldo Mendez RC	5.00
96	Junior Spivey RC	8.00

P.O.A. Milestone Bat

		NM/M
Common Player:		5.00
Golds:		3-5X
Production 35 Sets		
JB	Jeff Bagwell	8.00
BB	Barry Bonds	20.00
RB	Russell Branyan	5.00
JB	Jeromy Burnitz	5.00

Griffey hit a pair of homers on 7/13/00 at Colorado.

RC	Roger Clemens	20.00
DE	Darin Erstad	5.00
LG	Luis Gonzalez	5.00
KG	Ken Griffey Jr.	12.00
TH	Todd Helton	8.00
Chj	Chipper Jones	10.00
MP	Mike Piazza	10.00
CR	Cal Ripken Jr.	30.00
AR	Alex Rodriguez	15.00
GS	Gary Sheffield	5.00
SS	Sammy Sosa	10.00
IS	Ichiro Suzuki/203	80.00
FT	Frank Thomas	8.00
JT	Jim Thome	8.00

P.O.A. Int. Conn. Bat

		NM/M
Common Player:		5.00
Golds:		3-5X
Production 35 Sets		
RA	Roberto Alomar	6.00
AB	Adrian Beltre	5.00
RF	Rafael Furcal	5.00
JG	Juan Gonzalez	6.00
AJ	Andruw Jones	8.00
PM	Pedro Martinez	10.00
HN	Hideo Nomo/203	40.00
MO	Magglio Ordonez	5.00
CP	Chan Ho Park	5.00
JP	Jorge Posada	10.00
AP	Albert Pujols	70.00
MR	Manny Ramirez	8.00
TS	Tsuyoshi Shinjo	8.00
IS	Ichiro Suzuki/273	80.00
MT	Miguel Tejada	6.00
OV	Omar Vizquel	5.00

P.O.A. BFH Bat

Fred McGriff • Devil Rays™

	NM/M
Common Player:	5.00

Golds:

		2-3X
Production 35 Sets		
BB	Barry Bonds	20.00
RC	Roger Clemens/203	25.00
CD	Carlos Delgado	5.00
JG	Jason Giambi	5.00
KG	Ken Griffey Jr.	15.00
TGw	Tony Gwynn	15.00
GM	Greg Maddux	12.00
EM	Edgar Martinez	6.00
FM	Fred McGriff	6.00
RP	Rafael Palmeiro	8.00
MP	Mike Piazza	10.00
CR	Cal Ripken Jr.	30.00
AR	Alex Rodriguez	15.00
IR	Ivan Rodriguez	8.00
SS	Sammy Sosa	10.00

P.O.A. Autograph Bat

Gonzalez tied a Major League record with 13 RBI in April 2001.

		NM/M
Common Autograph:		15.00
Inserted 1:100		
RB	Russell Branyan	15.00
CD	Carlos Delgado/97	35.00
JDr	J.D. Drew	20.00
JDy	Jermaine Dye	15.00
LG	Luis Gonzalez	20.00
JK	Jason Kendall	15.00
JK	Jeff Kent/194	35.00
AR	Alex Rodriguez/97	120.00
GS	Gary Sheffield/194	40.00
IS	Ichiro Suzuki/53	800.00
MT	Miguel Tejada	40.00
JV	Jose Vidro	15.00
PW	Preston Wilson	15.00

P.O.A. Triple Bat

		NM/M
Common Card:		15.00
Inserted 1:50		
GRS	Ken Griffey Jr., Alex Rodriguez, Sammy Sosa	40.00
JJF	Chipper Jones, Andruw Jones, Rafael Furcal	15.00
RRP	Alex Rodriguez, Ivan Rodriguez, Rafael Palmeiro	35.00
SGB	Gary Sheffield, Shawn Green, Adrian Beltre	15.00
TVA	Jim Thome, Omar Vizquel, Roberto Alomar	15.00
KGR	Jason Kendall, Brian Giles, Aramis Ramirez	15.00
OJC	Paul O'Neill, David Justice, Roger Clemens	35.00
CMG	Roger Clemens, Greg Maddux, Tom Glavine	40.00
VSA	Robin Ventura, Tsuyoshi Shinjo, Edgardo Alfonzo	15.00
OTA	Magglio Ordonez, Frank Thomas, Sandy Alomar	15.00
PWS	Kirby Puckett, Dave Winfield, Ozzie Smith	25.00
GRB	Tony Gwynn, Cal Ripken Jr., Barry Bonds	60.00
GBM	Ken Griffey Jr., Barry Bonds, Fred McGriff	35.00
SFR	Alfonso Soriano, Rafael Furcal, Alex Ramirez	25.00

P.O.A. Quad Bat

		NM/M
Common Card:		15.00
Inserted 1:50		
TVAL	Jim Thome, Omar Vizquel, Roberto Alomar, Kenny Lofton	25.00
RRPM	Alex Rodriguez, Ivan Rodriguez, Rafael Palmeiro, Ruben Mateo	50.00
OJCP	Paul O'Neill, David Justice, Roger Clemens, Jorge Posada	60.00
JJFM	Chipper Jones, Andruw Jones, Rafael Furcal, Greg Maddux	40.00
PWSG	Kirby Puckett, Dave Winfield, Ozzie Smith, Steve Garvey	30.00
GRSB	Ken Griffey Jr., Alex Rodriguez, Sammy Sosa, Barry Bonds	80.00
SGBP	Gary Sheffield, Shawn Green, Adrian Beltre, Chan Ho Park	15.00
GGRR	Ken Griffey Jr., Ken Griffey Jr., Alex Rodriguez, Alex Rodriguez	65.00
GRBM	Tony Gwynn, Cal Ripken Jr., Barry Bonds, Fred McGriff	70.00
TDTA	Frank Thomas, Jermaine Dye, Jim Thome, Roberto Alomar	25.00
GHSK	Luis Gonzalez, Todd Helton, Gary Sheffield, Jeff Kent	20.00
GDBS	Ken Griffey Jr., J.D. Drew, Jeromy Burnitz, Sammy Sosa	50.00
JVBW	Chipper Jones, Robin Ventura, Pat Burrell, Preston Wilson	30.00
RGGM	Troy Glaus, Jason Giambi, Edgar Martinez	40.00
ONRD	Paul O'Neill, Hideo Nomo, Cal Ripken Jr., Carlos Delgado	80.00

Slugging Sensations

	NM/M
Complete Set (12):	12.00
Common Player:	.50
Inserted 1:5	

SS1	Troy Glaus	.50
SS2	Mark McGwire	2.50
SS3	Sammy Sosa	1.50
SS4	Juan Gonzalez	.50
SS5	Barry Bonds	3.00
SS6	Jeff Bagwell	.75
SS7	Jason Giambi	.75
SS8	Ivan Rodriguez	.75
SS9	Mike Piazza	1.50
SS10	Chipper Jones	1.00
SS11	Ken Griffey Jr.	2.00
SS12	Gary Sheffield	.50

The Art of Hitting

		NM/M
Complete Set (12):		10.00
Common Player:		.50
Inserted 1:5		
AH1	Tony Gwynn	1.50
AH2	Manny Ramirez	1.00
AH3	Todd Helton	1.00
AH4	Nomar Garciaparra	1.00
AH5	Vladimir Guerrero	1.00
AH6	Ichiro Suzuki	1.50
AH7	Darin Erstad	.50
AH8	Alex Rodriguez	2.50
AH9	Carlos Delgado	.75
AH10	Edgar Martinez	.50
AH11	Luis Gonzalez	.50
AH12	Barry Bonds	3.00

The Trophy Room

		NM/M
Complete Set (6):		8.00
Common Player:		1.00
Inserted 1:10		
TR1	Sammy Sosa	1.50
TR2	Jason Giambi	1.00
TR3	Todd Helton	1.00
TR4	Alex Rodriguez	2.50
TR5	Mark McGwire	2.50
TR6	Ken Griffey Jr.	2.00

2001 SP Game-Used Edition

		NM/M
Common Player:		.50
Common SP (61-90):		5.00
Production 500		
Pack (3):		30.00
Box (6):		150.00
1	Garret Anderson	.50
2	Troy Glaus	1.00
3	Darin Erstad	.75
4	Jason Giambi	1.50
5	Tim Hudson	.75
6	Johnny Damon	2.00
7	Carlos Delgado	1.00
8	Greg Vaughn	.50
9	Juan Gonzalez	.75

10	Roberto Alomar	1.00
11	Jim Thome	1.50
12	Edgar Martinez	.50
13	Cal Ripken Jr.	5.00
14	Andres Galarraga	.50
15	Alex Rodriguez	4.00
16	Rafael Palmeiro	1.25
17	Ivan Rodriguez	1.50
18	Manny Ramirez	1.50
19	Nomar Garciaparra	1.50
20	Pedro Martinez	2.00
21	Jermaine Dye	.50
22	Dean Palmer	.50
23	Matt Lawton	.50
24	Frank Thomas	1.50
25	David Wells	.50
26	Magglio Ordonez	.50
27	Derek Jeter	5.00
28	Bernie Williams	.50
29	Roger Clemens	4.00
30	Jeff Bagwell	1.50
31	Richard Hidalgo	.50
32	Chipper Jones	2.00
33	Andruw Jones	1.50
34	Greg Maddux	3.00
35	Jeffrey Hammonds	.50
36	Mark McGwire	4.00
37	Jim Edmonds	.75
38	Sammy Sosa	2.00
39	Corey Patterson	.50
40	Randy Johnson	1.50
41	Luis Gonzalez	.50
42	Gary Sheffield	.75
43	Shawn Green	.75
44	Kevin Brown	.50
45	Vladimir Guerrero	1.50
46	Barry Bonds	5.00
47	Jeff Kent	.75
48	Preston Wilson	.50
49	Charles Johnson	.50
50	Mike Piazza	2.00
51	Edgardo Alfonzo	.50
52	Tony Gwynn	2.00
53	Scott Rolen	1.50
54	Pat Burrell	1.00
55	Brian Giles	.50
56	Jason Kendall	.50
57	Ken Griffey Jr.	3.00
58	Mike Hampton	.50
59	Todd Helton	1.50
60	Larry Walker	.75
61	Wilson Betemit RC	10.00
62	Travis Hafner RC	20.00
63	Ichiro Suzuki RC	60.00
64	Juan Diaz RC	5.00
65	Morgan Ensberg RC	15.00
66	Horacio Ramirez RC	10.00
67	Ricardo Rodriguez RC	5.00
68	Sean Douglass RC	5.00
69	Brandon Duckworth RC	5.00
70	Jackson Melian RC	5.00
71	Adrian Hernandez RC	5.00
72	Kyle Kessel RC	5.00
73	Jason Michaels RC	5.00
74	Esix Snead RC	5.00
75	Jason Smith RC	5.00
76	Tyler Walker RC	5.00
77	Juan Uribe RC	8.00
78	Adam Pettyjohn RC	5.00
79	Tsuyoshi Shinjo RC	5.00
80	Mike Penney RC	5.00
81	Josh Towers RC	8.00
82	Erick Almonte RC	5.00
83	Ryan Freel RC	8.00
84	Juan Pena RC	5.00
85	Albert Pujols RC	220.00
86	Henry Mateo RC	5.00
87	Greg Miller RC	5.00
88	Jose Mieses RC	5.00
89	Jack Wilson RC	10.00
90	Carlos Valderrama RC	5.00

Authentic Fabric Jersey

		NM/M
Common Player:		4.00
Inserted 1:1		
EA	Edgardo Alfonzo	4.00
RA	Roberto Alomar	6.00
RA	Rick Ankiel	4.00
TB	Tony Batista/SP	4.00
BB	Barry Bonds	25.00
KB	Kevin Brown	4.00
JB	Jeromy Burnitz	6.00
PB	Pat Burrell	6.00
JC(B)	Jose Canseco/BLC	8.00
JC(H)	Jose Canseco/Yanks	8.00
EC	Eric Chavez	6.00
JCi	Jeff Cirillo	4.00
RC	Roger Clemens	20.00
CD	Carlos Delgado/SP	10.00
JDi	Joe DiMaggio/SP/50	160.00
JDr	J.D. Drew	5.00
JDy	Jermaine Dye/SP	8.00
JE	Jim Edmonds	6.00
DE	Darin Erstad	5.00
JG	Jason Giambi	8.00
BG	Brian Giles/SP	8.00
TGI	Troy Glaus	6.00
ToG	Tom Glavine	6.00
LG	Luis Gonzalez	6.00
MG	Mark Grace	8.00
SG	Shawn Green	6.00
KG(H)	Ken Griffey/Reds	12.00
KG(M)	Ken Griffey/M's	12.00
KG(R)	Ken Griffey/Reds	12.00
TGw	Tony Gwynn	10.00
MH	Mike Hampton	4.00
THe	Todd Helton	8.00
TrH	Trevor Hoffman	4.00
TH	Tim Hudson	6.00
AH	Aubrey Huff	4.00
JI	J. Isringhausen/SP	8.00
CJo	Charles Johnson	4.00
RJ	Randy Johnson	10.00
AJ	Andruw Jones	8.00
CJ	Chipper Jones	10.00
JK	Jason Kendall	4.00
JK	Jeff Kent	5.00
BL	Barry Larkin	6.00
AL	Al Leiter	4.00
KL	Kenny Lofton	5.00
TL	Terrence Long	4.00
GM	Greg Maddux	10.00
MM	Mickey Mantle/SP/50	250.00
RM	Roger Maris/SP	75.00
EM	Edgar Martinez	6.00
TM	Tino Martinez	6.00
FM	Fred McGriff	5.00
KM	Kevin Millwood	4.00
PN	Phil Nevin	4.00
JO	John Olerud	5.00
MO	Magglio Ordonez	6.00
AP	Adam Piatt	4.00
CR	Cal Ripken Jr.	25.00
MR	Mariano Rivera	6.00
AR(H)	Alex Rodriguez/Rangers	10.00
AR(M)	Alex Rodriguez/M's	10.00
IR	Ivan Rodriguez	8.00
SR	Scott Rolen	8.00
NR	Nolan Ryan/SP/50	50.00
TS	Tom Seaver/SP/50	30.00
GS	Gary Sheffield	4.00
SS(H)	Sammy Sosa	15.00
SS(R)	Sammy Sosa	15.00
FTa	Fernando Tatis	4.00
MT	Miguel Tejada	6.00
FTh	Frank Thomas	8.00
JT	Jim Thome	8.00

GV	Greg Vaughn	4.00
RV	Robin Ventura	4.00
JV	Jose Vidro	4.00
DW	David Wells/SP	8.00
MW	Matt Williams	5.00
PW	Preston Wilson	4.00
DY	Dmitri Young	4.00
TZ	Todd Zeile	4.00

Authentic Fabric Jersey Autograph

		NM/M
Production 50 Sets		
EA	Edgardo Alfonzo	25.00
RA	Rick Ankiel	15.00
BB	Barry Bonds/50	200.00
JC	Jose Canseco	40.00
CD	Carlos Delgado/50	40.00
JDr	J.D. Drew/50	40.00
JG	Jason Giambi/50	40.00
TGI	Troy Glaus/50	50.00
KG	Ken Griffey Jr.	150.00
TH	Tim Hudson/50	50.00
RJ	Randy Johnson	100.00
AJ	Andruw Jones	50.00
CJ	Chipper Jones	80.00
CR	Cal Ripken/50	200.00
AR	Alex Rodriguez	150.00
IR	Ivan Rodriguez	75.00
NR	Nolan Ryan/50	200.00
TS	Tom Seaver/50	80.00
SS	Sammy Sosa/50	120.00
FTh	Frank Thomas	75.00
DW	David Wells/50	25.00

2-Player Authentic Fabric Jersey

		NM/M
Common Card:		25.00
Production 50 Sets		
R-R	Alex Rodriguez, Ivan Rodriguez	50.00
M-D	Mickey Mantle, Joe DiMaggio	400.00
M-M	Mickey Mantle, Roger Maris	400.00
R-S	Nolan Ryan, Tom Seaver	100.00
B-C	Barry Bonds, Jose Canseco	70.00
S-G	Gary Sheffield, Shawn Green	25.00
J-J	Chipper Jones, Andruw Jones	40.00
C-W	Roger Clemens, Bernie Williams	40.00
J-R	Randy Johnson, Nolan Ryan	75.00
S-T	Sammy Sosa, Frank Thomas	35.00
G-S	Ken Griffey Jr., Sammy Sosa	50.00
G-R	Ken Griffey Jr., Alex Rodriguez	50.00
S-R	Sammy Sosa, Alex Rodriguez	40.00
H-G	Tim Hudson, Jason Giambi	30.00

3-Player Authentic Fabric Jersey

		NM/M
Production 25 Sets		
GRS	Ken Griffey Jr., Alex Rodriguez, Sammy Sosa	100.00
MJJ	Greg Maddux, Chipper Jones, Andruw Jones	80.00

		NM/M
JBS	Andruw Jones, Barry Bonds, Sammy Sosa	120.00
JSM	Randy Johnson, Tom Seaver, Greg Maddux	80.00

2001 SP Legendary Cuts

		NM/M
Complete Set (90):		25.00
Common Player:		.40
Pack (4):		16.00
Box (18):		250.00
1	Al Simmons	.40
2	Jimmie Foxx (Height, weight and birthplace incorrect.)	1.00
3	Mickey Cochrane	.40
4	Phil Niekro	.40
5	Eddie Mathews	1.00
6	Gary Matthews	.40
7	Hank Aaron	2.50
8	Joe Adcock	.40
9	Warren Spahn	.75
10	George Sisler	.40
11	Stan Musial	1.00
12	Dizzy Dean	.75
13	Frankie Frisch	.40
14	Harvey Haddix	.40
15	Johnny Mize	.40
16	Ken Boyer	.40
17	Rogers Hornsby	.75
18	Cap Anson	.40
19	Andre Dawson	.40
20	Billy Williams	.40
21	Billy Herman	.40
22	Hack Wilson	.40
23	Ron Santo	.40
24	Ryne Sandberg	1.50
25	Ernie Banks	1.50
26	Burleigh Grimes	.40
27	Don Drysdale	.75
28	Gil Hodges	.40
29	Jackie Robinson	2.00
30	Tommy Lasorda	.40
31	Pee Wee Reese	.40
32	Roy Campanella	.75
33	Tommy Davis	.40
34	Branch Rickey	.75
35	Leo Durocher	.40
36	Walt Alston	.40
37	Bill Terry	.40
38	Carl Hubbell	.40
39	Eddie Stanky	.40
40	George Kelly	.40
41	Mel Ott	.75
42	Juan Marichal	.40
43	Rube Marquard	.40
44	Travis Jackson	.40
45	Bob Feller	.40
46	Earl Averill	.40
47	Elmer Flick	.40
48	Ken Keltner	.40
49	Lou Boudreau	.40
50	Early Wynn	.40
51	Satchel Paige	1.50
52	Ron Hunt	.40
53	Tom Seaver	1.00
54	Richie Ashburn	.40
55	Mike Schmidt	1.00
56	Honus Wagner	1.00
57	Lloyd Waner	.40
58	Max Carey	.40
59	Paul Waner	.40
60	Roberto Clemente	2.50
61	Nolan Ryan	3.00
62	Bobby Doerr	.40
63	Carlton Fisk	.75
64	Joe Cronin	.40
65	Smokey Joe Wood	.40
66	Tony Conigliaro	.40

67	Edd Roush	.40
68	Johnny Vander Meer	.40
69	Walter Johnson	.75
70	Charlie Gehringer	.40
71	Al Kaline	1.00
72	Ty Cobb	2.00
73	Tony Oliva	.40
74	Luke Appling	.40
75	Minnie Minoso	.40
76	Nellie Fox	.40
77	Shoeless Joe Jackson	2.00
78	Babe Ruth	3.00
79	Bill Dickey	.40
80	Elston Howard	.40
81	Joe DiMaggio	2.50
82	Lefty Gomez	.40
83	Lou Gehrig	2.50
84	Mickey Mantle	3.00
85	Reggie Jackson	1.00
86	Roger Maris	1.00
87	Whitey Ford	.40
88	Waite Hoyt	.40
89	Yogi Berra	1.00
90	Casey Stengel	.40

Bat

		NM/M
Common Player:		4.00
Inserted 1:18		
HA	Hank Aaron/SP	40.00
YB	Yogi Berra	10.00
WB	Wade Boggs	8.00
GB	George Brett	15.00
RCa	Roy Campanella/SP	40.00
RC	Rico Carty	4.00
RCl	Roberto Clemente	60.00
TC	Ty Cobb/SP	125.00
KC	Kiki Cuyler	8.00
TD	Tommy Davis/SP	40.00
AD	Andre Dawson	8.00
JD	Joe DiMaggio/SP	100.00
DD	Don Drysdale/SP	25.00
CF	Carlton Fisk	10.00
NF	Nellie Fox	10.00
JF	Jimmie Foxx	40.00
GH	Gil Hodges/SP	40.00
THo	Tommy Holmes (Photo on front is Eddie Mathews.)	8.00
RJ	Reggie Jackson	15.00
DJ	Davey Johnson	4.00
MM	Mickey Mantle/SP	120.00
RM	Roger Maris/SP	60.00
EM	Eddie Mathews	25.00
WMc	Willie McCovey	8.00
PM	Paul Molitor	15.00
MM	Manny Mota	4.00
MO	Mel Ott/SP	50.00
VP	Vada Pinson	4.00
JR	Jackie Robinson/SP	50.00
BR	Babe Ruth/SP	165.00
NR	Nolan Ryan	40.00
RS	Ryne Sandberg	20.00
AS	Al Simmons/SP	25.00
BT	Bill Terry/SP	40.00
MW	Maury Wills	8.00
RY	Robin Yount	15.00

Combo Bat

No pricing due to scarcity.
Production 25 Sets

Debut Bat

		NM/M
Common Player:		5.00
Inserted 1:18		
JA	Joe Adcock/SP	15.00
LA	Luke Appling/SP	25.00
RA	Richie Ashburn/SP	25.00
BB	Bobby Bonds	5.00
LB	Lou Boudreau	10.00

KB	Ken Boyer/SP	15.00
BB	Bill Buckner	5.00
MC	Mickey Cochrane	60.00
TC	Tony Conigliaro/SP	15.00
JC	Joe Cronin	10.00
BD	Bobby Doerr/SP	15.00
BF	Bob Feller/SP	15.00
BF	Bill Freehan	5.00
FF	Frankie Frisch/SP	15.00
CG	Charlie Gehringer	15.00
BH	Billy Herman/SP	15.00
WH	Willie Horton	6.00
EH	Elston Howard/SP	15.00
RH	Ron Hunt	5.00
JJ	Joe Jackson	300.00
GL	Greg Luzinski	5.00
GM	Gary Matthews	5.00
MM	Minnie Minoso/SP	15.00
TO	Tony Oliva	8.00
WP	Wes Parker	5.00
BR	Bobby Richardson/SP	15.00
SS	Steve Sax	5.00
GS	George Sisler	20.00
ES	Eddie Stanky	5.00
AT	Alan Trammell	5.00
PW	Paul Waner/SP	60.00
HW	Hack Wilson/SP	70.00
SY	Steve Yeager	5.00

Game Jersey

		NM/M
Common Player:		5.00
Inserted 1:18		
YB	Yogi Berra	15.00
WB	Wade Boggs	5.00
RC	Roberto Clemente	80.00
TC	Ty Cobb/SP	
TC	Tony Conigliaro	8.00
BD	Bill Dickey	25.00
JD	Joe DiMaggio/SP	350.00
LD	Leo Durocher	8.00
WF	Whitey Ford	15.00
NF	Nellie Fox	8.00
JF	Jim Fregosi	5.00
GH	Gil Hodges	10.00
THo	Tommy Holmes	5.00
RJ	Reggie Jackson	15.00
TK	Ted Kluszewski	5.00
BL	Bob Lemon	5.00
VL	Vic Lombardi	5.00
MM	Mickey Mantle/SP	275.00
JM	Juan Marichal	10.00
RM	Roger Maris/SP	150.00
WM	Willie McCovey	10.00
JN	Joe Nuxhall	8.00
GP	Gaylord Perry	5.00
BR	Bobby Richardson	5.00
BRo	Brooks Robinson	15.00
BR	Babe Ruth/SP	600.00
NR	Nolan Ryan	40.00
TS	Tom Seaver/SP	100.00
CS	Casey Stengel	15.00
BT	Bobby Thomson	5.00
HW	Honus Wagner/SP	750.00
BW	Billy Williams	6.00
MW	Maury Wills	5.00
RY	Robin Yount	15.00

Signatures

		NM/M
Inserted 1:252		
WA	Walt Alston/34	175.00
CA	Cap Anson/2 (11/01 Auction)	10,000
LA	Luke Appling/45	205.00
EA	Earl Averill/189	100.00
EB	E.G. Barrow/16	600.00
MC	Max Carey/73	145.00
TC	Ty Cobb/24	2,500
JC	Jocko Conlan/12	1,200
SC	Stanley Coveleski/42	315.00
MC	Mickey Cochrane	60.00
JC	Joe Cronin/12	1,200
KC	Kiki Cuyler/6	4,000
DDe	Dizzy Dean/56	410.00
BD	Bill Dickey/28	275.00
JD	Joe DiMaggio/25	650.00
JD	Joe DiMaggio/50	400.00
JD	Joe DiMaggio/150	400.00
JD	Joe DiMaggio/275	350.00
DDr	Don Drysdale/12	1,500
LD	Leo Durocher/45	260.00
RF	Rick Ferrell/8	750.00
EF	Elmer Flick/22	400.00
NF	Nellie Fox/9	750.00
JF	Jimmie Foxx/16	2,500
FF	Ford Frick/21	750.00
FF	Frankie Frisch/3	3,500
LGe	Lou Gehrig/7	6,000
WG	Warren Giles/10	800.00
LGo	Lefty Gomez/85	195.00
BG	Burleigh Grimes/18	500.00
LG	Lefty Grove/34	600.00
HH	Harvey Haddix/4	3,000
BH	Bucky Harris/10	500.00
GH	Gabby Hartnett/32	380.00
BH	Billy Herman/88	140.00
GH	Gil Hodges/6	1,050
HH	Harry Hooper/14	800.00
WH	Waite Hoyt/38	245.00
CH	Carl Hubbell/30	375.00
TJ	Travis Jackson/85	225.00
JJ	Judy Johnson/9	650.00
WJ	Walter Johnson/113	510.00
CK	Charlie Keller/16	365.00
GK	George Kelly/52	140.00
KK	Ken Keltner/11	500.00
MK	Mark Koenig/30	275.00
BL	Bob Lemon/23	225.00
EL	Eddie Lopat/22	275.00
TL	Ted Lyons/59	185.00
SM	Sal Maglie/19	400.00
MM	Mickey Mantle/3	5,000
HM	Heinie Manush/50	185.00
RoM	Roger Maris/15	1,675
RuM	Rube Marquard/23	375.00
JMc	Joe McCarthy/40	340.00
JM	Joe Medwick/18	750.00
BM	Bob Meusel/23	400.00
JMi	Johnny Mize/84	160.00
MO	Mel Ott/38	4,000
SP	Satchel Paige/36	900.00
RP	Roger Peckinpaugh/45	200.00
VR	Vic Raschi/29	175.00
BRi	Branch Rickey/16	1,350
JR	Jackie Robinson/147	700.00
ER	Edd Roush/83	170.00
RR	Red Ruffing/5	2,250
BRu	Babe Ruth/7	9,000
GS	George Selkirk/15	450.00
JS	Joe Sewell/55	130.00
RS	Rip Sewell/39	155.00
BS	Bob Shawkey/39	165.00
CS	Casey Stengel/10	1,500
BT	Bill Terry/184	125.00
VM	Johnny Vander Meer/65	125.00
HW	Honus Wagner/24	2,200
BW	Bucky Walters/13	400.00
LW	Lloyd Waner/217	105.00
PW	Paul Waner/4	2,250
HW	Hack Wilson/4	6,000
JW	Smokey Joe Wood/43	215.00

2001 SPx

		NM/M
Complete Set (150):		
Common Player:		.25
Common Young Star (91-190):		4.00
Production 2,000		
Common Prospect Jersey (121-135):		6.00
Common Prosp. Auto. Jersey (136-150):		10.00
Pack (4):		12.00
Box (18):		200.00
1	Darin Erstad	.50
2	Troy Glaus	.50
3	Mo Vaughn	.25

#	Player	Price
4	Johnny Damon	1.00
5	Jason Giambi	.75
6	Tim Hudson	.50
7	Miguel Tejada	.50
8	Carlos Delgado	.75
9	Raul Mondesi	.25
10	Tony Batista	.25
11	Ben Grieve	.25
12	Greg Vaughn	.25
13	Juan Gonzalez	.75
14	Jim Thome	.75
15	Roberto Alomar	.50
16	John Olerud	.25
17	Edgar Martinez	.25
18	Albert Belle	.25
19	Cal Ripken Jr.	3.00
20	Ivan Rodriguez	.75
21	Rafael Palmeiro	.75
22	Alex Rodriguez	2.50
23	Nomar Garciaparra	1.50
24	Pedro J. Martinez	1.00
25	Manny Ramirez	1.00
26	Jermaine Dye	.25
27	Mark Quinn	.25
28	Carlos Beltran	.75
29	Tony Clark	.25
30	Bobby Higginson	.25
31	Eric Milton	.25
32	Matt Lawton	.25
33	Frank Thomas	1.00
34	Magglio Ordonez	.25
35	Ray Durham	.25
36	David Wells	.25
37	Derek Jeter	3.00
38	Bernie Williams	.50
39	Roger Clemens	2.00
40	David Justice	.25
41	Jeff Bagwell	.75
42	Richard Hidalgo	.25
43	Moises Alou	.40
44	Chipper Jones	1.00
45	Andruw Jones	1.00
46	Greg Maddux	2.00
47	Rafael Furcal	.50
48	Jeromy Burnitz	.25
49	Geoff Jenkins	.25
50	Mark McGwire	2.00
51	Jim Edmonds	.50
52	Rick Ankiel	.25
53	Edgar Renteria	.25
54	Sammy Sosa	1.50
55	Kerry Wood	.50
56	Rondell White	.25
57	Randy Johnson	1.00
58	Steve Finley	.25
59	Matt Williams	.25
60	Luis Gonzalez	.25
61	Kevin Brown	.25
62	Gary Sheffield	.50
63	Shawn Green	.50
64	Vladimir Guerrero	1.00
65	Jose Vidro	.25
66	Barry Bonds	3.00
67	Jeff Kent	.40
68	Livan Hernandez	.25
69	Preston Wilson	.25
70	Charles Johnson	.25
71	Cliff Floyd	.25
72	Mike Piazza	1.50
73	Edgardo Alfonzo	.25
74	Jay Payton	.25
75	Robin Ventura	.25
76	Tony Gwynn	1.50
77	Phil Nevin	.25
78	Ryan Klesko	.25
79	Scott Rolen	.75
80	Pat Burrell	.50
81	Bob Abreu	.50
82	Brian Giles	.25
83	Kris Benson	.25
84	Jason Kendall	.25
85	Ken Griffey Jr.	2.00
86	Barry Larkin	.50
87	Sean Casey	.40
88	Todd Helton	.75
89	Larry Walker	.25
90	Mike Hampton	.25
91	Billy Sylvester RC	4.00
92	Josh Towers RC	8.00
93	Zach Day RC	6.00
94	Martin Vargas RC	4.00
95	Adam Pettyjohn RC	4.00
96	Andres Torres RC	4.00
97	Kris Keller RC	4.00
98	Blaine Neal RC	4.00
99	Kyle Kessel RC	4.00
100	Greg Miller RC	4.00
101	Shawn Sonnier RC	4.00
102	Alexis Gomez RC	4.00
103	Grant Balfour RC	4.00
104	Henry Mateo RC	4.00
105	Wilkin Ruan RC	4.00
106	Nick Maness RC	4.00
107	Jason Michaels RC	4.00
108	Esix Snead RC	4.00
109	William Ortega RC	4.00
110	David Elder RC	4.00
111	Jackson Melian RC	4.00
112	Nate Teut RC	4.00
113	Jason Smith RC	4.00
114	Mike Penney RC	4.00
115	Jose Mieses RC	4.00
116	Juan Pena	4.00
117	Brian Lawrence RC	6.00
118	Jeremy Owens RC	6.00
119	Carlos Valderrama RC	4.00
120	Rafael Soriano RC	6.00
121	Horacio Ramirez RC	10.00
122	Ricardo Rodriguez RC	6.00
123	Juan Diaz RC	6.00
124	Donnie Bridges	6.00
125	Tyler Walker RC	6.00
126	Erick Almonte RC	6.00
127	Jesus Colome	6.00
128	Ryan Freel RC	8.00
129	Elpidio Guzman RC	6.00
130	Jack Cust	8.00
131	Eric Hinske RC	10.00
132	Josh Fogg RC	6.00
133	Juan Uribe RC	10.00
134	Bert Snow RC	6.00
135	Pedro Feliz	6.00
136	Wilson Betemit RC	25.00
137	Sean Douglass RC	10.00
138	Dernell Stenson	10.00
139	Brandon Inge	10.00
140	Morgan Ensberg RC	15.00
141	Brian Cole	10.00
142	Adrian Hernandez RC	10.00
143	Brandon Duckworth RC	10.00
144	Jack Wilson RC	15.00
145	Travis Hafner RC	75.00
146	Carlos Pena	20.00
147	Corey Patterson	15.00
148	Xavier Nady RC	10.00
149	Jason Hart	10.00
150	Ichiro Suzuki RC	750.00

Spectrum

Stars (1-90):	10-20X
SP's (91-120):	1-1.5X
Production 50 Sets	

Foundations

	NM/M
Complete Set (12):	15.00
Common Player:	1.00
Inserted 1:8	
F1 Mark McGwire	3.00
F2 Jeff Bagwell	1.00
F3 Alex Rodriguez	3.00
F4 Ken Griffey Jr.	2.00
F5 Andruw Jones	1.00
F6 Cal Ripken Jr.	4.00
F7 Barry Bonds	4.00
F8 Derek Jeter	4.00
F9 Frank Thomas	1.00
F10 Sammy Sosa	2.00
F11 Tony Gwynn	1.50
F12 Vladimir Guerrero	1.50

SPXcitement

	NM/M
Complete Set (12):	15.00
Common Player:	.75
Inserted 1:8	
X1 Alex Rodriguez	3.00
X2 Jason Giambi	.75
X3 Ken Griffey Jr.	2.00
X4 Sammy Sosa	1.50
X5 Frank Thomas	1.00
X6 Todd Helton	1.00
X7 Mark McGwire	2.00
X8 Mike Piazza	1.50
X9 Derek Jeter	4.00
X10 Vladimir Guerrero	1.50
X11 Carlos Delgado	.75
X12 Chipper Jones	1.50

Untouchable Talents

	NM/M
Complete Set (6):	10.00
Inserted 1:15	
UT1 Ken Griffey Jr.	2.00
UT2 Mike Piazza	2.00
UT3 Mark McGwire	2.50
UT4 Alex Rodriguez	2.50
UT5 Sammy Sosa	1.50
UT6 Derek Jeter	3.00

Winning Materials Base

	NM/M
Common Duo:	40.00
Production 50	
Trios:	No Pricing
Production 25	
MG Mark McGwire, Ken Griffey Jr.	40.00
MS Mark McGwire, Sammy Sosa	50.00
MR Mark McGwire, Alex Rodriguez	40.00

GJ	Nomar Garciaparra, Derek Jeter	50.00
TR	Frank Thomas, Alex Rodriguez	40.00
JG	Derek Jeter, Jason Giambi	40.00
PB	Mike Piazza, Barry Bonds	40.00
RJ	Alex Rodriguez, Derek Jeter	50.00
PM	Mike Piazza, Mark McGwire	40.00
JP	Derek Jeter, Mike Piazza	40.00
MGS	Mark McGwire, Ken Griffey Jr., Sammy Sosa	80.00
JRG	Derek Jeter, Alex Rodriguez, Nomar Garciaparra	100.00
PJW	Mike Piazza, Derek Jeter, Bernie Williams	80.00
BMS	Barry Bonds, Mark McGwire, Sammy Sosa	100.00
GJR	Ken Griffey Jr., Derek Jeter, Alex Rodriguez	100.00

Winning Materials Base/Ball

		NM/M
Common Player:		10.00
Production 250 Sets		
BB	Barry Bonds	50.00
NG	Nomar Garciaparra	20.00
KG	Ken Griffey Jr.	30.00
VG	Vladimir Guerrero	15.00
DJ	Derek Jeter	50.00
AJ	Andruw Jones	10.00
CJ	Chipper Jones	15.00
PM	Pedro Martinez	15.00
MM	Mark McGwire	75.00
MP	Mike Piazza	20.00
AR	Alex Rodriguez	20.00
SS	Sammy Sosa	20.00
FT	Frank Thomas	15.00

Winning Materials Jersey Combo

		NM/M
Common Duo:		25.00
Production 50		
Common Trio:		
Production 25		
KG-AR	Ken Griffey Jr., Alex Rodriguez	50.00
KG-BB	Ken Griffey Jr., Barry Bonds	50.00
KG-RJ	Ken Griffey Jr., Randy Johnson	50.00
CJ-DW	Chipper Jones, David Wells	25.00
BB-SS	Barry Bonds, Sammy Sosa	50.00
KG-JD	Ken Griffey Jr., Joe DiMaggio	180.00
KG-SS	Ken Griffey Jr., Sammy Sosa	50.00
SS-CD	Sammy Sosa, Carlos Delgado	25.00
SS-FT	Sammy Sosa, Frank Thomas	25.00
IR-AR	Ivan Rodriguez, Alex Rodriguez	40.00
AR-CR	Alex Rodriguez, Cal Ripken Jr.	60.00
AJ-CJ	Andruw Jones, Chipper Jones	25.00

KG-KG	Ken Griffey Jr., Ken Griffey Jr.	40.00
G-R-B	Ken Griffey Jr., Alex Rodriguez, Barry Bonds	100.00
S-G-C	Sammy Sosa, Ken Griffey Jr., Chipper Jones	60.00
B-G-J	Barry Bonds, Ken Griffey Jr., Andruw Jones	100.00
R-R-D	Alex Rodriguez, Ivan Rodriguez, Carlos Delgado	60.00
D-B-S	Carlos Delgado, Barry Bonds, Sammy Sosa	60.00
R-J-D	Cal Ripken Jr., Chipper Jones, Carlos Delgado	100.00

Winning Materials Jersey/Bat

		NM/M
Common Player:		8.00
Inserted 1:18		
RA	Rick Ankiel	8.00
BB1	Barry Bonds	25.00
BB2	Barry Bonds	25.00
CD	Carlos Delgado	10.00
JD	Joe DiMaggio	150.00
JE	Jim Edmonds	8.00
KG1	Ken Griffey Jr.	15.00
KG2	Ken Griffey Jr.	15.00
RJ1	Randy Johnson	15.00
RJ2	Randy Johnson	15.00
AJ1	Andruw Jones	10.00
AJ2	Andruw Jones	10.00
CJ1	Chipper Jones	15.00
CJ2	Chipper Jones	15.00
CR	Cal Ripken Jr.	40.00
AR1	Alex Rodriguez	15.00
AR2	Alex Rodriguez	15.00
IR1	Ivan Rodriguez	10.00
IR2	Ivan Rodriguez	10.00
SS	Sammy Sosa	15.00
FT	Frank Thomas	10.00

2002 SP Authentic

		NM/M
Complete Set (170):		
Common Player:		.25
Common SP (91-135):		4.00
Production 1,999		
Common SP Auto.		
(136-170):		10.00
Production 999		
Pack (5):		3.50
Box (24):		75.00
1	Troy Glaus	.50
2	Darin Erstad	.40
3	Barry Zito	.40
4	Eric Chavez	.40
5	Tim Hudson	.50
6	Miguel Tejada	.50
7	Carlos Delgado	.60
8	Shannon Stewart	.25
9	Ben Grieve	.25
10	Jim Thome	.75
11	C.C. Sabathia	.25

12	Ichiro Suzuki	2.00
13	Freddy Garcia	.25
14	Edgar Martinez	.25
15	Bret Boone	.25
16	Jeff Conine	.25
17	Alex Rodriguez	2.00
18	Juan Gonzalez	.50
19	Ivan Rodriguez	.75
20	Rafael Palmeiro	.75
21	Hank Blalock	.50
22	Pedro J. Martinez	1.00
23	Manny Ramirez	1.00
24	Nomar Garciaparra	1.00
25	Carlos Beltran	.75
26	Mike Sweeney	.25
27	Randall Simon	.25
28	Dmitri Young	.25
29	Bobby Higginson	.25
30	Corey Koskie	.25
31	Eric Milton	.25
32	Torii Hunter	.25
33	Joe Mays	.25
34	Frank Thomas	.75
35	Mark Buehrle	.40
36	Magglio Ordonez	.25
37	Kenny Lofton	.25
38	Roger Clemens	2.00
39	Derek Jeter	2.50
40	Jason Giambi	.75
41	Bernie Williams	.50
42	Alfonso Soriano	.75
43	Lance Berkman	.50
44	Roy Oswalt	.50
45	Jeff Bagwell	.75
46	Craig Biggio	.50
47	Chipper Jones	1.00
48	Greg Maddux	1.50
49	Gary Sheffield	.50
50	Andruw Jones	.75
51	Ben Sheets	.40
52	Richie Sexson	.50
53	Albert Pujols	2.50
54	Matt Morris	.25
55	J.D. Drew	.40
56	Sammy Sosa	1.00
57	Kerry Wood	.50
58	Corey Patterson	.25
59	Mark Prior	.75
60	Randy Johnson	.75
61	Luis Gonzalez	.40
62	Curt Schilling	.75
63	Shawn Green	.50
64	Kevin Brown	.25
65	Hideo Nomo	.75
66	Vladimir Guerrero	.75
67	Jose Vidro	.25
68	Barry Bonds	2.50
69	Jeff Kent	.40
70	Rich Aurilia	.25
71	Preston Wilson	.25
72	Josh Beckett	.40
73	Mike Lowell	.25
74	Roberto Alomar	.40
75	Mo Vaughn	.25
76	Jeromy Burnitz	.25
77	Mike Piazza	1.50
78	Sean Burroughs	.25
79	Phil Nevin	.25
80	Bobby Abreu	.50
81	Pat Burrell	.40
82	Scott Rolen	.75
83	Jason Kendall	.25
84	Brian Giles	.25
85	Ken Griffey Jr.	1.50
86	Adam Dunn	.75
87	Sean Casey	.40
88	Todd Helton	.75
89	Larry Walker	.25
90	Mike Hampton	.25
91	Brandon Puffer RC	4.00
92	Tom Shearn RC	4.00
93	Chris Baker RC	4.00
94	Gustavo Chacin RC	10.00
95	Joe Orloski RC	4.00
96	Mike Smith RC	4.00
97	John Ennis RC	4.00
98	John Foster RC	4.00
99	Kevin Gryboski RC	4.00
100	Brian Mallette RC	4.00
101	Takahito Nomura RC	4.00
102	So Taguchi RC	10.00
103	Jeremy Lambert RC	4.00
104	Jason Simontacchi RC	4.00
105	Jorge Sosa RC	4.00
106	Brandon Backe RC	8.00
107	P.J. Bevis RC	4.00
108	Jeremy Ward RC	4.00
109	Doug DeVore RC	4.00
110	Ron Chiavacci RC	4.00
111	Ron Calloway RC	4.00
112	Nelson Castro RC	4.00
113	Deivis Santos RC	4.00
114	Earl Snyder RC	4.00
115	Julio Mateo RC	4.00

116	J.J. Putz RC	4.00
117	Allan Simpson RC	4.00
118	Satoru Komiyama RC	4.00
119	Adam Walker RC	4.00
120	Oliver Perez RC	10.00
121	Clifford Bartosh RC	4.00
122	Todd Donovan RC	4.00
123	Elio Serrano RC	4.00
124	Peter Zamora RC	4.00
125	Mike Gonzalez RC	4.00
126	Travis Hughes RC	4.00
127	Jorge de la Rosa RC	4.00
128	Anastacio Martinez RC	4.00
129	Colin Young RC	4.00
130	Nate Field RC	4.00
131	Tim Kalita RC	4.00
132	Julius Matos RC	4.00
133	Terry Pearson RC	4.00
134	Kyle Kane RC	4.00
135	Mitch Wylie RC	4.00
136	Rodrigo Rosario RC	10.00
137	Franklyn German RC	10.00
138	Reed Johnson RC	15.00
139	Luis Martinez RC	10.00
140	Michael Crudale RC	10.00
141	Francis Beltran RC	10.00
142	Steve Kent RC	10.00
143	Felix Escalona RC	10.00
144	Jose Valverde RC	15.00
145	Victor Alvarez RC	10.00
146	Kazuhisa Ishii/ 249 RC	25.00
147	Jorge Nunez RC	10.00
148	Eric Good RC	10.00
149	Luis Ugueto RC	10.00
150	Matt Thornton RC	10.00
151	Wilson Valdez RC	10.00
152	Hansel Izquierdo/ 249 RC	25.00
153	Jaime Cerda RC	10.00
154	Mark Corey RC	10.00
155	Tyler Yates RC	10.00
156	Steve Bechler RC	10.00
157	Ben Howard/249 RC	20.00
158	Anderson Machado RC	10.00
159	Jorge Padilla RC	15.00
160	Eric Junge RC	10.00
161	Adrian Burnside RC	10.00
162	Josh Hancock RC	10.00
163	Chris Booker RC	10.00
164	Cam Esslinger RC	10.00
165	Rene Reyes RC	10.00
166	Aaron Cook RC	10.00
167	Juan Brito RC	10.00
168	Miguel Ascencio RC	10.00
169	Kevin Frederick RC	10.00
170	Edwin Almonte RC	10.00

Limited

Stars (1-90):	5-10X
Cards (91-135):	.5-1X
Cards (136-170):	.5-1X
Production 125 Sets	
Golds (1-90):	10-20X
Golds (91-135):	.75-1.5X
Golds (136-170):	.75-1.5X
Production 50 Sets	

Big Mac Missing Link

Production 25 Sets

MMC	Mark McGwire/1998
MM	Mark McGwire/1999
MAM	Mark McGwire/2000
SPMM	Mark McGwire/2001
MAMC	Mark McGwire/2002

Signed SP Big Mac

		NM/M
Quantity signed listed		
MM6	Mark McGwire/70	250.00

Chirography

		NM/M
Common Autograph:		10.00
Inserted 1:72		
HB	Hank Blalock/282	25.00
BB	Barry Bonds/112	180.00
BBo	Bret Boone/500	15.00
MB	Milton Bradley/470	15.00
JB	John Buck/427	10.00
MB	Mark Buehrle/438	15.00
SB	Sean Burroughs/275	15.00
AD	Adam Dunn/348	30.00
DE	Darin Erstad/80	15.00
CF	Cliff Floyd/313	10.00
FG	Freddy Garcia/456	15.00
JG	Jason Giambi/244	25.00
TG	Tom Glavine/376	25.00
AG	Alex Graman/418	10.00
KG	Ken Griffey Jr/238	100.00
TG	Tony Gwynn/75	40.00
JL	Jon Lieber/462	15.00
JM	Joe Mays/469	15.00
MM	Mark McGwire/50	300.00
DM	Doug Mientkiewicz/478	15.00
AR	Alex Rodriguez/391	90.00
CS	C.C. Sabathia/442	15.00
RS	Richie Sexson/483	15.00
SS	Sammy Sosa/247	100.00
IS	Ichiro Suzuki/78	350.00
MS	Mike Sweeney/265	15.00
BZ	Barry Zito/419	20.00

Chirography Gold

		NM/M
Quantity produced listed		
MB	Mark Buehrle/56	25.00
AD	Adam Dunn/44	40.00
CF	Cliff Floyd/30	20.00
FG	Freddy Garcia/34	35.00
TG	Tom Glavine/47	50.00
AG	Alex Graman/76	15.00
KG	Ken Griffey Jr./30	200.00
JL	Jon Lieber/32	20.00
CS	C.C. Sabathia/52	20.00
MS	Mike Sweeney/29	40.00
BZ	Barry Zito/75	25.00

Excellence

	NM/M
Production 25	
AE-1 Ken Griffey Jr., Sammy Sosa, Cal Ripken Jr., Jason Giambi, Mark McGwire, Ichiro Suzuki	1,500

Future USA Watch

		NM/M
Common Player:		4.00
Production 1,999 Sets		
USA1	Chad Cordero	5.00
USA2	Philip Humber	10.00
USA3	Grant Johnson	5.00
USA4	Wes Littleton	5.00
USA5	Kyle Sleeth	10.00
USA6	Huston Street	15.00
USA7	Brad Sullivan	5.00
USA8	Bob Zimmermann	5.00
USA9	Abe Alvarez	5.00
USA10	Kyle Bakker	5.00
USA11	Landon Powell	5.00
USA12	Clint Sammons	5.00
USA13	Michael Aubrey	10.00

USA14	Aaron Hill	5.00
USA15	Conor Jackson	20.00
USA16	Eric Patterson	5.00
USA17	Dustin Pedroia	10.00
USA18	Rickie Weeks	25.00
USA19	Shane Costa	5.00
USA20	Mark Jurich	5.00
USA21	Sam Fuld	5.00
USA22	Carlos Quentin	20.00

Game Jerseys

MADDUX

SP GAME JERSEY

		NM/M
Common Player:		5.00
Inserted 1:24		
RA	Roberto Alomar	8.00
JB	Jeff Bagwell	10.00
JB	Jeromy Burnitz/SP	5.00
RC	Roger Clemens	15.00
CD	Carlos Delgado	6.00
JE	Jim Edmonds	8.00
DE	Darin Erstad	8.00
JGi	Jason Giambi	8.00
JGo	Juan Gonzalez	8.00
SG	Shawn Green	6.00
KG	Ken Griffey Jr/95	40.00
TH	Todd Helton	8.00
KI	Kazuhisa Ishii	10.00
RJ	Randy Johnson	10.00
AJ	Andruw Jones	8.00
CJ	Chipper Jones	10.00
JK	Jason Kendall	5.00
GM	Greg Maddux	10.00
MM	Mark McGwire/SP	100.00
MO	Magglio Ordonez	8.00
AP	Andy Pettitte	10.00
MP	Mike Piazza	15.00
MR	Manny Ramirez	10.00
AR	Alex Rodriguez	15.00
IR	Ivan Rodriguez	8.00
SR	Scott Rolen	10.00
CC	C.C. Sabathia	5.00
CS	Curt Schilling	10.00
GS	Gary Sheffield	6.00
TS	Tsuyoshi Shinjo	5.00
SS	Sammy Sosa	15.00
IS	Ichiro Suzuki/SP	50.00
JT	Jim Thome	10.00
RV	Robin Ventura	5.00
OV	Omar Vizquel	5.00
BW	Bernie Williams	8.00
PW	Preston Wilson	5.00
BZ	Barry Zito	6.00

Game Jersey Gold

Quantity produced listed

KG	Ken Griffey Jr./30	65.00
RJ	Randy Johnson/51	25.00
GM	Greg Maddux/31	50.00
MO	Magglio Ordonez/30	15.00
AP	Andy Pettitte/46	20.00
MP	Mike Piazza/93	50.00
CC	C.C. Sabathia/52	10.00
CS	Curt Schilling/38	30.00
IS	Ichiro Suzuki/51	85.00
BW	Bernie Williams/51	20.00
PW	Preston Wilson/44	10.00
BZ	Barry Zito/75	10.00

Prospect Signatures

		NM/M
Common Autograph:		5.00
Inserted 1:36		
JC	Jose Cueto	5.00
JDe	Jeff Deardorff	5.00
JDi	Jose Diaz	8.00
AG	Alex Graman	5.00
MG	Matt Guerrier	5.00
BH	Bill Hall	15.00
KH	Ken Huckaby	5.00
DM	Dustan Mohr	5.00
XN	Xavier Nady	8.00
MS	Marco Scutaro	5.00
ST	Steve Torrealba	6.00
DW	Danny Wright	5.00

Signs of Greatness

1/1

NM/M

Babe Ruth, Joe DiMaggio, Mickey Mantle, Ken Griffey Jr., Sammy Sosa (2/03 Auction) 30,000

2002 SP Legendary Cuts

YANKEES' CATCHER

		NM/M
Complete Set (90):		30.00
Common Player:		.40
Pack (4):		10.00
Box (12):		100.00
1	Al Kaline	.75
2	Alvin Dark	.40
3	Andre Dawson	.75
4	Babe Ruth	3.00
5	Ernie Banks	1.00
6	Bob Lemon	.40
7	Bobby Bonds	.40
8	Carl Erskine	.40
9	Carl Hubbell	.40
10	Casey Stengel	.40
11	Charlie Gehringer	.40
12	Christy Mathewson	.75
13	Dale Murphy	.75
14	Dave Concepcion	.40
15	Dave Parker	.40
16	Dazzy Vance	.40
17	Dizzy Dean	.75
18	Don Baylor	.40
19	Don Drysdale	.75
20	Duke Snider	1.00
21	Earl Averill	.40
22	Early Wynn	.40
23	Edd Roush	.40
24	Elston Howard	.40
25	Ferguson Jenkins	.75
26	Frank Crosetti	.40
27	Frankie Frisch	.40
28	Gaylord Perry	.40
29	George Foster	.40
30	George Kell	.40
31	Gil Hodges	.75
32	Hank Greenberg	.75
33	Phil Niekro	.40
34	Harvey Haddix	.40
35	Harvey Kuenn	.40
36	Honus Wagner	1.50
37	Jackie Robinson	2.00
38	Orlando Cepeda	.40
39	Joe Adcock	.40
40	Joe Cronin	.40
41	Joe DiMaggio	2.50
42	Joe Morgan	.75
43	Johnny Mize	.40
44	Lefty Gomez	.75
45	Lefty Grove	.40
46	Jim Palmer	.75
47	Lou Boudreau	.40
48	Lou Gehrig	2.50
49	Luke Appling	.40
50	Mark McGwire	2.00
51	Mel Ott	.75
52	Mickey Cochrane	.40
53	Mickey Mantle	3.00
54	Minnie Minoso	.40
55	Brooks Robinson	1.00
56	Nellie Fox	.40
57	Nolan Ryan	3.00
58	Rollie Fingers	.40
59	Pee Wee Reese	.40
60	Phil Rizzuto	.75
61	Ralph Kiner	.75
62	Ray Dandridge	.40
63	Richie Ashburn	.40
64	Robin Yount	.75
65	Rocky Colavito	.40
66	Roger Maris	2.00
67	Rogers Hornsby	.75
68	Ron Santo	.40
69	Ryne Sandberg	1.50
70	Stan Musial	1.50
71	Sam McDowell	.40
72	Satchel Paige	1.00
73	Willie McCovey	.40
74	Steve Garvey	.40
75	Ted Kluszewski	.40
76	Catfish Hunter	.40
77	Terry Moore	.40
78	Thurman Munson	1.00
79	Tom Seaver	1.00
80	Tommy John	.40
81	Tony Gwynn	1.00
82	Tony Kubek	.40
83	Tony Lazzeri	.40
84	Ty Cobb	2.00
85	Wade Boggs	1.00
86	Waite Hoyt	.40
87	Walter Johnson	1.00
88	Willie Stargell	.75
89	Yogi Berra	1.00
90	Zack Wheat	.40

Bat

ANDRE DAWSON

		NM/M
Common Player:		6.00
Inserted 1:8		
DBa	Don Baylor	6.00
YBe	Yogi Berra/SP	20.00
BBo	Bobby Bonds	6.00
RCo	Rocky Colavito	12.00
ADa	Alvin Dark	6.00
AnD	Andre Dawson	8.00
GFo	George Foster	6.00
NFo	Nellie Fox	15.00
SGa	Steve Garvey	6.00
HGr	Hank Greenberg/SP	40.00
LGr	Lefty Grove	15.00
TGw	Tony Gwynn	12.00
EHo	Elston Howard/SP	15.00
GKe	George Kell	8.00
RKi	Ralph Kiner	10.00
TKu	Tonk (Tony) Kubek	8.00
TLa	Tony Lazzeri	10.00
MMa	Mickey Mantle/SP	120.00
RMa	Roger Maris/SP	50.00
MMc	Mark McGwire	60.00
JMi	Johnny Mize	12.00
TMu	Thurman Munson	25.00
DMu	Dale Murphy	10.00
DPa	Dave Parker	6.00
GPe	Gaylord Perry	8.00
PWe	Pee Wee Reese	10.00
CRi	Cal Ripken Jr.	25.00
JaR	Jackie Robinson/SP	50.00
BRu	Babe Ruth/SP	150.00
NRy	Nolan Ryan	30.00
RSa	Ryne Sandberg	12.00
TSe	Tom Seaver/SP	20.00
DSn	Duke Snider	12.00
WSt	Willie Stargell	8.00
RYo	Robin Yount	10.00
EWy	Early Wynn	8.00

Bat Barrel

NM/M

Many not priced due to scarcity.

BB-ADa	Alvin Dark/4	800.00
BB-AnD	Andre Dawson/4	750.00
BB-GFo	George Foster/5	250.00
BB-LGr	Lefty Grove/1 (8/03 Auction)	10,000
BB-TGw	Tony Gwynn/11	650.00
BB-MMa	Mickey Mantle/7 (8/04 Auction)	3,000
BB-MMc	Mark McGwire/4	2,000
BB-JMi	Johnny Mize/2	1,275
BB-DMu	Dale Murphy/3	600.00
BB-PWe	Pee Wee Reese/4	1,500
BB-BRu	Babe Ruth/3 (8/05 Auction)	9,500
BB-NRy	Nolan Ryan/9	1,500
BB-RSa	Ryne Sandberg/3	2,250
BB-DSn	Duke Snider/2	1,500
BB-RYo	Robin Yount/8	750.00

Jersey

		NM/M
Common Player:		6.00
Inserted 1:24		
DBa	Don Baylor	6.00
YBe	Yogi Berra	20.00
BBo	Bobby Bonds	6.00
FCr	Frank Crosetti	10.00
AnD	Andre Dawson	8.00
GFo	George Foster	6.00
SGa	Steve Garvey	8.00
MMa	Mickey Mantle/SP	100.00
RMa	Roger Maris	40.00
DPa	Dave Parker	6.00
PWe	Pee Wee Reese	12.00
JRo	Jackie Robinson/SP	45.00
NRy	Nolan Ryan	30.00
RSa	Ryne Sandberg	25.00
TSe	Tom Seaver	10.00

Signatures

		NM/M
Quantity signed listed		
JAd	Joe Adcock/48	145.00
LAp	Luke Appling/53	150.00
RAs	Richie Ashburn/10	550.00
EAv	Earl Averill/22	275.00
JBe	Johnny Berardino/1	450.00
LBo	Lou Boudreau/85	120.00
GBu	Guy Bush/38	125.00
GCa	George Case/36	180.00
HCh	Happy Chandler/96	95.00
SCh	Spud Chandler/17	350.00
TyC	Ty Cobb/2	5,500
MCo	Mickey Cochrane/2	5,000
JCo	Johnny Cooney/64	75.00
SCo	Stan Coveleski/85	150.00
JCr	Joe Cronin/185	120.00
BDa	Babe Dahlgren/51	180.00
RDa	Ray Dandridge/179	85.00
DDe	Dizzy Dean/4	2,000
JDi	Joe DiMaggio/103	175.00
DDo	Dick Donovan/23	200.00
TDo	Taylor Douthit/60	165.00
DDr	Don Drysdale/14	650.00
JDu	Joe Dugan/39	140.00
BFa	Bibb Falk/44	150.00
RFe	Rick Ferrell/19	225.00
NFo	Nellie Fox/1 (12/02 Auction)	3,100
FoF	Ford Frick/1 (10/03 Auction)	4,000
FFr	Frankie Frisch/35	
LGe	Lou Gehrig/3 (6/04 Auction)	7,500
CGe	Charlie Gehringer/3	700.00
LGo	Lefty Gomez/3	750.00
BGo	Billy Goodman/53	140.00
HGr	Hank Greenberg/94	425.00
LGr	Lefty Grove/190	240.00
SHa	Stan Hack/36	200.00
HHa	Harvey Haddix/37	250.00
BHa	Buddy Hassett/56	200.00
WHo	Waite Hoyt/62	175.00
CHu	Carl Hubbell/17	475.00
LJa	Larry Jackson/37	125.00
NJa	Newton "Bucky" Jacobs/44	150.00
EJo	Earl Johnson/31	200.00
JJo	Judy Johnson/86	150.00
WJo	Walter Johnson/20	2,000
BKa	Bob Kahle/53	150.00
WKa	Willie Kamm/57	110.00
CKe	Charlie Keller/29	280.00
KKe	Ken Keltner/11	415.00
TKl	Ted Kluszewski/23	300.00
MKo	Mark Koenig/22	260.00
HKu	Harvey Kuenn/23	230.00
CLa	Cookie Lavagetto/22	200.00
BiL	Billy Lee/40	150.00
BoL	Bob Lemon/91	110.00
ELo	Ed Lopat/58	150.00

SMa	Sal Maglie/29	200.00
HMa	Hank Majeski/21	300.00
MMa	Mickey Mantle/2	
	(10/04 Auction)	6,000
ChrM	Christy Mathewson/2	
	(5/03 Auction)	2,000
RMc	Roy McMillan/18	250.00
JMi	Johnny Mize/3	2,500
JMo	Johnny Moore/22	250.00
TMo	Terry Moore/86	95.00
ChM	Chet Morgan/27	185.00
HNe	Hal Newhouser/81	135.00
VRa	Vic Raschi/98	110.00
PWe	Pee Wee Reese/23	450.00
PRe	Pete Reiser/73	140.00
RRe	Rip Repulski/19	275.00
LRi	Lance Richbourg/3	1,800
ORo	Oscar Roettger/9	700.00
ERo	Edd Roush/101	100.00
ERo2	Edd Roush/99	100.00
BRu	Babe Ruth/3	
	(6/04 Auction)	12,500
BSc	Bob Scheffing/19	200.00
WSc	Willard Schmidt/10	350.00
HSc	Hal Schumacher/17	300.00
BSe	Bill Serena/16	275.00
JSe	Joe Sewell/136	125.00
BSh	Bob Shawkey/120	120.00
BSh	Bill Sherdel/10	450.00
BSz	Bill Shantz/17	300.00
WSt	Willie Stargell/153	95.00
CSt	Casey Stengel/8	750.00
BVe	Bill Veeck/11	500.00
HWa	Honus Wagner/6	
	(2/05 Auction)	5,000
BWa	Bucky Walters/31	165.00
VWe	Vic Wertz/17	300.00
ZWh	Zack Wheat/127	150.00
PWi	Pete Whisenant/13	300.00
EWy	Early Wynn/4	1,650

Swatches

		NM/M
Common Player:		6.00
Inserted 1:24		
DBa	Don Baylor	6.00
WBo	Wade Boggs	8.00
FCr	Frank Crosetti	8.00
DDr	Don Drysdale	20.00
CEr	Carl Erskine	8.00
TGw	Tony Gwynn	10.00
FJe	Ferguson Jenkins	8.00
TJo	Tommy John	6.00
SMc	Sam McDowell	6.00
MMi	Minnie Minoso	8.00
JMo	Joe Morgan	8.00
MOt	Mel Ott	25.00
DPa	Dave Parker	6.00
CRj	Cal Ripken Jr.	25.00
RSa	Ron Santo	10.00

2002 SPx

	NM/M
Common Player:	.25
Common SP (91-120):	4.00
Production 1,800	
Common SP Auto.	
(121-150):	10.00
Common SP Auto	
(151-190):	5.00
Production 800	

Pack (4):		4.00
Box (18):		60.00
1	Troy Glaus	.50
2	Darin Erstad	.40
3	David Justice	.25
4	Tim Hudson	.50
5	Miguel Tejada	.75
6	Barry Zito	.40
7	Carlos Delgado	.50
8	Shannon Stewart	.25
9	Greg Vaughn	.25
10	Toby Hall	.25
11	Jim Thome	.75
12	C.C. Sabathia	.25
13	Ichiro Suzuki	2.00
14	Edgar Martinez	.25
15	Freddy Garcia	.25
16	Mike Cameron	.25
17	Jeff Conine	.25
18	Tony Batista	.25
19	Alex Rodriguez	2.00
20	Rafael Palmeiro	.75
21	Ivan Rodriguez	.75
22	Carl Everett	.25
23	Pedro J. Martinez	1.00
24	Manny Ramirez	1.00
25	Nomar Garciaparra	1.00
26	Johnny Damon	1.00
27	Mike Sweeney	.25
28	Carlos Beltran	.25
29	Dmitri Young	.25
30	Joe Mays	.25
31	Doug Mientkiewicz	.25
32	Cristian Guzman	.25
33	Corey Koskie	.25
34	Frank Thomas	.75
35	Magglio Ordonez	.25
36	Mark Buehrle	.25
37	Bernie Williams	.50
38	Roger Clemens	2.00
39	Derek Jeter	2.50
40	Jason Giambi	.50
41	Mike Mussina	.50
42	Lance Berkman	.50
43	Jeff Bagwell	.50
44	Roy Oswalt	.50
45	Greg Maddux	2.00
46	Chipper Jones	1.00
47	Andruw Jones	.75
48	Gary Sheffield	.50
49	Geoff Jenkins	.25
50	Richie Sexson	.50
51	Ben Sheets	.40
52	Albert Pujols	2.50
53	J.D. Drew	.40
54	Jim Edmonds	.50
55	Sammy Sosa	1.50
56	Moises Alou	.25
57	Kerry Wood	.25
58	Jon Lieber	.25
59	Fred McGriff	.40
60	Randy Johnson	.75
61	Luis Gonzalez	.35
62	Curt Schilling	.75
63	Kevin Brown	.25
64	Hideo Nomo	.50
65	Shawn Green	.40
66	Vladimir Guerrero	1.00
67	Jose Vidro	.25
68	Barry Bonds	2.50
69	Jeff Kent	.40
70	Rich Aurilia	.25
71	Cliff Floyd	.25
72	Josh Beckett	.40
73	Preston Wilson	.25
74	Mike Piazza	1.00
75	Mo Vaughn	.25
76	Jeromy Burnitz	.25
77	Roberto Alomar	.50
78	Phil Nevin	.25
79	Ryan Klesko	.25
80	Scott Rolen	.75
81	Bobby Abreu	.50
82	Jimmy Rollins	.50
83	Brian Giles	.25
84	Aramis Ramirez	.50
85	Ken Griffey Jr.	1.50
86	Sean Casey	.40
87	Barry Larkin	.50
88	Mike Hampton	.25
89	Larry Walker	.40
90	Todd Helton	.75
91	Ron Calloway RC	4.00
92	Joe Orloski RC	4.00
93	Anderson Machado RC	6.00
94	Eric Good RC	4.00
95	Reed Johnson RC	8.00
96	Brendan Donnelly RC	4.00
97	Chris Baker RC	4.00
98	Wilson Valdez RC	4.00
99	Scotty Layfield RC	4.00
100	P.J. Bevis RC	4.00
101	Edwin Almonte RC	4.00
102	Francis Beltran RC	4.00

103	Valentino Pasucci	4.00
104	Nelson Castro RC	4.00
105	Michael Crudale RC	4.00
106	Colin Young RC	4.00
107	Todd Donovan RC	4.00
108	Felix Escalona RC	4.00
109	Brandon Backe RC	8.00
110	Corey Thurman RC	4.00
111	Kyle Kane RC	4.00
112	Allan Simpson RC	4.00
113	Jose Valverde RC	4.00
114	Chris Booker RC	4.00
115	Brandon Puffer RC	4.00
116	John Foster RC	4.00
117	Clifford Bartosh RC	4.00
118	Gustavo Chacin RC	8.00
119	Steve Kent RC	4.00
120	Nate Field RC	4.00
121	Victor Alvarez RC	10.00
122	Steve Bechler RC	10.00
123	Adrian Burnside RC	10.00
124	Marlon Byrd	15.00
125	Jaime Cerda RC	10.00
126	Brandon Claussen	10.00
127	Mark Corey RC	10.00
128	Doug DeVore RC	10.00
129	Kazuhisa Ishii RC	40.00
130	John Ennis RC	10.00
131	Kevin Frederick RC	10.00
132	Josh Hancock RC	10.00
133	Ben Howard RC	10.00
134	Orlando Hudson	15.00
135	Hansel Izquierdo RC	10.00
136	Eric Junge RC	10.00
137	Austin Kearns	15.00
138	Victor Martinez	25.00
139	Luis Martinez RC	10.00
140	Danny Mota RC	10.00
141	Jorge Padilla RC	10.00
142	Andy Pratt RC	10.00
143	Rene Reyes RC	10.00
144	Rodrigo Rosario RC	10.00
145	Tom Shearn RC	10.00
146	So Taguchi RC	30.00
147	Dennis Tankersley	15.00
148	Matt Thornton	10.00
149	Jeremy Ward RC	10.00
150	Mitch Wylie RC	10.00
151	Pedro Martinez	8.00
152	Cal Ripken Jr.	25.00
153	Roger Clemens	15.00
154	Bernie Williams	6.00
155	Jason Giambi	8.00
156	Robin Ventura	5.00
157	Carlos Delgado	6.00
158	Frank Thomas	8.00
159	Magglio Ordonez	5.00
160	Jim Thome	10.00
161	Darin Erstad	5.00
162	Tim Salmon	5.00
163	Tim Hudson	5.00
164	Barry Zito	5.00
165	Ichiro Suzuki	30.00
166	Edgar Martinez	8.00
167	Alex Rodriguez	15.00
168	Ivan Rodriguez	8.00
169	Juan Gonzalez	6.00
170	Greg Maddux	12.00
171	Chipper Jones	10.00
172	Andruw Jones	8.00
173	Tom Glavine	6.00
174	Mike Piazza	15.00
175	Roberto Alomar	8.00
176	Scott Rolen	12.00
177	Sammy Sosa	15.00
178	Moises Alou	8.00
179	Ken Griffey Jr.	15.00
180	Jeff Bagwell	8.00
181	Jim Edmonds	6.00
182	J.D. Drew	5.00
183	Brian Giles	5.00
184	Randy Johnson	10.00
185	Curt Schilling	5.00
186	Luis Gonzalez	5.00
187	Todd Helton	8.00
188	Shawn Green	6.00
189	David Wells	5.00
190	Jeff Kent	5.00

SuperStar Swatch Gold

Jersey (151-190):	.75-1.5X
Production 150	

SuperStar Swatch Silver

Jersey (151-190):	.5-1X
Production 400	

Sweet Spot Bat Barrel

No Pricing

Winning Materials Base Combo

		NM/M
Common Card:		15.00
Production 200		
PE	Mike Piazza,	
	Jim Edmonds	20.00
RJ	Alex Rodriguez,	
	Derek Jeter	40.00
BG	Barry Bonds,	
	Shawn Green	20.00
IM	Ichiro Suzuki,	
	Edgar Martinez	50.00
SG	Sammy Sosa,	
	Luis Gonzalez	25.00
GR	Troy Glaus,	
	Alex Rodriguez	20.00
WJ	Bernie Williams,	
	Derek Jeter	30.00
GS	Ken Griffey Jr.,	
	Sammy Sosa	30.00
PI	Albert Pujols,	
	Ichiro Suzuki	60.00
SR	Kazuhiro Sasaki,	
	Mariano Rivera	20.00

Winning Materials Base/Patch Combo

No Pricing
Production 25 Sets

Winning Materials Ball/Patch Combo

No Pricing
Production 25 Sets

Winning Materials Jersey Combo

		NM/M
Common Card:		8.00
Inserted 1:18		
AR	Alex Rodriguez,	
	Ivan Rodriguez	20.00
GC	Ken Griffey Jr.,	
	Sean Casey/SP	20.00
BR	Jeff Bagwell,	
	Alex Rodriguez	15.00

WG Bernie Williams, Jason Giambi 10.00
JS Randy Johnson, Curt Schilling 15.00
MJ Greg Maddux, Chipper Jones 20.00
MC Edgar Martinez, Mike Cameron 10.00
SP Sammy Sosa, Corey Patterson 20.00
ED Jim Edmonds, J.D. Drew 10.00
PA Mike Piazza, Roberto Alomar 15.00
DH Jermaine Dye, Tim Hudson 8.00
RA Scott Rolen, Bobby Abreu 15.00
TO Frank Thomas, Magglio Ordonez 15.00
HW Mike Hampton, Larry Walker 8.00
TS Jim Thome, C.C. Sabathia 15.00
GK Shawn Green, Eric Karros 10.00
KG Jason Kendall, Brian Giles 8.00
WP David Wells, Jorge Posada 10.00
NM Hideo Nomo, Pedro Martinez/SP 20.00
RP Ivan Rodriguez, Chan Ho Park 10.00
LH Al Leiter, Mike Hampton 8.00
BA Jeromy Burnitz, Edgardo Alfonzo 8.00
DS Carlos Delgado, Shannon Stewart 10.00
BG Jeff Bagwell, Juan Gonzalez 10.00
GR Juan Gonzalez, Ivan Rodriguez 10.00
VR Omar Vizquel, Alex Rodriguez 15.00
SE Aaron Sele, Darin Erstad 8.00
JJ Chipper Jones, Andruw Jones 15.00
SH Kazuhiro Sasaki, Shigetoshi Hasegawa 8.00

Winning Materials USA Jersey Combo

NM/M
Common Card: 10.00
Production 150
AH Brent Abernathy, Orlando Hudson 8.00
BT Sean Burroughs, Mark Teixeira 25.00
GB Jason Giambi, Sean Burroughs 15.00
HD Orlando Hudson, Jeff Deardorff 10.00
GT Jason Giambi, Mark Teixeira 20.00
HOU Roy Oswalt, Adam Everett 10.00
HP Dustin Hermanson, Mark Prior 15.00
JC Jacque Jones, Michael Cuddyer 10.00
KB Austin Kearns, Sean Burroughs 15.00
KC Austin Kearns, Michael Cuddyer 15.00
MG Doug Mientkiewicz, Jason Giambi 15.00
MIN Doug Mientkiewicz, Michael Cuddyer 10.00
MO Matt Morris, Roy Oswalt 15.00
MP Matt Morris, Mark Prior 15.00
AW Matt Anderson, Jeff Weaver 10.00
MW Matt Morris, Jeff Weaver 10.00
PB Mark Prior, Dewon Brazelton 15.00
RE Brian Roberts, Adam Everett 10.00
SD Mark Kotsay, Sean Burroughs 10.00
TB Brent Abernathy, Dewon Brazelton 10.00
TP Mark Teixeira, Mark Prior 25.00
WB Jeff Weaver, Dewon Brazelton 10.00
WH Jeff Weaver, Dustin Hermanson 10.00

2003 SP Authentic

NM/M
Complete Set (189):
Common Player: .25
Common Rk Archives (91-123): 1.00
Production 2,500
Common Back to '93 (124-150): 1.50
Production 1,993
Common Future Watch (150-180): 4.00
Production 2,003
Pack (5): 3.50
Box (24): 70.00
1 Darin Erstad .40
2 Garret Anderson .40
3 Troy Glaus .50
4 Eric Chavez .40
5 Barry Zito .50
6 Miguel Tejada .50
7 Eric Hinske .25
8 Carlos Delgado .50
9 Josh Phelps .25
10 Ben Grieve .25
11 Carl Crawford .40
12 Omar Vizquel .25
13 Matt Lawton .25
14 C.C. Sabathia .25
15 Ichiro Suzuki 1.50
16 John Olerud .40
17 Freddy Garcia .25
18 Jay Gibbons .25
19 Tony Batista .25
20 Melvin Mora .25
21 Alex Rodriguez 2.00
22 Rafael Palmeiro .50
23 Hank Blalock .50
24 Nomar Garciaparra 1.00
25 Pedro J. Martinez .75
26 Johnny Damon .75
27 Mike Sweeney .25
28 Carlos Febles .25
29 Carlos Beltran .50
30 Carlos Pena .25
31 Eric Munson .25
32 Bobby Higginson .25
33 Torii Hunter .40
34 Doug Mientkiewicz .25
35 Jacque Jones .25
36 Paul Konerko .50
37 Bartolo Colon .25
38 Magglio Ordonez .40
39 Derek Jeter 2.00
40 Bernie Williams .50
41 Jason Giambi .50
42 Alfonso Soriano .75
43 Roger Clemens 1.50
44 Jeff Bagwell .50
45 Jeff Kent .40
46 Lance Berkman .40
47 Chipper Jones .75
48 Andruw Jones .50
49 Gary Sheffield .50
50 Ben Sheets .40
51 Richie Sexson .50
52 Geoff Jenkins .25
53 Jim Edmonds .40
54 Albert Pujols 2.00
55 Scott Rolen .75
56 Sammy Sosa 1.00
57 Kerry Wood .75
58 Eric Karros .25
59 Luis Gonzalez .40
60 Randy Johnson .75
61 Curt Schilling .75
62 Fred McGriff .40
63 Shawn Green .40
64 Paul LoDuca .25
65 Vladimir Guerrero .75
66 Jose Vidro .25
67 Barry Bonds 2.00
68 Rich Aurilia .25
69 Edgardo Alfonzo .25
70 Ivan Rodriguez .50
71 Mike Lowell .40
72 Derrek Lee .50
73 Tom Glavine .50
74 Mike Piazza 1.00
75 Roberto Alomar .50
76 Ryan Klesko .25
77 Phil Nevin .25
78 Mark Kotsay .25
79 Jim Thome .75
80 Pat Burrell .40
81 Bobby Abreu .40
82 Jason Kendall .40
83 Brian Giles .40
84 Aramis Ramirez .40
85 Austin Kearns .40
86 Ken Griffey Jr. 1.00
87 Adam Dunn .50
88 Larry Walker .40
89 Todd Helton .50
90 Preston Wilson .40
91 Derek Jeter 6.00
92 Johnny Damon 3.00
93 Chipper Jones 3.00
94 Manny Ramirez 3.00
95 Trot Nixon 1.00
96 Alex Rodriguez 5.00
97 Chan Ho Park 1.00
98 Brad Fullmer 1.00
99 Billy Wagner 1.00
100 Hideo Nomo 2.00
101 Freddy Garcia 1.00
102 Darin Erstad 1.00
103 Jose Cruz Jr. 1.00
104 Nomar Garciaparra 4.00
105 Magglio Ordonez 1.50
106 Kerry Wood 2.00
107 Troy Glaus 1.50
108 J.D. Drew 1.00
109 Alfonso Soriano 3.00
110 Danys Baez 1.00
111 Kazuhiro Sasaki 1.00
112 Barry Zito 2.00
113 Brent Abernathy 1.00
114 Ben Diggins 1.00
115 Ben Sheets 2.00
116 Brad Wilkerson 1.00
117 Juan Pierre 1.00
118 Jon Rauch 1.00
119 Ichiro Suzuki 5.00
120 Albert Pujols 6.00
121 Mark Prior 2.00
122 Mark Teixeira 2.00
123 Kazuhisa Ishii 1.00
124 Troy Glaus 1.50
125 Randy Johnson 3.00
126 Curt Schilling 3.00
127 Chipper Jones 3.00
128 Greg Maddux 4.00
129 Nomar Garciaparra 3.00
130 Pedro J. Martinez 3.00
131 Sammy Sosa 3.00
132 Mark Prior 2.00
133 Ken Griffey Jr. 2.00
134 Adam Dunn 2.00
135 Jeff Bagwell 2.00
136 Vladimir Guerrero 3.00
137 Mike Piazza 4.00
138 Tom Glavine 1.50
139 Derek Jeter 8.00
140 Roger Clemens 6.00
141 Jason Giambi 2.00
142 Alfonso Soriano 3.00
143 Miguel Tejada 2.00
144 Barry Zito 1.50
145 Jim Thome 3.00
146 Barry Bonds 8.00
147 Ichiro Suzuki 5.00
148 Albert Pujols 5.00
149 Alex Rodriguez 6.00
150 Carlos Delgado 2.00
151 Richard Fischer RC 4.00
152 Brandon Webb RC 10.00
153 Rob Hammock RC 4.00
154 Matt Kata RC 4.00
155 Tim Olson RC 4.00
156 Oscar Villarreal RC 4.00
157 Michael Hessman RC 4.00
158 Daniel Cabrera RC 6.00
159 Jon Leicester RC 4.00
160 Todd Wellemeyer RC 4.00
161 Felix Sanchez RC 4.00
162 David Sanders RC 4.00
163 Josh Stewart RC 4.00
164 Arnie Munoz RC 4.00
165 Ryan Cameron RC 4.00
166 Clint Barmes RC 5.00
167 Josh Willingham RC 10.00
168 .25
169 Willie Eyre RC 4.00
170 Brent Hoard RC 4.00
171 Terrmel Sledge RC 4.00
172 Phil Seibel RC 4.00
173 Craig Brazell RC 4.00
174 Jeff Duncan RC 6.00
175 .25
176 Bernie Castro RC 4.00
177 Mike Nicolas RC 4.00
178 Rett Johnson RC 4.00
179 Bobby Madritsch RC 6.00
180 Chris Capuano RC 15.00
181 Hideki Matsui/ Auto./500 RC 240.00
181 H. Matsui/Bronze/ Auto./75 275.00
182 Jose Contreras/ Auto./500 RC 35.00
183 Lew Ford/Auto./ 500 RC 15.00
184 Jeremy Griffiths/ Auto./500 15.00
185 Guillermo Quiroz/ Auto./500 RC 15.00
186 Alejandro Machado/ Auto./500 RC 10.00
187 Francisco Cruceta/ Auto./500 RC 15.00
188 Prentice Redman/ Auto./500 RC 15.00
189 Shane Bazzell/ Auto./500 RC 15.00

Chirography

NM/M
Common Autograph: 10.00
Varying quantities produced
Bronze Autos.: 1X
Production 100
Silver Autos.: 1-1.5X
Production 50
Gold Autos.: No Pricing
Production 10
GA1 Garret Anderson/245 15.00
BA Jeff Bagwell/175 50.00
JD Johnny Damon/245 35.00
AD Adam Dunn/170 25.00
JE2 Jim Edmonds/350 20.00
FL Cliff Floyd/125 12.00
FC Rafael Furcal/150 15.00
FG Freddy Garcia/345 15.00
GI Jason Giambi/250 15.00
GL Brian Giles/225 15.00
LG1 Luis Gonzalez/195 15.00
GJ Ken Griffey Jr./350 85.00
JR Ken Griffey Jr./350 85.00
TO Torii Hunter/245 15.00
KE Jason Kendall/145 10.00
MM Mark McGwire/50 275.00
MP Mark Prior/150 40.00
CR Cal Ripken Jr./250 100.00
RO Scott Rolen/345 35.00
TS Tim Salmon/350 20.00
RS Richie Sexson/245 15.00
SA Sammy Sosa/335 75.00
SO Sammy Sosa/335 75.00
IC Ichiro Suzuki/85 350.00
IS Ichiro Suzuki/75 350.00
SW Mike Sweeney/125 15.00
JT1 Jim Thome/250 35.00

Chirography Dodger Stars

NM/M
Common Autograph: 8.00
Bronze Autos.: 1X
Production 100
Silver Autos.: 1-1.5X
Production 50
Gold Autos.: No Pricing
Production 10
BB Bill Buckner/245 10.00
CE Ron Cey/345 15.00
SG Steve Garvey/320 20.00
JN Tommy John/175 15.00
DL Davey Lopes/245 8.00
DN Don Newcombe/345 15.00
BI Bill Russell/245 15.00
DS Duke Snider/345 30.00
SU Don Sutton/345 15.00
MW Maury Wills/320 10.00
SY Steve Yeager/345 15.00

Chirography Double

		NM/M
		40.00
Common Duo Auto.:		40.00
FB	Yogi Berra, Whitey Ford/75	150.00
FE	Carlton Fisk, Dwight Evans/75	65.00
FM	Carlton Fisk, Bill Mazeroski/75	40.00
GG	Jason Giambi, Ken Griffey Jr.	125.00
GR	Steve Garvey, Ron Cey/75	50.00
JI	Ken Griffey Jr., Ichiro Suzuki	350.00
KR	Tony Kubek, Bobby Richardson/75	80.00
KT	Tom Seaver, Jerry Koosman/75	80.00
MG	Don Mattingly, Jason Giambi/25	150.00
MS	Mark McGwire, Sammy Sosa/15	500.00
SJ	Sammy Sosa, Jason Giambi/25	125.00
WB	Bill Buckner, Mookie Wilson/150	40.00

Chirography Flash Backs

		NM/M
Common Autograph:		8.00
Bronze Autos.:		1X
Production 100		
Silver Autos:		1-1.5X
Production 50		
Gold Autos.:		No Pricing
No Pricing		
JE1	Jim Edmonds/350	15.00
CF1	Cliff Floyd/350	8.00
JA	Jason Giambi/350	15.00
BN	Brian Giles/245	10.00
LA	Luis Gonzalez/200	15.00
GM	Ken Griffey Jr./350	80.00
MA	Mark McGwire/55	280.00
SR	Sammy Sosa/350	100.00

Chirography Hall of Famers

		NM/M
Common Autograph:		15.00
Bronze Autos.:		1X
Production 100		
Silver Autos.:		1-1.5X
Production 50		
Gold Autos.:		No Pricing
Production 10		
JB1	Johnny Bench/350	40.00
GC1	Gary Carter/350	20.00
OC	Orlando Cepeda/245	20.00
RF	Rollie Fingers/170	15.00
CF	Carlton Fisk/240	35.00
WF	Whitey Ford/150	40.00
BG	Bob Gibson/245	35.00
TP	Tony Perez/320	20.00
RR	Robin Roberts/170	30.00
NR	Nolan Ryan/170	140.00
TS	Tom Seaver/170	40.00
DS	Duke Snider/250	30.00
DW2	Dave Winfield/350	25.00

Chirography Triple

		NM/M
Quantity produced listed		
BKR	Bobby Richardson, Yogi Berra, Tony Kubek/75	120.00
FCG	Carlton Fisk, Gary Carter, Kirk Gibson/75	75.00

058/150

SP CHIROGRAPHY

GIS	Sammy Sosa, Ichiro Suzuki, Ken Griffey Jr./75	400.00
GLC	Davey Lopes, Ron Cey, Steve Garvey/75	65.00
GRC	Steve Garvey, Ron Cey, Bill Russell/75	60.00
GSG	Sammy Sosa, Jason Giambi, Ken Griffey Jr./75	250.00
GSJ	Ken Griffey Jr., Jason Giambi, Sammy Sosa/75	250.00
ISG	Sammy Sosa, Jason Giambi, Ichiro Suzuki/75	300.00
SEA	Tim Salmon, Garret Anderson, Darin Erstad/75	100.00
SKM	Tom Seaver, Tug McGraw, Jerry Koosman/75	125.00

Chirography Yankee Stars

		NM/M
Common Autograph:		8.00
Bronze Autos.:		1X
Production 100		
Silver Autos.:		1-1.5X
Production 50		
Gold Autos.:		No Pricing
Production 10		
YB	Yogi Berra/320	35.00
JB	Jim Bouton/345	10.00
RC	Roger Clemens/210	100.00
JG	Jason Giambi/275	15.00
KS	Ken Griffey Sr./350	10.00
TH	Tommy Henrich/345	15.00
HK	Ralph Houk/245	12.00
TJ	Tommy John/245	15.00
TK	Tony Kubek/345	20.00
SL	Sparky Lyle/345	10.00
DM	Don Mattingly/295	60.00
BR	Bobby Richardson/320	20.00
ST	Mel Stottlemyre/345	10.00
DW1	Dave Winfield/350	25.00

Chirography Young Stars

		NM/M
Common Autograph:		6.00
Bronze Autos.:		1X
Production 100		
Silver Autos.:		1-1.5X
Production 50		
Gold Autos.:		No Pricing
Production 10		
HB	Hank Blalock/245	25.00
BO	Joe Borchard/245	8.00
SB	Sean Burroughs/245	8.00
MB	Marlon Byrd/245	8.00
HC	Hee Seop Choi/245	20.00
DI1	Ben Diggins/350	8.00
DH	Drew Henson/245	15.00
EH	Eric Hinske/245	10.00
OH	Orlando Hudson/245	15.00
JJ	Jacque Jones/245	15.00
JJ1	Jimmy Journell/350	10.00
JL	Jason Lane/245	6.00
JO	Joe Mays/245	6.00
MI	Doug Mientkiewicz/245	15.00
MY	Brett Myers/245	10.00
CP	Corey Patterson/245	15.00
PE	Carlos Pena/245	10.00
OP	Oliver Perez/245	10.00
JP	Josh Phelps/245	8.00
BP1	Brandon Phillips/350	10.00
AP	A.J. Pierzynski/245	15.00
FS1	Freddy Sanchez/350	15.00

TX	Mark Teixeira/245	25.00
BZ	Barry Zito/350	20.00

Chirography World Series Heroes

		NM/M
Common Autograph:		10.00
Bronze Autos.:		1X
Production 100		
Silver Autos.:		1-1.5X
Production 50		
Gold Autos.:		No Pricing
Production 10		
GA	Garret Anderson/245	15.00
GC	Gary Carter/345	20.00
DE	Darin Erstad/245	15.00
CF	Carlton Fisk/200	40.00
KG	Kirk Gibson/145	15.00
GO	Luis Gonzalez/225	15.00
GS	Ken Griffey Sr./295	10.00
AJ1	Andruw Jones/350	20.00
DJ	David Justice/170	20.00
JK	Jerry Koosman/170	15.00
BM	Bill Mazeroski/245	30.00
TM	Tug McGraw/170	25.00
JP	Jorge Posada/350	35.00
ER	Edgar Renteria/220	15.00
CR	Cal Ripken Jr./295	100.00
TI	Tim Salmon/245	15.00
CS	Curt Schilling/345	30.00

Simply Splendid

		NM/M
Complete Set (30):		200.00
Common Williams:		8.00
Production 406 Sets		

Splendid Jerseys

		NM/M
Production 406 Sets		
TW	Mickey Mantle, Ted Williams	180.00
SJ-TW	Ted Williams	100.00
TW-IS	Ted Williams, Ichiro Suzuki	100.00
TW-JG	Ted Williams, Jason Giambi	60.00
TW-KG	Ted Williams, Ken Griffey Jr.	75.00

TW-MM	Mark McGwire, Ted Williams	110.00
TW-SS	Ted Williams, Sammy Sosa	80.00
TW-NM1	Ted Williams, Nomar Garciaparra	80.00
TW-NM2	Nomar Garciaparra, Ted Williams	80.00

Splendid Signatures

		NM/M
Hand Numbered to 5 or 3.		
GA	Nomar Garciaparra/406	100.00
TW-NM3	Ted Williams, Nomar Garciaparra/3 (10/03 Auction)	2,400

Superstar Flashback

		NM/M
Complete Set (60):		65.00
Common Player:		1.00
Production 2,003 Sets		
SF1	Tim Salmon	1.00
SF2	Darin Erstad	1.00
SF3	Troy Glaus	1.50
SF4	Randy Johnson	2.00
SF5	Curt Schilling	1.50
SF6	Steve Finley	1.00
SF7	Greg Maddux	3.00
SF8	Chipper Jones	3.00
SF9	Andruw Jones	1.50
SF10	Gary Sheffield	1.00
SF11	Manny Ramirez	2.00
SF12	Pedro J. Martinez	2.00
SF13	Nomar Garciaparra	2.50
SF14	Sammy Sosa	3.00
SF15	Frank Thomas	1.50
SF16	Kerry Wood	1.50
SF17	Paul Konerko	1.00
SF18	Corey Patterson	1.00
SF19	Mark Prior	2.00
SF20	Ken Griffey Jr.	3.00
SF21	Adam Dunn	1.50
SF22	Larry Walker	1.00
SF23	Preston Wilson	1.00
SF24	Todd Helton	1.50
SF25	Ivan Rodriguez	1.50
SF26	Josh Beckett	1.00
SF27	Jeff Bagwell	1.50
SF28	Jeff Kent	1.00
SF29	Lance Berkman	1.00
SF30	Carlos Beltran	1.50
SF31	Shawn Green	1.00
SF32	Richie Sexson	1.00
SF33	Vladimir Guerrero	1.50
SF34	Mike Piazza	4.00
SF35	Roberto Alomar	1.50
SF36	Roger Clemens	4.00
SF37	Derek Jeter	6.00
SF38	Jason Giambi	1.50
SF39	Bernie Williams	1.50
SF40	Nick Johnson	1.00
SF41	Alfonso Soriano	3.00
SF42	Miguel Tejada	1.50
SF43	Eric Chavez	1.00
SF44	Barry Zito	1.50
SF45	Jim Thome	1.50
SF46	Pat Burrell	1.00
SF47	Marlon Byrd	1.00
SF48	Jason Kendall	1.00

SF49	Aramis Ramirez	1.50
SF50	Brian Giles	1.00
SF51	Phil Nevin	1.00
SF52	Barry Bonds	6.00
SF53	Ichiro Suzuki	4.00
SF54	Scott Rolen	2.00
SF55	J.D. Drew	1.00
SF56	Albert Pujols	6.00
SF57	Mark Teixeira	1.50
SF58	Hank Blalock	2.00
SF59	Carlos Delgado	1.50
SF60	Roy Halladay	1.00

500 Home Run Club

NM/M

Production 25
500HR Ted Williams,
Barry Bonds,
Mark McGwire,
Sammy Sosa,
Mickey Mantle 325.00

2003 SP Legendary Cuts

NM/M

Complete Set (130):		
Common Player:		.25
Common SP:		3.00
Production 1,299		
Pack (4):		8.00
Box (12):		85.00
1	Luis Aparicio	.25
2	Al Barlick	.25
3	Al Lopez	.25
4	Ernie Banks	1.00
5	Alexander Cartwright	.25
6	Lou Brock	.50
7	Babe Ruth/SP	10.00
8	Bill Dickey	.50
9	Bill Mazeroski	.25
10	Bob Feller	.50
11	Billy Herman	.25
12	Billy Williams	.25
13	Bob Gibson/SP	4.00
14	Bob Lemon	.25
15	Bobby Doerr	.25
16	Branch Rickey	.25
17	Gary Carter	.50
18	Burleigh Grimes	.25
19	Cap Anson	.25
20	Carl Hubbell	.25
21	Carlton Fisk	.50
22	Casey Stengel	.50
23	Charlie Gehringer	.25
24	Chief Bender	.25
25	Christy Mathewson/SP	5.00
26	Cy Young	1.00
27	Dave Winfield	.50
28	Dazzy Vance	.25
29	Dizzy Dean/SP	4.00

30	Don Drysdale/SP	4.00
31	Duke Snider/SP	4.00
32	Earl Averill	.25
33	Earle Combs	.25
34	Edd Roush	.25
35	Earl Weaver	.25
36	Eddie Collins	.25
37	Eddie Plank	.25
38	Elmer Flick	.25
39	Enos Slaughter	.25
40	Ernie Lombardi	.25
41	Ford Frick	.25
42	Jim "Catfish" Hunter	.25
43	Frankie Frisch	.25
44	Gabby Hartnett	.25
45	George Kell	.25
46	Early Wynn	.25
47	Ferguson Jenkins	.25
48	Al Kaline	1.00
49	Harmon Killebrew	1.00
50	Hal Newhouser	.25
51	Hank Greenberg/SP	5.00
52	Harry Caray	.25
53	Tommy Lasorda	.25
54	Honus Wagner/SP	6.00
55	Hoyt Wilhelm/SP	3.00
56	Jackie Robinson/SP	6.00
57	Jim Bottomley	.25
58	Jim Bunning/SP	3.00
59	Jimmie Foxx/SP	6.00
60	Eddie Mathews	1.00
61	Joe Cronin	.25
62	Joe DiMaggio/SP	8.00
63	Joe McCarthy/SP	3.00
64	Joe Morgan/SP	3.00
65	Willie McCovey	.50
66	Joe Tinker	.25
67	Johnny Bench/SP	6.00
68	Johnny Evers/SP	3.00
69	Johnny Mize/SP	3.00
70	Josh Gibson/SP	5.00
71	Juan Marichal	.50
72	Judy Johnson	.25
73	Stan Musial	1.50
74	Kiki Cuyler	.25
75	Larry Doby	.75
76	Nap Lajoie	.25
77	Larry MacPhail	.25
78	Phil Niekro	.25
79	Lefty Gomez/SP	3.00
80	Lefty Grove/SP	3.00
81	Leo Durocher/SP	3.00
82	Leon Day	.25
83	Gaylord Perry/SP	3.00
84	Lou Boudreau	.25
85	Lou Gehrig	3.00
86	Luke Appling	.25
87	Max Carey	.25
88	Mel Allen/SP	3.00
89	Mel Ott/SP	5.00
90	Mickey Cochrane	.50
91	Mickey Mantle	4.00
92	Brooks Robinson	1.00
93	Monte Irvin	.50
94	Nellie Fox	.50
95	Nolan Ryan/SP	10.00
96	Ozzie Smith/SP	6.00
97	Mike Schmidt	2.00
98	Pee Wee Reese/SP	3.00
99	Phil Rizzuto	.75
100	Ralph Kiner	.50
101	Ray Dandridge	.25
102	Richie Ashburn	.50
103	Rick Ferrell	.25
104	Roberto Clemente	2.00
105	Robin Roberts	.25
106	Robin Yount	1.00
107	Rogers Hornsby	.50
108	Rollie Fingers	.25
109	Roy Campanella	.50
110	Rube Marquard	.25
111	Sam Crawford	.25
112	Steve Carlton	.50
113	Satchel Paige/SP	5.00
114	Sparky Anderson	.25
115	Stan Coveleski	.25
116	Red Schoendienst	.25
117	Ted Williams	3.00
118	Tom Seaver	1.00
119	Tom Yawkey	.25
120	Tony Lazzeri	.25
121	Tony Perez	.25
122	Tris Speaker	.25
123	Ty Cobb	2.00
124	Waite Hoyt/SP	3.00
125	Walter Alston	.25
126	Walter Johnson	.75
127	Warren Spahn	1.00
128	Whitey Ford	.75
129	Willie Stargell	.50
130	Yogi Berra	.75

Blue

Non SP's (1-130):		2-4X
SP's:		1-2X
Production 275 Sets		

Green

No pricing due to scarcity.
Production 25 Sets

Autographs

NM/M

Common Player:		
Inserted 1:196		
Many not priced due to scarcity.		
AL	Alexander Cartwright/1	
	(6/05 Auction)	7,800
BD	Bill Dickey/25	
BG	Burleigh Grimes/34	250.00
BI	Billy Herman/30	150.00
BL	Bob Lemon/34	150.00
BL1	Bob Lemon/41	150.00
CH	Carl Hubbell/47	300.00
CH1	Carl Hubbell/63	300.00
EA	Earl Averill/96	125.00
EC	Earle Combs/45	150.00
ES	Enos Slaughter/30	200.00
HC	Harry Caray/29	225.00
HC1	Harry Caray/35	225.00
HG	Hank Greenberg/30	375.00
JD	Joe DiMaggio/50	375.00
JD1	Joe DiMaggio/28	400.00
LB	Lou Boudreau/82	110.00
LB1	Lou Boudreau/49	120.00
LU	Luke Appling/52	150.00
RM	Rube Marquard/40	200.00

Autographs Blue

NM/M

Many not priced due to scarcity.		
EA	Earl Averill/50	125.00
HC1	Harry Caray/35	240.00
HN1	Hal Newhouser	
	B2B/29	125.00
JD1	Joe DiMaggio/40	375.00

Combo Cuts

No Pricing
Production One Set

Etched in Time

NM/M

Common Player:		3.00
Production 400 Sets		
Etched 300:		.5-1X
Production 300		
Etched 175:		.75-1.5X
Production 175		
ME	Mel Allen	3.00
RA	Richie Ashburn	4.00
AB	Al Barlick	3.00
LB	Lou Boudreau	3.00
RO	Roy Campanella	4.00
AC	Alexander Cartwright	3.00
HC	Harry Caray	3.00
RC	Roberto Clemente	10.00
TC	Ty Cobb	6.00
EC	Eddie Collins	3.00
DD	Dizzy Dean	3.00
JD	Joe DiMaggio	8.00
DO	Don Drysdale	3.00
LD	Leo Durocher	3.00
JF	Jimmie Foxx	5.00
LO	Lou Gehrig	8.00
CG	Charlie Gehringer	3.00
JG	Josh Gibson	5.00
LG	Lefty Gomez	3.00
HG	Hank Greenberg	5.00
LE	Lefty Grove	3.00
GH	Gabby Hartnett	3.00
RH	Rogers Hornsby	4.00
CH	Carl Hubbell	3.00
TL	Tony Lazzeri	3.00
EL	Ernie Lombardi	3.00
MM	Mickey Mantle	15.00

CM	Christy Mathewson	8.00
JM	Joe McCarthy	3.00
JO	Johnny Mize	3.00
MO	Mel Ott	4.00
SP	Satchel Paige	5.00
PR	Pee Wee Reese	3.00
JR	Jackie Robinson	5.00
BR	Babe Ruth	10.00
TS	Tris Speaker	3.00
CS	Casey Stengel	3.00
HW	Honus Wagner	5.00
TW	Ted Williams	8.00
CY	Cy Young	5.00

Hall Marks Autographs

NM/M

Inserted 1:196		
Many not priced due to scarcity.		
Greens:		No Pricing
Production 10		
BD1	Bobby Doerr/	
	Black/50	40.00
BM1	Bill Mazeroski/	
	Black/50	40.00
CF1	Carlton Fisk/Black/50	50.00
CY1	Carl Yastrzemski/	
	Black/45	75.00
DS1	Duke Snider/	
	Black/50	40.00
GC1	Gary Carter/Black/50	30.00
GK1	George Kell/Black/50	20.00
JM1	Juan Marichal/	
	Black/50	35.00
JO1	Joe Morgan/Black/75	30.00
LA1	Luis Aparicio/	
	Black/45	30.00
MI1	Monte Irvin/Black/85	30.00
OS1	Ozzie Smith/	
	Black/45	75.00
PR1	Phil Rizzuto/Black/50	40.00
RF1	Rollie Fingers/	
	Black/99	20.00
RK1	Ralph Kiner/Black/50	30.00
RR1	Robin Roberts/	
	Black/55	40.00
RY1	Robin Yount/	
	Black/45	75.00
TP1	Tony Perez/	
	Black/50	30.00
WS1	Warren Spahn/	
	Black/35	70.00
YB1	Yogi Berra/Black/50	60.00

Historic Impressions

NM/M

Common Player:		3.00
Production 350 Sets		
Golds:		1X
Production 200 Sets		
Golds 75:		1.5-2X
Production 75		
Silvers:		1X
Production 250 Sets		
MA	Mel Allen	3.00
RA	Richie Ashburn	5.00
LB	Lou Boudreau	3.00
RO	Roy Campanella	5.00
AC	Alexander Cartwright	3.00
HC	Harry Caray	4.00
RC	Roberto Clemente	15.00
TY	Ty Cobb	8.00

MC	Mickey Cochrane	5.00
EC	Eddie Collins	3.00
DD	Dizzy Dean	5.00
JD	Joe DiMaggio	8.00
DO	Don Drysdale	3.00
LD	Leo Durocher	3.00
JF	Jimmie Foxx	8.00
LO	Lou Gehrig	10.00
CG	Charlie Gehringer	3.00
LG	Lefty Gomez	3.00
HG	Hank Greenberg	6.00
LE	Lefty Grove	6.00
GH	Gabby Hartnett	3.00
RH	Rogers Hornsby	6.00
CH	Carl Hubbell	6.00
TL	Tony Lazzeri	3.00
MM	Mickey Mantle	25.00
CM	Christy Mathewson	6.00
JO	Joe McCarthy	3.00
JM	Johnny Mize	3.00
MO	Mel Ott	6.00
SP	Satchel Paige	6.00
PR	Pee Wee Reese	6.00
JR	Jackie Robinson	8.00
BR	Babe Ruth	15.00
ES	Enos Slaughter	3.00
TS	Tris Speaker	5.00
CS	Casey Stengel	4.00
HW	Honus Wagner	8.00
HO	Hoyt Wilhelm	3.00
TW	Ted Williams	15.00
CY	Cy Young	8.00

Historic Swatches

		NM/M
Common Player:		5.00
Inserted 1:12		
Blues:		.75-1.5X
Production 50 Sets		
Greens:		.75-1X
Production 160 to 250		
Purples:		.75-1.5X
Production 75 to 150		
BG	Bob Gibson CO/ Jsy/350	10.00
BM	Bill Mazeroski/ Pants/50	15.00
BW	Billy Williams/Jsy/190	5.00
CF	Carlton Fisk/ Pants/350	8.00
CM	Christy Mathewson/ Pants/300	100.00
CS	Casey Stengel/ Jsy/275	10.00
CY	Carl Yastrzemski/ Jsy/350	20.00
CY1	Carl Yastrzemski/ Pants/350	20.00
DS	Duke Snider/Jsy/350	10.00
DW1	Dave Winfield/ Twins Jsy/300	8.00
FR	Frank Robinson/ O's Jsy/350	10.00
FR1	Frank Robinson/ Angels Jsy/350	10.00
GC	Gary Carter/ Mets Jsy/350	5.00
GC1	Gary Carter/ Expos Jsy/350	5.00
HW	Honus Wagner/ Pants/275	120.00
JB	Johnny Bench/ Jsy/150	10.00
JM	Joe Morgan/Jsy/350	5.00
JN	Juan Marichal/ Pants/225	5.00
JN1	Juan Marichal/Jsy/48	5.00
LA	Luis Aparicio/Jsy/230	5.00
LB	Lou Boudreau/Jsy/265	5.00
MM	Mickey Mantle/ Pants/350	100.00
NR	Nolan Ryan/ Rgr. Pants/350	25.00
NR1	Nolan Ryan/ Astro Pants/350	25.00
OS	Ozzie Smith/Jsy/85	25.00
RF	Rollie Fingers/ Jsy/105	5.00
RY	Robin Yount/ Portrait/Jsy/350	10.00
RY1	Robin Yount/ Swing/Jsy/350	10.00

SA	Sparky Anderson/ Jsy/350	5.00
SC	Steve Carlton/ Jsy/350	10.00
SM	Stan Musial/Jsy/350	25.00
TC	Ty Cobb/Pants/350	90.00
TP	Tony Perez/Jsy/350	5.00
TS	Tom Seaver/Jsy/350	10.00
TS1	Tom Seaver/ Pants/350	10.00
TW	Ted Williams/ Jsy/250	85.00
WA	Walter Alston/ Look Left/Jsy/350	5.00
WA1	Walter Alston/ Ahead/Jsy/350	5.00
WI	Willie Stargell/Jsy/55	15.00
WS	Warren Spahn/ CO/Jsy/350	15.00
YB	Yogi Berra/Jsy/300	10.00

Historic Lumber

		NM/M
Common Player:		6.00
Inserted 1:12		
BR	Babe Ruth/ Away/150	125.00
BR1	Babe Ruth/ Home/150	125.00
CF	Carlton Fisk/ Red Sox/50	15.00
CF1	Carlton Fisk/ White Sox/50	15.00
CY	Carl Yastrzemski/ w/Bat/300	20.00
CY1	Carl Yastrzemski/ w/Cap/350	20.00
CY2	Carl Yastrzemski/ w/Helmet/350	20.00
DW	Dave Winfield/ Padres/350	10.00
DW1	Dave Winfield/ Yanks/350	10.00
FR	Frank Robinson/ O's/300	10.00
FR1	Frank Robinson/ Reds/350	10.00
FR2	Frank Robinson/ Angels/350	10.00
GC	Gary Carter/Mets/300	6.00
GC1	Gary Carter/ Helmet Expos/100	6.00
GC2	Gary Carter/ Cap Expos/100	6.00
HK	Harmon Killebrew/ 350	10.00
JB	Johnny Bench/ w/Bat/350	10.00
JB1	Johnny Bench/ Swing/350	10.00
JM	Joe Morgan/Reds/350	6.00
JM1	Joe Morgan/ Astros/350	6.00
MM	Mickey Mantle/300	100.00
NR	Nolan Ryan/Rgr./225	25.00
OS	Ozzie Smith/ Cards/300	15.00
OS1	Ozzie Smith/ Padres/350	15.00
RS	Red Schoendienst/ Look Right/165	6.00
RS1	Red Schoendienst/ Look Left/165	6.00
SC	Steve Carlton/350	8.00
TP	Tony Perez/Swing/350	6.00
TP1	Tony Perez/ Portrait/350	6.00
TS	Tom Seaver/100	10.00
TW	Ted Williams/ w/3 Bats/150	75.00
TW1	Ted Williams/ Portrait/150	75.00
WS	Willie Stargell/ Arms Down/150	8.00
WS1	Willie Stargell/ Arms Up/150	8.00
YB	Yogi Berra/Shout/350	10.00
YB1	Yogi Berra/w/Bat/350	10.00

Historic Lumber Green

		NM/M
Common Player:		

BR	Babe Ruth/Away/75	140.00
BR1	Babe Ruth/Home/75	140.00
CY	Carl Yastrzemski/ w/Bat/125	25.00
CY1	Carl Yastrzemski/ w/Cap/125	25.00
CY2	Carl Yastrzemski/ w/Helmet/125	25.00
DW	Dave Winfield/ Padres/125	10.00
DW1	Dave Winfield/ Yanks/125	10.00
FR	Frank Robinson/ O's/125	10.00
FR1	Frank Robinson/ Reds/125	10.00
FR2	Frank Robinson/ Angels/125	10.00
GC	Gary Carter/Mets/125	6.00
GC1	Gary Carter/ Helmet Expos/125	6.00
GC2	Gary Carter/ Cap Expos/125	6.00
HK	Harmon Killebrew/125	10.00
JB	Johnny Bench/ w/Bat/125	10.00
JB1	Johnny Bench/ Swing/125	10.00
JM	Joe Morgan/Reds/125	6.00
JM1	Joe Morgan/ Astros/125	6.00
MM	Mickey Mantle/75	120.00
NR	Nolan Ryan/ Astros/50	50.00
OS	Ozzie Smith/ Cards/125	20.00
OS1	Ozzie Smith/ Padres/125	20.00
RS	Red Schoendienst/ Look Right/125	8.00
RS1	Red Schoendienst/ Look Left/125	8.00
SC	Steve Carlton/125	10.00
TP	Tony Perez/Swing/125	6.00
TP1	Tony Perez/ Portrait/125	6.00
TS	Tom Seaver/50	15.00
TW	Ted Williams/ w/3 Bats/75	75.00
TW1	Ted Williams/ Portrait/75	75.00
WS	Willie Stargell/ Arms Down/125	10.00
WS1	Willie Stargell/ Arms Up/125	10.00
YB	Yogi Berra/Shout/125	10.00
YB1	Yogi Berra/w/Bat/125	10.00

Presidential Cut Signatures

Production between 1-3.
No Pricing

2003 SPx

		NM/M
Complete Set (178):		
Common Player:		.25
Common SP (126-160):		4.00
Production 999		
Common Jsy Auto.		
(161-178):		10.00
Production 1,224 unless noted.		
Pack (4):		6.00
Box (18):		90.00
1	Darin Erstad	.50
2	Garret Anderson	.50
3	Tim Salmon	.50
4	Troy Glaus/SP	2.00
5	Luis Gonzalez	.50
6	Randy Johnson	1.50
7	Curt Schilling	1.00
8	Lyle Overbay	.25
9	Andruw Jones/SP	3.00
10	Gary Sheffield	.75
11	Rafael Furcal	.40
12	Greg Maddux	2.00
13	Chipper Jones/SP	3.00
14	Tony Batista	.25
15	Rodrigo Lopez	.25
16	Jay Gibbons	.25
17	Byung-Hyun Kim	.25

18	Johnny Damon	1.00
19	Derek Lowe	.25
20	Nomar Garciaparra/ SP	4.00
21	Pedro J. Martinez	1.50
22	Manny Ramirez/SP	4.00
23	Mark Prior	1.00
24	Kerry Wood	.50
25	Corey Patterson	.50
26	Sammy Sosa/SP	5.00
27	Moises Alou	.50
28	Magglio Ordonez	.50
29	Frank Thomas	1.00
30	Paul Konerko	.50
31	Bartolo Colon	.25
32	Adam Dunn	1.00
33	Austin Kearns	.50
34	Aaron Boone	.25
35	Ken Griffey Jr./SP	5.00
36	Omar Vizquel	.50
37	C.C. Sabathia	.25
38	Jason Davis	.25
39	Travis Hafner	.75
40	Brandon Phillips	.25
41	Larry Walker	.50
42	Preston Wilson	.50
43	Jay Payton	.25
44	Todd Helton	.75
45	Carlos Pena	.25
46	Eric Munson	.25
47	Ivan Rodriguez	1.00
48	Josh Beckett	.50
49	Alex Gonzalez	.25
50	Roy Oswalt	.50
51	Craig Biggio	.50
52	Jeff Bagwell	.75
53	Dontrelle Willis/SP	2.00
54	Mike Sweeney	.25
55	Carlos Beltran	1.00
56	Brent Mayne	.25
57	Hideo Nomo	.75
58	Rickey Henderson	.75
59	Adrian Beltre	.50
60	Miguel Cabrera/SP	4.00
61	Kazuhisa Ishii	.25
62	Ben Sheets	.50
63	Richie Sexson	.50
64	Torii Hunter/SP	2.00
65	Jacque Jones	.25
66	Joe Mays	.25
67	Corey Koskie	.25
68	A.J. Pierzynski	.25
69	Jose Vidro	.25
70	Vladimir Guerrero/SP	4.00
71	Tom Glavine	.50
72	Jose Reyes/SP	4.00
73	Aaron Heilman	.25
74	Mike Piazza	2.00
75	Jorge Posada	.75
76	Mike Mussina	.75
77	Robin Ventura	.25
78	Mariano Rivera	.75
79	Roger Clemens/SP	6.00
80	Jason Giambi	.75
81	Bernie Williams	.75
82	Alfonso Soriano/SP	4.00
83	Derek Jeter	3.00
84	Miguel Tejada/SP	3.00
85	Eric Chavez	.50
86	Tim Hudson	.50
87	Barry Zito	.50
88	Mark Mulder	.50
89	Erubiel Durazo	.25
90	Pat Burrell	.50
91	Jim Thome/SP	3.00
92	Bobby Abreu	.50
93	Brian Giles	.50
94	Reggie Sanders/SP	2.00
95	Kenny Lofton	.50
96	Ryan Klesko	.25
97	Sean Burroughs	.25
98	Edgardo Alfonzo	.25
99	Rich Aurilia	.25
100	Jose Cruz Jr.	.25
101	Barry Bonds/SP	8.00
102	Mike Cameron	.25
103	Kazuhiro Sasaki	.25
104	Bret Boone	.25
105	Ichiro Suzuki/SP	5.00
106	J.D. Drew	.50
107	Jim Edmonds	.50
108	Scott Rolen/SP	3.00
109	Matt Morris	.25
110	Tino Martinez	.25
111	Albert Pujols/SP	8.00
112	Damian Rolls	.25
113	Carl Crawford	.50
114	Rocco Baldelli/SP	2.00
115	Hank Blalock	.50
116	Alex Rodriguez/SP	5.00
117	Kevin Mench	.25
118	Rafael Palmeiro	.75
119	Mark Teixeira	.75
120	Shannon Stewart	.25

121	Vernon Wells	.50
122	Josh Phelps	.25
123	Eric Hinske	.25
124	Orlando Hudson	.25
125	Carlos Delgado/SP	3.00
126	Jason Roach RC	4.00
127	Dan Haren	10.00
128	Luis Ayala RC	4.00
129	Bo Hart RC	4.00
130	Wilfredo Ledezma RC	4.00
131	Rick Roberts RC	4.00
132	Miguel Ojeda RC	4.00
133	Aquilino Lopez RC	4.00
134	Roger Deago RC	4.00
135	Arnie Munoz RC	4.00
136	Brent Hoard RC	4.00
137	Terrmel Sledge RC	4.00
138	Ryan Cameron RC	4.00
139	Prentice Redman RC	6.00
140	Clint Barmes RC	6.00
141	Jeremy Griffiths RC	4.00
142	Jon Leicester RC	4.00
143	Brandon Webb RC	15.00
144	Todd Wellemeyer RC	4.00
145	Felix Sanchez RC	4.00
146	Anthony Ferrari RC	4.00
147	Ian Ferguson RC	4.00
148	Micheal Nakamura RC	4.00
149	Lew Ford RC	8.00
150	Nate Bland RC	4.00
151	Dave Matranga RC	4.00
152	Edgar Gonzalez RC	4.00
153	Carlos Mendez RC	4.00
154	Jason Gilfillan RC	4.00
155	Mike Neu RC	4.00
156	Jason Shiell RC	4.00
157	Jeff Duncan RC	4.00
158	Oscar Villarreal RC	4.00
159	Diegomar Markwell RC	4.00
160	Joe Valentine RC	4.00
161	Hideki Matsui/864 RC	300.00
162	Jose Contreras/800 RC	20.00
163	Willie Eyre RC	10.00
164	Matt Bruback RC	10.00
165	Rett Johnson RC	15.00
166	Jeremy Griffiths RC	15.00
167	Francisco Cruceta RC	10.00
168	Fernando Cabrera RC	10.00
169	Jhonny Peralta RC	25.00
170	Shane Bazzell RC	10.00
171	Bobby Madritsch RC	20.00
172	Phil Seibel RC	10.00
173	Josh Willingham RC	20.00
174	Robby Hammock RC	10.00
175	Alejandro Machado RC	10.00
176	David Sanders RC	10.00
177	Matt Kata RC	15.00
178	Heath Bell RC	4.00

Spectrum

Stars (1-125) print run 51-99: 3-6X
Stars (1-125) p/r 26-50: 6-12X
Print run 25 or less not priced.
Numbered to jersey number.
SP's (126-160): .75-1.5X
Production 125

SPX Combos

NM/M
Common Duo: 20.00
Quantity produced listed

MJ	Hideki Matsui, Derek Jeter/90	100.00
RC	Nolan Ryan, Roger Clemens/90	120.00
SJ	Curt Schilling, Randy Johnson/90	
EG	Darin Erstad, Troy Glaus/90	20.00
GC	Greg Maddux, Chipper Jones/90	50.00
GS	Jason Giambi, Alfonso Soriano/90	30.00
BK	Jeff Bagwell, Jeff Kent/90	25.00
GD	Ken Griffey Jr., Adam Dunn/90	50.00
GR	Ken Griffey Jr., Sammy Sosa/90	50.00
SP	Sammy Sosa, Rafael Palmeiro/90	40.00
MG	Pedro Martinez, Nomar Garciaparra/90	40.00
RY	Nolan Ryan, Pedro Martinez/10	
RG	Alex Rodriguez, Nomar Garciaparra/90	40.00
CM	Jose Contreras, Pedro Martinez/90	40.00
FC	Carlton Fisk, Gary Carter/90	30.00
RR	Cal Ripken Jr., Scott Rolen/90	80.00
JJ	Chipper Jones, Andruw Jones/90	30.00
PM	Rafael Palmeiro, Fred McGriff/90	30.00
RT	Alex Rodriguez, Miguel Tejada/90	30.00
SB	Sammy Sosa, Barry Bonds/90	50.00
SN	Ichiro Suzuki, Hideo Nomo/90	175.00
MS	Hideki Matsui, Ichiro Suzuki/50	350.00
MW	Mickey Mantle, Ted Williams/50	300.00
CC	Jose Contreras, Roger Clemens/50	40.00
CL	Cal Ripken Jr., Lou Gehrig/90	300.00
HJ	Hideki Matsui, Jason Giambi/50	75.00
CA	Cal Ripken Jr., Alex Rodriguez/50	150.00
IA	Ichiro Suzuki, Albert Pujols/50	250.00
NI	Hideo Nomo, Kazuhisa Ishii/50	50.00
MD	Mickey Mantle, Derek Jeter/50	180.00
BT	Barry Bonds, Ted Williams/50	180.00
BM	Barry Bonds, Roger Maris/50	80.00
MB	Mickey Mantle, Barry Bonds/50	150.00
PS	Rafael Palmeiro, Sammy Sosa/90	40.00
RS	Nolan Ryan, Tom Seaver/90	110.00

Stars

NM/M
Common Player: 20.00
Quantity produced listed

LB	Lance Berkman/590	30.00
PB	Pat Burrell/590	25.00
NM	Nomar Garciaparra/195	80.00
JG	Jason Giambi/315	30.00
TG	Troy Glaus/490	25.00
LG	Luis Gonzalez/790	20.00
KG	Ken Griffey Jr./690	80.00
VG	Vladimir Guerrero/390	50.00
CJ	Chipper Jones/195	50.00
MP	Mark Prior/490	40.00
CS	Curt Schilling/490	40.00

Winning Materials

NM/M
Common Player: 5.00
Version 1 Production 375
Golds: 1X
Production 250
Version 2 Production 175
Golds: 1-2X
Production 50

RA1	Roberto Alomar	8.00
RA2	Roberto Alomar	10.00
JB1	Jeff Bagwell	6.00
JB2	Jeff Bagwell	8.00
LB1	Lance Berkman	5.00
LB2	Lance Berkman	5.00
PB1	Pat Burrell	6.00
PB2	Pat Burrell	8.00
RC1	Roger Clemens	15.00
RC2	Roger Clemens	15.00
CD1	Carlos Delgado	6.00
CD2	Carlos Delgado	8.00
RF1	Rafael Furcal	6.00
RF2	Rafael Furcal	8.00
JG1	Jason Giambi	8.00
JG2	Jason Giambi	8.00
TR1	Troy Glaus	6.00
TG2	Troy Glaus	8.00
TG1	Tom Glavine	5.00
TG2	Tom Glavine	6.00
LG1	Luis Gonzalez	5.00
LG2	Luis Gonzalez	5.00
SG1	Shawn Green	5.00
SG2	Shawn Green	5.00
KG1	Ken Griffey Jr.	15.00
KG2	Ken Griffey Jr.	15.00
VG1	Vladimir Guerrero	10.00
VG2	Vladimir Guerrero	12.00
TO1	Todd Helton	8.00
TH2	Todd Helton	10.00
TH1	Torii Hunter	8.00
RJ1	Randy Johnson	10.00
RJ2	Randy Johnson	12.00
AJ1	Andruw Jones	8.00
AJ2	Andruw Jones	8.00
CJ1	Chipper Jones	10.00
CJ2	Chipper Jones	15.00
JK1	Jeff Kent	5.00
JK2	Jeff Kent	5.00
GM1	Greg Maddux	15.00
GM2	Greg Maddux	15.00
MM2	Mickey Mantle	120.00
PM1	Pedro Martinez	10.00
PM2	Pedro Martinez	15.00
HM1	Hideki Matsui	30.00
HM2	Hideki Matsui	30.00
HN1	Hideo Nomo	15.00
HN2	Hideo Nomo	20.00
MP1	Mike Piazza	10.00
MP2	Mike Piazza	15.00
MA1	Mark Prior	10.00
MP2	Mark Prior	10.00
AP1	Albert Pujols	20.00
AP2	Albert Pujols	20.00
MR1	Manny Ramirez	10.00
MR2	Manny Ramirez	10.00
AR1	Alex Rodriguez	10.00
AR2	Alex Rodriguez	12.00
IR1	Ivan Rodriguez	8.00
IR2	Ivan Rodriguez	10.00
CS1	Curt Schilling	8.00
CS2	Curt Schilling	10.00
GS1	Gary Sheffield	6.00
GS2	Gary Sheffield	8.00
AS1	Alfonso Soriano	10.00
AS2	Alfonso Soriano	12.00
SS1	Sammy Sosa	10.00
SS2	Sammy Sosa	15.00
IS1	Ichiro Suzuki	25.00
IS2	Ichiro Suzuki	35.00
MT1	Miguel Tejada	6.00
MT2	Miguel Tejada	8.00
FT1	Frank Thomas	8.00
FT2	Frank Thomas	10.00
JT1	Jim Thome	8.00
JT2	Jim Thome	10.00
BW1	Bernie Williams	8.00
BW2	Bernie Williams	10.00
TW2	Ted Williams	80.00
TW2	Ted Williams/Gold/50	200.00
BZ1	Barry Zito	6.00
BZ2	Barry Zito	8.00

Young Stars

NM/M
Common Player: 8.00
Production 1,295 unless noted.

KA	Kurt Ainsworth/1,460	8.00
RB	Rocco Baldelli	8.00
JBa	Josh Bard	8.00
HB	Hank Blalock	20.00
SB	Sean Burroughs	8.00
MD	Michael Cuddyer/1,156	10.00
AD	Adam Dunn	20.00
CG	Chris George/1,260	8.00
EH	Eric Hinske	8.00
JA	Jason Jennings	8.00
NJ	Nick Johnson	8.00
JJ	Jacque Jones/1,260	12.00
AK	Austin Kearns/964	15.00
MK	Mike Kinkade	8.00
BM	Brett Myers	8.00
RO	Roy Oswalt	15.00
JP	Josh Phelps	10.00
BP	Brandon Phillips	10.00
KS	Kirk Saarloos	8.00
MT	Mark Teixeira	25.00

2004 SP Authentic

NM/M

Complete Set (191):		
Common (1-90):		.25
Common RC		
(91-132, 178-191):		4.00
Production 999		
Common SP (133-177):		2.00
Production 999		
Pack (5):		5.00
Box (24):		100.00
1	Bret Boone	.25
2	Gary Sheffield	.50
3	Rafael Palmeiro	.75
4	Jorge Posada	.50
5	Derek Jeter	3.00
6	Garret Anderson	.50
7	Bartolo Colon	.40
8	Kevin Brown	.40
9	Shea Hillenbrand	.25
10	Ryan Klesko	.25
11	Bobby Abreu	.50
12	Scott Rolen	1.00
13	Alfonso Soriano	.75
14	Jason Giambi	1.00
15	Tom Glavine	.50
16	Hideo Nomo	.50
17	Johan Santana	.75
18	Sammy Sosa	1.00
19	Rickie Weeks	.50
20	Barry Zito	.50
21	Kerry Wood	.50
22	Austin Kearns	.40
23	Shawn Green	.40
24	Miguel Cabrera	1.00
25	Richard Hidalgo	.25
26	Andruw Jones	.75
27	Randy Wolf	.25
28	David Ortiz	1.00
29	Roy Oswalt	.50
30	Vernon Wells	.50
31	Ben Sheets	.50
32	Mike Lowell	.25
33	Todd Helton	.75
34	Jacque Jones	.25
35	Mike Sweeney	.25
36	Hank Blalock	.50
37	Jason Schmidt	.50
38	Jeff Kent	.40
39	Josh Beckett	.50
40	Manny Ramirez	1.00
41	Torii Hunter	.50
42	Brian Giles	.40
43	Javier Vazquez	.25
44	Jim Edmonds	.50
45	Dmitri Young	.25
46	Preston Wilson	.25
47	Jeff Bagwell	.75
48	Pedro J. Martinez	1.00
49	Eric Chavez	.40
50	Ken Griffey Jr.	2.00
51	Shannon Stewart	.25
52	Rafael Furcal	.40
53	Brandon Webb	.25
54	Juan Pierre	.25
55	Roger Clemens	2.00
56	Geoff Jenkins	.25
57	Lance Berkman	.50
58	Albert Pujols	3.00
59	Frank Thomas	.75
60	Edgar Martinez	.40
61	Tim Hudson	.50
62	Eric Gagne	.50
63	Richie Sexson	.50
64	Corey Patterson	.25
65	Nomar Garciaparra	1.00
66	Hideki Matsui	2.00

#	Player	Price
67	Mark Teixeira	.75
68	Troy Glaus	.50
69	Carlos Lee	.40
70	Mike Mussina	.75
71	Magglio Ordonez	.50
72	Roy Halladay	.50
73	Ichiro Suzuki	2.00
74	Randy Johnson	1.00
75	Luis Gonzalez	.40
76	Mark Prior	.75
77	Carlos Beltran	.50
78	Ivan Rodriguez	.75
79	Alex Rodriguez	2.50
80	Dontrelle Willis	.50
81	Mike Piazza	1.00
82	Curt Schilling	.75
83	Vladimir Guerrero	1.00
84	Greg Maddux	1.50
85	Jim Thome	1.00
86	Miguel Tejada	.50
87	Carlos Delgado	.50
88	Jose Reyes	.75
89	Matt Morris	.25
90	Mark Mulder	.40
91	Angel Chavez RC	4.00
92	Brandon Medders RC	4.00
93	Carlos Vasquez RC	4.00
94	Chris Aguila RC	4.00
95	Colby Miller RC	4.00
96	David Crouthers	4.00
97	Dennis Sarfate RC	4.00
98	Donnie Kelly RC	4.00
99	Merkin Valdez RC	6.00
100	Eddy Rodriguez RC	4.00
101	Edwin Moreno RC	4.00
102	Enemencio Pacheco RC	4.00
103	Roberto Novoa RC	4.00
104	Greg Dobbs RC	4.00
105	Hector Gimenez RC	4.00
106	Ian Snell RC	10.00
107	Jake Woods	4.00
108	Jamie Brown RC	4.00
109	Jason Frasor RC	4.00
110	Jerome Gamble RC	4.00
111	Jerry Gil RC	6.00
112	Jesse Harper RC	4.00
113	Jorge Vasquez RC	4.00
114	Jose Capellan RC	6.00
115	Josh Labandeira RC	4.00
116	Justin Hampson RC	4.00
117	Justin Huisman RC	4.00
118	Justin Leone RC	6.00
119	Lincoln Holdzkom RC	4.00
120	Lino Urdaneta RC	4.00
121	Mike Gosling RC	4.00
122	Mike Johnston RC	4.00
123	Mike Rouse	4.00
124	Scott Proctor RC	4.00
125	Roman Colon RC	4.00
126	Ronny Cedeno RC	10.00
127	Ryan Meaux RC	4.00
128	Scott Dohmann RC	4.00
129	Sean Henn	6.00
130	Tim Bausher RC	4.00
131	Tim Bittner RC	4.00
132	William Bergolla RC	6.00
133	Rick Ferrell	2.00
134	Joe DiMaggio	6.00
135	Bob Feller	2.00
136	Ted Williams	6.00
137	Stan Musial	5.00
138	Larry Doby	2.00
139	Red Schoendienst	2.00
140	Enos Slaughter	2.00
141	Stan Musial	5.00
142	Mickey Mantle	8.00
143	Ted Williams	6.00
144	Mickey Mantle	8.00
145	Stan Musial	5.00
146	Tom Seaver	3.00
147	Willie McCovey	2.00
148	Bob Gibson	3.00
149	Frank Robinson	3.00
150	Joe Morgan	2.00
151	Billy Williams	2.00
152	Catfish Hunter	2.00
153	Joe Morgan	2.00
154	Joe Morgan	2.00
155	Mike Schmidt	5.00
156	Tommy Lasorda	2.00
157	Robin Yount	4.00
158	Nolan Ryan	8.00
159	John Franco	2.00
160	Nolan Ryan	8.00
161	Ken Griffey Jr.	4.00
162	Cal Ripken Jr.	8.00
163	Ken Griffey Jr.	5.00
164	Gary Sheffield	2.00
165	Fred McGriff	2.00
166	Hideo Nomo	2.00
167	Mike Piazza	2.00
168	Sandy Alomar Jr.	2.00
169	Roberto Alomar	2.00
170	Ted Williams	6.00
171	Pedro J. Martinez	4.00
172	Derek Jeter	8.00
173	Cal Ripken Jr.	8.00
174	Torii Hunter	2.00
175	Alfonso Soriano	3.00
176	Hank Blalock	2.00
177	Ichiro Suzuki	4.00
178	Orlando Rodriguez RC	4.00
179	Ramon Ramirez RC	4.00
180	Kazuo Matsui RC	6.00
181	Kevin Cave RC	4.00
182	John Gall RC	4.00
183	Freddy Guzman RC	4.00
184	Chris Oxspring RC	4.00
185	Rusty Tucker RC	4.00
186	Jorge Sequea RC	4.00
187	Carlos Hines RC	4.00
188	Luis Gonzalez	4.00
189	Ryan Wing	4.00
190	Jeff Bennett RC	4.00
191	Luis Gonzalez	4.00

Silver

Stars (1-90): 2-4X
Production 499
SP (91-132, 178-191): 1X
Production 249

Gold

Stars (1-90): 4-8X
Gold SP (91-132, 178-191): 2X
Production 99
Gold (133-177): 1-1.5X
Production 499

Future Watch Autograph

NM/M

#	Player	Price
	Production 295	8.00
91	Angel Chavez	8.00
92	Brandon Medders	8.00
93	Carlos Vasquez	10.00
94	Chris Aguila	8.00
95	Colby Miller	10.00
96	David Crouthers	10.00
97	Dennis Sarfate	8.00
98	Donnie Kelly	10.00
99	Merkin Valdez	15.00
100	Eddy Rodriguez	15.00
101	Edwin Moreno	10.00
102	Enemencio Pacheco	10.00
103	Roberto Novoa	8.00
104	Greg Dobbs	8.00
105	Hector Gimenez	8.00
106	Ian Snell	30.00
107	Jake Woods	10.00
108	Jamie Brown	8.00
109	Jason Frasor	10.00
110	Jerome Gamble	8.00
111	Jerry Gil	12.00
112	Jesse Harper	8.00
113	Jorge Vasquez	12.00
114	Jose Capellan	10.00
115	Josh Labandeira	10.00
116	Justin Hampson	8.00
117	Justin Huisman	8.00
118	Justin Leone	15.00
119	Lincoln Holdzkom	8.00
120	Lino Urdaneta	10.00
121	Mike Gosling	10.00
122	Mike Johnston	10.00
123	Mike Rouse	10.00
124	Scott Proctor	15.00
125	Roman Colon	10.00
126	Ronny Cedeno	15.00
127	Ryan Meaux	10.00
128	Scott Dohmann	8.00
129	Sean Henn	15.00
130	Tim Bausher	10.00
131	Tim Bittner	8.00
132	William Bergolla	10.00
178	Orlando Rodriguez	10.00
179	Ramon Ramirez	10.00
180	Kazuo Matsui	10.00
181	Kevin Cave	10.00
182	John Gall	15.00
183	Freddy Guzman	10.00
184	Chris Oxspring	10.00
185	Rusty Tucker	10.00
186	Jorge Sequea	10.00
187	Carlos Hines	8.00
188	Luis Gonzalez	10.00
189	Ryan Wing	10.00
190	Jeff Bennett	10.00
191	Luis Gonzalez	10.00

Chirography

NM/M

Bronze: 1X — Production 65
Bronze Duo Tone: 1X — Production 60
Gold: 1-1.5X — Production 40
Gold Duo Tone: No Pricing — Production 20
Silver: 1X — Production 30
Silver Duo Tone: 1.5-2X — Production 30
Duo Tone: 1X — Production 75

Code	Player	Price
AB	Bobby Abreu	15.00
GA	Garret Anderson	15.00
RB	Rocco Baldelli	20.00
JB	Josh Beckett	20.00
CB	Carlos Beltran	30.00
HB	Hank Blalock	20.00
BB	Bret Boone	20.00
MC	Miguel Cabrera	40.00
EC	Eric Chavez	20.00
DE	Dennis Eckersley	30.00
WE	Willie Eyre	8.00
EG	Eric Gagne	30.00
JG	Juan Gonzalez	20.00
KG	Ken Griffey Jr.	120.00
TH	Travis Hafner	15.00
HY	Roy Halladay	20.00
HA	Robby Hammock	10.00
BH	Bo Hart	8.00
HE	Runelvys Hernandez	8.00
HI	Bobby Hill	10.00
DJ	Derek Jeter	150.00
JJ	Jacque Jones	15.00
AK	Austin Kearns	15.00
CL	Cliff Lee	15.00
AL	Al Leiter	15.00
PL	Paul LoDuca	15.00
JL	Javy Lopez	15.00
ML	Mike Lowell	15.00
EM	Edgar Martinez	25.00
RO	Roy Oswalt	20.00
PA	Corey Patterson	15.00
PI	Mike Piazza	125.00
CP	Colin Porter	10.00
JP	Jorge Posada	25.00
MP	Mark Prior	30.00
HR	Horacio Ramirez	15.00
JR	Jose Reyes	35.00
CR	Cal Ripken Jr.	100.00
JS	Jae Weong Seo	15.00
BS	Ben Sheets	20.00
SM	John Smoltz	60.00
MT	Mark Teixeira	25.00
JV	Javier Vazquez	20.00
CW	Chien-Ming Wang	125.00
RW	Rickie Weeks	20.00
BW	Brandon Webb	15.00
VW	Vernon Wells	15.00
JW	Jerome Williams	10.00
DW	Dontrelle Willis	30.00
KW	Kerry Wood	25.00
DY	Delmon Young	25.00
BZ	Barry Zito	20.00

Chirography Dual

NM/M

Common Duo: 40.00
Production 50 Sets

Code	Players	Price
BC	Bret Boone, Eric Chavez	50.00
BL	Mike Lowell, Josh Beckett	50.00
BP	Corey Patterson, Carlos Beltran	50.00
BT	Hank Blalock, Mark Teixeira	50.00
EG	Dennis Eckersley, Eric Gagne	50.00
HW	Vernon Wells, Roy Halladay	40.00
JM	Johnny Bench, Mike Piazza	200.00
KG	Ken Griffey Jr., Austin Kearns	100.00
PB	Yogi Berra, Jorge Posada	100.00
RR	Alex Rodriguez, Cal Ripken Jr.	400.00
SG	Ken Griffey Jr., Ichiro Suzuki	375.00
SM	Stan Musial, Ozzie Smith	175.00
WC	Miguel Cabrera, Dontrelle Willis	70.00
WJ	Chien-Ming Wang, Derek Jeter	350.00
WR	Nolan Ryan, Kerry Wood	225.00
WW	Dontrelle Willis, Brandon Webb	50.00
YW	Delmon Young, Rickie Weeks	50.00
ZC	Eric Chavez, Barry Zito	50.00

Chirography Quad

No Pricing
Production 10 Sets

Chirography Triple

NM/M

Production 25 Sets

Code	Players	Price
BWR	Kerry Wood, Nolan Ryan, Josh Beckett	250.00
FBB	Johnny Bench, Carlton Fisk, Yogi Berra	300.00
GSM	Bob Gibson, Stan Musial, Ozzie Smith	220.00
JVB	Derek Jeter, Yogi Berra, Javier Vazquez	250.00
PRC	Jose Reyes, Miguel Cabrera, Colin Porter	100.00
RBT	Hank Blalock, Mark Teixeira, Alex Rodriguez	250.00
RRR	Alex Rodriguez, Cal Ripken Jr., Phil Rizzuto	400.00
SJB	Rocco Baldelli, Jacque Jones, Ichiro Suzuki	275.00
WLE	Chien-Ming Wang, Willie Eyre, Cliff Lee	275.00
WPB	Mark Prior, Josh Beckett, Brandon Webb	250.00
YYM	Robin Yount, Carl Yastrzemski, Stan Musial	300.00
ZHO	Barry Zito, Roy Oswalt, Roy Halladay	200.00

Chirography Hall of Famers

NM/M

Production 40 Sets
Duo Tone: No Pricing
Production 25

Code	Player	Price
LA	Luis Aparicio	20.00
JB	Johnny Bench	60.00
YB	Yogi Berra	50.00

BD	Bobby Doerr	30.00
DE	Dennis Eckersley	30.00
CF	Carlton Fisk	30.00
BG	Bob Gibson	40.00
MI	Monte Irvin	20.00
AK	Al Kaline	50.00
HK	Harmon Killebrew	65.00
RK	Ralph Kiner	25.00
PM	Paul Molitor	30.00
SM	Stan Musial	100.00
TP	Tony Perez	30.00
KP	Kirby Puckett	100.00
PR	Phil Rizzuto	40.00
RR	Robin Roberts	40.00
BR	Brooks Robinson	40.00
NR	Nolan Ryan	120.00
MS	Mike Schmidt	120.00
TS	Tom Seaver	40.00
OS	Ozzie Smith	65.00
DS	Duke Snider	30.00
CY	Carl Yastrzemski	75.00
RY	Robin Yount	75.00

USA Signature

NM/M

Production 445 Sets

Reds:		1.5X
Production 50		
USA-1	Ernie Young	6.00
USA-2	Chris Burke	12.00
USA-3	Jesse Crain	15.00
USA-4	Justin Duchscherer	15.00
USA-5	J.D. Durbin	10.00
USA-6	Gerald Laird	10.00
USA-7	John Grabow	8.00
USA-8	Gabe Gross	15.00
USA-9	J.J. Hardy	15.00
USA-10	Jeremy Reed	15.00
USA-11	Graham Koonce	10.00
USA-12	Mike Lamb	10.00
USA-13	Justin Leone	15.00
USA-14	Ryan Madson	12.00
USA-15	Joe Mauer	40.00
USA-16	Todd Williams	6.00
USA-17	Horacio Ramirez	15.00
USA-18	Mike Rouse	15.00
USA-19	Jason Stanford	10.00
USA-20	John Van Benschoten	10.00
USA-21	Grady Sizemore	40.00

2004 SP Game-Used Patch

NM/M

Complete Set (119):		
Common (1-60):		2.00
Common (61-90):		2.00
Quantity produced listed		
Common (91-119):		6.00
Production 375		
Box (1:Pack):		125.00
1	Miguel Cabrera	4.00
2	Alex Rodriguez	10.00
3	Edgar Renteria	2.50
4	Juan Gonzalez	2.50
5	Mike Lowell	2.50
6	Andruw Jones	3.00
7	Eric Chavez	2.00
8	Jim Edmonds	2.00
9	Mike Piazza	5.00
10	Angel Berroa	2.00
11	Eric Gagne	3.00
12	Jody Gerut	2.00
13	Orlando Cabrera	2.00
14	Austin Kearns	2.00
15	Frank Thomas	3.00
16	Johan Santana	3.00
17	Randy Johnson	4.00
18	Preston Wilson	2.00
19	Garret Anderson	2.50

20	Jorge Posada	3.00
21	Rich Harden	2.00
22	Barry Zito	2.50
23	Gary Sheffield	3.00
24	Jose Reyes	3.00
25	Roy Halladay	2.00
26	Ben Sheets	2.00
27	Geoff Jenkins	2.00
28	Josh Beckett	3.00
29	Roy Oswalt	2.50
30	Bobby Abreu	2.50
31	Hank Blalock	2.50
32	Kerry Wood	2.50
33	Ryan Klesko	2.00
34	Rafael Furcal	2.00
35	Tom Glavine	2.50
36	Kevin Brown	2.00
37	Scott Rolen	3.00
38	Bret Boone	2.00
39	Ichiro Suzuki	6.00
40	Lance Berkman	3.00
41	Tim Hudson	2.00
42	Carlos Delgado	3.00
43	Ivan Rodriguez	3.00
44	Luis Gonzalez	2.00
45	Torii Hunter	2.00
46	Carlos Lee	2.00
47	Jacque Jones	2.00
48	Manny Ramirez	3.00
49	Troy Glaus	2.50
50	Corey Patterson	2.00
51	Jason Schmidt	2.50
52	Mark Mulder	2.00
53	Vernon Wells	2.00
54	Curt Schilling	4.00
55	Javy Lopez	2.50
56	Mark Prior	3.50
57	Dontrelle Willis	2.00
58	Derek Jeter	10.00
59	Jeff Bagwell	3.00
60	Marlon Byrd	2.00
61	Rafael Palmeiro/500	3.00
62	Kevin Millwood/165	2.00
63	Greg Maddux/273	6.00
64	Adam Dunn/400	3.00
65	Richie Sexson/469	3.00
66	Magglio Ordonez/567	2.00
67	Hideo Nomo/236	2.00
68	Albert Pujols/194	10.00
69	Rocco Baldelli/368	3.00
70	Mark Teixeira/86	4.00
71	Jason Giambi/660	3.00
72	Alfonso Soriano/230	4.00
73	Roger Clemens/307	8.00
74	Miguel Tejada/359	2.00
75	Jeff Kent/684	2.00
76	Bernie Williams/342	3.00
77	Sammy Sosa/470	6.00
78	Mike Mussina/641	3.00
79	Jim Thome/334	4.00
80	Brian Giles/506	2.00
81	Shawn Green/234	2.00
82	Mike Sweeney/340	2.00
83	John Smoltz/262	3.00
84	Carlos Beltran/319	3.00
85	Todd Helton/384	3.00
86	Nomar Garciaparra/372	4.00
87	Ken Griffey Jr./481	8.00
88	Chipper Jones/633	4.00
89	Vladimir Guerrero/226	4.00
90	Pedro Martinez/313	5.00
91	Brandon Medders RC	6.00
92	Colby Miller RC	6.00
93	David Crouthers RC	6.00
94	Dennis Sarfate RC	8.00
95	Donald Kelly RC	6.00
96	Alec Zumwalt RC	6.00
97	Chris Aguila RC	6.00
98	Greg Dobbs RC	6.00
99	Ian Snell RC	10.00
100	Jake Woods	6.00
101	Jamie Brown RC	6.00
102	Jason Frasor RC	6.00
103	Jerome Gamble RC	6.00
104	Jesse Harper RC	6.00
105	Josh Labandeira RC	6.00
106	Justin Hampson RC	6.00
107	Justin Huisman RC	6.00
108	Justin Leone RC	6.00
109	Lincoln Holdzkom RC	6.00
110	Mike Bumatay RC	6.00
111	Mike Gosling RC	6.00
112	Mike Johnston RC	6.00
113	Mike Rouse	6.00
114	Nick Regilio RC	6.00
115	Ryan Meaux RC	6.00
116	Scott Dohmann RC	6.00
117	Sean Henn	8.00
118	Tim Bausher RC	6.00
119	Tim Bittner RC	6.00

All-Star Patch Autograph

Production 10 Sets

All-Star Patch Auto-Dual

Production 10 Sets

All-Star Patch Gold

NM/M

Production 50 Sets

AP	Albert Pujols	75.00
AR	Alex Rodriguez	50.00
AS	Alfonso Soriano	25.00
BZ	Barry Zito	25.00
CD	Carlos Delgado	20.00
CJ	Chipper Jones	30.00
CS	Curt Schilling	35.00
DJ	Derek Jeter	85.00
EC	Eric Chavez	20.00
FT	Frank Thomas	30.00
GS	Gary Sheffield	20.00
HE	Todd Helton	25.00
HN	Hideo Nomo	50.00
IS	Ichiro Suzuki	80.00
JG	Juan Gonzalez	20.00
JT	Jim Thome	30.00
KG	Ken Griffey Jr.	50.00
MP	Mark Prior	30.00
SS	Sammy Sosa	40.00
TH	Tim Hudson	25.00
VW	Vernon Wells	20.00

All-Star Patch Number

NM/M

Quantity produced listed

AJ	Andruw Jones/25	30.00
AP	Andy Pettitte/46	25.00
BZ	Barry Zito/50	30.00
CD	Carlos Delgado/25	25.00
CS	Curt Schilling/38	40.00
FT	Frank Thomas/35	40.00
GM	Greg Maddux/31	50.00
IS	Ichiro Suzuki/50	65.00
JG	Juan Gonzalez/19	35.00
JP	Jorge Posada/20	30.00
JT	Jim Thome/25	30.00
KG	Ken Griffey Jr./30	60.00
MM	Mike Mussina/35	30.00
MO	Magglio Ordonez/30	25.00
PM	Pedro Martinez/45	35.00
RC	Roger Clemens/22	50.00
RH	Roy Halladay/32	25.00
RP	Rafael Palmeiro/25	30.00
SG	Shawn Green/15	30.00
SR	Scott Rolen/27	35.00
SS	Sammy Sosa/21	80.00

Famous Nicknames

NM/M

Quantity produced listed

BR	Brooks Robinson/23	25.00
CR	Cal Ripken Jr./21	140.00
CY	Carl Yastrzemski/23	70.00
DM	Don Mattingly/14	50.00
DS	Darryl Strawberry/17	25.00
ES	Duke Snider/18	45.00
FT	Frank Thomas/14	40.00
GA	Sparky Anderson/27	25.00
GC	Gary Carter/19	30.00
HK	Harmon Killebrew/22	50.00
JF	Nellie Fox/19	120.00
JG	Juan Gonzalez/15	35.00
JH	"Catfish" Hunter/15	35.00
KG	Ken Griffey Jr./15	80.00
LB	Yogi Berra/19	50.00
MM	Mike Mussina/13	35.00
NR	Nolan Ryan/27	60.00
OC	Orlando Cepeda/17	25.00
OS	Ozzie Smith/19	60.00

PN	Phil Niekro/24	25.00
RC	Roger Clemens/20	60.00
RI	Phil Rizzuto/13	50.00
RJ	Randy Johnson/16	40.00
RY	Robin Yount/20	40.00
TS	Tom Seaver/20	60.00
SM	Stan Musial/22	85.00
SS	Sammy Sosa/15	50.00
WS	Willie Stargell/21	40.00

Famous Nicknames Autograph

NM/M

Production 50 Sets

AD	Andre Dawson	45.00
AR	Alex Rodriguez	150.00
BM	Bill Mazeroski	65.00
BR	Brooks Robinson	60.00
DM	Don Mattingly	120.00
FT	Frank Thomas	70.00
HK	Harmon Killebrew	70.00
HM	Hideki Matsui	350.00
JB	Jeff Bagwell	80.00
JG	Juan Gonzalez	50.00
KG	Ken Griffey Jr.	160.00
LJ	Chipper Jones	80.00
MM	Mike Mussina	60.00
NR	Nolan Ryan	125.00
OS	Ozzie Smith	90.00
PN	Phil Niekro	45.00
RC	Roger Clemens	150.00
RY	Robin Yount	80.00
TS	Tom Seaver	65.00
WI	Dontrelle Willis	60.00

Hall of Fame Numbers

NM/M

Quantity produced listed

AJ	Andruw Jones/25	30.00
BG	Bob Gibson/45	35.00
BW	Billy Williams/26	20.00
CD	Carlos Delgado/25	25.00
CH	Jim "Catfish" Hunter/27	40.00
CL	Roger Clemens/22	50.00
CS	Curt Schilling/38	25.00
DD	Don Drysdale/50	35.00
DS	Don Sutton/20	75.00
EG	Eric Gagne/38	25.00
EM	Eddie Mathews/41	50.00
FR	Frank Robinson/20	25.00
FT	Frank Thomas/35	40.00
GL	Tom Glavine/47	25.00
GM	Greg Maddux/31	45.00
GO	Juan Gonzalez/35	35.00
GP	Gaylord Perry/36	25.00
HE	Todd Helton/17	35.00
IS	Ichiro Suzuki/50	65.00
JC	Jose Canseco/33	25.00
JG	Jason Giambi/25	30.00
JI	Jim Thome/25	30.00
JP	Jim Palmer/22	35.00
KG	Ken Griffey Jr./30	60.00
MA	Juan Marichal/27	25.00
MP	Mike Piazza/31	40.00
MR	Manny Ramirez/24	30.00
MS	Mike Schmidt/20	60.00
MZ	Pedro Martinez/45	25.00
NR	Nolan Ryan/34	70.00
OC	Orlando Cepeda/30	20.00
PI	Mark Prior/22	40.00
RC	Roberto Clemente/21	200.00
RF	Rollie Fingers/34	25.00
RH	Rickey Henderson/25	40.00
RP	Rafael Palmeiro/25	30.00
RY	Robin Yount/19	45.00
SC	Steve Carlton/32	30.00
SG	Shawn Green/15	25.00
SR	Scott Rolen/27	30.00
SS	Sammy Sosa/21	50.00
TG	Tony Gwynn/19	45.00
TH	Tim Hudson/15	25.00
TS	Tom Seaver/41	25.00
WB	Wade Boggs/26	30.00
WS	Warren Spahn/21	65.00

Hall of Fame Numbers Autograph

Production 10 Sets

Hall of Fame Numbers Autograph Dual

Production 10 Sets

Historic Cut Signatures

Production One Set

Legendary Fabrics

		NM/M
Production 50 unless noted.		20.00
BE	Johnny Bench	25.00
BG	Bob Gibson	30.00
BW	Billy Williams	25.00
CH	"Catfish" Hunter	25.00
CR	Cal Ripken Jr.	60.00
CY	Carl Yastrzemski/31	45.00
EM	Eddie Mathews	35.00
FR	Frank Robinson	25.00
GP	Gaylord Perry	20.00
HK	Harmon Killebrew	40.00
JC	Jose Canseco	40.00
JM	Joe Morgan	20.00
JT	Joe Torre	25.00
LA	Luis Aparicio	25.00
LD	Leo Durocher	30.00
MS	Mike Schmidt	40.00
NR	Nolan Ryan	50.00
OC	Orlando Cepeda	20.00
OS	Ozzie Smith	35.00
PO	Paul O'Neill	20.00
RF	Rollie Fingers	20.00
RY	Robin Yount	35.00
SC	Steve Carlton	25.00
TS	Tom Seaver	30.00
WS	Warren Spahn	40.00

Legendary Fabrics Autograph Dual

		NM/M
Production 25 unless noted.		
AD	Andre Dawson	60.00
BE	Johnny Bench	90.00
BM	Bill Mazeroski/10	
BR	Brooks Robinson	90.00
BW	Billy Williams	65.00
CR	Cal Ripken Jr.	275.00
CY	Carl Yastrzemski/17	125.00
DE	Dwight Evans	60.00
DM	Don Mattingly	150.00
DS	Don Sutton	65.00
FL	Fred Lynn	70.00
FR	Frank Robinson	75.00
GP	Gaylord Perry	40.00
HK	Harmon Killebrew	100.00
JC	Jose Canseco	100.00
JM	Joe Morgan	50.00
JP	Jim Palmer	60.00
JT	Joe Torre	70.00
KP	Kirby Puckett	100.00
LA	Luis Aparicio	70.00
LB	Lou Brock/13	125.00
NR	Nolan Ryan	200.00
OC	Orlando Cepeda	50.00
OS	Ozzie Smith	100.00
PM	Paul Molitor	75.00
PO	Paul O'Neill	70.00
RC	Roger Clemens	150.00
RF	Rollie Fingers	65.00
RY	Robin Yount	120.00
SG	Steve Garvey	60.00
ST	Darryl Strawberry	65.00
TG	Tony Gwynn	120.00
TS	Tom Seaver	85.00
WB	Wade Boggs	100.00
WI	Maury Wills	50.00

Legendary Combo Cuts

Production One Set

Logo Threads

No Pricing
Production One Set

Logo Threads Autograph

Masters

No Pricing
Production One Set

		NM/M
Quantity produced listed		
AJ	Andruw Jones/25	25.00
BE	Josh Beckett/25	40.00
CD	Carlos Delgado/25	25.00
CS	Curt Schilling/38	25.00
FT	Frank Thomas/35	30.00
GM	Greg Maddux/31	45.00
GO	Juan Gonzalez/19	30.00
HE	Todd Helton/17	35.00
IS	Ichiro Suzuki/50	65.00
JG	Jason Giambi/25	30.00
JP	Jorge Posada/20	30.00
JT	Jim Thome/25	30.00
KG	Ken Griffey Jr./30	60.00
MO	Magglio Ordonez/30	20.00
MP	Mark Prior/22	30.00
MR	Manny Ramirez/24	25.00
PI	Mike Piazza/31	40.00
PM	Pedro Martinez/45	25.00
RC	Roger Clemens/22	50.00
RH	Roy Halladay/32	25.00
SG	Shawn Green/31	25.00
SR	Scott Rolen/27	30.00
SS	Sammy Sosa/21	50.00
TH	Tim Hudson/15	25.00
VW	Vernon Wells/10	

MVP Patch

		NM/M
Production 25 Sets		
AR	Alex Rodriguez	60.00
BR	Brooks Robinson	50.00
BW	Bernie Williams	35.00
CJ	Chipper Jones	40.00
CR	Cal Ripken Jr.	90.00
CS	Curt Schilling	35.00
DJ	Derek Jeter	75.00
FT	Frank Thomas	40.00
GA	Garret Anderson	30.00
IS	Ichiro Suzuki	75.00
IV	Ivan Rodriguez	40.00
JB	Josh Beckett	30.00
JG	Jason Giambi	30.00
KG	Ken Griffey Jr.	60.00
MP	Mike Piazza	50.00
MT	Miguel Tejada	40.00
PM	Pedro Martinez	45.00
RC	Roger Clemens	60.00
RJ	Randy Johnson	40.00
SS	Sammy Sosa	40.00
TG	Troy Glaus	25.00

Premium Patch

		NM/M
Production 50 unless noted.		
AD	Adam Dunn	30.00
AP	Albert Pujols	50.00
AR	Alex Rodriguez	50.00
AR1	Alex Rodriguez/Yankees	65.00
AS	Alfonso Soriano/34	35.00
BE	Josh Beckett	25.00
BW	Bernie Williams	25.00
BZ	Barry Zito	25.00
CD	Carlos Delgado	25.00
CJ	Chipper Jones	35.00
CS	Curt Schilling	25.00
DJ	Derek Jeter	60.00
DW	Dontrelle Willis	25.00
EC	Eric Chavez	20.00
FT	Frank Thomas	40.00
GM	Greg Maddux	40.00
GO	Juan Gonzalez	25.00
HM	Hideki Matsui/17	120.00
IR	Ivan Rodriguez	30.00
IS	Ichiro Suzuki	65.00
JB	Jeff Bagwell	30.00

		NM/M
JG	Jason Giambi	30.00
JP	Jorge Posada	30.00
JT	Jim Thome	30.00
KB	Kevin Brown	20.00
KG	Ken Griffey Jr.	50.00
MO	Magglio Ordonez	20.00
MP	Mark Prior	30.00
MR	Manny Ramirez	30.00
MT	Miguel Tejada	20.00
PI	Mike Piazza	35.00
NR	Nolan Ryan	50.00
PM	Pedro Martinez	30.00
RC	Roger Clemens	40.00
RH	Roy Halladay	20.00
RI	Mariano Rivera	30.00
RJ	Randy Johnson	30.00
RP	Rafael Palmeiro	30.00
SG	Shawn Green	20.00
SR	Scott Rolen	30.00
SS	Sammy Sosa	35.00
TE	Mark Teixeira	20.00
TG	Tom Glavine	25.00
TH	Tim Hudson	25.00

Premium Patch Autograph

		NM/M
Production 50 unless noted.		
AK	Austin Kearns	45.00
AR	Alex Rodriguez	150.00
BZ	Barry Zito	60.00
CD	Carlos Delgado	50.00
DW	Dontrelle Willis	60.00
EC	Eric Chavez	40.00
EG	Eric Gagne	60.00
HM	Hideki Matsui	350.00
IR	Ivan Rodriguez	80.00
IS	Ichiro Suzuki	300.00
KB	Kevin Brown	45.00
KG	Ken Griffey Jr.	160.00
MP	Mark Prior	60.00
MT	Miguel Tejada	50.00
NG	Nomar Garciaparra/33	140.00
RC	Roger Clemens	150.00
SG	Shawn Green	50.00
TH	Tim Hudson	50.00
TG	Troy Glaus	50.00
VG	Vladimir Guerrero	75.00

Significant Numbers

		NM/M
Quantity produced listed		
CR	Cal Ripken Jr./21	120.00
CS	Curt Schilling/16	40.00
CY	Carl Yastrzemski/23	65.00
DS	Darryl Strawberry/17	25.00
EM	Eddie Mathews/17	50.00
FT	Frank Thomas/14	50.00
GM	Greg Maddux/18	50.00
GO	Juan Gonzalez/15	40.00
GS	Gary Sheffield/16	30.00
JB	Jeff Bagwell/13	50.00
KG	Ken Griffey Jr./15	75.00
NR	Nolan Ryan/27	60.00
PO	Paul O'Neill/17	25.00
RC	Roger Clemens/20	50.00
RF	Rollie Fingers/17	25.00
RJ	Randy Johnson/16	35.00
RP	Rafael Palmeiro/18	40.00
SN	Duke Snider/18	50.00
SS	Sammy Sosa/15	60.00
TG	Tom Glavine/17	30.00
TS	Tom Seaver/20	40.00

Significant Numbers Autograph

		NM/M
Production 50 unless noted.		
AR	Alex Rodriguez	150.00
BA	Bobby Abreu	40.00
BG	Brian Giles	40.00
BW	Bernie Williams	100.00
BZ	Barry Zito	60.00
CD	Carlos Delgado	50.00
CJ	Chipper Jones	90.00
EC	Eric Chavez	40.00
EG	Eric Gagne	60.00
GM	Greg Maddux	110.00
HE	Todd Helton	60.00
GO	Juan Gonzalez	50.00
HM	Hideki Matsui	350.00
KB	Kevin Brown	45.00
KG	Ken Griffey Jr.	160.00
KP	Kirby Puckett/3	
LB	Lou Brock/16	60.00
LG	Luis Gonzalez	50.00
MM	Mike Mussina	60.00
MP	Mike Piazza	185.00
MS	Mike Schmidt	90.00
MT	Miguel Tejada	50.00
NR	Nolan Ryan	140.00

		NM/M
PB	Pat Burrell	40.00
PO	Paul O'Neill	65.00
PR	Mark Prior	60.00
RA	Roberto Alomar	60.00
RB	Rocco Baldelli	55.00
RF	Rollie Fingers	40.00
RO	Roy Oswalt	60.00
RP	Rafael Palmeiro	70.00
RS	Ryne Sandberg	90.00
SG	Shawn Green	50.00
TG	Tom Glavine	60.00
TH	Tim Hudson	50.00
VG	Vladimir Guerrero	75.00

Significant Numbers Autograph Dual

		NM/M
Production 25 unless noted.		
AR	Alex Rodriguez	200.00
BA	Bobby Abreu	50.00
BG	Brian Giles	50.00
BW	Bernie Williams	120.00
BZ	Barry Zito	80.00
CD	Carlos Delgado	70.00
CJ	Chipper Jones	100.00
DW	Dontrelle Willis	60.00
EC	Eric Chavez	65.00
EG	Eric Gagne	80.00
GI	Bob Gibson	100.00
GL	Troy Glaus	70.00
GM	Greg Maddux	140.00
HE	Todd Helton	85.00
GO	Juan Gonzalez	60.00
HM	Hideki Matsui	500.00
KB	Kevin Brown	65.00
KG	Ken Griffey Jr.	200.00
KP	Kirby Puckett	100.00
LB	Lou Brock/14	85.00
LG	Luis Gonzalez	50.00
MM	Mike Mussina	80.00
MP	Mike Piazza	200.00
MS	Mike Schmidt	160.00
MT	Miguel Tejada	50.00
NR	Nolan Ryan	200.00
PB	Pat Burrell	50.00
PO	Paul O'Neill	80.00
RA	Roberto Alomar	80.00
RF	Rollie Fingers	65.00
RP	Rafael Palmeiro	100.00
RS	Ryne Sandberg	150.00
SG	Shawn Green	60.00
TG	Tom Glavine	80.00
TH	Tim Hudson	75.00
VG	Vladimir Guerrero	100.00
TO	Tony Gwynn	120.00
TS	Tom Seaver	85.00

Star Potential Patch

		NM/M
Quantity produced listed		
BW	Brandon Webb/50	25.00
CP	Corey Patterson/20	25.00
DW	Dontrelle Willis/35	30.00
HA	Roy Halladay/32	30.00
IS	Ichiro Suzuki/50	65.00
HB	Josh Beckett/21	30.00
LB	Lance Berkman/17	30.00
MM	Mark Mulder/20	30.00
MP	Mark Prior/22	30.00
MT	Mark Teixeira/23	25.00
RH	Rich Harden/40	25.00
RO	Roy Oswalt/44	25.00
RW	Rickie Weeks/23	25.00
TG	Troy Glaus/25	30.00
TH	Tim Hudson/15	30.00

Stellar Combos

		NM/M
Production 25 unless noted.		
AD	Derek Jeter, Alfonso Soriano	75.00
AJ	Alex Rodriguez, Juan Gonzalez	50.00
AT	Jim Thome, Bobby Abreu	40.00
BK	Jeff Bagwell, Jeff Kent	30.00
BT	Mark Teixeira, Hank Blalock	40.00
CA	Roberto Alomar, Joe Carter	60.00

CO	Roger Clemens, Roy Oswalt	60.00
CR	Randy Johnson, Curt Schilling	40.00
DG	Jason Giambi, Carlos Delgado	40.00
DK	Austin Kearns, Adam Dunn	40.00
GH	Eric Gagne, Trevor Hoffman	40.00
GT	Greg Maddux, Tom Glavine	65.00
JJ	Andruw Jones, Chipper Jones	50.00
KR	Nolan Ryan, Jerry Koosman	100.00
LP	Mike Piazza, Al Leiter	50.00
LS	Fred Lynn, Ichiro Suzuki	75.00
MG	Don Mattingly, Jason Giambi	80.00
MT	Frank Thomas, Edgar Martinez	50.00
MY	Paul Molitor, Robin Yount	60.00
NB	Hideo Nomo, Kevin Brown	40.00
NY	Alfonso Soriano, Jose Reyes	40.00
PC	Mark Prior, Roger Clemens	60.00
PE	Albert Pujols, Jim Edmonds	80.00
PM	Mike Mussina, Andy Pettitte	50.00
PP	Mike Piazza, Jorge Posada	60.00
PS	Sammy Sosa, Rafael Palmeiro	50.00
RB	Ivan Rodriguez, Josh Beckett	50.00
RJ	Alex Rodriguez, Derek Jeter	100.00
RR	Alex Rodriguez, Cal Ripken Jr.	180.00
RS	Mike Schmidt, Brooks Robinson	85.00
SG	Shawn Green, Duke Snider	40.00
SJ	Randy Johnson, Gary Sheffield	40.00
SM	Pedro Martinez, Curt Schilling	50.00
SR	Nolan Ryan, Curt Schilling	75.00
TO	Frank Thomas, Magglio Ordonez	60.00
WC	Roger Clemens, David Wells	50.00
WH	Larry Walker, Todd Helton	45.00
WS	Sammy Sosa, Billy Williams	60.00
ZH	Barry Zito, Tim Hudson	50.00
RJ	Alex Rodriguez, Derek Jeter	100.00
RG	Cal Ripken Jr., Lou Gehrig	350.00
SC	Ty Cobb, Ichiro Suzuki	180.00

Team Threads
Production 10 unless noted.

Triple Authentic
Production 10

World Series Stars
NM/M
Production 50 unless noted.

AJ	Andruw Jones	25.00
AP	Andy Pettitte/15	40.00
AS	Alfonso Soriano/15	35.00
BL	Barry Larkin	25.00
BW	Bernie Williams	25.00
CA	Jose Canseco	30.00
CJ	Chipper Jones	30.00
CS	Curt Schilling	25.00
CY	Carl Yastrzemski/31	95.00
DW	Dontrelle Willis	20.00
GA	Garret Anderson	25.00
GL	Troy Glaus	30.00
GM	Greg Maddux	40.00
HM	Hideki Matsui/17	140.00
IR	Ivan Rodriguez	30.00
JB	Josh Beckett	25.00
JE	Derek Jeter	60.00
JM	Joe Morgan	25.00
JP	Jorge Posada	30.00
JT	Jim Thome	25.00
KB	Kevin Brown	20.00
MM	Mike Mussina/43	25.00
MP	Mike Piazza	35.00
MR	Mariano Rivera	30.00
MS	Mike Schmidt	40.00
PM	Paul Molitor	30.00
PO	Paul O'Neill	20.00
RC	Roger Clemens	40.00
RF	Rollie Fingers	25.00
RJ	Randy Johnson	30.00
TG	Tom Glavine	25.00

World Series Stars Autograph
No Pricing
Production One Set

300 Win Club
Production 10 Sets

Autographed 300 Win Club
Production 10 Sets

3000 Hit Club
Production 10 Sets

3000 Hit Club Autograph
Production 10 Sets

500 HR Club
Production 10 Sets

Autographed 500 HR Club
Production 10 Sets

500 HR Club Triple Patches
Production 10 Sets

2004 SP Legendary Cuts

NM/M

Complete Set (126):		
Common Player:		.40
Pack (4):		12.00
Box (12):		120.00
1	Al Kaline	1.00
2	Al Lopez	.40
3	Alan Trammell	.40
4	Andre Dawson	.40
5	Babe Ruth	3.00
6	Bert Campaneris	.40
7	Bill Mazeroski	.40
8	Bill Russell	.40
9	Billy Williams	.40
10	Bob Feller	.50
11	Bob Gibson	.75
12	Bob Lemon	.40
13	Bobby Doerr	.40
14	Brooks Robinson	1.00
15	Cal Ripken Jr.	3.00
16	Carl Yastrzemski	1.00
17	Carlton Fisk	.40
18	Jim "Catfish" Hunter	.40
19	Dale Murphy	.40
20	Darryl Strawberry	.40
21	Dave Concepcion	.40
22	Dave Winfield	.50
23	Dennis Eckersley	.40
24	Denny McLain	.40
25	Don Drysdale	.50
26	Don Larsen	.50
27	Don Mattingly	2.00
28	Don Sutton	.40
29	Duke Snider	1.00
30	Dusty Baker	.40
31	Dwight Gooden	.40
32	Earl Weaver	.40
33	Early Wynn	.40
34	Eddie Mathews	1.00
35	Eddie Murray	.75
36	Enos Slaughter	.40
37	Ernie Banks	1.50
38	Fergie Jenkins	.40
39	Frank Robinson	.75
40	Fred Lynn	.40
41	Gary Carter	.50
42	Gaylord Perry	.40
43	George Brett	2.00
44	George Foster	.40
45	George Kell	.40
46	Greg Luzinski	.40
47	Hal Newhouser	.40
48	Hank Greenberg	1.00
49	Harmon Killebrew	1.00
50	Honus Wagner	1.00
51	Hoyt Wilhelm	.40
52	Jackie Robinson	1.50
53	Jim Bunning	.40
54	Jim Palmer	.75
55	Jimmie Foxx	1.00
56	Joe Carter	.40
57	Joe DiMaggio	2.00
58	Joe Morgan	.40
59	Joe Torre	.40
60	Johnny Bench	1.00
61	Johnny Podres	.40
62	John Roseboro	.40
63	Johnny Sain	.40
64	Juan Marichal	.50
65	Keith Hernandez	.40
66	Kirby Puckett	.75
67	Kirk Gibson	.40
68	Will Clark	.50
69	Jim Rice	.40
70	Larry Doby	.40
71	Lou Boudreau	.40
72	Lou Brock	.50
73	Lou Gehrig	2.50
74	Lou Piniella	.40
75	Luis Aparicio	.40
76	Mark Grace	.50
77	Mel Ott	.40
78	Mickey Lolich	.40
79	Mickey Mantle	3.00
80	Mike Greenwell	.40
81	Mike Schmidt	2.00
82	Monte Irvin	.40
83	Nellie Fox	.50
84	Nolan Ryan	3.00
85	Orlando Cepeda	.40
86	Ozzie Smith	1.00
87	Paul Molitor	.75
88	Pee Wee Reese	.40
89	Phil Niekro	.40
90	Phil Rizzuto	.75
91	Ralph Kiner	.75
92	Red Rolfe	.40
93	Red Schoendienst	.40
94	Reggie Smith	.40
95	Rich "Goose" Gossage	.40
96	Richie Ashburn	.40
97	Rick Ferrell	.40
98	Elston Howard	.40
99	Roberto Clemente	2.00
100	Robin Roberts	.40
101	Robin Yount	1.00
102	Roger Maris	2.00
103	Rollie Fingers	.40
104	Ron Santo	.40
105	Roy Campanella	.75
106	Ryne Sandberg	1.50
107	Sparky Anderson	.40
108	Sparky Lyle	.40
109	Stan Musial	2.00
110	Steve Carlton	.50
111	Steve Garvey	.40
112	Ted Williams	2.50
113	Thurman Munson	1.00
114	Tom Seaver	1.00
115	Tommy Henrich	.40
116	Tommy Lasorda	.40
117	Tony Gwynn	1.00
118	Tony Perez	.40
119	Ty Cobb	1.50
120	Wade Boggs	.50
121	Warren Spahn	.75
122	Whitey Ford	.75
123	Willie McCovey	.40
124	Willie Randolph	.40
125	Willie Stargell	.50
126	Yogi Berra	.75

All-Time Autographs
NM/M
Production 50 Sets

LA	Luis Aparicio	20.00
YB	Yogi Berra	65.00
WB	Wade Boggs	40.00
SC	Steve Carlton	20.00
GC	Gary Carter	25.00
JC	Joe Carter	20.00
OC	Orlando Cepeda	25.00
WC	Will Clark	40.00
BD	Bobby Doerr	20.00
DE	Dennis Eckersley	20.00
RF	Rollie Fingers	20.00
CF	Carlton Fisk	30.00
WF	Whitey Ford	40.00
TG	Tony Gwynn	50.00
MI	Monte Irvin	25.00
FJ	Fergie Jenkins	20.00
AK	Al Kaline	40.00
GK	George Kell	25.00
HK	Harmon Killebrew	40.00
FL	Fred Lynn	15.00
MA	Don Mattingly	60.00
BM	Bill Mazeroski	50.00
WM	Willie McCovey	40.00
MC	Denny McLain	30.00
DM	Dale Murphy	30.00
SM	Stan Musial	80.00
DN	Don Newcombe	25.00
PN	Phil Niekro	20.00
TP	Tony Perez	25.00
GP	Gaylord Perry	20.00
JP	Johnny Podres	20.00
CR	Cal Ripken Jr.	125.00
RR	Robin Roberts	30.00
NR	Nolan Ryan	125.00
SA	Ryne Sandberg	75.00
RS	Red Schoendienst	25.00
TS	Tom Seaver	50.00
DS	Don Sutton	15.00
BW	Billy Williams	20.00
MW	Maury Willis	20.00
RY	Robin Yount	75.00

Game Graphs
NM/M
Production 25 Sets
Gold: No Pricing
Production 10 Sets

LA	Luis Aparicio	25.00
EB	Ernie Banks	75.00
JB	Johnny Bench	80.00
YB	Yogi Berra	80.00
WB	Wade Boggs	50.00
GB	George Brett	100.00
LB	Lou Brock	40.00
SC	Steve Carlton	30.00
GC	Gary Carter	35.00
JC	Joe Carter	30.00
RF	Rollie Fingers	25.00
CF	Carlton Fisk	50.00
BG	Bob Gibson	40.00
TG	Tony Gwynn	65.00
AK	Al Kaline	50.00
HK	Harmon Killebrew	50.00
JM	Juan Marichal	35.00
MA	Don Mattingly	80.00
BM	Bill Mazeroski	50.00
WM	Willie McCovey	50.00
PM	Paul Molitor	40.00
MO	Joe Morgan	40.00
DM	Dale Murphy	40.00
EM	Eddie Murray	85.00
SM	Stan Musial	100.00
PN	Phil Niekro	30.00
KP	Kirby Puckett	75.00
CR	Cal Ripken Jr.	180.00
PR	Phil Rizzuto	40.00
BR	Brooks Robinson	50.00
FR	Frank Robinson	40.00
NR	Nolan Ryan	175.00
RS	Ryne Sandberg	85.00
MS	Mike Schmidt	80.00
TS	Tom Seaver	60.00
OS	Ozzie Smith	75.00
SN	Duke Snider	50.00
DS	Don Sutton	20.00
BW	Billy Williams	25.00
DW	Dave Winfield	35.00
CY	Carl Yastrzemski	80.00
RY	Robin Yount	85.00

Historic Patches
NM/M
Production 25 Sets

EB	Ernie Banks	50.00
JB	Johnny Bench	
GB	George Brett	60.00
DD	Don Drysdale	40.00
BG	Bob Gibson	25.00
TG	Tony Gwynn	50.00
EM	Eddie Mathews	30.00
SM	Stan Musial	60.00
CR	Cal Ripken Jr.	100.00
NR	Nolan Ryan	75.00
TS	Tom Seaver	50.00
DS	Duke Snider	50.00
CY	Carl Yastrzemski	60.00
RY	Robin Yount	50.00

Historic Quads
No Pricing
Production 10 Sets

Historic Swatches

		NM/M
	Common Swatch:	4.00
	Golds:	2-3X
Production 25 Sets		
AN	Sparky Anderson	4.00
JB	Johnny Bench/SP	10.00
GB	George Brett	12.00
LB	Lou Brock	8.00
GC	Gary Carter	6.00
JC	Joe Carter	6.00
DC	Dave Concepcion	4.00
DD	Don Drysdale	8.00
RF	Rollie Fingers	6.00
CF	Carlton Fisk	8.00
GF	George Foster	4.00
SG	Steve Garvey	4.00
CH	Jim "Catfish" Hunter	6.00
FJ	Fergie Jenkins	8.00
HK	Harmon Killebrew	10.00
DL	Don Larsen SP	10.00
ML	Mickey Lolich	4.00
SL	Sparky Lyle	4.00
MA	Eddie Mathews	10.00
DM	Don Mattingly	15.00
PM	Paul Molitor	6.00
JM	Joe Morgan	6.00
TM	Thurman Munson	12.00
MU	Dale Murphy	8.00
EM	Eddie Murray/SP	10.00
SM	Stan Musial	20.00
PN	Phil Niekro	6.00
GP	Gaylord Perry	6.00
JP	Johnny Podres	6.00
KP	Kirby Puckett	10.00
JR	Jim Rice	8.00
CR	Cal Ripken Jr.	20.00
BR	Brooks Robinson	8.00
NR	Nolan Ryan	20.00
TS	Tom Seaver	8.00
OS	Ozzie Smith	10.00
DS	Don Sutton	4.00
HW	Hoyt Wilhelm	4.00
DW	Dave Winfield	6.00
RY	Robin Yount	8.00

Historical Cuts

Quantity Produced Listed
No Pricing

Legendary Cuts

		NM/M
Quantity produced listed		
WA	Walter Alston/74	200.00
LU	Luke Appling/108	150.00
RA	Richie Ashburn/31	350.00
LB	Lou Boudreau/199	125.00
EC	Earle Combs/27	350.00
ST	Stan Coveleski/102	150.00
RD	Ray Dandridge/199	125.00
DD	Dizzy Dean/33	650.00
BD	Bill Dickey/82	250.00
JD	Joe DiMaggio/111	500.00
DO	Larry Doby/14	400.00
DR	Don Drysdale/66	450.00
LD	Leo Durocher/75	400.00
RF	Rick Ferrell/44	160.00
WF	Wes Ferrell/36	200.00
FF	Frankie Frisch/57	450.00
CG	Charlie Gehringer/171	200.00
LG	Lefty Gomez/98	325.00
HG	Hank Greenberg/37	500.00
BU	Burleigh Grimes/83	200.00
GR	Lefty Grove/75	375.00
GH	Gabby Hartnett/19	475.00
BH	Billy Herman/134	125.00
WH	Waite Hoyt/106	200.00
CH	Carl Hubbell/199	180.00
JH	Jim "Catfish" Hunter/25	220.00
BJ	"Indian" Bob Johnson/32	200.00
HK	Harvey Kuenn/49	150.00
BL	Bob Lemon/199	100.00
EL	Ernie Lombardi/39	450.00
TL	Ted Lyons/199	150.00
RU	Rube Marquard/59	220.00
JM	Joe Medwick/32	450.00
MI	Johnny Mize/171	140.00
HN	Hal Newhouser/51	140.00
KN	Kid Nichols/4	2,500

SP	Satchel Paige/28	1,325
GP	George Pipgras/46	200.00
PR	Pee Wee Reese/35	350.00
SR	Sam Rice/28	500.00
ER	Edd Roush/129	125.00
RR	Red Ruffing/30	500.00
JS	Joe Sewell/199	140.00
GS	George Sisler/32	850.00
ES	Enos Slaughter/147	125.00
WS	Willie Stargell/39	220.00
WM	Hoyt Wilhelm/115	100.00
SW	"Smokey" Joe Wood/79	400.00
EW	Early Wynn/54	200.00

Legendary Duels

		NM/M
Production 25 Sets		
BG	George Brett, Rich "Goose" Gossage	40.00
DW	Joe DiMaggio, Ted Williams	150.00
EG	Dennis Eckersley, Kirk Gibson	25.00
FM	Joe Morgan, Carlton Fisk	30.00
GL	Bob Gibson, Mickey Lolich	30.00
MW	Mickey Mantle, Ted Williams	200.00
PL	Johnny Podres, Don Larsen	30.00
RM	Juan Marichal, John Roseboro	25.00
RR	Pee Wee Reese, Phil Rizzuto	35.00
SM	Duke Snider, Mickey Mantle	125.00
SS	Ryne Sandberg, Ozzie Smith	80.00
WB	Ernie Banks, Honus Wagner	125.00

Legendary Duels Patch

No Pricing
Production 15 Sets

Legendary Duos

		NM/M
Production 25 Sets		
CM	Joe Morgan, Dave Concepcion	20.00
DM	Joe DiMaggio, Mickey Mantle	200.00
LB	Yogi Berra, Don Larsen	60.00
MB	Yogi Berra, Mickey Mantle	200.00
MM	Mickey Mantle, Roger Maris	200.00
MY	Paul Molitor, Robin Yount	30.00
PJ	Jackie Robinson, Pee Wee Reese	75.00
RR	Cal Ripken Jr., Brooks Robinson	65.00
RS	Tom Seaver, Nolan Ryan	75.00
SC	Roy Campanella, Duke Snider	40.00
SS	Johnny Sain, Warren Spahn	40.00
WB	Ernie Banks, Billy Williams	40.00

Legendary Duos Patch

No Pricing
Production 15 Sets

Legendary Sigs

		NM/M
Production 50 Sets		
LA	Luis Aparicio	20.00
EB	Ernie Banks	60.00
JB	Johnny Bench	60.00
WB	Wade Boggs	40.00
GC	Gary Carter	25.00
JC	Joe Carter	20.00
WC	Will Clark	40.00
BD	Bobby Doerr	20.00
DE	Dennis Eckersley	25.00
BF	Bob Feller	30.00
RF	Rollie Fingers	20.00
BG	Bob Gibson	35.00
TG	Tony Gwynn	50.00
MI	Monte Irvin	25.00
AK	Al Kaline	40.00
GK	George Kell	25.00
HK	Harmon Killebrew	40.00
RK	Ralph Kiner	30.00
FL	Fred Lynn	15.00

JM	Juan Marichal	30.00
MA	Don Mattingly	60.00
WM	Willie McCovey	40.00
MC	Denny McLain	30.00
DM	Dale Murphy	30.00
EM	Eddie Murray	80.00
DN	Don Newcombe	25.00
PA	Jim Palmer	30.00
GP	Gaylord Perry	20.00
JP	Johnny Podres	25.00
CR	Cal Ripken Jr.	125.00
PR	Phil Rizzuto	25.00
RR	Robin Roberts	30.00
BR	Brooks Robinson	40.00
SA	Ryne Sandberg	75.00
MS	Mike Schmidt	60.00
RS	Red Schoendienst	25.00
OS	Ozzie Smith	65.00
SN	Duke Snider	40.00
DS	Don Sutton	15.00
MW	Maury Wills	20.00
CY	Carl Yastrzemski	75.00

Legendary Swatches

		NM/M
	Common Swatch:	4.00
	Golds:	No Pricing
Production 15 Sets		
EB	Ernie Banks/SP	15.00
JB	Johnny Bench	10.00
YB	Yogi Berra	12.00
WB	Wade Boggs	6.00
GB	George Brett	12.00
RC	Roy Campanella	10.00
SC	Steve Carlton	6.00
OC	Orlando Cepeda	6.00
BD	Bobby Doerr	8.00
DD	Don Drysdale	8.00
CF	Carlton Fisk	8.00
NF	Nellie Fox	10.00
BG	Bob Gibson	8.00
TG	Tony Gwynn	10.00
EH	Elston Howard	8.00
CH	Jim "Catfish" Hunter	10.00
AK	Al Kaline	10.00
HK	Harmon Killebrew	10.00
MA	Juan Marichal	8.00
EM	Eddie Mathews	10.00
DM	Don Mattingly	15.00
WM	Willie McCovey	6.00
TM	Thurman Munson	12.00
SM	Stan Musial	15.00
TP	Tony Perez	4.00
PO	Johnny Podres	6.00
PR	Pee Wee Reese	8.00
JR	Jim Rice	8.00
CR	Cal Ripken Jr.	20.00
RI	Phil Rizzuto	10.00
FR	Frank Robinson	6.00
NR	Nolan Ryan	20.00
MS	Mike Schmidt	15.00
TS	Tom Seaver	8.00
DS	Duke Snider	10.00
WS	Warren Spahn	10.00
ST	Willie Stargell	8.00
BW	Billy Williams	4.00
DW	Dave Winfield	6.00
CY	Carl Yastrzemski	10.00
RY	Robin Yount	6.00

Marked for the Hall

		NM/M
Production 50 Sets		
LA	Luis Aparicio	20.00
EB	Ernie Banks	60.00
JB	Johnny Bench	60.00
YB	Yogi Berra	65.00
GB	George Brett	75.00
LB	Lou Brock	30.00
SC	Steve Carlton	20.00
GC	Gary Carter	25.00
OC	Orlando Cepeda	25.00

BD	Bobby Doerr	20.00
BF	Bob Feller	30.00
CF	Carlton Fisk	35.00
WF	Whitey Ford	40.00
BG	Bob Gibson	35.00
AK	Al Kaline	40.00
HK	Harmon Killebrew	40.00
RK	Ralph Kiner	30.00
MA	Juan Marichal	30.00
BM	Bill Mazeroski	50.00
WM	Willie McCovey	40.00
PM	Paul Molitor	40.00
JM	Joe Morgan	35.00
EM	Eddie Murray	80.00
SM	Stan Musial	80.00
PN	Phil Niekro	20.00
JP	Jim Palmer	30.00
TP	Tony Perez	25.00
GP	Gaylord Perry	20.00
KP	Kirby Puckett	60.00
PR	Phil Rizzuto	25.00
RR	Robin Roberts	30.00
BR	Brooks Robinson	40.00
FR	Frank Robinson	30.00
NR	Nolan Ryan	125.00
MS	Mike Schmidt	60.00
TS	Tom Seaver	50.00
OS	Ozzie Smith	65.00
DS	Duke Snider	40.00
BW	Billy Williams	20.00
DW	Dave Winfield	30.00
CY	Carl Yastrzemski	75.00
RY	Robin Yount	75.00

Marks of Greatness

		NM/M
Production 50 Sets		
EB	Ernie Banks	60.00
JB	Johnny Bench	60.00
YB	Yogi Berra	65.00
WB	Wade Boggs	40.00
GB	George Brett	75.00
LB	Lou Brock	30.00
SC	Steve Carlton	20.00
JC	Joe Carter	20.00
OC	Orlando Cepeda	25.00
WC	Will Clark	40.00
RF	Rollie Fingers	20.00
CF	Carlton Fisk	35.00
WF	Whitey Ford	40.00
BG	Bob Gibson	35.00
TG	Tony Gwynn	50.00
FJ	Fergie Jenkins	20.00
AK	Al Kaline	40.00
HK	Harmon Killebrew	40.00
FL	Fred Lynn	15.00
MA	Don Mattingly	50.00
MC	Denny McLain	30.00
PM	Paul Molitor	40.00
JM	Joe Morgan	35.00
DM	Dale Murphy	30.00
SM	Stan Musial	80.00
DN	Don Newcombe	25.00
PN	Phil Niekro	20.00
JP	Jim Palmer	30.00
TP	Tony Perez	25.00
KP	Kirby Puckett	60.00
CR	Cal Ripken Jr.	125.00
BR	Brooks Robinson	40.00
FR	Frank Robinson	30.00
NR	Nolan Ryan	125.00
RS	Ryne Sandberg	75.00
MS	Mike Schmidt	60.00
TS	Tom Seaver	40.00
OZ	Ozzie Smith	65.00
DS	Duke Snider	40.00
BW	Billy Williams	20.00
DW	Dave Winfield	30.00
RY	Robin Yount	75.00

Significant Swatches

		NM/M
	Common Swatch:	4.00

Golds: 2-3X
Production 25 Sets
SA	Sparky Anderson	4.00
EB	Ernie Banks/SP	10.00
LB	Lou Brock/SP	4.00
GC	Gary Carter	4.00
JC	Joe Carter	4.00
OC	Orlando Cepeda	6.00
DC	Dave Concepcion	4.00
BD	Bobby Doerr	8.00
DD	Don Drysdale	8.00
RF	Rollie Fingers	6.00
CF	Carlton Fisk	8.00
GF	George Foster	4.00
SG	Steve Garvey	4.00
CH	Jim "Catfish" Hunter	8.00
FJ	Fergie Jenkins	4.00
SL	Sparky Lyle	4.00
RM	Roger Maris	30.00
ED	Eddie Mathews	10.00
MA	Don Mattingly	15.00
BM	Bill Mazeroski	8.00
WM	Willie McCovey	6.00
PM	Paul Molitor	6.00
TM	Thurman Munson	12.00
DM	Dale Murphy	8.00
EM	Eddie Murray/SP	8.00
PN	Phil Niekro	4.00
TP	Tony Perez	4.00
GP	Gaylord Perry	6.00
JP	Johnny Podres	6.00
CR	Cal Ripken Jr.	20.00
FR	Frank Robinson	6.00
NR	Nolan Ryan	20.00
MS	Mike Schmidt	15.00
TS	Tom Seaver	8.00
SN	Duke Snider	10.00
WS	Warren Spahn	10.00
ST	Willie Stargell	8.00
DS	Don Sutton	4.00
HW	Hoyt Wilhelm	4.00
DW	Dave Winfield	6.00
CY	Carl Yastrzemski	10.00
RY	Robin Yount	8.00

Significant Trips

No Pricing
Production 15 Sets

Significant Trips Patch

No Pricing
Production 10 Sets

Ultimate Autographs

NM/M

Production 25 Sets
EB	Ernie Banks	60.00
JB	Johnny Bench	60.00
YB	Yogi Berra	60.00
GB	George Brett	90.00
LB	Lou Brock	35.00
SC	Steve Carlton	25.00
DE	Dennis Eckersley	25.00
BF	Bob Feller	35.00
WF	Whitey Ford	40.00
BG	Bob Gibson	40.00
MI	Monte Irvin	30.00
FJ	Fergie Jenkins	30.00
AK	Al Kaline	50.00
GK	George Kell	25.00
HK	Harmon Killebrew	50.00
RK	Ralph Kiner	40.00
MA	Juan Marichal	30.00
DM	Don Mattingly	75.00
BM	Bill Mazeroski	40.00
PM	Paul Molitor	40.00
JM	Joe Morgan	35.00
EM	Eddie Murray	80.00
SM	Stan Musial	80.00
PA	Jim Palmer	40.00
JP	Johnny Podres	25.00
KP	Kirby Puckett	70.00
PR	Phil Rizzuto	35.00

BR	Brooks Robinson	40.00
FR	Frank Robinson	40.00
NR	Nolan Ryan	120.00
SA	Ryne Sandberg	80.00
MS	Mike Schmidt	75.00
RS	Red Schoendienst	25.00
TS	Tom Seaver	50.00
OS	Ozzie Smith	60.00
SN	Duke Snider	50.00
DS	Don Sutton	20.00
MW	Maury Willis	25.00
DW	Dave Winfield	30.00
CY	Carl Yastrzemski	80.00
RY	Robin Yount	60.00

Ultimate Swatches

NM/M

Common Swatch:		6.00
Golds:		No Pricing

Production 10 Sets
EB	Ernie Banks	12.00
JB	Johnny Bench	10.00
YB	Yogi Berra	12.00
WB	Wade Boggs	6.00
GB	George Brett	12.00
RC	Roy Campanella	10.00
SC	Steve Carlton	6.00
JD	Joe DiMaggio/SP	75.00
DD	Don Drysdale	8.00
NF	Nellie Fox	12.00
BG	Bob Gibson	8.00
HG	Hank Greenberg	20.00
TG	Tony Gwynn	10.00
CH	Jim "Catfish" Hunter	6.00
HK	Harmon Killebrew	10.00
MM	Mickey Mantle/SP	125.00
MA	Juan Marichal	8.00
RM	Roger Maris	30.00
EM	Eddie Mathews	10.00
DM	Don Mattingly	15.00
WM	Willie McCovey	6.00
TM	Thurman Munson	10.00
SM	Stan Musial	15.00
KP	Kirby Puckett	10.00
PR	Pee Wee Reese	8.00
CR	Cal Ripken Jr.	20.00
BR	Brooks Robinson	8.00
FR	Frank Robinson	6.00
JR	Jackie Robinson	40.00
NR	Nolan Ryan	20.00
MS	Mike Schmidt	15.00
TS	Tom Seaver	10.00
OS	Ozzie Smith	10.00
DS	Duke Snider/SP	10.00
WS	Warren Spahn	10.00
HW	Honus Wagner/SP	140.00
BW	Billy Williams	6.00
TW	Ted Williams	60.00
DW	Dave Winfield	6.00
CY	Carl Yastrzemski	10.00
RY	Robin Yount	8.00

2004 SP Prospects

NM/M

Complete Set (447):		9.00
Common SP (1-90):		.50
1:Pack		
Common Rookie (91-290):		1.00
Common Rookie Auto.		
(291-447):		8.00
Production 400 unless noted.		
Overall Autos. 1:5		
Pack (5):		9.00
Box (24):		200.00
1	Roger Clemens	3.00
2	Melvin Mora	.50
3	Dontrelle Willis	.50
4	Jose Vidro	.50
5	Oliver Perez	.50
6	Carlos Zambrano	.50
7	Chipper Jones	1.00
8	Greg Maddux	1.50
9	Curt Schilling	1.00

10	Jose Reyes	.75
11	David Ortiz	1.00
12	Mike Piazza	2.00
13	Jason Schmidt	.50
14	Randy Johnson	1.00
15	Magglio Ordonez	.50
16	Mike Mussina	1.00
17	Jake Peavy	.50
18	Jim Edmonds	.75
19	Ken Griffey Jr.	1.50
20	Jason Giambi	.75
21	Mike Sweeney	.50
22	Carlos Lee	.50
23	Craig Wilson	.50
24	Pedro Martinez	1.00
25	Bobby Abreu	.50
26	Mike Lowell	.50
27	Miguel Cabrera	1.00
28	Hank Blalock	.50
29	Frank Thomas	.75
30	Manny Ramirez	1.00
31	Mark Mulder	.50
32	Scott Podsednik	.50
33	Albert Pujols	3.00
34	Preston Wilson	.50
35	Todd Helton	.75
36	Victor Martinez	.50
37	Kerry Wood	.50
38	Carlos Beltran	1.00
39	Vernon Wells	.50
40	Sammy Sosa	1.00
41	Pat Burrell	.50
42	Tim Hudson	.50
43	Eric Gagne	.75
44	Jim Thome	1.00
45	Vladimir Guerrero	1.00
46	Travis Hafner	.75
47	Rickie Weeks	.50
48	Miguel Tejada	.75
49	Ivan Rodriguez	.75
50	J.D. Drew	.50
51	Ben Sheets	.50
52	Garret Anderson	.50
53	Aubrey Huff	.50
54	Nomar Garciaparra	1.00
55	Luis Gonzalez	.50
56	Lance Berkman	.50
57	Ichiro Suzuki	2.00
58	Torii Hunter	.50
59	Adam Dunn	.75
60	Mark Teixeira	.75
61	Bret Boone	.50
62	Roy Oswalt	.50
63	Joe Mauer	.75
64	Scott Rolen	1.00
65	Hideki Matsui	2.00
66	Richie Sexson	.50
67	Jeff Kent	.50
68	Barry Zito	.50
69	C.C. Sabathia	.50
70	Carlos Delgado	.50
71	Gary Sheffield	.75
72	Shawn Green	.50
73	Jason Bay	.50
74	Andruw Jones	.75
75	Jeff Bagwell	.75
76	Rafael Palmeiro	.75
77	Alex Rodriguez	3.00
78	Adrian Beltre	.50
79	Troy Glaus	.50
80	Tom Glavine	.50
81	Paul Konerko	.50
82	Alfonso Soriano	1.00
83	Roy Halladay	.50
84	Derek Jeter	3.00
85	Josh Beckett	.50
86	Delmon Young	.50
87	Brian Giles	.50
88	Eric Chavez	.50
89	Lyle Overbay	.50
90	Mark Prior	.75
91	Shawn Camp RC	1.00
92	Travis Smith	1.00

93	Juan Padilla RC	1.00
94	Brad Halsey RC	1.00
95	Scott Kazmir	6.00
96	Sam Narron RC	1.00
97	Frank Francisco RC	1.00
98	Mike Johnston RC	1.00
99	Sam McConnell RC	1.00
100	Josh Labandeira RC	1.00
101	Kazuhito Tadano RC	1.00
102	Hector Gimenez RC	1.00
103	David Aardsma RC	1.00
104	Charles Thomas RC	2.00
105	Ian Snell RC	2.50
106	Jeff Keppinger RC	1.00
107	Michael Vento RC	2.00
108	Jerry Gil RC	1.00
109	Marty McLeary RC	1.00
110	Donnie Kelly RC	1.00
111	Roman Colon RC	1.00
112	Travis Blackley RC	1.00
113	Edwardo Sierra RC	1.00
114	Chris Shelton RC	2.00
115	Bartolome Fortunato RC	1.00
116	Brandon Medders RC	1.00
117	Merkin Valdez RC	2.00
118	Carlos Vasquez RC	1.00
119	Shingo Takatsu RC	1.50
120	Aarom Baldiris RC	1.00
121	Chris Aguila RC	1.00
122	Jimmy Serrano RC	1.00
123	Mike Gosling RC	1.00
124	Brian Dallimore RC	1.00
125	Ronald Belisario RC	1.00
126	George Sherrill RC	1.00
127	Fernando Nieve RC	1.00
128	Abe Alvarez RC	1.50
129	Jeff Bennett RC	1.00
130	Ryan Meaux RC	1.00
131	Edwin Moreno RC	1.00
132	Jesse Crain RC	2.00
133	Scott Dohmann RC	1.00
134	Ronny Cedeno RC	1.00
135	Orlando Rodriguez RC	1.00
136	Mike Wuertz RC	1.00
137	Justin Hampson RC	1.00
138	Matt Treanor RC	1.00
139	Andy Green RC	1.00
140	Yadier Molina RC	2.50
141	Joe Nelson RC	1.00
142	Justin Lehr RC	1.00
143	Ryan Wing RC	1.00
144	Kevin Cave RC	1.50
145	Evan Rust RC	1.00
146	Mike Rouse RC	1.00
147	Lance Cormier RC	1.00
148	Eduardo Villacis RC	1.00
149	Justin Knoedler RC	1.00
150	Freddy Guzman RC	1.00
151	Casey Daigle RC	1.00
152	Joey Gathright RC	2.00
153	Tim Bittner RC	1.00
154	Scott Atchison RC	1.00
155	Ivan Ochoa RC	1.50
156	Lincoln Holdzkom RC	1.00
157	Onil Joseph RC	1.00
158	Jason Bartlett RC	1.00
159	Jon Knott RC	1.00
160	Jake Woods RC	1.00
161	Jerome Gamble RC	1.00
162	Sean Henn RC	1.50
163	Kazuo Matsui RC	1.50
164	Roberto Novoa RC	1.00
165	Eddy Rodriguez RC	1.00
166	Ramon Ramirez RC	1.00
167	Enemencio Pacheco RC	1.00
168	Chad Bentz RC	1.00
169	Chris Oxspring RC	1.00
170	Justin Leone RC	1.00
171	Joe Horgan RC	1.00
172	Jose Capellan RC	1.00
173	Greg Dobbs RC	1.00
174	Jason Frasor RC	1.00
175	Shawn Hill RC	1.00
176	Carlos Hines RC	1.00
177	John Gall RC	1.00
178	Steve Andrade RC	1.00
179	Scott Proctor RC	1.00
180	Rusty Tucker RC	1.00
181	David Crouthers RC	1.00
182	Franklyn Gracesqui RC	1.00
183	Justin Germano RC	1.00
184	Alfredo Simon RC	1.50
185	Jorge Sequea RC	1.00
186	Nick Regilio RC	1.00
187	Justin Huisman RC	1.00
188	Akinori Otsuka RC	1.50
189	Luis Gonzalez RC	1.50
190	Renyel Pinto RC	1.00
191	Josh LeBlanc RC	1.50
192	Devin Ivany RC	1.00
193	Chad Blackwell RC	1.50
194	Brandon Burgess RC	1.50

#	Player	Price
195	Cory Patton RC	1.50
196	Daniel Batz RC	1.50
197	Adam Russell RC	1.00
198	Jarrett Plouffpauir RC	1.50
199	Patrick Bryant RC	1.00
200	Sean Gamble RC	1.50
201	Jermaine Brock RC	1.50
202	Benjamin Zobrist RC	1.50
203	Cla Meredith RC	1.50
204	Derek Tharpe RC	1.00
205	Brad McCann RC	2.00
206	Justin Hedrick RC	1.00
207	Clint Sammons RC	2.50
208	Richard Steik RC	1.00
209	Fernando Perez RC	1.00
210	Mark Jecmen RC	1.00
211	Benjamin Harrison RC	1.00
212	Jason Quarles RC	1.00
213	William Layman RC	1.00
214	Koley Kolberg RC	1.00
215	Randy Dicken RC	1.00
216	Barry Richmond RC	1.00
217	Timothy Murphey RC	1.50
218	John Hardy RC	1.50
219	Sebastien Boucher RC	1.00
220	Andrew Alvarado RC	1.00
221	Patrick Perry RC	1.00
222	Jarod McAuliff RC	1.00
223	Jared Gaston RC	1.00
224	William Thompson RC	1.50
225	Lucas French RC	1.00
226	Brandon Parillo RC	1.00
227	Greg Goetz RC	1.00
228	David Haehnel RC	1.50
229	James Miller RC	1.00
230	Mark Roberts RC	1.00
231	Eric Ridener RC	1.00
232	Freddy Sandoval RC	1.00
234	Carlos Medero-Stullz RC	1.00
235	Matt Shepherd RC	1.00
236	Thomas Hubbard RC	1.00
237	Kyle Bono RC	1.00
238	Craig Moldrem RC	1.00
239	Brandon Timm RC	1.00
241	Mike Carp RC	2.50
242	Joseph Muro RC	1.00
243	Derek Decarlo RC	1.50
244	Chris Niesel RC	1.00
245	Trevor Lawhorn RC	1.50
246	Joey Howell RC	1.00
247	Dustin Hahn RC	1.00
248	Jim Fasano RC	2.00
249	Hainley Statia RC	1.00
250	Brandon Conway RC	1.00
251	Christopher McConnell RC	2.00
252	Austin Shappi RC	1.50
253	Joey Metropoulos RC	2.00
254	David Nicholson RC	1.50
255	Ryan McCarthy RC	2.00
256	Michael Parisi RC	1.00
257	Andrew Macfarlane RC	1.00
258	Jeffery Dominguez RC	1.50
259	Troy Patton RC	4.00
260	Ryan Norwood RC	1.00
261	Chad Boyd RC	1.00
262	Grant Plumley RC	1.00
263	Jeffrey Katz RC	2.00
264	Cory Middleton RC	1.00
265	Andrew Moffitt RC	1.00
266	Jarrett Grube RC	1.00
267	Derek Hankins RC	1.00
268	Douglas Reinhardt RC	1.00
269	Duron Legrande RC	1.00
270	Steven Jackson RC	1.00
271	Brian Hall RC	2.00
272	Cory Wade RC	1.50
273	John Grogan RC	1.00
274	Robert Asanovich RC	1.50
275	Kevin Hart RC	1.50
276	Matt Guillory RC	1.00
277	Cliff Remole RC	1.00
278	David Trahan RC	1.00
279	Kristian Bell RC	1.00
280	Chris Westervelt RC	1.00
281	Garry Bakker RC	1.00
282	Jonny Ash RC	1.00
283	Ryan Phillips RC	1.00
284	Wes Letson RC	1.00
285	Jeff Landing RC	1.00
286	Mark Worrell RC	1.00
287	Sean Gallagher RC	5.00
288	Nick Blasi RC	1.00
289	Kevin Frandsen RC	2.00
290	Richard Mercado RC	1.00
291	Matt Bush RC	30.00
292	Mark Rogers RC	25.00
293	Homer Bailey RC	100.00
294	Chris Nelson RC	40.00
295	Thomas Diamond RC	30.00
296	Neil Walker RC	85.00
297	Bill Bray RC	15.00
298	David Purcey RC	25.00
299	Scott Elbert RC	60.00
300	Josh Fields RC	80.00
301	Chris Lambert RC	20.00
302	Trevor Plouffe RC	40.00
303	Greg Golson RC	25.00
304	Phillip Hughes RC	250.00
305	Kyle Waldrop RC	30.00
306	Richie Robnett/350 RC	30.00
307	Taylor Tankersley RC	20.00
308	Blake Dewitt RC	40.00
309	Eric Hurley RC	80.00
310	James Howell RC	20.00
311	Zachary Jackson RC	15.00
312	Justin Orenduff RC	20.00
313	Tyler Lumsden RC	25.00
314	Matt Fox/600 RC	10.00
315	Dan Putnam/450 RC	20.00
316	Jon Poterson RC	20.00
317	Gio Gonzalez RC	80.00
318	Jay Rainville/475 RC	25.00
319	Huston Street RC	40.00
320	Jeff Marquez RC	20.00
321	Eric Beattie/500 RC	20.00
322	Reid Brignac/325 RC	125.00
323	Yovani Gallardo RC	150.00
324	Justin Hoyman RC	20.00
325	Brandon Szymanski RC	25.00
326	Seth Smith/600 RC	35.00
327	Karl Herren/600 RC	20.00
328	Brian Bixler/600 RC	15.00
329	Wes Whisler/600 RC	15.00
330	Erick San Pedro RC	10.00
331	Billy Buckner RC	20.00
332	Jon Zeringue RC	20.00
333	Curtis Thigpen RC	20.00
334	Blake Johnson RC	15.00
335	Donny Lucy RC	10.00
336	Mike Ferris/600 RC	15.00
337	Anthony Swarzak/600 RC	30.00
338	Jason Jaramillo RC	15.00
339	Hunter Pence/600 RC	250.00
340	Dustin Pedroia RC	100.00
341	Grant Johnson RC	15.00
342	Kurt Suzuki RC	30.00
343	Jason Vargas/600 RC	25.00
344	Ray Liotta RC	20.00
346	Eric Campbell RC	40.00
347	Jeff Frazier RC	15.00
348	Gaby Hernandez RC	40.00
349	Wade Davis/600 RC	75.00
350	Josh Wahpepah RC	15.00
351	Scott Lewis RC	25.00
352	Jeff Fiorentino RC	15.00
353	Steven Register/600 RC	10.00
354	Michael Schlact RC	15.00
355	Eddie Prasch RC	15.00
356	Adam Lind RC	75.00
357	Ian Desmond RC	30.00
358	Josh Johnson/575 RC	15.00
359	Garrett Mock/600 RC	15.00
360	Danny Hill/600 RC	10.00
361	Cory Dunlap/600 RC	25.00
362	Grant Hansen/600 RC	12.00
363	Eric Haberer RC	15.00
364	Eduardo Morlan RC	20.00
365	James Happ/600 RC	15.00
366	Matt Tuiasosopo/600 RC	40.00
367	Jordan Parraz RC	20.00
368	Andrew Dobies RC	20.00
369	Mark Reed RC	30.00
370	Jason Windsor RC	30.00
371	Gregory Burns/600 RC	20.00
372	Christian Garcia/600 RC	25.00
373	John Bowker/575 RC	20.00
374	John Holt/550 RC	15.00
375	Daryl Jones RC	25.00
376	Colin Mahoney RC	10.00
377	Aaron Hathaway RC	15.00
378	Matt Spring RC	10.00
379	Josh Baker RC	10.00
380	Charles Lofgren RC	60.00
381	Rafael Gonzalez RC	15.00
382	Bradley Bergesen/575 RC	10.00
383	Brandon Boggs/500 RC	15.00
384	Joseph Bauserman RC	15.00
385	Collin Balester/500 RC	40.00
386	James Moore/600 RC	10.00
387	Robert Janssen RC	20.00
388	Luis Guerra RC	15.00
389	Lucas Harrell/550 RC	15.00
390	Donnie Smith/500 RC	15.00
391	Mark Robinson/525 RC	15.00
392	Louis Marson/550 RC	20.00
393	Robert Johnson/600 RC	10.00
394	Lou Santangelo/600 RC	12.00
395	Tommy Hottovy RC	10.00
396	Ryan Webb RC	15.00
397	Jamar Walton RC	15.00
398	Jason Jones RC	20.00
399	Clay Timpner/600 RC	15.00
400	James Parr RC	20.00
401	Sean Kazmar RC	20.00
402	Andrew Kown RC	15.00
403	Jacob McGee/600 RC	80.00
404	Mike Butia/600 RC	20.00
405	Paul Janish/500 RC	20.00
406	Matt Macri RC	25.00
407	Mike Nickeas/500 RC	15.00
408	Kyle Bloom/550 RC	10.00
409	Luis Rivera/500 RC	15.00
410	William Bunn/600 RC	15.00
411	Enrique Barrera RC	20.00
412	Ryan Klosterman RC	15.00
413	John Raglani/515 RC	15.00
414	Brandon Allen/500 RC	20.00
415	Andy Baldwin/600 RC	15.00
416	Mark Lowe RC	20.00
417	Mitch Einertson RC	20.00
418	Ryan Schroyer/600 RC	10.00
419	Brad Davis RC	15.00
420	Jesse Hoover/500 RC	15.00
421	Garrett Broshuis RC	15.00
422	Peter Pope RC	30.00
423	Brent Dlugach RC	15.00
424	Ryan Coultas RC	15.00
425	Ryan Royster RC	75.00
426	Stephen Chapman RC	15.00
427	Bryce Chamberlin RC	25.00
428	Joe Koshansky/550 RC	50.00
429	William Susdorf RC	15.00
430	A.J. Johnson RC	15.00
431	Jeremy Sowers RC	50.00
432	Justin Pekarek RC	15.00
433	Brett Smith RC	15.00
434	Matt Durkin RC	15.00
435	Daniel Barone RC	15.00
436	Scott Hyde RC	15.00
437	Thomas Everidge RC	25.00
444	Mark Trumbo RC	25.00
446	Eric Patterson RC	30.00
447	Mike Rozier RC	15.00

Gold

Gold (291-447): No Pricing
Production 10 Sets

Platinum

No Pricing
Production One Set

Draft Class

No Pricing
Production 10 Sets

Draft Duos

NM/M

Common Dual Autograph: 15.00
Production 175 Sets

Code	Players	Price
LK	Adam Lind, Ryan Klosterman	40.00
BB	Bill Bray, Collin Balester	25.00
BI	Bill Bray, Ian Desmond	25.00
BM	William Buckner, James Moore	15.00
JH	James Howell, Josh Johnson	15.00
DB	Blake Dewitt, Daniel Batz	25.00
SJ	Brandon Szymanski, Paul Janish	25.00
SH	Brett Smith, Phillip Hughes	60.00
LS	Chris Lambert, Donnie Smith	15.00
LF	Chris Lambert, Mike Ferris	15.00
NS	Chris Nelson, Seth Smith	25.00
NM	Chris Nelson, Matt Macri	30.00
DG	Cory Dunlap, Luis Guerra	30.00
BN	Matt Bush, Chris Nelson	30.00
TH	Curtis Thigpen, Danny Hill	15.00
PT	Dan Putnam, Derek Tharpe	15.00
PJ	David Purcey, Robert Janssen	15.00
DZ	David Purcey, Zachary Jackson	20.00
LH	Donny Lucy, Grant Hansen	15.00
PD	Dustin Pedroia, Andrew Dobies	30.00
MR	Eduardo Morlan, Mark Robinson	15.00
PB	Eddie Prasch, Joseph Bauserman	20.00
EA	Eric Beattie, Andrew Kown	20.00
EJ	Eric Campbell, John Holt	25.00
EM	Eric Hurley, Mike Nickeas	25.00
PI	Erick San Pedro, Devin Ivany	15.00
HH	Gaby Hernandez, Aaron Hathaway	25.00
SK	Seth Smith, Joe Koshansky	30.00
GM	Gio Gonzalez, Timothy Murphey	25.00
BH	Matt Bush, Phillip Hughes	60.00
JR	Grant Johnson, Mark Reed	25.00
GH	Greg Golson, James Happ	20.00
GG	Greg Golson, Sean Gamble	15.00
BS	Homer Bailey, Brandon Szymanski	40.00
BG	Homer Bailey, Rafael Gonzalez	50.00
HJ	Hunter Pence, Jordan Parraz	80.00
SS	Huston Street, Kurt Suzuki	40.00
SW	Huston Street, Ryan Webb	30.00
HB	James Howell, Chad Blackwell	20.00
JM	Jason Jaramillo, Louis Marson	15.00
RS	Jay Rainville, Anthony Swarzak	20.00
JP	Jay Rainville, Patrick Bryant	20.00
FM	Jeff Frazier, Colin Mahoney	15.00
MS	Jeff Marquez, Brett Smith	20.00
MH	Jeff Marquez, Jesse Hoover	25.00
SL	Jeremy Sowers, Charles Lofgren	35.00
JS	Jeremy Sowers, Scott Lewis	25.00
JJ	Jon Poterson, Jason Jones	25.00
ZM	Jon Zeringue, Garrett Mock	20.00
FH	Josh Fields, Lucas Harrell	30.00
FW	Josh Fields, Wes Whisler	40.00
WB	Josh Wahpepah, Josh Baker	15.00
CL	Justin Hoyman, Jeremy Sowers	25.00
OJ	Justin Orenduff, Blake Johnson	25.00
OG	Justin Orenduff, Luis Guerra	20.00
HS	Karl Herren, Michael Schlact	20.00
WF	Kyle Waldrop, Matt Fox	20.00
KB	Kyle Waldrop, Patrick Bryant	25.00
RW	Richie Robnett, Jason Windsor	25.00
SR	Richie Robnett, Kurt Suzuki	25.00
RB	Mark Rogers, Josh Baker	30.00
RG	Mark Rogers, Yovani Gallardo	50.00

BK	Matt Bush, Sean Kazmar	25.00
WE	William Buckner, Enrique Barrera	15.00
WJ	William Buckner, James Howell	20.00
KH	Matt Durkin, Aaron Hathaway	20.00
NB	Neil Walker, Brian Bixler	25.00
NK	Neil Walker, Kyle Bloom	25.00
HG	Phillip Hughes, Christian Garcia	50.00
HP	Phillip Hughes, Jon Poterson	60.00
LA	Ray Liotta, Brandon Allen	25.00
BR	Reid Brignac, Ryan Royster	40.00
RP	Richie Robnett, Dan Putnam	25.00
RH	Richie Robnett, Huston Street	30.00
CO	Steven Register, Seth Smith	25.00
TD	Taylor Tankersley, Brad Davis	15.00
TV	Taylor Tankersley, Jason Vargas	20.00
BT	Thomas Diamond, Brandon Boggs	30.00
DH	Thomas Diamond, Eric Hurley	30.00
ED	Scott Elbert, Blake Dewitt	35.00
ER	Scott Elbert, John Raglani	25.00
PW	Trevor Plouffe, Kyle Waldrop	30.00
PR	Trevor Plouffe, Mark Robinson	25.00
LR	Tyler Lumsden, Adam Russell	15.00
LG	Tyler Lumsden, Gio Gonzalez	25.00
JB	William Buckner, Josh Johnson	20.00
BJ	Matt Bush, Daryl Jones	30.00
GW	Yovani Gallardo, Josh Wahpepah	40.00
JK	Zachary Jackson, Ryan Klosterman	15.00
DR	Blake Dewitt, John Raglani	25.00
GB	Homer Bailey, Greg Goetz	50.00
WR	Reid Brignac, Wade Davis	40.00
HM	Jeff Marquez, Phillip Hughes	60.00
PZ	Jordan Parraz, Benjamin Zobrist	25.00
RL	Luis Rivera, William Layman	15.00
EC	Eric Beattie, Collin Mahoney	15.00
JE	Jeff Frazier, Eric Beattie	15.00
BP	Matt Bush, Trevor Plouffe	30.00
CH	Ryan Coultas, Aaron Hathaway	15.00
SB	Jeremy Sowers, Homer Bailey	60.00
FB	Jeff Fiorentino, Bradley Bergesen	25.00
CF	Bryce Chamberlin, Jeff Fiorentino	20.00
RD	Cory Dunlap, John Raglani	20.00
ZP	Hunter Pence, Benjamin Zobrist	80.00

Draft Picks Autographs

		NM/M
	Common Autograph:	8.00
	Golds:	No Pricing
	Production 10 Sets	
	Platinum:	No Pricing
	Production One Set	
AA	Andrew Alvarado/400	8.00
RA	Robert Asanovich/400	15.00
JA	Jonny Ash/400	15.00
GB	Garry Bakker/400	10.00
DB	Daniel Batz/400	10.00
KB	Kristian Bell/400	8.00
BL	Chad Blackwell/400	15.00
NB	Nick Blasi/400	15.00
BO	Kyle Bono/400	10.00

SB	Sebastien Boucher/325	15.00
CB	Chad Boyd/475	8.00
JB	Jermaine Brock/400	8.00
PB	Patrick Bryant/400	10.00
BB	Brandon Burgess/400	10.00
CA	Mike Carp/400	25.00
BC	Brandon Conway/400	8.00
DD	Derek Decarlo/400	10.00
RD	Randy Dicken/475	8.00
JD	Jeffery Dominguez/400	15.00
JF	Jim Fasano/400	15.00
KF	Kevin Frandsen/400	30.00
LF	Lucas French/400	15.00
SE	Sean Gallagher/400	50.00
SG	Sean Gamble/400	10.00
GA	Jared Gaston/400	10.00
GG	Greg Goetz/400	15.00
GR	John Grogan/475	10.00
JG	Jarrett Grube/400	8.00
MG	Matt Guillory/400	10.00
DA	David Haehnel/475	12.00
HA	Dustin Hahn/400	8.00
BH	Brian Hall/400	15.00
DH	Derek Hankins/400	8.00
JO	John Hardy/475	10.00
BE	Benjamin Harrison/387	20.00
KH	Kevin Hart/400	10.00
HE	Justin Hedrick/400	15.00
JH	Jarrett Hoffpauir/400	15.00
HO	Joey Howell/400	15.00
TH	Thomas Hubbard/400	15.00
DI	Devin Ivany/550	15.00
SJ	Steven Jackson/475	15.00
MJ	Mark Jecmen/600	8.00
JK	Jeffrey Katz/400	10.00
KK	Koley Kolberg/400	10.00
LA	Jeff Landing/400	10.00
TL	Trevor Lawhorn/475	10.00
WL	William Layman/400	8.00
JL	Josh LeBlanc/400	10.00
DL	Duron Legrande/400	8.00
LE	Wes Letson/400	10.00
MA	Andrew Macfarlane/400	8.00
MC	Jarod McAuliff/400	15.00
BM	Brad McCann/400	25.00
RM	Ryan McCarthy/400	15.00
CH	Christopher McConnell/400	25.00
ME	Carlos Medero-Stullz/400	8.00
RI	Richard Mercado/475	12.00
CL	Cla Meredith/400	25.00
JM	Joey Metropoulos/400	15.00
CM	Cory Middleton/400	20.00
MI	James Miller/475	12.00
AM	Andrew Moffitt/400	15.00
MO	Craig Molldrem/400	12.00
MU	Joseph Muro/400	8.00
TM	Timothy Murphey/400	10.00
DN	David Nicholson/475	10.00
CN	Chris Niesel/475	15.00
RN	Ryan Norwood/400	25.00
BP	Brandon Parillo/475	15.00
MP	Michael Parisi/475	15.00
CP	Cory Patton/400	15.00
TP	Troy Patton/400	85.00
FP	Fernando Perez/400	20.00
PP	Patrick Perry/400	15.00
RP	Ryan Phillips/400	15.00
GP	Grant Plumley/475	10.00
JQ	Jason Quarles/400	8.00
DR	Douglas Reinhardt/400	8.00
CR	Cliff Remole/400	15.00
BR	Barry Richmond/400	20.00
ER	Eric Ridener/475	10.00

MR	Mark Roberts/400	8.00
AR	Adam Russell/550	8.00
CS	Clint Sammons/400	15.00
FS	Freddy Sandoval/400	10.00
AS	Austin Shappi/475	15.00
MS	Matt Shepherd/400	10.00
HS	Hainley Statia/400	20.00
RS	Richard Steik/400	8.00
DT	Derek Tharpe/400	8.00
WT	William Thompson/475	10.00
BT	Brandon Timm/475	15.00
TR	David Trahan/400	10.00
CW	Cory Wade/400	15.00
WE	Chris Westervelt/400	15.00
MW	Mark Worrell/400	15.00
BZ	Benjamin Zobrist/600	25.00

Draft Generations Triple Autograph

No Pricing
Production 25 Sets

Link to the Future Dual Autograph

		NM/M
	Common Dual Auto.	10.00
	Production 100 Sets	
BD	Adrian Beltre, Blake Dewitt	40.00
RF	Scott Rolen, Mike Ferris	40.00
JR	Andruw Jones, Richie Robnett	30.00
KB	Scott Kazmir, Reid Brignac	50.00
JB	Jason Kendall, Brian Bixler	20.00
SR	Ben Sheets, Mark Rogers	40.00
GP	Brian Giles, Dan Putnam	20.00
BG	Carlos Beltran, Greg Golson	30.00
SJ	Johan Santana, Jay Rainville	40.00
WT	Dontrelle Willis, Taylor Tankersley	15.00
JJ	Edwin Jackson, Blake Johnson	15.00
EJ	Eric Chavez, Josh Fields	40.00
QT	Guillermo Quiroz, Curtis Thigpen	10.00
KW	Jason Kendall, Neil Walker	40.00
VM	Javier Vazquez, Jeff Marquez	20.00
MP	Joe Mauer, Trevor Plouffe	50.00
SW	Johan Santana, Kyle Waldrop	40.00
VP	Javier Vazquez, Jon Poterson	20.00
GS	Ken Griffey Jr., Brandon Szymanski	75.00
WB	Kerry Wood, Homer Bailey	50.00
MS	Mike Mussina, Brett Smith	50.00
HS	Todd Helton, Seth Smith	30.00
GZ	Luis Gonzalez, Jon Zeringue	20.00
OH	Magglio Ordonez, Karl Herren	20.00
MB	Mark Mulder, Bill Bray	20.00
PJ	Mark Prior, Grant Johnson	40.00
CF	Matt Clement, Matt Fox	15.00
TN	Miguel Tejada, Chris Nelson	40.00
MH	Mike Mussina, Phillip Hughes	85.00
GB	Nomar Garciaparra, Matt Bush	80.00
PE	Odalis Perez, Scott Elbert	20.00
LS	Paul LoDuca, Erick San Pedro	20.00

HW	Rich Harden, Kyle Waldrop	25.00
CD	Roger Clemens, Thomas Diamond	100.00
RP	Alexis Rios, David Purcey	25.00
RE	Roy Oswalt, Eric Hurley	25.00
RL	Scott Rolen, Chris Lambert	40.00
TS	Tim Hudson, Huston Street	40.00
TJ	Tom Glavine, Jeremy Sowers	35.00
VD	Victor Martinez, Donny Lucy	25.00
BH	Angel Berroa, James Howell	15.00

Link to the Past Dual Autograph

Common Dual Autograph
Production 50 Sets

MB	Bill Mazeroski, Brian Bixler	35.00
FL	Carlton Fisk, Tyler Lumsden	35.00
WJ	Dave Winfield, Zachary Jackson	35.00
BW	Johnny Bench, Neil Walker	40.00
JD	Jose Canseco, Dan Putnam	50.00
AS	Billy Williams, Richie Robnett	40.00
RB	Nolan Ryan, Homer Bailey	180.00
PD	Gaylord Perry, Thomas Diamond	50.00
WR	Wade Boggs, Reid Brignac	60.00
WB	Whitey Ford, Brett Smith	30.00
WP	Whitey Ford, Phillip Hughes	75.00

Link to the Future Triple Autograph

		NM/M
	Common Triple Auto.	
	Production 50 Sets	
BHH	Hank Blalock, Eric Hurley, Benjamin Harrison	40.00
KBS	Scott Kazmir, Reid Brignac, Matt Spring	75.00
SRB	Ben Sheets, Mark Rogers, Josh Baker	50.00
JJB	Edwin Jackson, Blake Johnson, Daniel Batz	20.00
SWM	Johan Santana, Kyle Waldrop, Eduardo Morlan	60.00
VBB	Jose Vidro, Bill Bray, Collin Balester	30.00
GSJ	Ken Griffey Jr., Brandon Szymanski, Paul Janish	60.00
MSH	Mike Mussina, Brett Smith, Jesse Hoover	50.00
OFA	Magglio Ordonez, Josh Fields, Brandon Allen	30.00
PJR	Mark Prior, Grant Johnson, Mark Reed	100.00
GHM	Juan Gonzalez, James Howell, James Moore	40.00
HSW	Rich Harden, Huston Street, Jason Windsor	50.00
GMZ	Luis Gonzalez, Garrett Mock, Jon Zeringue	25.00
HRW	Tim Hudson, Richie Robnett, Ryan Webb	60.00
MSL	Victor Martinez, Jeremy Sowers, Charles Lofgren	
GTR	Vladimir Guerrero, Mark Trumbo, Luis Rivera	75.00

National Honors

		NM/M
	Common Player:	4.00
	Inserted 1:12	
DB	Daniel Bard	8.00
TB	Travis Buck	8.00
JC	Jeff Clement	8.00
BC	Brent Cox	8.00

Code	Player	Price
TC	Trevor Crowe	4.00
JD	Joey Devine	4.00
AG	Alex Gordon	20.00
BH	Brett Hayes	4.00
LH	Luke Hochevar	8.00
SK	Stephen Kahn	4.00
IK	Ian Kennedy	8.00
JL	Jed Lowrie	4.00
JM	John Mayberry Jr.	8.00
MP	Mike Pelfrey	15.00
CR	Cesar Ramos	8.00
MR	Mark Romanczuk	4.00
RR	Ricky Romero	4.00
DS	Drew Stubbs	8.00
TE	Taylor Teagarden	6.00
TT	Troy Tulowitzki	15.00
CV	Chris Valaika	4.00
RZ	Ryan Zimmerman	15.00

2004 SPx

	NM/M
Complete Set (202):	
Common Player:	.25
Common SP (111-145):	3.00
Production 1,599	
Common SP (146-154):	5.00
Production 499	
Common SP (155-160):	8.00
Production 299	
Common Jersey Auto.	
(161-202):	8.00
Production 799	
Pack (4):	5.00
Box (18):	75.00
1	Alfonso Soriano	1.00
2	Todd Helton	.75
3	Andruw Jones	.75
4	Eric Gagne	.50
5	Craig Wilson	.25
6	Brian Giles	.25
7	Miguel Tejada	.50
8	Kevin Brown	.25
9	Shawn Green	.50
10	Ben Sheets	.50
11	John Smoltz	.50
12	Tim Hudson	.50
13	Jason Schmidt	.50
14	Paul Konerko	.50
15	Randy Johnson	1.00
16	Roy Oswalt	.50
17	Mike Lowell	.25
18	Carlos Lee	.50
19	Sean Burroughs	.25
20	Edgar Renteria	.50
21	Michael Young	.25
22	Jose Vidro	.25
23	Scott Rolen	1.00
24	Rafael Furcal	.50
25	Tom Glavine	.75
26	Scott Podsednik	.25
27	Gary Sheffield	.75
28	Eric Chavez	.50
29	Mark Prior	.75
30	Chipper Jones	1.00
31	Frank Thomas	1.00
32	Victor Martinez	.50
33	Jake Peavy	.50
34	Carlos Beltran	1.00
35	Roy Halladay	.50
36	Mark Teixeira	.75
37	Jacque Jones	.25
38	Mike Sweeney	.25
39	Troy Glaus	.50
40	Pat Burrell	.50
41	Ichiro Suzuki	2.00
42	Vladimir Guerrero	1.00
43	Bobby Abreu	.50
44	Jim Edmonds	.50
45	Garret Anderson	.40
46	J.D. Drew	.40
47	C.C. Sabathia	.25
48	Joe Mauer	.50
49	Phil Nevin	.25
50	Hank Blalock	.50
51	Carlos Zambrano	.50
52	Mike Piazza	1.50
53	Manny Ramirez	1.00
54	Lance Berkman	.50
55	Delmon Young	.50
56	Nomar Garciaparra	1.00
57	Alex Rodriguez	2.50
58	Rickie Weeks	.50
59	Adrian Beltre	.50
60	Albert Pujols	2.50
61	Richie Sexson	.50
62	Magglio Ordonez	.50
63	Derrek Lee	.75
64	Sammy Sosa	1.50
65	Jason Giambi	.75
66	Curt Schilling	.50
67	Jorge Posada	.50
68	Rafael Palmeiro	.50
69	Jeff Kent	.50
70	Jose Reyes	.50
71	David Ortiz	1.00
72	Aubrey Huff	.25
73	Jim Thome	1.00
74	Andy Pettitte	.50
75	Barry Zito	.50
76	Carlos Delgado	.50
77	Hideki Matsui	2.00
78	Sean Casey	.25
79	Luis Gonzalez	.25
80	Marcus Giles	.25
81	Preston Wilson	.25
82	Javy Lopez	.25
83	Mark Mulder	.50
84	Derek Jeter	2.50
85	Miguel Cabrera	1.00
86	Vernon Wells	.50
87	Roger Clemens	2.50
88	Lyle Overbay	.25
89	Bret Boone	.25
90	Melvin Mora	.25
91	Greg Maddux	2.00
92	Kerry Wood	.50
93	Ivan Rodriguez	.75
94	Pedro J. Martinez	1.00
95	Jeff Bagwell	.75
96	Torii Hunter	.50
97	Ken Griffey Jr.	2.00
98	Mike Mussina	.75
99	Oliver Perez	.25
100	Josh Beckett	.50
101	Bob Gibson	4.00
102	Cal Ripken Jr.	8.00
103	Ted Williams	8.00
104	Nolan Ryan	8.00
105	Mickey Mantle	10.00
106	Ernie Banks	5.00
107	Joe DiMaggio	6.00
108	Stan Musial	5.00
109	Tom Seaver	4.00
110	Mike Schmidt	6.00
111	Jerry Gil RC	3.00
112	Dioner Navarro RC	8.00
113	Bartolome Fortunato RC	3.00
114	Carlos Hines RC	3.00
115	Franklyn Gracesqui RC	3.00
116	Aarom Baldiris RC	5.00
117	Casey Daigle RC	3.00
118	Joey Gathright RC	5.00
119	William Bergolla RC	3.00
120	Jeff Bennett RC	3.00
121	Lincoln Holdzkom RC	3.00
122	Jorge Sosa RC	3.00
123	Donnie Kelly RC	3.00
124	Yadier Molina RC	8.00
125	Ryan Wing RC	3.00
126	Justin Germano RC	3.00
127	Freddy Guzman RC	3.00
128	Onil Joseph RC	3.00
129	Roman Colon RC	3.00
130	Roberto Novoa RC	5.00
131	Renyel Pinto RC	5.00
132	Evan Rust RC	3.00
133	Orlando Rodriguez RC	3.00
134	Edwardo Sierra RC	5.00
135	Mike Rose RC	3.00
136	Phil Stockman RC	3.00
137	Greg Dobbs RC	3.00
138	Brad Halsey RC	3.00
139	David Aardsma RC	5.00
140	Joe Hietpas RC	3.00
141	Josh Labandeira RC	3.00
142	Mariano Gomez RC	3.00
143	Jeff Bajenaru RC	3.00
144	Travis Blackley RC	3.00
145	Abe Alvarez RC	5.00
146	Ramon Ramirez RC	5.00
147	Edwin Moreno RC	5.00
148	Ronny Cedeno RC	8.00
149	Hector Gimenez RC	5.00
150	Carlos Vasquez RC	8.00
151	Jesse Crain	8.00
152	Logan Kensing RC	5.00
153	Sean Henn	5.00
154	Rusty Tucker RC	5.00
155	Justin Lehr RC	5.00
156	Ian Snell RC	15.00
157	Merkin Valdez RC	10.00
158	Scott Proctor RC	8.00
159	Jose Capellan RC	8.00
160	Kazuo Matsui RC	8.00
161	Chris Oxspring RC	8.00
162	Jimmy Serrano RC	10.00
163	Jeff Keppinger RC	12.00
164	Brandon Medders RC	8.00
165	Brian Dallimore RC	10.00
166	Chad Bentz RC	12.00
167	Chris Aguila RC	10.00
168	Chris Saenz RC	10.00
169	Frank Francisco RC	10.00
170	Colby Miller RC	12.00
171	David Crouthers RC	10.00
172	Charles Thomas RC	15.00
173	Dennis Sarfate RC	12.00
174	Lance Cormier RC	10.00
175	Joe Horgan RC	10.00
176	Fernando Nieve RC	10.00
177	Jake Woods	12.00
178	Matt Treanor RC	12.00
179	Jerome Gamble RC	15.00
180	John Gall RC	15.00
181	Jorge Sequea RC	10.00
182	Justin Hampson RC	10.00
183	Justin Huisman RC	15.00
184	Justin Knoedler RC	12.00
185	Justin Leone RC	15.00
186	Scott Atchison RC	12.00
187	Jon Knott RC	15.00
188	Kevin Cave RC	10.00
189	Jason Frasor RC	10.00
190	George Sherrill RC	12.00
191	Mike Gosling RC	10.00
192	Mike Johnston RC	10.00
193	Mike Rouse RC	10.00
194	Nick Regilio RC	10.00
195	Ryan Meaux RC	10.00
196	Scott Dohmann RC	15.00
197	Shawn Camp RC	10.00
198	Shawn Hill RC	10.00
199	Shingo Takatsu RC	15.00
200	Tim Bausher RC	10.00
201	Tim Bittner RC	10.00
202	Scott Kazmir	60.00

Spectrum

Stars (1-100):	5-10X
SP's (101-202):	2-3X
Production 25 Sets	

Master Player Prints

No Pricing
Production One Set

Superscripts

	NM/M
Common Player:	8.00
Inserted 1:18	
JB	Josh Beckett	20.00
MC	Miguel Cabrera	25.00
EC	Eric Chavez	15.00
BC	Bobby Crosby	15.00
BF	Bartolome Fortunato	10.00
NG	Nomar	
	Garciaparra/SP	80.00
MG	Mariano Gomez	10.00
KG	Ken Griffey Jr.	75.00
RH	Rich Harden	15.00
SH	Sean Henn	10.00
CH	Carlos Hines	8.00
LH	Lincoln Holdzkom	10.00
EJ	Edwin Jackson	10.00
DJ	Derek Jeter/SP	200.00
DK	Donnie Kelly	8.00
LA	Josh Labandeira	8.00
JL	Justin Lehr	8.00
JM	Joe Mauer	35.00
IO	Ivan Ochoa	8.00
RO	Roy Oswalt	20.00
MP	Mark Prior	40.00
SP	Scott Proctor	8.00
AP	Albert Pujols/SP	240.00
RR	Ramon Ramirez	12.00
JR	Jose Reyes	35.00
CR	Cal Ripken Jr./SP	125.00
RU	Evan Rust	10.00
NR	Nolan Ryan/SP	
ES	Edwardo Sierra	10.00
AS	Alfredo Simon	10.00
IS	Ian Snell	25.00
PS	Phil Stockman	10.00
TE	Miguel Tejada	35.00
MT	Mark Teixeira	30.00
MV	Merkin Valdez	12.00
CV	Carlos Vasquez	10.00
VE	Michael Vento	15.00
BW	Brandon Webb	10.00
RW	Rickie Weeks	15.00
DW	Dontrelle Willis	25.00
DY	Delmon Young	25.00

Swatch Supremecy Cut Signatures

No pricing due to scarcity.

Swatch Supremecy Signatures

	NM/M
Common Player:	8.00
Production 999 unless noted.	
Spectrum:	1.5-3X
Production 25 Sets	
GA	Garret Anderson/275	20.00
RB	Rocco Baldelli	20.00
JB	Josh Beckett	15.00
AB	Angel Berroa	10.00
HB	Hank Blalock	15.00
SB	Sean Burroughs	10.00
MC	Miguel Cabrera	30.00
EC	Eric Chavez/275	20.00
CC	Chad Cordero	10.00
BC	Bobby Crosby	15.00
AE	Adam Eaton	10.00
NG	Nomar	
	Garciaparra/275	60.00
MG	Marcus Giles	15.00
GR	Khalil Greene	25.00
KG	Ken Griffey Jr./275	85.00
RH	Rich Harden	20.00
DJ	Derek Jeter/275	180.00
CK	Casey Kotchman	20.00
CL	Cliff Lee	10.00
DL	Derrek Lee/275	30.00
JM	Joe Mauer	40.00
RO	Roy Oswalt	20.00
LO	Lyle Overbay	15.00
CP	Corey Patterson	20.00
JP	Jake Peavy	35.00
SP	Scott Podsednik	20.00
MP	Mark Prior/275	40.00
AP	Albert Pujols/275	240.00
HR	Horacio Ramirez	10.00
JR	Jose Reyes	35.00
CR	Cal Ripken Jr./275	140.00
NR	Nolan Ryan/275	120.00
BS	Ben Sheets	20.00
MT	Mark Teixeira	25.00
BW	Brandon Webb	25.00
RW	Rickie Weeks	15.00
DW	Dontrelle Willis	25.00
JW	Jerome Williams	15.00
MY	Michael Young	15.00

Winning Materials

	NM/M
Common Player:	8.00
Inserted 1:18	
Spectrum:	2-3X
Production 25 Sets	
JB	Jeff Bagwell	10.00
BE	Josh Beckett	10.00
HB	Hank Blalock	10.00
KB	Kevin Brown	8.00
EC	Eric Chavez	8.00
RC	Roger Clemens	20.00
CD	Carlos Delgado	10.00
JG	Jason Giambi	12.00
TG	Troy Glaus	8.00
SG	Shawn Green	8.00
VG	Vladimir Guerrero	12.00
DJ	Derek Jeter	35.00
CJ	Chipper Jones	10.00
GM	Greg Maddux	15.00
HM	Hideki Matsui	30.00
MM	Mike Mussina	10.00
RP	Rafael Palmeiro	10.00
PI	Mike Piazza	15.00
JP	Jorge Posada	10.00
MP	Mark Prior	10.00
AP	Albert Pujols	30.00
MR	Manny Ramirez	15.00
JR	Jose Reyes	15.00
SR	Scott Rolen	15.00
GS	Gary Sheffield	10.00
SS	Sammy Sosa	15.00
IS	Ichiro Suzuki	30.00
TE	Miguel Tejada	10.00
JT	Jim Thome	12.00

Winning Materials (continued codes)

BW	Brandon Webb	10.00
RW	Rickie Weeks	15.00
DW	Dontrelle Willis	25.00
DY	Delmon Young	25.00

2005 SP Collection

		NM/M
Complete SPx Set (100):		25.00
Common Player:		.25
Pack (5):		6.00
Box (20):		100.00
1	Aaron Harang	.25
2	Aaron Rowand	.25
3	Aaron Miles	.25
4	Adrian Gonzalez	.25
5	Alex Rios	.25
6	Angel Berroa	.25
7	B.J. Upton	.25
8	Brandon Claussen	.25
9	Andy Marte	.25
10	Brandon Webb	.25
11	Bronson Arroyo	.25
12	Casey Kotchman	.25
13	Cesar Izturis	.25
14	Chad Cordero	.25
15	Chad Tracy	.25
16	Charles Thomas	.25
17	Chase Utley	.50
18	Chone Figgins	.25
19	Chris Burke	.25
20	Cliff Lee	.25
21	Clint Barmes	.25
22	Coco Crisp	.25
23	Bill Hall	.25
24	Dallas McPherson	.25
25	Brad Halsey	.25
26	Daniel Cabrera	.25
27	Danny Haren	.25
28	David Bush	.25
29	David DeJesus	.25
30	D.J. Houlton	.25
31	Derek Lee	3.00
32	Dewon Brazelton	.25
33	Edwin Jackson	.25
34	Brad Hawpe	.25
35	Brandon Inge	.25
36	Brett Myers	.25
37	Garrett Atkins	.25
38	Gavin Floyd	.25
39	Grady Sizemore	.50
40	Guillermo Mota	.25
41	Carlos Guillen	.25
42	Gustavo Chacin	.25
43	Huston Street	.25
44	Chris Duffy	.25
45	J.D. Closser	.25
46	J.J. Hardy	.25
47	Jason Bartlett	.25
48	Jason Dubois	.25
49	Chris Shelton	.25
50	Jason Lane	.25
51	Jayson Werth	.25
52	Jeff Baker	.25
53	Jeff Francis	.25
54	Jeremy Bonderman	.25
55	Jeremy Reed	.25
56	Jerome Williams	.25
57	Jesse Crain	.25
58	Chris Young	.25
59	Jhonny Peralta	.25
60	Joe Blanton	.25
61	Joe Crede	.25
62	Joel Pineiro	.25
63	Joey Gathright	.25
64	John Buck	.25
65	Jonny Gomes	.25
66	Jorge Cantu	.25
67	Dan Johnson	.25
68	Jose Valverde	.25
69	Ervin Santana	.25
70	Justin Morneau	.50
71	Keiichi Yabu	.25
72	Ken Griffey Jr.	2.00
73	Jason Repko	.25
74	Kevin Youkilis	.25
75	Koyie Hill	.25
76	Laynce Nix	.25
77	Luke Scott RC	1.00
78	Juan Rivera	.25
79	Justin Duchscherer	.25
80	Mark Teahen	.25
81	Lance Niekro	.25
82	Michael Cuddyer	.25
83	Nick Swisher	.25
84	Noah Lowry	.25
85	Matt Holliday	.50
86	Reed Johnson	.25
87	Rich Harden	.25
88	Robb Quinlan	.25
89	Nick Johnson	.25
90	Ryan Howard	1.00
91	Nook Logan	.25
92	Steve Schmoll	.25
93	Tadahito Iguchi	.25
94	Willy Taveras	.25
95	Wily Mo Pena	.25
96	Xavier Nady	.25
97	Yadier Molina	.25
98	Yhency Brazoban	.25
99	Ryan Freel	.25
100	Zack Greinke	.25

Complete SP Authentic Set (100): 25.00
Common Player: .25

1	A.J. Burnett	.25
2	Aaron Rowand	.25
3	Adam Dunn	.75
4	Adrian Beltre	.50
5	Adrian Gonzalez	.25
6	Akinori Otsuka	.25
7	Albert Pujols	3.00
8	Andre Dawson	.50
9	Andruw Jones	.50
10	Aramis Ramirez	.50
11	Barry Larkin	.50
12	Ben Sheets	.50
13	Bo Jackson	.50
14	Bobby Abreu	.50
15	Bobby Crosby	.50
16	Bronson Arroyo	.25
17	Cal Ripken Jr.	4.00
18	Carl Crawford	.25
19	Carlos Zambrano	.50
20	Casey Kotchman	.25
21	Cesar Izturis	.25
22	Chone Figgins	.25
23	Corey Patterson	.25
24	Craig Biggio	.50
25	Dale Murphy	.50
26	Dallas McPherson	.25
27	Danny Haren	.25
28	Darryl Strawberry	.25
29	David Ortiz	1.00
30	David Wright	1.00
31	Derek Jeter	3.00
32	Derek Lee	.50
33	Don Mattingly	1.50
34	Dwight Gooden	.25
35	Edgar Renteria	.50
36	Eric Chavez	.50
37	Eric Gagne	.25
38	Gary Sheffield	.50
39	Gavin Floyd	.25
40	Pedro Martinez	1.00
41	Greg Maddux	2.00
42	Hank Blalock	.50
43	Huston Street	.25
44	J.D. Drew	.25
45	Jake Peavy	.50
46	Jake Westbrook	.25
47	Jason Bay	.25
48	Austin Kearns	.25
49	Jeremy Reed	.25
50	Jim Rice	.50
51	Jimmy Rollins	.50
52	Joe Blanton	.25
53	Joe Mauer	.50
54	Johan Santana	1.00
55	John Smoltz	.50
56	Johnny Estrada	.25
57	Jose Reyes	.50
58	Ken Griffey Jr.	2.00
59	Kerry Wood	.50
60	Khalil Greene	.50
61	Marcus Giles	.25
62	Melvin Mora	.25
63	Mark Grace	.50
64	Mark Mulder	.50
65	Mark Prior	1.00
66	Mark Teixeira	.50
67	Matt Clement	.25
68	Michael Young	.25
69	Miguel Cabrera	1.00
70	Miguel Tejada	.75
71	Mike Piazza	1.50
72	Mike Schmidt	2.00
73	Nolan Ryan	3.00
74	Oliver Perez	.25
75	Nick Johnson	.25
76	Paul Molitor	.75
77	Rafael Palmeiro	.50
78	Randy Johnson	1.00
79	Reggie Jackson	1.00
80	Rich Harden	.25
81	Rickie Weeks	.50
82	Robin Yount	1.00
83	Roger Clemens	3.00
84	Roy Oswalt	.25
85	Ryan Howard	1.00
86	Ryne Sandberg	2.00
87	Scott Kazmir	.25
88	Scott Rolen	1.00
89	Sean Burroughs	.25
90	Sean Casey	.25
91	Shingo Takatsu	.25
92	Tim Hudson	.50
93	Tony Gwynn	1.00
94	Torii Hunter	.50
95	Travis Hafner	.25
96	Victor Martinez	.25
97	Vladimir Guerrero	1.00
98	Wade Boggs	.50
99	Will Clark	.50
100	Yadier Molina	.25

SP Authentic Chirography
No Pricing
Production 15 Sets

SP Authentic Chirography Triple
No Pricing
Production 5 Sets

SP Authentic Honors

		NM/M
Common Player:		1.00
Production 299 Sets		
JB	Jason Bay	1.50
AB	Adrian Beltre	1.50
WB	Wade Boggs	1.50
BO	Jeremy Bonderman	1.00
CA	Miguel Cabrera	2.00
WC	Will Clark	1.50
RC	Roger Clemens	6.00
CC	Carl Crawford	1.00
BC	Bobby Crosby	1.50
MG	Marcus Giles	1.00
DG	Dwight Gooden	1.50
GR	Khalil Greene	2.00
ZG	Zack Greinke	1.00
KG	Ken Griffey Jr.	4.00
TG	Tony Gwynn	2.00
TH	Travis Hafner	1.00
RH	Rich Harden	1.00
BJ	Bo Jackson	2.00
DJ	Derek Jeter	6.00
SK	Scott Kazmir	1.00
BL	Barry Larkin	1.50
VM	Victor Martinez	1.00
JM	Joe Mauer	1.50
MC	Dallas McPherson	1.00
PM	Paul Molitor	2.00
MO	Justin Morneau	1.00
DM	Dale Murphy	1.50
DO	David Ortiz	2.00
CP	Corey Patterson	1.00
JP	Jake Peavy	1.50
OP	Oliver Perez	1.00
AP	Albert Pujols	6.00
AR	Aramis Ramirez	1.50
RE	Jose Reyes	1.00
CR	Cal Ripken Jr.	8.00
JR	Jimmy Rollins	1.50
NR	Nolan Ryan	6.00
RS	Ryne Sandberg	4.00
JS	Johan Santana	2.00
MS	Mike Schmidt	4.00
BS	Ben Sheets	1.50
SM	John Smoltz	1.50
ST	Shingo Takatsu	1.50
MT	Mark Teixeira	1.50
TE	Miguel Tejada	2.00
BU	B.J. Upton	1.00
JW	Jake Westbrook	1.00
DW	David Wright	3.00
MY	Michael Young	1.00
CZ	Carlos Zambrano	1.50

SP Authentic Honors Jersey

		NM/M
Common Player:		4.00
Production 130 Sets		
JB	Jason Bay	4.00
AB	Adrian Beltre	6.00
WB	Wade Boggs	8.00
BO	Jeremy Bonderman	4.00
CA	Miguel Cabrera	8.00
WC	Will Clark	6.00
RC	Roger Clemens	10.00
CC	Carl Crawford	4.00
BC	Bobby Crosby	4.00
MG	Marcus Giles	4.00
DG	Dwight Gooden	6.00
GR	Khalil Greene	8.00
ZG	Zack Greinke	4.00
KG	Ken Griffey Jr.	15.00
TG	Tony Gwynn	8.00
TH	Travis Hafner	4.00
RH	Rich Harden	4.00
BJ	Bo Jackson	10.00
DJ	Derek Jeter	15.00
SK	Scott Kazmir	4.00
BL	Barry Larkin	6.00
VM	Victor Martinez	4.00
JM	Joe Mauer	6.00
MC	Dallas McPherson	4.00
PM	Paul Molitor	8.00
MO	Justin Morneau	4.00
DM	Dale Murphy	8.00
DO	David Ortiz	8.00
CP	Corey Patterson	4.00
JP	Jake Peavy	6.00
OP	Oliver Perez	4.00
AP	Albert Pujols	15.00
AR	Aramis Ramirez	6.00
RE	Jose Reyes	6.00
CR	Cal Ripken Jr.	20.00
JR	Jimmy Rollins	6.00
NR	Nolan Ryan	15.00
RS	Ryne Sandberg	10.00
JS	Johan Santana	8.00
MS	Mike Schmidt	8.00
BS	Ben Sheets	4.00
SM	John Smoltz	6.00
ST	Shingo Takatsu	4.00
MT	Mark Teixeira	6.00
TE	Miguel Tejada	6.00
BU	B.J. Upton	6.00
JW	Jake Westbrook	4.00
DW	David Wright	15.00
MY	Michael Young	4.00
CZ	Carlos Zambrano	6.00

SP Authentic Honors Signatures
No Pricing
Production 5 Sets

SP Authentic Materials

		NM/M
Common Player:		
Production 199 Sets		
Gold:		1X
Production 99 Sets		
1	A.J. Burnett	4.00
2	Aaron Rowand	4.00
3	Adam Dunn	6.00
4	Adrian Beltre	6.00
5	Adrian Gonzalez	4.00
6	Akinori Otsuka	4.00
7	Albert Pujols	15.00
8	Andre Dawson	6.00
9	Andruw Jones	6.00
10	Aramis Ramirez	6.00
11	Barry Larkin	6.00
12	Ben Sheets	4.00
13	Bo Jackson	8.00
14	Bobby Abreu	4.00
15	Bobby Crosby	6.00
16	Bronson Arroyo	6.00
17	Cal Ripken Jr.	20.00
18	Carl Crawford	4.00
19	Carlos Zambrano	4.00
20	Casey Kotchman	4.00
21	Cesar Izturis	4.00
22	Chone Figgins	4.00
23	Corey Patterson	4.00
24	Craig Biggio	6.00
25	Dale Murphy	6.00
26	Dallas McPherson	4.00
27	Danny Haren	4.00
28	Darryl Strawberry	4.00
29	David Ortiz	8.00
30	David Wright	10.00
31	Derek Jeter	15.00
32	Derek Lee	8.00
33	Don Mattingly	10.00
34	Dwight Gooden	6.00
35	Edgar Renteria	6.00
36	Eric Chavez	4.00
37	Eric Gagne	4.00
38	Gary Sheffield	4.00
39	Gavin Floyd	4.00
40	Pedro Martinez	8.00
41	Greg Maddux	10.00
42	Hank Blalock	4.00
43	Huston Street	4.00
44	J.D. Drew	4.00
45	Jake Peavy	4.00
46	Jake Westbrook	4.00
47	Jason Bay	4.00
48	Austin Kearns	4.00
49	Jeremy Reed	4.00

50	Jim Rice	6.00
51	Jimmy Rollins	6.00
52	Joe Blanton	4.00
53	Joe Mauer	6.00
54	Johan Santana	6.00
55	John Smoltz	6.00
56	Johnny Estrada	4.00
57	Jose Reyes	6.00
58	Ken Griffey Jr.	12.00
59	Kerry Wood	6.00
60	Khalil Greene	6.00
61	Marcus Giles	4.00
62	Melvin Mora	4.00
63	Mark Grace	6.00
64	Mark Mulder	4.00
65	Mark Prior	8.00
66	Mark Teixeira	6.00
67	Matt Clement	4.00
68	Michael Young	4.00
69	Miguel Cabrera	6.00
70	Miguel Tejada	6.00
71	Mike Piazza	8.00
72	Mike Schmidt	8.00
73	Nolan Ryan	15.00
74	Oliver Perez	4.00
75	Nick Johnson	4.00
76	Paul Molitor	8.00
77	Rafael Palmeiro	6.00
78	Randy Johnson	8.00
79	Reggie Jackson	8.00
80	Rich Harden	6.00
81	Rickie Weeks	6.00
82	Robin Yount	8.00
83	Roger Clemens	10.00
84	Roy Oswalt	4.00
85	Ryan Howard	15.00
86	Ryne Sandberg	8.00
87	Scott Kazmir	4.00
88	Scott Rolen	6.00
89	Sean Burroughs	4.00
90	Sean Casey	4.00
91	Shingo Takatsu	4.00
92	Tim Hudson	6.00
93	Tony Gwynn	8.00
94	Torii Hunter	6.00
95	Travis Hafner	4.00
96	Victor Martinez	4.00
97	Vladimir Guerrero	8.00
98	Wade Boggs	6.00
99	Will Clark	6.00
100	Yadier Molina	4.00

SP Authentic Signature Materials

No Pricing
Production 10 Sets

SP Authentic Signatures

NM/M
Production 25-550
Gold: No Pricing
Production 10 Sets

2	Aaron Rowand/550	20.00
3	Adam Dunn/25	20.00
4	Adrian Beltre/125	15.00
5	Adrian Gonzalez/550	10.00
6	Akinori Otsuka/475	15.00
8	Andre Dawson/125	15.00
10	Aramis Ramirez/475	15.00
11	Barry Larkin/125	20.00
12	Ben Sheets/350	12.00
15	Bobby Crosby/350	10.00
16	Bronson Arroyo/550	15.00
18	Carl Crawford/475	12.00
20	Casey Kotchman/550	8.00
21	Cesar Izturis/550	8.00
22	Chone Figgins/550	10.00
23	Corey Patterson/350	10.00
24	Craig Biggio/125	30.00
25	Dale Murphy/25	20.00
26	Dallas McPherson/550	10.00
27	Danny Haren/550	10.00
28	Darryl Strawberry/125	12.00
30	David Wright/350	60.00
31	Derek Jeter 150	140.00
32	Derrek Lee/125	15.00
34	Dwight Gooden/475	15.00
36	Eric Chavez 75	12.00
39	Gavin Floyd/550	8.00
43	Huston Street/550	25.00
45	Jake Peavy/475	15.00
46	Jake Westbrook/550	10.00
47	Jason Bay/475	12.00
48	Austin Kearns/550	10.00
49	Jeremy Reed/550	15.00
50	Jim Rice/350	15.00
52	Joe Blanton/550	10.00
53	Joe Mauer/350	20.00
57	Jose Reyes/475	35.00
60	Khalil Greene/350	20.00
62	Melvin Mora/475	12.00

64	Mark Mulder/350	15.00
66	Mark Teixeira/125	25.00
67	Matt Clement/350	20.00
68	Michael Young/475	15.00
69	Miguel Cabrera/125	25.00
74	Oliver Perez/475	15.00
75	Nick Johnson/550	10.00
84	Roy Oswalt/125	20.00
85	Ryan Howard/550	70.00
86	Ryne Sandberg/25	125.00
87	Scott Kazmir/475	15.00
89	Sean Burroughs/475	10.00
91	Shingo Takatsu/550	10.00

SP Collection of Stars

NM/M
Common Player: 1.00
Production 299 Sets

BR	Bronson Arroyo	1.00
GA	Garrett Atkins	1.00
JE	Jeff Baker	1.00
BA	Clint Barmes	1.00
JB	Jason Bartlett	1.00
JA	Jason Bay	1.00
BE	Adrian Beltre	1.50
BL	Joe Blanton	1.00
BO	Jeremy Bonderman	1.00
YB	Yhency Brazoban	1.00
CB	Chris Burke	1.50
AB	A.J. Burnett	1.00
DB	David Bush	1.00
DC	Daniel Cabrera	1.00
MC	Miguel Cabrera	2.00
CA	Jorge Cantu	1.00
GC	Gustavo Chacin	1.00
RC	Roger Clemens	6.00
JD	J.D. Closser	1.00
CH	Chad Cordero	1.00
JC	Jesse Crain	1.00
CC	Carl Crawford	1.00
CO	Coco Crisp	1.00
DD	David DeJesus	1.00
DU	Jason Dubois	1.00
CD	Chris Duffy	1.00
CF	Chone Figgins	1.00
GF	Gavin Floyd	1.00
JF	Jeff Francis	1.00
RF	Ryan Freel	1.00
JG	Joey Gathright	1.00
GO	Jonny Gomes	1.00
AG	Adrian Gonzalez	1.00
GR	Khalil Greene	2.00
ZG	Zack Greinke	1.00
KG	Ken Griffey Jr.	4.00
CG	Carlos Guillen	1.00
TR	Travis Hafner	1.00
BH	Bill Hall	1.00
RH	Rich Harden	1.50
DH	Danny Haren	1.00
MH	Matt Holliday	1.00
HO	Ryan Howard	2.00
BI	Brandon Inge	1.00
CI	Cesar Izturis	1.00
EJ	Edwin Jackson	1.00
DJ	Derek Jeter	6.00
NJ	Nick Johnson	1.00
RJ	Reed Johnson	1.00
SK	Scott Kazmir	1.00
CK	Casey Kotchman	1.00
JL	Jason Lane	1.00
LE	Brandon League	1.00
CL	Cliff Lee	1.00
GM	Greg Maddux	4.00
AM	Andy Marte	1.00
JM	Joe Mauer	1.50
YM	Yadier Molina	1.00
MM	Melvin Mora	1.00
MO	Guillermo Mota	1.00
BM	Brett Myers	1.00
DO	David Ortiz	2.00
CP	Corey Patterson	1.00

JP	Jake Peavy	1.50
WM	Wily Mo Pena	1.00
OP	Oliver Perez	1.00
PI	Joel Pineiro	1.00
MP	Mark Prior	2.00
AP	Albert Pujols	6.00
RQ	Robb Quinlan	1.00
RA	Aramis Ramirez	1.50
JR	Jeremy Reed	1.00
RE	Jose Reyes	1.50
RI	Alex Rios	1.00
CR	Cal Ripken Jr.	8.00
RO	Jimmy Rollins	1.50
AR	Aaron Rowand	1.00
JS	Johan Santana	2.00
MS	Mike Schmidt	4.00
LS	Luke Scott	1.00
CS	Chris Shelton	1.00
GS	Grady Sizemore	1.50
SM	John Smoltz	1.50
HS	Huston Street	1.00
NS	Nick Swisher	1.00
ST	Shingo Takatsu	1.00
WT	Willy Taveras	1.00
MT	Mark Teahen	1.00
TE	Mark Teixeira	1.50
MI	Miguel Tejada	1.50
TH	Charles Thomas	1.00
CT	Chad Tracy	1.00
BU	B.J. Upton	1.50
WE	Jayson Werth	1.00
JW	Jake Westbrook	1.00
DW	David Wright	3.00
KY	Kevin Youkilis	1.00
MY	Michael Young	1.00
CZ	Carlos Zambrano	1.50

SP Collection of Stars Jersey

NM/M
Production 130 Sets

BR	Bronson Arroyo	4.00
GA	Garrett Atkins	4.00
JE	Jeff Baker	4.00
BA	Clint Barmes	6.00
JB	Jason Bartlett	4.00
JA	Jason Bay	4.00
BE	Adrian Beltre	6.00
BL	Joe Blanton	4.00
BO	Jeremy Bonderman	4.00
YB	Yhency Brazoban	4.00
CB	Chris Burke	4.00
AB	A.J. Burnett	4.00
DB	David Bush	4.00
DC	Daniel Cabrera	4.00
MC	Miguel Cabrera	8.00
CA	Jorge Cantu	4.00
GC	Gustavo Chacin	4.00
RC	Roger Clemens	10.00
JD	J.D. Closser	4.00
CH	Chad Cordero	4.00
JC	Jesse Crain	4.00
CC	Carl Crawford	4.00
CO	Coco Crisp	4.00
DD	David DeJesus	4.00
DU	Jason Dubois	4.00
CD	Chris Duffy	6.00
CF	Chone Figgins	4.00
GF	Gavin Floyd	4.00
JF	Jeff Francis	4.00
RF	Ryan Freel	4.00
JG	Joey Gathright	4.00
GO	Jonny Gomes	6.00
AG	Adrian Gonzalez	4.00
GR	Khalil Greene	6.00
ZG	Zack Greinke	4.00
KG	Ken Griffey Jr.	15.00
CG	Carlos Guillen	4.00
TR	Travis Hafner	4.00
BH	Bill Hall	4.00
RH	Rich Harden	4.00
DH	Danny Haren	4.00
MH	Matt Holliday	8.00
HO	Ryan Howard	15.00
BI	Brandon Inge	4.00
CI	Cesar Izturis	4.00
EJ	Edwin Jackson	4.00
DJ	Derek Jeter	15.00
NJ	Nick Johnson	4.00
RJ	Reed Johnson	4.00
SK	Scott Kazmir	4.00
CK	Casey Kotchman	4.00
JL	Jason Lane	4.00
LE	Brandon League	4.00
CL	Cliff Lee	4.00
GM	Greg Maddux	10.00
AM	Andy Marte	4.00
JM	Joe Mauer	6.00
DM	Dallas McPherson	4.00
YM	Yadier Molina	4.00
MM	Melvin Mora	4.00
MO	Guillermo Mota	4.00
BM	Brett Myers	4.00

DO	David Ortiz	8.00
CP	Corey Patterson	4.00
JP	Jake Peavy	6.00
WM	Wily Mo Pena	4.00
OP	Oliver Perez	4.00
PI	Joel Pineiro	4.00
MP	Mark Prior	6.00
AP	Albert Pujols	15.00
RQ	Robb Quinlan	4.00
RA	Aramis Ramirez	6.00
JR	Jeremy Reed	4.00
RE	Jose Reyes	6.00
RI	Alex Rios	4.00
CR	Cal Ripken Jr.	20.00
RO	Jimmy Rollins	6.00
AR	Aaron Rowand	6.00
JS	Johan Santana	8.00
MS	Mike Schmidt	10.00
LS	Luke Scott	4.00
CS	Chris Shelton	4.00
GS	Grady Sizemore	6.00
SM	John Smoltz	6.00
HS	Huston Street	6.00
NS	Nick Swisher	4.00
ST	Shingo Takatsu	4.00
WT	Willy Taveras	4.00
MT	Mark Teahen	4.00
TE	Mark Teixeira	6.00
MI	Miguel Tejada	6.00
TH	Charles Thomas	4.00
CT	Chad Tracy	4.00
BU	B.J. Upton	4.00
WE	Jayson Werth	4.00
JW	Jake Westbrook	4.00
DW	David Wright	10.00
KY	Kevin Youkilis	4.00
MY	Michael Young	4.00
CZ	Carlos Zambrano	6.00

SP Collection of Stars Signatures

No Pricing
Production 5 Sets

SPx Materials

NM/M
Common Player: 3.00
Production 199 Sets
Spectrum: 1X
Production 99 Sets

1	Aaron Harang	3.00
2	Aaron Rowand	5.00
3	Aaron Miles	3.00
4	Adrian Gonzalez	5.00
5	Alex Rios	3.00
6	Angel Berroa	3.00
7	B.J. Upton	5.00
8	Brandon Claussen	3.00
9	Andy Marte	5.00
10	Brandon Webb	5.00
11	Bronson Arroyo	5.00
12	Casey Kotchman	3.00
13	Cesar Izturis	3.00
14	Chad Cordero	3.00
15	Chad Tracy	3.00
16	Charles Thomas	3.00
17	Chase Utley	8.00
18	Chone Figgins	3.00
19	Chris Burke	5.00
20	Cliff Lee	3.00
21	Clint Barmes	5.00
22	Coco Crisp	3.00
23	Bill Hall	3.00
24	Dallas McPherson	5.00
25	Brad Halsey	3.00
26	Daniel Cabrera	3.00
27	Danny Haren	3.00
28	David Bush	3.00
29	David DeJesus	3.00
30	D.J. Houlton	3.00
31	Derek Jeter	20.00
32	Dewon Brazelton	3.00
33	Edwin Jackson	3.00
34	Brad Hawpe	3.00
35	Brandon Inge	3.00
36	Brett Myers	3.00
37	Garrett Atkins	3.00
38	Gavin Floyd	3.00
39	Grady Sizemore	10.00
40	Guillermo Mota	3.00
41	Carlos Guillen	3.00
42	Gustavo Chacin	3.00
43	Huston Street	5.00
44	Chris Duffy	3.00
45	J.D. Closser	3.00
46	J.J. Hardy	3.00
47	Jason Bartlett	3.00
48	Jason Dubois	3.00
49	Chris Shelton	3.00
50	Jason Lane	3.00
51	Jayson Werth	3.00
52	Jeff Baker	3.00
53	Jeff Francis	3.00

54	Jeremy Bonderman	3.00
55	Jeremy Reed	3.00
56	Jerome Williams	3.00
57	Jesse Crain	3.00
58	Chris Young	3.00
59	Jhonny Peralta	3.00
60	Joe Blanton	3.00
61	Joe Crede	3.00
62	Joel Pineiro	3.00
63	Joey Gathright	3.00
64	John Buck	3.00
65	Jonny Gomes	8.00
66	Jorge Cantu	8.00
67	Dan Johnson	3.00
68	Jose Valverde	3.00
69	Ervin Santana	3.00
70	Justin Morneau	5.00
71	Keiichi Yabu	5.00
72	Ken Griffey Jr.	15.00
73	Jason Repko	5.00
74	Kevin Youkilis	3.00
75	Koyie Hill	3.00
76	Laynce Nix	3.00
77	Luke Scott	3.00
78	Juan Rivera	3.00
79	Justin Duchscherer	3.00
80	Mark Teahen	3.00
81	Lance Niekro	3.00
82	Michael Cuddyer	3.00
83	Nick Swisher	3.00
84	Noah Lowry	3.00
85	Matt Holliday	8.00
86	Reed Johnson	3.00
87	Rich Harden	5.00
88	Robb Quinlan	3.00
89	Nick Johnson	3.00
90	Ryan Howard	20.00
91	Nook Logan	3.00
92	Steve Schmoll	3.00
93	Tadahito Iguchi	20.00
94	Willy Taveras	3.00
95	Wily Mo Pena	3.00
96	Xavier Nady	3.00
97	Yadier Molina	3.00
98	Yhency Brazoban	3.00
99	Ryan Freel	3.00
100	Zack Greinke	3.00

SPx Signatures

NM/M

Production 50-350
Spectrum: No Pricing
Production 10 Sets
Jersey Auto.: No Pricing
Production 10 Sets

1	Aaron Harang/350	8.00
2	Aaron Rowand/150	20.00
4	Adrian Gonzalez/225	15.00
6	Angel Berroa/150	8.00
7	B.J. Upton/50	12.00
8	Brandon Claussen/350	8.00
9	Andy Marte/350	10.00
11	Bronson Arroyo/350	20.00
12	Casey Kotchman/225	8.00
13	Cesar Izturis/150	8.00
14	Chad Cordero/350	10.00
15	Chad Tracy/350	10.00
16	Charles Thomas/350	5.00
17	Chase Utley/50	40.00
18	Chone Figgins/150	8.00
19	Chris Burke/350	15.00
20	Cliff Lee/225	10.00
21	Clint Barmes/350	12.00
22	Coco Crisp/225	15.00
23	Bill Hall/350	8.00
24	Dallas McPherson/150	10.00
25	Brad Halsey/350	8.00
26	Daniel Cabrera/350	15.00
27	Danny Haren/225	10.00
28	David Bush/350	10.00
29	David DeJesus/225	8.00
30	D.J. Houlton/350	8.00
31	Derek Zumsteg/50	150.00
32	Dewon Brazelton/350	8.00
33	Edwin Jackson/150	8.00
34	Brad Hawpe/350	8.00
35	Brandon Inge/350	10.00
36	Brett Myers/150	8.00
37	Garrett Atkins/350	15.00
38	Gavin Floyd/150	8.00
39	Grady Sizemore/350	40.00
40	Guillermo Mota/225	8.00
41	Carlos Guillen/150	8.00
42	Gustavo Chacin/350	10.00
43	Huston Street/350	25.00
44	Chris Duffy/225	15.00
45	J.D. Closser/350	8.00
46	J.J. Hardy/50	10.00
47	Jason Bartlett/350	8.00
48	Jason Dubois/350	10.00
50	Jason Lane/350	8.00
51	Jayson Werth/350	12.00

52	Jeff Baker/350	8.00
53	Jeff Francis/150	10.00
54	Jeremy Bonderman/50	20.00
55	Jeremy Reed/150	10.00
56	Jeremy Williams/50	8.00
57	Jesse Crain/350	10.00
59	Jhonny Peralta/350	15.00
60	Joe Blanton/350	8.00
61	Joe Crede/350	25.00
62	Joel Pineiro/150	12.00
63	Joey Gathright/350	8.00
64	John Buck/350	8.00
65	Jonny Gomes/350	15.00
66	Jorge Cantu/350	15.00
67	Dan Johnson/350	15.00
68	Jose Valverde/350	15.00
69	Ervin Santana/350	15.00
71	Keiichi Yabu/350	25.00
73	Jason Repko/350	25.00
74	Kevin Youkilis/225	12.00
75	Koyie Hill/350	10.00
76	Laynce Nix/150	8.00
77	Luke Scott/350	40.00
78	Juan Rivera/225	8.00
79	Justin Duchscherer/350	10.00
80	Mark Teahen/350	8.00
81	Lance Niekro/350	10.00
82	Michael Cuddyer/350	8.00
83	Nick Swisher	
84	Noah Lowry/150	15.00
85	Matt Holliday/225	25.00
86	Reed Johnson/350	8.00
87	Rich Harden	
88	Robb Quinlan/350	5.00
89	Nick Johnson/150	8.00
90	Ryan Howard/225	80.00
91	Nook Logan/350	8.00
92	Steve Schmoll/350	5.00
93	Tadahito Iguchi/50	200.00
95	Wily Mo Pena/150	8.00
96	Xavier Nady/150	10.00
98	Yhency Brazoban/350	8.00
100	Zack Greinke/150	

SPx Superscripts Signatures

No Pricing
Production 15 Sets

SPx Superscripts Triple Signature

No Pricing
Production 5 Sets

SPx Winning Materials Dual

No Pricing
Production 20 Sets
Dual Auto.: No Pricing
Production 5 Sets

SPXtreme Stats

NM/M

Common Player: 1.00
Production 299 Sets

BA	Bobby Abreu	1.50
AB	Adrian Beltre	1.50
CB	Craig Biggio	1.50
HB	Hank Blalock	1.50
MC	Miguel Cabrera	2.00
SC	Sean Casey	1.00
EC	Eric Chavez	1.00
RC	Roger Clemens	6.00
CC	Carl Crawford	1.00
BC	Bobby Crosby	1.00
JD	J.D. Drew	1.00
AD	Adam Dunn	1.50
EG	Eric Gagne	1.00
GR	Khalil Greene	1.50
KG	Ken Griffey Jr.	4.00
VG	Vladimir Guerrero	2.00
TH	Tim Hudson	1.50
HU	Torii Hunter	1.00
DJ	Derek Jeter	6.00
RJ	Randy Johnson	2.00
AJ	Andruw Jones	1.50
DL	Derrek Lee	1.50
GM	Greg Maddux	4.00
VM	Victor Martinez	1.00

JM	Joe Mauer	1.50
MO	Melvin Mora	1.00
MM	Mark Mulder	1.50
DO	David Ortiz	2.00
RO	Roy Oswalt	1.50
RP	Rafael Palmeiro	1.50
CP	Corey Patterson	1.00
JP	Jake Peavy	1.50
OP	Oliver Perez	1.00
PI	Mike Piazza	3.00
MP	Mark Prior	2.00
AP	Albert Pujols	6.00
AR	Aramis Ramirez	1.50
ER	Edgar Renteria	1.00
JR	Jose Reyes	1.50
SR	Scott Rolen	2.00
SA	Johan Santana	2.00
BS	Ben Sheets	1.00
GS	Gary Sheffield	1.50
SM	John Smoltz	1.50
MT	Mark Teixeira	1.50
TE	Miguel Tejada	1.50
KW	Kerry Wood	1.50
MY	Michael Young	1.50
DW	David Wright	3.00
CZ	Carlos Zambrano	1.50

SPXtreme Stats Jersey

NM/M

BA	Bobby Abreu	6.00
AB	Adrian Beltre	6.00
CB	Craig Biggio	6.00
HB	Hank Blalock	4.00
MC	Miguel Cabrera	8.00
SC	Sean Casey	4.00
EC	Eric Chavez	4.00
RC	Roger Clemens	10.00
CC	Carl Crawford	4.00
BC	Bobby Crosby	4.00
JD	J.D. Drew	4.00
AD	Adam Dunn	6.00
EG	Eric Gagne	4.00
GR	Khalil Greene	4.00
KG	Ken Griffey Jr.	15.00
VG	Vladimir Guerrero	8.00
TH	Tim Hudson	4.00
HU	Torii Hunter	4.00
DJ	Derek Jeter	15.00
RJ	Randy Johnson	8.00
AJ	Andruw Jones	6.00
DL	Derrek Lee	6.00
GM	Greg Maddux	10.00
VM	Victor Martinez	4.00
JM	Joe Mauer	6.00
MO	Melvin Mora	4.00
MM	Mark Mulder	6.00
DO	David Ortiz	8.00
RO	Roy Oswalt	6.00
RP	Rafael Palmeiro	6.00
CP	Corey Patterson	4.00
JP	Jake Peavy	6.00
OP	Oliver Perez	4.00
PI	Mike Piazza	8.00
MP	Mark Prior	6.00
AP	Albert Pujols	15.00
AR	Aramis Ramirez	4.00
ER	Edgar Renteria	4.00
JR	Jose Reyes	66.00
SR	Scott Rolen	6.00
SA	Johan Santana	8.00
BS	Ben Sheets	6.00
GS	Gary Sheffield	6.00
SM	John Smoltz	6.00
MT	Mark Teixeira	6.00
TE	Miguel Tejada	6.00
KW	Kerry Wood	6.00
DW	David Wright	6.00
MY	Michael Young	4.00
CZ	Carlos Zambrano	6.00

SPXtreme Stats Signatures

No Pricing
Production 5 Sets

2005 SP Legendary Cuts

NM/M

Complete Set (90):		25.00
Common Player:		.25
Pack (4):		14.00
Box (12):		150.00
1	Al Kaline	1.00
2	Babe Ruth	3.00
3	Bill Mazeroski	.25
4	Billy Williams	.25
5	Bob Feller	.50
6	Bob Gibson	1.00
7	Bob Lemon	.25
8	Bobby Doerr	.25
9	Brooks Robinson	1.00
10	Carl Yastrzemski	1.50

11	Carlton Fisk	.75
12	Casey Stengel	.50
13	Jim "Catfish" Hunter	.25
14	Christy Mathewson	1.00
15	Cy Young	.50
16	Dennis Eckersley	.25
17	Dizzy Dean	.50
18	Don Drysdale	.25
19	Don Sutton	.25
20	Duke Snider	.75
21	Early Wynn	.25
22	Eddie Mathews	1.00
23	Eddie Murray	.75
24	Enos Slaughter	.25
25	Ernie Banks	1.00
26	Fergie Jenkins	.25
27	Frank Robinson	.25
28	Gary Carter	.25
29	Gaylord Perry	.25
30	Reggie Jackson	1.00
31	George Kell	.25
32	George Sisler	.25
33	Hal Newhouser	.25
34	Harmon Killebrew	1.00
35	Honus Wagner	1.00
36	Jackie Robinson	.50
37	Jim Bunning	.25
38	Jim Palmer	.50
39	Jimmie Foxx	.75
40	Joe DiMaggio	2.00
41	Joe Morgan	.50
42	Johnny Bench	1.00
43	Johnny Mize	.25
44	Juan Marichal	.50
45	Kirby Puckett	.75
46	Larry Doby	.25
47	Lefty Grove	.25
48	Lou Boudreau	.25
49	Lou Brock	.50
50	Lou Gehrig	2.00
51	Luis Aparicio	.25
52	Mel Ott	.50
53	Mickey Cochrane	.25
54	Mickey Mantle	4.00
55	Mike Schmidt	1.50
56	Monte Irvin	.50
57	Nolan Ryan	2.00
58	Orlando Cepeda	.25
59	Ozzie Smith	1.00
60	Paul Molitor	.50
61	Pee Wee Reese	.25
62	Phil Niekro	.25
63	Phil Rizzuto	.50
64	Ralph Kiner	.25
65	Red Schoendienst	.25
66	Richie Ashburn	.25
67	Rick Ferrell	.25
68	Robin Roberts	.25
69	Robin Yount	1.00
70	Rod Carew	.50
71	Rogers Hornsby	.50
72	Rollie Fingers	.25
73	Roy Campanella	.50
74	Ryne Sandberg	1.00
75	Satchel Paige	1.00
76	Stan Musial	1.00
77	Steve Carlton	.25
78	Ted Williams	2.00
79	Thurman Munson	1.00
80	Tom Seaver	1.00
81	Tony Gwynn	1.00
82	Tony Perez	.25
83	Ty Cobb	1.50
84	Wade Boggs	.50
85	Walter Johnson	1.00
86	Warren Spahn	1.00
87	Whitey Ford	1.00
88	Willie McCovey	.50
89	Willie Stargell	.75
90	Yogi Berra	1.00

Holofoil

Holofoil: 3-5X
Production 50 Sets

Classic Careers

NM/M

Common Player:		2.00
Production 399 Sets		
Gold:		1-2X
Production 75 Sets		
Platinum:		No Pricing
Production One Set		
LA	Luis Aparicio	2.00
HB	Harold Baines	2.00
JB	Jay Buhner	2.00
CA	Jose Canseco	3.00
GC	Gary Carter	2.00
OC	Orlando Cepeda	2.00
JC	Jack Clark	2.00
WC	Will Clark	3.00
DC	David Cone	2.00
AD	Andre Dawson	2.00
BD	Bobby Doerr	2.00

LD	Lenny Dykstra	2.00
CE	Carl Erskine	2.00
SF	Sid Fernandez	2.00
CF	Carlton Fisk	3.00
GF	George Foster	2.00
BF	Bill Freehan	2.00
DG	Dwight Gooden	2.00
GG	Rich "Goose" Gossage	2.00
MG	Mark Grace	3.00
RG	Ron Guidry	2.00
GU	Don Gullett	2.00
KH	Keith Hernandez	2.00
BH	Bob Horner	2.00
FJ	Fergie Jenkins	2.00
BL	Barry Larkin	3.00
SL	Sparky Lyle	2.00
BM	Bill Madlock	2.00
DE	Dennis Martinez	2.00
GM	Gary Mathews	2.00
MA	Don Mattingly	5.00
JM	Jack Morris	2.00
MU	Bobby Murcer	2.00
DM	Dale Murphy	3.00
GN	Graig Nettles	2.00
PN	Phil Niekro	2.00
TO	Tony Oliva	2.00
GP	Gaylord Perry	2.00
JP	Johnny Podres	2.00
TR	Tim Raines	2.00
JR	Jim Rice	2.00
CR	Cal Ripken Jr.	8.00
AR	Al Rosen	2.00
ST	Dave Stewart	2.00
DS	Darryl Strawberry	2.00
SU	Bruce Sutter	2.00
DO	Don Sutton	2.00
LT	Luis Tiant	2.00
AV	Andy Van Slyke	2.00
CY	Carl Yastrzemski	4.00

Classic Careers Autograph

NM/M

Common Player: 15.00
Production 25 Sets
Gold: No Pricing
Production 10 Sets
Platinum: No Pricing
Production One Set

LA	Luis Aparicio	20.00
HB	Harold Baines	25.00
JB	Jay Buhner	30.00
CA	Jose Canseco	40.00
GC	Gary Carter	20.00
OC	Orlando Cepeda	30.00
JC	Jack Clark	20.00
WC	Will Clark	25.00
DC	David Cone	20.00
AD	Andre Dawson	20.00
BD	Bobby Doerr	20.00
LD	Lenny Dykstra	20.00
CE	Carl Erskine	20.00
SF	Sid Fernandez	15.00
CF	Carlton Fisk	35.00
GF	George Foster	25.00
BF	Bill Freehan	25.00
DG	Dwight Gooden	15.00
GG	Rich "Goose" Gossage	20.00
MG	Mark Grace	30.00
RG	Ron Guidry	35.00
GU	Don Gullett	15.00
KH	Keith Hernandez	20.00
BH	Bob Horner	15.00
FJ	Fergie Jenkins	25.00
BL	Barry Larkin	40.00
SL	Sparky Lyle	20.00
BM	Bill Madlock	20.00
DE	Dennis Martinez	15.00
GM	Gary Mathews	15.00
MA	Don Mattingly	60.00
JM	Jack Morris	20.00
MU	Bobby Murcer	30.00
DM	Dale Murphy	35.00
PN	Phil Niekro	20.00
GN	Graig Nettles	20.00
TO	Tony Oliva	20.00
GP	Gaylord Perry	20.00
JP	Johnny Podres	15.00
TR	Tim Raines	20.00
JR	Jim Rice	25.00
CR	Cal Ripken Jr.	125.00
AR	Al Rosen	20.00
ST	Dave Stewart	15.00
DS	Darryl Strawberry	20.00
SU	Bruce Sutter	25.00
DO	Don Sutton	20.00
LT	Luis Tiant	20.00
AV	Andy Van Slyke	30.00
CY	Carl Yastrzemski	50.00

Classic Careers Jersey Autograph

NM/M

Production 25 Sets
Gold: No Pricing
Production 10 Sets
Platinum: No Pricing
Production One Set

LA	Luis Aparicio	20.00
HB	Harold Baines	25.00
JB	Jay Buhner	30.00
GC	Gary Carter	20.00
OC	Orlando Cepeda	30.00
JC	Jack Clark	20.00
WC	Will Clark	25.00
DC	David Cone	20.00
AD	Andre Dawson	20.00
BD	Bobby Doerr	20.00
LD	Lenny Dykstra	20.00
CE	Carl Erskine	20.00
SF	Sid Fernandez	15.00
GF	George Foster	25.00
BF	Bill Freehan	25.00
DG	Dwight Gooden	15.00
GG	Rich "Goose" Gossage	20.00
MG	Mark Grace	30.00
RG	Ron Guidry	35.00
GU	Don Gullett	15.00
KH	Keith Hernandez	20.00
BH	Bob Horner	15.00
FJ	Fergie Jenkins	25.00
BL	Barry Larkin	40.00
SL	Sparky Lyle	20.00
BM	Bill Madlock	20.00
DE	Dennis Martinez	15.00
GM	Gary Mathews	15.00
MA	Don Mattingly	60.00
JM	Jack Morris	20.00
MU	Bobby Murcer	30.00
DM	Dale Murphy	35.00
PN	Phil Niekro	20.00
GN	Graig Nettles	20.00
TO	Tony Oliva	20.00
GP	Gaylord Perry	20.00
JP	Johnny Podres	15.00
TR	Tim Raines	20.00
JR	Jim Rice	25.00
CR	Cal Ripken Jr.	125.00
AR	Al Rosen	20.00
ST	Dave Stewart	15.00
DS	Darryl Strawberry	20.00
SU	Bruce Sutter	25.00
LT	Luis Tiant	20.00
AV	Andy Van Slyke	30.00
CY	Carl Yastrzemski	50.00

Classic Careers Patch Autograph

NM/M

Production 25 Sets
Gold: No Pricing
Production 5 Sets
Platinum: No Pricing
Production One Set

HB	Harold Baines	40.00
JB	Jay Buhner	50.00
JC	Jack Clark	35.00
WC	Will Clark	40.00
DC	David Cone	35.00
AD	Andre Dawson	35.00
BD	Bobby Doerr	35.00
LD	Lenny Dykstra	35.00
SF	Sid Fernandez	25.00
GF	George Foster	40.00
BF	Bill Freehan	25.00
DG	Dwight Gooden	25.00
GG	Rich "Goose" Gossage	35.00
MG	Mark Grace	50.00
GU	Don Gullett	25.00
KH	Keith Hernandez	35.00
BL	Barry Larkin	60.00
DE	Dennis Martinez	25.00
GM	Gary Mathews	25.00
JM	Jack Morris	35.00
GN	Graig Nettles	35.00
TO	Tony Oliva	35.00
GP	Gaylord Perry	30.00
TR	Tim Raines	30.00
JR	Jim Rice	40.00
CR	Cal Ripken Jr.	200.00
ST	Dave Stewart	25.00
DS	Darryl Strawberry	30.00
AV	Andy Van Slyke	40.00

Classic Careers Jersey

NM/M

Common Player: 4.00
Gold: 1X

Production 75 Sets
Platinum: No Pricing
Production One Set

LA	Luis Aparicio	6.00
HB	Harold Baines	6.00
JB	Jay Buhner	6.00
CA	Jose Canseco	8.00
GC	Gary Carter	4.00
OC	Orlando Cepeda	6.00
JC	Jack Clark	4.00
WC	Will Clark	6.00
DC	David Cone	4.00
AD	Andre Dawson	6.00
BD	Bobby Doerr	6.00
LD	Lenny Dykstra	6.00
CE	Carl Erskine	4.00
SF	Sid Fernandez	4.00
CF	Carlton Fisk	6.00
GF	George Foster	4.00
BF	Bill Freehan	6.00
DG	Dwight Gooden	4.00
GG	Rich "Goose" Gossage	6.00
MG	Mark Grace	8.00
RG	Ron Guidry	6.00
GU	Don Gullett	4.00
KH	Keith Hernandez	4.00
BH	Bob Horner	4.00
FJ	Fergie Jenkins	6.00
BL	Barry Larkin	6.00
SL	Sparky Lyle	4.00
BM	Bill Madlock	4.00
DE	Dennis Martinez	4.00
GM	Gary Mathews	4.00
MA	Don Mattingly	12.00
JM	Jack Morris	4.00
MU	Bobby Murcer	4.00
DM	Dale Murphy	8.00
PN	Phil Niekro	4.00
GN	Graig Nettles	4.00
TO	Tony Oliva	4.00
GP	Gaylord Perry	4.00
JP	Johnny Podres	6.00
TR	Tim Raines	4.00
JR	Jim Rice	6.00
CR	Cal Ripken Jr.	20.00
AR	Al Rosen	6.00
ST	Dave Stewart	4.00
DS	Darryl Strawberry	6.00
SU	Bruce Sutter	4.00
DO	Don Sutton	4.00
LT	Luis Tiant	4.00
AV	Andy Van Slyke	4.00
CY	Carl Yastrzemski	15.00

Classic Careers Patch

NM/M

Production 50 Sets
Gold: No Pricing
Production 10 Sets
Platinum: No Pricing
Production One Set

HB	Harold Baines	10.00
JB	Jay Buhner	
CA	Jose Canseco	15.00
JC	Jack Clark	10.00
WC	Will Clark	20.00
DC	David Cone	15.00
AD	Andre Dawson	15.00
BD	Bobby Doerr	15.00
LD	Lenny Dykstra	15.00
SF	Sid Fernandez	10.00
GF	George Foster	10.00
BF	Bill Freehan	12.00
DG	Dwight Gooden	15.00
GG	Rich "Goose" Gossage	12.00
MG	Mark Grace	20.00
KH	Keith Hernandez	12.00
BL	Barry Larkin	25.00
DE	Dennis Martinez	10.00
GM	Gary Mathews	10.00
JM	Jack Morris	10.00
GN	Graig Nettles	10.00
GP	Gaylord Perry	12.00
TR	Tim Raines	10.00
JR	Jim Rice	15.00
CR	Cal Ripken Jr.	40.00
AV	Andy Van Slyke	15.00
ST	Dave Stewart	10.00
DS	Darryl Strawberry	12.00

Dual Legendary Cuts

Production 1-10

Glory Days

NM/M

Common Player: 2.00
Production 399 Sets
Gold: 1-2X
Production 75 Sets
Platinum: No Pricing
Production One Set
HB Harold Baines 2.00

YB	Yogi Berra	4.00
LB	Lou Brock	2.00
JB	Jay Buhner	2.00
CA	Jose Canseco	3.00
JC	Jack Clark	2.00
WC	Will Clark	3.00
DC	David Cone	2.00
AD	Andre Dawson	2.00
BD	Bobby Doerr	2.00
LD	Lenny Dykstra	2.00
SF	Sid Fernandez	2.00
WF	Whitey Ford	3.00
GF	George Foster	2.00
BF	Bill Freehan	2.00
KG	Kirk Gibson	2.00
DG	Dwight Gooden	2.00
RG	Ron Guidry	3.00
GU	Don Gullett	2.00
TG	Tony Gwynn	4.00
KH	Keith Hernandez	2.00
BH	Bob Horner	2.00
FJ	Fergie Jenkins	2.00
BL	Barry Larkin	3.00
SL	Sparky Lyle	2.00
FL	Fred Lynn	2.00
BM	Bill Madlock	2.00
MA	Juan Marichal	3.00
DE	Dennis Martinez	2.00
GM	Gary Mathews	2.00
PM	Paul Molitor	4.00
JM	Jack Morris	2.00
MU	Bobby Murcer	2.00
DM	Dale Murphy	3.00
GN	Graig Nettles	2.00
TO	Tony Oliva	2.00
JP	Jim Palmer	3.00
TR	Tim Raines	2.00
JR	Jim Rice	2.00
CR	Cal Ripken Jr.	8.00
AR	Al Rosen	2.00
NR	Nolan Ryan	8.00
RS	Red Schoendienst	2.00
SN	Duke Snider	3.00
ST	Dave Stewart	2.00
DS	Darryl Strawberry	2.00
BS	Bruce Sutter	2.00
LT	Luis Tiant	2.00
AV	Andy Van Slyke	2.00
RY	Robin Yount	4.00

Glory Days Autograph

NM/M

Common Player: 15.00
Production 25 Sets
Gold: No Pricing
Production 10 Sets
Platinum: No Pricing
Production One Set

HB	Harold Baines	25.00
YB	Yogi Berra	50.00
LB	Lou Brock	30.00
JB	Jay Buhner	30.00
CA	Jose Canseco	40.00
JC	Jack Clark	20.00
WC	Will Clark	25.00
DC	David Cone	20.00
AD	Andre Dawson	20.00
BD	Bobby Doerr	20.00
LD	Lenny Dykstra	20.00
SF	Sid Fernandez	15.00
WF	Whitey Ford	40.00
GF	George Foster	25.00
BF	Bill Freehan	25.00
KG	Kirk Gibson	20.00
DG	Dwight Gooden	15.00
RG	Ron Guidry	35.00
GU	Don Gullett	15.00
TG	Tony Gwynn	40.00
KH	Keith Hernandez	20.00
BH	Bob Horner	15.00
FJ	Fergie Jenkins	25.00
BL	Barry Larkin	40.00
SL	Sparky Lyle	20.00
FL	Fred Lynn	15.00
BM	Bill Madlock	20.00
MA	Juan Marichal	25.00
DE	Dennis Martinez	20.00
GM	Gary Mathews	15.00
PM	Paul Molitor	40.00
JM	Jack Morris	20.00
MU	Bobby Murcer	25.00
DM	Dale Murphy	35.00
GN	Graig Nettles	20.00
TO	Tony Oliva	20.00
JP	Jim Palmer	25.00
TR	Tim Raines	20.00
JR	Jim Rice	25.00
CR	Cal Ripken Jr.	125.00
AR	Al Rosen	20.00
NR	Nolan Ryan	100.00
RS	Red Schoendienst	20.00
SN	Duke Snider	40.00
ST	Dave Stewart	15.00
DS	Darryl Strawberry	20.00

BS	Bruce Sutter	25.00
LT	Luis Tiant	20.00
AV	Andy Van Slyke	30.00
RY	Robin Yount	50.00

Glory Days Patch Autograph

NM/M

Production 25 Sets
Gold: No Pricing
Production 5 Sets
Platinum: No Pricing
Production One Set

HB	Harold Baines	40.00
JB	Jay Buhner	50.00
JC	Jack Clark	35.00
DC	David Cone	35.00
AD	Andre Dawson	35.00
BD	Bobby Doerr	35.00
LD	Lenny Dykstra	35.00
SF	Sid Fernandez	25.00
GF	George Foster	40.00
DG	Dwight Gooden	25.00
KH	Keith Hernandez	35.00
BH	Bob Horner	25.00
FJ	Fergie Jenkins	40.00
BL	Barry Larkin	60.00
BM	Bill Madlock	25.00
DE	Dennis Martinez	25.00
GM	Gary Mathews	25.00
JM	Jack Morris	35.00
DM	Dale Murphy	40.00
GN	Graig Nettles	35.00
TO	Tony Oliva	35.00
JP	Jim Palmer	40.00
TR	Tim Raines	30.00
JR	Jim Rice	40.00
RS	Red Schoendienst	30.00
DS	Darryl Strawberry	30.00
BS	Bruce Sutter	25.00
LT	Luis Tiant	25.00
AV	Andy Van Slyke	40.00

Glory Days Jersey

NM/M

Common Player: 4.00
Gold: 1X
Production 75 Sets
Platinum: No Pricing
Production One Set

HB	Harold Baines	6.00
YB	Yogi Berra	10.00
LB	Lou Brock	6.00
JB	Jay Buhner	6.00
CA	Jose Canseco	8.00
JC	Jack Clark	4.00
WC	Will Clark	6.00
DC	David Cone	4.00
AD	Andre Dawson	6.00
BD	Bobby Doerr	6.00
LD	Lenny Dykstra	6.00
SF	Sid Fernandez	4.00
WF	Whitey Ford	10.00
GF	George Foster	4.00
BF	Bill Freehan	6.00
KG	Kirk Gibson	4.00
DG	Dwight Gooden	4.00
RG	Ron Guidry	6.00
GU	Don Gullett	4.00
TG	Tony Gwynn	8.00
KH	Keith Hernandez	4.00
BH	Bob Horner	4.00
FJ	Fergie Jenkins	6.00
BL	Barry Larkin	6.00
SL	Sparky Lyle	4.00
FL	Fred Lynn	4.00
BM	Bill Madlock	4.00
MA	Juan Marichal	6.00
DE	Dennis Martinez	4.00
GM	Gary Mathews	4.00
PM	Paul Molitor	6.00
JM	Jack Morris	4.00
MU	Bobby Murcer	4.00
DM	Dale Murphy	8.00
GN	Graig Nettles	4.00
TO	Tony Oliva	4.00
JP	Jim Palmer	6.00
TR	Tim Raines	4.00
JR	Jim Rice	6.00
CR	Cal Ripken Jr.	20.00
AR	Al Rosen	6.00
NR	Nolan Ryan	15.00
RS	Red Schoendienst	4.00
SN	Duke Snider	8.00
ST	Dave Stewart	4.00
DS	Darryl Strawberry	6.00
BS	Bruce Sutter	4.00
LT	Luis Tiant	4.00
AV	Andy Van Slyke	4.00
RY	Robin Yount	10.00

Glory Days Memorabilia Autograph

NM/M

Production 25 Sets
Gold: No Pricing
Production 10 Sets
Platinum: No Pricing
Production One Set

HB	Harold Baines	25.00
YB	Yogi Berra	50.00
JB	Jay Buhner	30.00
JC	Jack Clark	20.00
WC	Will Clark	25.00
DC	David Cone	20.00
AD	Andre Dawson	20.00
BD	Bobby Doerr	20.00
LD	Lenny Dykstra	20.00
SF	Sid Fernandez	20.00
WF	Whitey Ford	40.00
GF	George Foster	25.00
BF	Bill Freehan	25.00
KG	Kirk Gibson	20.00
DG	Dwight Gooden	15.00
BG	Ron Guidry	35.00
GU	Don Gullett	15.00
TG	Tony Gwynn	40.00
KH	Keith Hernandez	20.00
BH	Bob Horner	15.00
FJ	Fergie Jenkins	25.00
BL	Barry Larkin	40.00
SL	Sparky Lyle	20.00
FL	Fred Lynn	15.00
BM	Bill Madlock	20.00
MA	Juan Marichal	25.00
DE	Dennis Martinez	15.00
GM	Gary Mathews	15.00
PM	Paul Molitor	40.00
JM	Jack Morris	20.00
MU	Bobby Murcer	25.00
DM	Dale Murphy	35.00
GN	Graig Nettles	20.00
TO	Tony Oliva	20.00
JP	Jim Palmer	25.00
TR	Tim Raines	20.00
JR	Jim Rice	25.00
AR	Al Rosen	20.00
NR	Nolan Ryan	100.00
RS	Red Schoendienst	20.00
SN	Duke Snider	40.00
ST	Dave Stewart	15.00
DS	Darryl Strawberry	20.00
BS	Bruce Sutter	25.00
LT	Luis Tiant	20.00
AV	Andy Van Slyke	30.00
RY	Robin Yount	50.00

Glory Days Patch

NM/M

Production 50 Sets
Gold: No Pricing
Production 10 Sets
Platinum: No Pricing
Production One Set

HB	Harold Baines	10.00
JC	Jack Clark	10.00
DC	David Cone	15.00
AD	Andre Dawson	15.00
BD	Bobby Doerr	15.00
LD	Lenny Dykstra	15.00
SF	Sid Fernandez	10.00
GF	George Foster	15.00
DG	Dwight Gooden	15.00
KH	Keith Hernandez	12.00
BH	Bob Horner	10.00
FJ	Fergie Jenkins	15.00
BL	Barry Larkin	25.00
GM	Gary Mathews	10.00
JM	Jack Morris	10.00
DM	Dale Murphy	20.00
GN	Graig Nettles	10.00
JP	Jim Palmer	15.00
TR	Tim Raines	10.00
RS	Red Schoendienst	15.00
DS	Darryl Strawberry	12.00
BS	Bruce Sutter	15.00
LT	Luis Tiant	15.00
AV	Andy Van Slyke	15.00

Historic Cuts

No Pricing
Production One Set

Historic Quads Material

No Pricing
Production 5 Sets
Patch: No Pricing
Production One Set

Historic Quads Autograph

No Pricing
Production 5 Sets

Lasting Legends

NM/M

Common Player: 2.00
Production 399 Sets
Gold: 1-2X
Production 75 Sets
Platinum: No Pricing
Production One Set

LA	Luis Aparicio	2.00
EB	Ernie Banks	4.00
BE	Johnny Bench	4.00
YB	Yogi Berra	4.00
WB	Wade Boggs	3.00
LB	Lou Brock	3.00
RC	Rod Carew	3.00
SC	Steve Carlton	2.00
GC	Gary Carter	2.00
OC	Orlando Cepeda	2.00
BD	Bobby Doerr	2.00
DE	Dennis Eckersley	2.00
RF	Rollie Fingers	2.00
CF	Carlton Fisk	3.00
WF	Whitey Ford	3.00
BG	Bob Gibson	3.00
DG	Dwight Gooden	2.00
TG	Tony Gwynn	3.00
KH	Keith Hernandez	2.00
FJ	Fergie Jenkins	2.00
AK	Al Kaline	3.00
BL	Barry Larkin	3.00
MA	Juan Marichal	2.00
DM	Don Mattingly	5.00
BM	Bill Mazeroski	2.00
PM	Paul Molitor	3.00
JM	Joe Morgan	2.00
MU	Dale Murphy	3.00
EM	Eddie Murray	3.00
SM	Stan Musial	4.00
PN	Phil Niekro	2.00
GN	Graig Nettles	2.00
JP	Jim Palmer	3.00
TP	Tony Perez	2.00
GP	Gaylord Perry	2.00
KP	Kirby Puckett	3.00
JR	Jim Rice	2.00
CR	Cal Ripken Jr.	8.00
BR	Brooks Robinson	3.00
FR	Frank Robinson	3.00
NR	Nolan Ryan	6.00
SA	Ryne Sandberg	4.00
RS	Red Schoendienst	3.00
OS	Ozzie Smith	3.00
SN	Duke Snider	3.00
BS	Bruce Sutter	2.00
DS	Don Sutton	2.00
CY	Carl Yastrzemski	4.00
RY	Robin Yount	4.00

Lasting Legends Autograph

NM/M

Common Player:
Production 25 Sets
Gold: No Pricing
Production 10 Sets
Platinum: No Pricing
Production One Set

LA	Luis Aparicio	20.00
EB	Ernie Banks	60.00
BE	Johnny Bench	50.00
YB	Yogi Berra	60.00
WB	Wade Boggs	40.00
LB	Lou Brock	25.00
RC	Rod Carew	35.00
SC	Steve Carlton	25.00
GC	Gary Carter	25.00
OC	Orlando Cepeda	25.00
BD	Bobby Doerr	20.00
DE	Dennis Eckersley	25.00
RF	Rollie Fingers	20.00
CF	Carlton Fisk	35.00
WF	Whitey Ford	40.00
BG	Bob Gibson	40.00
DG	Dwight Gooden	15.00
TG	Tony Gwynn	50.00
KH	Keith Hernandez	20.00
FG	Fergie Jenkins	25.00
AK	Al Kaline	40.00
BL	Barry Larkin	40.00
MA	Juan Marichal	25.00
DM	Don Mattingly	60.00
BM	Bill Mazeroski	35.00
PM	Paul Molitor	40.00
JM	Joe Morgan	25.00
MU	Dale Murphy	40.00
EM	Eddie Murray	50.00

SM	Stan Musial	60.00
GN	Graig Nettles	20.00
PN	Phil Niekro	25.00
JP	Jim Palmer	25.00
TP	Tony Perez	20.00
GP	Gaylord Perry	20.00
KP	Kirby Puckett	50.00
JR	Jerry Rice	25.00
CR	Cal Ripken Jr.	125.00
BR	Brooks Robinson	40.00
FR	Frank Robinson	25.00
NR	Nolan Ryan	100.00
SA	Ryne Sandberg	50.00
MS	Mike Schmidt	50.00
RS	Red Schoendienst	20.00
OS	Ozzie Smith	60.00
SN	Duke Snider	40.00
BS	Bruce Sutter	25.00
DS	Don Sutton	20.00
CY	Carl Yastrzemski	50.00
RY	Robin Yount	50.00

Lasting Legends Jersey Autograph

NM/M

Production 25 Sets
Gold: No Pricing
Production 10 Sets
Platinum: No Pricing
Production One Set

LA	Luis Aparicio	20.00
EB	Ernie Banks	60.00
BE	Johnny Bench	50.00
YB	Yogi Berra	60.00
WB	Wade Boggs	40.00
LB	Lou Brock	25.00
RC	Rod Carew	40.00
SC	Steve Carlton	25.00
GC	Gary Carter	25.00
OC	Orlando Cepeda	25.00
BD	Bobby Doerr	20.00
DE	Dennis Eckersley	25.00
RF	Rollie Fingers	20.00
CF	Carlton Fisk	40.00
WF	Whitey Ford	40.00
BG	Bob Gibson	40.00
DG	Dwight Gooden	15.00
TG	Tony Gwynn	50.00
KH	Keith Hernandez	20.00
FG	Fergie Jenkins	25.00
AK	Al Kaline	50.00
BL	Barry Larkin	40.00
MA	Juan Marichal	25.00
DM	Don Mattingly	60.00
BM	Bill Mazeroski	40.00
PM	Paul Molitor	40.00
JM	Joe Morgan	25.00
MU	Dale Murphy	40.00
SM	Stan Musial	60.00
GN	Graig Nettles	20.00
PN	Phil Niekro	25.00
JP	Jim Palmer	25.00
TP	Tony Perez	20.00
GP	Gaylord Perry	20.00
JR	Jim Rice	25.00
CR	Cal Ripken Jr.	140.00
BR	Brooks Robinson	40.00
FR	Frank Robinson	25.00
NR	Nolan Ryan	100.00
SA	Ryne Sandberg	50.00
MS	Mike Schmidt	50.00
RS	Red Schoendienst	20.00
OS	Ozzie Smith	60.00
SN	Duke Snider	40.00
BS	Bruce Sutter	25.00
CY	Carl Yastrzemski	50.00
RY	Robin Yount	50.00

Lasting Legends Patch Autograph

NM/M

Production 25 Sets
Gold: No Pricing
Production 5 Sets
Platinum: No Pricing
Production One Set

WB	Wade Boggs	50.00
LB	Lou Brock	
RC	Rod Carew	50.00
SC	Steve Carlton	35.00
GC	Gary Carter	35.00
OC	Orlando Cepeda	30.00
DE	Dennis Eckersley	35.00
RF	Rollie Fingers	25.00
DG	Dwight Gooden	25.00
KH	Keith Hernandez	25.00
FJ	Fergie Jenkins	35.00
BL	Barry Larkin	50.00
MA	Juan Marichal	35.00
PM	Paul Molitor	50.00
JM	Joe Morgan	35.00
PN	Phil Niekro	35.00

JP	Jim Palmer	40.00
TP	Tony Perez	30.00
GP	Gaylord Perry	30.00
JR	Jim Rice	35.00
BR	Brooks Robinson	50.00
NR	Nolan Ryan	140.00
SA	Ryne Sandberg	80.00
OS	Ozzie Smith	75.00
BS	Bruce Sutter	30.00
RY	Robin Yount	65.00

Lasting Legends Material

NM/M
Common Player: 4.00
Gold: 1-1.5X
Production 75 Sets
Platinum: No Pricing
Production One Set

LA	Luis Aparicio	4.00
EB	Ernie Banks	10.00
BE	Johnny Bench	8.00
YB	Yogi Berra	8.00
WB	Wade Boggs	6.00
LB	Lou Brock	6.00
RC	Rod Carew	6.00
SC	Steve Carlton	4.00
GC	Gary Carter	4.00
OC	Orlando Cepeda	4.00
BD	Bobby Doerr	6.00
DE	Dennis Eckersley	6.00
RF	Rollie Fingers	4.00
CF	Carlton Fisk	6.00
WF	Whitey Ford	6.00
BG	Bob Gibson	8.00
DG	Dwight Gooden	4.00
TG	Tony Gwynn	8.00
KH	Keith Hernandez	4.00
FJ	Fergie Jenkins	4.00
AK	Al Kaline	10.00
BL	Barry Larkin	6.00
MA	Juan Marichal	6.00
DM	Don Mattingly	10.00
BM	Bill Mazeroski	6.00
PM	Paul Molitor	6.00
JM	Joe Morgan	4.00
MU	Dale Murphy	6.00
EM	Eddie Murray	6.00
SM	Stan Musial	10.00
GN	Graig Nettles	4.00
PN	Phil Niekro	4.00
JP	Jim Palmer	6.00
TP	Tony Perez	4.00
GP	Gaylord Perry	4.00
KP	Kirby Puckett	8.00
JR	Jim Rice	4.00
CR	Cal Ripken Jr.	20.00
BR	Brooks Robinson	6.00
FR	Frank Robinson	6.00
NR	Nolan Ryan	15.00
SA	Ryne Sandberg	8.00
MS	Mike Schmidt	10.00
RS	Red Schoendienst	4.00
OS	Ozzie Smith	8.00
SN	Duke Snider	6.00
BS	Bruce Sutter	4.00
DS	Don Sutton	4.00
CY	Carl Yastrzemski	15.00
RY	Robin Yount	8.00

Lasting Legends Patch

NM/M
Production 50 Sets
Gold: No Pricing
Production 10 Sets
Platinum: No Pricing
Production One Set

WB	Wade Boggs	20.00
LB	Lou Brock	15.00
RC	Rod Carew	15.00
SC	Steve Carlton	15.00
GC	Gary Carter	12.00
OC	Orlando Cepeda	15.00
DE	Dennis Eckersley	15.00
RF	Rollie Fingers	10.00
CF	Carlton Fisk	15.00
DG	Dwight Gooden	10.00
KH	Keith Hernandez	10.00
FJ	Fergie Jenkins	15.00
BL	Barry Larkin	25.00
MA	Juan Marichal	15.00
JM	Joe Morgan	15.00
PN	Phil Niekro	15.00
JP	Jim Palmer	15.00
TP	Tony Perez	15.00
GP	Gaylord Perry	12.00
KP	Kirby Puckett	25.00
JR	Jim Rice	15.00
BR	Brooks Robinson	20.00
FR	Frank Robinson	15.00
SA	Ryne Sandberg	25.00
OS	Ozzie Smith	25.00
BS	Bruce Sutter	15.00

DS	Don Sutton	12.00
RY	Robin Yount	25.00

Legendary Battery Cuts

NM/M
Production 6-99

SC	Stan Coveleski/25	140.00
BD	Bill Dickey/22	200.00
DD	Don Drysdale/31	200.00
LG	Lefty Gomez/77	160.00
JH	Jesse Haines/28	200.00
WH	Waite Hoyt/58	125.00
CH	Carl Hubbell/99	140.00
HN	Hal Newhouser/32	140.00
WS	Warren Spahn/43	150.00
EW	Early Wynn/32	125.00

Legendary Cornerstone Cuts

NM/M
Production 1-79

DC	Dolph Camilli/79	120.00
RD	Ray Dandridge/27	125.00
EM	Eddie Mathews/50	150.00
JM	Johnny Mize/44	150.00
WS	Willie Stargell/40	150.00

Legendary Cuts

NM/M
Production 1-108

LA	Luke Appling/55	125.00
RI	Richie Ashburn/83	150.00
EA	Earl Averill/91	90.00
JB	Cool Papa Bell/78	300.00
LB	Lou Boudreau/99	100.00
MC	Max Carey/84	140.00
HC	Happy Chandler/39	125.00
JC	Jocko Conlan/40	140.00
ST	Stan Coveleski/71	140.00
CR	Joe Cronin/76	140.00
RD	Ray Dandridge/76	100.00
BD	Bill Dickey/95	150.00
JD	Joe DiMaggio/56	500.00
LD	Larry Doby/32	200.00
DD	Don Drysdale/50	200.00
DU	Leo Durocher/57	150.00
FE	Rick Ferrell/80	125.00
CF	Carl Furillo/26	200.00
LG	Lou Gehrig/4	
CG	Charlie Gehringer/97	120.00
GO	Lefty Gomez/68	150.00
HG	Hank Greenberg/44	280.00
BU	Burleigh Grimes/71	125.00
GR	Lefty Grove/41	250.00
HA	Chick Hafey/52	150.00
JH	Jesse Haines/90	150.00
GH	Gabby Hartnett/50	180.00
BH	Billy Herman/99	90.00
WH	Waite Hoyt/99	140.00
CH	Carl Hubbell/99	150.00
HU	Jim "Catfish" Hunter/65	140.00
JJ	Jackie Jensen/48	180.00
JO	Judy Johnson/39	150.00
CK	Charlie Keller/98	140.00
HK	Harvey Kuenn/33	165.00
BL	Bob Lemon/108	100.00
LE	Buck Leonard/71	140.00
LI	Freddie Lindstrom/19	250.00
LO	Ernie Lombardi/29	200.00
HM	Heinie Manush/25	175.00
RU	Rube Marquard/80	150.00
EM	Eddie Mathews/80	150.00
RO	Roy McMillan/23	140.00
MI	Johnny Mize/92	125.00
HN	Hal Newhouser/96	125.00
PR	Pee Wee Reese/69	180.00
SR	Sam Rice/41	180.00
ER	Edd Roush/99	100.00
JS	Joe Sewell/76	140.00
ES	Enos Slaughter/99	100.00
WA	Warren Spahn/92	140.00
WS	Willie Stargell/63	165.00
CS	Casey Stengel/61	250.00
BW	Bucky Walters/34	150.00
JW	Hoyt Wilhelm/48	100.00
EW	Early Wynn/89	120.00

Legendary Cuts Material

NM/M
Production 75 unless noted.
Gold: No Pricing
Production 15 Sets

CA	Roy Campanella	40.00
RC	Roberto Clemente	80.00
TC	Ty Cobb	140.00
CO	Mickey Cochrane	50.00
CR	Joe Cronin	15.00
DE	Dizzy Dean	60.00
BD	Bill Dickey	35.00
JD	Joe DiMaggio	120.00
DD	Don Drysdale	15.00
JF	Jimmie Foxx	60.00
LG	Lou Gehrig	175.00
HG	Hank Greenberg	35.00
HO	Gil Hodges	40.00
RH	Rogers Hornsby	80.00
HU	Jim "Catfish" Hunter	10.00
TK	Ted Kluszewski	20.00
TL	Tony Lazerri	40.00
BL	Bob Lemon	25.00
MM	Mickey Mantle	150.00
RM	Roger Maris	60.00
EM	Eddie Mathews	40.00
CM	Christy Mathewson	125.00
MI	Johnny Mize	25.00
TM	Thurman Munson	35.00
MO	Mel Ott	50.00
SP	Satchel Paige	75.00
PR	Pee Wee Reese	25.00
JR	Jackie Robinson	65.00
BR	Babe Ruth	180.00
SI	George Sisler	35.00
ES	Enos Slaughter	15.00
WA	Warren Spahn	40.00
CS	Casey Stengel	40.00
HW	Honus Wagner/22	140.00
JW	Hoyt Wilhelm	15.00
TW	Ted Williams	75.00
EW	Early Wynn	10.00

Legendary Cuts Quad

No Pricing
Production One Set

Legendary Duels Material

NM/M
Production 25 Sets
Patch: No Pricing
Production 10 Sets

BM	Ernie Banks, Stan Musial	50.00
CC	Jose Canseco, Will Clark	40.00
DM	Paul Molitor, Lenny Dykstra	25.00
EG	Dennis Eckersley, Kirk Gibson	25.00
FB	Carlton Fisk, Johnny Bench	25.00
FR	George Foster, Jim Rice	15.00
JY	Reggie Jackson, Carl Yastrzemski	40.00
MC	Rod Carew, Paul Molitor	25.00
MH	Don Mattingly, Keith Hernandez	35.00
SF	Duke Snider, Whitey Ford	35.00
SG	Ron Guidry, Don Sutton	15.00
SS	Ozzie Smith, Ryne Sandberg	60.00
YS	Mike Schmidt, Robin Yount	35.00

Legendary Duels Autograph

No Pricing
Production 15 Sets

Legendary Duos Material

NM/M
Production 25 Sets
Patch: No Pricing
Production 10 Sets

CO	Tony Oliva, Rod Carew	20.00
ES	Duke Snider, Carl Erskine	15.00
FB	Yogi Berra, Whitey Ford	40.00
GS	Ryne Sandberg, Mark Grace	50.00
JG	Reggie Jackson, Ron Guidry	25.00
MB	Joe Morgan, Johnny Bench	35.00
MY	Robin Yount, Paul Molitor	40.00
RB	Wade Boggs, Jim Rice	20.00
RC	Will Clark, Cal Ripken Jr.	50.00
RM	Cal Ripken Jr., Eddie Murray	50.00
RR	Brooks Robinson, Frank Robinson	25.00
SC	Mike Schmidt, Steve Carlton	30.00
SG	Darryl Strawberry, Dwight Gooden	15.00

Legendary Duos Autograph

No Pricing
Production 15 Sets

Legendary Glovemen Cuts

NM/M

EA	Earl Averill/39	120.00
CP	Cool Papa Bell/29	350.00
MC	Max Carey/50	140.00
JD	Joe DiMaggio/75	400.00
ES	Enos Slaughter/65	120.00

Legendary Lineage

NM/M
Common Player: 2.00
Production 399 Sets
Gold: 1-2X
Production 75 Sets
Platinum: No Pricing
Production One Set

HB	Harold Baines	2.00
JB	Jay Buhner	2.00
CA	Jose Canseco	3.00
SC	Steve Carlton	3.00
JC	Jack Clark	2.00
WC	Will Clark	3.00
DC	David Cone	2.00
AD	Andre Dawson	2.00
BD	Bobby Doerr	2.00
LD	Lenny Dykstra	2.00
EC	Dennis Eckersley	2.00
SF	Sid Fernandez	2.00
BF	Bill Freehan	2.00
DG	Dwight Gooden	2.00
GG	Rich "Goose" Gossage	2.00
MG	Mark Grace	3.00
RG	Ron Guidry	2.00
GU	Don Gullett	2.00
TG	Tony Gwynn	4.00
KH	Keith Hernandez	2.00
BH	Bob Horner	2.00
RJ	Reggie Jackson	3.00
FJ	Fergie Jenkins	3.00
BL	Barry Larkin	3.00
SL	Sparky Lyle	2.00
BM	Bill Madlock	2.00
DE	Dennis Martinez	2.00
GM	Gary Matthews	2.00
MA	Don Mattingly	5.00
PM	Paul Molitor	3.00
JM	Jack Morris	2.00
MU	Bobby Murcer	2.00
DM	Dale Murphy	3.00
GN	Graig Nettles	2.00
TO	Tony Oliva	2.00
JP	Jim Palmer	3.00
KP	Kirby Puckett	4.00
TR	Tim Raines	2.00
JR	Jim Rice	2.00
CR	Cal Ripken Jr.	8.00
BR	Brooks Robinson	3.00
AR	Al Rosen	2.00
MS	Mike Schmidt	5.00
OS	Ozzie Smith	4.00
SN	Duke Snider	3.00
DS	Dave Stewart	2.00
ST	Darryl Strawberry	2.00
SU	Bruce Sutter	2.00
LT	Luis Tiant	2.00
AV	Andy Van Slyke	2.00

Legendary Lineage Autograph

NM/M
Common Player: 15.00
Production 25 Sets
Gold: No Pricing
Production 10 Sets
Platinum: No Pricing
Production One Set

HB	Harold Baines	25.00
JB	Jay Buhner	30.00
CA	Jose Canseco	40.00
SC	Steve Carlton	25.00
JC	Jack Clark	20.00
WC	Will Clark	25.00
DC	David Cone	20.00
AD	Andre Dawson	20.00
BD	Bobby Doerr	20.00
LD	Lenny Dykstra	20.00
EC	Dennis Eckersley	25.00
SF	Sid Fernandez	15.00

BF	Bill Freehan	25.00
DG	Dwight Gooden	15.00
GG	Rich "Goose" Gossage	20.00
MG	Mark Grace	30.00
RG	Ron Guidry	35.00
GU	Don Gullett	15.00
TG	Tony Gwynn	40.00
KH	Keith Hernandez	20.00
BH	Bob Horner	15.00
RJ	Reggie Jackson	40.00
FJ	Fergie Jenkins	25.00
BL	Barry Larkin	40.00
SL	Sparky Lyle	20.00
BM	Bill Madlock	20.00
DE	Dennis Martinez	15.00
GM	Gary Matthews	15.00
MA	Don Mattingly	60.00
PM	Paul Molitor	40.00
JM	Jack Morris	20.00
MU	Bobby Murcer	25.00
DM	Dale Murphy	35.00
GN	Graig Nettles	20.00
TO	Tony Oliva	20.00
JP	Jim Palmer	25.00
KP	Kirby Puckett	50.00
TR	Tim Raines	20.00
JR	Jim Rice	25.00
CR	Cal Ripken Jr.	125.00
BR	Brooks Robinson	40.00
AR	Al Rosen	20.00
MS	Mike Schmidt	60.00
OS	Ozzie Smith	50.00
SN	Duke Snider	40.00
DS	Dave Stewart	15.00
ST	Darryl Strawberry	20.00
SU	Bruce Sutter	25.00
LT	Luis Tiant	20.00
AV	Andy Van Slyke	30.00

Legendary Lineage Jersey Autograph

NM/M

Production 25 Sets
Gold: No Pricing
Production 10 Sets
Platinum: No Pricing
Production One Set

HB	Harold Baines	25.00
JB	Jay Buhner	30.00
CA	Jose Canseco	40.00
SC	Steve Carlton	25.00
JC	Jack Clark	20.00
WC	Will Clark	25.00
DC	David Cone	20.00
AD	Andre Dawson	25.00
BD	Bobby Doerr	25.00
LD	Lenny Dykstra	20.00
EC	Dennis Eckersley	25.00
SF	Sid Fernandez	15.00
BF	Bill Freehan	25.00
DG	Dwight Gooden	15.00
GG	Rich "Goose" Gossage	20.00
MG	Mark Grace	30.00
RG	Ron Guidry	35.00
GU	Don Gullett	15.00
TG	Tony Gwynn	40.00
KH	Keith Hernandez	20.00
BH	Bob Horner	15.00
RJ	Reggie Jackson	40.00
FJ	Fergie Jenkins	25.00
BL	Barry Larkin	40.00
SL	Sparky Lyle	20.00
BM	Bill Madlock	20.00
DE	Dennis Martinez	15.00
GM	Gary Matthews	15.00
MA	Don Mattingly	60.00
PM	Paul Molitor	40.00
JM	Jack Morris	20.00
MU	Bobby Murcer	25.00
DM	Dale Murphy	35.00
GN	Graig Nettles	20.00
TO	Tony Oliva	20.00
JP	Jim Palmer	25.00
KP	Kirby Puckett	50.00
TR	Tim Raines	20.00
JR	Jim Rice	25.00
CR	Cal Ripken Jr.	150.00
BR	Brooks Robinson	40.00
AR	Al Rosen	20.00
MS	Mike Schmidt	60.00
OS	Ozzie Smith	50.00
SN	Duke Snider	40.00
DS	Dave Stewart	20.00
ST	Darryl Strawberry	20.00
SU	Bruce Sutter	25.00
LT	Luis Tiant	20.00
AV	Andy Van Slyke	30.00

Legendary Lineage Patch Autograph

NM/M

Production 25 Sets

Gold: No Pricing
Production 5 Sets
Platinum: No Pricing
Production One Set

HB	Harold Baines	40.00
JB	Jay Buhner	50.00
JC	Jack Clark	35.00
WC	Will Clark	40.00
DC	David Cone	35.00
AD	Andre Dawson	35.00
BD	Bobby Doerr	35.00
BF	Bill Freehan	40.00
DG	Dwight Gooden	25.00
GG	Rich "Goose" Gossage	35.00
MG	Mark Grace	50.00
TG	Tony Gwynn	70.00
KH	Keith Hernandez	35.00
BH	Bob Horner	25.00
BL	Barry Larkin	60.00
BM	Bill Madlock	25.00
DE	Dennis Martinez	25.00
PM	Paul Molitor	50.00
JM	Jack Morris	35.00
DM	Dale Murphy	40.00
GN	Graig Nettles	35.00
TR	Tim Raines	30.00
JR	Jim Rice	40.00
CR	Cal Ripken Jr.	200.00
MS	Mike Schmidt	90.00
DS	Dave Stewart	25.00
ST	Darryl Strawberry	30.00
LT	Luis Tiant	25.00
AV	Andy Van Slyke	40.00

Legendary Lineage Jersey

NM/M

Common Player:	4.00
Gold:	1-1.5X

Production 75 Sets
Platinum: No Pricing
Production One Set

HB	Harold Baines	4.00
JB	Jay Buhner	4.00
CA	Jose Canseco	8.00
SC	Steve Carlton	6.00
JC	Jack Clark	4.00
WC	Will Clark	6.00
DC	David Cone	6.00
AD	Andre Dawson	6.00
BD	Bobby Doerr	6.00
LD	Lenny Dykstra	4.00
EC	Dennis Eckersley	6.00
SF	Sid Fernandez	4.00
BF	Bill Freehan	6.00
DG	Dwight Gooden	4.00
GG	Rich "Goose" Gossage	4.00
MG	Mark Grace	8.00
RG	Ron Guidry	4.00
GU	Don Gullett	4.00
TG	Tony Gwynn	8.00
KH	Keith Hernandez	4.00
BH	Bob Horner	4.00
RJ	Reggie Jackson	8.00
FJ	Fergie Jenkins	6.00
BL	Barry Larkin	4.00
SL	Sparky Lyle	4.00
BM	Bill Madlock	4.00
DE	Dennis Martinez	4.00
GM	Gary Matthews	4.00
MA	Don Mattingly	12.00
PM	Paul Molitor	6.00
JM	Jack Morris	4.00
MU	Bobby Murcer	4.00
DM	Dale Murphy	8.00
GN	Graig Nettles	4.00
TO	Tony Oliva	4.00
JP	Jim Palmer	6.00
KP	Kirby Puckett	8.00
TR	Tim Raines	4.00
JR	Jim Rice	6.00
CR	Cal Ripken Jr.	20.00
BR	Brooks Robinson	6.00
AR	Al Rosen	6.00
MS	Mike Schmidt	10.00
OS	Ozzie Smith	8.00
SN	Duke Snider	8.00
DS	Dave Stewart	4.00
ST	Darryl Strawberry	4.00
SU	Bruce Sutter	4.00
LT	Luis Tiant	4.00
AV	Andy Van Slyke	4.00

Legendary Lineage Patch

NM/M

Production 50 Sets
Gold: No Pricing
Production 10 Sets
Platinum: No Pricing
Production One Set

HB	Harold Baines	10.00
JB	Jay Buhner	15.00
JC	Jack Clark	10.00
WC	Will Clark	20.00
DC	David Cone	15.00
AD	Andre Dawson	15.00
BD	Bobby Doerr	15.00
BF	Bill Freehan	12.00
DG	Dwight Gooden	15.00
GG	Rich "Goose" Gossage	12.00
MG	Mark Grace	20.00
TG	Tony Gwynn	20.00
KH	Keith Hernandez	12.00
BH	Bob Horner	10.00
BL	Barry Larkin	25.00
BM	Bill Madlock	10.00
DE	Dennis Martinez	10.00
JM	Jack Morris	10.00
DM	Dale Murphy	20.00
GN	Graig Nettles	10.00
TR	Tim Raines	10.00
JR	Jim Rice	
CR	Cal Ripken Jr.	40.00
MS	Mike Schmidt	25.00
DS	Dave Stewart	10.00
ST	Darryl Strawberry	12.00
LT	Luis Tiant	10.00
AV	Andy Van Slyke	15.00

Middlemen Cuts

NM/M

Production 2-99

LA	Luke Appling/32	150.00
LB	Lou Boudreau/99	100.00
JC	Joe Cronin/30	140.00
CG	Charlie Gehringer/95	140.00
BH	Billy Herman/90	90.00
PW	Pee Wee Reese/39	200.00
JS	Joe Sewell/76	140.00

Significant Tips

No Pricing
Production 10 Sets
Patch: No Pricing
Production 5 Sets

Significant Trips Autograph

No Pricing
Production 10 Sets

2006 SP Authentic

RYAN HOWARD

NM/M

Complete Set (300):	
Common Player (1-100):	.25
Common SP (101-200):	2.00
Production 899	
Common Auto. (201-300):	8.00
Production 125-899	
Pack (5):	5.00
Box (24):	110.00
1 Erik Bedard	.25
2 Corey Patterson	.25
3 Ramon Hernandez	.25
4 Kris Benson	.25
5 Miguel Batista	.25
6 Orlando Hudson	.25
7 Shawn Green	.25
8 Jeff Francoeur	.40
9 Marcus Giles	.25

10 Edgar Renteria	.25
11 Tim Hudson	.40
12 Tim Wakefield	.25
13 Mark Loretta	.25
14 Kevin Youkilis	.25
15 Mike Lowell	.25
16 Coco Crisp	.25
17 Tadahito Iguchi	.25
18 Scott Podsednik	.25
19 Jermaine Dye	.25
20 Jose Contreras	.25
21 Carlos Zambrano	.40
22 Aramis Ramirez	.40
23 Jacque Jones	.25
24 Austin Kearns	.25
25 Felipe Lopez	.25
26 Brandon Phillips	.25
27 Aaron Harang	.25
28 Cliff Lee	.25
29 Jhonny Peralta	.25
30 Jason Michaels	.25
31 Clint Barmes	.25
32 Brad Hawpe	.25
33 Aaron Cook	.25
34 Kenny Rogers	.25
35 Carlos Guillen	.25
36 Brian Moehler	.25
37 Andy Pettitte	.40
38 Wandy Rodriguez	.25
39 Morgan Ensberg	.25
40 Preston Wilson	.25
41 Mark Grudzielanek	.25
42 Angel Berroa	.25
43 Jeremy Affeldt	.25
44 Zack Greinke	.25
45 Orlando Cabrera	.25
46 Garret Anderson	.25
47 Ervin Santana	.25
48 Derek Lowe	.25
49 Nomar Garciaparra	.75
50 J.D. Drew	.25
51 Rafael Furcal	.40
52 Rickie Weeks	.40
53 Geoff Jenkins	.25
54 Bill Hall	.25
55 Chris Capuano	.25
56 Derrick Turnbow	.25
57 Justin Morneau	.40
58 Michael Cuddyer	.25
59 Luis Castillo	.25
60 Hideki Matsui	1.00
61 Jason Giambi	.50
62 Jorge Posada	.50
63 Mariano Rivera	.50
64 Billy Wagner	.25
65 Carlos Delgado	.50
66 Jose Reyes	.75
67 Nick Swisher	.40
68 Bobby Crosby	.25
69 Frank Thomas	.50
70 Ryan Howard	2.00
71 Pat Burrell	.40
72 Jimmy Rollins	.50
73 Craig Wilson	.25
74 Freddy Sanchez	.25
75 Sean Casey	.25
76 Mike Piazza	1.00
77 Dave Roberts	.25
78 Chris Young	.25
79 Noah Lowry	.25
80 Armando Benitez	.25
81 Pedro Feliz	.25
82 Jose Lopez	.25
83 Adrian Beltre	.25
84 Jamie Moyer	.25
85 Jason Isringhausen	.25
86 Jason Marquis	.25
87 David Eckstein	.25
88 Juan Encarnacion	.25
89 Julio Lugo	.25
90 Ty Wigginton	.25
91 Jorge Cantu	.25
92 Akinori Otsuka	.25
93 Hank Blalock	.40
94 Kevin Mench	.25
95 Lyle Overbay	.25
96 Shea Hillenbrand	.25
97 B.J. Ryan	.25
98 Tony Armas	.25
99 Chad Cordero	.25
100 Jose Guillen	.25
101 Miguel Tejada	3.00
102 Brian Roberts	2.00
103 Melvin Mora	2.00
104 Brandon Webb	2.00
105 Chad Tracy	2.00
106 Luis Gonzalez	2.00
107 Andruw Jones	4.00
108 Chipper Jones	5.00
109 John Smoltz	3.00
110 Curt Schilling	4.00
111 Josh Beckett	3.00
112 David Ortiz	5.00
113 Manny Ramirez	4.00

114 Jason Varitek 4.00
115 Jim Thome 4.00
116 Paul Konerko 4.00
117 Javier Vazquez 2.00
118 Mark Prior 4.00
119 Derrek Lee 4.00
120 Greg Maddux 6.00
121 Ken Griffey Jr. 6.00
122 Adam Dunn 3.00
123 Bronson Arroyo 2.00
124 Travis Hafner 3.00
125 Victor Martinez 2.00
126 Grady Sizemore 3.00
127 C.C. Sabathia 2.00
128 Todd Helton 3.00
129 Matt Holliday 2.00
130 Garrett Atkins 2.00
131 Jeff Francis 2.00
132 Jeremy Bonderman 3.00
133 Ivan Rodriguez 4.00
134 Chris Shelton 2.00
135 Magglio Ordonez 2.00
136 Dontrelle Willis 3.00
137 Miguel Cabrera 5.00
138 Roger Clemens 8.00
139 Roy Oswalt 3.00
140 Lance Berkman 3.00
141 Reggie Sanders 2.00
142 Vladimir Guerrero 5.00
143 Bartolo Colon 2.00
144 Chone Figgins 2.00
145 Francisco Rodriguez 2.00
146 Brad Penny 2.00
147 Jeff Kent 3.00
148 Eric Gagne 2.00
149 Carlos Lee 2.00
150 Ben Sheets 2.00
151 Johan Santana 4.00
152 Torii Hunter 2.00
153 Joe Nathan 2.00
154 Alex Rodriguez 6.00
155 Derek Jeter 8.00
156 Randy Johnson 4.00
157 Johnny Damon 4.00
158 Mike Mussina 3.00
159 Pedro Martinez 4.00
160 Tom Glavine 3.00
161 David Wright 5.00
162 Carlos Beltran 4.00
163 Rich Harden 2.00
164 Barry Zito 3.00
165 Eric Chavez 2.00
166 Huston Street 2.00
167 Bobby Abreu 3.00
168 Chase Utley 3.00
169 Brett Myers 2.00
170 Jason Bay 3.00
171 Zachary Duke 2.00
172 Jake Peavy 3.00
173 Brian Giles 2.00
174 Khalil Greene 2.00
175 Trevor Hoffman 2.00
176 Jason Schmidt 2.00
177 Randy Winn 2.00
178 Omar Vizquel 2.00
179 Kenji Johjima 5.00
180 Ichiro Suzuki 6.00
181 Richie Sexson 3.00
182 Felix Hernandez 2.00
183 Albert Pujols 8.00
184 Chris Carpenter 3.00
185 Jim Edmonds 3.00
186 Scott Rolen 4.00
187 Carl Crawford 3.00
188 Scott Kazmir 2.00
189 Jonny Gomes 2.00
190 Mark Teixeira 3.00
191 Michael Young 2.00
192 Kevin Millwood 2.00
193 Vernon Wells 3.00
194 Troy Glaus 3.00
195 Roy Halladay 2.00
196 Alex Rios 2.00
197 Nick Johnson 2.00
198 Livan Hernandez 2.00
199 Alfonso Soriano 4.00
200 Jose Vidro 2.00
201 Aaron Rakers/ 399 (RC) 10.00
202 Angel Pagan/ 399 (RC) 15.00
203 Ben Hendrickson/ 399 (RC) 10.00
204 Bobby Livingston/ 399 (RC) 8.00
205 Darrell Rasner/ 399 (RC) 10.00
206 Brian Bannister/ 399 (RC) 20.00
207 Brian Wilson/899 RC 15.00
208 Bobby Keppel/ 199 (RC) 8.00
209 Choo Freeman/ 399 (RC) 10.00

210 Chris Booker/899 (RC) 8.00
211 Chris Britton/399 RC 15.00
212 Chris Demaria/329 RC 12.00
213 Chris Resop/899 (RC) 8.00
214 Tony Gwynn Jr./ 399 (RC) 30.00
215 Eric Reed/399 (RC) 8.00
216 Fabio Castro/399 RC 15.00
217 Fernando Nieve/ 299 (RC) 10.00
218 Freddie Bynum/ 899 (RC) 10.00
219 Guillermo Quiroz/ 399 (RC) 8.00
220 Hong-Chih Kuo/ 899 (RC) 25.00
221 Ryan Theriot/ 399 (RC) 60.00
222 Jack Taschner/ 899 (RC) 8.00
223 Jason Bergmann/ 899 RC 15.00
224 Jason Hammel/ 899 (RC) 8.00
225 Jeff Harris/399 RC 8.00
226 Jeremy Accardo/ 399 (RC) 15.00
227 Ty Taubenheim/ 399 RC 15.00
228 Joel Zumaya/ 399 (RC) 25.00
229 John Koronka/ 399 (RC) 10.00
230 Erick Aybar/399 (RC) 15.00
231 Jordan Tata/399 RC 20.00
232 Russell Martin/ 399 (RC) 40.00
233 Josh Rupe/399 (RC) 10.00
234 Kevin Frandsen/ 399 (RC) 10.00
235 Martin Prado/ 399 (RC) 20.00
236 Matt Capps/399 (RC) 15.00
237 Agustin Montero/ 199 (RC) 10.00
238 Mike Thompson/ 399 RC 10.00
239 Nate McLouth/ 399 (RC) 15.00
240 Peter Moylan/399 RC 15.00
241 Reggie Abercrombie/ 399 (RC) 15.00
242 Carlos Quentin/ 399 (RC) 20.00
243 Ron Flores/399 RC 10.00
244 Ryan Shealy/399 (RC) 15.00
245 Mike Rouse/399 (RC) 10.00
246 Santiago Ramirez/ 399 (RC) 10.00
247 Clay Hensley/ 899 (RC) 15.00
248 Skip Schumaker/ 399 (RC) 15.00
249 Eliezer Alfonzo/ 899 RC 15.00
250 Steve Stemle/399 RC 10.00
251 Tim Hamulack/ 399 (RC) 12.00
252 Tony Pena/299 (RC) 10.00
253 Emiliano Fruto/ 899 RC 10.00
254 Wilbert Nieves/ 399 (RC) 15.00
255 Joey Devine/399 RC 15.00
256 Adam Wainwright/ 399 (RC) 25.00
257 Andre Ethier/ 399 (RC) 20.00
258 Ben Johnson/ 399 (RC) 10.00
259 Boone Logan/399 RC 10.00
260 Chris Denorfia/ 899 (RC) 10.00
261 Alay Soler/299 RC 15.00
262 Cody Ross/899 (RC) 10.00
263 Dave Gassner/ 399 (RC) 15.00
264 Fausto Carmona/ 399 (RC) 25.00
265 Jeremy Sowers/ 299 (RC) 15.00
266 Jason Kubel/399 (RC) 15.00
267 John Van Benschoten/399 (RC) 10.00
268 Jose Capellan/ 399 (RC) 10.00
269 Josh Wilson/399 (RC) 8.00
270 Kelly Shoppach/ 399 (RC) 10.00
271 Macay McBride/ 399 (RC) 15.00
272 Matt Cain/399 (RC) 25.00
273 Mike Jacobs/399 (RC) 15.00

274 Paul Maholm/ 399 (RC) 15.00
275 Chad Billingsley/ 399 (RC) 25.00
276 Ruddy Lugo/399 (RC) 15.00
277 Jon Lester/399 (RC) 30.00
278 Sean Marshall/ 383 (RC) 15.00
279 Melky Cabrera/ 399 (RC) 30.00
280 Yusmeiro Petit/ 399 (RC) 15.00
281 Anderson Hernandez/ 299 (RC) 10.00
282 Brian Anderson/ 699 (RC) 15.00
283 Cole Hamels/ 299 (RC) 50.00
284 Boof Bonser/299 (RC) 20.00
285 Dan Uggla/199 (RC) 30.00
286 Francisco Liriano/ 299 (RC) 30.00
287 Hanley Ramirez/ 199 (RC) 50.00
288 Ian Kinsler/299 (RC) 25.00
289 Jeremy Hermida/ 299 (RC) 20.00
290 Jonathan Papelbon/ 199 (RC) 60.00
291 Jered Weaver/ 199 (RC) 30.00
292 Josh Johnson/ 299 (RC) 15.00
293 Josh Willingham/ 199 (RC) 20.00
294 Justin Verlander/ 199 (RC) 60.00
295 Stephen Drew/ 299 (RC) 25.00
296 Prince Fielder/ 125 (RC) 125.00
297 Ryan Zimmerman/ 199 (RC) 50.00
298 Takashi Saito/283 RC 40.00
299 Taylor Buchholz/ 399 (RC) 10.00
300 Conor Jackson/ 299 (RC) 15.00

By The Letter

NM/M

Production 4-200
JB Jason Bay/110 50.00
JB2 Jason Bay/50 50.00
CB Craig Biggio/55 125.00
BI Chad Billingsley/75 40.00
HB Hank Blalock/50 50.00
AB A.J. Burnett/50 50.00
MC Miguel Cabrera/35 85.00
EC Eric Chavez/75 40.00
AD Adam Dunn/50 60.00
MG Marcus Giles/136 30.00
JG Jonny Gomes/175 30.00
KH Khalil Greene/75 40.00
KG Ken Griffey Jr./25 200.00
KG2 Ken Griffey Jr./25 200.00
KG3 Ken Griffey Jr./25 200.00
KG4 Ken Griffey Jr./25 200.00
VG Vladimir Guerrero/25 120.00
AG Tony Gwynn Jr./150 50.00
CO Cole Hamels/120 65.00
CH Craig Hansen/30 50.00
DH Danny Haren/180 35.00
JH Jeremy Hermida/125 35.00
FH Felix Hernandez/40 50.00
FH2 Felix Hernandez/75 50.00
MH Matt Holliday/37 60.00
HU Tim Hudson/50 40.00
TI Tadahito Iguchi/20 120.00
HK Howie Kendrick/75 50.00
IK Ian Kinsler/125 50.00
DL Derrek Lee/200 65.00
FL Francisco Liriano/77 40.00
GM Greg Maddux/25 140.00
GM2 Greg Maddux/25 140.00
VM Victor Martinez/75 40.00
JM Joe Mauer/25 75.00
MO Justin Morneau/75 50.00
MM Mark Mulder/50 40.00
JN Joe Nathan/100 35.00
RO Roy Oswalt/50 60.00
JP Jonathan Papelbon/100 80.00
PE Jake Peavy/100 40.00
HR Hanley Ramirez/125 40.00
JR Jose Reyes/75 65.00
AR Alex Rios/100 50.00
CS C.C. Sabathia/40 40.00
BS Ben Sheets/125 35.00
SM John Smoltz/75 75.00
JS Jeremy Sowers/60 60.00
HS Huston Street/75 40.00

NS Nick Swisher/170 35.00
TE Miguel Tejada/25 50.00
JT Jim Thome/30 100.00
DU Dan Uggla/100 40.00
BU B.J. Upton/20 50.00
CU Chase Utley/25 100.00
JW Jered Weaver/40 60.00
RW Rickie Weeks/100 50.00
WI Josh Willingham/75 40.00
DW Dontrelle Willis/150 40.00
MY Michael Young/50 45.00
CZ Carlos Zambrano/17 100.00
RZ Ryan Zimmerman/17 120.00
JZ Joel Zumaya/125 85.00

Chirography

NM/M

Production 75 unless noted.
AN Brian Anderson 10.00
GA Garret Anderson 15.00
BB Brandon Backe 15.00
BA Brian Bannister 25.00
DB Denny Bautista 10.00
CB Craig Biggio 60.00
BI Chad Billingsley 25.00
HB Hank Blalock 15.00
JB Joe Blanton 15.00
BO Boof Bonser 25.00
TB Taylor Buchholz 8.00
MC Matt Cain 30.00
JC Jose Capellan 8.00
FC Fausto Carmona 20.00
SC Sean Casey 25.00
BC Bobby Crosby 10.00
DD David DeJesus 15.00
CD Chris Denorfia 15.00
JD Joey Devine 10.00
SD Stephen Drew 30.00
JE Johnny Estrada 10.00
AE Andre Ethier 25.00
KF Keith Foulke 20.00
JF Jeff Francis 10.00
CF Choo Freeman 8.00
DG Dave Gassner 8.00
KG Khalil Greene 30.00
GR Ken Griffey Jr. 80.00
CG Carlos Guillen 15.00
AG Tony Gwynn Jr. 40.00
TH Travis Hafner 20.00
CH Cole Hamels 50.00
RH Rich Harden 15.00
HA Jeff Harris 15.00
JH Jeremy Hermida 15.00
AH Anderson Hernandez 15.00
FH Felix Hernandez/25 40.00
CJ Conor Jackson 15.00
DJ Derek Jeter 160.00
JJ Josh Johnson 15.00
JQ Jacque Jones 10.00
SK Scott Kazmir/25 20.00
IK Ian Kinsler 25.00
CK Casey Kotchman 15.00
JK Jason Kubel 15.00
HK Hong-Chih Kuo 60.00
CL Cliff Lee 8.00
JL Jon Lester 35.00
LI Francisco Liriano 35.00
BL Boone Logan 20.00
FL Felipe Lopez 15.00
ML Mark Loretta 10.00
PM Paul Maholm 15.00
SM Sean Marshall 20.00
VM Victor Martinez 15.00
MM Macay McBride 15.00
KM Kevin Mench 15.00
JN Joe Nathan 15.00
LO Lyle Overbay/40 15.00
VP Vicente Padilla 8.00
JP Jonathan Papelbon 40.00
CP Corey Patterson 10.00
TP Tony Pena 8.00
WM Wily Mo Pena 10.00
OP Oliver Perez 20.00
YP Yusmeiro Petit 15.00
MP Mark Prior/55 20.00
HR Hanley Ramirez 40.00
RE Eric Reed 10.00
ER Edgar Renteria 15.00
AR Alex Rios 15.00
IR Ivan Rodriguez 30.00
CR Cody Ross 15.00
JR Josh Rupe 10.00
CS C.C. Sabathia 20.00
TS Takashi Saito 50.00
BS Ben Sheets 15.00
SH Chris Shelton 15.00
KS Kelly Shoppach 15.00
SO Alay Soler 20.00
AS Alfonso Soriano 40.00
JS Jeremy Sowers 20.00
NS Nick Swisher 20.00
FT Frank Thomas 65.00
DU Dan Uggla 25.00

CU	Chase Utley	50.00
VA	John Van Benschoten	15.00
JV	Jason Varitek	50.00
VE	Justin Verlander	40.00
AW	Adam Wainwright	30.00
WE	Jered Weaver	40.00
JW	Josh Willingham	15.00
DW	Dontrelle Willis	30.00
WI	Josh Wilson	10.00
KY	Kevin Youkilis	15.00
RZ	Ryan Zimmerman	40.00

Chirography Dual Signatures

NM/M
Production 25 Sets

CE	Eric Reed, Cody Ross	25.00
FJ	Conor Jackson, Prince Fielder	40.00
GB	Khalil Greene, Josh Barfield	25.00
HA	Jeremy Hermida, Reggie Abercrombie	25.00
HK	Cole Hamels, Scott Kazmir	50.00
KH	Anderson Hernandez, Ian Kinsler	40.00
KS	Takashi Saito, Hong-Chih Kuo	180.00
LB	Francisco Liriano, Boof Bonser	50.00
MH	Rich Hill, Sean Marshall	60.00
MW	Josh Willingham, Victor Martinez	25.00
PB	Freddie Bynum, Angel Pagan	25.00
PG	Ken Griffey Jr., Albert Pujols	350.00
PO	Jake Peavy, Roy Oswalt	40.00
PP	Tony Pena, Martin Prado	30.00
RC	Hanley Ramirez, Miguel Cabrera	50.00
RR	Jose Reyes, Hanley Ramirez	50.00
SC	Jose Capellan, Ben Sheets	25.00
UH	Cole Hamels, Chase Utley	65.00
WS	Josh Wilson, Ryan Shealy	25.00

Chirography Triple Signatures

No Pricing
Production 15 Sets

Heroes

NM/M
Common Player: .50

1	Albert Pujols	3.00
2	Andruw Jones	1.00
3	Aramis Ramirez	.75
4	Brian Roberts	.75
5	Carl Crawford	.75
6	Carlos Lee	.50
7	Vladimir Guerrero	1.00
8	Chris Carpenter	.75
9	Craig Biggio	.75
10	David Ortiz	1.50
11	David Wright	2.00
12	Derek Lee	.75
13	Dontrelle Willis	.75
14	Felix Hernandez	.75
15	Garrett Atkins	.50
16	Grady Sizemore	.75
17	Huston Street	.50
18	Jake Peavy	.50
19	Jason Bay	.75
20	Joe Mauer	1.00
21	John Smoltz	.75
22	Jonny Gomes	.50
23	Jorge Cantu	.50
24	Ken Griffey Jr.	2.00
25	Marcus Giles	.50
26	Mark Teixeira	.75
27	Matt Cain	.75
28	Michael Young	.50
29	Miguel Cabrera	1.00
30	Johan Santana	1.00
31	Nick Swisher	.50
32	Prince Fielder	1.00
33	Joe Blanton	.50
34	Roy Oswalt	.75
35	Ryan Howard	3.00
36	Scott Kazmir	.50
37	Tadahito Iguchi	.50
38	Travis Hafner	.75
39	Victor Martinez	.50
40	Jose Reyes	1.00
41	Chris Carpenter, Albert Pujols	3.00
42	Albert Pujols, Miguel Cabrera	3.00
43	Andruw Jones, Ken Griffey Jr.	2.00
44	Derrek Lee, Aramis Ramirez	.75
45	Ryan Howard, Prince Fielder	3.00
46	Jake Peavy, Roy Oswalt	.75
47	Morgan Ensberg, Craig Biggio	.75
48	David Ortiz, Travis Hafner	1.50
49	Derek Jeter, David Wright	3.00
50	Derek Jeter, Ken Griffey Jr.	3.00
51	Derek Jeter, Michael Young	3.00
52	Scott Kazmir, Dontrelle Willis	.50
53	Jason Bay, Grady Sizemore	.75
54	Michael Young, Mark Teixeira	.75
55	Brian Roberts, Tadahito Iguchi	.50
56	Matt Cain, Felix Hernandez, Chien-Ming Wang	2.00
57	Mark Teixeira, Derrek Lee, Albert Pujols	3.00
58	Albert Pujols, Ken Griffey Jr., Miguel Cabrera	3.00
59	Marcus Giles, Andruw Jones, John Smoltz	1.00
60	Derrek Lee, Kerry Wood, Aramis Ramirez	1.00
61	Aramis Ramirez, Morgan Ensberg, David Wright	2.00
62	Carl Crawford, Jorge Cantu, Jonny Gomes	.50
63	Jake Peavy, Chris Carpenter, John Smoltz	1.00
64	Travis Hafner, Grady Sizemore, Victor Martinez	.75
65	Ryan Howard, Prince Fielder, David Ortiz	3.00
66	Chris Carpenter, John Smoltz, Jake Peavy, Dontrelle Willis	.75
67	Ken Griffey Jr., Derek Jeter, David Ortiz, Albert Pujols	3.00
68	David Ortiz, Andruw Jones, Derrek Lee, Mark Teixeira	1.50
69	Brian Roberts, Marcus Giles, Craig Biggio, Tadahito Iguchi	.50
70	Jason Bay, David Wright, Mark Teixeira, Miguel Cabrera	2.00

Rookie Signatures Platinum

No Pricing
Production One Set

Sign of the Times

NM/M
Production 75 Sets

RA	Reggie Abercrombie	8.00
BA	Bobby Abreu	35.00
AN	Brian Anderson	10.00
BR	Brian Bannister	25.00
AB	Adrian Beltre	10.00
YB	Yuniesky Betancourt	15.00
BI	Chad Billingsley	25.00
BB	Boof Bonser	25.00
CB	Chris Booker	10.00
TB	Taylor Buchholz	8.00
ME	Melky Cabrera	25.00
MC	Miguel Cabrera	30.00
CA	Matt Cain	30.00
JC	Jose Capellan	8.00
FC	Fausto Carmona	8.00
CC	Carl Crawford	15.00
CD	Chris Demaria	15.00
DE	Chris Denorfia	15.00
JD	J.D. Drew	15.00
SD	Stephen Drew	30.00
AE	Andre Ethier	30.00
FR	Ron Flores	10.00
RF	Rafael Furcal	15.00
EG	Eric Gagne	20.00
DG	Dave Gassner	8.00
ZG	Zack Greinke	10.00
KG	Ken Griffey Jr.	80.00
VG	Vladimir Guerrero	50.00
JG	Jose Guillen	8.00
AG	Tony Gwynn Jr.	35.00
CH	Cole Hamels	50.00
JH	Jason Hammel	8.00
HA	Tim Hamulack	10.00
CY	Clay Hensley	10.00
HE	Jeremy Hermida	15.00
AH	Anderson Hernandez	8.00
RH	Ramon Hernandez	20.00
TH	Tim Hudson	15.00
JA	Conor Jackson	20.00
MJ	Mike Jacobs	15.00
DJ	Derek Jeter	160.00
BJ	Ben Johnson	10.00
JJ	Josh Johnson	20.00
RJ	Randy Johnson	50.00
AJ	Andruw Jones	25.00
JK	Jason Kendall	15.00
IK	Ian Kinsler	25.00
MK	Mark Kotsay	15.00
KU	Jason Kubel	15.00
CL	Carlos Lee	15.00
DL	Derrek Lee	25.00
FL	Francisco Liriano	35.00
BL	Boone Logan	20.00
LO	Derek Lowe	25.00
GM	Greg Maddux	140.00
PM	Paul Maholm	15.00
SM	Sean Marshall	20.00
RM	Russell Martin	20.00
JM	Joe Mauer	35.00
MA	Macay McBride	15.00
MO	Justin Morneau	25.00
MM	Mark Mulder	15.00
PA	Jonathan Papelbon	30.00
JP	Jake Peavy	20.00
TP	Tony Pena	8.00
PE	Joel Peralta	10.00
YP	Yusmeiro Petit	15.00
SP	Scott Podsednik	20.00
AR	Aramis Ramirez	20.00
HR	Hanley Ramirez	35.00
ER	Eric Reed	10.00
JR	Jose Reyes	40.00
SR	Scott Rolen	25.00
CR	Cody Ross	15.00
TS	Takashi Saito	50.00
CS	Curt Schilling	50.00
SS	Skip Schumaker	15.00
RS	Ryan Shealy	20.00
JS	John Smoltz	40.00
AS	Alay Soler	20.00
JY	Jeremy Sowers	20.00
ST	Steve Stemle	10.00
MT	Mark Teixeira	20.00
TE	Miguel Tejada	25.00
MI	Mike Thompson	10.00
DU	Dan Uggla	25.00
JV	John Van Benschoten	10.00
VE	Justin Verlander	40.00
AW	Adam Wainwright	30.00
JE	Jered Weaver	40.00
RW	Rickie Weeks	25.00
VW	Vernon Wells	20.00
JW	Josh Willingham	15.00
WI	Josh Wilson	10.00
RZ	Ryan Zimmerman	40.00

Sign of the Times Dual

NM/M
Production 25 Sets

BM	Nate McLouth, Jason Bay	25.00
CH	Jose Capellan, Ben Hendrickson	20.00
FW	Prince Fielder, Rickie Weeks	75.00
GP	Ken Griffey Jr., Albert Pujols	300.00
HD	Tim Hudson, Joey Devine	30.00
HF	Rich Harden, Ron Flores	20.00
KN	Michael Napoli, Howie Kendrick	40.00
LG	Dave Gassner, Francisco Liriano	30.00
MM	Sean Marshall, Greg Maddux	140.00
OB	Roy Oswalt, Taylor Buchholz	30.00
PB	Angel Pagan, Freddie Bynum	20.00
PT	Jake Peavy, Mike Thompson	20.00
RW	Josh Willingham, Hanley Ramirez	40.00
SC	Fausto Carmona, C.C. Sabathia	30.00
WM	Kendry Morales, Jered Weaver	40.00
ZH	Ryan Zimmerman, Brendan Harris	40.00

Signs of the Times Triple

No Pricing
Production 15 Sets

WBC Future Watch

NM/M
Common Player: 3.00
Production 999 Sets

1	Adrian Burnside	3.00
2	Gavin Fingleson	3.00
3	Bradley Harman	3.00
4	Brendan Kingman	3.00
5	Brett Roneberg	3.00
6	Paul Rutgers	3.00
7	Phil Stockman	3.00
8	Stubby Clapp	3.00
9	Steve Green	3.00
10	Pete LaForest	5.00
11	Adam Loewen	3.00
12	Ryan Radmanovich	3.00
13	Chenhao Li	3.00
14	Guangbiao Liu	3.00
15	Guogang Yang	3.00
16	Jingchao Wang	3.00
17	Lei Li	3.00
18	Lingfeng Sun	3.00
19	Nan Wang	3.00
20	Shuo Yang	3.00
21	Tao Bu	3.00
22	Wei Wang	3.00
23	Yi Feng	3.00
24	Chien-Ming Chiang	15.00
25	Yung-Chi Chen	20.00
26	Chia-Hsien Hseih	15.00
27	Chin-Lung Hu	15.00
28	En-Yu Lin	20.00
29	Wei-Lun Pan	10.00
30	Ariel Borrero	3.00
31	Yadel Marti	3.00
32	Yulieski Gourriel	20.00
33	Frederich Cepeda	3.00
34	Yadier Pedroso	3.00
35	Pedro Luis Lazo	3.00
36	Elier Sanchez	3.00
37	Norberto Gonzalez	3.00
38	Carlos Tabares	3.00
39	Eduardo Paret	3.00
40	Osmany Urrutia	3.00
41	Alexei Ramirez	3.00
42	Yoandy Garlobo	3.00
43	Vicyohandry Odelin	3.00
44	Michel Enriquez	3.00
45	Ormari Romero	3.00
46	Ariel Pestano	3.00
47	Francisco Liriano	5.00
48	Dustin Dellucchi	3.00
49	Tony Giarratano	3.00
50	Tom Gregorio	3.00
51	Mark Saccomanno	3.00
52	Takahiro Arai	8.00
53	Akinori Iwamura	15.00
54	Munenori Kawasaki	15.00
55	Nobuhiko Matsunaka	10.00
56	Daisuke Matsuzaka	100.00
57	Shinya Miyamoto	15.00
58	Tsuyoshi Nishioka	15.00
59	Tomoya Satozaki	8.00
60	Koji Uehara	15.00
61	Shunsuke Watanabe	15.00
62	Sadaharu Oh	20.00
63	Byung Kyu Lee	3.00
64	Ji Man Song	3.00
65	Jin Man Park	3.00
66	Jong Beom Lee	3.00
67	Jong Kook Kim	3.00
68	Min Han Son	3.00
69	Min Jae Kim	3.00
70	Seung-Yeop Lee	10.00
71	Luis A. Garcia	3.00
72	Mario Valenzuela	3.00
73	Sharnol Adriana	3.00
74	Rob Cordemans	3.00
75	Michael Duursma	3.00
76	Percy Isenia	3.00
77	Sidney de Jong	3.00
78	Dirk Klooster	3.00
79	Rayinoe Legito	3.00
80	Shairon Martis	5.00
81	Harvey Monte	3.00
82	Hainley Statia	3.00
83	Roger Deago	5.00

84	Audes De Leon	3.00
85	Freddy Herrera	3.00
86	Yoni Lasso	5.00
87	Orlando Miller	3.00
88	Len Picota	5.00
89	Federico Baez	3.00
90	Dicky Gonzalez	3.00
91	Josue Matos	3.00
92	Orlando Roman	3.00
93	Paul Bell	3.00
94	Kyle Botha	3.00
95	Jason Cook	3.00
96	Nicholas Dempsey	3.00
97	Victor Moreno	3.00
98	Ricardo Palma	3.00
99	Huston Street	3.00
100	Chase Utley	3.00

2006 SP Legendary Cuts

		NM/M
Complete Set (200):		
Common Player:		.25
Common SP (101-200):		2.00
Production 550		
Pack (4):		12.00
Box (12):		120.00
1	Juan Marichal	.50
2	Monte Irvin	.75
3	Will Clark	.75
4	Willie McCovey	.75
5	Eddie Gaedel	.25
6	Ken Williams	.25
7	Earl Battey	.25
8	Rick Ferrell	.25
9	Bob Gibson	1.00
10	Elmer Flick	.25
11	Joe Medwick	.25
12	Lou Brock	.75
13	Ozzie Smith	1.00
14	Red Schoendienst	.25
15	Stan Musial	2.00
16	Tony Oliva	.50
17	Phil Niekro	.25
18	Boog Powell	.25
19	Brooks Robinson	1.00
20	Cal Ripken Jr.	3.00
21	Eddie Murray	.75
22	Frank Robinson	1.00
23	Jim Palmer	.50
24	Jocko Conlon	.25
25	Carlton Fisk	.50
26	Dwight Evans	.25
27	Fred Lynn	.25
28	Jim Rice	.50
29	Ted Williams	2.00
30	Wade Boggs	.75
31	Hugh Duffy	.25
32	Kid Nichols	.25
33	Johnny Vander Meer	.25
34	Dolph Camilli	.25
35	Carl Yastrzemski	1.00
36	Chick Hafey	.25
37	Kirby Higbe	.25
38	Pee Wee Reese	.25
39	Pete Reiser	.25
40	Don Sutton	.25
41	Rod Carew	.75
42	Andre Dawson	.25
43	Billy Herman	.25
44	Billy Williams	.25
45	Charlie Root	.25
46	Hack Wilson	.25
47	Ernie Banks	1.00
48	Fergie Jenkins	.50
49	Gabby Hartnett	.25
50	Ken Hubbs	.25
51	Kiki Cuyler	.25
52	Mark Grace	.50
53	Ryne Sandberg	1.50
54	Harold Newhouser	.25
55	Charlie Robertson	.25

56	Harold Baines	.25
57	Luis Aparicio	.25
58	Luke Appling	.25
59	Nellie Fox	.50
60	Ray Schalk	.25
61	Red Faber	.25
62	Sloppy Thurston	.25
63	Freddie Lindstrom	.25
64	Vern Kennedy	.25
65	Barry Larkin	.50
66	Bucky Walters	.25
67	Dolf Luque	.25
68	Al Campanis	.25
69	Ernie Lombardi	.25
70	George Foster	.25
71	Joe Morgan	.75
72	Johnny Bench	1.00
73	Ken Griffey Sr.	.25
74	Ted Kluszewski	.25
75	Tony Perez	.50
76	Wally Post	.25
77	Bob Feller	.50
78	Bob Lemon	.25
79	Earl Averill	.25
80	Joe Sewell	.25
81	Johnny Hodapp	.25
82	Larry Doby	.25
83	Lou Boudreau	.25
84	Rocky Colavito	.25
85	Stan Coveleski	.25
86	Nap Lajoie	.50
87	Al Kaline	1.00
88	Alan Trammell	.50
89	Charlie Gehringer	.25
90	Denny McLain	.50
91	Hank Greenberg	.50
92	Jack Morris	.25
93	Mark Fidrych	.25
94	Ray Boone	.25
95	Rudy York	.25
96	Buck Leonard	.25
97	Bo Jackson	1.00
98	Zoilo Versalles	.25
99	John Kruk	.25
100	Don Drysdale	.50
101	Cecil Cooper	2.00
102	Vic Wertz	2.00
103	Kirk Gibson	2.00
104	Maury Wills	2.00
105	Steve Garvey	2.00
106	Warren Spahn	5.00
107	Paul Molitor	4.00
108	Robin Yount	5.00
109	Rollie Fingers	3.00
110	Bob Allison	2.00
111	Kirby Puckett	6.00
112	Tim Raines	2.00
113	George Pipgras	2.00
114	Eddie Grant	2.00
115	Hoyt Wilhelm	2.00
116	Sal Maglie	2.00
117	Ron Santo	3.00
118	Wally Joyner	2.00
119	Tom Seaver	5.00
120	Tommie Agee	2.00
121	Harmon Killebrew	4.00
122	Bill Dickey	3.00
123	Early Wynn	2.00
124	Bobby Murcer	4.00
125	Bucky Dent	2.00
126	Dave Winfield	4.00
127	Don Larsen	4.00
128	Don Mattingly	8.00
129	Earle Combs	2.00
130	Ed Lopat	2.00
131	Elston Howard	4.00
132	Everett Scott	2.00
133	Rich "Goose" Gossage	2.00
134	Graig Nettles	2.00
135	Joe DiMaggio	8.00
136	Lou Piniella	2.00
137	Bill "Moose" Skowron	2.00
138	Phil Rizzuto	3.00
139	Red Ruffing	2.00
140	Reggie Jackson	4.00
141	Roger Maris	6.00
142	Ron Guidry	3.00
143	Tiny Bonham	2.00
144	Bruce Sutter	2.00
145	Tony Lazzeri	2.00
146	Waite Hoyt	2.00
147	Whitey Ford	4.00
148	Steve Sax	2.00
149	Yogi Berra	5.00
150	Enos Slaughter	2.00
151	Jim "Catfish" Hunter	2.00
152	Dennis Eckersley	3.00
153	Jose Canseco	3.00
154	Al Rosen	2.00
155	Al Simmons	2.00
156	Chief Bender	2.00
157	Cy Williams	2.00
158	Mike Schmidt	5.00

159	Richie Ashburn	2.00
160	Robin Roberts	3.00
161	Steve Carlton	3.00
162	Judy Johnson	2.00
163	Al Oliver	2.00
164	Bill Mazeroski	3.00
165	Dave Parker	3.00
166	Max Carey	2.00
167	Pie Traynor	3.00
168	Ralph Kiner	2.00
169	Roberto Clemente	10.00
170	Willie Stargell	4.00
171	Gaylord Perry	2.00
172	Tony Gwynn	5.00
173	Nolan Ryan	8.00
174	Joe Carter	2.00
175	Frank Howard	2.00
176	George Kell	2.00
177	Heinie Manush	2.00
178	Sam Rice	2.00
179	Babe Ruth	10.00
180	Casey Stengel	3.00
181	Christy Mathewson	4.00
182	Cy Young	4.00
183	Dizzy Dean	4.00
184	Eddie Mathews	5.00
185	George Sisler	3.00
186	Honus Wagner	5.00
187	Jackie Robinson	6.00
188	Jimmie Foxx	5.00
189	Johnny Mize	2.00
190	Lefty Gomez	2.00
191	Lou Gehrig	8.00
192	Mel Ott	3.00
193	Mickey Cochrane	3.00
194	Rogers Hornsby	4.00
195	Roy Campanella	5.00
196	Satchel Paige	5.00
197	Thurman Munson	5.00
198	Ty Cobb	6.00
199	Walter Johnson	3.00
200	Lefty Grove	3.00

Gold

Gold (101-200):	2-4X
Production 99 Sets	

Baseball Chronology

		NM/M
Production 550 Sets		
Platinum:		1.5-2X
Production 99 Sets		
EB	Ernie Banks	5.00
EB2	Ernie Banks	5.00
JB	Johnny Bench	4.00
YB	Yogi Berra	4.00
WB	Wade Boggs	4.00
WB2	Wade Boggs	4.00
LB	Lou Boudreau	2.00
LO	Lou Brock	4.00
RC	Roy Campanella	4.00
CA	Rod Carew	3.00
SC	Steve Carlton	3.00
SC2	Steve Carlton	3.00
JC	Joe Carter	2.00
WC	Will Clark	4.00
CL	Roberto Clemente	10.00
TC	Ty Cobb	6.00
TC2	Ty Cobb	6.00
MC	Mickey Cochrane	3.00
CN	Joe Cronin	2.00
AD	Andre Dawson	3.00
DZ	Dizzy Dean	4.00
BD	Bucky Dent	2.00
JD	Joe DiMaggio	8.00
DD	Don Drysdale	3.00
DE	Dennis Eckersley	3.00
BF	Bob Feller	3.00
MF	Mark Fidrych	2.00
RF	Rollie Fingers	3.00
CF	Carlton Fisk	3.00
WF	Whitey Ford	4.00
JF	Jimmie Foxx	5.00
JF2	Jimmie Foxx	5.00
SG	Steve Garvey	2.00
LG	Lou Gehrig	8.00
LG2	Lou Gehrig	8.00
BG	Bob Gibson	3.00
KG	Kirk Gibson	3.00
HG	Hank Greenberg	3.00
TG	Tony Gwynn	4.00
GH	Gil Hodges	2.00
RH	Rogers Hornsby	4.00

CH	Jim "Catfish" Hunter	2.00
BO	Bo Jackson	4.00
RJ	Reggie Jackson	4.00
WJ	Walter Johnson	4.00
AK	Al Kaline	4.00
RK	Ralph Kiner	2.00
NL	Nap Lajoie	3.00
DL	Don Larsen	3.00
BL	Bob Lemon	2.00
FL	Fred Lynn	2.00
RM	Roger Maris	6.00
CM	Christy Mathewson	4.00
DM	Don Mattingly	6.00
BM	Bill Mazeroski	3.00
WM	Willie McCovey	3.00
JM	Johnny Mize	2.00
PM	Paul Molitor	3.00
JO	Joe Morgan	3.00
TM	Thurman Munson	5.00
EM	Eddie Murray	3.00
SM	Stan Musial	6.00
PN	Phil Niekro	2.00
MO	Mel Ott	3.00
SP	Satchel Paige	5.00
GP	Gaylord Perry	2.00
KP	Kirby Puckett	5.00
PW	Pee Wee Reese	3.00
RI	Jim Rice	3.00
CR	Cal Ripken Jr.	8.00
RO	Brooks Robinson	4.00
FR	Frank Robinson	4.00
JR	Jackie Robinson	6.00
BR	Babe Ruth	10.00
BR2	Babe Ruth	10.00
BR3	Babe Ruth	10.00
NR	Nolan Ryan	8.00
NR2	Nolan Ryan	8.00
NR3	Nolan Ryan	8.00
RS	Ryne Sandberg	4.00
MS	Mike Schmidt	5.00
TS	Tom Seaver	4.00
GS	George Sisler	3.00
ES	Enos Slaughter	2.00
OS	Ozzie Smith	5.00
WS	Warren Spahn	4.00
ST	Willie Stargell	4.00
CS	Casey Stengel	3.00
CS2	Casey Stengel	3.00
DS	Don Sutton	2.00
AT	Alan Trammell	3.00
HW	Honus Wagner	5.00
HY	Hoyt Wilhelm	3.00
BW	Billy Williams	2.00
TW	Ted Williams	8.00
TW2	Ted Williams	8.00
MW	Maury Wills	2.00
YZ	Carl Yastrzemski	4.00
CY	Cy Young	3.00
RY	Robin Yount	4.00

Baseball Chronology Materials

		NM/M
Common Player:		
EB	Ernie Banks	15.00
EB2	Ernie Banks/SP	20.00
JB	Johnny Bench	15.00
YB	Yogi Berra	20.00
WB	Wade Boggs	10.00
WB2	Wade Boggs	10.00
LB	Lou Boudreau	12.00
LO	Lou Brock	10.00
RC	Roy Campanella	20.00
CA	Rod Carew	10.00
SC	Steve Carlton	8.00
SC2	Steve Carlton	8.00
JC	Joe Carter	6.00
WC	Will Clark	10.00
CL	Roberto Clemente/SP	80.00
TC	Ty Cobb/SP	150.00
TC2	Ty Cobb/SP	150.00
CN	Joe Cronin	15.00
AD	Andre Dawson	8.00
DZ	Dizzy Dean/SP	60.00
BD	Bucky Dent	6.00
JD	Joe DiMaggio/SP	75.00
DD	Don Drysdale/SP	25.00
DE	Dennis Eckersley	10.00
BF	Bob Feller	10.00
MF	Mark Fidrych	10.00
RF	Rollie Fingers	8.00

CF Carlton Fisk 10.00
JF Jimmie Foxx/SP 40.00
JF2 Jimmie Foxx/SP 40.00
SG Steve Garvey 6.00
LG Lou Gehrig/SP 175.00
LG2 Lou Gehrig 175.00
BG Bob Gibson 10.00
HG Hank Greenberg 25.00
TG Tony Gwynn 12.00
GH Gil Hodges/SP 40.00
RH Rogers Hornsby/SP 50.00
CH Jim "Catfish" Hunter 10.00
BO Bo Jackson 12.00
RJ Reggie Jackson 12.00
AK Al Kaline 15.00
RK Ralph Kiner 12.00
DL Don Larsen 10.00
BL Bob Lemon 10.00
FL Fred Lynn 8.00
RM Roger Maris 30.00
CM Christy Mathewson/SP 240.00
DM Don Mattingly 15.00
BM Bill Mazeroski/SP 20.00
WM Willie McCovey 12.00
JM Johnny Mize 15.00
PM Paul Molitor 8.00
JO Joe Morgan 10.00
TM Thurman Munson 25.00
EM Eddie Murray 10.00
SM Stan Musial 20.00
PN Phil Niekro 8.00
MO Mel Ott SP 35.00
SP Satchel Paige/SP 75.00
GP Gaylord Perry 8.00
KP Kirby Puckett 15.00
PW Pee Wee Reese 10.00
RI Jim Rice 8.00
CR Cal Ripken Jr. 25.00
RO Brooks Robinson 12.00
FR Frank Robinson 10.00
JR Jackie Robinson/SP 60.00
BR Babe Ruth/SP 250.00
BR2 Babe Ruth/SP 250.00
BR3 Babe Ruth/SP 250.00
NR Nolan Ryan 20.00
NR2 Nolan Ryan 20.00
NR3 Nolan Ryan 20.00
RS Ryne Sandberg 15.00
MS Mike Schmidt 12.00
TS Tom Seaver 15.00
GS George Sisler/SP 35.00
ES Enos Slaughter 15.00
OS Ozzie Smith 12.00
WS Warren Spahn 15.00
ST Willie Stargell 15.00
CS Casey Stengel 25.00
CS2 Casey Stengel/SP 35.00
DS Don Sutton 8.00
AT Alan Trammell 8.00
HW Honus Wagner/SP 160.00
HY Hoyt Wilhelm/SP 15.00
BW Billy Williams 8.00
TW Ted Williams 40.00
TW2 Ted Williams 40.00
MW Maury Wills 8.00
YZ Carl Yastrzemski 15.00
RY Robin Yount 12.00

Dual Legendary Cuts
Production One Set

Historical Cut Signatures
Production One Set

Legendary Materials

NM/M
Production 225 unless noted.
Tier 1: .75-1.5X
Production 50-199
Tier 2: 1-2X

Production 25-99
Tier 3: No Pricing
Production 5-15
HB Harold Baines 6.00
EB Ernie Banks 20.00
JB Johnny Bench 15.00
YB Yogi Berra 15.00
WB Wade Boggs 10.00
LB Lou Brock 10.00
LB2 Lou Brock 10.00
JC Jose Canseco 10.00
CW Rod Carew 10.00
SC Steve Carlton 8.00
SC2 Steve Carlton 8.00
WC Will Clark 10.00
WC2 Will Clark 10.00
RC Rocky Colavito 20.00
DC Dave Concepcion 6.00
CC Cecil Cooper 10.00
AD Andre Dawson 8.00
BD Bucky Dent 8.00
JD Joe DiMaggio/99 75.00
DE Dennis Eckersley 8.00
DE2 Dennis Eckersley 8.00
EV Dwight Evans 8.00
BF Bob Feller 10.00
RF Rollie Fingers 8.00
CF Carlton Fisk 10.00
GF George Foster 6.00
SG Steve Garvey 6.00
BG Bob Gibson 10.00
KI Kirk Gibson 10.00
GG Rich "Goose" Gossage 8.00
MG Mark Grace 10.00
KG Ken Griffey Sr. 6.00
GU Ron Guidry 10.00
TG Tony Gwynn 15.00
FH Frank Howard 8.00
BO Bo Jackson 15.00
RJ Reggie Jackson 10.00
FJ Fergie Jenkins 8.00
WJ Wally Joyner 10.00
AK Al Kaline 12.00
RK Ralph Kiner 10.00
JK John Kruk 8.00
BL Barry Larkin 8.00
DL Don Larsen 12.00
FL Fred Lynn 6.00
JU Juan Marichal 10.00
MA Don Mattingly 20.00
BM Bill Mazeroski 10.00
WM Willie McCovey 10.00
PM Paul Molitor 8.00
JO Joe Morgan 10.00
JM Jack Morris 6.00
MU Bobby Murcer 8.00
EM Eddie Murray 10.00
SM Stan Musial 20.00
GN Graig Nettles 10.00
PN Phil Niekro 8.00
PN2 Phil Niekro 8.00
TO Tony Oliva 8.00
AO Al Oliver 8.00
JP Jim Palmer 10.00
JP2 Jim Palmer 10.00
DP Dave Parker 8.00
TP Tony Perez 8.00
GP Gaylord Perry 8.00
GP2 Gaylord Perry 8.00
LP Lou Piniella 8.00
BP Boog Powell 8.00
KP Kirby Puckett 15.00
JR Jim Rice 8.00
CR Cal Ripken Jr. 25.00
PR Phil Rizzuto/99 10.00
RR Robin Roberts 10.00
RO Brooks Robinson/175 10.00
FR Frank Robinson 10.00
FR2 Frank Robinson 10.00
AR Al Rosen 8.00
BR Babe Ruth/99 225.00
NR Nolan Ryan 20.00
RS Ryne Sandberg 15.00
RN Ron Santo/125 12.00
RN2 Ron Santo/125 12.00
SS Steve Sax 6.00
MS Mike Schmidt 12.00
RE Red Schoendienst/99 12.00
TS Tom Seaver 12.00
SK Bill "Moose" Skowron 8.00
OS Ozzie Smith 15.00
BS Bruce Sutter 8.00
SU Don Sutton 8.00
JT Joe Torre 10.00
BW Billy Williams 8.00
MW Maury Wills 6.00
DW Dave Winfield 8.00
CY Carl Yastrzemski 15.00
RY Robin Yount 10.00
MW 6.00

Legendary Cuts
NM/M
Production 1-90

JA Joe Adcock/47 120.00
GA Grover Alexander/1
MA Mel Allen/67 175.00
WA Walter Alston/27 160.00
LA Luke Appling/84 100.00
RA Richie Ashburn/22 200.00
EA Earl Averill/50 100.00
EB Ed Barrow/35 250.00
RB Ray Boone/51 120.00
LB Lou Boudreau/86 100.00
DC Dolph Camilli/58 100.00
MC Max Carey/79 140.00
EC Earle Combs/65 200.00
ST Stan Coveleski/81 120.00
JO Joe Cronin/30 125.00
RD Ray Dandridge/35 100.00
DD Dizzy Dean/21 600.00
BD Bill Dickey/34 240.00
DR Don Drysdale/45 200.00
DU Joe Dugan/25 160.00
DL Leo Durocher/22 150.00
CG Charlie Gehringer/76 100.00
LG Lefty Gomez/44 125.00
HG Hank Greenberg/60 250.00
BG Burleigh Grimes/33 150.00
HE Billy Herman/87 100.00
WH Waite Hoyt/49 125.00
CH Jim "Catfish" Hunter/24 150.00
JJ Judy Johnson/40 150.00
HK Harvey Kuenn/89 120.00
BL Bob Lemon/77 80.00
LO Ernie Lombardi/25 160.00
EL Ed Lopat/32 140.00
EM Eddie Mathews/59 150.00
JM Joe McCarthy/67 180.00
ME Joe Medwick/82 180.00
MI Johnny Mize/90 140.00
WP Wally Post/61 100.00
PR Pee Wee Reese/47 160.00
SR Sam Rice/31 180.00
ER Edd Roush/90 80.00
RR Red Ruffing/72 200.00
JS Joe Sewell/83 120.00
WS Warren Spahn/52 140.00
CS Casey Stengel/35 300.00
PT Pie Traynor/26 500.00
BW Bucky Walters/52 120.00
WI Hoyt Wilhelm/47 100.00

Place In History Signatures

NM/M
Production 99 unless noted.
LA Luis Aparicio 25.00
LA2 Luis Aparicio 25.00
HB Harold Baines/35 20.00
EB Ernie Banks/25 75.00
JB Johnny Bench/42 50.00
YB Yogi Berra/25
WB Wade Boggs/50 35.00
LB Lou Brock 25.00
LB2 Lou Brock 25.00
JC Jose Canseco 40.00
CA Rod Carew/50 25.00
SC Steve Carlton 25.00
SC2 Steve Carlton 25.00
WC Will Clark/92 25.00
WC2 Will Clark 25.00
CC Cecil Cooper 20.00
AD Andre Dawson 20.00
BD Bucky Dent 15.00
DE Dennis Eckersley 25.00
DE2 Dennis Eckersley
EV Dwight Evans 20.00
BF Bob Feller/35 40.00
RF Rollie Fingers/77 20.00
CF Carlton Fisk 30.00
WF Whitey Ford/35 60.00
GF George Foster/56 15.00
SG Steve Garvey 25.00
MG Mark Grace 25.00
KG Ken Griffey Sr. 25.00
TG Tony Gwynn/26 60.00
FH Frank Howard 25.00
BO Bo Jackson 50.00
RJ Reggie Jackson/25 60.00
FJ Fergie Jenkins 20.00
WJ Wally Joyner 25.00
BL Barry Larkin/49 40.00
FL Fred Lynn 15.00

JU Juan Marichal/29 35.00
MA Don Mattingly/50 100.00
BM Bill Mazeroski 35.00
MC Denny McLain/31 25.00
PM Paul Molitor 35.00
JO Joe Morgan/50 30.00
JM Jack Morris/82 20.00
SM Stan Musial/45 70.00
GN Graig Nettles 20.00
PN Phil Niekro/52 20.00
PN2 Phil Niekro/52 20.00
TO Tony Oliva 20.00
TO2 Tony Oliva 20.00
JP Jim Palmer 25.00
GP Gaylord Perry 20.00
GP2 Gaylord Perry 20.00
LP Lou Piniella 20.00
JY Johnny Podres/38 20.00
BP Boog Powell 20.00
KP Kirby Puckett 80.00
TR Tim Raines 25.00
JR Jim Rice 20.00
CR Cal Ripken Jr./50 140.00
PR Phil Rizzuto 40.00
RR Robin Roberts/55 25.00
BR Brooks Robinson/50 40.00
BR2 Brooks Robinson/50 40.00
FR Frank Robinson 40.00
FR2 Frank Robinson 40.00
AR Al Rosen 20.00
RO Ron Santo 60.00
RO2 Ron Santo 60.00
SS Steve Sax 20.00
MS Mike Schmidt/25 75.00
RD Red Schoendienst 35.00
TS Tom Seaver/55 50.00
SK Bill "Moose" Skowron 25.00
OS Ozzie Smith 50.00
BS Bruce Sutter 20.00
JT Joe Torre 40.00
BW Billy Williams 20.00
MW Maury Wills/96 20.00
CY Carl Yastrzemski 40.00
RY Robin Yount 40.00

Place In History Cut Signatures
NM/M
Production 1-98
BA Bob Allison/94 140.00
LA Luke Appling/94 100.00
EA Earl Averill/75 80.00
LB Lou Boudreau/88 100.00
HC Happy Chandler/61 100.00
CO Chuck Connors/25 450.00
JC Joe Cronin/30 125.00
RD Ray Dandridge/43 120.00
BD Bill Dickey/29 200.00
DL Leo Durocher/42 140.00
DU Joe Dugan/25 150.00
FF Ford Frick/30 150.00
CG Charlie Gehringer/57 120.00
WG Warren Giles/45 200.00
LG Lefty Gomez/30 125.00
HG Hank Greenberg/31 260.00
BG Burleigh Grimes/43 120.00
HI Harry Higbe/59 140.00
JH Johnny Hodapp/26 125.00
DH Dick Howser/28 160.00
JJ Judy Johnson/20 180.00
VK Vern Kennedy/61 120.00
BL Bob Lemon/47 90.00
SM Sal Maglie/73 120.00
EM Eddie Mathews/34 150.00
JM Joe McCarthy/58 200.00
ME Joe Medwick/60 200.00
PR Pee Wee Reese/57 180.00
RE Pete Reiser/75 125.00
RO Charlie Robertson/42 150.00
ER Edd Roush/98 100.00
JS Joe Sewell/87 100.00
GS George Sisler/42 450.00
WS Warren Spahn/41 140.00
WI Hoyt Wilhelm/65 100.00
CW Cy Williams/29 180.00
EW Early Wynn/36 100.00

Quadruple Legendary Cuts
Production One Set

Memorable Moments Swatch
NM/M
Common Player:
Production 225 Sets
JB Johnny Bench 15.00
CC Cesar Cedeno 8.00
RC Rocky Colavito 20.00
DC David Cone 8.00

CE	Cecil Cooper	10.00
AD	Andre Dawson	10.00
DE	Dwight Evans	8.00
BF	Bob Feller	12.00
RF	Rollie Fingers	8.00
CF	Carlton Fisk	10.00
GF	George Foster	8.00
SG	Steve Garvey	8.00
KG	Kirk Gibson	10.00
GG	Rich "Goose" Gossage	8.00
RG	Ron Guidry	12.00
TG	Tony Gwynn	12.00
BJ	Bo Jackson	15.00
RJ	Reggie Jackson	10.00
JK	John Kruk	10.00
BL	Barry Larkin	10.00
MA	Juan Marichal	10.00
EM	Eddie Mathews	15.00
DM	Don Mattingly	20.00
JM	Johnny Mize	15.00
MO	Joe Morgan	10.00
BM	Bobby Murcer	8.00
MU	Eddie Murray	10.00
SM	Stan Musial	20.00
PO	Paul O'Neill	10.00
DP	Dave Parker	8.00
GP	Gaylord Perry	8.00
TR	Tim Raines	8.00
PR	Phil Rizzuto	10.00
RS	Ron Santo	10.00
SS	Steve Sax	8.00
MS	Mike Schmidt	15.00
TS	Tom Seaver	12.00
OS	Ozzie Smith	15.00
BS	Bruce Sutter	10.00
DS	Don Sutton	8.00
RY	Robin Yount	12.00

Memorable Moments Autograph

NM/M

Production 1-99

CC	Cesar Cedeno/99	20.00
RC	Rocky Colavito/99	80.00
DC	David Cone/99	15.00
CE	Cecil Cooper/99	20.00
AD	Andre Dawson/99	20.00
DE	Dwight Evans/25	20.00
BF	Bob Feller/25	40.00
RF	Rollie Fingers/47	20.00
CF	Carlton Fisk/25	30.00
GF	George Foster/25	20.00
SG	Steve Garvey/25	35.00
KG	Kirk Gibson/25	30.00
TG	Tony Gwynn/25	75.00
BJ	Bo Jackson/25	50.00
JK	John Kruk/99	20.00
BL	Barry Larkin/50	40.00
MA	Juan Marichal/25	30.00
DM	Don Mattingly/50	100.00
MO	Joe Morgan/20	30.00
MU	Eddie Murray/45	20.00
GP	Gaylord Perry/99	20.00
TR	Tim Raines/50	30.00
PR	Phil Rizzuto/99	40.00
RS	Ron Santo/25	65.00
TS	Tom Seaver/44	40.00
OS	Ozzie Smith/25	50.00
RY	Robin Yount/25	60.00

When It Was A Game

NM/M

Production 550 Sets

Gold: 1.5-2X

Production 99 Sets

LA	Luis Aparicio	2.00
HB	Harold Baines	2.00
EB	Ernie Banks	5.00
JB	Johnny Bench	4.00
YB	Yogi Berra	4.00
WB	Wade Boggs	4.00

LB	Lou Brock	4.00
CA	Rod Carew	3.00
SC	Steve Carlton	3.00
SC2	Steve Carlton	3.00
WC	Will Clark	4.00
RC	Roberto Clemente	10.00
MC	Mickey Cochrane	3.00
CO	Rocky Colavito	3.00
AD	Andre Dawson	3.00
JD	Joe DiMaggio	8.00
DD	Don Drysdale	3.00
DE	Dennis Eckersley	3.00
EV	Dwight Evans	2.00
BF	Bob Feller	3.00
RF	Rollie Fingers	3.00
CF	Carlton Fisk	3.00
WF	Whitey Ford	4.00
JF	Jimmie Foxx	5.00
SG	Steve Garvey	2.00
LG	Lou Gehrig	8.00
BG	Bob Gibson	4.00
KI	Kirk Gibson	3.00
GG	Rich "Goose" Gossage	2.00
HG	Hank Greenberg	3.00
KG	Ken Griffey Sr.	2.00
GU	Ron Guidry	3.00
TG	Tony Gwynn	4.00
HO	Rogers Hornsby	4.00
FH	Frank Howard	2.00
RJ	Reggie Jackson	4.00
FJ	Fergie Jenkins	3.00
WJ	Wally Joyner	2.00
AK	Al Kaline	4.00
RK	Ralph Kiner	2.00
JK	John Kruk	2.00
DL	Don Larsen	3.00
FL	Fred Lynn	2.00
JU	Juan Marichal	3.00
EM	Eddie Mathews	3.00
MA	Don Mattingly	6.00
BM	Bill Mazeroski	3.00
WM	Willie McCovey	3.00
DY	Denny McLain	3.00
MZ	Johnny Mize	2.00
PM	Paul Molitor	3.00
JO	Joe Morgan	3.00
JM	Jack Morris	2.00
TM	Thurman Munson	5.00
MU	Bobby Murcer	3.00
ED	Eddie Murray	3.00
SM	Stan Musial	6.00
GN	Graig Nettles	2.00
PN	Phil Niekro	2.00
TO	Tony Oliva	2.00
TO2	Tony Oliva	3.00
MO	Mel Ott	3.00
SP	Satchel Paige	5.00
JP	Jim Palmer	3.00
DP	Dave Parker	2.00
TP	Tony Perez	2.00
GP	Gaylord Perry	2.00
LP	Lou Piniella	2.00
PS	Johnny Podres	2.00
KP	Kirby Puckett	5.00
TR	Tim Raines	2.00
RI	Jim Rice	3.00
CR	Cal Ripken Jr.	8.00
PR	Phil Rizzuto	3.00
RR	Robin Roberts	2.00
RO	Brooks Robinson	4.00
RO2	Brooks Robinson	4.00
FR	Frank Robinson	4.00
FR2	Frank Robinson	4.00
JR	Jackie Robinson	6.00
AR	Al Rosen	2.00
BR	Babe Ruth	10.00
NR	Nolan Ryan	8.00
SA	Ryne Sandberg	5.00
RN	Ron Santo	3.00
MS	Mike Schmidt	5.00
RS	Red Schoendienst	2.00
TS	Tom Seaver	4.00
GS	George Sisler	3.00
SK	Bill "Moose" Skowron	2.00
OS	Ozzie Smith	5.00
BS	Bruce Sutter	2.00
SU	Don Sutton	2.00
JT	Joe Torre	3.00
HW	Honus Wagner	5.00
BW	Billy Williams	2.00
MW	Maury Wills	2.00
YZ	Carl Yastrzemski	4.00
CY	Cy Young	3.00
RY	Robin Yount	4.00

When It Was A Game Used

NM/M

Production 75 unless noted.

LA	Luis Aparicio/25	10.00
HB	Harold Baines/25	10.00
EB	Ernie Banks	20.00

JB	Johnny Bench	15.00
YB	Yogi Berra	20.00
WB	Wade Boggs	10.00
LB	Lou Brock/25	12.00
CA	Rod Carew	12.00
SC	Steve Carlton	10.00
SC2	Steve Carlton	10.00
WC	Will Clark	12.00
RC	Roberto Clemente	80.00
MC	Mickey Cochrane/25	75.00
CO	Rocky Colavito	25.00
AD	Andre Dawson	10.00
JD	Joe DiMaggio	80.00
DD	Don Drysdale	15.00
DE	Dennis Eckersley	15.00
EV	Dwight Evans/25	15.00
BF	Bob Feller	10.00
RF	Rollie Fingers	12.00
CF	Carlton Fisk	12.00
JF	Jimmie Foxx	50.00
SG	Steve Garvey	8.00
LG	Lou Gehrig	140.00
BG	Bob Gibson	12.00
KI	Kirk Gibson	10.00
GG	Rich "Goose" Gossage/25	10.00
HG	Hank Greenberg	30.00
KG	Ken Griffey Sr.	8.00
GU	Ron Guidry	10.00
TG	Tony Gwynn	15.00
HO	Rogers Hornsby	50.00
FH	Frank Howard/25	20.00
RJ	Reggie Jackson/25	15.00
FJ	Fergie Jenkins	10.00
WJ	Wally Joyner	8.00
AK	Al Kaline/25	
RK	Ralph Kiner	12.00
JK	John Kruk	10.00
DL	Don Larsen	15.00
FL	Fred Lynn	8.00
JU	Juan Marichal	10.00
EM	Eddie Mathews	15.00
MA	Don Mattingly	15.00
BM	Bill Mazeroski	25.00
WM	Willie McCovey	10.00
MZ	Johnny Mize	10.00
PM	Paul Molitor	10.00
JO	Joe Morgan	10.00
JM	Jack Morris	10.00
TM	Thurman Munson	25.00
MU	Bobby Murcer	10.00
ED	Eddie Murray	12.00
SM	Stan Musial	25.00
GN	Graig Nettles	10.00
PN	Phil Niekro	10.00
TO	Tony Oliva	10.00
TO2	Tony Oliva	10.00
MO	Mel Ott	30.00
JP	Jim Palmer	10.00
DP	Dave Parker	8.00
TP	Tony Perez	10.00
GP	Gaylord Perry	10.00
LP	Lou Piniella	12.00
KP	Kirby Puckett	20.00
TR	Tim Raines	10.00
RI	Jim Rice	10.00
CR	Cal Ripken Jr.	25.00
PR	Phil Rizzuto/25	25.00
RR	Robin Roberts	15.00
RO	Brooks Robinson	20.00
RO2	Brooks Robinson/25	20.00
FR	Frank Robinson	15.00
FR2	Frank Robinson	15.00
JR	Jackie Robinson	50.00
AR	Al Rosen	10.00
BR	Babe Ruth	350.00
NR	Nolan Ryan/25	30.00
SA	Ryne Sandberg/25	20.00
RN	Ron Santo	10.00
MS	Mike Schmidt	20.00
RS	Red Schoendienst	10.00
TS	Tom Seaver	15.00
GS	George Sisler	30.00
SK	Bill "Moose" Skowron	10.00
OS	Ozzie Smith	15.00
BS	Bruce Sutter	10.00
SU	Don Sutton	8.00
JT	Joe Torre	10.00
BW	Billy Williams	10.00
MW	Maury Wills	10.00
YZ	Carl Yastrzemski	15.00
RY	Robin Yount	12.00

When It Was a Game Cut Signature

NM/M

Production 2-99

JA	Joe Adcock/18	150.00
LA	Luke Appling/83	100.00
EA	Earl Averill/67	80.00
EB	Earl Battey/71	175.00
RB	Ray Boone/68	120.00
LB	Lou Boudreau/50	100.00

AC	Al Campanis/30	250.00
MC	Max Carey/71	140.00
HC	Happy Chandler/64	100.00
SC	Stan Coveleski/91	100.00
CR	Joe Cronin/34	120.00
RD	Ray Dandridge/75	120.00
JD	Joe Dugan/30	150.00
DU	Leo Durocher/25	160.00
RF	Rick Ferrell/25	150.00
EF	Elmer Flick/25	150.00
FF	Ford Frick/30	150.00
CG	Charlie Gehringer/64	120.00
LG	Lefty Gomez/36	125.00
HG	Hank Greenberg/21	260.00
BG	Burleigh Grimes/56	140.00
HE	Billy Herman/99	140.00
WH	Waite Hoyt/70	100.00
CH	Carl Hubbell/80	140.00
HU	Jim "Catfish" Hunter/34	150.00
JJ	Judy Johnson/20	180.00
VK	Vern Kennedy/58	120.00
TK	Ted Kluszewski/50	140.00
BL	Bob Lemon/79	90.00
FL	Freddie Lindstrom/25	200.00
EL	Ernie Lombardi/24	150.00
LO	Ed Lopat/28	140.00
SM	Sal Maglie/68	120.00
EM	Eddie Mathews/33	150.00
JM	Joe McCarthy/51	200.00
ME	Joe Medwick/57	240.00
MI	Johnny Mize/70	120.00
GP	George Pipgras/25	180.00
WP	Wally Post/66	120.00
PR	Pee Wee Reese/52	180.00
SR	Sam Rice/33	175.00
ER	Edd Roush/98	100.00
RR	Red Ruffing/44	180.00
SE	George Selkirk/175	175.00
JS	Joe Sewell/78	100.00
GS	George Sisler/37	450.00
WS	Warren Spahn/78	125.00
ST	Willie Stargell/27	160.00
JV	Johnny Vander Meer/45	150.00
VW	Vic Wertz/30	160.00
HW	Hoyt Wilhelm/56	170.00
EW	Early Wynn/40	100.00

2006 SPx

NM/M

Complete Set (160):	.25
Common Player (1-100):	.25
Common Auto. (101-160):	10.00
Production 190-999	
Pack (4):	8.00
Box (18):	125.00

1	Luis Gonzalez	.25
2	Chad Tracy	.25
3	Brandon Webb	.50
4	Andruw Jones	1.00
5	Chipper Jones	1.00
6	John Smoltz	.75
7	Tim Hudson	.50
8	Miguel Tejada	.75
9	Brian Roberts	.25
10	Ramon Hernandez	.25
11	Curt Schilling	1.00
12	David Ortiz	1.50
13	Manny Ramirez	1.00
14	Jason Varitek	1.00
15	Josh Beckett	.50
16	Greg Maddux	2.00
17	Derrek Lee	.75
18	Mark Prior	.75
19	Aramis Ramirez	.50
20	Jim Thome	.75
21	Paul Konerko	.75
22	Scott Podsednik	.25
23	Jose Contreras	.25
24	Ken Griffey Jr.	2.00
25	Adam Dunn	.75
26	Felipe Lopez	.25
27	Travis Hafner	.75
28	Victor Martinez	.75
29	Grady Sizemore	.75
30	Jhonny Peralta	.25
31	Todd Helton	.75
32	Garrett Atkins	.25
33	Clint Barmes	.25
34	Ivan Rodriguez	.75

35	Chris Shelton	.25
36	Jeremy Bonderman	.50
37	Miguel Cabrera	1.00
38	Dontrelle Willis	.50
39	Lance Berkman	.50
40	Morgan Ensberg	.25
41	Roy Oswalt	.50
42	Reggie Sanders	.25
43	Mike Sweeney	.25
44	Vladimir Guerrero	1.00
45	Bartolo Colon	.25
46	Chone Figgins	.25
47	Nomar Garciaparra	1.00
48	Jeff Kent	.50
49	J.D. Drew	.25
50	Carlos Lee	.50
51	Ben Sheets	.50
52	Rickie Weeks	.25
53	Johan Santana	1.00
54	Torii Hunter	.50
55	Joe Mauer	.50
56	Pedro Martinez	1.00
57	David Wright	2.00
58	Carlos Beltran	.75
59	Carlos Delgado	.75
60	Jose Reyes	.75
61	Derek Jeter	3.00
62	Alex Rodriguez	3.00
63	Randy Johnson	1.00
64	Hideki Matsui	2.00
65	Gary Sheffield	.75
66	Rich Harden	.50
67	Eric Chavez	.50
68	Huston Street	.25
69	Bobby Crosby	.25
70	Bobby Abreu	.50
71	Ryan Howard	2.00
72	Chase Utley	.75
73	Pat Burrell	.50
74	Jason Bay	.50
75	Sean Casey	.25
76	Mike Piazza	1.00
77	Jake Peavy	.50
78	Brian Giles	.25
79	Milton Bradley	.25
80	Omar Vizquel	.25
81	Jason Schmidt	.25
82	Ichiro Suzuki	2.00
83	Felix Hernandez	.50
84	Richie Sexson	.50
85	Albert Pujols	3.00
86	Chris Carpenter	.75
87	Scott Rolen	1.00
88	Jim Edmonds	.50
89	Carl Crawford	.50
90	Jonny Gomes	.25
91	Scott Kazmir	.50
92	Mark Teixeira	.75
93	Michael Young	.25
94	Phil Nevin	.25
95	Vernon Wells	.25
96	Roy Halladay	.50
97	Troy Glaus	.50
98	Alfonso Soriano	.75
99	Nick Johnson	.25
100	Jose Vidro	.25
101	Conor Jackson/ 999 (RC)	15.00
102	Jered Weaver/ 299 (RC)	40.00
103	Macay McBride/ 999 (RC)	10.00
104	Aaron Rakers/ 499 (RC)	15.00
105	Jonathan Papelbon/ 499 (RC)	50.00
106	Jason Bergmann/ 999 RC	15.00
107	Stephen Drew/ 350 (RC)	40.00
108	Chris Denorfia/ 999 (RC)	10.00
109	Kelly Shoppach/ 999 (RC)	15.00
110	Ryan Shealy/999 (RC)	15.00
111	Josh Wilson/999 (RC)	10.00
112	Brian Anderson/ 999 (RC)	10.00
113	Justin Verlander/ 749 (RC)	40.00
114	Jeremy Hermida/ 999 (RC)	15.00
115	Mike Jacobs/999 (RC)	15.00
116	Josh Johnson/ 999 (RC)	15.00
117	Hanley Ramirez/ 659 (RC)	30.00
118	Chris Resop/999 (RC)	10.00
119	Josh Willingham/ 999 (RC)	15.00
120	Cole Hamels/ 499 (RC)	50.00
121	Matt Cain/999 (RC)	30.00
122	Steve Stemle/999 RC	10.00
123	Tim Hamulack/ 999 (RC)	10.00
124	Choo Freeman/ 999 (RC)	10.00
125	Hong-Chih Kuo/ 999 (RC)	30.00
126	Cody Ross/999 (RC)	15.00
127	Jose Capellan/ 999 (RC)	10.00
128	Prince Fielder/ 190 (RC)	120.00
129	David Gassner/ 999 (RC)	10.00
130	Jason Kubel/999 (RC)	15.00
131	Francisco Liriano/ 299 (RC)	40.00
132	Anderson Hernandez/ 999 (RC)	10.00
133	Joey Devine/499 RC	15.00
134	Chris Booker/ 999 (RC)	10.00
135	Matt Capps/999 (RC)	15.00
136	Paul Maholm/ 999 (RC)	10.00
137	Nate McLouth/ 999 (RC)	10.00
138	John Van Benschoten/ 999 (RC)	10.00
139	Jeff Harris/999 RC	10.00
140	Ben Johnson/ 999 (RC)	10.00
141	Wilbert Nieves/ 999 (RC)	15.00
142	Guillermo Quiroz/ 999 (RC)	10.00
143	Josh Rupe/500 (RC)	15.00
144	Skip Schumaker/ 999 (RC)	15.00
145	Jack Taschner/ 999 (RC)	10.00
146	Adam Wainwright/ 999 (RC)	25.00
147	Alay Soler/499 RC	15.00
148	Kendry Morales/ 999 (RC)	15.00
149	Ian Kinsler/999 (RC)	20.00
150	Jason Hammel/ 999 (RC)	10.00
151	Chad Billingsley/ 499 (RC)	30.00
152	Boof Bonser/999 (RC)	20.00
153	Peter Moylan/999 RC	10.00
154	Chris Britton/999 RC	10.00
155	Takashi Saito/999 RC	30.00
156	Scott Dunn (RC)	10.00
157	Joel Zumaya/ 299 (RC)	25.00
158	Dan Uggla/999 (RC)	25.00
159	Taylor Buchholz/ 999 (RC)	10.00
160	Melky Cabrera/ 499 (RC)	40.00

Spectrum

Stars (1-100): 2-3X
Inserted 1:3

Next in Line

Ben Johnson / OF

		NM/M
	Common Player:	1.00
BA	Brian Anderson	1.00
BB	Brian Bannister	1.00
JB	Josh Barfield	1.00
TB	Taylor Buchholz	1.00
MC	Matt Cain	1.50
RC	Ryan Church	1.00
PF	Prince Fielder	3.00
JH	Jeremy Hermida	1.00
FH	Felix Hernandez	1.50
RH	Ryan Howard	3.00
TI	Travis Ishikawa	1.00
CJ	Conor Jackson	1.00
MJ	Mike Jacobs	1.00
BJ	Ben Johnson	1.00
IK	Ian Kinsler	1.00
LE	Jon Lester	3.00
FL	Francisco Liriano	3.00
JL	James Loney	1.00
SO	Scott Olsen	1.00
JP	Jonathan Papelbon	3.00
HR	Hanley Ramirez	1.50
NM	Alay Soler	1.00
JS	Jeremy Sowers	1.00
HS	Huston Street	1.00
DU	Dan Uggla	1.00
JV	Justin Verlander	3.00
AW	Adam Wainwright	1.00
JE	Jered Weaver	3.00
JW	Josh Willingham	1.00
RZ	Ryan Zimmerman	3.00

Rookie Signature Platinum

No Pricing
Production One Set

Rookie Signature Gold

No Pricing
Production Five Sets

Rookie Signature Printing Plates

No Pricing
Production one set per color.

SPxciting Signatures

		NM/M
Production 30 unless noted.		
JA	Jeremy Accardo	10.00
BA	Brian Anderson	20.00
BY	Jason Bay	30.00
BI	Craig Biggio	40.00
CH	Chad Billingsley	35.00
HB	Hank Blalock	20.00
BR	Chris Britton	15.00
MI	Miguel Cabrera	40.00
MC	Matt Cain	40.00
CA	Matt Capps	15.00
RC	Roger Clemens	165.00
CW	Carl Crawford	30.00
SD	Scott Dunn	10.00
EG	Eric Gagne	35.00
GR	Khalil Greene	30.00
KG	Ken Griffey Jr.	100.00
HT	Travis Hafner	25.00
HA	Jason Hammel	15.00
TH	Tim Hamulack	20.00
JH	Jeff Harris	12.00
HE	Jeremy Hermida	30.00
TR	Trevor Hoffman	50.00
CJ	Conor Jackson	20.00
KU	Jason Kubel	25.00
HK	Hong-Chih Kuo	180.00
CL	Cliff Lee	15.00
PM	Paul Maholm	15.00
VM	Victor Martinez	20.00
MM	Macay McBride	20.00
NM	Nate McLouth	15.00
MU	Mark Mulder	20.00
WN	Wilbert Nieves	35.00
JP	Jonathan Papelbon	100.00
CP	Corey Patterson	20.00
PE	Jake Peavy	25.00
OP	Oliver Perez	15.00
HR	Hanley Ramirez	40.00
CR	Chris Resop	10.00
RO	Cody Ross	30.00
TS	Takashi Saito	140.00
SS	Skip Schumaker	30.00
RS	Ryan Shealy	20.00
KS	Kelly Shoppach	25.00
DU	Dan Uggla	75.00
JV	John Van Benschoten	15.00
VE	Justin Verlander	90.00
AW	Adam Wainwright	50.00
JW	Josh Willingham	30.00
WI	Josh Wilson	15.00

SPxtra Info

DONTRELLE WILLIS / P

		NM/M
	Common Player:	.50
BA	Bobby Abreu	.75
JB	Jason Bay	.75
EC	Eric Chavez	.50
CC	Carl Crawford	.75
BG	Brian Giles	.50
LG	Luis Gonzalez	.50
KG	Ken Griffey Jr.	2.00
VG	Vladimir Guerrero	1.00
TH	Travis Hafner	.75
HE	Todd Helton	.75
DJ	Derek Jeter	3.00
NJ	Nick Johnson	.50
AJ	Andruw Jones	1.00
JK	Jeff Kent	.50
CL	Carlos Lee	.75
DL	Derrek Lee	1.00
PM	Pedro Martinez	1.00
DO	David Ortiz	1.50
RO	Roy Oswalt	.75
AP	Albert Pujols	3.00
IR	Ivan Rodriguez	.75
RS	Reggie Sanders	.50
JS	Johan Santana	1.00
SC	Jason Schmidt	.50
IS	Ichiro Suzuki	2.00
TE	Mark Teixeira	.75
MT	Miguel Tejada	.75
JT	Jim Thome	1.00
VW	Vernon Wells	.50
DW	Dontrelle Willis	.75

SPxtreme Team

		NM/M
	Common Player:	.50
BA	Bobby Abreu	.75
JB	Jason Bay	.75
LB	Lance Berkman	.75
MC	Miguel Cabrera	1.00
CC	Chris Carpenter	.75
CR	Carl Crawford	.75
CD	Carlos Delgado	.75
AD	Adam Dunn	.75
PF	Prince Fielder	3.00
KG	Ken Griffey Jr.	2.00
VG	Vladimir Guerrero	1.00
HA	Travis Hafner	.75
RH	Rich Harden	.50
TH	Todd Helton	.75
HO	Ryan Howard	2.00
DJ	Derek Jeter	3.00
AJ	Andruw Jones	1.00
JK	Jeff Kent	.50
PK	Paul Konerko	.75
CL	Carlos Lee	.75
DL	Derrek Lee	1.00
PM	Pedro Martinez	1.00
VM	Victor Martinez	.50
HM	Hideki Matsui	2.00
DO	David Ortiz	1.50
JP	Jake Peavy	.50
AP	Albert Pujols	3.00
MR	Manny Ramirez	1.00
JR	Jose Reyes	.75
AR	Alex Rodriguez	3.00
JS	Johan Santana	1.00
GS	Grady Sizemore	.75
AS	Alfonso Soriano	1.00
IS	Ichiro Suzuki	2.00
MT	Mark Teixeira	.75
TE	Miguel Tejada	.75
JT	Jim Thome	1.00
VW	Vernon Wells	.75
DW	David Wright	2.00
MY	Michael Young	.50

Winning Materials

		NM/M
	Common Player:	5.00
BA	Bobby Abreu	6.00
JB	Jason Bay	10.00
CB	Carlos Beltran	10.00
MC	Miguel Cabrera	10.00
FC	Frederich Cepeda	5.00
HC	Hee Seop Choi	5.00
RC	Roger Clemens	15.00

JD	Johnny Damon	10.00
CD	Carlos Delgado	6.00
ME	Michel Enriquez	5.00
MF	Maikel Folch	5.00
YG	Yulieski Gourriel	8.00
KG	Ken Griffey Jr.	20.00
AI	Akinori Iwamura	25.00
AJ	Andruw Jones	8.00
MK	Munenori Kawasaki	20.00
PL	Pedro Luis Lazo	8.00
DL	Derrek Lee	8.00
JL	Jong Beom Lee	5.00
VM	Victor Martinez	5.00
NM	Nobuhiko Matsunaka	20.00
YM	Yuneiski Maya	5.00
TN	Tsuyoshi Nishioka	25.00
VO	Vicyohandry Odelin	5.00
MO	Michihiro Ogasawara	5.00
DO	David Ortiz	15.00
EP	Eduardo Paret	5.00
AP	Ariel Pestano	5.00
MP	Mike Piazza	15.00
PU	Albert Pujols	20.00
AR	Alex Rodriguez	20.00
JS	Johan Santana	10.00
NS	Naoyuki Shimizu	25.00
MS	Min Han Son	8.00
AS	Alfonso Soriano	10.00
IS	Ichiro Suzuki	90.00
HT	Hitoshi Tamura	20.00
MT	Miguel Tejada	10.00
KU	Koji Uehara	30.00
OU	Osmany Urrutia	8.00
TW	Tsuyoshi Wada	20.00
SW	Shunsuke Watanabe	20.00

Winning Big Materials

NM/M

Production 5-55

BA	Bobby Abreu/40	75.00
MA	Moises Alou/53	50.00
JB	Jason Bay/40	80.00
EB	Erik Bedard/40	50.00
CB	Carlos Beltran/40	75.00
AB	Adrian Beltre/40	50.00
MC	Miguel Cabrera/40	80.00
FC	Frederich Cepeda/30	65.00
HC	Hee Seop Choi/32	75.00
JD	Johnny Damon/40	100.00
CD	Carlos Delgado/40	65.00
ME	Michel Enriquez/30	50.00
MF	Maikel Folch/30	60.00
JF	Jeff Francis/40	50.00
YG	Yulieski Gourriel/30	100.00
AI	Akinori Iwamura/30	275.00
AJ	Andruw Jones/40	80.00
MK	Munenori Kawasaki/30	350.00
PL	Pedro Luis Lazo/30	80.00
CL	Carlos Lee/40	60.00
DL	Derrek Lee/40	75.00
JL	Jong Beom Lee/20	75.00
WL	Wei-Chu Lin/45	350.00
LO	Javy Lopez/40	50.00
VM	Victor Martinez/40	75.00
NM	Nobuhiko Matsunaka/30	300.00
YM	Yuneiski Maya/30	60.00
JM	Justin Morneau/25	60.00
TN	Tsuyoshi Nishioka/30	375.00
VO	Vicyohandry Odelin/30	75.00
MO	Michihiro Ogasawara/30	350.00
DO	David Ortiz/30	300.00
WP	Wei-Lun Pan/38	300.00
EP	Eduardo Paret/30	50.00
PE	Wily Mo Pena/60	50.00
AP	Ariel Pestano/30	50.00
MP	Mike Piazza/40	100.00
AR	Alex Rios/55	50.00
IR	Ivan Rodriguez/40	60.00
JS	Johan Santana/40	75.00
NS	Naoyuki Shimizu/30	250.00
AS	Alfonso Soriano/40	90.00
HT	Hitoshi Tamura/40	300.00
MT	Miguel Tejada/40	60.00
KU	Koji Uehara/30	300.00
OU	Osmany Urrutia/30	65.00
JV	Jason Varitek/40	120.00
TW	Tsuyoshi Wada/30	250.00
SW	Shunsuke Watanabe/30	260.00
BW	Bernie Williams/40	75.00
GY	Guogang Yang/52	50.00
CZ	Carlos Zambrano/40	50.00

WBC All-World Team

NM/M

Common Player:		.50
1	Brett Willemburg	.50
2	Bradley Harman	.50
3	Adam Stern	1.00

4	Jason Bay	1.00
5	Adam Loewen	.50
6	Wei Wang	2.00
7	Yi Feng	1.00
8	Yung-Chi Chen	6.00
9	Chin-Lung Hu	6.00
10	Wei-Lun Pan	5.00
11	Yoandy Garlobo	.50
12	Frederich Cepeda	.50
13	Osmany Urrutia	1.00
14	Yulieski Gourriel	2.00
15	Yadel Marti	.50
16	Pedro Luis Lazo	.50
17	Adrian Beltre	.50
18	David Ortiz	2.00
19	Albert Pujols	4.00
20	Bartolo Colon	.50
21	Miguel Tejada	1.00
22	Mike Piazza	1.50
23	Jason Grilli	1.00
24	Nobuhiko Matsunaka	3.00
25	Tomoya Satozaki	3.00
26	Ichiro Suzuki	3.00
27	Hitoshi Tamura	3.00
28	Daisuke Matsuzaka	8.00
29	Koji Uehara	3.00
30	Jong Beom Lee	.50
31	Seung-Yeop Lee	.50
32	Jae Weong Seo	.50
33	Min Han Son	.50
34	Chan Ho Park	.50
35	Jorge Cantu	.50
36	Miguel Ojeda	.50
37	Andruw Jones	1.00
38	Shairon Martis	.50
39	Carlos Lee	.75
40	Carlos Beltran	1.00
41	Javy Lopez	.50
42	Javier Vazquez	.50
43	Ken Griffey Jr.	3.00
44	Derek Jeter	4.00
45	Alex Rodriguez	4.00
46	Derrek Lee	1.50
47	Roger Clemens	3.00
48	Miguel Cabrera	1.50
49	Victor Martinez	1.50
50	Johan Santana	1.50

2007 SP Authentic

NM/M

Common Player:		.25
Common RC Letter Auto.:		15.00
Pack (5):		5.00
Box (24):		100.00
1	Chipper Jones	1.00
2	Andruw Jones	.50
3	John Smoltz	.50
4	Carlos Quentin	.25
5	Randy Johnson	1.00
6	Brandon Webb	.50
7	Alfonso Soriano	1.00
8	Derrek Lee	.75
9	Aramis Ramirez	.50
10	Carlos Zambrano	.50
11	Ken Griffey Jr.	2.00
12	Adam Dunn	.50
13	Josh Hamilton	.50
14	Todd Helton	.50
15	Jeff Francis	.25
16	Matt Holliday	.50
17	Hanley Ramirez	1.00
18	Dontrelle Willis	.50
19	Miguel Cabrera	1.00
20	Lance Berkman	.50
21	Roy Oswalt	.50
22	Carlos Lee	.50
23	Nomar Garciaparra	.75
24	Derek Lowe	.25
25	Juan Pierre	.50
26	Rafael Furcal	.50
27	Rickie Weeks	.25
28	Prince Fielder	1.50

29	Ben Sheets	.25
30	David Wright	1.50
31	Jose Reyes	1.00
32	Tom Glavine	.50
33	Carlos Beltran	.75
34	Cole Hamels	.75
35	Jimmy Rollins	.75
36	Ryan Howard	2.00
37	Jason Bay	.50
38	Freddy Sanchez	.25
39	Ian Snell	.25
40	Jake Peavy	.50
41	Greg Maddux	2.00
42	Trevor Hoffman	.25
43	Matt Cain	.50
44	Barry Zito	.25
45	Ray Durham	.25
46	Albert Pujols	3.00
47	Chris Carpenter	.50
48	Jim Edmonds	.50
49	Scott Rolen	.50
50	Ryan Zimmerman	.50
51	Felipe Lopez	.25
52	Austin Kearns	.25
53	Miguel Tejada	.50
54	Erik Bedard	.50
55	Daniel Cabrera	.25
56	David Ortiz	1.00
57	Curt Schilling	.75
58	Manny Ramirez	1.00
59	Jonathan Papelbon	.75
60	Jim Thome	.75
61	Paul Konerko	.50
62	Bobby Jenks	.25
63	Grady Sizemore	1.00
64	Victor Martinez	.50
65	Travis Hafner	.50
66	Ivan Rodriguez	.75
67	Justin Verlander	.50
68	Joel Zumaya	.25
69	Jeremy Bonderman	.25
70	Gil Meche	.25
71	Mike Sweeney	.25
72	Mark Teahen	.25
73	Vladimir Guerrero	1.00
74	Howie Kendrick	.25
75	Francisco Rodriguez	.50
76	Johan Santana	1.00
77	Justin Morneau	.50
78	Joe Mauer	.50
79	Joe Nathan	.25
80	Alex Rodriguez	3.00
81	Derek Jeter	3.00
82	Johnny Damon	.75
83	Chien-Ming Wang	1.00
84	Rich Harden	.25
85	Mike Piazza	1.00
86	Danny Haren	.25
87	Ichiro Suzuki	2.00
88	Felix Hernandez	.50
89	Kenji Johjima	.25
90	Adrian Beltre	.25
91	Carl Crawford	.50
92	Scott Kazmir	.50
93	Delmon Young	.50
94	Michael Young	.50
95	Mark Teixeira	.50
96	Eric Gagne	.25
97	Hank Blalock	.25
98	Vernon Wells	.50
99	Roy Halladay	.50
100	Frank Thomas	.75
101	Joaquin Arias/75 (RC)	15.00
102	Jeff Baker/ Redemp (RC)	15.00
103	Michael Bourn/ 75 (RC)	20.00
104	Brian Burres/75 (RC)	20.00
105	Jared Burton/75 RC	20.00
106	Ryan Braun/50 (RC)	75.00
107	Yovani Gallardo/ 75 (RC)	60.00
107	Yovani Gallardo/ 35 (RC)	60.00
108	Hector Gimenez/ 75 (RC)	15.00
108	Hector Gimenez/ 50 (RC)	15.00
109	Alex Gordon/50 RC	60.00
109	Josh Hamilton/ 50 (RC)	30.00
110	Josh Hamilton/ 35 (RC)	30.00
111	Justin Hampson/ 50 (RC)	15.00
111	Justin Hampson/ 75 (RC)	15.00
112	Sean Henn/75 (RC)	20.00
113	Phil Hughes/ Redemp. (RC)	75.00
114	Kei Igawa/25 RC	60.00
115	Akinori Iwamura/ 20 RC	60.00
116	Mark Reynolds/75 RC	30.00

116	Mark Reynolds/35 RC	30.00
117	Homer Bailey/75 (RC)	40.00
117	Homer Bailey/50 (RC)	40.00
118	Kevin Kouzmanoff/ 75 (RC)	20.00
118	Kevin Kouzmanoff/ 40 (RC)	20.00
119	Adam Lind/75 (RC)	20.00
120	Carlos Gomez/75 RC	50.00
120	Carlos Gomez/50 RC	50.00
121	Glen Perkins/75 (RC)	20.00
121	Glen Perkins/50 (RC)	20.00
122	Rick Vanden Hurk/ 75 RC	20.00
122	Rick Vanden Hurk/ 35 RC	20.00
123	Brad Salmon/75 RC	15.00
124	Zack Segovia/75 (RC)	20.00
124	Zack Segovia/50 (RC)	20.00
125	Kurt Suzuki/75 (RC)	20.00
125	Kurt Suzuki/50 (RC)	20.00
126	Chris Stewart/75 (RC)	15.00
126	Chris Stewart/50 (RC)	15.00
127	Cesar Jimenez/75 (RC)	15.00
128	Ryan Sweeney/ 50 (RC)	20.00
128	Ryan Sweeney/ 40 (RC)	20.00
129	Troy Tulowitzki/ Redmp. (RC)	60.00
130	Chase Wright/75 RC	20.00
131	Delmon Young/ 20 (RC)	40.00
132	Tony Abreu/75 (RC)	20.00
132	Tony Abreu/50 (RC)	20.00
133	Brian Barden/75 RC	15.00
134	Curtis Thigpen/ 75 (RC)	20.00
134	Curtis Thigpen/ 40 (RC)	20.00
135	Jon Coutlangus/ 75 (RC)	15.00
135	Jon Coutlangus/ 55 (RC)	15.00
136	Kevin Cameron/75 RC	15.00
136	Kevin Cameron/50 RC	15.00
137	Billy Butler/75 (RC)	30.00
138	Alexi Casilla/75 RC	20.00
138	Alexi Casilla/50 RC	20.00
139	Kory Casto/75 (RC)	20.00
140	Matt Chico/75 (RC)	20.00
141	John Danks/75 RC	20.00
142	Andrew Miller/50 RC	40.00
143	Ben Francisco/ 75 (RC)	15.00
143	Ben Francisco/ 40 (RC)	15.00
144	Andy Gonzalez/75 RC	15.00
144	Andy Gonzalez/50 RC	15.00
145	Devern Hansack/ Redemp. RC	20.00
146	Mike Rabelo/75 RC	15.00
147	Tim Lincecum/50 RC	75.00
147	Tim Lincecum/25 RC	75.00
148	Matt Lindstrom/ 75 (RC)	15.00
148	Matt Lindstrom/ 40 (RC)	15.00
149	Jay Marshall/75 RC	15.00
149	Jay Marshall/50 RC	15.00
150	Daisuke Matsuzaka/ Redemp RC	350.00
151	Miguel Montero/ 75 (RC)	20.00
151	Miguel Montero/ 50 (RC)	20.00
152	Micah Owings/ 75 (RC)	35.00
153	Hunter Pence/ 75 (RC)	50.00
154	Brandon Wood/ 75 (RC)	20.00
155	Felix Pie/75 (RC)	20.00
155	Felix Pie/70 (RC)	20.00
156	Danny Putnam/ 75 (RC)	15.00
157	Andy LaRoche/ 50 (RC)	25.00
157	Andy LaRoche/ 40 (RC)	25.00
158	Jarrod Saltalamacchia/ 75 (RC)	30.00
158	Jarrod Saltalamacchia/ 25 (RC)	30.00
159	Doug Slaten/75 RC	20.00
160	Joe Smith/75 RC	20.00
161	Justin Upton/120 RC	75.00
162	Joba Chamberlain/ 60 RC	200.00

Autograph Parallel

Production 5 Sets

Authentic Power

		NM/M
Common Player:		.50
1	Adam Dunn	1.00
2	Albert Pujols	4.00
3	Alex Rodriguez	4.00
4	Alfonso Soriano	1.50
5	Andruw Jones	.75
6	Aramis Ramirez	.75
7	Bill Hall	.50
8	Carlos Beltran	1.00
9	Carlos Delgado	.75
10	Carlos Lee	.75
11	Chase Utley	1.50
12	Chipper Jones	1.50
13	Dan Uggla	.50
14	David Ortiz	1.50
15	David Wright	2.00
16	Derrek Lee	.75
17	Eric Chavez	.50
18	Frank Thomas	1.00
19	Garrett Atkins	.50
20	Gary Sheffield	1.00
21	Hideki Matsui	2.50
22	J.D. Drew	.75
23	Jason Bay	.75
24	Jason Giambi	1.00
25	Jeff Francoeur	1.50
26	Jermaine Dye	.75
27	Jim Thome	1.00
28	Justin Morneau	1.00
29	Ken Griffey Jr.	3.00
30	Lance Berkman	.75
31	Magglio Ordonez	.75
32	Manny Ramirez	1.00
33	Mark Teixeira	1.00
34	Matt Holliday	1.00
35	Miguel Cabrera	1.50
36	Miguel Tejada	.75
37	Mike Piazza	1.50
38	Nick Swisher	.75
39	Pat Burrell	.75
40	Paul Konerko	1.00
41	Prince Fielder	2.00
42	Richie Sexson	.75
43	Ryan Howard	2.50
44	Sammy Sosa	1.00
45	Todd Helton	1.00
46	Travis Hafner	.75
47	Troy Glaus	.75
48	Vernon Wells	.75
49	Victor Martinez	.75
50	Vladimir Guerrero	1.50

Authentic Speed

		NM/M
Common Player:		.50
1	Alex Rios	.75
2	Alex Rodriguez	4.00
3	Alfonso Soriano	1.50
4	B.J. Upton	.75
5	Bobby Abreu	.75
6	Brandon Phillips	.50
7	Brian Roberts	.75
8	Carl Crawford	.75
9	Carlos Beltran	1.00
10	Chase Utley	1.50
11	Chone Figgins	.75
12	Chris Burke	.50
13	Chris Duffy	.50
14	Coco Crisp	.50
15	Corey Patterson	.50
16	Dave Roberts	.50
17	David Wright	2.00
18	Derek Jeter	4.00
19	Edgar Renteria	.50
20	Eric Byrnes	.75
21	Felipe Lopez	.50
22	Gary Matthews	.50
23	Grady Sizemore	2.00
24	Hanley Ramirez	1.50
25	Ian Kinsler	.75
26	Ichiro Suzuki	3.00
27	Jacque Jones	.50
28	Jimmy Rollins	1.00
29	Johnny Damon	1.00
30	Jose Reyes	2.00
31	Juan Pierre	.50
32	Julio Lugo	.50
33	Kenny Lofton	.50
34	Luis Castillo	.50
35	Marcus Giles	.50
36	Melky Cabrera	1.00
37	Mike Cameron	.50
38	Orlando Cabrera	.75
39	Rafael Furcal	.75
40	Randy Winn	.50
41	Rickie Weeks	.50
42	Rocco Baldelli	.50
43	Ryan Freel	.50
44	Ryan Theriot	1.00
45	Scott Podsednik	.50
46	Shane Victorino	.50
47	Tadahito Iguchi	.50
48	Torii Hunter	.75
49	Vernon Wells	.75
50	Willy Taveras	.50

By The Letter Signatures

		NM/M
Common Player:		
1	Derek Jeter/Redemp.	250.00
2	Ken Griffey Jr./25	125.00
2	Ken Griffey Jr./20	125.00
4	Justin Verlander/50	50.00
4	Justin Verlander/15	50.00
6	Adrian Gonzalez/60	20.00
6	Adrian Gonzalez/50	20.00
8	Josh Beckett/15	100.00
10	Aramis Ramirez/25	50.00
11	Austin Kearns/50	15.00
12	B.J. Upton/25	35.00
12	B.J. Upton/15	35.00
13	Boof Bonser/75	15.00
13	Boof Bonser/50	15.00
14	Bronson Arroyo/75	20.00
15	Troy Tulowitzki/Redemp.	50.00
16	Felix Pie/75	25.00
17	Alex Gordon/25	60.00
18	Chris Duffy/Redemp.	15.00
19	Chris Young/75	20.00
19	Chris Young/50	20.00
20	Cliff Lee/75	20.00
20	Cliff Lee/50	20.00
21	Cole Hamels/25	50.00
21	Cole Hamels/15	50.00
22	Adam Lind/75	20.00
23	Akinori Iwamura/25	60.00
23	Akinori Iwamura/15	60.00
24	Dan Uggla/25	25.00
25	Danny Haren/25	30.00
26	David Ortiz/10	125.00
27	Felix Hernandez/75	75.00
28	Tony Gwynn Jr./Redemp.	25.00
29	Josh Hamilton/75	30.00
29	Josh Hamilton/50	30.00
30	Phil Hughes/Redemp.	65.00
31	Khalil Greene/25	30.00
32	Dontrelle Willis/25	30.00
32	Dontrelle Willis/20	30.00
33	Hanley Ramirez/50	35.00
33	Hanley Ramirez/25	35.00
34	Howie Kendrick/60	20.00
34	Howie Kendrick/50	20.00
35	Huston Street/50	20.00
35	Huston Street/25	20.00
36	Ian Kinsler/Redemp.	20.00
37	Jason Bay/50	25.00
37	Jason Bay/25	25.00
41	Joe Mauer/Redemp.	50.00
41	Jonathan Papelbon/40	50.00
42	Tim Lincecum/50	75.00
42	Tim Lincecum/40	75.00
43	Matt Cain/75	40.00
43	Matt Cain/40	40.00
44	Victor Martinez/25	40.00
46	Ryan Zimmerman/25	50.00
47	Stephen Drew/25	30.00
48	Travis Hafner/25	30.00
49	Josh Willingham/50	15.00
49	Josh Willingham/Redemp.	15.00
50	Torii Hunter/25	30.00
51	Billy Butler/50	30.00
52	Justin Morneau/40	40.00
52	Justin Morneau/15	40.00
53	Andy LaRoche/75	25.00
53	Andy LaRoche/60	25.00
53	Andy LaRoche/25	25.00
54	Brandon Wood/75	20.00
54	Brandon Wood/50	20.00
55	Hunter Pence/50	50.00
56	Devern Hansack/Redemp.	20.00
56	Devern Hansack/75	20.00
58	Derrek Lee/25	40.00
59	Prince Fielder/25	50.00
60	Kevin Kouzmanoff/50	20.00

By The Letter RC Signatures Full Redemption

No Pricing

By The Letter Signatures Full Redemption

No Pricing

Chirography Dual Signatures

		NM/M
Common Dual Auto.:		25.00
CG	Eric Chavez, Alex Gordon/75	50.00
CL	Matt Cain, Tim Lincecum/175	80.00
DR	Stephen Drew, Hanley Ramirez/75	35.00
HD	Travis Hafner, Adam Dunn/75	30.00
HW	Danny Haren, Jered Weaver/175	30.00
KH	Scott Kazmir, Cole Hamels/175	40.00
MI	Daisuke Matsuzaka, Akinori Iwamura/75	300.00
ML	Andrew Miller, Tim Lincecum/175	100.00
MZ	Nicholas Markakis, Ryan Zimmerman/75	40.00
RJ	Cal Ripken Jr., Derek Jeter/75	200.00
VH	Justin Verlander, Felix Hernandez/175	50.00
WH	Vernon Wells, Torii Hunter/75	25.00
WK	Rickie Weeks, Ian Kinsler/175	25.00

Chirography Quad Signatures

Production 5 Sets

Sign of the Times Dual Signatures

		NM/M
Common Dual Auto.:		20.00
BP	Josh Beckett, Jonathan Papelbon/75	120.00
CH	Eric Chavez, Rich Harden/75	20.00
CJ	Roger Clemens, Derek Jeter/75	200.00
CL	Matt Cain, Tim Lincecum/175	80.00
FL	Rafael Furcal, Andy LaRoche/175	20.00
GD	Ken Griffey Jr., Adam Dunn/75	100.00
HM	Travis Hafner, Victor Martinez/75	50.00
SW	Ben Sheets, Rickie Weeks/75	20.00
TK	Mark Teixeira, Ian Kinsler/75	20.00
UY	B.J. Upton, Delmon Young/75	35.00
VM	Justin Verlander, Andrew Miller/75	50.00

Sign of the Times Triple Signatures

No Pricing

Sign of the Times Quad Signatures

Production 5 Sets

2007 SP Legendary Cuts

		NM/M
Complete Set (200):		
Common Player (1-100):		.25
Common SP (101-200):		3.00
Production 550 Sets		
Pack (4):		10.00
Box (12):		100.00
1	Phil Niekro	.25
2	Brooks Robinson	1.00
3	Frank Robinson	1.00
4	Jim Palmer	.50
5	Cal Ripken Jr.	3.00
6	Warren Spahn	1.00
7	Cy Young	1.00
8	Carl Yastrzemski	1.00
9	Wade Boggs	1.00
10	Carlton Fisk	.50
11	Joe Cronin	.25
12	Bobby Doerr	.50
13	Roy Campanella	1.00
14	Pee Wee Reese	.25
15	Rod Carew	.75
16	Ernie Banks	1.00
17	Fergie Jenkins	.50
18	Billy Williams	.50
19	Gabby Hartnett	.25
20	Luis Aparicio	.25

21	Nellie Fox	.25
22	Luke Appling	.25
23	Joe Morgan	.50
24	Johnny Bench	1.00
25	Tony Perez	.50
26	George Foster	.25
27	Johnny Vander Meer	.25
28	Bob Feller	.50
29	Bob Lemon	.25
30	Lou Boudreau	.25
31	Early Wynn	.25
32	Charlie Gehringer	.25
33	George Kell	.25
34	Hal Newhouser	.25
35	Al Kaline	1.00
36	Ted Kluszewski	.25
38	Maury Wills	.25
39	Don Drysdale	.50
40	Don Sutton	.50
41	Eddie Mathews	1.00
42	Joe Adcock	.25
43	Paul Molitor	.75
44	Kirby Puckett	1.50
45	Harmon Killebrew	1.00
46	Monte Irvin	.50
47	Ralph Kiner	.50
48	Christy Mathewson	1.00
49	Hoyt Wilhelm	.25
50	Tom Seaver	1.00
51	Allie Reynolds	.25
52	Joe DiMaggio	2.00
53	Lou Gehrig	2.00
54	Babe Ruth	3.00
55	Casey Stengel	1.00
56	Phil Rizzuto	1.00
57	Thurman Munson	1.00
58	Johnny Mize	.50
59	Yogi Berra	1.00
61	Don Mattingly	1.00
62	Ray Dandridge	.25
63	Rollie Fingers	.50
64	Roberto Clemente	2.00
65	Reggie Jackson	1.00
66	Dennis Eckersley	.50
67	Robin Yount	1.00
68	Jimmie Foxx	1.00
69	Lefty Grove	.50
70	Richie Ashburn	.25
71	Jim Bunning	.25
72	Steve Carlton	.50
73	Robin Roberts	.50
74	Mike Schmidt	1.00
75	Willie Stargell	1.00
76	Ozzie Smith	1.00
77	Bill Mazeroski	.50
78	Honus Wagner	1.00
79	Pie Traynor	.50
80	Tony Gwynn	1.00
81	Willie McCovey	.50
82	Gaylord Perry	.25
83	Juan Marichal	.50
84	Orlando Cepeda	.50
85	Satchel Paige	1.00
86	George Sisler	.50
87	Ken Boyer	.25
88	Joe Medwick	.25
89	Travis Jackson	.25
90	Stan Musial	1.50
91	Dizzy Dean	1.00
92	Bob Gibson	1.00
93	Red Schoendienst	.50
94	Lou Brock	.75
95	Enos Slaughter	.25
96	Nolan Ryan	3.00
97	Smoky Burgess	.25
98	Mickey Vernon	.25
99	Vern Stephens	.25
100	Rick Ferrell	.25
101	Phil Niekro	3.00
102	Brooks Robinson	6.00
103	Frank Robinson	6.00
104	Jim Palmer	5.00
105	Cal Ripken Jr.	15.00
106	Warren Spahn	6.00
107	Cy Young	5.00
108	Nellie Fox	6.00
109	Carl Yastrzemski	6.00
110	Joe Sewell	4.00
111	Wade Boggs	5.00
112	Carlton Fisk	5.00
113	Jackie Robinson	8.00
114	Roy Campanella	6.00
115	Pee Wee Reese	5.00
116	Earl Averill	3.00
117	Rod Carew	5.00
118	Ernie Banks	5.00
119	Fergie Jenkins	3.00
120	Billy Williams	3.00
121	Al Lopez	3.00
122	Luis Aparicio	3.00
123	Luke Appling	3.00
124	Joe Morgan	5.00
125	Johnny Bench	6.00
126	Tony Perez	5.00

127 George Foster 3.00
128 Bob Feller 5.00
129 Bob Lemon 3.00
130 Larry Doby 5.00
131 Lou Boudreau
132 George Kell 3.00
133 Hal Newhouser 3.00
134 Al Kaline 8.00
135 Ty Cobb 8.00
137 Buck Leonard 5.00
138 Maury Wills 3.00
139 Don Drysdale 5.00
140 Don Sutton 5.00
141 Eddie Mathews 6.00
142 Paul Molitor 5.00
143 Kirby Puckett 8.00
144 Harmon Killebrew 8.00
145 Monte Irvin 5.00
146 Mel Ott 5.00
147 Charlie Gehringer 5.00
148 Hoyt Wilhelm 3.00
149 Tom Seaver 6.00
150 Ted Kluszewski 3.00
151 Joe DiMaggio 8.00
152 Lou Gehrig 8.00
153 Babe Ruth 10.00
154 Casey Stengel 5.00
155 Phil Rizzuto 5.00
156 Thurman Munson 5.00
157 Johnny Mize 3.00
158 Yogi Berra 6.00
159 Roger Maris 6.00
160 Early Wynn 3.00
161 Bobby Doerr 5.00
162 Joe Cronin 5.00
163 Don Mattingly 8.00
164 Ray Dandridge 3.00
165 Rollie Fingers 3.00
166 Christy Mathewson 5.00
167 Reggie Jackson 5.00
168 Dennis Eckersley 3.00
169 Mickey Cochrane 3.00
170 Jimmie Foxx 5.00
171 Lefty Gomez 3.00
172 Jim Bunning 3.00
173 Steve Carlton 3.00
174 Robin Roberts 3.00
175 Richie Ashburn 5.00
176 Mike Schmidt 6.00
177 Ralph Kiner 3.00
178 Willie Stargell 5.00
179 Roberto Clemente 10.00
180 Bill Mazeroski 5.00
181 Honus Wagner 8.00
182 Pie Traynor 3.00
183 Tony Gwynn 5.00
184 Willie McCovey 3.00
185 Gaylord Perry 3.00
186 Juan Marichal 3.00
187 Orlando Cepeda 5.00
188 Satchel Paige 5.00
189 George Sisler 3.00
190 Rogers Hornsby 5.00
191 Stan Musial 8.00
192 Dizzy Dean 5.00
193 Bob Gibson 5.00
194 Red Schoendienst 5.00
195 Lou Brock 5.00
196 Enos Slaughter 3.00
197 Nolan Ryan 8.00
198 Mickey Vernon 3.00
199 Walter Johnson 5.00
200 Rick Ferrell 3.00

A Stitch In Time
NM/M
Common Player: 5.00
BG Bob Gibson 8.00
BR Brooks Robinson 10.00
BW Billy Williams 5.00
CR Cal Ripken Jr. 20.00
DE Dwight Evans 5.00
DM Don Mattingly 10.00
EM Eddie Murray 8.00
GP Gaylord Perry 5.00
HK Harmon Killebrew 10.00
JB Johnny Bench 10.00
JR Jim Rice 5.00
KP Kirby Puckett 15.00
MS Mike Schmidt 10.00
PM Paul Molitor 8.00
RC Rod Carew 8.00
RJ Reggie Jackson 10.00
TG Tony Gwynn 10.00

Cut Signatures
NM/M
Production 1-133
AB Al Barlick/49 75.00
AH Happy Chandler/44 75.00
AR Allie Reynolds/40 150.00
BA Bob Allison/31 90.00
BD Bill Dickey/50 125.00
BG Burleigh Grimes/52 125.00

BH Babe Herman/99 100.00
BV Bill Veeck/47 250.00
CA Max Carey/40 80.00
CG Charlie Gehringer/50 75.00
CH Carl Hubbell/54 100.00
DC Dolph Camilli/25 75.00
DI Joe DiMaggio/52 400.00
DU Leo Durocher/84 140.00
EA Earl Averill/62 80.00
EL Ed Lopat/66 100.00
EM Eddie Mathews/69 125.00
ER Edd Roush/50 60.00
ES Enos Slaughter/47 80.00
EW Early Wynn/40 100.00
FF Ford Frick/88 140.00
FL Freddy Lindstrom/45 200.00
GH Gabby Hartnett/50 160.00
GP George Pipgras/70 90.00
GR Lefty Grove/66 220.00
HG Hank Greenberg/59 200.00
HO Gil Hodges/25 450.00
JA Joe Adcock/49 100.00
JD Joe Dugan/46 120.00
JO Judy Johnson/54 150.00
JS Joe Sewell/110 80.00
JV Johnny Vander Meer/49 140.00
KB Ken Boyer/19 275.00
LA Luke Appling/92 80.00
LD Larry Doby/50 100.00
MI Johnny Mize/133 100.00
PR Pee Wee Reese/39 160.00
RA Richie Ashburn/50 150.00
RD Ray Dandridge/50 85.00
RS Ray Schalk/44 275.00
SC Stan Coveleski/84 80.00
SW Warren Spahn/95 100.00
WA Walter Alston/48 140.00
WH Waite Hoyt/79 90.00
WI Hoyt Wilhelm/60 80.00
WS Willie Stargell/71 180.00

Hall of Fame Cuts
NM/M
Production 1-86
AB Al Barlick/44 100.00
BL Bob Lemon/53 75.00
CG Charlie Gehringer/65 85.00
CH Carl Hubbell/31 100.00
EC Earle Combs/27 250.00
ER Edd Roush/65 100.00
GH Gabby Hartnett/31 180.00
HN Hal Newhouser/40 80.00
JC Joe Cronin/86 90.00
LA Luke Appling/45 80.00
LB Lou Boudreau/30 80.00
WH Waite Hoyt/33 100.00
WS Warren Spahn/35 125.00

Historical Cuts
Production One Set

Inside the Numbers Cuts
NM/M
Production 4-119
BD Bill Dickey/28 150.00
BH Babe Herman/99 100.00
BL Bob Lemon/75 75.00
CG Charlie Gehringer/60 120.00
CH Carl Hubbell/70 100.00
EA Earl Averill/57 65.00
EL Ernie Lombardi/52 200.00
EM Eddie Mathews/70 125.00
ES Enos Slaughter/69 80.00
EW Early Wynn/34 100.00
FS Fred Snodgrass/75 150.00
GH Gabby Hartnett/50 160.00
GR Lefty Grove/73 220.00
HG Hank Greenberg/25 250.00
JC Joe Cronin/29 100.00
JM Joe Medwick/119 140.00
JV Johnny Vander Meer/39 140.00
LA Luke Appling/59 80.00
LG Lefty Gomez/75 125.00
SC Stan Coveleski/72 65.00
WH Waite Hoyt/65 100.00

WI Hoyt Wilhelm/55 80.00
WS Warren Spahn/55 100.00

Legendary Americana
NM/M
Common Card: 5.00
Production 550 Sets
1 George Washington Carver
3 Frederick Douglass 5.00
4 Crazy Horse 5.00
6 Abraham Lincoln 5.00
7 Thomas Edison 5.00
8 Andrew Carnegie 5.00
9 Eli Whitney 5.00
11 Davy Crockett 5.00
12 Robert E. Lee 5.00
13 John D. Rockefeller 5.00
14 Billy the Kid 5.00
15 Ulysses S. Grant 5.00
18 Kit Carson 5.00
19 Francis Scott Key 5.00
20 Franklin D. Roosevelt 5.00
21 Mark Twain 5.00
24 Alexander Graham Bell 5.00
27 Eleanor Roosevelt 5.00
28 John F. Kennedy 8.00
30 Frank Lloyd Wright 5.00
34 Henry Ford 5.00
35 Dwight D. Eisenhower 5.00
36 Daniel Boone 5.00
38 William Randolph Hearst 5.00
42 Wyatt Earp 5.00
47 Abner Doubleday 5.00
48 Harry S. Truman 5.00
49 Amelia Earhart 5.00
53 Orville Wright 5.00
55 Jack London 5.00
59 Andrew Jackson 5.00
60 Zachary Taylor 5.00
62 Jefferson Davis 5.00
63 Sitting Bull 10.00
64 Clara Barton 5.00
66 Booker T. Washington 5.00
68 Samuel F. B. Morse 5.00
69 Alexander Cartwright 5.00
72 Andrew Johnson 5.00
73 Rutherford B. Hayes 5.00
74 James A. Garfield 5.00
75 Chester Arthur 5.00
76 Grover Cleveland 5.00
78 William McKinley 5.00
79 William H. Taft 5.00
80 Woodrow Wilson 5.00
81 Warren G. Harding 5.00
82 Calvin Coolidge 5.00
83 Herbert Hoover 5.00
84 Lyndon B. Johnson 5.00
85 Richard M. Nixon 5.00
86 Gerald Ford 5.00
88 Ronald Reagan 5.00
92 Babe Ruth 10.00
93 Jackie Robinson 8.00

Legendary Dual Cuts
Production One Set

Legendary Materials
NM/M
Common Player: 5.00
Production 199 Sets
AO Al Oliver 5.00
BJ Bo Jackson 15.00
BL Barry Larkin 8.00
BS Bruce Sutter 5.00
BW Billy Williams 15.00
CA Roy Campanella 10.00
DD Don Drysdale 8.00
DE Dwight Evans 5.00
DP Dave Parker 5.00
DS Don Sutton 5.00
EC Dennis Eckersley 5.00
FJ Fergie Jenkins 5.00
FR Frank Robinson 10.00
GF George Foster 5.00
GG Rich "Goose" Gossage 5.00
HB Harold Baines 5.00
JP Jim Palmer 8.00
JT Joe Torre 10.00
KG Ken Griffey Sr. 5.00
LA Luis Aparicio 5.00
MA Bill Madlock 5.00
MG Mark Grace 10.00
PN Phil Niekro 5.00
PO Paul O'Neill 5.00
PW Pee Wee Reese 5.00
RA Roberto Alomar 10.00
RC Roberto Clemente 50.00
RF Rollie Fingers 5.00
RG Ron Guidry 20.00
RM Roger Maris 25.00
RS Ryne Sandberg 15.00

SC Red Schoendienst 10.00
TO Tony Oliva 8.00
TP Tony Perez 8.00
AD1 Andre Dawson 8.00
AD2 Andre Dawson 8.00
AK1 Al Kaline 15.00
AK2 Al Kaline 15.00
BR1 Brooks Robinson 15.00
BR2 Brooks Robinson 15.00
CF1 Carlton Fisk 10.00
CF2 Carlton Fisk 10.00
CR1 Cal Ripken Jr. 25.00
CR2 Cal Ripken Jr. 25.00
CY1 Carl Yastrzemski 15.00
CY2 Carl Yastrzemski 15.00
DM1 Don Mattingly 20.00
DM2 Don Mattingly 20.00
DW1 Dave Winfield 8.00
DW2 Dave Winfield 8.00
EM1 Eddie Murray 8.00
EM2 Eddie Murray 8.00
FL1 Fred Lynn 5.00
FL2 Fred Lynn 5.00
GP1 Gaylord Perry 5.00
GP2 Gaylord Perry 5.00
HK1 Harmon Killebrew 15.00
HK2 Harmon Killebrew 15.00
JB1 Johnny Bench 15.00
JB2 Johnny Bench 15.00
JM1 Jack Morris 5.00
JM2 Jack Morris 5.00
JR1 Jim Rice 5.00
J2 Jim Rice 8.00
KG1 Kirk Gibson 5.00
KG2 Kirk Gibson 5.00
KP1 Kirby Puckett 25.00
KP2 Kirby Puckett 25.00
LB1 Lou Brock 10.00
LB2 Lou Brock 10.00
MS1 Mike Schmidt 15.00
MS2 Mike Schmidt 15.00
NR1 Nolan Ryan 25.00
NR2 Nolan Ryan 25.00
OS1 Ozzie Smith 20.00
OS2 Ozzie Smith 20.00
PM1 Paul Molitor 8.00
PM2 Paul Molitor 8.00
RC1 Rod Carew 8.00
RC2 Rod Carew 8.00
RJ1 Reggie Jackson 10.00
RJ2 Reggie Jackson 10.00
RY1 Robin Yount 20.00
RY2 Robin Yount 20.00
SC1 Steve Carlton 8.00
SC2 Steve Carlton 8.00
SG1 Steve Garvey 5.00
SG2 Steve Garvey 5.00
TG1 Tony Gwynn 15.00
TG2 Tony Gwynn 15.00
WB1 Wade Boggs 8.00
WB2 Wade Boggs 8.00
WC1 Will Clark 8.00
WC2 Will Clark 8.00

Legendary Quad Cuts
Production One Set

Legendary Signatures
NM/M
Production 15-199
JT Joe Torre/99 40.00
KG Kirk Gibson/199 15.00
AD1 Andre Dawson/199 20.00
AD2 Andre Dawson/199 20.00
AK1 Al Kaline/199 25.00
AK2 Al Kaline/199 25.00
BF1 Bob Feller/199 20.00
BF2 Bob Feller/199 20.00
BF3 Bob Feller/189 20.00
BG1 Bob Gibson/50 25.00
BG2 Bob Gibson/50 25.00
BG3 Bob Gibson/40 25.00
BJ1 Bo Jackson/100 50.00
BJ2 Bo Jackson/100 50.00
BM1 Bill Mazeroski/189 30.00
BM2 Bill Mazeroski/199 30.00
BR1 Brooks Robinson/150 30.00
BR2 Brooks Robinson/140 30.00
BW1 Billy Williams/199 20.00
BW2 Billy Williams/189 20.00
CF1 Carlton Fisk/75 25.00
CF2 Carlton Fisk/75 25.00
CF3 Carlton Fisk/65 25.00
CR1 Cal Ripken Jr./99 100.00
CR2 Cal Ripken Jr./50 10.00
DM1 Don Mattingly/25 75.00
DM2 Don Mattingly/25 75.00
EB1 Ernie Banks/35 60.00
EB2 Ernie Banks/35 60.00
EM1 Eddie Murray/25 50.00
EM2 Eddie Murray/25 50.00
FJ1 Fergie Jenkins/125 20.00

FJ2	Fergie Jenkins/125	20.00
FJ3	Fergie Jenkins/125	20.00
FR1	Frank Robinson/50	25.00
FR2	Frank Robinson/50	25.00
FR3	Frank Robinson/40	25.00
GP1	Gaylord Perry/199	15.00
GP2	Gaylord Perry/199	15.00
HK1	Harmon Killebrew/100	75.00
HK2	Harmon Killebrew/90	75.00
JM1	Juan Marichal/199	20.00
JM2	Juan Marichal/199	20.00
JM3	Juan Marichal/189	20.00
JP1	Jim Palmer/199	20.00
JP2	Jim Palmer/199	20.00
JP3	Jim Palmer/199	20.00
LA1	Luis Aparicio/199	20.00
LA2	Luis Aparicio/186	20.00
MS1	Mike Schmidt/35	50.00
MS2	Mike Schmidt/35	50.00
MS3	Mike Schmidt/35	60.00
NR1	Nolan Ryan/25	100.00
NR2	Nolan Ryan/25	10.00
OS1	Ozzie Smith/100	40.00
OS2	Ozzie Smith/100	40.00
OS3	Ozzie Smith/100	40.00
PM1	Paul Molitor/100	25.00
PM2	Paul Molitor/90	25.00
RC1	Rod Carew/35	40.00
RC2	Rod Carew/35	40.00
RJ1	Reggie Jackson/25	60.00
RS1	Ryne Sandberg/25	60.00
RS2	Ryne Sandberg/25	60.00
RS3	Ryne Sandberg/25	60.00
RY1	Robin Yount/35	60.00
RY2	Robin Yount/35	60.00
RY3	Robin Yount/25	60.00
SC1	Steve Carlton/199	20.00
SC2	Steve Carlton/199	20.00
SC3	Steve Carlton/189	20.00
TP1	Tony Perez/199	20.00
TP2	Tony Perez/199	20.00
WB1	Wade Boggs/35	50.00
WB2	Wade Boggs/35	50.00
WB3	Wade Boggs/35	50.00
WC1	Will Clark/199	20.00
WC2	Will Clark/199	20.00
WM1	Willie McCovey/25	50.00
WM2	Willie McCovey/25	50.00

Legendary Team Cuts

Production One Set

Masterful Material

NM/M

Common Player:		5.00
AD	Andre Dawson	5.00
BJ	Bo Jackson	10.00
BL	Barry Larkin	8.00
BM	Bill Madlock	5.00
BR	Brooks Robinson	8.00
BS	Bruce Sutter	5.00
CF	Carlton Fisk	8.00
CR	Cal Ripken Jr.	20.00
CY	Carl Yastrzemski	10.00
DE	Dwight Evans	5.00
DM	Don Mattingly	15.00
DP	Dave Parker	5.00
DS	Don Sutton	5.00
DW	Dave Winfield	8.00
EM	Eddie Mathews	10.00
FL	Fred Lynn	5.00
FR	Frank Robinson	8.00
GP	Gaylord Perry	5.00
JB	Johnny Bench	10.00
JR	Jim Rice	5.00
KG	Ken Griffey Sr.	5.00
KP	Kirby Puckett	15.00
MS	Mike Schmidt	10.00
MU	Eddie Murray	8.00
NR	Nolan Ryan	20.00
PM	Paul Molitor	8.00
RJ	Reggie Jackson	10.00
RS	Ryne Sandberg	10.00
RY	Robin Yount	10.00
SC	Steve Carlton	8.00
SG	Steve Garvey	5.00
TG	Tony Gwynn	10.00
WB	Wade Boggs	8.00
WC	Will Clark	8.00
WM	Willie McCovey	8.00
YB	Yogi Berra	15.00

Material Cuts

No Pricing
Production 1-5

Material Signatures

No Pricing
Production 10 Sets

Quotation Cuts

NM/M

Production 1-109

BL	Bob Lemon/80	75.00
CS	Casey Stengel/36	275.00
HC	Happy Chandler/44	75.00
JM	Joe McCarthy/109	140.00
LB	Lou Boudreau/28	60.00
MI	Johnny Mize/45	80.00
RA	Richie Ashburn/48	175.00
RD	Ray Dandridge/72	90.00
SC	Stan Coveleski/71	75.00
WA	Walter Alston/31	80.00
WI	Hoyt Wilhelm/37	90.00
WS	Warren Spahn/60	100.00

Reel History Film Frame

BR	Babe Ruth
LG	Lou Gehrig

Signature Cuts

Production One Set

When It Was A Game - Memorabilia

NM/M

Common Player:		5.00
AT	Alan Trammell	5.00
BF	Bob Feller	8.00
BG	Bob Gibson	10.00
BM	Bill Mazeroski	8.00
BW	Billy Williams	5.00
CF	Carlton Fisk	8.00
CY	Carl Yastrzemski	10.00
DE	Dennis Eckersley	5.00
DM	Don Mattingly	15.00
DW	Dave Winfield	8.00
EM	Eddie Murray	8.00
FJ	Fergie Jenkins	5.00
FL	Fred Lynn	5.00
FR	Frank Robinson	8.00
GP	Gaylord Perry	5.00
HK	Harmon Killebrew	10.00
JP	Jim Palmer	8.00
JR	Jim Rice	5.00
KG	Kirk Gibson	5.00
KP	Kirby Puckett	15.00
LB	Lou Brock	8.00
MS	Mike Schmidt	10.00
NR	Nolan Ryan	20.00
PM	Paul Molitor	8.00
PW	Pee Wee Reese	10.00
RF	Rollie Fingers	5.00
RJ	Reggie Jackson	10.00
RM	Roger Maris	25.00
RS	Red Schoendienst	8.00
TG	Tony Gwynn	10.00

2007 SPX

NM/M

Complete Set (150):		
Common Player (1-100):		.25
(101-150):		10.00
Pack (3):		20.00
Box (10):		180.00
1	Miguel Tejada	.75
2	Brian Roberts	.50
3	Melvin Mora	.25
4	David Ortiz	1.00
5	Manny Ramirez	1.00
6	Jason Varitek	.50
7	Curt Schilling	1.00
8	Jim Thome	.75
9	Paul Konerko	.50
10	Jermaine Dye	.50
11	Travis Hafner	.50
12	Victor Martinez	.50
13	Grady Sizemore	.75
14	C.C. Sabathia	.50
15	Ivan Rodriguez	.50
16	Magglio Ordonez	.50
17	Carlos Guillen	.25
18	Justin Verlander	.75
19	Shane Costa	.25
20	Emil Brown	.25
21	Mark Teahen	.25
22	Vladimir Guerrero	1.00
23	Jered Weaver	.50
24	Juan Rivera	.25
25	Justin Morneau	.75
26	Joe Mauer	.50
27	Torii Hunter	.50
28	Johan Santana	.75

29	Derek Jeter	3.00
30	Alex Rodriguez	3.00
31	Johnny Damon	1.00
32	Jason Giambi	.75
33	Bobby Crosby	.25
34	Nick Swisher	.50
35	Eric Chavez	.25
36	Ichiro Suzuki	2.00
37	Raul Ibanez	.25
38	Richie Sexson	.50
39	Carl Crawford	.50
40	Rocco Baldelli	.25
41	Scott Kazmir	.50
42	Michael Young	.50
43	Mark Teixeira	.75
44	Ian Kinsler	.25
45	Troy Glaus	.50
46	Vernon Wells	.50
47	Roy Halladay	.50
48	Lyle Overbay	.25
49	Brandon Webb	.50
50	Conor Jackson	.25
51	Stephen Drew	.50
52	Chipper Jones	1.00
53	Andruw Jones	.75
54	Adam LaRoche	.25
55	John Smoltz	.50
56	Derrek Lee	.75
57	Aramis Ramirez	.50
58	Carlos Zambrano	.50
59	Ken Griffey Jr.	2.00
60	Adam Dunn	.50
61	Aaron Harang	.25
62	Todd Helton	.75
63	Matt Holliday	.50
64	Garrett Atkins	.25
65	Miguel Cabrera	1.00
66	Hanley Ramirez	.50
67	Dontrelle Willis	.50
68	Lance Berkman	.50
69	Roy Oswalt	.50
70	Craig Biggio	.50
71	J.D. Drew	.25
72	Nomar Garciaparra	1.00
73	Rafael Furcal	.50
74	Jeff Kent	.50
75	Prince Fielder	1.00
76	Bill Hall	.50
77	Rickie Weeks	.50
78	Jose Reyes	1.00
79	David Wright	1.00
80	Carlos Delgado	.75
81	Carlos Beltran	.75
82	Ryan Howard	2.00
83	Chase Utley	1.00
84	Jimmy Rollins	.50
85	Jason Bay	.50
86	Freddy Sanchez	.25
87	Zachary Duke	.25
88	Trevor Hoffman	.25
89	Adrian Gonzalez	.50
90	Chris Young	.25
91	Ray Durham	.25
92	Omar Vizquel	.25
93	Jason Schmidt	.50
94	Albert Pujols	3.00
95	Scott Rolen	.75
96	Jim Edmonds	.50
97	Chris Carpenter	.75
98	Alfonso Soriano	.75
99	Ryan Zimmerman	.50
100	Nick Johnson	.25
101	Delmon Young (RC)	20.00
102	Andrew Miller RC	30.00
103	Troy Tulowitzki (RC)	35.00
104	Jeff Fiorentino (RC)	10.00
105	David Murphy (RC)	15.00
106	Tim Lincecum RC	160.00
107	Phil Hughes (RC)	75.00
108	Kevin Kouzmanoff (RC)	15.00
109	Adam Lind (RC)	15.00
110	Mark Reynolds RC	50.00
111	Kevin Hooper (RC)	10.00
112	Mitch Maier RC	10.00
113	Homer Bailey (RC)	50.00
114	Dennis Sarfate (RC)	10.00
115	Drew Anderson (RC)	10.00
116	Miguel Montero (RC)	10.00
117	Glen Perkins (RC)	10.00
118	Kevin Slowey (RC)	40.00
119	Tim Gradoville RC	10.00
120	Ryan Braun (RC)	120.00
121	Chris Narveson (RC)	10.00
122	Patrick Misch (RC)	10.00
123	Juan Salas (RC)	10.00
124	Beltran Perez (RC)	10.00
125	Joaquin Arias (RC)	10.00
126	Philip Humber (RC)	15.00
127	Kei Igawa RC	25.00
128	Daisuke Matsuzaka RC	300.00
129	Andy Cannizaro RC	10.00
130	Ubaldo Jimenez (RC)	10.00

131	Fred Lewis (RC)	15.00
132	Ryan Sweeney (RC)	10.00
133	Jeff Baker (RC)	10.00
134	Michael Bourn (RC)	15.00
135	Akinori Iwamura RC	30.00
136	Oswaldo Navarro RC	10.00
137	Hunter Pence (RC)	60.00
138	Jon Knott (RC)	10.00
139	Justin Hampson (RC)	10.00
140	Jeff Salazar (RC)	10.00
141	Juan Morillo (RC)	10.00
142	Delwyn Young (RC)	10.00
143	Brian Burres (RC)	10.00
144	Chris Stewart RC	10.00
145	Eric Stults RC	10.00
146	Carlos Maldonado (RC)	10.00
147	Angel Sanchez RC	10.00
148	Cesar Jimenez RC	10.00
149	Shawn Riggans (RC)	10.00
150	John Nelson (RC)	10.00

Printing Plates

No Pricing
Production one set per color.

Spectrum

Spectrum (101-150): No Pricing
Production 25 Sets

Autofacts Preview

NM/M

Common Autograph:		10.00
1:Hobby Box		
AI	Akinori Iwamura	25.00
AL	Adam Lind	15.00
AM	Andrew Miller/SP	40.00
AS	Angel Sanchez	10.00
BP	Beltran Perez	10.00
BR	Jeremy Brown	10.00
CM	Carlos Maldonado	15.00
CN	Chris Narveson	10.00
CR	Cal Ripken Jr./SP	220.00
DS	Dennis Sarfate	10.00
DW	Dewayne Wise	10.00
DY	Delmon Young	20.00
ES	Eric Stults	10.00
FL	Fred Lewis	15.00
GP	Glen Perkins	10.00
JA	Joaquin Arias	10.00
JB	Jeff Baker	10.00
JH	Justin Hampson	10.00
JK	Jon Knott	15.00
JM	Juan Morillo	10.00
JS	Juan Salas	10.00
JW	Jason Wood	10.00
KG	Ken Griffey Jr./SP	80.00
KH	Kevin Hooper	10.00
KI	Kei Igawa	25.00
KK	Kevin Kouzmanoff	15.00
MB	Michael Bourn	15.00
MM	Miguel Montero	15.00
PH	Philip Humber	15.00
PM	Patrick Misch	10.00
SA	Jeff Salazar	10.00
SR	Shawn Riggans	10.00
ST	Chris Stewart	10.00
TT	Troy Tulowitzki	25.00
YO	Delwyn Young	10.00

Iron Man

NM/M

Common Ripken (1-100):	5.00
Production 699 Sets	
Platinum:	No Pricing
Production One Set	
Printing Plates:	No Pricing
Production One Set	

Iron Man Memorabilia

NM/M

Common Ripken:	40.00

Production 25 Sets

Iron Man Autograph

Production One Set

Young Star Signatures

NM/M

Common Autograph:		10.00
Spectrum:		1-2X
Production 25 Sets		
AE	Andre Ethier	20.00
AG	Adrian Gonzalez	20.00
AS	Anibal Sanchez	20.00
BU	B.J. Upton	20.00
CA	Matt Cain/SP	20.00
CH	Cole Hamels/SP	30.00
CQ	Carlos Quentin	15.00
DJ	Derek Jeter	125.00
DU	Dan Uggla	20.00
DY	Delmon Young	20.00
FH	Felix Hernandez	25.00
FL	Francisco Liriano	25.00

HA	Rich Harden	15.00
HI	Rich Hill/SP	20.00
HK	Howie Kendrick	20.00
HR	Hanley Ramirez	20.00
JB	Jeremy Brown	10.00
JJ	Josh Johnson	15.00
JL	Jon Lester	25.00
JM	Joe Mauer	25.00
JP	Jonathan Papelbon	30.00
JR	Jose Reyes	50.00
JS	Jeremy Sowers	15.00
JV	Justin Verlander	30.00
JW	Jered Weaver/SP	20.00
JZ	Joel Zumaya	20.00
KG	Ken Griffey Jr.	75.00
KU	Hong-Chih Kuo	25.00
LO	James Loney	20.00
MO	Justin Morneau	25.00
NM	Nicholas Markakis	30.00
PH	Philip Humber	15.00
RW	Rickie Weeks	20.00
RZ	Ryan Zimmerman	30.00
SD	Stephen Drew	20.00
ST	Scott Thorman	15.00
TT	Troy Tulowitzki	30.00
WI	Josh Willingham	15.00

Winning Materials
Bronze 199

NM/M
Common Player:		5.00
Gold 199:		1X
Silver 199:		1X
Production 199 Sets		
Blue 175:		1X
Green 175:		1X
Production 175 Sets		
Gold 99:		1-1.5X
Silver 99:		1-1.5X
Production 99 Sets		
Dual Bronze:		No Pricing
Production 25 Sets		
Dual Gold:		1-1.5X
Dual Silver:		1-1.5X
Production 50 Sets		
Dual Green:		No Pricing
Production 15 Sets		
AB	A.J. Burnett	5.00
AD	Adam Dunn	6.00
AE	Andre Ethier	6.00
AJ	Andruw Jones	8.00
AL	Adam LaRoche	5.00
AP	Albert Pujols	20.00
AR	Aramis Ramirez	8.00
AS	Anibal Sanchez	5.00
BA	Bobby Abreu	6.00
BG	Brian Giles	5.00
BL	Joe Blanton	5.00
BM	Brian McCann	5.00
BO	Jeremy Bonderman	6.00
BR	Brian Roberts	5.00
BS	Ben Sheets	5.00
BU	B.J. Upton	5.00
CA	Miguel Cabrera	8.00
CB	Craig Biggio	5.00
CC	Chris Carpenter	8.00
CF	Chone Figgins	5.00
CH	Cole Hamels	10.00
CJ	Chipper Jones	8.00
CL	Roger Clemens	15.00
CN	Robinson Cano	10.00
CR	Carl Crawford	5.00
CU	Chase Utley	10.00
CW	Chien-Ming Wang	35.00
DJ	Derek Jeter	20.00
DJ2	Derek Jeter	20.00
DL	Derrek Lee	8.00
DO	David Ortiz	10.00
DU	Dan Uggla	5.00
DW	Dontrelle Willis	5.00
EC	Eric Chavez	5.00
FH	Felix Hernandez	6.00
FL	Francisco Liriano	5.00
FS	Freddy Sanchez	5.00
FT	Frank Thomas	8.00
GA	Garrett Atkins	5.00
HA	Travis Hafner	6.00
HE	Todd Helton	8.00
HK	Howie Kendrick	5.00
HN	Rich Harden	5.00
HR	Hanley Ramirez	8.00
HS	Huston Street	5.00
IK	Ian Kinsler	5.00
IR	Ivan Rodriguez	8.00
JB	Jason Bay	6.00
JE	Jim Edmonds	5.00
JF	Jeff Francoeur	8.00
JJ	Josh Johnson	5.00
JL	Chad Billingsley	5.00
JM	Joe Mauer	8.00
JN	Joe Nathan	5.00
JP	Jake Peavy	5.00
JR	Jose Reyes	10.00
JS	Jeremy Sowers	5.00

JT	Jim Thome	8.00
JV	Justin Verlander	8.00
JW	Jered Weaver	8.00
JZ	Joel Zumaya	5.00
KG	Ken Griffey Jr.	15.00
KG2	Ken Griffey Jr.	15.00
KH	Khalil Greene	5.00
KU	Hong-Chih Kuo	20.00
LE	Jon Lester	8.00
LG	Luis Gonzalez	5.00
MC	Matt Cain	5.00
ME	Melky Cabrera	6.00
MH	Matt Holliday	8.00
MO	Justin Morneau	8.00
MT	Mark Teixeira	8.00
NM	Nicholas Markakis	8.00
NS	Nick Swisher	5.00
PA	Jonathan Papelbon	15.00
PF	Prince Fielder	10.00
PL	Paul LoDuca	5.00
RC	Cal Ripken Jr.	20.00
RI	Alex Rios	5.00
RJ	Randy Johnson	8.00
RO	Roy Oswalt	6.00
RW	Rickie Weeks	5.00
RZ	Ryan Zimmerman	8.00
SA	Alfonso Soriano	8.00
SD	Stephen Drew	5.00
SH	James Shields	5.00
SK	Scott Kazmir	5.00
SM	John Smoltz	8.00
SO	Scott Olsen	5.00
SR	Scott Rolen	8.00
TE	Miguel Tejada	6.00
TG	Tom Glavine	5.00
TH	Trevor Hoffman	5.00
TO	Torii Hunter	6.00
VG	Vladimir Guerrero	8.00
VM	Victor Martinez	5.00
WE	David Wells	5.00
WI	Josh Willingham	5.00
YB	Yuniesky Betancourt	5.00

Winning Materials
Patch Gold

NM/M
Common Player:		10.00
Production 99 unless noted.		
Patch Silver:		1X
Production 3-99		
Patch Bronze:		1X
Production 50 Sets		
Triple Patch:		No Pricing
Production 25 Sets		
AB	A.J. Burnett	10.00
AD	Adam Dunn	15.00
AE	Andre Ethier	10.00
AJ	Andruw Jones	15.00
AL	Adam LaRoche	10.00
AP	Albert Pujols	40.00
AR	Aramis Ramirez	15.00
AS	Anibal Sanchez/54	10.00
BA	Bobby Abreu	15.00
BG	Brian Giles	10.00
BL	Joe Blanton	10.00
BM	Brian McCann	10.00
BO	Jeremy Bonderman	15.00
BR	Brian Roberts	10.00
BS	Ben Sheets	10.00
BU	B.J. Upton	10.00
CA	Miguel Cabrera	20.00
CB	Craig Biggio	15.00
CC	Chris Carpenter	20.00
CF	Chone Figgins	10.00
CH	Cole Hamels	20.00
CJ	Chipper Jones	20.00
CL	Roger Clemens	25.00
CN	Robinson Cano	20.00
CR	Carl Crawford	10.00
CU	Chase Utley	20.00
CW	Chien-Ming Wang	60.00
DJ	Derek Jeter	40.00
DJ2	Derek Jeter	40.00
DL	Derrek Lee	20.00
DO	David Ortiz	20.00
DU	Dan Uggla	10.00
DW	Dontrelle Willis	10.00
EC	Eric Chavez	10.00
FH	Felix Hernandez	15.00
FL	Francisco Liriano	15.00
FS	Freddy Sanchez	10.00
FT	Frank Thomas	20.00
GA	Garrett Atkins	10.00
HA	Travis Hafner	15.00
HE	Todd Helton	20.00
HK	Howie Kendrick/34	15.00
HN	Rich Harden	10.00
HR	Hanley Ramirez	20.00
HS	Huston Street	10.00
IK	Ian Kinsler	20.00
IR	Ivan Rodriguez	20.00
JB	Jason Bay	15.00
JE	Jim Edmonds	10.00

JF	Jeff Francoeur	20.00
JJ	Josh Johnson	10.00
JL	Chad Billingsley	10.00
JM	Joe Mauer	20.00
JN	Joe Nathan	10.00
JP	Jake Peavy	10.00
JR	Jose Reyes	25.00
JS	Jeremy Sowers	10.00
JT	Jim Thome	20.00
JW	Jered Weaver	20.00
JZ	Joel Zumaya	10.00
KG	Ken Griffey Jr.	30.00
KG2	Ken Griffey Jr.	30.00
KH	Khalil Greene	10.00
KU	Hong-Chih Kuo	40.00
LE	Jon Lester	20.00
LG	Luis Gonzalez	10.00
MC	Matt Cain	15.00
ME	Melky Cabrera	20.00
MH	Matt Holliday	20.00
MO	Justin Morneau	15.00
MT	Mark Teixeira	15.00
NM	Nicholas Markakis	15.00
NS	Nick Swisher	10.00
PA	Jonathan Papelbon	30.00
PF	Prince Fielder	20.00
PL	Paul LoDuca	10.00
RC	Cal Ripken Jr.	40.00
RI	Alex Rios	10.00
RJ	Randy Johnson	20.00
RO	Roy Oswalt	15.00
RW	Rickie Weeks	15.00
RZ	Ryan Zimmerman	15.00
SA	Alfonso Soriano	20.00
SD	Stephen Drew	15.00
SH	James Shields	10.00
SK	Scott Kazmir	10.00
SM	John Smoltz	20.00
SO	Scott Olsen	10.00
SR	Scott Rolen	15.00
TE	Miguel Tejada	15.00
TG	Tom Glavine	20.00
TH	Trevor Hoffman	10.00
TO	Torii Hunter	15.00
VG	Vladimir Guerrero	20.00
VM	Victor Martinez	10.00
WE	David Wells	10.00
WI	Josh Willingham	10.00
YB	Yuniesky Betancourt	10.00

Winning Materials
Triple Signatures

NM/M
Production 15-35		5.00
Platinum:		No Pricing
Production 3-10		
BR	Brian Roberts/35	35.00
EC	Eric Chavez/35	30.00
FH	Felix Hernandez/35	50.00
GA	Garrett Atkins/35	25.00
HA	Travis Hafner/35	35.00
HK	Howie Kendrick/35	30.00
JJ	Josh Johnson/35	20.00
JM	Joe Mauer/35	40.00
JP	Jake Peavy/35	35.00
JR	Jose Reyes/35	75.00
KU	Hong-Chih Kuo/35	120.00
LE	Jon Lester/35	40.00
TE	Miguel Tejada/35	30.00
TG	Tom Glavine/35	60.00

Winning Trios Gold

NM/M
Common Trio:	15.00
Production 75 Sets	
Silver:	1X
Production 50 Sets	
Bronze:	1-1.5X
Production 30 Sets	
Patch:	No Pricing
Production 8-25	
1 Ken Griffey Jr., Derek Jeter, Albert Pujols	40.00
2 Josh Willingham, Hanley Ramirez, Dan Uggla	15.00
3 Josh Johnson, Dontrelle Willis, Anibal Sanchez	15.00
4 Travis Hafner, David Ortiz, Lance Berkman	25.00
5 Ben Sheets, Roy Oswalt, Jake Peavy	15.00
6 Ivan Rodriguez, Jeremy Bonderman, Justin Verlander	25.00
7 Jose Reyes, Stephen Drew, Hanley Ramirez	25.00
8 Miguel Cabrera, Ryan Zimmerman, B.J. Upton	20.00

9 Justin Verlander, Jonathan Papelbon, Jered Weaver	40.00
10 Randy Johnson, Derek Jeter, Bobby Abreu	40.00
11 Craig Biggio, Lance Berkman, Morgan Ensberg	15.00
12 Brian McCann, Jeff Francoeur, Adam LaRoche	30.00
13 Victor Martinez, Joe Mauer, Brian McCann	20.00
14 Carl Crawford, Grady Sizemore, Jose Reyes	30.00
15 Freddy Garcia, Carlos Zambrano, Johan Santana	20.00
16 Vladimir Guerrero, Bobby Abreu, Alfonso Soriano	20.00
17 Justin Morneau, Johan Santana, Joe Mauer	25.00
18 Carlos Delgado, Carlos Beltran, Jose Reyes	25.00
19 Andre Ethier, Chad Billingsley, Matthew Kemp	25.00
20 Jim Thome, Jermaine Dye, Tadahito Iguchi	20.00
21 Jimmy Rollins, Chase Utley, Aaron Rowand	30.00
22 Ivan Rodriguez, Magglio Ordonez, Curtis Granderson	20.00
23 Chris Carpenter, Scott Rolen, Albert Pujols	30.00
24 Carl Crawford, B.J. Upton, James Shields	15.00
25 Howie Kendrick, Mike Napoli, Jered Weaver	15.00
26 Ian Kinsler, Dan Uggla, Howie Kendrick	20.00
27 Miguel Tejada, Brian Roberts, Nicholas Markakis	15.00
28 Justin Verlander, Jered Weaver, Mike Pelfrey	20.00
30 Randy Johnson, Derek Lowe, Anibal Sanchez	15.00
31 Prince Fielder, Ryan Zimmerman, Dan Uggla	25.00
32 Trevor Hoffman, Joe Nathan, Huston Street	15.00
33 Vernon Wells, Alex Rios, A.J. Burnett	15.00
34 Ben Sheets, Rickie Weeks, Prince Fielder	20.00
35 Adrian Beltre, Felix Hernandez, Yuniesky Betancourt	15.00
36 Jeremy Bonderman, Justin Verlander, Joel Zumaya	20.00
37 Billy Wagner, Paul LoDuca, Jose Reyes	20.00
38 Victor Martinez, Jeremy Sowers, C.C. Sabathia	15.00
39 Conor Jackson, Brandon Webb, Stephen Drew	20.00
40 Justin Verlander, Felix Hernandez, Jered Weaver	20.00
41 Ken Griffey Jr., Frank Thomas, Ivan Rodriguez	20.00
42 Cal Ripken Jr., Derek Jeter, Jose Reyes	50.00

1997 Sports Illustrated

NM/M
Complete Set (180):		20.00
Common Player:		.05
Pack (6):		1.25
Wax Box (24):		20.00
1	Bob Abreu	.10
2	Jaime Bluma	.05
3	Emil Brown	.05
4	Jose Cruz, Jr.	.05
5	Jason Dickson	.05
6	Nomar Garciaparra	1.00

7	Todd Greene	.05
8	Vladimir Guerrero	.75
9	Wilton Guerrero	.05
10	Jose Guillen	.05
11	Hideki Irabu	.05
12	Russ Johnson	.05
13	Andruw Jones	.75
14	Damon Mashore	.05
15	Jason McDonald	.05
16	Ryan McGuire	.05
17	Matt Morris	.05
18	Kevin Orie	.05
19	Dante Powell	.05
20	Pokey Reese	.05
21	Joe Roa	.05
22	Scott Rolen	.65
23	Glendon Rusch	.05
24	Scott Spiezio	.05
25	Bubba Trammell	.05
26	Todd Walker	.05
27	Jamey Wright	.05
28	Ken Griffey Jr.	.75
29	Tino Martinez	.05
30	Roger Clemens	.65
31	Hideki Irabu	.05
32	Kevin Brown	.05
33	Chipper Jones, Cal Ripken Jr.	.65
34	Sandy Alomar	.05
35	Ken Caminiti	.05
36	Randy Johnson	.40
37	Andy Ashby	.05
38	Jay Buhner	.05
39	Joe Carter	.05
40	Darren Daulton	.05
41	Jeff Fassero	.05
42	Andres Galarraga	.05
43	Rusty Greer	.05
44	Marquis Grissom	.05
45	Joey Hamilton	.05
46	Jimmy Key	.05
47	Ryan Klesko	.05
48	Eddie Murray	.75
49	Charles Nagy	.05
50	Dave Nilsson	.05
51	Ricardo Rincon	.05
52	Billy Wagner	.05
53	Dan Wilson	.05
54	Dmitri Young	.05
55	Roberto Alomar	.30
56	Sandy Alomar Jr.	.05
57	Scott Brosius	.05
58	Tony Clark	.05
59	Carlos Delgado	.45
60	Jermaine Dye	.05
61	Darin Erstad	.20
62	Derek Jeter	1.00
63	Jason Kendall	.05
64	Hideo Nomo	.20
65	Rey Ordonez	.05
66	Andy Pettitte	.10
67	Manny Ramirez	.75
68	Edgar Renteria	.05
69	Shane Reynolds	.05
70	Alex Rodriguez	1.00
71	Ivan Rodriguez	.65
72	Jose Rosado	.05
73	John Smoltz	.05
74	Tom Glavine	.35
75	Greg Maddux	1.00
76	Chipper Jones	1.00
77	Kenny Lofton	.05
78	Fred McGriff	.05
79	Kevin Brown	.05
80	Alex Fernandez	.05
81	Al Leiter	.05
82	Bobby Bonilla	.05
83	Gary Sheffield	.40
84	Moises Alou	.05
85	Henry Rodriguez	.05
86	Mark Grudzielanek	.05
87	Pedro Martinez	.75
88	Todd Hundley	.05

89	Bernard Gilkey	.05
90	Bobby Jones	.05
91	Curt Schilling	.35
92	Ricky Bottalico	.05
93	Mike Lieberthal	.05
94	Sammy Sosa	1.00
95	Ryne Sandberg	1.00
96	Mark Grace	.05
97	Deion Sanders	.05
98	Reggie Sanders	.05
99	Barry Larkin	.05
100	Craig Biggio	.05
101	Jeff Bagwell	.75
102	Derek Bell	.05
103	Brian Jordan	.05
104	Ray Lankford	.05
105	Ron Gant	.05
106	Al Martin	.05
107	Kevin Elster	.05
108	Jermaine Allensworth	.05
109	Vinny Castilla	.05
110	Dante Bichette	.05
111	Larry Walker	.05
112	Mike Piazza	1.25
113	Eric Karros	.05
114	Todd Hollandsworth	.05
115	Raul Mondesi	.05
116	Hideo Nomo	.40
117	Ramon Martinez	.05
118	Ken Caminiti	.05
119	Tony Gwynn	1.00
120	Steve Finley	.05
121	Barry Bonds	2.00
122	J.T. Snow	.05
123	Rod Beck	.05
124	Cal Ripken Jr.	2.00
125	Mike Mussina	.30
126	Brady Anderson	.05
127	Bernie Williams	.05
128	Derek Jeter	2.00
129	Tino Martinez	.05
130	Andy Pettitte	.30
131	David Cone	.05
132	Mariano Rivera	.15
133	Roger Clemens	1.00
134	Pat Hentgen	.05
135	Juan Guzman	.05
136	Bob Higginson	.05
137	Tony Clark	.05
138	Travis Fryman	.05
139	Mo Vaughn	.05
140	Tim Naehring	.05
141	John Valentin	.05
142	Matt Williams	.05
143	David Justice	.05
144	Jim Thome	.65
145	Chuck Knoblauch	.05
146	Paul Molitor	.75
147	Marty Cordova	.05
148	Frank Thomas	.85
149	Albert Belle	.05
150	Robin Ventura	.05
151	John Jaha	.05
152	Jeff Cirillo	.05
153	Jose Valentin	.05
154	Jay Bell	.05
155	Jeff King	.05
156	Kevin Appier	.05
157	Ken Griffey Jr.	1.25
158	Alex Rodriguez	1.50
158p	Alex Rodriguez/OPS	1.50
159	Randy Johnson	.75
160	Juan Gonzalez	.40
161	Will Clark	.05
162	Dean Palmer	.05
163	Tim Salmon	.05
164	Jim Edmonds	.05
165	Jim Leyritz	.05
166	Jose Canseco	.40
167	Jason Giambi	.50
168	Mark McGwire	1.50
169	Barry Bonds	1.00
170	Alex Rodriguez	.75
171	Roger Clemens	.65
172	Ken Griffey Jr.	.65
173	Greg Maddux	.50
174	Mike Piazza	.65
175	Will Clark, Mark McGwire	1.00
176	Hideo Nomo	.20
177	Cal Ripken Jr.	1.00
178	Ken Griffey Jr., Frank Thomas	.50
179	Alex Rodriguez, Derek Jeter	1.50
180	John Wetteland	.05
---	Jose Cruz Jr. Checklist	.05

Extra Edition

		NM/M
Complete Set (180):		150.00
Common Player:		1.00
Extra Edition Stars:		8X

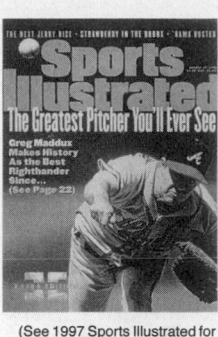

(See 1997 Sports Illustrated for checklist and base card values.)

Autographed Mini-Covers

	NM/M
Complete Set (6):	300.00
Common Player:	30.00
Alex Rodriguez	100.00
Cal Ripken Jr.	100.00
Kirby Puckett	80.00
Willie Mays	125.00
Frank Robinson	30.00
Hank Aaron	200.00

Box Topper

	NM/M
Alex Rodriguez	4.50

Cooperstown Collection

		NM/M
Complete Set (12):		27.50
Common Player:		2.00
1	Hank Aaron	6.00
2	Yogi Berra	3.00
3	Lou Brock	2.00
4	Rod Carew	2.00
5	Juan Marichal	2.00
6	Al Kaline	2.50
7	Joe Morgan	2.00
8	Brooks Robinson	3.00
9	Willie Stargell	2.00

10	Kirby Puckett	4.00
11	Willie Mays	6.00
12	Frank Robinson	3.00

Great Shots

		NM/M
Complete Set (25):		10.00
Common Player:		.20
(1)	Roberto Alomar	.30
(2)	Andy Ashby	.20
(3)	Albert Belle	.20
(4)	Barry Bonds	2.00
(5)	Jay Buhner	.20
(6)	Vinny Castilla, Andres Galarraga	.20
(7)	Darren Daulton	.20
(8)	Juan Gonzalez	.40
(9)	Ken Griffey Jr.	1.25
(10)	Derek Jeter	2.00
(11)	Randy Johnson	.75
(12)	Chipper Jones	1.00
(13)	Eric Karros	.20
(14)	Ryan Klesko	.20
(15)	Kenny Lofton	.20
(16)	Greg Maddux	1.00
(17)	Mark McGwire	1.50
(18)	Mike Piazza	1.25
(19)	Cal Ripken Jr.	2.00
(20)	Alex Rodriguez	1.50
(21)	Ryne Sandberg	1.00
(22)	Deion Sanders	.30
(23)	John Smoltz	.20
(24)	Frank Thomas	.75
(25)	Mo Vaughn	.20

1998 Sports Illustrated Then & Now

	NM/M
Complete Set (150):	15.00

Common Player:	.05
Pack (5):	1.00
Wax Box (24):	16.00
1 Luis Aparicio	.05
2 Richie Ashburn	.05
3 Ernie Banks	.50
4 Yogi Berra	.50
5 Lou Boudreau	.05
6 Lou Brock	.15
7 Jim Bunning	.05
8 Rod Carew	.15
9 Bob Feller	.25
10 Rollie Fingers	.05
11 Bob Gibson	.15
12 Fergie Jenkins	.05
13 Al Kaline	.25
14 George Kell	.05
15 Harmon Killebrew	.25
16 Ralph Kiner	.05
17 Tommy Lasorda	.05
18 Juan Marichal	.05
19 Eddie Mathews	.25
20 Willie Mays	1.00
21 Willie McCovey	.05
22 Joe Morgan	.15
23 Gaylord Perry	.05
24 Kirby Puckett	1.00
25 Pee Wee Reese	.25
26 Phil Rizzuto	.25
27 Robin Roberts	.05
28 Brooks Robinson	.35
29 Frank Robinson	.35
30 Red Schoendienst	.05
31 Enos Slaughter	.05
32 Warren Spahn	.25
33 Willie Stargell	.15
34 Earl Weaver	.05
35 Billy Williams	.15
36 Early Wynn	.05
37 Rickey Henderson	.75
38 Greg Maddux	1.00
39 Mike Mussina	.40
40 Cal Ripken Jr.	2.00
41 Albert Belle	.05
42 Frank Thomas	.75
43 Jeff Bagwell	.75
44 Paul Molitor	.75
45 Chuck Knoblauch	.05
46 Todd Hundley	.05
47 Bernie Williams	.05
48 Tony Gwynn	1.00
49 Barry Bonds	2.00
50 Ken Griffey Jr.	1.25
51 Randy Johnson	.75
52 Mark McGwire	1.50
53 Roger Clemens	1.00
54 Jose Cruz Jr.	.05
55 Roberto Alomar	.20
56 Sandy Alomar	.05
57 Brady Anderson	.05
58 Kevin Appier	.05
59 Jeff Bagwell	.75
60 Albert Belle	.05
61 Dante Bichette	.05
62 Craig Biggio	.05
63 Barry Bonds	2.00
64 Kevin Brown	.05
65 Jay Buhner	.05
66 Ellis Burks	.05
67 Ken Caminiti	.05
68 Jose Canseco	.50
69 Joe Carter	.05
70 Vinny Castilla	.05
71 Tony Clark	.05
72 Roger Clemens	1.00
73 David Cone	.05
74 Jose Cruz Jr.	.05
75 Jason Dickson	.05
76 Jim Edmonds	.05
77 Scott Erickson	.05
78 Darin Erstad	.20
79 Alex Fernandez	.05
80 Steve Finley	.05
81 Travis Fryman	.05
82 Andres Galarraga	.05
83 Nomar Garciaparra	1.00
84 Tom Glavine	.35
85 Juan Gonzalez	.40
86 Mark Grace	.05
87 Willie Greene	.05
88 Ken Griffey Jr.	1.25
89 Vladimir Guerrero	.75
90 Tony Gwynn	1.00
91 Livan Hernandez	.05
92 Bobby Higginson	.05
93 Derek Jeter	2.00
94 Charles Johnson	.05
95 Randy Johnson	.75
96 Andruw Jones	.75
97 Chipper Jones	1.00
98 David Justice	.05
99 Eric Karros	.05
100 Jason Kendall	.05
101 Jimmy Key	.05

102 Darryl Kile	.05
103 Chuck Knoblauch	.05
104 Ray Lankford	.05
105 Barry Larkin	.05
106 Kenny Lofton	.05
107 Greg Maddux	1.00
108 Al Martin	.05
109 Edgar Martinez	.05
110 Pedro Martinez	.75
111 Ramon Martinez	.05
112 Tino Martinez	.05
113 Mark McGwire	1.50
114 Raul Mondesi	.05
115 Matt Morris	.05
116 Charles Nagy	.05
117 Denny Neagle	.05
118 Hideo Nomo	.40
119 Dean Palmer	.05
120 Andy Pettitte	.25
121 Mike Piazza	1.25
122 Manny Ramirez	.75
123 Edgar Renteria	.05
124 Cal Ripken Jr.	2.00
125 Alex Rodriguez	1.50
126 Henry Rodriguez	.05
127 Ivan Rodriguez	.65
128 Scott Rolen	.65
129 Tim Salmon	.05
130 Curt Schilling	.35
131 Gary Sheffield	.45
132 John Smoltz	.05
133 Sammy Sosa	1.00
134 Frank Thomas	.75
135 Jim Thome	.65
136 Mo Vaughn	.05
137 Robin Ventura	.05
138 Larry Walker	.05
139 Bernie Williams	.05
140 Matt Williams	.05
141 Jaret Wright	.05
142 Michael Coleman	.05
143 Juan Encarnacion	.05
144 Brad Fullmer	.05
145 Ben Grieve	.05
146 Todd Helton	.75
147 Paul Konerko	.20
148 Derrek Lee	.50
149 Magglio Ordonez **RC**	1.50
150 Enrique Wilson	.05
--- Alex Rodriguez (Checklist)	1.00

Extra Edition

Willie Mays

	NM/M
Common Extra Edition:	1.00
Extra Edition Stars:	6X

Production 500 Sets
(See 1998 Sports Illustrated Then & Now for checklist and base card values.)

Art of the Game

"Brooks"

	NM/M
Complete Set (8):	11.00
Common Player:	1.00
Inserted 1:9	
1 Ken Griffey Jr./ It's Gone	1.50
2 Alex Rodriguez	2.00
3 Mike Piazza	1.50
4 Brooks Robinson	1.00
5 David Justice/AS	1.00
6 Cal Ripken Jr.	3.00
7 The Prospect and the Prospector	1.00
8 Barry Bonds	3.00

Autographs

Scott Rolen

	NM/M
Common Autograph:	15.00
Redemption Cards:	10%
Bob Gibson/500	15.00
Tony Gwynn/250	35.00
Roger Clemens/250	120.00
Scott Rolen/150	20.00
Willie Mays/250	90.00
Harmon Killebrew/500	25.00

Covers

	NM/M
Complete Set (12):	22.00
Common Player:	1.00
Inserted 1:18	
1 Lou Brock (10/16/67)	1.00
2 Kirby Puckett (4/6/92)	2.50
3 Harmon Killebrew (4/8/63 - Inside)	1.00
4 Eddie Mathews (8/16/54)	1.00
5 Willie Mays (5/22/72)	2.00
6 Frank Robinson (10/6/69)	1.00
7 Cal Ripken Jr. (9/11/95)	5.00
8 Roger Clemens (5/12/86)	2.50
9 Ken Griffey Jr. (10/16/95)	3.00
10 Mark McGwire (6/1/92)	4.00
11 Tony Gwynn (7/28/97)	2.50
12 Ivan Rodriguez (8/11/97)	1.50

Great Shots!

	NM/M
Complete Set (25):	7.50
Common Player:	.10
Inserted 1:1	
1 Ken Griffey Jr.	.65
2 Frank Thomas	.45
3 Alex Rodriguez	.75
4 Andruw Jones	.45
5 Chipper Jones	.50

6 Cal Ripken Jr.	1.00
7 Mark McGwire.	.75
8 Derek Jeter.	1.00
9 Greg Maddux.	.50
10 Jeff Bagwell.	.45
11 Mike Piazza.	.65
12 Scott Rolen.	.35
13 Nomar Garciaparra.	.50
14 Jose Cruz Jr.	.10
15 Charles Johnson.	.10
16 Fergie Jenkins.	.10
17 Lou Brock.	.10
18 Bob Gibson.	.10
19 Harmon Killebrew.	.10
20 Juan Marichal.	.10
21 Brooks Robinson.	.10
22 Rod Carew.	.10
23 Yogi Berra.	.25
24 Willie Mays.	.50
25 Kirby Puckett.	.50

Road to Cooperstown

KEN GRIFFEY, JR.

	NM/M
Complete Set (10):	10.00
Common Player:	.75
Inserted 1:24	
1 Barry Bonds	2.50
2 Roger Clemens	1.25
3 Ken Griffey Jr.	1.50
4 Tony Gwynn	1.00
5 Rickey Henderson	.75
6 Greg Maddux	1.00
7 Paul Molitor	.75
8 Mike Piazza	1.50
9 Cal Ripken Jr.	2.50
10 Frank Thomas	.75

1998 Sports Illustrated

Vladimir Guerrero

	NM/M
Complete Set (201):	20.00

Common Player:		.05
Pack (6):		1.50
Wax Box (24):		25.00
1	Edgardo Alfonzo	.05
2	Roberto Alomar	.20
3	Sandy Alomar	.05
4	Moises Alou	.05
5	Brady Anderson	.05
6	Garret Anderson	.05
7	Kevin Appier	.05
8	Jeff Bagwell	.75
9	Jay Bell	.05
10	Albert Belle	.05
11	Dante Bichette	.05
12	Craig Biggio	.05
13	Barry Bonds	2.00
14	Bobby Bonilla	.05
15	Kevin Brown	.05
16	Jay Buhner	.05
17	Ellis Burks	.05
18	Mike Cameron	.05
19	Ken Caminiti	.05
20	Jose Canseco	.45
21	Joe Carter	.05
22	Vinny Castilla	.05
23	Jeff Cirillo	.05
24	Tony Clark	.05
25	Will Clark	.05
26	Roger Clemens	1.00
27	David Cone	.05
28	Jose Cruz Jr.	.05
29	Carlos Delgado	.50
30	Jason Dickson	.05
31	Dennis Eckersley	.65
32	Jim Edmonds	.05
33	Scott Erickson	.05
34	Darin Erstad	.20
35	Shawn Estes	.05
36	Jeff Fassero	.05
37	Alex Fernandez	.05
38	Chuck Finley	.05
39	Steve Finley	.05
40	Travis Fryman	.05
41	Andres Galarraga	.05
42	Ron Gant	.05
43	Nomar Garciaparra	1.00
44	Jason Giambi	.50
45	Tom Glavine	.35
46	Juan Gonzalez	.40
47	Mark Grace	.05
48	Willie Green	.05
49	Rusty Greer	.05
50	Ben Grieve	.05
51	Ken Griffey Jr.	1.25
52	Mark Grudzielanek	.05
53	Vladimir Guerrero	.75
54	Juan Guzman	.05
55	Tony Gwynn	1.00
56	Joey Hamilton	.05
57	Rickey Henderson	.75
58	Pat Hentgen	.05
59	Livan Hernandez	.05
60	Bobby Higginson	.05
61	Todd Hundley	.05
62	Hideki Irabu	.05
63	John Jaha	.05
64	Derek Jeter	2.00
65	Charles Johnson	.05
66	Randy Johnson	.75
67	Andruw Jones	.75
68	Bobby Jones	.05
69	Chipper Jones	1.00
70	Brian Jordan	.05
71	David Justice	.05
72	Eric Karros	.05
73	Jeff Kent	.05
74	Jimmy Key	.05
75	Darryl Kile	.05
76	Jeff King	.05
77	Ryan Klesko	.05
78	Chuck Knoblauch	.05
79	Ray Lankford	.05
80	Barry Larkin	.05
81	Kenny Lofton	.05
82	Greg Maddux	1.00
83	Al Martin	.05
84	Edgar Martinez	.05
85	Pedro Martinez	.75
86	Tino Martinez	.05
87	Mark McGwire	1.50
88	Paul Molitor	.75
89	Raul Mondesi	.05
90	Jamie Moyer	.05
91	Mike Mussina	.30
92	Tim Naehring	.05
93	Charles Nagy	.05
94	Denny Neagle	.05
95	Dave Nilsson	.05
96	Hideo Nomo	.40
97	Rey Ordonez	.05
98	Dean Palmer	.05
99	Rafael Palmeiro	.65
100	Andy Pettitte	.30
101	Mike Piazza	1.25
102	Brad Radke	.05
103	Manny Ramirez	.75

104	Edgar Renteria	.05
105	Cal Ripken Jr.	2.00
106	Alex Rodriguez	1.50
106p	Alex Rodriguez./OPS	1.50
107	Henry Rodriguez	.05
108	Ivan Rodriguez	.65
109	Scott Rolen	.65
110	Tim Salmon	.05
111	Curt Schilling	.35
112	Gary Sheffield	.45
113	John Smoltz	.05
114	J.T. Snow	.05
115	Sammy Sosa	1.00
116	Matt Stairs	.05
117	Shannon Stewart	.05
118	Frank Thomas	.75
119	Jim Thome	.65
120	Justin Thompson	.05
121	Mo Vaughn	.05
122	Robin Ventura	.05
123	Larry Walker	.05
124	Rondell White	.05
125	Bernie Williams	.05
126	Matt Williams	.05
127	Tony Womack	.05
128	Jaret Wright	.05
129	Edgar Renteria	.05
130	Kenny Lofton	.05
131	Tony Gwynn	.50
132	Mark McGwire	.75
133	Craig Biggio	.05
134	Charles Johnson	.05
135	J.T. Snow	.05
136	Ken Caminiti	.05
137	Vladimir Guerrero	.40
138	Jim Edmonds	.05
139	Randy Johnson	.40
140	Darryl Kile	.05
141	John Smoltz	.05
142	Greg Maddux	.50
143	Andy Pettitte	.05
144	Ken Griffey Jr.	.65
145	Mike Piazza	.65
146	Todd Greene	.05
147	Vinny Castilla	.05
148	Derek Jeter	1.00
149	Robert Machado	.05
150	Mike Gulan	.05
151	Randall Simon	.05
152	Michael Coleman	.05
153	Brian Rose	.05
154	Scott Eyre RC	.05
155	Magglio Ordonez RC	1.50
156	Todd Helton	.65
157	Juan Encarnacion	.05
158	Mark Kotsay	.05
159	Josh Booty	.05
160	Melvin Rosario RC	.05
161	Shane Halter	.05
162	Paul Konerko	.25
163	Henry Blanco RC	.05
164	Antone Williamson	.05
165	Brad Fullmer	.05
166	Ricky Ledee	.05
167	Ben Grieve	.05
168	Frank Catalanotto RC	.25
169	Bobby Estalella	.05
170	Dennis Reyes	.05
171	Kevin Polcovich	.05
172	Jacob Cruz	.05
173	Ken Cloude	.05
174	Eli Marrero	.05
175	Fernando Tatis	.05
176	Tom Evans	.05
177	Carl Everett,	
	Nomar Garciaparra	
	(97 in Review)	.35
178	Eric Davis	
	(97 in Review)	.05
179	Roger Clemens	
	(97 in Review)	.60
180	Brett Butler, Eddie Murray	
	(97 in Review)	.30
181	Frank Thomas	
	(97 in Review)	.45
182	Curt Schilling	
	(97 in Review)	.15
183	Jeff Bagwell	
	(97 in Review)	.40
184	Mark McGwire,	
	Ken Griffey Jr.	
	(97 in Review)	.75
185	Kevin Brown	
	(97 in Review)	.05
186	Marty Cordova,	
	Ricardo Rincon	
	(97 in Review)	.05
187	Charles Johnson	
	(97 in Review)	.05
188	Hideki Irabu	
	(97 in Review)	.05
189	Tony Gwynn	
	(97 in Review)	.50
190	Sandy Alomar	
	(97 in Review)	.05

191	Ken Griffey Jr.	
	(97 in Review)	.65
192	Larry Walker	
	(97 in Review)	.05
193	Roger Clemens	
	(97 in Review)	.60
194	Pedro Martinez	
	(97 in Review)	.40
195	Nomar Garciaparra	
	(97 in Review)	.60
196	Scott Rolen	
	(97 in Review)	.40
197	Brian Anderson	
	(97 in Review)	.05
198	Tony Saunders	
	(97 in Review)	.05
199	Florida Celebration	
	(97 in Review)	.05
200	Livan Hernandez	
	(97 in Review)	.05
201	Travis Lee/SP	
	(One to Watch)	2.00

Extra Edition

NM/M

Common Player:	2.00
Extra Edition Stars:	8X
(See 1998 Sports Illustrated for checklist and base card values.)	

Autographs

PAUL KON...

NM/M

Common Player:	7.50
Lou Brock/500	40.00
Jose Cruz Jr./250	10.00
Rollie Fingers/500	10.00
Ben Grieve/250 (Exchange Card)	3.00
Ben Grieve (Signed Card)	7.50
Paul Konerko/250 (Exchange Card)	3.00
Paul Konerko (Signed Card)	20.00
Brooks Robinson/250	50.00

Covers

NM/M

Complete Set (10):	15.00
Common Player:	1.00

Inserted 1:9		
1	Ken Griffey Jr., Mike Piazza	2.00
2	Derek Jeter	3.00
3	Ken Griffey Jr.	2.50
4	Cal Ripken Jr.	3.00
5	Manny Ramirez	1.50
6	Jay Buhner	1.00
7	Matt Williams	1.00
8	Randy Johnson	1.50
9	Deion Sanders	1.00
10	Jose Canseco	1.50

Editor's Choice

NM/M

Complete Set (10):	20.00
Common Player:	1.00

Inserted 1:24		
1	Ken Griffey Jr.	3.00
2	Alex Rodriguez	4.00
3	Frank Thomas	1.50
4	Mark McGwire	4.00
5	Greg Maddux	2.00
6	Derek Jeter	5.00
7	Cal Ripken Jr.	5.00
8	Nomar Garciaparra	2.50
9	Jeff Bagwell	1.50
10	Jose Cruz Jr.	1.00

Mini-Posters

NM/M

Complete Set (30):	8.00
Common Player:	.10

Inserted 1:1		
1	Tim Salmon	.10
2	Travis Lee	.10
3	John Smoltz, Greg Maddux	.50
4	Cal Ripken Jr.	1.00
5	Nomar Garciaparra	.50
6	Sammy Sosa	.50
7	Frank Thomas	.45
8	Barry Larkin	.10
9	David Justice	.10
10	Larry Walker	.10
11	Tony Clark	.10
12	Livan Hernandez	.10
13	Jeff Bagwell	.45
14	Kevin Appier	.10
15	Mike Piazza	.65
16	Fernando Vina	.10
17	Chuck Knoblauch	.10
18	Vladimir Guerrero	.45
19	Rey Ordonez	.10
20	Bernie Williams	.10
21	Matt Stairs	.10
22	Curt Schilling	.30
23	Tony Womack	.10
24	Mark McGwire	.75
25	Tony Gwynn	.50
26	Barry Bonds	1.00

27	Ken Griffey Jr.	.65
28	Fred McGriff	.10
29	Juan Gonzalez, Alex Rodriguez	.50
30	Roger Clemens	.60

1998 Sports Illustrated World Series Fever

		NM/M
Complete Set (150):		10.00
Common Player:		.05
Pack (6):		1.00
Wax Box (24):		17.50
1	Mickey Mantle (Covers)	1.50
2	1957 World Series Preview (Covers)	.15
3	1958 World Series Preview (Covers)	.15
4	1959 World Series Preview (Covers)	.15
5	1962 World Series (Covers)	.10
6	Lou Brock (Covers)	.10
7	Brooks Robinson (Covers)	.25
8	Frank Robinson (Covers)	.25
9	1974 World Series (Covers)	.10
10	Reggie Jackson (Covers)	.60
11	1985 World Series (Covers)	.10
12	1987 World Series (Covers)	.10
13	Orel Hershiser (Covers)	.05
14	Rickey Henderson (Covers)	.40
15	1991 World Series (Covers)	.10
16	1992 World Series (Covers)	.05
17	Joe Carter (Covers)	.05
18	1995 World Series (Covers)	.10
19	1996 World Series (Covers)	.15
20	Edgar Renteria (Covers)	.05
21	Bill Mazeroski	.15
22	Joe Carter	.05
23	Carlton Fisk	.40
24	Bucky Dent	.15
25	Mookie Wilson	.05
26	Enos Slaughter	.05
27	Mickey Lolich	.05
28	Bobby Richardson	.05
29	Kirk Gibson	.05
30	Edgar Renteria	.05
31	Albert Belle	.05
32	Kevin Brown	.05
33	Brian Rose	.05
34	Ron Gant	.05
35	Jeromy Burnitz	.05
36	Andres Galarraga	.05
37	Jim Edmonds	.05
38	Jose Cruz Jr.	.05
39	Mark Grudzielanek	.05
40	Shawn Estes	.05
41	Mark Grace	.05
42	Nomar Garciaparra	.50
43	Juan Gonzalez	.20
44	Tom Glavine	.25
45	Brady Anderson	.05
46	Tony Clark	.05
47	Jeff Cirillo	.05
48	Dante Bichette	.05
49	Ben Grieve	.05
50	Ken Griffey Jr.	.65
51	Edgardo Alfonzo	.05
52	Roger Clemens	.60
53	Pat Hentgen	.05
54	Todd Helton	.30
55	Andy Benes	.05
56	Tony Gwynn	.50
57	Andruw Jones	.40
58	Bobby Higginson	.05
59	Bobby Jones	.05
60	Darryl Kile	.05
61	Chan Ho Park	.05
62	Charles Johnson	.05
63	Rusty Greer	.05
64	Travis Fryman	.05
65	Derek Jeter	1.00
66	Jay Buhner	.05
67	Chuck Knoblauch	.05
68	David Justice	.05
69	Brian Hunter	.05
70	Eric Karros	.05
71	Edgar Martinez	.05
72	Chipper Jones	.50
73	Barry Larkin	.05
74	Mike Lansing	.05
75	Craig Biggio	.05
76	Al Martin	.05
77	Barry Bonds	1.00
78	Randy Johnson	.40
79	Ryan Klesko	.05
80	Mark McGwire	.75
81	Fred McGriff	.05
82	Javy Lopez	.05
83	Kenny Lofton	.05
84	Sandy Alomar Jr.	.05
85	Matt Morris	.05
86	Paul Konerko	.10
87	Ray Lankford	.05
88	Kerry Wood	.30
89	Roberto Alomar	.20
90	Greg Maddux	.50
91	Travis Lee	.05
92	Moises Alou	.05
93	Dean Palmer	.05
94	Hideo Nomo	.20
95	Ken Caminiti	.05
96	Pedro Martinez	.40
97	Raul Mondesi	.05
98	Denny Neagle	.05
99	Tino Martinez	.05
100	Mike Mussina	.20
101	Kevin Appier	.05
102	Vinny Castilla	.05
103	Jeff Bagwell	.40
104	Paul O'Neill	.05
105	Rey Ordonez	.05
106	Vladimir Guerrero	.40
107	Rafael Palmeiro	.35
108	Alex Rodriguez	.75
109	Andy Pettitte	.15
110	Carl Pavano	.05
111	Henry Rodriguez	.05
112	Gary Sheffield	.40
113	Curt Schilling	.25
114	John Smoltz	.05
115	Reggie Sanders	.05
116	Scott Rolen	.35
117	Mike Piazza	.65
118	Manny Ramirez	.40
119	Cal Ripken Jr.	1.00
120	Brad Radke	.05
121	Tim Salmon	.05
122	Brett Tomko	.05
123	Robin Ventura	.05
124	Mo Vaughn	.05
125	A.J. Hinch	.05
126	Derrek Lee	.45
127	Orlando Hernandez **RC**	.40
128	Aramis Ramirez	.05
129	Frank Thomas	.40
130	J.T. Snow	.05
131	Magglio Ordonez **RC**	1.00
132	Bobby Bonilla	.05
133	Marquis Grissom	.05
134	Jim Thome	.45
135	Justin Thompson	.05
136	Matt Williams	.05
137	Matt Stairs	.05
138	Wade Boggs	.50
139	Chuck Finley	.05
140	Jaret Wright	.05
141	Ivan Rodriguez	.35
142	Brad Fullmer	.05
143	Bernie Williams	.05
144	Jason Giambi	.30
145	Larry Walker	.05
146	Tony Womack	.05
147	Sammy Sosa	.50
148	Rondell White	.05
149	Todd Stottlemyre	.05
150	Shane Reynolds	.05

Extra Edition

	NM/M
Common EE Player:	2.00
EE Stars:	15X
Production:	98 Sets
Common FE Player:	100.00
FE Stars:	Values Undetermined
1 of 1	

(See 1998 Sports Illustrated World Series Fever for checklist and base values.)

Autumn Excellence

		NM/M
Complete Set (10):		15.00
Common Player:		.50
Inserted 1:24		
Golds:		2X
Inserted 1:240		
AE1	Willie Mays	2.50
AE2	Kirby Puckett	2.00
AE3	Babe Ruth	4.00
AE4	Reggie Jackson	1.50
AE5	Whitey Ford	.50
AE6	Lou Brock	.50
AE7	Mickey Mantle	4.00
AE8	Yogi Berra	.75
AE9	Bob Gibson	.50
AE10	Don Larsen	1.00

MVP Collection

		NM/M
Complete Set (10):		1.00
Common Player:		.10
Inserted 1:4		
1	Frank Robinson	.25
2	Brooks Robinson	.25

3	Willie Stargell	.10
4	Bret Saberhagen	.10
5	Rollie Fingers	.10
6	Orel Hershiser	.10
7	Paul Molitor	.50
8	Tom Glavine	.15
9	John Wetteland	.10
10	Livan Hernandez	.10

Reggie Jackson Picks

		NM/M
Complete Set (15):		12.50
Common Player:		.25
Inserted 1:12		
1	Paul O'Neill	.25
2	Barry Bonds	2.50
3	Ken Griffey Jr.	1.50
4	Juan Gonzalez	.40
5	Greg Maddux	1.00
6	Mike Piazza	1.50
7	Larry Walker	.25
8	Mo Vaughn	.25
9	Roger Clemens	1.25
10	John Smoltz	.25
11	Alex Rodriguez	2.00
12	Frank Thomas	.75
13	Mark McGwire	2.00
14	Jeff Bagwell	.75
15	Randy Johnson	.75

1999 Sports Illustrated

		NM/M
Complete Set (180):		15.00
Common Player:		.05
Wax Pack (6):		1.00
Hobby Box (24):		15.00
Retail Box (16):		10.00
1	Yankees	.25
2	Scott Brosius	.05
3	David Wells	.05
4	Sterling Hitchcock	.05
5	David Justice	.05
6	David Cone	.05
7	Greg Maddux	.50
8	Jim Leyritz	.05
9	Gary Gaetti	.05
10	Mark McGwire	.75
11	Sammy Sosa	.50
12	Larry Walker	.05
13	Tony Womack	.05
14	Tom Glavine	.10
15	Curt Schilling	.10
16	Greg Maddux	.50
17	Trevor Hoffman	.05
18	Kerry Wood	.20
19	Tom Glavine	.10
20	Sammy Sosa	.50
21	Travis Lee	.05
22	Roberto Alomar	.05
23	Roger Clemens	.60
24	Barry Bonds	1.00

25	Paul Molitor	.45
26	Todd Stottlemyre	.05
27	Chris Hoiles	.05
28	Albert Belle	.05
29	Tony Clark	.05
30	Kerry Wood	.20
31	David Wells	.05
32	Dennis Eckersley	.40
33	Mark McGwire	.75
34	Cal Ripken Jr.	1.00
35	Ken Griffey Jr.	.65
36	Alex Rodriguez	.75
37	Craig Biggio	.05
38	Sammy Sosa	.50
39	Dennis Martinez	.05
40	Curt Schilling	.10
41	Orlando Hernandez	.05
42	Troy Glaus, Ben Molina, Todd Greene ("Team" 2000)	.45
43	Mitch Meluskey, Daryle Ward, Mike Grzanich ("Team" 2000)	.05
44	Eric Chavez, Mike Neill, Steve Connelly RC ("Team" 2000)	.10
45	Roy Halladay, Tom Evans, Kevin Witt ("Team" 2000)	.05
46	George Lombard, Adam Butler, Bruce Chen ("Team" 2000)	.05
47	Ronnie Belliard, Valerio de los Santos, Rafael Roque RC ("Team" 2000)	.05
48	J.D. Drew, Placido Polanco, Mark Little RC ("Team" 2000)	.50
49	Jason Maxwell, Jose Nieves, Jeremi Gonzalez ("Team" 2000)	.05
50	Scott McClain, Kerry Robinson, Mike Duvall RC ("Team" 2000)	.05
51	Ben Ford, Bryan Corey, Danny Klassen ("Team" 2000)	.05
52	Angel Pena, Jeff Kubenka, Paul LoDuca ("Team" 2000)	.05
53	Kirk Bullinger, Fernando Seguignol, Tim Young ("Team" 2000)	.05
54	Ramon Martinez, Wilson Delgado, Armando Rios ("Team" 2000)	.05
55	Russ Branyon, Jolbert Cabrera, Jason Rakers ("Team" 2000)	.05
56	Carlos Guillen, David Holdridge, Giomar Guevara RC ("Team" 2000)	.10
57	Alex Gonzalez, Joe Fontenot, Preston Wilson ("Team" 2000)	.05
58	Mike Kinkade, Jay Payton, Masato Yoshii ("Team" 2000)	.05
59	Willis Otanez, Ryan Minor, Calvin Pickering ("Team" 2000)	.05
60	Ben Davis, Matt Clement, Stan Spencer ("Team" 2000)	.05
61	Marlon Anderson, Mike Welch, Gary Bennett RC ("Team" 2000)	.05
62	Abraham Nunez, Sean Lawrence, Aramis Ramirez ("Team" 2000)	.05
63	Jonathan Johnson, Rob Sasser, Scott Sheldon RC ("Team" 2000)	.05
64	Keith Glauber, Guillermo Garcia, Eddie Priest ("Team" 2000)	.05
65	Brian Barkley, Jin Ho Cho, Donnie Sadler ("Team" 2000)	.05
66	Derrick Gibson, Mark Strittmatter, Edgard Clemente RC ("Team" 2000)	.05

67	Jeremy Giambi, Dermal Brown, Chris Hatcher RC ("Team" 2000)	.05
68	Rob Fick, Gabe Kapler, Marino Santana ("Team" 2000)	.10
69	Corey Koskie, A.J. Pierzynski, Benj Sampson ("Team" 2000)	.05
70	Brian Simmons, Mark Johnson, Craig Wilson ("Team" 2000)	.05
71	Ryan Bradley, Mike Lowell, Jay Tessmer ("Team" 2000)	.05
72	Ben Grieve	.05
73	Shawn Green	.45
74	Rafael Palmeiro	.65
75	Juan Gonzalez	.40
76	Mike Piazza	1.25
77	Devon White	.05
78	Jim Thome	.65
79	Barry Larkin	.05
80	Scott Rolen	.65
81	Raul Mondesi	.05
82	Jason Giambi	.50
83	Jose Canseco	.45
84	Tony Gwynn	1.00
85	Cal Ripken Jr.	2.00
86	Andy Pettitte	.15
87	Carlos Delgado	.50
88	Jeff Cirillo	.05
89	Bret Saberhagen	.05
90	John Olerud	.05
91	Ron Coomer	.05
92	Todd Helton	.65
93	Ray Lankford	.05
94	Tim Salmon	.05
95	Fred McGriff	.05
96	Matt Stairs	.05
97	Ken Griffey Jr.	1.25
98	Chipper Jones	1.00
99	Mark Grace	.05
100	Ivan Rodriguez	.65
101	Jeromy Burnitz	.05
102	Kenny Rogers	.05
103	Kevin Millwood	.05
104	Vinny Castilla	.05
105	Jim Edmonds	.05
106	Craig Biggio	.05
107	Andres Galarraga	.05
108	Sammy Sosa	1.00
109	Juan Encarnacion	.05
110	Larry Walker	.05
111	John Smoltz	.05
112	Randy Johnson	.75
113	Bobby Higginson	.05
114	Albert Belle	.05
115	Jaret Wright	.05
116	Edgar Renteria	.05
117	Andruw Jones	.75
118	Barry Bonds	2.00
119	Rondell White	.05
120	Jamie Moyer	.05
121	Darin Erstad	.20
122	Al Leiter	.05
123	Mark McGwire	1.50
124	Mo Vaughn	.05
125	Livan Hernandez	.05
126	Jason Kendall	.05
127	Frank Thomas	.75
128	Denny Neagle	.05
129	Johnny Damon	.35
130	Derek Bell	.05
131	Jeff Kent	.05
132	Tony Womack	.05
133	Trevor Hoffman	.05
134	Gary Sheffield	.40
135	Tino Martinez	.05
136	Travis Fryman	.05
137	Rolando Arrojo	.05
138	Dante Bichette	.05
139	Nomar Garciaparra	1.00
140	Moises Alou	.05
141	Chuck Knoblauch	.05
142	Robin Ventura	.05
143	Scott Erickson	.05
144	David Cone	.05
145	Greg Vaughn	.05
146	Wade Boggs	1.00
147	Mike Mussina	.30
148	Tony Clark	.05
149	Alex Rodriguez	1.50
150	Javy Lopez	.05
151	Bartolo Colon	.05
152	Derek Jeter	2.00
153	Greg Maddux	1.00
154	Kevin Brown	.05
155	Curt Schilling	.35
156	Jeff King	.05
157	Bernie Williams	.05

158	Roberto Alomar	.20
159	Travis Lee	.05
160	Kerry Wood	.50
160p	Kerry Wood/OPS	1.00
161	Jeff Bagwell	.75
162	Roger Clemens	1.00
163	Matt Williams	.05
164	Chan Ho Park	.05
165	Damion Easley	.05
166	Manny Ramirez	.75
167	Quinton McCracken	.05
168	Todd Walker	.05
169	Eric Karros	.05
170	Will Clark	.05
171	Edgar Martinez	.05
172	Cliff Floyd	.05
173	Vladimir Guerrero	.75
174	Tom Glavine	.35
175	Pedro Martinez	.75
176	Chuck Finley	.05
177	Dean Palmer	.05
178	Omar Vizquel	.05
179	Checklist	.05
180	Checklist	.05

Diamond Dominators

Complete Set (10):		30.00
Common Player:		1.50
Pitchers inserted 1:90		
Hitters inserted 1:180		
1DD	Kerry Wood	1.50
2DD	Roger Clemens	3.00
3DD	Randy Johnson	2.00
4DD	Greg Maddux	2.50
5DD	Pedro Martinez	2.00
6DD	Ken Griffey Jr.	5.00
7DD	Sammy Sosa	2.50
8DD	Nomar Garciaparra	2.50
9DD	Mark McGwire	6.00
10DD	Alex Rodriguez	6.00

Fabulous 40s

Complete Set (13):		9.00
Common Player:		.25
Inserted 1:20		
1FF	Mark McGwire	2.00
2FF	Sammy Sosa	1.25
3FF	Ken Griffey Jr.	1.50
4FF	Greg Vaughn	.25
5FF	Albert Belle	.25
6FF	Jose Canseco	.50
7FF	Vinny Castilla	.25
8FF	Juan Gonzalez	.50
9FF	Manny Ramirez	1.00
10FF	Andres Galarraga	.25
11FF	Rafael Palmeiro	.75
12FF	Alex Rodriguez	2.00
13FF	Mo Vaughn	.25

Fabulous 40s Extra

Common Player:		12.00
Numbered to amount of HRs.		
1FF	Mark McGwire/70	60.00
2FF	Sammy Sosa/66	40.00
3FF	Ken Griffey Jr./56	35.00
4FF	Greg Vaughn/50	12.00
5FF	Albert Belle/49	12.00
6FF	Jose Canseco/46	25.00
7FF	Vinny Castilla/46	12.00
8FF	Juan Gonzalez/45	20.00
9FF	Manny Ramirez/45	30.00
10FF	Andres Galarraga/44	12.00
11FF	Rafael Palmeiro/43	25.00
12FF	Alex Rodriguez/42	45.00
13FF	Mo Vaughn/40	12.00

Headliners

Complete Set (25):		10.00
Common Player:		.25
Inserted 1:4		
1H	Vladimir Guerrero	.40
2H	Randy Johnson	.40
3H	Mo Vaughn	.25
4H	Chipper Jones	.50
5H	Jeff Bagwell	.40
6H	Juan Gonzalez	.30
7H	Mark McGwire	.75
8H	Cal Ripken Jr.	1.00
9H	Frank Thomas	.40
10H	Manny Ramirez	.40
11H	Ken Griffey Jr.	.65
12H	Scott Rolen	.35
13H	Alex Rodriguez	.75
14H	Barry Bonds	1.00
15H	Roger Clemens	.55
16H	Darin Erstad	.30
17H	Nomar Garciaparra	.50
18H	Mike Piazza	.65
19H	Greg Maddux	.50
20H	Ivan Rodriguez	.35
21H	Derek Jeter	1.00
22H	Sammy Sosa	.50
23H	Andruw Jones	.40
24H	Pedro Martinez	.40
25H	Kerry Wood	.35

Ones To Watch

		NM/M
Complete Set (15):		5.00
Common Player:		.25
Inserted 1:12		
1OW	J.D. Drew	.65
2OW	Marlon Anderson	.25
3OW	Roy Halladay	.35
4OW	Ben Grieve	.25
5OW	Todd Helton	.75

ONES TO WATCH — ERIC CHAVEZ - 3B

6OW	Gabe Kapler	.25
7OW	Troy Glaus	.75
8OW	Ben Davis	.25
9OW	Eric Chavez	.35
10OW	Richie Sexson	.25
11OW	Fernando Seguignol	.25
12OW	Kerry Wood	.50
13OW	Bobby Smith	.25
14OW	Ryan Minor	.25
15OW	Jeremy Giambi	.25
	J.D. Drew/	
	Auto./250	15.00

1999 Sports Illustrated Greats of the Game

Frank Thomas — Outfield

		NM/M
Complete Set (90):		12.00
Common Player:		.05
Pack (7):		15.00
Wax Box (12):		150.00
1	Jimmie Foxx	.25
2	Red Schoendienst	.05
3	Babe Ruth	3.00
4	Lou Gehrig	2.00
5	Mel Ott	.05
6	Stan Musial	.05
7	Mickey Mantle	3.00
8	Carl Yastrzemski	.15
9	Enos Slaughter	.05
10	Andre Dawson	.05
11	Luis Aparicio	.05
12	Ferguson Jenkins	.05
13	Christy Mathewson	.25
14	Ernie Banks	.15
15	Johnny Podres	.05
16	George Foster	.05
17	Jerry Koosman	.05
18	Curt Simmons	.05
19	Bob Feller	.05
20	Frank Robinson	.05
21	Gary Carter	.05
22	Frank Thomas	.05
23	Bill Lee	.05
24	Willie Mays	1.00
25	Tommie Agee	.05
26	Boog Powell	.05
27	Jimmy Wynn	.05
28	Sparky Lyle	.05
29	Bo Belinsky	.05
30	Maury Wills	.05
31	Bill Buckner	.05
32	Steve Carlton	.05
33	Harmon Killebrew	.05
34	Nolan Ryan	1.00
35	Randy Jones	.05
36	Robin Roberts	.05
37	Al Oliver	.05
38	Rico Petrocelli	.05
39	Dave Parker	.05
40	Eddie Mathews	.05
41	Earl Weaver	.05
42	Jackie Robinson	1.50
43	Lou Brock	.05
44	Reggie Jackson	.15
45	Bob Gibson	.05
46	Jeff Burroughs	.05
47	Jim Bouton	.05
48	Bob Forsch	.05
49	Ron Guidry	.05
50	Ty Cobb	2.00
51	Roy White	.05
52	Joe Rudi	.05
53	Moose Skowron	.05
54	Goose Gossage	.05
55	Ed Kranepool	.05
56	Paul Blair	.05
57	Kent Hrbek	.05
58	Orlando Cepeda	.05
59	Buck O'Neil	.05
60	Al Kaline	.05
61	Vida Blue	.05
62	Sam McDowell	.05
63	Jesse Barfield	.05
64	Dave Kingman	.05
65	Ron Santo	.05
66	Steve Garvey	.05
67	Gaylord Perry	.05
68	Darrell Evans	.05
69	Rollie Fingers	.05
70	Walter Johnson	.25
71	Al Hrabosky	.05
72	Mickey Rivers	.05
73	Mike Torrez	.05
74	Hank Bauer	.05
75	Tug McGraw	.05
76	David Clyde	.05
77	Jim Lonborg	.05
78	Clete Boyer	.05
79	Harry Walker	.05
80	Cy Young	.25
81	Bud Harrelson	.05
82	Paul Splittorff	.05
83	Bert Campaneris	.05
84	Joe Niekro	.05
85	Bob Horner	.05
86	Jerry Royster	.05
87	Tommy John	.05
88	Mark Fidrych	.05
89	Dick Williams	.05
90	Graig Nettles	.05

Autographs

Bob Horner — Third Base

		NM/M
Common Player:		4.00
Inserted 1:1		
(1)	Tommie Agee	8.00
(2)	Luis Aparicio	12.00
(3)	Ernie Banks	25.00
(4)	Jesse Barfield	6.00
(5)	Hank Bauer	10.00
(6)	Bo Belinsky	6.00
(7)	Paul Blair	6.00
(8)	Vida Blue	10.00
(9)	Jim Bouton	10.00
(10)	Clete Boyer	10.00
(11)	Lou Brock	15.00
(12)	Bill Buckner	10.00
(13)	Jeff Burroughs	5.00
(14)	Bert Campaneris	8.00
(15)	Steve Carlton	20.00
(16)	Gary Carter	10.00
(17)	Orlando Cepeda	12.00
(18)	David Clyde	5.00
(19)	Andre Dawson	10.00
(20)	Darrell Evans	8.00
(21)	Bob Feller	15.00
(22)	Mark Fidrych	15.00
(23)	Rollie Fingers	10.00
(24)	Bob Forsch	6.00
(25)	George Foster	10.00
(26)	Steve Garvey	10.00
(27)	Bob Gibson	15.00
(28)	Goose Gossage	10.00
(29)	Ron Guidry	20.00
(30)	Bud Harrelson	10.00
(31)	Bob Horner	10.00
(32)	Al Hrabosky	8.00
(33)	Kent Hrbek	10.00
(34a)	Reggie Jackson	150.00
(34b)	Reggie Jackson ("Mr. October")	200.00
(34c)	Reggie Jackson ("HoF 93")	200.00
(35)	Ferguson Jenkins	10.00
(36)	Tommy John	8.00
(37)	Randy Jones	4.00
(38)	Al Kaline	25.00
(39)	Harmon Killebrew	25.00
(40)	Dave Kingman	8.00
(41)	Jerry Koosman	8.00
(42)	Ed Kranepool	8.00
(43)	Bill Lee	10.00
(44)	Jim Lonborg	5.00
(45)	Sparky Lyle	8.00
(46)	Eddie Mathews	60.00
(47)	Willie Mays	125.00
(48)	Sam McDowell	8.00
(49)	Tug McGraw	25.00
(50)	Stan Musial	100.00
(51)	Graig Nettles	10.00
(52)	Joe Niekro	8.00
(53)	Buck O'Neil	20.00
(54)	Al Oliver	10.00
(55)	Dave Parker	10.00
(56)	Gaylord Perry	10.00
(57)	Rico Petrocelli	10.00
(58)	Johnny Podres	20.00
(59)	Boog Powell	10.00
(60)	Mickey Rivers	8.00
(61)	Robin Roberts	20.00
(62)	Frank Robinson	20.00
(63)	Jerry Royster	4.00
(64)	Joe Rudi	8.00
(65)	Nolan Ryan	200.00
(66)	Ron Santo	15.00
(67)	Red Schoendienst	12.00
(68)	Curt Simmons	6.00
(69)	Moose Skowron	15.00
(70)	Enos Slaughter	20.00
(71)	Paul Splittorff	6.00
(72)	Frank Thomas	8.00
(73)	Mike Torrez	4.00
(74)	Harry Walker	4.00
(75)	Earl Weaver	10.00
(76)	Roy White	8.00
(77)	Dick Williams	10.00
(78)	Maury Wills	10.00
(79)	Jimmy Wynn	10.00
(80)	Carl Yastrzemski	50.00

Cover Collection

		NM/M
Complete Set (50):		25.00
Common Player:		.50
Inserted 1:1		
1	Johnny Podres	.50
2	Mickey Mantle	5.00
3	Stan Musial	.50
4	Eddie Mathews	.50
5	Frank Thomas	.50
6	Willie Mays	1.00
7	Red Schoendienst	.50
8	Luis Aparicio	.50
9	Mickey Mantle	3.00
10	Al Kaline	.50
11	Maury Wills	.50
12	Sam McDowell	.50
13	Harry Walker	.50
14	Carl Yastrzemski	.50
15	Carl Yastrzemski	.50
16	Lou Brock	.50
17	Ron Santo	.50
18	Reggie Jackson	.50
19	Frank Robinson	.50
20	Jerry Koosman	.50
21	Bud Harrelson	.50
22	Vida Blue	.50
23	Ferguson Jenkins	.50
24	Sparky Lyle	.50
25	Steve Carlton	.50
26	Bert Campaneris	.50
27	Jimmy Wynn	.50
28	Steve Garvey	.50
29	Nolan Ryan	1.00
30	Randy Jones	.50
31	Reggie Jackson	.50
32	Joe Rudi	.50
33	Reggie Jackson	.50
34	Dave Parker	.50
35	Mark Fidrych	.50
36	Earl Weaver	.50
37	Nolan Ryan	1.00
38	Steve Carlton	.50
39	Reggie Jackson	.50
40	Rollie Fingers	.50
41	Gary Carter	.50
42	Graig Nettles	.50
43	Gaylord Perry	.50
44	Kent Hrbek	.50
45	Gary Carter	.50
46	Steve Garvey	.50
47	Steve Carlton	.50
48	Nolan Ryan	1.00
49	Nolan Ryan	1.00
50	Mickey Mantle	3.00

Record Breakers

CHRISTY MATHEWSON — NEW YORK GIANTS • P

		NM/M
Complete Set (10):		40.00
Common Player:		2.00
Inserted 1:12		
Golds:		
Inserted 1:120		
Golds:		6X
1	Mickey Mantle	8.00
2	Stan Musial	3.50
3	Babe Ruth	8.00
4	Christy Mathewson	2.00
5	Cy Young	2.00
6	Nolan Ryan	7.50
7	Jackie Robinson	6.00
8	Lou Gehrig	7.00
9	Ty Cobb	3.50
10	Walter Johnson	2.00

1991 Stadium Club

		NM/M
Complete Set (600):		20.00
Common Player:		.05
Series 1 or 2 Pack (13):		.60
Series 1 or 2 Box (36):		15.00
1	Dave Stewart	.05
2	Wally Joyner	.05
3	Shawon Dunston	.05
4	Darren Daulton	.05
5	Will Clark	.05

No.	Player	Value
6	Sammy Sosa	1.00
7	Dan Plesac	.05
8	Marquis Grissom	.05
9	Erik Hanson	.05
10	Geno Petralli	.05
11	Jose Rijo	.05
12	Carlos Quintana	.05
13	Junior Ortiz	.05
14	Bob Walk	.05
15	Mike Macfarlane	.05
16	Eric Yelding	.05
17	Bryn Smith	.05
18	Bip Roberts	.05
19	Mike Scioscia	.05
20	Mark Williamson	.05
21	Don Mattingly	1.00
22	John Franco	.05
23	Chet Lemon	.05
24	Tom Henke	.05
25	Jerry Browne	.05
26	Dave Justice	.05
27	Mark Langston	.05
28	Damon Berryhill	.05
29	Kevin Bass	.05
30	Scott Fletcher	.05
31	Moises Alou	.05
32	Dave Valle	.05
33	Jody Reed	.05
34	Dave West	.05
35	Kevin McReynolds	.05
36	Pat Combs	.05
37	Eric Davis	.05
38	Bret Saberhagen	.05
39	Stan Javier	.05
40	Chuck Cary	.05
41	Tony Phillips	.05
42	Lee Smith	.05
43	Tim Teufel	.05
44	Lance Dickson	.05
45	Greg Litton	.05
46	Teddy Higuera	.05
47	Edgar Martinez	.05
48	Steve Avery	.05
49	Walt Weiss	.05
50	David Segui	.05
51	Andy Benes	.05
52	Karl Rhodes	.05
53	Neal Heaton	.05
54	Dan Gladden	.05
55	Luis Rivera	.05
56	Kevin Brown	.05
57	Frank Thomas	.75
58	Terry Mulholland	.05
59	Dick Schofield	.05
60	Ron Darling	.05
61	Sandy Alomar, Jr.	.05
62	Dave Stieb	.05
63	Alan Trammell	.05
64	Matt Nokes	.05
65	Lenny Harris	.05
66	Milt Thompson	.05
67	Storm Davis	.05
68	Joe Oliver	.05
69	Andres Galarraga	.05
70	Ozzie Guillen	.05
71	Ken Howell	.05
72	Garry Templeton	.05
73	Derrick May	.05
74	Xavier Hernandez	.05
75	Dave Parker	.05
76	Rick Aguilera	.05
77	Robby Thompson	.05
78	Pete Incaviglia	.05
79	Bob Welch	.05
80	Randy Milligan	.05
81	Chuck Finley	.05
82	Alvin Davis	.05
83	Tim Naehring	.05
84	Jay Bell	.05
85	Joe Magrane	.05
86	Howard Johnson	.05
87	Jack McDowell	.05
88	Kevin Seitzer	.05
89	Bruce Ruffin	.05
90	Fernando Valenzuela	.05
91	Terry Kennedy	.05
92	Barry Larkin	.05
93	Larry Walker	.05
94	Luis Salazar	.05
95	Gary Sheffield	.45
96	Bobby Witt	.05
97	Lonnie Smith	.05
98	Bryan Harvey	.05
99	Mookie Wilson	.05
100	Dwight Gooden	.05
101	Lou Whitaker	.05
102	Ron Karkovice	.05
103	Jesse Barfield	.05
104	Jose DeJesus	.05
105	Benito Santiago	.05
106	Brian Holman	.05
107	Rafael Ramirez	.05
108	Ellis Burks	.05
109	Mike Bielecki	.05
110	Kirby Puckett	1.00
111	Terry Shumpert	.05
112	Chuck Crim	.05
113	Todd Benzinger	.05
114	Brian Barnes	.05
115	Carlos Baerga	.05
116	Kal Daniels	.05
117	Dave Johnson	.05
118	Andy Van Slyke	.05
119	John Burkett	.05
120	Rickey Henderson	.75
121	Tim Jones	.05
122	Daryl Irvine	.05
123	Ruben Sierra	.05
124	Jim Abbott	.05
125	Daryl Boston	.05
126	Greg Maddux	1.00
127	Von Hayes	.05
128	Mike Fitzgerald	.05
129	Wayne Edwards	.05
130	Greg Briley	.05
131	Rob Dibble	.05
132	Gene Larkin	.05
133	David Wells	.05
134	Steve Balboni	.05
135	Greg Vaughn	.05
136	Mark Davis	.05
137	Dave Rohde	.05
138	Eric Show	.05
139	Bobby Bonilla	.05
140	Dana Kiecker	.05
141	Gary Pettis	.05
142	Dennis Boyd	.05
143	Mike Benjamin	.05
144	Luis Polonia	.05
145	Doug Jones	.05
146	Al Newman	.05
147	Alex Fernandez	.05
148	Bill Doran	.05
149	Kevin Elster	.05
150	Len Dykstra	.05
151	Mike Gallego	.05
152	Tim Belcher	.05
153	Jay Buhner	.05
154	Ozzie Smith	1.00
155	Jose Canseco	.50
156	Gregg Olson	.05
157	Charlie O'Brien	.05
158	Frank Tanana	.05
159	George Brett	1.00
160	Jeff Huson	.05
161	Kevin Tapani	.05
162	Jerome Walton	.05
163	Charlie Hayes	.05
164	Chris Bosio	.05
165	Chris Sabo	.05
166	Lance Parrish	.05
167	Don Robinson	.05
168	Manuel Lee	.05
169	Dennis Rasmussen	.05
170	Wade Boggs	1.00
171	Bob Geren	.05
172	Mackey Sasser	.05
173	Julio Franco	.05
174	Otis Nixon	.05
175	Bert Blyleven	.05
176	Craig Biggio	.05
177	Eddie Murray	.75
178	Randy Tomlin	.05
179	Tino Martinez	.05
180	Carlton Fisk	.75
181	Dwight Smith	.05
182	Scott Garrelts	.05
183	Jim Gantner	.05
184	Dickie Thon	.05
185	John Farrell	.05
186	Cecil Fielder	.05
187	Glenn Braggs	.05
188	Allan Anderson	.05
189	Kurt Stillwell	.05
190	Jose Oquendo	.05
191	Joe Orsulak	.05
192	Ricky Jordan	.05
193	Kelly Downs	.05
194	Delino DeShields	.05
195	Omar Vizquel	.05
196	Mark Carreon	.05
197	Mike Harkey	.05
198	Jack Howell	.05
199	Lance Johnson	.05
200	Nolan Ryan	2.00
201	John Marzano	.05
202	Doug Drabek	.05
203	Mark Lemke	.05
204	Steve Sax	.05
205	Greg Harris	.05
206	B.J. Surhoff	.05
207	Todd Burns	.05
208	Jose Gonzalez	.05
209	Mike Scott	.05
210	Dave Magadan	.05
211	Dante Bichette	.05
212	Trevor Wilson	.05
213	Hector Villanueva	.05
214	Dan Pasqua	.05
215	Greg Colbrunn	.05
216	Mike Jeffcoat	.05
217	Harold Reynolds	.05
218	Paul O'Neill	.05
219	Mark Guthrie	.05
220	Barry Bonds	2.00
221	Jimmy Key	.05
222	Billy Ripken	.05
223	Tom Pagnozzi	.05
224	Bo Jackson	.10
225	Sid Fernandez	.05
226	Mike Marshall	.05
227	John Kruk	.05
228	Mike Fetters	.05
229	Eric Anthony	.05
230	Ryne Sandberg	1.00
231	Carney Lansford	.05
232	Melido Perez	.05
233	Jose Lind	.05
234	Darryl Hamilton	.05
235	Tom Browning	.05
236	Spike Owen	.05
237	Juan Gonzalez	.40
238	Felix Fermin	.05
239	Keith Miller	.05
240	Mark Gubicza	.05
241	Kent Anderson	.05
242	Alvaro Espinoza	.05
243	Dale Murphy	.20
244	Orel Hershiser	.05
245	Paul Molitor	.75
246	Eddie Whitson	.05
247	Joe Girardi	.05
248	Kent Hrbek	.05
249	Bill Sampen	.05
250	Kevin Mitchell	.05
251	Mariano Duncan	.05
252	Scott Bradley	.05
253	Mike Greenwell	.05
254	Tom Gordon	.05
255	Todd Zeile	.05
256	Bobby Thigpen	.05
257	Gregg Jefferies	.05
258	Kenny Rogers	.05
259	Shane Mack	.05
260	Zane Smith	.05
261	Mitch Williams	.05
262	Jim DeShaies	.05
263	Dave Winfield	.75
264	Ben McDonald	.05
265	Randy Ready	.05
266	Pat Borders	.05
267	Jose Uribe	.05
268	Derek Lilliquist	.05
269	Greg Brock	.05
270	Ken Griffey Jr.	1.25
271	Jeff Gray	.05
272	Danny Tartabull	.05
273	Dennis Martinez	.05
274	Robin Ventura	.05
275	Randy Myers	.05
276	Jack Daugherty	.05
277	Greg Gagne	.05
278	Jay Howell	.05
279	Mike LaValliere	.05
280	Rex Hudler	.05
281	Mike Simms	.05
282	Kevin Maas	.05
283	Jeff Ballard	.05
284	Dave Henderson	.05
285	Pete O'Brien	.05
286	Brook Jacoby	.05
287	Mike Henneman	.05
288	Greg Olson	.05
289	Greg Myers	.05
290	Mark Grace	.05
291	Shawn Abner	.05
292	Frank Viola	.05
293	Lee Stevens	.05
294	Jason Grimsley	.05
295	Matt Williams	.05
296	Ron Robinson	.05
297	Tom Brunansky	.05
298	Checklist	.05
299	Checklist	.05
300	Checklist	.05
301	Darryl Strawberry	.05
302	Bud Black	.05
303	Harold Baines	.05
304	Roberto Alomar	.20
305	Norm Charlton	.05
306	Gary Thurman	.05
307	Mike Felder	.05
308	Tony Gwynn	1.00
309	Roger Clemens	1.00
310	Andre Dawson	.25
311	Scott Radinsky	.05
312	Bob Melvin	.05
313	Kirk McCaskill	.05
314	Pedro Guerrero	.05
315	Walt Terrell	.05
316	Sam Horn	.05
317	Wes Chamberlain RC	.05
318	Pedro Munoz RC	.05
319	Roberto Kelly	.05
320	Mark Portugal	.05
321	Tim McIntosh	.05
322	Jesse Orosco	.05
323	Gary Green	.05
324	Greg Harris	.05
325	Hubie Brooks	.05
326	Chris Nabholz	.05
327	Terry Pendleton	.05
328	Eric King	.05
329	Chili Davis	.05
330	Anthony Telford	.05
331	Kelly Gruber	.05
332	Dennis Eckersley	.65
333	Mel Hall	.05
334	Bob Kipper	.05
335	Willie McGee	.05
336	Steve Olin	.05
337	Steve Buechele	.05
338	Scott Leius	.05
339	Hal Morris	.05
340	Jose Offerman	.05
341	Kent Mercker	.05
342	Ken Griffey	.05
343	Pete Harnisch	.05
344	Kirk Gibson	.05
345	Dave Smith	.05
346	Dave Martinez	.05
347	Atlee Hammaker	.05
348	Brian Downing	.05
349	Todd Hundley	.05
350	Candy Maldonado	.05
351	Dwight Evans	.05
352	Steve Searcy	.05
353	Gary Gaetti	.05
354	Jeff Reardon	.05
355	Travis Fryman	.05
356	Dave Righetti	.05
357	Fred McGriff	.05
358	Don Slaught	.05
359	Gene Nelson	.05
360	Billy Spiers	.05
361	Lee Guetterman	.05
362	Darren Lewis	.05
363	Duane Ward	.05
364	Lloyd Moseby	.05
365	John Smoltz	.05
366	Felix Jose	.05
367	David Cone	.05
368	Wally Backman	.05
369	Jeff Montgomery	.05
370	Rich Garces	.05
371	Billy Hatcher	.05
372	Bill Swift	.05
373	Jim Eisenreich	.05
374	Rob Ducey	.05
375	Tim Crews	.05
376	Steve Finley	.05
377	Jeff Blauser	.05
378	Willie Wilson	.05
379	Gerald Perry	.05
380	Jose Mesa	.05
381	Pat Kelly	.05
382	Matt Merullo	.05
383	Ivan Calderon	.05
384	Scott Chiamparino	.05
385	Lloyd McClendon	.05
386	Dave Bergman	.05
387	Ed Sprague	.05
388	Jeff Bagwell RC	3.00
389	Brett Butler	.05
390	Larry Andersen	.05
391	Glenn Davis	.05
392	Alex Cole (Photo is Otis Nixon.)	.05
393	Mike Heath	.05
394	Danny Darwin	.05
395	Steve Lake	.05
396	Tim Layana	.05
397	Terry Leach	.05
398	Bill Wegman	.05
399	Mark McGwire	1.50
400	Mike Boddicker	.05
401	Steve Howe	.05
402	Bernard Gilkey	.05
403	Thomas Howard	.05
404	Rafael Belliard	.05
405	Tom Candiotti	.05
406	Rene Gonzalez	.05
407	Chuck McElroy	.05
408	Paul Sorrento	.05
409	Randy Johnson	.75
410	Brady Anderson	.05
411	Dennis Cook	.05
412	Mickey Tettleton	.05
413	Mike Stanton	.05
414	Ken Oberkfell	.05
415	Rick Honeycutt	.05
416	Nelson Santovenia	.05
417	Bob Tewksbury	.05
418	Brent Mayne	.05

ABBREVIATIONS

OPS - Overprint
"Promotional Sample"
SP - Short Print

419	Steve Farr	.05
420	Phil Stephenson	.05
421	Jeff Russell	.05
422	Chris James	.05
423	Tim Leary	.05
424	Gary Carter	.75
425	Glenallen Hill	.05
426	Matt Young	.05
427	Sid Bream	.05
428	Greg Swindell	.05
429	Scott Aldred	.05
430	Cal Ripken, Jr.	2.00
431	Bill Landrum	.05
432	Ernie Riles	.05
433	Danny Jackson	.05
434	Casey Candaele	.05
435	Ken Hill	.05
436	Jaime Navarro	.05
437	Lance Blankenship	.05
438	Randy Velarde	.05
439	Frank DiPino	.05
440	Carl Nichols	.05
441	Jeff Robinson	.05
442	Deion Sanders	.05
443	Vincente Palacios	.05
444	Devon White	.05
445	John Cerutti	.05
446	Tracy Jones	.05
447	Jack Morris	.05
448	Mitch Webster	.05
449	Bob Ojeda	.05
450	Oscar Azocar	.05
451	Luis Aquino	.05
452	Mark Whiten	.05
453	Stan Belinda	.05
454	Ron Gant	.05
455	Jose DeLeon	.05
456	Mark Salas	.05
457	Junior Felix	.05
458	Wally Whitehurst	.05
459	Phil Plantier RC	.05
460	Juan Berenguer	.05
461	Franklin Stubbs	.05
462	Joe Boever	.05
463	Tim Wallach	.05
464	Mike Moore	.05
465	Albert Belle	.05
466	Mike Witt	.05
467	Craig Worthington	.05
468	Jerald Clark	.05
469	Scott Terry	.05
470	Milt Cuyler	.05
471	John Smiley	.05
472	Charles Nagy	.05
473	Alan Mills	.05
474	John Russell	.05
475	Bruce Hurst	.05
476	Andujar Cedeno	.05
477	Dave Eiland	.05
478	Brian McRae RC	.10
479	Mike LaCoss	.05
480	Chris Gwynn	.05
481	Jamie Moyer	.05
482	John Olerud	.05
483	Efrain Valdez	.05
484	Sil Campusano	.05
485	Pascual Perez	.05
486	Gary Redus	.05
487	Andy Hawkins	.05
488	Cory Snyder	.05
489	Chris Hoiles	.05
490	Ron Hassey	.05
491	Gary Wayne	.05
492	Mark Lewis	.05
493	Scott Coolbaugh	.05
494	Gerald Young	.05
495	Juan Samuel	.05
496	Willie Fraser	.05
497	Jeff Treadway	.05
498	Vince Coleman	.05
499	Cris Carpenter	.05
500	Jack Clark	.05
501	Kevin Appier	.05
502	Rafael Palmeiro	.65
503	Hensley Meulens	.05
504	George Bell	.05
505	Tony Pena	.05
506	Roger McDowell	.05
507	Luis Sojo	.05
508	Mike Schooler	.05
509	Robin Yount	.75
510	Jack Armstrong	.05
511	Rick Cerone	.05
512	Curt Wilkerson	.05
513	Joe Carter	.05
514	Tim Burke	.05
515	Tony Fernandez	.05
516	Ramon Martinez	.05
517	Tim Hulett	.05
518	Tim Steinbach	.05
519	Pete Smith	.05
520	Ken Caminiti	.05
521	Shawn Boskie	.05
522	Mike Pagliarulo	.05

523	Tim Raines	.05
524	Alfredo Griffin	.05
525	Henry Cotto	.05
526	Mike Stanley	.05
527	Charlie Leibrandt	.05
528	Jeff King	.05
529	Eric Plunk	.05
530	Tom Lampkin	.05
531	Steve Bedrosian	.05
532	Tom Herr	.05
533	Craig Lefferts	.05
534	Jeff Reed	.05
535	Mickey Morandini	.05
536	Greg Cadaret	.05
537	Ray Lankford	.05
538	John Candelaria	.05
539	Rob Deer	.05
540	Brad Arnsberg	.05
541	Mike Sharperson	.05
542	Jeff Robinson	.05
543	Mo Vaughn	.05
544	Jeff Parrett	.05
545	Willie Randolph	.05
546	Herm Winningham	.05
547	Jeff Innis	.05
548	Chuck Knoblauch	.05
549	Tommy Greene	.05
550	Jeff Hamilton	.05
551	Barry Jones	.05
552	Ken Dayley	.05
553	Rick Dempsey	.05
554	Greg Smith	.05
555	Mike Devereaux	.05
556	Keith Comstock	.05
557	Paul Faries	.05
558	Tom Glavine	.35
559	Craig Grebeck	.05
560	Scott Erickson	.05
561	Joel Skinner	.05
562	Mike Morgan	.05
563	Dave Gallagher	.05
564	Todd Stottlemyre	.05
565	Rich Rodriguez	.05
566	Craig Wilson RC	.05
567	Jeff Brantley	.05
568	Scott Kamieniecki	.05
569	Steve Decker	.05
570	Juan Agosto	.05
571	Tommy Gregg	.05
572	Kevin Wickander	.05
573	Jamie Quirk	.05
574	Jerry Don Gleaton	.05
575	Chris Hammond	.05
576	Luis Gonzalez RC	1.00
577	Russ Swan	.05
578	Jeff Conine RC	.50
579	Charlie Hough	.05
580	Jeff Kunkel	.05
581	Darrel Akerfelds	.05
582	Jeff Manto	.05
583	Alejandro Pena	.05
584	Mark Davidson	.05
585	Bob MacDonald	.05
586	Paul Assenmacher	.05
587	Dan Wilson	.05
588	Tom Bolton	.05
589	Brian Harper	.05
590	John Habyan	.05
591	John Orton	.05
592	Mark Gardner	.05
593	Turner Ward	.05
594	Bob Patterson	.05
595	Edwin Nunez	.05
596	Gary Scott	.05
597	Scott Bankhead	.05
598	Checklist	.05
599	Checklist	.05
600	Checklist	.05

1992 Stadium Club

KENNY LOFTON

	NM/M
Complete Set (900):	20.00
Common Player:	.05
Series 1, 2, 3 Pack (15):	.75
Series 1, 2, 3 Box (36):	15.00

1	Cal Ripken, Jr.	1.50
2	Eric Yelding	.05
3	Geno Petralli	.05
4	Wally Backman	.05
5	Milt Cuyler	.05
6	Kevin Bass	.05
7	Dante Bichette	.05
8	Ray Lankford	.05
9	Mel Hall	.05
10	Joe Carter	.05
11	Juan Samuel	.05
12	Jeff Montgomery	.05
13	Glenn Braggs	.05
14	Henry Cotto	.05
15	Deion Sanders	.05
16	Dick Schofield	.05
17	David Cone	.05
18	Chili Davis	.05
19	Tom Foley	.05
20	Ozzie Guillen	.05
21	Luis Salazar	.05
22	Terry Steinbach	.05
23	Chris James	.05
24	Jeff King	.05
25	Carlos Quintana	.05
26	Mike Maddux	.05
27	Tommy Greene	.05
28	Jeff Russell	.05
29	Steve Finley	.05
30	Mike Flanagan	.05
31	Darren Lewis	.05
32	Mark Lee	.05
33	Willie Fraser	.05
34	Mike Henneman	.05
35	Kevin Maas	.05
36	Dave Hansen	.05
37	Erik Hanson	.05
38	Bill Doran	.05
39	Mike Boddicker	.05
40	Vince Coleman	.05
41	Devon White	.05
42	Mark Gardner	.05
43	Scott Lewis	.05
44	Juan Berenguer	.05
45	Carney Lansford	.05
46	Curt Wilkerson	.05
47	Shane Mack	.05
48	Bip Roberts	.05
49	Greg Harris	.05
50	Ryne Sandberg	.75
51	Mark Whiten	.05
52	Jack McDowell	.05
53	Jimmy Jones	.05
54	Steve Lake	.05
55	Bud Black	.05
56	Dave Valle	.05
57	Kevin Reimer	.05
58	Rich Gedman	.05
59	Travis Fryman	.05
60	Steve Avery	.05
61	Francisco de la Rosa	.05
62	Scott Hemond	.05
63	Hal Morris	.05
64	Hensley Meulens	.05
65	Frank Castillo	.05
66	Gene Larkin	.05
67	Jose DeLeon	.05
68	Al Osuna	.05
69	Dave Cochrane	.05
70	Robin Ventura	.05
71	John Cerutti	.05
72	Kevin Gross	.05
73	Ivan Calderon	.05
74	Mike Macfarlane	.05
75	Stan Belinda	.05
76	Shawn Hillegas	.05

77	Pat Borders	.05
78	Jim Vatcher	.05
79	Bobby Rose	.05
80	Roger Clemens	.85
81	Craig Worthington	.05
82	Jeff Treadway	.05
83	Jamie Quirk	.05
84	Randy Bush	.05
85	Anthony Young	.05
86	Trevor Wilson	.05
87	Jaime Navarro	.05
88	Les Lancaster	.05
89	Pat Kelly	.05
90	Alvin Davis	.05
91	Larry Andersen	.05
92	Rob Deer	.05
93	Mike Sharperson	.05
94	Lance Parrish	.05
95	Cecil Espy	.05
96	Tim Spehr	.05
97	Dave Stieb	.05
98	Terry Mulholland	.05
99	Dennis Boyd	.05
100	Barry Larkin	.05
101	Ryan Bowen	.05
102	Felix Fermin	.05
103	Luis Alicea	.05
104	Tim Hulett	.05
105	Rafael Belliard	.05
106	Mike Gallego	.05
107	Dave Righetti	.05
108	Jeff Schaefer	.05
109	Ricky Bones	.05
110	Scott Erickson	.05
111	Matt Nokes	.05
112	Bob Scanlan	.05
113	Tom Candiotti	.05
114	Sean Berry	.05
115	Kevin Morton	.05
116	Scott Fletcher	.05
117	B.J. Surhoff	.05
118	Dave Magadan	.05
119	Bill Gullickson	.05
120	Marquis Grissom	.05
121	Lenny Harris	.05
122	Wally Joyner	.05
123	Kevin Brown	.05
124	Braulio Castillo	.05
125	Eric King	.05
126	Mark Portugal	.05
127	Calvin Jones	.05
128	Mike Heath	.05
129	Todd Van Poppel	.05
130	Benny Santiago	.05
131	Gary Thurman	.05
132	Joe Girardi	.05
133	Dave Eiland	.05
134	Orlando Merced	.05
135	Joe Orsulak	.05
136	John Burkett	.05
137	Ken Dayley	.05
138	Ken Hill	.05
139	Walt Terrell	.05
140	Mike Scioscia	.05
141	Junior Felix	.05
142	Ken Caminiti	.05
143	Carlos Baerga	.05
144	Tony Fossas	.05
145	Craig Grebeck	.05
146	Scott Bradley	.05
147	Kent Mercker	.05
148	Derrick May	.05
149	Jerald Clark	.05
150	George Brett	.85
151	Luis Quinones	.05
152	Mike Pagliarulo	.05
153	Jose Guzman	.05
154	Charlie O'Brien	.05
155	Darren Holmes	.05
156	Joe Boever	.05
157	Rich Monteleone	.05
158	Reggie Harris	.05
159	Roberto Alomar	.20
160	Robby Thompson	.05
161	Chris Hoiles	.05
162	Tom Pagnozzi	.05
163	Omar Vizquel	.05
164	John Candelaria	.05
165	Terry Shumpert	.05
166	Andy Mota	.05
167	Scott Bailes	.05
168	Jeff Blauser	.05
169	Steve Olin	.05
170	Doug Drabek	.05
171	Dave Bergman	.05
172	Eddie Whitson	.05
173	Gilberto Reyes	.05
174	Mark Grace	.05
175	Paul O'Neill	.05
176	Greg Cadaret	.05
177	Mark Williamson	.05
178	Casey Candaele	.05
179	Candy Maldonado	.05
180	Lee Smith	.05

Nolan Ryan Bronze

CHARTER MEMBER

	NM/M
Nolan Ryan/Bronze	15.00

#	Player	Value		#	Player	Value		#	Player	Value		#	Player	Value
181	Harold Reynolds	.05		285	Kevin Seitzer	.05		387	Ruben Sierra	.05		491	Andres Santana	.05
182	Dave Justice	.05		286	Stan Royer	.05		388	Tom Gordon	.05		492	Chris Beasley	.05
183	Lenny Webster	.05		287	John Dopson	.05		389	Charles Nagy	.05		493	Mike Timlin	.05
184	Donn Pall	.05		288	Scott Bullett	.05		390	Dave Stewart	.05		494	Brian Downing	.05
185	Gerald Alexander	.05		289	Ken Patterson	.05		391	Pete Harnisch	.05		495	Kirk Gibson	.05
186	Jack Clark	.05		290	Todd Hundley	.05		392	Tim Burke	.05		496	Scott Sanderson	.05
187	Stan Javier	.05		291	Tim Leary	.05		393	Roberto Kelly	.05		497	Nick Esasky	.05
188	Ricky Jordan	.05		292	Brett Butler	.05		394	Freddie Benavides	.05		498	Johnny Guzman RC	.05
189	Franklin Stubbs	.05		293	Gregg Olson	.05		395	Tom Glavine	.35		499	Mitch Williams	.05
190	Dennis Eckersley	.60		294	Jeff Brantley	.05		396	Wes Chamberlain	.05		500	Kirby Puckett	.75
191	Danny Tartabull	.05		295	Brian Holman	.05		397	Eric Gunderson	.05		501	Mike Harkey	.05
192	Pete O'Brien	.05		296	Brian Harper	.05		398	Dave West	.05		502	Jim Gantner	.05
193	Mark Lewis	.05		297	Brian Bohanon	.05		399	Ellis Burks	.05		503	Bruce Egloff	.05
194	Mike Felder	.05		298	Checklist 1-100	.05		400	Ken Griffey Jr.	1.00		504	Josias Manzanillo	.05
195	Mickey Tettleton	.05		299	Checklist 101-200	.05		401	Thomas Howard	.05		505	Delino DeShields	.05
196	Dwight Smith	.05		300	Checklist 201-300	.05		402	Juan Guzman	.05		506	Rheal Cormier	.05
197	Shawn Abner	.05		301	Frank Thomas	.65		403	Mitch Webster	.05		507	Jay Bell	.05
198	Jim Leyritz	.05		302	Lloyd McClendon	.05		404	Matt Merullo	.05		508	Rich Rowland	.05
199	Mike Devereaux	.05		303	Brady Anderson	.05		405	Steve Buechele	.05		509	Scott Servais	.05
200	Craig Biggio	.05		304	Julio Valera	.05		406	Danny Jackson	.05		510	Terry Pendleton	.05
201	Kevin Elster	.05		305	Mike Aldrete	.05		407	Felix Jose	.05		511	Rich DeLucia	.05
202	Rance Mulliniks	.05		306	Joe Oliver	.05		408	Doug Piatt	.05		512	Warren Newson	.05
203	Tony Fernandez	.05		307	Todd Stottlemyre	.05		409	Jim Eisenreich	.05		513	Paul Faries	.05
204	Allan Anderson	.05		308	Rey Sanchez	.05		410	Bryan Harvey	.05		514	Kal Daniels	.05
205	Herm Winningham	.05		309	Gary Sheffield	.35		411	Jim Austin	.05		515	Jarvis Brown	.05
206	Tim Jones	.05		310	Andujar Cedeno	.05		412	Jim Poole	.05		516	Rafael Palmeiro	.60
207	Ramon Martinez	.05		311	Kenny Rogers	.05		413	Glenallen Hill	.05		517	Kelly Downs	.05
208	Teddy Higuera	.05		312	Bruce Hurst	.05		414	Gene Nelson	.05		518	Steve Chitren	.05
209	John Kruk	.05		313	Mike Schooler	.05		415	Ivan Rodriguez	.60		519	Moises Alou	.05
210	Jim Abbott	.05		314	Mike Benjamin	.05		416	Frank Tanana	.05		520	Wade Boggs	.75
211	Dean Palmer	.05		315	Chuck Finley	.05		417	Steve Decker	.05		521	Pete Schourek	.05
212	Mark Davis	.05		316	Mark Lemke	.05		418	Jason Grimsley	.05		522	Scott Terry	.05
213	Jay Buhner	.05		317	Scott Livingstone	.05		419	Tim Layana	.05		523	Kevin Appier	.05
214	Jesse Barfield	.05		318	Chris Nabholz	.05		420	Don Mattingly	.85		524	Gary Redus	.05
215	Kevin Mitchell	.05		319	Mike Humphreys	.05		421	Jerome Walton	.05		525	George Bell	.05
216	Mike LaValliere	.05		320	Pedro Guerrero	.05		422	Rob Ducey	.05		526	Jeff Kaiser	.05
217	Mark Wohlers	.05		321	Willie Banks	.05		423	Andy Benes	.05		527	Alvaro Espinoza	.05
218	Dave Henderson	.05		322	Tom Goodwin	.05		424	John Marzano	.05		528	Luis Polonia	.05
219	Dave Smith	.05		323	Hector Wagner	.05		425	Gene Harris	.05		529	Darren Daulton	.05
220	Albert Belle	.05		324	Wally Ritchie	.05		426	Tim Raines	.05		530	Norm Charlton	.05
221	Spike Owen	.05		325	Mo Vaughn	.05		427	Bret Barberie	.05		531	John Olerud	.05
222	Jeff Gray	.05		326	Joe Klink	.05		428	Harvey Pulliam	.05		532	Dan Plesac	.05
223	Paul Gibson	.05		327	Cal Eldred	.05		429	Cris Carpenter	.05		533	Billy Ripken	.05
224	Bobby Thigpen	.05		328	Daryl Boston	.05		430	Howard Johnson	.05		534	Rod Nichols	.05
225	Mike Mussina	.30		329	Mike Huff	.05		431	Orel Hershiser	.05		535	Joey Cora	.05
226	Darrin Jackson	.05		330	Jeff Bagwell	.65		432	Brian Hunter	.05		536	Harold Baines	.05
227	Luis Gonzalez	.05		331	Bob Milacki	.05		433	Kevin Tapani	.05		537	Bob Ojeda	.05
228	Greg Briley	.05		332	Tom Prince	.05		434	Rick Reed	.05		538	Mark Leonard	.05
229	Brent Mayne	.05		333	Pat Tabler	.05		435	Ron Witmeyer	.05		539	Danny Darwin	.05
230	Paul Molitor	.65		334	Ced Landrum	.05		436	Gary Gaetti	.05		540	Shawon Dunston	.05
231	Al Leiter	.05		335	Reggie Jefferson	.05		437	Alex Cole	.05		541	Pedro Munoz	.05
232	Andy Van Slyke	.05		336	Mo Sanford	.05		438	Chito Martinez	.05		542	Mark Gubicza	.05
233	Ron Tingley	.05		337	Kevin Ritz	.05		439	Greg Litton	.05		543	Kevin Baez	.05
234	Bernard Gilkey	.05		338	Gerald Perry	.05		440	Julio Franco	.05		544	Todd Zeile	.05
235	Kent Hrbek	.05		339	Jeff Hamilton	.05		441	Mike Munoz	.05		545	Don Slaught	.05
236	Eric Karros	.05		340	Tim Wallach	.05		442	Erik Pappas	.05		546	Tony Eusebio	.05
237	Randy Velarde	.05		341	Jeff Huson	.05		443	Pat Combs	.05		547	Alonzo Powell	.05
238	Andy Allanson	.05		342	Jose Melendez	.05		444	Lance Johnson	.05		548	Gary Pettis	.05
239	Willie McGee	.05		343	Willie Wilson	.05		445	Ed Sprague	.05		549	Brian Barnes	.05
240	Juan Gonzalez	.35		344	Mike Stanton	.05		446	Mike Greenwell	.05		550	Lou Whitaker	.05
241	Karl Rhodes	.05		345	Joel Johnston	.05		447	Milt Thompson	.05		551	Keith Mitchell	.05
242	Luis Mercedes	.05		346	Lee Guetterman	.05		448	Mike Magnante	.05		552	Oscar Azocar	.05
243	Billy Swift	.05		347	Francisco Olivares	.05		449	Chris Haney	.05		553	Stu Cole	.05
244	Tommy Gregg	.05		348	Dave Burba	.05		450	Robin Yount	.65		554	Steve Wapnick	.05
245	David Howard	.05		349	Tim Crews	.05		451	Rafael Ramirez	.05		555	Derek Bell	.05
246	Dave Hollins	.05		350	Scott Leius	.05		452	Gino Minutelli	.05		556	Luis Lopez	.05
247	Kip Gross	.05		351	Danny Cox	.05		453	Tom Lampkin	.05		557	Anthony Telford	.05
248	Walt Weiss	.05		352	Wayne Housie	.05		454	Tony Perezchica	.05		558	Tim Mauser	.05
249	Mackey Sasser	.05		353	Chris Donnels	.05		455	Dwight Gooden	.05		559	Glenn Sutko	.05
250	Cecil Fielder	.05		354	Chris George	.05		456	Mark Guthrie	.05		560	Darryl Strawberry	.05
251	Jerry Browne	.05		355	Gerald Young	.05		457	Jay Howell	.05		561	Tom Bolton	.05
252	Doug Dascenzo	.05		356	Roberto Hernandez	.05		458	Gary DiSarcina	.05		562	Cliff Young	.05
253	Darryl Hamilton	.05		357	Neal Heaton	.05		459	John Smoltz	.05		563	Bruce Walton	.05
254	Dann Bilardello	.05		358	Todd Frohwirth	.05		460	Will Clark	.05		564	Chico Walker	.05
255	Luis Rivera	.05		359	Jose Vizcaino	.05		461	Dave Otto	.05		565	John Franco	.05
256	Larry Walker	.05		360	Jim Thome	.60		462	Rob Maurer	.05		566	Paul McClellan	.05
257	Ron Karkovice	.05		361	Craig Wilson	.05		463	Dwight Evans	.05		567	Paul Abbott	.05
258	Bob Tewksbury	.05		362	Dave Haas	.05		464	Tom Brunansky	.05		568	Gary Varsho	.05
259	Jimmy Key	.05		363	Billy Hatcher	.05		465	Shawn Hare RC	.05		569	Carlos Maldonado	.05
260	Bernie Williams	.05		364	John Barfield	.05		466	Geronimo Pena	.05		570	Kelly Gruber	.05
261	Gary Wayne	.05		365	Luis Aquino	.05		467	Alex Fernandez	.05		571	Jose Oquendo	.05
262	Mike Simms	.05		366	Charlie Leibrandt	.05		468	Greg Myers	.05		572	Steve Frey	.05
263	John Orton	.05		367	Howard Farmer	.05		469	Jeff Fassero	.05		573	Tino Martinez	.05
264	Marvin Freeman	.05		368	Bryn Smith	.05		470	Len Dykstra	.05		574	Bill Haselman	.05
265	Mike Jeffcoat	.05		369	Mickey Morandini	.05		471	Jeff Johnson	.05		575	Eric Anthony	.05
266	Roger Mason	.05		370	Jose Canseco (Members Choice, should have been #597.)	.35		472	Russ Swan	.05		576	John Habyan	.05
267	Edgar Martinez	.05						473	Archie Corbin	.05		577	Jeffrey McNeely	.05
268	Henry Rodriguez	.05						474	Chuck McElroy	.05		578	Chris Bosio	.05
269	Sam Horn	.05		371	Jose Uribe	.05		475	Mark McGwire	1.25		579	Joe Grahe	.05
270	Brian McRae	.05		372	Bob MacDonald	.05		476	Wally Whitehurst	.05		580	Fred McGriff	.05
271	Kirt Manwaring	.05		373	Luis Sojo	.05		477	Tim McIntosh	.05		581	Rick Honeycutt	.05
272	Mike Bordick	.05		374	Craig Shipley	.05		478	Sid Bream	.05		582	Matt Williams	.05
273	Chris Sabo	.05		375	Scott Bankhead	.05		479	Jeff Juden	.05		583	Cliff Brantley	.05
274	Jim Olander	.05		376	Greg Gagne	.05		480	Carlton Fisk	.65		584	Rob Dibble	.05
275	Greg Harris	.05		377	Scott Cooper	.05		481	Jeff Plympton	.05		585	Skeeter Barnes	.05
276	Dan Gakeler	.05		378	Jose Offerman	.05		482	Carlos Martinez	.05		586	Greg Hibbard	.05
277	Bill Sampen	.05		379	Billy Spiers	.05		483	Jim Gott	.05		587	Randy Milligan	.05
278	Joel Skinner	.05		380	John Smiley	.05		484	Bob McClure	.05		588	Checklist 301-400	.05
279	Curt Schilling	.35		381	Jeff Carter	.05		485	Tim Teufel	.05		589	Checklist 401-500	.05
280	Dale Murphy	.25		382	Heathcliff Slocumb	.05		486	Vicente Palacios	.05		590	Checklist 501-600	.05
281	Lee Stevens	.05		383	Jeff Tackett	.05		487	Jeff Reed	.05		591	Frank Thomas	.35
282	Lonnie Smith	.05		384	John Kiely	.05		488	Tony Phillips	.05		592	Dave Justice	.05
283	Manuel Lee	.05		385	John Vander Wal	.05		489	Mel Rojas	.05		593	Roger Clemens	.45
284	Shawn Boskie	.05		386	Omar Olivares	.05		490	Ben McDonald	.05		594	Steve Avery	.05

595 Cal Ripken, Jr.	.75	
596 Barry Larkin	.05	
597 Not issued (See #370)	.05	
598 Will Clark	.05	
599 Cecil Fielder	.05	
600 Ryne Sandberg	.40	
601 Chuck Knoblauch	.05	
602 Dwight Gooden	.05	
603 Ken Griffey Jr.	.65	
604 Barry Bonds	.75	
605 Nolan Ryan	.75	
606 Jeff Bagwell	.35	
607 Robin Yount	.30	
608 Bobby Bonilla	.05	
609 George Brett	.50	
610 Howard Johnson	.05	
611 Esteban Beltre	.05	
612 Mike Christopher	.05	
613 Troy Afenir	.05	
614 Mariano Duncan	.05	
615 Doug Henry	.05	
616 Doug Jones	.05	
617 Alvin Davis	.05	
618 Craig Lefferts	.05	
619 Kevin McReynolds	.05	
620 Barry Bonds	1.50	
621 Turner Ward	.05	
622 Joe Magrane	.05	
623 Mark Parent	.05	
624 Tom Browning	.05	
625 John Smiley	.05	
626 Steve Wilson	.05	
627 Mike Gallego	.05	
628 Sammy Sosa	.75	
629 Rico Rossy	.05	
630 Royce Clayton	.05	
631 Clay Parker	.05	
632 Pete Smith	.05	
633 Jeff McKnight	.05	
634 Jack Daugherty	.05	
635 Steve Sax	.05	
636 Joe Hesketh	.05	
637 Vince Horsman	.05	
638 Eric King	.05	
639 Joe Boever	.05	
640 Jack Morris	.05	
641 Arthur Rhodes	.05	
642 Bob Melvin	.05	
643 Rick Wilkins	.05	
644 Scott Scudder	.05	
645 Bip Roberts	.05	
646 Julio Valera	.05	
647 Kevin Campbell	.05	
648 Steve Searcy	.05	
649 Scott Kamieniecki	.05	
650 Kurt Stillwell	.05	
651 Bob Welch	.05	
652 Andres Galarraga	.05	
653 Mike Jackson	.05	
654 Bo Jackson	.10	
655 Sid Fernandez	.05	
656 Mike Bielecki	.05	
657 Jeff Reardon	.05	
658 Wayne Rosenthal	.05	
659 Eric Bullock	.05	
660 Eric Davis	.05	
661 Randy Tomlin	.05	
662 Tom Edens	.05	
663 Rob Murphy	.05	
664 Leo Gomez	.05	
665 Greg Maddux	.75	
666 Greg Vaughn	.05	
667 Wade Taylor	.05	
668 Brad Arnsberg	.05	
669 Mike Moore	.05	
670 Mark Langston	.05	
671 Barry Jones	.05	
672 Bill Landrum	.05	
673 Greg Swindell	.05	
674 Wayne Edwards	.05	
675 Greg Olson	.05	
676 Bill Pulsipher RC	.05	
677 Bobby Witt	.05	
678 Mark Carreon	.05	
679 Patrick Lennon	.05	
680 Ozzie Smith	.75	
681 John Briscoe	.05	
682 Matt Young	.05	
683 Jeff Conine	.05	
684 Phil Stephenson	.05	
685 Ron Darling	.05	
686 Bryan Hickerson	.05	
687 Dale Sveum	.05	
688 Kirk McCaskill	.05	
689 Rich Amaral	.05	
690 Danny Tartabull	.05	
691 Donald Harris	.05	
692 Doug Davis	.05	
693 John Farrell	.05	
694 Paul Gibson	.05	
695 Kenny Lofton	.05	
696 Mike Fetters	.05	
697 Rosario Rodriguez	.05	
698 Chris Jones	.05	

699 Jeff Manto	.05	
700 Rick Sutcliffe	.05	
701 Scott Bankhead	.05	
702 Donnie Hill	.05	
703 Todd Worrell	.05	
704 Rene Gonzales	.05	
705 Rick Cerone	.05	
706 Tony Pena	.05	
707 Paul Sorrento	.05	
708 Gary Scott	.05	
709 Junior Noboa	.05	
710 Wally Joyner	.05	
711 Charlie Hayes	.05	
712 Rich Rodriguez	.05	
713 Rudy Seanez	.05	
714 Jim Bullinger	.05	
715 Jeff Robinson	.05	
716 Jeff Branson	.05	
717 Andy Ashby	.05	
718 Dave Burba	.05	
719 Rich Gossage	.05	
720 Randy Johnson	.65	
721 David Wells	.05	
722 Paul Kilgus	.05	
723 Dave Martinez	.05	
724 Denny Neagle	.05	
725 Andy Stankiewicz	.05	
726 Rick Aguilera	.05	
727 Junior Ortiz	.05	
728 Storm Davis	.05	
729 Don Robinson	.05	
730 Ron Gant	.05	
731 Paul Assenmacher	.05	
732 Mark Gardiner	.05	
733 Milt Hill	.05	
734 Jeremy Hernandez	.05	
735 Ken Hill	.05	
736 Xavier Hernandez	.05	
737 Gregg Jefferies	.05	
738 Dick Schofield	.05	
739 Ron Robinson	.05	
740 Sandy Alomar	.05	
741 Mike Stanley	.05	
742 Butch Henry	.05	
743 Floyd Bannister	.05	
744 Brian Drahman	.05	
745 Dave Winfield	.65	
746 Bob Walk	.05	
747 Chris James	.05	
748 Don Prybylinski	.05	
749 Dennis Rasmussen	.05	
750 Rickey Henderson	.65	
751 Chris Hammond	.05	
752 Bob Kipper	.05	
753 Dave Rohde	.05	
754 Hubie Brooks	.05	
755 Bret Saberhagen	.05	
756 Jeff Robinson	.05	
757 Pat Listach RC	.05	
758 Bill Wegman	.05	
759 John Wetteland	.05	
760 Phil Plantier	.05	
761 Wilson Alvarez	.05	
762 Scott Aldred	.05	
763 Armando Reynoso RC	.05	
764 Todd Benzinger	.05	
765 Kevin Mitchell	.05	
766 Gary Sheffield	.35	
767 Allan Anderson	.05	
768 Rusty Meacham	.05	
769 Rick Parker	.05	
770 Nolan Ryan	1.50	
771 Jeff Ballard	.05	
772 Cory Snyder	.05	
773 Denis Boucher	.05	
774 Jose Gonzales	.05	
775 Juan Guerrero	.05	
776 Ed Nunez	.05	
777 Scott Ruskin	.05	
778 Terry Leach	.05	
779 Carl Willis	.05	
780 Bobby Bonilla	.05	
781 Duane Ward	.05	
782 Joe Slusarski	.05	
783 David Segui	.05	
784 Kirk Gibson	.05	
785 Frank Viola	.05	
786 Keith Miller	.05	
787 Mike Morgan	.05	
788 Kim Batiste	.05	
789 Sergio Valdez	.05	
790 Charlie Leibrandt	.05	
791 Jack Armstrong	.05	
792 Scott Chiamparino	.05	
793 Steve Farr	.05	
794 Dan Pasqua	.05	
795 Eddie Murray	.65	
796 John Morris	.05	
797 Francisco Cabrera	.05	
798 Mike Perez	.05	
799 Ted Wood	.05	
800 Jose Rijo	.05	
801 Danny Gladden	.05	
802 Arci Cianfrocco	.05	

803 Monty Fariss	.05
804 Roger McDowell	.05
805 Randy Myers	.05
806 Kirk Dressendorfer	.05
807 Zane Smith	.05
808 Glenn Davis	.05
809 Torey Lovullo	.05
810 Andre Dawson	.25
811 Bill Pecota	.05
812 Ted Power	.05
813 Willie Blair	.05
814 Dave Fleming	.05
815 Chris Gwynn	.05
816 Jody Reed	.05
817 Mark Dewey	.05
818 Kyle Abbott	.05
819 Tom Henke	.05
820 Kevin Seitzer	.05
821 Al Newman	.05
822 Tim Sherrill	.05
823 Chuck Crim	.05
824 Darren Reed	.05
825 Tony Gwynn	.75
826 Steve Foster	.05
827 Steve Howe	.05
828 Brook Jacoby	.05
829 Rodney McCray	.05
830 Chuck Knoblauch	.05
831 John Wehner	.05
832 Scott Garrelts	.05
833 Alejandro Pena	.05
834 Jeff Parrett	.05
835 Juan Bell	.05
836 Lance Dickson	.05
837 Darryl Kile	.05
838 Efrain Valdez	.05
839 Bob Zupcic RC	.05
840 George Bell	.05
841 Dave Gallagher	.05
842 Tim Belcher	.05
843 Jeff Shaw	.05
844 Mike Fitzgerald	.05
845 Gary Carter	.65
846 John Russell	.05
847 Eric Hillman RC	.05
848 Mike Witt	.05
849 Curt Wilkerson	.05
850 Alan Trammell	.05
851 Rex Hudler	.05
852 Michael Walkden RC	.05
853 Kevin Ward	.05
854 Tim Naehring	.05
855 Bill Swift	.05
856 Damon Berryhill	.05
857 Mark Eichhorn	.05
858 Hector Villanueva	.05
859 Jose Lind	.05
860 Denny Martinez	.05
861 Bill Krueger	.05
862 Mike Kingery	.05
863 Jeff Innis	.05
864 Derek Lilliquist	.05
865 Reggie Sanders	.05
866 Ramon Garcia	.05
867 Bruce Ruffin	.05
868 Dickie Thon	.05
869 Melido Perez	.05
870 Ruben Amaro	.05
871 Alan Mills	.05
872 Matt Sinatro	.05
873 Eddie Zosky	.05
874 Pete Incaviglia	.05
875 Tom Candiotti	.05
876 Bob Patterson	.05
877 Neal Heaton	.05
878 Terrel Hansen RC	.05
879 Dave Eiland	.05
880 Von Hayes	.05
881 Tim Scott	.05
882 Otis Nixon	.05
883 Herm Winningham	.05
884 Dion James	.05
885 Dave Wainhouse	.05
886 Frank DiPino	.05
887 Dennis Cook	.05
888 Jose Mesa	.05
889 Mark Leiter	.05
890 Willie Randolph	.05
891 Craig Colbert	.05
892 Dwayne Henry	.05
893 Jim Lindeman	.05
894 Charlie Hough	.05
895 Gil Heredia	.05
896 Scott Chiamparino	.05
897 Lance Blankenship	.05
898 Checklist 601-700	.05
899 Checklist 701-800	.05
900 Checklist 801-900	.05

Master Photos

	NM/M
Complete Set (15):	20.00
Common Player:	.50
(1) Wade Boggs	2.25

(2)	Barry Bonds	4.00
(3)	Jose Canseco	1.00
(4)	Will Clark	.50
(5)	Cecil Fielder	.50
(6)	Dwight Gooden	.50
(7)	Ken Griffey Jr.	3.00
(8)	Rickey Henderson	2.00
(9)	Lance Johnson	.50
(10)	Cal Ripken, Jr.	4.00
(11)	Nolan Ryan	4.00
(12)	Deion Sanders	.50
(13)	Darryl Strawberry	.50
(14)	Danny Tartabull	.50
(15)	Frank Thomas	2.00

SkyDome

	NM/M
Unopened Factory Set (200):	15.00
Complete Set (200):	10.00
Common Player:	.05
1 Terry Adams RC	.05
2 Tommy Adams	.05
3 Rick Aguilera	.05
4 Ron Allen	.05
5 Roberto Alomar/AS	.20
6 Sandy Alomar	.05
7 Greg Anthony	.05
8 James Austin	.05
9 Steve Avery	.05
10 Harold Baines	.05
11 Brian Barber RC	.05
12 Jon Barnes	.05
13 George Bell	.05
14 Doug Bennett	.05
15 Sean Bergman	.05
16 Craig Biggio	.05
17 Bill Bliss	.05
18 Wade Boggs/AS	.60
19 Bobby Bonilla/AS	.05
20 Russell Brock	.05
21 Tarrik Brock	.05
22 Tom Browning	.05
23 Brett Butler	.05
24 Ivan Calderon	.05
25 Joe Carter	.05
26 Joe Caruso	.05
27 Dan Cholowsky	.05
28 Will Clark/AS	.05
29 Roger Clemens/AS	.65
30 Shawn Curran	.05
31 Chris Curtis	.05
32 Chili Davis	.05
33 Andre Dawson	.25
34 Joe DeBerry	.05
35 John Dettmer	.05
36 Rob Dibble	.05
37 John Donati RC	.05
38 Dave Doorneweerd	.05
39 Darren Dreifort	.05
40 Mike Durant	.05

No.	Player	Price
41	Chris Durkin	.05
42	Dennis Eckersley	.40
43	Brian Edmondson RC	.05
44	Vaughn Eshelman RC	.05
45	Shawn Estes RC	.50
46	Jorge Fabregas RC	.10
47	Jon Farrell	.05
48	Cecil Fielder/AS	.05
49	Carlton Fisk	.50
50	Tim Flannelly	.05
51	Cliff Floyd RC	.50
52	Julio Franco	.05
53	Greg Gagne	.05
54	Chris Gambs RC	.05
55	Ron Gant	.05
56	Brent Gates	.05
57	Dwayne Gerald	.05
58	Jason Giambi	1.50
59	Benji Gil RC	.05
60	Mark Gipner	.05
61	Danny Gladden	.05
62	Tom Glavine	.35
63	Jimmy Gonzalez	.05
64	Jeff Granger	.05
65	Dan Grapenthien	.05
66	Dennis Gray	.05
67	Shawn Green RC	2.00
68	Tyler Green	.05
69	Todd Greene	.05
70	Ken Griffey Jr./AS	.75
71	Kelly Gruber	.05
72	Ozzie Guillen	.05
73	Tony Gwynn/AS	.60
74	Shane Halter	.05
75	Jeffrey Hammonds	.05
76	Larry Hanlon	.05
77	Pete Harnisch	.05
78	Mike Harrison	.05
79	Bryan Harvey	.05
80	Scott Hatteberg	.05
81	Rick Helling	.05
82	Dave Henderson	.05
83	Rickey Henderson/AS	.50
84	Tyrone Hill	.05
85	Todd Hollandsworth RC	.10
86	Brian Holliday	.05
87	Terry Horn	.05
88	Jeff Hostetler	.05
89	Kent Hrbek	.05
90	Mark Hubbard	.05
91	Charles Johnson	.05
92	Howard Johnson	.05
93	Todd Johnson	.05
94	Bobby Jones RC	.10
95	Dan Jones	.05
96	Felix Jose	.05
97	Dave Justice	.05
98	Jimmy Key	.05
99	Marc Kroom RC	.05
100	John Kruk	.05
101	Mark Langston	.05
102	Barry Larkin	.05
103	Mike LaValliere	.05
104a	Scott Leius (1991 N.L. All-Star - Error)	.05
104b	Scott Leius (1991 World Series - Correct)	.25
105	Mark Lemke	.05
106	Donnie Leshnock	.05
107	Jimmy Lewis	.05
108	Shawn Livesy	.05
109	Ryan Long	.05
110	Trevor Mallory	.05
111	Denny Martinez	.05
112	Justin Mashore	.05
113	Jason McDonald	.05
114	Jack McDowell	.05
115	Tom McKinnon	.05
116	Billy McKinnon	.05
117	Buck McNabb RC	.05
118	Jim Mecir	.05
119	Dan Melendez	.05
120	Shawn Miller RC	.05
121	Trever Miller	.05
122	Paul Molitor	.50
123	Vincent Moore	.05
124	Mike Morgan	.05
125	Jack Morris	.05
126	Jack Morris/AS	.05
127	Sean Mulligan	.05
128	Eddie Murray	.50
129	Mike Neill	.05
130	Phil Nevin	.05
131	Mark O'Brien	.05
132	Alex Ochoa RC	.05
133	Chad Ogea RC	.05
134	Greg Olson	.05
135	Paul O'Neill	.05
136a	Jared Osentowski (1991 World Series - Error)	.05
136b	Jared Osentowski (Draft Pick - Correct)	.25
137	Mike Pagliarulo	.05
138	Rafael Palmeiro	.40
139	Rodney Pedraza	.05
140	Tony Phillips	.05
141	Scott Pisciotta RC	.05
142	Chris Pritchett	.05
143	Jason Pruitt	.05
144a	Kirby Puckett (1991 N.L. All-Star - Error)	.60
144b	Kirby Puckett (1991 World Series - Correct)	3.00
145	Kirby Puckett/AS	.60
146	Manny Ramirez RC	5.00
147	Eddie Ramos	.05
148	Mark Ratekin	.05
149	Jeff Reardon	.05
150	Sean Rees	.05
151	Calvin Reese RC	.50
152	Desmond Relaford RC	.10
153	Eric Richardson	.05
154	Cal Ripken, Jr./AS	1.50
155	Chris Roberts	.05
156	Mike Robertson	.05
157	Steve Rodriguez	.05
158	Mike Rossiter	.05
159	Scott Ruffcorn	.05
160a	Chris Sabo (1991 World Series - Error)	.05
160b	Chris Sabo (1991 N.L. All-Star - Correct)	.25
161	Juan Samuel	.05
162	Ryne Sandberg/AS	.60
163	Scott Sanderson	.05
164	Benito Santiago	.05
165	Gene Schall RC	.05
166	Chad Schoenvogel	.05
167	Chris Seelbach RC	.05
168	Aaron Sele RC	.50
169	Basil Shabazz	.05
170	Al Shirley RC	.05
171	Paul Shuey	.05
172	Ruben Sierra	.05
173	John Smiley	.05
174	Lee Smith	.05
175	Ozzie Smith	.60
176	Tim Smith	.05
177	Zane Smith	.05
178	John Smoltz	.05
179	Scott Stahoviak	.05
180	Kennie Steenstra	.05
181	Kevin Stocker	.05
182	Chris Stynes RC	.05
183	Danny Tartabull	.05
184	Brien Taylor	.05
185	Todd Taylor	.05
186	Larry Thomas	.05
187a	Ozzie Timmons RC	.05
187b	David Tuttle (Should be #188.)	.05
188	Not Issued	.05
189	Andy Van Slyke	.05
190a	Frank Viola (1991 World Series - Error)	.05
190b	Frank Viola (1991 N.L. All-Star - Correct)	.25
191	Michael Walkden	.05
192	Jeff Ware	.05
193	Allen Watson RC	.05
194	Steve Whitaker	.05
195a	Jerry Willard (1991 Draft Pick - Error)	.05
195b	Jerry Willard (1991 World Series - Correct)	.25
196	Craig Wilson	.05
197	Chris Wimmer	.05
198	Steve Wojciechowski RC	.05
199	Joel Wolfe	.05
200	Ivan Zweig	.05

1993 Stadium Club

JEFF BAGWELL

	NM/M
Complete Set (750):	25.00
Common Player:	.05
First Day:	8X
Pack (15):	.75

No.	Player	Price
Wax Box (24):		10.00
1	Pat Borders	.05
2	Greg Maddux	.85
3	Daryl Boston	.05
4	Bob Ayrault	.05
5	Tony Phillips	.05
6	Damion Easley	.05
7	Kip Gross	.05
8	Jim Thome	.65
9	Tim Belcher	.05
10	Gary Wayne	.05
11	Sam Militello	.05
12	Mike Magnante	.05
13	Tim Wakefield	.05
14	Tim Hulett	.05
15	Rheal Cormier	.05
16	Juan Guerrero	.05
17	Rich Gossage	.05
18	Tim Laker	.05
19	Darrin Jackson	.05
20	Jack Clark	.05
21	Roberto Hernandez	.05
22	Dean Palmer	.05
23	Harold Reynolds	.05
24	Dan Plesac	.05
25	Brent Mayne	.05
26	Pat Hentgen	.05
27	Luis Sojo	.05
28	Ron Gant	.05
29	Paul Gibson	.05
30	Bip Roberts	.05
31	Mickey Tettleton	.05
32	Randy Velarde	.05
33	Brian McRae	.05
34	Wes Chamberlain	.05
35	Wayne Kirby	.05
36	Rey Sanchez	.05
37	Jesse Orosco	.05
38	Mike Stanton	.05
39	Royce Clayton	.05
40	Cal Ripken, Jr.	2.50
41	John Dopson	.05
42	Gene Larkin	.05
43	Tim Raines	.05
44	Randy Myers	.05
45	Clay Parker	.05
46	Mike Scioscia	.05
47	Pete Incaviglia	.05
48	Todd Van Poppel	.05
49	Ray Lankford	.05
50	Eddie Murray	.75
51	Barry Bonds	2.50
52	Gary Thurman	.05
53	Bob Wickman	.05
54	Joey Cora	.05
55	Kenny Rogers	.05
56	Mike Devereaux	.05
57	Kevin Seitzer	.05
58	Rafael Belliard	.05
59	David Wells	.05
60	Mark Clark	.05
61	Carlos Baerga	.05
62	Scott Brosius	.05
63	Jeff Grotewold	.05
64	Rick Wrona	.05
65	Kurt Knudsen	.05
66	Lloyd McClendon	.05
67	Omar Vizquel	.05
68	Jose Vizcaino	.05
69	Rob Ducey	.05
70	Casey Candaele	.05
71	Ramon Martinez	.05
72	Todd Hundley	.05
73	John Marzano	.05
74	Derek Parks	.05
75	Jack McDowell	.05
76	Tim Scott	.05
77	Mike Mussina	.40
78	Delino DeShields	.05
79	Chris Bosio	.05
80	Mike Bordick	.05
81	Rod Beck	.05
82	Ted Power	.05
83	John Kruk	.05
84	Steve Shifflett	.05
85	Danny Tartabull	.05
86	Mike Greenwell	.05
87	Jose Melendez	.05
88	Craig Wilson	.05
89	Melvin Nieves	.05
90	Ed Sprague	.05
91	Willie McGee	.05
92	Joe Orsulak	.05
93	Jeff King	.05
94	Dan Pasqua	.05
95	Brian Harper	.05
96	Joe Oliver	.05
97	Shane Turner	.05
98	Lenny Harris	.05
99	Jeff Parrett	.05
100	Luis Polonia	.05
101	Kent Bottenfield	.05
102	Albert Belle	.05
103	Mike Maddux	.05
104	Randy Tomlin	.05
105	Andy Stankiewicz	.05
106	Rico Rossy	.05
107	Joe Hesketh	.05
108	Dennis Powell	.05
109	Derrick May	.05
110	Pete Harnisch	.05
111	Kent Mercker	.05
112	Scott Fletcher	.05
113	Rex Hudler	.05
114	Chico Walker	.05
115	Rafael Palmeiro	.65
116	Mark Leiter	.05
117	Pedro Munoz	.05
118	Jim Bullinger	.05
119	Ivan Calderon	.05
120	Mike Timlin	.05
121	Rene Gonzales	.05
122	Greg Vaughn	.05
123	Mike Flanagan	.05
124	Mike Hartley	.05
125	Jeff Montgomery	.05
126	Mike Gallego	.05
127	Don Slaught	.05
128	Charlie O'Brien	.05
129a	Jose Offerman (Home: Blank)	2.00
129b	Jose Offerman (Home: S.P. de MACORIS, D.R.)	.05
130	Mark Wohlers	.05
131	Eric Fox	.05
132	Doug Strange	.05
133	Jeff Frye	.05
134	Wade Boggs	.85
135	Lou Whitaker	.05
136	Craig Grebeck	.05
137	Rich Rodriguez	.05
138	Jay Bell	.05
139	Felix Fermin	.05
140	Denny Martinez	.05
141	Eric Anthony	.05
142	Roberto Alomar	.20
143	Darren Lewis	.05
144	Mike Blowers	.05
145	Scott Bankhead	.05
146	Jeff Reboulet	.05
147	Frank Viola	.05
148	Bill Pecota	.05
149	Carlos Hernandez	.05
150	Bobby Witt	.05
151	Sid Bream	.05
152	Todd Zeile	.05
153	Dennis Cook	.05
154	Brian Bohanon	.05
155	Pat Kelly	.05
156	Milt Cuyler	.05
157	Juan Bell	.05
158	Randy Milligan	.05
159	Mark Gardner	.05
160	Pat Tabler	.05
161	Jeff Reardon	.05
162	Ken Patterson	.05
163	Bobby Bonilla	.05
164	Tony Pena	.05
165	Greg Swindell	.05
166	Kirk McCaskill	.05
167	Doug Drabek	.05
168	Franklin Stubbs	.05
169	Ron Tingley	.05
170	Willie Banks	.05
171	Sergio Valdez	.05
172	Mark Lemke	.05
173	Robin Yount	.75
174	Storm Davis	.05
175	Dan Walters	.05
176	Steve Farr	.05
177	Curt Wilkerson	.05
178	Luis Alicea	.05
179	Russ Swan	.05
180	Mitch Williams	.05
181	Wilson Alvarez	.05
182	Carl Willis	.05
183	Craig Biggio	.05
184	Sean Berry	.05
185	Trevor Wilson	.05
186	Jeff Tackett	.05
187	Ellis Burks	.05
188	Jeff Branson	.05
189	Matt Nokes	.05
190	John Smiley	.05
191	Danny Gladden	.05
192	Mike Boddicker	.05
193	Roger Pavlik	.05
194	Paul Sorrento	.05
195	Vince Coleman	.05
196	Gary DiSarcina	.05
197	Rafael Bournigal	.05
198	Mike Schooler	.05
199	Scott Ruskin	.05
200	Frank Thomas	.75
201	Kyle Abbott	.05
202	Mike Perez	.05
203	Andre Dawson	.25
204	Bill Swift	.05

#	Player	Price	#	Player	Price	#	Player	Price	#	Player	Price
205	Alejandro Pena	.05	309	Marvin Freeman	.05	413	Lance Blankenship	.05	517	Ozzie Guillen	.05
206	Dave Winfield	.75	310	Jay Buhner	.05	414	Jeff Parrett	.05	518	Darryl Kile	.05
207	Andujar Cedeno	.05	311	Butch Henry	.05	415	Barry Larkin	.05	519	Rich Rowland	.05
208	Terry Steinbach	.05	312	Greg Harris	.05	416	Alan Trammell	.05	520	Carlos Delgado	.50
209	Chris Hammond	.05	313	Darren Daulton	.05	417	Mark Kiefer	.05	521	Doug Henry	.05
210	Todd Burns	.05	314	Chuck Knoblauch	.05	418	Gregg Olson	.05	522	Greg Colbrunn	.05
211	Hipolito Pichardo	.05	315	Greg Harris	.05	419	Mark Grace	.05	523	Tom Gordon	.05
212	John Kiely	.05	316	John Franco	.05	420	Shane Mack	.05	524	Ivan Rodriguez	.65
213	Tim Teufel	.05	317	John Wehner	.05	421	Bob Walk	.05	525	Kent Hrbek	.05
214	Lee Guetterman	.05	318	Donald Harris	.05	422	Curt Schilling	.25	526	Eric Young	.05
215	Geronimo Pena	.05	319	Benny Santiago	.05	423	Erik Hanson	.05	527	Rod Brewer	.05
216	Brett Butler	.05	320	Larry Walker	.05	424	George Brett	1.25	528	Eric Karros	.05
217	Bryan Hickerson	.05	321	Randy Knorr	.05	425	Reggie Jefferson	.05	529	Marquis Grissom	.05
218	Rick Trlicek	.05	322	Ramon D. Martinez RC	.05	426	Mark Portugal	.05	530	Rico Brogna	.05
219	Lee Stevens	.05	323	Mike Stanley	.05	427	Ron Karkovice	.05	531	Sammy Sosa	1.00
220	Roger Clemens	1.25	324	Bill Wegman	.05	428	Matt Young	.05	532	Bret Boone	.05
221	Carlton Fisk	.75	325	Tom Candiotti	.05	429	Troy Neel	.05	533	Luis Rivera	.05
222	Chili Davis	.05	326	Glenn Davis	.05	430	Hector Fajardo	.05	534	Hal Morris	.05
223	Walt Terrell	.05	327	Chuck Crim	.05	431	Dave Righetti	.05	535	Monty Fariss	.05
224	Jim Eisenreich	.05	328	Scott Livingstone	.05	432	Pat Listach	.05	536	Leo Gomez	.05
225	Ricky Bones	.05	329	Eddie Taubensee	.05	433	Jeff Innis	.05	537	Wally Joyner	.05
226	Henry Rodriguez	.05	330	George Bell	.05	434	Bob MacDonald	.05	538	Tony Gwynn	.85
227	Ken Hill	.05	331	Edgar Martinez	.05	435	Brian Jordan	.05	539	Mike Williams	.05
228	Rick Wilkins	.05	332	Paul Assenmacher	.05	436	Jeff Blauser	.05	540	Juan Gonzalez	.40
229	Ricky Jordan	.05	333	Steve Hosey	.05	437	Mike Myers RC	.05	541	Ryan Klesko	.05
230	Bernard Gilkey	.05	334	Mo Vaughn	.05	438	Frank Seminara	.05	542	Ryan Thompson	.05
231	Tim Fortugno	.05	335	Bret Saberhagen	.05	439	Rusty Meacham	.05	543	Chad Curtis	.05
232	Geno Petralli	.05	336	Mike Trombley	.05	440	Greg Briley	.05	544	Orel Hershiser	.05
233	Jose Rijo	.05	337	Mark Lewis	.05	441	Derek Lilliquist	.05	545	Carlos Garcia	.05
234	Jim Leyritz	.05	338	Terry Pendleton	.05	442	John Vander Wal	.05	546	Bob Welch	.05
235	Kevin Campbell	.05	339	Dave Hollins	.05	443	Scott Erickson	.05	547	Vinny Castilla	.05
236	Al Osuna	.05	340	Jeff Conine	.05	444	Bob Scanlan	.05	548	Ozzie Smith	.85
237	Pete Smith	.05	341	Bob Tewksbury	.05	445	Todd Frohwirth	.05	549	Luis Salazar	.05
238	Pete Schourek	.05	342	Billy Ashley	.05	446	Tom Goodwin	.05	550	Mark Guthrie	.05
239	Moises Alou	.05	343	Zane Smith	.05	447	William Pennyfeather	.05	551	Charles Nagy	.05
240	Donn Pall	.05	344	John Wetteland	.05	448	Travis Fryman	.05	552	Alex Fernandez	.05
241	Denny Neagle	.05	345	Chris Hoiles	.05	449	Mickey Morandini	.05	553	Mel Rojas	.05
242	Dan Peltier	.05	346	Frank Castillo	.05	450	Greg Olson	.05	554	Orestes Destrade	.05
243	Scott Scudder	.05	347	Bruce Hurst	.05	451	Trevor Hoffman	.05	555	Mark Gubicza	.05
244	Juan Guzman	.05	348	Kevin McReynolds	.05	452	Dave Magadan	.05	556	Steve Finley	.05
245	Dave Burba	.05	349	Dave Henderson	.05	453	Shawn Jeter	.05	557	Don Mattingly	1.25
246	Rick Sutcliffe	.05	350	Ryan Bowen	.05	454	Andres Galarraga	.05	558	Rickey Henderson	.75
247	Tony Fossas	.05	351	Sid Fernandez	.05	455	Ted Wood	.05	559	Tommy Greene	.05
248	Mike Munoz	.05	352	Mark Whiten	.05	456	Freddie Benavides	.05	560	Arthur Rhodes	.05
249	Tim Salmon	.05	353	Nolan Ryan	2.50	457	Junior Felix	.05	561	Alfredo Griffin	.05
250	Rob Murphy	.05	354	Rick Aguilera	.05	458	Alex Cole	.05	562	Will Clark	.05
251	Roger McDowell	.05	355	Mark Langston	.05	459	John Orton	.05	563	Bob Zupcic	.05
252	Lance Parrish	.05	356	Jack Morris	.05	460	Eddie Zosky	.05	564	Chuck Carr	.05
253	Cliff Brantley	.05	357	Rob Deer	.05	461	Dennis Eckersley	.65	565	Henry Cotto	.05
254	Scott Leius	.05	358	Dave Fleming	.05	462	Lee Smith	.05	566	Billy Spiers	.05
255	Carlos Martinez	.05	359	Lance Johnson	.05	463	John Smoltz	.05	567	Jack Armstrong	.05
256	Vince Horsman	.05	360	Joe Millette	.05	464	Ken Caminiti	.05	568	Kurt Stillwell	.05
257	Oscar Azocar	.05	361	Wil Cordero	.05	465	Melido Perez	.05	569	David McCarty	.05
258	Craig Shipley	.05	362	Chito Martinez	.05	466	Tom Marsh	.05	570	Joe Vitiello	.05
259	Ben McDonald	.05	363	Scott Servais	.05	467	Jeff Nelson	.05	571	Gerald Williams	.05
260	Jeff Brantley	.05	364	Bernie Williams	.05	468	Jesse Levis	.05	572	Dale Murphy	.25
261	Damon Berryhill	.05	365	Pedro Martinez	.75	469	Chris Nabholz	.05	573	Scott Aldred	.05
262	Joe Grahe	.05	366	Ryne Sandberg	.85	470	Mike Mcfarlane	.05	574	Bill Gullickson	.05
263	Dave Hansen	.05	367	Brad Ausmus	.05	471	Reggie Sanders	.05	575	Bobby Thigpen	.05
264	Rich Amaral	.05	368	Scott Cooper	.05	472	Chuck McElroy	.05	576	Glenallen Hill	.05
265	Tim Pugh RC	.05	369	Rob Dibble	.05	473	Kevin Gross	.05	577	Dwayne Henry	.05
266	Dion James	.05	370	Walt Weiss	.05	474	Matt Whiteside RC	.05	578	Calvin Jones	.05
267	Frank Tanana	.05	371	Mark Davis	.05	475	Cal Eldred	.05	579	Al Martin	.05
268	Stan Belinda	.05	372	Orlando Merced	.05	476	Dave Gallagher	.05	580	Ruben Sierra	.05
269	Jeff Kent	.05	373	Mike Jackson	.05	477	Len Dykstra	.05	581	Andy Benes	.05
270	Bruce Ruffin	.05	374	Kevin Appier	.05	478	Mark McGwire	2.00	582	Anthony Young	.05
271	Xavier Hernandez	.05	375	Esteban Beltre	.05	479	David Segui	.05	583	Shawn Boskie	.05
272	Darrin Fletcher	.05	376	Joe Slusarski	.05	480	Mike Henneman	.05	584	Scott Pose RC	.05
273	Tino Martinez	.05	377	William Suero	.05	481	Bret Barberie	.05	585	Mike Piazza	1.50
274	Benny Santiago	.05	378	Pete O'Brien	.05	482	Steve Sax	.05	586	Donovan Osborne	.05
275	Scott Radinsky	.05	379	Alan Embree	.05	483	Dave Valle	.05	587	James Austin	.05
276	Mariano Duncan	.05	380	Lenny Webster	.05	484	Danny Darwin	.05	588	Checklist 301-400	.05
277	Kenny Lofton	.05	381	Eric Davis	.05	485	Devon White	.05	589	Checklist 401-500	.05
278	Dwight Smith	.05	382	Duane Ward	.05	486	Eric Plunk	.05	590	Checklist 501-600	.05
279	Joe Carter	.05	383	John Habyan	.05	487	Jim Gott	.05	591	Ken Griffey Jr.	.75
280	Tim Jones	.05	384	Jeff Bagwell	.75	488	Scooter Tucker	.05	592	Ivan Rodriguez	.40
281	Jeff Huson	.05	385	Ruben Amaro	.05	489	Omar Oliveres	.05	593	Carlos Baerga	.05
282	Phil Plantier	.05	386	Julio Valera	.05	490	Greg Myers	.05	594	Fred McGriff	.05
283	Kirby Puckett	.85	387	Robin Ventura	.05	491	Brian Hunter	.05	595	Mark McGwire	1.00
284	Johnny Guzman	.05	388	Archi Cianfrocco	.05	492	Kevin Tapani	.05	596	Roberto Alomar	.10
285	Mike Morgan	.05	389	Skeeter Barnes	.05	493	Rich Monteleone	.05	597	Kirby Puckett	.45
286	Chris Sabo	.05	390	Tim Costo	.05	494	Steve Buechele	.05	598	Marquis Grissom	.05
287	Matt Williams	.05	391	Luis Mercedes	.05	495	Bo Jackson	.10	599	John Smoltz	.05
288	Checklist 1-100	.05	392	Jeremy Hernandez	.05	496	Mike LaValliere	.05	600	Ryne Sandberg	.45
289	Checklist 101-200	.05	393	Shawon Dunston	.05	497	Mark Leonard	.05	601	Wade Boggs	.85
290	Checklist 201-300	.05	394	Andy Van Slyke	.05	498	Daryl Boston	.05	602	Jeff Reardon	.05
291	Dennis Eckersley	.30	395	Kevin Maas	.05	499	Jose Canseco	.45	603	Billy Ripken	.05
292	Eric Karros	.05	396	Kevin Brown	.05	500	Brian Barnes	.05	604	Bryan Harvey	.05
293	Pat Listach	.05	397	J.T. Bruett	.05	501	Randy Johnson	.75	605	Carlos Quintana	.05
294	Andy Van Slyke	.05	398	Darryl Strawberry	.05	502	Tim McIntosh	.05	606	Greg Hibbard	.05
295	Robin Ventura	.05	399	Tom Pagnozzi	.05	503	Cecil Fielder	.05	607	Ellis Burks	.05
296	Tom Glavine	.05	400	Sandy Alomar	.05	504	Derek Bell	.05	608	Greg Swindell	.05
297	Juan Gonzalez	.20	401	Keith Miller	.05	505	Kevin Koslofski	.05	609	Dave Winfield	.75
298	Travis Fryman	.05	402	Rich DeLucia	.05	506	Darren Holmes	.05	610	Charlie Hough	.05
299	Larry Walker	.05	403	Shawn Abner	.05	507	Brady Anderson	.05	611	Chili Davis	.05
300	Gary Sheffield	.20	404	Howard Johnson	.05	508	John Valentin	.05	612	Jody Reed	.05
301	Chuck Finley	.05	405	Mike Benjamin	.05	509	Jerry Browne	.05	613	Mark Williamson	.05
302	Luis Gonzalez	.05	406	Roberto Mejia RC	.05	510	Fred McGriff	.05	614	Phil Plantier	.05
303	Darryl Hamilton	.05	407	Mike Butcher	.05	511	Pedro Astacio	.05	615	Jim Abbott	.05
304	Bien Figueroa	.05	408	Deion Sanders	.05	512	Gary Gaetti	.05	616	Dante Bichette	.05
305	Ron Darling	.05	409	Todd Stottlemyre	.05	513	John Burke RC	.05	617	Mark Eichhorn	.05
306	Jonathan Hurst	.05	410	Scott Kamieniecki	.05	514	Dwight Gooden	.05	618	Gary Sheffield	.45
307	Mike Sharperson	.05	411	Doug Jones	.05	515	Thomas Howard	.05	619	Richie Lewis RC	.05
308	Mike Christopher	.05	412	John Burkett	.05	516	Darrell Whitmore RC	.05	620	Joe Girardi	.05

621	Jaime Navarro	.05
622	Willie Wilson	.05
623	Scott Fletcher	.05
624	Bud Black	.05
625	Tom Brunansky	.05
626	Steve Avery	.05
627	Paul Molitor	.75
628	Gregg Jefferies	.05
629	Dave Stewart	.05
630	Javier Lopez	.05
631	Greg Gagne	.05
632	Bobby Kelly	.05
633	Mike Fetters	.05
634	Ozzie Canseco	.05
635	Jeff Russell	.05
636	Pete Incaviglia	.05
637	Tom Henke	.05
638	Chipper Jones	1.00
639	Jimmy Key	.05
640	Dave Martinez	.05
641	Dave Stieb	.05
642	Milt Thompson	.05
643	Alan Mills	.05
644	Tony Fernandez	.05
645	Randy Bush	.05
646	Joe Magrane	.05
647	Ivan Calderon	.05
648	Jose Guzman	.05
649	John Olerud	.05
650	Tom Glavine	.25
651	Julio Franco	.05
652	Armando Reynoso	.05
653	Felix Jose	.05
654	Ben Rivera	.05
655	Andre Dawson	.25
656	Mike Harkey	.05
657	Kevin Seitzer	.05
658	Lonnie Smith	.05
659	Norm Charlton	.05
660	Dave Justice	.05
661	Fernando Valenzuela	.05
662	Dan Wilson	.05
663	Mark Gardner	.05
664	Doug Dascenzo	.05
665	Greg Maddux	.85
666	Harold Baines	.05
667	Randy Myers	.05
668	Harold Reynolds	.05
669	Candy Maldonado	.05
670	Al Leiter	.05
671	Jerald Clark	.05
672	Doug Drabek	.05
673	Kirk Gibson	.05
674	Steve Reed RC	.05
675	Mike Felder	.05
676	Ricky Gutierrez	.05
677	Spike Owen	.05
678	Otis Nixon	.05
679	Scott Sanderson	.05
680	Mark Carreon	.05
681	Troy Percival	.05
682	Kevin Stocker	.05
683	Jim Converse RC	.05
684	Barry Bonds	2.50
685	Greg Gohr	.05
686	Tim Wallach	.05
687	Matt Mieske	.05
688	Robby Thompson	.05
689	Brien Taylor	.05
690	Kirt Manwaring	.05
691	Mike Lansing RC	.25
692	Steve Decker	.05
693	Mike Moore	.05
694	Kevin Mitchell	.05
695	Phil Hiatt	.05
696	Tony Tarasco RC	.05
697	Benji Gil	.05
698	Jeff Juden	.05
699	Kevin Reimer	.05
700	Andy Ashby	.05
701	John Jaha	.05
702	Tim Bogar RC	.05
703	David Cone	.05
704	Willie Greene	.05
705	David Hulse RC	.05
706	Cris Carpenter	.05
707	Ken Griffey Jr.	1.50
708	Steve Bedrosian	.05
709	Dave Nilsson	.05
710	Paul Wagner	.05
711	B.J. Surhoff	.05
712	Rene Arocha RC	.05
713	Manny Lee	.05
714	Brian Williams	.05
715	Sherman Obando RC	.05
716	Terry Mulholland	.05
717	Paul O'Neill	.05
718	David Nied	.05
719	J.T. Snow RC	.50
720	Nigel Wilson	.05
721	Mike Bielecki	.05
722	Kevin Young	.05
723	Charlie Leibrandt	.05
724	Frank Bolick	.05

725	Jon Shave RC	.05
726	Steve Cooke	.05
727	Domingo Martinez RC	.05
728	Todd Worrell	.05
729	Jose Lind	.05
730	Jim Tatum RC	.05
731	Mike Hampton	.05
732	Mike Draper	.05
733	Henry Mercedes	.05
734	John Johnstone RC	.05
735	Mitch Webster	.05
736	Russ Springer	.05
737	Rob Natal	.05
738	Steve Howe	.05
739	Darrell Sherman RC	.05
740	Pat Mahomes	.05
741	Alex Arias	.05
742	Damon Buford	.05
743	Charlie Hayes	.05
744	Guillermo Velasquez	.05
745	Checklist 601-750	.05
746	Frank Thomas	.40
747	Barry Bonds	1.50
748	Roger Clemens	.50
749	Joe Carter	.05
750	Greg Maddux	.45

1st Day Production

Common Player:		1.00
1st Day Stars:		8X

(See 1993 Stadium Club for checklist and base card values.)

Series 1 Inserts

		NM/M
Complete Set (4):		3.00
Common Player:		.25
1	Robin Yount (3,000 Hits)	1.00
2	George Brett (3,000 Hits)	2.00
3	David Nied (#1 Pick)	.25
4	Nigel Wilson (#1 Pick)	.25

Series 2 Inserts

		NM/M
Complete Set (4):		5.00
Common Card:		1.50
1	Will Clark, Mark McGwire Pacific Terrific	2.00
2	Dwight Gooden, Don Mattingly Broadway Stars	1.50
3	Ryne Sandberg, Frank Thomas Second City Sluggers	1.50

4	Ken Griffey Jr., Darryl Strawberry Pacific Terrific	1.50

Series 3 Inserts

		NM/M
Complete Set (2):		.50
Common Player:		.25
1	David Nied	.25
2	Charlie Hough	.25

Master Photos

		NM/M
Complete Set (30):		15.00
Common Player:		.20
Series 1		
(1)	Carlos Baerga	.20
(2)	Delino DeShields	.20
(3)	Brian McRae	.20
(4)	Sam Militello	.20
(5)	Joe Oliver	.20
(6)	Kirby Puckett	1.50
(7)	Cal Ripken Jr.	4.00
(8)	Bip Roberts	.20
(9)	Mike Scioscia	.20
(10)	Rick Sutcliffe	.20
(11)	Danny Tartabull	.20
(12)	Tim Wakefield	.20
Series 2		
(13)	George Brett	3.00
(14)	Jose Canseco	.50
(15)	Will Clark	.20
(16)	Travis Fryman	.20
(17)	Dwight Gooden	.20
(18)	Mark Grace	.30
(19)	Rickey Henderson	1.00
(20)	Mark McGwire	2.50
(21)	Nolan Ryan	4.00
(22)	Ruben Sierra	.20
(23)	Darryl Strawberry	.20
(24)	Larry Walker	.20
Series 3		
(25)	Barry Bonds	5.00
(26)	Ken Griffey Jr.	2.50
(27)	Greg Maddux	2.00
(28)	David Nied	.20
(29)	J.T. Snow	.20
(30)	Brien Taylor	.20
Redemption Card:		3X

Special

		NM/M
Unopened Set (200):		45.00
Complete Set (200):		40.00
Common Player:		.05
1	Dave Winfield	.75
2	Juan Guzman	.05
3	Tony Gwynn	.85
4	Chris Roberts	.05
5	Benny Santiago	.05
6	Sherard Clinkscales	.05
7	Jonathan Nunnally RC	.05
8	Chuck Knoblauch	.05
9	Bob Wolcott RC	.05
10	Steve Rodriguez	.05
11	Mark Williams RC	.05
12	Danny Clyburn RC	.05
13	Darren Dreifort	.05
14	Andy Van Slyke	.05
15	Wade Boggs	.85
16	Scott Patton	.05
17	Gary Sheffield	.45
18	Ron Villone	.05
19	Roberto Alomar	.20
20	Marc Valdes	.05
21	Daron Kirkreit	.05
22	Jeff Granger	.05
23	Levon Largusa	.05
24	Jimmy Key	.05
25	Kevin Pearson	.05
26	Michael Moore	.05
27	Preston Wilson RC	1.00
28	Kirby Puckett	.85
29	Tim Crabtree RC	.05
30	Bip Roberts	.05
31	Kelly Gruber	.05
32	Tony Fernandez	.05
33	Jason Angel	.05
34	Calvin Murray	.05
35	Chad McConnell	.05
36	Jason Moler	.05
37	Mark Lemke	.05
38	Tom Knauss	.05
39	Larry Mitchell	.05
40	Doug Mirabelli	.05
41	Everett Stull II	.05
42	Chris Wimmer	.05
43	Dan Serafini RC	.05
44	Ryne Sandberg	.85
45	Steve Lyons	.05
46	Ryan Freeburg	.05
47	Ruben Sierra	.05
48	David Mysel	.05
49	Joe Hamilton	.05
50	Steve Rodriguez	.05
51	Tim Wakefield	.05
52	Scott Gentile	.05
53	Doug Jones	.05
54	Willie Brown	.05
55	Chad Mottola RC	.05
56	Ken Griffey Jr.	1.50
57	Jon Lieber RC	.50
58	Denny Martinez	.05
59	Joe Petcka	.05
60	Benji Simonton	.05
61	Brett Backlund	.05
62	Damon Berryhill	.05
63	Juan Guzman	.05
64	Doug Hecker	.05
65	Jamie Arnold	.05
66	Bob Tewksbury	.05
67	Tim Leger	.05
68	Todd Etler	.05
69	Lloyd McClendon	.05
70	Kurt Ehmann	.05
71	Rick Magdaleno	.05
72	Tom Pagnozzi	.05
73	Jeffrey Hammonds	.05
74	Joe Carter	.05
75	Chris Holt	.05
76	Charles Johnson	.05
77	Bob Walk	.05

No.	Player	Price
78	Fred McGriff	.05
79	Tom Evans	.05
80	Scott Klingenbeck	.05
81	Chad McConnell	.05
82	Chris Eddy	.05
83	Phil Nevin	.05
84	John Kruk	.05
85	Tony Sheffield	.05
86	John Smoltz	.05
87	Trevor Humphry	.05
88	Charles Nagy	.05
89	Sean Runyan	.05
90	Mike Gulan	.05
91	Darren Daulton	.05
92	Otis Nixon	.05
93	Nomar Garciaparra	8.00
94	Larry Walker	.05
95	Hut Smith	.05
96	Rick Helling	.05
97	Roger Clemens	1.00
98	Ron Gant	.05
99	Kenny Felder	.05
100	Steve Murphy	.05
101	Mike Smith	.05
102	Terry Pendleton	.05
103	Tim Davis	.05
104	Jeff Patzke	.05
105	Craig Wilson	.05
106	Tom Glavine	.35
107	Mark Langston	.05
108	Mark Thompson	.05
109	Eric Owens RC	.05
110	Keith Johnson	.05
111	Robin Ventura	.05
112	Ed Sprague	.05
113	Jeff Schmidt RC	.05
114	Don Wengert	.05
115	Craig Biggio	.05
116	Kenny Carlyle	.05
117	Derek Jeter RC	30.00
118	Manuel Lee	.05
119	Jeff Haas	.05
120	Roger Bailey	.05
121	Sean Lowe	.05
122	Rick Aguilera	.05
123	Sandy Alomar	.05
124	Derek Wallace	.05
125	B.J. Wallace	.05
126	Greg Maddux	.85
127	Tim Moore	.05
128	Lee Smith	.05
129	Todd Steverson	.05
130	Chris Widger	.05
131	Paul Molitor	.75
132	Chris Smith	.05
133	Chris Gomez RC	.05
134	Jimmy Baron	.05
135	John Smoltz	.05
136	Pat Borders	.05
137	Donnie Leshnock	.05
138	Gus Gandarillos	.05
139	Will Clark	.05
140	Ryan Luzinski RC	.05
141	Cal Ripken, Jr.	2.50
142	B.J. Wallace	.05
143	Trey Beamon RC	.05
144	Norm Charlton	.05
145	Mike Mussina	.30
146	Billy Owens	.05
147	Ozzie Smith	.85
148	Jason Kendall RC	1.00
149	Mike Matthews RC	.05
150	David Spykstra	.05
151	Benji Grigsby	.05
152	Sean Smith	.05
153	Mark McGwire	2.00
154	David Cone	.05
155	Shon Walker RC	.05
156	Jason Giambi	.50
157	Jack McDowell	.05
158	Paxton Briley	.05
159	Edgar Martinez	.05
160	Brian Sackinsky	.05
161	Barry Bonds	2.50
162	Roberto Kelly	.05
163	Jeff Alkire	.05
164	Mike Sharperson	.05
165	Jamie Taylor	.05
166	John Saffer	.05
167	Jerry Browne	.05
168	Travis Fryman	.05
169	Brady Anderson	.05
170	Chris Roberts	.05
171	Lloyd Peever	.05
172	Francisco Cabrera	.05
173	Ramiro Martinez	.05
174	Jeff Alkire	.05
175	Ivan Rodriguez	.65
176	Kevin Brown	.05
177	Chad Roper	.05
178	Rod Henderson	.05
179	Dennis Eckersley	.65
180	Shannon Stewart RC	1.00
181	DeShawn Warren	.05
182	Lonnie Smith	.05
183	Willie Adams	.05
184	Jerry Montgomery	.05
185	Damon Hollins	.05
186	Byron Matthews	.05
187	Harold Baines	.05
188	Rick Greene	.05
189	Carlos Baerga	.05
190	Brandon Cromer	.05
191	Roberto Alomar	.20
192	Rich Ireland	.05
193	Steve Montgomery	.05
194	Brant Brown	.05
195	Ritchie Moody	.05
196	Michael Tucker	.05
197	Jason Varitek RC	6.00
198	David Manning	.05
199	Marquis Riley	.05
200	Jason Giambi	.60

1994 Stadium Club

cecil FIELDER

	NM/M
Complete Set (720):	20.00
Common Player:	.05
1st Day:	8X
Golden Rainbow:	2X
Series 1, 2, 3 Pack (12):	1.00
Series 1, 2, 3 Wax	
Box (24):	15.00

No.	Player	Price
1	Robin Yount	.65
2	Rick Wilkins	.05
3	Steve Scarsone	.05
4	Gary Sheffield	.40
5	George Brett	1.00
6	Al Martin	.05
7	Joe Oliver	.05
8	Stan Belinda	.05
9	Denny Hocking	.05
10	Roberto Alomar	.20
11	Luis Polonia	.05
12	Scott Hemond	.05
13	Joey Reed	.05
14	Mel Rojas	.05
15	Junior Ortiz	.05
16	Harold Baines	.05
17	Brad Pennington	.05
18	Jay Bell	.05
19	Tom Henke	.05
20	Jeff Branson	.05
21	Roberto Mejia	.05
22	Pedro Munoz	.05
23	Matt Nokes	.05
24	Jack McDowell	.05
25	Cecil Fielder	.05
26	Tony Fossas	.05
27	Jim Eisenreich	.05
28	Anthony Young	.05
29	Chuck Carr	.05
30	Jeff Treadway	.05
31	Chris Nabholz	.05
32	Tom Candiotti	.05
33	Mike Maddux	.05
34	Nolan Ryan	2.00
35	Luis Gonzalez	.05
36	Tim Salmon	.05
37	Mark Whiten	.05
38	Roger McDowell	.05
39	Royce Clayton	.05
40	Troy Neel	.05
41	Mike Harkey	.05
42	Darrin Fletcher	.05
43	Wayne Kirby	.05
44	Rich Amaral	.05
45	Rob Nen	.05
46	Tim Teufel	.05
47	Steve Cooke	.05
48	Jeff McNeely	.05
49	Jeff Montgomery	.05
50	Skeeter Barnes	.05
51	Scott Stahoviak	.05
52	Pat Kelly	.05
53	Brady Anderson	.05
54	Mariano Duncan	.05
55	Brian Bohanon	.05
56	Jerry Spradlin	.05
57	Ron Karkovice	.05
58	Jeff Gardner	.05
59	Bobby Bonilla	.05
60	Tino Martinez	.05
61	Todd Benzinger	.05
62	Steve Trachsel RC	.25
63	Brian Jordan	.05
64	Steve Bedrosian	.05
65	Brent Gates	.05
66	Shawn Green	.35
67	Sean Berry	.05
68	Joe Klink	.05
69	Fernando Valenzuela	.05
70	Andy Tomberlin	.05
71	Tony Pena	.05
72	Eric Young	.05
73	Chris Gomez	.05
74	Paul O'Neill	.05
75	Ricky Gutierrez	.05
76	Brad Holman	.05
77	Lance Painter	.05
78	Mike Butcher	.05
79	Sid Bream	.05
80	Sammy Sosa	.75
81	Felix Fermin	.05
82	Todd Hundley	.05
83	Kevin Higgins	.05
84	Todd Pratt	.05
85	Ken Griffey Jr.	1.25
86	John O'Donoghue	.05
87	Rick Renteria	.05
88	John Burkett	.05
89	Jose Vizcaino	.05
90	Kevin Seitzer	.05
91	Bobby Witt	.05
92	Chris Turner	.05
93	Omar Vizquel	.05
94	Dave Justice	.05
95	David Segui	.05
96	Dave Hollins	.05
97	Doug Strange	.05
98	Jerald Clark	.05
99	Mike Moore	.05
100	Joey Cora	.05
101	Scott Kamieniecki	.05
102	Andy Benes	.05
103	Chris Bosio	.05
104	Rey Sanchez	.05
105	John Jaha	.05
106	Otis Nixon	.05
107	Rickey Henderson	.65
108	Jeff Bagwell	.65
109	Gregg Jefferies	.05
110	Roberto Alomar, Paul Molitor, John Olerud Topps Trios	.25
111	Ron Gant, David Justice, Fred McGriff Topps Trios	.05
112	Juan Gonzalez, Rafael Palmeiro, Dean Palmer Topps Trios	.25
113	Greg Swindell	.05
114	Bill Hasleman	.05
115	Phil Plantier	.05
116	Ivan Rodriguez	.60
117	Kevin Tapani	.05
118	Mike LaValliere	.05
119	Tim Costo	.05
120	Mickey Morandini	.05
121	Brett Butler	.05
122	Tom Pagnozzi	.05
123	Ron Gant	.05
124	Damion Easley	.05
125	Dennis Eckersley	.60
126	Matt Mieske	.05
127	Cliff Floyd	.05
128	Julian Tavarez RC	.05
129	Arthur Rhodes	.05
130	Dave West	.05
131	Tim Naehring	.05
132	Freddie Benavides	.05
133	Paul Assenmacher	.05
134	David McCarty	.05
135	Jose Lind	.05
136	Reggie Sanders	.05
137	Don Slaught	.05
138	Andujar Cedeno	.05
139	Rob Deer	.05
140	Mike Piazza	1.25
141	Moises Alou	.05
142	Tom Foley	.05
143	Benny Santiago	.05
144	Sandy Alomar	.05
145	Carlos Hernandez	.05
146	Luis Alicea	.05
147	Tom Lampkin	.05
148	Ryan Klesko	.05
149	Juan Guzman	.05
150	Scott Servais	.05
151	Tony Gwynn	.75
152	Tim Wakefield	.05
153	David Nied	.05
154	Chris Haney	.05
155	Danny Bautista	.05
156	Randy Velarde	.05
157	Darrin Jackson	.05
158	J.R. Phillips RC	.05
159	Greg Gagne	.05
160	Luis Aquino	.05
161	John Vander Wal	.05
162	Randy Myers	.05
163	Ted Power	.05
164	Scott Brosius	.05
165	Len Dykstra	.05
166	Jacob Brumfield	.05
167	Bo Jackson	.10
168	Eddie Taubensee	.05
169	Carlos Baerga	.05
170	Tim Bogar	.05
171	Jose Canseco	.50
172	Greg Blosser	.05
173	Chili Davis	.05
174	Randy Knorr	.05
175	Mike Perez	.05
176	Henry Rodriguez	.05
177	Brian Turang RC	.05
178	Roger Pavlik	.05
179	Aaron Sele	.05
180	Fred McGriff, Gary Sheffield Tale of 2 Players	.05
181	J.T. Snow, Tim Salmon Tale of 2 Players	.05
182	Roberto Hernandez	.05
183	Jeff Reboulet	.05
184	John Doherty	.05
185	Danny Sheaffer	.05
186	Bip Roberts	.05
187	Denny Martinez	.05
188	Darryl Hamilton	.05
189	Eduardo Perez	.05
190	Pete Harnisch	.05
191	Rick Gossage	.05
192	Mickey Tettleton	.05
193	Lenny Webster	.05
194	Lance Johnson	.05
195	Don Mattingly	1.00
196	Gregg Olson	.05
197	Mark Gubicza	.05
198	Scott Fletcher	.05
199	Jon Shave	.05
200	Tim Mauser	.05
201	Jeromy Burnitz	.05
202	Rob Dibble	.05
203	Will Clark	.05
204	Steve Buechele	.05
205	Brian Williams	.05
206	Carlos Garcia	.05
207	Mark Clark	.05
208	Rafael Palmeiro	.60
209	Eric Davis	.05
210	Pat Meares	.05
211	Chuck Finley	.05
212	Jason Bere	.05
213	Gary DiSarcina	.05
214	Tony Fernandez	.05
215	B.J. Surhoff	.05
216	Lee Guetterman	.05
217	Tim Wallach	.05
218	Kirt Manwaring	.05
219	Albert Belle	.05
220	Dwight Gooden	.05
221	Archi Cianfrocco	.05
222	Terry Mulholland	.05
223	Hipolito Pichardo	.05
224	Kent Hrbek	.05
225	Criag Grebeck	.05
226	Todd Jones	.05
227	Mike Bordick	.05
228	John Olerud	.05
229	Jeff Blauser	.05
230	Alex Arias	.05
231	Bernard Gilkey	.05
232	Denny Neagle	.05
233	Pedro Borbon RC	.05
234	Dick Schofield	.05
235	Matias Carrillo	.05
236	Juan Bell	.05
237	Mike Hampton	.05
238	Barry Bonds	2.00
239	Cris Carpenter	.05
240	Eric Karros	.05
241	Greg McMichael	.05
242	Pat Hentgen	.05
243	Tim Pugh	.05
244	Vinny Castilla	.05
245	Charlie Hough	.05
246	Bobby Munoz	.05
247	Kevin Baez	.05
248	Todd Frohwirth	.05
249	Charlie Hayes	.05
250	Mike Macfarlane	.05
251	Danny Darwin	.05

#	Player	Price
252	Ben Rivera	.05
253	Dave Henderson	.05
254	Steve Avery	.05
255	Tim Belcher	.05
256	Dan Plesac	.05
257	Jim Thome	.60
258	Albert Belle	.05
259	Barry Bonds	1.00
260	Ron Gant	.05
261	Juan Gonzalez	.20
262	Ken Griffey Jr.	.65
263	Dave Justice	.05
264	Fred McGriff	.05
265	Rafael Palmeiro	.20
266	Mike Piazza	.65
267	Frank Thomas	.35
268	Matt Williams	.05
269a	Checklist 1-135	.05
269b	Checklist 271-408	.05
270a	Checklist 136-270	.05
270b	Checklist 409-540	.05
271	Mike Stanley	.05
272	Tony Tarasco	.05
273	Teddy Higuera	.05
274	Ryan Thompson	.05
275	Rick Aguilera	.05
276	Ramon Martinez	.05
277	Orlando Merced	.05
278	Guillermo Velasquez	.05
279	Mark Hutton	.05
280	Larry Walker	.05
281	Kevin Gross	.05
282	Jose Offerman	.05
283	Jim Leyritz	.05
284	Jamie Moyer	.05
285	Frank Thomas	.65
286	Derek Bell	.05
287	Derrick May	.05
288	Dave Winfield	.65
289	Curt Schilling	.35
290	Carlos Quintana	.05
291	Bob Natal	.05
292	David Cone	.05
293	Al Osuna	.05
294	Bob Hamelin	.05
295	Chad Curtis	.05
296	Danny Jackson	.05
297	Bob Welch	.05
298	Felix Jose	.05
299	Jay Buhner	.05
300	Joe Carter	.05
301	Kenny Lofton	.05
302	Kirk Rueter RC	.15
303	Kim Batiste	.05
304	Mike Morgan	.05
305	Pat Borders	.05
306	Rene Arocha	.05
307	Ruben Sierra	.05
308	Steve Finley	.05
309	Travis Fryman	.05
310	Zane Smith	.05
311	Willie Wilson	.05
312	Trevor Hoffman	.05
313	Terry Pendleton	.05
314	Salomon Torres	.05
315	Robin Ventura	.05
316	Randy Tomlin	.05
317	Dave Stewart	.05
318	Mike Benjamin	.05
319	Matt Turner	.05
320	Manny Ramirez	.65
321	Kevin Young	.05
322	Ken Caminiti	.05
323	Joe Girardi	.05
324	Jeff McKnight	.05
325	Gene Harris	.05
326	Devon White	.05
327	Darryl Kile	.05
328	Craig Paquette	.05
329	Cal Eldred	.05
330	Bill Swift	.05
331	Alan Trammell	.05
332	Armando Reynoso	.05
333	Brent Mayne	.05
334	Chris Donnels	.05
335	Darryl Strawberry	.05
336	Dean Palmer	.05
337	Frank Castillo	.05
338	Jeff King	.05
339	John Franco	.05
340	Kevin Appier	.05
341	Lance Blankenship	.05
342	Mark McLemore	.05
343	Pedro Astacio	.05
344	Rich Batchelor	.05
345	Ryan Bowen	.05
346	Terry Steinbach	.05
347	Troy O'Leary	.05
348	Willie Blair	.05
349	Wade Boggs	.75
350	Tim Raines	.05
351	Scott Livingstone	.05
352	Rod Carreia	.05
353	Ray Lankford	.05
354	Pat Listach	.05
355	Milt Thompson	.05
356	Miguel Jimenez	.05
357	Marc Newfield	.05
358	Mark McGwire	1.50
359	Kirby Puckett	.75
360	Kent Mercker	.05
361	John Kruk	.05
362	Jeff Kent	.05
363	Hal Morris	.05
364	Edgar Martinez	.05
365	Dave Magadan	.05
366	Dante Bichette	.05
367	Chris Hammond	.05
368	Bret Saberhagen	.05
369	Billy Ripken	.05
370	Bill Gullickson	.05
371	Andre Dawson	.35
372	Bobby Kelly	.05
373	Cal Ripken, Jr.	2.00
374	Craig Biggio	.05
375	Dan Pasqua	.05
376	Dave Nilsson	.05
377	Duane Ward	.05
378	Greg Vaughn	.05
379	Jeff Fassero	.05
380	Jerry Dipoto	.05
381	John Patterson	.05
382	Kevin Brown	.05
383	Kevin Roberson	.05
384	Joe Orsulak	.05
385	Hilly Hathaway	.05
386	Mike Greenwell	.05
387	Orestes Destrade	.05
388	Mike Gallego	.05
389	Ozzie Guillen	.05
390	Raul Mondesi	.05
391	Scott Lydy	.05
392	Tom Urbani	.05
393	Wil Cordero	.05
394	Tony Longmire	.05
395	Todd Zeile	.05
396	Scott Cooper	.05
397	Ryne Sandberg	.75
398	Ricky Bones	.05
399	Phil Clark	.05
400	Orel Hershiser	.05
401	Mike Henneman	.05
402	Mark Lemke	.05
403	Mark Grace	.05
404	Ken Ryan	.05
405	John Smoltz	.05
406	Jeff Conine	.05
407	Greg Harris	.05
408	Doug Drabek	.05
409	Dave Fleming	.05
410	Danny Tartabull	.05
411	Chad Kreuter	.05
412	Brad Ausmus	.05
413	Ben McDonald	.05
414	Barry Larkin	.05
415	Bret Barberie	.05
416	Chuck Knoblauch	.05
417	Ozzie Smith	.75
418	Ed Sprague	.05
419	Matt Williams	.05
420	Jeremy Hernandez	.05
421	Jose Bautista	.05
422	Kevin Mitchell	.05
423	Manuel Lee	.05
424	Mike Devereaux	.05
425	Omar Olivares	.05
426	Rafael Belliard	.05
427	Richie Lewis	.05
428	Ron Darling	.05
429	Shane Mack	.05
430	Tim Hulett	.05
431	Wally Joyner	.05
432	Wes Chamberlain	.05
433	Tom Browning	.05
434	Scott Radinsky	.05
435	Rondell White	.05
436	Rod Beck	.05
437	Rheal Cormier	.05
438	Randy Johnson	.65
439	Pete Schourek	.05
440	Mo Vaughn	.05
441	Mike Timlin	.05
442	Mark Langston	.05
443	Lou Whitaker	.05
444	Kevin Stocker	.05
445	Ken Hill	.05
446	John Wetteland	.05
447	J.T. Snow	.05
448	Erik Pappas	.05
449	David Hulse	.05
450	Darren Daulton	.05
451	Chris Hoiles	.05
452	Bryan Harvey	.05
453	Darren Lewis	.05
454	Andres Galarraga	.05
455	Joe Hesketh	.05
456	Jose Valentin	.05
457	Dan Peltier	.05
458	Joe Boever	.05
459	Kevin Rogers	.05
460	Craig Shipley	.05
461	Alvaro Espinoza	.05
462	Wilson Alvarez	.05
463	Cory Snyder	.05
464	Candy Maldonado	.05
465	Blas Minor	.05
466	Rod Bolton	.05
467	Kenny Rogers	.05
468	Greg Myers	.05
469	Jimmy Key	.05
470	Tony Castillo	.05
471	Mike Stanton	.05
472	Deion Sanders	.05
473	Tito Navarro	.05
474	Mike Gardiner	.05
475	Steve Reed	.05
476	John Roper	.05
477	Mike Trombley	.05
478	Charles Nagy	.05
479	Larry Casian	.05
480	Eric Hillman	.05
481	Bill Wertz	.05
482	Jeff Schwarz	.05
483	John Valentin	.05
484	Carl Willis	.05
485	Gary Gaetti	.05
486	Bill Pecota	.05
487	John Smiley	.05
488	Mike Mussina	.35
489	Mike Ignasiak RC	.05
490	Billy Brewer	.05
491	Jack Voigt	.05
492	Mike Munoz	.05
493	Lee Tinsley	.05
494	Bob Wickman	.05
495	Roger Salkeld	.05
496	Thomas Howard	.05
497	Mark Davis	.05
498	Dave Clark	.05
499	Turk Wendell	.05
500	Rafael Bournigal	.05
501	Chip Hale	.05
502	Matt Whiteside	.05
503	Brian Koelling	.05
504	Jeff Reed	.05
505	Paul Wagner	.05
506	Torey Lovullo	.05
507	Curtis Leskanic	.05
508	Derek Lilliquist	.05
509	Joe Magrane	.05
510	Mackey Sasser	.05
511	Lloyd McClendon	.05
512	Jayhawk Owens RC	.05
513	Woody Williams RC	.05
514	Gary Redus	.05
515	Tim Spehr	.05
516	Jim Abbott	.05
517	Lou Frazier	.05
518	Erik Plantenberg	.05
519	Tim Worrell	.05
520	Brian McRae	.05
521	Chan Ho Park RC	1.00
522	Mark Wohlers	.05
523	Geronimo Pena	.05
524	Andy Ashby	.05
525	Tim Raines, Andre Dawson Tale of 2 Players	.05
526	Paul Molitor, Dave Winfield Tale of 2 Players	.05
527	Joe Carter (RBI Leader)	.05
528	Frank Thomas	.35
529	Ken Griffey Jr.	.65
530	Dave Justice	.05
531	Gregg Jefferies	.05
532	Barry Bonds	1.00
533	John Kruk	.05
534	Roger Clemens	.50
535	Cecil Fielder	.05
536	Ruben Sierra	.05
537	Tony Gwynn	.40
538	Tom Glavine	.10
539	Not Issued, See #269	
540	Not Issued, See #270	
541	Ozzie Smith	.40
542	Eddie Murray	.30
543a	Lee Smith	.05
543b	Lonnie Smith (Should be #643.)	.05
544	Greg Maddux	.75
545	Denis Boucher	.05
546	Mark Gardner	.05
547	Bo Jackson	.10
548	Eric Anthony	.05
549	Delino DeShields	.05
550	Turner Ward	.05
551	Scott Sanderson	.05
552	Hector Carrasco	.05
553	Tony Phillips	.05
554	Melido Perez	.05
555	Mike Felder	.05
556	Jack Morris	.05
557	Rafael Palmeiro	.60
558	Shane Reynolds	.05
559	Pete Incaviglia	.05
560	Greg Harris	.05
561	Matt Walbeck	.05
562	Todd Van Poppel	.05
563	Todd Stottlemyre	.05
564	Ricky Bones	.05
565	Mike Jackson	.05
566	Kevin McReynolds	.05
567	Melvin Nieves	.05
568	Juan Gonzalez	.35
569	Frank Viola	.05
570	Vince Coleman	.05
571	Brian Anderson RC	.25
572	Omar Vizquel	.05
573	Bernie Williams	.05
574	Tom Glavine	.35
575	Mitch Williams	.05
576	Shawon Dunston	.05
577	Mike Lansing	.05
578	Greg Pirkl	.05
579	Sid Fernandez	.05
580	Doug Jones	.05
581	Walt Weiss	.05
582	Tim Belcher	.05
583	Alex Fernandez	.05
584	Alex Cole	.05
585	Greg Cadaret	.05
586	Bob Tewksbury	.05
587	Dave Hansen	.05
588	Kurt Abbott RC	.25
589	Rick White RC	.05
590	Kevin Bass	.05
591	Geronimo Berroa	.05
592	Jaime Navarro	.05
593	Steve Farr	.05
594	Jack Armstrong	.05
595	Steve Howe	.05
596	Jose Rijo	.05
597	Otis Nixon	.05
598	Robby Thompson	.05
599	Kelly Stinnett	.05
600	Carlos Delgado	.50
601	Brian Johnson RC	.05
602	Gregg Olson	.05
603	Jim Edmonds	.05
604	Mike Blowers	.05
605	Lee Smith	.05
606	Pat Rapp	.05
607	Mike Magnante	.05
608	Karl Rhodes	.05
609	Jeff Juden	.05
610	Rusty Meacham	.05
611	Pedro Martinez	.65
612	Todd Worrell	.05
613	Stan Javier	.05
614	Mike Hampton	.05
615	Jose Guzman	.05
616	Xavier Hernandez	.05
617	David Wells	.05
618	John Habyan	.05
619	Chris Nabholz	.05
620	Bobby Jones	.05
621	Chris James	.05
622	Ellis Burks	.05
623	Erik Hanson	.05
624	Pat Meares	.05
625	Harold Reynolds	.05
626	Bob Hamelin	.05
627	Manny Ramirez	.30
628	Ryan Klesko	.30
629	Carlos Delgado	.30
630	Javier Lopez	.05
631	Steve Karsay	.05
632	Rick Helling	.05
633	Steve Trachsel	.05
634	Hector Carrasco	.05
635	Andy Stankiewicz	.05
636	Paul Sorrento	.05
637	Scott Erickson	.05
638	Chipper Jones	.75
639	Luis Polonia	.05
640	Howard Johnson	.05
641	John Dopson	.05
642	Jody Reed	.05
643	Not issued, see #543.	
644	Mark Portugal	.05
645	Paul Molitor	.65
646	Paul Assenmacher	.05
647	Hubie Brooks	.05
648	Gary Wayne	.05
649	Sean Berry	.05
650	Roger Clemens	1.00
651	Brian Hunter	.05
652	Wally Whitehurst	.05
653	Allen Watson	.05
654	Rickey Henderson	.65
655	Sid Bream	.05
656	Dan Wilson	.05
657	Ricky Jordan	.05
658	Sterling Hitchcock	.05
659	Darrin Jackson	.05
660	Junior Felix	.05
661	Tom Brunansky	.05

662	Jose Vizcaino	.05
663	Mark Leiter	.05
664	Gil Heredia	.05
665	Fred McGriff	.05
666	Will Clark	.05
667	Al Leiter	.05
668	James Mouton	.05
669	Billy Bean	.05
670	Scott Leius	.05
671	Bret Boone	.05
672	Darren Holmes	.05
673	Dave Weathers	.05
674	Eddie Murray	.65
675	Felix Fermin	.05
676	Chris Sabo	.05
677	Billy Spiers	.05
678	Aaron Sele	.05
679	Juan Samuel	.05
680	Julio Franco	.05
681	Heathcliff Slocumb	.05
682	Denny Martinez	.05
683	Jerry Browne	.05
684	Pedro A. Martinez RC	.05
685	Rex Hudler	.05
686	Willie McGee	.05
687	Andy Van Slyke	.05
688	Pat Mahomes	.05
689	Dave Henderson	.05
690	Tony Eusebio	.05
691	Rick Sutcliffe	.05
692	Willie Banks	.05
693	Alan Mills	.05
694	Jeff Treadway	.05
695	Alex Gonzalez	.05
696	David Segui	.05
697	Rick Helling	.05
698	Bip Roberts	.05
699	Jeff Cirillo RC	.25
700	Terry Mulholland	.05
701	Marvin Freeman	.05
702	Jason Bere	.05
703	Javier Lopez	.05
704	Greg Hibbard	.05
705	Tommy Greene	.05
706	Marquis Grissom	.05
707	Brian Harper	.05
708	Steve Karsay	.05
709	Jeff Brantley	.05
710	Jeff Russell	.05
711	Bryan Harvey	.05
712	Jim Pittsley RC	.05
713	Bobby Ayala	.05
714	John Smoltz	.05
715	Jose Rijo	.05
716	Greg Maddux	.40
717	Matt Williams	.05
718	Frank Thomas	.35
719	Ryne Sandberg	.40
720	Checklist	.05

1st Day Issue

	NM/M
Common Player:	1.00
Stars:	8X

(See 1994 Stadium Club for checklist and base card values.)

Golden Rainbow

	NM/M
Complete Set (720):	60.00
Common Player:	.25
Stars:	2X

(See 1994 Stadium Club for checklist and base card values.)

Dugout Dirt

		NM/M
Complete Set (12):		5.00
Common Player:		.25
1	Mike Piazza (Catch of the Day)	1.00
2	Dave Winfield (The Road to 3,000)	.65
3	John Kruk (From Coal Mine to Gold Mine)	.25
4	Cal Ripken, Jr. (On Track)	2.00
5	Jack McDowell (Chin Music)	.25
6	Barry Bonds (The Bonds Market)	2.00
7	Ken Griffey Jr. (Gold Gloves/All-Star)	1.00
8	Tim Salmon (The Salmon Run)	.25
9	Frank Thomas (Big Hurt)	.65
10	Jeff Kent (Super Kent)	.25
11	Randy Johnson (High Heat)	.65
12	Darren Daulton (Daulton's Gym)	.25

Finest

		NM/M
Complete Set (10):		11.00
Common Player:		.50
1	Jeff Bagwell	1.25
2	Albert Belle	.50
3	Barry Bonds	3.00
4	Juan Gonzalez	.75

5	Ken Griffey Jr.	2.00
6	Marquis Grissom	.50
7	David Justice	.50
8	Mike Piazza	2.00
9	Tim Salmon	.50
10	Frank Thomas	1.50

Finest Jumbo

		NM/M
Complete Set (10):		30.00
Common Player:		2.00
1	Jeff Bagwell	4.00
2	Albert Belle	2.00
3	Barry Bonds	6.50
4	Juan Gonzalez	3.00
5	Ken Griffey Jr.	5.00
6	Marquis Grissom	2.00
7	David Justice	2.00
8	Mike Piazza	5.00
9	Tim Salmon	2.00
10	Frank Thomas	4.00

Super Teams

		NM/M
Complete Set (28):		25.00
Common Team:		.70
Expired Jan. 31, 1996.		
1	Atlanta Braves	5.00
2	Chicago Cubs	.70
3	Cincinnati Reds	1.25
4	Colorado Rockies	1.00
5	Florida Marlins	.70
6	Houston Astros	1.00
7	Los Angeles Dodgers	1.75
8	Montreal Expos	1.00
9	New York Mets	.70
10	Philadelphia Phillies	.70
11	Pittsburgh Pirates	.70
12	St. Louis Cardinals	.70
13	San Diego Padres	.70
14	San Francisco Giants	1.25
15	Baltimore Orioles	1.25
16	Boston Red Sox	1.00
17	California Angels	.70
18	Chicago White Sox	1.50
19	Cleveland Indians	2.00
20	Detroit Tigers	.70
21	Kansas City Royals	1.00
22	Milwaukee Brewers	.70
23	Minnesota Twins	1.00
24	New York Yankees	1.50
25	Oakland Athletics	1.00
26	Seattle Mariners	2.00
27	Texas Rangers	1.00
28	Toronto Blue Jays	1.00

1994 Stadium Club Draft Picks

	NM/M
Complete Set (90):	7.50

Common Player:		.05
Wax Box (24):		9.00
1	Jacob Shumate	.05
2	C.J. Nitkowski	.05
3	Doug Million	.05
4	Matt Smith	.05
5	Kevin Lovinger	.05
6	Alberto Castillo	.05
7	Mike Russell	.05
8	Dan Lock	.05
9	Tom Szimanski	.05
10	Aaron Boone	.25
11	Jayson Peterson	.05
12	Mark Johnson	.05
13	Cade Gaspar	.05
14	George Lombard	.10
15	Russ Johnson	.10
16	Travis Miller	.10
17	Jay Payton	.50
18	Brian Buchanan	.10
19	Jacob Cruz	.10
20	Gary Rath	.05
21	Ramon Castro	.05
22	Tommy Davis	.05
23	Tony Terry	.05
24	Jerry Whittaker	.05
25	Mike Darr	.05
26	Doug Webb	.05
27	Jason Camilli	.05
28	Brad Rigby	.05
29	Ryan Nye	.05
30	Carl Dale	.05
31	Andy Taulbee	.05
32	Trey Moore	.05
33	John Crowther	.05
34	Joe Giuliano	.05
35	Brian Rose	.05
36	Paul Failla	.05
37	Brian Meadows	.05
38	Oscar Robles	.05
39	Mike Metcalff	.05
40	Larry Barnes	.05
41	Paul Ottavinia	.05
42	Chris McBride	.05
43	Ricky Stone	.05
44	Billy Blythe	.05
45	Eddie Priest	.05
46	Scott Forster	.05
47	Eric Pickett	.05
48	Matt Beaumont	.05
49	Darrell Nicolas	.05
50	Mike Hampton	.05
51	Paul O'Malley	.05
52	Steve Shoemaker	.05
53	Jason Sikes	.05
54	Bryan Farson	.05
55	Yates Hall	.05
56	Troy Brohawn	.05
57	Dan Hower	.05
58	Clay Caruthers	.05
59	Pepe McNeal	.05
60	Ray Ricken	.05
61	Scott Shores	.05
62	Eddie Brooks	.05
63	Dave Kauflin	.05
64	David Meyer	.05
65	Geoff Blum	.05
66	Roy Marsh	.05
67	Ryan Beeney	.05
68	Derek Dukart	.05
69	Nomar Garciaparra	6.00
70	Jason Kelley	.05
71	Jesse Ibarra	.05
72	Bucky Buckles	.05
73	Mark Little	.05
74	Heath Murray	.05
75	Greg Morris	.05
76	Mike Halperin	.05
77	Wes Helms	.05
78	Ray Brown	.05
79	Kevin Brown	.05
80	Paul Konerko	.50
81	Mike Thurman	.05
82	Paul Wilson	.10

83	Terrence Long	.25
84	Ben Grieve	.50
85	Mark Farris	.05
86	Bret Wagner	.05
87	Dustin Hermanson	.05
88	Kevin Witt	.05
89	Corey Pointer	.05
90	Tim Grieve	.05

First Day Issue

	NM/M
Complete Set (90):	150.00
Common Player:	1.00
Stars:	15X

(See 1994 Stadium Club Draft Picks for checklist and base card values.)

1995 Stadium Club

	NM/M
Complete Set (630):	25.00
Common Player:	.05
Series 1 or 2 Pack (14):	1.25
Series 1 or 2 Wax Box (24):	20.00
Series 3 Pack (13):	1.25
Series 3 Wax Box (24):	20.00

1	Cal Ripken Jr.	2.50
2	Bo Jackson	.10
3	Bryan Harvey	.05
4	Curt Schilling	.35
5	Bruce Ruffin	.05
6	Travis Fryman	.05
7	Jim Abbott	.05
8	David McCarty	.05
9	Gary Gaetti	.05
10	Roger Clemens	1.25
11	Carlos Garcia	.05
12	Lee Smith	.05
13	Bobby Ayala	.05
14	Charles Nagy	.05
15	Lou Frazier	.05
16	Rene Arocha	.05
17	Carlos Delgado	.50
18	Steve Finley	.05
19	Ryan Klesko	.05
20	Cal Eldred	.05
21	Rey Sanchez	.05
22	Ken Hill	.05
23	Benny Santiago	.05
24	Julian Tavarez	.05
25	Jose Vizcaino	.05
26	Andy Benes	.05
27	Mariano Duncan	.05
28	Checklist A	.05
29	Shawon Dunston	.05
30	Rafael Palmeiro	.65
31	Dean Palmer	.05
32	Andres Galarraga	.05
33	Joey Cora	.05
34	Mickey Tettleton	.05
35	Barry Larkin	.05
36	Carlos Baerga	.05
37	Orel Hershiser	.05
38	Jody Reed	.05
39	Paul Molitor	.75
40	Jim Edmonds	.05
41	Bob Tewksbury	.05
42	John Patterson	.05
43	Ray McDavid	.05
44	Zane Smith	.05
45	Bret Saberhagen	.05
46	Greg Maddux	1.00
47	Frank Thomas	.75
48	Carlos Baerga	.05
49	Billy Spiers	.05
50	Stan Javier	.05
51	Rex Hudler	.05
52	Denny Hocking	.05
53	Todd Worrell	.05
54	Mark Clark	.05
55	Hipilito Pichardo	.05
56	Bob Wickman	.05
57	Raul Mondesi	.05
58	Steve Cooke	.05
59	Rod Beck	.05
60	Tim Davis	.05
61	Jeff Kent	.05
62	John Valentin	.05
63	Alex Arias	.05
64	Steve Reed	.05
65	Ozzie Smith	1.00
66	Terry Pendleton	.05
67	Kenny Rogers	.05
68	Vince Coleman	.05
69	Tom Pagnozzi	.05
70	Roberto Alomar	.20
71	Darrin Jackson	.05
72	Dennis Eckersley	.65
73	Jay Buhner	.05
74	Darren Lewis	.05
75	Dave Weathers	.05
76	Matt Walbeck	.05
77	Brad Ausmus	.05
78	Danny Bautista	.05
79	Bob Hamelin	.05
80	Steve Traschel	.05
81	Ken Ryan	.05
82	Chris Turner	.05
83	David Segui	.05
84	Ben McDonald	.05
85	Wade Boggs	1.00
86	John Vander Wal	.05
87	Sandy Alomar	.05
88	Ron Karkovice	.05
89	Doug Jones	.05
90	Gary Sheffield	.40
91	Ken Caminiti	.05
92	Chris Bosio	.05
93	Kevin Tapani	.05
94	Walt Weiss	.05
95	Erik Hanson	.05
96	Ruben Sierra	.05
97	Nomar Garciaparra	1.00
98	Terrence Long	.05
99	Jacob Shumate	.05
100	Paul Wilson	.05
101	Kevin Witt	.05
102	Paul Konerko	.15
103	Ben Grieve	.05
104	Mark Johnson RC	.05
105	Cade Gaspar RC	.05
106	Mark Farris	.05
107	Dustin Hermanson	.05
108	Scott Elarton RC	.15
109	Doug Million	.05
110	Matt Smith	.05
111	Brian Buchanan RC	.05
112	Jayson Peterson RC	.05
113	Bret Wagner	.05
114	C.J. Nitkowski	.05
115	Ramon Castro RC	.05
116	Rafael Bournigal	.05
117	Jeff Fassero	.05
118	Bobby Bonilla	.05
119	Ricky Gutierrez	.05
120	Roger Pavlik	.05
121	Mike Greenwell	.05
122	Deion Sanders	.05
123	Charlie Hayes	.05
124	Paul O'Neill	.05
125	Jay Bell	.05
126	Royce Clayton	.05
127	Willie Banks	.05
128	Mark Wohlers	.05
129	Todd Jones	.05
130	Todd Stottlemyre	.05
131	Will Clark	.05
132	Wilson Alvarez	.05
133	Chili Davis	.05
134	Dave Burba	.05
135	Chris Hoiles	.05
136	Jeff Blauser	.05
137	Jeff Reboulet	.05
138	Bret Saberhagen	.05
139	Kirk Rueter	.05
140	Dave Nilsson	.05
141	Pat Borders	.05
142	Ron Darling	.05
143	Derek Bell	.05
144	Dave Hollins	.05
145	Juan Gonzalez	.40
146	Andre Dawson	.25
147	Jim Thome	.65
148	Larry Walker	.05
149	Mike Piazza	1.50
150	Mike Perez	.05
151	Steve Avery	.05
152	Dan Wilson	.05
153	Andy Van Slyke	.05
154	Junior Felix	.05
155	Jack McDowell	.05
156	Danny Tartabull	.05
157	Willie Blair	.05
158	William Van Landingham	.05
159	Robb Nen	.05
160	Lee Tinsley	.05
161	Ismael Valdes	.05
162	Juan Guzman	.05
163	Scott Servais	.05
164	Cliff Floyd	.05
165	Allen Watson	.05
166	Eddie Taubensee	.05
167	Scott Hemond	.05
168	Jeff Tackett	.05
169	Chad Curtis	.05
170	Rico Brogna	.05
171	Luis Polonia	.05
172	Checklist B	.05
173	Lance Johnson	.05
174	Sammy Sosa	1.00
175	Mike MacFarlane	.05
176	Darryl Hamilton	.05
177	Rick Aguilera	.05
178	Dave West	.05
179	Mike Gallego	.05
180	Marc Newfield	.05
181	Steve Buechele	.05
182	David Wells	.05
183	Tom Glavine	.35
184	Joe Girardi	.05
185	Craig Biggio	.05
186	Eddie Murray	.75
187	Kevin Gross	.05
188	Sid Fernandez	.05
189	John Franco	.05
190	Bernard Gilkey	.05
191	Matt Williams	.05
192	Darrin Fletcher	.05
193	Jeff Conine	.05
194	Ed Sprague	.05
195	Eduardo Perez	.05
196	Scott Livingstone	.05
197	Ivan Rodriguez	.65
198	Orlando Merced	.05
199	Ricky Bones	.05
200	Javier Lopez	.05
201	Miguel Jimenez	.05
202	Terry McGriff	.05
203	Mike Lieberthal	.05
204	David Cone	.05
205	Todd Hundley	.05
206	Ozzie Guillen	.05
207	Alex Cole	.05
208	Tony Phillips	.05
209	Jim Eisenreich	.05
210	Greg Vaughn	.05
211	Barry Larkin	.05
212	Don Mattingly	1.00
213	Mark Grace	.05
214	Jose Canseco	.50
215	Joe Carter	.05
216	David Cone	.05
217	Sandy Alomar	.05
218	Al Martin	.05
219	Roberto Kelly	.05
220	Paul Sorrento	.05
221	Tony Fernandez	.05
222	Stan Belinda	.05
223	Mike Stanley	.05
224	Doug Drabek	.05
225	Todd Van Poppel	.05
226	Matt Mieske	.05
227	Tino Martinez	.05
228	Andy Ashby	.05
229	Midre Cummings	.05
230	Jeff Frye	.05
231	Hal Morris	.05
232	Jose Lind	.05
233	Shawn Green	.30
234	Rafael Belliard	.05
235	Randy Myers	.05
236	Frank Thomas	.45
237	Darren Daulton	.05
238	Sammy Sosa	.65
239	Cal Ripken Jr.	1.00
240	Jeff Bagwell	.40
241	Ken Griffey Jr.	1.50
242	Brett Butler	.05
243	Derrick May	.05
244	Pat Listach	.05
245	Mike Bordick	.05
246	Mark Langston	.05
247	Randy Velarde	.05
248	Julio Franco	.05
249	Chuck Knoblauch	.05
250	Bill Gullickson	.05
251	Dave Henderson	.05
252	Bret Boone	.05
253	Al Martin	.05
254	Armando Benitez	.05
255	Wil Cordero	.05
256	Al Leiter	.05
257	Luis Gonzalez	.05
258	Charlie O'Brien	.05
259	Tim Wallach	.05
260	Scott Sanders	.05
261	Tom Henke	.05
262	Otis Nixon	.05
263	Darren Daulton	.05
264	Manny Ramirez	.75
265	Bret Barberie	.05
266	Mel Rojas	.05
267	John Burkett	.05
268	Brady Anderson	.05
269	John Roper	.05
270	Shane Reynolds	.05
271	Barry Bonds	2.50
272	Alex Fernandez	.05
273	Brian McRae	.05
274	Todd Zeile	.05
275	Greg Swindell	.05
276	Johnny Ruffin	.05
277	Troy Neel	.05
278	Eric Karros	.05
279	John Hudek	.05
280	Thomas Howard	.05
281	Joe Carter	.05
282	Mike Devereaux	.05
283	Butch Henry	.05
284	Reggie Jefferson	.05
285	Mark Lemke	.05
286	Jeff Montgomery	.05
287	Ryan Thompson	.05
288	Paul Shuey	.05
289	Mark McGwire	2.00
290	Bernie Williams	.05
291	Mickey Morandini	.05
292	Scott Leius	.05
293	David Hulse	.05
294	Greg Gagne	.05
295	Moises Alou	.05
296	Geronimo Berroa	.05
297	Eddie Zambrano	.05
298	Alan Trammell	.05
299	Don Slaught	.05
300	Jose Rijo	.05
301	Joe Ausanio	.05
302	Tim Raines	.05
303	Melido Perez	.05
304	Kent Mercker	.05
305	James Mouton	.05
306	Luis Lopez	.05
307	Mike Kingery	.05
308	Willie Greene	.05
309	Cecil Fielder	.05
310	Scott Kamieniecki	.05
311	Mike Greenwell	.05
312	Bobby Bonilla	.05
313	Andres Galarraga	.05
314	Cal Ripken Jr.	1.25
315	Matt Williams	.05
316	Tom Pagnozzi	.05
317	Len Dykstra	.05
318	Frank Thomas	.40
319	Kirby Puckett	.50
320	Mike Piazza	1.00
321	Jason Jacome	.05
322	Brian Hunter	.05
323	Brent Gates	.05
324	Jim Converse	.05
325	Damion Easley	.05
326	Dante Bichette	.05
327	Kurt Abbott	.05
328	Scott Cooper	.05
329	Mike Henneman	.05
330	Orlando Miller	.05
331	John Kruk	.05
332	Jose Oliva	.05
333	Reggie Sanders	.05
334	Omar Vizquel	.05
335	Devon White	.05
336	Mike Morgan	.05
337	J.R. Phillips	.05
338	Gary DiSarcina	.05
339	Joey Hamilton	.05
340	Randy Johnson	.75
341	Jim Leyritz	.05
342	Bobby Jones	.05
343	Jaime Navarro	.05
344	Bip Roberts	.05
345	Steve Karsay	.05

346 Kevin Stocker	.05
347 Jose Canseco	.50
348 Bill Wegman	.05
349 Rondell White	.05
350 Mo Vaughn	.05
351 Joe Orsulak	.05
352 Pat Meares	.05
353 Albie Lopez	.05
354 Edgar Martinez	.05
355 Brian Jordan	.05
356 Tommy Greene	.05
357 Chuck Carr	.05
358 Pedro Astacio	.05
359 Russ Davis	.05
360 Chris Hammond	.05
361 Gregg Jefferies	.05
362 Shane Mack	.05
363 Fred McGriff	.05
364 Pat Rapp	.05
365 Bill Swift	.05
366 Checklist	.05
367 Robin Ventura	.05
368 Bobby Witt	.05
369 Karl Rhodes	.05
370 Eddie Williams	.05
371 John Jaha	.05
372 Steve Howe	.05
373 Leo Gomez	.05
374 Hector Fajardo	.05
375 Jeff Bagwell	.75
376 Mark Acre	.05
377 Wayne Kirby	.05
378 Mark Portugal	.05
379 Jesus Tavarez	.05
380 Jim Lindeman	.05
381 Don Mattingly	1.25
382 Trevor Hoffman	.05
383 Chris Gomez	.05
384 Garret Anderson	.05
385 Bobby Munoz	.05
386 Jon Lieber	.05
387 Rick Helling	.05
388 Marvin Freeman	.05
389 Juan Castillo	.05
390 Jeff Cirillo	.05
391 Sean Berry	.05
392 Hector Carrasco	.05
393 Mark Grace	.05
394 Pat Kelly	.05
395 Tim Naehring	.05
396 Greg Pirkl	.05
397 John Smoltz	.05
398 Robby Thompson	.05
399 Rick White	.05
400 Frank Thomas	.75
401 Jeff Conine	.05
402 Jose Valentin	.05
403 Carlos Baerga	.05
404 Rick Aguilera	.05
405 Wilson Alvarez	.05
406 Juan Gonzalez	.20
407 Barry Larkin	.05
408 Ken Hill	.05
409 Chuck Carr	.05
410 Tim Raines	.05
411 Bryan Eversgerd	.05
412 Phil Plantier	.05
413 Josias Manzanillo	.05
414 Roberto Kelly	.05
415 Rickey Henderson	.75
416 John Smiley	.05
417 Kevin Brown	.05
418 Jimmy Key	.05
419 Wally Joyner	.05
420 Roberto Hernandez	.05
421 Felix Fermin	.05
422 Checklist	.05
423 Greg Vaughn	.05
424 Ray Lankford	.05
425 Greg Maddux	1.00
426 Mike Mussina	.30
427 Geronimo Pena	.05
428 David Nied	.05
429 Scott Erickson	.05
430 Kevin Mitchell	.05
431 Mike Lansing	.05
432 Brian Anderson	.05
433 Jeff King	.05
434 Ramon Martinez	.05
435 Kevin Seitzer	.05
436 Salomon Torres	.05
437 Brian Hunter	.05
438 Melvin Nieves	.05
439 Mike Kelly	.05
440 Marquis Grissom	.05
441 Chuck Finley	.05
442 Len Dykstra	.05
443 Ellis Burks	.05
444 Harold Baines	.05
445 Kevin Appier	.05
446 Dave Justice	.05
447 Darryl Kile	.05
448 John Olerud	.05
449 Greg McMichael	.05

450 Kirby Puckett	1.00
451 Jose Valentin	.05
452 Rick Wilkins	.05
453 Arthur Rhodes	.05
454 Pat Hentgen	.05
455 Tom Gordon	.05
456 Tom Candiotti	.05
457 Jason Bere	.05
458 Wes Chamberlain	.05
459 Greg Colbrunn	.05
460 John Doherty	.05
461 Kevin Foster	.05
462 Mark Whiten	.05
463 Terry Steinbach	.05
464 Aaron Sele	.05
465 Kirt Manwaring	.05
466 Darren Hall	.05
467 Delino DeShields	.05
468 Andujar Cedeno	.05
469 Billy Ashley	.05
470 Kenny Lofton	.05
471 Pedro Munoz	.05
472 John Wetteland	.05
473 Tim Salmon	.05
474 Denny Neagle	.05
475 Tony Gwynn	1.00
476 Vinny Castilla	.05
477 Steve Dreyer	.05
478 Jeff Shaw	.05
479 Chad Ogea	.05
480 Scott Ruffcorn	.05
481 Lou Whitaker	.05
482 J.T. Snow	.05
483 Rich Rowland	.05
484 Dennis Martinez	.05
485 Pedro Martinez	.75
486 Rusty Greer	.05
487 Dave Fleming	.05
488 John Dettmer	.05
489 Albert Belle	.05
490 Ravelo Manzanillo	.05
491 Henry Rodriguez	.05
492 Andrew Lorraine	.05
493 Dwayne Hosey	.05
494 Mike Blowers	.05
495 Turner Ward	.05
496 Fred McGriff	.05
497 Sammy Sosa	.50
498 Barry Larkin	.05
499 Andres Galarraga	.05
500 Gary Sheffield	.15
501 Jeff Bagwell	.40
502 Mike Piazza	1.00
503 Moises Alou	.05
504 Bobby Bonilla	.05
505 Darren Daulton	.05
506 Jeff King	.05
507 Ray Lankford	.05
508 Tony Gwynn	.50
509 Barry Bonds	1.25
510 Cal Ripken Jr.	1.25
511 Mo Vaughn	.05
512 Tim Salmon	.05
513 Frank Thomas	.45
514 Albert Belle	.05
515 Cecil Fielder	.05
516 Kevin Appier	.05
517 Greg Vaughn	.05
518 Kirby Puckett	.50
519 Paul O'Neill	.05
520 Ruben Sierra	.05
521 Ken Griffey Jr.	.75
522 Will Clark	.05
523 Joe Carter	.05
524 Antonio Osuna	.05
525 Glenallen Hill	.05
526 Alex Gonzalez	.05
527 Dave Stewart	.05
528 Ron Gant	.05
529 Jason Bates	.05
530 Mike Macfarlane	.05
531 Esteban Loaiza	.05
532 Joe Randa	.05
533 Dave Winfield	.75
534 Danny Darwin	.05
535 Pete Harnisch	.05
536 Joey Cora	.05
537 Jaime Navarro	.05
538 Marty Cordova	.05
539 Andujar Cedeno	.05
540 Mickey Tettleton	.05
541 Andy Van Slyke	.05
542 Carlos Perez RC	.05
543 Chipper Jones	1.00
544 Tony Fernandez	.05
545 Tom Henke	.05
546 Pat Borders	.05
547 Chad Curtis	.05
548 Ray Durham	.05
549 Joe Oliver	.05
550 Jose Mesa	.05
551 Steve Finley	.05
552 Otis Nixon	.05
553 Jacob Brumfield	.05
554 Bill Swift	.05

555 Quilvio Veras	.05
556 Hideo Nomo RC	1.50
557 Joe Vitiello	.05
558 Mike Perez	.05
559 Charlie Hayes	.05
560 Brad Radke RC	.25
561 Darren Bragg	.05
562 Orel Hershiser	.05
563 Edgardo Alfonzo	.05
564 Doug Jones	.05
565 Andy Pettitte	.05
566 Benito Santiago	.05
567 John Burkett	.05
568 Brad Clontz	.05
569 Jim Abbott	.05
570 Joe Rosselli	.05
571 Mark Grudzielanek RC	.25
572 Dustin Hermanson	.05
573 Benji Gil	.05
574 Mark Whiten	.05
575 Mike Ignasiak	.05
576 Kevin Ritz	.05
577 Paul Quantrill	.05
578 Andre Dawson	.25
579 Jerald Clark	.05
580 Frank Rodriguez	.05
581 Mark Kiefer	.05
582 Trevor Wilson	.05
583 Gary Wilson RC	.05
584 Andy Stankiewicz	.05
585 Felipe Lira	.05
586 Mike Mimbs RC	.05
587 Jon Nunnally	.05
588 Tomas Perez RC	.05
589 Checklist	.05
590 Todd Hollandsworth	.05
591 Roberto Petagine	.05
592 Mariano Rivera	.15
593 Mark McLemore	.05
594 Bobby Witt	.05
595 Jose Offerman	.05
596 Jason Christiansen	.05
597 Jeff Manto	.05
598 Jim Dougherty	.05
599 Juan Acevedo	.05
600 Troy O'Leary	.05
601 Ron Villone	.05
602 Tripp Cromer	.05
603 Steve Scarsone	.05
604 Lance Parrish	.05
605 Ozzie Timmons	.05
606 Ray Holbert	.05
607 Tony Phillips	.05
608 Phil Plantier	.05
609 Shane Andrews	.05
610 Heathcliff Slocumb	.05
611 Bobby Higginson RC	.25
612 Bob Tewksbury	.05
613 Terry Pendleton	.05
614 Scott Cooper	.05
615 John Wetteland	.05
616 Ken Hill	.05
617 Marquis Grissom	.05
618 Larry Walker	.05
619 Derek Bell	.05
620 David Cone	.05
621 Ken Caminiti	.05
622 Jack McDowell	.05
623 Vaughn Eshelman	.05
624 Brian McRae	.05
625 Gregg Jefferies	.05
626 Kevin Brown	.05
627 Lee Smith	.05
628 Tony Tarasco	.05
629 Brett Butler	.05
630 Jose Canseco	.35

Clear Cut

	NM/M
Complete Set (28):	20.00
Common Player:	.65
1 Mike Piazza	3.00
2 Ruben Sierra	.65
3 Tony Gwynn	2.50
4 Frank Thomas	2.00
5 Fred McGriff	.65
6 Rafael Palmeiro	1.50
7 Bobby Bonilla	.65
8 Chili Davis	.65
9 Hal Morris	.65
10 Jose Canseco	1.00
11 Jay Bell	.65
12 Kirby Puckett	2.50
13 Gary Sheffield	1.00
14 Bob Hamelin	.65
15 Jeff Bagwell	2.00
16 Albert Belle	.65
17 Sammy Sosa	2.50
18 Ken Griffey Jr.	3.00
19 Todd Zeile	.65
20 Mo Vaughn	.65
21 Moises Alou	.65
22 Paul O'Neill	.65
23 Andres Galarraga	.65
24 Greg Vaughn	.65
25 Len Dykstra	.65
26 Joe Carter	.65
27 Barry Bonds	4.50
28 Cecil Fielder	.65

Crunch Time

	NM/M
Complete Set (20):	15.00
Common Player:	1.00
1 Jeff Bagwell	2.50
2 Kirby Puckett	3.00
3 Frank Thomas	2.50
4 Albert Belle	1.00
5 Julio Franco	1.00
6 Jose Canseco	1.50
7 Paul Molitor	2.50
8 Joe Carter	1.00
9 Ken Griffey Jr.	4.00
10 Larry Walker	1.00
11 Dante Bichette	1.00
12 Carlos Baerga	1.00
13 Fred McGriff	1.00
14 Ruben Sierra	1.00
15 Will Clark	1.00
16 Moises Alou	1.00
17 Rafael Palmeiro	2.00
18 Travis Fryman	1.00
19 Barry Bonds	5.00
20 Cal Ripken Jr.	5.00

1st Day Issue

	NM/M
Common Player:	.50
Stars:	7X

(See 1995 Stadium Club #1-270 for checklist and base card values.)

Crystal Ball

	NM/M
Complete Set (15):	15.00

Common Player: .75
1 Chipper Jones 5.00
2 Dustin Hermanson .75
3 Ray Durham .75
4 Phil Nevin .75
5 Billy Ashley .75
6 Shawn Green 2.50
7 Jason Bates .75
8 Benji Gil .75
9 Marty Cordova .75
10 Quilvio Veras .75
11 Mark Grudzielanek .75
12 Ruben Rivera .75
13 Bill Pulsipher .75
14 Derek Jeter 7.50
15 LaTroy Hawkins .75

Power Zone

NM/M
Complete Set (12): 9.00
Common Player: .50
1 Jeff Bagwell 1.00
2 Albert Belle .50
3 Barry Bonds 3.00
4 Joe Carter .50
5 Cecil Fielder .50
6 Andres Galarraga .50
7 Ken Griffey Jr. 2.00
8 Paul Molitor 1.00
9 Fred McGriff .50
10 Rafael Palmeiro .75
11 Frank Thomas 1.00
12 Matt Williams .50

Ring Leaders

NM/M
Complete Set (40): 70.00
Common Player: .75
1 Jeff Bagwell 3.00
2 Mark McGwire 7.50
3 Ozzie Smith 4.00
4 Paul Molitor 3.00
5 Darryl Strawberry .75
6 Eddie Murray 3.00
7 Tony Gwynn 4.00
8 Jose Canseco 2.00
9 Howard Johnson .75
10 Andre Dawson 1.25
11 Matt Williams .75
12 Tim Raines .75
13 Fred McGriff .75
14 Ken Griffey Jr. 6.00
15 Gary Sheffield 2.00
16 Dennis Eckersley 2.50
17 Kevin Mitchell .75
18 Will Clark .75
19 Darren Daulton .75
20 Paul O'Neill .75
21 Julio Franco .75
22 Albert Belle .75

23 Juan Gonzalez 1.50
24 Kirby Puckett 4.00
25 Joe Carter .75
26 Frank Thomas 3.00
27 Cal Ripken Jr. 9.00
28 John Olerud .75
29 Ruben Sierra .75
30 Barry Bonds 9.00
31 Cecil Fielder .75
32 Roger Clemens 5.00
33 Don Mattingly 5.00
34 Terry Pendleton .75
35 Rickey Henderson 3.00
36 Dave Winfield 3.00
37 Edgar Martinez .75
38 Wade Boggs 4.00
39 Willie McGee .75
40 Andres Galarraga .75

Super Skills

NM/M
Complete Set (20): 30.00
Common Player: .75
1 Roberto Alomar 1.00
2 Barry Bonds 10.00
3 Jay Buhner .75
4 Chuck Carr .75
5 Don Mattingly 5.00
6 Raul Mondesi .75
7 Tim Salmon .75
8 Deion Sanders .75
9 Devon White .75
10 Mark Whiten .75
11 Ken Griffey Jr. 7.50
12 Marquis Grissom .75
13 Paul O'Neill .75
14 Kenny Lofton .75
15 Larry Walker .75
16 Scott Cooper .75
17 Barry Larkin .75
18 Matt Williams .75
19 John Wetteland .75
20 Randy Johnson 2.50

Virtual Reality

NM/M
Complete Set (270): 35.00
Common Player: .10
1 Cal Ripken Jr. 2.50
2 Travis Fryman .10
3 Jim Abbott .10
4 Gary Gaetti .10
5 Roger Clemens 1.25
6 Carlos Garcia .10
7 Lee Smith .10
8 Bobby Ayala .10
9 Charles Nagy .10
10 Rene Arocha .10
11 Carlos Delgado .50
12 Steve Finley .10
13 Ryan Klesko .10
14 Cal Eldred .10
15 Rey Sanchez .10
16 Ken Hill .10
17 Jose Vizcaino .10
18 Andy Benes .10
19 Shawon Dunston .10
20 Rafael Palmeiro .65
21 Dean Palmer .10
22 Joey Cora .10
23 Mickey Tettleton .10

24 Barry Larkin .10
25 Carlos Baerga .10
26 Orel Hershiser .10
27 Jody Reed .10
28 Paul Molitor .75
29 Jim Edmonds .10
30 Bob Tewksbury .10
31 Ray McDavid .10
32 Stan Javier .10
33 Todd Worrell .10
34 Bob Wickman .10
35 Raul Mondesi .10
36 Rod Beck .10
37 Jeff Kent .10
38 John Valentin .10
39 Ozzie Smith 1.00
40 Terry Pendleton .10
41 Kenny Rogers .10
42 Vince Coleman .10
43 Roberto Alomar .20
44 Darrin Jackson .10
45 Dennis Eckersley .65
46 Jay Buhner .10
47 Dave Weathers .10
48 Danny Bautista .10
49 Bob Hamelin .10
50 Steve Trachsel .10
51 Ben McDonald .10
52 Wade Boggs 1.00
53 Sandy Alomar .10
54 Ron Karkovice .10
55 Doug Jones .10
56 Gary Sheffield .40
57 Ken Caminiti .10
58 Kevin Tapani .10
59 Ruben Sierra .10
60 Bobby Bonilla .10
61 Deion Sanders .10
62 Charlie Hayes .10
63 Paul O'Neill .10
64 Jay Bell .10
65 Todd Jones .10
66 Todd Stottlemyre .10
67 Will Clark .10
68 Wilson Alvarez .10
69 Chili Davis .10
70 Chris Hoiles .10
71 Bret Saberhagen .10
72 Dave Nilsson .10
73 Derek Bell .10
74 Juan Gonzalez .40
75 Andre Dawson .30
76 Jim Thome .65
77 Larry Walker .10
78 Mike Piazza 1.50
79 Dan Wilson .10
80 Junior Felix .10
81 Jack McDowell .10
82 Danny Tartabull .10
83 William
Van Landingham .10
84 Robb Nen .10
85 Ismael Valdes .10
86 Juan Guzman .10
87 Cliff Floyd .10
88 Rico Brogna .10
89 Luis Polonia .10
90 Lance Johnson .10
91 Sammy Sosa 1.00
92 Dave West .10
93 Tom Glavine .35
94 Joe Girardi .10
95 Craig Biggio .10
96 Eddie Murray .75
97 Kevin Gross .10
98 John Franco .10
99 Matt Williams .10
100 Darrin Fletcher .10
101 Jeff Conine .10
102 Ed Sprague .10
103 Ivan Rodriguez .65
104 Orlando Merced .10
105 Ricky Bones .10
106 David Cone .10
107 Todd Hundley .10
108 Alex Cole .10
109 Tony Phillips .10
110 Jim Eisenreich .10
111 Paul Sorrento .10
112 Mike Stanley .10
113 Doug Drabek .10
114 Matt Mieske .10
115 Tino Martinez .10
116 Midre Cummings .10
117 Hal Morris .10
118 Shawn Green .40
119 Randy Myers .10
120 Ken Griffey Jr. 1.50
121 Brett Butler .10
122 Julio Franco .10
123 Chuck Knoblauch .10
124 Bret Boone .10
125 Wil Cordero .10
126 Luis Gonzalez .10

127 Tim Wallach .10
128 Scott Sanders .10
129 Tom Henke .10
130 Otis Nixon .10
131 Darren Daulton .10
132 Manny Ramirez .75
133 Bret Barberie .10
134 Brady Anderson .10
135 Shane Reynolds .10
136 Barry Bonds 2.50
137 Alex Fernandez .10
138 Brian McRae .10
139 Todd Zeile .10
140 Greg Swindell .10
141 Troy Neel .10
142 Eric Karros .10
143 John Hudek .10
144 Joe Carter .10
145 Mike Devereaux .10
146 Butch Henry .10
147 Mark Lemke .10
148 Jeff Montgomery .10
149 Ryan Thompson .10
150 Bernie Williams .10
151 Scott Leius .10
152 Greg Gagne .10
153 Moises Alou .10
154 Geronimo Berroa .10
155 Alan Trammell .10
156 Don Slaught .10
157 Jose Rijo .10
158 Tim Raines .10
159 Melido Perez .10
160 Kent Mercker .10
161 James Mouton .10
162 Luis Lopez .10
163 Mike Kingery .10
164 Cecil Fielder .10
165 Scott Kamieniecki .10
166 Brent Gates .10
167 Jason Jacome .10
168 Dante Bichette .10
169 Kurt Abbott .10
170 Mike Henneman .10
171 John Kruk .10
172 Jose Oliva .10
173 Reggie Sanders .10
174 Omar Vizquel .10
175 Devon White .10
176 Mark McGwire 2.00
177 Gary DiSarcina .10
178 Joey Hamilton .10
179 Randy Johnson .75
180 Jim Leyritz .10
181 Bobby Jones .10
182 Bip Roberts .10
183 Jose Canseco .40
184 Mo Vaughn .10
185 Edgar Martinez .10
186 Tommy Greene .10
187 Chuck Carr .10
188 Pedro Astacio .10
189 Shane Mack .10
190 Fred McGriff .10
191 Pat Rapp .10
192 Bill Swift .10
193 Robin Ventura .10
194 Bobby Witt .10
195 Steve Howe .10
196 Leo Gomez .10
197 Hector Fajardo .10
198 Jeff Bagwell .75
199 Rondell White .10
200 Don Mattingly 1.25
201 Trevor Hoffman .10
202 Chris Gomez .10
203 Bobby Munoz .10
204 Marvin Freeman .10
205 Sean Berry .10
206 Mark Grace .10
207 Pat Kelly .10
208 Eddie Williams .10
209 Frank Thomas .75
210 Bryan Eversgerd .10
211 Phil Plantier .10
212 Roberto Kelly .10
213 Rickey Henderson .75
214 John Smiley .10
215 Kevin Brown .10
216 Jimmy Key .10
217 Wally Joyner .10
218 Roberto Hernandez .10
219 Felix Fermin .10
220 Greg Vaughn .10
221 Ray Lankford .10
222 Greg Maddux 1.00
223 Mike Mussina .30
224 David Nied .10
225 Scott Erickson .10
226 Kevin Mitchell .10
227 Brian Anderson .10
228 Jeff King .10
229 Ramon Martinez .10
230 Kevin Seitzer .10

231	Marquis Grissom	.10
232	Chuck Finley	.10
233	Len Dykstra	.10
234	Ellis Burks	.10
235	Harold Baines	.10
236	Kevin Appier	.10
237	Dave Justice	.10
238	Darryl Kile	.10
239	John Olerud	.10
240	Greg McMichael	.10
241	Kirby Puckett	1.00
242	Jose Valentin	.10
243	Rick Wilkins	.10
244	Pat Hentgen	.10
245	Tom Gordon	.10
246	Tom Candiotti	.10
247	Jason Bere	.10
248	Wes Chamberlain	.10
249	Jeff Cirillo	.10
250	Kevin Foster	.10
251	Mark Whiten	.10
252	Terry Steinbach	.10
253	Aaron Sele	.10
254	Kirt Manwaring	.10
255	Delino DeShields	.10
256	Andujar Cedeno	.10
257	Kenny Lofton	.10
258	John Wetteland	.10
259	Tim Salmon	.10
260	Denny Neagle	.10
261	Tony Gwynn	1.00
262	Lou Whitaker	.10
263	J.T. Snow	.10
264	Dennis Martinez	.10
265	Pedro Martinez	.75
266	Rusty Greer	.10
267	Dave Fleming	.10
268	John Dettmer	.10
269	Albert Belle	.10
270	Henry Rodriguez	.10

VR Extremist

		NM/M
Complete Set (10):		25.00
Common Player:		1.50
1	Barry Bonds	7.50
2	Ken Griffey Jr.	6.00
3	Jeff Bagwell	3.50
4	Albert Belle	1.50
5	Frank Thomas	3.50
6	Tony Gwynn	4.50
7	Kenny Lofton	1.50
8	Deion Sanders	1.50
9	Ken Hill	1.50
10	Jimmy Key	1.50

World Series Winners

	NM/M
Complete Set (585):	40.00
Common Player:	.25

Stars: 3X
(See 1995 Stadium Club for checklist and base card values.)

1996 Stadium Club

		NM/M
Complete Set (450):		25.00
Common Player:		.05
Series 1 or 2 Pack (10):		1.00
Series 1 or 2 Wax Box (24):		20.00
1	Hideo Nomo	.40
2	Paul Molitor	.75
3	Garret Anderson	.05
4	Jose Mesa	.05
5	Vinny Castilla	.05
6	Mike Mussina	.30
7	Ray Durham	.05
8	Jack McDowell	.05
9	Juan Gonzalez	.40
10	Chipper Jones	1.00
11	Deion Sanders	.05
12	Rondell White	.05
13	Tom Henke	.05
14	Derek Bell	.05
15	Randy Myers	.05
16	Randy Johnson	.75
17	Len Dykstra	.05
18	Bill Pulsipher	.05
19	Greg Colbrunn	.05
20	David Wells	.05
21	Chad Curtis	.05
22	Roberto Hernandez	.05
23	Kirby Puckett	1.00
24	Joe Vitiello	.05
25	Roger Clemens	1.25
26	Al Martin	.05
27	Chad Ogea	.05
28	David Segui	.05
29	Joey Hamilton	.05
30	Dan Wilson	.05
31	Chad Fonville	.05
32	Bernard Gilkey	.05
33	Kevin Seitzer	.05
34	Shawn Green	.35
35	Rick Aguilera	.05
36	Gary DiSarcina	.05
37	Jaime Navarro	.05
38	Doug Jones	.05
39	Brent Gates	.05
40	Dean Palmer	.05
41	Pat Rapp	.05
42	Tony Clark	.05
43	Bill Swift	.05
44	Randy Velarde	.05
45	Matt Williams	.05
46	John Mabry	.05
47	Mike Fetters	.05
48	Orlando Miller	.05
49	Tom Glavine	.35
50	Delino DeShields	.05
51	Scott Erickson	.05
52	Andy Van Slyke	.05
53	Jim Bullinger	.05
54	Lyle Mouton	.05
55	Bret Saberhagen	.05
56	Benito Santiago	.05
57	Dan Miceli	.05
58	Carl Everett	.05
59	Rod Beck	.05
60	Phil Nevin	.05
61	Jason Giambi	.50
62	Paul Menhart	.05
63	Eric Karros	.05
64	Allen Watson	.05
65	Jeff Cirillo	.05
66	Lee Smith	.05
67	Sean Berry	.05
68	Luis Sojo	.05
69	Jeff Montgomery	.05
70	Todd Hundley	.05
71	John Burkett	.05

72	Mark Gubicza	.05
73	Don Mattingly	1.25
74	Jeff Brantley	.05
75	Matt Walbeck	.05
76	Steve Parris	.05
77	Ken Caminiti	.05
78	Kirt Manwaring	.05
79	Greg Vaughn	.05
80	Pedro Martinez	.75
81	Benji Gil	.05
82	Heathcliff Slocumb	.05
83	Joe Girardi	.05
84	Sean Bergman	.05
85	Matt Karchner	.05
86	Butch Huskey	.05
87	Mike Morgan	.05
88	Todd Worrell	.05
89	Mike Bordick	.05
90	Bip Roberts	.05
91	Mike Hampton	.05
92	Troy O'Leary	.05
93	Wally Joyner	.05
94	Dave Stevens	.05
95	Cecil Fielder	.05
96	Wade Boggs	1.00
97	Hal Morris	.05
98	Mickey Tettleton	.05
99	Jeff Kent	.05
100	Denny Martinez	.05
101	Luis Gonzalez	.05
102	John Jaha	.05
103	Javy Lopez	.05
104	Mark McGwire	2.00
105	Ken Griffey Jr.	1.50
106	Darren Daulton	.05
107	Bryan Rekar	.05
108	Mike Macfarlane	.05
109	Gary Gaetti	.05
110	Shane Reynolds	.05
111	Pat Meares	.05
112	Jason Schmidt	.05
113	Otis Nixon	.05
114	John Franco	.05
115	Marc Newfield	.05
116	Andy Benes	.05
117	Ozzie Guillen	.05
118	Brian Jordan	.05
119	Terry Pendleton	.05
120	Chuck Finley	.05
121	Scott Stahoviak	.05
122	Sid Fernandez	.05
123	Derek Jeter	3.00
124	John Smiley	.05
125	David Bell	.05
126	Brett Butler	.05
127	Doug Drabek	.05
128	J.T. Snow	.05
129	Joe Carter	.05
130	Dennis Eckersley	.65
131	Marty Cordova	.05
132	Greg Maddux	1.00
133	Tom Goodwin	.05
134	Andy Ashby	.05
135	Paul Sorrento	.05
136	Ricky Bones	.05
137	Shawon Dunston	.05
138	Moises Alou	.05
139	Mickey Morandini	.05
140	Ramon Martinez	.05
141	Royce Clayton	.05
142	Brad Ausmus	.05
143	Kenny Rogers	.05
144	Tim Naehring	.05
145	Chris Gomez	.05
146	Bobby Bonilla	.05
147	Wilson Alvarez	.05
148	Johnny Damon	.35
149	Pat Hentgen	.05
150	Andres Galarraga	.05
151	David Cone	.05
152	Lance Johnson	.05
153	Carlos Garcia	.05
154	Doug Johns	.05
155	Midre Cummings	.05
156	Steve Sparks	.05
157	Sandy Martinez RC	.05
158	William Van Landingham	.05
159	Dave Justice	.05
160	Mark Grace	.05
161	Robb Nen	.05
162	Mike Greenwell	.05
163	Brad Radke	.05
164	Edgardo Alfonzo	.05
165	Mark Leiter	.05
166	Walt Weiss	.05
167	Mel Rojas	.05
168	Bret Boone	.05
169	Ricky Bottalico	.05
170	Bobby Higginson	.05
171	Trevor Hoffman	.05
172	Jay Bell	.05
173	Gabe White	.05
174	Curtis Goodwin	.05

175	Tyler Green	.05
176	Roberto Alomar	.20
177	Sterling Hitchcock	.05
178	Ryan Klesko	.05
179	Donne Wall RC	.05
180	Brian McRae	.05
181	Will Clark	.05
182	Frank Thomas	.60
183	Jeff Bagwell	.60
184	Mo Vaughn	.05
185	Tino Martinez	.05
186	Craig Biggio	.05
187	Chuck Knoblauch	.05
188	Carlos Baerga	.05
189	Quilvio Veras	.05
190	Luis Alicea	.05
191	Jim Thome	.40
192	Mike Blowers	.05
193	Robin Ventura	.05
194	Jeff King	.05
195	Tony Phillips	.05
196	John Valentin	.05
197	Barry Larkin	.05
198	Cal Ripken Jr.	2.00
199	Omar Vizquel	.05
200	Kurt Abbott	.05
201	Albert Belle	.05
202	Barry Bonds	2.00
203	Ron Gant	.05
204	Dante Bichette	.05
205	Jeff Conine	.05
206	Jim Edmonds	.05
207	Stan Javier	.05
208	Kenny Lofton	.05
209	Ray Lankford	.05
210	Bernie Williams	.05
211	Jay Buhner	.05
212	Paul O'Neill	.05
213	Tim Salmon	.05
214	Reggie Sanders	.05
215	Manny Ramirez	.60
216	Mike Piazza	1.50
217	Mike Stanley	.05
218	Tony Eusebio	.05
219	Chris Hoiles	.05
220	Ron Karkovice	.05
221	Edgar Martinez	.05
222	Chili Davis	.05
223	Jose Canseco	.35
224	Eddie Murray	.60
225	Geronimo Berroa	.05
226	Chipper Jones	.75
227	Garret Anderson	.05
228	Marty Cordova	.05
229	Jon Nunnally	.05
230	Brian Hunter	.05
231	Shawn Green	.20
232	Ray Durham	.05
233	Alex Gonzalez	.05
234	Bobby Higginson	.05
235	Randy Johnson	.60
236	Al Leiter	.05
237	Tom Glavine	.10
238	Kenny Rogers	.05
239	Mike Hampton	.05
240	David Wells	.05
241	Jim Abbott	.05
242	Denny Neagle	.05
243	Wilson Alvarez	.05
244	John Smiley	.05
245	Greg Maddux	.75
246	Andy Ashby	.05
247	Hideo Nomo	.30
248	Pat Rapp	.05
249	Tim Wakefield	.05
250	John Smoltz	.05
251	Joey Hamilton	.05
252	Frank Castillo	.05
253	Denny Martinez	.05
254	Jaime Navarro	.05
255	Karim Garcia	.05
256	Bob Abreu	.05
257	Butch Huskey	.05
258	Ruben Rivera	.05
259	Johnny Damon	.20
260	Derek Jeter	2.00
261	Dennis Eckersley	.50
262	Jose Mesa	.05
263	Tom Henke	.05
264	Rick Aguilera	.05
265	Randy Myers	.05
266	John Franco	.05
267	Jeff Brantley	.05
268	John Wetteland	.05
269	Mark Wohlers	.05
270	Rod Beck	.05
271	Barry Larkin	.05
272	Paul O'Neill	.05
273	Bobby Jones	.05
274	Will Clark	.05
275	Steve Avery	.05
276	Jim Edmonds	.05
277	John Olerud	.05
278	Carlos Perez	.05

279	Chris Hoiles	.05
280	Jeff Conine	.05
281	Jim Eisenreich	.05
282	Jason Jacome	.05
283	Ray Lankford	.05
284	John Wasdin	.05
285	Frank Thomas	.75
286	Jason Isringhausen	.05
287	Glenallen Hill RC	.05
288	Esteban Loaiza	.05
289	Bernie Williams	.05
290	Curtis Leskanic	.05
291	Scott Cooper	.05
292	Curt Schilling	.35
293	Eddie Murray	.75
294	Rick Krivda	.05
295	Domingo Cedeno	.05
296	Jeff Fassero	.05
297	Albert Belle	.05
298	Craig Biggio	.05
299	Fernando Vina	.05
300	Edgar Martinez	.05
301	Tony Gwynn	1.00
302	Felipe Lira	.05
303	Mo Vaughn	.05
304	Alex Fernandez	.05
305	Keith Lockhart	.05
306	Roger Pavlik	.05
307	Lee Tinsley	.05
308	Omar Vizquel	.05
309	Scott Servais	.05
310	Danny Tartabull	.05
311	Chili Davis	.05
312	Cal Eldred	.05
313	Roger Cedeno	.05
314	Chris Hammond	.05
315	Rusty Greer	.05
316	Brady Anderson	.05
317	Ron Villone	.05
318	Mark Carreon	.05
319	Larry Walker	.05
320	Pete Harnisch	.05
321	Robin Ventura	.05
322	Tim Belcher	.05
323	Tony Tarasco	.05
324	Juan Guzman	.05
325	Kenny Lofton	.05
326	Kevin Foster	.05
327	Wil Cordero	.05
328	Troy Percival	.05
329	Turk Wendell	.05
330	Thomas Howard	.05
331	Carlos Baerga	.05
332	B.J. Surhoff	.05
333	Jay Buhner	.05
334	Andujar Cedeno	.05
335	Jeff King	.05
336	Dante Bichette	.05
337	Alan Trammell	.05
338	Scott Leius	.05
339	Chris Snopek	.05
340	Roger Bailey	.05
341	Jacob Brumfield	.05
342	Jose Canseco	.50
343	Rafael Palmeiro	.65
344	Quilvio Veras	.05
345	Darrin Fletcher	.05
346	Carlos Delgado	.50
347	Tony Eusebio	.05
348	Ismael Valdes	.05
349	Terry Steinbach	.05
350	Orel Hershiser	.05
351	Kurt Abbott	.05
352	Jody Reed	.05
353	David Howard	.05
354	Ruben Sierra	.05
355	John Ericks	.05
356	Buck Showalter	.05
357	Jim Thome	.65
358	Geronimo Berroa	.05
359	Robby Thompson	.05
360	Jose Vizcaino	.05
361	Jeff Frye	.05
362	Kevin Appier	.05
363	Pat Kelly	.05
364	Ron Gant	.05
365	Luis Alicea	.05
366	Armando Benitez	.05
367	Rico Brogna	.05
368	Manny Ramirez	.75
369	Mike Lansing	.05
370	Sammy Sosa	1.00
371	Don Wengert	.05
372	Dave Nilsson	.05
373	Sandy Alomar	.05
374	Joey Cora	.05
375	Larry Thomas	.05
376	John Valentin	.05
377	Kevin Ritz	.05
378	Steve Finley	.05
379	Frank Rodriguez	.05
380	Ivan Rodriguez	.65
381	Alex Ochoa	.05
382	Mark Lemke	.05
383	Scott Brosius	.05
384	James Mouton	.05
385	Mark Langston	.05
386	Ed Sprague	.05
387	Joe Oliver	.05
388	Steve Ontiveros	.05
389	Rey Sanchez	.05
390	Mike Henneman	.05
391	Jose Valentin RC	.05
392	Tom Candiotti	.05
393	Damon Buford	.05
394	Erik Hanson	.05
395	Mark Smith	.05
396	Pete Schourek	.05
397	John Flaherty	.05
398	Dave Martinez	.05
399	Tommy Greene	.05
400	Gary Sheffield	.45
401	Glenn Dishman	.05
402	Barry Bonds	3.00
403	Tom Pagnozzi	.05
404	Todd Stottlemyre	.05
405	Tim Salmon	.05
406	John Hudek	.05
407	Fred McGriff	.05
408	Orlando Merced	.05
409	Brian Barber	.05
410	Ryan Thompson	.05
411	Mariano Rivera	.10
412	Eric Young	.05
413	Chris Bosio	.05
414	Chuck Knoblauch	.05
415	Jamie Moyer	.05
416	Chan Ho Park	.05
417	Mark Portugal	.05
418	Tim Raines	.05
419	Antonio Osuna	.05
420	Todd Zeile	.05
421	Steve Wojciechowski	.05
422	Marquis Grissom	.05
423	Norm Charlton	.05
424	Cal Ripken Jr.	3.00
425	Gregg Jefferies	.05
426	Mike Stanton	.05
427	Tony Fernandez	.05
428	Jose Rijo	.05
429	Jeff Bagwell	.75
430	Raul Mondesi	.05
431	Travis Fryman	.05
432	Ron Karkovice	.05
433	Alan Benes	.05
434	Tony Phillips	.05
435	Reggie Sanders	.05
436	Andy Pettitte	.25
437	Matt Lawton RC	.25
438	Jeff Blauser	.05
439	Michael Tucker	.05
440	Mark Loretta	.05
441	Charlie Hayes	.05
442	Mike Piazza	1.50
443	Shane Andrews	.05
444	Jeff Suppan	.05
445	Steve Rodriguez	.05
446	Mike Matheny	.05
447	Trenidad Hubbard	.05
448	Denny Hocking	.05
449	Mark Grudzielanek	.05
450	Joe Randa	.05

Bash & Burn

		NM/M
Complete Set (10):		10.00
Common Player:		.75
1	Sammy Sosa	3.50
2	Barry Bonds	6.00
3	Reggie Sanders	.75
4	Craig Biggio	.75
5	Raul Mondesi	.75
6	Ron Gant	.75
7	Ray Lankford	.75
8	Glenallen Hill	.75
9	Chad Curtis	.75
10	John Valentin	.75

Mega Heroes

ANDRES GALARRAGA

		NM/M
Complete Set (10):		10.00
Common Player:		1.00
1	Frank Thomas	1.50
2	Ken Griffey Jr.	3.00
3	Hideo Nomo	1.25
4	Ozzie Smith	1.75
5	Will Clark	1.00
6	Jack McDowell	1.00
7	Andres Galarraga	1.00
8	Roger Clemens	2.00
9	Deion Sanders	1.00
10	Mo Vaughn	1.00

Metalists

FRANK THOMAS

		NM/M
Complete Set (8):		12.00
Common Player:		1.00
1	Jeff Bagwell	1.25
2	Barry Bonds	3.50
3	Jose Canseco	1.00
4	Roger Clemens	2.50
5	Dennis Eckersley	1.00
6	Greg Maddux	2.00
7	Cal Ripken Jr.	3.50
8	Frank Thomas	1.25

Mickey Mantle Retrospective

MICKEY MANTLE

		NM/M
Complete Set (19):		35.00
Common Series 1:		4.00
Common Series 2:		2.00
1	Mickey Mantle/1950 (Minor League)	4.00
2	Mickey Mantle/1951	4.00
3	Mickey Mantle/1951	4.00

4	Mickey Mantle/1953	4.00
5	Mickey Mantle/1954 (W/Yogi Berra.)	
6	Mickey Mantle/1956	4.00
7	Mickey Mantle/1957	4.00
8	Mickey Mantle/1958 (W/Casey Stengel.)	4.00
9	Mickey Mantle/1959	4.00
10	Mickey Mantle/1960 (W/Elston Howard.)	2.00
11	Mickey Mantle/1961	2.00
12	Mickey Mantle/1961 (W/Roger Maris.)	2.00
13	Mickey Mantle/1962	4.00
14	Mickey Mantle/1963	2.00
15	Mickey Mantle/1964	2.00
16	Mickey Mantle	2.00
17	Mickey Mantle/1968	2.00
18	Mickey Mantle/1969	2.00
19	Mickey Mantle (In Memoriam)	3.50

Mickey Mantle "Cereal Box" Set

	NM/M
Unopened Set:	30.00
Common Player:	.10

(See 1996 Stadium Club for checklist and values.)

Midsummer Matchups

		NM/M
Complete Set (10):		20.00
Common Player:		1.00
1	Hideo Nomo, Randy Johnson	2.00
2	Mike Piazza, Ivan Rodriguez	4.00
3	Fred McGriff, Frank Thomas	2.00
4	Craig Biggio, Carlos Baerga	1.00
5	Vinny Castilla, Wade Boggs	2.50
6	Barry Larkin, Cal Ripken Jr.	5.00
7	Barry Bonds, Albert Belle	5.00
8	Len Dykstra, Kenny Lofton	1.00
9	Tony Gwynn, Kirby Puckett	3.00
10	Ron Gant, Edgar Martinez	1.00

Power Packed

		NM/M
Complete Set (15):		15.00
Common Player:		1.00
1	Albert Belle	1.00

2	Mark McGwire	4.00
3	Jose Canseco	1.75
4	Mike Piazza	3.00
5	Ron Gant	1.00
6	Ken Griffey Jr.	3.00
7	Mo Vaughn	1.00
8	Cecil Fielder	1.00
9	Tim Salmon	1.00
10	Frank Thomas	2.50
11	Juan Gonzalez	1.50
12	Andres Galarraga	1.00
13	Fred McGriff	1.00
14	Jay Buhner	1.00
15	Dante Bichette	1.00

Power Streak

		NM/M
Complete Set (15):		20.00
Common Player:		1.00
1	Randy Johnson	2.00
2	Hideo Nomo	1.25
3	Albert Belle	1.00
4	Dante Bichette	1.00
5	Jay Buhner	1.00
6	Frank Thomas	2.00
7	Mark McGwire	4.00
8	Rafael Palmeiro	1.50
9	Mo Vaughn	1.00
10	Sammy Sosa	3.00
11	Larry Walker	1.00
12	Gary Gaetti	1.00
13	Tim Salmon	1.00
14	Barry Bonds	5.00
15	Jim Edmonds	1.00

Prime Cuts

		NM/M
Complete Set (8):		20.00
Common Player:		1.50
1	Albert Belle	1.50
2	Barry Bonds	6.00
3	Ken Griffey Jr.	4.00
4	Tony Gwynn	3.00
5	Edgar Martinez	1.50
6	Rafael Palmeiro	2.00
7	Mike Piazza	4.00
8	Frank Thomas	2.50

TSC Awards

		NM/M
Complete Set (10):		15.00
Common Player:		.50
1	Cal Ripken Jr.	5.00
2	Albert Belle	.60
3	Tom Glavine	1.00
4		.50
5	Ken Griffey Jr.	4.00
6	Hideo Nomo	1.25
7	Greg Maddux	3.00
8	Chipper Jones	3.00

9	Randy Johnson	2.00
10	Jose Mesa	.50

1997 Stadium Club

		NM/M
Complete Set (390):		35.00
Common Player:		.05
Series 1 or 2 Pack (9):		1.50
Series 1 or 2 Wax		
Box (24):		27.50
1	Chipper Jones	1.50
2	Gary Sheffield	.50
3	Kenny Lofton	.05
4	Brian Jordan	.05
5	Mark McGwire	2.50
6	Charles Nagy	.05
7	Tim Salmon	.05
8	Cal Ripken Jr.	3.00
9	Jeff Conine	.05
10	Paul Molitor	1.00
11	Mariano Rivera	.15
12	Pedro Martinez	1.00
13	Jeff Bagwell	1.00
14	Bobby Bonilla	.05
15	Barry Bonds	3.00
16	Ryan Klesko	.05
17	Barry Larkin	.05
18	Jim Thome	.65
19	Jay Buhner	.05
20	Juan Gonzalez	.50
21	Mike Mussina	.30
22	Kevin Appier	.05
23	Eric Karros	.05
24	Steve Finley	.05
25	Ed Sprague	.05
26	Bernard Gilkey	.05
27	Tony Phillips	.05
28	Henry Rodriguez	.05
29	John Smoltz	.05
30	Dante Bichette	.05
31	Mike Piazza	2.00
32	Paul O'Neill	.05
33	Billy Wagner	.05
34	Reggie Sanders	.05
35	John Jaha	.05
36	Eddie Murray	1.00
37	Eric Young	.05
38	Roberto Hernandez	.05
39	Pat Hentgen	.05
40	Sammy Sosa	1.50
41	Todd Hundley	.05
42	Mo Vaughn	.05
43	Robin Ventura	.05
44	Mark Grudzielanek	.05
45	Shane Reynolds	.05
46	Andy Pettitte	.25
47	Fred McGriff	.05
48	Rey Ordonez	.05
49	Will Clark	.05
50	Ken Griffey Jr.	2.00
51	Todd Worrell	.05
52	Rusty Greer	.05
53	Mark Grace	.05
54	Tom Glavine	.35
55	Derek Jeter	3.00
56	Rafael Palmeiro	.75
57	Bernie Williams	.05
58	Marty Cordova	.05
59	Andres Galarraga	.05
60	Ken Caminiti	.05
61	Garret Anderson	.05
62	Denny Martinez	.05
63	Mike Greenwell	.05
64	David Segui	.05
65	Julio Franco	.05
66	Rickey Henderson	1.00
67	Ozzie Guillen	.05
68	Pete Harnisch	.05
69	Chan Ho Park	.05
70	Harold Baines	.05
71	Mark Clark	.05
72	Steve Avery	.05
73	Brian Hunter	.05
74	Pedro Astacio	.05
75	Jack McDowell	.05
76	Gregg Jefferies	.05
77	Jason Kendall	.05
78	Todd Walker	.05
79	B.J. Surhoff	.05
80	Moises Alou	.05
81	Fernando Vina	.05
82	Darryl Strawberry	.05
83	Jose Rosado	.05
84	Chris Gomez	.05
85	Chili Davis	.05
86	Alan Benes	.05
87	Todd Hollandsworth	.05
88	Jose Vizcaino	.05
89	Edgardo Alfonzo	.05
90	Ruben Rivera	.05
91	Donovan Osborne	.05
92	Doug Glanville	.05
93	Gary DiSarcina	.05
94	Brooks Kieschnick	.05
95	Bobby Jones	.05
96	Raul Casanova	.05
97	Jermaine Allensworth	.05
98	Kenny Rogers	.05
99	Mark McLemore	.05
100	Jeff Fassero	.05
101	Sandy Alomar	.05
102	Chuck Finley	.05
103	Eric Owens	.05
104	Billy McMillon	.05
105	Dwight Gooden	.05
106	Sterling Hitchcock	.05
107	Doug Drabek	.05
108	Paul Wilson	.05
109	Chris Snopek	.05
110	Al Leiter	.05
111	Bob Tewksbury	.05
112	Todd Greene	.05
113	Jose Valentin	.05
114	Delino DeShields	.05
115	Mike Bordick	.05
116	Pat Meares	.05
117	Mariano Duncan	.05
118	Steve Trachsel	.05
119	Luis Castillo	.05
120	Andy Benes	.05
121	Donne Wall	.05
122	Alex Gonzalez	.05
123	Dan Wilson	.05
124	Omar Vizquel	.05
125	Devon White	.05
126	Darryl Hamilton	.05
127	Orlando Merced	.05
128	Royce Clayton	.05
129	William Van Landingham	.05
130	Terry Steinbach	.05
131	Jeff Blauser	.05
132	Jeff Cirillo	.05
133	Roger Pavlik	.05
134	Danny Tartabull	.05
135	Jeff Montgomery	.05
136	Bobby Higginson	.05
137	Mike Grace	.05
138	Kevin Elster	.05
139	Brian Giles RC	1.00
140	Rod Beck	.05
141	Ismael Valdes	.05
142	Scott Brosius	.05
143	Mike Fetters	.05
144	Gary Gaetti	.05
145	Mike Lansing	.05
146	Glenallen Hill	.05
147	Shawn Green	.35
148	Mel Rojas	.05
149	Joey Cora	.05
150	John Smiley	.05
151	Marvin Benard	.05
152	Curt Schilling	.35
153	Dave Nilsson	.05
154	Edgar Renteria	.05
155	Joey Hamilton	.05
156	Carlos Garcia	.05
157	Nomar Garciaparra	2.00
158	Kevin Ritz	.05
159	Keith Lockhart	.05
160	Justin Thompson	.05
161	Terry Adams	.05
162	Jamey Wright	.05
163	Otis Nixon	.05
164	Michael Tucker	.05
165	Mike Stanley	.05
166	Ben McDonald	.05
167	John Mabry	.05
168	Troy O'Leary	.05
169	Mel Nieves	.05
170	Bret Boone	.05
171	Mike Timlin	.05
172	Scott Rolen	.75
173	Reggie Jefferson	.05
174	Neifi Perez	.05
175	Brian McRae	.05
176	Tom Goodwin	.05
177	Aaron Sele	.05
178	Benny Santiago	.05
179	Frank Rodriguez	.05
180	Eric Davis	.05
181	Andruw Jones	.75
182	Todd Walker	.15
183	Wes Helms	.15
184	Nelson Figueroa RC	.15
185	Vladimir Guerrero	.75
186	Billy McMillon	.15
187	Todd Helton	.65
188	Nomar Garciaparra	2.00
189	Katsuhiro Maeda	.15
190	Russell Branyan	.15
191	Glendon Rusch	.15
192	Bartolo Colon	.15
193	Scott Rolen	.50
194	Angel Echevarria	.15
195	Bob Abreu	.20
196	Greg Maddux	1.50
197	Joe Carter	.05
198	Alex Ochoa	.05
199	Ellis Burks	.05
200	Ivan Rodriguez	.75
201	Marquis Grissom	.05
202	Trevor Hoffman	.05
203	Matt Williams	.05
204	Carlos Delgado	.50
205	Ramon Martinez	.05
206	Chuck Knoblauch	.05
207	Juan Guzman	.05
208	Derek Bell	.05
209	Roger Clemens	1.75
210	Vladimir Guerrero	1.00
211	Cecil Fielder	.05
212	Hideo Nomo	.50
213	Frank Thomas	1.00
214	Greg Vaughn	.05
215	Javy Lopez	.05
216	Raul Mondesi	.05
217	Wade Boggs	1.50
218	Carlos Baerga	.05
219	Tony Gwynn	1.50
220	Tino Martinez	.05
221	Vinny Castilla	.05
222	Lance Johnson	.05
223	David Justice	.05
224	Rondell White	.05
225	Dean Palmer	.05
226	Jim Edmonds	.05
227	Albert Belle	.05
228	Alex Fernandez	.05
229	Ryne Sandberg	1.50
230	Jose Mesa	.05
231	David Cone	.05
232	Troy Percival	.05
233	Edgar Martinez	.05
234	Jose Canseco	.50
235	Kevin Brown	.05
236	Ray Lankford	.05
237	Karim Garcia	.05
238	J.T. Snow	.05
239	Dennis Eckersley	.75
240	Roberto Alomar	.35
241	John Valentin	.05
242	Ron Gant	.05
243	Geronimo Berroa	.05
244	Manny Ramirez	1.00
245	Travis Fryman	.05
246	Denny Neagle	.05
247	Randy Johnson	1.00
248	Darin Erstad	.15
249	Mark Wohlers	.05
250	Ken Hill	.05
251	Larry Walker	.05
252	Craig Biggio	.05
253	Brady Anderson	.05
254	John Wetteland	.05
255	Andruw Jones	1.00
256	Turk Wendell	.05
257	Jason Isringhausen	.05
258	Jaime Navarro	.05
259	Sean Berry	.05
260	Albie Lopez	.05

261	Jay Bell	.05
262	Bobby Witt	.05
263	Tony Clark	.05
264	Tim Wakefield	.05
265	Brad Radke	.05
266	Tim Belcher	.05
267	Mark Lewis	.05
268	Roger Cedeno	.05
269	Tim Naehring	.05
270	Kevin Tapani	.05
271	Joe Randa	.05
272	Randy Myers	.05
273	Dave Burba	.05
274a	Mike Sweeney	.05
274b	Tom Pagnozzi	.05
	(Should be #374.)	
275	Danny Graves	.05
276	Chad Mottola	.05
277	Ruben Sierra	.05
278	Norm Charlton	.05
279	Scott Servais	.05
280	Jacob Cruz	.05
281	Mike Macfarlane	.05
282	Rich Becker	.05
283	Shannon Stewart	.05
284	Gerald Williams	.05
285	Jody Reed	.05
286	Jeff D'Amico	.05
287	Walt Weiss	.05
288	Jim Leyritz	.05
289	Francisco Cordova	.05
290	F.P. Santangelo	.05
291	Scott Erickson	.05
292	Hal Morris	.05
293	Ray Durham	.05
294	Andy Ashby	.05
295	Darryl Kile	.05
296	Jose Paniagua	.05
297	Mickey Tettleton	.05
298	Joe Girardi	.05
299	Rocky Coppinger	.05
300	Bob Abreu	.05
301	John Olerud	.05
302	Paul Shuey	.05
303	Jeff Brantley	.05
304	Bob Wells	.05
305	Kevin Seitzer	.05
306	Shawon Dunston	.05
307	Jose Herrera	.05
308	Butch Huskey	.05
309	Jose Offerman	.05
310	Rick Aguilera	.05
311	Greg Gagne	.05
312	John Burkett	.05
313	Mark Thompson	.05
314	Alvaro Espinoza	.05
315	Todd Stottlemyre	.05
316	Al Martin	.05
317	James Baldwin	.05
318	Cal Eldred	.05
319	Sid Fernandez	.05
320	Mickey Morandini	.05
321	Robb Nen	.05
322	Mark Lemke	.05
323	Pete Schourek	.05
324	Marcus Jensen	.05
325	Rich Aurilia	.05
326	Jeff King	.05
327	Scott Stahoviak	.05
328	Ricky Otero	.05
329	Antonio Osuna	.05
330	Chris Hoiles	.05
331	Luis Gonzalez	.05
332	Wil Cordero	.05
333	Johnny Damon	.35
334	Mark Langston	.05
335	Orlando Miller	.05
336	Jason Giambi	.50
337	Damian Jackson	.05
338	David Wells	.05
339	Bip Roberts	.05
340	Matt Ruebel	.05
341	Tom Candiotti	.05
342	Wally Joyner	.05
343	Jimmy Key	.05
344	Tony Batista	.05
345	Paul Sorrento	.05
346	Ron Karkovice	.05
347	Wilson Alvarez	.05
348	John Flaherty	.05
349	Rey Sanchez	.05
350	John Vander Wal	.05
351a	Jermaine Dye	.05
351b	Brant Brown	.05
	(Should be #361.)	
352	Mike Hampton	.05
353	Greg Colbrunn	.05
354	Heathcliff Slocumb	.05
355	Ricky Bottalico	.05
356	Marty Janzen	.05
357	Orel Hershiser	.05
358	Rex Hudler	.05
359	Amaury Telemaco	.05
360	Darrin Fletcher	.05
361	Not Issued - see #351	
362	Russ Davis	.05

363	Allen Watson	.05
364	Mike Lieberthal	.05
365	Dave Stevens	.05
366	Jay Powell	.05
367	Tony Fossas	.05
368	Bob Wolcott	.05
369	Mark Loretta	.05
370	Shawn Estes	.05
371	Sandy Martinez	.05
372	Wendell Magee Jr.	.05
373	John Franco	.05
374	Not Issued - see #274	
375	Willie Adams	.05
376	Chipper Jones	2.00
377	Mo Vaughn	.15
378	Frank Thomas	1.50
379	Albert Belle	.15
380	Andres Galarraga	.15
381	Gary Sheffield	.85
382	Jeff Bagwell	1.50
383	Mike Piazza	3.00
384	Mark McGwire	3.00
385	Ken Griffey Jr.	2.50
386	Barry Bonds	3.50
387	Juan Gonzalez	.40
388	Brady Anderson	.15
389	Ken Caminiti	.15
390	Jay Buhner	.15

Co-Signers

		NM/M
Complete Set (10):		200.00
Common Card:		5.00
CO1	Andy Pettitte, Derek Jeter	100.00
CO2	Paul Wilson, Todd Hundley	5.00
CO3	Jermaine Dye, Mark Wohlers	6.00
CO4	Scott Rolen, Gregg Jefferies	15.00
CO5	Todd Hollandsworth, Jason Kendall	8.00
CO6	Alan Benes, Robin Ventura	8.00
CO7	Eric Karros, Raul Mondesi	15.00
CO8	Rey Ordonez, Nomar Garciaparra	45.00
CO9	Rondell White, Marty Cordova	6.00
CO10	Tony Gwynn, Karim Garcia	30.00

Firebrand

		NM/M
Complete Set (12):		25.00
Common Player:		1.00
1	Jeff Bagwell	2.50
2	Albert Belle	1.00
3	Barry Bonds	6.50
4	Andres Galarraga	1.00
5	Ken Griffey Jr.	4.50
6	Brady Anderson	1.00
7	Mark McGwire	5.50
8	Chipper Jones	3.50
9	Frank Thomas	2.50
10	Mike Piazza	4.50
11	Mo Vaughn	1.00
12	Juan Gonzalez	1.50

Instavision

		NM/M
Complete Set (22):		10.00
Common Player:		.35
11	Eddie Murray	.75
12	Paul Molitor	.75
13	Todd Hundley	.35
14	Roger Clemens	1.50
15	Barry Bonds	3.00
16	Mark McGwire	2.00
17	Brady Anderson	.35
18	Barry Larkin	.35
19	Ken Caminiti	.35
110	Hideo Nomo	.45
111	Bernie Williams	.35
112	Juan Gonzalez	.45
113	Andy Pettitte	.45
114	Albert Belle	.35
115	John Smoltz	.35
116	Brian Jordan	.35
117	Derek Jeter	3.00
118	Ken Caminiti	.35
119	John Wetteland	.35
120	Brady Anderson	.35
121	Andruw Jones	.75
122	Jim Leyritz	.35

Millennium

		NM/M
Complete Set (40):		12.50
Common Player:		.25
1	Derek Jeter	5.00
2	Mark Grudzielanek	.25
3	Jacob Cruz	.25
4	Ray Durham	.25
5	Tony Clark	.25
6	Chipper Jones	2.50
7	Luis Castillo	.25
8	Carlos Delgado	.50
9	Brant Brown	.25
10	Jason Kendall	.25
11	Alan Benes	.25
12	Rey Ordonez	.25
13	Justin Thompson	.25
14	Jermaine Allensworth	.25
15	Brian Hunter	.25
16	Marty Cordova	.25
17	Edgar Renteria	.25
18	Karim Garcia	.25
19	Todd Greene	.25
20	Paul Wilson	.25
21	Andruw Jones	1.50
22	Todd Walker	.25
23	Alex Ochoa	.25
24	Bartolo Colon	.25
25	Wendell Magee Jr.	.25
26	Jose Rosado	.25
27	Katsuhiro Maeda	.25
28	Bob Abreu	.25
29	Brooks Kieschnick	.25
30	Derrick Gibson	.25
31	Mike Sweeney	.25
32	Jeff D'Amico	.25
33	Chad Mottola	.25
34	Chris Snopek	.25
35	Jaime Bluma	.25
36	Vladimir Guerrero	1.50
37	Nomar Garciaparra	2.50
38	Scott Rolen	1.25
39	Dmitri Young	.25
40	Neifi Perez	.25

Patent Leather

		NM/M
Complete Set (13):		25.00
Common Player:		1.00
1	Ivan Rodriguez	3.00
2	Ken Caminiti	1.00
3	Barry Bonds	6.00
4	Ken Griffey Jr.	5.00
5	Greg Maddux	4.00
6	Craig Biggio	1.00
7	Andres Galarraga	1.00
8	Kenny Lofton	1.00
9	Barry Larkin	1.00
10	Mark Grace	1.00
11	Rey Ordonez	1.00
12	Roberto Alomar	1.25
13	Derek Jeter	6.00

Pure Gold

		NM/M
Complete Set (20):		60.00
Common Player:		1.25
1	Brady Anderson	1.25
2	Albert Belle	1.25
3	Dante Bichette	1.25
4	Barry Bonds	12.00
5	Jay Buhner	1.25
6	Tony Gwynn	6.00
7	Chipper Jones	6.00
8	Mark McGwire	9.00
9	Gary Sheffield	2.25
10	Frank Thomas	4.50
11	Juan Gonzalez	2.50
12	Ken Caminiti	1.25
13	Kenny Lofton	1.25
14	Jeff Bagwell	4.50
15	Ken Griffey Jr.	7.50
16	Cal Ripken Jr.	12.00
17	Mo Vaughn	1.25
18	Mike Piazza	7.50
19	Derek Jeter	12.00
20	Andres Galarraga	1.25

TSC Matrix

		NM/M
Complete Set (120):		70.00
Common Player:		.50
1	Chipper Jones	2.50
2	Gary Sheffield	1.00
3	Kenny Lofton	.50
4	Brian Jordan	.50
5	Mark McGwire	4.25
6	Charles Nagy	.50
7	Tim Salmon	.50
8	Cal Ripken Jr.	5.00
9	Jeff Conine	.50
10	Paul Molitor	1.75
11	Mariano Rivera	.65
12	Pedro Martinez	1.75
13	Jeff Bagwell	1.75

#	Player	Price
14	Bobby Bonilla	.50
15	Barry Bonds	5.00
16	Ryan Klesko	.50
17	Barry Larkin	.50
18	Jim Thome	1.50
19	Jay Buhner	.50
20	Juan Gonzalez	1.00
21	Mike Mussina	.75
22	Kevin Appier	.50
23	Eric Karros	.50
24	Steve Finley	.50
25	Ed Sprague	.50
26	Bernard Gilkey	.50
27	Tony Phillips	.50
28	Henry Rodriguez	.50
29	John Smoltz	.50
30	Dante Bichette	.50
31	Mike Piazza	3.25
32	Paul O'Neill	.50
33	Billy Wagner	.50
34	Reggie Sanders	.50
35	John Jaha	.50
36	Eddie Murray	1.75
37	Eric Young	.50
38	Roberto Hernandez	.50
39	Pat Hentgen	.50
40	Sammy Sosa	2.50
41	Todd Hundley	.50
42	Mo Vaughn	.50
43	Robin Ventura	.50
44	Mark Grudzielanek	.50
45	Shane Reynolds	.50
46	Andy Pettitte	.65
47	Fred McGriff	.50
48	Rey Ordonez	.50
49	Will Clark	.50
50	Ken Griffey Jr.	3.25
51	Todd Worrell	.50
52	Rusty Greer	.50
53	Mark Grace	.50
54	Tom Glavine	.75
55	Derek Jeter	5.00
56	Rafael Palmeiro	1.50
57	Bernie Williams	.50
58	Marty Cordova	.50
59	Andres Galarraga	.50
60	Ken Caminiti	.50
196	Greg Maddux	2.50
197	Joe Carter	.50
198	Alex Ochoa	.50
199	Ellis Burks	.50
200	Ivan Rodriguez	1.50
201	Marquis Grissom	.50
202	Trevor Hoffman	.50
203	Matt Williams	.50
204	Carlos Delgado	1.25
205	Ramon Martinez	.50
206	Chuck Knoblauch	.50
207	Juan Guzman	.50
208	Derek Bell	.50
209	Roger Clemens	3.00
210	Vladimir Guerrero	1.75
211	Cecil Fielder	.50
212	Hideo Nomo	1.00
213	Frank Thomas	1.75
214	Greg Vaughn	.50
215	Javy Lopez	.50
216	Raul Mondesi	.50
217	Wade Boggs	2.50
218	Carlos Baerga	.50
219	Tony Gwynn	2.50
220	Tino Martinez	.50
221	Vinny Castilla	.50
222	Lance Johnson	.50
223	David Justice	.50
224	Rondell White	.50
225	Dean Palmer	.50
226	Jim Edmonds	.50
227	Albert Belle	.50
228	Alex Fernandez	.50
229	Ryne Sandberg	2.50
230	Jose Mesa	.50
231	David Cone	.50
232	Troy Percival	.50
233	Edgar Martinez	.50
234	Jose Canseco	1.25
235	Kevin Brown	.50
236	Ray Lankford	.50
237	Karim Garcia	.50
238	J.T. Snow	.50
239	Dennis Eckersley	1.50
240	Roberto Alomar	.75
241	John Valentin	.50
242	Ron Gant	.50
243	Geronimo Berroa	.50
244	Manny Ramirez	1.75
245	Travis Fryman	.50
246	Denny Neagle	.50
247	Randy Johnson	1.75
248	Darin Erstad	.65
249	Mark Wohlers	.50
250	Ken Hill	.50
251	Larry Walker	.50
252	Craig Biggio	.50
253	Brady Anderson	.50
254	John Wetteland	.50
255	Andruw Jones	1.75

1998 Stadium Club

		NM/M
Complete Set (400):		30.00
Common Player:		.05
Hobby Pack (10):		1.50
Retail Pack (7):		1.50
Home Team Adv. Pack (16):		4.00
Hobby Box (24):		30.00
1	Chipper Jones	1.00
2	Frank Thomas	.75
3	Vladimir Guerrero	.75
4	Ellis Burks	.05
5	John Franco	.05
6	Paul Molitor	.75
7	Rusty Greer	.05
8	Todd Hundley	.05
9	Brett Tomko	.05
10	Eric Karros	.05
11	Mike Cameron	.05
12	Jim Edmonds	.05
13	Bernie Williams	.05
14	Denny Neagle	.05
15	Jason Dickson	.05
16	Sammy Sosa	1.00
17	Brian Jordan	.05
18	Jose Vidro	.05
19	Scott Spiezio	.05
20	Jay Buhner	.05
21	Jim Thome	.65
22	Sandy Alomar	.05
23	Devon White	.05
24	Roberto Alomar	.20
25	John Flaherty	.05
26	John Wetteland	.05
27	Willie Greene	.05
28	Gregg Jefferies	.05
29	Johnny Damon	.35
30	Barry Larkin	.05
31	Chuck Knoblauch	.05
32	Mo Vaughn	.05
33	Tony Clark	.05
34	Marty Cordova	.05
35	Vinny Castilla	.05
36	Jeff King	.05
37	Reggie Jefferson	.05
38	Mariano Rivera	.15
39	Jermaine Allensworth	.05
40	Livan Hernandez	.05
41	Heathcliff Slocumb	.05
42	Jacob Cruz	.05
43	Barry Bonds	2.50
44	Dave Magadan	.05
45	Chan Ho Park	.05
46	Jeremi Gonzalez	.05
47	Jeff Cirillo	.05
48	Delino DeShields	.05
49	Craig Biggio	.05
50	Benito Santiago	.05
51	Mark Clark	.05
52	Fernando Vina	.05
53	F.P. Santangelo	.05
54	Pep Harris RC	.05
55	Edgar Renteria	.05
56	Jeff Bagwell	.75
57	Jimmy Key	.05
58	Bartolo Colon	.05
59	Curt Schilling	.35
60	Steve Finley	.05
61	Andy Ashby	.05
62	John Burkett	.05
63	Orel Hershiser	.05
64	Pokey Reese	.05
65	Scott Servais	.05
66	Todd Jones	.05
67	Javy Lopez	.05
68	Robin Ventura	.05
69	Miguel Tejada	.15
70	Raul Casanova	.05
71	Reggie Sanders	.05
72	Edgardo Alfonzo	.05
73	Dean Palmer	.05
74	Todd Stottlemyre	.05
75	David Wells	.05
76	Troy Percival	.05
77	Albert Belle	.05
78	Pat Hentgen	.05
79	Brian Hunter	.05
80	Richard Hidalgo	.05
81	Darren Oliver	.05
82	Mark Wohlers	.05
83	Cal Ripken Jr.	2.50
84	Hideo Nomo	.40
85	Derrek Lee	.50
86	Stan Javier	.05
87	Rey Ordonez	.05
88	Randy Johnson	.75
89	Jeff Kent	.05
90	Brian McRae	.05
91	Manny Ramirez	.75
92	Trevor Hoffman	.05
93	Doug Glanville	.05
94	Todd Walker	.05
95	Andy Benes	.05
96	Jason Schmidt	.05
97	Mike Matheny	.05
98	Tim Naehring	.05
99	Jeff Blauser	.05
100	Jose Rosado	.05
101	Roger Clemens	1.25
102	Pedro Astacio	.05
103	Mark Bellhorn	.05
104	Paul O'Neill	.05
105	Darin Erstad	.15
106	Mike Lieberthal	.05
107	Wilson Alvarez	.05
108	Mike Mussina	.30
109	George Williams	.05
110	Cliff Floyd	.05
111	Shawn Estes	.05
112	Mark Grudzielanek	.05
113	Tony Gwynn	1.00
114	Alan Benes	.05
115	Terry Steinbach	.05
116	Greg Maddux	1.00
117	Andy Pettitte	.25
118	Dave Nilsson	.05
119	Deivi Cruz	.05
120	Carlos Delgado	.50
121	Scott Hatteberg	.05
122	John Olerud	.05
123	Moises Alou	.05
124	Garret Anderson	.05
125	Royce Clayton	.05
126	Dante Powell	.05
127	Tom Glavine	.35
128	Gary DiSarcina	.05
129	Terry Adams	.05
130	Raul Mondesi	.05
131	Dan Wilson	.05
132	Al Martin	.05
133	Mickey Morandini	.05
134	Rafael Palmeiro	.65
135	Juan Encarnacion	.05
136	Jim Pittsley	.05
137	Magglio Ordonez RC	1.00
138	Will Clark	.05
139	Todd Helton	.65
140	Kelvim Escobar	.05
141	Esteban Loaiza	.05
142	John Jaha	.05
143	Jeff Fassero	.05
144	Harold Baines	.05
145	Butch Huskey	.05
146	Pat Meares	.05
147	Brian Giles	.05
148	Ramiro Mendoza	.05
149	John Smoltz	.05
150	Felix Martinez	.05
151	Jose Valentin	.05
152	Brad Rigby	.05
153	Ed Sprague	.05
154	Mike Hampton	.05
155	Mike Lansing	.05
156	Ray Lankford	.05
157	Bobby Bonilla	.05
158	Bill Mueller	.05
159	Jeffrey Hammonds	.05
160	Charles Nagy	.05
161	Rich Loiselle	.05
162	Al Leiter	.05
163	Larry Walker	.05
164	Chris Hoiles	.05
165	Jeff Montgomery	.05
166	Francisco Cordova	.05
167	James Baldwin	.05
168	Mark McLemore	.05
169	Kevin Appier	.05
170	Jamey Wright	.05
171	Nomar Garciaparra	1.00
172	Matt Franco	.05
173	Jeromy Burnitz	.05
174	Armando Benitez	.05
175	Ismael Valdes	.05
176	Lance Johnson	.05
177	Paul Sorrento	.05
178	Rondell White	.05
179	Kevin Elster	.05
180	Jason Giambi	.50
181	Carlos Baerga	.05
182	Russ Davis	.05
183	Ryan McGuire	.05
184	Eric Young	.05
185	Ron Gant	.05
186	Manny Alexander	.05
187	Scott Karl	.05
188	Brady Anderson	.05
189	Randall Simon	.05
190	Tim Belcher	.05
191	Jaret Wright	.05
192	Dante Bichette	.05
193	John Valentin	.05
194	Darren Bragg	.05
195	Mike Sweeney	.05
196	Craig Counsell	.05
197	Jaime Navarro	.05
198	Todd Dunn	.05
199	Ken Griffey Jr.	1.50
200	Juan Gonzalez	.40
201	Billy Wagner	.05
202	Tino Martinez	.05
203	Mark McGwire	2.00
204	Jeff D'Amico	.05
205	Rico Brogna	.05
206	Todd Hollandsworth	.05
207	Chad Curtis	.05
208	Tom Goodwin	.05
209	Neifi Perez	.05
210	Derek Bell	.05
211	Quilvio Veras	.05
212	Greg Vaughn	.05
213	Roberto Hernandez	.05
214	Arthur Rhodes	.05
215	Cal Eldred	.05
216	Bill Taylor	.05
217	Todd Greene	.05
218	Mario Valdez	.05
219	Ricky Bottalico	.05
220	Frank Rodriguez	.05
221	Rich Becker	.05
222	Roberto Duran	.05
223	Ivan Rodriguez	.65
224	Mike Jackson	.05
225	Deion Sanders	.05
226	Tony Womack	.05
227	Mark Kotsay	.05
228	Steve Trachsel	.05
229	Ryan Klesko	.05
230	Ken Cloude	.05
231	Luis Gonzalez	.05
232	Gary Gaetti	.05
233	Michael Tucker	.05
234	Shawn Green	.35
235	Ariel Prieto	.05
236	Kirt Manwaring	.05
237	Omar Vizquel	.05
238	Matt Beech	.05
239	Justin Thompson	.05
240	Bret Boone	.05
241	Derek Jeter	2.50
242	Ken Caminiti	.05
243	Jay Bell	.05
244	Kevin Tapani	.05
245	Jason Kendall	.05
246	Jose Guillen	.05
247	Mike Bordick	.05
248	Dustin Hermanson	.05
249	Darrin Fletcher	.05
250	Dave Hollins	.05
251	Ramon Martinez	.05
252	Hideki Irabu	.05
253	Mark Grace	.05
254	Jason Isringhausen	.05
255	Jose Cruz Jr.	.05
256	Brian Johnson	.05
257	Brad Ausmus	.05
258	Andruw Jones	.75
259	Doug Jones	.05
260	Jeff Shaw	.05
261	Chuck Finley	.05
262	Gary Sheffield	.45

263	David Segui	.05
264	John Smiley	.05
265	Tim Salmon	.05
266	J.T. Snow Jr.	.05
267	Alex Fernandez	.05
268	Matt Stairs	.05
269	B.J. Surhoff	.05
270	Keith Foulke	.05
271	Edgar Martinez	.05
272	Shannon Stewart	.05
273	Eduardo Perez	.05
274	Wally Joyner	.05
275	Kevin Young	.05
276	Eli Marrero	.05
277	Brad Radke	.05
278	Jamie Moyer	.05
279	Joe Girardi	.05
280	Troy O'Leary	.05
281	Aaron Sele	.05
282	Jose Offerman	.05
283	Scott Erickson	.05
284	Sean Berry	.05
285	Shigetosi Hasegawa	.05
286	Felix Heredia	.05
287	Willie McGee	.05
288	Alex Rodriguez	2.00
289	Ugueth Urbina	.05
290	Jon Lieber	.05
291	Fernando Tatis	.05
292	Chris Stynes	.05
293	Bernard Gilkey	.05
294	Joey Hamilton	.05
295	Matt Karchner	.05
296	Paul Wilson	.05
297	Mel Nieves	.05
298	Kevin Millwood RC	.75
299	Quinton McCracken	.05
300	Jerry DiPoto	.05
301	Jermaine Dye	.05
302	Travis Lee	.05
303	Ron Coomer	.05
304	Matt Williams	.05
305	Bobby Higginson	.05
306	Jorge Fabregas	.05
307	Hal Morris	.05
308	Jay Bell	.05
309	Joe Randa	.05
310	Andy Benes	.05
311	Sterling Hitchcock	.05
312	Jeff Suppan	.05
313	Shane Reynolds	.05
314	Willie Blair	.05
315	Scott Rolen	.65
316	Wilson Alvarez	.05
317	David Justice	.05
318	Fred McGriff	.05
319	Bobby Jones	.05
320	Wade Boggs	1.00
321	Tim Wakefield	.05
322	Tony Saunders	.05
323	David Cone	.05
324	Roberto Hernandez	.05
325	Jose Canseco	.45
326	Kevin Stocker	.05
327	Gerald Williams	.05
328	Quinton McCracken	.05
329	Mark Gardner	.05
330	Ben Grieve	.05
331	Kevin Brown	.05
332	Mike Lowell RC	1.00
333	Jed Hansen	.05
334	Abraham Nunez	.05
335	John Thomson	.05
336	Derrek Lee	.05
337	Mike Piazza	1.50
338	Brad Fullmer	.05
339	Ray Durham	.05
340	Kerry Wood	.50
341	Kevin Polcovich RC	.05
342	Russ Johnson	.05
343	Darryl Hamilton	.05
344	David Ortiz	.45
345	Kevin Orie	.05
346	Sean Casey	.25
347	Juan Guzman	.05
348	Ruben Rivera	.05
349	Rick Aguilera	.05
350	Bobby Estalella	.05
351	Bobby Witt	.05
352	Paul Konerko	.25
353	Matt Morris	.05
354	Carl Pavano	.05
355	Todd Zeile	.05
356	Kevin Brown	.05
357	Alex Gonzalez	.05
358	Chuck Knoblauch	.05
359	Joey Cora	.05
360	Mike Lansing	.05
361	Adrian Beltre	.45
362	Dennis Eckersley	.65
363	A.J. Hinch	.05
364	Kenny Lofton	.05
365	Alex Gonzalez	.05
366	Henry Rodriguez	.05
367	Mike Stoner RC	.05
368	Darryl Kile	.05

369	Carl Pavano	.05
370	Walt Weiss	.05
371	Kris Benson	.05
372	Cecil Fielder	.05
373	Dermal Brown	.05
374	Rod Beck	.05
375	Eric Milton	.05
376	Travis Fryman	.05
377	Preston Wilson	.10
378	Chili Davis	.05
379	Travis Lee	.10
380	Jim Leyritz	.05
381	Vernon Wells	.05
382	Joe Carter	.05
383	J.J. Davis	.05
384	Marquis Grissom	.05
385	Mike Cuddyer RC	.50
386	Rickey Henderson	.75
387	Chris Enochs RC	.10
388	Andres Galarraga	.05
389	Jason Dellaero	.05
390	Robb Nen	.05
391	Mark Mangum	.05
392	Jeff Blauser	.05
393	Adam Kennedy	.05
394	Bob Abreu	.05
395	Jack Cust RC	1.00
396	Jose Vizcaino	.05
397	Jon Garland	.05
398	Pedro Martinez	.75
399	Aaron Akin	.05
400	Jeff Conine	.05

One of a Kind

	NM/M
Common Player:	2.00
Stars:	12X
Production 150 Sets	
(See 1998 Stadium Club for	
checklist and base card values.)	

First Day Issue

	NM/M
Common Player:	2.00
Stars:	10X
Production 200 Sets	
(See 1998 Stadium Club for	
checklist and base card values.)	

Printing Plates

	NM/M
Common Player:	25.00
(See 1998 Stadium Club for	
checklist.)	

Bowman Preview

		NM/M
Complete Set (10):		10.00
Common Player:		.25
Inserted 1:12		
BP1	Nomar Garciaparra	1.00
BP2	Scott Rolen	.65
BP3	Ken Griffey Jr.	1.50
BP4	Frank Thomas	.75
BP5	Larry Walker	.25
BP6	Mike Piazza	1.50
BP7	Chipper Jones	1.00
BP8	Tino Martinez	.25
BP9	Mark McGwire	2.00
BP10	Barry Bonds	2.50

Bowman Prospect Preview

		NM/M
Complete Set (10):		3.00
Common Player:		.25
Inserted 1:12		
BP1	Ben Grieve	.25
BP2	Brad Fullmer	.25
BP3	Ryan Anderson	.25
BP4	Mark Kotsay	.25
BP5	Bobby Estalella	.25
BP6	Juan Encarnacion	.25
BP7	Todd Helton	2.00
BP8	Mike Lowell	.25
BP9	A.J. Hinch	.25
BP10	Richard Hidalgo	.25

Co-Signers

		NM/M
Common Card:		10.00
Group A 1:4,372		
Group B 1:1,457		
Group C 1:121		
CS1	Nomar Garciaparra, Scott Rolen/A	120.00
CS2	Nomar Garciaparra, Derek Jeter/B	250.00
CS3	Nomar Garciaparra, Eric Karros/C	60.00
CS4	Scott Rolen, Derek Jeter/C	100.00
CS5	Scott Rolen, Eric Karros/B	40.00
CS6	Derek Jeter, Eric Karros/A	150.00
CS7	Travis Lee, Jose Cruz Jr./B	15.00
CS8	Travis Lee, Mark Kotsay/C	10.00
CS9	Travis Lee, Paul Konerko/A	25.00
CS10	Jose Cruz Jr., Mark Kotsay/A	25.00
CS11	Jose Cruz Jr., Paul Konerko/C	12.00
CS12	Mark Kotsay, Paul Konerko/B	20.00
CS13	Tony Gwynn, Larry Walker/A	120.00
CS14	Tony Gwynn, Mark Grudzielanek/C	30.00
CS15	Tony Gwynn, Andres Galarraga/B	60.00
CS16	Larry Walker, Mark Grudzielanek/B	40.00
CS17	Larry Walker, Andres Galarraga/C	30.00
CS18	Mark Grudzielanek, Andres Galarraga/A	25.00
CS19	Sandy Alomar, Roberto Alomar/A	75.00
CS20	Sandy Alomar, Andy Pettitte/C	20.00
CS21	Sandy Alomar, Tino Martinez/B	40.00
CS22	Roberto Alomar, Andy Pettitte/B	50.00
CS23	Roberto Alomar, Tino Martinez/C	25.00
CS24	Andy Pettitte, Tino Martinez/A	75.00
CS25	Tony Clark, Todd Hundley/A	25.00
CS26	Tony Clark, Tim Salmon/B	30.00
CS27	Tony Clark, Robin Ventura/C	10.00
CS28	Todd Hundley, Tim Salmon/C	15.00
CS29	Todd Hundley, Robin Ventura/B	12.00
CS30	Tim Salmon, Robin Ventura/A	50.00
CS31	Roger Clemens, Randy Johnson/B	175.00
CS32	Roger Clemens, Jaret Wright/A	140.00
CS33	Roger Clemens, Matt Morris/C	100.00
CS34	Randy Johnson, Jaret Wright/C	50.00
CS35	Randy Johnson, Matt Morris/A	85.00
CS36	Jaret Wright, Matt Morris/B	20.00

In the Wings

ELI MARRERO

		NM/M
Complete Set (15):		6.00
Common Player:		.50
Inserted 1:36		
W1	Juan Encarnacion	.50
W2	Brad Fullmer	.50
W3	Ben Grieve	.50
W4	Todd Helton	3.00
W5	Richard Hidalgo	.50
W6	Russ Johnson	.50
W7	Paul Konerko	.75
W8	Mark Kotsay	.50
W9	Derrek Lee	1.00
W10	Travis Lee	.50
W11	Eli Marrero	.50
W12	David Ortiz	.75
W13	Randall Simon	.50
W14	Shannon Stewart	.50
W15	Fernando Tatis	.50

Never Compromise

		NM/M
Complete Set (20):		10.00
Common Player:		.15
Inserted 1:12		
NC1	Cal Ripken Jr.	2.00
NC2	Ivan Rodriguez	.50
NC3	Ken Griffey Jr.	1.00
NC4	Frank Thomas	.60
NC5	Tony Gwynn	.75
NC6	Mike Piazza	1.00
NC7	Randy Johnson	.60
NC8	Greg Maddux	.75
NC9	Roger Clemens	.85

		NM/M
NC10	Derek Jeter	2.00
NC11	Chipper Jones	.75
NC12	Barry Bonds	2.00
NC13	Larry Walker	.15
NC14	Jeff Bagwell	.60
NC15	Barry Larkin	.15
NC16	Ken Caminiti	.15
NC17	Mark McGwire	1.50
NC18	Manny Ramirez	.60
NC19	Tim Salmon	.15
NC20	Paul Molitor	.60

Playing with Passion

		NM/M
Complete Set (10):		10.00
Common Player:		.35
Inserted 1:12		
P1	Bernie Williams	.35
P2	Jim Edmonds	.35
P3	Chipper Jones	1.00
P4	Cal Ripken Jr.	3.00
P5	Craig Biggio	.35
P6	Juan Gonzalez	.45
P7	Alex Rodriguez	2.25
P8	Tino Martinez	.35
P9	Mike Piazza	1.50
P10	Ken Griffey Jr.	1.50

Royal Court

		NM/M
Complete Set (15):		15.00
Common Player:		.50
Inserted 1:36		
RC1	Ken Griffey Jr.	2.00
RC2	Frank Thomas	1.25
RC3	Mike Piazza	2.00
RC4	Chipper Jones	1.50
RC5	Mark McGwire	2.50
RC6	Cal Ripken Jr.	3.00

RC7	Jeff Bagwell	1.25
RC8	Barry Bonds	3.00
RC9	Juan Gonzalez	.85
RC10	Alex Rodriguez	2.50
RC11	Travis Lee	.50
RC12	Paul Konerko	.75
RC13	Todd Helton	1.00
RC14	Ben Grieve	.50
RC15	Mark Kotsay	.50

Screen Plays Sound Chips

		NM/M
SC1	Cal Ripken Jr.	5.00

Triumvirate

		NM/M
Complete Set (54):		70.00
Complete Series 1 (24):		30.00
Complete Series 2 (30):		40.00
Common Player:		.50
Luminous 1:48		
Luminescents 1:192:		1.5X
Illuminators 1:384:		2.5X
T1a	Chipper Jones	2.50
T1b	Andruw Jones	2.00
T1c	Kenny Lofton	.50
T2a	Derek Jeter	5.00
T2b	Bernie Williams	.50
T2c	Tino Martinez	.50
T3a	Jay Buhner	.50
T3b	Edgar Martinez	.50
T3c	Ken Griffey Jr.	3.00
T4a	Albert Belle	.50
T4b	Robin Ventura	.50
T4c	Frank Thomas	2.00
T5a	Brady Anderson	.50
T5b	Cal Ripken Jr.	5.00
T5c	Rafael Palmeiro	1.50
T6a	Mike Piazza	3.00
T6b	Raul Mondesi	.50
T6c	Eric Karros	.50
T7a	Vinny Castilla	.50
T7b	Andres Galarraga	.50
T7c	Larry Walker	.50
T8a	Jim Thome	1.50
T8b	Manny Ramirez	2.00
T8c	David Justice	.50
T9a	Mike Mussina	.75
T9b	Greg Maddux	2.50
T9c	Randy Johnson	2.00
T10a	Mike Piazza	3.00
T10b	Sandy Alomar	.50
T10c	Ivan Rodriguez	1.50
T11a	Mark McGwire	4.00
T11b	Tino Martinez	.50
T11c	Frank Thomas	2.00
T12a	Roberto Alomar	.75
T12b	Chuck Knoblauch	.50
T12c	Craig Biggio	.50
T13a	Cal Ripken Jr.	5.00
T13b	Chipper Jones	2.50
T13c	Ken Caminiti	.50
T14a	Derek Jeter	5.00
T14b	Nomar Garciaparra	2.50
T14c	Alex Rodriguez	4.00
T15a	Barry Bonds	5.00
T15b	David Justice	.50
T15c	Albert Belle	.50
T16a	Bernie Williams	.50

T16b	Ken Griffey Jr.	3.00
T16c	Ray Lankford	.50
T17a	Tim Salmon	.50
T17b	Larry Walker	.50
T17c	Tony Gwynn	2.50
T18a	Paul Molitor	2.00
T18b	Edgar Martinez	.50
T18c	Juan Gonzalez	1.00

1999 Stadium Club

		NM/M
Complete Set (355):		40.00
Complete Series 1 (170):		20.00
Complete Series 2 (185):		20.00
Common Player:		.05
Common SP		
(141-160; 336-355):		.50
Inserted 1:3		
Pack (6):		1.25
Wax Box (24):		25.00
1	Alex Rodriguez	2.00
2	Chipper Jones	1.50
3	Rusty Greer	.05
4	Jim Edmonds	.05
5	Ron Gant	.05
6	Kevin Polcovich	.05
7	Darryl Strawberry	.05
8	Bill Mueller	.05
9	Vinny Castilla	.05
10	Wade Boggs	1.50
11	Jose Lima	.05
12	Darren Dreifort	.05
13	Jay Bell	.05
14	Ben Grieve	.05
15	Shawn Green	.35
16	Andres Galarraga	.05
17	Bartolo Colon	.05
18	Francisco Cordova	.05
19	Paul O'Neill	.05
20	Trevor Hoffman	.05
21	Darren Oliver	.05
22	John Franco	.05
23	Eli Marrero	.05
24	Roberto Hernandez	.05
25	Craig Biggio	.05
26	Brad Fullmer	.05
27	Scott Erickson	.05
28	Tom Gordon	.05
29	Brian Hunter	.05
30	Raul Mondesi	.05
31	Rick Reed	.05
32	Jose Canseco	.50
33	Robb Nen	.05
34	Turner Ward	.05
35	Bret Boone	.05
36	Jose Offerman	.05
37	Matt Lawton	.05
38	David Wells	.05
39	Bob Abreu	.10
40	Jeromy Burnitz	.05
41	Deivi Cruz	.05
42	Mike Cameron	.05
43	Rico Brogna	.05
44	Dmitri Young	.05
45	Chuck Knoblauch	.05
46	Johnny Damon	.35
47	Brian Meadows	.05
48	Jeremi Gonzalez	.05
49	Gary DiSarcina	.05
50	Frank Thomas	1.00
51	F.P. Santangelo	.05
52	Tom Candiotti	.05
53	Shane Reynolds	.05
54	Rod Beck	.05
55	Rey Ordonez	.05
56	Todd Helton	.75
57	Mickey Morandini	.05
58	Jorge Posada	.05
59	Mike Mussina	.30
60	Bobby Bonilla	.05
61	David Segui	.05
62	Brian McRae	.05

63	Fred McGriff	.05
64	Brett Tomko	.05
65	Derek Jeter	2.50
66	Sammy Sosa	1.50
67	Kenny Rogers	.05
68	Dave Nilsson	.05
69	Eric Young	.05
70	Mark McGwire	2.00
71	Kenny Lofton	.05
72	Tom Glavine	.35
73	Joey Hamilton	.05
74	John Valentin	.05
75	Mariano Rivera	.15
76	Ray Durham	.05
77	Tony Clark	.05
78	Livan Hernandez	.05
79	Rickey Henderson	1.00
80	Vladimir Guerrero	1.00
81	J.T. Snow Jr.	.05
82	Juan Guzman	.05
83	Darryl Hamilton	.05
84	Matt Anderson	.05
85	Travis Lee	.05
86	Joe Randa	.05
87	Dave Dellucci	.05
88	Moises Alou	.05
89	Alex Gonzalez	.05
90	Tony Womack	.05
91	Neifi Perez	.05
92	Travis Fryman	.05
93	Masato Yoshii	.05
94	Woody Williams	.05
95	Ray Lankford	.05
96	Roger Clemens	1.50
97	Dustin Hermanson	.05
98	Joe Carter	.05
99	Jason Schmidt	.05
100	Greg Maddux	1.50
101	Kevin Tapani	.05
102	Charles Johnson	.05
103	Derrek Lee	.50
104	Pete Harnisch	.05
105	Dante Bichette	.05
106	Scott Brosius	.05
107	Mike Caruso	.05
108	Eddie Taubensee	.05
109	Jeff Fassero	.05
110	Marquis Grissom	.05
111	Jose Hernandez	.05
112	Chan Ho Park	.05
113	Wally Joyner	.05
114	Bobby Estalella	.05
115	Pedro Martinez	1.00
116	Shawn Estes	.05
117	Walt Weiss	.05
118	John Mabry	.05
119	Brian Johnson	.05
120	Jim Thome	.65
121	Bill Spiers	.05
122	John Olerud	.05
123	Jeff King	.05
124	Tim Belcher	.05
125	John Wetteland	.05
126	Tony Gwynn	1.50
127	Brady Anderson	.05
128	Randy Winn	.05
129	Devon White	.05
130	Eric Karros	.05
131	Kevin Millwood	.05
132	Andy Benes	.05
133	Andy Ashby	.05
134	Ron Comer	.05
135	Juan Gonzalez	.50
136	Randy Johnson	1.00
137	Aaron Sele	.05
138	Edgardo Alfonzo	.05
139	B.J. Surhoff	.05
140	Jose Vizcaino	.05
141	Chad Moeller RC	.75
142	Mike Zwicka RC	.50
143	Angel Pena	.50
144	Nick Johnson RC	2.00
145	Giuseppe Chiaramonte RC	.50
146	Kit Pellow RC	.50
147	Clayton Andrews RC	.50
148	Jerry Hairston Jr. RC	.75
149	Jason Tyner RC	.50
150	Chip Ambres RC	.50
151	Pat Burrell RC	2.00
152	Josh McKinley RC	.75
153	Choo Freeman RC	.75
154	Rick Elder RC	.50
155	Eric Valent RC	.75
156	Jeff Winchester RC	.50
157	Mike Nannini RC	.50
158	Mamon Tucker RC	.50
159	Nate Bump RC	.50
160	Andy Brown RC	.50
161	Troy Glaus	1.00
162	Adrian Beltre	.45
163	Mitch Meluskey	.05
164	Alex Gonzalez	.05
165	George Lombard	.05
166	Eric Chavez	.25
167	Ruben Mateo	.05

168	Calvin Pickering	.05
169	Gabe Kapler	.05
170	Bruce Chen	.05
171	Darin Erstad	.15
172	Sandy Alomar	.05
173	Miguel Cairo	.05
174	Jason Kendall	.05
175	Cal Ripken Jr.	2.50
176	Darryl Kile	.05
177	David Cone	.05
178	Mike Sweeney	.05
179	Royce Clayton	.05
180	Curt Schilling	.25
181	Barry Larkin	.05
182	Eric Milton	.05
183	Ellis Burks	.05
184	A.J. Hinch	.05
185	Garret Anderson	.05
186	Sean Bergman	.05
187	Shannon Stewart	.05
188	Bernard Gilkey	.05
189	Jeff Blauser	.05
190	Andruw Jones	1.00
191	Omar Daal	.05
192	Jeff Kent	.05
193	Mark Kotsay	.05
194	Dave Burba	.05
195	Bobby Higginson	.05
196	Hideki Irabu	.05
197	Jamie Moyer	.05
198	Doug Glanville	.05
199	Quinton McCracken	.05
200	Ken Griffey Jr.	1.75
201	Mike Lieberthal	.05
202	Carl Everett	.05
203	Omar Vizquel	.05
204	Mike Lansing	.05
205	Manny Ramirez	1.00
206	Ryan Klesko	.05
207	Jeff Montgomery	.05
208	Chad Curtis	.05
209	Rick Helling	.05
210	Justin Thompson	.05
211	Tom Goodwin	.05
212	Todd Dunwoody	.05
213	Kevin Young	.05
214	Tony Saunders	.05
215	Gary Sheffield	.45
216	Jaret Wright	.05
217	Quilvio Veras	.05
218	Marty Cordova	.05
219	Tino Martinez	.05
220	Scott Rolen	.75
221	Fernando Tatis	.05
222	Damion Easley	.05
223	Aramis Ramirez	.05
224	Brad Radke	.05
225	Nomar Garciaparra	1.50
226	Magglio Ordonez	.05
227	Andy Pettitte	.20
228	David Ortiz	.45
229	Todd Jones	.05
230	Larry Walker	.05
231	Tim Wakefield	.05
232	Jose Guillen	.05
233	Gregg Olson	.05
234	Ricky Gutierrez	.05
235	Todd Walker	.05
236	Abraham Nunez	.05
237	Sean Casey	.15
238	Greg Norton	.05
239	Bret Saberhagen	.05
240	Bernie Williams	.05
241	Tim Salmon	.05
242	Jason Giambi	.50
243	Fernando Vina	.05
244	Darrin Fletcher	.05
245	Greg Vaughn	.05
246	Dennis Reyes	.05
247	Hideo Nomo	.50
248	Reggie Sanders	.05
249	Mike Hampton	.05
250	Kerry Wood	.50
251	Ismael Valdes	.05
252	Pat Hentgen	.05
253	Scott Spiezio	.05
254	Chuck Finley	.05
255	Troy Glaus	.75
256	Bobby Jones	.05
257	Wayne Gomes	.05
258	Rondell White	.05
259	Todd Zeile	.05
260	Matt Williams	.05
261	Henry Rodriguez	.05
262	Matt Stairs	.05
263	Jose Valentin	.05
264	David Justice	.05
265	Javy Lopez	.05
266	Matt Morris	.05
267	Steve Trachsel	.05
268	Edgar Martinez	.05
269	Al Martin	.05
270	Ivan Rodriguez	.75
271	Carlos Delgado	.50
272	Mark Grace	.05
273	Ugueth Urbina	.05

274	Jay Buhner	.05
275	Mike Piazza	1.75
276	Rick Aguilera	.05
277	Javier Valentin	.05
278	Brian Anderson	.05
279	Cliff Floyd	.05
280	Barry Bonds	2.50
281	Troy O'Leary	.05
282	Seth Greisinger	.05
283	Mark Grudzielanek	.05
284	Jose Cruz Jr.	.05
285	Jeff Bagwell	1.00
286	John Smoltz	.05
287	Jeff Cirillo	.05
288	Richie Sexson	.05
289	Charles Nagy	.05
290	Pedro Martinez	1.00
291	Juan Encarnacion	.05
292	Phil Nevin	.05
293	Terry Steinbach	.05
294	Miguel Tejada	.15
295	Dan Wilson	.05
296	Chris Peters	.05
297	Brian Moehler	.05
298	Jason Christiansen	.05
299	Kelly Stinnett	.05
300	Dwight Gooden	.05
301	Randy Velarde	.05
302	Kirt Manwaring	.05
303	Jeff Abbott	.05
304	Dave Hollins	.05
305	Kerry Ligtenberg	.05
306	Aaron Boone	.05
307	Carlos Hernandez	.05
308	Mike DiFelice	.05
309	Brian Meadows	.05
310	Tim Bogar	.05
311	Greg Vaughn	.05
312	Brant Brown	.05
313	Steve Finley	.05
314	Bret Boone	.05
315	Albert Belle	.05
316	Robin Ventura	.05
317	Eric Davis	.05
318	Todd Hundley	.05
319	Jose Offerman	.05
320	Kevin Brown	.05
321	Denny Neagle	.05
322	Brian Jordan	.05
323	Brian Giles	.05
324	Bobby Bonilla	.05
325	Roberto Alomar	.20
326	Ken Caminiti	.05
327	Todd Stottlemyre	.05
328	Randy Johnson	1.00
329	Luis Gonzalez	.05
330	Rafael Palmeiro	.75
331	Devon White	.05
332	Will Clark	.05
333	Dean Palmer	.05
334	Gregg Jefferies	.05
335	Mo Vaughn	.05
336	Brad Lidge RC	2.00
337	Chris George RC	.75
338	Austin Kearns RC	1.50
339	Matt Belisle RC	.75
340	Nate Cornejo RC	.75
341	Matt Holliday RC	5.00
342	J.M. Gold RC	.50
343	Matt Roney RC	.50
344	Seth Etherton RC	.75
345	Adam Everett RC	.75
346	Marlon Anderson	.50
347	Ron Belliard	.50
348	Fernando Seguignol	.50
349	Michael Barrett	.50
350	Dernell Stenson	.50
351	Ryan Anderson	.50
352	Ramon Hernandez	.50
353	Jeremy Giambi	.50
354	Ricky Ledee	.50
355	Carlos Lee	1.00

First Day Issue

	NM/M
Common Player:	10.00
Inserted 1:1,107	
1 Alex Rodriguez	75.00
2 Chipper Jones	30.00
3 Barry Bonds	150.00
4 Tino Martinez	25.00
5 Ben Grieve	10.00
6 Juan Gonzalez	15.00
7 Vladimir Guerrero	30.00
8 Albert Belle	15.00
9 Kerry Wood	25.00
10 Todd Helton	20.00

	NM/M
Common Player:	2.00
Stars:	8X
SP Stars:	4X

(See 1999 Stadium Club for checklist and base card values.)

One of a Kind

	NM/M
Common Player:	2.00
Stars:	8X
SP Stars:	4X

(See 1999 Stadium Club for checklist and base card values.)

Printing Plates

	NM/M
Common Player:	25.00

(See 1999 Stadium Club for checklist.)

Autographs

Caption: CHIPPER JONES

	NM/M
Common Player:	10.00
Inserted 1:1,107	
1 Alex Rodriguez	75.00
2 Chipper Jones	30.00
3 Barry Bonds	150.00
4 Tino Martinez	25.00
5 Ben Grieve	10.00
6 Juan Gonzalez	15.00
7 Vladimir Guerrero	30.00
8 Albert Belle	15.00
9 Kerry Wood	25.00
10 Todd Helton	20.00

Chrome

Caption: MANNY RAMIREZ

	NM/M
Complete Set (40):	45.00
Common Player:	.50
Inserted 1:24	
Refractors:	2X
Inserted 1:96	
1 Nomar Garciaparra	2.00
2 Kerry Wood	1.00
3 Jeff Bagwell	1.50
4 Ivan Rodriguez	1.25
5 Albert Belle	.50
6 Gary Sheffield	1.00
7 Andruw Jones	1.50
8 Kevin Brown	.50
9 David Cone	.50
10 Darin Erstad	.75
11 Manny Ramirez	1.50
12 Larry Walker	.50
13 Mike Piazza	2.50
14 Cal Ripken Jr.	4.00
15 Pedro Martinez	1.50
16 Greg Vaughn	.50
17 Barry Bonds	4.00
18 Mo Vaughn	.50
19 Bernie Williams	.50
20 Ken Griffey Jr.	2.50
21 Alex Rodriguez	3.00
22 Chipper Jones	2.00
23 Ben Grieve	.50
24 Frank Thomas	1.50
25 Derek Jeter	4.00
26 Sammy Sosa	2.00
27 Mark McGwire	3.00
28 Vladimir Guerrero	1.50
29 Greg Maddux	2.00
30 Juan Gonzalez	.75
31 Troy Glaus	1.25
32 Adrian Beltre	1.25
33 Mitch Meluskey	.50
34 Alex Gonzalez	.50
35 George Lombard	.50
36 Eric Chavez	.75
37 Ruben Mateo	.50
38 Calvin Pickering	.50
39 Gabe Kapler	.50
40 Bruce Chen	.50

Co-Signers

	NM/M
Common Group A:	90.00
Inserted 1:18,085	
Common Group B:	20.00
Inserted 1:9043	
Common Group C:	9.00
Inserted 1:3014	
Common Group D:	6.00
Inserted 1:254	
CS1 Ben Grieve, Richie Sexson/D	15.00
CS2 Todd Helton, Troy Glaus/D	50.00
CS3 Alex Rodriguez, Scott Rolen/D	85.00
CS4 Derek Jeter, Chipper Jones/D	150.00
CS5 Cliff Floyd, Eli Marrero/D	6.00
CS6 Jay Buhner, Kevin Young/D	8.00

CS7	Ben Grieve, Troy Glaus/C	40.00
CS8	Todd Helton, Richie Sexson/C	40.00
CS9	Alex Rodriguez, Chipper Jones/C	125.00
CS10	Derek Jeter, Scott Rolen/C	125.00
CS11	Cliff Floyd, Kevin Young/C	10.00
CS12	Jay Buhner, Eli Marrero/B	10.00
CS13	Ben Grieve, Todd Helton/B	50.00
CS14	Richie Sexson, Troy Glaus/B	40.00
CS15	Alex Rodriguez, Derek Jeter/B	350.00
CS16	Chipper Jones, Scott Rolen/B	150.00
CS17	Cliff Floyd, Jay Buhner/B	15.00
CS18	Eli Marrero, Kevin Young/B	20.00
CS19	Ben Grieve, Todd Helton, Richie Sexson, Troy Glaus/A	180.00
CS20	Alex Rodriguez, Derek Jeter, Chipper Jones, Scott Rolen/A	2,500
CS21	Cliff Floyd, Jay Buhner, Eli Marrero, Kevin Young/A	100.00
CS22	Edgardo Alfonzo, Jose Guillen/D	15.00
CS23	Mike Lowell, Ricardo Rincon/D	10.00
CS24	Juan Gonzalez, Vinny Castilla/D	20.00
CS25	Moises Alou, Roger Clemens/D	60.00
CS26	Scott Spezio, Tony Womack/D	10.00
CS27	Fernando Vina, Quilvio Veras/D	10.00
CS28	Edgardo Alfonzo, Ricardo Rincon/C	10.00
CS29	Jose Guillen, Mike Lowell/C	10.00
CS30	Juan Gonzalez, Moises Alou/C	25.00
CS31	Roger Clemens, Vinny Castilla/C	85.00
CS32	Scott Spezio, Fernando Vina/C	10.00
CS33	Tony Womack, Quilvio Veras/B	20.00
CS34	Edgardo Alfonzo, Mike Lowell/B	30.00
CS35	Jose Guillen, Ricardo Rincon/B	30.00
CS36	Juan Gonzalez, Roger Clemens/B	135.00
CS37	Moises Alou, Vinny Castilla/B	30.00
CS38	Scott Spezio, Quilvio Veras/B	20.00
CS39	Tony Womack, Fernando Vina/B	20.00
CS40	Edgardo Alfonzo, Jose Guillen, Mike Lowell, Ricardo Rincon/A	90.00
CS41	Juan Gonzalez, Moises Alou, Roger Clemens, Vinny Castilla/A	900.00
CS42	Scott Spezio, Tony Womack, Fernando Vina, Quilvio Veras/A	90.00

Never Compromise

	NM/M
Complete Set (20):	10.00
Common Player:	.25
Inserted 1:12	
NC1 Mark McGwire	1.00
NC2 Sammy Sosa	.65
NC3 Ken Griffey Jr.	.75
NC4 Greg Maddux	.65
NC5 Barry Bonds	1.50
NC6 Alex Rodriguez	1.00
NC7 Darin Erstad	.35
NC8 Roger Clemens	.65
NC9 Nomar Garciaparra	.65
NC10 Derek Jeter	1.50
NC11 Cal Ripken Jr.	1.50
NC12 Mike Piazza	.75
NC13 Greg Vaughn	.25
NC14 Andres Galarraga	.25
NC15 Vinny Castilla	.25
NC16 Jeff Bagwell	.50
NC17 Chipper Jones	.65
NC18 Eric Chavez	.35
NC19 Orlando Hernandez	.25
NC20 Troy Glaus	.40

Photography

	NM/M
Complete Set (10):	200.00
Common Player:	20.00
1 Alex Rodriguez	20.00
65 Derek Jeter	20.00
66 Sammy Sosa	20.00
135 Juan Gonzalez	20.00
NC1 Mark McGwire	20.00
NC3 Ken Griffey Jr.	20.00
SCA5 Ben Grieve	20.00
SCC1 Nomar Garciaparra	20.00
SCC2 Kerry Wood	20.00
SCC13 Mike Piazza	20.00

Triumvirate

	NM/M
Complete Set (48):	75.00
Common Player:	.50
Inserted 1:36	
Luminescents:	1.5X
Inserted 1:144	
Illuminators:	2.5X
Inserted 1:288	
T1A Greg Vaughn	.50
T1B Ken Caminiti	.50
T1C Tony Gwynn	2.50
T2A Andruw Jones	2.00
T2B Chipper Jones	2.50
T2C Andres Galarraga	.50
T3A Jay Buhner	.50
T3B Ken Griffey Jr.	3.00
T3C Alex Rodriguez	4.00
T4A Derek Jeter	6.00
T4B Tino Martinez	.50
T4C Bernie Williams	.50
T5A Brian Jordan	.50
T5B Ray Lankford	.50
T5C Mark McGwire	4.00
T6A Jeff Bagwell	2.00
T6B Craig Biggio	.50
T6C Randy Johnson	2.00
T7A Nomar Garciaparra	2.50
T7B Pedro Martinez	2.00
T7C Mo Vaughn	.50
T8A Mark Grace	.50
T8B Sammy Sosa	2.50
T8C Kerry Wood	1.00
T9A Alex Rodriguez	4.00
T9B Nomar Garciaparra	2.50
T9C Derek Jeter	6.00
T10A Todd Helton	1.50
T10B Travis Lee	.50
T10C Pat Burrell	1.50
T11A Greg Maddux	2.50
T11B Kerry Wood	1.00
T11C Tom Glavine	.75
T12A Chipper Jones	2.50
T12B Vinny Castilla	.50
T12C Scott Rolen	1.50
T13A Juan Gonzalez	1.00
T13B Ken Griffey Jr.	3.00
T13C Ben Grieve	.50
T14A Sammy Sosa	3.00
T14B Vladimir Guerrero	2.00
T14C Barry Bonds	6.00
T15A Frank Thomas	2.00
T15B Jim Thome	1.50
T15C Tino Martinez	.50
T16A Mark McGwire	4.00
T16B Andres Galarraga	.50
T16C Jeff Bagwell	2.00

Video Replay

	NM/M
Complete Set (5):	4.50
Common Player:	.75
Inserted 1:12	
VR1 Mark McGwire	1.50
VR2 Sammy Sosa	1.00
VR3 Ken Griffey Jr.	1.25
VR4 Kerry Wood	.75
VR5 Alex Rodriguez	.75

2000 Stadium Club

	NM/M
Complete Set (250):	80.00
Common Player:	.15
Common SP (201-250):	2.00
Inserted 1:5	
Pack (6):	1.50
Wax Box (24):	30.00
1 Nomar Garciaparra	1.25
2 Brian Jordan	.15
3 Mark Grace	.25
4 Jeromy Burnitz	.15
5 Shane Reynolds	.15
6 Alex Gonzalez	.15
7 Jose Offerman	.15
8 Orlando Hernandez	.15
9 Mike Caruso	.15
10 Tony Clark	.15
11 Sean Casey	.25
12 Johnny Damon	.25
13 Dante Bichette	.15
14 Kevin Young	.15
15 Juan Gonzalez	.75
16 Chipper Jones	1.00
17 Quilvio Veras	.15
18 Trevor Hoffman	.15
19 Roger Cedeno	.15
20 Ellis Burks	.15
21 Richie Sexson	.15
22 Gary Sheffield	.40
23 Delino DeShields	.15
24 Wade Boggs	1.00
25 Ray Lankford	.15
26 Kevin Appier	.15
27 Roy Halladay	.15
28 Harold Baines	.15
29 Todd Zeile	.15
30 Barry Larkin	.15
31 Ron Coomer	.15
32 Jorge Posada	.15
33 Magglio Ordonez	.15
34 Brian Giles	.15
35 Jeff Kent	.15
36 Henry Rodriguez	.15
37 Fred McGriff	.15
38 Shawn Green	.50
39 Derek Bell	.15
40 Ben Grieve	.15
41 Dave Nilsson	.15
42 Mo Vaughn	.15
43 Rondell White	.15
44 Doug Glanville	.15
45 Paul O'Neill	.15
46 Carlos Lee	.15
47 Vinny Castilla	.15
48 Mike Sweeney	.15
49 Rico Brogna	.15
50 Alex Rodriguez	1.50
51 Luis Castillo	.15
52 Kevin Brown	.15
53 Jose Vidro	.15
54 John Smoltz	.15
55 Garret Anderson	.15
56 Matt Stairs	.15
57 Omar Vizquel	.15
58 Tom Goodwin	.15
59 Scott Brosius	.15
60 Robin Ventura	.15
61 B.J. Surhoff	.15
62 Andy Ashby	.15
63 Chris Widger	.15
64 Tim Hudson	.40
65 Javy Lopez	.15
66 Tim Salmon	.25
67 Warren Morris	.15
68 John Wetteland	.15
69 Gabe Kapler	.15
70 Bernie Williams	.30
71 Rickey Henderson	.75
72 Andruw Jones	.75
73 Eric Young	.15
74 Bob Abreu	.15
75 David Cone	.15
76 Rusty Greer	.15
77 Ron Belliard	.15
78 Troy Glaus	.75
79 Mike Hampton	.15
80 Miguel Tejada	.30
81 Jeff Cirillo	.15
82 Todd Hundley	.15
83 Roberto Alomar	.40
84 Charles Johnson	.15
85 Rafael Palmeiro	.65
86 Doug Mientkiewicz	.15
87 Mariano Rivera	.25
88 Neifi Perez	.15
89 Jermaine Dye	.15
90 Ivan Rodriguez	.65
91 Jay Buhner	.15
92 Pokey Reese	.15
93 John Olerud	.15
94 Brady Anderson	.15
95 Manny Ramirez	.75
96 Keith Osik	.15
97 Mickey Morandini	.15
98 Matt Williams	.15
99 Eric Karros	.15
100 Ken Griffey Jr.	1.25
101 Bret Boone	.15
102 Ryan Klesko	.15
103 Craig Biggio	.15
104 John Jaha	.15
105 Vladimir Guerrero	.75
106 Devon White	.15
107 Tony Womack	.15
108 Marvin Benard	.15
109 Kenny Lofton	.15
110 Preston Wilson	.15
111 Al Leiter	.15
112 Reggie Sanders	.15
113 Scott Williamson	.15
114 Deivi Cruz	.15
115 Carlos Beltran	.50
116 Ray Durham	.15
117 Ricky Ledee	.15
118 Torii Hunter	.15
119 John Valentin	.15
120 Scott Rolen	.65
121 Jason Kendall	.15
122 Dave Martinez	.15
123 Jim Thome	.65
124 David Bell	.15
125 Jose Canseco	.45
126 Jose Lima	.15
127 Carl Everett	.15
128 Kevin Millwood	.15
129 Bill Spiers	.15
130 Omar Daal	.15
131 Miguel Cairo	.15
132 Mark Grudzielanek	.15
133 David Justice	.15
134 Russ Ortiz	.15
135 Mike Piazza	1.25
136 Brian Meadows	.15
137 Tony Gwynn	1.00
138 Cal Ripken Jr.	2.00
139 Kris Benson	.15
140 Larry Walker	.15

141	Cristian Guzman	.15
142	Tino Martinez	.25
143	Chris Singleton	.15
144	Lee Stevens	.15
145	Rey Ordonez	.15
146	Russ Davis	.15
147	J.T. Snow Jr.	.15
148	Luis Gonzalez	.25
149	Marquis Grissom	.15
150	Greg Maddux	1.00
151	Fernando Tatis	.15
152	Jason Giambi	.50
153	Carlos Delgado	.50
154	Joe McEwing	.15
155	Raul Mondesi	.15
156	Rich Aurilia	.15
157	Alex Fernandez	.15
158	Albert Belle	.25
159	Pat Meares	.15
160	Mike Lieberthal	.15
161	Mike Cameron	.15
162	Juan Encarnacion	.15
163	Chuck Knoblauch	.15
164	Pedro Martinez	.75
165	Randy Johnson	.75
166	Shannon Stewart	.15
167	Jeff Bagwell	.75
168	Edgar Renteria	.15
169	Barry Bonds	2.00
170	Steve Finley	.15
171	Brian Hunter	.15
172	Tom Glavine	.35
173	Mark Kotsay	.15
174	Tony Fernandez	.15
175	Sammy Sosa	1.25
176	Geoff Jenkins	.15
177	Adrian Beltre	.15
178	Jay Bell	.15
179	Mike Bordick	.15
180	Ed Sprague	.15
181	Dave Roberts	.15
182	Greg Vaughn	.15
183	Brian Daubach	.15
184	Damion Easley	.15
185	Carlos Febles	.15
186	Kevin Tapani	.15
187	Frank Thomas	.75
188	Roger Clemens	1.00
189	Mike Benjamin	.15
190	Curt Schilling	.40
191	Edgardo Alfonzo	.15
192	Mike Mussina	.40
193	Todd Helton	.75
194	Todd Jones	.15
195	Dean Palmer	.15
196	John Flaherty	.15
197	Derek Jeter	2.00
198	Todd Walker	.15
199	Brad Ausmus	.15
200	Mark McGwire	1.50
201	Erubiel Durazo	2.00
202	Nick Johnson	2.50
203	Ruben Mateo	2.00
204	Lance Berkman	2.50
205	Pat Burrell	3.00
206	Pablo Ozuna	2.00
207	Roosevelt Brown	2.00
208	Alfonso Soriano	4.00
209	A.J. Burnett	2.00
210	Rafael Furcal	2.00
211	Scott Morgan	2.00
212	Adam Piatt	2.00
213	Dee Brown	2.00
214	Corey Patterson	2.50
215	Mickey Lopez	2.00
216	Rob Ryan	2.00
217	Sean Burroughs	2.00
218	Jack Cust	2.00
219	John Patterson	2.00
220	Kit Pellow	2.00
221	Chad Hermansen	2.00
222	Daryle Ward	2.00
223	Jayson Werth	2.00
224	Jason Standridge	2.00
225	Mark Mulder	2.50
226	Peter Bergeron	2.00
227	Willi Mo Pena	2.00
228	Aramis Ramirez	2.00
229	John Sneed RC	2.00
230	Wilton Veras	2.00
231	Josh Hamilton	2.00
232	Eric Munson	2.00
233	Bobby Bradley RC	2.00
234	Larry Bigbie RC	2.00
235	B.J. Garbe RC	2.00
236	Brett Myers RC	6.00
237	Jason Stumm RC	2.00
238	Corey Myers RC	2.00
239	Ryan Christianson RC	2.00
240	David Walling	2.00
241	Josh Girdley	2.00
242	Omar Ortiz	2.00
243	Jason Jennings	2.00
244	Kyle Snyder RC	2.00

245	Jay Gehrke	2.00
246	Mike Paradis RC	2.00
247	Chance Caple RC	2.00
248	Ben Christiansen RC	2.00
249	Brad Baker RC	2.00
250	Rick Asadoorian RC	2.00
---	Nomar Garciaparra Checklist	.25

One of a Kind

Stars: 5-10X
Short-Prints: 2-3X
Production 150 Sets H
(See 2000 Stadium Club for checklist and base card values.)

First Day Issue

Stars: 5-10X
Short-Prints: 2-3X
Production 150 Sets R
(See 2000 Stadium Club for checklist and base card values.)

Printing Plates

	NM/M
Common Player:	60.00

(See 2000 Stadium Club for checklist.)

Bats of Brilliance

		NM/M
Complete Set (10):		10.00
Common Player:		.50
Inserted 1:12		
1	Mark McGwire	2.50
2	Sammy Sosa	1.50
3	Jose Canseco	.50
4	Jeff Bagwell	.75
5	Ken Griffey Jr.	1.50
6	Nomar Garciaparra	1.50
7	Mike Piazza	1.50
8	Alex Rodriguez	2.50
9	Vladimir Guerrero	.75
10	Chipper Jones	1.50

Capture The Action

		NM/M
Complete Set (20):		20.00
Common Player:		.50
Inserted 1:12		
Game View Stars:		3-6X
Production 100 Sets H		
1	Josh Hamilton	.50
2	Pat Burrell	.75
3	Erubiel Durazo	.50
4	Alfonso Soriano	1.00
5	A.J. Burnett	.50
6	Alex Rodriguez	3.00
7	Sean Casey	.50
8	Derek Jeter	4.00
9	Vladimir Guerrero	1.00

10	Nomar Garciaparra	2.00
11	Mike Piazza	2.00
12	Ken Griffey Jr.	2.00
13	Sammy Sosa	2.00
14	Juan Gonzalez	1.00
15	Mark McGwire	3.00
16	Ivan Rodriguez	.75
17	Barry Bonds	4.00
18	Wade Boggs	1.50
19	Tony Gwynn	1.50
20	Cal Ripken Jr.	4.00

Chrome Preview

		NM/M
Complete Set (20):		40.00
Common Player:		1.00
Inserted 1:24		
Refractors:		2-3X
Inserted 1:120		
1	Nomar Garciaparra	3.00
2	Juan Gonzalez	1.50
3	Chipper Jones	2.00
4	Alex Rodriguez	4.50
5	Ivan Rodriguez	1.25
6	Manny Ramirez	1.50
7	Ken Griffey Jr.	3.00
8	Vladimir Guerrero	1.50
9	Mike Piazza	3.00
10	Pedro Martinez	2.00
11	Jeff Bagwell	1.50
12	Barry Bonds	6.00
13	Sammy Sosa	3.00
14	Derek Jeter	6.00
15	Mark McGwire	4.50
16	Erubiel Durazo	1.00
17	Nick Johnson	1.00
18	Pat Burrell	1.00
19	Alfonso Soriano	1.50
20	Adam Piatt	1.00

Co-Signers

		NM/M
Common Card:		15.00
Group A 1:10,184		
Group B 1:5,092		
Group C 1:508		
1	Alex Rodriguez, Derek Jeter	400.00

2	Derek Jeter, Omar Vizquel	150.00
3	Alex Rodriguez, Rey Ordonez	100.00
4	Derek Jeter, Rey Ordonez	150.00
5	Omar Vizquel, Alex Rodriguez	100.00
6	Rey Ordonez, Omar Vizquel	15.00
7	Wade Boggs, Robin Ventura	30.00
8	Randy Johnson, Mike Mussina	90.00
9	Pat Burrell, Magglio Ordonez	40.00
10	Chad Hermansen, Pat Burrell	20.00
11	Magglio Ordonez, Chad Hermansen	20.00
12	Josh Hamilton, Corey Myers	20.00
13	B.J. Garbe, Josh Hamilton	20.00
14	Corey Myers, B.J. Garbe	15.00
15	Tino Martinez, Fred McGriff	60.00

Lone Star Signatures

		NM/M
Common Player:		8.00
Group 1 1:1,979		
Group 2 1:2,374		
Group 3 1:1,979		
Group 4 1:424		
1	Derek Jeter	100.00
2	Alex Rodriguez	100.00
3	Wade Boggs	25.00
4	Robin Ventura	15.00
5	Randy Johnson	60.00
6	Mike Mussina	25.00
7	Tino Martinez	35.00
8	Fred McGriff	25.00
9	Omar Vizquel	15.00
10	Rey Ordonez	8.00
11	Pat Burrell	15.00
12	Chad Hermansen	8.00
13	Magglio Ordonez	10.00
14	Josh Hamilton	20.00
15	Corey Myers	8.00
16	B.J. Garbe	8.00

Onyx Extreme

	NM/M
Complete Set (10):	10.00
Common Player:	.40
Inserted 1:12	
Die-Cuts:	2-3X
Inserted 1:60	

1	Ken Griffey Jr.	1.50
2	Derek Jeter	3.00
3	Vladimir Guerrero	1.00
4	Nomar Garciaparra	1.50
5	Barry Bonds	3.00
6	Alex Rodriguez	2.50
7	Sammy Sosa	1.50
8	Ivan Rodriguez	.75
9	Larry Walker	.40
10	Andruw Jones	1.00

Scenes

		NM/M
Complete Set (9):		10.00
Common Player:		.50
Inserted 1:Box		
1	Mark McGwire	2.50
2	Alex Rodriguez	2.50
3	Cal Ripken Jr.	3.00
4	Sammy Sosa	2.00
5	Derek Jeter	3.00
6	Ken Griffey Jr.	2.00
7	Raul Mondesi	.50
8	Chipper Jones	1.50
9	Nomar Garciaparra	2.00

Souvenirs

		NM/M
Complete Set (3):		35.00
Common Player:		8.00
Inserted 2:339		
1	Wade Boggs	20.00
2	Randy Johnson	20.00
3	Robin Ventura	8.00

3 X 3

		NM/M
Complete Set (30):		40.00
Common Player:		.75
Inserted 1:18		
Luminescent:		2X
Inserted 1:72		
Illuminator:		3-4X
Inserted 1:144		
1A	Randy Johnson	1.50
1B	Pedro Martinez	1.50
1C	Greg Maddux	2.00
2A	Mike Piazza	3.00
2B	Ivan Rodriguez	1.25
2C	Mike Lieberthal	.75
3A	Mark McGwire	4.50
3B	Jeff Bagwell	1.50
3C	Sean Casey	.75
4A	Craig Biggio	.75
4B	Roberto Alomar	1.00
4C	Jay Bell	.75
5A	Chipper Jones	2.00
5B	Matt Williams	.75
5C	Robin Ventura	.75
6A	Alex Rodriguez	4.50
6B	Derek Jeter	6.00
6C	Nomar Garciaparra	3.00
7A	Barry Bonds	6.00
7B	Luis Gonzalez	1.00
7C	Dante Bichette	.75
8A	Ken Griffey Jr.	3.00
8B	Bernie Williams	1.00
8C	Andruw Jones	1.50
9A	Manny Ramirez	1.50
9B	Sammy Sosa	3.00
9C	Juan Gonzalez	1.50
10A	Jose Canseco	1.00
10B	Frank Thomas	1.50
10C	Rafael Palmeiro	1.00

2000 Stadium Club Chrome

		NM/M
Complete Set (250):		40.00
Common Player:		.15
Pack (11):		1.50
Wax Box (36):		40.00
1	Nomar Garciaparra	1.50
2	Brian Jordan	.15
3	Mark Grace	.25
4	Jeromy Burnitz	.15
5	Shane Reynolds	.15
6	Alex Gonzalez	.15
7	Jose Offerman	.15
8	Orlando Hernandez	.15
9	Mike Caruso	.15
10	Tony Clark	.15
11	Sean Casey	.25
12	Johnny Damon	.25
13	Dante Bichette	.15
14	Kevin Young	.15
15	Juan Gonzalez	.75
16	Chipper Jones	1.00
17	Quilvio Veras	.15
18	Trevor Hoffman	.15
19	Roger Cedeno	.15
20	Ellis Burks	.15
21	Richie Sexson	.15
22	Gary Sheffield	.45
23	Delino DeShields	.15
24	Wade Boggs	1.00
25	Ray Lankford	.15
26	Kevin Appier	.15
27	Roy Halladay	.15
28	Harold Baines	.15
29	Todd Zeile	.15
30	Barry Larkin	.15
31	Ron Coomer	.15
32	Jorge Posada	.15
33	Magglio Ordonez	.15
34	Brian Giles	.15
35	Jeff Kent	.15
36	Henry Rodriguez	.15
37	Fred McGriff	.15
38	Shawn Green	.50
39	Derek Bell	.15
40	Ben Grieve	.15
41	Dave Nilsson	.15
42	Mo Vaughn	.15
43	Rondell White	.15
44	Doug Glanville	.15
45	Paul O'Neill	.15
46	Carlos Lee	.15
47	Vinny Castilla	.15
48	Mike Sweeney	.15
49	Rico Brogna	.15
50	Alex Rodriguez	2.50
51	Luis Castillo	.15
52	Kevin Brown	.15
53	Jose Vidro	.15
54	John Smoltz	.15
55	Garret Anderson	.15
56	Matt Stairs	.15
57	Omar Vizquel	.15
58	Tom Goodwin	.15
59	Scott Brosius	.15
60	Robin Ventura	.15
61	B.J. Surhoff	.15
62	Andy Ashby	.15
63	Chris Widger	.15
64	Tim Hudson	.40
65	Javy Lopez	.15
66	Tim Salmon	.25
67	Warren Morris	.15
68	John Wetteland	.15
69	Gabe Kapler	.15
70	Bernie Williams	.25
71	Rickey Henderson	.75
72	Andruw Jones	.75
73	Eric Young	.15
74	Bobby Abreu	.15
75	David Cone	.15
76	Rusty Greer	.15
77	Ron Belliard	.15
78	Troy Glaus	.75
79	Mike Hampton	.15
80	Miguel Tejada	.30
81	Jeff Cirillo	.15
82	Todd Hundley	.15
83	Roberto Alomar	.35
84	Charles Johnson	.15
85	Rafael Palmeiro	.65
86	Doug Mientkiewicz	.15
87	Mariano Rivera	.25
88	Neifi Perez	.15
89	Jermaine Dye	.15
90	Ivan Rodriguez	.65
91	Jay Buhner	.15
92	Pokey Reese	.15
93	John Olerud	.15
94	Brady Anderson	.15
95	Manny Ramirez	.75
96	Keith Osik	.15
97	Mickey Morandini	.15
98	Matt Williams	.15
99	Eric Karros	.15
100	Ken Griffey Jr.	1.50
101	Bret Boone	.15
102	Ryan Klesko	.15
103	Craig Biggio	.15
104	John Jaha	.15
105	Vladimir Guerrero	.75
106	Devon White	.15
107	Tony Womack	.15
108	Marvin Benard	.15
109	Kenny Lofton	.15
110	Preston Wilson	.15
111	Al Leiter	.15
112	Reggie Sanders	.15
113	Scott Williamson	.15
114	Deivi Cruz	.15
115	Carlos Beltran	.50
116	Ray Durham	.15
117	Ricky Ledee	.15
118	Torii Hunter	.15
119	John Valentin	.15
120	Scott Rolen	.65
121	Jason Kendall	.15
122	Dave Martinez	.15
123	Jim Thome	.65
124	David Bell	.15
125	Jose Canseco	.50
126	Jose Lima	.15
127	Carl Everett	.15
128	Kevin Millwood	.15
129	Bill Spiers	.15
130	Omar Daal	.15
131	Miguel Cairo	.15
132	Mark Grudzielanek	.15
133	David Justice	.15
134	Russ Ortiz	.15
135	Mike Piazza	1.50
136	Brian Meadows	.15
137	Tony Gwynn	1.00
138	Cal Ripken Jr.	3.00
139	Kris Benson	.15
140	Larry Walker	.15
141	Cristian Guzman	.15
142	Tino Martinez	.15
143	Chris Singleton	.15
144	Lee Stevens	.15
145	Rey Ordonez	.15
146	Russ Davis	.15
147	J.T. Snow Jr.	.15
148	Luis Gonzalez	.25
149	Marquis Grissom	.15
150	Greg Maddux	1.00
151	Fernando Tatis	.15
152	Jason Giambi	.50
153	Carlos Delgado	.50
154	Joe McEwing	.15
155	Raul Mondesi	.15
156	Rich Aurilia	.15
157	Alex Fernandez	.15
158	Albert Belle	.25
159	Pat Meares	.15
160	Mike Lieberthal	.15
161	Mike Cameron	.15
162	Juan Encarnacion	.15
163	Chuck Knoblauch	.15
164	Pedro Martinez	.75
165	Randy Johnson	.75
166	Shannon Stewart	.15
167	Jeff Bagwell	.75
168	Edgar Renteria	.15
169	Barry Bonds	3.00
170	Steve Finley	.15
171	Brian Hunter	.15
172	Tom Glavine	.40
173	Mark Kotsay	.15
174	Tony Fernandez	.15
175	Sammy Sosa	1.50
176	Geoff Jenkins	.15
177	Adrian Beltre	.45
178	Jay Bell	.15
179	Mike Bordick	.15
180	Ed Sprague	.15
181	Dave Roberts	.15
182	Greg Vaughn	.15
183	Brian Daubach	.15
184	Damion Easley	.15
185	Carlos Febles	.15
186	Kevin Tapani	.15
187	Frank Thomas	.75
188	Roger Clemens	1.25
189	Mike Benjamin	.15
190	Curt Schilling	.40
191	Edgardo Alfonzo	.15
192	Mike Mussina	.45
193	Todd Helton	.75
194	Todd Jones	.15
195	Dean Palmer	.15
196	John Flaherty	.15
197	Derek Jeter	3.00
198	Todd Walker	.15
199	Brad Ausmus	.15
200	Mark McGwire	2.50
201	Erubiel Durazo	.15
202	Nick Johnson	.15
203	Ruben Mateo	.15
204	Lance Berkman	.15
205	Pat Burrell	.65
206	Pablo Ozuna	.15
207	Roosevelt Brown	.15
208	Alfonso Soriano	1.00
209	A.J. Burnett	.15
210	Rafael Furcal	.15
211	Scott Morgan	.15
212	Adam Piatt	.15
213	Dee Brown	.15
214	Corey Patterson	.15
215	Mickey Lopez	.15
216	Rob Ryan	.15
217	Sean Burroughs	.15
218	Jack Cust	.15
219	John Patterson	.15
220	Kit Pellow	.15
221	Chad Hermansen	.15
222	Daryle Ward	.15
223	Jayson Werth	.15
224	Jason Standridge	.15
225	Mark Mulder	.15
226	Peter Bergeron	.15
227	Willi Mo Pena	.15
228	Aramis Ramirez	.15
229	John Sneed	.15
230	Wilton Veras	.15
231	Josh Hamilton	.15
232	Eric Munson	.15
233	Bobby Bradley RC	1.00
234	Larry Bigbie RC	1.00
235	B.J. Garbe RC	1.00
236	Brett Myers RC	4.00
237	Jason Stumm RC	1.00
238	Corey Myers RC	1.00
239	Ryan Christianson RC	1.00
240	David Walling	.15
241	Josh Girdley	.15
242	Omar Ortiz	.15
243	Jason Jennings	.15
244	Kyle Snyder	.15
245	Jay Gehrke	.15
246	Mike Paradis	.15
247	Chance Caple RC	1.00
248	Ben Christensen RC	1.00
249	Brad Baker RC	1.00
250	Rick Asadoorian RC	1.00

Refractor

Stars:	2-4X
Rookies:	1-2X
Inserted 1:12	

First Day Issue

Stars:	4-8X
Rookies:	1-3X
Production 100 Sets	
Refractor:	25-40X
Rookies:	5-10X
Production 25 Sets	

Capture The Action

		NM/M
Complete Set (20):		40.00
Common Player:		1.00
Inserted 1:18		
Refractors:		2-3X
Inserted 1:90		
1	Josh Hamilton	1.00
2	Pat Burrell	1.50
3	Erubiel Durazo	1.00
4	Alfonso Soriano	1.50
5	A.J. Burnett	1.00
6	Alex Rodriguez	5.00
7	Sean Casey	1.00
8	Derek Jeter	6.00
9	Vladimir Guerrero	1.50
10	Nomar Garciaparra	3.00
11	Mike Piazza	3.00
12	Ken Griffey Jr.	3.00
13	Sammy Sosa	3.00
14	Juan Gonzalez	1.50
15	Mark McGwire	5.00
16	Ivan Rodriguez	1.50
17	Barry Bonds	6.00
18	Wade Boggs	2.00
19	Tony Gwynn	2.00
20	Cal Ripken Jr.	6.00

Clear Shots

	NM/M
Complete Set (10):	10.00

Common Player:	.50
Inserted 1:24	
Refractor:	2-3X
Inserted 1:120	
1	Derek Jeter	4.00
2	Bernie Williams	.50
3	Roger Clemens	2.50
4	Chipper Jones	2.00
5	Greg Maddux	2.00
6	Andruw Jones	1.00
7	Juan Gonzalez	1.00
8	Manny Ramirez	1.00
9	Ken Griffey Jr.	3.00
10	Josh Hamilton	.50

Eyes of the Game

		NM/M
Complete Set (10):		10.00
Common Player:		.50
Inserted 1:16		
Refractors:		2-3X
Inserted 1:80		
1	Randy Johnson	1.00
2	Mike Piazza	1.50
3	Nomar Garciaparra	1.50
4	Mark McGwire	2.50
5	Alex Rodriguez	2.50
6	Derek Jeter	3.00
7	Tony Gwynn	1.00
8	Sammy Sosa	1.50
9	Larry Walker	.50
10	Ken Griffey Jr.	1.50

True Colors

		NM/M
Complete Set (10):		15.00
Common Player:		1.00
Inserted 1:32		
Refractors:		2-3X
Inserted 1:160		
1	Sammy Sosa	2.00
2	Nomar Garciaparra	2.00
3	Alex Rodriguez	3.00
4	Derek Jeter	4.00
5	Mark McGwire	3.00
6	Chipper Jones	1.50
7	Mike Piazza	2.00
8	Ken Griffey Jr.	2.00
9	Manny Ramirez	1.00
10	Vladimir Guerrero	1.00

Visionaries

		NM/M
Complete Set (20):		17.50
Common Player:		1.00
Inserted 1:18		
Refractors:		2X
Inserted 1:90		
1	Alfonso Soriano	3.00
2	Josh Hamilton	1.00
3	A.J. Burnett	1.50

4	Pat Burrell	2.50
5	Ruben Salazar	1.00
6	Aaron Rowand	1.00
7	Adam Piatt	1.00
8	Nick Johnson	1.00
9	Rafael Furcal	1.00
10	Jack Cust	1.00
11	Corey Patterson	1.00
12	Sean Burroughs	1.50
13	Pablo Ozuna	1.00
14	Dee Brown	1.00
15	John Patterson	1.00
16	Willi Mo Pena	1.00
17	Mark Mulder	1.00
18	Eric Munson	1.00
19	Alex Escobar	1.00
20	Rob Ryan	1.00

2001 Stadium Club

		NM/M
Complete Set (200):		65.00
Common Player:		.15
Common SP:		1.50
Inserted 1:6		
Pack (7):		2.00
Box (24):		35.00
1	Nomar Garciaparra	1.25
2	Chipper Jones	1.00
3	Jeff Bagwell	.75
4	Chad Kreuter	.15
5	Randy Johnson	.75
6	Mike Hampton	.15
7	Barry Larkin	.15
8	Bernie Williams	.30
9	Chris Singleton	.15
10	Larry Walker	.15
11	Brad Ausmus	.15
12	Ron Coomer	.15
13	Edgardo Alfonzo	.15
14	Delino DeShields	.15
15	Tony Gwynn	1.00
16	Andruw Jones	.75
17	Raul Mondesi	.15
18	Troy Glaus	.75
19	Ben Grieve	.15
20	Sammy Sosa	1.25
21	Fernando Vina	.15
22	Jeromy Burnitz	.15
23	Jay Bell	.15
24	Pete Harnisch	.15
25	Barry Bonds	2.00
26	Eric Karros	.15
27	Alex Gonzalez	.15
28	Mike Lieberthal	.15
29	Juan Encarnacion	.15
30	Derek Jeter	2.00
31	Bruce Aven	.15
32	Eric Milton	.15
33	Aaron Boone	.15
34	Roberto Alomar	.40
35	John Olerud	.15

36	Orlando Cabrera	.15
37	Shawn Green	.45
38	Roger Cedeno	.15
39	Garret Anderson	.15
40	Jim Thome	.65
41	Gabe Kapler	.15
42	Mo Vaughn	.15
43	Sean Casey	.25
44	Preston Wilson	.15
45	Javy Lopez	.15
46	Ryan Klesko	.15
47	Ray Durham	.15
48	Dean Palmer	.15
49	Jorge Posada	.15
50	Alex Rodriguez	1.50
51	Tom Glavine	.40
52	Ray Lankford	.15
53	Jose Canseco	.40
54	Tim Salmon	.25
55	Cal Ripken Jr.	2.00
56	Bob Abreu	.15
57	Robin Ventura	.15
58	Damion Easley	.15
59	Paul O'Neill	.15
60	Ivan Rodriguez	.65
61	Carl Everett	.15
62	Doug Glanville	.15
63	Jeff Kent	.15
64	Jay Buhner	.15
65	Cliff Floyd	.15
66	Rick Ankiel	.15
67	Mark Grace	.25
68	Brian Jordan	.15
69	Craig Biggio	.15
70	Carlos Delgado	.50
71	Brad Radke	.15
72	Greg Maddux	1.00
73	Al Leiter	.15
74	Pokey Reese	.15
75	Todd Helton	.75
76	Mariano Rivera	.25
77	Shane Spencer	.15
78	Jason Kendall	.15
79	Chuck Knoblauch	.15
80	Scott Rolen	.65
81	Jose Offerman	.15
82	J.T. Snow Jr.	.15
83	Pat Meares	.15
84	Quilvio Veras	.15
85	Edgar Renteria	.15
86	Luis Matos	.15
87	Adrian Beltre	.15
88	Luis Gonzalez	.25
89	Rickey Henderson	.75
90	Brian Giles	.15
91	Carlos Febles	.15
92	Tino Martinez	.15
93	Magglio Ordonez	.15
94	Rafael Furcal	.15
95	Mike Mussina	.30
96	Gary Sheffield	.40
97	Kenny Lofton	.15
98	Fred McGriff	.15
99	Ken Caminiti	.15
100	Mark McGwire	1.50
101	Tom Goodwin	.15
102	Mark Grudzielanek	.15
103	Derek Bell	.15
104	Mike Lowell	.15
105	Jeff Cirillo	.15
106	Orlando Hernandez	.15
107	Jose Valentin	.15
108	Warren Morris	.15
109	Mike Williams	.15
110	Gregg Zaun	.15
111	Jose Vidro	.15
112	Omar Vizquel	.15
113	Vinny Castilla	.15
114	Gregg Jefferies	.15
115	Kevin Brown	.15
116	Shannon Stewart	.15
117	Marquis Grissom	.15
118	Manny Ramirez	.75
119	Albert Belle	.15
120	Bret Boone	.15
121	Johnny Damon	.25
122	Juan Gonzalez	.75
123	David Justice	.15
124	Jeffrey Hammonds	.15
125	Ken Griffey Jr.	1.25
126	Mike Sweeney	.15
127	Tony Clark	.15
128	Todd Zeile	.15
129	Mark Johnson	.15
130	Matt Williams	.15
131	Geoff Jenkins	.15
132	Jason Giambi	.50
133	Steve Finley	.15
134	Derrek Lee	.15
135	Royce Clayton	.15
136	Joe Randa	.15
137	Rafael Palmeiro	.65
138	Kevin Young	.15
139	Curt Schilling	.40

140	Vladimir Guerrero	.75
141	Greg Vaughn	.15
142	Jermaine Dye	.15
143	Roger Clemens	1.00
144	Denny Hocking	.15
145	Frank Thomas	.75
146	Carlos Beltran	.50
147	Eric Young	.15
148	Pat Burrell	.50
149	Pedro Martinez	.75
150	Mike Piazza	1.25
151	Adrian Gonzalez	.50
152	Adam Johnson	.15
153	Luis Montanez **RC**	1.50
154	Mike Stodolka	.15
155	Phil Dumatrait	.15
156	Sean Burnett	1.50
157	Dominic Rich **RC**	1.50
158	Adam Wainwright	.50
159	Scott Thorman	.15
160	Scott Heard	.25
161	Chad Petty **RC**	1.50
162	Matt Wheatland	2.00
163	Brad Digby	.15
164	Rocco Baldelli	1.00
165	Grady Sizemore	1.00
166	Brian Sellier **RC**	1.50
167	Rick Brosseau **RC**	1.50
168	Shawn Fagan **RC**	1.50
169	Sean Smith	1.50
170	Chris Bass **RC**	1.50
171	Corey Patterson	.25
172	Sean Burroughs	.25
173	Ben Petrick	.15
174	Mike Glendenning	.15
175	Barry Zito	.50
176	Milton Bradley	.15
177	Bobby Bradley	.15
178	Jason Hart	.15
179	Ryan Anderson	.15
180	Ben Sheets	.25
181	Adam Everett	.15
182	Alfonso Soriano	.75
183	Josh Hamilton	.25
184	Eric Munson	.15
185	Chin-Feng Chen	.25
186	Tim Christman **RC**	1.50
187	J.R. House	2.00
188	Brandon Parker **RC**	1.50
189	Sean Fesh **RC**	1.50
190	Joel Pieniero **RC**	2.00
191	Oscar Ramirez **RC**	1.50
192	Alex Santos **RC**	1.50
193	Eddy Reyes **RC**	1.50
194	Mike Jacobs **RC**	1.50
195	Erick Almonte **RC**	2.00
196	Brandon Claussen **RC**	2.00
197	Kris Keller **RC**	1.50
198	Wilson Betemit **RC**	1.50
199	Andy Phillips **RC**	1.50
200	Adam Pettyjohn **RC**	1.50
---	Derek Jeter (Checklist)	.25

Beam Team

NM/M

Complete Set (30):		100.00
Common Player:		1.50
Production 500 Sets		
1	Sammy Sosa	6.00
2	Mark McGwire	8.00
3	Vladimir Guerrero	3.00
4	Chipper Jones	4.50
5	Manny Ramirez	3.00
6	Derek Jeter	10.00
7	Alex Rodriguez	8.00
8	Cal Ripken Jr.	10.00
9	Ken Griffey Jr.	6.00
10	Greg Maddux	4.50
11	Barry Bonds	10.00
12	Pedro Martinez	3.00
13	Nomar Garciaparra	6.00
14	Randy Johnson	3.00
15	Frank Thomas	3.00
16	Ivan Rodriguez	2.50
17	Jeff Bagwell	3.00
18	Mike Piazza	6.00
19	Todd Helton	3.00
20	Shawn Green	2.00
21	Juan Gonzalez	3.00
22	Larry Walker	1.50
23	Tony Gwynn	4.50
24	Pat Burrell	2.00
25	Rafael Furcal	1.50
26	Corey Patterson	1.50
27	Chin-Feng Chen	1.50
28	Sean Burroughs	1.50
29	Ryan Anderson	1.50
30	Josh Hamilton	4.00

Capture The Action

NM/M

Complete Set (15):		15.00
Common Player:		1.00
Inserted 1:8		

CAPTURE THE ACTION!

DEREK JETER

1	Cal Ripken Jr.	3.00
2	Alex Rodriguez	2.50
3	Mike Piazza	2.00
4	Mark McGwire	2.50
5	Greg Maddux	1.50
6	Derek Jeter	3.00
7	Chipper Jones	1.50
8	Pedro Martinez	1.00
9	Ken Griffey Jr.	2.00
10	Nomar Garciaparra	2.00
11	Randy Johnson	1.00
12	Sammy Sosa	2.00
13	Vladimir Guerrero	1.00
14	Barry Bonds	3.00
15	Ivan Rodriguez	1.00

Capture The Action Game View

CAPTURE THE ACTION GAMEVIEW

Barry Bonds

NM/M

Common Player:		10.00
Production 100 Sets		
1	Cal Ripken Jr.	30.00
2	Alex Rodriguez	25.00
3	Mike Piazza	20.00
4	Mark McGwire	25.00
5	Greg Maddux	15.00
6	Derek Jeter	30.00
7	Chipper Jones	15.00
8	Pedro Martinez	10.00
9	Ken Griffey Jr.	20.00
10	Nomar Garciaparra	20.00
11	Randy Johnson	10.00
12	Sammy Sosa	20.00
13	Vladimir Guerrero	10.00
14	Barry Bonds	30.00
15	Ivan Rodriguez	10.00

Co-Signers

CO-SIGNERS

NM/M

Common Duo:		15.00
Inserted 1:1,117		
1	Nomar Garciaparra, Derek Jeter	400.00
2	Roberto Alomar, Edgardo Alfonso	50.00
3	Rick Ankiel, Kevin Millwood	15.00
4	Chipper Jones, Troy Glaus	65.00
5	Magglio Ordonez, Bobby Abreu	20.00
6	Adam Piatt, Sean Burroughs	20.00
7	Corey Patterson, Nick Johnson	40.00
8	Adrian Gonzalez, Rocco Baldelli	40.00
9	Adam Johnson, Mike Stodolka	15.00

Diamond Pearls

TODD HELTON
DP19

NM/M

Complete Set (20):		20.00
Common Player:		.65
Inserted 1:8		
1	Ken Griffey Jr.	2.00
2	Alex Rodriguez	2.50
3	Derek Jeter	3.00
4	Chipper Jones	1.50
5	Nomar Garciaparra	2.00
6	Vladimir Guerrero	1.00
7	Jeff Bagwell	1.00
8	Cal Ripken Jr.	3.00
9	Sammy Sosa	2.00
10	Mark McGwire	2.50
11	Frank Thomas	1.00
12	Pedro Martinez	1.00
13	Manny Ramirez	1.00
14	Randy Johnson	1.00
15	Barry Bonds	3.00
16	Ivan Rodriguez	.75
17	Greg Maddux	1.50
18	Mike Piazza	2.00
19	Todd Helton	1.00
20	Shawn Green	.65

Game-Used Cards

PROSPECT PERFORMANCE

BEN SHEETS

NM/M

Common Player:		5.00
Inserted 1:285		
1	Chin-Feng Chen	20.00
2	Bobby Bradley	5.00
3	Tomokazu Ohka	5.00
4	Kurt Ainsworth	5.00
5	Craig Anderson	5.00
6	Josh Hamilton	10.00
7	Felipe Lopez	5.00
8	Ryan Anderson	5.00
9	Alex Escobar	5.00
10	Ben Sheets	8.00
11	Ntema Ndungidi	5.00
12	Eric Munson	5.00
13	Aaron Myette	5.00
14	Jack Cust	5.00
15	Julio Zuleta	5.00
16	Corey Patterson	10.00
17	Carlos Pena	5.00
18	Marcus Giles	5.00
19	Travis Wilson	5.00
20	Barry Zito	8.00

King of the Hill

NM/M

Complete Set (5):		30.00
Common Player:		3.00
Inserted 1:21		
1	Pedro Martinez	10.00
2	Randy Johnson	10.00
3	Greg Maddux	15.00
4	Rick Ankiel	3.00
5	Kevin Brown	3.00

Lone Star Signatures

NM/M

Common Player:		6.00
Inserted 1:196		
1	Nomar Garciaparra	100.00
2	Derek Jeter	120.00
3	Edgardo Alfonso	20.00
4	Roberto Alomar	40.00

5	Magglio Ordonez	20.00
6	Bobby Abreu	40.00
7	Chipper Jones	40.00
8	Troy Glaus	30.00
9	Nick Johnson	15.00
10	Adam Piatt	6.00
11	Sean Burroughs	8.00
12	Corey Patterson	15.00
13	Rick Ankiel	6.00
14	Kevin Millwood	10.00
15	Adrian Gonzalez	15.00
16	Adam Johnson	6.00
17	Rocco Baldelli	25.00
18	Mike Stodolka	6.00

Play at the Plate

KEN GRIFFEY JR.
CINCINNATI REDS

NM/M

Common Player:		10.00
Inserted 1:11		
1	Mark McGwire	20.00
2	Sammy Sosa	15.00
3	Vladimir Guerrero	8.00
4	Ken Griffey Jr.	15.00
5	Mike Piazza	15.00
6	Chipper Jones	10.00
7	Barry Bonds	25.00
8	Alex Rodriguez	20.00
9	Jeff Bagwell	8.00
10	Nomar Garciaparra	15.00

Souvenirs

JOSE VIDRO

NM/M

Common Player:		4.00
1	Scott Rolen/Bat	8.00
2	Larry Walker/Bat	5.00
3	Rafael Furcal/Bat	5.00
4	Darin Erstad/Bat	5.00
5	Mike Sweeney/Jsy	4.00
6	Matt Lawton/Jsy	4.00
7	Jose Vidro/Jsy	4.00
8	Pat Burrell/Jsy	6.00

Super Teams

NM/M

Common Card:		1.00
STP1	Troy Glaus/ Anaheim Angels	2.00
STP2	Jeff Bagwell/ Houston Astros	2.00
STP3	Jason Giambi/ Oakland A's	1.25
STP4	Carlos Delgado/ Toronto Blue Jays	1.00
STP5	Chipper Jones/ Atlanta Braves	2.50
STP6	Geoff Jenkins/ Milwaukee Brewers	1.00
STP7	Mark McGwire/ St. Louis Cardinals	4.00
STP8	Sammy Sosa/ Chicago Cubs	3.00

STP9	Greg Vaughn/Tampa Bay Devil Rays	1.00
STP10	Luis Gonzalez/Arizona Diamondbacks	1.00
STP11	Shawn Green/ L.A. Dodgers	1.00
STP12	Vladimir Guerrero/ Montreal Expos	1.50
STP13	Barry Bonds/ S.F. Giants	5.00
STP14	Roberto Alomar/ Cleveland Indians	1.00
STP15	Alex Rodriguez/ Seattle Mariners	4.00
STP16	Preston Wilson/ Florida Marlins	1.00
STP17	Mike Piazza/ N.Y. Mets	3.00
STP18	Mike Mussina/ Baltimore Orioles	1.00
STP19	Tony Gwynn/ S.D. Padres	2.00
STP20	Scott Rolen/ Philadelphia Phillies	1.25
STP21	Jason Kendall/ Pittsburgh Pirates	1.00
STP22	Ivan Rodriguez/ Texas Rangers	1.25
STP23	Nomar Garciaparra/ Boston Red Sox	3.00
STP24	Ken Griffey Jr./ Cincinnati Reds	3.00
STP25	Todd Helton/ Colorado Rockies	1.50
STP26	Mike Sweeney/ K.C. Royals	1.00
STP27	Juan Gonzalez/ Detroit Tigers	1.50
STP28	Brad Radke Minnesota Twins	1.00
STP29	Frank Thomas/ Chicago White Sox	1.50
STP30	Derek Jeter/ N.Y. Yankees	5.00

2002 Stadium Club
Relic Edition

NM/M

Complete Set (125):		
Common Player:		.15
Common SP (101-125):		5.00
Production 2,999		
Pack (6):		1.50
Box (24):		30.00
1	Pedro Martinez	.75
2	Derek Jeter	2.00
3	Chipper Jones	1.00
4	Roberto Alomar	.40
5	Albert Pujols	1.50
6	Bret Boone	.15
7	Alex Rodriguez	1.50
8	Jose Cruz	.15
9	Mike Hampton	.15
10	Vladimir Guerrero	.75
11	Jim Edmonds	.25
12	Luis Gonzalez	.25
13	Jeff Kent	.15
14	Mike Piazza	1.25
15	Ben Sheets	.15
16	Tsuyoshi Shinjo	.15
17	Pat Burrell	.40
18	Jermaine Dye	.15
19	Rafael Furcal	.15
20	Randy Johnson	.75
21	Carlos Delgado	.50
22	Roger Clemens	1.00
23	Eric Chavez	.25
24	Nomar Garciaparra	1.25
25	Ivan Rodriguez	.65
26	Juan Gonzalez	.75
27	Reggie Sanders	.15
28	Jeff Bagwell	.75
29	Kazuhiro Sasaki	.15
30	Larry Walker	.15
31	Ben Grieve	.15
32	David Justice	.15
33	David Wells	.15
34	Kevin Brown	.15
35	Miguel Tejada	.25
36	Jorge Posada	.15
37	Javy Lopez	.15
38	Cliff Floyd	.15
39	Carlos Lee	.15
40	Manny Ramirez	.75
41	Jim Thome	.65
42	Pokey Reese	.15
43	Scott Rolen	.65
44	Richie Sexson	.15
45	Dean Palmer	.15
46	Rafael Palmeiro	.65
47	Alfonso Soriano	.75
48	Craig Biggio	.15
49	Troy Glaus	.75
50	Andruw Jones	.75
51	Ichiro Suzuki	1.50
52	Kenny Lofton	.15
53	Hideo Nomo	.75
54	Magglio Ordonez	.15
55	Brad Penny	.15
56	Omar Vizquel	.15
57	Mike Sweeney	.15
58	Gary Sheffield	.25
59	Ken Griffey Jr.	1.25
60	Curt Schilling	.40
61	Bobby Higginson	.15
62	Terrence Long	.15
63	Moises Alou	.15
64	Sandy Alomar	.15
65	Cristian Guzman	.15
66	Sammy Sosa	1.25
67	Jose Vidro	.15
68	Edgar Martinez	.15
69	Jason Giambi	.50
70	Mark McGwire	1.50
71	Barry Bonds	2.00
72	Greg Vaughn	.15
73	Phil Nevin	.15
74	Jason Kendall	.15
75	Greg Maddux	1.00
76	Jeromy Burnitz	.15
77	Mike Mussina	.40
78	Johnny Damon	.25
79	Shawn Green	.40
80	Jimmy Rollins	.25
81	Edgardo Alfonzo	.15
82	Barry Larkin	.15
83	Raul Mondesi	.15
84	Preston Wilson	.15
85	Mike Lieberthal	.15
86	J.D. Drew	.40
87	Ryan Klesko	.15
88	David Segui	.15
89	Derek Bell	.15
90	Bernie Williams	.40
91	Doug Mientkiewicz	.15
92	Rich Aurilia	.15
93	Ellis Burks	.15
94	Placido Polanco	.15
95	Darin Erstad	.25
96	Brian Giles	.15
97	Geoff Jenkins	.15
98	Kerry Wood	.65
99	Mariano Rivera	.40
100	Todd Helton	.75
101	Adam Dunn	15.00
102	Grant Balfour	5.00
103	Jae Weong Seo	5.00
104	Hank Blalock	10.00
105	Chris George	5.00
106	Jack Cust	5.00
107	Juan Cruz	5.00
108	Adrian Gonzalez	5.00
109	Nick Johnson	5.00
110	Jeff Devanon RC	5.00
111	Juan Diaz	5.00
112	Brandon Duckworth	5.00
113	Jason Lane	5.00
114	Seung Jun Song	5.00
115	Morgan Ensberg	5.00
116	Marlyn Tisdale RC	5.00
117	Jason Botts RC	5.00
118	Henry Pichardo RC	5.00
119	John Rodriguez RC	5.00
120	Mike Peeples RC	5.00
121	Rob Bowen RC	5.00
122	Jeremy Affeldt	5.00
123	Jorge Buret RC	5.00
124	Manny Ravelo RC	5.00
125	Eudy Lajara RC	5.00

All-Star Relics

NM/M

Common Player:		5.00
RA	Roberto Alomar	7.50
MA	Moises Alou	5.00
BB	Barry Bonds	40.00
BRB	Bret Boone	5.00
MC	Mike Cameron	5.00
SC	Sean Casey	7.50
CF	Cliff Floyd	5.00
BG	Brian Giles	5.00
JG	Juan Gonzalez	12.00
LG3	Luis Gonzalez	5.00
CG	Cristian Guzman	5.00
TG	Tony Gwynn	15.00
MH	Mike Hampton	5.00
TH	Todd Helton	12.00
RJ	Randy Johnson	12.00
CJ	Chipper Jones	15.00
JK	Jeff Kent	5.00
RK	Ryan Klesko	5.00
EM	Edgar Martinez	5.00
ERM	Eric Milton	5.00
JO	John Olerud	5.00
MO	Magglio Ordonez	5.00
MP	Mike Piazza	20.00
JP	Jorge Posada	5.00
AP	Albert Pujols	30.00
MR	Manny Ramirez	12.00
CR	Cal Ripken Jr.	
IR	Ivan Rodriguez	10.00
KS	Kazuhiro Sasaki	5.00
MS	Mike Sweeney	5.00
LW	Larry Walker	5.00

Barry Bonds
Autograph Ball

NM/M

Inserted as a redemption.
Barry Bonds 200.00

Chasing 500-500

NM/M

Common Player:		
BB1	Barry Bonds/Dual	40.00
BB2	Barry Bonds/Jsy/600	30.00
BB3	Barry Bonds/Mult/200	75.00

Passport to the Majors

NM/M

Common Player:		5.00
Jsy 1:84		
Bat 1:795		
BA	Bobby Abreu/400	6.00
EA	Edgardo Alfonzo	5.00
RA	Roberto Alomar	6.00
WB	Wilson Betemit/325	5.00
BC	Bartolo Colon	5.00
RF	Rafael Furcal	5.00
AG	Andres Galarraga	5.00
JG	Juan Gonzalez	8.00
SH	Shigetoshi Hasegawa	5.00
AJ	Andruw Jones	8.00
CL	Carlos Lee	5.00
JL	Javy Lopez	5.00
PM	Pedro Martinez	10.00
RM	Raul Mondesi	5.00
MO	Magglio Ordonez	5.00
RP	Rafael Palmeiro	8.00
CP	Chan Ho Park	5.00
AP	Albert Pujols/450	40.00
MR	Manny Ramirez	10.00
IR	Ivan Rodriguez	10.00
KS	Kazuhiro Sasaki	5.00
TS	Tsuyoshi Shinjo/400	6.00
AS	Alfonso Soriano/400	10.00
MT	Miguel Tejada/375	6.00
LW	Larry Walker	5.00

Reel Time

NM/M

Complete Set (20):		25.00
Common Player:		.50
Inserted 1:8		
RT1	Luis Gonzalez	.50
RT2	Derek Jeter	4.00
RT3	Ken Griffey Jr.	2.50
RT4	Alex Rodriguez	3.00
RT5	Barry Bonds	4.00
RT6	Ichiro Suzuki	2.50
RT7	Carlos Delgado	1.00
RT8	Manny Ramirez	1.50
RT9	Mike Piazza	2.50
RT10	Mark McGwire	3.00
RT11	Todd Helton	1.50
RT12	Vladimir Guerrero	1.50

RT13	Jim Thome	1.50
RT14	Rich Aurilia	.50
RT15	Bret Boone	.50
RT16	Roberto Alomar	.75
RT17	Jason Giambi	1.00
RT18	Chipper Jones	2.00
RT19	Albert Pujols	3.00
RT20	Sammy Sosa	2.50

Stadium Shots

NM/M

Complete Set (10):		15.00
Common Player:		1.50
Inserted 1:12		
SS1	Sammy Sosa	2.00
SS2	Manny Ramirez	1.50
SS3	Jason Giambi	1.00
SS4	Mike Piazza	2.00
SS5	Barry Bonds	4.00
SS6	Ken Griffey Jr.	2.00
SS7	Juan Gonzalez	1.50
SS8	Jeff Bagwell	1.50
SS9	Jim Thome	1.00
SS10	Mark McGwire	3.00

Stadium Slices Handle

NM/M

Common Player:		15.00
BB	Barry Bonds	50.00
LG	Luis Gonzalez	15.00
AP	Albert Pujols	50.00
IR	Ivan Rodriguez	20.00
BW	Bernie Williams	15.00

Stadium Slices Barrel

NM/M

Common Player:		15.00
BB	Barry Bonds	75.00
LG	Luis Gonzalez	15.00
AP	Albert Pujols	75.00
IR	Ivan Rodriguez	35.00
BW	Bernie Williams	25.00

Stadium Slices
Trademark

NM/M

Common Player:		15.00
BB	Barry Bonds	60.00

LG	Luis Gonzalez	15.00
AP	Albert Pujols	60.00
IR	Ivan Rodriguez	20.00
BW	Bernie Williams	15.00

World Champions Relics

NM/M

Common Player:		4.00
Jersey 1:106		
Bat 1:94		
Pants 1:795		
Spikes 1:38,400		
RA	Roberto Alomar	15.00
MA	Moises Alou	8.00
DB	Don Baylor	8.00
JB	Johnny Bench	20.00
BB	Bert Blyleven	8.00
WB	Wade Boggs	15.00
BRB	Bob Boone	4.00
GB	George Brett	50.00
SB	Scott Brosius	10.00
AB	Al Bumbry	4.00
JC1	Jose Canseco	15.00
JC2	Jose Canseco	15.00
GC1	Gary Carter	15.00
GC2	Gary Carter	15.00
JC	Joe Carter	10.00
RC	Ron Cey	10.00
CC	Chris Chambliss	8.00
DC	Dave Concepcion	8.00
ED	Eric Davis	10.00
BD	Bucky Dent	8.00
GF	George Foster	8.00
PG	Phil Garner	4.00
KG1	Kirk Gibson	10.00
KG2	Kirk Gibson	10.00
TG	Tom Glavine	15.00
KG	Ken Griffey Sr.	15.00
RH	Rickey Henderson/50	80.00
GH	George Hendrick	6.00
KH	Keith Hernandez	15.00
WH	Willie Hernandez	8.00
OH	Orel Hershiser	10.00
RJ	Reggie Jackson	15.00
CWJ	Chipper Jones	15.00
DJ	David Justice	15.00
CK	Chuck Knoblauch	4.00
AL	Al Leiter	8.00
DL	Davey Lopes	8.00
JL	Javy Lopez	8.00
GL	Greg Luzinski	6.00
GM	Greg Maddux	30.00
BM	Bill Madlock	8.00
TLM	Tino Martinez	15.00
HM	Hal McCrae	8.00
FM	Fred McGriff	10.00
PM	Paul Molitor	15.00
TM	Thurman Munson	50.00
EM1	Eddie Murray	15.00
EM2	Eddie Murray	15.00
JO	John Olerud	6.00
PO	Paul O'Neill	15.00
DP	Dave Parker	10.00
TP	Tony Perez	10.00
LVP	Lou Pinella	15.00
JP	Jorge Posada	10.00
KP	Kirby Puckett	20.00
WR	Willie Randolph	10.00
MJS	Mike Schmidt	50.00
MS	Mike Scoscia	10.00
OS	Ozzie Smith	30.00
JS	John Smoltz	10.00
ES	Ed Sprague	4.00
WS	Willie Stargell	15.00
AT	Alan Trammell	10.00
LW	Lou Whitaker	10.00
BW	Bernie Williams	15.00
MW	Mookie Wilson	10.00
DW	Dave Winfield	10.00
FV	Fernando Valenzuela	10.00
JV	Jose Vizcaino	4.00

2003 Stadium Club

NM/M

Complete Set (125):		30.00
Common Player:		.15
Hobby Pack (6):		1.50
Hobby Box (24):		30.00
1	Rafael Furcal	.15
2	Randy Winn	.15
3	Eric Chavez	.25

4	Fernando Vina	.15
5	Pat Burrell	.25
6	Derek Jeter	2.00
7	Ivan Rodriguez	.65
8	Eric Hinske	.15
9	Roberto Alomar	.40
10	Tony Batista	.15
11	Jacque Jones	.15
12	Alfonso Soriano	.75
13	Omar Vizquel	.15
14	Paul Konerko	.25
15	Shawn Green	.45
16	Garret Anderson	.15
17	Darin Erstad	.25
18	Johnny Damon	.25
19	Juan Gonzalez	.75
20	Luis Gonzalez	.25
21	Sean Burroughs	.15
22	Mark Prior	.75
23	Javier Vazquez	.15
24	Shannon Stewart	.15
25	Jay Gibbons	.15
26	A.J. Pierzynski	.15
27	Vladimir Guerrero	.75
28	Austin Kearns	.25
29	Shea Hillenbrand	.15
30	Magglio Ordonez	.15
31	Mike Cameron	.15
32	Tim Salmon	.25
33	Brian Jordan	.15
34	Moises Alou	.15
35	Rich Aurilia	.15
36	Nick Johnson	.15
37	Junior Spivey	.15
38	Curt Schilling	.40
39	Jose Vidro	.15
40	Orlando Cabrera	.15
41	Jeff Bagwell	.75
42	Mo Vaughn	.15
43	Luis Castillo	.15
44	Vicente Padilla	.15
45	Pedro J. Martinez	.75
46	John Olerud	.15
47	Tom Glavine	.40
48	Torii Hunter	.15
49	J.D. Drew	.25
50	Alex Rodriguez	1.50
51	Randy Johnson	.75
52	Richie Sexson	.15
53	Jimmy Rollins	.25
54	Cristian Guzman	.15
55	Tim Hudson	.25
56	Mark Buehrle	.15
57	Paul LoDuca	.15
58	Aramis Ramirez	.25
59	Todd Helton	.75
60	Lance Berkman	.15
61	Josh Beckett	.25
62	Bret Boone	.15
63	Miguel Tejada	.35
64	Nomar Garciaparra	1.25
65	Albert Pujols	1.50
66	Chipper Jones	1.00
67	Scott Rolen	.65
68	Kerry Wood	.65
69	Jorge Posada	.15
70	Ichiro Suzuki	1.50
71	Jeff Kent	.15
72	David Eckstein	.15
73	Phil Nevin	.15
74	Brian Giles	.15
75	Barry Zito	.25
76	Andruw Jones	.75
77	Jim Thome	.65
78	Robert Fick	.15
79	Rafael Palmeiro	.65
80	Barry Bonds	2.00
81	Gary Sheffield	.40
82	Jim Edmonds	.25
83	Kazuhisa Ishii	.15
84	Jose Hernandez	.15
85	Jason Giambi	.40

86	Mark Mulder	.15
87	Roger Clemens	1.00
88	Troy Glaus	.75
89	Carlos Delgado	.50
90	Mike Sweeney	.15
91	Ken Griffey Jr.	1.25
92	Manny Ramirez	.75
93	Ryan Klesko	.15
94	Larry Walker	.15
95	Adam Dunn	.65
96	Raul Ibanez	.15
97	Preston Wilson	.15
98	Roy Oswalt	.15
99	Sammy Sosa	1.25
100	Mike Piazza	1.25
101	Jose Reyes	.50
102	Ed Rogers	.15
103	Hank Blalock	.75
104	Mark Teixeira	.65
105	Orlando Hudson	.15
106	Drew Henson	.25
107	Joe Mauer	.75
108	Carl Crawford	.15
109	Marlon Byrd	.15
110	Jason Stokes	.15
111	Miguel Cabrera	.50
112	Wilson Betemit	.15
113	Jerome Williams	.15
114	Walter Young	.15
115	Juan Camacho **RC**	.15
116	Chris Duncan **RC**	3.00
117	Franklin Gutierrez **RC**	3.00
118	Adam LaRoche	.50
119	Manuel Ramirez **RC**	.50
120	Il Kim **RC**	.50
121	Wayne Lydon **RC**	.50
122	Daryl Clark **RC**	.50
123	Sean Pierce	.15
124	Andy Marte **RC**	3.00
125	Matthew Peterson **RC**	.75

Photographer's Proof

Stars (1-100):	4-8X
Cards (101-125):	2-4X
Production 299 Sets	

Royal Gold

Stars:	1-3X
Inserted 1:1	

Beam Team

NM/M

Complete Set (20):		50.00
Common Player:		1.00
Inserted 1:12		
BT1	Larry Walker	1.00
BT2	Miguel Tejada	1.50
BT3	Ichiro Suzuki	5.00
BT4	Sammy Sosa	5.00
BT5	Ivan Rodriguez	2.50
BT6	Alex Rodriguez	6.00
BT7	Mike Piazza	5.00
BT8	Jeff Kent	1.00
BT9	Chipper Jones	4.00
BT10	Derek Jeter	8.00
BT11	Todd Helton	3.00
BT12	Vladimir Guerrero	3.00
BT13	Shawn Green	1.50
BT14	Brian Giles	1.00
BT15	Jason Giambi	2.00
BT16	Nomar Garciaparra	5.00
BT17	Adam Dunn	2.00
BT18	Carlos Delgado	1.50
BT19	Barry Bonds	8.00
BT20	Lance Berkman	1.00

Born In The USA

NM/M

Common Player:		5.00
Jerseys Inserted 1:52		
Bats Inserted 1:76		
RA	Rich Aurilia/Jsy	5.00
JB	Jeff Bagwell/Jsy	12.00
CB	Craig Biggio/Jsy	8.00
BB	Bret Boone/Jsy	5.00
AB	A.J. Burnett/Jsy	5.00
JNB	Jeromy Burnitz/Bat	6.00
PB	Pat Burrell/Bat	10.00
SB	Sean Burroughs/Bat	6.00
EC	Eric Chavez/Jsy	6.00
TC	Tony Clark/Bat	5.00
JD	Johnny Damon/Bat	8.00
JDD	J.D. Drew/Bat	6.00
AD	Adam Dunn/Bat	12.00
JE	Jim Edmonds/Jsy	8.00
CF	Cliff Floyd/Bat	5.00
BF	Brad Fullmer/Bat	5.00
NG	Nomar Garciaparra/Bat	20.00
LG	Luis Gonzalez/Bat	6.00
MG	Mark Grace/Jsy	12.00
SG	Shawn Green/Bat	6.00
TJH	Toby Hall	5.00
JH	Josh Hamilton/Bat	8.00
TH	Todd Helton/Bat	8.00
RH	Rickey Henderson/Bat	15.00
RJ	Randy Johnson/Bat	12.00
CJ	Chipper Jones/Jsy	12.00
RK	Ryan Klesko/Bat	5.00
PK	Paul Konerko/Bat	8.00
BL	Barry Larkin/Jsy	10.00
TRL	Travis Lee/Bat	5.00
TL	Terrence Long/Jsy	5.00
GM	Greg Maddux/Jsy	15.00
TM	Tino Martinez/Bat	10.00
WM	Willie Mays/Bat	40.00
EM	Eric Milton/Jsy	6.00
JO	John Olerud/Jsy	6.00
CP	Corey Patterson/Bat	8.00
MP	Mike Piazza/Jsy	15.00
AR	Alex Rodriguez/Bat	15.00
SR	Scott Rolen/Bat	15.00
RS	Richie Sexson/Bat	6.00
GS	Gary Sheffield/Bat	8.00
JS	John Smoltz/Jsy	6.00
FT	Frank Thomas/Bat	8.00
JT	Jim Thome/Jsy	15.00
MV	Mo Vaughn/Bat	6.00
RV	Robin Ventura/Bat	8.00
MW	Matt Williams/Bat	8.00
PW	Preston Wilson/Jsy	5.00
KW	Kerry Wood/Bat	10.00

Co-Signers

NM/M

HTA Exclusive		
MI	Masanori Murakami, Kazuhisa Ishii	180.00
AM	Hank Aaron, Willie Mays	400.00

Clubhouse Exclusive

NM/M
Jersey Inserted 1:488
Jersey & Bat 1:2,073
Jersey, Bat & Spikes 1:2,750
CE1	Albert Pujols/Jsy	15.00
CE2	Albert Pujols/Bat/Jsy	35.00
CE3	Albert Pujols/ Jsy/Bat/Spike	100.00

License To Drive

NM/M
Common Player: 5.00
Inserted 1:98
RA	Roberto Alomar	8.00
MA	Moises Alou	6.00
AB	Adrian Beltre	8.00
LB	Lance Berkman	6.00
EC	Eric Chavez	6.00
AD	Adam Dunn	8.00
NG	Nomar Garciaparra	15.00
JG	Juan Gonzalez	8.00
LG	Luis Gonzalez	6.00
SG	Shawn Green	8.00
TH	Todd Helton	10.00
AJ	Andruw Jones	10.00
CJ	Chipper Jones	12.00
TM	Tino Martinez	6.00
RP	Rafael Palmeiro	8.00
MP	Mike Piazza	15.00
AP	Albert Pujols	25.00
ANR	Aramis Ramirez	6.00
AR	Alex Rodriguez	20.00
IR	Ivan Rodriguez	8.00
SR	Scott Rolen	10.00
GS	Gary Sheffield	8.00
FT	Frank Thomas	10.00
LW	Larry Walker	6.00
BW	Bernie Williams	6.00

MLB Match-Ups

NM/M
Inserted 1:485
BB	Bret Boone	15.00
TH	Todd Helton	15.00
AJ	Andruw Jones	12.00
GM	Greg Maddux	30.00
AP	Albert Pujols	30.00

Stadium Shots

NM/M
Complete Set (10): 25.00
Common Player: 1.00
Inserted 1:24
SS1	Lance Berkman	1.00
SS2	Barry Bonds	6.00

SS3	Jason Giambi	2.50
SS4	Shawn Green	1.50
SS5	Vladimir Guerrero	3.00
SS6	Paul Konerko	1.00
SS7	Mike Piazza	4.50
SS8	Alex Rodriguez	6.00
SS9	Sammy Sosa	4.50
SS10	Jim Thome	2.00

Stadium Slices Handle

NM/M
Common Player: 5.00
Inserted 1:237
Trademarks: 1-1.5X
Inserted 1:415
Barrels: 1.5-2X
Inserted 1:550
RA	Roberto Alomar	15.00
CD	Carlos Delgado	8.00
NG	Nomar Garciaparra	20.00
TH	Todd Helton	10.00
AJ	Andruw Jones	8.00
RP	Rafael Palmeiro	10.00
MP	Mike Piazza	15.00
AP	Albert Pujols	20.00
AR	Alex Rodriguez	15.00
GS	Gary Sheffield	10.00

World Stage

NM/M
Common Player: 5.00
Jerseys Inserted 1:118
Bats Inserted 1:809
AB	Adrian Beltre/Jsy	6.00
KI	Kazuhisa Ishii/Jsy	5.00
BK	Byung-Hyun Kim/Jsy	5.00
HN	Hideo Nomo/Bat	20.00
AP	Albert Pujols/Jsy	15.00
IR	Ivan Rodriguez/Jsy	8.00
KS	Kazuhiro Sasaki/Jsy	5.00
TS	Tsuyoshi Shinjo/Bat	5.00
AS	Alfonso Soriano/Bat	15.00
MT	Miguel Tejada/Jsy	8.00

1991 Studio

IVAN CALDERON, LF

NM/M
Complete Set (264): 7.50
Common Player: .05
Foil Pack (10): .50
Foil Box (48): 12.50
1	Glenn Davis	.05
2	Dwight Evans	.05
3	Leo Gomez	.05
4	Chris Hoiles	.05
5	Sam Horn	.05
6	Ben McDonald	.05
7	Randy Milligan	.05
8	Gregg Olson	.05
9	Cal Ripken, Jr.	1.00

10	David Segui	.05
11	Wade Boggs	.40
12	Ellis Burks	.05
13	Jack Clark	.05
14	Roger Clemens	.45
15	Mike Greenwell	.05
16	Tim Naehring	.05
17	Tony Pena	.05
18	Phil Plantier **RC**	.05
19	Jeff Reardon	.05
20	Mo Vaughn	.05
21	Jimmy Reese	.05
22	Jim Abbott	.05
23	Bert Blyleven	.05
24	Chuck Finley	.05
25	Gary Gaetti	.05
26	Wally Joyner	.05
27	Mark Langston	.05
28	Kirk McCaskill	.05
29	Lance Parrish	.05
30	Dave Winfield	.30
31	Alex Fernandez	.05
32	Carlton Fisk	.30
33	Scott Fletcher	.05
34	Greg Hibbard	.05
35	Charlie Hough	.05
36	Jack McDowell	.05
37	Tim Raines	.05
38	Sammy Sosa	.40
39	Bobby Thigpen	.05
40	Frank Thomas	.30
41	Sandy Alomar	.05
42	John Farrell	.05
43	Glenallen Hill	.05
44	Brook Jacoby	.05
45	Chris James	.05
46	Doug Jones	.05
47	Eric King	.05
48	Mark Lewis	.05
49	Greg Swindell	.05
50	Mark Whiten	.05
51	Milt Cuyler	.05
52	Rob Deer	.05
53	Cecil Fielder	.05
54	Travis Fryman	.05
55	Bill Gullickson	.05
56	Lloyd Moseby	.05
57	Frank Tanana	.05
58	Mickey Tettleton	.05
59	Alan Trammell	.05
60	Lou Whitaker	.05
61	Mike Boddicker	.05
62	George Brett	.45
63	Jeff Conine	.05
64	Warren Cromartie	.05
65	Storm Davis	.05
66	Kirk Gibson	.05
67	Mark Gubicza	.05
68	Brian McRae **RC**	.05
69	Bret Saberhagen	.05
70	Kurt Stillwell	.05
71	Tim McIntosh	.05
72	Candy Maldonado	.05
73	Paul Molitor	.30
74	Willie Randolph	.05
75	Ron Robinson	.05
76	Gary Sheffield	.20
77	Franklin Stubbs	.05
78	B.J. Surhoff	.05
79	Greg Vaughn	.05
80	Robin Yount	.30
81	Rick Aguilera	.05
82	Steve Bedrosian	.05
83	Scott Erickson	.05
84	Greg Gagne	.05
85	Dan Gladden	.05
86	Brian Harper	.05
87	Kent Hrbek	.05
88	Shane Mack	.05
89	Jack Morris	.05
90	Kirby Puckett	.40
91	Jesse Barfield	.05
92	Steve Farr	.05
93	Steve Howe	.05
94	Roberto Kelly	.05
95	Tim Leary	.05
96	Kevin Maas	.05
97	Don Mattingly	.45
98	Hensley Meulens	.05
99	Scott Sanderson	.05
100	Steve Sax	.05
101	Jose Canseco	.20
102	Dennis Eckersley	.25
103	Dave Henderson	.05
104	Rickey Henderson	.30
105	Rick Honeycutt	.05
106	Mark McGwire	.75
107	Dave Stewart	.05
108	Eric Show	.05
109	Todd Van Poppel **RC**	.05
110	Bob Welch	.05
111	Alvin Davis	.05
112	Ken Griffey Jr.	.50
113	Ken Griffey Sr.	.05

114	Erik Hanson	.05
115	Brian Holman	.05
116	Randy Johnson	.30
117	Edgar Martinez	.05
118	Tino Martinez	.05
119	Harold Reynolds	.05
120	David Valle	.05
121	Kevin Belcher	.05
122	Scott Chiamparino	.05
123	Julio Franco	.05
124	Juan Gonzalez	.20
125	Rich Gossage	.05
126	Jeff Kunkel	.05
127	Rafael Palmeiro	.25
128	Nolan Ryan	1.00
129	Ruben Sierra	.05
130	Bobby Witt	.05
131	Roberto Alomar	.10
132	Tom Candiotti	.05
133	Joe Carter	.05
134	Ken Dayley	.05
135	Kelly Gruber	.05
136	John Olerud	.05
137	Dave Stieb	.05
138	Turner Ward	.05
139	Devon White	.05
140	Mookie Wilson	.05
141	Steve Avery	.05
142	Sid Bream	.05
143	Nick Esasky	.05
144	Ron Gant	.05
145	Tom Glavine	.20
146	Dave Justice	.05
147	Kelly Mann	.05
148	Terry Pendleton	.05
149	John Smoltz	.05
150	Jeff Treadway	.05
151	George Bell	.05
152	Shawn Boskie	.05
153	Andre Dawson	.20
154	Lance Dickson	.05
155	Shawon Dunston	.05
156	Joe Girardi	.05
157	Mark Grace	.05
158	Ryne Sandberg	.40
159	Gary Scott	.05
160	Dave Smith	.05
161	Tom Browning	.05
162	Eric Davis	.05
163	Rob Dibble	.05
164	Mariano Duncan	.05
165	Chris Hammond	.05
166	Billy Hatcher	.05
167	Barry Larkin	.05
168	Hal Morris	.05
169	Paul O'Neill	.05
170	Chris Sabo	.05
171	Eric Anthony	.05
172	Jeff Bagwell **RC**	1.50
173	Craig Biggio	.05
174	Ken Caminitti	.05
175	Jim Deshaies	.05
176	Steve Finley	.05
177	Pete Harnisch	.05
178	Darryl Kile	.05
179	Curt Schilling	.20
180	Mike Scott	.05
181	Brett Butler	.05
182	Gary Carter	.30
183	Orel Hershiser	.05
184	Ramon Martinez	.05
185	Eddie Murray	.30
186	Jose Offerman	.05
187	Bob Ojeda	.05
188	Juan Samuel	.05
189	Mike Scioscia	.05
190	Darryl Strawberry	.05
191	Moises Alou	.05
192	Brian Barnes	.05
193	Oil Can Boyd	.05
194	Ivan Calderon	.05
195	Delino DeShields	.05
196	Mike Fitzgerald	.05
197	Andres Galarraga	.05
198	Marquis Grissom	.05
199	Bill Sampen	.05
200	Tim Wallach	.05
201	Daryl Boston	.05
202	Vince Coleman	.05
203	John Franco	.05
204	Dwight Gooden	.05
205	Tom Herr	.05
206	Gregg Jefferies	.05
207	Howard Johnson	.05
208	Dave Magadan	.05
209	Kevin McReynolds	.05
210	Frank Viola	.05
211	Wes Chamberlain	.05
212	Darren Daulton	.05
213	Len Dykstra	.05
214	Charlie Hayes	.05
215	Ricky Jordan	.05
216	Steve Lake	.05
217	Roger McDowell	.05

#	Player	Price
218	Mickey Morandini	.05
219	Terry Mulholland	.05
220	Dale Murphy	.15
221	Jay Bell	.05
222	Barry Bonds	1.00
223	Bobby Bonilla	.05
224	Doug Drabek	.05
225	Bill Landrum	.05
226	Mike LaValliere	.05
227	Jose Lind	.05
228	Don Slaught	.05
229	John Smiley	.05
230	Andy Van Slyke	.05
231	Bernard Gilkey	.05
232	Pedro Guerrero	.05
233	Rex Hudler	.05
234	Ray Lankford	.05
235	Joe Magrane	.05
236	Jose Oquendo	.05
237	Lee Smith	.05
238	Ozzie Smith	.40
239	Milt Thompson	.05
240	Todd Zeile	.05
241	Larry Andersen	.05
242	Andy Benes	.05
243	Paul Faries	.05
244	Tony Fernandez	.05
245	Tony Gwynn	.40
246	Atlee Hammaker	.05
247	Fred McGriff	.05
248	Bip Roberts	.05
249	Benito Santiago	.05
250	Ed Whitson	.05
251	Dave Anderson	.05
252	Mike Benjamin	.05
253	John Burkett	.05
254	Will Clark	.05
255	Scott Garrelts	.05
256	Willie McGee	.05
257	Kevin Mitchell	.05
258	Dave Righetti	.05
259	Matt Williams	.05
260	Bud Black, Steve Decker/ Black & Decker	.10
261	Checklist	.03
262	Checklist	.03
263	Checklist	.03
---	Header Card	.03

1991 Studio Preview

		NM/M
Complete Set (18):		5.00
Common Player:		.50
1	Juan Bell	.50
2	Roger Clemens	3.00
3	Dave Parker	.50
4	Tim Raines	.50
5	Kevin Seitzer	.50
6	Teddy Higuera	.50
7	Bernie Williams	.50
8	Harold Baines	.50
9	Gary Pettis	.50
10	Dave Justice	.50
11	Eric Davis	.50
12	Andujar Cedeno	.50
13	Tom Foley	.50
14	Dwight Gooden	.50
15	Doug Drabek	.50
16	Steve Decker	.50
17	Joe Torre	.75
18	Header Card	.10

1992 Studio

		NM/M
Complete Set (264):		8.00
Common Player:		.05
Pack (10):		.65
Wax Box (48):		15.00
1	Steve Avery	.05
2	Sid Bream	.05
3	Ron Gant	.05
4	Tom Glavine	.25

PETE HARNISCH   RHP
Houston Astros

#	Player	Price
5	Dave Justice	.05
6	Mark Lemke	.05
7	Greg Olson	.05
8	Terry Pendleton	.05
9	Deion Sanders	.05
10	John Smoltz	.05
11	Doug Dascenzo	.05
12	Andre Dawson	.25
13	Joe Girardi	.05
14	Mark Grace	.05
15	Greg Maddux	.50
16	Chuck McElroy	.05
17	Mike Morgan	.05
18	Ryne Sandberg	.50
19	Gary Scott	.05
20	Sammy Sosa	.50
21	Norm Charlton	.05
22	Rob Dibble	.05
23	Barry Larkin	.05
24	Hal Morris	.05
25	Paul O'Neill	.05
26	Jose Rijo	.05
27	Bip Roberts	.05
28	Chris Sabo	.05
29	Reggie Sanders	.05
30	Greg Swindell	.05
31	Jeff Bagwell	.45
32	Craig Biggio	.05
33	Ken Caminiti	.05
34	Andujar Cedeno	.05
35	Steve Finley	.05
36	Pete Harnisch	.05
37	Butch Henry	.05
38	Doug Jones	.05
39	Darryl Kile	.05
40	Eddie Taubensee	.05
41	Brett Butler	.05
42	Tom Candiotti	.05
43	Eric Davis	.05
44	Orel Hershiser	.05
45	Eric Karros	.05
46	Ramon Martinez	.05
47	Jose Offerman	.05
48	Mike Scioscia	.05
49	Mike Sharperson	.05
50	Darryl Strawberry	.05
51	Bret Barbarie	.05
52	Ivan Calderon	.05
53	Gary Carter	.45
54	Delino DeShields	.05
55	Marquis Grissom	.05
56	Ken Hill	.05
57	Dennis Martinez	.05
58	Spike Owen	.05
59	Larry Walker	.05
60	Tim Wallach	.05
61	Bobby Bonilla	.05
62	Tim Burke	.05
63	Vince Coleman	.05
64	John Franco	.05
65	Dwight Gooden	.05
66	Todd Hundley	.05
67	Howard Johnson	.05
68	Eddie Murray	.45
69	Bret Saberhagen	.05
70	Anthony Young	.05
71	Kim Batiste	.05
72	Wes Chamberlain	.05
73	Darren Daulton	.05
74	Mariano Duncan	.05
75	Len Dykstra	.05
76	John Kruk	.05
77	Mickey Morandini	.05
78	Terry Mulholland	.05
79	Dale Murphy	.20
80	Mitch Williams	.05
81	Jay Bell	.05
82	Barry Bonds	1.00
83	Steve Buechele	.05
84	Doug Drabek	.05
85	Mike LaValliere	.05
86	Jose Lind	.05
87	Denny Neagle	.05
88	Randy Tomlin	.05
89	Andy Van Slyke	.05
90	Gary Varsho	.05
91	Pedro Guerrero	.05
92	Rex Hudler	.05
93	Brian Jordan	.05
94	Felix Jose	.05
95	Donovan Osborne	.05
96	Tom Pagnozzi	.05
97	Lee Smith	.05
98	Ozzie Smith	.50
99	Todd Worrell	.05
100	Todd Zeile	.05
101	Andy Benes	.05
102	Jerald Clark	.05
103	Tony Fernandez	.05
104	Tony Gwynn	.50
105	Greg Harris	.05
106	Fred McGriff	.05
107	Benito Santiago	.05
108	Gary Sheffield	.30
109	Kurt Stillwell	.05
110	Tim Teufel	.05
111	Kevin Bass	.05
112	Jeff Brantley	.05
113	John Burkett	.05
114	Will Clark	.05
115	Royce Clayton	.05
116	Mike Jackson	.05
117	Darren Lewis	.05
118	Bill Swift	.05
119	Robby Thompson	.05
120	Matt Williams	.05
121	Brady Anderson	.05
122	Glenn Davis	.05
123	Mike Devereaux	.05
124	Chris Hoiles	.05
125	Sam Horn	.05
126	Ben McDonald	.05
127	Mike Mussina	.25
128	Gregg Olson	.05
129	Cal Ripken, Jr.	1.00
130	Rick Sutcliffe	.05
131	Wade Boggs	.05
132	Roger Clemens	.60
133	Greg Harris	.05
134	Tim Naehring	.05
135	Tony Pena	.05
136	Phil Plantier	.05
137	Jeff Reardon	.05
138	Jody Reed	.05
139	Mo Vaughn	.05
140	Frank Viola	.05
141	Jim Abbott	.05
142	Hubie Brooks	.05
143	Chad Curtis RC	.05
144	Gary DiSarcina	.05
145	Chuck Finley	.05
146	Bryan Harvey	.05
147	Von Hayes	.05
148	Mark Langston	.05
149	Lance Parrish	.05
150	Lee Stevens	.05
151	George Bell	.05
152	Alex Fernandez	.05
153	Greg Hibbard	.05
154	Lance Johnson	.05
155	Kirk McCaskill	.05
156	Tim Raines	.05
157	Steve Sax	.05
158	Bobby Thigpen	.05
159	Frank Thomas	.45
160	Robin Ventura	.05
161	Sandy Alomar, Jr.	.05
162	Jack Armstrong	.05
163	Carlos Baerga	.05
164	Albert Belle	.05
165	Alex Cole	.05
166	Glenallen Hill	.05
167	Mark Lewis	.05
168	Kenny Lofton	.05
169	Paul Sorrento	.05
170	Mark Whiten	.05
171	Milt Cuyler (Color photo is Lou Whitaker.)	.05
172	Rob Deer	.05
173	Cecil Fielder	.05
174	Travis Fryman	.05
175	Mike Henneman	.05
176	Tony Phillips	.05
177	Frank Tanana	.05
178	Mickey Tettleton	.05
179	Alan Trammell	.05
180	Lou Whitaker	.05
181	George Brett	.60
182	Tom Gordon	.05
183	Mark Gubicza	.05
184	Gregg Jefferies	.05
185	Wally Joyner	.05
186	Brent Mayne	.05
187	Brian McRae	.05
188	Kevin McReynolds	.05
189	Keith Miller	.05
190	Jeff Montgomery	.05
191	Dante Bichette	.05
192	Ricky Bones	.05
193	Scott Fletcher	.05
194	Paul Molitor	.45
195	Jaime Navarro	.05
196	Franklin Stubbs	.05
197	B.J. Surhoff	.05
198	Greg Vaughn	.05
199	Bill Wegman	.05
200	Robin Yount	.45
201	Rick Aguilera	.05
202	Scott Erickson	.05
203	Greg Gagne	.05
204	Brian Harper	.05
205	Kent Hrbek	.05
206	Scott Leius	.05
207	Shane Mack	.05
208	Pat Mahomes	.05
209	Kirby Puckett	.50
210	John Smiley	.05
211	Mike Gallego	.05
212	Charlie Hayes	.05
213	Pat Kelly	.05
214	Roberto Kelly	.05
215	Kevin Maas	.05
216	Don Mattingly	.60
217	Matt Nokes	.05
218	Melido Perez	.05
219	Scott Sanderson	.05
220	Danny Tartabull	.05
221	Harold Baines	.05
222	Jose Canseco	.30
223	Dennis Eckersley	.35
224	Dave Henderson	.05
225	Carney Lansford	.05
226	Mark McGwire	.75
227	Mike Moore	.05
228	Randy Ready	.05
229	Terry Steinbach	.05
230	Dave Stewart	.05
231	Jay Buhner	.05
232	Ken Griffey Jr.	.65
233	Erik Hanson	.05
234	Randy Johnson	.45
235	Edgar Martinez	.05
236	Tino Martinez	.05
237	Kevin Mitchell	.05
238	Pete O'Brien	.05
239	Harold Reynolds	.05
240	David Valle	.05
241	Julio Franco	.05
242	Juan Gonzalez	.25
243	Jose Guzman	.05
244	Rafael Palmeiro	.35
245	Dean Palmer	.05
246	Ivan Rodriguez	.35
247	Jeff Russell	.05
248	Nolan Ryan	1.00
249	Ruben Sierra	.05
250	Dickie Thon	.05
251	Roberto Alomar	.20
252	Derek Bell	.05
253	Pat Borders	.05
254	Joe Carter	.05
255	Kelly Gruber	.05
256	Juan Guzman	.05
257	Jack Morris	.05
258	John Olerud	.05
259	Devon White	.05
260	Dave Winfield	.45
261	Checklist	.05
262	Checklist	.05
263	Checklist	.05
264	History Card	.05

1992 Studio Preview

CAL RIPKEN, JR.   PREVIEW
Baltimore Orioles

		NM/M
Complete Set (22):		75.00
Common Player:		1.50
1	Ruben Sierra	1.50
2	Kirby Puckett	6.00
3	Ryne Sandberg	6.00

4	John Kruk	1.50
5	Cal Ripken, Jr.	12.00
6	Robin Yount	4.50
7	Dwight Gooden	1.50
8	David Justice	1.50
9	Don Mattingly	7.50
10	Wally Joyner	1.50
11	Will Clark	1.50
12	Rob Dibble	1.50
13	Roberto Alomar	2.50
14	Wade Boggs	6.00
15	Barry Bonds	12.00
16	Jeff Bagwell	4.50
17	Mark McGwire	9.00
18	Frank Thomas	6.00
19	Brett Butler	1.50
20	Ozzie Smith	6.00
21	Jim Abbott	1.50
22	Tony Gwynn	6.00

Heritage

RYNE SANDBERG

		NM/M
Complete Set (14):		6.00
Common Player:		.50
1	Ryne Sandberg	1.00
2	Carlton Fisk	.75
3	Wade Boggs	1.00
4	Jose Canseco	.65
5	Don Mattingly	1.25
6	Darryl Strawberry	.50
7	Cal Ripken, Jr.	1.50
8	Will Clark	.50
9	Andre Dawson	.50
10	Andy Van Slyke	.50
11	Paul Molitor	.75
12	Jeff Bagwell	.75
13	Darren Daulton	.50
14	Kirby Puckett	1.00

1993 Studio

		NM/M
Complete Set (220):		15.00
Common Player:		.05
Pack (12):		.75
Wax Box (36):		12.50
1	Dennis Eckersley	.35
2	Chad Curtis	.05
3	Eric Anthony	.05
4	Roberto Alomar	.20
5	Steve Avery	.05
6	Cal Eldred	.05
7	Bernard Gilkey	.05
8	Steve Buechele	.05
9	Brett Butler	.05
10	Terry Mulholland	.05
11	Moises Alou	.05
12	Barry Bonds	1.00
13	Sandy Alomar Jr.	.05
14	Chris Bosio	.05
15	Scott Sanderson	.05
16	Bobby Bonilla	.05
17	Brady Anderson	.05
18	Derek Bell	.05
19	Wes Chamberlain	.05
20	Jay Bell	.05
21	Kevin Brown	.05
22	Roger Clemens	.60
23	Roberto Kelly	.05
24	Dante Bichette	.05
25	George Brett	.60
26	Rob Deer	.05
27	Brian Harper	.05
28	George Bell	.05
29	Jim Abbott	.05
30	Dave Henderson	.05
31	Wade Boggs	.50
32	Chili Davis	.05
33	Ellis Burks	.05
34	Jeff Bagwell	.40
35	Kent Hrbek	.05
36	Pat Borders	.05
37	Cecil Fielder	.05
38	Sid Bream	.05
39	Greg Gagne	.05
40	Darryl Hamilton	.05
41	Jerald Clark	.05
42	Mark Grace	.05
43	Barry Larkin	.05
44	John Burkett	.05
45	Scott Cooper	.05
46	Mike Lansing RC	.25
47	Jose Canseco	.30
48	Will Clark	.05
49	Carlos Garcia	.05
50	Carlos Baerga	.05
51	Darren Daulton	.05
52	Jay Buhner	.05
53	Andy Benes	.05
54	Jeff Conine	.05
55	Mike Devereaux	.05
56	Vince Coleman	.05
57	Terry Steinbach	.05
58	J.T. Snow RC	.40
59	Greg Swindell	.05
60	Devon White	.05
61	John Smoltz	.05
62	Todd Zeile	.05
63	Rick Wilkins	.05
64	Tim Wallach	.05
65	John Wetteland	.05
66	Matt Williams	.05
67	Paul Sorrento	.05
68	David Valle	.05
69	Walt Weiss	.05
70	John Franco	.05
71	Nolan Ryan	1.00
72	Frank Viola	.05
73	Chris Sabo	.05
74	David Nied	.05
75	Kevin McReynolds	.05
76	Lou Whitaker	.05
77	Dave Winfield	.40
78	Robin Ventura	.05
79	Spike Owen	.05
80	Cal Ripken, Jr.	1.00
81	Dan Walter	.05
82	Mitch Williams	.05
83	Tim Wakefield	.05
84	Rickey Henderson	.40
85	Gary DiSarcina	.05
86	Craig Biggio	.05
87	Joe Carter	.05
88	Ron Gant	.05
89	John Jaha	.05
90	Gregg Jefferies	.05
91	Jose Guzman	.05
92	Eric Karros	.05
93	Wil Cordero	.05
94	Royce Clayton	.05
95	Albert Belle	.65
96	Ken Griffey Jr.	.65
97	Orestes Destrade	.05
98	Tony Fernandez	.05
99	Leo Gomez	.05
100	Tony Gwynn	.50
101	Len Dykstra	.05
102	Jeff King	.05
103	Julio Franco	.05
104	Andre Dawson	.25
105	Randy Milligan	.05
106	Alex Cole	.05
107	Phil Hiatt	.05
108	Travis Fryman	.05
109	Chuck Knoblauch	.05
110	Bo Jackson	.10
111	Pat Kelly	.05
112	Bret Saberhagen	.05
113	Ruben Sierra	.05
114	Tim Salmon	.05
115	Doug Jones	.05
116	Ed Sprague	.05
117	Terry Pendleton	.05
118	Robin Yount	.40
119	Mark Whiten	.05
120	Checklist	.05
121	Sammy Sosa	.50
122	Darryl Strawberry	.05
123	Larry Walker	.05
124	Robby Thompson	.05
125	Carlos Martinez	.05
126	Edgar Martinez	.05
127	Benito Santiago	.05
128	Howard Johnson	.05
129	Harold Reynolds	.05
130	Craig Shipley	.05
131	Curt Schilling	.30
132	Andy Van Slyke	.05
133	Ivan Rodriguez	.35
134	Mo Vaughn	.05
135	Bip Roberts	.05
136	Charlie Hayes	.05
137	Brian McRae	.05
138	Mickey Tettleton	.05
139	Frank Thomas	.40
140	Paul O'Neill	.05
141	Mark McGwire	.75
142	Damion Easley	.05
143	Ken Caminiti	.05
144	Juan Guzman	.05
145	Tom Glavine	.25
146	Pat Listach	.05
147	Lee Smith	.05
148	Derrick May	.05
149	Ramon Martinez	.05
150	Delino DeShields	.05
151	Kirt Manwaring	.05
152	Reggie Jefferson	.05
153	Randy Johnson	.40
154	Dave Magadan	.05
155	Dwight Gooden	.05
156	Chris Hoiles	.05
157	Fred McGriff	.05
158	Dave Hollins	.05
159	Al Martin	.05
160	Juan Gonzalez	.20
161	Mike Greenwell	.05
162	Kevin Mitchell	.05
163	Andres Galarraga	.05
164	Wally Joyner	.05
165	Kirk Gibson	.05
166	Pedro Munoz	.05
167	Ozzie Guillen	.05
168	Jimmy Key	.05
169	Kevin Seitzer	.05
170	Luis Polonia	.05
171	Luis Gonzalez	.05
172	Paul Molitor	.40
173	Dave Justice	.05
174	B.J. Surhoff	.05
175	Ray Lankford	.05
176	Ryne Sandberg	.50
177	Jody Reed	.05
178	Marquis Grissom	.05
179	Willie McGee	.05
180	Kenny Lofton	.05
181	Junior Felix	.05
182	Jose Offerman	.05
183	John Kruk	.05
184	Orlando Merced	.05
185	Rafael Palmeiro	.35
186	Billy Hatcher	.05
187	Joe Oliver	.05
188	Joe Girardi	.05
189	Jose Lind	.05
190	Harold Baines	.05
191	Mike Pagliarulo	.05
192	Lance Johnson	.05
193	Don Mattingly	.60
194	Doug Drabek	.05
195	John Olerud	.05
196	Greg Maddux	.50
197	Greg Vaughn	.05
198	Tom Pagnozzi	.05
199	Willie Wilson	.05
200	Jack McDowell	.05
201	Mike Piazza	.65
202	Mike Mussina	.30
203	Charles Nagy	.05
204	Tino Martinez	.05
205	Charlie Hough	.05
206	Todd Hundley	.05
207	Gary Sheffield	.30
208	Mickey Morandini	.05
209	Don Slaught	.05
210	Dean Palmer	.05
211	Jose Rijo	.05
212	Vinny Castilla	.05
213	Tony Phillips	.05
214	Kirby Puckett	.50
215	Tim Raines	.05
216	Otis Nixon	.05
217	Ozzie Smith	.50
218	Jose Vizcaino	.05
220	Checklist	.05

Frank Thomas

FRANK THOMAS

		NM/M
Complete Set (5):		5.00
Common Card:		1.00
1	Childhood	1.00
2	Baseball Memories	1.00
3	Importance of Family	1.00
4	Performance	1.00
5	On Being a Role Model	1.00

Heritage

OZZIE SMITH

		NM/M
Complete Set (12):		12.00
Common Player:		.50
1	George Brett	2.00
2	Juan Gonzalez	.75
3	Roger Clemens	2.00
4	Mark McGwire	4.00
5	Mark Grace	.50
6	Ozzie Smith	1.50
7	Barry Larkin	.50
8	Frank Thomas	1.00
9	Carlos Baerga	.50
10	Eric Karros	.50
11	J.T. Snow	.50
12	John Kruk	.50

Silhouettes

JEFF BLAUSER

		NM/M
Complete Set (10):		7.00
Common Player:		.15
1	Frank Thomas	.65
2	Barry Bonds	3.00
3	Jeff Bagwell	.65
4	Juan Gonzalez	.40
5	Travis Fryman	.15
6	J.T. Snow	.15
7	John Kruk	.15
8	Jeff Blauser	.15
9	Mike Piazza	2.00
10	Nolan Ryan	3.00

Superstars on Canvas

		NM/M
Complete Set (10):		8.00
Common Player:		.25
1	Ken Griffey Jr.	1.50
2	Jose Canseco	.60
3	Mark McGwire	2.00
4	Mike Mussina	.50
5	Joe Carter	.25
6	Frank Thomas	1.00
7	Darren Daulton	.25
8	Mark Grace	.25
9	Andres Galarraga	.25
10	Barry Bonds	2.50

1994 Studio

		NM/M
Complete Set (220):		7.50
Common Player:		.05
Pack (12):		.45
Wax Box (36):		10.00
1	Dennis Eckersley	.45
2	Brent Gates	.05
3	Rickey Henderson	.55
4	Mark McGwire	1.00
5	Troy Neel	.05
6	Ruben Sierra	.05
7	Terry Steinbach	.05
8	Chad Curtis	.05
9	Chili Davis	.05
10	Gary DiSarcina	.05
11	Damion Easley	.05
12	Bo Jackson	.10
13	Mark Langston	.05
14	Eduardo Perez	.05
15	Tim Salmon	.05
16	Jeff Bagwell	.55
17	Craig Biggio	.05
18	Ken Caminiti	.05
19	Andujar Cedeno	.05
20	Doug Drabek	.05
21	Steve Finley	.05
22	Luis Gonzalez	.05
23	Darryl Kile	.05
24	Roberto Alomar	.20
25	Pat Borders	.05
26	Joe Carter	.05
27	Carlos Delgado	.40
28	Pat Hentgen	.05
29	Paul Molitor	.55
30	John Olerud	.05
31	Ed Sprague	.05
32	Devon White	.05
33	Steve Avery	.05
34	Tom Glavine	.25
35	David Justice	.05
36	Roberto Kelly	.05
37	Ryan Klesko	.05
38	Javier Lopez	.05
39	Greg Maddux	.60
40	Fred McGriff	.05
41	Terry Pendleton	.05
42	Ricky Bones	.05
43	Darryl Hamilton	.05
44	Brian Harper	.05
45	John Jaha	.05
46	Dave Nilsson	.05
47	Kevin Seitzer	.05
48	Greg Vaughn	.05
49	Turner Ward	.05
50	Bernard Gilkey	.05
51	Gregg Jefferies	.05
52	Ray Lankford	.05
53	Tom Pagnozzi	.05
54	Ozzie Smith	.60
55	Bob Tewksbury	.05
56	Mark Whiten	.05
57	Todd Zeile	.05
58	Steve Buechele	.05
59	Shawon Dunston	.05
60	Mark Grace	.05
61	Derrick May	.05
62	Tuffy Rhodes	.05
63	Ryne Sandberg	.60
64	Sammy Sosa	.60
65	Rick Wilkins	.05
66	Brett Butler	.05
67	Delino DeShields	.05
68	Orel Hershiser	.05
69	Eric Karros	.05
70	Raul Mondesi	.05
71	Jose Offerman	.05
72	Mike Piazza	.75
73	Tim Wallach	.05
74	Moises Alou	.05
75	Sean Berry	.05
76	Wil Cordero	.05
77	Cliff Floyd	.05
78	Marquis Grissom	.05
79	Ken Hill	.05
80	Larry Walker	.05
81	John Wetteland	.05
82	Rod Beck	.05
83	Barry Bonds	1.50
84	Royce Clayton	.05
85	Darren Lewis	.05
86	Willie McGee	.05
87	Bill Swift	.05
88	Robby Thompson	.05
89	Matt Williams	.05
90	Sandy Alomar Jr.	.05
91	Carlos Baerga	.05
92	Albert Belle	.05
93	Kenny Lofton	.05
94	Eddie Murray	.55
95	Manny Ramirez	.55
96	Paul Sorrento	.05
97	Jim Thome	.45
98	Rich Amaral	.05
99	Eric Anthony	.05
100	Jay Buhner	.05
101	Ken Griffey Jr.	.75
102	Randy Johnson	.55
103	Edgar Martinez	.05
104	Tino Martinez	.05
105	Kurt Abbott RC	.05
106	Bret Barberie	.05
107	Chuck Carr	.05
108	Jeff Conine	.05
109	Chris Hammond	.05
110	Bryan Harvey	.05
111	Benito Santiago	.05
112	Gary Sheffield	.30
113	Bobby Bonilla	.05
114	Dwight Gooden	.05
115	Todd Hundley	.05
116	Bobby Jones	.05
117	Jeff Kent	.05
118	Kevin McReynolds	.05
119	Bret Saberhagen	.05
120	Ryan Thompson	.05
121	Harold Baines	.05
122	Mike Devereaux	.05
123	Jeffrey Hammonds	.05
124	Ben McDonald	.05
125	Mike Mussina	.25
126	Rafael Palmeiro	.45
127	Cal Ripken, Jr.	1.50
128	Lee Smith	.05
129	Brad Ausmus	.05
130	Derek Bell	.05
131	Andy Benes	.05
132	Tony Gwynn	.60
133	Trevor Hoffman	.05
134	Scott Livingstone	.05
135	Phil Plantier	.05
136	Darren Daulton	.05
137	Mariano Duncan	.05
138	Len Dykstra	.05
139	Dave Hollins	.05
140	Pete Incaviglia	.05
141	Danny Jackson	.05
142	John Kruk	.05
143	Kevin Stocker	.05
144	Jay Bell	.05
145	Carlos Garcia	.05
146	Jeff King	.05
147	Al Martin	.05
148	Orlando Merced	.05
149	Don Slaught	.05
150	Andy Van Slyke	.05
151	Kevin Brown	.05
152	Jose Canseco	.40
153	Will Clark	.05
154	Juan Gonzalez	.30
155	David Hulse	.05
156	Dean Palmer	.05
157	Ivan Rodriguez	.45
158	Kenny Rogers	.05
159	Roger Clemens	.65
160	Scott Cooper	.05
161	Andre Dawson	.25
162	Mike Greenwell	.05
163	Otis Nixon	.05
164	Aaron Sele	.05
165	John Valentin	.05
166	Mo Vaughn	.05
167	Bret Boone	.05
168	Barry Larkin	.05
169	Kevin Mitchell	.05
170	Hal Morris	.05
171	Jose Rijo	.05
172	Deion Sanders	.05
173	Reggie Sanders	.05
174	John Smiley	.05
175	Dante Bichette	.05
176	Ellis Burks	.05
177	Andres Galarraga	.05
178	Joe Girardi	.05
179	Charlie Hayes	.05
180	Roberto Mejia	.05
181	Walt Weiss	.05
182	David Cone	.05
183	Gary Gaetti	.05
184	Greg Gagne	.05
185	Felix Jose	.05
186	Wally Joyner	.05
187	Mike Macfarlane	.05
188	Brian McRae	.05
189	Eric Davis	.05
190	Cecil Fielder	.05
191	Travis Fryman	.05
192	Tony Phillips	.05
193	Mickey Tettleton	.05
194	Alan Trammell	.05
195	Lou Whitaker	.05
196	Kent Hrbek	.05
197	Chuck Knoblauch	.05
198	Shane Mack	.05
199	Pat Meares	.05
200	Kirby Puckett	.60
201	Matt Walbeck	.05
202	Dave Winfield	.55
203	Wilson Alvarez	.05
204	Alex Fernandez	.05
205	Julio Franco	.05
206	Ozzie Guillen	.05
207	Jack McDowell	.05
208	Tim Raines	.05
209	Frank Thomas	.55
210	Robin Ventura	.05
211	Jim Abbott	.05
212	Wade Boggs	.60
213	Pat Kelly	.05
214	Jimmy Key	.05
215	Don Mattingly	.65
216	Paul O'Neill	.05
217	Mike Stanley	.05
218	Danny Tartabull	.05
219	Checklist	.05
220	Checklist	.05

Gold Stars

		NM/M
Complete Set (10):		80.00
Common Player:		4.50
1	Tony Gwynn	9.00
2	Barry Bonds	16.00
3	Frank Thomas	7.50
4	Ken Griffey Jr.	12.50
5	Joe Carter	4.50
6	Mike Piazza	12.50
7	Cal Ripken, Jr.	16.00
8	Greg Maddux	9.00
9	Juan Gonzalez	5.00
10	Don Mattingly	10.00

Silver Stars

		NM/M
Complete Set (10):		35.00
Common Player:		1.50
1	Tony Gwynn	3.50
2	Barry Bonds	7.50
3	Frank Thomas	2.50
4	Ken Griffey Jr.	4.50
5	Joe Carter	1.50
6	Mike Piazza	4.50
7	Cal Ripken, Jr.	7.50
8	Greg Maddux	3.50
9	Juan Gonzalez	2.00
10	Don Mattingly	4.00

Editor's Choice

		NM/M
Complete Set (8):		12.00
Common Player:		.50
1	Barry Bonds	3.00
2	Frank Thomas	1.50
3	Ken Griffey Jr.	2.50
4	Andres Galarraga	.50
5	Juan Gonzalez	.75
6	Tim Salmon	.50
7	Paul O'Neill	.50
8	Mike Piazza	2.50

Heritage

	NM/M
Complete Set (8):	9.00

Common Player:		.50
1	Barry Bonds	4.00
2	Frank Thomas	1.50
3	Joe Carter	.50
4	Don Mattingly	3.00
5	Ryne Sandberg	2.00
6	Javier Lopez	.50
7	Gregg Jefferies	.50
8	Mike Mussina	.65

1995 Studio

		NM/M
Complete Set (200):		25.00
Common Player:		.05
Pack (5):		1.00
Wax Box (36):		20.00
1	Frank Thomas	.75
2	Jeff Bagwell	.75
3	Don Mattingly	1.25
4	Mike Piazza	1.50
5	Ken Griffey Jr.	1.50
6	Greg Maddux	1.00
7	Barry Bonds	2.50
8	Cal Ripken Jr.	2.50
9	Jose Canseco	.40
10	Paul Molitor	.75
11	Kenny Lofton	.05
12	Will Clark	.05
13	Tim Salmon	.05
14	Joe Carter	.05
15	Albert Belle	.05
16	Roger Clemens	1.25
17	Roberto Alomar	.30
18	Alex Rodriguez	2.00
19	Raul Mondesi	.05
20	Deion Sanders	.05
21	Juan Gonzalez	.40
22	Kirby Puckett	1.00
23	Fred McGriff	.05
24	Matt Williams	.05
25	Tony Gwynn	1.00
26	Cliff Floyd	.05
27	Travis Fryman	.05
28	Shawn Green	.30
29	Mike Mussina	.35
30	Bob Hamelin	.05
31	Dave Justice	.05
32	Manny Ramirez	.75
33	David Cone	.05
34	Marquis Grissom	.05
35	Moises Alou	.05
36	Carlos Baerga	.05
37	Barry Larkin	.05
38	Robin Ventura	.05
39	Mo Vaughn	.05
40	Jeffrey Hammonds	.05
41	Ozzie Smith	1.00
42	Andres Galarraga	.05
43	Carlos Delgado	.50
44	Lenny Dykstra	.05
45	Cecil Fielder	.05
46	Wade Boggs	1.00
47	Gregg Jefferies	.05
48	Randy Johnson	.75
49	Rafael Palmeiro	.65
50	Craig Biggio	.05
51	Steve Avery	.05
52	Ricky Bottalico	.05
53	Chris Gomez	.05
54	Carlos Garcia	.05
55	Brian Anderson	.05
56	Wilson Alvarez	.05
57	Roberto Kelly	.05
58	Larry Walker	.05
59	Dean Palmer	.05
60	Rick Aguilera	.05
61	Javy Lopez	.05
62	Shawon Dunston	.05
63	William Van Landingham	.05
64	Jeff Kent	.05
65	David McCarty	.05
66	Armando Benitez	.05
67	Brett Butler	.05
68	Bernard Gilkey	.05
69	Joey Hamilton	.05
70	Chad Curtis	.05
71	Dante Bichette	.05
72	Chuck Carr	.05
73	Pedro Martinez	.75
74	Ramon Martinez	.05
75	Rondell White	.05

76	Alex Fernandez	.05
77	Dennis Martinez	.05
78	Sammy Sosa	1.00
79	Bernie Williams	.05
80	Lou Whitaker	.05
81	Kurt Abbott	.05
82	Tino Martinez	.05
83	Willie Greene	.05
84	Garret Anderson	.05
85	Jose Rijo	.05
86	Jeff Montgomery	.05
87	Mark Langston	.05
88	Reggie Sanders	.05
89	Rusty Greer	.05
90	Delino DeShields	.05
91	Jason Bere	.05
92	Lee Smith	.05
93	Devon White	.05
94	John Wetteland	.05
95	Luis Gonzalez	.05
96	Greg Vaughn	.05
97	Lance Johnson	.05
98	Alan Trammell	.05
99	Bret Saberhagen	.05
100	Jack McDowell	.05
101	Trevor Hoffman	.05
102	Dave Nilsson	.05
103	Bryan Harvey	.05
104	Chuck Knoblauch	.05
105	Bobby Bonilla	.05
106	Hal Morris	.05
107	Mark Whiten	.05
108	Phil Plantier	.05
109	Ryan Klesko	.05
110	Greg Gagne	.05
111	Ruben Sierra	.05
112	J.R. Phillips	.05
113	Terry Steinbach	.05
114	Jay Buhner	.05
115	Ken Caminiti	.05
116	Gary DiSarcina	.05
117	Ivan Rodriguez	.65
118	Bip Roberts	.05
119	Jay Bell	.05
120	Ken Hill	.05
121	Mike Greenwell	.05
122	Rick Wilkins	.05
123	Rickey Henderson	.75
124	Dave Hollins	.05
125	Terry Pendleton	.05
126	Rich Becker	.05
127	Billy Ashley	.05
128	Derek Bell	.05
129	Dennis Eckersley	.65
130	Andujar Cedeno	.05
131	John Jaha	.05
132	Chuck Finley	.05
133	Steve Finley	.05
134	Danny Tartabull	.05
135	Jeff Conine	.05
136	Jon Lieber	.05
137	Jim Abbott	.05
138	Steve Traschel	.05
139	Bret Boone	.05
140	Charles Johnson	.05
141	Mark McGwire	2.00
142	Eddie Murray	.75
143	Doug Drabek	.05
144	Steve Cooke	.05
145	Kevin Seitzer	.05
146	Rod Beck	.05
147	Eric Karros	.05
148	Tim Raines	.05
149	Joe Girardi	.05
150	Aaron Sele	.05
151	Robby Thompson	.05
152	Chan Ho Park	.05
153	Ellis Burks	.05
154	Brian McRae	.05
155	Jimmy Key	.05
156	Rico Brogna	.05
157	Ozzie Guillen	.05
158	Chili Davis	.05
159	Darren Daulton	.05
160	Chipper Jones	1.00
161	Walt Weiss	.05
162	Paul O'Neill	.05
163	Al Martin	.05
164	John Valentin	.05
165	Tim Wallach	.05
166	Scott Erickson	.05
167	Ryan Thompson	.05
168	Todd Zeile	.05
169	Scott Cooper	.05
170	Matt Mieske	.05
171	Allen Watson	.05
172	Brian Hunter	.05
173	Kevin Stocker	.05
174	Cal Eldred	.05
175	Tony Phillips	.05
176	Ben McDonald	.05
177	Mark Grace	.05
178	Midre Cummings	.05
179	Orlando Merced	.05

180	Jeff King	.05
181	Gary Sheffield	.40
182	Tom Glavine	.35
183	Edgar Martinez	.05
184	Steve Karsay	.05
185	Pat Listach	.05
186	Wil Cordero	.05
187	Brady Anderson	.05
188	Bobby Jones	.05
189	Andy Benes	.05
190	Ray Lankford	.05
191	John Doherty	.05
192	Wally Joyner	.05
193	Jim Thome	.65
194	Royce Clayton	.05
195	John Olerud	.05
196	Steve Buechele	.05
197	Harold Baines	.05
198	Geronimo Berroa	.05
199	Checklist	.05
200	Checklist	.05

Gold

		NM/M
Complete Set (50):		25.00
Common Player:		.15
1	Frank Thomas	1.00
2	Jeff Bagwell	1.00
3	Don Mattingly	1.75
4	Mike Piazza	2.00
5	Ken Griffey Jr.	2.00
6	Greg Maddux	1.50
7	Barry Bonds	3.00
8	Cal Ripken Jr.	3.00
9	Jose Canseco	.50
10	Paul Molitor	1.00
11	Kenny Lofton	.15
12	Will Clark	.15
13	Tim Salmon	.15
14	Joe Carter	.15
15	Albert Belle	.15
16	Roger Clemens	1.75
17	Roberto Alomar	.35
18	Alex Rodriguez	2.50
19	Raul Mondesi	.15
20	Deion Sanders	.15
21	Juan Gonzalez	.50
22	Kirby Puckett	1.50
23	Fred McGriff	.15
24	Matt Williams	.15
25	Tony Gwynn	1.50
26	Cliff Floyd	.15
27	Travis Fryman	.15
28	Shawn Green	.40
29	Mike Mussina	.35
30	Bob Hamelin	.15
31	Dave Justice	.15
32	Manny Ramirez	1.00
33	David Cone	.15
34	Marquis Grissom	.15
35	Moises Alou	.15
36	Carlos Baerga	.15
37	Barry Larkin	.15
38	Robin Ventura	.15
39	Mo Vaughn	.15
40	Jeffrey Hammonds	.15
41	Ozzie Smith	1.50
42	Andres Galarraga	.15
43	Carlos Delgado	.50
44	Lenny Dykstra	.15
45	Cecil Fielder	.15
46	Wade Boggs	1.50
47	Gregg Jefferies	.15
48	Randy Johnson	1.00
49	Rafael Palmeiro	.75
50	Craig Biggio	.15

Platinum

		NM/M
Complete Set (25):		25.00
Common Player:		.50

1	Frank Thomas	2.00
2	Jeff Bagwell	2.00
3	Don Mattingly	3.25
4	Mike Piazza	3.50
5	Ken Griffey Jr.	3.50
6	Greg Maddux	3.00
7	Barry Bonds	5.00
8	Cal Ripken Jr.	5.00
9	Jose Canseco	1.00
10	Paul Molitor	2.00
11	Kenny Lofton	.50
12	Will Clark	.50
13	Tim Salmon	.50
14	Joe Carter	.50
15	Albert Belle	.50
16	Roger Clemens	3.25
17	Roberto Alomar	.75
18	Alex Rodriguez	4.00
19	Raul Mondesi	.50
20	Deion Sanders	.50
21	Juan Gonzalez	1.00
22	Kirby Puckett	3.00
23	Fred McGriff	.50
24	Matt Williams	.50
25	Tony Gwynn	3.00

1996 Studio

		NM/M
Complete Set (150):		9.00
Common Player:		.05
Pack (7):		1.25
Wax Box (24):		20.00
1	Cal Ripken Jr.	1.50
2	Alex Gonzalez	.05
3	Roger Cedeno	.05
4	Todd Hollandsworth	.05
5	Gregg Jefferies	.05
6	Ryne Sandberg	.65
7	Eric Karros	.05
8	Jeff Conine	.05
9	Rafael Palmeiro	.45
10	Bip Roberts	.05
11	Roger Clemens	.70
12	Tom Glavine	.30
13	Jason Giambi	.40
14	Rey Ordonez	.05
15	Chan Ho Park	.05
16	Vinny Castilla	.05
17	Butch Huskey	.05
18	Greg Maddux	.65
19	Bernard Gilkey	.05
20	Marquis Grissom	.05
21	Chuck Knoblauch	.05
22	Ozzie Smith	.65
23	Garret Anderson	.05
24	J.T. Snow	.05
25	John Valentin	.05
26	Barry Larkin	.05
27	Bobby Bonilla	.05
28	Todd Zeile	.05
29	Roberto Alomar	.20
30	Ramon Martinez	.05
31	Jeff King	.05
32	Dennis Eckersley	.45
33	Derek Jeter	1.50
34	Edgar Martinez	.05
35	Geronimo Berroa	.05
36	Hal Morris	.05
37	Troy Percival	.05
38	Jason Isringhausen	.05
39	Greg Vaughn	.05
40	Robin Ventura	.05
41	Craig Biggio	.05
42	Will Clark	.05
43	Sammy Sosa	.65
44	Bernie Williams	.05
45	Kenny Lofton	.05
46	Wade Boggs	.65
47	Javy Lopez	.05
48	Reggie Sanders	.05
49	Jeff Bagwell	.55
50	Fred McGriff	.05
51	Charles Johnson	.05

52	Darren Daulton	.05
53	Jose Canseco	.40
54	Cecil Fielder	.05
55	Hideo Nomo	.30
56	Tim Salmon	.05
57	Carlos Delgado	.40
58	David Cone	.05
59	Tim Raines	.05
60	Lyle Mouton	.05
61	Wally Joyner	.05
62	Bret Boone	.05
63	Raul Mondesi	.05
64	Gary Sheffield	.35
65	Alex Rodriguez	1.00
66	Russ Davis	.05
67	Checklist	
68	Marty Cordova	.05
69	Ruben Sierra	.05
70	Jose Mesa	.05
71	Matt Williams	.05
72	Chipper Jones	.65
73	Randy Johnson	.55
74	Kirby Puckett	.65
75	Jim Edmonds	.05
76	Barry Bonds	1.50
77	David Segui	.05
78	Larry Walker	.05
79	Jason Kendall	.05
80	Mike Piazza	.75
81	Brian Hunter	.05
82	Julio Franco	.05
83	Jay Bell	.05
84	Kevin Seitzer	.05
85	John Smoltz	.05
86	Joe Carter	.05
87	Ray Durham	.05
88	Carlos Baerga	.05
89	Ron Gant	.05
90	Orlando Merced	.05
91	Lee Smith	.05
92	Pedro Martinez	.55
93	Frank Thomas	.55
94	Al Martin	.05
95	Chad Curtis	.05
96	Eddie Murray	.55
97	Rusty Greer	.05
98	Jay Buhner	.05
99	Rico Brogna	.05
100	Todd Hundley	.05
101	Moises Alou	.05
102	Chili Davis	.05
103	Ismael Valdes	.05
104	Mo Vaughn	.05
105	Juan Gonzalez	.30
106	Mark Grudzielanek	.05
107	Derek Bell	.05
108	Shawn Green	.30
109	David Justice	.05
110	Paul O'Neill	.05
111	Kevin Appier	.05
112	Ray Lankford	.05
113	Travis Fryman	.05
114	Manny Ramirez	.55
115	Brooks Kieschnick	.05
116	Ken Griffey Jr.	.75
117	Jeffrey Hammonds	.05
118	Mark McGwire	1.00
119	Denny Neagle	.05
120	Quilvio Veras	.05
121	Alan Benes	.05
122	Rondell White	.05
123	Osvaldo Fernandez RC	.20
124	Andres Galarraga	.05
125	Johnny Damon	.35
126	Lenny Dykstra	.05
127	Jason Schmidt	.05
128	Mike Mussina	.30
129	Ken Caminiti	.05
130	Michael Tucker	.05
131	LaTroy Hawkins	.05
132	Checklist	
133	Delino DeShields	.05
134	Dave Nilsson	.05
135	Jack McDowell	.05
136	Joey Hamilton	.05
137	Dante Bichette	.05
138	Paul Molitor	.55
139	Ivan Rodriguez	.45
140	Mark Grace	.05
141	Paul Wilson	.05
142	Orel Hershiser	.05
143	Albert Belle	.05
144	Tino Martinez	.05
145	Tony Gwynn	.65
146	George Arias	.05
147	Brian Jordan	.05
148	Brian McRae	.05
149	Rickey Henderson	.55
150	Ryan Klesko	.05

Press Proofs

	NM/M
Common Player, Bronze:	.50
Bronze Stars:	3X

Common Player, Gold:	1.00
Gold Stars:	7X
Common Player, Silver:	4.00
Silver Stars:	25X

(See 1996 Studio for checklist, base card values.)

Hit Parade

		NM/M
Complete Set (10):		10.00
Common Player:		.75
1	Tony Gwynn	1.50
2	Ken Griffey Jr.	2.00
3	Frank Thomas	1.00
4	Jeff Bagwell	1.00
5	Kirby Puckett	1.50
6	Mike Piazza	2.00
7	Barry Bonds	2.50
8	Albert Belle	.75
9	Tim Salmon	.75
10	Mo Vaughn	.75

Masterstrokes

		NM/M
Complete Set (8):		30.00
Common Player:		4.00
Samples:		75 Percent
1	Tony Gwynn	6.00
2	Mike Piazza	8.00
3	Jeff Bagwell	4.00
4	Manny Ramirez	4.00
5	Cal Ripken Jr.	12.00
6	Frank Thomas	4.00
7	Ken Griffey Jr.	8.00
8	Greg Maddux	6.00

Stained Glass Stars

		NM/M
Complete Set (12):		24.00
Common Player:		1.00
1	Cal Ripken Jr.	5.00
2	Ken Griffey Jr.	3.50
3	Frank Thomas	2.00
4	Greg Maddux	2.50
5	Chipper Jones	2.50
6	Mike Piazza	3.50
7	Albert Belle	1.00
8	Jeff Bagwell	2.00
9	Hideo Nomo	1.50
10	Barry Bonds	5.00
11	Manny Ramirez	2.00
12	Kenny Lofton	1.00

1997 Studio

		NM/M
Complete Set (165):		17.50
Common Player:		.05
Pack (5):		3.00
Wax Box (18):		40.00
1	Frank Thomas	.65
2	Gary Sheffield	.45
3	Jason Isringhausen	.05
4	Ron Gant	.05
5	Andy Pettitte	.25
6	Todd Hollandsworth	.05
7	Troy Percival	.05
8	Mark McGwire	1.50
9	Barry Larkin	.05
10	Ken Caminiti	.05
11	Paul Molitor	.65
12	Travis Fryman	.05
13	Kevin Brown	.05
14	Robin Ventura	.05
15	Andres Galarraga	.05
16	Ken Griffey Jr.	1.00
17	Roger Clemens	.85
18	Alan Benes	.05
19	David Justice	.05
20	Damon Buford	.05
21	Mike Piazza	1.00
22	Ray Durham	.05
23	Billy Wagner	.05
24	Dean Palmer	.05
25	David Cone	.05
26	Ruben Sierra	.05
27	Henry Rodriguez	.05
28	Ray Lankford	.05
29	Jamey Wright	.05
30	Brady Anderson	.05
31	Tino Martinez	.05
32	Manny Ramirez	.65
33	Jeff Conine	.05
34	Dante Bichette	.05
35	Jose Canseco	.50
36	Mo Vaughn	.05
37	Sammy Sosa	.75
38	Mark Grudzielanek	.05
39	Mike Mussina	.35
40	Bill Pulsipher	.05
41	Ryne Sandberg	.75
42	Rickey Henderson	.65
43	Alex Rodriguez	1.50
44	Eddie Murray	.65
45	Ernie Young	.05
46	Joey Hamilton	.05
47	Wade Boggs	.75
48	Rusty Greer	.05
49	Carlos Delgado	.50
50	Ellis Burks	.05
51	Cal Ripken Jr.	2.00

52	Alex Fernandez	.05
53	Wally Joyner	.05
54	James Baldwin	.05
55	Juan Gonzalez	.35
56	John Smoltz	.05
57	Omar Vizquel	.05
58	Shane Reynolds	.05
59	Barry Bonds	2.00
60	Jason Kendall	.05
61	Marty Cordova	.05
62	Charles Johnson	.05
63	John Jaha	.05
64	Chan Ho Park	.05
65	Jermaine Allensworth	.05
66	Mark Grace	.05
67	Tim Salmon	.05
68	Edgar Martinez	.05
69	Marquis Grissom	.05
70	Craig Biggio	.05
71	Bobby Higginson	.05
72	Kevin Seitzer	.05
73	Hideo Nomo	.35
74	Dennis Eckersley	.60
75	Bobby Bonilla	.05
76	Dwight Gooden	.05
77	Jeff Cirillo	.05
78	Brian McRae	.05
79	Chipper Jones	.75
80	Jeff Fassero	.05
81	Fred McGriff	.05
82	Garret Anderson	.05
83	Eric Karros	.05
84	Derek Bell	.05
85	Kenny Lofton	.05
86	John Mabry	.05
87	Pat Hentgen	.05
88	Greg Maddux	.75
89	Jason Giambi	.45
90	Al Martin	.05
91	Derek Jeter	2.00
92	Rey Ordonez	.05
93	Will Clark	.05
94	Kevin Appier	.05
95	Roberto Alomar	.30
96	Joe Carter	.05
97	Bernie Williams	.05
98	Albert Belle	.05
99	Greg Vaughn	.05
100	Tony Clark	.05
101	Matt Williams	.05
102	Jeff Bagwell	.65
103	Reggie Sanders	.05
104	Mariano Rivera	.15
105	Larry Walker	.05
106	Shawn Green	.30
107	Alex Ochoa	.05
108	Ivan Rodriguez	.60
109	Eric Young	.05
110	Javier Lopez	.05
111	Brian Hunter	.05
112	Raul Mondesi	.05
113	Randy Johnson	.65
114	Tony Phillips	.05
115	Carlos Garcia	.05
116	Moises Alou	.05
117	Paul O'Neill	.05
118	Jim Thome	.60
119	Jermaine Dye	.05
120	Wilson Alvarez	.05
121	Rondell White	.05
122	Michael Tucker	.05
123	Mike Lansing	.05
124	Tony Gwynn	.75
125	Ryan Klesko	.05
126	Jim Edmonds	.05
127	Chuck Knoblauch	.05
128	Rafael Palmeiro	.60
129	Jay Buhner	.05
130	Tom Glavine	.35
131	Julio Franco	.05
132	Cecil Fielder	.05
133	Paul Wilson	.05
134	Deion Sanders	.05
135	Alex Gonzalez	.05
136	Charles Nagy	.05
137	Andy Ashby	.05
138	Edgar Renteria	.05
139	Pedro Martinez	.65
140	Brian Jordan	.05
141	Todd Hundley	.05
142	Marc Newfield	.05
143	Darryl Strawberry	.05
144	Dan Wilson	.05
145	Brian Giles RC	.50
146	Bartolo Colon	.05
147	Shannon Stewart	.05
148	Scott Spiezio	.05
149	Andruw Jones	.65
150	Karim Garcia	.05
151	Vladimir Guerrero	.65
152	George Arias	.05
153	Brooks Kieschnick	.05
154	Todd Walker	.05
155	Scott Rolen	.60

156	Todd Greene	.05
157	Dmitri Young	.05
158	Ruben Rivera	.05
159	Trey Beamon	.05
160	Nomar Garciaparra	.75
161	Bob Abreu	.05
162	Darin Erstad	.15
163	Ken Griffey Jr. (Checklist)	.50
164	Frank Thomas (Checklist)	.35
165	Alex Rodriguez (Checklist)	.75

Press Proofs

John Smoltz

		NM/M
Common Player, Silver:		.50
Silver Stars:		4X
Common Player, Gold:		1.00
Gold Stars:		8X
(See 1997 Studio for checklist and base card values.)		

Hard Hats

		NM/M
Complete Set (24):		50.00
Common Player:		1.50
1	Ivan Rodriguez	3.00
2	Albert Belle	1.50
3	Ken Griffey Jr.	6.00
4	Chuck Knoblauch	1.50
5	Frank Thomas	4.00
6	Cal Ripken Jr.	8.00
7	Todd Walker	1.50
8	Alex Rodriguez	7.00
9	Jim Thome	3.00
10	Mike Piazza	6.00
11	Barry Larkin	1.50
12	Chipper Jones	5.00
13	Derek Jeter	8.00
14	Jermaine Dye	1.50
15	Jason Giambi	2.00
16	Tim Salmon	1.50
17	Brady Anderson	1.50
18	Rondell White	1.50
19	Bernie Williams	1.50
20	Juan Gonzalez	2.00
21	Karim Garcia	1.50
22	Scott Rolen	3.00
23	Darin Erstad	2.00
24	Brian Jordan	1.50

Master Strokes

		NM/M
Complete Set (24):		120.00
Common Player:		2.00
1	Derek Jeter	12.00
2	Jeff Bagwell	4.50
3	Ken Griffey Jr.	8.00
4	Barry Bonds	12.00
5	Frank Thomas	4.50
6	Andy Pettitte	2.25
7	Mo Vaughn	2.00
8	Alex Rodriguez	10.00
9	Andruw Jones	4.50
10	Kenny Lofton	2.00
11	Cal Ripken Jr.	12.00
12	Greg Maddux	6.00
13	Manny Ramirez	4.50

14	Mike Piazza	8.00
14p	Mike Piazza (Promo)	3.50
15	Vladimir Guerrero	4.50
16	Albert Belle	2.00
17	Chipper Jones	6.00
18	Hideo Nomo	2.50
19	Sammy Sosa	6.00
20	Tony Gwynn	6.00
21	Gary Sheffield	2.50
22	Mark McGwire	10.00
23	Juan Gonzalez	2.50
24	Paul Molitor	4.50

Master Strokes 8x10

Alex Rodriguez • Mariners

		NM/M
Complete Set (24):		45.00
Common Player:		.75
1	Derek Jeter	5.00
2	Jeff Bagwell	2.00
3	Ken Griffey Jr.	3.00
4	Barry Bonds	5.00
5	Frank Thomas	2.00
6	Andy Pettitte	1.00
7	Mo Vaughn	.75
8	Alex Rodriguez	4.00
9	Andruw Jones	2.00
10	Kenny Lofton	.75
11	Cal Ripken Jr.	5.00
12	Greg Maddux	2.50
13	Manny Ramirez	2.00
14	Mike Piazza	3.00
15	Vladimir Guerrero	2.00
16	Albert Belle	.75
17	Chipper Jones	2.50
18	Hideo Nomo	1.50
19	Sammy Sosa	2.50
20	Tony Gwynn	2.50
21	Gary Sheffield	1.50
22	Mark McGwire	4.00
23	Juan Gonzalez	1.50
24	Paul Molitor	2.00

Portraits

Hideo Nomo

	NM/M
Complete Set (24):	10.00

Common Player:		.25
1	Ken Griffey Jr.	1.00
1s	Frank Thomas/OPS	.75
2	Frank Thomas	.65
3	Alex Rodriguez	1.50
4	Andruw Jones	.65
5	Cal Ripken Jr.	2.00
6	Greg Maddux	.75
7	Mike Piazza	1.00
8	Chipper Jones	.75
9	Albert Belle	.25
10	Derek Jeter	2.00
11	Juan Gonzalez	.45
12	Todd Walker	.25
12a	Todd Walker (Autographed edition of 1,250.)	10.00
13	Mark McGwire	1.50
14	Barry Bonds	2.00
15	Jeff Bagwell	.65
16	Manny Ramirez	.65
17	Kenny Lofton	.25
18	Mo Vaughn	.25
19	Hideo Nomo	.45
20	Tony Gwynn	.75
21	Vladimir Guerrero	.65
21a	Vladimir Guerrero (Autographed edition of 500.)	30.00
22	Gary Sheffield	.45
23	Ryne Sandberg	.75
24	Scott Rolen	.50
24a	Scott Rolen (Autographed edition of 1,000.)	12.00

Portrait Collection

	NM/M
Complete Set, Studio Portrait (24):	2,850
Complete Set, Master Strokes (24):	5,250
Common Plaque, Studio Portrait:	125.00
Common Plaque, Master Strokes:	225.00
P1 Ken Griffey Jr.	125.00
P2 Frank Thomas	125.00
P3 Alex Rodriguez	125.00
P4 Andruw Jones	125.00
P5 Cal Ripken Jr.	125.00
P6 Greg Maddux	125.00
P7 Mike Piazza	125.00
P8 Chipper Jones	125.00
P9 Albert Belle	125.00
P10 Derek Jeter	125.00
P11 Juan Gonzalez	125.00
P12 Todd Walker	125.00
P13 Mark McGwire	125.00
P14 Barry Bonds	125.00
P15 Jeff Bagwell	125.00
P16 Manny	125.00
P17 Kenny Lofton	125.00
P18 Mo Vaughn	125.00
P19 Hideo Nomo	125.00
P20 Tony Gwynn	125.00
P21 Vladimir Guerrero	125.00
P22 Gary Sheffield	125.00
P23 Ryne Sandberg	125.00
P24 Scott Rolen	125.00
M1 Derek Jeter	225.00
M2 Jeff Bagwell	225.00
M3 Ken Griffey Jr.	225.00
M4 Barry Bonds	225.00
M5 Frank Thomas	225.00
M6 Andy Pettitte	225.00
M7 Mo Vaughn	225.00
M8 Alex Rodriguez	225.00
M9 Andruw Jones	225.00
M10 Kenny Lofton	225.00
M11 Cal Ripken Jr.	225.00
M12 Greg Maddux	225.00
M13 Manny Ramirez	225.00
M14 Mike Piazza	225.00
M15 Vladimir Guerrero	225.00
M16 Albert Belle	225.00
M17 Chipper Jones	225.00
M18 Hideo Nomo	225.00
M19 Sammy Sosa	225.00
M20 Tony Gwynn	225.00
M21 Gary Sheffield	225.00
M22 Mark McGwire	225.00
M23 Juan Gonzalez	225.00
M24 Paul Molitor	225.00

1998 Studio

		NM/M
Complete Set (220):		25.00
Common Player:		.05
Pack (7 Cards+8x10)		2.00
Wax Box (18):		20.00
1	Tony Clark	.05
2	Jose Cruz Jr.	.65
3	Ivan Rodriguez	.65
4	Mo Vaughn	.05
5	Kenny Lofton	.05

Andruw Jones

6	Will Clark	.05
7	Barry Larkin	.05
8	Jay Bell	.05
9	Kevin Young	.05
10	Francisco Cordova	.05
11	Justin Thompson	.05
12	Paul Molitor	.75
13	Jeff Bagwell	.75
14	Jose Canseco	.45
15	Scott Rolen	.65
16	Wilton Guerrero	.05
17	Shannon Stewart	.05
18	Hideki Irabu	.05
19	Michael Tucker	.05
20	Joe Carter	.05
21	Gabe Alvarez	.05
22	Ricky Ledee	.05
23	Karim Garcia	.05
24	Eli Marrero	.05
25	Scott Elarton	.05
26	Mario Valdez	.05
27	Ben Grieve	.05
28	Paul Konerko	.15
29	Esteban Yan RC	.05
30	Esteban Loaiza	.05
31	Delino DeShields	.05
32	Bernie Williams	.05
33	Joe Randa	.05
34	Randy Johnson	.75
35	Brett Tomko	.05
36	Todd Erdos RC	.05
37	Bobby Higginson	.05
38	Jason Kendall	.05
39	Ray Lankford	.05
40	Mark Grace	.05
41	Andy Pettitte	.25
42	Alex Rodriguez	2.00
43	Hideo Nomo	.45
44	Sammy Sosa	1.00
45	J.T. Snow	.05
46	Jason Varitek	.05
47	Vinny Castilla	.05
48	Neifi Perez	.05
49	Todd Walker	.05
50	Mike Cameron	.05
51	Jeffrey Hammonds	.05
52	Deivi Cruz	.05
53	Brian Hunter	.05
54	Al Martin	.05
55	Ron Coomer	.05
56	Chan Ho Park	.05
57	Pedro Martinez	.75
58	Darin Erstad	.15
59	Albert Belle	.05
60	Nomar Garciaparra	1.00
61	Tony Gwynn	1.00
62	Mike Piazza	1.50
63	Todd Helton	.65
64	David Ortiz	.45
65	Todd Dunwoody	.05
66	Orlando Cabrera	.05
67	Ken Cloude	.05
68	Andy Benes	.05
69	Mariano Rivera	.15
70	Cecil Fielder	.05
71	Brian Jordan	.05
72	Darryl Kile	.05
73	Reggie Jefferson	.05
74	Shawn Estes	.05
75	Bobby Bonilla	.05
76	Denny Neagle	.05
77	Robin Ventura	.05
78	Omar Vizquel	.05
79	Craig Biggio	.05
80	Moises Alou	.05
81	Garret Anderson	.05
82	Eric Karros	.05
83	Dante Bichette	.05
84	Charles Johnson	.05
85	Rusty Greer	.05
86	Travis Fryman	.05
87	Fernando Tatis	.05
88	Wilson Alvarez	.05

89	Carl Pavano	.05
90	Brian Rose	.05
91	Geoff Jenkins	.05
92	Magglio Ordonez RC	1.50
93	David Segui	.05
94	David Cone	.05
95	John Smoltz	.05
96	Jim Thome	.65
97	Gary Sheffield	.45
98	Barry Bonds	2.50
99	Andres Galarraga	.05
100	Brad Fullmer	.05
101	Bobby Estalella	.05
102	Enrique Wilson	.05
103	Frank Catalanotto RC	.25
104	Mike Lowell RC	1.00
105	Kevin Orie	.05
106	Matt Morris	.05
107	Pokey Reese	.05
108	Shawn Green	.35
109	Tony Womack	.05
110	Ken Caminiti	.05
111	Roberto Alomar	.20
112	Ken Griffey Jr.	1.50
113	Cal Ripken Jr.	2.50
114	Lou Collier	.05
115	Larry Walker	.05
116	Fred McGriff	.05
117	Jim Edmonds	.05
118	Edgar Martinez	.05
119	Matt Williams	.05
120	Ismael Valdes	.05
121	Bartolo Colon	.05
122	Jeff Cirillo	.05
123	Steve Woodard RC	.25
124	Kevin Millwood RC	1.00
125	Derrick Gibson	.05
126	Jacob Cruz	.05
127	Russell Branyan	.05
128	Sean Casey	.15
129	Derrek Lee	.50
130	Paul O'Neill	.05
131	Brad Radke	.05
132	Kevin Appier	.05
133	John Olerud	.05
134	Alan Benes	.05
135	Todd Greene	.05
136	Carlos Mendoza RC	.05
137	Wade Boggs	1.00
138	Jose Guillen	.05
139	Tino Martinez	.05
140	Aaron Boone	.05
141	Abraham Nunez	.05
142	Preston Wilson	.05
143	Randall Simon	.05
144	Dennis Reyes	.05
145	Mark Kotsay	.05
146	Richard Hidalgo	.05
147	Travis Lee	.05
148	Hanley Frias RC	.05
149	Ruben Rivera	.05
150	Rafael Medina	.05
151	Dave Nilsson	.05
152	Curt Schilling	.35
153	Brady Anderson	.05
154	Carlos Delgado	.50
155	Jason Giambi	.45
156	Pat Hentgen	.05
157	Tom Glavine	.35
158	Ryan Klesko	.05
159	Chipper Jones	1.00
160	Juan Gonzalez	.45
161	Mark McGwire	2.00
162	Vladimir Guerrero	.75
163	Derek Jeter	2.50
164	Manny Ramirez	.75
165	Mike Mussina	.30
166	Rafael Palmeiro	.65
167	Henry Rodriguez	.05
168	Jeff Suppan	.05
169	Eric Milton	.05
170	Scott Spiezio	.05
171	Wilson Delgado	.05
172	Bubba Trammell	.05
173	Ellis Burks	.05
174	Jason Dickson	.05
175	Butch Huskey	.05
176	Edgardo Alfonzo	.05
177	Eric Young	.05
178	Marquis Grissom	.05
179	Lance Johnson	.05
180	Kevin Brown	.05
181	Sandy Alomar Jr.	.05
182	Todd Hundley	.05
183	Rondell White	.05
184	Javier Lopez	.05
185	Damian Jackson	.05
186	Raul Mondesi	.05
187	Rickey Henderson	.75
188	David Justice	.05
189	Jay Buhner	.05
190	Jaret Wright	.05
191	Miguel Tejada	.25
192	Ron Wright	.05
193	Livan Hernandez	.05
194	A.J. Hinch	.05
195	Richie Sexson	.05
196	Bob Abreu	.05
197	Luis Castillo	.05
198	Michael Coleman	.05
199	Greg Maddux	1.00
200	Frank Thomas	.75
201	Andruw Jones	.75
202	Roger Clemens	1.25
203	Tim Salmon	.05
204	Chuck Knoblauch	.05
205	Wes Helms	.05
206	Juan Encarnacion	.05
207	Russ Davis	.05
208	John Valentin	.05
209	Tony Saunders	.05
210	Mike Sweeney	.05
211	Steve Finley	.05
212	David Dellucci RC	.25
213	Edgar Renteria	.05
214	Jeremi Gonzalez	.05
215	Jeff Bagwell Checklist	.40
216	Mike Piazza Checklist	1.00
217	Greg Maddux Checklist	.50
218	Cal Ripken Jr. Checklist	1.25
219	Frank Thomas Checklist	.45
220	Ken Griffey Jr. Checklist	.75

Gold Proofs

	NM/M
Common Player:	3.00
Stars:	6X

(See 1998 Studio for checklist and base card values.)

Silver Proofs

	NM/M
Common Player:	1.00
Silver Stars:	3X

(See 1998 Studio for checklist, base cardvalues.)

Autographs

		NM/M
1	Travis Lee/500	20.00
2	Todd Helton/1,000	20.00
3	Ben Grieve/1,000	10.00

Freeze Frame

		NM/M
Complete Set (30):		75.00
Common Player:		1.25
Production 4,500 Sets		
Die-Cuts:		1.5X
Production 500 Sets		
1	Ken Griffey Jr.	5.00

2	Derek Jeter	7.50
3	Ben Grieve	1.25
4	Cal Ripken Jr.	7.50
5	Alex Rodriguez	6.00
6	Greg Maddux	4.00
7	David Justice	1.25
8	Mike Piazza	5.00
9	Chipper Jones	4.00
10	Randy Johnson	3.00
11	Jeff Bagwell	3.00
12	Nomar Garciaparra	4.00
13	Andruw Jones	3.00
14	Frank Thomas	3.00
15	Scott Rolen	2.50
16	Barry Bonds	7.50
17	Kenny Lofton	1.25
18	Ivan Rodriguez	2.50
19	Chuck Knoblauch	1.25
20	Jose Cruz Jr.	1.25
21	Bernie Williams	1.25
22	Tony Gwynn	4.00
23	Juan Gonzalez	2.00
24	Gary Sheffield	2.25
25	Roger Clemens	4.50
26	Travis Lee	1.25
27	Brad Fullmer	1.25
28	Tim Salmon	1.25
29	Raul Mondesi	1.25
30	Roberto Alomar	2.00

Hit Parade

		NM/M
Complete Set (20):		30.00
Common Player:		1.00
Production 5,000 Sets		
1	Tony Gwynn	2.50
2	Larry Walker	1.00
3	Mike Piazza	3.00
4	Frank Thomas	2.00
5	Manny Ramirez	2.00
6	Ken Griffey Jr.	3.00
7	Todd Helton	1.50
8	Vladimir Guerrero	2.00
9	Albert Belle	1.00
10	Jeff Bagwell	2.00
11	Juan Gonzalez	1.25
12	Jim Thome	1.50
13	Scott Rolen	1.50
14	Tino Martinez	1.00
15	Mark McGwire	4.00
16	Barry Bonds	5.00
17	Tony Clark	1.00
18	Mo Vaughn	1.00
19	Darin Erstad	1.25
20	Paul Konerko	1.25

Masterstrokes

	NM/M
Complete Set (20):	95.00
Common Player:	2.00
Production 1,000 Sets	

Samples:		3X
1	Travis Lee	2.00
2	Kenny Lofton	2.00
3	Mo Vaughn	2.00
4	Ivan Rodriguez	3.50
5	Roger Clemens	6.50
6	Mark McGwire	10.00
7	Hideo Nomo	2.50
8	Andruw Jones	4.50
9	Nomar Garciaparra	6.00
10	Juan Gonzalez	2.50
11	Jeff Bagwell	4.50
12	Derek Jeter	12.50
13	Tony Gwynn	6.00
14	Chipper Jones	6.00
15	Mike Piazza	7.50
16	Greg Maddux	6.00
17	Alex Rodriguez	10.00
18	Cal Ripken Jr.	12.50
19	Frank Thomas	4.50
20	Ken Griffey Jr.	7.50

Sony MLB 99

		NM/M
Complete Set (20):		8.00
Common Player:		.15
1	Cal Ripken Jr.	1.50
2	Nomar Garciaparra	.75
3	Barry Bonds	1.50
4	Mike Mussina	.35
5	Pedro Martinez	.60
6	Derek Jeter	1.50
7	Andruw Jones	.60
8	Kenny Lofton	.15
9	Gary Sheffield	.45
10	Raul Mondesi	.15
11	Jeff Bagwell	.60
12	Tim Salmon	.15
13	Tom Glavine	.35
14	Ben Grieve	.15
15	Matt Williams	.15
16	Juan Gonzalez	.35
17	Mark McGwire	1.00
18	Bernie Williams	.15
19	Andres Galarraga	.15
20	Jose Cruz Jr.	.15

8x10 Portraits

		NM/M
Complete Set (36):		65.00
Common Player:		.50
Inserted 1:1		
1	Travis Lee	.50
2	Todd Helton	1.50
3	Ben Grieve	.50
4	Paul Konerko	.65
5	Jeff Bagwell	2.00
6	Derek Jeter	7.00
7	Ivan Rodriguez	1.50
8	Cal Ripken Jr.	7.00

9	Mike Piazza	4.00
10	Chipper Jones	3.00
11	Frank Thomas	2.00
12	Tony Gwynn	3.00
13	Nomar Garciaparra	3.00
14	Juan Gonzalez	1.00
15	Greg Maddux	3.00
16	Hideo Nomo	1.00
17	Scott Rolen	1.50
18	Barry Bonds	7.00
19	Ken Griffey Jr.	4.00
20	Alex Rodriguez	5.00
21	Roger Clemens	3.50
22	Mark McGwire	5.00
23	Jose Cruz Jr.	.50
24	Andruw Jones	2.00
25	Tino Martinez	.50
26	Mo Vaughn	.50
27	Vladimir Guerrero	2.00
28	Tony Clark	.50
29	Andy Pettitte	.65
30	Jaret Wright	.50
31	Paul Molitor	2.00
32	Darin Erstad	.65
33	Chuck Knoblauch	.50
34	Chuck Knoblauch	.50
35	Barry Larkin	.50
36	Kenny Lofton	.50

8x10 Portraits Gold Proofs

	NM/M
Common Player:	5.00
Stars:	6X

(See 1998 Studio 8X10 Portraits for checklist and base card values.)

1995 Summit

	NM/M
Complete Set (200):	10.00
Common Player:	.05
Pack (7):	1.00
Wax Box (24):	12.50
1	Ken Griffey Jr.	1.00
2	Alex Fernandez	.05
3	Fred McGriff	.05
4	Ben McDonald	.05
5	Rafael Palmeiro	.60
6	Tony Gwynn	.75
7	Jim Thome	.60
8	Ken Hill	.05
9	Barry Bonds	2.00
10	Barry Larkin	.05
11	Albert Belle	.05
12	Billy Ashley	.05
13	Matt Williams	.05
14	Andy Benes	.05
15	Midre Cummings	.05
16	J.R. Phillips	.05
17	Edgar Martinez	.05
18	Manny Ramirez	.65
19	Jose Canseco	.40

20	Chili Davis	.05
21	Don Mattingly	.85
22	Bernie Williams	.05
23	Tom Glavine	.35
24	Robin Ventura	.05
25	Jeff Conine	.05
26	Mark Grace	.05
27	Mark McGwire	1.50
28	Carlos Delgado	.45
29	Greg Colbrunn	.05
30	Greg Maddux	.75
31	Craig Biggio	.05
32	Kirby Puckett	.75
33	Derek Bell	.05
34	Lenny Dykstra	.05
35	Tim Salmon	.05
36	Deion Sanders	.05
37	Moises Alou	.05
38	Ray Lankford	.05
39	Willie Greene	.05
40	Ozzie Smith	.75
41	Roger Clemens	.85
42	Andres Galarraga	.05
43	Gary Sheffield	.35
44	Sammy Sosa	.75
45	Larry Walker	.05
46	Kevin Appier	.05
47	Raul Mondesi	.05
48	Kenny Lofton	.05
49	Darryl Hamilton	.05
50	Roberto Alomar	.20
51	Hal Morris	.05
52	Cliff Floyd	.05
53	Brent Gates	.05
54	Rickey Henderson	.65
55	John Olerud	.05
56	Gregg Jefferies	.05
57	Cecil Fielder	.05
58	Paul Molitor	.65
59	Bret Boone	.05
60	Greg Vaughn	.05
61	Wally Joyner	.05
62	Jeffrey Hammonds	.05
63	James Mouton	.05
64	Omar Vizquel	.05
65	Wade Boggs	.75
66	Terry Steinbach	.05
67	Wil Cordero	.05
68	Joey Hamilton	.05
69	Rico Brogna	.05
70	Darren Daulton	.05
71	Chuck Knoblauch	.05
72	Bob Hamelin	.05
73	Carl Everett	.05
74	Joe Carter	.05
75	Dave Winfield	.65
76	Bobby Bonilla	.05
77	Paul O'Neill	.05
78	Javier Lopez	.05
79	Cal Ripken Jr.	2.00
80	David Cone	.05
81	Bernard Gilkey	.05
82	Ivan Rodriguez	.60
83	Dean Palmer	.05
84	Jason Bere	.05
85	Will Clark	.05
86	Scott Cooper	.05
87	Royce Clayton	.05
88	Mike Piazza	1.00
89	Ryan Klesko	.05
90	Juan Gonzalez	.35
91	Travis Fryman	.05
92	Frank Thomas	.65
93	Eduardo Perez	.05
94	Mo Vaughn	.05
95	Jay Bell	.05
96	Jeff Bagwell	.65
97	Randy Johnson	.65
98	Jimmy Key	.05
99	Dennis Eckersley	.60
100	Carlos Baerga	.05
101	Eddie Murray	.65
102	Mike Mussina	.30
103	Brian Anderson	.05
104	Jeff Cirillo	.05
105	Dante Bichette	.05
106	Bret Saberhagen	.05
107	Jeff Kent	.05
108	Ruben Sierra	.05
109	Kirk Gibson	.05
110	Reggie Sanders	.05
111	Dave Justice	.05
112	Benji Gil	.05
113	Vaughn Eshelman	.05
114	Carlos Perez RC	.05
115	Chipper Jones	.75
116	Shane Andrews	.05
117	Orlando Miller	.05
118	Scott Ruffcorn	.05
119	Jose Oliva	.05
120	Joe Vitiello	.05
121	Jon Nunnally	.05
122	Garret Anderson	.05
123	Curtis Goodwin	.05

124	Mark Grudzielanek RC	.25
125	Alex Gonzalez	.05
126	David Bell	.05
127	Dustin Hermanson	.05
128	Dave Nilsson	.05
129	Wilson Heredia	.05
130	Charles Johnson	.05
131	Frank Rodriguez	.05
132	Alex Ochoa	.05
133	Alex Rodriguez	1.50
134	Bobby Higginson RC	.25
135	Edgardo Alfonzo	.05
136	Armando Benitez	.05
137	Rich Aude	.05
138	Tim Naehring	.05
139	Joe Randa	.05
140	Quilvio Veras	.05
141	Hideo Nomo RC	1.00
142	Ray Holbert	.05
143	Michael Tucker	.05
144	Chad Mottola	.05
145	John Valentin	.05
146	James Baldwin	.05
147	Esteban Loaiza	.05
148	Marty Cordova	.05
149	Juan Acevedo RC	.05
150	Tim Unroe RC	.05
151	Brad Clontz	.05
152	Steve Rodriguez	.05
153	Rudy Pemberton	.05
154	Ozzie Timmons	.05
155	Ricky Otero	.05
156	Allen Battle	.05
157	Joe Roselli	.05
158	Roberto Petagine	.05
159	Todd Hollandsworth	.05
160	Shannon Penn	.05
161	Antonio Osuna	.05
162	Russ Davis	.05
163	Jason Giambi	.40
164	Terry Bradshaw	.05
165	Ray Durham	.05
166	Todd Steverson	.05
167	Tim Belk	.05
168	Andy Pettitte	.25
169	Roger Cedeno	.05
170	Jose Parra	.05
171	Scott Sullivan	.05
172	LaTroy Hawkins	.05
173	Jeff McCurry	.05
174	Ken Griffey Jr.	.50
175	Frank Thomas	.30
176	Cal Ripken Jr.	1.00
177	Jeff Bagwell	.30
178	Mike Piazza	.50
179	Barry Bonds	1.00
180	Matt Williams	.05
181	Don Mattingly	.45
182	Will Clark	.05
183	Tony Gwynn	.40
184	Kirby Puckett	.40
185	Jose Canseco	.25
186	Paul Molitor	.30
187	Albert Belle	.05
188	Joe Carter	.05
189	Greg Maddux	.40
190	Roger Clemens	.45
191	David Cone	.05
192	Mike Mussina	.15
193	Randy Johnson	.30
194	Frank Thomas Checklist	.30
195	Ken Griffey Jr. Checklist	.50
196	Cal Ripken Jr. Checklist	.75
197	Jeff Bagwell Checklist	.30
198	Mike Piazza Checklist	.50
199	Barry Bonds Checklist	.75
200	Mo Vaughn, Matt Williams Checklist	.05

Nth Degree

	NM/M
Complete Set (200):	50.00
Common Player:	.25
Stars:	2X

(See 1995 Summit for checklist, base cardvalues.)

Big Bang

	NM/M
Complete Set (20):	45.00
Common Player:	1.00
1	Ken Griffey Jr.	6.00
2	Frank Thomas	3.25
3	Cal Ripken Jr.	8.00
4	Jeff Bagwell	3.25
5	Mike Piazza	6.00
6	Barry Bonds	8.00
7	Matt Williams	1.00
8	Don Mattingly	4.50
9	Will Clark	1.00
10	Tony Gwynn	4.00
11	Kirby Puckett	4.00
12	Jose Canseco	2.00
13	Paul Molitor	3.25
14	Albert Belle	1.00
15	Joe Carter	1.00
16	Rafael Palmeiro	3.00
17	Fred McGriff	1.00
18	Dave Justice	1.00
19	Tim Salmon	1.00
20	Mo Vaughn	1.00

New Age

	NM/M
Complete Set (15):	10.00
Common Player:	.25
1	Cliff Floyd	.25
2	Manny Ramirez	2.00
3	Raul Mondesi	.25
4	Alex Rodriguez	5.00
5	Billy Ashley	.25
6	Alex Gonzalez	.25
7	Michael Tucker	.25
8	Charles Johnson	.25
9	Carlos Delgado	1.00
10	Benji Gil	.25
11	Chipper Jones	3.00
12	Todd Hollandsworth	.25
13	Frank Rodriguez	.25
14	Shawn Green	.60
15	Ray Durham	.25

21 Club

	NM/M
Complete Set (9):	4.00
Common Player:	.50
1	Bob Abreu	.65
2	Pokey Reese	.50
3	Edgardo Alfonzo	.50

4	Jim Pittsley	.50
5	Ruben Rivera	.50
6	Chan Ho Park	.50
7	Julian Tavarez	.50
8	Ismael Valdes	.50
9	Dmitri Young	.50

1996 Summit

		NM/M
Complete Set (200):		10.00
Common Player:		.05
Pack (7):		1.25
Wax Box (18):		15.00
1	Mike Piazza	1.25
2	Matt Williams	.05
3	Tino Martinez	.05
4	Reggie Sanders	.05
5	Ray Durham	.05
6	Brad Radke	.05
7	Jeff Bagwell	.65
8	Ron Gant	.05
9	Lance Johnson	.05
10	Kevin Seitzer	.05
11	Dante Bichette	.05
12	Ivan Rodriguez	.60
13	Jim Abbott	.05
14	Greg Colbrunn	.05
15	Rondell White	.05
16	Shawn Green	.40
17	Gregg Jefferies	.05
18	Omar Vizquel	.05
19	Cal Ripken Jr.	2.00
20	Mark McGwire	1.50
21	Wally Joyner	.05
22	Chili Davis	.05
23	Jose Canseco	.40
24	Royce Clayton	.05
25	Jay Bell	.05
26	Travis Fryman	.05
27	Jeff King	.05
28	Todd Hundley	.05
29	Joe Vitiello	.05
30	Russ Davis	.05
31	Mo Vaughn	.05
32	Raul Mondesi	.05
33	Ray Lankford	.05
34	Mike Stanley	.05
35	B.J. Surhoff	.05
36	Greg Vaughn	.05
37	Todd Stottlemyre	.05
38	Carlos Delgado	.50
39	Kenny Lofton	.05
40	Hideo Nomo	.35
41	Sterling Hitchcock	.05
42	Pete Schourek	.05
43	Edgardo Alfonzo	.05
44	Ken Hill	.05
45	Ken Caminiti	.05
46	Bobby Higginson	.05
47	Michael Tucker	.05
48	David Cone	.05
49	Cecil Fielder	.05
50	Brian Hunter	.05
51	Charles Johnson	.05
52	Bobby Bonilla	.05
53	Eddie Murray	.65
54	Kenny Rogers	.05
55	Jim Edmonds	.05
56	Trevor Hoffman	.05
57	Kevin Mitchell	.05
58	Ruben Sierra	.05
59	Benji Gil	.05
60	Juan Gonzalez	.35
61	Larry Walker	.05
62	Jack McDowell	.05
63	Shawon Dunston	.05
64	Andy Benes	.05
65	Jay Buhner	.05
66	Rickey Henderson	.65
67	Alex Gonzalez	.05
68	Mike Kelly	.05
69	Fred McGriff	.05

70	Ryne Sandberg	.75
71	Ernie Young	.05
72	Kevin Appier	.05
73	Moises Alou	.05
74	John Jaha	.05
75	J.T. Snow	.05
76	Jim Thome	.60
77	Kirby Puckett	.75
78	Hal Morris	.05
79	Robin Ventura	.05
80	Ben McDonald	.05
81	Tim Salmon	.05
82	Albert Belle	.05
83	Marquis Grissom	.05
84	Alex Rodriguez	1.50
85	Manny Ramirez	.65
86	Ken Griffey Jr.	1.25
87	Sammy Sosa	.75
88	Frank Thomas	.65
89	Lee Smith	.05
90	Marty Cordova	.05
91	Greg Maddux	.75
92	Lenny Dykstra	.05
93	Butch Huskey	.05
94	Garret Anderson	.05
95	Mike Bordick	.05
96	Dave Justice	.05
97	Chad Curtis	.05
98	Carlos Baerga	.05
99	Jason Isringhausen	.05
100	Gary Sheffield	.35
101	Roger Clemens	1.00
102	Ozzie Smith	.75
103	Ramon Martinez	.05
104	Paul O'Neill	.05
105	Will Clark	.05
106	Tom Glavine	.35
107	Barry Bonds	2.00
108	Barry Larkin	.05
109	Derek Bell	.05
110	Randy Johnson	.65
111	Jeff Conine	.05
112	John Mabry	.05
113	Julian Tavarez	.05
114	Gary DiSarcina	.05
115	Andres Galarraga	.05
116	Marc Newfield	.05
117	Frank Rodriguez	.05
118	Brady Anderson	.05
119	Mike Mussina	.30
120	Orlando Merced	.05
121	Melvin Nieves	.05
122	Brian Jordan	.05
123	Rafael Palmeiro	.60
124	Johnny Damon	.35
125	Wil Cordero	.05
126	Chipper Jones	.75
127	Eric Karros	.05
128	Darren Daulton	.05
129	Vinny Castilla	.05
130	Joe Carter	.05
131	Bernie Williams	.05
132	Bernard Gilkey	.05
133	Bret Boone	.05
134	Tony Gwynn	.75
135	Dave Nilsson	.05
136	Ryan Klesko	.05
137	Paul Molitor	.65
138	John Olerud	.05
139	Craig Biggio	.05
140	John Valentin	.05
141	Chuck Knoblauch	.05
142	Edgar Martinez	.05
143	Rico Brogna	.05
144	Dean Palmer	.05
145	Mark Grace	.05
146	Roberto Alomar	.20
147	Alex Fernandez	.05
148	Andre Dawson	.25
149	Wade Boggs	.75
150	Mark Lewis	.05
151	Gary Gaetti	.05
152	Paul Wilson,	
	Roger Clemens	.45
153	Rey Ordonez,	
	Ozzie Smith	.35
154	Derek Jeter,	
	Cal Ripken Jr.	1.00
155	Alan Benes,	
	Andy Benes	.05
156	Jason Kendall,	
	Mike Piazza	.75
157	Ryan Klesko,	
	Frank Thomas	.30
158	Johnny Damon,	
	Ken Griffey Jr.	.65
159	Karim Garcia,	
	Sammy Sosa	.40
160	Raul Mondesi,	
	Tim Salmon	.40
161	Chipper Jones,	
	Matt Williams	.40
162	Rey Ordonez	.05
163	Bob Wolcott	.05

164	Brooks Kieschnick	.05
165	Steve Gibralter	.05
166	Bob Abreu	.05
167	Gregg Zaun	.05
168	Tavo Alvarez	.05
169	Sal Fasano	.05
170	George Arias	.05
171	Derek Jeter	2.00
172	Livan Hernandez **RC**	.25
173	Alan Benes	.05
174	George Williams	.05
175	John Wasdin	.05
176	Chan Ho Park	.05
177	Paul Wilson	.05
178	Jeff Suppan	.05
179	Quinton McCracken	.05
180	Wilton Guerrero **RC**	.05
181	Eric Owens	.05
182	Felipe Crespo	.05
183	LaTroy Hawkins	.05
184	Jason Schmidt	.05
185	Terrell Wade	.05
186	Mike Grace **RC**	.05
187	Chris Snopek	.05
188	Jason Kendall	.05
189	Todd Hollandsworth	.05
190	Jim Pittsley	.05
191	Jermaine Dye	.05
192	Mike Busby **RC**	.05
193	Richard Hidalgo	.05
194	Tyler Houston	.05
195	Jimmy Haynes	.05
196	Karim Garcia	.05
197	Ken Griffey Jr.	
	(Checklist)	.50
198	Frank Thomas	
	(Checklist)	.30
199	Greg Maddux	
	(Checklist)	.40
200	Cal Ripken Jr.	
	(Checklist)	1.00

Above & Beyond

	NM/M
Complete Set (200):	50.00
Common Player:	.25
Stars:	3X
(See 1996 Summit for	
checklist, base card values.)	

Artist's Proof

	NM/M
Complete Set (200):	100.00
Common Player:	1.00
Stars:	8X
(See 1996 Summit for	
checklist, base cardvalues.)	

Foil

	NM/M
Complete Set (200):	30.00

Common Player:	.25
Stars:	3X
(See 1996 Summit for checklist	
and base card values.)	

Ballparks

		NM/M
Complete Set (18):		45.00
Common Player:		1.00
1	Cal Ripken Jr.	7.50
2	Albert Belle	1.00
3	Dante Bichette	1.00
4	Mo Vaughn	1.00
5	Ken Griffey Jr.	6.00
6	Derek Jeter	7.50
7	Juan Gonzalez	1.50
8	Greg Maddux	4.00
9	Frank Thomas	3.00
10	Ryne Sandberg	4.00
11	Mike Piazza	6.00
12	Johnny Damon	1.50
13	Barry Bonds	7.50
14	Jeff Bagwell	3.00
15	Paul Wilson	1.00
16	Tim Salmon	1.00
17	Kirby Puckett	4.00
18	Tony Gwynn	4.00

Big Bang

Mike Piazza

		NM/M
Complete Set (16):		60.00
Common Player:		1.50
1	Frank Thomas	4.00
2	Ken Griffey Jr.	7.50
3	Albert Belle	1.50
4	Mo Vaughn	1.50
5	Barry Bonds	12.00
6	Cal Ripken Jr.	12.00
7	Jeff Bagwell	4.00
8	Mike Piazza	7.50
9	Ryan Klesko	1.50
10	Manny Ramirez	4.00
11	Tim Salmon	1.50
12	Dante Bichette	1.50
13	Sammy Sosa	6.00
14	Raul Mondesi	1.50
15	Chipper Jones	6.00
16	Garret Anderson	1.50

Hitters, Inc.

		NM/M
Complete Set (16):		40.00
Common Player:		1.25
1	Tony Gwynn	4.00
2	Mo Vaughn	1.25
3	Tim Salmon	1.25
4	Ken Griffey Jr.	5.00
5	Sammy Sosa	4.00
6	Frank Thomas	3.00
7	Wade Boggs	4.00
8	Albert Belle	1.25
9	Cal Ripken Jr.	8.00
10	Manny Ramirez	3.00
11	Ryan Klesko	1.25
11p	Ryan Klesko/OPS	1.25
12	Dante Bichette	1.25
13	Mike Piazza	5.00
14	Chipper Jones	4.00
15	Ryne Sandberg	4.00
16	Matt Williams	1.25

Positions

		NM/M
Complete Set (9):		100.00
Common Card:		6.00
1	Jeff Bagwell, Mo Vaughn, Frank Thomas (First Base)	10.00
2	Roberto Alomar, Craig Biggio, Chuck Knoblauch (Second Base)	6.00
3	Matt Williams, Jim Thome, Chipper Jones (Third Base)	12.50
4	Barry Larkin, Cal Ripken Jr., Alex Rodriguez (Short Stop)	20.00
5	Mike Piazza, Ivan Rodriguez, Charles Johnson/ Catcher	15.00
6	Hideo Nomo, Greg Maddux, Randy Johnson/ Pitcher	12.50
7	Barry Bonds, Albert Belle, Ryan Klesko/ Left Field	20.00
8	Johnny Damon, Jim Edmonds, Ken Griffey Jr./ Center Field	15.00
9	Manny Ramirez, Gary Sheffield, Sammy Sosa (Right Field)	12.50

T

1981 Topps

	NM/M
Complete Set (726):	37.00
Common Player:	.08
Wax Pack (15):	3.00
Wax Box (36):	85.00

Cello Pack (28):		3.00
Cello Box (24):		75.00
Rack Pack (48):		6.00
Rack Box (24):		120.00
Vending Box (500):		40.00
1	George Brett, Bill Buckner Batting Leaders	.60
2	Reggie Jackson, Ben Oglivie, Mike Schmidt Home Run Leaders	.60
3	Cecil Cooper, Mike Schmidt RBI Leaders	.20
4	Rickey Henderson, Ron LeFlore Stolen Base Leaders	.40
5	Steve Carlton, Steve Stone Victory Leaders	.11
6	Len Barker, Steve Carlton Strikeout Leaders	.11
7	Rudy May, Don Sutton ERA Leaders	.08
8	Rollie Fingers, Tom Hume, Dan Quisenberry Leading Firemen	.08
9	Pete LaCock/DP	.08
10	Mike Flanagan	.08
11	Jim Wohlford/DP	.08
12	Mark Clear	.08
13	Joe Charboneau RC	.40
14	John Tudor RC	.15
15	Larry Parrish	.08
16	Ron Davis	.08
17	Cliff Johnson	.08
18	Glenn Adams	.08
19	Jim Clancy	.08
20	Jeff Burroughs	.08
21	Ron Oester	.08
22	Danny Darwin	.08
23	Alex Trevino	.08
24	Don Stanhouse	.08
25	Sixto Lezcano	.08
26	U.L. Washington	.08
27	Champ Summers/DP	.08
28	Enrique Romo	.08
29	Gene Tenace	.08
30	Jack Clark	.08
31	Checklist 1-121/DP	.08
32	Ken Oberkfell	.08
33	Rick Honeycutt	.08
34	Aurelio Rodriguez	.08
35	Mitchell Page	.08
36	Ed Farmer	.08
37	Gary Roenicke	.08
38	Win Remmerswaal	.08
39	Tom Veryzer	.08
40	Tug McGraw	.08
41	Bob Babcock, John Butcher, Jerry Don Gleaton Rangers Future Stars	.08
42	Jerry White/DP	.08
43	Jose Morales	.08
44	Larry McWilliams	.08
45	Enos Cabell	.08
46	Rick Bosetti	.08
47	Ken Brett	.08
48	Dave Skaggs	.08
49	Bob Shirley	.08
50	Dave Lopes	.08
51	Bill Robinson/DP	.08
52	Hector Cruz	.08
53	Kevin Saucier	.08
54	Ivan DeJesus	.08
55	Mike Norris	.08
56	Buck Martinez	.08
57	Dave Roberts	.08
58	Joel Youngblood	.08
59	Dan Petry	.08
60	Willie Randolph	.08
61	Butch Wynegar	.08
62	Joe Pettini	.08
63	Steve Renko/DP	.08
64	Brian Asselstine	.08

65	Scott McGregor	.08
66	Manny Castillo, Tim Ireland, Mike Jones Royals Future Stars	.08
67	Ken Kravec	.08
68	Matt Alexander/DP	.08
69	Ed Halicki	.08
70	Al Oliver/DP	.08
71	Hal Dues	.08
72	Barry Evans/DP	.08
73	Doug Bair	.08
74	Mike Hargrove	.08
75	Reggie Smith	.08
76	Mario Mendoza	.08
77	Mike Barlow	.08
78	Steve Dillard	.08
79	Bruce Robbins	.08
80	Rusty Staub	.11
81	Dave Stapleton	.08
82	Danny Heep, Alan Knicely, Bobby Sprowl/Astros Future Stars/DP	.08
83	Mike Proly	.08
84	Johnnie LeMaster	.08
85	Mike Caldwell	.08
86	Wayne Gross	.08
87	Rick Camp	.08
88	Joe Lefebvre	.08
89	Darrell Jackson	.08
90	Bake McBride	.08
91	Tim Stoddard/DP	.08
92	Mike Easler	.08
93	Ed Glynn/DP	.08
94	Harry Spilman/DP	.08
95	Jim Sundberg	.08
96	Dave Beard, Ernie Camacho, Pat Dempsey/ A's Future Stars	.08
97	Chris Speier	.08
98	Clint Hurdle	.08
99	Eric Wilkins	.08
100	Rod Carew	1.50
101	Benny Ayala	.08
102	Dave Tobik	.08
103	Jerry Martin	.08
104	Terry Forster	.08
105	Jose Cruz	.08
106	Don Money	.08
107	Rich Wortham	.08
108	Bruce Benedict	.08
109	Mike Scott	.08
110	Carl Yastrzemski	1.50
111	Greg Minton	.08
112	Rusty Kuntz, Fran Mullins, Leo Sutherland/ White Sox Future Stars	.08
113	Mike Phillips	.08
114	Tom Underwood	.08
115	Roy Smalley	.08
116	Joe Simpson	.08
117	Pete Falcone	.08
118	Kurt Bevacqua	.08
119	Tippy Martinez	.08
120	Larry Bowa	.08
121	Larry Harlow	.08
122	John Denny	.08
123	Al Cowens	.08
124	Jerry Garvin	.08
125	Andre Dawson	1.25
126	Charlie Leibrandt RC	.30
127	Rudy Law	.08
128	Gary Allenson/DP	.08
129	Art Howe	.08
130	Larry Gura	.08
131	Keith Moreland RC	.15
132	Tommy Boggs	.08
133	Jeff Cox	.08
134	Steve Mura	.08
135	Gorman Thomas	.08
136	Doug Capilla	.08
137	Hosken Powell	.08
138	Rich Dotson/DP RC	.15
139	Oscar Gamble	.08
140	Bob Forsch	.08
141	Miguel Dilone	.08
142	Jackson Todd	.08
143	Dan Meyer	.08
144	Allen Ripley	.08
145	Mickey Rivers	.08
146	Bobby Castillo	.08
147	Dale Berra	.08
148	Randy Niemann	.08
149	Joe Nolan	.08
150	Mark Fidrych	.11
151	Claudell Washington/DP	.08
152	John Urrea	.08
153	Tom Poquette	.08
154	Rick Langford	.08
155	Chris Chambliss	.08
156	Bob McClure	.08
157	John Wathan	.08
158	Fergie Jenkins	.70

159	Brian Doyle	.08
160	Garry Maddox	.08
161	Dan Graham	.08
162	Doug Corbett	.08
163	Billy Almon	.08
164	Lamarr Hoyt (LaMarr) RC	.11
165	Tony Scott	.08
166	Floyd Bannister	.08
167	Terry Whitfield	.08
168	Don Robinson/DP	.08
169	John Mayberry	.08
170	Ross Grimsley	.08
171	Gene Richards	.08
172	Gary Woods	.08
173	Bump Wills	.08
174	Doug Rau	.08
175	Dave Collins	.08
176	Mike Krukow	.08
177	Rick Peters	.08
178	Jim Essian/DP	.08
179	Rudy May	.08
180	Pete Rose	3.75
181	Elias Sosa	.08
182	Bob Grich	.08
183	Dick Davis/DP	.08
184	Jim Dwyer	.08
185	Dennis Leonard	.08
186	Wayne Nordhagen	.08
187	Mike Parrott	.08
188	Doug DeCinces	.08
189	Craig Swan	.08
190	Cesar Cedeno	.08
191	Rick Sutcliffe	.08
192	Terry Harper, Ed Miller, Rafael Ramirez RC Braves Future Stars	.08
193	Pete Vuckovich	.08
194	Rod Scurry RC	.08
195	Rich Murray	.08
196	Duffy Dyer	.08
197	Jim Kern	.08
198	Jerry Dybzinski	.08
199	Chuck Rainey	.08
200	George Foster	.08
201	Johnny Bench (Record Breaker)	.35
202	Steve Carlton (Record Breaker)	.20
203	Bill Gullickson (Record Breaker)	.08
204	Ron LeFlore, Rodney Scott (Record Breaker)	.08
205	Pete Rose (Record Breaker)	1.25
206	Mike Schmidt (Record Breaker)	.70
207	Ozzie Smith (Record Breaker)	.70
208	Willie Wilson (Record Breaker)	.08
209	Dickie Thon (DP)	.08
210	Jim Palmer	1.25
211	Derrel Thomas	.08
212	Steve Nicosia	.08
213	Al Holland RC	.08
214	Ralph Botting, Jim Dorsey, John Harris/ Angels Future Stars	.08
215	Larry Hisle	.08
216	John Henry Johnson	.08
217	Rich Hebner	.08
218	Paul Splittorff	.08
219	Ken Landreaux	.08
220	Tom Seaver	1.50
221	Bob Davis	.08
222	Jorge Orta	.08
223	Roy Lee Jackson	.08
224	Pat Zachry	.08
225	Ruppert Jones	.08
226	Manny Sanguillen/DP	.08
227	Fred Martinez	.08
228	Tom Paciorek	.08
229	Rollie Fingers	.70
230	George Hendrick	.08
231	Joe Beckwith	.08
232	Mickey Klutts	.08
233	Skip Lockwood	.08
234	Lou Whitaker	.08
235	Scott Sanderson	.08
236	Mike Ivie	.08
237	Charlie Moore	.08
238	Willie Hernandez	.08
239	Rick Miller/DP	.08
240	Nolan Ryan	3.75
241	Checklist 122-242/DP	.08
242	Chet Lemon	.08
243	Sal Butera	.08
244	Tito Landrum, Al Olmsted, Andy Rincon Cardinals Future Stars	.08
245	Ed Figueroa	.08
246	Ed Ott/DP	.08
247	Glenn Hubbard/DP	.08

No.	Player	Value
248	Joey McLaughlin	.08
249	Larry Cox	.08
250	Ron Guidry	.11
251	Tom Brookens	.08
252	Victor Cruz	.08
253	Dave Bergman	.08
254	Ozzie Smith	2.25
255	Mark Littell	.08
256	Bombo Rivera	.08
257	Rennie Stennett	.08
258	Joe Price RC	.08
259	Juan Berenguer, Hubie Brooks, Mookie Wilson RC Mets Future Stars	.60
260	Ron Cey	.08
261	Rickey Henderson	3.50
262	Sammy Stewart	.08
263	Brian Downing	.08
264	Jim Norris	.08
265	John Candelaria	.08
266	Tom Herr	.08
267	Stan Bahnsen	.08
268	Jerry Royster	.08
269	Ken Forsch	.08
270	Greg Luzinski	.08
271	Bill Castro	.08
272	Bruce Kimm	.08
273	Stan Papi	.08
274	Craig Chamberlain	.08
275	Dwight Evans	.08
276	Dan Spillner	.08
277	Alfredo Griffin	.08
278	Rick Sofield	.08
279	Bob Knepper	.08
280	Ken Griffey	.08
281	Fred Stanley	.08
282	Rick Anderson, Greg Biercevicz, Rodney Craig Mariners Future Stars	.08
283	Billy Sample	.08
284	Brian Kingman	.08
285	Jerry Turner	.08
286	Dave Frost	.08
287	Lenn Sakata	.08
288	Bob Clark	.08
289	Mickey Hatcher	.08
290	Bob Boone/DP	.08
291	Aurelio Lopez	.08
292	Mike Squires	.08
293	Charlie Lea RC	.11
294	Mike Tyson/DP	.08
295	Hal McRae	.08
296	Bill Nahorodny/DP	.08
297	Bob Bailor	.08
298	Buddy Solomon	.08
299	Elliott Maddox	.08
300	Paul Molitor	1.50
301	Matt Keough	.08
302	Jack Perconte, Mike Scioscia, Fernando Valenzuela RC Dodgers Future Stars	1.50
303	Johnny Oates	.08
304	John Castino	.08
305	Ken Clay	.08
306	Juan Beniquez/DP	.08
307	Gene Garber	.08
308	Rick Manning	.08
309	Luis Salazar RC	.08
310	Vida Blue/DP	.08
311	Freddie Patek	.08
312	Rick Rhoden	.08
313	Luis Pujols	.08
314	Rich Dauer	.08
315	Kirk Gibson RC	3.75
316	Craig Minetto	.08
317	Lonnie Smith	.08
318	Steve Yeager	.08
319	Rowland Office	.08
320	Tom Burgmeier	.08
321	Leon Durham RC	.11
322	Neil Allen	.08
323	Jim Morrison/DP	.08
324	Mike Willis	.08
325	Ray Knight	.08
326	Biff Pocoroba	.08
327	Moose Haas	.08
328	Dave Engle, Greg Johnston, Gary Ward Twins Future Stars	.11
329	Joaquin Andujar	.08
330	Frank White	.08
331	Dennis Lamp	.08
332	Lee Lacy/DP	.08
333	Sid Monge	.08
334	Dane Iorg	.08
335	Rick Cerone	.08
336	Eddie Whitson	.08
337	Lynn Jones	.08
338	Checklist 243-363	.08
339	John Ellis	.08
340	Bruce Kison	.08
341	Dwayne Murphy	.08
342	Eric Rasmussen/DP	.08
343	Frank Taveras	.08
344	Byron McLaughlin	.08
345	Warren Cromartie	.08
346	Larry Christenson/DP	.08
347	Harold Baines RC	3.00
348	Bob Sykes	.08
349	Glenn Hoffman	.08
350	J.R. Richard	.08
351	Otto Velez	.08
352	Dick Tidrow/DP	.08
353	Terry Kennedy	.08
354	Mario Soto	.08
355	Bob Horner	.08
356	George Stablein, Craig Stimac, Tom Tellmann Padres Future Stars	.08
357	Jim Slaton	.08
358	Mark Wagner	.08
359	Tom Hausman	.08
360	Willie Wilson	.08
361	Joe Strain	.08
362	Bo Diaz	.08
363	Geoff Zahn	.08
364	Mike Davis RC	.08
365	Graig Nettles/DP	.11
366	Mike Ramsey	.08
367	Denny Martinez	.08
368	Leon Roberts	.08
369	Frank Tanana	.08
370	Dave Winfield	1.50
371	Charlie Hough	.08
372	Jay Johnstone	.08
373	Pat Underwood	.08
374	Tom Hutton	.08
375	Dave Concepcion	.08
376	Ron Reed	.08
377	Jerry Morales	.08
378	Dave Rader	.08
379	Lary Sorensen	.08
380	Willie Stargell	1.50
381	Carlos Lezcano, Steve Macko, Randy Martz Cubs Future Stars	.08
382	Paul Mirabella RC	.08
383	Eric Soderholm/DP	.08
384	Mike Sadek	.08
385	Joe Sambito	.08
386	Dave Edwards	.08
387	Phil Niekro	.70
388	Andre Thornton	.08
389	Marty Pattin	.08
390	Cesar Geronimo	.08
391	Dave Lemanczyk/DP	.08
392	Lance Parrish	.08
393	Broderick Perkins	.08
394	Woodie Fryman	.08
395	Scot Thompson	.08
396	Bill Campbell	.08
397	Julio Cruz	.08
398	Ross Baumgarten	.08
399	Mike Boddicker, Mark Corey, Floyd Rayford RC Orioles Future Stars	.15
400	Reggie Jackson	2.25
401	A.L. Championships (Royals Sweep Yankees)	.40
402	N.L. Championships (Phillies Squeak Past Astros)	.20
403	World Series (Phillies Beat Royals In 6)	.20
404	World Series Summary (Phillies Win First World Series)	.20
405	Nino Espinosa	.08
406	Dickie Noles	.08
407	Ernie Whitt	.08
408	Fernando Arroyo	.08
409	Larry Herndon	.08
410	Bert Campaneris	.08
411	Terry Puhl	.08
412	Britt Burns RC	.08
413	Tony Bernazard	.08
414	John Pacella/DP	.08
415	Ben Oglivie	.08
416	Gary Alexander	.08
417	Dan Schatzeder	.08
418	Bobby Brown	.08
419	Tom Hume	.08
420	Keith Hernandez	.08
421	Bob Stanley	.08
422	Dan Ford	.08
423	Shane Rawley	.08
424	Tim Lollar, Bruce Robinson, Dennis Werth Yankees Future Stars	.08
425	Al Bumbry	.08
426	Warren Brusstar	.08
427	John D'Acquisto	.08
428	John Stearns	.08
429	Mick Kelleher	.08
430	Jim Bibby	.08
431	Dave Roberts	.08
432	Len Barker	.08
433	Rance Mulliniks	.08
434	Roger Erickson	.08
435	Jim Spencer	.08
436	Gary Lucas	.08
437	Mike Heath/DP	.08
438	John Montefusco	.08
439	Denny Walling	.08
440	Jerry Reuss	.08
441	Ken Reitz	.08
442	Ron Pruitt	.08
443	Jim Beattie/DP	.08
444	Garth Iorg	.08
445	Ellis Valentine	.08
446	Checklist 364-484	.08
447	Junior Kennedy/DP	.08
448	Tim Corcoran	.08
449	Paul Mitchell	.08
450	Dave Kingman/DP	.08
451	Chris Bando, Tom Brennan, Sandy Wihtol Indians Future Stars	.08
452	Renie Martin	.08
453	Rob Wilfong/DP	.08
454	Andy Hassler	.08
455	Rick Burleson	.08
456	Jeff Reardon RC	1.25
457	Mike Lum	.08
458	Randy Jones	.08
459	Greg Gross	.08
460	Rich Gossage	.08
461	Dave McKay	.08
462	Jack Brohamer	.08
463	Milt May	.08
464	Adrian Devine	.08
465	Bill Russell	.08
466	Bob Molinaro	.08
467	Dave Stieb	.08
468	Johnny Wockenfuss	.08
469	Jeff Leonard	.08
470	Manny Trillo	.08
471	Mike Vail	.08
472	Dyar Miller/DP	.08
473	Jose Cardenal	.08
474	Mike LaCoss	.08
475	Buddy Bell	.08
476	Jerry Koosman	.08
477	Luis Gomez	.08
478	Juan Eichelberger	.08
479	Bobby Pate, Tim Raines, Roberto Ramos RC Expos Future Stars	2.25
480	Carlton Fisk	1.50
481	Bob Lacey/DP	.08
482	Jim Gantner	.08
483	Mike Griffin	.08
484	Max Venable/DP	.08
485	Garry Templeton	.08
486	Marc Hill	.08
487	Dewey Robinson	.08
488	Damaso Garcia RC	.08
489	John Littlefield (Photo actually Mark Riggins.)	.08
490	Eddie Murray	1.50
491	Gordy Pladson	.08
492	Barry Foote	.08
493	Dan Quisenberry	.08
494	Bob Walk RC	.15
495	Dusty Baker	.11
496	Paul Dade	.08
497	Fred Norman	.08
498	Pat Putnam	.08
499	Frank Pastore	.08
500	Jim Rice	.20
501	Tim Foli/DP	.08
502	Chris Bourjos, Al Hargesheimer, Mike Rowland Giants Future Stars	.08
503	Steve McCatty	.08
504	Dale Murphy	.60
505	Jason Thompson	.08
506	Phil Huffman	.08
507	Jamie Quirk	.08
508	Rob Dressler	.08
509	Pete Mackanin	.08
510	Lee Mazzilli	.08
511	Wayne Garland	.08
512	Gary Thomasson	.08
513	Frank LaCorte	.08
514	George Riley	.08
515	Robin Yount	1.50
516	Doug Bird	.08
517	Richie Zisk	.08
518	Grant Jackson	.08
519	John Tamargo/DP	.08
520	Steve Stone	.08
521	Sam Mejias	.08
522	Mike Colbern	.08
523	John Fulgham	.08
524	Willie Aikens	.08
525	Mike Torrez	.08
526	Marty Bystrom, Jay Loviglio, Jim Wright Phillies Future Stars	.08
527	Danny Goodwin	.08
528	Gary Matthews	.08
529	Dave LaRoche	.08
530	Steve Garvey	.60
531	John Curtis	.08
532	Bill Stein	.08
533	Jesus Figueroa	.08
534	Dave Smith RC	.08
535	Omar Moreno	.08
536	Bob Owchinko/DP	.08
537	Ron Hodges	.08
538	Tom Griffin	.08
539	Rodney Scott	.08
540	Mike Schmidt/DP	2.25
541	Steve Swisher	.08
542	Larry Bradford/DP	.08
543	Terry Crowley	.08
544	Rich Gale	.08
545	Johnny Grubb	.08
546	Paul Moskau	.08
547	Mario Guerrero	.08
548	Dave Goltz	.08
549	Jerry Remy	.08
550	Tommy John	.15
551	Vance Law, Tony Pena, Pascual Perez RC Pirates Future Stars	.60
552	Steve Trout	.08
553	Tim Blackwell	.08
554	Bert Blyleven	.08
555	Cecil Cooper	.08
556	Jerry Mumphrey	.08
557	Chris Knapp	.08
558	Barry Bonnell	.08
559	Willie Montanez	.08
560	Joe Morgan	1.50
561	Dennis Littlejohn	.08
562	Checklist 485-605	.08
563	Jim Kaat	.11
564	Ron Hassey/DP	.08
565	Burt Hooton	.08
566	Del Unser	.08
567	Mark Bomback	.08
568	Dave Revering	.08
569	Al Williams/DP	.08
570	Ken Singleton	.08
571	Todd Cruz	.08
572	Jack Morris	.08
573	Phil Garner	.08
574	Bill Caudill	.08
575	Tony Perez	.70
576	Reggie Cleveland	.08
577	Luis Leal, Brian Milner, Ken Schrom RC Blue Jays Future Stars	.08
578	Bill Gullickson RC	.15
579	Tim Flannery	.08
580	Don Baylor	.11
581	Roy Howell	.08
582	Gaylord Perry	.70
583	Larry Milbourne	.08
584	Randy Lerch	.08
585	Amos Otis	.08
586	Silvio Martinez	.08
587	Jeff Newman	.08
588	Gary Lavelle	.08
589	Lamar Johnson	.08
590	Bruce Sutter	.70
591	John Lowenstein	.08
592	Steve Comer	.08
593	Steve Kemp	.08
594	Preston Hanna/DP	.08
595	Butch Hobson	.08
596	Jerry Augustine	.08
597	Rafael Landestoy	.08
598	George Vukovich/DP	.08
599	Dennis Kinney	.08
600	Johnny Bench	1.50
601	Don Aase	.08
602	Bobby Murcer	.08
603	John Verhoeven	.08
604	Rob Picciolo	.08
605	Don Sutton	.70
606	Bruce Berenyi, Geoff Combe, Paul Householder Reds Future Stars/DP	.08
607	Dave Palmer	.08
608	Greg Pryor	.08
609	Lynn McGlothen	.08
610	Darrell Porter	.08
611	Rick Matula/DP	.08
612	Duane Kuiper	.08
613	Jim Anderson	.08
614	Dave Rozema	.08
615	Rick Dempsey	.08
616	Rick Wise	.08
617	Craig Reynolds	.08
618	John Milner	.08

619	Steve Henderson	.08
620	Dennis Eckersley	.70
621	Tom Donohue	.08
622	Randy Moffitt	.08
623	Sal Bando	.08
624	Bob Welch	.08
625	Bill Buckner	.08
626	Dave Steffen, Jerry Ujdur, Roger Weaver Tigers Future Stars	.08
627	Luis Tiant	.08
628	Vic Correll	.08
629	Tony Armas	.08
630	Steve Carlton	1.50
631	Ron Jackson	.08
632	Alan Bannister	.08
633	Bill Lee	.08
634	Doug Flynn	.08
635	Bobby Bonds	.08
636	Al Hrabosky	.08
637	Jerry Narron	.08
638	Checklist 606	.08
639	Carney Lansford	.08
640	Dave Parker	.08
641	Mark Belanger	.08
642	Vern Ruhle	.08
643	Lloyd Moseby **RC**	.15
644	Ramon Aviles/DP	.08
645	Rick Reuschel	.08
646	Marvis Foley	.08
647	Dick Drago	.08
648	Darrell Evans	.08
649	Manny Sarmiento	.08
650	Bucky Dent	.08
651	Pedro Guerrero	.08
652	John Montague	.08
653	Bill Fahey	.08
654	Ray Burris	.08
655	Dan Driessen	.08
656	Jon Matlack	.08
657	Mike Cubbage/DP	.08
658	Milt Wilcox	.08
659	John Flinn, Ed Romero, Ned Yost Brewers Future Stars	.08
660	Gary Carter	1.50
661	Earl Weaver Orioles Team	.20
662	Ralph Houk Red Sox Team	.15
663	Jim Fregosi Angels Team	.08
664	Tony LaRussa White Sox Team	.20
665	Dave Garcia Indians Team	.08
666	Sparky Anderson Tigers Team	.20
667	Jim Frey Royals Team	.08
668	Bob Rodgers Brewers Team	.08
669	John Goryl Twins Team	.08
670	Gene Michael Yankees Team	.11
671	Billy Martin A's Team	.20
672	Maury Wills Mariners Team	.15
673	Don Zimmer Rangers Team	.15
674	Bobby Mattick Blue Jays Team	.08
675	Bobby Cox Braves Team	.20
676	Joe Amalfitano Cubs Team	.08
677	John McNamara Reds Team	.08
678	Bill Virdon Astros Team	.08
679	Tom Lasorda Dodgers Team	.20
680	Dick Williams Expos Team	.15
681	Joe Torre Mets Team	.20
682	Dallas Green Phillies Team	.11
683	Chuck Tanner Pirates Team	.08
684	Whitey Herzog Cardinals Team	.11
685	Frank Howard Padres Team	.15
686	Dave Bristol Giants Team	.08
687	Jeff Jones	.08
688	Kiko Garcia	.08
689	Bruce Hurst, Keith MacWhorter, Reid Nichols **RC** Red Sox Future Stars	.25
690	Bob Watson	.08
691	Dick Ruthven	.08
692	Lenny Randle	.08
693	Steve Howe **RC**	.15
694	Bud Harrelson/DP	.08

695	Kent Tekulve	.08
696	Alan Ashby	.08
697	Rick Waits	.08
698	Mike Jorgensen	.08
699	Glenn Abbott	.08
700	George Brett	2.75
701	Joe Rudi	.08
702	George Medich	.08
703	Alvis Woods	.08
704	Bill Travers/DP	.08
705	Ted Simmons	.08
706	Dave Ford	.08
707	Dave Cash	.08
708	Doyle Alexander	.08
709	Alan Trammell/DP	.08
710	Ron LeFlore/DP	.08
711	Joe Ferguson	.08
712	Bill Bonham	.08
713	Bill North	.08
714	Pete Redfern	.08
715	Bill Madlock	.08
716	Glenn Borgmann	.08
717	Jim Barr/DP	.08
718	Larry Biittner	.08
719	Sparky Lyle	.08
720	Fred Lynn	.08
721	Toby Harrah	.08
722	Joe Niekro	.08
723	Bruce Bochte	.08
724	Lou Piniella	.11
725	Steve Rogers	.08
726	Rick Monday	.08

Traded

NM/M

Complete Set (132):
Common Player:

727	Danny Ainge **(RC)**	1.50
728	Doyle Alexander	.11
729	Gary Alexander	.11
730	Billy Almon	.11
731	Joaquin Andujar	.11
732	Bob Bailor	.11
733	Juan Beniquez	.11
734	Dave Bergman	.11
735	Tony Bernazard	.11
736	Larry Biittner	.11
737	Doug Bird	.11
738	Bert Blyleven	.20
739	Mark Bomback	.11
740	Bobby Bonds	.11
741	Rick Bosetti	.11
742	Hubie Brooks	.11
743	Rick Burleson	.11
744	Ray Burris	.11
745	Jeff Burroughs	.11
746	Enos Cabell	.11
747	Ken Clay	.11
748	Mark Clear	.11
749	Larry Cox	.11
750	Hector Cruz	.11
751	Victor Cruz	.11
752	Mike Cubbage	.11
753	Dick Davis	.11
754	Brian Doyle	.11
755	Dick Drago	.11
756	Leon Durham	.11
757	Jim Dwyer	.11
758	Dave Edwards	.11
759	Jim Essian	.11
760	Bill Fahey	.11
761	Rollie Fingers	.70
762	Carlton Fisk	1.50
763	Barry Foote	.11
764	Ken Forsch	.11
765	Kiko Garcia	.11
766	Cesar Geronimo	.11
767	Gary Gray	.11
768	Mickey Hatcher	.11
769	Steve Henderson	.11
770	Marc Hill	.11
771	Butch Hobson	.11
772	Rick Honeycutt	.11

773	Roy Howell	.11
774	Mike Ivie	.11
775	Roy Lee Jackson	.11
776	Cliff Johnson	.11
777	Randy Jones	.11
778	Ruppert Jones	.11
779	Mick Kelleher	.11
780	Terry Kennedy	.11
781	Dave Kingman	.11
782	Bob Knepper	.11
783	Ken Kravec	.11
784	Bob Lacey	.11
785	Dennis Lamp	.11
786	Rafael Landestoy	.11
787	Ken Landreaux	.11
788	Carney Lansford	.11
789	Dave LaRoche	.11
790	Joe Lefebvre	.11
791	Ron LeFlore	.11
792	Randy Lerch	.11
793	Sixto Lezcano	.11
794	John Littlefield	.11
795	Mike Lum	.11
796	Greg Luzinski	.11
797	Fred Lynn	.11
798	Jerry Martin	.11
799	Buck Martinez	.11
800	Gary Matthews	.11
801	Mario Mendoza	.11
802	Larry Milbourne	.11
803	Rick Miller	.11
804	John Montefusco	.11
805	Jerry Morales	.11
806	Jose Morales	.11
807	Joe Morgan	1.50
808	Jerry Mumphrey	.11
809	Gene Nelson **RC**	.11
810	Ed Ott	.11
811	Bob Owchinko	.11
812	Gaylord Perry	.70
813	Mike Phillips	.11
814	Darrell Porter	.11
815	Mike Proly	.11
816	Tim Raines	2.25
817	Lenny Randle	.11
818	Doug Rau	.11
819	Jeff Reardon	.11
820	Ken Reitz	.11
821	Steve Renko	.11
822	Rick Reuschel	.11
823	Dave Revering	.11
824	Dave Roberts	.11
825	Leon Roberts	.11
826	Joe Rudi	.11
827	Kevin Saucier	.11
828	Tony Scott	.11
829	Bob Shirley	.11
830	Ted Simmons	.11
831	Lary Sorensen	.11
832	Jim Spencer	.11
833	Harry Spilman	.11
834	Fred Stanley	.11
835	Rusty Staub	.20
836	Bill Stein	.11
837	Joe Strain	.11
838	Bruce Sutter	.70
839	Don Sutton	.70
840	Steve Swisher	.11
841	Frank Tanana	.11
842	Gene Tenace	.11
843	Jason Thompson	.11
844	Dickie Thon	.11
845	Bill Travers	.11
846	Tom Underwood	.11
847	John Urrea	.11
848	Mike Vail	.11
849	Ellis Valentine	.11
850	Fernando Valenzuela	1.50
851	Pete Vuckovich	.11
852	Mark Wagner	.11
853	Bob Walk	.11
854	Claudell Washington	.11
855	Dave Winfield	3.00
856	Geoff Zahn	.11
857	Richie Zisk	.11
858	Checklist 727-858	.04

1982 Topps

NM/M

	Unopened Fact. Set (792):	180.00
	Complete Set (792):	70.00
	Common Player:	.10
	Wax Pack (15):	5.00
	Wax Box (36):	140.00
	Cello Pack (28):	6.00
	Cello Box (24):	130.00
	Rack Pack (51):	8.00
	Rack Box (24):	210.00
	Vending Box (500):	60.00
1	Steve Carlton (1981 Highlight)	.25
2	Ron Davis (1981 Highlight)	.10

BRAVES
OUTFIELD DALE MURPHY

3	Tim Raines (1981 Highlight)	.10
4	Pete Rose (1981 Highlight)	.75
5	Nolan Ryan (1981 Highlight)	3.00
6	Fernando Valenzuela (1981 Highlight)	.10
7	Scott Sanderson	.10
8	Rich Dauer	.10
9	Ron Guidry	.15
10	Ron Guidry/IA	.10
11	Gary Alexander	.10
12	Moose Haas	.10
13	Lamar Johnson	.10
14	Steve Howe	.10
15	Ellis Valentine	.10
16	Steve Comer	.10
17	Darrell Evans	.10
18	Fernando Arroyo	.10
19	Ernie Whitt	.10
20	Garry Maddox	.10
21	Bob Bonner, Cal Ripken, Jr., Jeff Schneider **RC** Orioles Future Stars	50.00
22	Jim Beattie	.10
23	Willie Hernandez	.10
24	Dave Frost	.10
25	Jerry Remy	.10
26	Jorge Orta	.10
27	Tom Herr	.10
28	John Urrea	.10
29	Dwayne Murphy	.10
30	Tom Seaver	1.50
31	Tom Seaver/IA	1.00
32	Gene Garber	.10
33	Jerry Morales	.10
34	Joe Sambito	.10
35	Willie Aikens	.10
36	George Medich, Al Oliver Rangers Btg/Pitching Leaders	.10
37	Dan Graham	.10
38	Charlie Lea	.10
39	Lou Whitaker	.10
40	Dave Parker	.10
41	Dave Parker/IA	.10
42	Rick Sofield	.10
43	Mike Cubbage	.10
44	Britt Burns	.10
45	Rick Cerone	.10
46	Jerry Augustine	.10
47	Jeff Leonard	.10
48	Bobby Castillo	.10
49	Alvis Woods	.10
50	Buddy Bell	.10
51	Jay Howell, Carlos Lezcano, Ty Waller **RC** Chicago Cubs Future Stars	.40
52	Larry Andersen	.10
53	Greg Gross	.10
54	Ron Hassey	.10
55	Rick Burleson	.10
56	Mark Littell	.10
57	Craig Reynolds	.10
58	John D'Acquisto	.10
59	Rich Gedman **RC**	.10
60	Tony Armas	.10
61	Tommy Boggs	.10
62	Mike Tyson	.10
63	Mario Soto	.10
64	Lynn Jones	.10
65	Terry Kennedy	.10
66	Art Howe, Nolan Ryan Astros Batting/ Pitching Leaders	.75
67	Rich Gale	.10
68	Roy Howell	.10
69	Al Williams	.10
70	Tim Raines	.50

71	Roy Lee Jackson	.10
72	Rick Auerbach	.10
73	Buddy Solomon	.10
74	Bob Clark	.10
75	Tommy John	.20
76	Greg Pryor	.10
77	Miguel Dilone	.10
78	George Medich	.10
79	Bob Bailor	.10
80	Jim Palmer	1.00
81	Jim Palmer/In Action	.30
82	Bob Welch	.10
83	Steve Balboni, Andy McGaffigan, Andre Robertson RC Yankees Future Stars	.15
84	Rennie Stennett	.10
85	Lynn McGlothen	.10
86	Dane Iorg	.10
87	Matt Keough	.10
88	Biff Pocoroba	.10
89	Steve Henderson	.10
90	Nolan Ryan	4.00
91	Carney Lansford	.10
92	Brad Havens	.10
93	Larry Hisle	.10
94	Andy Hassler	.10
95	Ozzie Smith	2.00
96	George Brett, Larry Gura Royals Batting/ Pitching Leaders	.35
97	Paul Moskau	.10
98	Terry Bulling	.10
99	Barry Bonnell	.10
100	Mike Schmidt	3.00
101	Mike Schmidt (In Action)	1.50
102	Dan Briggs	.10
103	Bob Lacey	.10
104	Rance Mulliniks	.10
105	Kirk Gibson	.10
106	Enrique Romo	.10
107	Wayne Krenchicki	.10
108	Bob Sykes	.10
109	Dave Revering	.10
110	Carlton Fisk	1.50
111	Carlton Fisk/IA	.65
112	Billy Sample	.10
113	Steve McCatty	.10
114	Ken Landreaux	.10
115	Gaylord Perry	1.00
116	Jim Wohlford	.10
117	Rawly Eastwick	.10
118	Terry Francona, Brad Mills, Bryn Smith RC Expos Future Stars	.20
119	Joe Pittman	.10
120	Gary Lucas	.10
121	Ed Lynch	.10
122	Jamie Easterly	.10
123	Danny Goodwin	.10
124	Reid Nichols	.10
125	Danny Ainge	1.00
126	Rick Mahler, Claudell Washington Braves Btg/Pitching Leaders	.10
127	Lonnie Smith	.10
128	Frank Pastore	.10
129	Checklist 1-132	.10
130	Julio Cruz	.10
131	Stan Bahnsen	.10
132	Lee May	.10
133	Pat Underwood	.10
134	Dan Ford	.10
135	Andy Rincon	.10
136	Lenn Sakata	.10
137	George Cappuzzello	.10
138	Tony Pena	.10
139	Jeff Jones	.10
140	Ron LeFlore	.10
141	Chris Bando, Tom Brennan, Von Hayes RC Indians Future Stars	.20
142	Dave LaRoche	.10
143	Mookie Wilson	.10
144	Fred Breining	.10
145	Bob Horner	.10
146	Mike Griffin	.10
147	Denny Walling	.10
148	Mickey Klutts	.10
149	Pat Putnam	.10
150	Ted Simmons	.10
151	Dave Edwards	.10
152	Ramon Aviles	.10
153	Roger Erickson	.10
154	Dennis Werth	.10
155	Otto Velez	.10
156	Rickey Henderson, Steve McCatty A's Btg/ Pitching Leaders	.10
157	Steve Crawford	.10
158	Brian Downing	.10
159	Larry Biittner	.10
160	Luis Tiant	.10

161	Carney Lansford, Bill Madlock Btg Leaders	.10
162	Tony Armas, Dwight Evans, Bobby Grich, Eddie Murray, Mike Schmidt Home Run Leaders	.25
163	Eddie Murray, Mike Schmidt RBI Leaders	.40
164	Rickey Henderson, Tim Raines Stolen Base Leaders	.35
165	Denny Martinez, Steve McCatty, Jack Morris, Tom Seaver, Pete Vuckovich Victory Leaders	.10
166	Len Barker, Fernando Valenzuela Strikeout Leaders	.10
167	Steve McCatty, Nolan Ryan ERA Leaders	1.50
168	Rollie Fingers, Bruce Sutter Leading Relievers	.15
169	Charlie Leibrandt	.10
170	Jim Bibby	.10
171	Bob Brenly, Chili Davis, Bob Tufts RC Giants Future Stars	2.00
172	Bill Gullickson	.10
173	Jamie Quirk	.10
174	Dave Ford	.10
175	Jerry Mumphrey	.10
176	Dewey Robinson	.10
177	John Ellis	.10
178	Dyar Miller	.10
179	Steve Garvey	.75
180	Steve Garvey (In Action)	.30
181	Silvio Martinez	.10
182	Larry Herndon	.10
183	Mike Proly	.10
184	Mick Kelleher	.10
185	Phil Niekro	1.00
186	Bob Forsch, Keith Hernandez Cardinals Btg/Pitching Leaders	.10
187	Jeff Newman	.10
188	Randy Martz	.10
189	Glenn Hoffman	.10
190	J.R. Richard	.05
191	Tim Wallach RC	2.00
192	Broderick Perkins	.10
193	Darrell Jackson	.10
194	Mike Vail	.10
195	Paul Molitor	1.50
196	Willie Upshaw	.10
197	Shane Rawley	.10
198	Chris Speier	.10
199	Don Aase	.10
200	George Brett	3.00
201	George Brett/IA	2.00
202	Rick Manning	.10
203	Jesse Barfield, Brian Milner, Boomer Wells Blue Jays Future Stars	.50
204	Gary Roenicke	.10
205	Neil Allen	.10
206	Tony Bernazard	.10
207	Rod Scurry	.10
208	Bobby Murcer	.10
209	Gary Lavelle	.10
210	Keith Hernandez	.10
211	Dan Petry	.10
212	Mario Mendoza	.10
213	Dave Stewart RC	4.00
214	Brian Asselstine	.10
215	Mike Krukow	.10
216	Dennis Lamp, Chet Lemon White Sox Btg/Pitching Leaders	.10
217	Bo McLaughlin	.10
218	Dave Roberts	.10
219	John Curtis	.10
220	Manny Trillo	.10
221	Jim Slaton	.10
222	Butch Wynegar	.10
223	Lloyd Moseby	.10
224	Bruce Bochte	.10
225	Mike Torrez	.10
226	Checklist 133-264	.10
227	Ray Burris	.10
228	Sam Mejias	.10
229	Geoff Zahn	.10
230	Willie Wilson	.10
231	Mark Davis, Bob Dernier, Ozzie Virgil RC Phillies Future Stars	.20
232	Terry Crowley	.10
233	Duane Kuiper	.10
234	Ron Hodges	.10
235	Mike Easler	.10
236	John Martin	.10

237	Rusty Kuntz	.10
238	Kevin Saucier	.10
239	Jon Matlack	.10
240	Bucky Dent	.10
241	Bucky Dent/IA	.10
242	Milt May	.10
243	Bob Owchinko	.10
244	Rufino Linares	.10
245	Ken Reitz	.10
246	Hubie Brooks, Mike Scott Mets Btg/Pitching Leaders	.10
247	Pedro Guerrero	.10
248	Frank LaCorte	.10
249	Tim Flannery	.10
250	Tug McGraw	.10
251	Fred Lynn	.10
252	Fred Lynn/IA	.10
253	Chuck Baker	.10
254	George Bell RC	1.00
255	Tony Perez	1.00
256	Tony Perez/IA	.10
257	Larry Harlow	.10
258	Bo Diaz	.10
259	Rodney Scott	.10
260	Bruce Sutter	1.00
261	Howard Bailey, Marty Castillo, Dave Rucker Tigers Future Stars	.10
262	Doug Bair	.10
263	Victor Cruz	.10
264	Dan Quisenberry	.10
265	Al Bumbry	.10
266	Rick Leach	.10
267	Kurt Bevacqua	.10
268	Rickey Keeton	.10
269	Jim Essian	.10
270	Rusty Staub	.15
271	Larry Bradford	.10
272	Bump Wills	.10
273	Doug Bird	.10
274	Bob Ojeda RC	.50
275	Bob Watson	.10
276	Rod Carew, Ken Forsch Angels Batting/Pitching Leaders	.25
277	Terry Puhl	.10
278	John Littlefield	.10
279	Bill Russell	.10
280	Ben Oglivie	.10
281	John Verhoeven	.10
282	Ken Macha	.10
283	Brian Allard	.10
284	Bob Grich	.10
285	Sparky Lyle	.10
286	Bill Fahey	.10
287	Alan Bannister	.10
288	Garry Templeton	.10
289	Bob Stanley	.10
290	Ken Singleton	.10
291	Vance Law, Bob Long, Johnny Ray RC Pirates Future Stars	.15
292	Dave Palmer	.10
293	Rob Picciolo	.10
294	Mike LaCoss	.10
295	Jason Thompson	.10
296	Bob Walk	.10
297	Clint Hurdle	.10
298	Danny Darwin	.10
299	Steve Trout	.10
300	Reggie Jackson	2.00
301	Reggie Jackson/IA	1.50
302	Doug Flynn	.10
303	Bill Caudill	.10
304	Johnnie LeMaster	.10
305	Don Sutton	1.00
306	Don Sutton/IA	.20
307	Randy Bass	.10
308	Charlie Moore	.10
309	Pete Redfern	.10
310	Mike Hargrove	.10
311	Dusty Baker, Burt Hooton Dodgers Btg/Pitching Leaders	.10
312	Lenny Randle	.10
313	John Harris	.10
314	Buck Martinez	.10
315	Burt Hooton	.10
316	Steve Braun	.10
317	Dick Ruthven	.10
318	Mike Heath	.10
319	Dave Rozema	.10
320	Chris Chambliss	.10
321	Chris Chambliss/IA	.10
322	Garry Hancock	.10
323	Bill Lee	.10
324	Steve Dillard	.10
325	Jose Cruz	.10
326	Pete Falcone	.10
327	Joe Nolan	.10
328	Ed Farmer	.10
329	U.L. Washington	.10

330	Rick Wise	.10
331	Benny Ayala	.10
332	Don Robinson	.10
333	Frank DiPino, Marshall Edwards, Chuck Porter Brewers Future Stars	.10
334	Aurelio Rodriguez	.10
335	Jim Sundberg	.10
336	Glenn Abbott, Tom Paciorek Mariners Btg/Pitching Leaders	.10
337	Pete Rose/AS	1.50
338	Dave Lopes/AS	.10
339	Mike Schmidt/AS	1.00
340	Dave Concepcion/AS	.10
341	Andre Dawson/AS	.25
342a	George Foster (All-Star no autograph)	2.00
342b	George Foster (All-Star autograph on front)	.10
343	Dave Parker/AS	.10
344	Gary Carter/AS	.60
345	Fernando Valenzuela/AS	.10
346	Tom Seaver/AS	.75
347	Bruce Sutter/AS	.50
348	Derrel Thomas	.10
349	George Frazier	.10
350	Thad Bosley	.10
351	Scott Brown, Geoff Combe, Paul Householder Reds Future Stars	.10
352	Dick Davis	.10
353	Jack O'Connor	.10
354	Roberto Ramos	.10
355	Dwight Evans	.10
356	Denny Lewallyn	.10
357	Butch Hobson	.10
358	Mike Parrott	.10
359	Jim Dwyer	.10
360	Len Barker	.10
361	Rafael Landestoy	.10
362	Jim Wright	.10
363	Bob Molinaro	.10
364	Doyle Alexander	.10
365	Bill Madlock	.10
366	Juan Eichelberger, Luis Salazar Padres Btg/Pitching Leaders	.10
367	Jim Kaat	.10
368	Alex Trevino	.10
369	Champ Summers	.10
370	Mike Norris	.10
371	Jerry Don Gleaton	.10
372	Luis Gomez	.10
373	Gene Nelson RC	.10
374	Tim Blackwell	.10
375	Dusty Baker	.15
376	Chris Welsh	.10
377	Kiko Garcia	.10
378	Mike Caldwell	.10
379	Rob Wilfong	.10
380	Dave Stieb	.10
381	Bruce Hurst, Dave Schmidt, Julio Valdez Red Sox Future Stars	.25
382	Joe Simpson	.10
383a	Pascual Perez (No position on front.)	20.00
383b	Pascual Perez ("Pitcher" on front.)	.10
384	Keith Moreland	.10
385	Ken Forsch	.10
386	Jerry White	.10
387	Tom Veryzer	.10
388	Joe Rudi	.10
389	George Vukovich	.10
390	Eddie Murray	1.50
391	Dave Tobik	.10
392	Rick Bosetti	.10
393	Al Hrabosky	.10
394	Checklist 265-396	.10
395	Omar Moreno	.10
396	Fernando Arroyo, John Castino Twins Btg/Pitching Leaders	.10
397	Ken Brett	.10
398	Mike Squires	.10
399	Pat Zachry	.10
400	Johnny Bench	1.50
401	Johnny Bench/IA	.45
402	Bill Stein	.10
403	Jim Tracy	.10
404	Dickie Thon	.10
405	Rick Reuschel	.10
406	Al Holland	.10
407	Danny Boone	.10
408	Ed Romero	.10
409	Don Cooper	.10
410	Ron Cey	.10
411	Ron Cey/IA	.10
412	Luis Leal	.10
413	Dan Meyer	.10

#	Player	Price
414	Elias Sosa	.10
415	Don Baylor	.15
416	Marty Bystrom	.10
417	Pat Kelly	.10
418	John Butcher, Bobby Johnson, Dave Schmidt RC Rangers Future Stars	.10
419	Steve Stone	.10
420	George Hendrick	.10
421	Mark Clear	.10
422	Cliff Johnson	.10
423	Stan Papi	.10
424	Bruce Benedict	.10
425	John Candelaria	.10
426	Eddie Murray, Sammy Stewart Orioles Btg/Pitching Leaders	.25
427	Ron Oester	.10
428	Lamarr Hoyt (LaMarr)	.10
429	John Wathan	.10
430	Vida Blue	.10
431	Vida Blue/IA	.10
432	Mike Scott	.10
433	Alan Ashby	.10
434	Joe Lefebvre	.10
435	Robin Yount	1.50
436	Joe Strain	.10
437	Juan Berenguer	.10
438	Pete Mackanin	.10
439	Dave Righetti RC	.75
440	Jeff Burroughs	.10
441	Danny Heep, Billy Smith, Bobby Sprowl Astros Future Stars	.10
442	Bruce Kison	.10
443	Mark Wagner	.10
444	Terry Forster	.10
445	Larry Parrish	.10
446	Wayne Garland	.10
447	Darrell Porter	.10
448	Darrell Porter/IA	.10
449	Luis Aguayo RC	.10
450	Jack Morris	.10
451	Ed Miller	.10
452	Lee Smith RC	4.00
453	Art Howe	.10
454	Rick Langford	.10
455	Tom Burgmeier	.10
456	Bill Buckner, Randy Martz Cubs Btg & Pitching Leaders	.10
457	Tim Stoddard	.10
458	Willie Montanez	.10
459	Bruce Berenyi	.10
460	Jack Clark	.10
461	Rich Dotson	.10
462	Dave Chalk	.10
463	Jim Kern	.10
464	Juan Bonilla	.10
465	Lee Mazzilli	.10
466	Randy Lerch	.10
467	Mickey Hatcher	.10
468	Floyd Bannister	.10
469	Ed Ott	.10
470	John Mayberry	.10
471	Atlee Hammaker, Mike Jones, Darryl Motley Royals Future Stars	.15
472	Oscar Gamble	.10
473	Mike Stanton	.10
474	Ken Oberkfell	.10
475	Alan Trammell	.10
476	Brian Kingman	.10
477	Steve Yeager	.10
478	Ray Searage	.10
479	Rowland Office	.10
480	Steve Carlton	1.50
481	Steve Carlton/IA	.40
482	Glenn Hubbard	.10
483	Gary Woods	.10
484	Ivan DeJesus	.10
485	Kent Tekulve	.10
486	Tommy John, Jerry Mumphrey Yankees Btg & Pitching Ldrs.	.10
487	Bob McClure	.10
488	Ron Jackson	.10
489	Rick Dempsey	.10
490	Dennis Eckersley	1.00
491	Checklist 397-528	.10
492	Joe Price	.10
493	Chet Lemon	.10
494	Hubie Brooks	.10
495	Dennis Leonard	.10
496	Johnny Grubb	.10
497	Jim Anderson	.10
498	Dave Bergman	.10
499	Paul Mirabella	.10
500	Rod Carew	1.50
501	Rod Carew/IA	.40
502	Steve Bedrosian, Brett Butler, Larry Owen Braves Future Stars	2.00
503	Julio Gonzalez	.10
504	Rick Peters	.10
505	Graig Nettles	.10
506	Graig Nettles/IA	.10
507	Terry Harper	.10
508	Jody Davis RC	.15
509	Harry Spilman	.10
510	Fernando Valenzuela	.10
511	Ruppert Jones	.10
512	Jerry Dybzinski	.10
513	Rick Rhoden	.10
514	Joe Ferguson	.10
515	Larry Bowa	.10
516	Larry Bowa/IA	.10
517	Mark Brouhard	.10
518	Garth Iorg	.10
519	Glenn Adams	.10
520	Mike Flanagan	.10
521	Billy Almon	.10
522	Chuck Rainey	.10
523	Gary Gray	.10
524	Tom Hausman	.10
525	Ray Knight	.10
526	Warren Cromartie, Bill Gullickson Expos Btg & Pitching Ldrs.	.10
527	John Henry Johnson	.10
528	Matt Alexander	.10
529	Allen Ripley	.10
530	Dickie Noles	.10
531	Rich Bordi, Mark Budaska, Kelvin Moore A's Future Stars	.10
532	Toby Harrah	.10
533	Joaquin Andujar	.10
534	Dave McKay	.10
535	Lance Parrish	.10
536	Rafael Ramirez	.10
537	Doug Capilla	.10
538	Lou Piniella	.10
539	Vern Ruhle	.10
540	Andre Dawson	.75
541	Barry Evans	.10
542	Ned Yost	.10
543	Bill Robinson	.10
544	Larry Christenson	.10
545	Reggie Smith	.10
546	Reggie Smith/IA	.10
547	Rod Carew/AS	.25
548	Willie Randolph/AS	.10
549	George Brett/AS	1.50
550	Bucky Dent/AS	.10
551	Reggie Jackson/AS	.75
552	Ken Singleton/AS	.10
553	Dave Winfield/AS	.60
554	Carlton Fisk/AS	.25
555	Scott McGregor/AS	.10
556	Jack Morris/AS	.10
557	Rich Gossage/AS	.10
558	John Tudor	.10
559	Bert Blyleven, Mike Hargrove Indians Btg & Pitching Leaders	.10
560	Doug Corbett	.10
561	Glenn Brummer, Luis DeLeon, Gene Roof Cardinals Future Stars	.10
562	Mike O'Berry	.10
563	Ross Baumgarten	.10
564	Doug DeCinces	.10
565	Jackson Todd	.10
566	Mike Jorgensen	.10
567	Bob Babcock	.10
568	Joe Pettini	.10
569	Willie Randolph	.10
570	Willie Randolph/IA	.10
571	Glenn Abbott	.10
572	Juan Beniquez	.10
573	Rick Waits	.10
574	Mike Ramsey	.10
575	Al Cowens	.10
576	Vida Blue, Milt May Giants Batting & Pitching Ldrs.	.10
577	Rick Monday	.10
578	Shooty Babitt	.10
579	Rick Mahler RC	.10
580	Bobby Bonds	.10
581	Ron Reed	.10
582	Luis Pujols	.10
583	Tippy Martinez	.10
584	Hosken Powell	.10
585	Rollie Fingers	1.00
586	Rollie Fingers/IA	.15
587	Tim Lollar	.10
588	Dale Berra	.10
589	Dave Stapleton	.10
590	Al Oliver	.10
591	Al Oliver/IA	.10
592	Craig Swan	.10
593	Billy Smith	.10
594	Renie Martin	.10
595	Dave Collins	.10
596	Damaso Garcia	.10
597	Wayne Nordhagen	.10
598	Bob Galasso	.10
599	Jay Loviglio, Reggie Patterson, Leo Sutherland White Sox Future Stars	.10
600	Dave Winfield	1.50
601	Sid Monge	.10
602	Freddie Patek	.10
603	Rich Hebner	.10
604	Orlando Sanchez	.10
605	Steve Rogers	.10
606	John Mayberry, Dave Stieb Blue Jays Btg & Pitching Leaders	.10
607	Leon Durham	.10
608	Jerry Royster	.10
609	Rick Sutcliffe	.10
610	Rickey Henderson	1.50
611	Joe Niekro	.10
612	Gary Ward	.10
613	Jim Gantner	.10
614	Juan Eichelberger	.10
615	Bob Boone	.10
616	Bob Boone/IA	.10
617	Scott McGregor	.10
618	Tim Foli	.10
619	Bill Campbell	.10
620	Ken Griffey	.10
621	Ken Griffey/IA	.10
622	Dennis Lamp	.10
623	Ron Gardenhire, Terry Leach, Tim Leary RC Mets Future Stars	.20
624	Fergie Jenkins	1.00
625	Hal McRae	.10
626	Randy Jones	.10
627	Enos Cabell	.10
628	Bill Travers	.10
629	Johnny Wockenfuss	.10
630	Joe Charboneau	.10
631	Gene Tenace	.10
632	Bryan Clark	.10
633	Mitchell Page	.10
634	Checklist 529-660	.10
635	Ron Davis	.10
636	Steve Carlton, Pete Rose Phillies Btg & Pitching Leaders	.50
637	Rick Camp	.10
638	John Milner	.10
639	Ken Kravec	.10
640	Cesar Cedeno	.10
641	Steve Mura	.10
642	Mike Scioscia	.10
643	Pete Vuckovich	.10
644	John Castino	.10
645	Frank White	.10
646	Frank White/IA	.10
647	Warren Brusstar	.10
648	Jose Morales	.10
649	Ken Clay	.10
650	Carl Yastrzemski	1.50
651	Carl Yastrzemski/IA	.65
652	Steve Nicosia	.10
653	Tom Brunansky, Luis Sanchez, Daryl Sconiers RC Angels Future Stars	.40
654	Jim Morrison	.10
655	Joel Youngblood	.10
656	Eddie Whitson	.10
657	Tom Poquette	.10
658	Tito Landrum	.10
659	Fred Martinez	.10
660	Dave Concepcion	.10
661	Dave Concepcion/IA	.10
662	Luis Salazar	.10
663	Hector Cruz	.10
664	Dan Spillner	.10
665	Jim Clancy	.10
666	Steve Kemp, Dan Petry Tigers Btg & Pitching Leaders	.10
667	Jeff Reardon	.15
668	Dale Murphy	.75
669	Larry Milbourne	.10
670	Steve Kemp	.10
671	Mike Davis	.10
672	Bob Knepper	.10
673	Keith Drumright	.10
674	Dave Goltz	.10
675	Cecil Cooper	.10
676	Sal Butera	.10
677	Alfredo Griffin	.10
678	Tom Paciorek	.10
679	Sammy Stewart	.10
680	Gary Matthews	.10
681	Mike Marshall, Ron Roenicke, Steve Sax RC Dodgers Future Stars	.75
682	Jesse Jefferson	.10
683	Phil Garner	.10
684	Harold Baines	.05
685	Bert Blyleven	.10
686	Gary Allenson	.10
687	Greg Minton	.10
688	Leon Roberts	.10
689	Lary Sorensen	.10
690	Dave Kingman	.10
691	Dan Schatzeder	.10
692	Wayne Gross	.10
693	Cesar Geronimo	.10
694	Dave Wehrmeister	.10
695	Warren Cromartie	.10
696	Bill Madlock, Buddy Solomon Pirates Btg & Pitching Leaders	.10
697	John Montefusco	.10
698	Tony Scott	.10
699	Dick Tidrow	.10
700	George Foster	.10
701	George Foster/IA	.10
702	Steve Renko	.10
703	Cecil Cooper, Pete Vuckovich Brewers Btg & Pitching Leaders	.10
704	Mickey Rivers	.10
705	Mickey Rivers/IA	.10
706	Barry Foote	.10
707	Mark Bomback	.10
708	Gene Richards	.10
709	Don Money	.10
710	Jerry Reuss	.10
711	Dave Edler, Dave Henderson, Reggie Walton RC Mariners Future Stars	.25
712	Denny Martinez	.10
713	Del Unser	.10
714	Jerry Koosman	.10
715	Willie Stargell	1.50
716	Willie Stargell/IA	.30
717	Rick Miller	.10
718	Charlie Hough	.10
719	Jerry Narron	.10
720	Greg Luzinski	.10
721	Greg Luzinski/IA	.10
722	Jerry Martin	.10
723	Junior Kennedy	.10
724	Dave Rosello	.10
725	Amos Otis	.10
726	Amos Otis/IA	.10
727	Sixto Lezcano	.10
728	Aurelio Lopez	.10
729	Jim Spencer	.10
730	Gary Carter	1.50
731	Mike Armstrong, Doug Gwosdz, Fred Kuhaulua Padres Future Stars	.10
732	Mike Lum	.10
733	Larry McWilliams	.10
734	Mike Ivie	.10
735	Rudy May	.10
736	Jerry Turner	.10
737	Reggie Cleveland	.10
738	Dave Engle	.10
739	Joey McLaughlin	.10
740	Dave Lopes	.10
741	Dave Lopes/IA	.10
742	Dick Drago	.10
743	John Stearns	.10
744	Mike Witt RC	.25
745	Bake McBride	.10
746	Andre Thornton	.10
747	John Lowenstein	.10
748	Marc Hill	.10
749	Bob Shirley	.10
750	Jim Rice	.20
751	Rick Honeycutt	.10
752	Lee Lacy	.10
753	Tom Brookens	.10
754	Joe Morgan	1.50
755	Joe Morgan/IA	.25
756	Ken Griffey, Tom Seaver Reds Btg & Pitching Leaders	.25
757	Tom Underwood	.10
758	Claudell Washington	.10
759	Paul Splittorff	.10
760	Bill Buckner	.10
761	Dave Smith	.10
762	Mike Phillips	.10
763	Tom Hume	.10
764	Steve Swisher	.10
765	Gorman Thomas	.10
766	Lenny Faedo, Kent Hrbek, Tim Laudner RC Twins Future Stars	2.00
767	Roy Smalley	.10
768	Jerry Garvin	.10
769	Richie Zisk	.10
770	Rich Gossage	.10
771	Rich Gossage/IA	.10
772	Bert Campaneris	.10
773	John Denny	.10
774	Jay Johnstone	.10

775	Bob Forsch	.10
776	Mark Belanger	.10
777	Tom Griffin	.10
778	Kevin Hickey	.10
779	Grant Jackson	.10
780	Pete Rose	3.50
781	Pete Rose/IA	2.00
782	Frank Taveras	.10
783	Greg Harris RC	.10
784	Milt Wilcox	.10
785	Dan Driessen	.10
786	Carney Lansford, Mike Torrez Red Sox Btg & Pitching Leaders	.10
787	Fred Stanley	.10
788	Woodie Fryman	.10
789	Checklist 661-792	.10
790	Larry Gura	.10
791	Bobby Brown	.10
792	Frank Tanana	.10

Traded

OZZIE SMITH — CARDINALS SHORTSTOP

		NM/M
	Complete Set (132):	175.00
	Common Player:	.10
1T	Doyle Alexander	.10
2T	Jesse Barfield	.10
3T	Ross Baumgarten	.10
4T	Steve Bedrosian	.10
5T	Mark Belanger	.10
6T	Kurt Bevacqua	.10
7T	Tim Blackwell	.10
8T	Vida Blue	.10
9T	Bob Boone	.30
10T	Larry Bowa	.10
11T	Dan Briggs	.10
12T	Bobby Brown	.10
13T	Tom Brunansky	.10
14T	Jeff Burroughs	.10
15T	Enos Cabell	.10
16T	Bill Campbell	.10
17T	Bobby Castillo	.10
18T	Bill Caudill	.10
19T	Cesar Cedeno	.10
20T	Dave Collins	.10
21T	Doug Corbett	.10
22T	Al Cowens	.10
23T	Chili Davis	.50
24T	Dick Davis	.10
25T	Ron Davis	.10
26T	Doug DeCinces	.10
27T	Ivan DeJesus	.10
28T	Bob Dernier	.10
29T	Bo Diaz	.10
30T	Roger Erickson	.10
31T	Jim Essian	.10
32T	Ed Farmer	.10
33T	Doug Flynn	.10
34T	Tim Foli	.10
35T	Dan Ford	.10
36T	George Foster	.10
37T	Dave Frost	.10
38T	Rich Gale	.10
39T	Ron Gardenhire	.10
40T	Ken Griffey	.10
41T	Greg Harris	.10
42T	Von Hayes	.10
43T	Larry Herndon	.10
44T	Kent Hrbek	2.00
45T	Mike Ivie	.10
46T	Grant Jackson	.10
47T	Reggie Jackson	5.00
48T	Ron Jackson	.10
49T	Fergie Jenkins	2.00
50T	Lamar Johnson	.10
51T	Randy Johnson	.10
52T	Jay Johnstone	.10
53T	Mick Kelleher	.10
54T	Steve Kemp	.10
55T	Junior Kennedy	.10
56T	Jim Kern	.10
57T	Ray Knight	.10
58T	Wayne Krenchicki	.10
59T	Mike Krukow	.10
60T	Duane Kuiper	.10
61T	Mike LaCoss	.10
62T	Chet Lemon	.10
63T	Sixto Lezcano	.10
64T	Dave Lopes	.10
65T	Jerry Martin	.10
66T	Renie Martin	.10
67T	John Mayberry	.10
68T	Lee Mazzilli	.10
69T	Bake McBride	.10
70T	Dan Meyer	.10
71T	Larry Milbourne	.10
72T	Eddie Milner	.10
73T	Sid Monge	.10
74T	John Montefusco	.10
75T	Jose Morales	.10
76T	Keith Moreland	.10
77T	Jim Morrison	.10
78T	Rance Mulliniks	.10
79T	Steve Mura	.10
80T	Gene Nelson	.10
81T	Joe Nolan	.10
82T	Dickie Noles	.10
83T	Al Oliver	.10
84T	Jorge Orta	.10
85T	Tom Paciorek	.10
86T	Larry Parrish	.10
87T	Jack Perconte	.10
88T	Gaylord Perry	2.00
89T	Rob Picciolo	.10
90T	Joe Pittman	.10
91T	Hosken Powell	.10
92T	Mike Proly	.10
93T	Greg Pryor	.10
94T	Charlie Puleo	.10
95T	Shane Rawley	.10
96T	Johnny Ray	.10
97T	Dave Revering	.10
98T	Cal Ripken, Jr.	140.00
99T	Allen Ripley	.10
100T	Bill Robinson	.10
101T	Aurelio Rodriguez	.10
102T	Joe Rudi	.10
103T	Steve Sax	.50
104T	Dan Schatzeder	.10
105T	Bob Shirley	.10
106T	Eric Show	.10
107T	Roy Smalley	.10
108T	Lonnie Smith	.10
109T	Ozzie Smith	20.00
110T	Reggie Smith	.10
111T	Lary Sorensen	.10
112T	Elias Sosa	.10
113T	Mike Stanton	.10
114T	Steve Stroughter	.10
115T	Champ Summers	.10
116T	Rick Sutcliffe	.10
117T	Frank Tanana	.10
118T	Frank Taveras	.10
119T	Garry Templeton	.10
120T	Alex Trevino	.10
121T	Jerry Turner	.10
122T	Ed Vande Berg	.10
123T	Tom Veryzer	.10
124T	Ron Washington	.10
125T	Bob Watson	.10
126T	Dennis Werth	.10
127T	Eddie Whitson	.10
128T	Rob Wilfong	.10
129T	Bump Wills	.10
130T	Gary Woods	.10
131T	Butch Wynegar	.10
132T	Checklist 1-132	.10

1983 Topps

WADE BOGGS — 1st BASE-3rd BASE — RED SOX

	NM/M
Complete Set (792):	60.00
Common Player:	.05
Wax Pack (15):	3.00
Wax Box (36):	110.00
Crimp-End Test Pack (15):	4.00
Crimp-end Test Box (36):	110.00
Cello Pack (28):	5.00
Cello Box (24):	125.00
Rack Pack (51):	7.50
Rack Box (24):	175.00
Vending Box (500):	65.00

1	Tony Armas (Record Breaker)	.05
2	Rickey Henderson (Record Breaker)	.75
3	Greg Minton (Record Breaker)	.05
4	Lance Parrish (Record Breaker)	.05
5	Manny Trillo (Record Breaker)	.05
6	John Wathan (Record Breaker)	.05
7	Gene Richards	.05
8	Steve Balboni	.05
9	Joey McLaughlin	.05
10	Gorman Thomas	.05
11	Billy Gardner	.05
12	Paul Mirabella	.05
13	Larry Herndon	.05
14	Frank LaCorte	.05
15	Ron Cey	.05
16	George Vukovich	.05
17	Kent Tekulve	.05
18	Kent Tekulve (Super Veteran)	.05
19	Oscar Gamble	.05
20	Carlton Fisk	2.00
21	Eddie Murray, Jim Palmer Orioles Btg & Pitching Leaders	.25
22	Randy Martz	.05
23	Mike Heath	.05
24	Steve Mura	.05
25	Hal McRae	.05
26	Jerry Royster	.05
27	Doug Corbett	.05
28	Bruce Bochte	.05
29	Randy Jones	.05
30	Jim Rice	.15
31	Bill Gullickson	.05
32	Dave Bergman	.05
33	Jack O'Connor	.05
34	Paul Householder	.05
35	Rollie Fingers	.75
36	Rollie Fingers (Super Veteran)	.15
37	Darrell Johnson	.05
38	Tim Flannery	.05
39	Terry Puhl	.05
40	Fernando Valenzuela	.05
41	Jerry Turner	.05
42	Dale Murray	.05
43	Bob Dernier	.05
44	Don Robinson	.05
45	John Mayberry	.05
46	Richard Dotson	.05
47	Dave McKay	.05
48	Lary Sorensen	.05
49	Willie McGee RC	1.50
50	Bob Horner	.05
51	Leon Durham, Fergie Jenkins Cubs Btg & Pitching Leaders	.05
52	Onix Concepcion RC	.05
53	Mike Witt	.05
54	Jim Maler	.05
55	Mookie Wilson	.05
56	Chuck Rainey	.05
57	Tim Blackwell	.05
58	Al Holland	.05
59	Benny Ayala	.05
60	Johnny Bench	2.00
61	Johnny Bench (Super Veteran)	.75
62	Bob McClure	.05
63	Rick Monday	.05
64	Bill Stein	.05
65	Jack Morris	.05
66	Bob Lillis	.05
67	Sal Butera	.05
68	Eric Show RC	.15
69	Lee Lacy	.05
70	Steve Carlton	2.00
71	Steve Carlton (Super Veteran)	.30
72	Tom Paciorek	.05
73	Allen Ripley	.05
74	Julio Gonzalez	.05
75	Amos Otis	.05
76	Rick Mahler	.05
77	Hosken Powell	.05
78	Bill Caudill	.05
79	Mick Kelleher	.05
80	George Foster	.05
81	Jerry Mumphrey, Dave Righetti/Yankees Btg & Pitching Leaders	.05
82	Bruce Hurst	.05
83	Ryne Sandberg RC	15.00
84	Milt May	.05
85	Ken Singleton	.05
86	Tom Hume	.05
87	Joe Rudi	.05
88	Jim Gantner	.05
89	Leon Roberts	.05
90	Jerry Reuss	.05
91	Larry Milbourne	.05
92	Mike LaCoss	.05
93	John Castino	.05
94	Dave Edwards	.05
95	Alan Trammell	.05
96	Dick Howser	.05
97	Ross Baumgarten	.05
98	Vance Law	.05
99	Dickie Noles	.05
100	Pete Rose	4.00
101	Pete Rose (Super Veteran)	2.00
102	Dave Beard	.05
103	Darrell Porter	.05
104	Bob Walk	.05
105	Don Baylor	.15
106	Gene Nelson	.05
107	Mike Jorgensen	.05
108	Glenn Hoffman	.05
109	Luis Leal	.05
110	Ken Griffey	.05
111	Al Oliver, Steve Rogers Expos Btg & Pitching Leaders	.05
112	Bob Shirley	.05
113	Ron Roenicke	.05
114	Jim Slaton	.05
115	Chili Davis	.05
116	Dave Schmidt	.05
117	Alan Knicely	.05
118	Chris Welsh	.05
119	Tom Brookens	.05
120	Len Barker	.05
121	Mickey Hatcher	.05
122	Jimmy Smith	.05
123	George Frazier	.05
124	Marc Hill	.05
125	Leon Durham	.05
126	Joe Torre	.25
127	Preston Hanna	.05
128	Mike Ramsey	.05
129	Checklist 1-132	.05
130	Dave Stieb	.05
131	Ed Ott	.05
132	Todd Cruz	.05
133	Jim Barr	.05
134	Hubie Brooks	.05
135	Dwight Evans	.05
136	Willie Aikens	.05
137	Woodie Fryman	.05
138	Rick Dempsey	.05
139	Bruce Berenyi	.05
140	Willie Randolph	.05
141	Toby Harrah, Rick Sutcliffe Indians Btg & Pitching Leaders	.05
142	Mike Caldwell	.05
143	Joe Pettini	.05
144	Mark Wagner	.05
145	Don Sutton	.75
146	Don Sutton (Super Veteran)	.20
147	Rick Leach	.05
148	Dave Roberts	.05
149	Johnny Ray	.05
150	Bruce Sutter	.75
151	Bruce Sutter (Super Veteran)	.50
152	Jay Johnstone	.05
153	Jerry Koosman	.05
154	Johnnie LeMaster	.05
155	Dan Quisenberry	.05
156	Billy Martin	.15
157	Steve Bedrosian	.05
158	Rob Wilfong	.05
159	Mike Stanton	.05
160	Dave Kingman	.05
161	Dave Kingman (Super Veteran)	.05
162	Mark Clear	.05
163	Cal Ripken, Jr.	6.00
164	Dave Palmer	.05
165	Dan Driessen	.05
166	John Pacella	.05
167	Mark Brouhard	.05
168	Juan Eichelberger	.05
169	Doug Flynn	.05
170	Steve Howe	.05
171	Bill Laskey, Joe Morgan Giants Btg & Pitching Leaders	.05
172	Vern Ruhle	.05
173	Jim Morrison	.05
174	Jerry Ujdur	.05
175	Bo Diaz	.05
176	Dave Righetti	.05

No.	Name	Price
177	Harold Baines	.05
178	Luis Tiant	.05
179	Luis Tiant (Super Veteran)	.05
180	Rickey Henderson	2.00
181	Terry Felton	.05
182	Mike Fischlin	.05
183	Ed Vande Berg RC	.05
184	Bob Clark	.05
185	Tim Lollar	.05
186	Whitey Herzog	.05
187	Terry Leach	.05
188	Rick Miller	.05
189	Dan Schatzeder	.05
190	Cecil Cooper	.05
191	Joe Price	.05
192	Floyd Rayford	.05
193	Harry Spilman	.05
194	Cesar Geronimo	.05
195	Bob Stoddard	.05
196	Bill Fahey	.05
197	Jim Eisenreich RC	.50
198	Kiko Garcia	.05
199	Marty Bystrom	.05
200	Rod Carew	2.00
201	Rod Carew (Super Veteran)	.35
202	Damaso Garcia, Dave Stieb Blue Jays Btg & Pitching Leaders	.05
203	Mike Morgan	.05
204	Junior Kennedy	.05
205	Dave Parker	.05
206	Ken Oberkfell	.05
207	Rick Camp	.05
208	Dan Meyer	.05
209	Mike Moore RC	.15
210	Jack Clark	.05
211	John Denny	.05
212	John Stearns	.05
213	Tom Burgmeier	.05
214	Jerry White	.05
215	Mario Soto	.05
216	Tony LaRussa	.05
217	Tim Stoddard	.05
218	Roy Howell	.05
219	Mike Armstrong	.05
220	Dusty Baker	.05
221	Joe Niekro	.05
222	Damaso Garcia	.05
223	John Montefusco	.05
224	Mickey Rivers	.05
225	Enos Cabell	.05
226	Enrique Romo	.05
227	Chris Bando	.05
228	Joaquin Andujar	.05
229	Steve Carlton, Bo Diaz Phillies Btg/Pitching Leaders	.15
230	Fergie Jenkins	.75
231	Fergie Jenkins (Super Veteran)	.20
232	Tom Brunansky	.05
233	Wayne Gross	.05
234	Larry Andersen	.05
235	Claudell Washington	.05
236	Steve Renko	.05
237	Dan Norman	.05
238	Bud Black RC	.25
239	Dave Stapleton	.05
240	Rich Gossage	.05
241	Rich Gossage (Super Veteran)	.05
242	Joe Nolan	.05
243	Duane Walker	.05
244	Dwight Bernard	.05
245	Steve Sax	.05
246	George Bamberger	.05
247	Dave Smith	.05
248	Bake McBride	.05
249	Checklist 133-264	.05
250	Bill Buckner	.05
251	Alan Wiggins RC	.05
252	Luis Aguayo	.05
253	Larry McWilliams	.05
254	Rick Cerone	.05
255	Gene Garber	.05
256	Gene Garber (Super Veteran)	.05
257	Jesse Barfield	.05
258	Manny Castillo	.05
259	Jeff Jones	.05
260	Steve Kemp	.05
261	Larry Herndon, Dan Petry Tigers Btg & Pitching Leaders	.05
262	Ron Jackson	.05
263	Renie Martin	.05
264	Jamie Quirk	.05
265	Joel Youngblood	.05
266	Paul Boris	.05
267	Terry Francona	.05
268	Storm Davis RC	.05
269	Ron Oester	.05
270	Dennis Eckersley	.75
271	Ed Romero	.05
272	Frank Tanana	.05
273	Mark Belanger	.05
274	Terry Kennedy	.05
275	Ray Knight	.05
276	Gene Mauch	.05
277	Rance Mulliniks	.05
278	Kevin Hickey	.05
279	Greg Gross	.05
280	Bert Blyleven	.05
281	Andre Robertson	.05
282	Reggie Smith	.05
283	Reggie Smith (Super Veteran)	.05
284	Jeff Lahti	.05
285	Lance Parrish	.05
286	Rick Langford	.05
287	Bobby Brown	.05
288	Joe Cowley RC	.05
289	Jerry Dybzinski	.05
290	Jeff Reardon	.05
291	John Candelaria, Bill Madlock Pirates Btg & Pitching Leaders	.05
292	Craig Swan	.05
293	Glenn Gulliver	.05
294	Dave Engle	.05
295	Jerry Remy	.05
296	Greg Harris	.05
297	Ned Yost	.05
298	Floyd Chiffer	.05
299	George Wright	.05
300	Mike Schmidt	3.00
301	Mike Schmidt (Super Veteran)	1.50
302	Ernie Whitt	.05
303	Miguel Dilone	.05
304	Dave Rucker	.05
305	Larry Bowa	.05
306	Tom Lasorda	.25
307	Lou Piniella	.05
308	Jesus Vega	.05
309	Jeff Leonard	.05
310	Greg Luzinski	.05
311	Glenn Brummer	.05
312	Brian Kingman	.05
313	Gary Gray	.05
314	Ken Dayley	.05
315	Rick Burleson	.05
316	Paul Splittorff	.05
317	Gary Rajsich	.05
318	John Tudor	.05
319	Lenn Sakata	.05
320	Steve Rogers	.05
321	Pete Vuckovich, Robin Yount Brewers Btg & Pitching Leaders	.10
322	Dave Van Gorder	.05
323	Luis DeLeon	.05
324	Mike Marshall	.05
325	Von Hayes	.05
326	Garth Iorg	.05
327	Bobby Castillo	.05
328	Craig Reynolds	.05
329	Randy Niemann	.05
330	Buddy Bell	.05
331	Mike Krukow	.05
332	Glenn Wilson RC	.05
333	Dave LaRoche	.05
334	Dave LaRoche (Super Veteran)	.05
335	Steve Henderson	.05
336	Rene Lachemann	.05
337	Tito Landrum	.05
338	Bob Owchinko	.05
339	Terry Harper	.05
340	Larry Gura	.05
341	Doug DeCinces	.05
342	Atlee Hammaker	.05
343	Bob Bailor	.05
344	Roger LaFrancois	.05
345	Jim Clancy	.05
346	Joe Pittman	.05
347	Sammy Stewart	.05
348	Alan Bannister	.05
349	Checklist 265-396	.05
350	Robin Yount	2.00
351	Cesar Cedeno, Mario Soto Reds Btg & Pitching Leaders	.05
352	Mike Scioscia	.05
353	Steve Comer	.05
354	Randy S. Johnson	.05
355	Jim Bibby	.05
356	Gary Woods	.05
357	Len Matuszek RC	.05
358	Jerry Garvin	.05
359	Dave Collins	.05
360	Nolan Ryan	5.00
361	Nolan Ryan (Super Veteran)	4.00
362	Bill Almon	.05
363	John Stuper RC	.05
364	Brett Butler	.05
365	Dave Lopes	.05
366	Dick Williams	.05
367	Bud Anderson	.05
368	Richie Zisk	.05
369	Jesse Orosco	.05
370	Gary Carter	2.00
371	Mike Richardt	.05
372	Terry Crowley	.05
373	Kevin Saucier	.05
374	Wayne Krenchicki	.05
375	Pete Vuckovich	.05
376	Ken Landreaux	.05
377	Lee May	.05
378	Lee May (Super Veteran)	.05
379	Guy Sularz	.05
380	Ron Davis	.05
381	Jim Rice, Bob Stanley Red Sox Btg & Pitching Leaders	.05
382	Bob Knepper	.05
383	Ozzie Virgil	.05
384	Dave Dravecky RC	.50
385	Mike Easler	.05
386	Rod Carew/AS	.35
387	Bob Grich/AS	.05
388	George Brett/AS	1.50
389	Robin Yount/AS	.60
390	Reggie Jackson/AS	1.00
391	Rickey Henderson/AS	.50
392	Fred Lynn/AS	.05
393	Carlton Fisk/AS	.35
394	Pete Vuckovich/AS	.05
395	Larry Gura/AS	.05
396	Dan Quisenberry/AS	.05
397	Pete Rose/AS	2.00
398	Manny Trillo/AS	.05
399	Mike Schmidt/AS	1.50
400	Dave Concepcion/AS	.05
401	Dale Murphy/AS	.20
402	Andre Dawson/AS	.35
403	Tim Raines/AS	.05
404	Gary Carter/AS	.35
405	Steve Rogers/AS	.05
406	Steve Carlton/AS	.30
407	Bruce Sutter/AS	.25
408	Rudy May	.05
409	Marvis Foley	.05
410	Phil Niekro	.75
411	Phil Niekro (Super Veteran)	.25
412	Buddy Bell, Charlie Hough Rangers Batting & Pitching Leaders	.05
413	Matt Keough	.05
414	Julio Cruz	.05
415	Bob Forsch	.05
416	Joe Ferguson	.05
417	Tom Hausman	.05
418	Greg Pryor	.05
419	Steve Crawford	.05
420	Al Oliver	.05
421	Al Oliver (Super Veteran)	.05
422	George Cappuzzello	.05
423	Tom Lawless RC	.05
424	Jerry Augustine	.05
425	Pedro Guerrero	.05
426	Earl Weaver	.25
427	Roy Lee Jackson	.05
428	Champ Summers	.05
429	Eddie Whitson	.05
430	Kirk Gibson	.05
431	Gary Gaetti RC	.75
432	Porfirio Altamirano	.05
433	Dale Berra	.05
434	Dennis Lamp	.05
435	Tony Armas	.05
436	Bill Campbell	.05
437	Rick Sweet	.05
438	Dave LaPoint RC	.05
439	Rafael Ramirez	.05
440	Ron Guidry	.20
441	Ray Knight, Joe Niekro Astros Btg & Pitching Leaders	.05
442	Brian Downing	.05
443	Don Hood	.05
444	Wally Backman	.05
445	Mike Flanagan	.05
446	Reid Nichols	.05
447	Bryn Smith	.05
448	Darrell Evans	.05
449	Eddie Milner RC	.05
450	Ted Simmons	.05
451	Ted Simmons (Super Veteran)	.05
452	Lloyd Moseby	.05
453	Lamar Johnson	.05
454	Bob Welch	.05
455	Sixto Lezcano	.05
456	Lee Elia	.05
457	Milt Wilcox	.05
458	Ron Washington	.05
459	Ed Farmer	.05
460	Roy Smalley	.05
461	Steve Trout	.05
462	Steve Nicosia	.05
463	Gaylord Perry	.75
464	Gaylord Perry (Super Veteran)	.20
465	Lonnie Smith	.05
466	Tom Underwood	.05
467	Rufino Linares	.05
468	Dave Goltz	.05
469	Ron Gardenhire	.05
470	Greg Minton	.05
471	Vida Blue, Willie Wilson Royals Btg & Pitching Leaders	.05
472	Gary Allenson	.05
473	John Lowenstein	.05
474	Ray Burris	.05
475	Cesar Cedeno	.05
476	Rob Picciolo	.05
477	Tom Niedenfuer	.05
478	Phil Garner	.05
479	Charlie Hough	.05
480	Toby Harrah	.05
481	Scot Thompson	.05
482	Tony Gwynn RC	25.00
483	Lynn Jones	.05
484	Dick Ruthven	.05
485	Omar Moreno	.05
486	Clyde King	.05
487	Jerry Hairston Sr.	.05
488	Alfredo Griffin	.05
489	Tom Herr	.05
490	Jim Palmer	1.50
491	Jim Palmer (Super Veteran)	.20
492	Paul Serna	.05
493	Steve McCatty	.05
494	Bob Brenly	.05
495	Warren Cromartie	.05
496	Tom Veryzer	.05
497	Rick Sutcliffe	.05
498	Wade Boggs RC	15.00
499	Jeff Little	.05
500	Reggie Jackson	2.00
501	Reggie Jackson (Super Veteran)	.75
502	Dale Murphy, Phil Niekro Braves Batting & Pitching Leaders	.20
503	Moose Haas	.05
504	Don Werner	.05
505	Garry Templeton	.05
506	Jim Gott RC	.25
507	Tony Scott	.05
508	Tom Filer	.05
509	Lou Whitaker	.05
510	Tug McGraw	.05
511	Tug McGraw (Super Veteran)	.05
512	Doyle Alexander	.05
513	Fred Stanley	.05
514	Rudy Law	.05
515	Gene Tenace	.05
516	Bill Virdon	.05
517	Gary Ward	.05
518	Bill Laskey	.05
519	Terry Bulling	.05
520	Fred Lynn	.05
521	Bruce Benedict	.05
522	Pat Zachry	.05
523	Carney Lansford	.05
524	Tom Brennan	.05
525	Frank White	.05
526	Checklist 397-528	.05
527	Larry Biittner	.05
528	Jamie Easterly	.05
529	Tim Laudner	.05
530	Eddie Murray	2.00
531	Rickey Henderson, Rick Langford Athletics Btg & Pitching Leaders	.15
532	Dave Stewart	.05
533	Luis Salazar	.05
534	John Butcher	.05
535	Manny Trillo	.05
536	Johnny Wockenfuss	.05
537	Rod Scurry	.05
538	Danny Heep	.05
539	Roger Erickson	.05
540	Ozzie Smith	2.00
541	Britt Burns	.05
542	Jody Davis	.05
543	Alan Fowlkes	.05
544	Larry Whisenton	.05
545	Floyd Bannister	.05
546	Dave Garcia	.05
547	Geoff Zahn	.05
548	Brian Giles	.05
549	Charlie Puleo RC	.05
550	Carl Yastrzemski	2.00

551	Carl Yastrzemski (Super Veteran)	.50
552	Tim Wallach	.05
553	Denny Martinez	.05
554	Mike Vail	.05
555	Steve Yeager	.05
556	Willie Upshaw	.05
557	Rick Honeycutt	.05
558	Dickie Thon	.05
559	Pete Redfern	.05
560	Ron LeFlore	.05
561	Joaquin Andujar, Lonnie Smith Cardinals Btg & Pitching Leaders	.05
562	Dave Rozema	.05
563	Juan Bonilla	.05
564	Sid Monge	.05
565	Bucky Dent	.05
566	Manny Sarmiento	.05
567	Joe Simpson	.05
568	Willie Hernandez	.05
569	Jack Perconte	.05
570	Vida Blue	.05
571	Mickey Klutts	.05
572	Bob Watson	.05
573	Andy Hassler	.05
574	Glenn Adams	.05
575	Neil Allen	.05
576	Frank Robinson	.25
577	Luis Aponte	.05
578	David Green	.05
579	Rich Dauer	.05
580	Tom Seaver	2.00
581	Tom Seaver (Super Veteran)	.50
582	Marshall Edwards	.05
583	Terry Forster	.05
584	Dave Hostetler	.05
585	Jose Cruz	.05
586	Frank Viola **RC**	1.50
587	Ivan DeJesus	.05
588	Pat Underwood	.05
589	Alvis Woods	.05
590	Tony Pena	.05
591	LaMarr Hoyt, Greg Luzinski White Sox Batting & Pitching Leaders	.05
592	Shane Rawley	.05
593	Broderick Perkins	.05
594	Eric Rasmussen	.05
595	Tim Raines	.05
596	Randy S. Johnson	.05
597	Mike Proly	.05
598	Dwayne Murphy	.05
599	Don Aase	.05
600	George Brett	3.00
601	Ed Lynch	.05
602	Rich Gedman	.05
603	Joe Morgan	2.00
604	Joe Morgan (Super Veteran)	.35
605	Gary Roenicke	.05
606	Bobby Cox	.05
607	Charlie Leibrandt	.05
608	Don Money	.05
609	Danny Darwin	.05
610	Steve Garvey	.50
611	Bert McGraw	.05
612	Steve Swisher	.05
613	Mike Ivie	.05
614	Ed Glynn	.05
615	Garry Maddox	.05
616	Bill Nahorodny	.05
617	Butch Wynegar	.05
618	LaMarr Hoyt	.05
619	Keith Moreland	.05
620	Mike Norris	.05
621	Craig Swan, Mookie Wilson Mets Btg & Pitching Leaders	.05
622	Dave Edler	.05
623	Luis Sanchez	.05
624	Glenn Hubbard	.05
625	Ken Forsch	.05
626	Jerry Martin	.05
627	Doug Bair	.05
628	Julio Valdez	.05
629	Charlie Lea	.05
630	Paul Molitor	2.00
631	Tippy Martinez	.05
632	Alex Trevino	.05
633	Vicente Romo	.05
634	Max Venable	.05
635	Graig Nettles	.05
636	Graig Nettles (Super Veteran)	.05
637	Pat Corrales	.05
638	Dan Petry	.05
639	Art Howe	.05
640	Andre Thornton	.05
641	Billy Sample	.05
642	Checklist 529-660	.05
643	Bump Wills	.05
644	Joe Lefebvre	.05
645	Bill Madlock	.05
646	Jim Essian	.05
647	Bobby Mitchell	.05
648	Jeff Burroughs	.05
649	Tommy Boggs	.05
650	George Hendrick	.05
651	Rod Carew, Mike Witt Angels Btg & Pitching Leaders	.05
652	Butch Hobson	.05
653	Ellis Valentine	.05
654	Bob Ojeda	.05
655	Al Bumbry	.05
656	Dave Frost	.05
657	Mike Gates	.05
658	Frank Pastore	.05
659	Charlie Moore	.05
660	Mike Hargrove	.05
661	Bill Russell	.05
662	Joe Sambito	.05
663	Tom O'Malley	.05
664	Bob Molinaro	.05
665	Jim Sundberg	.05
666	Sparky Anderson	.25
667	Dick Davis	.05
668	Larry Christenson	.05
669	Mike Squires	.05
670	Jerry Mumphrey	.05
671	Lenny Faedo	.05
672	Jim Kaat	.10
673	Jim Kaat (Super Veteran)	.05
674	Kurt Bevacqua	.05
675	Jim Beattie	.05
676	Biff Pocoroba	.05
677	Dave Revering	.05
678	Juan Beniquez	.05
679	Mike Scott	.05
680	Andre Dawson	.60
681	Pedro Guerrero, Fernando Valenzuela Dodgers Batting & Pitching Leaders	.05
682	Bob Stanley	.05
683	Dan Ford	.05
684	Rafael Landestoy	.05
685	Lee Mazzilli	.05
686	Randy Lerch	.05
687	U.L. Washington	.05
688	Jim Wohlford	.05
689	Ron Hassey	.05
690	Kent Hrbek	.05
691	Dave Tobik	.05
692	Denny Walling	.05
693	Sparky Lyle	.05
694	Sparky Lyle (Super Veteran)	.05
695	Ruppert Jones	.05
696	Chuck Tanner	.05
697	Barry Foote	.05
698	Tony Bernazard	.05
699	Lee Smith	.05
700	Keith Hernandez	.05
701	Al Oliver, Willie Wilson Batting Leaders	.05
702	Reggie Jackson, Dave Kingman, Gorman Thomas Home Run Leaders	.15
703	Hal McRae, Dale Murphy, Al Oliver Runs Batted In Leaders	.05
704	Rickey Henderson, Tim Raines Stolen Base Leaders	.10
705	Steve Carlton, LaMarr Hoyt Victory Leaders	.05
706	Floyd Bannister, Steve Carlton Strikeout Leaders	.05
707	Steve Rogers, Rick Sutcliffe Earned Run Average Leaders	.05
708	Dan Quisenberry, Bruce Sutter Leading Firemen	.10
709	Jimmy Sexton	.05
710	Willie Wilson	.05
711	Jim Beattie, Bruce Bochte Mariners Batting & Pitching Leaders	.05
712	Bruce Kison	.05
713	Ron Hodges	.05
714	Wayne Nordhagen	.05
715	Tony Perez	1.50
716	Tony Perez (Super Veteran)	.05
717	Scott Sanderson	.05
718	Jim Dwyer	.05
719	Rich Gale	.05
720	Dave Concepcion	.05
721	John Martin	.05
722	Jorge Orta	.05
723	Randy Moffitt	.05
724	Johnny Grubb	.05
725	Dan Spillner	.05
726	Harvey Kuenn	.05
727	Chet Lemon	.05
728	Ron Reed	.05
729	Jerry Morales	.05
730	Jason Thompson	.05
731	Al Williams	.05
732	Dave Henderson	.05
733	Buck Martinez	.05
734	Steve Braun	.05
735	Tommy John	.20
736	Tommy John (Super Veteran)	.05
737	Mitchell Page	.05
738	Tim Foli	.05
739	Rick Ownbey	.05
740	Rusty Staub	.05
741	Rusty Staub (Super Veteran)	.05
742	Terry Kennedy, Tim Lollar Padres Batting & Pitching Leaders	.05
743	Mike Torrez	.05
744	Brad Mills	.05
745	Scott McGregor	.05
746	John Wathan	.05
747	Fred Breining	.05
748	Derrel Thomas	.05
749	Jon Matlack	.05
750	Ben Oglivie	.05
751	Brad Havens	.05
752	Luis Pujols	.05
753	Elias Sosa	.05
754	Bill Robinson	.05
755	John Candelaria	.05
756	Russ Nixon	.05
757	Rick Manning	.05
758	Aurelio Rodriguez	.05
759	Doug Bird	.05
760	Dale Murphy	.60
761	Gary Lucas	.05
762	Cliff Johnson	.05
763	Al Cowens	.05
764	Pete Falcone	.05
765	Bob Boone	.05
766	Barry Bonnell	.05
767	Duane Kuiper	.05
768	Chris Speier	.05
769	Checklist 661-792	.05
770	Dave Winfield	2.00
771	Bobby Castillo, Kent Hrbek Twins Batting & Pitching Leaders	.05
772	Jim Kern	.05
773	Larry Hisle	.05
774	Alan Ashby	.05
775	Burt Hooton	.05
776	Larry Parrish	.05
777	John Curtis	.05
778	Rich Hebner	.05
779	Rick Waits	.05
780	Gary Matthews	.05
781	Rick Rhoden	.05
782	Bobby Murcer	.05
783	Bobby Murcer (Super Veteran)	.05
784	Jeff Newman	.05
785	Dennis Leonard	.05
786	Ralph Houk	.05
787	Dick Tidrow	.05
788	Dane Iorg	.05
789	Bryan Clark	.05
790	Bob Grich	.05
791	Gary Lavelle	.05
792	Chris Chambliss	.05

Traded

RON CEY
3rd BASE
CUBS

NM/M

Complete Set (132):		20.00
Common Player:		.05
1T	Neil Allen	.05
2T	Bill Almon	.05
3T	Joe Altobelli	.05
4T	Tony Armas	.05
5T	Doug Bair	.05
6T	Steve Baker	.05
7T	Floyd Bannister	.05
8T	Don Baylor	.25
9T	Tony Bernazard	.05
10T	Larry Biittner	.05
11T	Dann Bilardello	.05
12T	Doug Bird	.05
13T	Steve Boros	.05
14T	Greg Brock	.05
15T	Mike Brown	.05
16T	Tom Burgmeier	.05
17T	Randy Bush	.05
18T	Bert Campaneris	.05
19T	Ron Cey	.05
20T	Chris Codiroli **(RC)**	.05
21T	Dave Collins	.05
22T	Terry Crowley	.05
23T	Julio Cruz	.05
24T	Mike Davis	.05
25T	Frank DiPino	.05
26T	Bill Doran **(RC)**	.05
27T	Jerry Dybzinski	.05
28T	Jamie Easterly	.05
29T	Juan Eichelberger	.05
30T	Jim Essian	.05
31T	Pete Falcone	.05
32T	Mike Ferraro	.05
33T	Terry Forster	.05
34T	Julio Franco **RC**	3.00
35T	Rich Gale	.05
36T	Kiko Garcia	.05
37T	Steve Garvey	1.00
38T	Johnny Grubb	.05
39T	Mel Hall	.05
40T	Von Hayes	.05
41T	Danny Heep	.05
42T	Steve Henderson	.05
43T	Keith Hernandez	.15
44T	Leo Hernandez	.05
45T	Willie Hernandez	.05
46T	Al Holland	.05
47T	Frank Howard	.05
48T	Bobby Johnson	.05
49T	Cliff Johnson	.05
50T	Odell Jones	.05
51T	Mike Jorgensen	.05
52T	Bob Kearney	.05
53T	Steve Kemp	.05
54T	Matt Keough	.05
55T	Ron Kittle **(RC)**	.05
56T	Mickey Klutts	.05
57T	Alan Knicely	.05
58T	Mike Krukow	.05
59T	Rafael Landestoy	.05
60T	Carney Lansford	.05
61T	Joe Lefebvre	.05
62T	Bryan Little	.05
63T	Aurelio Lopez	.05
64T	Mike Madden	.05
65T	Rick Manning	.05
66T	Billy Martin	.25
67T	Lee Mazzilli	.05
68T	Andy McGaffigan	.05
69T	Craig McMurtry	.05
70T	John McNamara	.05
71T	Orlando Mercado	.05
72T	Larry Milbourne	.05
73T	Randy Moffitt	.05
74T	Sid Monge	.05
75T	Jose Morales	.05
76T	Omar Moreno	.05
77T	Joe Morgan	4.00
78T	Mike Morgan	.05
79T	Dale Murray	.05
80T	Jeff Newman	.05
81T	Pete O'Brien	.05
82T	Jorge Orta	.05
83T	Alejandro Pena	.05
84T	Pascual Perez	.05
85T	Tony Perez	1.00
86T	Broderick Perkins	.05
87T	Tony Phillips **RC**	.15
88T	Charlie Puleo	.05
89T	Pat Putnam	.05
90T	Jamie Quirk	.05
91T	Doug Rader	.05
92T	Chuck Rainey	.05
93T	Bobby Ramos	.05
94T	Gary Redus	.05
95T	Steve Renko	.05
96T	Leon Roberts	.05
97T	Aurelio Rodriguez	.05
98T	Dick Ruthven	.05
99T	Daryl Sconiers	.05
100T	Mike Scott	.05
101T	Tom Seaver	6.00
102T	John Shelby	.05
103T	Bob Shirley	.05
104T	Joe Simpson	.05
105T	Doug Sisk	.05

106T	Mike Smithson	.05
107T	Elias Sosa	.05
108T	Darryl Strawberry RC	10.00
109T	Tom Tellmann	.05
110T	Gene Tenace	.05
111T	Gorman Thomas	.05
112T	Dick Tidrow	.05
113T	Dave Tobik	.05
114T	Wayne Tolleson	.05
115T	Mike Torrez	.05
116T	Manny Trillo	.05
117T	Steve Trout	.05
118T	Lee Tunnell	.05
120T	Ellis Valentine	.05
121T	Tom Veryzer	.05
122T	George Vukovich	.05
123T	Rick Waits	.05
124T	Greg Walker	.05
125T	Chris Welsh	.05
126T	Len Whitehouse	.05
127T	Eddie Whitson	.05
128T	Jim Wohlford	.05
129T	Matt Young	.05
130T	Joel Youngblood	.05
131T	Pat Zachry	.05
132T	Checklist 1-132	.05

1984 Topps

CARDINALS

WILLIE McGEE OF

	NM/M
Complete Set (792):	40.00
Common Player:	.05
Wax Pack (15):	2.00
Wax Box (36):	50.00
Cello Pack (28):	2.50
Cello Box (24):	50.00
Rack Pack (54+1):	3.50
Rack Box (24):	60.00
Vending Box (500):	20.00

1	Steve Carlton (1983 Highlight)	.25
2	Rickey Henderson (1983 Highlight)	.25
3	Dan Quisenberry (1983 Highlight)	.05
4	Steve Carlton, Gaylord Perry, Nolan Ryan (1983 Highlight)	.50
5	Bob Forsch, Dave Righetti, Mike Warren (1983 Highlight)	.05
6	Johnny Bench, Gaylord Perry, Carl Yastrzemski (1983 Highlight)	.25
7	Gary Lucas	.05
8	Don Mattingly RC	15.00
9	Jim Gott	.05
10	Robin Yount	1.00
11	Kent Hrbek, Ken Schrom Twins Batting & Pitching Leaders	.05
12	Billy Sample	.05
13	Scott Holman	.05
14	Tom Brookens	.05
15	Burt Hooton	.05
16	Omar Moreno	.05
17	John Denny	.05
18	Dale Berra	.05
19	Ray Fontenot RC	.05
20	Greg Luzinski	.05
21	Joe Altobelli	.05
22	Bryan Clark	.05
23	Keith Moreland	.05
24	John Martin	.05
25	Glenn Hubbard	.05
26	Bud Black	.05
27	Daryl Sconiers	.05
28	Frank Viola	.05
29	Danny Heep	.05
30	Wade Boggs	3.00
31	Andy McGaffigan	.05
32	Bobby Ramos	.05
33	Tom Burgmeier	.05
34	Eddie Milner	.05
35	Don Sutton	.65
36	Denny Walling	.05
37	Buddy Bell, Rick Honeycutt Rangers Batting & Pitching Leaders	.05
38	Luis DeLeon	.05
39	Garth Iorg	.05
40	Dusty Baker	.05
41	Tony Bernazard	.05
42	Johnny Grubb	.05
43	Ron Reed	.05
44	Jim Morrison	.05
45	Jerry Mumphrey	.05
46	Ray Smith	.05
47	Rudy Law	.05
48	Julio Franco	.05
49	John Stuper	.05
50	Chris Chambliss	.05
51	Jim Frey	.05
52	Paul Splittorff	.05
53	Juan Beniquez	.05
54	Jesse Orosco	.05
55	Dave Concepcion	.05
56	Gary Allenson	.05
57	Dan Schatzeder	.05
58	Max Venable	.05
59	Sammy Stewart	.05
60	Paul Molitor	1.00
61	Chris Codiroli RC	.05
62	Dave Hostetler	.05
63	Ed Vande Berg	.05
64	Mike Scioscia	.05
65	Kirk Gibson	.05
66	Jose Cruz, Nolan Ryan Astros Batting & Pitching Leaders	.25
67	Gary Ward	.05
68	Luis Salazar	.05
69	Rod Scurry	.05
70	Gary Matthews	.05
71	Leo Hernandez	.05
72	Mike Squires	.05
73	Jody Davis	.05
74	Jerry Martin	.05
75	Bob Forsch	.05
76	Alfredo Griffin	.05
77	Brett Butler	.05
78	Mike Torrez	.05
79	Rob Wilfong	.05
80	Steve Rogers	.05
81	Billy Martin	.15
82	Doug Bird	.05
83	Richie Zisk	.05
84	Lenny Faedo	.05
85	Atlee Hammaker	.05
86	John Shelby RC	.05
87	Frank Pastore	.05
88	Rob Picciolo	.05
89	Mike Smithson RC	.05
90	Pedro Guerrero	.05
91	Dan Spillner	.05
92	Lloyd Moseby	.05
93	Bob Knepper	.05
94	Mario Ramirez	.05
95	Aurelio Lopez	.05
96	Larry Gura, Hal McRae Royals Batting & Pitching Leaders	.05
97	LaMarr Hoyt	.05
98	Steve Nicosia	.05
99	Craig Lefferts RC	.25
100	Reggie Jackson	1.50
101	Porfirio Altamirano	.05
102	Ken Oberkfell	.05
103	Dwayne Murphy	.05
104	Ken Dayley	.05
105	Tony Armas	.05
106	Tim Stoddard	.05
107	Ned Yost	.05
108	Randy Moffitt	.05
109	Brad Wellman	.05
110	Ron Guidry	.05
111	Bill Virdon	.05
112	Tom Niedenfuer	.05
113	Kelly Paris	.05
114	Checklist 1-132	.05
115	Andre Thornton	.05
116	George Bjorkman	.05
117	Tom Veryzer	.05
118	Charlie Hough	.05
119	Johnny Wockenfuss	.05
120	Keith Hernandez	.05

ABBREVIATIONS

DP - Double Print
OPS - Overprint
"Promotional Sample"

121	Pat Sheridan RC	.05
122	Cecilio Guante	.05
123	Butch Wynegar	.05
124	Damaso Garcia	.05
125	Britt Burns	.05
126	Craig McMurtry, Dale Murphy Braves Batting & Pitching Leaders	.05
127	Mike Madden	.05
128	Rick Manning	.05
129	Bill Laskey	.05
130	Ozzie Smith	2.00
131	Wade Boggs, Bill Madlock Batting Leaders	.25
132	Jim Rice, Mike Schmidt Home Run Leaders	.25
133	Cecil Cooper, Dale Murphy, Jim Rice RBI Leaders	.10
134	Rickey Henderson, Tim Raines Stolen Base Leaders	.25
135	John Denny, LaMarr Hoyt Victory Leaders	.05
136	Steve Carlton, Jack Morris Strikeout Leaders	.05
137	Atlee Hammaker, Rick Honeycutt Earned Run Average Leaders	.05
138	Al Holland, Dan Quisenberry Leading Firemen	.05
139	Bert Campaneris	.05
140	Storm Davis	.05
141	Pat Corrales	.05
142	Rich Gale	.05
143	Jose Morales	.05
144	Brian Harper RC	.20
145	Gary Lavelle	.05
146	Ed Romero	.05
147	Dan Petry	.05
148	Joe Lefebvre	.05
149	Jon Matlack	.05
150	Dale Murphy	.50
151	Steve Trout	.05
152	Glenn Brummer	.05
153	Dick Tidrow	.05
154	Dave Henderson	.05
155	Frank White	.05
156	Tim Conroy, Rickey Henderson Athletics Batting & Pitching Leaders	.15
157	Gary Gaetti	.05
158	John Curtis	.05
159	Darryl Cias	.05
160	Mario Soto	.05
161	Junior Ortiz RC	.05
162	Bob Ojeda	.05
163	Lorenzo Gray	.05
164	Scott Sanderson	.05
165	Ken Singleton	.05
166	Jamie Nelson	.05
167	Marshall Edwards	.05
168	Juan Bonilla	.05
169	Larry Parrish	.05
170	Jerry Reuss	.05
171	Frank Robinson	.25
172	Frank DiPino	.05
173	Marvell Wynne RC	.05
174	Juan Berenguer	.05
175	Graig Nettles	.05
176	Lee Smith	.05
177	Jerry Hairston Sr.	.05
178	Bill Krueger	.05
179	Buck Martinez	.05
180	Manny Trillo	.05
181	Roy Thomas	.05
182	Darryl Strawberry	.25
183	Al Williams	.05
184	Mike O'Berry	.05
185	Sixto Lezcano	.05
186	Lonnie Smith, John Stuper Cardinals Batting & Pitching Leaders	.05
187	Luis Aponte	.05
188	Bryan Little	.05
189	Tim Conroy RC	.05
190	Ben Oglivie	.05
191	Mike Boddicker	.05
192	Nick Esasky RC	.05
193	Darrell Brown	.05
194	Domingo Ramos	.05
195	Jack Morris	.05
196	Don Slaught	.05
197	Garry Hancock	.05
198	Bill Doran RC	.05
199	Willie Hernandez	.05
200	Andre Dawson	.60
201	Bruce Kison	.05
202	Bobby Cox	.05
203	Matt Keough	.05
204	Bobby Meacham RC	.05
205	Greg Minton	.05
206	Andy Van Slyke RC	.75
207	Donnie Moore	.05
208	Jose Oquendo RC	.05
209	Manny Sarmiento	.05
210	Joe Morgan	1.00
211	Rick Sweet	.05
212	Broderick Perkins	.05
213	Bruce Hurst	.05
214	Paul Householder	.05
215	Tippy Martinez	.05
216	Richard Dotson, Carlton Fisk White Sox Batting & Pitching Leaders	.05
217	Alan Ashby	.05
218	Rick Waits	.05
219	Joe Simpson	.05
220	Fernando Valenzuela	.05
221	Cliff Johnson	.05
222	Rick Honeycutt	.05
223	Wayne Krenchicki	.05
224	Sid Monge	.05
225	Lee Mazzilli	.05
226	Juan Eichelberger	.05
227	Steve Braun	.05
228	John Rabb	.05
229	Paul Owens	.05
230	Rickey Henderson	1.00
231	Gary Woods	.05
232	Tim Wallach	.05
233	Checklist 133-264	.05
234	Rafael Ramirez	.05
235	Matt Young RC	.05
236	Ellis Valentine	.05
237	John Castino	.05
238	Reid Nichols	.05
239	Jay Howell	.05
240	Eddie Murray	1.00
241	Billy Almon	.05
242	Alex Trevino	.05
243	Pete Ladd	.05
244	Candy Maldonado	.05
245	Rick Sutcliffe	.05
246	Tom Seaver, Mookie Wilson Mets Batting & Pitching Leaders	.25
247	Onix Concepcion	.05
248	Bill Dawley RC	.05
249	Jay Johnstone	.05
250	Bill Madlock	.05
251	Tony Gwynn	4.00
252	Larry Christenson	.05
253	Jim Wohlford	.05
254	Shane Rawley	.05
255	Bruce Benedict	.05
256	Dave Geisel	.05
257	Julio Cruz	.05
258	Luis Sanchez	.05
259	Sparky Anderson	.15
260	Scott McGregor	.05
261	Bobby Brown	.05
262	Tom Candiotti RC	.25
263	Jack Fimple	.05
264	Doug Frobel	.05
265	Donnie Hill RC	.05
266	Steve Lubratich	.05
267	Carmelo Martinez RC	.05
268	Jack O'Connor	.05
269	Aurelio Rodriguez	.05
270	Jeff Russell RC	.05
271	Moose Haas	.05
272	Rick Dempsey	.05
273	Charlie Puleo	.05
274	Rick Monday	.05
275	Len Matuszek	.05
276	Rod Carew, Geoff Zahn Angels Batting & Pitching Leaders	.10
277	Eddie Whitson	.05
278	Jorge Bell	.05
279	Ivan DeJesus	.05
280	Floyd Bannister	.05
281	Larry Milbourne	.05
282	Jim Barr	.05
283	Larry Biittner	.05
284	Howard Bailey	.05
285	Darrell Porter	.05
286	Lary Sorensen	.05
287	Warren Cromartie	.05
288	Jim Beattie	.05
289	Randy S. Johnson	.05
290	Dave Dravecky	.05
291	Chuck Tanner	.05
292	Tony Scott	.05
293	Ed Lynch	.05
294	U.L. Washington	.05
295	Mike Flanagan	.05
296	Jeff Newman	.05
297	Bruce Berenyi	.05
298	Jim Gantner	.05
299	John Butcher	.05
300	Pete Rose	5.00
301	Frank LaCorte	.05
302	Barry Bonnell	.05

#	Player	Price
303	Marty Castillo	.05
304	Warren Brusstar	.05
305	Roy Smalley	.05
306	Pedro Guerrero,Bob Welch Dodgers Batting & Pitching Leaders	.05
307	Bobby Mitchell	.05
308	Ron Hassey	.05
309	Tony Phillips	.05
310	Willie McGee	.05
311	Jerry Koosman	.05
312	Jorge Orta	.05
313	Mike Jorgensen	.05
314	Orlando Mercado	.05
315	Bob Grich	.05
316	Mark Bradley	.05
317	Greg Pryor	.05
318	Bill Gullickson	.05
319	Al Bumbry	.05
320	Bob Stanley	.05
321	Harvey Kuenn	.05
322	Ken Schrom	.05
323	Alan Knicely	.05
324	Alejandro Pena RC	.05
325	Darrell Evans	.05
326	Bob Kearney	.05
327	Ruppert Jones	.05
328	Vern Ruhle	.05
329	Pat Tabler	.05
330	John Candelaria	.05
331	Bucky Dent	.05
332	Kevin Gross RC	.05
333	Larry Herndon	.05
334	Chuck Rainey	.05
335	Don Baylor	.15
336	Pat Putnam, Matt Young Mariners Batting & Pitching Leaders	.05
337	Kevin Hagen	.05
338	Mike Warren	.05
339	Roy Lee Jackson	.05
340	Hal McRae	.05
341	Dave Tobik	.05
342	Tim Foli	.05
343	Mark Davis	.05
344	Rick Miller	.05
345	Kent Hrbek	.05
346	Kurt Bevacqua	.05
347	Allan Ramirez	.05
348	Toby Harrah	.05
349	Bob L. Gibson	.05
350	George Foster	.05
351	Russ Nixon	.05
352	Dave Stewart	.05
353	Jim Anderson	.05
354	Jeff Burroughs	.05
355	Jason Thompson	.05
356	Glenn Abbott	.05
357	Ron Cey	.05
358	Bob Dernier	.05
359	Jim Acker RC	.05
360	Willie Randolph	.05
361	Dave Smith	.05
362	David Green	.05
363	Tim Laudner	.05
364	Scott Fletcher	.05
365	Steve Bedrosian	.05
366	Dave Dravecky, Terry Kennedy Padres Batting & Pitching Leaders	.05
367	Jamie Easterly	.05
368	Hubie Brooks	.05
369	Steve McCatty	.05
370	Tim Raines	.05
371	Dave Gumpert	.05
372	Gary Roenicke	.05
373	Bill Scherrer	.05
374	Don Money	.05
375	Dennis Leonard	.05
376	Dave Anderson RC	.05
377	Danny Darwin	.05
378	Bob Brenly	.05
379	Checklist 265-396	.05
380	Steve Garvey	.45
381	Ralph Houk	.05
382	Chris Nyman	.05
383	Terry Puhl	.05
384	Lee Tunnell RC	.05
385	Tony Perez	1.00
386	George Hendrick/AS	.05
387	Johnny Ray/AS	.05
388	Mike Schmidt/AS	.75
389	Ozzie Smith/AS	.50
390	Tim Raines/AS	.05
391	Dale Murphy/AS	.20
392	Andre Dawson/AS	.25
393	Gary Carter/AS	.30
394	Steve Rogers/AS	.05
395	Steve Carlton/AS	.25
396	Jesse Orosco/AS	.05
397	Eddie Murray/AS	.40
398	Lou Whitaker/AS	.05
399	George Brett/AS	.75
400	Cal Ripken, Jr./AS	4.00
401	Jim Rice/AS	.05
402	Dave Winfield/AS	.30
403	Lloyd Moseby/AS	.05
404	Ted Simmons/AS	.05
405	LaMarr Hoyt/AS	.05
406	Ron Guidry/AS	.05
407	Dan Quisenberry/AS	.05
408	Lou Piniella	.05
409	Juan Agosto RC	.05
410	Claudell Washington	.05
411	Houston Jimenez	.05
412	Doug Rader	.05
413	Spike Owen RC	.05
414	Mitchell Page	.05
415	Tommy John	.15
416	Dane Iorg	.05
417	Mike Armstrong	.05
418	Ron Hodges	.05
419	John Henry Johnson	.05
420	Cecil Cooper	.05
421	Charlie Lea	.05
422	Jose Cruz	.05
423	Mike Morgan	.05
424	Dann Bilardello RC	.05
425	Steve Howe	.05
426	Mike Boddicker, Cal Ripken, Jr. Orioles Batting & Pitching Leaders	.50
427	Rick Leach	.05
428	Fred Breining	.05
429	Randy Bush RC	.05
430	Rusty Staub	.05
431	Chris Bando	.05
432	Charlie Hudson RC	.05
433	Rich Hebner	.05
434	Harold Baines	.05
435	Neil Allen	.05
436	Rick Peters	.05
437	Mike Proly	.05
438	Biff Pocoroba	.05
439	Bob Stoddard	.05
440	Steve Kemp	.05
441	Bob Lillis	.05
442	Byron McLaughlin	.05
443	Benny Ayala	.05
444	Steve Renko	.05
445	Jerry Remy	.05
446	Luis Pujols	.05
447	Tom Brunansky	.05
448	Ben Hayes	.05
449	Joe Pettini	.05
450	Gary Carter	1.00
451	Bob Jones	.05
452	Chuck Porter	.05
453	Willie Upshaw	.05
454	Joe Beckwith	.05
455	Terry Kennedy	.05
456	Fergie Jenkins, Keith Moreland Cubs Batting & Pitching Leaders	.05
457	Dave Rozema	.05
458	Kiko Garcia	.05
459	Kevin Hickey	.05
460	Dave Winfield	1.00
461	Jim Maler	.05
462	Lee Lacy	.05
463	Dave Engle	.05
464	Jeff Jones	.05
465	Mookie Wilson	.05
466	Gene Garber	.05
467	Mike Ramsey	.05
468	Geoff Zahn	.05
469	Tom O'Malley	.05
470	Nolan Ryan	6.00
471	Dick Howser	.05
472	Mike Brown	.05
473	Jim Dwyer	.05
474	Greg Bargar	.05
475	Gary Redus RC	.05
476	Tom Tellmann	.05
477	Rafael Landestoy	.05
478	Alan Bannister	.05
479	Frank Tanana	.05
480	Ron Kittle	.05
481	Mark Thurmond RC	.05
482	Enos Cabell	.05
483	Fergie Jenkins	.65
484	Ozzie Virgil	.05
485	Rick Rhoden	.05
486	Don Baylor, Ron Guidry Yankees Batting & Pitching Leaders	.05
487	Ricky Adams	.05
488	Jesse Barfield	.05
489	Joe Von Ohlen	.05
490	Cal Ripken, Jr.	6.00
491	Bobby Castillo	.05
492	Tucker Ashford	.05
493	Mike Norris	.05
494	Chili Davis	.05
495	Rollie Fingers	.65
496	Terry Francona	.05
497	Bud Anderson	.05
498	Rich Gedman	.05
499	Mike Witt	.05
500	George Brett	2.00
501	Steve Henderson	.05
502	Joe Torre	.05
503	Elias Sosa	.05
504	Mickey Rivers	.05
505	Pete Vuckovich	.05
506	Ernie Whitt	.05
507	Mike LaCoss	.05
508	Mel Hall	.05
509	Brad Havens	.05
510	Alan Trammell	.05
511	Marty Bystrom	.05
512	Oscar Gamble	.05
513	Dave Beard	.05
514	Floyd Rayford	.05
515	Gorman Thomas	.05
516	Charlie Lea, Al Oliver Expos Batting & Pitching Leaders	.05
517	John Moses	.05
518	Greg Walker RC	.05
519	Ron Davis	.05
520	Bob Boone	.05
521	Pete Falcone	.05
522	Dave Bergman	.05
523	Glenn Hoffman	.05
524	Carlos Diaz	.05
525	Willie Wilson	.05
526	Ron Oester	.05
527	Checklist 397-528	.05
528	Mark Brouhard	.05
529	Keith Atherton RC	.05
530	Dan Ford	.05
531	Steve Boros	.05
532	Eric Show	.05
533	Ken Landreaux	.05
534	Pete O'Brien	.05
535	Bo Diaz	.05
536	Doug Bair	.05
537	Johnny Ray	.05
538	Kevin Bass	.05
539	George Frazier	.05
540	George Hendrick	.05
541	Dennis Lamp	.05
542	Duane Kuiper	.05
543	Craig McMurtry RC	.05
544	Cesar Geronimo	.05
545	Bill Buckner	.05
546	Mike Hargrove, Lary Sorensen Indians Batting & Pitching Leaders	.05
547	Mike Moore	.05
548	Ron Jackson	.05
549	Walt Terrell RC	.05
550	Jim Rice	.15
551	Scott Ullger	.05
552	Ray Burris	.05
553	Joe Nolan	.05
554	Ted Power	.05
555	Greg Brock	.05
556	Joey McLaughlin	.05
557	Wayne Tolleson	.05
558	Mike Davis	.05
559	Mike Scott	.05
560	Carlton Fisk	1.00
561	Whitey Herzog	.05
562	Manny Castillo	.05
563	Glenn Wilson	.05
564	Al Holland	.05
565	Leon Durham	.05
566	Jim Bibby	.05
567	Mike Heath	.05
568	Pete Filson	.05
569	Bake McBride	.05
570	Dan Quisenberry	.05
571	Bruce Bochy	.05
572	Jerry Royster	.05
573	Dave Kingman	.05
574	Brian Downing	.05
575	Jim Clancy	.05
576	Atlee Hammaker, Jeff Leonard Giants Batting & Pitching Leaders	.05
577	Mark Clear	.05
578	Lenn Sakata	.05
579	Bob James	.05
580	Lonnie Smith	.05
581	Jose DeLeon RC	.05
582	Bob McClure	.05
583	Derrel Thomas	.05
584	Dave Schmidt	.05
585	Dan Driessen	.05
586	Joe Niekro	.05
587	Von Hayes	.05
588	Milt Wilcox	.05
589	Mike Easler	.05
590	Dave Stieb	.05
591	Tony LaRussa	.05
592	Andre Robertson	.05
593	Jeff Lahti	.05
594	Gene Richards	.05
595	Jeff Reardon	.05
596	Ryne Sandberg	3.00
597	Rick Camp	.05
598	Rusty Kuntz	.05
599	Doug Sisk RC	.05
600	Rod Carew	1.00
601	John Tudor	.05
602	John Wathan	.05
603	Renie Martin	.05
604	John Lowenstein	.05
605	Mike Caldwell	.05
606	Lloyd Moseby, Dave Stieb Blue Jays Batting & Pitching Leaders	.05
607	Tom Hume	.05
608	Bobby Johnson	.05
609	Dan Meyer	.05
610	Steve Sax	.05
611	Chet Lemon	.05
612	Harry Spilman	.05
613	Greg Gross	.05
614	Len Barker	.05
615	Garry Templeton	.05
616	Don Robinson	.05
617	Rick Cerone	.05
618	Dickie Noles	.05
619	Jerry Dybzinski	.05
620	Al Oliver	.05
621	Frank Howard	.05
622	Al Cowens	.05
623	Ron Washington	.05
624	Terry Harper	.05
625	Larry Gura	.05
626	Bob Clark	.05
627	Dave LaPoint	.05
628	Ed Jurak	.05
629	Rick Langford	.05
630	Ted Simmons	.05
631	Denny Martinez	.05
632	Tom Foley	.05
633	Mike Krukow	.05
634	Mike Marshall	.05
635	Dave Righetti	.05
636	Pat Putnam	.05
637	John Denny, Gary Matthews Phillies Batting & Pitching Leaders	.05
638	George Vukovich	.05
639	Rick Lysander	.05
640	Lance Parrish	.05
641	Mike Richardt	.05
642	Tom Underwood	.05
643	Mike Brown	.05
644	Tim Lollar	.05
645	Tony Pena	.05
646	Checklist 529-660	.05
647	Ron Roenicke	.05
648	Len Whitehouse	.05
649	Tom Herr	.05
650	Phil Niekro	.65
651	John McNamara	.05
652	Rudy May	.05
653	Dave Stapleton	.05
654	Bob Bailor	.05
655	Amos Otis	.05
656	Bryn Smith	.05
657	Thad Bosley	.05
658	Jerry Augustine	.05
659	Duane Walker	.05
660	Ray Knight	.05
661	Steve Yeager	.05
662	Tom Brennan	.05
663	Johnnie LeMaster	.05
664	Dave Stegman	.05
665	Buddy Bell	.05
666	Jack Morris, Lou Whitaker Tigers Batting & Pitching Leaders	.05
667	Vance Law	.05
668	Larry McWilliams	.05
669	Dave Lopes	.05
670	Rich Gossage	.05
671	Jamie Quirk	.05
672	Ricky Nelson	.05
673	Mike Walters	.05
674	Tim Flannery	.05
675	Pascual Perez	.05
676	Brian Giles	.05
677	Doyle Alexander	.05
678	Chris Speier	.05
679	Art Howe	.05
680	Fred Lynn	.05
681	Tom Lasorda	.15
682	Dan Morogiello	.05
683	Marty Barrett RC	.05
684	Bob Shirley	.05
685	Willie Aikens	.05
686	Joe Price	.05
687	Roy Howell	.05
688	George Wright	.05
689	Mike Fischlin	.05
690	Jack Clark	.05
691	Steve Lake RC	.05

692	Dickie Thon	.05
693	Alan Wiggins	.05
694	Mike Stanton	.05
695	Lou Whitaker	.05
696	Bill Madlock, Rick Rhoden Pirates Batting & Pitching Leaders	.05
697	Dale Murray	.05
698	Marc Hill	.05
699	Dave Rucker	.05
700	Mike Schmidt	2.00
701	Bill Madlock, Dave Parker, Pete Rose NL Active Career Batting Leaders	.25
702	Tony Perez, Pete Rose, Rusty Staub NL Active Career Hit Leaders	.25
703	Dave Kingman, Tony Perez, Mike Schmidt NL Active Career Home Run Leaders	.15
704	Al Oliver, Tony Perez, Rusty Staub NL Active Career RBI Leaders	.05
705	Larry Bowa, Cesar Cedeno, Joe Morgan NL Active Career Stolen Bases Leaders	.05
706	Steve Carlton, Fergie Jenkins, Tom Seaver NL Active Career Victory Leaders	.05
707	Steve Carlton, Nolan Ryan, Tom Seaver NL Active Career Strikeout Leaders	.35
708	Steve Carlton, Steve Rogers, Tom Seaver NL Active Career ERA Leaders	.05
709	Gene Garber, Tug McGraw, Bruce Sutter NL Active Career Save Leaders	.10
710	George Brett, Rod Carew, Cecil Cooper AL Active Career Batting Leaders	.25
711	Bert Campaneris, Rod Carew, Reggie Jackson AL Active Career Hit Leaders	.15
712	Reggie Jackson, Greg Luzinski, Graig Nettles AL Active Career Home Run Leaders	.15
713	Reggie Jackson, Graig Nettles, Ted Simmons AL Active Career RBI Leaders	.15
714	Bert Campaneris, Dave Lopes, Omar Moreno AL Active Career Stolen Bases Leaders	.05
715	Tommy John, Jim Palmer, Don Sutton AL Active Career Victory Leaders	.05
716	Bert Blyleven, Jerry Koosman, Don Sutton AL Active Strikeout Leaders	.05
717	Rollie Fingers, Ron Guidry, Jim Palmer AL Active Career ERA Leaders	.05
718	Rollie Fingers, Rich Gossage, Dan Quisenberry AL Active Career Save Leaders	.05
719	Andy Hassler	.05
720	Dwight Evans	.05
721	Del Crandall	.05
722	Bob Welch	.05
723	Rich Dauer	.05
724	Eric Rasmussen	.05
725	Cesar Cedeno	.05
726	Moose Haas, Ted Simmons Brewers Batting & Pitching Leaders	.05
727	Joel Youngblood	.05
728	Tug McGraw	.05
729	Gene Tenace	.05
730	Bruce Sutter	.75
731	Lynn Jones	.05
732	Terry Crowley	.05
733	Dave Collins	.05
734	Odell Jones	.05
735	Rick Burleson	.05
736	Dick Ruthven	.05
737	Jim Essian	.05
738	Bill Schroeder RC	.05
739	Bob Watson	.05
740	Tom Seaver	1.00
741	Wayne Gross	.05
742	Dick Williams	.05
743	Don Hood	.05
744	Jamie Allen	.05

745	Dennis Eckersley	.65
746	Mickey Hatcher	.05
747	Pat Zachry	.05
748	Jeff Leonard	.05
749	Doug Flynn	.05
750a	Jim Palmer	1.00
750b	Jim Palmer (Missing 1980-82 losses on back.)	3.00
750c	Jim Palmer (Missing 1979-83 losses on back.)	4.00
751	Charlie Moore	.05
752	Phil Garner	.05
753	Doug Gwosdz	.05
754	Kent Tekulve	.05
755	Garry Maddox	.05
756	Ron Oester, Mario Soto Reds Batting & Pitching Leaders	.05
757	Larry Bowa	.05
758	Bill Stein	.05
759	Richard Dotson	.05
760	Bob Horner	.05
761	John Montefusco	.05
762	Rance Mulliniks	.05
763	Craig Swan	.05
764	Mike Hargrove	.05
765	Ken Forsch	.05
766	Mike Vail	.05
767	Carney Lansford	.05
768	Champ Summers	.05
769	Bill Caudill	.05
770	Ken Griffey	.05
771	Billy Gardner	.05
772	Jim Slaton	.05
773	Todd Cruz	.05
774	Tom Gorman	.05
775	Dave Parker	.05
776	Craig Reynolds	.05
777	Tom Paciorek	.05
778	Andy Hawkins RC	.05
779	Jim Sundberg	.05
780	Steve Carlton	1.00
781	Checklist 661-792	.05
782	Steve Balboni	.05
783	Luis Leal	.05
784	Leon Roberts	.05
785	Joaquin Andujar	.05
786	Wade Boggs, Bob Ojeda Red Sox Batting & Pitching Leaders	.25
787	Bill Campbell	.05
788	Milt May	.05
789	Bert Blyleven	.05
790	Doug DeCinces	.05
791	Terry Forster	.05
792	Bill Russell	.05

1984 Topps Tiffany

	NM/M
Unopened Set (792):	175.00
Complete Set (792):	95.00
Common Player:	.15
Stars:	6X
8 Don Mattingly	80.00

(See 1984 Topps for checklist and base card values.)

Traded

	NM/M
Complete Set (132):	17.50
Common Player:	.05
1T	Willie Aikens	.05
2T	Luis Aponte	.05
3T	Mike Armstrong	.05
4T	Bob Bailor	.05
5T	Dusty Baker	.15
6T	Steve Balboni	.05
7T	Alan Bannister	.05
8T	Dave Beard	.05
9T	Joe Beckwith	.05
10T	Bruce Berenyi	.05
11T	Dave Bergman	.05

12T	Tony Bernazard	.05
13T	Yogi Berra	.25
14T	Barry Bonnell	.05
15T	Phil Bradley	.05
16T	Fred Breining	.05
17T	Bill Buckner	.05
18T	Ray Burris	.05
19T	John Butcher	.05
20T	Brett Butler	.05
21T	Enos Cabell	.05
22T	Bill Campbell	.05
23T	Bill Caudill	.05
24T	Bob Clark	.05
25T	Bryan Clark	.05
26T	Jaime Cocanower	.05
27T	Ron Darling RC	.50
28T	Alvin Davis RC	.05
29T	Ken Dayley	.05
30T	Jeff Dedmon	.05
31T	Bob Dernier	.05
32T	Carlos Diaz	.05
33T	Mike Easler	.05
34T	Dennis Eckersley	1.50
35T	Jim Essian	.05
36T	Darrell Evans	.05
37T	Mike Fitzgerald	.05
38T	Tim Foli	.05
39T	George Frazier	.05
40T	Rich Gale	.05
41T	Barbaro Garbey	.05
12T	Dwight Gooden RC	3.00
43T	Rich Gossage	.05
44T	Wayne Gross	.05
45T	Mark Gubicza RC	.25
46T	Jackie Gutierrez	.05
47T	Mel Hall	.05
48T	Toby Harrah	.05
49T	Ron Hassey	.05
50T	Rich Hebner	.05
51T	Willie Hernandez	.05
52T	Ricky Horton	.05
53T	Art Howe	.05
54T	Dane Iorg	.05
55T	Brook Jacoby	.05
56T	Mike Jeffcoat	.05
57T	Dave Johnson	.05
58T	Lynn Jones	.05
59T	Ruppert Jones	.05
60T	Mike Jorgensen	.05
61T	Bob Kearney	.05
62T	Jimmy Key RC	.50
63T	Dave Kingman	.05
64T	Jerry Koosman	.05
65T	Wayne Krenchicki	.05
66T	Rusty Kuntz	.05
67T	Rene Lachemann	.05
68T	Frank LaCorte	.05
69T	Dennis Lamp	.05
70T	Mark Langston RC	.50
71T	Rick Leach	.05
72T	Craig Lefferts	.05
73T	Gary Lucas	.05
74T	Jerry Martin	.05
75T	Carmelo Martinez	.05
76T	Mike Mason (RC)	.05
77T	Gary Matthews	.05
78T	Andy McGaffigan	.05
79T	Larry Milbourne	.05
80T	Sid Monge	.05
81T	Jackie Moore	.05
82T	Joe Morgan	2.00
83T	Graig Nettles	.05
84T	Phil Niekro	1.00
85T	Ken Oberkfell	.05
86T	Mike O'Berry	.05
87T	Al Oliver	.05
88T	Jorge Orta	.05
89T	Amos Otis	.05
90T	Dave Parker	.05
91T	Tony Perez	1.00
92T	Gerald Perry	.05
93T	Gary Pettis	.05
94T	Rob Picciolo	.05
95T	Vern Rapp	.05
96T	Floyd Rayford	.05
97T	Randy Ready	.05
98T	Ron Reed	.05
99T	Gene Richards	.05
100T	Jose Rijo RC	.25
101T	Jeff Robinson	.05
102T	Ron Romanick	.05
103T	Pete Rose	7.50
104T	Bret Saberhagen RC	3.00
105T	Juan Samuel	.05
106T	Scott Sanderson	.05
107T	Dick Schofield	.05
108T	Tom Seaver	3.00
109T	Jim Slaton	.05
110T	Mike Smithson	.05
111T	Lary Sorensen	.05
112T	Tim Stoddard	.05
113T	Champ Summers	.05
114T	Jim Sundberg	.05
115T	Rick Sutcliffe	.05

116T	Craig Swan	.05
117T	Tim Teufel	.05
118T	Derrel Thomas	.05
119T	Gorman Thomas	.05
120T	Alex Trevino	.05
121T	Manny Trillo	.05
122T	John Tudor	.05
123T	Tom Underwood	.05
124T	Mike Vail	.05
125T	Tom Waddell	.05
126T	Gary Ward	.05
127T	Curt Wilkerson	.05
128T	Frank Williams	.05
129T	Glenn Wilson	.05
130T	Johnny Wockenfuss	.05
131T	Ned Yost	.05
132T	Checklist 1-132	.05

Topps Traded Tiffany

	NM/M
Complete Set (132):	35.00
Common Player:	.25
Stars:	2X

(See 1984 Topps Traded for checklist and base card values.)

1985 Topps

	NM/M
Unopened Fact. Set (792):	140.00
Complete Set (792):	70.00
Common Player:	.05
Wax Pack (15):	4.50
Wax Box (36):	150.00
Cello Pack (28):	6.50
Cello Box (24):	150.00
Rack Pack (51+1):	9.00
Rack Box (24):	180.00
Vending Box (500):	60.00
1	Carlton Fisk	.25
2	Steve Garvey	.05
3	Dwight Gooden	.05
4	Cliff Johnson	.05
5	Joe Morgan	.10
6	Pete Rose	.50
7	Nolan Ryan	1.50
8	Juan Samuel	.05
9	Bruce Sutter	.10
10	Don Sutton	.05
11	Ralph Houk	.05
12	Dave Lopes	.05
13	Tim Lollar	.05
14	Chris Bando	.05
15	Jerry Koosman	.05
16	Bobby Meacham	.05
17	Mike Scott	.05
18	Mickey Hatcher	.05
19	George Frazier	.05
20	Chet Lemon	.05
21	Lee Tunnell	.05
22	Duane Kuiper	.05
23	Bret Saberhagen	.05
24	Jesse Barfield	.05
25	Steve Bedrosian	.05
26	Roy Smalley	.05
27	Bruce Berenyi	.05
28	Dann Bilardello	.05
29	Odell Jones	.05
30	Cal Ripken, Jr.	4.00
31	Terry Whitfield	.05
32	Chuck Porter	.05
33	Tito Landrum	.05
34	Ed Nunez (RC)	.05
35	Graig Nettles	.05
36	Fred Breining	.05
37	Reid Nichols	.05
38	Jackie Moore	.05
39	Johnny Wockenfuss	.05
40	Phil Niekro	.60
41	Mike Fischlin	.05
42	Luis Sanchez	.05
43	Andre David	.05

#	Player	Price
44	Dickie Thon	.05
45	Greg Minton	.05
46	Gary Woods	.05
47	Dave Rozema	.05
48	Tony Fernandez	.05
49	Butch Davis	.05
50	John Candelaria	.05
51	Bob Watson	.05
52	Jerry Dybzinski	.05
53	Tom Gorman	.05
54	Cesar Cedeno	.05
55	Frank Tanana	.05
56	Jim Dwyer	.05
57	Pat Zachry	.05
58	Orlando Mercado	.05
59	Rick Waits	.05
60	George Hendrick	.05
61	Curt Kaufman	.05
62	Mike Ramsey	.05
63	Steve McCatty	.05
64	Mark Bailey RC	.05
65	Bill Buckner	.05
66	Dick Williams	.05
67	Rafael Santana RC	.05
68	Von Hayes	.05
69	Jim Winn RC	.05
70	Don Baylor	.10
71	Tim Laudner	.05
72	Rick Sutcliffe	.05
73	Rusty Kuntz	.05
74	Mike Krukow	.05
75	Willie Upshaw	.05
76	Alan Bannister	.05
77	Joe Beckwith	.05
78	Scott Fletcher	.05
79	Rick Mahler	.05
80	Keith Hernandez	.05
81	Lenn Sakata	.05
82	Joe Price	.05
83	Charlie Moore	.05
84	Spike Owen	.05
85	Mike Marshall	.05
86	Don Aase	.05
87	David Green	.05
88	Bryn Smith	.05
89	Jackie Gutierrez	.05
90	Rich Gossage	.05
91	Jeff Burroughs	.05
92	Paul Owens	.05
93	Don Schulze RC	.05
94	Toby Harrah	.05
95	Jose Cruz	.05
96	Johnny Ray	.05
97	Pete Filson	.05
98	Steve Lake	.05
99	Milt Wilcox	.05
100	George Brett	3.00
101	Jim Acker	.05
102	Tommy Dunbar	.05
103	Randy Lerch	.05
104	Mike Fitzgerald	.05
105	Ron Kittle	.05
106	Pascual Perez	.05
107	Tom Foley	.05
108	Darnell Coles	.05
109	Gary Roenicke	.05
110	Alejandro Pena	.05
111	Doug DeCinces	.05
112	Tom Tellmann	.05
113	Tom Herr	.05
114	Bob James	.05
115	Rickey Henderson	.75
116	Dennis Boyd	.05
117	Greg Gross	.05
118	Eric Show	.05
119	Pat Corrales	.05
120	Steve Kemp	.05
121	Checklist 1-132	.05
122	Tom Brunansky	.05
123	Dave Smith	.05
124	Rich Hebner	.05
125	Kent Tekulve	.05
126	Ruppert Jones	.05
127	Mark Gubicza	.05
128	Ernie Whitt	.05
129	Gene Garber	.05
130	Al Oliver	.05
131	Buddy Bell, Gus Bell / Father - Son	.05
132	Dale Berra, Yogi Berra / Father - Son	.10
133	Bob Boone, Ray Boone / Father - Son	.05
134	Terry Francona, Tito Francona / Father - Son	.05
135	Bob Kennedy, Terry Kennedy / Father - Son	.05
136	Bill Kunkel, Jeff Kunkel / Father - Son	.05
137	Vance Law, Vern Law / Father - Son	.05
138	Dick Schofield, Dick Schofield, Jr. / Father - Son	.05
139	Bob Skinner, Joel Skinner / Father - Son	.05
140	Roy Smalley, Jr., Roy Smalley III / Father - Son	.05
141	Dave Stenhouse, Mike Stenhouse / Father - Son	.05
142	Dizzy Trout, Steve Trout Father - Son	.05
143	Ozzie Virgil, Ozzie Virgil / Father - Son	.05
144	Ron Gardenhire	.05
145	Alvin Davis	.05
146	Gary Redus	.05
147	Bill Swaggerty	.05
148	Steve Yeager	.05
149	Dickie Noles	.05
150	Jim Rice	.15
151	Moose Haas	.05
152	Steve Braun	.05
153	Frank LaCorte	.05
154	Argenis Salazar	.05
155	Yogi Berra	.10
156	Craig Reynolds	.05
157	Tug McGraw	.05
158	Pat Tabler	.05
159	Carlos Diaz	.05
160	Lance Parrish	.05
161	Ken Schrom	.05
162	Benny Distefano RC	.05
163	Dennis Eckersley	.60
164	Jorge Orta	.05
165	Dusty Baker	.05
166	Keith Atherton	.05
167	Rufino Linares	.05
168	Garth Iorg	.05
169	Dan Spillner	.05
170	George Foster	.05
171	Bill Stein	.05
172	Jack Perconte	.05
173	Mike Young	.05
174	Rick Honeycutt	.05
175	Dave Parker	.05
176	Bill Schroeder	.05
177	Dave Von Ohlen	.05
178	Miguel Dilone	.05
179	Tommy John	.10
180	Dave Winfield	.75
181	Roger Clemens	30.00
182	Tim Flannery	.05
183	Larry McWilliams	.05
184	Carmen Castillo	.05
185	Al Holland	.05
186	Bob Lillis	.05
187	Mike Walters	.05
188	Greg Pryor	.05
189	Warren Brusstar	.05
190	Rusty Staub	.05
191	Steve Nicosia	.05
192	Howard Johnson	.05
193	Jimmy Key	.05
194	Dave Stegman	.05
195	Glenn Hubbard	.05
196	Pete O'Brien	.05
197	Mike Warren	.05
198	Eddie Milner	.05
199	Denny Martinez	.05
200	Reggie Jackson	2.00
201	Burt Hooton	.05
202	Gorman Thomas	.05
203	Bob McClure	.05
204	Art Howe	.05
205	Steve Rogers	.05
206	Phil Garner	.05
207	Mark Clear	.05
208	Champ Summers	.05
209	Bill Campbell	.05
210	Gary Matthews	.05
211	Clay Christiansen	.05
212	George Vukovich	.05
213	Billy Gardner	.05
214	John Tudor	.05
215	Bob Brenly	.05
216	Jerry Don Gleaton	.05
217	Leon Roberts	.05
218	Doyle Alexander	.05
219	Gerald Perry	.05
220	Fred Lynn	.05
221	Ron Reed	.05
222	Hubie Brooks	.05
223	Tom Hume	.05
224	Al Cowens	.05
225	Mike Boddicker	.05
226	Juan Beniquez	.05
227	Danny Darwin	.05
228	Dion James	.05
229	Dave LaPoint	.05
230	Gary Carter	.75
231	Dwayne Murphy	.05
232	Dave Beard	.05
233	Ed Jurak	.05
234	Jerry Narron	.05
235	Garry Maddox	.05
236	Mark Thurmond	.05
237	Julio Franco	.05
238	Jose Rijo	.05
239	Tim Teufel	.05
240	Dave Stieb	.05
241	Jim Frey	.05
242	Greg Harris	.05
243	Barbaro Garbey	.05
244	Mike Jones	.05
245	Chili Davis	.05
246	Mike Norris	.05
247	Wayne Tolleson	.05
248	Terry Forster	.05
249	Harold Baines	.05
250	Jesse Orosco	.05
251	Brad Gulden	.05
252	Dan Ford	.05
253	Sid Bream RC	.10
254	Pete Vuckovich	.05
255	Lonnie Smith	.05
256	Mike Stanton	.05
257	Brian Little (Bryan)	.05
258	Mike Brown	.05
259	Gary Allenson	.05
260	Dave Righetti	.05
261	Checklist 133-264	.05
262	Greg Booker RC	.05
263	Mel Hall	.05
264	Joe Sambito	.05
265	Juan Samuel	.05
266	Frank Viola	.05
267	Henry Cotto RC	.05
268	Chuck Tanner	.05
269	Doug Baker RC	.05
270	Dan Quisenberry	.05
271	Tim Foli	.05
272	Jeff Burroughs	.05
273	Bill Almon	.05
274	Floyd Bannister	.05
275	Harold Baines	.10
276	Bob Horner	.10
277	Al Chambers	.05
278	Darryl Strawberry	.30
279	Mike Moore	.05
280	Shawon Dunston RC	.40
281	Tim Belcher RC	.30
282	Shawn Abner RC	.05
283	Fran Mullins	.05
284	Marty Bystrom	.05
285	Dan Driessen	.05
286	Rudy Law	.05
287	Walt Terrell	.05
288	Jeff Kunkel (RC) RC	.05
289	Tom Underwood	.05
290	Cecil Cooper	.05
291	Bob Welch	.05
292	Brad Komminsk	.05
293	Curt Young RC	.05
294	Tom Nieto RC	.05
295	Joe Niekro	.05
296	Ricky Nelson	.05
297	Gary Lucas	.05
298	Marty Barrett	.05
299	Andy Hawkins	.05
300	Rod Carew	.75
301	John Montefusco	.05
302	Tim Corcoran	.05
303	Mike Jeffcoat RC	.05
304	Gary Gaetti	.05
305	Dale Berra	.05
306	Rick Reuschel	.05
307	Sparky Anderson	.10
308	John Wathan	.05
309	Mike Witt	.05
310	Manny Trillo	.05
311	Jim Gott	.05
312	Marc Hill	.05
313	Dave Schmidt	.05
314	Ron Oester	.05
315	Doug Sisk	.05
316	John Lowenstein	.05
317	Jack Lazorko (RC) RC	.05
318	Ted Simmons	.05
319	Jeff Jones	.05
320	Dale Murphy	.35
321	Ricky Horton RC	.05
322	Dave Stapleton	.05
323	Andy McGaffigan	.05
324	Bruce Bochy	.05
325	John Denny	.05
326	Kevin Bass	.05
327	Brook Jacoby	.05
328	Bob Shirley	.05
329	Ron Washington	.05
330	Leon Durham	.05
331	Bill Laskey	.05
332	Brian Harper	.05
333	Willie Hernandez	.05
334	Dick Howser	.05
335	Bruce Benedict	.05
336	Rance Mulliniks	.05
337	Billy Sample	.05
338	Britt Burns	.05
339	Danny Heep	.05
340	Robin Yount	.75
341	Floyd Rayford	.05
342	Ted Power	.05
343	Bill Russell	.05
344	Dave Henderson	.05
345	Charlie Lea	.05
346	Terry Pendleton RC	.75
347	Rick Langford	.05
348	Bob Boone	.05
349	Domingo Ramos	.05
350	Wade Boggs	1.00
351	Juan Agosto	.05
352	Joe Morgan	.75
353	Julio Solano	.05
354	Andre Robertson	.05
355	Bert Blyleven	.05
356	Dave Meier	.05
357	Rich Bordi	.05
358	Tony Pena	.05
359	Pat Sheridan	.05
360	Steve Carlton	.75
361	Alfredo Griffin	.05
362	Craig McMurtry	.05
363	Ron Hodges	.05
364	Richard Dotson	.05
365	Danny Ozark	.05
366	Todd Cruz	.05
367	Keefe Cato	.05
368	Dave Bergman	.05
369	R.J. Reynolds RC	.05
370	Bruce Sutter	.65
371	Mickey Rivers	.05
372	Roy Howell	.05
373	Mike Moore	.05
374	Brian Downing	.05
375	Jeff Reardon	.05
376	Jeff Newman	.05
377	Checklist 265-396	.05
378	Alan Wiggins	.05
379	Charles Hudson	.05
380	Ken Griffey	.05
381	Roy Smith	.05
382	Denny Walling	.05
383	Rick Lysander	.05
384	Jody Davis	.05
385	Jose DeLeon	.05
386	Dan Gladden RC	.30
387	Buddy Biancalana RC	.05
388	Bert Roberge	.05
389	Rod Dedeaux	.05
390	Sid Akins	.05
391	Flavio Alfaro	.05
392	Don August	.05
393	Scott Bankhead RC	.10
394	Bob Caffrey	.05
395	Mike Dunne	.05
396	Gary Green	.05
397	John Hoover	.05
398	Shane Mack RC	.10
399	John Marzano	.05
400	Oddibe McDowell	.05
401	Mark McGwire RC	20.00
402	Pat Pacillo	.05
403	Cory Snyder RC	.30
404	Billy Swift RC	.40
405	Tom Veryzer	.05
406	Len Whitehouse	.05
407	Bobby Ramos	.05
408	Sid Monge	.05
409	Brad Wellman	.05
410	Bob Horner	.05
411	Bobby Cox	.05
412	Bud Black	.05
413	Vance Law	.05
414	Gary Ward	.05
415	Ron Darling	.05
416	Wayne Gross	.05
417	John Franco	.50
418	Ken Landreaux	.05
419	Mike Caldwell	.05
420	Andre Dawson	.50
421	Dave Rucker	.05
422	Carney Lansford	.05
423	Barry Bonnell	.05
424	Al Nipper (RC) RC	.05
425	Mike Hargrove	.05
426	Verne Ruhle	.05
427	Mario Ramirez	.05
428	Larry Andersen	.05

ABBREVIATIONS

AS - All-Star
DP - Double Print
IA - In-Action
OPS - Overprint
"Promotional Sample"

No.	Player	Price
429	Rick Cerone	.05
430	Ron Davis	.05
431	U.L. Washington	.05
432	Thad Bosley	.05
433	Jim Morrison	.05
434	Gene Richards	.05
435	Dan Petry	.05
436	Willie Aikens	.05
437	Al Jones	.05
438	Joe Torre	.10
439	Junior Ortiz	.05
440	Fernando Valenzuela	.05
441	Duane Walker	.05
442	Ken Forsch	.05
443	George Wright	.05
444	Tony Phillips	.05
445	Tippy Martinez	.05
446	Jim Sundberg	.05
447	Jeff Lahti	.05
448	Derrel Thomas	.05
449	Phil Bradley RC	.10
450	Steve Garvey	.25
451	Bruce Hurst	.05
452	John Castino	.05
453	Tom Waddell	.05
454	Glenn Wilson	.05
455	Bob Knepper	.05
456	Tim Foli	.05
457	Cecilio Guante	.05
458	Randy S. Johnson	.05
459	Charlie Leibrandt	.05
460	Ryne Sandberg	1.00
461	Marty Castillo	.05
462	Gary Lavelle	.05
463	Dave Collins	.05
464	Mike Mason RC	.05
465	Bob Grich	.05
466	Tony LaRussa	.10
467	Ed Lynch	.05
468	Wayne Krenchicki	.05
469	Sammy Stewart	.05
470	Steve Sax	.05
471	Pete Ladd	.05
472	Jim Essian	.05
473	Tim Wallach	.05
474	Kurt Kepshire	.05
475	Andre Thornton	.05
476	Jeff Stone RC	.05
477	Bob Ojeda	.05
478	Kurt Bevacqua	.05
479	Mike Madden	.05
480	Lou Whitaker	.05
481	Dale Murray	.05
482	Harry Spilman	.05
483	Mike Smithson	.05
484	Larry Bowa	.05
485	Matt Young	.05
486	Steve Balboni	.05
487	Frank Williams RC	.05
488	Joel Skinner	.05
489	Bryan Clark	.05
490	Jason Thompson	.05
491	Rick Camp	.05
492	Dave Johnson	.05
493	Orel Hershiser RC	2.00
494	Rich Dauer	.05
495	Mario Soto	.05
496	Donnie Scott	.05
497	Gary Pettis	.05
498	Ed Romero	.05
499	Danny Cox	.05
500	Mike Schmidt	2.00
501	Dan Schatzeder	.05
502	Rick Miller	.05
503	Tim Conroy	.05
504	Jerry Willard	.05
505	Jim Beattie	.05
506	Franklin Stubbs RC	.05
507	Ray Fontenot	.05
508	John Shelby	.05
509	Milt May	.05
510	Kent Hrbek	.05
511	Lee Smith	.05
512	Tom Brookens	.05
513	Lynn Jones	.05
514	Jeff Cornell	.05
515	Dave Concepcion	.05
516	Roy Lee Jackson	.05
517	Jerry Martin	.05
518	Chris Chambliss	.05
519	Doug Rader	.05
520	LaMarr Hoyt	.05
521	Rick Dempsey	.05
522	Paul Molitor	.75
523	Candy Maldonado	.05
524	Rob Wilfong	.05
525	Darrell Porter	.05
526	Dave Palmer	.05
527	Checklist 397-528	.05
528	Bill Krueger	.05
529	Rich Gedman	.05
530	Dave Dravecky	.05
531	Joe Lefebvre	.05
532	Frank DiPino	.05
533	Tony Bernazard	.05
534	Brian Dayett	.05
535	Pat Putnam	.05
536	Kirby Puckett	10.00
537	Don Robinson	.05
538	Keith Moreland	.05
539	Aurelio Lopez	.05
540	Claudell Washington	.05
541	Mark Davis	.05
542	Don Slaught	.05
543	Mike Squires	.05
544	Bruce Kison	.05
545	Lloyd Moseby	.05
546	Brent Gaff	.05
547	Pete Rose	1.50
548	Larry Parrish	.05
549	Mike Scioscia	.05
550	Scott McGregor	.05
551	Andy Van Slyke	.05
552	Chris Codiroli	.05
553	Bob Clark	.05
554	Doug Flynn	.05
555	Bob Stanley	.05
556	Sixto Lezcano	.05
557	Len Barker	.05
558	Carmelo Martinez	.05
559	Jay Howell	.05
560	Bill Madlock	.05
561	Darryl Motley	.05
562	Houston Jimenez	.05
563	Dick Ruthven	.05
564	Alan Ashby	.05
565	Kirk Gibson	.05
566	Ed Vande Berg	.05
567	Joel Youngblood	.05
568	Cliff Johnson	.05
569	Ken Oberkfell	.05
570	Darryl Strawberry	.10
571	Charlie Hough	.05
572	Tom Paciorek	.05
573	Jay Tibbs RC	.05
574	Joe Altobelli	.05
575	Pedro Guerrero	.05
576	Jaime Cocanower	.05
577	Chris Speier	.05
578	Terry Francona	.05
579	Ron Romanick RC	.05
580	Dwight Evans	.05
581	Mark Wagner	.05
582	Ken Phelps	.05
583	Bobby Brown	.05
584	Kevin Gross	.05
585	Butch Wynegar	.05
586	Bill Scherrer	.05
587	Doug Frobel	.05
588	Bobby Castillo	.05
589	Bob Dernier	.05
590	Ray Knight	.05
591	Larry Herndon	.05
592	Jeff Robinson RC	.05
593	Rick Leach	.05
594	Curt Wilkerson	.05
595	Larry Gura	.05
596	Jerry Hairston Sr.	.05
597	Brad Lesley	.05
598	Jose Oquendo	.05
599	Storm Davis	.05
600	Pete Rose	3.00
601	Tom Lasorda	.10
602	Jeff Dedmon RC	.05
603	Rick Manning	.05
604	Daryl Sconiers	.05
605	Ozzie Smith	1.00
606	Rich Gale	.05
607	Bill Almon	.05
608	Craig Lefferts	.05
609	Broderick Perkins	.05
610	Jack Morris	.05
611	Ozzie Virgil	.05
612	Mike Armstrong	.05
613	Terry Puhl	.05
614	Al Williams	.05
615	Marvell Wynne	.05
616	Scott Sanderson	.05
617	Willie Wilson	.05
618	Pete Falcone	.05
619	Jeff Leonard	.05
620	Dwight Gooden	.50
621	Marvis Foley	.05
622	Luis Leal	.05
623	Greg Walker	.05
624	Benny Ayala	.05
625	Mark Langston	.05
626	German Rivera	.05
627	Eric Davis RC	1.00
628	Rene Lachemann	.05
629	Dick Schofield	.05
630	Tim Raines	.05
631	Bob Forsch	.05
632	Bruce Bochte	.05
633	Glenn Hoffman	.05
634	Bill Dawley	.05
635	Terry Kennedy	.05
636	Shane Rawley	.05
637	Brett Butler	.05
638	Mike Pagliarulo RC	.10
639	Ed Hodge	.05
640	Steve Henderson	.05
641	Rod Scurry	.05
642	Dave Owen	.05
643	Johnny Grubb	.05
644	Mark Huismann	.05
645	Damaso Garcia	.05
646	Scot Thompson	.05
647	Rafael Ramirez	.05
648	Bob Jones	.05
649	Sid Fernandez	.05
650	Greg Luzinski	.05
651	Jeff Russell	.05
652	Joe Nolan	.05
653	Mark Brouhard	.05
654	Dave Anderson	.05
655	Joaquin Andujar	.05
656	Chuck Cottier	.05
657	Jim Slaton	.05
658	Mike Stenhouse	.05
659	Checklist 529-660	.05
660	Tony Gwynn	1.00
661	Steve Crawford	.05
662	Mike Heath	.05
663	Luis Aguayo	.05
664	Steve Farr RC	.05
665	Don Mattingly	3.00
666	Mike LaCoss	.05
667	Dave Engle	.05
668	Steve Trout	.05
669	Lee Lacy	.05
670	Tom Seaver	.75
671	Dane Iorg	.05
672	Juan Berenguer	.05
673	Buck Martinez	.05
674	Atlee Hammaker	.05
675	Tony Perez	.75
676	Albert Hall (RC) RC	.05
677	Wally Backman	.05
678	Joey McLaughlin	.05
679	Bob Kearney	.05
680	Jerry Reuss	.05
681	Ben Oglivie	.05
682	Doug Corbett	.05
683	Whitey Herzog	.05
684	Bill Doran	.05
685	Bill Caudill	.05
686	Mike Easler	.05
687	Bill Gullickson	.05
688	Len Matuszek	.05
689	Luis DeLeon	.05
690	Alan Trammell	.05
691	Dennis Rasmussen	.05
692	Randy Bush	.05
693	Tim Stoddard	.05
694	Joe Carter	.05
695	Rick Rhoden	.05
696	John Rabb	.05
697	Onix Concepcion	.05
698	Jorge Bell	.05
699	Donnie Moore	.05
700	Eddie Murray	.75
701	Eddie Murray/AS	.40
702	Damaso Garcia/AS	.05
703	George Brett/AS	.50
704	Cal Ripken, Jr./AS	1.50
705	Dave Winfield/AS	.40
706	Rickey Henderson/AS	.40
707	Tony Armas/AS	.05
708	Lance Parrish/AS	.05
709	Mike Boddicker/AS	.05
710	Frank Viola/AS	.05
711	Dan Quisenberry/AS	.05
712	Keith Hernandez/AS	.05
713	Ryne Sandberg/AS)	.40
714	Mike Schmidt/AS	.75
715	Ozzie Smith/AS	.50
716	Dale Murphy/AS	.15
717	Tony Gwynn/AS	.75
718	Jeff Leonard/AS	.05
719	Gary Carter/AS	.40
720	Rick Sutcliffe/AS	.05
721	Bob Knepper/AS	.05
722	Bruce Sutter/AS	.30
723	Dave Stewart	.05
724	Oscar Gamble	.05
725	Floyd Bannister	.05
726	Al Bumbry	.05
727	Frank Pastore	.05
728	Bob Bailor	.05
729	Don Sutton	.60
730	Dave Kingman	.05
731	Neil Allen	.05
732	John McNamara	.05
733	Tony Scott	.05
734	John Henry Johnson	.05
735	Garry Templeton	.05
736	Jerry Mumphrey	.05
737	Bo Diaz	.05
738	Omar Moreno	.05
739	Ernie Camacho	.05
740	Jack Clark	.05
741	John Butcher	.05
742	Ron Hassey	.05
743	Frank White	.05
744	Doug Bair	.05
745	Buddy Bell	.05
746	Jim Clancy	.05
747	Alex Trevino	.05
748	Lee Mazzilli	.05
749	Julio Cruz	.05
750	Rollie Fingers	.60
751	Kelvin Chapman	.05
752	Bob Owchinko	.05
753	Greg Brock	.05
754	Larry Milbourne	.05
755	Ken Singleton	.05
756	Rob Picciolo	.05
757	Willie McGee	.05
758	Ray Burris	.05
759	Jim Fanning	.05
760	Nolan Ryan	4.00
761	Jerry Remy	.05
762	Eddie Whitson	.05
763	Kiko Garcia	.05
764	Jamie Easterly	.05
765	Willie Randolph	.05
766	Paul Mirabella	.05
767	Darrell Brown	.05
768	Ron Cey	.05
769	Joe Cowley	.05
770	Carlton Fisk	.75
771	Geoff Zahn	.05
772	Johnnie LeMaster	.05
773	Hal McRae	.05
774	Dennis Lamp	.05
775	Mookie Wilson	.05
776	Jerry Royster	.05
777	Ned Yost	.05
778	Mike Davis	.05
779	Nick Esasky	.05
780	Mike Flanagan	.05
781	Jim Gantner	.05
782	Tom Niedenfuer	.05
783	Mike Jorgensen	.05
784	Checklist 661-792	.05
785	Tony Armas	.05
786	Enos Cabell	.05
787	Jim Wohlford	.05
788	Steve Comer	.05
789	Luis Salazar	.05
790	Ron Guidry	.10
791	Ivan DeJesus	.05
792	Darrell Evans	.05

Tiffany

	NM/M
Complete Unopened Set (792):	500.00
Complete Set, Opened (792):	325.00
Common Player:	.25
Stars:	4X
181 Roger Clemens	150.00
401 Mark McGwire	80.00

(See 1985 Topps for checklist and base card values.)

Traded

	NM/M
Complete Set (132):	10.00
Common Player:	.05
Wax Test Pack (8):	10.00
Wax Test Wax Box (36):	150.00
1 Don Aase	.05
2 Bill Almon	.05
3 Benny Ayala	.05
4 Dusty Baker	.25
5 George Bamberger	.05
6 Dale Berra	.05
7 Rich Bordi	.05
8 Daryl Boston	.05
9 Hubie Brooks	.05
10 Chris Brown	.05

No.	Player	Price
11	Tom Browning	.05
12	Al Bumbry	.05
13	Ray Burris	.05
14	Jeff Burroughs	.05
15	Bill Campbell	.05
16	Don Carman	.05
17	Gary Carter	1.50
18	Bobby Castillo	.05
19	Bill Caudill	.05
20	Rick Cerone	.05
21	Bryan Clark	.05
22	Jack Clark	.05
23	Pat Clements	.05
24	Vince Coleman RC	.50
25	Dave Collins	.05
26	Danny Darwin	.05
27	Jim Davenport	.05
28	Jerry Davis	.05
29	Brian Dayett	.05
30	Ivan DeJesus	.05
31	Ken Dixon	.05
32	Mariano Duncan	.05
33	John Felske	.05
34	Mike Fitzgerald	.05
35	Ray Fontenot	.05
36	Greg Gagne	.05
37	Oscar Gamble	.05
38	Scott Garrelts	.05
39	Bob L. Gibson	.05
40	Jim Gott	.05
41	David Green	.05
42	Alfredo Griffin	.05
43	Ozzie Guillen RC	3.00
44	Eddie Haas	.05
45	Terry Harper	.05
46	Toby Harrah	.05
47	Greg Harris	.05
48	Ron Hassey	.05
49	Rickey Henderson	2.50
50	Steve Henderson	.05
51	George Hendrick	.05
52	Joe Hesketh	.05
53	Teddy Higuera	.05
54	Donnie Hill	.05
55	Al Holland	.05
56	Burt Hooton	.05
57	Jay Howell	.05
58	Ken Howell	.05
59	LaMarr Hoyt	.05
60	Tim Hulett	.05
61	Bob James	.05
62	Steve Jeltz	.05
63	Cliff Johnson	.05
64	Howard Johnson	.05
65	Ruppert Jones	.05
66	Steve Kemp	.05
67	Bruce Kison	.05
68	Alan Knicely	.05
69	Mike LaCoss	.05
70	Lee Lacy	.05
71	Dave LaPoint	.05
72	Gary Lavelle	.05
73	Vance Law	.05
74	Johnnie LeMaster	.05
75	Sixto Lezcano	.05
76	Tim Lollar	.05
77	Fred Lynn	.05
78	Billy Martin	.25
79	Ron Mathis	.05
80	Len Matuszek	.05
81	Gene Mauch	.05
82	Oddibe McDowell	.05
83	Roger McDowell	.05
84	John McNamara	.05
85	Donnie Moore	.05
86	Gene Nelson	.05
87	Steve Nicosia	.05
88	Al Oliver	.05
89	Joe Orsulak	.05
90	Rob Picciolo	.05
91	Chris Pittaro	.05
92	Jim Presley	.05
93	Rick Reuschel	.05
94	Bert Roberge	.05
95	Bob Rodgers	.05
96	Jerry Royster	.05
97	Dave Rozema	.05
98	Dave Rucker	.05
99	Vern Ruhle	.05
100	Paul Runge	.05
101	Mark Salas	.05
102	Luis Salazar	.05
103	Joe Sambito	.05
104	Rick Schu	.05
105	Donnie Scott	.05
106	Larry Sheets	.05
107	Don Slaught	.05
108	Roy Smalley	.05
109	Lonnie Smith	.05
110	Nate Snell	.05
111	Chris Speier	.05
112	Mike Stenhouse	.05
113	Tim Stoddard	.05
114	Jim Sundberg	.05
115	Bruce Sutter	1.00
116	Don Sutton	.50
117	Kent Tekulve	.05
118	Tom Tellmann	.05
119	Walt Terrell	.05
120	Mickey Tettleton RC	1.00
121	Derrel Thomas	.05
122	Rich Thompson	.05
123	Alex Trevino	.05
124	John Tudor	.05
125	Jose Uribe	.05
126	Bobby Valentine	.05
127	Dave Von Ohlen	.05
128	U.L. Washington	.05
129	Earl Weaver	.30
130	Eddie Whitson	.05
131	Herm Winningham	.05
132	Checklist 1-132	.05

1986 Topps

GARY CARTER

	NM/M
Unopened Fact. Set, Retail (792):	65.00
Unopened Fact. Set, Hobby (792):	30.00
Complete Set (792):	25.00
Common Player:	.05
Wax Pack (15):	.75
Wax Box (36):	20.00
Cello Pack (28):	1.00
Cello Box (24):	20.00
Rack Pack (51):	1.25
Rack Box (24):	25.00
Vending Box (500):	10.00

No.	Player	Price
1	Pete Rose	1.50
2	Pete Rose (Special 1963-66)	.50
3	Pete Rose (Special 1967-70)	.50
4	Pete Rose (Special 1971-74)	.50
5	Pete Rose (Special 1975-78)	.50
6	Pete Rose (Special 1972-82)	.50
7	Pete Rose (Special 1983-85)	.50
8	Dwayne Murphy	.05
9	Roy Smith	.05
10	Tony Gwynn	.75
11	Bob Ojeda	.05
12	Jose Uribe RC	.05
13	Bob Kearney	.05
14	Julio Cruz	.05
15	Eddie Whitson	.05
16	Rick Schu	.05
17	Mike Stenhouse	.05
18	Brent Gaff	.05
19	Rich Hebner	.05
20	Lou Whitaker	.05
21	George Bamberger	.05
22	Duane Walker	.05
23	Manny Lee RC	.05
24	Len Barker	.05
25	Willie Wilson	.05
26	Frank DiPino	.05
27	Ray Knight	.05
28	Eric Davis	.05
29	Tony Phillips	.05
30	Eddie Murray	.50
31	Jamie Easterly	.05
32	Steve Yeager	.05
33	Jeff Lahti	.05
34	Ken Phelps	.05
35	Jeff Reardon	.05
36	Lance Parrish Tigers Leaders	.05
37	Mark Thurmond	.05
38	Glenn Hoffman	.05
39	Dave Rucker	.05
40	Ken Griffey	.05
41	Brad Wellman	.05
42	Geoff Zahn	.05
43	Dave Engle	.05
44	Lance McCullers RC	.05
45	Damaso Garcia	.05
46	Billy Hatcher	.05
47	Juan Berenguer	.05
48	Bill Almon	.05
49	Rick Manning	.05
50	Dan Quisenberry	.05
51	Not Issued, See #57	
52	Chris Welsh	.05
53	Len Dykstra RC	.50
54	John Franco	.05
55	Fred Lynn	.05
56	Tom Niedenfuer	.05
57a	Bill Doran	.05
57b	Bobby Wine (Supposed to be #51.)	.05
58	Bill Krueger	.05
59	Andre Thornton	.05
60	Dwight Evans	.05
61	Karl Best	.05
62	Bob Boone	.05
63	Ron Roenicke	.05
64	Floyd Bannister	.05
65	Dan Driessen	.05
66	Bob Forsch Cardinals Leaders	.05
67	Carmelo Martinez	.05
68	Ed Lynch	.05
69	Luis Aguayo	.05
70	Dave Winfield	.50
71	Ken Schrom	.05
72	Shawon Dunston	.05
73	Randy O'Neal	.05
74	Rance Mulliniks	.05
75	Jose DeLeon	.05
76	Dion James	.05
77	Charlie Leibrandt	.05
78	Bruce Benedict	.05
79	Dave Schmidt	.05
80	Darryl Strawberry	.05
81	Gene Mauch	.05
82	Tippy Martinez	.05
83	Phil Garner	.05
84	Curt Young	.05
85	Tony Perez	.40
86	Tom Waddell	.05
87	Candy Maldonado	.05
88	Tom Nieto	.05
89	Randy St. Claire	.05
90	Garry Templeton	.05
91	Steve Crawford	.05
92	Al Cowens	.05
93	Scot Thompson	.05
94	Rich Bordi	.05
95	Ozzie Virgil	.05
96	Jim Clancy/ Blue Jay Leaders	.05
97	Gary Gaetti	.05
98	Dick Ruthven	.05
99	Buddy Biancalana	.05
100	Nolan Ryan	2.00
101	Dave Bergman	.05
102	Joe Orsulak RC	.15
103	Luis Salazar	.05
104	Sid Fernandez	.05
105	Gary Ward	.05
106	Ray Burris	.05
107	Rafael Ramirez	.05
108	Ted Power	.05
109	Len Matuszek	.05
110	Scott McGregor	.05
111	Roger Craig	.05
112	Bill Campbell	.05
113	U.L. Washington	.05
114	Mike Brown	.05
115	Jay Howell	.05
116	Brook Jacoby	.05
117	Bruce Kison	.05
118	Jerry Royster	.05
119	Barry Bonnell	.05
120	Steve Carlton	.50
121	Nelson Simmons	.05
122	Pete Filson	.05
123	Greg Walker	.05
124	Luis Sanchez	.05
125	Dave Lopes	.05
126	Mookie Wilson/ Mets Leaders	.05
127	Jack Howell RC	.05
128	John Wathan	.05
129	Jeff Dedmon	.05
130	Alan Trammell	.05
131	Checklist 1-132	.05
132	Razor Shines	.05
133	Andy McGaffigan	.05
134	Carney Lansford	.05
135	Joe Niekro	.05
136	Mike Hargrove	.05
137	Charlie Moore	.05
138	Mark Davis	.05
139	Daryl Boston	.05
140	John Candelaria	.05
141a	Chuck Cottier	.05
141b	Bob Rodgers (Supposed to be #171.)	.05
142	Bob Jones	.05
143	Dave Van Gorder	.05
144	Doug Sisk	.05
145	Pedro Guerrero	.05
146	Jack Perconte	.05
147	Larry Sheets	.05
148	Mike Heath	.05
149	Brett Butler	.05
150	Joaquin Andujar	.05
151	Dave Stapleton	.05
152	Mike Morgan	.05
153	Ricky Adams	.05
154	Bert Roberge	.05
155	Bob Grich	.05
156	Richard Dotson/ White Sox Leaders	.05
157	Ron Hassey	.05
158	Derrel Thomas	.05
159	Orel Hershiser	.05
160	Chet Lemon	.05
161	Lee Tunnell	.05
162	Greg Gagne	.05
163	Pete Ladd	.05
164	Steve Balboni	.05
165	Mike Davis	.05
166	Dickie Thon	.05
167	Zane Smith	.05
168	Jeff Burroughs	.05
169	George Wright	.05
170	Gary Carter	.50
171	Not Issued, See #141	
172	Jerry Reed	.05
173	Wayne Gross	.05
174	Brian Snyder	.05
175	Steve Sax	.05
176	Jay Tibbs	.05
177	Joel Youngblood	.05
178	Ivan DeJesus	.05
179	Stu Cliburn RC	.05
180	Don Mattingly	1.00
181	Al Nipper	.05
182	Bobby Brown	.05
183	Larry Andersen	.05
184	Tim Laudner	.05
185	Rollie Fingers	.40
186	Jose Cruz/ Astros Leaders	.05
187	Scott Fletcher	.05
188	Bob Dernier	.05
189	Mike Mason	.05
190	George Hendrick	.05
191	Wally Backman	.05
192	Milt Wilcox	.05
193	Daryl Sconiers	.05
194	Craig McMurtry	.05
195	Dave Concepcion	.05
196	Doyle Alexander	.05
197	Enos Cabell	.05
198	Ken Dixon	.05
199	Dick Howser	.05
200	Mike Schmidt	1.00
201	Vince Coleman	.05
202	Dwight Gooden	.05
203	Keith Hernandez	.05
204	Phil Niekro	.05
205	Tony Perez	.05
206	Pete Rose	.25
207	Fernando Valenzuela (Record Breaker)	.05
208	Ramon Romero	.05
209	Randy Ready	.05
210	Calvin Schiraldi	.05
211	Ed Wojna	.05
212	Chris Speier	.05
213	Bob Shirley	.05
214	Randy Bush	.05
215	Frank White	.05
216	Dwayne Murphy/ A's Leaders	.05
217	Bill Scherrer	.05
218	Randy Hunt	.05
219	Dennis Lamp	.05
220	Bob Horner	.05
221	Dave Henderson	.05
222	Craig Gerber	.05
223	Atlee Hammaker	.05
224	Cesar Cedeno	.05
225	Ron Darling	.05
226	Lee Lacy	.05
227	Al Jones	.05
228	Tom Lawless	.05
229	Bill Gullickson	.05
230	Terry Kennedy	.05
231	Jim Frey	.05
232	Rick Rhoden	.05
233	Steve Lyons	.05
234	Doug Corbett	.05
235	Butch Wynegar	.05
236	Frank Eufemia	.05
237	Ted Simmons	.05
238	Larry Parrish	.05

#	Player	Price	#	Player	Price	#	Player	Price	#	Player	Price
239	Joel Skinner	.05	339	Bruce Berenyi	.05	440	Alvin Davis	.05	541	Jorge Orta	.05
240	Tommy John	.10	340	Cal Ripken, Jr.	2.00	441	Whitey Herzog	.05	542	Don Schulze	.05
241	Tony Fernandez	.05	341	Frank Williams	.05	442	Ron Robinson	.05	543	Jerry Narron	.05
242	Rich Thompson	.05	342	Gary Redus	.05	443	Bill Buckner	.05	544	Eddie Milner	.05
243	Johnny Grubb	.05	343	Carlos Diaz	.05	444	Alex Trevino	.05	545	Jimmy Key	.05
244	Craig Lefferts	.05	344	Jim Wohlford	.05	445	Bert Blyleven	.05	546	Dave Henderson/ Mariners Leaders	.05
245	Jim Sundberg	.05	345	Donnie Moore	.05	446	Lenn Sakata	.05	547	Roger McDowell	.05
246	Steve Carlton/ Phillies Leaders	.10	346	Bryan Little	.05	447	Jerry Don Gleaton	.05	548	Mike Young	.05
247	Terry Harper	.05	347	Teddy Higuera RC	.10	448	Herm Winningham RC	.05	549	Bob Welch	.05
248	Spike Owen	.05	348	Cliff Johnson	.05	449	Rod Scurry	.05	550	Tom Herr	.05
249	Rob Deer	.05	349	Mark Clear	.05	450	Graig Nettles	.05	551	Dave LaPoint	.05
250	Dwight Gooden	.05	350	Jack Clark	.05	451	Mark Brown	.05	552	Marc Hill	.05
251	Rich Dauer	.05	351	Chuck Tanner	.05	452	Bob Clark	.05	553	Jim Morrison	.05
252	Bobby Castillo	.05	352	Harry Spilman	.05	453	Steve Jeltz	.05	554	Paul Householder	.05
253	Dann Bilardello	.05	353	Keith Atherton	.05	454	Burt Hooton	.05	555	Hubie Brooks	.05
254	Ozzie Guillen RC	.30	354	Tony Bernazard	.05	455	Willie Randolph	.05	556	John Denny	.05
255	Tony Armas	.05	355	Lee Smith	.05	456	Dale Murphy/ Braves Leaders	.10	557	Gerald Perry	.05
256	Kurt Kepshire	.05	356	Mickey Hatcher	.05	457	Mickey Tettleton	.05	558	Tim Stoddard	.05
257	Doug DeCinces	.05	357	Ed Vande Berg	.05	458	Kevin Bass	.05	559	Tommy Dunbar	.05
258	Tim Burke RC	.05	358	Rick Dempsey	.05	459	Luis Leal	.05	560	Dave Righetti	.05
259	Dan Pasqua	.05	359	Mike LaCoss	.05	460	Leon Durham	.05	561	Bob Lillis	.05
260	Tony Pena	.05	360	Lloyd Moseby	.05	461	Walt Terrell	.05	562	Joe Beckwith	.05
261	Bobby Valentine	.05	361	Shane Rawley	.05	462	Domingo Ramos	.05	563	Alejandro Sanchez	.05
262	Mario Ramirez	.05	362	Tom Paciorek	.05	463	Jim Gott	.05	564	Warren Brusstar	.05
263	Checklist 133-264	.05	363	Terry Forster	.05	464	Ruppert Jones	.05	565	Tom Brunansky	.05
264	Darren Daulton	.05	364	Reid Nichols	.05	465	Jesse Orosco	.05	566	Alfredo Griffin	.05
265	Ron Davis	.05	365	Mike Flanagan	.05	466	Tom Foley	.05	567	Jeff Barkley	.05
266	Keith Moreland	.05	366	Dave Concepcion/ Reds Leaders	.05	467	Bob James	.05	568	Donnie Scott	.05
267	Paul Molitor	.50	367	Aurelio Lopez	.05	468	Mike Scioscia	.05	569	Jim Acker	.05
268	Mike Scott	.05	368	Greg Brock	.05	469	Storm Davis	.05	570	Rusty Staub	.10
269	Dane Iorg	.05	369	Al Holland	.05	470	Bill Madlock	.05	571	Mike Jeffcoat	.05
270	Jack Morris	.05	370	Vince Coleman RC	.35	471	Bobby Cox	.05	572	Paul Zuvella	.05
271	Dave Collins	.05	371	Bill Stein	.05	472	Joe Hesketh	.05	573	Tom Hume	.05
272	Tim Tolman	.05	372	Ben Oglivie	.05	473	Mark Brouhard	.05	574	Ron Kittle	.05
273	Jerry Willard	.05	373	Urbano Lugo RC	.05	474	John Tudor	.05	575	Mike Boddicker	.05
274	Ron Gardenhire	.05	374	Terry Francona	.05	475	Juan Samuel	.05	576	Andre Dawson/ Expos Leaders	.05
275	Charlie Hough	.05	375	Rich Gedman	.05	476	Ron Mathis	.05	577	Jerry Reuss	.05
276	Willie Randolph/ Yankees Leaders	.05	376	Bill Dawley	.05	477	Mike Easler	.05	578	Lee Mazzilli	.05
277	Jaime Cocanower	.05	377	Joe Carter	.05	478	Andy Hawkins	.05	579	Jim Slaton	.05
278	Sixto Lezcano	.05	378	Bruce Bochte	.05	479	Bob Melvin RC	.05	580	Willie McGee	.05
279	Al Pardo	.05	379	Bobby Meacham	.05	480	Oddibe McDowell RC	.05	581	Bruce Hurst	.05
280	Tim Raines	.05	380	LaMarr Hoyt	.05	481	Scott Bradley	.05	582	Jim Gantner	.05
281	Steve Mura	.05	381	Ray Miller	.05	482	Rick Lysander	.05	583	Al Bumbry	.05
282	Jerry Mumphrey	.05	382	Ivan Calderon RC	.05	483	George Vukovich	.05	584	Brian Fisher RC	.05
283	Mike Fischlin	.05	383	Chris Brown RC	.05	484	Donnie Hill	.05	585	Garry Maddox	.05
284	Brian Dayett	.05	384	Steve Trout	.05	485	Gary Matthews	.05	586	Greg Harris	.05
285	Buddy Bell	.05	385	Cecil Cooper	.05	486	Bob Grich/ Angels Leaders	.05	587	Rafael Santana	.05
286	Luis DeLeon	.05	386	Cecil Fielder RC	.75	487	Bret Saberhagen	.05	588	Steve Lake	.05
287	John Christensen RC	.05	387	Steve Kemp	.05	488	Lou Thornton	.05	589	Sid Bream	.05
288	Don Aase	.05	388	Dickie Noles	.05	489	Jim Winn	.05	590	Bob Knepper	.05
289	Johnnie LeMaster	.05	389	Glenn Davis	.05	490	Jeff Leonard	.05	591	Jackie Moore	.05
290	Carlton Fisk	.50	390	Tom Seaver	.60	491	Pascual Perez	.05	592	Frank Tanana	.05
291	Tom Lasorda	.10	391	Julio Franco	.05	492	Kelvin Chapman	.05	593	Jesse Barfield	.05
292	Chuck Porter	.05	392	John Russell	.05	493	Gene Nelson	.05	594	Chris Bando	.05
293	Chris Chambliss	.05	393	Chris Pittaro	.05	494	Gary Roenicke	.05	595	Dave Parker	.05
294	Danny Cox	.05	394	Checklist 265-396	.05	495	Mark Langston	.05	596	Onix Concepcion	.05
295	Kirk Gibson	.05	395	Scott Garrelts	.05	496	Jay Johnstone	.05	597	Sammy Stewart	.05
296	Geno Petralli	.05	396	Dwight Evans/ Red Sox Leaders	.05	497	John Stuper	.05	598	Jim Presley	.05
297	Tim Lollar	.05	397	Steve Buechele RC	.10	498	Tito Landrum	.05	599	Rick Aguilera RC	.25
298	Craig Reynolds	.05	398	Earnie Riles RC	.05	499	Bob L. Gibson	.05	600	Dale Murphy	.25
299	Bryn Smith	.05	399	Bill Swift	.05	500	Rickey Henderson	.50	601	Gary Lucas	.05
300	George Brett	1.00	400	Rod Carew	.50	501	Dave Johnson	.05	602	Mariano Duncan	.05
301	Dennis Rasmussen	.05	401	Fernando Valenzuela	.05	502	Glen Cook	.05	603	Bill Laskey	.05
302	Greg Gross	.05	402	Tom Seaver	.25	503	Mike Fitzgerald	.05	604	Gary Pettis	.05
303	Curt Wardle	.05	403	Willie Mays	.35	504	Denny Walling	.05	605	Dennis Boyd	.05
304	Mike Gallego RC	.10	404	Frank Robinson	.10	505	Jerry Koosman	.05	606	Hal McRae/ Royals Leaders	.05
305	Phil Bradley	.05	405	Roger Maris	.30	506	Bill Russell	.05	607	Ken Dayley	.05
306	Terry Kennedy Padres Leaders	.05	406	Scott Sanderson	.05	507	Steve Ontiveros RC	.05	608	Bruce Bochy	.05
307	Dave Sax	.05	407	Sal Butera	.05	508	Alan Wiggins	.05	609	Barbaro Garbey	.05
308	Ray Fontenot	.05	408	Dave Smith	.05	509	Ernie Camacho	.05	610	Ron Guidry	.05
309	John Shelby	.05	409	Paul Runge RC	.05	510	Wade Boggs	.75	611	Gary Woods	.05
310	Greg Minton	.05	410	Dave Kingman	.05	511	Ed Nunez	.05	612	Richard Dotson	.05
311	Dick Schofield	.05	411	Sparky Anderson	.10	512	Thad Bosley	.05	613	Roy Smalley	.05
312	Tom Filer	.05	412	Jim Clancy	.05	513	Ron Washington	.05	614	Rick Waits	.05
313	Joe DeSa	.05	413	Tim Flannery	.05	514	Mike Jones	.05	615	Johnny Ray	.05
314	Frank Pastore	.05	414	Tom Gorman	.05	515	Darrell Evans	.05	616	Glenn Brummer	.05
315	Mookie Wilson	.05	415	Hal McRae	.05	516	Greg Minton/ Giants Leaders	.05	617	Lonnie Smith	.05
316	Sammy Khalifa	.05	416	Denny Martinez	.05	517	Milt Thompson RC	.05	618	Jim Pankovits	.05
317	Ed Romero	.05	417	R.J. Reynolds	.05	518	Buck Martinez	.05	619	Danny Heep	.05
318	Terry Whitfield	.05	418	Alan Knicely	.05	519	Danny Darwin	.05	620	Bruce Sutter	.40
319	Rick Camp	.05	419	Frank Wills	.05	520	Keith Hernandez	.05	621	John Felske	.05
320	Jim Rice	.15	420	Von Hayes	.05	521	Nate Snell	.05	622	Gary Lavelle	.05
321	Earl Weaver	.10	421	Dave Palmer	.05	522	Bob Bailor	.05	623	Floyd Rayford	.05
322	Bob Forsch	.05	422	Mike Jorgensen	.05	523	Joe Price	.05	624	Steve McCatty	.05
323	Jerry Davis	.05	423	Dan Spillner	.05	524	Darrell Miller	.05	625	Bob Brenly	.05
324	Dan Schatzeder	.05	424	Rick Miller	.05	525	Marvell Wynne	.05	626	Roy Thomas	.05
325	Juan Beniquez	.05	425	Larry McWilliams	.05	526	Charlie Lea	.05	627	Ron Oester	.05
326	Kent Tekulve	.05	426	Charlie Moore/ Brewers Leaders	.05	527	Checklist 397-528	.05	628	Kirk McCaskill RC	.15
327	Mike Pagliarulo	.05	427	Joe Cowley	.05	528	Terry Pendleton	.05	629	Mitch Webster RC	.05
328	Pete O'Brien	.05	428	Max Venable	.05	529	Marc Sullivan	.05	630	Fernando Valenzuela	.05
329	Kirby Puckett	.75	429	Greg Booker	.05	530	Rich Gossage	.05	631	Steve Braun	.05
330	Rick Sutcliffe	.05	430	Kent Hrbek	.05	531	Tony LaRussa	.05	632	Dave Von Ohlen	.05
331	Alan Ashby	.05	431	George Frazier	.05	532	Don Carman RC	.05	633	Jackie Gutierrez	.05
332	Darryl Motley	.05	432	Mark Bailey	.05	533	Billy Sample	.05	634	Roy Lee Jackson	.05
333	Tom Henke	.05	433	Chris Codiroli	.05	534	Jeff Calhoun	.05	635	Jason Thompson	.05
334	Ken Oberkfell	.05	434	Curt Wilkerson	.05	535	Toby Harrah	.05	636	Lee Smith/ Cubs Leaders	.05
335	Don Sutton	.40	435	Bill Caudill	.05	536	Jose Rijo	.05	637	Rudy Law	.05
336	Andre Thornton/ Indians Leaders	.05	436	Doug Flynn	.05	537	Mark Salas	.05	638	John Butcher	.05
337	Darnell Coles	.05	437	Rick Mahler	.05	538	Dennis Eckersley	.40	639	Bo Diaz	.05
338	Jorge Bell	.05	438	Clint Hurdle	.05	539	Glenn Hubbard	.05	640	Jose Cruz	.05
			439	Rick Honeycutt	.05	540	Dan Petry	.05			

641	Wayne Tolleson	.05
642	Ray Searage	.05
643	Tom Brookens	.05
644	Mark Gubicza	.05
645	Dusty Baker	.05
646	Mike Moore	.05
647	Mel Hall	.05
648	Steve Bedrosian	.05
649	Ronn Reynolds	.05
650	Dave Stieb	.05
651	Billy Martin	.10
652	Tom Browning	.05
653	Jim Dwyer	.05
654	Ken Howell	.05
655	Manny Trillo	.05
656	Brian Harper	.05
657	Juan Agosto	.05
658	Rob Wilfong	.05
659	Checklist 529-660	.05
660	Steve Garvey	.20
661	Roger Clemens	3.00
661	Roger Clemens (Blue streak upper-right.)	7.50
662	Bill Schroeder	.05
663	Neil Allen	.05
664	Tim Corcoran	.05
665	Alejandro Pena	.05
666	Charlie Hough Rangers Leaders	.05
667	Tim Teufel	.05
668	Cecilio Guante	.05
669	Ron Cey	.05
670	Willie Hernandez	.05
671	Lynn Jones	.05
672	Rob Picciolo	.05
673	Ernie Whitt	.05
674	Pat Tabler	.05
675	Claudell Washington	.05
676	Matt Young	.05
677	Nick Esasky	.05
678	Dan Gladden	.05
679	Britt Burns	.05
680	George Foster	.05
681	Dick Williams	.05
682	Junior Ortiz	.05
683	Andy Van Slyke	.05
684	Bob McClure	.05
685	Tim Wallach	.05
686	Jeff Stone	.05
687	Mike Trujillo	.05
688	Larry Herndon	.05
689	Dave Stewart	.05
690	Ryne Sandberg	.75
691	Mike Madden	.05
692	Dale Berra	.05
693	Tom Tellmann	.05
694	Garth Iorg	.05
695	Mike Smithson	.05
696	Bill Russell Dodgers Leaders	.05
697	Bud Black	.05
698	Brad Komminsk	.05
699	Pat Corrales	.05
700	Reggie Jackson	.75
701	Keith Hernandez/AS	.05
702	Tom Herr/AS	.05
703	Tim Wallach/AS	.05
704	Ozzie Smith/AS	.35
705	Dale Murphy/AS	.10
706	Pedro Guerrero/AS	.05
707	Willie McGee/AS	.05
708	Gary Carter/AS	.25
709	Dwight Gooden/AS	.05
710	John Tudor/AS	.05
711	Jeff Reardon/AS	.05
712	Don Mattingly/AS	.50
713	Damaso Garcia/AS	.05
714	George Brett/AS	.45
715	Cal Ripken, Jr./AS	1.00
716	Rickey Henderson/AS	.25
717	Dave Winfield/AS	.25
718	George Bell/AS	.05
719	Carlton Fisk/AS	.20
720	Bret Saberhagen/AS	.05
721	Ron Guidry/AS	.05
722	Dan Quisenberry/AS	.05
723	Marty Bystrom	.05
724	Tim Hulett	.05
725	Mario Soto	.05
726	Rick Dempsey Orioles Leaders	.05
727	David Green	.05
728	Mike Marshall	.05
729	Jim Beattie	.05
730	Ozzie Smith	.75
731	Don Robinson	.05
732	Floyd Youmans RC	.05
733	Ron Romanick	.05
734	Marty Barrett	.05
735	Dave Dravecky	.05
736	Glenn Wilson	.05
737	Pete Vuckovich	.05
738	Andre Robertson	.05
739	Dave Rozema	.05

740	Lance Parrish	.05
741	Pete Rose	1.00
742	Frank Viola	.05
743	Pat Sheridan	.05
744	Lary Sorensen	.05
745	Willie Upshaw	.05
746	Denny Gonzalez	.05
747	Rick Cerone	.05
748	Steve Henderson	.05
749	Ed Jurak	.05
750	Gorman Thomas	.05
751	Howard Johnson	.05
752	Mike Krukow	.05
753	Dan Ford	.05
754	Pat Clements RC	.05
755	Harold Baines	.05
756	Rick Rhoden Pirates Leaders	.05
757	Darrell Porter	.05
758	Dave Anderson	.05
759	Moose Haas	.05
760	Andre Dawson	.30
761	Don Slaught	.05
762	Eric Show	.05
763	Terry Puhl	.05
764	Kevin Gross	.05
765	Don Baylor	.05
766	Rick Langford	.05
767	Jody Davis	.05
768	Vern Ruhle	.05
769	Harold Reynolds RC	.25
770	Vida Blue	.05
771	John McNamara	.05
772	Brian Downing	.05
773	Greg Pryor	.05
774	Terry Leach	.05
775	Al Oliver	.05
776	Gene Garber	.05
777	Wayne Krenchicki	.05
778	Jerry Hairston Sr.	.05
779	Rick Reuschel	.05
780	Robin Yount	.50
781	Joe Nolan	.05
782	Ken Landreaux	.05
783	Ricky Horton	.05
784	Alan Bannister	.05
785	Bob Stanley	.05
786	Mickey Hatcher Twins Leaders	.05
787	Vance Law	.05
788	Marty Castillo	.05
789	Kurt Bevacqua	.05
790	Phil Niekro	.40
791	Checklist 661-792	.05
792	Charles Hudson	.05

Tiffany

	NM/M
Unopened Set (792):	100.00
Complete Set (792):	45.00
Common Player:	.25

(Star cards valued at 4X corresponding cards in regular 1986 Topps issue.)

Traded

JOSE CANSECO

	NM/M
Unopened Set (132):	30.00
Complete Set (132):	25.00
Common Player:	.05

1T	Andy Allanson	.05
2T	Neil Allen	.05
3T	Joaquin Andujar	.05
4T	Paul Assenmacher	.05
5T	Scott Bailes	.05
6T	Don Baylor	.15
7T	Steve Bedrosian	.05
8T	Juan Beniquez	.05
9T	Juan Berenguer	.05
10T	Mike Bielecki	.05
11T	Barry Bonds RC	20.00
12T	Bobby Bonilla RC	.50

13T	Juan Bonilla	.05
14T	Rich Bordi	.05
15T	Steve Boros	.05
16T	Rick Burleson	.05
17T	Bill Campbell	.05
18T	Tom Candiotti	.05
19T	John Cangelosi	.05
20T	Jose Canseco RC	4.00
21T	Carmen Castillo	.05
22T	Rick Cerone	.05
23T	John Cerutti	.05
24T	Will Clark RC	1.50
25T	Mark Clear	.05
26T	Darnell Coles	.05
27T	Dave Collins	.05
28T	Tim Conroy	.05
29T	Joe Cowley	.05
30T	Joel Davis	.05
31T	Rob Deer	.05
32T	John Denny	.05
33T	Mike Easler	.05
34T	Mark Eichhorn	.05
35T	Steve Farr	.05
36T	Scott Fletcher	.05
37T	Terry Forster	.05
38T	Terry Francona	.05
39T	Jim Fregosi	.05
40T	Andres Galarraga	.35
41T	Ken Griffey	.05
42T	Bill Gullickson	.05
43T	Jose Guzman	.05
44T	Moose Haas	.05
45T	Billy Hatcher	.05
46T	Mike Heath	.05
47T	Tom Hume	.05
48T	Pete Incaviglia RC	.20
49T	Dane Iorg	.05
50T	Bo Jackson RC	3.00
51T	Wally Joyner RC	.40
52T	Charlie Kerfeld	.05
53T	Eric King	.05
54T	Bob Kipper	.05
55T	Wayne Krenchicki	.05
56T	John Kruk RC	.35
57T	Mike LaCoss	.05
58T	Pete Ladd	.05
59T	Mike Laga	.05
60T	Hal Lanier	.05
61T	Dave LaPoint	.05
62T	Rudy Law	.05
63T	Rick Leach	.05
64T	Tim Leary	.05
65T	Dennis Leonard	.05
66T	Jim Leyland	.05
67T	Steve Lyons	.05
68T	Mickey Mahler	.05
69T	Candy Maldonado	.05
70T	Roger Mason	.05
71T	Bob McClure	.05
72T	Andy McGaffigan	.05
73T	Gene Michael	.05
74T	Kevin Mitchell RC	.25
75T	Omar Moreno	.05
76T	Jerry Mumphrey	.05
77T	Phil Niekro	.25
78T	Randy Niemann	.05
79T	Juan Nieves	.05
80T	Otis Nixon	.05
81T	Bob Ojeda	.05
82T	Jose Oquendo	.05
83T	Tom Paciorek	.05
84T	Dave Palmer	.05
85T	Frank Pastore	.05
86T	Lou Piniella	.05
87T	Dan Plesac	.05
88T	Darrell Porter	.05
89T	Rey Quinones	.05
90T	Gary Redus	.05
91T	Bip Roberts	.05
92T	Billy Jo Robidoux	.05
93T	Jeff Robinson	.05
94T	Gary Roenicke	.05
95T	Ed Romero	.05
96T	Argenis Salazar	.05
97T	Joe Sambito	.05
98T	Billy Sample	.05
99T	Dave Schmidt	.05
100T	Ken Schrom	.05
101T	Tom Seaver	.50
102T	Ted Simmons	.05
103T	Sammy Stewart	.05
104T	Kurt Stillwell	.05
105T	Franklin Stubbs	.05
106T	Dale Sveum	.05
107T	Chuck Tanner	.05
108T	Danny Tartabull	.05
109T	Tim Teufel	.05
110T	Bob Tewksbury	.05
111T	Andres Thomas	.05
112T	Milt Thompson	.05
113T	Robby Thompson	.05
114T	Jay Tibbs	.05
115T	Wayne Tolleson	.05
116T	Alex Trevino	.05
117T	Manny Trillo	.05

118T	Ed Vande Berg	.05
119T	Ozzie Virgil	.05
120T	Bob Walk	.05
121T	Gene Walter	.05
122T	Claudell Washington	.05
123T	Bill Wegman	.05
124T	Dick Williams	.05
125T	Mitch Williams	.05
126T	Bobby Witt	.05
127T	Todd Worrell	.05
128T	George Wright	.05
129T	Ricky Wright	.05
130T	Steve Yeager	.05
131T	Paul Zuvella	.05
132T	Checklist	.05

Traded Tiffany

	NM/M
Unopened Set (132):	700.00
Complete Set (132):	450.00
Common Player:	.25
11T Barry Bonds	200.00

(Star cards valued at 4X corresponding cards in regular Topps Traded.)

1987 Topps

	NM/M
Unopened Factory Set, Retail (792):	30.00
Unopened Factory Set, Hobby (792):	25.00
Complete Set (792):	20.00
Uncut Sheet of (6):	45.00
Common Player:	.05
Wax Pack (15):	.75
Wax Box (36):	20.00
Cello Pack (31):	1.00
Cello Box (24):	20.00
Rack Pack (49):	1.50
Rack Box (24):	25.00
Vending Box (500):	12.00

1	Roger Clemens	.45
2	Jim Deshaies	.05
3	Dwight Evans	.05
4	Dave Lopes	.05
5	Dave Righetti	.05
6	Ruben Sierra	.05
7	Todd Worrell	.05
8	Terry Pendleton	.05
9	Jay Tibbs	.05
10	Cecil Cooper	.05
11	Jack Aker, Chris Bando, Phil Niekro Indians Leaders	.05
12	Jeff Sellers RC	.05
13	Nick Esasky	.05
14	Dave Stewart	.05
15	Claudell Washington	.05
16	Pat Clements	.05
17	Pete O'Brien	.05
18	Dick Howser	.05
19	Matt Young	.05
20	Gary Carter	.40
21	Mark Davis	.05
22	Doug DeCinces	.05
23	Lee Smith	.05
24	Tony Walker	.05
25	Bert Blyleven	.05
26	Greg Brock	.05
27	Joe Cowley	.05
28	Rick Dempsey	.05
29	Jimmy Key	.05
30	Tim Raines	.05
31	Glenn Hubbard, Rafael Ramirez Braves Leaders	.05
32	Tim Leary	.05
33	Andy Van Slyke	.05
34	Jose Rijo	.05
35	Sid Bream	.05
36	Eric King RC	.05

No.	Player	Price
37	Marvell Wynne	.05
38	Dennis Leonard	.05
39	Marty Barrett	.05
40	Dave Righetti	.05
41	Bo Diaz	.05
42	Gary Redus	.05
43	Gene Michael	.05
44	Greg Harris	.05
45	Jim Presley	.05
46	Danny Gladden	.05
47	Dennis Powell	.05
48	Wally Backman	.05
49	Terry Harper	.05
50	Dave Smith	.05
51	Mel Hall	.05
52	Keith Atherton	.05
53	Ruppert Jones	.05
54	Bill Dawley	.05
55	Tim Wallach	.05
56	Jamie Cocanower, Paul Molitor, Charlie Moore, Herm Starrette Brewers Leaders	.10
57	Scott Nielsen RC	.05
58	Thad Bosley	.05
59	Ken Dayley	.05
60	Tony Pena	.05
61	Bobby Thigpen RC	.05
62	Bobby Meacham	.05
63	Fred Toliver	.05
64	Harry Spilman	.05
65	Tom Browning	.05
66	Marc Sullivan	.05
67	Bill Swift	.05
68	Tony LaRussa	.05
69	Lonnie Smith	.05
70	Charlie Hough	.05
71	Mike Aldrete RC	.05
72	Walt Terrell	.05
73	Dave Anderson	.05
74	Dan Pasqua	.05
75	Ron Darling	.05
76	Rafael Ramirez	.05
77	Bryan Oelkers	.05
78	Tom Foley	.05
79	Juan Nieves	.05
80	Wally Joyner RC	.35
81	Andy Hawkins, Terry Kennedy Padres Leaders	.05
82	Rob Murphy RC	.05
83	Mike Davis	.05
84	Steve Lake	.05
85	Kevin Bass	.05
86	Nate Snell	.05
87	Mark Salas	.05
88	Ed Wojna	.05
89	Ozzie Guillen	.05
90	Dave Stieb	.05
91	Harold Reynolds	.05
92a	Urbano Lugo (No trademark on front.)	.10
92b	Urbano Lugo (Trademark on front.)	.05
93	Jim Leyland	.05
94	Calvin Schiraldi	.05
95	Oddibe McDowell	.05
96	Frank Williams	.05
97	Glenn Wilson	.05
98	Bill Scherrer	.05
99	Darryl Motley	.05
100	Steve Garvey	.15
101	Carl Willis RC	.05
102	Paul Zuvella	.05
103	Rick Aguilera	.05
104	Billy Sample	.05
105	Floyd Youmans	.05
106	George Bell, Willie Upshaw Blue Jays Leaders	.05
107	John Butcher	.05
108	Jim Gantner (Photo reversed.)	.05
109	R.J. Reynolds	.05
110	John Tudor	.05
111	Alfredo Griffin	.05
112	Alan Ashby	.05
113	Neil Allen	.05
114	Billy Beane	.05
115	Donnie Moore	.05
116	Mike Stanley RC	.05
117	Jim Beattie	.05
118	Bobby Valentine	.05
119	Ron Robinson	.05
120	Eddie Murray	.40
121	Kevin Romine RC	.05
122	Jim Clancy	.05
123	John Kruk	.05
124	Ray Fontenot	.05
125	Bob Brenly	.05
126	Mike Loynd RC	.05
127	Vance Law	.05
128	Checklist 1-132	.05
129	Rick Cerone	.05
130	Dwight Gooden	.05
131	Sid Bream, Tony Pena Pirates Leaders	.05
132	Paul Assenmacher RC	.05
133	Jose Oquendo	.05
134	Rich Yett RC	.05
135	Mike Easler	.05
136	Ron Romanick	.05
137	Jerry Willard	.05
138	Roy Lee Jackson	.05
139	Devon White RC	.40
140	Bret Saberhagen	.05
141	Herm Winningham	.05
142	Rick Sutcliffe	.05
143	Steve Boros	.05
144	Mike Scioscia	.05
145	Charlie Kerfeld	.05
146	Tracy Jones RC	.05
147	Randy Niemann	.05
148	Dave Collins	.05
149	Ray Searage	.05
150	Wade Boggs	.45
151	Mike LaCoss	.05
152	Toby Harrah	.05
153	Duane Ward RC	.05
154	Tom O'Malley	.05
155	Eddie Whitson	.05
156	Bob Kearney, Phil Regan, Matt Young Mariners Leaders	.05
157	Danny Darwin	.05
158	Tim Teufel	.05
159	Ed Olwine	.05
160	Julio Franco	.05
161	Steve Ontiveros	.05
162	Mike LaValliere RC	.10
163	Kevin Gross	.05
164	Sammy Khalifa	.05
165	Jeff Reardon	.05
166	Bob Boone	.05
167	Jim Deshaies RC	.10
168	Lou Piniella	.05
169	Ron Washington	.05
170	Bo Jackson (Future Stars)	1.50
171	Chuck Cary RC	.05
172	Ron Oester	.05
173	Alex Trevino	.05
174	Henry Cotto	.05
175	Bob Stanley	.05
176	Steve Buechele	.05
177	Keith Moreland	.05
178	Cecil Fielder	.05
179	Bill Wegman	.05
180	Chris Brown	.05
181	Mike LaValliere, Ozzie Smith, Ray Soff Cardinals Leaders	.10
182	Lee Lacy	.05
183	Andy Hawkins	.05
184	Bobby Bonilla	.05
185	Roger McDowell	.05
186	Bruce Benedict	.05
187	Mark Huismann	.05
188	Tony Phillips	.05
189	Joe Hesketh	.05
190	Jim Sundberg	.05
191	Charles Hudson	.05
192	Cory Snyder	.05
193	Roger Craig	.05
194	Kirk McCaskill	.05
195	Mike Pagliarulo	.05
196	Randy O'Neal	.05
197	Mark Bailey	.05
198	Lee Mazzilli	.05
199	Mariano Duncan	.05
200	Pete Rose	.75
201	John Cangelosi RC	.05
202	Ricky Wright	.05
203	Mike Kingery RC	.05
204	Sammy Stewart	.05
205	Graig Nettles	.05
206	Tim Laudner, Frank Viola Twins Leaders	.05
207	George Frazier	.05
208	John Shelby	.05
209	Rick Schu	.05
210	Lloyd Moseby	.05
211	John Morris	.05
212	Mike Fitzgerald	.05
213	Randy Myers RC	.20
214	Omar Moreno	.05
215	Mark Langston	.05
216	B.J. Surhoff RC (Future Stars)	.20
217	Chris Codiroli	.05
218	Sparky Anderson	.10
219	Cecilio Guante	.05
220	Joe Carter	.05
221	Vern Ruhle	.05
222	Denny Walling	.05
223	Charlie Leibrandt	.05
224	Wayne Tolleson	.05
225	Mike Smithson	.05
226	Max Venable	.05
227	Jamie Moyer RC	.05
228	Curt Wilkerson	.05
229	Mike Birkbeck RC	.05
230	Don Baylor	.05
231	Bob Brenly, Mike Krukow Giants Leaders	.05
232	Reggie Williams RC	.05
233	Russ Morman RC	.05
234	Pat Sheridan	.05
235	Alvin Davis	.05
236	Tommy John	.10
237	Jim Morrison	.05
238	Bill Krueger	.05
239	Juan Espino	.05
240	Steve Balboni	.05
241	Danny Heep	.05
242	Rick Mahler	.05
243	Whitey Herzog	.05
244	Dickie Noles	.05
245	Willie Upshaw	.05
246	Jim Dwyer	.05
247	Jeff Reed	.05
248	Gene Walter	.05
249	Jim Pankovits	.05
250	Teddy Higuera	.05
251	Rob Wilfong	.05
252	Denny Martinez	.05
253	Eddie Milner	.05
254	Bob Tewksbury RC	.20
255	Juan Samuel	.05
256	George Brett, Frank White Royals Leaders	.15
257	Bob Forsch	.05
258	Steve Yeager	.05
259	Mike Greenwell RC	.25
260	Vida Blue	.05
261	Ruben Sierra	.05
262	Jim Winn	.05
263	Stan Javier	.05
264	Checklist 133-264	.05
265	Darrell Evans	.05
266	Jeff Hamilton RC	.05
267	Howard Johnson	.05
268	Pat Corrales	.05
269	Cliff Speck	.05
270	Jody Davis	.05
271	Mike Brown	.05
272	Andres Galarraga	.05
273	Gene Nelson	.05
274	Jeff Hearron RC	.05
275	LaMarr Hoyt	.05
276	Jackie Gutierrez	.05
277	Juan Agosto	.05
278	Gary Pettis	.05
279	Dan Plesac RC	.05
280	Jeffrey Leonard	.05
281	Bo Diaz, Bill Gullickson, Pete Rose Reds Leaders	.10
282	Jeff Calhoun	.05
283	Doug Drabek RC	.25
284	John Moses	.05
285	Dennis Boyd	.05
286	Mike Woodard	.05
287	Dave Von Ohlen	.05
288	Tito Landrum	.05
289	Bob Kipper	.05
290	Leon Durham	.05
291	Mitch Williams	.05
292	Franklin Stubbs	.05
293	Bob Rodgers	.05
294	Steve Jeltz	.05
295	Len Dykstra	.05
296	Andres Thomas RC	.05
297	Don Schulze	.05
298	Larry Herndon	.05
299	Joel Davis	.05
300	Reggie Jackson	.50
301	Luis Aquino RC	.05
302	Bill Schroeder	.05
303	Juan Berenguer	.05
304	Phil Garner	.05
305	John Franco	.05
306	Rich Gedman, John McNamara, Tom Seaver Red Sox Leaders	.10
307	Lee Guetterman RC	.05
308	Don Slaught	.05
309	Mike Young	.05
310	Frank Viola	.05
311	Rickey Henderson	.10
312	Reggie Jackson	.10
313	Roberto Clemente	.50
314	Carl Yastrzemski	.10
315	Maury Wills	.05
316	Brian Fisher	.05
317	Clint Hurdle	.05
318	Jim Fregosi	.05
319	Greg Swindell RC	.10
320	Barry Bonds	8.00
321	Mike Laga	.05
322	Chris Bando	.05
323	Al Newman RC	.05
324	Dave Palmer	.05
325	Garry Templeton	.05
326	Mark Gubicza	.05
327	Dale Sveum RC	.05
328	Bob Welch	.05
329	Ron Roenicke	.05
330	Mike Scott	.05
331	Gary Carter, Keith Hernandez, Dave Johnson, Darryl Strawberry Mets Leaders	.10
332	Joe Price	.05
333	Ken Phelps	.05
334	Ed Correa RC	.05
335	Candy Maldonado	.05
336	Allan Anderson RC	.05
337	Darrell Miller	.05
338	Tim Conroy	.05
339	Donnie Hill	.05
340	Roger Clemens	.65
341	Mike Brown	.05
342	Bob James	.05
343	Hal Lanier	.05
344a	Joe Niekro (Copyright outside yellow on back.)	.25
344b	Joe Niekro (Copyright inside yellow on back.)	.05
345	Andre Dawson	.25
346	Shawon Dunston	.05
347	Mickey Brantley	.05
348	Carmelo Martinez	.05
349	Storm Davis	.05
350	Keith Hernandez	.05
351	Gene Garber	.05
352	Mike Felder	.05
353	Ernie Camacho	.05
354	Jamie Quirk	.05
355	Don Carman	.05
356	Ed Brinkman, Julio Cruz White Sox Leaders	.05
357	Steve Fireovid RC	.05
358	Sal Butera	.05
359	Doug Corbett	.05
360	Pedro Guerrero	.05
361	Mark Thurmond	.05
362	Luis Quinones RC	.05
363	Jose Guzman	.05
364	Randy Bush	.05
365	Rick Rhoden	.05
366	Mark McGwire	3.00
367	Jeff Lahti	.05
368	John McNamara	.05
369	Brian Dayett	.05
370	Fred Lynn	.05
371	Mark Eichhorn RC	.05
372	Jerry Mumphrey	.05
373	Jeff Dedmon	.05
374	Glenn Hoffman	.05
375	Ron Guidry	.10
376	Scott Bradley	.05
377	John Henry Johnson	.05
378	Rafael Santana	.05
379	John Russell	.05
380	Rich Gossage	.05
381	Mike Fitzgerald, Bob Rodgers Expos Leaders	.05
382	Rudy Law	.05
383	Ron Davis	.05
384	Johnny Grubb	.05
385	Orel Hershiser	.05
386	Dickie Thon	.05
387	T.R. Bryden RC	.05
388	Geno Petralli	.05
389	Jeff Robinson	.05
390	Gary Matthews	.05
391	Jay Howell	.05
392	Checklist 265-396	.05
393	Pete Rose	.60
394	Mike Bielecki	.05
395	Damaso Garcia	.05
396	Tim Lollar	.05
397	Greg Walker	.05
398	Brad Havens	.05
399	Curt Ford	.05
400	George Brett	.50
401	Billy Jo Robidoux	.05
402	Mike Trujillo	.05
403	Jerry Royster	.05
404	Doug Sisk	.05
405	Brook Jacoby	.05
406	Rickey Henderson, Don Mattingly Yankees Leaders	.25
407	Jim Acker	.05
408	John Mizerock	.05
409	Milt Thompson	.05
410	Fernando Valenzuela	.05
411	Darnell Coles	.05
412	Eric Davis	.05
413	Moose Haas	.05
414	Joe Orsulak	.05

#	Player	Price
415	Bobby Witt RC	.05
416	Tom Nieto	.05
417	Pat Perry	.05
418	Dick Williams	.05
419	Mark Portugal RC	.10
420	Will Clark	.40
421	Jose DeLeon	.05
422	Jack Howell	.05
423	Jaime Cocanower	.05
424	Chris Speier	.05
425	Tom Seaver	.40
426	Floyd Rayford	.05
427	Ed Nunez	.05
428	Bruce Bochy	.05
429	Tim Pyznarski RC (Future Stars)	.05
430	Mike Schmidt	.50
431	Tom Niedenfuer, Ron Perranoski, Alex Trevino Dodgers Leaders	.05
432	Jim Slaton	.05
433	Ed Hearn RC	.05
434	Mike Fischlin	.05
435	Bruce Sutter	.35
436	Andy Allanson RC	.05
437	Ted Power	.05
438	Kelly Downs RC	.05
439	Karl Best	.05
440	Willie McGee	.05
441	Dave Leiper RC	.05
442	Mitch Webster	.05
443	John Felske	.05
444	Jeff Russell	.05
445	Dave Lopes	.05
446	Chuck Finley RC	.25
447	Bill Almon	.05
448	Chris Bosio RC	.10
449	Pat Dodson RC (Future Stars)	.05
450	Kirby Puckett	.45
451	Joe Sambito	.05
452	Dave Henderson	.05
453	Scott Terry RC	.05
454	Luis Salazar	.05
455	Mike Boddicker	.05
456	Carney Lansford, Tony LaRussa, Mickey Tettleton, Dave Von Ohlen A's Leaders	.05
457	Len Matuszek	.05
458	Kelly Gruber (RC)	.05
459	Dennis Eckersley	.35
460	Darryl Strawberry	.05
461	Craig McMurtry	.05
462	Scott Fletcher	.05
463	Tom Candiotti	.05
464	Butch Wynegar	.05
465	Todd Worrell	.05
466	Kal Daniels	.05
467	Randy St. Claire	.05
468	George Bamberger	.05
469	Mike Diaz RC	.05
470	Dave Dravecky	.05
471	Ronn Reynolds	.05
472	Bill Doran	.05
473	Steve Farr	.05
474	Jerry Narron	.05
475	Scott Garrelts	.05
476	Danny Tartabull	.05
477	Ken Howell	.05
478	Tim Laudner	.05
479	Bob Sebra RC	.05
480	Jim Rice	.15
481	Von Hayes, Juan Samuel, Glenn Wilson Phillies Leaders	.05
482	Daryl Boston	.05
483	Dwight Lowry	.05
484	Jim Traber	.05
485	Tony Fernandez	.05
486	Otis Nixon	.05
487	Dave Gumpert	.05
488	Ray Knight	.05
489	Bill Gullickson	.05
490	Dale Murphy	.20
491	Ron Karkovice RC	.05
492	Mike Heath	.05
493	Tom Lasorda	.10
494	Barry Jones RC	.05
495	Gorman Thomas	.05
496	Bruce Bochte	.05
497	Dale Mohorcic RC	.05
498	Bob Kearney	.05
499	Bruce Ruffin RC	.05
500	Don Mattingly	.65
501	Craig Lefferts	.05
502	Dick Schofield	.05
503	Larry Andersen	.05
504	Mickey Hatcher	.05
505	Bryn Smith	.05
506	Rich Bordi, Rick Dempsey, Earl Weaver Orioles Leaders	.05
507	Dave Stapleton	.05
508	Scott Bankhead RC	.05
509	Enos Cabell	.05
510	Tom Henke	.05
511	Steve Lyons	.05
512	Dave Magadan RC (Future Stars)	.20
513	Carmen Castillo	.05
514	Orlando Mercado	.05
515	Willie Hernandez	.05
516	Ted Simmons	.05
517	Mario Soto	.05
518	Gene Mauch	.05
519	Curt Young	.05
520	Jack Clark	.05
521	Rick Reuschel	.05
522	Checklist 397-528	.05
523	Earnie Riles	.05
524	Bob Shirley	.05
525	Phil Bradley	.05
526	Roger Mason	.05
527	Jim Wohlford	.05
528	Ken Dixon	.05
529	Alvaro Espinoza RC	.05
530	Tony Gwynn	.45
531	Yogi Berra, Hal Lanier, Denis Menke, Gene Tenace Astros Leaders	.05
532	Jeff Stone	.05
533	Argenis Salazar	.05
534	Scott Sanderson	.05
535	Tony Armas	.05
536	Terry Mulholland RC	.15
537	Rance Mulliniks	.05
538	Tom Niedenfuer	.05
539	Reid Nichols	.05
540	Terry Kennedy	.05
541	Rafael Belliard RC	.05
542	Ricky Horton	.05
543	Dave Johnson	.05
544	Zane Smith	.05
545	Buddy Bell	.05
546	Mike Morgan	.05
547	Rob Deer	.05
548	Bill Mooneyham RC	.05
549	Bob Melvin	.05
550	Pete Incaviglia	.05
551	Frank Wills	.05
552	Larry Sheets	.05
553	Mike Maddux RC	.05
554	Buddy Biancalana	.05
555	Dennis Rasmussen	.05
556	Bob Boone, Marcel Lachemann, Mike Witt Angels Leaders	.05
557	John Cerutti RC	.05
558	Greg Gagne	.05
559	Lance McCullers	.05
560	Glenn Davis	.05
561	Rey Quinones RC	.05
562	Bryan Clutterbuck RC	.05
563	John Stefero	.05
564	Larry McWilliams	.05
565	Dusty Baker	.05
566	Tim Hulett	.05
567	Greg Mathews RC	.05
568	Earl Weaver	.10
569	Wade Rowdon	.05
570	Sid Fernandez	.05
571	Ozzie Virgil	.05
572	Pete Ladd	.05
573	Hal McRae	.05
574	Manny Lee	.05
575	Pat Tabler	.05
576	Frank Pastore	.05
577	Dann Bilardello	.05
578	Billy Hatcher	.05
579	Rick Burleson	.05
580	Mike Krukow	.05
581	Ron Cey, Steve Trout Cubs Leaders	.05
582	Bruce Berenyi	.05
583	Junior Ortiz	.05
584	Ron Kittle	.05
585	Scott Bailes RC	.05
586	Ben Oglivie	.05
587	Eric Plunk	.05
588	Wallace Johnson	.05
589	Steve Crawford	.05
590	Vince Coleman	.05
591	Spike Owen	.05
592	Chris Welsh	.05
593	Chuck Tanner	.05
594	Rick Anderson	.05
595	Keith Hernandez/AS	.05
596	Steve Sax/AS	.05
597	Mike Schmidt/AS	.35
598	Ozzie Smith/AS	.30
599	Tony Gwynn/AS	.30
600	Dave Parker/AS	.05
601	Darryl Strawberry/AS	.05
602	Gary Carter/AS	.25
603a	Dwight Gooden/AS (No trademark on front.)	.25
603b	Dwight Gooden/AS (Trademark on front.)	.05
604	Fernando Valenzuela/AS	.05
605	Todd Worrell/AS	.05
606a	Don Mattingly/AS (No trademark on front.)	.75
606b	Don Mattingly/AS (Trademark on front.)	.35
607	Tony Bernazard/AS	.05
608	Wade Boggs/AS	.30
609	Cal Ripken, Jr./AS	.45
610	Jim Rice/AS	.05
611	Kirby Puckett/AS	.30
612	George Bell/AS	.05
613	Lance Parrish/AS	.05
614	Roger Clemens/AS	.35
615	Teddy Higuera/AS	.05
616	Dave Righetti/AS	.05
617	Al Nipper	.05
618	Tom Kelly	.05
619	Jerry Reed	.05
620	Jose Canseco	.60
621	Danny Cox	.05
622	Glenn Braggs RC	.05
623	Kurt Stillwell RC	.05
624	Tim Burke	.05
625	Mookie Wilson	.05
626	Joel Skinner	.05
627	Ken Oberkfell	.05
628	Bob Walk	.05
629	Larry Parrish	.05
630	John Candelaria	.05
631	Sparky Anderson, Mike Heath, Willie Hernandez Tigers Leaders	.05
632	Rob Woodward	.05
633	Jose Uribe	.05
634	Rafael Palmeiro RC	2.00
635	Ken Schrom	.05
636	Darren Daulton	.05
637	Bip Roberts RC	.10
638	Rich Bordi	.05
639	Gerald Perry	.05
640	Mark Clear	.05
641	Domingo Ramos	.05
642	Al Pulido	.05
643	Ron Shepherd	.05
644	John Denny	.05
645	Dwight Evans	.05
646	Mike Mason	.05
647	Tom Lawless	.05
648	Barry Larkin RC	.60
649	Mickey Tettleton	.05
650	Hubie Brooks	.05
651	Benny Distefano	.05
652	Terry Forster	.05
653	Kevin Mitchell	.05
654	Checklist 529-660	.05
655	Jesse Barfield	.05
656	Bobby Valentine, Rickey Wright Rangers Leaders	.05
657	Tom Waddell	.05
658	Robby Thompson RC	.05
659	Aurelio Lopez	.05
660	Bob Horner	.05
661	Lou Whitaker	.05
662	Frank DiPino	.05
663	Cliff Johnson	.05
664	Mike Marshall	.05
665	Rod Scurry	.05
666	Von Hayes	.05
667	Ron Hassey	.05
668	Juan Bonilla	.05
669	Bud Black	.05
670	Jose Cruz	.05
671a	Ray Soff (No "D*" before copyright line.)	.20
671b	Ray Soff ("D*" before copyright line.)	.05
672	Chili Davis	.05
673	Don Sutton	.35
674	Bill Campbell	.05
675	Ed Romero	.05
676	Charlie Moore	.05
677	Bob Grich	.05
678	Carney Lansford	.05
679	Kent Hrbek	.05
680	Ryne Sandberg	.45
681	George Bell	.05
682	Jerry Reuss	.05
683	Gary Roenicke	.05
684	Kent Tekulve	.05
685	Jerry Hairston Sr.	.05
686	Doyle Alexander	.05
687	Alan Trammell	.05
688	Juan Beniquez	.05
689	Darrell Porter	.05
690	Dane Iorg	.05
691	Dave Parker	.05
692	Frank White	.05
693	Terry Puhl	.05
694	Phil Niekro	.35
695	Chico Walker	.05
696	Gary Lucas	.05
697	Ed Lynch	.05
698	Ernie Whitt	.05
699	Ken Landreaux	.05
700	Dave Bergman	.05
701	Willie Randolph	.05
702	Greg Gross	.05
703	Dave Schmidt	.05
704	Jesse Orosco	.05
705	Bruce Hurst	.05
706	Rick Manning	.05
707	Bob McClure	.05
708	Scott McGregor	.05
709	Dave Kingman	.05
710	Gary Gaetti	.05
711	Ken Griffey	.05
712	Don Robinson	.05
713	Tom Brookens	.05
714	Dan Quisenberry	.05
715	Bob Dernier	.05
716	Rick Leach	.05
717	Ed Vande Berg	.05
718	Steve Carlton	.40
719	Tom Hume	.05
720	Richard Dotson	.05
721	Tom Herr	.05
722	Bob Knepper	.05
723	Brett Butler	.05
724	Greg Minton	.05
725	George Hendrick	.05
726	Frank Tanana	.05
727	Mike Moore	.05
728	Tippy Martinez	.05
729	Tom Paciorek	.05
730	Eric Show	.05
731	Dave Concepcion	.05
732	Manny Trillo	.05
733	Bill Caudill	.05
734	Bill Madlock	.05
735	Rickey Henderson	.40
736	Steve Bedrosian	.05
737	Floyd Bannister	.05
738	Jorge Orta	.05
739	Chet Lemon	.05
740	Rich Gedman	.05
741	Paul Molitor	.40
742	Andy McGaffigan	.05
743	Dwayne Murphy	.05
744	Roy Smalley	.05
745	Glenn Hubbard	.05
746	Bob Ojeda	.05
747	Johnny Ray	.05
748	Mike Flanagan	.05
749	Ozzie Smith	.45
750	Steve Trout	.05
751	Garth Iorg	.05
752	Dan Petry	.05
753	Rick Honeycutt	.05
754	Dave LaPoint	.05
755	Luis Aguayo	.05
756	Carlton Fisk	.40
757	Nolan Ryan	.75
758	Tony Bernazard	.05
759	Joel Youngblood	.05
760	Mike Witt	.05
761	Greg Pryor	.05
762	Gary Ward	.05
763	Tim Flannery	.05
764	Bill Buckner	.05
765	Kirk Gibson	.05
766	Don Aase	.05
767	Ron Cey	.05
768	Dennis Lamp	.05
769	Steve Sax	.05
770	Dave Winfield	.40
771	Shane Rawley	.05
772	Harold Baines	.05
773	Robin Yount	.40
774	Wayne Krenchicki	.05
775	Joaquin Andujar	.05
776	Tom Brunansky	.05
777	Chris Chambliss	.05
778	Jack Morris	.05
779	Craig Reynolds	.05
780	Andre Thornton	.05
781	Atlee Hammaker	.05
782	Brian Downing	.05
783	Willie Wilson	.05
784	Cal Ripken, Jr.	.75
785	Terry Francona	.05
786	Jimy Williams	.05
787	Alejandro Pena	.05
788	Tim Stoddard	.05
789	Dan Schatzeder	.05
790	Julio Cruz	.05
791	Lance Parrish	.05
792	Checklist 661-792	.05

1987 Topps Tiffany

	NM/M
Unopened Set (792):	90.00
Complete Set (792):	50.00
Common Player:	.15
320 Barry Bonds	35.00

(Star cards valued at 4X corresponding cards in regular 1987 Topps.)

Traded

KEVIN McREYNOLDS

	NM/M
Complete Set (132):	4.00
Common Player:	.05
1 Bill Almon	.05
2 Scott Bankhead	.05
3 Eric Bell	.05
4 Juan Beniquez	.05
5 Juan Berenguer	.05
6 Greg Booker	.05
7 Thad Bosley	.05
8 Larry Bowa	.05
9 Greg Brock	.05
10 Bob Brower	.05
11 Jerry Browne	.05
12 Ralph Bryant	.05
13 DeWayne Buice	.05
14 Ellis Burks RC	.50
15 Ivan Calderon	.05
16 Jeff Calhoun	.05
17 Casey Candaele	.05
18 John Cangelosi	.05
19 Steve Carlton	.25
20 Juan Castillo	.05
21 Rick Cerone	.05
22 Ron Cey	.05
23 John Christensen	.05
24 Dave Cone	.15
25 Chuck Crim	.05
26 Storm Davis	.05
27 Andre Dawson	.25
28 Rick Dempsey	.05
29 Doug Drabek	.05
30 Mike Dunne	.05
31 Dennis Eckersley	.25
32 Lee Elia	.05
33 Brian Fisher	.05
34 Terry Francona	.05
35 Willie Fraser	.05
36 Billy Gardner	.05
37 Ken Gerhart	.05
38 Danny Gladden	.05
39 Jim Gott	.05
40 Cecilio Guante	.05
41 Albert Hall	.05
42 Terry Harper	.05
43 Mickey Hatcher	.05
44 Brad Havens	.05
45 Neal Heaton	.05
46 Mike Henneman RC	.20
47 Donnie Hill	.05
48 Guy Hoffman	.05
49 Brian Holton	.05
50 Charles Hudson	.05
51 Danny Jackson	.05
52 Reggie Jackson	.40
53 Chris James	.05
54 Dion James	.05
55 Stan Jefferson	.05
56 Joe Johnson	.05
57 Terry Kennedy	.05
58 Mike Kingery	.05
59 Ray Knight	.05
60 Gene Larkin	.05
61 Mike LaValliere	.05
62 Jack Lazorko	.05
63 Terry Leach	.05
64 Tim Leary	.05
65 Jim Lindeman	.05
66 Steve Lombardozzi	.05
67 Bill Long	.05
68 Barry Lyons	.05
69 Shane Mack RC	.05
70 Greg Maddux RC	3.00
71 Bill Madlock	.05
72 Joe Magrane	.05
73 Dave Martinez	.05
74 Fred McGriff	.25
75 Mark McLemore	.05
76 Kevin McReynolds	.05
77 Dave Meads	.05
78 Eddie Milner	.05
79 Greg Minton	.05
80 John Mitchell	.05
81 Kevin Mitchell	.05
82 Charlie Moore	.05
83 Jeff Musselman	.05
84 Gene Nelson	.05
85 Graig Nettles	.05
86 Al Newman	.05
87 Reid Nichols	.05
88 Tom Niedenfuer	.05
89 Joe Niekro	.05
90 Tom Nieto	.05
91 Matt Nokes RC	.10
92 Dickie Noles	.05
93 Pat Pacillo	.05
94 Lance Parrish	.05
95 Tony Pena	.05
96 Luis Polonia	.05
97 Randy Ready	.05
98 Jeff Reardon	.05
99 Gary Redus	.05
100 Jeff Reed	.05
101 Rick Rhoden	.05
102 Cal Ripken, Sr.	.05
103 Wally Ritchie	.05
104 Jeff Robinson	.05
105 Gary Roenicke	.05
106 Jerry Royster	.05
107 Mark Salas	.05
108 Luis Salazar	.05
109 Benny Santiago	.15
110 Dave Schmidt	.05
111 Kevin Seitzer	.05
112 John Shelby	.05
113 Steve Shields	.05
114 John Smiley RC	.20
115 Chris Speier	.05
116 Mike Stanley	.05
117 Terry Steinbach	.15
118 Les Straker	.05
119 Jim Sundberg	.05
120 Danny Tartabull	.05
121 Tom Trebelhorn	.05
122 Dave Valle	.05
123 Ed Vande Berg	.05
124 Andy Van Slyke	.05
125 Gary Ward	.05
126 Alan Wiggins	.05
127 Bill Wilkinson	.05
128 Frank Williams	.05
129 Matt Williams RC	.75
130 Jim Winn	.05
131 Matt Young	.05
132 Checklist 1T-132T	.05

Traded Tiffany

	NM/M
Complete Set (132):	30.00
Common Player:	.15

(Star cards valued at 2X corresponding cards in regular Topps Traded.)

1988 Topps

WHITE SOX — CARLTON FISK

	NM/M
Unopened Factory Set, Retail (792):	15.00
Unopened Factory Set, Hobby (792):	15.00
Complete Set (792):	12.00
Common Player:	.05
Wax Pack (15):	.40
Wax Box (36):	15.00
Cello Pack (28):	.70
Cello Box (24):	13.50
Rack Pack (43):	.75
Rack Box (24):	15.00
Vending Box (500):	7.50
1 Vince Coleman	.05
2 Don Mattingly	.25
3a Mark McGwire (White triangle by left foot.)	1.00
3b Mark McGwire (No white triangle.)	.40
4a Eddie Murray (No mention of record on front.)	.25
4b Eddie Murray (Record in box on front.)	.20
5 Joe Niekro, Phil Niekro	.05
6 Nolan Ryan	.40
7 Benito Santiago	.05
8 Kevin Elster (Future Stars)	.05
9 Andy Hawkins	.05
10 Ryne Sandberg	.50
11 Mike Young	.05
12 Bill Schroeder	.05
13 Andres Thomas	.05
14 Sparky Anderson	.10
15 Chili Davis	.05
16 Kirk McCaskill	.05
17 Ron Oester	.05
18a Al Leiter RC (No "NY" on shirt, photo actually Steve George.)	.40
18b Al Leiter RC ("NY" on shirt, correct photo.)	.20
19 Mark Davidson RC	.05
20 Kevin Gross	.05
21 Wade Boggs, Spike Owen Red Sox Leaders	.10
22 Greg Swindell	.05
23 Ken Landreaux	.05
24 Jim Deshaies	.05
25 Andres Galarraga	.05
26 Mitch Williams	.05
27 R.J. Reynolds	.05
28 Jose Nunez RC	.05
29 Argenis Salazar	.05
30 Sid Fernandez	.05
31 Bruce Bochy	.05
32 Mike Morgan	.05
33 Rob Deer	.05
34 Ricky Horton	.05
35 Harold Baines	.05
36 Jamie Moyer	.05
37 Ed Romero	.05
38 Jeff Calhoun	.05
39 Gerald Perry	.05
40 Orel Hershiser	.05
41 Bob Melvin	.05
42 Bill Landrum RC	.05
43 Dick Schofield	.05
44 Lou Piniella	.05
45 Kent Hrbek	.05
46 Darnell Coles	.05
47 Joaquin Andujar	.05
48 Alan Ashby	.05
49 Dave Clark	.05
50 Hubie Brooks	.05
51 Eddie Murray, Cal Ripken, Jr. Orioles Leaders	.25
52 Don Robinson	.05
53 Curt Wilkerson	.05
54 Jim Clancy	.05
55 Phil Bradley	.05
56 Ed Hearn	.05
57 Tim Crews RC	.05
58 Dave Magadan	.05
59 Danny Cox	.05
60 Rickey Henderson	.40
61 Mark Knudson RC	.05
62 Jeff Hamilton	.05
63 Jimmy Jones	.05
64 Ken Caminiti RC	.25
65 Leon Durham	.05
66 Shane Rawley	.05
67 Ken Oberkfell	.05
68 Dave Dravecky	.05
69 Mike Hart RC	.05
70 Roger Clemens	.60
71 Gary Pettis	.05
72 Dennis Eckersley	.30
73 Randy Bush	.05
74 Tom Lasorda	.05
75 Joe Carter	.05
76 Denny Martinez	.05
77 Tom O'Malley	.05
78 Dan Petry	.05
79 Ernie Whitt	.05
80 Mark Langston	.05
81 John Franco, Ron Robinson Reds Leaders	.05
82 Darrel Akerfelds RC	.05
83 Jose Oquendo	.05
84 Cecilio Guante	.05
85 Howard Johnson	.05
86 Ron Karkovice	.05
87 Mike Mason	.05
88 Earnie Riles	.05
89 Gary Thurman RC	.05
90 Dale Murphy	.20
91 Joey Cora RC	.10
92 Len Matuszek	.05
93 Bob Sebra	.05
94 Chuck Jackson RC	.05
95 Lance Parrish	.05
96 Todd Benzinger RC	.05
97 Scott Garrelts	.05
98 Rene Gonzales RC	.05
99 Chuck Finley	.05
100 Jack Clark	.05
101 Allan Anderson	.05
102 Barry Larkin	.05
103 Curt Young	.05
104 Dick Williams	.05
105 Jesse Orosco	.05
106 Jim Walewander RC	.05
107 Scott Bailes	.05
108 Steve Lyons	.05
109 Joel Skinner	.05
110 Teddy Higuera	.05
111 Hubie Brooks, Vance Law Expos Leaders	.05
112 Les Lancaster RC	.05
113 Kelly Gruber	.05
114 Jeff Russell	.05
115 Johnny Ray	.05
116 Jerry Don Gleaton	.05
117 James Steels RC	.05
118 Bob Welch	.05
119 Robbie Wine RC	.05
120 Kirby Puckett	.50
121 Checklist 1-132	.05
122 Tony Bernazard	.05
123 Tom Candiotti	.05
124 Ray Knight	.05
125 Bruce Hurst	.05
126 Steve Jeltz	.05
127 Jim Gott	.05
128 Johnny Grubb	.05
129 Greg Minton	.05
130 Buddy Bell	.05
131 Don Schulze	.05
132 Donnie Hill	.05
133 Greg Mathews	.05
134 Chuck Tanner	.05
135 Dennis Rasmussen	.05
136 Brian Dayett	.05
137 Chris Bosio	.05
138 Mitch Webster	.05
139 Jerry Browne	.05
140 Jesse Barfield	.05
141 George Brett, Bret Saberhagen Royals Leaders	.20
142 Andy Van Slyke	.05
143 Mickey Tettleton	.05
144 Don Gordon RC	.05
145 Bill Madlock	.05
146 Donell Nixon RC	.05
147 Bill Buckner	.05
148 Carmelo Martinez	.05
149 Ken Howell	.05
150 Eric Davis	.05
151 Bob Knepper	.05
152 Jody Reed RC	.10
153 John Habyan	.05
154 Jeff Stone	.05
155 Bruce Sutter	.30
156 Gary Matthews	.05
157 Atlee Hammaker	.05
158 Tim Hulett	.05
159 Brad Arnsberg RC	.05
160 Willie McGee	.05
161 Bryn Smith	.05
162 Mark McLemore	.05
163 Dale Mohorcic	.05
164 Dave Johnson	.05
165 Robin Yount	.40
166 Rick Rodriguez RC	.05
167 Rance Mulliniks	.05
168 Barry Jones	.05
169 Ross Jones RC	.05
170 Rich Gossage	.05
171 Shawon Dunston, Manny Trillo Cubs Leaders	.05
172 Lloyd McClendon RC	.05
173 Eric Plunk	.05
174 Phil Garner	.05
175 Kevin Bass	.05
176 Jeff Reed	.05
177 Frank Tanana	.05
178 Dwayne Henry	.05
179 Charlie Puleo	.05
180 Terry Kennedy	.05
181 Dave Cone	.05

No.	Player	Price
182	Ken Phelps	.05
183	Tom Lawless	.05
184	Ivan Calderon	.05
185	Rick Rhoden	.05
186	Rafael Palmeiro	.35
187	Steve Kiefer	.05
188	John Russell	.05
189	Wes Gardner RC	.05
190	Candy Maldonado	.05
191	John Cerutti	.05
192	Devon White	.05
193	Brian Fisher	.05
194	Tom Kelly	.05
195	Dan Quisenberry	.05
196	Dave Engle	.05
197	Lance McCullers	.05
198	Franklin Stubbs	.05
199	Dave Meads RC	.05
200	Wade Boggs	.50
201	Steve Buechele, Pete Incaviglia, Pete O'Brien, Bobby Valentine Rangers Leaders	.05
202	Glenn Hoffman	.05
203	Fred Toliver	.05
204	Paul O'Neill	.05
205	Nelson Liriano RC	.05
206	Domingo Ramos	.05
207	John Mitchell RC	.05
208	Steve Lake	.05
209	Richard Dotson	.05
210	Willie Randolph	.05
211	Frank DiPino	.05
212	Greg Brock	.05
213	Albert Hall	.05
214	Dave Schmidt	.05
215	Von Hayes	.05
216	Jerry Reuss	.05
217	Harry Spilman	.05
218	Dan Schatzeder	.05
219	Mike Stanley	.05
220	Tom Henke	.05
221	Rafael Belliard	.05
222	Steve Farr	.05
223	Stan Jefferson	.05
224	Tom Trebelhorn	.05
225	Mike Scioscia	.05
226	Dave Lopes	.05
227	Ed Correa	.05
228	Wallace Johnson	.05
229	Jeff Musselman	.05
230	Pat Tabler	.05
231	Barry Bonds, Bobby Bonilla Pirates Leaders	.50
232	Bob James	.05
233	Rafael Santana	.05
234	Ken Dayley	.05
235	Gary Ward	.05
236	Ted Power	.05
237	Mike Heath	.05
238	Luis Polonia RC	.10
239	Roy Smalley	.05
240	Lee Smith	.05
241	Damaso Garcia	.05
242	Tom Niedenfuer	.05
243	Mark Ryal	.05
244	Jeff Robinson	.05
245	Rich Gedman	.05
246	Mike Campbell RC (Future Stars)	.05
247	Thad Bosley	.05
248	Storm Davis	.05
249	Mike Marshall	.05
250	Nolan Ryan	.75
251	Tom Foley	.05
252	Bob Brower	.05
253	Checklist 133-264	.05
254	Lee Elia	.05
255	Mookie Wilson	.05
256	Ken Schrom	.05
257	Jerry Royster	.05
258	Ed Nunez	.05
259	Ron Kittle	.05
260	Vince Coleman	.05
261	Will Clark, Candy Maldonado, Kevin Mitchell, Robby Thompson, Jose Uribe Giants Leaders	.05
262	Drew Hall	.05
263	Glenn Braggs	.05
264	Les Straker RC	.05
265	Bo Diaz	.05
266	Paul Assenmacher	.05
267	Billy Bean RC	.05
268	Bruce Ruffin	.05
269	Ellis Burks	.05
270	Mike Witt	.05
271	Ken Gerhart	.05
272	Steve Ontiveros	.05
273	Garth Iorg	.05
274	Junior Ortiz	.05
275	Kevin Seitzer	.05
276	Luis Salazar	.05
277	Alejandro Pena	.05
278	Jose Cruz	.05
279	Randy St. Claire	.05
280	Pete Incaviglia	.05
281	Jerry Hairston Sr.	.05
282	Pat Perry	.05
283	Phil Lombardi	.05
284	Larry Bowa	.05
285	Jim Presley	.05
286	Chuck Crim RC	.05
287	Manny Trillo	.05
288	Pat Pacillo RC	.05
289	Dave Bergman	.05
290	Tony Fernandez	.05
291	Kevin Bass, Billy Hatcher Astros Leaders	.05
292	Carney Lansford	.05
293	Doug Jones RC	.05
294	Al Pedrique RC	.05
295	Bert Blyleven	.05
296	Floyd Rayford	.05
297	Zane Smith	.05
298	Milt Thompson	.05
299	Steve Crawford	.05
300	Don Mattingly	.60
301	Bud Black	.05
302	Jose Uribe	.05
303	Eric Show	.05
304	George Hendrick	.05
305	Steve Sax	.05
306	Billy Hatcher	.05
307	Mike Trujillo	.05
308	Lee Mazzilli	.05
309	Bill Long RC	.05
310	Tom Herr	.05
311	Scott Sanderson	.05
312	Joey Meyer (Future Stars)	.05
313	Bob McClure	.05
314	Jimy Williams	.05
315	Dave Parker	.05
316	Jose Rijo	.05
317	Tom Nieto	.05
318	Mel Hall	.05
319	Mike Loynd	.05
320	Alan Trammell	.05
321	Harold Baines, Carlton Fisk White Sox Leaders	.05
322	Vicente Palacios RC	.05
323	Rick Leach	.05
324	Danny Jackson	.05
325	Glenn Hubbard	.05
326	Al Nipper	.05
327	Larry Sheets	.05
328	Greg Cadaret RC	.05
329	Chris Speier	.05
330	Eddie Whitson	.05
331	Brian Downing	.05
332	Jerry Reed	.05
333	Wally Backman	.05
334	Dave LaPoint	.05
335	Claudell Washington	.05
336	Ed Lynch	.05
337	Jim Gantner	.05
338	Brian Holton	.05
339	Kurt Stillwell	.05
340	Jack Morris	.05
341	Carmen Castillo	.05
342	Larry Andersen	.05
343	Greg Gagne	.05
344	Tony LaRussa	.05
345	Scott Fletcher	.05
346	Vance Law	.05
347	Joe Johnson	.05
348	Jim Eisenreich	.05
349	Bob Walk	.05
350	Will Clark	.05
351	Tony Pena, Red Schoendienst Cardinals Leaders	.05
352	Billy Ripken RC	.05
353	Ed Olwine	.05
354	Marc Sullivan	.05
355	Roger McDowell	.05
356	Luis Aguayo	.05
357	Floyd Bannister	.05
358	Rey Quinones	.05
359	Tim Stoddard	.05
360	Tony Gwynn	.50
361	Greg Maddux	.50
362	Juan Castillo	.05
363	Willie Fraser	.05
364	Nick Esasky	.05
365	Floyd Youmans	.05
366	Chet Lemon	.05
367	Tim Leary	.05
368	Gerald Young RC	.05
369	Greg Harris	.05
370	Jose Canseco	.25
371	Joe Hesketh	.05
372	Matt Williams	.05
373	Checklist 265-396	.05
374	Doc Edwards	.05
375	Tom Brunansky	.05
376	Bill Wilkinson RC	.05
377	Sam Horn RC	.05
378	Todd Frohwirth RC	.05
379	Rafael Ramirez	.05
380	Joe Magrane RC	.05
381	Jack Howell, Wally Joyner Angels Leaders	.05
382	Keith Miller RC	.05
383	Eric Bell	.05
384	Neil Allen	.05
385	Carlton Fisk	.40
386	Don Mattingly/AS	.30
387	Willie Randolph/AS	.05
388	Wade Boggs/AS	.20
389	Alan Trammell/AS	.05
390	George Bell/AS	.05
391	Kirby Puckett/AS	.25
392	Dave Winfield/AS	.20
393	Matt Nokes/AS	.05
394	Roger Clemens/AS	.35
395	Jimmy Key/AS	.05
396	Tom Henke/AS	.05
397	Jack Clark/AS	.05
398	Juan Samuel/AS	.05
399	Tim Wallach/AS	.05
400	Ozzie Smith/AS	.25
401	Andre Dawson/AS	.15
402	Tony Gwynn/AS	.25
403	Tim Raines/AS	.05
404	Benny Santiago/AS	.05
405	Dwight Gooden/AS	.05
406	Shane Rawley/AS	.05
407	Steve Bedrosian/AS	.05
408	Dion James	.05
409	Joel McKeon	.05
410	Tony Pena	.05
411	Wayne Tolleson	.05
412	Randy Myers	.05
413	John Christensen	.05
414	John McNamara	.05
415	Don Carman	.05
416	Keith Moreland	.05
417	Mark Ciardi RC	.05
418	Joel Youngblood	.05
419	Scott McGregor	.05
420	Wally Joyner	.05
421	Ed Vande Berg	.05
422	Dave Concepcion	.05
423	John Smiley	.05
424	Dwayne Murphy	.05
425	Jeff Reardon	.05
426	Randy Ready	.05
427	Paul Kilgus RC	.05
428	John Shelby	.05
429	Kirk Gibson, Alan Trammell Tigers Leaders	.05
430	Glenn Davis	.05
431	Casey Candaele	.05
432	Mike Moore	.05
433	Bill Pecota RC	.05
434	Rick Aguilera	.05
435	Mike Pagliarulo	.05
436	Mike Bielecki	.05
437	Fred Manrique RC	.05
438	Rob Ducey RC	.05
439	Dave Martinez	.05
440	Steve Bedrosian	.05
441	Rick Manning	.05
442	Tom Bolton RC	.05
443	Ken Griffey	.05
444	Cal Ripken, Sr.	.05
445	Mike Krukow	.05
446	Doug DeCinces	.05
447	Jeff Montgomery RC	.20
448	Mike Davis	.05
449	Jeff Robinson RC	.05
450	Barry Bonds	.75
451	Keith Atherton	.05
452	Willie Wilson	.05
453	Dennis Powell	.05
454	Marvell Wynne	.05
455	Shawn Hillegas RC	.05
456	Dave Anderson	.05
457	Terry Leach	.05
458	Ron Hassey	.05
459	Willie Randolph, Dave Winfield Yankees Leaders	.05
460	Ozzie Smith	.50
461	Danny Darwin	.05
462	Don Slaught	.05
463	Fred McGriff	.05
464	Jay Tibbs	.05
465	Paul Molitor	.40
466	Jerry Mumphrey	.05
467	Don Aase	.05
468	Darren Daulton	.05
469	Jeff Dedmon	.05
470	Dwight Evans	.05
471	Donnie Moore	.05
472	Robby Thompson	.05
473	Joe Niekro	.05
474	Tom Brookens	.05
475	Pete Rose	.65
476	Dave Stewart	.05
477	Jamie Quirk	.05
478	Sid Bream	.05
479	Brett Butler	.05
480	Dwight Gooden	.05
481	Mariano Duncan	.05
482	Mark Davis	.05
483	Rod Booker RC	.05
484	Pat Clements	.05
485	Harold Reynolds	.05
486	Pat Keedy RC	.05
487	Jim Pankovits	.05
488	Andy McGaffigan	.05
489	Pedro Guerrero, Fernando Valenzuela Dodgers Leaders	.05
490	Larry Parrish	.05
491	B.J. Surhoff	.05
492	Doyle Alexander	.05
493	Mike Greenwell	.05
494	Wally Ritchie RC	.05
495	Eddie Murray	.40
496	Guy Hoffman	.05
497	Kevin Mitchell	.05
498	Bob Boone	.05
499	Eric King	.05
500	Andre Dawson	.25
501	Tim Birtsas	.05
502	Danny Gladden	.05
503	Junior Noboa RC	.05
504	Bob Rodgers	.05
505	Willie Upshaw	.05
506	John Cangelosi	.05
507	Mark Gubicza	.05
508	Tim Teufel	.05
509	Bill Dawley	.05
510	Dave Winfield	.40
511	Joel Davis	.05
512	Alex Trevino	.05
513	Tim Flannery	.05
514	Pat Sheridan	.05
515	Juan Nieves	.05
516	Jim Sundberg	.05
517	Ron Robinson	.05
518	Greg Gross	.05
519	Phil Bradley, Harold Reynolds Mariners Leaders	.05
520	Dave Smith	.05
521	Jim Dwyer	.05
522	Bob Patterson RC	.05
523	Gary Roenicke	.05
524	Gary Lucas	.05
525	Marty Barrett	.05
526	Juan Berenguer	.05
527	Steve Henderson	.05
528a	Checklist 397-528 (#455 is Steve Carlton)	.05
528b	Checklist 397-528 (#455 is Shawn Hillegas)	.05
529	Tim Burke	.05
530	Gary Carter	.40
531	Rich Yett	.05
532	Mike Kingery	.05
533	John Farrell RC	.05
534	John Wathan	.05
535	Ron Guidry	.05
536	John Morris	.05
537	Steve Buechele	.05
538	Bill Wegman	.05
539	Mike LaValliere	.05
540	Bret Saberhagen	.05
541	Juan Beniquez	.05
542	Paul Noce RC	.05
543	Kent Tekulve	.05
544	Jim Traber	.05
545	Don Baylor	.05
546	John Candelaria	.05
547	Felix Fermin RC	.05
548	Shane Mack	.05
549	Ken Griffey, Dion James, Dale Murphy, Gerald Perry Braves Leaders	.05
550	Pedro Guerrero	.05
551	Terry Steinbach	.05
552	Mark Thurmond	.05
553	Tracy Jones	.05
554	Mike Smithson	.05
555	Brook Jacoby	.05
556	Stan Clarke RC	.05
557	Craig Reynolds	.05
558	Bob Ojeda	.05
559	Ken Williams RC	.05
560	Tim Wallach	.05
561	Rick Cerone	.05
562	Jim Lindeman	.05
563	Jose Guzman	.05
564	Frank Lucchesi	.05
565	Lloyd Moseby	.05
566	Charlie O'Brien RC	.05
567	Mike Diaz	.05
568	Chris Brown	.05

569	Charlie Leibrandt	.05
570	Jeffrey Leonard	.05
571	Mark Williamson RC	.05
572	Chris James	.05
573	Bob Stanley	.05
574	Graig Nettles	.05
575	Don Sutton	.30
576	Tommy Hinzo RC	.05
577	Tom Browning	.05
578	Gary Gaetti	.05
579	Gary Carter, Kevin McReynolds Mets Leaders	.05
580	Mark McGwire	.65
581	Tito Landrum	.05
582	Mike Henneman	.05
583	Dave Valle	.05
584	Steve Trout	.05
585	Ozzie Guillen	.05
586	Bob Forsch	.05
587	Terry Puhl	.05
588	Jeff Parrett RC	.05
589	Geno Petralli	.05
590	George Bell	.05
591	Doug Drabek	.05
592	Dale Sveum	.05
593	Bob Tewksbury	.05
594	Bobby Valentine	.05
595	Frank White	.05
596	John Kruk	.05
597	Gene Garber	.05
598	Lee Lacy	.05
599	Calvin Schiraldi	.05
600	Mike Schmidt	.60
601	Jack Lazorko	.05
602	Mike Aldrete	.05
603	Rob Murphy	.05
604	Chris Bando	.05
605	Kirk Gibson	.05
606	Moose Haas	.05
607	Mickey Hatcher	.05
608	Charlie Kerfeld	.05
609	Gary Gaetti, Kent Hrbek Twins Leaders	.05
610	Keith Hernandez	.05
611	Tommy John	.05
612	Curt Ford	.05
613	Bobby Thigpen	.05
614	Herm Winningham	.05
615	Jody Davis	.05
616	Jay Aldrich RC	.05
617	Oddibe McDowell	.05
618	Cecil Fielder	.05
619	Mike Dunne RC	.05
620	Cory Snyder	.05
621	Gene Nelson	.05
622	Kal Daniels	.05
623	Mike Flanagan	.05
624	Jim Leyland	.05
625	Frank Viola	.05
626	Glenn Wilson	.05
627	Joe Boever RC	.05
628	Dave Henderson	.05
629	Kelly Downs	.05
630	Darrell Evans	.05
631	Jack Howell	.05
632	Steve Shields RC	.05
633	Barry Lyons RC	.05
634	Jose DeLeon	.05
635	Terry Pendleton	.05
636	Charles Hudson	.05
637	Jay Bell RC	.25
638	Steve Balboni	.05
639	Glenn Braggs, Tony Muser Brewers Leaders	.05
640	Garry Templeton	.05
641	Rick Honeycutt	.05
642	Bob Dernier	.05
643	Rocky Childress RC	.05
644	Terry McGriff	.05
645	Matt Nokes	.05
646	Checklist 529-660	.05
647	Pascual Perez	.05
648	Al Newman	.05
649	DeWayne Buice RC	.05
650	Cal Ripken, Jr.	.75
651	Mike Jackson RC	.05
652	Bruce Benedict	.05
653	Jeff Sellers	.05
654	Roger Craig	.05
655	Len Dykstra	.05
656	Lee Guetterman	.05
657	Gary Redus	.05
658	Tim Conroy	.05
659	Bobby Meacham	.05
660	Rick Reuschel	.05
661	Nolan Ryan	.35
662	Jim Rice	.05
663	Ron Blomberg	.05
664	Bob Gibson	.10
665	Stan Musial	.20
666	Mario Soto	.05
667	Luis Quinones	.05
668	Walt Terrell	.05

669	Lance Parrish, Mike Ryan Phillies Leaders	.05
670	Dan Plesac	.05
671	Tim Laudner	.05
672	John Davis RC	.05
673	Tony Phillips	.05
674	Mike Fitzgerald	.05
675	Jim Rice	.20
676	Ken Dixon	.05
677	Eddie Milner	.05
678	Jim Acker	.05
679	Darrell Miller	.05
680	Charlie Hough	.05
681	Bobby Bonilla	.05
682	Jimmy Key	.05
683	Julio Franco	.05
684	Hal Lanier	.05
685	Ron Darling	.05
686	Terry Francona	.05
687	Mickey Brantley	.05
688	Jim Winn	.05
689	Tom Pagnozzi RC	.05
690	Jay Howell	.05
691	Dan Pasqua	.05
692	Mike Birkbeck	.05
693	Benny Santiago	.05
694	Eric Nolte RC	.05
695	Shawon Dunston	.05
696	Duane Ward	.05
697	Steve Lombardozzi	.05
698	Brad Havens	.05
699	Tony Gwynn, Benny Santiago Padres Leaders	.15
700	George Brett	.60
701	Sammy Stewart	.05
702	Mike Gallego	.05
703	Bob Brenly	.05
704	Dennis Boyd	.05
705	Juan Samuel	.05
706	Rick Mahler	.05
707	Fred Lynn	.05
708	Gus Polidor	.05
709	George Frazier	.05
710	Darryl Strawberry	.05
711	Bill Gullickson	.05
712	John Moses	.05
713	Willie Hernandez	.05
714	Jim Fregosi	.05
715	Todd Worrell	.05
716	Lenn Sakata	.05
717	Jay Baller	.05
718	Mike Felder	.05
719	Denny Walling	.05
720	Tim Raines	.05
721	Pete O'Brien	.05
722	Manny Lee	.05
723	Bob Kipper	.05
724	Danny Tartabull	.05
725	Mike Boddicker	.05
726	Alfredo Griffin	.05
727	Greg Booker	.05
728	Andy Allanson	.05
729	George Bell, Fred McGriff Blue Jays Leaders	.05
730	John Franco	.05
731	Rick Schu	.05
732	Dave Palmer	.05
733	Spike Owen	.05
734	Craig Lefferts	.05
735	Kevin McReynolds	.05
736	Matt Young	.05
737	Butch Wynegar	.05
738	Scott Bankhead	.05
739	Daryl Boston	.05
740	Rick Sutcliffe	.05
741	Mike Easler	.05
742	Mark Clear	.05
743	Larry Herndon	.05
744	Whitey Herzog	.05
745	Bill Doran	.05
746	Gene Larkin RC	.05
747	Bobby Witt	.05
748	Reid Nichols	.05
749	Mark Eichhorn	.05
750	Bo Jackson	.10
751	Jim Morrison	.05
752	Mark Grant	.05
753	Danny Heep	.05
754	Mike LaCoss	.05
755	Ozzie Virgil	.05
756	Mike Maddux	.05
757	John Marzano RC	.05
758	Eddie Williams RC	.05
759	Jose Canseco, Mark McGwire A's Leaders	.35
760	Mike Scott	.05
761	Tony Armas	.05
762	Scott Bradley	.05
763	Doug Sisk	.05
764	Greg Walker	.05
765	Neal Heaton	.05
766	Henry Cotto	.05

767	Jose Lind RC	.10
768	Dickie Noles	.05
769	Cecil Cooper	.05
770	Lou Whitaker	.05
771	Ruben Sierra	.05
772	Sal Butera	.05
773	Frank Williams	.05
774	Gene Mauch	.05
775	Dave Stieb	.05
776	Checklist 661-792	.05
777	Lonnie Smith	.05
778a	Keith Comstock RC (White team letters.)	.40
778b	Keith Comstock RC (Blue team letters, white name.)	.10
778c	Keith Comstock RC (Blue team letters, yellow name.)	2.00
779	Tom Glavine RC	1.50
780	Fernando Valenzuela	.05
781	Keith Hughes RC	.05
782	Jeff Ballard RC	.05
783	Ron Roenicke	.05
784	Joe Sambito	.05
785	Alvin Davis	.05
786	Joe Price	.05
787	Bill Almon	.05
788	Ray Searage	.05
789	Joe Carter, Cory Snyder Indians Leaders	.05
790	Dave Righetti	.05
791	Ted Simmons	.05
792	John Tudor	.05

Tiffany

	NM/M
Complete Set (792):	40.00
Common Player:	.15

(Star cards valued at 3X corresponding cards in regular 1988 Topps issue.)

Traded

	NM/M
Complete Set (132):	5.00
Common Player:	.05
1	Jim Abbott RC (USA)	.25
2	Juan Agosto	.05
3	Luis Alicea	.05
4	Roberto Alomar RC	1.50
5	Brady Anderson RC	.25
6	Jack Armstrong	.05
7	Don August	.05
8	Floyd Bannister	.05
9	Bret Barberie (USA)	.05
10	Jose Bautista	.05
11	Don Baylor	.05
12	Tim Belcher	.05
13	Buddy Bell	.05
14	Andy Benes RC (USA)	.25
15	Damon Berryhill	.05
16	Bud Black	.05
17	Pat Borders	.05
18	Phil Bradley	.05
19	Jeff Branson (USA)	.05
20	Tom Brunansky	.05
21	Jay Buhner RC	.75
22	Brett Butler	.05
23	Jim Campanis (USA)	.05
24	Sil Campusano	.05
25	John Candelaria	.05
26	Jose Cecena	.05
27	Rick Cerone	.05
28	Jack Clark	.05
29	Kevin Coffman	.05
30	Pat Combs (USA)	.05
31	Henry Cotto	.05
32	Chili Davis	.05
33	Mike Davis	.05
34	Jose DeLeon	.05
35	Richard Dotson	.05
36	Cecil Espy	.05
37	Tom Filer	.05

38	Mike Fiore (USA)	.05
39	Ron Gant RC	.25
40	Kirk Gibson	.05
41	Rich Gossage	.05
42	Mark Grace RC	1.00
43	Alfredo Griffin	.05
44	Ty Griffin (USA)	.05
45	Bryan Harvey	.05
46	Ron Hassey	.05
47	Ray Hayward	.05
48	Dave Henderson	.05
49	Tom Herr	.05
50	Bob Horner	.05
51	Ricky Horton	.05
52	Jay Howell	.05
53	Glenn Hubbard	.05
54	Jeff Innis	.05
55	Danny Jackson	.05
56	Darrin Jackson	.05
57	Roberto Kelly	.05
58	Ron Kittle	.05
59	Ray Knight	.05
60	Vance Law	.05
61	Jeffrey Leonard	.05
62	Mike Macfarlane RC	.05
63	Scotti Madison	.05
64	Kirt Manwaring	.05
65	Mark Marquess (USA)	.05
66	Tino Martinez RC (USA)	.75
67	Billy Masse (USA)	.05
68	Jack McDowell RC	.25
69	Jack McKeon	.05
70	Larry McWilliams	.05
71	Mickey Morandini (USA)	.05
72	Keith Moreland	.05
73	Mike Morgan	.05
74	Charles Nagy (USA)	.10
75	Al Nipper	.05
76	Russ Nixon	.05
77	Jesse Orosco	.05
78	Joe Orsulak	.05
79	Dave Palmer	.05
80	Mark Parent	.05
81	Dave Parker	.05
82	Dan Pasqua	.05
83	Melido Perez	.05
84	Steve Peters	.05
85	Dan Petry	.05
86	Gary Pettis	.05
87	Jeff Pico	.05
88	Jim Poole (USA)	.05
89	Ted Power	.05
90	Rafael Ramirez	.05
91	Dennis Rasmussen	.05
92	Jose Rijo	.05
93	Earnie Riles	.05
94	Luis Rivera	.05
95	Doug Robbins (USA)	.05
96	Frank Robinson	.15
97	Cookie Rojas	.05
98	Chris Sabo RC	.10
99	Mark Salas	.05
100	Luis Salazar	.05
101	Rafael Santana	.05
102	Nelson Santovenia	.05
103	Mackey Sasser	.05
104	Calvin Schiraldi	.05
105	Mike Schooler	.05
106	Scott Servais (USA)	.05
107	Dave Silvestri (USA)	.05
108	Don Slaught	.05
109	Joe Slusarski (USA)	.05
110	Lee Smith	.05
111	Pete Smith	.05
112	Jim Snyder	.05
113	Ed Sprague (USA)	.05
114	Pete Stanicek	.05
115	Kurt Stillwell	.05
116	Todd Stottlemyre	.05
117	Bill Swift	.05
118	Pat Tabler	.05
119	Scott Terry	.05
120	Mickey Tettleton	.05
121	Dickie Thon	.05
122	Jeff Treadway	.05
123	Willie Upshaw	.05
124	Robin Ventura RC	.25
125	Ron Washington	.05
126	Walt Weiss	.05
127	Bob Welch	.05
128	David Wells	.25
129	Glenn Wilson	.05
130	Ted Wood (USA)	.05
131	Don Zimmer	.05
132	Checklist 1T-132T	.05

Traded Tiffany

	NM/M
Complete Set (132):	25.00
Common Player:	.15

(Star cards valued at 3X corresponding cards in regular Topps Traded issue.)

1989 Topps

RUBEN SIERRA

		NM/M
Unopened Factory Set, Retail (792):		25.00
Unopened Factory Set, Hobby (792):		25.00
Complete Set (792):		15.00
Common Player:		.05
Wax Pack (15):		.75
Wax Box (36):		12.00
Cello Pack (29):		1.00
Cello Box (24):		18.00
Rack Pack (43):		.75
Rack Box (24):		15.00
Vending Box (500):		6.00

1	George Bell	.05
2	Wade Boggs	.25
3	Gary Carter	.20
4	Andre Dawson	.10
5	Orel Hershiser	.05
6	Doug Jones	.05
7	Kevin McReynolds	.05
8	Dave Eiland RC	.05
9	Tim Teufel	.05
10	Andre Dawson	.25
11	Bruce Sutter	.35
12	Dale Sveum	.05
13	Doug Sisk	.05
14	Tom Kelly	.05
15	Robby Thompson	.05
16	Ron Robinson	.05
17	Brian Downing	.05
18	Rick Rhoden	.05
19	Greg Gagne	.05
20	Steve Bedrosian	.05
21	Greg Walker	.05
	White Sox Leaders	.05
22	Tim Crews	.05
23	Mike Fitzgerald	.05
24	Larry Andersen	.05
25	Frank White	.05
26	Dale Mohorcic	.05
27	Orestes Destrade RC	.05
28	Mike Moore	.05
29	Kelly Gruber	.05
30	Dwight Gooden	.05
31	Terry Francona	.05
32	Dennis Rasmussen	.05
33	B.J. Surhoff	.05
34	Ken Williams	.05
35	John Tudor	.05
36	Mitch Webster	.05
37	Bob Stanley	.05
38	Paul Runge	.05
39	Mike Maddux	.05
40	Steve Sax	.05
41	Terry Mulholland	.05
42	Jim Eppard	.05
43	Guillermo Hernandez	.05
44	Jim Snyder	.05
45	Kal Daniels	.05
46	Mark Portugal	.05
47	Carney Lansford	.05
48	Tim Burke	.05
49	Craig Biggio	.05
50	George Bell	.05
51	Mark McLemore	.05
	Angels Leaders	.05
52	Bob Brenly	.05
53	Ruben Sierra	.05
54	Steve Trout	.05
55	Julio Franco	.05
56	Pat Tabler	.05
57	Alejandro Pena	.05
58	Lee Mazzilli	.05
59	Mark Davis	.05
60	Tom Brunansky	.05
61	Neil Allen	.05
62	Alfredo Griffin	.05
63	Mark Clear	.05
64	Alex Trevino	.05

65	Rick Reuschel	.05
66	Manny Trillo	.05
67	Dave Palmer	.05
68	Darrell Miller	.05
69	Jeff Ballard	.05
70	Mark McGwire	.65
71	Mike Boddicker	.05
72	John Moses	.05
73	Pascual Perez	.05
74	Nick Leyva	.05
75	Tom Henke	.05
76	Terry Blocker RC	.05
77	Doyle Alexander	.05
78	Jim Sundberg	.05
79	Scott Bankhead	.05
80	Cory Snyder	.05
81	Tim Raines	
	Expos Leaders	.05
82	Dave Leiper	.05
83	Jeff Blauser	.05
84	Bill Bene RC (#1 Draft Pick)	.05
85	Kevin McReynolds	.05
86	Al Nipper	.05
87	Larry Owen	.05
88	Darryl Hamilton RC	.05
89	Dave LaPoint	.05
90	Vince Coleman	.05
91	Floyd Youmans	.05
92	Jeff Kunkel	.05
93	Ken Howell	.05
94	Chris Speier	.05
95	Gerald Young	.05
96	Rick Cerone	.05
97	Greg Mathews	.05
98	Larry Sheets	.05
99	Sherman Corbett RC	.05
100	Mike Schmidt	.50
101	Les Straker	.05
102	Mike Gallego	.05
103	Tim Birtsas	.05
104	Dallas Green	.05
105	Ron Darling	.05
106	Willie Upshaw	.05
107	Jose DeLeon	.05
108	Fred Manrique	.05
109	Hipolito Pena RC	.05
110	Paul Molitor	.40
111	Eric Davis	
	Reds Leaders	.05
112	Jim Presley	.05
113	Lloyd Moseby	.05
114	Bob Kipper	.05
115	Jody Davis	.05
116	Jeff Montgomery	.05
117	Dave Anderson	.05
118	Checklist 1-132	.05
119	Terry Puhl	.05
120	Frank Viola	.05
121	Garry Templeton	.05
122	Lance Johnson	.05
123	Spike Owen	.05
124	Jim Traber	.05
125	Mike Krukow	.05
126	Sid Bream	.05
127	Walt Terrell	.05
128	Milt Thompson	.05
129	Terry Clark RC	.05
130	Gerald Perry	.05
131	Dave Otto	.05
132	Curt Ford	.05
133	Bill Long	.05
134	Don Zimmer	.05
135	Jose Rijo	.05
136	Joey Meyer	.05
137	Geno Petralli	.05
138	Wallace Johnson	.05
139	Mike Flanagan	.05
140	Shawon Dunston	.05
141	Brook Jacoby	
	Indians Leaders	.05
142	Mike Diaz	.05
143	Mike Campbell	.05
144	Jay Bell	.05
145	Dave Stewart	.05
146	Gary Pettis	.05
147	DeWayne Buice	.05
148	Bill Pecota	.05
149	Doug Dascenzo RC	.05
150	Fernando Valenzuela	.05
151	Terry McGriff	.05
152	Mark Thurmond	.05
153	Jim Pankovits	.05
154	Don Carman	.05
155	Marty Barrett	.05
156	Dave Gallagher RC	.05
157	Tom Glavine	.25
158	Mike Aldrete	.05
159	Pat Clements	.05
160	Jeffrey Leonard	.05
161	Gregg Olson RC (#1 Draft Pick)	.05
162	John Davis	.05
163	Bob Forsch	.05

164	Hal Lanier	.05
165	Mike Dunne	.05
166	Doug Jennings RC	.05
167	Steve Searcy RC	.05
168	Willie Wilson	.05
169	Mike Jackson	.05
170	Tony Fernandez	.05
171	Andres Thomas Braves Leaders	.05
172	Frank Williams	.05
173	Mel Hall	.05
174	Todd Burns RC	.05
175	John Shelby	.05
176	Jeff Parrett	.05
177	Monty Fariss RC (#1 Draft Pick)	.05
178	Mark Grant	.05
179	Ozzie Virgil	.05
180	Mike Scott	.05
181	Craig Worthington RC	.05
182	Bob McClure	.05
183	Oddibe McDowell	.05
184	John Costello RC	.05
185	Claudell Washington	.05
186	Pat Perry	.05
187	Darren Daulton	.05
188	Dennis Lamp	.05
189	Kevin Mitchell	.05
190	Mike Witt	.05
191	Sil Campusano RC	.05
192	Paul Mirabella	.05
193	Sparky Anderson	.10
194	Greg Harris RC	.05
195	Ozzie Guillen	.05
196	Denny Walling	.05
197	Neal Heaton	.05
198	Danny Heep	.05
199	Mike Schooler RC	.05
200	George Brett	.50
201	Kelly Gruber Blue Jays Leaders	.05
202	Brad Moore RC	.05
203	Rob Ducey	.05
204	Brad Havens	.05
205	Dwight Evans	.05
206	Roberto Alomar	.35
207	Terry Leach	.05
208	Tom Pagnozzi	.05
209	Jeff Bittiger RC	.05
210	Dale Murphy	.15
211	Mike Pagliarulo	.05
212	Scott Sanderson	.05
213	Rene Gonzales	.05
214	Charlie O'Brien	.05
215	Kevin Gross	.05
216	Jack Howell	.05
217	Joe Price	.05
218	Mike LaValliere	.05
219	Jim Clancy	.05
220	Gary Gaetti	.05
221	Cecil Espy	.05
222	Mark Lewis RC (#1 Draft Pick)	.05
223	Jay Buhner	.05
224	Tony LaRussa	.05
225	Ramon Martinez RC	.25
226	Bill Doran	.05
227	John Farrell	.05
228	Nelson Santovenia RC	.05
229	Jimmy Key	.05
230	Ozzie Smith	.45
231	Roberto Alomar Padres Leaders	.05
232	Ricky Horton	.05
233	Gregg Jefferies	.20
234	Tom Browning	.05
235	John Kruk	.05
236	Charles Hudson	.05
237	Glenn Hubbard	.05
238	Eric King	.05
239	Tim Laudner	.05
240	Greg Maddux	.45
241	Brett Butler	.05
242	Ed Vande Berg	.05
243	Bob Boone	.05
244	Jim Acker	.05
245	Jim Rice	.15
246	Rey Quinones	.05
247	Shawn Hillegas	.05
248	Tony Phillips	.05
249	Tim Leary	.05
250	Cal Ripken, Jr.	.75
251	John Dopson RC	.05
252	Billy Hatcher	.05
253	Jose Alvarez RC	.05
254	Tom LaSorda	.05
255	Ron Guidry	.10
256	Benny Santiago	.05
257	Rick Aguilera	.05
258	Checklist 133-264	.05
259	Larry McWilliams	.05
260	Dave Winfield	.40
261	Tom Brunansky Cardinals Leaders	.05

262	Jeff Pico RC	.05
263	Mike Felder	.05
264	Rob Dibble RC	.10
265	Kent Hrbek	.05
266	Luis Aquino	.05
267	Jeff Robinson	.05
268	Keith Miller	.05
269	Tom Bolton	.05
270	Wally Joyner	.05
271	Jay Tibbs	.05
272	Ron Hassey	.05
273	Jose Lind	.05
274	Mark Eichhorn	.05
275	Danny Tartabull	.05
276	Paul Kilgus	.05
277	Mike Davis	.05
278	Andy McGaffigan	.05
279	Scott Bradley	.05
280	Bob Knepper	.05
281	Gary Redus	.05
282	Cris Carpenter RC	.05
283	Andy Allanson	.05
284	Jim Leyland	.05
285	John Candelaria	.05
286	Darrin Jackson	.05
287	Juan Nieves	.05
288	Pat Sheridan	.05
289	Ernie Whitt	.05
290	John Franco	.05
291	Darryl Strawberry Mets Leaders	.05
292	Jim Corsi RC	.05
293	Glenn Wilson	.05
294	Juan Berenguer	.05
295	Scott Fletcher	.05
296	Ron Gant	.05
297	Oswald Peraza RC	.05
298	Chris James	.05
299	Steve Ellsworth RC	.05
300	Darryl Strawberry	.05
301	Charlie Leibrandt	.05
302	Gary Ward	.05
303	Felix Fermin	.05
304	Joel Youngblood	.05
305	Dave Smith	.05
306	Tracy Woodson	.05
307	Lance McCullers	.05
308	Ron Karkovice	.05
309	Mario Diaz (RC)	.05
310	Rafael Palmeiro	.35
311	Chris Bosio	.05
312	Tom Lawless	.05
313	Denny Martinez	.05
314	Bobby Valentine	.05
315	Greg Swindell	.05
316	Walt Weiss	.05
317	Jack Armstrong RC	.05
318	Gene Larkin	.05
319	Greg Booker	.05
320	Lou Whitaker	.05
321	Jody Reed Red Sox Leaders	.05
322	John Smiley	.05
323	Gary Thurman	.05
324	Bob Milacki RC	.05
325	Jesse Barfield	.05
326	Dennis Boyd	.05
327	Mark Lemke RC	.05
328	Rick Honeycutt	.05
329	Bob Melvin	.05
330	Eric Davis	.05
331	Curt Wilkerson	.05
332	Tony Armas	.05
333	Bob Ojeda	.05
334	Steve Lyons	.05
335	Dave Righetti	.05
336	Steve Balboni	.05
337	Calvin Schiraldi	.05
338	Jim Adduci	.05
339	Scott Bailes	.05
340	Kirk Gibson	.05
341	Jim Deshaies	.05
342	Tom Brookens	.05
343	Gary Sheffield RC	1.50
344	Tom Trebelhorn	.05
345	Charlie Hough	.05
346	Rex Hudler	.05
347	John Cerutti	.05
348	Ed Hearn	.05
349	Ron Jones RC	.05
350	Andy Van Slyke	.05
351	Bob Melvin Giants Leaders	.05
352	Rick Schu	.05
353	Marvell Wynne	.05
354	Larry Parrish	.05
355	Mark Langston	.05
356	Kevin Elster	.05
357	Jerry Reuss	.05
358	Ricky Jordan RC	.05
359	Tommy John	.10
360	Ryne Sandberg	.45
361	Kelly Downs	.05
362	Jack Lazorko	.05

No.	Player	Value
363	Rich Yett	.05
364	Rob Deer	.05
365	Mike Henneman	.05
366	Herm Winningham	.05
367	Johnny Paredes RC	.05
368	Brian Holton	.05
369	Ken Caminiti	.05
370	Dennis Eckersley	.35
371	Manny Lee	.05
372	Craig Lefferts	.05
373	Tracy Jones	.05
374	John Wathan	.05
375	Terry Pendleton	.05
376	Steve Lombardozzi	.05
377	Mike Smithson	.05
378	Checklist 265-396	.05
379	Tim Flannery	.05
380	Rickey Henderson	.40
381	Larry Sheets Orioles Leaders	.05
382	John Smoltz	.50
383	Howard Johnson	.05
384	Mark Salas	.05
385	Von Hayes	.05
386	Andres Galarraga/AS	.05
387	Ryne Sandberg/AS	.20
388	Bobby Bonilla/AS	.05
389	Ozzie Smith/AS	.25
390	Darryl Strawberry/AS	.05
391	Andre Dawson/AS	.05
392	Andy Van Slyke/AS	.05
393	Gary Carter/AS	.05
394	Orel Hershiser/AS	.05
395	Danny Jackson/AS	.05
396	Kirk Gibson/AS	.05
397	Don Mattingly/AS	.30
398	Julio Franco/AS	.05
399	Wade Boggs/AS	.20
400	Alan Trammell/AS	.05
401	Jose Canseco/AS	.15
402	Mike Greenwell/AS	.05
403	Kirby Puckett/AS	.25
404	Bob Boone/AS	.05
405	Roger Clemens/AS	.30
406	Frank Viola/AS	.05
407	Dave Winfield/AS	.20
408	Greg Walker	.05
409	Ken Dayley	.05
410	Jack Clark	.05
411	Mitch Williams	.05
412	Barry Lyons	.05
413	Mike Kingery	.05
414	Jim Fregosi	.05
415	Rich Gossage	.05
416	Fred Lynn	.05
417	Mike LaCoss	.05
418	Bob Dernier	.05
419	Tom Filer	.05
420	Joe Carter	.05
421	Kirk McCaskill	.05
422	Bo Diaz	.05
423	Brian Fisher	.05
424	Luis Polonia	.05
425	Jay Howell	.05
426	Danny Gladden	.05
427	Eric Show	.05
428	Craig Reynolds	.05
429	Greg Gagne Twins Leaders	.05
430	Mark Gubicza	.05
431	Luis Rivera	.05
432	Chad Kreuter RC	.10
433	Albert Hall	.05
434	Ken Patterson RC	.05
435	Len Dykstra	.05
436	Bobby Meacham	.05
437	Andy Benes (#1 Draft Pick)	.05
438	Greg Gross	.05
439	Frank DiPino	.05
440	Bobby Bonilla	.05
441	Jerry Reed	.05
442	Jose Oquendo	.05
443	Rod Nichols RC	.05
444	Moose Stubing	.05
445	Matt Nokes	.05
446	Rob Murphy	.05
447	Donell Nixon	.05
448	Eric Plunk	.05
449	Carmelo Martinez	.05
450	Roger Clemens	.50
451	Mark Davidson	.05
452	Israel Sanchez RC	.05
453	Tom Prince	.05
454	Paul Assenmacher	.05
455	Johnny Ray	.05
456	Tim Belcher	.05
457	Mackey Sasser	.05
458	Donn Pall RC	.05
459	Dave Valle Mariners Leaders	.05
460	Dave Stieb	.05
461	Buddy Bell	.05
462	Jose Guzman	.05
463	Steve Lake	.05
464	Bryn Smith	.05
465	Mark Grace	.05
466	Chuck Crim	.05
467	Jim Walewander	.05
468	Henry Cotto	.05
469	Jose Bautista RC	.05
470	Lance Parrish	.05
471	Steve Curry RC	.05
472	Brian Harper	.05
473	Don Robinson	.05
474	Bob Rodgers	.05
475	Dave Parker	.05
476	Jon Perlman	.05
477	Dick Schofield	.05
478	Doug Drabek	.05
479	Mike Macfarlane	.05
480	Keith Hernandez	.05
481	Chris Brown	.05
482	Steve Peters RC	.05
483	Mickey Hatcher	.05
484	Steve Shields	.05
485	Hubie Brooks	.05
486	Jack McDowell	.05
487	Scott Lusader	.05
488	Kevin Coffman	.05
489	Mike Schmidt Phillies Leaders	.15
490	Chris Sabo	.05
491	Mike Birkbeck	.05
492	Alan Ashby	.05
493	Todd Benzinger	.05
494	Shane Rawley	.05
495	Candy Maldonado	.05
496	Dwayne Henry	.05
497	Pete Stanicek	.05
498	Dave Valle	.05
499	Don Heinkel RC	.05
500	Jose Canseco	.35
501	Vance Law	.05
502	Duane Ward	.05
503	Al Newman	.05
504	Bob Walk	.05
505	Pete Rose	.75
506	Kirt Manwaring	.05
507	Steve Farr	.05
508	Wally Backman	.05
509	Bud Black	.05
510	Bob Horner	.05
511	Richard Dotson	.05
512	Donnie Hill	.05
513	Jesse Orosco	.05
514	Chet Lemon	.05
515	Barry Larkin	.05
516	Eddie Whitson	.05
517	Greg Brock	.05
518	Bruce Ruffin	.05
519	Willie Randolph Yankees Leaders	.05
520	Rick Sutcliffe	.05
521	Mickey Tettleton	.05
522	Randy Kramer RC	.05
523	Andres Thomas	.05
524	Checklist 397-528	.05
525	Chili Davis	.05
526	Wes Gardner	.05
527	Dave Henderson	.05
528	Luis Medina RC	.05
529	Tom Foley	.05
530	Nolan Ryan	.75
531	Dave Hengel	.05
532	Jerry Browne	.05
533	Andy Hawkins	.05
534	Doc Edwards	.05
535	Todd Worrell	.05
536	Joel Skinner	.05
537	Pete Smith	.05
538	Juan Castillo	.05
539	Barry Jones	.05
540	Bo Jackson	.10
541	Cecil Fielder	.05
542	Todd Frohwirth	.05
543	Damon Berryhill	.05
544	Jeff Sellers	.05
545	Mookie Wilson	.05
546	Mark Williamson	.05
547	Mark McLemore	.05
548	Bobby Witt	.05
549	Jamie Moyer Cubs Leaders	.05
550	Orel Hershiser	.05
551	Randy Ready	.05
552	Greg Cadaret	.05
553	Luis Salazar	.05
554	Nick Esasky	.05
555	Bert Blyleven	.05
556	Bruce Fields	.05
557	Keith Miller RC	.05
558	Dan Pasqua	.05
559	Juan Agosto	.05
560	Tim Raines	.05
561	Luis Aguayo	.05
562	Danny Cox	.05
563	Bill Schroeder	.05
564	Russ Nixon	.05
565	Jeff Russell	.05
566	Al Pedrique	.05
567	David Wells	.05
568	Mickey Brantley	.05
569	German Jimenez RC	.05
570	Tony Gwynn	.45
571	Billy Ripken	.05
572	Atlee Hammaker	.05
573	Jim Abbott (#1 Draft Pick)	.10
574	Dave Clark	.05
575	Juan Samuel	.05
576	Greg Minton	.05
577	Randy Bush	.05
578	John Morris	.05
579	Glenn Davis Astros Leaders	.05
580	Harold Reynolds	.05
581	Gene Nelson	.05
582	Mike Marshall	.05
583	Paul Gibson RC	.05
584	Randy Velarde	.05
585	Harold Baines	.05
586	Joe Boever	.05
587	Mike Stanley	.05
588	Luis Alicea RC	.05
589	Dave Meads	.05
590	Andres Galarraga	.05
591	Jeff Musselman	.05
592	John Cangelosi	.05
593	Drew Hall	.05
594	Jimy Williams	.05
595	Teddy Higuera	.05
596	Kurt Stillwell	.05
597	Terry Taylor (RC) RC	.05
598	Ken Gerhart	.05
599	Tom Candiotti	.05
600	Wade Boggs	.45
601	Dave Dravecky	.05
602	Devon White	.05
603	Frank Tanana	.05
604	Paul O'Neill	.05
605a	Bob Welch (Missing Complete Major League Pitching Record line.)	3.00
605b	Bob Welch (Contains Complete Major League Pitching Record line.)	.05
606	Rick Dempsey	.05
607	Willie Ansley RC (#1 Draft Pick)	.05
608	Phil Bradley	.05
609	Frank Tanana Tigers Leaders	.05
610	Randy Myers	.05
611	Don Slaught	.05
612	Dan Quisenberry	.05
613	Gary Varsho RC	.05
614	Joe Hesketh	.05
615	Robin Yount	.40
616	Steve Rosenberg RC	.05
617	Mark Parent RC	.05
618	Rance Mulliniks	.05
619	Checklist 529-660	.05
620	Barry Bonds	.75
621	Rick Mahler	.05
622	Stan Javier	.05
623	Fred Toliver	.05
624	Jack McKeon	.05
625	Eddie Murray	.40
626	Jeff Reed	.05
627	Greg Harris	.05
628	Matt Williams	.05
629	Pete O'Brien	.05
630	Mike Greenwell	.05
631	Dave Bergman	.05
632	Bryan Harvey RC	.10
633	Daryl Boston	.05
634	Marvin Freeman	.05
635	Willie Randolph	.05
636	Bill Wilkinson	.05
637	Carmen Castillo	.05
638	Floyd Bannister	.05
639	Walt Weiss Athletics Leaders	.05
640	Willie McGee	.05
641	Curt Young	.05
642	Argenis Salazar	.05
643	Louie Meadows RC	.05
644	Lloyd McClendon	.05
645	Jack Morris	.05
646	Kevin Bass	.05
647	Randy Johnson RC	3.00
648	Sandy Alomar RC	.25
649	Stewart Cliburn	.05
650	Kirby Puckett	.45
651	Tom Niedenfuer	.05
652	Rich Gedman	.05
653	Tommy Barrett RC	.05
654	Whitey Herzog	.05
655	Dave Magadan	.05
656	Ivan Calderon	.05
657	Joe Magrane	.05
658	R.J. Reynolds	.05
659	Al Leiter	.05
660	Will Clark	.05
661	Dwight Gooden	.05
662	Lou Brock	.05
663	Hank Aaron	.15
664	Gil Hodges	.05
665a	Tony Oliva (No copyright line.)	12.50
665b	Tony Oliva (With copyright line.)	.05
666	Randy St. Claire	.05
667	Dwayne Murphy	.05
668	Mike Bielecki	.05
669	Orel Hershiser Dodgers Leaders	.05
670	Kevin Seitzer	.05
671	Jim Gantner	.05
672	Allan Anderson	.05
673	Don Baylor	.05
674	Otis Nixon	.05
675	Bruce Hurst	.05
676	Ernie Riles	.05
677	Dave Schmidt	.05
678	Dion James	.05
679	Willie Fraser	.05
680	Gary Carter	.40
681	Jeff Robinson	.05
682	Rick Leach	.05
683	Jose Cecena RC	.05
684	Dave Johnson	.05
685	Jeff Treadway	.05
686	Scott Terry	.05
687	Alvin Davis	.05
688	Zane Smith	.05
689a	Stan Jefferson (Pink triangle at bottom-left photo.)	.05
689b	Stan Jefferson (Pink/purple triangle.)	.05
689c	Stan Jefferson (Purple triangle.)	.05
690	Doug Jones	.05
691	Roberto Kelly	.05
692	Steve Ontiveros	.05
693	Pat Borders RC	.05
694	Les Lancaster	.05
695	Carlton Fisk	.40
696	Don August	.05
697	Franklin Stubbs	.05
698	Keith Atherton	.05
699	Al Pedrique Pirates Leaders	.05
700	Don Mattingly	.50
701	Storm Davis	.05
702	Jamie Quirk	.05
703	Scott Garrelts	.05
704	Carlos Quintana RC	.05
705	Terry Kennedy	.05
706	Pete Incaviglia	.05
707	Steve Jeltz	.05
708	Chuck Finley	.05
709	Tom Herr	.05
710	Dave Cone	.05
711	Candy Sierra RC	.05
712	Bill Swift	.05
713	Ty Griffin RC (#1 Draft Pick)	.05
714	Joe M. Morgan	.05
715	Tony Pena	.05
716	Wayne Tolleson	.05
717	Jamie Moyer	.05
718	Glenn Braggs	.05
719	Danny Darwin	.05
720	Tim Wallach	.05
721	Ron Tingley RC	.05
722	Todd Stottlemyre	.05
723	Rafael Belliard	.05
724	Jerry Don Gleaton	.05
725	Terry Steinbach	.05
726	Dickie Thon	.05
727	Joe Orsulak	.05
728	Charlie Puleo	.05
729	Steve Buechele Rangers Leaders	.05
730	Danny Jackson	.05
731	Mike Young	.05
732	Steve Buechele	.05
733	Randy Bockus RC	.05
734	Jody Reed	.05
735	Roger McDowell	.05
736	Jeff Hamilton	.05
737	Norm Charlton RC	.05
738	Darnell Coles	.05
739	Brook Jacoby	.05
740	Dan Plesac	.05
741	Ken Phelps	.05
742	Mike Harkey RC	.05
743	Mike Heath	.05
744	Roger Craig	.05
745	Fred McGriff	.05
746	German Gonzalez RC	.05
747	Wil Tejada	.05
748	Jimmy Jones	.05

749	Rafael Ramirez	.05
750	Bret Saberhagen	.05
751	Ken Oberkfell	.05
752	Jim Gott	.05
753	Jose Uribe	.05
754	Bob Brower	.05
755	Mike Scioscia	.05
756	Scott Medvin RC	.05
757	Brady Anderson	.05
758	Gene Walter	.05
759	Rob Deer	
	Brewers Leaders	.05
760	Lee Smith	.05
761	Dante Bichette RC	.25
762	Bobby Thigpen	.05
763	Dave Martinez	.05
764	Robin Ventura	
	(#1 Draft Pick)	.25
765	Glenn Davis	.05
766	Cecilio Guante	.05
767	Mike Capel (RC) RC	.05
768	Bill Wegman	.05
769	Junior Ortiz	.05
770	Alan Trammell	.05
771	Ron Kittle	.05
772	Ron Oester	.05
773	Keith Moreland	.05
774	Frank Robinson	.15
775	Jeff Reardon	.05
776	Nelson Liriano	.05
777	Ted Power	.05
778	Bruce Benedict	.05
779	Craig McMurtry	.05
780	Pedro Guerrero	.05
781	Greg Briley RC	.05
782	Checklist 661-792	.05
783	Trevor Wilson RC	.05
784	Steve Avery RC	
	(#1 Draft Pick)	.15
785	Ellis Burks	.05
786	Melido Perez	.05
787	Dave West RC	.05
788	Mike Morgan	.05
789	Bo Jackson	
	Royals Leaders	.05
790	Sid Fernandez	.05
791	Jim Lindeman	.05
792	Rafael Santana	.05

Tiffany

	NM/M
Unopened Set (792):	75.00
Complete Set (792):	40.00
Common Player:	.10

(Star cards valued at 3X corresponding cards in regular 1989 Topps issue.)

1990 Topps 1989 Major League Debut

MIKE BLOWERS

	NM/M
Complete Set (150):	10.00
Common Player:	.05
1	Jim Abbott	.05
2	Beau Allred	.05
3	Wilson Alvarez	.05
4	Kent Anderson	.05
5	Eric Anthony	.05
6	Kevin Appier	.05
7	Larry Arndt	.05
8	John Barfield	.05
9	Billy Bates	.05
10	Kevin Batiste	.05
11	Blaine Beatty	.05
12	Stan Belinda	.05
13	Juan Bell	.05
14	Joey Belle	.25
15	Andy Benes	.05
16	Mike Benjamin	.05
17	Geronimo Berroa	.05
18	Mike Blowers	

19	Brian Brady	.05
20	Francisco Cabrera	.05
21	George Canale	.05
22	Jose Cano	.05
23	Steve Carter	.05
24	Pat Combs	.05
25	Scott Coolbaugh	.05
26	Steve Cummings	.05
27	Pete Dalena	.05
28	Jeff Datz	.05
29	Bobby Davidson	.05
30	Drew Denson	.05
31	Gary DiSarcina	.05
32	Brian DuBois	.05
33	Mike Dyer	.05
34	Wayne Edwards	.05
35	Junior Felix	.05
36	Mike Fetters	.05
37	Steve Finley	.05
38	Darren Fletcher	.05
39	LaVel Freeman	.05
40	Steve Frey	.05
41	Mark Gardner	.05
42	Joe Girardi	.05
43	Juan Gonzalez	.50
44	Goose Gozzo	.05
45	Tommy Greene	.05
46	Ken Griffey Jr.	3.00
47	Jason Grimsley	.05
48	Marquis Grissom	.05
49	Mark Guthrie	.05
50	Chip Hale	.05
51	John Hardy	.05
52	Gene Harris	.05
53	Mike Hartley	.05
54	Scott Hemond	.05
55	Xavier Hernandez	.05
56	Eric Hetzel	.05
57	Greg Hibbard	.05
58	Mark Higgins	.05
59	Glenallen Hill	.05
60	Chris Hoiles	.05
61	Shawn Holman	.05
62	Dann Howitt	.05
63	Mike Huff	.05
64	Terry Jorgenson	.05
65	Dave Justice	.25
66	Jeff King	.05
67	Matt Kinzer	.05
68	Joe Kraemer	.05
69	Marcus Lawton	.05
70	Derek Lilliquist	.05
71	Scott Little	.05
72	Greg Litton	.05
73	Rick Lueken	.05
74	Julio Machado	.05
75	Tom Magrann	.05
76	Kelly Mann	.05
77	Randy McCament	.05
78	Ben McDonald	.05
79	Chuck McElroy	.05
80	Jeff McKnight	.05
81	Kent Mercker	.05
82	Matt Merullo	.05
83	Hensley Meulens	.05
84	Kevin Mmahat	.05
85	Mike Munoz	.05
86	Dan Murphy	.05
87	Jaime Navarro	.05
88	Randy Nosek	.05
89	John Olerud	.15
90	Steve Olin	.05
91	Joe Oliver	.05
92	Francisco Oliveras	.05
93	Greg Olson	.05
94	John Orton	.05
95	Dean Palmer	.05
96	Ramon Pena	.05
97	Jeff Peterek	.05
98	Marty Pevey	.05
99	Rusty Richards	.05
100	Jeff Richardson	.05
101	Rob Richie	.05
102	Kevin Ritz	.05
103	Rosario Rodriguez	.05
104	Mike Roesler	.05
105	Kenny Rogers	.05
106	Bobby Rose	.05
107	Alex Sanchez	.05
108	Deion Sanders	.25
109	Jeff Schaefer	.05
110	Jeff Schulz	.05
111	Mike Schwabe	.05
112	Dick Scott	.05
113	Scott Scudder	.05
114	Rudy Seanez	.05
115	Joe Skalski	.05
116	Dwight Smith	.05
117	Greg Smith	.05
118	Mike Smith	.05
119	Paul Sorrento	.05
120	Sammy Sosa	3.00
121	Billy Spiers	.05
122	Mike Stanton	.05

123	Phil Stephenson	.05
124	Doug Strange	.05
125	Russ Swan	.05
126	Kevin Tapani	.05
127	Stu Tate	.05
128	Greg Vaughn	.05
129	Robin Ventura	.15
130	Randy Veres	.05
131	Jose Vizcaino	.05
132	Omar Vizquel	.05
133	Larry Walker	.25
134	Jerome Walton	.05
135	Gary Wayne	.05
136	Lenny Webster	.05
137	Mickey Weston	.05
138	Jeff Wetherby	.05
139	John Wetteland	.05
140	Ed Whited	.05
141	Wally Whitehurst	.05
142	Kevin Wickander	.05
143	Dean Wilkins	.05
144	Dana Williams	.05
145	Paul Wilmet	.05
146	Craig Wilson	.05
147	Matt Winters	.05
148	Eric Yelding	.05
149	Clint Zavaras	.05
150	Todd Zeile	.05
----	Checklist (1 of 2)	.05
----	Checklist (2 of 2)	.05

Traded

	NM/M
Unopened Set, Retail (132):	12.50
Unopened Set, Hobby (132):	10.00
Complete Set (132):	7.50
Common Player:	.05
1T	Don Aase	.05
2T	Jim Abbott	.05
3T	Kent Anderson	.05
4T	Keith Atherton	.05
5T	Wally Backman	.05
6T	Steve Balboni	.05
7T	Jesse Barfield	.05
8T	Steve Bedrosian	.05
9T	Todd Benzinger	.05
10T	Geronimo Berroa	.05
11T	Bert Blyleven	.05
12T	Bob Boone	.05
13T	Phil Bradley	.05
14T	Jeff Brantley RC	.05
15T	Kevin Brown	.05
16T	Jerry Browne	.05
17T	Chuck Cary	.05
18T	Carmen Castillo	.05
19T	Jim Clancy	.05
20T	Jack Clark	.05
21T	Bryan Clutterbuck	.05
22T	Jody Davis	.05
23T	Mike Devereaux	.05
24T	Frank DiPino	.05
25T	Benny Distefano	.05
26T	John Dopson	.05
27T	Len Dykstra	.05
28T	Jim Eisenreich	.05
29T	Nick Esasky	.05
30T	Alvaro Espinoza	.05
31T	Darrell Evans	.05
32T	Junior Felix	.05
33T	Felix Fermin	.05
34T	Julio Franco	.05
35T	Terry Francona	.05
36T	Cito Gaston	.05
37T	Bob Geren (Photo actually Mike Fennell.)	.05
38T	Tom Gordon RC	.10
39T	Tommy Gregg	.05
40T	Ken Griffey	.05
41T	Ken Griffey Jr. RC	6.00
42T	Kevin Gross	.05

43T	Lee Guetterman	.05
44T	Mel Hall	.05
45T	Erik Hanson	.05
46T	Gene Harris	.05
47T	Andy Hawkins	.05
48T	Rickey Henderson	.40
49T	Tom Herr	.05
50T	Ken Hill RC	.05
51T	Brian Holman	.05
52T	Brian Holton	.05
53T	Art Howe	.05
54T	Ken Howell	.05
55T	Bruce Hurst	.05
56T	Chris James	.05
57T	Randy Johnson	1.50
58T	Jimmy Jones	.05
59T	Terry Kennedy	.05
60T	Paul Kilgus	.05
61T	Eric King	.05
62T	Ron Kittle	.05
63T	John Kruk	.05
64T	Randy Kutcher	.05
65T	Steve Lake	.05
66T	Mark Langston	.05
67T	Dave LaPoint	.05
68T	Rick Leach	.05
69T	Terry Leach	.05
70T	Jim Levebvre	.05
71T	Al Leiter	.05
72T	Jeffrey Leonard	.05
73T	Derek Lilliquist	.05
74T	Rick Mahler	.05
75T	Tom McCarthy	.05
76T	Lloyd McClendon	.05
77T	Lance McCullers	.05
78T	Oddibe McDowell	.05
79T	Roger McDowell	.05
80T	Larry McWilliams	.05
81T	Randy Milligan	.05
82T	Mike Moore	.05
83T	Keith Moreland	.05
84T	Mike Morgan	.05
85T	Jamie Moyer	.05
86T	Rob Murphy	.05
87T	Eddie Murray	.40
88T	Pete O'Brien	.05
89T	Gregg Olson	.05
90T	Steve Ontiveros	.05
91T	Jesse Orosco	.05
92T	Spike Owen	.05
93T	Rafael Palmeiro	.35
94T	Clay Parker	.05
95T	Jeff Parrett	.05
96T	Lance Parrish	.05
97T	Dennis Powell	.05
98T	Rey Quinones	.05
99T	Doug Rader	.05
100T	Willie Randolph	.05
101T	Shane Rawley	.05
102T	Randy Ready	.05
103T	Bip Roberts	.05
104T	Kenny Rogers RC	.10
105T	Ed Romero	.05
106T	Nolan Ryan	1.00
107T	Luis Salazar	.05
108T	Juan Samuel	.05
109T	Alex Sanchez	.05
110T	Deion Sanders RC	.50
111T	Steve Sax	.05
112T	Rick Schu	.05
113T	Dwight Smith	.05
114T	Lonnie Smith	.05
115T	Billy Spiers	.05
116T	Kent Tekulve	.05
117T	Walt Terrell	.05
118T	Milt Thompson	.05
119T	Dickie Thon	.05
120T	Jeff Torborg	.05
121T	Jeff Treadway	.05
122T	Omar Vizquel RC	.50
123T	Jerome Walton	.05
124T	Gary Ward	.05
125T	Claudell Washington	.05
126T	Curt Wilkerson	.05
127T	Eddie Williams	.05
128T	Frank Williams	.05
129T	Ken Williams	.05
130T	Mitch Williams	.05
131T	Steve Wilson	.05

1989 Topps Traded Tiffany

	NM/M
Unopened Set (132):	85.00
Complete Set (132):	50.00
Common Player:	.10

(Star cards valued at 3X corresponding cards in regular Topps Traded issue.)

1990 Topps

JOEY BELLE

		NM/M
Unopened Factory Set, Retail (792):		25.00
Unopened Factory Set, Hobby (792):		20.00
Complete Set (792):		15.00
Common Player:		.05
Wax Pack (16):		.60
Wax Box (36):		12.00
Cello Pack (31):		1.00
Cello Box (24):		15.00
Rack Pack (45):		1.00
Rack Box (24):		16.00
Vending Box (500):		7.50
1	Nolan Ryan	.75
2	Nolan Ryan/Mets	.35
3	Nolan Ryan/Angels	.25
4	Nolan Ryan/Astros	.25
5	Nolan Ryan/Rangers	.25
6	Vince Coleman (Record Breaker)	.05
7	Rickey Henderson (Record Breaker)	.20
8	Cal Ripken, Jr. (Record Breaker)	.40
9	Eric Plunk	.05
10	Barry Larkin	.05
11	Paul Gibson	.05
12	Joe Girardi	.05
13	Mark Williamson	.05
14	Mike Fetters RC	.05
15	Teddy Higuera	.05
16	Kent Anderson RC	.05
17	Kelly Downs	.05
18	Carlos Quintana	.05
19	Al Newman	.05
20	Mark Gubicza	.05
21	Jeff Torborg	.05
22	Bruce Ruffin	.05
23	Randy Velarde	.05
24	Joe Hesketh	.05
25	Willie Randolph	.05
26	Don Slaught	.05
27	Rick Leach	.05
28	Duane Ward	.05
29	John Cangelosi	.05
30	David Cone	.05
31	Henry Cotto	.05
32	John Farrell	.05
33	Greg Walker	.05
34	Tony Fossas RC	.05
35	Benito Santiago	.05
36	John Costello	.05
37	Domingo Ramos	.05
38	Wes Gardner	.05
39	Curt Ford	.05
40	Jay Howell	.05
41	Matt Williams	.05
42	Jeff Robinson	.05
43	Dante Bichette	.05
44	Roger Salkeld RC (#1 Draft Pick)	.10
45	Dave Parker	.05
46	Rob Dibble	.05
47	Brian Harper	.05
48	Zane Smith	.05
49	Tom Lawless	.05
50	Glenn Davis	.05
51	Doug Rader	.05
52	Jack Daugherty RC	.05
53	Mike LaCoss	.05
54	Joel Skinner	.05
55	Darrell Evans	.05
56	Franklin Stubbs	.05
57	Greg Vaughn	.05
58	Keith Miller	.05
59	Ted Power	.05
60	George Brett	.50
61	Deion Sanders	.10
62	Ramon Martinez	.05
63	Mike Pagliarulo	.05
64	Danny Darwin	.05
65	Devon White	.05
66	Greg Litton RC	.05
67	Scott Sanderson	.05
68	Dave Henderson	.05
69	Todd Frohwirth	.05
70	Mike Greenwell	.05
71	Allan Anderson	.05
72	Jeff Huson RC	.05
73	Bob Milacki	.05
74	Jeff Jackson RC (#1 Draft Pick)	.05
75	Doug Jones	.05
76	Dave Valle	.05
77	Dave Bergman	.05
78	Mike Flanagan	.05
79	Ron Kittle	.05
80	Jeff Russell	.05
81	Bob Rodgers	.05
82	Scott Terry	.05
83	Hensley Meulens	.05
84	Ray Searage	.05
85	Juan Samuel	.05
86	Paul Kilgus	.05
87	Rick Luecken RC	.05
88	Glenn Braggs	.05
89	Clint Zavaras RC	.05
90	Jack Clark	.05
91	Steve Frey RC	.05
92	Mike Stanley	.05
93	Shawn Hillegas	.05
94	Herm Winningham	.05
95	Todd Worrell	.05
96	Jody Reed	.05
97	Curt Schilling	.25
98	Jose Gonzalez	.05
99	Rich Monteleone RC	.05
100	Will Clark	.05
101	Shane Rawley	.05
102	Stan Javier	.05
103	Marvin Freeman	.05
104	Bob Knepper	.05
105	Randy Myers	.05
106	Charlie O'Brien	.05
107	Fred Lynn	.05
108	Rod Nichols	.05
109	Roberto Kelly	.05
110	Tommy Helms	.05
111	Ed Whited	.05
112	Glenn Wilson	.05
113	Manny Lee	.05
114	Mike Bielecki	.05
115	Tony Pena	.05
116	Floyd Bannister	.05
117	Mike Sharperson	.05
118	Erik Hanson	.05
119	Billy Hatcher	.05
120	John Franco	.05
121	Robin Ventura	.05
122	Shawn Abner	.05
123	Rich Gedman	.05
124	Dave Dravecky	.05
125	Kent Hrbek	.05
126	Randy Kramer	.05
127	Mike Devereaux	.05
128	Checklist 1-132	.05
129	Ron Jones	.05
130	Bert Blyleven	.05
131	Matt Nokes	.05
132	Lance Blankenship	.05
133	Ricky Horton	.05
134	Earl Cunningham RC (#1 Draft Pick)	.05
135	Dave Magadan	.05
136	Kevin Brown	.05
137	Marty Pevey RC	.05
138	Al Leiter	.05
139	Greg Brock	.05
140	Andre Dawson	.25
141	John Hart	.05
142	Jeff Wetherby RC	.05
143	Rafael Belliard	.05
144	Bud Black	.05
145	Terry Steinbach	.05
146	Rob Richie RC	.05
147	Chuck Finley	.05
148	Edgar Martinez	.05
149	Steve Farr	.05
150	Kirk Gibson	.05
151	Rick Mahler	.05
152	Lonnie Smith	.05
153	Randy Milligan	.05
154	Mike Maddux	.05
155	Ellis Burks	.05
156	Ken Patterson	.05
157	Craig Biggio	.05
158	Craig Lefferts	.05
159	Mike Felder	.05
160	Dave Righetti	.05
161	Harold Reynolds	.05
162	Todd Zeile RC	.20
163	Phil Bradley	.05
164	Jeff Juden RC (#1 Draft Pick)	.05
165	Walt Weiss	.05
166	Bobby Witt	.05
167	Kevin Appier	.05
168	Jose Lind	.05
169	Richard Dotson	.05
170	George Bell	.05
171	Russ Nixon	.05
172	Tom Lampkin	.05
173	Tim Belcher	.05
174	Jeff Kunkel	.05
175	Mike Moore	.05
176	Luis Quinones	.05
177	Mike Henneman	.05
178	Chris James	.05
179	Brian Holton	.05
180	Rock Raines	.05
181	Juan Agosto	.05
182	Mookie Wilson	.05
183	Steve Lake	.05
184	Danny Cox	.05
185	Ruben Sierra	.05
186	Dave LaPoint	.05
187	Rick Wrona RC	.05
188	Mike Smithson	.05
189	Dick Schofield	.05
190	Rick Reuschel	.05
191	Pat Borders	.05
192	Don August	.05
193	Andy Benes	.05
194	Glenallen Hill	.05
195	Tim Burke	.05
196	Gerald Young	.05
197	Doug Drabek	.05
198	Mike Marshall	.05
199	Sergio Valdez RC	.05
200	Don Mattingly	.50
201	Cito Gaston	.05
202	Mike Macfarlane	.05
203	Mike Roesler RC	.05
204	Bob Dernier	.05
205	Mark Davis	.05
206	Nick Esasky	.05
207	Bob Ojeda	.05
208	Brook Jacoby	.05
209	Greg Mathews	.05
210	Ryne Sandberg	.45
211	John Cerutti	.05
212	Joe Orsulak	.05
213	Scott Bankhead	.05
214	Terry Francona	.05
215	Kirk McCaskill	.05
216	Ricky Jordan	.05
217	Don Robinson	.05
218	Wally Backman	.05
219	Donn Pall	.05
220	Barry Bonds	.75
221	Gary Mielke RC	.05
222	Kurt Stillwell	.05
223	Tommy Gregg	.05
224	Delino DeShields RC	.15
225	Jim Deshaies	.05
226	Mickey Hatcher	.05
227	Kevin Tapani RC	.15
228	Dave Martinez	.05
229	David Wells	.05
230	Keith Hernandez	.05
231	Jack McKeon	.05
232	Darnell Coles	.05
233	Ken Hill	.05
234	Mariano Duncan	.05
235	Jeff Reardon	.05
236	Hal Morris	.05
237	Kevin Ritz RC	.05
238	Felix Jose	.05
239	Eric Show	.05
240	Mark Grace	.05
241	Mike Krukow	.05
242	Fred Manrique	.05
243	Barry Jones	.05
244	Bill Schroeder	.05
245	Roger Clemens	.50
246	Jim Eisenreich	.05
247	Jerry Reed	.05
248	Dave Anderson	.05
249	Mike Smith RC	.05
250	Jose Canseco	.25
251	Jeff Blauser	.05
252	Otis Nixon	.05
253	Mark Portugal	.05
254	Francisco Cabrera	.05
255	Bobby Thigpen	.05
256	Marvell Wynne	.05
257	Jose DeLeon	.05
258	Barry Lyons	.05
259	Lance McCullers	.05
260	Eric Davis	.05
261	Whitey Herzog	.05
262	Checklist 133-264	.05
263	Mel Stottlemyre, Jr. RC	.10
264	Bryan Clutterbuck	.05
265	Pete O'Brien	.05
266	German Gonzalez	.05
267	Mark Davidson	.05
268	Rob Murphy	.05
269	Dickie Thon	.05
270	Dave Stewart	.05
271	Chet Lemon	.05
272	Bryan Harvey	.05
273	Bobby Bonilla	.05
274	Goose Gozzo RC	.05
275	Mickey Tettleton	.05
276	Gary Thurman	.05
277	Lenny Harris	.05
278	Pascual Perez	.05
279	Steve Buechele	.05
280	Lou Whitaker	.05
281	Kevin Bass	.05
282	Derek Lilliquist	.05
283	Albert Belle	.15
284	Mark Gardner RC	.05
285	Willie McGee	.05
286	Lee Guetterman	.05
287	Vance Law	.05
288	Greg Briley	.05
289	Norm Charlton	.05
290	Robin Yount	.35
291	Dave Johnson	.05
292	Jim Gott	.05
293	Mike Gallego	.05
294	Craig McMurtry	.05
295	Fred McGriff	.05
296	Jeff Ballard	.05
297	Tom Herr	.05
298	Danny Gladden	.05
299	Adam Peterson	.05
300	Bo Jackson	.10
301	Don Aase	.05
302	Marcus Lawton RC	.05
303	Rick Cerone	.05
304	Marty Clary	.05
305	Eddie Murray	.35
306	Tom Niedenfuer	.05
307	Bip Roberts	.05
308	Jose Guzman	.05
309	Eric Yelding RC	.05
310	Steve Bedrosian	.05
311	Dwight Smith	.05
312	Dan Quisenberry	.05
313	Gus Polidor	.05
314	Donald Harris RC (#1 Draft Pick)	.05
315	Bruce Hurst	.05
316	Carney Lansford	.05
317	Mark Guthrie RC	.05
318	Wallace Johnson	.05
319	Dion James	.05
320	Dave Steib	.05
321	Joe M. Morgan	.05
322	Junior Ortiz	.05
323	Willie Wilson	.05
324	Pete Harnisch	.05
325	Robby Thompson	.05
326	Tom McCarthy RC	.05
327	Ken Williams	.05
328	Curt Young	.05
329	Oddibe McDowell	.05
330	Ron Darling	.05
331	Juan Gonzalez RC	1.50
332	Paul O'Neill	.05
333	Bill Wegman	.05
334	Johnny Ray	.05
335	Andy Hawkins	.05
336	Ken Griffey Jr.	.75
337	Lloyd McClendon	.05
338	Dennis Lamp	.05
339	Dave Clark	.05
340	Fernando Valenzuela	.05
341	Tom Foley	.05
342	Alex Trevino	.05
343	Frank Tanana	.05
344	George Canale RC	.05
345	Harold Baines	.05
346	Jim Presley	.05
347	Junior Felix RC	.05
348	Gary Wayne RC	.05
349	Steve Finley RC	.15
350	Bret Saberhagen	.05
351	Roger Craig	.05
352	Bryn Smith	.05
353	Sandy Alomar	.05
354	Stan Belinda RC	.05
355	Marty Barrett	.05
356	Randy Ready	.05
357	Dave West	.05
358	Andres Thomas	.05
359	Jimmy Jones	.05
360	Paul Molitor	.35
361	Randy McCament RC	.05
362	Damon Berryhill	.05
363	Dan Petry	.05
364	Rolando Roomes	.05
365	Ozzie Guillen	.05
366	Mike Heath	.05
367	Mike Morgan	.05
368	Bill Doran	.05
369	Todd Burns	.05

370 Tim Wallach	.05
371 Jimmy Key	.05
372 Terry Kennedy	.05
373 Alvin Davis	.05
374 Steve Cummings **RC**	.05
375 Dwight Evans	.05
376 Checklist 265-396	.05
377 Mickey Weston **RC**	.05
378 Luis Salazar	.05
379 Steve Rosenberg	.05
380 Dave Winfield	.35
381 Frank Robinson	.10
382 Jeff Musselman	.05
383 John Morris	.05
384 Pat Combs **RC**	.05
385 Fred McGriff/AS	.05
386 Julio Franco/AS	.05
387 Wade Boggs/AS	.20
388 Cal Ripken, Jr./AS	.40
389 Robin Yount/AS	.20
390 Ruben Sierra/AS	.05
391 Kirby Puckett/AS	.25
392 Carlton Fisk/AS	.05
393 Bret Saberhagen/AS	.05
394 Jeff Ballard/AS	.05
395 Jeff Russell/AS	.05
396 A. Bartlett Giamatti	.20
397 Will Clark/AS	.05
398 Ryne Sandberg/AS	.05
399 Howard Johnson/AS	.05
400 Ozzie Smith/AS	.20
401 Kevin Mitchell/AS	.05
402 Eric Davis/AS	.05
403 Tony Gwynn/AS	.25
404 Craig Biggio/AS	.05
405 Mike Scott/AS	.05
406 Joe Magrane/AS	.05
407 Mark Davis/AS	.05
408 Trevor Wilson	.05
409 Tom Brunansky	.05
410 Joe Boever	.05
411 Ken Phelps	.05
412 Jamie Moyer	.05
413 Brian DuBois **RC**	.05
414a Frank Thomas	
(No Name **RC**)	
(No name on front.)	500.00
414b Frank Thomas **RC**	
(Name on front.)	3.00
415 Shawon Dunston	.05
416 Dave Johnson **RC**	.05
417 Jim Gantner	.05
418 Tom Browning	.05
419 Beau Allred **RC**	.05
420 Carlton Fisk	.35
421 Greg Minton	.05
422 Pat Sheridan	.05
423 Fred Toliver	.05
424 Jerry Reuss	.05
425 Bill Landrum	.05
426 Jeff Hamilton	.05
427 Carmem Castillo	.05
428 Steve Davis **RC**	.05
429 Tom Kelly	.05
430 Pete Incaviglia	.05
431 Randy Johnson	.35
432 Damaso Garcia	.05
433 Steve Olin **RC**	.05
434 Mark Carreon	.05
435 Kevin Seitzer	.05
436 Mel Hall	.05
437 Les Lancaster	.05
438 Greg Myers	.05
439 Jeff Parrett	.05
440 Alan Trammell	.05
441 Bob Kipper	.05
442 Jerry Browne	.05
443 Cris Carpenter	.05
444 Kyle Abbott **RC** (FDP)	.10
445 Danny Jackson	.05
446 Dan Pasqua	.05
447 Atlee Hammaker	.05
448 Greg Gagne	.05
449 Dennis Rasmussen	.05
450 Rickey Henderson	.35
451 Mark Lemke	.05
452 Luis de los Santos	.05
453 Jody Davis	.05
454a Jeff King	
(No white on back.)	100.00
454b Jeff King	
(Correct use of white.)	.05
455 Jeffrey Leonard	.05
456 Chris Gwynn	.05
457 Gregg Jefferies	.05
458 Bob McClure	.05
459 Jim Lefebvre	.05
460 Mike Scott	.05
461 Carlos Martinez **RC**	.05
462 Denny Walling	.05
463 Drew Hall	.05
464 Jerome Walton **RC**	.05
465 Kevin Gross	.05
466 Rance Mulliniks	.05

467 Juan Nieves	.05
468 Billy Ripken	.05
469 John Kruk	.05
470 Frank Viola	.05
471 Mike Brumley	.05
472 Jose Uribe	.05
473 Joe Price	.05
474 Rich Thompson	.05
475 Bob Welch	.05
476 Brad Komminsk	.05
477 Willie Fraser	.05
478 Mike LaValliere	.05
479 Frank White	.05
480 Sid Fernandez	.05
481 Garry Templeton	.05
482 Steve Carter **RC**	.05
483 Alejandro Pena	.05
484 Mike Fitzgerald	.05
485 John Candelaria	.05
486 Jeff Treadway	.05
487 Steve Searcy	.05
488 Ken Oberkfell	.05
489 Nick Leyva	.05
490 Dan Plesac	.05
491 Dave Cochrane **RC**	.05
492 Ron Oester	.05
493 Jason Grimsley **RC**	.05
494 Terry Puhl	.05
495 Lee Smith	.05
496 Cecil Espy	.05
497 Dave Schmidt	.05
498 Rick Schu	.05
499 Bill Long	.05
500 Kevin Mitchell	.05
501 Matt Young	.05
502 Mitch Webster	.05
503 Randy St. Claire	.05
504 Tom O'Malley	.05
505 Kelly Gruber	.05
506 Tom Glavine	.25
507 Gary Redus	.05
508 Terry Leach	.05
509 Tom Pagnozzi	.05
510 Dwight Gooden	.05
511 Clay Parker	.05
512 Gary Pettis	.05
513 Mark Eichhorn	.05
514 Andy Allanson	.05
515 Len Dykstra	.05
516 Tim Leary	.05
517 Roberto Alomar	.15
518 Bill Krueger	.05
519 Bucky Dent	.05
520 Mitch Williams	.05
521 Craig Worthington	.05
522 Mike Dunne	.05
523 Jay Bell	.05
524 Daryl Boston	.05
525 Wally Joyner	.05
526 Checklist 397-528	.05
527 Ron Hassey	.05
528 Kevin Wickander **RC**	.05
529 Greg Harris	.05
530 Mark Langston	.05
531 Ken Caminiti	.05
532 Cecilio Guante	.05
533 Tim Jones	.05
534 Louie Meadows	.05
535 John Smoltz	.05
536 Bob Geren **RC**	.05
537 Mark Grant	.05
538 Billy Spiers **RC**	.05
539 Neal Heaton	.05
540 Danny Tartabull	.05
541 Pat Perry	.05
542 Darren Daulton	.05
543 Nelson Liriano	.05
544 Dennis Boyd	.05
545 Kevin McReynolds	.05
546 Kevin Hickey	.05
547 Jack Howell	.05
548 Pat Clements	.05
549 Don Zimmer	.05
550 Julio Franco	.05
551 Tim Crews	.05
552 Mike Smith **RC**	.05
553 Scott Scudder **RC**	.05
554 Jay Buhner	.05
555 Jack Morris	.05
556 Gene Larkin	.05
557 Jeff Innis **RC**	.05
558 Rafael Ramirez	.05
559 Andy McGaffigan	.05
560 Steve Sax	.05
561 Ken Dayley	.05
562 Chad Kreuter	.05
563 Alex Sanchez	.05
564 Tyler Houston **RC**	
(#1 Draft Pick)	.10
565 Scott Fletcher	.05
566 Mark Knudson	.05
567 Ron Gant	.05
568 John Smiley	.05
569 Ivan Calderon	.05

570 Cal Ripken, Jr.	.75
571 Brett Butler	.05
572 Greg Harris	.05
573 Danny Heep	.05
574 Bill Swift	.05
575 Lance Parrish	.05
576 Mike Dyer **RC**	.05
577 Charlie Hayes	.05
578 Joe Magrane	.05
579 Art Howe	.05
580 Joe Carter	.05
581 Ken Griffey	.05
582 Rick Honeycutt	.05
583 Bruce Benedict	.05
584 Phil Stephenson **RC**	.05
585 Kal Daniels	.05
586 Ed Nunez	.05
587 Lance Johnson	.05
588 Rick Rhoden	.05
589 Mike Aldrete	.05
590 Ozzie Smith	.45
591 Todd Stottlemyre	.05
592 R.J. Reynolds	.05
593 Scott Bradley	.05
594 Luis Sojo **RC**	.05
595 Greg Swindell	.05
596 Jose DeJesus	.05
597 Chris Bosio	.05
598 Brady Anderson	.05
599 Frank Williams	.05
600 Darryl Strawberry	.05
601 Luis Rivera	.05
602 Scott Garrelts	.05
603 Tony Armas	.05
604 Ron Robinson	.05
605 Mike Scioscia	.05
606 Storm Davis	.05
607 Steve Jeltz	.05
608 Eric Anthony **RC**	.10
609 Sparky Anderson	.10
610 Pedro Guerrero	.05
611 Walt Terrell	.05
612 Dave Gallagher	.05
613 Jeff Pico	.05
614 Nelson Santovenia	.05
615 Rob Deer	.05
616 Brian Holman	.05
617 Geronimo Berroa	.05
618 Eddie Whitson	.05
619 Rob Ducey	.05
620 Tony Castillo **RC**	.05
621 Melido Perez	.05
622 Sid Bream	.05
623 Jim Corsi	.05
624 Darrin Jackson	.05
625 Roger McDowell	.05
626 Bob Melvin	.05
627 Jose Rijo	.05
628 Candy Maldonado	.05
629 Eric Hetzel	.05
630 Gary Gaetti	.05
631 John Wetteland **RC**	.15
632 Scott Lusader	.05
633 Dennis Cook	.05
634 Luis Polonia	.05
635 Brian Downing	.05
636 Jesse Orosco	.05
637 Craig Reynolds	.05
638 Jeff Montgomery	.05
639 Tony LaRussa	.05
640 Rick Sutcliffe	.05
641 Doug Strange **RC**	.05
642 Jack Armstrong	.05
643 Alfredo Griffin	.05
644 Paul Assenmacher	.05
645 Jose Oquendo	.05
646 Checklist 529-660	.05
647 Rex Hudler	.05
648 Jim Clancy	.05
649 Dan Murphy **RC**	.05
650 Mike Witt	.05
651 Rafael Santana	.05
652 Mike Boddicker	.05
653 John Moses	.05
654 Paul Coleman **RC**	
(#1 Draft Pick)	.05
655 Gregg Olson	.05
656 Mackey Sasser	.05
657 Terry Mulholland	.05
658 Donell Nixon	.05
659 Greg Cadaret	.05
660 Vince Coleman	.05
661 Dick Howser	.05
662 Mike Schmidt	.10
663 Fred Lynn	.05
664 Johnny Bench	.05
665 Sandy Koufax	.15
666 Brian Fisher	.05
667 Curt Wilkerson	.05
668 Joe Oliver **RC**	.05
669 Tom Lasorda	.05
670 Dennis Eckersley	.30
671 Bob Boone	.05
672 Roy Smith	.05

673 Joey Meyer	.05
674 Spike Owen	.05
675 Jim Abbott	.05
676 Randy Kutcher	.05
677 Jay Tibbs	.05
678 Kirt Manwaring	.05
679 Gary Ward	.05
680 Howard Johnson	.05
681 Mike Schooler	.05
682 Dann Bilardello	.05
683 Kenny Rogers	.05
684 Julio Machado **RC**	.05
685 Tony Fernandez	.05
686 Carmelo Martinez	.05
687 Tim Birtsas	.05
688 Milt Thompson	.05
689 Rich Yett	.05
690 Mark McGwire	.65
691 Chuck Cary	.05
692 Sammy Sosa **RC**	4.00
693 Calvin Schiraldi	.05
694 Mike Stanton **RC**	.05
695 Tom Henke	.05
696 B.J. Surhoff	.05
697 Mike Davis	.05
698 Omar Vizquel	.05
699 Jim Leyland	.05
700 Kirby Puckett	.45
701 Bernie Williams **RC**	1.00
702 Tony Phillips	.05
703 Jeff Brantley	.05
704 Chip Hale **RC**	.05
705 Claudell Washington	.05
706 Geno Petralli	.05
707 Luis Aquino	.05
708 Larry Sheets	.05
709 Juan Berneguer	.05
710 Von Hayes	.05
711 Rick Aguilera	.05
712 Todd Benzinger	.05
713 Tim Drummond **RC**	.05
714 Marquis Grissom **RC**	.25
715 Greg Maddux	.45
716 Steve Balboni	.05
717 Ron Kakovice	.05
718 Gary Sheffield	.30
719 Wally Whitehurst **RC**	.05
720 Andres Galarraga	.05
721 Lee Mazzilli	.05
722 Felix Fermin	.05
723 Jeff Robinson	.05
724 Juan Bell	.05
725 Terry Pendleton	.05
726 Gene Nelson	.05
727 Pat Tabler	.05
728 Jim Acker	.05
729 Bobby Valentine	.05
730 Tony Gwynn	.45
731 Don Carman	.05
732 Ernie Riles	.05
733 John Dopson	.05
734 Kevin Elster	.05
735 Charlie Hough	.05
736 Rick Dempsey	.05
737 Chris Sabo	.05
738 Gene Harris **RC**	.05
739 Dale Sveum	.05
740 Jesse Barfield	.05
741 Steve Wilson	.05
742 Ernie Whitt	.05
743 Tom Candiotti	.05
744 Kelly Mann **RC**	.05
745 Hubie Brooks	.05
746 Dave Smith	.05
747 Randy Bush	.05
748 Doyle Alexander	.05
749 Mark Parent	.05
750 Dale Murphy	.15
751 Steve Lyons	.05
752 Tom Gordon	.05
753 Chris Speier	.05
754 Bob Walk	.05
755 Rafael Palmeiro	.30
756 Ken Howell	.05
757 Larry Walker **RC**	.75
758 Mark Thurmond	.05
759 Tom Trebelhorn	.05
760 Wade Boggs	.45
761 Mike Jackson	.05
762 Doug Dascenzo	.05
763 Denny Martinez	.05
764 Tim Teufel	.05
765 Chili Davis	.05
766 Brian Meyer	.05
767 Tracy Jones	.05
768 Chuck Crim	.05
769 Greg Hibbard **RC**	.05
770 Cory Snyder	.05
771 Pete Smith	.05
772 Jeff Reed	.05
773 Dave Leiper	.05
774 Ben McDonald **RC**	.20
775 Andy Van Slyke	.05
776 Charlie Leibrandt	.05

777 Tim Laudner .05
778 Mike Jeffcoat .05
779 Lloyd Moseby .05
780 Orel Hershiser .05
781 Mario Diaz .05
782 Jose Alvarez .05
783 Checklist 661-792 .05
784 Scott Bailes .05
785 Jim Rice .15
786 Eric King .05
787 Rene Gonzales .05
788 Frank DiPino .05
789 John Wathan .05
790 Gary Carter .35
791 Alvaro Espinoza .05
792 Gerald Perry .05

Tiffany

NM/M
Unopened Set (792): 115.00
Complete Set (792): 90.00
Common Player: .10
(Star cards valued at 5X corresponding cards in regular Topps issue.)

Traded

NM/M
Complete Set, Retail (132): 6.00
Complete Set, Hobby (132): 4.00
Common Player: .05
Wax Pack (7): .75
Wax Box (36): 9.00
1 Darrel Akerfelds .05
2 Sandy Alomar, Jr. .05
3 Brad Arnsberg .05
4 Steve Avery .05
5 Wally Backman .05
6 Carlos Baerga RC .10
7 Kevin Bass .05
8 Willie Blair .05
9 Mike Blowers .05
10 Shawn Boskie .05
11 Daryl Boston .05
12 Dennis Boyd .05
13 Glenn Braggs .05
14 Hubie Brooks .05
15 Tom Brunansky .05
16 John Burkett .05
17 Casey Candaele .05
18 John Candelaria .05
19 Gary Carter .75
20 Joe Carter .05
21 Rick Cerone .05
22 Scott Coolbaugh .05
23 Bobby Cox .05
24 Mark Davis .05
25 Storm Davis .05
26 Edgar Diaz .05
27 Wayne Edwards .05
28 Mark Eichhorn .05
29 Scott Erickson .05
30 Nick Esasky .05
31 Cecil Fielder .05
32 John Franco .05
33 Travis Fryman RC .25
34 Bill Gullickson .05
35 Darryl Hamilton .05
36 Mike Harkey .05
37 Bud Harrelson .05
38 Billy Hatcher .05
39 Keith Hernandez .05
40 Joe Hesketh .05
41 Dave Hollins .05
42 Sam Horn .05
43 Steve Howard .05
44 Todd Hundley RC .15
45 Jeff Huson .05
46 Chris James .05
47 Stan Javier .05
48 Dave Justice RC .75
49 Jeff Kaiser .05

50 Dana Kiecker .05
51 Joe Klink .05
52 Brent Knackert .05
53 Brad Komminsk .05
54 Mark Langston .05
55 Tim Layana .05
56 Rick Leach .05
57 Terry Leach .05
58 Tim Leary .05
59 Craig Lefferts .05
60 Charlie Leibrandt .05
61 Jim Leyritz .05
62 Fred Lynn .05
63 Kevin Maas .05
64 Shane Mack .05
65 Candy Maldonado .05
66 Fred Manrique .05
67 Mike Marshall .05
68 Carmelo Martinez .05
69 John Marzano .05
70 Ben McDonald .05
71 Jack McDowell .05
72 John McNamara .05
73 Orlando Mercado .05
74 Stump Merrill .05
75 Alan Mills .05
76 Hal Morris .05
77 Lloyd Moseby .05
78 Randy Myers .05
79 Tim Naehring .05
80 Junior Noboa .05
81 Matt Nokes .05
82 Pete O'Brien .05
83 John Olerud RC .75
84 Greg Olson .05
85 Junior Ortiz .05
86 Dave Parker .05
87 Rick Parker .05
88 Bob Patterson .05
89 Alejandro Pena .05
90 Tony Pena .05
91 Pascual Perez .05
92 Gerald Perry .05
93 Dan Petry .05
94 Gary Pettis .05
95 Tony Phillips .05
96 Lou Pinella .05
97 Luis Polonia .05
98 Jim Presley .05
99 Scott Radinsky .05
100 Willie Randolph .05
101 Jeff Reardon .05
102 Greg Riddoch .05
103 Jeff Robinson .05
104 Ron Robinson .05
105 Kevin Romine .05
106 Scott Ruskin .05
107 John Russell .05
108 Bill Sampen .05
109 Juan Samuel .05
110 Scott Sanderson .05
111 Jack Savage .05
112 Dave Schmidt .05
113 Red Schoendienst .10
114 Terry Shumpert .05
115 Matt Sinatro .05
116 Don Slaught .05
117 Bryn Smith .05
118 Lee Smith .05
119 Paul Sorrento .05
120 Franklin Stubbs .05
121 Russ Swan .05
122 Bob Tewksbury .05
123 Wayne Tolleson .05
124 John Tudor .05
125 Randy Veres .05
126 Hector Villanueva .05
127 Mitch Webster .05
128 Ernie Whitt .05
129 Frank Wills .05
130 Dave Winfield .75
131 Matt Young .05
132 Checklist .05

Traded Tiffany

NM/M
Complete Set (132): 25.00
Common Player: .15
(Star cards valued at 4X corresponding cards in regular Topps Traded issue.)

1991 Topps 1990 Major League Debut

NM/M
Complete Set (171): 5.00
Common Player: .05
1 Paul Abbott .05
2 Steve Adkins .05
3 Scott Aldred .05
4 Gerald Alexander .05
5 Moises Alou .25
6 Steve Avery .05
7 Oscar Azocar .05
8 Carlos Baerga .05

9 Kevin Baez .05
10 Jeff Baldwin .05
11 Brian Barnes .05
12 Kevin Bearse .05
13 Kevin Belcher .05
14 Mike Bell .05
15 Sean Berry .05
16 Joe Bitker .05
17 Willie Blair .05
18 Brian Bohanon .05
19 Mike Bordick .05
20 Shawn Boskie .05
21 Rod Brewer .05
22 Kevin Brown .10
23 Dave Burba .05
24 Jim Campbell .05
25 Ozzie Canseco .05
26 Chuck Carr .05
27 Larry Casian .05
28 Andujar Cedeno .05
29 Wes Chamberlain .05
30 Scott Chiamparino .05
31 Steve Chitren .05
32 Pete Coachman .05
33 Alex Cole .05
34 Jeff Conine .10
35 Scott Cooper .05
36 Milt Cuyler .05
37 Steve Decker .05
38 Rich DeLucia .05
39 Delino DeShields .05
40 Mark Dewey .05
41 Carlos Diaz .05
42 Lance Dickson .05
43 Narciso Elvira .05
44 Luis Encarnacion .05
45 Scott Erickson .05
46 Paul Faries .05
47 Howard Farmer .05
48 Alex Fernandez .05
49 Travis Fryman .05
50 Rich Garces .05
51 Carlos Garcia .05
52 Mike Gardiner .05
53 Bernard Gilkey .05
54 Tom Gilles .05
55 Jerry Goff .05
56 Leo Gomez .05
57 Luis Gonzalez .75
58 Joe Grahe .05
59 Craig Grebeck .05
60 Kip Gross .05
61 Eric Gunderson .05
62 Chris Hammond .05
63 Dave Hansen .05
64 Reggie Harris .05
65 Bill Haselman .05
66 Randy Hennis .05
67 Carlos Hernandez .05
68 Howard Hilton .05
69 Dave Hollins .05
70 Darren Holmes .05
71 John Hoover .05
72 Steve Howard .05
73 Thomas Howard .05
74 Todd Hundley .05
75 Daryl Irvine .05
76 Chris Jelic .05
77 Dana Kiecker .05
78 Brent Knackert .05
79 Jimmy Kremers .05
80 Jerry Kutzler .05
81 Ray Lankford .05
82 Tim Layana .05
83 Terry Lee .05
84 Mark Leiter .05
85 Scott Leius .05
86 Mark Leonard .05
87 Darren Lewis .05
88 Scott Lewis .05
89 Jim Leyritz .05
90 Dave Liddell .05
91 Luis Lopez .05
92 Kevin Maas .05

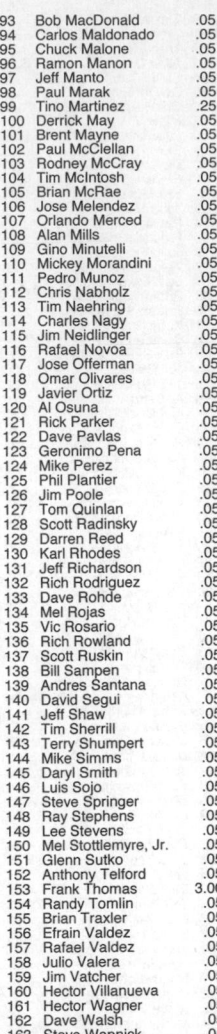

93 Bob MacDonald .05
94 Carlos Maldonado .05
95 Chuck Malone .05
96 Ramon Manon .05
97 Jeff Manto .05
98 Paul Marak .05
99 Tino Martinez .25
100 Derrick May .05
101 Brent Mayne .05
102 Paul McClellan .05
103 Rodney McCray .05
104 Tim McIntosh .05
105 Brian McRae .05
106 Jose Melendez .05
107 Orlando Merced .05
108 Alan Mills .05
109 Gino Minutelli .05
110 Mickey Morandini .05
111 Pedro Munoz .05
112 Chris Nabholz .05
113 Tim Naehring .05
114 Charles Nagy .05
115 Jim Neidlinger .05
116 Rafael Novoa .05
117 Jose Offerman .05
118 Omar Olivares .05
119 Javier Ortiz .05
120 Al Osuna .05
121 Rick Parker .05
122 Dave Pavlas .05
123 Geronimo Pena .05
124 Mike Perez .05
125 Phil Plantier .05
126 Jim Poole .05
127 Tom Quinlan .05
128 Scott Radinsky .05
129 Darren Reed .05
130 Karl Rhodes .05
131 Jeff Richardson .05
132 Rich Rodriguez .05
133 Dave Rohde .05
134 Mel Rojas .05
135 Vic Rosario .05
136 Rich Rowland .05
137 Scott Ruskin .05
138 Bill Sampen .05
139 Andres Santana .05
140 David Segui .05
141 Jeff Shaw .05
142 Tim Sherrill .05
143 Terry Shumpert .05
144 Mike Simms .05
145 Daryl Smith .05
146 Luis Sojo .05
147 Steve Springer .05
148 Ray Stephens .05
149 Lee Stevens .05
150 Mel Stottlemyre, Jr. .05
151 Glenn Sutko .05
152 Anthony Telford .05
153 Frank Thomas 3.00
154 Randy Tomlin .05
155 Brian Traxler .05
156 Efrain Valdez .05
157 Rafael Valdez .05
158 Julio Valera .05
159 Jim Vatcher .05
160 Hector Villanueva .05
161 Hector Wagner .05
162 Dave Walsh .05
163 Steve Wapnick .05
164 Colby Ward .05
165 Turner Ward .05
166 Terry Wells .05
167 Mark Whiten .05
168 Mike York .05
169 Cliff Young .05
170 Checklist .05
171 Checklist .05

1991 Topps

NM/M
Unopened Factory Set, Retail (792): 30.00

No.	Player	Price
	Unopened Factory Set, Hobby (792):	25.00
	Complete Set (792):	20.00
	Common Player:	.05
	Wax Pack (15):	.50
	Wax Box (36):	12.50
	Cello Pack (34):	1.00
	Cello Box (24):	15.00
	Rack Pack (45):	1.00
	Rack Box (24):	15.00
	Vending Box (500):	7.50
1	Nolan Ryan	.75
2	George Brett	.25
3	Carlton Fisk	.20
4	Kevin Maas	.05
5	Cal Ripken, Jr.	.40
6	Nolan Ryan	.40
7	Ryne Sandberg	.30
8	Bobby Thigpen	.05
9	Darrin Fletcher	.05
10	Gregg Olson	.05
11	Roberto Kelly	.05
12	Paul Assenmacher	.05
13	Mariano Duncan	.05
14	Dennis Lamp	.05
15	Von Hayes	.05
16	Mike Heath	.05
17	Jeff Brantley	.05
18	Nelson Liriano	.05
19	Jeff Robinson	.05
20	Pedro Guerrero	.05
21	Joe M. Morgan	.05
22	Storm Davis	.05
23	Jim Gantner	.05
24	Dave Martinez	.05
25	Tim Belcher	.05
26	Luis Sojo	.05
27	Bobby Witt	.05
28	Alvaro Espinoza	.05
29	Bob Walk	.05
30	Gregg Jefferies	.05
31	Colby Ward RC	.05
32	Mike Simms RC	.05
33	Barry Jones	.05
34	Atlee Hammaker	.05
35	Greg Maddux	.50
36	Donnie Hill	.05
37	Tom Bolton	.05
38	Scott Bradley	.05
39	Jim Neidlinger RC	.05
40	Kevin Mitchell	.05
41	Ken Dayley	.05
42a	Chris Hoiles RC (White inner photo frame.)	.20
42b	Chris Hoiles RC (Gray inner photo frame.)	.10
43	Roger McDowell	.05
44	Mike Felder	.05
45	Chris Sabo	.05
46	Tim Drummond	.05
47	Brook Jacoby	.05
48	Dennis Boyd	.05
49a	Pat Borders (40 stolen bases in Kinston 1986)	.20
49b	Pat Borders (0 stolen bases in Kinston 1986)	.10
50	Bob Welch	.05
51	Art Howe	.05
52	Francisco Oliveras RC	.05
53	Mike Sharperson	.05
54	Gary Mielke	.05
55	Jeffrey Leonard	.05
56	Jeff Parrett	.05
57	Jack Howell	.05
58	Mel Stottlemyre	.05
59	Eric Yelding	.05
60	Frank Viola	.05
61	Stan Javier	.05
62	Lee Guetterman	.05
63	Milt Thompson	.05
64	Tom Herr	.05
65	Bruce Hurst	.05
66	Terry Kennedy	.05
67	Rick Honeycutt	.05
68	Gary Sheffield	.25
69	Steve Wilson	.05
70	Ellis Burks	.05
71	Jim Acker	.05
72	Junior Ortiz	.05
73	Craig Worthington	.05
74	Shane Andrews RC (#1 Draft Pick)	.10
75	Jack Morris	.05
76	Jerry Browne	.05
77	Drew Hall	.05
78	Geno Petralli	.05
79	Frank Thomas	.35
80a	Fernando Valenzuela (No diamond after 104 ER in 1990.)	.25
80b	Fernando Valenzuela (Diamond after 104 ER in 1990.)	.05
81	Cito Gaston	.05
82	Tom Glavine	.20
83	Daryl Boston	.05
84	Bob McClure	.05
85	Jesse Barfield	.05
86	Les Lancaster	.05
87	Tracy Jones	.05
88	Bob Tewksbury	.05
89	Darren Daulton	.05
90	Danny Tartabull	.05
91	Greg Colbrunn RC	.05
92	Danny Jackson	.05
93	Ivan Calderon	.05
94	John Dopson	.05
95	Paul Molitor	.35
96	Trevor Wilson	.05
97a	Brady Anderson (3H, 2RBI in Sept. scoreboard)	.25
97b	Brady Anderson (14H, 3 RBI in Sept. scoreboard)	.05
98	Sergio Valdez	.05
99	Chris Gwynn	.05
100a	Don Mattingly (10 hits 1990)	.50
100b	Don Mattingly (101 hits in 1990)	.50
101	Rob Ducey	.05
102	Gene Larkin	.05
103	Tim Costo RC (#1 Draft Pick)	.05
104	Don Robinson	.05
105	Kevin McReynolds	.05
106	Ed Nunez	.05
107	Luis Polonia	.05
108	Matt Young	.05
109	Greg Riddoch	.05
110	Tom Henke	.05
111	Andres Thomas	.05
112	Frank DiPino	.05
113	Carl Everett RC (#1 Draft Pick)	.50
114	Lance Dickson RC	.05
115	Hubie Brooks	.05
116	Mark Davis	.05
117	Dion James	.05
118	Tom Edens RC	.05
119	Carl Nichols	.05
120	Joe Carter	.05
121	Eric King	.05
122	Paul O'Neill	.05
123	Greg Harris	.05
124	Randy Bush	.05
125	Steve Bedrosian	.05
126	Bernard Gilkey RC	.10
127	Joe Price	.05
128	Travis Fryman	.05
129	Mark Eichhorn	.05
130	Ozzie Smith	.50
131a	Checklist 1 (Phil Bradley #727.)	.05
131b	Checklist 1 (Phil Bradley #717.)	.05
132	Jamie Quirk	.05
133	Greg Briley	.05
134	Kevin Elster	.05
135	Jerome Walton	.05
136	Dave Schmidt	.05
137	Randy Ready	.05
138	Jamie Moyer	.05
139	Jeff Treadway	.05
140	Fred McGriff	.05
141	Nick Leyva	.05
142	Curtis Wilkerson	.05
143	John Smiley	.05
144	Dave Henderson	.05
145	Lou Whitaker	.05
146	Dan Plesac	.05
147	Carlos Baerga	.05
148	Rey Palacios	.05
149	Al Osuna RC	.05
150	Cal Ripken, Jr.	.75
151	Tom Browning	.05
152	Mickey Hatcher	.05
153	Bryan Harvey	.05
154	Jay Buhner	.05
155a	Dwight Evans (Diamond after 162 G 1982.)	.10
155b	Dwight Evans (No diamond after 162 G 1982.)	.05
156	Carlos Martinez	.05
157	John Smoltz	.05
158	Jose Uribe	.05
159	Joe Boever	.05
160	Vince Coleman	.05
161	Tim Leary	.05
162	Ozzie Canseco RC	.10
163	Dave Johnson	.05
164	Edgar Diaz	.05
165	Sandy Alomar	.05
166	Harold Baines	.05
167a	Randy Tomlin RC ("Harriburg" 1989-90.)	.10
167b	Randy Tomlin RC ("Harrisburg" 1989-90.)	.05
168	John Olerud	.05
169	Luis Aquino	.05
170	Carlton Fisk	.35
171	Tony LaRussa	.05
172	Pete Incaviglia	.05
173	Jason Grimsley	.05
174	Ken Caminiti	.05
175	Jack Armstrong	.05
176	John Orton	.05
177	Reggie Harris RC	.05
178	Dave Valle	.05
179	Pete Harnisch	.05
180	Tony Gwynn	.50
181	Duane Ward	.05
182	Junior Noboa	.05
183	Clay Parker	.05
184	Gary Green	.05
185	Joe Magrane	.05
186	Rod Booker	.05
187	Greg Cadaret	.05
188	Damon Berryhill	.05
189	Daryl Irvine RC	.05
190	Matt Williams	.05
191	Willie Blair RC	.05
192	Rob Deer	.05
193	Felix Fermin	.05
194	Xavier Hernandez	.05
195	Wally Joyner	.05
196	Jim Vatcher RC	.05
197	Chris Nabholz RC	.05
198	R.J. Reynolds	.05
199	Mike Hartley	.05
200	Darryl Strawberry	.05
201	Tom Kelly	.05
202	Jim Leyritz RC	.20
203	Gene Harris	.05
204	Herm Winningham	.05
205	Mike Perez RC	.05
206	Carlos Quintana	.05
207	Gary Wayne	.05
208	Willie Wilson	.05
209	Ken Howell	.05
210	Lance Parrish	.05
211	Brian Barnes RC	.05
212	Steve Finley	.05
213	Frank Wills	.05
214	Joe Girardi	.05
215	Dave Smith	.05
216	Greg Gagne	.05
217	Chris Bosio	.05
218	Rick Parker RC	.05
219	Jack McDowell	.05
220	Tim Wallach	.05
221	Don Slaught	.05
222	Brian McRae RC	.10
223	Allan Anderson	.05
224	Juan Gonzalez	.20
225	Randy Johnson	.35
226	Alfredo Griffin	.05
227	Steve Avery	.05
228	Rex Hudler	.05
229	Rance Mulliniks	.05
230	Sid Fernandez	.05
231	Doug Rader	.05
232	Jose DeJesus	.05
233	Al Leiter	.05
234	Scott Erickson RC	.10
235	Dave Parker	.05
236a	Frank Tanana (No diamond after 269 SO 1975.)	.10
236b	Frank Tanana (Diamond after 269 SO 1975.)	.05
237	Rick Cerone	.05
238	Mike Dunne	.05
239	Darren Lewis RC	.05
240	Mike Scott	.05
241	Dave Clark	.05
242	Mike LaCoss	.05
243	Lance Johnson	.05
244	Mike Jeffcoat	.05
245	Kal Daniels	.05
246	Kevin Wickander	.05
247	Jody Reed	.05
248	Tom Gordon	.05
249	Bob Melvin	.05
250	Dennis Eckersley	.30
251	Mark Lemke	.05
252	Mel Rojas RC	.05
253	Garry Templeton	.05
254	Shawn Boskie RC	.05
255	Brian Downing	.05
256	Greg Hibbard	.05
257	Tom O'Malley	.05
258	Chris Hammond	.05
259	Hensley Meulens	.05
260	Harold Reynolds	.05
261	Bud Harrelson	.05
262	Tim Jones	.05
263	Checklist 2	.05
264	Dave Hollins RC	.05
265	Mark Gubicza	.05
266	Carmen Castillo	.05
267	Mark Knudson	.05
268	Tom Brookens	.05
269	Joe Hesketh	.05
270a	Mark McGwire (1987 SLG .618)	.75
270b	Mark McGwire (1987 SLG 618)	.75
271	Omar Olivares RC	.05
272	Jeff King	.05
273	Johnny Ray	.05
274	Ken Williams	.05
275	Alan Trammell	.05
276	Bill Swift	.05
277	Scott Coolbaugh	.05
278	Alex Fernandez RC (#1 Draft Pick)	.10
279a	Jose Gonzalez (Photo of Billy Bean, left-handed batter.)	.75
279b	Jose Gonzalez (Correct photo, right-handed batter.)	.05
280	Bret Saberhagen	.05
281	Larry Sheets	.05
282	Don Carman	.05
283	Marquis Grissom	.05
284	Bill Spiers	.05
285	Jim Abbott	.05
286	Ken Oberkfell	.05
287	Mark Grant	.05
288	Derrick May	.05
289	Tim Birtsas	.05
290	Steve Sax	.05
291	John Wathan	.05
292	Bud Black	.05
293	Jay Bell	.05
294	Mike Moore	.05
295	Rafael Palmeiro	.30
296	Mark Williamson	.05
297	Manny Lee	.05
298	Omar Vizquel	.05
299	Scott Radinsky RC	.05
300	Kirby Puckett	.50
301	Steve Farr	.05
302	Tim Teufel	.05
303	Mike Boddicker	.05
304	Kevin Reimer	.05
305	Mike Scioscia	.05
306a	Lonnie Smith (136 G 1990)	.10
306b	Lonnie Smith (135 G 1990)	.05
307	Andy Benes	.05
308	Tom Pagnozzi	.05
309	Norm Charlton	.05
310	Gary Carter	.35
311	Jeff Pico	.05
312	Charlie Hayes	.05
313	Ron Robinson	.05
314	Gary Pettis	.05
315	Roberto Alomar	.15
316	Gene Nelson	.05
317	Mike Fitzgerald	.05
318	Rick Aguilera	.05
319	Jeff McKnight	.05
320	Tony Fernandez	.05
321	Bob Rodgers	.05
322	Terry Shumpert RC	.05
323	Cory Snyder	.05
324a	Ron Kittle ("6 Home Runs" in career summary)	.10
324b	Ron Kittle ("7 Home Runs" in career summary)	.05
325	Brett Butler	.05
326	Ken Patterson	.05
327	Ron Hassey	.05
328	Walt Terrell	.05
329	Dave Justice	.05
330	Dwight Gooden	.05
331	Eric Anthony	.05
332	Kenny Rogers	.05
333	Chipper Jones RC (#1 Draft Pick)	2.00
334	Todd Benzinger	.05
335	Mitch Williams	.05
336	Matt Nokes	.05
337a	Keith Comstock (Mariners logo.)	.05
337b	Keith Comstock (Cubs logo.)	1.50
338	Luis Rivera	.05
339	Larry Walker	.05
340	Ramon Martinez	.05
341	John Moses	.05
342	Mickey Morandini RC	.10
343	Jose Oquendo	.05
344	Jeff Russell	.05
345	Len Dykstra	.05
346	Jesse Orosco	.05
347	Greg Vaughn	.05
348	Todd Stottlemyre	.05
349	Dave Gallagher	.05
350	Glenn Davis	.05
351	Joe Torre	.05
352	Frank White	.05
353	Tony Castillo	.05

No.	Player	Value
354	Sid Bream	.05
355	Chili Davis	.05
356	Mike Marshall	.05
357	Jack Savage	.05
358	Mark Parent	.05
359	Chuck Cary	.05
360	Tim Raines	.05
361	Scott Garrelts	.05
362	Hector Villanueva RC	.05
363	Rick Mahler	.05
364	Dan Pasqua	.05
365	Mike Schooler	.05
366a	Checklist 3 (Carl Nichols #19.)	.05
366b	Checklist 3 (Carl Nichols #119.)	.05
367	Dave Walsh RC	.05
368	Felix Jose	.05
369	Steve Searcy	.05
370	Kelly Gruber	.05
371	Jeff Montgomery	.05
372	Spike Owen	.05
373	Darrin Jackson	.05
374	Larry Casian RC	.05
375	Tony Pena	.05
376	Mike Harkey	.05
377	Rene Gonzales	.05
378a	Wilson Alvarez RC (No 1989 Port Charlotte stats.)	.50
378b	Wilson Alvarez RC (1989 Port Charlotte stats)	.20
379	Randy Velarde	.05
380	Willie McGee	.05
381	Jim Leyland	.05
382	Mackey Sasser	.05
383	Pete Smith	.05
384	Gerald Perry	.05
385	Mickey Tettleton	.05
386	Cecil Fielder/AS	.05
387	Julio Franco/AS	.05
388	Kelly Gruber/AS	.05
389	Alan Trammell/AS	.05
390	Jose Canseco/AS	.15
391	Rickey Henderson/AS	.20
392	Ken Griffey Jr./AS	.35
393	Carlton Fisk/AS	.20
394	Bob Welch/AS	.05
395	Chuck Finley/AS	.05
396	Bobby Thigpen/AS	.05
397	Eddie Murray/AS	.20
398	Ryne Sandberg/AS	.30
399	Matt Williams/AS	.05
400	Barry Larkin/AS	.05
401	Barry Bonds/AS	.40
402	Darryl Strawberry/AS	.05
403	Bobby Bonilla/AS	.05
404	Mike Scoscia/AS	.05
405	Doug Drabek/AS	.05
406	Frank Viola/AS	.05
407	John Franco/AS	.05
408	Ernie Riles	.05
409	Mike Stanley	.05
410	Dave Righetti	.05
411	Lance Blankenship	.05
412	Dave Bergman	.05
413	Terry Mulholland	.05
414	Sammy Sosa	.60
415	Rick Sutcliffe	.05
416	Randy Milligan	.05
417	Bill Krueger	.05
418	Nick Esasky	.05
419	Jeff Reed	.05
420	Bobby Thigpen	.05
421	Alex Cole	.05
422	Rick Rueschel	.05
423	Rafael Ramirez	.05
424	Calvin Schiraldi	.05
425	Andy Van Slyke	.05
426	Joe Grahe RC	.05
427	Rick Dempsey	.05
428	John Barfield RC	.05
429	Stump Merrill	.05
430	Gary Gaetti	.05
431	Paul Gibson	.05
432	Delino DeShields	.05
433	Pat Tabler	.05
434	Julio Machado	.05
435	Kevin Maas	.05
436	Scott Bankhead	.05
437	Doug Dascenzo	.05
438	Vicente Palacios	.05
439	Dickie Thon	.05
440	George Bell	.05
441	Zane Smith	.05
442	Charlie O'Brien	.05
443	Jeff Innis	.05
444	Glenn Braggs	.05
445	Greg Swindell	.05
446	Craig Grebeck RC	.05
447	John Burkett	.05
448	Craig Lefferts	.05
449	Juan Berenguer	.05
450	Wade Boggs	.50
451	Neal Heaton	.05
452	Bill Schroeder	.05
453	Lenny Harris	.05
454a	Kevin Appier (No 1990 Omaha stats.)	.15
454b	Kevin Appier (1990 Omaha stats)	.05
455	Walt Weiss	.05
456	Charlie Leibrandt	.05
457	Todd Hundley	.05
458	Brian Holman	.05
459	Tom Trebelhorn	.05
460	Dave Steib	.05
461a	Robin Ventura (Gray inner photo frame at left.)	.15
461b	Robin Ventura (Red inner photo frame at left.)	.05
462	Steve Frey	.05
463	Dwight Smith	.05
464	Steve Buechele	.05
465	Ken Griffey	.05
466	Charles Nagy	.05
467	Dennis Cook	.05
468	Tim Hulett	.05
469	Chet Lemon	.05
470	Howard Johnson	.05
471	Mike Lieberthal RC (#1 Draft Pick)	.50
472	Kirt Manwaring	.05
473	Curt Young	.05
474	Phil Plantier RC	.10
475	Teddy Higuera	.05
476	Glenn Wilson	.05
477	Mike Fetters	.05
478	Kurt Stillwell	.05
479	Bob Patterson	.05
480	Dave Magadan	.05
481	Eddie Whitson	.05
482	Tino Martinez	.05
483	Mike Aldrete	.05
484	Dave LaPoint	.05
485	Terry Pendleton	.05
486	Tommy Greene	.05
487	Rafael Belliard	.05
488	Jeff Manto	.05
489	Bobby Valentine	.05
490	Kirk Gibson	.05
491	Kurt Miller RC (#1 Draft Pick)	.05
492	Ernie Whitt	.05
493	Jose Rijo	.05
494	Chris James	.05
495	Charlie Hough	.05
496	Marty Barrett	.05
497	Ben McDonald	.05
498	Mark Salas	.05
499	Melido Perez	.05
500	Will Clark	.05
501	Mike Bielecki	.05
502	Carney Lansford	.05
503	Roy Smith	.05
504	Julio Valera RC	.05
505	Chuck Finley	.05
506	Darnell Coles	.05
507	Steve Jeltz	.05
508	Mike York RC	.05
509	Glenallen Hill	.05
510	John Franco	.05
511	Steve Balboni	.05
512	Jose Mesa	.05
513	Jerald Clark	.05
514	Mike Stanton	.05
515	Alvin Davis	.05
516	Karl Rhodes RC	.05
517	Joe Oliver	.05
518	Cris Carpenter	.05
519	Sparky Anderson	.10
520	Mark Grace	.05
521	Joe Orsulak	.05
522	Stan Belinda	.05
523	Rodney McCray RC	.05
524	Darrel Akerfelds	.05
525	Willie Randolph	.05
526a	Moises Alou (37 R 1990 Pirates)	.20
526b	Moises Alou (0 R 1990 Pirates)	.15
527a	Checklist 4 (Kevin McReynolds #719)	.05
527b	Checklist 4 (Kevin McReynolds #105)	.05
528	Denny Martinez	.05
529	Mark Newfield RC (#1 Draft Pick)	.05
530	Roger Clemens	.60
531	Dave Rhode RC	.05
532	Kirk McCaskill	.05
533	Oddibe McDowell	.05
534	Mike Jackson	.05
535	Ruben Sierra	.05
536	Mike Witt	.05
537	Jose Lind	.05
538	Bip Roberts	.05
539	Scott Terry	.05
540	George Brett	.60
541	Domingo Ramos	.05
542	Rob Murphy	.05
543	Junior Felix	.05
544	Alejandro Pena	.05
545	Dale Murphy	.15
546	Jeff Ballard	.05
547	Mike Pagliarulo	.05
548	Jaime Navarro	.05
549	John McNamara	.05
550	Eric Davis	.05
551	Bob Kipper	.05
552	Jeff Hamilton	.05
553	Joe Klink RC	.05
554	Brian Harper	.05
555	Turner Ward RC	.05
556	Gary Ward	.05
557	Wally Whitehurst	.05
558	Otis Nixon	.05
559	Adam Peterson	.05
560	Greg Smith	.05
561	Tim McIntosh	.05
562	Jeff Kunkel	.05
563	Brent Knackert RC	.05
564	Dante Bichette	.05
565	Craig Biggio	.05
566	Craig Wilson RC	.05
567	Dwayne Henry	.05
568	Ron Karkovice	.05
569	Curt Schilling	.05
570	Barry Bonds	.75
571	Pat Combs	.05
572	Dave Anderson	.05
573	Rich Rodriguez RC	.05
574	John Marzano	.05
575	Robin Yount	.35
576	Jeff Kaiser	.05
577	Bill Doran	.05
578	Dave West	.05
579	Roger Craig	.05
580	Dave Stewart	.05
581	Luis Quinones	.05
582	Marty Clary	.05
583	Tony Phillips	.05
584	Kevin Brown	.05
585	Pete O'Brien	.05
586	Fred Lynn	.05
587	Jose Offerman	.05
588a	Mark Whiten (Hand inside left border.)	.05
588b	Mark Whiten (Hand over left border.)	.20
589	Scott Ruskin RC	.05
590	Eddie Murray	.35
591	Ken Hill	.05
592	B.J. Surhoff	.05
593a	Mike Walker RC (No 1990 Canton-Akron stats.)	.15
593b	Mike Walker RC (1990 Canton-Akron stats)	.05
594	Rich Garces RC	.05
595	Bill Landrum	.05
596	Ronnie Walden RC (#1 Draft Pick)	.05
597	Jerry Don Gleaton	.05
598	Sam Horn	.05
599a	Greg Myers (No 1990 Syracuse stats.)	.10
599b	Greg Myers (1990 Syracuse stats)	.05
600	Bo Jackson	.10
601	Bob Ojeda	.05
602	Casey Candaele	.05
603a	Wes Chamberlain RC (Photo of Louie Meadows, no bat.)	.75
603b	Wes Chamberlain RC (Correct photo, holding bat.)	.05
604	Billy Hatcher	.05
605	Jeff Reardon	.05
606	Jim Gott	.05
607	Edgar Martinez	.05
608	Todd Burns	.05
609	Jeff Torborg	.05
610	Andres Galarraga	.05
611	Dave Eiland	.05
612	Steve Lyons	.05
613	Eric Show	.05
614	Luis Salazar	.05
615	Bert Blyleven	.05
616	Todd Zeile	.05
617	Bill Wegman	.05
618	Sil Campusano	.05
619	David Wells	.05
620	Ozzie Guillen	.05
621	Ted Power	.05
622	Jack Daugherty	.05
623	Jeff Blauser	.05
624	Tom Candiotti	.05
625	Terry Steinbach	.05
626	Gerald Young	.05
627	Tim Layana RC	.05
628	Greg Litton	.05
629	Wes Gardner	.05
630	Dave Winfield	.35
631	Mike Morgan	.05
632	Lloyd Moseby	.05
633	Kevin Tapani	.05
634	Henry Cotto	.05
635	Andy Hawkins	.05
636	Geronimo Pena	.05
637	Bruce Ruffin	.05
638	Mike Macfarlane	.05
639	Frank Robinson	.05
640	Andre Dawson	.20
641	Mike Henneman	.05
642	Hal Morris	.05
643	Jim Presley	.05
644	Chuck Crim	.05
645	Juan Samuel	.05
646	Andujar Cedeno RC	.05
647	Mark Portugal	.05
648	Lee Stevens	.05
649	Bill Sampen RC	.05
650	Jack Clark	.05
651	Alan Mills RC	.05
652	Kevin Romine	.05
653	Anthony Telford RC	.05
654	Paul Sorrento	.05
655	Erik Hanson	.05
656a	Checklist 5 (Vincente Palacios #348.)	.05
656b	Checklist 5 (Palacios #433.)	.05
656c	Checklist 5 (Palacios #438.)	.05
657	Mike Kingery	.05
658	Scott Aldred RC	.05
659	Oscar Azocar RC	.05
660	Lee Smith	.05
661	Steve Lake	.05
662	Rob Dibble	.05
663	Greg Brock	.05
664	John Farrell	.05
665	Mike LaValliere	.05
666	Danny Darwin	.05
667	Kent Anderson	.05
668	Bill Long	.05
669	Lou Pinella	.05
670	Rickey Henderson	.35
671	Andy McGaffigan	.05
672	Shane Mack	.05
673	Greg Olson RC	.05
674a	Kevin Gross (No diamond after 89 BB 1988.)	.10
674b	Kevin Gross (Diamond after 89 BB 1988.)	.05
675	Tom Brunansky	.05
676	Scott Chiamparino RC	.05
677	Billy Ripken	.05
678	Mark Davidson	.05
679	Bill Bathe	.05
680	David Cone	.05
681	Jeff Schaefer RC	.05
682	Ray Lankford RC	.15
683	Derek Lilliquist	.05
684	Milt Cuyler	.05
685	Doug Drabek	.05
686	Mike Gallego	.05
687a	John Cerutti (4.46 ERA 1990)	.05
687b	John Cerutti (4.76 ERA 1990)	.05
688	Rosario Rodriguez RC	.05
689	John Kruk	.05
690	Orel Hershiser	.05
691	Mike Blowers	.05
692a	Efrain Valdez RC (No text below stats.)	.15
692b	Efrain Valdez RC (Two lines of text below stats.)	.05
693	Francisco Cabrera	.05
694	Randy Veres	.05
695	Kevin Seitzer	.05
696	Steve Olin	.05
697	Shawn Abner	.05
698	Mark Guthrie	.05
699	Jim Lefebvre	.05
700	Jose Canseco	.25
701	Pascual Perez	.05
702	Tim Naehring RC	.05
703	Juan Agosto	.05
704	Devon White	.05
705	Robby Thompson	.05
706a	Brad Arnsberg (68.2 IP Rangers 1990)	.05
706b	Brad Arnsberg (62.2 IP Rangers 1990)	.05
707	Jim Eisenreich	.05
708	John Mitchell	.05
709	Matt Sinatro	.05
710	Kent Hrbek	.05
711	Jose DeLeon	.05
712	Ricky Jordan	.05
713	Scott Scudder	.05
714	Marvell Wynne	.05
715	Tim Burke	.05
716	Bob Geren	.05

717	Phil Bradley	.05
718	Steve Crawford	.05
719	Keith Miller	.05
720	Cecil Fielder	.05
721	Mark Lee RC	.05
722	Wally Backman	.05
723	Candy Maldonado	.05
724	David Segui RC	.10
725	Ron Gant	.05
726	Phil Stephenson	.05
727	Mookie Wilson	.05
728	Scott Sanderson	.05
729	Don Zimmer	.05
730	Barry Larkin	.05
731	Jeff Gray RC	.05
732	Franklin Stubbs	.05
733	Kelly Downs	.05
734	John Russell	.05
735	Ron Darling	.05
736	Dick Schofield	.05
737	Tim Crews	.05
738	Mel Hall	.05
739	Russ Swan RC	.05
740	Ryne Sandberg	.50
741	Jimmy Key	.05
742	Tommy Gregg	.05
743	Bryn Smith	.05
744	Nelson Santovenia	.05
745	Doug Jones	.05
746	John Shelby	.05
747	Tony Fossas	.05
748	Al Newman	.05
749	Greg Harris	.05
750	Bobby Bonilla	.05
751	Wayne Edwards RC	.05
752	Kevin Bass	.05
753	Paul Marak RC	.05
754	Bill Pecota	.05
755	Mark Langston	.05
756	Jeff Huson	.05
757	Mark Gardner	.05
758	Mike Devereaux	.05
759	Bobby Cox	.05
760	Benny Santiago	.05
761	Larry Andersen	.05
762	Mitch Webster	.05
763	Dana Kiecker RC	.05
764	Mark Carreon	.05
765	Shawon Dunston	.05
766	Jeff Robinson	.05
767	Dan Wilson RC (#1 Draft Pick)	.10
768	Donn Pall	.05
769	Tim Sherrill RC	.05
770	Jay Howell	.05
771	Gary Redus	.05
772	Kent Mercker	.05
773	Tom Foley	.05
774	Dennis Rasmussen	.05
775	Julio Franco	.05
776	Brent Mayne	.05
777	John Candelaria	.05
778	Danny Gladden	.05
779	Carmelo Martinez	.05
780a	Randy Myers (Career losses 15.)	.10
780b	Randy Myers (Career losses 19.)	.05
781	Darryl Hamilton	.05
782	Jim Deshaies	.05
783	Joel Skinner	.05
784	Willie Fraser	.05
785	Scott Fletcher	.05
786	Eric Plunk	.05
787	Checklist 6	.05
788	Bob Milacki	.05
789	Tom Lasorda	.05
790	Ken Griffey Jr.	.60
791	Mike Benjamin (RC)	.05
792	Mike Greenwell	.05

Tiffany

	NM/M
Unopened Set (792):	135.00
Complete Set (792):	85.00
Common Player:	.10

(Star cards valued at 3X corresponding regular issue Topps cards.)

Traded

	NM/M
Unopened Retail or Hobby Set (132):	12.00
Complete Set (132):	10.00
Common Player:	.05
Wax Pack (7):	.65
Wax Box (36):	15.00

1	Juan Agosto	.05
2	Roberto Alomar	.15
3	Wally Backman	.05
4	Jeff Bagwell RC	3.00
5	Skeeter Barnes	.05
6	Steve Bedrosian	.05
7	Derek Bell	.05
8	George Bell	.05
9	Rafael Belliard	.05
10	Dante Bichette	.05
11	Bud Black	.05
12	Mike Boddicker	.05
13	Sid Bream	.05
14	Hubie Brooks	.05
15	Brett Butler	.05
16	Ivan Calderon	.05
17	John Candelaria	.05
18	Tom Candiotti	.05
19	Gary Carter	.50
20	Joe Carter	.05
21	Rick Cerone	.05
22	Jack Clark	.05
23	Vince Coleman	.05
24	Scott Coolbaugh	.05
25	Danny Cox	.05
26	Danny Darwin	.05
27	Chili Davis	.05
28	Glenn Davis	.05
29	Steve Decker	.05
30	Rob Deer	.05
31	Rich DeLucia	.05
32	John Dettmer RC (USA)	.05
33	Brian Downing	.05
34	Darren Dreifort RC (USA)	.25
35	Kirk Dressendorfer (USA)	.05
36	Jim Essian	.05
37	Dwight Evans	.05
38	Steve Farr	.05
39	Jeff Fassero	.05
40	Junior Felix	.05
41	Tony Fernandez	.05
42	Steve Finley	.05
43	Jim Fregosi	.05
44	Gary Gaetti	.05
45	Jason Giambi RC (USA)	4.00
46	Kirk Gibson	.05
47	Leo Gomez	.05
48	Luis Gonzalez RC	1.00
49	Jeff Granger RC (USA)	.10
50	Todd Greene RC (USA)	.15
51	Jeffrey Hammonds RC (USA)	.15
52	Mike Hargrove	.05
53	Pete Harnisch	.05
54	Rick Helling RC (USA)	.10
55	Glenallen Hill	.05
56	Charlie Hough	.05
57	Pete Incaviglia	.05
58	Bo Jackson	.10
59	Danny Jackson	.05
60	Reggie Jefferson	.05
61	Charles Johnson RC (USA)	.15
62	Jeff Johnson	.05
63	Todd Johnson RC (USA)	.05
64	Barry Jones	.05
65	Chris Jones	.05
66	Scott Kamieniecki	.05
67	Pat Kelly RC	.05
68	Darryl Kile	.05
69	Chuck Knoblauch	.05
70	Bill Krueger	.05
71	Scott Leius	.05
72	Donnie Leshnock RC (USA)	.05
73	Mark Lewis	.05
74	Candy Maldonado	.05
75	Jason McDonald RC (USA)	.05
76	Willie McGee	.05
77	Fred McGriff	.05
78	Billy McMillon RC (USA)	.05
79	Hal McRae	.05
80	Dan Melendez RC (USA)	.05
81	Orlando Merced	.05
82	Jack Morris	.05
83	Phil Nevin RC (USA)	.50
84	Otis Nixon	.05
85	Johnny Oates	.05
86	Bob Ojeda	.05
87	Mike Pagliarulo	.05
88	Dean Palmer	.05
89	Dave Parker	.05
90	Terry Pendleton	.05
91	Tony Phillips RC (USA)	.10
92	Doug Piatt	.05
93	Ron Polk (U.S.A.)	.05
94	Tim Raines	.05
95	Willie Randolph	.05
96	Dave Righetti	.05
97	Ernie Riles	.05
98	Chris Roberts RC (USA)	.05
99	Jeff Robinson/Angels	.05
100	Jeff Robinson/Orioles	.05
101	Ivan Rodriguez RC	3.00
102	Steve Rodriguez RC (USA)	.05
103	Tom Runnells	.05
104	Scott Sanderson	.05
105	Bob Scanlan	.05
106	Pete Schourek RC	.10
107	Gary Scott	.05
108	Paul Shuey RC (USA)	.10
109	Doug Simons RC	.05
110	Dave Smith	.05
111	Cory Snyder	.05
112	Luis Sojo	.05
113	Kennie Steenstra RC (USA)	.05
114	Darryl Strawberry	.05
115	Franklin Stubbs	.05
116	Todd Taylor RC (USA)	.05
117	Wade Taylor	.05
118	Garry Templeton	.05
119	Mickey Tettleton	.05
120	Tim Teufel	.05
121	Mike Timlin	.05
122	David Tuttle RC (USA)	.05
123	Mo Vaughn	.25
124	Jeff Ware RC (USA)	.05
125	Devon White	.05
126	Mark Whiten	.05
127	Mitch Williams	.05
128	Craig Wilson RC (USA)	.05
129	Willie Wilson	.05
130	Chris Wimmer RC (USA)	.05
131	Ivan Zweig RC (USA)	.05
132	Checklist	.05

Traded Tiffany

	NM/M
Unopened Set (132):	165.00
Complete Set (132):	90.00
Common Player:	.25
Stars and Rookies:	4X

(See 1991 Topps Traded for checklist and base card values.)

1992 Topps 1991 Major League Debut

	NM/M
Complete Set (194):	12.50
Common Player:	.05

1	Kyle Abbott	.05
2	Dana Allison	.05
3	Rich Amaral	.05
4	Ruben Amaro	.05
5	Andy Ashby	.05
6	Jim Austin	.05
7	Jeff Bagwell	4.00
8	Jeff Bateman	.05
9	Willie Banks	.05
10	Bret Barberie	.05
11	Kim Batiste	.05
12	Chris Beasley	.05
13	Rod Beck	.05
14	Derek Bell	.05
15	Esteban Beltre	.05
16	Freddie Benavides	.05
17	Rickey Bones	.05
18	Denis Boucher	.05
19	Ryan Bowen	.05
20	Cliff Brantley	.05
21	John Briscoe	.05
22	Scott Brosius	.05
23	Terry Bross	.05
24	Jarvis Brown	.05
25	Scott Bullett	.05
26	Kevin Campbell	.05
27	Amalio Carreno	.05
28	Matias Carrillo	.05
29	Jeff Carter	.05
30	Vinny Castilla	.05
31	Braulio Castillo	.05
32	Frank Castillo	.05
33	Darrin Chapin	.05
34	Mike Christopher	.05
35	Mark Clark	.05
36	Royce Clayton	.05
37	Stu Cole	.05
38	Gary Cooper	.05
39	Archie Corbin	.05
40	Rheal Cormier	.05
41	Chris Cron	.05
42	Mike Dalton	.05
43	Mark Davis	.05
44	Francisco de la Rosa	.05
45	Chris Donnels	.05
46	Brian Drahman	.05
47	Tom Drees	.05
48	Kirk Dressendorfer	.05
49	Bruce Egloff	.05
50	Cal Eldred	.05
51	Jose Escobar	.05
52	Tony Eusebio	.05
53	Hector Fajardo	.05
54	Monty Farriss	.05
55	Jeff Fassero	.05
56	Dave Fleming	.05
57	Kevin Flora	.05
58	Steve Foster	.05
59	Dan Gakeler	.05
60	Ramon Garcia	.05
61	Chris Gardner	.05
62	Jeff Gardner	.05
63	Chris George	.05
64	Ray Giannelli	.05
65	Tom Goodwin	.05
66	Mark Grater	.05
67	Johnny Guzman	.05
68	Juan Guzman	.05
69	Dave Haas	.05
70	Chris Haney	.05
71	Shawn Hare	.05
72	Donald Harris	.05
73	Doug Henry	.05
74	Pat Hentgen	.05
75	Gil Heredia	.05
76	Jeremy Hernandez	.05
77	Jose Hernandez	.05
78	Roberto Hernandez	.05
79	Bryan Hickerson	.05
80	Milt Hill	.05
81	Vince Horsman	.05
82	Wayne Housie	.05
83	Chris Howard	.05
84	David Howard	.05
85	Mike Humphreys	.05
86	Brian Hunter	.05
87	Jim Hunter	.05
88	Mike Ignasiak	.05
89	Reggie Jefferson	.05
90	Jeff Johnson	.05
91	Joel Johnson	.05
92	Calvin Jones	.05
93	Chris Jones	.05
94	Stacy Jones	.05
95	Jeff Juden	.05
96	Scott Kamienecki	.05
97	Eric Karros	.05
98	Pat Kelly	.05
99	John Kiely	.05
100	Darryl Kile	.05
101	Wayne Kirby	.05
102	Garland Kiser	.05
103	Chuck Knoblauch	.05
104	Randy Knorr	.05
105	Tom Kramer	.05
106	Ced Landrum	.05
107	Patrick Lennon	.05
108	Jim Lewis	.05
109	Mark Lewis	.05
110	Doug Lindsey	.05
111	Scott Livingstone	.05
112	Kenny Lofton	.10
113	Ever Magallanes	.05
114	Mike Magnante	.05
115	Barry Manuel	.05
116	Josias Manzanillo	.05
117	Chito Martinez	.05
118	Terry Mathews	.05
119	Rob Mauer	.05
120	Tim Mauser	.05

#	Player	Price
121	Terry McDaniel	.05
122	Rusty Meacham	.05
123	Luis Mercedes	.05
124	Paul Miller	.05
125	Keith Mitchell	.05
126	Bobby Moore	.05
127	Kevin Morton	.05
128	Andy Mota	.05
129	Jose Mota	.05
130	Mike Mussina	2.00
131	Jeff Mutis	.05
132	Denny Neagle	.05
133	Warren Newson	.05
134	Jim Olander	.05
135	Erik Pappas	.05
136	Jorge Pedre	.05
137	Yorkis Perez	.05
138	Mark Petkovsek	.05
139	Doug Piatt	.05
140	Jeff Plympton	.05
141	Harvey Pulliam	.05
142	John Ramos	.05
143	Mike Remlinger	.05
144	Laddie Renfroe	.05
145	Armando Reynoso	.05
146	Arthur Rhodes	.05
147	Pat Rice	.05
148	Nikco Riesgo	.05
149	Carlos Rodriguez	.05
150	Ivan Rodriguez	3.00
151	Wayne Rosenthal	.05
152	Rico Rossy	.05
153	Stan Royer	.05
154	Rey Sanchez	.05
155	Reggie Sanders	.05
156	Mo Sanford	.05
157	Bob Scanlan	.05
158	Pete Schourek	.05
159	Gary Scott	.05
160	Tim Scott	.05
161	Tony Scruggs	.05
162	Scott Servais	.05
163	Doug Simons	.05
164	Heathcliff Slocumb	.05
165	Joe Slusarski	.05
166	Tim Spehr	.05
167	Ed Sprague	.05
168	Jeff Tackett	.05
169	Eddie Taubensee	.05
170	Wade Taylor	.05
171	Jim Thome	2.50
172	Mike Timlin	.05
173	Jose Tolentino	.05
174	John Vander Wal	.05
175	Todd Van Poppel	.05
176	Mo Vaughn	.50
177	Dave Wainhouse	.05
178	Don Wakamatsu	.05
179	Bruce Walton	.05
180	Kevin Ward	.05
181	Dave Weathers	.05
182	Eric Wedge	.05
183	John Wehner	.05
184	Rick Wilkins	.05
185	Bernie Williams	.50
186	Brian Williams	.05
187	Ron Witmeyer	.05
188	Mark Wohlers	.05
189	Ted Wood	.05
190	Anthony Young	.05
191	Eddie Zosky	.05
192	Bob Zupcic	.05
193	Checklist	.05
194	Checklist	.05

1992 Topps

	NM/M
Unopened Fact. Set (802):	30.00
Complete Set (792):	20.00
Common Player:	.05
Wax Pack (14):	.50
Wax Box (36):	12.50
Cello Pack (34):	1.00
Cello Box (24):	16.00

#	Player	Price
	Vending Box (500):	6.00
1	Nolan Ryan	.75
2	Rickey Henderson	.20
3	Jeff Reardon	.05
4	Nolan Ryan	.40
5	Dave Winfield	.20
6	Brien Taylor RC	.05
7	Jim Olander RC	.05
8	Bryan Hickerson RC	.05
9	John Farrell	.05
10	Wade Boggs	.45
11	Jack McDowell	.05
12	Luis Gonzalez	.05
13	Mike Scioscia	.05
14	Wes Chamberlain	.05
15	Denny Martinez	.05
16	Jeff Montgomery	.05
17	Randy Milligan	.05
18	Greg Cadaret	.05
19	Jamie Quirk	.05
20	Bip Roberts	.05
21	Buck Rodgers	.05
22	Bill Wegman	.05
23	Chuck Knoblauch	.05
24	Randy Myers	.05
25	Ron Gant	.05
26	Mike Bielecki	.05
27	Juan Gonzalez	.20
28	Mike Schooler	.05
29	Mickey Tettleton	.05
30	John Kruk	.05
31	Bryn Smith	.05
32	Chris Nabholz	.05
33	Carlos Baerga	.05
34	Jeff Juden	.05
35	Dave Righetti	.05
36	Scott Ruffcorn RC	.05
37	Luis Polonia	.05
38	Tom Candiotti	.05
39	Greg Olson	.05
40	Cal Ripken, Jr.	.75
41	Craig Lefferts	.05
42	Mike Macfarlane	.05
43	Jose Lind	.05
44	Rick Aguilera	.05
45	Gary Carter	.35
46	Steve Farr	.05
47	Rex Hudler	.05
48	Scott Scudder	.05
49	Damon Berryhill	.05
50	Ken Griffey Jr.	.55
51	Tom Runnells	.05
52	Juan Bell	.05
53	Tommy Gregg	.05
54	David Wells	.05
55	Rafael Palmeiro	.30
56	Charlie O'Brien	.05
57	Donn Pall	.05
58	Brad Ausmus, Jim Campanis, Dave Nilsson, Doug Robbins RC Top Prospects-Catchers	.15
59	Mo Vaughn	.05
60	Tony Fernandez	.05
61	Paul O'Neill	.05
62	Gene Nelson	.05
63	Randy Ready	.05
64	Bob Kipper	.05
65	Willie McGee	.05
66	Scott Stahoviak RC	.05
67	Luis Salazar	.05
68	Marvin Freeman	.05
69	Kenny Lofton	.05
70	Gary Gaetti	.05
71	Erik Hanson	.05
72	Eddie Zosky	.05
73	Brian Barnes	.05
74	Scott Leius	.05
75	Bret Saberhagen	.05
76	Mike Gallego	.05
77	Jack Armstrong	.05
78	Ivan Rodriguez	.35
79	Jesse Orosco	.05
80	Dave Justice	.05
81	Ced Landrum RC	.05
82	Doug Simons RC	.05
83	Tommy Greene	.05
84	Leo Gomez	.05
85	Jose DeLeon	.05
86	Steve Finley	.05
87	Bob MacDonald RC	.05
88	Darrin Jackson	.05
89	Neal Heaton	.05
90	Robin Yount	.35
91	Jeff Reed	.05
92	Lenny Harris	.05
93	Reggie Jefferson	.05
94	Sammy Sosa	.45
95	Scott Bailes	.05
96	Tom McKinnon RC	.05
97	Luis Rivera	.05
98	Mike Harkey	.05
99	Jeff Treadway	.05

#	Player	Price
100	Jose Canseco	.25
101	Omar Vizquel	.05
102	Scott Kamieniecki RC	.05
103	Ricky Jordan	.05
104	Jeff Ballard	.05
105	Felix Jose	.05
106	Mike Boddicker	.05
107	Dan Pasqua	.05
108	Mike Timlin RC	.10
109	Roger Craig	.05
110	Ryne Sandberg	.45
111	Mark Carreon	.05
112	Oscar Azocar	.05
113	Mike Greenwell	.05
114	Mark Portugal	.05
115	Terry Pendleton	.05
116	Willie Randolph	.05
117	Scott Terry	.05
118	Chili Davis	.05
119	Mark Gardner	.05
120	Alan Trammell	.05
121	Derek Bell	.05
122	Gary Varsho	.05
123	Bob Ojeda	.05
124	Shawn Livsey RC	.05
125	Chris Hoiles	.05
126	Rico Brogna, John Jaha, Ryan Klesko, Dave Staton Top Prospects-1st Baseman	.05
127	Carlos Quintana	.05
128	Kurt Stillwell	.05
129	Melido Perez	.05
130	Alvin Davis	.05
131	Checklist 1	.05
132	Eric Show	.05
133	Rance Mulliniks	.05
134	Darryl Kile	.05
135	Von Hayes	.05
136	Bill Doran	.05
137	Jeff Robinson	.05
138	Monty Fariss	.05
139	Jeff Innis	.05
140	Mark Grace	.05
141	Jim Leyland	.05
142	Todd Van Poppel	.05
143	Paul Gibson	.05
144	Bill Swift	.05
145	Danny Tartabull	.05
146	Al Newman	.05
147	Cris Carpenter	.05
148	Anthony Young RC	.05
149	Brian Bohanon RC	.05
150	Roger Clemens	.50
151	Jeff Hamilton	.05
152	Charlie Leibrandt	.05
153	Ron Karkovice	.05
154	Hensley Meulens	.05
155	Scott Bankhead	.05
156	Manny Ramirez RC	3.00
157	Keith Miller	.05
158	Todd Frohwirth	.05
159	Darrin Fletcher	.05
160	Bobby Bonilla	.05
161	Casey Candaele	.05
162	Paul Faries (RC)	.05
163	Dana Kiecker	.05
164	Shane Mack	.05
165	Mark Langston	.05
166	Geronimo Pena	.05
167	Andy Allanson	.05
168	Dwight Smith	.05
169	Chuck Crim	.05
170	Alex Cole	.05
171	Bill Plummer	.05
172	Juan Berenguer	.05
173	Brian Downing	.05
174	Steve Frey	.05
175	Orel Hershiser	.05
176	Ramon Garcia RC	.05
177	Danny Gladden	.05
178	Jim Acker	.05
179	Cesar Bernhardt, Bobby DeJardin, Armando Moreno, Andy Stankiewicz RC Top Prospects-2nd Baseman	.05
180	Kevin Mitchell	.05
181	Hector Villanueva	.05
182	Jeff Reardon	.05
183	Brent Mayne	.05
184	Jimmy Jones	.05
185	Benny Santiago	.05
186	Cliff Floyd RC	.50
187	Ernie Riles	.05
188	Jose Guzman	.05
189	Junior Felix	.05
190	Glenn Davis	.05
191	Charlie Hough	.05
192	Dave Fleming RC	.05
193	Omar Oliveras	.05
194	Eric Karros	.05
195	David Cone	.05

#	Player	Price
196	Frank Castillo RC	.05
197	Glenn Braggs	.05
198	Scott Aldred	.05
199	Jeff Blauser	.05
200	Len Dykstra	.05
201	Buck Showalter	.05
202	Rick Honeycutt	.05
203	Greg Myers	.05
204	Trevor Wilson	.05
205	Jay Howell	.05
206	Luis Sojo	.05
207	Jack Clark	.05
208	Julio Machado	.05
209	Lloyd McClendon	.05
210	Ozzie Guillen	.05
211	Jeremy Hernandez RC	.05
212	Randy Velarde	.05
213	Les Lancaster	.05
214	Andy Mota RC	.05
215	Rich Gossage	.05
216	Brent Gates RC	.05
217	Brian Harper	.05
218	Mike Flanagan	.05
219	Jerry Browne	.05
220	Jose Rijo	.05
221	Skeeter Barnes	.05
222	Jaime Navarro	.05
223	Mel Hall	.05
224	Brett Barberie RC	.05
225	Roberto Alomar	.15
226	Pete Smith	.05
227	Daryl Boston	.05
228	Eddie Whitson	.05
229	Shawn Boskie	.05
230	Dick Schofield	.05
231	Brian Drahman RC	.05
232	John Smiley	.05
233	Mitch Webster	.05
234	Terry Steinbach	.05
235	Jack Morris	.05
236	Bill Pecota	.05
237	Jose Hernandez RC	.05
238	Greg Litton	.05
239	Brian Holman	.05
240	Andres Galarraga	.05
241	Gerald Young	.05
242	Mike Mussina	.30
243	Alvaro Espinoza	.05
244	Darren Daulton	.05
245	John Smoltz	.05
246	Jason Pruitt RC	.05
247	Chuck Finley	.05
248	Jim Gantner	.05
249	Tony Fossas	.05
250	Ken Griffey	.05
251	Kevin Elster	.05
252	Dennis Rasmussen	.05
253	Terry Kennedy	.05
254	Ryan Bowen RC	.05
255	Robin Ventura	.05
256	Mike Aldrete	.05
257	Jeff Russell	.05
258	Jim Lindeman	.05
259	Ron Darling	.05
260	Devon White	.05
261	Tom Lasorda	.05
262	Terry Lee (RC)	.05
263	Bob Patterson	.05
264	Checklist 2	.05
265	Teddy Higuera	.05
266	Roberto Kelly	.05
267	Steve Bedrosian	.05
268	Brady Anderson	.05
269	Ruben Amaro RC	.05
270	Tony Gwynn	.45
271	Tracy Jones	.05
272	Jerry Don Gleaton	.05
273	Craig Grebeck	.05
274	Bob Scanlan RC	.05
275	Todd Zeile	.05
276	Shawn Green RC	1.50
277	Scott Chiamparino	.05
278	Darryl Hamilton	.05
279	Jim Clancy	.05
280	Carlos Martinez	.05
281	Kevin Appier	.05
282	John Wehner RC	.05
283	Reggie Sanders	.05
284	Gene Larkin	.05
285	Bob Welch	.05
286	Gilberto Reyes	.05
287	Pete Schourek	.05
288	Andujar Cedeno	.05
289	Mike Morgan	.05
290	Bo Jackson	.10
291	Phil Garner	.05
292	Ray Lankford	.05
293	Mike Henneman	.05
294	Dave Valle	.05
295	Alonzo Powell	.05
296	Tom Brunansky	.05
297	Kevin Brown	.05
298	Kelly Gruber	.05
299	Charles Nagy	.05

#	Player	Price	#	Player	Price	#	Player	Price	#	Player	Price
300	Don Mattingly	.50	404	Matt Nokes/AS	.05	504	Aaron Sele RC	.25	601	Dave Smith	.05
301	Kirk McCaskill	.05	405	Roger Clemens/AS	.25	505	Bobby Thigpen	.05	602	Mike Fetters	.05
302	Joey Cora	.05	406	Jim Abbott/AS	.05	506	Todd Benzinger	.05	603	Luis Mercedes RC	.05
303	Dan Plesac	.05	407	Bryan Harvey/AS	.05	507	Candy Maldonado	.05	604	Chris Gwynn	.05
304	Joe Oliver	.05	408	Bob Milacki	.05	508	Bill Gullickson	.05	605	Scott Erickson	.05
305	Tom Glavine	.25	409	Geno Petralli	.05	509	Doug Dascenzo	.05	606	Brook Jacoby	.05
306	Al Shirley RC	.05	410	Dave Stewart	.05	510	Frank Viola	.05	607	Todd Stottlemyre	.05
307	Bruce Ruffin	.05	411	Mike Jackson	.05	511	Kenny Rogers	.05	608	Scott Bradley	.05
308	Craig Shipley RC	.05	412	Luis Aquino	.05	512	Mike Heath	.05	609	Mike Hargrove	.05
309	Dave Martinez	.05	413	Tim Teufel	.05	513	Kevin Bass	.05	610	Eric Davis	.05
310	Jose Mesa	.05	414	Jeff Ware	.05	514	Kim Batiste RC	.05	611	Brian Hunter RC	.05
311	Henry Cotto	.05	415	Jim Deshaies	.05	515	Delino DeShields	.05	612	Pat Kelly	.05
312	Mike LaValliere	.05	416	Ellis Burks	.05	516	Ed Sprague RC	.05	613	Pedro Munoz	.05
313	Kevin Tapani	.05	417	Allan Anderson	.05	517	Jim Gott	.05	614	Al Osuna	.05
314	Jeff Huson	.05	418	Alfredo Griffin	.05	518	Jose Melendez RC	.05	615	Matt Merullo	.05
315	Juan Samuel	.05	419	Wally Whitehurst	.05	519	Hal McRae	.05	616	Larry Andersen	.05
316	Curt Schilling	.25	420	Sandy Alomar	.05	520	Jeff Bagwell	.35	617	Junior Ortiz	.05
317	Mike Bordick	.05	421	Juan Agosto	.05	521	Joe Hesketh	.05	618	Cesar Hernandez, Steve Hosey, Dan Peltier, Jeff McNeely RC Top Prospects-Outfielders	.10
318	Steve Howe	.05	422	Sam Horn	.05	522	Milt Cuyler	.05			
319	Tony Phillips	.05	423	Jeff Fassero RC	.05	523	Shawn Hillegas	.05			
320	George Bell	.05	424	Paul McClellan RC	.05	524	Don Slaught	.05			
321	Lou Pinella	.05	425	Cecil Fielder	.05	525	Randy Johnson	.35	619	Danny Jackson	.05
322	Tim Burke	.05	426	Tim Raines	.05	526	Doug Piatt RC	.05	620	George Brett	.50
323	Milt Thompson	.05	427	Eddie Taubensee RC	.05	527	Checklist 4	.05	621	Dan Gakeler RC	.05
324	Danny Darwin	.05	428	Dennis Boyd	.05	528	Steve Foster RC	.05	622	Steve Buechele	.05
325	Joe Orsulak	.05	429	Tony LaRussa	.05	529	Joe Girardi	.05	623	Bob Tewksbury	.05
326	Eric King	.05	430	Steve Sax	.05	530	Jim Abbott	.05	624	Shawn Estes RC	.25
327	Jay Buhner	.05	431	Tom Gordon	.05	531	Larry Walker	.05	625	Kevin McReynolds	.05
328	Joel Johnston RC	.05	432	Billy Hatcher	.05	532	Mike Huff	.05	626	Chris Haney RC	.05
329	Franklin Stubbs	.05	433	Cal Eldred	.05	533	Mackey Sasser	.05	627	Mike Sharperson	.05
330	Will Clark	.05	434	Wally Backman	.05	534	Benji Gil RC	.05	628	Mark Williamson	.05
331	Steve Lake	.05	435	Mark Eichhorn	.05	535	Dave Stieb	.05	629	Wally Joyner	.05
332	Chris Jones RC	.05	436	Mookie Wilson	.05	536	Willie Wilson	.05	630	Carlton Fisk	.35
333	Pat Tabler	.05	437	Scott Servais RC	.10	537	Mark Leiter RC	.05	631	Armando Reynoso RC	.05
334	Kevin Gross	.05	438	Mike Maddux	.05	538	Jose Uribe	.05	632	Felix Fermin	.05
335	Dave Henderson	.05	439	Chico Walker RC	.05	539	Thomas Howard	.05	633	Mitch Williams	.05
336	Greg Anthony RC	.05	440	Doug Drabek	.05	540	Ben McDonald	.05	634	Manuel Lee	.05
337	Alejandro Pena	.05	441	Rob Deer	.05	541	Jose Tolentino RC	.05	635	Harold Baines	.05
338	Shawn Abner	.05	442	Dave West	.05	542	Keith Mitchell RC	.05	636	Greg Harris	.05
339	Tom Browning	.05	443	Spike Owen	.05	543	Jerome Walton	.05	637	Orlando Merced	.05
340	Otis Nixon	.05	444	Tyrone Hill RC	.05	544	Cliff Brantley RC	.05	638	Chris Bosio	.05
341	Bob Geren	.05	445	Matt Williams	.05	545	Andy Van Slyke	.05	639	Wayne Housie	.05
342	Tim Spehr RC	.05	446	Mark Lewis	.05	546	Paul Sorrento	.05	640	Xavier Hernandez	.05
343	Jon Vander Wal RC	.20	447	David Segui	.05	547	Herm Winningham	.05	641	David Howard RC	.05
344	Jack Daugherty	.05	448	Tom Pagnozzi	.05	548	Mark Guthrie	.05	642	Tim Crews	.05
345	Zane Smith	.05	449	Jeff Johnson RC	.05	549	Joe Torre	.05	643	Rick Cerone	.05
346	Rheal Cormier RC	.05	450	Mark McGwire	.65	550	Darryl Strawberry	.05	644	Terry Leach	.05
347	Kent Hrbek	.05	451	Tom Henke	.05	551	Manny Alexander, Alex Arias, Wil Cordero, Chipper Jones Top Prospects-Shortstops	.25	645	Deion Sanders	.10
348	Rick Wilkins RC	.10	452	Wilson Alvarez	.05				646	Craig Wilson	.05
349	Steve Lyons	.05	453	Gary Redus	.05				647	Marquis Grissom	.05
350	Gregg Olson	.05	454	Darren Holmes	.05				648	Scott Fletcher	.05
351	Greg Riddoch	.05	455	Pete O'Brien	.05	552	Dave Gallagher	.05	649	Norm Charlton	.05
352	Ed Nunez	.05	456	Pat Combs	.05	553	Edgar Martinez	.05	650	Jesse Barfield	.05
353	Braulio Castillo RC	.05	457	Hubie Brooks	.05	554	Donald Harris	.05	651	Joe Slusarski RC	.05
354	Dave Bergman	.05	458	Frank Tanana	.05	555	Frank Thomas	.35	652	Bobby Rose	.05
355	Warren Newson RC	.05	459	Tom Kelly	.05	556	Storm Davis	.05	653	Dennis Lamp	.05
356	Luis Quinones	.05	460	Andre Dawson	.25	557	Dickie Thon	.05	654	Allen Watson RC	.05
357	Mike Witt	.05	461	Doug Jones	.05	558	Scott Garrelts	.05	655	Brett Butler	.05
358	Ted Wood RC	.05	462	Rich Rodriguez	.05	559	Steve Olin	.05	656	Rudy Pemberton, Henry Rodriguez, Lee Tinsley, Gerald Williams RC Top Prospects-Outfielders	.10
359	Mike Moore	.05	463	Mike Simms RC	.05	560	Rickey Henderson	.35			
360	Lance Parrish	.05	464	Mike Jeffcoat	.05	561	Jose Vizcaino	.05			
361	Barry Jones	.05	465	Barry Larkin	.05	562	Wade Taylor RC	.05			
362	Javier Ortiz RC	.05	466	Stan Belinda	.05	563	Pat Borders	.05	657	Dave Johnson	.05
363	John Candelaria	.05	467	Lonnie Smith	.05	564	Jimmy Gonzalez RC	.05	658	Checklist 5	.05
364	Glenallen Hill	.05	468	Greg Harris	.05	565	Lee Smith	.05	659	Brian McRae	.05
365	Duane Ward	.05	469	Jim Eisenreich	.05	566	Bill Sampen	.05	660	Fred McGriff	.05
366	Checklist 3	.05	470	Pedro Guerrero	.05	567	Dean Palmer	.05	661	Bill Landrum	.05
367	Rafael Belliard	.05	471	Jose DeJesus	.05	568	Bryan Harvey	.05	662	Juan Guzman	.05
368	Bill Krueger	.05	472	Rich Rowland RC	.05	569	Tony Pena	.05	663	Greg Gagne	.05
369	Steve Whitaker RC	.05	473	Frank Bolick, Craig Paquette, Tom Redington, Paul Russo RC Top Prospects- 3rd Baseman	.05	570	Lou Whitaker	.05	664	Ken Hill	.05
370	Shawon Dunston	.05				571	Randy Tomlin	.05	665	Dave Haas RC	.05
371	Dante Bichette	.05				572	Greg Vaughn	.05	666	Tom Foley	.05
372	Kip Gross RC	.05				573	Kelly Downs	.05	667	Roberto Hernandez RC	.10
373	Don Robinson	.05				574	Steve Avery	.05	668	Dwayne Henry	.05
374	Bernie Williams	.05	474	Mike Rossiter RC	.05	575	Kirby Puckett	.45	669	Jim Fregosi	.05
375	Bert Blyleven	.05	475	Robby Thompson	.05	576	Heathcliff Slocumb RC	.05	670	Harold Reynolds	.05
376	Chris Donnels RC	.05	476	Randy Bush	.05	577	Kevin Seitzer	.05	671	Mark Whiten	.05
377	Bob Zupcic RC	.05	477	Greg Hibbard	.05	578	Lee Guetterman	.05	672	Eric Plunk	.05
378	Joel Skinner	.05	478	Dale Sveum	.05	579	Johnny Oates	.05	673	Todd Hundley	.05
379	Steve Chitren	.05	479	Chito Martinez RC	.05	580	Greg Maddux	.45	674	Mo Sanford RC	.05
380	Barry Bonds	.75	480	Scott Sanderson	.05	581	Stan Javier	.05	675	Bobby Witt	.05
381	Sparky Anderson	.10	481	Tino Martinez	.05	582	Vicente Palacios	.05	676	Pat Mahomes, Sam Militello, Roger Salkeld, Turk Wendell RC Top Prospects-Pitchers	.15
382	Sid Fernandez	.05	482	Jimmy Key	.05	583	Mel Rojas	.05			
383	Dave Hollins	.05	483	Terry Shumpert	.05	584	Wayne Rosenthal RC	.05			
384	Mark Lee	.05	484	Mike Hartley	.05	585	Lenny Webster	.05			
385	Tim Wallach	.05	485	Chris Sabo	.05	586	Rod Nichols	.05			
386	Will Clark/AS	.05	486	Bob Walk	.05	587	Mickey Morandini	.05	677	John Marzano	.05
387	Ryne Sandberg/AS	.20	487	John Cerutti	.05	588	Russ Swan	.05	678	Joe Klink	.05
388	Howard Johnson/AS	.05	488	Scott Cooper	.05	589	Mariano Duncan	.05	679	Pete Incaviglia	.05
389	Barry Larkin/AS	.05	489	Bobby Cox	.05	590	Howard Johnson	.05	680	Dale Murphy	.15
390	Barry Bonds/AS	.40	490	Julio Franco	.05	591	Jacob Brumfield, Jeromy Burnitz, Alan Cockrell, D.J. Dozier Top Prospects-Outfielders	.25	681	Rene Gonzales	.05
391	Ron Gant/AS	.05	491	Jeff Brantley	.05				682	Andy Benes	.05
392	Bobby Bonilla/AS	.05	492	Mike Devereaux	.05				683	Jim Poole	.05
393	Craig Biggio/AS	.05	493	Jose Offerman	.05				684	Trever Miller RC	.10
394	Denny Martinez/AS	.05	494	Gary Thurman	.05	592	Denny Neagle RC	.10	685	Scott Livingstone RC	.05
395	Tom Glavine/AS	.05	495	Carney Lansford	.05	593	Steve Decker	.05	686	Rich DeLucia	.05
396	Lee Smith/AS	.05	496	Joe Grahe	.05	594	Brian Barber RC	.05	687	Harvey Pulliam RC	.05
397	Cecil Fielder/AS	.05	497	Andy Ashby RC	.10	595	Bruce Hurst	.05	688	Tim Belcher	.05
398	Julio Franco/AS	.05	498	Gerald Perry	.05	596	Kent Mercker	.05	689	Mark Lemke	.05
399	Wade Boggs/AS	.20	499	Dave Otto	.05	597	Mike Magnante RC	.05	690	John Franco	.05
400	Cal Ripken, Jr./AS	.40	500	Vince Coleman	.05	598	Jody Reed	.05	691	Walt Weiss	.05
401	Jose Canseco/AS	.15	501	Mark Malicoat RC	.05	599	Steve Searcy	.05	692	Scott Ruskin	.05
402	Joe Carter/AS	.05	502	Greg Briley	.05	600	Paul Molitor	.35	693	Jeff King	.05
403	Ruben Sierra/AS	.05	503	Pascual Perez	.05						

694	Mike Gardiner	.05
695	Gary Sheffield	.30
696	Joe Boever	.05
697	Mike Felder	.05
698	John Habyan	.05
699	Cito Gaston	.05
700	Ruben Sierra	.05
701	Scott Radinsky	.05
702	Lee Stevens	.05
703	Mark Wohlers RC	.05
704	Curt Young	.05
705	Dwight Evans	.05
706	Rob Murphy	.05
707	Gregg Jefferies	.05
708	Tom Bolton	.05
709	Chris James	.05
710	Kevin Maas	.05
711	Ricky Bones RC	.05
712	Curt Wilkerson	.05
713	Roger McDowell	.05
714	Calvin Reese RC	.10
715	Craig Biggio	.05
716	Kirk Dressendorfer RC	.05
717	Ken Dayley	.05
718	B.J. Surhoff	.05
719	Terry Mulholland	.05
720	Kirk Gibson	.05
721	Mike Pagliarulo	.05
722	Walt Terrell	.05
723	Jose Oquendo	.05
724	Kevin Morton	.05
725	Dwight Gooden	.05
726	Kirt Manwaring	.05
727	Chuck McElroy	.05
728	Dave Burba	.05
729	Art Howe	.05
730	Ramon Martinez	.05
731	Donnie Hill	.05
732	Nelson Santovenia	.05
733	Bob Melvin	.05
734	Scott Hatteberg RC	.10
735	Greg Swindell	.05
736	Lance Johnson	.05
737	Kevin Reimer	.05
738	Dennis Eckersley	.35
739	Rob Ducey	.05
740	Ken Caminiti	.05
741	Mark Gubicza	.05
742	Billy Spiers	.05
743	Darren Lewis	.05
744	Chris Hammond	.05
745	Dave Magadan	.05
746	Bernard Gilkey	.05
747	Willie Banks	.05
748	Matt Nokes	.05
749	Jerald Clark	.05
750	Travis Fryman	.05
751	Steve Wilson	.05
752	Billy Ripken	.05
753	Paul Assenmacher	.05
754	Charlie Hayes	.05
755	Alex Fernandez	.05
756	Gary Pettis	.05
757	Rob Dibble	.05
758	Tim Naehring	.05
759	Jeff Torborg	.05
760	Ozzie Smith	.45
761	Mike Fitzgerald	.05
762	John Burkett	.05
763	Kyle Abbott	.05
764	Tyler Green RC	.05
765	Pete Harnisch	.05
766	Mark Davis	.05
767	Kal Daniels	.05
768	Jim Thome	.35
769	Jack Howell	.05
770	Sid Bream	.05
771	Arthur Rhodes RC	.10
772	Garry Templeton	.05
773	Hal Morris	.05
774	Bud Black	.05
775	Ivan Calderon	.05
776	Doug Henry RC	.05
777	John Olerud	.05
778	Tim Leary	.05
779	Jay Bell	.05
780	Eddie Murray	.35
781	Paul Abbott	.05
782	Phil Plantier	.05
783	Joe Magrane	.05
784	Ken Patterson	.05
785	Albert Belle	.05
786	Royce Clayton	.05
787	Checklist 6	.05
788	Mike Stanton	.05
789	Bobby Valentine	.05
790	Joe Carter	.05
791	Danny Cox	.05
792	Dave Winfield	.35

1992 Topps Gold

NM/M

Unopened Fact. Set (793):		75.00
Complete Set (792):		35.00
Common Player:		.20

(Star cards valued at 4X corresponding cards in regular-issue 1992 Topps.)

793	Brien Taylor (Autographed edition of 12,000; factory sets only.)	7.50

Traded

NM/M

Complete Set (132):		50.00
Common Player:		.05
Golds:		2-4X
1	Willie Adams RC (USA)	.05
2	Jeff Alkire (USA)	.05
3	Felipe Alou	.05
4	Moises Alou	.10
5	Ruben Amaro	.05
6	Jack Armstrong	.05
7	Scott Bankhead	.05
8	Tim Belcher	.05
9	George Bell	.05
10	Freddie Benavides	.05
11	Todd Benzinger	.05
12	Joe Boever	.05
13	Ricky Bones	.05
14	Bobby Bonilla	.05
15	Hubie Brooks	.05
16	Jerry Browne	.05
17	Jim Bullinger	.05
18	Dave Burba	.05
19	Kevin Campbell	.05
20	Tom Candiotti	.05
21	Mark Carreon	.05
22	Gary Carter	.75
23	Archi Cianfrocco	.05
24	Phil Clark	.05
25	Chad Curtis RC	.50
26	Eric Davis	.05
27	Tim Davis (USA)	.05
28	Gary DiSarcina	.05
29	Darren Dreifort (USA)	.05
30	Mariano Duncan	.05
31	Mike Fitzgerald	.05
32	John Flaherty	.05
33	Darrin Fletcher	.05
34	Scott Fletcher	.05
35	Ron Fraser (USA)	.05
36	Andres Galarraga	.05
37	Dave Gallagher	.05
38	Mike Gallego	.05
39	Nomar Garciaparra RC (USA)	30.00
40	Jason Giambi (USA)	1.00
41	Danny Gladden	.05
42	Rene Gonzales	.05

43	Jeff Granger (USA)	.05
44	Rick Greene (USA)	.05
45	Jeffrey Hammonds (USA)	.05
46	Charlie Hayes	.05
47	Von Hayes	.05
48	Rick Helling (USA)	.05
49	Butch Henry	.05
50	Carlos Hernandez	.05
51	Ken Hill	.05
52	Butch Hobson	.05
53	Vince Horsman	.05
54	Pete Incaviglia	.05
55	Gregg Jefferies	.05
56	Charles Johnson (USA)	.05
57	Doug Jones	.05
58	Brian Jordan RC	2.00
59	Wally Joyner	.05
60	Daron Kirkreit RC (USA)	.20
61	Bill Krueger	.05
62	Gene Lamont	.05
63	Jim Lefebvre	.05
64	Danny Leon RC	.05
65	Pat Listach	.05
66	Kenny Lofton	.05
67	Dave Martinez	.05
68	Derrick May	.05
69	Kirk McCaskill	.05
70	Chad McConnell RC (USA)	.05
71	Kevin McReynolds	.05
72	Rusty Meacham	.05
73	Keith Miller	.05
74	Kevin Mitchell	.05
75	Jason Moler RC (USA)	.05
76	Mike Morgan	.05
77	Jack Morris	.05
78	Calvin Murray RC (USA)	.05
79	Eddie Murray	.75
80	Randy Myers	.05
81	Denny Neagle	.05
82	Phil Nevin (USA)	.10
83	Dave Nilsson	.05
84	Junior Ortiz	.05
85	Donovan Osborne	.05
86	Bill Pecota	.05
87	Melido Perez	.05
88	Mike Perez	.05
89	Hipolito Pena	.05
90	Willie Randolph	.05
91	Darren Reed	.05
92	Bip Roberts	.05
93	Chris Roberts (USA)	.05
94	Steve Rodriguez (USA)	.05
95	Bruce Ruffin	.05
96	Scott Ruskin	.05
97	Bret Saberhagen	.05
98	Rey Sanchez	.05
99	Steve Sax	.05
100	Curt Schilling	.25
101	Dick Schofield	.05
102	Gary Scott	.05
103	Kevin Seitzer	.05
104	Frank Seminara	.05
105	Gary Sheffield	.35
106	John Smiley	.05
107	Cory Snyder	.05
108	Paul Sorrento	.05
109	Sammy Sosa	1.50
110	Matt Stairs RC	.25
111	Andy Stankiewicz	.05
112	Kurt Stillwell	.05
113	Rick Sutcliffe	.05
114	Bill Swift	.05
115	Jeff Tackett	.05
116	Danny Tartabull	.05
117	Eddie Taubensee	.05
118	Dickie Thon	.05
119	Michael Tucker RC (USA)	.25
120	Scooter Tucker	.05
121	Marc Valdes RC (USA)	.05
122	Julio Valera	.05
123	Jason Varitek RC (USA)	15.00
124	Ron Villone RC (USA)	.05
125	Frank Viola	.05
126	B.J. Wallace RC (USA)	.05
127	Dan Walters (RC)	.05
128	Craig Wilson (USA)	.05
129	Chris Wimmer (USA)	.05
130	Dave Winfield	.75
131	Herm Winningham	.05
132	Checklist	

Traded Gold

NM/M

Complete Unopened Set (132):		75.00
Complete Set (132):		65.00
Common Player:		.25
Stars/Rookies:		4X

(See 1992 Topps Traded for checklist and base card values.)

1993 Topps

Andy Van Slyke — Pirates

NM/M

Unopened Fact. Set (847):		40.00
Complete Set (825):		30.00
Common Player:		.05
Series 1 Wax Pack (15):		1.00
Series 1 Wax Box (36):		25.00
Series 2 Wax Pack (15):		.75
Series 2 Wax Box (36):		15.00
Series 1 Jumbo Pack (41):		2.00
Series 1 Jumbo Box (24):		30.00
Series 2 Jumbo Pack (41):		1.50
Series 2 Jumbo Box (24):		20.00
1	Robin Yount	.50
2	Barry Bonds	1.00
3	Ryne Sandberg	.60
4	Roger Clemens	.65
5	Tony Gwynn	.60
6	Jeff Tackett RC	.05
7	Pete Incaviglia	.05
8	Mark Wohlers	.05
9	Kent Hrbek	.05
10	Will Clark	.05
11	Eric Karros	.05
12	Lee Smith	.05
13	Esteban Beltre	.05
14	Greg Briley	.05
15	Marquis Grissom	.05
16	Dan Plesac	.05
17	Dave Hollins	.05
18	Terry Steinbach	.05
19	Ed Nunez	.05
20	Tim Salmon	.05
21	Luis Salazar	.05
22	Jim Eisenreich	.05
23	Todd Stottlemyre	.05
24	Tim Naehring	.05
25	John Franco	.05
26	Skeeter Barnes	.05
27	Carlos Garcia RC	.05
28	Joe Orsulak	.05
29	Dwayne Henry	.05
30	Fred McGriff	.05
31	Derek Lilliquist	.05
32	Don Mattingly	.65
33	B.J. Wallace (1992 Draft Pick)	.05
34	Juan Gonzalez	.25
35	John Smoltz	.05
36	Scott Servais	.05
37	Lenny Webster	.05
38	Chris James	.05
39	Roger McDowell	.05
40	Ozzie Smith	.60
41	Alex Fernandez	.05
42	Spike Owen	.05
43	Ruben Amaro	.05
44	Kevin Seitzer	.05

#	Player	Price
45	Dave Fleming	.05
46	Eric Fox **RC**	.05
47	Bob Scanlan	.05
48	Bert Blyleven	.05
49	Brian McRae	.05
50	Roberto Alomar	.20
51	Mo Vaughn	.05
52	Bobby Bonilla	.05
53	Frank Tanana	.05
54	Mike LaValliere	.05
55	Mark McLemore	.05
56	Chad Mottola **RC** (1992 Draft Pick)	.10
57	Norm Charlton	.05
58	Jose Melendez	.05
59	Carlos Martinez	.05
60	Roberto Kelly	.05
61	Gene Larkin	.05
62	Rafael Belliard	.05
63	Al Osuna	.05
64	Scott Chiamparino	.05
65	Brett Butler	.05
66	John Burkett	.05
67	Felix Jose	.05
68	Omar Vizquel	.05
69	John Vander Wal	.05
70	Roberto Hernandez	.05
71	Ricky Bones	.05
72	Jeff Grotewold **RC**	.05
73	Mike Moore	.05
74	Steve Buechele	.05
75	Juan Guzman	.05
76	Kevin Appier	.05
77	Junior Felix	.05
78	Greg Harris	.05
79	Dick Schofield	.05
80	Cecil Fielder	.05
81	Lloyd McClendon	.05
82	David Segui	.05
83	Reggie Sanders	.05
84	Kurt Stillwell	.05
85	Sandy Alomar	.05
86	John Habyan	.05
87	Kevin Reimer	.05
88	Mike Stanton	.05
89	Eric Anthony	.05
90	Scott Erickson	.05
91	Craig Colbert	.05
92	Tom Pagnozzi	.05
93	Pedro Astacio **RC**	.10
94	Lance Johnson	.05
95	Larry Walker	.05
96	Russ Swan	.05
97	Scott Fletcher	.05
98	Derek Jeter **RC** (1992 Draft Pick)	10.00
99	Mike Williams **RC**	.05
100	Mark McGwire	.85
101	Jim Bullinger **RC**	.05
102	Brian Hunter	.05
103	Jody Reed	.05
104	Mike Butcher **RC**	.05
105	Gregg Jefferies	.05
106	Howard Johnson	.05
107	John Kiely **RC**	.05
108	Jose Lind	.05
109	Sam Horn	.05
110	Barry Larkin	.05
111	Bruce Hurst	.05
112	Brian Barnes	.05
113	Thomas Howard	.05
114	Mel Hall	.05
115	Robby Thompson	.05
116	Mark Lemke	.05
117	Eddie Taubensee	.05
118	David Hulse	.05
119	Pedro Munoz	.05
120	Ramon Martinez	.05
121	Todd Worrell	.05
122	Joey Cora	.05
123	Moises Alou	.05
124	Franklin Stubbs	.05
125	Pete O'Brien	.05
126	Bob Ayrault **RC**	.05
127	Carney Lansford	.05
128	Kal Daniels	.05
129	Joe Grahe	.05
130	Jeff Montgomery	.05
131	Dave Winfield	.50
132	Preston Wilson **RC** (1992 Draft Pick)	.75
133	Steve Wilson	.05
134	Lee Guetterman	.05
135	Mickey Tettleton	.05
136	Jeff King	.05
137	Alan Mills	.05
138	Joe Oliver	.05
139	Gary Gaetti	.05
140	Gary Sheffield	.30
141	Dennis Cook	.05
142	Charlie Hayes	.05
143	Jeff Huson	.05
144	Kent Mercker	.05
145	Eric Young **RC**	.10
146	Scott Leius	.05
147	Bryan Hickerson	.05
148	Steve Finley	.05
149	Rheal Cormier	.05
150	Frank Thomas	.50
151	Archi Cianfrocco **RC**	.05
152	Rich DeLucia	.05
153	Greg Vaughn	.05
154	Wes Chamberlain	.05
155	Dennis Eckersley	.40
156	Sammy Sosa	.60
157	Gary DiSarcina	.05
158	Kevin Koslofski **RC**	.05
159	Doug Linton **RC**	.05
160	Lou Whitaker	.05
161	Chad McDonnell (1992 Draft Pick)	.05
162	Joe Hesketh	.05
163	Tim Wakefield **RC**	.10
164	Leo Gomez	.05
165	Jose Rijo	.05
166	Tim Scott **RC**	.05
167	Steve Olin	.05
168	Kevin Maas	.05
169	Kenny Rogers	.05
170	Dave Justice	.05
171	Doug Jones	.05
172	Jeff Reboulet **RC**	.05
173	Andres Galarraga	.05
174	Randy Velarde	.05
175	Kirk McCaskill	.05
176	Darren Lewis	.05
177	Lenny Harris	.05
178	Jeff Fassero	.05
179	Ken Griffey Jr.	.75
180	Darren Daulton	.05
181	John Jaha	.05
182	Ron Darling	.05
183	Greg Maddux	.60
184	Damion Easley **RC**	.10
185	Jack Morris	.05
186	Mike Magnante	.05
187	John Dopson	.05
188	Sid Fernandez	.05
189	Tony Phillips	.05
190	Doug Drabek	.05
191	Sean Lowe **RC** (1992 Draft Pick)	.05
192	Bob Milacki	.05
193	Steve Foster **RC**	.05
194	Jerald Clark	.05
195	Pete Harnisch	.05
196	Pat Kelly	.05
197	Jeff Frye	.05
198	Alejandro Pena	.05
199	Junior Ortiz	.05
200	Kirby Puckett	.60
201	Jose Uribe	.05
202	Mike Scioscia	.05
203	Bernard Gilkey	.05
204	Dan Pasqua	.05
205	Gary Carter	.50
206	Henry Cotto	.05
207	Paul Molitor	.50
208	Mike Hartley	.05
209	Jeff Parrett	.05
210	Mark Langston	.05
211	Doug Dascenzo	.05
212	Rick Reed	.05
213	Candy Maldonado	.05
214	Danny Darwin	.05
215	Pat Howell **(RC) RC**	.05
216	Mark Leiter	.05
217	Kevin Mitchell	.05
218	Ben McDonald	.05
219	Bip Roberts	.05
220	Benny Santiago	.05
221	Carlos Baerga	.05
222	Bernie Williams	.05
223	Roger Pavlik **RC**	.05
224	Sid Bream	.05
225	Matt Williams	.05
226	Willie Banks	.05
227	Jeff Bagwell	.50
228	Tom Goodwin	.05
229	Mike Perez	.05
230	Carlton Fisk	.50
231	John Wetteland	.05
232	Tino Martinez	.05
233	Rick Greene **RC** (1992 Draft Pick)	.05
234	Tim McIntosh	.05
235	Mitch Williams	.05
236	Kevin Campbell **RC**	.05
237	Jose Vizcaino	.05
238	Chris Donnels	.05
239	Mike Boddicker	.05
240	John Olerud	.05
241	Mike Gardiner	.05
242	Charlie O'Brien	.05
243	Rob Deer	.05
244	Denny Neagle	.05
245	Chris Sabo	.05
246	Gregg Olson	.05
247	Frank Seminara	.05
248	Scott Scudder	.05
249	Tim Burke	.05
250	Chuck Knoblauch	.05
251	Mike Bielecki	.05
252	Xavier Hernandez	.05
253	Jose Guzman	.05
254	Cory Snyder	.05
255	Orel Hershiser	.05
256	Wil Cordero	.05
257	Luis Alicea	.05
258	Mike Schooler	.05
259	Craig Grebeck	.05
260	Duane Ward	.05
261	Bill Wegman	.05
262	Mickey Morandini	.05
263	Vince Horsman **RC**	.05
264	Paul Sorrento	.05
265	Andre Dawson	.25
266	Rene Gonzales	.05
267	Keith Miller	.05
268	Derek Bell	.05
269	Todd Steverson **RC** (1992 Draft Pick)	.05
270	Frank Viola	.05
271	Wally Whitehurst	.05
272	Kurt Knudsen **RC**	.05
273	Dan Walters **RC**	.05
274	Rick Sutcliffe	.05
275	Andy Van Slyke	.05
276	Paul O'Neill	.05
277	Mark Whiten	.05
278	Chris Nabholz	.05
279	Todd Burns	.05
280	Tom Glavine	.25
281	Butch Henry **RC**	.05
282	Shane Mack	.05
283	Mike Jackson	.05
284	Henry Rodriguez	.05
285	Bob Tewksbury	.05
286	Ron Karkovice	.05
287	Mike Gallego	.05
288	Dave Cochrane	.05
289	Jesse Orosco	.05
290	Dave Stewart	.05
291	Tommy Greene	.05
292	Rey Sanchez	.05
293	Rob Ducey	.05
294	Brent Mayne	.05
295	Dave Stieb	.05
296	Luis Rivera	.05
297	Jeff Innis	.05
298	Scott Livingstone	.05
299	Bob Patterson	.05
300	Cal Ripken, Jr.	1.00
301	Cesar Hernandez	.05
302	Randy Myers	.05
303	Brook Jacoby	.05
304	Melido Perez	.05
305	Rafael Palmeiro	.40
306	Damon Berryhill	.05
307	Dan Serafini **RC** (1992 Draft Pick)	.05
308	Darryl Kile	.05
309	J.T. Bruett **RC**	.05
310	Dave Righetti	.05
311	Jay Howell	.05
312	Geronimo Pena	.05
313	Greg Hibbard	.05
314	Mark Gardner	.05
315	Edgar Martinez	.05
316	Dave Nilsson	.05
317	Kyle Abbott	.05
318	Willie Wilson	.05
319	Paul Assenmacher	.05
320	Tim Fortugno **RC**	.05
321	Rusty Meacham	.05
322	Pat Borders	.05
323	Mike Greenwell	.05
324	Willie Randolph	.05
325	Bill Gullickson	.05
326	Gary Varsho	.05
327	Tim Hulett	.05
328	Scott Ruskin	.05
329	Mike Maddux	.05
330	Danny Tartabull	.05
331	Kenny Lofton	.05
332	Geno Petralli	.05
333	Otis Nixon	.05
334	Jason Kendall **RC** (1992 Draft Pick)	.50
335	Mark Portugal	.05
336	Mike Pagliarulo	.05
337	Kirt Manwaring	.05
338	Bob Ojeda	.05
339	Mark Clark **RC**	.05
340	John Kruk	.05
341	Mel Rojas	.05
342	Erik Hanson	.05
343	Doug Henry	.05
344	Jack McDowell	.05
345	Harold Baines	.05
346	Chuck McElroy	.05
347	Luis Sojo	.05
348	Andy Stankiewicz	.05
349	Hipolito Pichardo **RC**	.05
350	Joe Carter	.05
351	Ellis Burks	.05
352	Pete Schourek	.05
353	Buddy Groom **RC**	.05
354	Jay Bell	.05
355	Brady Anderson	.05
356	Freddie Benavides	.05
357	Phil Stephenson	.05
358	Kevin Wickander	.05
359	Mike Stanley	.05
360	Ivan Rodriguez	.40
361	Scott Bankhead	.05
362	Luis Gonzalez	.05
363	John Smiley	.05
364	Trevor Wilson	.05
365	Tom Candiotti	.05
366	Craig Wilson	.05
367	Steve Sax	.05
368	Delino Deshields	.05
369	Jaime Navarro	.05
370	Dave Valle	.05
371	Mariano Duncan	.05
372	Rod Nichols	.05
373	Mike Morgan	.05
374	Julio Valera	.05
375	Wally Joyner	.05
376	Tom Henke	.05
377	Herm Winningham	.05
378	Orlando Merced	.05
379	Mike Munoz	.05
380	Todd Hundley	.05
381	Mike Flanagan	.05
382	Tim Belcher	.05
383	Jerry Browne	.05
384	Mike Benjamin	.05
385	Jim Leyritz	.05
386	Ray Lankford	.05
387	Devon White	.05
388	Jeremy Hernandez	.05
389	Brian Harper	.05
390	Wade Boggs	.60
391	Derrick May	.05
392	Travis Fryman	.05
393	Ron Gant	.05
394	Checklist 1-132	.05
395	Checklist 133-264	.05
396	Checklist 265-396	.05
397	George Brett	.65
398	Bobby Witt	.05
399	Daryl Boston	.05
400	Bo Jackson	.10
401	Fred McGriff, Frank Thomas/AS	.20
402	Ryne Sandberg, Carlos Baerga/AS	.30
403	Gary Sheffield, Edgar Martinez/AS	.05
404	Barry Larkin, Travis Fryman/AS	.05
405	Andy Van Slyke, Ken Griffey Jr./AS	.40
406	Larry Walker, Kirby Puckett/AS	.20
407	Barry Bonds, Joe Carter/AS	.50
408	Darren Daulton, Brian Harper/AS	.05
409	Greg Maddux, Roger Clemens/AS	.25
410	Tom Glavine, Dave Fleming/AS	.05
411	Lee Smith, Dennis Eckersley/AS	.15
412	Jamie McAndrew	.05
413	Pete Smith	.05
414	Juan Guerrero	.05
415	Todd Frohwirth	.05
416	Randy Tomlin	.05
417	B.J. Surhoff	.05
418	Jim Gott	.05
419	Mark Thompson (1992 Draft Pick)	.05
420	Kevin Tapani	.05
421	Curt Schilling	.25
422	J.T. Snow **RC**	.40
423	Ryan Klesko, Ivan Cruz, Bubba Smith, Larry Sutton Top Prospects 1B	.05
424	John Valentin	.05
425	Joe Girardi	.05
426	Nigel Wilson **RC**	.05
427	Bob MacDonald	.05
428	Todd Zeile	.05
429	Milt Cuyler	.05
430	Eddie Murray	.50
431	Rich Amaral	.05
432	Pete Young	.05
433	Roger Bailey, Tom Schmidt Rockies Future Stars	
434	Jack Armstrong	.05
435	Willie McGee	.05
436	Greg Harris	.05

#	Name	Value
437	Chris Hammond	.05
438	Ritchie Moody RC	
	(1992 Draft Pick)	.05
439	Bryan Harvey	.05
440	Ruben Sierra	.05
441	Don Lemon, Todd Pridy	
	Marlins Future Stars	.05
442	Kevin McReynolds	.05
443	Terry Leach	.05
444	David Nied	.05
445	Dale Murphy	.15
446	Luis Mercedes	.05
447	Keith Shepherd RC	.05
448	Ken Caminiti	.05
449	James Austin	.05
450	Darryl Strawberry	.05
451	Ramon Caraballo,	
	Jon Shave, Brent Gates,	
	Quinton McCracken RC	
	Top Prospects 2B	.10
452	Bob Wickman	.05
453	Victor Cole	.05
454	John Johnstone RC	.05
455	Chili Davis	.05
456	Scott Taylor	.05
457	Tracy Woodson	.05
458	David Wells	.05
459	Derek Wallace RC	
	(1992 Draft Pick)	.05
460	Randy Johnson	.50
461	Steve Reed RC	.05
462	Felix Fermin	.05
463	Scott Aldred	.05
464	Greg Colbrunn	.05
465	Tony Fernandez	.05
466	Mike Felder	.05
467	Lee Stevens	.05
468	Matt Whiteside	.05
469	Dave Hansen	.05
470	Rob Dibble	.05
471	Dave Gallagher	.05
472	Chris Gwynn	.05
473	Dave Henderson	.05
474	Ozzie Guillen	.05
475	Jeff Reardon	.05
476	Mark Voisard, Will Scalzitti	
	Rockies Future Stars	.05
477	Jimmy Jones	.05
478	Greg Cadaret	.05
479	Todd Pratt	.05
480	Pat Listach	.05
481	Ryan Luzinski RC	
	(1992 Draft Pick)	.05
482	Darren Reed	.05
483	Brian Griffiths RC	.05
484	John Wehner	.05
485	Glenn Davis	.05
486	Eric Wedge RC	.05
487	Jesse Hollins	.05
488	Manuel Lee	.05
489	Scott Fredrickson RC	.05
490	Omar Olivares	.05
491	Shawn Hare	.05
492	Tom Lampkin	.05
493	Jeff Nelson	.05
494	Kevin Young,	
	Adell Davenport,	
	Eduardo Perez, Lou Lucca	
	Top Prospects 3B	.05
495	Ken Hill	.05
496	Reggie Jefferson	.05
497	Matt Petersen, Willie Brown	
	Marlins Future Stars	.05
498	Bud Black	.05
499	Chuck Crim	.05
500	Jose Canseco	.30
501	Johnny Oates, Bobby Cox	
	Major League Managers	.05
502	Butch Hobson,	
	Jim Lefebvre Major	
	League Managers	.05
503	Buck Rodgers, Tony Perez	
	Major League Managers	.05
504	Gene Lamont, Don Baylor	
	Major League Managers	.05
505	Mike Hargrove,	
	Rene Lachemann Major	
	League Managers	.05
506	Sparky Anderson, Art Howe	
	Major League Managers	.10
507	Hal McRae, Tommy Lasorda	
	Major League Managers	.05
508	Phil Garner, Felipe Alou	
	Major League Manager	.05
509	Tom Kelly, Jeff Torborg	
	Major League Managers	.05
510	Buck Showalter, Jim Fregosi	
	Major League Managers	.05
511	Tony LaRussa, Jim Leyland	
	Major League Managers	.05
512	Lou Piniella, Joe Torre Major	
	League Managers	.10
513	Toby Harrah, Jim Riggleman	
	Major League Managers	.05

#	Name	Value
514	Cito Gaston, Dusty Baker	
	Major League Managers	.05
515	Greg Swindell	.05
516	Alex Arias	.05
517	Bill Pecota	.05
518	Benji Grigsby RC	
	(1992 Draft Pick)	.05
519	David Howard	.05
520	Charlie Hough	.05
521	Kevin Flora	.05
522	Shane Reynolds	.05
523	Doug Bochtler RC	.05
524	Chris Hoiles	.05
525	Scott Sanderson	.05
526	Mike Sharperson	.05
527	Mike Fetters	.05
528	Paul Quantrill	.05
529	Dave Silvestri,	
	Chipper Jones, Benji Gil,	
	Jeff Patzke	
	Top Propsects SS	.25
530	Sterling Hitchcock	.05
531	Joe Millette	.05
532	Tom Brunansky	.05
533	Frank Castillo	.05
534	Randy Knorr	.05
535	Jose Oquendo	.05
536	Dave Haas	.05
537	Jason Hutchins,	
	Ryan Turner	
	Rockies Future Stars	.05
538	Jimmy Baron	
	(1992 Draft Pick)	.05
539	Kerry Woodson	.05
540	Ivan Calderon	.05
541	Denis Boucher	.05
542	Royce Clayton	.05
543	Reggie Williams	.05
544	Steve Decker	.05
545	Dean Palmer	.05
546	Hal Morris	.05
547	Ryan Thompson RC	.05
548	Lance Blankenship	.05
549	Hensley Meulens	.05
550	Scott Radinsky	.05
551	Eric Young RC	.10
552	Jeff Blauser	.05
553	Andujar Cedeno	.05
554	Arthur Rhodes	.05
555	Terry Mulholland	.05
556	Darryl Hamilton	.05
557	Pedro Martinez	.50
558	Ryan Whitman,	
	Mark Skeels	
	Marlins Future Stars	.05
559	Jamie Arnold RC	
	(1992 Draft Pick)	.05
560	Zane Smith	.05
561	Matt Nokes	.05
562	Bob Zupcic	.05
563	Shawn Boskie	.05
564	Mike Timlin	.05
565	Jerald Clark	.05
566	Rod Brewer	.05
567	Mark Carreon	.05
568	Andy Benes	.05
569	Shawn Barton	.05
570	Tim Wallach	.05
571	Dave Mlicki	.05
572	Trevor Hoffman	.05
573	John Patterson	.05
574	DeShawn Warren	
	(1992 Draft Pick)	.05
575	Monty Fariss	.05
576	Darrell Sherman,	
	Damon Buford, Cliff Floyd,	
	Michael Moore Top	
	Prospects OF	.05
577	Tim Costo	.05
578	Dave Magadan	.05
579	Neil Garret, Jason Bates	
	Rockies Future Stars	.05
580	Walt Weiss	.05
581	Chris Haney	.05
582	Shawn Abner	.05
583	Marvin Freeman	.05
584	Casey Candaele	.05
585	Ricky Jordan	.05
586	Jeff Tabaka	.05
587	Manny Alexander	.05
588	Mike Trombley	.05
589	Carlos Hernandez	.05
590	Cal Eldred	.05
591	Alex Cole	.05
592	Phil Plantier	.05
593	Brett Merriman	.05
594	Jerry Nielsen	.05
595	Shawon Dunston	.05
596	Jimmy Key	.05
597	Gerald Perry	.05
598	Rico Brogna	.05
599	Clemente Nunez,	
	Dan Robinson	
	Marlins Future Stars	.05

#	Name	Value
600	Bret Saberhagen	.05
601	Craig Shipley	.05
602	Henry Mercedes	.05
603	Jim Thome	.40
604	Rod Beck	.05
605	Chuck Finley	.05
606	J. Owens	.05
607	Dan Smith	.05
608	Bill Doran	.05
609	Lance Parrish	.05
610	Denny Martinez	.05
611	Tom Gordon	.05
612	Byron Mathews	
	(1992 Draft Pick)	.05
613	Joel Adamson	.05
614	Brian Williams	.05
615	Steve Avery	.05
616	Matt Mieske,	
	Tracy Sanders,	
	Midre Cummings,	
	Ryan Freeburg	
	Top Prospects OF	.05
617	Craig Lefferts	.05
618	Tony Pena	.05
619	Billy Spiers	.05
620	Todd Benzinger	.05
621	Mike Kotarski, Greg Boyd	
	Rockies Future Stars	.05
622	Ben Rivera	.05
623	Al Martin	.05
624	Sam Militello	.05
625	Rick Aguilera	.05
626	Danny Gladden	.05
627	Andres Berumen	.05
628	Kelly Gruber	.05
629	Cris Carpenter	.05
630	Mark Grace	.05
631	Jeff Brantley	.05
632	Chris Widger	
	(1992 Draft Pick)	.05
633	Rodolf Razjigaev,	
	Evgenyi Puchkov,	
	Ilya Bogatyrev Russian	
	Angels	.10
634	Mo Sanford	.05
635	Albert Belle	.05
636	Tim Teufel	.05
637	Greg Myers	.05
638	Brian Bohanon	.05
639	Mike Bordick	.05
640	Dwight Gooden	.05
641	Pat Leahy, Gavin Baugh	
	Marlins Future Stars	.05
642	Milt Hill	.05
643	Luis Aquino	.05
644	Dante Bichette	.05
645	Bobby Thigpen	.05
646	Rich Scheid	.05
647	Brian Sackinsky	
	(1992 Draft Pick)	.05
648	Ryan Hawblitzel	.05
649	Tom Marsh	.05
650	Terry Pendleton	.05
651	Rafael Bournigal RC	.05
652	Dave West	.05
653	Steve Hosey	.05
654	Gerald Williams	.05
655	Scott Cooper	.05
656	Gary Scott	.05
657	Mike Harkey	.05
658	Jeromy Burnitz,	
	Melvin Nieves,	
	Rich Becker, Shon Walker	
	Top Prospects OF	.05
659	Ed Sprague	.05
660	Alan Trammell	.05
661	Garvin Alston, Mike Case	
	Rockies Future Stars	.05
662	Donovan Osborne	.05
663	Jeff Gardner	.05
664	Calvin Jones	.05
665	Darrin Fletcher	.05
666	Glenallen Hill	.05
667	Jim Rosenbohm	
	(1992 Draft Pick)	.05
668	Scott Lewis	.05
669	Kip Yaughn	.05
670	Julio Franco	.05
671	Dave Martinez	.05
672	Kevin Bass	.05
673	Todd Van Poppel	.05
674	Mark Gubicza	.05
675	Tim Raines	.05
676	Rudy Seanez	.05
677	Charlie Leibrandt	.05
678	Randy Milligan	.05
679	Kim Batiste	.05
680	Craig Biggio	.05
681	Darren Holmes	.05
682	John Candelaria	.05
683	Jerry Stafford,	
	Eddie Christian	
	Marlins Future Stars	.05
684	Pat Mahomes	.05

#	Name	Value
685	Bob Walk	.05
686	Russ Springer	.05
687	Tony Sheffield	
	(1992 Draft Picks)	.05
688	Dwight Smith	.05
689	Eddie Zosky	.05
690	Bien Figueroa	.05
691	Jim Tatum	.05
692	Chad Kreuter	.05
693	Rich Rodriguez	.05
694	Shane Turner	.05
695	Kent Bottenfield	.05
696	Jose Mesa	.05
697	Darrell Whitmore RC	.05
698	Ted Wood	.05
699	Chad Curtis	.05
700	Nolan Ryan	1.00
701	Mike Piazza,	
	Carlos Delgado,	
	Brook Fordyce,	
	Donnie Leshnock	
	Top Prospects C	.85
702	Tim Pugh RC	.05
703	Jeff Kent	.05
704	Jon Goodrich,	
	Danny Figueroa	
	Rockies Future Stars	.05
705	Bob Welch	.05
706	Sherard Clinkscales	
	(1992 Draft Pick)	.05
707	Donn Pall	.05
708	Greg Olson	.05
709	Jeff Juden	.05
710	Mike Mussina	.30
711	Scott Chiamparino	.05
712	Stan Javier	.05
713	John Doherty	.05
714	Kevin Gross	.05
715	Greg Gagne	.05
716	Steve Cooke	.05
717	Steve Farr	.05
718	Jay Buhner	.05
719	Butch Henry	.05
720	David Cone	.05
721	Rick Wilkins	.05
722	Chuck Carr	.05
723	Kenny Felder RC	
	(1992 Draft Pick)	.05
724	Guillermo Velasquez	.05
725	Billy Hatcher	.05
726	Mike Veneziale,	
	Ken Kendrena	
	Marlins Future Stars	.05
727	Jonathan Hurst	.05
728	Steve Frey	.05
729	Mark Leonard	.05
730	Charles Nagy	.05
731	Donald Harris	.05
732	Travis Buckley	.05
733	Tom Browning	.05
734	Anthony Young	.05
735	Steve Shifflett	.05
736	Jeff Russell	.05
737	Wilson Alvarez	.05
738	Lance Painter	.05
739	Dave Weathers	.05
740	Len Dykstra	.05
741	Mike Devereaux	.05
742	Rene Arocha,	
	Alan Embree,	
	Tim Crabtree, Brien Taylor	
	Top Prospects/SP	.05
743	Dave Landaker	
	(1992 Draft Pick)	.05
744	Chris George	.05
745	Eric Davis	.05
746	Mark Strittmatter,	
	LaMarr Rogers Rockies	
	Future Stars	.05
747	Carl Willis	.05
748	Stan Belinda	.05
749	Scott Kamieniecki	.05
750	Rickey Henderson	.50
751	Eric Hillman	.05
752	Pat Hentgen	.05
753	Jim Corsi	.05
754	Brian Jordan	.05
755	Bill Swift	.05
756	Mike Henneman	.05
757	Harold Reynolds	.05
758	Sean Berry	.05
759	Charlie Hayes	.05
760	Luis Polonia	.05
761	Darrin Jackson	.05
762	Mark Lewis	.05
763	Rob Maurer	.05
764	Willie Greene	.05
765	Vince Coleman	.05
766	Todd Revenig	.05
767	Rich Ireland	
	(1992 Draft Pick)	.05
768	Mike MacFarlane	.05
769	Francisco Cabrera	.05
770	Robin Ventura	.05

771	Kevin Ritz	.05
772	Chito Martinez	.05
773	Cliff Brantley	.05
774	Curtis Leskanic	.05
775	Chris Bosio	.05
776	Jose Offerman	.05
777	Mark Guthrie	.05
778	Don Slaught	.05
779	Rich Monteleone	.05
780	Jim Abbott	.05
781	Jack Clark	.05
782	Rafael Mendoza, Dan Roman Marlins Future Stars	.05
783	Heathcliff Slocumb	.05
784	Jeff Branson	.05
785	Kevin Brown	.05
786	Mike Christopher, Ken Ryan, Aaron Taylor, Gus Gandarillas Top Prospects RP	.05
787	Mike Matthews (1992 Draft Pick)	.05
788	Mackey Sasser	.05
789	Jeff Conine	.05
790	George Bell	.05
791	Pat Rapp	.05
792	Joe Boever	.05
793	Jim Poole	.05
794	Andy Ashby	.05
795	Deion Sanders	.10
796	Scott Brosius	.05
797	Brad Pennington	.05
798	Greg Blosser	.05
799	Jim Edmonds RC	1.00
800	Shawn Jeter	.05
801	Jesse Levis	.05
802	Phil Clark	.05
803	Ed Pierce	.05
804	Jose Valentin RC	.05
805	Terry Jorgensen	.05
806	Mark Hutton	.05
807	Troy Neel	.05
808	Bret Boone	.05
809	Chris Colon	.05
810	Domingo Martinez RC	.05
811	Javier Lopez	.05
812	Matt Walbeck	.05
813	Dan Wilson	.05
814	Scooter Tucker	.05
815	Billy Ashley RC	.05
816	Tim Laker RC	.05
817	Bobby Jones	.05
818	Brad Brink	.05
819	William Pennyfeather	.05
820	Stan Royer	.05
821	Doug Brocail	.05
822	Kevin Rogers	.05
823	Checklist 397-528	.05
824	Checklist 541-691	.05
825	Checklist 692-825	.05

1993 Topps Gold

NM/M

Complete Set (825): 40.00
Common Player: .15
(Star cards valued at 3X corresponding cards in regular 1993 Topps issue.)

394	Bernardo Brito	.25
395	Jim McNamara	.25
396	Rich Sauveur	.25
823	Keith Brown	.25
824	Russ McGinnis	.25
825	Mike Walker	.25

Black Gold

NM/M

Complete Set (44): 7.50
Common Player: .10
Winner A (1-11): 1.00
Winner B (12-22): 1.00

JOE OLIVER

	Winner C (23-33):	1.00
	Winner D (34-44):	1.00
	Winner AB (1-22):	3.00
	Winner CD (23-44):	3.00
	Winner ABCD (1-44):	5.00
1	Barry Bonds	1.50
2	Will Clark	.10
3	Darren Daulton	.10
4	Andre Dawson	.25
5	Delino DeShields	.10
6	Tom Glavine	.20
7	Marquis Grissom	.10
8	Tony Gwynn	.75
9	Eric Karros	.10
10	Ray Lankford	.10
11	Barry Larkin	.10
12	Greg Maddux	.75
13	Fred McGriff	.10
14	Joe Oliver	.10
15	Terry Pendleton	.10
16	Bip Roberts	.10
17	Ryne Sandberg	.75
18	Gary Sheffield	.40
19	Lee Smith	.10
20	Ozzie Smith	.75
21	Andy Van Slyke	.10
22	Larry Walker	.10
23	Roberto Alomar	.20
24	Brady Anderson	.10
25	Carlos Baerga	.10
26	Joe Carter	.10
27	Roger Clemens	.85
28	Mike Devereaux	.10
29	Dennis Eckersley	.60
30	Cecil Fielder	.10
31	Travis Fryman	.10
32	Juan Gonzalez	.35
33	Ken Griffey Jr.	1.00
34	Brian Harper	.10
35	Pat Listach	.10
36	Kenny Lofton	.10
37	Edgar Martinez	.10
38	Jack McDowell	.10
39	Mark McGwire	1.00
40	Kirby Puckett	.75
41	Mickey Tettleton	.10
42	Frank Thomas	.65
43	Robin Ventura	.10
44	Dave Winfield	.65

Traded

GREGG JEFFERIES
CARDINALS

NM/M

Complete Set (132): 20.00
Common Player: .05

1	Barry Bonds	2.00
2	Rich Renteria	.05
3	Aaron Sele	.05
4	Carlton Loewer RC (USA)	.10
5	Erik Pappas	.05
6	Greg McMichael RC	.05
7	Freddie Benavides	.05
8	Kirk Gibson	.05
9	Tony Fernandez	.05
10	Jay Gainer RC (USA)	.05
11	Orestes Destrade	.05
12	A.J. Hinch RC (USA)	.40
13	Bobby Munoz	.05
14	Tom Henke	.05
15	Rob Butler	.05
16	Gary Wayne	.05
17	David McCarty	.05
18	Walt Weiss	.05
19	Todd Helton RC (USA)	15.00
20	Mark Whiten	.05
21	Ricky Gutierrez	.05
22	Dustin Hermanson RC (USA)	.40
23	Sherman Obando RC	.05
24	Mike Piazza	2.00
26	Jason Bere	.05
27	Jack Voight RC	.05
28	Chris Bosio	.05
29	Phil Hiatt	.05
30	Matt Beaumont RC (USA)	.05
31	Andres Galarraga	.05
32	Greg Swindell	.05
33	Vinny Castilla	.05
34	Pat Clougherty RC (USA)	.05
35	Greg Briley	.05
36	Dallas Green, Davey Johnson	.05
37	Tyler Green	.05
38	Craig Paquette	.05
39	Danny Sheaffer	.05
40	Jim Converse	.05
41	Terry Harvey	.05
42	Phil Plantier	.05
43	Doug Saunders RC	.05
44	Benny Santiago	.05
45	Dante Powell RC (USA)	.10
46	Jeff Parrett	.05
47	Wade Boggs	.85
48	Paul Molitor	.75
49	Turk Wendell	.05
50	David Wells	.05
51	Gary Sheffield	.35
52	Kevin Young	.05
53	Nelson Liriano	.05
54	Greg Maddux	.85
55	Derek Bell	.05
56	Matt Turner RC	.05
57	Charlie Nelson RC (USA)	.05
58	Mike Hampton	.05
59	Troy O'Leary RC	.10
60	Benji Gil	.05
61	Mitch Lyden RC	.05
62	J.T. Snow	.05
63	Damon Buford	.05
64	Gene Harris	.05
65	Randy Myers	.05
66	Felix Jose	.05
67	Todd Dunn RC (USA)	.05
68	Jimmy Key	.05
69	Pedro Castellano	.05
70	Mark Merila RC (USA)	.05
71	Rich Rodriguez	.05
72	Matt Mieske	.05
73	Pete Incaviglia	.05
74	Carl Everett	.05
75	Jim Abbott	.05
76	Luis Aquino	.05
77	Rene Arocha RC	.05
78	Jon Shave RC	.05
79	Todd Walker RC (USA)	1.00
80	Jack Armstrong	.05
81	Jeff Richardson	.05
82	Blas Minor	.05
83	Dave Winfield	.75
84	Paul O'Neill	.05
85	Steve Reich RC (USA)	.10
86	Chris Hammond	.05
87	Hilly Hathaway RC	.05
88	Fred McGriff	.05
89	Dave Telgheder RC	.05
90	Richie Lewis RC	.05
91	Brent Gates	.05
92	Andre Dawson	.15
93	Andy Barkett RC (USA)	.05
94	Doug Drabek	.05
95	Joe Klink	.05
96	Willie Blair	.05
97	Danny Graves RC (USA)	.05
98	Pat Meares	.05
99	Mike Lansing	.05
100	Marcos Armas RC	.05
101	Darren Grass RC (USA)	.05
102	Chris Jones	.05
103	Ken Ryan RC	.05
104	Ellis Burks	.05
105	Bobby Kelly	.05
106	Dave Magadan	.05
107	Paul Wilson RC (USA)	.25
108	Rob Natal	.05
109	Paul Wagner	.05
110	Jeromy Burnitz	.05
111	Monty Fariss	.05
112	Kevin Mitchell	.05
113	Scott Pose RC	.05
114	Dave Stewart	.05
115	Russ Johnson RC (USA)	.10
116	Armando Reynoso	.05
117	Geronimo Berroa	.05
118	Woody Williams RC	.15
119	Tim Bogar RC	.05
120	Bob Scafa RC (USA)	.05
121	Henry Cotto	.05
122	Gregg Jefferies	.05
123	Norm Charlton	.05
124	Bret Wagner RC (USA)	.05
125	David Cone	.05
126	Daryl Boston	.05
127	Tim Wallach	.05
128	Mike Martin RC (USA)	.05
129	John Cummings RC	.05
130	Ryan Bowen	.05
131	John Powell RC (USA)	.05
132	Checklist	.05

1994 Topps

Mike Piazza
DODGERS
C

NM/M

Unopened Retail Set (818): 60.00
Unopened Hobby Set (808): 50.00
Complete Set (792): 35.00
Common Player: .05
Golds: 2X
Series 1 or 2 Pack (12): .50
Series 1 or 2 Wax Box (36): 15.00

1	Mike Piazza	.85
2	Bernie Williams	.05
3	Kevin Rogers	.05
4	Paul Carey	.05
5	Ozzie Guillen	.05
6	Derrick May	.05
7	Jose Mesa	.05
8	Todd Hundley	.05
9	Chris Haney	.05
10	John Olerud	.05
11	Andujar Cedeno	.05
12	John Smiley	.05
13	Phil Plantier	.05
14	Willie Banks	.05
15	Jay Bell	.05
16	Doug Henry	.05
17	Lance Blankenship	.05
18	Greg Harris	.05
19	Scott Livingstone	.05
20	Bryan Harvey	.05
21	Wil Cordero	.05
22	Roger Pavlik	.05
23	Mark Lemke	.05
24	Jeff Nelson	.05
25	Todd Zeile	.05
26	Billy Hatcher	.05
27	Joe Magrane	.05
28	Tony Longmire	.05
29	Omar Daal	.05
30	Kirt Manwaring	.05
31	Melido Perez	.05
32	Tim Hulett	.05
33	Jeff Schwarz	.05
34	Nolan Ryan	1.00
35	Jose Guzman	.05
36	Felix Fermin	.05
37	Jeff Innis	.05
38	Brent Mayne	.05
39	Huck Flener RC	.05
40	Jeff Bagwell	.50
41	Kevin Wickander	.05

No.	Player	Price
42	Ricky Gutierrez	.05
43	Pat Mahomes	.05
44	Jeff King	.05
45	Cal Eldred	.05
46	Craig Paquette	.05
47	Richie Lewis	.05
48	Tony Phillips	.05
49	Armando Reynoso	.05
50	Moises Alou	.05
51	Manuel Lee	.05
52	Otis Nixon	.05
53	Billy Ashley	.05
54	Mark Whiten	.05
55	Jeff Russell	.05
56	Chad Curtis	.05
57	Kevin Stocker	.05
58	Mike Jackson	.05
59	Matt Nokes	.05
60	Chris Bosio	.05
61	Damon Buford	.05
62	Tim Belcher	.05
63	Glenallen Hill	.05
64	Bill Wertz	.05
65	Eddie Murray	.50
66	Tom Gordon	.05
67	Alex Gonzalez	.05
68	Eddie Taubensee	.05
69	Jacob Brumfield	.05
70	Andy Benes	.05
71	Rich Becker	.05
72	Steve Cooke	.05
73	Billy Spiers	.05
74	Scott Brosius	.05
75	Alan Trammell	.05
76	Luis Aquino	.05
77	Jerald Clark	.05
78	Mel Rojas	.05
79	Billy Masse, Stanton Cameron, Tim Clark, Craig McClure OF Prospects	.05
80	Jose Canseco	.30
81	Greg McMichael	.05
82	Brian Turang	.05
83	Tom Urban	.05
84	Garret Anderson	.05
85	Tony Pena	.05
86	Ricky Jordan	.05
87	Jim Gott	.05
88	Pat Kelly	.05
89	Bud Black	.05
90	Robin Ventura	.05
91	Rick Sutcliffe	.05
92	Jose Bautista	.05
93	Bob Ojeda	.05
94	Phil Hiatt	.05
95	Tim Pugh	.05
96	Randy Knorr	.05
97	Todd Jones	.05
98	Ryan Thompson	.05
99	Tim Mauser	.05
100	Kirby Puckett	.60
101	Mark Dewey	.05
102	B.J. Surhoff	.05
103	Sterling Hitchcock	.05
104	Alex Arias	.05
105	David Wells	.05
106	Daryl Boston	.05
107	Mike Stanton	.05
108	Gary Redus	.05
109a	Delino DeShields (Red "Expos, 2B.")	2.00
109b	Delino DeShields (Yellow "Expos, 2B.")	.05
110	Lee Smith	.05
111	Greg Litton	.05
112	Frank Rodriguez	.05
113	Russ Springer	.05
114	Mitch Williams	.05
115	Eric Karros	.05
116	Jeff Brantley	.05
117	Jack Voight	.05
118	Jason Bere	.05
119	Kevin Roberson	.05
120	Jimmy Key	.05
121	Reggie Jefferson	.05
122	Jeromy Burnitz	.05
123	Billy Brewer	.05
124	Willie Canate	.05
125	Greg Swindell	.05
126	Hal Morris	.05
127	Brad Ausmus	.05
128	George Tsamis	.05
129	Denny Neagle	.05
130	Pat Listach	.05
131	Steve Karsay	.05
132	Bret Barberie	.05
133	Mark Leiter	.05
134	Greg Colbrunn	.05
135	David Nied	.05
136	Dean Palmer	.05
137	Steve Avery	.05
138	Bill Haselman	.05
139	Tripp Cromer	.05
140	Frank Viola	.05
141	Rene Gonzales	.05
142	Curt Schilling	.25
143	Tim Wallach	.05
144	Bobby Munoz	.05
145	Brady Anderson	.05
146	Rod Beck	.05
147	Mike LaValliere	.05
148	Greg Hibbard	.05
149	Kenny Lofton	.05
150	Dwight Gooden	.05
151	Greg Gagne	.05
152	Ray McDavid	.05
153	Chris Donnels	.05
154	Dan Wilson	.05
155	Todd Stottlemyre	.05
156	David McCarty	.05
157	Paul Wagner	.05
158	Orlando Miller, Brandon Wilson, Derek Jeter, Mike Neal SS Prospects	1.00
159	Mike Fetters	.05
160	Scott Lydy	.05
161	Darrell Whitmore	.05
162	Bob MacDonald	.05
163	Vinny Castilla	.05
164	Denis Boucher	.05
165	Ivan Rodriguez	.40
166	Ron Gant	.05
167	Tim Davis	.05
168	Steve Dixon	.05
169	Scott Fletcher	.05
170	Terry Mulholland	.05
171	Greg Myers	.05
172	Brett Butler	.05
173	Bob Wickman	.05
174	Dave Martinez	.05
175	Fernando Valenzuela	.05
176	Craig Grebeck	.05
177	Shawn Boskie	.05
178	Albie Lopez	.05
179	Butch Huskey	.05
180	George Brett	.65
181	Juan Guzman	.05
182	Eric Anthony	.05
183	Bob Dibble	.05
184	Craig Shipley	.05
185	Kevin Tapani	.05
186	Marcus Moore	.05
187	Graeme Lloyd	.05
188	Mike Bordick	.05
189	Chris Hammond	.05
190	Cecil Fielder	.05
191	Curtis Leskanic	.05
192	Lou Frazier	.05
193	Steve Dreyer	.05
194	Javier Lopez	.05
195	Edgar Martinez	.05
196	Allen Watson	.05
197	John Flaherty	.05
198	Kurt Stillwell	.05
199	Danny Jackson	.05
200	Cal Ripken, Jr.	1.00
201	Mike Bell	.05
202	Alan Benes RC	.10
203	Matt Farner	.05
204	Jeff Granger RC	.05
205	Brooks Kieschnick RC	.05
206	Jeremy Lee	.05
207	Charles Peterson RC	.05
208	Andy Rice	.05
209	Billy Wagner RC	.25
210	Kelly Wunsch	.05
211	Tom Candiotti	.05
212	Domingo Jean	.05
213	John Burkett	.05
214	George Bell	.05
215	Dan Plesac	.05
216	Manny Ramirez	.60
217	Mike Maddux	.05
218	Kevin McReynolds	.05
219	Pat Borders	.05
220	Doug Drabek	.05
221	Larry Luebbers	.05
222	Trevor Hoffman	.05
223	Pat Meares	.05
224	Danny Miceli	.05
225	Greg Vaughn	.05
226	Scott Hemond	.05
227	Pat Rapp	.05
228	Kirk Gibson	.05
229	Lance Painter	.05
230	Larry Walker	.05
231	Benji Gil	.05
232	Mark Wohlers	.05
233	Rich Amaral	.05
234	Erik Pappas	.05
235	Scott Cooper	.05
236	Mike Butcher	.05
237	Curtis Pride, Shawn Green, Mark Sweeney, Eddie Davis OF Prospects	.35
238	Kim Batiste	.05
239	Paul Assenmacher	.05
240	Will Clark	.05
241	Jose Offerman	.05
242	Todd Frohwirth	.05
243	Tim Raines	.05
244	Rick Wilkins	.05
245	Bret Saberhagen	.05
246	Thomas Howard	.05
247	Stan Belinda	.05
248	Rickey Henderson	.50
249	Brian Williams	.05
250	Barry Larkin	.05
251	Jose Valentin	.05
252	Lenny Webster	.05
253	Blas Minor	.05
254	Tim Teufel	.05
255	Bobby Witt	.05
256	Walt Weiss	.05
257	Chad Kreuter	.05
258	Roberto Mejia	.05
259	Cliff Floyd	.05
260	Julio Franco	.05
261	Rafael Belliard	.05
262	Marc Newfield	.05
263	Gerald Perry	.05
264	Ken Ryan	.05
265	Chili Davis	.05
266	Dave West	.05
267	Royce Clayton	.05
268	Pedro Martinez	.50
269	Mark Hutton	.05
270	Frank Thomas	.50
271	Brad Pennington	.05
272	Mike Harkey	.05
273	Sandy Alomar	.05
274	Dave Gallagher	.05
275	Wally Joyner	.05
276	Ricky Trlicek	.05
277	Al Osuna	.05
278	Calvin Reese	.05
279	Kevin Higgins	.05
280	Rick Aguilera	.05
281	Orlando Merced	.05
282	Mike Mohler	.05
283	John Jaha	.05
284	Robb Nen	.05
285	Travis Fryman	.05
286	Mark Thompson	.05
287	Mike Lansing	.05
288	Craig Lefferts	.05
289	Damon Berryhill	.05
290	Randy Johnson	.50
291	Jeff Reed	.05
292	Danny Darwin	.05
293	J.T. Snow	.05
294	Tyler Green	.05
295	Chris Hoiles	.05
296	Roger McDowell	.05
297	Spike Owen	.05
298	Salomon Torres	.05
299	Wilson Alvarez	.05
300	Ryne Sandberg	.60
301	Derek Lilliquist	.05
302	Howard Johnson	.05
303	Greg Cadaret	.05
304	Pat Hentgen	.05
305	Craig Biggio	.05
306	Scott Service	.05
307	Melvin Nieves	.05
308	Mike Trombley	.05
309	Carlos Garcia	.05
310	Robin Yount	.50
311	Marcos Armas	.05
312	Rich Rodriguez	.05
313	Justin Thompson	.05
314	Danny Sheaffer	.05
315	Ken Hill	.05
316	Chad Ogea, Duff Brumley, Terrell Wade, Chris Michalak RC P Propsects	.10
317	Cris Carpenter	.05
318	Jeff Blauser	.05
319	Ted Power	.05
320	Ozzie Smith	.60
321	John Dopson	.05
322	Chris Turner	.05
323	Pete Incaviglia	.05
324	Alan Mills	.05
325	Jody Reed	.05
326	Rich Monteleone	.05
327	Mark Carreon	.05
328	Donn Pall	.05
329	Matt Walbeck	.05
330	Charles Nagy	.05
331	Jeff McKnight	.05
332	Jose Lind	.05
333	Mike Timlin	.05
334	Doug Jones	.05
335	Kevin Mitchell	.05
336	Luis Lopez	.05
337	Shane Mack	.05
338	Randy Tomlin	.05
339	Matt Mieske	.05
340	Mark McGwire	.85
341	Nigel Wilson	.05
342	Danny Gladden	.05
343	Mo Sanford	.05
344	Sean Berry	.05
345	Kevin Brown	.05
346	Greg Olson	.05
347	Dave Magadan	.05
348	Rene Arocha	.05
349	Carlos Quintana	.05
350	Jim Abbott	.05
351	Gary DiSarcina	.05
352	Ben Rivera	.05
353	Carlos Hernandez	.05
354	Darren Lewis	.05
355	Harold Reynolds	.05
356	Scott Ruffcorn	.05
357	Mark Gubicza	.05
358	Paul Sorrento	.05
359	Anthony Young	.05
360	Mark Grace	.05
361	Rob Butler	.05
362	Kevin Bass	.05
363	Eric Helfand	.05
364	Derek Bell	.05
365	Scott Erickson	.05
366	Al Martin	.05
367	Ricky Bones	.05
368	Jeff Branson	.05
369	Luis Ortiz, David Bell, Jason Giambi, George Arias RC 3B Prospects	.30
370a	Benny Santiago	.05
370b	Mark McLemore (Originally checklisted as #379.)	.05
371	John Doherty	.05
372	Joe Girardi	.05
373	Tim Scott	.05
374	Marvin Freeman	.05
375	Deion Sanders	.10
376	Roger Salkeld	.05
377	Bernard Gilkey	.05
378	Tony Fossas	.05
379	(Not issued, see #370.)	
380	Darren Daulton	.05
381	Chuck Finley	.05
382	Mitch Webster	.05
383	Gerald Williams	.05
384	Frank Thomas, Fred McGriff/AS	.30
385	Roberto Alomar, Robby Thompson/AS	.05
386	Wade Boggs, Matt Williams/AS	.35
387	Cal Ripken, Jr., Jeff Blauser/AS	.50
388	Ken Griffey Jr., Len Dykstra/AS	.40
389	Juan Gonzalez, Dave Justice/AS	.10
390	Albert Belle, Barry Bonds/AS	.45
391	Mike Stanley, Mike Piazza/AS	.45
392	Jack McDowell, Greg Maddux/AS	.35
393	Jimmy Key, Tom Glavine/AS	.05
394	Jeff Montgomery, Randy Myers/AS	.05
395	Checklist 1	.05
396	Checklist 2	.05
397	Tim Salmon	.10
398	Todd Benzinger	.05
399	Frank Castillo	.05
400	Ken Griffey Jr.	.75
401	John Kruk	.05
402	Dave Telgheder	.05
403	Gary Gaetti	.05
404	Jim Edmonds	.05
405	Don Slaught	.05
406	Jose Oquendo	.05
407	Bruce Ruffin	.05
408	Phil Clark	.05
409	Joe Klink	.05
410	Lou Whitaker	.05
411	Kevin Seitzer	.05
412	Darrin Fletcher	.05
413	Kenny Rogers	.05
414	Bill Pecota	.05
415	Dave Fleming	.05
416	Luis Alicea	.05
417	Paul Quantrill	.05
418	Damion Easley	.05
419	Wes Chamberlain	.05
420	Harold Baines	.05
421	Scott Radinsky	.05
422	Rey Sanchez	.05
423	Junior Ortiz	.05
424	Jeff Kent	.05
425	Brian McRae	.05
426	Ed Sprague	.05

427	Tom Edens	.05
428	Willie Greene	.05
429	Bryan Hickerson	.05
430	Dave Winfield	.50
431	Pedro Astacio	.05
432	Mike Gallego	.05
433	Dave Burba	.05
434	Bob Walk	.05
435	Darryl Hamilton	.05
436	Vince Horsman	.05
437	Bob Natal	.05
438	Mike Henneman	.05
439	Willie Blair	.05
440	Denny Martinez	.05
441	Dan Peltier	.05
442	Tony Tarasco	.05
443	John Cummings	.05
444	Geronimo Pena	.05
445	Aaron Sele	.05
446	Stan Javier	.05
447	Mike Williams	.05
448	Greg Pirkl, Roberto Petagine, D.J. Boston, Shawn Wooten 1B Prospects	.05
449	Jim Poole	.05
450	Carlos Baerga	.05
451	Bob Scanlan	.05
452	Lance Johnson	.05
453	Eric Hillman	.05
454	Keith Miller	.05
455	Dave Stewart	.05
456	Pete Harnisch	.05
457	Roberto Kelly	.05
458	Tim Worrell	.05
459	Pedro Munoz	.05
460	Orel Hershiser	.05
461	Randy Velarde	.05
462	Trevor Wilson	.05
463	Jerry Goff	.05
464	Bill Wegman	.05
465	Dennis Eckersley	.40
466	Jeff Conine	.05
467	Joe Boever	.05
468	Dante Bichette	.05
469	Jeff Shaw	.05
470	Rafael Palmeiro	.40
471	Phil Leftwich RC	.05
472	Jay Buhner	.05
473	Bob Tewksbury	.05
474	Tim Naehring	.05
475	Tom Glavine	.25
476	Dave Hollins	.05
477	Arthur Rhodes	.05
478	Joey Cora	.05
479	Mike Morgan	.05
480	Albert Belle	.05
481	John Franco	.05
482	Hipolito Pichardo	.05
483	Duane Ward	.05
484	Luis Gonzalez	.05
485	Joe Oliver	.05
486	Wally Whitehurst	.05
487	Mike Benjamin	.05
488	Eric Davis	.05
489	Scott Kamieniecki	.05
490	Kent Hrbek	.05
491	John Hope RC	.05
492	Jesse Orosco	.05
493	Troy Neel	.05
494	Ryan Bowen	.05
495	Mickey Tettleton	.05
496	Chris Jones	.05
497	John Wetteland	.05
498	David Hulse	.05
499	Greg Maddux	.60
500	Bo Jackson	.10
501	Donovan Osborne	.05
502	Mike Greenwell	.05
503	Steve Frey	.05
504	Jim Eisenreich	.05
505	Robby Thompson	.05
506	Leo Gomez	.05
507	Dave Staton	.05
508	Wayne Kirby	.05
509	Tim Bogar	.05
510	David Cone	.05
511	Devon White	.05
512	Xavier Hernandez	.05
513	Tim Costo	.05
514	Gene Harris	.05
515	Jack McDowell	.05
516	Kevin Gross	.05
517	Scott Leius	.05
518	Lloyd McClendon	.05
519	Alex Diaz RC	.05
520	Wade Boggs	.60
521	Bob Welch	.05
522	Henry Cotto	.05
523	Mike Moore	.05
524	Tim Laker	.05
525	Andres Galarraga	.05
526	Jamie Moyer	.05

527	Norberto Martin, Ruben Santana, Jason Hardtke, Chris Sexton 2B Prospects	.05
528	Sid Bream	.05
529	Erik Hanson	.05
530	Ray Lankford	.05
531	Rob Deer	.05
532	Rod Correia	.05
533	Roger Mason	.05
534	Mike Devereaux	.05
535	Jeff Montgomery	.05
536	Dwight Smith	.05
537	Jeremy Hernandez	.05
538	Ellis Burks	.05
539	Bobby Jones	.05
540	Paul Molitor	.50
541	Jeff Juden	.05
542	Chris Sabo	.05
543	Larry Casian	.05
544	Jeff Gardner	.05
545	Ramon Martinez	.05
546	Paul O'Neill	.05
547	Steve Hosey	.05
548	Dave Nilsson	.05
549	Ron Darling	.05
550	Matt Williams	.05
551	Jack Armstrong	.05
552	Bill Krueger	.05
553	Freddie Benavides	.05
554	Jeff Fassero	.05
555	Chuck Knoblauch	.05
556	Guillermo Velasquez	.05
557	Joel Johnston	.05
558	Tom Lampkin	.05
559	Todd Van Poppel	.05
560	Gary Sheffield	.30
561	Skeeter Barnes	.05
562	Darren Holmes	.05
563	John Vander Wal	.05
564	Mike Ignasiak	.05
565	Fred McGriff	.05
566	Luis Polonia	.05
567	Mike Perez	.05
568	John Valentin	.05
569	Mike Felder	.05
570	Tommy Greene	.05
571	David Segui	.05
572	Roberto Hernandez	.05
573	Steve Wilson	.05
574	Willie McGee	.05
575	Randy Myers	.05
576	Darrin Jackson	.05
577	Eric Plunk	.05
578	Mike MacFarlane	.05
579	Doug Brocail	.05
580	Steve Finley	.05
581	John Roper	.05
582	Danny Cox	.05
583	Chip Hale	.05
584	Scott Bullett	.05
585	Kevin Reimer	.05
586	Brent Gates	.05
587	Matt Turner	.05
588	Rich Rowland	.05
589	Kent Bottenfield	.05
590	Marquis Grissom	.05
591	Doug Strange	.05
592	Jay Howell	.05
593	Omar Vizquel	.05
594	Rheal Cormier	.05
595	Andre Dawson	.25
596	Hilly Hathaway	.05
597	Todd Pratt	.05
598	Mike Mussina	.30
599	Alex Fernandez	.05
600	Don Mattingly	.65
601	Frank Thomas	.25
602	Ryne Sandberg	.30
603	Wade Boggs	.30
604	Cal Ripken, Jr.	.50
605	Barry Bonds	.50
606	Ken Griffey Jr.	.40
607	Kirby Puckett	.35
608	Darren Daulton	.05
609	Paul Molitor	.25
610	Terry Steinbach	.05
611	Todd Worrell	.05
612	Jim Thome	.40
613	Chuck McElroy	.05
614	John Habyan	.05
615	Sid Fernandez	.05
616	Eddie Zambrano, Glenn Murray, Chad Mottola, Jermaine Allensworth RC OF Prospects	.05
617	Steve Bedrosian	.05
618	Rob Ducey	.05
619	Tom Browning	.05
620	Tony Gwynn	.60
621	Carl Willis	.05
622	Kevin Young	.05

623	Rafael Novoa	.05
624	Jerry Browne	.05
625	Charlie Hough	.05
626	Chris Gomez	.05
627	Steve Reed	.05
628	Kirk Rueter	.05
629	Matt Whiteside	.05
630	Dave Justice	.05
631	Brad Holman	.05
632	Brian Jordan	.05
633	Scott Bankhead	.05
634	Torey Lovullo	.05
635	Len Dykstra	.05
636	Ben McDonald	.05
637	Steve Howe	.05
638	Jose Vizcaino	.05
639	Bill Swift	.05
640	Darryl Strawberry	.05
641	Steve Farr	.05
642	Tom Kramer	.05
643	Joe Orsulak	.05
644	Tom Henke	.05
645	Joe Carter	.05
646	Ken Caminiti	.05
647	Reggie Sanders	.05
648	Andy Ashby	.05
649	Derek Parks	.05
650	Andy Van Slyke	.05
651	Juan Bell	.05
652	Roger Smithberg	.05
653	Chuck Carr	.05
654	Bill Gullickson	.05
655	Charlie Hayes	.05
656	Chris Nabholz	.05
657	Karl Rhodes	.05
658	Pete Smith	.05
659	Bret Boone	.05
660	Gregg Jefferies	.05
661	Bob Zupcic	.05
662	Steve Sax	.05
663	Mariano Duncan	.05
664	Jeff Tackett	.05
665	Mark Langston	.05
666	Steve Buechele	.05
667	Candy Maldonado	.05
668	Woody Williams	.05
669	Tim Wakefield	.05
670	Danny Tartabull	.05
671	Charlie O'Brien	.05
672	Felix Jose	.05
673	Bobby Ayala	.05
674	Scott Servais	.05
675	Roberto Alomar	.15
676	Pedro Martinez	.05
677	Eddie Guardado	.05
678	Mark Lewis	.05
679	Jaime Navarro	.05
680	Ruben Sierra	.05
681	Rick Renteria	.05
682	Storm Davis	.05
683	Cory Snyder	.05
684	Ron Karkovice	.05
685	Juan Gonzalez	.25
686	Chris Howard, Carlos Delgado, Jason Kendall, Paul Bako C Prospects	.40
687	John Smoltz	.05
688	Brian Dorsett	.05
689	Omar Olivares	.05
690	Mo Vaughn	.05
691	Joe Grahe	.05
692	Mickey Morandini	.05
693	Tino Martinez	.05
694	Brian Barnes	.05
695	Mike Stanton	.05
696	Mark Clark	.05
697	Dave Hansen	.05
698	Willie Wilson	.05
699	Pete Schourek	.05
700	Barry Bonds	1.00
701	Kevin Appier	.05
702	Tony Fernandez	.05
703	Darryl Kile	.05
704	Archi Cianfrocco	.05
705	Jose Rijo	.05
706	Brian Harper	.05
707	Zane Smith	.05
708	Dave Henderson	.05
709	Angel Miranda	.05
710	Orestes Destrade	.05
711	Greg Gohr	.05
712	Eric Young	.05
713	Todd Williams, Ron Watson, Kirk Bullinger, Mike Welch P Prospects	.05
714	Tim Spehr	.05
715	Hank Aaron (20th Anniversary #715)	.50
716	Nate Minchey	.05
717	Mike Blowers	.05
718	Kent Mercker	.05
719	Tom Pagnozzi	.05

720	Roger Clemens	.65
721	Eduardo Perez	.05
722	Milt Thompson	.05
723	Gregg Olson	.05
724	Kirk McCaskill	.05
725	Sammy Sosa	.60
726	Alvaro Espinoza	.05
727	Henry Rodriguez	.05
728	Jim Leyritz	.05
729	Steve Scarsone	.05
730	Bobby Bonilla	.05
731	Chris Gwynn	.05
732	Al Leiter	.05
733	Bip Roberts	.05
734	Mark Portugal	.05
735	Terry Pendleton	.05
736	Dave Valle	.05
737	Paul Kilgus	.05
738	Greg Harris	.05
739	Jon Ratliff RC	.05
740	Kirk Presley RC	.05
741	Josue Estrada RC	.05
742	Wayne Gomes RC	.10
743	Pat Watkins RC	.05
744	Jamey Wright RC	.05
745	Jay Powell RC	.05
746	Ryan McGuire RC	.05
747	Marc Barcelo RC	.05
748	Sloan Smith RC	.05
749	John Wasdin RC	.05
750	Marc Valdes	.05
751	Dan Ehler RC	.05
752	Andre King RC	.05
753	Greg Keagle RC	.05
754	Jason Myers RC	.05
755	Dax Winslett RC	.05
756	Casey Whitten RC	.05
757	Tony Fuduric RC	.05
758	Greg Norton RC	.05
759	Jeff D'Amico RC	.05
760	Ryan Hancock RC	.05
761	David Cooper RC	.05
762	Kevin Orie RC	.05
763	John O'Donoghue, Mike Oquist	.05
764	Cory Bailey, Scott Hatteberg	.05
765	Mark Holzemer, Paul Swingle	.05
766	James Baldwin, Rod Bolton	.05
767	Jerry DiPoto, Julian Tavarez RC	.10
768	Danny Bautista, Sean Bergman	.05
769	Bob Hamelin, Joe Vitiello	.05
770	Mark Kiefer, Troy O'Leary	.05
771	Denny Hocking, Oscar Munoz	.05
772	Russ Davis, Brien Taylor	.05
773	Kurt Abbott, Miguel Jimenez	.05
774	Kevin King, Eric Plantenberg	.05
775	Jon Shave, Desi Wilson	.05
776	Domingo Cedeno, Paul Spoljaric	.05
777	Chipper Jones, Ryan Klesko	.60
778	Steve Trachsel, Turk Wendell	.05
779	Johnny Ruffin, Jerry Spradlin	.05
780	Jason Bates, John Burke	.05
781	Carl Everett, Dave Weathers	.05
782	Gary Mota, James Mouton	.05
783	Raul Mondesi, Ben Van Ryn	.05
784	Gabe White, Rondell White	.05
785	Brook Fordyce, Bill Pulsipher	.05
786	Kevin Foster, Gene Schall	.05
787	Rich Aude, Midre Cummings	.05
788	Brian Barber, Richard Batchelor	.05
789	Brian Johnson, Scott Sanders	.05
790	Rikkert Faneyte, J.R. Phillips	.05
791	Checklist 3	.05
792	Checklist 4	.05

Gold

	NM/M
Complete Set (792):	50.00
Common Player:	.15

(Star cards valued at 2X corresponding cards in regular Topps issue.)

Black Gold

	NM/M
Complete Set (44):	10.00
Complete Series 1 (22):	6.00
Complete Series 2 (22):	4.00
Common Player:	.10
1 Roberto Alomar	.20
2 Carlos Baerga	.10
3 Albert Belle	.10
4 Joe Carter	.10
5 Cecil Fielder	.10
6 Travis Fryman	.10
7 Juan Gonzalez	.25
8 Ken Griffey Jr.	.75
9 Chris Hoiles	.10
10 Randy Johnson	.45
11 Kenny Lofton	.10
12 Jack McDowell	.10
13 Paul Molitor	.45
14 Jeff Montgomery	.10
15 John Olerud	.10
16 Rafael Palmeiro	.45
17 Kirby Puckett	.60
18 Cal Ripken, Jr.	1.50
19 Tim Salmon	.10
20 Mike Stanley	.10
21 Frank Thomas	.50
22 Robin Ventura	.10
23 Jeff Bagwell	.45
24 Jay Bell	.10
25 Craig Biggio	.10
26 Jeff Blauser	.10
27 Barry Bonds	1.50
28 Darren Daulton	.10
29 Len Dykstra	.10
30 Andres Galarraga	.10
31 Ron Gant	.10
32 Tom Glavine	.10
33 Mark Grace	.10
34 Marquis Grissom	.10
35 Gregg Jefferies	.10
36 Dave Justice	.10
37 John Kruk	.10
38 Greg Maddux	.60
39 Fred McGriff	.10
40 Randy Myers	.10
41 Mike Piazza	1.00
42 Sammy Sosa	.60
43 Robby Thompson	.10
44 Matt Williams	.10
--- Winner A	.50
--- Winner B	.50
--- Winner C	.50
--- Winner D	.50
--- Winner A/B	.60
--- Winner C/D	.60
--- Winner A/B/C/D	.75

Traded

	NM/M
Complete Set (140):	30.00
Common Player:	.05
1 Paul Wilson	.05
2 Bill Taylor	.05
3 Dan Wilson	.05
4 Mark Smith	.05
5 Toby Borland	.05
6 Dave Clark	.05
7 Denny Martinez	.05
8 Dave Gallagher	.05
9 Josias Manzanillo	.05
10 Brian Anderson	.05
11 Damon Berryhill	.05
12 Alex Cole	.05
13 Jacob Shumate	.05
14 Oddibe McDowell	.05
15 Willie Banks	.05
16 Jerry Browne	.05
17 Donnie Elliott	.05
18 Ellis Burks	.05
19 Chuck McElroy	.05
20 Luis Polonia	.05
21 Brian Harper	.05
22 Mark Portugal	.05
23 Dave Henderson	.05
24 Mark Acre	.05
25 Julio Franco	.05
26 Darren Hall	.05
27 Eric Anthony	.05
28 Sid Fernandez	.05
29 Rusty Greer RC	.25
30 Riccardo Ingram	.05
31 Gabe White	.05
32 Tim Belcher	.05
33 Terrence Long RC	1.00
34 Mark Dalesandro RC	.05
35 Mike Kelly	.05
36 Jack Morris	.05
37 Jeff Brantley	.05
38 Larry Barnes RC	.05
39 Brian Hunter	.05
40 Otis Nixon	.05
41 Bret Wagner	.05
42 Pedro Martinez, Delino DeShields Anatomy of a Trade	.25
43 Heathcliff Slocumb	.05
44 Ben Grieve RC	.35
45 John Hudek	.05
46 Shawon Dunston	.05
47 Greg Colbrunn	.05
48 Joey Hamilton	.05
49 Marvin Freeman	.05
50 Terry Mulholland	.05
51 Keith Mitchell	.05
52 Dwight Smith	.05
53 Shawn Boskie	.05
54 Kevin Witt RC	.05
55 Ron Gant	.05
56 Trenidad Hubbard, Jason Schmidt, Larry Sutton, Stephen Larkin 1994 Prospects	10.00
57 Jody Reed	.05
58 Rick Helling	.05
59 John Powell	.05
60 Eddie Murray	.60
61 Joe Hall	.05
62 Jorge Fabregas	.05
63 Mike Mordecai	.05
64 Ed Vosberg	.05
65 Rickey Henderson	.60
66 Tim Grieve	.05
67 Jon Lieber	.05
68 Chris Howard	.05
69 Matt Walbeck	.05
70 Chan Ho Park	.15
71 Bryan Eversgerd	.05
72 John Dettmer	.05
73 Erik Hanson	.05
74 Mike Thurman	.05
75 Bobby Ayala	.05
76 Rafael Palmeiro	.50
77 Bret Boone	.05
78 Paul Shuey	.05
79 Kevin Foster	.05
80 Dave Magadan	.05
81 Bip Roberts	.05
82 Howard Johnson	.05
83 Xavier Hernandez	.05
84 Ross Powell	.05
85 Doug Million RC	.05
86 Geronimo Berroa	.05
87 Mark Farris RC	.05
88 Butch Henry	.05
89 Junior Felix	.05
90 Bo Jackson	.10
91 Hector Carrasco	.05
92 Charlie O'Brien	.05
93 Omar Vizquel	.05
94 David Segui	.05
95 Dustin Hermanson	.05
96 Gar Finnvold	.05
97 Dave Stevens	.05
98 Corey Pointer	.05
99 Felix Fermin	.05
100 Lee Smith	.05
101 Reid Ryan	.15
102 Bobby Munoz	.05
103 Deion Sanders, Roberto Kelly Anatomy of a Trade	.05
104 Turner Ward	.05
105 William Van Landingham	.05
106 Vince Coleman	.05
107 Stan Javier	.05
108 Darrin Jackson	.05
109 C.J. Nitkowski	.05
110 Anthony Young	.05
111 Kurt Miller	.05
112 Paul Konerko RC	15.00
113 Walt Weiss	.05
114 Daryl Boston	.05
115 Will Clark	.05
116 Matt Smith RC	.05
117 Mark Leiter	.05
118 Gregg Olson	.05
119 Tony Pena	.05
120 Jose Vizcaino	.05
121 Rick White	.05
122 Rich Rowland	.05
123 Jeff Reboulet	.05
124 Greg Hibbard	.05
125 Chris Sabo	.05
126 Doug Jones	.05
127 Tony Fernandez	.05
128 Carlos Reyes	.05
129 Kevin Brown	.05
130 Ryne Sandberg Commemorative	1.00
131 Ryne Sandberg Commemorative	1.00
132 Checklist 1-132	

Traded Finest Inserts

	NM/M
Complete Set (8):	6.00
Common Player:	.25
1 Greg Maddux	1.50
2 Mike Piazza	2.00
3 Matt Williams	.25
4 Raul Mondesi	.25
5 Ken Griffey Jr.	2.00
6 Kenny Lofton	.25
7 Frank Thomas	1.25
8 Manny Ramirez	1.00

1995 Topps

	NM/M
Unopened Hobby Set (677):	100.00
Unopened Retail Set (684):	75.00
Unopened Retail Set (677):	85.00
Complete Set (660):	45.00
Common Player:	.05
Series 1 or 2 Pack (15):	1.25
Series 1 or 2 Wax Box (36):	25.00
1 Frank Thomas	.75
2 Mickey Morandini	.05
3a Babe Ruth (100th Birthday, no gold "Topps" logo)	2.00
3b Babe Ruth (100th Birthday, gold "Topps" logo)	2.00
4 Scott Cooper	.05
5 David Cone	.05
6 Jacob Shumate	.05
7 Trevor Hoffman	.05
8 Shane Mack	.05
9 Delino DeShields	.05
10 Matt Williams	.05
11 Sammy Sosa	1.00
12 Gary DiSarcina	.05
13 Kenny Rogers	.05
14 Jose Vizcaino	.05
15 Lou Whitaker	.05
16 Ron Darling	.05
17 Dave Nilsson	.05
18 Chris Hammond	.05
19 Sid Bream	.05
20 Denny Martinez	.05
21 Orlando Merced	.05
22 John Wetteland	.05
23 Mike Devereaux	.05
24 Rene Arocha	.05
25 Jay Buhner	.05
26 Darren Holmes	.05
27 Hal Morris	.05
28 Brian Buchanan RC	.10
29 Keith Miller	.05
30 Paul Molitor	.75
31 Dave West	.05
32 Tony Tarasco	.05
33 Scott Sanders	.05
34 Eddie Zambrano	.05
35 Ricky Bones	.05
36 John Valentin	.05
37 Kevin Tapani	.05
38 Tim Wallach	.05
39 Darren Lewis	.05
40 Travis Fryman	.05
41 Mark Leiter	.05
42 Jose Bautista	.05
43 Pete Smith	.05
44 Bret Barberie	.05
45 Dennis Eckersley	.65
46 Ken Hill	.05
47 Chad Ogea (Star Track)	.05
48 Pete Harnisch	.05
49 James Baldwin	.05
50 Mike Mussina	.45
51 Al Martin	.05
52 Mark Thompson (Star Track)	.05
53 Matt Smith	.05
54 Joey Hamilton (All Star Rookie)	.05
55 Edgar Martinez	.05
56 John Smiley	.05
57 Rey Sanchez	.05
58 Mike Timlin	.05
59 Ricky Bottalico (Star Track)	.05
60 Jim Abbott	.05
61 Mike Kelly	.05
62 Brian Jordan	.05
63 Ken Ryan	.05
64 Matt Mieske	.05

#	Player	Price	#	Player	Price	#	Player	Price	#	Player	Price
65	Rick Aguilera	.05	162	Luis Gonzalez	.05	261	Dwight Smith	.05	352	Scott Kamieniecki	.05
66	Ismael Valdes	.05	163	Alex Fernandez	.05	262	Allen Watson	.05	353	Gary Gaetti	.05
67	Royce Clayton	.05	164	Freddie Benavides	.05	263	Dan Wilson	.05	354	Todd Stottlemyre	.05
68	Junior Felix	.05	165	Ben McDonald	.05	264	Brent Mayne	.05	355	Fred McGriff	.05
69	Harold Reynolds	.05	166	Blas Minor	.05	265	Bip Roberts	.05	356	Tim Mauser	.05
70	Juan Gonzalez	.35	167	Bret Wagner	.05	266	Sterling Hitchcock	.05	357	Chris Gwynn	.05
71	Kelly Stinnett	.05	168	Mac Suzuki	.05	267	Alex Gonzalez (Star Track)	.05	358	Frank Castillo	.05
72	Carlos Reyes	.05	169	Roberto Mejia	.05	268	Greg Harris	.05	359	Jeff Reboulet	.05
73	Dave Weathers	.05	170	Wade Boggs	1.00	269	Ricky Jordan	.05	360	Roger Clemens	1.00
74	Mel Rojas	.05	171	Calvin Reese	.05	270	Johnny Ruffin	.05	361	Mark Carreon	.05
75	Doug Drabek	.05	172	Hipolito Pichardo	.05	271	Mike Stanton	.05	362	Chad Kreuter	.05
76	Charles Nagy	.05	173	Kim Batiste	.05	272	Rich Rowland	.05	363	Mark Farris	.05
77	Tim Raines	.05	174	Darren Hall	.05	273	Steve Trachsel	.05	364	Bob Welch	.05
78	Midre Cummings	.05	175	Tom Glavine	.25	274	Pedro Munoz	.05	365	Dean Palmer	.05
79	Gene Schall, Scott Talanoa, Harold Williams, Ray Brown RC 1B Prospects	.05	176	Phil Plantier	.05	275	Ramon Martinez	.05	366	Jeromy Burnitz	.05
			177	Chris Howard	.05	276	Dave Henderson	.05	367	B.J. Surhoff	.05
80	Rafael Palmeiro	.65	178	Karl Rhodes	.05	277	Chris Gomez (All Star Rookie)	.05	368	Mike Butcher	.05
81	Charlie Hayes	.05	179	LaTroy Hawkins	.05	278	Joe Grahe	.05	369	Brad Clontz, Steve Phoenix, Scott Gentile, Bucky Buckles RP Prospects	.05
82	Ray Lankford	.05	180	Raul Mondesi (All Star Rookie)	.05	279	Rusty Greer	.05			
83	Tim Davis	.05	181	Jeff Reed	.05	280	John Franco	.05	370	Eddie Murray	.75
84	C.J. Nitkowski RC	.05	182	Milt Cuyler	.05	281	Mike Bordick	.05	371	Orlando Miller (Star Track)	.05
85	Andy Ashby	.05	183	Jim Edmonds	.05	282	Jeff D'Amico	.05	372	Ron Karkovice	.05
86	Gerald Williams	.05	184	Hector Fajardo	.05	283	Dave Magadan	.05	373	Richie Lewis	.05
87	Terry Shumpert	.05	185	Jeff Kent	.05	284	Tony Pena	.05	374	Lenny Webster	.05
88	Heathcliff Slocumb	.05	186	Wilson Alvarez	.05	285	Greg Swindell	.05	375	Jeff Tackett	.05
89	Domingo Cedeno	.05	187	Geronimo Berroa	.05	286	Doug Million	.05	376	Tom Urbani	.05
90	Mark Grace	.05	188	Billy Spiers	.05	287	Gabe White (Star Track)	.05	377	Tino Martinez	.05
91	Brad Woodall RC (Star Track)	.10	189	Derek Lilliquist	.05	288	Trey Beamon	.05	378	Mark Dewey	.05
92	Gar Finnvold	.05	190	Craig Biggio	.05	289	Arthur Rhodes	.05	379	Charlie O'Brien	.05
93	Jaime Navarro	.05	191	Roberto Hernandez	.05	290	Juan Guzman	.05	380	Terry Mulholland	.05
94	Carlos Hernandez	.05	192	Bob Natal	.05	291	Jose Oquendo	.05	381	Thomas Howard	.05
95	Mark Langston	.05	193	Bobby Ayala	.05	292	Willie Blair	.05	382	Chris Haney	.05
96	Chuck Carr	.05	194	Travis Miller RC	.10	293	Eddie Taubensee	.05	383	Billy Hatcher	.05
97	Mike Gardiner	.05	195	Bob Tewksbury	.05	294	Steve Howe	.05	384	Jeff Bagwell, Frank Thomas/AS	.45
98	David McCarty	.05	196	Rondell White	.05	295	Greg Maddux	1.00	385	Bret Boone, Carlos Baerga/AS	.05
99	Cris Carpenter	.05	197	Steve Cooke	.05	296	Mike MacFarlane	.05	386	Matt Williams, Wade Boggs/AS	.30
100	Barry Bonds	2.00	198	Jeff Branson	.05	297	Curt Schilling	.25	387	Wil Cordero, Cal Ripken Jr./AS	1.00
101	David Segui	.05	199	Derek Jeter	2.00	298	Phil Clark	.05	388	Barry Bonds, Ken Griffey Jr./AS	1.00
102	Scott Brosius	.05	200	Tim Salmon	.05	299	Woody Williams	.05	389	Tony Gwynn, Albert Belle/AS	.50
103	Mariano Duncan	.05	201	Steve Frey	.05	300	Jose Canseco	.40	390	Dante Bichette, Kirby Puckett/AS	.50
104	Kenny Lofton	.05	202	Kent Mercker	.05	301	Aaron Sele	.05	391	Mike Piazza, Mike Stanley/AS	.75
105	Ken Caminiti	.05	203	Randy Johnson	.75	302	Carl Willis	.05	392	Greg Maddux, David Cone/AS	.50
106	Darrin Jackson	.05	204	Todd Worrell	.05	303	Steve Buechele	.05	393	Danny Jackson, Jimmy Key/AS	.05
107	Jim Poole	.05	205	Mo Vaughn	.05	304	Dave Burba	.05	394	John Franco, Lee Smith/AS	.05
108	Wil Cordero	.05	206	Howard Johnson	.05	305	Orel Hershiser	.05	395	Checklist 1-198	.05
109	Danny Miceli	.05	207	John Wasdin	.05	306	Damion Easley	.05	396	Checklist 199-396	.05
110	Walt Weiss	.05	208	Eddie Williams	.05	307	Mike Henneman	.05	397	Ken Griffey Jr.	1.25
111	Tom Pagnozzi	.05	209	Tim Belcher	.05	308	Josias Manzanillo	.05	398	Rick Heiserman RC	.05
112	Terrence Long	.05	210	Jeff Montgomery	.05	309	Kevin Seitzer	.05	399	Don Mattingly	1.00
113	Bret Boone	.05	211	Kirt Manwaring	.05	310	Ruben Sierra	.05	400	Henry Rodriguez	.05
114	Daryl Boston	.05	212	Ben Grieve	.05	311	Bryan Harvey	.05	401	Lenny Harris	.05
115	Wally Joyner	.05	213	Pat Hentgen	.05	312	Jim Thome	.45	402	Ryan Thompson	.05
116	Rob Butler	.05	214	Shawon Dunston	.05	313	Ramon Castro RC	.05	403	Darren Oliver	.05
117	Rafael Belliard	.05	215	Mike Greenwell	.05	314	Lance Johnson	.05	404	Omar Vizquel	.05
118	Luis Lopez	.05	216	Alex Diaz	.05	315	Marquis Grissom	.05	405	Jeff Bagwell	.75
119	Tony Fossas	.05	217	Pat Mahomes	.05	316	Terrell Wade, Juan Acevedo, Matt Arrandale, Eddie Priest RC/SP Prospects	.05	406	Doug Webb RC	.05
120	Len Dykstra	.05	218	Dave Hanson	.05				407	Todd Van Poppel	.05
121	Mike Morgan	.05	219	Kevin Rogers	.05	317	Paul Wagner	.05	408	Leo Gomez	.05
122	Denny Hocking	.05	220	Cecil Fielder	.05	318	Jamie Moyer	.05	409	Mark Whiten	.05
123	Kevin Gross	.05	221	Andrew Lorraine (Star Track)	.05	319	Todd Zeile	.05	410	Pedro Martinez	.05
124	Todd Benzinger	.05	222	Jack Armstrong	.05	320	Chris Bosio	.05	411	Reggie Sanders	.05
125	John Doherty	.05	223	Todd Hundley	.05	321	Steve Reed	.05	412	Kevin Foster	.05
126	Eduardo Perez	.05	224	Mark Acre	.05	322	Erik Hanson	.05	413	Danny Tartabull	.05
127	Dan Smith	.05	225	Darrell Whitmore	.05	323	Luis Polonia	.05	414	Jeff Blauser	.05
128	Joe Orsulak	.05	226	Randy Milligan	.05	324	Ryan Klesko	.05	415	Mike Magnante	.05
129	Brent Gates	.05	227	Wayne Kirby	.05	325	Kevin Appier	.05	416	Tom Candiotti	.05
130	Jeff Conine	.05	228	Darryl Kile	.05	326	Jim Eisenreich	.05	417	Rod Beck	.05
131	Doug Henry	.05	229	Bob Zupcic	.05	327	Randy Knorr	.05	418	Jody Reed	.05
132	Paul Sorrento	.05	230	Jay Bell	.05	328	Craig Shipley	.05	419	Vince Coleman	.05
133	Mike Hampton	.05	231	Dustin Hermanson	.05	329	Tim Naehring	.05	420	Danny Jackson	.05
134	Tim Spehr	.05	232	Harold Baines	.05	330	Randy Myers	.05	421	Ryan Nye RC	.05
135	Julio Franco	.05	233	Alan Benes	.05	331	Alex Cole	.05	422	Larry Walker	.05
136	Mike Dyer	.05	234	Felix Fermin	.05	332	Jim Gott	.05	423	Russ Johnson	.05
137	Chris Sabo	.05	235	Ellis Burks	.05	333	Mike Jackson	.05	424	Pat Borders	.05
138	Rheal Cormier	.05	236	Jeff Brantley	.05	334	John Flaherty	.05	425	Lee Smith	.05
139	Paul Konerko	.25	237	Brian Hunter, Jose Malave, Shane Pullen, Karim Garcia RC OF Prospects	.40	335	Chili Davis	.05	426	Paul O'Neill	.05
140	Dante Bichette	.05				336	Benji Gil (Star Track)	.05	427	Devon White	.05
141	Chuck McElroy	.05	238	Matt Nokes	.05	337a	Jason Jacome (No Diamond Vision logo on back photo.)	.25	428	Jim Bullinger	.05
142	Mike Stanley	.05	239	Ben Rivera	.05	337b	Jason Jacome (Diamond Vision logo on back photo.)	.05	429	Greg Hansell, Brian Sackinsky, Carey Paige, Rob Welch SP Prospects	.05
143	Bob Hamelin (All Star Rookie)	.05	240	Joe Carter	.05	338	Stan Javier	.05			
144	Tommy Greene	.05	241	Jeff Granger (Star Track)	.05	339	Mike Fetters	.05	430	Steve Avery	.05
145	John Smoltz	.05	242	Terry Pendleton	.05	340	Rick Renteria	.05	431	Tony Gwynn	1.00
146	Ed Sprague	.05	243	Melvin Nieves	.05	341	Kevin Witt	.05	432	Pat Meares	.05
147	Ray McDavid (Star Track)	.05	244	Frank Rodriguez	.05	342	Scott Servais	.05	433	Bill Swift	.05
148	Otis Nixon	.05	245	Darryl Hamilton	.05	343	Craig Grebeck	.05	434	David Wells	.05
149	Turk Wendell	.05	246	Brooks Kieschnick	.05	344	Kirk Rueter	.05	435	John Briscoe	.05
150	Chris James	.05	247	Todd Hollandsworth	.05	345	Don Slaught	.05	436	Roger Pavlik	.05
151	Derek Parks	.05	248	Joe Rosselli	.05	346	Armando Benitez RC (Star Track)	.15			
152	Jose Offerman	.05	249	Bill Gullickson	.05	347	Ozzie Smith	1.00			
153	Tony Clark	.05	250	Chuck Knoblauch	.05	348	Mike Blowers	.05			
154	Chad Curtis	.05	251	Kurt Abbott (Star Track)	.05	349	Armando Reynoso	.05			
155	Mark Portugal	.05	252	Bobby Jones	.05	350	Barry Larkin	.05			
156	Bill Pulsipher	.05	253	Lance Blankenship	.05	351	Mike Williams	.05			
157	Troy Neel	.05	254	Matt Whiteside	.05						
158	Dave Winfield	.75	255	Darrin Fletcher	.05						
159	Bill Wegman	.05	256	Eric Plunk	.05						
160	Benny Santiago	.05	257	Shane Reynolds	.05						
161	Jose Mesa	.05	258	Norberto Martin	.05						
			259	Mike Thurman	.05						
			260	Andy Van Slyke	.05						

No.	Player	Price
437	Jayson Peterson RC	.05
438	Roberto Alomar	.15
439	Billy Brewer	.05
440	Gary Sheffield	.40
441	Lou Frazier	.05
442	Terry Steinbach	.05
443	Jay Payton RC	.25
444	Jason Bere	.05
445	Denny Neagle	.05
446	Andres Galarraga	.05
447	Hector Carrasco	.05
448	Bill Risley	.05
449	Andy Benes	.05
450	Jim Leyritz	.05
451	Jose Oliva	.05
452	Greg Vaughn	.05
453	Rich Monteleone	.05
454	Tony Eusebio	.05
455	Chuck Finley	.05
456	Kevin Brown	.05
457	Joe Boever	.05
458	Bobby Munoz	.05
459	Bret Saberhagen	.05
460	Kurt Abbott	.05
461	Bobby Witt	.05
462	Cliff Floyd	.05
463	Mark Clark	.05
464	Andujar Cedeno	.05
465	Marvin Freeman	.05
466	Mike Piazza	1.25
467	Willie Greene	.05
468	Pat Kelly	.05
469	Carlos Delgado	.40
470	Willie Banks	.05
471	Matt Walbeck	.05
472	Mark McGwire	1.50
473	McKay Christensen	.05
474	Alan Trammell	.05
475	Tom Gordon	.05
476	Greg Colbrunn	.05
477	Darren Daulton	.05
478	Albie Lopez	.05
479	Robin Ventura	.05
480	Eddie Perez, Jason Kendall, Einar Diaz, Bret Hemphill C Prospects	.20
481	Bryan Eversgerd	.05
482	Dave Fleming	.05
483	Scott Livingstone	.05
484	Pete Schourek	.05
485	Bernie Williams	.05
486	Mark Lemke	.05
487	Eric Karros	.05
488	Scott Ruffcorn	.05
489	Billy Ashley	.05
490	Rico Brogna	.05
491	John Burkett	.05
492	Cade Gaspar RC	.05
493	Jorge Fabregas	.05
494	Greg Gagne	.05
495	Doug Jones	.05
496	Troy O'Leary	.05
497	Pat Rapp	.05
498	Butch Henry	.05
499	John Olerud	.05
500	John Hudek	.05
501	Jeff King	.05
502	Bobby Bonilla	.05
503	Albert Belle	.05
504	Rick Wilkins	.05
505	John Jaha	.05
506	Nigel Wilson	.05
507	Sid Fernandez	.05
508	Deion Sanders	.05
509	Gil Heredia	.05
510	Scott Elarton RC	.10
511	Melido Perez	.05
512	Greg McMichael	.05
513	Rusty Meacham	.05
514	Shawn Green	.35
515	Carlos Garcia	.05
516	Dave Stevens	.05
517	Eric Young	.05
518	Omar Daal	.05
519	Kirk Gibson	.05
520	Spike Owen	.05
521	Jacob Cruz RC	.05
522	Sandy Alomar	.05
523	Steve Bedrosian	.05
524	Ricky Gutierrez	.05
525	Dave Veres	.05
526	Gregg Jefferies	.05
527	Jose Valentin	.05
528	Robb Nen	.05
529	Jose Rijo	.05
530	Sean Berry	.05
531	Mike Gallego	.05
532	Roberto Kelly	.05
533	Kevin Stocker	.05
534	Kirby Puckett	1.00
535	Chipper Jones	1.00
536	Russ Davis	.05
537	Jon Lieber	.05
538	Trey Moore RC	.05
539	Joe Girardi	.05
540	Quilvio Veras, Arquimedez Pozo, Miguel Cairo, Jason Camilli 2B Prospects	.05
541	Tony Phillips	.05
542	Brian Anderson	.05
543	Ivan Rodriguez	.65
544	Jeff Cirillo	.05
545	Joey Cora	.05
546	Chris Hoiles	.05
547	Bernard Gilkey	.05
548	Mike Lansing	.05
549	Jimmy Key	.05
550	Mark Wohlers	.05
551	Chris Clemons RC	.05
552	Vinny Castilla	.05
553	Mark Guthrie	.05
554	Mike Lieberthal	.05
555	Tommy Davis RC	.05
556	Robby Thompson	.05
557	Danny Bautista	.05
558	Will Clark	.05
559	Rickey Henderson	.75
560	Todd Jones	.05
561	Jack McDowell	.05
562	Carlos Rodriguez	.05
563	Mark Eichhorn	.05
564	Jeff Nelson	.05
565	Eric Anthony	.05
566	Randy Velarde	.05
567	Javy Lopez	.05
568	Kevin Mitchell	.05
569	Steve Karsay	.05
570	Brian Meadows RC	.10
571	Rey Ordonez, Mike Metcalfe, Ray Holbert, Kevin Orie SS Propects	.40
572	John Kruk	.05
573	Scott Leius	.05
574	John Patterson	.05
575	Kevin Brown	.05
576	Mike Moore	.05
577	Manny Ramirez	.75
578	Jose Lind	.05
579	Derrick May	.05
580	Cal Eldred	.05
581	David Bell, Joel Chelmis, Lino Diaz, Aaron Boone RC 3B Prospects	.15
582	J.T. Snow	.05
583	Luis Sojo	.05
584	Moises Alou	.05
585	Dave Clark	.05
586	Dave Hollins	.05
587	Nomar Garciaparra	2.00
588	Cal Ripken Jr.	2.00
589	Pedro Astacio	.05
590	J.R. Phillips	.05
591	Jeff Frye	.05
592	Bo Jackson	.10
593	Steve Ontiveros	.05
594	David Nied	.05
595	Brad Ausmus	.05
596	Carlos Baerga	.05
597	James Mouton	.05
598	Ozzie Guillen	.05
599	Ozzie Timmons, Curtis Goodwin, Johnny Damon, Jeff Abbott RC OF Prospects	.25
600	Yorkis Perez	.05
601	Rich Rodriguez	.05
602	Mark McLemore	.05
603	Jeff Fassero	.05
604	John Roper	.05
605	Mark Johnson RC	.10
606	Wes Chamberlain	.05
607	Felix Jose	.05
608	Tony Longmire	.05
609	Duane Ward	.05
610	Brett Butler	.05
611	William Van Landingham	.05
612	Mickey Tettleton	.05
613	Brady Anderson	.05
614	Reggie Jefferson	.05
615	Mike Kingery	.05
616	Derek Bell	.05
617	Scott Erickson	.05
618	Bob Wickman	.05
619	Phil Leftwich	.05
620	Dave Justice	.05
621	Paul Wilson	.05
622	Pedro Martinez	.75
623	Terry Mathews	.05
624	Brian McRae	.05
625	Bruce Ruffin	.05
626	Steve Finley	.05
627	Ron Gant	.05
628	Rafael Bournigal	.05
629	Darryl Strawberry	.05
630	Luis Alicea	.05
631	Mark Smith, Scott Klingenbeck	.05
632	Cory Bailey, Scott Hatteberg	.05
633	Todd Greene, Troy Percival	.05
634	Rod Bolton, Olmedo Saenz	.05
635	Herb Perry, Steve Kline	.05
636	Sean Bergman, Shannon Penn	.05
637	Joe Vitiello, Joe Randa	.05
638	Jose Mercedes, Duane Singleton	.05
639	Marty Cordova, Marc Barcelo	.10
640	Ruben Rivera, Andy Pettitte	.10
641	Willie Adams, Scott Spiezio	.05
642	Eddie Diaz, Desi Relaford	.05
643	Jon Shave, Terrell Lowery	.05
644	Paul Spoljaric, Angel Martinez	.05
645	Damon Hollins, Tony Graffanino	.05
646	Darron Cox, Doug Glanville	.05
647	Tim Belk, Pat Watkins	.05
648	Rod Pedraza, Phil Schneider	.05
649	Marc Valdes, Vic Darensbourg	.05
650	Rick Huisman, Roberto Petagine	.05
651	Ron Coomer, Roger Cedeno	.05
652	Carlos Perez, Shane Andrews	.10
653	Jason Isringhausen, Chris Roberts	.05
654	Kevin Jordan, Wayne Gomes	.05
655	Esteban Loaiza, Steve Pegues	.05
656	John Frascatore, Terry Bradshaw	.05
657	Bryce Florie, Andres Berumen	.05
658	Keith Williams, Dan Carlson	.05
659	Checklist	
660	Checklist	

Cyberstats

2B/OF—SAN DIEGO PADRES

No.	Player	NM/M
	Complete Set (396):	25.00
	Common Player:	.10
1	Frank Thomas	.75
2	Mickey Morandini	.10
3	Todd Worrell	.10
4	David Cone	.10
5	Trevor Hoffman	.10
6	Shane Mack	.10
7	Delino DeShields	.10
8	Matt Williams	.10
9	Sammy Sosa	1.00
10	Gary DiSarcina	.10
11	Kenny Rogers	.10
12	Jose Vizcaino	.10
13	Lou Whitaker	.10
14	Ron Darling	.10
15	Dave Nilsson	.10
16	Dennis Martinez	.10
17	Orlando Merced	.10
18	John Wetteland	.10
19	Mike Devereaux	.10
20	Rene Arocha	.10
21	Jay Buhner	.10
22	Hal Morris	.10
23	Paul Molitor	.75
24	Dave West	.10
25	Scott Sanders	.10
26	Eddie Zambrano	.10
27	Ricky Bones	.10
28	John Valentin	.10
29	Kevin Tapani	.10
30	Tim Wallach	.10
31	Darren Lewis	.10
32	Travis Fryman	.10
33	Bret Barberie	.10
34	Dennis Eckersley	.65
35	Ken Hill	.10
36	Pete Harnisch	.10
37	Mike Mussina	.50
38	Dave Winfield	.75
39	Joey Hamilton	.10
40	Edgar Martinez	.10
41	John Smiley	.10
42	Jim Abbott	.10
43	Mike Kelly	.10
44	Brian Jordan	.10
45	Ken Ryan	.10
46	Matt Mieske	.10
47	Rick Aguilera	.10
48	Ismael Valdes	.10
49	Royce Clayton	.10
50	Juan Gonzalez	.35
51	Mel Rojas	.10
52	Doug Drabek	.10
53	Charles Nagy	.10
54	Tim Raines	.10
55	Midre Cummings	.10
56	Rafael Palmeiro	.65
57	Charlie Hayes	.10
58	Ray Lankford	.10
59	Tim Davis	.10
60	Andy Ashby	.10
61	Mark Grace	.10
62	Mark Langston	.10
63	Chuck Carr	.10
64	Barry Bonds	2.00
65	David Segui	.10
66	Mariano Duncan	.10
67	Kenny Lofton	.10
68	Ken Caminiti	.10
69	Darrin Jackson	.10
70	Wil Cordero	.10
71	Walt Weiss	.10
72	Tom Pagnozzi	.10
73	Bret Boone	.10
74	Wally Joyner	.10
75	Luis Lopez	.10
76	Len Dykstra	.10
77	Pedro Munoz	.10
78	Kevin Gross	.10
79	Eduardo Perez	.10
80	Brent Gates	.10
81	Jeff Conine	.10
82	Paul Sorrento	.10
83	Julio Franco	.10
84	Chris Sabo	.10
85	Dante Bichette	.10
86	Mike Stanley	.10
87	Bob Hamelin	.10
88	Tommy Greene	.10
89	Jeff Brantley	.10
90	Ed Sprague	.10
91	Otis Nixon	.10
92	Chad Curtis	.10
93	Chuck McElroy	.10
94	Troy Neel	.10
95	Benito Santiago	.10
96	Jose Mesa	.10
97	Luis Gonzalez	.10
98	Alex Fernandez	.10
99	Ben McDonald	.10
100	Wade Boggs	1.00
101	Tom Glavine	.35
102	Phil Plantier	.10
103	Raul Mondesi	.10
104	Jim Edmonds	.10
105	Jeff Kent	.10
106	Wilson Alvarez	.10
107	Geronimo Berroa	.10
108	Craig Biggio	.10
109	Roberto Hernandez	.10
110	Bobby Ayala	.10
111	Bob Tewksbury	.10
112	Rondell White	.10
113	Steve Cooke	.10
114	Tim Salmon	.10
115	Kent Mercker	.10
116	Randy Johnson	.75
117	Mo Vaughn	.10
118	Eddie Williams	.10
119	Jeff Montgomery	.10
120	Kirt Manwaring	.10
121	Pat Hentgen	.10
122	Shawon Dunston	.10
123	Tim Belcher	.10
124	Cecil Fielder	.10
125	Todd Hundley	.10
126	Mark Acre	.10

127	Darrell Whitmore	.10
128	Darryl Kile	.10
129	Jay Bell	.10
130	Harold Baines	.10
131	Felix Fermin	.10
132	Ellis Burks	.10
133	Joe Carter	.10
134	Terry Pendleton	.10
135	Junior Felix	.10
136	Bill Gullickson	.10
137	Melvin Nieves	.10
138	Chuck Knoblauch	.10
139	Bobby Jones	.10
140	Darrin Fletcher	.10
141	Andy Van Slyke	.10
142	Allen Watson	.10
143	Dan Wilson	.10
144	Bip Roberts	.10
145	Sterling Hitchcock	.10
146	Johnny Ruffin	.10
147	Steve Trachsel	.10
148	Ramon Martinez	.10
149	Dave Henderson	.10
150	Chris Gomez	.10
151	Rusty Greer	.10
152	John Franco	.10
153	Mike Bordick	.10
154	Dave Magadan	.10
155	Greg Swindell	.10
156	Arthur Rhodes	.10
157	Juan Guzman	.10
158	Greg Maddux	1.00
159	Mike Macfarlane	.10
160	Curt Schilling	.35
161	Jose Canseco	.40
162	Aaron Sele	.10
163	Steve Buechele	.10
164	Orel Hershiser	.10
165	Mike Henneman	.10
166	Kevin Seitzer	.10
167	Ruben Sierra	.10
168	Alex Cole	.10
169	Jim Thome	.65
170	Lance Johnson	.10
171	Marquis Grissom	.10
172	Jamie Moyer	.10
173	Todd Zeile	.10
174	Chris Bosio	.10
175	Steve Howe	.10
176	Luis Polonia	.10
177	Ryan Klesko	.10
178	Kevin Appier	.10
179	Tim Naehring	.10
180	Randy Myers	.10
181	Mike Jackson	.10
182	Chili Davis	.10
183	Jason Jacome	.10
184	Stan Javier	.10
185	Scott Servais	.10
186	Kirk Rueter	.10
187	Don Slaught	.10
188	Ozzie Smith	1.00
189	Barry Larkin	.10
190	Gary Gaetti	.10
191	Fred McGriff	.75
192	Roger Clemens	1.00
193	Dean Palmer	.10
194	Jeromy Burnitz	.10
195	Scott Kamieniecki	.10
196	Eddie Murray	.75
197	Ron Karkovice	.10
198	Tino Martinez	.10
199	Ken Griffey Jr.	1.25
200	Don Mattingly	1.00
201	Henry Rodriguez	.10
202	Lenny Harris	.10
203	Ryan Thompson	.10
204	Darren Oliver	.10
205	Omar Vizquel	.10
206	Jeff Bagwell	.75
207	Todd Van Poppel	.10
208	Leo Gomez	.10
209	Mark Whiten	.10
210	Pedro Martinez	.10
211	Reggie Sanders	.10
212	Kevin Foster	.10
213	Danny Tartabull	.10
214	Jeff Blauser	.10
215	Mike Magnante	.10
216	Tom Candiotti	.10
217	Rod Beck	.10
218	Jody Reed	.10
219	Vince Coleman	.10
220	Danny Jackson	.10
221	Larry Walker	.10
222	Pat Borders	.10
223	Lee Smith	.10
224	Paul O'Neill	.10
225	Devon White	.10
226	Jim Bullinger	.10
227	Steve Avery	.10
228	Tony Gwynn	1.00
229	Pat Meares	.10
230	Bill Swift	.10

231	David Wells	.10
232	John Briscoe	.10
233	Roger Pavlik	.10
234	Roberto Alomar	.30
235	Billy Brewer	.10
236	Gary Sheffield	.40
237	Lou Frazier	.10
238	Terry Steinbach	.10
239	Omar Daal	.10
240	Jason Bere	.10
241	Denny Neagle	.10
242	Danny Bautista	.10
243	Hector Carrasco	.10
244	Bill Risley	.10
245	Andy Benes	.10
246	Jim Leyritz	.10
247	Jose Oliva	.10
248	Greg Vaughn	.10
249	Rich Monteleone	.10
250	Tony Eusebio	.10
251	Chuck Finley	.10
252	Joe Boever	.10
253	Bobby Munoz	.10
254	Bret Saberhagen	.10
255	Kurt Abbott	.10
256	Bobby Witt	.10
257	Cliff Floyd	.10
258	Mark Clark	.10
259	Andujar Cedeno	.10
260	Marvin Freeman	.10
261	Mike Piazza	1.25
262	Pat Kelly	.10
263	Carlos Delgado	.45
264	Willie Banks	.10
265	Matt Walbeck	.10
266	Mark McGwire	1.50
267	Alan Trammell	.10
268	Tom Gordon	.10
269	Greg Colbrunn	.10
270	Darren Daulton	.10
271	Albie Lopez	.10
272	Robin Ventura	.10
273	Bryan Eversgerd	.10
274	Dave Fleming	.10
275	Scott Livingstone	.10
276	Pete Schourek	.10
277	Bernie Williams	.10
278	Mark Lemke	.10
279	Eric Karros	.10
280	Billy Ashley	.10
281	Rico Brogna	.10
282	John Burkett	.10
283	Jorge Fabregas	.10
284	Greg Gagne	.10
285	Doug Jones	.10
286	Troy O'Leary	.10
287	Pat Rapp	.10
288	Butch Henry	.10
289	John Olerud	.10
290	John Hudek	.10
291	Jeff King	.10
292	Bobby Bonilla	.10
293	Albert Belle	.10
294	Rick Wilkins	.10
295	John Jaha	.10
296	Sid Fernandez	.10
297	Deion Sanders	.10
298	Gil Heredia	.10
299	Melido Perez	.10
300	Greg McMichael	.10
301	Rusty Meacham	.10
302	Shawn Green	.35
303	Carlos Garcia	.10
304	Dave Stevens	.10
305	Eric Young	.10
306	Kirk Gibson	.10
307	Spike Owen	.10
308	Sandy Alomar	.10
309	Ricky Gutierrez	.10
310	Dave Veres	.10
311	Gregg Jefferies	.10
312	Jose Valentin	.10
313	Robb Nen	.10
314	Jose Rijo	.10
315	Sean Berry	.10
316	Mike Gallego	.10
317	Roberto Kelly	.10
318	Kevin Stocker	.10
319	Kirby Puckett	1.00
320	Jon Lieber	.10
321	Joe Girardi	.10
322	Tony Phillips	.10
323	Brian Anderson	.10
324	Ivan Rodriguez	.65
325	Jeff Cirillo	.10
326	Joey Cora	.10
327	Chris Hoiles	.10
328	Bernard Gilkey	.10
329	Mike Lansing	.10
330	Jimmy Key	.10
331	Vinny Castilla	.10
332	Mark Guthrie	.10
333	Mike Lieberthal	.10
334	Will Clark	.10

335	Rickey Henderson	.75
336	Todd Jones	.10
337	Jack McDowell	.10
338	Carlos Rodriguez	.10
339	Mark Eichhorn	.10
340	Jeff Nelson	.10
341	Eric Anthony	.10
342	Randy Velarde	.10
343	Javier Lopez	.10
344	Kevin Mitchell	.10
345	Steve Bedrosian	.10
346	John Kruk	.10
347	Scott Leius	.10
348	John Patterson	.10
349	Kevin Brown	.10
350	Mike Moore	.10
351	Manny Ramirez	.75
352	Jose Lind	.10
353	Derrick May	.10
354	Cal Eldred	.10
355	J.T. Snow	.10
356	Luis Sojo	.10
357	Moises Alou	.10
358	Dave Clark	.10
359	Dave Hollins	.10
360	Cal Ripken Jr.	2.00
361	Pedro Astacio	.10
362	Tony Longmire	.10
363	Jeff Frye	.10
364	Bo Jackson	.20
365	Steve Ontiveros	.10
366	David Nied	.10
367	Brad Ausmus	.10
368	Carlos Baerga	.10
369	James Mouton	.10
370	Ozzie Guillen	.10
371	Yorkis Perez	.10
372	Rich Rodriguez	.10
373	Mark McLemore	.10
374	Jeff Fassero	.10
375	John Roper	.10
376	Wes Chamberlain	.10
377	Felix Jose	.10
378	Brett Butler	.10
379	William Van Landingham	.10
380	Mickey Tettleton	.10
381	Brady Anderson	.10
382	Reggie Jefferson	.10
383	Mike Kingery	.10
384	Derek Bell	.10
385	Scott Erickson	.10
386	Bob Wickman	.10
387	Phil Leftwich	.10
388	Dave Justice	.10
389	Pedro Martinez	.75
390	Terry Mathews	.10
391	Brian McRae	.10
392	Bruce Ruffin	.10
393	Steve Finley	.10
394	Rafael Bournigal	.10
395	Darryl Strawberry	.10
396	Luis Alicea	.10

Cyberstat Season in Review

Juan Gonzalez

			NM/M
	Complete Set (7):		10.00
	Common Player:		1.00
1	Barry Bonds (61 Home Runs)		6.00
2	Jose Canseco (AL West One-Game Playoff)		2.00
3	Juan Gonzalez (AL Divisional Playoffs)		1.50
4	Fred McGriff (NL Divisional Playoffs)		1.00
5	Carlos Baerga (ALCS MVP)		1.00
6	Ryan Klesko (NLCS MVP)		1.00
7	Kenny Lofton (World Series MVP)		1.00

League Leaders

DEION SANDERS

		NM/M
	Complete Set (50):	20.00
	Common Player:	.15
1	Albert Belle	.15
2	Kevin Mitchell	.15
3	Wade Boggs	1.50
4	Tony Gwynn	1.50
5	Moises Alou	.15
6	Andres Galarraga	.15
7	Matt Williams	.15
8	Barry Bonds	4.00
9	Frank Thomas	.75
10	Jose Canseco	.50
11	Jeff Bagwell	.75
12	Kirby Puckett	1.50
13	Julio Franco	.15
14	Albert Belle	.15
15	Fred McGriff	.15
16	Kenny Lofton	.15
17	Otis Nixon	.15
18	Brady Anderson	.15
19	Deion Sanders	.15
20	Chuck Carr	.15
21	Pat Hentgen	.15
22	Andy Benes	.15
23	Roger Clemens	1.75
24	Greg Maddux	1.50
25	Pedro Martinez	.75
26	Paul O'Neill	.15
27	Jeff Bagwell	.75
28	Frank Thomas	.75
29	Hal Morris	.15
30	Kenny Lofton	.15
31	Ken Griffey Jr.	2.00
32	Jeff Bagwell	.75
33	Albert Belle	.15
34	Fred McGriff	.15
35	Cecil Fielder	.15
36	Matt Williams	.15
37	Joe Carter	.15
38	Dante Bichette	.15
39	Frank Thomas	.75
40	Mike Piazza	2.00
41	Craig Biggio	.15
42	Vince Coleman	.15
43	Marquis Grissom	.15
44	Chuck Knoblauch	.15
45	Darren Lewis	.15
46	Randy Johnson	.75
47	Jose Rijo	.15
48	Chuck Finley	.15
49	Bret Saberhagen	.15
50	Kevin Appier	.15

Opening Day

Devon White

		NM/M
	Complete Set (10):	7.50
	Common Player:	.75
1	Kevin Appier	.75

2	Dante Bichette	.75
3	Ken Griffey Jr.	3.50
4	Todd Hundley	.75
5	John Jaha	.75
6	Fred McGriff	.75
7	Raul Mondesi	.75
8	Manny Ramirez	2.50
9	Danny Tartabull	.75
10	Devon White	.75

Total Bases Finest

		NM/M
Complete Set (15):		12.00
Common Player:		.50
1	Jeff Bagwell	1.25
2	Albert Belle	.50
3	Ken Griffey Jr.	2.00
4	Frank Thomas	1.25
5	Matt Williams	.50
6	Dante Bichette	.50
7	Barry Bonds	2.50
8	Moises Alou	.50
9	Andres Galarraga	.50
10	Kenny Lofton	.50
11	Rafael Palmeiro	1.00
12	Tony Gwynn	1.50
13	Kirby Puckett	1.50
14	Jose Canseco	.75
15	Jeff Conine	.50

1995 Topps Embossed

		NM/M
Complete Set (140):		7.50
Common Player:		.10
Wax Pack (6+1):		1.50
Wax Box (24):		22.50
1	Kenny Lofton	.10
2	Gary Sheffield	.35
3	Hal Morris	.10
4	Cliff Floyd	.10
5	Pat Hentgen	.10
6	Tony Gwynn	.75
7	Jose Valentin	.10
8	Jason Bere	.10
9	Jeff Kent	.10
10	John Valentin	.10
11	Brian Anderson	.10
12	Deion Sanders	.10
13	Ryan Thompson	.10
14	Ruben Sierra	.10
15	Jay Bell	.10
16	Chuck Carr	.10
17	Brent Gates	.10
18	Bret Boone	.10
19	Paul Molitor	.60
20	Chili Davis	.10
21	Ryan Klesko	.10
22	Will Clark	.10
23	Greg Vaughn	.10
24	Moises Alou	.10
25	Ray Lankford	.10
26	Jose Rijo	.10
27	Bobby Jones	.10
28	Rick Wilkins	.10
29	Cal Eldred	.10
30	Juan Gonzalez	.30
31	Royce Clayton	.10
32	Bryan Harvey	.10
33	Dave Nilsson	.10
34	Chris Hoiles	.10
35	David Nied	.10
36	Javy Lopez	.10
37	Tim Wallach	.10
38	Bobby Bonilla	.10
39	Danny Tartabull	.10
40	Andy Benes	.10
41	Dean Palmer	.10
42	Chris Gomez	.10
43	Kevin Appier	.10
44	Brady Anderson	.10
45	Alex Fernandez	.10
46	Roberto Kelly	.10
47	Dave Hollins	.10
48	Chuck Finley	.10
49	Wade Boggs	.75
50	Travis Fryman	.10
51	Ken Griffey Jr.	1.00
52	John Olerud	.10
53	Delino DeShields	.10
54	Ivan Rodriguez	.50
55	Tommy Greene	.10
56	Tom Pagnozzi	.10
57	Bip Roberts	.10
58	Luis Gonzalez	.10
59	Rey Sanchez	.10
60	Ken Ryan	.10
61	Darren Daulton	.10
62	Rick Aguilera	.10
63	Wally Joyner	.10
64	Mike Greenwell	.10
65	Jay Buhner	.10
66	Craig Biggio	.10
67	Charles Nagy	.10
68	Devon White	.10
69	Randy Johnson	.60
70	Shawon Dunston	.10
71	Kirby Puckett	.75
72	Paul O'Neill	.10
73	Tino Martinez	.10
74	Carlos Garcia	.10
75	Ozzie Smith	.75
76	Cecil Fielder	.10
77	Mike Stanley	.10
78	Lance Johnson	.10
79	Tony Phillips	.10
80	Bobby Munoz	.10
81	Kevin Tapani	.10
82	William Van Landingham	.10
83	Dante Bichette	.10
84	Tom Candiotti	.10
85	Wil Cordero	.10
86	Jeff Conine	.10
87	Joey Hamilton	.10
88	Mark Whiten	.10
89	Jeff Montgomery	.10
90	Andres Galarraga	.10
91	Roberto Alomar	.20
92	Orlando Merced	.10
93	Mike Mussina	.35
94	Pedro Martinez	.60
95	Carlos Baerga	.10
96	Steve Trachsel	.10
97	Lou Whitaker	.10
98	David Cone	.10
99	Chuck Knoblauch	.10
100	Frank Thomas	.60
101	Dave Justice	.10
102	Raul Mondesi	.10
103	Rickey Henderson	.60
104	Doug Drabek	.10
105	Sandy Alomar	.10
106	Roger Clemens	.10
107	Mark McGwire	1.20
108	Tim Salmon	.10
109	Greg Maddux	.75
110	Mike Piazza	1.00
111	Tom Glavine	.30
112	Walt Weiss	.10
113	Cal Ripken Jr.	1.50
114	Eddie Murray	.60
115	Don Mattingly	.85
116	Ozzie Guillen	.10
117	Bob Hamelin	.10
118	Jeff Bagwell	.60
119	Eric Karros	.10
120	Barry Bonds	1.50
121	Mickey Tettleton	.10
122	Mark Langston	.10
123	Robin Ventura	.10
124	Bret Saberhagen	.10
125	Albert Belle	.50
126	Rafael Palmeiro	.50
127	Fred McGriff	.10
128	Jimmy Key	.10
129	Barry Larkin	.10
130	Tim Raines	.10
131	Len Dykstra	.10
132	Todd Zeile	.10
133	Joe Carter	.10
134	Matt Williams	.10
135	Terry Steinbach	.10
136	Manny Ramirez	.60
137	John Wetteland	.10
138	Rod Beck	.10
139	Mo Vaughn	.10
140	Darren Lewis	.10

Golden Idols

		NM/M
Complete Set (140):		25.00
Common Player:		.25

(Star cards valued at 2X corresponding regular Embossed cards.)

1995 Topps DIII

		NM/M
Complete Set (59):		10.00
Common Player:		.15
Retail Pack (3):		.50
Retail Wax Box (24):		9.00
Hobby Pack (5):		.65
Hobby Wax Box (24):		12.50
1	Dave Justice	.15
2	Cal Ripken Jr.	2.50
3	Ruben Sierra	.15
4	Roberto Alomar	.25
5	Dennis Martinez	.15
6	Todd Zeile	.15
7	Albert Belle	.15
8	Chuck Knoblauch	.15
9	Roger Clemens	1.25
10	Cal Eldred	.15
11	Dennis Eckersley	.75
12	Andy Benes	.15
13	Moises Alou	.15
14	Andres Galarraga	.15
15	Jim Thome	.65
16	Tim Salmon	.15
17	Carlos Garcia	.15
18	Scott Leius	.15
19	Jeff Montgomery	.15
20	Brian Anderson	.15
21	Will Clark	.15
22	Bobby Bonilla	.15
23	Mike Stanley	.15
24	Barry Bonds	2.50
25	Jeff Conine	.15
26	Paul O'Neill	.15
27	Mike Piazza	1.50
28	Tom Glavine	.35
29	Jim Edmonds	.15
30	Lou Whitaker	.15
31	Jeff Frye	.15
32	Ivan Rodriguez	.75
33	Bret Boone	.15
34	Mike Greenwell	.15
35	Mark Grace	.15
36	Darren Lewis	.15
37	Don Mattingly	1.25
38	Jose Rijo	.15
39	Robin Ventura	.15
40	Bob Hamelin	.15
41	Tim Wallach	.15
42	Tony Gwynn	1.00
43	Ken Griffey Jr.	1.50
44	Doug Drabek	.15
45	Rafael Palmeiro	.75
46	Dean Palmer	.15
47	Bip Roberts	.15
48	Barry Larkin	.15
49	Dave Nilsson	.15
50	Wil Cordero	.15
51	Travis Fryman	.15
52	Chuck Carr	.15
53	Rey Sanchez	.15
54	Walt Weiss	.15
55	Joe Carter	.15
56	Len Dykstra	.15
57	Orlando Merced	.15
58	Ozzie Smith	1.00
59	Chris Gomez	.15

Zone

		NM/M
Complete Set (6):		4.00
Common Player:		.50
1	Frank Thomas	1.00
2	Kirby Puckett	1.50
3	Jeff Bagwell	1.00
4	Fred McGriff	.50
5	Raul Mondesi	.50
6	Kenny Lofton	.50

Traded and Rookies

		NM/M
Complete Set (165):		30.00
Common Player:		.05
Pack (11):		2.50
Wax Box (36):		60.00
1	Frank Thomas	.50
2	Ken Griffey Jr.	.65
3	Barry Bonds	1.00
4	Albert Belle	.05
5	Cal Ripken Jr.	1.00
6	Mike Piazza	.75
7	Tony Gwynn	.60
8	Jeff Bagwell	.45
9	Mo Vaughn	.05
10	Matt Williams	.05
11	Ray Durham	.05
12	Juan LeBron (Photo Carlos Beltran.)	5.00
13	Shawn Green (Rookie of the Year Candidate)	.50
14	Kevin Gross	.05
15	Jon Nunnally	.05

16	Brian Maxcy RC	.05
17	Mark Kiefer	.05
18	Carlos Beltran RC (Photo actually Juan Beltran.)	15.00
19	Mike Mimbs RC	.05
20	Larry Walker	.05
21	Chad Curtis	.05
22	Jeff Barry	.05
23	Joe Oliver	.05
24	Tomas Perez RC	.05
25	Michael Barrett RC	1.50
26	Brian McRae	.05
27	Derek Bell	.05
28	Ray Durham (Rookie of the Year Candidate)	.05
29	Todd Williams	.05
30	Ryan Jaroncyk RC	.05
31	Todd Steverson	.05
32	Mike Devereaux	.05
33	Rheal Cormier	.05
34	Benny Santiago	.05
35	Bobby Higginson RC	.50
36	Jack McDowell	.05
37	Mike Macfarlane	.05
38	Tony McKnight RC	.05
39	Brian Hunter (Rookie of the Year Candidate)	.05
40	Hideo Nomo RC (Star Track)	2.00
41	Brett Butler	.05
42	Donovan Osborne	.05
43	Scott Karl	.05
44	Tony Phillips	.05
45	Marty Cordova (Rookie of the Year Candidate)	.20
46	Dave Mlicki	.05
47	Bronson Arroyo RC	4.00
48	John Burkett	.05
49	J.D. Smart RC	.05
50	Mickey Tettleton	.05
51	Todd Stottlemyre	.05
52	Mike Perez	.05
53	Terry Mulholland	.05
54	Edgardo Alfonzo	.05
55	Zane Smith	.05
56	Jacob Brumfield	.05
57	Andujar Cedeno	.05
58	Jose Parra	.05
59	Manny Alexander	.05
60	Tony Tarasco	.05
61	Orel Hershiser	.05
62	Tim Scott	.05
63	Felix Rodriguez RC	.05
64	Ken Hill	.05
65	Marquis Grissom	.05
66	Lee Smith	.05
67	Jason Bates (Rookie of the Year Candidate)	.05
68	Felipe Lira	.05
69	Alex Hernandez RC	.10
70	Tony Fernandez	.05
71	Scott Radinsky	.05
72	Jose Canseco	.50
73	Mark Grudzielanek RC	.50
74	Ben Davis RC	.25
75	Jim Abbott	.05
76	Roger Bailey	.05
77	Gregg Jefferies	.05
78	Erik Hanson	.05
79	Brad Radke RC	1.50
80	Jaime Navarro	.05
81	John Wetteland	.05
82	Chad Fonville RC	.10
83	John Mabry	.05
84	Glenallen Hill	.05
85	Ken Caminiti	.05
86	Tom Goodwin	.05
87	Darren Bragg	.05
88	Pat Ahearne, Gary Rath, Larry Wimberly, Robbie Bell RC 1995 Prospects/Pitchers	.10
89	Jeff Russell	.05
90	Dave Gallagher	.05
91	Steve Finley	.05
92	Vaughn Eshelman	.05
93	Kevin Jarvis	.05
94	Mark Gubicza	.05
95	Tim Wakefield	.05
96	Bob Tewksbury	.05
97	Sid Roberson RC	.05
98	Tom Henke	.05
99	Michael Tucker	.05
100	Jason Bates	.05
101	Otis Nixon	.05
102	Mark Whiten	.05
103	Dilson Torres	.05
104	Melvin Bunch RC	.05
105	Terry Pendleton	.05
106	Corey Jenkins RC	.05
107	Glenn Dishman, Rob Grable RC On Deck	.05
108	Reggie Taylor RC	.05

109	Curtis Goodwin (Rookie of the Year Candidate)	.05
110	David Cone	.05
111	Antonio Osuna	.05
112	Paul Shuey	.05
113	Doug Jones	.05
114	Mark McLemore	.05
115	Kevin Ritz	.05
116	John Kruk	.05
117	Trevor Wilson	.05
118	Jerald Clark	.05
119	Julian Tavarez	.05
120	Tim Pugh	.05
121	Todd Zeile	.05
122	Mark Sweeney, George Arias, Richie Sexson, Brian Schneider RC 1995 Prospects/Fielders	4.00
123	Bobby Witt	.05
124	Hideo Nomo (Rookie of the Year Candidate)	1.00
125	Joey Cora	.05
126	Jim Scharrer RC	.05
127	Paul Quantrill	.05
128	Chipper Jones (Rookie of the Year Candidate)	.75
129	Kenny James RC	.05
130	Lyle Mouton, Mariano Rivera On Deck	.15
131	Tyler Green (Rookie of the Year Candidate)	.05
132	Brad Clontz	.05
133	Jon Nunnally (Rookie of the Year Candidate)	.05
134	Dave Magadan	.05
135	Al Leiter	.05
136	Bret Barberie	.05
137	Bill Swift	.05
138	Scott Cooper	.05
139	Roberto Kelly	.05
140	Charlie Hayes	.05
141	Pete Harnisch	.05
142	Rich Amaral	.05
143	Rudy Seanez	.05
144	Pat Listach	.05
145	Quilvio Veras (Rookie of the Year Candidate)	.05
146	Jose Olmeda RC	.05
147	Roberto Petagine	.05
148	Kevin Brown	.05
149	Phil Plantier	.05
150	Carlos Perez RC (Rookie of the Year Candidate)	.05
151	Pat Borders	.05
152	Tyler Green	.05
153	Stan Belinda	.05
154	Dave Stewart	.05
155	Andre Dawson	.25
156	Frank Thomas, Fred McGriff/AS	.30
157	Carlos Baerga, Craig Biggio/AS	.05
158	Wade Boggs, Matt Williams/AS	.35
159	Cal Ripken Jr., Ozzie Smith/AS	.75
160	Ken Griffey Jr., Tony Gwynn/AS	.40
161	Albert Belle, Barry Bonds/AS	.75
162	Kirby Puckett, Len Dykstra/AS	.35
163	Ivan Rodriguez, Mike Piazza/AS	.40
164	Randy Johnson, Hideo Nomo/AS	.25
165	Checklist	

Traded and Rookies Power Boosters

	NM/M
Complete Set (10):	20.00
Common Player:	.75
1 Frank Thomas	1.50
2 Ken Griffey Jr.	3.00
3 Barry Bonds	5.00
4 Albert Belle	.75
5 Cal Ripken Jr.	5.00
6 Mike Piazza	3.00
7 Tony Gwynn	2.50
8 Jeff Bagwell	1.50
9 Mo Vaughn	.75
10 Matt Williams	.75

1996 Topps

MO VAUGHN

	NM/M
Unopened Hobby Set (449):	40.00
Unopened Retail Set (450):	40.00
Unopened Cereal Box Set (444):	35.00
Complete Set (440):	25.00
Common Player:	.05
Wax Pack (12):	1.50
Wax Box (36):	35.00
Cello Pack (17):	2.50
Cello Box (24):	40.00
Vending Box (500):	12.50
1 Tony Gwynn	.50
2 Mike Piazza	.75
3 Greg Maddux	.50
4 Jeff Bagwell	.40
5 Larry Walker	.05
6 Barry Larkin	.05
7 Mickey Mantle (Commemorative)	4.00
8 Tom Glavine	.05
9 Craig Biggio	.05
10 Barry Bonds	1.00
11 Heathcliff Slocumb	.05
12 Matt Williams	.05
13 Todd Helton	.75
14 Mark Redman	.05
15 Michael Barrett	.05
16 Ben Davis	.05
17 Juan LeBron	.05
18 Tony McKnight	.05
19 Ryan Jaroncyk	.05
20 Corey Jenkins	.05
21 Jim Scharrer	.05
22 Mark Bellhorn RC	.10
23 Jarrod Washburn RC	.05
24 Geoff Jenkins RC	1.00
25 Sean Casey RC	3.00
26 Brett Tomko RC	.10
27 Tony Fernandez	.05
28 Rich Becker	.05
29 Andujar Cedeno	.05
30 Paul Molitor	.75
31 Brent Gates	.05
32 Glenallen Hill	.05
33 Mike MacFarlane	.05
34 Manny Alexander	.05
35 Todd Zeile	.05
36 Joe Girardi	.05
37 Tony Tarasco	.05
38 Tim Belcher	.05
39 Tom Goodwin	.05
40 Orel Hershiser	.05
41 Tripp Cromer	.05
42 Sean Bergman	.05
43 Troy Percival	.05
44 Kevin Stocker	.05
45 Albert Belle	.05
46 Tony Eusebio	.05
47 Sid Roberson	.05
48 Todd Hollandsworth	.05
49 Mark Wohlers	.05
50 Kirby Puckett	1.00
51 Darren Holmes	.05
52 Ron Karkovice	.05
53 Al Martin	.05

54	Pat Rapp	.05
55	Mark Grace	.05
56	Greg Gagne	.05
57	Stan Javier	.05
58	Scott Sanders	.05
59	J.T. Snow	.05
60	David Justice	.05
61	Royce Clayton	.05
62	Kevin Foster	.05
63	Tim Naehring	.05
64	Orlando Miller	.05
65	Mike Mussina	.35
66	Jim Eisenreich	.05
67	Felix Fermin	.05
68	Bernie Williams	.05
69	Robb Nen	.05
70	Ron Gant	.05
71	Felipe Lira	.05
72	Jacob Brumfield	.05
73	John Mabry	.05
74	Mark Carreon	.05
75	Carlos Baerga	.05
76	Jim Dougherty	.05
77	Ryan Thompson	.05
78	Scott Leius	.05
79	Roger Pavlik	.05
80	Gary Sheffield	.45
81	Julian Tavarez	.05
82	Andy Ashby	.05
83	Mark Lemke	.05
84	Omar Vizquel	.05
85	Darren Daulton	.05
86	Mike Lansing	.05
87	Rusty Greer	.05
88	Dave Stevens	.05
89	Jose Offerman	.05
90	Tom Henke	.05
91	Troy O'Leary	.05
92	Michael Tucker	.05
93	Marvin Freeman	.05
94	Alex Diaz	.05
95	John Wetteland	.05
96	Cal Ripken Jr. (Tribute Card)	1.00
97	Mike Mimbs	.05
98	Bobby Higginson	.05
99	Edgardo Alfonzo	.05
100	Frank Thomas	.75
101	Steve Gibralter, Bob Abreu (AAA Stars)	.05
102	Brian Givens, T.J. Mathews (AAA Stars)	.05
103	Chris Pritchett, Trenidad Hubbard (AAA Stars)	.05
104	Eric Owens, Butch Huskey (AAA Stars)	.05
105	Doug Drabek	.05
106	Tomas Perez	.05
107	Mark Leiter	.05
108	Joe Oliver	.05
109	Tony Castillo	.05
110	Checklist	.05
111	Kevin Seitzer	.05
112	Pete Schourek	.05
113	Sean Berry	.05
114	Todd Stottlemyre	.05
115	Joe Carter	.05
116	Jeff King	.05
117	Dan Wilson	.05
118	Kurt Abbott	.05
119	Lyle Mouton	.05
120	Jose Rijo	.05
121	Curtis Goodwin	.05
122	Jose Valentin RC	.05
123	Ellis Burks	.05
124	David Cone	.05
125	Eddie Murray	.75
126	Brian Jordan	.05
127	Darrin Fletcher	.05
128	Curt Schilling	.25
129	Ozzie Guillen	.05
130	Kenny Rogers	.05
131	Tom Pagnozzi	.05
132	Garret Anderson	.05
133	Bobby Jones	.05
134	Chris Gomez	.05
135	Mike Stanley	.05
136	Hideo Nomo	.35
137	Jon Nunnally	.05
138	Tim Wakefield	.05
139	Steve Finley	.05
140	Ivan Rodriguez	.65
141	Quilvio Veras	.05
142	Mike Fetters	.05
143	Mike Greenwell	.05
144	Bill Pulsipher	.05
145	Mark McGwire	1.50
146	Frank Castillo	.05
147	Greg Vaughn	.05
148	Pat Hentgen	.05
149	Walt Weiss	.05
150	Randy Johnson	.75
151	David Segui	.05

152 Benji Gil	.05	256 Bernard Gilkey	.05
153 Tom Candiotti	.05	257 John Smiley	.05
154 Geronimo Berroa	.05	258 Brady Anderson	.05
155 John Franco	.05	259 Rico Brogna	.05
156 Jay Bell	.05	260 Kirt Manwaring	.05
157 Mark Gubicza	.05	261 Len Dykstra	.05
158 Hal Morris	.05	262 Tom Glavine	.25
159 Wilson Alvarez	.05	263 Vince Coleman	.05
160 Derek Bell	.05	264 John Olerud	.05
161 Ricky Bottalico	.05	265 Orlando Merced	.05
162 Bret Boone	.05	266 Kent Mercker	.05
163 Brad Radke	.05	267 Terry Steinbach	.05
164 John Valentin	.05	268 Brian Hunter	.05
165 Steve Avery	.05	269 Jeff Fassero	.05
166 Mark McLemore	.05	270 Jay Buhner	.05
167 Danny Jackson	.05	271 Jeff Brantley	.05
168 Tino Martinez	.05	272 Tim Raines	.05
169 Shane Reynolds	.05	273 Jimmy Key	.05
170 Terry Pendleton	.05	274 Mo Vaughn	.25
171 Jim Edmonds	.05	275 Andre Dawson	.25
172 Esteban Loaiza	.05	276 Jose Mesa	.05
173 Ray Durham	.05	277 Brett Butler	.05
174 Carlos Perez	.05	278 Luis Gonzalez	.05
175 Raul Mondesi	.05	279 Steve Sparks	.05
176 Steve Ontiveros	.05	280 Chili Davis	.05
177 Chipper Jones	1.00	281 Carl Everett	.05
178 Otis Nixon	.05	282 Jeff Cirillo	.05
179 John Burkett	.05	283 Thomas Howard	.05
180 Gregg Jefferies	.05	284 Paul O'Neill	.05
181 Denny Martinez	.05	285 Pat Meares	.05
182 Ken Caminiti	.05	286 Mickey Tettleton	.05
183 Doug Jones	.05	287 Rey Sanchez	.05
184 Brian McRae	.05	288 Bip Roberts	.05
185 Don Mattingly	1.00	289 Roberto Alomar	.15
186 Mel Rojas	.05	290 Ruben Sierra	.05
187 Marty Cordova	.05	291 John Flaherty	.05
188 Vinny Castilla	.05	292 Bret Saberhagen	.05
189 John Smoltz	.05	293 Barry Larkin	.05
190 Travis Fryman	.05	294 Sandy Alomar	.05
191 Chris Hoiles	.05	295 Ed Sprague	.05
192 Chuck Finley	.05	296 Gary DiSarcina	.05
193 Ryan Klesko	.05	297 Marquis Grissom	.05
194 Alex Fernandez	.05	298 John Frascatore	.05
195 Dante Bichette	.05	299 Will Clark	.05
196 Eric Karros	.05	300 Barry Bonds	2.00
197 Roger Clemens	1.00	301 Ozzie Smith	1.00
198 Randy Myers	.05	302 Dave Nilsson	.05
199 Tony Phillips	.05	303 Pedro Martinez	.75
200 Cal Ripken Jr.	2.00	304 Joey Cora	.05
201 Rod Beck	.05	305 Rick Aguilera	.05
202 Chad Curtis	.05	306 Craig Biggio	.05
203 Jack McDowell	.05	307 Jose Vizcaino	.05
204 Gary Gaetti	.05	308 Jeff Montgomery	.05
205 Ken Griffey Jr.	1.25	309 Moises Alou	.05
206 Ramon Martinez	.05	310 Robin Ventura	.05
207 Jeff Kent	.05	311 David Wells	.05
208 Brad Ausmus	.05	312 Delino DeShields	.05
209 Devon White	.05	313 Trevor Hoffman	.05
210 Jason Giambi	.45	314 Andy Benes	.05
211 Nomar Garciaparra	1.00	315 Deion Sanders	.05
212 Billy Wagner	.05	316 Jim Bullinger	.05
213 Todd Greene	.05	317 John Jaha	.05
214 Paul Wilson	.05	318 Greg Maddux	1.00
215 Johnny Damon	.25	319 Tim Salmon	.05
216 Alan Benes	.05	320 Ben McDonald	.05
217 Karim Garcia	.10	321 Sandy Martinez RC	.05
218 Dustin Hermanson	.05	322 Dan Miceli	.05
219 Derek Jeter	2.00	323 Wade Boggs	1.00
220 Checklist	.05	324 Ismael Valdes	.05
221 Kirby Puckett	.50	325 Juan Gonzalez	.35
222 Cal Ripken Jr.	1.00	326 Charles Nagy	.05
223 Albert Belle	.05	327 Ray Lankford	.05
224 Randy Johnson	.40	328 Mark Portugal	.05
225 Wade Boggs	.50	329 Bobby Bonilla	.05
226 Carlos Baerga	.05	330 Reggie Sanders	.05
227 Ivan Rodriguez	.30	331 Jamie Brewington	.05
228 Mike Mussina	.25	332 Aaron Sele	.05
229 Frank Thomas	.40	333 Pete Harnisch	.05
230 Ken Griffey Jr.	.75	334 Cliff Floyd	.05
231 Jose Mesa	.05	335 Cal Eldred	.05
232 Matt Morris RC	1.00	336 Jason Bates	.05
233 Craig Wilson RC	.50	337 Tony Clark	.05
234 Alvie Shepherd RC	.05	338 Jose Herrera	.05
235 Randy Winn RC	.05	339 Alex Ochoa	.05
236 David Yocum RC	.05	340 Mark Loretta	.05
237 Jason Brester RC	.05	341 Donne Wall RC	.05
238 Shane Monahan RC	.05	342 Jason Kendall	.05
239 Brian McNichol RC	.05	343 Shannon Stewart	.05
240 Reggie Taylor	.05	344 Brooks Kieschnick	.05
241 Garrett Long	.05	345 Chris Snopek	.05
242 Jonathan Johnson RC	.05	346 Ruben Rivera	.05
243 Jeff Liefer RC	.05	347 Jeff Suppan	.05
244 Brian Powell RC	.05	348 Phil Nevin	.05
245 Brian Buchanan	.05	349 John Wasdin	.05
246 Mike Piazza	1.25	350 Jay Payton	.05
247 Edgar Martinez	.05	351 Tim Crabtree	.05
248 Chuck Knoblauch	.05	352 Rick Krivda	.05
249 Andres Galarraga	.05	353 Bob Wolcott	.05
250 Tony Gwynn	1.00	354 Jimmy Haynes	.05
251 Lee Smith	.05	355 Herb Perry	.05
252 Sammy Sosa	1.00	356 Ryne Sandberg	1.00
253 Jim Thome	.45	357 Harold Baines	.05
254 Frank Rodriguez	.05	358 Chad Ogea	.05
255 Charlie Hayes	.05	359 Lee Tinsley	.05

360 Matt Williams	.05
361 Randy Velarde	.05
362 Jose Canseco	.40
363 Larry Walker	.05
364 Kevin Appier	.05
365 Darryl Hamilton	.05
366 Jose Lima	.05
367 Javy Lopez	.05
368 Dennis Eckersley	.65
369 Jason Isringhausen	.05
370 Mickey Morandini	.05
371 Scott Cooper	.05
372 Jim Abbott	.05
373 Paul Sorrento	.05
374 Chris Hammond	.05
375 Lance Johnson	.05
376 Kevin Brown	.05
377 Luis Alicea	.05
378 Andy Pettitte	.25
379 Dean Palmer	.05
380 Jeff Bagwell	.75
381 Jaime Navarro	.05
382 Rondell White	.05
383 Erik Hanson	.05
384 Pedro Munoz	.05
385 Heathcliff Slocumb	.05
386 Wally Joyner	.05
387 Bob Tewksbury	.05
388 David Bell	.05
389 Fred McGriff	.05
390 Mike Henneman	.05
391 Robby Thompson	.05
392 Norm Charlton	.05
393 Cecil Fielder	.05
394 Benito Santiago	.05
395 Rafael Palmeiro	.65
396 Ricky Bones	.05
397 Rickey Henderson	.75
398 C.J. Nitkowski	.05
399 Shawon Dunston	.05
400 Manny Ramirez	.75
401 Bill Swift	.05
402 Chad Fonville	.05
403 Joey Hamilton	.05
404 Alex Gonzalez	.05
405 Roberto Hernandez	.05
406 Jeff Blauser	.05
407 LaTroy Hawkins	.05
408 Greg Colbrunn	.05
409 Todd Hundley	.05
410 Glenn Dishman	.05
411 Joe Vitiello	.05
412 Todd Worrell	.05
413 Wil Cordero	.05
414 Ken Hill	.05
415 Carlos Garcia	.05
416 Bryan Rekar	.05
417 Shawn Green (Topps Rookie All-Star)	.40
418 Tyler Green	.05
419 Mike Blowers	.05
420 Kenny Lofton	.05
421 Denny Neagle	.05
422 Jeff Conine	.05
423 Mark Langston	.05
424 Steve Cox, Jesse Ibarra, Derrek Lee, Ron Wright RC	.10
425 Jim Bonnici, Billy Owens, Richie Sexson, Daryle Ward RC	.10
426 Kevin Jordan, Bobby Morris, Desi Relaford, Adam Riggs RC	.10
427 Tim Harkrider, Rey Ordonez, Neifi Perez, Enrique Wilson	.05
428 Bartolo Colon, Doug Million, Rafael Orellano, Ray Ricken RC	.05
429 Jeff D'Amico, Marty Janzen, Gary Rath, Clint Sodowsky	.05
430 Matt Drews, Rich Hunter, Matt Ruebel, Bret Wagner	.05
431 Jaime Bluma, Dave Coggin, Steve Montgomery, Brandon Reed	.05
432 Mike Figga, Raul Ibanez, Paul Konerko, Julio Mosquera	.25
433 Brian Barber, Marc Kroon, Marc Valdes, Don Wengert	.05
434 George Arias, Chris Haas, Scott Rolen, Scott Spiezio	.50

435 Brian Banks, Vladimir Guerrero, Andruw Jones, Billy McMillon	.50
436 Roger Cedeno, Derrick Gibson, Ben Grieve, Shane Spencer RC	.50
437 Anton French, Demond Smith, Darond Stovall, Keith Williams	.05
438 Michael Coleman, Jacob Cruz, Richard Hidalgo, Charles Peterson	.10
439 Trey Beamon, Yamil Benitez, Jermaine Dye, Angel Echevarria	.05
440 Checklist	.05

Classic Confrontations

	NM/M
Complete Set (15):	3.50
Common Player:	.06
1 Ken Griffey Jr.	.65
2 Cal Ripken Jr.	1.00
3 Edgar Martinez	.05
4 Kirby Puckett	.45
5 Frank Thomas	.35
6 Barry Bonds	1.00
7 Reggie Sanders	.05
8 Andres Galarraga	.05
9 Tony Gwynn	.45
10 Mike Piazza	.65
11 Randy Johnson	.35
12 Mike Mussina	.25
13 Roger Clemens	.50
14 Tom Glavine	.25
15 Greg Maddux	.45

League Leaders Finest Bronze

	NM/M
Complete Set (6):	75.00
Common Player:	10.00
(1) Mo Vaughn (A.L. MVP)	10.00
(2) Barry Larkin (N.L. MVP)	10.00
(3) Randy Johnson (A.L. CY)	15.00
(4) Greg Maddux (N.L. CY)	30.00
(5) Marty Cordova (A.L. ROY)	10.00
(6) Hideo Nomo (N.L. ROY)	15.00

Masters of the Game

	NM/M
Complete Set (20):	20.00
Common Player:	.35
1 Dennis Eckersley	.75
2 Denny Martinez	.35
3 Eddie Murray	1.00
4 Paul Molitor	1.00

5	Ozzie Smith	1.50
6	Rickey Henderson	1.00
7	Tim Raines	.35
8	Lee Smith	.35
9	Cal Ripken Jr.	4.00
10	Chili Davis	.35
11	Wade Boggs	1.50
12	Tony Gwynn	1.50
13	Don Mattingly	2.00
14	Bret Saberhagen	.35
15	Kirby Puckett	1.50
16	Joe Carter	.35
17	Roger Clemens	2.00
18	Barry Bonds	4.00
19	Greg Maddux	1.50
20	Frank Thomas	1.00

Mickey Mantle Reprints

		NM/M
Complete Set (19):		90.00
Common Mantle:		5.00
Common SP Mantle (15-19):		8.00
1	1951 Bowman #253	15.00
2	1952 Topps #311	15.00
3	1953 Topps #82	5.00
4	1954 Bowman #65	5.00
5	1955 Bowman #202	5.00
6	1956 Topps #135	5.00
7	1957 Topps #95	5.00
8	1958 Topps #150	5.00
9	1959 Topps #10	5.00
10	1960 Topps #350	5.00
11	1961 Topps #300	5.00
12	1962 Topps #200	5.00
13	1963 Topps #200	5.00
14	1964 Topps #50	5.00
15	1965 Topps #350	8.00
16	1966 Topps #50	8.00
17	1967 Topps #150	8.00
18	1968 Topps #280	8.00
19	1969 Topps #500	8.00

Mickey Mantle Finest Reprints

		NM/M
Complete Set (19):		90.00
Common Card (1-14):		6.00
Common Shortprint (15-19):		8.00
Refractors:		3X
Inserted 1:144		
1	1951 Bowman #253	15.00
2	1952 Topps #311	15.00
3	1953 Topps #82	6.00
4	1954 Bowman #65	6.00
5	1955 Bowman #202	6.00
6	1956 Topps #135	6.00
7	1957 Topps #95	6.00
8	1958 Topps #150	6.00
9	1959 Topps #10	6.00

10	1960 Topps #350	6.00
11	1961 Topps #300	6.00
12	1962 Topps #200	6.00
13	1963 Topps #200	6.00
14	1964 Topps #50	6.00
15	1965 Topps #350	8.00
16	1966 Topps #50	8.00
17	1967 Topps #150	8.00
18	1968 Topps #280	8.00
19	1969 Topps #500	8.00

Mickey Mantle Commemorative Card Sheet

	NM/M
Framed Sheet:	80.00
Mickey Mantle	

Mickey Mantle Commemorative Last Day

		NM/M
7	Mickey Mantle	5.00

Mickey Mantle Case Inserts

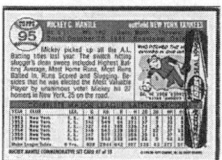

		NM/M
Complete Set (19):		375.00
Common Mantle:		20.00
Common SP Mantle		
(15-19):		30.00
1	1951 Bowman #253	60.00
2	1952 Topps #311	60.00
3	1953 Topps #82	30.00
4	1954 Bowman #65	20.00
5	1955 Bowman #202	20.00
6	1956 Topps #135	20.00
7	1957 Topps #95	20.00
8	1958 Topps #150	20.00
9	1959 Topps #10	20.00
10	1960 Topps #350	20.00
11	1961 Topps #300	20.00
12	1962 Topps #200	20.00
13	1963 Topps #200	20.00
14	1964 Topps #50	20.00
15	1965 Topps #350	30.00
16	1966 Topps #50	30.00
17	1967 Topps #150	30.00
18	1968 Topps #280	30.00
19	1969 Topps #500	30.00

Mystery Finest

		NM/M
Complete Set (21):		25.00
Common Player:		.50
Refractors:		1.5X
M1	Hideo Nomo	1.00
M2	Greg Maddux	2.00
M3	Randy Johnson	1.50
M4	Chipper Jones	2.00
M5	Marty Cordova	.50
M6	Garret Anderson	.50
M7	Cal Ripken Jr.	4.00
M8	Kirby Puckett	2.00
M9	Tony Gwynn	2.00
M10	Manny Ramirez	1.50
M11	Jim Edmonds	.50

M12	Mike Piazza	2.50
M13	Barry Bonds	4.00
M14	Raul Mondesi	.50
M15	Sammy Sosa	2.00
M16	Ken Griffey Jr.	2.50
M17	Albert Belle	.50
M18	Dante Bichette	.50
M19	Mo Vaughn	.50
M20	Jeff Bagwell	1.50
M21	Frank Thomas	1.50

Power Boosters

		NM/M
Complete Set (26):		30.00
Common Player:		1.00
1	Tony Gwynn	2.00
2	Mike Piazza	3.00
3	Greg Maddux	2.00
4	Jeff Bagwell	1.50
5	Larry Walker	1.00
6	Barry Larkin	1.00
7	Tom Glavine	1.25
8	Craig Biggio	1.00
9	Barry Bonds	4.00
10	Heathcliff Slocumb	1.00
11	Matt Williams	1.00
12	Todd Helton	4.00
13	Mark Redman	1.00
14	Michael Barrett	1.00
15	Ben Davis	1.00
16	Juan LeBron	1.00
17	Tony McKnight	1.00
18	Ryan Jaroncyk	1.00
19	Corey Jenkins	1.00
20	Jim Scharrer	1.00
21	Mark Bellhorn	1.00
22	Jarrod Washburn	1.00
23	Geoff Jenkins	1.00
24	Sean Casey	2.00
25	Brett Tomko	1.00

Profiles-AL

		NM/M
Complete Set (20):		8.00
Common Player:		.25
1	Roberto Alomar	.30
2	Carlos Baerga	.25
3	Albert Belle	.25
4	Cecil Fielder	.25
5	Ken Griffey Jr.	1.00
6	Randy Johnson	.60
7	Paul O'Neill	.25
8	Cal Ripken Jr.	1.50
9	Frank Thomas	.60
10	Mo Vaughn	.25
11	Jay Buhner	.25
12	Marty Cordova	.25
13	Jim Edmonds	.25
14	Juan Gonzalez	.35
15	Kenny Lofton	.25
16	Edgar Martinez	.25

17	Don Mattingly	.75
18	Mark McGwire	1.25
19	Rafael Palmeiro	.50
20	Tim Salmon	.25

Profiles-NL

		NM/M
Complete Set (20):		7.00
Common Player:		.25
1	Jeff Bagwell	.60
2	Derek Bell	.25
3	Barry Bonds	1.50
4	Greg Maddux	.75
5	Fred McGriff	.25
6	Raul Mondesi	.25
7	Mike Piazza	1.00
8	Reggie Sanders	.25
9	Sammy Sosa	.75
10	Larry Walker	.25
11	Dante Bichette	.25
12	Andres Galarraga	.25
13	Ron Gant	.25
14	Tom Glavine	.35
15	Chipper Jones	.75
16	David Justice	.25
17	Barry Larkin	.25
18	Hideo Nomo	.40
19	Gary Sheffield	.40
20	Matt Williams	.25

Road Warriors

		NM/M
Complete Set (20):		9.00
Common Player:		.25
1	Derek Bell	.25
2	Albert Belle	.25
3	Craig Biggio	.25
4	Barry Bonds	2.50
5	Jay Buhner	.25

6	Jim Edmonds	.25
7	Gary Gaetti	.25
8	Ron Gant	.25
9	Edgar Martinez	.25
10	Tino Martinez	.25
11	Mark McGwire	1.50
12	Mike Piazza	1.25
13	Manny Ramirez	1.00
14	Tim Salmon	.25
15	Reggie Sanders	.25
16	Frank Thomas	1.00
17	John Valentin	.25
18	Mo Vaughn	.25
19	Robin Ventura	.25
20	Matt Williams	.25

Wrecking Crew

		NM/M
Complete Set (15):		20.00
Common Player:		.50
1	Jeff Bagwell	1.50
2	Albert Belle	.50
3	Barry Bonds	5.00
4	Jose Canseco	.75
5	Joe Carter	.50
6	Cecil Fielder	.50
7	Ron Gant	.50
8	Juan Gonzalez	.75
9	Ken Griffey Jr.	3.00
10	Fred McGriff	.50
11	Mark McGwire	4.00
12	Mike Piazza	3.00
13	Frank Thomas	1.50
14	Mo Vaughn	.50
15	Matt Williams	.50

5-Star Mystery Finest

		NM/M
Complete Set (5):		12.50
Common Player:		2.00
Refractors:		2X
M22	Hideo Nomo	2.00
M23	Cal Ripken Jr.	5.00
M24	Mike Piazza	3.00
M25	Ken Griffey Jr.	3.00
M26	Frank Thomas	2.50

1996 Topps Chrome

		NM/M
Complete Set (165):		40.00
Common Player:		.10
Refractors:		3X
Pack (4):		2.00
Wax Box (24):		30.00
1	Tony Gwynn	1.00
2	Mike Piazza	1.25
3	Greg Maddux	1.00
4	Jeff Bagwell	.75
5	Larry Walker	.10
6	Barry Larkin	.10

JAY BUHNER

7	Mickey Mantle	9.00
8	Tom Glavine	.10
9	Craig Biggio	.10
10	Barry Bonds	2.00
11	Heathcliff Slocumb	.10
12	Matt Williams (Star Power)	.10
13	Todd Helton	2.00
14	Paul Molitor	1.50
15	Glenallen Hill	.10
16	Troy Percival	.10
17	Albert Belle	.10
18	Mark Wohlers	.10
19	Kirby Puckett	2.00
20	Mark Grace	.10
21	J.T. Snow	.10
22	David Justice	.10
23	Mike Mussina	.75
24	Bernie Williams	.10
25	Ron Gant	.10
26	Carlos Baerga	.10
27	Gary Sheffield	.65
28	Cal Ripken Jr. (Tribute Card)	2.00
29	Frank Thomas	1.50
30	Kevin Seitzer	.10
31	Joe Carter	.10
32	Jeff King	.10
33	David Cone	.10
34	Eddie Murray	1.50
35	Brian Jordan	.10
36	Garret Anderson	.10
37	Hideo Nomo	.75
38	Steve Finley	.10
39	Ivan Rodriguez	1.25
40	Quilvio Veras	.10
41	Mark McGwire	3.00
42	Greg Vaughn	.10
43	Randy Johnson	1.50
44	David Segui	.10
45	Derek Bell	.10
46	John Valentin	.10
47	Steve Avery	.10
48	Tino Martinez	.10
49	Shane Reynolds	.10
50	Jim Edmonds	.10
51	Raul Mondesi	.10
52	Chipper Jones	2.00
53	Gregg Jefferies	.10
54	Ken Caminiti	.10
55	Brian McRae	.10
56	Don Mattingly	2.25
57	Marty Cordova	.10
58	Vinny Castilla	.10
59	John Smoltz	.10
60	Travis Fryman	.10
61	Ryan Klesko	.10
62	Alex Fernandez	.10
63	Dante Bichette	.10
64	Eric Karros	.10
65	Roger Clemens	2.25
66	Randy Myers	.10
67	Cal Ripken Jr.	4.00
68	Rod Beck	.10
69	Jack McDowell	.10
70	Ken Griffey Jr.	2.50
71	Ramon Martinez	.10
72	Jason Giambi	.75
73	Nomar Garciaparra	2.00
74	Billy Wagner	.10
75	Todd Greene	.10
76	Paul Wilson	.10
77	Johnny Damon	.35
78	Alan Benes	.10
79	Karim Garcia	.25
80	Derek Jeter	4.00
81	Kirby Puckett	1.00
82	Cal Ripken Jr.	2.00
83	Albert Belle	.10
84	Randy Johnson	.40
85	Wade Boggs	1.00
86	Carlos Baerga	.10

87	Ivan Rodriguez (Star Power)	.35
88	Mike Mussina	.30
89	Frank Thomas	.75
90	Ken Griffey Jr.	1.25
91	Jose Mesa	.10
92	Matt Morris RC	1.00
93	Mike Piazza	2.50
94	Edgar Martinez	.10
95	Chuck Knoblauch	.10
96	Andres Galarraga	.10
97	Tony Gwynn	2.00
98	Lee Smith	.10
99	Sammy Sosa	2.00
100	Jim Thome	1.25
101	Bernard Gilkey	.10
102	Brady Anderson	.10
103	Rico Brogna	.10
104	Lenny Dykstra	.10
105	Tom Glavine	.35
106	John Olerud	.10
107	Terry Steinbach	.10
108	Brian Hunter	.10
109	Jay Buhner	.10
110	Mo Vaughn	.10
111	Jose Mesa	.10
112	Brett Butler	.10
113	Chili Davis	.10
114	Paul O'Neill	.10
115	Roberto Alomar	.35
116	Barry Larkin	.10
117	Marquis Grissom	.10
118	Will Clark	.10
119	Barry Bonds	4.00
120	Ozzie Smith	2.00
121	Pedro Martinez	1.50
122	Craig Biggio	.10
123	Moises Alou	.10
124	Robin Ventura	.10
125	Greg Maddux	2.00
126	Tim Salmon	.10
127	Wade Boggs	2.00
128	Ismael Valdes	.10
129	Juan Gonzalez	.75
130	Ray Lankford	.10
131	Bobby Bonilla	.10
132	Reggie Sanders	.10
133	Alex Ochoa	.10
134	Mark Loretta	.10
135	Jason Kendall	.10
136	Brooks Kieschnick	.10
137	Chris Snopek	.10
138	Ruben Rivera	.10
139	Jeff Suppan	.10
140	John Wasdin	.10
141	Jay Payton	.10
142	Rick Krivda	.10
143	Jimmy Haynes	.10
144	Ryne Sandberg	2.00
145	Matt Williams	.10
146	Jose Canseco	.65
147	Larry Walker	.10
148	Kevin Appier	.10
149	Javy Lopez	.10
150	Dennis Eckersley	1.25
151	Jason Isringhausen	.10
152	Dean Palmer	.10
153	Jeff Bagwell	1.50
154	Rondell White	.10
155	Wally Joyner	.10
156	Fred McGriff	.10
157	Cecil Fielder	.10
158	Rafael Palmeiro	1.25
159	Rickey Henderson	1.50
160	Shawon Dunston	.10
161	Manny Ramirez	1.50
162	Alex Gonzalez	.10
163	Shawn Green	.45
164	Kenny Lofton	.10
165	Jeff Conine	.10

Wrecking Crew

		NM/M
Complete Set (15):		25.00
Common Player:		1.00
Refractors:		1.5X
1	Jeff Bagwell	2.50
2	Albert Belle	1.00
3	Barry Bonds	5.00
4	Jose Canseco	1.50
5	Joe Carter	1.00
6	Cecil Fielder	1.00
7	Ron Gant	1.00
8	Juan Gonzalez	1.25
9	Ken Griffey Jr.	3.50
10	Fred McGriff	1.00
11	Mark McGwire	4.00
12	Mike Piazza	4.00
13	Frank Thomas	2.50
14	Mo Vaughn	1.00
15	Matt Williams	1.00

Masters of the Game

		NM/M
Complete Set (20):		35.00
Common Player:		1.00
Refractors:		1.5X
1	Dennis Eckersley	2.00
2	Denny Martinez	1.00
3	Eddie Murray	2.50
4	Paul Molitor	2.50
5	Ozzie Smith	3.50
6	Rickey Henderson	2.50
7	Tim Raines	1.00
8	Lee Smith	1.00
9	Cal Ripken Jr.	6.00
10	Chili Davis	1.00
11	Wade Boggs	3.50
12	Tony Gwynn	3.50
13	Don Mattingly	4.00
14	Bret Saberhagen	1.00
15	Kirby Puckett	3.50
16	Joe Carter	1.00
17	Roger Clemens	4.00
18	Barry Bonds	6.00
19	Greg Maddux	3.50
20	Frank Thomas	2.50

1996 Topps Gallery

MARQUIS GRISSOM

		NM/M
Complete Set (180):		20.00
Common Player:		.10
Pack (8):		1.50
Wax Box (24):		27.50
1	Tom Glavine	.35
2	Carlos Baerga	.10
3	Dante Bichette	.10
4	Mark Langston	.10
5	Ray Lankford	.10
6	Moises Alou	.10
7	Marquis Grissom	.10
8	Ramon Martinez	.10
8p	Ramon Martinez (Unmarked promo, "Pitcher" spelled out under photo on back.)	2.50
9	Steve Finley	.10
10	Todd Hundley	.10
11	Brady Anderson	.10
12	John Valentin	.10
13	Heathcliff Slocumb	.10
14	Ruben Sierra	.10

15	Jeff Conine	.10
16	Jay Buhner	.10
16p	Jay Buhner (Unmarked promo; height, weight and "Bats" on same line.)	2.50
17	Sammy Sosa	1.00
18	Doug Drabek	.10
19	Jose Mesa	.10
20	Jeff King	.10
21	Mickey Tettleton	.10
22	Jeff Montgomery	.10
23	Alex Fernandez	.10
24	Greg Vaughn	.10
25	Chuck Finley	.10
26	Terry Steinbach	.10
27	Rod Beck	.10
28	Jack McDowell	.10
29	Mark Wohlers	.10
30	Lenny Dykstra	.10
31	Bernie Williams	.10
32	Travis Fryman	.10
33	Jose Canseco	.45
34	Ken Caminiti	.10
35	Devon White	.10
36	Bobby Bonilla	.10
37	Paul Sorrento	.10
38	Ryne Sandberg	1.00
39	Derek Bell	.10
40	Bobby Jones	.10
41	J.T. Snow	.10
42	Denny Neagle	.10
43	Tim Wakefield	.10
44	Andres Galarraga	.10
45	David Segui	.10
46	Lee Smith	.10
47	Mel Rojas	.10
48	John Franco	.10
49	Pete Schourek	.10
50	John Wetteland	.10
51	Paul Molitor	.75
52	Ivan Rodriguez	.65
53	Chris Hoiles	.10
54	Mike Greenwell	.10
55	Orel Hershiser	.10
56	Brian McRae	.10
57	Geronimo Berroa	.10
58	Craig Biggio	.10
59	David Justice	.10
59p	David Justice (Unmarked promo; height, weight and "Bats" on same line.)	2.50
60	Lance Johnson	.10
61	Andy Ashby	.10
62	Randy Myers	.10
63	Gregg Jefferies	.10
64	Kevin Appier	.10
65	Rick Aguilera	.10
66	Shane Reynolds	.10
67	John Smoltz	.10
68	Ron Gant	.10
69	Eric Karros	.10
70	Jim Thome	.65
71	Terry Pendleton	.10
72	Kenny Rogers	.10
73	Robin Ventura	.10
74	Dave Nilsson	.10
75	Brian Jordan	.10
76	Glenallen Hill	.10
77	Greg Colbrunn	.10
78	Roberto Alomar	.25
79	Rickey Henderson	.75
80	Carlos Garcia	.10
81	Dean Palmer	.10
82	Mike Stanley	.10
83	Hal Morris	.10
84	Wade Boggs	1.00
85	Chad Curtis	.10
86	Roberto Hernandez	.10
87	John Olerud	.10
88	Frank Castillo	.10
89	Rafael Palmeiro	.65
90	Trevor Hoffman	.10
91	Marty Cordova	.10
92	Hideo Nomo	.35
93	Johnny Damon	.30
94	Bill Pulsipher	.10
95	Garret Anderson	.10
96	Ray Durham	.10
97	Ricky Bottalico	.10
98	Carlos Perez	.10
99	Troy Percival	.10
100	Chipper Jones	1.00
101	Esteban Loaiza	.10
102	John Mabry	.10
103	Jon Nunnally	.10
104	Andy Pettitte	.35
105	Lyle Mouton	.10
106	Jason Isringhausen	.10
107	Brian Hunter	.10
108	Quilvio Veras	.10
109	Jim Edmonds	.10
110	Ryan Klesko	.10
111	Pedro Martinez	.75
112	Joey Hamilton	.10

113	Vinny Castilla	.10
114	Alex Gonzalez	.10
115	Raul Mondesi	.10
116	Rondell White	.10
117	Dan Miceli	.10
118	Tom Goodwin	.10
119	Bret Boone	.10
120	Shawn Green	.35
121	Jeff Cirillo	.10
122	Rico Brogna	.10
123	Chris Gomez	.10
124	Ismael Valdes	.10
125	Javy Lopez	.10
126	Manny Ramirez	.75
127	Paul Wilson	.10
128	Billy Wagner	.10
129	Eric Owens	.10
130	Todd Greene	.10
131	Karim Garcia	.10
132	Jimmy Haynes	.10
133	Michael Tucker	.10
134	John Wasdin	.10
135	Brooks Kieschnick	.10
136	Alex Ochoa	.10
137	Ariel Prieto	.10
138	Tony Clark	.10
139	Mark Loretta	.10
140	Rey Ordonez	.10
141	Chris Snopek	.10
142	Roger Cedeno	.10
143	Derek Jeter	2.00
144	Jeff Suppan	.10
145	Greg Maddux	1.00
146	Ken Griffey Jr.	1.25
147	Tony Gwynn	1.00
148	Darren Daulton	.10
149	Will Clark	.10
150	Mo Vaughn	.10
151	Reggie Sanders	.10
152	Kirby Puckett	1.00
153	Paul O'Neill	.10
154	Tim Salmon	.10
155	Mark McGwire	1.50
156	Barry Bonds	2.00
157	Albert Belle	.10
158	Edgar Martinez	.10
159	Mike Mussina	.35
160	Cecil Fielder	.10
161	Kenny Lofton	.10
162	Randy Johnson	.75
163	Juan Gonzalez	.35
164	Jeff Bagwell	.75
165	Joe Carter	.10
166	Mike Piazza	1.25
167	Eddie Murray	.75
168	Cal Ripken Jr.	2.00
169	Barry Larkin	.10
170	Chuck Knoblauch	.10
171	Chili Davis	.10
172	Fred McGriff	.10
173	Matt Williams	.10
174	Roger Clemens	1.00
175	Frank Thomas	.75
176	Dennis Eckersley	.10
177	Gary Sheffield	.40
178	David Cone	.10
179	Larry Walker	.10
180	Mark Grace	.10

Players Private Issue

	NM/M
Complete Set (180):	200.00
Common Player:	1.00
Stars:	8X

(See 1996 Topps Gallery for checklist and base card values.)

Expressionists

		NM/M
Complete Set (20):		20.00
Common Player:		.35
1	Mike Piazza	3.00
2	J.T. Snow	.35
3	Ken Griffey Jr.	3.00
4	Kirby Puckett	2.00
5	Carlos Baerga	.35
6	Chipper Jones	2.00
7	Hideo Nomo	.75
8	Mark McGwire	4.00
9	Gary Sheffield	.75
10	Randy Johnson	1.25
11	Ray Lankford	.35
12	Sammy Sosa	2.00
13	Denny Martinez	.35
14	Jose Canseco	.75
15	Tony Gwynn	2.00
16	Edgar Martinez	.35
17	Reggie Sanders	.35
18	Andres Galarraga	.35
19	Albert Belle	.35
20	Barry Larkin	.35

Masterpiece

		NM/M
MP1	Mickey Mantle	6.00

Photo Gallery

		NM/M
Complete Set (15):		20.00
Common Player:		.75
1	Eddie Murray	2.00
2	Randy Johnson	2.00
3	Cal Ripken Jr.	5.00
4	Bret Boone	.75
5	Frank Thomas	2.00
6	Jeff Conine	.75
7	Johnny Damon	.85
8	Roger Clemens	3.00
9	Albert Belle	.75
10	Ken Griffey Jr.	4.00
11	Kirby Puckett	2.50
12	David Justice	.75
13	Bobby Bonilla	.75
14	Larry Walker, Andres Galarraga, Vinny Castilla, Dante Bichette	1.00
15	Mark Wohlers, Javier Lopez	.75

1996 Topps Laser

		NM/M
Complete Set (128):		27.50
Common Player:		.10
Series 1 or 2 Pack (4):		1.50
Series 1 or 2 Wax Box (24):		22.50
1	Moises Alou	.10
2	Derek Bell	.10
3	Joe Carter	.10
4	Jeff Conine	.10
5	Darren Daulton	.10
6	Jim Edmonds	.10
7	Ron Gant	.10
8	Juan Gonzalez	.50
9	Brian Jordan	.10
10	Ryan Klesko	.10
11	Paul Molitor	1.00
12	Tony Phillips	.10
13	Manny Ramirez	1.00
14	Sammy Sosa	1.50
15	Devon White	.10
16	Bernie Williams	.10
17	Garret Anderson	.10
18	Jay Bell	.10
19	Craig Biggio	.10
20	Bobby Bonilla	.10
21	Ken Caminiti	.10
22	Shawon Dunston	.10
23	Mark Grace	.10
23p	Mark Grace (Unmarked promo, plain, rather than brushed, gold foil.)	2.00
24	Gregg Jefferies	.10
25	Jeff King	.10
26	Javy Lopez	.10
27	Edgar Martinez	.10
28	Dean Palmer	.10
29	J.T. Snow	.10
30	Mike Stanley	.10
30p	Mike Stanley (Unmarked promo; plain, rather than brushed, gold foil.)	1.00
31	Terry Steinbach	.10
32	Robin Ventura	.10
33	Roberto Alomar	.20
34	Jeff Bagwell	1.00
35	Dante Bichette	.10
36	Wade Boggs	1.50
37	Barry Bonds	3.00
38	Jose Canseco	.50
39	Vinny Castilla	.10
40	Will Clark	.10
41	Marty Cordova	.10
42	Ken Griffey Jr.	2.00
43	Tony Gwynn	1.50
44	Rickey Henderson	1.00
45	Chipper Jones	1.50
46	Mark McGwire	2.50
47	Brian McRae	.10
48	Ryne Sandberg	1.50
49	Andy Ashby	.10
50	Alan Benes	.10
51	Andy Benes	.10
52	Roger Clemens	1.75
53	Doug Drabek	.10
54	Dennis Eckersley	.75
55	Tom Glavine	.35
56	Randy Johnson	1.00
57	Mark Langston	.10
58	Denny Martinez	.10
59	Jack McDowell	.10
60	Hideo Nomo	.50
61	Shane Reynolds	.10
62	John Smoltz	.10
63	Paul Wilson	.10
64	Mark Wohlers	.10
65	Shawn Green	.35
66	Marquis Grissom	.10
67	Dave Hollins	.10
68	Todd Hundley	.10
69	David Justice	.10

70	Eric Karros	.10
71	Ray Lankford	.10
72	Fred McGriff	.10
73	Hal Morris	.10
74	Eddie Murray	1.00
75	Paul O'Neill	.10
76	Rey Ordonez	.10
77	Reggie Sanders	.10
78	Gary Sheffield	.45
79	Jim Thome	.75
80	Rondell White	.10
81	Travis Fryman	.10
82	Derek Jeter	3.00
83	Chuck Knoblauch	.10
84	Barry Larkin	.10
85	Tino Martinez	.10
86	Raul Mondesi	.10
87	John Olerud	.10
88	Rafael Palmeiro	.75
89	Mike Piazza	2.00
90	Cal Ripken Jr.	3.00
91	Ivan Rodriguez	.75
92	Frank Thomas	1.00
93	John Valentin	.10
94	Mo Vaughn	.10
95	Quilvio Veras	.10
96	Matt Williams	.10
97	Brady Anderson	.10
98	Carlos Baerga	.10
99	Albert Belle	.10
100	Jay Buhner	.10
101	Johnny Damon	.35
102	Chili Davis	.10
103	Ray Durham	.10
104	Lenny Dykstra	.10
105	Cecil Fielder	.10
106	Andres Galarraga	.10
107	Brian Hunter	.10
108	Kenny Lofton	.10
109	Kirby Puckett	1.50
110	Tim Salmon	.10
111	Greg Vaughn	.10
112	Larry Walker	.10
113	Rick Aguilera	.10
114	Kevin Appier	.10
115	Kevin Brown	.10
116	David Cone	.10
117	Alex Fernandez	.10
118	Chuck Finley	.10
119	Joey Hamilton	.10
120	Jason Isringhausen	.10
121	Greg Maddux	1.50
122	Pedro Martinez	1.00
123	Jose Mesa	.10
124	Jeff Montgomery	.10
125	Mike Mussina	.50
126	Randy Myers	.10
127	Kenny Rogers	.10
128	Ismael Valdes	.10

Bright Spots

		NM/M
Complete Set (16):		17.50
Common Player:		.50
1	Brian Hunter	.50
2	Derek Jeter	4.50
3	Jason Kendall	.50
4	Brooks Kieschnick	.50
5	Rey Ordonez	.50
6	Jason Schmidt	.50
7	Chris Snopek	.50
8	Bob Wolcott	.50
9	Alan Benes	.50
10	Marty Cordova	.50
11	Jimmy Haynes	.50
12	Todd Hollandsworth	.50
13	Derek Jeter	4.50
14	Chipper Jones	3.00
15	Hideo Nomo	1.00
16	Paul Wilson	.50

Power Cuts

	NM/M
Complete Set (16):	20.00

Common Player:		.75
1	Albert Belle	.75
2	Jay Buhner	.75
3	Fred McGriff	.75
4	Mike Piazza	3.00
5	Tim Salmon	.75
6	Frank Thomas	2.00
7	Mo Vaughn	.75
8	Matt Williams	.75
9	Jeff Bagwell	2.00
10	Barry Bonds	5.00
11	Jose Canseco	1.00
12	Cecil Fielder	.75
13	Juan Gonzalez	1.00
14	Ken Griffey Jr.	3.00
15	Sammy Sosa	2.50
16	Larry Walker	.75

Stadium Stars

		NM/M
Complete Set (16):		45.00
Common Player:		1.50
1	Carlos Baerga	1.50
2	Barry Bonds	10.00
3	Andres Galarraga	1.50
4	Ken Griffey Jr.	7.50
5	Barry Larkin	1.50
6	Raul Mondesi	1.50
7	Kirby Puckett	5.00
8	Cal Ripken Jr.	10.00
9	Will Clark	1.50
10	Roger Clemens	6.00
11	Tony Gwynn	5.00
12	Randy Johnson	4.00
13	Kenny Lofton	1.50
14	Edgar Martinez	1.50
15	Ryne Sandberg	5.00
16	Frank Thomas	4.00

1997 Topps

		NM/M
Unopened Fact. Set (504):		110.00
Unopened Fact. Set (503):		145.00
Complete Set (495):		65.00
Common Player:		.05
Ser. 1 or 2 Pack (11):		.75
Ser. 1 or 2 Wax Box (36):		20.00
Ser. 1 or 2 Vending Box (500):		12.00
1	Barry Bonds	2.00

2	Tom Pagnozzi	.05
3	Terrell Wade	.05
4	Jose Valentin	.05
5	Mark Clark	.05
6	Brady Anderson	.05
7	Not Issued	
8	Wade Boggs	1.00
9	Scott Stahoviak	.05
10	Andres Galarraga	.05
11	Steve Avery	.05
12	Rusty Greer	.05
13	Derek Jeter	2.00
14	Ricky Bottalico	.05
15	Andy Ashby	.05
16	Paul Shuey	.05
17	F.P. Santangelo	.05
18	Royce Clayton	.05
19	Mike Mohler	.05
20	Mike Piazza	1.50
21	Jaime Navarro	.05
22	Billy Wagner	.05
23	Mike Timlin	.05
24	Garret Anderson	.05
25	Ben McDonald	.05
26	Mel Rojas	.05
27	John Burkett	.05
28	Jeff King	.05
29	Reggie Jefferson	.05
30	Kevin Appier	.05
31	Felipe Lira	.05
32	Kevin Tapani	.05
33	Mark Portugal	.05
34	Carlos Garcia	.05
35	Joey Cora	.05
36	David Segui	.05
37	Mark Grace	.05
38	Erik Hanson	.05
39	Jeff D'Amico	.05
40	Jay Buhner	.05
41	B.J. Surhoff	.05
42	Jackie Robinson	1.50
43	Roger Pavlik	.05
44	Hal Morris	.05
45	Mariano Duncan	.05
46	Harold Baines	.05
47	Jorge Fabregas	.05
48	Jose Herrera	.05
49	Jeff Cirillo	.05
50	Tom Glavine	.25
51	Pedro Astacio	.05
52	Mark Gardner	.05
53	Arthur Rhodes	.05
54	Troy O'Leary	.05
55	Bip Roberts	.05
56	Mike Lieberthal	.05
57	Shane Andrews	.05
58	Scott Karl	.05
59	Gary DiSarcina	.05
60	Andy Pettitte	.25
61a	Kevin Elster	.05
61b	Mike Fetters (Should be #84.)	.05
62	Mark McGwire	1.75
63	Dan Wilson	.05
64	Mickey Morandini	.05
65	Chuck Knoblauch	.05
66	Tim Wakefield	.05
67	Raul Mondesi	.05
68	Todd Jones	.05
69	Albert Belle	.05
70	Trevor Hoffman	.05
71	Eric Young	.05
72	Robert Perez	.05
73	Butch Huskey	.05
74	Brian McRae	.05
75	Jim Edmonds	.05
76	Mike Henneman	.05
77	Frank Rodriguez	.05
78	Danny Tartabull	.05
79	Robby Nen	.05
80	Reggie Sanders	.05
81	Ron Karkovice	.05
82	Benny Santiago	.05
83	Mike Lansing	.05
84	Not Issued - See #61b	
85	Craig Biggio	.05
86	Mike Bordick	.05
87	Ray Lankford	.05
88	Charles Nagy	.05
89	Paul Wilson	.05
90	John Wetteland	.05
91	Tom Candiotti	.05
92	Carlos Delgado	.45
93	Derek Bell	.05
94	Mark Lemke	.05
95	Edgar Martinez	.05
96	Rickey Henderson	.75
97	Greg Myers	.05
98	Jim Leyritz	.05
99	Mark Johnson	.05
100	Dwight Gooden	.05
101	Al Leiter	.05
102a	John Mabry (Last line on back ends "... Mabry.")	.05

102b	John Mabry (Last line on back ends "...walked.")	.05
103	Alex Ochoa	.05
104	Mike Piazza	.75
105	Jim Thome	.65
106	Ricky Otero	.05
107	Jamey Wright	.05
108	Frank Thomas	.75
109	Jody Reed	.05
110	Orel Hershiser	.05
111	Terry Steinbach	.05
112	Mark Loretta	.05
113	Turk Wendell	.05
114	Marvin Benard	.05
115	Kevin Brown	.05
116	Robert Person	.05
117	Joey Hamilton	.05
118	Francisco Cordova	.05
119	John Smiley	.05
120	Travis Fryman	.05
121	Jimmy Key	.05
122	Tom Goodwin	.05
123	Mike Greenwell	.05
124	Juan Gonzalez	.35
125	Pete Harnisch	.05
126	Roger Cedeno	.05
127	Ron Gant	.05
128	Mark Langston	.05
129	Tim Crabtree	.05
130	Greg Maddux	1.00
131	William Van Landingham	.05
132	Wally Joyner	.05
133	Randy Myers	.05
134	John Valentin	.05
135	Bret Boone	.05
136	Bruce Ruffin	.05
137	Chris Snopek	.05
138	Paul Molitor	.75
139	Mark McLemore	.05
140	Rafael Palmeiro	.65
141	Herb Perry	.05
142	Luis Gonzalez	.05
143	Doug Drabek	.05
144	Ken Ryan	.05
145	Todd Hundley	.05
146	Ellis Burks	.05
147	Ozzie Guillen	.05
148	Rich Becker	.05
149	Sterling Hitchcock	.05
150	Bernie Williams	.05
151	Mike Stanley	.05
152	Roberto Alomar	.25
153	Jose Mesa	.05
154	Steve Trachsel	.05
155	Alex Gonzalez	.05
156	Troy Percival	.05
157	John Smoltz	.05
158	Pedro Martinez	.75
159	Jeff Conine	.05
160	Bernard Gilkey	.05
161	Jim Eisenreich	.05
162	Mickey Tettleton	.05
163	Justin Thompson	.05
164	Jose Offerman	.05
165	Tony Phillips	.05
166	Ismael Valdes	.05
167	Ryne Sandberg	1.00
168	Matt Mieske	.05
169	Geronimo Berroa	.05
170	Otis Nixon	.05
171	John Mabry	.05
172	Shawon Dunston	.05
173	Omar Vizquel	.05
174	Chris Holles	.05
175	Doc Gooden	.05
176	Wilson Alvarez	.05
177	Todd Hollandsworth	.05
178	Roger Salkeld	.05
179	Rey Sanchez	.05
180	Rey Ordonez	.05
181	Denny Martinez	.05
182	Ramon Martinez	.05
183	Dave Nilsson	.05
184	Marquis Grissom	.05
185	Randy Velarde	.05
186	Ron Coomer	.05
187	Tino Martinez	.05
188	Jeff Brantley	.05
189	Steve Finley	.05
190	Andy Benes	.05
191	Terry Adams	.05
192	Mike Blowers	.05
193	Russ Davis	.05
194	Darryl Hamilton	.05
195	Jason Kendall	.05
196	Johnny Damon	.25
197	Dave Martinez	.05
198	Mike Macfarlane	.05
199	Norm Charlton	.05
200	Doug Million, Damian Moss, Bobby Rodgers	.05

201	Geoff Jenkins, Raul Ibanez, Mike Cameron	.05
202	Sean Casey, Jim Bonnici, Dmitri Young	.15
203	Jed Hansen, Homer Bush, Felipe Crespo	.05
204	Kevin Orie, Gabe Alvarez, Aaron Boone	.05
205	Ben Davis, Kevin Brown, Bobby Estalella	.05
206	Billy McMillon, Bubba Trammell, Dante Powell	.25
207	Jarrod Washburn, Marc Wilkins, Glendon Rusch	.05
208	Brian Hunter	.05
209	Jason Giambi	.45
210	Henry Rodriguez	.05
211	Edgar Renteria	.05
212	Edgardo Alfonzo	.05
213	Fernando Vina	.05
214	Shawn Green	.40
215	Ray Durham	.05
216	Joe Randa	.05
217	Armando Reynoso	.05
218	Eric Davis	.05
219	Bob Tewksbury	.05
220	Jacob Cruz	.05
221	Glenallen Hill	.05
222	Gary Gaetti	.05
223	Donne Wall	.05
224	Brad Clontz	.05
225	Marty Janzen	.05
226	Todd Worrell	.05
227	John Franco	.05
228	David Wells	.05
229	Gregg Jefferies	.05
230	Tim Naehring	.05
231	Thomas Howard	.05
232	Roberto Hernandez	.05
233	Kevin Ritz	.05
234	Julian Tavarez	.05
235	Ken Hill	.05
236	Greg Gagne	.05
237	Bobby Chouinard	.05
238	Joe Carter	.05
239	Jermaine Dye	.05
240	Antonio Osuna	.05
241	Julio Franco	.05
242	Mike Grace	.05
243	Aaron Sele	.05
244	David Justice	.05
245	Sandy Alomar	.05
246	Jose Canseco	.45
247	Paul O'Neill	.05
248	Sean Berry	.05
249	Nick Bierbrodt, Kevin Sweeney RC	.05
250	Larry Rodriguez, Vladimir Nunez RC	.10
251	Ron Hartman, David Hayman	.05
252	Alex Sanchez, Matt Quatraro (Devil Rays)	.05
253	Ronni Seberino, Pablo Ortega RC (Devil Rays)	.05
254	Rex Hudler	.05
255	Orlando Miller	.05
256	Mariano Rivera	.10
257	Brad Radke	.05
258	Bobby Higginson	.05
259	Jay Bell	.05
260	Mark Grudzielanek	.05
261	Lance Johnson	.05
262	Ken Caminiti	.05
263	J.T. Snow	.05
264	Gary Sheffield	.45
265	Darrin Fletcher	.05
266	Eric Owens	.05
267	Luis Castillo	.05
268	Scott Rolen	.65
269	Todd Noel, John Oliver	.05
270	Robert Stratton, Corey Lee RC	.05
271	Gil Meche, Matt Halloran RC	.50
272	Eric Milton, Dermal Brown	.25
273	Josh Garrett, Chris Reitsma RC	.10
274	A.J. Zapp, Jason Marquis RC	.50
275	Checklist	
276a	Checklist	.05
276b	Chipper Jones (Should be #277.)	1.00
277	Not Issued	
278	Orlando Merced	.05
279	Ariel Prieto	.05
280	Al Leiter	.05
281	Pat Meares	.05

282	Darryl Strawberry	.05
283	Jamie Moyer	.05
284	Scott Servais	.05
285	Delino DeShields	.05
286	Danny Graves	.05
287	Gerald Williams	.05
288	Todd Greene	.05
289	Rico Brogna	.05
290	Derrick Gibson	.05
291	Joe Girardi	.05
292	Darren Lewis	.05
293	Nomar Garciaparra	1.00
294	Greg Colbrunn	.05
295	Jeff Bagwell	.75
296	Brent Gates	.05
297	Jose Vizcaino	.05
298	Alex Ochoa	.05
299	Sid Fernandez	.05
300	Ken Griffey Jr.	1.50
301	Chris Gomez	.05
302	Wendell Magee	.05
303	Darren Oliver	.05
304	Mel Nieves	.05
305	Sammy Sosa	1.00
306	George Arias	.05
307	Jack McDowell	.05
308	Stan Javier	.05
309	Kimera Bartee	.05
310	James Baldwin	.05
311	Rocky Coppinger	.05
312	Keith Lockhart	.05
313	C.J. Nitkowski	.05
314	Allen Watson	.05
315	Darryl Kile	.05
316	Amaury Telemaco	.05
317	Jason Isringhausen	.05
318	Manny Ramirez	.75
319	Terry Pendleton	.05
320	Tim Salmon	.05
321	Eric Karros	.05
322	Mark Whiten	.05
323	Rick Krivda	.05
324	Brett Butler	.05
325	Randy Johnson	.75
326	Eddie Taubensee	.05
327	Mark Leiter	.05
328	Kevin Gross	.05
329	Ernie Young	.05
330	Pat Hentgen	.05
331	Rondell White	.05
332	Bobby Witt	.05
333	Eddie Murray	.75
334	Tim Raines	.05
335	Jeff Fassero	.05
336	Chuck Finley	.05
337	Willie Adams	.05
338	Chan Ho Park	.05
339	Jay Powell	.05
340	Ivan Rodriguez	.65
341	Jermaine Allensworth	.05
342	Jay Payton	.05
343	T.J. Mathews	.05
344	Tony Batista	.05
345	Ed Sprague	.05
346	Jeff Kent	.05
347	Scott Erickson	.05
348	Jeff Suppan	.05
349	Pete Schourek	.05
350	Kenny Lofton	.05
351	Alan Benes	.05
352	Fred McGriff	.05
353	Charlie O'Brien	.05
354	Darren Bragg	.05
355	Alex Fernandez	.05
356	Al Martin	.05
357	Bob Wells	.05
358	Chad Mottola	.05
359	Devon White	.05
360	David Cone	.05
361	Bobby Jones	.05
362	Scott Sanders	.05
363	Karim Garcia	.15
364	Kirt Manwaring	.05
365	Chili Davis	.05
366	Mike Hampton	.05
367	Chad Ogea	.05
368	Curt Schilling	.25
369	Phil Nevin	.05
370	Roger Clemens	1.25
371	Willie Greene	.05
372	Kenny Rogers	.05
373	Jose Rijo	.05
374	Bobby Bonilla	.05
375	Mike Mussina	.35
376	Curtis Pride	.05
377	Todd Walker	.05
378	Jason Bere	.05
379	Heathcliff Slocumb	.05
380	Dante Bichette	.05
381	Carlos Baerga	.05
382	Livan Hernandez	.05
383	Jason Schmidt	.05
384	Kevin Stocker	.05
385	Matt Williams	.05
386	Bartolo Colon	.05

387	Will Clark	.05
388	Dennis Eckersley	.65
389	Brooks Kieschnick	.05
390	Ryan Klesko	.05
391	Mark Carreon	.05
392	Tim Worrell	.05
393	Dean Palmer	.05
394	Wil Cordero	.05
395	Javy Lopez	.05
396	Rich Aurilia	.05
397	Greg Vaughn	.05
398	Vinny Castilla	.05
399	Jeff Montgomery	.05
400	Cal Ripken Jr.	2.00
401	Walt Weiss	.05
402	Brad Ausmus	.05
403	Ruben Rivera	.05
404	Mark Wohlers	.05
405	Rick Aguilera	.05
406	Tony Clark	.05
407	Lyle Mouton	.05
408	Bill Pulsipher	.05
409	Jose Rosado	.05
410	Tony Gwynn	1.00
411	Cecil Fielder	.05
412	John Flaherty	.05
413	Lenny Dykstra	.05
414	Ugueth Urbina	.05
415	Brian Jordan	.05
416	Bob Abreu	.05
417	Craig Paquette	.05
418	Sandy Martinez	.05
419	Jeff Blauser	.05
420	Barry Larkin	.05
421	Kevin Seitzer	.05
422	Tim Belcher	.05
423	Paul Sorrento	.05
424	Cal Eldred	.05
425	Robin Ventura	.05
426	John Olerud	.05
427	Bob Wolcott	.05
428	Matt Lawton	.05
429	Rod Beck	.05
430	Shane Reynolds	.05
431	Mike James	.05
432	Steve Wojciechowski	.05
433	Vladimir Guerrero	.75
434	Dustin Hermanson	.05
435	Marty Cordova	.05
436	Marc Newfield	.05
437	Todd Stottlemyre	.05
438	Jeffrey Hammonds	.05
439	Dave Stevens	.05
440	Hideo Nomo	.35
441	Mark Thompson	.05
442	Mark Lewis	.05
443	Quinton McCracken	.05
444	Cliff Floyd	.05
445	Denny Neagle	.05
446	John Jaha	.05
447	Mike Sweeney	.05
448	John Wasdin	.05
449	Chad Curtis	.05
450	Mo Vaughn	.05
451	Donovan Osborne	.05
452	Ruben Sierra	.05
453	Michael Tucker	.05
454	Kurt Abbott	.05
455	Andruw Jones	.75
456	Shannon Stewart	.05
457	Scott Brosius	.05
458	Juan Guzman	.05
459	Ron Villone	.05
460	Moises Alou	.05
461	Larry Walker	.05
462	Eddie Murray	.40
463	Paul Molitor	.40
464	Hideo Nomo	.20
465	Barry Bonds	1.00
466	Todd Hundley	.05
467	Rheal Cormier	.05
468	Jason Conti RC	.05
469	Rod Barajas RC	.05
470	Jared Sandberg, Cedric Bowers RC	.05
471	Paul Wilders, Chie Gunner RC	.05
472	Mike Decelle, Marcus McCain RC	.05
473	Todd Zeile	.05
474	Neifi Perez	.05
475	Jeromy Burnitz	.05
476	Trey Beamon	.05
477	John Patterson, Braden Looper RC	.15
478	Danny Peoples, Jake Westbrook RC	.25
479	Eric Chavez, Adam Eaton	.75
480	Joe Lawrence, Pete Tucci	.05
481	Kris Benson, Billy Koch RC	.25
482	John Nicholson, Andy Prater	.05
483	Mark Kotsay, Mark Johnson	.25

484	Armando Benitez	.05
485	Mike Matheny	.05
486	Jeff Reed	.05
487	Mark Bellhorn, Russ Johnson, Enrique Wilson	.05
488	Ben Grieve, Richard Hidalgo, Scott Morgan RC	.05
489	Paul Konerko, Derrek Lee, Ron Wright	.50
490	Wes Helms, Bill Mueller, Brad Seitzer	.50
491	Jeff Abbott, Shane Monahan, Edgard Velazquez	.05
492	Jimmy Anderson, Ron Blazier, Gerald Witasick Jr.	.05
493	Darin Blood, Heath Murray, Carl Pavano	.05
494	Mark Redman, Mike Villano, Nelson Figueroa	.05
495	Checklist	.05
496	Checklist	.05

All-Stars

Ivan Rodriguez

		NM/M
Complete Set (22):		12.00
Common Player:		.25
1	Ivan Rodriguez	.75
2	Todd Hundley	.25
3	Frank Thomas	1.00
4	Andres Galarraga	.25
5	Chuck Knoblauch	.25
6	Eric Young	.25
7	Jim Thome	.75
8	Chipper Jones	1.50
9	Cal Ripken Jr.	3.00
10	Barry Larkin	.25
11	Albert Belle	.25
12	Barry Bonds	3.00
13	Ken Griffey Jr.	2.00
14	Ellis Burks	.25
15	Juan Gonzalez	.60
16	Gary Sheffield	.50
17	Andy Pettitte	.35
18	Tom Glavine	.35
19	Pat Hentgen	.25
20	John Smoltz	.25
21	Roberto Hernandez	.25
22	Mark Wohlers	.25

Awesome Impact

Mariano Rivera

		NM/M
Complete Set (20):		20.00
Common Player:		.40
1	Jaime Bluma	.40
2	Tony Clark	.40
3	Jermaine Dye	.40
4	Nomar Garciaparra	4.50

5	Vladimir Guerrero	3.00
6	Todd Hollandsworth	.40
7	Derek Jeter	6.00
8	Andruw Jones	3.00
9	Chipper Jones	4.50
10	Jason Kendall	.40
11	Brooks Kieschnick	.40
12	Alex Ochoa	.40
13	Rey Ordonez	.40
14	Neifi Perez	.40
15	Edgar Renteria	.40
16	Mariano Rivera	.50
17	Ruben Rivera	.40
18	Scott Rolen	2.25
19	Billy Wagner	.40
20	Todd Walker	.40

Derek Jeter Autograph

	NM/M
Derek Jeter	130.00

Hobby Masters

		NM/M
Complete Set (20):		30.00
Common Player:		.75
1	Ken Griffey Jr.	3.00
2	Cal Ripken Jr.	4.50
3	Greg Maddux	2.25
4	Albert Belle	.75
5	Tony Gwynn	2.25
6	Jeff Bagwell	1.50
7	Randy Johnson	1.50
8	Raul Mondesi	.75
9	Juan Gonzalez	1.00
10	Kenny Lofton	.75
11	Frank Thomas	1.50
12	Mike Piazza	3.00
13	Chipper Jones	2.25
14	Brady Anderson	.75
15	Ken Caminiti	.75
16	Barry Bonds	4.50
17	Mo Vaughn	.75
18	Derek Jeter	4.50
19	Sammy Sosa	2.25
20	Andres Galarraga	.75

Inter-League Match Ups

		NM/M
Complete Set (14):		16.00
Common Card:		.50
Refractors:		1.5X
1	Mark McGwire, Barry Bonds	3.00
2	Tim Salmon, Mike Piazza	2.00
3	Ken Griffey Jr., Dante Bichette	2.00
4	Juan Gonzalez, Tony Gwynn	1.50

5	Frank Thomas, Sammy Sosa	1.50
6	Albert Belle, Barry Larkin	.50
7	Johnny Damon, Brian Jordan	.75
8	Paul Molitor, Jeff King	1.00
9	John Jaha, Jeff Bagwell	1.00
10	Bernie Williams, Todd Hundley	.50
11	Joe Carter, Henry Rodriguez	.50
12	Cal Ripken Jr., Gregg Jefferies	3.00
13	Mo Vaughn, Chipper Jones	1.50
14	Travis Fryman, Gary Sheffield	.75

Mickey Mantle Reprints

	NM/M
Complete Set (16):	60.00
Common Mantle:	5.00
Inserted 1:12 Series 1	

Mickey Mantle Finest

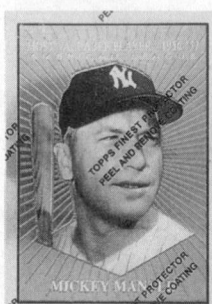

		NM/M
Complete Set (16):		70.00
Common Card:		5.00
Inserted 1:24 Series 2		
Refractor:		4X
Inserted 1:216		
21	1953 Bowman #44	5.00
22	1953 Bowman #59	7.50
23	1957 Topps #407	5.00
24	1958 Topps #418	5.00
25	1958 Topps #487	5.00
26	1959 Topps #461	5.00
27	1959 Topps #564	5.00
28	1960 Topps #160	5.00
29	1960 Topps #563	5.00
30	1961 Topps #406	5.00
31	1961 Topps #475	5.00
32	1961 Topps #578	5.00
33	1962 Topps #18	5.00
34	1962 Topps #318	5.00
35	1962 Topps #471	5.00
36	1964 Topps #331	5.00

1997 Topps Mickey Mantle Case Inserts

World Series Batting Foes
MICKEY MANTLE · HANK AARON

		NM/M
Complete Set (16):		160.00
Common Mantle:		12.50
21	1953 Bowman #44	12.50
22	1953 Bowman #59	18.00
23	1957 Topps #407	12.50
24	1958 Topps #418	12.50
25	1958 Topps #487	12.50
26	1959 Topps #461	12.50
27	1959 Topps #564	12.50
28	1960 Topps #160	12.50
29	1960 Topps #563	12.50
30	1961 Topps #406	12.50
31	1961 Topps #475	12.50
32	1961 Topps #578	12.50
33	1962 Topps #18	12.50
34	1962 Topps #318	12.50
35	1962 Topps #471	12.50
36	1964 Topps #331	12.50

Season's Best

		NM/M
Complete Set (25):		12.00
Common Player:		.25
1	Tony Gwynn	1.50
2	Frank Thomas	1.25
3	Ellis Burks	.25
4	Paul Molitor	1.25
5	Chuck Knoblauch	.25
6	Mark McGwire	3.00
7	Brady Anderson	.25
8	Ken Griffey Jr.	2.00
9	Albert Belle	.25
10	Andres Galarraga	.25
11	Andres Galarraga	.25
12	Albert Belle	.25
13	Juan Gonzalez	.75
14	Mo Vaughn	.25
15	Rafael Palmeiro	1.00
16	John Smoltz	.25
17	Andy Pettitte	.50
18	Pat Hentgen	.25
19	Mike Mussina	.50
20	Andy Benes	.25
21	Kenny Lofton	.25
22	Tom Goodwin	.25
23	Otis Nixon	.25

24	Eric Young	.25
25	Lance Johnson	.25

Sweet Strokes

		NM/M
Complete Set (15):		15.00
Common Player:		.35
1	Roberto Alomar	.50
2	Jeff Bagwell	1.25
3	Albert Belle	.35
4	Barry Bonds	3.00
5	Mark Grace	.35
6	Ken Griffey Jr.	2.00
7	Tony Gwynn	1.50
8	Chipper Jones	1.50
9	Edgar Martinez	.35
10	Mark McGwire	2.50
11	Rafael Palmeiro	.50
12	Mike Piazza	2.00
13	Gary Sheffield	.75
14	Frank Thomas	1.25
15	Mo Vaughn	.35

Team Timber

		NM/M
Complete Set (16):		24.00
Common Player:		.50
1	Ken Griffey Jr.	3.00
2	Ken Caminiti	.50
3	Bernie Williams	.50
4	Jeff Bagwell	1.50
5	Frank Thomas	1.50
6	Andres Galarraga	.50
7	Barry Bonds	5.00
8	Rafael Palmeiro	1.25
9	Brady Anderson	.50
10	Juan Gonzalez	.75
11	Mo Vaughn	.50
12	Mark McGwire	4.00
13	Gary Sheffield	.90
14	Albert Belle	.50
15	Chipper Jones	2.50
16	Mike Piazza	3.00

Willie Mays Reprints

WILLIE MAYS outfield

	NM/M
Complete Set (27):	50.00
Common Card:	3.00

Autographed Card:		120.00
1	1951 Bowman #305	6.00
2	1952 Topps #261	4.00
3	1953 Topps #244	3.00
4	1954 Bowman #89	3.00
5	1954 Topps #90	3.00
6	1955 Bowman #184	3.00
7	1955 Topps #194	3.00
8	1956 Topps #130	3.00
9	1957 Topps #10	3.00
10	1958 Topps #5	3.00
11	1959 Topps #50	3.00
12	1960 Topps #200	3.00
13	1960 Topps #564	3.00
14	1961 Topps #150	3.00
15	1961 Topps #579	3.00
16	1962 Topps #300	3.00
17	1963 Topps #300	3.00
18	1964 Topps #150	3.00
19	1965 Topps #250	3.00
20	1966 Topps #1	3.00
21	1967 Topps #200	3.00
22	1968 Topps #50	3.00
23	1969 Topps #190	3.00
24	1970 Topps #600	3.00
25	1971 Topps #600	3.00
26	1972 Topps #49	3.00
27	1973 Topps #305	3.00

Willie Mays Reprint Autographs

		NM/M
Common Card:		120.00
1	1951 Bowman #305	150.00
2	1952 Topps #261	120.00
3	1953 Topps #244	120.00
6	1955 Bowman #184	120.00
7	1955 Topps #194	120.00
9	1957 Topps #10	120.00
10	1958 Topps #5	120.00
12	1960 Topps #200	120.00
13	1960 Topps #564	120.00
14	1961 Topps #150	120.00
15	1961 Topps #579	120.00
17	1963 Topps #300	120.00
18	1964 Topps #150	120.00
19	1965 Topps #250	120.00
20	1966 Topps #1	120.00
23	1969 Topps #190	120.00
24	1970 Topps #600	120.00
26	1972 Topps #49	120.00
27	1973 Topps #305	120.00

Willie Mays Finest

		NM/M
Complete Set (27):		60.00
Common Card:		3.00
Refractor:		3X
Inserted 1:180		
1	1951 Bowman #305	6.00
2	1952 Topps #261	4.00
3	1953 Topps #244	3.00
4	1954 Bowman #89	3.00
5	1954 Topps #90	3.00
6	1955 Bowman #184	3.00
7	1955 Topps #194	3.00
8	1956 Topps #130	3.00
9	1957 Topps #10	3.00
10	1958 Topps #5	3.00
11	1959 Topps #50	3.00
12	1960 Topps #200	3.00
13	1960 Topps #564	3.00
14	1961 Topps #150	3.00
15	1961 Topps #579	3.00
16	1962 Topps #300	3.00
17	1963 Topps #300	3.00
18	1964 Topps #150	3.00
19	1965 Topps #250	3.00
20	1966 Topps #1	3.00
21	1967 Topps #200	3.00
22	1968 Topps #50	3.00
23	1969 Topps #190	3.00
24	1970 Topps #600	3.00
25	1971 Topps #600	3.00
26	1972 Topps #49	3.00
27	1973 Topps #305	3.00

1997 Topps Chrome

JOSE VALENTIN

		NM/M
Complete Set (165):		35.00
Common Player:		.10
Refractors:		2X
Pack (4):		1.50
Wax Box (24):		25.00
1	Barry Bonds	3.00
2	Jose Valentin	.10
3	Brady Anderson	.10
4	Wade Boggs	1.50
5	Andres Galarraga	.10
6	Rusty Greer	.10
7	Derek Jeter	3.00
8	Ricky Bottalico	.10
9	Mike Piazza	2.00
10	Garret Anderson	.10
11	Jeff King	.10
12	Kevin Appier	.10
13	Mark Grace	.10
14	Jeff D'Amico	.10
15	Jay Buhner	.10
16	Hal Morris	.10
17	Harold Baines	.10
18	Jeff Cirillo	.10
19	Tom Glavine	.35
20	Andy Pettitte	.35
21	Mark McGwire	2.50
22	Chuck Knoblauch	.10
23	Raul Mondesi	.10
24	Albert Belle	.10
25	Trevor Hoffman	.10
26	Eric Young	.10
27	Brian McRae	.10
28	Jim Edmonds	.10
29	Robb Nen	.10
30	Reggie Sanders	.10
31	Mike Lansing	.10
32	Craig Biggio	.10
33	Ray Lankford	.10
34	Charles Nagy	.10
35	Paul Wilson	.10
36	John Wetteland	.10
37	Derek Bell	.10
38	Edgar Martinez	.10
39	Rickey Henderson	1.00
40	Jim Thome	.75
41	Frank Thomas	1.00
42	Jackie Robinson (Tribute)	2.00
43	Terry Steinbach	.10
44	Kevin Brown	.10
45	Joey Hamilton	.10
46	Travis Fryman	.10
47	Juan Gonzalez	.50
48	Ron Gant	.10
49	Greg Maddux	1.50
50	Wally Joyner	.10
51	John Valentin	.10
42	Bret Boone	.10
53	Paul Molitor	1.00
54	Rafael Palmeiro	.75
55	Todd Hundley	.10
56	Ellis Burks	.10
57	Bernie Williams	.10
58	Roberto Alomar	.25
59	Jose Mesa	.10
60	Troy Percival	.10
61	John Smoltz	.10
62	Jeff Conine	.10
63	Bernard Gilkey	.10
64	Mickey Tettleton	.10
65	Justin Thompson	.10
66	Tony Phillips	.10
67	Ryne Sandberg	1.50
68	Geronimo Berroa	.10
69	Todd Hollandsworth	.10
70	Rey Ordonez	.10
71	Marquis Grissom	.10
72	Tino Martinez	.10
73	Steve Finley	.10
74	Andy Benes	.10
75	Jason Kendall	.10
76	Johnny Damon	.35
77	Jason Giambi	.50
78	Henry Rodriguez	.10
79	Edgar Renteria	.10
80	Ray Durham	.10
81	Gregg Jefferies	.10
82	Roberto Hernandez	.10
83	Joe Carter	.10
84	Jermaine Dye	.10
85	Julio Franco	.10
86	David Justice	.10
87	Jose Canseco	.50
88	Paul O'Neill	.10
89	Mariano Rivera	.15
90	Bobby Higginson	.10
91	Mark Grudzielanek	.10
92	Lance Johnson	.10
93	Ken Caminiti	.10
94	Gary Sheffield	.50
95	Luis Castillo	.10
96	Scott Rolen	.75
97	Chipper Jones	1.50
98	Darryl Strawberry	.10
99	Nomar Garciaparra	1.50
100	Jeff Bagwell	1.00
101	Ken Griffey Jr.	2.00
102	Sammy Sosa	1.50
103	Jack McDowell	.10
104	James Baldwin	.10
105	Rocky Coppinger	.10
106	Manny Ramirez	1.00
107	Tim Salmon	.10
108	Eric Karros	.10
109	Brett Butler	.10
110	Randy Johnson	1.00
111	Pat Hentgen	.10
112	Rondell White	.10
113	Eddie Murray	1.00
114	Ivan Rodriguez	.75
115	Jermaine Allensworth	.10
116	Ed Sprague	.10
117	Kenny Lofton	.10
118	Alan Benes	.10
119	Fred McGriff	.10
120	Alex Fernandez	.10
121	Al Martin	.10
122	Devon White	.10
123	David Cone	.10
124	Karim Garcia	.25
125	Chili Davis	.10
126	Roger Clemens	1.75
127	Bobby Bonilla	.10
128	Mike Mussina	.50
129	Todd Walker	.10
130	Dante Bichette	.10
131	Carlos Baerga	.10
132	Matt Williams	.10
133	Will Clark	.10
134	Dennis Eckersley	.75
135	Ryan Klesko	.10
136	Dean Palmer	.10
137	Javy Lopez	.10
138	Greg Vaughn	.10
139	Vinny Castilla	.10
140	Cal Ripken Jr.	3.00
141	Ruben Rivera	.10
142	Mark Wohlers	.10
143	Tony Clark	.10
144	Jose Rosado	.10
145	Tony Gwynn	1.50
146	Cecil Fielder	.10
147	Brian Jordan	.10
148	Bob Abreu	.10
149	Barry Larkin	.10
150	Robin Ventura	.10
151	John Olerud	.10
152	Rod Beck	.10
153	Vladimir Guerrero	1.00
154	Marty Cordova	.10
155	Todd Stottlemyre	.10
156	Hideo Nomo	.50
157	Denny Neagle	.10
158	John Jaha	.10
159	Mo Vaughn	.10
160	Andruw Jones	1.00
161	Moises Alou	.10
162	Larry Walker	.10
163	Eddie Murray	.75
164	Paul Molitor	.75
165	Checklist	.10

Jumbos

		NM/M
Complete Set (6):		10.00
Common Player:		.75
9	Mike Piazza	2.00
94	Gary Sheffield	.75
97	Chipper Jones	1.50
101	Ken Griffey Jr.	2.00

MIKE PIAZZA

102	Sammy Sosa	1.50
140	Cal Ripken Jr.	3.00

All-Stars

Eric Young

		NM/M
Complete Set (22):		25.00
Common Player:		.75
Refractors:		1.5X
1	Ivan Rodriguez	1.50
2	Todd Hundley	.75
3	Frank Thomas	2.00
4	Andres Galarraga	.75
5	Chuck Knoblauch	.75
6	Eric Young	.75
7	Jim Thome	1.50
8	Chipper Jones	3.00
9	Cal Ripken Jr.	6.00
10	Barry Larkin	.75
11	Albert Belle	.75
12	Barry Bonds	6.00
13	Ken Griffey Jr.	4.00
14	Ellis Burks	.75
15	Juan Gonzalez	1.00
16	Gary Sheffield	1.25
17	Andy Pettitte	1.00
18	Tom Glavine	1.00
19	Pat Hentgen	.75
20	John Smoltz	.75
21	Roberto Hernandez	.75
22	Mark Wohlers	.75

Diamond Duos

DIAMOND DUOS

Mike Piazza

		NM/M
Complete Set (10):		17.50
Common Player:		.50
Refractors:		1.5X
1	Chipper Jones, Andruw Jones	2.00
2	Derek Jeter, Bernie Williams	4.00

3	Ken Griffey Jr., Jay Buhner	2.50
4	Kenny Lofton, Manny Ramirez	1.50
5	Jeff Bagwell, Craig Biggio	1.50
6	Juan Gonzalez, Ivan Rodriguez	1.25
7	Cal Ripken Jr., Brady Anderson	4.00
8	Mike Piazza, Hideo Nomo	2.50
9	Andres Galarraga, Dante Bichette	.50
10	Frank Thomas, Albert Belle	1.50

Season's Best

		NM/M
Complete Set (25):		17.50
Common Player:		.50
Refractors:		1.5X
1	Tony Gwynn	2.00
2	Frank Thomas	1.50
3	Ellis Burks	.50
4	Paul Molitor	1.50
5	Chuck Knoblauch	.50
6	Mark McGwire	4.00
7	Brady Anderson	.50
8	Ken Griffey Jr.	3.00
9	Albert Belle	.50
10	Andres Galarraga	.50
11	Andres Galarraga	.50
12	Albert Belle	.50
13	Juan Gonzalez	.75
14	Mo Vaughn	.50
15	Rafael Palmeiro	1.25
16	John Smoltz	.50
17	Andy Pettitte	.75
18	Pat Hentgen	.50
19	Mike Mussina	.75
20	Andy Benes	.50
21	Kenny Lofton	.50
22	Tom Goodwin	.50
23	Otis Nixon	.50
24	Eric Young	.50
25	Lance Johnson	.50

1997 Topps Gallery

		NM/M
Complete Set (180):		20.00
Common Player:		.10
Pack (8):		1.50
Wax Box (24):		25.00
1	Paul Molitor	.75
2	Devon White	.10
3	Andres Galarraga	.10
4	Cal Ripken Jr.	3.00
5	Tony Gwynn	1.50
6	Mike Stanley	.10
7	Orel Hershiser	.10
8	Jose Canseco	.50
9	Chili Davis	.10
10	Harold Baines	.10
11	Rickey Henderson	.75
12	Darryl Strawberry	.10
13	Todd Worrell	.10
14	Cecil Fielder	.10
15	Gary Gaetti	.10
16	Bobby Bonilla	.10
17	Will Clark	.10
18	Kevin Brown	.10
19	Tom Glavine	.35
20	Wade Boggs	1.50
21	Edgar Martinez	.10
22	Lance Johnson	.10
23	Gregg Jefferies	.10
24	Bip Roberts	.10
25	Tony Phillips	.10
26	Greg Maddux	1.50
27	Mickey Tettleton	.10
28	Terry Steinbach	.10
29	Ryne Sandberg	1.50
30	Wally Joyner	.10
31	Joe Carter	.10
32	Ellis Burks	.10
33	Fred McGriff	.10
34	Barry Larkin	.10
35	John Franco	.10
36	Rafael Palmeiro	.65
37	Mark McGwire	2.50
38	Ken Caminiti	.10
39	David Cone	.10
40	Julio Franco	.10
41	Roger Clemens	1.75
42	Barry Bonds	3.00
43	Dennis Eckersley	.65
44	Eddie Murray	.75
45	Paul O'Neill	.10
46	Craig Biggio	.10
47	Roberto Alomar	.20
48	Mark Grace	.10
49	Matt Williams	.10
50	Jay Buhner	.10
51	John Smoltz	.10
52	Randy Johnson	.75
53	Ramon Martinez	.10
54	Curt Schilling	.35
55	Gary Sheffield	.50
56	Jack McDowell	.10
57	Brady Anderson	.10
58	Dante Bichette	.10
59	Ron Gant	.10
60	Alex Fernandez	.10
61	Moises Alou	.10
62	Travis Fryman	.10
63	Dean Palmer	.10
64	Todd Hundley	.10
65	Jeff Brantley	.10
66	Bernard Gilkey	.10
67	Geronimo Berroa	.10
68	John Wetteland	.10
69	Robin Ventura	.10
70	Ray Lankford	.10
71	Kevin Appier	.10
72	Larry Walker	.10
73	Juan Gonzalez	.40
74	Jeff King	.10
75	Greg Vaughn	.10
76	Steve Finley	.10
77	Brian McRae	.10
78	Paul Sorrento	.10
79	Ken Griffey Jr.	2.00
80	Omar Vizquel	.10
81	Jose Mesa	.10
82	Albert Belle	.10
83	Glenallen Hill	.10
84	Sammy Sosa	1.50
85	Andy Benes	.10
86	David Justice	.10
87	Marquis Grissom	.10
88	John Olerud	.10
89	Tino Martinez	.10
90	Frank Thomas	.75
91	Raul Mondesi	.10
92	Steve Trachsel	.10
93	Jim Edmonds	.10
94	Rusty Greer	.10
95	Joey Hamilton	.10
96	Ismael Valdes	.10
97	Dave Nilsson	.10
98	John Jaha	.10
99	Alex Gonzalez	.10
100	Javy Lopez	.10
101	Ryan Klesko	.10
102	Tim Salmon	.10
103	Bernie Williams	.10
104	Roberto Hernandez	.10
105	Chuck Knoblauch	.10
106	Mike Lansing	.10
107	Vinny Castilla	.10
108	Reggie Sanders	.10
109	Mo Vaughn	.10
110	Rondell White	.10
111	Ivan Rodriguez	.65
112	Mike Mussina	.40
113	Carlos Baerga	.10
114	Jeff Conine	.10
115	Jim Thome	.65
116	Manny Ramirez	.75
117	Kenny Lofton	.10
118	Wilson Alvarez	.10
119	Eric Karros	.10
120	Robb Nen	.10
121	Mark Wohlers	.10
122	Ed Sprague	.10
123	Pat Hentgen	.10
124	Juan Guzman	.10
125	Derek Bell	.10
126	Jeff Bagwell	.75
127	Eric Young	.10
128	John Valentin	.10
129	Al Martin (Photo actually Javy Lopez.)	
130	Trevor Hoffman	.10
131	Henry Rodriguez	.10
132	Pedro Martinez	.75
133	Mike Piazza	2.00
134	Brian Jordan	.10
135	Jose Valentin	.10
136	Jeff Cirillo	.10
137	Chipper Jones	1.50
138	Ricky Bottalico	.10
139	Hideo Nomo	.40
140	Troy Percival	.10
141	Rey Ordonez	.10
142	Edgar Renteria	.10
143	Luis Castillo	.10
144	Vladimir Guerrero	.75
145	Jeff D'Amico	.10
146	Andruw Jones	.75
147	Darin Erstad	.25
148	Bob Abreu	.10
149	Carlos Delgado	.45
150	Jamey Wright	.10
151	Nomar Garciaparra	1.50
152	Jason Kendall	.10
153	Jermaine Allensworth	.10
154	Scott Rolen	.65
155	Rocky Coppinger	.10
156	Paul Wilson	.10
157	Garret Anderson	.10
158	Mariano Rivera	.15
159	Ruben Rivera	.10
160	Andy Pettitte	.35
161	Derek Jeter	3.00
162	Neifi Perez	.10
163	Ray Durham	.10
164	James Baldwin	.10
165	Marty Cordova	.10
166	Tony Clark	.10
167	Michael Tucker	.10
168	Mike Sweeney	.10
169	Johnny Damon	.25
170	Jermaine Dye	.10
171	Alex Ochoa	.10
172	Jason Isringhausen	.10
173	Mark Grudzielanek	.10
174	Jose Rosado	.10
175	Todd Hollandsworth	.10
176	Alan Benes	.10
177	Jason Giambi	.45
178	Billy Wagner	.10
179	Justin Thompson	.10
180	Todd Walker	.10

Players Private Issue

	NM/M
Common Player:	1.00
Stars:	5X

(See 1997 Topps/Gallery for checklist and base card values.)

Peter Max

		NM/M
Complete Set (10):		60.00
Common Player:		2.00
Peter Max Autographed:		100.00
1	Derek Jeter	10.00
2	Albert Belle	3.00
3	Ken Caminiti	3.00
4	Chipper Jones	6.00
5	Ken Griffey Jr.	7.50
6	Frank Thomas	5.00
7	Cal Ripken Jr.	10.00
8	Mark McGwire	9.00
9	Barry Bonds	10.00
10	Mike Piazza	7.50

Photo Gallery

		NM/M
Complete Set (16):		15.00
Common Player:		.50
1	World Series	.50
2	Paul Molitor	1.00
3	Eddie Murray	1.00
4	Ken Griffey Jr.	2.50
5	Chipper Jones	1.50
6	Derek Jeter	3.50
7	Frank Thomas	1.00
8	Mark McGwire	3.00
9	Kenny Lofton	.50
10	Gary Sheffield	.65
11	Mike Piazza	2.50
12	Vinny Castilla	.50
13	Andres Galarraga	.50
14	Andy Pettitte	.50
15	Robin Ventura	.50
16	Barry Larkin	.50

Gallery of Heroes

		NM/M
Complete Set (10):		30.00
Common Player:		1.50
1	Derek Jeter	6.00
2	Chipper Jones	3.00
3	Frank Thomas	2.50
4	Ken Griffey Jr.	4.00
5	Cal Ripken Jr.	6.00
6	Mark McGwire	5.00
7	Mike Piazza	4.00
8	Jeff Bagwell	2.50
9	Tony Gwynn	3.00
10	Mo Vaughn	1.50

1997 Topps Screenplays

		NM/M
Complete Set (20):		25.00
Common Player:		1.00
Pack (1):		2.50
Wax Box (21):		30.00
(1)	Jeff Bagwell	2.00
(2)	Albert Belle	1.00
(3)	Barry Bonds	5.00
(4)	Andres Galarraga	1.00

(5)	Nomar Garciaparra	2.50
(6)	Juan Gonzalez	1.25
(7)	Ken Griffey Jr.	3.00
(8)	Tony Gwynn	2.50
(9)	Derek Jeter	5.00
(10)	Randy Johnson	2.00
(11)	Andruw Jones	2.00
(12)	Chipper Jones	2.50
(13)	Kenny Lofton	1.00
(14)	Mark McGwire	4.00
(15)	Paul Molitor	2.00
(16)	Hideo Nomo	1.25
(17)	Cal Ripken Jr.	5.00
(18)	Sammy Sosa	2.50
(19)	Frank Thomas	2.00
(20)	Jim Thome	1.50

Inserts

		NM/M
	Complete Set (6):	35.00
	Common Player:	2.00
1	Larry Walker	2.00
2	Cal Ripken Jr.	12.50
3	Chipper Jones	6.00
4	Frank Thomas	5.00
5	Mike Piazza	7.50
6	Ken Griffey Jr.	7.50

1997 Topps Stars

		NM/M
	Complete Set (125):	30.00
	Common Player:	.10
	Pack (7):	3.00
	Wax Box (24):	65.00
1	Larry Walker	.10
2	Tino Martinez	.10
3	Cal Ripken Jr.	3.00
4	Ken Griffey Jr.	2.00
5	Chipper Jones	1.50
6	David Justice	.10
7	Mike Piazza	2.00
8	Jeff Bagwell	1.00
9	Ron Gant	.10
10	Sammy Sosa	2.00
11	Tony Gwynn	1.50
12	Carlos Baerga	.10
13	Frank Thomas	1.00
14	Moises Alou	.10
15	Barry Larkin	.10
16	Ivan Rodriguez	.75
17	Greg Maddux	1.50
18	Jim Edmonds	.10
19	Jose Canseco	.50
20	Rafael Palmeiro	.75
21	Paul Molitor	1.00
22	Kevin Appier	.10
23	Raul Mondesi	.10
24	Lance Johnson	.10
25	Edgar Martinez	.10
26	Andres Galarraga	.10
27	Mo Vaughn	.10
28	Ken Caminiti	.10
29	Cecil Fielder	.10
30	Harold Baines	.10
31	Roberto Alomar	.25
32	Shawn Estes	.10
33	Tom Glavine	.35
34	Dennis Eckersley	.75
35	Manny Ramirez	1.00
36	John Olerud	.10
37	Juan Gonzalez	.50
38	Chuck Knoblauch	.10
39	Albert Belle	.10
40	Vinny Castilla	.10
41	John Smoltz	.10
42	Barry Bonds	3.00
43	Randy Johnson	1.00
44	Brady Anderson	.10
45	Jeff Blauser	.10
46	Craig Biggio	.10
47	Jeff Conine	.10
48	Marquis Grissom	.10

49	Mark Grace	.10
50	Roger Clemens	1.75
51	Mark McGwire	2.50
52	Fred McGriff	.10
53	Gary Sheffield	.50
54	Bobby Jones	.10
55	Eric Young	.10
56	Robin Ventura	.10
57	Wade Boggs	1.50
58	Joe Carter	.10
59	Ryne Sandberg	1.50
60	Matt Williams	.10
61	Todd Hundley	.10
62	Dante Bichette	.10
63	Chili Davis	.10
64	Kenny Lofton	.10
65	Jay Buhner	.10
66	Will Clark	.10
67	Travis Fryman	.10
68	Pat Hentgen	.10
69	Ellis Burks	.10
70	Mike Mussina	.40
71	Hideo Nomo	.50
72	Sandy Alomar	.10
73	Bobby Bonilla	.10
74	Rickey Henderson	1.00
75	David Cone	.10
76	Terry Steinbach	.10
77	Pedro Martinez	1.00
78	Jim Thome	.75
79	Rod Beck	.10
80	Randy Myers	.10
81	Charles Nagy	.10
82	Mark Wohlers	.10
83	Paul O'Neill	.10
84	Curt Schilling	.35
85	Joey Cora	.10
86	John Franco	.10
87	Kevin Brown	.10
88	Benito Santiago	.10
89	Ray Lankford	.10
90	Bernie Williams	.10
91	Jason Dickson	.10
92	Jeff Cirillo	.10
93	Nomar Garciaparra	2.00
94	Mariano Rivera	.15
95	Javy Lopez	.10
96	Tony Womack RC	.25
97	Jose Rosado	.10
98	Denny Neagle	.10
99	Darryl Kile	.10
100	Justin Thompson	.10
101	Juan Encarnacion	.10
102	Brad Fullmer	.10
103	Kris Benson RC	.75
104	Todd Helton	1.00
105	Paul Konerko	.10
106	Travis Lee RC	1.00
107	Todd Greene	.10
108	Mark Kotsay RC	.50
109	Carl Pavano	.10
110	Kerry Wood RC	4.00
111	Jason Romano RC	.10
112	Geoff Goetz RC	.10
113	Scott Hodges RC	.10
114	Aaron Akin RC	.10
115	Vernon Wells RC	6.00
116	Chris Stowe RC	.10
117	Brett Caradonna RC	.10
118	Adam Kennedy RC	1.00
119	Jayson Werth RC	.10
120	Glenn Davis RC	.10
121	Troy Cameron RC	.10
122	J.J. Davis RC	.10
123	Jason Dellaero RC	.10
124	Jason Standridge RC	.10
125	Lance Berkman RC	2.00

Always Mint

	NM/M
Complete Set (125):	250.00
Common Player:	.50

	Stars/Rookies:	8X

(See 1997 Topps Stars for checklist and base card values.)

All-Star Memories

		NM/M
	Complete Set (10):	20.00
	Common Player:	1.00
1	Cal Ripken Jr.	6.00
2	Jeff Conine	1.00
3	Mike Piazza	4.00
4	Randy Johnson	2.00
5	Ken Griffey Jr.	4.00
6	Fred McGriff	1.00
7	Moises Alou	1.00
8	Hideo Nomo	1.25
9	Larry Walker	1.00
10	Sandy Alomar	1.00

Autographed Rookie Reprints

		NM/M
	Common Player:	15.00
(1)	Luis Aparicio	20.00
(3)	Jim Bunning	30.00
(4)	Bob Feller	35.00
(5)	Rollie Fingers	15.00
(6)	Monte Irvin	15.00
(7)	Al Kaline	30.00
(8)	Ralph Kiner	25.00
(9)	Eddie Mathews	75.00
(10)	Hal Newhouser	40.00
(11)	Gaylord Perry	15.00
(12)	Robin Roberts	30.00
(13)	Brooks Robinson	40.00
(14)	Enos Slaughter	30.00
(15)	Earl Weaver	20.00

Future All-Stars

		NM/M
	Complete Set (15):	17.50
	Common Player:	.75
1	Derek Jeter	4.00
2	Andruw Jones	2.50
3	Vladimir Guerrero	3.00
4	Scott Rolen	2.50
5	Jose Guillen	.75
6	Jose Cruz, Jr.	.75
7	Darin Erstad	2.50
8	Tony Clark	.75
9	Scott Spiezio	.75
10	Kevin Orie	.75
11	Calvin Reese	.75
12	Billy Wagner	.75
13	Matt Morris	.75
14	Jeremi Gonzalez	.75
15	Hideki Irabu	.75

Rookie Reprints

		NM/M
	Complete Set (15):	25.00
	Common Player:	2.00
(1)	Luis Aparicio	2.00
(2)	Richie Ashburn	2.00
(3)	Jim Bunning	2.00
(4)	Bob Feller	2.00
(5)	Rollie Fingers	2.00
(6)	Monte Irvin	2.00
(7)	Al Kaline	3.00
(8)	Ralph Kiner	2.00
(9)	Eddie Mathews	3.00
(10)	Hal Newhouser	2.00
(11)	Gaylord Perry	2.00
(12)	Robin Roberts	2.00
(13)	Brooks Robinson	3.00
(14)	Enos Slaughter	2.00
(15)	Earl Weaver	2.00

1997 All-Stars

		NM/M
	Complete Set (20):	60.00
	Common Player:	1.50
1	Greg Maddux	6.00
2	Randy Johnson	4.50
3	Tino Martinez	1.50
4	Jeff Bagwell	4.50
5	Ivan Rodriguez	3.50
6	Mike Piazza	7.50
7	Cal Ripken Jr.	12.00
8	Ken Caminiti	1.50
9	Tony Gwynn	6.00
10	Edgar Martinez	1.50
11	Craig Biggio	1.50
12	Roberto Alomar	2.00
13	Larry Walker	1.50
14	Brady Anderson	1.50
15	Barry Bonds	12.00
16	Ken Griffey Jr.	7.50
17	Ray Lankford	1.50

18	Paul O'Neill	1.50
19	Jeff Blauser	1.50
20	Sandy Alomar	1.50

1998 Topps

		NM/M
Unopened Fact. Set (511):		85.00
Complete Set (503):		40.00
Common Player:		.05
Series 1 or 2 Pack (11):		1.00
Series 1 or 2 Wax		
	Box (36):	25.00
1	Tony Gwynn	1.00
2	Larry Walker	.05
3	Billy Wagner	.05
4	Denny Neagle	.05
5	Vladimir Guerrero	.75
6	Kevin Brown	.05
7	Not Issued	
8	Mariano Rivera	.10
9	Tony Clark	.05
10	Deion Sanders	.05
11	Francisco Cordova	.05
12	Matt Williams	.05
13	Carlos Baerga	.05
14	Mo Vaughn	.05
15	Bobby Witt	.05
16	Matt Stairs	.05
17	Chan Ho Park	.05
18	Mike Bordick	.05
19	Michael Tucker	.05
20	Frank Thomas	.75
21	Roberto Clemente	1.50
22	Dmitri Young	.05
23	Steve Trachsel	.05
24	Jeff Kent	.05
25	Scott Rolen	.50
26	John Thomson	.05
27	Joe Vitiello	.05
28	Eddie Guardado	.05
29	Charlie Hayes	.05
30	Juan Gonzalez	.40
31	Garret Anderson	.05
32	John Jaha	.05
33	Omar Vizquel	.05
34	Brian Hunter	.05
35	Jeff Bagwell	.75
36	Mark Lemke	.05
37	Doug Glanville	.05
38	Dan Wilson	.05
39	Steve Cooke	.05
40	Chili Davis	.05
41	Mike Cameron	.05
42	F.P. Santangelo	.05
43	Brad Ausmus	.05
44	Gary DiSarcina	.05
45	Pat Hentgen	.05
46	Wilton Guerrero	.05
47	Devon White	.05
48	Danny Patterson	.05
49	Pat Meares	.05
50	Rafael Palmeiro	.65
51	Mark Gardner	.05
52	Jeff Blauser	.05
53	Dave Hollins	.05
54	Carlos Garcia	.05
55	Ben McDonald	.05
56	John Mabry	.05
57	Trevor Hoffman	.05
58	Tony Fernandez	.05
59	Rich Loiselle	.05
60	Mark Leiter	.05
61	Pat Kelly	.05
62	John Flaherty	.05
63	Roger Bailey	.05
64	Tom Gordon	.05
65	Ryan Klesko	.05
66	Darryl Hamilton	.05
67	Jim Eisenreich	.05
68	Butch Huskey	.05
69	Mark Grudzielanek	.05
70	Marquis Grissom	.05
71	Mark McLemore	.05

72	Gary Gaetti	.05
73	Greg Gagne	.05
74	Lyle Mouton	.05
75	Jim Edmonds	.05
76	Shawn Green	.25
77	Greg Vaughn	.05
78	Terry Adams	.05
79	Kevin Polcovich **RC**	.05
80	Troy O'Leary	.05
81	Jeff Shaw	.05
82	Rich Becker	.05
83	David Wells	.05
84	Steve Karsay	.05
85	Charles Nagy	.05
86	B.J. Surhoff	.05
87	Jamey Wright	.05
88	James Baldwin	.05
89	Edgardo Alfonzo	.05
90	Jay Buhner	.05
91	Brady Anderson	.05
92	Scott Servais	.05
93	Edgar Renteria	.05
94	Mike Lieberthal	.05
95	Rick Aguilera	.05
96	Walt Weiss	.05
97	Deivi Cruz	.05
98	Kurt Abbott	.05
99	Henry Rodriguez	.05
100	Mike Piazza	1.25
101	Bill Taylor	.05
102	Todd Zeile	.05
103	Rey Ordonez	.05
104	Willie Greene	.05
105	Tony Womack	.05
106	Mike Sweeney	.05
107	Jeffrey Hammonds	.05
108	Kevin Orie	.05
109	Alex Gonzalez	.05
110	Jose Canseco	.50
111	Paul Sorrento	.05
112	Joey Hamilton	.05
113	Brad Radke	.05
114	Steve Avery	.05
115	Esteban Loaiza	.05
116	Stan Javier	.05
117	Chris Gomez	.05
118	Royce Clayton	.05
119	Orlando Merced	.05
120	Kevin Appier	.05
121	Mel Nieves	.05
122	Joe Girardi	.05
123	Rico Brogna	.05
124	Kent Mercker	.05
125	Manny Ramirez	.75
126	Jeromy Burnitz	.05
127	Kevin Foster	.05
128	Matt Morris	.05
129	Jason Dickson	.05
130	Tom Glavine	.25
131	Wally Joyner	.05
132	Rick Reed	.05
133	Todd Jones	.05
134	Dave Martinez	.05
135	Sandy Alomar	.05
136	Mike Lansing	.05
137	Sean Berry	.05
138	Doug Jones	.05
139	Todd Stottlemyre	.05
140	Jay Bell	.05
141	Jaime Navarro	.05
142	Chris Hoiles	.05
143	Joey Cora	.05
144	Scott Spiezio	.05
145	Joe Carter	.05
146	Jose Guillen	.05
147	Damion Easley	.05
148	Lee Stevens	.05
149	Alex Fernandez	.05
150	Randy Johnson	.75
151	J.T. Snow	.05
152	Chuck Finley	.05
153	Bernard Gilkey	.05
154	David Segui	.05
155	Dante Bichette	.05
156	Kevin Stocker	.05
157	Carl Everett	.05
158	Jose Valentin	.05
159	Pokey Reese	.05
160	Derek Jeter	2.00
161	Roger Pavlik	.05
162	Mark Wohlers	.05
163	Ricky Bottalico	.05
164	Ozzie Guillen	.05
165	Mike Mussina	.50
166	Gary Sheffield	.50
167	Hideo Nomo	.40
168	Mark Grace	.05
169	Aaron Sele	.05
170	Darryl Kile	.05
171	Shawn Estes	.05
172	Vinny Castilla	.05
173	Ron Coomer	.05
174	Jose Rosado	.05
175	Kenny Lofton	.05
176	Jason Giambi	.50
177	Hal Morris	.05

178	Darren Bragg	.05
179	Orel Hershiser	.05
180	Ray Lankford	.05
181	Hideki Irabu	.05
182	Kevin Young	.05
183	Javy Lopez	.05
184	Jeff Montgomery	.05
185	Mike Holtz	.05
186	George Williams	.05
187	Cal Eldred	.05
188	Tom Candiotti	.05
189	Glenallen Hill	.05
190	Brian Giles	.05
191	Dave Mlicki	.05
192	Garrett Stephenson	.05
193	Jeff Frye	.05
194	Joe Oliver	.05
195	Bob Hamelin	.05
196	Luis Sojo	.05
197	LaTroy Hawkins	.05
198	Kevin Elster	.05
199	Jeff Reed	.05
200	Dennis Eckersley	.65
201	Bill Mueller	.05
202	Russ Davis	.05
203	Armando Benitez	.05
204	Quilvio Veras	.05
205	Tim Naehring	.05
206	Quinton McCracken	.05
207	Raul Casanova	.05
208	Matt Lawton	.05
209	Luis Alicea	.05
210	Luis Gonzalez	.05
211	Allen Watson	.05
212	Gerald Williams	.05
213	David Bell	.05
214	Todd Hollandsworth	.05
215	Wade Boggs	1.00
216	Jose Mesa	.05
217	Jamie Moyer	.05
218	Darren Daulton	.05
219	Mickey Morandini	.05
220	Rusty Greer	.05
221	Jim Bullinger	.05
222	Jose Offerman	.05
223	Matt Karchner	.05
224	Woody Williams	.05
225	Mark Loretta	.05
226	Mike Hampton	.05
227	Willie Adams	.05
228	Scott Hatteberg	.05
229	Rich Amaral	.05
230	Terry Steinbach	.05
231	Glendon Rusch	.05
232	Bret Boone	.05
233	Robert Person	.05
234	Jose Hernandez	.05
235	Doug Drabek	.05
236	Jason McDonald	.05
237	Chris Widger	.05
238	Tom Martin **RC**	.05
239	Dave Burba	.05
240	Pete Rose II	.05
241	Bobby Ayala	.05
242	Tim Wakefield	.05
243	Dennis Springer	.05
244	Tim Belcher	.05
245	Jon Garland,	
	Geoff Goetz	.05
246	Glenn Davis,	
	Lance Berkman	.05
247	Vernon Wells,	
	Aaron Akin	.10
248	Adam Kennedy,	
	Jason Romano	.10
249	Jason Dellaero,	
	Troy Cameron	.05
250	Alex Sanchez,	
	Jared Sandberg **RC**	.10
251	Pablo Ortega,	
	Jim Manias	.05
252	Jason Conti,	
	Mike Stoner **RC**	.10
253	John Patterson,	
	Larry Rodriguez	.05
254	Adrian Beltre, Ryan Minor,	
	Aaron Boone	.15
255	Ben Grieve,	
	Brian Buchanan,	
	Dermal Brown	.05
256	Carl Pavano, Kerry Wood,	
	Gil Meche	.15
257	David Ortiz, Daryle Ward,	
	Richie Sexson	.50
258	Randy Winn,	
	Juan Encarnacion,	
	Andrew Vessel	.10
259	Kris Benson, Travis Smith,	
	Courtney Duncan	.05
260	Chad Hermansen,	
	Brent Butler,	
	Warren Morris **RC**	.10
261	Ben Davis, Elieser Marrero,	
	Ramon Hernandez	.05

262	Eric Chavez,	
	Russell Branyan,	
	Russ Johnson	.20
263	Todd Dunwoody,	
	John Barnes,	
	Ryan Jackson **RC**	.10
264	Matt Clement,	
	Roy Halladay,	
	Brian Fuentes **RC**	.05
265	Randy Johnson	.15
266	Kevin Brown	.05
267	Ricardo Rincon,	
	Francisco Cordova	.05
268	Nomar Garciaparra	.50
269	Tino Martinez	.05
270	Chuck Knoblauch	.05
271	Pedro Martinez	.40
272	Denny Neagle	.05
273	Juan Gonzalez	.20
274	Andres Galarraga	.05
275	Checklist	.05
276	Checklist	.05
277	Moises Alou	.05
278	Sandy Alomar	.05
279	Gary Sheffield	.05
280	Matt Williams	.05
281	Livan Hernandez	.05
282	Chad Ogea	.05
283	Marlins Win	.05
284	Tino Martinez	.05
285	Roberto Alomar	.20
286	Jeff King	.05
287	Brian Jordan	.05
288	Darin Erstad	.15
289	Ken Caminiti	.05
290	Jim Thome	.60
291	Paul Molitor	.75
292	Ivan Rodriguez	.65
293	Bernie Williams	.05
294	Todd Hundley	.05
295	Andres Galarraga	.05
296	Greg Maddux	1.00
297	Edgar Martinez	.05
298	Ron Gant	.05
299	Derek Bell	.05
300	Roger Clemens	1.00
301	Rondell White	.05
302	Barry Larkin	.05
303	Robin Ventura	.05
304	Jason Kendall	.05
305	Chipper Jones	1.00
306	John Franco	.05
307	Sammy Sosa	1.00
308	Troy Percival	.05
309	Chuck Knoblauch	.05
310	Ellis Burks	.05
311	Al Martin	.05
312	Tim Salmon	.05
313	Moises Alou	.05
314	Lance Johnson	.05
315	Justin Thompson	.05
316	Will Clark	.05
317	Barry Bonds	2.00
318	Craig Biggio	.05
319	John Smoltz	.05
320	Cal Ripken Jr.	2.00
321	Ken Griffey Jr.	1.25
322	Paul O'Neill	.05
323	Todd Helton	.65
324	John Olerud	.05
325	Mark McGwire	1.50
326	Jose Cruz Jr.	.05
327	Jeff Cirillo	.05
328	Dean Palmer	.05
329	John Wetteland	.05
330	Steve Finley	.05
331	Albert Belle	.05
332	Curt Schilling	.25
333	Raul Mondesi	.05
334	Andruw Jones	.75
335	Nomar Garciaparra	1.00
336	David Justice	.05
337	Andy Pettitte	.25
338	Pedro Martinez	.75
339	Travis Miller	.05
340	Chris Stynes	.05
341	Gregg Jefferies	.05
342	Jeff Fassero	.05
343	Craig Counsell	.05
344	Wilson Alvarez	.05
345	Bip Roberts	.05
346	Kelvim Escobar	.05
347	Mark Bellhorn	.05
348	Cory Lidle **RC**	.05
349	Fred McGriff	.05
350	Chuck Carr	.05
351	Bob Abreu	.05
352	Juan Guzman	.05
353	Fernando Vina	.05
354	Andy Benes	.05
355	Dave Nilsson	.05
356	Bobby Bonilla	.05
357	Ismael Valdes	.05
358	Carlos Perez	.05
359	Kirk Rueter	.05
360	Bartolo Colon	.05

361	Mel Rojas	.05
362	Johnny Damon	.25
363	Geronimo Berroa	.05
364	Reggie Sanders	.05
365	Jermaine Allensworth	.05
366	Orlando Cabrera	.05
367	Jorge Fabregas	.05
368	Scott Stahoviak	.05
369	Ken Cloude	.05
370	Donovan Osborne	.05
371	Roger Cedeno	.05
372	Neifi Perez	.05
373	Chris Holt	.05
374	Cecil Fielder	.05
375	Marty Cordova	.05
376	Tom Goodwin	.05
377	Jeff Suppan	.05
378	Jeff Brantley	.05
379	Mark Langston	.05
380	Shane Reynolds	.05
381	Mike Fetters	.05
382	Todd Greene	.05
383	Ray Durham	.05
384	Carlos Delgado	.30
385	Jeff D'Amico	.05
386	Brian McRae	.05
387	Alan Benes	.05
388	Heathcliff Slocumb	.05
389	Eric Young	.05
390	Travis Fryman	.05
391	David Cone	.05
392	Otis Nixon	.05
393	Jeremi Gonzalez	.05
394	Jeff Juden	.05
395	Jose Vizcaino	.05
396	Ugueth Urbina	.05
397	Ramon Martinez	.05
398	Robb Nen	.05
399	Harold Baines	.05
400	Delino DeShields	.05
401	John Burkett	.05
402	Sterling Hitchcock	.05
403	Mark Clark	.05
404	Terrell Wade	.05
405	Scott Brosius	.05
406	Chad Curtis	.05
407	Brian Johnson	.05
408	Roberto Kelly	.05
409	Dave Dellucci RC	.15
410	Michael Tucker	.05
411	Mark Kotsay	.05
412	Mark Lewis	.05
413	Ryan McGuire	.05
414	Shawon Dunston	.05
415	Brad Rigby	.05
416	Scott Erickson	.05
417	Bobby Jones	.05
418	Darren Oliver	.05
419	John Smiley	.05
420	T.J. Mathews	.05
421	Dustin Hermanson	.05
422	Mike Timlin	.05
423	Willie Blair	.05
424	Manny Alexander	.05
425	Bob Tewksbury	.05
426	Pete Schourek	.05
427	Reggie Jefferson	.05
428	Ed Sprague	.05
429	Jeff Conine	.05
430	Roberto Hernandez	.05
431	Tom Pagnozzi	.05
432	Jaret Wright	.05
433	Livan Hernandez	.05
434	Andy Ashby	.05
435	Todd Dunn	.05
436	Bobby Higginson	.05
437	Rod Beck	.05
438	Jim Leyritz	.05
439	Matt Williams	.05
440	Brett Tomko	.05
441	Joe Randa	.05
442	Chris Carpenter	.05
443	Dennis Reyes	.05
444	Al Leiter	.05
445	Jason Schmidt	.05
446	Ken Hill	.05
447	Shannon Stewart	.05
448	Enrique Wilson	.05
449	Fernando Tatis	.05
450	Jimmy Key	.05
451	Darrin Fletcher	.05
452	John Valentin	.05
453	Kevin Tapani	.05
454	Eric Karros	.05
455	Jay Bell	.05
456	Walt Weiss	.05
457	Devon White	.05
458	Carl Pavano	.05
459	Mike Lansing	.05
460	John Flaherty	.05
461	Richard Hidalgo	.05
462	Quinton McCracken	.05
463	Karim Garcia	.15
464	Miguel Cairo	.05
465	Edwin Diaz	.05
466	Bobby Smith	.05

467	Yamil Benitez	.05
468	Rich Butler RC	.05
469	Ben Ford RC	.05
470	Bubba Trammell	.05
471	Brent Brede	.05
472	Brooks Kieschnick	.05
473	Carlos Castillo	.05
474	Brad Radke	.05
475	Roger Clemens	.50
476	Curt Schilling	.05
477	John Olerud	.05
478	Mark McGwire	.75
479	Mike Piazza, Ken Griffey Jr.	.75
480	Jeff Bagwell, Frank Thomas	.50
481	Chipper Jones, Nomar Garciaparra	.65
482	Larry Walker, Juan Gonzalez	.30
483	Gary Sheffield, Tino Martinez	.05
484	Derrick Gibson, Michael Coleman, Norm Hutchins	.05
485	Braden Looper, Cliff Politte, Brian Rose	.05
486	Eric Milton, Jason Marquis, Corey Lee	.05
487	A.J. Hinch, Mark Osborne, Robert Fick RC	.10
488	Aramis Ramirez, Alex Gonzalez, Sean Casey	.15
489	Donnie Bridges, Tim Drew RC	.10
490	Ntema Ndungidi, Darnell McDonald RC	.10
491	Ryan Anderson, Mark Mangum	.25
492	J.J. Davis, Troy Glaus RC	2.00
493	Jayson Werth, Dan Reichert RC	.10
494	John Curtice, Mike Cuddyer RC	.25
495	Jack Cust, Jason Standridge	1.00
496	Brian Anderson	.05
497	Tony Saunders	.05
498	Vladimir Nunez, Jhensy Sandoval RC	.10
499	Brad Penny, Nick Bierbrodt	.05
500	Dustin Carr, Luis Cruz RC	.05
501	Marcus McCain, Cedrick Bowers RC	.05
502	Checklist	.05
503	Checklist	.05
504	Alex Rodriguez	1.50

Minted in Cooperstown

		NM/M
Common Card:		.50
Stars/Rookies:		6X
(See 1998 Topps for checklist and base card values.)		

Baby Boomers

		NM/M
Complete Set (15):		15.00
Common Player:		.75
Inserted 1:36 Retail		
1	Derek Jeter	6.00
2	Scott Rolen	1.00
3	Nomar Garciaparra	3.50
4	Jose Cruz Jr.	.75
5	Darin Erstad	.85
6	Todd Helton	1.50
7	Tony Clark	.75
8	Jose Guillen	.75
9	Andruw Jones	1.00

10	Vladimir Guerrero	1.50
11	Mark Kotsay	.75
12	Todd Greene	.75
13	Andy Pettitte	.85
14	Justin Thompson	.75
15	Alan Benes	.75

Clout 9

		NM/M
Complete Set (9):		17.50
Common Player:		1.00
Inserted 1:72		
1	Edgar Martinez	1.00
2	Mike Piazza	5.00
3	Frank Thomas	2.00
4	Craig Biggio	1.00
5	Vinny Castilla	1.00
6	Jeff Blauser	1.00
7	Barry Bonds	7.50
8	Ken Griffey Jr.	5.00
9	Larry Walker	1.00

Etch-A-Sketch

		NM/M
Complete Set (9):		20.00
Common Player:		1.00
Inserted 1:36		
1	Albert Belle	1.00
2	Barry Bonds	6.00
3	Ken Griffey Jr.	4.00
4	Greg Maddux	3.00
5	Hideo Nomo	1.50
6	Mike Piazza	4.00
7	Cal Ripken Jr.	6.00
8	Frank Thomas	2.00
9	Mo Vaughn	1.00

Flashback

		NM/M
Complete Set (10):		22.50
Common Player:		1.00
Inserted 1:72		
1	Barry Bonds	7.50
2	Ken Griffey Jr.	5.00
3	Paul Molitor	2.00
4	Randy Johnson	2.00
5	Cal Ripken Jr.	7.50
6	Tony Gwynn	3.00
7	Kenny Lofton	1.00
8	Gary Sheffield	1.50

9	Deion Sanders	1.00
10	Brady Anderson	1.00

Focal Point

		NM/M
Complete Set (15):		25.00
Common Player:		.75
Inserted 1:36		
1	Juan Gonzalez	.85
2	Nomar Garciaparra	2.50
3	Jose Cruz Jr.	.75
4	Cal Ripken Jr.	5.00
5	Ken Griffey Jr.	3.50
6	Ivan Rodriguez	1.00
7	Larry Walker	.75
8	Barry Bonds	5.00
9	Roger Clemens	3.00
10	Frank Thomas	1.50
11	Chuck Knoblauch	.75
12	Mike Piazza	3.50
13	Greg Maddux	2.50
14	Vladimir Guerrero	1.50
15	Andruw Jones	1.50

Hallbound

		NM/M
Complete Set (15):		45.00
Common Player:		1.50
1	Paul Molitor	2.50
2	Tony Gwynn	3.50
3	Wade Boggs	3.50
4	Roger Clemens	4.00
5	Dennis Eckersley	2.00
6	Cal Ripken Jr.	7.50
7	Greg Maddux	3.50
8	Rickey Henderson	2.50
9	Ken Griffey Jr.	5.00
10	Frank Thomas	2.50
11	Mark McGwire	6.00
12	Barry Bonds	7.50
13	Mike Piazza	5.00

14	Juan Gonzalez	1.50
15	Randy Johnson	2.50

Inter-League Mystery Finest

		NM/M
Complete Set (20):		35.00
Common Player:		.75
Inserted 1:36		
Refractors:		1.5X
Inserted 1:144		
1	Chipper Jones	3.00
2	Cal Ripken Jr.	6.50
3	Greg Maddux	3.00
4	Rafael Palmeiro	1.50
5	Todd Hundley	.75
6	Derek Jeter	6.50
7	John Olerud	.75
8	Tino Martinez	.75
9	Larry Walker	.75
10	Ken Griffey Jr.	4.00
11	Andres Galarraga	.75
12	Randy Johnson	2.00
13	Mike Piazza	4.00
14	Jim Edmonds	.75
15	Eric Karros	.75
16	Tim Salmon	.75
17	Sammy Sosa	3.00
18	Frank Thomas	2.00
19	Mark Grace	.75
20	Albert Belle	.75

Milestones

		NM/M
Complete Set (10):		17.50
Common Player:		.75
MS1	Barry Bonds	5.00
MS2	Roger Clemens	2.50
MS3	Dennis Eckersley	1.00
MS4	Juan Gonzalez	.75
MS5	Ken Griffey Jr.	3.00
MS6	Tony Gwynn	2.00
MS7	Greg Maddux	2.00
MS8	Mark McGwire	4.00
MS9	Cal Ripken Jr.	5.00
MS10	Frank Thomas	1.25

Mystery Finest

	NM/M
Complete Set (20):	25.00

Common Player:		.50
Inserted 1:36		
Borderless 1:72:		1.5X
Bordered Refractors 1:108:		1.5X
Borderless Refractors 1:288:		2X
1	Nomar Garciaparra	1.50
2	Chipper Jones	1.50
3	Scott Rolen	.75
4	Albert Belle	.50
5	Mo Vaughn	.50
6	Jose Cruz Jr.	.50
7	Mark McGwire	3.00
8	Derek Jeter	3.50
9	Tony Gwynn	1.50
10	Frank Thomas	1.00
11	Tino Martinez	.50
12	Greg Maddux	1.50
13	Juan Gonzalez	.75
14	Larry Walker	.50
15	Mike Piazza	2.50
16	Cal Ripken Jr.	3.50
17	Jeff Bagwell	1.00
18	Andruw Jones	1.00
19	Barry Bonds	3.50
20	Ken Griffey Jr.	2.50

Roberto Clemente Finest

	NM/M
Complete Set (19):	60.00
Common Clemente:	4.00
Inserted 1:72	
Refractors:	2X
Inserted 1:288	

Roberto Clemente Reprints

	NM/M
Complete Set (19):	50.00
Common Clemente:	2.50
Inserted 1:18	

Values quoted in this guide reflect the retail price of a card, the price a collector can expect to pay when buying a card from a dealer.

Roberto Clemente Tribute

	NM/M
Complete Set (5):	3.00
Common Clemente:	.75
Inserted 1:12	

Rookie Class

		NM/M
Complete Set (10):		4.00
Common Player:		.25
Inserted 1:12		
1	Travis Lee	.50
2	Richard Hidalgo	.25
3	Todd Helton	2.00
4	Paul Konerko	.75
5	Mark Kotsay	.25
6	Derrek Lee	1.50
7	Eli Marrero	.25
8	Fernando Tatis	.25
9	Juan Encarnacion	.25
10	Ben Grieve	.25

1998 Topps Chrome

		NM/M
Complete Set (502):		100.00
Common Player:		.10
Foil Pack (4):		1.50
Foil Box (24):		25.00
1	Tony Gwynn	2.00
2	Larry Walker	.10
3	Billy Wagner	.10
4	Denny Neagle	.10
5	Vladimir Guerrero	1.50
6	Kevin Brown	.10
7	Not Issued	
8	Mariano Rivera	.10
9	Tony Clark	.10
10	Deion Sanders	.10
11	Francisco Cordova	.10
12	Matt Williams	.10
13	Carlos Baerga	.10
14	Mo Vaughn	.10
15	Bobby Witt	.10
16	Matt Stairs	.10
17	Chan Ho Park	.10
18	Mike Bordick	.10
19	Michael Tucker	.10
20	Frank Thomas	1.50
21	Roberto Clemente (Tribute)	2.50
22	Dmitri Young	.10
23	Steve Trachsel	.10
24	Jeff Kent	.10
25	Scott Rolen	.75
26	John Thomson	.10
27	Joe Vitiello	.10
28	Eddie Guardado	.10
29	Charlie Hayes	.10
30	Juan Gonzalez	.75
31	Garret Anderson	.10
32	John Jaha	.10
33	Omar Vizquel	.10
34	Brian Hunter	.10
35	Jeff Bagwell	1.50
36	Mark Lemke	.10
37	Doug Glanville	.10
38	Dan Wilson	.10
39	Steve Cooke	.10
40	Chili Davis	.10
41	Mike Cameron	.10
42	F.P. Santangelo	.10
43	Brad Ausmus	.10
44	Gary DiSarcina	.10
45	Pat Hentgen	.10
46	Wilton Guerrero	.10
47	Devon White	.10
48	Danny Patterson	.10
49	Pat Meares	.10
50	Rafael Palmeiro	1.00
51	Mark Gardner	.10
52	Jeff Blauser	.10
53	Dave Hollins	.10
54	Carlos Garcia	.10
55	Ben McDonald	.10
56	John Mabry	.10
57	Trevor Hoffman	.10
58	Tony Fernandez	.10
59	Rich Loiselle	.10
60	Mark Leiter	.10
61	Pat Kelly	.10
62	John Flaherty	.10
63	Roger Bailey	.10
64	Tom Gordon	.10
65	Ryan Klesko	.10
66	Darryl Hamilton	.10
67	Jim Eisenreich	.10
68	Butch Huskey	.10
69	Mark Grudzielanek	.10
70	Marquis Grissom	.10
71	Mark McLemore	.10
72	Gary Gaetti	.10
73	Greg Gagne	.10
74	Lyle Mouton	.10
75	Jim Edmonds	.10
76	Shawn Green	.35
77	Terry Vaughn	.10
78	Terry Adams	.10
79	Kevin Polcovich **RC**	.10
80	Troy O'Leary	.10
81	Jeff Shaw	.10
82	Rich Becker	.10
83	David Wells	.10
84	Steve Karsay	.10
85	Charles Nagy	.10
86	B.J. Surhoff	.10
87	Jamey Wright	.10
88	James Baldwin	.10
89	Edgardo Alfonzo	.10
90	Jay Buhner	.10
91	Brady Anderson	.10
92	Scott Servais	.10
93	Edgar Renteria	.10
94	Mike Lieberthal	.10
95	Rick Aguilera	.10
96	Walt Weiss	.10
97	Deivi Cruz	.10
98	Kurt Abbott	.10
99	Henry Rodriguez	.10
100	Mike Piazza	2.25
101	Bill Taylor	.10
102	Todd Zeile	.10
103	Rey Ordonez	.10
104	Willie Greene	.10
105	Tony Womack	.10
106	Mike Sweeney	.10
107	Jeffrey Hammonds	.10
108	Kevin Orie	.10
109	Alex Gonzalez	.10
110	Jose Canseco	.60
111	Paul Sorrento	.10

No.	Player	Price
112	Joey Hamilton	.10
113	Brad Radke	.10
114	Steve Avery	.10
115	Esteban Loaiza	.10
116	Stan Javier	.10
117	Chris Gomez	.10
118	Royce Clayton	.10
119	Orlando Merced	.10
120	Kevin Appier	.10
121	Mel Nieves	.10
122	Joe Girardi	.10
123	Rico Brogna	.10
124	Kent Mercker	.10
125	Manny Ramirez	1.50
126	Jeromy Burnitz	.10
127	Kevin Foster	.10
128	Matt Morris	.10
129	Jason Dickson	.10
130	Tom Glavine	.35
131	Wally Joyner	.10
132	Rick Reed	.10
133	Todd Jones	.10
134	Dave Martinez	.10
135	Sandy Alomar	.10
136	Mike Lansing	.10
137	Sean Berry	.10
138	Doug Jones	.10
139	Todd Stottlemyre	.10
140	Jay Bell	.10
141	Jaime Navarro	.10
142	Chris Hoiles	.10
143	Joey Cora	.10
144	Scott Spiezio	.10
145	Joe Carter	.10
146	Jose Guillen	.10
147	Damion Easley	.10
148	Lee Stevens	.10
149	Alex Fernandez	.10
150	Randy Johnson	1.50
151	J.T. Snow	.10
152	Chuck Finley	.10
153	Bernard Gilkey	.10
154	David Segui	.10
155	Dante Bichette	.10
156	Kevin Stocker	.10
157	Carl Everett	.10
158	Jose Valentin	.10
159	Pokey Reese	.10
160	Derek Jeter	3.00
161	Roger Pavlik	.10
162	Mark Wohlers	.10
163	Ricky Bottalico	.10
164	Ozzie Guillen	.10
165	Mike Mussina	.60
166	Gary Sheffield	.50
167	Hideo Nomo	.75
168	Mark Grace	.10
169	Aaron Sele	.10
170	Darryl Kile	.10
171	Shawn Estes	.10
172	Vinny Castilla	.10
173	Ron Coomer	.10
174	Jose Rosado	.10
175	Kenny Lofton	.10
176	Jason Giambi	.65
177	Hal Morris	.10
178	Darren Bragg	.10
179	Orel Hershiser	.10
180	Ray Lankford	.10
181	Hideki Irabu	.10
182	Kevin Young	.10
183	Javy Lopez	.10
184	Jeff Montgomery	.10
185	Mike Holtz	.10
186	George Williams	.10
187	Cal Eldred	.10
188	Tom Candiotti	.10
189	Glenallen Hill	.10
190	Brian Giles	.10
191	Dave Mlicki	.10
192	Garrett Stephenson	.10
193	Jeff Frye	.10
194	Joe Oliver	.10
195	Bob Hamelin	.10
196	Luis Sojo	.10
197	LaTroy Hawkins	.10
198	Kevin Elster	.10
199	Jeff Reed	.10
200	Dennis Eckersley	1.00
201	Bill Mueller	.10
202	Russ Davis	.10
203	Armando Benitez	.10
204	Quilvio Veras	.10
205	Tim Naehring	.10
206	Quinton McCracken	.10
207	Raul Casanova	.10
208	Matt Lawton	.10
209	Luis Alicea	.10
210	Luis Gonzalez	.10
211	Allen Watson	.10
212	Gerald Williams	.10
213	David Bell	.10
214	Todd Hollandsworth	.10
215	Wade Boggs	2.00
216	Jose Mesa	.10
217	Jamie Moyer	.10
218	Darren Daulton	.10
219	Mickey Morandini	.10
220	Rusty Greer	.10
221	Jim Bullinger	.10
222	Jose Offerman	.10
223	Matt Karchner	.10
224	Woody Williams	.10
225	Mark Loretta	.10
226	Mike Hampton	.10
227	Willie Adams	.10
228	Scott Hatteberg	.10
229	Rich Amaral	.10
230	Terry Steinbach	.10
231	Glendon Rusch	.10
232	Bret Boone	.10
233	Robert Person	.10
234	Jose Hernandez	.10
235	Doug Drabek	.10
236	Jason McDonald	.10
237	Chris Widger	.10
238	Tom Martin RC	.10
239	Dave Burba	.10
240	Pete Rose	.10
241	Bobby Ayala	.10
242	Tim Wakefield	.10
243	Dennis Springer	.10
244	Tim Belcher	.10
245	Jon Garland, Geoff Goetz	.10
246	Glenn Davis, Lance Berkman	.25
247	Vernon Wells, Aaron Akin	.15
248	Adam Kennedy, Jason Romano	.25
249	Jason Dellaero, Troy Cameron	.10
250	Alex Sanchez, Jared Sandberg RC	.25
251	Pablo Ortega, James Manias RC	.10
252	Jason Conti, Mike Stoner RC	.10
253	John Patterson, Larry Rodriguez	.10
254	Adrian Beltre, Ryan Minor, Aaron Boone	.25
255	Ben Grieve, Brian Buchanan, Dermal Brown	.10
256	Carl Pavano, Kerry Wood, Gil Meche	.75
257	David Ortiz, Daryle Ward, Richie Sexson	.65
258	Randy Winn, Juan Encarnacion, Andrew Vessel	.10
259	Kris Benson, Travis Smith, Courtney Duncan	.15
260	Chad Hermansen, Brent Butler, Warren Morris RC	.15
261	Ben Davis, Elieser Marrero, Ramon Hernandez	.10
262	Eric Chavez, Russell Branyan, Russ Johnson	.25
263	Todd Dunwoody, John Barnes, Ryan Jackson RC	.15
264	Matt Clement, Roy Halladay, Brian Fuentes	.20
265	Randy Johnson	.50
266	Kevin Brown	.10
267	Francisco Cordova, Ricardo Rincon	.10
268	Nomar Garciaparra	.75
269	Tino Martinez	.10
270	Chuck Knoblauch	.10
271	Pedro Martinez	.40
272	Denny Neagle	.10
273	Juan Gonzalez	.20
274	Andres Galarraga	.10
275	Checklist	.10
276	Checklist	.10
277	Moises Alou	.10
278	Sandy Alomar	.10
279	Gary Sheffield	.10
280	Matt Williams	.10
281	Livan Hernandez	.10
282	Chad Ogea	.10
283	Marlins Win	.10
284	Tino Martinez	.10
285	Roberto Alomar	.35
286	Kit King	.10
287	Brian Jordan	.10
288	Darin Erstad	.30
289	Ken Caminiti	.10
290	Jim Thome	.90
291	Paul Molitor	1.50
292	Ivan Rodriguez	1.00
293	Bernie Williams	.10
294	Todd Hundley	.10
295	Andres Galarraga	.10
296	Greg Maddux	2.00
297	Edgar Martinez	.10
298	Ron Gant	.10
299	Derek Bell	.10
300	Roger Clemens	2.00
301	Rondell White	.10
302	Barry Larkin	.10
303	Robin Ventura	.10
304	Jason Kendall	.10
305	Chipper Jones	2.00
306	John Franco	.10
307	Sammy Sosa	2.00
308	Troy Percival	.10
309	Chuck Knoblauch	.10
310	Ellis Burks	.10
311	Al Martin	.10
312	Tim Salmon	.10
313	Moises Alou	.10
314	Lance Johnson	.10
315	Justin Thompson	.10
316	Will Clark	.10
317	Barry Bonds	3.00
318	Craig Biggio	.10
319	John Smoltz	.10
320	Cal Ripken Jr.	3.00
321	Ken Griffey Jr.	2.25
322	Paul O'Neill	.10
323	Todd Helton	1.50
324	John Olerud	.10
325	Mark McGwire	2.50
326	Jose Cruz Jr.	.10
327	Jeff Cirillo	.10
328	Dean Palmer	.10
329	John Wetteland	.10
330	Steve Finley	.10
331	Albert Belle	.10
332	Curt Schilling	.35
333	Raul Mondesi	.10
334	Andruw Jones	1.50
335	Nomar Garciaparra	2.00
336	David Justice	.10
337	Andy Pettitte	.30
338	Pedro Martinez	1.50
339	Travis Miller	.10
340	Chris Stynes	.10
341	Gregg Jefferies	.10
342	Jeff Fassero	.10
343	Craig Counsell	.10
344	Wilson Alvarez	.10
345	Bip Roberts	.10
346	Kelvim Escobar	.10
347	Mark Bellhorn	.10
348	Cory Lidle	.10
349	Fred McGriff	.10
350	Chuck Carr	.10
351	Bob Abreu	.10
352	Juan Guzman	.10
353	Fernando Vina	.10
354	Andy Benes	.10
355	Dave Nilsson	.10
356	Bobby Bonilla	.10
357	Ismael Valdes	.10
358	Carlos Perez	.10
359	Kirk Rueter	.10
360	Bartolo Colon	.10
361	Mel Rojas	.10
362	Johnny Damon	.35
363	Geronimo Berroa	.10
364	Reggie Sanders	.10
365	Jermaine Allensworth	.10
366	Orlando Cabrera	.10
367	Jorge Fabregas	.10
368	Scott Stahoviak	.10
369	Ken Cloude	.10
370	Donovan Osborne	.10
371	Roger Cedeno	.10
372	Neifi Perez	.10
373	Chris Holt	.10
374	Cecil Fielder	.10
375	Marty Cordova	.10
376	Tom Goodwin	.10
377	Jeff Suppan	.10
378	Jeff Brantley	.10
379	Mark Langston	.10
380	Shane Reynolds	.10
381	Mike Fetters	.10
382	Todd Greene	.10
383	Ray Durham	.10
384	Carlos Delgado	.35
385	Jeff D'Amico	.10
386	Ben McRae	.10
387	Alan Benes	.10
388	Heathcliff Slocumb	.10
389	Eric Young	.10
390	Travis Fryman	.10
391	David Cone	.10
392	Otis Nixon	.10
393	Jeremi Gonzalez	.10
394	Jeff Juden	.10
395	Jose Vizcaino	.10
396	Ugueth Urbina	.10
397	Ramon Martinez	.10
398	Robb Nen	.10
399	Harold Baines	.10
400	Delino DeShields	.10
401	John Burkett	.10
402	Sterling Hitchcock	.10
403	Mark Clark	.10
404	Terrell Wade	.10
405	Scott Brosius	.10
406	Chad Curtis	.10
407	Brian Johnson	.10
408	Roberto Kelly	.10
409	Dave Dellucci RC	.25
410	Michael Tucker	.10
411	Mark Kotsay	.10
412	Mark Lewis	.10
413	Ryan McGuire	.10
414	Shawon Dunston	.10
415	Brad Rigby	.10
416	Scott Erickson	.10
417	Bobby Jones	.10
418	Darren Oliver	.10
419	John Smiley	.10
420	T.J. Mathews	.10
421	Dustin Hermanson	.10
422	Mike Timlin	.10
423	Willie Blair	.10
424	Manny Alexander	.10
425	Bob Tewksbury	.10
426	Pete Schourek	.10
427	Reggie Jefferson	.10
428	Ed Sprague	.10
429	Jeff Conine	.10
430	Roberto Hernandez	.10
431	Tom Pagnozzi	.10
432	Jaret Wright	.10
433	Livan Hernandez	.10
434	Andy Ashby	.10
435	Todd Dunn	.10
436	Bobby Higginson	.10
437	Rod Beck	.10
438	Jim Leyritz	.10
439	Matt Williams	.10
440	Brett Tomko	.10
441	Joe Randa	.10
442	Chris Carpenter	.10
443	Dennis Reyes	.10
444	Al Leiter	.10
445	Jason Schmidt	.10
446	Ken Hill	.10
447	Shannon Stewart	.10
448	Enrique Wilson	.10
449	Fernando Tatis	.10
450	Jimmy Key	.10
451	Darrin Fletcher	.10
452	John Valentin	.10
453	Kevin Tapani	.10
454	Eric Karros	.10
455	Jay Bell	.10
456	Walt Weiss	.10
457	Devon White	.10
458	Carl Pavano	.10
459	Mike Lansing	.10
460	John Flaherty	.10
461	Richard Hidalgo	.10
462	Quinton McCracken	.10
463	Karim Garcia	.20
464	Miguel Cairo	.10
465	Edwin Diaz	.10
466	Bobby Smith	.10
467	Yamil Benitez	.10
468	Rich Butler RC	.10
469	Ben Ford RC	.10
470	Bubba Trammell	.10
471	Brent Brede	.10
472	Brooks Kieschnick	.10
473	Carlos Castillo	.10
474	Brad Radke	.10
475	Roger Clemens	1.00
476	Curt Schilling	.15
477	John Olerud	.10
478	Mark McGwire	1.25
479	Mike Piazza, Ken Griffey Jr.	1.25
480	Jeff Bagwell, Frank Thomas	1.00
481	Chipper Jones, Nomar Garciaparra	1.00
482	Larry Walker, Juan Gonzalez	.20
483	Gary Sheffield, Tino Martinez	.10
484	Derrick Gibson, Michael Coleman, Norm Hutchins	.10
485	Braden Looper, Cliff Politte, Brian Rose	.15
486	Eric Milton, Jason Marquis, Corey Lee	.25
487	A.J. Hinch, Mark Osborne, Robert Fick RC	.25
488	Aramis Ramirez, Alex Gonzalez, Sean Casey	.25
489	Donnie Bridges, Tim Drew RC	.20
490	Ntema Ndungidi, Darnell McDonald RC	.10
491	Ryan Anderson, Mark Mangum	.50

492	J.J. Davis,	
	Troy Glaus RC	3.00
493	Jayson Werth,	
	Dan Reichert	.10
494	John Curtice,	
	Mike Cuddyer RC	.50
495	Jack Cust,	
	Jason Standridge	4.00
496	Brian Anderson	.10
497	Tony Saunders	.10
498	Vladimir Nunez,	
	Jhensy Sandoval RC	.10
499	Brad Penny,	
	Nick Bierbrodt	.10
500	Dustin Carr,	
	Luis Cruz RC	.10
501	Marcus McCain,	
	Cedrick Bowers RC	.10
502	Checklist	.10
503	Checklist	.10
504	Alex Rodriguez	2.50

Refractors

	NM/M
Common Player:	.50
Stars/Rookies:	5X

(See 1998 Topps Chrome for checklist and base card values.)

Baby Boomers

	NM/M
Complete Set (15):	16.00
Common Player:	.75
Inserted 1:24	
Refractors:	1.5X
Inserted 1:72	
1 Derek Jeter	6.00
2 Scott Rolen	.90
3 Nomar Garciaparra	3.50
4 Jose Cruz Jr.	.75
5 Darin Erstad	.90
6 Todd Helton	1.50
7 Tony Clark	.75
8 Jose Guillen	.75
9 Andruw Jones	1.50
10 Vladimir Guerrero	1.50
11 Mark Kotsay	.75
12 Todd Greene	.75
13 Andy Pettitte	.90
14 Justin Thompson	.75
15 Alan Benes	.75

Clout 9

	NM/M
Complete Set (9):	15.00
Common Player:	.75
Inserted 1:24	
Refractors:	1.5X
Inserted 1:72	
1 Edgar Martinez	.75
2 Mike Piazza	3.50

3	Frank Thomas	1.50
4	Craig Biggio	.75
5	Vinny Castilla	.75
6	Jeff Blauser	.75
7	Barry Bonds	6.00
8	Ken Griffey Jr.	3.50
9	Larry Walker	.75

Flashback

	NM/M
Complete Set (10):	16.00
Common Player:	.75
Inserted 1:24	
Refractors:	1.5X
Inserted 1:72	
1 Barry Bonds	6.00
2 Ken Griffey Jr.	3.50
3 Paul Molitor	1.50
4 Randy Johnson	1.50
5 Cal Ripken Jr.	6.00
6 Tony Gwynn	2.50
7 Kenny Lofton	.75
8 Gary Sheffield	.85
9 Deion Sanders	.75
10 Brady Anderson	.75

Hallbound

	NM/M
Complete Set (15):	35.00
Common Player:	1.50
Inserted 1:24	
Refractors:	1.5X
Inserted 1:72	
1 Paul Molitor	2.00
2 Tony Gwynn	2.50
3 Wade Boggs	2.50
4 Roger Clemens	3.00
5 Dennis Eckersley	1.50
6 Cal Ripken Jr.	6.00
7 Greg Maddux	2.50
8 Rickey Henderson	2.00
9 Ken Griffey Jr.	3.50
10 Frank Thomas	2.00
11 Mark McGwire	4.50
12 Barry Bonds	6.00
13 Mike Piazza	3.50
14 Juan Gonzalez	1.50
15 Randy Johnson	2.00

Milestones

	NM/M
Complete Set (10):	25.00
Common Player:	1.00
Inserted 1:24	
Refractors:	1.5X
Inserted 1:72	
1 Barry Bonds	6.00
2 Roger Clemens	3.00
3 Dennis Eckersley	1.00
4 Juan Gonzalez	1.00
5 Ken Griffey Jr.	3.50
6 Tony Gwynn	2.50

7	Greg Maddux	2.50
8	Mark McGwire	4.50
9	Cal Ripken Jr.	6.00
10	Frank Thomas	1.50

Rookie Class

	NM/M
Complete Set (10):	10.00
Common Player:	.75
Inserted 1:12	
Refractors:	1.5X
Inserted 1:24	
1 Travis Lee	1.00
2 Richard Hidalgo	.75
3 Todd Helton	4.50
4 Paul Konerko	1.50
5 Mark Kotsay	.75
6 Derrek Lee	3.00
7 Eli Marrero	.75
8 Fernando Tatis	.75
9 Juan Encarnacion	.75
10 Ben Grieve	.75

1998 Topps Gallery

	NM/M
Complete Set (150):	15.00
Common Player:	.10
Pack (6):	1.50
Wax Box (24):	25.00
1 Andruw Jones	1.00
2 Fred McGriff	.10
3 Wade Boggs	1.50
4 Pedro Martinez	1.00
5 Matt Williams	.10
6 Wilson Alvarez	.10
7 Henry Rodriguez	.10
8 Jay Bell	.10
9 Marquis Grissom	.10
10 Darryl Kile	.10
11 Chuck Knoblauch	.10
12 Kenny Lofton	.10
13 Quinton McCracken	.10
14 Andres Galarraga	.10
15 Brian Jordan	.10
16 Mike Lansing	.10
17 Travis Fryman	.10
18 Tony Saunders	.10
19 Moises Alou	.10
20 Travis Lee	.10
21 Garret Anderson	.10
22 Ken Caminiti	.10
23 Pedro Astacio	.10
24 Ellis Burks	.10
25 Albert Belle	.10
26 Alan Benes	.10
27 Jay Buhner	.10
28 Derek Bell	.10
29 Jeromy Burnitz	.10
30 Kevin Appier	.10
31 Jeff Cirillo	.10
32 Bernard Gilkey	.10
33 David Cone	.10
34 Jason Dickson	.10
35 Jose Cruz Jr.	.10
36 Marty Cordova	.10
37 Ray Durham	.10
38 Jaret Wright	.10
39 Billy Wagner	.10
40 Roger Clemens	1.75
41 Juan Gonzalez	.50
42 Jeremi Gonzalez	.10
43 Mark Grudzielanek	.10
44 Tom Glavine	.35
45 Barry Larkin	.10
46 Lance Johnson	.10
47 Bobby Higginson	.10
48 Mike Mussina	.50
49 Al Martin	.10
50 Mark McGwire	2.50
51 Todd Hundley	.10
52 Ray Lankford	.10
53 Jason Kendall	.10
54 Javy Lopez	.10

55	Ben Grieve	.10
56	Randy Johnson	1.00
57	Jeff King	.10
58	Mark Grace	.10
59	Rusty Greer	.10
60	Greg Maddux	1.50
61	Jeff Kent	.10
62	Rey Ordonez	.10
63	Hideo Nomo	.50
64	Charles Nagy	.10
65	Rondell White	.10
66	Todd Helton	.75
67	Jim Thome	.75
68	Denny Neagle	.10
69	Ivan Rodriguez	.75
70	Vladimir Guerrero	1.00
71	Jorge Posada	.10
72	J.T. Snow Jr.	.10
73	Reggie Sanders	.10
74	Scott Rolen	.75
75	Robin Ventura	.10
76	Mariano Rivera	.15
77	Cal Ripken Jr.	3.00
78	Justin Thompson	.10
79	Mike Piazza	2.00
80	Kevin Brown	.10
81	Sandy Alomar	.10
82	Craig Biggio	.10
83	Vinny Castilla	.10
84	Eric Young	.10
85	Bernie Williams	.10
86	Brady Anderson	.10
87	Bobby Bonilla	.10
88	Tony Clark	.10
89	Dan Wilson	.10
90	John Wetteland	.10
91	Barry Bonds	3.00
92	Chan Ho Park	.10
93	Carlos Delgado	.35
94	David Justice	.10
95	Chipper Jones	1.50
96	Shawn Estes	.10
97	Jason Giambi	.60
98	Ron Gant	.10
99	John Olerud	.10
100	Frank Thomas	1.00
101	Jose Guillen	.10
102	Brad Radke	.10
103	Troy Percival	.10
104	John Smoltz	.10
105	Edgardo Alfonzo	.10
106	Dante Bichette	.10
107	Larry Walker	.10
108	John Valentin	.10
109	Roberto Alomar	.30
110	Mike Cameron	.10
111	Eric Davis	.10
112	Johnny Damon	.35
113	Darin Erstad	.30
114	Omar Vizquel	.10
115	Derek Jeter	3.00
116	Tony Womack	.10
117	Edgar Renteria	.10
118	Raul Mondesi	.10
119	Tony Gwynn	1.50
120	Ken Griffey Jr.	2.00
121	Jim Edmonds	.10
122	Brian Hunter	.10
123	Neifi Perez	.10
124	Dean Palmer	.10
125	Alex Rodriguez	2.50
126	Tim Salmon	.10
127	Curt Schilling	.35
128	Kevin Orie	.10
129	Andy Pettitte	.30
130	Gary Sheffield	.50
131	Jose Rosado	.10
132	Manny Ramirez	1.00
133	Rafael Palmeiro	.75
134	Sammy Sosa	1.50
135	Jeff Bagwell	1.00
136	Delino DeShields	.10
137	Ryan Klesko	.10
138	Mo Vaughn	.10
139	Steve Finley	.10
140	Nomar Garciaparra	1.50
141	Paul Molitor	1.00
142	Pat Hentgen	.10
143	Eric Karros	.10
144	Bobby Jones	.10
145	Tino Martinez	.10
146	Matt Morris	.10
147	Livan Hernandez	.10
148	Edgar Martinez	.10
149	Paul O'Neill	.10
150	Checklist	.10

Printing Plates

	NM/M
Common Player, Front:	50.00
Common Player, Back:	35.00

PLATE I.D.
BACK - BLACK

NEIFI
PEREZ
COLORADO ROCKIES

(See 1998 Topps Gallery for checklist.)

Player's Private Issue

	NM/M
Common Player:	1.00
Stars/Rookies:	4X

Production 250 Sets
(See 1998 Topps Gallery for checklist and base card values.)

Player's Private Issue Auction Cards

	NM/M
Complete Set (150):	60.00
Common Player:	.25
Stars/Rookies:	1.5X

(See 1998 Topps Gallery for checklist and base values.)

Awards Gallery

		NM/M
Complete Set (10):		18.00
Common Player:		1.00
Inserted 1:24		
1	Ken Griffey Jr.	4.00
2	Larry Walker	1.00
3	Roger Clemens	2.50
4	Pedro Martinez	1.50
5	Nomar Garciaparra	2.00
6	Scott Rolen	1.00
7	Frank Thomas	1.50
8	Tony Gwynn	2.00
9	Mark McGwire	5.00
10	Livan Hernandez	1.00

Gallery Proofs

	NM/M
Common Player:	1.50
Stars/Rookies:	4X

Production 125 Sets
(See 1998 Topps Gallery for checklist and base card values.)

Gallery of Heroes

		NM/M
Complete Set (15):		80.00
Common Player:		1.25
Inserted 1:24		
Jumbo Version (1:24):		75%
1	Ken Griffey Jr.	8.00
2	Derek Jeter	15.00
3	Barry Bonds	15.00
4	Alex Rodriguez	12.00
5	Frank Thomas	4.00
6	Nomar Garciaparra	6.00
7	Mark McGwire	12.00
8	Mike Piazza	8.00
9	Cal Ripken Jr.	15.00
10	Jose Cruz Jr.	1.25
11	Jeff Bagwell	4.00
12	Chipper Jones	6.00
13	Juan Gonzalez	2.00
14	Hideo Nomo	2.00
15	Greg Maddux	6.00

Photo Gallery

		NM/M
Complete Set (10):		25.00
Common Player:		1.00
Inserted 1:24		
1	Alex Rodriguez	3.00
2	Frank Thomas	2.00
3	Derek Jeter	4.00
4	Cal Ripken Jr.	4.00
5	Ken Griffey Jr.	2.50
6	Mike Piazza	2.50
7	Nomar Garciaparra	2.25
8	Tim Salmon	1.00
9	Jeff Bagwell	2.00
10	Barry Bonds	4.00

1998 Topps Gold Label Class 1 (Fielding, Follow-Thru)

	NM/M
Complete Set (100):	12.00
Gold Label Common Player:	.10
Black Label Common Player:	.35
Black Label Stars/RC's:	4X
Red Label Common Player:	1.50
Red Label Stars/RC's:	12X
Pack (5):	2.00
Wax Box (24):	40.00

1	Kevin Brown	.10
2	Greg Maddux	1.25
3	Albert Belle	.10
4	Andres Galarraga	.10
5	Craig Biggio	.10
6	Matt Williams	.10
7	Derek Jeter	3.00
8	Randy Johnson	1.00
9	Jay Bell	.10
10	Jim Thome	.75
11	Roberto Alomar	.30

Jim Thome

12	Tom Glavine	.35
13	Reggie Sanders	.10
14	Tony Gwynn	1.25
15	Mark McGwire	2.00
16	Jeromy Burnitz	.10
17	Andruw Jones	1.00
18	Jay Buhner	.10
19	Robin Ventura	.10
20	Jeff Bagwell	1.00
21	Roger Clemens	1.25
22	Masato Yoshii RC	.25
23	Travis Fryman	.10
24	Rafael Palmeiro	.75
25	Alex Rodriguez	2.00
26	Sandy Alomar	.10
27	Chipper Jones	1.25
28	Rusty Greer	.10
29	Cal Ripken Jr.	3.00
30	Tony Clark	.10
31	Derek Bell	.10
32	Fred McGriff	.10
33	Paul O'Neill	.10
34	Moises Alou	.10
35	Henry Rodriguez	.10
36	Steve Finley	.10
37	Marquis Grissom	.10
38	Jason Giambi	.60
39	Javy Lopez	.10
40	Damion Easley	.10
41	Mariano Rivera	.15
42	Mo Vaughn	.10
43	Mike Mussina	.40
44	Jason Kendall	.10
45	Pedro Martinez	1.00
46	Frank Thomas	1.00
47	Jim Edmonds	.10
48	Hideki Irabu	.10
49	Eric Karros	.10
50	Juan Gonzalez	.50
51	Ellis Burks	.10
52	Dean Palmer	.10
53	Scott Rolen	.60
54	Raul Mondesi	.10
55	Quinton McCracken	.10
56	John Olerud	.10
57	Ken Caminiti	.10
58	Brian Jordan	.10
59	Wade Boggs	1.25
60	Mike Piazza	1.50
61	Darin Erstad	.30
62	Curt Schilling	.35
63	David Justice	.10
64	Kenny Lofton	.10
65	Barry Bonds	3.00
66	Ray Lankford	.10
67	Brian Hunter	.10
68	Chuck Knoblauch	.10
69	Vinny Castilla	.10
70	Vladimir Guerrero	1.00
71	Tim Salmon	.10
72	Larry Walker	.10
73	Paul Molitor	1.00
74	Barry Larkin	.10
75	Edgar Martinez	.10
76	Bernie Williams	.10
77	Dante Bichette	.10
78	Nomar Garciaparra	1.25
79	Ben Grieve	.10
80	Ivan Rodriguez	.75
81	Todd Helton	.75
82	Ryan Klesko	.10
83	Sammy Sosa	1.25
84	Travis Lee	.10
85	Jose Cruz	.10
86	Mark Kotsay	.10
87	Richard Hidalgo	.10
88	Rondell White	.10
89	Greg Vaughn	.10
90	Gary Sheffield	.50
91	Paul Konerko	.25
92	Mark Grace	.10
93	Kevin Millwood RC	1.00
94	Manny Ramirez	1.00
95	Tino Martinez	.10
96	Brad Fullmer	.10
97	Todd Walker	.10
98	Carlos Delgado	.45
99	Kerry Wood	.60
100	Ken Griffey Jr.	1.50

Class 2 (Running, Set Position)

Jim Thome

	NM/M
Complete Set (100):	50.00
Gold Label Common Player:	.35
Gold Label Stars/RC's:	2X
Black Label Common Player:	1.00
Black Label Stars/RC's:	4X
Red Label Common Player:	4.00
Red Label Stars/RC's:	25X

(See 1998 Topps Gold Label Class 1 for checklist and base card values.)

Class 3 (Hitting, Throwing)

	NM/M
Complete Set (100):	120.00
Common Player:	.75
Gold Label Stars/RC's:	2.5X
Black Label Common Player:	2.00
Black Label Stars/RC's:	6X
Red Label Common Player:	6.00
Red Label Stars/RC's:	35X

(See 1998 Topps Gold Label Class 1 for checklist and base card values.)

Home Run Race

		NM/M
Complete Set (4):		7.50
Common Player:		2.00
Black Label:		2X
Red Label:		4X
HR1	Roger Maris	3.00
HR2	Mark McGwire	3.00
HR3	Ken Griffey Jr.	2.50
HR4	Sammy Sosa	2.00

1998 Topps Stars

	NM/M
Complete Set, Red or Bronze (150):	24.00
Common Player, Red or Bronze:	.10

Production 9,799 sets each.

		NM/M
Pack (6):		1.25
Wax Box (24):		25.00
1	Greg Maddux	1.50
2	Darryl Kile	.10
3	Rod Beck	.10
4	Ellis Burks	.10

5	Gary Sheffield	.40
6	David Ortiz	.10
7	Marquis Grissom	.10
8	Tony Womack	.10
9	Mike Mussina	.60
10	Bernie Williams	.10
11	Andy Benes	.10
12	Rusty Greer	.10
13	Carlos Delgado	.35
14	Jim Edmonds	.10
15	Raul Mondesi	.10
16	Andres Galarraga	.10
17	Wade Boggs	1.50
18	Paul O'Neill	.10
19	Edgar Renteria	.10
20	Tony Clark	.10
21	Vladimir Guerrero	1.00
22	Moises Alou	.10
23	Bernard Gilkey	.10
24	Lance Johnson	.10
25	Ben Grieve	.10
26	Sandy Alomar	.10
27	Ray Durham	.10
28	Shawn Estes	.10
29	David Segui	.10
30	Javy Lopez	.10
31	Steve Finley	.10
32	Rey Ordonez	.10
33	Derek Jeter	3.00
34	Henry Rodriguez	.10
35	Mo Vaughn	.10
36	Richard Hidalgo	.10
37	Omar Vizquel	.10
38	Johnny Damon	.35
39	Brian Hunter	.10
40	Matt Williams	.10
41	Chuck Finley	.10
42	Jeromy Burnitz	.10
43	Livan Hernandez	.10
44	Delino DeShields	.10
45	Charles Nagy	.10
46	Scott Rolen	.75
47	Neifi Perez	.10
48	John Wetteland	.10
49	Eric Milton	.10
50	Mike Piazza	2.00
51	Cal Ripken Jr.	3.00
52	Mariano Rivera	.25
53	Butch Huskey	.10
54	Quinton McCracken	.10
55	Jose Cruz Jr.	.10
56	Brian Jordan	.10
57	Hideo Nomo	.50
58	Masato Yoshii	.10
59	Cliff Floyd	.10
60	Jose Guillen	.10
61	Jeff Shaw	.10
62	Edgar Martinez	.10
63	Rondell White	.10
64	Hal Morris	.10
65	Barry Larkin	.10
66	Eric Young	.10
67	Ray Lankford	.10
68	Derek Bell	.10
69	Charles Johnson	.10
70	Robin Ventura	.10
71	Chuck Knoblauch	.10
72	Kevin Brown	.10
73	Jose Valentin	.10
74	Jay Buhner	.10
75	Tony Gwynn	1.50
76	Andy Pettitte	.30
77	Edgardo Alfonzo	.10
78	Kerry Wood	.40
79	Darin Erstad	.30
80	Paul Konerko	.15
81	Jason Kendall	.10
82	Tino Martinez	.10
83	Brad Radke	.10
84	Jeff King	.10
85	Travis Lee	.10
86	Jeff Kent	.10
87	Trevor Hoffman	.10
88	David Cone	.10
89	Jose Canseco	.40
90	Juan Gonzalez	.50
91	Todd Hundley	.10
92	John Valentin	.10
93	Sammy Sosa	1.50
94	Jason Giambi	.40
95	Chipper Jones	1.50
96	Jeff Blauser	.10
97	Brad Fullmer	.10
98	Derek Lee	.60
99	Denny Neagle	.10
100	Ken Griffey Jr.	2.00
101	David Justice	.10
102	Tim Salmon	.10
103	J.T. Snow	.10
104	Fred McGriff	.10
105	Brady Anderson	.10
106	Larry Walker	.10
107	Jeff Cirillo	.10
108	Andruw Jones	1.00
109	Manny Ramirez	1.00

110	Justin Thompson	.10
111	Vinny Castilla	.10
112	Chan Ho Park	.10
113	Mark Grudzielanek	.10
114	Mark Grace	.10
115	Ken Caminiti	.10
116	Ryan Klesko	.10
117	Rafael Palmeiro	.75
118	Pat Hentgen	.10
119	Eric Karros	.10
120	Randy Johnson	1.00
121	Roberto Alomar	.25
122	John Olerud	.10
123	Paul Molitor	1.00
124	Dean Palmer	.10
125	Nomar Garciaparra	1.50
126	Curt Schilling	.30
127	Jay Bell	.10
128	Craig Biggio	.10
129	Marty Cordova	.10
130	Ivan Rodriguez	.75
131	Todd Helton	.75
132	Jim Thome	.65
133	Albert Belle	.10
134	Mike Lansing	.10
135	Mark McGwire	2.50
136	Roger Clemens	1.75
137	Tom Glavine	.30
138	Ron Gant	.10
139	Alex Rodriguez	2.50
140	Jeff Bagwell	1.00
141	John Smoltz	.10
142	Kenny Lofton	.10
143	Dante Bichette	.10
144	Pedro Martinez	1.00
145	Travis Fryman	.10
146	Bobby Jones	.10
147	Bobby Higginson	.10
148	Reggie Sanders	.10
149		
150	Frank Thomas	1.00

Silver

	NM/M
Common Silver:	.50
Silver Stars:	1.5X
Production 4,399 Sets	
(See 1998 Topps Stars for	
checklist and base card values.)	

Gold

	NM/M
Common Gold:	1.00
Gold Stars:	2X
Production 2,299 Sets	
(See 1998 Topps Stars for	
checklist and base card values.)	

Gold Rainbow

| | NM/M |
| Common Gold Rainbow: | 4.00 |

Gold Rainbow Stars:	8X
Production 99 Sets	
(See 1998 Topps Stars for	
checklist and base card values.)	

Galaxy

	NM/M
Complete Set (10):	150.00
Common Player:	7.50
Production 100 Sets	
Silvers:	1.5X
Production 75 Sets	
Golds:	2X
Production 50 Sets	
Gold Rainbows:	
	Values Undetermined
Production 5 Sets	
G1	Barry Bonds	40.00
G2	Jeff Bagwell	15.00
G3	Nomar Garciaparra	20.00
G4	Chipper Jones	20.00
G5	Ken Griffey Jr.	25.00
G6	Sammy Sosa	20.00
G7	Larry Walker	7.50
G8	Alex Rodriguez	35.00
G9	Craig Biggio	7.50
G10	Raul Mondesi	7.50

Luminaries

	NM/M
Complete Set (15):	140.00
Common Player:	4.00
Production 100 Sets	
Silver (75 Sets):	1.5X
Gold (50 Sets):	1.5X
Gold Rainbow (Five	
Sets): Values Undetermined	
L1	Ken Griffey Jr.	15.00
L2	Mark McGwire	20.00
L3	Juan Gonzalez	5.00
L4	Tony Gwynn	12.50
L5	Frank Thomas	10.00
L6	Mike Piazza	15.00
L7	Chuck Knoblauch	4.00
L8	Kenny Lofton	4.00
L9	Barry Bonds	25.00
L10	Matt Williams	4.00
L11	Raul Mondesi	4.00
L12	Ivan Rodriguez	7.50
L13	Alex Rodriguez	20.00
L14	Nomar Garciaparra	12.50
L15	Ken Caminiti	4.00

Rookie Reprints

	NM/M
Complete Set (5):	7.00
Common Player:	1.50
1968	Johnny Bench	1.50
1953	Whitey Ford	1.50
1965	Joe Morgan	1.50
1973	Mike Schmidt	2.50
1960	Carl Yastrzemski	2.00

Rookie Reprints Autographs

	NM/M
Complete Set (5):	175.00
Common Player:	25.00
1968	Johnny Bench	75.00
1953	Whitey Ford	50.00
1965	Joe Morgan	25.00
1973	Mike Schmidt	90.00
1960	Carl Yastrzemski	90.00

Supernovas

	NM/M
Complete Set (10):	35.00
Common Player:	2.00
Production 100 Sets	
Silver:	1.5X
Production 75 Sets	
Gold:	1.5X
Production 50 Sets	
Gold Rainbow:	
	Values Undetermined
Production 5 Sets	
S1	Ben Grieve	2.00
S2	Travis Lee	2.00
S3	Todd Helton	10.00
S4	Adrian Beltre	2.50
S5	Derrek Lee	6.00
S6	David Ortiz	6.00
S7	Brad Fullmer	2.00
S8	Mark Kotsay	2.00
S9	Paul Konerko	2.50
S10	Kerry Wood	6.00

1998 Topps Super Chrome

	NM/M
Complete Set (36):	20.00
Common Player:	.25
Refractors:	1.5X
Inserted 1:12	
Pack (3):	2.50
Wax Box (12):	25.00
1	Tony Gwynn	1.00
2	Larry Walker	.25

3	Vladimir Guerrero	.75
4	Mo Vaughn	.25
5	Frank Thomas	.75
6	Barry Larkin	.25
7	Scott Rolen	.65
8	Juan Gonzalez	.75
9	Jeff Bagwell	.75
10	Ryan Klesko	.25
11	Mike Piazza	1.50
12	Randy Johnson	.75
13	Derek Jeter	3.00
14	Gary Sheffield	.50
15	Hideo Nomo	.50
16	Tino Martinez	.25
17	Ivan Rodriguez	.65
18	Bernie Williams	.25
19	Greg Maddux	1.00
20	Roger Clemens	1.25
21	Roberto Clemente	2.00
22	Chipper Jones	1.00
23	Sammy Sosa	1.00
24	Tony Clark	.25
25	Barry Bonds	3.00
26	Craig Biggio	.25
27	Cal Ripken Jr.	3.00
28	Ken Griffey Jr.	1.50
29	Todd Helton	.65
30	Mark McGwire	2.00
31	Jose Cruz	.25
32	Albert Belle	.25
33	Andruw Jones	.75
34	Nomar Garciaparra	1.00
35	Andy Pettitte	.45
36	Alex Rodriguez	2.00

1998 Topps Stars 'N Steel

		NM/M
Complete Set (44):		40.00
Common Player:		.25
Golds:		2X
Holographics:		7X
Pack (3):		3.50
Wax Box (12):		30.00
1	Roberto Alomar	.50
2	Jeff Bagwell	1.25
3	Albert Belle	.25
4	Dante Bichette	.25
5	Barry Bonds	4.00
6	Jay Buhner	.25
7	Ken Caminiti	.25
8	Vinny Castilla	.25
9	Roger Clemens	2.25
10	Jose Cruz Jr.	.25
11	Andres Galarraga	.25
12	Nomar Garciaparra	2.00
13	Juan Gonzalez	.65
14	Mark Grace	.25
15	Ken Griffey Jr.	2.50
16	Tony Gwynn	2.00
17	Todd Hundley	.25
18	Derek Jeter	4.00
19	Randy Johnson	1.25
20	Andruw Jones	1.25
21	Chipper Jones	2.00
22	David Justice	.25
23	Ray Lankford	.25
24	Barry Larkin	.25
25	Kenny Lofton	.25
26	Greg Maddux	2.00
27	Edgar Martinez	.25
28	Tino Martinez	.25
29	Mark McGwire	3.00
30	Paul Molitor	1.25
31	Rafael Palmeiro	1.00
32	Mike Piazza	2.50
33	Manny Ramirez	1.25
34	Cal Ripken Jr.	4.00
35	Ivan Rodriguez	1.00
36	Scott Rolen	.75
37	Tim Salmon	.25
38	Gary Sheffield	.50
39	Sammy Sosa	2.00
40	Frank Thomas	1.25
41	Jim Thome	1.00
42	Mo Vaughn	.25
43	Larry Walker	.25
44	Bernie Williams	.25

1998 Topps TEK

		NM/M
Complete Set (90):		75.00
Common Player:		.25
Pack (4):		4.00
Wax Box (20):		80.00
1	Ben Grieve	.25
2	Kerry Wood	1.50
3	Barry Bonds	8.00
4	John Olerud	.25
5	Ivan Rodriguez	2.00
6	Frank Thomas	2.50
7	Bernie Williams	.25
8	Dante Bichette	.25
9	Alex Rodriguez	6.00
10	Tom Glavine	.50
11	Eric Karros	.25
12	Craig Biggio	.25
13	Mark McGwire	6.00
14	Derek Jeter	8.00
15	Nomar Garciaparra	4.00
16	Brady Anderson	.25
17	Vladimir Guerrero	2.50
18	David Justice	.25
19	Chipper Jones	4.00
20	Jim Edmonds	.25
21	Roger Clemens	4.50
22	Mark Kotsay	.25
23	Tony Gwynn	4.00
24	Todd Walker	.25
25	Tino Martinez	.25
26	Andruw Jones	2.50
27	Sandy Alomar	.25
28	Sammy Sosa	4.00
29	Gary Sheffield	1.50
30	Ken Griffey Jr.	5.00
31	Aramis Ramirez	.25
32	Curt Schilling	.50
33	Robin Ventura	.25
34	Larry Walker	.25
35	Darin Erstad	1.25
36	Todd Dunwoody	.25
37	Paul O'Neill	.25
38	Vinny Castilla	.25
39	Randy Johnson	2.50
40	Rafael Palmeiro	2.00
41	Pedro Martinez	2.50
42	Derek Bell	.25
43	Carlos Delgado	.50
44	Matt Williams	.25
45	Kenny Lofton	.25
46	Edgar Renteria	.25
47	Albert Belle	.25
48	Jeromy Burnitz	.25
49	Adrian Beltre	.40
50	Greg Maddux	4.00
51	Cal Ripken Jr.	8.00
52	Jason Kendall	.25
53	Ellis Burks	.25
54	Paul Molitor	2.50
55	Moises Alou	.25
56	Raul Mondesi	.25
57	Barry Larkin	.25
58	Tony Clark	.25
59	Travis Lee	.25
60	Juan Gonzalez	1.25
61	Troy Glaus RC	3.00
62	Jose Cruz Jr.	.25
63	Paul Konerko	.40
64	Edgar Martinez	.25
65	Javy Lopez	.25
66	Manny Ramirez	2.50
67	Roberto Alomar	.75
68	Ken Caminiti	.25
69	Todd Helton	1.50
70	Chuck Knoblauch	.25
71	Kevin Brown	.25
72	Tim Salmon	.25
73	Orlando Hernandez **RC**	1.00
74	Jeff Bagwell	2.50
75	Brian Jordan	.25
76	Derek Lee	1.50
77	Brad Fullmer	.25
78	Mark Grace	.25
79	Jeff King	.25
80	Mike Mussina	1.50
81	Jay Buhner	.25
82	Quinton McCracken	.25
83	A.J. Hinch	.25
84	Richard Hidalgo	.25
85	Andres Galarraga	.25
86	Mike Piazza	5.00
87	Mo Vaughn	.25
88	Scott Rolen	1.50
89	Jim Thome	2.00
90	Ray Lankford	.25

Diffraction

		NM/M
Complete Set (90):		400.00
Common Player:		4.00
Stars/RC's:		4X

(See 1998 Topps TEK for checklist and base card values.)

1999 Topps

		NM/M
Unop. Hobby Set (462):		40.00
Unop. Retail Set (463):		50.00
Complete Set (462):		35.00
Common Player:		.05
Ser. 1 or 2 Hobby Pack (11):		1.25
Ser. 1 or 2 Hobby Box (36):		40.00
Ser. 1 or 2 Retail Pack (8):		1.00
Ser. 1 or 2 Retail Box (22):		20.00
Ser. 1 or 2 Jumbo Pack (40):		3.50
Ser. 1 or 2 Jumbo Box (12):		30.00
1	Roger Clemens	1.00
2	Andres Galarraga	.05
3	Scott Brosius	.05
4	John Flaherty	.05
5	Jim Leyritz	.05
6	Ray Durham	.05
7	Not Issued	
8	Joe Vizcaino	.05
9	Will Clark	.05
10	David Wells	.05
11	Jose Guillen	.05
12	Scott Hatteberg	.05
13	Edgardo Alfonzo	.05
14	Mike Bordick	.05
15	Manny Ramirez	.75
16	Greg Maddux	1.00
17	David Segui	.05
18	Darryl Strawberry	.05
19	Brad Radke	.05
20	Kerry Wood	.40
21	Matt Anderson	.05
22	Derek Lee	.60
23	Mickey Morandini	.05
24	Paul Konerko	.15
25	Travis Lee	.15
26	Ken Hill	.05
27	Kenny Rogers	.05
28	Paul Sorrento	.05
29	Quilvio Veras	.05
30	Todd Walker	.05
31	Ryan Jackson	.05
32	John Olerud	.05
33	Doug Glanville	.05
34	Nolan Ryan	2.00
35	Ray Lankford	.05
36	Mark Loretta	.05
37	Jason Dickson	.05
38	Sean Bergman	.05
39	Quinton McCracken	.05
40	Bartolo Colon	.05
41	Brady Anderson	.05
42	Chris Stynes	.05
43	Jorge Posada	.05
44	Justin Thompson	.05
45	Johnny Damon	.30
46	Armando Benitez	.05
47	Brant Brown	.05
48	Charlie Hayes	.05
49	Darren Dreifort	.05
50	Juan Gonzalez	.40
51	Chuck Knoblauch	.05
52	Todd Helton (Rookie All-Star)	.75
53	Rick Reed	.05
54	Chris Gomez	.05
55	Gary Sheffield	.45
56	Rod Beck	.05
57	Rey Sanchez	.05
58	Garret Anderson	.05
59	Jimmy Haynes	.05
60	Steve Woodard	.05
61	Rondell White	.05
62	Vladimir Guerrero	.75
63	Eric Karros	.05
64	Russ Davis	.05
65	Mo Vaughn	.05
66	Sammy Sosa	1.00
67	Troy Percival	.05
68	Kenny Lofton	.05
69	Bill Taylor	.05
70	Mark McGwire	1.50
71	Roger Cedeno	.05
72	Javy Lopez	.05
73	Damion Easley	.05
74	Andy Pettitte	.25
75	Tony Gwynn	1.00
76	Ricardo Rincon	.05
77	F.P. Santangelo	.05
78	Jay Bell	.05
79	Scott Servais	.05
80	Jose Canseco	.40
81	Roberto Hernandez	.05
82	Todd Dunwoody	.05
83	John Wetteland	.05
84	Mike Caruso (Rookie All-Star)	.05
85	Derek Jeter	2.00
86	Aaron Sele	.05
87	Jose Lima	.05
88	Ryan Christenson	.05
89	Jeff Cirillo	.05
90	Jose Hernandez	.05
91	Mark Kotsay (Rookie All-Star)	.05
92	Darren Bragg	.05
93	Albert Belle	.05
94	Matt Lawton	.05
95	Pedro Martinez	.75
96	Greg Vaughn	.05
97	Neifi Perez	.05
98	Gerald Williams	.05
99	Derek Bell	.05
100	Ken Griffey Jr.	1.25
101	David Cone	.05
102	Brian Johnson	.05
103	Dean Palmer	.05
104	Javier Valentin	.05
105	Trevor Hoffman	.05
106	Butch Huskey	.05
107	Dave Martinez	.05
108	Billy Wagner	.05
109	Shawn Green	.30
110	Ben Grieve (Rookie All-Star)	.05
111	Tom Goodwin	.05
112	Jaret Wright	.05
113	Aramis Ramirez	.05

114 Dmitri Young	.05	
115 Hideki Irabu	.05	
116 Roberto Kelly	.05	
117 Jeff Fassero	.05	
118 Mark Clark	.05	
119 Jason McDonald	.05	
120 Matt Williams	.05	
121 Dave Burba	.05	
122 Bret Saberhagen	.05	
123 Deivi Cruz	.05	
124 Chad Curtis	.05	
125 Scott Rolen	.65	
126 Lee Stevens	.05	
127 J.T. Snow Jr.	.05	
128 Rusty Greer	.05	
129 Brian Meadows	.05	
130 Jim Edmonds	.05	
131 Ron Gant	.05	
132 A.J. Hinch (Rookie All-Star)	.05	
133 Shannon Stewart	.05	
134 Brad Fullmer	.05	
135 Cal Eldred	.05	
136 Matt Walbeck	.05	
137 Carl Everett	.05	
138 Walt Weiss	.05	
139 Fred McGriff	.05	
140 Darin Erstad	.25	
141 Dave Nilsson	.05	
142 Eric Young	.05	
143 Dan Wilson	.05	
144 Jeff Reed	.05	
145 Brett Tomko	.05	
146 Terry Steinbach	.05	
147 Seth Greisinger	.05	
148 Pat Meares	.05	
149 Livan Hernandez	.05	
150 Jeff Bagwell	.75	
151 Bob Wickman	.05	
152 Omar Vizquel	.05	
153 Eric Davis	.05	
154 Larry Sutton	.05	
155 Magglio Ordonez (Rookie All-Star)	.40	
156 Eric Milton	.05	
157 Darren Lewis	.05	
158 Rick Aguilera	.05	
159 Mike Lieberthal	.05	
160 Robb Nen	.05	
161 Brian Giles	.05	
162 Jeff Brantley	.05	
163 Gary DiSarcina	.05	
164 John Valentin	.05	
165 David Dellucci	.05	
166 Chan Ho Park	.05	
167 Masato Yoshii	.05	
168 Jason Schmidt	.05	
169 LaTroy Hawkins	.05	
170 Bret Boone	.05	
171 Jerry DiPoto	.05	
172 Mariano Rivera	.10	
173 Mike Cameron	.05	
174 Scott Erickson	.05	
175 Charles Johnson	.05	
176 Bobby Jones	.05	
177 Francisco Cordova	.05	
178 Todd Jones	.05	
179 Jeff Montgomery	.05	
180 Mike Mussina	.40	
181 Bob Abreu	.05	
182 Ismael Valdes	.05	
183 Andy Fox	.05	
184 Woody Williams	.05	
185 Denny Neagle	.05	
186 Jose Valentin	.05	
187 Darrin Fletcher	.05	
188 Gabe Alvarez	.05	
189 Eddie Taubensee	.05	
190 Edgar Martinez	.05	
191 Jason Kendall	.05	
192 Darryl Kile	.05	
193 Jeff King	.05	
194 Rey Ordonez	.05	
195 Andruw Jones	.75	
196 Tony Fernandez	.05	
197 Jamey Wright	.05	
198 B.J. Surhoff	.05	
199 Vinny Castilla	.05	
200 David Wells	.05	
201 Mark McGwire	.75	
202 Sammy Sosa	.50	
203 Roger Clemens	.50	
204 Kerry Wood	.15	
205 Lance Berkman, Mike Frank, Gabe Kapler	.15	
206 Alex Escobar, Ricky Ledee, Mike Stoner	.25	
207 Peter Bergeron, Jeremy Giambi, George Lombard	.30	
208 Michael Barrett, Ben Davis, Robert Fick	.05	
209 Pat Cline, Ramon Hernandez, Jayson Werth	.05	
210 Bruce Chen, Chris Enochs, Ryan Anderson	.05	
211 Mike Lincoln, Octavio Dotel, Brad Penny	.05	
212 Brent Butler, Danny Klassen, Chuck Abbott	.05	
213 Chris Jones, Jeff Urban RC	.05	
214 Arturo McDowell, Tony Torcato RC	.25	
215 Josh McKinley, Jason Tyner RC	.25	
216 Matt Burch, Seth Etherton RC	.25	
217 Mamon Tucker, Rick Elder RC	.10	
218 J.M. Gold, Ryan Mills RC	.10	
219 Adam Brown, Choo Freeman RC	.25	
220 M. McGwire Home Run Record #1	20.00	
220 M. McGwire HR Record #2-60	6.00	
220 M. McGwire HR Record #61-62	10.00	
220 M. McGwire HR Record #63-69	15.00	
220 Mark McGwire HR Record #70	40.00	
221 Larry Walker	.05	
222 Bernie Williams	.05	
223 Mark McGwire	.75	
224 Ken Griffey Jr.	.65	
225 Sammy Sosa	.50	
226 Juan Gonzalez	.20	
227 Dante Bichette	.05	
228 Alex Rodriguez	.75	
229 Sammy Sosa	.50	
230 Derek Jeter	1.00	
231 Greg Maddux	.50	
232 Roger Clemens	.50	
233 Ricky Ledee	.05	
234 Chuck Knoblauch	.05	
235 Bernie Williams	.05	
236 Tino Martinez	.05	
237 Orlando Hernandez	.05	
238 Scott Brosius	.05	
239 Andy Pettitte	.05	
240 Mariano Rivera	.05	
241 Checklist		
242 Checklist		
243 Tom Glavine	.25	
244 Andy Benes	.05	
245 Sandy Alomar	.05	
246 Wilton Guerrero	.05	
247 Alex Gonzalez	.05	
248 Roberto Alomar	.30	
249 Ruben Rivera	.05	
250 Eric Chavez	.15	
251 Ellis Burks	.05	
252 Richie Sexson	.05	
253 Steve Finley	.05	
254 Dwight Gooden	.05	
255 Dustin Hermanson	.05	
256 Kirk Rueter	.05	
257 Steve Trachsel	.05	
258 Gregg Jefferies	.05	
259 Matt Stairs	.05	
260 Shane Reynolds	.05	
261 Gregg Olson	.05	
262 Kevin Tapani	.05	
263 Matt Morris	.05	
264 Carl Pavano	.05	
265 Nomar Garciaparra	1.00	
266 Kevin Young	.05	
267 Rick Helling	.05	
268 Mark Leiter	.05	
269 Brian McRae	.05	
270 Cal Ripken Jr.	2.00	
271 Jeff Abbott	.05	
272 Tony Batista	.05	
273 Bill Simas	.05	
274 Brian Hunter	.05	
275 John Franco	.05	
276 Devon White	.05	
277 Rickey Henderson	.75	
278 Chuck Finley	.05	
279 Mike Blowers	.05	
280 Mark Grace	.50	
281 Randy Winn	.05	
282 Bobby Bonilla	.05	
283 David Justice	.05	
284 Shane Monahan	.05	
285 Kevin Brown	.05	
286 Todd Zeile	.05	
287 Al Martin	.05	
288 Troy O'Leary	.05	
289 Darryl Hamilton	.05	
290 Tino Martinez	.05	
291 David Ortiz	.45	
292 Tony Clark	.05	
293 Ryan Minor	.05	
294 Reggie Sanders	.05	
295 Wally Joyner	.05	
296 Cliff Floyd	.05	
297 Shawn Estes	.05	
298 Pat Hentgen	.05	
299 Scott Elarton	.05	
300 Alex Rodriguez	1.50	
301 Ozzie Guillen	.05	
302 Manny Martinez	.05	
303 Ryan McGuire	.05	
304 Brad Ausmus	.05	
305 Alex Gonzalez	.05	
306 Brian Jordan	.05	
307 John Jaha	.05	
308 Mark Grudzielanek	.05	
309 Juan Guzman	.05	
310 Tony Womack	.05	
311 Dennis Reyes	.05	
312 Marty Cordova	.05	
313 Ramiro Mendoza	.05	
314 Robin Ventura	.05	
315 Rafael Palmeiro	.60	
316 Ramon Martinez	.05	
317 John Mabry	.05	
318 Dave Hollins	.05	
319 Tom Candiotti	.05	
320 Al Leiter	.05	
321 Rico Brogna	.05	
322 Jimmy Key	.05	
323 Bernard Gilkey	.05	
324 Jason Giambi	.45	
325 Craig Biggio	.05	
326 Troy Glaus	.65	
327 Delino DeShields	.05	
328 Fernando Vina	.05	
329 John Smoltz	.05	
330 Jeff Kent	.05	
331 Roy Halladay	.05	
332 Andy Ashby	.05	
333 Tim Wakefield	.05	
334 Tim Belcher	.05	
335 Bernie Williams	.05	
336 Desi Relaford	.05	
337 John Burkett	.05	
338 Mike Hampton	.05	
339 Royce Clayton	.05	
340 Mike Piazza	1.25	
341 Jeremi Gonzalez	.05	
342 Mike Lansing	.05	
343 Jamie Moyer	.05	
344 Ron Coomer	.05	
345 Barry Larkin	.05	
346 Fernando Tatis	.05	
347 Chili Davis	.05	
348 Bobby Higginson	.05	
349 Hal Morris	.05	
350 Larry Walker	.05	
351 Carlos Guillen	.05	
352 Miguel Tejada	.05	
353 Travis Fryman	.05	
354 Jarrod Washburn	.05	
355 Chipper Jones	1.00	
356 Todd Stottlemyre	.05	
357 Henry Rodriguez	.05	
358 Eli Marrero	.05	
359 Alan Benes	.05	
360 Tim Salmon	.05	
361 Luis Gonzalez	.05	
362 Scott Spiezio	.05	
363 Chris Carpenter	.05	
364 Bobby Howry	.05	
365 Raul Mondesi	.05	
366 Ugueth Urbina	.05	
367 Tom Evans	.05	
368 Kerry Ligtenberg RC	.15	
369 Adrian Beltre	.15	
370 Ryan Klesko	.05	
371 Wilson Alvarez	.05	
372 John Thomson	.05	
373 Tony Saunders	.05	
374 Mike Stanley	.05	
375 Ken Caminiti	.05	
376 Jay Buhner	.05	
377 Bill Mueller	.05	
378 Jeff Blauser	.05	
379 Edgar Renteria	.05	
380 Jim Thome	.60	
381 Joey Hamilton	.05	
382 Calvin Pickering	.05	
383 Marquis Grissom	.05	
384 Omar Daal	.05	
385 Curt Schilling	.25	
386 Jose Cruz Jr.	.05	
387 Chris Widger	.05	
388 Pete Harnisch	.05	
389 Charles Nagy	.05	
390 Tom Gordon	.05	
391 Bobby Smith	.05	
392 Derrick Gibson	.05	
393 Jeff Conine	.05	
394 Carlos Perez	.05	
395 Barry Bonds	2.00	
396 Mark McLemore	.05	
397 Juan Encarnacion	.05	
398 Wade Boggs	1.00	
399 Ivan Rodriguez	.65	
400 Moises Alou	.05	
401 Jeromy Burnitz	.05	
402 Sean Casey	.10	
403 Jose Offerman	.05	
404 Joe Fontenot	.05	
405 Kevin Millwood	.05	
406 Lance Johnson	.05	
407 Richard Hidalgo	.05	
408 Mike Jackson	.05	
409 Brian Anderson	.05	
410 Jeff Shaw	.05	
411 Preston Wilson	.05	
412 Todd Hundley	.05	
413 Jim Parque	.05	
414 Justin Baughman	.05	
415 Dante Bichette	.05	
416 Paul O'Neill	.05	
417 Miguel Cairo	.05	
418 Randy Johnson	.75	
419 Jesus Sanchez	.05	
420 Carlos Delgado	.30	
421 Ricky Ledee	.05	
422 Orlando Hernandez	.05	
423 Frank Thomas	.75	
424 Pokey Reese	.05	
425 Carlos Lee, Mike Lowell, Kit Pellow RC	.25	
426 Michael Cuddyer, Mark DeRosa, Jerry Hairston Jr.	.05	
427 Marlon Anderson, Ron Belliard, Orlando Cabrera	.10	
428 Micah Bowie, Phil Norton, Randy Wolf	.10	
429 Jack Cressend, Jason Rakers, John Rocker	.10	
430 Ruben Mateo, Scott Morgan, Mike Zywica RC	.10	
431 Jason LaRue, Matt LeCroy, Mitch Meluskey	.10	
432 Gabe Kapler, Armando Rios, Fernando Seguignol	.05	
433 Adam Kennedy, Mickey Lopez, Jackie Rexrode	.10	
434 Jose Fernandez, Jeff Liefer, Chris Truby	.10	
435 Corey Koskie, Doug Mientkiewicz, Damon Minor	.10	
436 Roosevelt Brown, Dernell Stenson, Vernon Wells	.10	
437 A.J. Burnett, John Nicholson, Billy Koch	.25	
438 Matt Belisle, Matt Roney RC	.10	
439 Austin Kearns, Chris George RC	2.50	
440 Nate Bump, Nate Cornejo RC	.40	
441 Brad Lidge, Mike Nannini RC	.25	
442 Matt Holiday, Jeff Winchester RC	.25	
443 Adam Everett, Chip Ambres RC	.25	
444 Pat Burrell, Eric Valent RC	1.50	
445 Roger Clemens	.50	
446 Kerry Wood	.15	
447 Curt Schilling	.05	
448 Randy Johnson	.40	
449 Pedro Martinez	.40	
450 Jeff Bagwell, Andres Galarraga, Mark McGwire	.50	
451 John Olerud, Jim Thome, Tino Martinez	.30	
452 Alex Rodriguez, Nomar Garciaparra, Derek Jeter	.60	
453 Vinny Castilla, Chipper Jones, Scott Rolen	.40	
454 Sammy Sosa, Ken Griffey Jr., Juan Gonzalez	.50	
455 Barry Bonds, Manny Ramirez, Larry Walker	.60	

456	Frank Thomas, Tim Salmon, David Justice	.30
457	Travis Lee, Todd Helton, Ben Grieve	.30
458	Vladimir Guerrero, Greg Vaughn, Bernie Williams	.25
459	Mike Piazza, Ivan Rodriguez, Jason Kendall	.50
460	Roger Clemens, Kerry Wood, Greg Maddux	.45
461	Sammy Sosa Home Run Parade #1	10.00
461	Sammy Sosa HR Parade #2-60	4.00
461	Sammy Sosa HR Parade #61-62	10.00
461	Sammy Sosa HR Parade #63-65	6.00
461	Sammy Sosa HR Parade #66	20.00
462	Checklist	.05
463	Checklist	.05

MVP Promotion

		NM/M
Common Player:		3.00
Stars/Rookies:		20X

(See 1999 Topps for checklist and base card values.)

All-Matrix

		NM/M
Complete Set (30):		45.00
Common Player:		.75
Inserted 1:18		
AM1	Mark McGwire	6.00
AM2	Sammy Sosa	3.50
AM3	Ken Griffey Jr.	4.50
AM4	Greg Vaughn	.75
AM5	Albert Belle	.75
AM6	Vinny Castilla	.75
AM7	Jose Canseco	1.25
AM8	Juan Gonzalez	1.25
AM9	Manny Ramirez	2.50
AM10	Andres Galarraga	.75
AM11	Rafael Palmeiro	2.00
AM12	Alex Rodriguez	6.00
AM13	Mo Vaughn	.75
AM14	Eric Chavez	1.25
AM15	Gabe Kapler	.75
AM16	Calvin Pickering	.75
AM17	Ruben Mateo	.75
AM18	Roy Halladay	1.25
AM19	Jeremy Giambi	.75
AM20	Alex Gonzalez	.75
AM21	Ron Belliard	.75
AM22	Marlon Anderson	.75
AM23	Carlos Lee	.75
AM24	Kerry Wood	1.25
AM25	Roger Clemens	3.50
AM26	Curt Schilling	1.25
AM27	Kevin Brown	.75
AM28	Randy Johnson	2.50
AM29	Pedro Martinez	2.50
AM30	Orlando Hernandez	.75

All-Topps Mystery Finest

		NM/M
Complete Set (33):		100.00
Common Player:		1.00
Inserted 1:36		
Refractors:		1.5X
Inserted 1:144		
M1	Jeff Bagwell	4.25
M2	Andres Galarraga	1.00
M3	Mark McGwire	9.00
M4	John Olerud	1.00
M5	Jim Thome	2.50
M6	Tino Martinez	1.00
M7	Alex Rodriguez	9.00
M8	Nomar Garciaparra	5.00
M9	Derek Jeter	12.50
M10	Vinny Castilla	1.00
M11	Chipper Jones	5.00
M12	Scott Rolen	3.00
M13	Sammy Sosa	5.00
M14	Ken Griffey Jr.	7.50
M15	Juan Gonzalez	2.00
M16	Barry Bonds	12.50
M17	Manny Ramirez	4.50
M18	Larry Walker	1.00
M19	Frank Thomas	4.50
M20	Tim Salmon	1.00
M21	David Justice	1.00
M22	Travis Lee	1.50
M23	Todd Helton	4.50
M24	Ben Grieve	1.00
M25	Vladimir Guerrero	4.50
M26	Greg Vaughn	1.00
M27	Bernie Williams	1.00
M28	Mike Piazza	7.50
M29	Ivan Rodriguez	3.50
M30	Jason Kendall	1.00
M31	Roger Clemens	6.00
M32	Kerry Wood	2.00
M33	Greg Maddux	5.00

Autographs

		NM/M
Common Player:		8.00
Series 1 Inserted 1:532 H		
Series 2 Inserted 1:501 H		
A1	Roger Clemens	100.00
A2	Chipper Jones	40.00
A3	Scott Rolen	25.00
A4	Alex Rodriguez	100.00
A5	Andres Galarraga	8.00
A6	Rondell White	8.00
A7	Ben Grieve	8.00
A8	Troy Glaus	20.00
A9	Moises Alou	15.00
A10	Barry Bonds	180.00
A11	Vladimir Guerrero	35.00
A12	Andruw Jones	20.00
A13	Darin Erstad	12.00
A14	Shawn Green	16.00
A15	Eric Chavez	20.00
A16	Pat Burrell	25.00

Hall of Fame

		NM/M
Complete Set (10):		8.00
Common Player:		.50
Inserted 1:12 H		
HOF1	Mike Schmidt	1.50
HOF2	Brooks Robinson	.75
HOF3	Stan Musial	1.50
HOF4	Willie McCovey	.50
HOF5	Eddie Mathews	.75
HOF6	Reggie Jackson	1.50
HOF7	Ernie Banks	1.00
HOF8	Whitey Ford	.75
HOF9	Bob Feller	.50
HOF10	Yogi Berra	1.00

Lords of the Diamond

		NM/M
Complete Set (15):		13.00
Common Player:		.25
Inserted 1:18		
LD1	Ken Griffey Jr.	1.25
LD2	Chipper Jones	1.00
LD3	Sammy Sosa	1.00
LD4	Frank Thomas	.75
LD5	Mark McGwire	1.50
LD6	Jeff Bagwell	.75
LD7	Alex Rodriguez	1.50
LD8	Juan Gonzalez	.40
LD9	Barry Bonds	2.00
LD10	Nomar Garciaparra	1.00
LD11	Darin Erstad	.35
LD12	Tony Gwynn	1.00
LD13	Andres Galarraga	.25
LD14	Mike Piazza	1.25
LD15	Greg Maddux	1.00

New Breed

		NM/M
Complete Set (15):		9.00
Common Player:		.25
Inserted 1:18		
NB1	Darin Erstad	.50
NB2	Brad Fullmer	.25
NB3	Kerry Wood	.50

NB4	Nomar Garciaparra	1.50
NB5	Travis Lee	.35
NB6	Scott Rolen	.75
NB7	Todd Helton	.75
NB8	Vladimir Guerrero	1.00
NB9	Derek Jeter	3.00
NB10	Alex Rodriguez	2.00
NB11	Ben Grieve	.25
NB12	Andruw Jones	1.00
NB13	Paul Konerko	.40
NB14	Aramis Ramirez	.25
NB15	Adrian Beltre	.35

Nolan Ryan Reprints

		NM/M
Complete Set (27):		40.00
Common Ryan:		3.00
Inserted 1:18		
Nolan Ryan Autograph:		150.00

Nolan Ryan Finest Reprints

		NM/M
Complete Set (27):		125.00
Common Ryan:		5.00
Inserted 1:72		
Refractors:		2X
Inserted 1:288		

Nolan Ryan Reprint Autographs

		NM/M
Common Card:		150.00
1	Nolan Ryan/1968	200.00

2	Nolan Ryan/1969	150.00
3	Nolan Ryan/1970	150.00
4	Nolan Ryan/1971	150.00
5	Nolan Ryan/1972	150.00
6	Nolan Ryan/1973	150.00
7	Nolan Ryan/1974	150.00
8	Nolan Ryan/1975	150.00
9	Nolan Ryan/1976	150.00
10	Nolan Ryan/1977	150.00
11	Nolan Ryan/1978	150.00
12	Nolan Ryan/1979	150.00
13	Nolan Ryan/1980	150.00
14	Nolan Ryan/1981	150.00
15	Nolan Ryan/1982	150.00
16	Nolan Ryan/1983	150.00
17	Nolan Ryan/1984	150.00
18	Nolan Ryan/1985	150.00
19	Nolan Ryan/1986	150.00
20	Nolan Ryan/1987	150.00
21	Nolan Ryan/1988	150.00
22	Nolan Ryan/1989	150.00
23	Nolan Ryan/1990	150.00
24	Nolan Ryan/1991	150.00
25	Nolan Ryan/1992	150.00
26	Nolan Ryan/1993	150.00
27	Nolan Ryan/1994	150.00

Picture Perfect

		NM/M
Complete Set (10):		5.00
Common Player:		.25
Inserted 1:8		
P1	Ken Griffey Jr.	.75
P2	Kerry Wood	.30
P3	Pedro Martinez	.45
P4	Mark McGwire	.90
P5	Greg Maddux	.60
P6	Sammy Sosa	.60
P7	Greg Vaughn	.25
P8	Juan Gonzalez	.30
P9	Jeff Bagwell	.45
P10	Derek Jeter	1.50

Power Brokers

		NM/M
Complete Set (20):		20.00
Common Player:		.25
Inserted 1:36		
Refractors:		1.5X
Inserted 1:144		
PB1	Mark McGwire	3.00
PB2	Andres Galarraga	.25
PB3	Ken Griffey Jr.	2.00
PB4	Sammy Sosa	1.50
PB5	Juan Gonzalez	.50
PB6	Alex Rodriguez	3.00
PB7	Frank Thomas	1.00
PB8	Jeff Bagwell	1.00
PB9	Vinny Castilla	.25
PB10	Mike Piazza	2.00
PB11	Greg Vaughn	.25

PB12	Barry Bonds	4.00
PB13	Mo Vaughn	.25
PB14	Jim Thome	.65
PB15	Larry Walker	.25
PB16	Chipper Jones	1.50
PB17	Nomar Garciaparra	1.50
PB18	Manny Ramirez	1.00
PB19	Roger Clemens	1.75
PB20	Kerry Wood	.65

Record Numbers

		NM/M
Complete Set (10):		8.00
Common Player:		.50
Inserted 1:8		
RN1	Mark McGwire	1.50
RN2	Mike Piazza	1.00
RN3	Curt Schilling	.75
RN4	Ken Griffey Jr.	1.50
RN5	Sammy Sosa	.75
RN6	Nomar Garciaparra	.75
RN7	Kerry Wood	.50
RN8	Roger Clemens	1.50
RN9	Cal Ripken Jr.	2.00
RN10	Mark McGwire	1.50

Record Numbers Gold

		NM/M
Common Player:		8.00
RN1	Mark McGwire/70	40.00
RN2	Mike Piazza/362	15.00
RN3	Curt Schilling/319	8.00
RN4	Ken Griffey Jr./350	20.00
RN5	Sammy Sosa/20	20.00
RN6	Nomar Garciaparra/30	20.00
RN7	Kerry Wood/20	15.00
RN8	Roger Clemens/20	40.00
RN9	Cal Ripken Jr./2,632	15.00
RN10	Mark McGwire/162	20.00

1999 Topps Traded and Rookies

		NM/M
Unopened Set (122):		30.00
Complete Set, No Autograph (121):		10.00
Common Player:		.10
1	Seth Etherton	.10
2	Mark Harriger RC	.10
3	Matt Wise RC	.25
4	Carlos Hernandez RC	.15
5	Julio Lugo RC	.25
6	Mike Nannini	.10
7	Justin Bowles RC	.10
8	Mark Mulder RC	.75
9	Roberto Vaz RC	.10
10	Felipe Lopez RC	.75
11	Matt Belisle	.10

12	Micah Bowie	.10
13	Ruben Quevedo RC	.10
14	Jose Garcia RC	.10
15	David Kelton RC	.25
16	Phillip Norton	.10
17	Corey Patterson RC	.75
18	Ron Walker RC	.10
19	Paul Hoover RC	.10
20	Ryan Rupe RC	.15
21	J.D. Closser RC	.10
22	Rob Ryan RC	.10
23	Steve Colyer RC	.10
24	Bubba Crosby RC	.50
25	Luke Prokopec RC	.10
26	Matt Blank RC	.10
27	Josh McKinley	.10
28	Nate Bump	.10
29	Giuseppe Chiaramonte RC	.10
30	Arturo McDowell	.10
31	Tony Torcato	.10
32	Dave Roberts	.10
33	C.C. Sabathia RC	1.50
34	Sean Spencer RC	.10
35	Chip Ambres	.10
36	A.J. Burnett	.15
37	Mo Bruce RC	.10
38	Jason Tyner	.10
39	Mamon Tucker	.10
40	Sean Burroughs RC	.25
41	Kevin Eberwein RC	.10
42	Junior Herndon RC	.10
43	Bryan Wolff RC	.10
44	Pat Burrell	.50
45	Eric Valent	.10
46	Carlos Pena RC	1.00
47	Mike Zywica	.10
48	Adam Everett	.10
49	Juan Pena RC	.50
50	Adam Dunn RC	3.00
51	Austin Kearns	.75
52	Jacobo Sequea RC	.10
53	Choo Freeman	.10
54	Jeff Winchester	.10
55	Matt Burch	.10
56	Chris George	.10
57	Scott Mullen RC	.10
58	Kit Pellow	.10
59	Mark Quinn RC	.15
60	Nate Cornejo	.10
61	Ryan Mills RC	.25
62	Kevin Beirne RC	.10
63	Kip Wells RC	.50
64	Juan Rivera RC	.25
65	Alfonso Soriano RC	4.00
66	Josh Hamilton RC	4.00
67	Josh Girdley RC	.10
68	Kyle Snyder RC	.15
69	Mike Paradis RC	.10
70	Jason Jennings RC	.25
71	David Walling RC	.10
72	Omar Ortiz RC	.10
73	Jay Gehrke RC	.10
74	Casey Burns RC	.10
75	Carl Crawford RC	2.00
76	Reggie Sanders	.10
77	Will Clark	.10
78	David Wells	.10
79	Paul Konerko	.20
80	Armando Benitez	.10
81	Brant Brown	.10
82	Mo Vaughn	.10
83	Jose Canseco	.25
84	Albert Belle	.25
85	Dean Palmer	.10
86	Greg Vaughn	.10
87	Mark Clark	.10
88	Pat Meares	.10
89	Eric Davis	.10
90	Brian Giles	.10
91	Jeff Brantley	.10
92	Bret Boone	.10
93	Ron Gant	.10

94	Mike Cameron	.10
95	Charles Johnson	.10
96	Denny Neagle	.10
97	Brian Hunter	.10
98	Jose Hernandez	.10
99	Rick Aguilera	.10
100	Tony Batista	.10
101	Roger Cedeno	.10
102	Creighton Gubanich	.10
103	Tim Belcher	.10
104	Bruce Aven	.10
105	Brian Daubach RC	.25
106	Ed Sprague	.10
107	Michael Tucker	.10
108	Homer Bush	.10
109	Armando Reynoso	.10
110	Brook Fordyce	.10
111	Matt Mantei	.10
112	Jose Guillen	.10
113	Kenny Rogers	.10
114	Livan Hernandez	.10
115	Butch Huskey	.10
116	David Segui	.10
117	Darryl Hamilton	.10
118	Jim Leyritz	.10
119	Randy Velarde	.10
120	Bill Taylor	.10
121	Kevin Appier	.10

Autographs

		NM/M
Common Player:		3.00
Inserted 1:Set		
1	Seth Etherton	3.00
2	Mark Harriger	3.00
3	Matt Wise	5.00
4	Carlos Hernandez	5.00
5	Julio Lugo	20.00
6	Mike Nannini	3.00
7	Justin Bowles	3.00
8	Mark Mulder	20.00
9	Roberto Vaz	3.00
10	Felipe Lopez	20.00
11	Matt Belisle	3.00
12	Micah Bowie	5.00
13	Ruben Quevedo	5.00
14	Jose Garcia	5.00
15	David Kelton	10.00
16	Phillip Norton	3.00
17	Corey Patterson	25.00
18	Ron Walker	3.00
19	Paul Hoover	3.00
20	Ryan Rupe	4.00
21	J.D. Closser	8.00
22	Rob Ryan	3.00
23	Steve Colyer	5.00
24	Bubba Crosby	15.00
25	Luke Prokopec	3.00
26	Matt Blank	5.00
27	Josh McKinley	5.00
28	Nate Bump	5.00
29	Giuseppe Chiaramonte	3.00
30	Arturo McDowell	3.00
31	Tony Torcato	5.00
32	Dave Roberts	10.00
33	C.C. Sabathia	75.00
34	Sean Spencer	3.00
35	Chip Ambres	3.00
36	A.J. Burnett	25.00
37	Mo Bruce	3.00
38	Jason Tyner	3.00
39	Mamon Tucker	3.00
40	Sean Burroughs	10.00
41	Kevin Eberwein	3.00
42	Junior Herndon	3.00
43	Bryan Wolff	3.00
44	Pat Burrell	25.00
45	Eric Valent	8.00
46	Carlos Pena	30.00
47	Mike Zywica	3.00

#	Player	Price
48	Adam Everett	15.00
49	Juan Pena	5.00
50	Adam Dunn	100.00
51	Austin Kearns	25.00
52	Jacobo Sequea	3.00
53	Choo Freeman	8.00
54	Jeff Winchester	3.00
55	Matt Burch	3.00
56	Chris George	4.00
57	Scott Mullen	3.00
58	Kit Pellow	3.00
59	Mark Quinn	3.00
60	Nate Cornejo	8.00
61	Ryan Mills	3.00
62	Kevin Beirne	4.00
63	Kip Wells	8.00
64	Juan Rivera	10.00
65	Alfonso Soriano	160.00
66	Josh Hamilton	100.00
67	Josh Girdley	3.00
68	Kyle Snyder	5.00
69	Mike Paradis	3.00
70	Jason Jennings	10.00
71	David Walling	3.00
72	Omar Ortiz	3.00
73	Jay Gehrke	5.00
74	Casey Burns	3.00
75	Carl Crawford	100.00

1999 Topps Chrome

	NM/M
Complete Set (461):	75.00
Common Player:	.15
Refractors:	4X
Inserted 1:12	
Ser. 1 or 2 Pack (4):	1.50
Ser. 1 or 2 Box (24):	30.00

#	Player	Price
1	Roger Clemens	1.75
2	Andres Galarraga	.15
3	Scott Brosius	.15
4	John Flaherty	.15
5	Jim Leyritz	.15
6	Ray Durham	.15
7	Not Issued	
8	Joe Vizcaino	.15
9	Will Clark	.15
10	David Wells	.15
11	Jose Guillen	.15
12	Scott Hatteberg	.15
13	Edgardo Alfonzo	.15
14	Mike Bordick	.15
15	Manny Ramirez	1.00
16	Greg Maddux	1.50
17	David Segui	.15
18	Darryl Strawberry	.15
19	Brad Radke	.15
20	Kerry Wood	.40
21	Matt Anderson	.15
22	Derrek Lee	.60
23	Mickey Morandini	.15
24	Paul Konerko	.30
25	Travis Lee	.15
26	Ken Hill	.15
27	Kenny Rogers	.15
28	Paul Sorrento	.15
29	Quilvio Veras	.15
30	Todd Walker	.15
31	Ryan Jackson	.15
32	John Olerud	.15
33	Doug Glanville	.15
34	Nolan Ryan	3.00
35	Ray Lankford	.15
36	Mark Loretta	.15
37	Jason Dickson	.15
38	Sean Bergman	.15
39	Quinton McCracken	.15
40	Bartolo Colon	.15
41	Brady Anderson	.15
42	Chris Stynes	.15
43	Jorge Posada	.15
44	Justin Thompson	.15
45	Johnny Damon	.40
46	Armando Benitez	.15

#	Player	Price
47	Brant Brown	.15
48	Charlie Hayes	.15
49	Darren Dreifort	.15
50	Juan Gonzalez	.50
51	Chuck Knoblauch	.15
52	Todd Helton (Rookie All-Star)	1.00
53	Rick Reed	.15
54	Chris Gomez	.15
55	Gary Sheffield	.50
56	Rod Beck	.15
57	Rey Sanchez	.15
58	Garret Anderson	.15
59	Jimmy Haynes	.15
60	Steve Woodard	.15
61	Rondell White	.15
62	Vladimir Guerrero	1.00
63	Eric Karros	.15
64	Russ Davis	.15
65	Mo Vaughn	.15
66	Sammy Sosa	1.50
67	Troy Percival	.15
68	Kenny Lofton	.15
69	Bill Taylor	.15
70	Mark McGwire	2.50
71	Roger Cedeno	.15
72	Javy Lopez	.15
73	Damion Easley	.15
74	Andy Pettitte	.35
75	Tony Gwynn	1.50
76	Ricardo Rincon	.15
77	F.P. Santangelo	.15
78	Jay Bell	.15
79	Scott Servais	.15
80	Jose Canseco	.50
81	Roberto Hernandez	.15
82	Todd Dunwoody	.15
83	John Wetteland	.15
84	Mike Caruso (Rookie All-Star)	.15
85	Derek Jeter	3.00
86	Aaron Sele	.15
87	Jose Lima	.15
88	Ryan Christenson	.15
89	Jeff Cirillo	.15
90	Jose Hernandez	.15
91	Mark Kotsay (Rookie All-Star)	.15
92	Darren Bragg	.15
93	Albert Belle	.15
94	Matt Lawton	.15
95	Pedro Martinez	1.00
96	Greg Vaughn	.15
97	Neifi Perez	.15
98	Gerald Williams	.15
99	Derek Bell	.15
100	Ken Griffey Jr.	2.00
101	David Cone	.15
102	Brian Johnson	.15
103	Dean Palmer	.15
104	Javier Valentin	.15
105	Trevor Hoffman	.15
106	Butch Huskey	.15
107	Dave Martinez	.15
108	Billy Wagner	.15
109	Shawn Green	.35
110	Ben Grieve (Rookie All-Star)	.15
111	Tom Goodwin	.15
112	Jaret Wright	.15
113	Aramis Ramirez	.15
114	Dmitri Young	.15
115	Hideki Irabu	.15
116	Roberto Kelly	.15
117	Jeff Fassero	.15
118	Mark Clark	.15
119	Jason McDonald	.15
120	Matt Williams	.15
121	Dave Burba	.15
122	Bret Saberhagen	.15
123	Deivi Cruz	.15
124	Chad Curtis	.15
125	Scott Rolen	.75
126	Lee Stevens	.15
127	J.T. Snow Jr.	.15
128	Rusty Greer	.15
129	Brian Meadows	.15
130	Jim Edmonds	.15
131	Ron Gant	.15
132	A.J. Hinch	.15
133	Shannon Stewart	.15
134	Brad Fullmer	.15
135	Cal Eldred	.15
136	Matt Walbeck	.15
137	Carl Everett	.15
138	Walt Weiss	.15
139	Fred McGriff	.15
140	Darin Erstad	.40
141	Dave Nilsson	.15
142	Eric Young	.15
143	Dan Wilson	.15
144	Jeff Reed	.15
145	Brett Tomko	.15
146	Terry Steinbach	.15

#	Player	Price
147	Seth Greisinger	.15
148	Pat Meares	.15
149	Livan Hernandez	.15
150	Jeff Bagwell	1.00
151	Bob Wickman	.15
152	Omar Vizquel	.15
153	Eric Davis	.15
154	Larry Sutton	.15
155	Magglio Ordonez	.45
156	Eric Milton	.15
157	Darren Lewis	.15
158	Rick Aguilera	.15
159	Mike Lieberthal	.15
160	Robb Nen	.15
161	Brian Giles	.15
162	Jeff Brantley	.15
163	Gary DiSarcina	.15
164	John Valentin	.15
165	David Dellucci	.15
166	Chan Ho Park	.15
167	Masato Yoshii	.15
168	Jason Schmidt	.15
169	LaTroy Hawkins	.15
170	Bret Boone	.15
171	Jerry DiPoto	.15
172	Mariano Rivera	.25
173	Mike Cameron	.15
174	Scott Erickson	.15
175	Charles Johnson	.15
176	Bobby Jones	.15
177	Francisco Cordova	.15
178	Todd Jones	.15
179	Jeff Montgomery	.15
180	Mike Mussina	.50
181	Bob Abreu	.15
182	Ismael Valdes	.15
183	Andy Fox	.15
184	Woody Williams	.15
185	Denny Neagle	.15
186	Jose Valentin	.15
187	Darrin Fletcher	.15
188	Gabe Alvarez	.15
189	Eddie Taubensee	.15
190	Edgar Martinez	.15
191	Jason Kendall	.15
192	Darryl Kile	.15
193	Jeff King	.15
194	Rey Ordonez	.15
195	Andruw Jones	1.00
196	Tony Fernandez	.15
197	Jamey Wright	.15
198	B.J. Surhoff	.15
199	Vinny Castilla	.15
200	David Wells	.15
201	Mark McGwire	1.25
202	Sammy Sosa	.75
203	Roger Clemens	.85
204	Kerry Wood	.20
205	Lance Berkman, Mike Frank, Gabe Kapler	.15
206	Alex Escobar, Ricky Ledee, Mike Stoner	.50
207	Peter Bergeron, Jeremy Giambi, George Lombard	.50
208	Michael Barrett, Ben Davis, Robert Fick	.15
209	Pat Cline, Ramon Hernandez, Jayson Werth	.20
210	Bruce Chen, Chris Enochs, Ryan Anderson	.15
211	Mike Lincoln, Octavio Dotel, Brad Penny	.15
212	Chuck Abbott, Brent Butler, Danny Klassen	.15
213	Chris Jones, Jeff Urban **RC**	.15
214	Arturo McDowell, Tony Torcato **RC**	.25
215	Josh McKinley, Jason Tyner **RC**	.30
216	Matt Burch, Seth Etherton **RC**	.15
217	Mamon Tucker, Rick Elder **RC**	.20
218	J.M. Gold, Ryan Mills **RC**	.15
219	Adam Brown, Choo Freeman **RC**	.20
220	Mark McGwire HR #1 (Record Breaker)	15.00
220	Mark McGwire HR #2-60	10.00
220	McGwire HR #61-62	15.00
220	McGwire HR #63-69	12.50
220	McGwire HR #70	40.00
221	Larry Walker	.15
222	Bernie Williams	.15
223	Mark McGwire	1.25
224	Ken Griffey Jr.	1.00
225	Sammy Sosa	.75

#	Player	Price
226	Juan Gonzalez	.35
227	Dante Bichette	.15
228	Alex Rodriguez	1.25
229	Sammy Sosa	.75
230	Derek Jeter	1.50
231	Greg Maddux	.75
232	Roger Clemens	.75
233	Ricky Ledee	.15
234	Chuck Knoblauch	.15
235	Bernie Williams	.15
236	Tino Martinez	.15
237	Orlando Hernandez	.15
238	Scott Brosius	.15
239	Andy Pettitte	.15
240	Mariano Rivera	.15
241	Checklist	.15
242	Checklist	.15
243	Tom Glavine	.35
244	Andy Benes	.15
245	Sandy Alomar	.15
246	Wilton Guerrero	.15
247	Alex Gonzalez	.15
248	Roberto Alomar	.30
249	Ruben Rivera	.15
250	Eric Chavez	.15
251	Ellis Burks	.15
252	Richie Sexson	.15
253	Steve Finley	.15
254	Dwight Gooden	.15
255	Dustin Hermanson	.15
256	Kirk Rueter	.15
257	Steve Trachsel	.15
258	Gregg Jefferies	.15
259	Matt Stairs	.15
260	Shane Reynolds	.15
261	Gregg Olson	.15
262	Kevin Tapani	.15
263	Matt Morris	.15
264	Carl Pavano	.15
265	Nomar Garciaparra	1.50
266	Kevin Young	.15
267	Rick Helling	.15
268	Matt Franco	.15
269	Brian McRae	.15
270	Cal Ripken Jr.	3.00
271	Jeff Abbott	.15
272	Tony Batista	.15
273	Bill Simas	.15
274	Brian Hunter	.15
275	John Franco	.15
276	Devon White	.15
277	Rickey Henderson	1.00
278	Chuck Finley	.15
279	Mike Blowers	.15
280	Mark Grace	.15
281	Randy Winn	.15
282	Bobby Bonilla	.15
283	David Justice	.15
284	Shane Monahan	.15
285	Kevin Brown	.15
286	Todd Zeile	.15
287	Al Martin	.15
288	Troy O'Leary	.15
289	Darryl Hamilton	.15
290	Tino Martinez	.15
291	David Ortiz	.50
292	Tony Clark	.15
293	Ryan Minor	.15
294	Reggie Sanders	.15
295	Wally Joyner	.15
296	Cliff Floyd	.15
297	Shawn Estes	.15
298	Pat Hentgen	.15
299	Scott Elarton	.15
300	Alex Rodriguez	2.50
301	Ozzie Guillen	.15
302	Hideo Martinez	.15
303	Ryan McGuire	.15
304	Brad Ausmus	.15
305	Alex Gonzalez	.15
306	Brian Jordan	.15
307	John Jaha	.15
308	Mark Grudzielanek	.15
309	Juan Guzman	.15
310	Tony Womack	.15
311	Dennis Reyes	.15
312	Marty Cordova	.15
313	Ramiro Mendoza	.15
314	Robin Ventura	.15
315	Rafael Palmeiro	.65
316	Ramon Martinez	.15
317	Pedro Astacio	.15
318	Dave Hollins	.15
319	Tom Candiotti	.15
320	Al Leiter	.15
321	Rico Brogna	.15
322	Reggie Jefferson	.15
323	Bernard Gilkey	.15
324	Jason Giambi	.40
325	Craig Biggio	.15
326	Troy Glaus	.75
327	Delino DeShields	.15
328	Fernando Vina	.15
329	John Smoltz	.15

330	Jeff Kent	.15
331	Roy Halladay	.15
332	Andy Ashby	.15
333	Tim Wakefield	.15
334	Roger Clemens	1.75
335	Bernie Williams	.15
336	Desi Relaford	.15
337	John Burkett	.15
338	Mike Hampton	.15
339	Royce Clayton	.15
340	Mike Piazza	2.00
341	Jeremi Gonzalez	.15
342	Mike Lansing	.15
343	Jamie Moyer	.15
344	Ron Coomer	.15
345	Barry Larkin	.15
346	Fernando Tatis	.15
347	Chili Davis	.15
348	Bobby Higginson	.15
349	Hal Morris	.15
350	Larry Walker	.15
351	Carlos Guillen	.15
352	Miguel Tejada	.30
353	Travis Fryman	.15
354	Jarrod Washburn	.15
355	Chipper Jones	1.50
356	Todd Stottlemyre	.15
357	Henry Rodriguez	.15
358	Eli Marrero	.15
359	Alan Benes	.15
360	Tim Salmon	.15
361	Luis Gonzalez	.15
362	Scott Spiezio	.15
363	Chris Carpenter	.15
364	Bobby Howry	.15
365	Raul Mondesi	.15
366	Ugueth Urbina	.15
367	Tom Evans	.15
368	Kerry Ligtenberg RC	.40
369	Adrian Beltre	.35
370	Ryan Klesko	.15
371	Wilson Alvarez	.15
372	John Thomson	.15
373	Tony Saunders	.15
374	Mike Stanley	.15
375	Ken Caminiti	.15
376	Jay Buhner	.15
377	Bill Mueller	.15
378	Jeff Blauser	.15
379	Edgar Renteria	.15
380	Jim Thome	.60
381	Joey Hamilton	.15
382	Calvin Pickering	.15
383	Marquis Grissom	.15
384	Omar Daal	.15
385	Curt Schilling	.35
386	Jose Cruz Jr.	.15
387	Chris Widger	.15
388	Pete Harnisch	.15
389	Charles Nagy	.15
390	Tom Gordon	.15
391	Bobby Smith	.15
392	Derrick Gibson	.15
393	Jeff Conine	.15
394	Carlos Perez	.15
395	Barry Bonds	3.00
396	Mark McLemore	.15
397	Juan Encarnacion	.15
398	Wade Boggs	1.50
399	Ivan Rodriguez	.75
400	Moises Alou	.15
401	Jeromy Burnitz	.15
402	Sean Casey	.25
403	Jose Offerman	.15
404	Joe Fontenot	.15
405	Kevin Millwood	.15
406	Lance Johnson	.15
407	Richard Hidalgo	.15
408	Mike Jackson	.15
409	Brian Anderson	.15
410	Jeff Shaw	.15
411	Preston Wilson	.15
412	Todd Hundley	.15
413	Jim Parque	.15
414	Justin Baughman	.15
415	Dante Bichette	.15
416	Paul O'Neill	.15
417	Miguel Cairo	.15
418	Randy Johnson	1.00
419	Jesus Sanchez	.15
420	Carlos Delgado	.35
421	Ricky Ledee	.15
422	Orlando Hernandez	.15
423	Frank Thomas	1.00
424	Pokey Reese	.15
425	Carlos Lee, Mike Lowell, Kit Pellow RC	.30
426	Michael Cuddyer, Mark DeRosa, Jerry Hairston Jr. RC	.60
427	Marlon Anderson, Ron Belliard, Orlando Cabrera	.45

428	Micah Bowie, Phil Norton, Randy Wolf	.35
429	Jack Cressend, Jason Rakers, John Rocker	.25
430	Ruben Mateo, Scott Morgan, Mike Zywica RC	.25
431	Jason LaRue, Matt LeCroy, Mitch Meluskey RC	.25
432	Gabe Kapler, Armando Rios, Fernando Seguignol	.25
433	Adam Kennedy, Mickey Lopez, Jackie Rexrode	.25
434	Jose Fernandez, Jeff Liefer, Chris Truby	.25
435	Corey Koskie, Doug Mientkiewicz, Damon Minor	.60
436	Roosevelt Brown, Dernell Stenson, Vernon Wells	.25
437	A.J. Burnett, John Nicholson, Billy Koch	.75
438	Matt Belisle, Matt Roney RC	.30
439	Austin Kearns, Chris George RC	3.00
440	Nate Bump, Nate Cornejo RC	.40
441	Brad Lidge, Mike Nannini RC	.60
442	Matt Holliday, Jeff Winchester RC	8.00
443	Adam Everett, Chip Ambres RC	.30
444	Pat Burrell, Eric Valent RC	3.00
445	Roger Clemens	.85
446	Kerry Wood	.20
447	Curt Schilling	.15
448	Randy Johnson	.50
449	Pedro Martinez	.50
450	Jeff Bagwell, Andres Galarraga, Mark McGwire	1.25
451	John Olerud, Jim Thome, Tino Martinez	.40
452	Alex Rodriguez, Nomar Garciaparra, Derek Jeter	1.50
453	Vinny Castilla, Chipper Jones, Scott Rolen	.75
454	Sammy Sosa, Ken Griffey Jr., Juan Gonzalez	1.00
455	Barry Bonds, Manny Ramirez, Larry Walker	1.50
456	Frank Thomas, Tim Salmon, David Justice	.60
457	Travis Lee, Todd Helton, Ben Grieve	.50
458	Vladimir Guerrero, Greg Vaughn, Bernie Williams	.50
459	Mike Piazza, Ivan Rodriguez, Jason Kendall	1.00
460	Roger Clemens, Kerry Wood, Greg Maddux	1.00
461	Sammy Sosa #1 (Home Run Parade)	10.00
461	Sammy Sosa HR #2-60	6.00
461	S. Sosa HR #61-62	10.00
461	S. Sosa HR #63-65	7.50
461	S. Sosa HR #66	20.00
---	Checklist 1-100	.15
---	Checklist - inserts	.15

All-Etch

		NM/M
Complete Set (30):		15.00
Common Player:		.35
Inserted 1:6		
Refractors:		1.5X
Inserted 1:24		
1	Mark McGwire	3.00
2	Sammy Sosa	1.50
3	Ken Griffey Jr.	2.00
4	Greg Vaughn	.25
5	Albert Belle	.25
6	Vinny Castilla	.25
7	Jose Canseco	.50
8	Juan Gonzalez	.50
9	Manny Ramirez	1.00
10	Andres Galarraga	.25

11	Rafael Palmeiro	.75
12	Alex Rodriguez	3.00
13	Mo Vaughn	.25
14	Eric Chavez	.40
15	Gabe Kapler	.25
16	Calvin Pickering	.25
17	Ruben Mateo	.25
18	Roy Halladay	.40
19	Jeremy Giambi	.25
20	Alex Gonzalez	.25
21	Ron Belliard	.25
22	Marlon Anderson	.25
23	Carlos Lee	.25
24	Kerry Wood	.50
25	Roger Clemens	1.50
26	Curt Schilling	.50
27	Kevin Brown	.25
28	Randy Johnson	1.00
29	Pedro Martinez	1.00
30	Orlando Hernandez	.25

Early Road to the Hall

		NM/M
Complete Set (10):		12.00
Common Player:		.50
Inserted 1:12		
Refractors (#'d to 100):		6X
ER1	Nomar Garciaparra	1.50
ER2	Derek Jeter	3.00
ER3	Alex Rodriguez	2.50
ER4	Juan Gonzalez	.50
ER5	Ken Griffey Jr.	2.00
ER6	Chipper Jones	1.50
ER7	Vladimir Guerrero	1.00
ER8	Jeff Bagwell	1.00
ER9	Ivan Rodriguez	.75
ER10	Frank Thomas	1.00

Fortune 15

		NM/M
Complete Set (15):		17.50
Common Player:		.50
Inserted 1:12		
Refractors (#'d to 100):		4X
1	Alex Rodriguez	2.25
2	Nomar Garciaparra	1.25
3	Derek Jeter	3.00
4	Troy Glaus	.75
5	Ken Griffey Jr.	1.50
6	Vladimir Guerrero	1.00
7	Kerry Wood	.65
8	Eric Chavez	.65
9	Greg Maddux	1.25
10	Mike Piazza	1.50
11	Sammy Sosa	1.25
12	Mark McGwire	2.25
13	Ben Grieve	.50
14	Chipper Jones	1.25
15	Manny Ramirez	1.00

Lords of the Diamond

		NM/M
Complete Set (15):		20.00
Common Player:		.40
Inserted 1:8		
Refractors:		2X
Inserted 1:24		
LD1	Ken Griffey Jr.	2.00
LD2	Chipper Jones	1.50
LD3	Sammy Sosa	1.50
LD4	Frank Thomas	1.25
LD5	Mark McGwire	2.50
LD6	Jeff Bagwell	1.25
LD7	Alex Rodriguez	2.25
LD8	Juan Gonzalez	.65
LD9	Barry Bonds	3.00
LD10	Nomar Garciaparra	1.50
LD11	Darin Erstad	.50
LD12	Tony Gwynn	1.50
LD13	Andres Galarraga	.40
LD14	Mike Piazza	2.00
LD15	Greg Maddux	1.50

New Breed

		NM/M
Complete Set (15):		30.00
Common Player:		.50
Inserted 1:24		
Refractors:		1.5X
Inserted 1:72		
NB1	Darin Erstad	.75
NB2	Brad Fullmer	.50
NB3	Kerry Wood	.75
NB4	Nomar Garciaparra	5.00
NB5	Travis Lee	.65
NB6	Scott Rolen	2.00
NB7	Todd Helton	3.00
NB8	Vladimir Guerrero	3.00
NB9	Derek Jeter	7.50
NB10	Alex Rodriguez	6.00

NB11	Ben Grieve	.50
NB12	Andruw Jones	3.00
NB13	Paul Konerko	.75
NB14	Aramis Ramirez	.50
NB15	Adrian Beltre	.75

Record Numbers

		NM/M
Complete Set (10):		20.00
Common Player:		.50
Inserted 1:36		
Refractors:		1.5X
Inserted 1:144		
1	Mark McGwire	3.00
2	Craig Biggio	.50
3	Barry Bonds	4.00
4	Ken Griffey Jr.	2.50
5	Sammy Sosa	2.00
6	Alex Rodriguez	3.00
7	Kerry Wood	1.00
8	Roger Clemens	2.00
9	Cal Ripken Jr.	4.00
10	Mark McGwire	3.00

1999 Topps Chrome Traded and Rookies

		NM/M
Complete Set (121):		60.00
Common Player:		.15
1	Seth Etherton	.15
2	Mark Harriger RC	.25
3	Matt Wise RC	.50
4	Carlos Hernandez RC	.50
5	Julio Lugo RC	1.50
6	Mike Nannini	.15
7	Justin Bowles RC	.25
8	Mark Mulder RC	3.00
9	Roberto Vaz RC	.15
10	Felipe Lopez RC	3.00
11	Matt Belisle	.15
12	Micah Bowie	.15
13	Ruben Quevedo RC	.25
14	Jose Garcia RC	.15
15	David Kelton RC	1.00
16	Phillip Norton	.15
17	Corey Patterson RC	2.50
18	Ron Walker RC	.15
19	Paul Hoover RC	.15
20	Ryan Rupe RC	.25
21	J.D. Closser RC	.15
22	Rob Ryan RC	.15
23	Steve Colyer RC	.15
24	Bubba Crosby RC	1.00
25	Luke Prokopec RC	.15
26	Matt Blank RC	.15
27	Josh McKinley	.15
28	Nate Bump	.15
29	Giuseppe Chiaramonte RC	.15
30	Arturo McDowell	.15
31	Tony Torcato	.15
32	Dave Roberts	.15
33	C.C. Sabathia RC	4.00
34	Sean Spencer RC	.15
35	Chip Ambres	.15
36	A.J. Burnett	.50
37	Mo Bruce RC	.15
38	Jason Tyner	.15
39	Mamon Tucker	.15
40	Sean Burroughs RC	.75
41	Kevin Eberwein RC	.15
42	Junior Herndon RC	.25
43	Bryan Wolff RC	.15
44	Pat Burrell	1.00
45	Eric Valent	.15
46	Carlos Pena RC	3.00
47	Mike Zywica	.15
48	Adam Everett	.15
49	Juan Pena RC	.75
50	Adam Dunn RC	10.00
51	Austin Kearns	2.00
52	Jacobo Sequea RC	.15
53	Choo Freeman	.50
54	Jeff Winchester	.15
55	Matt Burch	.15
56	Chris George	.25
57	Scott Mullen RC	.15
58	Kit Pellow	.15
59	Mark Quinn RC	.75
60	Nate Cornejo	.15
61	Ryan Mills RC	.15
62	Kevin Beirne RC	.15
63	Kip Wells RC	.75
64	Juan Rivera RC	1.00
65	Alfonso Soriano RC	10.00
66	Josh Hamilton RC	12.00
67	Josh Girdley RC	.15
68	Kyle Snyder RC	.25
69	Mike Paradis RC	.25
70	Jason Jennings RC	.25
71	David Walling RC	.25
72	Omar Ortiz RC	.15
73	Jay Gehrke RC	.15
74	Casey Burns RC	.15
75	Carl Crawford RC	8.00
76	Reggie Sanders	.15
77	Will Clark	.15
78	David Wells	.15
79	Paul Konerko	.30
80	Armando Benitez	.15
81	Brant Brown	.15
82	Mo Vaughn	.15
83	Jose Canseco	.75
84	Albert Belle	.15
85	Dean Palmer	.15
86	Greg Vaughn	.15
87	Mark Clark	.15
88	Pat Meares	.15
89	Eric Davis	.15
90	Brian Giles	.15
91	Jeff Brantley	.15
92	Bret Boone	.15
93	Ron Gant	.15
94	Mike Cameron	.15
95	Charles Johnson	.15
96	Denny Neagle	.15
97	Brian Hunter	.15
98	Jose Hernandez	.15
99	Rick Aguilera	.15
100	Tony Batista	.15
101	Roger Cedeno	.15
102	Creighton Gubanich	.15
103	Tim Belcher	.15
104	Bruce Aven	.15
105	Brian Daubach RC	.75
106	Ed Sprague	.15
107	Michael Tucker	.15
108	Homer Bush	.15
109	Armando Reynoso	.15
110	Brook Fordyce	.15
111	Matt Mantei	.15
112	Jose Guillen	.15
113	Kenny Rogers	.15
114	Livan Hernandez	.15
115	Butch Huskey	.15
116	David Segui	.15
117	Darryl Hamilton	.15
118	Jim Leyritz	.15
119	Randy Velarde	.15
120	Bill Taylor	.15
121	Kevin Appier	.15

1999 Topps Gallery

		NM/M
Complete Set (150):		60.00
Common Player (1-100):		.10
Common Player (101-150):		.25
Pack (6):		3.00
Wax Box (24):		45.00
1	Mark McGwire	1.50
2	Jim Thome	.35
3	Bernie Williams	.10
4	Larry Walker	.10
5	Juan Gonzalez	.30
6	Ken Griffey Jr.	1.00
7	Raul Mondesi	.10

TODD HELTON

8	Sammy Sosa	.75
9	Greg Maddux	.75
10	Jeff Bagwell	.60
11	Vladimir Guerrero	.60
12	Scott Rolen	.50
13	Nomar Garciaparra	.75
14	Mike Piazza	1.00
15	Travis Lee	.15
16	Carlos Delgado	.35
17	Darin Erstad	.25
18	David Justice	.10
19	Cal Ripken Jr.	2.00
20	Derek Jeter	2.00
21	Tony Clark	.10
22	Barry Larkin	.10
23	Greg Vaughn	.10
24	Jeff Kent	.10
25	Wade Boggs	.75
26	Andres Galarraga	.10
27	Ken Caminiti	.10
28	Jason Kendall	.10
29	Todd Helton	.60
30	Chuck Knoblauch	.10
31	Roger Clemens	.85
32	Jeromy Burnitz	.10
33	Javy Lopez	.10
34	Roberto Alomar	.25
35	Eric Karros	.10
36	Ben Grieve	.10
37	Eric Davis	.10
38	Rondell White	.10
39	Dmitri Young	.10
40	Ivan Rodriguez	.50
41	Paul O'Neill	.10
42	Jeff Cirillo	.10
43	Kerry Wood	.30
44	Albert Belle	.10
45	Frank Thomas	.60
46	Manny Ramirez	.60
47	Tom Glavine	.25
48	Mo Vaughn	.10
49	Jose Cruz Jr.	.10
50	Sandy Alomar	.10
51	Edgar Martinez	.10
52	John Olerud	.10
53	Todd Walker	.10
54	Tim Salmon	.10
55	Derek Bell	.10
56	Matt Williams	.10
57	Alex Rodriguez	1.50
58	Rusty Greer	.10
59	Vinny Castilla	.10
60	Jason Giambi	.30
61	Mark Grace	.10
62	Jose Canseco	.40
63	Gary Sheffield	.40
64	Brad Fullmer	.10
65	Trevor Hoffman	.10
66	Mark Kotsay	.10
67	Mike Mussina	.25
68	Johnny Damon	.30
69	Tino Martinez	.10
70	Curt Schilling	.25
71	Jay Buhner	.10
72	Kenny Lofton	.10
73	Randy Johnson	.60
74	Kevin Brown	.10
75	Brian Jordan	.10
76	Craig Biggio	.10
77	Barry Bonds	2.00
78	Tony Gwynn	.75
79	Jim Edmonds	.10
80	Shawn Green	.35
81	Todd Hundley	.10
82	Cliff Floyd	.10
83	Jose Guillen	.10
84	Dante Bichette	.10
85	Moises Alou	.10
86	Chipper Jones	.75
87	Ray Lankford	.10
88	Fred McGriff	.10
89	Rod Beck	.10
90	Dean Palmer	.10
91	Pedro Martinez	.60
92	Andruw Jones	.60
93	Robin Ventura	.10
94	Ugueth Urbina	.10
95	Orlando Hernandez	.10
96	Sean Casey	.15
97	Denny Neagle	.10
98	Troy Glaus	.60
99	John Smoltz	.10
100	Al Leiter	.10
101	Ken Griffey Jr.	1.50
102	Frank Thomas	.75
103	Mark McGwire	2.00
104	Sammy Sosa	1.00
105	Chipper Jones	1.00
106	Alex Rodriguez	2.00
107	Nomar Garciaparra	1.00
108	Juan Gonzalez	.40
109	Derek Jeter	3.00
110	Mike Piazza	1.50
111	Barry Bonds	3.00
112	Tony Gwynn	1.00
113	Cal Ripken Jr.	3.00
114	Greg Maddux	1.00
115	Roger Clemens	1.25
116	Brad Fullmer	.25
117	Kerry Wood	.50
118	Ben Grieve	.25
119	Todd Helton	.65
120	Kevin Millwood	.25
121	Sean Casey	.35
122	Vladimir Guerrero	.75
123	Travis Lee	.25
124	Troy Glaus	.65
125	Bartolo Colon	.25
126	Andruw Jones	.75
127	Scott Rolen	.25
128	Alfonso Soriano RC	4.00
129	Nick Johnson RC	1.00
130	Matt Belisle RC	.25
131	Jorge Toca RC	.25
132	Masao Kida RC	.25
133	Carlos Pena RC	1.50
134	Adrian Beltre	.40
135	Eric Chavez	.40
136	Carlos Beltran	.65
137	Alex Gonzalez	.25
138	Ryan Anderson	.25
139	Ruben Mateo	.25
140	Bruce Chen	.25
141	Pat Burrell RC	3.00
142	Michael Barrett	.25
143	Carlos Lee	.25
144	Mark Mulder RC	1.00
145	Choo Freeman RC	.50
146	Gabe Kapler	.25
147	Juan Encarnacion	.25
148	Jeremy Giambi	.25
149	Jason Tyner	.35
150	George Lombard	.25
		.10
Checklist Folder 1 (1:3 Packs)		
Checklist Folder 2 (1:3)		.10
Checklist Folder 3 (1:3)		.10
Checklist Folder 4 (1:12)		.25
Checklist Folder 5 (1:240)		1.50
Checklist Folder 6 (1:640)		3.00

Player's Private Issue

ANDRES GALARRAGA
1B ATLANTA BRAVES

	NM/M
Common Player:	1.00
Stars:	5X
SP's:	3X
Production 250 Sets	

(See 1999 Topps Gallery for checklist and base card values.)

Press Plates

NM/M
Common Player: 25.00
(See 1999 Topps Gallery for checklist.)

Autograph Cards

NM/M
Common Player: 10.00
Inserted 1:209
GA1 Troy Glaus 15.00
GA2 Adrian Beltre 10.00
GA3 Eric Chavez 10.00

Awards Gallery

NM/M
Complete Set (10): 12.50
Common Player: .50
Inserted 1:12
AG1 Kerry Wood .75
AG2 Ben Grieve .50
AG3 Roger Clemens 2.50
AG4 Tom Glavine .75
AG5 Juan Gonzalez .75
AG6 Sammy Sosa 3.00
AG7 Ken Griffey Jr. 3.00
AG8 Mark McGwire 4.00
AG9 Bernie Williams .50
AG10 Larry Walker .50

Exhibitions

NM/M
Complete Set (20): 75.00
Common Player: 2.00
Inserted 1:48
E1 Sammy Sosa 4.50
E2 Mark McGwire 7.50
E3 Greg Maddux 4.50

E4 Roger Clemens 5.00
E5 Ben Grieve 2.00
E6 Kerry Wood 2.25
E7 Ken Griffey Jr. 6.00
E8 Tony Gwynn 4.50
E9 Cal Ripken Jr. 10.00
E10 Frank Thomas 4.00
E11 Jeff Bagwell 4.00
E12 Derek Jeter 10.00
E13 Alex Rodriguez 7.50
E14 Nomar Garciaparra 4.50
E15 Manny Ramirez 4.00
E16 Vladimir Guerrero 4.00
E17 Darin Erstad 2.25
E18 Scott Rolen 3.00
E19 Mike Piazza 6.00
E20 Andres Galarraga 2.00

Gallery of Heroes

NM/M
Complete Set (10): 30.00
Common Player: .75
Inserted 1:24
GH1 Mark McGwire 6.00
GH2 Sammy Sosa 3.50
GH3 Ken Griffey Jr. 4.50
GH4 Mike Piazza 4.50
GH5 Derek Jeter 7.50
GH6 Nomar Garciaparra 4.50
GH7 Kerry Wood 1.50
GH8 Ben Grieve .75
GH9 Chipper Jones 3.50
GH10 Alex Rodriguez 6.00

Heritage

NM/M
Complete Set (20): 100.00
Common Player: 2.50
Inserted 1:12
Heritage Proofs: 1.5X

Inserted 1:48
TH1 Hank Aaron 10.00
TH2 Ben Grieve 2.50
TH3 Nomar Garciaparra 7.50
TH4 Roger Clemens 8.50
TH5 Travis Lee 2.50
TH6 Tony Gwynn 7.50
TH7 Alex Rodriguez 12.50
TH8 Ken Griffey Jr. 10.00
TH9 Derek Jeter 15.00
TH10 Sammy Sosa 7.50
TH11 Scott Rolen 2.50
TH12 Chipper Jones 7.50
TH13 Cal Ripken Jr. 15.00
TH14 Kerry Wood 3.00
TH15 Barry Bonds 15.00
TH16 Juan Gonzalez 3.00
TH17 Mike Piazza 10.00
TH18 Greg Maddux 7.50
TH19 Frank Thomas 6.00
TH20 Mark McGwire 12.50

Heritage Lithographs

NM/M
Complete Set (8): 480.00
Single Player: 60.00
(1) Roger Clemens 60.00
(2) Nomar Garciaparra 60.00
(3) Ken Griffey Jr. 60.00
(4) Derek Jeter 60.00
(5) Mark McGwire 60.00
(6) Mike Piazza 60.00
(7) Cal Ripken Jr. 60.00
(8) Sammy Sosa 60.00

Heritage Auction Original Art

NM/M
TH3 Nomar Garciaparra
(6/01 Auction) 1,375
TH13 Cal Ripken Jr.
(6/01 Auction) 3,950

1999 Topps Gold Label Class 1

Pedro Martinez

		NM/M
Complete Set (100):		30.00
Common Gold Label:		.10
Common Black Label:		.50
Black Label Stars:		3X
Common Red Label:		2.00
Red Label Stars:		12X
Pack (5):		3.00
Wax Box (24):		50.00
1	Mike Piazza	2.00
2	Andres Galarraga	.10
3	Mark Grace	.10
4	Tony Clark	.10
5	Jim Thome	.60
6	Tony Gwynn	1.50
7	Kelly Dransfeldt RC	.15
8	Eric Chavez	.25
9	Brian Jordan	.10
10	Todd Hundley	.10
11	Rondell White	.10
12	Dmitri Young	.10
13	Jeff Kent	.10
14	Derek Bell	.10
15	Todd Helton	.75
16	Chipper Jones	1.50
17	Albert Belle	.10
18	Barry Larkin	.10
19	Dante Bichette	.10
20	Gary Sheffield	.50
21	Cliff Floyd	.10
22	Derek Jeter	3.00
23	Jason Giambi	.50
24	Ray Lankford	.10
25	Alex Rodriguez	2.50
26	Ruben Mateo	.10
27	Wade Boggs	1.50
28	Carlos Delgado	.45
29	Tim Salmon	.10
30	Alfonso Soriano RC	5.00
31	Javy Lopez	.10
32	Jason Kendall	.10
33	Nick Johnson RC	1.00
34	A.J. Burnett RC	1.00
35	Troy Glaus	.75
36	Pat Burrell RC	3.00
37	Jeff Cirillo	.10
38	David Justice	.10
39	Ivan Rodriguez	.75
40	Bernie Williams	.10
41	Jay Buhner	.10
42	Mo Vaughn	.10
43	Randy Johnson	1.00
44	Pedro Martinez	1.00
45	Larry Walker	.10
46	Todd Walker	.10
47	Roberto Alomar	.25
48	Kevin Brown	.10
49	Mike Mussina	.40
50	Tom Glavine	.25
51	Curt Schilling	.25
52	Ken Caminiti	.10
53	Brad Fullmer	.10
54	Bobby Seay RC	.10
55	Orlando Hernandez	.10
56	Sean Casey	.10
57	Al Leiter	.10
58	Sandy Alomar	.10
59	Mark Kotsay	.10
60	Matt Williams	.10
61	Raul Mondesi	.10
62	Joe Crede RC	5.00
63	Jim Edmonds	.10
64	Jose Cruz Jr.	.10
65	Juan Gonzalez	.50
66	Sammy Sosa	1.50
67	Cal Ripken Jr.	3.00
68	Vinny Castilla	.10
69	Craig Biggio	.10
70	Mark McGwire	2.50
71	Greg Vaughn	.10
72	Greg Maddux	1.50
73	Paul O'Neill	.10
74	Scott Rolen	.65
75	Ben Grieve	.10
76	Vladimir Guerrero	1.00
77	John Olerud	.10
78	Eric Karros	.10
79	Jeromy Burnitz	.10
80	Jeff Bagwell	1.00
81	Kenny Lofton	.10
82	Manny Ramirez	1.00
83	Andruw Jones	1.00
84	Travis Lee	.15
85	Darin Erstad	.25
86	Nomar Garciaparra	1.50
87	Frank Thomas	1.00
88	Moises Alou	.10
89	Tino Martinez	.10
90	Carlos Pena RC	1.50
91	Shawn Green	.40
92	Rusty Greer	.10
93	Matt Belisle RC	.25
94	Adrian Beltre	.25
95	Roger Clemens	1.75
96	John Smoltz	.10
97	Mark Mulder RC	1.00

98	Kerry Wood	.50
99	Barry Bonds	3.00
100	Ken Griffey Jr.	2.00

Class 2

Joe Crede

	NM/M
Complete Set (100):	75.00
Common Gold Label:	.25
Gold Label Stars:	1.5X
Common Black Label:	2.00
Black Label Stars:	4X
Common Red Label:	6.00
Red Label Stars:	15X

(See 1999 Topps Gold Label Class 1 for checklist and base card values.)

Class 3

Complete Set (100):	125.00
Common Gold Label:	.50
Gold Label Stars:	2
Common Black Label:	3.00
Black Label Stars:	6X
Common Red Label:	12.00
Red Label Stars:	35X

(See 1999 Topps Gold Label Class 1 for checklist and base card values.)

One to One

Nomar Garciaparra

	NM/M
Common Player, Base Set:	50.00
Common Player, Race to Aaron:	150.00

(Star/rookie card values cannot be determined due to scarcity.)

Race to Aaron

Vladimir Guerrero
Race to Aaron

		NM/M
	Complete Set (10):	20.00
	Common Player:	1.00
	Blacks:	2X
	Reds:	12X
1	Mark McGwire	4.50
2	Ken Griffey Jr.	3.00
3	Alex Rodriguez	4.50
4	Vladimir Guerrero	1.50
5	Albert Belle	1.00
6	Nomar Garciaparra	2.50
7	Ken Griffey Jr.	3.00
8	Alex Rodriguez	4.50
9	Juan Gonzalez	1.00
10	Barry Bonds	7.50

1999 Topps Stars

		NM/M
	Complete Set (180):	20.00
	Common Player:	.05
	Pack (6):	1.50
	Wax Box (24):	25.00
1	Ken Griffey Jr.	.75
2	Chipper Jones	.50
3	Mike Piazza	.75
4	Nomar Garciaparra	.50
5	Derek Jeter	1.50
6	Frank Thomas	.40
7	Ben Grieve	.05
8	Mark McGwire	1.00
9	Sammy Sosa	.50
10	Alex Rodriguez	1.00
11	Troy Glaus	.35
12	Eric Chavez	.25
13	Kerry Wood	.30
14	Barry Bonds	1.50
15	Vladimir Guerrero	.40
16	Albert Belle	.05
17	Juan Gonzalez	.20
18	Roger Clemens	.60
19	Ruben Mateo	.05
20	Cal Ripken Jr.	1.50
21	Darin Erstad	.25
22	Jeff Bagwell	.40
23	Roy Halladay	.10
24	Todd Helton	.35
25	Michael Barrett	.05
26	Manny Ramirez	.40
27	Fernando Seguignol	.05
28	Pat Burrell RC	2.00
29	Andruw Jones	.40
30	Randy Johnson	.40
31	Jose Canseco	.30
32	Brad Fullmer	.05
33	Alex Escobar RC	.10
34	Alfonso Soriano RC	3.00
35	Larry Walker	.05
36	Matt Clement	.05
37	Mo Vaughn	.05
38	Bruce Chen	.05
39	Travis Lee	.20
40	Adrian Beltre	.10
41	Alex Gonzalez	.05
42	Jason Tyner RC	.10
43	George Lombard	.05
44	Scott Rolen	.25
45	Mark Mulder RC	.50
46	Gabe Kapler	.05
47	Choo Freeman RC	.10
48	Tony Gwynn	.50
49	A.J. Burnett RC	.25
50	Matt Belisle RC	.10
51	Greg Maddux	.50
52	John Smoltz	.05
53	Mark Grace	.05
54	Wade Boggs	.50
55	Bernie Williams	.05
56	Pedro Martinez	.40
57	Barry Larkin	.05
58	Orlando Hernandez	.05
59	Jason Kendall	.05
60	Mark Kotsay	.05
61	Jim Thome	.35
62	Gary Sheffield	.30
63	Preston Wilson	.05
64	Rafael Palmeiro	.35
65	David Wells	.05
66	Shawn Green	.30
67	Tom Glavine	.25
68	Jeromy Burnitz	.05
69	Kevin Brown	.05
70	Rondell White	.05
71	Roberto Alomar	.25
72	Cliff Floyd	.05
73	Craig Biggio	.05
74	Greg Vaughn	.05
75	Ivan Rodriguez	.35
76	Vinny Castilla	.05
77	Todd Walker	.05
78	Paul Konerko	.15
79	Andy Brown RC	.05
80	Todd Hundley	.05
81	Dmitri Young	.05
82	Tony Clark	.05
83	Nick Johnson RC	.50
84	Mike Caruso	.05
85	David Ortiz	.35
86	Matt Williams	.05
87	Raul Mondesi	.05
88	Kenny Lofton	.05
89	Miguel Tejada	.10
90	Dante Bichette	.05
91	Jorge Posada	.05
92	Carlos Beltran	.25
93	Carlos Delgado	.30
94	Javy Lopez	.05
95	Aramis Ramirez	.05
96	Neifi Perez	.05
97	Marlon Anderson	.05
98	David Cone	.05
99	Moises Alou	.05
100	John Olerud	.05
101	Tim Salmon	.05
102	Jason Giambi	.30
103	Sandy Alomar	.05
104	Curt Schilling	.25
105	Andres Galarraga	.05
106	Rusty Greer	.05
107	Bobby Seay RC	.05
108	Eric Young	.05
109	Brian Jordan	.05
110	Eric Davis	.05
111	Will Clark	.05
112	Andy Ashby	.05
113	Edgardo Alfonzo	.05
114	Paul O'Neill	.05
115	Denny Neagle	.05
116	Eric Karros	.05
117	Ken Caminiti	.05
118	Garret Anderson	.05
119	Todd Stottlemyre	.05
120	David Justice	.05
121	Francisco Cordova	.05
122	Robin Ventura	.05
123	Mike Mussina	.25
124	Hideki Irabu	.05
125	Justin Thompson	.05
126	Mariano Rivera	.15
127	Delino DeShields	.05
128	Steve Finley	.05
129	Jose Cruz Jr.	.05
130	Ray Lankford	.05
131	Jim Edmonds	.05
132	Charles Johnson	.05
133	Al Leiter	.05
134	Jose Offerman	.05
135	Eric Milton	.05
136	Dean Palmer	.05
137	Johnny Damon	.25
138	Andy Pettitte	.20
139	Ray Durham	.05
140	Ugueth Urbina	.05
141	Marquis Grissom	.05
142	Ryan Klesko	.05
143	Brady Anderson	.05
144	Bobby Higginson	.05
145	Chuck Knoblauch	.05
146	Rickey Henderson	.40
147	Kevin Millwood	.05
148	Fred McGriff	.05
149	Damion Easley	.05
150	Tino Martinez	.05
151	Greg Maddux	.30
152	Scott Rolen	.20
153	Pat Burrell	.75
154	Roger Clemens	.35
155	Albert Belle	.05
156	Troy Glaus	.25
157	Cal Ripken Jr.	.75
158	Alfonso Soriano	.75
159	Manny Ramirez	.25
160	Eric Chavez	.10
161	Kerry Wood	.20
162	Tony Gwynn	.30
163	Barry Bonds	.75
164	Ruben Mateo	.05
165	Todd Helton	.20
166	Darin Erstad	.05
167	Jeff Bagwell	.25
168	Juan Gonzalez	.15
169	Mo Vaughn	.05
170	Vladimir Guerrero	.25
171	Nomar Garciaparra	.35
172	Derek Jeter	.75
173	Alex Rodriguez	.50
174	Ben Grieve	.05
175	Mike Piazza	.40
176	Chipper Jones	.35
177	Frank Thomas	.25
178	Ken Griffey Jr.	.40
179	Sammy Sosa	.35
180	Mark McGwire	.50

One-Star

Alex Rodriguez

		NM/M
	Complete Set (100):	25.00
	Common Player:	.10
	Foils (249 Each):	2X
1	Ken Griffey Jr.	1.25
2	Chipper Jones	1.00
3	Mike Piazza	1.25
4	Nomar Garciaparra	1.00
5	Derek Jeter	2.00
6	Frank Thomas	.75
7	Ben Grieve	.10
8	Mark McGwire	1.50
9	Sammy Sosa	1.00
10	Alex Rodriguez	1.50
11	Troy Glaus	.65
12	Eric Chavez	.25
13	Kerry Wood	.35
14	Barry Bonds	2.00
15	Vladimir Guerrero	.75
16	Albert Belle	.10
17	Juan Gonzalez	.40
18	Roger Clemens	1.00
19	Ruben Mateo	.10
20	Cal Ripken Jr.	2.00
21	Darin Erstad	.30
22	Jeff Bagwell	.75
23	Roy Halladay	.20
24	Todd Helton	.65
25	Michael Barrett	.10
26	Manny Ramirez	.75
27	Fernando Seguignol	.10
28	Pat Burrell	1.00
29	Andruw Jones	.75
30	Randy Johnson	.75
31	Jose Canseco	.40
32	Brad Fullmer	.10
33	Alex Escobar	.10
34	Alfonso Soriano	1.00
35	Larry Walker	.10
36	Matt Clement	.25
37	Mo Vaughn	.10
38	Bruce Chen	.10
39	Travis Lee	.15
40	Adrian Beltre	.20
41	Alex Gonzalez	.10
42	Jason Tyner	.10
43	George Lombard	.10
44	Scott Rolen	.50
45	Mark Mulder	.50
46	Gabe Kapler	.10
47	Choo Freeman	.10
48	Tony Gwynn	1.00
49	A.J. Burnett	.15
50	Matt Belisle	.10
51	Greg Maddux	1.00
52	John Smoltz	.10
53	Mark Grace	.10
54	Wade Boggs	1.00
55	Bernie Williams	.10
56	Pedro Martinez	.75
57	Barry Larkin	.10
58	Orlando Hernandez	.10
59	Jason Kendall	.10
60	Mark Kotsay	.10
61	Jim Thome	.45
62	Gary Sheffield	.40

63	Preston Wilson	.10
64	Rafael Palmeiro	.60
65	David Wells	.10
66	Shawn Green	.30
67	Tom Glavine	.30
68	Jeromy Burnitz	.10
69	Kevin Brown	.10
70	Rondell White	.10
71	Roberto Alomar	.25
72	Cliff Floyd	.10
73	Craig Biggio	.10
74	Greg Vaughn	.10
75	Ivan Rodriguez	.60
76	Vinny Castilla	.10
77	Todd Walker	.10
78	Paul Konerko	.20
79	Andy Brown	.10
80	Todd Hundley	.10
81	Dmitri Young	.10
82	Tony Clark	.10
83	Nick Johnson	.50
84	Mike Caruso	.10
85	David Ortiz	.40
86	Matt Williams	.10
87	Raul Mondesi	.10
88	Kenny Lofton	.10
89	Miguel Tejada	.20
90	Dante Bichette	.10
91	Jorge Posada	.10
92	Carlos Beltran	.20
93	Carlos Delgado	.25
94	Javy Lopez	.10
95	Aramis Ramirez	.10
96	Neifi Perez	.10
97	Marlon Anderson	.10
98	David Cone	.10
99	Moises Alou	.10
100	John Olerud	.10

Two-Star

		NM/M
Complete Set (50):		50.00
Common Player:		.25
Foils:		3X
1	Ken Griffey Jr.	2.00
2	Chipper Jones	1.50
3	Mike Piazza	2.00
4	Nomar Garciaparra	1.50
5	Derek Jeter	3.00
6	Frank Thomas	1.00
7	Ben Grieve	.25
8	Mark McGwire	2.50
9	Sammy Sosa	1.50
10	Alex Rodriguez	2.50
11	Troy Glaus	.75
12	Eric Chavez	.30
13	Kerry Wood	.40
14	Barry Bonds	3.00
15	Vladimir Guerrero	1.00
16	Albert Belle	.25
17	Juan Gonzalez	.50
18	Roger Clemens	1.75
19	Ruben Mateo	.25
20	Cal Ripken Jr.	3.00
21	Darin Erstad	.75
22	Jeff Bagwell	1.00
23	Roy Halladay	.40
24	Todd Helton	.75
25	Michael Barrett	.25
26	Manny Ramirez	1.00
27	Fernando Seguignol	.25
28	Pat Burrell	1.50
29	Andruw Jones	1.00
30	Randy Johnson	1.00
31	Jose Canseco	.50
32	Brad Fullmer	.25
33	Alex Escobar	.25
34	Alfonso Soriano	1.50
35	Larry Walker	.25
36	Matt Clement	.30
37	Mo Vaughn	.25
38	Bruce Chen	.25
39	Travis Lee	.30

40	Adrian Beltre	.30
41	Alex Gonzalez	.25
42	Jason Tyner	.25
43	George Lombard	.25
44	Scott Rolen	.65
45	Mark Mulder	.45
46	Gabe Kapler	.25
47	Choo Freeman	.25
48	Tony Gwynn	1.50
49	A.J. Burnett	.30
50	Matt Belisle	.25

Three-Star

KERRY WOOD

		NM/M
Complete Set (20):		30.00
Common Player:		.50
Foils:		4X
1	Ken Griffey Jr.	2.50
2	Chipper Jones	2.00
3	Mike Piazza	2.50
4	Nomar Garciaparra	2.00
5	Derek Jeter	4.00
6	Frank Thomas	1.50
7	Ben Grieve	.50
8	Mark McGwire	3.00
9	Sammy Sosa	2.00
10	Alex Rodriguez	3.00
11	Troy Glaus	1.25
12	Eric Chavez	.60
13	Kerry Wood	.75
14	Barry Bonds	4.00
15	Vladimir Guerrero	1.50
16	Albert Belle	.50
17	Juan Gonzalez	.75
18	Roger Clemens	2.25
19	Ruben Mateo	.50
20	Cal Ripken Jr.	4.00

Four-Star

		NM/M
Complete Set (10):		30.00
Common Player:		1.00
Foils:		2X
1	Ken Griffey Jr.	4.00
2	Chipper Jones	3.00
3	Mike Piazza	4.00
4	Nomar Garciaparra	3.00
5	Derek Jeter	6.00
6	Frank Thomas	2.50
7	Ben Grieve	1.00
8	Mark McGwire	5.00
9	Sammy Sosa	3.00
10	Alex Rodriguez	5.00

Foil

MIGUEL TEJADA

		NM/M
Complete Base Set (180):		90.00
Common Foil Player:		.15
Foil Stars:		3X
(See 1999 Topps Stars for checklist and base card values.)		

Bright Futures

BRIGHT FUTURES

		NM/M
Complete Set (10):		20.00
Common Player:		1.50
Production 1,999 Sets		
Foil (30 Each):		8X
1	Troy Glaus	3.00
2	Eric Chavez	2.00
3	Adrian Beltre	2.00
4	Michael Barrett	1.50
5	Fernando Seguignol	1.50
6	Alex Gonzalez	1.50
7	Matt Clement	1.50
8	Pat Burrell	6.00
9	Ruben Mateo	1.50
10	Alfonso Soriano	6.00

Galaxy

Galaxy

Mark McGwire

		NM/M
Complete Set (10):		25.00
Common Player:		1.00
Production 1,999 Sets		
Foil (30 Each):		8X
1	Mark McGwire	5.00
2	Roger Clemens	3.00
3	Nomar Garciaparra	4.00
4	Alex Rodriguez	5.00
5	Kerry Wood	1.50
6	Ben Grieve	1.00
7	Derek Jeter	6.00
8	Vladimir Guerrero	2.50
9	Ken Griffey Jr.	4.00
10	Sammy Sosa	3.00

Rookie Reprints

bob gibson

ST. LOUIS CARDINALS
PITCHER

		NM/M
Complete Set (5):		10.00
Common Player:		2.00
Production 2,500 Sets		

1	Frank Robinson	2.00
2	Ernie Banks	3.00
3	Yogi Berra	3.00
4	Bob Gibson	2.00
5	Tom Seaver	3.00

Rookie Reprints Autographs

METS 1967 ROOKIE STARS
BILL DENEHY • P   TOM SEAVER • P

		NM/M
Complete Set (5):		150.00
Common Player:		20.00
Inserted 1:406		
Banks Inserted 1:812		
1	Frank Robinson	25.00
2	Ernie Banks	70.00
3	Yogi Berra	35.00
4	Bob Gibson	20.00
5	Tom Seaver	65.00

1999 Topps Stars 'N Steel

IVAN RODRIGUEZ

		NM/M
Complete Set (44):		65.00
Common Player:		.50
Gold:		4X
Inserted 1:12		
Holographic Dome:		6X
Inserted 1:24		
Pack (3):		4.00
Wax Box (12):		40.00
1	Kerry Wood	1.00
2	Ben Grieve	.50
3	Chipper Jones	3.00
4	Alex Rodriguez	5.00
5	Mo Vaughn	.50
6	Bernie Williams	.50
7	Juan Gonzalez	1.00
8	Vinny Castilla	.50
9	Tony Gwynn	3.00
10	Manny Ramirez	2.00
11	Raul Mondesi	.50
12	Roger Clemens	3.50
13	Darin Erstad	.75
14	Barry Bonds	6.00
15	Cal Ripken Jr.	6.00
16	Barry Larkin	.50
17	Scott Rolen	1.00
18	Albert Belle	.50
19	Craig Biggio	.50
20	Tony Clark	.50
21	Mark McGwire	5.00
22	Andres Galarraga	.50
23	Kenny Lofton	.50
24	Pedro Martinez	2.00
25	Paul O'Neill	.50
26	Ken Griffey Jr.	4.00
27	Travis Lee	75.00
28	Tim Salmon	.50
29	Frank Thomas	2.00
30	Larry Walker	.50
31	Moises Alou	.50
32	Vladimir Guerrero	2.00
33	Ivan Rodriguez	1.50
34	Derek Jeter	6.00
35	Greg Vaughn	.50
36	Gary Sheffield	1.00
37	Carlos Delgado	1.00
38	Greg Maddux	3.00
39	Sammy Sosa	3.00

40 Mike Piazza 4.00
41 Nomar Garciaparra 3.00
42 Dante Bichette .50
43 Jeff Bagwell 2.00
44 Jim Thome 1.50

1999 Topps TEK

Pat Burrell

	NM/M
Complete Set (45):	30.00
Common Player:	.25
Common Player (10 Each Variation):	2.00
Gold Stars:	10X
Pack (4):	3.00
Wax Box (20):	45.00

1 Ben Grieve .25
2 Andres Galarraga .25
3 Travis Lee .35
4 Larry Walker .25
5 Ken Griffey Jr. 2.50
6 Sammy Sosa 2.00
7 Mark McGwire 3.00
8 Roberto Alomar .40
9 Wade Boggs 2.00
10 Troy Glaus .75
11 Craig Biggio .25
12 Kerry Wood .50
13 Vladimir Guerrero 1.00
14 Albert Belle .25
15 Mike Piazza 2.50
16 Chipper Jones 2.00
17 Randy Johnson 1.00
18 Adrian Beltre .45
19 Barry Bonds 4.00
20 Jim Thome .65
21 Greg Vaughn .25
22 Scott Rolen .65
23 Ivan Rodriguez .75
24 Derek Jeter 4.00
25 Cal Ripken Jr. 4.00
26 Mark Grace .25
27 Bernie Williams .25
28 Darin Erstad .75
29 Eric Chavez .35
30 Tom Glavine .75
31 Jeff Bagwell 1.00
32 Manny Ramirez 1.00
33 Tino Martinez .25
34 Todd Helton .75
35 Jason Kendall .25
36 Pat Burrell RC 2.50
37 Tony Gwynn 2.00
38 Nomar Garciaparra 2.00
39 Frank Thomas 1.00
40 Orlando Hernandez .25
41 Juan Gonzalez .50
42 Alex Rodriguez 3.00
43 Greg Maddux 2.00
44 Mo Vaughn .25
45 Roger Clemens 2.25

Version A Checklist Folder (Orange) .05
Version B Checklist Folder (Green) .05

Values quoted in this guide reflect the retail price of a card, the price a collector can expect to pay when buying a card from a dealer.

Gold

Travis Lee

	NM/M
Common Gold:	2.00
Gold Stars:	10X

(See 1999 Topps TEK for checklist, base card values.)

Fantastek Phenoms

Eric Chavez

	NM/M
Complete Set (10):	15.00
Common Player:	.75
Inserted 1:18	

F1 Eric Chavez 1.50
F2 Troy Glaus 4.00
F3 Pat Burrell 4.00
F4 Alex Gonzalez .75
F5 Carlos Lee 1.00
F6 Ruben Mateo .75
F7 Carlos Beltran 2.00
F8 Adrian Beltre 1.50
F9 Bruce Chen .75
F10 Ryan Anderson .75

Teknicians

Mark McGwire

	NM/M
Complete Set (10):	24.00
Common Player:	1.00
Inserted 1:18	

T1 Ken Griffey Jr. 3.00
T2 Mark McGwire 4.00
T3 Kerry Wood 1.00
T4 Brien Grieve 1.00
T5 Sammy Sosa 2.50
T6 Derek Jeter 6.00
T7 Alex Rodriguez 4.00
T8 Roger Clemens 2.50
T9 Nomar Garciaparra 2.50
T10 Vladimir Guerrero 1.50

2000 Topps

JEFF BAGWELL

	NM/M
Complete Set (478):	50.00
Complete Series I Set (239):	25.00
Complete Series II Set (239):	25.00
Common Player:	.10
MVP Stars:	20-40X
Yng Stars & RC's:	10-20X
Production 100 Sets	
5 Versions for 236-240, 475-479	
Pack (11):	1.00
Wax Box (36):	30.00

1 Mark McGwire 1.00
2 Tony Gwynn .75
3 Wade Boggs .75
4 Cal Ripken Jr. 1.50
5 Matt Williams .10
6 Jay Buhner .10
7 Not Issued
8 Jeff Conine .10
9 Todd Greene .10
10 Mike Lieberthal .10
11 Steve Avery .10
12 Bret Saberhagen .10
13 Magglio Ordonez .20
14 Brad Radke .10
15 Derek Jeter 1.50
16 Javy Lopez .10
17 Russ David .10
18 Armando Benitez .10
19 B.J. Surhoff .10
20 Darryl Kile .10
21 Mark Lewis .10
22 Mike Williams .10
23 Mark McLemore .10
24 Sterling Hitchcock .10
25 Darin Erstad .20
26 Ricky Gutierrez .10
27 John Jaha .10
28 Homer Bush .10
29 Darrin Fletcher .10
30 Mark Grace .10
31 Fred McGriff .10
32 Omar Daal .10
33 Eric Karros .10
34 Orlando Cabrera .15
35 J.T. Snow Jr. .10
36 Luis Castillo .10
37 Rey Ordonez .10
38 Bob Abreu .20
39 Warren Morris .10
40 Juan Gonzalez .20
41 Mike Lansing .10
42 Chili Davis .10
43 Dean Palmer .10
44 Hank Aaron 1.00
45 Jeff Bagwell .60
46 Jose Valentin .10
47 Shannon Stewart .10
48 Kent Bottenfield .10
49 Jeff Shaw .10
50 Sammy Sosa .75
51 Randy Johnson .60
52 Benny Agbayani .10
53 Dante Bichette .10
54 Pete Harnisch .10
55 Frank Thomas .60
56 Jorge Posada .10
57 Todd Walker .10
58 Juan Encarnacion .15
59 Mike Sweeney .10
60 Pedro Martinez .60
61 Lee Stevens .10
62 Brian Giles .10
63 Chad Ogea .10
64 Ivan Rodriguez .50
65 Roger Cedeno .10
66 David Justice .10
67 Steve Trachsel .10
68 Eli Marrero .10

69 Dave Nilsson .10
70 Ken Caminiti .10
71 Tim Raines .10
72 Brian Jordan .10
73 Jeff Blauser .10
74 Bernard Gilkey .10
75 John Flaherty .10
76 Brent Mayne .10
77 Jose Vidro .10
78 Jeff Fassero .10
79 Bruce Aven .10
80 John Olerud .10
81 Pokey Reese .10
82 Woody Williams .10
83 Ed Sprague .10
84 Joe Girardi .10
85 Barry Larkin .10
86 Mike Caruso .10
87 Bobby Higginson .10
88 Roberto Kelly .10
89 Edgar Martinez .10
90 Mark Kotsay .10
91 Paul Sorrento .10
92 Eric Young .10
93 Carlos Delgado .40
94 Troy Glaus .50
95 Ben Grieve .10
96 Jose Lima .10
97 Garret Anderson .10
98 Luis Gonzalez .10
99 Carl Pavano .10
100 Alex Rodriguez 1.25
101 Preston Wilson .10
102 Ron Gant .10
103 Harold Baines .10
104 Rickey Henderson .60
105 Gary Sheffield .40
106 Mickey Morandini .10
107 Jim Edmonds .10
108 Kris Benson .10
109 Adrian Beltre .20
110 Alex Fernandez .10
111 Dan Wilson .10
112 Mark Clark .10
113 Greg Vaughn .10
114 Neifi Perez .10
115 Paul O'Neill .10
116 Jermaine Dye .10
117 Todd Jones .10
118 Terry Steinbach .10
119 Greg Norton .10
120 Curt Schilling .25
121 Todd Zeile .10
122 Edgardo Alfonzo .10
123 Ryan McGuire .10
124 Stan Javier .10
125 John Smoltz .10
126 Bob Wickman .10
127 Richard Hidalgo .10
128 Chuck Finley .10
129 Billy Wagner .10
130 Todd Hundley .10
131 Dwight Gooden .10
132 Russ Ortiz .10
133 Mike Lowell .10
134 Reggie Sanders .10
135 John Valentin .10
136 Brad Ausmus .10
137 Chad Kreuter .10
138 David Cone .10
139 Brook Fordyce .10
140 Roberto Alomar .25
141 Charles Nagy .10
142 Brian Hunter .10
143 Mike Mussina .30
144 Robin Ventura .10
145 Kevin Brown .10
146 Pat Hentgen .10
147 Ryan Klesko .10
148 Derek Bell .10
149 Andy Sheets .10
150 Larry Walker .10
151 Scott Williamson .10
152 Jose Offerman .10
153 Doug Mientkiewicz .10
154 John Snyder RC .10
155 Sandy Alomar .10
156 Joe Nathan .10
157 Lance Johnson .10
158 Odalis Perez .10
159 Hideo Nomo .25
160 Steve Finley .10
161 Dave Martinez .10
162 Matt Walbeck .10
163 Bill Spiers .10
164 Fernando Tatis .10
165 Kenny Lofton .10
166 Paul Byrd .10
167 Aaron Sele .10
168 Eddie Taubensee .10
169 Reggie Jefferson .10
170 Roger Clemens .85
171 Francisco Cordova .10
172 Mike Bordick .10

#	Player	Price
173	Wally Joyner	.10
174	Marvin Benard	.10
175	Jason Kendall	.10
176	Mike Stanley	.10
177	Chad Allen	.10
178	Carlos Beltran	.25
179	Deivi Cruz	.10
180	Chipper Jones	.75
181	Vladimir Guerrero	.60
182	Dave Burba	.10
183	Tom Goodwin	.10
184	Brian Daubach	.10
185	Jay Bell	.10
186	Roy Halladay	.25
187	Miguel Tejada	.25
188	Armando Rios	.10
189	Fernando Vina	.10
190	Eric Davis	.10
191	Henry Rodriguez	.10
192	Joe McEwing	.10
193	Jeff Kent	.10
194	Mike Jackson	.10
195	Mike Morgan	.10
196	Jeff Montgomery	.10
197	Jeff Zimmerman	.10
198	Tony Fernandez	.10
199	Jason Giambi	.40
200	Jose Canseco	.40
201	Alex Gonzalez	.10
202	Jack Cust, Mike Colangelo, Dee Brown	.10
203	Felipe Lopez, Alfonso Soriano, Pablo Ozuna	.75
204	Erubiel Durazo, Pat Burrell, Nick Johnson	.25
205	John Sneed, Kip Wells, Matt Blank	.10
206	Josh Kalinowski, Michael Tejera, Chris Mears	.10
207	Roosevelt Brown, Corey Patterson, Lance Berkman	.25
208	Kit Pellow, Kevin Barker, Russ Branyan	.10
209	B.J. Garbe, Larry Bigbie **RC**	1.00
210	Eric Munson, Bobby Bradley **RC**	.25
211	Josh Girdley, Kyle Snyder	.10
212	Chance Caple, Jason Jennings	.25
213	Ryan Christiansen, Brett Myers **RC**	1.50
214	Jason Stumm, Rob Purvis **RC**	.25
215	David Walling, Mike Paradis	.10
216	Omar Ortiz, Jay Gehrke	.10
217	David Cone	.10
218	Jose Jimenez	.10
219	Chris Singleton	.10
220	Fernando Tatis	.10
221	Todd Helton	.20
222	Kevin Millwood	.15
223	Todd Pratt	.10
224	Orlando Hernandez	.20
225	(Post-Season Highlights)	.10
226	(Post-Season Highlights)	.10
227	Bernie Williams	.25
228	Mariano Rivera	.20
229	Tony Gwynn	.50
230	Wade Boggs	.25
231	Tim Raines	.10
232	Mark McGwire	2.00
233	Rickey Henderson	.25
234	Rickey Henderson	.25
235	Roger Clemens	1.50
236	Mark McGwire	2.00
237	Hank Aaron	2.00
238	Cal Ripken Jr.	3.00
239	Wade Boggs	.75
240	Tony Gwynn	1.00
	Series 1 checklist (1-201)	.05
	Series 1 checklist (202-240, inserts)	.05
241	Tom Glavine	.25
242	David Wells	.10
243	Kevin Appier	.10
244	Troy Percival	.10
245	Ray Lankford	.10
246	Marquis Grissom	.10
247	Randy Winn	.10
248	Miguel Batista	.10
249	Darren Dreifort	.10
250	Barry Bonds	1.50
251	Harold Baines	.10
252	Cliff Floyd	.10
253	Freddy Garcia	.10
254	Kenny Rogers	.10
255	Ben Davis	.10
256	Charles Johnson	.10
257	John Burkett	.10
258	Deivi Relaford	.10
259	Al Martin	.10
260	Andy Pettitte	.20
261	Carlos Lee	.10
262	Matt Lawton	.10
263	Andy Fox	.10
264	Chan Ho Park	.10
265	Billy Koch	.10
266	Dave Roberts	.10
267	Carl Everett	.10
268	Orel Hershiser	.10
269	Trot Nixon	.10
270	Rusty Greer	.10
271	Will Clark	.10
272	Quilvio Veras	.10
273	Rico Brogna	.10
274	Devon White	.10
275	Tim Hudson	.25
276	Mike Hampton	.10
277	Miguel Cairo	.10
278	Darren Oliver	.10
279	Jeff Cirillo	.10
280	Al Leiter	.10
281	Brant Brown	.10
282	Carlos Febles	.10
283	Pedro Astacio	.10
284	Juan Guzman	.10
285	Orlando Hernandez	.20
286	Paul Konerko	.15
287	Tony Clark	.10
288	Aaron Boone	.10
289	Ismael Valdes	.10
290	Moises Alou	.10
291	Kevin Tapani	.10
292	John Franco	.10
293	Todd Zeile	.10
294	Jason Schmidt	.15
295	Johnny Damon	.25
296	Scott Brosius	.10
297	Travis Fryman	.10
298	Jose Vizcaino	.10
299	Eric Chavez	.20
300	Mike Piazza	1.00
301	Matt Clement	.10
302	Cristian Guzman	.10
303	Darryl Strawberry	.10
304	Jeff Abbott	.10
305	Brett Tomko	.10
306	Mike Lansing	.10
307	Eric Owens	.10
308	Livan Hernandez	.10
309	Rondell White	.10
310	Todd Stottlemyre	.10
311	Chris Carpenter	.10
312	Ken Hill	.10
313	Mark Loretta	.10
314	John Rocker	.10
315	Richie Sexson	.25
316	Ruben Mateo	.10
317	Joe Randa	.10
318	Mike Sirotka	.10
319	Jose Rosado	.10
320	Matt Mantei	.10
321	Kevin Millwood	.10
322	Gary DiSarcina	.10
323	Dustin Hermanson	.10
324	Mike Stanton	.10
325	Kirk Rueter	.10
326	Damian Miller	.10
327	Doug Glanville	.10
328	Scott Rolen	.50
329	Ray Durham	.10
330	Butch Huskey	.10
331	Mariano Rivera	.20
332	Darren Lewis	.10
333	Ramiro Mendoza	.10
334	Mark Grudzielanek	.10
335	Mike Cameron	.10
336	Kelvim Escobar	.10
337	Bret Boone	.10
338	Mo Vaughn	.10
339	Craig Biggio	.10
340	Michael Barrett	.10
341	Marlon Anderson	.10
342	Bobby Jones	.10
343	John Halama	.10
344	Todd Ritchie	.10
345	Chuck Knoblauch	.10
346	Rick Reed	.10
347	Kelly Stinnett	.10
348	Tim Salmon	.10
349	A.J. Hinch	.10
350	Jose Cruz Jr.	.10
351	Roberto Hernandez	.10
352	Edgar Renteria	.10
353	Jose Hernandez	.10
354	Brad Fullmer	.10
355	Trevor Hoffman	.10
356	Troy O'Leary	.10
357	Justin Thompson	.10
358	Kevin Young	.10
359	Hideki Irabu	.10
360	Jim Thome	.50
361	Todd Dunwoody	.10
362	Octavio Dotel	.10
363	Omar Vizquel	.10
364	Raul Mondesi	.10
365	Shane Reynolds	.10
366	Bartolo Colon	.10
367	Chris Widger	.10
368	Gabe Kapler	.10
369	Bill Simas	.10
370	Tino Martinez	.10
371	John Thomson	.10
372	Delino DeShields	.10
373	Carlos Perez	.10
374	Eddie Perez	.10
375	Jeromy Burnitz	.10
376	Jimmy Haynes	.10
377	Travis Lee	.10
378	Darryl Hamilton	.10
379	Jamie Moyer	.10
380	Alex Gonzalez	.10
381	John Wetteland	.10
382	Vinny Castilla	.10
383	Jeff Suppan	.10
384	Chad Curtis	.10
385	Robb Nen	.10
386	Wilson Alvarez	.10
387	Andres Galarraga	.10
388	Mike Remlinger	.10
389	Geoff Jenkins	.10
390	Matt Stairs	.10
391	Bill Mueller	.10
392	Mike Lowell	.10
393	Andy Ashby	.10
394	Ruben Rivera	.10
395	Todd Helton	.50
396	Bernie Williams	.10
397	Royce Clayton	.10
398	Manny Ramirez	.60
399	Kerry Wood	.25
400	Ken Griffey Jr.	.75
401	Enrique Wilson	.10
402	Joey Hamilton	.10
403	Shawn Estes	.10
404	Ugueth Urbina	.10
405	Albert Belle	.10
406	Rick Helling	.10
407	Steve Parris	.10
408	Eric Milton	.10
409	Dave Mlicki	.10
410	Shawn Green	.25
411	Jaret Wright	.10
412	Tony Womack	.10
413	Vernon Wells	.15
414	Ron Belliard	.10
415	Ellis Burks	.10
416	Scott Erickson	.10
417	Rafael Palmeiro	.35
418	Damion Easley	.10
419	Jamey Wright	.10
420	Corey Koskie	.10
421	Bobby Howry	.10
422	Ricky Ledee	.10
423	Dmitri Young	.10
424	Sidney Ponson	.10
425	Greg Maddux	.75
426	Jose Guillen	.10
427	Jon Lieber	.10
428	Andy Benes	.10
429	Randy Velarde	.10
430	Sean Casey	.20
431	Torii Hunter	.20
432	Ryan Rupe	.10
433	David Segui	.10
434	Rich Aurilia	.10
435	Nomar Garciaparra	.75
436	Denny Neagle	.10
437	Ron Coomer	.10
438	Chris Singleton	.10
439	Tony Batista	.10
440	Andruw Jones	.60
441	Adam Piatt, Aubrey Huff, Sean Burroughs	.20
442	Rafael Furcal, Jason Dallero, Travis Dawkins	.20
443	Wilton Veras, Joe Crede, Mike Lamb **RC**	.10
444	Julio Zuleta, Dernell Stenson, Jorge Toca	.20
445	Tim Raines Jr., Gary Mathews Jr., Garry Maddox Jr. **RC**	.20
446	Matt Riley, Mark Mulder, C.C. Sabathia	.10
447	Scott Downs, Chris George, Matt Belisle	.10
448	Doug Mirabelli, Ben Petrick, Jayson Werth	.10
449	Josh Hamilton, Corey Myers **RC**	.25
450	Ben Christensen, Brett Myers	.20
451	Barry Zito, Ben Sheets **RC**	2.00
452	Ty Howington, Kurt Ainsworth **RC**	.25
453	Rick Asadoorian, Vince Faison **RC**	.10
454	Keith Reed, Jeff Heaverlo **RC**	.20
455	Mike MacDougal, Jay Gehrke	.25
456	Mark McGwire	.75
457	Cal Ripken Jr.	1.00
458	Wade Boggs	.25
459	Tony Gwynn	.50
460	Jesse Orosco	.10
461	Nomar Garciaparra, Larry Walker	.50
462	Mark McGwire, Ken Griffey Jr.	.50
463	Mark McGwire, Manny Ramirez	.50
464	Randy Johnson, Pedro Martinez	.25
465	Randy Johnson, Pedro Martinez	.25
466	Luis Gonzalez, Derek Jeter	.50
467	Manny Ramirez, Larry Walker	.25
468	Tony Gwynn	.75
469	Mark McGwire	2.00
470	Frank Thomas	.50
471	Harold Baines	.10
472	Roger Clemens	.75
473	John Franco	.10
474	John Franco	.10
475	Ken Griffey Jr.	1.50
476	Barry Bonds	2.00
477	Sammy Sosa	1.25
478	Derek Jeter	2.50
479	Alex Rodriguez	2.00

Limited Edition

NM/M

Complete Factory Set (619):	100.00
Common Player:	.50
Stars/Rookies:	1-2X
Inserts:	1X

(See 2000 Topps and inserts for checklists and base card values.)

All-Star Rookie Team

NM/M

Complete Set (10):	10.00
Common Player:	.25
Inserted 1:36	
"Limited Edition" 4,000 Sets:	1X

#	Player	Price
1	Mark McGwire	3.00
2	Chuck Knoblauch	.25
3	Chipper Jones	2.00
4	Cal Ripken Jr.	4.00
5	Manny Ramirez	1.00
6	Jose Canseco	.75
7	Ken Griffey Jr.	2.00
8	Mike Piazza	2.00
9	Dwight Gooden	.25
10	Billy Wagner	.25

All-Topps Team

CRAIG BIGGIO
All-Topps NL Team

		NM/M
Complete Set (20):		15.00
Common Player:		.25
Inserted 1:12		
"Limited Edition" 4,000 Sets:		1X
1	Greg Maddux	1.50
2	Mike Piazza	1.50
3	Mark McGwire	2.50
4	Craig Biggio	.40
5	Chipper Jones	1.50
6	Barry Larkin	.40
7	Barry Bonds	2.50
8	Andruw Jones	.75
9	Sammy Sosa	1.50
10	Larry Walker	.40
11	Pedro Martinez	1.00
12	Ivan Rodriguez	.50
13	Rafael Palmeiro	.50
14	Roberto Alomar	.50
15	Cal Ripken Jr.	3.00
16	Derek Jeter	3.00
17	Albert Belle	.25
18	Ken Griffey Jr.	1.50
19	Manny Ramirez	.75
20	Jose Canseco	.50

Autographs

VINNY CASTILLA

		NM/M
Common Player:		8.00
Group A 1:7,589		
Group B 1:4,553		
Group C 1:518		
Group D 1:911		
Group E 1:1,138		
1	Alex Rodriguez/A	100.00
2	Tony Gwynn/A	50.00
3	Vinny Castilla/B	15.00
4	Sean Casey/B	15.00
5	Shawn Green/C	25.00
6	Rey Ordonez/C	8.00
7	Matt Lawton/C	15.00
8	Tony Womack/C	8.00
9	Gabe Kapler/D	10.00
10	Pat Burrell/D	20.00
11	Preston Wilson/D	15.00
12	Troy Glaus/D	30.00
13	Carlos Beltran/D	40.00
14	Josh Girdley/E	8.00
15	B.J. Garbe/E	8.00
16	Alex Rodriguez/B	125.00
17	Cal Ripken Jr./A	150.00
18	Ivan Rodriguez/B	40.00
19	Rafael Palmeiro/B	40.00
20	Vladimir Guerrero/E	45.00
21	Raul Mondesi/C	15.00
22	Scott Rolen/C	40.00
23	Billy Wagner/C	10.00
24	Fernando Tatis/C	8.00
25	Ruben Mateo/D	8.00

26	Carlos Febles/D	8.00
27	Mike Sweeney/E	10.00
28	Alex Gonzalez/D	10.00
29	Miguel Tejada/D	40.00
30	Josh Hamilton/E	30.00

Century Best

20th century's best
1944
1954
1970
1937
1983
henderson
1944
PHILS

		NM/M
Common Player:		2.00
Ser. 1 1:869 H		
Ser. 2 1:362		
CB1	Tony Gwynn/339	8.00
CB2	Wade Boggs/578	4.00
CB3	Lance Johnson/117	2.00
CB4	Mark McGwire/522	20.00
CB5	Rickey Henderson/ 1,334	4.00
CB6	Rickey Henderson/ 2,103	4.00
CB7	Roger Clemens/247	12.00
CB8	Tony Gwynn/3,067	6.00
CB9	Mark McGwire/587	20.00
CB10	Frank Thomas/440	6.00
CB11	Harold Baines/ 1,583	2.00
CB12	Roger Clemens/ 3,316	8.00
CB13	John Franco/264	2.00
CB14	John Franco/416	2.00

Combos

DIAMOND
Strikeout Kings
RANDY JOHNSON • PEDRO MARTINEZ

		NM/M
Complete Set (10):		15.00
Common Card:		1.00
Inserted 1:18		
"Limited Edition" 4,000 Sets:		1X
1	Roberto Alomar, Manny Ramirez, Kenny Lofton, Jim Thome	1.00
2	Tom Glavine, Greg Maddux, John Smoltz	1.50
3	Derek Jeter, Bernie Williams, Tino Martinez	3.00
4	Ivan Rodriguez, Mike Piazza	1.50
5	Nomar Garciaparra, Alex Rodriguez, Derek Jeter	3.00
6	Sammy Sosa, Mark McGwire	3.00
7	Pedro Martinez, Randy Johnson	1.00
8	Barry Bonds, Ken Griffey Jr.	2.50
9	Chipper Jones, Ivan Rodriguez	1.50

10	Cal Ripken Jr., Tony Gwynn, Wade Boggs	3.00

Hands of Gold

Hands of Gold
Omar Vizquel

		NM/M
Complete Set (7):		5.00
Common Player:		.25
Inserted 1:18		
"Limited Edition" 4,000 Sets:		1X
1	Barry Bonds	2.50
2	Ivan Rodriguez	.75
3	Ken Griffey Jr.	1.50
4	Roberto Alomar	.75
5	Tony Gwynn	1.00
6	Omar Vizquel	.25
7	Greg Maddux	1.50

Hank Aaron Reprints

BRAVES
HANK AARON outfield

		NM/M
Complete Set (23):		60.00
Common Aaron:		3.00
Inserted 1:18		
Autographed:		300.00
"Limited Edition" 4,000 Sets:		1X

Hank Aaron Chrome Reprints

HANK AARON • OUTFIELD
Henry Aaron
BRAVES

		NM/M
Complete Set (23):		90.00
Common Aaron:		5.00
Inserted 1:72		
Refractors:		3X
Inserted 1:288		

Mark McGwire 1985 Rookie Reprint

USA 1984 UNITED STATES BASEBALL TEAM
USA
MARK McGWIRE FIRST BASE

		NM/M
Complete Set (1):		6.00
	Mark McGwire	6.00

Own the Game

TITANS
OWN THE GAME
SCOTT WILLIAMSON

		NM/M
Complete Set (30):		15.00
Common Player:		.15
Inserted 1:12		
"Limited Edition" 4,000 Sets:		1X
1	Derek Jeter	2.00
2	B.J. Surhoff	.15
3	Luis Gonzalez	.25
4	Manny Ramirez	.50
5	Rafael Palmeiro	.40
6	Mark McGwire	1.50
7	Mark McGwire	1.50
8	Sammy Sosa	1.00
9	Ken Griffey Jr.	1.00
10	Larry Walker	.25
11	Nomar Garciaparra	1.50
12	Derek Jeter	2.00
13	Larry Walker	.25
14	Mark McGwire	1.50
15	Manny Ramirez	.50
16	Pedro Martinez	.75
17	Randy Johnson	.75
18	Kevin Millwood	.25
19	Pedro Martinez	.75
20	Randy Johnson	.75
21	Kevin Brown	.25
22	Chipper Jones	1.00
23	Ivan Rodriguez	.50
24	Mariano Rivera	.25
25	Scott Williamson	.15
26	Carlos Beltran	.25
27	Randy Johnson	.75
28	Pedro Martinez	.75
29	Sammy Sosa	1.00
30	Manny Ramirez	.50

Perennial All-Stars

		NM/M
Complete Set (10):		10.00
Common Player:		.50
Inserted 1:18		
"Limited Edition" 4,000 Sets:		1X
1	Ken Griffey Jr.	1.00
2	Derek Jeter	2.00
3	Sammy Sosa	1.00
4	Cal Ripken Jr.	2.00
5	Mike Piazza	1.00
6	Nomar Garciaparra	1.50
7	Jeff Bagwell	.50
8	Barry Bonds	1.50

9	Alex Rodriguez	1.50
10	Mark McGwire	1.50

Power Players

		NM/M
Complete Set (20):		10.00
Common Player:		.25
Inserted 1:8		
"Limited Edition" 4,000 Sets:		1X
1	Juan Gonzalez	.50
2	Ken Griffey Jr.	1.00
3	Mark McGwire	1.50
4	Nomar Garciaparra	1.50
5	Barry Bonds	1.50
6	Mo Vaughn	.25
7	Larry Walker	.25
8	Alex Rodriguez	1.50
9	Jose Canseco	.25
10	Jeff Bagwell	.50
11	Manny Ramirez	.50
12	Albert Belle	.25
13	Frank Thomas	.50
14	Mike Piazza	1.00
15	Chipper Jones	1.00
16	Sammy Sosa	1.00
17	Vladimir Guerrero	.50
18	Scott Rolen	.50
19	Raul Mondesi	.25
20	Derek Jeter	2.00

Stadium Relics

		NM/M
Common Player:		40.00
Inserted 1:165 HTA		
1	Don Mattingly	150.00
2	Carl Yastrzemski	100.00
3	Ernie Banks	75.00
4	Johnny Bench	75.00
5	Willie Mays	150.00
6	Mike Schmidt	100.00
7	Lou Brock	50.00
8	Al Kaline	75.00
9	Paul Molitor	60.00
10	Eddie Mathews	75.00

21st Century Topps

	NM/M
Complete Set (10):	5.00

Common Player:		.25
Inserted 1:18		
"Limited Edition" 4,000 Sets:		1X
1	Ben Grieve	.25
2	Alex Gonzalez	.25
3	Derek Jeter	2.00
4	Sean Casey	.25
5	Nomar Garciaparra	1.50
6	Alex Rodriguez	1.50
7	Scott Rolen	.50
8	Andruw Jones	.50
9	Vladimir Guerrero	.50
10	Todd Helton	.50

2000 Topps Traded and Rookies

		NM/M
Complete Set (135):		25.00
Common Player:		.10
Unopened Set (136):		50.00
1	Mike MacDougal RC	.20
2	Andy Tracy RC	.20
3	Brandon Phillips RC	.75
4	Brandon Inge RC	.75
5	Robbie Morrison RC	.25
6	Josh Pressley RC	.20
7	Todd Moser RC	.25
8	Rob Purvis RC	.25
9	Chance Caple RC	.25
10	Ben Sheets RC	.75
11	Russ Jacobson RC	.10
12	Brian Cole RC	.10
13	Brad Baker RC	.25
14	Alex Cintron RC	.40
15	Lyle Overbay RC	1.00
16	Mike Edwards RC	.20
17	Sean McGowan RC	.25
18	Jose Molina RC	.25
19	Marcos Castillo RC	.20
20	Josue Espada RC	.20
21	Alex Gordon RC	.10
22	Rob Pugmire RC	.10
23	Jason Stumm RC	.25
24	Ty Howington RC	.40
25	Brett Myers RC	.50
26	Maicer Izturis RC	.10
27	John McDonald RC	.10
28	Wilfredo Rodriguez RC	.25
29	Carlos Zambrano RC	3.00
30	Alejandro Diaz RC	.20
31	Geraldo Guzman RC	.20
32	J.R. House RC	.50
33	Elvin Nina RC	.10
34	Juan Pierre RC	.50
35	Ben Johnson RC	.50
36	Jeff Bailey RC	.20
37	Miguel Olivo RC	.10
38	Francisco Rodriguez RC	2.00
39	Tony Pena Jr. RC	.25
40	Miguel Cabrera RC	15.00
41	Asdrubal Oropeza RC	.10
42	Junior Zamora RC	.10
43	Jovanny Cedeno RC	.25
44	John Sneed RC	.10
45	Josh Kalinowski RC	.10
46	Mike Young RC	3.00
47	Rico Washington RC	.10
48	Chad Durbin RC	.40
49	Junior Brignac RC	.25
50	Carlos Hernandez RC	.40
51	Cesar Izturis RC	.50
52	Oscar Salazar RC	.25
53	Pat Strange RC	.25
54	Rick Asadoorian RC	.15
55	Keith Reed RC	.25
56	Leo Estrella RC	.10
57	Wascar Serrano RC	.10
58	Richard Gomez RC	.25
59	Ramon Santiago RC	.25
60	Jovanny Sosa RC	.25
61	Aaron Rowand RC	.50
62	Junior Guerrero RC	.25
63	Luis Terrero RC	.25
64	Brian Sanches RC	.10
65	Scott Sobkowiak RC	.25
66	Gary Majewski RC	.10
67	Barry Zito	1.00
68	Ryan Christianson RC	.40
69	Cristian Guerrero RC	.40
70	Tomas de la Rosa RC	.10
71	Andrew Beinbrink RC	.25
72	Ryan Knox RC	.10
73	Alex Graman RC	.25
74	Juan Guzman RC	.10
75	Ruben Salazar RC	.40
76	Luis Matos RC	.40
77	Tony Mota RC	.10
78	Doug Davis RC	.50
79	Ben Christensen RC	.25
80	Mike Lamb RC	.10
81	Adrian Gonzalez RC	1.50
82	Mike Stodolka RC	.25
83	Adam Johnson RC	.25
84	Matt Wheatland RC	.25
85	Corey Smith RC	.50
86	Rocco Baldelli RC	1.50
87	Keith Bucktrot RC	.25
88	Adam Wainwright RC	1.50
89	Scott Thorman RC	1.50
90	Tripper Johnson RC	.50
91	Jim Edmonds	.25
92	Masato Yoshii	.10
93	Adam Kennedy	.10
94	Darryl Kile	.10
95	Mark McLemore	.10
96	Ricky Gutierrez	.10
97	Juan Gonzalez	.40
98	Melvin Mora	.10
99	Dante Bichette	.10
100	Lee Stevens	.10
101	Roger Cedeno	.10
102	John Olerud	.25
103	Eric Young	.10
104	Mickey Morandini	.10
105	Travis Lee	.10
106	Greg Vaughn	.10
107	Todd Zeile	.10
108	Chuck Finley	.10
109	Ismael Valdes	.10
110	Ron Henika	.10
111	Pat Hentgen	.10
112	Ryan Klesko	.10
113	Derek Bell	.10
114	Hideo Nomo	.40
115	Aaron Sele	.10
116	Fernando Vina	.10
117	Wally Joyner	.10
118	Brian Hunter	.10
119	Joe Girardi	.10
120	Omar Daal	.10
121	Brook Fordyce	.10
122	Jose Valentin	.10
123	Curt Schilling	.40
124	B.J. Surhoff	.10
125	Henry Rodriguez	.10
126	Mike Bordick	.10
127	David Justice	.25
128	Charles Johnson	.10
129	Will Clark	.25
130	Dwight Gooden	.10
131	David Segui	.10
132	Denny Neagle	.10
133	Andy Ashby	.10
134	Bruce Chen	.10
135	Jason Bere	.10

Autographs

		NM/M
Common Player:		4.00
Inserted 1:Set		
1	Mike MacDougal	8.00
2	Andy Tracy	8.00
3	Brandon Phillips	50.00

4	Brandon Inge	25.00
5	Robbie Morrison	4.00
6	Josh Pressley	4.00
7	Todd Moser	4.00
8	Rob Purvis	4.00
9	Chance Caple	4.00
10	Ben Sheets	40.00
11	Russ Jacobson	4.00
12	Brian Cole	4.00
13	Brad Baker	4.00
14	Alex Cintron	10.00
15	Lyle Overbay	30.00
16	Mike Edwards	4.00
17	Sean McGowan	4.00
18	Jose Molina	4.00
19	Marcos Castillo	4.00
20	Josue Espada	4.00
21	Alex Gordon	4.00
22	Rob Pugmire	4.00
23	Jason Stumm	4.00
24	Ty Howington	8.00
25	Brett Myers	25.00
26	Maicer Izturis	8.00
27	John McDonald	4.00
28	Wilfredo Rodriguez	4.00
29	Carlos Zambrano	140.00
30	Alejandro Diaz	4.00
31	Geraldo Guzman	8.00
32	J.R. House	8.00
33	Elvin Nina	4.00
34	Juan Pierre	25.00
35	Ben Johnson	10.00
36	Jeff Bailey	4.00
37	Miguel Olivo	4.00
38	Francisco Rodriguez	50.00
39	Tony Pena Jr.	4.00
40	Miguel Cabrera	500.00
41	Asdrubal Oropeza	4.00
42	Junior Zamora	4.00
43	Jovanny Cedeno	4.00
44	John Sneed	4.00
45	Josh Kalinowski	8.00
46	Mike Young	100.00
47	Rico Washington	4.00
48	Chad Durbin	4.00
49	Junior Brignac	4.00
50	Carlos Hernandez	8.00
51	Cesar Izturis	10.00
52	Oscar Salazar	4.00
53	Pat Strange	4.00
54	Rick Asadoorian	4.00
55	Keith Reed	4.00
56	Leo Estrella	4.00
57	Wascar Serrano	4.00
58	Richard Gomez	4.00
59	Ramon Santiago	4.00
60	Jovanny Sosa	4.00
61	Aaron Rowand	30.00
62	Junior Guerrero	4.00
63	Luis Terrero	10.00
64	Brian Sanches	4.00
65	Scott Sobkowiak	8.00
66	Gary Majewski	8.00
67	Barry Zito	30.00
68	Ryan Christianson	8.00
69	Cristian Guerrero	8.00
70	Tomas de la Rosa	4.00
71	Andrew Beinbrink	4.00
72	Ryan Knox	4.00
73	Alex Graman	4.00
74	Juan Guzman	4.00
75	Ruben Salazar	4.00
76	Luis Matos	10.00
77	Tony Mota	4.00
78	Doug Davis	15.00
79	Ben Christensen	4.00
80	Mike Lamb	10.00

2000 Topps Chrome

	NM/M
Complete Set (478):	100.00
Complete Series I Set (239):	50.00

JOSE CANSECO

Complete Series II Set		
(239):		50.00
Common Player:		.25
Pack (4):		1.50
Wax Box (24):		30.00
1	Mark McGwire	3.00
2	Tony Gwynn	1.50
3	Wade Boggs	.75
4	Cal Ripken Jr.	4.00
5	Matt Williams	.40
6	Jay Buhner	.40
7	Not Issued	
8	Jeff Conine	.25
9	Todd Greene	.25
10	Mike Lieberthal	.25
11	Steve Avery	.25
12	Bret Saberhagen	.25
13	Magglio Ordonez	.50
14	Brad Radke	.25
15	Derek Jeter	4.00
16	Javy Lopez	.50
17	Russ David	.25
18	Armando Benitez	.25
19	B.J. Surhoff	.25
20	Darryl Kile	.25
21	Mark Lewis	.25
22	Mike Williams	.25
23	Mark McLemore	.25
24	Sterling Hitchcock	.25
25	Darin Erstad	.50
26	Ricky Gutierrez	.25
27	John Jaha	.25
28	Homer Bush	.25
29	Darrin Fletcher	.25
30	Mark Grace	.75
31	Fred McGriff	.25
32	Omar Daal	.25
33	Eric Karros	.40
34	Orlando Cabrera	.40
35	J.T. Snow Jr.	.25
36	Luis Castillo	.25
37	Rey Ordonez	.25
38	Bob Abreu	.40
39	Warren Morris	.25
40	Juan Gonzalez	1.00
41	Mike Lansing	.25
42	Chili Davis	.25
43	Dean Palmer	.25
44	Hank Aaron	3.00
45	Jeff Bagwell	1.00
46	Jose Valentin	.25
47	Shannon Stewart	.25
48	Kent Bottenfield	.25
49	Jeff Shaw	.25
50	Sammy Sosa	2.00
51	Randy Johnson	1.50
52	Benny Agbayani	.25
53	Dante Bichette	.25
54	Pete Harnisch	.25
55	Frank Thomas	1.00
56	Jorge Posada	.75
57	Todd Walker	.25
58	Juan Encarnacion	.40
59	Mike Sweeney	.25
60	Pedro Martinez	1.50
61	Lee Stevens	.25
62	Brian Giles	.50
63	Chad Ogea	.25
64	Ivan Rodriguez	1.00
65	Roger Cedeno	.25
66	David Justice	.50
67	Steve Trachsel	.25
68	Eli Marrero	.25
69	Dave Nilsson	.25
70	Ken Caminiti	.25
71	Tim Raines	.25
72	Brian Jordan	.25
73	Jeff Blauser	.25
74	Bernard Gilkey	.25
75	John Flaherty	.25
76	Brent Mayne	.25
77	Jose Vidro	.25
78	Jeff Fassero	.25

79	Bruce Aven	.25
80	John Olerud	.50
81	Juan Guzman	.25
82	Woody Williams	.25
83	Ed Sprague	.25
84	Joe Girardi	.25
85	Barry Larkin	.50
86	Mike Caruso	.25
87	Bobby Higginson	.25
88	Roberto Kelly	.25
89	Edgar Martinez	.40
90	Mark Kotsay	.25
91	Paul Sorrento	.25
92	Eric Young	.25
93	Carlos Delgado	1.00
94	Troy Glaus	1.00
95	Ben Grieve	.25
96	Jose Lima	.25
97	Garret Anderson	.25
98	Luis Gonzalez	.50
99	Carl Pavano	.25
100	Alex Rodriguez	3.00
101	Preston Wilson	.40
102	Ron Gant	.40
103	Harold Baines	.25
104	Rickey Henderson	.50
105	Gary Sheffield	.75
106	Mickey Morandini	.25
107	Jim Edmonds	.50
108	Kris Benson	.25
109	Adrian Beltre	.25
110	Alex Fernandez	.25
111	Dan Wilson	.25
112	Mark Clark	.25
113	Greg Vaughn	.25
114	Neifi Perez	.25
115	Paul O'Neill	.50
116	Jermaine Dye	.25
117	Todd Jones	.25
118	Terry Steinbach	.25
119	Greg Norton	.25
120	Curt Schilling	.75
121	Todd Zeile	.25
122	Edgardo Alfonzo	.25
123	Ryan McGuire	.25
124	Stan Javier	.25
125	John Smoltz	.40
126	Bob Wickman	.25
127	Richard Hidalgo	.25
128	Chuck Finley	.25
129	Billy Wagner	.25
130	Todd Hundley	.25
131	Dwight Gooden	.40
132	Russ Ortiz	.25
133	Mike Lowell	.25
134	Reggie Sanders	.25
135	John Valentin	.25
136	Brad Ausmus	.25
137	Chad Kreuter	.25
138	David Cone	.40
139	Brook Fordyce	.25
140	Roberto Alomar	.75
141	Charles Nagy	.25
142	Brian Hunter	.25
143	Mike Mussina	.75
144	Robin Ventura	.40
145	Kevin Brown	.40
146	Pat Hentgen	.25
147	Ryan Klesko	.40
148	Derek Bell	.25
149	Andy Sheets	.25
150	Larry Walker	.50
151	Scott Williamson	.25
152	Jose Offerman	.25
153	Doug Mientkiewicz	.25
154	John Snyder RC	.40
155	Sandy Alomar	.25
156	Joe Nathan	.25
157	Lance Johnson	.25
158	Odalis Perez	.25
159	Hideo Nomo	.75
160	Steve Finley	.25
161	Dave Martinez	.25
162	Matt Walbeck	.25
163	Bill Spiers	.25
164	Fernando Tatis	.25
165	Kenny Lofton	.40
166	Paul Byrd	.25
167	Aaron Sele	.25
168	Eddie Taubensee	.25
169	Reggie Jefferson	.25
170	Roger Clemens	2.50
171	Francisco Cordova	.25
172	Mike Bordick	.25
173	Wally Joyner	.25
174	Marvin Benard	.25
175	Jason Kendall	.40
176	Mike Stanley	.25
177	Chad Allen	.25
178	Carlos Beltran	.50
179	Deivi Cruz	.25
180	Chipper Jones	2.00
181	Vladimir Guerrero	1.50
182	Dave Burba	.25

183	Tom Goodwin	.25
184	Brian Daubach	.25
185	Jay Bell	.25
186	Roy Halladay	.50
187	Miguel Tejada	.50
188	Armando Rios	.25
189	Fernando Vina	.25
190	Eric Davis	.40
191	Henry Rodriguez	.25
192	Joe McEwing	.25
193	Jeff Kent	.50
194	Mike Jackson	.25
195	Mike Morgan	.25
196	Jeff Montgomery	.25
197	Jeff Zimmerman	.25
198	Tony Fernandez	.25
199	Jason Giambi	1.00
200	Jose Canseco	.75
201	Alex Gonzalez	.25
202	Jack Cust, Mike Colangelo, Dee Brown	.50
203	Felipe Lopez, Alfonso Soriano, Pablo Ozuna	3.00
204	Erubiel Durazo, Pat Burrell, Nick Johnson	.75
205	John Sneed, Kip Wells, Matt Blank	.50
206	Josh Kalinowski, Michael Tejera, Chris Mears	.50
207	Roosevelt Brown, Corey Patterson, Lance Berkman	.50
208	Kit Pellow, Kevin Barker, Russ Branyan	.40
209	B.J. Garbe, Larry Bigbie RC	3.00
210	Eric Munson, Bobby Bradley RC	.75
211	Josh Girdley, Kyle Snyder	.50
212	Chance Caple, Jason Jennings	.50
213	Ryan Christiansen, Brett Myers RC	6.00
214	Jason Stumm, Rob Purvis RC	.75
215	David Walling, Mike Paradis	.40
216	Omar Ortiz, Jay Gehrke	.40
217	David Cone	.40
218	Jose Jimenez	.25
219	Chris Singleton	.25
220	Fernando Tatis	.25
221	Todd Helton	1.00
222	Kevin Millwood	.50
223	Todd Pratt	.25
224	Orlando Hernandez	.25
225	Post-Season Highlights	.25
226	Post-Season Highlights	.25
227	Bernie Williams	.75
228	Mariano Rivera	.25
229	Tony Gwynn	1.50
230	Wade Boggs	.50
231	Tim Raines	.25
232	Mark McGwire	3.00
233	Rickey Henderson	.75
234	Rickey Henderson	.75
235	Roger Clemens	2.00
236	Mark McGwire	5.00
237	Hank Aaron	5.00
238	Cal Ripken Jr.	6.00
239	Wade Boggs	1.00
240	Tony Gwynn	3.00
	Series 1 checklist (1-201)	.05
	Series 1 checklist (202-240, inserts)	.05
241	Tom Glavine	.50
242	David Wells	.25
243	Kevin Appier	.25
244	Troy Percival	.25
245	Ray Lankford	.25
246	Marquis Grissom	.25
247	Randy Winn	.25
248	Miguel Batista	.25
249	Darren Dreifort	.25
250	Barry Bonds	3.00
251	Harold Baines	.25
252	Cliff Floyd	.25
253	Freddy Garcia	.40
254	Kenny Rogers	.25
255	Ben Davis	.25
256	Charles Johnson	.25
257	John Burkett	.25
258	Desi Relaford	.25
259	Al Martin	.25
260	Andy Pettitte	.50
261	Carlos Lee	.25
262	Matt Lawton	.25
263	Andy Fox	.25
264	Chan Ho Park	.25
265	Billy Koch	.25
266	Dave Roberts	.25
267	Carl Everett	.25

268	Orel Hershiser	.25
269	Trot Nixon	.25
270	Rusty Greer	.25
271	Will Clark	.75
272	Quilvio Veras	.25
273	Rico Brogna	.25
274	Devon White	.25
275	Tim Hudson	.50
276	Mike Hampton	.25
277	Miguel Cairo	.25
278	Darren Oliver	.25
279	Jeff Cirillo	.25
280	Al Leiter	.25
281	Brant Brown	.25
282	Carlos Febles	.25
283	Pedro Astacio	.25
284	Juan Guzman	.25
285	Orlando Hernandez	.25
286	Paul Konerko	.25
287	Tony Clark	.25
288	Aaron Boone	.50
289	Ismael Valdes	.25
290	Moises Alou	.50
291	Kevin Tapani	.25
292	John Franco	.25
293	Todd Zeile	.25
294	Jason Schmidt	.25
295	Johnny Damon	.40
296	Scott Brosius	.25
297	Travis Fryman	.40
298	Jose Vizcaino	.25
299	Eric Chavez	.50
300	Mike Piazza	2.00
301	Matt Clement	.25
302	Cristian Guzman	.25
303	Darryl Strawberry	.40
304	Jeff Abbott	.25
305	Brett Tomko	.25
306	Mike Lansing	.25
307	Eric Owens	.25
308	Livan Hernandez	.25
309	Rondell White	.40
310	Todd Stottlemyre	.25
311	Chris Carpenter	.25
312	Ken Hill	.25
313	Mark Loretta	.25
314	John Rocker	.25
315	Richie Sexson	.75
316	Ruben Mateo	.25
317	Ramon Martinez	.25
318	Mike Sirotka	.25
319	Jose Rosado	.25
320	Matt Mantei	.25
321	Kevin Millwood	.50
322	Gary DiSarcina	.25
323	Dustin Hermanson	.25
324	Mike Stanton	.25
325	Kirk Rueter	.25
326	Damian Miller	.25
327	Doug Glanville	.25
328	Scott Rolen	1.00
329	Ray Durham	.25
330	Butch Huskey	.25
331	Mariano Rivera	.50
332	Darren Lewis	.25
333	Ramiro Mendoza	.25
334	Mark Grudzielanek	.25
335	Mike Cameron	.25
336	Kelvim Escobar	.25
337	Bret Boone	.40
338	Mo Vaughn	.40
339	Craig Biggio	.40
340	Michael Barrett	.25
341	Marlon Anderson	.25
342	Bobby Jones	.25
343	John Halama	.25
344	Todd Ritchie	.25
345	Chuck Knoblauch	.25
346	Rick Reed	.25
347	Kelly Stinnett	.25
348	Tim Salmon	.50
349	A.J. Hinch	.25
350	Jose Cruz Jr.	.25
351	Roberto Hernandez	.25
352	Edgar Renteria	.25
353	Jose Hernandez	.25
354	Brad Fullmer	.25
355	Trevor Hoffman	.25
356	Troy O'Leary	.25
357	Justin Thompson	.25
358	Kevin Young	.25
359	Hideki Irabu	.25
360	Jim Thome	1.00
361	Todd Dunwoody	.25
362	Octavio Dotel	.25
363	Omar Vizquel	.40
364	Raul Mondesi	.40
365	Shane Reynolds	.25
366	Bartolo Colon	.25
367	Chris Widger	.25
368	Gabe Kapler	.25
369	Bill Simas	.25
370	Tino Martinez	.50
371	John Thomson	.25
372	Delino DeShields	.25
373	Carlos Perez	.25

374	Eddie Perez	.25
375	Jeromy Burnitz	.25
376	Jimmy Haynes	.25
377	Travis Lee	.25
378	Darryl Hamilton	.25
379	Jamie Moyer	.25
380	Alex Gonzalez	.25
381	John Wetteland	.25
382	Vinny Castilla	.40
383	Jeff Suppan	.25
384	Chad Curtis	.25
385	Robb Nen	.25
386	Wilson Alvarez	.25
387	Andres Galarraga	.50
388	Mike Remlinger	.25
389	Geoff Jenkins	.40
390	Matt Stairs	.25
391	Bill Mueller	.25
392	Mike Lowell	.25
393	Andy Ashby	.25
394	Ruben Rivera	.25
395	Todd Helton	1.00
396	Bernie Williams	.75
397	Royce Clayton	.25
398	Manny Ramirez	1.00
399	Kerry Wood	.75
400	Ken Griffey Jr.	2.00
401	Enrique Wilson	.25
402	Joey Hamilton	.25
403	Shawn Estes	.25
404	Ugueth Urbina	.25
405	Albert Belle	.30
406	Rick Helling	.25
407	Steve Parris	.25
408	Eric Milton	.25
409	Dave Mlicki	.25
410	Shawn Green	.50
411	Jaret Wright	.25
412	Tony Womack	.25
413	Vernon Wells	.50
414	Ron Belliard	.25
415	Ellis Burks	.25
416	Scott Erickson	.25
417	Rafael Palmeiro	.75
418	Damion Easley	.25
419	Jamey Wright	.25
420	Corey Koskie	.25
421	Bobby Howry	.25
422	Ricky Ledee	.25
423	Dmitri Young	.25
424	Sidney Ponson	.25
425	Greg Maddux	2.00
426	Jose Guillen	.25
427	Jon Lieber	.25
428	Andy Benes	.25
429	Randy Velarde	.25
430	Sean Casey	.40
431	Torii Hunter	.50
432	Ryan Rupe	.25
433	David Segui	.25
434	Rich Aurilia	.25
435	Nomar Garciaparra	3.00
436	Denny Neagle	.25
437	Ron Coomer	.25
438	Chris Singleton	.25
439	Tony Batista	.25
440	Andruw Jones	1.00
441	Adam Piatt, Aubrey Huff, Sean Burroughs	.50
442	Rafael Furcal, Jason Dallero, Travis Dawkins	.50
443	Wilton Veras, Joe Crede, Mike Lamb RC	.25
444	Julio Zuleta, Dernell Stenson, Jorge Toca	.25
445	Tim Raines Jr., Gary Mathews Jr., Garry Maddox Jr. RC	.50
446	Matt Riley, Mark Mulder, C.C. Sabathia	.25
447	Scott Downs, Chris George, Matt Belisle	.50
448	Doug Mirabelli, Ben Petrick, Jayson Werth	.25
449	Josh Hamilton, Corey Myers RC	.50
450	Ben Christensen, Brett Myers	.50
451	Barry Zito, Ben Sheets RC	10.00
452	Ty Howington, Kurt Ainsworth RC	2.00
453	Rick Asadoorian, Vince Faison RC	.50
454	Keith Reed, Jeff Heaverlo RC	.50
455	Mike MacDougal, Jay Gehrke	1.50
456	Mark McGwire	3.00
457	Cal Ripken Jr.	4.00
458	Wade Boggs	.75
459	Tony Gwynn	1.50
460	Jesse Orosco	.25
461	Nomar Garciaparra, Larry Walker	1.50
462	Mark McGwire, Ken Griffey Jr.	1.50
463	Mark McGwire, Manny Ramirez	1.50
464	Randy Johnson, Pedro Martinez	1.00
465	Randy Johnson, Pedro Martinez	1.00
466	Luis Gonzalez, Derek Jeter	2.00
467	Manny Ramirez, Larry Walker	.75
468	Tony Gwynn	1.50
469	Mark McGwire	3.00
470	Frank Thomas	.75
471	Harold Baines	.25
472	Roger Clemens	1.50
473	John Franco	.25
474	John Franco	.25
475	Ken Griffey Jr.	3.00
476	Barry Bonds	5.00
477	Sammy Sosa	4.00
478	Derek Jeter	6.00
479	Alex Rodriguez	5.00

Refractors

KEVIN MILLWOOD

Stars:	3-5X
Young Stars/RC's:	1-2X

Inserted 1:12
(See 2000 Topps Chrome for checklist and base card values.)

Allegiance

		NM/M
Complete Set (20):		30.00
Common Player:		.75
Inserted 1:16		
Refractors:		5X
Inserted 1:424		
1	Derek Jeter	6.00
2	Ivan Rodriguez	1.00
3	Alex Rodriguez	5.00
4	Cal Ripken Jr.	6.00
5	Mark Grace	1.00
6	Tony Gwynn	2.00
7	Juan Gonzalez	1.50
8	Frank Thomas	1.50
9	Manny Ramirez	1.50
10	Barry Larkin	.75
11	Bernie Williams	1.50
12	Raul Mondesi	.75
13	Vladimir Guerrero	1.50
14	Craig Biggio	.75
15	Nomar Garciaparra	4.00
16	Andruw Jones	1.50
17	Jim Thome	1.50
18	Scott Rolen	1.50
19	Chipper Jones	3.00
20	Ken Griffey Jr.	3.00

All-Star Rookie Team

		NM/M
Complete Set (10):		10.00
Common Player:		.50
Inserted 1:16		
Refractors:		2-3X
Inserted 1:80		
1	Mark McGwire	3.00
2	Chuck Knoblauch	.50
3	Chipper Jones	2.00
4	Cal Ripken Jr.	4.00
5	Manny Ramirez	1.00
6	Jose Canseco	.75
7	Ken Griffey Jr.	2.00
8	Mike Piazza	2.00
9	Dwight Gooden	.50
10	Billy Wagner	.50

All-Topps Team

LARRY WALKER
All-Topps N1 Team

		NM/M
Complete Set (20):		40.00
Complete Series I Set (10):		20.00
Complete Series II Set (10):		20.00
Common Player:		.50
Inserted 1:32		
Refractors:		2-3X
Inserted 1:160		
1	Greg Maddux	3.00
2	Mike Piazza	3.00
3	Mark McGwire	5.00
4	Craig Biggio	1.00
5	Chipper Jones	3.00
6	Barry Larkin	1.00
7	Barry Bonds	5.00
8	Andruw Jones	1.50
9	Sammy Sosa	3.00
10	Larry Walker	1.00
11	Pedro Martinez	2.00
12	Ivan Rodriguez	1.00
13	Rafael Palmeiro	1.00
14	Roberto Alomar	1.00
15	Cal Ripken Jr.	6.00
16	Derek Jeter	6.00
17	Albert Belle	.50
18	Ken Griffey Jr.	3.00
19	Manny Ramirez	1.50
20	Jose Canseco	1.00

Combos

		NM/M
Complete Set (10):		20.00
Common Player:		1.00
Inserted 1:16		
Refractors:		2-3X
Inserted 1:80		
1	Roberto Alomar, Manny Ramirez, Kenny Lofton, Jim Thome	1.00

Strikeout Kings
RANDY JOHNSON · PEDRO MARTINEZ

2	Tom Glavine, Greg Maddux, John Smoltz	2.00
3	Derek Jeter, Bernie Williams, Tino Martinez	4.00
4	Ivan Rodriguez, Mike Piazza	2.00
5	Nomar Garciaparra, Alex Rodriguez, Derek Jeter	4.00
6	Sammy Sosa, Mark McGwire	4.00
7	Pedro Martinez, Randy Johnson	1.50
8	Barry Bonds, Ken Griffey Jr.	3.00
9	Chipper Jones, Ivan Rodriguez	2.00
10	Cal Ripken Jr., Tony Gwynn, Wade Boggs	4.00

Kings

		NM/M
Complete Set (10):		25.00
Common Player:		1.50
Inserted 1:32		
1	Mark McGwire	5.00
2	Sammy Sosa	3.00
3	Ken Griffey Jr.	3.00
4	Mike Piazza	3.00
5	Alex Rodriguez	5.00
6	Manny Ramirez	1.50
7	Barry Bonds	6.00
8	Nomar Garciaparra	4.00
9	Chipper Jones	3.00
10	Vladimir Guerrero	1.50

Mark McGwire 1985 Rookie Reprint

	NM/M
Complete Set (1):	5.00

Inserted 1:32
Refractor: 50.00
Production 70 cards.
Mark McGwire 5.00

Millennium Stars

		NM/M
Complete Set (10):		10.00
Common Player:		.50
Inserted 1:32		
Refractors:		2-3X
Inserted 1:160		
1	Nomar Garciaparra	4.00
2	Vladimir Guerrero	1.50
3	Sean Casey	.75
4	Richie Sexson	1.00
5	Todd Helton	1.50
6	Carlos Beltran	.75
7	Kevin Millwood	.75
8	Ruben Mateo	.50
9	Pat Burrell	1.00
10	Alfonso Soriano	2.00

Own the Game

		NM/M
Complete Set (30):		30.00
Common Player:		.25
Inserted 1:12		
Refractors:		2-3X
Inserted 1:55		
1	Derek Jeter	4.00
2	B.J. Surhoff	.25
3	Luis Gonzalez	.50
4	Manny Ramirez	1.00
5	Rafael Palmeiro	1.00
6	Mark McGwire	3.00
7	Mark McGwire	3.00
8	Sammy Sosa	2.00
9	Ken Griffey Jr.	2.00
10	Larry Walker	.50
11	Nomar Garciaparra	3.00
12	Derek Jeter	4.00
13	Larry Walker	.50
14	Mark McGwire	3.00
15	Manny Ramirez	1.00
16	Pedro Martinez	1.50
17	Randy Johnson	1.50
18	Kevin Millwood	.50
19	Pedro Martinez	1.50
20	Randy Johnson	1.50
21	Kevin Brown	.50
22	Chipper Jones	2.00
23	Ivan Rodriguez	1.00
24	Mariano Rivera	.50
25	Scott Williamson	.25
26	Carlos Beltran	.50
27	Randy Johnson	1.50
28	Pedro Martinez	1.50
29	Sammy Sosa	2.00
30	Manny Ramirez	1.00

Power Players

		NM/M
Complete Set (20):		25.00
Common Player:		.25
Inserted 1:8		
Refractors:		2-3X
Inserted 1:40		
1	Juan Gonzalez	1.00
2	Ken Griffey Jr.	2.00
3	Mark McGwire	3.00
4	Nomar Garciaparra	3.00
5	Barry Bonds	3.00
6	Mo Vaughn	.40
7	Larry Walker	.50
8	Alex Rodriguez	3.00
9	Jose Canseco	.75
10	Jeff Bagwell	1.00
11	Manny Ramirez	1.00
12	Albert Belle	.25
13	Frank Thomas	1.00
14	Mike Piazza	2.00
15	Chipper Jones	2.00
16	Sammy Sosa	2.00
17	Vladimir Guerrero	1.00
18	Scott Rolen	1.00
19	Raul Mondesi	.40
20	Derek Jeter	4.00

21st Century Topps

		NM/M
Complete Set (10):		10.00
Common Player:		.25
Inserted 1:16		
Refractors:		2-3X
Inserted 1:80		
1	Ben Grieve	.25
2	Alex Gonzalez	.25
3	Derek Jeter	4.00
4	Sean Casey	.50
5	Nomar Garciaparra	3.00
6	Alex Rodriguez	3.00
7	Scott Rolen	1.00
8	Andruw Jones	1.00
9	Vladimir Guerrero	1.00
10	Todd Helton	1.00

2000 Topps Chrome Traded and Rookies

		NM/M
Complete Set (135):		60.00
Common Player:		.25
1	Mike MacDougal RC	1.00
2	Andy Tracy RC	.50
3	Brandon Phillips RC	3.00
4	Brandon Inge RC	1.50
5	Robbie Morrison RC	.50
6	Josh Pressley RC	.50
7	Todd Moser RC	.50
8	Rob Purvis RC	.50
9	Chance Caple RC	.50
10	Ben Sheets	2.00
11	Russ Jacobson RC	.50
12	Brian Cole RC	.50
13	Brad Baker RC	.50
14	Alex Cintron RC	.75
15	Lyle Overbay RC	2.00
16	Mike Edwards RC	.50
17	Sean McGowan RC	.50
18	Jose Molina RC	.50
19	Marcos Castillo RC	.50
20	Josue Espada RC	.50
21	Alex Gordon RC	.50
22	Rob Pugmire RC	.50
23	Jason Stumm RC	.50
24	Ty Howington RC	1.00
25	Brett Myers RC	1.00
26	Maicer Izturis RC	.50
27	John McDonald RC	.50
28	Wilfredo Rodriguez RC	.50
29	Carlos Zambrano RC	6.00
30	Alejandro Diaz RC	.50
31	Geraldo Guzman RC	.50
32	J.R. House RC	.75
33	Elvin Nina RC	.50
34	Juan Pierre RC	2.00
35	Ben Johnson RC	1.00
36	Jeff Bailey RC	.50
37	Miguel Olivo RC	.50
38	Francisco Rodriguez RC	4.00
39	Tony Pena Jr. RC	.50
40	Miguel Cabrera RC	50.00
41	Asdrubal Oropeza RC	.50
42	Junior Zamora RC	.50
43	Jovanny Cedeno RC	.50
44	John Sneed RC	.50
45	Josh Kalinowski RC	.50
46	Mike Young RC	8.00
47	Rico Washington RC	.50
48	Chad Durbin RC	.50
49	Junior Brignac RC	.50
50	Carlos Hernandez RC	.50
51	Cesar Izturis RC	1.00
52	Oscar Salazar RC	.50
53	Pat Strange RC	.50
54	Rick Asadoorian RC	.50
55	Keith Reed RC	.50
56	Leo Estrella RC	.50
57	Wascar Serrano RC	.50
58	Richard Gomez RC	.50
59	Ramon Santiago RC	.50
60	Jovanny Sosa RC	.50
61	Aaron Rowand RC	3.00
62	Junior Guerrero RC	.50
63	Luis Terrero RC	.75
64	Brian Sanches RC	.50
65	Scott Sobkowiak RC	.50
66	Gary Majewski RC	.50
67	Barry Zito RC	2.00
68	Ryan Christianson RC	.50
69	Cristian Guerrero RC	.50
70	Tomas de la Rosa RC	.50
71	Andrew Beinbrink RC	.50
72	Ryan Knox RC	.50
73	Alex Graman RC	.50
74	Juan Guzman RC	.50
75	Ruben Salazar RC	.50
76	Luis Matos RC	.75
77	Tony Mota RC	.50
78	Doug Davis RC	.75
79	Ben Christensen RC	.50
80	Mike Lamb RC	.50
81	Adrian Gonzalez RC	5.00
82	Mike Stodolka RC	.50
83	Adam Johnson RC	.50
84	Matt Wheatland RC	.50
85	Corey Smith RC	.75
86	Rocco Baldelli RC	4.00
87	Keith Bucktrot RC	.50
88	Adam Wainwright RC	5.00
89	Scott Thorman RC	2.00
90	Tripper Johnson RC	.75
91	Jim Edmonds	.50
92	Masato Yoshii	.25
93	Adam Kennedy	.25
94	Darryl Kile	.25
95	Mark McLemore	.25
96	Ricky Gutierrez	.25
97	Juan Gonzalez	.50
98	Melvin Mora	.25
99	Dante Bichette	.25
100	Lee Stevens	.25
101	Roger Cedeno	.25
102	John Olerud	.40
103	Eric Young	.25
104	Mickey Morandini	.25
105	Travis Lee	.25
106	Greg Vaughn	.25
107	Todd Zeile	.25
108	Chuck Finley	.25
109	Ismael Valdes	.25
110	Ron Henika	.25
111	Pat Hentgen	.25
112	Ryan Klesko	.40
113	Derek Bell	.25
114	Hideo Nomo	1.00
115	Aaron Sele	.25
116	Fernando Vina	.25
117	Wally Joyner	.25
118	Brian Hunter	.25
119	Joe Girardi	.25
120	Omar Daal	.25
121	Brook Fordyce	.25
122	Jose Valentin	.25
123	Curt Schilling	.75
124	B.J. Surhoff	.25
125	Henry Rodriguez	.25
126	Mike Bordick	.25
127	David Justice	.50
128	Charles Johnson	.25
129	Will Clark	.75
130	Dwight Gooden	.25
131	David Segui	.25
132	Denny Neagle	.25
133	Andy Ashby	.25
134	Bruce Chen	.25
135	Jason Bere	.25

2000 Topps Gallery

		NM/M
Complete Set (150):		40.00
Common Player:		.15
Common (101-150):		.50
Inserted 1:1		
Pack (6):		2.00
Wax Box (24):		40.00
1	Nomar Garciaparra	1.50
2	Kevin Millwood	.25
3	Jay Bell	.15
4	Rusty Greer	.15
5	Bernie Williams	.50
6	Barry Larkin	.25
7	Carlos Beltran	.25
8	Damion Easley	.15
9	Magglio Ordonez	.25
10	Matt Williams	.20
11	Shannon Stewart	.15
12	Ray Lankford	.15
13	Vinny Castilla	.20
14	Miguel Tejada	.25
15	Craig Biggio	.25
16	Chipper Jones	1.00
17	Albert Belle	.20
18	Doug Glanville	.15
19	Brian Giles	.25
20	Shawn Green	.25
21	J.T. Snow Jr.	.15
22	Luis Gonzalez	.25
23	Carlos Delgado	.50
24	J.D. Drew	.25
25	Ivan Rodriguez	.50
26	Tino Martinez	.25
27	Erubiel Durazo	.20
28	Scott Rolen	.50
29	Gary Sheffield	.40
30	Manny Ramirez	.50
31	Luis Castillo	.15
32	Fernando Tatis	.15
33	Darin Erstad	.25
34	Tim Hudson	.25
35	Sammy Sosa	1.00
36	Jason Kendall	.25
37	Todd Walker	.15
38	Orlando Hernandez	.25
39	Pokey Reese	.15
40	Mike Piazza	1.00
41	B.J. Surhoff	.15
42	Tony Gwynn	.75
43	Kevin Brown	.25
44	Preston Wilson	.25
45	Kenny Lofton	.25
46	Rondell White	.20
47	Frank Thomas	.50
48	Neifi Perez	.15
49	Edgardo Alfonzo	.25
50	Ken Griffey Jr.	1.00
51	Barry Bonds	1.50

52	Brian Jordan	.15
53	Raul Mondesi	.25
54	Troy Glaus	.50
55	Curt Schilling	.40
56	Mike Mussina	.50
57	Brian Daubach	.15
58	Roger Clemens	1.00
59	Carlos Febles	.15
60	Todd Helton	.50
61	Mark Grace	.40
62	Randy Johnson	.75
63	Jeff Bagwell	.50
64	Tom Glavine	.25
65	Adrian Beltre	.20
66	Rafael Palmeiro	.50
67	Paul O'Neill	.25
68	Robin Ventura	.25
69	Ray Durham	.15
70	Mark McGwire	1.50
71	Greg Vaughn	.15
72	Javy Lopez	.25
73	Jeromy Burnitz	.15
74	Mike Lieberthal	.15
75	Cal Ripken Jr.	2.00
76	Juan Gonzalez	.50
77	Sean Casey	.25
78	Jermaine Dye	.15
79	John Olerud	.25
80	Jose Canseco	.40
81	Eric Karros	.20
82	Roberto Alomar	.40
83	Ben Grieve	.15
84	Greg Maddux	1.00
85	Pedro Martinez	.75
86	Tony Clark	.15
87	Richie Sexson	.25
88	Cliff Floyd	.15
89	Eric Chavez	.25
90	Andruw Jones	.50
91	Vladimir Guerrero	.50
92	Alex Gonzalez	.15
93	Jim Thome	.50
94	Bob Abreu	.25
95	Derek Jeter	2.00
96	Larry Walker	.25
97	John Smoltz	.25
98	Mo Vaughn	.20
99	Jason Giambi	.50
100	Alex Rodriguez	1.50
101	Mark McGwire	2.50
102	Sammy Sosa	1.50
103	Alex Rodriguez	2.50
104	Derek Jeter	3.00
105	Greg Maddux	1.50
106	Jeff Bagwell	.75
107	Nomar Garciaparra	2.00
108	Mike Piazza	1.50
109	Pedro Martinez	1.00
110	Chipper Jones	1.50
111	Randy Johnson	1.00
112	Barry Bonds	2.50
113	Ken Griffey Jr.	1.50
114	Manny Ramirez	.75
115	Ivan Rodriguez	.75
116	Juan Gonzalez	.75
117	Vladimir Guerrero	.75
118	Tony Gwynn	1.00
119	Larry Walker	.50
120	Cal Ripken Jr.	3.00
121	Josh Hamilton	.50
122	Corey Patterson	.50
123	Pat Burrell	.50
124	Nick Johnson	.50
125	Adam Piatt	.50
126	Rick Ankiel	.50
127	A.J. Burnett	.50
128	Ben Petrick	.50
129	Rafael Furcal	.75
130	Alfonso Soriano	2.00
131	Dee Brown	.50
132	Ruben Mateo	.50
133	Pablo Ozuna	.50
134	Sean Burroughs	.75
135	Mark Mulder	.75
136	Jason Jennings	.50
137	Eric Munson	.50
138	Vernon Wells	.75
139	Brett Myers **RC**	3.00
140	Ben Christensen **RC**	.50
141	Bobby Bradley **RC**	.50
142	Ruben Salazar **RC**	.50
143	Ryan Christianson **RC**	.50
144	Corey Myers **RC**	.50
145	Aaron Rowand **RC**	1.00
146	Julio Zuleta **RC**	.50
147	Kurt Ainsworth **RC**	1.00
148	Scott Downs **RC**	.50
149	Larry Bigbie **RC**	1.50
150	Chance Caple **RC**	.50

Press Plates

NM/M
Common Player: 50.00
(See 2000 Topps Gallery for
checklist.)

Players Private Issue

Stars (1-100): 4-8X
SPs (101-150): 2-4X
Production 250 Sets

Autographs

NM/M
Common Player: 5.00
Inserted 1:153

RA	Rick Ankiel	15.00
RM	Ruben Mateo	5.00
CP	Corey Patterson	15.00
BP	Ben Petrick	5.00
VW	Vernon Wells	20.00

Gallery Exhibits

NM/M
Complete Set (30): 50.00
Common Player: .50
Inserted 1:18

1	Mark McGwire	5.00
2	Jeff Bagwell	1.50
3	Mike Piazza	3.00
4	Alex Rodriguez	5.00
5	Nomar Garciaparra	4.00
6	Ivan Rodriguez	1.50
7	Chipper Jones	3.00
8	Cal Ripken Jr.	6.00
9	Tony Gwynn	2.00
10	Jose Canseco	1.00
11	Albert Belle	.50
12	Greg Maddux	3.00

13	Barry Bonds	5.00
14	Ken Griffey Jr.	3.00
15	Juan Gonzalez	1.50
16	Rickey Henderson	1.00
17	Craig Biggio	.75
18	Vladimir Guerrero	1.50
19	Rey Ordonez	.50
20	Roberto Alomar	1.00
21	Derek Jeter	6.00
22	Manny Ramirez	1.50
23	Shawn Green	1.00
24	Sammy Sosa	3.00
25	Larry Walker	1.00
26	Pedro Martinez	2.00
27	Randy Johnson	2.00
28	Pat Burrell	1.00
29	Josh Hamilton	1.00
30	Corey Patterson	1.00

Lithos

NM/M
Complete Set (8): 675.00
Common Player: 80.00

(1)	Shawn Green	80.00
(2)	Ken Griffey Jr.	80.00
(3)	Chipper Jones	80.00
(4)	Pedro Martinez	80.00
(5)	Alex Rodriguez	80.00
(6)	Ivan Rodriguez	80.00
(7)	Nomar Garciaparra, Alex Rodriguez, Derek Jeter Three of a Kind	100.00
(8)	Paul O'Neill, Derek Jeter, Bernie Williams, Tino Martinez Torre's Terrors	100.00

Gallery of Heroes

NM/M
Complete Set (10): 20.00
Common Player: 1.00
Inserted 1:24

1	Alex Rodriguez	3.00
2	Chipper Jones	2.00
3	Pedro Martinez	1.50
4	Sammy Sosa	2.00
5	Mark McGwire	3.00
6	Nomar Garciaparra	3.00
7	Vladimir Guerrero	1.00
8	Ken Griffey Jr.	2.00
9	Mike Piazza	2.00
10	Derek Jeter	4.00

Proof Positive

NM/M
Complete Set (10): 40.00
Common Player: 3.00
Inserted 1:48

1	Ken Griffey Jr., Ruben Mateo	4.00

2	Derek Jeter, Alfonso Soriano	6.00
3	Mark McGwire, Pat Burrell	6.00
4	Pedro Martinez, A.J. Burnett	3.00
5	Alex Rodriguez, Rafael Furcal	6.00
6	Sammy Sosa, Corey Patterson	4.00
7	Randy Johnson, Rick Ankiel	3.00
8	Chipper Jones, Adam Piatt	4.00
9	Nomar Garciaparra, Pablo Ozuna	6.00
10	Mike Piazza, Eric Munson	4.00

Topps Heritage

NM/M
Complete Set (20): 100.00
Common Player: 2.00
Inserted 1:12
Proofs: 1-2X
Inserted 1:27

1	Mark McGwire	12.00
2	Sammy Sosa	8.00
3	Greg Maddux	8.00
4	Mike Piazza	8.00
5	Ivan Rodriguez	4.00
6	Manny Ramirez	4.00
7	Jeff Bagwell	4.00
8	Sean Casey	2.00
9	Orlando Hernandez	2.00
10	Randy Johnson	5.00
11	Pedro Martinez	5.00
12	Vladimir Guerrero	4.00
13	Shawn Green	2.50
14	Ken Griffey Jr.	8.00
15	Alex Rodriguez	12.00
16	Nomar Garciaparra	10.00
17	Derek Jeter	15.00
18	Tony Gwynn	5.00
19	Chipper Jones	8.00
20	Cal Ripken Jr.	15.00

2000 Topps Gold Label
Class 1

NM/M
Complete Set (100): 25.00
Common Player: .25
Gold Parallel: 4-8X
Production 100 Sets
Pack (3): 2.00
Wax Box (24): 30.00

1	Sammy Sosa	1.50
2	Greg Maddux	1.50
3	Dee Brown	.25
4	Rondell White	.40
5	Fernando Tatis	.25
6	Troy Glaus	.75
7	Nick Johnson	.40
8	Albert Belle	.30
9	Scott Rolen	.75
10	Rafael Palmeiro	.50
11	Tony Gwynn	1.00
12	Kevin Brown	.40
13	Roberto Alomar	.50

14	John Olerud	.40
15	Rick Ankiel	.25
16	Chipper Jones	1.50
17	Craig Biggio	.40
18	Mark Mulder	.40
19	Carlos Delgado	.75
20	Alex Gonzalez	.25
21	Gabe Kapler	.25
22	Derek Jeter	3.00
23	Carlos Beltran	.40
24	Todd Helton	.75
25	Mark McGwire	2.50
26	Ben Grieve	.25
27	Rafael Furcal	.40
28	Vernon Wells	.40
29	Greg Vaughn	.25
30	Vladimir Guerrero	.75
31	Mike Piazza	1.50
32	Roger Clemens	2.00
33	Barry Larkin	.40
34	Pedro Martinez	1.00
35	Matt Williams	.30
36	Mo Vaughn	.30
37	Tim Hudson	.40
38	Andruw Jones	.75
39	Vinny Castilla	.25
40	Frank Thomas	.75
41	Pokey Reese	.25
42	Corey Patterson	.40
43	Jeromy Burnitz	.25
44	Preston Wilson	.40
45	Juan Gonzalez	.75
46	Brian Giles	.40
47	Todd Walker	.25
48	Magglio Ordonez	.40
49	Alfonso Soriano	1.00
50	Ken Griffey Jr.	1.50
51	Michael Barrett	.25
52	Shawn Green	.50
53	Erubiel Durazo	.40
54	Adam Piatt	.25
55	Pat Burrell	.50
56	Mike Mussina	.50
57	Bernie Williams	.75
58	Sean Casey	.40
59	Randy Johnson	1.00
60	Jeff Bagwell	.75
61	Eric Chavez	.50
62	Josh Hamilton	.50
63	A.J. Burnett	.25
64	Jim Thome	.75
65	Raul Mondesi	.40
66	Jason Kendall	.40
67	Mike Lieberthal	.25
68	Robin Ventura	.40
69	Ivan Rodriguez	.50
70	Larry Walker	.40
71	Eric Munson	.25
72	Brian Jordan	.25
73	Edgardo Alfonzo	.25
74	Curt Schilling	.50
75	Nomar Garciaparra	2.00
76	Mark Grace	.50
77	Shannon Stewart	.25
78	J.D. Drew	.40
79	Jack Cust	.25
80	Cal Ripken Jr.	3.00
81	Bob Abreu	.40
82	Ruben Mateo	.25
83	Orlando Hernandez	.25
84	Kris Benson	.25
85	Barry Bonds	2.50
86	Manny Ramirez	.75
87	Jose Canseco	.50
88	Sean Burroughs	.25
89	Kevin Millwood	.40
90	Alex Rodriguez	2.50
91	Brett Myers RC	3.00
92	Rick Asadoorian RC	.40
93	Ben Christensen RC	.40
94	Bobby Bradley RC	.50
95	Corey Myers RC	.50
96	Brad Baisley RC	.50

97	Aaron McNeal RC	.50
98	Aaron Rowand RC	.75
99	Scott Downs RC	.40
100	Michael Tejera RC	.40

Class 2

	NM/M
Same prices as Class 1.	
Gold Parallel:	4-8X

Class 3

Same prices as Class 1.

Gold Parallel:	4-8X
Production 100 Sets	

Bullion

Complete Set (10):		125.00
Common Player:		4.00
Inserted 1:53		
1	Jim Thome, Manny Ramirez, Roberto Alomar	6.00
2	Derek Jeter, Orlando Hernandez, Bernie Williams	15.00
3	Chipper Jones, Andruw Jones, Greg Maddux	12.00
4	Alex Rodriguez, Jay Buhner, John Olerud	20.00
5	Nomar Garciaparra, Pedro Martinez, Brian Daubach	15.00
6	Mark McGwire, J.D. Drew, Rick Ankiel	20.00
7	Sammy Sosa, Mark Grace, Kerry Wood	15.00
8	Ken Griffey Jr., Sean Casey, Barry Larkin	20.00
9	Mike Piazza, Edgardo Alfonzo, Robin Ventura	15.00
10	Randy Johnson, Matt Williams, Erubiel Durazo	6.00

End of the Rainbow

	NM/M
Complete Set (15):	8.00
Common Player:	.50
Inserted 1:11	
1	Pat Burrell	1.50
2	Corey Patterson	1.00
3	Josh Hamilton	1.00
4	Eric Munson	.50
5	Sean Burroughs	.75
6	Jack Cust	.50
7	Rafael Furcal	.75
8	Ruben Salazar	.50
9	Brett Myers	1.00

10	Wes Anderson	.50
11	Nick Johnson	1.00
12	Scott Downs	.50
13	Choo Freeman	.50
14	Brad Baisley	.50
15	A.J. Burnett	.75

Prospector's Dream

	NM/M
Complete Set (10):	15.00
Common Player:	.50
Inserted 1:26	
1	Mark McGwire	3.00
2	Alex Rodriguez	3.00
3	Nomar Garciaparra	3.00
4	Pat Burrell	.75
5	Todd Helton	1.00
6	Derek Jeter	4.00
7	Adam Piatt	.50
8	Chipper Jones	2.00
9	Shawn Green	.75
10	Josh Hamilton	1.00

The Treasury

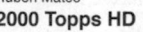

	NM/M
Complete Set (25):	40.00
Common Player:	.50
Inserted 1:21	
1	Ken Griffey Jr.	3.00
2	Derek Jeter	6.00
3	Chipper Jones	3.00
4	Manny Ramirez	1.50
5	Nomar Garciaparra	4.00
6	Sammy Sosa	3.00
7	Cal Ripken Jr.	6.00
8	Alex Rodriguez	5.00
9	Mike Piazza	3.00
10	Pedro Martinez	2.00
11	Vladimir Guerrero	1.50
12	Jeff Bagwell	1.50
13	Shawn Green	1.00
14	Greg Maddux	3.00
15	Mark McGwire	5.00
16	Josh Hamilton	1.00
17	Corey Patterson	1.00
18	Dee Brown	.50
19	Rafael Furcal	.75
20	Pat Burrell	1.00
21	Alfonso Soriano	3.00
22	Adam Piatt	.50
23	A.J. Burnett	.75
24	Mark Mulder	.75
25	Ruben Mateo	.50

2000 Topps HD

	NM/M
Complete Set (100):	30.00
Common Player:	.25
Platinums:	4-8X
Production 99 Sets	
Pack (4):	1.50
Wax Box (20):	30.00

1	Derek Jeter	3.00
2	Andruw Jones	.75
3	Ben Grieve	.25
4	Carlos Beltran	.25
5	Randy Johnson	1.00
6	Javy Lopez	.40
7	Gary Sheffield	.50
8	John Olerud	.40
9	Vinny Castilla	.25
10	Barry Larkin	.40
11	Tony Clark	.25
12	Roberto Alomar	.50
13	Brian Jordan	.25
14	Wade Boggs	.50
15	Carlos Febles	.25
16	Alfonso Soriano	1.50
17	A.J. Burnett	.25
18	Matt Williams	.25
19	Alex Gonzalez	.25
20	Larry Walker	.40
21	Jeff Bagwell	.75
22	Al Leiter	.25
23	Ken Griffey Jr.	1.50
24	Ruben Mateo	.25
25	Mark Grace	.50
26	Carlos Delgado	.75
27	Vladimir Guerrero	.75
28	Kenny Lofton	.40
29	Rusty Greer	.25
30	Pedro Martinez	1.00
31	Todd Helton	.75
32	Ray Lankford	.25
33	Jose Canseco	.50
34	Raul Mondesi	.40
35	Mo Vaughn	.40
36	Eric Chavez	.40
37	Manny Ramirez	.75
38	Jason Kendall	.40
39	Mike Mussina	.50
40	Dante Bichette	.25
41	Troy Glaus	.75
42	Rickey Henderson	.50
43	Pablo Ozuna	.25
44	Michael Barrett	.25
45	Tony Gwynn	1.00
46	John Smoltz	.40
47	Rafael Palmeiro	.50
48	Curt Schilling	.50
49	Todd Walker	.25
50	Greg Vaughn	.25
51	Orlando Hernandez	.25
52	Jim Thome	.75
53	Pat Burrell	.50
54	Tim Salmon	.40
55	Tom Glavine	.40
56	Travis Lee	.25
57	Gabe Kapler	.25
58	Greg Maddux	1.50
59	Scott Rolen	.75
60	Cal Ripken Jr.	3.00
61	Preston Wilson	.40
62	Ivan Rodriguez	.50
63	Johnny Damon	.40
64	Bernie Williams	.50
65	Barry Bonds	2.50
66	Sammy Sosa	1.50
67	Robin Ventura	.40
68	Tony Fernandez	.25
69	Jay Bell	.25
70	Mark McGwire	2.50
71	Jeromy Burnitz	.25
72	Chipper Jones	1.50
73	Josh Hamilton	.25
74	Darin Erstad	.40
75	Alex Rodriguez	2.50
76	Sean Casey	.40
77	Tino Martinez	.40
78	Juan Gonzalez	.75
79	Cliff Floyd	.25
80	Craig Biggio	.40
81	Shawn Green	.50
82	Adrian Beltre	.25
83	Mike Piazza	1.50
84	Nomar Garciaparra	2.00

85	Kevin Brown	.40
86	Roger Clemens	2.00
87	Frank Thomas	.75
88	Albert Belle	.25
89	Erubiel Durazo	.25
90	David Walling	.25
91	John Sneed RC	.50
92	Larry Bigbie RC	1.50
93	B.J. Garbe RC	.50
94	Bobby Bradley RC	.50
95	Ryan Christiansen RC	.50
96	Jay Gerhke RC	.50
97	Jason Stumm RC	.50
98	Brett Myers RC	4.00
99	Chance Caple RC	.50
100	Corey Myers RC	.75

Autographs

		NM/M
Jeter 1:859		
Ripken 1:4,386		
1	Derek Jeter	150.00
2	Cal Ripken Jr.	250.00

Ballpark Figures

		NM/M
Complete Set (10):		15.00
Common Player:		.50
Inserted 1:11		
1	Mark McGwire	3.00
2	Ken Griffey Jr.	2.00
3	Nomar Garciaparra	3.00
4	Derek Jeter	4.00
5	Sammy Sosa	2.00
6	Mike Piazza	2.00
7	Juan Gonzalez	1.00
8	Larry Walker	.75
9	Ben Grieve	.50
10	Barry Bonds	3.00

Clearly Refined

		NM/M
Complete Set (10):		8.00
Common Player:		.50
Inserted 1:20		
1	Alfonso Soriano	3.00
2	Ruben Mateo	.50
3	Josh Hamilton	.75
4	Chad Hermansen	.50
5	Ryan Anderson	.50
6	Nick Johnson	1.00
7	Octavio Dotel	.50
8	Peter Bergeron	.50
9	Adam Piatt	.50
10	Pat Burrell	2.00

Image

		NM/M
Complete Set (10):		30.00
Common Player:		1.00
Inserted 1:44		
1	Sammy Sosa	3.00
2	Mark McGwire	5.00
3	Derek Jeter	6.00
4	Albert Belle	1.00
5	Vladimir Guerrero	1.50
6	Ken Griffey Jr.	3.00
7	Mike Piazza	3.00
8	Alex Rodriguez	5.00
9	Barry Bonds	5.00
10	Nomar Garciaparra	4.00

On The Cutting Edge

		NM/M
Complete Set (10):		15.00
Common Player:		.50
Inserted 1:22		
1	Andruw Jones	1.00
2	Nomar Garciaparra	3.00
3	Barry Bonds	3.00
4	Larry Walker	.50
5	Vladimir Guerrero	1.00
6	Jeff Bagwell	1.00
7	Derek Jeter	4.00
8	Sammy Sosa	2.00
9	Alex Rodriguez	3.00
10	Ken Griffey Jr.	2.00

2000 Topps Opening Day

PAUL BYRD

		NM/M
Complete Set (165):		30.00
Common Player:		.15
Pack (8):		1.00
Wax Box (36):		25.00
1	Mark McGwire	2.00
2	Tony Gwynn	1.00
3	Wade Boggs	.40
4	Cal Ripken Jr.	2.50
5	Matt Williams	.20
6	Jay Buhner	.15
7	Mike Lieberthal	.15
8	Magglio Ordonez	.25
9	Derek Jeter	2.00
10	Javy Lopez	.25
11	Armando Benitez	.15
12	Darin Erstad	.25
13	Mark Grace	.25
14	Eric Karros	.15
15	J.T. Snow Jr.	.15
16	Luis Castillo	.15
17	Rey Ordonez	.15
18	Bob Abreu	.25
19	Warren Morris	.15
20	Juan Gonzalez	.75
21	Dean Palmer	.15
22	Hank Aaron	2.00
23	Jeff Bagwell	.75
24	Sammy Sosa	1.50
25	Randy Johnson	.75
26	Dante Bichette	.15
27	Frank Thomas	.75
28	Pedro Martinez	.75
29	Brian Giles	.20
30	Ivan Rodriguez	.50
31	Roger Cedeno	.15
32	David Justice	.25
33	Ken Caminiti	.15
34	Brian Jordan	.15
35	John Olerud	.25
36	Pokey Reese	.15
37	Barry Larkin	.25
38	Edgar Martinez	.15
39	Carlos Delgado	.50
40	Troy Glaus	.40
41	Ben Grieve	.15
42	Jose Lima	.15
43	Luis Gonzalez	.15
44	Alex Rodriguez	2.00
45	Preston Wilson	.20
46	Rickey Henderson	.40
47	Gary Sheffield	.25
48	Jim Edmonds	.25
49	Greg Vaughn	.15
50	Neifi Perez	.15
51	Paul O'Neill	.25
52	Jermaine Dye	.15
53	Curt Schilling	.25
54	Edgardo Alfonzo	.15
55	John Smoltz	.20
56	Chuck Finley	.15
57	Billy Wagner	.15
58	David Cone	.25
59	Roberto Alomar	.50
60	Charles Nagy	.15
61	Mike Mussina	.50
62	Robin Ventura	.25
63	Kevin Brown	.15
64	Pat Hentgen	.15
65	Ryan Klesko	.15
66	Derek Bell	.15
67	Larry Walker	.25
68	Scott Williamson	.15
69	Jose Offerman	.15
70	Doug Mientkiewicz	.15
71	John Snyder	.15
72	Sandy Alomar	.15
73	Joe Nathan	.15
74	Steve Finley	.15
75	Dave Martinez	.15
76	Fernando Tatis	.15
77	Kenny Lofton	.20
78	Paul Byrd	.15
79	Aaron Sele	.15
80	Roger Clemens	1.50
81	Francisco Cordova	.15
82	Wally Joyner	.15
83	Jason Kendall	.25
84	Carlos Beltran	.15
85	Chipper Jones	1.50
86	Vladimir Guerrero	.75
87	Tom Goodwin	.15
88	Brian Daubach	.15
89	Jay Bell	.15
90	Roy Halladay	.25
91	Miguel Tejada	.40
92	Eric Davis	.15
93	Henry Rodriguez	.15
94	Joe McEwing	.15
95	Jeff Kent	.25
96	Jeff Zimmerman	.15
97	Tony Fernandez	.15
98	Jason Giambi	.75
99	Jose Canseco	.40
100	Alex Gonzalez	.15
101	Erubiel Durazo, Pat Burrell, Nick Johnson	.40
102	Corey Patterson, Roosevelt Brown, Lance Berkman	.25
103	Eric Munson, Bobby Bradley RC	.25
104	Josh Hamilton, Corey Myers RC	.25
105	Mark McGwire	2.00
106	Hank Aaron	2.00
107	Cal Ripken Jr.	2.50
108	Wade Boggs	.40
109	Tony Gwynn	1.00
(110)	Hank Aaron	2.00
111	Tom Glavine	.40
112	Mo Vaughn	.20
113	Tino Martinez	.25
114	Craig Biggio	.25
115	Tim Hudson	.25
116	John Wetteland	.15
117	Ellis Burks	.15
118	David Wells	.15
119	Rico Brogna	.15
120	Greg Maddux	1.50
121	Jeromy Burnitz	.15
122	Raul Mondesi	.25
123	Rondell White	.25
124	Barry Bonds	2.00
125	Orlando Hernandez	.25
126	Bartolo Colon	.15
127	Tim Salmon	.25
128	Kevin Young	.15
129	Troy O'Leary	.15
130	Jim Thome	.50
131	Ray Durham	.15
132	Tony Clark	.15
133	Mariano Rivera	.25
134	Omar Vizquel	.15
135	Ken Griffey Jr.	1.50
136	Shawn Green	.40
137	Cliff Floyd	.15
138	Al Leiter	.15
139	Mike Hampton	.15
140	Mike Piazza	1.50
141	Andy Pettitte	.25
142	Albert Belle	.20
143	Scott Rolen	.75
144	Rusty Greer	.15
145	Kevin Millwood	.25
146	Ivan Rodriguez	.75
147	Nomar Garciaparra	1.50
148	Denny Neagle	.15
149	Manny Ramirez	.75
150	Vinny Castilla	.15
151	Andruw Jones	.50
152	Johnny Damon	.15
153	Eric Milton	.15
154	Todd Helton	.50
155	Rafael Palmeiro	.50
156	Damion Easley	.15
157	Carlos Febles	.15
158	Paul Konerko	.25
159	Bernie Williams	.50
160	Ken Griffey Jr.	1.50
161	Barry Bonds	2.00
162	Sammy Sosa	2.00
163	Derek Jeter	2.00
164	Alex Rodriguez	2.00
165	Checklist	.15

Autographs

		NM/M
Common Player:		25.00
1	Edgardo Alfonzo	25.00
2	Wade Boggs	60.00
3	Robin Ventura	25.00
4	Josh Hamilton	25.00
5	Vernon Wells	30.00

2000 Topps Opening Day 2K

		NM/M
Complete Set (8):		6.00
Common Player:		.50
1	Mark McGwire	2.00
2	Barry Bonds	.75
3	Ivan Rodriguez	.75
4	Sean Casey	.65
5	Derek Jeter	1.00
6	Vladimir Guerrero	1.00

Ivan Rodriguez
Texas Rangers

7	Preston Wilson	.65
8	Ben Grieve	.50

2000 Topps Stars

		NM/M
	Complete Set (200):	35.00
	Common Player:	.10
	Pack (6):	2.00
	Box (24):	40.00
1	Vladimir Guerrero	.75
2	Eric Karros	.10
3	Omar Vizquel	.20
4	Ken Griffey Jr.	1.50
5	Preston Wilson	.20
6	Albert Belle	.20
7	Ryan Klesko	.10
8	Bob Abreu	.10
9	Warren Morris	.10
10	Rafael Palmeiro	.40
11	Nomar Garciaparra	2.00
12	Dante Bichette	.10
13	Jeff Cirillo	.10
14	Carlos Beltran	.10
15	Tony Clark	.10
16	Ray Durham	.10
17	Mark McGwire	2.00
18	Jim Thome	.50
19	Todd Walker	.10
20	Richie Sexson	.40
21	Adrian Beltre	.10
22	Jay Bell	.10
23	Craig Biggio	.25
24	Ben Grieve	.15
25	Greg Maddux	1.50
26	Fernando Tatis	.10
27	Jeromy Burnitz	.10
28	Vinny Castilla	.10
29	Mark Grace	.25
30	Derek Jeter	2.00
31	Larry Walker	.25
32	Ivan Rodriguez	.50
33	Curt Schilling	.40
34	Mike Lamb RC	.25
35	Kevin Brown	.25
36	Andruw Jones	.40
37	Chris Mears RC	.10
38	Bartolo Colon	.10
39	Edgardo Alfonzo	.15
40	Brady Anderson	.20
41	Andres Galarraga	.25
42	Scott Rolen	.50
43	Manny Ramirez	.75
44	Carlos Delgado	.50
45	David Cone	.10
46	Carl Everett	.10
47	Chipper Jones	1.50
48	Barry Bonds	2.00
49	Dean Palmer	.10
50	Frank Thomas	.75
51	Paul O'Neill	.25
52	Mo Vaughn	.20

53	Todd Helton	.75
54	Jason Giambi	1.00
55	Brian Jordan	.10
56	Luis Gonzalez	.25
57	Alex Rodriguez	2.00
58	J.D. Drew	.10
59	Javy Lopez	.20
60	Tony Gwynn	1.00
61	Jason Kendall	.20
62	Pedro Martinez	.75
63	Matt Williams	.20
64	Gary Sheffield	.40
65	Roberto Alomar	.50
66	Lyle Overbay RC	1.00
67	Jeff Bagwell	.75
68	Tim Hudson	.40
69	Sammy Sosa	1.50
70	Keith Reed RC	.10
71	Robin Ventura	.20
72	Cal Ripken Jr.	2.50
73	Alex Gonzalez	.10
74	Aaron McNeal RC	.10
75	Mike Lieberthal	.10
76	Brian Giles	.25
77	Kevin Millwood	.10
78	Troy O'Leary	.10
79	Raul Mondesi	.20
80	John Olerud	.20
81	David Justice	.25
82	Erubiel Durazo	.10
83	Shawn Green	.40
84	Tino Martinez	.20
85	Greg Vaughn	.15
86	Tom Glavine	.25
87	Jose Canseco	.40
88	Kenny Lofton	.25
89	Brian Daubach	.10
90	Mike Piazza	1.50
91	Randy Johnson	.75
92	Pokey Reese	.10
93	Troy Glaus	.50
94	Kerry Wood	.25
95	Sean Casey	.20
96	Magglio Ordonez	.40
97	Bernie Williams	.50
98	Juan Gonzalez	.75
99	Barry Larkin	.25
100	Orlando Hernandez	.20
101	Roger Clemens	1.50
102	Bob Gibson	.40
103	Gary Carter	.10
104	Willie Stargell	.10
105	Joe Morgan	.40
106	Brooks Robinson	.50
107	Ozzie Smith	.50
108	Carl Yastrzemski	.25
109	Al Kaline	.40
110	Frank Robinson	.50
111	Lance Berkman	.10
112	Adam Piatt	.20
113	Vernon Wells	.25
114	Rafael Furcal	.25
115	Rick Ankiel	.20
116	Corey Patterson	.25
117	Josh Hamilton	.25
118	Jack Cust	.20
119	Josh Girdley	.10
120	Pablo Ozuna	.10
121	Sean Burroughs	.25
122	Pat Burrell	.25
123	Chad Hermansen	.10
124	Ruben Mateo	.10
125	Ben Petrick	.10
126	Dee Brown	.10
127	Eric Munson	.10
128	Ruben Salazar	.10
129	Kip Wells	.10
130	Alfonso Soriano	1.00
131	Mark Mulder	.25
132	Roosevelt Brown	.10
133	Nick Johnson	.25
134	Kyle Snyder	.10
135	David Walling	.10
136	Geraldo Guzman RC	.25
137	John Sneed RC	.25
138	Ben Christensen RC	.40
139	Corey Myers RC	.25
140	Jose Ortiz RC	3.00
141	Ryan Christianson RC	.25
142	Brett Myers RC	3.00
143	Bobby Bradley RC	.25
144	Rick Asadoorian RC	.25
145	Julio Zuleta RC	.40
146	Ty Howington RC	1.00
147	Josh Kalinowski RC	.40
148	B.J. Garbe RC	.40
149	Scott Downs RC	.40
150	Dan Wright RC	.25
151	Jeff Bagwell	.40
152	Vladimir Guerrero	.50
153	Mike Piazza	1.00
154	Juan Gonzalez	.40
155	Ivan Rodriguez	.40
156	Manny Ramirez	.40

157	Sammy Sosa	1.00
158	Chipper Jones	.75
159	Shawn Green	.20
160	Ken Griffey Jr.	.75
161	Cal Ripken Jr.	1.25
162	Nomar Garciaparra	1.00
163	Derek Jeter	1.00
164	Barry Bonds	1.00
165	Greg Maddux	.75
166	Mark McGwire	1.00
167	Roberto Alomar	.25
168	Alex Rodriguez	1.25
169	Randy Johnson	.40
170	Tony Gwynn	.50
171	Pedro Martinez	.40
172	Bob Gibson	.25
173	Gary Carter	.10
174	Willie Stargell	.25
175	Joe Morgan	.25
176	Brooks Robinson	.40
177	Ozzie Smith	.50
178	Carl Yastrzemski	.20
179	Al Kaline	.25
180	Frank Robinson	.40
181	Adam Piatt	.20
182	Alfonso Soriano	.75
183	Corey Patterson	.25
184	Vernon Wells	.40
185	Pat Burrell	.20
186	Mark Mulder	.10
187	Eric Munson	.10
188	Rafael Furcal	.15
189	Rick Ankiel	.20
190	Ruben Mateo	.10
191	Sean Burroughs	.20
192	Josh Hamilton	.40
193	Brett Myers	1.00
194	Ben Christensen	.20
195	Ty Howington	.25
196	Rick Asadoorian	.20
197	Josh Kalinowski	.20
198	Corey Myers	.25
199	Ryan Christianson	.25
200	John Sneed	.25

Blue

	NM/M
Stars (1-150):	3-5X
Production 299 Sets	
Stars (151-180):	4-8X
Rookies (180-200):	2-4X
Production 99 Sets	

All-Star Authority

Manny Ramirez

		NM/M
	Complete Set (14):	25.00
	Common Player:	1.00
	Inserted 1:13	
1	Mark McGwire	3.00
2	Sammy Sosa	2.00
3	Ken Griffey Jr.	2.00
4	Cal Ripken Jr.	4.00

5	Tony Gwynn	1.50
6	Barry Bonds	4.00
7	Mike Piazza	2.00
8	Pedro Martinez	1.50
9	Chipper Jones	2.00
10	Manny Ramirez	1.00
11	Alex Rodriguez	3.00
12	Derek Jeter	4.00
13	Nomar Garciaparra	3.00
14	Roberto Alomar	1.00

Autographs

		NM/M
	Common Player:	10.00
	Group A 1:382	
	Group B 1:1,636	
RA	Rick Ankiel/A	10.00
GC	Gary Carter/B	60.00
RF	Rafael Furcal/A	15.00
BG	Bob Gibson/A	25.00
DJ	Derek Jeter/A	90.00
AK	Al Kaline/B	50.00
KM	Kevin Millwood/A	15.00
JM	Joe Morgan/B	40.00
BR	Brooks Robinson/B	40.00
FR	Frank Robinson/B	20.00
OS	Ozzie Smith/B	35.00
WS	Willie Stargell/B	50.00
CY	Carl Yastrzemski/B	65.00

Game Gear Jersey

		NM/M
	Common Player:	10.00
	Inserted 1:382	
1	Kevin Millwood	10.00
2	Brad Penny	10.00
3	J.D. Drew	15.00

Game Gear Bats

		NM/M
	Common Player:	10.00
	Group A 1:2,289	
	Group B 1:1,153	
	Group C 1:409	
1	Rafael Furcal/C	10.00
2	Sean Burroughs/B	10.00
3	Corey Patterson/B	10.00
4	Chipper Jones/B	40.00
5	Vernon Wells/C	15.00
6	Alfonso Soriano/B	25.00
7	Eric Munson/C	10.00
8	Ben Petrick/B	10.00
9	Dee Brown/C	10.00
10	Lance Berkman/C	15.00

Progression

		NM/M
	Complete Set (9):	15.00
	Common Player:	1.00
	Inserted 1:13	
1	Bob Gibson, Pedro Martinez, Rick Ankiel	1.50
2	Gary Carter, Mike Piazza, Ben Petrick	2.00
3	Willie Stargell, Mark McGwire, Pat Burrell	3.00

4	Joe Morgan, Roberto Alomar, Ruben Salazar	1.00
5	Brooks Robinson, Chipper Jones, Sean Burroughs	2.00
6	Ozzie Smith, Derek Jeter, Rafael Furcal	3.00
7	Carl Yastrzemski, Barry Bonds, Josh Hamilton	4.00
8	Al Kaline, Ken Griffey Jr., Ruben Mateo	2.00
9	Frank Robinson, Manny Ramirez, Corey Patterson	1.50

Walk of Fame

	NM/M
Complete Set (15):	15.00
Common Player:	.75
Inserted 1:8	
1 Cal Ripken Jr.	3.00
2 Ken Griffey Jr.	1.50
3 Mark McGwire	2.00
4 Sammy Sosa	1.50
5 Alex Rodriguez	2.00
6 Derek Jeter	2.50
7 Nomar Garciaparra	2.00
8 Chipper Jones	1.50
9 Manny Ramirez	1.00
10 Mike Piazza	1.50
11 Vladimir Guerrero	1.00
12 Barry Bonds	3.00
13 Tony Gwynn	1.00
14 Roberto Alomar	.75
15 Pedro Martinez	1.00

2000 Topps Subway Series

Rick Reed
2000 New York City Subway Series

	NM/M
Complete Fact. Set (101):	70.00
Complete Set (100):	20.00
Common Player:	.20
1 Mike Piazza	3.00
2 Jay Payton	.20
3 Edgardo Alfonzo	.40
4 Todd Pratt	.20
5 Todd Zeile	.20
6 Mike Bordick	.20
7 Robin Ventura	.40
8 Benny Agbayani	.20
9 Timo Perez	.50
10 Kurt Abbott	.20
11 Matt Franco	.20
12 Bubba Trammell	.20
13 Darryl Hamilton	.20
14 Lenny Harris	.20
15 Joe McEwing	.20
16 Mike Hampton	.40

17 Al Leiter	.40
18 Rick Reed	.20
19 Bobby Jones	.20
20 Glendon Rusch	.20
21 Armando Benitez	.20
22 John Franco	.20
23 Rick White	.20
24 Dennis Cook	.20
25 Turk Wendell	.20
26 Bobby Valentine	.20
27 Derek Jeter	4.00
28 Chuck Knoblauch	.40
29 Tino Martinez	.30
30 Jorge Posada	.40
31 Luis Sojo	.20
32 Scott Brosius	.20
33 Chris Turner	.20
34 Bernie Williams	.75
35 David Justice	.75
36 Paul O'Neill	.40
37 Glenallen Hill	.20
38 Jose Vizcaino	.20
39 Luis Polonia	.20
40 Clay Bellinger	.20
41 Orlando Hernandez	.40
42 Roger Clemens	1.50
43 Andy Pettitte	.50
44 Denny Neagle	.20
45 Dwight Gooden	.30
46 David Cone	.20
47 Mariano Rivera	.50
48 Jeff Nelson	.20
49 Mike Stanton	.20
50 Jason Grimsley	.20
51 Jose Canseco	.75
52 Joe Torre	.50
53 Edgardo Alfonzo	.40
54 Darryl Hamilton	.20
55 John Franco	.20
56 Benny Agbayani	.20
57 Bobby Jones	.20
58 New York Mets	.20
59 Bobby Valentine	.20
60 Mike Piazza	3.00
61 Armando Benitez	.20
62 Mike Piazza	3.00
63 Mike Piazza	3.00
64 Todd Zeile	.20
65 Timo Perez	.50
66 Timo Perez	.50
67 Mike Hampton	.40
68 Andy Pettitte	.50
69 Tino Martinez	.30
70 Joe Torre	.50
71 New York Yankees	.40
72 Orlando Hernandez	.40
73 Bernie Williams	.75
74 Andy Pettitte	.50
75 Mariano Rivera	.50
76 New York Yankees	.40
77 Roger Clemens	1.50
78 Derek Jeter	4.00
79 David Justice	.75
80 Mariano Rivera	.50
81 Tino Martinez	.30
82 New York Yankees	.40
83 Jorge Posada	.40
84 Chuck Knoblauch	.40
85 Jose Vizcaino	.20
86 Roger Clemens	1.50
87 Mike Piazza	3.00
88 Clay Bellinger	.20
89 Robin Ventura	.40
90 Benny Agbayani	.20
91 Orlando Hernandez	.40
92 Derek Jeter	4.00
93 Mike Piazza	3.00
94 Mariano Rivera	.50
95 Derek Jeter	3.00
96 Luis Sojo	.20
97 New York Yankees	.40
98 Mike Hampton	.40
99 David Justice	.75
100 Derek Jeter	4.00

Fan Fare

Mike Piazza
Catcher

	NM/M
Common Player:	25.00
Inserted 1:Set	
1 Timo Perez	35.00
2 Edgardo Alfonzo	40.00
3 Mike Piazza	120.00
4 Robin Ventura	35.00

5 Todd Zeile	25.00
6 Benny Agbayani	25.00
7 Jay Payton	25.00
8 Mike Bordick	25.00
9 Matt Franco	25.00
10 Mike Hampton	40.00
11 Al Leiter	40.00
12 Rick Reed	25.00
13 Bobby Jones	25.00
14 Glendon Rusch	25.00
15 Darryl Hamilton	25.00
16 Turk Wendell	25.00
17 John Franco	25.00
18 Armando Benitez	25.00
19 Chuck Knoblauch	35.00
20 Derek Jeter	200.00
21 David Justice	40.00
22 Bernie Williams	50.00
23 Jorge Posada	40.00
24 Paul O'Neill	50.00
25 Tino Martinez	35.00
26 Luis Sojo	25.00
27 Scott Brosius	25.00
28 Jose Canseco	50.00
29 Orlando Hernandez	35.00
30 Roger Clemens	100.00
31 Andy Pettitte	40.00
32 Denny Neagle	25.00
33 David Cone	25.00
34 Jeff Nelson	25.00
35 Mike Stanton	25.00
36 Mariano Rivera	60.00

2000 Topps TEK

	NM/M
Complete Set (45):	25.00
Common Player:	.40
Common Rookie (41-45):	.75
2,000 serial numbered rookies.	
Pack (4):	2.00
Box (20):	30.00
1 Mike Piazza	1.50
2 Chipper Jones	1.50
3 Juan Gonzalez	.75
4 Ivan Rodriguez	.50
5 Cal Ripken Jr.	3.00
6 A.J. Burnett	.40
7 Jim Thome	.75
8 Mo Vaughn	.40
9 Andruw Jones	.75
10 Mark McGwire	2.00
11 Jose Canseco	.50
12 Shawn Green	.50
13 Barry Bonds	3.00
14 Bernie Williams	.50
15 Manny Ramirez	.75
16 Greg Maddux	1.50
17 Carlos Beltran	.40
18 Pedro Martinez	1.00
19 Jeff Bagwell	.75
20 Sammy Sosa	2.00
21 J.D. Drew	.40
22 Randy Johnson	1.00
23 Larry Walker	.40
24 Frank Thomas	.75
25 Orlando Hernandez	.40
26 Scott Rolen	.75
27 Tony Gwynn	1.00
28 Rick Ankiel	.40
29 Roberto Alomar	.75
30 Ken Griffey Jr.	1.50
31 Vladimir Guerrero	1.00
32 Derek Jeter	3.00
33 Nomar Garciaparra	2.00
34 Alex Rodriguez	2.50
35 Sean Casey	.40
36 Adam Piatt	.40
37 Corey Patterson	.40
38 Josh Hamilton	.40
39 Pat Burrell	.50
40 Eric Munson	.40
41 Ruben Salazar RC	.75

42 John Sneed RC	.75
43 Josh Girdley RC	.75
44 Brett Myers RC	4.00
45 Rick Asadoorian RC	.75

Color

Patterns 16-20:	1-2X
Inserted 1:10	

Gold

Stars:	8-15X
Rookies:	4-8X
Production 10 Sets	

ArchiTEKs

	NM/M
Complete Set (18):	20.00
Common Player:	.50
Inserted 1:5	
1 Nomar Garciaparra	2.00
2 Derek Jeter	3.00
3 Chipper Jones	1.50
4 Vladimir Guerrero	1.00
5 Mark McGwire	2.50
6 Ken Griffey Jr.	1.50
7 Mike Piazza	1.50
8 Jeff Bagwell	1.00
9 Larry Walker	.50
10 Manny Ramirez	1.00
11 Alex Rodriguez	2.00
12 Sammy Sosa	2.00
13 Shawn Green	.50
14 Juan Gonzalez	.75
15 Barry Bonds	3.00
16 Pedro Martinez	1.00
17 Cal Ripken Jr.	3.00
18 Ivan Rodriguez	.75

DramaTEK Performers

		NM/M
Complete Set (9):		15.00
Common Player:		1.00
Inserted 1:10		
1	Mark McGwire	3.00
2	Sammy Sosa	2.50
3	Ken Griffey Jr.	2.00
4	Nomar Garciaparra	3.00
5	Chipper Jones	2.00
6	Mike Piazza	2.00
7	Alex Rodriguez	3.00
8	Derek Jeter	3.00
9	Vladimir Guerrero	1.50

TEKtonics

		NM/M
Complete Set (9):		35.00
Common Player:		4.00
Inserted 1:30		
1	Derek Jeter	6.00
2	Mark McGwire	6.00
3	Ken Griffey Jr.	4.00
4	Mike Piazza	4.00
5	Alex Rodriguez	6.00
6	Chipper Jones	4.00
7	Nomar Garciaparra	6.00
8	Sammy Sosa	5.00
9	Cal Ripken Jr.	8.00

2001 Topps

		NM/M
Complete Set (790):		70.00
Complete Ser. 1 Set (405):		30.00
Complete Ser. 2 Set (385):		40.00
Common Player:		.10
Complete Factory Set, Blue (795):		75.00

#	Player	Price
	Complete Factory Set, Gold (795):	75.00
	Ser. 1 Pack (10):	1.50
	Ser. 1 Box (36):	45.00
	Ser. 2 Pack (10):	1.50
	Ser. 2 Box (36):	45.00
1	Cal Ripken Jr.	1.50
2	Chipper Jones	1.00
3	Roger Cedeno	.10
4	Garret Anderson	.10
5	Robin Ventura	.20
6	Daryle Ward	.10
7	Not Issued	
8	Ron Gant	.20
9	Phil Nevin	.10
10	Jermaine Dye	.10
11	Chris Singleton	.10
12	Mike Stanton	.10
13	Brian Hunter	.10
14	Mike Redmond	.10
15	Jim Thome	.25
16	Brian Jordan	.10
17	Joe Girardi	.10
18	Steve Woodard	.10
19	Dustin Hermanson	.10
20	Shawn Green	.30
21	Todd Stottlemyre	.10
22	Dan Wilson	.10
23	Todd Pratt	.10
24	Derek Lowe	.10
25	Juan Gonzalez	.40
26	Clay Bellinger	.10
27	Jeff Fassero	.10
28	Pat Meares	.10
29	Eddie Taubensee	.10
30	Paul O'Neill	.25
31	Jeffrey Hammonds	.10
32	Pokey Reese	.10
33	Mike Mussina	.30
34	Rico Brogna	.10
35	Jay Buhner	.10
36	Steve Cox	.10
37	Quilvio Veras	.10
38	Marquis Grissom	.10
39	Shigetoshi Hasegawa	.10
40	Shane Reynolds	.10
41	Adam Piatt	.10
42	Luis Polonia	.10
43	Brook Fordyce	.10
44	Preston Wilson	.10
45	Ellis Burks	.10
46	Armando Rios	.10
47	Chuck Finley	.10
48	Dan Plesac	.10
49	Shannon Stewart	.10
50	Mark McGwire	1.00
51	Mark Loretta	.10
52	Gerald Williams	.10
53	Eric Young	.10
54	Peter Bergeron	.10
55	Dave Hansen	.10
56	Arthur Rhodes	.10
57	Bobby Jones	.10
58	Matt Clement	.10
59	Mike Benjamin	.10
60	Pedro Martinez	.50
61	Jose Canseco	.40
62	Matt Anderson	.10
63	Torii Hunter	.10
64	Carlos Lee	.10
65	David Cone	.10
66	Ray Sanchez	.10
67	Eric Chavez	.20
68	Rick Helling	.10
69	Manny Alexander	.10
70	John Franco	.10
71	Mike Bordick	.10
72	Andres Galarraga	.25
73	Jose Cruz Jr.	.10
74	Mike Matheny	.10
75	Randy Johnson	.50
76	Richie Sexson	.10
77	Vladimir Nunez	.10
78	Harold Baines	.10
79	Aaron Boone	.10
80	Darin Erstad	.40
81	Alex Gonzalez	.10
82	Gil Heredia	.10
83	Shane Andrews	.10
84	Todd Hundley	.10
85	Bill Mueller	.10
86	Mark McLemore	.10
87	Scott Spiezio	.10
88	Kevin McGlinchy	.10
89	Bubba Trammell	.10
90	Manny Ramirez	.50
91	Mike Lamb	.10
92	Scott Karl	.10
93	Brian Buchanan	.10
94	Chris Turner	.10
95	Mike Sweeney	.10
96	John Wetteland	.10
97	Rob Bell	.10
98	Pat Rapp	.10
99	John Burkett	.10
100	Derek Jeter	1.50
101	J.D. Drew	.25
102	Jose Offerman	.10
103	Rick Reed	.10
104	Will Clark	.30
105	Rickey Henderson	.25
106	Dave Berg	.10
107	Kirk Rueter	.10
108	Lee Stevens	.10
109	Jay Bell	.10
110	Fred McGriff	.20
111	Julio Zuleta	.10
112	Brian Anderson	.10
113	Orlando Cabrera	.10
114	Alex Fernandez	.10
115	Derek Bell	.10
116	Eric Owens	.10
117	Brian Bohannon	.10
118	Dennys Reyes	.10
119	Mike Stanley	.10
120	Jorge Posada	.20
121	Rich Becker	.10
122	Paul Konerko	.10
123	Mike Remlinger	.10
124	Travis Lee	.10
125	Ken Caminiti	.10
126	Kevin Barker	.10
127	Paul Quantrill	.10
128	Ozzie Guillen	.10
129	Kevin Tapani	.10
130	Mark Johnson	.10
131	Randy Wolf	.10
132	Michael Tucker	.10
133	Darren Lewis	.10
134	Joe Randa	.10
135	Jeff Cirillo	.10
136	David Ortiz	.10
137	Herb Perry	.10
138	Jeff Nelson	.10
139	Chris Stynes	.10
140	Johnny Damon	.10
141	Desi Relaford	.10
142	Jason Schmidt	.10
143	Charles Johnson	.10
144	Pat Burrell	.40
145	Gary Sheffield	.25
146	Tom Glavine	.25
147	Jason Isringhausen	.10
148	Chris Carpenter	.10
149	Jeff Suppan	.10
150	Ivan Rodriguez	.50
151	Luis Sojo	.10
152	Ron Villone	.10
153	Mike Sirotka	.10
154	Chuck Knoblauch	.20
155	Jason Kendall	.10
156	Dennis Cook	.10
157	Bobby Estalella	.10
158	Jose Guillen	.10
159	Thomas Howard	.10
160	Carlos Delgado	.50
161	Benji Gil	.10
162	Tim Bogar	.10
163	Kevin Elster	.10
164	Scott Downs	.10
165	Andy Benes	.10
166	Adrian Beltre	.10
167	David Bell	.10
168	Turk Wendell	.10
169	Pete Harnisch	.10
170	Roger Clemens	.75
171	Scott Williamson	.10
172	Kevin Jordan	.10
173	Brad Penny	.10
174	John Flaherty	.10
175	Troy Glaus	.50
176	Kevin Appier	.10
177	Walt Weiss	.10
178	Tyler Houston	.10
179	Michael Barrett	.10
180	Mike Hampton	.10
181	Francisco Cordova	.10
182	Mike Jackson	.10
183	David Segui	.10
184	Carlos Febles	.10
185	Roy Halladay	.10
186	Seth Etherton	.10
187	Charlie Hayes	.10
188	Fernando Tatis	.10
189	Steve Trachsel	.10
190	Livan Hernandez	.10
191	Joe Oliver	.10
192	Stan Javier	.10
193	B.J. Surhoff	.10
194	Rob Ducey	.10
195	Barry Larkin	.25
196	Danny Patterson	.10
197	Bobby Howry	.10
198	Dmitri Young	.10
199	Brian Hunter	.10
200	Alex Rodriguez	1.00
201	Hideo Nomo	.25
202	Luis Alicea	.10
203	Warren Morris	.10
204	Antonio Alfonseca	.10
205	Edgardo Alfonzo	.20
206	Mark Grudzielanek	.10
207	Fernando Vina	.10
208	Willie Greene	.10
209	Homer Bush	.10
210	Jason Giambi	.30
211	Mike Morgan	.10
212	Steve Karsay	.10
213	Matt Lawton	.10
214	Wendell Magee Jr.	.10
215	Rusty Greer	.10
216	Keith Lockhart	.10
217	Billy Koch	.10
218	Todd Hollandsworth	.10
219	Raul Ibanez	.10
220	Tony Gwynn	.75
221	Carl Everett	.20
222	Hector Carrasco	.10
223	Jose Valentin	.10
224	Deivi Cruz	.10
225	Bret Boone	.10
226	Kurt Abbott	.10
227	Melvin Mora	.10
228	Danny Graves	.10
229	Jose Jimenez	.10
230	James Baldwin	.10
231	C.J. Nitkowski	.10
232	Jeff Zimmerman	.10
233	Mike Lowell	.10
234	Hideki Irabu	.10
235	Greg Vaughn	.20
236	Omar Daal	.10
237	Darren Dreifort	.10
238	Gil Meche	.10
239	Damian Jackson	.10
240	Frank Thomas	.75
241	Travis Miller	.10
242	Jeff Frye	.10
243	Dave Magadan	.10
244	Luis Castillo	.10
245	Bartolo Colon	.10
246	Steve Kline	.10
247	Shawon Dunston	.10
248	Rick Aguilera	.10
249	Omar Olivares	.10
250	Craig Biggio	.20
251	Scott Schoeneweis	.10
252	Dave Veres	.10
253	Ramon Martinez	.10
254	Jose Vidro	.10
255	Todd Helton	.50
256	Greg Norton	.10
257	Jacque Jones	.10
258	Jason Grimsley	.10
259	Dan Reichert	.10
260	Robb Nen	.10
261	Mark Clark	.10
262	Scott Hatteberg	.10
263	Doug Brocail	.10
264	Mark Johnson	.10
265	Eric Davis	.20
266	Terry Shumpert	.10
267	Kevin Millar	.10
268	Ismael Valdes	.10
269	Richard Hidalgo	.20
270	Randy Velarde	.10
271	Bengie Molina	.10
272	Tony Womack	.10
273	Enrique Wilson	.10
274	Jeff Brantley	.10
275	Rick Ankiel	.25
276	Terry Mulholland	.10
277	Ron Belliard	.10
278	Terrence Long	.10
279	Alberto Castillo	.10
280	Royce Clayton	.10
281	Joe McEwing	.10
282	Jason McDonald	.10
283	Ricky Bottalico	.10
284	Keith Foulke	.10
285	Brad Radke	.10
286	Gabe Kapler	.10
287	Pedro Astacio	.10
288	Armando Reynoso	.10
289	Darryl Kile	.10
290	Reggie Sanders	.10
291	Esteban Yan	.10
292	Joe Nathan	.10
293	Jay Payton	.10
294	Francisco Cordero	.10
295	Gregg Jefferies	.10
296	LaTroy Hawkins	.10
297	Jeff Tam	.10
298	Jacob Cruz	.10
299	Chris Holt	.10
300	Vladimir Guerrero	.75
301	Marvin Benard	.10
302	Matt Franco	.10
303	Mike Williams	.10
304	Sean Bergman	.10
305	Juan Encarnacion	.10
306	Russ Davis	.10

No.	Player	Value
307	Hanley Frias	.10
308	Ramon Hernandez	.10
309	Matt Walbeck	.10
310	Bill Spiers	.10
311	Bob Wickman	.10
312	Sandy Alomar	.10
313	Eddie Guardado	.10
314	Shane Halter	.10
315	Geoff Jenkins	.20
316	Gerald Witasick	.10
317	Damian Miller	.10
318	Darrin Fletcher	.10
319	Rafael Furcal	.25
320	Mark Grace	.25
321	Mark Mulder	.10
322	Joe Torre	.10
323	Bobby Cox	.10
324	Mike Scioscia	.10
325	Mike Hargrove	.10
326	Jimy Williams	.10
327	Jerry Manuel	.10
328	Buck Showalter	.10
329	Charlie Manuel	.10
330	Don Baylor	.10
331	Phil Garner	.10
332	Jack McKeon	.10
333	Tony Muser	.10
334	Buddy Bell	.10
335	Tom Kelly	.10
336	John Boles	.10
337	Art Howe	.10
338	Larry Dierker	.10
339	Lou Pinella	.10
340	Davey Johnson	.10
341	Larry Rothschild	.10
342	Davey Lopes	.10
343	Johnny Oates	.10
344	Felipe Alou	.10
345	Jim Fregosi	.10
346	Bobby Valentine	.10
347	Terry Francona	.10
348	Gene Lamont	.10
349	Tony LaRussa	.10
350	Bruce Bochy	.10
351	Dusty Baker	.10
352	Adrian Gonzalez, Adam Johnson	.75
353	Matt Wheatland, Brian Digby	.40
354	Tripper Johnson, Scott Thorman	.40
355	Phil Dumatrait, Adam Wainwright	.50
356	Scott Heard, David Parrish RC	.40
357	Rocco Baldelli, Mark Folsom RC	.40
358	Dominic Rich, Aaron Herr	.40
359	Mike Stodolka, Sean Burnett	.25
360	Derek Thompson, Corey Smith	.40
361	Danny Borrell, Jason Bourgeois RC	.40
362	Chin-Feng Chen, Corey Patterson, Josh Hamilton	.25
363	Ryan Anderson, Barry Zito, C.C. Sabathia	.50
364	Scott Sobkowiak, David Walling, Ben Sheets	.50
365	Ty Howington, Josh Kalinowski, Josh Girdley	.10
366	Hee Seop Choi, Aaron McNeal, Jason Hart	1.00
367	Bobby Bradley, Kurt Ainsworth, Chin-Hui Tsao	.40
368	Mike Glendenning, Kenny Kelly, Juan Silvestri RC	.25
369	J.R. House, Ramon Castro, Ben Davis	.25
370	Chance Caple, Rafael Soriano, Pasqual Coco	.50
371	Travis Hafner, Eric Munson, Bucky Jacobsen	1.50
372	Jason Conti, Chris Wakeland, Brian Cole	.20
373	Scott Seabol, Aubrey Huff, Joe Crede	.40
374	Adam Everett, Jose Ortiz, Keith Ginter	.25
375	Carlos Hernandez, Geraldo Guzman, Adam Eaton	.25
376	Bobby Kielty, Milton Bradley, Juan Rivera	.25
377	Mark McGwire	.75
378	Don Larsen	.20
379	Bobby Thomson	.10
380	Bill Mazeroski	.20
381	Reggie Jackson	.40
382	Kirk Gibson	.10
383	Roger Maris	.40
384	Cal Ripken Jr.	.75
385	Hank Aaron	.75
386	Joe Carter	.10
387	Cal Ripken Jr.	.75
388	Randy Johnson	.30
389	Ken Griffey Jr.	.50
390	Troy Glaus	.30
391	Kazuhiro Sasaki	.40
392	Sammy Sosa, Troy Glaus	.50
393	Todd Helton, Edgar Martinez	.25
394	Nomar Garciaparra, Todd Helton	.50
395	Barry Bonds, Jason Giambi	.40
396	Todd Helton, Manny Ramirez	.25
397	Todd Helton, Darin Erstad	.25
398	Kevin Brown, Pedro Martinez	.25
399	Randy Johnson, Pedro Martinez	.25
400	Will Clark (Playoff Highlights)	.20
401	NY Mets Divisional Highlight	.10
402	NY Yankees Divisional Highlight	.10
403	Seattle Mariners Divisional Highlight	.10
404	Mike Hampton (Playoff Highlights)	.10
405	NY Yankees ALCS Highlight	.75
406	World Series Highlight	1.00
407	Jeff Bagwell	.50
408	Brant Brown	.10
409	Brad Fullmer	.10
410	Dean Palmer	.10
411	Gregg Zaun	.10
412	Jose Vizcaino	.10
413	Jeff Abbott	.10
414	Travis Fryman	.15
415	Mike Cameron	.10
416	Matt Mantei	.10
417	Alan Benes	.10
418	Mickey Morandini	.10
419	Troy Percival	.10
420	Eddie Perez	.10
421	Vernon Wells	.10
422	Ricky Gutierrez	.10
423	Carlos Hernandez	.10
424	Chan Ho Park	.15
425	Armando Benitez	.10
426	Sidney Ponson	.10
427	Adrian Brown	.10
428	Ruben Mateo	.20
429	Alex Ochoa	.10
430	Jose Rosado	.10
431	Masato Yoshii	.10
432	Corey Koskie	.10
433	Andy Pettitte	.20
434	Brian Daubach	.10
435	Sterling Hitchcock	.10
436	Timo Perez	.10
437	Shawn Estes	.10
438	Tony Armas Jr.	.10
439	Danny Bautista	.10
440	Randy Winn	.10
441	Wilson Alvarez	.10
442	Rondell White	.15
443	Jeromy Burnitz	.10
444	Kelvim Escobar	.10
445	Paul Bako	.10
446	Javier Vazquez	.10
447	Eric Gagne	.10
448	Kenny Lofton	.20
449	Mark Kotsay	.10
450	Jamie Moyer	.10
451	Delino DeShields	.10
452	Rey Ordonez	.10
453	Russ Ortiz	.10
454	Dave Burba	.10
455	Eric Karros	.15
456	Felix Martinez	.10
457	Tony Batista	.10
458	Bobby Higginson	.10
459	Jeff D'Amico	.10
460	Shane Spencer	.10
461	Brent Mayne	.10
462	Glendon Rusch	.10
463	Chris Gomez	.10
464	Jeff Shaw	.10
465	Damon Buford	.10
466	Mike DiFelice	.10
467	Jimmy Haynes	.10
468	Billy Wagner	.10
469	A.J. Hinch	.10
470	Gary DiSarcina	.10
471	Tom Lampkin	.10
472	Adam Eaton	.10
473	Brian Giles	.15
474	John Thomson	.10
475	Cal Eldred	.10
476	Ramiro Mendoza	.10
477	Scott Sullivan	.10
478	Scott Rolen	.25
479	Todd Ritchie	.10
480	Pablo Ozuna	.10
481	Carl Pavano	.10
482	Matt Morris	.10
483	Matt Stairs	.10
484	Tim Belcher	.10
485	Lance Berkman	.15
486	Brian Meadows	.10
487	Bobby Abreu	.10
488	John Vander Wal	.10
489	Donnie Sadler	.10
490	Damion Easley	.10
491	David Justice	.25
492	Ray Durham	.10
493	Todd Zeile	.10
494	Desi Relaford	.10
495	Cliff Floyd	.10
496	Scott Downs	.10
497	Barry Bonds	1.00
498	Jeff D'Amico	.10
499	Octavio Dotel	.10
500	Kent Mercker	.10
501	Craig Grebeck	.10
502	Roberto Hernandez	.10
503	Matt Williams	.15
504	Bruce Aven	.10
505	Brett Tomko	.10
506	Kris Benson	.10
507	Neifi Perez	.10
508	Alfonso Soriano	.50
509	Keith Osik	.10
510	Matt Franco	.10
511	Steve Finley	.10
512	Olmedo Saenz	.10
513	Esteban Loaiza	.10
514	Adam Kennedy	.10
515	Scott Elarton	.10
516	Moises Alou	.15
517	Bryan Rekar	.10
518	Darryl Hamilton	.10
519	Osvaldo Fernandez	.10
520	Kip Wells	.10
521	Bernie Williams	.40
522	Mike Darr	.10
523	Marlon Anderson	.10
524	Derrek Lee	.10
525	Ugueth Urbina	.10
526	Vinny Castilla	.10
527	David Wells	.10
528	Jason Marquis	.10
529	Orlando Palmeiro	.10
530	Carlos Perez	.10
531	J.T. Snow Jr.	.10
532	Al Leiter	.15
533	Jimmy Anderson	.10
534	Brett Laxton	.10
535	Butch Huskey	.10
536	Orlando Hernandez	.20
537	Magglio Ordonez	.15
538	Willie Blair	.10
539	Kevin Sefcik	.10
540	Chad Curtis	.10
541	John Halama	.10
542	Andy Fox	.10
543	Juan Guzman	.10
544	Frank Menechino	.10
545	Raul Mondesi	.15
546	Tim Salmon	.15
547	Ryan Rupe	.10
548	Jeff Reed	.10
549	Mike Mordecai	.10
550	Jeff Kent	.15
551	Wiki Gonzalez	.10
552	Kenny Rogers	.10
553	Kevin Young	.10
554	Brian Johnson	.10
555	Tom Goodwin	.10
556	Tony Clark	.10
557	Mac Suzuki	.10
558	Brian Moehler	.10
559	Jim Parque	.10
560	Mariano Rivera	.20
561	Trot Nixon	.10
562	Mike Mussina	.30
563	Nelson Figueroa	.10
564	Alex Gonzalez	.10
565	Benny Agbayani	.10
566	Ed Sprague	.10
567	Scott Erickson	.10
568	Abraham Nunez	.10
569	Jerry DiPoto	.10
570	Sean Casey	.10
571	Wilton Veras	.10
572	Joe Mays	.10
573	Bill Simas	.10
574	Doug Glanville	.10
575	Scott Sauerbeck	.10
576	Ben Davis	.10
577	Jesus Sanchez	.10
578	Ricardo Rincon	.10
579	John Olerud	.15
580	Curt Schilling	.15
581	Alex Cora	.10
582	Pat Hentgen	.10
583	Javy Lopez	.15
584	Ben Grieve	.15
585	Frank Castillo	.10
586	Kevin Stocker	.10
587	Mark Sweeney	.10
588	Ray Lankford	.10
589	Turner Ward	.10
590	Felipe Crespo	.10
591	Omar Vizquel	.15
592	Mike Lieberthal	.10
593	Ken Griffey Jr.	1.00
594	Troy O'Leary	.10
595	Dave Mlicki (Front photo actually Brian Moehler)	.10
596	Manny Ramirez	.50
597	Mike Lansing	.10
598	Rich Aurilia	.10
599	Russ Branyan	.10
600	Russ Johnson	.10
601	Gregg Colbrunn	.10
602	Andruw Jones	.40
603	Henry Blanco	.10
604	Jarrod Washburn	.10
605	Tony Eusebio	.10
606	Aaron Sele	.10
607	Charles Nagy	.10
608	Ryan Klesko	.10
609	Dante Bichette	.10
610	Bill Haselman	.10
611	Jerry Spradlin	.10
612	Alex Rodriguez	1.00
613	Jose Silva	.10
614	Darren Oliver	.10
615	Pat Mahomes	.10
616	Roberto Alomar	.40
617	Edgar Renteria	.10
618	Jon Lieber	.10
619	John Rocker	.10
620	Miguel Tejada	.15
621	Mo Vaughn	.15
622	Jose Lima	.10
623	Kerry Wood	.15
624	Mike Timlin	.10
625	Wil Cordero	.10
626	Albert Belle	.15
627	Bobby Jones	.10
628	Doug Mirabelli	.10
629	Jason Tyner	.10
630	Andy Ashby	.10
631	Jose Hernandez	.10
632	Devon White	.10
633	Ruben Rivera	.10
634	Steve Parris	.10
635	David McCarty	.10
636	Jose Canseco	.25
637	Todd Walker	.10
638	Stan Spencer	.10
639	Wayne Gomes	.10
640	Freddy Garcia	.10
641	Jeremy Giambi	.10
642	Luis Lopez	.10
643	John Smoltz	.10
644	Kelly Stinnett	.10
645	Kevin Brown	.10
646	Wilton Guerrero	.10
647	Al Martin	.10
648	Woody Williams	.10
649	Brian Rose	.10
650	Rafael Palmeiro	.30
651	Pete Schourek	.10
652	Kevin Jarvis	.10
653	Mark Redman	.10
654	Ricky Ledee	.10
655	Larry Walker	.20
656	Paul Byrd	.10
657	Jason Bere	.10
658	Rick White	.10
659	Calvin Murray	.10
660	Greg Maddux	1.00
661	Ron Gant	.10
662	Eli Marrero	.10
663	Graeme Lloyd	.10
664	Trevor Hoffman	.10
665	Nomar Garciaparra	1.00
666	Glenallen Hill	.10
667	Matt LeCroy	.10
668	Justin Thompson	.10
669	Brady Anderson	.10
670	Miguel Batista	.10

671	Erubiel Durazo	.10
672	Kevin Millwood	.10
673	Mitch Meluskey	.10
674	Luis Gonzalez	.15
675	Edgar Martinez	.10
676	Robert Person	.10
677	Benito Santiago	.10
678	Todd Jones	.10
679	Tino Martinez	.15
680	Carlos Beltran	.10
681	Gabe White	.10
682	Bret Saberhagen	.10
683	Jeff Conine	.10
684	Jaret Wright	.10
685	Bernard Gilkey	.10
686	Garrett Stephenson	.10
687	Jamey Wright	.10
688	Sammy Sosa	1.00
689	John Jaha	.10
690	Ramon Martinez	.10
691	Robert Fick	.10
692	Eric Milton	.10
693	Denny Neagle	.10
694	Ron Coomer	.10
695	John Valentin	.10
696	Placido Polanco	.10
697	Tim Hudson	.15
698	Marty Cordova	.10
699	Chad Kreuter	.10
700	Frank Catalanotto	.10
701	Tim Wakefield	.10
702	Jim Edmonds	.15
703	Michael Tucker	.10
704	Cristian Guzman	.10
705	Joey Hamilton	.10
706	Mike Piazza	1.00
707	Dave Martinez	.10
708	Mike Hampton	.15
709	Bobby Bonilla	.10
710	Juan Pierre	.10
711	John Parrish	.10
712	Kory DeHaan	.10
713	Brian Tollberg	.10
714	Chris Truby	.10
715	Emil Brown	.10
716	Ryan Dempster	.10
717	Rich Garces	.10
718	Mike Myers	.10
719	Luis Ordaz	.10
720	Kazuhiro Sasaki	.10
721	Mark Quinn	.10
722	Ramon Ortiz	.10
723	Kerry Ligtenberg	.10
724	Rolando Arrojo	.10
725	Tsuyoshi Shinjo RC	1.00
726	Ichiro Suzuki RC	15.00
727	Roy Oswalt, Pat Strange, Jon Rauch	.25
728	Phil Wilson, Jake Peavy, Darwin Cubillan RC	.75
729	Steve Smyth, Mike Bynum, Nathan Haynes	.40
730	Michael Cuddyer, Joe Lawrence, Choo Freeman	.10
731	Carlos Pena, Larry Barnes, Dewayne Wise	.10
732	Gookie Dawkins, Erick Almonte, Felipe Lopez	.40
733	Alex Escobar, Eric Valent, Brad Wilkerson	.10
734	Toby Hall, Rod Barajas, Jeff Goldbach RC	.10
735	Jason Romano, Marcus Giles, Pablo Ozuna	.10
736	Dee Brown, Jack Cust, Vernon Wells	.10
737	David Espinosa, Luis Montanez RC	.40
738	John Lackey, Justin Wayne RC	.50
739	Josh Axelson, Carmen Cali RC	.50
740	Shaun Boyd, Chris Morris RC	.50
741	Tommy Arko, Dan Moylan RC	.50
742	Luis Cotto, Luis Escobar	.40
743	Brandon Mims, Blake Williams RC	.40
744	Chris Russ, Bryan Edwards	.40
745	Joe Torres, Ben Diggins	.10
746	Mark Dalesandro, Edwin Encarnacion RC	.50
747	Brian Bass, Odannis Ayala RC	.40
748	Jason Kaanoi, Michael Mathews RC	.10
749	Stuart McFarland, Adam Sterrett RC	.40
750	David Krynzel, Grady Sizemore	.50
751	Keith Bucktrot, Dane Sardinha	.10
752	Anaheim Angels	.10
753	Arizona Diamondbacks	.10
754	Atlanta Braves	.10
755	Baltimore Orioles	.10
756	Boston Red Sox	.10
757	Chicago Cubs	.10
758	Chicago White Sox	.10
759	Cincinnati Reds	.10
760	Cleveland Indians	.10
761	Colorado Rockies	.10
762	Detroit Tigers	.10
763	Florida Marlins	.10
764	Houston Astros	.10
765	Kansas City Royals	.10
766	Los Angeles Dodgers	.10
767	Milwaukee Brewers	.10
768	Minnesota Twins	.10
769	Montreal Expos	.10
770	New York Mets	.10
771	New York Yankees	.75
772	Oakland Athletics	.10
773	Philadelphia Phillies	.10
774	Pittsburgh Pirates	.10
775	San Diego Padres	.10
776	San Francisco Giants	.10
777	Seattle Mariners	.10
778	St. Louis Cardinals	.10
779	Tampa Bay Devil Rays	.10
780	Texas Rangers	.10
781	Toronto Blue Jays	.10
782	Bucky Dent	.10
783	Jackie Robinson	1.00
784	Roberto Clemente	1.00
785	Nolan Ryan	1.50
786	Kerry Wood	.10
787	Rickey Henderson	.20
788	Lou Brock	.25
789	David Wells	.10
790	Andruw Jones	.25
791	Carlton Fisk	.10

Gold

Stars: 8-15X
Prospects and RC's: 3-6X
Inserted 1:17

Autographs

NM/M

Common Player:
Group A 1:22,866
Group B 1:3,054
Group C 1:1,431
Group D 1:18,339
Group E 1:13,737
Group F 1:11,015

Group G 1:625		
HA	Hank Aaron	250.00
DA	Dick Allen	25.00
RA	Rick Ankiel	10.00
RB	Rocco Baldelli	30.00
EB	Ernie Banks	100.00
YB	Yogi Berra	80.00
LB	Lou Brock	50.00
PB	Pat Burrell	15.00
RC	Rod Carew	50.00
MC	Mike Cuellar	15.00
WF	Whitey Ford	40.00
RF	Rafael Furcal	25.00
BG	Bob Gibson	40.00
AG	Adrian Gonzalez	15.00
SH	Scott Heard	15.00
WH	Willie Hernandez	10.00
AJ	Adam Johnson	10.00
CJ	Chipper Jones	80.00
SK	Sandy Koufax	500.00
ML	Mike Lamb	10.00
VL	Vernon Law	15.00
JM	Jason Marquis	10.00
WM	Willie Mays	250.00
MO	Magglio Ordonez	20.00
AP	Andy Pafko	30.00
BR	Brooks Robinson	80.00
JR	Joe Rudi	15.00
MS	Mike Schmidt	100.00
MS	Mike Stodolka	15.00
RS	Ron Swoboda	30.00
GT	Garry Templeton	30.00
JV	Jose Vidro	20.00
MW	Matt Wheatland	20.00
TZ	Todd Zeile	20.00

Autographs Series 2

NM/M

Common Player:		10.00
DA	Denny Abreu	10.00
TA	Tony Alvarez	10.00
RB	Rocco Baldelli	30.00
GB	George Bell	10.00
JB	Johnny Bench	60.00
BB	Barry Bonds	180.00
MB	Milton Bradley	15.00
GHB	George Brett	175.00
MAB	Mike Bynum	10.00
EB	Eric Byrnes	10.00
JC	Jorge Cantu	10.00
CC	Chris Clapinski	10.00
WD	Willie Davis	40.00
JDD	J.D. Drew	30.00
TDLR	Tomas de la Rosa	10.00
CD	Chad Durbin	10.00
CE	Carl Erskine	25.00
BE	Brian Esposito	15.00
WF	Whitey Ford	40.00
EF	Eddy Furniss	10.00
BG	Bob Gibson	40.00
MG	Mike Glendenning	15.00
AG	Adrian Gonzalez	20.00
NG	Nick Green	10.00
KG	Kevin Gregg	10.00
DG	Dick Groat	25.00
GG	Geraldo Guzman	10.00
YH	Yamid Haad	10.00
TH	Todd Helton	40.00
AH	Aaron Herr	15.00
KH	Ken Holtzman	20.00
RJ	Reggie Jackson	100.00
NJ	Neil Jenkins	15.00
AJ	Adam Johnson	10.00
TJ	Tripper Johnson	15.00
BK	Bobby Kielty	10.00
JL	John Lackey	10.00
ML	Matt Lawton	10.00
CL	Colby Lewis	10.00
MFL	Mike Lockwood	10.00
GM	Gary Matthews	20.00
LM	Luis Montanez	10.00
EM	Eric Munson	15.00
SM	Stan Musial	150.00
BO	Ben Oglivie	15.00
AO	Augie Ojeda	10.00
ER	Erasmo Ramirez	15.00
CR	Chris Richard	15.00
JR	Juan Rincon	10.00
LR	Luis Rivas	20.00
SR	Scott Rolen	35.00
NR	Nolan Ryan	200.00
JS	Juan Salas	10.00
TS	Tom Seaver	150.00
CS	Carlos Silva	10.00
GS	Grady Sizemore	125.00
CCS	Corey Smith	10.00
MS	Mike Stodolka	10.00
MS	Mike Sweeney	10.00
KT	Kent Tekulve	20.00
DT	Derek Thompson	10.00
ST	Scott Thorman	10.00
BT	Brian Tollberg	15.00
JW	Justin Wayne	20.00
MW	Michael Wenner	15.00
MJW	Matt Wheatland	15.00
WW	Wilbur Wood	20.00
CY	Carl Yastrzemski	75.00

A Look Ahead

NM/M

Complete Set (10):		15.00
Common Player:		.50
Inserted 1:25		
1	Vladimir Guerrero	1.50
2	Derek Jeter	4.00
3	Todd Helton	1.00
4	Alex Rodriguez	3.00
5	Ken Griffey Jr.	2.00
6	Nomar Garciaparra	3.00
7	Chipper Jones	2.00
8	Ivan Rodriguez	1.00
9	Pedro Martinez	1.50
10	Rick Ankiel	.50

A Tradition Continued

NM/M

Complete Set (30):		50.00
Common Player:		.50
Inserted 1:17		
1	Chipper Jones	3.00
2	Cal Ripken Jr.	6.00
3	Mike Piazza	3.00
4	Ken Griffey Jr.	3.00
5	Randy Johnson	1.50
6	Derek Jeter	5.00
7	Scott Rolen	1.50
8	Nomar Garciaparra	4.00
9	Roberto Alomar	1.00
10	Greg Maddux	1.50
11	Ivan Rodriguez	1.50
12	Jeff Bagwell	1.50
13	Luis Montanez	1.50
14	Pedro Martinez	2.00
15	Sammy Sosa	4.00

16	Jim Edmonds	1.00
17	Mo Vaughn	.50
18	Barry Bonds	5.00
19	Larry Walker	.75
20	Mark McGwire	4.00
21	Vladimir Guerrero	2.00
22	Andruw Jones	1.50
23	Todd Helton	1.50
24	Kevin Brown	.75
25	Tony Gwynn	2.00
26	Manny Ramirez	1.50
27	Roger Clemens	4.00
28	Frank Thomas	1.50
29	Shawn Green	.75
30	Jim Thome	1.50

Base Hit

		NM/M
	Complete Set (28):	450.00
	Common Player:	25.00
BH1	Mike Scioscia	35.00
BH2	Larry Dierker	25.00
BH3	Art Howe	25.00
BH4	Jim Fregosi	25.00
BH5	Bobby Cox	35.00
BH6	Davey Lopes	25.00
BH7	Tony LaRussa	30.00
BH8	Don Baylor	35.00
BH9	Larry Rothschild	25.00
BH10	Buck Showalter	30.00
BH11	Davey Johnson	30.00
BH12	Felipe Alou	30.00
BH13	Charlie Manuel	25.00
BH14	Lou Piniella	30.00
BH15	John Boles	25.00
BH16	Bobby Valentine	30.00
BH17	Mike Hargrove	25.00
BH18	Bruce Bochy	25.00
BH19	Terry Francona	25.00
BH20	Gene Lamont	25.00
BH21	Johnny Oates	25.00
BH22	Jimy Williams	25.00
BH23	Jack McKeon	25.00
BH24	Buddy Bell	25.00
BH25	Tony Muser	25.00
BH26	Phil Garner	25.00
BH27	Tom Kelly	25.00
BH28	Jerry Manuel	25.00

Before There Was Topps

Lou Gehrig

		NM/M
	Complete Set (10):	20.00
	Common Player:	1.50
	Inserted 1:25	
BT1	Lou Gehrig	4.00
BT2	Babe Ruth	5.00
BT3	Cy Young	2.00
BT4	Walter Johnson	2.00
BT5	Ty Cobb	4.00
BT6	Tris Speaker	1.50
BT7	Honus Wagner	2.00
BT8	Christy Mathewson	1.50
BT9	Grover Alexander	1.50
BT0	Joe DiMaggio	4.00

Combos

	NM/M
Complete Set (20):	25.00
Common Player:	1.50

LATIN HEAT

VLADIMIR GUERRERO — ROBERTO CLEMENTE

		NM/M
	Inserted 1:12	
1	Yogi Berra, Whitey Ford, Reggie Jackson, Don Mattingly, Derek Jeter	3.00
2	Brooks Robinson, Cal Ripken Jr.	3.00
3	Barry Bonds, Willie Mays	3.00
4	Bob Gibson, Pedro Martinez	1.50
5	Ivan Rodriguez, Johnny Bench	2.00
6	Ernie Banks, Alex Rodriguez	2.50
7	Joe Morgan, Ken Griffey Jr., Barry Larkin, Johnny Bench	2.50
8	Vladimir Guerrero, Roberto Clemente	2.50
9	Ted Williams, Carl Yastrzemski, Nomar Garciaparra	3.00
10	Joe Torre, Casey Stengel	1.50
11	Kevin Brown, Sandy Koufax, Don Drysdale	3.00
12	Mark McGwire, Sammy Sosa, Roger Maris, Babe Ruth	3.00
13	Ted Williams, Carl Yastrzemski, Nomar Garciaparra	3.00
14	Greg Maddux, Roger Clemens, Cy Young	2.00
15	Tony Gwynn, Ted Williams	3.00
16	Cal Ripken Jr., Lou Gehrig	4.00
17	Sandy Koufax, Randy Johnson, Warren Spahn, Steve Carlton	3.00
18	Mike Piazza, Josh Gibson	2.00
19	Barry Bonds, Willie Mays	3.00
20	Jackie Robinson, Larry Doby	2.50

Golden Anniversary

GOLD NUGGETS

CAL RIPKEN

		NM/M
	Complete Set (50):	60.00
	Common Player:	.50
	Inserted 1:10	
1	Hank Aaron	3.00
2	Ernie Banks	1.50
3	Mike Schmidt	3.00

4	Willie Mays	4.00
5	Johnny Bench	1.50
6	Tom Seaver	1.00
7	Frank Robinson	1.00
8	Sandy Koufax	3.00
9	Bob Gibson	1.00
10	Ted Williams	4.00
11	Cal Ripken Jr.	5.00
12	Tony Gwynn	1.50
13	Mark McGwire	3.00
14	Ken Griffey Jr.	2.00
15	Greg Maddux	2.00
16	Roger Clemens	3.00
17	Barry Bonds	4.00
18	Rickey Henderson	.75
19	Mike Piazza	2.00
20	Jose Canseco	1.00
21	Derek Jeter	4.00
22	Nomar Garciaparra	3.00
23	Alex Rodriguez	3.00
24	Sammy Sosa	2.50
25	Ivan Rodriguez	1.00
26	Vladimir Guerrero	1.50
27	Chipper Jones	2.00
28	Jeff Bagwell	1.00
29	Pedro Martinez	1.50
30	Randy Johnson	1.50
31	Pat Burrell	1.00
32	Josh Hamilton	.50
33	Nick Johnson	.50
34	Corey Patterson	.50
35	Eric Munson	.50
36	Sean Burroughs	.50
37	Alfonso Soriano	1.50
38	Chin-Feng Chen	.50
39	Barry Zito	.75
40	Adrian Gonzalez	.50
41	Mark McGwire	3.00
42	Nomar Garciaparra	3.00
43	Todd Helton	1.00
44	Matt Williams	.50
45	Troy Glaus	.75
46	Geoff Jenkins	.50
47	Frank Thomas	1.00
48	Mo Vaughn	.50
49	Barry Larkin	.75
50	J.D. Drew	.50

Hit Parade

Reggie Jackson

		NM/M
	Complete Set (6):	
	Common Player:	25.00
	1:2,600 Retail	
HP1	Reggie Jackson	40.00
HP2	Dave Winfield	25.00
HP3	Eddie Murray	25.00
HP4	Rickey Henderson	25.00
HP5	Robin Yount	25.00
HP6	Carl Yastrzemski	65.00

2001 Topps Home Team Advantage

Common Player:	
Star:	+25 Percent
(See 2001 Topps for checklist and base card values.)	

King of Kings

		NM/M
	Common Card:	25.00
	Inserted 1:2,056	
1	Hank Aaron	75.00
2	Nolan Ryan	75.00
3	Rickey Henderson	30.00
5	Bob Gibson	25.00
6	Nolan Ryan	75.00

King of Kings Golden Edition

	NM/M
Production 50 cards.	
KKGE Hank Aaron, Nolan Ryan, Rickey Henderson	250.00

Noteworthy

bob gibson

		NM/M
	Complete Set (50):	40.00
	Common Player:	.50
	Inserted 1:8	
TN1	Mark McGwire	2.00
TN2	Derek Jeter	2.50
TN3	Sammy Sosa	2.00
TN4	Todd Helton	1.00
TN5	Alex Rodriguez	2.00
TN6	Chipper Jones	1.50
TN7	Barry Bonds	3.00
TN8	Ken Griffey Jr.	1.50
TN9	Nomar Garciaparra	2.00
TN10	Frank Thomas	1.00
TN11	Randy Johnson	1.00
TN12	Cal Ripken Jr.	3.00
TN13	Mike Piazza	1.50
TN14	Ivan Rodriguez	1.00
TN15	Jeff Bagwell	1.00
TN16	Vladimir Guerrero	1.00
TN17	Greg Maddux	1.50
TN18	Tony Gwynn	1.00
TN19	Larry Walker	.50
TN20	Juan Gonzalez	.75
TN21	Scott Rolen	1.00
TN22	Jason Giambi	1.00
TN23	Jeff Kent	.50
TN24	Pat Burrell	.75
TN25	Pedro Martinez	1.00

TN26	Willie Mays	2.00
TN27	Whitey Ford	.75
TN28	Jackie Robinson	2.00
TN29	Ted Williams	2.50
TN30	Babe Ruth	3.00
TN31	Warren Spahn	1.00
TN32	Nolan Ryan	3.00
TN33	Yogi Berra	1.00
TN34	Mike Schmidt	2.00
TN35	Steve Carlton	.75
TN36	Brooks Robinson	1.00
TN37	Bob Gibson	1.00
TN38	Reggie Jackson	1.00
TN39	Johnny Bench	1.50
TN40	Ernie Banks	1.00
TN41	Eddie Mathews	.50
TN42	Don Mattingly	2.50
TN43	Duke Snider	.75
TN44	Hank Aaron	2.00
TN45	Roberto Clemente	2.00
TN46	Harmon Killebrew	1.00
TN47	Frank Robinson	1.00
TN48	Stan Musial	2.00
TN49	Lou Brock	.50
TN50	Joe Morgan	.50

Originals

		NM/M
Common Player:		10.00
Series 1 1:1,172		
Series 2 1:1,023		
1	Roberto Clemente/ 1955	80.00
2	Carl Yastrzemski/ 1960	30.00
3	Mike Schmidt/1974	30.00
4	Wade Boggs/1983	10.00
5	Chipper Jones/1991	15.00
6	Willie Mays	40.00
7	Lou Brock	15.00
8	Dave Parker	10.00
9	Barry Bonds	40.00
10	Alex Rodriguez	25.00

The Shot Heard Round
The World Autograph

		NM/M
B. Thomson/R. Branca		
Ralph Branca,		
Bobby Thomson		40.00

Through the Years

DON MATTINGLY OF-1B

		NM/M
Complete Set (50):		100.00
Common Player:		1.50
Inserted 1:8		
1	Yogi Berra	2.00
2	Roy Campanella	2.00

3	Willie Mays	5.00
4	Andy Pafko	1.50
5	Jackie Robinson	4.00
6	Stan Musial	4.00
7	Duke Snider	2.00
8	Warren Spahn	2.50
9	Ted Williams	6.00
10	Eddie Matthews	2.00
11	Willie McCovey	1.50
12	Frank Robinson	2.00
13	Ernie Banks	3.00
14	Hank Aaron	5.00
15	Sandy Koufax	4.00
16	Bob Gibson	2.00
17	Harmon Killebrew	2.00
18	Whitey Ford	2.00
19	Roberto Clemente	5.00
20	Juan Marichal	1.50
21	Johnny Bench	3.00
22	Willie Stargell	1.50
23	Joe Morgan	1.50
24	Carl Yastrzemski	2.00
25	Reggie Jackson	2.00
26	Tom Seaver	2.00
27	Steve Carlton	1.50
28	Jim Palmer	1.50
29	Rod Carew	1.50
30	George Brett	5.00
31	Roger Clemens	4.00
32	Don Mattingly	5.00
33	Ryne Sandberg	3.00
34	Mike Schmidt	4.00
35	Cal Ripken Jr.	6.00
36	Tony Gwynn	2.00
37	Ozzie Smith	3.00
38	Wade Boggs	1.50
39	Nolan Ryan	6.00
40	Robin Yount	2.00
41	Mark McGwire	5.00
42	Ken Griffey Jr.	4.00
43	Sammy Sosa	4.00
44	Alex Rodriguez	4.00
45	Barry Bonds	6.00
46	Mike Piazza	3.00
47	Chipper Jones	3.00
48	Greg Maddux	3.00
49	Nomar Garciaparra	4.00
50	Derek Jeter	5.00

Two of a Kind

		NM/M
Inserted 1:30,167		
TK	Bo Jackson, Deion Sanders	75.00

What Could've Been

		NM/M
Complete Set (10):		15.00
Common Player:		1.00
Inserted 1:25		
WCB1	Josh Gibson	3.00
WCB2	Leroy "Satchel" Paige	3.00
WCB3	Walter "Buck" Leonard	2.00
WCB4	James "Cool Papa" Bell	2.00
WCB5	Andrew "Rube" Foster	2.00
WCB6	Martin Dihigo	1.00
WCB7	William "Judy" Johnson	1.50
WCB8	Mule Suttles	1.00
WCB9	Ray Dandridge	1.00
WCB10	John Henry "Pop" Lloyd	2.00

2001 Topps Traded & Rookies

	NM/M
Complete Topps Set (265):	140.00

Common Player:		.10
Chrome Cards:		2-3X
Pack (8 + 2 Chrome):		8.00
Box (24):		175.00
T1	Sandy Alomar Jr.	.10
T2	Kevin Appier	.10
T3	Brad Ausmus	.10
T4	Derek Bell	.10
T5	Bret Boone	.20
T6	Rico Brogna	.10
T7	Ellis Burks	.10
T8	Ken Caminiti	.10
T9	Roger Cedeno	.10
T10	Royce Clayton	.10
T11	Enrique Wilson	.10
T12	Rheal Cormier	.10
T13	Eric Davis	.10
T14	Shawon Duston	.10
T15	Andres Galarraga	.20
T16	Tom Gordon	.10
T17	Mark Grace	.50
T18	Jeffrey Hammonds	.10
T19	Dustin Hermanson	.10
T20	Quinton McCracken	.10
T21	Todd Hundley	.10
T22	Charles Johnson	.10
T23	Marquis Grissom	.10
T24	Jose Mesa	.10
T25	Terry Mulholland	.10
T26	John Rocker	.10
T27	Jeff Frye	.10
T28	Reggie Sanders	.10
T29	David Segui	.10
T30	Mike Sirotka	.10
T31	Fernando Tatis	.10
T32	Steve Trachsel	.10
T33	Ismael Valdes	.10
T34	Randy Velarde	.10
T35	Brian Boehringer	.10
T36	Mike Bordick	.10
T37	Ken Bottenfield	.10
T38	Pat Rapp	.10
T39	Jeff Nelson	.10
T40	Ricky Bottalico	.10
T41	Deion Sanders	.20
T42	Hideo Nomo	.50
T43	Bill Mueller	.10
T44	Roberto Kelly	.10
T45	Chris Holt	.10
T46	Mike Jackson	.10
T47	Devon White	.10
T48	Gerald Williams	.10
T49	Eddie Taubensee	.10
T50	Brian Hunter	.10
T51	Nelson Cruz	.10
T52	Jeff Fassero	.10
T53	Bubba Trammell	.10
T54	Bo Porter	.10
T55	Greg Norton	.10
T56	Benito Santiago	.10
T57	Ruben Rivera	.10
T58	Dee Brown	.10
T59	Jose Canseco	.50
T60	Chris Michalak	.10
T61	Tim Worrell	.10
T62	Matt Clement	.10
T63	Bill Pulsipher	.10
T64	Troy Brohawn	.10
T65	Mark Kotsay	.10
T66	Jose Lima	.10
T67	Shea Hillenbrand	.10
T68	Ted Lilly	.10
T69	Jermaine Dye	.10
T70	Jerry Hairston Jr.	.10
T71	John Mabry	.10
T72	Kurt Abbott	.10
T73	Eric Owens	.10
T74	Jeff Brantley	.10
T75	Vinny Castilla	.10
T76	Ron Villone	.10
T77	Ricky Henderson	.40
T78	Jason Grimsley	.10
T79	Christian Parker RC	.10
T80	Donnie Wall	.10
T81	Alex Arias	.10
T82	Willis Roberts	.10
T83	Ryan Minor	.10
T84	Jason LaRue	.10
T85	Ruben Sierra	.10
T86	Johnny Damon	.75
T87	Juan Gonzalez	.40
T88	Mac Suzuki	.10
T89	Tony Batista	.10
T90	Jay Witasick	.10
T91	Brent Abernathy	.10
T92	Paul LoDuca	.10
T93	Wes Helms	.10
T94	Milton Bradley	.10
T95	Matt LeCroy	.10
T96	A.J. Hinch	.10
T97	Bud Smith RC	.10
T98	Adam Dunn	.50
T99	Albert Pujols, Ichiro Suzuki	15.00

T100	Carlton Fisk	.25
T101	Tim Raines	.25
T102	Juan Marichal	.25
T103	Dave Winfield	.50
T104	Reggie Jackson	1.00
T105	Cal Ripken Jr.	3.00
T106	Ozzie Smith	1.00
T107	Tom Seaver	1.00
T108	Lou Piniella	.25
T109	Dwight Gooden	.25
T110	Bret Saberhagen	.25
T111	Gary Carter	.25
T112	Jack Clark	.25
T113	Rickey Henderson	.75
T114	Barry Bonds	3.00
T115	Bobby Bonilla	.25
T116	Jose Canseco	.75
T117	Will Clark	.50
T118	Andres Galarraga	.25
T119	Bo Jackson	.75
T120	Wally Joyner	.25
T121	Ellis Burks	.25
T122	David Cone	.25
T123	Greg Maddux	1.00
T124	Willie Randolph	.25
T125	Dennis Eckersley	.25
T126	Matt Williams	.40
T127	Joe Morgan	.50
T128	Fred McGriff	.40
T129	Roberto Alomar	.50
T130	Lee Smith	.25
T131	David Wells	.25
T132	Ken Griffey Jr.	2.00
T133	Deion Sanders	.50
T134	Nolan Ryan	2.00
T135	David Justice	.25
T136	Joe Carter	.25
T137	Jack Morris	.10
T138	Mike Piazza	1.50
T139	Barry Bonds	2.00
T140	Terrence Long	.10
T141	Ben Grieve	.10
T142	Richie Sexson	.25
T143	Sean Burroughs	.10
T144	Alfonso Soriano	.50
T145	Bob Boone	.10
T146	Larry Bowa	.10
T147	Bob Brenly	.10
T148	Buck Martinez	.10
T149	Lloyd McClendon	.10
T150	Jim Tracy	.10
T151	Jared Abruzzo RC	.50
T152	Kurt Ainsworth	.10
T153	Willie Bloomquist	.10
T154	Ben Broussard	.10
T155	Bobby Bradley	.10
T156	Mike Bynum	.10
T157	Ken Harvey	.10
T158	Ryan Christianson	.10
T159	Ryan Kohlmeier	.10
T160	Joe Crede	.50
T161	Jack Cust	.10
T162	Ben Diggins	.10
T163	Phil Dumatrait	.10
T164	Alex Escobar	.10
T165	Miguel Olivo	.10
T166	Chris George	.10
T167	Marcus Giles	.10
T168	Keith Ginter	.10
T169	Josh Girdley	.10
T170	Tony Alvarez	.10
T171	Scott Seabol	.10
T172	Josh Hamilton	.25
T173	Jason Hart	.10
T174	Israel Alcantara	.10
T175	Jake Peavy	2.50
T176	Stubby Clapp RC	.40
T177	D'Angelo Jimenez	.10
T178	Nick Johnson	.25
T179	Ben Johnson	.10
T180	Larry Bigbie	.10
T181	Allen Levrault	.10
T182	Felipe Lopez	.10
T183	Sean Burnett	.10
T184	Nick Neugebauer	.10
T185	Austin Kearns	.25
T186	Corey Patterson	.25
T187	Carlos Pena	.10
T188	Ricardo Rodriguez RC	.50
T189	Juan Rivera	.10
T190	Grant Roberts	.10
T191	Adam Pettyjohn RC	.25
T192	Jared Sandberg	.10
T193	Xavier Nady	.25
T194	Dane Sardinha	.10
T195	Shawn Sonnier	.10
T196	Rafael Soriano	.25
T197	Brian Specht RC	.25
T198	Aaron Myette	.10
T199	Juan Uribe RC	.40
T200	Jayson Werth	.10
T201	Brad Wilkerson	.10
T202	Horacio Estrada	.10
T203	Joel Pineiro	.10

T204	Matt LeCroy	.10
T205	Michael Coleman	.10
T206	Ben Sheets	.40
T207	Eric Byrnes	.10
T208	Sean Burroughs	.10
T209	Ken Harvey	.10
T210	Travis Hafner	2.50
T211	Erick Almonte	.10
T212	Jason Belcher RC	.50
T213	Wilson Betemit RC	.75
T214	Hank Blalock RC	2.00
T215	Danny Borrell	.10
T216	John Buck RC	.50
T217	Freddie Bynum RC	.50
T218	Noel Devarez RC	.25
T219	Juan Diaz RC	.25
T220	Felix Diaz RC	.25
T221	Josh Fogg RC	.50
T222	Matt Ford RC	.25
T223	Scott Heard	.10
T224	Ben Hendrickson RC	.25
T225	Cody Ross RC	.50
T226	Adrian Hernandez RC	.40
T227	Alfredo Amezaga RC	.50
T228	Bob Keppel RC	.25
T229	Ryan Madson RC	.50
T230	Octavio Martinez RC	.25
T231	Hee Seop Choi	.40
T232	Thomas Mitchell	.10
T233	Luis Montanez	.40
T234	Andy Morales RC	.40
T235	Justin Morneau RC	5.00
T236	Greg "Toe" Nash RC	.25
T237	Valentino Pasucci RC	.25
T238	Roy Smith RC	.40
T239	Antonio Perez RC	.40
T240	Chad Petty RC	.50
T241	Steve Smyth	.10
T242	Jose Reyes RC	20.00
T243	Eric Reynolds RC	.40
T244	Dominic Rich	.10
T245	Jason Richardson RC	.25
T246	Ed Rogers RC	.40
T247	Albert Pujols RC	50.00
T248	Esix Snead RC	.25
T249	Luis Torres RC	.25
T250	Matt White RC	.40
T251	Blake Williams	.10
T252	Chris Russ	.10
T253	Joe Kennedy RC	.25
T254	Jeff Randazzo RC	.25
T255	Beau Hale RC	.25
256	Brad Hennessey RC	.25
257	Jake Gautreau RC	.25
258	Jeff Mathis RC	.75
259	Aaron Heilman RC	.50
260	Bronson Sardinha RC	.50
261	Irvin Guzman RC	4.00
262	Gabe Gross RC	.50
263	J.D. Martin RC	.40
264	Chris Smith RC	.25
265	Kenny Baugh RC	.40

Autographs

		NM/M
Common Autograph:		15.00
JD	Johnny Damon	30.00
MM	Mike Mussina	25.00

Dual-Traded Relics

		NM/M
Common Player:		4.00

DB	Derek Bell	4.00
MG	Mark Grace	10.00
BG	Ben Grieve	4.00
DH	Dustin Hermanson	4.00
MR	Manny Ramirez	15.00

Farewell Dual Relic

		NM/M
Inserted 1:4,693		
RG	Cal Ripken,	
	Tony Gwynn	80.00

Hall of Fame Relics

		NM/M
Complete Set (1):		
PW	Kirby Puckett,	
	Dave Winfield	40.00

Legends Autographs

		NM/M
Common Player:		
TT51	Ralph Branca	15.00
TTF47	Frank Howard	25.00
TTF50	Mickey Lolich	15.00
TT37	Tug McGraw	15.00
TT48F	Bobby Richardson	20.00
TT36F	Enos Slaughter	25.00
TT13	Warren Spahn	40.00
TT43	Bobby Thomson	20.00

Relics

		NM/M
Common Player:		4.00
Inserted 1:29		
SA	Sandy Alomar Jr.	4.00
DB	Derek Bell	4.00
BB	Bobby Bonilla	4.00
BB	Bret Boone	4.00
RB	Rico Brogna	4.00
KC	Ken Caminiti	4.00
JC	Jose Canseco	8.00
ROC	Roger Cedeno	4.00
RSC	Royce Clayton	4.00
JD	Johnny Damon	10.00
ED	Eric Davis	4.00
JD	Jermaine Dye	4.00
AG	Andres Galarraga	4.00
RG	Ron Gant	4.00
JG	Juan Gonzalez	6.00
MG	Mark Grace	8.00
MG	Marquis Grissom	4.00
JH	Jeffrey Hammonds	4.00
MH	Mike Hampton	4.00
DH	Dustin Hermanson	4.00
TH	Todd Hundley	4.00
CJ	Charles Johnson	4.00
FM	Fred McGriff	5.00
BM	Bill Mueller	4.00
DN	Denny Neagle	4.00
HR	Hideo Nomo	25.00
NP	Neifi Perez	4.00

TR	Tim Raines	4.00
RS	Ruben Sierra	4.00
MS	Matt Stairs	4.00
KS	Kelly Stinnett	4.00
FT	Fernando Tatis	4.00
DW	David Wells	4.00
GW	Gerald Williams	4.00
EW	Enrique Wilson	4.00

Rookie Relics

		NM/M
Common Player:		4.00
Inserted 1:91		
AP	Albert Pujols	150.00
TS	Tsuyoshi Shinjo	4.00
AB	Angel Berroa	6.00
BO	Bill Ortega	4.00
HC	Humberto Cota	4.00
JL	Jason Lane	4.00
JS	Jamal Strong	4.00
JV	Jose Valverde	4.00
JY	Jason Young	4.00
NC	Nate Cornejo	4.00
NN	Nick Neugebauer	4.00
PF	Pedro Feliz	4.00
RS	Richard Stahl	4.00
SB	Sean Burroughs	4.00
SS	Jae Weong Seo	6.00
WB	Wilson Betemit	8.00
WR	Wilken Ruan	4.00

Who Would Have Thought

		NM/M
Complete Set (20):		15.00
Common Player:		.75
Inserted 1:8		
WWH1	Nolan Ryan	3.00
WWH2	Ozzie Smith	1.50
WWH3	Tom Seaver	1.50
WWH4	Steve Carlton	.75
WWH5	Reggie Jackson	1.50
WWH6	Frank Robinson	1.00
WWH7	Keith Hernandez	.75
WWH8	Andre Dawson	.75
WWH9	Lou Brock	.75
WWH10	Dennis Eckersley	.75
WWH11	Dave Winfield	1.00
WWH12	Rod Carew	1.00
WWH13	Willie Randolph	.75
WWH14	Doc Gooden	.75
WWH15	Carlton Fisk	1.00
WWH16	Dale Murphy	.75
WWH17	Paul Molitor	1.00
WWH18	Gary Carter	.75
WWH19	Wade Boggs	.75
WWH20	Willie Mays	3.00

2001 Topps American Pie

		NM/M
Complete Set (150):		30.00
Common Player:		.20
Pack (5):		3.00
Box (24):		50.00
1	Al Kaline	.40
2	Al Oliver	.20
3	Andre Dawson	.20
4	Bert Blyleven	.20
5	Bill Buckner	.20
6	Bill Mazeroski	.20
7	Bob Gibson	.50
8	Bill Freeman	.20
9	Bobby Grich	.20
10	Bobby Murcer	.20
11	Bobby Richardson	.20
12	Boog Powell	.20
13	Brooks Robinson	.50
14	Carl Yastrzemski	.75
15	Carlton Fisk	.40
16	Clete Boyer	.20
17	Curt Flood	.20
18	Dale Murphy	.30
19	Tony Conigliaro	.20
20	Dave Parker	.20
21	Dave Winfield	.50
22	Dick Allen	.20
23	Dick Groat	.20
24	Don Drysdale	.50
25	Don Sutton	.20
26	Dwight Evans	.20
27	Eddie Mathews	.75
28	Elston Howard	.20
29	Frank Howard	.20
30	Frank Robinson	.50
31	Fred Lynn	.20
32	Gary Carter	.20
33	Gaylord Perry	.20
34	Norm Cash	.20
35	George Brett	1.50
36	George Foster	.20
37	Goose Gossage	.20
38	Graig Nettles	.20
39	Greg Luzinski	.20
41	Harmon Killebrew	.75
42	Jack Clark	.20
43	Jack Morris	.20
44	Jim Wynn	.20
45	Jim Kaat	.20
46	Jim Palmer	.20
47	Joe Pepitone	.20
48	Joe Rudi	.20
49	Johnny Bench	1.00
50	Juan Marichal	.40
51	Keith Hernandez	.20
52	Bucky Dent	.20
53	Lou Brock	.40
54	Ron Cey	.20
55	Luis Aparicio	.20
56	Luis Tiant	.20
57	Mark Fidrych	.20
58	Maury Wills	.20
59	Mickey Lolich	.20
60	Mickey Rivers	.20
61	Mike Schmidt	1.00
62	Moose Skowron	.20
63	Nolan Ryan	3.00
64	Orlando Cepeda	.20
65	Ozzie Smith	.75
66	Phil Niekro	.20
67	Reggie Jackson	.75
68	Reggie Smith	.20
69	Rico Carty	.20
70	Roberto Clemente	2.00
71	Robin Yount	.75
72	Roger Maris	1.50
73	Rollie Fingers	.20
74	Ron Guidry	.20
75	Ron Santo	.20
76	Ron Swoboda	.20
77	Sal Bando	.20
78	Sam McDowell	.20
79	Steve Carlton	.40
80	Thurman Munson	1.00
81	Tim McCarver	.20
82	Tom Seaver	.75
83	Mike Cuellar	.20
84	Tony Kubek	.20
85	Tommy John	.20
86	Tony Perez	.20
87	Tug McGraw	.20
88	Vida Blue	.20
89	Warren Spahn	.75
90	Whitey Ford	.50
91	Willie Mays	2.00
92	Willie McCovey	.50
93	Willie Stargell	.50
94	Yogi Berra	1.00
95	Stan Musial	1.00
96	Jim Piersall	.20
97	Duke Snider	.50
98	Bruce Sutter	.30
99	Dave Concepcion	.20
100	Darrell Evans	.20

101	Dennis Eckersley	.40
102	Hoyt Wilhelm	.20
103	Minnie Minoso	.20
104	Don Newcombe	.20
105	Richie Ashburn	.20
106	Alan Trammell	.20
107	Jim "Catfish" Hunter	.20
108	Lou Whitaker	.20
109	Johnny Podres	.20
110	Denny Martinez	.20
111	Willie Horton	.20
112	Dean Chance	.20
113	Fergie Jenkins	.20
114	Cecil Cooper	.20
115	Rick Reuschel	.20
116	Space Race	.20
117	Man On The Moon	.50
118	Woodstock	.50
119	Peace Movement/Flower Power	.20
120	N.Y. Worlds Fair	.20
121	Vietnam War	.20
122	Vietnam Cease Fire	.20
123	Kennedy Elected President	.50
124	Kennedy Assassination	.20
125	Malcom X	.20
126	Nixon Elected President	.20
127	Watergate	.20
128	Nixon Resigns	.20
129	Cuban Missile Crisis	.20
130	Astrodome	.20
131	Secretariat	.20
132	Lyndon Johnson Signs Civil Rights Bill	.20
133	Atomic Bomb Test Ban Treaty	.20
134	Bi Centennial	.20
135	String Bikini	.20
136	Birth Control Pill	.20
137	Studio 54	.20
138	Motown	.20
139	Microsoft Started	.20
140	Internet Developed	.20
141	John F. Kennedy	1.50
142	Marilyn Monroe	1.50
143	Elvis Presley	1.00
144	Jimi Hendrix	1.00
145	Arthur Ashe	.20
146	Richard Nixon	.20
147	James Dean	.20
148	Janis Joplin	.50
149	Frank Sinatra	1.00
150	Malcom X	.50

Autoproofs Baseball Legends

No pricing due to scarcity.
Production 25 Sets

Decade Leaders

		NM/M
Complete Set (10):		15.00
Common Player:		1.00
Inserted 1:12		
DL1	Willie Stargell	1.50
DL2	Harmon Killebrew	1.50
DL3	Johnny Bench	2.00
DL4	Hank Aaron	3.00
DL5	Rod Carew	1.00
DL6	Roberto Clemente	3.00
DL7	Nolan Ryan	4.00
DL8	Bob Gibson	1.50
DL9	Jim Palmer	1.00
DL10	Juan Marichal	1.00

Entertainment Stars

		NM/M
Production 500 Sets		
1	Lou Ferrigno (Incredible Hulk)	50.00

2	Adam West (Batman)	60.00
3	Danny Bonaduce (Partridge Family)	30.00

Legends Autographs

		NM/M
Common Player:		10.00
Inserted 1:211		
TT1R	Willie Mays	100.00
TT14R	Johnny Bench	60.00
TT48R	Bobby Richardson	20.00
TT8R	Carl Yastrzemski	50.00
TT13R	Warren Spahn	25.00
TT15R	Reggie Jackson	50.00
TT18R	Bob Gibson	20.00
TT25R	Luis Tiant	10.00
TT29R	Moose Skowron	10.00
TT31R	Clete Boyer	10.00
TT33R	Vida Blue	15.00
TT35R	Joe Pepitone	10.00
TT37R	Tug McGraw	15.00
TT47R	Frank Howard	10.00
TT49R	Tony Kubek	40.00
TT50R	Mickey Lolich	10.00

Piece of American Pie Relics

		NM/M
Common Card:		10.00
Inserted 1:29		
PAPM1	Frank Sinatra	60.00
PAPM2	JFK/Berlin Wall	10.00
PAPM3	Elvis Presley	100.00
PAPM4	Janis Joplin	90.00
PAPM5	Jimi Hendrix	

Profiles In Courage

		NM/M
Complete Set (20):		25.00
Common Player:		1.00
Inserted 1:8		
PIC1	Roger Maris	2.00
PIC2	Lou Brock	1.00
PIC3	Brooks Robinson	1.50
PIC4	Carl Yastrzemski	1.50
PIC5	Mike Schmidt	2.50
PIC6	Hank Aaron	3.00
PIC7	Tom Seaver	1.50
PIC8	Willie Mays	3.00
PIC9	Graig Nettles	1.00
PIC10	Frank Robinson	1.50
PIC11	Rollie Fingers	1.00
PIC12	Tony Perez	1.00
PIC13	George Brett	3.00
PIC14	Robin Yount	1.50
PIC15	Nolan Ryan	4.00
PIC16	Warren Spahn	1.50
PIC17	Johnny Bench	2.00
PIC18	Vida Blue	1.00
PIC19	Roberto Clemente	3.00
PIC20	Thurman Munson	2.00

Rookie Reprint Relics

		NM/M
Common Player:		10.00
Inserted 1:116		
JB	Johnny Bench	20.00
GB	George Brett	40.00
SC	Steve Carlton	15.00
GC	Gary Carter	10.00
AD	Andre Dawson	10.00
DE	Dennis Eckersley	10.00
MF	Mark Fidrych	10.00
BG	Bobby Grich	10.00
RJ	Reggie Jackson	15.00
JK	Jim Kaat	10.00
TMC	Tim McCarver	10.00
TM	Thurman Munson	35.00
BM	Bobby Murcer	10.00
AO	Al Oliver	10.00
BP	Boog Powell	10.00
OS	Ozzie Smith	20.00
DS	Don Sutton	10.00
DW	Dave Winfield	10.00
RY	Robin Yount	20.00

Timeless Classics Relics

		NM/M
Common Player:		8.00
Inserted 1:80		
	Sam McDowell	8.00
	Frank Howard	8.00
	Dick Groat	8.00
	Roger Maris	50.00
	Orlando Cepeda	10.00
	Willie Mays	40.00
	Carl Yastrzemski	30.00
	Roberto Clemente	60.00
	Harmon Killebrew	20.00
	Brooks Robinson	20.00
	Tony Conigliaro	15.00
	Frank Robinson	15.00
	Hank Aaron	40.00
	Willie McCovey	15.00
	Rico Carty	8.00
	Johnny Bench	20.00
	Willie Stargell	15.00
	Steve Carlton	15.00
	Norm Cash	8.00
	Reggie Jackson	15.00
	Mike Schmidt	30.00
	Mickey Rivers	8.00
	Tom Seaver	20.00
	George Brett	40.00
	George Foster	8.00
	Graig Nettles	8.00

	Nolan Ryan	40.00
	Dave Parker	10.00
	Dick Allen	8.00
	Fred Lynn	8.00
	Keith Hernandez	8.00
	Dave Winfield	15.00

Woodstock Relics

		NM/M
Common Player:		8.00
Inserted 1:138		
GB	George Brett	40.00
BB	Bill Buckner	8.00
OC	Orlando Cepeda	10.00
DE	Dwight Evans	8.00
CF	Carlton Fisk	15.00
BF	Bill Freehan	8.00
DG	Dick Groat	8.00
RJ	Reggie Jackson	15.00
TK	Ted Kluszewski	8.00
FL	Fred Lynn	8.00
WM	Willie Mays	45.00
SM	Stan Musial	40.00
TP	Tony Perez	8.00
JP	Jimmy Piersall	8.00
BR	Brooks Robinson	15.00
FR	Frank Robinson	15.00
JR	Joe Rudi	8.00
DS	Duke Snider	15.00
WS	Willie Stargell	15.00
MW	Maury Wills	8.00
DW	Dave Winfield	8.00
WS	Woodstock	15.00
JW	Jim Wynn	8.00
CY	Carl Yastrzemski	30.00
RY	Robin Yount	20.00

2001 Topps Archives

		NM/M
Complete Set (450):		150.00
Complete Series 1 (225):		75.00
Complete Series 2 (225):		75.00
Common Player:		.40
Pack (8):		4.50
Box (20):		80.00
1	Johnny Antonelli	.40
2	Yogi Berra	2.50
3	Dom DiMaggio	.40
4	Carl Erskine	.40
5	Joe Garagiola	.50
6	Monte Irvin	.40
7	Vernon Law	.40
8	Eddie Mathews	2.00
9	Willie Mays	5.00
10	Gil McDougald	.40
11	Andy Pafko	.40
12	Phil Rizzuto	.75
13	Preacher Roe	.40
14	Hank Sauer	.50
15	Bobby Shantz	.40
16	Enos Slaughter	.50
17	Warren Spahn	2.00
18	Mickey Vernon	.40
19	Early Wynn	.40
20	Whitey Ford	1.00
21	Johnny Podres	.40
22	Ernie Banks	2.00
23	Moose Skowron	.40
24	Harmon Killebrew	2.00
25	Ted Williams	6.00
26	Jimmy Piersall	.40
27	Frank Thomas	.40
28	Bill Mazeroski	.50
29	Bobby Richardson	.40
30	Frank Robinson	1.50
31	Stan Musial	3.00
32	Johnny Callison	.40
33	Bob Gibson	2.00
34	Frank Howard	.50
35	Willie McCovey	.40
36	Carl Yastrzemski	2.00
37	Jim Maloney	.40

#	Player	Price	#	Player	Price	#	Player	Price	#	Player	Price
38	Ron Santo	.40	142	Bobby Shantz	.40	227	Ralph Branca	.40	331	Bobby Thomson	.40
39	Lou Brock	.75	143	Nellie Fox	.50	228	Joe Garagiola	.75	332	Carl Furillo	.40
40	Tim McCarver	.50	144	Elston Howard	.40	229	Bob Feller	2.00	333	Hank Bauer	.40
41	Joe Pepitone	.40	145	Jackie Jensen	.40	230	Dick Groat	.40	334	Herb Score	.40
42	Boog Powell	.50	146	Al Rosen	.40	231	George Kell	.40	335	Richie Ashburn	.40
43	Bill Freehan	.40	147	Dick Allen	.40	232	Bob Boone	.40	336	Billy Pierce	.40
44	Dick Allen	.40	148	Bill Freehan	.40	233	Minnie Minoso	.40	337	Duke Snider	2.00
45	Willie Horton	.40	149	Boog Powell	.40	234	Billy Pierce	.40	338	Harvey Haddix	.40
46	Mickey Lolich	.40	150	Lou Brock	.75	235	Robin Roberts	.50	339	Robin Roberts	.40
47	Wilbur Wood	.40	151	Rod Carew	.75	236	Johnny Sain	.40	340	Dick Groat	.40
48	Bert Campaneris	.40	152	Wilbur Wood	.40	237	Red Schoendienst	.40	341	Curt Simmons	.40
49	Rod Carew	1.50	153	Thurman Munson	1.50	238	Curt Simmons	.40	342	Bob Uecker	1.00
50	Tug McGraw	.40	154	Ken Holtzman	.40	239	Duke Snider	2.00	343	Smoky Burgess	.40
51	Tony Perez	.75	155	Willie Horton	.40	240	Bobby Thomson	.40	344	Jim Bouton	.40
52	Luis Tiant	.40	156	Mickey Lolich	.40	241	Hoyt Wilhelm	.40	345	Elroy Face	.40
53	Bobby Murcer	.40	157	Tim McCarver	.40	242	Elroy Face	.40	346	Don Drysdale	1.00
54	Don Sutton	.75	158	Willie McCovey	.40	243	Ralph Kiner	.75	347	Bob Allison	.40
55	Ken Holtzman	.40	159	Roy White	.40	244	Hank Aaron	4.00	348	Clete Boyer	.40
56	Reggie Smith	.40	160	Bobby Murcer	.40	245	Al Kaline	2.00	349	Dean Chance	.40
57	Hal McRae	.40	161	Joe Rudi	.40	246	Don Larsen	1.50	350	Tony Conigliaro	.40
58	Roy White	.40	162	Reggie Smith	.40	247	Tug McGraw	.40	351	Curt Flood	.40
59	Reggie Jackson	3.00	163	Luis Tiant	.40	248	Don Newcombe	.75	352	Hoyt Wilhelm	.40
60	Graig Nettles	.40	164	Bert Campaneris	.40	249	Herb Score	.40	353	Ron Swoboda	.40
61	Joe Rudi	.40	165	Frank Howard	.40	250	Clete Boyer	.40	354	Roberto Clemente	3.00
62	Vida Blue	.50	166	Harvey Kuenn	.50	251	Lindy McDaniel	.40	355	Tug McGraw	.40
63	Darrell Evans	.40	167	Greg Luzinski	.40	252	Brooks Robinson	2.50	356	Orlando Cepeda	.40
64	David Concepcion	.40	168	Tug McGraw	.40	253	Orlando Cepeda	.60	357	Joe Garagiola	.40
65	Bobby Grich	.40	169	Willie Mays	3.00	254	Larry Bowa	.40	358	Juan Marichal	.50
66	Greg Luzinski	.40	170	Roger Maris	2.00	255	Mike Cuellar	.40	359	Sam McDowell	.40
67	Cecil Cooper	.40	171	Vida Blue	.40	256	Jim Perry	.40	360	Johnny Sain	.40
68	George Hendrick	.40	172	Bobby Grich	.40	257	Dave Parker	.40	361	Ted Kluszewski	.40
69	Dwight Evans	.40	173	Reggie Jackson	2.00	258	Maury Wills	.40	362	Al Kaline	2.00
70	Gary Matthews	.40	174	Hal McRae	.40	259	Willie Davis	.40	363	Lindy McDaniel	.40
71	Mike Schmidt	3.00	175	Carl Yastrzemski	1.00	260	Juan Marichal	.60	364	Don Newcombe	.40
72	Dave Parker	.40	176	David Concepcion	.40	261	Jim Bouton	.40	365	Jim Perry	.40
73	Dave Winfield	1.00	177	Cecil Cooper	.40	262	Dean Chance	.40	366	Hank Aaron	4.00
74	Gary Carter	.40	178	George Hendrick	.40	263	Sam McDowell	.40	367	Don Larsen	1.00
75	Dennis Eckersley	.75	179	Gary Matthews	.40	264	Whitey Ford	3.00	368	Mike Cuellar	.40
76	Kent Tekulve	.40	180	Stan Musial	2.00	265	Bob Uecker	2.00	369	Willie Davis	.40
77	Andre Dawson	.75	181	Graig Nettles	.40	266	Willie Stargell	2.00	370	Ralph Kiner	.50
78	Denny Martinez	.40	182	Don Sutton	.50	267	Rico Carty	.40	371	Minnie Minoso	.40
79	Bruce Sutter	.75	183	Kent Tekulve	.40	268	Tommy John	.40	372	Larry Bowa	.40
80	Jack Morris	.40	184	Bruce Sutter	.75	269	Phil Niekro	.60	373	Brooks Robinson	1.00
81	Ozzie Smith	1.50	185	Darrell Evans	.40	270	Paul Blair	.40	374	Bob Boone	.40
82	Lee Smith	.40	186	Mike Schmidt	2.00	271	Steve Carlton	3.00	375	Jim Lonborg	.40
83	Don Mattingly	4.00	187	Dave Parker	.40	272	Jim Lonborg	.40	376	Paul Blair	.40
84	Joe Carter	.40	188	Dwight Evans	.40	273	Tony Perez	.60	377	Rico Carty	.40
85	Kirby Puckett	3.00	189	Gary Carter	.40	274	Ron Swoboda	.40	378	Sal Bando	.40
86	Joe Adcock	.40	190	Jack Morris	.40	275	Fergie Jenkins	.75	379	Mark Fidrych	.40
87	Gus Bell	.40	191	Tony Perez	.50	276	Jim Palmer	1.50	380	Al Hrabosky	.40
88	Roy Campanella	2.00	192	Dave Winfield	.75	277	Sal Bando	.40	381	Willie Stargell	1.00
89	Jackie Jensen	.40	193	Andre Dawson	.50	278	Tom Seaver	4.00	382	Johnny Bench	2.50
90	Johnny Mize	.75	194	Lee Smith	.40	279	Johnny Bench	4.00	383	Dave Parker	.40
91	Allie Reynolds	.40	195	Ozzie Smith	1.00	280	Nolan Ryan	6.00	384	Sparky Lyle	.40
92	Al Rosen	.40	196	Denny Martinez	.40	281	Rollie Fingers	.50	385	Fergie Jenkins	.50
93	Hal Newhouser	.40	197	Don Mattingly	2.50	282	Sparky Lyle	.40	386	Jim Palmer	1.00
94	Harvey Kuenn	.40	198	Joe Carter	.40	283	Al Oliver	.40	387	Whitey Ford	2.00
95	Nellie Fox	.75	199	Dennis Eckersley	.75	284	Bob Watson	.40	388	Tony Perez	.40
96	Elston Howard	.40	200	Kirby Puckett	2.00	285	Bill Buckner	.40	389	Mickey Rivers	.40
97	Sal Maglie	.40	201	Walter Alston	.40	286	Bert Blyleven	.40	390	Bob Watson	.40
98	Roger Maris	3.00	202	Casey Stengel	.75	287	George Foster	.40	391	Rollie Fingers	.40
99	Norm Cash	.40	203	Sparky Anderson	.40	288	Al Hrabosky	.40	392	George Foster	.40
100	Thurman Munson	2.50	204	Tommy Lasorda	.75	289	Cecil Cooper	.40	393	Al Oliver	.40
101	Roy Campanella	1.50	205	Whitey Herzog	.40	290	Carlton Fisk	1.00	394	Tom Seaver	3.00
102	Joe Garagiola	.75	206	Harmon Killebrew, Frank Howard, Reggie Jackson	.40	291	Mickey Rivers	.40	395	Maury Wills	.40
103	Dom DiMaggio	.40				292	Goose Gossage	.40	396	Steve Carlton	1.00
104	Johnny Mize	.50	207	Hank Aaron, Early Wynn, Ron Santo, Willie McCovey	2.50	293	Rick Reuschel	.40	397	Cecil Cooper	.40
105	Allie Reynolds	.40				294	Bucky Dent	.40	398	Bill Buckner	.40
106	Preacher Roe	.40	208	Frank Robinson, Harmon Killebrew, Boog Powell	1.50	295	Frank Tanana	.40	399	Phil Niekro	.40
107	Hal Newhouser	.40				296	George Brett	4.00	400	Red Schoendienst	.40
108	Monte Irvin	.40	209	Tony Oliva, Frank Robinson, Frank Howard	.75	297	Keith Hernandez	.40	401	Ron Guidry	.40
109	Carl Erskine	.40				298	Fred Lynn	.40	402	Willie Hernandez	.40
110	Enos Slaughter	.40	210	Hank Aaron, Willie McCovey, Willie Mays, Orlando Cepeda	2.50	299	Robin Yount	3.00	403	Tommy John	.40
111	Gil McDougald	.40				300	Ron Guidry	.40	404	Gil Hodges	.40
112	Andy Pafko	.40	211	Hank Aaron, Frank Robinson, Willie Mays, Ernie Banks	2.50	301	Jack Clark	.40	405	Bucky Dent	.40
113	Sal Maglie	.40				302	Mark Fidrych	.40	406	Keith Hernandez	.40
114	Johnny Antonelli	.40	212	Carl Yastrzemski, Harmon Killebrew, Frank Howard	1.50	303	Dale Murphy	1.50	407	Dan Quisenberry	.40
115	Phil Rizzuto	.50				304	Willie Hernandez	.40	408	Fred Lynn	.40
116	Yogi Berra	1.50	213	Ernie Banks	1.50	305	Lou Whitaker	.40	409	Rick Reuschel	.40
117	Early Wynn	.40	214	Hank Aaron	2.50	306	Kirk Gibson	.75	410	Jackie Robinson	3.00
118	Mickey Vernon	.40	215	Willie Mays	2.50	307	Wade Boggs	3.00	411	Goose Gossage	.40
119	Gus Bell	.40	216	Al Kaline	.75	308	Ryne Sandberg	4.00	412	Bert Blyleven	.40
120	Ted Williams	4.00	217	Stan Musial	2.00	309	Orel Hershiser	.40	413	Jack Clark	.40
121	Frank Thomas	.40	218	Duke Snider	.75	310	Jimmy Key	.40	414	Carlton Fisk	.50
122	Bobby Richardson	.40	219	Frank Robinson, Hank Bauer, Frank Robinson	.50	311	Richie Ashburn	.40	415	Dale Murphy	.75
123	Whitey Ford	1.00				312	Smoky Burgess	.40	416	Frank Tanana	.40
124	Vernon Law	.40	220	Willie Mays, Stan Musial	1.50	313	Gil Hodges	1.50	417	George Brett	3.00
125	Jimmy Piersall	.40	221	Whitey Ford	.75	314	Ted Kluszewski	.40	418	Robin Yount	2.50
126	Moose Skowron	.40	222	Jerry Koosman	.40	315	Pee Wee Reese	1.00	419	Kirk Gibson	.50
127	Joe Adcock	.40	223	Bob Gibson	.75	316	Jackie Robinson	4.00	420	Lou Whitaker	.40
128	Johnny Podres	.40	224	Gil Hodges	.40	317	Harvey Haddix	.40	421	Ryne Sandberg	2.50
129	Ernie Banks	1.50	225	Reggie Jackson	1.50	318	Satchel Paige	3.00	422	Jimmy Key	.40
130	Jim Maloney	.40	226	Hank Bauer	.40	319	Roberto Clemente	5.00	423	Nolan Ryan	5.00
131	Johnny Callison	.40				320	Carl Furillo	.40	424	Wade Boggs	.75
132	Eddie Mathews	1.50				321	Don Drysdale	2.00	425	Orel Hershiser	.40
133	Joe Pepitone	.40				322	Curt Flood	.40	426	Billy Martin	.40
134	Warren Spahn	1.50				323	Bob Allison	.40	427	Ralph Houk	.40
135	Bill Mazeroski	.40				324	Tony Conigliaro	.40	428	Chuck Tanner	.40
136	Norm Cash	.40				325	Dan Quisenberry	.40	429	Earl Weaver	.40
137	Bob Gibson	1.00				326	Ralph Branca	.40	430	Leo Durocher	.40
138	Harmon Killebrew	1.50				327	Bob Feller	1.00	431	Tony Conigliaro, Norm Cash, Willie Horton	.40
139	Frank Robinson	1.00				328	Satchel Paige	3.00			
140	Ron Santo	.40				329	George Kell	.40			
141	Hank Sauer	.40				330	Pee Wee Reese	1.00			

432	Ernie Banks, Hank Aaron, Eddie Mathews, Clete Boyer	1.50
433	Norm Cash, Frank Howard, Al Kaline, Jimmy Piersall	.40
434	Goose Gossage, Rollie Fingers	.40
435	Nolan Ryan, Tom Seaver	.40
436	Reggie Jackson, Willie Stargell	.75
437	Johnny Bench, Dick Allen	.75
438	Roger Maris	3.00
439	Carl Yastrzemski	2.00
440	Nolan Ryan	4.00
441	Cincinnati Reds	.75
442	Tony Perez	.40
443	Steve Carlton	.75
444	Wade Boggs	.75
445	Andre Dawson	.40
446	Whitey Ford	1.50
447	Hank Aaron	4.00
448	Bob Gibson	.75
449	Roberto Clemente	4.00
450	Orioles/Jackie Robinson	1.50

Baseball Bucks

NM/M
Valid to 3/02 for Topps merchandise:

TB1	Willie Mays ($1/15,000)	2.00
TB2	Roberto Clemente ($5/1,000)	4.00
TB3	Jackie Robinson ($10/500)	10.00

Autographs

NM/M
Common Player: 10.00
Inserted 1:Box

TAA1	Johnny Antonelli	15.00
TAA2	Hank Bauer	20.00
TAA3	Yogi Berra/50	350.00
TAA4	Ralph Branca	20.00
TAA5	Dom DiMaggio	50.00
TAA6	Joe Garagiola	40.00
TAA7	Carl Erskine	25.00
TAA8	Bob Feller	25.00
TAA10	Dick Groat	50.00
TAA11	Monte Irvin	20.00
TAA12	George Kell	20.00
TAA13	Vernon Law	15.00
TAA14	Bob Boone	10.00
TAA16	Willie Mays/50	500.00
TAA17	Gil McDougald	20.00
TAA18	Minnie Minoso	30.00
TAA19	Andy Pafko	30.00
TAA20	Billy Pierce	10.00
TAA21	Phil Rizzuto/200	100.00
TAA22	Robin Roberts	40.00
TAA23	Preacher Roe	20.00
TAA24	Johnny Sain	20.00
TAA25	Hank Sauer	20.00
TAA26	Red Schoendienst	25.00
TAA27	Bobby Shantz	10.00
TAA28	Curt Simmons	10.00
TAA29	Enos Slaughter	30.00
TAA30	Duke Snider	80.00
TAA31	Warren Spahn	120.00
TAA32	Bobby Thomson	20.00
TAA33	Mickey Vernon	15.00
TAA34	Hoyt Wilhelm	30.00
TAA35	Jim Wynn	10.00
TAA36	Elroy Face	10.00
TAA37	Gaylord Perry	35.00
TAA38	Ralph Kiner	50.00
TAA39	Johnny Podres	10.00
TAA40	Hank Aaron/50	500.00
TAA41	Ernie Banks/50	450.00
TAA42	Al Kaline	150.00
TAA43	Moose Skowron	15.00
TAA44	Don Larsen	180.00
TAA45	Harmon Killebrew	140.00
TAA46	Tug McGraw	30.00
TAA48	Don Newcombe	20.00
TAA49	Jimmy Piersall	15.00
TAA50	Herb Score	15.00
TAA51	Frank Thomas	10.00
TAA52	Clete Boyer	15.00
TAA53	Bill Mazeroski	60.00
TAA54	Lindy McDaniel	10.00
TAA55	Bobby Richardson	15.00
TAA56	Brooks Robinson/SP	200.00
TAA57	Frank Robinson	80.00
TAA58	Orlando Cepeda	75.00
TAA59	Stan Musial/50	300.00
TAA60	Larry Bowa	25.00
TAA61	Johnny Callison	10.00
TAA62	Mike Cuellar	15.00
TAA63	Bob Gibson/SP/50	180.00
TAA64	Jim Perry	10.00
TAA65	Frank Howard	15.00
TAA66	David Palmer	15.00
TAA67	Willie McCovey	80.00
TAA68	Maury Wills	15.00
TAA69	Carl Yastrzemski	200.00
TAA70	Willie Davis	10.00
TAA71	Jim Maloney	10.00
TAA73	Ron Santo	30.00
TAA74	Jim Bouton	25.00
TAA75	Lou Brock/50	180.00
TAA76	Dean Chance	10.00
TAA77	Tim McCarver/200	50.00
TAA78	Sam McDowell	15.00
TAA79	Joe Pepitone	20.00
TAA80	Whitey Ford	120.00
TAA81	Boog Powell	20.00
TAA83	Bill Freehan	10.00
TAA85	Dick Allen	30.00
TAA86	Rico Carty	10.00
TAA87	Willie Horton	10.00
TAA88	Tommy John	15.00
TAA89	Mickey Lolich	10.00
TAA90	Phil Niekro	30.00
TAA91	Wilbur Wood	10.00
TAA92	Paul Blair	10.00
TAA93	Bert Campaneris	10.00
TAA94	Steve Carlton	40.00
TAA96	Jim Lonborg	10.00
TAA97	Luis Aparicio	40.00
TAA98	Tony Perez	40.00
TAA99	Joe Morgan/200	60.00
TAA100	Ron Swoboda	25.00
TAA101	Luis Tiant	15.00
TAA102	Fergie Jenkins	30.00
TAA103	Bobby Murcer	30.00
TAA104	Jim Palmer	75.00
TAA106	Sal Bando	10.00
TAA107	Ken Holtzman	40.00
TAA108	Tom Seaver/50	200.00
TAA110	Johnny Bench	225.00
TAA111	Hal McRae	10.00
TAA112	Nolan Ryan	400.00
TAA113	Roy White	10.00
TAA114	Rollie Fingers	25.00
TAA115	Reggie Jackson/50	200.00
TAA116	Sparky Lyle	15.00
TAA117	Graig Nettles	20.00
TAA118	Al Oliver	10.00
TAA119	Joe Rudi	15.00
TAA120	Bob Watson	10.00
TAA121	Vida Blue	10.00
TAA122	Bill Buckner	10.00
TAA123	Darrell Evans	10.00
TAA124	Bert Blyleven	25.00
TAA125	David Concepcion	15.00
TAA126	George Foster	10.00
TAA127	Bobby Grich	10.00
TAA128	Al Hrabosky	10.00
TAA129	Greg Luzinski	20.00
TAA130	Cecil Cooper	10.00
TAA131	Ron Cey	10.00
TAA132	Carlton Fisk	90.00
TAA133	George Hendrick	10.00
TAA134	Mickey Rivers	10.00
TAA135	Dwight Evans	20.00
TAA136	Goose Gossage	10.00
TAA137	Gary Matthews	10.00
TAA138	Rick Reuschel	10.00
TAA139	Mike Schmidt	300.00
TAA140	Bucky Dent	25.00
TAA141	Jim Kaat	25.00
TAA142	Frank Tanana	10.00
TAA143	Dave Winfield/200	90.00
TAA144	George Brett	300.00
TAA145	Gary Carter/200	60.00
TAA146	Keith Hernandez	25.00
TAA147	Fred Lynn	25.00
TAA148	Robin Yount SP/200	150.00
TAA149	Dennis Eckersley/SP/200	80.00
TAA150	Ron Guidry	25.00
TAA151	Kent Tekulve	15.00
TAA152	Jack Clark	10.00
TAA153	Andre Dawson/SP/200	60.00
TAA154	Mark Fidrych	20.00
TAA155	Denny Martinez/SP/200	40.00
TAA156	Dale Murphy	50.00
TAA157	Bruce Sutter	35.00
TAA158	Willie Hernandez	10.00
TAA160	Lou Whitaker	15.00
TAA162	Kirk Gibson	30.00
TAA163	Lee Smith	15.00
TAA164	Wade Boggs	80.00
TAA165	Ryne Sandberg/SP/200	160.00
TAA166	Don Mattingly	125.00
TAA167	Joe Carter/SP/200	30.00
TAA168	Orel Hershiser	40.00
TAA169	Kirby Puckett	150.00
TAA170	Jimmy Key	30.00

Game-Used Bat

NM/M

	Common Player:	15.00
1	Johnny Bench	30.00
2	George Brett	50.00
3	Fred Lynn	15.00
4	Reggie Jackson	15.00
5	Mike Schmidt	50.00
6	Willie Stargell	20.00

Game-Used Bat Autograph

NM/M
Common Player: 120.00
Production 25 Sets

1	Johnny Bench	150.00
2	George Brett	200.00
3	Fred Lynn	75.00

Topps Final Autoproof

NM/M

Common Player:	30.00
Carlton Fisk	60.00
Wade Boggs	40.00
Willie Mays	120.00
Willie McCovey	30.00
Jim Palmer	30.00
Robin Roberts	30.00
Duke Snider	40.00
Warren Spahn	40.00
Hoyt Wilhelm	30.00
Carl Yastrzemski	80.00

2001 Topps Archives Reserve

NM/M
Complete Set (100): 90.00
Common Player: .75
Hobby Pack (5): 8.00
Hobby Box (10 + Auto. Ball): 125.00

1	Joe Adcock	.75
2	Brooks Robinson	3.00
3	Luis Aparicio	.75
4	Richie Ashburn	.75
5	Hank Bauer	.75
6	Johnny Bench	4.00
7	Wade Boggs	2.00
8	Moose Skowron	.75
9	George Brett	5.00
10	Lou Brock	2.00
11	Roy Campanella	4.00
12	Willie Hernandez	.75
13	Steve Carlton	2.00
14	Gary Carter	.75
15	Hoyt Wilhelm	.75
16	Orlando Cepeda	.75
17	Roberto Clemente	8.00
18	Dale Murphy	1.50
19	Dave Concepcion	.75
20	Dom DiMaggio	.75
21	Larry Doby	.75
22	Don Drysdale	4.00
23	Dennis Eckersley	.75
24	Bob Feller	2.00
25	Rollie Fingers	.75
26	Carlton Fisk	2.00
27	Nellie Fox	1.50
28	Mickey Rivers	.75
29	Tommy John	.75
30	Johnny Sain	.75
31	Keith Hernandez	.75
32	Gil Hodges	.75
33	Elston Howard	3.00
34	Frank Howard	.75
35	Bob Gibson	5.00
36	Fergie Jenkins	.75
37	Jackie Jensen	.75
38	Al Kaline	3.00
39	Harmon Killebrew	5.00
40	Ralph Kiner	.75
41	Dick Groat	.75
42	Don Larsen	.75
43	Ralph Branca	.75
44	Mickey Lolich	.75
45	Juan Marichal	3.00
46	Roger Maris	6.00
47	Bobby Thomson	.75
48	Eddie Mathews	4.00
49	Don Mattingly	8.00
50	Willie McCovey	2.00
51	Gil McDougald	.75
52	Tug McGraw	.75
53	Billy Pierce	.75
54	Minnie Minoso	.75
55	Johnny Mize	2.00

56	Elroy Face	.75
57	Joe Morgan	1.50
58	Thurman Munson	5.00
59	Stan Musial	5.00
60	Phil Niekro	.75
61	Paul Blair	.75
62	Andy Pafko	.75
63	Satchel Paige	5.00
64	Tony Perez	.75
65	Sal Bando	.75
66	Jimmy Piersall	.75
67	Kirby Puckett	5.00
68	Phil Rizzuto	3.00
69	Robin Roberts	.75
70	Jackie Robinson	8.00
71	Ryne Sandberg	3.00
72	Mike Schmidt	4.00
73	Red Schoendienst	.75
74	Herb Score	.75
75	Enos Slaughter	.75
76	Ozzie Smith	3.00
77	Warren Spahn	2.00
78	Don Sutton	.75
79	Luis Tiant	.75
80	Ted Kluszewski	.75
81	Whitey Ford	3.00
82	Maury Wills	.75
83	Dave Winfield	2.00
84	Early Wynn	.75
85	Carl Yastrzemski	3.00
86	Robin Yount	4.00
87	Bob Allison	.75
88	Clete Boyer	.75
89	Reggie Jackson	3.00
90	Yogi Berra	5.00
91	Willie Mays	8.00
92	Jim Palmer	.75
93	Pee Wee Reese	2.00
94	Frank Robinson	2.00
95	Boog Powell	.75
96	Willie Stargell	3.00
97	Nolan Ryan	10.00
98	Tom Seaver	4.00
99	Duke Snider	3.00
100	Bill Mazeroski	.75

Autographs

NM/M
Common Autograph: 10.00
Inserted 1:10

1	Willie Mays	160.00
2	Whitey Ford	60.00
3	Nolan Ryan	175.00
4	Carl Yastrzemski	90.00
5	Frank Robinson	40.00
6	Tom Seaver	80.00
7	Warren Spahn	75.00
8	Johnny Bench	100.00
9	Reggie Jackson	80.00
10	Bob Gibson	40.00
11	Bob Feller	20.00
12	Gil McDougald	15.00
13	Luis Tiant	10.00
14	Minnie Minoso	10.00
16	Herb Score	10.00
17	Moose Skowron	15.00
18	Maury Wills	10.00
19	Clete Boyer	15.00
21	Don Larsen	20.00
23	Tug McGraw	20.00
25	Robin Roberts	20.00
26	Frank Howard	20.00
27	Mickey Lolich	10.00
29	Tommy John	10.00
32	Dick Groat	15.00
34	Paul Blair	10.00

Autographed Baseball

NM/M
Common Autograph: 15.00
Inserted 1:Box

1	Johnny Bench/100	80.00
2	Paul Blair/1,000	15.00
3	Clete Boyer/1,000	15.00
4	Ralph Branca/400	25.00
5	Elroy Face/1,000	15.00
6	Bob Feller/1,000	25.00
7	Whitey Ford/100	60.00
8	Bob Gibson/1,000	30.00
9	Dick Groat/1,000	15.00
10	Frank Howard/1,000	15.00
11	Reggie Jackson/100	75.00
12	Don Larsen/100	30.00
13	Mickey Lolich/500	15.00
14	Willie Mays/100	150.00
15	Gil McDougald/500	20.00
16	Tug McGraw/1,000	15.00
17	Minnie Minoso/1,000	15.00
18	Andy Pafko/500	25.00
19	Joe Pepitone/1,000	15.00
20	Robin Roberts/1,000	25.00
21	Frank Robinson/100	50.00
22	Nolan Ryan/100	150.00
23	Herb Score/500	20.00
24	Tom Seaver/100	80.00
25	Moose Skowron/1,000	15.00
26	Warren Spahn/100	50.00
27	Bobby Thomson/400	20.00
28	Luis Tiant/500	20.00
29	Carl Yastrzemski/100	100.00
30	Maury Wills/1,000	20.00

Bat Relics

NM/M
Common Player: 8.00
Overall Relic Odds 1:10

21	Al Kaline	20.00
22	Carl Yastrzemski	25.00
23	Carlton Fisk	15.00
24	Dale Murphy	15.00
25	Dave Winfield	10.00
26	Dick Groat	8.00
27	Dom DiMaggio	15.00
28	Don Mattingly	40.00
29	Gary Carter	8.00
30	George Kell	15.00
31	Harmon Killebrew	20.00
32	Jackie Jensen	15.00
33	Jackie Robinson	75.00
34	Jimmy Piersall	8.00
35	Joe Adcock	8.00
36	Joe Carter	8.00
37	Johnny Mize	10.00
38	Kirk Gibson	8.00
39	Mickey Vernon	8.00
40	Mike Schmidt	40.00
41	Ryne Sandberg	40.00
42	Ozzie Smith	20.00
43	Ted Kluszewski	10.00
44	Wade Boggs	15.00
45	Willie Mays	60.00
46	Duke Snider	15.00
47	Harvey Kuenn	8.00
48	Robin Yount	20.00
49	Red Schoendienst	8.00

50	Elston Howard	10.00
51	Bob Allison	8.00

Jersey Relics

NM/M
Common Player: 8.00
Overall Relic Odds 1:10

1	Brooks Robinson	15.00
2	Tony Conigliaro	15.00
3	Frank Howard	8.00
4	Don Sutton	10.00
5	Ferguson Jenkins	8.00
6	Frank Robinson	15.00
7	Don Mattingly	40.00
8	Willie Stargell	15.00
9	Moose Skowron	15.00
10	Fred Lynn	8.00
11	George Brett	40.00
12	Nolan Ryan	50.00
13	Orlando Cepeda	10.00
14	Reggie Jackson	15.00
15	Steve Carlton	15.00
16	Tom Seaver	20.00
17	Thurman Munson	25.00
18	Yogi Berra	20.00
19	Willie McCovey	10.00
20	Robin Yount	20.00

2001 Topps Chrome

NM/M
Complete Set (660): 225.00
Complete Series 1 (330): 100.00
Complete Series 2 (330): 125.00
Common Player: .25
Series 1 Pack (4): 2.00
Series 1 Box (24): 40.00
Series 2 Pack (4): 6.00
Series 2 Box (24): 120.00

1	Cal Ripken Jr.	3.00
2	Chipper Jones	1.00
3	Roger Cedeno	.25
4	Garret Anderson	.50
5	Robin Ventura	.40
6	Daryle Ward	.25
7	Not Issued (Retired)	
8	Phil Nevin	.25
9	Jermaine Dye	.25
10	Chris Singleton	.25
11	Mike Redmond	.25
12	Jim Thome	1.00
13	Brian Jordan	.25
14	Dustin Hermanson	.25
15	Shawn Green	.50
16	Todd Stottlemyre	.25
17	Dan Wilson	.25
18	Derek Lowe	.25
19	Juan Gonzalez	.75
20	Pat Meares	.25
21	Paul O'Neill	.50
22	Jeffrey Hammonds	.25
23	Pokey Reese	.25
24	Mike Mussina	.75
25	Rico Brogna	.25
26	Jay Buhner	.25
27	Steve Cox	.25
28	Quilvio Veras	.25
29	Marquis Grissom	.25
30	Shigetoshi Hasegawa	.25
31	Shane Reynolds	.25
32	Adam Piatt	.25
33	Preston Wilson	.25

34	Ellis Burks	.25
35	Armando Rios	.25
36	Chuck Finley	.25
37	Shannon Stewart	.25
38	Mark McGwire	2.50
39	Gerald Williams	.25
40	Eric Young	.25
41	Peter Bergeron	.25
42	Arthur Rhodes	.25
43	Bobby Jones	.25
44	Matt Clement	.25
45	Pedro Martinez	1.00
46	Jose Canseco	.75
47	Matt Anderson	.25
48	Torii Hunter	.50
49	Carlos Lee	.50
50	Eric Chavez	.50
51	Rick Helling	.25
52	John Franco	.25
53	Mike Bordick	.25
54	Andres Galarraga	.40
55	Jose Cruz Jr.	.25
56	Mike Matheny	.25
57	Randy Johnson	1.00
58	Richie Sexson	.75
59	Vladimir Nunez	.25
60	Aaron Boone	.25
61	Darin Erstad	.50
62	Alex Gonzalez	.25
63	Gil Heredia	.25
64	Shane Andrews	.25
65	Todd Hundley	.25
66	Bill Mueller	.25
67	Mark McLemore	.25
68	Scott Spiezio	.25
69	Kevin McGlinchy	.25
70	Manny Ramirez	1.00
71	Mike Lamb	.25
72	Brian Buchanan	.25
73	Mike Sweeney	.25
74	John Wetteland	.25
75	Rob Bell	.25
76	John Burkett	.25
77	Derek Jeter	3.00
78	J.D. Drew	.50
79	Jose Offerman	.25
80	Rick Reed	.25
81	Will Clark	.75
82	Rickey Henderson	.75
83	Kirk Rueter	.25
84	Lee Stevens	.25
85	Jay Bell	.25
86	Fred McGriff	.50
87	Julio Zuleta	.25
88	Brian Anderson	.25
89	Orlando Cabrera	.25
90	Alex Fernandez	.25
91	Derek Bell	.25
92	Eric Owens	.25
93	Dennys Reyes	.25
94	Mike Stanley	.25
95	Jorge Posada	.75
96	Paul Konerko	.50
97	Mike Remlinger	.25
98	Travis Lee	.25
99	Ken Caminiti	.25
100	Kevin Barker	.25
101	Ozzie Guillen	.25
102	Randy Wolf	.25
103	Michael Tucker	.25
104	Darren Lewis	.25
105	Joe Randa	.25
106	Jeff Cirillo	.25
107	David Ortiz	1.00
108	Herb Perry	.25
109	Jeff Nelson	.25
110	Chris Stynes	.25
111	Johnny Damon	1.00
112	Jason Schmidt	.50
113	Charles Johnson	.25
114	Pat Burrell	.50
115	Gary Sheffield	.75
116	Tom Glavine	.50
117	Jason Isringhausen	.25
118	Chris Carpenter	.50
119	Jeff Suppan	.25
120	Ivan Rodriguez	1.00
121	Luis Sojo	.25
122	Ron Villone	.25
123	Mike Sirotka	.25
124	Chuck Knoblauch	.25
125	Jason Kendall	.25
126	Bobby Estalella	.25
127	Jose Guillen	.25
128	Carlos Delgado	1.00
129	Benji Gil	.25
130	Einar Diaz	.25
131	Andy Benes	.25
132	Adrian Beltre	.50
133	Roger Clemens	3.00
134	Scott Williamson	.25
135	Brad Penny	.25
136	Troy Glaus	.50
137	Kevin Appier	.25

#	Player	Value
138	Walt Weiss	.25
139	Michael Barrett	.25
140	Mike Hampton	.25
141	Francisco Cordova	.25
142	David Segui	.25
143	Carlos Febles	.25
144	Roy Halladay	.50
145	Seth Etherton	.25
146	Fernando Tatis	.25
147	Livan Hernandez	.25
148	B.J. Surhoff	.25
149	Barry Larkin	.50
150	Bobby Howry	.25
151	Dmitri Young	.25
152	Brian Hunter	.25
153	Alex Rodriguez	3.00
154	Hideo Nomo	.75
155	Warren Morris	.25
156	Antonio Alfonseca	.25
157	Edgardo Alfonzo	.25
158	Mark Grudzielanek	.25
159	Fernando Vina	.25
160	Homer Bush	.25
161	Jason Giambi	1.00
162	Steve Karsay	.25
163	Matt Lawton	.25
164	Rusty Greer	.25
165	Billy Koch	.25
166	Todd Hollandsworth	.25
167	Raul Ibanez	.25
168	Tony Gwynn	1.00
169	Carl Everett	.25
170	Hector Carrasco	.25
171	Jose Valentin	.25
172	Deivi Cruz	.25
173	Bret Boone	.25
174	Melvin Mora	.25
175	Danny Graves	.25
176	Jose Jimenez	.25
177	James Baldwin	.25
178	C.J. Nitkowski	.25
179	Jeff Zimmerman	.25
180	Mike Lowell	.25
181	Hideki Irabu	.25
182	Greg Vaughn	.25
183	Omar Daal	.25
184	Darren Dreifort	.25
185	Gil Meche	.25
186	Damian Jackson	.25
187	Frank Thomas	1.00
188	Luis Castillo	.25
189	Bartolo Colon	.50
190	Craig Biggio	.50
191	Scott Schoeneweis	.25
192	Dave Veres	.25
193	Ramon Martinez	.25
194	Jose Vidro	.25
195	Todd Helton	.75
196	Greg Norton	.25
197	Jacque Jones	.25
198	Jason Grimsley	.25
199	Dan Reichert	.25
200	Robb Nen	.25
201	Scott Hatteberg	.25
202	Terry Shumpert	.25
203	Kevin Millar	.25
204	Ismael Valdes	.25
205	Richard Hidalgo	.25
206	Randy Velarde	.25
207	Bengie Molina	.25
208	Tony Womack	.25
209	Enrique Wilson	.25
210	Jeff Brantley	.25
211	Rick Ankiel	.25
212	Terry Mulholland	.25
213	Ron Belliard	.25
214	Terrence Long	.25
215	Alberto Castillo	.25
216	Royce Clayton	.25
217	Joe McEwing	.25
218	Jason McDonald	.25
219	Ricky Bottalico	.25
220	Keith Foulke	.25
221	Brad Radke	.25
222	Gabe Kapler	.25
223	Pedro Astacio	.25
224	Armando Reynoso	.25
225	Darryl Kile	.25
226	Reggie Sanders	.25
227	Esteban Yan	.25
228	Joe Nathan	.25
229	Jay Payton	.25
230	Francisco Cordero	.25
231	Gregg Jefferies	.25
232	LaTroy Hawkins	.25
233	Jacob Cruz	.25
234	Chris Holt	.25
235	Vladimir Guerrero	1.00
236	Marvin Benard	.25
237	Alex Ramirez	.25
238	Mike Williams	.25
239	Sean Bergman	.25
240	Juan Encarnacion	.25
241	Russ Davis	.25
242	Ramon Hernandez	.25
243	Sandy Alomar	.25
244	Eddie Guardado	.25
245	Shane Halter	.25
246	Geoff Jenkins	.50
247	Brian Meadows	.25
248	Damian Miller	.25
249	Darrin Fletcher	.25
250	Rafael Furcal	.50
251	Mark Grace	.75
252	Mark Mulder	.50
253	Joe Torre	.75
254	Bobby Cox	.25
255	Mike Scioscia	.25
256	Mike Hargrove	.25
257	Jimy Williams	.25
258	Jerry Manuel	.25
259	Charlie Manuel	.25
260	Don Baylor	.25
261	Phil Garner	.25
262	Tony Muser	.25
263	Buddy Bell	.25
264	Tom Kelly	.25
265	John Boles	.25
266	Art Howe	.25
267	Larry Dierker	.25
268	Lou Pinella	.25
269	Larry Rothschild	.25
270	Davey Lopes	.25
271	Johnny Oates	.25
272	Felipe Alou	.25
273	Bobby Valentine	.25
274	Tony LaRussa	.25
275	Bruce Bochy	.25
276	Dusty Baker	.25
277	Adrian Gonzalez, Adam Johnson	1.00
278	Matt Wheatland, Brian Digby	.50
279	Tripper Johnson, Scott Thorman	1.00
280	Phil Dumatrait, Adam Wainwright	1.00
281	Scott Heard, David Parrish RC	.75
282	Rocco Baldelli, Mark Folsom RC	1.00
283	Dominic Rich, Aaron Herr	.75
284	Mike Stodolka, Sean Burnett	.75
285	Derek Thompson, Corey Smith	.75
286	Danny Borrell, Jason Bourgeois RC	.75
287	Chin-Feng Chen, Corey Patterson, Josh Hamilton	.75
288	Ryan Anderson, Barry Zito, C.C. Sabathia	.75
289	Scott Sobkowiak, David Walling, Ben Sheets	.75
290	Ty Howington, Josh Kalinowski, Josh Girdley	.50
291	Hee Seop Choi, Aaron McNeal, Jason Hart	1.00
292	Bobby Bradley, Kurt Ainsworth, Chin-Hui Tsao	.75
293	Mike Glendenning, Kenny Kelly, Juan Silvestri	.50
294	J.R. House, Ramon Castro, Ben Davis	.50
295	Chance Caple, Rafael Soriano, Pascual Coco	1.00
296	Travis Hafner, Eric Munson, Bucky Jacobsen	6.00
297	Jason Conti, Chris Wakeland, Brian Cole	.75
298	Scott Seabol, Aubrey Huff, Joe Crede	.50
299	Adam Everett, Jose Ortiz, Keith Ginter	.50
300	Carlos Hernandez, Geraldo Guzman, Adam Eaton	.75
301	Bobby Kielty, Milton Bradley, Juan Rivera	.50
302	Mark McGwire	2.00
303	Don Larsen	.75
304	Bobby Thomson	.25
305	Bill Mazeroski	.25
306	Reggie Jackson	1.00
307	Kirk Gibson	.25
308	Roger Maris	1.50
309	Cal Ripken Jr.	3.00
310	Hank Aaron	3.00
311	Joe Carter	.25
312	Cal Ripken Jr.	3.00
313	Randy Johnson	1.00
314	Ken Griffey Jr.	2.00
315	Troy Glaus	.75
316	Kazuhiro Sasaki	.25
317	Sammy Sosa, Troy Glaus	1.00
318	Todd Helton, Edgar Martinez	.50
319	Todd Helton, Nomar Garciaparra	1.00
320	Barry Bonds, Jason Giambi	1.50
321	Todd Helton, Manny Ramirez	.50
322	Todd Helton, Darin Erstad	.50
323	Kevin Brown, Pedro Martinez	.75
324	Randy Johnson, Pedro Martinez	.75
325	Will Clark	.40
326	New York Mets	.25
327	New York Yankees	1.00
328	Seattle Mariners	.25
329	Mike Hampton	.25
330	New York Yankees	1.00
331	World Series	1.50
332	Jeff Bagwell	1.00
333	Andy Pettitte	.75
334	Tony Armas Jr.	.25
335	Jeromy Burnitz	.25
336	Javier Vazquez	.25
337	Eric Karros	.25
338	Brian Giles	.50
339	Scott Rolen	1.00
340	David Justice	.50
341	Ray Durham	.25
342	Todd Zeile	.25
343	Cliff Floyd	.25
344	Barry Bonds	3.00
345	Matt Williams	.50
346	Steve Finley	.25
347	Scott Elarton	.25
348	Bernie Williams	.75
349	David Wells	.25
350	J.T. Snow	.25
351	Al Leiter	.40
352	Magglio Ordonez	.50
353	Raul Mondesi	.25
354	Tim Salmon	.50
355	Jeff Kent	.40
356	Mariano Rivera	.50
357	John Olerud	.50
358	Javy Lopez	.50
359	Ben Grieve	.25
360	Ray Lankford	.25
361	Ken Griffey Jr.	2.00
362	Rich Aurilia	.25
363	Andruw Jones	1.00
364	Ryan Klesko	.50
365	Roberto Alomar	.75
366	Miguel Tejada	.50
367	Mo Vaughn	.25
368	Albert Belle	.25
369	Jose Canseco	.75
370	Kevin Brown	.50
371	Rafael Palmeiro	.75
372	Mark Redman	.25
373	Larry Walker	.50
374	Greg Maddux	2.00
375	Nomar Garciaparra	1.00
376	Kevin Millwood	.50
377	Edgar Martinez	.50
378	Sammy Sosa	1.50
379	Tim Hudson	.50
380	Jim Edmonds	.50
381	Mike Piazza	1.50
382	Brant Brown	.25
383	Brad Fullmer	.25
384	Alan Benes	.25
385	Mickey Morandini	.25
386	Troy Percival	.25
387	Eddie Perez	.25
388	Vernon Wells	.50
389	Ricky Gutierrez	.25
390	Rondell White	.25
391	Kevin Escobar	.25
392	Tony Batista	.25
393	Jimmy Haynes	.25
394	Billy Wagner	.50
395	A.J. Hinch	.25
396	Matt Morris	.25
397	Lance Berkman	.75
398	Jeff D'Amico	.25
399	Octavio Dotel	.25
400	Olmedo Saenz	.25
401	Esteban Loaiza	.25
402	Adam Kennedy	.25
403	Moises Alou	.50
404	Orlando Palmeiro	.25
405	Kevin Young	.25
406	Tom Goodwin	.25
407	Mac Suzuki	.25
408	Pat Hentgen	.25
409	Kevin Stocker	.25
410	Mark Sweeney	.25
411	Tony Eusebio	.25
412	Edgar Renteria	.25
413	John Rocker	.25
414	Jose Lima	.25
415	Kerry Wood	.50
416	Mike Timlin	.25
417	Jose Hernandez	.25
418	Jeremy Giambi	.25
419	Luis Lopez	.25
420	Mitch Meluskey	.25
421	Garrett Stephenson	.25
422	Jamey Wright	.25
423	John Jaha	.25
424	Placido Polanco	.25
425	Marty Cordova	.25
426	Joey Hamilton	.25
427	Travis Fryman	.25
428	Mike Cameron	.25
429	Matt Mantei	.25
430	Chan Ho Park	.25
431	Shawn Estes	.25
432	Danny Bautista	.25
433	Wilson Alvarez	.25
434	Kenny Lofton	.40
435	Russ Ortiz	.25
436	Dave Burba	.25
437	Felix Martinez	.25
438	Jeff Shaw	.25
439	Mike Difelice	.25
440	Roberto Hernandez	.25
441	Bryan Rekar	.25
442	Ugueth Urbina	.25
443	Vinny Castilla	.25
444	Carlos Perez	.25
445	Juan Guzman	.25
446	Ryan Rupe	.25
447	Mike Mordecai	.25
448	Ricardo Rincon	.25
449	Curt Schilling	1.00
450	Alex Cora	.25
451	Turner Ward	.25
452	Omar Vizquel	.40
453	Russ Branyan	.25
454	Russ Johnson	.25
455	Gregg Colbrunn	.25
456	Charles Nagy	.25
457	Wil Cordero	.25
458	Jason Tyner	.25
459	Devon White	.25
460	Kelly Stinnett	.25
461	Wilton Guerrero	.25
462	Jason Bere	.25
463	Calvin Murray	.25
464	Miguel Batista	.25
465	Erubiel Durazo	.25
466	Luis Gonzalez	.50
467	Jaret Wright	.25
468	Chad Kreuter	.25
469	Armando Benitez	.25
470	Sidney Ponson	.25
471	Adrian Brown	.25
472	Sterling Hitchcock	.25
473	Timoniel Perez	.25
474	Jamie Moyer	.25
475	Delino DeShields	.25
476	Glendon Rusch	.25
477	Chris Gomez	.25
478	Adam Eaton	.25
479	Pablo Ozuna	.25
480	Bob Abreu	.50
481	Kris Benson	.25
482	Keith Osik	.25
483	Darryl Hamilton	.25
484	Marlon Anderson	.25
485	Jimmy Anderson	.25
486	John Halama	.25
487	Nelson Figueroa	.25
488	Alex Gonzalez	.25
489	Benny Agbayani	.25
490	Ed Sprague	.25
491	Scott Erickson	.25
492	Doug Glanville	.25
493	Jesus Sanchez	.25
494	Mike Lieberthal	.25
495	Aaron Sele	.25
496	Pat Mahomes	.25
497	Ruben Rivera	.25
498	Wayne Gomes	.25
499	Freddy Garcia	.25
500	Al Martin	.25
501	Woody Williams	.25
502	Paul Byrd	.25
503	Rick White	.25
504	Trevor Hoffman	.25
505	Brady Anderson	.25
506	Robert Person	.25
507	Jeff Conine	.25
508	Chris Truby	.25
509	Emil Brown	.25

510	Ryan Dempster	.25
511	Ruben Mateo	.25
512	Alex Ochoa	.25
513	Jose Rosado	.25
514	Masato Yoshii	.25
515	Brian Daubach	.25
516	Jeff D'Amico	.25
517	Brent Mayne	.25
518	John Thomson	.25
519	Todd Ritchie	.25
520	John Vander Wal	.25
521	Neifi Perez	.25
522	Chad Curtis	.25
523	Kenny Rogers	.25
524	Trot Nixon	.25
525	Sean Casey	.25
526	Wilton Veras	.25
527	Troy O'Leary	.25
528	Dante Bichette	.25
529	Jose Silva	.25
530	Darren Oliver	.25
531	Steve Parris	.25
532	David McCarty	.25
533	Todd Walker	.25
534	Brian Rose	.25
535	Pete Schourek	.25
536	Ricky Ledee	.25
537	Justin Thompson	.25
538	Benito Santiago	.25
539	Carlos Beltran	.40
540	Gabe White	.25
541	Bret Saberhagen	.25
542	Ramon Martinez	.25
543	John Valentin	.25
544	Frank Catalanotto	.25
545	Tim Wakefield	.25
546	Manuel Tucker	.25
547	Juan Pierre	.25
548	Rich Garces	.25
549	Luis Ordaz	.25
550	Jerry Spradlin	.25
551	Corey Koskie	.25
552	Cal Eldred	.25
553	Alfonso Soriano	1.00
554	Kip Wells	.25
555	Orlando Hernandez	.40
556	Bill Simas	.25
557	Jim Parque	.25
558	Joe Mays	.25
559	Tim Belcher	.25
560	Shane Spencer	.25
561	Glenallen Hill	.25
562	Matt LeCroy	.25
563	Tino Martinez	.25
564	Eric Milton	.25
565	Ron Coomer	.25
566	Cristian Guzman	.25
567	Kazuhiro Sasaki	.25
568	Mark Quinn	.25
569	Eric Gagne	.25
570	Kerry Ligtenberg	.25
571	Rolando Arrojo	.25
572	Jon Lieber	.25
573	Jose Vizcaino	.25
574	Jeff Abbott	.25
575	Carlos Hernandez	.25
576	Scott Sullivan	.25
577	Matt Stairs	.25
578	Tom Lampkin	.25
579	Donnie Sadler	.25
580	Desi Relaford	.25
581	Scott Downs	.25
582	Mike Mussina	.75
583	Ramon Ortiz	.25
584	Mike Myers	.25
585	Frank Castillo	.25
586	Manny Ramirez	1.00
587	Alex Rodriguez	3.00
588	Andy Ashby	.25
589	Felipe Crespo	.25
590	Bobby Bonilla	.25
591	Denny Neagle	.25
592	Dave Martinez	.25
593	Mike Hampton	.25
594	Gary DiSarcina	.25
595	Tsuyoshi Shinjo RC	.75
596	Albert Pujols RC	80.00
597	Roy Oswalt, Pat Strange, Jon Rauch	.75
598	Phil Wilson, Jake Peavy, Darwin Cubillan RC	10.00
599	Nathan Haynes, Steve Smyth, Mike Bynum	.75
600	Joe Lawrence, Choo Freeman, Michael Cuddyer	.50
601	Larry Barnes, Dewayne Wise, Carlos Pena	.25

602	Felipe Lopez, Gookie Dawkins, Erick Almonte RC	1.00
603	Brad Wilkerson, Alex Escobar, Eric Valent	.25
604	Jeff Goldbach, Toby Hall, Rod Barajas	.25
605	Marcus Giles, Pablo Ozuna, Jason Romano	.25
606	Vernon Wells, Jack Cust, Dee Brown	.25
607	Luis Montanez, David Espinosa	1.00
608	John Lackey, Justin Wayne RC	1.00
609	Josh Axelson, Carmen Cali RC	1.00
610	Shaun Boyd, Chris Morris RC	1.00
611	Dan Moylan, Tommy Arko RC	1.00
612	Luis Cotto, Luis Escobar	1.00
613	Blake Williams, Brandon Mims RC	1.00
614	Chris Russ, Bryan Edwards	1.00
615	Joe Torres, Ben Diggins	.25
616	Mark Dalesandro, Edwin Encarnacion RC	5.00
617	Brian Bass, Odannis Ayala RC	1.00
618	Jason Kaanoi, Michael Mathews RC	.50
619	Stuart McFarland, Adam Sterrett RC	1.00
620	David Krynzel, Grady Sizemore	1.00
621	Keith Bucktrot, Dane Sardinha	.25
622	Anaheim Angels	.25
623	Arizona Diamondbacks	.25
624	Atlanta Braves	.25
625	Baltimore Orioles	.25
626	Boston Red Sox	.25
627	Chicago Cubs	.25
628	Chicago White Sox	.25
629	Cincinnati Reds	.25
630	Cleveland Indians	.25
631	Colorado Rockies	.25
632	Detroit Tigers	.25
633	Florida Marlins	.25
634	Houston Astros	.25
635	Kansas City Royals	.25
636	Los Angeles Dodgers	.25
637	Milwaukee Brewers	.25
638	Minnesota Twins	.25
639	Montreal Expos	.25
640	New York Mets	.25
641	New York Yankees	1.50
642	Oakland Athletics	.25
643	Philadelphia Phillies	.25
644	Pittsburgh Pirates	.25
645	San Diego Padres	.25
646	San Francisco Giants	.25
647	Seattle Mariners	.25
648	St. Louis Cardinals	.25
649	Tampa Bay Devil Rays	.25
650	Texas Rangers	.25
651	Toronto Blue Jays	.25
652	Bucky Dent	.25
653	Jackie Robinson	1.50
654	Roberto Clemente	1.50
655	Nolan Ryan	2.50
656	Kerry Wood	.50
657	Rickey Henderson	.75
658	Lou Brock	.50
659	David Wells	.25
660	Andruw Jones	.75
661	Carlton Fisk	.25

Retrofractors

Stars:	3-5X
Inserted 1:12	

Before There Was Topps

		NM/M
Complete Set (10):		40.00
Common Player:		3.00
Inserted 1:20		
Refractors:		2-4X
Inserted 1:200		
BT1	Lou Gehrig	8.00
BT2	Babe Ruth	10.00
BT3	Cy Young	5.00
BT4	Walter Johnson	3.00
BT5	Ty Cobb	8.00
BT6	Rogers Hornsby	3.00

Joe DiMaggio

BT7	Honus Wagner	4.00
BT8	Christy Mathewson	3.00
BT9	Grover Alexander	3.00
BT10	Joe DiMaggio	8.00

Combos

MOUND MARKSMEN
BOB GIBSON   PEDRO MARTINEZ

		NM/M
Complete Set (20):		80.00
Common Card:		2.00
Inserted 1:12		
Refractors:		2-4X
Inserted 1:120		
1	Derek Jeter, Yogi Berra, Whitey Ford, Don Mattingly, Reggie Jackson	6.00
2	Chipper Jones, Mike Schmidt	6.00
3	Brooks Robinson, Cal Ripken Jr.	8.00
4	Bob Gibson, Pedro Martinez	3.00
5	Ivan Rodriguez, Johnny Bench	4.00
6	Ernie Banks, Alex Rodriguez	6.00
7	Joe Morgan, Ken Griffey Jr., Barry Larkin	5.00
8	Vladimir Guerrero, Roberto Clemente	6.00
9	Ken Griffey Jr., Hank Aaron	6.00
10	Casey Stengel, Joe Torre	2.00
TC11	Kevin Brown, Sandy Koufax, Don Drysdale	5.00
TC12	Mark McGwire, Sammy Sosa, Roger Marris, Babe Ruth	8.00
TC13	Ted Williams, Carl Yastrzemski, Nomar Garciaparra	8.00
TC14	Greg Maddux, Roger Clemens, Cy Young	5.00
TC15	Tony Gwynn, Ted Williams	6.00
TC16	Cal Ripken Jr., Lou Gehrig	10.00
TC17	Sandy Koufax, Randy Johnson, Warren Spahn, Steve Carlton	4.00
TC18	Mike Piazza, Josh Gibson	5.00
TC19	Barry Bonds, Willie Mays	8.00
TC20	Jackie Robinson, Larry Doby	5.00

Golden Anniversary

HANK AARON

		NM/M
Complete Set (50):		120.00
Common Player:		1.00
Inserted 1:10		
Refractors:		2-4X
Inserted 1:100		
1	Hank Aaron	6.00
2	Ernie Banks	3.00
3	Mike Schmidt	5.00
4	Willie Mays	6.00
5	Johnny Bench	4.00
6	Tom Seaver	3.00
7	Frank Robinson	2.00
8	Sandy Koufax	5.00
9	Bob Gibson	3.00
10	Ted Williams	8.00
11	Cal Ripken Jr.	8.00
12	Tony Gwynn	3.00
13	Mark McGwire	6.00
14	Ken Griffey Jr.	4.00
15	Greg Maddux	4.00
16	Roger Clemens	6.00
17	Barry Bonds	8.00
18	Rickey Henderson	1.50
19	Mike Piazza	4.00
20	Jose Canseco	2.00
21	Derek Jeter	5.00
22	Nomar Garciaparra	5.00
23	Alex Rodriguez	5.00
24	Sammy Sosa	5.00
25	Ivan Rodriguez	2.00
26	Vladimir Guerrero	3.00
27	Chipper Jones	4.00
28	Jeff Bagwell	2.00
29	Pedro Martinez	3.00
30	Randy Johnson	3.00
31	Pat Burrell	1.50
32	Josh Hamilton	1.00
33	Ryan Anderson	1.00
34	Corey Patterson	1.50
35	Eric Munson	1.00
36	Sean Burroughs	1.00
37	C.C. Sabathia	1.00
38	Chin-Feng Chen	1.00
39	Barry Zito	1.50
40	Adrian Gonzalez	1.00
41	Mark McGwire	6.00
42	Nomar Garciaparra	5.00
43	Todd Helton	2.00
44	Matt Williams	1.00
45	Troy Glaus	1.50
46	Geoff Jenkins	1.00
47	Frank Thomas	2.00
48	Mo Vaughn	1.00
49	Barry Larkin	1.50
50	J.D. Drew	1.00

King of Kings

	NM/M
Common Player:	40.00
Inserted 1:5,175 H	
Inserted 1:5,209 R	
KKR1	Hank Aaron	80.00
KKR2	Nolan Ryan	120.00
KKR3	Rickey Henderson	40.00
KKR5	Bob Gibson	40.00
KKR6	Nolan Ryan	120.00

King of Kings Golden Edition

Inserted 1:59,220 H
KKGE Hank Aaron, Nolan Ryan, Rickey Henderson

Past To Present

	NM/M
Complete Set (10):	20.00
Common Player:	1.50
Inserted 1:18	
Refractors:	1.5-3X

Inserted 1:180
1	Phil Rizzuto, Derek Jeter	6.00
2	Warren Spahn, Greg Maddux	4.00
3	Yogi Berra, Jorge Posada	3.00
4	Willie Mays, Barry Bonds	6.00
5	Red Schoendienst, Fernando Vina	1.50
6	Duke Snider, Shawn Green	2.00
7	Bob Feller, Bartolo Colon	1.50
8	Johnny Mize, Tino Martinez	1.50
9	Larry Doby, Manny Ramirez	2.00
10	Eddie Mathews, Chipper Jones	3.00

Through The Years

NM/M
Complete Set (50): 200.00
Common Player: 2.00
Inserted 1:10
Refractors: 2-4X
Inserted 1:100
1	Yogi Berra	4.00
2	Roy Campanella	4.00
3	Willie Mays	8.00
4	Andy Pafko	2.00
5	Jackie Robinson	8.00
6	Stan Musial	5.00
7	Duke Snider	4.00
8	Warren Spahn	4.00
9	Ted Williams	10.00
10	Eddie Matthews	4.00
11	Willie McCovey	2.00
12	Frank Robinson	3.00
13	Ernie Banks	5.00
14	Hank Aaron	8.00
15	Sandy Koufax	6.00
16	Bob Gibson	4.00
17	Harmon Killebrew	3.00
18	Whitey Ford	3.00
19	Roberto Clemente	8.00
20	Juan Marichal	2.00
21	Johnny Bench	5.00
22	Willie Stargell	3.00
23	Joe Morgan	2.00
24	Carl Yastrzemski	5.00
25	Reggie Jackson	4.00
26	Tom Seaver	4.00
27	Steve Carlton	3.00
28	Jim Palmer	2.00
29	Rod Carew	3.00
30	George Brett	8.00
31	Roger Clemens	8.00
32	Don Mattingly	8.00
33	Ryne Sandberg	6.00
34	Mike Schmidt	8.00
35	Cal Ripken Jr.	10.00
36	Tony Gwynn	4.00
37	Ozzie Smith	5.00
38	Wade Boggs	3.00
39	Nolan Ryan	10.00
40	Robin Yount	4.00
41	Mark McGwire	8.00
42	Ken Griffey Jr.	5.00
43	Sammy Sosa	6.00
44	Alex Rodriguez	6.00
45	Barry Bonds	8.00
46	Mike Piazza	5.00
47	Chipper Jones	5.00
48	Greg Maddux	5.00
49	Nomar Garciaparra	6.00
50	Derek Jeter	8.00

Topps Originals

NM/M
Common Player: 15.00
Inserted 1:1,783 H
Inserted 1:1,788 R
Refractors 10 sets produced.
1	Roberto Clemente	180.00
2	Carl Yastrzemski	60.00
3	Mike Schmidt	75.00
4	Wade Boggs	20.00
5	Chipper Jones	40.00
6	Willie Mays	
7	Lou Brock	20.00
8	Dave Parker	15.00
9	Barry Bonds	80.00
10	Alex Rodriguez	50.00

What Could've Been

NM/M
Complete Set (10): 25.00
Common Player: 2.00
Inserted 1:30
Refractors: 2-4X
Inserted 1:300
WCB1	Josh Gibson	6.00
WCB2	Satchel Paige	6.00
WCB3	Buck Leonard	3.00
WCB4	James "Cool Pap Bell	4.00
WCB5	Andrew "Rube" Foster	3.00
WCB6	Martin Dihigo	2.00
WCB7	William "Judy" Johnson	3.00
WCB8	Mule Suttles	2.00
WCB9	Ray Dandridge	2.00
WCB10	John Henry Lloyd	2.00

2001 Topps Chrome Traded & Rookies

NM/M
Complete Chrome Set (265): 150.00

	Common Player:	.25
T1	Sandy Alomar Jr.	.25
T2	Kevin Appier	.25
T3	Brad Ausmus	.25
T4	Derek Bell	.25
T5	Bret Boone	.40
T6	Rico Brogna	.25
T7	Ellis Burks	.25
T8	Ken Caminiti	.25
T9	Roger Cedeno	.25
T10	Royce Clayton	.25
T11	Enrique Wilson	.25
T12	Rheal Cormier	.25
T13	Eric Davis	.25
T14	Shawon Duston	.25
T15	Andres Galarraga	.40
T16	Tom Gordon	.25
T17	Mark Grace	1.00
T18	Jeffrey Hammonds	.25
T19	Dustin Hermanson	.25
T20	Quinton McCracken	.25
T21	Todd Hundley	.25
T22	Charles Johnson	.25
T23	Marquis Grissom	.25
T24	Jose Mesa	.25
T25	Terry Mulholland	.25
T26	John Rocker	.25
T27	Jeff Frye	.25
T28	Reggie Sanders	.25
T29	David Segui	.25
T30	Mike Sirotka	.25
T31	Fernando Tatis	.25
T32	Steve Trachsel	.25
T33	Ismael Valdes	.25
T34	Randy Velarde	.25
T35	Brian Boehringer	.25
T36	Mike Bordick	.25
T37	Ken Bottenfield	.25
T38	Pat Rapp	.25
T39	Jeff Nelson	.25
T40	Ricky Bottalico	.25
T41	Deion Sanders	.50
T42	Hideo Nomo	1.00
T43	Bill Mueller	.25
T44	Roberto Kelly	.25
T45	Chris Holt	.25
T46	Mike Jackson	.25
T47	Devon White	.25
T48	Gerald Williams	.25
T49	Eddie Taubensee	.25
T50	Brian Hunter	.25
T51	Nelson Cruz	.25
T52	Jeff Fassero	.25
T53	Bubba Trammell	.25
T54	Bo Porter	.25
T55	Greg Norton	.25
T56	Benito Santiago	.25
T57	Ruben Rivera	.25
T58	Dee Brown	.25
T59	Jose Canseco	1.00
T60	Chris Michalak	.25
T61	Tim Worrell	.25
T62	Matt Clement	.25
T63	Bill Pulsipher	.25
T64	Troy Brohawn	.25
T65	Mark Kotsay	.25
T66	Jose Lima	.25
T67	Shea Hillenbrand	.25
T68	Ted Lilly	.25
T69	Jermaine Dye	.25
T70	Jerry Hairston Jr.	.25
T71	John Mabry	.25
T72	Kurt Abbott	.25
T73	Eric Owens	.25
T74	Jeff Brantley	.25
T75	Vinny Castilla	.25
T76	Ron Villone	.25
T77	Rickey Henderson	.75
T78	Jason Grimsley	.25
T79	Christian Parker RC	.50
T80	Donnie Wall	.25
T81	Alex Arias	.25
T82	Willis Roberts	.25
T83	Ryan Minor	.25
T84	Jason LaRue	.25
T85	Ruben Sierra	.25
T86	Johnny Damon	1.50
T87	Juan Gonzalez	.75
T88	Mac Suzuki	.25
T89	Tony Batista	.25
T90	Jay Witasick	.25
T91	Brent Abernathy	.25
T92	Paul LoDuca	.25
T93	Wes Helms	.25
T94	Milton Bradley	.25
T95	Matt LeCroy	.25
T96	A.J. Hinch	.25
T97	Bud Smith RC	.25
T98	Adam Dunn	1.00
T99	Albert Pujols, Ichiro Suzuki	25.00
T100	Carlton Fisk	.50
T101	Tim Raines	.50
T102	Juan Marichal	.50
T103	Dave Winfield	.75
T104	Reggie Jackson	1.50
T105	Cal Ripken Jr.	4.00
T106	Ozzie Smith	1.50
T107	Tom Seaver	1.50
T108	Lou Piniella	.50
T109	Dwight Gooden	.50
T110	Bret Saberhagen	.25
T111	Gary Carter	.50
T112	Jack Clark	.25
T113	Rickey Henderson	1.00
T114	Barry Bonds	4.00
T115	Bobby Bonilla	.25
T116	Jose Canseco	1.00
T117	Will Clark	1.00
T118	Andres Galarraga	.25
T119	Bo Jackson	1.00
T120	Wally Joyner	.25
T121	Ellis Burks	.25
T122	David Cone	.25
T123	Greg Maddux	2.00
T124	Willie Randolph	.25
T125	Dennis Eckersley	.50
T126	Matt Williams	.75
T127	Joe Morgan	.75
T128	Fred McGriff	.75
T129	Roberto Alomar	.75
T130	Lee Smith	.50
T131	David Wells	.50
T132	Ken Griffey Jr.	3.00
T133	Deion Sanders	1.00
T134	Nolan Ryan	3.00
T135	David Justice	.50
T136	Joe Carter	.50
T137	Jack Morris	.25
T138	Mike Piazza	2.00
T139	Barry Bonds	3.00
T140	Terrence Long	.25
T141	Ben Grieve	.25
T142	Richie Sexson	.50
T143	Sean Burroughs	.25
T144	Alfonso Soriano	1.00
T145	Bob Boone	.25
T146	Larry Bowa	.25
T147	Bob Brenly	.25
T148	Buck Martinez	.25
T149	Lloyd McClendon	.25
T150	Jim Tracy	.25
T151	Jared Abruzzo RC	.75
T152	Kurt Ainsworth	.25
T153	Willie Bloomquist	.25
T154	Ben Broussard	.25
T155	Bobby Bradley	.25
T156	Mike Bynum	.25
T157	Ken Harvey	.25
T158	Ryan Christianson	.25
T159	Ryan Kohlmeier	.25
T160	Joe Crede	1.50
T161	Jack Cust	.25
T162	Ben Diggins	.25
T163	Phil Dumatrait	.25
T164	Alex Escobar	.25
T165	Miguel Olivo	.25
T166	Chris George	.25
T167	Marcus Giles	.25
T168	Keith Ginter	.25
T169	Josh Girdley	.25
T170	Tony Alvarez	.25
T171	Scott Seabol	.25
T172	Josh Hamilton	.25
T173	Jason Hart	.25
T174	Israel Alcantara	.25
T175	Jake Peavy	4.00
T176	Stubby Clapp RC	.75
T177	D'Angelo Jimenez	.25
T178	Nick Johnson	.25
T179	Ben Johnson	.50
T180	Larry Bigbie	.25
T181	Allen Levrault	.25
T182	Felipe Lopez	.25
T183	Sean Burnett	.25
T184	Nick Neugebauer	.25
T185	Austin Kearns	.50
T186	Corey Patterson	.50
T187	Carlos Pena	.25
T188	Ricardo Rodriguez RC	.75
T189	Juan Rivera	.25
T190	Grant Roberts	.25
T191	Adam Pettyjohn RC	.50
T192	Jared Sandberg	.25
T193	Xavier Nady	.25
T194	Dane Sardinha	.25
T195	Shawn Sonnier	.25
T196	Rafael Soriano	.25
T197	Brian Specht RC	.50
T198	Aaron Myette	.25
T199	Juan Uribe RC	.75
T200	Jayson Werth	.25
T201	Brad Wilkerson	.25
T202	Horacio Estrada	.25
T203	Joel Pineiro	.25
T204	Matt LeCroy	.25
T205	Michael Coleman	.25
T206	Ben Sheets	1.00

T207	Eric Byrnes	.25
T208	Sean Burroughs	.25
T209	Ken Harvey	.25
T210	Travis Hafner	6.00
T211	Erick Almonte	.25
T212	Jason Belcher RC	1.00
T213	Wilson Betemit RC	2.50
T214	Hank Blalock RC	4.00
T215	Danny Borrell	.25
T216	John Buck RC	.75
T217	Freddie Bynum RC	.75
T218	Noel Devarez RC	.50
T219	Juan Diaz RC	.50
T220	Felix Diaz RC	.50
T221	Josh Fogg RC	1.00
T222	Matt Ford RC	.50
T223	Scott Heard	.25
T224	Ben Hendrickson RC	.50
T225	Cody Ross RC	1.00
T226	Adrian Hernandez RC	.75
T227	Alfredo Amezaga RC	.75
T228	Bob Keppel RC	.50
T229	Ryan Madson RC	1.00
T230	Octavio Martinez RC	.50
T231	Hee Seop Choi	.50
T232	Thomas Mitchell	.50
T233	Luis Montanez	.25
T234	Andy Morales RC	.75
T235	Justin Morneau RC	15.00
T236	Greg "Toe" Nash RC	.50
T237	Valentino Pasucci RC	.50
T238	Roy Smith RC	.75
T239	Antonio Perez RC	.75
T240	Chad Petty RC	.50
T241	Steve Smyth	.25
T242	Jose Reyes RC	30.00
T243	Eric Reynolds RC	.75
T244	Dominic Rich	.50
T245	Jason Richardson RC	.50
T246	Ed Rogers RC	.75
T247	Albert Pujols RC	75.00
T248	Esix Snead RC	.50
T249	Luis Torres RC	.50
T250	Matt White RC	.75
T251	Blake Williams	.25
T252	Chris Russ	.25
T253	Joe Kennedy RC	.50
T254	Jeff Randazzo RC	.50
T255	Beau Hale RC	.50
256	Brad Hennessey RC	.75
257	Jace Gautreau RC	.50
258	Jeff Mathis RC	1.00
259	Aaron Heilman RC	.75
260	Bronson Sardinha RC	.75
261	Irvin Guzman RC	6.00
262	Gabe Gross RC	1.00
263	J.D. Martin RC	.75
264	Chris Smith RC	.50
265	Kenny Baugh RC	.50
266	Ichiro Suzuki RC	25.00

2001 Topps Fusion

		NM/M
Complete Set (250):		100.00
Common Player:		.25
Pack (5):		2.50
Box (24):		50.00
1	Albert Belle	.25
2	Albert Belle	.25
3	Albert Belle	.25
4	Nick Bierbrodt	.25
5	Alex Rodriguez	2.50
6	Alex Rodriguez	2.50
7	Alex Rodriguez	2.50
8	Alex Rodriguez	2.50
9	Eric Munson	.25
10	Barry Bonds	3.00
11	Andruw Jones	.75
12	Antonio Alfonseca	.25
13	Andres Galarraga	.40
14	Joe Crede	.25
15	Barry Larkin	.40

16	Barry Bonds	3.00
17	Barry Bonds	3.00
18	Andruw Jones	.75
19	C.C. Sabathia	.25
20	Bobby Higginson	.25
21	Barry Larkin	.40
22	Ben Grieve	.25
23	Barry Bonds	3.00
24	Corey Patterson	.25
25	Carlos Delgado	.75
26	Bernie Williams	.50
27	Brian Giles	.40
28	Barry Larkin	.40
29	Gookie Dawkins	.25
30	Chipper Jones	1.50
31	Brian Giles	.40
32	Carlos Delgado	.75
33	Ben Grieve	.25
34	Geoff Goetz	.25
35	Cristian Guzman	.25
36	Cal Ripken Jr.	3.00
37	Chipper Jones	1.50
38	Bernie Williams	.50
39	Pablo Ozuna	.25
40	Dante Bichette	.25
41	Carlos Delgado	.75
42	Craig Biggio	.50
43	Cal Ripken Jr.	3.00
44	Tim Redding	.25
45	Darin Erstad	.50
46	Chipper Jones	1.50
47	Darin Erstad	.50
48	Carlos Delgado	.75
49	Josh Hamilton	.25
50	Derek Jeter	3.00
51	Darin Erstad	.50
52	Dean Palmer	.25
53	Chipper Jones	1.50
54	Chin-Feng Chen	.25
55	Edgar Martinez	.25
56	Derek Jeter	3.00
57	Derek Jeter	3.00
58	Craig Biggio	.25
59	Keith Ginter	.25
60	Edgardo Alfonzo	.25
61	Edgar Martinez	.25
62	Edgardo Alfonzo	.25
63	David Justice	.50
64	Roy Oswalt	.25
65	Eric Karros	.25
66	Edgardo Alfonzo	.25
67	Frank Thomas	1.00
68	Dean Palmer	.25
69	Alfonso Soriano	1.00
70	Fernando Vina	.25
71	Frank Thomas	1.00
72	Garret Anderson	.40
73	Derek Jeter	3.00
74	Bobby Bradley	.25
75	Frank Thomas	1.00
76	Gary Sheffield	.50
77	Geoff Jenkins	.25
78	Edgar Martinez	.25
79	Nick Johnson	.25
80	Fred McGriff	.40
81	Geoff Jenkins	.25
82	Greg Maddux	1.50
83	Edgardo Alfonzo	.25
84	Hee Seop Choi RC	2.00
85	Garret Anderson	.50
86	Greg Maddux	1.50
87	Ivan Rodriguez	.75
88	Eric Karros	.25
89	Scott Seabol	.25
90	Ivan Rodriguez	.75
91	Ivan Rodriguez	.75
92	J.D. Drew	.25
93	Frank Thomas	1.00
94	Ryan Anderson	.25
95	Jason Giambi	.75
96	Jason Giambi	.75
97	Jason Kendall	.25
98	Gary Sheffield	.50
99	Milton Bradley	.25
100	Jason Kendall	.25
101	Jason Kendall	.25
102	Jeff Bagwell	.75
103	Greg Maddux	1.50
104	Sean Burroughs	.25
105	Jay Bell	.25
106	Jeff Bagwell	.75
107	Jeffrey Hammonds	.25
108	Ivan Rodriguez	.75
109	Ben Petrick	.25
110	Jeff Bagwell	.75
111	Jeff Cirillo	.25
112	Jermaine Dye	.25
113	J.T. Snow Jr.	.25
114	Ben Davis	.25
115	Jeff Cirillo	.25
116	Jeff Kent	.25
117	Jeromy Burnitz	.25
118	Jay Bell	.25
119	Jason Hart	.25

120	Jeff Kent	.25
121	Jermaine Dye	.25
122	John Olerud	.25
123	Jeff Bagwell	.75
124	Jeff Segar RC	.50
125	Jeromy Burnitz	.25
126	Jeromy Burnitz	.25
127	Johnny Damon	.25
128	Jim Edmonds	.40
129	Tim Christman RC	.50
130	Jim Thome	.75
131	Jim Edmonds	.40
132	Jorge Posada	.50
133	Jim Thome	.75
134	Danny Borrell RC	.50
135	Johnny Damon	.25
136	Jim Thome	.75
137	Jose Vidro	.25
138	Ken Griffey Jr.	1.50
139	Sean Burnett	.25
140	Larry Walker	.40
141	Jose Vidro	.25
142	Ken Griffey Jr.	1.50
143	Larry Walker	.40
144	Robert Keppell RC	1.00
145	Luis Castillo	.25
146	Ken Griffey Jr.	1.50
147	Kevin Brown	.40
148	Manny Ramirez	.75
149	David Parrish RC	.25
150	Manny Ramirez	.75
151	Kevin Brown	.40
152	Luis Castillo	.25
153	Mark Grace	.50
154	Mike Jacobs RC	.50
155	Mark Grace	.50
156	Larry Walker	.40
157	Magglio Ordonez	.40
158	Mark McGwire	2.00
159	Adam Johnson	.25
160	Mark McGwire	2.00
161	Magglio Ordonez	.50
162	Mark McGwire	2.00
163	Matt Williams	.40
164	Oscar Ramirez RC	.50
165	Mike Piazza	1.50
166	Manny Ramirez	.75
167	Mike Piazza	1.50
168	Mike Mussina	.50
169	Odannis Ayala RC	.25
170	Mike Sweeney	.25
171	Mark McGwire	2.00
172	Nomar Garciaparra	2.50
173	Mike Piazza	1.50
174	J.R. House	.25
175	Neifi Perez	.25
176	Mike Piazza	1.50
177	Pedro Martinez	1.00
178	Mo Vaughn	.25
179	Shawn Fagan RC	.50
180	Nomar Garciaparra	2.50
181	Mo Vaughn	.25
182	Rafael Palmeiro	.50
183	Nomar Garciaparra	2.50
184	Chris Bass RC	.75
185	Raul Mondesi	.25
186	Nomar Garciaparra	2.50
187	Randy Johnson	1.00
188	Omar Vizquel	.25
189	Erick Almonte RC	1.00
190	Ray Durham	.25
191	Pedro Martinez	1.00
192	Robb Nen	.25
193	Pedro Martinez	1.00
194	Luis Montanez RC	1.00
195	Ray Lankford	.25
196	Rafael Palmeiro	.50
197	Roberto Alomar	.75
198	Rafael Palmeiro	.50
199	Chad Petty RC	.50
200	Richard Hidalgo	.25
201	Randy Johnson	1.00
202	Robin Ventura	.25
203	Randy Johnson	1.00
204	Derek Thompson	.25
205	Sammy Sosa	2.00
206	Roberto Alomar	.75
207	Sammy Sosa	2.00
208	Raul Mondesi	.25
209	Scott Heard	.25
210	Scott Rolen	.75
211	Sammy Sosa	2.00
212	Scott Rolen	.75
213	Roberto Alomar	.75
214	Dominic Rich RC	.50
215	Sean Casey	.25
216	Scott Rolen	.75
217	Sean Casey	.25
218	Robin Ventura	.25
219	William Smith RC	.50
220	Tim Salmon	.40
221	Sean Casey	.25
222	Shannon Stewart	.25
223	Sammy Sosa	2.00

224	Joel Pieniero RC	.50
225	Tino Martinez	.25
226	Shawn Green	.40
227	Shawn Green	.40
228	Scott Rolen	.50
229	Greg Morrison RC	.50
230	Tony Gwynn	1.00
231	Todd Helton	.75
232	Steve Finley	.25
233	Scott Williamson	.25
234	Talmadge Nunnari	.25
235	Tony Womack	.25
236	Tony Batista	.25
237	Tim Salmon	.40
238	Shawn Green	.40
239	Carlos Villalobos RC	.50
240	Troy Glaus	.50
241	Troy Glaus	.50
242	Todd Helton	.75
243	Tim Salmon	.40
244	Marco Scutaro RC	.50
245	Troy O'Leary	.25
246	Vladimir Guerrero	1.00
247	Vladimir Guerrero	1.00
248	Vladimir Guerrero	1.00
249	Horacio Estrada	.25
250	Vladimir Guerrero	1.00

Autographs

		NM/M
Common Player:		5.00
Inserted 1:23		
1	Rafael Furcal	10.00
2	Mike Lamb	5.00
3	Jason Marquis	5.00
4	Milton Bradley	5.00
5	Barry Zito	20.00
6	Derrek Lee	20.00
7	Corey Patterson	10.00
8	Josh Hamilton	30.00
9	Sean Burroughs	8.00
10	Jason Hart	5.00
11	Luis Montanez	5.00
12	Robert Keppell	5.00
13	Blake Williams	10.00
14	Phil Wilson	5.00
15	Jake Peavy	40.00
16	Alex Rodriguez	70.00
17	Ivan Rodriguez	20.00
18	Don Larsen	20.00
19	Todd Helton	20.00
20	Carlos Delgado	15.00
21	Geoff Jenkins	10.00
22	Willie Stargell	30.00
23	Frank Robinson	30.00
24	Warren Spahn	40.00
25	Harmon Killebrew	30.00
26	Chipper Jones	30.00
27	Chipper Jones	30.00
28	Chipper Jones	30.00
29	Chipper Jones	30.00
30	Chipper Jones	30.00
31	Rocco Baldelli	25.00
32	Keith Ginter	5.00
33	J.R. House	8.00
34	Alex Cabrera	5.00
35	Tony Alvarez	5.00
36	Pablo Ozuna	5.00
37	Juan Salas	5.00

Double Feature

		NM/M
Common Duo:		10.00
1	Ivan Rodriguez, Rickey Henderson	40.00
2	John Smoltz, Tom Glavine	15.00
3	Willie Stargell, Frank Thomas	20.00
4	Carlos Delgado, Todd Helton	15.00

5	Adrian Gonzalez, Pat Burrell	15.00
6	Jose Vidro, Roberto Alomar	15.00
7	Chipper Jones, Robin Ventura	20.00
8	J.D. Drew, Matt Lawton	10.00
9	Josh Hamilton, Chin-Feng Chen	25.00
10	Rafael Furcal, Miguel Tejada	15.00
11	Josh Beckett, Ryan Anderson	15.00

Feature

		NM/M
	Common Player:	4.00
	Inserted 1:51	
1	Ivan Rodriguez	8.00
2	Rickey Henderson	15.00
3	John Smoltz	5.00
4	Tom Glavine	8.00
5	Willie Stargell	8.00
6	Frank Thomas	8.00
7	Carlos Delgado	8.00
8	Todd Helton	8.00
9	Adrian Gonzalez	5.00
10	Pat Burrell	4.00
11	Jose Vidro	4.00
12	Roberto Alomar	8.00
13	Chipper Jones	10.00
14	Robin Ventura	5.00
15	J.D. Drew	5.00
16	Matt Lawton	4.00
17	Josh Hamilton	4.00
18	Chin-Feng Chen	25.00
19	Rafael Furcal	8.00
20	Miguel Tejada	8.00
21	Josh Beckett	8.00
22	Ryan Anderson	4.00

2001 Topps Gallery

		NM/M
	Complete Set (152):	120.00
	Common Player:	.15
	Common Rookie:	1.50
	Inserted 1:3.5	
	Common Prospect:	.50
	Inserted 1:2.5	
	Common Retired:	1.00
	Inserted 1:5	
	Pack (6):	5.00
	Box (24):	100.00

Set price includes one Suzuki rookie.

1	Darin Erstad	.40
2	Chipper Jones	1.50
3	Nomar Garciaparra	2.50
4	Fernando Vina	.15
5	Bartolo Colon	.25
6	Bobby Higginson	.15
7	Antonio Alfonseca	.15
8	Mike Sweeney	.15
9	Kevin Brown	.25
10	Jose Vidro	.15
11	Derek Jeter	3.00
12	Jason Giambi	.75
13	Pat Burrell	.50
14	Jeff Kent	.25
15	Alex Rodriguez	2.50
16	Rafael Palmeiro	.50
17	Garret Anderson	.40
18	Brad Fullmer	.15
19	Doug Glanville	.15
20	Mark Quinn	.15
21	Mo Vaughn	.25
22	Andruw Jones	.75
23	Pedro Martinez	1.00
24	Ken Griffey Jr.	1.50
25	Roberto Alomar	.75
26	Dean Palmer	.15
27	Jeff Bagwell	.75
28	Jermaine Dye	.15
29	Chan Ho Park	.15
30	Vladimir Guerrero	1.00
31	Bernie Williams	.50
32	Ben Grieve	.15
33	Jason Kendall	.15
34	Barry Bonds	3.00
35	Jim Edmonds	.40
36	Ivan Rodriguez	.75
37	Javy Lopez	.25
38	J.T. Snow	.15
39	Erubiel Durazo	.15
40	Terrence Long	.15
41	Tim Salmon	.25
42	Greg Maddux	1.50
43	Sammy Sosa	2.00
44	Sean Casey	.25
45	Jeff Cirillo	.15
46	Juan Gonzalez	.75
47	Richard Hidalgo	.25
48	Shawn Green	.25
49	Jeromy Burnitz	.15
50	Willie Mays	15.00
51	David Justice	.25
52	Tim Hudson	.40
53	Brian Giles	.25
54	Robb Nen	.15
55	Fernando Tatis	.15
56	Tony Batista	.15
57	Pokey Reese	.15
58	Ray Durham	.15
59	Greg Vaughn	.15
60	Kazuhiro Sasaki	.15
61	Troy Glaus	.50
62	Rafael Furcal	.40
63	Magglio Ordonez	.40
64	Jim Thome	.75
65	Todd Helton	.75
66	Preston Wilson	.15
67	Moises Alou	.25
68	Gary Sheffield	.40
69	Geoff Jenkins	.25
70	Mike Piazza	1.50
71	Jorge Posada	.50
72	Bobby Abreu	.25
73	Phil Nevin	.15
74	John Olerud	.25
75	Mark McGwire	2.00
76	Jose Cruz Jr.	.15
77	David Segui	.15
78	Neifi Perez	.15
79	Omar Vizquel	.25
80	Rick Ankiel	.15
81	Randy Johnson	1.00
82	Albert Belle	.15
83	Frank Thomas	.75
84	Manny Ramirez	.75
85	Larry Walker	.25
86	Luis Castillo	.15
87	Johnny Damon	.25
88	Adrian Beltre	.15
89	Cristian Guzman	.15
90	Jay Payton	.15
91	Miguel Tejada	.40
92	Scott Rolen	.75
93	Ryan Klesko	.40
94	Edgar Martinez	.25
95	Fred McGriff	.25
96	Carlos Delgado	.75
97	Barry Zito	.50
98	Mike Lieberthal	.15
99	Trevor Hoffman	.15
100	Gabe Kapler	.15
101	Edgardo Alfonzo	.15
102	Corey Patterson	.50
103	Alfonso Soriano	1.00
104	Keith Ginter	.50
105	Keith Reed	.50
106	Nick Johnson	.50
107	Carlos Pena	.50
108	Vernon Wells	.50
109	Roy Oswalt	.75
110	Alex Escobar	.50
111	Adam Everett	.50
112	Jimmy Rollins	.50
113	Marcus Giles	.50
114	Jack Cust	.50
115	Chin-Feng Chen	1.00
116	Pablo Ozuna	.50
117	Ben Sheets	.50
118	Adrian Gonzalez	.50
119	Ben Davis	.50
120	Eric Valent	.50
121	Scott Heard	.50
122	David Parrish RC	1.50
123	Sean Burnett	.50
124	Derek Thompson	.50
125	Tim Christman RC	1.50
126	Mike Jacobs RC	1.00
127	Luis Montanez RC	1.50
128	Chris Bass RC	1.50
129	William Smith RC	1.50
130	Justin Wayne RC	2.00
131	Shawn Fagan RC	1.50
132	Chad Petty RC	1.50
133	J.R. House	.50
134	Joel Pineiro	.50
135	Albert Pujols RC	75.00
136	Carmen Cali RC	1.50
137	Steve Smyth RC	1.50
138	John Lackey	.50
139	Bob Keppel RC	1.50
140	Dominic Rich RC	1.50
141	Josh Hamilton	.50
142	Nolan Ryan	5.00
143	Tom Seaver	1.50
144	Reggie Jackson	1.50
145	Johnny Bench	1.50
146	Warren Spahn	1.50
147	Brooks Robinson	1.50
148	Carl Yastrzemski	1.00
149	Al Kaline	1.00
150	Bob Feller	1.00
151a	Ichiro Suzuki/ English RC	25.00
151b	Ichiro Suzuki/ Japanese RC	25.00

Press Plates

NM/M
Common Player: 50.00

(See 2001 Topps Gallery for checklist.)

Autographs

		NM/M
	Common Autograph:	15.00
	Inserted 1:232	
RA	Rick Ankiel	15.00
BB	Barry Bonds	150.00
PB	Pat Burrell	20.00
AG	Adrian Gonzalez	15.00
AR	Alex Rodriguez	100.00
IR	Ivan Rodriguez	50.00

Heritage

		NM/M
	Complete Set (10):	30.00
	Common Player:	2.00
	Inserted 1:12	
1	Todd Helton	3.00
2	Greg Maddux	4.00
3	Pedro Martinez	3.00
4	Orlando Cepeda	2.00
5	Willie McCovey	2.00
6	Ken Griffey Jr.	4.00
7	Alex Rodriguez	6.00
8	Derek Jeter	8.00
9	Mark McGwire	6.00
10	Vladimir Guerrero	3.00

Heritage Relic

	NM/M
Common Player:	10.00
Inserted 1:133	
Orlando Cepeda	10.00
Greg Maddux	25.00
Pedro Martinez	20.00
Willie McCovey	10.00

Heritage Autographed Relic

	NM/M
Production 25 Sets	
Orlando Cepeda	75.00
Willie McCovey	100.00

Originals Relics

		NM/M
	Common Player:	8.00
	Inserted 1:133	
RA	Roberto Alomar	10.00
JD	Jermaine Dye	8.00
DE	Darin Erstad	8.00
JG	Jason Giambi	10.00
AG	Adrian Gonzalez	8.00
SG	Shawn Green	10.00
AJ	Andruw Jones	10.00
JK	Jason Kendall	8.00
JFK	Jeff Kent	8.00
RP	Rafael Palmeiro	10.00
PR	Pokey Reese	8.00
SS	Sammy Sosa	20.00

RV	Robin Ventura	8.00
BW	Bernie Williams	10.00
PW	Preston Wilson	8.00

Star Gallery

	NM/M
Complete Set (10):	15.00
Common Player:	1.00
Inserted 1:8.	
1 Vladimir Guerrero.	1.00
2 Alex Rodriguez.	2.50
3 Derek Jeter.	3.00
4 Nomar Garciaparra.	2.50
5 Ken Griffey Jr.	1.50
6 Mark McGwire.	2.00
7 Chipper Jones.	1.50
8 Sammy Sosa.	2.00
9 Barry Bonds.	3.00
10 Mike Piazza.	1.50

Team Topps Legends Autographs

	NM/M
Common Autograph:	10.00
Inserted 1:286	
23R Gil McDougald	10.00
27F Andy Pafko	20.00
10R Frank Robinson	20.00
28F Herb Score	10.00
25R Luis Tiant	10.00

2001 Topps Gold Label

	NM/M
Complete Set (115):	80.00
Common Player:	.25
Common Rookie:	4.00
Production 999	
Golds:	2-3X
Production 999	

Gold Rookies:		2-3X
Production 99		
Pack (5):		3.00
Box (24):		50.00
1	Adrian Beltre	.40
2	Danny Borrell RC	4.00
3	Albert Belle	.25
4	Alex Cabrera	.25
5	Alex Rodriguez	2.50
6	Andruw Jones	.75
7	Antonio Alfonseca	.25
8	Barry Bonds	3.00
9	Barry Larkin	.50
10	Ben Grieve	.25
11	Ben Molina	.25
12	Bernie Williams	.50
13	Bobby Abreu	.40
14	Bobby Higginson	.25
15	Brad Fullmer	.25
16	Brian Giles	.40
17	Cal Ripken Jr.	3.00
18	Carlos Delgado	.75
19	Chad Petty RC	4.00
20	Charles Johnson	.25
21	Chipper Jones	1.50
22	Cristian Guzman	.25
23	Darin Erstad	.40
24	David Justice	.40
25	David Segui	.25
26	Derek Jeter	2.50
27	Edgar Martinez	.40
28	Edgardo Alfonzo	.25
29	Fernando Tatis	.25
30	Eric Karros	.25
31	Eric Munson	.25
32	Eric Young	.25
33	Frank Thomas	.75
34	Fernando Vina	.25
35	Garret Anderson	.40
36	Gary Sheffield	.50
37	Geoff Jenkins	.40
38	Greg Maddux	1.50
39	Ivan Rodriguez	.75
40	J.D. Drew	.40
41	J.R. House	.25
42	J.T. Snow Jr.	.25
43	Jason Giambi	.75
44	Jason Kendall	.40
45	Jay Payton	.25
46	Jeff Bagwell	.75
47	Jeff Cirillo	.25
48	Jeff Kent	.25
49	Chan Ho Park	.25
50	Jermaine Dye	.25
51	Jeromy Burnitz	.25
52	Jim Edmonds	.50
53	Jim Thome	.75
54	John Olerud	.50
55	Johnny Damon	.40
56	Jorge Posada	.50
57	Jose Cruz Jr.	.25
58	Jose Vidro	.25
59	Josh Hamilton	.25
60	Juan Gonzalez	.75
61	Steve Smyth RC	4.00
62	Justin Wayne RC	8.00
63	Kazuhiro Sasaki	.25
64	Ken Griffey Jr.	1.50
65	Kevin Brown	.40
66	Kevin Young	.25
67	Larry Walker	.50
68	Luis Castillo	.25
69	Steve Finley	.25
70	Magglio Ordonez	.50
71	Manny Ramirez	.75
72	Mark McGwire	2.50
73	Mark Quinn	.25
74	Miguel Tejada	.50
75	Mike Piazza	1.50
76	Mike Sweeney	.25
77	Mo Vaughn	.40
78	Moises Alou	.40
79	Nomar Garciaparra	2.00
80	Pat Burrell	.50
81	Paul Konerko	.25
82	Pedro Martinez	1.00
83	Phil Nevin	.25
84	Preston Wilson	.25
85	Rafael Furcal	.25
86	Todd Zeile	.25
87	Randy Johnson	1.00
88	Travis Lee	.25
89	Carl Everett	.25
90	Quilvio Veras	.25
91	Rick Ankiel	.25
92	Rick Brosseau RC	4.00
93	Robert Keppell RC	4.00
94	Roberto Alomar	.50
95	Ryan Klesko	.40
96	Sammy Sosa	2.00
97	Scott Heard	4.00
98	Scott Rolen	.75
99	Sean Casey	.50
100	Shawn Green	.40
101	Terrence Long	.25
102	Tim Salmon	.40
103	Todd Helton	.75
104	Tom Glavine	.50
105	Tony Batista	.25
106	Travis Baptist RC	4.00
107	Troy Glaus	.50
108	Victor Hall RC	4.00
109	Vladimir Guerrero	1.00
110	Tim Hudson	.40
111	Brian Roberts RC	2.00
112	Virgil Chevalier RC	4.00
113	Fernando Rodney RC	4.00
114	Paul Phillips RC	4.00
115	Cesar Bolivar RC	4.00

Class 2

Stars:	1-2X
Inserted 1:4	
Rookies:	1-1.5X
Production 699	
Golds:	2-3X
Production 699	
Gold Rookies:	2-3X
Production 69	
(See 2001 Topps Gold Label for checklist and base card values.)	

Class 3

Stars:	2-3X
Inserted 1:12	
Rookies:	1-2X
Production 299	
Golds:	3-5X
Production 299	
Gold Rookies:	2-4X
Production 29	
(See 2001 Topps Gold Label for checklist and base card values.)	

Masterpiece

	NM/M
Common Player:	50.00
(See 2001 Topps Gold Label for checklist.)	

Gold Fixtures

	NM/M
Complete Set (10):	150.00
Common Player:	8.00
Inserted 1:374	
1 Alex Rodriguez	20.00
2 Mark McGwire	20.00
3 Derek Jeter	25.00
4 Nomar Garciaparra	20.00
5 Chipper Jones	15.00
6 Sammy Sosa	20.00
7 Ken Griffey Jr.	15.00
8 Carlos Delgado	8.00
9 Frank Thomas	10.00
10 Barry Bonds	25.00

MLB Awards Ceremony

		NM/M
Common Player:		4.00
Inserted 1:24		
SA	Sandy Alomar/Bat	4.00
JB	Jeff Bagwell/Bat	8.00
AB	Albert Belle/Bat	4.00
CB	Carlos Beltran/Bat	4.00
DB	Dante Bichette	4.00
BB	Barry Bonds/Jsy	25.00
BB	Barry Bonds/Bat	25.00
SB	Scott Brosius/Bat	5.00
JC	Jose Canseco/Jsy	6.00
JC	Jose Canseco/Bat	6.00
WC	Will Clark/Bat	6.00
RC	Roger Clemens/Jsy	20.00
MC	Marty Cordova/Bat	4.00
RF	Rafael Furcal/Bat	6.00
AG	Andres Galarraga/Bat	4.00
NG	Nomar Garciaparra/Jsy	20.00
NG	Nomar Garciaparra/Bat	20.00
JG	Jason Giambi/Bat	8.00
TG	Troy Glaus/Bat	8.00
TG	Tom Glavine/Jsy	6.00
JG	Juan Gonzalez/Jsy	8.00
JG	Juan Gonzalez/Bat	8.00
DG	Dwight Gooden/Jsy	4.00
BG	Ben Grieve/Jsy	4.00
KG	Ken Griffey Jr./Jsy	15.00
KG	Ken Griffey Jr./Bat	15.00
TG	Tony Gwynn/Bat	10.00
TH	Todd Helton/Bat	8.00
RH	Rickey Henderson/Jsy	15.00
TH	Todd Hollandsworth/Bat	4.00
DJ	Derek Jeter/Bat	25.00
RJ	Randy Johnson/Jsy	10.00
CJ	Chipper Jones/Jsy	10.00
DJ	David Justice/Jsy	5.00
JK	Jeff Kent/Bat	4.00
CK	Chuck Knoblauch/Bat	4.00
BL	Barry Larkin/Bat	8.00
GM	Greg Maddux/Jsy	15.00
EM	Edgar Martinez/Bat	6.00
PM	Pedro Martinez/Jsy	10.00

FM Fred McGriff/Bat 5.00
MM Mark McGwire/Bat 60.00
MM Mark McGwire/Jsy 60.00
RM Raul Mondesi/Bat 4.00
HN Hideo Nomo/Jsy 25.00
JO John Olerud/Bat 4.00
PO Paul O'Neill/Bat 5.00
MP Mike Piazza/Bat 12.00
CR Cal Ripken Jr./Jsy 35.00
AR Alex Rodriguez/Jsy 15.00
IR Ivan Rodriguez/Jsy 8.00
SR Scott Rolen/Jsy 8.00
TS Tim Salmon/Jsy 4.00
KS Kazuhiro Sasaki/Jsy 5.00
GS Gary Sheffield/Bat 6.00
JS John Smoltz/Jsy 4.00
SS Sammy Sosa/Jsy 15.00
SS Sammy Sosa/Jsy 15.00
DS Darryl Strawberry/Jsy 4.00
DS Darryl Strawberry/Bat 4.00
FT Frank Thomas/Bat 8.00
FT Frank Thomas/Jsy 8.00
MV Mo Vaughn/Jsy 4.00
MV Mo Vaughn/Bat 4.00
LW Larry Walker/Bat 5.00
LW Larry Walker/Jsy 5.00
JW John Wetteland/Jsy 4.00
BW Bernie Williams/Jsy 8.00
MW Matt Williams/Bat 5.00

2001 Topps Heritage

MANNY RAMIREZ

	NM/M
Complete Set (407):	275.00
Complete Master Set (487):	320.00
Common Player:	.50
Common SP (311-407):	2.50
Inserted 1:2	
Pack (8):	13.00
Box (24):	275.00

1 Kris Benson .50
2 Brian Jordan .50
3 Fernando Vina .50
4 Mike Sweeney .50
5 Rafael Palmeiro 2.00
6 Paul O'Neill 1.00
7 Todd Helton 2.50
8 Ramiro Mendoza .50
9 Kevin Millwood 1.00
10 Chuck Knoblauch .75
11 Derek Jeter 10.00
12 Alex Rodriguez 8.00
13 Geoff Jenkins .75
14 David Justice 1.00
15 David Cone .50
16 Andres Galarraga 1.00
17 Garret Anderson 1.00
18 Roger Cedeno .50
19 Randy Velarde .50
20 Carlos Delgado 2.00
21 Quilvio Veras .50
22 Jose Vidro .50
23 Corey Patterson .75
24 Jorge Posada 1.00
25 Eddie Perez .50
26 Jack Cust .50
27 Sean Burroughs .75
28 Randy Wolf .50
29 Mike Lamb .50
30 Rafael Furcal .75
31 Barry Bonds 8.00
32 Tim Hudson .75
33 Tom Glavine 1.50
34 Javy Lopez .75
35 Aubrey Huff .50
36 Wally Joyner .50
37 Magglio Ordonez 1.00
38 Matt Lawton .50
39 Mariano Rivera 1.00
40 Andy Ashby .50
41 Mark Buehrle 3.00
42 Esteban Loaiza .50

43 Mark Redman .50
44 Mark Quinn .50
45 Tino Martinez .75
46 Joe Mays .50
47 Walt Weiss .50
48 Roger Clemens 6.00
49 Greg Maddux 5.00
50 Richard Hidalgo .75
51 Orlando Hernandez .75
52 Chipper Jones 5.00
53 Ben Grieve .50
54 Jimmy Haynes .50
55 Ken Caminiti .50
56 Tim Salmon 1.00
57 Andy Pettitte 1.00
58 Darin Erstad 1.00
59 Marquis Grissom .50
60 Raul Mondesi .75
61 Bengie Molina .50
62 Miguel Tejada 1.00
63 Jose Cruz Jr. .50
64 Billy Koch .50
65 Troy Glaus 2.00
66 Cliff Floyd .50
67 Tony Batista .50
68 Jeff Bagwell 2.50
69 Billy Wagner .50
70 Eric Chavez .75
71 Troy Percival .50
72 Andruw Jones 2.50
73 Shane Reynolds .50
74 Barry Zito 2.50
75 Roy Halladay 1.00
76 David Wells .50
77 Jason Giambi 1.50
78 Scott Elarton .50
79 Moises Alou .75
80 Adam Piatt .75
81 Wilton Veras .50
82 Darryl Kile .50
83 Johnny Damon .50
84 Tony Armas Jr. .50
85 Ellis Burks .50
86 Jamey Wright .50
87 Jose Vizcaino .50
88 Bartolo Colon .50
89 Carmen Cali RC .50
90 Kevin Brown .75
91 Josh Hamilton .50
92 Jay Buhner .50
93 Scott Pratt RC .50
94 Alex Cora .50
95 Luis Montanez RC 1.00
96 Dmitri Young .50
97 J.T. Snow Jr. .50
98 Damion Easley .50
99 Greg Norton .50
100 Matt Wheatland .50
101 Chin-Feng Chen .50
102 Tony Womack .50
103 Adam Kennedy .50
104 J.D. Drew .50
105 Carlos Febles .50
106 Jim Thome 1.00
107 Danny Graves .50
108 Dave Mlicki .50
109 Ron Coomer .50
110 James Baldwin .50
111 Shaun Boyd RC .75
112 Brian Bohannon .50
113 Jacque Jones .50
114 Alfonso Soriano 1.50
115 Tony Clark .50
116 Terrence Long .50
117 Todd Hundley .50
118 Kazuhiro Sasaki .50
119 Brian Sellier RC .50
120 John Olerud .75
121 Javier Vazquez .50
122 Sean Burnett .50
123 Matt LeCroy .50
124 Erubiel Durazo .50
125 Juan Encarnacion .50
126 Pablo Ozuna .50
127 Russ Ortiz .50
128 David Segui .50
129 Mark McGwire 3.00
130 Mark Grace 1.00
131 Fred McGriff .75
132 Carl Pavano .50
133 Derek Thompson .50
134 Shawn Green .75
135 B.J. Surhoff .50
136 Michael Tucker .50
137 Jason Isringhausen .50
138 Eric Milton .50
139 Mike Stodolka .50
140 Milton Bradley .50
141 Curt Schilling .75
142 Sandy Alomar .50
143 Brent Mayne .50
144 Todd Jones .50
145 Charles Johnson .50
146 Dean Palmer .50

147 Masato Yoshii .50
148 Edgar Renteria .50
149 Joe Randa .50
150 Adam Johnson .50
151 Greg Vaughn .50
152 Adrian Beltre .75
153 Glenallen Hill .50
154 David Parrish RC .75
155 Neifi Perez .50
156 Pete Harnisch .50
157 Paul Konerko .50
158 Dennys Reyes .50
159 Jose Lima .50
160 Eddie Taubensee .50
161 Miguel Cairo .50
162 Jeff Kent .75
163 Dustin Hermanson .50
164 Alex Gonzalez .50
165 Hideo Nomo .50
166 Sammy Sosa 2.00
167 C.J. Nitkowski .50
168 Cal Eldred .50
169 Jeff Abbott .50
170 Jim Edmonds .75
171 Mark Mulder .75
172 Dominic Rich RC .50
173 Ray Lankford .50
174 Danny Borrell RC .75
175 Rick Aguilera .50
176 Shannon Stewart .50
177 Steve Finley .50
178 Jim Parque .50
179 Kevin Appier .50
180 Adrian Gonzalez .75
181 Tom Goodwin .50
182 Kevin Tapani .50
183 Fernando Tatis .50
184 Mark Grudzielanek .50
185 Ryan Anderson .50
186 Jeffrey Hammonds .50
187 Corey Koskie .50
188 Brad Fullmer .50
189 Rey Sanchez .50
190 Michael Barrett .50
191 Rickey Henderson 1.00
192 Jermaine Dye .50
193 Scott Brosius .50
194 Matt Anderson .50
195 Brian Buchanan .50
196 Derrek Lee .50
197 Larry Walker .75
198 David Krynzel .50
199 Vinny Castilla .50
200 Ken Griffey Jr. 2.00
201 Matt Stairs .50
202 Ty Howington .50
203 Andy Benes .50
204 Luis Gonzalez .75
205 Brian Moehler .50
206 Harold Baines .50
207 Pedro Astacio .50
208 Cristian Guzman .50
209 Kip Wells .50
210 Frank Thomas 1.00
211 Jose Rosado .50
212 Vernon Wells .50
213 Bobby Higginson .50
214 Juan Gonzalez 1.00
215 Omar Vizquel .75
216 Bernie Williams 1.00
217 Aaron Sele .50
218 Shawn Estes .50
219 Roberto Alomar 1.00
220 Rick Ankiel .50
221 Josh Kalinowski .50
222 David Bell .50
223 Keith Foulke .50
224 Craig Biggio .75
225 Shawn Fagan RC .50
226 Scott Williamson .50
227 Ron Belliard .50
228 Chris Singleton .50
229 Alex Serrano .50
230 Deivi Cruz .50
231 Eric Munson .50
232 Luis Castillo .50
233 Edgar Martinez .75
234 Jeff Shaw .50
235 Jeromy Burnitz .50
236 Richie Sexson .75
237 Will Clark 1.00
238 Ron Villone .50
239 Kerry Wood 1.00
240 Rich Aurilia .50
241 Mo Vaughn .50
242 Travis Fryman .75
243 Manny Ramirez 1.00
244 Chris Stynes .50
245 Ray Durham .50
246 Juan Uribe RC .50
247 Juan Guzman .50
248 Lee Stevens .50
249 Devon White .50
250 Kyle Lohse RC 1.50

251 Bryan Wolff .50
252 Rick Brousseau RC .50
253 Eric Young .50
254 Freddy Garcia .50
255 Jay Bell .50
256 Steve Cox .50
257 Torii Hunter .75
258 Jose Canseco .75
259 Brad Ausmus .50
260 Jeff Cirillo .50
261 Brad Penny .50
262 Antonio Alfonseca .50
263 Russ Branyan .50
264 Scott Heard .50
265 John Lackey .50
266 Justin Wayne RC 1.00
267 Brad Radke .50
268 Todd Stottlemyre .50
269 Mark Loretta .50
270 Matt Williams .50
271 Kenny Lofton .50
272 Jeff D'Amico .50
273 Jamie Moyer .50
274 Darren Dreifort .50
275 Denny Neagle .50
276 Orlando Cabrera .50
277 Chuck Finley .50
278 Miguel Batista .50
279 Carlos Beltran .50
280 Eric Karros .50
281 Mark Kotsay .50
282 Ryan Dempster .50
283 Barry Larkin .75
284 Jeff Suppan .50
285 Gary Sheffield .75
286 Jose Valentin .50
287 Robb Nen .50
288 Chan Ho Park .50
289 John Halama .50
290 Steve Smyth RC .50
291 Gerald Williams .50
292 Preston Wilson .50
293 Victor Hall RC .75
294 Ben Sheets .50
295 Eric Davis .50
296 Kirk Rueter .50
297 Chad Petty RC .75
298 Kevin Millar .50
299 Marvin Benard .50
300 Vladimir Guerrero 1.00
301 Livan Hernandez .50
302 Travis Baptist RC .75
303 Bill Mueller .50
304 Mike Cameron .50
305 Randy Johnson 1.50
306 Alan Mahaffey RC .50
307 Timo Perez (No facsimile autograph.) .50
308 Pokey Reese .50
309 Ryan Rupe .50
310 Carlos Lee .50
311 Doug Glanville 2.50
312 Jay Payton 2.50
313 Troy O'Leary 2.50
314 Francisco Cordero 2.50
315 Rusty Greer 2.50
316 Cal Ripken Jr. 25.00
317 Ricky Ledee 2.50
318 Brian Daubach 2.50
319 Robin Ventura 3.00
320 Todd Zeile 3.00
321 Francisco Cordova 2.50
322 Henry Rodriguez 2.50
323 Pat Meares 2.50
324 Glendon Rusch 2.50
325 Keith Osik 2.50
326 Robert Keppell RC 4.00
327 Bobby Jones 2.50
328 Alex Ramirez 2.50
329 Robert Person 2.50
330 Ruben Mateo 2.50
331 Rob Bell 2.50
332 Carl Everett 2.50
333 Jason Schmidt 3.00
334 Scott Rolen 5.00
335 Jimmy Anderson 2.50
336 Bret Boone 3.00
337 Delino DeShields 2.50
338 Trevor Hoffman 2.50
339 Bob Abreu 3.00
340 Mike Williams 2.50
341 Mike Hampton 3.00
342 John Wetteland 2.50
343 Scott Erickson 2.50
344 Enrique Wilson 2.50
345 Tim Wakefield 2.50
346 Mike Lowell 2.50
347 Todd Pratt 2.50
348 Brook Fordyce 2.50
349 Benny Agbayani 2.50
350 Gabe Kapler 3.00
351 Sean Casey 3.00
352 Darren Oliver 2.50
353 Todd Ritchie 2.50

354	Kenny Rogers	2.50
355	Jason Kendall	3.00
356	John Vander Wal	2.50
357	Ramon Martinez	2.50
358	Edgardo Alfonzo	2.50
359	Phil Nevin	2.50
360	Albert Belle	2.50
361	Ruben Rivera	2.50
362	Pedro Martinez	10.00
363	Derek Lowe	2.50
364	Pat Burrell	5.00
365	Mike Mussina	5.00
366	Brady Anderson	2.50
367	Darren Lewis	2.50
368	Sidney Ponson	2.50
369	Adam Eaton	2.50
370	Eric Owens	2.50
371	Aaron Boone	2.50
372	Matt Clement	2.50
373	Derek Bell	2.50
374	Trot Nixon	2.50
375	Travis Lee	2.50
376	Mike Benjamin	2.50
377	Jeff Zimmerman	2.50
378	Mike Lieberthal	2.50
379	Rick Reed	2.50
380	Nomar Garciaparra	15.00
381	Omar Daal	2.50
382	Ryan Klesko	3.00
383	Rey Ordonez	2.50
384	Kevin Young	2.50
385	Rick Helling	2.50
386	Brian Giles	4.00
387	Tony Gwynn	8.00
388	Ed Sprague	2.50
389	J.R. House	2.50
390	Scott Hatteberg	2.50
391	John Valentin	2.50
392	Melvin Mora	2.50
393	Royce Clayton	2.50
394	Jeff Fassero	2.50
395	Manny Alexander	2.50
396	John Franco	2.50
397	Luis Alicea	2.50
398	Ivan Rodriguez	5.00
399	Kevin Jordan	2.50
400	Jose Offerman	2.50
401	Jeff Conine	2.50
402	Seth Etherton	2.50
403	Mike Bordick	2.50
404	Al Leiter	3.00
405	Mike Piazza	10.00
406	Armando Benitez	2.50
407	Warren Morris	2.50

Chrome

DAVID WELLS

		NM/M
Common Player:		3.00
Production 552 Sets		
1	Cal Ripken Jr.	40.00
2	Jim Thome	10.00
3	Derek Jeter	40.00
4	Andres Galarraga	4.00
5	Carlos Delgado	8.00
6	Roberto Alomar	8.00
7	Tom Glavine	8.00
8	Gary Sheffield	5.00
9	Mo Vaughn	3.00
10	Preston Wilson	3.00
11	Mike Mussina	8.00
12	Greg Maddux	30.00
13	Ivan Rodriguez	10.00
14	Al Leiter	3.00
15	Seth Etherton	3.00
16	Edgardo Alfonzo	3.00
17	Richie Sexson	3.00
18	Andruw Jones	10.00
19	Bartolo Colon	3.00
20	Darin Erstad	5.00
21	Kevin Brown	4.00
22	Mike Sweeney	3.00
23	Mike Piazza	30.00
24	Rafael Palmeiro	10.00

25	Terrence Long	3.00
26	Kazuhiro Sasaki	3.00
27	John Olerud	5.00
28	Mark McGwire	30.00
29	Fred McGriff	5.00
30	Todd Helton	10.00
31	Curt Schilling	5.00
32	Alex Rodriguez	30.00
33	Jeff Kent	4.00
34	Pat Burrell	8.00
35	Jim Edmonds	6.00
36	Mark Mulder	3.00
37	Troy Glaus	8.00
38	Jay Payton	3.00
39	Jermaine Dye	3.00
40	Larry Walker	5.00
41	Ken Griffey Jr.	30.00
42	Jeff Bagwell	10.00
43	Rick Ankiel	3.00
44	Mark Redman	3.00
45	Edgar Martinez	3.00
46	Mike Hampton	4.00
47	Manny Ramirez	10.00
48	Ray Durham	3.00
49	Rafael Furcal	3.00
50	Sean Casey	4.00
51	Jose Canseco	10.00
52	Barry Bonds	40.00
53	Tim Hudson	5.00
54	Barry Zito	10.00
55	Chuck Finley	3.00
56	Magglio Ordonez	4.00
57	David Wells	3.00
58	Jason Giambi	8.00
59	Tony Gwynn	15.00
60	Vladimir Guerrero	15.00
61	Randy Johnson	15.00
62	Bernie Williams	8.00
63	Craig Biggio	5.00
64	Jason Kendall	3.00
65	Pedro Martinez	15.00
66	Mark Quinn	3.00
67	Frank Thomas	15.00
68	Nomar Garciaparra	30.00
69	Brian Giles	5.00
70	Shawn Green	5.00
71	Roger Clemens	25.00
72	Sammy Sosa	30.00
73	Juan Gonzalez	10.00
74	Orlando Hernandez	4.00
75	Chipper Jones	20.00
76	Josh Hamilton	3.00
77	Adam Johnson	3.00
78	Shaun Boyd	3.00
79	Alfonso Soriano	15.00
80	Derek Thompson	3.00
81	Adrian Gonzalez	3.00
82	Ryan Anderson	3.00
83	Corey Patterson	5.00
84	J.R. House	3.00
85	Sean Burroughs	3.00
86	Scott Heard	3.00
87	John Lackey	3.00
88	Ben Sheets	4.00
89	Wilson Betemit	3.00
90	Robert Keppell	3.00
91	Luis Montanez	3.00
92	Sean Burnett	3.00
93	Justin Wayne	5.00
94	Eric Munson	3.00
95	Steve Smyth	3.00
96	Rick Brousseau	3.00
97	Carmen Cali	3.00
98	Brian Sellier	3.00
99	David Parrish	3.00
100	Danny Borrell	3.00
101	Chad Petty	3.00
102	Dominic Rich	3.00
103	Shawn Fagan	3.00
104	Alex Serrano	3.00
105	Juan Uribe	3.00
106	Travis Baptist	3.00
107	Alan Mahaffey	3.00
108	Kyle Lohse	4.00
109	Victor Hall	3.00
110	Scott Pratt	3.00

Classic Renditions

		NM/M
Complete Set (10):		15.00
Common Player:		1.00
Inserted 1:5		
1	Mark McGwire	2.50
2	Nomar Garciaparra	2.00
3	Barry Bonds	3.00
4	Sammy Sosa	2.00
5	Chipper Jones	1.50
6	Pat Burrell	1.00
7	Frank Thomas	1.00
8	Manny Ramirez	1.00

Classic Renditions

Nomar Garciaparra
Boston Red Sox

9	Derek Jeter	3.00
10	Ken Griffey Jr.	2.00

Classic Renditions Autogtraphs

Production 25 Sets		
BB	Barry Bonds	650.00
CJ	Chipper Jones	350.00
NG	Nomar Garciaparra	450.00

Clubhouse Collection Game-Used

CLUBHOUSE COLLECTION

CHIPPER JONES

		NM/M
Common Player:		25.00
MM	Minnie Monoso	25.00
RS	Red Schoendienst	30.00
DS	Duke Snider	40.00
EM	Eddie Mathews	40.00
CJ	Chipper Jones	40.00
RA	Richie Ashburn	30.00
FT	Frank Thomas	40.00
FV	Fernando Vina	25.00
SG	Shawn Green	30.00
WM	Willie Mays	150.00
BB	Barry Bonds	80.00
SR	Scott Rolen	40.00

Clubhouse Collection Dual Game-Used

		NM/M
Common Card:		75.00
Production 52 Sets		
MMFT	Minnie Monoso, Frank Thomas	100.00
RSFV	Red Schoendienst, Fernando Vina	75.00
DSSG	Duke Snider, Shawn Green	150.00
RAPB	Richie Ashburn, Scott Rolen	100.00
EMCJ	Eddie Mathews, Chipper Jones	125.00
WMBB	Willie Mays, Barry Bonds	250.00

Clubhouse Collection Autographs

		NM/M
Common Player:		
MM	Minnie Monoso/25	120.00
RS	Red Schoendienst/25	150.00

Grandstand Glory

GRANDSTAND GLORY

		NM/M
Common Player:		20.00
Inserted 1:211		
PR	Phil Rizzuto	30.00
YB	Yogi Berra	30.00
RA	Richie Ashburn	20.00
RR	Robin Roberts	20.00
WM	Willie Mays	60.00
NF	Nellie Fox	20.00
JR	Jackie Robinson	50.00

New Age Performers

new age performers

Derek Jeter
NEW YORK YANKEES

		NM/M
Complete Set (15):		20.00
Common Player:		1.00
Inserted 1:8		
1	Mike Piazza	1.50
2	Sammy Sosa	2.00
3	Alex Rodriguez	2.50
4	Barry Bonds	3.00
5	Ken Griffey Jr.	1.50
6	Chipper Jones	1.50
7	Randy Johnson	1.00
8	Derek Jeter	3.00
9	Nomar Garciaparra	2.00
10	Mark McGwire	2.50
11	Jeff Bagwell	1.00
12	Pedro Martinez	1.00
13	Todd Helton	1.00
14	Vladimir Guerrero	1.00
15	Greg Maddux	2.00

Real One Autographs

GIANTS

BARRY BONDS

	NM/M
Common Player:	30.00
Current MLB Players	
200 Blue-Inked Produced	
52 Red-Inked Produced	

Prices listed for Blue Sigs

RH	Richard Hidalgo	30.00
TL	Terrence Long	30.00
CD	Carlos Delgado	60.00
CJ	Chipper Jones	150.00
TG	Tom Glavine	100.00
GJ	Geoff Jenkins	40.00
JM	Joe Mays	30.00
FV	Fernando Vina	30.00
CP	Corey Patterson	40.00
JV	Jose Vidro	30.00
BB	Barry Bonds	275.00
AR	Alex Rodriguez	200.00
AH	Aubrey Huff	40.00
SPB	Sean Burroughs	30.00
RW	Randy Wolf	30.00
KB	Kris Benson	30.00
ML	Mike Lamb	30.00
TH	Todd Helton	80.00
MQ	Mark Quinn	30.00
MS	Mike Sweeney	30.00
ML	Matt Lawton	35.00
MO	Magglio Ordonez	40.00
MB	Mark Buehrle	50.00
MR	Mark Redman	30.00
CF	Cliff Floyd	30.00
NG	Nomar Garciaparra	150.00

1952 MLB Players

MV	Mickey Vernon	40.00
HB	Hank Bauer	80.00
DD	Dom DiMaggio	100.00
LD	Larry Doby	90.00
JG	Joe Garagiola	75.00
DG	Dick Groat	60.00
MI	Monte Irvin	75.00
VL	Vernon Law	50.00
EM	Eddie Matthews	200.00
WM	Willie Mays	200.00
GM	Gil McDougald	60.00
MM	Minnie Monoso	80.00
AP	Andy Pafko	75.00
PFR	Phil Rizzuto	120.00
PR	Preacher Roe	100.00
JS	Johnny Sain	60.00
HS	Hank Sauer	60.00
RS	Red Schoendienst	75.00
BS	Bobby Shantz	40.00
CS	Curt Simmons	40.00
ES	Enos Slaughter	100.00
DS	Duke Snider	180.00
WS	Warren Spahn	120.00
BT	Bobby Thomson	85.00
HW	Hoyt Wilhelm	90.00
RR	Robin Roberts	80.00

Then and Now

Then and Now

Pee Wee Reese — Brooklyn Dodgers®
Nomar Garciaparra — Boston Red Sox®

		NM/M
Complete Set (10):		15.00
Common Player:		1.50
Inserted 1:8		
1	Yogi Berra, Mike Piazza	1.50
2	Duke Snider, Sammy Sosa	2.00
3	Willie Mays, Ken Griffey Jr.	2.00
4	Phil Rizzuto, Derek Jeter	3.00
5	Pee Wee Reese, Nomar Garciaparra	2.00
6	Jackie Robinson, Alex Rodriguez	2.50
7	Johnny Mize, Mark McGwire	2.50
8	Bob Feller, Pedro Martinez	1.50
9	Robin Roberts, Greg Maddux	2.00
10	Warren Spahn, Randy Johnson	1.50

Time Capsule

	NM/M
Common Player:	20.00

TED WILLIAMS

Inserted 1:369		
WM	Willie Mays	75.00
TW	Ted Williams	85.00
DN	Don Newcombe	20.00
WF	Whitey Ford	30.00
WMTW	Ted Williams, Willie Mays/52	200.00

2001 Topps HD

ANDRES GALARRAGA

	NM/M
Complete Set (120):	50.00
Common Player:	.25
Common (101-120):	1.00
Inserted 1:6	
Pack (4):	2.50
Box (20):	40.00
1 Derek Jeter	3.00
2 Magglio Ordonez	.50
3 Eric Munson	.25
4 Jermaine Dye	.25
5 Larry Walker	.40
6 Pokey Reese	.25
7 Pedro Martinez	1.00
8 Rafael Palmeiro	.75
9 Jason Kendall	.40
10 Mike Lieberthal	.25
11 Ryan Klesko	.40
12 Cal Ripken Jr.	3.00
13 Mike Piazza	1.50
14 Adam Sterrett RC	.75
15 John Olerud	.40
16 Manny Ramirez	.75
17 Chad Petty RC	.75
18 Vladimir Guerrero	1.00
19 Kevin Brown	.40
20 Luis Cotto RC	.50
21 Josh Hamilton	.25
22 Mark Grace	.50
23 Mark McGwire	2.50
24 Jeromy Burnitz	.25
25 Andruw Jones	.75
26 Raul Mondesi	.40
27 Stuart McFarland RC	.50
28 Craig Biggio	.40
29 Troy Glaus	.50
30 Carlos Delgado	.75
31 Rafael Furcal	.40
32 J.D. Drew	.25
33 Corey Patterson	.40
34 Gary Sheffield	.50
35 Jeff Kent	.40
36 Alex Rodriguez	2.50
37 Edgardo Alfonzo	.25
38 Jeff Segar RC	.50
39 Bobby Abreu	.40
40 Brian Giles	.40
41 Jason Smith RC	.40
42 Mo Vaughn	.25
43 Pat Burrell	.50
44 Barry Larkin	.50
45 Carlos Beltran	.50
46 Eric Mosley RC	.50
47 Alfonso Soriano	1.00
48 Tim Salmon	.40
49 Jason Giambi	.75
50 Greg Maddux	1.50
51 Randy Johnson	1.00
52 Jose Vidro	.25
53 Edgar Martinez	.40
54 Albert Belle	.25
55 Ivan Rodriguez	.75

56	Sean Casey	.25
57	Jorge Posada	.50
58	Preston Wilson	.25
59	Paul Konerko	.25
60	Todd Helton	.75
61	Dominic Rich RC	.50
62	Tony Gwynn	1.00
63	Bernie Williams	.75
64	Anthony Brewer RC	.50
65	Shawn Green	.50
66	Jeff Bagwell	.75
67	Jose Cruz Jr.	.25
68	Darin Erstad	.40
69	Jim Edmonds	.50
70	Frank Thomas	.75
71	Ryan Anderson	.25
72	Scott Rolen	.75
73	Jeff Cirillo	.25
74	Chris Bass RC	.50
75	William Smith RC	.50
76	Trot Nixon	.25
77	Bobby Bradley	.25
78	Odannis Ayala RC	.50
79	Jim Thome	.75
80	Sammy Sosa	2.00
81	Geoff Jenkins	.40
82	Ben Grieve	.25
83	Andres Galarraga	.40
84	Rick Ankiel	.25
85	Barry Bonds	3.00
86	Alex Gonzalez	.25
87	Sean Burroughs	.25
88	Nomar Garciaparra	2.00
89	Ken Griffey Jr.	1.50
90	Tim Hudson	.50
91	Chipper Jones	1.50
92	Matt Williams	.40
93	Roberto Alomar	.75
94	Adrian Gonzalez	.40
95	Juan Gonzalez	.75
96	Brian Bass RC	.50
97	Rick Brosseau RC	.50
98	Mariano Rivera	.40
99	James Baldwin	.25
100	Dean Palmer	.25
101	Pedro Martinez	2.00
102	Randy Johnson	2.00
103	Greg Maddux	3.00
104	Sammy Sosa	4.00
105	Mark McGwire	5.00
106	Ivan Rodriguez	1.50
107	Mike Piazza	3.00
108	Chipper Jones	3.00
109	Vladimir Guerrero	2.00
110	Alex Rodriguez	5.00
111	Ken Griffey Jr.	3.00
112	Cal Ripken Jr.	6.00
113	Derek Jeter	6.00
114	Barry Bonds	6.00
115	Nomar Garciaparra	4.00
116	Jeff Bagwell	1.50
117	Todd Helton	1.50
118	Darin Erstad	1.00
119	Shawn Green	1.00
120	Roberto Alomar	1.00

Platinum

Stars (1-100):	4-8X
Stars (101-120):	2-4X
Production 199 Sets	

Autographed Cards

	NM/M
Common Player:	10.00
Inserted 1:431	
1 Todd Helton	25.00
2 Rick Ankiel	10.00
3 Mark Quinn	10.00
4 Adrian Gonzalez	10.00

Game Defined

THE GAME DEFINED

SAMMY SOSA

	NM/M
Complete Set (10):	25.00

Common Player:	1.50
Inserted 1:24	
Platinum:	1.5-2X
Inserted 1:72	
1 Ken Griffey Jr.	3.00
2 Derek Jeter	5.00
3 Sammy Sosa	3.00
4 Mark McGwire	4.00
5 Todd Helton	1.50
6 Mike Piazza	3.00
7 Chipper Jones	2.50
8 Vladimir Guerrero	1.50
9 Alex Rodriguez	4.00
10 Nomar Garciaparra	3.00

Game-Worn Jersey

	NM/M
Common Card:	5.00
Inserted 1:108	
Cards 5-8 are redemptions.	
1 Grant Roberts	5.00
2 Vernon Wells	10.00
3 Travis Dawkins	5.00
4 Ramon Ortiz	5.00
5 Steve Finley	5.00
6 Ramon Hernandez	5.00
7 Jay Payton	8.00
8 Jeromy Burnitz	5.00

Images of Excellence

IMAGES OF EXCELLENCE

REGGIE JACKSON

	NM/M
Complete Set (10):	15.00
Common Player:	1.00
Inserted 1:8	
Platinum:	1.5-2X
Inserted 1:24	
1 Willie Mays	2.50
2 Reggie Jackson	1.00
3 Ernie Banks	1.50
4 Hank Aaron	2.50
5 Ted Williams	2.50
6 Mike Schmidt	2.00
7 Tom Seaver	1.00
8 Johnny Bench	1.50
9 George Brett	2.50
10 Nolan Ryan	3.00

20-20

20 20

SAMMY — SOSA

	NM/M
Complete Set (10):	15.00
Common Player:	.50
Inserted 1:12	
Platinum:	1.5-2X
Inserted 1:36	
1 Barry Bonds	4.00
2 Chipper Jones	2.00
3 Ken Griffey Jr.	2.00
4 Alex Rodriguez	3.00
5 Ivan Rodriguez	1.00
6 Sammy Sosa	2.50
7 Roberto Alomar	.75
8 Larry Walker	.50
9 Shawn Green	.75
10 Jeff Bagwell	1.00

2001 Topps Opening Day

	NM/M
Complete Set (165):	35.00

Common Player: .15
Pack (7): 1.00
Box (24): 20.00
1	Cal Ripken Jr.	2.50
2	Chipper Jones	1.50
3	Garret Anderson	.40
4	Robin Ventura	.20
5	Jermaine Dye	.15
6	Jim Thome	.75
7	Brian Jordan	.15
8	Shawn Green	.40
9	Juan Gonzalez	.75
10	Paul O'Neill	.25
11	Pokey Reese	.15
12	Mike Mussina	.40
13	Jay Buhner	.15
14	Shane Reynolds	.15
15	Adam Piatt	.15
16	Preston Wilson	.15
17	Ellis Burks	.15
18	Chuck Finley	.15
19	Shannon Stewart	.15
20	Mark McGwire	2.00
21	Mark Loretta	.15
22	Bobby Jones	.15
23	Matt Clement	.15
24	Pedro J. Martinez	1.00
25	Carlos Lee	.15
26	John Franco	.15
27	Andres Galarraga	.15
28	Jose Cruz Jr.	.15
29	Randy Johnson	.75
30	Richie Sexson	.40
31	Darin Erstad	.30
32	Manny Ramirez	.75
33	Mike Sweeney	.15
34	John Wetteland	.15
35	Derek Jeter	2.50
36	J.D. Drew	.15
37	Rick Reed	.15
38	Jay Bell	.15
39	Fred McGriff	.25
40	Orlando Cabrera	.15
41	Eric Owens	.15
42	Jorge Posada	.40
43	Jeff Cirillo	.15
44	Johnny Damon	.25
45	Charles Johnson	.15
46	Pat Burrell	.40
47	Gary Sheffield	.40
48	Tom Glavine	.30
49	Ivan Rodriguez	.75
50	Chuck Knoblauch	.15
51	Jason Kendall	.15
52	Carlos Delgado	.60
53	Roger Clemens	1.50
54	Brad Penny	.15
55	Troy Glaus	.75
56	Mike Hampton	.15
57	Carlos Febles	.15
58	Seth Etherton	.15
59	Fernando Tatis	.15
60	Livan Hernandez	.15
61	Barry Larkin	.30
62	Alex Rodriguez	2.00
63	Warren Morris	.15
64	Antonio Alfonseca	.15
65	Edgardo Alfonzo	.15
66	Fernando Vina	.15
67	Jason Giambi	.75
68	Matt Lawton	.15
69	Rusty Greer	.15
70	Tony Gwynn	1.00
71	Carl Everett	.15
72	Bret Boone	.25
73	James Baldwin	.15
74	Greg Vaughn	.15
75	Darren Dreifort	.15
76	Frank Thomas	1.00
77	Luis Castillo	.15
78	Bartolo Colon	.25
79	Craig Biggio	.25
80	Jose Vidro	.15

81	Todd Helton	.75
82	Jacque Jones	.15
83	Robb Nen	.15
84	Richard Hidalgo	.15
85	Tony Womack	.15
86	Rick Ankiel	.15
87	Terrence Long	.15
88	Brad Radke	.15
89	Gabe Kapler	.15
90	Pedro Astacio	.15
91	Darryl Kile	.15
92	Jay Payton	.15
93	Vladimir Guerrero	1.00
94	Juan Encarnacion	.15
95	Ramon Hernandez	.15
96	Sandy Alomar	.15
97	Geoff Jenkins	.25
98	Rafael Furcal	.25
99	Mark Grace	.25
100	Mark Mulder	.25
101	Jim Edmonds	.40
102	Tim Salmon	.25
103	Jeff Bagwell	.75
104	Jose Canseco	.40
105	Ben Grieve	.15
106	Ryan Klesko	.25
107	Javy Lopez	.25
108	Greg Maddux	1.50
109	Andruw Jones	.50
110	Jeromy Burnitz	.15
111	Ray Lankford	.15
112	Sammy Sosa	1.50
113	Raul Mondesi	.25
114	Mike Piazza	1.50
115	Todd Zeile	.15
116	Eric Karros	.15
117	Barry Bonds	2.50
118	J.T. Snow	.15
119	Jeff Kent	.15
120	David Justice	.25
121	Matt Williams	.25
122	Brian Giles	.25
123	Edgar Martinez	.15
124	Ken Griffey Jr.	1.50
125	Al Leiter	.25
126	Kevin Brown	.25
127	John Olerud	.25
128	Roberto Alomar	.50
129	Rafael Palmeiro	.40
130	Steve Finley	.15
131	Tim Hudson	.40
132	Scott Rolen	.75
133	Nomar Garciaparra	1.50
134	Mo Vaughn	.15
135	Larry Walker	.30
136	Albert Belle	.15
137	Ray Durham	.15
138	Andy Pettitte	.40
139	Mariano Rivera	.25
140	Bernie Williams	.50
141	David Wells	.15
142	Magglio Ordonez	.40
143	Kevin Millwood	.15
144	Cliff Floyd	.15
145	Rich Aurilia	.15
146	Eric Chavez	.15
147	Scott Elarton	.15
148	Tony Armas Jr.	.15
149	Mark Redman	.15
150	Javier Vazquez	.15
151	Adrian Gonzalez, Adam Johnson	.50
152	Mike Stodolka, Sean Burnett	.15
153	David Walling, Ben Sheets	.50
154	Chin-Feng Chen, Corey Patterson, Josh Hamilton	.25
155	Mark McGwire	1.00
156	Bobby Thomson	.15
157	Bill Mazeroski	.15
158	Cal Ripken Jr.	1.00
159	Hank Aaron	1.00
160	Bucky Dent	.15
161	Jackie Robinson	1.00
162	Roberto Clemente	1.00
163	Nolan Ryan	1.00
164	Kerry Wood	.25
165	Checklist	.15

Autographs

NM/M
Common Autograph: 20.00
TH	Todd Helton	40.00
CJ	Chipper Jones	100.00
MO	Magglio Ordonez	25.00
CP	Corey Patterson	20.00

Team Logo Stickers

NM/M
Complete Set (30): 6.00
Sticker: .25
Each team represented.

2001 Topps Reserve

NM/M
Complete Set (151):
Common Player: .40
Common SP (101-150): 4.00
Production 1,500
Sealed Hobby Box (10): 150.00
1	Darin Erstad	.50
2	Moises Alou	.40
3	Tony Batista	.40
4	Andruw Jones	.75
5	Edgar Renteria	.40
6	Eric Young	.40
7	Steve Finley	.40
8	Adrian Beltre	.40
9	Vladimir Guerrero	1.00
10	Barry Bonds	3.00
11	Juan Gonzalez	.75
12	Jay Buhner	.40
13	Luis Castillo	.40
14	Cal Ripken Jr.	3.00
15	Bob Abreu	.40
16	Ivan Rodriguez	.75
17	Nomar Garciaparra	2.00
18	Todd Helton	.75
19	Bobby Higginson	.40
20	Jorge Posada	.50
21	Tim Salmon	.50
22	Jason Giambi	.75
23	Jose Cruz Jr.	.40
24	Chipper Jones	1.50
25	Jim Edmonds	.50
26	Gerald Williams	.40
27	Randy Johnson	1.00
28	Gary Sheffield	.50
29	Jeff Kent	.40
30	Jim Thome	.75
31	John Olerud	.50
32	Cliff Floyd	.40
33	Mike Lowell	.40
34	Phil Nevin	.40
35	Scott Rolen	.75
36	Alex Rodriguez	2.50
37	Ken Griffey Jr.	2.00
38	Neifi Perez	.40
39	Christian Guzman	.40
40	Mariano Rivera	.50
41	Troy Glaus	.75
42	Johnny Damon	.40
43	Rafael Furcal	.40
44	Jeromy Burnitz	.40
45	Mark McGwire	2.00
46	Fred McGriff	.40
47	Matt Williams	.40
48	Kevin Brown	.40
49	J.T. Snow	.40
50	Kenny Lofton	.40
51	Al Martin	.40
52	Antonio Alfonseca	.40
53	Edgardo Alfonzo	.40
54	Ryan Klesko	.40
55	Pat Burrell	.50
56	Rafael Palmeiro	.75
57	Sean Casey	.40
58	Jeff Cirillo	.40
59	Ray Durham	.40
60	Derek Jeter	3.00
61	Jeff Bagwell	.75
62	Carlos Delgado	.75
63	Tom Glavine	.50
64	Richie Sexson	.50
65	J.D. Drew	.40
66	Ben Grieve	.40
67	Mark Grace	.50
68	Shawn Green	.40
69	Robb Nen	.40
70	Omar Vizquel	.40
71	Edgar Martinez	.40
72	Preston Wilson	.40
73	Mike Piazza	1.50
74	Tony Gwynn	1.00
75	Jason Kendall	.40

76	Manny Ramirez	.75
77	Pokey Reese	.40
78	Mike Sweeney	.40
79	Magglio Ordonez	.50
80	Bernie Williams	.75
81	Richard Hidalgo	.40
82	Brad Fullmer	.40
83	Greg Maddux	2.00
84	Geoff Jenkins	.40
85	Sammy Sosa	2.00
86	Luis Gonzalez	.50
87	Eric Karros	.40
88	Jose Vidro	.40
89	Rich Aurilia	.40
90	Roberto Alomar	.75
91	Mike Cameron	.40
92	Mike Mussina	.60
93	Albert Belle	.40
94	Mike Lieberthal	.40
95	Brian Giles	.40
96	Pedro Martinez	1.00
97	Barry Larkin	.50
98	Jermaine Dye	.40
99	Frank Thomas	.75
100	David Justice	.50
101	Gary Johnson RC	4.00
102	Matt Ford RC	4.00
103	Albert Pujols RC	140.00
104	Brad Cresse	4.00
105	Valentino Pascucci RC	4.00
106	Bob Keppel RC	4.00
107	Luis Torres RC	4.00
108	Tony Blanco RC	6.00
109	Ronnie Corona RC	4.00
110	Phil Wilson RC	4.00
111	John Buck RC	4.00
112	Jim Journell RC	4.00
113	Victor Hall RC	4.00
114	Jeff Andra RC	4.00
115	Greg Nash RC	4.00
116	Travis Hafner RC	25.00
117	Casey Fossum RC	4.00
118	Miguel Olivo	4.00
119	Elpidio Guzman RC	4.00
120	Jason Belcher RC	4.00
121	Esix Snead RC	4.00
122	Joe Thurston RC	4.00
123	Rafael Soriano RC	6.00
124	Ed Rogers RC	4.00
125	Omar Beltre RC	4.00
126	Brett Gray RC	4.00
127	Deivi Mendez RC	4.00
128	Freddie Bynum RC	4.00
129	David Krynzel RC	4.00
130	Blake Williams RC	4.00
131	Reggie Abercrombie RC	8.00
132	Miguel Villilo RC	4.00
133	Ryan Madson RC	10.00
134	Matt Thompson RC	4.00
135	Mark Burnett RC	4.00
136	Andy Beal RC	4.00
137	Ryan Ludwick RC	6.00
138	Roberto Miniel RC	4.00
139	Steve Smyth RC	4.00
140	Ben Washburn RC	4.00
141	Marvin Seale RC	4.00
142	Reggie Griggs RC	4.00
143	Seung Song RC	4.00
144	Chad Petty RC	4.00
145	Noel Devarez RC	4.00
146	Matt Butler RC	4.00
147	Brett Evert RC	4.00
148	Cesar Izturis	4.00
149	Troy Farnsworth RC	4.00
150	Brian Schmitt RC	4.00
151	Ichiro Suzuki RC	50.00

Game-Worn Uniform

NM/M
Common Player: 4.00
Inserted 1:Box
RA	Roberto Alomar	8.00
BB	Barry Bonds	25.00
CD	Carlos Delgado	8.00
JE	Jim Edmonds	6.00
NG	Nomar Garciaparra	15.00
JG	Juan Gonzalez	8.00
SG	Shawn Green	5.00
VG	Vladimir Guerrero	8.00
TG	Tony Gwynn	10.00
TH	Todd Helton	8.00
RJ	Randy Johnson	8.00

CJ	Chipper Jones	10.00
DJ	David Justice	4.00
GM	Greg Maddux	15.00
PM	Pedro Martinez	8.00
RP	Rafael Palmeiro	8.00
AR	Alex Rodriguez	15.00
IR	Ivan Rodriguez	8.00
SR	Scott Rolen	8.00
FT	Frank Thomas	8.00

Game-Used Bat

	NM/M
Common Player:	4.00
Inserted 1:Box	
JB	Jeff Bagwell	8.00
BB	Barry Bonds	25.00
CD	Carlos Delgado	6.00
JE	Jim Edmonds	6.00
DE	Darin Erstad	4.00
RF	Rafael Furcal	4.00
NG	Nomar Garciaparra	20.00
VG	Vladimir Guerrero	10.00
TG	Tony Gwynn	10.00
CJ	Chipper Jones	10.00
MP	Mike Piazza	15.00
AR	Alex Rodriguez	15.00
IR	Ivan Rodriguez	8.00
BW	Bernie Williams	8.00

Rookie Graded Autograph

	NM/M
Common Rookie:	10.00
Inserted 1:Box	
Prices for PSA 8	
PSA 9's:	1.5X
Reggie Abercrombie	10.00
Jeff Andra	10.00
Andy Beal	10.00
Jason Belcher	10.00
Omar Beltre	10.00
Tony Blanco	10.00
John Buck	10.00
Mark Burnett	10.00
Freddie Bynum	10.00
Ronnie Corona	10.00
Noel Devarez	10.00
Matt Ford	10.00
Casey Fossum	15.00
Brett Gray	10.00
Reggie Griggs	10.00
Elpidio Guzman	10.00
Travis Hafner	65.00
Victor Hall	10.00
Gary Johnson	10.00
Jim Journell	10.00
David Krynzel	10.00
Ryan Ludwick	20.00
Ryan Madson	10.00
Deivi Mendez	10.00
Roberto Miniel	10.00
Greg Nash	10.00
Miguel Olivo	10.00
Valentino Pascucci	10.00
Chad Petty	10.00

	Albert Pujols	375.00
	Ed Rogers	10.00
	Marvin Seale	10.00
	Steve Smyth	10.00
	Esix Snead	10.00
	Seung Song	10.00
	Rafael Soriano	15.00
	Matt Thompson	10.00
	Joe Thurston	15.00
	Luis Torres	10.00
	Miguel Villilo	10.00
	Ben Washburn	10.00
	Blake Williams	10.00
	Phil Wilson	10.00

Rookie Autographed Baseballs

	NM/M
Common Player:	10.00
Inserted 1:Box w/holder.	
Reggie Abercrombie	10.00
Jeff Andra	10.00
Andy Beal	10.00
Jason Belcher	10.00
Omar Beltre	10.00
Tony Blanco	10.00
John Buck	15.00
Mark Burnett	10.00
Freddie Bynum	10.00
Ronnie Corona	10.00
Noel Devarez	10.00
Matt Ford	10.00
Casey Fossum	15.00
Brett Gray	10.00
Reggie Griggs	10.00
Elpidio Guzman	10.00
Travis Hafner	60.00
Victor Hall	10.00
Gary Johnson	10.00
Jim Journell	10.00
Bob Keppel	10.00
David Krynzel	15.00
Ryan Ludwick	15.00
Ryan Madson	10.00
Deivi Mendez	10.00
Roberto Miniel	10.00
Greg Nash	10.00
Chad Petty	10.00
Albert Pujols	400.00
Ed Rogers	10.00
Marvin Seale	10.00
Steve Smyth	10.00
Esix Snead	10.00
Seung Song	10.00
Rafael Soriano	15.00
Matt Thompson	10.00
Joe Thurston	10.00
Luis Torres	10.00
Miguel Villilo	10.00
Ben Washburn	10.00

2001 Topps Stars

	NM/M
Complete Set (200):	90.00
Common Player:	.15
Pack (6):	5.00

Box (24):		100.00
1	Darin Erstad	.25
2	Luis Gonzalez	.25
3	Rafael Furcal	.25
4	Dante Bichette	.15
5	Sammy Sosa	1.25
6	Ken Griffey Jr.	1.00
7	Jim Thome	.50
8	Bobby Higginson	.15
9	Cliff Floyd	.15
10	Lance Berkman	.25
11	Eric Karros	.15
12	Jeromy Burnitz	.15
13	Jose Vidro	.15
14	Benny Agbayani	.15
15	Jorge Posada	.40
16	Ramon Hernandez	.15
17	Jason Kendall	.25
18	Jeff Kent	.25
19	John Olerud	.25
20	Al Martin	.15
21	Gerald Williams	.15
22	Gabe Kapler	.15
23	Carlos Delgado	.50
24	Mariano Rivera	.25
25	Javy Lopez	.25
26	Paul Konerko	.15
27	Daryle Ward	.15
28	Mike Lieberthal	.15
29	Tom Goodwin	.15
30	Garret Anderson	.40
31	Steve Finley	.15
32	Brian Jordan	.15
33	Nomar Garciaparra	1.50
34	Ray Durham	.15
35	Sean Casey	.25
36	Kenny Lofton	.25
37	Dean Palmer	.15
38	Jeff Bagwell	.50
39	Mike Sweeney	.15
40	Adrian Beltre	.25
41	Richie Sexson	.40
42	Vladimir Guerrero	.75
43	Derek Jeter	2.00
44	Miguel Tejada	.25
45	Doug Glanville	.15
46	Brian Giles	.25
47	Marvin Benard	.15
48	Edgar Martinez	.25
49	Edgar Renteria	.15
50	Fred McGriff	.25
51	Ivan Rodriguez	.50
52	Brad Fullmer	.15
53	Antonio Alfonseca	.15
54	Tom Glavine	.40
55	Warren Morris	.15
56	Johnny Damon	.25
57	Dmitri Young	.15
58	Mo Vaughn	.15
59	Randy Johnson	.75
60	Greg Maddux	1.00
61	Carl Everett	.15
62	Magglio Ordonez	.25
63	Pokey Reese	.15
64	Todd Helton	.50
65	Preston Wilson	.15
66	Richard Hidalgo	.15
67	Jermaine Dye	.15
68	Gary Sheffield	.40
69	Geoff Jenkins	.15
70	Edgardo Alfonzo	.15
71	Paul O'Neill	.25
72	Terrence Long	.15
73	Bob Abreu	.25
74	Kevin Young	.15
75	J.T. Snow	.15
76	Alex Rodriguez	1.50
77	Jim Edmonds	.25
78	Mark McGwire	1.50
79	Tony Batista	.15
80	Darrin Fletcher	.15
81	Robb Nen	.15
82	Jose Offerman	.15
83	Travis Fryman	.25
84	Joe Randa	.15
85	Omar Vizquel	.25
86	Tim Salmon	.25
87	Andruw Jones	.50
88	Albert Belle	.15
89	Manny Ramirez	.50
90	Frank Thomas	.50
91	Barry Larkin	.40
92	Neifi Perez	.15
93	Luis Castillo	.15
94	Moises Alou	.25
95	Mark Quinn	.15
96	Kevin Brown	.25
97	Cristian Guzman	.15
98	Mike Piazza	1.00
99	Bernie Williams	.40
100	Jason Giambi	.50
101	Scott Rolen	.75
102	Phil Nevin	.15
103	Rich Aurilia	.15
104	Mike Cameron	.15
105	Fernando Vina	.15
106	Greg Vaughn	.15
107	Jose Cruz	.15
108	Raul Mondesi	.15
109	Ben Molina	.15
110	Pedro Martinez	.75
111	Todd Hollandsworth	.15
112	Jacque Jones	.15
113	Rickey Henderson	.25
114	Troy Glaus	.40
115	Chipper Jones	1.00
116	Delino DeShields	.15
117	Eric Young	.15
118	Jose Valentin	.15
119	Roberto Alomar	.40
120	Jeff Cirillo	.15
121	Mike Lowell	.15
122	Julio Lugo	.15
123	Shawn Green	.25
124	Marquis Grissom	.15
125	Matt Lawton	.15
126	Jay Payton	.15
127	David Justice	.25
128	Eric Chavez	.25
129	Pat Burrell	.50
130	Ryan Klesko	.25
131	Barry Bonds	2.00
132	Jay Buhner	.15
133	J.D. Drew	.25
134	Rafael Palmeiro	.50
135	Shannon Stewart	.15
136	Juan Gonzalez	.50
137	Tony Womack	.15
138	Carlos Lee	.15
139	Derrek Lee	.15
140	Ben Grieve	.15
141	Ron Belliard	.15
142	Stan Musial	1.50
143	Ernie Banks	1.00
144	Jim Palmer	.50
145	Tony Perez	.25
146	Duke Snider	.50
147	Rod Carew	.40
148	Warren Spahn	.75
149	Yogi Berra	.75
150	Juan Marichal	.25
151	Eric Munson	.15
152	Carlos Pena	.15
153	Joe Crede	.15
154	Ryan Anderson	.15
155	Milton Bradley	.15
156	Sean Burroughs	.15
157	Corey Patterson	.25
158	C.C. Sabathia	.15
159	Ben Petrick	.15
160	Aubrey Huff	.15
161	Gookie Dawkins	.15
162	Ben Sheets	.25
163	Pablo Ozuna	.15
164	Eric Valent	.15
165	Rod Barajas	.15
166	Chin-Feng Chen	.40
167	Josh Hamilton	.25
168	Keith Ginter	.15
169	Vernon Wells	.15
170	Dernell Stenson	.15
171	Alfonso Soriano	.75
172	Jason Marquis	.15
173	Nick Johnson	.15
174	Adam Everett	.15
175	Jimmy Rollins	.25
176	Ben Diggins	.15
177	John Lackey	.15
178	Scott Heard	.15
179	Brian Hitchcox RC	.50
180	Odannis Ayala RC	.15
181	Scott Pratt RC	.50
182	Greg Runser RC	.50
183	Chris Russ RC	.50
184	Derek Thompson RC	.50
185	Jason Jones RC	.50
186	Dominic Rich RC	.50
187	Chad Petty RC	.50
188	Steve Smyth RC	.50
189	Bryan Hebson RC	.50
190	Danny Borrell RC	.50
191	Bob Keppel RC	.50
192	Justin Wayne RC	1.00
193	Reggie Abercrombie RC	1.00
194	Travis Baptist RC	.50
195	Shawn Fagan RC	.50
196	Jose Reyes RC	25.00
197	Chris Bass RC	.50
198	Albert Pujols RC	75.00
199	Luis Cotto RC	.50
200	Jake Peavy RC	4.00

Gold

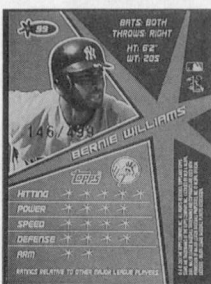

Stars: 2-5X
Production 499 Sets

Onyx

Stars: 6-12X
Rookies: 4-6X
Production 99 Sets

Autographs

		NM/M
Common Player:		15.00
Inserted 1:353		
EB	Ernie Banks	50.00
YB	Yogi Berra	40.00
RC	Rod Carew	30.00
CD	Carlos Delgado	15.00
TH	Todd Helton	30.00
JM	Juan Marichal	30.00
EM	Eric Munson	10.00
SM	Stan Musial	80.00
JP	Jim Palmer	25.00
TP	Tony Perez	25.00
IR	Ivan Rodriguez	30.00
DS	Duke Snider	35.00
WS	Warren Spahn	40.00

Elimination

Stars: 5-10X
Production 100 Sets
Redemp. deadline 10/19/01.

Game Gear Bats

		NM/M
Common Player:		5.00
Inserted 1:187		
AB	Adrian Beltre	5.00
LB	Lance Berkman	6.00
SB	Sean Burroughs	5.00
MC	Michael Cuddyer	5.00
BD	Ben Davis	5.00
JDD	J.D. Drew	5.00
ED	Erubiel Durazo	5.00
JE	Juan Encarnacion	5.00
RF	Rafael Furcal	8.00
AK	Adam Kennedy	5.00
GL	George Lombard	5.00
TL	Terrence Long	5.00
FL	Felipe Lopez	5.00
GM	Gary Mathews	5.00

CP	Corey Patterson	8.00
NP	Neifi Perez	5.00
AP	Adam Piatt	5.00
SR	Scott Rolen	15.00
FS	Fernando Seguignol	5.00
RS	Richie Sexson	10.00

Game Gear Bats Autographs

Inserted 1:12,240
No pricing due to scarcity.

Game Gear Jerseys

		NM/M
Common Player:		4.00
Inserted 1:61		
EA	Edgardo Alfonzo	4.00
RA	Roberto Alomar	8.00
BB	Barry Bonds	25.00
LC	Luis Castillo	4.00
TG	Tony Gwynn	10.00
TH	Todd Helton	8.00
AJ	Andruw Jones	8.00
CJ	Chipper Jones	10.00
EM	Edgar Martinez	8.00
MO	Magglio Ordonez	5.00
MP	Mike Piazza	15.00
SS	Sammy Sosa	25.00
SHS	Shannon Stewart	4.00
FT	Frank Thomas	8.00
JV	Jose Vidro	4.00

Game Gear Jerseys Autographs

Inserted 1:19,288
No pricing due to scarcity.

Player Choice Awards Relics

		NM/M
Common Player:		10.00
Inserted 1:1,530		
1	Carlos Delgado	15.00
2	Eric Davis	10.00
3	Carlos Delgado	15.00
4	Pedro Martinez	25.00
5	Terrence Long	10.00
6	Frank Thomas	20.00
7	Todd Helton	15.00
8	Randy Johnson	25.00
9	Rafael Furcal	15.00
10	Andres Galarraga	10.00

Players Choice Award Nominees

	NM/M
Complete Set (10):	15.00
Common Player:	1.50

			NM/M
Inserted 1:12			
1	Barry Bonds, Carlos Delgado, Todd Helton		4.00
2	Gary Sheffield, Eric Davis, Turk Wendell		1.50
3	Alex Rodriguez, Carlos Delgado, Frank Thomas		3.00
4	David Wells, Pedro Martinez, Andy Pettitte		2.00
5	Mark Quinn, Terrence Long, Kazuhiro Sasaki		1.50
6	Jay Buhner, Frank Thomas, Bobby Higginson		1.50
7	Barry Bonds, Todd Helton, Jeff Kent		4.00
8	Tom Glavine, Randy Johnson, Greg Maddux		2.50
9	Rick Ankiel, Rafael Furcal, Jay Payton		1.50
10	Moises Alou, Andres Galarraga, Jeff D'Amico		1.50

Progression

			NM/M
Complete Set (9):			10.00
Common Player:			1.00
Inserted 1:8			
P1	Ernie Banks, Alex Rodriguez, Felipe Lopez		3.00
P2	Yogi Berra, Ivan Rodriguez, Ramon Hernandez		2.00
P3	Tony Perez, Carlos Delgado, Eric Munson		1.00
P4	Rod Carew, Roberto Alomar, Jose Ortiz		1.00
P5	Stan Musial, Darin Erstad, Alex Escobar		2.00
P6	Jim Palmer, Kevin Brown, Kurt Ainsworth		1.00
P7	Duke Snider, Jim Edmonds, Vernon Wells		1.00
P8	Warren Spahn, Randy Johnson, Ryan Anderson		1.50
P9	Juan Marichal, Bartolo Colon, Bobby Bradley		1.00

2001 Topps Tribute

	NM/M
Complete Set (90):	300.00
Common Player:	2.00
Pack (3):	75.00
Box (6):	425.00
1 Pee Wee Reese	2.00
2 Babe Ruth	15.00
3 Ralph Kiner	2.00
4 Brooks Robinson	5.00
5 Don Sutton	2.00
6 Carl Yastrzemski	8.00
7 Roger Maris	10.00
8 Andre Dawson	2.00
9 Luis Aparicio	2.00
10 Wade Boggs	4.00
11 Johnny Bench	8.00
12 Ernie Banks	6.00
13 Thurman Munson	5.00
14 Harmon Killebrew	5.00
15 Ted Kluszewski	2.00
16 Bob Feller	3.00
17 Mike Schmidt	10.00
18 Warren Spahn	4.00
19 Jim Palmer	3.00
20 Don Mattingly	12.00
21 Willie Mays	10.00
22 Gil Hodges	2.00
23 Juan Marichal	2.00
24 Robin Yount	6.00
25 Nolan Ryan	12.00
26 Dave Winfield	3.00
27 Hank Greenberg	2.00
28 Honus Wagner	8.00
29 Nolan Ryan	12.00
30 Phil Niekro	2.00
31 Robin Roberts	2.00
32 Casey Stengel	3.00
33 Willie McCovey	2.00
34 Roy Campanella	4.00
35 Rollie Fingers	2.00
36 Tom Seaver	5.00
37 Jackie Robinson	10.00
38 Hank Aaron	10.00
39 Bob Gibson	4.00
40 Carlton Fisk	4.00
41 Hank Aaron	10.00
42 George Brett	10.00
43 Orlando Cepeda	2.00
44 Red Schoendienst	2.00
45 Don Drysdale	4.00
46 Mel Ott	4.00
47 Casey Stengel	3.00
48 Al Kaline	4.00
49 Reggie Jackson	6.00
50 Tony Perez	2.00
51 Ozzie Smith	6.00
52 Billy Martin	4.00
53 Bill Dickey	2.00
54 Catfish Hunter	2.00
55 Duke Snider	4.00
56 Dale Murphy	2.00
57 Bobby Doerr	2.00
58 Earl Averill	2.00
59 Carlton Fisk	4.00
60 Tom Lasorda	2.00
61 Lou Gehrig	12.00
62 Enos Slaughter	2.00
63 Jim Bunning	2.00
64 Rollie Fingers	2.00
65 Frank Robinson	4.00
66 Earl Weaver	2.00
67 Eddie Mathews	5.00
68 Kirby Puckett	5.00
69 Phil Rizzuto	4.00
70 Lou Brock	4.00
71 Walt Alston	2.00
72 Bill Pierce	2.00
73 Joe Morgan	2.00
74 Roberto Clemente	12.00
75 Whitey Ford	4.00
76 Richie Ashburn	2.00
77 Elston Howard	2.00
78 Gary Carter	2.00
79 Carl Hubbell	2.00
80 Yogi Berra	6.00
81 Ken Boyer	2.00
82 Nolan Ryan	12.00
83 Bill Mazeroski	2.00
84 Dizzy Dean	4.00
85 Nellie Fox	2.00
86 Stan Musial	10.00
87 Steve Carlton	4.00
88 Willie Stargell	4.00
89 Hal Newhouser	2.00
90 Frank Robinson	4.00

Casey Stengel Dual Relic

	NM/M
Inserted 1:860	

CS Casey Stengel 100.00

Franchise Figures

NM/M

Inserted 1:34

AL	Walt Alston, Tommy Lasorda	50.00
AFF	Luis Aparicio, Nellie Fox, Carlton Fisk	125.00
BPKR	Johnny Bench, Tony Perez, Ted Kluszewski, Frank Robinson, Joe Morgan	150.00
CD	Gary Carter, Andre Dawson	40.00
HDB	Bill Dickey, Elston Howard, Yogi Berra	150.00
FY	Carlton Fisk, Carl Yastrzemski	150.00
HSS	Gil Hodges, Casey Stengel, Tom Seaver	150.00
JM	Reggie Jackson, Billy Martin	125.00
KG	Al Kaline, Hank Greenberg	150.00
MMC	Willie Mays, Willie McCovey, Orlando Cepeda	200.00
MCS	Bill Mazeroski, Roberto Clemente, Willie Stargell	185.00
MM	Thurman Munson, Don Mattingly	200.00
MMA	Dale Murphy, Ed Mathews, Hank Aaron	185.00
PK	Kirby Puckett, Harmon Killebrew	100.00
RSC	Pee Wee Reese, Duke Snider, Roy Campanella	160.00
RR	Brooks Robinson, Frank Robinson	75.00
RG	Babe Ruth, Lou Gehrig	500.00
SAC	Mike Schmidt, Richie Ashburn, Steve Carlton	125.00
SBSM	Ozzie Smith, Lou Brock, Red Schoendienst, Stan Musial	125.00

Frank Robinson Dual Relic

NM/M

Inserted 1:860

FR-RO Frank Robinson 90.00

Game-Used Bat Relics

NM/M

Common Player: 20.00
Inserted 1:2

HA	Hank Aaron	50.00
LA	Luis Aparicio	20.00
RA	Richie Ashburn	25.00
KB	Ken Boyer	20.00
GB	George Brett	40.00

LB	Lou Brock	20.00
RC	Roy Campanella	30.00
RCL	Roberto Clemente	80.00
CF	Carlton Fisk	25.00
LG	Lou Gehrig	160.00
HG	Hank Greenberg	50.00
GH	Gil Hodges	25.00
RJ	Reggie Jackson	30.00
AK	Al Kaline	30.00
HK	Harmon Killebrew	30.00
RM	Roger Maris	50.00
BM	Billy Martin	20.00
DM	Don Mattingly	50.00
WM	Willie McCovey	25.00
TM	Thurman Munson	35.00
PWR	Pee Wee Reese	20.00
BRO	Brooks Robinson	30.00
FRR	Frank Robinson	30.00
JR	Jackie Robinson	
BR	Babe Ruth	200.00
OS	Ozzie Smith	35.00
CS	Casey Stengel	20.00
HW	Honus Wagner	200.00
CY	Carl Yastrzemski	40.00

Game-Worn Patch And Number Relics

NM/M

Common Player: 60.00
Inserted 1:61

WA	Walt Alston	60.00
JB	Johnny Bench	180.00
YB	Yogi Berra	150.00
WB	Wade Boggs	80.00
LB	Lou Brock	60.00
BD	Bill Dickey	150.00
BDO	Bobby Doerr	100.00
HK	Harmon Killebrew	250.00
TL	Tom Lasorda	80.00
JM	Juan Marichal	75.00
EM	Eddie Mathews	150.00
KB	Kirby Puckett	250.00
NR	Nolan Ryan	300.00
MS	Mike Schmidt	250.00
RS	Red Schoendienst	80.00
DW	Dave Winfield	80.00
CY	Carl Yastrzemski	200.00
RY	Robin Yount	100.00

Nolan Ryan Tri-Relic

NM/M

Randomly inserted.

NR Nolan Ryan 475.00

Retired Game-Worn Relics

NM/M

Common Player: 20.00

Inserted 1:2

WA	Walt Alston	20.00
EB	Ernie Banks	30.00
EBA	Ernie Banks	30.00
JB	Johnny Bench	30.00
YB	Yogi Berra	30.00
WB	Wade Boggs	20.00
GB	George Brett	50.00
LB	Lou Brock	25.00
SC	Steve Carlton	25.00
DD	Dizzy Dean	40.00
BD	Bill Dickey	20.00
BDO	Bobby Doerr	25.00
NF	Nellie Fox	20.00
HK	Harmon Killebrew	30.00
TL	Tom Lasorda	20.00
JMG	Juan Marichal	30.00
EM	Eddie Mathews	30.00
DM	Don Mattingly	50.00
WMF	Willie Mays	75.00
WMW	Willie Mays	75.00
SM	Stan Musial	75.00
JP	Jim Palmer	20.00
KP	Kirby Puckett	30.00
FR	Frank Robinson	25.00
NRA	Nolan Ryan	80.00
NRH	Nolan Ryan	80.00
NRR	Nolan Ryan	80.00
MSB	Mike Schmidt	50.00
MSW	Mike Schmidt	50.00
RS	Red Schoendienst	20.00
WST	Willie Stargell	20.00
CS	Casey Stengel	20.00
DW	Dave Winfield	20.00
CY	Carl Yastrzemski/ White	40.00
CYA	Carl Yastrzemski/ Gray	40.00
RY	Robin Yount	30.00

Vintage Buy-Back Cards

No pricing due to scarcity.

2002 Topps

NM/M

Complete Set (718):		70.00
Complete Factory Set (723):		80.00
Complete Series 1 (365):		35.00
Complete Series 2 (354):		35.00
Common Player:		.10
Pack (10):		1.50
Box (36):		40.00
1	Pedro Martinez	.50
2	Mike Stanton	.10
3	Brad Penny	.10
4	Mike Matheny	.10
5	Johnny Damon	.20
6	Bret Boone	.20
7	Not Issued (Retired)	.10
8	Chris Truby	.10
9	B.J. Surhoff	.10
10	Mike Hampton	.10
11	Juan Pierre	.10
12	Mark Buehrle	.10
13	Bob Abreu	.20
14	David Cone	.10
15	Aaron Sele	.10
16	Fernando Tatis	.10
17	Bobby Jones	.10
18	Rick Helling	.10
19	Dmitri Young	.10
20	Mike Mussina	.40
21	Mike Sweeney	.10
22	Cristian Guzman	.10
23	Ryan Kohlmeier	.10
24	Adam Kennedy	.10
25	Larry Walker	.25
26	Eric Davis	.10
27	Jason Tyner	.10
28	Eric Young	.10

29	Jason Marquis	.10
30	Luis Gonzalez	.20
31	Kevin Tapani	.10
32	Orlando Cabrera	.10
33	Marty Cordova	.10
34	Brad Ausmus	.10
35	Livan Hernandez	.10
36	Alex Gonzalez	.10
37	Edgar Renteria	.20
38	Bengie Molina	.10
39	Frank Menechino	.10
40	Rafael Palmeiro	.40
41	Brad Fullmer	.10
42	Julio Zuleta	.10
43	Darren Dreifort	.10
44	Trot Nixon	.10
45	Trevor Hoffman	.10
46	Vladimir Nunez	.10
47	Mark Kotsay	.10
48	Kenny Rogers	.10
49	Ben Petrick	.10
50	Jeff Bagwell	.40
51	Juan Encarnacion	.10
52	Ramiro Mendoza	.10
53	Brian Meadows	.10
54	Chad Curtis	.10
55	Aramis Ramirez	.25
56	Mark McLemore	.10
57	Dante Bichette	.10
58	Scott Schoeneweis	.10
59	Jose Cruz Jr.	.10
60	Roger Clemens	1.00
61	Jose Guillen	.10
62	Darren Oliver	.10
63	Chris Reitsma	.10
64	Jeff Abbott	.10
65	Robin Ventura	.10
66	Denny Neagle	.10
67	Al Martin	.10
68	Benito Santiago	.10
69	Roy Oswalt	.20
70	Juan Gonzalez	.40
71	Garret Anderson	.25
72	Bobby Bonilla	.10
73	Danny Bautista	.10
74	J.T. Snow Jr.	.10
75	Derek Jeter	1.50
76	John Olerud	.20
77	Kevin Appier	.10
78	Phil Nevin	.20
79	Sean Casey	.20
80	Troy Glaus	.40
81	Joe Randa	.10
82	Jose Valentin	.10
83	Ricky Bottalico	.10
84	Todd Zeile	.10
85	Barry Larkin	.25
86	Bob Wickman	.10
87	Jeff Shaw	.10
88	Greg Vaughn	.10
89	Fernando Vina	.10
90	Mark Mulder	.25
91	Paul Bako	.10
92	Aaron Boone	.10
93	Esteban Loaiza	.10
94	Richie Sexson	.40
95	Alfonso Soriano	.50
96	Tony Womack	.10
97	Paul Shuey	.10
98	Melvin Mora	.10
99	Tony Gwynn	.50
100	Vladimir Guerrero	.50
101	Keith Osik	.10
102	Randy Velarde	.10
103	Scott Williamson	.10
104	Daryle Ward	.10
105	Doug Mientkiewicz	.10
106	Stan Javier	.10
107	Russ Ortiz	.10
108	Wade Miller	.10
109	Luke Prokopec	.10
110	Andruw Jones	.40
111	Ron Coomer	.10
112	Dan Wilson	.10
113	Luis Castillo	.10
114	Derek Bell	.10
115	Gary Sheffield	.20
116	Ruben Rivera	.10
117	Paul O'Neill	.20
118	Craig Paquette	.10
119	Chris Michalak	.10
120	Brad Radke	.10
121	Jorge Fabregas	.10
122	Randy Winn	.10
123	Tom Goodwin	.10
124	Jaret Wright	.10
125	Manny Ramirez	.40
126	Al Leiter	.20
127	Ben Davis	.10
128	Frank Catalanotto	.10
129	Jose Cabrera	.10
130	Magglio Ordonez	.20
131	Jose Macias	.10
132	Ted Lilly	.10

No.	Player	Value
133	Chris Holt	.10
134	Eric Milton	.10
135	Shannon Stewart	.10
136	Omar Olivares	.10
137	David Segui	.10
138	Jeff Nelson	.10
139	Matt Williams	.25
140	Ellis Burks	.10
141	Jason Bere	.10
142	Jimmy Haynes	.10
143	Ramon Hernandez	.10
144	Craig Counsell (Front photo actually Greg Colbrunn.)	.10
145	John Smoltz	.10
146	Homer Bush	.10
147	Quilvio Veras	.10
148	Esteban Yan	.10
149	Ramon Ortiz	.10
150	Carlos Delgado	.30
151	Lee Stevens	.10
152	Wil Cordero	.10
153	Mike Bordick	.10
154	John Flaherty	.10
155	Omar Daal	.10
156	Todd Ritchie	.10
157	Carl Everett	.10
158	Scott Sullivan	.10
159	Deivi Cruz	.10
160a	Albert Pujols (Back photo is Placido Polanco.) (In cap.)	1.00
160b	Albert Pujols (Back photo corrected) (No cap.)	10.00
161	Royce Clayton	.10
162	Jeff Suppan	.10
163	C.C. Sabathia	.10
164	Jimmy Rollins	.25
165	Rickey Henderson	.25
166	Rey Ordonez	.10
167	Shawn Estes	.10
168	Reggie Sanders	.10
169	Jon Lieber	.10
170	Armando Benitez	.10
171	Mike Remlinger	.10
172	Billy Wagner	.10
173	Troy Percival	.10
174	Devon White	.10
175	Ivan Rodriguez	.40
176	Dustin Hermanson	.10
177	Brian Anderson	.10
178	Graeme Lloyd	.10
179	Russ Branyan	.10
180	Bobby Higginson	.10
181	Alex Gonzalez	.10
182	John Franco	.10
183	Sidney Ponson	.10
184	Jose Mesa	.10
185	Todd Hollandsworth	.10
186	Kevin Young	.10
187	Tim Wakefield	.10
188	Craig Biggio	.20
189	Jason Isringhausen	.10
190	Mark Quinn	.10
191	Glendon Rusch	.10
192	Damian Miller	.10
193	Sandy Alomar	.10
194	Scott Brosius	.10
195	Dave Martinez	.10
196	Danny Graves	.10
197	Shea Hillenbrand	.10
198	Jimmy Anderson	.10
199	Travis Lee	.10
200	Randy Johnson	.50
201	Carlos Beltran	.25
202	Jerry Hairston Jr.	.10
203	Jesus Sanchez	.10
204	Eddie Taubensee	.10
205	David Wells	.10
206	Russ Davis	.10
207	Michael Barrett	.10
208	Marquis Grissom	.10
209	Byung-Hyun Kim	.10
210	Hideo Nomo	.25
211	Ryan Rupe	.10
212	Ricky Gutierrez	.10
213	Darryl Kile	.10
214	Rico Brogna	.10
215	Terrence Long	.10
216	Mike Jackson	.10
217	Jamey Wright	.10
218	Adrian Beltre	.20
219	Benny Agbayani	.10
220	Chuck Knoblauch	.10
221	Randy Wolf	.10
222	Andy Ashby	.10
223	Corey Koskie	.10
224	Roger Cedeno	.10
225	Ichiro Suzuki	1.00
226	Keith Foulke	.10
227	Ryan Minor	.10
228	Shawon Dunston	.10
229	Alex Cora	.10
230	Jeromy Burnitz	.10
231	Mark Grace	.25
232	Aubrey Huff	.10
233	Jeffrey Hammonds	.10
234	Olmedo Saenz	.10
235	Brian Jordan	.10
236	Jeremy Giambi	.10
237	Joe Girardi	.10
238	Eric Gagne	.25
239	Masato Yoshii	.10
240	Greg Maddux	.75
241	Bryan Rekar	.10
242	Ray Durham	.10
243	Torii Hunter	.20
244	Derrek Lee	.20
245	Jim Edmonds	.25
246	Einar Diaz	.10
247	Brian Bohanon	.10
248	Ron Belliard	.10
249	Mike Lowell	.20
250	Sammy Sosa	1.00
251	Richard Hidalgo	.10
252	Bartolo Colon	.10
253	Jorge Posada	.25
254	LaTroy Hawkins	.10
255	Paul LoDuca	.10
256	Carlos Febles	.10
257	Nelson Cruz	.10
258	Edgardo Alfonzo	.10
259	Joey Hamilton	.10
260	Cliff Floyd	.10
261	Wes Helms	.10
262	Jay Bell	.10
263	Mike Cameron	.10
264	Paul Konerko	.10
265	Jeff Kent	.20
266	Robert Fick	.10
267	Allen Levrault	.10
268	Placido Polanco	.10
269	Marlon Anderson	.10
270	Mariano Rivera	.20
271	Chan Ho Park	.10
272	Jose Vizcaino	.10
273	Jeff D'Amico	.10
274	Mark Gardner	.10
275	Travis Fryman	.10
276	Darren Lewis	.10
277	Bruce Bochy	.10
278	Jerry Manuel	.10
279	Bob Brenly	.10
280	Don Baylor	.10
281	Davey Lopes	.10
282	Jerry Narron	.10
283	Tony Muser	.10
284	Hal McRae	.10
285	Bobby Cox	.10
286	Larry Dierker	.10
287	Phil Garner	.10
288	Jimy Williams	.10
289	Bobby Valentine	.10
290	Dusty Baker	.10
291	Lloyd McLendon	.10
292	Mike Scioscia	.10
293	Buck Martinez	.10
294	Larry Bowa	.10
295	Tony LaRussa	.10
296	Jeff Torborg	.10
297	Tom Kelly	.10
298	Mike Hargrove	.10
299	Art Howe	.10
300	Lou Pinella	.10
301	Charlie Manuel	.10
302	Buddy Bell	.10
303	Tony Perez	.10
304	Bob Boone	.10
305	Joe Torre	.25
306	Jim Tracy	.10
307	Jason Lane	.10
308	Chris George	.10
309	Hank Blalock	.25
310	Joe Borchard	.10
311	Marlon Byrd	.10
312	Raymond Cabrera RC	.25
313	Freddy Sanchez RC	.40
314	Scott Wiggins RC	.40
315	Jason Maule RC	.30
316	Dionys Cesar RC	.40
317	Boof Bonser	.10
318	Juan Tolentino RC	.40
319	Earl Snyder RC	.10
320	Travis Wade RC	.25
321	Napoleon Calzado RC	.10
322	Eric Glaser RC	.40
323	Craig Kuzmic RC	.40
324	Nic Jackson RC	.50
325	Mike Rivera	.10
326	Jason Bay RC	1.00
327	Chris Smith	.10
328	Jake Gautreau	.10
329	Gabe Gross	.10
330	Kenny Baugh	.10
331	J.D. Martin	.10
332	Barry Bonds	1.00
333	Rickey Henderson	.25
334	Bud Smith	.10
335	Rickey Henderson	.25
336	Barry Bonds	1.00
337	Ichiro Suzuki, Jason Giambi, Roberto Alomar	.50
338	Alex Rodriguez, Ichiro Suzuki, Bret Boone	.50
339	Alex Rodriguez, Jim Thome, Rafael Palmeiro	.40
340	Bret Boone, Juan Gonzalez, Alex Rodriguez	.40
341	Freddy Garcia, Mike Mussina, Joe Mays	.15
342	Hideo Nomo, Mike Mussina, Roger Clemens	.40
343	Larry Walker, Todd Helton, Moises Alou	.25
344	Sammy Sosa, Todd Helton, Barry Bonds	.40
345	Barry Bonds, Sammy Sosa, Luis Gonzalez	.40
346	Sammy Sosa, Todd Helton, Luis Gonzalez	.40
347	Curt Schilling, Randy Johnson, John Burkett	.20
348	Randy Johnson, Curt Schilling, Chan Ho Park	.20
349	Seattle Mariners	.25
350	Oakland A's	.10
351	New York Yankees	.50
352	Cleveland Indians	.10
353	Arizona Diamondbacks	.10
354	Atlanta Braves	.10
355	St. Louis Cardinals	.10
356	Houston Astros	.10
357	D'backs vs. Rockies	.10
358	Mets vs. Pirates	.10
359	Braves vs. Phillies	.10
360	D'backs vs. Phillies	.10
361	Yankees vs. White Sox	.10
362	Cubs vs. Reds	.10
363	Angels vs. Mariners	.10
364	Astros vs. Giants	.10
365	Barry Bonds Race to 70 #1	10.00
365	Barry Bonds HR #2-69	8.00
365	Barry Bonds HR #70	15.00
365	Barry Bonds HR #71	10.00
365	Barry Bonds HR #72	10.00
365	Barry Bonds HR #73	50.00
366	Pat Meares	.10
367	Mike Lieberthal	.10
368	Scott Erickson	.10
369	Ron Gant	.10
370	Moises Alou	.25
371	Chad Kreuter	.10
372	Willis Roberts	.10
373	Toby Hall	.10
374	Miguel Batista	.10
375	John Burkett	.10
376	Cory Lidle	.10
377	Nick Neugebauer	.10
378	Jay Payton	.10
379	Steve Karsay	.10
380	Eric Chavez	.20
381	Kelly Stinnett	.10
382	Jarrod Washburn	.10
383	C.J. Nitkowski	.10
384	Jeff Conine	.10
385	Fred McGriff	.10
386	Marvin Benard	.10
387	Dave Burba	.10
388	Dennis Cook	.10
389	Rick Reed	.10
390	Tom Glavine	.25
391	Rondell White	.15
392	Matt Morris	.20
393	Pat Rapp	.10
394	Robert Person	.10
395	Omar Vizquel	.15
396	Jeff Cirillo	.10
397	Dave Mlicki	.10
398	Jose Ortiz	.10
399	Ryan Dempster	.10
400	Curt Schilling	.25
401	Peter Bergeron	.10
402	Kyle Lohse	.10
403	Craig Wilson	.10
404	David Justice	.20
405	Darin Erstad	.20
406	Jose Mercedes	.10
407	Carl Pavano	.10
408	Albie Lopez	.10
409	Alex Ochoa	.10
410	Chipper Jones	.50
411	Tyler Houston	.10
412	Dean Palmer	.10
413	Damian Jackson	.10
414	Josh Towers	.10
415	Rafael Furcal	.20
416	Ken Caminiti	.10
417	Herb Perry	.10
418	Mike Sirotka	.10
419	Mark Wohlers	.10
420	Nomar Garciaparra	1.00
421	Felipe Lopez	.10
422	Joe McEwing	.10
423	Jacque Jones	.10
424	Julio Franco	.10
425	Frank Thomas	.40
426	So Taguchi RC	.50
427	Kazuhisa Ishii RC	1.00
428	D'Angelo Jimenez	.10
429	Chris Stynes	.10
430	Kerry Wood	.50
431	Chris Singleton	.10
432	Erubiel Durazo	.10
433	Matt Lawton	.10
434	Bill Mueller	.10
435	Jose Canseco	.25
436	Ben Grieve	.10
437	Terry Mulholland	.10
438	David Bell	.10
439	A.J. Pierzynski	.10
440	Adam Dunn	.40
441	Jon Garland	.10
442	Jeff Fassero	.10
443	Julio Lugo	.10
444	Carlos Guillen	.10
445	Orlando Hernandez	.20
446	Mark Loretta	.10
447	Scott Spiezio	.10
448	Kevin Millwood	.20
449	Jamie Moyer	.10
450	Todd Helton	.40
451	Todd Walker	.10
452	Jose Lima	.10
453	Brook Fordyce	.10
454	Aaron Rowand	.10
455	Barry Zito	.20
456	Eric Owens	.10
457	Charles Nagy	.10
458	Raul Ibanez	.10
459	Joe Mays	.10
460	Jim Thome	.50
461	Adam Eaton	.10
462	Felix Martinez	.10
463	Vernon Wells	.10
464	Donnie Sadler	.10
465	Tony Clark	.10
466	Jose Hernandez	.10
467	Ramon Martinez	.10
468	Rusty Greer	.10
469	Rod Barajas	.10
470	Lance Berkman	.25
471	Brady Anderson	.10
472	Pedro Astacio	.10
473	Shane Halter	.10
474	Bret Prinz	.10
475	Edgar Martinez	.20
476	Steve Trachsel	.10
477	Gary Matthews Jr.	.10
478	Ismael Valdes	.10
479	Juan Uribe	.10
480	Shawn Green	.20
481	Kirk Rueter	.10
482	Damion Easley	.10
483	Chris Carpenter	.10
484	Kris Benson	.10
485	Antonio Alfonseca	.10
486	Kyle Farnsworth	.10
487	Brandon Lyon	.10
488	Hideki Irabu	.10
489	David Ortiz	.25
490	Mike Piazza	1.00
491	Derek Lowe	.10
492	Chris Gomez	.10
493	Mark Johnson	.10
494	John Rocker	.10
495	Eric Karros	.10
496	Bill Haselman	.10
497	Dave Veres	.10
498	Gil Heredia	.10
499	Tomokazu Ohka	.10
500	Barry Bonds	1.50
501	David Dellucci	.10
502	Ed Sprague	.10
503	Tom Gordon	.10
504	Javier Vazquez	.10
505	Ben Sheets	.25
506	Wilton Guerrero	.10
507	John Halama	.10
508	Mark Redman	.10
509	Jack Wilson	.10
510	Bernie Williams	.40
511	Miguel Cairo	.10
512	Denny Hocking	.10
513	Tony Batista	.10
514	Mark Grudzielanek	.10
515	Jose Vidro	.10

#	Player	Price
516	Sterling Hitchcock	.10
517	Billy Koch	.10
518	Matt Clement	.10
519	Bruce Chen	.10
520	Roberto Alomar	.40
521	Orlando Palmeiro	.10
522	Steve Finley	.10
523	Danny Patterson	.10
524	Terry Adams	.10
525	Tino Martinez	.10
526	Tony Armas Jr.	.10
527	Geoff Jenkins	.20
528	Chris Michalak	.10
529	Corey Patterson	.20
530	Brian Giles	.20
531	Jose Jimenez	.10
532	Joe Kennedy	.10
533	Armando Rios	.10
534	Osvaldo Fernandez	.10
535	Ruben Sierra	.10
536	Octavio Dotel	.10
537	Luis Sojo	.10
538	Brent Butler	.10
539	Pablo Ozuna	.10
540	Freddy Garcia	.10
541	Chad Durbin	.10
542	Orlando Merced	.10
543	Michael Tucker	.10
544	Roberto Hernandez	.10
545	Pat Burrell	.25
546	A.J. Burnett	.10
547	Bubba Trammell	.10
548	Scott Elarton	.10
549	Mike Darr	.10
550	Ken Griffey Jr.	1.00
551	Ugueth Urbina	.10
552	Todd Jones	.10
553	Delino DeShields	.10
554	Adam Piatt	.10
555	Jason Kendall	.10
556	Hector Ortiz	.10
557	Turk Wendell	.10
558	Rob Bell	.10
559	Sun-Woo Kim	.10
560	Raul Mondesi	.10
561	Brent Abernathy	.10
562	Seth Etherton	.10
563	Shawn Wooten	.10
564	Jay Buhner	.10
565	Andres Galarraga	.10
566	Shane Reynolds	.10
567	Rod Beck	.10
568	Dee Brown	.10
569	Pedro Feliz	.10
570	Ryan Klesko	.10
571	John Vander Wal	.10
572	Nick Bierbrodt	.10
573	Joe Nathan	.10
574	James Baldwin	.10
575	J.D. Drew	.20
576	Greg Colbrunn	.10
577	Doug Glanville	.10
578	Rey Sanchez	.10
579	Todd Van Poppel	.10
580	Rich Aurilia	.10
581	Chuck Finley	.10
582	Abraham Nunez	.10
583	Kenny Lofton	.20
584	Brian Daubach	.10
585	Miguel Tejada	.25
586	Nate Cornejo	.10
587	Kazuhiro Sasaki	.10
588	Chris Richard	.10
589	Armando Reynoso	.10
590	Tim Hudson	.20
591	Neifi Perez	.10
592	Steve Cox	.10
593	Henry Blanco	.10
594	Ricky Ledee	.10
595	Tim Salmon	.20
596	Luis Rivas	.10
597	Jeff Zimmerman	.10
598	Matt Stairs	.10
599	Preston Wilson	.10
600	Mark McGwire	1.50
601	Timo Perez	.10
602	Matt Anderson	.10
603	Todd Hundley	.10
604	Rick Ankiel	.10
605	Tsuyoshi Shinjo	.10
606	Woody Williams	.10
607	Jason LaRue	.10
608	Carlos Lee	.10
609	Russ Johnson	.10
610	Scott Rolen	.50
611	Brent Mayne	.10
612	Darrin Fletcher	.10
613	Ray Lankford	.10
614	Troy O'Leary	.10
615	Javier Lopez	.20
616	Randy Velarde	.10
617	Vinny Castilla	.10
618	Milton Bradley	.10
619	Ruben Mateo	.10
620	Jason Giambi	.40
621	Andy Benes	.10
622	Tony Eusebio	.10
623	Andy Pettitte	.20
624	Jose Offerman	.10
625	Mo Vaughn	.20
626	Steve Sparks	.10
627	Mike Matthews	.10
628	Robb Nen	.10
629	Kip Wells	.10
630	Kevin Brown	.20
631	Arthur Rhodes	.10
632	Gabe Kapler	.10
633	Jermaine Dye	.10
634	Josh Beckett	.25
635	Pokey Reese	.10
636	Benji Gil	.10
637	Marcus Giles	.10
638	Julian Tavarez	.10
639	Jason Schmidt	.25
640	Alex Rodriguez	1.25
641	Anaheim Angels	.10
642	Arizona Diamondbacks	.10
643	Atlanta Braves	.10
644	Baltimore Orioles	.10
645	Boston Red Sox	.10
646	Chicago Cubs	.10
647	Chicago White Sox	.10
648	Cincinnati Reds	.10
649	Cleveland Indians	.10
650	Colorado Rockies	.10
651	Detroit Tigers	.10
652	Florida Marlins	.10
653	Houston Astros	.10
654	Kansas City Royals	.10
655	Los Angeles Dodgers	.10
656	Milwaukee Brewers	.10
657	Minnesota Twins	.10
658	Montreal Expos	.10
659	New York Mets	.10
660	New York Yankees	.10
661	Oakland Athletics	.10
662	Philadelphia Phillies	.10
663	Pittsburgh Pirates	.10
664	San Diego Padres	.10
665	San Francisco Giants	.10
666	Seattle Mariners	.10
667	St. Louis Cardinals	.10
668	Tampa Bay Devil Rays	.10
669	Texas Rangers	.10
670	Toronto Blue Jays	.10
671	Juan Cruz	.25
672	Kevin Cash RC	.50
673	Jimmy Gobble RC	.75
674	Mike Hill RC	.40
675	Taylor Buchholz RC	.40
676	Bill Hall	.10
677	Brett Roneberg RC	.40
678	Royce Huffman RC	.40
679	Chris Tritle RC	.40
680	Nate Espy RC	.40
681	Nick Alvarez RC	.50
682	Jason Botts RC	.40
683	Ryan Gripp RC	.40
684	Dan Phillips RC	.50
685	Pablo Arias RC	.50
686	John Rodriguez RC	.40
687	Rich Harden RC	3.00
688	Neal Frendling RC	.50
689	Rich Thompson RC	.40
690	Greg Montalbano RC	.40
691	Leonard Dinardo RC	.40
692	Ryan Raburn RC	.40
693	Josh Barfield RC	1.00
694	David Bacani RC	.40
695	Dan Johnson RC	.50
696	Mike Mussina	.25
697	Ivan Rodriguez	.25
698	Doug Mientkiewicz	.10
699	Roberto Alomar	.25
700	Eric Chavez	.15
701	Omar Vizquel	.10
702	Mike Cameron	.10
703	Torii Hunter	.10
704	Ichiro Suzuki	.50
705	Greg Maddux	.50
706	Brad Ausmus	.10
707	Todd Helton	.25
708	Fernando Vina	.10
709	Scott Rolen	.40
710	Orlando Cabrera	.10
711	Andruw Jones	.15
712	Jim Edmonds	.10
713	Larry Walker	.15
714	Roger Clemens	.50
715	Randy Johnson	.25
716	Ichiro Suzuki	.50
717	Barry Bonds	.75
718	Ichiro Suzuki	.50
719	Albert Pujols	.50

Gold

	NM/M
Complete Set (659):	700.00
Stars:	5-10X
Production 2,002 Sets	

2002 Topps Limited

	NM/M
Complete Set (790):	165.00

Includes all 73 B. Bonds #365 HR cards.

Aces

		NM/M
Common Player:		10.00
Inserted 1:1,180		
MH	Mike Hampton	10.00
RJ	Randy Johnson	20.00
GM	Greg Maddux	30.00
PM	Pedro Martinez	20.00
MM	Mark Mulder	10.00

All-World Team

		NM/M
Complete Set (25):		25.00
Common Player:		.50
Inserted 1:12		
AW-1	Ichiro Suzuki	3.00
AW-2	Barry Bonds	4.00
AW-3	Pedro Martinez	1.50
AW-4	Juan Gonzalez	1.00
AW-5	Larry Walker	.50
AW-6	Sammy Sosa	3.00
AW-7	Mariano Rivera	.75
AW-8	Vladimir Guerrero	1.50
AW-9	Alex Rodriguez	3.00
AW-10	Albert Pujols	3.00
AW-11	Luis Gonzalez	.50
AW-12	Ken Griffey Jr.	2.50
AW-13	Kazuhiro Sasaki	.50
AW-14	Bob Abreu	.50
AW-15	Todd Helton	1.00
AW-16	Nomar Garciaparra	2.50
AW-17	Miguel Tejada	.75
AW-18	Roger Clemens	3.00
AW-19	Mike Piazza	2.50
AW-20	Carlos Delgado	1.00
AW-21	Derek Jeter	4.00
AW-22	Hideo Nomo	.75
AW-23	Randy Johnson	1.50
AW-24	Ivan Rodriguez	1.00
AW-25	Chan Ho Park	.50

Autographs

		NM/M
Common Player:		10.00
TA1	Carlos Delgado	40.00
TA2	Ivan Rodriguez	50.00
TA3	Miguel Tejada	30.00
TA4	Geoff Jenkins	10.00
TA5	Johnny Damon	40.00
TA6	Tim Hudson	25.00
TA7	Terrence Long	10.00
TA8	Gabe Kapler	10.00
TA9	Magglio Ordonez	20.00
TA10	Barry Bonds	180.00
TA11	Pat Burrell	20.00
TA12	Mike Mussina	40.00
TA13	Eric Valent	5.00
TA14	Xavier Nady	8.00
TA15	Cristian Guerrero	5.00
TA16	Ben Sheets	15.00
TA17	Corey Patterson	15.00
TA18	Carlos Pena	5.00
TA19	Alex Rodriguez	80.00
Series 2		
TA-AB	Adrian Beltre	25.00
TA-JD	Jermaine Dye	15.00
TA-AE	Alex Escobar	8.00
TA-CF	Cliff Floyd	15.00
TA-RF	Rafael Furcal	20.00
TA-BG	Brian Giles	20.00
TA-KG	Keith Ginter	8.00
TA-TG	Troy Glaus	40.00
TA-BGR	Ben Grieve	15.00
TA-CG	Cristian Guzman	15.00
TA-JH	Josh Hamilton	25.00
TA-NJ	Nick Johnson	5.00
TA-RK	Ryan Klesko	20.00
TA-JO	Jose Ortiz	5.00
TA-RO	Roy Oswalt	15.00
TA-RP	Rafael Palmeiro	50.00
TA-AR	Alex Rodriguez	80.00
TA-JR	Jimmy Rollins	25.00
TA-RS	Richie Sexson	25.00
TA-MS	Mike Sweeney	20.00
TA-JW	Justin Wayne	10.00
TA-BW	Brad Wilkerson	10.00

Battery Mates Relic

		NM/M
Inserted 1:4,401		
ML	Greg Maddux, Javy Lopez	30.00
LP	Al Leiter, Mike Piazza	30.00

Coaches Collection Relics

		NM/M
Common Card		8.00
Inserted 1:236 Retail		
AH	Art Howe	8.00
AT	Alan Trammell	15.00
BB	Bruce Bochy	8.00
BM	Buck Martinez	8.00
BV	Bobby Valentine	15.00
BW	Billy Williams	15.00
BBE	Buddy Bell	15.00
BBR	Bob Brenly	15.00
DB	Dusty Baker	20.00
DL	Davey Lopes	15.00
DBA	Don Baylor	15.00
EH	Elrod Hendricks	8.00
EM	Eddie Murray	40.00
FW	Frank White	15.00
HM	Hal McRae	8.00
JT	Joe Torre	10.00
KG	Ken Griffey Sr.	8.00
LB	Larry Bowa	15.00
LP	Lance Parrish	15.00
MH	Mike Hargrove	10.00
MS	Mike Scioscia	15.00
MW	Mookie Wilson	15.00
PG	Phil Garner	10.00
PM	Paul Molitor	40.00
TP	Tony Perez	10.00
WR	Willie Randolph	15.00

Draft Picks

		NM/M
Complete Set (10):		40.00
1-5 in Green Factory Sets		
6-10 in Holiday Factory Sets		
1	Scott Moore	6.00
2	Val Majewski	6.00
3	Brian Slocum	4.00
4	Chris Gruler	6.00
5	Mark Schramek	6.00
6	Joe Saunders	4.00
7	Jeff Francis	8.00
8	Royce Ring	6.00
9	Greg Miller	8.00
10	Brandon Weeden	4.00

Dueces Are Wild

		NM/M
Common Card:		15.00
Inserted 1:1,962		
JG	Randy Johnson, Luis Gonzalez	30.00
BK	Barry Bonds, Jeff Kent	40.00

TA	Jim Thome, Roberto Alomar	30.00
WH	Larry Walker, Todd Helton	25.00
BG	Bret Boone, Freddy Garcia	15.00

Dual Ebbets/Yankee Seat Relic

No Pricing

Dual Ebbets/Yankee Autographed Seat Relic

No Pricing

East Meets West

NM/M

Complete Set (8):		6.00
Common Player:		1.00
Inserted 1:24		
EW-HN	Hideo Nomo, Masanori Murakami	2.00
EW-HI	Hideki Irabu, Masanori Murakami	1.00
EW-SH	Shigetoshi Hasegawa, Masanori Murakami	1.00
EW-MY	Masato Yoshii, Masanori Murakami	1.00
EW-TS	Tsuyoshi Shinjo, Masanori Murakami	1.00
EW-KS	Kazuhiro Sasaki, Masanori Murakami	1.00
EW-MS	Mac Suzuki, Masanori Murakami	1.00
EW-TO	Tomo Ohka, Masanori Murakami	1.00

East Meets West Relics

NM/M

Common Player:		15.00
Inserted 1:3,419		
HN	Hideo Nomo	40.00
KS	Kazuhiro Sasaki	15.00
TS	Tsuyoshi Shinjo	15.00

Ebbets Field Seat Relics

NM/M

Inserted 1:9,116		
JB	Joe Black	100.00
RC	Roy Campanella	250.00
BC	Billy Cox	100.00
CF	Carl Furillo	100.00
GH	Gil Hodges	250.00
AP	Andy Pafko	100.00
PWR	Pee Wee Reese	250.00
JR	Jackie Robinson	250.00
DS	Duke Snider	250.00

Ebbets Field/Yankee Stadium Seat Dual Relic

No Pricing

Hall of Fame Vintage BuyBacks AutoProofs

NM/M

Common Autograph:		15.00
BR16	Brooks Robinson 82 KM/200	50.00
EW10	Earl Weaver 87/100	15.00
FJ33	Fergie Jenkins 84/100	15.00
GP26	Gaylord Perry 82/100	15.00
GP29	Gaylord Perry 83/100	15.00
GP30	Gaylord Perry 83 SV/200	15.00
OC1	Orlando Cepeda 82 KM/200	15.00
RF15	Rollie Fingers 81/300	15.00
RF16	Rollie Fingers 81 LL/100	15.00
RF18	Rollie Fingers 82/100	15.00
RF19	Rollie Fingers 82 IA/200	15.00
RF21	Rollie Fingers 82 KM/300	15.00
RF22	Rollie Fingers 83/200	15.00
RF24	Rollie Fingers 84/200	15.00
RF27	Rollie Fingers 85/300	15.00
RF28	Rollie Fingers 86/100	15.00
SC5	Steve Carlton 84 LL/100	25.00
SC6	Steve Carlton 85/200	25.00
SC8	Steve Carlton 87/200	25.00

Heart of the Order Relic

NM/M

Inserted 1:4,247		
KBA	Jeff Kent, Barry Bonds, Rich Aurilia	75.00
TGA	Jim Thome, Juan Gonzalez, Roberto Alomar	50.00
ARB	Bob Abreu, Scott Rolen, Pat Burrell	50.00
OWM	Paul O'Neill, Bernie Williams, Tino Martinez	50.00

Hit and Run Relic

NM/M

Inserted 1:4,241		
JD	Johnny Damon	10.00
DE	Darin Erstad	10.00
RF	Rafael Furcal	10.00

Hobby Masters

NM/M

Complete Set (20):		40.00
Common Player:		1.00
Inserted 1:25		
1	Mark McGwire	5.00
2	Derek Jeter	5.00
3	Chipper Jones	2.00
4	Roger Clemens	4.00
5	Vladimir Guerrero	2.00
6	Ichiro Suzuki	3.00
7	Todd Helton	1.50
8	Alex Rodriguez	4.00
9	Albert Pujols	4.00
10	Sammy Sosa	3.00
11	Ken Griffey Jr.	3.00
12	Randy Johnson	2.00
13	Nomar Garciaparra	3.00
14	Ivan Rodriguez	1.50
15	Manny Ramirez	1.50
16	Barry Bonds	5.00
17	Mike Piazza	3.00
18	Pedro Martinez	1.50
19	Jeff Bagwell	1.50
20	Luis Gonzalez	1.00

Jack of All Trades

NM/M

Inserted 1:1,350		
RO	Roberto Alomar/Bat	20.00
BB	Barry Bonds/Jsy	35.00
AJ	Andruw Jones/Jsy	10.00
IR	Ivan Rodriguez/Jsy	15.00
BW	Bernie Williams/Jsy	15.00

Kings of the Clubhouse

NM/M

Common Player:		10.00
Inserted 1:1,449 Ser. 2		
TG	Tom Glavine/Jsy	15.00
TH	Todd Helton/Jsy	15.00
RJ	Randy Johnson/Jsy	20.00
EM	Edgar Martinez/Jsy	10.00
PO	Paul O'Neill/Bat	20.00

Like Father Like Son Relic

NM/M

Common Duo:		
Inserted 1:1,304 Retail		
AL	Roberto Alomar, Sandy Alomar, Sandy Alomar Jr.	40.00
BE	Dale Berra, Yogi Berra	50.00
BON	Bobby Bonds, Barry Bonds	80.00
BOO	Bob Boone, Bret Boone, Aaron Boone	40.00
CR	Jose Cruz, Jose Cruz Jr.	40.00

Own The Game

NM/M

Complete Set (30):		25.00
Common Player:		.50
Inserted 1:12		
OG1	Moises Alou	.75
OG2	Roberto Alomar	.75
OG3	Luis Gonzalez	.50
OG4	Bret Boone	.75
OG5	Barry Bonds	4.00
OG6	Jim Thome	1.50
OG7	Jimmy Rollins	.75
OG8	Cristian Guzman	.50
OG9	Lance Berkman	.75
OG10	Mike Sweeney	.50
OG11	Rich Aurilia	.50
OG12	Ichiro Suzuki	2.50
OG13	Luis Gonzalez	.50
OG14	Ichiro Suzuki	2.50
OG15	Jimmy Rollins	.75
OG16	Roger Cedeno	.50
OG17	Barry Bonds	4.00
OG18	Jim Thome	1.50
OG19	Curt Schilling	1.00
OG20	Roger Clemens	3.00
OG21	Curt Schilling	1.00
OG22	Brad Radke	.50
OG23	Greg Maddux	2.00
OG24	Mark Mulder	.75
OG25	Jeff Shaw	.50
OG26	Mariano Rivera	.75
OG27	Randy Johnson	1.50
OG28	Pedro Martinez	1.50
OG29	John Burkett	.50
OG30	Tim Hudson	.75

Prime Cuts Pine Tar Series

NM/M

Common Player:		15.00
Inserted 1:4,420		
BB	Barry Bonds	60.00
LG	Luis Gonzalez	20.00
TG	Tony Gwynn	40.00
TH	Todd Helton	25.00
AP	Albert Pujols	40.00
Series 2		
Inserted 1:1,043		
Trademark Series:		1.5-2X
Inserted 1:2,087 Ser. 2		
Prime Cuts Barrel:		2-4X
Inserted 1:7,824 Ser. 2		
WB	Wilson Betemit	15.00
SB	Sean Burroughs	15.00
JC	Joe Crede	20.00
AD	Adam Dunn	30.00
AE	Alex Escobar	15.00
MG	Marcus Giles	15.00
AG	Alexis Gomez	15.00
TH	Toby Hall	15.00
JH	Josh Hamilton	15.00
NJ	Nick Johnson	15.00
XN	Xavier Nady	15.00
CP	Corey Patterson	20.00
CPE	Carlos Pena	15.00
AR	Aaron Rowand	25.00
RS	Ruben Salazar	15.00

Prime Cuts Autograph Series

No Pricing

Ring Masters

NM/M

Complete Set (10):		15.00
Common Player:		.50
Inserted 1:25		
1	Derek Jeter	4.00
2	Mark McGwire	4.00
3	Mariano Rivera	1.00
4	Gary Sheffield	.75
5	Al Leiter	.50
6	Chipper Jones	1.50
7	Roger Clemens	3.00
8	Greg Maddux	2.00
9	Roberto Alomar	1.00
10	Paul O'Neill	.50

Team Topps Legends Autographs

NM/M

Common Player:		25.00
TT6R	Whitey Ford	60.00
TT8R	Bob Gibson	40.00
TT47R	Frank Howard	25.00
TT46F	Robin Roberts	25.00
TT13F	Warren Spahn	40.00
Series 2		
	Gil McDougald	
	Joe Pepitone	
	Frank Robinson	
	Enos Slaughter	
	Luis Tiant	

Three of a Kind

NM/M

Common Card:		
Inserted 1:2,039		
SPA	Tsuyoshi Shinjo, Mike Piazza, Edgardo Alfonzo	50.00
LOC	Carlos Lee, Magglio Ordonez, Jose Canseco	50.00
FBJ	Rafael Furcal, Wilson Betemit, Andruw Jones	40.00
PSW	Jorge Posada, Alfonso Soriano, Bernie Williams	50.00
BDB	A.J. Burnett, Ryan Dempster, Josh Beckett	40.00

Turn Two Relic

NM/M

Inserted 1:4,401		
TW	Alan Trammell, Lou Whitaker	40.00
VA	Omar Vizquel, Roberto Alomar	40.00

Yankee Stadium Seat Relics

NM/M

Inserted 1:579		
HB	Hank Bauer	100.00
YB	Yogi Berra	250.00
JC	Joe Collins	100.00
BM	Billy Martin	250.00
GM	Gil McDougald	100.00
JM	Johnny Mize	100.00
AR	Allie Reynolds	100.00
PR	Phil Rizzuto	250.00
GW	Gene Woodling	100.00

1952 Player Autographs

NM/M

Inserted 1:7,524		
HBA	Hank Bauer	75.00
YBA	Yogi Berra	100.00
PRA	Preacher Roe	70.00

1952 Reprint Autographs

NM/M

Common Autograph:		25.00
Inserted 1:10,268		
JBA	Joe Black	90.00
CEA	Carl Erskine	50.00
GMA	Gil McDougal	40.00
APA	Andy Pafko	60.00
PRA	Phil Rizzuto	80.00
DSA	Duke Snider	100.00

1952 World Series Tribute

BILLY COX
Billy Cox

NM/M

Complete Set (19):		50.00
Common Player:		3.00
Inserted 1:25		
1	Roy Campanella	4.00
2	Duke Snider	4.00
3	Carl Erskine	3.00
4	Andy Pafko	3.00
5	Johnny Mize	3.00
6	Billy Martin	4.00
7	Phil Rizzuto	4.00
8	Gil McDougal	3.00
9	Allie Reynolds	4.00
10	Jackie Robinson	4.00
Series 2		
11	Preacher Roe	3.00

12	Gil Hodges	3.00
13	Billy Cox	3.00
14	Yogi Berra	4.00
15	Gene Woodling	3.00
16	Jerry Sain	3.00
17	Ralph Houk	3.00
18	Joe Collins	3.00
19	Hank Bauer	3.00

1952 World Series Highlights

	NM/M
Complete Set (7):	10.00
Common Player:	2.00
Inserted 1:25	
52WS-1	Dodgers' Game 1 Starting Line Up	3.00
52WS-2	Dodgers Celebrate Game 3 Win!	2.00
52WS-3	Carl Erskine Wins Game 5	2.00
Series 2	
52WS-2	Game 2	2.00
52WS-4	Game 4	2.00
52WS-6	Game 6	2.00
52WS-7	Game 7	2.00

2 Bagger Relic

	NM/M
Inserted 1:3,733	
TG	Tony Gwynn	30.00
TH	Todd Helton	20.00
SR	Scott Rolen	20.00

2002 Topps Traded & Rookies

	NM/M
Complete Set (275):	125.00
Common Player:	.15
Common SP (1-110):	.50
Chrome Cards:	2-4X
2:Pack	
Pack (10):	3.00
Box (24):	60.00
T1	Jeff Weaver	.50
T2	Jay Powell	.50
T3	Alex Gonzalez	.50
T4	Jason Isringhausen	.50
T5	Darren Oliver	.50
T6	Hector Ortiz	.50
T7	Chuck Knoblauch	.50
T8	Brian L. Hunter	.50
T9	Dustan Mohr	.50
T10	Eric Hinske	.50
T11	Roger Cedeno	.50
T12	Eddie Perez	.50
T13	Jeromy Burnitz	.50
T14	Bartolo Colon	.50
T15	Rick Helling	.50

T16	Dan Plesac	.50
T17	Scott Strickland	.50
T18	Antonio Alfonseca	.50
T19	Ricky Gutierrez	.50
T20	John Valentin	.50
T21	Raul Mondesi	.50
T22	Ben Davis	.50
T23	Nelson Figueroa	.50
T24	Earl Snyder	.50
T25	Robin Ventura	.50
T26	Jimmy Haynes	.50
T27	Kenny Kelly	.50
T28	Morgan Ensberg	.50
T29	Reggie Sanders	.50
T30	Shigetoshi Hasegawa	.50
T31	Allen Levrault	.50
T32	Russell Branyan	.50
T33	Jose Guillen	.50
T34	Jose Paniagua	.50
T35	Kent Mercker	.50
T36	Jesse Orosco	.50
T37	Gregg Zaun	.50
T38	Reggie Taylor	.50
T39	Andres Galarraga	.50
T40	Chris Truby	.50
T41	Bruce Chen	.50
T42	Darren Lewis	.50
T43	Ryan Kohlmeier	.50
T44	John McDonald	.50
T45	Omar Daal	.50
T46	Matt Clement	.50
T47	Glendon Rusch	.50
T48	Chan Ho Park	.50
T49	Benny Agbayani	.50
T50	Juan Gonzalez	1.50
T51	Carlos Baerga	.50
T52	Tim Raines	.50
T53	Kevin Appier	.50
T54	Marty Cordoua	.50
T55	Jeff D'Amico	.50
T56	Dmitri Young	.50
T57	Roosevelt Brown	.50
T58	Dustin Hermanson	.50
T59	Jose Rijo	.50
T60	Todd Ritchie	.50
T61	Lee Stevens	.50
T62	Shane Heams	.50
T63	Eric Young	.50
T64	Chuck Finley	.50
T65	Dicky Gonzalez	.50
T66	Jose Macias	.50
T67	Gabe Kapler	.50
T68	Sandy Alomar Jr.	.50
T69	Henry Blanco	.50
T70	Julian Tavarez	.50
T71	Paul Bako	.50
T72	Dave Burba	.50
T73	Brian Jordan	.50
T74	Rickey Henderson	1.00
T75	Kevin Mench	.50
T76	Hideo Nomo	1.00
T77	Mark Sweeney	.50
T78	Brad Fullmer	.50
T79	Carl Everett	.50
T80	David Wells	.50
T81	Aaron Sele	.50
T82	Todd Hollandsworth	.50
T83	Vicente Padilla	.50
T84	Chris Latham	.50
T85	Corky Miller	.50
T86	Josh Fogg	.50
T87	Calvin Murray	.50
T88	Craig Paquette	.50
T89	Jay Payton	.50
T90	Carlos Pena	.50
T91	Juan Encarnacion	.50
T92	Rey Sanchez	.50
T93	Ryan Dempster	.50
T94	Mario Encarnacion	.50
T95	Jorge Julio	.50
T96	John Mabry	.50
T97	Todd Zeile	.50
T98	Johnny Damon	.50
T99	Deivi Cruz	.50
T100	Gary Sheffield	1.00
T101	Ted Lilly	.50
T102	Todd Van Poppel	.50
T103	Shawn Estes	.50
T104	Cesar Izturis	.50
T105	Ron Coomer	.50
T106	Grady Little	.50
T107	Jimy Williams	.50
T108	Tony Pena	.50
T109	Frank Robinson	.50
T110	Ron Gardenhire	.50
T111	Dennis Tankersley	.15
T112	Alejandro Cadena RC	.25
T113	Justin Kubel RC	.25
T114	Nate Field RC	.25
T115	Rene Reyes RC	.25
T116	Nelson Castro RC	.25
T117	Miguel Olivo	.15
T118	David Espinosa	.15
T119	Chris Bootcheck RC	.40

T120	Rob Henkel RC	.25
T121	Steve Bechler RC	.25
T122	Mark Outlaw RC	.25
T123	Henry Pichardo RC	.25
T124	Michael Floyd RC	.25
T125	Richard Lane RC	.25
T126	Peter Zamora RC	.25
T127	Javier Colina	.15
T128	Greg Sain RC	.25
T129	Ronnie Merrill	.25
T130	Gavin Floyd	1.50
T131	Josh Bonifay RC	.25
T132	Tommy Marx RC	.25
T133	Gary Cates Jr. RC	.25
T134	Neal Cotts	.50
T135	Angel Berroa	.25
T136	Elio Serrano RC	.25
T137	J.J. Putz RC	.25
T138	Ruben Gotay RC	.25
T139	Eddie Rogers RC	.25
T140	Wily Mo Pena	.25
T141	Tyler Yates RC	.25
T142	Colin Young RC	.25
T143	Chance Caple	.15
T144	Ben Howard RC	.25
T145	Ryan Bukvich RC	.25
T146	Clifford Bartosh RC	.25
T147	Brandon Claussen	.25
T148	Cristian Guerrero	.15
T149	Derrick Lewis	.15
T150	Eric Miller RC	.25
T151	Justin Huber RC	.75
T152	Adrian Gonzalez	.15
T153	Brian West RC	.25
T154	Chris Baker RC	.25
T155	Drew Henson	.15
T156	Scott Hairston	.75
T157	Jason Simontacchi RC	.75
T158	Jason Arnold	.40
T159	Brandon Phillips	.15
T160	Adam Roller RC	.25
T161	Scotty Layfield RC	.25
T162	Freddie Money RC	.25
T163	Noochie Varner RC	.50
T164	Terrance Hill RC	.25
T165	Jeremy Hill RC	.25
T166	Carlos Cabrera RC	.25
T167	Jose Morban RC	.25
T168	Kevin Frederick RC	.25
T169	Mark Teixeira	.40
T170	Brian Rogers	.15
T171	Anastacio Martinez RC	.25
T172	Bobby Jenks RC	.75
T173	David Gil RC	.25
T174	Andres Torres	.15
T175	James Barrett RC	.25
T176	Jimmy Journell	.15
T177	Brett Kay RC	.25
T178	Jason Young RC	.25
T179	Mark Hamilton RC	.25
T180	Jose Bautista RC	.50
T181	Blake McGinley RC	.25
T182	Ryan Mottl RC	.25
T183	Jeff Austin RC	.25
T184	Xavier Nady	.15
T185	Kyle Kane RC	.25
T186	Travis Foley	.15
T187	Nathan Kaup RC	.25
T188	Eric Cyr RC	.25
T189	Josh Cisneros RC	.25
T190	Brad Nelson RC	.75
T191	Clint Weibl RC	.25
T192	Ron Calloway RC	.25
T193	Jung Bong	.15
T194	Rolando Viera RC	.25
T195	Jason Bulger RC	.25
T196	Chone Figgins RC	.75
T197	Jimmy Alvarez RC	.25
T198	Joel Crump RC	.25
T199	Ryan Doumit RC	1.50
T200	Demetrius Heath RC	.25
T201	John Ennis RC	.25
T202	Doug Sessions RC	.25
T203	Clinton Hosford RC	.25
T204	Chris Narveson RC	.25
T205	Ross Peeples RC	.25
T206	Alexander Requena RC	.25
T207	Matt Erickson RC	.25
T208	Brian Forystek RC	.25
T209	Dewon Brazelton	.15
T210	Nathan Haynes	.15
T211	Jack Cust	.15
T212	Jesse Foppert	.75
T213	Jesus Cota RC	.25
T214	Juan Gonzalez	.15
T215	Tim Kalita RC	.25
T216	Manny Delcarmen RC	2.00
T217	Jim Kavourias	.15
T218	C.J. Wilson RC	.25
T219	Edwin Yan RC	.25
T220	Andy Van Hekken	.15
T221	Michael Cuddyer	.15
T222	Jeff Verplancke RC	.25
T223	Mike Wilson RC	.25

T224	Corwin Malone	.15
T225	Chris Snelling RC	.50
T226	Joe Rogers RC	.25
T227	Jason Bay	.50
T228	Ezequiel Astacio RC	.25
T229	Joey Hammond RC	.25
T230	Chris Duffy RC	.25
T231	Mark Prior	1.00
T232	Hansel Izquierdo RC	.25
T233	Franklyn German RC	.25
T234	Alexis Gomez	.15
T235	Jorge Padilla RC	.25
T236	Ryan Snare RC	.25
T237	Deivis Santos	.15
T238	Taggert Bozied RC	1.00
T239	Mike Peeples RC	.25
T240	Ronald Acuna RC	.25
T241	Koyie Hill	.15
T242	Garrett Guzman RC	.25
T243	Ryan Church RC	1.00
T244	Tony Fontana RC	.25
T245	Keto Anderson RC	.25
T246	Brad Bouras RC	.25
T247	Jason Dubois RC	1.00
T248	Angel Guzman RC	2.00
T249	Joel Hanrahan RC	.50
T250	Joe Jiannetti RC	.25
T251	Sean Pierce RC	.25
T252	Jake Mauer RC	.25
T253	Marshall McDougall RC	.50
T254	Edwin Almonte RC	.25
T255	Shawn Riggans RC	.25
T256	Steven Shell	.15
T257	Kevin Hooper RC	.40
T258	Michael Frick RC	.25
T259	Travis Chapman RC	.40
T260	Tim Hummel RC	.25
T261	Adam Morrissey RC	.25
T262	Dontrelle Willis RC	5.00
T263	Justin Sherrod RC	.25
T264	Gerald Smiley RC	.25
T265	Tony Miller RC	.25
T266	Nolan Ryan	1.50
T267	Reggie Jackson	.50
T268	Steve Garvey	.15
T269	Wade Boggs	.50
T270	Sammy Sosa	1.00
T271	Curt Schilling	.25
T272	Mark Grace	.25
T273	Jason Giambi	.50
T274	Ken Griffey Jr.	.75
T275	Roberto Alomar	.40

Gold

Gold Stars:	2-4X
Production 2,002 Sets	
Chrome Refractors:	3-5X
Inserted 1:12	

Tools of the Trade Relics

	NM/M
Common Player:	5.00
Bat Relics 1:34	
Jersey Relics 1:426	
RAB	Roberto Alomar/Bat	8.00
MA	Moises Alou/Bat	8.00
DB	David Bell/Bat	5.00
JBU	Jeromy Burnitz/Bat	5.00

JC	Jose Canseco/Bat	10.00
VC	Vinny Castilla/Bat	5.00
JCI	Jeff Cirillo/Bat	5.00
TC	Tony Clark/Bat	5.00
JDB	Johnny Damon/Bat	6.00
CE	Carl Everett/Bat	5.00
BF	Brad Fullmer/Bat	5.00
AG	Andres Galarraga/Bat	6.00
JG	Juan Gonzalez/Jsy	8.00
RHB	Rickey Henderson/Bat	10.00
BJ	Brian Jordan/Bat	5.00
DJ	David Justice/Bat	5.00
CK	Chuck Knoblauch/Bat	5.00
MLB	Matt Lawton/Bat	5.00
KL	Kenny Lofton/Bat	5.00
TM	Tino Martinez/Bat	6.00
CP	Carlos Pena/Bat	8.00
JP	Josh Phelps/Jsy	6.00
TR	Tim Raines/Bat	5.00
RS	Reggie Sanders/Bat	5.00
GS	Gary Sheffield/Bat	5.00
TS	Tsuyoshi Shinjo/Bat	5.00
RSI	Ruben Sierra/Bat	5.00
MT	Michael Tucker/Bat	5.00
MV	Mo Vaughn/Jsy	6.00
MVB	Mo Vaughn/Bat	6.00
RV	Robin Ventura/Bat	6.00
RW	Rondell White/Bat	5.00
EY	Eric Young/Bat	5.00

Tools of the Trade
Dual Relics

		NM/M
Common Card:		8.00
Inserted 1:539		
MA	Moises Alou	10.00
HN	Hideo Nomo	35.00
CP	Chan Ho Park	8.00

Farewell Relics

		NM/M
Randomly inserted.		
JC	Jose Canseco	10.00

Hall of Fame Relics

		NM/M
Randomly inserted.		
HOF-OS	Ozzie Smith	25.00

Legends Autographs

		NM/M
Common Autograph:		10.00
Inserted 1:1,097		
	Johnny Bench	40.00
	Vida Blue	10.00
	Clete Boyer	12.00
	Whitey Ford	30.00
	Bob Gibson	25.00
	Joe Pepitone	10.00
	Bobby Richardson	10.00
	Bill "Moose" Skowron	10.00
	Enos Slaughter	18.00
	Carl Yastrzemski	60.00

Signature Moves
Autographs

		NM/M
Common Autograph:		8.00
Inserted 1:91		
RA	Roberto Alomar	30.00
MA	Moises Alou	15.00
TBL	Tony Blanco	8.00
BB	Boof Bonser	8.00
AC	Antoine Cameron	10.00
BC	Brandon Claussen	15.00
MC	Matt Cooper	8.00
JD	Johnny Damon	30.00
JDA	Jeff DaVanon	8.00
VD	Victor Diaz	12.00
RH	Ryan Hannaman	8.00
KI	Kazuhisa Ishii	40.00
FJ	Forrest Johnson	8.00
TL	Todd Linden	15.00
CM	Corwin Malone	8.00
JM	Jake Mauer	8.00
AM	Andy Morales	8.00
RM	Ramon Moreta	8.00
JMO	Justin Morneau	30.00
JP	Juan Pena	8.00
JS	Juan Silvestre	8.00
CS	Chris Smith	8.00
DT	Dennis Tankersley	8.00
MT	Marcus Thames	8.00
CU	Chase Utley	70.00
JW	Justin Wayne	8.00

2002 Topps American
Pie Spirit of America

		NM/M
Complete Set (150):		30.00
Common Player:		.25

Pack (7):		5.00
Box (24):		100.00
1	Warren Spahn	.75
2	Reggie Jackson	.75
3	Bill Mazeroski	.25
4	Carl Yastrzemski	.75
5	Whitey Ford	.75
6	Ralph Houk	.25
7	Rod Carew	.50
8	Kirk Gibson	.25
9	Bobby Thomson	.25
10	Don Newcombe	.25
11	Gaylord Perry	.25
12	Bruce Sutter	.40
13	Bob Gibson	.50
14	Brooks Robinson	1.00
15	Steve Carlton	.50
16	Robin Yount	1.00
17	Ernie Banks	.75
18	Lou Brock	.25
19	Al Kaline	.75
20	Carlton Fisk	.75
21	Frank Robinson	.75
22	Bobby Bonds	.25
23	Andre Dawson	.25
24	Rich "Goose" Gossage	.25
25	Fred Lynn	.25
26	Keith Hernandez	.25
27	Rollie Fingers	.25
28	Juan Marichal	.25
29	Maury Wills	.25
30	Dave Winfield	.50
31	Frank Howard	.25
32	Tony Gwynn	1.00
33	Jim Palmer	.50
34	Mike Schmidt	1.50
35	Bo Jackson	.75
36	Ferguson Jenkins	.25
37	Bobby Richardson	.25
38	Harmon Killebrew	.75
39	Monte Irvin	.25
40	Jim Abbott	.50
41	Wade Boggs	.75
42	Jackie Robinson	2.00
43	Ralph Branca	.25
44	Minnie Minoso	.25
45	Tug McGraw	.25
46	Willie Mays	2.00
47	Nolan Ryan	3.00
48	Duke Snider	1.00
49	Tom Seaver	1.00
50	Casey Stengel	.50
51	D-Day	.75
52	Gulf War	.25
53	Vietnam War	.25
54	Korean War	.25
55	Secret Service	.25
56	Crayons	.25
57	Hoover Dam	.25
58	Penicillin	.25
59	Polio Vaccine	.25
60	Empire State Building	.25
61	Television	.25
62	Free Speech	.25
63	Voyager Mission	.25
64	Space Shuttle	.25
65	Ellis Island	.25
66	Statue of Liberty	.25
67	Battle of the Bulge	.25
68	Battle of Midway	.25
69	Iwo Jima	.25
70	Panama Canal	.25
71	Spirit of St. Louis/Lindbergh	.25
72	Civil Rights/We Shall Overcome	.25
73	Space Race	.25
74	Alaska Pipeline	.25
75	Teddy Bear	.25
76	Sea Biscuit	.25
77	Bazooka Joe	.25
78	Mt. Rushmore	.25
79	Yellowstone Park	.25

80	Niagara Falls	.25
81	Grand Canyon	.25
82	Hoola Hoop	.25
83	George Patton	.50
84	Audie Murphy	.25
85	Amelia Earhart	.25
86	Glen Miller	.25
87	Rick Monday	.25
88	Buzz Aldrin	.25
89	Rosa Parks	.25
90	Edward R. Murrow	.25
91	Susan B. Anthony	.25
92	Bobby Kennedy	.25
93	Gloria Steinem	.25
94	Hank Greenberg	.75
95	Jimmy Doolittle	.25
96	Thurgood Marshall	.25
97	Ernest Hemingway	.75
98	Henry Ford	.25
99	Wright Brothers	.25
100	Thomas Edison	.75
101	Albert Einstein	.75
102	Will Rogers	.25
103	George Gershwin	.25
104	Irving Berlin	.25
105	Frank Lloyd Wright	.25
106	Howard Hughes	.25
107	George M. Cohan	.25
108	Jack Kerouac	.25
109	Harry Houdini	.25
110	Helen Keller	.25
111	John McCain	.25
112	Andrew Carnegie	.25
113	Sandra Day O'Connor	.25
114	Brooklyn Bridge	.25
115	Douglas MacArthur	.25
116	Elvis Presley	1.00
117	George Burns	.25
118	Judy Garland	.50
119	Buddy Holly	.25
120	Don McLean	.25
121	Marilyn Monroe	1.00
122	Humphrey Bogart	.50
123	Gary Cooper	.25
124	The Andrews Sisters	.25
125	Jim Thorpe	1.00
126	Joe Louis	.75
127	Jesse Owens	.50
128	Kate Smith	.25
129	W.C. Fields	.25
130	Bette Davis	.25
131	Jayne Mansfield	.25
132	Teddy Roosevelt	.50
133	Franklin D. Roosevelt	.75
134	Harry Truman	.50
135	Dwight Eisenhower	.50
136	George H.W. Bush	.50
137	George W. Bush	.50
138	John F. Kennedy	1.00
139	Lyndon B. Johnson	.25
140	William Taft	.25
141	Horace Harding	.25
142	Woodrow Wilson	.25
143	Richard Nixon	.25
144	Bill Clinton	.25
145	Jimmy Carter	.25
146	Herbert Hoover	.25
147	Gerald Ford	.25
148	Ronald Reagan	.25
149	Calvin Coolidge	.25
150	William McKinley	.25

Piece of American Pie

		NM/M
Common Card:		25.00
Inserted 1:119		
HB	Humphrey Bogart	120.00
GB	George Burns	60.00
GC	Gary Cooper	60.00
JD	Judy Garland	80.00
MM	Marilyn Monroe	350.00
EP	Elvis Presley/Shirt	150.00
EP2	Elvis Presley/Coat	150.00
RR	Ronald Reagan/Berlin Wall	25.00
JM	Jayne Mansfield	80.00
BD	Bette Davis	25.00

American Sluggers

		NM/M
Complete Set (25):		25.00
Common Player:		.50
Inserted 1:1		

Each card issued in blue, gold, silver and red; no value differential.

AD	Andre Dawson	.50
AK	Al Kaline	1.00
BR	Brooks Robinson	1.00
CC	Cecil Cooper	.50
CF	Carlton Fisk	1.00
CY	Carl Yastrzemski	2.00
DS	Duke Snider	1.00
DW	Dave Winfield	1.00
EM	Eddie Mathews	1.00
FH	Frank Howard	.50
FL	Fred Lynn	.50
FR	Frank Robinson	1.00
GB	George Brett	3.00
GF	George Foster	.50
HK	Harmon Killebrew	1.00
JC	Jack Clark	.50
JCC	Joe Carter	.50
KG	Kirk Gibson	.50
MI	Monte Irvin	.50
MS	Mike Schmidt	3.00
RC	Rod Carew	1.00
RJ	Reggie Jackson	2.50
RS	Ryne Sandberg	2.00
TK	Ted Kluszewski	1.00
WM	Willie Mays	4.00

Presidential First
Pitch Relics

		NM/M
Common Player:		10.00
Inserted 1:32		
GHWB	George H.W. Bush	10.00
GWB	George W. Bush	30.00
BC	Bill Clinton	40.00
CC	Calvin Coolidge	10.00
DE	Dwight Eisenhower	20.00
GF	Gerald Ford	20.00
WH	Warren Harding	10.00
HH	Herbert Hoover	10.00
LBJ	Lyndon B. Johnson	15.00
JFK	John F. Kennedy	35.00
RN	Richard Nixon	30.00
RR	Ronald Reagan	40.00
FDR	Franklin D. Roosevelt	15.00
WT	William Taft	10.00
HT	Harry Truman	20.00
WW	Woodrow Wilson	10.00

Through the Years
Relics

Common Player:		8.00
Inserted 1:11		
JA	Jim Abbott	15.00
DA	Dick Allen	8.00
JB	Johnny Bench	20.00
WB	Wade Boggs	10.00

BB	Bill Buckner	8.00
JC	Jack Clark	8.00
AD	Andre Dawson	10.00
KT	Jim Kaat	10.00
EM	Eddie Mathews	15.00
DM	Don Mattingly	40.00
WM	Willie Mays	40.00
MM	Minnie Minoso	15.00
RM	Rick Monday	10.00
JM	Joe Morgan	10.00
TM	Thurman Munson	30.00
AL	Al Oliver	8.00
DP	Dave Parker	10.00
GP	Gaylord Perry	10.00
FR	Frank Robinson	15.00
JR	Joe Rudi	10.00
NR	Nolan Ryan	40.00
TS	Tom Seaver	20.00
WS	Willie Stargell	15.00
DS	Darryl Strawberry	15.00
DW	Dave Winfield	12.00
CY	Carl Yastrzemski	20.00

2002 Topps Archives

		NM/M
Complete Set (200):		70.00
Common Player:		.40
Pack (8):		3.00
Box (20):		50.00
1	Willie Mays	3.00
2	Dale Murphy	.40
3	Dave Winfield	.75
4	Roger Maris	2.00
5	Ron Cey	.40
6	Lee Smith	.40
7	Len Dykstra	.40
8	Ray Fosse	.40
9	Warren Spahn	1.00
10	Herb Score	.40
11	Jim Wynn	.40
12	Sam McDowell	.40
13	Fred Lynn	.40
14	Yogi Berra	1.50
15	Ron Santo	.40
16	Alvin Dark	.40
17	Bill Buckner	.40
18	Rollie Fingers	.60
19	Tony Gwynn	1.50
20	Red Schoendienst	.40
21	Gaylord Perry	.40
22	Jose Cruz	.40
23	Dennis Martinez	.40
24	Dave McNally	.40
25	Norm Cash	.40
26	Ted Kluszewski	.40
27	Rick Reuschel	.40
28	Bruce Sutter	.75
29	Don Larsen	.40
30	Claudell Washington	.40
31	Luis Aparicio	.40
32	Clete Boyer	.40
33	Rich "Goose" Gossage	.40
34	Ray Knight	.40
35	Roy Campanella	1.50
36	Tug McGraw	.40
37	Bob Lemon	.40
38	Willie Stargell	1.00
39	Roberto Clemente	3.00
40	Jim Fregosi	.40
41	Reggie Smith	.40
42	Dave Parker	.40
43	Darrell Evans	.40
44	Ryne Sandberg	2.00
45	Manny Mota	.40
46	Dennis Eckersley	.60
47	Nellie Fox	.40
48	Gil Hodges	.40
49	Reggie Jackson	1.50
50	Bobby Shantz	.40
51	Cecil Cooper	.40
52	Jim Kaat	.40
53	George Hendrick	.40
54	Johnny Podres	.40
55	Bob Gibson	1.00
56	Vern Law	.40
57	Joe Adcock	.40
58	Jack Clark	.40
59	Bill Mazeroski	.40
60	Carl Yastrzemski	1.50
61	Bobby Murcer	.40
62	Davey Johnson	.40
63	Jim Palmer	.75
64	Roy Face	.40
65	Dean Chance	.40
66	Bill "Moose" Skowron	.40
67	Dwight Evans	.40
68	Kirk Gibson	.40
69	Sal Bando	.40
70	Mike Schmidt	2.00
71	Bo Jackson	.75
72	Chris Chambliss	.40
73	Fergie Jenkins	.75
74	Brooks Robinson	1.50
75	Bobby Richardson	.40
76	Duke Snider	1.50
77	Allie Reynolds	.40
78	Harmon Killebrew	1.50
79	Steve Carlton	1.00
80	Bert Blyleven	.40
81	Phil Niekro	.40
82	Lew Burdette	.40
83	Hoyt Wilhelm	.40
84	Curt Flood	.40
85	Guillermo Hernandez	.40
86	Robin Yount	1.50
87	Robin Roberts	.40
88	Whitey Ford	1.00
89	Tony Oliva	.75
90	Don Newcombe	.40
91	Al Oliver	.40
92	Mike Cuellar	.40
93	Mike Scott	.40
94	Dick Allen	.40
95	Jimmy Piersall	.40
96	Bill Freehan	.40
97	Willie Horton	.40
98	Bob Friend	.40
99	Ken Holtzman	.40
100	Rico Carty	.40
101	Gil McDougald	.40
102	Lee May	.40
103	Joe Pepitone	.40
104	Gene Tenace	.40
105	Gary Carter	.40
106	Tim McCarver	.40
107	Ernie Banks	1.50
108	George Foster	.40
109	Lou Brock	1.00
110	Dick Groat	.40
111	Graig Nettles	.40
112	Boog Powell	.40
113	Joe Carter	.40
114	Juan Marichal	.75
115	Larry Doby	.40
116	Fernando Valenzuela	.40
117	Luis Tiant	.40
118	Early Wynn	.40
119	Bill Madlock	.40
120	Eddie Mathews	1.50
121	George Brett	3.00
122	Al Kaline	1.50
123	Frank Howard	.40
124	Mickey Lolich	.40
125	Kirby Puckett	3.00
126	Bob Cerv	.40
127	Will Clark	1.00
128	Vida Blue	.40
129	Kevin Mitchell	.40
130	Bucky Dent	.40
131	Tom Seaver	2.00
132	Jerry Koosman	.40
133	Orlando Cepeda	.40
134	Nolan Ryan	4.00
135	Tony Kubek	.40
136	Don Drysdale	1.00
137	Paul Blair	.40
138	Elston Howard	.40
139	Joe Rudi	.40
140	Tommie Agee	.40
141	Richie Ashburn	.40
142	Jim Bunning	.40
143	Hank Sauer	.40
144	Greg Luzinski	.40
145	Ron Guidry	.40
146	Rod Carew	1.00
147	Andre Dawson	.75
148	Keith Hernandez	.40
149	Carlton Fisk	1.00
150	Cleon Jones	.40
151	Don Mattingly	3.00
152	Vada Pinson	.40
153	Ozzie Smith	1.50
154	Dave Concepcion	.40
155	Al Rosen	.40
156	Tommy John	.40
157	Bob Ojeda	.40
158	Frank Robinson	1.50
159	Darryl Strawberry	.40
160	Bobby Bonds	.40
161	Bert Campaneris	.40
162	Jim "Catfish" Hunter	.40
163	Bud Harrelson	.40
164	Dwight Gooden	.40
165	Wade Boggs	1.00
166	Joe Morgan	1.00
167	Ron Swoboda	.40
168	Hank Aaron	4.00
169	Steve Garvey	.40
170	Mickey Rivers	.40
171	Johnny Bench	3.00
172	Ralph Terry	.40
173	Billy Pierce	.40
174	Thurman Munson	2.50
175	Don Sutton	.40
176	Sparky Anderson	.40
177	Gil Hodges	.40
178	Davey Johnson	.40
179	Frank Robinson	1.50
180	Red Schoendienst	.40
181	Roger Maris	2.00
182	Willie Mays	3.00
183	Luis Aparicio	.40
184	Nellie Fox	.40
185	Ernie Banks	1.50
186	Orlando Cepeda	.75
187	Whitey Ford	1.00
188	Bob Gibson	1.00
189	Bill Mazeroski	.40
190	Hank Aaron	3.00
191	Elston Howard, Harmon Killebrew, Carl Yastrzemski League Leaders	.75
192	Orlando Cepeda, Jackie Robinson, Willie Mays League Leaders	2.00
193	Hank Aaron, Roberto Clemente, Dick Allen League Leaders	2.00
194	Tom Seaver, Phil Niekro, Fergie Jenkins, Juan Marichal League Leaders	1.00
195	Jim Palmer, Jim Hunter, Dennis Eckersley League Leaders	.65
196	Hank Aaron	3.00
197	Brooks Robinson	1.50
198	Tom Seaver	1.50
199	Jim Palmer	.75
200	Lou Brock	1.00

Autographs

		NM/M
Common Autograph:		10.00
Inserted 1:22		
HA	Hank Aaron	250.00
DA	Dick Allen	25.00
SB	Sal Bando	20.00
EB	Ernie Banks	125.00
BB	Bobby Bonds	25.00
GB	George Brett	250.00
JBU	Jim Bunning	40.00
LB	Lew Burdette	20.00
BC	Bert Campaneris	10.00
GC	Gary Carter	50.00
RCE	Ron Cey	15.00
CC	Chris Chambliss	15.00
JCR	Jose Cruz	15.00
AD	Alvin Dark	25.00
BD	Bucky Dent	20.00
LD	Len Dykstra	20.00
DEV	Darrell Evans	15.00
GF	George Foster	15.00
JF	Jim Fregosi	10.00
SG	Steve Garvey	15.00
DG	Dwight Gooden	25.00
DGR	Dick Groat	15.00
BH	Bud Harrelson	15.00
WH	Willie Horton	10.00
KH	Keith Hernandez	40.00
BJ	Bo Jackson	80.00
FJ	Fergie Jenkins	20.00
TJ	Tommy John	15.00
JK	Jim Kaat	20.00
AK	Al Kaline	125.00
HK	Harmon Killebrew	110.00
JKO	Jerry Koosman	65.00
GL	Greg Luzinski	20.00
FL	Fred Lynn	20.00
DM	Dave McNally	20.00
KM	Kevin Mitchell	20.00
DN	Don Newcombe	15.00
TO	Tony Oliva	30.00
JP	Jim Palmer	50.00
DP	Dave Parker	20.00
GP	Gaylord Perry	20.00
BP	Billy Pierce	10.00
JPI	Jimmy Piersall	15.00
JPO	Johnny Podres	15.00
BPO	Boog Powell	25.00
KP	Kirby Puckett	150.00
MR	Mickey Rivers	10.00
BRO	Brooks Robinson	80.00
JR	Joe Rudi	15.00
RS	Ron Santo	30.00
MS	Mike Schmidt	150.00
LS	Lee Smith	20.00
RSM	Reggie Smith	15.00
BS	Bruce Sutter	35.00
RT	Ralph Terry	25.00
HW	Hoyt Wilhelm	20.00
DW	Dave Winfield	85.00
RY	Robin Yount	100.00

AutoProofs

		NM/M
Quantity produced listed		
1	Gary Carter/80	40.00
2	Jose Cruz/95	25.00
4	Bo Jackson/300	50.00
5	Kevin Mitchell/65	25.00
6	Kirby Puckett/65	75.00
7	Mike Schmidt/147	90.00
8	Ozzie Smith/105	75.00
9	Darryl Strawberry/181	40.00
11	Robin Yount/39	100.00

Game-Used Bat

		NM/M
Common Player:		8.00
Group A 1:106		
Group B 1:282		
JB	Johnny Bench	20.00
GB	George Brett	40.00
GC	Gary Carter	10.00
JC	Joe Carter	10.00
NC	Norm Cash	10.00
AD	Andre Dawson	8.00
DE	Dwight Evans	8.00
BF	Bill Freehan	8.00
WH	Willie Horton	10.00
RJ	Reggie Jackson	15.00
DM	Don Mattingly	50.00
RM	Roger Maris	50.00
JM	Joe Morgan	10.00
DP	Dave Parker	10.00
BR	Brooks Robinson	20.00
RS	Ron Santo	20.00
WS	Willie Stargell	15.00
CY	Carl Yastrzemski	40.00
RY	Robin Yount	20.00

Game-Worn Uniform

		NM/M
Common Player:		8.00
Inserted 1:28		
SA	Sparky Anderson	10.00
WB	Wade Boggs	15.00
BB	Bobby Bonds	8.00
GB	George Brett	30.00
OC	Orlando Cepeda	10.00
WC	Will Clark	20.00
DC	Dave Concepcion	8.00
DE	Dennis Eckersley	10.00
SG	Steve Garvey	10.00
FL	Fred Lynn	8.00
DM	Dale Murphy	20.00
PN	Phil Niekro	10.00
GP	Gaylord Perry	20.00
KP	Kirby Puckett	20.00
FR	Frank Robinson	15.00
NR	Nolan Ryan	40.00
RS	Ryne Sandberg	30.00
OS	Ozzie Smith	20.00
DS	Don Sutton	10.00
DW	Dave Winfield	10.00

Stadium Seat

	NM/M
Common Player:	8.00

RA	Richie Ashburn	15.00
SA	Sparky Anderson	10.00
EB	Ernie Banks	25.00
YB	Yogi Berra	20.00
JB	Jim Bunning	10.00
RC	Rod Carew	20.00
JC	Joe Carter	10.00
NF	Nellie Fox	15.00
RG	Ron Guidry	10.00
TK	Ted Kluszewski	15.00
BL	Bob Lemon	10.00
ML	Mickey Lolich	10.00
EM	Eddie Mathews	20.00
SM	Sam McDowell	8.00
JP	Jim Palmer	10.00
DP	Dave Parker	10.00
HS	Herb Score	10.00
DS	Duke Snider	20.00
WS	Warren Spahn	15.00

2002 Topps Archives Reserve

HANK Aaron MILWAUKEE BRAVES OUTFIELD

		NM/M
Complete Set (100):		100.00
Common Player:		.75
Box (10 Packs + Auto. Baseball):		125.00
1	Lee Smith	.75
2	Gaylord Perry	.75
3	Al Oliver	.75
4	Rich "Goose" Gossage	.75
5	Bill Madlock	.75
6	Rod Carew	1.50
7	Fred Lynn	.75
8	Frank Robinson	2.00
9	Al Kaline	2.50
10	Len Dykstra	.75
11	Carlton Fisk	1.50
12	Nellie Fox	1.00
13	Reggie Jackson	3.00
14	Bob Gibson	2.00
15	Bill Buckner	.75
16	Harmon Killebrew	2.00
17	Gary Carter	1.50
18	Dave Winfield	1.50
19	Ozzie Smith	2.50
20	Dwight Evans	.75
21	Dave Concepcion	.75
22	Joe Morgan	1.00
23	Clete Boyer	.75
24	Will Clark	1.50
25	Lee May	.75
26	Kevin Mitchell	.75
27	Roger Maris	3.00
28	Mickey Lolich	.75
29	Luis Aparicio	.75
30	George Foster	.75
31	Don Mattingly	6.00
32	Fernando Valenzuela	.75
33	Bobby Bonds	.75
34	Jim Palmer	1.50
35	Dennis Eckersley	1.00
36	Kirby Puckett	3.00
37	Jose Cruz	.75
38	Richie Ashburn	.75
39	Whitey Ford	2.00
40	Robin Roberts	.75
41	Don Newcombe	.75
42	Roy Campanella	2.50
43	Dennis Martinez	.75
44	Larry Doby	1.00
45	Steve Garvey	.75
46	Thurman Munson	3.00
47	Dale Murphy	1.50
48	Bill "Moose" Skowron	.75
49	Tom Seaver	3.00
50	Orlando Cepeda	.75
51	Graig Nettles	.75
52	Willie Stargell	1.50
53	Yogi Berra	2.50
54	Steve Carlton	1.50
55	Don Sutton	.75
56	Brooks Robinson	1.50
57	Vida Blue	.75
58	Rollie Fingers	1.00
59	Jim Bunning	.75
60	Nolan Ryan	8.00
61	Hank Aaron	6.00
62	Fergie Jenkins	.75
63	Andre Dawson	1.00
64	Ernie Banks	2.50
65	Early Wynn	.75
66	Duke Snider	1.50
67	Red Schoendienst	.75
68	Don Drysdale	1.00
69	Jim "Catfish" Hunter	1.00
70	George Brett	6.00
71	Elston Howard	1.00
72	Wade Boggs	1.50
73	Keith Hernandez	.75
74	Billy Pierce	.75
75	Ted Kluszewski	.75
76	Carl Yastrzemski	4.00
77	Bert Blyleven	.75
78	Tony Oliva	.75
79	Joe Carter	.75
80	Johnny Bench	3.00
81	Tony Gwynn	3.00
82	Mike Schmidt	4.00
83	Phil Niekro	.75
84	Juan Marichal	.75
85	Eddie Mathews	2.50
86	Boog Powell	.75
87	Dwight Gooden	.75
88	Darryl Strawberry	.75
89	Roberto Clemente	6.00
90	Ryne Sandberg	5.00
91	Jack Clark	.75
92	Willie Mays	6.00
93	Ron Guidry	.75
94	Kirk Gibson	.75
95	Lou Brock	1.00
96	Robin Yount	2.50
97	Bill Mazeroski	.75
98	Dave Parker	.75
99	Hoyt Wilhelm	.75
100	Warren Spahn	1.50

Autographed Baseballs

	NM/M
Common Auto. Ball:	15.00
Inserted 1:Box	
Luis Aparicio/1,600	25.00
Ernie Banks/50	75.00
Yogi Berra/100	85.00
Lou Brock/400	40.00
Jim Bunning/500	35.00
Gary Carter/500	40.00
Rich Gossage/500	20.00
Fergie Jenkins/ 1,000	20.00
Al Kaline/250	75.00
Harmon Killebrew/ 250	60.00
Joe Morgan/250	40.00
Graig Nettles/1,600	15.00
Jim Palmer/400	25.00
Gaylord Perry/500	15.00
Brooks Robinson/ 500	40.00
Mike Schmidt/250	125.00
Duke Snider/100	65.00
Dave Winfield/ 1,650	30.00
Robin Yount/250	90.00

Best Years Autographs

		NM/M
Common Autograph:		12.00
Inserted 1:15 Hobby		
LA	Luis Aparicio	15.00
EB	Ernie Banks	70.00
YB	Yogi Berra	60.00
LB	Lou Brock	25.00
GC	Gary Carter	20.00
FJ	Fergie Jenkins	12.00

AK	Al Kaline	40.00
HK	Harmon Killebrew	40.00
WM	Willie Mays	120.00
JM	Joe Morgan	25.00
GN	Graig Nettles	12.00
GP	Gaylord Perry	15.00
BR	Brooks Robinson	25.00
MS	Mike Schmidt	125.00
LS	Lee Smith	12.00
DS	Duke Snider	60.00
RY	Robin Yount	80.00

Best Years Game-Worn Uniform

		NM/M
Common Player:		10.00
Inserted 1:7 Hobby		
EB	Ernie Banks	25.00
JBU	Johnny Bench	15.00
WBJ	Wade Boggs	10.00
GCJ	Gary Carter	12.00
WC	Will Clark	15.00
NF	Nellie Fox	15.00
TG	Tony Gwynn	15.00
JM	Juan Marichal	12.00
WM	Willie Mays	35.00
KPJ	Kirby Puckett	15.00
BR	Brooks Robinson	12.00
NR	Nolan Ryan	30.00
RSJ	Red Schoendienst	10.00
WS	Willie Stargell	15.00
RYU	Robin Yount	12.00

Best Years Game-Used Bat

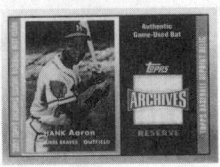

		NM/M
Common Player:		10.00
Inserted 1:22		
HAB	Hank Aaron	40.00
GBB	George Brett	25.00
OC	Orlando Cepeda	10.00
CF	Carlton Fisk	10.00
RM	Roger Maris	70.00
EMB	Eddie Mathews	20.00
DMB	Don Mattingly	30.00
TM	Thurman Munson	30.00
DW	Dave Winfield	10.00
CYB	Carl Yastrzemski	25.00

Team Topps Legends Autographs

	NM/M
Common Player:	
Rich "Goose" Gossage	10.00
Graig Nettles	10.00

Jim Palmer	15.00
Gaylord Perry	15.00

2002 Topps Chrome

TODD HELTON

		NM/M
Complete Set (685):		200.00
Common Player:		.25
Pack (4):		2.00
Box (24):		40.00
1	Pedro Martinez	1.25
2	Mike Stanton	.25
3	Brad Penny	.25
4	Mike Matheny	.25
5	Johnny Damon	.40
6	Bret Boone	.40
7	Retired # not issued	.25
8	Chris Truby	.25
9	B.J. Surhoff	.25
10	Mike Hampton	.40
11	Juan Pierre	.25
12	Mark Buehrle	.25
13	Bob Abreu	.50
14	David Cone	.25
15	Aaron Sele	.25
16	Fernando Tatis	.25
17	Bobby Jones	.25
18	Rick Helling	.25
19	Dmitri Young	.25
20	Mike Mussina	1.00
21	Mike Sweeney	.25
22	Cristian Guzman	.25
23	Ryan Kohlmeier	.25
24	Adam Kennedy	.25
25	Larry Walker	.50
26	Eric Davis	.40
27	Jason Tyner	.25
28	Eric Young	.25
29	Jason Marquis	.25
30	Luis Gonzalez	.50
31	Kevin Tapani	.25
32	Orlando Cabrera	.25
33	Marty Cordova	.25
34	Brad Ausmus	.25
35	Livan Hernandez	.25
36	Alex Gonzalez	.25
37	Edgar Renteria	.50
38	Bengie Molina	.25
39	Frank Menechino	.25
40	Rafael Palmeiro	1.00
41	Brad Fullmer	.25
42	Julio Zuleta	.25
43	Darren Dreifort	.25
44	Trot Nixon	.50
45	Trevor Hoffman	.25
46	Vladimir Nunez	.25
47	Mark Kotsay	.25
48	Kenny Rogers	.25
49	Ben Petrick	.25
50	Jeff Bagwell	1.00
51	Juan Encarnacion	.25
52	Ramiro Mendoza	.25

#	Player	Price	#	Player	Price	#	Player	Price	#	Player	Price
53	Brian Meadows	.25	157	Carl Everett	.25	261	Wes Helms	.25	399	Ryan Dempster	.25
54	Chad Curtis	.25	158	Scott Sullivan	.25	262	Jay Bell	.25	400	Curt Schilling	.75
55	Aramis Ramirez	.50	159	Deivi Cruz	.25	263	Mike Cameron	.25	401	Peter Bergeron	.25
56	Mark McLemore	.25	160	Albert Pujols	3.00	264	Paul Konerko	.25	402	Kyle Lohse	.25
57	Dante Bichette	.25	161	Royce Clayton	.25	265	Jeff Kent	.50	403	Craig Wilson	.25
58	Scott Schoeneweis	.25	162	Jeff Suppan	.25	266	Robert Fick	.25	404	David Justice	.75
59	Jose Cruz	.25	163	C.C. Sabathia	.25	267	Allen Levrault	.25	405	Darin Erstad	.50
60	Roger Clemens	3.00	164	Jimmy Rollins	.50	268	Placido Polanco	.25	406	Jose Mercedes	.25
61	Jose Guillen	.25	165	Rickey Henderson	.50	269	Marlon Anderson	.25	407	Carl Pavano	.25
62	Darren Oliver	.25	166	Rey Ordonez	.25	270	Mariano Rivera	.50	408	Albie Lopez	.25
63	Chris Reitsma	.25	167	Shawn Estes	.25	271	Chan Ho Park	.25	409	Alex Ochoa	.25
64	Jeff Abbott	.25	168	Reggie Sanders	.25	272	Jose Vizcaino	.25	410	Chipper Jones	1.50
65	Robin Ventura	.25	169	Jon Lieber	.25	273	Jeff D'Amico	.25	411	Tyler Houston	.25
66	Denny Neagle	.25	170	Armando Benitez	.25	274	Mark Gardner	.25	412	Dean Palmer	.25
67	Al Martin	.25	171	Mike Remlinger	.25	275	Travis Fryman	.25	413	Damian Jackson	.25
68	Benito Santiago	.25	172	Billy Wagner	.25	276	Darren Lewis	.25	414	Josh Towers	.25
69	Roy Oswalt	.50	173	Troy Percival	.25	277	Bruce Bochy	.25	415	Rafael Furcal	.50
70	Juan Gonzalez	1.00	174	Devon White	.25	278	Jerry Manuel	.25	416	Mike Morgan	.25
71	Garret Anderson	.75	175	Ivan Rodriguez	1.00	279	Bob Brenly	.25	417	Herb Perry	.25
72	Bobby Bonilla	.25	176	Dustin Hermanson	.25	280	Don Baylor	.25	418	Mike Sirotka	.25
73	Danny Bautista	.25	177	Brian Anderson	.25	281	Davey Lopes	.25	419	Mark Wohlers	.25
74	J.T. Snow	.25	178	Graeme Lloyd	.25	282	Jerry Narron	.25	420	Nomar Garciaparra	2.50
75	Derek Jeter	4.00	179	Russell Branyan	.25	283	Tony Muser	.25	421	Felipe Lopez	.25
76	John Olerud	.50	180	Bobby Higginson	.25	284	Hal McRae	.25	422	Joe McEwing	.25
77	Kevin Appier	.25	181	Alex Gonzalez	.25	285	Bobby Cox	.25	423	Jacque Jones	.25
78	Phil Nevin	.25	182	John Franco	.25	286	Larry Dierker	.25	424	Julio Franco	.25
79	Sean Casey	.50	183	Sidney Ponson	.25	287	Phil Garner	.25	425	Frank Thomas	1.00
80	Troy Glaus	.75	184	Jose Mesa	.25	288	Jimy Williams	.25	426	Kent Bottenfield	.25
81	Joe Randa	.25	185	Todd Hollandsworth	.25	289	Bobby Valentine	.25	427	Mac Suzuki	.25
82	Jose Valentin	.25	186	Kevin Young	.25	290	Dusty Baker	.25	428	D'Angelo Jimenez	.25
83	Ricky Bottalico	.25	187	Tim Wakefield	.25	291	Lloyd McLendon	.25	429	Chris Stynes	.25
84	Todd Zeile	.25	188	Craig Biggio	.50	292	Mike Scioscia	.25	430	Kerry Wood	1.50
85	Barry Larkin	.75	189	Jason Isringhausen	.25	293	Buck Martinez	.25	431	Chris Singleton	.25
86	Bob Wickman	.25	190	Mark Quinn	.25	294	Larry Bowa	.25	432	Erubiel Durazo	.25
87	Jeff Shaw	.25	191	Glendon Rusch	.25	295	Tony LaRussa	.25	433	Matt Lawton	.25
88	Greg Vaughn	.25	192	Damian Miller	.25	296	Jeff Torborg	.25	434	Bill Mueller	.25
89	Fernando Vina	.25	193	Sandy Alomar	.25	297	Tom Kelly	.25	435	Jose Canseco	.50
90	Mark Mulder	.50	194	Scott Brosius	.25	298	Mike Hargrove	.25	436	Ben Grieve	.25
91	Paul Bako	.25	195	Dave Martinez	.25	299	Art Howe	.25	437	Terry Mulholland	.25
92	Aaron Boone	.25	196	Danny Graves	.25	300	Lou Piniella	.25	438	David Bell	.25
93	Esteban Loaiza	.25	197	Shea Hillenbrand	.25	301	Charlie Manuel	.25	439	A.J. Pierzynski	.25
94	Richie Sexson	.75	198	Jimmy Anderson	.25	302	Buddy Bell	.25	440	Adam Dunn	1.00
95	Alfonso Soriano	1.00	199	Travis Lee	.25	303	Tony Perez	.25	441	Jon Garland	.25
96	Tony Womack	.25	200	Randy Johnson	1.50	304	Bob Boone	.25	442	Jeff Fassero	.25
97	Paul Shuey	.25	201	Carlos Beltran	.50	305	Joe Torre	.25	443	Julio Lugo	.25
98	Melvin Mora	.25	202	Jerry Hairston Jr.	.25	306	Jim Tracy	.25	444	Carlos Guillen	.25
99	Tony Gwynn	1.50	203	Jesus Sanchez	.25	307	Jason Lane	1.00	445	Orlando Hernandez	.25
100	Vladimir Guerrero	1.50	204	Eddie Taubensee	.25	308	Chris George	.25	446	Mark Loretta	.25
101	Keith Osik	.25	205	David Wells	.25	309	Hank Blalock	2.00	447	Scott Spiezio	.25
102	Randy Velarde	.25	206	Russ Davis	.25	310	Joe Borchard	.25	448	Kevin Millwood	.50
103	Scott Williamson	.25	207	Michael Barrett	.25	311	Marlon Byrd	.50	449	Jamie Moyer	.25
104	Daryle Ward	.25	208	Marquis Grissom	.25	312	Raymond Cabrera RC	1.00	450	Todd Helton	1.00
105	Doug Mientkiewicz	.25	209	Byung-Hyun Kim	.25	313	Freddy Sanchez RC	4.00	451	Todd Walker	.25
106	Stan Javier	.25	210	Hideo Nomo	.75	314	Scott Wiggins RC	1.00	452	Jose Lima	.25
107	Russ Ortiz	.25	211	Ryan Rupe	.25	315	Jason Maule RC	1.00	453	Brook Fordyce	.25
108	Wade Miller	.25	212	Ricky Gutierrez	.25	316	Dionys Cesar RC	1.50	454	Aaron Rowand	.25
109	Luke Prokopec	.25	213	Darryl Kile	.25	317	Boof Bonser	.25	455	Barry Zito	.50
110	Andruw Jones	1.00	214	Rico Brogna	.25	318	Juan Tolentino RC	1.50	456	Eric Owens	.25
111	Ron Coomer	.25	215	Terrence Long	.25	319	Earl Snyder RC	1.50	457	Charles Nagy	.25
112	Dan Wilson	.25	216	Mike Jackson	.25	320	Travis Wade RC	1.50	458	Raul Ibanez	.25
113	Luis Castillo	.25	217	Jamey Wright	.25	321	Napoleon Calzado RC	1.50	459	Joe Mays	.25
114	Derek Bell	.25	218	Adrian Beltre	.50	322	Eric Glaser RC	1.50	460	Jim Thome	1.50
115	Gary Sheffield	.75	219	Benny Agbayani	.25	323	Craig Kuzmic RC	1.50	461	Adam Eaton	.25
116	Ruben Rivera	.25	220	Chuck Knoblauch	.25	324	Nic Jackson RC	1.50	462	Felix Martinez	.25
117	Paul O'Neill	.50	221	Randy Wolf	.25	325	Mike Rivera	.25	463	Vernon Wells	.25
118	Craig Paquette	.25	222	Andy Ashby	.25	326	Jason Bay RC	8.00	464	Donnie Sadler	.25
119	Kelvim Escobar	.25	223	Corey Koskie	.25	327	Chris Smith	.25	465	Tony Clark	.25
120	Brad Radke	.25	224	Roger Cedeno	.25	328	Jake Gautreau	.25	466	Jose Hernandez	.25
121	Jorge Fabregas	.25	225	Ichiro Suzuki	3.00	329	Gabe Gross	.25	467	Ramon Martinez	.25
122	Randy Winn	.25	226	Keith Foulke	.25	330	Kenny Baugh	.25	468	Rusty Greer	.25
123	Tom Goodwin	.25	227	Ryan Minor	.25	331	J.D. Martin	.25	469	Rod Barajas	.25
124	Jaret Wright	.25	228	Shawon Dunston	.25	366	Pat Meares	.25	470	Lance Berkman	.75
125	Bonds-Race to 73	40.00	229	Alex Cora	.25	367	Mike Lieberthal	.25	471	Brady Anderson	.25
126	Al Leiter	.50	230	Jeromy Burnitz	.25	368	Scott Erickson	.25	472	Pedro Astacio	.25
127	Ben Davis	.25	231	Mark Grace	.75	369	Ron Gant	.25	473	Shane Halter	.25
128	Frank Catalanotto	.25	232	Aubrey Huff	.25	370	Moises Alou	.50	474	Bret Prinz	.25
129	Jose Cabrera	.25	233	Jeffrey Hammonds	.25	371	Chad Kreuter	.25	475	Edgar Martinez	.50
130	Magglio Ordonez	.50	234	Olmedo Saenz	.25	372	Willis Roberts	.25	476	Steve Trachsel	.25
131	Jose Macias	.25	235	Brian Jordan	.25	373	Toby Hall	.25	477	Gary Matthews Jr.	.25
132	Ted Lilly	.25	236	Jeremy Giambi	.25	374	Miguel Batista	.25	478	Ismael Valdes	.25
133	Chris Holt	.25	237	Joe Girardi	.25	375	John Burkett	.25	479	Juan Uribe	.25
134	Eric Milton	.25	238	Eric Gagne	.50	376	Cory Lidle	.25	480	Shawn Green	.75
135	Shannon Stewart	.25	239	Masato Yoshii	.25	377	Nick Neugebauer	.25	481	Kirk Rueter	.25
136	Omar Olivares	.25	240	Greg Maddux	2.00	378	Jay Payton	.25	482	Damion Easley	.25
137	David Segui	.25	241	Bryan Rekar	.25	379	Steve Karsay	.25	483	Chris Carpenter	.25
138	Jeff Nelson	.25	242	Ray Durham	.25	380	Eric Chavez	.50	484	Kris Benson	.25
139	Matt Williams	.25	243	Torii Hunter	.50	381	Kelly Stinnett	.25	485	Antonio Alfonseca	.25
140	Ellis Burks	.25	244	Derrek Lee	.50	382	Jarrod Washburn	.25	486	Kyle Farnsworth	.25
141	Jason Bere	.25	245	Jim Edmonds	.75	383	C.J. Nitkowski	.25	487	Brandon Lyon	.25
142	Jimmy Haynes	.25	246	Einar Diaz	.25	384	Jeff Conine	.25	488	Hideki Irabu	.25
143	Ramon Hernandez	.25	247	Brian Bohanon	.25	385	Fred McGriff	.50	489	David Ortiz	.50
144	Craig Counsell	.25	248	Ron Belliard	.25	386	Marvin Benard	.25	490	Mike Piazza	2.50
145	John Smoltz	.50	249	Mike Lowell	.50	387	Dave Burba	.25	491	Derek Lowe	.25
146	Homer Bush	.25	250	Sammy Sosa	2.50	388	Dennis Cook	.25	492	Chris Gomez	.25
147	Quilvio Veras	.25	251	Richard Hidalgo	.40	389	Rick Reed	.25	493	Mark Johnson	.25
148	Esteban Yan	.25	252	Bartolo Colon	.25	390	Tom Glavine	.75	494	John Rocker	.25
149	Ramon Ortiz	.25	253	Jorge Posada	.50	391	Rondell White	.25	495	Eric Karros	.25
150	Carlos Delgado	.75	254	LaTroy Hawkins	.25	392	Matt Morris	.50	496	Bill Haselman	.25
151	Lee Stevens	.25	255	Paul LoDuca	.25	393	Pat Rapp	.25	497	Dave Veres	.25
152	Wil Cordero	.25	256	Carlos Febles	.25	394	Robert Person	.25	498	Gil Heredia	.25
153	Mike Bordick	.25	257	Nelson Cruz	.25	395	Omar Vizquel	.40	499	Tomokazu Ohka	.25
154	John Flaherty	.25	258	Edgardo Alfonzo	.25	396	Jeff Cirillo	.25	500	Barry Bonds	4.00
155	Omar Daal	.25	259	Joey Hamilton	.25	397	Dave Mlicki	.25	501	David Dellucci	.25
156	Todd Ritchie	.25	260	Cliff Floyd	.25	398	Jose Ortiz	.25	502	Ed Sprague	.25

#	Player	Price
503	Tom Gordon	.25
504	Javier Vazquez	.25
505	Ben Sheets	.75
506	Wilton Guerrero	.25
507	John Halama	.25
508	Mark Redman	.25
509	Jack Wilson	.25
510	Bernie Williams	.75
511	Miguel Cairo	.25
512	Denny Hocking	.25
513	Tony Batista	.25
514	Mark Grudzielanek	.25
515	Jose Vidro	.25
516	Sterling Hitchcock	.25
517	Billy Koch	.25
518	Matt Clement	.25
519	Bruce Chen	.25
520	Roberto Alomar	1.00
521	Orlando Palmeiro	.25
522	Steve Finley	.25
523	Danny Patterson	.25
524	Terry Adams	.25
525	Tino Martinez	.25
526	Tony Armas Jr.	.25
527	Geoff Jenkins	.50
528	Chris Michalak	.25
529	Corey Patterson	.50
530	Brian Giles	.50
531	Jose Jimenez	.25
532	Joe Kennedy	.25
533	Armando Rios	.25
534	Osvaldo Fernandez	.25
535	Ruben Sierra	.25
536	Octavio Dotel	.25
537	Luis Sojo	.25
538	Brent Butler	.25
539	Pablo Ozuna	.25
540	Freddy Garcia	.25
541	Chad Durbin	.25
542	Orlando Merced	.25
543	Michael Tucker	.25
544	Roberto Hernandez	.25
545	Pat Burrell	.50
546	A.J. Burnett	.25
547	Bubba Trammell	.25
548	Scott Elarton	.25
549	Mike Darr	.25
550	Ken Griffey Jr.	2.00
551	Ugueth Urbina	.25
552	Todd Jones	.25
553	Delino DeShields	.25
554	Adam Piatt	.25
555	Jason Kendall	.25
556	Hector Ortiz	.25
557	Turk Wendell	.25
558	Rob Bell	.25
559	Sun-Woo Kim	.25
560	Raul Mondesi	.50
561	Brent Abernathy	.25
562	Seth Etherton	.25
563	Shawn Wooten	.25
564	Jay Buhner	.25
565	Andres Galarraga	.50
566	Shane Reynolds	.25
567	Rod Beck	.25
568	Dee Brown	.25
569	Pedro Feliz	.25
570	Ryan Klesko	.25
571	John Vander Wal	.25
572	Nick Bierbrodt	.25
573	Joe Nathan	.25
574	James Baldwin	.25
575	J.D. Drew	.75
576	Greg Colbrunn	.25
577	Doug Glanville	.25
578	Rey Sanchez	.25
579	Todd Van Poppel	.25
580	Rich Aurilia	.25
581	Chuck Finley	.25
582	Abraham Nunez	.25
583	Kenny Lofton	.50
584	Brian Daubach	.25
585	Miguel Tejada	.75
586	Nate Cornejo	.25
587	Kazuhiro Sasaki	.50
588	Chris Richard	.25
589	Armando Reynoso	.25
590	Tim Hudson	.75
591	Neifi Perez	.25
592	Steve Cox	.25
593	Henry Blanco	.25
594	Ricky Ledee	.25
595	Tim Salmon	.50
596	Luis Rivas	.25
597	Jeff Zimmerman	.25
598	Matt Stairs	.25
599	Preston Wilson	.25
600	Mark McGwire	4.00
601	Timo Perez	.25
602	Matt Anderson	.25
603	Todd Hundley	.25
604	Rick Ankiel	.75
605	Tsuyoshi Shinjo	.25
606	Woody Williams	.25
607	Jason LaRue	.25
608	Carlos Lee	.25
609	Russ Johnson	.25
610	Scott Rolen	1.50
611	Brent Mayne	.25
612	Darrin Fletcher	.25
613	Ray Lankford	.25
614	Troy O'Leary	.25
615	Javier Lopez	.50
616	Randy Velarde	.25
617	Vinny Castilla	.25
618	Milton Bradley	.25
619	Ruben Mateo	.25
620	Jason Giambi	1.00
621	Andy Benes	.25
622	Joe Mauer RC	12.00
623	Andy Pettitte	.75
624	Jose Offerman	.25
625	Mo Vaughn	.50
626	Steve Sparks	.25
627	Mike Matthews	.25
628	Robb Nen	.25
629	Kip Wells	.25
630	Kevin Brown	.50
631	Arthur Rhodes	.25
632	Gabe Kapler	.25
633	Jermaine Dye	.25
634	Josh Beckett	.75
635	Pokey Reese	.25
636	Benji Gil	.25
637	Marcus Giles	.25
638	Julian Tavarez	.25
639	Jason Schmidt	.50
640	Alex Rodriguez	3.00
641	Anaheim Angels	.25
642	Arizona Diamondbacks	.25
643	Atlanta Braves	.25
644	Baltimore Orioles	.25
645	Boston Red Sox	.25
646	Chicago Cubs	.25
647	Chicago White Sox	.25
648	Cincinnati Reds	.25
649	Cleveland Indians	.25
650	Colorado Rockies	.25
651	Detroit Tigers	.25
652	Florida Marlins	.25
653	Houston Astros	.25
654	Kansas City Royals	.25
655	Los Angeles Dodgers	.25
656	Milwaukee Brewers	.25
657	Minnesota Twins	.25
658	Montreal Expos	.25
659	New York Mets	.25
660	New York Yankees	1.00
661	Oakland Athletics	.25
662	Philadelphia Phillies	.25
663	Pittsburgh Pirates	.25
664	San Diego Padres	.25
665	San Francisco Giants	.25
666	Seattle Mariners	.25
667	St. Louis Cardinals	.25
668	Tampa Bay Devil Rays	.25
669	Texas Rangers	.25
670	Toronto Blue Jays	.25
671	Juan Cruz	.25
672	Kevin Cash RC	1.00
673	Jimmy Gobble RC	3.00
674	Mike Hill RC	.75
675	Taylor Buchholz RC	.75
676	Bill Hall	.75
677	Brett Roneberg RC	.75
678	Royce Huffman RC	.75
679	Chris Tritle RC	1.00
680	Nate Espy RC	.50
681	Nick Alvarez RC	1.00
682	Jason Botts RC	1.50
683	Ryan Gripp RC	.75
684	Dan Phillips RC	.50
685	Pablo Arias RC	.75
686	John Rodriguez RC	.75
687	Rich Harden RC	10.00
688	Neal Frendling RC	1.00
689	Rich Thompson RC	.50
690	Greg Montalbano RC	1.00
691	Leonard Dinardo RC	.75
692	Ryan Raburn RC	.50
693	Josh Barfield RC	5.00
694	David Bacani RC	.75
695	Dan Johnson RC	2.00
696	Mike Mussina	.50
697	Ivan Rodriguez	.50
698	Doug Mientkiewicz	.25
699	Roberto Alomar	.50
700	Eric Chavez	.25
701	Omar Vizquel	.25
702	Mike Cameron	.25
703	Torii Hunter	.25
704	Ichiro Suzuki	1.50
705	Greg Maddux	1.00
706	Brad Ausmus	.25
707	Todd Helton	.75
708	Fernando Vina	.25
709	Scott Rolen	.75
710	Orlando Cabrera	.25
711	Andruw Jones	.50
712	Jim Edmonds	.25
713	Larry Walker	.25
714	Roger Clemens	1.50
715	Randy Johnson	.75
716	Ichiro Suzuki	1.50
717	Barry Bonds	2.00
718	Ichiro Suzuki	1.50
719	Albert Pujols	1.50

Black Refractor

Stars: 5-10X
Production 50 Sets

Gold Refractor

Stars: 2-4X
Inserted 1:4

Aces

		NM/M
Common Player:		10.00
KB	Kevin Brown	10.00
TH	Tim Hudson	10.00
AL	Al Leiter	10.00
CS	Curt Schilling	15.00
BZ	Barry Zito	10.00

Batterymates

		NM/M
Inserted 1:349		
GL	Tom Glavine, Javy Lopez	20.00
HP	Mike Hampton, Ben Petrick	10.00

Deuces Are Wild

		NM/M
Common Card:		
Inserted 1:428		
CA	Andruw Jones, Chipper Jones	40.00
BT	Bernie Williams, Tino Martinez	25.00
RC	Ryan Dempster, Cliff Floyd	10.00

Jack of All Trades

		NM/M
Common Player:		10.00
CJ	Chipper Jones	20.00
MO	Magglio Ordonez	10.00
AR	Alex Rodriguez	25.00

Kings of the Clubhouse

		NM/M
Common Player:		15.00
JB	Jeff Bagwell	15.00
TG	Tony Gwynn	20.00
AR	Alex Rodriguez	25.00

Like Father, Like Son Relics

		NM/M
Inserted 1:790		
WI	Preston Wilson, Mookie Wilson	10.00

Top Of The Order

		NM/M
Common Player:		8.00
Inserted 1:106		
BA	Benny Agbayani/Jsy	8.00
PB	Peter Bergeron/Jsy	8.00
CB	Craig Biggio/Jsy	15.00
JD	Johnny Damon/Bat	10.00
RF	Rafael Furcal/Bat	10.00
RH	Rickey Henderson/Bat	20.00
JK	Jason Kendall/Bat	10.00
CK	Chuck Knoblauch/Bat	8.00
PL	Paul LoDuca/Bat	10.00
KL	Kenny Lofton/Jsy	10.00
JP	Juan Pierre/Bat	10.00
SS	Shannon Stewart/Jsy	10.00

Three of a Kind

		NM/M
Common Card		
AIR	Alex Rodriguez, Ivan Rodriguez, Rafael Palmeiro	50.00
BEJ	Bret Boone, Edgar Martinez, John Olerud	25.00
JCL	Jeff Bagwell, Craig Biggio, Lance Berkman	40.00

1952 Player Reprints

		NM/M
Complete Set (19):		50.00
Common Card:		3.00
Inserted 1:8		
Refractors:		2X
Inserted 1:24		
52R-1	Roy Campanella	4.00
52R-2	Duke Snider	4.00
52R-3	Carl Erskine	3.00
52R-4	Andy Pafko	3.00
52R-5	Johnny Mize	3.00
52R-6	Billy Martin	4.00
52R-7	Phil Rizzuto	4.00
52R-8	Gil McDougald	3.00
52R-9	Allie Reynolds	3.00
52R-10	Jackie Robinson	5.00
52R-11	Preacher Roe	3.00
52R-12	Gil Hodges	3.00
52R-13	Billy Cox	3.00
52R-14	Yogi Berra	4.00
52R-15	Gene Woodling	3.00
52R-16	Johnny Sain	3.00
52R-17	Ralph Houk	3.00
52R-18	Joe Collins	3.00
52R-19	Hank Bauer	3.00

2002 Topps Gallery

		NM/M
Complete Set (200):		60.00
Common Player:		.25
Common (151-200):		.75
Inserted 1:1		
Pack (6):		1.50
Box (24):		30.00
1	Jason Giambi	.50
2	Mark Grace	.40
3	Bret Boone	.40
4	Antonio Alfonseca	.25
5	Kevin Brown	.40
6	Cristian Guzman	.25
7	Magglio Ordonez	.40
8	Luis Gonzalez	.40

9	Jorge Posada	.40
10	Roberto Alomar	.50
11	Mike Sweeney	.25
12	Jeff Kent	.40
13	Matt Morris	.40
14	Alfonso Soriano	.75
15	Adam Dunn	.50
16	Neifi Perez	.25
17	Todd Walker	.25
18	J.D. Drew	.40
19	Eric Chavez	.40
20	Alex Rodriguez	1.50
21	Ray Lankford	.25
22	Roger Cedeno	.25
23	Chipper Jones	.75
24	Jose Canseco	.75
25	Mike Piazza	1.50
26	Freddy Garcia	.25
27	Todd Helton	.50
28	Tino Martinez	.40
29	Kazuhiro Sasaki	.25
30	Curt Schilling	.50
31	Mark Buehrle	.25
32	John Olerud	.40
33	Brad Radke	.25
34	Steve Sparks	.25
35	Jason Tyner	.25
36	Jeff Shaw	.25
37	Mariano Rivera	.40
38	Russ Ortiz	.25
39	Richard Hidalgo	.25
40	Barry Bonds	2.00
41	John Burkett	.25
42	Tim Hudson	.40
43	Mike Hampton	.25
44	Orlando Cabrera	.25
45	Barry Zito	.40
46	C.C. Sabathia	.25
47	Chan Ho Park	.40
48	Tom Glavine	.50
49	Aramis Ramirez	.40
50	Lance Berkman	.40
51	Al Leiter	.25
52	Phil Nevin	.25
53	Javier Vazquez	.25
54	Troy Glaus	.40
55	Tsuyoshi Shinjo	.40
56	Albert Pujols	1.50
57	John Smoltz	.40
58	Derek Jeter	2.00
59	Robb Nen	.25
60	Jason Kendall	.25
61	Eric Gagne	.50
62	Vladimir Guerrero	.75
63	Corey Patterson	.40
64	Rickey Henderson	.50
65	Jack Wilson	.25
66	Jason LaRue	.25
67	Sammy Sosa	1.50
68	Ken Griffey Jr.	1.00
69	Randy Johnson	.75
70	Nomar Garciaparra	1.50
71	Ivan Rodriguez	.50
72	J.T. Snow	.25
73	Darryl Kile	.25
74	Andruw Jones	.50
75	Brian Giles	.25
76	Pedro Martinez	.75
77	Jeff Bagwell	.50
78	Rafael Palmeiro	.50
79	Ryan Dempster	.25
80	Jeff Cirillo	.25
81	Geoff Jenkins	.40
82	Brandon Duckworth	.25
83	Roger Clemens	1.50
84	Fred McGriff	.50
85	Hideo Nomo	.50
86	Larry Walker	.40
87	Sean Casey	.40
88	Trevor Hoffman	.25
89	Robert Fick	.25
90	Armando Benitez	.25
91	Jeromy Burnitz	.25
92	Bernie Williams	.50
93	Carlos Delgado	.50
94	Troy Percival	.25
95	Nate Cornejo	.25
96	Derrek Lee	.40
97	Jose Ortiz	.25
98	Brian Jordan	.25

99	Jose Cruz	.25
100	Ichiro Suzuki	1.50
101	Jose Mesa	.25
102	Tim Salmon	.40
103	Bud Smith	.25
104	Paul LoDuca	.25
105	Juan Pierre	.25
106	Ben Grieve	.25
107	Russell Branyan	.25
108	Bobby Abreu	.40
109	Moises Alou	.40
110	Richie Sexson	.50
111	Jerry Hairston Jr.	.25
112	Marlon Anderson	.25
113	Juan Gonzalez	.50
114	Craig Biggio	.40
115	Carlos Beltran	.50
116	Eric Milton	.25
117	Cliff Floyd	.25
118	Rich Aurilia	.25
119	Adrian Beltre	.40
120	Jason Bere	.25
121	Darin Erstad	.40
122	Ben Sheets	.40
123	Johnny Damon	.40
124	Jimmy Rollins	.40
125	Shawn Green	.40
126	Greg Maddux	1.00
127	Mark Mulder	.40
128	Bartolo Colon	.25
129	Shannon Stewart	.25
130	Ramon Ortiz	.25
131	Kerry Wood	.75
132	Ryan Klesko	.25
133	Preston Wilson	.25
134	Roy Oswalt	.40
135	Rafael Furcal	.25
136	Eric Karros	.25
137	Nick Neugebauer	.25
138	Doug Mientkiewicz	.25
139	Paul Konerko	.40
140	Bobby Higginson	.25
141	Garret Anderson	.40
142	Wes Helms	.25
143	Brent Abernathy	.25
144	Scott Rolen	.75
145	Dmitri Young	.25
146	Jim Thome	.75
147	Raul Mondesi	.25
148	Pat Burrell	.40
149	Gary Sheffield	.40
150	Miguel Tejada	.40
151	Brandon Inge	.75
152	Carlos Pena	.75
153	Jason Lane	.75
154	Nathan Haynes	.75
155	Hank Blalock	1.50
156	Juan Cruz	.75
157	Morgan Ensberg	.75
158	Sean Burroughs	.75
159	Ed Rogers	.75
160	Nick Johnson	.75
161	Orlando Hudson	.75
162	Anastacio Martinez RC	.75
163	Jeremy Affeldt	.75
164	Brandon Claussen	.75
165	Deivis Santos	.75
166	Mike Rivera	.75
167	Carlos Silva	.75
168	Valentino Pascucci	.75
169	Xavier Nady	.75
170	David Espinosa	.75
171	Dan Phillips RC	.75
172	Tony Fontana RC	.75
173	Juan Silvestre	.75
174	Henry Pichardo RC	.75
175	Pablo Arias RC	.75
176	Brett Roneberg RC	.75
177	Chad Qualls RC	.75
178	Greg Sain RC	.75
179	Rene Reyes RC	.75
180	So Taguchi RC	2.00
181	Dan Johnson RC	2.50
182	Justin Backsmeyer RC	.75
183	Juan Gonzalez	.75
184	Jason Ellison RC	.75
185	Kazuhisa Ishii RC	3.00
186	Joe Mauer RC	8.00
187	James Shanks RC	.75
188	Kevin Cash RC	.75
189	J.J. Trujillo RC	.75
190	Jorge Padilla RC	1.00
191	Nolan Ryan	4.00
192	George Brett	3.00
193	Ryne Sandberg	2.00
194	Robin Yount	1.50
195	Tom Seaver	1.00
196	Mike Schmidt	2.00
197	Frank Robinson	1.00
198	Harmon Killebrew	1.00
199	Kirby Puckett	2.00
200	Don Mattingly	4.00

Press Plates

	NM/M
Common Player:	50.00

(See 2002 Topps Gallery for checklist.)

Autographs

		NM/M
Common Player:		8.00

Inserted 1:192

LB	Lance Berkman	30.00
BBO	Bret Boone	20.00
JD	J.D. Drew	25.00
LG	Luis Gonzalez	20.00
SG	Shawn Green	25.00
JL	Jason Lane	8.00
MO	Magglio Ordonez	20.00
JP	Jorge Posada	40.00
JS	Juan Silvestre	8.00

Heritage

	NM/M
Complete Set (25):	100.00
Common Player:	2.00

Inserted 1:12

RA	Roberto Alomar	4.00
BBO	Bret Boone	2.00
RC	Roger Clemens	8.00
JG	Jason Giambi	3.00
LG	Luis Gonzalez	2.00
SG	Shawn Green	3.00
KG	Ken Griffey Jr.	6.00
TG	Tony Gwynn	4.00
RJ	Reggie Jackson	4.00
CJ	Chipper Jones	4.00
AK	Al Kaline	4.00
GM	Greg Maddux	5.00
PM	Pedro Martinez	4.00
MM	Mark McGwire	10.00
SM	Stan Musial	5.00
MP	Mike Piazza	6.00
BR	Brooks Robinson	4.00
AR	Alex Rodriguez	8.00
NR	Nolan Ryan	10.00
MS	Mike Schmidt	6.00
TS	Tom Seaver	4.00
TSH	Tsuyoshi Shinjo	2.00
SS	Sammy Sosa	8.00
CY	Carl Yastrzemski	5.00
RY	Robin Yount	5.00

Heritage Autographs

	NM/M

Inserted 1:240

BBO	Bret Boone	20.00
LG	Luis Gonzalez	25.00
SG	Shawn Green	25.00

Heritage Relics

	NM/M
Common Player:	8.00

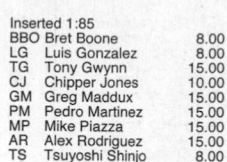

Inserted 1:85

BBO	Bret Boone	8.00
LG	Luis Gonzalez	8.00
TG	Tony Gwynn	15.00
CJ	Chipper Jones	10.00
GM	Greg Maddux	15.00
PM	Pedro Martinez	15.00
MP	Mike Piazza	15.00
AR	Alex Rodriguez	8.00
TS	Tsuyoshi Shinjo	8.00

Originals Relics

	NM/M
Common Player:	8.00

Inserted 1:169

BBO	Bret Boone	8.00
JC	Jose Canseco	10.00
CD	Carlos Delgado	8.00
JG	Juan Gonzalez	10.00
LG	Luis Gonzalez	8.00
TG	Tony Gwynn	15.00
TH	Todd Helton	12.00
AJ	Andruw Jones	8.00
CJ	Chipper Jones	10.00
TM	Tino Martinez	10.00
MP	Mike Piazza	20.00
AP	Albert Pujols	35.00
AR	Alex Rodriguez	15.00
AS	Alfonso Soriano	10.00
BW	Bernie Williams	10.00

Team Topps Legends
Autographs

	NM/M

Inserted 1:1,019

	Luis Aparicio	15.00
	Jim Bunning	20.00
	Fergie Jenkins	15.00
	Carl Yastrzemski	65.00

2002 Topps Gold Label

	NM/M
Complete Set (200):	60.00
Common Player:	.25
Pack (4):	3.00
Box (18):	40.00

1	Alex Rodriguez	1.50
2	Derek Jeter	2.00
3	Luis Gonzalez	.40
4	Troy Glaus	.40
5	Albert Pujols	1.50
6	Lance Berkman	.40
7	J.D. Drew	.40
8	Chipper Jones	.75
9	Miguel Tejada	.40
10	Randy Johnson	.75
11	Mike Cameron	.25
12	Brian Giles	.40
13	Roger Cedeno	.25
14	Kerry Wood	.75
15	Ken Griffey Jr.	1.00
16	Carlos Lee	.25
17	Todd Helton	.50
18	Gary Sheffield	.40
19	Richie Sexson	.40
20	Vladimir Guerrero	.75
21	Bobby Higginson	.25
22	Roger Clemens	1.50
23	Barry Zito	.40
24	Juan Pierre	.25

25	Pedro Martinez	.75
26	Sean Casey	.40
27	David Segui	.25
28	Jose Garcia	.25
29	Curt Schilling	.50
30	Bernie Williams	.40
31	Ben Grieve	.25
32	Hideo Nomo	.40
33	Aramis Ramirez	.40
34	Cristian Guzman	.25
35	Rich Aurilia	.25
36	Greg Maddux	1.00
37	Eric Chavez	.40
38	Shawn Green	.40
39	Luis Rivas	.25
40	Magglio Ordonez	.40
41	Jose Vidro	.25
42	Mariano Rivera	.40
43	Chris Tritle RC	.50
44	C.C. Sabathia	.25
45	Larry Walker	.40
46	Raul Mondesi	.25
47	Kevin Brown	.40
48	Jeff Bagwell	.50
49	Earl Snyder RC	.50
50	Jason Giambi	.50
51	Ichiro Suzuki	1.50
52	Andruw Jones	.50
53	Ivan Rodriguez	.50
54	Jim Edmonds	.40
55	Preston Wilson	.25
56	Greg Vaughn	.25
57	Jon Lieber	.25
58	Justin Sherrod RC	.50
59	Marcus Giles	.40
60	Roberto Alomar	.40
61	Pat Burrell	.40
62	Doug Mientkiewicz	.25
63	Mark Mulder	.40
64	Mike Hampton	.25
65	Adam Dunn	.50
66	Moises Alou	.40
67	Jose Cruz Jr.	.25
68	Derek Bell	.25
69	Sammy Sosa	1.50
70	Joe Mays	.25
71	Phil Nevin	.25
72	Edgardo Alfonzo	.25
73	Barry Bonds	2.00
74	Edgar Martinez	.40
75	Juan Encarnacion	.25
76	Jason Tyner	.25
77	Edgar Renteria	.40
78	Bret Boone	.40
79	Scott Rolen	.75
80	Nomar Garciaparra	1.50
81	Frank Thomas	.50
82	Roy Oswalt	.40
83	Tsuyoshi Shinjo	.40
84	Ben Sheets	.40
85	Hank Blalock	.40
86	Carlos Delgado	.50
87	Tim Hudson	.40
88	Alfonso Soriano	.75
89	Michael Hill RC	.75
90	Jim Thome	.75
91	Craig Biggio	.25
92	Ryan Klesko	.25
93	Geoff Jenkins	.40
94	Matt Morris	.40
95	Jorge Posada	.40
96	Cliff Floyd	.40
97	Jimmy Rollins	.40
98	Mike Sweeney	.25
99	Frank Catalanotto	.25
100	Mike Piazza	1.25
101	Mark Quinn	.25
102	Torii Hunter	.25
103	Lee Stevens	.25
104	Byung-Hyug Kim	.25
105	Freddy Sanchez RC	.50
106	David Cone	.25
107	Jerry Hairston Jr.	.25
108	Kyle Farnsworth	.25
109	Rafael Furcal	.25
110	Bartolo Colon	.25
111	Juan Rivera	.25
112	Kevin Young	.25
113	Chris Narveson RC	1.00
114	Richard Hidalgo	.25
115	Andy Pettitte	.40
116	Darin Erstad	.40
117	Corey Koskie	.25
118	Rickey Henderson	.50
119	Derrek Lee	.25
120	Sean Burroughs	.25
121	Paul Konerko	.25
122	Ross Peeples RC	.50
123	Terrence Long	.25
124	John Smoltz	.40
125	Brandon Duckworth	.25
126	Luis Maza	.25
127	Morgan Ensberg	.25
128	Eric Valent	.25
129	Shannon Stewart	.25
130	D'Angelo Jimenez	.25
131	Jeff Cirillo	.25
132	Jack Cust	.25
133	Dmitri Young	.25
134	Darryl Kile	.25
135	Reggie Sanders	.25
136	Marlon Byrd	.25
137	Napoleon Calzado RC	.50
138	Javy Lopez	.40
139	Orlando Cabrera	.25
140	Mike Mussina	.40
141	Josh Beckett	.40
142	Kazuhiro Sasaki	.25
143	Jermaine Dye	.25
144	Carlos Beltran	.40
145	Trevor Hoffman	.25
146	Kazuhisa Ishii RC	2.00
147	Alex Gonzalez	.25
148	Marty Cordova	.25
149	Kevin Deaton RC	.50
150	Toby Hall	.25
151	Rafael Palmeiro	.50
152	John Olerud	.40
153	David Eckstein	.25
154	Doug Glanville	.25
155	Johnny Damon	.40
156	Javier Vazquez	.25
157	Jason Bay RC	2.00
158	Robb Nen	.25
159	Rafael Soriano	.25
160	Placido Polanco	.25
161	Garret Anderson	.40
162	Aaron Boone	.25
163	Mike Lieberthal	.25
164	Joe Mauer RC	10.00
165	Matt Lawton	.25
166	Juan Tolentino RC	.50
167	Alex Gonzalez	.25
168	Steve Finley	.25
169	Troy Percival	.25
170	Bud Smith	.25
171	Freddie Garcia	.25
172	Ray Lankford	.25
173	Tim Redding	.25
174	Ryan Dempster	.25
175	Travis Lee	.25
176	Jeff Kent	.40
177	Ramon Hernandez	.25
178	Carl Everett	.25
179	Tom Glavine	.40
180	Juan Gonzalez	.50
181	Nick Johnson	.40
182	Mike Lowell	.40
183	Al Leiter	.25
184	Jason Maule RC	.50
185	Wilson Betemit	.25
186	Tino Martinez	.25
187	Jason Standridge	.25
188	Mike Peeples RC	.50
189	Jason Kendall	.40
190	Fred McGriff	.40
191	John Rodriguez RC	.50
192	Brett Roneberg RC	.50
193	Marlyn Tisdale RC	.50
194	J.T. Snow	.25
195	Craig Kuzmic RC	.75
196	Cory Lidle	.25
197	Alex Cintron	.25
198	Fernando Vina	.25
199	Austin Kearns	.50
200	Paul LoDuca	.25

Class One Gold

JUAN TOLENTINO 315/500

Stars: 2-4X
Production 500 Sets

Class Two Platinum

JUAN ENCARNACION 469/250

Stars: 4-8X
Production 250 Sets

Class Three Titanium

Stars: 6-10X
Production 100 Sets

Platinum Memorabilia

	NM/M
Platinum:	.75-1.5X
Titanium Memorabilia:	1-2X

All-Star MVP Winners

		NM/M
Common Player:		8.00
RA	Roberto Alomar	10.00
SA	Sandy Alomar	8.00
BLB	Bobby Bonds	8.00
DC	Dave Concepcion	8.00
SG2	Steve Garvey	10.00
KG	Ken Griffey Sr.	8.00
BM1	Bill Madlock	8.00
FM	Fred McGriff	10.00
DP3	Dave Parker	8.00
TP	Tony Perez	10.00
MP	Mike Piazza	15.00
KP2	Kirby Puckett	15.00
TR	Tim Raines	8.00

Batting Average

		NM/M
Common Player:		8.00
WB	Wade Boggs	15.00
BB	Bill Buckner	8.00
RC2	Rod Carew	15.00
RAC	Rico Carty	8.00
NC	Norm Cash	15.00
TG1	Tony Gwynn	15.00
TG2	Tony Gwynn	15.00
BM2	Bill Madlock	8.00
DP4	Dave Parker	8.00
KP3	Kirby Puckett	15.00
LW	Larry Walker	8.00
CY2	Carl Yastrzemski	30.00

Cy Young Winners

		NM/M
Common Player:		8.00
RWC	Roger Clemens	15.00
DE	Dennis Eckersley	8.00
RJ	Randy Johnson	12.00
BS	Bret Saberhagen	8.00
JS	John Smoltz	8.00

Home Run Champions

		NM/M
Common Player:		8.00
BB2	Barry Bonds	20.00
GF	George Foster	8.00
TK2	Ted Kluszewski	15.00
KM2	Kevin Mitchell	8.00
DM2	Dale Murphy	40.00
AR	Alex Rodriguez	15.00
DS1	Darryl Strawberry	10.00

League Championship MVP Winners

		NM/M
Common Player:		8.00
GB2	George Brett	40.00
WC	Will Clark	15.00
CC	Craig Counsell	8.00
RH	Rickey Henderson	15.00
JL	Javier Lopez	8.00
AEP	Andy Pettitte	12.00
KP1	Kirby Puckett	15.00
FW	Frank White	8.00
BFW	Bernie Williams	10.00

MLB Moments in Time

	NM/M
Common Player:	8.00

BLB	Barry Bonds	20.00
BB1	Bret Boone	8.00
BB2	Bret Boone	8.00
CD	Carlos Delgado	8.00
TG	Tony Gwynn	15.00
TH	Toby Hall	8.00
CL	Carlos Lee	8.00
JL	Javy Lopez	8.00
MO	Magglio Ordonez	10.00
RP1	Rafael Palmeiro	10.00
RP2	Rafael Palmeiro	10.00
AR	Alex Rodriguez	15.00

MVP Winners

		NM/M
Common Player:		8.00
EB	Ernie Banks	20.00
DB	Don Baylor	8.00
YB	Yogi Berra	15.00
BB1	Barry Bonds	20.00
GB1	George Brett	40.00
SG1	Steve Garvey	8.00
KHG	Kirk Gibson	8.00
KH	Keith Hernandez	10.00
RJ1	Reggie Jackson	15.00
DM	Don Mattingly	40.00
KM1	Kevin Mitchell	8.00
JM	Joe Morgan	8.00
DM1	Dale Murphy	40.00
DP1	Dave Parker	8.00
BR	Brooks Robinson	15.00
FR	Frank Robinson	12.00
RS	Ryne Sandberg	40.00
HS	Hank Sauer	8.00
WS	Willie Stargell	15.00
JT	Joe Torre	10.00
MW	Maury Wills	8.00
CY1	Carl Yastrzemski	30.00
RY	Robin Yount	20.00

Rookie of the Year Winners

		NM/M
Common Player:		8.00
DA	Dick Allen	15.00
AB	Al Bumbry	8.00
RC1	Rod Carew	15.00
CF	Carlton Fisk	15.00
MH	Mike Hargrove	8.00
DJ	Dave Justice	10.00
EM2	Eddie Murray	12.00
LP	Lou Piniella	10.00
AP	Albert Pujols	20.00
DS2	Darryl Strawberry	15.00
FV	Fernando Valenzuela	8.00
BW	Billy Williams	10.00

RBI Leaders

		NM/M
Common Player:		8.00
BRB	Bret Boone	8.00
BRB2	Bret Boone	8.00
GC	Gary Carter	8.00
GL	Greg Luzinski	8.00
EM1	Eddie Murray	12.00
AO	Al Oliver	8.00
DP2	Dave Parker	8.00
DW	Dave Winfield	12.00

World Series MVP Winners

		NM/M
Common Player:		8.00
JB	Johnny Bench	15.00
RCC	Ron Cey	8.00
RJ2	Reggie Jackson	15.00
PM	Paul Molitor	15.00
MR	Mariano Rivera	10.00

2002 Topps Heritage

	NM/M
Complete Set (440)	325.00
Common Player:	.25
Common (364-446)	3.00
Inserted 1:2	
Pack (8):	4.00
Box (24):	90.00
1 Ichiro Suzuki/SP	10.00
2 Darin Erstad	.50
3 Rod Beck	.25

KERRY WOOD
pitcher CHICAGO CUBS

#	Player	Value
4	Doug Mientkiewicz	.25
5	Mike Sweeney	.25
6	Roger Clemens	2.50
7	Jason Tyner	.25
8	Alex Gonzalez	.25
9	Eric Young	.25
10	Randy Johnson	1.50
10	Randy Johnson/SP	6.00
11	Aaron Sele	.25
12	Tony Clark	.25
13	C.C. Sabathia	.25
14	Melvin Mora	.25
15	Tim Hudson	.50
16	Ben Petrick	.25
17	Tom Glavine	.75
18	Jason Lane	.25
19	Larry Walker	.50
20	Mark Mulder	.50
21	Steve Finley	.25
22	Bengie Molina	.25
23	Rob Bell	.25
24	Nathan Haynes	.25
25	Rafael Furcal	.50
25	Rafael Furcal/SP	3.00
26	Mike Mussina	1.00
27	Paul LoDuca	.25
28	Torii Hunter	.50
29	Carlos Lee	.25
30	Jimmy Rollins	.50
31	Arthur Rhodes	.25
32	Ivan Rodriguez	1.00
33	Wes Helms	.25
34	Cliff Floyd	.25
35	Julian Tavarez	.25
36	Mark McGwire	4.00
37	Chipper Jones/SP	6.00
38	Denny Neagle	.25
39	Odalis Perez	.25
40	Antonio Alfonseca	.25
41	Edgar Renteria	.50
42	Troy Glaus	.75
43	Scott Brosius	.25
44	Abraham Nunez	.25
45	Jamey Wright	.25
46	Bobby Bonilla	.25
47	Ismael Valdes	.25
48	Chris Reitsma	.25
49	Neifi Perez	.25
50	Juan Cruz	.25
51	Kevin Brown	.50
52	Ben Grieve	.25
53	Alex Rodriguez/SP	10.00
54	Charles Nagy	.25
55	Reggie Sanders	.25
56	Nelson Figueroa	.25
57	Felipe Lopez	.25
58	Bill Ortega	.25
59	Mac Suzuki	.25
60	Johnny Estrada	.25
61	Bob Wickman	.25
62	Doug Glanville	.25
63	Jeff Cirillo	.25
63	Jeff Cirillo/SP	3.00
64	Corey Patterson	.50
65	Aaron Myette	.25
66	Magglio Ordonez	.50
67	Ellis Burks	.25
68	Miguel Tejada	.50
69	John Olerud	.50
69	John Olerud/SP	4.00
70	Greg Vaughn	.25
71	Andy Pettitte	.75
72	Mike Matheny	.25
73	Brandon Duckworth	.25
74	Scott Schoeneweis	.25
75	Mike Lowell	.50
76	Einar Diaz	.25
77	Tino Martinez	.50
78	Matt Williams	.25
79	Jason Young **RC**	1.00
80	Nate Cornejo	.25
81	Andres Galarraga	.40
82	Bernie Williams/SP	6.00
83	Ryan Klesko	.25
84	Dan Wilson	.25
85	Henry Pichardo **RC**	.50
86	Ray Durham	.25
87	Omar Daal	.25
88	Derrek Lee	.50
89	Al Leiter	.50
90	Darrin Fletcher	.25
91	Josh Beckett	.75
92	Johnny Damon	.25
92	Johnny Damon/SP	5.00
93	Abraham Nunez	.25
94	Ricky Ledee	.25
95	Richie Sexson	.75
96	Adam Kennedy	.25
97	Raul Mondesi	.25
98	John Burkett	.25
99	Ben Sheets	.50
99	Ben Sheets/SP	4.00
100	Preston Wilson	.25
100	Preston Wilson/SP	3.00
101	Boof Bonser	.25
102	Shigetoshi Hasegawa	.25
103	Carlos Febles	.25
104	Jorge Posada/SP	5.00
105	Michael Tucker	.25
106	Roberto Hernandez	.25
107	John Rodriguez **RC**	.75
108	Danny Graves	.25
109	Rich Aurilia	.25
110	Jon Lieber	.25
111	Tim Hummel **RC**	.50
112	J.T. Snow	.25
113	Kris Benson	.25
114	Derek Jeter	4.00
115	John Franco	.25
116	Matt Stairs	.25
117	Ben Davis	.25
118	Darryl Kile	.25
119	Mike Peeples **RC**	.50
120	Kevin Tapani	.25
121	Armando Benitez	.25
122	Damian Miller	.25
123	Jose Jimenez	.25
124	Pedro Astacio	.25
125	Marlyn Tisdale **RC**	.50
126	Deivi Cruz	.25
127	Paul O'Neill	.75
128	Jermaine Dye	.25
129	Marcus Giles	.25
130	Mark Loretta	.25
131	Garret Anderson	.50
132	Todd Ritchie	.25
133	Joe Crede	.25
134	Kevin Millwood	.50
135	Shane Reynolds	.25
136	Mark Grace	.75
137	Shannon Stewart	.25
138	Nick Neugebauer	.25
139	Nic Jackson **RC**	.75
140	Robb Nen	.25
141	Dmitri Young	.25
142	Kevin Appier	.25
143	Jack Cust	.25
144	Andres Torres	.25
145	Frank Thomas	1.00
146	Jason Kendall	.25
147	Greg Maddux	2.00
148	David Justice	.50
149	Hideo Nomo	.75
150	Bret Boone	.50
151	Wade Miller	.25
152	Jeff Kent	.50
153	Scott Williamson	.25
154	Julio Lugo	.25
155	Bobby Higginson	.25
156	Geoff Jenkins	.50
157	Darren Dreifort	.25
158	Freddy Sanchez **RC**	.75
159	Bud Smith	.25
160	Phil Nevin	.25
161	Cesar Izturis	.25
162	Sean Casey	.50
163	Jose Ortiz	.25
164	Brent Abernathy	.25
165	Kevin Young	.25
166	Daryle Ward	.25
167	Trevor Hoffman	.25
168	Rondell White	.25
169	Kip Wells	.25
170	John Vander Wal	.25
171	Jose Lima	.25
172	Wilton Guerrero	.25
173	Aaron Dean	.25
174	Rick Helling	.25
175	Juan Pierre	.25
176	Jay Bell	.25
177	Craig House	.25
178	David Bell	.25
179	Pat Burrell	.50
180	Eric Gagne	.75
181	Adam Pettyjohn	.25
182	Ugueth Urbina	.25
183	Peter Bergeron	.25
184	Adrian Gonzalez	.25
184	Adrian Gonzalez/SP	4.00
185	Damion Easley	.25
186	Gookie Dawkins	.25
187	Matt Lawton	.25
188	Frank Catalanotto	.25
189	David Wells	.25
190	Roger Cedeno	.25
191	Brian Giles	.50
192	Julio Zuleta	.25
193	Timo Perez	.25
194	Billy Wagner	.25
195	Craig Counsell	.25
196	Bart Miadich	.25
197	Gary Sheffield	.75
198	Richard Hidalgo	.50
199	Juan Uribe	.25
200	Curt Schilling	1.00
201	Javy Lopez	.50
202	Jimmy Haynes	.25
203	Jim Edmonds	.75
204	Pokey Reese	.25
204	Pokey Reese SP	3.00
205	Matt Clement	.25
206	Dean Palmer	.25
207	Nick Johnson	.25
208	Nate Espy **RC**	.75
209	Pedro Feliz	.25
210	Aaron Rowand	.25
211	Masato Yoshii	.25
212	Jose Cruz	.25
213	Paul Byrd	.25
214	Mark Phillips **RC**	1.00
215	Benny Agbayani	.25
216	Frank Menechino	.25
217	John Flaherty	.25
218	Brian Boehringer	.25
219	Todd Hollandsworth	.25
220	Sammy Sosa/SP	8.00
221	Steve Sparks	.25
222	Homer Bush	.25
223	Mike Hampton	.50
224	Bobby Abreu	.50
225	Barry Larkin	.75
226	Ryan Rupe	.25
227	Bubba Trammell	.25
228	Todd Zeile	.25
229	Jeff Shaw	.25
230	Alex Ochoa	.25
231	Orlando Cabrera	.25
232	Jeremy Giambi	.25
233	Tomo Ohka	.25
234	Luis Castillo	.25
235	Chris Holt	.25
236	Shawn Green	.50
237	Sidney Ponson	.25
238	Lee Stevens	.25
239	Hank Blalock	.50
240	Randy Winn	.25
241	Pedro Martinez	1.50
242	Vinny Castilla	.25
243	Steve Karsay	.25
244	Barry Bonds/SP	15.00
245	Jason Bere	.25
246	Scott Rolen	1.50
246	Scott Rolen/SP	6.00
247	Ryan Kohlmeier	.25
248	Kerry Wood	1.50
249	Aramis Ramirez	.50
250	Lance Berkman	.75
251	Omar Vizquel	.50
252	Juan Encarnacion	.25
253	David Segui	.25
254	Brian Anderson	.25
255	Jay Payton	.25
256	Mark Grudzielanek	.25
257	Jimmy Anderson	.25
258	Eric Valent	.25
259	Chad Durbin	.25
260	Alex Gonzalez	.25
261	Scott Dunn	.25
262	Scott Elarton	.25
263	Tom Gordon	.25
265	Moises Alou	.50
266	Mark Buehrle	.25
269	Jerry Hairston Jr.	.25
270	Luke Prokopec	.25
272	Graeme Lloyd	.25
273	Bret Prinz	.25
274	Ryan Minor	.25
276	Chris Carpenter	.25
277	Jeff D'Amico	.25
278	Raul Ibanez	.25
279	Joe Mays	.25
280	Livan Hernandez	.25
281	Robin Ventura	.40
282	Gabe Kapler	.40
283	Tony Batista	.25
284	Ramon Hernandez	.25
285	Craig Paquette	.25
286	Mark Kotsay	.25
287	Mike Lieberthal	.25
288	Joe Borchard	.25
290	Cristian Guzman	.25
291	Craig Biggio	.50
292	Joaquin Benoit	.25
293	Ken Caminiti	.25
294	Sean Burroughs	.50
295	Eric Karros	.50
296	Eric Chavez	.50
297	LaTroy Hawkins	.25
298	Alfonso Soriano	1.00
299	John Smoltz	.50
300	Adam Dunn	1.00
301	Ryan Dempster	.25
302	Travis Hafner	.50
303	Russell Branyan	.25
304	Dustin Hermanson	.25
305	Jim Thome	1.50
306	Carlos Beltran	.75
307	Jason Botts **RC**	.75
308	David Cone	.25
309	Ivanon Coffie	.25
310	Brian Jordan	.25
311	Todd Walker	.25
312	Jeromy Burnitz	.25
313	Tony Armas	.25
314	Jeff Conine	.25
315	Todd Jones	.25
316	Roy Oswalt	.50
317	Aubrey Huff	.25
318	Josh Fogg	.25
319	Jose Vidro	.25
320	Jace Brewer	.25
321	Mike Redmond	.25
322	Noochie Varner **RC**	1.00
323	Russ Ortiz	.25
324	Edgardo Alfonzo	.25
325	Ruben Sierra	.25
326	Calvin Murray	.25
327	Marlon Anderson	.25
328	Albie Lopez	.25
329	Chris Gomez	.25
330	Fernando Tatis	.25
331	Stubby Clapp	.25
332	Rickey Henderson	.75
333	Brad Radke	.25
334	Brent Mayne	.25
335	Cory Lidle	.25
336	Edgar Martinez	.50
337	Aaron Boone	.25
338	Jay Witasick	.25
339	Benito Santiago	.25
340	Jose Mercedes	.25
341	Fernando Vina	.25
342	A.J. Pierzynski	.25
343	Jeff Bagwell	1.00
344	Brian Bohanon	.25
345	Adrian Beltre	.50
346	Troy Percival	.25
347	Napoleon Calzado **RC**	.75
348	Ruben Rivera	.25
349	Rafael Soriano	.25
350	Damian Jackson	.25
351	Joe Randa	.25
352	Chan Ho Park	.25
353	Dante Bichette	.25
354	Bartolo Colon	.25
355	Jason Bay **RC**	5.00
356	Shea Hillenbrand	.25
357	Matt Morris	.50
358	Brad Penny	.25
359	Mark Quinn	.25
360	Marquis Grissom	.25
361	Henry Blanco	.25
362	Billy Koch	.25
363	Mike Cameron	.25
364	Albert Pujols	10.00
365	Paul Konerko	3.00
366	Eric Milton	3.00
367	Nick Bierbrodt	3.00
368	Rafael Palmeiro	5.00
369	Jorge Padilla **RC**	4.00
370	Jason Giambi	4.00
371	Mike Piazza	10.00
372	Alex Cora	3.00
373	Todd Helton	6.00
374	Juan Gonzalez	6.00
375	Mariano Rivera	4.00
376	Jason LaRue	3.00
377	Tony Gwynn	9.00
378	Wilson Betemit	3.00
379	J.J. Trujillo **RC**	3.00
380	Brad Ausmus	3.00
381	Chris George	3.00
382	Jose Canseco	5.00
383	Ramon Ortiz	3.00
384	John Rocker	3.00
385	Rey Ordonez	3.00
386	Ken Griffey Jr.	10.00
387	Juan Pena	3.00
388	Michael Barrett	3.00
389	J.D. Drew	4.00
390	Corey Koskie	3.00
391	Vernon Wells	3.00
392	Juan Tolentino **RC**	3.00
393	Luis Gonzalez	4.00
394	Terrance Long	3.00

395	Travis Lee	3.00
396	Earl Snyder RC	3.00
397	Nomar Garciaparra	10.00
398	Jason Schmidt	4.00
399	David Espinosa	3.00
400	Steve Green	3.00
401	Jack Wilson	3.00
402	Chris Tritle RC	3.00
403	Angel Berroa	3.00
404	Josh Towers	3.00
405	Andruw Jones	4.00
406	Brent Butler	3.00
407	Craig Kuzmic RC	3.00
408	Derek Bell	3.00
409	Eric Glaser RC	3.00
410	Joel Pineiro	3.00
411	Alexis Gomez	3.00
412	Mike Rivera	3.00
413	Shawn Estes	3.00
414	Milton Bradley	3.00
415	Carl Everett	3.00
416	Kazuhiro Sasaki	3.00
417	Tony Fontana RC	3.00
418	Josh Pearce	3.00
419	Gary Matthews Jr.	3.00
420	Raymond Cabrera RC	3.00
421	Joe Kennedy	3.00
422	Jason Maule RC	3.00
423	Casey Fossum	3.00
424	Christian Parker	3.00
425	Laynce Nix RC	5.00
426	Byung-Hyun Kim	3.00
427	Freddy Garcia	3.00
428	Herbert Perry	3.00
429	Jason Marquis	3.00
430	Sandy Alomar Jr.	3.00
431	Roberto Alomar	5.00
432	Tsuyoshi Shinjo	3.00
433	Tim Wakefield	3.00
434	Robert Fick	3.00
435	Vladimir Guerrero	6.00
436	Jose Mesa	3.00
437	Scott Spiezio	3.00
438	Jose Hernandez	3.00
439	Jose Acevedo	3.00
440	Brian West RC	3.00
441	Barry Zito	4.00
442	Luis Maza	3.00
443	Marlon Byrd	4.00
444	A.J. Burnett	3.00
445	Dee Brown	3.00
446	Carlos Delgado	5.00

Chrome

Stars (1-100):	6-10X
RC's:	3-6X

Production 553 Sets

Classic Renditions

	NM/M
Complete Set (10):	10.00
Common Player:	.50
Inserted 1:12	
CR-1	Kerry Wood	2.00
CR-2	Brian Giles	1.00
CR-3	Roger Cedeno	.50
CR-4	Jason Giambi	1.50
CR-5	Albert Pujols	4.00
CR-6	Mark Buehrle	.50
CR-7	Cristian Guzman	.50
CR-8	Jimmy Rollins	.50
CR-9	Jim Thome	2.00
CR-10	Shawn Green	1.00

Classic Renditions Autographs

Production 25 Sets

Clubhouse Collection

	NM/M
Common Player:	15.00
Jersey 1:332	

	Bat 1:498	
RA	Rich Aurilia/Bat	15.00
YB	Yogi Berra/Jsy	40.00
BB	Barry Bonds/Bat	60.00
AD	Alvin Dark/Bat	25.00
NG	Nomar Garciaparra/Bat	50.00
GK	George Kell/Jsy	25.00
GM	Greg Maddux/Jsy	30.00
EM	Eddie Mathews/Jsy	35.00
WM	Willie Mays/Bat	75.00
CP	Corey Patterson/Bat	20.00
JP	Jorge Posada/Bat	25.00
HS	Hank Sauer/Bat	20.00

Clubhouse Collection Dual Relics

		NM/M
Production 53 Sets		
SM	Eddie Mathews, Greg Maddux	150.00
BP	Yogi Berra, Jorge Posada	125.00
SP	Hank Sauer, Corey Patterson	75.00
KR	George Kell, Nomar Garciaparra	100.00
DA	Alvin Dark, Rich Aurilia	100.00
MB	Willie Mays, Barry Bonds	200.00

Clubhouse Collection Auto. Relics

No Pricing
Production 25 Sets

Grandstand Glory Stadium Seat

		NM/M
Common Player:		10.00
Inserted 1:133		
RC	Roy Campanella	25.00
BF	Bob Feller	20.00
WF	Whitey Ford	20.00
TK	Ted Kluszewski	20.00
BM	Billy Martin	25.00
HN	Hal Newhouser	15.00
SP	Satchel Paige	40.00
BP	Billy Pierce	15.00
HS	Hank Sauer	10.00
BS	Bobby Shantz	15.00
WS	Warren Spahn	20.00
EW	Early Wynn	15.00

New Age Performers

		NM/M
Complete Set (15):		30.00
Common Player:		1.00
Inserted 1:15		
NA-1	Luis Gonzalez	1.00
NA-2	Mark McGwire	5.00
NA-3	Barry Bonds	5.00
NA-4	Ken Griffey Jr.	3.00
NA-5	Ichiro Suzuki	3.00
NA-6	Sammy Sosa	3.00
NA-7	Andruw Jones	1.00
NA-8	Derek Jeter	5.00
NA-9	Todd Helton	1.50
NA-10	Alex Rodriguez	4.00
NA-11	Jason Giambi	1.50
NA-12	Bret Boone	1.00
NA-13	Roberto Alomar	1.00
NA-14	Albert Pujols	4.00
NA-15	Vladimir Guerrero	1.50

Real One Autographs

	NM/M
Common Autograph:	20.00
Inserted 1:180	

	NM/M
Red Ink:	.75-1.5X
Production 53	
YB	Yogi Berra	100.00
JB	Joe Black	50.00
RB	Ray Boone	60.00
AC	Andy Carey	40.00
RCL	Roger Clemens	125.00
AD	Alvin Dark	60.00
DD	Dom DiMaggio	80.00
JE	Jim Edmonds	50.00
RF	Roy Face	60.00
BF	Bob Feller	60.00
WF	Whitey Ford	80.00
CG	Brian Giles	25.00
CG	Cristian Guzman	20.00
MI	Monte Irvin	60.00
GK	George Kell	60.00
WM	Willie Mays	200.00
GM	Gil McDougald	75.00
OM	Orestes Minoso	60.00
JP	John Podres	60.00
PR	Phil Rizzuto	80.00
ARO	Alex Rodriguez	140.00
PRO	Preacher Roe	60.00
AR	Al Rosen	75.00
ASC	Al Schoendienst	50.00
BS	Bobby Shantz	50.00
ES	Enos Slaughter	80.00
WS	Warren Spahn	100.00
HW	Hoyt Wilhelm	50.00

Team Topps Legends Autographs

	NM/M
Inserted 1:613	
Vida Blue	20.00
Frank Howard	30.00
Mickey Lolich	25.00
Frank Robinson	40.00
Bobby Thomson	30.00

Then and Now

		NM/M
Complete Set (10):		15.00
Common Player:		1.00
Inserted 1:15		
TN-1	Ed Mathews, Barry Bonds	4.00
TN-2	Al Rosen, Alex Rodriguez	4.00
TN-3	Carl Furillo, Larry Walker	1.00
TN-4	Mickey Vernon, Ichiro Suzuki	3.00
TN-5	Roy Campanella, Sammy Sosa	3.00
TN-6	Al Rosen, Bret Boone	1.00
TN-7	Warren Spahn, Randy Johnson	2.00
TN-8	Ed Lopat, Freddy Garcia	1.00
TN-9	Robin Roberts, Randy Johnson	2.00
TN-10	Billy Pierce, Hideo Nomo	1.50

2002 Topps Opening Day

	NM/M
Complete Set (165):	40.00

Common Player:	.10
Pack (7):	1.00
Box (36):	30.00
1	Roy Oswalt	.25
2	Derek Jeter	2.00
3	Dmitri Young	.10
4	Ramon Hernandez	.10
5	Albert Pujols	1.50
6	Sean Casey	.25
7	Joe Randa	.10
8	Craig Counsell	.10
9	John Olerud	.25
10	Troy Glaus	.40
11	Adam Kennedy	.10
12	Carlos Delgado	.40
13	Bobby Abreu	.20
14	J.T. Snow Jr.	.10
15	Ivan Rodriguez	.50
16	Mike Lowell	.25
17	Juan Pierre	.10
18	Magglio Ordonez	.30
19	Greg Maddux	1.00
20	Jorge Posada	.25
21	Johnny Damon	.20
22	Mike Hampton	.10
23	Paul LoDuca	.10
24	Terrence Long	.10
25	Jeff Bagwell	.50
26	Shannon Stewart	.10
27	Brad Radke	.10
28	Brian Jordan	.10
29	Lee Stevens	.10
30	Cliff Floyd	.10
31	Roger Clemens	1.00
32	Mike Matheny	.10
33	Alfonso Soriano	.50
34	Randy Johnson	.75
35	Mike Sweeney	.10
36	Jose Cruz Jr.	.20
37	Fernando Tatis	.10
38	Eric Young	.10
39	Ruben Rivera	.10
40	Mike Mussina	.50
41	Alex Gonzalez	.10
42	Edgardo Alfonzo	.10
43	Torii Hunter	.25
44	Richie Sexson	.25
45	Bret Boone	.20
46	John Smoltz	.20
47	Bengie Molina	.10
48	Trot Nixon	.10
49	Mike Cameron	.10
50	Mariano Rivera	.20
51	Ichiro Suzuki	1.50
52	Cristian Guzman	.10
53	Andruw Jones	.40
54	Jerry Hairston Jr.	.10
55	Brad Fullmer	.10
56	Luis Gonzalez	.25
57	Placido Polanco	.10
58	Jason Tyner	.10
59	Dan Wilson	.10
60	Jim Edmonds	.25
61	Larry Walker	.25
62	Edgar Renteria	.25
63	Orlando Cabrera	.10
64	Sammy Sosa	1.50
65	Derrek Lee	.20
66	C.C. Sabathia	.10
67	Aaron Boone	.10
68	Royce Clayton	.10
69	Darryl Kile	.10
70	Vladimir Guerrero	.75
71	Bud Smith	.10
72	Adrian Beltre	.20
73	Barry Bonds	15.00
74	Ben Petrick	.10
75	Derek Bell	.10
76	Jeff Kent	.20
77	Ricky Gutierrez	.10
78	Rafael Palmeiro	.50
79	Doug Mientkiewicz	.10

80	Fernando Vina	.10
81	Mark Mulder	.20
82	Carlos Beltran	.25
83	Juan Encarnacion	.10
84	Jimmy Rollins	.20
85	Pedro J. Martinez	.50
86	Aramis Ramirez	.25
87	Reggie Sanders	.10
88	Gary Sheffield	.25
89	Bartolo Colon	.10
90	Jose Macias	.10
91	Bobby Higginson	.10
92	Craig Biggio	.20
93	Al Leiter	.20
94	Juan Gonzalez	.50
95	Jose Valentin	.10
96	Jon Lieber	.10
97	Alex Gonzalez	.10
98	Jose Mesa	.10
99	Sandy Alomar	.10
100	Barry Bonds	2.00
101	Todd Walker	.10
102	Kevin Young	.10
103	Ken Griffey Jr.	1.00
104	Mark McGwire	2.00
105	Jason Giambi	.50
106	Todd Helton	.50
107	Mike Piazza	1.00
108	Nomar Garciaparra	1.50
109	Bernie Williams	.40
110	Shawn Wooten	.10
111	Eric Chavez	.20
112	Curt Schilling	.40
113	Roberto Alomar	.50
114	Chipper Jones	.75
115	Edgar Martinez	.20
116	Shawn Green	.20
117	Ben Grieve	.10
118	Jermaine Dye	.10
119	Steve Finley	.10
120	Adam Dunn	.25
121	Preston Wilson	.10
122	Lance Berkman	.20
123	Ben Sheets	.25
124	Ryan Klesko	.10
125	Brian Giles	.25
126	Marcus Giles	.10
127	Craig Wilson	.10
128	Miguel Tejada	.25
129	Andres Galarraga	.20
130	Alex Rodriguez	1.50
131	David Justice	.25
132	Barry Zito	.25
133	Scott Rolen	.75
134	Brent Abernathy	.10
135	Raul Mondesi	.20
136	Josh Towers	.10
137	Rafael Furcal	.10
138	Gabe Kapler	.10
139	Fred McGriff	.25
140	Jeff Conine	.10
141	Mike Lieberthal	.10
142	Frank Thomas	.50
143	Jason Kendall	.10
144	Toby Hall	.10
145	Pat Burrell	.30
146	J.D. Drew	.25
147	Javier Lopez	.25
148	Carlos Lee	.10
149	Doug Glanville	.10
150	Ruben Sierra	.10
151	Julio Franco	.10
152	Tim Hudson	.20
153	Rich Aurilia	.10
154	Geoff Jenkins	.10
155	Tsuyoshi Shinjo	.10
156	Moises Alou	.20
157	Jim Thome	.75
158	Steve Cox	.10
159	Kevin Brown	.20
160	Barry Bonds	.50
161	Rickey Henderson	.20
162	Bud Smith	.10
163	Rickey Henderson	.20
164	Barry Bonds	.50
165	Checklist	.10

Autographs

		NM/M
	Common Auto.:	10.00
GJ	Geoff Jenkins	15.00
NJ	Nick Johnson	10.00
BS	Ben Sheets	25.00

2002 Topps Pristine

		NM/M
	Common Player:	.75
	Common Uncommon RC:	3.00
	Production 1,999	
	Common Rare RC:	5.00
	Production 799	
	Pack (8):	30.00
	Box (5):	125.00
1	Alex Rodriguez	5.00

SAMMY SOSA
CHICAGO CUBS

2	Carlos Delgado	1.50
3	Jimmy Rollins	.75
4	Jason Kendall	.75
5	John Olerud	1.00
6	Albert Pujols	5.00
7	Curt Schilling	2.00
8	Gary Sheffield	1.00
9	Johnny Damon	1.00
10	Ichiro Suzuki	4.00
11	Pat Burrell	1.00
12	Garret Anderson	1.00
13	Andruw Jones	1.50
14	Kerry Wood	2.00
15	Kenny Lofton	1.00
16	Adam Dunn	1.50
17	Juan Pierre	.75
18	Josh Beckett	1.00
19	Roy Oswalt	1.00
20	Derek Jeter	6.00
21	Jose Vidro	.75
22	Richie Sexson	1.50
23	Mike Sweeney	.75
24	Jeff Kent	1.00
25	Jason Giambi	1.50
26	Bret Boone	1.00
27	J.D. Drew	1.00
28	Shannon Stewart	.75
29	Miguel Tejada	1.00
30	Barry Bonds	6.00
31	Randy Johnson	2.00
32	Pedro J. Martinez	2.00
33	Magglio Ordonez	1.00
34	Todd Helton	1.50
35	Craig Biggio	1.00
36	Shawn Green	1.00
37	Vladimir Guerrero	2.00
38	Mo Vaughn	1.00
39	Alfonso Soriano	2.00
40	Barry Zito	1.00
41	Aramis Ramirez	1.00
42	Ryan Klesko	1.00
43	Ruben Sierra	.75
44	Tino Martinez	.75
45	Toby Hall	.75
46	Ivan Rodriguez	1.50
47	Raul Mondesi	.75
48	Carlos Pena	.75
49	Darin Erstad	1.00
50	Sammy Sosa	4.00
51	Bartolo Colon	1.00
52	Robert Fick	.75
53	Cliff Floyd	.75
54	Brian Jordan	.75
55	Torii Hunter	1.00
56	Roberto Alomar	1.00
57	Roger Clemens	4.00
58	Mark Mulder	1.00
59	Brian Giles	1.00
60	Mike Piazza	4.00
61	Rich Aurilia	.75
62	Freddy Garcia	.75
63	Jim Edmonds	1.50
64	Eric Hinske	.75
65	Jeremy Giambi	.75
66	Javier Vazquez	.75
67	Cristian Guzman	.75
68	Paul LoDuca	.75
69	Bobby Abreu	1.00
70	Nomar Garciaparra	4.00
71	Troy Glaus	1.00
72	Chipper Jones	2.00
73	Scott Rolen	2.00
74	Lance Berkman	1.00
75	C.C. Sabathia	.75
76	Bernie Williams	1.00
77	Rafael Palmeiro	1.50
78	Phil Nevin	.75
79	Kazuhiro Sasaki	.75
80	Eric Chavez	1.00
81	Jorge Posada	1.00
82	Edgardo Alfonzo	.75
83	Geoff Jenkins	1.00
84	Preston Wilson	.75

85	Jim Thome	2.00
86	Frank Thomas	1.50
87	Jeff Bagwell	1.50
88	Greg Maddux	3.00
89	Mark Prior	3.00
90	Larry Walker	1.00
91	Luis Gonzalez	1.00
92	Tim Hudson	1.00
93	Tsuyoshi Shinjo	.75
94	Juan Gonzalez	1.50
95	Shea Hillenbrand	.75
96	Paul Konerko	.75
97	Tom Glavine	1.50
98	Marty Cordova	.75
99	Moises Alou	1.00
100	Ken Griffey Jr.	4.00
101	Hank Blalock	1.50
102	Matt Morris	1.00
103	Robb Nen	.75
104	Mike Cameron	.75
105	Mark Buehrle	.75
106	Sean Burroughs	.75
107	Orlando Cabrera	.75
108	Jeromy Burnitz	.75
109	Juan Uribe	.75
110	Eric Milton	.75
111	Carlos Lee	.75
112	Jose Mesa	.75
113	Morgan Ensberg	.75
114	Mike Rivera	.75
115	Juan Cruz	.75
116	Mike Lieberthal	.75
117	Armando Benitez	.75
118	Vinny Castilla	.75
119	Russ Ortiz	.75
120	Mike Lowell	1.00
121	Corey Patterson	1.00
122	Mike Mussina	1.50
123	Rafael Furcal	.75
124	Mark Grace	1.50
125	Ben Sheets	1.00
126	John Smoltz	1.00
127	Fred McGriff	1.00
128	Nick Johnson	.75
129	J.T. Snow	.75
130	Jeff Cirillo	.75
131	Trevor Hoffman	.75
132	Kevin Brown	1.00
133	Mariano Rivera	1.50
134	Marlon Anderson	.75
135	Al Leiter	.75
136	Doug Mientkiewicz	.75
137	Eric Karros	.75
138	Bobby Higginson	.75
139	Sean Casey	1.00
140	Troy Percival	.75
141	Willie Mays	5.00
142	Carl Yastrzemski	3.00
143	Stan Musial	4.00
144	Harmon Killebrew	3.00
145	Mike Schmidt	5.00
146	Duke Snider	2.00
147	Brooks Robinson	3.00
148	Frank Robinson	2.00
149	Nolan Ryan	8.00
150	Reggie Jackson	3.00
151	Joe Mauer/C RC	20.00
152	Joe Mauer/U RC	25.00
153	Joe Mauer/R RC	35.00
154	Colt Griffin/C	3.00
155	Colt Griffin/U	5.00
156	Colt Griffin/R	8.00
157	Jason Simontacchi/ C RC	2.00
158	Jason Simontacchi/ U RC	3.00
159	Jason Simontacchi/ R RC	5.00
160	Casey Kotchman/C	5.00
161	Casey Kotchman/U	8.00
162	Casey Kotchman/R	15.00
163	Greg Sain/C RC	1.50
164	Greg Sain/U RC	3.00
165	Greg Sain/R RC	5.00
166	David Wright/C	40.00
167	David Wright/U	50.00
168	David Wright/R	60.00
169	Scott Hairston/C	4.00
170	Scott Hairston/U	6.00
171	Scott Hairston/R	10.00
172	Rolando Viera/C RC	1.50
173	Rolando Viera/U RC	3.00
174	Rolando Viera/R RC	5.00
175	Tyrell Godwin/C	1.50
176	Tyrell Godwin/U	3.00
177	Tyrell Godwin/R	5.00
178	Jesus Cota/C RC	1.50
179	Jesus Cota/U RC	3.00
180	Jesus Cota/R RC	5.00
181	Dan Johnson/C RC	5.00
182	Dan Johnson/U RC	10.00
183	Dan Johnson/R RC	15.00
184	Mario Ramos/C	1.50
185	Mario Ramos/U	3.00

186	Mario Ramos/R	5.00
187	Jason Dubois/C RC	4.00
188	Jason Dubois/U RC	6.00
189	Jason Dubois/R RC	10.00
190	Jonny Gomes/C RC	8.00
191	Jonny Gomes/U RC	15.00
192	Jonny Gomes/R RC	20.00
193	Chris Snelling/C RC	2.00
194	Chris Snelling/U RC	4.00
195	Chris Snelling/R RC	6.00
196	Hansel Izquierdo/C RC	2.00
197	Hansel Izquierdo/U RC	4.00
198	Hansel Izquierdo/R RC	6.00
199	So Taguchi/C RC	3.00
200	So Taguchi/U RC	5.00
201	So Taguchi/R RC	8.00
202	Kazuhisa Ishii/C RC	3.00
203	Kazuhisa Ishii/U RC	5.00
204	Kazuhisa Ishii/R RC	8.00
205	Jorge Padilla/C RC	1.50
206	Jorge Padilla/U RC	3.00
207	Jorge Padilla/R RC	5.00
208	Earl Snyder/C RC	2.00
209	Earl Snyder/U RC	4.00
210	Earl Snyder/R RC	6.00

Refractors

JAVIER VAZQUEZ
MONTREAL EXPOS

Stars (1-150):	2-4X
Production 149	
Common Rookies:	.75-1.5X
Production 1,999	
Uncommon Rookies:	1-2X
Production 799	
Rare Rookies:	2-3X
Production 149	
Gold Refractors (1-150):	3-5X
Gold Common RC's:	4-8X
Gold Uncommon RC's:	2-4X
Gold Rare RC's:	1-2X
Production 70 Sets	
All Refractors are uncirculated.	

Fall Memories

FALL MEMORIES

		NM/M
	Common Player:	5.00
	Varying quantities produced	
JB	Johnny Bench	15.00
BB	Barry Bonds	30.00
GB	George Brett	25.00
TG	Tom Glavine	8.00
LG	Luis Gonzalez	5.00
MG	Mark Grace	12.00
SG	Shawn Green	6.00
TH	Todd Helton	8.00
RJ	Reggie Jackson	15.00
AJ	Andruw Jones	8.00
CP	Chipper Jones	10.00
TM	Tino Martinez	8.00
WM	Willie Mays	40.00
EM	Eddie Murray	15.00
JP	Jorge Posada	8.00
KP	Kirby Puckett	15.00
CS	Curt Schilling	8.00
GS	Gary Sheffield	5.00
AS	Alfonso Soriano	10.00
BW	Bernie Williams	8.00

In The Gap

	NM/M
Common Player:	5.00
Varying quantities produced	

BERNIE WILLIAMS

RA	Roberto Alomar	10.00
LB	Lance Berkman	8.00
WBE	Wilson Betemit	5.00
WB	Wade Boggs	8.00
BBO	Barry Bonds	25.00
BB	Bret Boone	6.00
EC	Eric Chavez	8.00
CD	Carlos Delgado	6.00
AD	Adam Dunn	10.00
JE	Jim Edmonds	6.00
DE	Darin Erstad	5.00
NG	Nomar Garciaparra	15.00
TG	Tony Gwynn	15.00
TH	Todd Helton	8.00
RH	Rickey Henderson	10.00
AJ	Andruw Jones	10.00
JK	Jeff Kent	5.00
RK	Ryan Klesko	8.00
PL	Paul LoDuca	10.00
RP	Rafael Palmeiro	10.00
MP	Mike Piazza	15.00
AP	Albert Pujols	15.00
ARA	Aramis Ramirez	8.00
AR	Alex Rodriguez	15.00
IR	Ivan Rodriguez	8.00
TS	Tsuyoshi Shinjo	5.00
AS	Alfonso Soriano	10.00
LW	Larry Walker	5.00
BW	Bernie Williams	15.00
PW	Preston Wilson	5.00

Patches

No Pricing
Production 25 Sets

Personal Endorsements

		NM/M
Common Autograph:		8.00
Inserted 1:Box		
RA	Roberto Alomar	30.00
KB	Kenny Baugh	8.00
LB	Lance Berkman	30.00
BB	Barry Bonds	180.00
DB	Dewon Brazelton	15.00
JD	Johnny Damon	30.00
GF	Gavin Floyd	25.00
CG	Cristian Guzman	10.00
IG	Irvin Guzman	10.00
OH	Orlando Hudson	10.00
KI	Kazuhisa Ishii	30.00
CK	Casey Kotchman	20.00
JL	Jason Lane	8.00
CW	Corwin Malone	8.00
NN	Nick Neugebauer	8.00
AP	Albert Pujols	125.00
JR	Jimmy Rollins	20.00
BS	Ben Sheets	20.00
JS	Juan Silvestre	8.00
ST	So Taguchi	15.00
MT	Marcus Thames	8.00

Popular Demand

		NM/M
Common Player:		5.00
Varying quantities produced		
RA	Roberto Alomar	10.00
JB	Jeff Bagwell	10.00
WB	Wade Boggs	8.00
BBO	Barry Bonds	25.00
BB	Bret Boone	5.00
CD	Carlos Delgado	5.00
AD	Adam Dunn	8.00
NG	Nomar Garciaparra	15.00
SG	Shawn Green	5.00
TG	Tony Gwynn	12.00
TH	Todd Helton	8.00
CJ	Chipper Jones	12.00
DM	Don Mattingly	35.00
MP	Mike Piazza	15.00

AP	Albert Pujols	20.00
AR	Alex Rodriguez	15.00
IR	Ivan Rodriguez	8.00
CS	Curt Schilling	8.00
FT	Frank Thomas	10.00
LW	Larry Walker	5.00

Portions

PRISTINE PORTIONS
BRET BOONE // SECOND BASE // SEATTLE MARINERS

		NM/M
Common Player:		5.00
Varying quantities produced		
RA	Roberto Alomar	10.00
JB	Jeff Bagwell	10.00
LB	Lance Berkman	10.00
CB	Craig Biggio	8.00
BBO	Barry Bonds	20.00
BB	Bret Boone	5.00
CD	Carlos Delgado	5.00
RD	Ryan Dempster	5.00
AD	Adam Dunn	8.00
CF	Cliff Floyd	5.00
RF	Rafael Furcal	5.00
NG	Nomar Garciaparra	15.00
CG	Cristian Guzman	5.00
TH	Todd Helton	8.00
NJ	Nick Johnson	5.00
LD	Paul LoDuca	5.00
GM	Greg Maddux	10.00
EM	Edgar Martinez	10.00
MM	Mike Mussina	10.00
MO	Magglio Ordonez	5.00
RP	Rafael Palmeiro	8.00
MP	Mike Piazza	15.00
JP	Jorge Posada	8.00
AP	Albert Pujols	15.00
AR	Alex Rodriguez	15.00
IR	Ivan Rodriguez	8.00
NR	Nolan Ryan	30.00
KS	Kazuhiro Sasaki	5.00

2002 Topps Reserve

KEARNS

	NM/M
Complete Set (150):	120.00
Common Player:	.25
Common (136-150):	4.00
Production 999	
Silver Parallel (1-135):	4-8X
Silver (136-150):	.75-1.5X
Production 150	
Box:10 Packs & 1	
Auto. Helmet:	100.00
1	Alex Rodriguez	2.50

1	Alex Rodriguez	2.50
2	Tsuyoshi Shinjo	.25
3	Craig Biggio	.40
4	Troy Glaus	.50
5	Mike Rivera	.25
6	Curt Schilling	.75
7	Garret Anderson	.50
8	Ben Sheets	.50
9	Todd Helton	.75
10	Paul Konerko	.50
11	Sammy Sosa	2.00
12	Bud Smith	.25
13	Jeff Bagwell	.75
14	Albert Pujols	2.00
15	Jose Vidro	.25
16	Carlos Delgado	.50
17	Torii Hunter	.50
18	Jerry Hairston Jr.	.25
19	Troy Percival	.25
20	Vladimir Guerrero	1.00
21	Geoff Jenkins	.40
22	Carlos Pena	.25
23	Juan Gonzalez	.75
24	Raul Mondesi	.25
25	Jimmy Rollins	.40
26	Mariano Rivera	.50
27	Jorge Posada	.50
28	Magglio Ordonez	.50
29	Roberto Alomar	.50
30	Randy Johnson	1.00
31	Xavier Nady	.25
32	Terrence Long	.25
33	Chipper Jones	1.00
34	Rich Aurilia	.25
35	Aramis Ramirez	.25
36	Jim Thome	1.00
37	Bret Boone	.50
38	Angel Berroa	.25
39	Jeff Conine	.25
40	Cliff Floyd	.25
41	Pedro J. Martinez	1.00
42	J.D. Drew	.50
43	Kazuhiro Sasaki	.25
44	Jon Rauch	.25
45	Orlando Hudson	.25
46	Scott Rolen	1.00
47	Rafael Furcal	.25
48	Brad Penny	.25
49	Miguel Tejada	.50
50	Orlando Cabrera	.25
51	Bobby Abreu	.50
52	Darin Erstad	.50
53	Edgar Martinez	.40
54	Ben Grieve	.25
55	Shawn Green	.50
56	Ivan Rodriguez	.75
57	Josh Beckett	.50
58	Ray Durham	.25
59	Jason Hart	.25
60	Nathan Haynes	.25
61	Jason Giambi	.75
62	Eric Chavez	.50
63	Matt Morris	.40
64	Lance Berkman	.50
65	Jeff Kent	.40
66	Andruw Jones	.50
67	Brian Giles	.50
68	Morgan Ensberg	.25
69	Pat Burrell	.50
70	Ken Griffey Jr.	2.00
71	Carlos Beltran	.50
72	Ichiro Suzuki	2.00
73	Larry Walker	.50
74	J.J. Putz RC	.50
75	Mike Piazza	2.00
76	Rafael Palmeiro	.75
77	Mark Prior	2.00
78	Toby Hall	.25
79	Pokey Reese	.25
80	Mike Mussina	.50
81	Omar Vizquel	.25
82	Shannon Stewart	.25
83	Jeromy Burnitz	.25
84	Bernie Williams	.50
85	C.C. Sabathia	.25
86	Mike Hampton	.25
87	Kevin Brown	.50
88	Juan Cruz	.25
89	Jeff Weaver	.25
90	Jason Lane	.25
91	Adam Dunn	.75
92	Jose Cruz Jr.	.25
93	Marlon Anderson	.25
94	Jeff Cirillo	.25
95	Mark Buehrle	.25
96	Austin Kearns	.50
97	Tim Hudson	.50
98	Brian Jordan	.25
99	Phil Nevin	.25
100	Barry Bonds	3.00
101	Derek Jeter	3.00
102	Javier Vazquez	.25
103	Jason Kendall	.40
104	Jim Edmonds	.50
105	Kenny Kelly	.25
106	Juan Pena	.25
107	Mark Grace	.50
108	Roger Clemens	2.00
109	Barry Zito	.50
110	Greg Vaughn	.25
111	Greg Maddux	1.50
112	Richie Sexson	.50
113	Jermaine Dye	.25
114	Kerry Wood	1.00
115	Matt Lawton	.25
116	Sean Casey	.50
117	Gary Sheffield	.50
118	Preston Wilson	.25
119	Cristian Guzman	.25
120	Mike Sweeney	.25
121	Neifi Perez	.25
122	Paul LoDuca	.25
123	Luis Gonzalez	.50
124	Ryan Klesko	.25

125	Alfonso Soriano	1.00
126	Bobby Higginson	.25
127	Juan Pierre	.25
128	Moises Alou	.50
129	Roy Oswalt	.50
130	Nomar Garciaparra	2.00
131	Fred McGriff	.40
132	Edgardo Alfonzo	.25
133	Johnny Damon	.40
134	Dewon Brazelton	.25
135	Mark Mulder	.50
136	So Taguchi RC	8.00
137	Mario Ramos	4.00
138	Dan Johnson RC	15.00
139	Hansel Izquierdo RC	5.00
140	Kazuhisa Ishii RC	10.00
141	Jon Switzer	4.00
142	Chris Tritle RC	6.00
143	Chris Snelling RC	8.00
144	Chone Figgins RC	8.00
145	Dan Phillips RC	4.00
146	John Rodriguez RC	4.00
147	Colt Griffin	8.00
148	Jonny Gomes RC	15.00
149	Josh Barfield	10.00
150	Joe Mauer RC	30.00

Silver

Stars (1-135):	4-8X
SP's (136-150):	.75-1.5X

Autographed Mini-Helmets

		NM/M
Common Helmet:		20.00
1:Box		
Gold Ink Autographs: No Pricing		
Production 25		
	Roberto Alomar	45.00
	Moises Alou	25.00
	Lance Berkman	35.00
	Bret Boone	25.00
	Eric Chavez	30.00
	Adam Dunn	40.00
	Cliff Floyd	20.00
	Troy Glaus	40.00
	Luis Gonzalez	30.00
	Todd Helton	50.00
	Magglio Ordonez	25.00
	Rafael Palmeiro	40.00
	Albert Pujols	200.00
	Alex Rodriguez	125.00
	Scott Rolen	35.00
	Jimmy Rollins	30.00
	Alfonso Soriano	50.00
	Barry Zito	30.00

Game-Used Baseball

		NM/M
Inserted 1:1,761		
AR	Alex Rodriguez	
I	Ichiro Suzuki	65.00

Game-Used Bat

AUTHENTIC GAME-USED BAT

BAGWELL

		NM/M
Common Player:		5.00
Inserted 1:12		
RA	Roberto Alomar	10.00
JB	Jeff Bagwell	10.00
BB	Barry Bonds	20.00
CD	Carlos Delgado	8.00
JG	Juan Gonzalez	8.00
LG	Luis Gonzalez	5.00
TG	Tony Gwynn	12.00
RH	Rickey Henderson	10.00
CJ	Chipper Jones	10.00
AJ	Andruw Jones	8.00
TM	Tino Martinez	8.00

RP	Rafael Palmeiro	8.00
MB	Mike Piazza	15.00
AP	Albert Pujols	15.00
AR	Alex Rodriguez	12.00
IR	Ivan Rodriguez	8.00
TS	Tsuyoshi Shinjo	5.00
AS	Alfonso Soriano	10.00
FT	Frank Thomas	8.00
BW	Bernie Williams	8.00

Game-Worn Patch
No Pricing
Production 25 Sets

Game-Worn Uniform

		NM/M
Common Player:		5.00
Inserted 1:5		
BB	Barry Bonds	20.00
BBO	Bret Boone	5.00
DE	Darin Erstad	5.00
NG	Nomar Garciaparra	15.00
LG	Luis Gonzalez	5.00
TG	Tony Gwynn	10.00
TH	Todd Helton	8.00
RJ	Randy Johnson	10.00
AJ	Andruw Jones	6.00
CJ	Chipper Jones	10.00
GM	Greg Maddux	12.00
PM	Pedro Martinez	10.00
MM	Mark Mulder	5.00
MO	Magglio Ordonez	5.00
RP	Rafael Palmeiro	8.00
MP	Mike Piazza	12.00
AP	Albert Pujols	15.00
AR	Alex Rodriguez	12.00
IR	Ivan Rodriguez	8.00
SR	Scott Rolen	10.00
KS	Kazuhiro Sasaki	5.00
CS	Curt Schilling	8.00
FT	Frank Thomas	8.00
KW	Kerry Wood	10.00

2002 Topps Super Teams

		NM/M
Complete Set:		40.00
Common Player:		.25
Pack (7):		3.50
Box (20):		60.00
1	Leo Durocher	.25
2	Whitey Lockman	.25
3	Alvin Dark	.25
4	Monte Irvin	.50
5	Willie Mays	2.50
6	Wes Westrum	.25
7	Johnny Antonelli	.25
8	Sal Maglie	.25
9	Dusty Rhodes	.25
10	Davey Williams	.25
11	Hoyt Wilhelm	.25
12	Don Mueller	.25
13	Dusty Rhodes	.25
14	Willie Mays, Monte Irvin, Dusty Rhodes	.75
15	Walt Alston	.25
16	Gil Hodges	.75
17	Jim Gilliam	.25
18	Pee Wee Reese	.50
19	Jackie Robinson	2.00
20	Duke Snider	1.00
21	Carl Furillo	.25
22	Roy Campanella	1.00
23	Don Newcombe	.25
24	Don Hoak	.25
25	Johnny Podres	.25
26	Clem Labine	.25
27	Johnny Podres	.25
28	Pee Wee Reese, Jackie Robinson, Duke Snider	1.00
29	Fred Haney	.25
30	Joe Adcock	.25
31	Frank Torre	.25
32	Red Schoendienst	.25
33	Johnny Logan	.25
34	Eddie Mathews	1.00
35	Hank Aaron	3.00
36	Andy Pafko	.25
37	Wes Covington	.25
38	Lew Burdette	.25
39	Warren Spahn	1.00
40	Del Crandall	.25
41	Lew Burdette	.25
42	Warren Spahn, Eddie Mathews, Hank Aaron	1.50
43	Danny Murtaugh	.25
44	Dick Stuart	.25
45	Bill Mazeroski	.25
46	Dick Groat	.25
47	Don Hoak	.25
48	Gino Cimoli	.25
49	Bill Virdon	.25
50	Roberto Clemente	2.50
51	Smoky Burgess	.25
52	Bob Friend	.25
53	Vernon Law	.25
55	Roy Face	.25
56	Bill Mazeroski	.25
57	Roberto Clemente, Bill Mazeroski, Dick Groat	1.00
58	Ralph Houk	.25
59	Bill "Moose" Skowron	.50
60	Bobby Richardson	.25
61	Tony Kubek	.25
62	Clete Boyer	.25
63	Yogi Berra	1.50
64	Bob Cerv	.25
65	Roger Maris	1.50
66	Elston Howard	.25
67	Whitey Ford	1.00
68	Ralph Terry	.25
69	Johnny Blanchard	.25
70	Whitey Ford	1.00
71	Yogi Berra, Roger Maris, Elston Howard, Bill "Moose" Skowron	1.00
72	Red Schoendienst	.25
73	Orlando Cepeda	.40
74	Julian Javier	.25
75	Dal Maxvill	.25
76	Mike Shannon	.25
77	Lou Brock	.75
78	Roger Maris	1.50
79	Curt Flood	.25
80	Tim McCarver	.25
81	Steve Carlton	.75
82	Bob Gibson	1.00
83	Nelson Briles	.25
84	Bobby Tolan	.25
85	Bob Gibson	1.00
86	Bob Gibson, Steve Carlton, Orlando Cepeda, Lou Brock	.50
87	Gil Hodges	.25
88	Ed Kranepool	.25
89	Buddy Harrelson	.25
90	Wayne Garrett	.25
91	Cleon Jones	.25
92	Tommie Agee	.25
93	Ron Swoboda	.25
94	Al Weis	.25
95	Jerry Grote	.25
96	Tom Seaver	1.00
97	Jerry Koosman	.25
98	Tug McGraw	.25
99	Nolan Ryan	3.00
100	Donn Clendenon	.25
101	Tom Seaver, Jerry Koosman, Tug McGraw, Nolan Ryan	1.00
102	Earl Weaver	.25
103	Boog Powell	.25
104	Davey Johnson	.25
105	Mark Belanger	.25
106	Brooks Robinson	1.00
107	Don Buford	.25
108	Paul Blair	.25
109	Frank Robinson	1.00
110	Dick Hall	.25
111	Jim Palmer	.75
112	Mike Cuellar	.25
113	Dave McNally	.25
114	Andy Etchebarren	.25
115	Brooks Robinson	1.00
116	Dick Hall, Jim Palmer, Mike Cuellar, Dave McNally	.40
117	Alvin Dark	.25
118	Gene Tenace	.25
119	Dick Green	.25
120	Bert Campaneris	.25
121	Sal Bando	.25
122	Reggie Jackson	1.00
123	Joe Rudi	.25
124	Claudell Washington	.25
125	Ray Fosse	.25
126	Vida Blue	.40
127	Rollie Fingers	.25
128	Jim "Catfish" Hunter	.50
129	Ken Holtzman	.25
130	Rollie Fingers	.25
131	Jim "Catfish" Hunter, Sal Bando, Reggie Jackson, Rollie Fingers	.50
132	Davey Johnson	.25
133	Keith Hernandez	.25
134	Wally Backman	.25
135	Rafael Santana	.25
136	Ray Knight	.25
137	Len Dykstra	.25
138	Darryl Strawberry	.25
139	Kevin Mitchell	.25
140	Dwight Gooden	.25
141	Bob Ojeda	.25
142	Sid Fernandez	.25
143	Ron Darling	.25
144	Gary Carter	.25
145	Ray Knight	.25
146	Darryl Strawberry, Dwight Gooden, Keith Hernandez	.25

Retrofractor
Cards (1-146):	2-4X
#'d to year team won World Series	

Autographs
		NM/M
Common Autograph:		10.00
Inserted 1:19		
YB	Yogi Berra	60.00
VB	Vida Blue	15.00
CB	Clete Boyer	15.00
SC	Steve Carlton	25.00
MI	Monte Irvin	15.00
RJ	Reggie Jackson	50.00
TK	Tony Kubek	30.00
TM	Tug McGraw	15.00
AP	Andy Pafko	20.00
JP	Jim Palmer	25.00
JPO	Johnny Podres	15.00
BR	Bobby Richardson	15.00
BRO	Brooks Robinson	30.00
NR	Nolan Ryan	150.00
TS	Tom Seaver	40.00
MS	Bill "Moose" Skowron	20.00
WS	Warren Spahn	40.00
HW	Hoyt Wilhelm	15.00

A View To A Thrill Autograph Relics

		NM/M
# Produced listed		
WFA	Whitey Ford/61	100.00
BGA	Bob Gibson/67	60.00
WMA	Willie Mays/54	150.00
DSA	Duke Snider/55	80.00
WSA	Warren Spahn/57	60.00

A View To A Thrill Seat Relics
		NM/M
Common Player:		10.00
Inserted 1:30		
HA	Hank Aaron	20.00
YB	Yogi Berra	15.00
LB	Lew Burdette	10.00
RC	Roberto Clemente	50.00
WF	Whitey Ford	15.00
BG	Bob Gibson	15.00
RMB	Roger Maris/ Cardinals	20.00
RMY	Roger Maris/ Yankees	40.00
EM	Eddie Mathews	15.00
WM	Willie Mays	30.00
BM	Bill Mazeroski	10.00
JP	Jim Palmer	10.00
BP	Boog Powell	10.00
BR	Brooks Robinson	15.00
FR	Frank Robinson	15.00
RS	Red Schoendienst	10.00
DS	Duke Snider	15.00
WS	Warren Spahn	15.00

Classic Combos
		NM/M
Common Card:		40.00
Inserted 1:865		
AJ	Tommie Agee, Cleon Jones	40.00
JR	Reggie Jackson, Joe Rudi	40.00
RR	Brooks Robinson, Frank Robinson	50.00
SK	Tom Seaver, Jerry Koosman	50.00
SRBK	"Moose" Skowron, Bobby Richardson, Clete Boyer, Tony Kubek	80.00

Relics
		NM/M
Common Player:		10.00
TA	Tommie Agee/Bat	20.00
SBB	Sal Bando/Bat	10.00
SBJ	Sal Bando/Jsy	10.00
MB	Mark Belanger/Bat	10.00
PB	Paul Blair/Bat	10.00
CB	Clete Boyer/Bat	10.00
LB	Lew Burdette/Jsy	15.00
SB	Smoky Burgess/Bat	15.00
BC	Bert Campaneris/Bat	15.00
GC	Gary Carter/Jacket	20.00
GCB	Gary Carter/Bat	15.00
GCJ	Gary Carter/Jsy	15.00
OC	Orlando Cepeda/Bat	15.00
BCE	Bob Cerv/Bat	10.00
GCI	Gino Cimoli/Bat	10.00
DC	Del Crandel/Bat	10.00
MC	Mike Cuellar/Jsy	10.00
RD	Ron Darling/Jsy	10.00
LD	Len Dykstra/Bat	15.00
RF	Ray Fosse/Bat	10.00
BF	Bob Friend/Jsy	10.00
WG	Wayne Garrett/Bat	10.00
DG	Dwight Gooden/Jsy	15.00
DH	Don Hoak/Bat	10.00
RH	Ralph Houk/Jsy	10.00
RJ	Reggie Jackson/Bat	35.00
DJ	Davey Johnson/Bat	20.00
CJ	Cleon Jones/Bat	20.00
RK	Ray Knight/Bat	10.00
JK	Jerry Koosman/Jsy	10.00
EK	Ed Kranepool/Jsy	15.00
TK	Tony Kubek/Bat	25.00
TM	Tug McGraw/Jsy	15.00
DM	Dave McNally/Jsy	10.00
KM	Kevin Mitchell/Bat	10.00
AP	Andy Pafko/Bat	10.00
BR	Bobby Richardson/ Bat	25.00
BRO	Brooks Robinson/ Bat	25.00
FR	Frank Robinson/Bat	25.00
JR	Joe Rudi/Bat	10.00
NR	Nolan Ryan/Bat	75.00
RS	Red Schoendienst/ Bat	10.00
TS	Tom Seaver/Bat	20.00
MS	"Moose" Skowron/ Bat	20.00
DS	Darryl Strawberry/ Bat	20.00
CW	Claudell Washington/ Bat	10.00

Super Teammates
	NM/M
Complete Set (5):	10.00

Common Card:		2.00
Inserted 1:10		
BG	Lou Brock,	
	Bob Gibson	2.00
FB	Whitey Ford,	
	Yogi Berra	4.00
MI	Willie Mays,	
	Monte Irvin	4.00
RR	Brooks Robinson,	
	Frank Robinson	3.00
SRBK	Bill "Moose" Skowron,	
	Bobby Richardson,	
	Clete Boyer,	
	Tony Kubek	2.00

Super Teammates Autographs

		NM/M
Production 50 Sets		
BGA	Lou Brock,	
	Bob Gibson	100.00
FBA	Whitey Ford,	
	Yogi Berra	150.00
MIA	Willie Mays,	
	Monte Irvin	180.00
RRA	Brooks Robinson,	
	Frank Robinson	100.00
SRBKA	Bill "Moose" Skowron,	
	Bobby Richardson,	
	Clete Boyer,	
	Tony Kubek	200.00

2002 Topps Ten

		NM/M
Complete Set (200):		40.00
Common Player:		.15
Pack (7):		2.00
Box (24):		40.00
1	Ichiro Suzuki	1.00
2	Rich Aurilia	.15
3	Bret Boone	.25
4	Juan Pierre	.15
5	Shannon Stewart	.15
6	Alex Rodriguez	1.00
7	Luis Gonzalez	.25
8	Todd Helton	.50
9	Garret Anderson	.25
10	Albert Pujols	1.00
11	Lance Berkman	.25
12	Todd Helton	.50
13	Jeff Kent	.15
14	Bob Abreu	.25
15	Jason Giambi	.40
16	Albert Pujols	1.00
17	Mike Sweeney	.15
18	Vladimir Guerrero	.50
19	Cliff Floyd	.15
20	Shannon Stewart	.15
21	Cristian Guzman	.15
22	Roberto Alomar	.40

23	Carlos Beltran	.25
24	Jimmy Rollins	.25
25	Roger Cedeno	.15
26	Juan Pierre	.15
27	Juan Uribe	.15
28	Luis Castillo	.15
29	Ray Durham	.15
30	Mark McLemore	.15
31	Barry Bonds	1.50
32	Sammy Sosa	1.00
33	Luis Gonzalez	.25
34	Alex Rodriguez	1.00
35	Shawn Green	.25
36	Todd Helton	.50
37	Jim Thome	.50
38	Rafael Palmeiro	.40
39	Richie Sexson	.25
40	Phil Nevin	.15
41	Troy Glaus	.40
42	Sammy Sosa	1.00
43	Todd Helton	.50
44	Luis Gonzalez	.25
45	Bret Boone	.25
46	Juan Gonzalez	.40
47	Barry Bonds	1.50
48	Alex Rodriguez	1.00
49	Jeff Bagwell	.50
50	Albert Pujols	1.00
51	Phil Nevin	.15
52	Ichiro Suzuki	1.00
53	Larry Walker	.25
54	Jason Giambi	.40
55	Roberto Alomar	.40
56	Todd Helton	.50
57	Moises Alou	.25
58	Lance Berkman	.25
59	Bret Boone	.25
60	Frank Catalanotto	.15
61	Chipper Jones	.50
62	Barry Bonds	1.50
63	Sammy Sosa	1.00
64	Luis Gonzalez	.25
65	Todd Helton	.50
66	Larry Walker	.25
67	Jason Giambi	.40
68	Jim Thome	.50
69	Alex Rodriguez	1.00
70	Lance Berkman	.25
71	Albert Pujols	1.00
72	Ichiro Suzuki	1.00
73	Roger Cedeno	.15
74	Juan Pierre	.15
75	Jimmy Rollins	.25
76	Alfonso Soriano	.50
77	Mark McLemore	.15
78	Chuck Knoblauch	.15
79	Vladimir Guerrero	.50
80	Bob Abreu	.25
81	Mike Cameron	.15
82	Sammy Sosa	1.00
83	Alex Rodriguez	1.00
84	Todd Helton	.50
85	Barry Bonds	1.50
86	Luis Gonzalez	.25
87	Ichiro Suzuki	1.00
88	Jeff Bagwell	.50
89	Cliff Floyd	.15
90	Shawn Green	.25
91	Craig Biggio	.25
92	Juan Pierre	.15
93	Fernando Vina	.15
94	Paul LoDuca	.15
95	Mark Grace	.25
96	Eric Young	.15
97	Placido Polanco	.15
98	Jason Kendall	.15
99	Ichiro Suzuki	1.00
100	Orlando Cabrera	.15
101	Rey Sanchez	.15
102	Ichiro Suzuki	1.00
103	Edgar Martinez	.25
104	Bret Boone	.25
105	Barry Bonds	1.50
106	Ivan Rodriguez	.40
107	Mike Piazza	1.00
108	Sammy Sosa	1.00
109	John Olerud	.25
110	Roberto Alomar	.40
111	Roberto Alomar	.40
112	Mark McGwire	1.50
113	Barry Larkin	.25
114	Ken Griffey Jr.	1.00
115	Rickey Henderson	.25
116	Barry Bonds	1.50
117	Ivan Rodriguez	.40
118	Mike Piazza	1.00
119	Roger Clemens	1.00
120	Randy Johnson	.50
121	Albert Pujols	1.00
122	Ichiro Suzuki	1.00
123	Roy Oswalt	.25
124	C.C. Sabathia	.15
125	Jimmy Rollins	.25
126	Alfonso Soriano	.50

127	David Eckstein	.15
128	Adam Dunn	.50
129	Bud Smith	.15
130	Tsuyoshi Shinjo	.15
131	Matt Morris	.15
132	Curt Schilling	.25
133	Randy Johnson	.50
134	Mark Mulder	.25
135	Roger Clemens	1.00
136	Jon Lieber	.15
137	Jamie Moyer	.15
138	Freddy Garcia	.15
139	Tim Hudson	.25
140	C.C. Sabathia	.15
141	Randy Johnson	.50
142	Curt Schilling	.25
143	John Burkett	.15
144	Freddy Garcia	.15
145	Greg Maddux	.75
146	Darryl Kile	.15
147	Mike Mussina	.40
148	Joe Mays	.15
149	Matt Morris	.25
150	Russ Ortiz	.15
151	Randy Johnson	.50
152	Curt Schilling	.25
153	Hideo Nomo	.15
154	Chan Ho Park	.15
155	Kerry Wood	.50
156	Mike Mussina	.40
157	Roger Clemens	1.00
158	Javier Vazquez	.15
159	Barry Zito	.25
160	Bartolo Colon	.15
161	Mariano Rivera	.25
162	Robb Nen	.15
163	Kazuhiro Sasaki	.15
164	Armando Benitez	.15
165	Trevor Hoffman	.15
166	Jeff Shaw	.15
167	Keith Foulke	.15
168	Jose Mesa	.15
169	Troy Percival	.15
170	Billy Wagner	.15
171	Pat Burrell	.25
172	Raul Mondesi	.15
173	Gary Sheffield	.25
174	Carlos Beltran	.25
175	Vladimir Guerrero	.50
176	Torii Hunter	.25
177	Jeromy Burnitz	.15
178	Tim Salmon	.15
179	Jim Edmonds	.25
180	Tsuyoshi Shinjo	.15
181	Greg Maddux	.75
182	Roberto Alomar	.40
183	Ken Griffey Jr.	1.00
184	Ivan Rodriguez	.40
185	Omar Vizquel	.15
186	Barry Bonds	1.50
187	Devon White	.15
188	J.T. Snow	.15
189	Larry Walker	.25
190	Robin Ventura	.15
191	Mark Phillips RC	3.00
192	Clint Nageotte RC	2.00
193	Mauricio Lara RC	.75
194	Nic Jackson RC	.75
195	Chris Tritle RC	.75
196	Ryan Gripp RC	.75
197	Greg Montalbano RC	.75
198	Noochie Varner RC	.75
199	Nick Alvarez RC	.75
200	Craig Kuzmic RC	.75

Die-Cut

Stars (1-200):	2-4X
Inserted 1:4	

Autographs

	NM/M
Common Autograph:	10.00
Inserted 1:67	
BB	Barry Bonds	180.00
BBO	Bret Boone	20.00
RCL	Roger Clemens	100.00
JE	Jim Edmonds	25.00
CF	Cliff Floyd	10.00
LG	Luis Gonzalez	15.00
CG	Cristian Guzman	10.00
RO	Roy Oswalt	15.00
JR	Jimmy Rollins	15.00
BZ	Barry Zito	20.00

Relics

	NM/M
Common Player:	8.00
Bat Relic 1:27	
Jersey Relic 1:26	
BA	Bob Abreu/Bat	12.00
RA	Roberto Alomar/Bat	15.00
MA	Moises Alou/Bat	8.00
GA	Garret Anderson/Bat	10.00
JBA	Jeff Bagwell/Jsy	15.00

CB	Carlos Beltran/Bat	10.00
AB	Armando Benitez/Jsy	8.00
LB	Lance Berkman/Bat	15.00
CBI	Craig Biggio/Jsy	15.00
BB	Barry Bonds/Jsy	25.00
BBO	Bret Boone/Bat	10.00
JBU	John Burkett/Jsy	8.00
JB	Jeromy Burnitz/Jsy	8.00
MC	Mike Cameron/Bat	10.00
LC	Luis Castillo/Bat	8.00
RC	Roger Cedeno/Bat	8.00
BC	Bartolo Colon/Jsy	8.00
RD	Ray Durham/Bat	8.00
JE	Jim Edmonds/Bat	15.00
CF	Cliff Floyd/Bat	8.00
FG	Freddy Garcia/Jsy	8.00
JGO	Juan Gonzalez/Bat	10.00
LG	Luis Gonzalez/Jsy	10.00
MG	Mark Grace/Bat	20.00
SG	Shawn Green/Bat	10.00
CG	Cristian Guzman/Bat	10.00
TH	Todd Helton/Bat	15.00
THO	Trevor Hoffman/Jsy	10.00
THU	Torii Hunter/Bat	15.00
RJ	Randy Johnson/Jsy	20.00
CJ	Chipper Jones/Bat	20.00
JK	Jason Kendall/Jsy	10.00
JKE	Jeff Kent/Jsy	10.00
CK	Chuck Knoblauch/Bat	10.00
PL	Paul LoDuca/Jsy	10.00
GM	Greg Maddux/Jsy	20.00
EM	Edgar Martinez/Jsy	10.00
MM	Mark McLemore/Bat	8.00
PM	Raul Mondesi/Bat	8.00
PN	Phil Nevin/Bat	8.00
JO	John Olerud/Jsy	8.00
RP	Rafael Palmeiro/Jsy	12.00
CP	Chan Ho Park/Jsy	8.00
MP	Mike Piazza/Jsy	20.00
JP	Juan Pierre/Jsy	10.00
PP	Placido Polanco/Bat	10.00
AP	Albert Pujols/Bat	25.00
AR	Alex Rodriguez/Jsy	10.00
TS	Tim Salmon/Bat	10.00
CS	Curt Schilling/Jsy	15.00
RS	Richie Sexson/Jsy	10.00
GS	Gary Sheffield/Jsy	10.00
TSH	Tsuyoshi Shinjo/Bat	10.00
JS	J.T. Snow/Bat	10.00
AS	Alfonso Soriano/Bat	15.00
SS	Shannon Stewart/Bat	8.00
MS	Mike Sweeney/Bat	15.00
JT	Jim Thome/Bat	20.00
RV	Robin Ventura/Bat	8.00
FV	Fernando Vina/Bat	10.00
OV	Omar Vizquel/Bat	10.00
BW	Billy Wagner/Jsy	10.00
LW	Larry Walker/Bat	10.00
DW	Devon White/Bat	8.00
BZ	Barry Zito/Jsy	10.00

Team Topps Legends Autographs

	NM/M
Common Player:	
Carl Yastrzemski	65.00

2002 Topps Total

	NM/M
Complete Set (990):	125.00

Common Player:	.10
Pack (10):	1.00
Box (36):	30.00

No.	Player	Price	No.	Player	Price	No.	Player	Price	No.	Player	Price
1	Joe Mauer RC	5.00	102	Danny Graves	.10	206	Russ Ortiz	.10	310	Jorge Posada	.25
2	Derek Jeter	2.00	103	Brandon Berger RC	.10	207	Nate Rolison	.10	311	Jason Conti	.10
3	Shawn Green	.25	104	Carlos Garcia	.10	208	Jose Cruz Jr.	.10	312	Kevin Millar	.10
4	Vladimir Guerrero	.50	105	Alfonso Soriano	.75	209	Bill Ortega	.10	313	Paul Shuey	.10
5	Mike Piazza	1.50	106	Allan Simpson RC	.25	210	Carl Everett	.10	314	Jake Mauer RC	.75
6	Brandon Duckworth	.10	107	Brad Thomas	.10	211	Luis Lopez	.10	315	Luke Hudson	.10
7	Aramis Ramirez	.10	108	Devon White	.10	212	Brian Wolfe RC	.25	316	Angel Berroa	.10
8	Josh Barfield	1.00	109	Scott Chiasson	.10	213	Doug Davis	.10	317	Fred Bastardo RC	.25
9	Troy Glaus	.40	110	Cliff Floyd	.10	214	Troy Mattes	.10	318	Shawn Estes	.10
10	Sammy Sosa	1.00	111	Scott Williamson	.10	215	Al Leiter	.10	319	Andy Ashby	.10
11	Rod Barajas	.10	112	Julio Zuleta	.10	216	Joe Mays	.10	320	Ryan Klesko	.10
12	Tsuyoshi Shinjo	.25	113	Terry Adams	.10	217	Bobby Smith	.10	321	Kevin Appier	.10
13	Larry Bigbie	.10	114	Zach Day	.10	218	J.J. Trujillo RC	.25	322	Juan Pena	.10
14	Tino Martinez	.10	115	Ben Grieve	.10	219	Hideo Nomo	.25	323	Alex Herrera	.10
15	Craig Biggio	.25	116	Mark Ellis	.10	220	Jimmy Rollins	.25	324	Robb Nen	.10
16	Anastacio Martinez RC	.40	117	Bobby Jenks RC	.75	221	Bobby Seay	.10	325	Orlando Hudson	.10
17	John McDonald	.10	118	LaTroy Hawkins	.10	222	Mike Thurman	.10	326	Lyle Overbay	.10
18	Kyle Kane RC	.30	119	Tim Raines Jr.	.10	223	Bartolo Colon	.10	327	Ben Sheets	.25
19	Aubrey Huff	.10	120	Juan Uribe	.10	224	Jesus Sanchez	.10	328	Mike DiFelice	.10
20	Juan Cruz	.10	121	Bob Scanlan	.10	225	Ray Durham	.10	329	Pablo Arias RC	.25
21	Doug Creek	.10	122	Brad Nelson RC	1.50	226	Juan Diaz	.10	330	Mike Sweeney	.10
22	Luther Hackman	.10	123	Adam Johnson	.10	227	Lee Stevens	.10	331	Rick Ankiel	.10
23	Rafael Furcal	.10	124	Raul Casanova	.10	228	Ben Howard RC	.75	332	Tomas De La Rosa	.25
24	Andres Torres	.10	125	Jeff D'Amico	.10	229	James Moulton	.10	333	Kazuhisa Ishii RC	1.00
25	Jason Giambi	.50	126	Aaron Cook RC	.50	230	Paul Quantrill	.10	334	Jose Reyes	.10
26	Jose Paniagua	.10	127	Alan Benes	.10	231	Randy Knorr	.10	335	Jeremy Giambi	.10
27	Jose Offerman	.10	128	Mark Little	.10	232	Abraham Nunez	.10	336	Jose Mesa	.10
28	Alex Arias	.10	129	Randy Wolf	.10	233	Mike Fetters	.10	337	Ralph Roberts RC	.25
29	J.M. Gold	.10	130	Phil Nevin	.10	234	Mario Encarnacion	.10	338	Jose Nunez	.10
30	Jeff Bagwell	.50	131	Guillermo Mota	.10	235	Jeremy Fikac	.10	339	Curt Schilling	.40
31	Brent Cookson RC	.20	132	Nick Neugebauer	.10	236	Travis Lee	.10	340	Sean Casey	.20
32	Kelly Wunsch	.10	133	Pedro Borbon	.10	237	Bob File	.10	341	Bob Wells	.10
33	Larry Walker	.25	134	Doug Mientkiewicz	.10	238	Pete Harnisch	.10	342	Carlos Beltran	.10
34	Luis Gonzalez	.25	135	Edgardo Alfonzo	.10	239	Randy Galvez RC	.25	343	Alexis Gomez	.10
35	John Franco	.10	136	Dustan Mohr	.10	240	Geoff Goetz	.10	344	Brandon Claussen	.25
36	Roy Oswalt	.25	137	Dan Reichert	.10	241	Gary Glover	.10	345	Buddy Groom	.10
37	Tom Glavine	.25	138	Dewon Brazelton	.10	242	Troy Percival	.10	346	Mark Phillips RC	.50
38	C.C. Sabathia	.10	139	Orlando Cabrera	.10	243	Lenny Dinardo RC	.40	347	Francisco Cordova	.10
39	Jay Gibbons	.10	140	Todd Hollandsworth	.10	244	Jonny Gomes RC	2.00	348	Joe Oliver	.10
40	Wilson Betemit	.10	141	Darren Dreifort	.10	245	Jesus Medrano RC	.25	349	Danny Patterson	.10
41	Tony Armas	.10	142	Jose Valentin	.10	246	Rey Ordonez	.10	350	Joel Pineiro	.10
42	Mo Vaughn	.10	143	Josh Kalinowski	.10	247	Juan Gonzalez	.50	351	J.R. House	.10
43	Gerard Oakes RC	.40	144	Randy Keisler	.10	248	Jose Guillen	.10	352	Benny Agbayani	.10
44	Dmitri Young	.10	145	Bret Boone	.10	249	Franklin German RC	.25	353	Jose Vidro	.10
45	Tim Salmon	.10	146	Roosevelt Brown	.10	250	Mike Mussina	.40	354	Reed Johnson RC	.10
46	Barry Zito	.10	147	Brent Abernathy	.10	251	Ugueth Urbina	.10	355	Mike Lowell	.10
47	Adrian Gonzalez	.10	148	Jorge Julio	.10	252	Melvin Mora	.10	356	Scott Schoeneweis	.10
48	Joe Davenport	.10	149	Alex Gonzalez	.10	253	Gerald Williams	.10	357	Brian Jordan	.10
49	Adrian Hernandez	.10	150	Juan Pierre	.10	254	Jared Sandberg	.10	358	Steve Finley	.10
50	Randy Johnson	.50	151	Roger Cedeno	.10	255	Darrin Fletcher	.10	359	Randy Choate	.10
51	Benito Baez	.10	152	Javier Vazquez	.10	256	A.J. Pierzynski	.10	360	Jose Lima	.10
52	Adam Pettyjohn	.10	153	Armando Benitez	.10	257	Lenny Harris	.10	361	Miguel Olivo	.10
53	Alex Escobar	.10	154	Dave Burba	.10	258	Blaine Neal	.10	362	Kenny Rogers	.10
54	Stevenson Agosto RC	.25	155	Brad Penny	.10	259	Denny Neagle	.10	363	David Justice	.20
55	Omar Daal	.10	156	Ryan Jensen	.10	260	Jason Hart	.10	364	Brandon Knight	.10
56	Mike Buddie	.10	157	Jeromy Burnitz	.10	261	Henry Mateo	.10	365	Joe Kennedy	.10
57	Dave Williams	.10	158	Matt Childers RC	.40	262	Rheal Cormier	.10	366	Eric Valent	.10
58	Marquis Grissom	.10	159	Wilmy Caceres	.10	263	Luis Terrero	.10	367	Nelson Cruz	.10
59	Pat Burrell	.25	160	Roger Clemens	.10	264	Shigetoshi Hasegawa	.10	368	Brian Giles	.25
60	Mark Prior	2.00	161	Michael Tejera	.10	265	Bill Haselman	.10	369	Charles Gibson Jr.	.10
61	Mike Bynum	.10	162	Jason Christiansen	.10	266	Scott Hatteberg	.10	370	Juan Pena	.10
62	Mike Hill RC	.25	163	Pokey Reese	.10	267	Adam Hyzdu	.10	371	Mark Redman	.10
63	Brandon Backe RC	.25	164	Ivanon Coffie	.10	268	Mike Williams	.10	372	Billy Koch	.10
64	Dan Wilson	.10	165	Joaquin Benoit	.10	269	Marlon Anderson	.10	373	Ted Lilly	.10
65	Nick Johnson	.10	166	Mike Matheny	.10	270	Bruce Chen	.10	374	Craig Paquette	.10
66	Jason Grimsley	.10	167	Eric Cammack	.10	271	Eli Marrero	.10	375	Kevin Jarvis	.10
67	Russ Johnson	.10	168	Alex Graman	.10	272	Jimmy Haynes	.10	376	Scott Erickson	.10
68	Todd Walker	.10	169	Bronson Fordyce	.10	273	Bronson Arroyo	.10	377	Josh Paul	.10
69	Kyle Farnsworth	.10	170	Mike Lieberthal	.10	274	Kevin Jordan	.10	378	Darwin Cubillan	.10
70	Ben Broussard	.10	171	Giovanni Carrara	.10	275	Rick Helling	.10	379	Nelson Figueroa	.10
71	Garrett Guzman RC	.50	172	Antonio Perez	.10	276	Mark Loretta	.10	380	Darin Erstad	.20
72	Terry Mulholland	.10	173	Fernando Tatis	.10	277	Dustin Hermanson	.10	381	Jeremy Hill RC	.25
73	Tyler Houston	.10	174	Jason Bay RC	2.00	278	Pablo Ozuna	.10	382	Elvin Nina	.10
74	Jace Brewer	.10	175	Jason Botts RC	.50	279	Syketo Anderson RC	.25	383	David Wells	.25
75	Chris Baker RC	.25	176	Danys Baez	.10	280	Jermaine Dye	.10	384	Jay Caligiuri RC	.40
76	Frank Catalanotto	.10	177	Shea Hillenbrand	.10	281	Will Smith	.10	385	Freddy Garcia	.10
77	Mike Redmond	.10	178	Jack Cust	.10	282	Brian Daubach	.10	386	Damian Miller	.10
78	Matt Wise	.10	179	Clay Bellinger	.10	283	Eric Hinske	.10	387	Bobby Higginson	.10
79	Fernando Vina	.10	180	Roberto Alomar	.10	284	Joe Jiannetti RC	.40	388	Alejandro Giron RC	.25
80	Kevin Brown	.10	181	Graeme Lloyd	.10	285	Chan Ho Park	.10	389	Ivan Rodriguez	.40
81	Grant Balfour	.10	182	Clint Weibl RC	.40	286	Curtis Legendre RC	.25	390	Ed Rogers	.10
82	Clint Nageotte RC	.75	183	Royce Clayton	.10	287	Jeff Reboulet	.10	391	Andy Benes	.10
83	Jeff Tam	.10	184	Ben Davis	.10	288	Scott Rolen	.50	392	Matt Blank	.10
84	Steve Trachsel	.10	185	Brian Adams	.25	289	Chris Richard	.10	393	Ryan Vogelsong	.10
85	Tomokazu Ohka	.10	186	Jack Wilson	.10	290	Eric Chavez	.25	394	Kelly Ramos RC	.25
86	Keith McDonald	.10	187	David Coggin	.10	291	Scot Shields	.10	395	Eric Karros	.10
87	Jose Ortiz	.10	188	Derrick Turnbow	.10	292	Donnie Sadler	.10	396	Bobby Jones	.10
88	Rusty Greer	.10	189	Vladimir Nunez	.10	293	Dave Veres	.10	397	Omar Vizquel	.25
89	Jeff Suppan	.10	190	Mariano Rivera	.10	294	Craig Counsell	.10	398	Matt Perisho	.10
90	Moises Alou	.10	191	Wilson Guzman	.10	295	Armando Reynoso	.10	399	Delino DeShields	.10
91	Juan Encarnacion	.10	192	Michael Barrett	.10	296	Kyle Lohse	.10	400	Carlos Hernandez	.10
92	Tyler Yates RC	.40	193	Corey Patterson	.10	297	Arthur Rhodes	.10	401	Derek Lee	.10
93	Scott Strickland	.10	194	Luis Sojo	.10	298	Sidney Ponson	.10	402	Kirk Rueter	.10
94	Brent Butler	.10	195	Scott Elarton	.10	299	Trevor Hoffman	.10	403	David Wright	30.00
95	Jon Rauch	.10	196	Charles Thomas	.25	300	Kerry Wood	.25	404	Paul LoDuca	.10
96	Brian Mallette RC	.25	197	Ricky Bottalico	.10	301	Danny Bautista	.10	405	Brian Schneider	.10
97	Joe Randa	.10	198	Wilfredo Rodriguez	.10	302	Scott Sauerbeck	.10	406	Milton Bradley	.10
98	Cesar Crespo	.10	199	Ricardo Rincon	.10	303	Johnny Estrada	.10	407	Daryle Ward	.10
99	Felix Rodriguez	.10	200	John Smoltz	.10	304	Mike Timlin	.10	408	Cody Ransom	.10
100	Chipper Jones	.75	201	Travis Miller	.10	305	Orlando Hernandez	.25	409	Fernando Rodney	.10
101	Victor Martinez	.10	202	Ben Weber	.10	306	Tony Clark	.10	410	John Suomi RC	.20
			203	T.J. Tucker	.10	307	Tomas Perez	.10	411	Joe Girardi	.10
			204	Terry Shumpert	.10	308	Marcus Giles	.10	412	Demetrius Heath RC	.25
			205	Bernie Williams	.10	309	Mike Bordick	.10	413	John Foster RC	.25

#	Player	Price	#	Player	Price	#	Player	Price	#	Player	Price
414	Doug Glanville	.10	518	Doug Nickle	.10	622	Chad Hutchinson	.10	726	Mark Johnson	.10
415	Ryan Kohlmeier	.10	519	Ramon Ortiz	.10	623	Todd Greene	.10	727	B.J. Ryan	.10
416	Mike Matthews	.10	520	Greg Swindell	.10	624	David Eckstein	.10	728	Wendell Magee	.10
417	Craig Wilson	.10	521	J.J. Davis	.10	625	Greg Montalbano RC	1.00	729	Michael Coleman	.10
418	Jay Witasick	.10	522	Sandy Alomar	.10	626	Joe Beimel	.10	730	Mario Ramos	.50
419	Jay Payton	.10	523	Chris Carpenter	.10	627	Adrian Beltre	.20	731	Mike Stanton	.10
420	Andruw Jones	.40	524	Vance Wilson	.10	628	Charles Nagy	.10	732	Dee Brown	.10
421	Benji Gil	.10	525	Nomar Garciaparra	1.00	629	Cristian Guzman	.10	733	Brad Ausmus	.10
422	Jeff Liefer	.10	526	Jim Mecir	.10	630	Toby Hall	.10	734	Napoleon Calzado RC	.25
423	Kevin Young	.10	527	Taylor Buchholz RC	.25	631	Jose Hernandez	.10	735	Woody Williams	.10
424	Richie Sexson	.25	528	Brent Mayne	.10	632	Jose Macias	.10	736	Paxton Crawford	.10
425	Cory Lidle	.10	529	John Rodriguez RC	.25	633	Jaret Wright	.10	737	Jason Karnuth	.10
426	Shane Halter	.10	530	David Segui	.10	634	Steve Parris	.10	738	Michael Restovich	.10
427	Jesse Foppert	.40	531	Nate Cornejo	.10	635	Gene Kingsdale	.10	739	Ramon Castro	.10
428	Jose Molina	.10	532	Gil Heredia	.10	636	Tim Worrell	.10	740	Magglio Ordonez	.25
429	Nick Alvarez RC	.40	533	Esteban Loaiza	.10	637	Billy Martin	.10	741	Tom Gordon	.10
430	Brian L. Hunter	.10	534	Pat Mahomes	.10	638	Jovanny Cedeno	.10	742	Mark Grudzielanek	.10
431	Clifford Bartosh RC	.25	535	Matt Morris	.20	639	Curt Leskanic	.10	743	Jamie Moyer	.10
432	Junior Spivey	.10	536	Todd Stottlemyre	.10	640	Tim Hudson	.20	744	Marlyn Tisdale RC	.20
433	Eric Good RC	.25	537	Brian Lesher	.10	641	Juan Castro	.10	745	Steve Kline	.10
434	Chin-Feng Chen	.10	538	Arturo McDowell	.10	642	Rafael Soriano	.10	746	Adam Eaton	.10
435	T.J. Mathews	.10	539	Felix Diaz	.10	643	Juan Rincon	.10	747	Eric Glaser RC	.25
436	Rich Rodriguez	.10	540	Mark Mulder	.10	644	Mark DeRosa	.10	748	Sean DePaula	.10
437	Bobby Abreu	.20	541	Kevin Frederick RC	.25	645	Carlos Pena	.10	749	Greg Norton	.10
438	Joe McEwing	.10	542	Andy Fox	.10	646	Robin Ventura	.20	750	Steve Reed	.10
439	Michael Tucker	.10	543	Dionys Cesar RC	.10	647	Odalis Perez	.10	751	Ricardo Aramboles	.10
440	Preston Wilson	.10	544	Justin Miller	.10	648	Damion Easley	.10	752	Matt Mantei	.10
441	Mike MacDougal	.10	545	Keith Osik	.10	649	Benito Santiago	.10	753	Gene Stechschulte	.10
442	Shannon Stewart	.10	546	Shane Reynolds	.10	650	Alex Rodriguez	1.50	754	Chuck McElroy	.10
443	Bob Howry	.10	547	Mike Myers	.10	651	Aaron Rowand	.10	755	Barry Bonds	1.50
444	Mike Benjamin	.10	548	Raul Chavez RC	.25	652	Alex Cora	.10	756	Matt Anderson	.10
445	Erik Hiljus	.10	549	Joe Nathan	.10	653	Bobby Kielty	.10	757	Yorvit Torrealba	.10
446	Ryan Gripp RC	.25	550	Ryan Anderson	.10	654	Jose Rodriguez	.10	758	Jason Standridge	.10
447	Jose Vizcaino	.10	551	Jason Marquis	.10	655	Herbert Perry	.10	759	Desi Relaford	.10
448	Shawn Wooten	.10	552	Marty Cordova	.10	656	Jeff Urban	.10	760	Jolbert Cabrera	.10
449	Steve Kent RC	.25	553	Kevin Tapani	.10	657	Paul Bako	.10	761	Chris George	.10
450	Ramiro Mendoza	.10	554	Jimmy Anderson	.10	658	Shane Spencer	.10	762	Erubiel Durazo	.10
451	Jake Westbrook	.10	555	Pedro Martinez	.50	659	Pat Hentgen	.10	763	Paul Konerko	.25
452	Joe Lawrence	.10	556	Rocky Biddle	.10	660	Jeff Kent	.20	764	Tike Redman	.10
453	Jae Weong Seo	.10	557	Alex Ochoa	.10	661	Mark McLemore	.10	765	Chad Ricketts RC	.20
454	Ryan Fry RC	.20	558	D'Angelo Jimenez	.10	662	Chuck Knoblauch	.10	766	Roberto Hernandez	.10
455	Darren Lewis	.10	559	Wilkin Ruan	.10	663	Blake Stein	.10	767	Mark Lewis	.10
456	Brad Wilkerson	.10	560	Terrence Long	.10	664	Brett Roneberg RC	.25	768	Livan Hernandez	.10
457	Gustavo Chacin RC	.25	561	Mark Lukasiewicz	.10	665	Josh Phelps	.10	769	Carlos Brackley RC	.25
458	Adrian Brown	.10	562	Jose Santiago	.10	666	Byung-Hyun Kim	.10	770	Kazuhiro Sasaki	.10
459	Mike Cameron	.10	563	Brad Fullmer	.10	667	Dave Martinez	.10	771	Bill Hall	.10
460	Bud Smith	.10	564	Corky Miller	.10	668	Mike Maroth	.10	772	Nelson Castro RC	.25
461	Derrick Lewis	.10	565	Matt White	.10	669	Shawn Chacon	.10	773	Eric Milton	.10
462	Derek Lowe	.10	566	Mark Grace	.30	670	Billy Wagner	.10	774	Tom Davey	.10
463	Matt Williams	.10	567	Raul Ibanez	.10	671	Luis Alicea	.10	775	Todd Ritchie	.10
464	Jason Jennings	.10	568	Josh Towers	.10	672	Sterling Hitchcock	.10	776	Seth Etherton	.10
465	Albie Lopez	.10	569	Juan Gonzalez	.40	673	Adam Piatt	.10	777	Chris Singleton	.10
466	Felipe Lopez	.10	570	Brian Buchanan	.10	674	Ryan Franklin	.10	778	Robert Averette RC	.20
467	Luke Allen	.10	571	Ken Harvey	.10	675	Luke Prokopec	.10	779	Robert Person	.10
468	Brian Anderson	.10	572	Jeffrey Hammonds	.10	676	Alfredo Amezega	.10	780	Fred McGriff	.25
469	Matt Riley	.10	573	Wade Miller	.10	677	Gookie Dawkins	.10	781	Richard Hidalgo	.10
470	Ryan Dempster	.10	574	Elpidio Guzman	.10	678	Eric Byrnes	.10	782	Kris Wilson	.10
471	Matt Ginter	.10	575	Kevin Olsen	.10	679	Barry Larkin	.25	783	John Rocker	.10
472	David Ortiz	.10	576	Austin Kearns	.40	680	Albert Pujols	1.00	784	Justin Kaye	.10
473	Cole Barthel	.10	577	Tim Kalita RC	.40	681	Edwards Guzman	.10	785	Glendon Rusch	.10
474	Damian Jackson	.10	578	David Dellucci	.10	682	Jason Bere	.10	786	Greg Vaughn	.10
475	Andy Van Hekken	.10	579	Alex Gonzalez	.10	683	Adam Everett	.10	787	Mike Lamb	.10
476	Doug Brocail	.10	580	Joe Orloski RC	.20	684	Greg Colbrunn	.10	788	Greg Myers	.10
477	Denny Hocking	.10	581	Gary Matthews Jr.	.10	685	Brandon Puffer RC	.40	789	Nate Field RC	.25
478	Sean Douglass	.10	582	Ryan Mills	.10	686	Mark Kotsay	.10	790	Jim Edmonds	.25
479	Eric Owens	.10	583	Erick Almonte	.10	687	Willie Bloomquist	.10	791	Olmedo Saenz	.10
480	Ryan Ludwick	.10	584	Jeremy Affeldt	.10	688	Hank Blalock	.25	792	Jason Johnson	.10
481	Todd Pratt	.10	585	Chris Tritle RC	1.00	689	Travis Hafner	.10	793	Mike Lincoln	.10
482	Aaron Sele	.10	586	Michael Cuddyer	.10	690	Lance Berkman	.40	794	Todd Coffey	.10
483	Edgar Renteria	.10	587	Kris Foster	.10	691	Joe Crede	.10	795	Jesus Sanchez	.10
484	Raymond Cabrera RC	.25	588	Russell Branyan	.10	692	Chuck Finley	.10	796	Aaron Myette	.10
485	Brandon Lyon	.10	589	Darren Oliver	.10	693	John Grabow	.10	797	Tony Womack	.10
486	Chase Utley	.25	590	Freddie Money RC	.25	694	Randy Winn	.10	798	Chad Kreuter	.10
487	Robert Fick	.10	591	Carlos Lee	.10	695	Mike James	.10	799	Brady Clark	.10
488	Wilfredo Cordero	.10	592	Tim Wakefield	.10	696	Kris Benson	.10	800	Adam Dunn	.50
489	Octavio Dotel	.10	593	Bubba Trammell	.10	697	Bret Prinz	.10	801	Jacque Jones	.10
490	Paul Abbott	.10	594	John Koronka RC	3.00	698	Jeff Williams	.10	802	Kevin Millwood	.10
491	Jason Kendall	.10	595	Geoff Blum	.10	699	Eric Munson	.10	803	Mike Rivera	.10
492	Jarrod Washburn	.10	596	Darryl Kile	.10	700	Mike Hampton	.10	804	Jim Thome	.40
493	Dane Sardinha	.10	597	Neifi Perez	.10	701	Ramon E. Martinez	.10	805	Jeff Conine	.10
494	Jung Bong	.10	598	Torii Hunter	.10	702	Hansel Izquierdo RC	.25	806	Elmer Dessens	.10
495	J.D. Drew	.10	599	Luis Castillo	.10	703	Nathan Haynes	.10	807	Randy Velarde	.10
496	Jason Schmidt	.10	600	Mark Buehrle	.10	704	Eddie Taubensee	.10	808	Carlos Delgado	.30
497	Mike Magnante	.10	601	Jeff Zimmerman	.10	705	Esteban German	.10	809	Steve Karsay	.10
498	Jorge Padilla RC	.50	602	Mike DeJean	.10	706	Ross Gload	.10	810	Casey Fossum	.10
499	Eric Gagne	.10	603	Julio Lugo	.10	707	Matthew Merricks RC	.20	811	J.C. Romero	.10
500	Todd Helton	.50	604	Chad Hermansen	.10	708	Chris Piersoll RC	.25	812	Chris Truby	.10
501	Jeff Weaver	.10	605	Keith Foulke	.10	709	Seth Greisinger	.10	813	Tony Graffanino	.10
502	Alex Sanchez	.10	606	Lance Davis	.10	710	Ichiro Suzuki	1.00	814	Wascar Serrano	.10
503	Ken Griffey Jr.	.10	607	Jeff Austin RC	.25	711	Cesar Izturis	.10	815	Delvin James	.10
504	Abraham Nunez	.10	608	Brandon Inge	.10	712	Brad Cresse	.10	816	Pedro Feliz	.10
505	Reggie Sanders	.10	609	Orlando Merced	.10	713	Carl Pavano	.10	817	Damian Rolls	.10
506	Casey Kotchman	2.00	610	Johnny Damon	.10	714	Steve Sparks	.10	818	Scott Linebrink	.10
507	Jim Mann	.10	611	Doug Henry	.10	715	Dennis Tankersley	.10	819	Rafael Palmeiro	.40
508	Matt LeCroy	.10	612	Adam Kennedy	.10	716	Kelvim Escobar	.10	820	Javy Lopez	.10
509	Frank Castillo	.10	613	Wiki Gonzalez	.10	717	Jason LaRue	.10	821	Larry Barnes	.10
510	Geoff Jenkins	.20	614	Brian West RC	.25	718	Corey Koskie	.10	822	Brian Lawrence	.10
511	Jayson Durocher RC	.20	615	Andy Pettitte	.25	719	Vinny Castilla	.10	823	Scotty Layfield RC	.25
512	Ellis Burks	.10	616	Chone Figgins RC	.25	720	Tim Drew	.10	824	Jeff Cirillo	.10
513	Aaron Fultz	.10	617	Matt Lawton	.10	721	Chin-Hui Tsao	.10	825	Willis Roberts	.10
514	Hiram Bocachica	.10	618	Paul Rigdon	.10	722	Paul Byrd	.10	826	Rich Harden RC	4.00
515	Nate Espy RC	.10	619	Keith Lockhart	.10	723	Alex Cintron	.10	827	Chris Snelling RC	1.00
516	Placido Polanco	.10	620	Tim Redding	.10	724	Orlando Palmeiro	.10	828	Gary Sheffield	.25
517	Kerry Ligtenberg	.10	621	John Parrish	.10	725	Ramon Hernandez	.10	829	Jeff Heaverlo	.10

830	Matt Clement	.10
831	Rich Garces	.10
832	Rondell White	.10
833	Henry Pichardo RC	.25
834	Aaron Boone	.10
835	Ruben Sierra	.10
836	Deivis Santos	.10
837	Tony Batista	.10
838	Rob Bell	.10
839	Frank Thomas	.50
840	Jose Silva	.10
841	Dan Johnson RC	.50
842	Steve Cox	.10
843	Jose Acevedo	.10
844	Jay Bell	.10
845	Mike Sirotka	.10
846	Garret Anderson	.10
847	James Shanks RC	.25
848	Trot Nixon	.10
849	Keith Ginter	.10
850	Tim Spooneybarger	.10
851	Matt Stairs	.10
852	Chris Stynes	.10
853	Marvin Bernard	.10
854	Raul Mondesi	.20
855	Jeremy Owens	.10
856	Jon Garland	.10
857	Mitch Meluskey	.10
858	Chad Durbin	.10
859	John Burkett	.10
860	Jon Switzer	.10
861	Peter Bergeron	.10
862	Jesus Colome	.10
863	Todd Hundley	.10
864	Ben Petrick	.10
865	So Taguchi RC	.75
866	Ryan Drese	.10
867	Mike Trombley	.10
868	Rick Reed	.10
869	Mark Teixeira	.20
870	Corey Thurman RC	.10
871	Brian Roberts	.10
872	Mike Timlin	.10
873	Chris Reitsma	.10
874	Jeff Fassero	.10
875	Carlos Valderrama	.10
876	John Lackey	.10
877	Travis Fryman	.10
878	Ismael Valdes	.10
879	Rick White	.10
880	Edgar Martinez	.10
881	Dean Palmer	.10
882	Matt Allegra RC	.20
883	Greg Sain RC	.25
884	Carlos Silva	.10
885	Jose Valverde RC	.25
886	Dernell Stenson	.10
887	Todd Van Poppel	.10
888	Wes Anderson	.10
889	Bill Mueller	.10
890	Morgan Ensberg	.10
891	Marcus Thames	.10
892	Adam Walker RC	.10
893	John Halama	.10
894	Frank Menechino	.10
895	Greg Maddux	1.00
896	Gary Bennett	.10
897	Mauricio Lara RC	.25
898	Mike Young	.10
899	Travis Phelps	.10
900	Rich Aurilia	.10
901	Henry Blanco	.10
902	Carlos Febles	.10
903	Scott MacRae	.10
904	Lou Merloni	.10
905	Dicky Gonzalez	.10
906	Jeff DaVanon	.10
907	A.J. Burnett	.10
908	Einar Diaz	.10
909	Julio Franco	.10
910	John Olerud	.25
911	Mark Hamilton RC	.25
912	David Riske	.10
913	Jason Tyner	.10
914	Britt Reames	.10
915	Vernon Wells	.10
916	Eddie Perez	.10
917	Edwin Almonte RC	.25
918	Enrique Wilson	.10
919	Chris Gomez	.10
920	Jayson Werth	.10
921	Jeff Nelson	.10
922	Freddy Sanchez RC	.75
923	John Vander Wal	.10
924	Chad Qualls RC	.25
925	Gabe White	.10
926	Chad Harville	.10
927	Ricky Gutierrez	.10
928	Carlos Guillen	.10
929	B.J. Surhoff	.10
930	Chris Woodard	.10
931	Ricardo Rodriguez	.10
932	Jimmy Gobble RC	1.00
933	Jon Lieber	.10

934	Craig Kuzmic RC	.25
935	Eric Young	.10
936	Gregg Zaun	.10
937	Miguel Batista	.10
938	Danny Wright	.10
939	Todd Zeile	.10
940	Chad Zerbe	.10
941	Jason Young RC	.50
942	Ronnie Belliard	.10
943	John Ennis RC	.10
944	John Flaherty	.10
945	Jerry Hairston Jr.	.10
946	Al Levine	.10
947	Antonio Alfonseca	.10
948	Brian Moehler	.10
949	Calvin Murray	.10
950	Nick Bierbrodt	.10
951	Sun-Woo Kim	.10
952	Noochie Varner RC	.50
953	Luis Rivas	.10
954	Donnie Bridges	.10
955	Ramon Vazquez	.10
956	Luis Garcia	.10
957	Mark Quinn	.10
958	Armando Rios	.10
959	Chad Fox	.10
960	Hee Seop Choi	.10
961	Turk Wendell	.10
962	Adam Roller RC	.20
963	Grant Roberts	.10
964	Ben Molina	.10
965	Juan Rivera	.10
966	Matt Kinney	.10
967	Rod Beck	.10
968	Xavier Nady	.10
969	Masato Yoshii	.10
970	Miguel Tejada	.25
971	Danny Kolb	.10
972	Mike Remlinger	.10
973	Ray Lankford	.10
974	Ryan Minor	.10
975	J.T. Snow	.10
976	Brad Radke	.10
977	Jason Lane	.10
978	Jamey Wright	.10
979	Tom Goodwin	.10
980	Erik Bedard	.10
981	Gabe Kapler	.10
982	Brian Reith	.10
983	Nic Jackson RC	.50
984	Kurt Ainsworth	.10
985	Jason Isringhausen	.10
986	Willie Harris	.10
987	David Cone	.10
988	Bob Wickman	.10
989	Wes Helms	.10
990	Josh Beckett	.25

Award Winners

JORGE POSADA

		NM/M
Complete Set (30):		25.00
Common Player:		.75
Inserted 1:6		
AW1	Ichiro Suzuki	2.00
AW2	Albert Pujols	2.00
AW3	Barry Bonds	3.00
AW4	Ichiro Suzuki	2.00
AW5	Randy Johnson	1.00
AW6	Roger Clemens	2.00
AW7	Jason Giambi	.75
AW8	Bret Boone	.50
AW9	Troy Glaus	.75
AW10	Alex Rodriguez	2.50
AW11	Juan Gonzalez	.75
AW12	Ichiro Suzuki	2.00
AW13	Jorge Posada	.75
AW14	Edgar Martinez	.50
AW15	Todd Helton	.75
AW16	Jeff Kent	.50
AW17	Albert Pujols	2.00
AW18	Rich Aurilia	.50
AW19	Barry Bonds	3.00
AW20	Luis Gonzalez	.50

AW21	Sammy Sosa	2.00
AW22	Mike Piazza	2.00
AW23	Mike Hampton	.50
AW24	Ruben Sierra	.50
AW25	Matt Morris	.50
AW26	Curt Schilling	.75
AW27	Alex Rodriguez	2.50
AW28	Barry Bonds	3.00
AW29	Jim Thome	1.00
AW30	Barry Bonds	3.00

Total Production

MAGGLIO ORDONEZ

		NM/M
Complete Set (10):		15.00
Common Player:		.75
Inserted 1:12		
TP1	Alex Rodriguez	3.00
TP2	Barry Bonds	3.00
TP3	Ichiro Suzuki	2.00
TP4	Edgar Martinez	.75
TP5	Jason Giambi	1.00
TP6	Todd Helton	1.00
TP7	Nomar Garciaparra	2.50
TP8	Vladimir Guerrero	1.00
TP9	Sammy Sosa	2.00
TP10	Chipper Jones	2.00

Total Topps

		NM/M
Complete Set (50):		35.00
Common Player:		.50
Inserted 1:3		
TT1	Roberto Alomar	.75
TT2	Moises Alou	.50
TT3	Jeff Bagwell	1.00
TT4	Lance Berkman	.75
TT5	Barry Bonds	2.00
TT6	Bret Boone	.50
TT7	Kevin Brown	.50
TT8	Eric Chavez	.50
TT9	Roger Clemens	1.50
TT10	Carlos Delgado	.50
TT11	Cliff Floyd	.50
TT12	Nomar Garciaparra	2.50
TT13	Jason Giambi	1.00
TT14	Brian Giles	.75
TT15	Troy Glaus	.75
TT16	Tom Glavine	.50
TT17	Luis Gonzalez	.50
TT18	Juan Gonzalez	.75
TT19	Shawn Green	.50
TT20	Ken Griffey Jr.	2.50
TT21	Vladimir Guerrero	1.00
TT22	Jorge Posada	.50
TT23	Todd Helton	.75
TT24	Tim Hudson	.50
TT25	Derek Jeter	4.00
TT26	Randy Johnson	1.00
TT27	Andruw Jones	.75
TT28	Chipper Jones	2.00
TT29	Jeff Kent	.50
TT30	Greg Maddux	2.00
TT31	Edgar Martinez	.50
TT32	Pedro Martinez	1.00
TT33	Magglio Ordonez	.50
TT34	Rafael Palmeiro	.50
TT35	Mike Piazza	3.00
TT36	Albert Pujols	2.00
TT37	Aramis Ramirez	.50
TT38	Mariano Rivera	.50
TT39	Alex Rodriguez	3.00
TT40	Ivan Rodriguez	.75
TT41	Curt Schilling	.75
TT42	Gary Sheffield	.50
TT43	Sammy Sosa	2.00
TT44	Ichiro Suzuki	4.00
TT45	Miguel Tejada	.50
TT46	Frank Thomas	1.00
TT47	Jim Thome	.75
TT48	Larry Walker	.50
TT49	Bernie Williams	.50
TT50	Kerry Wood	.50

2002 Topps Tribute

		NM/M
Complete Set (90):		120.00
Common Player:		1.50
Pack (5):		35.00
Box (6):		150.00
1	Hank Aaron	6.00
2	Rogers Hornsby	2.50
3	Bobby Thomson	1.50
4	Eddie Collins	1.50
5	Joe Carter	1.50
6	Jim Palmer	1.50
7	Willie Mays	6.00
8	Willie Stargell	2.50
9	Vida Blue	1.50
10	Whitey Ford	3.00
11	Bob Gibson	3.00
12	Nellie Fox	2.00
13	Napoleon Lajoie	2.00
14	Frankie Frisch	1.50
15	Nolan Ryan	10.00
16	Brooks Robinson	2.50
17	Kirby Puckett	5.00
18	Fergie Jenkins	1.50
19	Edd Roush	1.50
20	Honus Wagner	6.00
21	Richie Ashburn	1.50
22	Bob Feller	1.50
23	Joe Morgan	1.50
24	Orlando Cepeda	1.50
25	Steve Garvey	1.50
26	Hank Greenberg	1.50
27	Stan Musial	5.00
28	Sam Crawford	1.50
29	Jim Rice	1.50
30	Hack Wilson	2.50
31	Lou Brock	1.50
32	Mickey Vernon	1.50
33	Chuck Klein	1.50
34	Joe Jackson	6.00
35	Duke Snider	3.00
36	Ryne Sandberg	5.00
37	Johnny Bench	5.00
38	Sam Rice	1.50
39	Lou Gehrig	8.00
40	Robin Yount	3.00
41	Don Sutton	1.50
42	Jim Bottomley	1.50
43	Billy Herman	1.50
44	Zach Wheat	1.50
45	Juan Marichal	1.50
46	Bert Blyleven	1.50
47	Jackie Robinson	6.00
48	Gil Hodges	1.50
49	Mike Schmidt	6.00
50	Dale Murphy	1.50
51	Phil Rizzuto	1.50
52	Ty Cobb	6.00
53	Andre Dawson	1.50
54	Fred Lindstrom	1.50
55	Roy Campanella	3.00
56	Don Larsen	2.00
57	Harry Heilmann	1.50
58	Jim "Catfish" Hunter	1.50
59	Frank Robinson	2.00
60	Bill Mazeroski	1.50
61	Roger Maris	6.00
62	Dave Winfield	2.50
63	Warren Spahn	2.50
64	Babe Ruth	10.00
65	Ernie Banks	4.00
66	Wade Boggs	2.00
67	Carl Yastrzemski	3.00
68	Ron Santo	1.50
69	Dennis Martinez	1.50
70	Yogi Berra	4.00
71	Paul Waner	1.50
72	George Brett	6.00
73	Eddie Mathews	1.50
74	Bill Dickey	1.50
75	Carlton Fisk	2.00
76	Thurman Munson	5.00

77	Reggie Jackson	4.00
78	Phil Niekro	1.50
79	Luis Aparicio	1.50
80	Steve Carlton	1.50
81	Tris Speaker	1.50
82	Johnny Mize	1.50
83	Tom Seaver	4.00
84	Heinie Manush	1.50
85	Tommy John	1.50
86	Joe Cronin	1.50
87	Don Mattingly	8.00
88	Kirk Gibson	1.50
89	Bo Jackson	3.00
90	Mel Ott	1.50

First Impressions

NM/M
Cards #'d 51-86: 3-5X
Cards #'d 26-50: 4-8X
#'d to last two digits of Rk year.
Lasting Impressions
Cards #'d 51-96: 3-5X
Cards #'d 26-50: 4-8X
#'d to last two digits of final
season
Production under 25 not priced.

Marks of Excellence

NM/M
Inserted 1:61
LB	Lou Brock	50.00
SC	Steve Carlton	50.00
DL	Don Larsen	50.00
SM	Stan Musial	100.00
MS	Mike Schmidt	85.00
WS	Warren Spahn	65.00

Marks of Excellence Relics

NM/M
Inserted 1:61
FJ	Fergie Jenkins	40.00
DM	Don Mattingly	120.00
JP	Jim Palmer	40.00
BR	Brooks Robinson	75.00
DS	Duke Snider	60.00
RY	Robin Yount	70.00

Matching Marks Dual

NM/M
Common Card: 10.00
Inserted 1:11
SBA	Ron Santo,	
	Ernie Banks	25.00
YK	Carl Yastrzemski,	
	Chuck Klein	65.00
WY	Dave Winfield,	
	Carl Yastrzemski	25.00
WYO	Dave Winfield,	
	Robin Yount	20.00
SM	Duke Snider,	
	Willie Mays	85.00
RJ	Frank Robinson,	
	Reggie Jackson	50.00
BMA	George Brett,	
	Don Mattingly	90.00
GH	Steve Garvey,	
	Gil Hodges	20.00
AR	Hank Aaron,	
	Babe Ruth	300.00

GA	Hank Greenberg,	
	Richie Ashburn	80.00
PJ	Jim Palmer,	
	Tommy John	20.00
NS	Phil Niekro,	
	Tom Seaver	15.00
SR	Willie Stargell,	
	Jim Rice	15.00
BF	Johnny Bench,	
	Carlton Fisk	50.00
RS	Nolan Ryan,	
	Tom Seaver	125.00
JS	Fergie Jenkins,	
	Tom Seaver	35.00
YP	Robin Yount,	
	Kirby Puckett	60.00
SB	Tris Speaker,	
	George Brett	100.00
BM	Vida Blue,	
	Dennis Martinez	10.00
BB	Wade Boggs,	
	George Brett	40.00
MA	Willie Mays,	
	Hank Aaron	200.00
BS	Bert Blyleven,	
	Don Sutton	15.00

Memorable Materials

NM/M
Common Player: 10.00
Season parallel: 1.5-3X
#'d to last two digits year event
occurred.
Jsy Number para.#'d
40-75: 1.5-3X
Under 40 not priced.
Numbered to jersey #.
HA	Hank Aaron	40.00
GB	George Brett	35.00
RC	Roy Campanella	30.00
JC	Joe Carter	10.00
CF	Carlton Fisk	20.00
KG	Kirk Gibson	15.00
BJ	Bo Jackson	25.00
RJ	Reggie Jackson	20.00
CK	Chuck Klein	25.00
RM	Roger Maris	75.00
DM	Don Mattingly	40.00
BM	Bill Mazeroski	15.00
JM	Joe Morgan	15.00
TM	Thurman Munson	50.00
KP	Kirby Puckett	30.00
PR	Phil Rizzuto	25.00
JR	Jackie Robinson	50.00
NR	Nolan Ryan	50.00
BT	Bobby Thomson	15.00
HW	Hack Wilson	40.00
CY	Carl Yastrzemski	30.00

Milestone Materials

NM/M
Common Player: 10.00
Inserted 1:4
Season parallel #'d 51-95:1.5-3X
#'d to last two digits milestone
season
Jersey Number par.
#'d 51-95: 1.5-3X
Numbered to Jersey Number.
Under 50 not priced yet.
LA	Luis Aparicio	15.00
EB	Ernie Banks	30.00
JB	Johnny Bench	20.00
YB	Yogi Berra	25.00
WB	Wade Boggs	15.00
JBO	Jim Bottomley	20.00
OC	Orlando Cepeda	15.00
TC	Ty Cobb	150.00
EC	Eddie Collins	30.00
SC	Sam Crawford	25.00
JC	Joe Cronin	20.00

AD	Andre Dawson	15.00
BD	Bill Dickey	15.00
BF	Bob Feller	15.00
WF	Whitey Ford	25.00
NF	Nellie Fox	30.00
FF	Frankie Frisch	25.00
LG	Lou Gehrig	150.00
BG	Bob Gibson	15.00
HH	Harry Heilmann	20.00
BH	Billy Herman	10.00
RH	Rogers Hornsby	50.00
CH	Jim "Catfish" Hunter	12.00
RJ	Reggie Jackson	20.00
NL	Napoleon Lajoie	60.00
FL	Fred Lindstrom	15.00
HM	Heinie Manush	20.00
JMA	Juan Marichal	15.00
EM	Eddie Mathews	20.00
WH	Willie Mays	45.00
JM	Johnny Mize	15.00
DM	Dale Murphy	20.00
MO	Mel Ott	40.00
JP	Jim Palmer	15.00
SR	Sam Rice	20.00
BRO	Brooks Robinson	20.00
FR	Frank Robinson	20.00
ER	Edd Roush	25.00
BR	Babe Ruth	160.00
NR	Nolan Ryan	50.00
RS	Ryne Sandberg	30.00
TS	Tom Seaver	15.00
DS	Duke Snider	20.00
TSP	Tris Speaker	65.00
WS	Willie Stargell	15.00
MV	Mickey Vernon	15.00
HW	Honus Wagner	140.00
PW	Paul Waner	30.00
ZW	Zach Wheat	40.00
RY	Robin Yount	25.00

Pasttime Patches

NM/M
Inserted 1:92
JB	Johnny Bench	125.00
WB	Wade Boggs	90.00
GB	George Brett	200.00
BD	Bill Dickey	100.00
EM	Eddie Mathews	125.00
DM	Don Mattingly	160.00
JP	Jim Palmer	75.00
KP	Kirby Puckett	125.00
NRA	Nolan Ryan	200.00
NRR	Nolan Ryan	200.00
DW	Dave Winfield	100.00
CY	Carl Yastrzemski	180.00
RY	Robin Yount	100.00

"The Catch" Dual

NM/M
Inserted 1:1,023
MW	Willie Mays,	
	Vic Wertz	250.00
MW	Willie Mays,	
	Vic Wertz/54	300.00

Signature Cuts

NM/M
Reported production 2 each.
Inserted 1:9,936
SC-TC	Ty Cobb	
	(4/04 Auction)	4,725

2002 Topps206

NM/M
Complete Set (456):	150.00
Common Player:	.20
Common	
(141-155, 271-285):	1.00
Inserted 1:2	
Series I Pack (8):	6.00
Series I Box (20):	100.00
Series II Pack (8):	4.00
Series II Box (20):	60.00
Series III Pack (8):	6.00
Series III Box (20):	100.00

1	Vladimir Guerrero	.75
2	Sammy Sosa	1.50
3	Garret Anderson	.40
4	Rafael Palmeiro	.50
5	Juan Gonzalez	.50
6	John Smoltz	.40
7	Mark Mulder	.40

SCHMIDT, Philadelphia

8	Jon Lieber	.20
9	Greg Maddux	1.00
10	Moises Alou	.40
11	Joe Randa	.20
12	Bobby Abreu	.40
13	Ryan Kohlmeier	.20
14	Kerry Wood	.75
15	Craig Biggio	.40
16	Curt Schilling	.50
17	Brian Jordan	.20
18	Edgardo Alfonzo	.20
19	Darren Dreifort	.20
20	Todd Helton	.50
21	Ramon Ortiz	.20
22	Ichiro Suzuki	1.50
23	Jimmy Rollins	.50
24	Darin Erstad	.40
25	Shawn Green	.40
26	Tino Martinez	.30
27	Bret Boone	.40
28	Alfonso Soriano	.75
29	Chan Ho Park	.40
30	Roger Clemens	1.50
31	Cliff Floyd	.20
32	Johnny Damon	.40
33	Frank Thomas	.50
34	Barry Bonds	2.00
35	Luis Gonzalez	.40
36	Carlos Lee	.20
37	Roberto Alomar	.50
38	Carlos Delgado	.50
39	Nomar Garciaparra	1.50
40	Jason Kendall	.40
41	Scott Rolen	.75
42	Tom Glavine	.40
43	Ryan Klesko	.20
44	Brian Giles	.20
45	Bud Smith	.20
46	Charles Nagy	.20
47	Tony Gwynn	.75
48	C.C. Sabathia	.20
49	Manny Ramirez	.75
50	Jerry Hairston Jr.	.20
51	Jeromy Burnitz	.20
52	David Justice	.40
53	Bartolo Colon	.20
54	Andres Galarraga	.30
55	Jeff Weaver	.20
56	Terrance Long	.20
57	Tsuyoshi Shinjo	.20
58	Barry Zito	.40
59	Mariano Rivera	.40
60	John Olerud	.20
61	Randy Johnson	.75
62	Kenny Lofton	.40
63	Jermaine Dye	.20
64	Troy Glaus	.50
65	Larry Walker	.40
66	Hideo Nomo	.40
67	Mike Mussina	.50
68	Paul LoDuca	.20
69	Magglio Ordonez	.40
70	Paul O'Neill	.40
71	Sean Casey	.40
72	Lance Berkman	.40
73	Adam Dunn	.50
74	Aramis Ramirez	.40
75	Rafael Furcal	.40
76	Gary Sheffield	.40
77	Todd Hollandsworth	.20
78	Chipper Jones	1.00
79	Bernie Williams	.50
80	Richard Hidalgo	.25
81	Eric Chavez	.40
82	Mike Piazza	1.50
83	J.D. Drew	.40
84	Ken Griffey Jr.	1.00
85	Joe Kennedy	.20
86	Joel Pineiro	.20
87	Josh Towers	.20
88	Andruw Jones	.50
89	Carlos Beltran	.40
90	Mike Cameron	.20

No.	Player	Price
91	Albert Pujols	1.50
92	Alex Rodriguez	1.50
93	Omar Vizquel	.30
94	Juan Encarnacion	.20
95	Jeff Bagwell	.50
96	Jose Canseco	.40
97	Ben Sheets	.40
98	Mark Grace	.40
99	Mike Sweeney	.20
100	Mark McGwire	2.00
101	Ivan Rodriguez	.75
102	Rich Aurilia	.20
103	Cristian Guzman	.20
104	Roy Oswalt	.40
105	Tim Hudson	.40
106	Brent Abernathy	.20
107	Mike Hampton	.20
108	Miguel Tejada	.40
109	Bobby Higginson	.20
110	Edgar Martinez	.20
111	Jorge Posada	.40
112	Jason Giambi	.50
113	Pedro Astacio	.20
114	Kazuhiro Sasaki	.20
115	Preston Wilson	.20
116	Jason Bere	.20
117	Mark Quinn	.20
118	Pokey Reese	.20
119	Derek Jeter	2.00
120	Shannon Stewart	.20
121	Jeff Kent	.40
122	Jeremy Giambi	.20
123	Pat Burrell	.40
124	Jim Edmonds	.40
125	Mark Buehrle	.40
126	Kevin Brown	.40
127	Raul Mondesi	.20
128	Pedro Martinez	.75
129	Jim Thome	.75
130	Russ Ortiz	.20
131	Brandon Duckworth	.20
132	Ryan Jamison RC	.50
133	Brandon Inge	.20
134	Felipe Lopez	.20
135	Jason Lane	.20
136	Forrest Johnson RC	.50
137	Greg Nash	.20
138	Covelli Crisp	.20
139	Nick Neugebauer	.20
140	Dustan Mohr	.20
141	Freddy Sanchez RC	1.00
142	Justin Backsmeyer RC	1.00
143	Jorge Julio	.20
144	Ryan Mottl RC	1.00
145	Chris Tritle RC	1.00
146	Noochie Varner RC	1.00
147	Brian Rogers	1.00
148	Michael Hill RC	1.00
149	Luis Pineda	1.00
150	Rich Thompson RC	1.00
151	Bill Hall	1.00
152	Jose Dominguez RC	1.50
153	Justin Woodrow RC	1.00
154	Nic Jackson RC	1.00
155	Laynce Nix RC	4.00
157	Hank Aaron	3.00
158	Johnny Bench	1.50
159	George Brett	4.00
160	Carlton Fisk	.50
161	Bob Gibson	.75
162	Reggie Jackson	1.00
163	Don Mattingly	4.00
164	Kirby Puckett	1.50
165	Frank Robinson	1.00
166	Nolan Ryan	5.00
167	Tom Seaver	1.00
168	Mike Schmidt	2.00
169	Dave Winfield	.50
170	Carl Yastrzemski	1.00
171	Frank Chance	.75
172	Ty Cobb	3.00
173	Sam Crawford	1.00
174	Johnny Evers	.75
175	John McGraw	1.00
176	Eddie Plank	.50
177	Tris Speaker	1.00
178	Joe Tinker	.50
179	Honus Wagner	5.00
180	Cy Young	2.50
181	Javier Vazquez	.20
182	Mark Mulder	.40
183	Roger Clemens	1.50
184	Kazuhisa Ishii RC	1.50
185	Roberto Alomar	.50
186	Lance Berkman	.40
187	Adam Dunn	.50
188	Aramis Ramirez	.40
189	Chuck Knoblauch	.20
190	Nomar Garciaparra	1.50
191	Brad Penny	.20
192	Gary Sheffield	.40
193	Alfonso Soriano	.75
194	Andruw Jones	.50
195	Randy Johnson	.75
196	Corey Patterson	.40
197	Milton Bradley	.20
198	Johnny Damon	.40
199	Paul LoDuca	.20
200	Albert Pujols	1.50
201	Scott Rolen	.75
202	J.D. Drew	.40
203	Vladimir Guerrero	.75
204	Jason Giambi	.50
205	Moises Alou	.20
206	Magglio Ordonez	.40
207	Carlos Febles	.20
208	So Taguchi RC	.75
209	Rafael Palmeiro	.50
210	David Wells	.50
211	Orlando Cabrera	.20
212	Sammy Sosa	1.50
213	Armando Benitez	.20
214	Wes Helms	.20
215	Mariano Rivera	.50
216	Jimmy Rollins	.50
217	Matt Lawton	.20
218	Shawn Green	.40
219	Bernie Williams	.50
220	Bret Boone	.40
221	Alex Rodriguez	2.00
222	Roger Cedeno	.20
223	Marty Cordova	.20
224	Fred McGriff	.40
225	Chipper Jones	.75
226	Kerry Wood	.75
227	Larry Walker	.40
228	Robin Ventura	.40
229	Robert Fick	.20
230	Tino Martinez	.40
231	Ben Petrick	.20
232	Neifi Perez	.20
233	Pedro Martinez	.75
234	Brian Jordan	.20
235	Freddy Garcia	.20
236	Derek Jeter	2.00
237	Ben Grieve	.20
238	Barry Bonds	2.00
239	Luis Gonzalez	.40
240	Shane Halter	.20
241	Brian Giles	.40
242	Bud Smith	.20
243	Richie Sexson	.20
244	Barry Zito	.40
245	Eric Milton	.20
246	Ivan Rodriguez	.50
247	Toby Hall	.20
248	Mike Piazza	1.50
249	Ruben Sierra	.20
250	Tsuyoshi Shinjo	.20
251	Jermaine Dye	.20
252	Roy Oswalt	.40
253	Todd Helton	.50
254	Adrian Beltre	.40
255	Doug Mientkiewicz	.20
256	Ichiro Suzuki	1.50
257	C.C. Sabathia	.20
258	Paul Konerko	.20
259	Ken Griffey Jr.	1.00
260	Jeromy Burnitz	.20
261	Hank Blalock	.50
262	Mark Prior	1.50
263	Josh Beckett	.50
264	Carlos Pena	.20
265	Sean Burroughs	.20
266	Austin Kearns	.40
267	Chin-Hui Tsao	.20
268	Dewon Brazelton	.20
269	J.D. Martin	.20
270	Marlon Byrd	.20
271	Joe Mauer RC	8.00
272	Jason Botts RC	1.00
273	Mauricio Lara RC	1.00
274	Jonny Gomes RC	3.00
275	Gavin Floyd	1.50
276	Alexander Requena RC	1.00
277	Jimmy Gobble RC	1.00
278	Chris Duffy RC	1.00
279	Colt Griffin	1.00
280	Ryan Church RC	1.50
281	Beltran Perez	1.00
282	Clint Nageotte RC	1.50
283	Justin Schuda RC	1.00
284	Scott Hairston	1.50
285	Mario Ramos	1.00
286	Tom Seaver	2.00
287	Hank Aaron	3.00
288	Mike Schmidt	3.00
289	Robin Yount	1.50
290	Joe Morgan	1.00
291	Frank Robinson	1.00
292	Reggie Jackson	2.00
293	Nolan Ryan	4.00
294	Dave Winfield	1.00
295	Willie Mays	3.00
296	Brooks Robinson	1.50
297	Mark McGwire	3.00
298	Honus Wagner	3.00
299	Sherry Magee	1.00
300	Frank Chance	1.00
301	Larry Doyle	1.00
302	John McGraw	2.00
303	Jimmy Collins	1.00
304	Buck Herzog	1.00
305	Sam Crawford	1.00
306	Cy Young	2.50
307	Honus Wagner	3.00
308	Alex Rodriguez	2.00
308	Alex Rodriguez/ SP Blue Jsy	4.00
309	Vernon Wells	.20
310	Barry Bonds	2.00
310	Barry Bonds/ SP Cream Jsy	6.00
311	Vicente Padilla	.20
312	Alfonso Soriano	.75
312	A.Soriano/ SP No Wristband	1.50
313	Mike Piazza	1.50
314	Jacque Jones	.20
315	Shawn Green/SP	1.50
316	Paul Byrd	.20
317	Lance Berkman	.40
318	Larry Walker	.40
319	Ken Griffey Jr./SP	3.00
320	Shea Hillenbrand	.20
321	Jay Gibbons	.20
322	Andruw Jones	.50
323	Luis Gonzalez/SP	1.50
324	Garret Anderson	.40
325	Roy Halladay	.40
326	Randy Winn	.20
327	Matt Morris	.40
328	Robb Nen	.20
329	Trevor Hoffman	.20
330	Kip Wells	.20
331	Orlando Hernandez	.30
332	Rey Ordonez	.20
333	Torii Hunter	.40
334	Geoff Jenkins	.40
335	Eric Karros	.20
336	Mike Lowell	.40
337	Nick Johnson	.20
338	Randall Simon	.20
339	Ellis Burks	.20
340	Sammy Sosa	1.50
340	Sammy Sosa/ SP Blue Jsy	4.00
341	Pedro J. Martinez	.75
342	Junior Spivey	.20
343	Vinny Castilla	.20
344	Randy Johnson/SP	2.00
345	Chipper Jones/SP	1.50
346	Orlando Hudson	.20
347	Albert Pujols/SP	5.00
348	Rondell White	.20
349	Vladimir Guerrero	.75
350	Mark Prior	1.00
350	Mark Prior/ SP Red background	3.00
351	Eric Gagne	.50
352	Todd Zeile	.20
353	Manny Ramirez/SP	2.00
354	Kevin Millwood	.40
355	Troy Percival	.20
356	Jason Giambi	.50
356	Jason Giambi/ SP White Jsy	1.50
357	Bartolo Colon	.20
358	Jeremy Giambi	.20
359	Jose Cruz Jr.	.20
360	Ichiro Suzuki	1.50
360	Ichiro/ SP Blue warm-up	3.00
361	Eddie Guardado	.20
362	Ivan Rodriguez	.50
363	Carl Crawford	.50
364	Jason Simontacchi RC	.50
365	Kenny Lofton	.40
366	Raul Mondesi	.20
367	A.J. Pierzynski	.20
368	Ugueth Urbina	.20
369	Rodrigo Lopez	.20
370	Nomar Garciaparra	1.50
370	N. Garciaparra/ SP 1 Bat	3.00
371	Craig Counsell	.20
372	Barry Larkin	.40
373	Carlos Pena	.20
374	Luis Castillo	.20
375	Raul Ibanez	.20
376	Kazuhisa Ishii/SP	1.50
377	Derek Lowe	.20
378	Curt Schilling	.50
379	Jim Thome	.75
380	Derek Jeter	2.00
380	D. Jeter/ SP Blue background	5.00
381	Pat Burrell	.50
382	Jamie Moyer	.20
383	Eric Hinske	.20
384	Scott Rolen	.75
385	Miguel Tejada/SP	1.50
386	Andy Pettitte	.40
387	Mike Lieberthal	.20
388	Al Leiter	.40
389	Todd Helton/SP	2.00
390	Adam Dunn	.50
390	Adam Dunn/ SP with bat	2.00
391	Cliff Floyd	.20
392	Tim Salmon	.40
393	Joe Torre	.50
394	Bobby Cox	.20
395	Tony LaRussa	.20
396	Art Howe	.20
397	Bob Brenly	.20
398	Ron Gardenhire	.20
399	Mike Cuddyer	.20
400	Joe Mauer	2.50
401	Mark Teixeira	.50
402	Hee Seop Choi	.20
403	Angel Berroa	.20
404	Jesse Foppert	.50
405	Bobby Crosby	.50
406	Jose Reyes	.50
407	Casey Kotchman	1.00
408	Aaron Heilman	.20
409	Adrian Gonzalez	.20
410	Delwyn Young RC	.75
411	Brett Myers	.20
412	Justin Huber RC	1.00
413	Drew Henson	.20
414	Taggert Bozied RC	1.00
415	Dontrelle Willis RC	6.00
416	Rocco Baldelli	.50
417	Jason Stokes RC	2.50
418	Brandon Phillips	.20
419	Jake Blalock/SP RC	1.00
420	Micah Schilling/SP RC	1.00
421	Denard Span/SP RC	1.00
422	James Loney/SP RC	4.00
423	Wes Bankston/SP RC	1.50
424	Jeremy Hermida/ SP RC	6.00
425	Curtis Granderson/ SP RC	3.00
426	Jason Pridie/SP RC	1.00
427	Larry Broadway/SP RC	1.00
428	Khalil Greene/SP RC	5.00
429	Joey Votto/SP RC	2.50
430	B.J. Upton/SP RC	8.00
431	Sergio Santos/SP RC	2.00
432	Brian Dopirak/SP RC	2.00
433	Ozzie Smith/SP	2.00
434	Wade Boggs/SP	1.00
435	Yogi Berra/SP	3.00
436	Al Kaline/SP	2.00
437	Robin Roberts/SP	1.00
438	Roberto Clemente/SP	8.00
439	Gary Carter/SP	1.00
440	Fergie Jenkins/SP	1.00
441	Orlando Cepeda/SP	1.00
442	Rod Carew/SP	1.50
443	Harmon Killebrew/SP	2.50
444	Duke Snider/SP	2.00
445	Stan Musial/SP	5.00
446	Hank Greenberg/SP	1.00
447	Lou Brock/SP	1.00
448	Jim Palmer/SP	.50
449	John McGraw	.75
450	Mordecai Brown	.50
451	Christy Mathewson	1.00
452	Sam Crawford	.50
453	Bill O'Hara	.50
454	Joe Tinker	.50
455	Napoleon Lajoie	.50
456	Honus Wagner	3.00

T206 Mini Parallel

	NM/M
Polar Bear:	2-3X
Tolstoi Black:	2-5X
Average 4:Box	
Tolstoi Red:	4-8X
Average 2:Box	
Cycle:	6-12X
Average 1:Box	
Series 2	
Polar Bear:	2-3X
Piedmont Black:	3-5X
Piedmont Red:	4-8X
Carolina Brights:	6-12X
Series 3	
Polar Bear:	2-3X
Sweet Caporal Red:	3-5X
Sweet Caporal Blue or Black:	4-6X
Uzit:	6-12X
Bazooka Backs:	No Pricing
Production 30	
Drum Backs:	No Pricing
Production 20	
Lenox Variations:	No Pricing
Production 10	

American Beauty

American Beauty
Variation: No Pricing
Production 5

Autographs

		NM/M
Common Player:		8.00
Inserted 1:41		
BB	Barry Bonds	200.00
RC	Roger Clemens	150.00
JE	Jim Edmonds	30.00
BG	Brian Giles	15.00
CG	Cristian Guzman	15.00
BI	Brandon Inge	10.00
RJ	Ryan Jamison	8.00
FJ	Forrest Johnson	8.00
JJ	Jorge Julio	10.00
FL	Felipe Lopez	15.00
GN	Greg Nash	8.00
MO	Magglio Ordonez	20.00
AR	Alex Rodriguez	100.00
JR	Jimmy Rollins	20.00
BZ	Barry Zito	20.00

Autographs Series 2

		NM/M
Common Player:		8.00
Inserted 1:55		
MA	Moises Alou	30.00
LB	Lance Berkman	35.00
HB	Hank Blalock	30.00
DB	Dewon Brazelton	8.00
MB	Marlon Byrd	10.00
EC	Eric Chavez	30.00
JD	Johnny Damon	25.00
GF	Gavin Floyd	20.00
LG	Luis Gonzalez	40.00
KI	Kazuhisa Ishii	40.00
JDM	J.D. Martin	8.00
JM	Joe Mauer	100.00
MP	Mark Prior	40.00
AP	Albert Pujols	140.00
SR	Scott Rolen	40.00
RS	Richie Sexson	15.00
BS	Ben Sheets	20.00
BSM	Bud Smith	10.00
ST	So Taguchi	25.00
CT	Chris Tritle	10.00

Autographs Series 3

		NM/M
Common Autograph:		8.00
MB	Milton Bradley	10.00
JC	Jose Cruz Jr.	15.00
DE	David Eckstein	8.00
DH	Drew Henson	15.00
ML	Mike Lamb	8.00
MT	Marcus Thames	8.00
JV	Jose Vidro	10.00

Relics

		NM/M
Common Player:		5.00
Overall Relics 1:11		
RA	Roberto Alomar/Jsy	10.00
JB	Jeff Bagwell/Jsy	10.00
CB	Craig Biggio/Jsy	8.00
BB	Barry Bonds/Jsy	25.00
BBO	Bret Boone/Jsy	8.00
MC	Mike Cameron/Jsy	5.00
JC	Jose Canseco/Bat	10.00
CD	Carlos Delgado/Jsy	8.00
JED	Jim Edmonds/Jsy	10.00
CF	Cliff Floyd/Jsy	5.00
JGI	Jason Giambi/Jsy	8.00
JG	Jeremy Giambi/Jsy	5.00
TG	Tom Glavine/Jsy	8.00
SG	Shawn Green/Jsy	8.00
TGW	Tony Gwynn/Jsy	15.00
TH	Todd Helton/Jsy	10.00
RJ	Randy Johnson/Jsy	15.00
AJ	Andruw Jones/Jsy	10.00
CJ	Chipper Jones/Jsy	10.00
CL	Carlos Lee/Jsy	5.00
KL	Kenny Lofton/Jsy	5.00
GM	Greg Maddux/Jsy	15.00
EM	Edgar Martinez/Jsy	10.00
TM	Tino Martinez/Jsy	10.00
JO	John Olerud/Jsy	5.00
PO	Paul O'Neill/Jsy	8.00
MO	Magglio Ordonez/Jsy	6.00
CP	Chan Ho Park/Bat	5.00
MP	Mike Piazza/Jsy	15.00
AP	Albert Pujols/Bat	25.00
IR	Ivan Rodriguez/Jsy	10.00
AS	Alfonso Soriano/Bat	10.00
SS	Shannon Stewart/Bat	10.00
FT	Frank Thomas/Jsy	10.00
JT	Jim Thome/Jsy	20.00
LW	Larry Walker/Jsy	8.00
JW	Jeff Weaver/Jsy	5.00
BW	Bernie Williams/Jsy	8.00
BZ	Barry Zito/Jsy	8.00

Relics Series 2

		NM/M
Common Player:		5.00
Jerseys 1:18		
Bats 1:40		
RA	Roberto Alomar/Bat	10.00
JB	Jeff Bagwell/Jsy	8.00
BB	Barry Bonds/Jsy	20.00
BBO	Bret Boone/Jsy	6.00
KB	Kevin Brown/Jsy	6.00
AB	A.J. Burnett/Jsy	5.00
SB	Sean Burroughs/Bat	8.00
EC	Eric Chavez/Bat	8.00
TC	Ty Cobb/Bat	420.00
JC	Jimmy Collins/Bat	45.00
SCR	Sam Crawford/Bat	50.00
JD	Johnny Damon/Bat	12.00
RD	Ryan Dempster/Jsy	5.00
BD	Brandon Duckworth/Jsy	5.00
AD	Adam Dunn/Bat	10.00
DE	Darin Erstad/Jsy	5.00
JEV	Johnny Evers/Bat	50.00
CF	Cliff Floyd/Jsy	5.00
TGL	Tom Glavine/Jsy	8.00
JG	Juan Gonzalez/Bat	5.00
MG	Mark Grace/Bat	10.00
SG	Shawn Green/Jsy	6.00
CG	Cristian Guzman/Jsy	5.00
TG	Tony Gwynn/Jsy	15.00
TH	Toby Hall/Jsy	5.00
JH	Josh Hamilton/Bat	10.00
THE	Todd Helton/Jsy	8.00
RH	Rickey Henderson/Bat	15.00
BH	Buck Herzog/Bat	30.00
JJ	Jason Jennings/Jsy	5.00
RJ	Randy Johnson/Jsy	10.00
AJ	Andruw Jones/Jsy	8.00
CJO	Chipper Jones/Jsy	10.00
JK	Jeff Kent/Jsy	5.00
BL	Barry Larkin/Jsy	8.00
TL	Travis Lee/Bat	5.00
GM	Greg Maddux/Jsy	12.00
EM	Edgar Martinez/Bat	8.00
TM	Tino Martinez/Jsy	10.00
JM	Joe Mays/Jsy	5.00
JMC	John McGraw/Bat	60.00
FM	Fred McGriff/Bat	8.00
JO	John Olerud/Jsy	5.00
RP	Rafael Palmeiro/Jsy	8.00
BP	Brad Penny/Jsy	5.00
MP	Mike Piazza/Jsy	15.00
AP	Albert Pujols/Jsy	15.00
ARA	Aramis Ramirez/Jsy	10.00
AR	Alex Rodriguez/Bat	20.00
IR	Ivan Rodriguez/Bat	8.00
CS	Curt Schilling/Bat	15.00
GS	Gary Sheffield/Jsy	8.00
TS	Tsuyoshi Shinjo/Jsy	5.00
AS	Alfonso Soriano/Bat	10.00

		NM/M
MT	Miguel Tejada/Bat	8.00
FT	Frank Thomas/Jsy	8.00
JTH	Jim Thome/Bat	15.00
JT	Joe Tinker/Bat	40.00
MV	Mo Vaughn/Bat	8.00
RV	Robin Ventura/Bat	5.00
HWA	Honus Wagner/Bat	400.00
LW	Larry Walker/Jsy	5.00
BW	Bernie Williams/Jsy	5.00
MW	Matt Williams/Jsy	5.00
PW	Preston Wilson/Jsy	5.00

Relics Series 3

		NM/M
Common Player:		5.00
RA	Roberto Alomar/Bat	8.00
JB	Jeff Bagwell/Bat	8.00
WB	Wilson Betemit/Bat	5.00
PB	Pat Burrell/Bat	10.00
EC	Eric Chavez/Bat	8.00
AD	Adam Dunn/Bat	10.00
JE	Jim Edmonds/Bat	8.00
NG	Nomar Garciaparra/Bat	20.00
LG	Luis Gonzalez/Jsy	5.00
TG	Tony Gwynn/Jsy	10.00
TH	Todd Helton/Jsy	8.00
RH	Rickey Henderson/Bat	15.00
NJ	Nick Johnson/Bat	5.00
RJ	Randy Johnson/Jsy	10.00
AJ	Andruw Jones/Jsy	8.00
CJ	Chipper Jones/Jsy	10.00
PM	Pedro Martinez/Jsy	12.00
DM	Doug Mientkiewicz/Jsy	6.00
RP	Rafael Palmeiro/Jsy	6.00
CP	Corey Patterson/Bat	6.00
MP	Mike Piazza/Jsy	15.00
AP	Albert Pujols/Bat	20.00
AR	Alex Rodriguez/Bat	15.00
IR	Ivan Rodriguez/Bat	10.00
SR	Scott Rolen/Bat	10.00
CS	Curt Schilling/Bat	8.00
GS	Gary Sheffield/Bat	8.00
TS	Tsuyoshi Shinjo/Bat	5.00
AS	Alfonso Soriano/Bat	10.00
MTE	Miguel Tejada/Jsy	5.00
FT	Frank Thomas/Jsy	8.00
JT	Jim Thome/Jsy	10.00
MV	Mo Vaughn/Jsy	5.00
HW	Honus Wagner/Bat/25	
BW	Bernie Williams/Jsy	8.00
BZ	Barry Zito/Jsy	6.00

Reprint Relics

		NM/M
Common Player:		75.00
SC	Sam Crawford	90.00
JE	Johnny Evers	90.00
JM	John McGraw	75.00
TS	Tris Speaker	140.00
HW	Honus Wagner	400.00

Team Topps Legends Autographs

		NM/M
Inserted 1:7,093		
	Nolan Ryan	400.00

Team Topps Legends Autographs Series 2

		NM/M
Inserted 1:260		
	Ralph Branca	25.00
	Andy Pafko	20.00
	Joe Pepitone	10.00
	Tom Seaver	60.00
	Warren Spahn	25.00
	Luis Tiant	10.00

Team 206

		NM/M
Complete Set (20):		10.00
Common Player:		.25
Inserted 1:Pack		
1	Barry Bonds	2.00
2	Ivan Rodriguez	.50
3	Luis Gonzalez	.25
4	Jason Giambi	.50
5	Pedro Martinez	.75
6	Larry Walker	.25
7	Bobby Abreu	.40
8	Derek Jeter	2.00
9	Bret Boone	.40
10	Mike Piazza	1.00
11	Alex Rodriguez	1.50
12	Roger Clemens	1.50
13	Albert Pujols	1.50
14	Randy Johnson	.75
15	Sammy Sosa	1.50
16	Cristian Guzman	.25

17	Shawn Green	.40
18	Curt Schilling	.50
19	Ichiro Suzuki	1.00
20	Chipper Jones	.75

Team 206 Series 2

		NM/M
Complete Set (25):		10.00
Common Player:		.25
Inserted 1:1		
1	Alex Rodriguez	1.50
2	Sammy Sosa	1.50
3	Jason Giambi	.50
4	Nomar Garciaparra	1.25
5	Ichiro Suzuki	1.00
6	Chipper Jones	.75
7	Derek Jeter	2.00
8	Barry Bonds	2.00
9	Mike Piazza	1.50
10	Randy Johnson	.75
11	Shawn Green	.25
12	Todd Helton	.50
13	Luis Gonzalez	.25
14	Albert Pujols	1.50
15	Curt Schilling	.50
16	Scott Rolen	.75
17	Ivan Rodriguez	.50
18	Roberto Alomar	.50
19	Cristian Guzman	.25
20	Bret Boone	.25
21	Barry Zito	.40
22	Larry Walker	.25
23	Eric Chavez	.25
24	Roger Clemens	1.50
25	Pedro Martinez	.75

Team 206 Series 3

		NM/M
Complete Set (30):		10.00
Common Player:		.25
Inserted 1:1		
1	Ichiro Suzuki	1.00
2	Kazuhisa Ishii	.25
3	Alex Rodriguez	1.50
4	Mark Prior	1.00
5	Derek Jeter	2.00
6	Sammy Sosa	1.50
7	Nomar Garciaparra	1.25
8	Mike Piazza	1.00
9	Jason Giambi	.50
10	Vladimir Guerrero	.75
11	Curt Schilling	.50
12	Jim Thome	.75
13	Adam Dunn	.50
14	Albert Pujols	1.50
15	Pat Burrell	.50
16	Chipper Jones	.75
17	Randy Johnson	.75
18	Todd Helton	.50
19	Luis Gonzalez	.25
20	Alfonso Soriano	.75
21	Shawn Green	.40
22	Pedro J. Martinez	.75
23	Lance Berkman	.40
24	Ivan Rodriguez	.50
25	Larry Walker	.25
26	Andruw Jones	.40
27	Ken Griffey Jr.	1.00
28	Eric Hinske	.25
29	Mike Sweeney	.25
30	Miguel Tejada	.50

2003 Topps

		NM/M
Complete Set (720):		70.00
Sealed Factory Set (725):		70.00
Complete Series 1 Set (366):		35.00
Complete Series 2 Set (355):		35.00
Common Player:		.10
Series 1 & 2 Pack (10):		1.50

Series 1 & 2 Box (36): 35.00
Series 2 Jumbo Box: 45.00
White Topps "throw-back" logo.
Series 1 (1:8852):
    Value Undetermined
Series 2 (1:4487):
    Value Undetermined

1a	Alex Rodriguez (Red Topps)	1.00
1b	Alex Rodriguez (White Topps)	
2	Dan Wilson	.10
3	Jimmy Rollins	.25
4	Jermaine Dye	.10
5	Steve Karsay	.10
6	Timoniel Perez	.10
7	Not Issued	
8	Jose Vidro	.10
9	Eddie Guardado	.10
10a	Mark Prior (Red Topps)	.50
10b	Mark Prior (White Topps)	
11a	Curt Schilling (Red Topps)	.40
11b	Curt Schilling (White Topps)	
12	Dennis Cook	.10
13	Andruw Jones	.40
14	David Segui	.10
15	Trot Nixon	.10
16	Antonio Alfonseca	.10
17	Magglio Ordonez	.20
18	Jason LaRue	.10
19	Danys Baez	.10
20a	Todd Helton (Red Topps)	.40
20b	Todd Helton (White Topps)	
21	Denny Neagle	.10
22	Dave Mlicki	.10
23	Roberto Hernandez	.10
24	Odalis Perez	.10
25	Nick Neugebauer	.10
26	David Ortiz	.10
27	Andres Galarraga	.15
28	Edgardo Alfonzo	.10
29	Chad Bradford	.10
30a	Jason Giambi (Red Topps)	.40
30b	Jason Giambi (White Topps)	
31	Brian Giles	.25
32	Deivi Cruz	.10
33	Robb Nen	.10
34	Jeff Nelson	.10
35	Edgar Renteria	.10
36	Aubrey Huff	.10
37	Brandon Duckworth	.10
38	Juan Gonzalez	.40
39	Sidney Ponson	.10
40	Eric Hinske	.10
41	Kevin Appier	.10
42	Danny Bautista	.10
43	Javier Lopez	.10
44	Jeff Conine	.10
45	Carlos Baerga	.10
46	Ugueth Urbina	.10
47	Mark Buehrle	.10
48	Aaron Boone	.10
49	Chuck Finley	.10
50a	Sammy Sosa (Red Topps)	1.00
50b	Sammy Sosa (White Topps)	
51	Jose Jimenez	.10
52	Chris Truby	.10
53	Luis Castillo	.10
54	Orlando Merced	.10
55	Brian Jordan	.10
56	Eric Young	.10
57	Bobby Kielty	.10
58	Luis Rivas	.10
59	Brad Wilkerson	.10
60	Roberto Alomar	.40

61a	Roger Clemens (Red Topps)	1.00
61b	Roger Clemens (White Topps)	
62	Scott Hatteberg	.10
63	Andy Ashby	.10
64	Mike Williams	.10
65	Ron Gant	.10
66	Benito Santiago	.10
67	Bret Boone	.10
68	Matt Morris	.10
69	Troy Glaus	.40
70	Austin Kearns	.25
71	Jim Thome	.40
72	Rickey Henderson	.40
73a	Luis Gonzalez (Red Topps)	.20
73b	Luis Gonzalez (White Topps)	
74	Brad Fullmer	.10
75	Benny Agbayani	.10
76	Randy Wolf	.10
77a	Miguel Tejada (Red Topps)	.25
77b	Miguel Tejada (White Topps)	
78	Jimmy Anderson	.10
79	Ramon Martinez	.10
80a	Ivan Rodriguez (Red Topps)	.40
80b	Ivan Rodriguez (White Topps)	
81	John Flaherty	.10
82	Shannon Stewart	.10
83	Orlando Palmeiro	.10
84	Rafael Furcal	.10
85	Kenny Rogers	.10
86	Bud Smith	.10
87	Mo Vaughn	.15
88	Jose Cruz Jr.	.10
89	Mike Matheny	.10
90a	Alfonso Soriano (Red Topps)	.50
90b	Alfonso Soriano (White Topps)	
91	Orlando Cabrera	.10
92	Jeffrey Hammonds	.10
93	Hideo Nomo	.25
94	Carlos Febles	.10
95	Billy Wagner	.10
96	Alex Gonzalez	.10
97	Todd Zeile	.10
98	Omar Vizquel	.20
99	Jose Rijo	.10
100a	Ichiro Suzuki (Red Topps)	1.00
100b	Ichiro Suzuki (White Topps)	
101	Steve Cox	.10
102	Hideki Irabu	.10
103	Roy Halladay	.10
104	David Eckstein	.10
105	Greg Maddux	.75
106	Chris Richard	.10
107	Travis Driskill	.10
108	Fred McGriff	.10
109	Frank Thomas	.50
110	Shawn Green	.20
111	Ruben Quevedo	.10
112	Jacque Jones	.10
113	Tomokazu Ohka	.10
114	Joe McEwing	.10
115	Ramiro Mendoza	.10
116	Mark Mulder	.20
117	Mike Lieberthal	.10
118	Jack Wilson	.10
119	Randall Simon	.10
120	Bernie Williams	.40
121	Marvin Benard	.10
122	Jamie Moyer	.10
123	Andy Benes	.10
124	Tino Martinez	.10
125	Esteban Yan	.10
126	Gabe Kapler	.10
127	Jason Isringhausen	.10
128	Chris Carpenter	.10
129	Mike Cameron	.10
130a	Gary Sheffield (Red Topps)	.25
130b	Gary Sheffield (White Topps)	
131	Geronimo Gil	.10
132	Brian Daubach	.10
133	Corey Patterson	.10
134	Aaron Rowand	.10
135	Chris Reitsma	.10
136	Bob Wickman	.10
137	Paul Shuey	.10
138	Jason Jennings	.10
139	Brandon Inge	.10
140	Larry Walker	.20
141	Ramon Santiago	.10
142	Hansel Izquierdo	.10
143	Jose Vizcaino	.10
144	Mark Quinn	.10

145	Michael Tucker	.10
146	Darren Dreifort	.10
147	Mark Loretta	.10
148	Corey Koskie	.10
149	Tony Armas Jr.	.10
150a	Kazuhisa Ishii (Red Topps)	.10
150b	Kazuhisa Ishii (White Topps)	
151	Al Leiter	.10
152	Steve Trachsel	.10
153	Mike Stanton	.10
154	David Justice	.15
155	Marlon Anderson	.10
156	Jason Kendall	.10
157	Brian Lawrence	.10
158	J.T. Snow Jr.	.10
159	Edgar Martinez	.10
160a	Pat Burrell (Red Topps)	.25
160b	Pat Burrell (White Topps)	
161	Kerry Robinson	.10
162	Greg Vaughn	.10
163	Carl Everett	.10
164	Vernon Wells	.10
165	Jose Mesa	.10
166	Troy Percival	.10
167	Erubiel Durazo	.10
168	Jason Marquis	.10
169	Jerry Hairston Jr.	.10
170a	Vladimir Guerrero (Red Topps)	.50
170b	Vladimir Guerrero (White Topps)	
171	Byung-Hyun Kim	.10
172	Marcus Giles	.10
173	Johnny Damon	.10
174	Jon Lieber	.10
175	Ray Durham	.10
176	Sean Casey	.10
177a	Adam Dunn (Red Topps)	.40
177b	Adam Dunn (White Topps)	
178	Juan Pierre	.10
179	Damion Easley	.10
180a	Barry Zito (Red Topps)	.25
180b	Barry Zito (White Topps)	
181	Abraham Nunez	.10
182	Pokey Reese	.10
183	Jeff Kent	.20
184	Russ Ortiz	.10
185	Ruben Sierra	.10
186	Brent Abernathy	.10
187	Ismael Valdes	.10
188	Darrin Fletcher	.10
189	Craig Counsell	.10
190	David Wells	.10
191	Ramon Hernandez	.10
192	Adam Kennedy	.10
193	Tony Womack	.10
194	Wes Helms	.10
195	Tony Batista	.10
196	Rolando Arrojo	.10
197	Matt Clement	.10
198	Sandy Alomar	.10
199	Scott Sullivan	.10
200a	Albert Pujols (Red Topps)	1.00
200b	Albert Pujols (White Topps)	
201	Kirk Rueter	.10
202	Phil Nevin	.10
203	Kip Wells	.10
204	Ron Coomer	.10
205	Jeromy Burnitz	.10
206	Kyle Lohse	.10
207	Paul Bako	.10
208	Paul LoDuca	.10
209	Carlos Beltran	.10
210	Roy Oswalt	.25
211	Mike Lowell	.10
212	Robert Fick	.10
213	Todd Jones	.10
214	C.C. Sabathia	.10
215	Danny Graves	.10
216	Todd Hundley	.10
217	Tim Wakefield	.10
218	Dustin Hermanson	.10
219	Kevin Millwood	.10
220	Jorge Posada	.25
221	Bobby Jones	.10
222	Carlos Guillen	.10
223	Fernando Vina	.10
224	Ryan Rupe	.10
225	Kelvim Escobar	.10
226	Ramon Ortiz	.10
227	Junior Spivey	.10
228	Juan Cruz	.10
229	Melvin Mora	.10
230a	Lance Berkman (Red Topps)	.25
230b	Lance Berkman (White Topps)	
231	Brent Butler	.10
232	Matt Anderson	.10
233	Derrek Lee	.10

234	Matt Lawton	.10
235	Chuck Knoblauch	.10
236	Eric Gagne	.10
237	Alex Sanchez	.10
238	Denny Hocking	.10
239	Rick Reed	.10
240	Rey Ordonez	.10
241	Orlando Hernandez	.10
242	Robert Person	.10
243	Sean Burroughs	.10
244	Jeff Cirillo	.10
245	Mike Lamb	.10
246	Jose Valentin	.10
247	Ellis Burks	.10
248	Shawn Chacon	.10
249	Josh Beckett	.10
250a	Nomar Garciaparra (Red Topps)	1.00
250b	Nomar Garciaparra (White Topps)	
251	Craig Biggio	.20
252	Joe Randa	.10
253	Mark Grudzielanek	.10
254	Glendon Rusch	.10
255	Michael Barrett	.10
256	Tyler Houston	.10
257	Ryan Dempster	.10
258	Wade Miller	.10
259	Adrian Beltre	.20
260	Vicente Padilla	.10
261	Kazuhiro Sasaki	.10
262	Mike Scioscia	.10
263	Bobby Cox	.10
264	Mike Hargrove	.10
265	Grady Little	.10
266	Alex Gonzalez	.10
267	Jerry Manuel	.10
268	Bob Boone	.10
269	Joel Skinner	.10
270	Clint Hurdle	.10
271	Luis Pujols	.10
272	Bob Brenly	.10
273	Jeff Torborg	.10
274	Jimy Williams	.10
275	Tony Pena	.10
276	Jim Tracy	.10
277	Jerry Royster	.10
278	Ron Gardenhire	.10
279	Frank Robinson	.10
280	Bobby Valentine	.10
281	Joe Torre	.10
282	Art Howe	.10
283	Larry Bowa	.10
284	Lloyd McClendon	.10
285	Bruce Bochy	.10
286	Dusty Baker	.10
287	Lou Pinella	.10
288	Tony LaRussa	.10
289	Hal McRae	.10
290	Jerry Narron	.10
291	Carlos Tosca	.10
292	Chris Duncan RC	2.00
293	Franklin Gutierrez RC	1.00
294	Adam LaRoche	.10
295	Manuel Ramirez RC	.10
296	Il Kim RC	.10
297	Wayne Lydon RC	.20
298	Daryl Clark RC	.25
299	Sean Pierce	.10
300a	Andy Marte RC (Red Topps)	1.00
200b	Andy Marte RC (White Topps)	
301	Matt Peterson RC	.25
302	Gonzalo Lopez RC	.25
303	Bernie Castro RC	.10
304	Cliff Lee	.10
305	Jason Perry RC	.50
306	Jaime Bubela RC	.10
307	Alexis Rios	.10
308	Brendan Harris RC	.50
309	Ramon Martinez	.25
310	Terry Tiffee RC	.40
311	Kevin Youkilis RC	1.00
312	Ruddy Lugo RC	.20
313	C.J. Wilson	.10
314	Mike McNutt RC	.10
315	Jeff Clark RC	.10
316	Mark Malaska RC	.10
317	Doug Waechter RC	.25
318	Derell McCall RC	.10
319	Scott Tyler	.10
320	Craig Brazell RC	.40
321a	Walter Young (Red Topps)	
321b	Walter Young (White Topps)	.10
322a	Marlon Byrd, Jorge Padilla (Red Topps)	
322b	Marlon Byrd, Jorge Padilla (White Topps)	
323	Chris Snelling, Shin-Soo Choo	.10

652	Pittsburgh Pirates	.10
653	San Diego Padres	.10
654	San Francisco Giants	.10
655	Seattle Mariners	.10
656	St. Louis Cardinals	.10
657	Tampa Bay Devil Rays	.10
658	Texas Rangers	.10
659	Toronto Blue Jays	.10
660	Bryan Bullington RC	1.00
661	Jeremy Guthrie	.10
662	Joey Gomes	.25
663	Evel Bastida-Martinez	.40
664	Brian Wright RC	.10
665	B.J. Upton	.10
666	Jeff Francis	.10
667	Drew Meyer	.10
668	Jeremy Hermida	.10
669	Khalil Greene	.75
670	Darrell Rasner	.10
671	Cole Hamels	.50
672	James Loney	.10
673	Sergio Santos	.10
674	Jason Pridie	.10
675	Brandon Phillips, Victor Martinez	.10
676	Hee Seop Choi, Nic Jackson	.10
677	Dontrelle Willis, Jason Stokes	.10
678	Chad Tracy, Lyle Overbay	.10
679	Joe Borchard, Corwin Malone	.10
680	Joe Mauer, Justin Morneau	.25
681	Drew Henson, Brandon Claussen	.10
682	Chase Utley, Gavin Floyd	.25
683	Taggert Bozied, Xavier Nady	.25
684	Aaron Heilman, Jose Reyes	.25
685	Kenny Rogers	.10
686	Bengie Molina	.10
687	John Olerud	.10
688	Bret Boone	.10
689	Eric Chavez	.15
690	Alex Rodriguez	.75
691	Darin Erstad	.15
692	Ichiro Suzuki	.50
693	Torii Hunter	.50
694	Greg Maddux	.50
695	Brad Ausmus	.10
696	Todd Helton	.20
697	Fernando Vina	.10
698	Scott Rolen	.25
699	Edgar Renteria	.10
700	Andruw Jones	.20
701	Larry Walker	.10
702	Jim Edmonds	.10
703	Barry Zito	.10
704	Randy Johnson	.40
705	Miguel Tejada	.15
706	Barry Bonds	.75
707	Eric Hinske	.10
708	Jason Jennings	.10
709	Todd Helton	.20
710	Jeff Kent	.10
711	Edgar Renteria	.10
712	Scott Rolen	.25
713	Barry Bonds	.75
714	Sammy Sosa	.50
715	Vladimir Guerrero	.40
716	Mike Piazza	.75
717	Curt Schilling	.20
718	Randy Johnson	.40
719	Bobby Cox	.10
720	World Series Card	.10
721	World Series Card	.10

Gold

JOHNNY DAMON

Stars:	3-6X
Production 2,003 Sets	

Black

Stars:	10-20X
Production 52 Sets	

All-Stars

		NM/M
Complete Set (20):		20.00
Common Player:		.50
Inserted 1:15		
TAS1	Alfonso Soriano	1.50
TAS2	Barry Bonds	4.00
TAS3	Ichiro Suzuki	2.00
TAS4	Alex Rodriguez	3.00
TAS5	Miguel Tejada	.75
TAS6	Nomar Garciaparra	2.50
TAS7	Jason Giambi	2.00
TAS8	Manny Ramirez	1.00
TAS9	Derek Jeter	4.00
TAS10	Garret Anderson	.50
TAS11	Barry Zito	.50
TAS12	Sammy Sosa	2.00
TAS13	Adam Dunn	1.00
TAS14	Vladimir Guerrero	1.50
TAS15	Mike Piazza	2.50
TAS16	Shawn Green	.50
TAS17	Luis Gonzalez	.50
TAS18	Todd Helton	.75
TAS19	Torii Hunter	.75
TAS20	Curt Schilling	.75

Autographs

		NM/M
Common Autograph:		8.00
HB	Hank Blalock	20.00
MB	Mark Buehrle	20.00
EC	Eric Chavez	25.00
DE	Darin Erstad	15.00
OH	Orlando Hudson	10.00
AJ	Andruw Jones	
AK	Austin Kearns	15.00
JL	Jason Lane	10.00
PL	Paul LoDuca	12.00
JDM	J.D. Martin	8.00
JM	Joe Mauer	40.00
EM	Eric Milton	10.00
NN	Nick Neugebauer	10.00
MP	Mark Prior	40.00
SR	Scott Rolen	50.00
BS	Ben Sheets	15.00
AS	Alfonso Soriano	
MTE	Mark Teixeira	20.00
MT	Miguel Tejada	
MTH	Marcus Thames	8.00

Autographs Series 2

		NM/M
Common Autograph:		8.00
JB	Josh Beckett	30.00
LB	Lance Berkman	40.00
CE	Clint Everts	8.00
CF	Cliff Floyd	20.00
BH	Brad Hawpe	8.00
EH	Eric Hinske	10.00
TH	Torii Hunter	20.00
AK	Austin Kearns	15.00
PK	Paul Konerko	20.00
PL	Paul LoDuca	15.00
MO	Magglio Ordonez	20.00
JPH	Josh Phelps	10.00
AP	Albert Pujols	120.00
MT	Miguel Tejada	30.00
BU	B.J. Upton	25.00
JV	Jose Vidro	10.00
DW	Dontrelle Willis	25.00
BZ	Barry Zito	30.00

Blue Backs

	NM/M
Complete Set (40):	50.00

Common Player:		.75
Inserted 1:12		
BB1	Albert Pujols	2.00
BB2	Barry Bonds	5.00
BB3	Ichiro Suzuki	3.00
BB4	Sammy Sosa	2.50
BB5	Kazuhisa Ishii	.75
BB6	Alex Rodriguez	4.00
BB7	Derek Jeter	5.00
BB8	Vladimir Guerrero	2.00
BB9	Ken Griffey Jr.	2.50
BB10	Jason Giambi	2.50
BB11	Todd Helton	1.00
BB12	Mike Piazza	3.00
BB13	Nomar Garciaparra	3.00
BB14	Chipper Jones	2.50
BB15	Ivan Rodriguez	1.00
BB16	Luis Gonzalez	.75
BB17	Pat Burrell	1.00
BB18	Mark Prior	1.50
BB19	Adam Dunn	1.50
BB20	Jeff Bagwell	1.50
BB21	Austin Kearns	1.00
BB22	Alfonso Soriano	2.00
BB23	Jim Thome	1.50
BB24	Bernie Williams	1.00
BB25	Pedro J. Martinez	2.00
BB26	Lance Berkman	1.00
BB27	Randy Johnson	2.00
BB28	Rafael Palmeiro	1.00
BB29	Richie Sexson	.75
BB30	Troy Glaus	1.50
BB31	Shawn Green	.75
BB32	Larry Walker	.75
BB33	Eric Hinske	.75
BB34	Andruw Jones	1.50
BB35	Carlos Delgado	1.00
BB36	Curt Schilling	1.50
BB37	Greg Maddux	2.50
BB38	Jimmy Rollins	.75
BB39	Eric Chavez	1.00
BB40	Scott Rolen	1.00

Draft Picks

		NM/M
Complete Set (10):		30.00
1-5 issued in retail sets		
6-10 issued in holiday sets		
1	Brandon Wood	10.00
2	Ryan Wagner	5.00
3	Sean Rodriguez	3.00
4	Chris Lubanski	5.00
5	Chad Billingsley	3.00
6	Javi Herrera	3.00
7	Brian McFall	3.00
8	Nicholas Markakis	5.00
9	Adam Miller	5.00
10	Daric Barton	5.00

Flashback

		NM/M
Complete Set (14):		50.00
Common Player:		2.00
HTA Exclusive		
GB	George Brett	6.00
LD	Lenny Dykstra	3.00
HK	Harmon Killebrew	6.00
BM	Bill Madlock	2.00
EM	Eddie Mathews	4.00
DM	Dale Murphy	5.00
JP	Jim Palmer	3.00
MP	Mike Piazza	6.00
RR	Robin Roberts	3.00
AR	Al Rosen	4.00
NR	Nolan Ryan	10.00
TS	Tom Seaver	5.00
WS	Warren Spahn	4.00
CY	Carl Yastrzemski	6.00

Futures Game

	NM/M
Complete Set (6):	5.00

ALFONSO SORIANO

Common Player:		.50
1	Alfonso Soriano	2.00
2	Pat Burrell	1.00
3	Adam Dunn	1.00
4	Barry Zito	.75
5	Mark Buehrle	.50
6	Rafael Furcal	.75

Hit Parade

		NM/M
Complete Set (30):		30.00
Common Player:		.50
Inserted 1:15		
HP1	Barry Bonds	4.00
HP2	Sammy Sosa	2.50
HP3	Rafael Palmeiro	1.00
HP4	Fred McGriff	.75
HP5	Ken Griffey Jr.	2.50
HP6	Juan Gonzalez	1.00
HP7	Andres Galarraga	.50
HP8	Jeff Bagwell	1.50
HP9	Frank Thomas	1.50
HP10	Matt Williams	.50
HP11	Barry Bonds	4.00
HP12	Rafael Palmeiro	1.00
HP13	Fred McGriff	.75
HP14	Andres Galarraga	.50
HP15	Ken Griffey Jr.	2.50
HP16	Sammy Sosa	2.50
HP17	Jeff Bagwell	1.50
HP18	Juan Gonzalez	1.00
HP19	Frank Thomas	1.50
HP20	Matt Williams	.50
HP21	Rickey Henderson	1.00
HP22	Rafael Palmeiro	1.00
HP23	Roberto Alomar	1.00
HP24	Barry Bonds	4.00
HP25	Mark Grace	1.00
HP26	Fred McGriff	.75
HP27	Julio Franco	.50
HP28	Craig Biggio	.50
HP29	Andres Galarraga	.50
HP30	Barry Larkin	.50

Hobby Masters

		NM/M
Complete Set (20):		40.00
Common Player:		1.00
Inserted 1:18		
HM1	Ichiro Suzuki	4.00
HM2	Kazuhisa Ishii	1.00
HM3	Derek Jeter	6.00
HM4	Barry Bonds	5.00
HM5	Sammy Sosa	3.00
HM6	Alex Rodriguez	5.00
HM7	Mike Piazza	4.00
HM8	Chipper Jones	3.00
HM9	Vladimir Guerrero	2.00
HM10	Nomar Garciaparra	4.00
HM11	Todd Helton	1.00
HM12	Jason Giambi	3.00

		NM/M
HM13	Ken Griffey Jr.	3.00
HM14	Albert Pujols	2.00
HM15	Ivan Rodriguez	1.00
HM16	Mark Prior	1.00
HM17	Adam Dunn	1.50
HM18	Randy Johnson	2.00
HM19	Pedro J. Martinez	2.00
HM20	Alfonso Soriano	3.00

Nolan Ryan No-Hitters

	NM/M
Complete Set (7):	45.00
Common Ryan (1-7):	8.00

Nolan Ryan Record Breakers Autographs

	NM/M
Inserted 1:1,894	
HTA Exclusive	
NR	Nolan Ryan	200.00
NRA	Nolan Ryan	200.00
NRR	Nolan Ryan	200.00

Own The Game

LUIS CASTILLO

		NM/M
Complete Set (30):		30.00
Common Player:		.50
Inserted 1:12		
OG1	Ichiro Suzuki	3.00
OG2	Barry Bonds	4.00
OG3	Todd Helton	.75
OG4	Larry Walker	.75
OG5	Mike Sweeney	.50
OG6	Sammy Sosa	2.50
OG7	Lance Berkman	.75
OG8	Alex Rodriguez	4.00
OG9	Jim Thome	1.25
OG10	Shawn Green	.75
OG11	Troy Glaus	1.00
OG12	Richie Sexson	.50
OG13	Paul Konerko	.50
OG14	Jason Giambi	2.50
OG15	Chipper Jones	2.50
OG16	Torii Hunter	.50
OG17	Albert Pujols	1.50
OG18	Jose Vidro	.50
OG19	Alfonso Soriano	2.00
OG20	Luis Castillo	.50
OG21	Mike Lowell	.50
OG22	Garret Anderson	.50
OG23	Jimmy Rollins	.50
OG24	Curt Schilling	1.00
OG25	Kazuhisa Ishii	.50
OG26	Randy Johnson	1.50
OG27	Tom Glavine	.75
OG28	Roger Clemens	2.50
OG29	Pedro J. Martinez	1.50
OG30	Derek Lowe	.50

Prime Cuts Pine Tar Series

	NM/M
Pine Tar Series	
Production 200 Sets	
Trademark Series:	1-1.5X
Production 100 Sets	
Prime Cuts Series:	1.5-2X
Production 50 Sets	
RA	Roberto Alomar	20.00
LB	Lance Berkman	15.00
EC	Eric Chavez	20.00
AD	Adam Dunn	25.00
DE	Darin Erstad	15.00
NG	Nomar Garciaparra	40.00
JG	Juan Gonzalez	15.00
TH	Todd Helton	25.00
AJ	Andruw Jones	20.00
CJ	Chipper Jones	30.00
RP	Rafael Palmeiro	20.00
MP	Mike Piazza	30.00
AP	Albert Pujols	40.00
AR	Alex Rodriguez	25.00
IR	Ivan Rodriguez	25.00
SR	Scott Rolen	25.00
AS	Alfonso Soriano	25.00
MT	Miguel Tejada	15.00
FT	Frank Thomas	30.00
MV	Mo Vaughn	10.00
BW	Bernie Williams	25.00
Pine Tar Series:	
Production 200	
RA	Roberto Alomar	20.00
LB	Lance Berkman	15.00
HB	Hank Blalock	25.00
BBO	Barry Bonds	40.00
EC	Eric Chavez	15.00
CD	Carlos Delgado	10.00
AD	Adam Dunn	25.00
NG	Nomar Garciaparra	30.00
LG	Luis Gonzalez	8.00
TG	Tony Gwynn	20.00
RH	Rickey Henderson	25.00
RJ	Randy Johnson	25.00
EM	Edgar Martinez	20.00
TM	Tino Martinez	15.00
MO	Magglio Ordonez	10.00
RP	Rafael Palmeiro	15.00
JP	Jorge Posada	15.00
AP	Albert Pujols	40.00
MP	Mark Prior	20.00
AR	Alex Rodriguez	25.00
AS	Alfonso Soriano	20.00
Trademark Series:	1-1.5X
Production 100	
Prime Cuts:	1.5-2.5X
Production 50	

Prime Cuts Autograph

		NM/M
Production 50 Sets		
EC	Eric Chavez	100.00
LB	Lance Berkman	120.00
AJ	Andruw Jones	100.00
CJ	Chipper Jones	150.00
MO	Magglio Ordonez	100.00
MT	Miguel Tejada	120.00

Record Breakers

		NM/M
Complete Set (50):		40.00
Common Player:		.50
Inserted 1:6		
JB	Jeff Bagwell	1.50
LBE	Lance Berkman	1.00
BB	Barry Bonds	5.00
GB	George Brett	2.50
LB	Lou Brock	.50
RCA	Rod Carew	.50
LC	Luis Castillo	.50
RC	Roger Clemens	2.50
CD	Carlos Delgado	.50
CF	Cliff Floyd	.50
GF	George Foster	.50
AG	Andres Galarraga	.50
JG	Jason Giambi	2.50
BG	Bob Gibson	1.00
TG	Troy Glaus	1.00
JGO	Juan Gonzalez	1.00
LGO	Luis Gonzalez	.50
SG	Shawn Green	.75
HG	Hank Greenberg	.50
KG	Ken Griffey Jr.	3.00
VG	Vladimir Guerrero	1.50
RG	Ron Guidry	.50
TH	Todd Helton	1.00
RH	Rickey Henderson	.75
FJ	Fergie Jenkins	.50
RJ	Randy Johnson	1.50
CJ	Chipper Jones	3.00
HK	Harmon Killebrew	1.00
CK	Chuck Klein	.50
JM	Juan Marichal	.50
PM	Pedro J. Martinez	1.50
EM	Eddie Mathews	1.00
DM	Don Mattingly	4.00
FM	Fred McGriff	.50
JO	John Olerud	.50
RP	Rafael Palmeiro	1.00
MP	Mike Piazza	3.00
FR	Frank Robinson	1.00
AR	Alex Rodriguez	4.00
NR	Nolan Ryan	6.00
MSC	Mike Schmidt	3.00
CS	Curt Schilling	1.00
TS	Tom Seaver	1.00
RS	Richie Sexson	.50
GS	Gary Sheffield	.50
SS	Sammy Sosa	3.00
MS	Mike Sweeney	.50
HW	Hack Wilson	.50
PW	Preston Wilson	.50
RY	Robin Yount	1.00

Record Breakers Autographs

		NM/M
Common Autograph:		
CF	Cliff Floyd	20.00
LG	Luis Gonzalez	30.00
FJ	Fergie Jenkins	25.00
CJ	Chipper Jones	75.00
HK	Harmon Killebrew	60.00
RP	Rafael Palmeiro	60.00
MS	Mike Schmidt	100.00
RS	Richie Sexson	30.00
MSW	Mike Sweeney	30.00
RY	Robin Yount	75.00

Record Breakers Relics

		NM/M
Common Player:		6.00
JB	Jeff Bagwell/Jsy	8.00
LB	Lance Berkman/Bat	10.00
GB	George Brett/Bat	25.00
LC	Luis Castillo/Bat	6.00
CD	Carlos Delgado/Jsy	8.00
LGO	Luis Gonzalez/Jsy	6.00
SG	Shawn Green/Jsy	8.00
HG	Hank Greenberg/Bat	30.00
TH	Todd Helton/Jsy	10.00
RH	Rickey Henderson/ Bat	15.00
CJ	Chipper Jones/Jsy	12.00
PM	Pedro Martinez/Jsy	10.00
DM	Don Mattingly/Bat	35.00
MP	Mike Piazza/Bat	15.00
FR	Frank Robinson/Bat	12.00
AR	Alex Rodriguez/Jsy	15.00
NR	Nolan Ryan/Jsy	35.00
MS	Mike Sweeney/Bat	8.00
HW	Hack Wilson/Bat	50.00
RY	Robin Yount/Jsy	15.00

Record Breakers Series 2

		NM/M
Complete Set (50):		40.00
Common Player:		.50
Inserted 1:6		
RA	Roberto Alomar	1.00
GA	Garret Anderson	.75
LA	Luis Aparicio	.50
JB	Jeff Bagwell	1.50
LB	Lance Berkman	1.00
CB	Craig Biggio	.75
WB	Wade Boggs	.75
BB	Barry Bonds	5.00
GB	George Brett	2.50
LBR	Lou Brock	.75
JD	Johnny Damon	.50
CD	Carlos Delgado	.50

51 2Bs in 1962
Cincinnati Reds ® Doubles Season Leader

LD	Lenny Dykstra	.50
DE	Darin Erstad	.50
BF	Bob Feller	.75
GF	George Foster	.50
NG	Nomar Garciaparra	3.00
LG	Luis Gonzalez	.50
DG	Dwight Gooden	.50
SG	Shawn Green	.75
KG	Ken Griffey Jr.	2.50
VG	Vladimir Guerrero	1.50
TG	Tony Gwynn	1.50
TH	Todd Helton	1.00
RH	Rickey Henderson	1.00
RJ	Randy Johnson	1.50
JK	Jeff Kent	.50
TK	Ted Kluszewski	.50
GM	Greg Maddux	2.50
JM	Juan Marichal	.50
EM	Edgar Martinez	.50
WM	Willie Mays	4.00
JME	Jose Mesa	.50
PM	Paul Molitor	1.00
JP	Jim Palmer	.75
TR	Tim Raines	.50
MR	Manny Ramirez	1.50
JR	Jim Rice	.50
FR	Frank Robinson	1.00
AR	Alex Rodriguez	4.00
TS	Tom Seaver	2.00
RS	Richie Sexson	.75
JS	John Smoltz	.50
SS	Sammy Sosa	2.50
WS	Willie Stargell	1.00
IS	Ichiro Suzuki	2.50
FT	Frank Thomas	1.50
JT	Jim Thome	1.50
LW	Larry Walker	.50
RY	Robin Yount	2.00

Record Breakers Autographs Series 2

		NM/M
Common Autograph:		25.00
Inserted 1:2,218		
LA	Luis Aparicio	40.00
LB	Lance Berkman	40.00
LBR	Lou Brock	40.00
GF	George Foster	25.00
JM	Juan Marichal	40.00
DM	Don Mattingly	125.00
WM	Willie Mays	150.00

Record Breaker Relics Series 2

		NM/M
Common Player:		5.00
WB	Wade Boggs/Bat	10.00
GB	George Brett/Bat	25.00
CD	Carlos Delgado/Jsy	6.00
DE	Darin Erstad/Bat	8.00
LG	Luis Gonzalez/Jsy	5.00
TH	Todd Helton/Jsy	8.00
RH	Rogers Hornsby/Bat	35.00
TK	Ted Kluszewski/Bat	15.00
EM	Edgar Martinez/Bat	12.00
JR	Jim Rice/Jsy	8.00
FR	Frank Robinson/Bat	12.00
AR	Alex Rodriguez/Jsy	15.00
NRA	Nolan Ryan/Jsy	30.00
RS	Richie Sexson/Jsy	8.00
FT	Frank Thomas/Bat	10.00
RY	Robin Yount	12.00

Red Backs

		NM/M
Complete Set (40):		50.00
Common Player:		.50
Inserted 1:12		
TRB1	Nomar Garciaparra	3.00
TRB2	Ichiro Suzuki	2.50
TRB3	Alex Rodriguez	4.00

TRB4	Sammy Sosa	2.50
TRB5	Barry Bonds	5.00
TRB6	Vladimir Guerrero	1.50
TRB7	Derek Jeter	5.00
TRB8	Miguel Tejada	1.00
TRB9	Alfonso Soriano	2.00
TRB10	Manny Ramirez	1.50
TRB11	Adam Dunn	1.50
TRB12	Jason Giambi	2.50
TRB13	Mike Piazza	3.00
TRB14	Scott Rolen	1.50
TRB15	Shawn Green	.75
TRB16	Randy Johnson	1.50
TRB17	Todd Helton	1.00
TRB18	Garret Anderson	.50
TRB19	Curt Schilling	1.00
TRB20	Albert Pujols	2.00
TRB21	Chipper Jones	2.50
TRB22	Luis Gonzalez	.50
TRB23	Mark Prior	1.50
TRB24	Jim Thome	1.50
TRB25	Ivan Rodriguez	1.00
TRB26	Torii Hunter	1.00
TRB27	Lance Berkman	1.00
TRB28	Troy Glaus	1.50
TRB29	Andruw Jones	1.00
TRB30	Barry Zito	.75
TRB31	Jeff Bagwell	1.50
TRB32	Magglio Ordonez	.75
TRB33	Pat Burrell	1.50
TRB34	Mike Sweeney	.50
TRB35	Rafael Palmeiro	1.00
TRB36	Larry Walker	.50
TRB37	Carlos Delgado	.50
TRB38	Brian Giles	.50
TRB39	Pedro J. Martinez	1.50
TRB40	Greg Maddux	2.50

Stadium Seat Relics

NM/M

Common Player: 15.00

Inserted 1:37 Series 2 HTA

JB	Johnny Bench	30.00
DC	Dave Concepcion	20.00
AD	Adam Dunn	20.00
KG	Ken Griffey Jr.	25.00
AK	Austin Kearns	20.00
BL	Barry Larkin	25.00
JM	Joe Morgan	15.00
PO	Paul O'Neill	15.00
TP	Tony Perez	20.00
TS	Tom Seaver	25.00

Team Topps Legends Autographs

WILLIE MAYS
SAN FRANCISCO GIANTS®

NM/M

Common Player:
	Vida Blue	20.00
	Bob Feller	25.00
	Willie Mays	125.00
	Gil McDougald	12.00

	Robin Roberts	25.00
	Bobby Thomson	20.00
	Luis Tiant	8.00
	Carl Yastrzemski	50.00

Turn Back The Clock Autographs

NM/M

Common Player:
LD	Lenny Dykstra	15.00
BM	Bill Madlock	10.00
DM	Dale Murphy	40.00
JP	Jim Palmer	20.00

2003 Topps Traded & Rookies

NM/M

Complete Set (275):		50.00
Common Player:		.15
Pack (8 + 2 Chrome):		2.00
Box (24):		40.00
Chrome Cards:		2-4X
T1	Juan Pierre	.15
T2	Mark Grudzielanek	.15
T3	Tanyon Sturtze	.15
T4	Greg Vaughn	.15
T5	Greg Myers	.15
T6	Randall Simon	.15
T7	Todd Hundley	.15
T8	Marlon Anderson	.15
T9	Jeff Reboulet	.15
T10	Alex Sanchez	.15
T11	Mike Rivera	.15
T12	Todd Walker	.15
T13	Ray King	.15
T14	Shawn Estes	.15
T15	Gary Mathews Jr.	.15
T16	Jaret Wright	.15
T17	Edgardo Alfonzo	.15
T18	Omar Daal	.15
T19	Ryan Rupe	.15
T20	Tony Clark	.15
T21	Damon Minor	.15
T22	Mike Stanton	.15
T23	Ramon Martinez	.15
T24	Armando Rios	.15
T25	Johnny Estrada	.15
T26	Joe Girardi	.15
T27	Ivan Rodriguez	.75
T28	Robert Fick	.15
T29	Rick White	.15
T30	Robert Person	.15
T31	Alan Benes	.15
T32	Chris Carpenter	.40
T33	Chris Widger	.15
T34	Travis Hafner	.40
T35	Mike Venafro	.15
T36	Jon Lieber	.15
T37	Orlando Hernandez	.15
T38	Aaron Myette	.15
T39	Paul Bako	.15
T40	Erubiel Durazo	.15
T41	Mark Guthrie	.15
T42	Steve Avery	.15
T43	Damian Jackson	.15
T44	Rey Ordonez	.15
T45	John Flaherty	.15
T46	Byung-Hyun Kim	.15
T47	Tom Goodwin	.15
T48	Elmer Dessens	.15
T49	Al Martin	.15
T50	Gene Kingsale	.15
T51	Lenny Harris	.15
T52	David Ortiz	.75
T53	John Rocker	.15
T54	Mike DiFelice	.15
T55	Nick Bierbrodt	.15
T56	Todd Zeile	.15
T57	Roberto Hernandez	.15
T58	Albie Lopez	.15
T59	Roberto Alomar	.50

T60	Russ Ortiz	.15
T61	Brian Daubach	.15
T62	Carl Everett	.15
T63	Jeromy Burnitz	.15
T64	Mark Bellhorn	.15
T65	Ruben Sierra	.15
T66	Mike Fetters	.15
T67	Armando Benitez	.15
T68	Deivi Cruz	.15
T69	Jose Cruz Jr.	.15
T70	Jeremy Fikac	.15
T71	Jeff Kent	.25
T72	Andres Galarraga	.25
T73	Rickey Henderson	.50
T74	Royce Clayton	.15
T75	Troy O'Leary	.15
T76	Ron Coomer	.15
T77	Greg Colbrunn	.15
T78	Wes Helms	.15
T79	Kevin Millwood	.25
T80	Damion Easley	.15
T81	Bobby Kielty	.15
T82	Keith Osik	.15
T83	Ramiro Mendoza	.15
T84	Shea Hillenbrand	.15
T85	Shannon Stewart	.15
T86	Eddie Perez	.15
T87	Ugueth Urbina	.15
T88	Orlando Palmeiro	.15
T89	Graeme Lloyd	.15
T90	John Vander Wal	.15
T91	Gary Bennett	.15
T92	Shane Reynolds	.15
T93	Steve Parris	.15
T94	Julio Lugo	.15
T95	John Halama	.15
T96	Carlos Baerga	.15
T97	Jim Parque	.15
T98	Mike Williams	.15
T99	Fred McGriff	.25
T100	Kenny Rogers	.15
T101	Matt Herges	.15
T102	Jay Bell	.15
T103	Esteban Yan	.15
T104	Eric Owens	.15
T105	Aaron Fultz	.15
T106	Rey Sanchez	.15
T107	Jim Thome	.75
T108	Aaron Boone	.25
T109	Raul Mondesi	.25
T110	Kenny Lofton	.25
T111	Jose Guillen	.15
T112	Aramis Ramirez	.40
T113	Sidney Ponson	.15
T114	Scott Williamson	.15
T115	Robin Ventura	.25
T116	Dusty Baker	.15
T117	Felipe Alou	.15
T118	Buck Showalter	.15
T119	Jack McKeon	.15
T120	Art Howe	.15
T121	Bobby Crosby	.40
T122	Adrian Gonzalez	.25
T123	Kevin Cash	.15
T124	Shin-Soo Choo	.15
T125	Chin-Feng Chen	.25
T126	Miguel Cabrera	.75
T127	Jason Young	.15
T128	Alex Herrera	.15
T129	Jason Dubois	.15
T130	Jeff Mathis	.15
T131	Casey Kotchman	.25
T132	Ed Rogers	.15
T133	Wilson Betemit	.15
T134	Jim Kavourias	.15
T135	Taylor Buchholz	.15
T136	Adam LaRoche	.15
T137	Dallas McPherson	.40
T138	Jesus Cota	.15
T139	Clint Nageotte	.15
T140	Boof Bonser	.15
T141	Walter Young	.15
T142	Joe Crede	.25
T143	Denny Bautista	.15
T144	Victor Diaz	.15
T145	Chris Narveson	.15
T146	Gabe Gross	.15
T147	Jimmy Journell	.15
T148	Rafael Soriano	.15
T149	Jerome Williams	.15
T150	Aaron Cook	.15
T151	Anastacio Martinez	.15
T152	Scott Hairston	.15
T153	John Buck	.15
T154	Ryan Ludwick	.15
T155	Chris Bootcheck	.15
T156	John Rheinecker	.15
T157	Jason Lane	.15
T158	Shelley Duncan	.15
T159	Adam Wainwright	.15
T160	Jason Arnold	.15
T161	Jonny Gomes	.15
T162	James Loney	.50
T163	Mike Fontenot	.15

T164	Khalil Greene	1.00
T165	Sean Burnett	.15
T166	David Martinez	.15
T167	Felix Pie RC	3.00
T168	Joe Valentine RC	.50
T169	Brandon Webb RC	1.50
T170	Matt Diaz RC	.25
T171	Lew Ford RC	.75
T172	Jeremy Griffiths	.25
T173	Matt Hensley RC	.25
T174	Charlie Manning RC	.25
T175	Elizardo Ramirez RC	.75
T176	Greg Aquino RC	.25
T177	Felix Sanchez RC	.50
T178	Kelly Shoppach RC	.75
T179	Bubba Nelson RC	.50
T180	Mike O'Keefe RC	.25
T181	Hanley Ramirez RC	5.00
T182	Todd Wellemeyer RC	.50
T183	Dustin Moseley RC	.25
T184	Eric Crozier RC	.50
T185	Ryan Shealy RC	1.00
T186	Jeremy Bonderman	2.00
T187	Thomari Story-Harden RC	.40
T188	Dusty Brown RC	.50
T189	Rob Hammock RC	.40
T190	Jorge Piedra RC	.25
T191	Chris De La Cruz RC	.25
T192	Eli Whiteside RC	.25
T193	Jason Kubel RC	1.00
T194	Jon Schuerholz RC	.25
T195	Stephen Randolph RC	.25
T196	Andy Sisco	.75
T197	Sean Smith	.15
T198	Jon-Mark Sprowl RC	.75
T199	Matt Kata RC	.40
T200	Robinson Cano RC	6.00
T201	Nook Logan RC	.25
T202	Ben Francisco RC	.50
T203	Arnie Munoz RC	.25
T204	Eric Chavez	.15
T205	Eric Riggs RC	.25
T206	Beau Kemp RC	.25
T207	Travis Wong RC	.50
T208	Dustin Yount RC	.25
T209	Brian McCann	4.00
T210	Wilton Reynolds RC	.25
T211	Matt Bruback RC	.50
T212	Andrew Brown RC	.50
T213	Edgar Gonzalez RC	.25
T214	Eider Torres RC	.25
T215	Aquilino Lopez RC	.25
T216	Bobby Basham RC	.50
T217	Tim Olson RC	.50
T218	Nathan Panther RC	.50
T219	Bryan Grace RC	.25
T220	Dusty Gomon RC	.25
T221	Wilfredo Ledezma RC	.25
T222	Josh Willingham RC	.75
T223	David Cash RC	.25
T224	Oscar Villarreal RC	.25
T225	Jeff Duncan RC	.25
T226	Kade Johnson RC	.25
T227	Luke Steidlmayer RC	.25
T228	Brandon Watson RC	.50
T229	Jose Morales RC	.50
T230	Mike Gallo RC	.25
T231	Tyler Adamczyk RC	.50
T232	Adam Stern	.15
T233	Brennan King RC	.25
T234	Dan Haren	1.00
T235	Michel Hernandez RC	.25
T236	Ben Fritz	.15
T237	Clay Hensley RC	.50
T238	Tyler Johnson RC	.25
T239	Pete LaForest RC	.25
T240	Tyler Martin RC	.25
T241	J.D. Durbin RC	.50
T242	Shane Victorino RC	.25
T243	Rajai Davis RC	.50
T244	Ismael Castro RC	.25
T245	Chien-Ming Wang RC	4.00
T246	Travis Ishikawa RC	.40
T247	Corey Shafer RC	.50
T248	Gary Schneidmiller RC	.25
T249	David Pember RC	.25
T250	Keith Stamler RC	.25
T251	Tyson Graham RC	.25
T252	Ryan Cameron RC	.25
T253	Eric Eckenstahler RC	.25
T254	Matthew Peterson RC	.25
T255	Dustin McGowan RC	1.00
T256	Prentice Redman RC	.40
T257	Haj Turay RC	.25
T258	Carlos Guzman RC	.40
T259	Matt DeMarco RC	.25
T260	Derek Michaelis RC	.25
T261	Brian Burgamy RC	.25
T262	Jay Sitzman RC	.25
T263	Chris Fallon RC	.25
T264	Mike Adams RC	.25
T265	Clint Barmes RC	.75
T266	Eric Reed RC	.50

T267	Willie Eyre RC	.25
T268	Carlos Duran RC	.40
T269	Nick Trzesniak RC	.25
T270	Ferdin Tejeda RC	.50
T271	Michael Garciaparra	.25
T272	Michael Hinckley RC	.75
T273	Branden Florence RC	.25
T274	Trent Oeltjen RC	.40
T275	Mike Neu RC	.25

Gold

Stars: 5-10X
Rookies: 1-2.5X
Production 2003 Sets

Chrome Refractor

Stars: 4-8X
Rookies: 2-4X
Inserted 1:12

Future Phenoms

		NM/M
	Common Player:	4.00
RB	Rocco Baldelli	6.00
WB	Wilson Betemit	4.00
HB	Hank Blalock	6.00
WPB	Willie Bloomquist	15.00
MB	Marlon Byrd	4.00
CC	Chin-Feng Chen	20.00
CDC	Carl Crawford	6.00
TH	Travis Hafner	6.00
TAH	Trey Hodges	4.00
JM	Justin Morneau	10.00
BP	Brandon Phillips	4.00
MR	Michael Restovich	6.00
CS	Chris Snelling	4.00
MT	Mark Teixeira	8.00
JT	Joe Thurston	4.00

Hall of Fame

		NM/M
	Common Player:	8.00
GC	Gary Carter	8.00
EM	Eddie Murray	15.00

Hall of Fame Dual

		NM/M
	Complete Set (1):	
CM	Gary Carter, Eddie Murray	25.00

Signature Moves

		NM/M
	Common Player:	8.00
EA	Erick Almonte	8.00
DB	David Bell	10.00
JB	Joe Borchard	8.00
BC	Bartolo Colon	12.00
JC	Jose Cruz Jr.	8.00
JJC	Jack Cust	10.00
RF	Robert Fick	8.00
CF	Cliff Floyd	15.00
JF	Jesse Foppert	10.00
JG	Joey Gomes	8.00
KG	Khalil Greene	25.00
JL	James Loney	25.00
VM	Victor Martinez	20.00
FP	Felix Pie	60.00
ER	Elizardo Ramirez	12.00
JR	Jose Reyes	40.00
JS	Jason Stokes	15.00
MT	Mark Teixeira	25.00
BU	B.J. Upton	25.00
WY	Walter Young	10.00

Tools of the Trade

		NM/M
	Common Player:	4.00
EA	Edgardo Alfonzo	4.00
DB	David Bell	4.00
JC	Jose Cruz Jr.	4.00
ED	Erubiel Durazo	4.00
RD	Ray Durham	4.00
RF	Robert Fick	4.00
CF	Cliff Floyd	4.00
AG	Andres Galarraga	5.00
JG	Jeremy Giambi	4.00
TG	Tom Glavine	6.00
EK	Eric Karros	5.00
JK	Jeff Kent	5.00
KL	Kenny Lofton	10.00
FL	Felipe Lopez	5.00
FM	Fred McGriff	6.00
KM	Kevin Millar	5.00
RO	Rey Ordonez	4.00
JP	Juan Pierre	5.00
SH	Tsuyoshi Shinjo	4.00
SS	Shane Spencer	4.00
JT	Jim Thome	10.00
BT	Bubba Trammell	4.00
RW	Rondell White	4.00
PW	Preston Wilson	4.00
TZ	Todd Zeile	6.00

Tools of the Trade Dual

		NM/M
	Common Player:	10.00
KM	Kevin Millwood	10.00
IR	Ivan Rodriguez	15.00
JT	Jim Thome	15.00

2003 Topps All-Time Fan Favorites

		NM/M
	Complete Set (150):	30.00
	Common Player:	.25
	Pack (6):	4.00
	Box (24):	75.00
1	Willie Mays	3.00
2	Whitey Ford	1.00
3	Stan Musial	2.50
4	Paul Blair	.25
5	Harold Reynolds	.25
6	Bob Friend	.25
7	Rod Carew	.75
8	Kirk Gibson	.25
9	Graig Nettles	.25
10	Ozzie Smith	1.00
11	Tony Perez	.25
12	Tim Wallach	.25
13	Bert Campaneris	.25
14	Cory Snyder	.25
15	Dave Parker	.25
16	Darrell Evans	.25
17	Joe Pepitone	.25
18	Don Sutton	.25
19	Dale Murphy	1.00
20	George Brett	2.50
21	Carlton Fisk	.50
22	Bob Watson	.25
23	Wally Joyner	.25
24	Paul Molitor	1.00
25	Keith Hernandez	.25
26	Jerry Koosman	.25
27	George Bell	.25
28	Boog Powell	.25
29	Bruce Sutter	.25
30	Ernie Banks	1.50
31	Steve Lyons	.25
32	Earl Weaver	.25
33	Dave Stieb	.25
34	Alan Trammell	.25
35	Bret Saberhagen	.25
36	J.R. Richard	.25
37	Mickey Rivers	.25
38	Juan Marichal	.75
39	Gaylord Perry	.25
40	Don Mattingly	3.00
41	Bobby Grich	.25
42	Steve Sax	.25
43	Sparky Anderson	.25
44	Luis Aparicio	.25
45	Fergie Jenkins	.50
46	Jim Palmer	.75
47	Howard Johnson	.25
48	Dwight Evans	.25
49	Bill Buckner	.25
50	Cal Ripken Jr.	4.00
51	Jose Cruz	.25
52	Tony Oliva	.25
53	Bobby Richardson	.25
54	Luis Tiant	.25
55	Warren Spahn	1.00
56	Phil Rizzuto	1.00
57	Eric Davis	.25
58	Vida Blue	.25
59	Steve Balboni	.25
60	Mike Schmidt	2.50
61	Ken Griffey Sr.	.25
62	Jim Abbott	.25
63	Whitey Herzog	.25
64	Rich "Goose" Gossage	.25
65	Tony Armas	.25
66	Bill "Moose" Skowron	.25
67	Don Newcombe	.25
68	Bill Madlock	.25
69	Lance Parrish	.25
70	Reggie Jackson	1.50
71	Willie Wilson	.25
72	Terry Pendleton	.25
73	Jimmy Piersall	.25
74	George Foster	.25
75	Bob Horner	.25
76	Chris Sabo	.25
77	Fred Lynn	.25
78	Jim Rice	.25
79	Maury Wills	.25
80	Yogi Berra	1.50
81	Johnny Sain	.25
82	Tom Lasorda	.50
83	Bill Mazeroski	.25
84	John Kruk	.25
85	Bob Feller	.75
86	Frank Robinson	.75
87	Red Schoendienst	.25
88	Gary Carter	.50
89	Andre Dawson	.50
90	Tim McCarver	.25
91	Robin Yount	1.00
92	Phil Niekro	.25
93	Joe Morgan	.25
94	Darren Daulton	.25
95	Bobby Thomson	.25
96	Alvin Davis	.25
97	Robin Roberts	.25
98	Kirby Puckett	1.50
99	Jack Clark	.25
100	Hank Aaron	3.00
101	Orlando Cepeda	.50
102	Vern Law	.25
103	Cecil Cooper	.25
104	Don Larsen	.50
105	Mario Mendoza	.25
106	Tony Gwynn	1.50
107	Ernie Harwell	.25
108a	Monte Irvin (No facsimile autograph).	.75
108b	Monte Irvin (W/facsimile autograph).	1.50
109	Tommy John	.25
110	Rollie Fingers	.75
111	Johnny Podres	.25
112	Jeff Reardon	.25
113	Buddy Bell	.25
114	Dwight Gooden	.50
115	Garry Templeton	.25
116	Johnny Bench	2.00
117	Joe Rudi	.25
118	Ron Guidry	.50
119	Vince Coleman	.25
120	Al Kaline	2.00
121	Carl Yastrzemski	1.50
122	Hank Bauer	.25
123	Mark Fidrych	.25
124	Paul O'Neill	.50
125	Ron Cey	.25
126	Willie McGee	.25
127	Harmon Killebrew	1.50
128	Dave Concepcion	.25
129	Harold Baines	.25
130	Lou Brock	.50
131	Lee Smith	.25
132	Willie McCovey	.75
133	Steve Garvey	.25
134	Kent Tekulve	.25
135	Tom Seaver	1.50
136	Bo Jackson	1.00
137	Walt Weiss	.25
138	Brook Jacoby	.25
139	Dennis Eckersley	.50
140	Duke Snider	1.00
141	Lenny Dykstra	.25
142	Greg Luzinski	.25
143	Jim Bunning	.25
144	Jose Canseco	.75
145	Ron Santo	.25
146	Bert Blyleven	.25
147	Wade Boggs	.75
148	Brooks Robinson	1.00
149	Ray Knight	.25
150	Nolan Ryan	4.00

Refractors

Cards (1-150): 3-6X
Production 299 Sets

Autographs

		NM/M
	Common Autograph:	8.00
	SP's Production 50	
HA	Hank Aaron/SP	250.00
JA	Jim Abbott	10.00
SA	Sparky Anderson/SP	30.00

Code	Name	Price
LA	Luis Aparicio	10.00
TA	Tony Armas	10.00
HBA	Harold Baines	15.00
SB	Steve Balboni	8.00
EB	Ernie Banks/SP	120.00
HB	Hank Bauer/SP	35.00
BBE	Buddy Bell	15.00
GB	George Bell	10.00
JBE	Johnny Bench/SP	100.00
YB	Yogi Berra/SP	100.00
BBI	Buddy Biancalana	8.00
PB	Paul Blair	10.00
VB	Vida Blue	15.00
BB	Bert Blyleven	15.00
WB	Wade Boggs/SP	75.00
GBR	George Brett/SP	250.00
LB	Lou Brock/SP	60.00
BBU	Bill Buckner	10.00
JB	Jim Bunning/SP	75.00
BC	Bert Campaneris	10.00
JOS	Jose Canseco/SP	60.00
RCA	Rod Carew/SP	75.00
GC	Gary Carter/SP	40.00
JCA	Joe Carter/SP	35.00
OC	Orlando Cepeda/SP	60.00
RCE	Ron Cey	10.00
JC	Jack Clark	15.00
VC	Vince Coleman	10.00
DC	Dave Concepcion/SP	35.00
CC	Cecil Cooper	10.00
JCR	Jose Cruz	10.00
RDA	Ron Darling	10.00
DD	Darren Daulton	15.00
AD	Alvin Davis	8.00
ED	Eric Davis	15.00
ADA	Andre Dawson/SP	50.00
DDE	Doug DeCinces	15.00
RD	Rob Dibble	15.00
LDU	Leon Durham	10.00
LD	Lenny Dykstra	10.00
DEC	Dennis Eckersley/SP	60.00
DE	Darrell Evans	10.00
DEV	Dwight Evans/SP	40.00
BF	Bob Feller	15.00
MF	Mark Fidrych	10.00
RF	Rollie Fingers/SP	40.00
CF	Carlton Fisk/SP	60.00
WF	Whitey Ford/SP	100.00
GF	George Foster	10.00
BFR	Bob Friend	10.00
SG	Steve Garvey	20.00
KGI	Kirk Gibson/SP	75.00
DG	Dwight Gooden/SP	30.00
RG	Rich "Goose" Gossage/SP	30.00
BGR	Bobby Grich	10.00
KG	Ken Griffey Sr./SP	30.00
RGU	Ron Guidry	15.00
TG	Tony Gwynn/SP	100.00
EH	Ernie Harwell	40.00
KH	Keith Hernandez/SP	60.00
WHE	Willie Hernandez	10.00
TH	Tom Herr	10.00
WH	Whitey Herzog	20.00
BH	Bob Horner	8.00
MI	Monte Irvin/SP	40.00
BJ	Bo Jackson/SP	100.00
RJ	Reggie Jackson/SP	100.00
BJA	Brook Jacoby	8.00
FJ	Fergie Jenkins	15.00
TJ	Tommy John	15.00
HJ	Howard Johnson	10.00
WJ	Wally Joyner	10.00
AK	Al Kaline/SP	75.00
HK	Harmon Killebrew/SP	80.00
RK	Ralph Kiner/SP	65.00
RKI	Ron Kittle	10.00
RY	Ray Knight	10.00
JK	Jerry Koosman	20.00
JKR	John Kruk/SP	60.00
CL	Carney Lansford	15.00
DL	Don Larsen	15.00
TL	Tom Lasorda/SP	40.00
VL	Vern Law	15.00
BL	Bill Lee	10.00
CLE	Chet Lemon	10.00
GL	Greg Luzinski	15.00
FL	Fred Lynn/SP	25.00
SL	Steve Lyons	15.00
BMA	Bill Madlock	10.00
JMA	Juan Marichal/SP	75.00
DON	Don Mattingly/SP	100.00
WM	Willie Mays/SP	150.00
BMZ	Bill Mazeroski/SP	50.00
TM	Tim McCarver/SP	40.00
WMC	Willie McCovey/SP	60.00
MCG	Willie McGee/SP	60.00
TMC	Tug McGraw	20.00
MM	Mario Mendoza	10.00
KM	Kevin Mitchell	10.00
PM	Paul Molitor/SP	60.00

Code	Name	Price
JMO	John Montefusco	10.00
JM	Joe Morgan/SP	30.00
DM	Dale Murphy/SP	60.00
SM	Stan Musial/SP	120.00
GN	Graig Nettles	15.00
DN	Don Newcombe/SP	40.00
PN	Phil Niekro/SP	40.00
AO	Al Oliver	10.00
PO	Paul O'Neill/SP	75.00
MP	Mike Pagliarulo	10.00
JP	Jim Palmer/SP	60.00
DP	Dave Parker/SP	40.00
LP	Lance Parrish	10.00
TP	Terry Pendleton	15.00
JPE	Joe Pepitone	10.00
TPE	Tony Perez/SP	65.00
GP	Gaylord Perry	25.00
BP	Boog Powell	15.00
KP	Kirby Puckett/SP	65.00
JRE	Jeff Reardon	10.00
HR	Harold Reynolds/SP	40.00
JRI	Jim Rice/SP	45.00
JR	J.R. Richard	10.00
CR	Cal Ripken Jr./SP	225.00
MR	Mickey Rivers	10.00
PR	Phil Rizzuto/SP	75.00
RR	Robin Roberts	25.00
BRO	Brooks Robinson/SP	100.00
FR	Frank Robinson/SP	75.00
JRU	Joe Rudi	10.00
NR	Nolan Ryan/SP	200.00
BSA	Bret Saberhagen/SP	40.00
CS	Chris Sabo	8.00
RSA	Ron Santo	25.00
SS	Steve Sax	8.00
MS	Mike Schmidt/SP	150.00
RS	Red Schoendienst	15.00
TSE	Tom Seaver/SP	100.00
KS	Kevin Seitzer	10.00
BS	Bill "Moose" Skowron	15.00
LS	Lee Smith	10.00
OS	Ozzie Smith/SP	100.00
DSN	Duke Snider/SP	60.00
CN	Cory Snyder	15.00
WS	Warren Spahn/SP	40.00
CSP	Chris Speier	10.00
DS	Dave Stieb	15.00
BSU	Bruce Sutter	35.00
DSU	Don Sutton/SP	40.00
KT	Kent Tekulve	10.00
GT	Garry Templeton	10.00
BT	Bobby Thomson/SP	25.00
LT	Luis Tiant/SP	40.00
AT	Alan Trammell	20.00
TW	Tim Wallach	10.00
BW	Bob Watson	10.00
EW	Earl Weaver	10.00
WW	Walt Weiss	8.00
MW	Maury Wills	10.00
WWI	Willie Wilson/SP	25.00
CY	Carl Yastrzemski/SP	150.00
SY	Steve Yeager	10.00
RYO	Robin Yount/SP	100.00

Best Seat Relics

AUTHENTIC STADIUM SEAT

PHIL NIEKRO · BOB DI RENEE · DALE MURPHY

BEST SEAT IN THE HOUSE

	NM/M
Common Card:	20.00
BS1	Jim Palmer, Frank Robinson, Brooks Robinson 25.00
BS2	Wally Joyner, Rod Carew, Bobby Grich 20.00
BS3	Phil Garner, Willie Stargell, Dave Parker, Kent Tekulve 20.00
BS4	Rollie Fingers, Robin Yount, Paul Molitor 25.00
BS5	Phil Niekro, Dale Murphy, Bob Horner 20.00

Relics

	NM/M
Common Player:	8.00
HBA	Harold Baines/Bat	12.00
GBR	George Brett/Jsy	25.00
JOS	Jose Canseco/Bat	12.00
RCA	Rod Carew/Bat	10.00
GC	Gary Carter/Bat	10.00
NC	Norm Cash/Jsy	25.00
VC	Vince Coleman/Bat	8.00
JCR	Jose Cruz/Bat	6.00
RDA	Ron Darling/Jsy	8.00
ADA	Andre Dawson/Bat	8.00
LD	Lenny Dykstra/Bat	8.00
DEC	Dennis Eckersley/Jsy	10.00
CF	Curt Flood/Bat	10.00
GF	George Foster/Bat	8.00
BFR	Bob Friend/Jsy	6.00
SG	Steve Garvey/Bat	6.00
KGI	Kirk Gibson/Bat	8.00
KH	Keith Hernandez/Bat	12.00
WHE	Willie Hernandez/Bat	8.00
BH	Bob Horner/Bat	6.00
BJ	Bo Jackson/Bat	20.00
WJ	Wally Joyner/Bat	8.00
GL	Greg Luzinski/Bat	6.00
FL	Fred Lynn/Bat	10.00
DON	Don Mattingly/Bat	30.00
MCG	Willie McGee/Bat	15.00
TMC	Tug McGraw/Jsy	10.00
KM	Kevin Mitchell/Bat	6.00
JM	Joe Morgan/Bat	10.00
DM	Dale Murphy/Bat	15.00
PO	Paul O'Neill/Bat	8.00
DP	Dave Parker/Bat	6.00
LP	Lance Parrish/Bat	12.00
KP	Kirby Puckett/Bat	15.00
HR	Harold Reynolds/Bat	6.00
JRI	Jim Rice/Bat	8.00
BR	Bobby Richardson/Bat	15.00
JRU	Joe Rudi/Bat	6.00
CS	Chris Sabo/Bat	8.00
MS	Mike Schmidt/Bat	25.00
WS	Willie Stargell/Bat	12.00
AT	Alan Trammell/Bat	15.00
MW	Maury Wills/Bat	6.00

Team Topps Legend Autograph

	NM/M
Common Autograph:	10.00
Ernie Banks	
Paul Blair	
Lou Brock	30.00
Jim Bunning	15.00
Gary Carter	30.00
Rich "Goose" Gossage	15.00
Al Kaline	50.00
Willie Mays	120.00
Joe Morgan	30.00
Stan Musial	75.00
Graig Nettles	15.00
Johnny Sain	15.00
Mike Schmidt	75.00
Robin Yount	

2003 Topps Bazooka

	NM/M
Complete Set (280):	40.00
Common Player:	.15
Pack (8):	2.00
Box (24):	40.00
Card #7 has 31 variations.	
1	Luis Castillo	.15
2	Randy Winn	.15
3	Orlando Hudson	.15
4	Fernando Vina	.15
5	Pat Burrell	.25
6	Brad Wilkerson	.15
7	Bazooka Joe	.25
8	Javy Lopez	.25
9	Juan Pierre	.15
10	Hideo Nomo	.40
11	Barry Larkin	.25
12	Alfonso Soriano	.75

13	Rodrigo Lopez	.15
14	Mark Ellis	.15
15	Tim Salmon	.25
16	Garret Anderson	.25
17	Aaron Boone	.15
18	Jason Kendall	.15
19	Hee Seop Choi	.15
20	Jorge Posada	.40
21	Sammy Sosa	1.50
22	Mark Prior	.75
23	Mark Teixeira	.50
24	Manny Ramirez	.50
25	Jim Thome	.75
26	A.J. Pierzynski	.15
27	Scott Rolen	.75
28	Austin Kearns	.25
29	Bret Boone	.15
30	Ken Griffey Jr.	1.00
31	Greg Maddux	1.00
32	Derek Lowe	.15
33	David Wells	.15
34	A.J. Burnett	.15
35	Randall Simon	.15
36	Nick Johnson	.15
37	Junior Spivey	.15
38	Eric Gagne	.40
39	Darin Erstad	.25
40	Marty Cordova	.15
41	Brett Myers	.15
42	Mo Vaughn	.15
43	Randy Wolf	.15
44	Vicente Padilla	.15
45	Elmer Dessens	.15
46	Jason Simontacchi	.15
47	John Mabry	.15
48	Torii Hunter	.25
49	Lyle Overbay	.15
50	Kirk Saarloos	.15
51	Bernie Williams	.50
52	Wade Miller	.15
53	Bobby Abreu	.25
54	Wilson Betemit	.15
55	Edwin Almonte	.15
56	Jarrod Washburn	.15
57	Drew Henson	.25
58	Tony Batista	.15
59	Juan Rivera	.15
60	Larry Walker	.25
61	Brandon Phillips	.15
62	Franklyn German	.15
63	Victor Martinez	.25
64	Moises Alou	.15
65	Nomar Garciaparra	1.00
66	Willie Harris	.15
67	Sean Casey	.25
68	Omar Vizquel	.25
69	Robert Fick	.15
70	Curt Schilling	.50
71	Adam Kennedy	.15
72	Scott Hairston	.15
73	Jimmy Journell	.15
74	Rafael Furcal	.25
75	Barry Zito	.25
76	Ed Rogers	.15
77	Cliff Floyd	.15
78	Matt Clement	.15
79	Mike Lowell	.25
80	Randy Johnson	.75
81	Craig Biggio	.25
82	Carlos Beltran	.50
83	Paul LoDuca	.15
84	Jose Vidro	.15
85	Gary Sheffield	.40
86	Jacque Jones	.15
87	Corey Hart	.15
88	Roberto Alomar	.40
89	Robin Ventura	.25
90	Pedro Martinez	.75
91	Scott Hatteberg	.15
92	Marlon Byrd	.15
93	Pokey Reese	.15
94	Sean Burroughs	.15
95	Magglio Ordonez	.25
96	Tsuyoshi Shinjo	.15
97	John Olerud	.15
98	Edgar Renteria	.25
99	Ben Grieve	.15
100	Mariano Rivera	.25
101	Ivan Rodriguez	.50
102	Josh Phelps	.15
103	Nobuaki Yoshida RC	.40
104	Roy Halladay	.25
105	Mark Buehrle	.15
106	Chan Ho Park	.15
107	Joe Kennedy	.15
108	Shin-Soo Choo	.15
109	Ryan Jensen	.15
110	Todd Helton	.50
111	Chris Duncan RC	1.00
112	Taggert Bozied	.15
113	Sean Burnett	.15
114	Mike Lieberthal	.15
115	Josh Beckett	.40
116	Andy Pettitte	.40

117	Jose Reyes	.25
118	Bartolo Colon	.15
119	Justin Morneau	.25
120	Lance Berkman	.25
121	Mike Wodnicki RC	.40
122	Craig Brazell RC	.50
123	Troy Glaus	.40
124	John Smoltz	.25
125	Mike Sweeney	.15
126	Jay Gibbons	.15
127	Kerry Wood	.75
128	Ellis Burks	.15
129	Carlos Pena	.15
130	Shawn Green	.25
131	Jason Stokes	.15
132	Raul Ibanez	.15
133	Francisco Rodriguez	.15
134	Adrian Beltre	.25
135	Richie Sexson	.40
136	Paul Byrd	.15
137	Bobby Kielty	.15
138	Dewon Brazelton	.15
139	Jeremy Griffiths	.15
140	Vladimir Guerrero	.75
141	Jake Peavy	.25
142	Bryan Bullington RC	1.00
143	Orlando Cabrera	.15
144	Scott Erickson	.15
145	Doug Mientkiewicz	.15
146	Derek Lee	.25
147	Daryl Clark RC	.40
148	Trevor Hoffman	.15
149	Gabe Gross	.15
150	Roger Clemens	1.50
151	Khalil Greene	1.00
152	Cory Doyne RC	.40
153	Brandon Roberson RC	.40
154	Josh Fogg	.15
155	Eric Chavez	.25
156	Kris Benson	.15
157	Billy Koch	.15
158	Jermaine Dye	.25
159	Kip Bouknight RC	.40
160	Brian Giles	.25
161	Justin Huber	.15
162	Mike Restovich	.15
163	Brandon Webb RC	.75
164	Odalis Perez	.15
165	Phil Nevin	.15
166	Dontrelle Willis	.25
167	Aaron Heilman	.15
168	Dustin Moseley RC	.50
169	Rylan Reed RC	.40
170	Miguel Tejada	.40
171	Nic Jackson	.15
172	Anthony Webster RC	.40
173	Jorge Julio	.15
174	Kevin Millwood	.25
175	Brian Jordan	.15
176	Terry Tiffee RC	.40
177	Dallas McPherson	.15
178	Freddy Garcia	.15
179	Jamie Moyer	.15
180	Rafael Palmeiro	.50
181	Mike O'Keefe RC	.40
182	Kevin Youkilis RC	1.00
183	Kip Wells	.15
184	Joe Mauer	.25
185	Edgar Martinez	.25
186	Jaime Bubela RC	.40
187	Jose Hernandez	.15
188	Josh Hamilton	.15
189	Matt Diaz RC	.40
190	Chipper Jones	.75
191	Kevin Mench	.15
192	Joey Gomes	.15
193	Shannon Stewart	.15
194	Damian Miller	.15
195	Mike Piazza	1.00
196	Damian Moss	.15
197	Mike Fontenot	.15
198	Shea Hillenbrand	.15
199	Evel Bastida-Martinez RC	.40
200	Jason Giambi	.40
201	Aron Weston RC	.40
202	Frank Thomas	.50
203	Carlos Lee	.15
204	C.C. Sabathia	.15
205	Jim Edmonds	.40
206	Jemel Spearman RC	.40
207	Jason Jennings	.15
208	Jeremy Bonderman	1.00
209	Preston Wilson	.15
210	Eric Hinske	.15
211	Will Smith	.15
212	Matthew Hagen RC	.40
213	Joe Randa	.15
214	James Loney	.15
215	Carlos Delgado	.25
216	Kris Kroski RC	.50
217	Cristian Guzman	.15
218	Tomokazu Ohka	.15
219	Al Leiter	.15

220	Adam Dunn	.50
221	Raul Mondesi	.25
222	Donald Hood RC	.40
223	Mark Mulder	.25
224	Mike Williams	.15
225	Ryan Klesko	.25
226	Rich Aurilia	.15
227	Chris Snelling	.15
228	Gary Schneidmiller RC	.40
229	Ichiro Suzuki	1.50
230	Luis Gonzalez	.25
231	Rocco Baldelli	.15
232	Callix Crabbe RC	.40
233	Adrian Gonzalez	.15
234	Corey Koskie	.15
235	Tom Glavine	.40
236	Kevin Beavers RC	.40
237	Frank Catalanotto	.15
238	Kevin Cash	.15
239	Nick Trzesniak RC	.50
240	Paul Konerko	.25
241	Jose Cruz Jr.	.15
242	Hank Blalock	.50
243	J.D. Drew	.25
244	Kazuhiro Sasaki	.15
245	Jeff Bagwell	.50
246	Jason Schmidt	.25
247	Xavier Nady	.15
248	Aramis Ramirez	.40
249	Jimmy Rollins	.20
250	Alex Rodriguez	1.50
251	Terrence Long	.15
252	Derek Jeter	2.00
253	Edgardo Alfonzo	.15
254	Toby Hall	.15
255	Kazuhisa Ishii	.15
256	Brad Nelson	.15
257	Kevin Brown	.25
258	Roy Oswalt	.25
259	Mike Cameron	.15
260	Juan Gonzalez	.40
261	Dmitri Young	.15
262	Jose Jimenez	.15
263	Wily Mo Pena	.25
264	Joe Borchard	.15
265	Mike Mussina	.50
266	Fred McGriff	.25
267	Johnny Damon	.25
268	Joel Pineiro	.15
269	Andruw Jones	.50
270	Tim Hudson	.25
271	Chad Tracy	.15
272	Brad Fullmer	.15
273	Boof Bonser	.15
274	Clint Nageotte	.15
275	Jeff Kent	.25
276	Tino Martinez	.25
277	Matt Morris	.15
278	Jonny Gomes	.15
279	Benito Santiago	.15
280	Albert Pujols	1.50

Silver

Stars:	1-3X
Inserted 1:1	

Mini

Stars:	1-3X
Inserted 1:1	

Blasts

		NM/M
	Common Player:	4.00
	Refractors:	3-4X
	Production 25 Sets	
RA	Roberto Alomar	6.00
LB	Lance Berkman	6.00
WB	Wilson Betemit	4.00
JD	Johnny Damon	6.00
CD	Carlos Delgado	5.00
JDD	J.D. Drew	8.00
DE	Darin Erstad	4.00
AG	Andres Galarraga	4.00
LG	Luis Gonzalez	4.00
SG	Shawn Green	6.00
TG	Tony Gwynn	8.00
RH	Rickey Henderson	10.00
DH	Drew Henson	4.00
NJ	Nick Johnson	4.00
CJ	Chipper Jones	10.00
RK	Ryan Klesko	4.00
PL	Paul LoDuca	4.00
EM	Edgar Martinez	8.00
TM	Tino Martinez	4.00
RM	Raul Mondesi	4.00
RP	Rafael Palmeiro	4.00
MP	Mike Piazza	12.00
JP	Jorge Posada	8.00
ANR	Aramis Ramirez	4.00
MR	Manny Ramirez	8.00
AR	Alex Rodriguez	12.00
IR	Ivan Rodriguez	8.00
GS	Gary Sheffield	8.00
TS	Tsuyoshi Shinjo	4.00
AS	Alfonso Soriano	10.00
MS	Mike Sweeney	4.00
RV	Robin Ventura	4.00
BW	Bernie Williams	10.00

Comics

		NM/M
	Complete Set (12):	4.00
	Common Player:	.25
	Inserted 1:4	
	Roger Clemens	.40
	Nomar Garciaparra	.60
	Jason Giambi	.40
	Derek Jeter	.75
	Randy Johnson	.30
	Chipper Jones	.40
	Mike Piazza	.50
	Albert Pujols	.30
	Alex Rodriguez	.60
	Alfonso Soriano	.40
	Sammy Sosa	.40
	Ichiro Suzuki	.50

Piece of Americana

CURT SCHILLING

		NM/M
	Common Player:	5.00
	Refractors:	3-4X
	Production 25 Sets	
JB	Jeff Bagwell	10.00
CB	Craig Biggio	5.00
BB	Bret Boone	5.00
DB	Dewon Brazelton	5.00
CD	Carlos Delgado	5.00
AD	Adam Dunn	10.00
JE	Jim Edmonds	6.00
RF	Rafael Furcal	5.00
NG	Nomar Garciaparra	15.00
SG	Shawn Green	6.00

CG	Cristian Guzman	5.00
TG	Tony Gwynn	10.00
THA	Toby Hall	5.00
TH	Todd Helton	6.00
AH	Aubrey Huff	5.00
AJ	Andruw Jones	5.00
CJ	Chipper Jones	10.00
JK	Jeff Kent	5.00
AL	Al Leiter	5.00
PL	Paul LoDuca	5.00
MM	Mike Mussina	8.00
MO	Magglio Ordonez	6.00
RP	Rafael Palmeiro	6.00
MP	Mike Piazza	12.00
PA	Albert Pujols	10.00
IR	Ivan Rodriguez	5.00
CS	Curt Schilling	8.00
FT	Frank Thomas	6.00
LW	Larry Walker	5.00
PW	Preston Wilson	5.00

Stand-Ups

JIM THOME
PHILADELPHIA PHILLIES® FIRST BASE

		NM/M
	Complete Set (25):	20.00
	Common Player:	.40
	Inserted 1:8	
1	Albert Pujols	2.50
2	Alfonso Soriano	1.00
3	Ichiro Suzuki	2.00
4	Sammy Sosa	2.00
5	Randy Johnson	1.00
6	Torii Hunter	.50
7	Vladimir Guerrero	1.00
8	Nomar Garciaparra	2.00
9	Alex Rodriguez	3.00
10	Troy Glaus	.50
11	Greg Maddux	1.50
12	Derek Jeter	3.00
13	Lance Berkman	.40
14	Larry Walker	.40
15	Adam Dunn	.50
16	Shawn Green	.50
17	Curt Schilling	.75
18	Todd Helton	.75
19	Pedro Martinez	1.00
20	Pat Burrell	.50
21	Miguel Tejada	.50
22	Manny Ramirez	1.00
23	Mike Piazza	1.50
24	Chipper Jones	1.00
25	Jason Giambi	1.00

4-On-1 Stickers

		NM/M
	Complete Set (55):	10.00
	Common Sticker:	.20
	Inserted 1:4	
1	Mark Prior, Roy Oswalt, Jarrod Washburn, Barry Zito	.30

2	Troy Glaus, Shea Hillenbrand, Eric Chavez, Eric Hinske .30
3	Orlando Hudson, Alfonso Soriano, Roberto Alomar, Jose Vidro .40
4	Nomar Garciaparra, Derek Jeter, Miguel Tejada, Alex Rodriguez .75
5	Jason Giambi, Jim Thome, Todd Helton, Rafael Palmeiro .40
6	Mike Williams, Trevor Hoffman, Billy Koch, John Smoltz .20
7	Jorge Posada, Mike Piazza, A.J. Pierzynski, Ivan Rodriguez .50
8	Vladimir Guerrero, Jim Edmonds, Manny Ramirez, Brad Wilkerson .40
9	Shawn Green, Sammy Sosa, Torii Hunter, Larry Walker .40
10	Bernie Williams, Ken Griffey Jr., Ichiro Suzuki, Adam Dunn .50
11	John Olerud, Mike Lieberthal, Terrence Long, Drew Henson .20
12	Edgar Martinez, Bret Boone, Mo Vaughn, Robert Fisk .20
13	Randy Johnson, Roger Clemens, Pedro Martinez, Greg Maddux .40
14	Curt Schilling, Tim Hudson, Tom Glavine, Kerry Wood .20
15	Paul Konerko, Mike Sweeney, Cristian Guzman, Scott Rolen .20
16	Josh Phelps, Brandon Phillips, Hee Seop Choi, Hank Blalock .20
17	Benito Santiago, Barry Larkin, Gary Sheffield, Carlos Delgado .20
18	Juan Rivera, Jose Reyes, Sean Burroughs, Carlos Pena .20
19	Tony Batista, Tim Salmon, Jeff Bagwell, Raul Ibanez .25
20	Edgardo Alfonzo, Nic Jackson, Luis Castillo, Damian Miller .20
21	David Wells, Ryan Klesko, Phil Nevin, Jeff Kent .20
22	Derek Lowe, Vicente Padilla, Kevin Millwood, Joel Pineiro .20
23	Fernando Vina, Darin Erstad, Jimmy Rollins, Doug Mientkiewicz .20
24	Joe Mauer, Justin Huber, Jason Stokes, Chad Tracy .20
25	Austin Kearns, Junior Spivey, Brett Myers, Victor Martinez .25
26	Khalil Greene, Gabe Gross, Kevin Cash, James Loney .20
27	Albert Pujols, Mark Buehrle, Chipper Jones, Lance Berkman .40
28	Adam Kennedy, Craig Biggio, Johnny Damon, Randy Winn .20
29	Brian Giles, J.D. Drew, Marlon Byrd, Joe Borchard .20
30	Al Leiter, Mike Mussina, Bartolo Colon, Freddy Garcia .20
31	Jason Kendall, Richie Sexson, Mike Lowell, Paul LoDuca .20

32	Pat Burrell, Garret Anderson, Cliff Floyd, Andruw Jones .25
33	Xavier Nady, Bobby Abreu, Taggert Bozied, Adrian Beltre .20
34	Rocco Baldelli, Dontrelle Willis, Chris Snelling, Mark Teixeira .20
35	Willie Harris, Nick Johnson, Jason Jennings, Kazuhisa Ishii .20
36	Mark Mulder, Sean Burnett, Paul Byrd, Josh Beckett .20
37	Corey Koskie, Aramis Ramirez, Tino Martinez, Moises Alou .20
38	Jose Cruz Jr., Roy Halliday, Dewon Brazelton, Jonny Gomes .20
39	Odalis Perez, Kevin Brown, Matt Clement, Randy Wolf .20
40	Eric Gagne, Jose Jimenez, Franklyn German, Edwin Almonte .20
41	Luis Gonzalez, Shannon Stewart, Brian Jordan, Juan Gonzalez .25
42	Toby Hall, Joe Kennedy, Javier Lopez, Damian Moss .20
43	Magglio Ordonez, Carlos Lee, Randall Simon, Dmitri Young .20
44	Sean Casey, Aaron Boone, Jacque Jones, Michael Restovich .20
45	Adrian Gonzalez, Corey Hart, Fred McGriff, Frank Thomas .25
46	C.C. Sabathia, Omar Vizquel, Andy Pettitte, Robin Ventura .20
47	Jason Schmidt, Ellis Burks, Joe Randa, Tsuyoshi Shinjo .20
48	Mike Cameron, Pokey Reese, Jermaine Dye, Preston Wilson .20
49	Chan Ho Park, Kazuhiro Sasaki, Tomokazu Ohka, Hideo Nomo .20
50	Jason Simontacchi, Kip Wells, Matt Morris, Rodrigo Lopez .20
51	Dallas McPherson, Josh Hamilton, Jeremy Bonderman, Aaron Heilman .20
52	Nobuaki Yoshida, Chris Duncan, Craig Brazell, Bryan Bullington .20
53	Daryl Clark, Brandon Webb, Dustin Moseley, Mike O'Keefe .20
54	Kevin Youkilis, Jaime Bubela, Matt Diaz, Joey Gomes .20
55	Kris Kroski, Donald Hood, Gary Schneidmiller, Callix Crabbe .20

2003 Topps Chrome

ADAM DUNN
of

		NM/M
	Complete Set (440):	160.00
	Common Player:	.25
	Series 1 & 2 Hobby Pack (4):	2.50
	Hobby Box (24):	50.00
1	Alex Rodriguez	4.00
2	Eddie Guardado	.25
3	Curt Schilling	1.50
4	Andruw Jones	1.00
5	Magglio Ordonez	.75
6	Todd Helton	1.00
7	Odalis Perez	.25
8	Edgardo Alfonzo	.25
9	Eric Hinske	.25
10	Danny Bautista	.25
11	Sammy Sosa	2.50
12	Roberto Alomar	1.00
13	Roger Clemens	3.00
14	Austin Kearns	1.00
15	Luis Gonzalez	.50
16	Mo Vaughn	.50
17	Alfonso Soriano	1.50
18	Orlando Cabrera	.25
19	Hideo Nomo	.75
20	Omar Vizquel	.25
21	Greg Maddux	2.50
22	Fred McGriff	.50
23	Frank Thomas	1.25
24	Shawn Green	.75
25	Jacque Jones	.25
26	Bernie Williams	1.00
27	Corey Patterson	.75
28	Cesar Izturis	.25
29	Larry Walker	.75
30	Darren Dreifort	.25
31	Al Leiter	.25
32	Jason Marquis	.25
33	Sean Casey	.25
34	Craig Counsell	.25
35	Albert Pujols	3.00
36	Kyle Lohse	.25
37	Paul LoDuca	.25
38	Roy Oswalt	.50
39	Danny Graves	.25
40	Kevin Millwood	.25
41	Lance Berkman	1.00
42	Denny Hocking	.25
43	Jose Valentin	.25
44	Josh Beckett	.75
45	Nomar Garciaparra	3.00
46	Craig Biggio	.50
47	Omar Daal	.25
48	Jimmy Rollins	.50
49	Jermaine Dye	.25
50	Edgar Renteria	.50
51	Brandon Duckworth	.25
52	Luis Castillo	.25
53	Andy Ashby	.25
54	Mike Williams	.25
55	Benito Santiago	.25
56	Bret Boone	.25
57	Randy Wolf	.25
58	Ivan Rodriguez	1.50
59	Shannon Stewart	.25
60	Jose Cruz Jr.	.25
61	Billy Wagner	.25
62	Alex Gonzalez	.25
63	Ichiro Suzuki	3.00
64	Joe McEwing	.25
65	Mark Mulder	.50
66	Mike Cameron	.25
67	Corey Koskie	.25
68	Marlon Anderson	.25
69	Jason Kendall	.25
70	J.T. Snow Jr.	.25
71	Edgar Martinez	.50
72	Vernon Wells	.50
73	Vladimir Guerrero	2.00
74	Adam Dunn	1.50
75	Barry Zito	.50
76	Jeff Kent	.50
77	Russ Ortiz	.25
78	Phil Nevin	.25
79	Carlos Beltran	1.00
80	Mike Lowell	.50
81	Bob Wickman	.25
82	Junior Spivey	.25
83	Melvin Mora	.25
84	Derek Lee	.50
85	Chuck Knoblauch	.25
86	Eric Gagne	.75
87	Orlando Hernandez	.50
88	Robert Person	.25
89	Elmer Dessens	.25
90	Wade Miller	.25
91	Adrian Beltre	.50
92	Kazuhiro Sasaki	.25
93	Timoniel Perez	.25
94	Jose Vidro	.25
95	Geronimo Gil	.25
96	Trot Nixon	.25
97	Denny Neagle	.25
98	Roberto Hernandez	.25

99	David Ortiz	1.50
100	Robb Nen	.25
101	Sidney Ponson	.25
102	Kevin Appier	.25
103	Javier Lopez	.50
104	Jeff Conine	.25
105	Mark Buehrle	.25
106	Jason Simontacchi	.25
107	Jose Jimenez	.25
108	Brian Jordan	.25
109	Brad Wilkerson	.25
110	Scott Hatteberg	.25
111	Matt Morris	.50
112	Miguel Tejada	.75
113	Rafael Furcal	.50
114	Steve Cox	.25
115	Roy Halladay	.25
116	David Eckstein	.25
117	Tomokazu Ohka	.25
118	Jack Wilson	.25
119	Randall Simon	.25
120	Jamie Moyer	.25
121	Andy Benes	.25
122	Tino Martinez	.50
123	Esteban Yan	.25
124	Jason Isringhausen	.25
125	Chris Carpenter	.25
126	Aaron Rowand	.25
127	Brandon Inge	.25
128	Jose Vizcaino	.25
129	Jose Mesa	.25
130	Troy Percival	.25
131	Jon Lieber	.25
132	Brian Giles	.50
133	Aaron Boone	.25
134	Bobby Higginson	.25
135	Luis Rivas	.25
136	Troy Glaus	1.00
137	Jim Thome	1.50
138	Ramon Martinez	.25
139	Jay Gibbons	.25
140	Mike Lieberthal	.25
141	Juan Uribe	.25
142	Gary Sheffield	.75
143	Ramon Santiago	.25
144	Ben Sheets	.50
145	Tony Armas Jr.	.25
146	Kazuhisa Ishii	.25
147	Erubiel Durazo	.25
148	Jerry Hairston Jr.	.25
149	Byung-Hyun Kim	.25
150	Marcus Giles	.25
151	Johnny Damon	.75
152	Terrence Long	.25
153	Juan Pierre	.25
154	Aramis Ramirez	.75
155	Brent Abernathy	.25
156	Ismael Valdes	.25
157	Mike Mussina	1.00
158	Ramon Hernandez	.25
159	Adam Kennedy	.25
160	Tony Womack	.25
161	Tony Batista	.25
162	Kip Wells	.25
163	Jeromy Burnitz	.25
164	Todd Hundley	.25
165	Tim Wakefield	.25
166	Derek Lowe	.25
167	Jorge Posada	.75
168	Ramon Ortiz	.25
169	Brent Butler	.25
170	Shane Halter	.25
171	Matt Lawton	.25
172	Alex Sanchez	.25
173	Eric Milton	.25
174	Vicente Padilla	.25
175	Steve Karsay	.25
176	Mark Prior	1.50
177	Kerry Wood	1.50
178	Jason LaRue	.25
179	Danys Baez	.25
180	Nick Neugebauer	.25
181	Andres Galarraga	.25
182	Jason Giambi	1.00
183	Aubrey Huff	.25
184	Juan Gonzalez	1.00
185	Ugueth Urbina	.25
186	Rickey Henderson	.75
187	Brad Fullmer	.25
188	Todd Zeile	.25
189	Jason Jennings	.25
190	Vladimir Nunez	.25
191	David Justice	.50
192	Brian Lawrence	.25
193	Pat Burrell	.50
194	Pokey Reese	.25
195	Robert Fick	.25
196	C.C. Sabathia	.25
197	Fernando Vina	.25
198	Sean Burroughs	.25
199	Ellis Burks	.25
200	Joe Randa	.25
201	Chris Duncan **RC**	8.00
202	Franklin Gutierrez **RC**	1.00

203	Adam LaRoche	.25
204	Manuel Ramirez **RC**	1.00
205	Il Kim **RC**	1.00
206	Daryl Clark **RC**	1.00
207	Sean Pierce	.25
208	Andy Marte **RC**	5.00
209	Bernie Castro **RC**	1.00
210	Jason Perry **RC**	1.00
211	Jaime Bubela **RC**	1.00
212	Alexis Rios	.25
213	Brendan Harris **RC**	2.00
214	Ramon A. Martinez **RC**	1.00
215	Terry Tiffee **RC**	1.00
216	Kevin Youkilis **RC**	4.00
217	Derell McCall **RC**	1.00
218	Scott Tyler **RC**	1.00
219	Craig Brazell **RC**	2.50
220	Walter Young **RC**	1.00
221	Francisco Rodriguez	.40
222	Chipper Jones	2.00
223	Chris Singleton	.25
224	Cliff Floyd	.25
225	Bobby Hill	.25
226	Antonio Osuna	.25
227	Barry Larkin	.50
228	Dean Palmer	.25
229	Eric Owens	.25
230	Randy Johnson	1.50
231	Jeff Suppan	.25
232	Eric Karros	.25
233	Johan Santana	.25
234	Javier Vazquez	.25
235	John Thomson	.25
236	Nick Johnson	.25
237	Mark Ellis	.25
238	Doug Glanville	.25
239	Ken Griffey Jr.	2.50
240	Bubba Trammell	.25
241	Livan Hernandez	.25
242	Desi Relaford	.25
243	Eli Marrero	.25
244	Jared Sandberg	.25
245	Barry Bonds	4.00
246	Aaron Sele	.25
247	Derek Jeter	5.00
248	Eric Byrnes	.25
249	Rich Aurilia	.25
250	Joel Pineiro	.25
251	Chuck Finley	.25
252	Bengie Molina	.25
253	Steve Finley	.25
254	Marty Cordova	.25
255	Shea Hillenbrand	.25
256	Milton Bradley	.25
257	Carlos Pena	.25
258	Brad Ausmus	.25
259	Carlos Delgado	.75
260	Kevin Mench	.25
261	Joe Kennedy	.25
262	Mark McLemore	.25
263	Bill Mueller	.25
264	Ricky Ledee	.25
265	Ted Lilly	.25
266	Sterling Hitchcock	.25
267	Scott Strickland	.25
268	Damion Easley	.25
269	Torii Hunter	.50
270	Brad Radke	.25
271	Geoff Jenkins	.25
272	Paul Byrd	.25
273	Morgan Ensberg	.25
274	Mike Hampton	.25
275	Flash Gordon	.25
276	John Burkett	.25
277	Rodrigo Lopez	.25
278	Tim Spooneybarger	.25
279	Quinton McCracken	.25
280	Tim Salmon	.50
281	Jarrod Washburn	.25
282	Pedro J. Martinez	1.50
283	Julio Lugo	.25
284	Armando Benitez	.25
285	Raul Mondesi	.50
286	Robin Ventura	.25
287	Bobby Abreu	.50
288	Josh Fogg	.25
289	Ryan Klesko	.50
290	Tsuyoshi Shinjo	.25
291	Jim Edmonds	.75
292	Chan Ho Park	.25
293	John Mabry	.25
294	Woody Williams	.25
295	Scott Schoeneweis	.25
296	Brian Anderson	.25
297	Brett Tomko	.25
298	Scott Erickson	.25
299	Tony Clark	.25
300	Danny Wright	.25
301	Jason Schmidt	.75
302	Scott Williamson	.25
303	Einar Diaz	.25
304	Jay Payton	.25
305	Juan Acevedo	.25
306	Ben Grieve	.25

307	Raul Ibanez	.25
308	Richie Sexson	.75
309	Rick Reed	.25
310	Pedro Astacio	.25
311	Bud Smith	.25
312	Tomas Perez	.25
313	Adam Eaton	.25
314	Rafael Palmeiro	1.50
315	Jason Tyner	.25
316	Scott Rolen	2.00
317	Randy Winn	.25
318	Ryan Jensen	.25
319	Trevor Hoffman	.25
320	Craig Wilson	.25
321	Jeremy Giambi	.25
322	Andy Pettitte	.50
323	John Franco	.25
324	Felipe Lopez	.25
325	Mike Piazza	3.00
326	Cristian Guzman	.25
327	Jose Hernandez	.25
328	Octavio Dotel	.25
329	Brad Penny	.25
330	Charles Johnson	.25
331	Ryan Dempster	.25
332	Joe Crede	.25
333	Chad Hermansen	.25
334	Gary Matthews Jr.	.25
335	Frank Catalanotto	.25
336	Darin Erstad	.50
337	Matt Williams	.25
338	B.J. Surhoff	.25
339	Kerry Ligtenberg	.25
340	Mike Bordick	.25
341	Joe Girardi	.25
342	D'Angelo Jimenez	.25
343	Paul Konerko	.25
344	Joe Mays	.25
345	Marquis Grissom	.25
346	Neifi Perez	.25
347	Preston Wilson	.25
348	Jeff Weaver	.25
349	Eric Chavez	.50
350	Placido Polanco	.25
351	Ray Lankford	.25
352	James Baldwin	.25
353	Toby Hall	.25
354	Benji Gil	.25
355	Damian Moss	.25
356	Jorge Julio	.25
357	Matt Clement	.25
358	Lee Stevens	.25
359	Dave Roberts	.25
360	J.C. Romero	.25
361	Bartolo Colon	.25
362	Roger Cedeno	.25
363	Mariano Rivera	.50
364	Billy Koch	.25
365	Manny Ramirez	1.50
366	Travis Lee	.25
367	Oliver Perez	.25
368	Rafael Soriano	.25
369	Damian Miller	.25
370	John Smoltz	.50
371	Willis Roberts	.25
372	Tim Hudson	.50
373	Moises Alou	.50
374	Corky Miller	.25
375	Ben Broussard	.25
376	Gabe Kapler	.25
377	Chris Woodward	.25
378	Todd Hollandsworth	.25
379	So Taguchi	.25
380	John Olerud	.50
381	Reggie Sanders	.25
382	Jake Peavy	.25
383	Kris Benson	.25
384	Ray Durham	.25
385	David Wells	.25
386	Tom Glavine	.75
387	Antonio Alfonseca	.25
388	Keith Foulke	.25
389	Shawn Estes	.25
390	Mark Grace	.50
391	Dmitri Young	.25
392	A.J. Burnett	.25
393	Richard Hidalgo	.25
394	Mike Sweeney	.25
395	Doug Mientkiewicz	.25
396	Cory Lidle	.25
397	Jeff Bagwell	1.50
398	Steve Sparks	.25
399	Sandy Alomar Jr.	.25
400	John Lackey	.25
401	Rick Helling	.25
402	Carlos Lee	.25
403	Garret Anderson	.50
404	Vinny Castilla	.25
405	David Bell	.25
406	Freddy Garcia	.25
407	Scott Spiezio	.25
408	Russell Branyan	.25
409	Jose Contreras **RC**	3.00
410	Kevin Brown	.50

411	Tyler Houston	.25
412	A.J. Pierzynski	.25
413	Peter Bergeron	.25
414	Brett Myers	.25
415	Kenny Lofton	.25
416	Ben Davis	.25
417	J.D. Drew	.50
418	Ricky Gutierrez	.25
419	Mark Redman	.25
420	Juan Encarnacion	.25
421	Bryan Bullington **RC**	4.00
422	Jeremy Guthrie	.25
423	Joey Gomes	.50
424	Evel Bastida-Martinez **RC**	1.50
425	Brian Wright **RC**	1.00
426	B.J. Upton	.25
427	Jeff Francis	.25
428	Jeremy Hermida	.25
429	Khalil Greene	3.00
430	Darrell Rasner	.25
431	Brandon Phillips, Victor Martinez	.75
432	Hee Seop Choi, Nic Jackson	.75
433	Dontrelle Willis, Jason Stokes	1.00
434	Chad Tracy, Lyle Overbay	.25
435	Joe Borchard, Corwin Malone	.25
436	Joe Mauer, Justin Morneau	1.00
437	Drew Henson, Brandon Claussen	.50
438	Chase Utley, Gavin Floyd	.50
439	Taggert Bozied, Xavier Nady	.25
440	Aaron Heilman, Jose Reyes	1.50

Refractors

JASON KENDALL

Stars:	1-2X
Production 699 Sets	
Gold Refractors:	1.5-3X
Production 449 Sets	
Black Refractors:	3-5X
Production 199 Sets	

Uncirculated X-Fractors

ADRIAN BELTRE

Stars:	5-10X
Inserted 1:Hobby Box	
Production 50 Sets	

Blue Backs Relics

	NM/M
Common Player:	6.00
Bat Relics Inserted 1:236	

RA	Roberto Alomar/Bat	10.00
JBA	Jeff Bagwell/Jsy	10.00
JB	Josh Beckett/Jsy	10.00
LB	Lance Berkman/Bat	8.00
EC	Eric Chavez/Jsy	8.00
AD	Adam Dunn/Jsy	15.00
NG	Nomar Garciaparra/Jsy	15.00
SG	Shawn Green/Jsy	6.00
NJ	Nick Johnson/Bat	8.00
PK	Paul Konerko/Jsy	8.00
MO	Magglio Ordonez/Jsy	8.00
MP	Mike Piazza/Jsy	15.00
AP	Albert Pujols/Jsy	15.00
AR	Alex Rodriguez/Bat	15.00
JR	Jimmy Rollins/Jsy	6.00
TS	Tsuyoshi Shinjo/Bat	8.00
AS	Alfonso Soriano/Bat	10.00
FT	Frank Thomas/Jsy	8.00
BW	Bernie Williams/Bat	10.00
KW	Kerry Wood/Jsy	8.00

Record Breakers Relics

RECORD BREAKERS

Slugged .643 In 1996
Texas Season Slugging % Leader
Juan Gonzalez

	NM/M
Common Player:	5.00
Bat Relics 1:364	

JB	Jeff Bagwell	10.00
CB	Craig Biggio	5.00
LB	Lou Brock	15.00
CD	Carlos Delgado	5.00
CF	Cliff Floyd	5.00
JG	Juan Gonzalez	8.00
LG	Luis Gonzalez	5.00
TH	Todd Helton	8.00
RH	Rickey Henderson	15.00
RJ	Randy Johnson	15.00
HK	Harmon Killebrew	15.00
JM	Joe Morgan	8.00
SM	Stan Musial	25.00
MP	Mike Piazza	15.00
AR	Alex Rodriguez	15.00
MS	Mike Schmidt	25.00
FT	Frank Thomas	8.00
KS	Kazuhiro Sasaki	5.00
LW	Larry Walker	5.00
RY	Robin Yount	15.00

Record Breakers Relics Series 2

	NM/M
Common Player:	5.00

JB	Jeff Bagwell	8.00
BB	Barry Bonds	20.00
BB2	Barry Bonds	20.00
BB3	Barry Bonds	20.00
JC	Jose Canseco	10.00
RC	Rod Carew	8.00
RC2	Rod Carew	8.00
DLE	Dennis Eckersley	8.00
DE	Darin Erstad	5.00
LG	Luis Gonzalez	5.00
RH	Rickey Henderson	15.00
RJ	Randy Johnson	8.00
DM	Don Mattingly	30.00
PM	Paul Molitor	15.00
MR	Manny Ramirez	15.00
HR	Harold Reynolds	5.00
AR	Alex Rodriguez	15.00
TS	Tom Seaver	20.00
JS	John Smoltz	8.00
SS	Sammy Sosa	15.00

Red Backs Relics

	NM/M
Common Player:	5.00
Inserted 1:49	

RA	Roberto Alomar	8.00
GA	Garret Anderson	8.00
JB	Jeff Bagwell	8.00
PB	Pat Burrell	5.00

AD	Adam Dunn	8.00
NG	Nomar Garciaparra	12.00
TH	Todd Helton	8.00
TKH	Torii Hunter	8.00
RJ	Randy Johnson	8.00
AJ	Andruw Jones	8.00
CJ	Chipper Jones	10.00
PM	Pedro J. Martinez	10.00
MP	Mike Piazza	10.00
AP	Albert Pujols	15.00
MR	Manny Ramirez	8.00
AR	Alex Rodriguez	10.00
SR	Scott Rolen	10.00
CS	Curt Schilling	8.00
AS	Alfonso Soriano	10.00
MS	Mike Sweeney	5.00

2003 Topps Gallery

		NM/M
Complete Set (200):		60.00
Common Player:		.25
SP's Inserted 1:20		
Pack (5):		2.50
Box (20):		45.00
1	Jason Giambi	.50
1	Jason Giambi/SP/ Drk Blue Jsy	2.00
2	Miguel Tejada	.50
3	Mike Lieberthal	.25
4	Jason Kendall	.40
5	Robb Nen	.25
6	Freddy Garcia	.25
7	Scott Rolen	.75
8	David Wells	.25
9	Rafael Palmeiro	.75
10	Garret Anderson	.50
11	Curt Schilling	.75
12	Greg Maddux	1.00
13	Rodrigo Lopez	.25
14	Nomar Garciaparra	1.50
14	N.Garciaparra/SP/ Navy Elbow Pad	4.00
15	Kerry Wood	.75
16	Frank Thomas	.75
17	Ken Griffey Jr.	1.00
18	Jim Thome	.75
19	Todd Helton	.75
20	Lance Berkman	.50
21	Robert Fick	.25
22	Kevin Brown	.40
23	Richie Sexson	.50
24	Eddie Guardado	.25
25	Vladimir Guerrero	1.00
26	Mike Piazza	1.50
27	Bernie Williams	.50
28	Eric Chavez	.40
29	Jimmy Rollins	.40
30	Ichiro Suzuki	1.50
30	Ichiro Suzuki/SP/ Black Long Shirt	3.00
31	J.D. Drew	.25
32	Nick Johnson	.25
33	Shannon Stewart	.25
34	Tim Salmon	.40
35	Andruw Jones	.75
36	Jay Gibbons	.25
37	Johnny Damon	.50
38	Fred McGriff	.40
39	Carlos Lee	.25
40	Adam Dunn	.75
40	Adam Dunn/SP/Red Sleeves & Helmet	1.50
41	Jason Jennings	.25
42	Mike Lowell	.40
43	Mike Sweeney	.25
44	Shawn Green	.25
45	Doug Mientkiewicz	.25
46	Bartolo Colon	.40
47	Edgardo Alfonzo	.25
48	Roger Clemens	2.00
49	Randy Wolf	.25
50	Alex Rodriguez	2.00

50	Alex Rodriguez/SP/ Red Undershirt	4.00
51	Vernon Wells	.40
52	Kenny Lofton	.40
53	Mariano Rivera	.40
54	Brian Jordan	.25
55	Roberto Alomar	.50
56	Carlos Pena	.25
57	Moises Alou	.40
58	John Smoltz	.50
59	Adam Kennedy	.25
60	Randy Johnson	1.00
61	Mark Buehrle	.25
62	C.C. Sabathia	.40
63	Craig Biggio	.40
64	Eric Karros	.25
65	Jose Vidro	.25
66	Tim Hudson	.40
67	Trevor Hoffman	.25
68	Bret Boone	.25
69	Carl Crawford	.40
70	Derek Jeter	2.50
71	Troy Percival	.25
72	Gary Sheffield	.50
73	Rickey Henderson	.50
74	Paul Konerko	.40
75	Larry Walker	.40
76	Pat Burrell	.50
77	Brian Giles	.40
78	Jeff Kent	.40
79	Kazuhiro Sasaki	.25
80	Chipper Jones	1.00
81	Darin Erstad	.40
82	Sean Casey	.40
83	Luis Gonzalez	.40
84	Roy Oswalt	.40
85	Dustan Mohr	.25
86	Al Leiter	.25
87	Mike Mussina	.50
88	Vicente Padilla	.25
89	Rich Aurilia	.25
90	Albert Pujols	2.00
91	John Olerud	.40
92	Ivan Rodriguez	.75
93	Eric Hinske	.25
94	Phil Nevin	.25
95	Barry Zito	.50
96	Armando Benitez	.25
97	Torii Hunter	.50
98	Paul LoDuca	.25
99	Preston Wilson	.40
100	Sammy Sosa	1.50
100	Sammy Sosa/SP/ No Shin Guard	4.00
101	Jarrod Washburn	.25
102	Steve Finley	.25
103	Cliff Floyd	.25
104	Mark Prior	1.00
105	Austin Kearns	.50
106	Jeff Bagwell	.75
107	A.J. Pierzynski	.25
108	Pedro J. Martinez	1.00
109	Orlando Cabrera	.25
110	Raul Mondesi	.25
111	Russ Ortiz	.25
112	Ruben Sierra	.25
113	Tino Martinez	.25
114	Manny Ramirez	.75
115	Troy Glaus	.50
116	Magglio Ordonez	.50
117	Omar Vizquel	.40
118	Carlos Beltran	.50
119	Jose Hernandez	.25
120	Javier Vazquez	.25
121	Jorge Posada	.50
122	Aramis Ramirez	.25
123	Jason Schmidt	.40
124	Jamie Moyer	.25
125	Jim Edmonds	.50
126	Aubrey Huff	.25
127	Carlos Delgado	.50
128	Junior Spivey	.25
129	Tom Glavine	.50
130	Marty Cordova	.25
131	Derek Lowe	.25
132	Ellis Burks	.25
133	Barry Bonds	2.50
134	Josh Beckett	.50
135	Raul Ibanez	.25
136	Kazuhisa Ishii	.25
137	Geoff Jenkins	.25
138	Eric Milton	.25
139	Mo Vaughn	.25
140	Mark Mulder	.40
141	Bobby Abreu	.40
142	Ryan Klesko	.40
143	Tsuyoshi Shinjo	.25
144	Jose Mesa	.25
145	Shea Hillenbrand	.25
146	Edgar Renteria	.25
147	Juan Gonzalez	.50
148	Edgar Martinez	.25
149	Matt Morris	.25
150	Alfonso Soriano	1.00

150	Alfonso Soriano/SP/ No Elbow Pad	2.50
151	Bryan Bullington RC	2.50
151	Bryan Bullington/SP/ Red Background RC	6.00
152	Andy Marte RC	3.00
152	Andy Marte/SP/ No Necklace RC	4.00
153	Brendan Harris RC	1.00
154	Juan Camacho RC	1.00
155	Byron Gettis RC	1.00
156	Daryl Clark RC	1.00
157	J.D. Durbin RC	1.50
158	Craig Brazell RC	1.50
158	Craig Brazell/SP/ Black Jersey RC	3.00
159	Jason Kubel RC	4.00
160	Brandon Roberson RC	1.00
161	Jose Contreras RC	2.00
162	Hanley Ramirez RC	5.00
163	Jaime Bubela RC	1.00
164	Chris Duncan RC	8.00
165	Tyler Johnson RC	1.00
166	Adam LaRoche	.25
167	Walter Young	.25
168	Ryan Kibler	.25
169	Tommy Whiteman RC	.25
170	Trey Hodges	.25
171	Francisco Rodriguez	.25
172	Jason Arnold	.25
173	Brett Myers	.25
174	Rocco Baldelli	.50
175	Adrian Gonzalez	.25
176	Dontrelle Willis	1.00
177	Kris Honel	.25
178	Marlon Byrd	.25
179	Aaron Heilman	.25
180	Casey Kotchman	.25
181	Miguel Cabrera	.50
182	Hee Seop Choi	.50
183	Drew Henson	.25
184	Jose Reyes	.50
185	Michael Cuddyer	.25
186	Brandon Phillips	.25
187	Victor Martinez	.25
188	Joe Mauer	.50
189	Hank Blalock	.75
190	Mark Teixeira	.25
191	Willie Mays	2.00
192	George Brett	2.00
193	Tony Gwynn	1.00
194	Carl Yastrzemski	1.00
195	Nolan Ryan	3.00
196	Reggie Jackson	.75
197	Mike Schmidt	1.50
198	Cal Ripken Jr.	3.00
199	Don Mattingly	2.00
200	Tom Seaver	.75

Rainbow Refractors

Stars (1-200):		2-3X
Inserted 1:1		
Rookies (151-165):		1X
Inserted 1:1		

Currency Collection

		NM/M
Common Player:		4.00
Inserted 1:Box		
BA	Bobby Abreu	6.00
HC	Hee Seop Choi	6.00
BC	Bartolo Colon	4.00
LG	Luis Gonzalez	4.00
VG	Vladimir Guerrero	12.00
KI	Kazuhisa Ishii	4.00
AJ	Andruw Jones	8.00

ABBREVIATIONS

SP - Short Print

RL	Rodrigo Lopez	6.00
PM	Pedro J. Martinez	10.00
RM	Raul Mondesi	4.00
MO	Magglio Ordonez	8.00
VP	Vicente Padilla	6.00
RP	Rafael Palmeiro	6.00
AP	Albert Pujols	20.00
MR	Manny Ramirez	8.00
ER	Edgar Renteria	6.00
JR	Jose Reyes	8.00
MRI	Mariano Rivera	10.00
FR	Francisco Rodriguez	4.00
KS	Kazuhiro Sasaki	4.00
AS	Alfonso Soriano	8.00
SS	Sammy Sosa	15.00
IS	Ichiro Suzuki	15.00
OV	Omar Vizquel	10.00
LW	Larry Walker	5.00

Heritage

		NM/M
Complete Set (25):		75.00
Common Player:		1.50
Inserted 1:10		
WB	Wade Boggs	1.50
GB	George Brett	8.00
JC	Jose Canseco	1.50
RC	Roger Clemens	6.00
AD	Adam Dunn	2.00
NG	Nomar Garciaparra	5.00
TG	Tom Glavine	1.50
SG	Shawn Green	1.50
TGW	Tony Gwynn	3.00
RH	Rickey Henderson	2.00
DJ	Derek Jeter	8.00
RJ	Randy Johnson	3.00
HK	Harmon Killebrew	4.00
KR	Jerry Koosman, Nolan Ryan	10.00
WM	Willie Mays	8.00
HN	Hideo Nomo	2.00
KP	Kirby Puckett	3.00
IR	Ivan Rodriguez	2.00
DS	Duke Snider	2.00
AS	Alfonso Soriano	3.00
IS	Ichiro Suzuki	5.00
MT	Miguel Tejada	1.50
JT	Jim Thome	2.00
BW	Bernie Williams	2.00
CY	Carl Yastrzemski	3.00

Heritage Autographed Relics

		NM/M
Inserted 1:3,260		
WB	Wade Boggs	70.00
KP	Kirby Puckett/25	80.00

Heritage Relics

	NM/M
Common Player:	5.00

WB	Wade Boggs	5.00
GB	George Brett	20.00
JC	Jose Canseco	8.00
RC	Roger Clemens	15.00
SG	Shawn Green	5.00
TG	Tony Gwynn	10.00
RH	Rickey Henderson	10.00
HK	Harmon Killebrew	25.00
HN	Hideo Nomo	15.00
KP	Kirby Puckett	15.00

Originals Relics

		NM/M
Common Player:		5.00
RA	Roberto Alomar	6.00
MA	Moises Alou	5.00
LB	Lance Berkman	5.00
BB	Bret Boone	5.00
AD	Adam Dunn	6.00
NG	Nomar Garciaparra	12.00
LG	Luis Gonzalez	5.00
SG	Shawn Green	5.00
TG	Tony Gwynn	8.00
TH	Todd Helton	8.00
RH	Rickey Henderson	8.00
DH	Drew Henson	5.00
THU	Torii Hunter	8.00
AJ	Andruw Jones	6.00
CJ	Chipper Jones	8.00
JM	Joe Mauer	10.00
MO	Magglio Ordonez	5.00
RP	Rafael Palmeiro	8.00
MP	Mike Piazza	10.00
AP	Albert Pujols	15.00
MR	Manny Ramirez	8.00
AR	Alex Rodriguez	10.00
IR	Ivan Rodriguez	8.00
GS	Gary Sheffield	6.00
AS	Alfonso Soriano	8.00
MT	Miguel Tejada	5.00
FT	Frank Thomas	8.00
JT	Jim Thome	8.00
BW	Bernie Williams	6.00
CY	Carl Yastrzemski	20.00

2003 Topps Gallery HOF Edition

	NM/M
Complete Set (74):	35.00

Common Player:		.40
SP Variations:		2-4X
Inserted 1:1		
Pack (5):		4.00
Box (20):		70.00
1	Willie Mays	2.00
2	Al Kaline	1.50
3	Hank Aaron	2.00
4	Carl Yastrzemski	1.00
5	Luis Aparicio	.40
6	Sam Crawford	.40
7	Tom Lasorda	.40
8	John McGraw	.40
9	Edd Roush	.40
10	Reggie Jackson	1.00
11	Jim "Catfish" Hunter	.40
12	Roberto Clemente	2.00
13	Ralph Kiner	.40
14	Frankie Frisch	.40
15	Nolan Ryan	4.00
16	Brooks Robinson	1.00
17	Phil Niekro	.40
18	Joe Cronin	.40
19	Joe Tinker	.40
20	Johnny Bench	1.50
21	Harry Heilmann	.40
22	Ernie Harwell	.40
23	Warren Spahn	1.00
24	George Kelly	.40
25	Phil Rizzuto	1.00
26	Robin Roberts	.40
27	Ozzie Smith	1.00
28	Jim Palmer	.40
29	Duke Snider	1.00
30	Bob Feller	.40
31	Buck Leonard	.40
32	Kirby Puckett	1.00
33	Monte Irvin	.40
34	Chuck Klein	.40
35	Willie Stargell	.75
36	Juan Marichal	.40
37	Lou Brock	.40
38	Bucky Harris	.40
39	Bobby Doerr	.40
40	Lee MacPhail	.40
41	Heinie Manush	.40
42	George Brett	1.50
43	Harmon Killebrew	1.50
44	Whitey Ford	1.00
45	Eddie Mathews	1.50
46	Gaylord Perry	.40
47	Red Schoendienst	.40
48	Earl Weaver	.40
49	Joe Morgan	.40
50	Mike Schmidt	2.00
51	Willie McCovey	.40
52	Stan Musial	2.00
53	Don Sutton	.40
54	Hank Greenberg	.40
55	Robin Yount	1.00
56	Tom Seaver	1.00
57	Tony Perez	.40
58	George Sisler	.40
59	Jim Bottomley	.40
60	Yogi Berra	1.50
61	Fred Lindstrom	.40
62	Napoleon Lajoie	.40
63	Frank Robinson	1.00
64	Carlton Fisk	.40
65	Orlando Cepeda	.40
66	Fergie Jenkins	.40
67	Ernie Banks	1.50
68	Bill Mazeroski	.40
69	Jim Bunning	.40
70	Rollie Fingers	.40
71	Jimmie Foxx	1.50
72	Rod Carew	.40
73	Sparky Anderson	.40
74	George Kell	.40

Refractors

Cards (1-74):		2-4X
Inserted 1:1		

SP Refractors:		4-8X
Inserted 1:Box		

Accent Mark Autograph

		NM/M
Common Player:		
Refractors:		1-2X
Production 25 Sets		
YB	Yogi Berra	65.00
BD	Bobby Doerr	40.00
LM	Lee MacPhail	40.00
RR	Robin Roberts	40.00
RS	Red Schoendienst	30.00
WS	Warren Spahn	30.00

ARTifact Relics

		NM/M
Common Player:		6.00
Refractors:		1.5-3X
Production 25 Sets		
HA	Hank Aaron/Bat	25.00
SA	Sparky Anderson/Jsy	8.00
LA	Luis Aparicio/Bat	15.00
EB	Ernie Banks/Jsy	30.00
JBE	Johnny Bench/Bat	12.00
JB	Jim Bottomley/Bat	15.00
GB	George Brett/Jsy	25.00
RCA	Rod Carew/Jsy	10.00
OC	Orlando Cepeda/Bat	8.00
TC	Ty Cobb/Bat	80.00
EC	Eddie Collins/Bat	12.00
SC	Sam Crawford/Bat	20.00
BD	Bobby Doerr/Jsy	15.00
CF	Carlton Fisk/Bat	8.00
FF	Frankie Frisch/Bat	15.00
LG	Lou Gehrig/Bat	125.00
HG	Hank Greenberg/Bat	25.00
BH	Bucky Harris/Bat	12.00
HH	Harry Heilmann/Bat	20.00
RJ	Reggie Jackson/Bat	10.00
AK	Al Kaline/Bat	15.00
GK	George Kelly/Bat	20.00
HK	Harmon Killebrew/Jsy	25.00
CK	Chuck Klein/Bat	15.00
TLA	Tom Lasorda/Jsy	15.00
HM	Heinie Manush/Jsy	15.00
EM	Eddie Mathews/Jsy	30.00
WM	Willie Mays/Jsy	45.00
WMC	Willie McCovey/Bat	8.00
JM	Joe Morgan/Bat	8.00
SM	Stan Musial/Bat	20.00
PN	Phil Niekro/Jsy	6.00
JP	Jim Palmer/Jsy	20.00
TP	Tony Perez/Bat	8.00
GP	Gaylord Perry/Jsy	8.00
KP	Kirby Puckett/Bat	12.00
BRO	Brooks Robinson/Bat	20.00
FR	Frank Robinson/Bat	10.00
JR	Jackie Robinson/Bat	35.00

ER	Edd Roush/Bat	20.00
BR	Babe Ruth/Bat	140.00
NR	Nolan Ryan/Bat	40.00
MS	Mike Schmidt/Jsy	25.00
RSC	Red Schoendienst/Jsy	
TS	Tom Seaver/Bat	25.00
GS	George Sisler/Bat	12.00
OS	Ozzie Smith/Bat	15.00
DS	Duke Snider/Bat	12.00
WS	Willie Stargell/Jsy	10.00
DSU	Don Sutton/Bat	8.00
JT	Joe Tinker/Bat	20.00
HW	Honus Wagner/Bat	140.00
PW	Paul Waner/Bat	20.00
HWI	Hoyt Wilhelm/Jsy	8.00
CY	Carl Yastrzemski/Bat	20.00
RY	Robin Yount/Bat	10.00

ARTifact Autograph Relics

		NM/M
Common Player:		30.00
Refractors:		1-1.5X
Production 25 Sets		
OC	Orlando Cepeda	30.00
BD	Bobby Doerr	45.00
AK	Al Kaline	75.00
HK	Harmon Killebrew	75.00
JM	Joe Morgan	40.00
JP	Jim Palmer	50.00
BRO	Brooks Robinson	60.00
MS	Mike Schmidt	225.00
RS	Red Schoendienst	30.00
DS	Duke Snider	50.00
RY	Robin Yount	125.00

Currency Connection

		NM/M
Common Player:		12.00
1:Box		
EB	Ernie Banks	20.00
OC	Orlando Cepeda	15.00
TC	Ty Cobb	40.00
BF	Bob Feller	25.00
LG	Lou Gehrig	35.00
HG	Hank Greenberg	20.00
WM	Willie Mays	20.00
WMA	Willie Mays	20.00
WMC	Willie McCovey	12.00
SM	Stan Musial	30.00
JR	Jackie Robinson	25.00
BR	Babe Ruth	60.00

Patch Relics

		NM/M
Common Player:		40.00
Production 25 Sets		
GB	George Brett	125.00
CH	Jim "Catfish" Hunter	40.00
FJ	Fergie Jenkins	40.00
HK	Harmon Killebrew	80.00
TL	Tom Lasorda	40.00
EM	Eddie Matthews	80.00
WM	Willie McCovey	40.00
JP	Jim Palmer	40.00
NR	Nolan Ryan	125.00
MS	Mike Schmidt	125.00
OS	Ozzie Smith	75.00
DS	Don Sutton	
CY	Carl Yastrzemski	80.00
RY	Robin Yount	85.00

Team Topps Legends Autographs

		NM/M
Common Player:		
	Vern Law	20.00
	Al Kaline	
	Johnny Sain	30.00

2003 Topps Heritage

RANDY JOHNSON
pitcher ARIZ. DIAMONDBACKS™

		NM/M
Complete Set (430):		350.00
Common Player:		.40
Common High # SP		
(364-430):		4.00
Pack (8):		5.00
Box (24):		100.00
1	Alex Rodriguez	3.00
1	Alex Rodriguez/	
	Black SP	10.00
2	Jose Cruz Jr.	.40
3	Ichiro Suzuki/SP	10.00
4	Rich Aurilia	.40
5	Trevor Hoffman	.40
6	Brian Giles	.75
6	Brian Giles/	
	Old Logo SP	5.00
7	Albert Pujols	2.00
7	Albert Pujols/	
	Black SP	10.00
8	Vicente Padilla	.40
9	Bobby Crosby	.40
10	Derek Jeter	4.00
10	Derek Jeter/	
	Old Logo SP	15.00
11	Pat Burrell	.50
11	Pat Burrell/	
	Old Logo SP	5.00
12	Armando Benitez	.40
13	Javier Vazquez	.40
14	Justin Morneau	.75
15	Doug Mientkiewicz	.40
16	Kevin Brown	.40
17	Alexis Gomez	.40
18	Lance Berkman	.75
18	Lance Berkman/	
	Black SP	5.00
19	Adrian Gonzalez	.50
20	Todd Helton	.75
20	Todd Helton/Black SP	6.00
21	Carlos Pena	.40
22	Matt Lawton	.40
23	Elmer Dessens	.40
24	Hee Seop Choi	.40
25	Chris Duncan/SP RC	12.00
26	Ugueth Urbina	.40
27	Rodrigo Lopez	.40
27	Rodrigo Lopez/	
	Old Logo SP	4.00
28	Damian Moss	.40
29	Steve Finley	.40
30	Sammy Sosa	1.50
30	Sammy Sosa/	
	Old Logo SP	6.00
31	Kevin Cash	.40
32	Kenny Rogers	.40
33	Ben Grieve	.40
34	Jason Simontacchi	.40
35	Shin-Soo Choo	.40
36	Freddy Garcia	.40
37	Jesse Foppert	.40
38	Tony LaRussa	.40
39	Mark Kotsay	.40
40	Barry Zito	.75
41	Josh Fogg	.40
42	Marlon Byrd	.40
43	Marcus Thames	.40
44	Al Leiter	.50
45	Michael Barrett	.40
46	Jake Peavy	.75
47	Dustan Mohr	.40
48	Alex Sanchez	.40
49	Chin-Feng Chen	.40
50	Kazuhisa Ishii	.40
50	Kazuhisa Ishii/	
	Black SP	5.00
51	Carlos Beltran	.75
52	Franklin Gutierrez RC	1.50
53	Miguel Cabrera	1.00
54	Roger Clemens	2.50
55	Juan Cruz	.40
56	Jason Young	.40
57	Alex Herrera	.40
58	Aaron Boone	.40
59	Mark Buehrle	.50
60	Larry Walker	.75
61	Morgan Ensberg	.40
62	Barry Larkin	.75
63	Joe Borchard	.40
64	Jason Dubois	.40
65	Juan Acevedo	.40
66	Jay Gibbons	.40
67	Vinny Castilla	.40
68	Jeff Mathis	.40
69	Curt Schilling	1.00
70	Garret Anderson	.50
71	Josh Phelps	.40
72	Chan Ho Park	.40
73	Edgar Renteria	.50
74	Kazuhiro Sasaki	.40
75	Lloyd McClendon	.40
76	Jon Lieber	.40
77	Rolando Viera	.40
78	Jeff Conine	.40
79	Kevin Millwood	.40
80	Randy Johnson	1.50
80	Randy Johnson/	
	Black SP	8.00
81	Troy Percival	.40
82	Cliff Floyd	.40
83	Tony Graffanino	.40
84	Austin Kearns	.50
85	Manuel Ramirez/	
	SP RC	5.00
86	Jim Tracy	.40
87	Rondell White	.40
88	Trot Nixon	.40
89	Carlos Lee	.50
90	Mike Lowell	.50
91	Raul Ibanez	.40
92	Ricardo Rodriguez	.40
93	Ben Sheets	.50
94	Jason Perry/SP RC	4.00
95	Mark Teixeira	.75
96	Brad Fullmer	.40
97	Casey Kotchman	.40
98	Craig Counsell	.40
99	Jason Marquis	.40
100	Nomar Garciaparra	2.00
100	Nomar Garciaparra/	
	Old Logo SP	10.00
101	Ed Rogers	.40
102	Wilson Betemit	.40
103	Wayne Lydon RC	1.00
104	Jack Cust	.40
105	Derrek Lee	.75
106	Jim Kavourias	.40
107	Joe Randa	.40
108	Taylor Buchholz	.40
109	Gabe Kapler	.40
110	Preston Wilson	.40
111	Craig Biggio	.50
112	Paul LoDuca	.40
113	Eddie Guardado	.40
114	Andres Galarraga	.40
115	Edgardo Alfonzo	.40
116	Robin Ventura	.40
117	Jeremy Giambi	.40
118	Ray Durham	.40
119	Mariano Rivera	.50
120	Jimmy Rollins	.50
121	Dennis Tankersley	.40
122	Jason Schmidt	.50
123	Bret Boone	.40
124	Josh Hamilton	.50
125	Scott Rolen	.75
126	Steve Cox	.40
127	Larry Bowa	.40
128	Adam LaRoche/SP	5.00
129	Ryan Klesko	.40
130	Tim Hudson	.50
131	Brandon Claussen	.40
132	Craig Brazell/SP RC	4.00
133	Grady Little	.40
134	Jarrod Washburn	.40
135	Lyle Overbay	.40
136	John Burkett	.40
137	Daryl Clark RC	.75
138	Kirk Rueter	.40
139	Joe Mauer,	
	Jake Mauer	1.00
139	Joe Mauer,	
	Jake Mauer/Black SP	8.00
140	Troy Glaus	.75
141	Trey Hodges/SP	4.00
142	Dallas McPherson	.40
143	Art Howe	.40
144	Jesus Cota	.40
145	J.R. House	.40
146	Reggie Sanders	.40
147	Clint Nageotte	.40
148	Jim Edmonds	.50
149	Carl Crawford	.50
150	Mike Piazza	2.00
150	Mike Piazza/	
	Black SP	10.00
151	Seung Jun Song	.40
152	Roberto Hernandez	.40
153	Marquis Grissom	.40
154	Billy Wagner	.40
155	Josh Beckett	.50
156	Randall Simon	.40
156	Randall Simon/	
	Old Logo SP	4.00
157	Ben Broussard	.40
158	Russell Branyan	.40
159	Frank Thomas	1.00
160	Alex Escobar	.40
161	Mark Bellhorn	.40
162	Melvin Mora	.40
163	Andruw Jones	.75
164	Danny Bautista	.40
165	Ramon Ortiz	.40
166	Wily Mo Pena	.50
167	Jose Jimenez	.40
168	Mark Redman	.40
169	Angel Berroa	.40
170	Andy Marte/SP RC	15.00
171	Juan Gonzalez	.75
172	Fernando Vina	.40
173	Joel Pineiro	.40
174	Boof Bonser	.40
175	Bernie Castro/SP RC	4.00
176	Bobby Cox	.40
177	Jeff Kent	.50
178	Oliver Perez	.40
179	Chase Utley	1.00
180	Mark Mulder	.50
181	Bobby Abreu	.50
182	Ramiro Mendoza	.40
183	Aaron Heilman	.40
184	A.J. Pierzynski	.40
185	Eric Gagne	.75
186	Kirk Saarloos	.40
187	Ron Gardenhire	.40
188	Dmitri Young	.40
189	Todd Zeile	.40
190	Jim Thome	1.00
190	Jim Thome/	
	Old Logo SP	8.00
191	Cliff Lee	.40
192	Matt Morris	.40
193	Robert Fick	.40
194	C.C. Sabathia	.40
195	Alexis Rios	.40
196	D'Angelo Jimenez	.40
197	Edgar Martinez	.50
198	Robb Nen	.40
199	Taggert Bozied	.40
200	Vladimir Guerrero/SP	8.00
201	Walter Young/SP	4.00
202	Brendan Harris RC	1.00
203	Mike Hargrove	.40
204	Vernon Wells	.50
205	Hank Blalock	.75
206	Mike Cameron	.40
207	Tony Batista	.40
208	Matt Williams	.40
209	Tony Womack	.40
210	Ramon A. Martinez RC	.40
211	Aaron Sele	.40
212	Mark Grace	.75
213	Joe Crede	.75
214	Ryan Dempster	.40
215	Omar Vizquel	.40
216	Juan Pierre	.40
217	Denny Bautista	.40
218	Chuck Knoblauch	.40
219	Eric Karros	.40
220	Victor Diaz	.40
221	Jacque Jones	.40
222	Jose Vidro	.40
223	Joe McEwing	.40
224	Nick Johnson	.40
225	Eric Chavez	.50
226	Jose Mesa	.40
227	Aramis Ramirez	.75
228	John Lackey	.40
229	David Bell	.40
230	John Olerud	.50
231	Tino Martinez	.40
232	Randy Winn	.40
233	Todd Hollandsworth	.40
234	Ruddy Lugo RC	.75
235	Carlos Delgado	.75
236	Chris Narveson	.40
237	Tim Salmon	.75
238	Orlando Palmeiro	.40
239	Jeff Clark/SP RC	4.00
240	Byung-Hyun Kim	.40
241	Mike Remlinger	.40
242	Johnny Damon	1.00
243	Corey Patterson	.50
244	Paul Konerko	.75
245	Danny Graves	.40
246	Ellis Burks	.40
247	Gavin Floyd	.40
248	Jaime Bubela RC	.75
249	Sean Burroughs	.40
250	Alex Rodriguez/SP	10.00
251	Gabe Gross	.40
252	Rafael Palmeiro	.75
253	Dewon Brazelton	.40
254	Jimmy Journell	.40
255	Rafael Soriano	.40
256	Jerome Williams	.40
257	Xavier Nady	.40
258	Mike Williams	.40
259	Randy Wolf	.40
260	Miguel Tejada	.75
260	Miguel Tejada/	
	Black SP	5.00
261	Juan Rivera	.40
262	Rey Ordonez	.40
263	Bartolo Colon	.40
264	Eric Milton	.40
265	Jeffrey Hammonds	.40
266	Odalis Perez	.40
267	Mike Sweeney	.40
268	Richard Hidalgo	.40
269	Alex Gonzalez	.40
270	Aaron Cook	.40
271	Earl Snyder	.40
272	Todd Walker	.40
273	Aaron Rowand	.40
274	Matt Clement	.40
275	Anastacio Martinez	.40
276	Mike Bordick	.40
277	John Smoltz	.50
278	Scott Hairston	.40
279	David Eckstein	.40
280	Shannon Stewart	.40
281	Carl Everett	.40
282	Aubrey Huff	.40
283	Mike Mussina	.75
284	Ruben Sierra	.40
285	Russ Ortiz	.40
286	Brian Lawrence	.40
287	Kip Wells	.40
288	Placido Polanco	.40
289	Ted Lilly	.40
290	Andy Pettitte	.50
291	John Buck	.40
292	Orlando Cabrera	.40
293	Cristian Guzman	.40
294	Ruben Quevedo	.40
295	Cesar Izturis	.40
296	Ryan Ludwick	.40
297	Roy Oswalt	.75
298	Jason Stokes	.40
299	Mike Hampton	.40
300	Pedro Martinez	1.50
301	Nic Jackson	.40
302	Magglio Ordonez	.50
302	Magglio Ordonez/	
	Old Logo SP	5.00
303	Manny Ramirez	1.00
304	Jorge Julio	.40
305	Javy Lopez	.50
306	Roy Halladay	.50
307	Kevin Mench	.40
308	Jason Isringhausen	.40
309	Carlos Guillen	.40
310	Tsuyoshi Shinjo	.40
311	Phil Nevin	.40
312	Pokey Reese	.40
313	Jorge Padilla	.40
314	Jermaine Dye	.40
315	David Wells	.40
316	Mo Vaughn	.40
317	Bernie Williams	.75
318	Michael Restovich	.40
319	Jose Hernandez	.40
320	Richie Sexson	.75
321	Daryle Ward	.40
322	Luis Castillo	.40
323	Rene Reyes	.40
324	Victor Martinez	.40
325	Adam Dunn	.75
325	Adam Dunn/	
	Old Logo SP	6.00
326	Corwin Malone	.40
327	Kerry Wood	.50
328	Rickey Henderson	.75
329	Marty Cordova	.40
330	Greg Maddux	2.00
331	Miguel Batista	.40
332	Chris Bootcheck	.40
333	Carlos Baerga	.40
334	Antonio Alfonseca	.40
335	Shane Halter	.40
336	Juan Encarnacion	.40
337	Flash Gordon	.40
338	Hideo Nomo	.75
339	Torii Hunter	.75
340	Alfonso Soriano	1.00
340	Alfonso Soriano/	
	Black SP	6.00
341	Roberto Alomar	.75
342	David Justice	.50
343	Mike Lieberthal	.40
344	Jeff Weaver	.40
345	Timoniel Perez	.40
346	Travis Lee	.40
347	Sean Casey	.40
348	Willie Harris	.40

349	Derek Lowe	.40
350	Tom Glavine	.75
351	Eric Hinske	.40
352	Rocco Baldelli	.40
353	J.D. Drew	.60
354	Jamie Moyer	.40
355	Todd Linden	.40
356	Benito Santiago	.40
357	Brad Baker	.40
358	Alex Gonzalez	.40
359	Brandon Duckworth	.40
360	John Rheinecker	.40
361	Orlando Hernandez	.40
362	Pedro Astacio	.40
363	Brad Wilkerson	.40
364	David Ortiz	8.00
365	Geoff Jenkins	4.00
366	Brian Jordan	4.00
367	Paul Byrd	4.00
368	Jason Lane	4.00
369	Jeff Bagwell	6.00
370	Bobby Higginson	4.00
371	Juan Uribe	4.00
372	Lee Stevens	4.00
373	Jimmy Haynes	4.00
374	Jose Valentin	4.00
375	Ken Griffey Jr.	10.00
376	Shea Hillenbrand	4.00
377	Gary Matthews Jr.	4.00
378	Gary Sheffield	5.00
379	Rick Helling	4.00
380	Junior Spivey	4.00
381	Francisco Rodriguez	4.00
382	Chipper Jones	6.00
383	Orlando Hudson	4.00
384	Ivan Rodriguez	6.00
385	Chris Snelling	4.00
386	Kenny Lofton	4.00
387	Eric Cyr	4.00
388	Jason Kendall	4.00
389	Marlon Anderson	4.00
390	Billy Koch	4.00
391	Shelly Duncan	4.00
392	Jose Reyes	6.00
393	Fernando Tatis	4.00
394	Michael Cuddyer	4.00
395	Mark Prior	6.00
396	Dontrelle Willis	4.00
397	Jay Payton	4.00
398	Brandon Phillips	4.00
399	Dustin Moseley RC	4.00
400	Jason Giambi	5.00
401	John Mabry	4.00
402	Ron Gant	4.00
403	J.T. Snow	4.00
404	Jeff Cirillo	4.00
405	Darin Erstad	4.00
406	Luis Gonzalez	4.00
407	Marcus Giles	4.00
408	Brian Daubach	4.00
409	Moises Alou	4.00
410	Raul Mondesi	4.00
411	Adrian Beltre	4.00
412	A.J. Burnett	4.00
413	Jason Jennings	4.00
414	Edwin Almonte	4.00
415	Fred McGriff	4.00
416	Tim Raines Jr.	4.00
417	Rafael Furcal	4.00
418	Erubiel Durazo	4.00
419	Drew Henson	4.00
420	Kevin Appier	4.00
421	Chad Tracy	4.00
422	Adam Wainwright	4.00
423	Choo Freeman	4.00
424	Sandy Alomar Jr.	4.00
425	Corey Koskie	4.00
426	Jeromy Burnitz	4.00
427	Jorge Posada	6.00
428	Jason Arnold	4.00
429	Brett Myers	4.00
430	Shawn Green	5.00

Chrome

		NM/M
Common Player:		1.00
Production 1,954 Sets		
Refractors:		1.5-2X
Production 554 Sets		
THC1	Alex Rodriguez	8.00
THC2	Ichiro Suzuki	8.00
THC3	Brian Giles	1.50
THC4	Albert Pujols	8.00
THC5	Derek Jeter	10.00
THC6	Pat Burrell	3.00
THC7	Lance Berkman	2.00
THC8	Todd Helton	2.00
THC9	Chris Duncan	20.00
THC10	Rodrigo Lopez	1.00
THC11	Sammy Sosa	5.00
THC12	Barry Zito	2.00
THC13	Marlon Byrd	1.00
THC14	Al Leiter	1.00
THC15	Kazuhisa Ishii	1.50
THC16	Franklin Gutierrez	1.00
THC17	Roger Clemens	5.00
THC18	Mark Buehrle	1.00
THC19	Larry Walker	1.50
THC20	Curt Schilling	2.50
THC21	Garret Anderson	1.50
THC22	Randy Johnson	3.00
THC23	Cliff Floyd	1.00
THC24	Austin Kearns	2.00
THC25	Manuel Ramirez	1.00
THC26	Raul Ibanez	1.00
THC27	Jason Perry	1.00
THC28	Mark Teixeira	2.00
THC29	Nomar Garciaparra	6.00
THC30	Wayne Lydon	1.00
THC31	Preston Wilson	1.00
THC32	Paul LoDuca	1.00
THC33	Edgardo Alfonzo	1.00
THC34	Jeremy Giambi	1.00
THC35	Mariano Rivera	1.50
THC36	Jimmy Rollins	2.00
THC37	Bret Boone	1.00
THC38	Scott Rolen	2.00
THC39	Adam LaRoche	1.00
THC40	Tim Hudson	1.50
THC41	Craig Brazell	1.00
THC42	Daryl Clark	1.00
THC43	Joe Mauer, Jake Mauer	3.00
THC44	Troy Glaus	2.50
THC45	Sean Pierce	1.00
THC46	Carl Crawford	1.00
THC47	Mike Piazza	6.00
THC48	Josh Beckett	1.00
THC49	Randall Simon	1.00
THC50	Frank Thomas	2.50
THC51	Andruw Jones	2.00
THC52	Andy Marte	4.00
THC53	Bernie Castro	1.00
THC54	Jim Thome	3.00
THC55	Alexis Rios	1.00
THC56	Vladimir Guerrero	4.00
THC57	Walter Young	1.00
THC58	Hank Blalock	1.50
THC59	Ramon A. Martinez	1.00
THC60	Jacque Jones	1.00
THC61	Nick Johnson	1.00
THC62	Ruddy Lugo	1.00
THC63	Carlos Delgado	1.50
THC64	Jeff Clark	1.00
THC65	Johnny Damon	1.00
THC66	Jaime Bubela	1.00
THC67	Alex Rodriguez	8.00
THC68	Rafael Palmeiro	2.00
THC69	Miguel Tejada	2.00
THC70	Bartolo Colon	1.00
THC71	Mike Sweeney	1.00
THC72	John Smoltz	1.00
THC73	Shannon Stewart	1.00
THC74	Mike Mussina	2.00
THC75	Roy Oswalt	1.50
THC76	Pedro Martinez	4.00
THC77	Magglio Ordonez	2.00
THC78	Manny Ramirez	3.00
THC79	David Wells	1.00
THC80	Richie Sexson	1.50
THC81	Adam Dunn	2.50
THC82	Greg Maddux	5.00
THC83	Alfonso Soriano	5.00
THC84	Roberto Alomar	2.00
THC85	Derek Lowe	1.00
THC86	Tom Glavine	2.00
THC87	Jeff Bagwell	2.50
THC88	Ken Griffey Jr.	6.00
THC89	Shea Hillenbrand	1.00
THC90	Gary Sheffield	1.50
THC91	Chipper Jones	5.00
THC92	Orlando Hudson	1.00
THC93	Jose Cruz Jr.	1.00
THC94	Mark Prior	2.50
THC95	Jason Giambi	5.00
THC96	Luis Gonzalez	1.50
THC97	Drew Henson	1.50
THC98	Cristian Guzman	1.00
THC99	Shawn Green	1.50
THC100	Jose Vidro	1.00

Clubhouse Collection Relics

		NM/M
Common Player:		10.00
EB	Ernie Banks.	25.00
AD	Adam Dunn.	15.00
JG	Jim Gilliam.	12.00
SG	Shawn Green.	10.00
CJ	Chipper Jones.	15.00
AK	Al Kaline.	25.00
EM	Eddie Mathews.	20.00
WM	Willie Mays.	40.00
AP	Albert Pujols.	15.00
AR	Alex Rodriguez.	15.00
DS	Duke Snider.	25.00
KW	Kerry Wood.	10.00

Clubhouse Collection Autographed

No Pricing
Production 25 Sets

Clubhouse Collection Dual Relics

		NM/M
Production 54 Sets		
SG	Duke Snider, Shawn Green	80.00
BW	Ernie Banks, Kerry Wood	80.00
MJ	Eddie Mathews, Chipper Jones	100.00

Flashbacks

RICHIE ASHBURN LEADS THE NATIONAL LEAGUE IN ON-BASE PERCENTAGE

		NM/M
Complete Set (10):		12.00
Common Player:		.75
Inserted 1:12		
F1	Willie Mays	3.00
F2	Yogi Berra	2.00
F3	Ted Kluszewski	.75
F4	Stan Musial	3.00
F5	Hank Aaron	3.00
F6	Duke Snider	1.50
F7	Richie Ashburn	.75
F8	Robin Roberts	.75
F9	Mickey Vernon	.75
F10	Don Larsen	.75

Flashbacks Autographs

Production 25:
WM Willie Mays

Grandstand Glory

	NM/M
Common Player:	10.00

RA	Richie Ashburn	15.00
EB	Ernie Banks	20.00
YB	Yogi Berra	20.00
DG	Dick Groat	12.00
AK	Al Kaline	15.00
TK	Ted Kluszewski	12.00
EM	Eddie Mathews	12.00
WM	Willie Mays	35.00
AP	Andy Pafko	10.00
PR	Phil Rizzuto	15.00
HS	Hank Sauer	10.00
DS	Duke Snider	15.00
WS	Warren Spahn	15.00

New Age Performers

NEW AGE PERFORMERS

		NM/M
Complete Set (15):		20.00
Common Player:		.75
Inserted 1:15		
NA1	Mike Piazza	3.00
NA2	Ichiro Suzuki	3.00
NA3	Derek Jeter	4.00
NA4	Alex Rodriguez	3.00
NA5	Sammy Sosa	2.00
NA6	Jason Giambi	2.00
NA7	Vladimir Guerrero	1.50
NA8	Albert Pujols	1.50
NA9	Todd Helton	.75
NA10	Nomar Garciaparra	2.50
NA11	Randy Johnson	1.50
NA12	Jim Thome	1.00
NA13	Andruw Jones	.75
NA14	Miguel Tejada	.75
NA15	Alfonso Soriano	1.50

Real One Autographs

		NM/M
Common Autograph:		15.00
Inserted 1:188		
Special Editions (Red Ink):		1.5-2X
Production 54		
HA	Hank Aaron	250.00
EB	Ernie Banks	150.00
MB	Matt Batts	25.00
HB	Hank Bauer	40.00
LB	Lance Berkman	50.00
YB	Yogi Berra	80.00
MBL	Mike Blyzka	25.00
JC	Jose Cruz Jr.	15.00
RF	Roy Face	40.00
WF	Whitey Ford	60.00
DG	Dick Groat	40.00
GH	Gene Hermanski	25.00
CH	Cal Hogue	25.00
MI	Monte Irvin	50.00
LJ	Larry Jansen	30.00
AK	Al Kaline	80.00
CK	Charlie Kress	25.00
DK	Dick Kryhoski	25.00
TL	Tom Lasorda	70.00
VL	Vern Law	30.00
DL	Don Lenhardt	25.00
DLU	Don Lund	25.00
EM	Eddie Mayo	25.00
WM	Willie Mays	200.00
MM	Mickey Micelotta	25.00
RM	Ray Murray	25.00
AP	Andy Pafko	60.00
PP	Paul Penson	30.00
JPO	Johnny Podres	40.00
JP	Joe Presko	25.00
PR	Phil Rizzuto	50.00
PRO	Preacher Roe	50.00
JR	Jimmy Rollins	25.00
BR	Bob Ross	25.00
JS	Johnny Sain	40.00
MS	Mike Sandlock	25.00
CS	Carl Scheib	25.00
BSH	Bobby Shantz	40.00
BS	Bill "Moose" Skowron	40.00
DS	Duke Snider	80.00

BT	Bob Talbot	25.00
JV	Jose Vidro	15.00
BWE	Bill Werle	25.00
LW	Leroy Wheat	25.00
JW	Jim Willis	25.00

Team Legends Autographs

		NM/M
Common Autograph:		35.00
	Luis Aparicio	35.00
	Jim Bunning	35.00
	Al Kaline	70.00
	Don Larsen	40.00
	Duke Snider	70.00

Then and Now

		NM/M
Complete Set (10):		12.00
Common Card:		.75
Inserted 1:15		
TN1	Ted Kluszewski, Alex Rodriguez	3.00
TN2	Ted Kluszewski, Alex Rodriguez	3.00
TN3	Robin Roberts, Randy Johnson	1.00
TN4	Don Mueller, Alfonso Soriano	1.50
TN5	Stan Musial, Garret Anderson	2.00
TN6	Minnie Minoso, Johnny Damon	.75
TN7	Robin Roberts, Randy Johnson	1.00
TN8	Duke Snider, Alex Rodriguez	3.00
TN9	Robin Roberts, Randy Johnson	1.00
TN10	Johnny Antonelli, Pedro Martinez	1.00

2003 Topps Pristine

		NM/M
Common Player:		1.00
Common Rookie:		1.00
Common Uncommon RC:		2.50
Production 1,499		
Common Rare RC:		5.00
Production 499		
Pack (8):		30.00
Box (5):		140.00
1	Pedro J. Martinez	2.50
2	Derek Jeter	6.00
3	Alex Rodriguez	6.00
4	Miguel Tejada	1.00
5	Nomar Garciaparra	2.50
6	Austin Kearns	1.50
7	Jose Vidro	1.00
8	Bret Boone	1.00
9	Scott Rolen	2.00
10	Mike Sweeney	1.00
11	Jason Schmidt	1.00
12	Alfonso Soriano	2.50
13	Tim Hudson	1.50
14	A.J. Pierzynski	1.00
15	Lance Berkman	2.00
16	Frank Thomas	2.00
17	Gary Sheffield	1.50
18	Jarrod Washburn	1.00
19	Hideo Nomo	1.50
20	Barry Zito	1.50
21	Kevin Millwood	1.50
22	Matt Morris	1.00
23	Carl Crawford	1.00
24	Carlos Delgado	2.00
25	Mike Piazza	3.00
26	Brad Radke	1.00
27	Richie Sexson	1.50
28	Kevin Brown	1.00
29	Carlos Beltran	2.00
30	Curt Schilling	2.00
31	Chipper Jones	3.00
32	Paul Konerko	1.50
33	Larry Walker	1.50
34	Jeff Bagwell	2.00
35	Jason Giambi	1.50
36	Mark Mulder	1.50
37	Vicente Padilla	1.00
38	Kris Benson	1.00
39	Bernie Williams	1.50
40	Jim Thome	2.00
41	Roger Clemens	5.00
42	Roberto Alomar	1.50
43	Torii Hunter	1.50
44	Bobby Abreu	1.00
45	Jeff Kent	1.00
46	Roy Oswalt	1.50
47	Bartolo Colon	1.00
48	Greg Maddux	4.00
49	Tom Glavine	1.50
50	Sammy Sosa	3.00
51	Ichiro Suzuki	4.00
52	Mark Prior	1.50
53	Manny Ramirez	2.00
54	Andruw Jones	1.50
55	Randy Johnson	3.00
56	Garret Anderson	1.50
57	Roy Halladay	1.00
58	Rafael Palmeiro	1.50
59	Rocco Baldelli	1.50
60	Albert Pujols	6.00
61	Edgar Renteria	1.00
62	John Olerud	1.00
63	Rich Aurilia	1.00
64	Ryan Klesko	1.00
65	Brian Giles	1.50
66	Eric Chavez	1.50
67	Jorge Posada	1.50
68	Cliff Floyd	1.00
69	Vladimir Guerrero	2.00
70	Cristian Guzman	1.00
71	Raul Ibanez	1.00
72	Paul LoDuca	1.00
73	A.J. Burnett	1.00
74	Ken Griffey Jr.	4.00
75	Mark Buehrle	1.50
76	Moises Alou	1.50
77	Adam Dunn	2.00
78	Tony Batista	1.00
79	Troy Glaus	1.50
80	Luis Gonzalez	1.00
81	Shea Hillenbrand	1.00
82	Kerry Wood	1.00
83	Magglio Ordonez	1.00
84	Omar Vizquel	1.00
85	Bobby Higginson	1.00
86	Mike Lowell	1.00
87	Runelvys Hernandez	1.00
88	Shawn Green	1.50
89	Erubiel Durazo	1.00
90	Pat Burrell	1.50
91	Todd Helton	2.00
92	Jim Edmonds	1.50
93	Aubrey Huff	1.00
94	Eric Hinske	1.00
95	Barry Bonds	6.00
96	Willie Mays	5.00
97	Bo Jackson	2.00
98	Carl Yastrzemski	2.00
99	Don Mattingly	3.00
100	Gary Carter	1.50
101	Jose Contreras/C RC	2.00
102	Jose Contreras/U RC	4.00
103	Jose Contreras/R RC	8.00
104	Dan Haren/C	4.00
105	Dan Haren/U	6.00
106	Dan Haren/R	10.00
107	Michel Hernandez/C RC	1.00
108	Michel Hernandez/U RC	2.50
109	Michel Hernandez/R RC	5.00
110	Bobby Basham/C RC	1.00
111	Bobby Basham/U RC	2.50
112	Bobby Basham/R RC	5.00
113	Bryan Bullington/C RC	1.50
114	Bryan Bullington/U RC	2.50
115	Bryan Bullington/R RC	5.00
116	Bernie Castro/C RC	1.00
117	Bernie Castro/U RC	2.50
118	Bernie Castro/R RC	5.00
119	Chien-Ming Wang/C RC	25.00
120	Chien-Ming Wang/U RC	30.00
121	Chien-Ming Wang/R RC	40.00
122	Eric Crozier/C RC	1.00
123	Eric Crozier/U RC	2.50
124	Eric Crozier/R RC	5.00
125	Michael Garciaparra/C	1.00
126	Michael Garciaparra/U	2.50
127	Michael Garciaparra/R	5.00
128	Joey Gomes/C	1.00
129	Joey Gomes/U	2.50
130	Joey Gomes/R	5.00
131	Wilfredo Ledezma/C RC	1.00
132	Wilfredo Ledezma/U RC	2.50
133	Wilfredo Ledezma/R RC	5.00
134	Branden Florence/C RC	1.00
135	Branden Florence/U RC	2.50
136	Branden Florence/R RC	5.00
137	Jeremy Bonderman/C	6.00
138	Jeremy Bonderman/U	10.00
139	Jeremy Bonderman/R	15.00
140	Travis Ishikawa/C RC	1.00
141	Travis Ishikawa/U RC	2.50
142	Travis Ishikawa/R RC	5.00
143	Ben Francisco/C RC	1.00
144	Ben Francisco/U RC	2.50
145	Ben Francisco/R RC	5.00
146	Jason Kubel/C RC	4.00
147	Jason Kubel/U RC	8.00
148	Jason Kubel/R RC	10.00
149	Tyler Martin/C RC	1.00
150	Tyler Martin/U RC	2.50
151	Tyler Martin/R RC	5.00
152	Jason Perry/C	1.50
153	Jason Perry/U	3.00
154	Jason Perry/R	5.00
155	Ryan Shealy/C RC	4.00
156	Ryan Shealy/U RC	6.00
157	Ryan Shealy/R RC	10.00
158	Hanley Ramirez/C RC	12.00
159	Hanley Ramirez/U RC	15.00
160	Hanley Ramirez/R RC	25.00
161	Rajai Davis/C RC	1.00
162	Rajai Davis/U RC	2.50
163	Rajai Davis/R RC	5.00
164	Gary Schneidmiller/C RC	1.00
165	Gary Schneidmiller/U RC	2.50
166	Gary Schneidmiller/R RC	5.00
167	Haj Turay/C RC	1.00
168	Haj Turay/U RC	2.50
169	Haj Turay/R RC	5.00
170	Kevin Youkilis/C RC	4.00
171	Kevin Youkilis/U RC	8.00
172	Kevin Youkilis/R RC	15.00
173	Shane Bazzell/C RC	1.00
174	Shane Bazzell/U RC	2.50
175	Shane Bazzell/R RC	5.00
176	Elizardo Ramirez/C RC	1.50
177	Elizardo Ramirez/U RC	3.00
178	Elizardo Ramirez/R RC	6.00
179	Robinson Cano/C RC	20.00
180	Robinson Cano/U RC	30.00
181	Robinson Cano/R RC	35.00
182	Nook Logan/C RC	1.00
183	Nook Logan/U RC	2.50
184	Nook Logan/R RC	5.00
185	Dustin McGowan/C RC	2.00
186	Dustin McGowan/U RC	5.00
187	Dustin McGowan/R RC	8.00
188	Ryan Howard/C	40.00
189	Ryan Howard/U	40.00
190	Ryan Howard/R	65.00

Refractors

Veterans (1-100):	4-6X
Production 99	
Common RC's:	.75-1.5X
Production 1,599	
Uncommon RC's:	1-2X
Production 499	
Rare RC's:	1.5-3X
Production 99	
Veteran Gold Refrac. (1-100):	4-8X

Rookie Golds (101-190):	2-4X
Production 69 Sets	

Plates

No pricing due to scarcity.
Four plates per player.

Bomb Squad

		NM/M
Common Player:		4.00
Refractors:		No Pricing
Production 25 Sets		
MO1	Moises Alou	4.00
MO2	Moises Alou	4.00
GA1	Garret Anderson	5.00
GA2	Garret Anderson	5.00
JRB	Jeff Bagwell	6.00
JB	Johnny Bench	10.00
LB1	Lance Berkman	5.00
LB2	Lance Berkman	5.00
HB	Hank Blalock	5.00
BB	Barry Bonds	15.00
GB1	George Brett	12.00
GB2	George Brett	12.00
GC	Gary Carter	5.00
EC1	Eric Chavez	4.00
EC2	Eric Chavez	4.00
CC	Carl Crawford	5.00
AD	Adam Dunn	6.00
DE1	Darin Erstad	4.00
DE2	Darin Erstad	4.00
CF	Cliff Floyd	4.00
NG1	Nomar Garciaparra	10.00
NG2	Nomar Garciaparra	10.00
JG	Jason Giambi	6.00
TG1	Troy Glaus	5.00
TG2	Troy Glaus	5.00
JAG	Juan Gonzalez	6.00
LG	Luis Gonzalez	4.00
SG	Shawn Green	5.00
VG1	Vladimir Guerrero	8.00
VG2	Vladimir Guerrero	8.00
TH	Todd Helton	6.00
RH	Rickey Henderson	10.00
AJ	Andruw Jones	6.00
CJ	Chipper Jones	8.00
JK	Jeff Kent	4.00
MO	Magglio Ordonez	5.00
RP	Rafael Palmeiro	6.00
MP	Mike Piazza	10.00
AP1	Albert Pujols	15.00
AP2	Albert Pujols	15.00
MR	Manny Ramirez	6.00
AR1	Alex Rodriguez	10.00
AR2	Alex Rodriguez	10.00
TS	Tim Salmon	4.00
MS1	Mike Schmidt	12.00
MS2	Mike Schmidt	12.00
GS	Gary Sheffield	5.00
AS	Alfonso Soriano	8.00
SS1	Sammy Sosa	10.00
SS2	Sammy Sosa	10.00
MT	Miguel Tejada	6.00
FT	Frank Thomas	6.00
JT	Jim Thome	10.00

Borders

	NM/M
Common Player:	4.00
Inserted 1:9	
Refractors:	No Pricing

Production 25 Sets

CC	Chin-Feng Chen	40.00
VG	Vladimir Guerrero	8.00
CG	Cristian Guzman	4.00
KI	Kazuhisa Ishii	4.00
AJ	Andruw Jones	6.00
PM	Pedro J. Martinez	8.00
MO	Magglio Ordonez	6.00
AP	Albert Pujols	15.00
MR	Manny Ramirez	6.00
IR	Ivan Rodriguez	6.00
TS	Tsuyoshi Shinjo	4.00
AS	Alfonso Soriano	8.00
SS	Sammy Sosa	10.00
MT	Miguel Tejada	4.00
BW	Bernie Williams	6.00

Corners

		NM/M
Common Duo:		6.00
Inserted 1:12		
Refractors:		No Pricing

Production 25 Sets

CD	Eric Chavez, Erubiel Durazo	6.00
VG	Robin Ventura, Jason Giambi	10.00
WG	Matt Williams, Mark Grace	8.00
RM	Scott Rolen, Tino Martinez	10.00
BM	Adrian Beltre, Fred McGriff	6.00
GS	Troy Glaus, Scott Spiezio	8.00
KM	Corey Koskie, Doug Mientkiewicz	6.00
BT	David Bell, Jim Thome	10.00
BK	Sean Burroughs, Ryan Klesko	6.00
AS	Edgardo Alfonzo, J.T. Snow	6.00
TP	Mark Teixeira, Rafael Palmeiro	10.00

Double Bonds

		NM/M
Common Duo:		25.00
Refractors:		No Pricing

Production 25

BJ	Barry Bonds, Randy Johnson	50.00
BT	Miguel Tejada, Barry Bonds	25.00
BM	Willie Mays, Barry Bonds	75.00
BR	Alex Rodriguez, Barry Bonds	35.00

Factor

	NM/M
Common Player:	4.00
Inserted 1:9	
Refractors:	No Pricing

Production 25 Sets

LB	Lance Berkman	4.00
AD	Adam Dunn	6.00
DE	Darin Erstad	4.00
NG	Nomar Garciaparra	10.00
JG	Jason Giambi	6.00
TG	Troy Glaus	5.00
VG	Vladimir Guerrero	8.00
TH	Todd Helton	6.00
TKH	Torii Hunter	5.00
MO	Magglio Ordonez	4.00
MP	Mike Piazza	10.00
MR	Manny Ramirez	6.00
AR	Alex Rodriguez	10.00
AS	Alfonso Soriano	8.00
SS	Sammy Sosa	10.00

Mini

		NM/M
Common Player:		1.00
RB	Rocco Baldelli	1.50
BWB	Bobby Basham	1.00
JB	Jeremy Bonderman	4.00
BB	Barry Bonds	6.00
BPB	Bryan Bullington	3.00
RJC	Robinson Cano	20.00
BC	Bernie Castro	1.00
EC	Eric Chavez	1.00
RC	Roger Clemens	5.00
JC	Jose Contreras	2.00
ELC	Eric Crozier	1.00
RD	Rajai Davis	1.00
NG	Nomar Garciaparra	5.00
JG	Jason Giambi	2.00
BG	Brian Giles	1.50
VG	Vladimir Guerrero	3.00
DH	Dan Haren	4.00
MH	Michel Hernandez	1.00
RH	Ryan Howard	60.00
DJ	Derek Jeter	6.00
AK	Austin Kearns	2.00
JK	Jeff Kent	1.50
JJK	Jason Kubel	4.00
WL	Wilfredo Ledezma	1.00
NL	Nook Logan	1.00
TM	Tyler Martin	1.00
DM	Dustin McGowan	3.00
MO	Magglio Ordonez	1.00
MJP	Mike Piazza	4.00
MP	Mark Prior	6.00
ER	Elizardo Ramirez	1.00
AR	Alex Rodriguez	6.00
RS	Ryan Shealy	3.00
AS	Alfonso Soriano	3.00
SS	Sammy Sosa	4.00
IS	Ichiro Suzuki	3.00
MT	Miguel Tejada	1.50
JT	Jim Thome	2.00
CW	Chien-Ming Wang	40.00
KY	Kevin Youkilis	6.00

Mini Autograph

	NM/M
Production 100	
RC	Roger Clemens	125.00

Personal Endorsements

	NM/M
Common Autograph:	6.00
Golds:	No Pricing

Production 25 Sets

AB	Andrew Brown	6.00
RYC	Ryan Church	10.00
DE	David Eckstein	10.00
LF	Lew Ford	10.00
JG	Jay Gibbons	10.00
RJH	Rich Harden	25.00
KH	Ken Harvey	6.00
PK	Paul Konerko	20.00
ML	Mike Lowell	10.00
VM	Victor Martinez	20.00
BM	Brett Myers	10.00
JP	Josh Phelps	8.00
SR	Scott Rolen	25.00
FS	Felix Sanchez	6.00
KS	Kelly Shoppach	15.00
MS	Mike Sweeney	10.00
FV	Fernando Vina	6.00

Primary Elements

	NM/M
Many not priced due to scarcity.	
Production 50 Sets	
Refractors:	No Pricing
Production 10	
MRO	Moises Alou	

BRB	Bret Boone	15.00
NG	Nomar Garciaparra	35.00
LG	Luis Gonzalez	10.00
SG	Shawn Green	10.00
TH	Todd Helton	20.00
TKH	Torii Hunter	20.00
KI	Kazuhisa Ishii	10.00
AJ	Andruw Jones	15.00
CJ	Chipper Jones	20.00
PM	Pedro J. Martinez	20.00
MO	Magglio Ordonez	10.00
RP	Rafael Palmeiro	15.00
MP	Mike Piazza	25.00
AR	Alex Rodriguez	50.00
MT	Miguel Tejada	15.00
BZ	Barry Zito	15.00

Solo Bonds

		NM/M
Common Bonds:		20.00
Refractors:		No Pricing
Production 25		
GG	Barry Bonds	20.00
HR	Barry Bonds	20.00
BB	Barry Bonds	20.00
MVP	Barry Bonds	20.00

2003 Topps Retired Signature Edition

	NM/M
Complete Set (110):	100.00
Common Player:	.50
Pack (5):	30.00
Box (5):	120.00
1	Willie Mays	4.00
2	Tony Perez	1.00
3	Tom Seaver	2.00
4	Johnny Bench	4.00
5	Rod Carew	1.50
6	Red Schoendienst	.50
7	Phil Rizzuto	1.00
8	Ozzie Smith	2.50
9	Maury Wills	.50
10	Hank Aaron	4.00
11	Jim Palmer	1.00
12	Jose Cruz	.50
13	Dave Parker	.50
14	Don Sutton	.75
15	Brooks Robinson	2.00
16	Bo Jackson	1.50
17	Andre Dawson	.75
18	Fergie Jenkins	.75
19	George Foster	.50
20	George Brett	5.00
21	Jerry Koosman	.50
22	John Kruk	.50
23	Kent Tekulve	.50
24	Lee Smith	.50
25	Nolan Ryan	6.00
26	Paul O'Neill	.50
27	Rich "Goose" Gossage	.50
28	Ron Santo	.50
29	Tom Lasorda	.75
30	Tony Gwynn	2.00
31	Vida Blue	.50
32	Whitey Herzog	.50
33	Willie McGee	.50
34	Bill Mazeroski	.50
35	Al Kaline	3.00
36	Bobby Richardson	.50
37	Carlton Fisk	1.00
38	Darrell Evans	.50
39	Dave Concepcion	.50
40	Cal Ripken Jr.	5.00
41	Dwight Evans	.50
42	Earl Weaver	.50
43	Fred Lynn	.50
44	Greg Luzinski	.50
45	Duke Snider	1.50
46	Hank Bauer	.50
47	Jim Rice	.50
48	Johnny Sain	.50

49	Lenny Dykstra	.50
50	Mike Schmidt	4.00
51	Orlando Cepeda	1.00
52	Ralph Kiner	.75
53	Robin Roberts	.50
54	Ron Guidry	.50
55	Steve Garvey	.50
56	Tony Oliva	.75
57	Whitey Ford	1.00
58	Willie McCovey	1.00
59	Phil Niekro	.50
60	Stan Musial	3.00
61	Rollie Fingers	1.00
62	Robin Yount	2.00
63	Alan Trammell	1.00
64	Bill Buckner	.50
65	Bob Feller	1.00
66	Bruce Sutter	.75
67	Dale Murphy	1.00
68	Dennis Eckersley	1.00
69	Don Newcombe	1.00
70	Don Mattingly	5.00
71	Dwight Gooden	.50
72	Frank Robinson	1.50
73	Gary Carter	.50
74	Graig Nettles	.50
75	Harmon Killebrew	2.00
76	Jim Bunning	.50
77	Joe Morgan	1.00
78	Joe Rudi	.50
79	Jose Canseco	1.00
80	Ernie Banks	3.00
81	Luis Aparicio	.50
82	Luis Tiant	.50
83	Mark Fidrych	.50
84	Kirk Gibson	.50
85	Lou Brock	1.00
86	Juan Marichal	1.00
87	Monte Irvin	1.00
88	Paul Molitor	1.00
89	Tommy John	.50
90	Warren Spahn	1.50
91	Wade Boggs	1.00
92	Reggie Jackson	2.00
93	Kirby Puckett	3.00
94	Boog Powell	.50
95	Carl Yastrzemski	2.00
96	Bobby Thomson	.50
97	Bill "Moose" Skowron	.50
98	Bill Madlock	.50
99	Sparky Anderson	.50
100	Yogi Berra	2.00
101	Bobby Doerr	.50
102	Gaylord Perry	.50
103	George Kell	.50
104	Harold Reynolds	.50
105	Joe Carter	.50
106	Johnny Podres	.50
107	Ron Cey	.50
108	Tim McCarver	.50
109	Tug McGraw	.50
110	Don Larsen	1.00

Black

Cards (1-110):	2-4X
Production 99 Sets	

Autographs

	NM/M
Common Autograph:	10.00
Inserted 1:1	
Refractors:	1-2.5X

Production 25 Sets

HA	Hank Aaron/30	300.00
JA	Jim Abbott	20.00
SA	Sparky Anderson	20.00
LA	Luis Aparicio	12.00
HB	Harold Baines	10.00
EB	Ernie Banks/24	175.00
HBA	Hank Bauer	20.00
JBE	Johnny Bench	65.00

Code	Player	Price
YB	Yogi Berra/25	150.00
VB	Vida Blue	15.00
BB	Bert Blyleven	10.00
WB	Wade Boggs/77	125.00
GB	George Brett/25	180.00
LB	Lou Brock/76	120.00
BBU	Bill Buckner	10.00
JB	Jim Bunning/76	100.00
JCA	Jose Canseco	40.00
RCA	Rod Carew	60.00
GC	Gary Carter/77	100.00
JC	Joe Carter	25.00
OC	Orlando Cepeda/75	180.00
RCE	Ron Cey	10.00
JCR	Jose Cruz	10.00
AD	Andre Dawson	20.00
BD	Bobby Doerr	20.00
LD	Lenny Dykstra	20.00
DEC	Dennis Eckersley	65.00
DE	Darrell Evans	10.00
DEV	Dwight Evans/78	80.00
BF	Bob Feller	20.00
MF	Mark Fidrych	20.00
RF	Rollie Fingers	25.00
CF	Carlton Fisk	65.00
WF	Whitey Ford	65.00
GF	George Foster	10.00
SG	Steve Garvey	15.00
KG	Kirk Gibson	40.00
DG	Dwight Gooden	30.00
RG	Rich "Goose" Gossage	15.00
BGR	Bobby Grich	15.00
KGR	Ken Griffey Sr.	25.00
RGU	Ron Guidry	35.00
TG	Tony Gwynn/25	165.00
WH	Whitey Herzog	15.00
BH	Bob Horner	10.00
MI	Monte Irvin	60.00
BJ	Bo Jackson	75.00
RJ	Reggie Jackson	100.00
FJ	Fergie Jenkins	20.00
TJ	Tommy John	25.00
AK	Al Kaline	75.00
GK	George Kell	30.00
HK	Harmon Killebrew/76	150.00
RK	Ralph Kiner	125.00
JK	Jerry Koosman	25.00
JKR	John Kruk	35.00
DL	Don Larsen	15.00
TL	Tom Lasorda/76	100.00
GL	Greg Luzinski	15.00
FL	Fred Lynn	20.00
BM	Bill Madlock	10.00
JMA	Juan Marichal	35.00
DON	Don Mattingly/81	175.00
WM	Willie Mays/25	
BMA	Bill Mazeroski	15.00
TM	Tim McCarver	25.00
WMC	Willie McCovey	50.00
WMG	Willie McGee	25.00
TMC	Tug McGraw	50.00
PM	Paul Molitor	75.00
JM	Joe Morgan	35.00
DM	Dale Murphy	40.00
SM	Stan Musial/28	185.00
PN	Phil Niekro	15.00
GN	Graig Nettles	10.00
DN	Don Newcombe	15.00
TO	Tony Oliva	25.00
PO	Paul O'Neill	50.00
JP	Jim Palmer	50.00
DP	Dave Parker	20.00
LP	Lance Parrish	10.00
TP	Terry Pendleton	10.00
TP	Tony Perez	40.00
GP	Gaylord Perry	10.00
JPI	Jimmy Piersall	10.00
JPO	Johnny Podres	10.00
BP	Boog Powell	10.00
KP	Kirby Puckett/75	
HR	Harold Reynolds	20.00
JR	Jim Rice	30.00
BR	Bobby Richardson	15.00
CR	Cal Ripken Jr./25	340.00
PR	Phil Rizzuto/70	140.00
RR	Robin Roberts	25.00
BRO	Brooks Robinson/75	140.00
FR	Frank Robinson	60.00
JRU	Joe Rudi	10.00
NR	Nolan Ryan/77	200.00
BSA	Bret Saberhagen	25.00
JS	Johnny Sain	
RSA	Ron Santo	20.00
MS	Mike Schmidt/83	200.00
RS	Red Schoendienst/83	100.00
TS	Tom Seaver	65.00
BS	Bill "Moose" Skowron	10.00
LS	Lee Smith	15.00
OS	Ozzie Smith	65.00
DSN	Duke Snider/75	100.00
WS	Warren Spahn	50.00
DS	Dave Stieb	15.00
BSU	Bruce Sutter	35.00
DSU	Don Sutton	20.00
KT	Kent Tekulve	20.00
BT	Bobby Thomson	10.00
LT	Luis Tiant	10.00
AT	Alan Trammell	20.00
BW	Bob Watson	10.00
EW	Earl Weaver	12.00
MW	Maury Wills	10.00
CY	Carl Yastrzemski	80.00
RY	Robin Yount/25	150.00

2003 Topps Total

Chien-Ming WANG

		NM/M
Complete Set (990):		125.00
Common Player:		.10
Pack (10):		1.00
Box (36):		25.00
1	Brent Abernathy	.10
2	Bobby Hill	.10
3	Victor Martinez	.10
4	Chip Ambres	.10
5	Matt Anderson	.10
6	Ricardo Aramboles	.10
7	Carlos Pena	.10
8	Aaron Guiel	.10
9	Luke Allen	.10
10	Francisco Rodriguez	.20
11	Jason Marquis	.10
12	Edwin Almonte	.10
13	Grant Balfour	.10
14	Adam Piatt	.10
15	Andy Phillips	.10
16	Adrian Beltre	.10
17	Brandon Backe	.10
18	Dave Berg	.10
19	Brett Myers	.10
20	Brian Meadows	.10
21	Chin-Feng Chen	.25
22	Blake Williams	.10
23	Josh Bard	.10
24	Josh Beckett	.10
25	Kip Bouknight RC	.20
26	Matt Childers	.10
27	Adam Everett	.10
28	Mike Bordick	.10
29	Antonio Alfonseca	.10
30	Doug Creek	.10
31	J.D. Drew	.20
32	Milton Bradley	.10
33	David Wells	.10
34	Vance Wilson	.10
35	Jeff Fassero	.10
36	Sandy Alomar	.10
37	Ryan Vogelsong	.10
38	Roger Clemens	1.25
39	Juan Gonzalez	.40
40	Dustin Hermanson	.10
41	Andy Ashby	.10
42	Adam Hyzdu	.10
43	Ben Broussard	.10
44	Ryan Klesko	.10
45	Chris Buglovsky	.10
46	Bud Smith	.10
47	Aaron Boone	.10
48	Cliff Floyd	.10
49	Alex Cora	.10
50	Curt Schilling	.40
51	Michael Cuddyer	.10
52	Mike Venafro	.10
53	Carlos Gullien	.10
54	Angel Berroa	.10
55	Eli Marrero	.10
56	A.J. Burnett	.10
57	Oliver Perez	.10
58	Matt Morris	.25
59	Valerio De Los Santos	.10
60	Austin Kearns	.50
61	Darren Dreifort	.10
62	Jason Standridge	.10
63	Carlos Silva	.10
64	Moises Alou	.20
65	Jason Anderson	.10
66	Russell Branyan	.10
67	B.J. Ryan	.10
68	Cory Aldridge	.10
69	Ellis Burks	.10
70	Troy Glaus	.50
71	Kelly Wunsch	.10
72	Brad Wilkerson	.10
73	Jayson Durocher	.10
74	Tony Fiore	.10
75	Brian Giles	.25
76	Billy Wagner	.10
77	Neifi Perez	.10
78	Jose Valverde	.10
79	Brent Butler	.10
80	Mario Ramos	.10
81	Kerry Robinson	.10
82	Brent Mayne	.10
83	Sean Casey	.10
84	Danys Baez	.10
85	Chase Utley	.25
86	Jared Sandberg	.10
87	Terrence Long	.10
88	Kevin Walker	.10
89	Royce Clayton	.10
90	Shea Hillenbrand	.10
91	Brad Lidge	.10
92	Shawn Chacon	.10
93	Kevin Frederick	.10
94	Chris Snelling	.10
95	Omar Vizquel	.20
96	Joe Borchard	.10
97	Matt Belisle	.10
98	Steve Smyth	.10
99	Raul Mondesi	.20
100	Chipper Jones	1.00
101	Victor Alvarez	.10
102	J.M. Gold	.10
103	Willis Roberts	.10
104	Eddie Guardado	.10
105	Brad Voyles	.10
106	Bronson Arroyo	.10
107	Juan Castro	.10
108	Dan Pleasac	.10
109	Ramon Castro	.10
110	Tim Salmon	.25
111	Damion Easley	.10
112	J.D. Closser	.10
113	Mark Buehrle	.10
114	Steve Karsay	.10
115	Cristian Guerrero	.10
116	Brad Ausmus	.10
117	Cristian Guzman	.10
118	Dan Wilson	.10
119	Jake Westbrook	.10
120	Manny Ramirez	.50
121	Jason Giambi	.75
122	Bob Wickman	.10
123	Aaron Cook	.10
124	Alfredo Amezaga	.10
125	Corey Thurman	.10
126	Brandon Puffer	.10
127	Hee Seop Choi	.25
128	Javier Vazquez	.10
129	Carlos Valderrama	.10
130	Jerome Williams	.10
131	Wilson Betemit	.10
132	Bruce Chen	.10
133	Esteban Yan	.10
134	Brandon Berger	.10
135	Bill Hall	.10
136	LaTroy Hawkins	.10
137	Nate Cornejo	.10
138	Jim Mecir	.10
139	Joe Crede	.10
140	Andres Galarraga	.10
141	Dave Williams	.10
142	Joey Eischen	.10
143	Mike Timlin	.10
144	Jose Cruz Jr.	.10
145	Wes Helms	.10
146	Brian Roberts	.10
147	Bret Prinz	.10
148	Brian Hunter	.10
149	Chad Hermansen	.10
150	Andruw Jones	.40
151	Kurt Ainsworth	.10
152	Clifford Bartosh	.10
153	Kyle Lohse	.10
154	Brian Jordan	.10
155	Coco Crisp	.10
156	Tomas Perez	.10
157	Keith Foulke	.10
158	Chris Carpenter	.10
159	Mike Remlinger	.10
160	Dewon Brazelton	.10
161	Brook Fordyce	.10
162	Rusty Greer	.10
163	Scott Downs	.10
164	Jason Dubois	.10
165	David Coggin	.10
166	Jose Hernandez	.10
167	Carlos Hernandez	.10
168	Matt Williams	.10
169	Rheal Cormier	.10
170	Duaner Sanchez	.10
171	Craig Counsell	.10
172	Edgar Martinez	.20
173	Zack Greinke	.10
174	Pedro Feliz	.10
175	Randy Choate	.10
176	Jon Garland	.10
177	Keith Ginter	.10
178	Carlos Febles	.10
179	Gregor Blanco RC	.10
180	Jack Cust	.10
181	Koyie Hill	.10
182	Ricky Gutierrez	.10
183	Ben Grieve	.10
184	Livan Hernandez	.10
185	Jason Isringhausen	.10
186	Gookie Dawkins	.10
187	Roberto Alomar	.40
188	Eric Junge	.10
189	Carlos Beltran	.10
190	Denny Hocking	.10
191	Jason Schmidt	.10
192	Cory Lidle	.10
193	Robert Mackowiak	.10
194	Charlton Jimerson RC	.10
195	Darin Erstad	.25
196	Jason Davis	.10
197	Luis Castillo	.10
198	Juan Encarnacion	.10
199	Jeffrey Hammonds	.10
199		.10
200	Nomar Garciaparra	1.50
201	Ryan Christianson	.10
202	Willie Banks	.10
203	Damian Moss	.10
204	Chris Richard	.10
205	Todd Hundley	.10
206	Paul Bako	.10
207	Adam Kennedy	.10
208	Scott Hatteberg	.10
209	Andy Pratt	.10
210	Ken Griffey Jr.	1.00
211	Chris George	.10
212	Lance Niekro	.10
213	Greg Colbrunn	.10
214	Herbert Perry	.10
215	Cody Ransom	.10
216	Craig Biggio	.25
217	Miguel Batista	.10
218	Alex Escobar	.10
219	Willie Harris	.10
220	Scott Strickland	.10
221	Felix Rodriguez	.10
222	Torii Hunter	.25
223	Tyler Houston	.10
224	Darrell May	.10
225	Benito Santiago	.10
226	Ryan Dempster	.10
227	Andy Fox	.10
228	Jung Bong	.10
229	Jose Macias	.10
230	Shannon Stewart	.10
231	Buddy Groom	.10
232	Eric Valent	.10
233	Scott Schoeneweis	.10
234	Corey Hart	.10
235	Brett Tomko	.10
236	Shane Bazzell RC	.20
237	Tim Hummel	.10
238	Al Reyes	.10
239	Daryle Ward	.10
240	Ismael Valdes	.10
241	Brian Fuentes	.10
242	Cesar Izturis	.10
243	Mark Bellhorn	.10
244	Geoff Jenkins	.10
245	Derek Jeter	2.00
246	Anderson Machado	.10
247	Dave Roberts	.10
248	Jaime Cerda	.10
249	Woody Williams	.10
250	Vernon Wells	.20
251	Jon Lieber	.10
252	Franklyn German	.10
253	David Segui	.10
254	Freddy Garcia	.10
255	James Baldwin	.10
256	Tony Alvarez	.10
257	Walter Young	.10
258	Alex Herrera	.10
259	Robert Fick	.10
260	Rob Bell	.10
261	Ross Gload	.10
262	Dee Brown	.10
263	Mike Bacsik	.10
264	Corey Patterson	.10
265	Marvin Bernard	.10
266	Eddie Rogers	.10
267	Elio Serrano	.10
268	D'Angelo Jimenez	.10
269	Adam Johnson	.10
270	Gregg Zaun	.10
271	Nick Johnson	.10
272	Geoff Goetz	.10
273	Ryan Drese	.10

#	Name		#	Name		#	Name		#	Name	
274	Eric DuBose	.10	380	Checklist	.10	486	Travis Lee	.10	592	Tomokazu Ohka	.10
275	Barry Zito	.25	381	Alex Gonzalez	.10	487	Bobby Bradley	.10	593	Brian Boehringer	.10
276	Mike Crudale	.10	382	Flash Gordon	.10	488	Marcus Giles	.10	594	Danny Patterson	.10
277	Paul Byrd	.10	383	John Buck	.10	489	Steve Trachsel	.10	595	Jeff Tam	.10
278	Eric Gagne	.10	384	Shigetoshi Hasegawa	.10	490	Derek Lowe	.10	596	Anastacio Martinez	.10
279	Aramis Ramirez	.10	385	Scott Stewart	.10	491	Hideo Nomo	.25	597	Rod Barajas	.10
280	Ray Durham	.10	386	Luke Hudson	.10	492	Brad Hawpe	.10	598	Octavio Dotel	.10
281	Tony Graffanino	.10	387	Todd Jones	.10	493	Jesus Medrano	.10	599	Jason Tyner	.10
282	Jeremy Guthrie	.10	388	Fred McGriff	.25	494	Rick Ankiel	.10	600	Gary Sheffield	.40
283	Erik Bedard	.10	389	Mike Sweeney	.10	495	Pasqual Coco	.10	601	Ruben Quevedo	.10
284	Vince Faison	.10	390	Marlon Anderson	.10	496	Michael Barrett	.10	602	Jay Payton	.10
285	Bobby Kielty	.10	391	Terry Adams	.10	497	Joe Beimel	.10	603	Mo Vaughn	.10
286	Francis Beltran	.10	392	Mark DeRosa	.10	498	Marty Cordova	.10	604	Pat Burrell	.40
287	Alexis Gomez	.10	393	Doug Mientkiewicz	.10	499	Aaron Sele	.10	605	Fernando Vina	.10
288	Vladimir Guerrero	.75	394	Miguel Cairo	.10	500	Sammy Sosa	1.00	606	Wes Anderson	.10
289	Kevin Appier	.10	395	Jamie Moyer	.10	501	Ivan Rodriguez	.40	607	Alex Gonzalez	.10
290	Gil Meche	.10	396	Josh Towers	.10	502	Keith Osik	.10	608	Ted Lilly	.10
291	Marquis Grissom	.10	397	Matt Clement	.10	503	Hank Blalock	.25	609	Nick Punto	.10
292	John Burkett	.10	398	Bengie Molina	.10	504	Craig Monroe	.10	610	Ryan Madson	.10
293	Vinny Castilla	.10	399	Marcus Thames	.10	505	Junior Spivey	.10	611	Odalis Perez	.10
294	Tyler Walker	.10	400	Nick Bierbrodt	.10	506	Edgardo Alfonzo	.10	612	Chris Woodward	.10
295	Shane Halter	.10	401	Tim Kalita	.10	507	Alex Graman	.10	613	John Olerud	.25
296	Geronimo Gil	.10	402	Corwin Malone	.10	508	J.J. Davis	.10	614	Brad Cresse	.10
297	Eric Hinske	.10	403	Jesse Orosco	.10	509	Roger Cedeno	.10	615	Chad Zerbe	.10
298	Adam Dunn	.50	404	Brandon Phillips	.10	510	Joe Roa	.10	616	Brad Penny	.10
299	Mike Kinkade	.10	405	Eric Cyr	.10	511	Wily Mo Pena	.10	617	Barry Larkin	.40
300	Mark Prior	.50	406	Jason Michaels	.10	512	Eric Munson	.10	618	Brandon Duckworth	.10
301	Corey Koskie	.10	407	Julio Lugo	.10	513	Arnie Munoz RC	.10	619	Brad Radke	.10
302	David Dellucci	.10	408	Gabe Kapler	.10	514	Miguel Asencio	.10	620	Giovanni Carrara	.10
303	Todd Helton	.40	409	Mark Mulder	.25	515	Andy Pettitte	.25	621	Juan Pierre	.10
304	Greg Miller	.10	410	Adam Eaton	.10	516	Jim Edmonds	.25	622	Rick Reed	.10
305	Delvin James	.10	411	Ken Harvey	.10	517	Jeff DaVanon	.10	623	Omar Daal	.10
306	Humberto Cota	.10	412	Jolbert Cabrera	.10	518	Aaron Myette	.10	624	Jose Hernandez	.10
307	Aaron Harang	.10	413	Eric Milton	.10	519	C.C. Sabathia	.10	625	Greg Maddux	1.00
308	Jeremy Hill	.10	414	Josh Hall RC	.20	520	Gerardo Garcia	.10	626	Henry Mateo	.10
309	Billy Koch	.10	415	Bob File	.10	521	Brian Schneider	.10	627	Kip Wells	.10
310	Brandon Claussen	.10	416	Brett Evert	.10	522	Wes Obermueller	.10	628	Kevin Cash	.10
311	Matt Ginter	.10	417	Ron Chiavacci	.10	523	John Mabry	.10	629	Mark Redman	.10
312	Jason Lane	.10	418	Jorge De La Rosa	.10	524	Casey Fossum	.10	630	Luis Gonzalez	.25
313	Ben Weber	.10	419	Quinton McCracken	.10	525	Toby Hall	.10	631	Jason Conti	.10
314	Alan Benes	.10	420	Luther Hackman	.10	526	Denny Neagle	.10	632	Ricardo Rincon	.10
315	Oscar Herinquez	.10	421	Gary Knotts	.10	527	Willie Bloomquist	.10	633	Mike Bynum	.10
316	Danny Graves	.10	422	Kevin Brown	.20	528	A.J. Pierzynski	.10	634	Mike Redmond	.10
317	Jason Johnson	.10	423	Jeff Cirillo	.10	529	Bartolo Colon	.10	635	Chance Capel	.10
318	Jason Grimsley	.10	424	Damaso Marte	.10	530	Chad Harville	.10	636	Chris Widger	.10
319	Steve Kline	.10	425	Chan Ho Park	.10	531	Blaine Neal	.10	637	Michael Restovich	.10
320	Johnny Damon	.10	426	Nathan Haynes	.10	532	Luis Terrero Jr.	.10	638	Mark Grudzielanek	.10
321	Jay Gibbons	.10	427	Matt Lawton	.10	533	Reggie Taylor	.10	639	Brandon Larson	.10
322	J.J. Putz	.10	428	Mike Stanton	.10	534	Melvin Mora	.10	640	Luis De Los Santos	.10
323	Stephen Randolph RC	.10	429	Bernie Williams	.40	535	Tino Martinez	.10	641	Javy Lopez	.20
324	Bobby Higginson	.10	430	Kevin Jarvis	.10	536	Peter Bergeron	.10	642	Rene Reyes	.10
325	Kazuhisa Ishii	.10	431	Joe McEwing	.10	537	Jorge Padilla	.10	643	Orlando Merced	.10
326	Carlos Lee	.10	432	Mark Kotsay	.10	538	Oscar Villarreal RC	.20	644	Jason Phillips	.10
327	J.R. House	.10	433	Juan Cruz	.10	539	David Weathers	.10	645	Luis Ugueto	.10
328	Mark Loretta	.10	434	Russ Ortiz	.10	540	Mike Lamb	.10	646	Ron Calloway	.10
329	Mike Matheny	.10	435	Jeff Nelson	.10	541	Greg Norton	.10	647	Josh Paul	.10
330	Ben Diggins	.10	436	Alan Embree	.10	542	Michael Tucker	.10	648	Todd Greene	.10
331	Seth Etherton	.10	437	Miguel Tejada	.25	543	Ben Kozlowski	.10	649	Joe Giradi	.10
332	Eli Whiteside RC	.20	438	Kirk Saarloos	.10	544	Alex Sanchez	.10	650	Todd Ritchie	.10
333	Juan Rivera	.10	439	Cliff Lee	.10	545	Trey Lunsford	.10	651	Lou Merloni	.10
334	Jeff Conine	.10	440	Ryan Ludwick	.10	546	Abraham Nunez	.10	652	Shawn Wooten	.10
335	John McDonald	.10	441	Derrek Lee	.10	547	Mike Lincoln	.10	653	David Riske	.10
336	Erik Hiljus	.10	442	Bobby Abreu	.20	548	Orlando Hernandez	.10	654	Luis Rivas	.10
337	David Eckstein	.10	443	Dustan Mohr	.10	549	Kevin Mench	.10	655	Roy Halladay	.10
338	Jeff Bagwell	.50	444	Nook Logan RC	.25	550	Garret Anderson	.25	656	Travis Driskill	.10
339	Matt Holliday	.25	445	Seth McClung	.10	551	Kyle Farnsworth	.10	657	Ricky Ledee	.10
340	Jeff Liefer	.10	446	Miguel Olivo	.10	552	Kevin Olsen	.10	658	Tony Perez	.10
341	Greg Myers	.10	447	Henry Blanco	.10	553	Joel Pineiro	.10	659	Fernando Rodney	.10
342	Scott Sauerbeck	.10	448	Seung Jun Song	.10	554	Jorge Julio	.10	660	Trevor Hoffman	.10
343	Omar Infante	.10	449	Kris Wilson	.10	555	Jose Mesa	.10	661	Pat Hentgen	.10
344	Ryan Langerhans	.10	450	Xavier Nady	.10	556	Jorge Posada	.40	662	Bret Boone	.10
345	Abraham Nunez	.10	451	Corky Miller	.10	557	Jose Ortiz	.10	663	Ryan Jensen	.10
346	Mike MacDougal	.10	452	Jim Thome	.50	558	Mike Tonis	.10	664	Ricardo Rodriguez	.10
347	Travis Phelps	.10	453	George Lombard	.10	559	Gabe White	.10	665	Jeremy Lambert	.10
348	Dan Reichert	.10	454	Rey Ordonez	.10	560	Rafael Furcal	.10	666	Troy Percival	.10
349	Alex Rodriguez	1.50	455	Deivis Santos	.10	561	Matt Franco	.10	667	Jon Rauch	.10
350	Bobby Seay	.10	456	Mike Myers	.10	562	Trey Hodges	.10	668	Mariano Rivera	.25
351	Ichiro Suzuki	1.00	457	Edgar Renteria	.10	563	Esteban German	.10	669	Jason LaRue	.10
352	Brandon Inge	.10	458	Braden Looper	.10	564	Josh Fogg	.10	670	J.C. Romero	.10
353	Jack Wilson	.10	459	Guillermo Mota	.10	565	Fernando Tatis	.10	671	Cody Ross	.10
354	John Ennis	.10	460	Scott Rolen	.50	566	Alex Cintron	.10	672	Eric Byrnes	.10
355	Jamal Strong	.10	461	Lance Berkman	.10	567	Grant Roberts	.10	673	Paul LoDuca	.10
356	Jason Jennings	.10	462	Jeff Heaverlo	.10	568	Gene Stechschulte	.10	674	Brad Fullmer	.10
357	Jeff Kent	.20	463	Ramon Hernandez	.10	569	Rafael Palmeiro	.25	675	Cliff Politte	.10
358	Scott Chiasson	.10	464	Jason Simontacchi	.10	570	Mike Hampton	.10	676	Justin Miller	.10
359	Jeremy Griffiths	.10	465	So Taguchi	.10	571	Ben Davis	.10	677	Nic Jackson	.10
360	Paul Konerko	.10	466	Dave Veres	.10	572	Dean Palmer	.10	678	Kris Benson	.10
361	Jeff Austin	.10	467	Shane Loux	.10	573	Jerrod Riggan	.10	679	Carl Sadler	.10
362	Todd Van Poppel	.10	468	Rodrigo Lopez	.10	574	Nate Frese	.10	680	Joe Nathan	.10
363	Sun-Woo Kim	.10	469	Bubba Trammell	.10	575	Josh Phelps	.10	681	Julio Santana	.10
364	Jerry Hairston	.10	470	Scott Sullivan	.10	576	Freddie Bynum	.10	682	Wade Miller	.10
365	Tony Torcato	.10	471	Mike Mussina	.40	577	Morgan Ensberg	.10	683	Josh Pearce	.10
366	Arthur Rhodes	.10	472	Ramon Ortiz	.10	578	Juan Rincon	.10	684	Tony Armas	.10
367	Jose Jimenez	.10	473	Lyle Overbay	.10	579	Kazuhiro Sasaki	.40	685	Al Leiter	.10
368	Matt LeCroy	.10	474	Mike Lowell	.10	580	Yorvit Torrealba	.10	686	Raul Ibanez	.10
369	Curtis Lesanic	.10	475	Greg Vaughn	.10	581	Tim Wakefield	.10	687	Danny Bautista	.10
370	Ramon Vasquez	.10	476	Larry Bigbie	.10	582	Sterling Hitchcock	.10	688	Travis Hafner	.10
371	Joe Randa	.10	477	Rey Sanchez	.10	583	Craig Paquette	.10	689	Rylan Reed RC	.20
372	John Franco	.10	478	Magglio Ordonez	.25	584	Kevin Millwood	.25	690	Pedro J. Martinez	.75
373	Charles Johnson	.10	479	Rondell White	.10	585	Damian Rolls	.10	691	Ramon Santiago	.10
374	Craig Wilson	.10	480	Jay Witasick	.10	586	Brad Baisley	.10	692	Felipe Lopez	.10
375	Michael Young	.10	481	Jimmy Rollins	.25	587	Kyle Snyder	.10	693	David Ross	.10
376	Mark Ellis	.10	482	Mike Maroth	.10	588	Paul Quantrill	.10	694	Chone Figgins	.10
377	Joe Mauer	.25	483	Mark Quinn	.10	589	Trot Nixon	.10	695	Antonio Osuna	.10
378	Checklist	.10	484	Nick Neugebauer	.10	590	J.T. Snow	.10	696	Jay Powell	.10
379	Jason Kendall	.10	485	Victor Zambrano	.10	591	Kevin Young	.10	697	Roy Smith	.10

698	Alexis Rios	.10
699	Tanyon Sturtze	.10
700	Turk Wendell	.10
701	Richard Hidalgo	.10
702	Joe Mays	.10
703	Jorge Sosa	.10
704	Eric Karros	.10
705	Steve Finley	.10
706	Sean Smith	.10
707	Jeremy Giambi	.10
708	Scott Hodges	.10
709	Vicente Padilla	.10
710	Bert Snow	.10
711	Aaron Rowand	.10
712	Dennis Tankersley	.10
713	Rick Bauer	.10
714	Tim Olson **RC**	.25
715	Jeff Urban	.10
716	Steve Sparks	.10
717	Glendon Rusch	.10
718	Ricky Stone	.10
719	Benji Gil	.10
720	Pete Walker	.10
721	Tim Worrell	.10
722	Michael Tejera	.10
723	David Kelton	.10
724	Britt Reames	.10
725	John Stephens	.10
726	Mark McLemore	.10
727	Jeff Zimmerman	.10
728	Checklist	.10
729	Andres Torres	.10
730	Checklist	.10
731	Johan Santana	.10
732	Dane Sardinha	.10
733	Rodrigo Rosario	.10
734	Frank Thomas	.50
735	Tom Glavine	.25
736	Doug Mirabelli	.10
737	Juan Uribe	.10
738	Ryan Anderson	.10
739	Sean Burroughs	.10
740	Eric Chavez	.25
741	Enrique Wilson	.10
742	Elmer Dessens	.10
743	Marlon Byrd	.10
744	Brendan Donnelly	.10
745	Gary Bennett	.10
746	Roy Oswalt	.25
747	Andy Van Hekken	.10
748	Jesus Colome	.10
749	Erick Almonte	.10
750	Frank Catalanotto	.10
751	Matt Herges	.10
752	Carlos Delgado	.40
753	Ryan Franklin	.10
754	Wilken Ruan	.10
755	Kelvim Escobar	.10
756	Tim Drew	.10
757	Jarrod Washburn	.10
758	Runelvys Hernandez	.10
759	Cory Vance	.10
760	Doug Glanville	.10
761	Ryan Rupe	.10
762	Jermaine Dye	.10
763	Mike Cameron	.10
764	Scott Erickson	.10
765	Richie Sexson	.25
766	Jose Vidro	.10
767	Brian West	.10
768	Shawn Estes	.10
769	Brian Tallet	.10
770	Larry Walker	.25
771	Josh Hamilton	.10
772	Orlando Hudson	.10
773	Justin Morneau	.20
774	Ryan Bukvich	.10
775	Mike Gonzalez	.10
776	Tsuyoshi Shinjo	.10
777	Matt Mantei	.10
778	Jimmy Journell	.10
779	Brian Lawrence	.10
780	Mike Lieberthal	.10
781	Scott Mullen	.10
782	Zach Day	.10
783	John Thomson	.10
784	Ben Sheets	.10
785	Damon Minor	.10
786	Jose Valentin	.10
787	Armando Benitez	.10
788	Jamie Walker	.10
789	Preston Wilson	.10
790	Josh Wilson	.10
791	Phil Nevin	.10
792	Roberto Hernandez	.10
793	Mike Williams	.10
794	Jake Peavy	.10
795	Paul Shuey	.10
796	Chad Bradford	.10
797	Bobby Jenks	.10
798	Sean Douglass	.10
799	Damian Miller	.10
800	Mark Wohlers	.10
801	Ty Wigginton	.10
802	Alfonso Soriano	1.00
803	Randy Johnson	.75

804	Placido Polanco	.10
805	Drew Henson	.10
806	Tony Womack	.10
807	Pokey Reese	.10
808	Albert Pujols	.75
809	Shane Reynolds	.10
810	Mike Rivera	.10
811	John Lackey	.10
812	Brian Wright **RC**	.20
813	Eric Good	.10
814	Dernell Stenson	.10
815	Kirk Rueter	.10
816	Todd Zeile	.10
817	Brad Thomas	.10
818	Shawn Sedlacek	.10
819	Garrett Stephenson	.10
820	Mark Teixeira	.25
821	Tim Hudson	.25
822	Mike Koplove	.10
823	Chris Reitsma	.10
824	Rafael Soriano	.10
825	Ugueth Urbina	.10
826	Matt White	.10
827	Colin Young	.10
828	Pat Strange	.10
829	Juan Pena	.10
830	Joe Thurston	.10
831	Shawn Green	.25
832	Pedro Astacio	.10
833	Danny Wright	.10
834	Weston O'Brien **RC**	.20
835	Luis Lopez	.10
836	Randall Simon	.10
837	Jaret Wright	.10
838	Jayson Werth	.10
839	Endy Chavez	.10
840	Checklist	.10
841	Chad Paronto	.10
842	Randy Winn	.10
843	Sidney Ponson	.10
844	Robin Ventura	.10
845	Rich Aurilia	.10
846	Joaquin Benoit	.10
847	Barry Bonds	2.00
848	Carl Crawford	.10
849	Jeromy Burnitz	.10
850	Orlando Cabrera	.10
851	Luis Vizcaino	.10
852	Randy Wolf	.10
853	Benny Agbayani	.10
854	Jeremy Affeldt	.10
855	Einar Diaz	.10
856	Carl Everett	.10
857	Wiki Gonzalez	.10
858	Steve Belcher	.10
859	Travis Harper	.10
860	Mike Piazza	1.25
861	Will Ohman	.10
862	Eric Young	.10
863	Jason Grabowski	.10
864	Rett Johnson **RC**	.20
865	Aubrey Huff	.10
866	John Smoltz	.10
867	Mickey Callaway	.10
868	Joe Kennedy	.10
869	Tim Redding	.10
870	Colby Lewis	.10
871	Salomon Torres	.10
872	Marco Scutaro	.10
873	Tony Batista	.10
874	Dmitri Young	.10
875	Scott Williamson	.10
876	Scott Spezio	.10
877	John Webb	.10
878	Jose Acevedo	.10
879	Kevin Orie	.10
880	Jacque Jones	.10
881	Ben Francisco **RC**	.25
882	Bobby Basham **RC**	.25
883	Corey Shafer **RC**	.20
884	J.D. Durbin **RC**	.10
885	Chien-Ming Wang **RC**	2.50
886	Adam Stern	.10
887	Wayne Lydon **RC**	.20
888	Derell McCall **RC**	.20
889	Jon Nelson **RC**	.20
890	Willie Eyre **RC**	.20
891	Ramon A. Martinez **RC**	.20
892	Adrian Myers **RC**	.20
893	Jamie Athas **RC**	.20
894	Ismael Castro **RC**	.20
895	David Martinez	.10
896	Terry Tiffee **RC**	.20
897	Nathan Panther **RC**	.25
898	Kyle Roat **RC**	.20
899	Kason Gabbard **RC**	.75
900	Hanley Ramirez **RC**	3.00
901	Bryan Grace **RC**	.15
902	B.J. Barns **RC**	.50
903	Greg Bruso **RC**	.15
904	Mike Neu **RC**	.15
905	Dustin Yount **RC**	.50
906	Shane Victorino **RC**	.20
907	Brian Burgamy **RC**	.20
908	Beau Kemp **RC**	.20
909	Eny Cabreja **RC**	.50

910	Dexter Cooper **RC**	.20
911	Chris Colton **RC**	.20
912	David Cash **RC**	.20
913	Bernie Castro **RC**	.20
914	Luis Hodge **RC**	.20
915	Jeff Clark **RC**	.20
916	Jason Kubel **RC**	1.00
917	T.J. Bohn **RC**	.20
918	Luke Steidlmayer **RC**	.20
919	Natthew Petterson	.10
920	Darrell Rasner	.10
921	Scott Tyler	.10
922	Gary Schneidmiller **RC**	.20
923	Kerry Wood	.40
924	Ryan Cameron **RC**	.20
925	Wilfredo Rodriguez	.10
926	Rajai Davis **RC**	.20
927	Evel Bastida-Martinez **RC**	.20
928	Chris Duncan **RC**	2.00
929	David Pember **RC**	.20
930	Branden Florence **RC**	.20
931	Eric Eckenstahler	.10
932	Hong-Chih Kuo **RC**	1.00
933	Il Kim **RC**	.20
934	Michael Garciaparra	.50
935	Tommy Whiteman **RC**	.10
936	Gary Harris **RC**	.20
937	Derry Hammond	.10
938	Joey Gomes	.10
939	Donald Hood **RC**	.20
940	Clay Hensley **RC**	.50
941	David Pahucki **RC**	.20
942	Wilton Reynolds **RC**	.20
943	Michael Hinckley **RC**	.20
944	Josh Willingham **RC**	.20
945	Pete LaForest **RC**	.20
946	Pete Smart **RC**	.10
947	Jay Stizman	.10
948	Mark Malaska **RC**	.20
949	Mike Gallo **RC**	.20
950	Tyler Martin **RC**	.20
951	Shane Victorino	.10
952	Ryan Howard	30.00
953	Daryl Clark **RC**	.20
954	Dayton Buller	.10
955	Carlos Zambrano	.10
956	Chris Booker	.10
957	Brandon Watson **RC**	.20
958	Matt DeMarco **RC**	.20
959	Doug Waechter **RC**	.75
960	Callix Crabbe **RC**	.20
961	Jairo Garcia **RC**	.20
962	Jason Perry **RC**	.20
963	Eric Riggs **RC**	.20
964	Travis Ishikawa **RC**	.40
965	Jorge Piedra **RC**	.20
966	Manuel Ramirez **RC**	.20
967	Tyler Johnson **RC**	.20
968	Jaime Bubela **RC**	.20
969	Haj Turay **RC**	.20
970	Tyson Graham **RC**	.20
971	David DeJesus **RC**	.20
972	Franklin Gutierrez **RC**	.20
973	Craig Brazell **RC**	1.00
974	Keith Stamler **RC**	.20
975	Jemel Spearman **RC**	.20
976	Kade Johnson **RC**	.10
977	Nick Trzesniak **RC**	.20
978	Bill Simon **RC**	.20
979	Matthew Hagen **RC**	.20
980	Kris Kroski **RC**	.20
981	Prentice Redman **RC**	.50
982	Kevin Randel **RC**	.20
983	Thomari Stori-Harden **RC**	.20
984	Brian Shackelford **RC**	.20
985	Mike Adams **RC**	.20
986	Brian McCann **RC**	5.00
987	Mike McNutt **RC**	.20
988	Aron Weston **RC**	.20
989	Dustin Moseley **RC**	.20
990	Bryan Bullington **RC**	1.50

Silver

Jim THOME

Stars (1-990):	1-2X
Inserted 1:1	

Award Winners

ALEX RODRIGUEZ

	NM/M
Complete Set (30):	20.00
Common Player:	.50
Inserted 1:12	
AW1	Barry Zito	.75
AW2	Randy Johnson	1.50
AW3	Miguel Tejada	.75
AW4	Barry Bonds	3.00
AW5	Sammy Sosa	2.00
AW6	Barry Bonds	3.00
AW7	Mike Piazza	2.50
AW8	Todd Helton	.75
AW9	Jeff Kent	.50
AW10	Edgar Renteria	.50
AW11	Scott Rolen	.75
AW12	Vladimir Guerrero	1.00
AW13	Mike Hampton	.50
AW14	Jason Giambi	1.50
AW15	Alfonso Soriano	1.50
AW16	Alex Rodriguez	3.00
AW17	Eric Chavez	.50
AW18	Jorge Posada	.50
AW19	Bernie Williams	.75
AW20	Magglio Ordonez	.50
AW21	Garret Anderson	.50
AW22	Manny Ramirez	1.00
AW23	Jason Jennings	.50
AW24	Eric Hinske	.50
AW25	Billy Koch	.50
AW26	John Smoltz	.50
AW27	Alex Rodriguez	3.00
AW28	Barry Bonds	3.00
AW29	Tony LaRussa	.50
AW30	Mike Scioscia	.50

Total Production

	NM/M
Complete Set (10):	10.00
Common Player:	.40
Inserted 1:18	
TP1	Barry Bonds	2.50
TP2	Manny Ramirez	.75
TP3	Albert Pujols	1.00
TP4	Jason Giambi	1.00
TP5	Magglio Ordonez	.40
TP6	Mike Piazza	1.50
TP7	Todd Helton	.75
TP8	Miguel Tejada	.50
TP9	Sammy Sosa	1.50
TP10	Alex Rodriguez	2.50

Total Signatures

	NM/M
Common Autograph:	
Inserted 1:176	
MB	Marlon Byrd	10.00

EM	Eli Marrero	8.00
BP	Brandon Phillips	10.00
MT	Marcus Thames	8.00
TT	Tony Torcato	8.00

Total Topps

		NM/M
Complete Set (50):		25.00
Common Player:		.25
Inserted 1:7		
TT1	Ichiro Suzuki	1.50
TT2	Alex Rodriguez	2.50
TT3	Barry Bonds	2.50
TT4	Jason Giambi	1.00
TT5	Troy Glaus	.75
TT6	Greg Maddux	1.50
TT7	Albert Pujols	1.00
TT8	Randy Johnson	1.00
TT9	Chipper Jones	1.50
TT10	Magglio Ordonez	.25
TT11	Jim Thome	.75
TT12	Jeff Kent	.50
TT13	Curt Schilling	.50
TT14	Alfonso Soriano	1.00
TT15	Rafael Palmeiro	.50
TT16	Carlos Delgado	.50
TT17	Torii Hunter	.50
TT18	Pat Burrell	.50
TT19	Adam Dunn	.75
TT20	Roberto Alomar	.50
TT21	Eric Chavez	.40
TT22	Derek Jeter	3.00
TT23	Nomar Garciaparra	2.00
TT24	Lance Berkman	.40
TT25	Jim Edmonds	.40
TT26	Todd Helton	.75
TT27	Sammy Sosa	1.50
TT28	Phil Nevin	.25
TT29	Andruw Jones	.40
TT30	Barry Zito	.40
TT31	Richie Sexson	.40
TT32	Ken Griffey Jr.	1.50
TT33	Gary Sheffield	.40
TT34	Shawn Green	.40
TT35	Mike Sweeney	.25
TT36	Mike Lowell	.25
TT37	Larry Walker	.25
TT38	Manny Ramirez	.75
TT39	Miguel Tejada	.40
TT40	Mike Piazza	2.00
TT41	Scott Rolen	.75
TT42	Brian Giles	.40
TT43	Garret Anderson	.40
TT44	Vladimir Guerrero	.75
TT45	Bartolo Colon	.25
TT46	Jorge Posada	.40
TT47	Ivan Rodriguez	.50
TT48	Ryan Klesko	.25
TT49	Jose Vidro	.25
TT50	Pedro J. Martinez	.75

2003 Topps Tribute

		NM/M
Complete Set (110):		300.00
Common Player:		1.00
Common Auto. (101-110):		10.00
Pack (5):		35.00
Box (6):		160.00
1	Jim Thome	2.50
2	Edgardo Alfonzo	1.00
3	Edgar Martinez	1.50
4	Scott Rolen	2.50
5	Eric Hinske	1.00
6	Mark Mulder	1.50
7	Jason Giambi	2.50
8	Bernie Williams	2.00
9	Cliff Floyd	1.00
10	Ichiro Suzuki	5.00
11	Pat Burrell	1.50
12	Garret Anderson	1.50
13	Gary Sheffield	1.50
14	Johnny Damon	3.00
15	Kerry Wood	1.50
16	Bartolo Colon	1.00
17	Adam Dunn	2.00
18	Omar Vizquel	1.50
19	Todd Helton	2.00
20	Nomar Garciaparra	4.00
21	A.J. Burnett	1.00
22	Craig Biggio	1.50
23	Carlos Beltran	2.50
24	Kazuhisa Ishii	1.00
25	Vladimir Guerrero	2.50
26	Roberto Alomar	2.00
27	Roger Clemens	6.00
28	Tim Hudson	2.00
29	Brian Giles	1.50
30	Barry Bonds	8.00
31	Jim Edmonds	1.50
32	Rafael Palmeiro	2.00
33	Francisco Rodriguez	1.00
34	Andruw Jones	2.00
35	Shea Hillenbrand	1.00
36	Moises Alou	1.50
37	Luis Gonzalez	1.00
38	Darin Erstad	1.00
39	John Smoltz	1.50
40	Derek Jeter	8.00
41	Aubrey Huff	1.50
42	Eric Chavez	1.50
43	Doug Mientkiewicz	1.00
44	Lance Berkman	2.00
45	Josh Beckett	1.50
46	Austin Kearns	1.50
47	Frank Thomas	2.50
48	Pedro J. Martinez	3.00
49	Tim Salmon	1.50
50	Alex Rodriguez	8.00
51	Ryan Klesko	1.00
52	Tom Glavine	1.50
53	Shawn Green	1.50
54	Jeff Kent	1.50
55	Carlos Pena	1.00
56	Paul Konerko	1.50
57	Troy Glaus	2.00
58	Manny Ramirez	2.50
59	Jason Jennings	1.00
60	Randy Johnson	3.00
61	Ivan Rodriguez	2.00
62	Roy Oswalt	1.50
63	Kevin Brown	1.50
64	Jose Vidro	1.00
65	Jorge Posada	1.50
66	Mike Piazza	5.00
67	Bret Boone	1.50
68	Carlos Delgado	2.00
69	Jimmy Rollins	2.00
70	Alfonso Soriano	3.00
71	Greg Maddux	5.00
72	Mark Prior	2.00
73	Jeff Bagwell	2.50
74	Richie Sexson	2.00
75	Sammy Sosa	4.00
76	Curt Schilling	2.00
77	Mike Sweeney	1.00
78	Torii Hunter	1.50
79	Larry Walker	1.50
80	Miguel Tejada	1.50
81	Rich Aurilia	1.00
82	Bobby Abreu	1.50
83	Phil Nevin	1.00
84	Rodrigo Lopez	1.00
85	Chipper Jones	3.00
86	Ken Griffey Jr.	5.00
87	Mike Lowell	1.00
88	Magglio Ordonez	1.50
89	Barry Zito	1.50
90	Albert Pujols	8.00
91	Corey Shafer RC	2.00
92	Dan Haren	5.00
93	Jeremy Bonderman	6.00
94	Branden Florence RC	2.00
95	Evel Bastida-Martinez RC	2.00
96	Brian Wright RC	2.00
97	Elizardo Ramirez RC	2.00
98	Michael Garciaparra	2.00
99	Clay Hensley RC	3.00
100	Bobby Basham RC	2.00
101	Jose Contreras RC	20.00
102	Bryan Bullington RC	20.00
103	Joey Gomes	10.00
104	Craig Brazell RC	15.00
105	Andy Marte RC	25.00
106	Hanley Ramirez RC	80.00
107	Ryan Shealy RC	25.00
108	Daryl Clark RC	10.00
109	Tyler Johnson RC	15.00
110	Ben Francisco RC	10.00

Red Proof

Stars (1-100):	2-4X
Production 225	
Autos (101-110):	1-2.5X
Production 50	

Gold Proof

Cards (1-100):	No Pricing
Production 25	
Autos. (101-110) are 1 of 1.	

Solo Bonds

		NM/M
Premiere Proof:		1.5X
Production 50		
SB	Barry Bonds	25.00

Double Bonds

		NM/M
Premiere Proof:		1.5X
Production 50		
BT-DB	Barry Bonds	40.00

Triple Bonds

		NM/M
Premiere Proof:		1.5X
Production 50		
TB	Barry Bonds	60.00

Matching Marks Dual Relics

		NM/M
Common Duo:		10.00
Premiere Proofs:		1.5X
Production 50		
PH	Rafael Palmeiro, Rickey Henderson	15.00
GR	Nomar Garciaparra, Alex Rodriguez	25.00
AP	Roberto Alomar, Rafael Palmeiro	15.00
MP	Fred McGriff, Rafael Palmeiro	10.00
HR	Rickey Henderson, Manny Ramirez	15.00
RP	Manny Ramirez, Mike Piazza	20.00
BG	Jeff Bagwell, Juan Gonzalez	10.00
BP	Barry Bonds, Rafael Palmeiro	35.00
SB	Sammy Sosa, Jeff Bagwell	20.00
SG	Alfonso Soriano, Vladimir Guerrero	15.00
PS	Rafael Palmeiro, Sammy Sosa	20.00
MG	Fred McGriff, Juan Gonzalez	10.00
PA	Rafael Palmeiro, Roberto Alomar	15.00

Memorable Materials

		NM/M
Common Player:		8.00
Premiere Proofs:		1.5X
Production 50		
BB	Barry Bonds	30.00
JG	Jason Giambi	8.00
JG2	Jason Giambi	8.00
TG	Troy Glaus	8.00
LG	Luis Gonzalez	8.00
SG	Shawn Green	8.00
VG	Vladimir Guerrero	10.00
RH	Rickey Henderson	8.00
TH	Torii Hunter	8.00
AJ	Andruw Jones	8.00
GM	Greg Maddux	15.00
AP	Albert Pujols	20.00
CR	Cal Ripken Jr.	45.00
AR	Alex Rodriguez	15.00
AS	Alfonso Soriano	10.00
SS	Sammy Sosa	15.00
SS2	Sammy Sosa	15.00
MT	Miguel Tejada	8.00
KW	Kerry Wood	8.00

Milestone Materials

		NM/M
Common Player:		8.00
Premiere Proofs:		1.5X
Production 50		
RA	Roberto Alomar	10.00
JB1	Jeff Bagwell	10.00
JB2	Jeff Bagwell	10.00
BB1	Barry Bonds	25.00
BB2	Barry Bonds	25.00
BB3	Barry Bonds	25.00
BB4	Barry Bonds	25.00
BB5	Barry Bonds	25.00
NG	Nomar Garciaparra	20.00
JG1	Juan Gonzalez	10.00
JG2	Juan Gonzalez	10.00
VG	Vladimir Guerrero	10.00
TH	Todd Helton	10.00
RH1	Rickey Henderson	10.00
RH2	Rickey Henderson	10.00
RH3	Rickey Henderson	10.00
RH4	Rickey Henderson	10.00
RH5	Rickey Henderson	10.00
CJ	Chipper Jones	12.00
FM1	Fred McGriff	8.00
FM2	Fred McGriff	8.00
FM3	Fred McGriff	8.00
RP1	Rafael Palmeiro	10.00
RP2	Rafael Palmeiro	10.00
RP3	Rafael Palmeiro	10.00
RP4	Rafael Palmeiro	10.00
MP1	Mike Piazza	15.00
MP2	Mike Piazza	15.00
MR1	Manny Ramirez	10.00
MR2	Manny Ramirez	10.00
AR	Alex Rodriguez	15.00
SS1	Sammy Sosa	15.00
SS2	Sammy Sosa	15.00
SS3	Sammy Sosa	15.00
FT	Frank Thomas	12.00

Modern Marks Autographs

		NM/M
Common Autograph:		10.00
Premiere Proofs:		1.5X
Production 50		
LB	Lance Berkman	20.00
RC	Roger Clemens	120.00
CF	Cliff Floyd	10.00
EH	Eric Hinske	10.00
TH	Torii Hunter	15.00
PK	Paul Konerko	15.00
PL	Paul LoDuca	15.00
MO	Magglio Ordonez	20.00
JP	Josh Phelps	

Perennial All-Stars Relics

		NM/M
Common Player:		8.00
Premiere Proofs:		1.5X
Production 50		
RA	Roberto Alomar	10.00
CB	Craig Biggio	8.00
BB	Barry Bonds	25.00
RC	Roger Clemens	20.00
RH	Rickey Henderson	15.00
CJ	Chipper Jones	10.00
GM	Greg Maddux	15.00
EM	Edgar Martinez	15.00
EM	Pedro J. Martinez	15.00
MM	Mike Mussina	10.00
MP	Mike Piazza	20.00
MR	Manny Ramirez	10.00
AR	Alex Rodriguez	15.00
IR	Ivan Rodriguez	8.00
BS	Benito Santiago	8.00
CS	Curt Schilling	8.00
GS	Gary Sheffield	8.00
JS	John Smoltz	8.00
SS	Sammy Sosa	20.00
FT	Frank Thomas	10.00
LW	Larry Walker	8.00
BW	Bernie Williams	10.00

Performance Tribute Doubles

		NM/M
Common Duo:		10.00
Premiere Proofs:		1.5X
Production 50		
ZJ	Barry Zito, Randy Johnson	15.00
SA	Alfonso Soriano, Roberto Alomar	15.00
RR	Cal Ripken Jr., Alex Rodriguez	60.00
RT	Alex Rodriguez, Miguel Tejada	15.00
GG	Luis Gonzalez, Troy Glaus	10.00
PW	Albert Pujols, Kerry Wood	25.00
RG	Alex Rodriguez, Nomar Garciaparra	30.00
BJ	Barry Bonds, Chipper Jones	25.00

		NM/M
SG	Sammy Sosa, Juan Gonzalez	15.00
PS	Mike Piazza, Benito Santiago	15.00
PR	Mike Piazza, Ivan Rodriguez	15.00
MM	Pedro J. Martinez, Greg Maddux	15.00
CM	Roger Clemens, Greg Maddux	35.00
JP	Chipper Jones, Mike Piazza	20.00

Performance Tribute Triples

		NM/M
Common Trio:		20.00
Premiere Proofs:		1.5X
Production 50		
SMP	Sammy Sosa, Rafael Palmeiro, Fred McGriff	25.00
CMJ	Roger Clemens, Greg Maddux, Randy Johnson	30.00
RHP	Manny Ramirez, Mike Piazza, Rickey Henderson	30.00
STB	Sammy Sosa, Frank Thomas, Jeff Bagwell	20.00
BMP	Barry Bonds, Fred McGriff, Rafael Palmeiro	30.00

Team Tribute Doubles

		NM/M
Common Duo:		10.00
Premiere Proofs:		1.5X
Production 50		
MS	Greg Maddux, John Smoltz	35.00
IN	Kazuhisa Ishii, Hideo Nomo	25.00
WH	Larry Walker, Todd Helton	10.00
BB	Craig Biggio, Jeff Bagwell	15.00
RP	Alex Rodriguez, Rafael Palmeiro	15.00
GR	Nomar Garciaparra, Manny Ramirez	20.00

Team Tribute Triples

		NM/M
Common Trio:		15.00
Premiere Proofs:		1.5X
Production 50		
JSJ	Andruw Jones, Gary Sheffield, Chipper Jones	30.00
GRM	Nomar Garciaparra, Manny Ramirez, Pedro J. Martinez	40.00
ASP	Moises Alou, Sammy Sosa, Corey Patterson	30.00
TOK	Frank Thomas, Magglio Ordonez, Paul Konerko	20.00
BBB	Craig Biggio, Lance Berkman, Jeff Bagwell	20.00
MHM	Joe Mauer, Torii Hunter, Doug Mientkiewicz	25.00
SGV	Alfonso Soriano, Jason Giambi, Robin Ventura	25.00
CTM	Eric Chavez, Miguel Tejada, Mark Mulder	15.00

		NM/M
HZM	Tim Hudson, Barry Zito, Mark Mulder	25.00
TBB	Jim Thome, Marlon Byrd, Pat Burrell	25.00
MOB	Edgar Martinez, John Olerud, Bret Boone	20.00
PER	Albert Pujols, Jim Edmonds, Scott Rolen	40.00
RGP	Alex Rodriguez, Juan Gonzalez, Rafael Palmeiro	25.00
RBT	Alex Rodriguez, Hank Blalock, Mark Teixeira	25.00

Tribute to the Stars

		NM/M
Common Player:		10.00
Premiere Proofs:		1.5X
Production 50		
RA	Roberto Alomar	15.00
GA	Garret Anderson	15.00
LB	Lance Berkman	10.00
BB	Barry Bonds	50.00
PB	Pat Burrell	15.00
EC	Eric Chavez	15.00
AD	Adam Dunn	15.00
NG	Nomar Garciaparra	40.00
TG	Troy Glaus	15.00
VG	Vladimir Guerrero	15.00
TH	Todd Helton	15.00
RH	Rickey Henderson	15.00
THU	Torii Hunter	10.00
AJ	Andruw Jones	10.00
CJ	Chipper Jones	15.00
GM	Greg Maddux	20.00
RP	Rafael Palmeiro	10.00
MP	Mike Piazza	20.00
AP	Albert Pujols	40.00
AR	Alex Rodriguez	30.00
AS	Alfonso Soriano	15.00
SS	Sammy Sosa	25.00
FT	Frank Thomas	15.00
JT	Jim Thome	15.00
LW	Larry Walker	10.00

Tribute to the Stars Patchworks

		NM/M
Common Player:		25.00
Production 50 Sets		
JB	Jeff Bagwell	35.00
BB	Barry Bonds	80.00
NG	Nomar Garciaparra	50.00
LG	Luis Gonzalez	25.00
SG	Shawn Green	25.00
TH	Todd Helton	35.00
THU	Torii Hunter	25.00
RJ	Randy Johnson	40.00
CJ	Chipper Jones	35.00
GM	Greg Maddux	50.00
PM	Pedro J. Martinez	40.00
RP	Rafael Palmeiro	30.00
AP	Albert Pujols	80.00
MR	Manny Ramirez	35.00
AR	Alex Rodriguez	50.00
AR2	Alex Rodriguez	50.00
CS	Curt Schilling	25.00
SS	Sammy Sosa	40.00
FT	Frank Thomas	35.00
KW	Kerry Wood	30.00

40/40 Club

		NM/M
Premiere Proof:		1.5X
Production 50		
CBR	Jose Canseco, Barry Bonds, Alex Rodriguez	85.00

600 HR Club Relic

		NM/M
Premiere Proofs:		1.5X
Production 50		
Gold:		No Pricing
Production One Set		
HA-600	Hank Aaron	35.00
BB-600	Barry Bonds	30.00
WM-600	Willie Mays	45.00
BR-600	Babe Ruth	125.00

600 HR Club Double Relic

		NM/M
Premiere Proofs:		1.5X
Production 50		
BA-600	Barry Bonds, Hank Aaron	80.00
BA-600	Barry Bonds, Willie Mays	80.00
BA-600	Barry Bonds, Babe Ruth	200.00

600 HR Club Quad Relic

		NM/M
Premiere Proof:		1X
Production 25		
BA-600	Hank Aaron, Babe Ruth, Willie Mays, Barry Bonds	625.00

2003 Topps Tribute All-Star Edition

		NM/M
Complete Set (50):		50.00
Common Player:		1.00
Pack (5):		40.00
Box (6):		200.00
1	Willie Mays	8.00
2	Don Mattingly	8.00
3	Hoyt Wilhelm	1.00
4	Hank Aaron	8.00
5	Hank Greenberg	1.00
6	Johnny Bench	5.00
7	Duke Snider	3.00
8	Carl Yastrzemski	3.00
9	Jim Palmer	1.00
10	Roberto Clemente	8.00
11	Mike Schmidt	8.00
12	Joe Cronin	1.00
13	Lou Brock	1.00
14	Orlando Cepeda	1.00
15	Bill Mazeroski	1.00
16	Whitey Ford	3.00
17	Rod Carew	1.00
18	Joe Morgan	1.00
19	Luis Aparicio	1.00
20	Nolan Ryan	10.00
21	Bobby Doerr	1.00
22	Dale Murphy	2.00
23	Bob Feller	1.00
24	Paul Molitor	2.00
25	Tom Seaver	3.00
26	Ozzie Smith	3.00
27	Stan Musial	6.00
28	Willie McCovey	1.00
29	Gary Carter	1.00
30	Reggie Jackson	3.00
31	Gaylord Perry	1.00
32	George Brett	8.00
33	Rocky Colavito	1.00
34	Wade Boggs	2.00
35	Cal Ripken Jr.	8.00
36	Carlton Fisk	1.00
37	Al Kaline	3.00
38	Kirby Puckett	4.00
39	Phil Rizzuto	2.00
40	Willie Stargell	1.00
41	Harmon Killebrew	3.00

42	Red Schoendienst	1.00
43	Tony Gwynn	3.00
44	Ralph Kiner	1.00
45	Yogi Berra	4.00
46	Jim "Catfish" Hunter	1.00
47	Frank Robinson	2.00
48	Ernie Banks	4.00
49	Warren Spahn	2.00
50	Brooks Robinson	3.00

Premier Proof

Cards (1-50): 4-8X
Numbered to last two digits of 1st
All-Star Year.

1st Class Cuts

		NM/M
Production One Set		
FC-TC	Ty Cobb (3/03 Auction)	7,600
FC-DD	Dizzy Dean	
FC-LG	Lou Gehrig	
FC-JR	Jackie Robinson (3/03 Auction)	3,500
FC-BR	Babe Ruth (6/04 Auction)	7,300
FC-TS	Tris Speaker	
FC-HW	Honus Wagner	

All-Star Signing

		NM/M
Common Autograph:		40.00
Premier Proofs:		1.5-2X
Production 25 Sets		
LB	Lou Brock	50.00
GC	Gary Carter	40.00
OC	Orlando Cepeda	40.00
AD	Andre Dawson	40.00
TG	Tony Gwynn	80.00
AK	Al Kaline	75.00
DMA	Don Mattingly	125.00
DM	Dale Murphy	75.00
JP	Jim Palmer	40.00
MS	Mike Schmidt	100.00
DSN	Duke Snider	45.00

Memorable Match-up Relic

		NM/M
Common Card:		50.00
Production 150 Sets		
Premier Proofs:		1.5-2X
Production 25 Sets		
YB	Carl Yastrzemski, Johnny Bench	70.00
BS	George Brett, Mike Schmidt	120.00
MJ	Willie Mays, Reggie Jackson	65.00
BF	Johnny Bench, Carlton Fisk	50.00
CM	Gary Carter, Don Mattingly	85.00
KA	Harmon Killebrew, Hank Aaron	125.00
BG	Wade Boggs, Tony Gwynn	60.00
PG	Kirby Puckett, Tony Gwynn	60.00
YBR	Carl Yastrzemski, Lou Brock	60.00

Perennial Patch Relics

		NM/M
Common Player:		40.00
Production 30 Sets		
WB	Wade Boggs	75.00
GB	George Brett	220.00
GC	Gary Carter	40.00
TG	Tony Gwynn	125.00
HK	Harmon Killebrew	90.00
WM	Willie McCovey	40.00
JM	Joe Morgan	40.00
DMU	Dale Murphy	120.00
CR	Cal Ripken Jr.	225.00
NR	Nolan Ryan/Rangers	200.00
NRA	Nolan Ryan/Astros	200.00
MS	Mike Schmidt	200.00
OS	Ozzie Smith	120.00
WS	Willie Stargell	75.00
CY	Carl Yastrzemski	190.00

Tribute Relics

		NM/M
Common Player:		10.00
Inserted 1:1		
HA	Hank Aaron	35.00
LA	Luis Aparicio	10.00
EB	Ernie Banks	20.00
JBE	Johnny Bench	20.00
YB	Yogi Berra	40.00
WB	Wade Boggs	15.00
GB	George Brett	20.00
LB	Lou Brock/bat	30.00
LBU	Lou Brock/Jersey	15.00
RCA	Roy Campanella	20.00
ROD	Rod Carew	15.00
GC	Gary Carter	10.00
OC	Orlando Cepeda	12.00
RC	Roberto Clemente	60.00
TC	Ty Cobb	100.00
JCR	Joe Cronin	15.00
AD	Andre Dawson	10.00
DD	Dizzy Dean	40.00
BD	Bobby Doerr	10.00
BF	Bob Feller	15.00
CF	Carlton Fisk	15.00
WF	Whitey Ford	30.00
JF	Jimmie Foxx	40.00
LG	Lou Gehrig	125.00
HG	Hank Greenberg	40.00
TG	Tony Gwynn	20.00
RH	Rogers Hornsby	40.00
CH	Jim "Catfish" Hunter	20.00
RJ	Reggie Jackson	15.00
AK	Al Kaline	25.00
HK	Harmon Killebrew	20.00
NL	Napoleon Lajoie	60.00
EM	Eddie Mathews	15.00
DMA	Don Mattingly	30.00
WM	Willie Mays	40.00
BM	Bill Mazeroski	20.00
WMC	Willie McCovey	18.00
JMI	Johnny Mize	30.00
PM	Paul Molitor	15.00
JMO	Joe Morgan	10.00
TM	Thurman Munson	30.00
DM	Dale Murphy	50.00
SM	Stan Musial	30.00
DN	Don Newcombe	10.00
MO	Mel Ott	30.00
JP	Jim Palmer	10.00
KP	Kirby Puckett	20.00
CRB	Cal Ripken Jr.	40.00
PR	Phil Rizzuto	15.00
BRO	Brooks Robinson	15.00
FR	Frank Robinson	10.00
JR	Jackie Robinson	40.00
BR	Babe Ruth	140.00
NR	Nolan Ryan/Rangers	40.00
NRA	Nolan Ryan/Astros	40.00
MS	Mike Schmidt	20.00
RS	Red Schoendienst	15.00
TSE	Tom Seaver	25.00
OS	Ozzie Smith	15.00
DSN	Duke Snider	20.00
TS	Tris Speaker	75.00
WST	Willie Stargell	20.00
HW	Honus Wagner	125.00
WHI	Hoyt Wilhelm	10.00
CY	Carl Yastrzemski	30.00

2003 Topps Tribute World Series

		NM/M
Complete Set (150):		150.00
Common Player:		1.00
Pack (5):		50.00
Box (5):		260.00
1	Willie Mays	8.00
2	Gary Carter	1.50
3	Yogi Berra	4.00
4	Dennis Eckersley	1.50
5	Willie McCovey	1.50
6	Willie Stargell	2.00
7	Mike Schmidt	8.00
8	Robin Yount	4.00
9	Bucky Harris	1.00
10	Carl Yastrzemski	4.00
11	Lenny Dykstra	1.00
12	Boog Powell	1.00
13	Bill Lee	1.00
14	Lou Brock	1.50
15	Bob Friend	1.00
16	Hank Greenberg	1.50
17	Maury Wills	1.00
18	Tommy Lasorda	1.00
19	Bill "Moose" Skowron	1.00
20	Frank Robinson	2.00
21	Rollie Fingers	1.00
22	Doug DeCinces	1.00
23	Eric Davis	1.00
24	Johnny Podres	1.00
25	Darrell Evans	1.00
26	Ron Cey	1.00
27	Ray Knight	1.00
28	Don Larsen	1.00
29	Harold Baines	1.00
30	Brooks Robinson	4.00
31	Wade Boggs	2.00
32	Joe Morgan	1.00
33	Kirk Gibson	1.00
34	Tommy John	1.00
35	Monte Irvin	2.00
36	Rich "Goose" Gossage	1.00
37	Tug McGraw	1.00
38	Walt Weiss	1.00
39	Bill Madlock	1.00
40	Juan Marichal	2.00
41	Willie McGee	1.00
42	Joe Cronin	1.00
43	Paul Blair	1.00
44	Norm Cash	1.00
45	Ken Griffey Sr.	1.00
46	Bret Saberhagen	1.00
47	Don Sutton	1.00
48	Kirby Puckett	4.00
49	Keith Hernandez	1.00
50	George Brett	8.00
51	Bobby Richardson	1.00
52	Jose Canseco	2.00
53	Greg Luzinski	1.00
54	Bill Mazeroski	1.00
55	Red Schoendienst	1.00
56	Graig Nettles	1.00
57	Jerry Koosman	1.00
58	Tony Perez	1.00
59	Jim Rice	1.00
60	Duke Snider	4.00
61	David Justice	1.00
62	Johnny Sain	1.00
63	Chuck Klein	1.00
64	Sparky Anderson	1.00
65	Alan Trammell	2.00
66	Willie Wilson	1.00
67	Hoyt Wilhelm	1.00
68	Joe Pepitone	1.00
69	Darren Daulton	1.00
70	Tom Seaver	4.00
71	Jim "Catfish" Hunter	1.00
72	Tim McCarver	1.00
73	Dave Parker	1.00
74	Earl Weaver	1.00
75	Ted Kluszewski	1.00
76	John Kruk	1.00
77	Dwight Evans	1.00
78	Ron Darling	1.00
79	Tony Oliva	1.00
80	Johnny Bench	5.00
81	Sam Crawford	1.00
82	Steve Yeager	1.00
83	Paul Molitor	2.00
84	Bert Campaneris	1.00
85	Mickey Rivers	1.00
86	Vince Coleman	1.00
87	Kent Tekulve	1.00
88	Dwight Gooden	1.00
89	Whitey Herzog	1.00
90	Whitey Ford	4.00
91	Warren Spahn	3.00
92	Fred Lynn	1.00
93	Joe Tinker	1.00
94	Bill Buckner	1.00
95	Bob Feller	2.00
96	Hank Bauer	1.00
97	Joe Rudi	1.00
98	Steve Sax	1.00
99	Bruce Sutter	1.50
100	Nolan Ryan	10.00
101	Bobby Thomson	1.00
102	Bob Watson	1.00
103	Vida Blue	1.00
104	Robin Roberts	1.00
105	Orlando Cepeda	2.00
106	Jim Bottomley	1.00
107	Heinie Manush	1.00
108	Jim Gilliam	1.00
109	Dave Concepcion	1.00
110	Al Kaline	5.00
111	Howard Johnson	1.00
112	Phil Rizzuto	2.00
113	Steve Garvey	1.00
114	George Foster	1.00
115	Carlton Fisk	2.00
116	Don Newcombe	1.00
117	Lance Parrish	1.00
118	Reggie Jackson	4.00
119	Luis Aparicio	1.00
120	Jim Palmer	1.50
121	Ron Guidry	1.00
122	Frankie Frisch	1.00
123	Chet Lemon	1.00
124	Cecil Cooper	1.00
125	Harmon Killebrew	4.00
126	Luis Tiant	1.00
127	John McGraw	1.00
128	Paul O'Neill	1.00
129	Jack Clark	1.00
130	Stan Musial	6.00
131	Mike Schmidt	4.00
132	Kirby Puckett	2.00
133	Carlton Fisk	1.50
134	Bill Mazeroski	1.00
135	Johnny Podres	1.00
136	Robin Yount	1.50
137	David Justice	1.00
138	Bobby Thomson	1.00
139	Joe Carter	1.00
140	Reggie Jackson	1.50
141	Kirk Gibson	1.00
142	Whitey Ford	1.50
143	Don Larsen	1.50
144	Duke Snider	1.50
145	Carl Yastrzemski	1.50
146	Johnny Bench	2.00
147	Lou Brock	1.00
148	Ted Kluszewski	1.00
149	Jim Palmer	1.00
150	Willie Mays	5.00

Gold

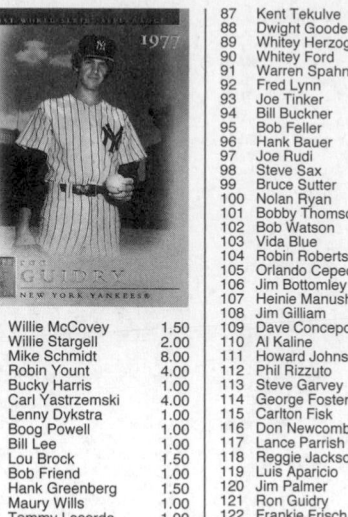

Golds (1-150): 4-8X
Production 100 Sets

Autographed Relic

	NM/M
Inserted 1:55	

Golds: No Pricing
Production 25 Sets

LB	Lou Brock	40.00
JC	Jose Canseco	40.00
CF	Carlton Fisk	120.00
HK	Harmon Killebrew	75.00
WM	Willie Mays	275.00
BM	Bill Mazeroski	60.00
MS	Mike Schmidt	100.00
BT	Bobby Thomson	40.00

Cut Signature Relic

No pricing due to scarcity.
Production One Set

Fan Fare Relic

	NM/M
Common Player:	10.00

Inserted 1:Box

HB	Hank Bauer	10.00
YB	Yogi Berra	20.00
WF	Whitey Ford	15.00
DJ	David Justice	10.00
DL	Don Larsen	15.00
BM	Billy Martin	15.00
DN	Don Newcombe	10.00
PO	Paul O'Neill	15.00
JP	Johnny Podres	15.00
PR	Phil Rizzuto	15.00
MS	Bill "Moose" Skowron	10.00
DS	Duke Snider	15.00

Memorabilia Match-Up Relic

	NM/M

Common Player:
Varying quantities produced

WC	Honus Wagner, Ty Cobb/9	
CR	Eddie Collins, Edd Roush/19	
GF	Hank Greenberg, Frankie Frisch/34	90.00
GK	Hank Greenberg, Chuck Klein/35	90.00
PR	Phil Rizzuto, Willie Mays/51	150.00
FS	Whitey Ford, Duke Snider/53	75.00
AS	Luis Aparicio, Duke Snider/59	35.00
MF	Bill Mazeroski, Whitey Ford/60	50.00
KB	Al Kaline, Lou Brock/68	75.00
RS	Frank Robinson, Tom Seaver/69	40.00
RBE	Brooks Robinson, Johnny Bench/70	55.00
AM	Sparky Anderson, Billy Martin/76	25.00
SP	Willie Stargell, Jim Palmer/79	40.00
SB	Mike Schmidt, George Brett/80	80.00
SY	Ozzie Smith, Robin Yount/82	50.00
SRI	Mike Schmidt, Cal Ripken Jr./83	120.00

TG	Alan Trammell, Tony Gwynn/84	50.00
WB	Mookie Wilson, Bill Buckner/86	40.00
EG	Dennis Eckersley, Kirk Gibson/88	35.00

Pastime Patches Relics

No pricing due to scarcity.
Production 15 Sets

Relic

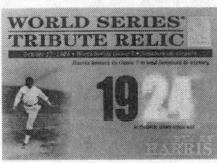

	NM/M
Common Player:	10.00

Production 425 unless noted.
Golds: No Pricing
Production 25

HA	Hank Aaron/50	60.00
HB	Hank Bauer/50	30.00
JBE	Johnny Bench	25.00
YB	Yogi Berra	20.00
WB	Wade Boggs	15.00
JB	Jim Bottomley/50	30.00
GB	George Brett	25.00
LB	Lou Brock	10.00
JC	Jose Canseco	15.00
NC	Norm Cash/50	25.00
OC	Orlando Cepeda/50	30.00
RC	Roberto Clemente/50	120.00
TC	Ty Cobb	120.00
SC	Sam Crawford/50	50.00
CF	Carlton Fisk	40.00
JF	Jimmie Foxx/50	80.00
FF	Frankie Frisch	15.00
LG	Lou Gehrig/50	185.00
HG	Hank Greenberg/50	60.00
TG	Tony Gwynn	20.00
BH	Bucky Harris	10.00
RH	Rogers Hornsby	35.00
CH	Jim "Catfish" Hunter	15.00
RJ	Reggie Jackson	15.00
HK	Harmon Killebrew	25.00
CK	Chuck Klein	10.00
TK	Ted Kluszewski	15.00
HM	Heinie Manush/50	35.00
JM	Juan Marichal	10.00
RM	Roger Maris/50	75.00
BMA	Billy Martin	15.00
WM	Willie Mays	50.00
BM	Bill Mazeroski	15.00
WMC	Willie McCovey	10.00
TM	Thurman Munson	30.00
SM	Stan Musial	30.00
KP	Kirby Puckett	20.00
CR	Cal Ripken Jr.	35.00
FR	Frank Robinson	15.00
JR	Jackie Robinson	40.00
ER	Edd Roush/50	40.00
BR	Babe Ruth	140.00
MS	Mike Schmidt	25.00
RS	Red Schoendienst	10.00
TS	Tom Seaver	15.00
OS	Ozzie Smith	20.00
TSP	Tris Speaker/50	90.00
WS	Willie Stargell/50	30.00
BT	Bobby Thomson	15.00
JT	Joe Tinker	30.00
HW	Honus Wagner/50	150.00
CY	Carl Yastrzemski/50	30.00
RY	Robin Yount	20.00

World Series Tribute Singles

	NM/M
Common Player:	8.00
Premiere Proofs:	1.5X

Production 50

TG	Troy Glaus	8.00
MR	Mariano Rivera	10.00

World Series Tribute Doubles

	NM/M
Common Duo:	10.00
Premiere Proofs:	1.5X

Production 50

PP	Jorge Posada, Andy Pettitte	15.00

WO	Bernie Williams, Paul O'Neill	15.00
LP	John Lackey, Troy Percival	10.00
SJ	Curt Schilling, Randy Johnson	15.00
BG	Barry Bonds, Troy Glaus	35.00
WG	Bernie Williams, Luis Gonzalez	10.00
PC	Mike Piazza, Roger Clemens	35.00

World Series Tribute Triples

	NM/M
Common Trio:	15.00
Premiere Proofs:	1.5X

Production 50

LGP	John Lackey, Troy Glaus, Troy Percival	15.00
EGS	Darin Erstad, Troy Glaus, Tim Salmon	15.00

Series Signatures

	NM/M

Common Autograph: 25.00
Golds: No Pricing
Production 25

SA	Sparky Anderson	25.00
JC	Joe Carter	25.00
WF	Whitey Ford	60.00
SG	Steve Garvey	25.00
KG	Kirk Gibson	30.00
DJ	David Justice	40.00
AK	Al Kaline	50.00
DN	Don Newcombe	40.00
JP	Jim Palmer	30.00
BR	Brooks Robinson	75.00
MS	Bill "Moose" Skowron	25.00
AT	Alan Trammell	25.00
EW	Earl Weaver	25.00
MW	Maury Wills	25.00
MWI	Mookie Wilson	30.00

Team Tribute Relic

	NM/M
Common Card:	15.00

Production 275 unless noted.

YLK	Carl Yastrzemski, Fred Lynn, Carlton Fisk	50.00
OSD	Paul O'Neill, Chris Sabo, Eric Davis	25.00
FPG	George Foster, Tony Perez, Ken Griffey Jr.	25.00
CPM	Dave Concepcion, Tony Perez, Joe Morgan	50.00
KCA	Al Kaline, Norm Cash	40.00
TA	Alan Trammell, Sparky Anderson	15.00
GT	Kirk Gibson, Alan Trammell	25.00
SB	Bret Saberhagen, George Brett	40.00
CYG	Ron Cey, Steve Yeager, Steve Garvey	30.00
YM	Robin Yount, Paul Molitor	35.00
SRK	Tom Seaver, Nolan Ryan, Jerry Koosman	50.00
HCD	Keith Hernandez, Gary Carter, Lenny Dykstra	30.00
GB	Lou Gehrig, Babe Ruth/25	500.00
EC	Dennis Eckersley, Jose Canseco	25.00
HJ	Jim "Catfish" Hunter, Reggie Jackson	30.00
SPM	Willie Stargell, Dave Parker, Bill Madlock	30.00
CM	Orlando Cepeda, Juan Marichal	30.00

MM	Willie Mays, Willie McCovey	50.00
SMC	Ozzie Smith, Willie McGee, Vince Coleman	40.00

2003 Topps 205

	NM/M
Complete Set (335):	150.00
Common Player:	.20

SP's inserted 1:5
25 variations in base set and minis.
Mini-Cards(316-335):Exclusive
Mini Cards
Price for minis (316-335) are
Polar Bear

Series 1 or 2 Pack (8):		4.00
Series 1 or 2 Box (20):		65.00
1	Barry Bonds	2.50
1	Barry Bonds/Variation	3.00
2	Bret Boone	.40
3	Albert Pujols	2.00
3	Albert Pujols/Variation	2.00
4	Carl Crawford	.20
5	Bartolo Colon	.20
6	Cliff Floyd	.20
7	John Olerud	.40
8	Jason Giambi	.50
8	Jason Giambi/Variation	.75
9	Edgardo Alfonzo	.20
10	Ivan Rodriguez	.50
11	Jim Edmonds	.50
12	Mike Piazza	1.50
12	Mike Piazza/Variation	2.00
13	Greg Maddux	1.50
14	Jose Vidro	.20
15	Vladimir Guerrero	.75
15	Vladimir Guerrero/Variation	1.00
16	Bernie Williams	.50
17	Roger Clemens	2.00
18	Miguel Tejada	.50
18	Miguel Tejada/Variation	.75
19	Carlos Delgado	.50
20	Alfonso Soriano	.75
20	Alfonso Soriano/Variation	.75
21	Bobby Cox	.20
22	Mike Scioscia	.20
23	John Smoltz	.40
24	Luis Gonzalez	.40
25	Shawn Green	.40
26	Raul Ibanez	.20
27	Andruw Jones	.50
28	Josh Beckett	.40
29	Derek Lowe	.20
30	Todd Helton	.75
31	Barry Larkin	.40
32	Jason Jennings	.20
33	Darin Erstad	.40
34	Magglio Ordonez	.40
35	Mike Sweeney	.20
36	Kazuhisa Ishii	.20
37	Ron Gardenhire	.20
38	Tim Hudson	.40
39	Tim Salmon	.50
40	Pat Burrell	.40
40	Pat Burrell/Variation	.50
41	Manny Ramirez	.75
42	Nick Johnson	.20
43	Tom Glavine	.40
44	Mark Mulder	.40
45	Brian Jordan	.20
46	Rafael Palmeiro	.50
47	Vernon Wells	.40
48	Bob Brenly	.20
49	C.C. Sabathia	.20
50	Alex Rodriguez	2.50
50	Alex Rodriguez/Variation	2.50
51	Sammy Sosa	1.50

51	Sammy Sosa/Variation	2.00	
52	Paul Konerko	.20	
53	Craig Biggio	.20	
54	Moises Alou	.40	
55	Johnny Damon	.50	
56	Torii Hunter	.40	
57	Omar Vizquel	.40	
58	Orlando Hernandez	.40	
59	Barry Zito	.40	
60	Lance Berkman	.50	
61	Carlos Beltran	.50	
62	Edgar Renteria	.40	
63	Ben Sheets	.40	
64	Doug Mientkiewicz	.20	
65	Troy Glaus	.50	
66	Preston Wilson	.20	
67	Kerry Wood	.75	
68	Frank Thomas	.75	
69	Jimmy Rollins	.40	
70	Brian Giles	.40	
71	Bobby Higginson	.20	
72	Larry Walker	.40	
73	Randy Johnson	1.00	
74	Tony LaRussa	.20	
75	Derek Jeter	3.00	
75	Derek Jeter/Variation	3.00	
76	Bobby Abreu	.40	
77	Adam Dunn	.75	
77	Adam Dunn/Variation	.75	
78	Ryan Klesko	.20	
79	Francisco Rodriguez	.20	
80	Scott Rolen	.75	
81	Roberto Alomar	.50	
82	Joe Torre	.50	
83	Jim Thome	.75	
84	Kevin Millwood	.40	
85	J.T. Snow	.20	
86	Trevor Hoffman	.20	
87	Jay Gibbons	.20	
88	Mark Prior	1.00	
88	Mark Prior/Variation	1.50	
89	Rich Aurilia	.20	
90	Chipper Jones	1.00	
91	Richie Sexson	.50	
92	Gary Sheffield	.50	
93	Pedro J. Martinez	1.00	
94	Rodrigo Lopez	.20	
95	Al Leiter	.20	
96	Jorge Posada	.50	
97	Luis Castillo	.20	
98	Aubrey Huff	.20	
99	A.J. Pierzynski	.20	
100	Ichiro Suzuki	2.00	
100	Ichiro Suzuki/Variation	2.00	
101	Eric Chavez	.40	
102	Brett Myers	.20	
103	Jason Kendall	.40	
104	Jeff Kent	.50	
105	Eric Hinske	.20	
106	Jacque Jones	.20	
107	Phil Nevin	.20	
108	Roy Oswalt	.40	
109	Curt Schilling	.75	
110	Nomar Garciaparra	2.00	
110	Nomar Garciaparra/Variation	2.00	
111	Garret Anderson	.40	
112	Eric Gagne	.40	
113	Javier Vazquez	.20	
114	Jeff Bagwell	.75	
115	Mike Lowell	.40	
116	Carlos Pena	.20	
117	Ken Griffey Jr.	1.50	
118	Tony Batista	.20	
119	Edgar Martinez	.20	
120	Austin Kearns	.50	
121	Jason Stokes	.20	
122	Jose Reyes	.50	
123	Rocco Baldelli	.40	
124	Joe Borchard	.20	
125	Joe Mauer	.50	
126	Gavin Floyd	.20	
127	Mark Teixeira	.50	
128	Jeremy Guthrie	.20	
129	B.J. Upton	.40	
130	Khalil Greene	.20	
131	Hanley Ramirez RC	3.00	
132	Andy Marte RC	3.00	
133	J.D. Durbin RC	1.00	
134	Jason Kubel RC	2.00	
135	Craig Brazell RC	.75	
136	Bryan Bullington RC	1.00	
137	Jose Contreras RC	.75	
138	Brian Burgamy RC	.75	
139	Evel Bastida-Martinez RC	.50	
140	Joey Gomes	1.00	
141	Ismael Castro RC	.75	
142	Travis Wong RC	.75	
143	Michael Garciaparra	.50	
144	Arnaldo Munoz RC	.50	
145	Louis Sockalexis	2.00	
146	Dick Hoblitzell	1.00	
147	George "Peaches" Graham	.50	
148	Hal Chase	.50	
149	John McGraw	1.00	
150	Bobby Wallace	.50	
151	Dave Shean	.20	
152	Dick Hoblitzell SP	3.00	
153	Hal Chase	.50	
154	George Wiltse	.20	
155	George Brett	2.00	
156	Willie Mays	3.00	
157	Honus Wagner SP	4.00	
158	Nolan Ryan	3.00	
159	Reggie Jackson	1.00	
160	Mike Schmidt	1.50	
161	Josh Barfield	.20	
162	Grady Sizemore	.40	
163	Justin Morneau	.40	
164	Laynce Nix	.20	
165	Zack Greinke	.20	
166	Victor Martinez	.20	
167	Jeff Mathis	.20	
168	Casey Kotchman	.20	
169	Gabe Gross	.20	
170	Edwin Jackson RC	1.50	
171	Delmon Young/SP RC	10.00	
172	Eric Duncan/SP	2.00	
173	Brian Snyder/SP	1.50	
174	Chris Lubanski/SP RC	4.00	
175	Ryan Harvey/SP RC	5.00	
176	Nicholas Markakis/SP RC	6.00	
177	Chad Billingsley/SP RC	3.00	
178	Elizardo Ramirez	.50	
179	Ben Francisco	.50	
180	Franklin Gutierrez/SP	4.00	
181	Aaron Hill/SP	2.00	
182	Kevin Correia	.50	
183	Kelly Shoppach RC	.75	
184	Felix Pie/SP RC	5.00	
185	Adam Loewen/SP RC	5.00	
186	Danny Garcia	.50	
187	Rickie Weeks/SP RC	8.00	
188	Robby Hammock/SP	.50	
189	Ryan Wagner/SP RC	2.00	
190	Matt Kata/SP	1.50	
191	Bo Hart/SP RC	2.00	
192	Brandon Webb/SP RC	3.00	
193	Bengie Molina	.20	
194	Junior Spivey	.20	
195	Gary Sheffield	.50	
196	Jason Johnson	.20	
197	David Ortiz	.75	
198	Roberto Alomar	.50	
199	Wily Mo Pena	.20	
200	Sammy Sosa	2.00	
201	Jay Payton	.20	
202	Dmitri Young	.20	
203	Derek Lee	.40	
204	Jeff Bagwell	.75	
204	Jeff Bagwell/Variation	.75	
205	Runelvys Hernandez	.20	
206	Kevin Brown	.40	
207	Wes Helms	.20	
208	Eddie Guardado	.20	
209	Orlando Cabrera	.20	
210	Alfonso Soriano	.75	
211	Ty Wigginton	.20	
212	Rich Harden	.40	
212	Rich Harden/Variation	.50	
213	Mike Lieberthal	.20	
214	Brian Giles	.40	
215	Jason Schmidt	.40	
216	Jamie Moyer	.20	
217	Matt Morris	.20	
218	Victor Zambrano	.20	
219	Roy Halladay	.50	
220	Mike Hampton	.20	
221	Kevin Millar	.20	
222	Hideo Nomo	.50	
223	Milton Bradley	.20	
224	Jose Guillen	.20	
225	Derek Jeter	3.00	
226	Rondell White	.20	
227	Hank Blalock	.50	
227	Hank Blalock/Variation	.50	
228	Shigetoshi Hasegawa	.20	
229	Mike Mussina	.50	
230	Cristian Guzman	.20	
231	Todd Helton	.75	
231	Todd Helton/Variation	.75	
232	Kenny Lofton	.40	
233	Carl Everett	.20	
234	Shea Hillenbrand	.20	
235	Brad Fullmer	.20	
236	Bernie Williams	.50	
237	Vicente Padilla	.20	
238	Tim Worrell	.20	
239	Juan Gonzalez	.40	
240	Ichiro Suzuki	2.00	
241	Aaron Boone	.20	
242	Shannon Stewart	.20	
243	Barry Zito	.40	
243	Barry Zito/Variation	.40	
244	Reggie Sanders	.20	
245	Scott Podsednik	.40	
246	Miguel Cabrera	.75	
247	Angel Berroa	.20	
248	Carlos Zambrano	.40	
249	Marlon Byrd	.20	
250	Mark Prior	1.00	
251	Esteban Loaiza	.20	
252	David Eckstein	.20	
253	Alex Cintron	.20	
254	Melvin Mora	.20	
255	Russ Ortiz	.20	
256	Carlos Lee	.20	
257	Tino Martinez	.20	
258	Randy Wolf	.20	
259	Jason Phillips	.20	
260	Vladimir Guerrero	1.00	
261	Brad Wilkerson	.20	
262	Ivan Rodriguez	.75	
263	Matt Lawton	.20	
264	Adam Dunn	.50	
265	Joe Borowski	.20	
266	Jody Gerut	.20	
267	Alex Rodriguez	2.50	
268	Brendan Donnelly	.20	
269	Randy Johnson	1.00	
269	Randy Johnson/Variation	1.00	
270	Nomar Garciaparra	2.50	
271	Javy Lopez	.50	
272	Travis Hafner	.20	
273	Juan Pierre	.20	
274	Morgan Ensberg	.20	
275	Albert Pujols	2.00	
276	Jason LaRue	.20	
277	Paul LoDuca	.20	
278	Andy Pettitte	.50	
279	Mike Piazza	1.50	
280	Jim Thome	1.00	
280	Jim Thome/Variation	1.00	
281	Marquis Grissom	.20	
282	Woody Williams	.20	
283	Curt Schilling	.75	
283	Curt Schilling/Variation	.75	
284	Chipper Jones	1.00	
284	Chipper Jones/Variation	1.00	
285	Deivi Cruz	.20	
286	Johnny Damon	.50	
287	Chin-Hui Tsao	.20	
288	Alex Gonzalez	.20	
289	Billy Wagner	.40	
290	Jason Giambi	.50	
291	Keith Foulke	.20	
292	Jerome Williams	.20	
293	Livan Hernandez	.20	
294	Aaron Guiel	.20	
295	Randall Simon	.20	
296	Byung-Hyun Kim	.20	
297	Jorge Julio	.20	
298	Miguel Batista	.20	
299	Rafael Furcal	.40	
300	Dontrelle Willis SP	1.00	
300	Dontrelle Willis/Variation	1.00	
301	Alex Sanchez	.20	
302	Shawn Chacon	.20	
303	Matt Clement	.20	
304	Luis Matos	.20	
305	Steve Finley	.20	
306	Marcus Giles	.40	
307	David Wells	.20	
308	Jeromy Burnitz	.20	
309	Mike MacDougal	.20	
310	Mariano Rivera	.40	
311	Adrian Beltre	.40	
312	Mark Loretta	.20	
313	Ugueth Urbina	.20	
314	Bill Mueller	.20	
315	Johan Santana	.50	
316	Willie Mays	2.00	
317	Delmon Young	.40	
318	Rickie Weeks	4.00	
319	Ryan Wagner	.50	
320	Brandon Webb	.50	
321	Chris Lubanski	1.00	
322	Ryan Harvey	3.00	
323	Nicholas Markakis	1.00	
324	Chad Billingsley	1.00	
325	Aaron Hill	.40	
326	Brian Snyder	.40	
327	Eric Duncan	.40	
328	Sammy Sosa	1.50	
329	Alfonso Soriano	1.00	
330	Ichiro Suzuki	2.00	
331	Alex Rodriguez	2.00	
332	Nomar Garciaparra	2.00	
333	Albert Pujols	2.00	
334	Jim Thome	1.00	
335	Dontrelle Willis	.50	

Mini Parallel

Polar Bear:	1-2X
Sovereign:	1-2X
Sovereign Green:	2-3X
American Beauty:	1-2X
Amer. Beauty Purple:	3-5X
Cycle:	1-2X
Cycle Purple:	3-5X
Drum:	2-4X
Honest:	1-2X
Honest Purple:	3-5X
Piedmont:	1-2X
Piedmont Purple:	3-5X
Sweet Caporal:	1-2X
Sweet Caporal Purple:	3-5X
Bazooka:	No Pricing
Production 5 Sets	
Brooklyn:	1.5-4X
Brooklyn: Varies for common, rare & Unc.	

T-205 Relics

		NM/M
	Common Player:	4.00
RA	Roberto Alomar/Bat	6.00
GA	Garret Anderson/Jsy	5.00
JB	Jeff Bagwell/Jsy	6.00
LB	Lance Berkman/Bat	8.00
BB	Barry Bonds	25.00
AB	A.J. Burnett/Jsy	4.00
LC	Luis Castillo/Jsy	4.00
EC	Eric Chavez/Bat	5.00
JD	Johnny Damon/Bat	6.00
AD	Adam Dunn/Jsy	4.00
RF	Rafael Furcal/Bat	6.00
EG	Eric Gagne/Jsy	8.00
NG	Nomar Garciaparra/Jsy	15.00
BG	Brian Giles/Bat	5.00
LG	Luis Gonzalez/Jsy	4.00
TH	Todd Helton/Jsy	10.00
KI	Kazuhisa Ishii/Jsy	6.00
JJ	Jason Jennings/Jsy	4.00
NJ	Nick Johnson/Bat	4.00
RJ	Randy Johnson/Jsy	8.00
JK	Jeff Kent/Bat	4.00
AL	Al Leiter/Jsy	4.00
KL	Kenny Lofton/Bat	4.00
DL	Derek Lowe/Jsy	4.00
GM	Greg Maddux/Jsy	15.00
PM	Pedro Martinez/Jsy	10.00
MO	Magglio Ordonez/Jsy	4.00
RO	Roy Oswalt/Jsy	4.00
RP	Rafael Palmeiro/Jsy	6.00
TP	Troy Percival/Jsy	4.00
MP	Mike Piazza/Bat	10.00
AP	Albert Pujols/Jsy	20.00
MR	Manny Ramirez/Bat	8.00
AR	Alex Rodriguez/Jsy	10.00
SR	Scott Rolen/Bat	15.00
CS	Curt Schilling/Jsy	6.00
JS	John Smoltz/Jsy	8.00
AS	Alfonso Soriano/Jsy	10.00
MS	Mike Sweeney/Bat	4.00
JT	Jim Thome/Bat	12.00
MV	Mo Vaughn/Jsy	4.00
BW	Bernie Williams/Bat	10.00
BZ	Barry Zito/Jsy	4.00
Series 2		4.00
RA	Roberto Alomar	4.00
JB	Jeff Bagwell	8.00
RBB	Rocco Baldelli/Bat	8.00
RB	Rocco Baldelli/Jsy	8.00
CB	Craig Biggio	4.00
HB	Hank Blalock	6.00
WB	Wade Boggs	15.00
BB	Bret Boone	10.00
GB	George Brett	25.00
KB	Kevin Brown	4.00
SB	Sean Burroughs	4.00
MC	Mike Cameron	4.00
JC	Jose Canseco	8.00
GC	Gary Carter	4.00
RC	Roger Clemens	15.00

CD	Carlos Delgado	6.00
BD	Brandon Duckworth	4.00
JE	Jim Edmonds	6.00
DE	Darin Erstad	4.00
RF	Rafael Furcal	4.00
NG	Nomar Garciaparra	10.00
JG	Jason Giambi	6.00
JGI	Jeremy Giambi	4.00
BG	Brian Giles	4.00
TG	Troy Glaus	6.00
JGO	Juan Gonzalez	6.00
LG	Luis Gonzalez	4.00
MG	Mark Grace	10.00
MGR	Marquis Grissom	4.00
VG	Vladimir Guerrero	8.00
CG	Cristian Guzman	4.00
RH	Rickey Henderson	8.00
RJ	Randy Johnson	8.00
AJ	Andruw Jones	6.00
CJB	Chipper Jones	8.00
KL	Kenny Lofton	4.00
GM	Greg Maddux	10.00
EM	Edgar Martinez	4.00
PM	Pedro J. Martinez	8.00
TM	Tino Martinez	6.00
FM	Fred McGriff	6.00
MM	Mark Mulder	4.00
EMU	Eddie Murray	25.00
JO	John Olerud	4.00
PO	Paul O'Neill	4.00
RP	Rafael Palmeiro	8.00
CP	Corey Patterson	10.00
BP	Brad Penny	4.00
MP	Mike Piazza	10.00
JP	Jorge Posada	15.00
APB	Albert Pujols/bat	20.00
AP	Albert Pujols/jersey	20.00
ARA	Aramis Ramirez	6.00
FR	Frank Robinson	15.00
AR	Alex Rodriguez	10.00
IR	Ivan Rodriguez	8.00
SR	Scott Rolen	8.00
NR	Nolan Ryan	40.00
CS	Curt Schilling	6.00
MS	Mike Schmidt	25.00
GS	Gary Sheffield	6.00
TS	Tsuyoshi Shinjo	4.00
AS	Alfonso Soriano	8.00
SS	Sammy Sosa	15.00
SST	Shannon Stewart	4.00
MT	Mark Teixeira	6.00
MTE	Miguel Tejada	6.00
FT	Frank Thomas	8.00
RV	Robin Ventura	4.00
LW	Larry Walker	4.00
VW	Vernon Wells	8.00
BW	Bernie Williams	6.00
DW	Dontrelle Willis	8.00

T-205 Autographs

		NM/M
	Common Autograph:	12.00
LB	Lance Berkman	25.00
MB	Marlon Byrd	10.00
CF	Cliff Floyd	15.00
TH	Torii Hunter	15.00
PL	Paul LoDuca	15.00
MO	Magglio Ordonez	20.00
JR	Jose Reyes	30.00
SR	Scott Rolen	40.00
MS	Mike Sweeney	20.00
Series 2		
HA	Hank Aaron/50	280.00
LC	Luis Castillo	10.00
ED	Eric Duncan	20.00
RH	Rich Harden	25.00
FP	Felix Pie	40.00
RWA	Ryan Wagner	15.00
JW	Jerome Williams	20.00
DW	Dontrelle Willis	25.00

Team Topps Legends Autographs

	NM/M
Common Player:	
Stan Musial	65.00
Jim Palmer	20.00
Gaylord Perry	10.00
Robin Yount	75.00

Triple Folder

	NM/M
Complete Set (100):	60.00
Common Card:	.25
Inserted 1:1	
Series 1 Brooklyn Variation:	4-8X
Inserted 1:72	
Series 2 Brooklyn Variation:	2-4X
Inserted 1:29	

TF1	Barry Bonds, Jason LaRue	1.50
TF2	Alfonso Soriano, Derek Jeter	1.50
TF3	Alex Rodriguez, Miguel Tejada	1.50
TF4	Nomar Garciaparra, Derek Jeter	2.00
TF5	Omar Vizquel, Alex Rodriguez	1.50
TF6	Paul Konerko, Omar Vizquel	.25
TF7	Paul Konerko, Magglio Ordonez	.25
TF8	Doug Mientkiewicz, Darin Erstad	.25
TF9	Jason Kendall, Jimmy Rollins	.25
TF10	Shawn Green, Roberto Alomar	.25
TF11	Derek Jeter, Roberto Alomar	1.50
TF12	Bobby Abreu, Luis Castillo	.25
TF13	Randy Johnson, Curt Schilling	.75
TF14	Mike Piazza, Kerry Wood	1.00
TF15	Roger Clemens, Jorge Posada	1.00
TF16	Ichiro Suzuki, Ryan Klesko	1.00
TF17	Alfonso Soriano, Chipper Jones	1.00
TF18	Barry Bonds, Nick Johnson	1.50
TF19	Chipper Jones, Andruw Jones	.75
TF20	Bobby Abreu, Paul Konerko	.25
TF21	Rafael Palmeiro, Alex Rodriguez	1.50
TF22	Eric Hinske, Carlos Delgado	.25
TF23	Nomar Garciaparra, Jay Gibbons	1.00
TF24	Mike Piazza, Luis Gonzalez	1.00
TF25	J.T. Snow, Vladimir Guerrero	.50
TF26	Jason Giambi, Bernie Williams	.75
TF27	Miguel Tejada, Richie Sexson	.25
TF28	Doug Mientkiewicz, Jimmy Rollins	.25
TF29	Eric Chavez, Derek Jeter	2.00
TF30	Alfonso Soriano, Bret Boone	1.00
TF31	Chipper Jones, Mike Piazza	1.00
TF32	Ichiro Suzuki, Bret Boone	1.00
TF33	Bobby Abreu, Mike Piazza	1.00
TF34	Jimmy Rollins, Pat Burrell	.25
TF35	Ichiro Suzuki, Miguel Tejada	1.00
TF36	Jason LaRue, Barry Bonds	1.50
TF37	Derek Jeter, Alfonso Soriano	1.50
TF38	Miguel Tejada, Alex Rodriguez	1.50
TF39	Derek Jeter, Nomar Garciaparra	2.00
TF40	Alex Rodriguez, Omar Vizquel	1.50
TF41	Curt Schilling, Randy Johnson	.75
TF42	Jorge Posada, Roger Clemens	1.50
TF43	Ryan Klesko, Ichiro Suzuki	1.00
TF44	Nick Johnson, Barry Bonds	1.50
TF45	Alex Rodriguez, Rafael Palmeiro	1.50
TF46	Vladimir Guerrero, J.T. Snow	.50
TF47	Derek Jeter, Eric Chavez	2.00
TF48	Bret Boone, Ichiro Suzuki	1.00
TF49	Mike Piazza, Bobby Abreu	1.00
TF50	Miguel Tejada, Ichiro Suzuki	1.00
TF51	Juan Pierre, Jim Thome	.50
TF52	Kevin Millwood, Jim Thome	.50
TF53	Hank Blalock, Jorge Posada	.40
TF54	Deivi Cruz, Hank Blalock	.25
TF55	Rafael Furcal, Ty Wigginton	.25
TF56	Jim Thome, Nomar Garciaparra	1.50
TF57	Craig Biggio, Jason Giambi	.75
TF58	Aaron Boone, Jason Giambi	.75
TF59	Jason Giambi, Bernie Williams	.75
TF60	Cristian Guzman, Jody Gerut	.25
TF61	Todd Helton, Jose Reyes	.50
TF62	Derek Jeter, Hank Blalock	2.00
TF63	Mike Piazza, Jimmy Rollins	1.00
TF64	Bernie Williams, Derek Jeter	2.00
TF65	Andruw Jones, Rafael Furcal	.50
TF66	Mike Piazza, Andruw Jones	1.00
TF67	Mike Piazza, Cliff Floyd	1.00
TF68	Jason Kendall, Albert Pujols	1.50
TF69	Nomar Garciaparra, Manny Ramirez	1.50
TF70	Jorge Posada, Alex Rodriguez	1.50
TF71	Derek Jeter, Alex Rodriguez	2.00
TF72	Mike Sweeney, Alex Rodriguez	1.50
TF73	Marquis Grissom, Ivan Rodriguez	.50
TF74	Jason Phillips, Gary Sheffield	.40
TF75	Chipper Jones, Gary Sheffield	1.00
TF76	Junior Spivey, Gary Sheffield	.40
TF77	Al Leiter, Ichiro Suzuki	1.00
TF78	Jose Vidro, Jim Thome	.75
TF79	Jimmy Rollins, Paul LoDuca	.25
TF80	Alex Rodriguez, Rafael Palmeiro	1.50
TF81	Albert Pujols, Jim Edmonds	1.50
TF82	Eric Chavez, Mike Sweeney	.25
TF83	Cristian Guzman, Jimmy Rollins	.25
TF84	Alfonso Soriano, Bernie Williams	.50
TF85	Ichiro Suzuki, Derek Jeter	2.00
TF86	Jimmy Rollins, Derek Lee	.25
TF87	Shawn Green, Paul LoDuca	.25
TF88	Carlos Delgado, Jorge Posada	.50
TF89	Dmitri Young, C.C. Sabathia	.25
TF90	Dontrelle Willis, Shawn Chacon	.25
TF91	Edgar Martinez, Alex Rodriguez	1.50
TF92	Edgar Martinez, Carlos Delgado	.50
TF93	Edgar Martinez, Esteban Loaiza	.25
TF94	Roy Halladay, C.C. Sabathia	.25
TF95	Ichiro Suzuki, Albert Pujols	1.50
TF96	Ichiro Suzuki, Shigetoshi Hasegawa	1.00
TF97	Geoff Jenkins, Aaron Boone	.25
TF98	Nomar Garciaparra, Alfonso Soriano	1.50
TF99	Jorge Posada, Alfonso Soriano	.75
TF100	Vernon Wells, Garret Anderson	.25

Triple Folder Autographs

		NM/M
Inserted 1:355		
RH	Rich Harden	40.00
RW	Ryan Wagner	40.00
JW	Jerome Williams	35.00
DW	Dontrelle Willis	40.00

2004 Topps

	NM/M
Complete Set (732):	60.00
Complete Team Factory Set (737):	75.00
Complete Factory Set (742):	75.00
Common Player:	.15
Pack (10):	2.00
Box (36):	55.00
Jumbo Box (12):	65.00

1	Jim Thome	.40
2	Aramis Ramirez	.25
3	Mark Kotsay	.15
4	Edgardo Alfonzo	.15
5	Ben Davis	.15
6	Mike Matheny	.15
8	Marlon Anderson	.15
9	Chan Ho Park	.15
10	Ichiro Suzuki	.75
11	Kevin Millwood	.25
12	Bengie Molina	.15
13	Tom Glavine	.25
14	Junior Spivey	.15
15	Marcus Giles	.15
16	David Segui	.15
17	Kevin Millar	.15
18	Corey Patterson	.15
19	Aaron Rowand	.15
20	Derek Jeter	1.00
21	Jason LaRue	.15
22	Chris Hammond	.15
23	Jay Payton	.15
24	Bobby Higginson	.15
25	Lance Berkman	.25
26	Juan Pierre	.15
27	Brent Mayne	.15
28	Fred McGriff	.25
29	Richie Sexson	.25
30	Tim Hudson	.25
31	Mike Piazza	.50
32	Brad Radke	.15
33	Jeff Weaver	.15
34	Ramon Hernandez	.15
35	David Bell	.15
36	Craig Wilson	.15
37	Jake Peavy	.15
38	Tim Worrell	.15

#	Player	Price
39	Gil Meche	.15
40	Albert Pujols	1.00
41	Michael Young	.15
42	Josh Phelps	.15
43	Brendan Donnelly	.15
44	Steve Finley	.15
45	John Smoltz	.15
46	Jay Gibbons	.15
47	Trot Nixon	.15
48	Carl Pavano	.15
49	Frank Thomas	.40
50	Mark Prior	1.00
51	Danny Graves	.15
52	Milton Bradley	.15
53	Jose Jimenez	.15
54	Shane Halter	.15
55	Mike Lowell	.15
56	Geoff Blum	.15
57	Michael Tucker	.15
58	Paul LoDuca	.15
59	Vicente Padilla	.15
60	Jacque Jones	.15
61	Fernando Tatis	.15
62	Ty Wigginton	.15
63	Pedro Astacio	.15
64	Andy Pettitte	.25
65	Terrence Long	.15
66	Cliff Floyd	.15
67	Mariano Rivera	.25
68	Mike Williams	.15
69	Marlon Byrd	.15
70	Mark Mulder	.25
71	Damian Moss	.15
72	Carlos Guillen	.15
73	Fernando Vina	.15
74	Lance Carter	.15
75	Hank Blalock	.25
76	Jimmy Rollins	.25
77	Kevin Appier	.15
78	Javy Lopez	.25
79	Jerry Hairston Jr.	.15
80	Andruw Jones	.40
81	Rodrigo Lopez	.15
82	Johnny Damon	.25
83	Hee Seop Choi	.15
84	Miguel Olivo	.15
85	Scott Sullivan	.15
86	Matt Lawton	.15
87	Juan Uribe	.15
88	Steve Sparks	.15
89	Tim Spooneybarger	.15
90	Jose Vidro	.15
91	Luis Rivas	.15
92	Hideo Nomo	.25
93	Javier Vazquez	.15
94	Al Leiter	.15
95	Darren Dreifort	.15
96	Mike DeJean	.15
97	Zach Day	.15
98	Jorge Posada	.25
99	John Halama	.15
100	Alex Rodriguez	1.00
101	Orlando Palmeiro	.15
102	Dave Berg	.15
103	Brad Fullmer	.15
104	Mike Hampton	.15
105	Willis Roberts	.15
106	Ramiro Mendoza	.15
107	Juan Cruz	.15
108	Esteban Loaiza	.15
109	Aaron Boone	.15
110	Todd Helton	.40
111	Braden Looper	.15
112	Octavio Dotel	.15
113	Mike MacDougal	.15
114	Cesar Izturis	.15
115	Johan Santana	.15
116	Jose Contreras	.25
117	Placido Polanco	.15
118	Kenny Lofton	.25
119	Adam Eaton	.15
120	Vernon Wells	.25
121	Ben Grieve	.15
122	Randy Winn	.15
123	Ismael Valdes	.15
124	Eric Owens	.15
125	Curt Schilling	.15
126	Russ Ortiz	.15
127	Mark Buehrle	.15
128	Danys Baez	.15
129	Dmitri Young	.15
130	Kazuhisa Ishii	.15
131	A.J. Pierzynski	.15
132	Michael Barrett	.15
133	Joe McEwing	.15
134	Robin Ventura	.15
135	Tom Wilson	.15
136	Carlos Zambrano	.15
137	Brett Tomko	.15
138	Jeff Nelson	.15
139	Jarrod Washburn	.15
140	Greg Maddux	.75
141	Craig Counsell	.15
142	Reggie Taylor	.15
143	Omar Vizquel	.25
144	Alex Gonzalez	.15
145	Billy Wagner	.15
146	Brian Jordan	.15
147	Wes Helms	.15
148	Kyle Lohse	.15
149	Timoniel Perez	.15
150	Jason Giambi	.50
151	Erubiel Durazo	.15
152	Mike Lieberthal	.15
153	Jason Kendall	.15
154	Xavier Nady	.15
155	Kirk Rueter	.15
156	Mike Cameron	.15
157	Miguel Cairo	.15
158	Woody Williams	.15
159	Toby Hall	.15
160	Bernie Williams	.40
161	Darin Erstad	.25
162	Matt Mantei	.15
163	Geronimo Gil	.15
164	Bill Mueller	.15
165	Damian Miller	.15
166	Tony Graffanino	.15
167	Sean Casey	.15
168	Brandon Phillips	.15
169	Mike Remlinger	.15
170	Adam Dunn	.25
171	Carlos Lee	.15
172	Juan Encarnacion	.15
173	Angel Berroa	.15
174	Desi Relaford	.15
175	Paul Quantrill	.15
176	Ben Sheets	.15
177	Eddie Guardado	.15
178	Rocky Biddle	.15
179	Mike Stanton	.15
180	Eric Chavez	.25
181	Jason Michaels	.15
182	Terry Adams	.15
183	Kip Wells	.15
184	Brian Lawrence	.15
185	Bret Boone	.25
186	Tino Martinez	.25
187	Aubrey Huff	.15
188	Kevin Mench	.15
189	Tim Salmon	.25
190	Carlos Delgado	.40
191	John Lackey	.15
192	Oscar Villarreal	.15
193	Sidney Ponson	.15
194	Derek Lowe	.15
195	Mark Grudzielanek	.15
196	Flash Gordon	.15
197	Matt Clement	.15
198	Scott Williamson	.15
199	Brandon Inge	.15
200	Nomar Garciaparra	1.00
201	Antonio Osuna	.15
202	Jose Mesa	.15
203	Randall Simon	.15
204	Jack Wilson	.15
205	Ray Durham	.15
206	Freddy Garcia	.15
207	J.D. Drew	.15
208	Einar Diaz	.15
209	Roy Halladay	.25
210	David Eckstein	.15
211	Jason Marquis	.15
212	Jorge Julio	.15
213	Tim Wakefield	.15
214	Moises Alou	.25
215	Bartolo Colon	.25
216	Jimmy Haynes	.15
217	Preston Wilson	.15
218	Luis Castillo	.15
219	Richard Hidalgo	.15
220	Manny Ramirez	.40
221	Mike Mussina	.40
222	Randy Wolf	.15
223	Kris Benson	.15
224	Ryan Klesko	.25
225	Rich Aurilia	.15
226	Kelvim Escobar	.15
227	Francisco Cordero	.15
228	Kazuhiro Sasaki	.15
229	Danny Bautista	.15
230	Rafael Furcal	.15
231	Travis Driskill	.15
232	Kyle Farnsworth	.15
233	Jose Valentin	.15
234	Felipe Lopez	.15
235	C.C. Sabathia	.15
236	Brad Penny	.15
237	Brad Ausmus	.15
238	Raul Ibanez	.15
239	Adrian Beltre	.15
240	Rocco Baldelli	.25
241	Orlando Hudson	.15
242	Dave Roberts	.15
243	Doug Mientkiewicz	.15
244	Brad Wilkerson	.15
245	Scott Strickland	.15
246	Sterling Hitchcock	.15
247	Chad Bradford	.15
248	Gary Bennett	.15
249	Jose Cruz Jr.	.15
250	Jeff Kent	.25
251	Josh Beckett	.25
252	Ramon Ortiz	.15
253	Miguel Batista	.15
254	Jung Bong	.15
255	Deivi Cruz	.15
256	Alex Gonzalez	.15
257	Shawn Chacon	.15
258	Runelvys Hernandez	.15
259	Joe Mays	.15
260	Eric Gagne	.15
261	Dustan Mohr	.15
262	Tomokazu Ohka	.15
263	Eric Byrnes	.15
264	Frank Catalanotto	.15
265	Cristian Guzman	.15
266	Orlando Cabrera	.15
267	Mike Scioscia	.15
268	Bob Brenly	.15
269	Bobby Cox	.15
270	Mike Hargrove	.15
271	Grady Little	.15
272	Dusty Baker	.15
273	Jerry Manuel	.15
274	Bob Boone	.15
275	Eric Wedge	.15
276	Clint Hurdle	.15
277	Alan Trammell	.15
278	Jack McKeon	.15
279	Jimy Williams	.15
280	Tony Pena	.15
281	Jim Tracy	.15
282	Ned Yost	.15
283	Ron Gardenhire	.15
284	Frank Robinson	.25
285	Art Howe	.15
286	Joe Torre	.25
287	Ken Macha	.15
288	Larry Bowa	.15
289	Lloyd McClendon	.15
290	Bruce Bochy	.15
291	Felipe Alou	.15
292	Bob Melvin	.15
293	Tony LaRussa	.15
294	Lou Piniella	.15
295	Buck Showalter	.15
296	Carlos Tosca	.15
297	Anthony Acevedo RC	.15
298	Anthony Lerew RC	.75
299	Blake Hawksworth RC	.50
300	Brayan Pena RC	.50
301	Casey Myers RC	.50
302	Craig Ansman RC	.50
303	David Murphy	.40
304	David Crouthers	.15
305	Dioner Navarro RC	.40
306	Donald Levinski	.15
307	Jesse Roman RC	.40
308	Sung Ki Jung RC	.25
309	Jon Knott RC	.40
310	Josh Labandeira RC	.25
311	Kenny Perez RC	.25
312	Khalid Ballouli RC	.25
313	Kyle Davies RC	.40
314	Marcus McBeth RC	.40
315	Matt Creighton RC	.40
316	Chris O'Riordan RC	.50
317	Mike Gosling	.15
318	Nic Ungs RC	.40
319	Omar Falcon RC	.40
320	Rodney Choy Foo RC	.40
321	Tim Frend RC	.50
322	Todd Self RC	.50
323	Tydus Meadows RC	.40
324	Yadier Molina RC	.50
325	Zachary Duke RC	2.00
326	Zach Miner RC	1.00
327	Bernie Castro, Khalil Greene	.15
328	Ryan Madson, Elizardo Ramirez	.15
329	Rich Harden, Bobby Crosby	.15
330	Zack Greinke, Jimmy Gobble	.15
331	Bobby Jenks, Casey Kotchman	.15
332	Sammy Sosa	.50
333	Kevin Millwood	.25
334	Rafael Palmeiro	.25
335	Roger Clemens	.75
336	Eric Gagne	.15
337	Bill Mueller, Manny Ramirez, Derek Jeter	.50
338	Vernon Wells, Ichiro Suzuki, Michael Young	.40
339	Alex Rodriguez, Frank Thomas, Carlos Delgado	.50
340	Carlos Delgado, Alex Rodriguez, Bret Boone	.50
341	Pedro Martinez, Tim Hudson, Esteban Loaiza	.25
342	Esteban Loaiza, Pedro Martinez, Roy Halladay	.25
343	Albert Pujols, Todd Helton, Edgar Renteria	.50
344	Albert Pujols, Todd Helton, Juan Pierre	.50
345	Jim Thome, Richie Sexson, Javy Lopez	.25
346	Preston Wilson, Gary Sheffield, Jim Thome	.25
347	Jason Schmidt, Kevin Brown, Mark Prior	.50
348	Kerry Wood, Mark Prior, Javier Vazquez	.50
349	AL Division Series	.15
350	NL Division Series	.15
351	NL Championship Series	.15
352	AL Championship Series	.25
353	AL & NL Division Series	.15
354	AL Championship Series	.15
355	World Series Highlights	.25
356	Carlos Delgado	.25
357	Bret Boone	.15
358	Alex Rodriguez	.50
359	Bill Mueller	.15
360	Vernon Wells	.15
361	Garret Anderson	.15
362	Magglio Ordonez	.15
363	Jorge Posada	.15
364	Roy Halladay	.15
365	Andy Pettitte	.15
366	Frank Thomas	.25
367	Jody Gerut	.15
368	Sammy Sosa	.75
369	Joe Crede	.15
370	Gary Sheffield	.25
371	Coco Crisp	.15
372	Torii Hunter	.25
373	Derrek Lee	.15
374	Adam Everett	.15
375	Miguel Tejada	.25
376	Jeremy Affeldt	.15
377	Robin Ventura	.15
378	Scott Podsednik	.40
379	Matthew LeCroy	.15
380	Vladimir Guerrero	.40
381	Tony Clark	.15
382	Jeff Nelson	.15
383	Chris Singleton	.15
384	Bobby Abreu	.25
385	Josh Fogg	.15
386	Trevor Hoffman	.15
387	Jesse Foppert	.15
388	Edgar Martinez	.25
389	Edgar Renteria	.25
390	Chipper Jones	.50
391	Eric Munson	.15
392	Dewon Brazelton	.15
393	John Thomson	.15
394	Chris Woodward	.15
395	Aaron Sele	.15
396	Elmer Dessens	.15
397	Johnny Estrada	.15
398	Damian Moss	.15
399	Gabe Kapler	.15
400	Dontrelle Willis	.40
401	Troy Glaus	.25
402	Raul Mondesi	.20
403	Shane Reynolds	.15
404	Kurt Ainsworth	.15
405	Pedro J. Martinez	.50
406	Eric Karros	.15
407	Billy Koch	.15
408	Scott Schoeneweis	.15
409	Paul Wilson	.15
410	Mike Sweeney	.15
411	Jason Bay	.15
412	Mark Redman	.15
413	Jason Jennings	.15
414	Rondell White	.25
415	Todd Hundley	.15
416	Shannon Stewart	.15
417	Jae Weong Seo	.15
418	Livan Hernandez	.15
419	Mark Ellis	.15
420	Pat Burrell	.25
421	Mark Loretta	.15
422	Robb Nen	.15
423	Joel Pineiro	.15
424	Jason Simontacchi	.15
425	Sterling Hitchcock	.15

426	Rey Ordonez	.15
427	Greg Myers	.15
428	Shane Spencer	.15
429	Carlos Baerga	.15
430	Garret Anderson	.25
431	Horacio Ramirez	.15
432	Brian Roberts	.15
433	Damian Jackson	.15
434	Doug Glanville	.15
435	Brian Daubach	.15
436	Alex Escobar	.15
437	Alex Sanchez	.15
438	Jeff Bagwell	.40
439	Darrell May	.15
440	Shawn Green	.25
441	Geoff Jenkins	.25
442	Endy Chavez	.15
443	Nick Johnson	.15
444	Jose Guillen	.15
445	Tomas Perez	.15
446	Phil Nevin	.25
447	Jason Schmidt	.25
448	Julio Mateo	.15
449	So Taguchi	.15
450	Randy Johnson	.40
451	Paul Byrd	.15
452	Chone Figgins	.15
453	Larry Bigbie	.15
454	Scott Williamson	.15
455	Ramon Martinez	.15
456	Roberto Alomar	.25
457	Ryan Dempster	.15
458	Ryan Ludwick	.15
459	Ramon Santiago	.15
460	Jeff Conine	.15
461	Brad Lidge	.15
462	Ken Harvey	.15
463	Guillermo Mota	.15
464	Rick Reed	.15
465	Joey Eischen	.15
466	Wade Miller	.15
467	Steve Karsay	.15
468	Chase Utley	.25
469	Matt Stairs	.15
470	Yorvit Torrealba	.15
471	Joe Kennedy	.15
472	Reed Johnson	.15
473	Victor Zambrano	.15
474	Jeff DaVanon	.15
475	Luis Gonzalez	.25
476	Rod Barajas	.15
477	Ray King	.15
478	Jack Cust	.15
479	Omar Daal	.15
480	Todd Walker	.15
481	Shawn Estes	.15
482	Chris Reitsma	.15
483	Jake Westbrook	.15
484	Jeremy Bonderman	.15
485	A.J. Burnett	.15
486	Roy Oswalt	.25
487	Kevin Brown	.25
488	Eric Milton	.15
489	Claudio Vargas	.15
490	Roger Cedeno	.15
491	David Wells	.15
492	Scott Hatteberg	.15
493	Ricky Ledee	.15
494	Eric Young	.15
495	Armando Benitez	.15
496	Dan Haren	.15
497	Carl Crawford	.15
498	Laynce Nix	.15
499	Eric Hinske	.15
500	Ivan Rodriguez	.40
501	Scot Shields	.15
502	Brandon Webb	.15
503	Mark DeRosa	.15
504	Jhonny Peralta	.15
505	Adam Kennedy	.15
506	Tony Batista	.15
507	Jeff Suppan	.15
508	Kenny Lofton	.25
509	Scott Sullivan	.15
510	Ken Griffey Jr.	.60
511	Billy Traber	.15
512	Larry Walker	.25
513	Mike Maroth	.15
514	Todd Hollandsworth	.15
515	Kirk Saarloos	.15
516	Carlos Beltran	.25
517	Andy Ashby	.15
518	Jose Macias	.15
519	Karim Garcia	.15
520	Jose Reyes	.40
521	Brandon Duckworth	.15
522	Brian Giles	.25
523	J.T. Snow Jr.	.15
524	Jamie Moyer	.15
525	Jason Isringhausen	.15
526	Julio Lugo	.15
527	Mark Teixeira	.25
528	Cory Lidle	.15
529	Lyle Overbay	.15
530	Troy Percival	.15
531	Robby Hammock	.15

532	Robert Fick	.15
533	Jason Johnson	.15
534	Brandon Lyon	.15
535	Antonio Alfonseca	.15
536	Tom Goodwin	.15
537	Paul Konerko	.15
538	D'Angelo Jimenez	.15
539	Ben Broussard	.15
540	Magglio Ordonez	.25
541	Ellis Burks	.15
542	Carlos Pena	.15
543	Chad Fox	.15
544	Jeriome Robertson	.15
545	Travis Hafner	.15
546	Joe Randa	.15
547	Wil Cordero	.15
548	Brady Clark	.15
549	Ruben Sierra	.15
550	Barry Zito	.25
551	Brett Myers	.15
552	Oliver Perez	.15
553	Trey Hodges	.15
554	Benito Santiago	.15
555	David Ross	.15
556	Ramon Vazquez	.15
557	Joe Nathan	.15
558	Dan Wilson	.15
559	Garrett Stephenson	.15
560	Jim Edmonds	.25
561	Shawn Wooten	.15
562	Matt Kata	.15
563	Vinny Castilla	.15
564	Marty Cordova	.15
565	Aramis Ramirez	.15
566	Carl Everett	.15
567	Ryan Freel	.15
568	Jason Davis	.15
569	Mark Bellhorn	.15
570	Craig Monroe	.15
571	Ugueth Urbina	.15
572	Tim Redding	.15
573	Kevin Appier	.15
574	Jeromy Burnitz	.15
575	Miguel Cabrera	.40
576	Orlando Hernandez	.15
577	Casey Blake	.15
578	Aaron Boone	.15
579	Jermaine Dye	.15
580	Jerome Williams	.15
581	John Olerud	.15
582	Scott Rolen	.40
583	Bobby Kielty	.15
584	Travis Lee	.15
585	Jeff Cirillo	.15
586	Scott Spiezio	.15
587	Stephen Randolph	.15
588	Melvin Mora	.15
589	Mike Timlin	.15
590	Kerry Wood	.50
591	Tony Womack	.15
592	Jody Gerut	.15
593	Franklyn German	.15
594	Morgan Ensberg	.15
595	Odalis Perez	.15
596	Michael Cuddyer	.15
597	Jon Lieber	.15
598	Mike Williams	.15
599	Jose Hernandez	.15
600	Alfonso Soriano	.50
601	Marquis Grissom	.15
602	Matt Morris	.25
603	Damian Rolls	.15
604	Juan Gonzalez	.25
605	Aquilino Lopez	.15
606	Jose Valverde	.15
607	Scott Sauerbeck	.15
608	Joe Borowski	.15
609	Josh Bard	.15
610	Austin Kearns	.25
611	Chin-Hui Tsao	.15
612	Wilfredo Ledezma	.15
613	Aaron Guiel	.15
614	LaTroy Hawkins	.15
615	Tony Armas Jr.	.15
616	Steve Trachsel	.15
617	Ted Lilly	.15
618	Todd Pratt	.15
619	Sean Burroughs	.15
620	Rafael Palmeiro	.40
621	Jeremi Gonzalez	.15
622	Quinton McCracken	.15
623	David Ortiz	.25
624	Randall Simon	.15
625	Wily Mo Pena	.15
626	Nate Cornejo	.15
627	Brian Anderson	.15
628	Corey Koskie	.15
629	Keith Foulke	.15
630	Rheal Cormier	.15
631	Sidney Ponson	.15
632	Gary Matthews Jr.	.15
633	Herbert Perry	.15
634	Shea Hillenbrand	.15
635	Craig Biggio	.25
636	Barry Larkin	.25
637	Orlando Merced	.15

638	Anaheim Angels	.15
639	Arizona Diamondbacks	.15
640	Atlanta Braves	.15
641	Baltimore Orioles	.15
642	Boston Red Sox	.25
643	Chicago Cubs	.40
644	Chicago White Sox	.15
645	Cincinnati Reds	.15
646	Cleveland Indians	.15
647	Colorado Rockies	.15
648	Detroit Tigers	.15
649	Florida Marlins	.15
650	Houston Astros	.15
651	Kansas City Royals	.15
652	Los Angeles Dodgers	.15
653	Milwaukee Brewers	.15
654	Minnesota Twins	.15
655	Montreal Expos	.15
656	New York Mets	.15
657	New York Yankees	.50
658	Oakland Athletics	.15
659	Philadelphia Phillies	.15
660	Pittsburgh Pirates	.15
661	San Diego Padres	.15
662	San Francisco Giants	.15
663	Seattle Mariners	.15
664	St. Louis Cardinals	.15
665	Tampa Bay Devil Rays	.15
666	Texas Rangers	.15
667	Toronto Blue Jays	.15
668	Kyle Sleeth	.15
669	Bradley Sullivan	.15
670	Carlos Quentin	.50
671	Conor Jackson	1.00
672	Jeffrey Allison	.15
673	Matthew Moses	.25
674	Tim Stauffer	.15
675	Estee Harris RC	.25
676	David Aardsma	.15
677	Omar Quintanilla	.25
678	Aaron Hill	.15
679	Tony Richie	.15
680	Lastings Milledge	3.00
681	Brad Snyder	.15
682	Jason Hirsh	.50
683	Logan Kensing RC	.40
684	Chris Lubanski	.15
685	Ryan Harvey	.15
686	Ryan Wagner	.15
687	Rickie Weeks	.50
688	Jeremy Guthrie, Grady Sizemore	.25
689	Edwin Jackson, Greg Miller	.15
690	Neal Cotts, Jeremy Reed	.15
691	Nicholas Markakis, Adam Loewen	.15
692	Delmon Young, B.J. Upton	.75
693	Nomar Garciaparra, Alfonso Soriano	.50
694	Ichiro Suzuki, Albert Pujols	.50
695	Jim Thome, Mike Schmidt	.40
696	Mike Mussina	.25
697	Bengie Molina	.15
698	John Olerud	.15
699	Bret Boone	.25
700	Eric Chavez	.25
701	Alex Rodriguez	.75
702	Mike Cameron	.15
703	Ichiro Suzuki	.75
704	Torii Hunter	.25
705	Mike Hampton	.15
706	Mike Matheny	.15
707	Derrek Lee	.15
708	Luis Castillo	.15
709	Scott Rolen	.40
710	Edgar Renteria	.25
711	Andruw Jones	.25
712	Jose Cruz Jr.	.15
713	Jim Edmonds	.25
714	Roy Halladay	.25
715	Eric Gagne	.25
716	Alex Rodriguez	.75
717	Angel Berroa	.15
718	Dontrelle Willis	.25
719	Todd Helton	.25
720	Marcus Giles	.15
721	Edgar Renteria	.25
722	Scott Rolen	.40
723	Albert Pujols	.75
724	Gary Sheffield	.25
725	Javy Lopez	.25
726	Eric Gagne	.25
727	Randy Wolf	.15
728	Bobby Cox	.15
729	Scott Podsednik	.15
730	World Series Game 4	.15
731	World Series Game 5	.15
732	World Series Game 6	.15
733	World Series MVP	.25

Gold

Stars (1-733):   5-10X
Production 2,004 Sets

Black

Black (1-733):   15-30X
Production 53 Sets

1st Edition

	NM/M
Stars:	3-5X
HTA Exclusive	
1st Edition Pack (10):	3.00
1st Edition Box (20):	55.00

2004 Topps Team Factory Sets

	NM/M
Complete Astros Set (737):	75.00
Complete Cubs Set (737):	75.00
Complete Red Sox Set (737):	75.00
Complete Yankees Set (737):	75.00

Astros Prospects

1	Brooks Conrad	1.00
2	Hector Giminez	1.00
3	Kevin Davidson	1.00
4	Chris Burke	3.00
5	John Buck	1.00

Cubs Prospects

1	Bobby Brownlie	2.00
2	Felix Pie	3.00
3	Jon Connolly	1.00
4	David Kelton	1.00
5	Ricky Nolasco	1.00

Red Sox Prospects

1	David Murphy	1.00
2	Kevin Youkilis	3.00
3	Juan Cedeno	1.00
4	Matt Murton	1.00
5	Kenny Perez	1.00

Yankees Prospects

1	Rudy Guillen	1.00
2	David Parrish	2.00
3	Brad Halsey	1.00
4	Hector Made	1.00
5	Robinson Cano	6.00

All-Stars

		NM/M
Complete Set (20):		20.00
Common Player:		.50
Inserted 1:16		
TAS1	Jason Giambi	1.50
TAS2	Ichiro Suzuki	2.50
TAS3	Alex Rodriguez	3.00
TAS4	Albert Pujols	3.00
TAS5	Alfonso Soriano	1.50
TAS6	Nomar Garciaparra	2.50
TAS7	Andruw Jones	1.00
TAS8	Carlos Delgado	.75
TAS9	Gary Sheffield	.75
TAS10	Jorge Posada	.75
TAS11	Magglio Ordonez	.75

TAS12	Kerry Wood	1.50
TAS13	Garret Anderson	.75
TAS14	Bret Boone	.50
TAS15	Hank Blalock	.75
TAS16	Mike Lowell	.50
TAS17	Todd Helton	1.00
TAS18	Vernon Wells	.50
TAS19	Roger Clemens	3.00
TAS20	Scott Rolen	1.50

All-Star Stitches

		NM/M
Common Player:		5.00
Inserted 1:137		
GA	Garret Anderson	6.00
HB	Hank Blalock	6.00
AB	Aaron Boone	5.00
BD	Brendan Donnelly	5.00
CE	Carl Everett	5.00
KF	Keith Foulke	5.00
RF	Rafael Furcal	8.00
EGA	Eric Gagne	8.00
NG	Nomar Garciaparra	15.00
TG	Troy Glaus	8.00
EG	Eddie Guardado	5.00
SH	Shigetoshi Hasegawa	5.00
TH	Todd Helton	8.00
RH	Ramon Hernandez	5.00
AJ	Andruw Jones	8.00
EL	Esteban Loaiza	5.00
PL	Paul LoDuca	5.00
JL	Javy Lopez	8.00
ML	Mike Lowell	5.00
EM	Edgar Martinez	8.00
MMO	Melvin Mora	5.00
JM	Jamie Moyer	5.00
MM	Mark Mulder	6.00
RO	Russ Ortiz	6.00
JP	Jorge Posada	8.00
ER	Edgar Renteria	5.00
AR	Alex Rodriguez	15.00
SR	Scott Rolen	10.00
JS	Jason Schmidt	6.00
JV	Jose Vidro	5.00
BW	Billy Wagner	5.00
VW	Vernon Wells	6.00
RWH	Rondell White	5.00
WW	Woody Williams	6.00
PW	Preston Wilson	5.00
RW	Randy Wolf	5.00
KW	Kerry Wood	8.00

All-Star Patch Relics

No Pricing
Inserted 1:7,698

American Treasures Cut Signatures

No Pricing
Inserted 1:658,152

American Treasures Dual

Complete Set (1):
AT-GB2 George H.W. Bush, George W. Bush

American Treasures Presidential Signatures

No Pricing
Production One Set

Autographs

		NM/M
Common Player:		
JB	Josh Beckett	50.00
HB	Hank Blalock	20.00
CF	Cliff Floyd	8.00
JG	Jay Gibbons	15.00
KG	Khalil Greene	10.00
EH	Eric Hinske	10.00
TH	Torii Hunter	25.00
AK	Austin Kearns	25.00
PK	Paul Konerko	15.00
PL	Paul LoDuca	10.00
ML	Mike Lowell	8.00
VM	Victor Martinez	20.00
MO	Magglio Ordonez	15.00
JP	Josh Phelps	8.00
MP	Mark Prior	40.00
ER	Elizardo Ramirez	8.00
BS	Benito Santiago	15.00
MS	Mike Sweeney	20.00
MT	Mark Teixeira	25.00
BU	B.J. Upton	20.00
JV	Jose Vidro	8.00
Series 2		
GA	Garret Anderson	35.00
LB	Lance Berkman	35.00
AB	Aaron Boone	35.00
BB	Bobby Brownlie	30.00
MC	Miguel Cabrera	40.00
ZG	Zack Greinke	20.00
AH	Aubrey Huff	20.00
DM	Dustin McGowan	15.00
SP	Scott Podsednik	25.00
JP	Jorge Posada	40.00
IR	Ivan Rodriguez	45.00
SR	Scott Rolen	30.00
DW	Dontrelle Willis	30.00

Derby Digs

		NM/M
Common Player:		8.00
Inserted 1:585		
GA	Garret Anderson	8.00
BB	Bret Boone	8.00
CD	Carlos Delgado	8.00
JE	Jim Edmonds	8.00
JG	Jason Giambi	15.00
AP	Albert Pujols	25.00
RS	Richie Sexson	8.00

Draft Pick Bonus

		NM/M
Complete Set (15):		50.00
Complete Holiday Set (10):		30.00
Complete Retail Set (5):		20.00
1	Josh Johnson	4.00
2	Donny Lucy	4.00
3	Greg Golson	6.00
4	K.C. Herren	4.00
5	Jeff Marquez	8.00
6	Mark Rogers	8.00
7	Eric Hurley	4.00
8	Gio Gonzalez	6.00
9	Thomas Diamond	6.00
10	Matt Bush	8.00
11	Kyle Waldrop	6.00
12	Neil Walker	6.00
13	Mike Ferris	4.00
14	Ray Liotta	6.00
15	Phillip Hughes	15.00

Fall Classic Covers

	NM/M
Complete Set (99):	125.00
Common World Series Card:	2.00
Inserted 1:12	

Hit Parade

	NM/M
Complete Set (30):	20.00
Common Player:	.50

Rafael Palmeiro

Inserted 1:7		
HP1	Sammy Sosa	3.00
HP2	Rafael Palmeiro	1.00
HP3	Fred McGriff	.50
HP4	Ken Griffey Jr.	2.00
HP5	Juan Gonzalez	1.00
HP6	Frank Thomas	1.00
HP7	Andres Galarraga	.50
HP8	Jim Thome	1.50
HP9	Jeff Bagwell	1.00
HP10	Mike Piazza	2.00
HP11	Rafael Palmeiro	1.00
HP12	Sammy Sosa	3.00
HP13	Fred McGriff	.50
HP14	Andres Galarraga	.50
HP15	Juan Gonzalez	1.00
HP16	Frank Thomas	1.00
HP17	Jeff Bagwell	1.00
HP18	Ken Griffey Jr.	2.00
HP19	Ruben Sierra	.50
HP20	Ellis Burks	.50
HP21	Rafael Palmeiro	1.00
HP22	Roberto Alomar	.75
HP23	Julio Franco	.50
HP24	Andres Galarraga	.50
HP25	Fred McGriff	.50
HP26	Craig Biggio	.75
HP27	Barry Larkin	.75
HP28	Edgar Martinez	.50
HP29	Ellis Burks	.50
HP30	Sammy Sosa	3.00

Hobby Masters

		NM/M
Complete Set (20):		40.00
Common Player:		.75
Inserted 1:12		
HM1	Albert Pujols	3.00
HM2	Mark Prior	4.00
HM3	Alex Rodriguez	4.00
HM4	Nomar Garciaparra	3.00
HM5	Barry Bonds	4.00
HM6	Sammy Sosa	3.00
HM7	Alfonso Soriano	2.00
HM8	Ichiro Suzuki	2.50
HM9	Derek Jeter	4.00
HM10	Jim Thome	1.50
HM11	Jason Giambi	1.50
HM12	Mike Piazza	2.50
HM13	Barry Zito	1.00
HM14	Randy Johnson	2.00
HM15	Adam Dunn	1.00
HM16	Vladimir Guerrero	2.00
HM17	Gary Sheffield	.75
HM18	Carlos Delgado	1.00
HM19	Chipper Jones	2.50
HM20	Dontrelle Willis	1.00

Own the Game

	NM/M
Complete Set (30):	25.00

GARRET ANDERSON

Common Player:		.50
Inserted 1:18		
OG1	Jim Thome	1.50
OG2	Albert Pujols	3.00
OG3	Alex Rodriguez	3.00
OG4	Barry Bonds	4.00
OG5	Ichiro Suzuki	2.00
OG6	Derek Jeter	3.00
OG7	Nomar Garciaparra	3.00
OG8	Alfonso Soriano	1.50
OG9	Gary Sheffield	.75
OG10	Jason Giambi	1.00
OG11	Todd Helton	1.00
OG12	Garret Anderson	.50
OG13	Carlos Delgado	1.00
OG14	Manny Ramirez	1.00
OG15	Richie Sexson	.75
OG16	Vernon Wells	.50
OG17	Preston Wilson	.50
OG18	Frank Thomas	1.00
OG19	Shawn Green	.75
OG20	Rafael Furcal	.50
OG21	Juan Pierre	.50
OG22	Javy Lopez	.50
OG23	Edgar Renteria	.50
OG24	Mark Prior	3.00
OG25	Pedro J. Martinez	1.50
OG26	Kerry Wood	1.00
OG27	Curt Schilling	.75
OG28	Roy Halladay	.50
OG29	Eric Gagne	.50
OG30	Brandon Webb	.50

Presidential Pastime

		NM/M
Complete Set (42):		100.00
Common President:		3.00
Inserted 1:6		
PP1	George Washington	8.00
PP2	John Adams	4.00
PP3	Thomas Jefferson	4.00
PP4	James Madison	4.00
PP5	James Monroe	4.00
PP6	John Quincy Adams	4.00
PP7	Andrew Jackson	3.00
PP8	Martin Van Buren	3.00
PP9	William H. Harrison	3.00
PP10	John Tyler	4.00
PP11	James K. Polk	4.00
PP12	Zachary Taylor	3.00
PP13	Millard Fillmore	3.00
PP14	Franklin Pierce	3.00
PP15	James Buchanan	3.00
PP16	Abraham Lincoln	6.00
PP17	Andrew Johnson	3.00
PP18	Ulysses S. Grant	5.00
PP19	Rutherford B. Hayes	3.00
PP20	James Garfield	4.00
PP21	Chester A. Arthur	3.00
PP22	Grover Cleveland	3.00
PP23	Benjamin Harrison	3.00
PP24	William McKinley	3.00
PP25	Theodore Roosevelt	4.00
PP26	William H. Taft	4.00
PP27	Woodrow Wilson	4.00
PP28	Warren Harding	4.00
PP29	Calvin Coolidge	3.00
PP30	Herbert Hoover	3.00
PP31	Franklin D. Roosevelt	4.00
PP32	Harry S. Truman	4.00

PP33 Dwight D.
     Eisenhower 4.00
PP34 John F. Kennedy 6.00
PP35 Lyndon B. Johnson 3.00
PP36 Richard Nixon 4.00
PP37 Gerald Ford 3.00
PP38 Jimmy Carter 3.00
PP39 Ronald Reagan 3.00
PP40 George H.W. Bush 3.00
PP41 Bill Clinton 4.00
PP42 George W. Bush 3.00

Presidential First Pitch Relics

		NM/M
Common Player:		15.00
Inserted 1:592		
GHB	George H.W. Bush	25.00
GB	George W. Bush	25.00
BC	Bill Clinton	40.00
CC	Calvin Coolidge	15.00
DE	Dwight D. Eisenhower	15.00
GF	Gerald Ford	30.00
WH	Warren Harding	30.00
HH	Herbert Hoover	30.00
LJ	Lyndon B. Johnson	20.00
JK	John F. Kennedy	50.00
RN	Richard Nixon	30.00
RR	Ronald Reagan	30.00
FR	Franklin D. Roosevelt	40.00
WT	William H. Taft	25.00
HT	Harry S. Truman	30.00
WW	Woodrow Wilson	25.00

Series Seats Relics

		NM/M
Common Player:		10.00
Inserted 1:316		
LA	Luis Aparicio	15.00
BF	Bob Feller	12.00
RJ	Reggie Jackson	20.00
AK	Al Kaline	20.00
HK	Harmon Killebrew	25.00
WM	Willie Mays	25.00
BM	Bill Mazeroski	20.00
PM	Paul Molitor	20.00
JP	Jim Palmer	15.00
LP	Lou Piniella	10.00
BP	Boog Powell	10.00
BR	Brooks Robinson	15.00
FR	Frank Robinson	15.00
WS	Warren Spahn	15.00
RY	Robin Yount	20.00

Series Stitches Relics

		NM/M
Common Player:		10.00
JBE	Josh Beckett	10.00
JB	Johnny Bench	25.00
GB	George Brett	30.00
JCA	Jose Canseco	15.00
GC	Gary Carter	12.00
JC	Joe Carter	10.00
RC	Roger Clemens	20.00
LD	Lenny Dykstra	15.00
SG	Steve Garvey	15.00
KG	Kirk Gibson	10.00
DG	Dwight Gooden	15.00
RJA	Reggie Jackson	20.00
RJ	Randy Johnson	10.00
CJ	Chipper Jones	15.00
DJ	David Justice	15.00
HK	Harmon Killebrew	30.00
WM	Willie Mays	50.00
PO	Paul O'Neill	20.00
KP	Kirby Puckett	25.00
FR	Frank Robinson	30.00
MS	Mike Schmidt	30.00
TS	Tom Seaver	25.00
AS	Alfonso Soriano	15.00
RY	Robin Yount	20.00

Team Topps Legends Autographs

		NM/M
Inserted 1:766		
SG	Steve Garvey	15.00
BP	Boog Powell	10.00

World Series Highlights

		NM/M
Complete Set (30):		35.00
Common Player:		1.00
Inserted 1:18		
LB	Lou Brock	1.00
CF	Carlton Fisk	1.50
KG	Kirk Gibson	1.00
RJ	Reggie Jackson	2.00
DL	Don Larsen	1.00
MM	Willie Mays	4.00
BM	Bill Mazeroski	1.00
SM	Stan Musial	3.00
JP	Jim Palmer	1.00
KP	Kirby Puckett	2.00
BR	Brooks Robinson	2.00
MS	Mike Schmidt	4.00
TS	Tom Seaver	2.00
CY	Carl Yastrzemski	2.00
RY	Robin Yount	2.00
Series 2		
DB	Dusty Baker	1.00
JB	Johnny Bench	2.50
JCA	Jose Canseco	1.50
JC	Joe Carter	1.00
WF	Whitey Ford	2.00
LG	Luis Gonzalez	1.00
AJ	Andruw Jones	1.50
DJ	David Justice	1.00
AK	Al Kaline	2.00
WM	Willie McCovey	1.00
JP	Johnny Podres	1.00
FR	Frank Robinson	1.50
OS	Ozzie Smith	2.00
DS	Duke Snider	1.50
BT	Bobby Thomson	1.00

World Series Highlights Autographs

		NM/M
Common Player:		
LB	Lou Brock	30.00
CF	Carlton Fisk	50.00
KG	Kirk Gibson	30.00
DL	Don Larsen	25.00
WM	Willie Mays	
BM	Bill Mazeroski	30.00
JP	Jim Palmer	25.00
BR	Brooks Robinson	40.00
MS	Mike Schmidt	65.00
TS	Tom Seaver	
RY	Robin Yount	50.00
Series 2		
DB	Dusty Baker	20.00
JB	Johnny Bench	50.00
WF	Whitey Ford	35.00
RJ	Reggie Jackson	40.00
DJ	David Justice	30.00
AK	Al Kaline	40.00
SM	Stan Musial	75.00
JP	Johnny Podres	15.00
DS	Duke Snider	35.00
BT	Bobby Thomson	20.00

2004 Topps Traded & Rookies

Alex RODRIGUEZ

	NM/M
Complete Set (220):	50.00

Common Player:		.10
Chrome Cards:		2-4X
Pack (10):		4.00
Box (24):		85.00
T1	Pokey Reese	.10
T2	Tony Womack	.10
T3	Michael Barrett	.10
T4	Juan Uribe	.10
T5	J.D. Drew	.25
T6	Marlon Anderson	.10
T7	Carlos Guillen	.10
T8	Royce Clayton	.10
T9	Fernando Vina	.10
T10	Milton Bradley	.10
T11	Eddie Perez	.10
T12	Ben Grieve	.10
T13	Brian Jordan	.10
T14	Tony Graffanino	.10
T15	Billy Wagner	.10
T16	Terrence Long	.10
T17	Casey Fossum	.10
T18	Denny Hocking	.10
T19	Reggie Sanders	.10
T20	Javy Lopez	.25
T21	Jay Payton	.10
T22	Cliff Politte	.10
T23	Eddie Guardado	.10
T24	Andy Pettitte	.50
T25	Richie Sexson	.40
T26	Ronnie Belliard	.10
T27	Michael Tucker	.10
T28	Brad Fullmer	.10
T29	Orlando Palmeiro	.10
T30	Bartolo Colon	.25
T31	Larry Walker	.40
T32	Mark Kotsay	.10
T33	Jason Marquis	.10
T34	Dustan Mohr	.10
T35	Javier Vazquez	.25
T36	Nomar Garciaparra	1.50
T37	Tino Martinez	.25
T38	Hee Seop Choi	.10
T39	Damian Miller	.10
T40	Jose Lima	.10
T41	Todd Zeile	.10
T42	Raul Ibanez	.10
T43	Danys Baez	.10
T44	Tony Clark	.10
T45	Greg Maddux	1.00
T46	Craig Counsell	.10
T47	Orlando Cabrera	.25
T48	Jose Cruz Jr.	.10
T49	Kris Benson	.10
T50	Alex Rodriguez	2.00
T51	Steve Finley	.10
T52	Ramon Hernandez	.10
T53	Esteban Loaiza	.10
T54	Ugueth Urbina	.10
T55	Jeff Weaver	.10
T56	Flash Gordon	.10
T57	Jose Contreras	.10
T58	Paul LoDuca	.10
T59	Junior Spivey	.10
T60	Curt Schilling	1.00
T61	Brad Penny	.10
T62	Braden Looper	.10
T63	Miguel Cairo	.10
T64	Juan Encarnacion	.10
T65	Miguel Batista	.10
T66	Terry Francona	.10
T67	Lee Mazzilli	.10
T68	Al Pedrique	.10
T69	Ozzie Guillen	.10
T70	Phil Garner	.10
T71	Matt Bush RC	1.50
T72	Homer Bailey RC	5.00
T73	Greg Dobson RC	2.00
T74	Kyle Waldrop RC	1.00
T75	Richie Robnett RC	1.00
T76	Jay Rainville RC	1.50
T77	Bill Bray RC	.50
T78	Phillip Hughes RC	10.00
T79	Scott Elbert RC	1.00
T80	Josh Fields RC	2.00
T81	Justin Orenduff RC	.75
T82	Dan Putnam RC	.75
T83	Chris Nelson RC	2.50
T84	Blake DeWitt RC	2.00
T85	J.P. Howell RC	1.00
T86	Huston Street RC	2.00
T87	Kurt Suzuki RC	1.50
T88	Erick San Pedro RC	1.00
T89	Matt Tuiasosopo RC	1.50
T90	Matt Macri RC	1.00
T91	Chad Tracy	.20
T92	Scott Hairston	.20
T93	Jonny Gomes	.20
T94	Chin-Feng Chen	.20
T95	Chien-Ming Wang	.50
T96	Dustin McGowan	.20
T97	Chris Burke	.20
T98	Denny Bautista	.20
T99	Preston Larrison	.20
T100	Kevin Youkilis	.40
T101	John Maine	.20
T102	Guillermo Quiroz	.20
T103	David Krynzel	.20
T104	David Kelton	.20
T105	Edwin Encarnacion	.20
T106	Chad Gaudin	.20
T107	Sergio Mitre	.20
T108	Laynce Nix	.20
T109	David Parrish	.20
T110	Brandon Claussen	.20
T111	Frank Francisco RC	.25
T112	Brian Dallimore RC	.25
T113	Jim Crowell RC	.25
T114	Andres Blanco RC	.50
T115	Eduardo Villacis RC	.50
T116	Kazuhito Tadano RC	.50
T117	Aarom Baldiris RC	.25
T118	Justin Germano RC	.25
T119	Joey Gathright RC	1.00
T120	Franklyn Gracesqui RC	.25
T121	Chin-Lung Hu RC	1.00
T122	Scott Olsen RC	1.00
T123	Tyler Davidson RC	.25
T124	Fausto Carmona RC	.50
T125	Tim Hutting RC	.25
T126	Ryan Meaux RC	.25
T127	Jon Connolly RC	.75
T128	Hector Made RC	.75
T129	Jamie Brown RC	.25
T130	Paul McAnulty RC	.50
T131	Chris Saenz RC	.25
T132	Marland Williams RC	.25
T133	Mike Huggins RC	.25
T134	Jesse Crain RC	.50
T135	Chad Bentz RC	.50
T136	Kazuo Matsui RC	.75
T137	Paul Maholm RC	.75
T138	Brock Jacobsen RC	.25
T139	Casey Daigle RC	.25
T140	Nyjer Morgan RC	.25
T141	Tom Mastny RC	.25
T142	Kody Kirkland RC	.50
T143	Jose Capellan RC	.50
T144	Felix Hernandez RC	5.00
T145	Shawn Hill RC	.25
T146	Danny Gonzalez RC	.25
T147	Scott Dohmann RC	.25
T148	Tommy Murphy RC	.50
T149	Akinori Otsuka RC	.25
T150	Miguel Perez RC	.50
T151	Mike Rouse RC	.25
T152	Ramon Ramirez RC	.50
T153	Luke Hughes RC	.25
T154	Howard Kendrick RC	5.00
T155	Ryan Budde RC	.25
T156	Charlie Zink RC	.25
T157	Warner Madrigal RC	.50
T158	Jason Szuminski RC	.25
T159	Chad Chop RC	.50
T160	Shingo Takatsu RC	.50
T161	Matt Lemanczyk RC	.25
T162	Wardell Starling RC	.25
T163	Nick Gorneault RC	.25
T164	Scott Proctor RC	.50
T165	Brooks Conrad RC	.50
T166	Hector Gimenez RC	.50
T167	Kevin Howard RC	.50
T168	Vince Perkins RC	.25
T169	Brock Peterson RC	.25
T170	Chris Shelton RC	1.00
T171	Erick Aybar RC	1.00
T172	Paul Bacot RC	.25
T173	Matt Capps RC	.25
T174	Kory Casto RC	.25
T175	Juan Cedeno RC	.25
T176	Vito Chiaravalloti RC	.50
T177	Alec Zumwalt RC	.25
T178	J.J. Furmaniak RC	.50
T179	Lee Gwaltney RC	.25
T180	Donald Kelly RC	.25
T181	Benji DeQuin RC	.25
T182	Brant Colamarino RC	.75
T183	Juan Gutierrez RC	.25
T184	Carl Loadenthal RC	.50
T185	Ricky Nolasco RC	1.25
T186	Jeff Salazar RC	1.00
T187	Rob Tejeda RC	.50
T188	Alex Romero RC	.25
T189	Yoann Torrealba RC	.25
T190	Carlos Sosa RC	.25
T191	Tim Bittner RC	.25
T192	Chris Aguila RC	.25
T193	Jason Frasor RC	.25
T194	Reid Gorecki RC	.50
T195	Dustin Nippert RC	.50
T196	Javier Guzman RC	.50
T197	Harvey Garcia RC	.25
T198	Ivan Ochoa RC	.25
T199	Dave Wallace RC	.25
T200	Joel Zumaya RC	2.50
T201	Casey Kopitzke RC	.25
T202	Lincoln Holdzkom RC	.25
T203	Chad Santos RC	.25
T204	Brian Pilkington RC	.25

T205 Terry Jones RC .25
T206 Jerome Gamble RC .25
T207 Brad Eldred RC .50
T208 David Pauley RC 1.00
T209 Kevin Davidson RC .25
T210 Damaso Espino RC .25
T211 Tom Farmer RC .50
T212 Michael Mooney RC .25
T213 James Tomlin RC .25
T214 Greg Thissen RC .25
T215 Calvin Hayes RC .25
T216 Fernando Cortez RC .25
T217 Sergio Silva RC .25
T218 Jon DeVries RC .25
T219 Don Sutton RC 1.00
T220 Leo Nunez RC .25
T221 Barry Bonds
HTA Redemption 5.00

Gold
Stars: 5-10X
Rookies: 2-3X
Production 2,004 Sets

X-Fractor
No Pricing
Production 20 Sets

Chrome Refractor
Stars: 4-8X
Rookies: 2-4X
Inserted 1:12

Blue Refractor
No Pricing
Production One Set

Printing Plates
No pricing due to scarcity.

Dual Transactions Relic
NM/M
Common Player:
Inserted 1:562
RP Rafael Palmeiro 15.00
AR Alex Rodriguez 25.00
CS Curt Schilling 15.00

Future Phenoms
NM/M
Common Player: 5.00
KC Kevin Cash 5.00
BC Bobby Crosby 10.00
ED Eric Duncan 5.00
AG Adrian Gonzalez 8.00
NG Nick Green 5.00
JH J.J. Hardy 5.00
EJ Edwin Jackson 5.00
MM Mark Malaska 5.00
VM Victor Martinez 8.00
KM Kazuo Matsui 10.00
LM Lastings Milledge 15.00
JM Justin Morneau 10.00
DN Dioner Navarro 8.00
RN Ramon Nivar 5.00
BU B.J. Upton 12.00
JW Jayson Werth 10.00
DY Delmon Young 10.00

Hall of Fame Relic
NM/M
Common Player:
DE Dennis Eckersley 10.00
PM Paul Molitor 15.00

Hall of Fame Dual Relic
NM/M
Inserted 1:3,388
ME Paul Molitor,
Dennis Eckersley 30.00

Signature Moves
NM/M
Common Autograph: 10.00
MB Milton Bradley 15.00
MK Mark Kotsay 10.00
EM Eli Marrero 10.00
MN Mike Neu 10.00
AR Alex Rodriguez 160.00
JV Javier Vazquez 15.00
FV Fernando Vina 10.00
AW Adam Wainwright 35.00

Signature Cuts
No Pricing
Production One Set

Transactions Relics

VLADIMIR GUERRERO • OF
ANAHEIM ANGELS

NM/M
Common Player: 5.00
Inserted 1:106
RA Roberto Alomar 8.00
JB Jeromy Burnitz 5.00
HC Hee Seop Choi 5.00
RC Roger Clemens 15.00
CE Carl Everett 5.00
JG Juan Gonzalez 8.00
VG Vladimir Guerrero 10.00
BJ Brian Jordan 5.00
KL Kenny Lofton 5.00
JL Javy Lopez 5.00
RP Rafael Palmeiro 8.00
AP Andy Pettitte 8.00
AR Alex Rodriguez 25.00
IR Ivan Rodriguez 10.00
RS Reggie Sanders 5.00
RLS Richie Sexson 8.00
GS Gary Sheffield 10.00
MT Miguel Tejada 8.00
RW Rondell White 5.00

2004 Topps All-Time Fan Favorites

CATCHER EXPOS GARY CARTER TOPPS

NM/M
Complete Set (150): 35.00
Common Player: .25
Pack (6): 4.00
Box (24): 80.00
1 Willie Mays 2.50
2 Bob Gibson .75
3 Dave Steib .25
4 Tim McCarver .25
5 Reggie Jackson .75
6 John Candelaria .25
7 Lenny Dykstra .25
8 Tony Oliva .50
9 Frank Viola .25
10 Don Mattingly 2.50
11 Garry Maddox .25
12 Randy Jones .25
13 Joe Carter .50
14 Orlando Cepeda .50
15 Bob Sheppard .25
16 Bobby Grich .25
17 George Scott .25
18 Mickey Rivers .25
19 Ron Santo .25
20 Mike Schmidt 2.00
21 Luis Aparicio .25
22 Cesar Geronimo .25
23 Jack Morris .25
24 Jeffrey Loria .25
25 George Brett 2.00
26 Paul O'Neill .25
27 Reggie Smith .25
28 Robin Yount 1.00
29 Andre Dawson .50
30 Whitey Ford .75
31 Ralph Kiner .50
32 Will Clark .50
33 Keith Hernandez .25
34 Tony Fernandez .25
35 Willie McGee .25
36 Harmon Killebrew .75
37 Dave Kingman .25
38 Kirk Gibson .25
39 Terry Steinbach .25

40 Frank Robinson .75
41 Chet Lemon .25
42 Mike Cuellar .25
43 Darrell Evans .25
44 Don Kessinger .25
45 Dave Concepcion .25
46 Sparky Anderson .25
47 Bret Saberhagen .25
48 Brett Butler .25
49 Kent Hrbek .25
50 Hank Aaron 2.50
51 Rudolph Giuliani .25
52 Clete Boyer .25
53 Mookie Wilson .25
54 Dave Stewart .25
55 Gary Matthews .25
56 Roy Face .25
57 Vida Blue .25
58 Jimmy Key .25
59 Al Hrabosky .25
60 Al Kaline .75
61 Mike Scott .25
62 Jack McDowell .25
63 Reggie Jackson .75
64 Earl Weaver .25
65 Ernie Harwell .25
66 David Justice .25
67 Wilbur Wood .25
68 Mike Boddicker .25
69 Don Zimmer .25
70 Jim Palmer .50
71 Doug DeCinces .25
72 Ryne Sandberg 1.00
73 Don Newcombe .25
74 Denny Martinez .25
75 Carl Yastrzemski 1.50
76 Bake McBride .25
77 Andy Van Slyke .25
78 Bruce Sutter .50
79 Bobby Valentine .25
80 Johnny Bench 1.50
81 Orel Hershiser .25
82 Danny Tartabull .25
83 Lou Whitaker .25
84 Alan Trammell .50
85 Sam McDowell .25
86 Ray Knight .25
87 Fernando Valenzuela .25
88 Ben Oglivie .25
89 Billy Beane .25
90 Yogi Berra 1.00
91 Jose Canseco .50
92 Bobby Bonilla .25
93 Darren Daulton .25
94 Harold Reynolds .25
95 Lou Brock .50
96 Pete Incaviglia .25
97 Eric Gregg .25
98 Devon White .25
99 Kelly Gruber .25
100 Nolan Ryan 3.00
101 Carlton Fisk .50
102 George Foster .25
103 Dennis Eckersley .25
104 Rick Sutcliffe .25
105 Cal Ripken Jr. 3.00
106 Norm Cash .25
107 Charlie Hough .25
108 Paul Molitor .75
109 Maury Wills .25
110 Tom Seaver 1.00
111 Brooks Robinson 1.00
112 Jim Rice .25
113 Dwight Gooden .25
114 Harold Baines .25
115 Tim Raines .25
116 Roy Smalley .25
117 Richie Allen .25
118 Ron Swoboda .25
119 Ron Guidry .25
120 Duke Snider .75
121 Ferguson Jenkins .50
122 Mark Fidrych .25
123 Buddy Bell .25
124 Bo Jackson .50
125 Stan Musial 1.50
126 Jesse Barfield .25
127 Tony Gwynn 1.00
128 Phil Garner .25
129 Dale Murphy .75
130 Wade Boggs .50
131 Sid Fernandez .25
132 Monte Irvin .25
133 Peter Ueberroth .25
134 Gary Gaetti .25
135 Gorman Thomas .25
136 Davey Lopes .25
137 Sy Berger .25
138 Buck O'Neil .25
139 Herb Score .25
140 Rod Carew .75
141 Joe Buck .25
142 Willie Horton .25
143 Hal McRae .25

144 Rollie Fingers .25
145 Tom Brunansky .25
146 Fay Vincent .25
147 Gary Carter .50
148 Bobby Richardson .25
149 Steve Garvey .25
150 Don Larsen .50

Refractor

KELLY GRUBER BlueJays

Cards (1-150): 3-6X
Production 299 Sets

Autographs

NOLAN RYAN P
ANGELS

NM/M
Common Autograph: 10.00
Inserted 2:Box
SP's Noted
HA Hank Aaron/50 350.00
RA Richie Allen 15.00
SA Sparky Anderson/100 20.00
LA Luis Aparicio/100 40.00
HB Harold Baines/100 20.00
JB Jesse Barfield 10.00
BB Billy Beane/100 25.00
BBE Buddy Bell 20.00
JBE Johnny Bench/100 150.00
SB Sy Berger 50.00
YB Yogi Berra/100 90.00
VB Vida Blue 15.00
MB Mike Boddicker 15.00
WB Wade Boggs/50 100.00
BMB Bobby Bonilla 20.00
GB George Brett/50 100.00
LB Lou Brock/100 60.00
TB Tom Brunansky 25.00
JB Joe Buck/100 30.00
JCA Jose Canseco/100 65.00
RC Rod Carew/100 60.00
GC Gary Carter/50 60.00
JC Joe Carter/100 45.00
OC Orlando Cepeda/100 65.00
DC Dave Concepcion/100 40.00
DD Darren Daulton 15.00
AD Andre Dawson/100 40.00
LD Lenny Dykstra/100 20.00
DEC Dennis Eckersley/100 40.00
DE Darrell Evans 10.00
SF Sid Fernandez/100 40.00
TF Tony Fernandez 15.00
MF Mark Fidrych/100 40.00
RF Rollie Fingers/100 40.00
WF Whitey Ford/100 100.00
GF George Foster 10.00
SG Steve Garvey/100 30.00
CG Cesar Geronimo/100 65.00
BG Bob Gibson/100 90.00
DG Dwight Gooden/50 60.00
EG Eric Gregg 15.00

BGR	Bobby Grich	10.00
RG	Ron Guidry/100	50.00
TG	Tony Gwynn/50	100.00
EH	Ernie Harwell	25.00
KH	Keith Hernandez/50	25.00
OH	Orel Hershiser	30.00
WH	Willie Horton	10.00
CH	Charlie Hough	15.00
AH	Al Hrabosky	15.00
PI	Pete Incaviglia	20.00
MI	Monte Irvin/100	25.00
BJ	Bo Jackson/50	100.00
RJ2	Reggie Jackson	80.00
FJ	Ferguson Jenkins	15.00
RJO	Randy Jones	10.00
DJ	David Justice	25.00
AK	Al Kaline/50	100.00
DKE	Don Kessinger	15.00
JK	Jimmy Key/100	45.00
HK	Harmon Killebrew/100	85.00
RK	Ralph Kiner	40.00
DK	Dave Kingman	40.00
RKN	Ray Knight/100	40.00
DLA	Don Larsen	15.00
CL	Chet Lemon	15.00
DL	Davey Lopes	10.00
GM	Gary Mathews	10.00
DON	Don Mattingly/50	125.00
WM	Willie Mays/50	225.00
TM	Tim McCarver	40.00
JM	Jack McDowell	15.00
SM	Sam McDowell/100	15.00
WMC	Willie McGee/100	50.00
PM	Paul Molitor/50	85.00
JMO	Jack Morris	10.00
DM	Dale Murphy/50	75.00
SM	Stan Musial/100	100.00
BO	Buck O'Neil	30.00
PO	Paul O'Neill/50	60.00
BO	Ben Oglivie	15.00
TO	Tony Oliva	30.00
JP	Jim Palmer/50	100.00
TR	Tim Raines	25.00
HR	Harold Reynolds/100	30.00
JR	Jim Rice/100	40.00
BR	Bobby Richardson	15.00
CR	Cal Ripken Jr./50	200.00
MR	Mickey Rivers	10.00
BRO	Brooks Robinson/50	100.00
FR	Frank Robinson/100	80.00
NR	Nolan Ryan	175.00
BS	Bret Saberhagen/100	45.00
RYN	Ryne Sandberg/100	100.00
RS	Ron Santo	30.00
MS	Mike Schmidt/50	120.00
GS	George Scott	15.00
MSC	Mike Scott	10.00
TSE	Tom Seaver/50	100.00
DSN	Duke Snider/100	75.00
DS	Dave Stewart	10.00
DST	Dave Stieb	25.00
RSU	Rick Sutcliffe/100	40.00
BSU	Bruce Sutter	35.00
RSW	Ron Swoboda	15.00
AT	Alan Trammell/100	60.00
PU	Peter Ueberroth/100	60.00
BV	Bobby Valentine/100	50.00
AV	Andy Van Slyke/100	65.00
FVI	Fay Vincent/100	50.00
EW	Earl Weaver	15.00
MW	Maury Wills	15.00
MWI	Mookie Wilson	10.00
WW	Wilbur Wood	15.00
CY	Carl Yastrzemski/50	100.00
RY	Robin Yount/100	100.00
DZ	Don Zimmer	30.00

Best Seat In The House

BEST SEAT IN THE HOUSE

		NM/M
Common Card:		15.00
BS1	Tom Seaver, Johnny Bench, George Foster	15.00
BS2	Frank Robinson, Jim Palmer, Brooks Robinson	15.00
BS3	Dave Parker, Bill Madlock, Bill Mazeroski	15.00
BS4	Kent Hrbek, Rod Carew, Harmon Killebrew	30.00

Relics

FRANK ROBINSON
OUTFIELD • BALTIMORE ORIOLES

		NM/M
Common Player:		5.00
WB	Wade Boggs	10.00
GB	George Brett	15.00
LB	Lou Brock	10.00
JC	Jose Canseco/Jsy	8.00
JCB	Jose Canseco/Bat	8.00
GC	Gary Carter	8.00
DE	Dennis Eckersley	5.00
CF	Carlton Fisk	10.00
GF	George Foster	5.00
KG	Kirk Gibson	5.00
KH	Keith Hernandez	8.00
RJ	Reggie Jackson	10.00
DJ	David Justice	5.00
HK	Harmon Killebrew	20.00
WM	Willie Mays	30.00
JM	Joe Morgan	5.00
GN	Graig Nettles	5.00
JP	Jim Palmer	8.00
DP	Dave Parker	5.00
KP	Kirby Puckett	10.00
HR	Harold Reynolds	5.00
JR	Jim Rice	5.00
BR	Brooks Robinson	12.00
FRB	Frank Robinson/Bat	8.00
FR	Frank Robinson/Jsy	8.00
NR	Nolan Ryan	25.00
BS	Bret Saberhagen	5.00
MS	Mike Schmidt	15.00
DS	Darryl Strawberry	8.00
EW	Earl Weaver	8.00
MW	Maury Wills	5.00
CY	Carl Yastrzemski	20.00

2004 Topps Bazooka

ANAHEIM ANGELS
BARTOLO COLON

		NM/M
Complete Set (300):		40.00
Common Player:		.15
Variations (30):		Same Price
Pack (8):		2.00
Box (24):		40.00
1	Bobby Abreu	.25
2	Jesse Foppert	.15
3	Shea Hillenbrand	.15
4	Jose Lima	.15
5	Manny Ramirez	.50
6	Denny Neagle	.15
7	Frank Thomas	.50
8	A.J. Burnett	.15
9	Carl Everett	.15
10	Scott Podsednik	.25
11	Travis Lee	.15
12	Mike Mussina	.40
13	Runelvys Hernandez	.15
14	Shannon Stewart	.15
15	Miguel Cabrera	.40
16	Edgardo Alfonzo	.15
17	Victor Zambrano	.15
18	Rafael Furcal	.25
19	Eric Hinske	.15
20	Paul LoDuca	.15
21	Phil Nevin	.15
22	Aramis Ramirez	.15
23	Jim Thome	.75
24	Jeromy Burnitz	.15
25	Mark Prior	1.50
26	Ramon Hernandez	.15
27	Cliff Lee	.15
28	Greg Myers	.15
29	Robert Fick	.15
30	Mike Sweeney	.15
31	Carlos Zambrano	.15
32	Roberto Alomar	.40
33	Orlando Cabrera	.25
34	Orlando Hudson	.15
35	Nomar Garciaparra	1.50
36	Esteban Loaiza	.15
37	Laynce Nix	.15
38	Joe Randa	.15
39	Juan Uribe	.15
40	Pat Burrell	.40
41	Steve Finley	.15
42	Livan Hernandez	.15
43	Al Leiter	.15
44	Brett Myers	.15
45	Jody Gerut	.15
46	Mark Teixeira	.40
47	Barry Zito	.40
48	Moises Alou	.25
49	Mike Cameron	.15
50	Albert Pujols	1.50
51	Tim Hudson	.25
52	Kenny Lofton	.25
53	Trot Nixon	.15
54	Tim Redding	.15
55	Marlon Byrd	.15
56	Javier Vazquez	.25
57	Sean Burroughs	.15
58	Cliff Floyd	.15
59	Juan Rivera	.15
60	Mike Lieberthal	.15
61	Xavier Nady	.15
62	Brad Radke	.15
63	Miguel Tejada	.40
64	Ichiro Suzuki	1.00
65	Garret Anderson	.25
66	Sean Casey	.15
67	Jason Giambi	.75
68	Aubrey Huff	.15
69	Javy Lopez	.25
70	Hideo Nomo	.25
71	Mark Redman	.15
72	Jose Vidro	.15
73	Rich Aurilia	.15
74	Luis Castillo	.15
75	Jay Gibbons	.15
76	Torii Hunter	.25
77	Derek Lowe	.15
78	Wes Obermueller	.15
79	Edgar Renteria	.15
80	Jeff Bagwell	.50
81	Fernando Vina	.15
82	Frank Catalanotto	.15
83	Marcus Giles	.15
84	Raul Ibanez	.15
85	Mike Lowell	.25
86	Tomokazu Ohka	.15
87	Jose Reyes	.25
88	Omar Vizquel	.25
89	Shawn Chacon	.15
90	Rocco Baldelli	.25
91	Brian Giles	.25
92	Kazuhisa Ishii	.15
93	Greg Maddux	1.00
94	John Olerud	.25
95	Eric Chavez	.25
96	Doug Waechter	.15
97	Tony Batista	.15
98	Jeriome Robertson	.15
99	Troy Glaus	.25
100	Eric Gagne	.25
101	Pedro J. Martinez	.75
102	Magglio Ordonez	.25
103	Alex Rodriguez	2.00
104	Jason Bay	.15
105	Larry Walker	.25
106	Matt Clement	.15
107	Tom Glavine	.25
108	Geoff Jenkins	.25
109	Victor Martinez	.15
110	David Ortiz	.15
111	Ivan Rodriguez	.40
112	Jarrod Washburn	.15
113	Josh Beckett	.25
114	Bartolo Colon	.25
115	Juan Gonzalez	.40
116	Derek Jeter	2.00
117	Edgar Martinez	.25
118	Ramon Ortiz	.15
119	Scott Rolen	.75
120	Brandon Webb	.15
121	Carlos Beltran	.25
122	Jose Contreras	.25
123	Luis Gonzalez	.25
124	Jason Johnson	.15
125	Luis Matos	.15
126	Russ Ortiz	.15
127	Damian Rolls	.15
128	David Wells	.15
129	Adrian Beltre	.15
130	Shawn Green	.25
131	Nate Cornejo	.15
132	Nick Johnson	.15
133	Joe Mays	.15
134	Roy Oswalt	.25
135	C.C. Sabathia	.15
136	Vernon Wells	.25
137	Kris Benson	.15
138	Carl Crawford	.15
139	Ken Griffey Jr.	1.00
140	Randy Johnson	.75
141	Fred McGriff	.25
142	Vicente Padilla	.15
143	Tim Salmon	.25
144	Kip Wells	.15
145	Lance Berkman	.25
146	Jose Cruz Jr.	.15
147	Marquis Grissom	.15
148	Jacque Jones	.15
149	Gil Meche	.15
150	Vladimir Guerrero	.75
151	Reggie Sanders	.15
152	Ty Wigginton	.15
153	Angel Berroa	.15
154	Johnny Damon	.25
155	Rafael Palmeiro	.50
156	Chipper Jones	.75
157	Kevin Millar	.15
158	Corey Patterson	.25
159	Johan Santana	.15
160	Bernie Williams	.40
161	Craig Biggio	.25
162	Carlos Delgado	.50
163	Aaron Guiel	.15
164	Wade Miller	.15
165	Andruw Jones	.50
166	Jay Payton	.15
167	Benito Santiago	.15
168	Woody Williams	.15
169	Casey Blake	.15
170	Adam Dunn	.40
171	Jose Guillen	.15
172	Brian Jordan	.15
173	Kevin Millwood	.25
174	Carlos Pena	.15
175	Curt Schilling	.50
176	Jerome Williams	.15
177	Hank Blalock	.25
178	Erubiel Durazo	.15
179	Cristian Guzman	.15
180	Austin Kearns	.40
181	Raul Mondesi	.15
182	Andy Pettitte	.25
183	Jason Schmidt	.25
184	Jeremy Bonderman	.15
185	Dontrelle Willis	.25
186	Ray Durham	.15
187	Jerry Hairston Jr.	.15
188	Jason Kendall	.15
189	Melvin Mora	.15
190	Jeff Kent	.25
191	Jae Weong Seo	.15
192	Jack Wilson	.15
193	Cesar Izturis	.15
194	Jermaine Dye	.15
195	Roy Halladay	.25
196	Jason Phillips	.15
197	Matt Morris	.25
198	Mike Piazza	1.00
199	Richie Sexson	.40
200	Alfonso Soriano	.75
201	Mark Mulder	.25
202	David Eckstein	.15
203	Mike Hampton	.15
204	Ryan Klesko	.25
205	Damian Moss	.15
206	Juan Pierre	.15
207	Ben Sheets	.25
208	Randy Winn	.15
209	Bret Boone	.25
210	Jim Edmonds	.25
211	Rich Harden	.15
212	Paul Konerko	.25
213	Jamie Moyer	.15
214	A.J. Pierzynski	.15
215	Gary Sheffield	.25
216	Randy Wolf	.15
217	Kevin Brown	.25
218	Morgan Ensberg	.15
219	Bo Hart	.15
220	Bill Mueller	.15
221	Corey Koskie	.15
222	Joel Pineiro	.15
223	Preston Wilson	.15
224	Aaron Boone	.15
225	Kerry Wood	.50

226	Darin Erstad	.25
227	Wes Helms	.15
228	Brian Lawrence	.15
229	Mark Buehrle	.15
230	Sammy Sosa	1.25
231	Sidney Ponson	.15
232	Dmitri Young	.15
233	Ellis Burks	.15
234	Kelvim Escobar	.15
235	Todd Helton	.50
236	Matt Lawton	.15
237	Eric Munson	.15
238	Jorge Posada	.50
239	Junior Spivey	.15
240	Michael Young	.15
241	Ramon Nivar	.15
242	Edwin Jackson	.15
243	Felix Pie	.15
244	Ryan Wagner	.15
245	Grady Sizemore	.25
246	Bobby Jenks	.15
247	Chad Billingsley	.15
248	Casey Kotchman	.15
249	Bobby Crosby	.15
250	Khalil Greene	.15
251	Danny Garcia	.15
252	Nicholas Markakis	.15
253	Bernie Castro	.15
254	Aaron Hill	.15
255	Josh Barfield	.15
256	Ryan Wagner	.15
257	Ryan Harvey	.15
258	Jimmy Gobble	.15
259	Ryan Madson	.15
260	Zack Greinke	.15
261	Rene Reyes	.15
262	Eric Duncan	.15
263	Chris Lubanski	.15
264	Jeff Mathis	.15
265	Rickie Weeks	.25
266	Justin Morneau	.25
267	Brian Snyder	.15
268	Neal Cotts	.15
269	Joe Borchard	.15
270	Larry Bigbie	.15
271	Marcus McBeth RC	.40
272	Tydus Meadows RC	.40
273	Zach Miner RC	.50
274	Anthony Lerew RC	.40
275	Yadier Molina RC	.40
276	Jon Knott RC	.40
277	Matthew Moses	.40
278	Sung Jung RC	.40
279	Mike Gosling	.15
280	David Murphy	.15
281	Tim Frend RC	.40
282	Casey Myers RC	.40
283	Brayan Pena RC	.40
284	Omar Falcon RC	.40
285	Blake Hawksworth RC	.40
286	Jesse Roman RC	.40
287	Kyle Davies RC	.40
288	Matt Creighton RC	.40
289	Rodney Choy Foo RC	.40
290	Kyle Sleeth	.15
291	Carlos Quentin	.50
292	Khalid Ballouli RC	.40
293	Tim Stauffer	.15
294	Craig Ansman RC	.40
295	Dioner Navarro RC	.40
296	Josh Labandeira RC	.40
297	Jeff Allison	.15
298	Anthony Acevedo RC	.40
299	Brad Sullivan	.15
300	Conor Jackson	.50

Red

Cards (1-300):		1-2X
Inserted 1:1		

Mini

Stars (1-300):		1-2X
Inserted 1:1		

Adventures

AUTHENTIC
CHIPPER JONES
REGULAR ISSUE GAME-WORN JERSEY

		NM/M
Common Player:		4.00
EA	Edgardo Alfonzo	4.00
JB	Jeff Bagwell	8.00
LB	Lance Berkman	6.00
CB	Craig Biggio	4.00
KB	Kevin Brown	4.00
PB	Pat Burrell	6.00
MB	Marlon Byrd	4.00
SC	Sean Casey	4.00
LC	Luis Castillo	4.00
EC	Eric Chavez	5.00
AD1	Adam Dunn	6.00
AD2	Adam Dunn	4.00
CE	Carl Everett	4.00
CF	Cliff Floyd	4.00
NG	Nomar Garciaparra	10.00
JG	Jason Giambi	8.00
JDG	Jeremy Giambi	4.00

TEG	Troy Glaus	5.00
TG	Tom Glavine	5.00
LG	Luis Gonzalez	4.00
SG	Shawn Green	5.00
BG	Ben Grieve	4.00
VG	Vladimir Guerrero	8.00
CG	Cristian Guzman	4.00
TH	Toby Hall	4.00
TAH1	Tim Hudson	4.00
TAH2	Tim Hudson	4.00
GJ	Geoff Jenkins	4.00
RJ	Randy Johnson	8.00
AJ	Andruw Jones	6.00
CJ	Chipper Jones	8.00
JK	Jason Kendall	4.00
PK	Paul Konerko	4.00
PL	Paul LoDuca	4.00
ML	Mike Lowell	4.00
GM	Greg Maddux	8.00
KM	Kevin Millwood	6.00
MM	Mark Mulder	5.00
MCM	Mike Mussina	6.00
HN	Hideo Nomo	8.00
JO	John Olerud	4.00
RP1	Rafael Palmeiro	6.00
RP2	Rafael Palmeiro	6.00
BP	Brad Penny	4.00
MP1	Mike Piazza	10.00
MP2	Mike Piazza	10.00
AP	Albert Pujols	15.00
MR	Manny Ramirez	6.00
AR1	Alex Rodriguez	10.00
AR2	Alex Rodriguez	10.00
TJS	Tim Salmon	5.00
CS	Curt Schilling	8.00
AS	Alfonso Soriano	6.00
MT	Miguel Tejada	6.00
JT	Jim Thome	8.00
LW	Larry Walker	4.00
JW	Jarrod Washburn	4.00
BW	Bernie Williams	6.00
DW	Dontrelle Willis	4.00
PW	Preston Wilson	4.00
KW	Kerry Wood	6.00
BZ	Barry Zito	6.00

Blasts

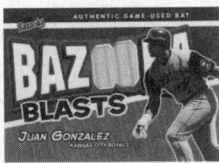

AUTHENTIC GAME-USED BAT
BAZOOKA BLASTS
JUAN GONZALEZ
KANSAS CITY ROYALS

		NM/M
Common Player:		4.00
RA	Roberto Alomar	6.00
MA	Moises Alou	4.00
RSA	Rich Aurilia	4.00
JB	Jeff Bagwell	8.00
RB	Rocco Baldelli	8.00
TB	Tony Batista	4.00
CIB	Carlos Beltran	4.00
LB	Lance Berkman	5.00
CB	Craig Biggio	4.00
HB	Hank Blalock	6.00
BB	Bret Boone	5.00
JNB	Jeromy Burnitz	4.00
SB	Sean Burroughs	4.00
CC	Carl Crawford	6.00
AD	Adam Dunn	6.00
CE	Carl Everett	4.00
BF	Brad Fullmer	4.00
RF	Rafael Furcal	4.00
AJG	Andres Galarraga	4.00
NG	Nomar Garciaparra	12.00
JG	Jason Giambi	8.00
TG	Troy Glaus	5.00

AG	Adrian Gonzalez	4.00
JAG	Juan Gonzalez	6.00
LG	Luis Gonzalez	4.00
SG	Shawn Green	6.00
MG	Marquis Grissom	4.00
VG	Vladimir Guerrero	8.00
CG	Cristian Guzman	4.00
NH	Nathan Haynes	4.00
TKH	Todd Helton	6.00
AH	Aubrey Huff	4.00
TH	Torii Hunter	5.00
CJ	Chipper Jones	8.00
PK	Paul Konerko	4.00
ML	Matt Lawton	4.00
CL	Carlos Lee	4.00
PL	Paul LoDuca	4.00
EM	Edgar Martinez	4.00
TM	Tino Martinez	6.00
FM	Fred McGriff	5.00
DM	Doug Mientkiewicz	4.00
JO	John Olerud	4.00
MO	Magglio Ordonez	4.00
RP	Rafael Palmeiro	4.00
CP	Corey Patterson	4.00
MP	Mike Piazza	10.00
JP	Jorge Posada	6.00
AP	Albert Pujols	15.00
ANR	Aramis Ramirez	4.00
MR	Manny Ramirez	6.00
JR	Juan Rivera	4.00
AR	Alex Rodriguez	10.00
IR	Ivan Rodriguez	8.00
SR	Scott Rolen	8.00
TJS	Tim Salmon	6.00
GS	Gary Sheffield	8.00
RS	Ruben Sierra	4.00
AS	Alfonso Soriano	8.00
SS	Shannon Stewart	4.00
ST	So Taguchi	5.00
MCT	Mark Teixeira	8.00
MT	Miguel Tejada	8.00
FT	Frank Thomas	8.00
MAT	Michael Tucker	4.00
MV	Mo Vaughn	6.00
OV	Omar Vizquel	4.00
LW	Larry Walker	5.00
VW	Vernon Wells	5.00
RW	Rondell White	4.00
BW	Bernie Williams	6.00

Comics

ALEX RODRIGUEZ
A-ROD YOUNGEST EVER TO HIT 300 HR

		NM/M
Complete Set (24):		6.00
Common Player:		.25
Inserted 1:4		
BC1	Garret Anderson	.25
BC2	Jeff Bagwell	.50
BC3	Hank Blalock	.25
BC4	Roy Halladay	.25
BC5	Dontrelle Willis	.25
BC6	Roger Clemens	.75
BC7	Carlos Delgado	.40
BC8	Rafael Furcal	.25
BC9	Eric Gagne	.25
BC10	Nomar Garciaparra	.75
BC11	Derek Jeter	.75
BC12	Esteban Loaiza	.25
BC13	Kevin Millwood	.25
BC14	Bill Mueller	.25
BC15	Rafael Palmeiro	.40
BC16	Albert Pujols	.75
BC17	Jose Reyes	.25
BC18	Alex Rodriguez	.75
BC19	Alfonso Soriano	.40
BC20	Sammy Sosa	.50
BC21	Ichiro Suzuki	.50
BC22	Frank Thomas	.40
BC23	Brad Wilkerson	.25
BC24	Houston Astros	.25

One-Liners

BAZOOKA ONE-LINERS
"RUN EVERYTHING OUT AND BE IN BY TWELVE."
RED SCHOENDIENST   ST. LOUIS CARDINALS

	NM/M
Common Player:	5.00
DA	Dick Allen	8.00
JB	Johnny Bench	10.00
BB	Bert Blyleven	5.00
WB1	Wade Boggs	6.00
WB2	Wade Boggs	6.00
GB	George Brett	20.00
BC	Bert Campaneris	5.00
RC	Rod Carew	8.00
GC	Gary Carter	5.00
JCA	Joe Carter	5.00
OC	Orlando Cepeda	5.00
RD	Ron Darling	5.00
AD	Andre Dawson	8.00
DE	Dennis Eckersley	10.00
KG1	Kirk Gibson	5.00
KG2	Kirk Gibson	5.00
DW	Dwight Gooden	5.00
KH	Keith Hernandez	5.00
RJ	Reggie Jackson	10.00
DJ1	David Justice	8.00
DJ2	David Justice	8.00
HK	Harmon Killebrew	20.00
JK	Jerry Koosman	5.00
BM	Bill Madlock	5.00
WM	Willie Mays	30.00
WMC	Willie McGee	8.00
TM	Tug McGraw	5.00
JM	Joe Morgan	8.00
DM	Dale Murphy	15.00
EM	Eddie Murray	10.00
PN	Phil Niekro	5.00
DP	Dave Parker	5.00
GP	Gaylord Perry	5.00
KP1	Kirby Puckett	10.00
KP2	Kirby Puckett	10.00
FR	Frank Robinson	10.00
NR	Nolan Ryan	15.00
BS	Bret Saberhagen	5.00
RSA	Ron Santo	10.00
MS	Mike Schmidt	15.00
RS	Red Schoendienst	5.00
TS	Tom Seaver	8.00
WS	Willie Stargell	8.00
CY	Carl Yastrzemski	15.00
RY	Robin Yount	10.00

Stand-Ups

VERNON WELLS
TORONTO BLUE JAYS   OUTFIELD

		NM/M
Complete Set (25):		20.00
Common Player:		.50
Inserted 1:8		
1	Jose Reyes	.50
2	Jim Thome	1.00
3	Roy Halladay	.50
4	Jason Giambi	1.00
5	Dontrelle Willis	.50
6	Mike Piazza	1.50
7	Chipper Jones	1.00
8	Mark Prior	2.00
9	Todd Helton	.75
10	Miguel Cabrera	.75
11	Derek Jeter	3.00
12	Nomar Garciaparra	2.00
13	Alex Rodriguez	3.00
14	Miguel Tejada	.50
15	Carlos Delgado	.75
16	Pedro J. Martinez	1.00
17	Sammy Sosa	2.00
18	Ichiro Suzuki	1.50
19	Vladimir Guerrero	1.00
20	Alfonso Soriano	1.00
21	Eric Chavez	.50
22	Albert Pujols	2.50
23	Ivan Rodriguez	.75
24	Vernon Wells	.50
25	Eric Gagne	.50

Tattoos

	NM/M
Complete Set (55):	8.00

Common Player: .15
Inserted 1:4

JB	Jeff Bagwell	.25
BAZ	Bazooka Logo	.15
LB	Lance Berkman	.15
CB	Craig Biggio	.15
KB	Kevin Brown	.15
PB	Pat Burrell	.15
MB	Marlon Byrd	.15
SC	Sean Casey	.15
LC	Luis Castillo	.15
EC	Eric Chavez	.15
AD	Adam Dunn	.15
CF	Cliff Floyd	.15
NG	Nomar Garciaparra	.75
JG	Jason Giambi	.40
TFG	Troy Glaus	.25
TG	Tom Glavine	.25
LG	Luis Gonzalez	.15
SG	Shawn Green	.15
VG	Vladimir Guerrero	.40
CG	Cristian Guzman	.15
TH	Toby Hall	.15
TAH	Tim Hudson	.15
GJ	Geoff Jenkins	.15
RJ	Randy Johnson	.40
AJ	Andruw Jones	.25
CJ	Chipper Jones	.40
JK	Jason Kendall	.15
PK	Paul Konerko	.15
PL	Paul LoDuca	.15
ML	Mike Lowell	.15
GM	Greg Maddux	.50
KM	Kevin Millwood	.15
MM	Mark Mulder	.15
MCM	Mike Mussina	.25
HN	Hideo Nomo	.15
JO	John Olerud	.15
RP	Rafael Palmeiro	.25
BP	Brad Penny	.15
MP	Mike Piazza	.50
AP	Albert Pujols	1.00
MR	Manny Ramirez	.25
AR	Alex Rodriguez	1.00
TJS	Tim Salmon	.25
CS	Curt Schilling	.15
AS	Alfonso Soriano	.40
MT	Miguel Tejada	.25
JT	Jim Thome	.40
TOP	Topps Logo	.15
LW	Larry Walker	.15
JW	Jarrod Washburn	.15
BW	Bernie Williams	.25
DW	Dontrelle Willis	.15
PW	Preston Wilson	.15
KW	Kerry Wood	.25
BZ	Barry Zito	.25

4-on-1 Stickers

NM/M
Complete Set (40): 8.00

Common Player: .20
Inserted 1:4

1 Rich Harden,
   Dontrelle Willis,
   Jerome Williams,
   Brandon Webb, .20
2 Eric Duncan, Derek Jeter,
   Alfonso Soriano,
   Jason Giambi, .75
3 Grady Sizemore,
   Rocco Baldelli,
   Ichiro Suzuki,
   Vladimir Guerrero .50
4 Roy Halladay,
   Pedro J. Martinez,
   Curt Schilling,
   Brett Myers .40
5 Alex Rodriguez,
   Angel Berroa, Jose Reyes,
   Khalil Greene .75
6 Kerry Wood, Adam Dunn,
   Jeff Kent, Scott Rolen .40
7 Miguel Cabrera,
   Scott Podsednik, Bo Hart,
   Mark Teixeira .20
8 Rickie Weeks,
   Josh Barfield, Albert Pujols,
   Vernon Wells .50
9 Torii Hunter,
   Garret Anderson,
   Bobby Abreu,
   Ken Griffey Jr. .40
10 Jay Gibbons,
   Chipper Jones,
   Mike Piazza,
   Mike Sweeney .50
11 David Ortiz, Nick Johnson,
   Carlos Delgado,
   Frank Thomas .40
12 Todd Helton, Jose Vidro,
   Mike Lowell,
   Miguel Tejada .40
13 Randy Wolf, Mark Mulder,
   Johan Santana,
   Randy Johnson .40
14 Bret Boone, Aubrey Huff,
   Eric Chavez,
   Javy Lopez .20
15 Jason Schmidt,
   Roy Oswalt, Joel Pineiro,
   Mark Prior .50
16 Kevin Millwood,
   Andy Pettitte, Matt Morris,
   Tim Hudson .20
17 Javier Vazquez,
   Esteban Loaiza,
   Orlando Cabrera,
   Roberto Alomar .20
18 Al Leiter, David Wells,
   Mike Hampton,
   Jarrod Washburn .20
19 Paul LoDuca,
   Mike Lieberthal,
   Brian Giles,
   Andruw Jones .20
20 Magglio Ordonez,
   Corey Patterson,
   Aaron Boone,
   Jeff Bagwell .40
21 Troy Glaus,
   Edgar Martinez,
   Manny Ramirez,
   Raul Ibanez .30
22 Sammy Sosa, Barry Zito,
   Bartolo Colon,
   Austin Kearns .50
23 Jim Edmonds,
   Gary Sheffield,
   Preston Wilson,
   Shawn Green .20
24 Bernie Williams,
   Juan Pierre, Josh Beckett,
   Mike Mussina .20
25 Ramon Hernandez,
   Jason Kendall,
   Jason Phillips,
   A.J. Pierzynski .20
26 Pat Burrell, Laynce Nix,
   Mike Cameron,
   Cliff Floyd .20
27 Eric Gagne, Carl Crawford,
   Jose Guillen,
   Steve Finley .20
28 Ellis Burks,
   Livan Hernandez,
   Derek Lowe,
   Kazuhisa Ishii .20
29 Jorge Posada, Jeff Mathis,
   Victor Martinez,
   Ivan Rodriguez .20
30 Jim Thome, Marcus Giles,
   Nomar Garciaparra,
   Hank Blalock .50

---

31 Edgar Renteria,
   Bobby Crosby, Neal Cotts,
   Russ Ortiz .20
32 Zack Greinke,
   Cristian Guzman,
   Cesar Izturis,
   Kevin Brown .20
33 Bobby Jenks,
   Ramon Nivar,
   Richie Sexson,
   Ryan Klesko .20
34 Omar Vizquel,
   Carlos Pena, Rafael Furcal,
   Gil Meche .20
35 Kenny Lofton, Tim Salmon,
   Marquis Grissom,
   Craig Biggio .20
36 Kyle Davies,
   Anthony Lerew,
   Brayan Pena,
   Sung Jung .20
37 Rodney Choy Foo,
   Craig Ansman,
   David Murphy,
   Matthew Moses .20
38 Carlos Quentin,
   Dioner Navarro,
   Marcus McBeth,
   Josh Labandeira .20
39 Kyle Sleeth,
   Conor Jackson,
   Brad Sullivan,
   Jeff Allison .20
40 Yadier Molina, Jon Knott,
   Blake Hawksworth,
   Tim Stauffer .20

2004 Topps Chrome

NM/M

Complete Set (466):
Common Player: .25
Common Rookie Auto.
  (221-246): 10.00
Inserted 1:21
Series 1 Pack (4): 3.50
Series 1 Box (20): 50.00
Series 2 Pack (4): 3.50
Series 2 Box (20): 50.00
1 Jim Thome 1.00
2 Reggie Sanders .25
3 Mark Kotsay .25
4 Edgardo Alfonzo .25
5 Tim Wakefield .25
6 Moises Alou .50
7 Jorge Julio .25
8 Bartolo Colon .50
9 Chan Ho Park .25
10 Ichiro Suzuki 3.00
11 Kevin Millwood .50
12 Preston Wilson .40
13 Tom Glavine .75
14 Junior Spivey .25
15 Marcus Giles .40
16 David Segui .25
17 Kevin Millar .25
18 Corey Patterson .40
19 Aaron Rowand .25
20 Derek Jeter 4.00
21 Luis Castillo .25
22 Manny Ramirez 1.50
23 Jay Payton .25
24 Bobby Higginson .25
25 Lance Berkman .75
26 Juan Pierre .25
27 Mike Mussina 1.00
28 Fred McGriff .50
29 Richie Sexson .75
30 Tim Hudson .50
31 Mike Piazza 2.00
32 Brad Radke .25
33 Jeff Weaver .25
34 Ramon Hernandez .25
35 David Bell .25

---

36 Randy Wolf .25
37 Jake Peavy .50
38 Tim Worrell .25
39 Gil Meche .25
40 Albert Pujols 4.00
41 Michael Young .25
42 Josh Phelps .25
43 Brendan Donnelly .25
44 Steve Finley .25
45 John Smoltz .50
46 Jay Gibbons .25
47 Trot Nixon .25
48 Carl Pavano .25
49 Frank Thomas 1.00
50 Mark Prior 1.00
51 Danny Graves .25
52 Milton Bradley .25
53 Kris Benson .25
54 Ryan Klesko .25
55 Mike Lowell .25
56 Geoff Blum .25
57 Michael Tucker .25
58 Paul LoDuca .25
59 Vicente Padilla .25
60 Jacque Jones .25
61 Fernando Tatis .25
62 Ty Wigginton .25
63 Rich Aurilia .25
64 Andy Pettitte .75
65 Terrence Long .25
66 Cliff Floyd .25
67 Mariano Rivera .50
68 Kelvim Escobar .25
69 Marlon Byrd .25
70 Mark Mulder .50
71 Francisco Cordero .25
72 Carlos Guillen .25
73 Fernando Vina .25
74 Lance Carter .25
75 Hank Blalock .75
76 Jimmy Rollins .50
77 Francisco Rodriguez .25
78 Javy Lopez .50
79 Jerry Hairston Jr. .25
80 Andruw Jones .75
81 Rodrigo Lopez .25
82 Johnny Damon 1.00
83 Hee Seop Choi .25
84 Kazuhiro Sasaki .25
85 Danny Bautista .25
86 Matt Lawton .25
87 Juan Uribe .25
88 Rafael Furcal .50
89 Kyle Farnsworth .25
90 Jose Vidro .25
91 Luis Rivas .25
92 Hideo Nomo .75
93 Javier Vazquez .50
94 Al Leiter .40
95 Jose Valentin .25
96 Alex Cintron .25
97 Zach Day .25
98 Jorge Posada .75
99 C.C. Sabathia .25
100 Alex Rodriguez 3.00
101 Brad Penny .25
102 Brad Ausmus .25
103 Raul Ibanez .25
104 Mike Hampton .25
105 Adrian Beltre .50
106 Ramiro Mendoza .25
107 Rocco Baldelli .75
108 Esteban Loaiza .25
109 Russell Branyan .25
110 Todd Helton 1.00
111 Braden Looper .25
112 Octavio Dotel .25
113 Mike MacDougal .25
114 Cesar Izturis .25
115 Johan Santana 1.00
116 Jose Contreras .50
117 Placido Polanco .25
118 Jason Phillips .25
119 Orlando Hudson .25
120 Vernon Wells .50
121 Ben Grieve .25
122 Dave Roberts .25
123 Ismael Valdes .25
124 Eric Owens .25
125 Curt Schilling 1.00
126 Russ Ortiz .25
127 Mark Buehrle .50
128 Doug Mientkiewicz .25
129 Dmitri Young .25
130 Kazuhisa Ishii .25
131 A.J. Pierzynski .25
132 Brad Wilkerson .25
133 Joe McEwing .25
134 Alex Cora .25
135 Jose Cruz Jr. .25
136 Carlos Zambrano .25
137 Jeff Kent .50
138 Shigetoshi Hasegawa .25
139 Jarrod Washburn .25

140	Greg Maddux	2.00
141	Josh Beckett	.75
142	Miguel Batista	.25
143	Omar Vizquel	.40
144	Alex Gonzalez	.25
145	Billy Wagner	.25
146	Brian Jordan	.25
147	Wes Helms	.25
148	Deivi Cruz	.25
149	Alex Gonzalez	.25
150	Jason Giambi	1.00
151	Erubiel Durazo	.25
152	Mike Lieberthal	.25
153	Jason Kendall	.25
154	Xavier Nady	.25
155	Kirk Rueter	.25
156	Mike Cameron	.25
157	Miguel Cairo	.25
158	Woody Williams	.25
159	Toby Hall	.25
160	Bernie Williams	.75
161	Darin Erstad	.50
162	Matt Mantei	.25
163	Shawn Chacon	.25
164	Bill Mueller	.25
165	Damian Miller	.25
166	Tony Graffanino	.25
167	Sean Casey	.25
168	Brandon Phillips	.25
169	Runelvys Hernandez	.25
170	Adam Dunn	.75
171	Carlos Lee	.50
172	Juan Encarnacion	.25
173	Angel Berroa	.25
174	Desi Relaford	.25
175	Joe Mays	.25
176	Ben Sheets	.50
177	Eddie Guardado	.25
178	Rocky Biddle	.25
179	Eric Gagne	.25
180	Eric Chavez	.50
181	Jason Michaels	.25
182	Dustan Mohr	.25
183	Kip Wells	.25
184	Brian Lawrence	.25
185	Bret Boone	.25
186	Tino Martinez	.40
187	Aubrey Huff	.25
188	Kevin Mench	.25
189	Tim Salmon	.50
190	Carlos Delgado	1.00
191	John Lackey	.25
192	Eric Byrnes	.25
193	Luis Matos	.25
194	Derek Lowe	.50
195	Mark Grudzielanek	.25
196	Flash Gordon	.25
197	Matt Clement	.25
198	Byung-Hyun Kim	.25
199	Brandon Inge	.25
200	Nomar Garciaparra	1.50
201	Frank Catalanotto	.25
202	Cristian Guzman	.25
203	Bo Hart	.25
204	Jack Wilson	.25
205	Ray Durham	.25
206	Freddy Garcia	.25
207	J.D. Drew	.50
208	Orlando Cabrera	.25
209	Roy Halladay	.50
210	David Eckstein	.25
211	Omar Falcon RC	2.00
212	Todd Self RC	2.00
213	David Murphy	3.00
214	Dioner Navarro RC	4.00
215	Marcus McBeth RC	2.00
216	Chris O'Riordan RC	2.00
217	Rodney Choy Foo RC	2.00
218	Tim Frend RC	2.00
219	Yadier Molina RC	6.00
220	Zachary Duke RC	3.00
221	Anthony Lerew/ Auto. RC	10.00
222	Blake Hawksworth/ Auto. RC	15.00
223	Brayan Pena/ Auto. RC	10.00
224	Craig Ansman/ Auto. RC	10.00
225	Jon Knott/Auto. RC	10.00
226	Josh Labandeira/ Auto. RC	10.00
227	Khalid Ballouli/ Auto. RC	10.00
228	Kyle Davies/ Auto. RC	15.00
229	Matt Creighton/ Auto. RC	15.00
230	Mike Gosling/Auto.	15.00
231	Nic Ungs/Auto. RC	10.00
232	Zach Miner/Auto. RC	10.00
233	Donald Levinski/Auto.	10.00
234	Bradley Sullivan	15.00
235	Carlos Quentin	25.00
236	Conor Jackson	25.00
237	Estee Harris RC	15.00
238	Jeffrey Allison	10.00
239	Kyle Sleeth	10.00
240	Matthew Moses	15.00
241	Tim Stauffer	15.00
242	Brad Snyder	10.00
243	Jason Hirsh	15.00
244	Lastings Milledge	30.00
245	Logan Kensing RC	15.00
246	Kory Casto	10.00
247	David Aardsma	1.50
248	Omar Quintanilla	2.00
249	Ervin Santana RC	2.00
250	Merkin Valdez RC	2.00
251	Vito Chiaravalloti RC	2.00
252	Travis Blackley RC	2.00
253	Chris Shelton RC	2.00
254	Rudy Guillen RC	3.00
255	Bobby Brownlie RC	2.00
256	Paul Maholm RC	4.00
257	Roger Clemens	3.00
258	Laynce Nix	.25
259	Eric Hinske	.25
260	Ivan Rodriguez	1.00
261	Brandon Webb	.50
262	Jhonny Peralta	.25
263	Adam Kennedy	.25
264	Tony Batista	.25
265	Jeff Suppan	.25
266	Kenny Lofton	.50
267	Scott Sullivan	.25
268	Ken Griffey Jr.	2.00
269	Billy Traber	.25
270	Larry Walker	.50
271	Todd Hollandsworth	.25
272	Carlos Beltran	1.00
273	Carl Crawford	.50
274	Karim Garcia	.25
275	Jose Reyes	.75
276	Brandon Duckworth	.25
277	Brian Giles	.50
278	J.T. Snow Jr.	.25
279	Jamie Moyer	.25
280	Julio Lugo	.25
281	Mark Teixeira	.75
282	Cory Lidle	.25
283	Lyle Overbay	.50
284	Troy Percival	.25
285	Robby Hammock	.25
286	Jason Johnson	.25
287	Brandon Lyon	.25
288	Antonio Alfonseca	.25
289	Tom Goodwin	.25
290	Paul Konerko	.50
291	D'Angelo Jimenez	.25
292	Ben Broussard	.25
293	Magglio Ordonez	.50
294	Carlos Pena	.25
295	Chad Fox	.25
296	Jeriome Robertson	.25
297	Travis Hafner	.50
298	Joe Randa	.25
299	Brady Clark	.25
300	Barry Zito	.75
301	Ruben Sierra	.25
302	Brett Myers	.25
303	Oliver Perez	.25
304	Benito Santiago	.25
305	David Ross	.25
306	Joe Nathan	.25
307	Jim Edmonds	.50
308	Matt Kata	.25
309	Vinny Castilla	.25
310	Marty Cordova	.25
311	Aramis Ramirez	.50
312	Carl Everett	.25
313	Ryan Freel	.25
314	Mark Bellhorn	.25
315	Ugueth Urbina	.25
316	Tim Redding	.25
317	Jeromy Burnitz	.25
318	Miguel Cabrera	1.00
319	Orlando Hernandez	.25
320	Casey Blake	.25
321	Aaron Boone	.25
322	Jermaine Dye	.25
323	Jerome Williams	.25
324	John Olerud	.50
325	Scott Rolen	1.00
326	Bobby Kielty	.25
327	Travis Lee	.25
328	Jeff Cirillo	.25
329	Scott Spiezio	.25
330	Melvin Mora	.25
331	Mike Timlin	.25
332	Kerry Wood	.50
333	Tony Womack	.25
334	Jody Gerut	.25
335	Morgan Ensberg	.25
336	Odalis Perez	.25
337	Michael Cuddyer	.25
338	Jose Hernandez	.25
339	LaTroy Hawkins	.25
340	Marquis Grissom	.25
341	Matt Morris	.50
342	Juan Gonzalez	.75
343	Jose Valverde	.25
344	Joe Borowski	.25
345	Josh Bard	.25
346	Austin Kearns	.50
347	Chin-Hui Tsao	.25
348	Wilfredo Ledezma	.25
349	Aaron Guiel	.25
350	Alfonso Soriano	1.00
351	Ted Lilly	.25
352	Sean Burroughs	.25
353	Rafael Palmeiro	.75
354	Quinton McCracken	.25
355	David Ortiz	1.00
356	Randall Simon	.25
357	Wily Mo Pena	.25
358	Brian Anderson	.25
359	Corey Koskie	.25
360	Keith Foulke	.25
361	Sidney Ponson	.25
362	Gary Matthews Jr.	.25
363	Herbert Perry	.25
364	Shea Hillenbrand	.25
365	Craig Biggio	.50
366	Barry Larkin	.50
367	Orlando Merced	.25
368	Sammy Sosa	1.50
369	Joe Crede	.50
370	Gary Sheffield	.75
371	Coco Crisp	.25
372	Torii Hunter	.50
373	Derrek Lee	.75
374	Adam Everett	.25
375	Miguel Tejada	.75
376	Jeremy Affeldt	.25
377	Robin Ventura	.25
378	Scott Podsednik	.75
379	Matthew LeCroy	.25
380	Vladimir Guerrero	1.50
381	Steve Karsay	.25
382	Jeff Nelson	.25
383	Chase Utley	.75
384	Bobby Abreu	.50
385	Josh Fogg	.25
386	Trevor Hoffman	.25
387	Matt Stairs	.25
388	Edgar Martinez	.50
389	Edgar Renteria	.25
390	Chipper Jones	1.50
391	Eric Munson	.25
392	Dewon Brazelton	.25
393	John Thomson	.25
394	Chris Woodward	.25
395	Joe Kennedy	.25
396	Reed Johnson	.25
397	Johnny Estrada	.25
398	Damian Moss	.25
399	Victor Zambrano	.25
400	Dontrelle Willis	.50
401	Troy Glaus	.75
402	Raul Mondesi	.25
403	Jeff DaVanon	.25
404	Kurt Ainsworth	.25
405	Pedro J. Martinez	1.50
406	Eric Karros	.25
407	Billy Koch	.25
408	Luis Gonzalez	.50
409	Jack Cust	.25
410	Mike Sweeney	.25
411	Jason Bay	.75
412	Mark Redman	.25
413	Jason Jennings	.25
414	Rondell White	.50
415	Todd Hundley	.25
416	Shannon Stewart	.25
417	Jae Weong Seo	.25
418	Livan Hernandez	.25
419	Mark Ellis	.25
420	Pat Burrell	.50
421	Mark Loretta	.25
422	Robb Nen	.25
423	Joel Pineiro	.25
424	Todd Walker	.25
425	Jeremy Bonderman	.50
426	A.J. Burnett	.25
427	Greg Myers	.25
428	Roy Oswalt	.50
429	Carlos Baerga	.25
430	Garret Anderson	.50
431	Horacio Ramirez	.25
432	Brian Roberts	.25
433	Kevin Brown	.25
434	Eric Milton	.25
435	Brian Daubach	.25
436	Alex Escobar	.25
437	Alex Sanchez	.25
438	Jeff Bagwell	1.00
439	Claudio Vargas	.25
440	Shawn Green	.50
441	Geoff Jenkins	.25
442	David Wells	.25
443	Nick Johnson	.25
444	Jose Guillen	.25
445	Scott Hatteberg	.25
446	Phil Nevin	.25
447	Jason Schmidt	.50
448	Ricky Ledee	.25
449	So Taguchi	.25
450	Randy Johnson	.75
451	Eric Young	.25
452	Chone Figgins	.25
453	Larry Bigbie	.25
454	Scott Williamson	.25
455	Ramon Martinez	.25
456	Roberto Alomar	.50
457	Ryan Dempster	.25
458	Ryan Ludwick	.25
459	Ramon Santiago	.25
460	Jeff Conine	.25
461	Brad Lidge	.25
462	Ken Harvey	.25
463	Guillermo Mota	.25
464	Rick Reed	.25
465	Armando Benitez	.25
466	Wade Miller	.25

Refractors

	NM/M
Cards (1-220, 247-466):	1-2X
Inserted 1:4	
Rookie Auto. (221-246):	1.5-2X
Production 100	
Gold Refractor (1-220):	1-2X
Inserted 1:5	
Rookie Gold Refractor	
(221-246):	2-3X
Production 50	
Black Refractor (1-220):	2-4X
Inserted 1:10	
Rookie Black	
Refractor:	No Pricing
Production 25	

Fashionably Great

		NM/M
Common Player:		5.00
Inserted 1:Box		
JB	Jeff Bagwell	10.00
CB	Craig Biggio	5.00
HB	Hank Blalock	8.00
JBO	Joe Borchard	5.00
KB	Kevin Brown	5.00
EC	Eric Chavez	6.00
CD	Carlos Delgado	6.00
AD	Adam Dunn	6.00
FG	Freddy Garcia	5.00
CF	Cliff Floyd	6.00
NG	Nomar Garciaparra	10.00
TH	Trevor Hoffman	5.00
TH	Tim Hudson	6.00
AJ	Andruw Jones	6.00
CJ	Chipper Jones	8.00
DL	Derek Lowe	6.00
PM	Pedro J. Martinez	8.00
FM	Fred McGriff	8.00
MM	Mark Mulder	6.00
BM	Brett Myers	5.00
JO	John Olerud	6.00
RP	Rafael Palmeiro	8.00
WP	Wily Mo Pena	5.00
MP	Mike Piazza	10.00
AP	Albert Pujols	15.00
MR	Manny Ramirez	8.00
JR	Juan Rivera	5.00
AR	Alex Rodriguez	12.00
IR	Ivan Rodriguez	8.00
CS	Curt Schilling	6.00
JS	John Smoltz	6.00
SS	Sammy Sosa	12.00
MS	Mike Sweeney	5.00
FT	Frank Thomas	10.00
JV	Jose Vidro	5.00
BW	Billy Wagner	6.00
VW	Vernon Wells	5.00

Handle With Care

No pricing due to scarcity.
Production 5 Sets

Presidential First Pitch Relics

		NM/M
Common President:		10.00
Inserted 1:15		
GHB	George H.W. Bush	20.00
GB	George W. Bush	25.00
BC	Bill Clinton	20.00
CC	Calvin Coolidge	20.00
DE	Dwight D. Eisenhower	20.00
GF	Gerald Ford	30.00
WH	Warren Harding	15.00
HH	Herbert Hoover	25.00
LJ	Lyndon B. Johnson	30.00
JK	John F. Kennedy	
RN	Richard Nixon	25.00
RR	Ronald Reagan	30.00
FR	Franklin D. Roosevelt	20.00
WT	William H. Taft	25.00
HT	Harry S. Truman	25.00
WW	Woodrow Wilson	10.00

Presidential Pastime

		NM/M
Common President:		3.00
X-Fractors:		3-5X
Inserted 1:400		
PP1	George Washington	10.00
PP2	John Adams	3.00
PP3	Thomas Jefferson	6.00
PP4	James Madison	4.00
PP5	James Monroe	4.00
PP6	John Quincy Adams	4.00
PP7	Andrew Jackson	3.00
PP8	Martin Van Buren	3.00
PP9	William H. Harrison	3.00
PP10	John Tyler	3.00
PP11	James K. Polk	3.00
PP12	Zachary Taylor	3.00
PP13	Millard Fillmore	3.00
PP14	Franklin Pierce	3.00
PP15	James Buchanan	3.00
PP16	Abraham Lincoln	8.00
PP17	Andrew Johnson	3.00
PP18	Ulysses S. Grant	5.00
PP19	Rutherford B. Hayes	3.00
PP20	James Garfield	3.00
PP21	Chester A. Arthur	3.00
PP22	Grover Cleveland	3.00
PP23	Benjamin Harrison	3.00
PP24	William McKinley	3.00
PP25	Theodore Roosevelt	5.00
PP26	William H. Taft	3.00
PP27	Woodrow Wilson	3.00
PP28	Warren Harding	3.00
PP29	Calvin Coolidge	3.00
PP30	Herbert Hoover	3.00
PP31	Franklin D. Roosevelt	5.00
PP32	Harry S. Truman	3.00
PP33	Dwight D. Eisenhower	3.00
PP34	John F. Kennedy	8.00
PP35	Lyndon B. Johnson	3.00
PP36	Richard Nixon	4.00
PP37	Gerald Ford	3.00
PP38	Jimmy Carter	3.00
PP39	Ronald Reagan	3.00
PP40	George H.W. Bush	3.00
PP41	Bill Clinton	4.00
PP42	George W. Bush	3.00

Town Heroes

		NM/M
Common Player:		5.00
LB	Lance Berkman	5.00
EC	Eric Chavez	5.00
NG	Nomar Garciaparra	12.00
JG	Jason Giambi	8.00
RH	Rich Harden	5.00
TH	Tim Hudson	5.00
CJ	Chipper Jones	8.00
MM	Mark Mulder	5.00
HN	Hideo Nomo	8.00
RP	Rafael Palmeiro	8.00
MP	Mark Prior	8.00
AP	Albert Pujols	15.00
MR	Manny Ramirez	8.00
JR	Jose Reyes	5.00
AR	Alex Rodriguez	10.00

CHROME-TOWN HEROES

CHICAGO CUBS®

PITCHER
KERRY WOOD

SS	Sammy Sosa	15.00
SST	Shannon Stewart	5.00
MT	Miguel Tejada	5.00
FT	Frank Thomas	8.00
KW	Kerry Wood	10.00
BZ	Barry Zito	6.00

2004 Topps Clubhouse Collection Relics

		NM/M
Common Player:		4.00
2 Relics Per Pack		
Pack (2):		18.00
Box (10):		140.00
HA	Hank Aaron/113	50.00
BA	Bobby Abreu	6.00
RA	Roberto Alomar	6.00
EA	Edgardo Alfonzo/286	4.00
TA	Tony Armas Jr.	4.00
JB	Jeff Bagwell	8.00
RB	Rocco Baldelli	6.00
TB	Tony Batista	4.00
HB	Hank Bauer	10.00
JPB	Josh Beckett/195	8.00
JBE	Johnny Bench	10.00
AB	Armando Benitez	4.00
LB	Lance Berkman	6.00
YB	Yogi Berra	10.00
HBL	Hank Blalock	6.00
WB	Wade Boggs/250	6.00
BB	Bret Boone	4.00
GB	George Brett	12.00
KB	Kevin Brown	6.00
JBU	Jeromy Burnitz	4.00
PB	Pat Burrell	6.00
MB	Marlon Byrd	4.00
MC	Miguel Cabrera	8.00
GC	Gary Carter/221	8.00
JCA	Joe Carter/259	6.00
RLC	Roger Cedeno	4.00
OC	Orlando Cepeda	8.00
RCE	Ron Cey	6.00
EC	Eric Chavez	6.00
CFC	Chin-Feng Chen	8.00
JC	Jeff Cirillo	4.00
WC	Will Clark	8.00
RC	Roberto Clemente	75.00
DC	Dave Concepcion	8.00
CCR	Carl Crawford	4.00
CD	Carlos Delgado/200	6.00
AD	Adam Dunn	8.00
DE	Dennis Eckersley	10.00
CE	Carl Everett	4.00
SF	Steve Finley	4.00
CFL	Cliff Floyd	4.00
WF	Whitey Ford/296	15.00
BF	Brad Fullmer/200	4.00
JF	Jonathan Fulton	4.00
RF	Rafael Furcal	4.00
EG	Eric Gagne	8.00
NG	Nomar Garciaparra	12.00
JG	Jason Giambi	6.00
TGL	Troy Glaus	6.00
TG	Tom Glavine	8.00
AG	Adrian Gonzalez	4.00
LG	Luis Gonzalez	6.00
JGO	Juan Gonzalez	8.00
MG	Mark Grace	8.00
SG	Shawn Green	6.00
KG	Ken Griffey Jr./200	15.00
MDG	Marquis Grissom	4.00
VG	Vladimir Guerrero	8.00
CG	Cristian Guzman	4.00
TGW	Tony Gwynn	10.00
MH	Mickey Hall	4.00
EH	Estee Harris/206	4.00
THE	Todd Helton	8.00
RHE	Rickey Henderson	10.00
RH	Ramon Hernandez	4.00
OH	Orel Hershiser	8.00
JH	James Houser/182	4.00
OHU	Orlando Hudson	4.00

TH	Tim Hudson	6.00
THU	Torii Hunter	6.00
KI	Kazuhisa Ishii	4.00
RJ	Reggie Jackson	10.00
DJ	Derek Jeter	20.00
AJ	Andruw Jones	6.00
CJ	Chipper Jones	8.00
AK	Al Kaline	15.00
JKE	Jeff Kent/200	8.00
PK	Paul Konerko	6.00
BL	Barry Larkin/200	10.00
AL	Al Leiter	4.00
SL	Steve Lerud	4.00
EL	Esteban Loaiza	4.00
PL	Paul LoDuca	4.00
JL	Javy Lopez	6.00
DL	Derek Lowe/200	4.00
CL	Chris Lubanski/209	8.00
GM	Greg Maddux	15.00
EMA	Edgar Martinez/200	6.00
PM	Pedro Martinez/200	10.00
TM	Tino Martinez	6.00
EM	Eddie Mathews/174	25.00
WM	Willie Mays	60.00
FM	Fred McGriff	6.00
KM	Kevin Millwood	4.00
MM	Mark Mulder	6.00
EMU	Eddie Murray	12.00
BM	Brett Myers	4.00
HN	Hideo Nomo/207	8.00
JO	John Olerud	6.00
MO	Magglio Ordonez	4.00
RP	Rafael Palmeiro/200	10.00
CP	Chan Ho Park	4.00
DP	Dave Parker/292	10.00
CPA	Corey Patterson/267	4.00
WP	Wily Mo Pena	8.00
TPE	Troy Percival	4.00
TP	Tony Perez	10.00
MP	Mike Piazza	10.00
JP	Jorge Posada/264	8.00
AP	Albert Pujols	15.00
ARA	Aramis Ramirez	8.00
MR	Manny Ramirez/207	8.00
JRE	Jose Reyes	6.00
CR	Cal Ripken Jr.	20.00
MRI	Mariano Rivera/239	8.00
FR	Frank Robinson	8.00
JR	Jackie Robinson/262	50.00
AR	Alex Rodriguez	10.00
IR	Ivan Rodriguez	8.00
SR	Scott Rolen	10.00
JRO	Jimmy Rollins	8.00
NR	Nolan Ryan	20.00
CS	C.C. Sabathia	4.00
TS	Tim Salmon	6.00
RSA	Ryne Sandberg	15.00
JS	Jay Sborz	6.00
CSC	Curt Schilling	8.00
MS	Mike Schmidt	15.00
RS	Richie Sexson/200	6.00
GS	Gary Sheffield	6.00
RSI	Ruben Sierra	10.00
OS	Ozzie Smith	15.00
JSM	John Smoltz	6.00
DS	Duke Snider	15.00
AS	Alfonso Soriano	6.00
SS	Sammy Sosa	12.00
WS	Willie Stargell/200	10.00
CST	Casey Stengel/217	10.00
MSW	Mike Sweeney	4.00
MTE	Miguel Tejada	4.00
MT	Mark Teixeira	6.00
FT	Frank Thomas	8.00
JT	Jim Thome	8.00
FV	Fernando Valenzuela	8.00
JVI	Jose Vidro	4.00
BWA	Billy Wagner	4.00
LW	Larry Walker	6.00
VW	Vernon Wells/200	4.00
BW	Bernie Williams	6.00
PW	Preston Wilson	4.00
JV	Javier Vazquez	6.00
CY	Carl Yastrzemski	15.00
RY	Robin Yount	12.00
BZ	Barry Zito/230	6.00

Copper

Copper:		.75-1.5X
Production 99 Sets		

Black

Black:		2-3X
Production 25 Sets		

Red

Red:		No Pricing
Production One Set		

All-Star Appeal Ball

No Pricing
Production 10 Sets

All-Star Appeal Ball Autograph

		NM/M
Production 30 Sets		
GA	Garret Anderson	30.00
HB	Hank Blalock	35.00
JP	Jorge Posada	50.00

All-Star Appeal Base

ALL-STAR APPEAL

GARRET ANDERSON
ANAHEIM ANGELS™

		NM/M
Common Player:		5.00
Production 65 Sets		
On Deck Circle:		1X
Production 90 Sets		
GA	Garret Anderson	8.00
HB	Hank Blalock	8.00
BB	Bret Boone	5.00
CD	Carlos Delgado	6.00
JE	Jim Edmonds	8.00
RF	Rafael Furcal	6.00
NG	Nomar Garciaparra	15.00
JG	Jason Giambi	8.00
TG	Troy Glaus	6.00
LG	Luis Gonzalez	6.00
TH	Todd Helton	8.00
AJ	Andruw Jones	6.00
JL	Javy Lopez	8.00
ML	Mike Lowell	6.00
EM	Edgar Martinez	6.00
MO	Magglio Ordonez	6.00
JP	Jorge Posada	8.00
AP	Albert Pujols	25.00
ER	Edgar Renteria	8.00
AR	Alex Rodriguez	15.00
SR	Scott Rolen	10.00
RS	Richie Sexson	6.00
GS	Gary Sheffield	8.00
AS	Alfonso Soriano	10.00
VW	Vernon Wells	6.00
PW	Preston Wilson	5.00

All-Star Appeal Base Autograph

		NM/M
Production 50 Sets		
GA	Garret Anderson	25.00
JP	Jorge Posada	35.00
GS	Gary Sheffield	25.00

All-Star Appeal On Deck Circle

		NM/M
Common Player:		5.00
Production 90 Sets		
GA	Garret Anderson	8.00
HB	Hank Blalock	8.00
AB	Aaron Boone	5.00
BB	Bret Boone	5.00
LC	Luis Castillo	6.00
CD	Carlos Delgado	6.00
JE	Jim Edmonds	5.00
CE	Carl Everett	5.00
RF	Rafael Furcal	6.00
NG	Nomar Garciaparra	15.00
JG	Jason Giambi	8.00
TG	Troy Glaus	6.00
LG	Luis Gonzalez	8.00
TH	Todd Helton	8.00
AJ	Andruw Jones	6.00
PL	Paul LoDuca	5.00
JL	Javy Lopez	8.00
ML	Mike Lowell	6.00
EM	Edgar Martinez	8.00
MM	Melvin Mora	5.00
MO	Magglio Ordonez	6.00
JP	Jorge Posada	8.00
AP	Albert Pujols	20.00
ER	Edgar Renteria	8.00
AR	Alex Rodriguez	15.00
SR	Scott Rolen	10.00

RS	Richie Sexson	6.00
GS	Gary Sheffield	8.00
AS	Alfonso Soriano	10.00
JV	Jose Vidro	5.00
VW	Vernon Wells	6.00
RW	Rondell White	5.00
PW	Preston Wilson	5.00

All-Star Appeal On Deck Autograph

NM/M
Quantity produced listed

GA	Garret Anderson/320	15.00
HB	Hank Blalock/920	15.00
JP	Jorge Posada/420	30.00
GS	Gary Sheffield/170	25.00

Career Legends Relics

NM/M
Common Player:

BR1	Babe Ruth/60	175.00
BR2	Babe Ruth/171	150.00
BR3	Babe Ruth/45	200.00
EB1	Ernie Banks/143	15.00
EB3	Ernie Banks/47	20.00
EB6	Ernie Banks/71	15.00
LG1	Lou Gehrig/49	125.00
LG2	Lou Gehrig/184	100.00
LG3	Lou Gehrig/52	125.00
TC3	Ty Cobb/47	120.00
WM1	Willie Mays/52	70.00
WM2	Willie Mays/141	60.00

Double Play Relics

NM/M
Production 75 Sets

CLE	Omar Vizquel, Brandon Phillips, Travis Hafner	10.00
NYM	Ty Wigginton, Jose Reyes, Mike Piazza	25.00
NYY	Derek Jeter, Alex Rodriguez, Jason Giambi	50.00
PHI	Jimmy Rollins, David Bell, Jim Thome	20.00
SDP	Khalil Greene, Sean Burroughs, Phil Nevin	10.00

Frozen Ropes Relics

NM/M

	Common Player:	5.00
	Production 50 Sets	
BA	Bobby Abreu	8.00
JB	Jeff Bagwell	10.00
RB	Rocco Baldelli	8.00
JBE	Johnny Bench	20.00
LB	Lance Berkman	5.00
CB	Craig Biggio	6.00
HB	Hank Blalock	10.00
WB	Wade Boggs	8.00
GC	Gary Carter	8.00
EC	Eric Chavez	8.00
ADA	Andre Dawson	8.00
AD	Adam Dunn	10.00
CE	Carl Everett	5.00
RF	Rafael Furcal	5.00
JG	Jason Giambi	8.00
LG	Luis Gonzalez	5.00
SG	Shawn Green	5.00
VG	Vladimir Guerrero	15.00
TH	Todd Helton	10.00
AH	Aubrey Huff	5.00
CJ	Chipper Jones	15.00
PK	Paul Konerko	5.00
EM	Edgar Martinez	8.00
DM	Don Mattingly	40.00
DMU	Dale Murphy	12.00
MO	Magglio Ordonez	5.00
RP	Rafael Palmeiro	10.00

MP	Mike Piazza	15.00
KP	Kirby Puckett	15.00
AP	Albert Pujols	25.00
MR	Manny Ramirez	10.00
JR	Jose Reyes	8.00
BR	Brooks Robinson	15.00
AR	Alex Rodriguez	15.00
IR	Ivan Rodriguez	10.00
RS	Ryne Sandberg	40.00
MS	Mike Schmidt	40.00
GS	Gary Sheffield	6.00
OS	Ozzie Smith	25.00
DS	Duke Snider	15.00
AS	Alfonso Soriano	10.00
SS	Sammy Sosa	15.00
MT	Miguel Tejada	8.00
JT	Jim Thome	10.00
BW	Bernie Williams	8.00
PW	Preston Wilson	8.00
CY	Carl Yastrzemski	20.00

Heart of theLine-Up Relics

NM/M
Production 100 unless noted.

ARI	Steve Finley, Richie Sexson, Luis Gonzalez	10.00
CHC	Sammy Sosa, Moises Alou, Aramis Ramirez	35.00
CHW	Magglio Ordonez, Frank Thomas, Carlos Lee/78	20.00
CIN	Ken Griffey Jr., Austin Kearns, Adam Dunn	25.00
COL	Todd Helton, Larry Walker, Preston Wilson	15.00
HOU	Jeff Bagwell, Jeff Kent, Lance Berkman	
NYY	Alex Rodriguez, Jason Giambi, Gary Sheffield	35.00
PHI	Jim Thome, Pat Burrell, Bobby Abreu	20.00
SEA	Edgar Martinez, Bret Boone, John Olerud	10.00
STL	Albert Pujols, Jim Edmonds, Scott Rolen	40.00
TEX	Alfonso Soriano, Mark Teixeira, Hank Blalock	20.00
TOR	Vernon Wells, Carlos Delgado, Eric Hinske	10.00

Patch Place Relics

No Pricing
Production 25 or less.

Pieces Relics

NM/M
Quantity produced listed

CD	Carlos Delgado/25	8.00
THU	Torii Hunter/48	8.00
AJ	Andruw Jones/25	10.00
PM	Pedro Martinez/45	10.00
WM	Willie Mays/24	85.00
BM	Brett Myers/39	5.00
BP	Brad Penny/31	5.00
MP	Mike Piazza/31	40.00
SR	Scott Rolen/27	
NR	Nolan Ryan/34	50.00
CS	Curt Schilling/38	8.00
BZ	Barry Zito/75	6.00

2004 Topps Cracker Jack

PUJOLS, St. Louis · Nationals

NM/M
Complete Set with SP's (250): 160.00
Common Player: .25
Common SP: 2.00
SP's inserted 1:3
Pack (8): 3.00
Box (24): 60.00

1	Jose Reyes/SP	2.00
2	Edgar Renteria	.25
3	Albert Pujols	2.00
3	Albert Pujols/SP/Swinging	6.00
4	Garret Anderson	.50
5	Bobby Abreu	.40
6	Andruw Jones	.75
7	Jeff Kent	.40
8	Magglio Ordonez	.50
9	Kris Benson	.25
10	Luis Gonzalez	.40
11	Corey Patterson	.50
12	Connie Mack	.25
13	Vernon Wells/SP	2.00
14	Jim Edmonds	.50
15	Bret Boone	.50
16	Travis Lee	.25
17	Alex Rodriguez/SP	6.00
No #	Alex Rodriguez	2.00
18	Erubiel Durazo	.25
19	Brett Myers	.25
20	Scott Rolen/SP	3.00
21	Paul LoDuca	.25
22	Geoff Jenkins	.50
23	Charles Comiskey	.25
24	Cliff Floyd	.25
25	Jim Thome	.75
25	Jim Thome/SP/Fielding	3.00
26	Russ Ortiz	.25
27	Bill Mueller	.25
28	Kenny Lofton	.40
29	Jay Gibbons	.40
30	Ken Griffey Jr.	1.50
31	Jeff Bagwell	.75
32	Jose Lima	.25
33	Brad Radke	.25
34	Ramon Hernandez	.25
35	Brian Giles/SP	2.00
36	Jeremy Bonderman	.25
37	Jerome Williams	.25
38	Rafael Palmeiro	.50
39	Scott Podsednik	.75
40	Rafael Furcal	.40
41	Roy Oswalt	.40
42	Orlando Hudson	.25
43	Todd Helton	.75
44	Kerry Wood	1.00
45	Tom Glavine	.40
46	David Eckstein	.25
47	Trot Nixon	.25
48	Preston Wilson	.25
50	Eric Gagne/SP	3.00
51	Ichiro Suzuki/SP	5.00
52	Juan Gonzalez	.75
53	Torii Hunter	.50
54	Bartolo Colon	.40
55	Dick Hoblitzell	.25
56	Al Leiter	.25
57	Johnny Damon	.40
58	Larry Walker	.40
59	Brian Jordan	.25
60	Richie Sexson/SP	3.00
61	Orlando Cabrera	.25
62	Jason Phillips	.25
63	Phil Nevin	.25
64	John Olerud	.40
65	Miguel Tejada	.50
66	Nap Lajoie	.50
67	C.C. Sabathia	.25
68	Ty Wigginton	.25
69	Troy Glaus	.50
70	Mike Piazza	1.50
71	Craig Biggio	.40
72	Cristian Guzman	.25
73	Dmitri Young	.25
74	Roger Clemens	2.00
75	Runelvys Hernandez	.25
76	Nomar Garciaparra	2.00
77	Mark Mulder	.40
78	Derek Lowe	.40
79	Paul Konerko	.25
80	Sammy Sosa/SP	5.00
81	Vladimir Guerrero	1.00
82	Xavier Nady	.25
83	Joel Pineiro	.25
84	Chipper Jones	1.50
85	Manny Ramirez	.75
86	Burt Shotton	.25
87	Raul Ibanez/SP	2.00
88	Eric Chavez	.25
89	Frank Catalanotto	.25
90	Dontrelle Willis	.50
91	Roy Halladay	.50
92	Jermaine Dye	.25
93	Jason Kendall	.25
94	Jacque Jones	.25
95	Gary Sheffield	.50
95	Gary Sheffield/SP/Yankees	3.00
96	Mike Lieberthal	.25
97	Adam Dunn	.50
98	Carl Crawford	.25
99	Reggie Sanders	.25
100	Mark Prior/SP	6.00
101	Luis Matos	.25
102	Barry Zito	.50
103	Randy Johnson	1.00
104	Kevin Brown	.50
105	Pat Burrell	.50
106	Steve Finley	.25
107	Moises Alou	.25
108	David Ortiz/SP	3.00
109	Austin Kearns/SP	2.00
110	Carlos Beltran	.50
111	Shawn Green	.40
112	Javier Vazquez	.50
113	Hideo Nomo	.50
114	Kazuhisa Ishii	.25
115	Corey Koskie	.25
116	Kevin Millwood	.50
117	Randy Wolf	.40
118	Darin Erstad	.25
119	Fernando Vina	.25
120	Pedro J. Martinez	1.00
121	Melvin Mora	.25
122	Carl Everett	.25
123	Matt Morris	.40
124	Greg Maddux	1.50
125	Jason Schmidt	.25
126	Mark Teixeira/SP	3.00
127	Randy Winn	.25
128	Rich Aurilia	.25
129	Vicente Padilla	.25
130	Tim Hudson	.50
131	Marlon Byrd	.25
132	Jae Weong Seo	.25
133	Branch Rickey	.25
134	A.J. Pierzynski	.25
135	Ryan Klesko	.40
136	Eric Hinske	.25
137	Mike Cameron	.25
138	Roberto Alomar	.50
139	Jarrod Washburn	.25
140	Curt Schilling	.75
140	Curt Schilling/SP/Red Sox	3.00
141	Omar Vizquel	.25
142	Mike Sweeney	.25
143	Wade Miller	.25
144	Jose Vidro	.25
145	Rich Harden/SP	2.00
146	Eric Munson	.25
147	Lance Berkman	.50
148	Mark Buehrle	.25
149	Carlos Delgado	.75
150	Sean Burroughs	.25
151	Kevin Millar	.25
152	Frank Thomas	.75
153	Adrian Beltre	.25
154	Shannon Stewart	.25
155	Johan Santana	.25
156	Edgardo Alfonzo	.25
157	Jose Cruz Jr.	.25
158	Sidney Ponson	.25
159	Edgar Martinez	.50
160	Jamie Moyer	.25
161	Tony Batista	.25
162	Wes Helms	.25
163	Brandon Webb/SP	2.00
164	Gil Meche	.25
165	Marcus Giles/SP	2.00
166	Angel Berroa/SP	2.00
167	Rocco Baldelli/SP	3.00
168	Michael Young	.25
169	Esteban Loaiza	.25
170	Casey Blake	.25
171	Jody Gerut	.25
172	Bo Hart/SP	2.00
173	Kelvim Escobar	.25
174	Aaron Guiel	.25
175	Javy Lopez/SP	3.00
176	Aubrey Huff	.25
177	Hank Blalock	.50
178	Edwin Jackson	.25
178	Edwin Jackson/SP/#104	2.00
179	Delmon Young/SP	3.00
180	Bobby Jenks	.25
181	Felix Pie	.25
181	Felix Pie/SP/#80	2.00
182	Jeremy Reed/SP	2.00
183	Aaron Hill	.25
184	Casey Kotchman/SP	2.00
185	Grady Sizemore	.50
186	Joe Mauer/SP	3.00
187	Ryan Harvey	.25
188	Neal Cotts	.25
189	Victor Martinez	.25
190	Rene Reyes	.25
191	Eric Duncan	.25

192	B.J. Upton/SP	3.00
193	Khalil Greene/SP	2.00
194	Bobby Crosby	.25
195	Rickie Weeks/SP	3.00
196	Zack Greinke/SP	2.00
197	Laynce Nix	.25
198	Vito Chiaravalloti/	
	SP RC	2.00
199	Estee Harris RC	.25
200	Jon Knott/SP RC	.75
201	Dioner Navarro RC	.75
201	Dioner Navarro/	
	SP/#236	2.00
202	Craig Ansman RC	.50
203	Travis Blackley RC	1.00
204	Yadier Molina RC	.50
205	Rodney Choy Foo RC	.50
206	Kyle Sleeth/SP	5.00
207	Jeff Allison	1.00
208	Josh Labandeira RC	.50
209	Lastings Milledge/SP	10.00
210	Rudy Guillen/SP RC	3.00
211	Blake	
	Hawksworth/SP RC	3.00
212	David Aardsma	.50
213	Shawn Hill RC	.50
214	Erick Aybar/SP RC	3.00
215	Ervin Santana RC	1.00
216	Tim Stauffer/SP	3.00
217	Merkin Valdez RC	1.00
218	Jack McKeon	.25
219	Derrek Lee	.50
220	Josh Beckett/SP	3.00
221	Luis Castillo	.25
222	Mike Lowell	.25
223	Juan Pierre	.40
224	Ivan Rodriguez	.75
224	Ivan Rodriguez/	
	SP/Tigers	3.00
225	A.J. Burnett	.25
226	Miguel Cabrera/SP	4.00
227	Jeffrey Loria	.25
228	Joe Torre	.50
229	Jason Giambi	.75
229	Jason Giambi/	
	SP/Fldg	3.00
230	Aaron Boone	.25
231	Jose Contreras	.25
232	Derek Jeter/SP	6.00
233	Nick Johnson	.25
234	Mike Mussina	.75
235	Andy Pettitte	.50
236	Jorge Posada/SP	3.00
237	Alfonso Soriano	.75
238	Bernie Williams	.50

Mini

BIGGIO, Houston – Nationals

Mini:	1-2X
Mini SP:	1X
Inserted 1:Pack	
Mini SPs Inserted 1:20	
SP's are same as in base set.	

Mini Blue

Mini Blue:	3-6X
Mini Blue SP:	1-2X
Inserted 1:10	
Mini Blue SP's Inserted 1:60	
SP's are same as in base set.	

Mini White

No Pricing
Production One Set

Mini Autograph

	NM/M
Common Autograph:	
Inserted 1:258	
95	Gary Sheffield/50	40.00
112	Javier Vazquez	15.00
163	Brandon Webb	15.00
165	Marcus Giles	12.00
221	Luis Castillo	8.00
226	Miguel Cabrera	35.00

Secret Surprise Signatures

		NM/M
Common Autograph:		8.00
CF	Cliff Floyd	15.00
BG	Brian Giles	15.00
AH	Aubrey Huff	15.00
ML	Mike Lamb	8.00
DM	Dustin McGowan	20.00
FP	Felix Pie	20.00
SP	Scott Podsednik	20.00
SR	Scott Rolen	30.00
MV	Merkin Valdez	15.00
JW	Jerome Williams	20.00
DW	Dontrelle Willis	30.00

Sticker

Stickers:	1X
SP Stickers:	.5X
Inserted 1:Surprise Pack	
SP's Inserted 1:10 Surprise Packs	

Take Me Out to/Ballgame Relics

HANK BLALOCK, Texas – Rangers

		NM/M
Common Player:		5.00
BA	Bobby Abreu	5.00
MA	Moises Alou	6.00
GA	Garret Anderson	8.00
JB	Jeff Bagwell	8.00
RB	Rocco Baldelli	8.00
LB	Lance Berkman	5.00
AB	Angel Berroa	5.00
CB	Craig Biggio	6.00
HB	Hank Blalock	6.00
BB1	Bret Boone/Bat	5.00
BB2	Bret Boone/Jsy	5.00
PB	Pat Burrell	6.00
MC	Miguel Cabrera	8.00
EC	Eric Chavez	5.00
AD	Adam Dunn	8.00
JE	Jim Edmonds	5.00
RF	Rafael Furcal	6.00
NG	Nomar	
	Garciaparra/Bat	10.00
NG	Nomar	
	Garciaparra/Jsy	10.00
JG	Jason Giambi	8.00
MG	Marcus Giles	5.00
TG	Troy Glaus	8.00
LG	Luis Gonzalez	5.00
SG	Shawn Green/Bat	6.00
SG	Shawn Green/Jsy	6.00
TH	Todd Helton	8.00
TKH	Torii Hunter	6.00
CJ	Chipper Jones	8.00
PL	Paul LoDuca	5.00
JL	Javy Lopez/Bat	6.00
JL	Javy Lopez/Jsy	6.00
MP	Mike Piazza	10.00
AP	Albert Pujols/Bat	15.00
AP	Albert Pujols/Jsy	15.00
MR	Manny Ramirez	8.00
JR	Jose Reyes	6.00
AR	Alex Rodriguez/	
	Bat/Yankees	15.00
AR	Alex Rodriguez/Jsy	10.00
IR	Ivan Rodriguez	8.00
JRO	Jimmy Rollins	5.00
AS	Alfonso Soriano/Bat	8.00
AS	Alfonso Soriano/Jsy	8.00
SS	Sammy Sosa/Bat	10.00
SS	Sammy Sosa/Jsy	10.00
MS	Mike Sweeney	5.00
MT	Mark Teixeira	6.00
MT	Miguel Tejada	6.00
JT	Jim Thome	8.00
LW	Larry Walker	5.00
VW	Vernon Wells	5.00
KW	Kerry Wood	8.00
MY	Michael Young	5.00

1,2,3 Strikes You're Out Relics

		NM/M
Common Player:		4.00
JB	Josh Beckett	8.00
KB	Kevin Brown	6.00
EG	Eric Gagne	8.00

RH	Rich Harden	4.00
RJ	Randy Johnson	8.00
DL	Derek Lowe	6.00
PM	Pedro J. Martinez	8.00
KM	Kevin Millwood	6.00
MAM	Mark Mulder	6.00
MM	Mike Mussina	15.00
BM	Brett Myers	4.00
HN	Hideo Nomo	8.00
CCS	C.C. Sabathia	4.00
CS	Curt Schilling	15.00
JS	John Smoltz	6.00
BW	Billy Wagner	4.00
KW	Kerry Wood	10.00
BZ	Barry Zito	6.00

2004 Topps Heritage

RAUL IBANEZ

		NM/M
Complete Set (475):		400.00
Common Player:		.40
Common SP (398-475):		4.00
Variations & SP's Inserted 1:2		
Pack (8):		5.00
Box (24):		100.00
1	Jim Thome	1.50
1	Jim Thome/SP/Htg	8.00
2	Nomar	
	Garciaparra/SP	10.00
3	Aramis Ramirez	.50
4	Rafael Palmeiro/SP	6.00
5	Danny Graves	.40
6	Casey Blake	.40
7	Juan Uribe	.40
8	Dmitri Young	.40
8	Dmitri Young/	
	SP/Old Logo	4.00
9	Billy Wagner	.40
10	Jason Giambi	.75
10	Jason Giambi/	
	SP/Batting Stance	6.00
11	Carlos Beltran	1.00
12	Chad Hermansen	.40
13	B.J. Upton	.75
14	Dustan Mohr	.40
15	Endy Chavez	.40
16	Cliff Floyd	.40
17	Bernie Williams	.75
18	Eric Chavez	.50
19	Chase Utley	.75
20	Randy Johnson	1.50
21	Vernon Wells	.50
22	Juan Gonzalez	.75
23	Joe Kennedy	.40
24	Bengie Molina	.40
25	Carlos Lee	.40
26	Horacio Ramirez	.40
27	Anthony Acevedo RC	1.00
28	Sammy Sosa/SP	10.00
29	Jon Garland	.40
30	Adam Dunn	1.00
30	Adam Dunn/SP/Htg	6.00
31	Aaron Rowand	.40
32	Jody Gerut	.40
33	Chin-Hui Tsao	.40
34	Alex Sanchez	.40
35	A.J. Burnett	.40
36	Brad Ausmus	.40
37	Blake Hawksworth RC	1.50
38	Francisco Rodriguez	.40
39	Alex Cintron	.40
40	Chipper Jones	1.50
40	Chipper Jones/	
	SP/Fielding	6.00
41	Deivi Cruz	.40
42	Bill Mueller	.40
43	Joe Borowski	.40
44	Jimmy Haynes	.40
45	Mark Loretta	.40
46	Jerome Williams	.40
47	Gary Sheffield/SP	6.00
48	Richard Hidalgo	.40
49	Jason Kendall	.40
49	Jason Kendall/	
	SP/Old Logo	4.00
50	Ichiro Suzuki/SP	8.00
51	Jim Edmonds	.75
52	Frank Catalanotto	.40
53	Jose Contreras	.40
54	Mo Vaughn	.40
55	Brendan Donnelly	.40
56	Luis Gonzalez	.50
57	Robert Fick	.40
58	Laynce Nix	.40

59	Johnny Damon	.75
60	Magglio Ordonez	.50
60	Magglio Ordonez/	
	SP/Hitting	6.00
61	Matt Clement	.40
62	Ryan Ludwick	.40
63	Luis Castillo	.40
64	David Crouthers	.40
65	Dave Berg	.40
66	Kyle Davies RC	3.00
67	Tim Salmon	.50
68	Marcus Giles	.40
69	Marty Cordova	.40
70	Todd Helton	1.00
70	Todd Helton/	
	SP/Purple Jersey	6.00
71	Jeff Kent	.50
72	Michael Tucker	.40
73	Cesar Izturis	.40
74	Paul Quantrill	.40
75	Conor Jackson	3.00
76	Placido Polanco	.40
77	Adam Eaton	.40
78	Ramon Hernandez	.40
79	Edgardo Alfonzo	.40
80	Dioner Navarro RC	1.00
81	Woody Williams	.40
82	Rey Ordonez	.40
83	Randy Winn	.40
84	Casey Myers RC	1.00
85	Rodney Choy Foo RC	2.00
85	Rodney Choy Foo/	
	SP/Old Logo	6.00
86	Ray Durham	.40
87	Sean Burroughs	.40
88	Tim Frend RC	3.00
89	Shigetoshi Hasegawa	.40
90	Jeff Allison	.40
91	Orlando Hudson	.40
92	Matt Creighton/SP RC	6.00
93	Tim Worrell	.40
94	Kris Benson	.40
95	Mike Lieberthal	.40
96	David Wells	.40
97	Jason Phillips	.40
98	Bobby Cox	.40
99	Johan Santana	.75
100	Alex Rodriguez	3.00
100	Alex Rodriguez/	
	SP/Throwing	10.00
101	John Vander Wal	.40
102	Orlando Cabrera	.50
103	Hideo Nomo	.75
104	Todd Walker	.40
105	Jason Johnson	.40
106	Matt Mantei	.40
107	Jarrod Washburn	.40
108	Preston Wilson	.40
109	Carl Pavano	.40
110	Geoff Blum	.40
111	Eric Gagne	.50
112	Geoff Jenkins	.50
113	Joe Torre	.50
114	Jon Knott RC	1.50
115	Hank Blalock	.75
116	John Olerud	.50
117	Pat Burrell	.75
117	Pat Burrell/Old Logo	5.00
118	Aaron Boone	.40
119	Zach Day	.40
120	Frank Thomas	1.00
120	Frank Thomas/	
	Old Logo	6.00
121	Kyle Farnsworth	.40
122	Derek Lowe	.50
123	Zach Miner/SP RC	6.00
124	Matt Moses/SP	8.00
125	Jesse Roman RC	1.50
126	Josh Phelps	.40
127	Nic Ungs RC	1.50
128	Dan Haren	.40
129	Kirk Rueter	.40
130	Jack McKeon	.40
131	Keith Foulke	.40
132	Garrett Stephenson	.40
133	Wes Helms	.40
134	Raul Ibanez	.50
135	Morgan Ensberg	.40
136	Jay Payton	.40
137	Billy Koch	.40
138	Mark Grudzielanek	.40
139	Rodrigo Lopez	.40
140	Corey Patterson	.40
141	Troy Percival	.40
142	Shea Hillenbrand	.40
143	Brad Fullmer	.40
144	Ricky Nolasco	1.50
145	Mark Teixeira	.75
146	Tydus Meadows RC	.40
147	Toby Hall	.40
148	Orlando Palmeiro	.40
149	Khalid Ballouli RC	1.50
150	Grady Little	.40
151	David Eckstein	.40

No.	Player	Price
152	Kenny Perez RC	1.50
153	Ben Grieve	.40
154	Ismael Valdes	.40
155	Bret Boone	.50
156	Jesse Foppert	.40
157	Vicente Padilla	.40
158	Bobby Abreu	.50
159	Scott Hatteberg	.40
160	Carlos Quentin	4.00
161	Anthony Lerew RC	1.50
162	Lance Carter	.40
163	Robb Nen	.40
164	Zachary Duke/SP RC	10.00
165	Xavier Nady	.40
166	Kip Wells	.40
167	Kevin Millwood	.75
168	Jon Lieber	.40
169	Jose Reyes	.50
170	Eric Byrnes	.40
171	Paul Konerko	.40
172	Chris Lubanski	.40
173	Jae Weong Seo	.40
174	Corey Koskie	.40
175	Tim Stauffer	.40
176	John Lackey	.40
177	Danny Bautista	.40
178	Shane Reynolds	.40
179	Jorge Julio	.40
180	Manny Ramirez	1.00
180	Manny Ramirez/ SP/Old Logo	6.00
181	Alex Gonzalez	.40
182	Moises Alou	.75
182	Moises Alou/ SP/Old Logo	6.00
183	Mark Buehrle	.40
184	Carlos Guillen	.40
185	Nate Cornejo	.40
186	Billy Traber	.40
187	Jason Jennings	.40
188	Eric Munson	.40
189	Braden Looper	.40
190	Juan Encarnacion	.40
191	Dusty Baker	.40
192	Travis Lee	.40
193	Miguel Cairo	.40
194	Rich Aurilia/SP	5.00
195	Flash Gordon	.40
196	Freddy Garcia	.40
197	Brian Lawrence	.40
198	Jorge Posada/SP	8.00
199	Javier Vazquez	.40
200	Albert Pujols	3.00
200	Albert Pujols/ SP/Old Logo	12.00
201	Victor Zambrano	.40
202	Eli Marrero	.40
203	Joel Pineiro	.40
204	Rondell White	.50
205	Craig Ansman RC	2.00
206	Michael Young	.40
207	Carlos Baerga	.40
208	Andruw Jones	1.00
209	Jerry Hairston Jr.	.40
210	Shawn Green/SP	6.00
211	Ron Gardenhire	.40
212	Darin Erstad	.50
213	Brandon Webb	.50
213	Brandon Webb/ SP/Glove In Air	6.00
214	Greg Maddux	2.00
215	Reed Johnson	.40
216	John Thomson	.40
217	Tino Martinez	.40
218	Mike Cameron	.40
219	Edgar Martinez	.50
220	Eric Young	.40
221	Reggie Sanders	.40
222	Randy Wolf	.40
223	Erubiel Durazo	.40
224	Mike Mussina	.75
225	Tom Glavine	.75
226	Troy Glaus	.75
227	Oscar Villarreal	.40
228	David Segui	.40
229	Jeff Suppan	.40
230	Kenny Lofton	.50
231	Esteban Loaiza	.40
232	Felipe Lopez	.40
233	Matt Lawton	.40
234	Mark Bellhorn	.40
235	Wilfredo Ledezma	.40
236	Todd Hollandsworth	.40
237	Octavio Dotel	.40
238	Darren Dreifort	.40
239	Paul LoDuca	.40
240	Richie Sexson	.75
241	Doug Mientkiewicz	.40
242	Luis Rivas	.40
243	Claudio Vargas	.40
244	Mark Ellis	.40
245	Brett Myers	.40
246	Jake Peavy	.40
247	Marquis Grissom	.40
248	Armando Benitez	.40
249	Ryan Franklin	.40
250	Alfonso Soriano	1.50
250	Alfonso Soriano/ SP/Fielding	6.00
251	Tim Hudson	.75
252	Shannon Stewart	.40
253	A.J. Pierzynski	.40
254	Runelvys Hernandez	.40
255	Roy Oswalt	.50
256	Shawn Chacon	.40
257	Tony Graffanino	.40
258	Tim Wakefield	.40
259	Damian Miller	.40
260	Joe Crede	.40
261	Jason LaRue	.40
262	Jose Jimenez	.40
263	Juan Pierre	.40
264	Wade Miller	.40
265	Odalis Perez	.40
266	Eddie Guardado	.40
267	Rocky Biddle	.40
268	Jeff Nelson	.40
269	Terrence Long	.40
270	Ramon Ortiz	.40
271	Raul Mondesi	.50
272	Ugueth Urbina	.40
273	Jeromy Burnitz	.40
274	Brad Radke	.40
275	Jose Vidro	.40
276	Bobby Jenks	.40
277	Ty Wigginton	.40
278	Jose Guillen	.40
279	Delmon Young	.75
280	Brian Giles	.50
281	Jason Schmidt	.50
282	Nicholas Markakis	.40
283	Felipe Alou	.40
284	Carl Crawford	.40
285	Neifi Perez	.40
286	Miguel Tejada	.75
287	Victor Martinez	.40
288	Adam Kennedy	.40
289	Kerry Ligtenberg	.40
290	Scott Williamson	.40
291	Tony Womack	.40
292	Travis Hafner	.40
293	Bobby Crosby	.40
294	Chad Billingsley	.40
295	Russ Ortiz	.40
296	John Burkett	.40
297	Carlos Zambrano	.40
298	Randall Simon	.40
299	Juan Castro	.40
300	Mike Lowell	.40
301	Fred McGriff	.50
302	Glendon Rusch	.40
303	Sung Ki Jung RC	.40
304	Rocco Baldelli	.75
305	Fernando Vina	.40
306	Gil Meche	.40
307	Jose Cruz Jr.	.40
308	Bernie Castro	.40
309	Scott Spiezio	.40
310	Paul Byrd	.40
311	Jay Gibbons	.50
311	Jay Gibbons/ SP/Old Logo	6.00
312	Trot Nixon	.40
313	Chris O'Riordan RC	1.50
314	Julio Lugo	.40
315	Ben Davis	.40
316	Mike Williams	.40
317	Trevor Hoffman	.40
318	Andy Pettitte	.75
319	Orlando Hernandez	.40
320	Juan Rivera	.40
321	Elizardo Ramirez	.40
322	Junior Spivey	.40
323	Tony Batista	.40
324	Mike Remlinger	.40
325	Alex Gonzalez	.40
326	Aaron Hill	.40
327	Steve Finley	.40
328	Vinny Castilla	.40
329	Eric Duncan	.40
330	Mike Gosling	.40
331	Eric Hinske	.40
332	Scott Rolen	1.50
333	Benito Santiago	.40
334	Jimmy Gobble	.40
335	Bobby Higginson	.40
336	Kelvim Escobar	.40
337	Mike DeJean	.40
338	Sidney Ponson	.40
339	Todd Self RC	1.50
340	Jeff Cirillo	.40
341	Jimmy Rollins	.50
342	Barry Zito	.75
342	Barry Zito/ SP/Green Jersey	6.00
343	Felix Pie	.40
344	Matt Morris	.40
345	Kazuhiro Sasaki	.40
346	Jack Wilson	.40
347	Nick Johnson	.40
348	Wil Cordero	.40
349	Ryan Madson	.40
350	Torii Hunter	.75
351	Andy Ashby	.40
352	Aubrey Huff	.40
353	Brad Lidge	.40
354	Derrek Lee	.40
355	Yadier Molina RC	2.00
356	Paul Wilson	.40
357	Omar Vizquel	.50
358	Rene Reyes	.40
359	Marlon Anderson	.40
360	Bobby Kielty	.40
361	Ryan Wagner	.40
361	Ryan Wagner/ SP/Old Logo	5.00
362	Justin Morneau	.50
363	Shane Spencer	.40
364	David Bell	.40
365	Matt Stairs	.40
366	Joe Borowski	.40
367	Mark Redman	.40
368	Dave Roberts	.40
369	Desi Relaford	.40
370	Rich Harden	.40
371	Fernando Tatis	.40
372	Eric Karros	.40
373	Eric Milton	.40
374	Mike Sweeney	.40
375	Brian Daubach	.40
376	Brian Snyder	.40
377	Chris Reitsma	.40
378	Kyle Lohse	.40
379	Livan Hernandez	.40
380	Robin Ventura	.40
381	Jacque Jones	.40
382	Danny Kolb	.40
383	Casey Kotchman	.40
384	Cristian Guzman	.40
385	Josh Beckett	1.00
386	Khalil Greene	.40
387	Greg Myers	.40
388	Francisco Cordero	.40
389	Donald Levinski	.40
390	Roy Halladay	.75
391	J.D. Drew	.40
392	Jamie Moyer	.40
393	Ken Macha	.40
394	Jeff DaVanon	.40
395	Matt Kata	.40
396	Jack Cust	.40
397	Mike Timlin	.40
398	Zack Greinke	4.00
399	Byung-Hyun Kim	4.00
400	Kazuhisa Ishii	4.00
401	Brayan Pena RC	4.00
402	Garret Anderson	6.00
403	Kyle Sleeth	4.00
404	Javy Lopez	4.00
405	Damian Moss	4.00
406	David Ortiz	4.00
407	Pedro J. Martinez	8.00
408	Hee Seop Choi	4.00
409	Carl Everett	4.00
410	Dontrelle Willis	5.00
411	Ryan Harvey	4.00
412	Russell Branyan	4.00
413	Milton Bradley	4.00
414	Marcus McBeth RC	4.00
415	Carlos Pena	4.00
416	Ivan Rodriguez	6.00
417	Craig Biggio	5.00
418	Angel Berroa	4.00
419	Brian Jordan	4.00
420	Scott Podsednik	4.00
421	Omar Falcon RC	4.00
422	Joe Mays	4.00
423	Brad Wilkerson	4.00
424	Al Leiter	4.00
425	Derek Jeter	15.00
426	Mark Mulder	4.00
427	Marlon Byrd	4.00
428	David Murphy	4.00
429	Phil Nevin	4.00
430	J.T. Snow Jr.	4.00
431	Brad Sullivan	4.00
432	Bo Hart	4.00
433	Josh Labandeira RC	4.00
434	Chan Ho Park	4.00
435	Carlos Delgado	6.00
436	Curt Schilling	6.00
437	John Smoltz	5.00
438	Luis Matos	4.00
439	Mark Prior	5.00
440	Roberto Alomar	6.00
441	Coco Crisp	4.00
442	Austin Kearns	4.00
443	Larry Walker	5.00
444	Neal Cotts	4.00
445	Jeff Bagwell	6.00
446	Adrian Beltre	4.00
447	Grady Sizemore	6.00
448	Keith Ginter	4.00
449	Vladimir Guerrero	8.00
450	Lyle Overbay	4.00
451	Rafael Furcal	4.00
452	Melvin Mora	4.00
453	Kerry Wood	4.00
454	Jose Valentin	4.00
455	Ken Griffey Jr.	8.00
456	Brandon Phillips	4.00
457	Miguel Cabrera	8.00
458	Edwin Jackson	4.00
459	Eric Owens	4.00
460	Miguel Batista	4.00
461	Mike Hampton	4.00
462	Kevin Millar	4.00
463	Bartolo Colon	4.00
464	Sean Casey	4.00
465	C.C. Sabathia	5.00
466	Rickie Weeks	4.00
467	Brad Penny	4.00
468	Mike MacDougal	4.00
469	Kevin Brown	4.00
470	Lance Berkman	5.00
471	Ben Sheets	4.00
472	Mariano Rivera	5.00
473	Mike Piazza	8.00
474	Ryan Klesko	4.00
475	Edgar Renteria	4.00

Chrome

NM/M

Complete Set (110):		
Common Player:		1.00
Production 1,955 Sets		
Refractor:		1.5-2X
Production 555 Sets		
Black Refractor:		2-4X
Production 55 Sets		
THC1	Sammy Sosa	8.00
THC2	Nomar Garciaparra	8.00
THC3	Ichiro Suzuki	6.00
THC4	Rafael Palmeiro	3.00
THC5	Carlos Delgado	2.50
THC6	Troy Glaus	2.00
THC7	Jay Gibbons	1.50
THC8	Frank Thomas	3.00
THC9	Pat Burrell	2.00
THC10	Albert Pujols	8.00
THC11	Brandon Webb	1.50
THC12	Chipper Jones	4.00
THC13	Magglio Ordonez	2.00
THC14	Adam Dunn	2.00
THC15	Todd Helton	2.50
THC16	Jason Giambi	3.00
THC17	Alfonso Soriano	3.00
THC18	Barry Zito	2.00
THC19	Jim Thome	3.00
THC20	Alex Rodriguez	8.00
THC21	Hee Seop Choi	1.00
THC22	Pedro J. Martinez	3.00
THC23	Kerry Wood	3.00
THC24	Bartolo Colon	1.50
THC25	Austin Kearns	2.00
THC26	Ken Griffey Jr.	5.00
THC27	Coco Crisp	1.00
THC28	Larry Walker	1.50
THC29	Ivan Rodriguez	2.50
THC30	Dontrelle Willis	2.00
THC31	Miguel Cabrera	2.50
THC32	Jeff Bagwell	2.50
THC33	Lance Berkman	1.50
THC34	Shawn Green	1.50
THC35	Kevin Brown	1.50
THC36	Vladimir Guerrero	3.00
THC37	Mike Piazza	5.00
THC38	Derek Jeter	10.00
THC39	John Smoltz	1.50
THC40	Mark Prior	8.00
THC41	Gary Sheffield	2.00
THC42	Curt Schilling	2.00
THC43	Randy Johnson	3.00
THC44	Luis Gonzalez	1.50
THC45	Andruw Jones	2.50
THC46	Greg Maddux	5.00
THC47	Tony Batista	1.00
THC48	Esteban Loaiza	1.00
THC49	Chin-Hui Tsao	1.00
THC50	Mike Lowell	1.50
THC51	Jeff Kent	1.50
THC52	Richie Sexson	2.00
THC53	Torii Hunter	2.00
THC54	Jose Vidro	1.00

THC55	Jose Reyes	3.00
THC56	Jimmy Rollins	1.00
THC57	Bret Boone	1.50
THC58	Rocco Baldelli	2.00
THC59	Hank Blalock	2.00
THC60	Rickie Weeks	2.00
THC61	Rodney Choy Foo	1.00
THC62	Zach Miner	3.00
THC63	Brayan Pena	1.00
THC64	David Murphy	1.00
THC65	Matt Creighton	1.00
THC66	Kyle Sleeth	1.00
THC67	Matthew Moses	1.00
THC68	Josh Labandeira	1.00
THC69	Grady Sizemore	2.00
THC70	Edwin Jackson	1.00
THC71	Marcus McBeth	1.00
THC72	Bradley Sullivan	1.00
THC73	Zachary Duke	25.00
THC74	Omar Falcon	1.00
THC75	Conor Jackson	2.00
THC76	Carlos Quentin	4.00
THC77	Craig Ansman	1.00
THC78	Mike Gosling	1.00
THC79	Kyle Davies	1.00
THC80	Anthony Lerew	1.00
THC81	Sung Jung	1.00
THC82	David Crouthers	1.00
THC83	Kenny Perez	1.00
THC84	Jeffrey Allison	1.00
THC85	Nic Ungs	1.00
THC86	Donald Levinski	1.00
THC87	Anthony Acevedo	1.00
THC88	Todd Self	1.00
THC89	Tim Frend	1.00
THC90	Tydus Meadows	1.00
THC91	Khalid Ballouli	1.00
THC92	Dioner Navarro	1.00
THC93	Casey Myers	1.00
THC94	Jon Knott	1.00
THC95	Tim Stauffer	1.00
THC96	Ricky Nolasco	2.00
THC97	Blake Hawksworth	1.00
THC98	Jesse Roman	1.00
THC99	Yadier Molina	1.00
THC100	Chris O'Riordan	1.00
THC101	Cliff Floyd	1.00
THC102	Nick Johnson	1.00
THC103	Edgar Martinez	1.50
THC104	Brett Myers	1.00
THC105	Francisco Rodriguez	1.00
THC106	Scott Rolen	3.00
THC107	Mark Teixeira	2.00
THC108	Miguel Tejada	2.00
THC109	Vernon Wells	1.50
THC110	Jerome Williams	1.00

Clubhouse Collection

		NM/M
	Common Player:	5.00
BA	Bobby Abreu	6.00
RB	Rocco Baldelli	12.00
LB	Lance Berkman	6.00
YB	Yogi Berra	35.00
HB	Hank Blalock	8.00
BB	Bret Boone	6.00
KB	Kevin Brown	6.00
EC	Eric Chavez	5.00
RC	Roger Clemens	10.00
JD	Johnny Damon	10.00
AD	Adam Dunn	6.00
RF	Rafael Furcal	6.00
EG	Eric Gagne	8.00
NG	Nomar Garciaparra	15.00
JG	Jason Giambi	8.00
MG	Marcus Giles	8.00
TG	Troy Glaus	6.00
LG	Luis Gonzalez	5.00
SG	Shawn Green	6.00
TH	Tim Hudson	6.00
THU	Torii Hunter	8.00
KI	Kazuhisa Ishii	6.00
RJ	Randy Johnson	10.00
AJ	Andruw Jones	6.00
CJ	Chipper Jones	8.00
AK	Al Kaline	25.00
HK	Harmon Killebrew	30.00
PL	Paul LoDuca	5.00
JL	Javy Lopez	6.00
GM	Greg Maddux	20.00
PM	Pedro J. Martinez	10.00
WM	Willie Mays	100.00
FM	Fred McGriff	6.00
MM	Mark Mulder	5.00
SM	Stan Musial	40.00
BM	Brett Myers	5.00
AP	Albert Pujols	15.00
MR	Manny Ramirez	8.00
JRE	Jose Reyes	8.00
AR	Alex Rodriguez	10.00
IR	Ivan Rodriguez	6.00
SRB	Scott Rolen/bat	8.00
SR	Scott Rolen/jsy	8.00
JR	Jimmy Rollins	6.00
CS	C.C. Sabathia	5.00
GS	Gary Sheffield	8.00
JS	John Smoltz	8.00
DS	Duke Snider	30.00
AS	Alfonso Soriano	10.00
SS	Sammy Sosa	15.00
MS	Mike Sweeney	5.00
MTE	Mark Teixeira	6.00
MT	Miguel Tejada/jsy	6.00
MTB	Miguel Tejada/bat	8.00
JT	Jim Thome	10.00
VW	Vernon Wells	6.00
KW	Kerry Wood	10.00
BZ	Barry Zito	6.00

Clubhouse Collection Autograph

Inserted 15,186
Production 25 Sets

		NM/M
WM	Willie Mays	400.00

Clubhouse Collection - Dual

		NM/M
	Production 55 Sets	
MP	Albert Pujols, Stan Musial	
BC	Yogi Berra, Roger Clemens	160.00
GS	Shawn Green, Duke Snider	150.00

Doubleheader

		NM/M
	Complete Set (30):	50.00
	Common Player:	.75
	Inserted 1:Box	
1	Alex Rodriguez	5.00
2	Nomar Garciaparra	4.00
3	Ichiro Suzuki	4.00
4	Albert Pujols	4.00
5	Sammy Sosa	4.00
6	Derek Jeter	6.00
7	Jim Thome	2.00
8	Adam Dunn	1.00
9	Jason Giambi	2.00
10	Ivan Rodriguez	1.50
11	Todd Helton	1.50
12	Luis Gonzalez	.75
13	Jeff Bagwell	1.50
14	Lance Berkman	1.00
15	Alfonso Soriano	2.00
16	Dontrelle Willis	1.00
17	Mark Prior	2.00
18	Vladimir Guerrero	2.00
19	Mike Piazza	3.00
20	Roger Clemens	4.00
21	Randy Johnson	2.00
22	Curt Schilling	1.50
23	Gary Sheffield	1.00
24	Pedro J. Martinez	2.00
25	Carlos Delgado	1.50
26	Jimmy Rollins	.75
27	Andruw Jones	1.50
28	Chipper Jones	3.00
29	Rocco Baldelli	1.50
30	Hank Blalock	1.00

Flashbacks

		NM/M
	Complete Set (10):	8.00
	Common Player:	.50
	Inserted 1:12	
F1	Duke Snider	1.50
F2	Whitey Ford	.50
F3	Don Newcombe	.50
F4	Al Kaline	1.50
F5	Willie Mays	4.00
F6	Stan Musial	3.00

F7	Harmon Killebrew	2.00
F8	Herb Score	.50
F9	Whitey Ford	1.00
F10	Robin Roberts	.50

Flashbacks Autograph

Inserted 1:30,373

Grandstand Glory

		NM/M
	Common Player:	20.00
YB	Yogi Berra	20.00
AK	Al Kaline	30.00
HK	Harmon Killebrew	30.00
WM	Willie Mays	
SM	Stan Musial	35.00
WS	Warren Spahn	20.00

New Age Performers

		NM/M
	Complete Set (15):	15.00
	Common Player:	.75
	Inserted 1:5	
NAP1	Jason Giambi	1.50
NAP2	Ichiro Suzuki	2.50
NAP3	Alex Rodriguez	3.00
NAP4	Alfonso Soriano	1.50
NAP5	Albert Pujols	3.00
NAP6	Nomar Garciaparra	3.00
NAP7	Mark Prior	3.00
NAP8	Derek Jeter	4.00
NAP9	Sammy Sosa	2.50
NAP10	Carlos Delgado	1.00
NAP11	Jim Thome	1.50
NAP12	Todd Helton	1.00
NAP13	Gary Sheffield	.75
NAP14	Vladimir Guerrero	1.50
NAP15	Josh Beckett	1.00

Real One Autograph

		NM/M
	Common Autograph:	30.00
	Inserted 1:230	
	Red Autograph:	1.5-2X
	Production 55	
GA	Gair Allie	50.00
EB	Ernie Banks	100.00
YB	Yogi Berra	100.00
BB	Bob Borkowski	40.00
BC	Billy Consolo	55.00
CF	Cliff Floyd	30.00
BG	Bill Glynn	45.00
JG	Johnny Gray	45.00
AH	Aubrey Huff	30.00
AK	Al Kaline	100.00
HK	Harmon Killebrew	90.00
TK	Thornton Kipper	45.00
BK	Bob Kline	45.00
SK	Steve Kraly	60.00
LL	Lou Limmer	60.00
ML	Mike Lowell	40.00
WM	Willie Mays	185.00
BM	Bob Milliken	45.00
SM	Stan Musial	140.00
DN	Don Newcombe	65.00
MO	Magglio Ordonez	35.00
JP	Jim Pearce	45.00
HP	Harry Perkowski	50.00
DP	Duane Pillette	40.00
JPO	Johnny Podres	45.00
SR	Scott Rolen	45.00
FS	Frank Smith	45.00
DS	Duke Snider	85.00
VT	"Jake" Thies	45.00
HV	Harold Valentine	45.00
DW	Dontrelle Willis	50.00
BW	Bill Wilson	40.00
TW	Tom Wright	45.00

Team Topps Legends

	NM/M
Inserted 1:505	
Davey Johnson	12.00
Joe Rudi	15.00

Then And Now

		NM/M
	Complete Set (6):	8.00
	Common Player:	1.00
	Inserted 1:15	
TN1	Willie Mays, Jim Thome	4.00
TN2	Al Kaline, Albert Pujols	4.00
TN3	Duke Snider, Carlos Delgado	1.50
TN4	Robin Roberts, Roy Halladay	1.00
TN5	Don Newcombe, Johan Santana	1.00
TN6	Herb Score, Kerry Wood	1.50

2004 Topps Opening Day

		NM/M
	Complete Set (165):	25.00
	Common Player:	.10
	Pack (6):	1.00
	Box (36):	30.00
1	Jim Thome	.50
2	Edgardo Alfonzo	.10
3	Marlon Anderson	.10
4	Ichiro Suzuki	1.00
5	Frank Thomas	.40
6	Tom Glavine	.25
7	Bo Hart	.10
8	Marcus Giles	.10
9	Kevin Millar	.10
10	Derek Jeter	1.50
11	Corey Patterson	.10
12	Jay Payton	.10
13	Lance Berkman	.20
14	Juan Pierre	.10
15	Mike Piazza	.75
16	Richie Sexson	.40
17	Tim Hudson	.25
18	Fred McGriff	.20
19	Brad Radke	.10
20	John Smoltz	.20
21	Jay Gibbons	.10

22	Michael Young	.10
23	Steve Finley	.10
24	Ramon Hernandez	.10
25	Albert Pujols	1.25
26	Trot Nixon	.10
27	Kevin Millwood	.25
28	Mark Prior	1.00
29	Mike Lowell	.20
30	Paul LoDuca	.10
31	Jacque Jones	.10
32	Ty Wigginton	.10
33	Cliff Floyd	.10
34	Marlon Byrd	.10
35	Mark Mulder	.20
36	Johnny Damon	.20
37	Jimmy Rollins	.25
38	Javy Lopez	.25
39	Andruw Jones	.40
40	Hank Blalock	.25
41	Hee Seop Choi	.10
42	Jose Vidro	.10
43	Hideo Nomo	.25
44	Javier Vazquez	.10
45	Jorge Posada	.25
46	Al Leiter	.10
47	Orlando Cabrera	.10
48	Mike Hampton	.10
49	Esteban Loaiza	.10
50	Todd Helton	.40
51	Jose Contreras	.20
52	Jason L. Phillips	.10
53	Vernon Wells	.20
54	Randy Winn	.10
55	Curt Schilling	.40
56	Mark Buehrle	.10
57	Dmitri Young	.10
58	Kazuhisa Ishii	.10
59	A.J. Pierzynski	.10
60	Greg Maddux	.75
61	Jarrod Washburn	.10
62	Omar Vizquel	.10
63	Alex Gonzalez	.10
64	Sean Casey	.10
65	Eric Chavez	.20
66	Mike Lieberthal	.10
67	Jason Kendall	.10
68	Mike Cameron	.10
69	Woody Williams	.10
70	Nomar Garciaparra	1.00
71	Bernie Williams	.20
72	Darin Erstad	.20
73	Bill Mueller	.10
74	Damian Miller	.10
75	Jason Giambi	.50
76	Adam Dunn	.25
77	Carlos Lee	.10
78	Angel Berroa	.10
79	Erubiel Durazo	.10
80	Bret Boone	.20
81	Aubrey Huff	.20
82	Carlos Delgado	.40
83	Toby Hall	.10
84	Roy Halladay	.25
85	Preston Wilson	.10
86	Bartolo Colon	.20
87	Moises Alou	.10
88	Luis Castillo	.10
89	Manny Ramirez	.40
90	Garret Anderson	.25
91	Ryan Klesko	.20
92	Rich Aurilia	.10
93	Rafael Furcal	.20
94	Rocco Baldelli	.20
95	Eric Gagne	.20
96	Jeff Kent	.20
97	Josh Beckett	.40
98	Alex Gonzalez	.10
99	Jose Cruz Jr.	.10
100	Alex Rodriguez	1.25
101	Troy Glaus	.20
102	Carlos Beltran	.20
103	Luis Gonzalez	.20
104	A.J. Burnett	.10
105	Gary Sheffield	.25
106	Benito Santiago	.10
107	Tony Batista	.10
108	David Ortiz	.20
109	Shannon Stewart	.10
110	Jim Edmonds	.25
111	Kenny Lofton	.20
112	Paul Konerko	.20
113	Rafael Palmeiro	.40
114	Pat Burrell	.25
115	Barry Zito	.25
116	Edgar Martinez	.20
117	Austin Kearns	.25
118	Geoff Jenkins	.20
119	Mike Mussina	.25
120	Alfonso Soriano	.50
121	Shea Hillenbrand	.20
122	Ivan Rodriguez	.40
123	Kerry Wood	.40
124	Scott Rolen	.50
125	Jeff Bagwell	.40
126	Roberto Alomar	.25
127	Carl Crawford	.25
128	Mike Sweeney	.10
129	Melvin Mora	.10
130	Larry Walker	.20
131	Matt Morris	.10
132	Shawn Green	.20
133	Scott Podsednik	.25
134	Phil Nevin	.10
135	Dontrelle Willis	.25
136	Torii Hunter	.25
137	Carl Everett	.10
138	Pedro J. Martinez	.50
139	Roy Oswalt	.25
140	Vladimir Guerrero	.50
141	Chipper Jones	.75
142	Jose Reyes	.25
143	Sammy Sosa	1.00
144	Nick Johnson	.10
145	Miguel Tejada	.25
146	Bobby Abreu	.20
147	Magglio Ordonez	.25
148	Sean Burroughs	.10
149	Jody Gerut	.10
150	Jermaine Dye	.10
151	Craig Biggio	.20
152	Randy Johnson	.50
153	Jeff Conine	.10
154	Edgar Renteria	.20
155	Mark Teixeira	.25
156	Eric Hinske	.10
157	Kevin Brown	.20
158	Ken Griffey Jr.	.75
159	Brandon Webb	.10
160	Brian Giles	.20
161	Jason Schmidt	.20
162	Aramis Ramirez	.10
163	Aaron Boone	.10
164	Miguel Cabrera	.40
165	Checklist	.10

Autograph

NM/M

Common Autograph: 10.00
Inserted 1:629

JD	Jeff Duncan	20.00
RH	Rich Harden	20.00
AT	Andres Torres	10.00
RW	Ryan Wagner	25.00
JW	Jerome Williams	
DW	Dontrelle Willis	30.00

2004 Topps Originals Signature Edition

WILLIE MAYS

NM/M

Common Autograph: 10.00
Pack (4): 45.00
Box (6): 220.00
Second number reflects quantity produced.

JA1	Jim Abbott 88 TR/339	20.00
SA5	Sparky Anderson 83 MG/67	15.00
SA6	Sparky Anderson 84 MG/97	15.00
SA7	Sparky Anderson 85 MG/73	15.00
LA9	Luis Aparicio 69/49	20.00
LA12	Luis Aparicio 72/15	30.00
HB2	Harold Baines 82/31	25.00
HB3	Harold Baines 83/19	30.00
HB5	Harold Baines 85/97	15.00
HB6	Harold Baines 86/93	15.00
HB7	Harold Baines 87/115	15.00
JB2	Jesse Barfield 83/45	15.00
JB4	Jesse Barfield 85/60	15.00
JB5	Jesse Barfield 86/37	15.00
JB6	Jesse Barfield 87/180	10.00
KB2	Kevin Bass 84/71	10.00
KB3	Kevin Bass 85/30	10.00
KB4	Kevin Bass 86/44	10.00
KB5	Kevin Bass 87/74	10.00
KB6	Kevin Bass 90 TR/35	10.00
BB5	Buddy Bell 79/135	15.00
BB8	Buddy Bell 82/34	15.00
BB9	Buddy Bell 83/83	10.00
BB10	Buddy Bell 84/22	15.00
BB12	Buddy Bell 86/32	15.00
GB2	George Bell 84/67	10.00
GB3	George Bell 85/32	15.00
GB4	George Bell 86/46	15.00
GB5	George Bell 87/204	10.00
JBE2	Johnny Bench 79/14	125.00
JBE5	Johnny Bench 82/16	125.00
YB10	Yogi Berra 85 MG/27	100.00
VB5	Vida Blue 79/21	20.00
VB7	Vida Blue 81/227	10.00
VB8	Vida Blue 82/53	15.00
VB9	Vida Blue 83/45	15.00
BBL4	Bert Blyleven 79/45	25.00
BBL6	Bert Blyleven 81/29	25.00
BBL8	Bert Blyleven 83/41	20.00
BBL10	Bert Blyleven 85/40	20.00
BBL11	Bert Blyleven 86/62	20.00
BBL12	Bert Blyleven 87/54	20.00
MB2	Mike Boddicker 84/56	15.00
MB3	Mike Boddicker 85/139	10.00
MB4	Mike Boddicker 86/66	10.00
MB5	Mike Boddicker 87/88	10.00
WB2	Wade Boggs 84/20	75.00
WB3	Wade Boggs 85/25	75.00
WB5	Wade Boggs 87/45	60.00
LB4	Lou Brock 70/20	50.00
LB13	Lou Brock 79/27	50.00
TB2	Tom Brunansky 83/27	15.00
TB3	Tom Brunansky 84/62	15.00
TB5	Tom Brunansky 86/28	15.00
TB6	Tom Brunansky 87/193	10.00
BU8	Bill Buckner 81/39	20.00
BU9	Bill Buckner 82/38	20.00
BU10	Bill Buckner 83/47	15.00
BU11	Bill Buckner 84/31	20.00
BU12	Bill Buckner 84 TR/24	20.00
BU13	Bill Buckner 85/80	15.00
BU14	Bill Buckner 86/63	15.00
BC5	Bert Campaneris 79/107	10.00
BC7	Bert Campaneris 84/28	15.00
JC2	John Candelaria 79/77	20.00
JC4	John Candelaria 81/19	30.00
JC5	John Candelaria 82/42	25.00
JC6	John Candelaria 83/77	20.00
JC8	John Candelaria 85/61	20.00
JC9	John Candelaria 86/36	20.00
JCA2	Jose Canseco 87/99	60.00
RC4	Rod Carew 79/29	60.00
RC6	Rod Carew 81/21	75.00
RC7	Rod Carew 82/18	75.00
GC3	Gary Carter 79/21	40.00
GC4	Gary Carter 80/24	40.00
GC5	Gary Carter 81/22	40.00
JCR2	Joe Carter 86/24	50.00
JCR3	Joe Carter 87/23	50.00
RCE3	Ron Cey 79/55	15.00
RCE6	Ron Cey 82/34	15.00
RCE7	Ron Cey 83/87	15.00
RCE8	Ron Cey 83 TR/68	15.00
RCE11	Ron Cey 86/43	15.00
VC2	Vince Coleman 87/299	15.00
VC3	Vince Coleman 88/34	20.00
VC4	Vince Coleman 91 TR/23	25.00
DC6	Dave Concepcion 80/21	40.00
DC8	Dave Concepcion 82/43	30.00
DC9	Dave Concepcion 83/34	30.00
DC10	Dave Concepcion 84/24	40.00
DC11	Dave Concepcion 85/41	30.00
DC12	Dave Concepcion 86/69	25.00
JCU8	Jose Cruz Sr. 82/28	15.00
JCU9	Jose Cruz Sr. 83/102	10.00
JCU10	Jose Cruz Sr. 84/67	10.00
JCU11	Jose Cruz Sr. 85/68	10.00
JCU12	Jose Cruz Sr. 86/31	15.00
RD3	Ron Darling 87/224	15.00
DD2	Darren Daulton 87/269	10.00
DD4	Darren Daulton 92/32	15.00
DD5	Darren Daulton 94/17	20.00
DD6	Darren Daulton 96/22	20.00
ED3	Eric Davis 87/336	15.00
AD3	Andre Dawson 80/27	25.00
AD4	Andre Dawson 81/37	25.00
AD5	Andre Dawson 82/55	20.00
AD6	Andre Dawson 83/47	20.00
AD7	Andre Dawson 84/25	25.00
AD8	Andre Dawson 85/22	25.00
AD9	Andre Dawson 86/24	25.00
DDE2	Doug DeCinces 79/38	20.00
DDE3	Doug DeCinces 80/24	20.00
DDE4	Doug DeCinces 81/24	20.00
DDE5	Doug DeCinces 82/42	20.00
DDE6	Doug DeCinces 83/75	15.00
DDE7	Doug DeCinces 84/19	20.00
DDE8	Doug DeCinces 85/54	15.00
DDE9	Doug DeCinces 86/74	15.00
BD6	Bucky Dent 82/49	20.00
BD7	Bucky Dent 83/92	15.00
BD8	Bucky Dent 84/63	15.00
RDI2	Rob Dibble 90/31	25.00
RDI3	Rob Dibble 91/62	20.00
RDI4	Rob Dibble 92/56	20.00
RDI6	Rob Dibble 93/47	15.00
RDI7	Rob Dibble 94/37	15.00
LD2	Leon Durham 82/51	10.00
LD3	Leon Durham 83/52	10.00
LD4	Leon Durham 84/151	10.00
LD7	Leon Durham 87/87	10.00
LDY2	Lenny Dykstra 87/200	15.00
LDY3	Lenny Dykstra 88/30	25.00
LDY4	Lenny Dykstra 89/17	30.00
DE3	Dennis Eckersley 79/44	40.00
DE4	Dennis Eckersley 80/40	40.00
DEV5	Darrell Evans 79/19	20.00
DEV7	Darrell Evans 81/15	20.00
DEV8	Darrell Evans 82/25	20.00
DEV9	Darrell Evans 83/63	15.00
DEV10	Darrell Evans 84/81	10.00
DEV11	Darrell Evans 85/48	15.00
DEV12	Darrell Evans 86/82	10.00
SF2	Sid Fernandez 86/18	30.00

Code	Player / Year	Price
SF3	Sid Fernandez 87/211	15.00
SF4	Sid Fernandez 93/20	25.00
TF2	Tony Fernandez 86/41	15.00
TF3	Tony Fernandez 87/228	10.00
MF3	Mark Fidrych 79/74	25.00
MF4	Mark Fidrych 80/16	40.00
CF2	Cecil Fielder 87/208	30.00
CF3	Cecil Fielder 88/26	50.00
CF4	Cecil Fielder 89/16	50.00
RF3	Rollie Fingers 79/52	20.00
RF4	Rollie Fingers 80/15	40.00
RF5	Rollie Fingers 81/18	40.00
CFI3	Carlton Fisk 79/24	60.00
CFI4	Carlton Fisk 80/32	50.00
CFI6	Carlton Fisk 82/30	50.00
GF6	George Foster 79/20	20.00
GF10	George Foster 83/39	15.00
GF11	George Foster 84/112	10.00
GF12	George Foster 85/76	10.00
GF13	George Foster 86/64	10.00
SG4	Steve Garvey 79/26	30.00
SG7	Steve Garvey 82/122	15.00
SG9	Steve Garvey 84/32	20.00
SG10	Steve Garvey 85/129	15.00
CG3	Cesar Geronimo 79/28	15.00
CG5	Cesar Geronimo 81/21	15.00
CG6	Cesar Geronimo 82/52	10.00
CG7	Cesar Geronimo 83/67	10.00
CG8	Cesar Geronimo 84/70	10.00
KGI2	Kirk Gibson 82/35	20.00
KGI3	Kirk Gibson 83/35	20.00
KGI5	Kirk Gibson 85/44	20.00
KGI6	Kirk Gibson 86/44	20.00
KGI7	Kirk Gibson 87/65	20.00
DG3	Dwight Gooden 87/52	30.00
RG7	Rich "Goose" Gossage 81/21	20.00
RG8	Rich "Goose" Gossage 82/30	20.00
RG9	Rich "Goose" Gossage 83/34	20.00
RG10	Rich "Goose" Gossage 84/90	15.00
RG12	Rich "Goose" Gossage 86/30	15.00
BG2	Bobby Grich 79/29	20.00
BG3	Bobby Grich 80/70	15.00
BG5	Bobby Grich 82/45	15.00
BG6	Bobby Grich 83/85	10.00
BG7	Bobby Grich 84/57	15.00
BG8	Bobby Grich 85/36	15.00
KG5	Ken Griffey Sr. 80/15	30.00
KG7	Ken Griffey Sr. 82/18	30.00
KG8	Ken Griffey Sr. 83/70	15.00
KG9	Ken Griffey Sr. 84/64	15.00
KG10	Ken Griffey Sr. 85/32	20.00
KG11	Ken Griffey Sr. 86 TR/32	20.00
KGU2	Kelly Gruber 88/77	10.00
KGU3	Kelly Gruber 89/44	10.00
KGU4	Kelly Gruber 90/86	10.00
KGU5	Kelly Gruber 91/52	10.00
KGU6	Kelly Gruber 92/55	10.00
KGU7	Kelly Gruber 93/26	15.00
RGU4	Ron Guidry 80/22	40.00
RGU5	Ron Guidry 81/104	20.00
RGU6	Ron Guidry 82/53	40.00
RGU7	Ron Guidry 83/46	40.00
RGU8	Ron Guidry 84/40	40.00
RGU9	Ron Guidry 85/50	40.00
TG2	Tony Gwynn 84/95	60.00
KH3	Keith Hernandez 80/78	50.00
KH4	Keith Hernandez 81/19	50.00
KH5	Keith Hernandez 82/156	20.00
KH6	Keith Hernandez 83/17	50.00
TH1	Tom Herr 80/1	
TH2	Tom Herr 81/22	15.00
TH3	Tom Herr 82/42	15.00
TH4	Tom Herr 83/80	10.00
TH5	Tom Herr 84/30	15.00
TH6	Tom Herr 85/17	15.00
TH7	Tom Herr 86/28	15.00
TH8	Tom Herr 87/134	10.00
OH2	Orel Hershiser 86/23	40.00
OH3	Orel Hershiser 87/218	20.00
WH4	Whitey Herzog 83 MG/63	10.00
WH5	Whitey Herzog 84 MG/85	10.00
WH6	Whitey Herzog 85 MG/75	10.00
WH7	Whitey Herzog 86 MG/66	10.00
WH8	Whitey Herzog 87 MG/29	15.00
WH9	Whitey Herzog 88 MG/35	15.00
BH5	Bob Horner 83/69	15.00
BH6	Bob Horner 84/63	15.00
BH8	Bob Horner 86/118	15.00
BH9	Bob Horner 87/38	15.00
CH2	Charlie Hough 83/19	20.00
CH3	Charlie Hough 84/50	10.00
CH4	Charlie Hough 85/57	10.00
CH5	Charlie Hough 86/66	10.00
CH6	Charlie Hough 87/46	10.00
CH7	Charlie Hough 88/19	20.00
CH8	Charlie Hough 91 TR/70	10.00
CH9	Charlie Hough 92/25	15.00
AH6	Al Hrabosky 78/20	20.00
AH7	Al Hrabosky 79/40	15.00
AH8	Al Hrabosky 80/61	10.00
AH9	Al Hrabosky 81/38	15.00
AH10	Al Hrabosky 82/62	10.00
AH11	Al Hrabosky 89 Sr./20	20.00
BJ2	Bo Jackson 87/100	60.00
RJ8	Reggie Jackson 82/21	75.00
RJ11	Reggie Jackson 85/17	75.00
RJ12	Reggie Jackson 86/17	75.00
BJA1	Brook Jacoby 85/1	
BJA2	Brook Jacoby 86/133	10.00
BJA3	Brook Jacoby 87/191	10.00
FJ8	Fergie Jenkins 78/17	40.00
FJ10	Fergie Jenkins 80/37	30.00
FJ11	Fergie Jenkins 81/32	30.00
FJ12	Fergie Jenkins 82/65	20.00
FJ13	Fergie Jenkins 83/22	30.00
FJ14	Fergie Jenkins 84/42	30.00
WJ2	Wally Joyner 87/335	15.00
DJ3	David Justice 93/32	20.00
AK10	Al Kaline 67/18	120.00
AK16	Al Kaline 73/25	140.00
JK2	Jimmy Key 86/21	10.00
JK3	Jimmy Key 87/263	10.00
JK5	Jimmy Key 92/37	20.00
DK4	Dave Kingman 81/25	30.00
DK6	Dave Kingman 83/32	30.00
DK7	Dave Kingman 86/32	30.00
RK1	Ron Kittle 84/1	
RK2	Ron Kittle 85/86	10.00
RK3	Ron Kittle 86/55	15.00
RK4	Ron Kittle 87/201	10.00
RKN5	Ray Knight 82/25	20.00
RKN6	Ray Knight 83/36	20.00
RKN7	Ray Knight 84/26	20.00
RKN8	Ray Knight 85/68	15.00
RKN9	Ray Knight 86/80	15.00
RKN10	Ray Knight 87 TR/90	15.00
JKR2	John Kruk 87/214	15.00
JKR3	John Kruk 92/22	35.00
CL3	Carney Lansford 81/184	10.00
CL5	Carney Lansford 83/40	15.00
CL6	Carney Lansford 85/35	15.00
CL7	Carney Lansford 86/76	10.00
CLE3	Chet Lemon 79/24	20.00
CLE6	Chet Lemon 82/23	20.00
CLE7	Chet Lemon 83/35	15.00
CLE8	Chet Lemon 84/42	15.00
CLE9	Chet Lemon 85/32	15.00
CLE10	Chet Lemon 86/136	10.00
CLE11	Chet Lemon 87/27	20.00
JL2	Jim Leyritz 91/38	10.00
JL3	Jim Leyritz 93/49	10.00
JL4	Jim Leyritz 94/16	20.00
JL6	Jim Leyritz 97/62	10.00
JL7	Jim Leyritz 98/20	10.00
JL8	Jim Leyritz 99/124	10.00
JL9	Jim Leyritz 00/40	10.00
DL4	Davey Lopes 79/71	10.00
DL5	Davey Lopes 80/19	15.00
DL7	Davey Lopes 82/17	15.00
DL8	Davey Lopes 83/65	10.00
DL10	Davey Lopes 85/24	15.00
DL11	Davey Lopes 86/40	10.00
DL12	Davey Lopes 01 MG/67	10.00
DL13	Davey Lopes 02 MG/19	15.00
GL7	Greg Luzinski 80/21	30.00
GL9	Greg Luzinski 82/34	20.00
GL10	Greg Luzinski 83/75	10.00
GL11	Greg Luzinski 84/85	10.00
GL12	Greg Luzinski 85/92	10.00
BM7	Bill Madlock 82/26	15.00
BM8	Bill Madlock 83/55	15.00
BM9	Bill Madlock 84/69	15.00
BM10	Bill Madlock 85/60	15.00
BM11	Bill Madlock 86/63	15.00
BM12	Bill Madlock 87/42	15.00
GM3	Gary Matthews Sr. 83/20	15.00
GM4	Gary Matthews Sr. 84/43	10.00
GM5	Gary Matthews Sr. 85/39	10.00
GM6	Gary Matthews Sr. 86/38	10.00
GM7	Gary Matthews Sr. 87/82	10.00
GM8	Gary Matthews Sr. 88/30	15.00
DM3	Don Mattingly 87/84	100.00
WM9	Willie Mays 72/25	300.00
TM5	Tim McCarver 79/22	20.00
JM2	Jack McDowell 89/36	20.00
JM3	Jack McDowell 90 TR/61	15.00
JM4	Jack McDowell 91/33	20.00
JM5	Jack McDowell 92/38	20.00
JM6	Jack McDowell 93/27	20.00
JM9	Jack McDowell 96/15	25.00
JM10	Jack McDowell 97/20	20.00
WMC2	Willie McGee 84/66	25.00
WMC3	Willie McGee 85/44	25.00
WMC4	Willie McGee 86/24	40.00
WMC5	Willie McGee 87/117	25.00
PM1	Paul Molitor 79/15	60.00
PM2	Paul Molitor 80/26	50.00
PM4	Paul Molitor 82/32	50.00
JMO9	Joe Morgan 81/32	30.00
JMO10	Joe Morgan 82/18	15.00
JMO11	Joe Morgan 83/49	25.00
JMO13	Joe Morgan 84/73	15.00
JMO14	Joe Morgan 85/20	15.00
DMU2	Dale Murphy 79/38	50.00
DMU6	Dale Murphy 84/29	40.00
DMU8	Dale Murphy 86/25	50.00
DMU9	Dale Murphy 87/91	25.00
SM5	Stan Musial 62/16	150.00
AO6	Al Oliver 79/42	15.00
AO8	Al Oliver 81/54	15.00
AO9	Al Oliver 82/45	15.00
AO10	Al Oliver 83/50	15.00
AO11	Al Oliver 84/51	15.00
AO12	Al Oliver 85/46	15.00
AO13	Al Oliver 86/44	15.00
PO2	Paul O'Neill 89/24	50.00
PO3	Paul O'Neill 90/18	50.00
PO4	Paul O'Neill 91/24	50.00
PO5	Paul O'Neill 97/33	40.00
JP3	Jim Palmer 80/33	30.00
JP4	Jim Palmer 81/23	30.00
JP5	Jim Palmer 82/24	30.00
DP6	Dave Parker 82/73	20.00
DP7	Dave Parker 83/30	30.00
DP9	Dave Parker 85/45	20.00
DP10	Dave Parker 86/29	30.00
BP9	Boog Powell 73/17	50.00
BP11	Boog Powell 75/19	40.00
TR2	Tim Raines 82/43	20.00
TR3	Tim Raines 83/26	25.00
TR5	Tim Raines 85/43	20.00
TR6	Tim Raines 86/21	25.00
TR7	Tim Raines 87/211	15.00
HR2	Harold Reynolds 87/255	10.00
JR7	Jim Rice 81/123	20.00
JR8	Jim Rice 82/24	35.00
JR9	Jim Rice 83/71	25.00
CR4	Cal Ripken Jr. 86/74	120.00
MR2	Mickey Rivers 79/35	15.00
MR5	Mickey Rivers 82/49	15.00
MR6	Mickey Rivers 83/79	10.00
MR7	Mickey Rivers 84/91	10.00
MR8	Mickey Rivers 85/34	15.00
BR11	Brooks Robinson 74/20	75.00
BR13	Brooks Robinson 76/17	75.00
JRU9	Joe Rudi 79/24	15.00
JRU10	Joe Rudi 80/45	15.00
JRU11	Joe Rudi 85/16	15.00
JRU12	Joe Rudi 87/8	15.00
NR5	Nolan Ryan 83/23	200.00
NR6	Nolan Ryan 84/20	200.00
NR8	Nolan Ryan 86/20	200.00
BS2	Bret Saberhagen 86/23	25.00
BS3	Bret Saberhagen 87/230	15.00
RS2	Ryne Sandberg 84/37	100.00
RS5	Ryne Sandberg 87/32	100.00
SS2	Steve Sax 83/34	15.00
SS4	Steve Sax 85/33	15.00
SS5	Steve Sax 86/45	15.00
SS6	Steve Sax 87/215	10.00
MS2	Mike Schmidt 80/100	60.00
MSC3	Mike Scott 82/32	15.00
MSC4	Mike Scott 83/55	15.00
MSC5	Mike Scott 84/28	15.00
MSC6	Mike Scott 86/73	10.00
MSC7	Mike Scott 87/36	15.00
MSC8	Mike Scott 88/21	15.00
TS2	Tom Seaver 79/44	85.00
TS4	Tom Seaver 81/16	100.00
TS5	Tom Seaver 82/25	100.00
KS2	Kevin Seitzer 88/88	15.00
KS3	Kevin Seitzer 89/39	10.00
KS4	Kevin Seitzer 90/18	15.00
KS5	Kevin Seitzer 91/39	10.00
KS6	Kevin Seitzer 92/49	10.00
KS9	Kevin Seitzer 93/38	10.00
KS10	Kevin Seitzer 94/22	15.00
KS13	Kevin Seitzer 97/24	15.00
LS5	Lee Smith 86/29	25.00
LS6	Lee Smith 87/237	15.00
LS7	Lee Smith 88/27	25.00
OS2	Ozzie Smith 81/28	60.00
OS3	Ozzie Smith 83/55	25.00
OS5	Ozzie Smith 84/19	75.00
OS6	Ozzie Smith 85/16	75.00
RM8	Reggie Smith 79/15	25.00
RM9	Reggie Smith 80/16	25.00
RM10	Reggie Smith 81/14	25.00
RM11	Reggie Smith 82/32	15.00
RM12	Reggie Smith 83/48	15.00
DS8	Duke Snider 64/18	150.00

CS2	Cory Snyder 87/291	10.00
CS3	Cory Snyder 91/39	15.00
DSW2	Dave Stewart 83/41	15.00
DSW3	Dave Stewart 84/60	15.00
DSW4	Dave Stewart 85/24	15.00
DSW5	Dave Stewart 86/53	15.00
DSW6	Dave Stewart 87/171	10.00
DSE2	Dave Stieb 81/21	35.00
DSE3	Dave Stieb 82/34	30.00
DSE4	Dave Stieb 83/70	25.00
DSE5	Dave Stieb 84/20	35.00
DSE6	Dave Stieb 85/55	25.00
DSE7	Dave Stieb 86/69	25.00
DSE8	Dave Stieb 87/75	25.00
DSR2	Darryl Strawberry 85/32	25.00
DSR3	Darryl Strawberry 86/24	25.00
DSR4	Darryl Strawberry 87/183	20.00
DSR5	Darryl Strawberry 87 AS/110	20.00
RU3	Rick Sutcliffe 82/53	20.00
RU4	Rick Sutcliffe 83/43	20.00
RU5	Rick Sutcliffe 84/33	20.00
RU6	Rick Sutcliffe 85/82	20.00
RU8	Rick Sutcliffe 87/19	25.00
BSU6	Bruce Sutter 82/111	20.00
BSU7	Bruce Sutter 83/45	25.00
BSU8	Bruce Sutter 84/24	30.00
BSU9	Bruce Sutter 85/19	35.00
BSU10	Bruce Sutter 86/78	20.00
BSU11	Bruce Sutter 87/36	25.00
KT5	Kent Tekulve 81/17	20.00
KT6	Kent Tekulve 82/36	15.00
KT7	Kent Tekulve 83/52	15.00
KT8	Kent Tekulve 84/71	15.00
KT9	Kent Tekulve 85/43	15.00
KT10	Kent Tekulve 86/57	15.00
KT11	Kent Tekulve 87/32	15.00
KT12	Kent Tekulve 88/20	20.00
LT2	Luis Tiant 68/16	40.00
LT11	Luis Tiant 79/22	30.00
LT12	Luis Tiant 80/23	30.00
LT13	Luis Tiant 81/20	30.00
LT14	Luis Tiant 82/51	15.00
LT15	Luis Tiant 83/58	15.00
AT2	Alan Trammell 80/17	30.00
AT3	Alan Trammell 81/26	30.00
AT4	Alan Trammell 82/40	30.00
AT5	Alan Trammell 83/21	30.00
AT6	Alan Trammell 84/57	30.00
AT7	Alan Trammell 85/39	30.00
AT8	Alan Trammell 86/23	30.00
AT9	Alan Trammell 87/15	30.00
AV2	Andy Van Slyke 85/35	35.00
AV3	Andy Van Slyke 86/37	35.00
AV4	Andy Van Slyke 87/178	25.00
AV5	Andy Van Slyke 87 TR/130	25.00
FV3	Frank Viola 85/25	25.00
FV4	Frank Viola 86/99	15.00
FV5	Frank Viola 87/209	15.00
TW2	Tim Wallach 83/49	15.00
TW4	Tim Wallach 85/46	15.00
TW5	Tim Wallach 86/44	15.00
TW6	Tim Wallach 87/197	15.00
BW3	Bob Watson 79/77	10.00
BW6	Bob Watson 82/23	20.00
BW7	Bob Watson 83/93	10.00
BW8	Bob Watson 84/64	10.00
BW9	Bob Watson 85/68	10.00
EW4	Earl Weaver 78 MG/52	15.00
EW5	Earl Weaver 83 MG/38	20.00
EW7	Earl Weaver 86 MG/107	15.00
EW8	Earl Weaver 87 MG/175	10.00
WW2	Walt Weiss 89/34	10.00
WW3	Walt Weiss 91/30	10.00
WW4	Walt Weiss 92/71	10.00
WW7	Walt Weiss 97/49	10.00
WW10	Walt Weiss 99/40	10.00
WW11	Walt Weiss 01/51	10.00
MW2	Mookie Wilson 82/20	20.00

MW3	Mookie Wilson 83/41	15.00
MW5	Mookie Wilson 85/51	15.00
MW6	Mookie Wilson 86/47	15.00
MW7	Mookie Wilson 87/67	15.00
CY4	Carl Yastrzemski 80/60	100.00
CY5	Carl Yastrzemski 81/35	120.00
SY5	Steve Yeager 79/23	25.00
SY9	Steve Yeager 83/80	10.00
SY12	Steve Yeager 86/47	15.00
SY13	Steve Yeager 86 TR/100	10.00
RY5	Robin Yount 80/18	100.00
RY6	Robin Yount 81/23	100.00
RY9	Robin Yount 84/15	125.00
RY11	Robin Yount 86/21	100.00

2004 Topps Pristine

NM/M

Complete Set (190):		
Common Player:		1.00
Common Rookie:		1.50
Common Uncommon RC:		3.00
Production 999		
Common Rare RC:		6.00
Production 499		
Pack (8):		35.00
Box (5):		140.00
1	Jim Thome	2.00
2	Ryan Klesko	1.00
3	Ichiro Suzuki	4.00
4	Rocco Baldelli	1.00
5	Vernon Wells	1.00
6	Javier Vazquez	1.00
7	Billy Wagner	1.00
8	Jose Reyes	1.00
9	Lance Berkman	1.00
10	Alex Rodriguez	6.00
11	Pat Burrell	1.00
12	Mark Mulder	1.00
13	Mike Piazza	3.00
14	Miguel Cabrera	2.00
15	Larry Walker	1.00
16	Carlos Lee	1.00
17	Mark Prior	2.00
18	Pedro J. Martinez	2.00
19	Melvin Mora	1.00
20	Sammy Sosa	4.00
21	Bartolo Colon	1.00
22	Luis Gonzalez	1.00
23	Marcus Giles	1.00
24	Ken Griffey Jr.	3.00
25	Ivan Rodriguez	1.50
26	Carlos Beltran	1.00
27	Geoff Jenkins	1.00
28	Nick Johnson	1.00
29	Gary Sheffield	1.50
30	Alfonso Soriano	2.00
31	Scott Rolen	2.00
32	Garret Anderson	1.00
33	Richie Sexson	1.00
34	Curt Schilling	1.50
35	Greg Maddux	3.00
36	Adam Dunn	1.50
37	Preston Wilson	1.00
38	Josh Beckett	1.50
39	Roy Oswalt	1.00
40	Derek Jeter	6.00
41	Jason Kendall	1.00
42	Bret Boone	1.00
43	Torii Hunter	1.00

44	Roy Halladay	1.00
45	Edgar Renteria	1.00
46	Troy Glaus	1.00
47	Chipper Jones	2.00
48	Manny Ramirez	1.50
49	C.C. Sabathia	1.00
50	Albert Pujols	5.00
51	Randy Wolf	1.00
52	Eric Chavez	1.00
53	Kevin Brown	1.00
54	Cliff Floyd	1.00
55	Jeff Bagwell	1.50
56	Frank Thomas	1.50
57	David Ortiz	1.50
58	Rafael Palmeiro	1.50
59	Randy Johnson	2.00
60	Vladimir Guerrero	2.00
61	Carlos Delgado	1.00
62	Hank Blalock	1.50
63	Jim Edmonds	1.00
64	Jason Schmidt	1.00
65	Mike Lieberthal	1.00
66	Tim Hudson	1.00
67	Jorge Posada	1.00
68	Jose Vidro	1.00
69	Eric Gagne	1.00
70	Roger Clemens	5.00
71	Mike Lowell	1.00
72	Dontrelle Willis	1.00
73	Austin Kearns	1.00
74	Kerry Wood	2.00
75	Miguel Tejada	1.50
76	Bobby Abreu	1.00
77	Edgar Martinez	1.00
78	Joe Mauer	1.00
79	Mike Sweeney	1.00
80	Jason Giambi	1.00
81	Mark Teixeira	1.00
82	Aubrey Huff	1.00
83	Brian Giles	1.00
84	Barry Zito	1.00
85	Mike Mussina	1.50
86	Brandon Webb	1.00
87	Andruw Jones	1.50
88	Javy Lopez	1.00
89	Bill Mueller	1.00
90	Scott Podsednik	1.00
91	Moises Alou	1.00
92	Esteban Loaiza	1.00
93	Magglio Ordonez	1.00
94	Jeff Kent	1.00
95	Todd Helton	1.50
96	Juan Pierre	1.00
97	Jody Gerut	1.00
98	Angel Berroa	1.00
99	Shawn Green	1.00
100	Nomar Garciaparra	3.00
101	David Aardsma/C	1.50
102	David Aardsma/U	4.00
103	David Aardsma/R	8.00
104	Erick Aybar/C RC	5.00
105	Erick Aybar/U RC	10.00
106	Erick Aybar/R RC	15.00
107	Chad Bentz/C RC	1.50
108	Chad Bentz/U RC	3.00
109	Chad Bentz/R RC	6.00
110	Travis Blackley/C RC	1.50
111	Travis Blackley/U RC	3.00
112	Travis Blackley/R RC	6.00
113	Bobby Brownlie/C RC	4.00
114	Bobby Brownlie/U RC	6.00
115	Bobby Brownlie/R RC	10.00
116	Alberto Callaspo/C RC	1.50
117	Alberto Callaspo/U RC	3.00
118	Alberto Callaspo/R RC	6.00
119	Kazuo Matsui/C RC	5.00
120	Kazuo Matsui/U RC	8.00
121	Kazuo Matsui/R RC	12.00
122	Jesse Crain/C	3.00
123	Jesse Crain/U	5.00
124	Jesse Crain/R	8.00
125	Howard Kendrick/C RC	15.00
126	Howard Kendrick/U RC	20.00
127	Howard Kendrick/R RC	25.00
128	Blake Hawksworth/C RC	1.50
129	Blake Hawksworth/U RC	3.00
130	Blake Hawksworth/R RC	6.00
131	Conor Jackson/C	6.00
132	Conor Jackson/U	8.00
133	Conor Jackson/R	12.00
134	Paul Maholm/C RC	1.50
135	Paul Maholm/U RC	3.00
136	Paul Maholm/R RC	6.00
137	Lastings Milledge/C	8.00
138	Lastings Milledge/U	15.00
139	Lastings Milledge/R	20.00
140	Matt Moses/C	4.00
141	Matt Moses/U	6.00
142	Matt Moses/R	10.00
143	David Murphy/C	1.50

144	David Murphy/U	3.00
145	David Murphy/R	6.00
146	Dioner Navarro/C RC	4.00
147	Dioner Navarro/U RC	8.00
148	Dioner Navarro/R RC	10.00
149	Dustin Nippert/C RC	1.50
150	Dustin Nippert/U RC	3.00
151	Dustin Nippert/R RC	6.00
152	Vito Chiaravalloti/C RC	3.00
153	Vito Chiaravalloti/U RC	6.00
154	Vito Chiaravalloti/R RC	8.00
155	Akinori Otsuka/C RC	3.00
156	Akinori Otsuka/U RC	5.00
157	Akinori Otsuka/R RC	8.00
158	Casey Daigle/C RC	1.50
159	Casey Daigle/U RC	3.00
160	Casey Daigle/R RC	6.00
161	Carlos Quentin/C	5.00
162	Carlos Quentin/U	10.00
163	Carlos Quentin	15.00
164	Omar Quintanilla/C	4.00
165	Omar Quintanilla/U	8.00
166	Omar Quintanilla/R	12.00
167	Chris Saenz/C RC	1.50
168	Chris Saenz/U RC	3.00
169	Chris Saenz/R RC	6.00
170	Ervin Santana/C RC	1.50
171	Ervin Santana/U RC	4.00
172	Ervin Santana/R RC	8.00
173	Chris Shelton/C RC	4.00
174	Chris Shelton/U RC	8.00
175	Chris Shelton/R RC	10.00
176	Kyle Sleeth/C	1.50
177	Kyle Sleeth/U	3.00
178	Kyle Sleeth/R	6.00
179	Brad Snyder/C	4.00
180	Brad Snyder/U	8.00
181	Brad Snyder/R	12.00
182	Tim Stauffer/C	4.00
183	Tim Stauffer/U	8.00
184	Tim Stauffer/R	12.00
185	Shingo Takatsu/C RC	4.00
186	Shingo Takatsu/U RC	8.00
187	Shingo Takatsu/R RC	12.00
188	Merkin Valdez/C RC	1.50
189	Merkin Valdez/U RC	3.00
190	Merkin Valdez/R RC	6.00

Refractors

Veterans (1-100):	4-8X
Production 49	
Common RC's:	.75-1.5X
Production 999	
UnCommon RC's:	1-2X
Production 399	
Rare RC's:	1.5-3X
Production 49	

Gold Refractors

Veterans (1-100):	4-8X
Common RC's:	4-8X
Uncommon RC's:	3-5X
Rare RC's:	1.5-3X
Production 41 Sets	

Fantasy Favorite Relics

NM/M

Common Player:	4.00

Refractor:		2-4X
Production 25 Sets		
MA	Moises Alou	6.00
JB	Jeff Bagwell	8.00
RB	Rocco Baldelli	6.00
AB	Angel Berroa	4.00
BB	Bret Boone	4.00
JD	Johnny Damon	8.00
CD	Carlos Delgado	5.00
RF	Rafael Furcal	4.00
RFJ	Rafael Furcal	4.00
EG	Eric Gagne	10.00
NG	Nomar Garciaparra	10.00
SG	Shawn Green	4.00
MG	Mark Grudzielanek	4.00
VG	Vladimir Guerrero	8.00
THE	Todd Helton	8.00
TH	Tim Hudson	6.00
DJ	Derek Jeter	20.00
AJ	Andruw Jones	6.00
CJ	Chipper Jones	8.00
CK	Corey Koskie	4.00
KL	Kenny Lofton	4.00
PM	Pedro J. Martinez	8.00
MPI	Mike Piazza	10.00
MP	Mark Prior	8.00
AP	Albert Pujols	15.00
AR	Alex Rodriguez	12.00
JR	Jimmy Rollins	4.00
MT	Mark Teixeira	4.00
FT	Frank Thomas	8.00
JT	Jim Thome	10.00
JV	Jose Vidro	4.00
LW	Larry Walker	4.00
BW	Brandon Webb	4.00
PW	Preston Wilson	4.00
KW	Kerry Wood	8.00

Going, Going, Gone! Relics

		NM/M
Common Player:		4.00
Refractor:		2-4X
Production 25 Sets		
LB	Lance Berkman	4.00
BB	Bret Boone	4.00
AD	Adam Dunn	8.00
JG	Juan Gonzalez	6.00
LG	Luis Gonzalez	4.00
VG	Vladimir Guerrero	8.00
TH	Todd Helton	8.00
CJ	Chipper Jones	8.00
JJ	Jacque Jones	4.00
JK	Jeff Kent	4.00
RK	Ryan Klesko	4.00
MO	Magglio Ordonez	4.00
DO	David Ortiz	10.00
MP	Mike Piazza	10.00
AP	Albert Pujols	15.00
MR	Manny Ramirez	8.00
AR	Alex Rodriguez	12.00
SR	Scott Rolen	8.00
AS	Alfonso Soriano	8.00
SS	Sammy Sosa	10.00
FT	Frank Thomas	8.00
JT	Jim Thome	10.00
VW	Vernon Wells	4.00

Key Acquisitions Relics

		NM/M
Common Player:		4.00
Inserted 1:8		
Refractors:		2-4X
Production 25 Sets		
HC	Hee Seop Choi	4.00
JG	Juan Gonzalez	6.00
VG	Vladimir Guerrero	8.00
JL	Javy Lopez	6.00
AR	Alex Rodriguez	12.00
IR	Ivan Rodriguez	8.00
GS	Gary Sheffield	6.00
AS	Alfonso Soriano	8.00

Mini

		NM/M
Common Player:		2.00
Inserted 1:5		
DA	David Aardsma	5.00
EA	Erick Aybar	4.00
VC	Vito Chiaravalloti	3.00
NG	Nomar Garciaparra	4.00
JG	Jason Giambi	2.00
VG	Vladimir Guerrero	4.00
BH	Blake Hawksworth	4.00
CJA	Conor Jackson	4.00
DJ	Derek Jeter	6.00
CJ	Chipper Jones	3.00
HK	Howard Kendrick	10.00
KM	Kazuo Matsui	4.00
LM	Lastings Milledge	6.00
MM	Matt Moses	6.00
DM	David Murphy	3.00
DN	Dioner Navarro	10.00
AO	Akinori Otsuka	3.00
MPI	Mike Piazza	4.00
MP	Mark Prior	3.00
AP	Albert Pujols	6.00
AR	Alex Rodriguez	6.00
KS	Kyle Sleeth	4.00
SS	Sammy Sosa	4.00
TS	Tim Stauffer	3.00
IS	Ichiro Suzuki	5.00
ST	Shingo Takatsu	4.00
JT	Jim Thome	3.00
MV	Merkin Valdez	3.00
DW	Dontrelle Willis	3.00
KW	Kerry Wood	4.00

Mini Relics

		NM/M
Common Player:		5.00
Inserted 1:51		
JB	Jeff Bagwell	20.00
EG	Eric Gagne	15.00
NG	Nomar Garciaparra	12.00
CJ	Chipper Jones	10.00
PM	Pedro J. Martinez	12.00
MPI	Mike Piazza	12.00
MP	Mark Prior	10.00
AP	Albert Pujols	25.00
PW	Preston Wilson	5.00
KW	Kerry Wood	10.00

Patch Place Relics

		NM/M
Common Player:		10.00
Refractor:		No Pricing
Production 10 Sets		
JB	Jeff Bagwell	12.00
RB	Rocco Baldelli	12.00
JBE	Josh Beckett	15.00
BB	Bret Boone	10.00
LC	Luis Castillo	10.00
CC	Chin-Feng Chen	40.00
CD	Carlos Delgado	10.00
AD	Adam Dunn	10.00
RF	Rafael Furcal	10.00
EG	Eric Gagne	15.00
NG	Nomar Garciaparra	40.00
LG	Luis Gonzalez	10.00
SG	Shawn Green	15.00
THE	Todd Helton	15.00
TH	Tim Hudson	10.00
RJ	Randy Johnson	20.00
AJ	Andruw Jones	10.00
CJ	Chipper Jones	15.00
AK	Austin Kearns	10.00
PL	Paul LoDuca	10.00
ML	Mike Lowell	10.00
PM	Pedro J. Martinez	20.00
MPI	Mike Piazza	35.00
MP	Mark Prior	15.00
AP	Albert Pujols	40.00
JR	Jose Reyes	15.00
JS	John Smoltz	15.00
SS	Sammy Sosa	20.00
FT	Frank Thomas	15.00
DW	Dontrelle Willis	10.00
PW	Preston Wilson	20.00
KW	Kerry Wood	20.00
BZ	Barry Zito	15.00

Personal Endorsements

		NM/M
Common Autograph:		6.00
Golds:		1.5-3X
Production 25 Sets		
DA	David Aardsma	15.00
GA	Garret Anderson	10.00
LB	Lance Berkman	20.00
HB	Hank Blalock	20.00
MC	Miguel Cabrera	30.00
VC	Vito Chiaravalloti	10.00
BC	Bobby Crosby	25.00
JF	Jennie Finch	120.00
MG	Marcus Giles	10.00
VG	Vladimir Guerrero	50.00
EH	Estee Harris	8.00
AH	Aubrey Huff	8.00
CJ	Conor Jackson	20.00
CL	Chris Lubanski	10.00
JM	Joe Mauer	35.00
WM	Willie Mays	200.00
DM	Dustin McGowan	6.00
BM	Brett Myers	10.00
SP	Scott Podsednik	10.00
JP	Jorge Posada	40.00
AR	Alex Rodriguez	150.00
IR	Ivan Rodriguez	40.00
ES	Ervin Santana	10.00
GS	Gary Sheffield	40.00
GS	Grady Sizemore	25.00
JV	Javier Vazquez	15.00
BW	Brandon Webb	6.00
DY	Delmon Young	15.00

Two of a Kind Autograph
Production 13

1, 2, 3 Triple Relics

	NM/M
Inserted 1:171	
Refractor:	1.5-2X
Production 25 Sets	
NYY Kenny Lofton, Derek Jeter, Alex Rodriguez	50.00
CHC Mark Grudzielanek, Alex Gonzalez, Sammy Sosa	40.00
BOS Johnny Damon, Bill Mueller, Nomar Garciaparra	40.00

2004 Topps Retired Signature Edition

		NM/M
Complete Set (110):		125.00
Common Player:		1.00
Pack (5):		35.00
Box (5):		140.00
1	Willie Mays	6.00
2	Tony Gwynn	3.00
3	Dale Murphy	2.00
4	Lenny Dykstra	1.00
5	Johnny Bench	4.00
6	Bill Buckner	1.00
7	Ferguson Jenkins	1.50
8	George Brett	6.00

9	Ralph Kiner	2.00
10	Ernie Banks	4.00
11	Hal McRae	1.00
12	Lou Brock	2.00
13	Keith Hernandez	1.00
14	Jose Canseco	2.00
15	Whitey Ford	2.50
16	Dave Kingman	1.00
17	Tim Raines	1.00
18	Paul O'Neill	1.50
19	Lou Whitaker	1.00
20	Mike Schmidt	5.00
21	Wally Joyner	1.00
22	Kirk Gibson	1.00
23	Ryne Sandberg	5.00
24	Luis Tiant	1.00
25	Al Kaline	4.00
26	Brooks Robinson	3.00
27	Don Zimmer	1.00
28	Nolan Ryan	6.00
29	Maury Wills	1.00
30	Stan Musial	4.00
31	Garry Maddox	1.00
32	Tom Brunansky	1.00
33	Don Mattingly	5.00
34	Earl Weaver	1.00
35	Bobby Grich	1.00
36	Orlando Cepeda	1.50
37	Alan Trammell	1.50
38	Al Hrabosky	1.00
39	Davey Lopes	1.00
40	Rod Carew	2.00
41	Robin Yount	4.00
42	Dwight Gooden	1.00
43	Andre Dawson	1.50
44	Hank Aaron	6.00
45	Norm Cash	1.00
46	Reggie Jackson	2.50
47	Jim Rice	1.00
48	Carlton Fisk	2.00
49	Dave Parker	1.00
50	Cal Ripken Jr.	6.00
51	Roy Face	1.00
52	Bob Gibson	2.50
53	Jimmy Key	1.00
54	Al Oliver	1.00
55	Don Larsen	1.50
56	Tom Seaver	3.00
57	Tony Armas	1.00
58	Dave Stieb	1.00
59	Will Clark	2.00
60	Duke Snider	2.50
61	Cesar Geronimo	1.00
62	Ron Kittle	1.00
63	Ron Santo	2.00
64	Mickey Rivers	1.00
65	Jimmy Piersall	1.00
66	Ron Swoboda	1.00
67	Kent Hrbek	1.00
68	Dennis Eckersley	2.00
69	Greg Luzinski	1.00
70	Harmon Killebrew	3.00
71	Ron Guidry	1.50
72	Steve Garvey	1.00
73	Andy Van Slyke	1.00
74	Rich "Goose" Gossage	1.00
75	Ozzie Smith	3.00
76	Richie Allen	1.00
77	Vida Blue	1.00
78	Tony Oliva	1.00
79	Darryl Strawberry	1.00
80	Frank Robinson	2.00
81	Bruce Sutter	1.50
82	Dave Concepcion	1.00
83	Darrell Evans	1.00
84	Jack Morris	1.00
85	Bo Jackson	2.00
86	Orel Hershiser	1.00
87	Rob Dibble	1.00
88	Wade Boggs	2.00
89	Fernando Valenzuela	1.00
90	Jim Palmer	2.00
91	George Foster	1.00
92	Mike Scott	1.00
93	Paul Molitor	2.50
94	Gary Carter	2.00
95	Bobby Richardson	1.00
96	Rollie Fingers	1.00
97	Tim McCarver	1.00
98	John Candelaria	1.00
99	Dave Winfield	2.00
100	Yogi Berra	3.00
101	Bill Madlock	1.00
102	Jack McDowell	1.00
103	Luis Aparicio	1.00
104	Graig Nettles	1.00
105	Dave Stewart	1.00
106	Darren Daulton	1.00
107	Gary Gaetti	1.00
108	Tony Fernandez	1.00
109	Buddy Bell	1.00
110	Carl Yastrzemski	4.00

Black

Black (1-110):	4-6X
Production 99 Sets	

Chrome Autographs

	NM/M
Common Autograph:	10.00
Inserted 1:1	
Refractor:	2-4X
SP Refractor:	.75-2X
Production 25 Sets	
HA	Hank Aaron/SP/50	320.00
TA	Tony Armas	10.00
EB	Ernie Banks/SP/50	180.00
BBE	Buddy Bell	12.00
JB	Johnny Bench/SP/75	80.00
YB	Yogi Berra/SP/75	80.00
VB	Vida Blue	10.00
WB	Wade Boggs	40.00
TB	Tom Brunansky	10.00
BB	Bill Buckner	12.00
JC	John Candelaria	20.00
JCA	Jose Canseco	35.00
RC	Rod Carew	35.00
GC	Gary Carter	20.00
OC	Orlando Cepeda	15.00
DD	Darren Daulton	10.00
BD	Bucky Dent	10.00
RD	Rob Dibble	12.00
DEC	Dennis Eckersley	30.00
DE	Darrell Evans	10.00
RF	Roy Face	15.00
TF	Tony Fernandez	10.00
WF	Whitey Ford/SP/75	90.00
RF	Rollie Fingers	15.00
CF	Carlton Fisk	40.00
GF	George Foster	12.00
CG	Cesar Geronimo	25.00
BG	Bob Gibson/SP/75	75.00
KG	Kirk Gibson	20.00
DG	Dwight Gooden/SP/75	40.00
GG	Rich "Goose" Gossage	15.00
BGR	Bobby Grich	10.00
TG	Tony Gwynn/SP/75	75.00
OH	Orel Hershiser	25.00
AH	Al Hrabosky	10.00
FJ	Ferguson Jenkins	15.00
WJ	Wally Joyner	10.00
JK	Jimmy Key	10.00
RK	Ralph Kiner	50.00
RKI	Ron Kittle	10.00
DL	Davey Lopes	10.00
GL	Greg Luzinski	15.00
BM	Bill Madlock	10.00
DM	Don Mattingly/SP/75	100.00
JM	Jack McDowell	10.00
PM	Paul Molitor	50.00
DM	Dale Murphy	25.00
SM	Stan Musial/SP/50	160.00
GN	Graig Nettles	12.00
TO	Tony Oliva	20.00
AO	Al Oliver	12.00
PO	Paul O'Neill	40.00
DP	Dave Parker	20.00
JP	Jimmy Piersall	15.00
BR	Bobby Richardson	15.00
CR	Cal Ripken Jr./SP/25	275.00
BRO	Brooks Robinson/SP/75	90.00
FR	Frank Robinson	30.00
NR	Nolan Ryan/SP/25	300.00
RSA	Ryne Sandberg	75.00
RS	Ron Santo	20.00
MS	Mike Schmidt/SP/75	150.00
TS	Tom Seaver/SP/75	75.00
OS	Ozzie Smith/SP/75	100.00
DSN	Duke Snider/SP/50	90.00
DST	Dave Stieb	12.00
DS	Darryl Strawberry	30.00
BS	Bruce Sutter	25.00
RS	Ron Swoboda	10.00
LT	Luis Tiant	10.00
AT	Alan Trammell	20.00
EW	Earl Weaver	10.00
MW	Maury Wills	10.00
CY	Carl Yastrzemski/SP/25	180.00
RY	Robin Yount/SP/50	125.00
DZ	Don Zimmer	20.00

Chrome Co-Signers

No Pricing
Production 25 Sets

2004 Topps Total

	NM/M
Complete Set (880):	100.00
Common Player:	.10
Pack (10):	1.00

Box (36):		30.00
1	Kevin Brown	.25
2	Mike Mordecai	.10
3	Seung Jun Song	.10
4	Mike Maroth	.10
5	Mike Lieberthal	.10
6	Billy Koch	.10
7	Mike Stanton	.10
8	Brad Penny	.10
9	Brooks Kieschnick	.10
10	Carlos Delgado	.40
11	Brady Clark	.10
12	Ramon Martinez	.10
13	Dan Wilson	.10
14	Guillermo Mota	.10
15	Trevor Hoffman	.10
16	Tony Batista	.10
17	Rusty Greer	.10
18	David Weathers	.10
19	Horacio Ramirez	.10
20	Aubrey Huff	.10
21	Casey Blake	.10
22	Ryan Bukvich	.10
23	Garrett Atkins	.10
24	Jose Contreras	.10
25	Chipper Jones	.75
26	Neifi Perez	.10
27	Scott Linebrink	.10
28	Matt Kinney	.10
29	Michael Restovich	.10
30	Scott Rolen	.75
31	John Franco	.10
32	Toby Hall	.10
33	Wily Mo Pena	.10
34	Dennis Tankersley	.10
35	Robb Nen	.10
36	Jose Valverde	.10
37	Chin-Feng Chen	.10
38	Gary Knotts	.10
39	Scott Elarton	.10
40	Bret Boone	.25
41	Josh Phelps	.10
42	Jason Larue	.10
43	Tim Redding	.10
44	Greg Myers	.10
45	Darin Erstad	.25
46	Kip Wells	.10
47	Matt Ford	.10
48	Jerome Williams	.10
49	Brian Meadows	.10
50	Albert Pujols	1.50
51	Kirk Saarloos	.10
52	Scott Eyre	.10
53	John Flaherty	.10
54	Rafael Soriano	.10
55	Shea Hillenbrand	.10
56	Kyle Farnsworth	.10
57	Nate Cornejo	.10
58	Kerry Robinson	.10
59	Yan Vogelsong	.10
60	Ryan Klesko	.20
61	Luke Hudson	.10
62	Justin Morneau	.20
63	Frank Catalanotto	.10
64	Derrick Turnbow	.10
65	Marcus Giles	.10
66	Mark Mulder	.25
67	Matt Anderson	.10
68	Mike Matheny	.10
69	Brian Lawrence	.10
70	Bobby Abreu	.10
71	Damian Moss	.10
72	Richard Hidalgo	.10
73	Mark Kotsay	.10
74	Mike Cameron	.10
75	Troy Glaus	.40
76	Matt Holliday	.25
77	Byung-Hyun Kim	.10
78	Aaron Sele	.10
79	Danny Graves	.10
80	Barry Zito	.40
81	Matt LeCroy	.10
82	Jason Isringhausen	.10

83	Colby Lewis	.10
84	Franklyn German	.10
85	Luis Matos	.10
86	Mike Timlin	.10
87	Miguel Batista	.10
88	John McDonald	.10
89	Joey Eischen	.10
90	Mike Mussina	.50
91	Jack Wilson	.20
92	Aaron Cook	.10
93	John Parrish	.10
94	Jose Valentin	.10
95	Johnny Damon	.20
96	Pat Burrell	.25
97	Brendan Donnelly	.10
98	Lance Carter	.10
99	Omar Daal	.10
100	Ichiro Suzuki	1.00
101	Robin Ventura	.10
102	Brian Shouse	.10
103	Kevin Jarvis	.10
104	Jason Young	.10
105	Moises Alou	.25
106	Wes Obermueller	.10
107	David Segui	.10
108	Mike MacDougal	.10
109	John Buck	.10
110	Gary Sheffield	.25
111	Yorvit Torrealba	.10
112	Matt Kata	.10
113	David Bell	.10
114	Juan Gonzalez	.40
115	Kelvim Escobar	.10
116	Ruben Sierra	.10
117	Todd Wellemeyer	.10
118	Jamie Walker	.10
119	Will Cunnane	.10
120	Cliff Floyd	.10
121	Aramis Ramirez	.40
122	Damaso Marte	.10
123	Juan Castro	.10
124	Chris Woodward	.10
125	Andruw Jones	.50
126	Ben Weber	.10
127	Dee Brown	.10
128	Steve Reed	.10
129	Gabe Kapler	.10
130	Miguel Cabrera	.75
131	Billy McMillon	.10
132	Julio Mateo	.10
133	Preston Wilson	.10
134	Tony Clark	.10
135	Carlos Lee	.20
136	Carlos Baerga	.10
137	Mike Crudale	.10
138	David Ross	.10
139	Josh Fogg	.10
140	Dmitri Young	.10
141	Cliff Lee	.10
142	Mike Lowell	.25
143	Jason Lane	.10
144	Pedro Feliz	.10
145	Ken Griffey Jr.	1.00
146	Dustin Hermanson	.10
147	Scott Hodges	.10
148	Aquilino Lopez	.10
149	Wes Helms	.10
150	Jason Giambi	.50
151	Erasmo Ramirez	.10
152	Sean Burroughs	.10
153	J.T. Snow	.10
154	Eddie Guardado	.10
155	C.C. Sabathia	.10
156	Kyle Lohse	.10
157	Roberto Hernandez	.10
158	Jason Simontacchi	.10
159	Tim Spooneybarger	.10
160	Alfonso Soriano	.50
161	Mike Gonzalez	.10
162	Alex Cora	.10
163	Kevin Gryboski	.10
164	Steve Cox	.10
165	Luis Castillo	.10
166	Odalis Perez	.10
167	Alex Sanchez	.10
168	Robert Mackowiak	.10
169	Francisco Rodriguez	.10
170	Roy Oswalt	.25
171	Omar Infante	.10
172	Ryan Jensen	.10
173	Ben Broussard	.10
174	Mark Hendrickson	.10
175	Manny Ramirez	.50
176	Rob Bell	.10
177	Adam Everett	.10
178	Chris George	.10
179	Ricky Gutierrez	.10
180	Eric Gagne	.40
181	Scott Schoeneweis	.10
182	Kris Benson	.10
183	Amaury Telemaco	.10
184	John Riedling	.10
185	Juan Pierre	.10
186	Ramon Ortiz	.10

187	Luis Rivas	.10
188	Larry Bigbie	.10
189	Robby Hammock	.10
190	Geoff Jenkins	.20
191	Chad Cordero	.10
192	Mark Ellis	.10
193	Mark Loretta	.10
194	Ryan Drese	.10
195	Lance Berkman	.10
196	Kevin Appier	.10
197	Enrique Calero (Kiko)	.10
198	Mickey Callaway	.10
199	Chase Utley	.25
200	Nomar Garciaparra	1.00
201	Kevin Cash	.10
202	Ramiro Mendoza	.10
203	Shane Reynolds	.10
204	Chris Spurling	.10
205	Aaron Guiel	.10
206	Mark Derosa	.10
207	Adam Kennedy	.10
208	Andy Pettitte	.25
209	Rafael Palmeiro	.50
210	Luis Gonzalez	.25
211	Ryan Franklin	.10
212	Bob Wickman	.10
213	Ron Calloway	.10
214	Jae Weong Seo	.10
215	Kazuhisa Ishii	.10
216	Sterling Hitchcock	.10
217	Jimmy Gobble	.10
218	Chad Moeller	.10
219	Jake Peavy	.10
220	John Smoltz	.25
221	Erick Almonte	.10
222	David Wells	.10
223	Brad Lidge	.10
224	Carlos Zambrano	.25
225	Kerry Wood	.75
226	Alex Cintron	.10
227	Javier Lopez	.25
228	Jeremy Griffiths	.10
229	Jon Garland	.10
230	Curt Schilling	.50
231	Alex Gonzalez	.10
232	Jay Gibbons	.10
233	Damian Jackson	.10
234	Jeriome Robertson	.10
235	Johan Santana	.10
236	Jose Guillen	.10
237	Jeff Connie	.10
238	Matt Roney	.10
239	Desi Relaford	.10
240	Frank Thomas	.50
241	Danny Patterson	.10
242	Kevin Mench	.10
243	Mike Redmond	.10
244	Jeff Suppan	.10
245	Carl Everett	.10
246	Jack Cressend	.10
247	Matt Mantei	.10
248	Enrique Wilson	.10
249	Craig Counsell	.10
250	Mark Prior	1.50
251	Jared Sandberg	.10
252	Scott Strickland	.10
253	Lew Ford	.10
254	Hee Seop Choi	.10
255	Jason Phillips	.10
256	Jason Jennings	.10
257	Todd Pratt	.10
258	Matt Herges	.10
259	Kerry Ligtenberg	.10
260	Austin Kearns	.25
261	Jay Witasick	.10
262	Tony Armas Jr.	.10
263	Tom Martin	.10
264	Oliver Perez	.10
265	Jorge Posada	.40
266	Joe Beimel	.10
267	Ben Hendrickson	.10
268	Reggie Sanders	.10
269	Julio Lugo	.10
270	Josh Beckett	.40
271	Kyle Snyder	.10
272	Felipe Lopez	.10
273	Kevin Millar	.10
274	Travis Hafner	.20
275	Magglio Ordonez	.25
276	Marlon Byrd	.10
277	Scott Spiezio	.10
278	Mark Corey	.10
279	Tim Salmon	.25
280	Alex Gonzalez	.10
281	Marquis Grissom	.20
282	Miguel Olivo	.10
283	Orlando Hudson	.10
284	Rondell White	.20
285	Jermaine Dye	.10
286	Paul Shuey	.10
287	Brandon Inge	.10
288	B.J. Surhoff	.10
289	Edgar Gonzalez	.10
290	Angel Berroa	.10

#	Name	Price	#	Name	Price	#	Name	Price	#	Name	Price
291	Claudio Vargas	.10	395	Melvin Mora	.10	499	Bobby Higginson	.10	603	J.C. Romero	.10
292	Cesar Izturis	.10	396	Morgan Ensberg	.10	500	Alex Rodriguez	1.50	604	Scott Sullivan	.10
293	Brandon Phillips	.10	397	Ramon Hernandez	.10	501	Octavio Dotel	.10	605	Brad Radke	.10
294	Jeff Duncan	.10	398	Juan Rincon	.10	502	Rheal Cormier	.10	606	Fernando Rodney	.10
295	Randy Wolf	.10	399	Ron Mahay	.10	503	Felix Heredia	.10	607	Jim Brower	.10
296	Barry Larkin	.25	400	Jeff Kent	.25	504	Dan Wright	.10	608	Josh Towers	.10
297	Felix Rodriguez	.10	401	Cal Eldred	.10	505	Michael Young	.10	609	Brad Fullmer	.10
298	Robb Quinlan	.10	402	Mike Difelice	.10	506	Wilfredo Ledezma	.10	610	Jose Reyes	.25
299	Brian Jordan	.10	403	Valerio De Los Santos	.10	507	Sun-Woo Kim	.10	611	Ryan Wagner	.10
300	Dontrelle Willis	.25	404	Steve Finley	.10	508	Michael Tejera	.10	612	Joe Mays	.10
301	Doug Davis	.10	405	Trot Nixon	.25	509	Herbert Perry	.10	613	Jung Bong	.10
302	Ricky Stone	.10	406	Kevin Walker	.10	510	Esteban Loaiza	.10	614	Curtis Leskanic	.10
303	Travis Harper	.10	407	John Vander Wal	.10	511	Alan Embree	.10	615	Al Leiter	.10
304	Jaret Wright	.10	408	Ray Durham	.10	512	Ben Davis	.10	616	Wade Miller	.10
305	Edgardo Alfonzo	.10	409	Aaron Heilman	.10	513	Greg Colbrunn	.10	617	Keith Foulke	.10
306	Quinton McCracken	.10	410	Edgar Renteria	.25	514	Josh Hall	.10	618	Casey Fossum	.10
307	Jason Bay	.10	411	Mike Hampton	.10	515	Raul Ibanez	.10	619	Craig Monroe	.10
308	Joe Randa	.10	412	Kirk Rueter	.10	516	Jayson Werth	.10	620	Hideo Nomo	.25
309	Steve Sparks	.10	413	Jim Mecir	.10	517	Corky Miller	.10	621	Bob File	.10
310	Roy Halladay	.25	414	Brian Roberts	.10	518	Jason Marquis	.10	622	Steve Kline	.10
311	Antonio Alfonseca	.10	415	Paul Konerko	.10	519	Roger Cedeno	.10	623	Bobby Kielty	.10
312	Michael Cuddyer	.10	416	Reed Johnson	.10	520	Adam Dunn	.50	624	Dewon Brazelton	.10
313	John Patterson	.10	417	Roger Clemens	1.50	521	Paul Byrd	.10	625	Eric Chavez	.25
314	Chris Widger	.10	418	Coco Crisp	.10	522	Sandy Alomar	.10	626	Chris Carpenter	.10
315	Shigetoshi Hasegawa	.10	419	Carlos Hernandez	.10	523	Salomon Torres	.10	627	Trever Miller	.10
316	Tim Wakefield	.10	420	Scott Podsednik	.40	524	John Halama	.10	628	Jason Davis	.10
317	Scott Hatteberg	.10	421	Miguel Cairo	.10	525	Mike Piazza	1.00	629	Jose Jimenez	.10
318	Mike Remlinger	.10	422	Abraham Nunez	.10	526	Buddy Groom	.10	630	Vernon Wells	.10
319	Jose Vizcaino	.10	423	Endy Chavez	.10	527	Adrian Beltre	.25	631	Kenny Lofton	.25
320	Rocco Baldelli	.25	424	Eric Munson	.10	528	Chad Harville	.10	632	Chad Bradford	.10
321	David Riske	.10	425	Torii Hunter	.25	529	Javier Vazquez	.20	633	Brad Wilkerson	.10
322	Steve Karsay	.10	426	Ben Howard	.10	530	Jody Gerut	.10	634	Pokey Reese	.10
323	Peter Bergeron	.10	427	Chris Gomez	.10	531	Elmer Dessens	.10	635	Richie Sexson	.40
324	Jeff Weaver	.10	428	Francisco Cordero	.10	532	B.J. Ryan	.10	636	Chin-Hui Tsao	.10
325	Larry Walker	.25	429	Jeffrey Hammonds	.10	533	Chad Durbin	.10	637	Eli Marrero	.10
326	Jack Cust	.10	430	Shannon Stewart	.10	534	Doug Mirabelli	.10	638	Chris Reitsma	.10
327	Bo Hart	.10	431	Einar Diaz	.10	535	Bernie Williams	.40	639	Daryle Ward	.10
328	Rod Beck	.10	432	Eric Byrnes	.10	536	Jeff Davanon	.10	640	Mark Teixeira	.25
329	Jose Acevedo	.10	433	Marty Cordova	.10	537	Dave Berg	.10	641	Corwin Malone	.10
330	Hank Blalock	.40	434	Matt Ginter	.10	538	Geoff Blum	.10	642	Adam Eaton	.10
331	Flash Gordon	.10	435	Victor Martinez	.10	539	John Thomson	.10	643	Jimmy Rollins	.25
332	Brian Fuentes	.10	436	Geronimo Gil	.10	540	Jeremy Bonderman	.10	644	Brian Anderson	.10
333	Tomas Perez	.10	437	Grant Balfour	.10	541	Jeff Zimmerman	.10	645	Bill Mueller	.10
334	Lenny Harris	.10	438	Ramon Vazquez	.10	542	Derek Lowe	.10	646	Jake Westbrook	.10
335	Matt Morris	.25	439	Jose Cruz	.10	543	Scot Shields	.10	647	Bengie Molina	.10
336	Jeremi Gonzalez	.10	440	Orlando Cabrera	.10	544	Michael Tucker	.10	648	Jorge Julio	.10
337	David Eckstein	.10	441	Joe Kennedy	.10	545	Tim Hudson	.40	649	Billy Traber	.10
338	Aaron Rowand	.10	442	Scott Williamson	.10	546	Ryan Ludwick	.10	650	Randy Johnson	.75
339	Rick Bauer	.10	443	Troy Percival	.10	547	Rick Reed	.10	651	Javy Lopez	.25
340	Jim Edmonds	.25	444	Derrek Lee	.25	548	Placido Polanco	.10	652	Doug Glanville	.10
341	Joe Borowski	.10	445	Runelvys Hernandez	.10	549	Tony Graffanino	.10	653	Jeff Cirillo	.10
342	Eric Dubose	.10	446	Mark Grudzielanek	.10	550	Garret Anderson	.40	654	Tino Martinez	.10
343	D'Angelo Jimenez	.10	447	Trey Hodges	.10	551	Timoniel Perez	.10	655	Mark Buehrle	.10
344	Tomokazu Ohka	.10	448	Jimmy Haynes	.10	552	Jesus Colome	.10	656	Jason Michaels	.10
345	Victor Zambrano	.10	449	Eric Milton	.10	553	R.A. Dickey	.10	657	Damian Rolls	.10
346	Joe McEwing	.10	450	Todd Helton	.50	554	Tim Worrell	.10	658	Rosman Garcia	.10
347	Jorge Sosa	.10	451	Gregg Zaun	.10	555	Jason Kendall	.10	659	Scott Hairston	.10
348	Keith Ginter	.10	452	Woody Williams	.10	556	Tom Goodwin	.10	660	Carl Crawford	.10
349	A.J. Pierzynski	.10	453	Todd Walker	.10	557	Joaquin Benoit	.10	661	Livan Hernandez	.10
350	Mike Sweeney	.10	454	Gary Matthews	.10	558	Stephen Randolph	.10	662	Danny Bautista	.10
351	Shawn Chacon	.10	455	Fernando Vina	.10	559	Miguel Tejada	.40	663	Brad Ausmus	.10
352	Matt Clement	.25	456	Omar Vizquel	.10	560	A.J. Burnett	.10	664	Juan Acevedo	.10
353	Vance Wilson	.10	457	Roberto Alomar	.40	561	Ben Diggins	.10	665	Sean Casey	.10
354	Benito Santiago	.10	458	Bill Hall	.10	562	Juan Cruz	.10	666	Pedro Martinez	.75
355	Eric Hinske	.10	459	Juan Rivera	.10	563	Zach Day	.10	667	Milton Bradley	.10
356	Vladimir Guerrero	.75	460	Tom Glavine	.40	564	Antonio Perez	.10	668	Braden Looper	.10
357	Kenny Rogers	.10	461	Ramon Castro	.10	565	Jason Schmidt	.25	669	Paul Abbott	.10
358	Aaron Boone	.10	462	Cory Vance	.10	566	Armando Benitez	.10	670	Joel Pinero	.10
359	Jay Powell	.10	463	Dan Miceli	.10	567	Denny Neagle	.10	671	Luis Terrero	.10
360	Phil Nevin	.10	464	Lyle Overbay	.25	568	Eric Eckenstahler	.10	672	Rodrigo Lopez	.10
361	Willie Harris	.10	465	Craig Biggio	.25	569	Chan Ho Park	.10	673	Joe Crede	.10
362	Ty Wigginton	.10	466	Ricky Ledee	.10	570	Carlos Beltran	.40	674	Mike Koplove	.10
363	Chad Fox	.10	467	Michael Barrett	.10	571	Brett Tomko	.10	675	Brian Giles	.25
364	Junior Spivey	.10	468	Jason Anderson	.10	572	Henry Mateo	.10	676	Jeff Nelson	.10
365	Brandon Webb	.10	469	Matt Stairs	.10	573	Ken Harvey	.10	677	Russell Branyan	.10
366	Brett Myers	.10	470	Jarrod Washburn	.10	574	Matt Lawton	.10	678	Mike DeJean	.10
367	Alexis Gomez	.10	471	Todd Hundley	.10	575	Mariano Rivera	.25	679	Brian Daubach	.10
368	Dave Roberts	.10	472	Grant Roberts	.10	576	Darrell May	.10	680	Ellis Burks	.10
369	LaTroy Hawkins	.10	473	Randy Winn	.10	577	Jamie Moyer	.10	681	Ryan Dempster	.10
370	Kevin Millwood	.25	474	Pat Hentgen	.10	578	Paul Bako	.10	682	Cliff Politte	.10
371	Brian Schneider	.10	475	Jose Vidro	.10	579	Cory Lidle	.10	683	Brian Reith	.10
372	Blaine Neal	.10	476	Tony Torcato	.10	580	Jacque Jones	.10	684	Scott Stewart	.10
373	Jeromy Burnitz	.10	477	Jeremy Affeldt	.10	581	Jolbert Cabrera	.10	685	Allan Simpson	.10
374	Ted Lilly	.10	478	Carlos Guillen	.10	582	Jason Grimsley	.10	686	Shawn Estes	.10
375	Shawn Green	.25	479	Paul Quantrill	.10	583	Danny Kolb	.10	687	Jason Johnson	.10
376	Carlos Pena	.10	480	Rafael Furcal	.10	584	Billy Wagner	.10	688	Wil Cordero	.10
377	Gil Meche	.10	481	Adam Melhuse	.10	585	Rich Aurilia	.10	689	Kelly Stinnett	.10
378	Jeff Bagwell	.50	482	Jerry Hairston	.10	586	Vicente Padilla	.10	690	Jose Lima	.10
379	Alex Escobar	.10	483	Adam Bernero	.10	587	Oscar Villarreal	.10	691	Gary Bennett	.10
380	Erubiel Durazo	.10	484	Terrence Long	.10	588	Rene Reyes	.10	692	T.J. Tucker	.10
381	Cristian Guzman	.10	485	Paul Lo Duca	.10	589	Jon Lieber	.10	693	Shane Spencer	.10
382	Rocky Biddle	.10	486	Corey Koskie	.10	590	Nick Johnson	.10	694	Chris Hammond	.10
383	Craig Wilson	.25	487	John Lackey	.10	591	Bobby Crosby	.10	695	Chris Singleton	.10
384	Rey Sanchez	.10	488	Chad Zerbe	.10	592	Steve Trachsel	.10	696	Xavier Nady	.10
385	Russ Ortiz	.10	489	Vinny Castilla	.10	593	Brian Boehringer	.10	697	Cody Ransom	.10
386	Freddy Garcia	.10	490	Corey Patterson	.20	594	Juan Uribe	.10	698	Ron Villone	.10
387	Luis Vizcaino	.10	491	John Olerud	.20	595	Bartolo Colon	.20	699	Brook Fordyce	.10
388	David Ortiz	.40	492	Josh Bard	.10	596	Bobby Hill	.10	700	Sammy Sosa	1.50
389	Jose Molina	.10	493	Darren Dreifort	.10	597	Andy Van Hekken	.10	701	Terry Adams	.10
390	Edgar Martinez	.25	494	Jason Standridge	.10	598	Carl Pavano	.10	702	Ricardo Rincon	.10
391	Nate Bump	.10	495	Ben Sheets	.25	599	Kurt Ainsworth	.10	703	Tike Redman	.10
392	Brent Mayne	.10	496	Jose Castillo	.10	600	Derek Jeter	2.00	704	Chris Stynes	.10
393	Ray King	.10	497	Jay Payton	.10	601	Doug Mientkiewicz	.10	705	Mark Redman	.10
394	Paul Wilson	.10	498	Rob Bowen	.10	602	Orlando Pameiro	.10	706	Juan Encarnacion	.10

707	Jhonny Peralta	.10
708	Denny Hocking	.10
709	Ivan Rodriguez	.50
710	Jose Hernandez	.10
711	Brandon Duckworth	.10
712	Dave Burba	.10
713	Joe Nathan	.10
714	Dan Smith	.10
715	Karim Garcia	.10
716	Arthur Rhodes	.10
717	Shawn Wooten	.10
718	Ramon Santiago	.10
719	Luis Ugueto	.10
720	Danys Baez	.10
721	Alfredo Amezaga	.10
722	Sidney Ponson	.10
723	Joe Mauer	.50
724	Jesse Foppert	.10
725	Todd Greene	.10
726	Dan Haren	.10
727	Brandon Larson	.10
728	Bobby Jenks	.10
729	Grady Sizemore	.25
730	Ben Grieve	.10
731	Khalil Greene	.10
732	Chad Gaudin	.10
733	Johnny Estrada	.10
734	Joe Valentine	.10
735	Tim Raines	.10
736	Brandon Claussen	.10
737	Sam Marsonek	.10
738	Delmon Young	.25
739	David Dellucci	.10
740	Sergio Mitre	.10
741	Nick Neugebauer	.10
742	Laynce Nix	.10
743	Joe Thurston	.10
744	Ryan Langerhans	.10
745	Pete LaForest	.10
746	Arnie Munoz	.10
747	Rickie Weeks	.25
748	Neal Cotts	.10
749	Jonny Gomes	.10
750	Jim Thome	.75
751	Jon Rauch	.10
752	Edwin Jackson	.10
753	Ryan Madson	.10
754	Chad Tracy	.10
755	Eddie Perez	.10
756	Joe Borchard	.10
757	Jeremy Guthrie	.10
758	Jose Mesa	.10
759	Doug Waechter	.10
760	J.D. Drew	.25
761	Adam LaRoche	.10
762	Rich Harden	.10
763	Justin Speier	.10
764	Todd Zeile	.10
765	Turk Wendell	.10
766	Mark Bellhorn	.10
767	Mike Jackson	.10
768	Chone Figgins	.10
769	Mike Neu	.10
770	Greg Maddux	.10
771	Frank Brooks	.10
772	Alec Zumwalt RC	.25
773	Glendon Rusch	.10
774	Dustan Mohr	.10
775	Shane Halter	.10
776	Tom Wilson	.10
777	So Taguchi	.10
778	Eric Karros	.10
779	Ramon Nivar	.10
780	Marlon Anderson	.10
781	Brayan Pena RC	.10
782	Chris O'Riordan	.10
783	Dioner Navarro RC	1.50
784	Alberto Callaspo RC	.50
785	Hector Gimenez RC	.25
786	Yadier Molina RC	.40
787	Kevin Richardson	.25
788	Brian Pilkington	.40
789	Adam Greenberg	.50
790	Ervin Santana RC	1.00
791	Brent Colamarino	.75
792	Ben Himes	.10
793	Todd Self RC	.25
794	Brad Vericker	.25
795	Donald Kelly RC	.25
796	Brock Jacobsen	.25
797	Brock Peterson	.25
798	Carlos Sosa	.25
799	Chad Chop	.10
800	Matt Moses	1.00
801	Chris Aguila RC	.25
802	David Murphy	.50
803	Don Sutton RC	1.00
804	Jereme Milons	.10
805	Jon Coutlangus	.10
806	Greg Thissen	.10
807	Jose Capellan RC	1.00
808	Chad Santos RC	.10
809	Wardell Starling RC	.10
810	Kevin Kouzmanoff	2.00

811	Kevin Davidson	.40
812	Michael Mooney	.10
813	Rodney Choy Foo	.10
814	Reid Gorecki	.10
815	Rudy Guillen RC	1.00
816	Harvey Garcia	.10
817	Warner Madrigal RC	.50
818	Kenny Perez	.10
819	Joaquin Arias RC	.10
820	Benji Dequin	.40
821	Lastings Milledge	2.00
822	Blake Hawksworth RC	.50
823	Estee Harris RC	.50
824	Bobby Brownlie RC	.75
825	Wanell Severino RC	.10
826	Bobby Madritsch	.10
827	Travis Hanson	.40
828	Brandon Medders RC	.40
829	Kevin Howard RC	.50
830	Brian Steffek	.10
831	Terry Jones	.10
832	Anthony Acevedo	.40
833	Kory Casto	.10
834	Brooks Conrad	.10
835	Juan Gutierrez RC	.50
836	Charlie Zink RC	.40
837	David Aardsma	.40
838	Carl Loadenthal	.10
839	Donald Levinski	.10
840	Dustin Nippert RC	.75
841	Calvin Hayes	.10
842	Felix Hernandez RC	4.00
843	Tyler Davidson	.50
844	George Sherrill RC	.10
845	Craig Ansman RC	.10
846	Jeffrey Allison	.50
847	Tommy Murphy RC	.10
848	Jerome Gamble RC	.40
849	Jesse English RC	.10
850	Alex Romero RC	.40
851	Joel Zumaya RC	2.00
852	Carlos Quentin	2.00
853	Jose Valdez	.25
854	J.J. Furmaniak RC	.75
855	Juan Cedeno RC	.25
856	Kyle Sleeth	1.00
857	Josh Labandeira RC	.25
858	Lee Gwaltney	.10
859	Lincoln Holdzkom RC	.25
860	Ivan Ochoa RC	.10
861	Luke Anderson	.10
862	Conor Jackson	1.00
863	Matt Capps RC	.75
864	Merkin Valdez RC	.75
865	Paul Bacot	.50
866	Erick Aybar RC	1.00
867	Scott Proctor RC	1.00
868	Tim Stauffer	.50
869	Matt Creighton RC	.50
870	Zach Miner RC	1.00
871	Danny Gonzalez RC	.10
872	Tom Farmer	.10
873	John Santor	.10
874	Logan Kensing RC	.25
875	Vito Chiaravalloti RC	.50
876	Checklist	.10
877	Checklist	.10
878	Checklist	.10
879	Checklist	.10
880	Checklist	.10

Silver

Stars:		2-3X
Inserted 1:1		

Press Plates

No Pricing
Production one for each color.

Autograph

	NM/M
Inserted 1:414	8.00

GB	Grant Balfour	8.00
LB	Larry Bigbie	10.00
BC	Rodney Claussen	8.00
TH	Toby Hall	8.00
JJ	Jimmy Journell	8.00

Award Winners

Tony Pena

	NM/M
Complete Set (30):	20.00
Common Player:	.50
Inserted 1:12	
AW1 Roy Halladay	.50
AW2 Eric Gagne	.50
AW3 Alex Rodriguez	3.00
AW4 Albert Pujols	3.00
AW5 Alex Rodriguez	3.00
AW6 Jorge Posada	.50
AW7 Javy Lopez	.50
AW8 Carlos Delgado	.50
AW9 Todd Helton	.75
AW10 Bret Boone	.50
AW11 Jose Vidro	.50
AW12 Bill Mueller	.50
AW13 Mike Lowell	.50
AW14 Alex Rodriguez	3.00
AW15 Edgar Renteria	.50
AW16 Garret Anderson	.50
AW17 Albert Pujols	3.00
AW18 Manny Ramirez	1.00
AW19 Vernon Wells	.50
AW20 Gary Sheffield	.50
AW21 Edgar Martinez	.50
AW22 Mike Hampton	.50
AW23 Angel Berroa	.50
AW24 Dontrelle Willis	.50
AW25 Keith Foulke	.50
AW26 Eric Gagne	.50
AW27 Alex Rodriguez	3.00
AW28 Albert Pujols	3.00
AW29 Tony Pena	.50
AW30 Jack McKeon	.50

Total Production

	NM/M
Complete Set (10):	10.00
Common Player:	.50
Inserted 1:18	
TP1 Alex Rodriguez	3.00
TP2 Albert Pujols	3.00
TP3 Sammy Sosa	2.50
TP4 Carlos Delgado	.50
TP5 Gary Sheffield	.50
TP6 Manny Ramirez	1.00
TP7 Jim Thome	1.00
TP8 Todd Helton	.75
TP9 Garret Anderson	.50
TP10 Nomar Garciaparra	2.00

Total Topps

	NM/M
Complete Set (50):	25.00

Mike Piazza

Common Player:	.50
Inserted 1:7	
TT1 Derek Jeter	3.00
TT2 Jose Reyes	.50
TT3 Miguel Tejada	.50
TT4 Larry Walker	.50
TT5 Frank Thomas	.75
TT6 Carlos Delgado	.50
TT7 Vernon Wells	.50
TT8 Jeff Bagwell	.75
TT9 Jason Giambi	.75
TT10 Mike Lowell	.50
TT11 Shannon Stewart	.50
TT12 Mike Piazza	1.50
TT13 Todd Helton	.75
TT14 Austin Kearns	.50
TT15 Jim Edmonds	.50
TT16 Jose Vidro	.50
TT17 Andruw Jones	.50
TT18 Gary Sheffield	.50
TT19 Eric Chavez	.50
TT20 Magglio Ordonez	.50
TT21 Geoff Jenkins	.50
TT22 Ken Griffey Jr.	1.50
TT23 Jeff Kent	.50
TT24 Jorge Posada	.50
TT25 Albert Pujols	2.00
TT26 Javy Lopez	.50
TT27 Alfonso Soriano	1.00
TT28 Brian Giles	.50
TT29 Mike Sweeney	.50
TT30 Miguel Cabrera	1.00
TT31 Luis Gonzalez	.50
TT32 Scott Rolen	1.00
TT33 Jim Thome	1.00
TT34 Garret Anderson	.75
TT35 Vladimir Guerrero	1.00
TT36 Shawn Green	.50
TT37 Hank Blalock	.75
TT38 Marcus Giles	.50
TT39 Torii Hunter	.50
TT40 Sammy Sosa	2.00
TT41 Nomar Garciaparra	2.00
TT42 Bobby Abreu	.50
TT43 Richie Sexson	.50
TT44 Manny Ramirez	.75
TT45 Troy Glaus	.75
TT46 Preston Wilson	.50
TT47 Ivan Rodriguez	.75
TT48 Ichiro Suzuki	1.50
TT49 Chipper Jones	1.00
TT50 Alex Rodriguez	3.00

2004 Topps Tribute HOF

1973
ROBERTO CLEMENTE
Pittsburgh Pirates® Outfield

	NM/M
Complete Set (80):	120.00
Common Player:	2.00
Pack (5):	50.00
Box (6):	260.00

1	Willie Mays	8.00
2	Richie Ashburn	2.00
3	Babe Ruth	10.00
4	Lou Gehrig	8.00
5	Carl Yastrzemski	5.00
6	Fergie Jenkins	2.00
7	Cool Papa Bell	3.00
8	Johnny Bench	4.00
9	Satchel Paige	4.00
10	Ty Cobb	6.00
11	Robin Roberts	2.00
12	Eddie Mathews	3.00
13	Tom Seaver	3.00
14	Kirby Puckett	3.00
15	Stan Musial	5.00
16	Ralph Kiner	2.00
17	Reggie Jackson	3.00
18	Walter Johnson	4.00
19	Phil Niekro	2.00
20	Mike Schmidt	6.00
21	Brooks Robinson	3.00
22	Jimmie Foxx	4.00
23	Nellie Fox	2.00
24	Joe Morgan	2.00
25	Cy Young	3.00
26	Hank Greenberg	3.00
27	Josh Gibson	3.00
28	Robin Yount	5.00
29	Hoyt Wilhelm	2.00
30	Yogi Berra	3.00
31	Rollie Fingers	2.00
32	Gaylord Perry	2.00
33	Ozzie Smith	4.00
34	Jim Palmer	2.00
35	Harmon Killebrew	4.00
36	Bob Feller	2.00
37	Chuck Klein	2.00
38	Mordecai Brown	2.00
39	Napoleon Lajoie	2.00
40	Al Kaline	3.00
41	Paul Molitor	3.00
42	Jackie Robinson	5.00
43	Mel Ott	3.00
44	Hank Aaron	8.00
45	Rod Carew	2.00
46	Rogers Hornsby	3.00
47	Bob Gibson	2.00
48	Juan Marichal	2.00
49	Bill Mazeroski	2.00
50	Roberto Clemente	8.00
51	Willie McCovey	2.00
52	Red Schoendienst	2.00
53	Nolan Ryan	8.00
54	Dennis Eckersley	2.00
55	Monte Irvin	2.00
56	George Kell	2.00
57	Gary Carter	2.00
58	Tony Perez	2.00
59	Carlton Fisk	2.00
60	Duke Snider	3.00
61	Bobby Doerr	2.00
62	John McGraw	2.00
63	George Sisler	2.00
64	Orlando Cepeda	2.00
65	Earl Weaver	2.00
66	Roy Campanella	3.00
67	Tris Speaker	3.00
68	Sparky Anderson	2.00
69	Willie Stargell	2.00
70	Honus Wagner	3.00
71	Lou Brock	2.00
72	Whitey Ford	3.00
73	George Brett	8.00
74	Luis Aparicio	2.00
75	Ernie Banks	4.00
76	Jim Bunning	2.00
77	Warren Spahn	3.00
78	Jim "Catfish" Hunter	2.00
79	Pee Wee Reese	2.00
80	Frank Robinson	2.00

Gold

Gold Print Run 61-99:	2-3X
Gold p/r 36-60:	2-4X
#'d to last 2 digits of HOF induction yr	

Cooperstown Cut Signatures

AUTHENTIC CUT SIGNATURE OF JIMMIE FOXX

NM/M

No Pricing
Production One Set

JF	Jimmie Foxx (10/05 Auction)	1,940
MO	Mel Ott (8/05 Auction)	2,025

Cooperstown Classmates Dual Cut Signature

No Pricing
Production One Set

Cooperstown Classmates Dual Relic

		NM/M
Common Duo:		20.00
Gold:		.75-1.5X
Production 25		
ME	Paul Molitor, Dennis Eckersley/75	35.00
KK	Chuck Klein, Al Kaline/75	35.00
RB	Nolan Ryan, George Brett/50	60.00
MP	Joe Morgan, Jim Palmer/75	20.00
SK	Duke Snider, Al Kaline/50	60.00
PC	Gaylord Perry, Rod Carew/50	30.00
BY	Johnny Bench, Carl Yastrzemski/75	50.00
CR	Orlando Cepeda, Nolan Ryan/75	60.00
MR	Juan Marichal, Brooks Robinson/50	35.00

Cut Signatures

No Pricing
Production One Set

Dual Cut Signatures

No Pricing
Production One Set

Hall of Fame Patches Relics

		NM/M
Common Player:		20.00
Gold:		.75-1.5X
Production 1-25		
No pricing for production 15 or less.		
GB	George Brett/50	40.00
RC	Rod Carew/100	25.00
DE	Dennis Eckersley/25	25.00
RJ	Reggie Jackson/50	25.00
FR	Frank Robinson/39	35.00
NR	Nolan Ryan/100	50.00
MS	Mike Schmidt/100	40.00
MS2	Mike Schmidt/100	40.00
RY	Robin Yount/35	40.00

Tribute Relics

HALL OF FAME

		NM/M
Common Player:		10.00
Golds:		1-3X
Production 25 Sets		
HA	Hank Aaron/Bat	30.00

JB	Johnny Bench/ Jsy/250	15.00
JB2	Johnny Bench/Jsy	10.00
GB	George Brett/Jsy	15.00
GBB	George Brett/Bat	15.00
LBB	Lou Brock/Bat	10.00
GC	Gary Carter/Jsy/200	10.00
GCU	Gary Carter/Jsy	10.00
OC	Orlando Cepeda/ Bat/100	20.00
RC	Roberto Clemente/Bat	50.00
TC	Ty Cobb/Jsy/20	275.00
TCB	Ty Cobb/Bat	75.00
CF	Carlton Fisk/ Wall/300	20.00
WF	Whitey Ford/Jsy/50	60.00
JF	Jimmie Foxx/ Bat/25	100.00
LG	Lou Gehrig/Bat/52	300.00
BG	Bob Gibson/Jsy	15.00
HG	Hank Greenberg/ Bat	20.00
RH	Rogers Hornsby/ Bat	40.00
RJ	Reggie Jackson/ Jsy/110	15.00
RJB	Reggie Jackson/ Bat/200	10.00
AK	Al Kaline/Jsy/125	20.00
AKB	Al Kaline/Bat	15.00
HK	Harmon Killebrew/ Bat/135	30.00
CK	Chuck Klein/ Bat/107	20.00
JMA	Juan Marichal/ Jsy/125	10.00
WM1	Willie Mays/ Glove/110	150.00
WM2	Willie Mays/Bat	30.00
WM3	Willie Mays/Bat	30.00
WM4	Willie Mays/Jsy	30.00
WM5	Willie Mays/Jsy	30.00
PM	Paul Molitor/Jsy	10.00
PMB	Paul Molitor/Bat	10.00
JM	Joe Morgan/Bat	10.00
SM	Stan Musial/Jsy	20.00
MO	Mel Ott/Bat/25	100.00
JP	Jim Palmer/Jsy	10.00
JP2	Jim Palmer/Jsy	10.00
KP	Kirby Puckett/ Jsy/175	15.00
KPB	Kirby Puckett/Bat	10.00
BRO	Brooks Robinson/ Bat	10.00
FR	Frank Robinson/Jsy	10.00
FRA	Frank Robinson/Jsy	10.00
FRB	Frank Robinson/Bat	10.00
JR	Jackie Robinson/ Bat	25.00
BR	Babe Ruth/Bat/163	150.00
NR	Nolan Ryan/Jsy	10.00
NRA	Nolan Ryan/Jsy/425	25.00
NRJ	Nolan Ryan/Jsy	25.00
MS	Mike Schmidt/ Jsy/50	30.00
MSB	Mike Schmidt/Bat	15.00
TS	Tom Seaver/Jsy	10.00
GS	George Sisler/ Bat/455	25.00
OS	Ozzie Smith/Bat	15.00
DS	Duke Snider/Bat	10.00
TSP	Tris Speaker/ Bat/85	120.00
HW	Honus Wagner/ Bat/118	120.00
EW	Earl Weaver/Jsy/25	20.00
CY	Carl Yastrzemski/ Wall/300	30.00
CYU	Carl Yastrzemski/ Jsy	15.00
RY	Robin Yount/Jsy/50	25.00

Tribute Relic Autographs

		NM/M
Common Player:		40.00
Gold:		No Pricing
Production 5 Sets		
AKB	Al Kaline/95	60.00
BRO	Brooks Robinson/95	50.00
NRJ	Nolan Ryan/95	140.00
EW	Earl Weaver/55	40.00
CYU	Carl Yastrzemski/95	85.00

2005 Topps

	NM/M
Complete Set (732):	75.00
Factory Set (742):	80.00
Factory Set (737):	80.00
Common Player:	.10
Pack (10):	2.00
Box (36):	60.00

BONDS

1	Alex Rodriguez	1.50
2	Placido Polanco	.10
3	Torii Hunter	.25
4	Lyle Overbay	.10
5	Johnny Damon	.40
6	Johnny Estrada	.10
7	Francisco Rodriguez	.10
8	Jason LaRue	.10
9	Sammy Sosa	1.00
10	Randy Wolf	.10
11	Jason Bay	.10
12	Tom Glavine	.25
13	Michael Tucker	.10
14	Brian Giles	.20
15	Dan Wilson	.10
16	Jim Edmonds	.40
17	Danys Baez	.10
18	Roy Halladay	.20
19	Hank Blalock	.50
20	Darin Erstad	.20
21	Robby Hammock	.10
22	Mike Hampton	.10
23	Mark Bellhorn	.10
24	Jim Thome	.50
25	Scott Schoeneweis	.10
26	Jody Gerut	.10
27	Vinny Castilla	.10
28	Luis Castillo	.10
29	Ivan Rodriguez	.50
30	Craig Biggio	.20
31	Joe Randa	.10
32	Dave Roberts	.10
33	Scott Podsednik	.10
34	Cliff Floyd	.10
35	Livan Hernandez	.10
36	Eric Byrnes	.10
37	Ricky Ledee	.10
38	Jack Wilson	.10
39	Gary Sheffield	.40
40	Chan Ho Park	.10
41	Carl Crawford	.25
42	Miguel Batista	.10
43	David Bell	.10
44	Jeff DaVanon	.10
45	Brandon Webb	.10
46	Bronson Arroyo	.10
47	Melvin Mora	.10
48	David Ortiz	.50
49	Andruw Jones	.40
50	Chone Figgins	.10
51	Danny Graves	.10
52	Preston Wilson	.10
53	Jeremy Bonderman	.10
54	Chad Fox	.10
55	Dan Miceli	.10
56	Jimmy Gobble	.10
57	Darren Dreifort	.10
58	Matt LeCroy	.10
59	Jose Vidro	.10
60	Al Leiter	.10
61	Javier Vazquez	.10
62	Erubiel Durazo	.10
63	Doug Glanville	.10
64	Scot Shields	.10
65	Edgardo Alfonzo	.10
66	Ryan Franklin	.10
67	Francisco Cordero	.10
68	Brett Myers	.10
69	Curt Schilling	.50
70	Matt Kata	.10
71	Mark DeRosa	.10
72	Rodrigo Lopez	.10
73	Tim Wakefield	.10
74	Frank Thomas	.50
75	Jimmy Rollins	.25
76	Barry Zito	.25
77	Hideo Nomo	.25
78	Brad Wilkerson	.10
79	Adam Dunn	.50
80	Billy Traber	.10
81	Fernando Vina	.10
82	Nate Robertson	.10
83	Brad Ausmus	.10

#	Player	Value
85	Mike Sweeney	.10
86	Kip Wells	.10
87	Doug Mientkiewicz	.10
88	Zach Day	.10
89	Tony Clark	.10
90	Bret Boone	.10
91	Mark Loretta	.10
92	Jerome Williams	.10
93	Randy Winn	.10
94	Marlon Anderson	.10
95	Aubrey Huff	.10
96	Kevin Mench	.10
97	Frank Catalanotto	.10
98	Flash Gordon	.10
99	Scott Hatteberg	.10
100	Albert Pujols	1.50
101	Jose Molina, Bengie Molina	.10
102	Oscar Villarreal	.10
103	Jay Gibbons	.10
104	Byung-Hyun Kim	.10
105	Joe Borowski	.10
106	Mark Grudzielanek	.10
107	Mark Buehrle	.10
108	Paul Wilson	.10
109	Ronnie Belliard	.10
110	Larry Walker	.40
111	Tim Redding	.10
112	Hee Seop Choi	.10
113	Darrell May	.10
114	Jose Hernandez	.10
115	Ben Sheets	.25
116	Johan Santana	.40
117	Billy Wagner	.20
118	Mariano Rivera	.25
119	Steve Trachsel	.10
120	Akinori Otsuka	.10
121	Bobby Kielty	.10
122	Felix Rodriguez	.10
123	Raul Ibanez	.10
124	Mike Matheny	.10
125	Vernon Wells	.10
126	Jason Isringhausen	.10
127	Jose Guillen	.10
128	Danny Bautista	.10
129	Marcus Giles	.10
130	Javy Lopez	.25
131	Kevin Millar	.10
132	Kyle Farnsworth	.10
133	Carl Pavano	.10
134	D'Angelo Jimenez	.10
135	Casey Blake	.10
136	Matt Holliday	.25
137	Bobby Higginson	.10
138	Ramon Castro	.10
139	Alex Gonzalez	.10
140	Jeff Kent	.20
141	Aaron Guiel	.10
142	Shawn Green	.25
143	Bill Hall	.10
144	Shannon Stewart	.10
145	Juan Rivera	.10
146	Ty Wigginton	.10
147	Mike Mussina	.50
148	Eric Chavez	.25
149	Randall Simon	.10
150	Vladimir Guerrero	.75
151	Alex Cintron	.10
152	Horacio Ramirez	.10
153	Sidney Ponson	.10
154	Trot Nixon	.10
155	Greg Maddux	1.00
156	Esteban Loaiza	.10
157	Ryan Freel	.10
158	Matt Lawton	.10
159	Shawn Chacon	.10
160	Josh Beckett	.25
161	Ken Harvey	.10
162	Juan Cruz	.10
163	Juan Encarnacion	.10
164	Wes Helms	.10
165	Brad Radke	.10
166	Claudio Vargas	.10
167	Mike Cameron	.10
168	Jose Contreras	.10
169	Bobby Crosby	.10
170	Mike Lieberthal	.10
171	Robert Mackowiak	.10
172	Sean Burroughs	.10
173	J.T. Snow Jr.	.10
174	Paul Konerko	.10
175	Luis Gonzalez	.10
176	John Lackey	.10
177	Antonio Alfonseca	.10
178	Brian Roberts	.10
179	Bill Mueller	.10
180	Carlos Lee	.10
181	Corey Patterson	.25
182	Sean Casey	.25
183	Cliff Lee	.10
184	Jason Jennings	.10
185	Dmitri Young	.10
186	Brad Penny	.10
187	Andy Pettitte	.25
188	Juan Gonzalez	.25
189	Paul LoDuca	.10
190	Jason Phillips	.10
191	Rocky Biddle	.10
192	Lew Ford	.10
193	Mark Mulder	.25
194	Bobby Abreu	.25
195	Jason Kendall	.10
196	Terrence Long	.10
197	A.J. Pierzynski	.10
198	Eddie Guardado	.10
199	So Taguchi	.10
200	Jason Giambi	.25
201	Tony Batista	.10
202	Kyle Lohse	.10
203	Trevor Hoffman	.10
204	Tike Redman	.10
205	Neifi Perez	.10
206	Gil Meche	.10
207	Chris Carpenter	.10
208	Josh Phelps	.10
209	Eric Young	.10
210	Doug Waechter	.10
211	Jarrod Washburn	.10
212	Chad Tracy	.10
213	John Smoltz	.25
214	Jorge Julio	.10
215	Alex Gonzalez	.10
216	Shingo Takatsu	.10
217	Jose Acevedo	.10
218	Jason Davis	.10
219	Shawn Estes	.10
220	Lance Berkman	.25
221	Carlos Quilen	.10
222	Jeremy Affeldt	.10
223	Cesar Izturis	.10
224	Scott Sullivan	.10
225	Kazuo Matsui	.25
226	Josh Fogg	.10
227	Jason Schmidt	.25
228	Jason Marquis	.10
229	Scott Spiezio	.10
230	Miguel Tejada	.40
231	Bartolo Colon	.10
232	Jose Valverde	.10
233	Derrek Lee	.25
234	Scott Williamson	.10
235	Joe Crede	.10
236	Cory Lidle	.10
237	Mike MacDougal	.10
238	Eric Gagne	.25
239	Alex Sanchez	.10
240	Miguel Cabrera	.75
241	Luis Rivas	.10
242	Adam Everett	.10
243	Jason Johnson	.10
244	Travis Hafner	.25
245	Jose Valentin	.10
246	Stephen Randolph	.10
247	Rafael Furcal	.25
248	Adam Kennedy	.10
249	Luis Matos	.10
250	Mark Prior	.75
251	Angel Berroa	.10
252	Phil Nevin	.10
253	Oliver Perez	.10
254	Orlando Hudson	.10
255	Victor Zambrano	.10
256	Khalil Greene	.25
257	Tim Worrell	.10
258	Carlos Zambrano	.25
259	Elmer Dessens	.10
260	Gerald Laird	.10
261	Jose Cruz Jr.	.10
262	Michael Barrett	.10
263	Michael Young (Uncorrected error - photo is Rod Barajas.)	.10
264	Toby Hall	.10
265	Woody Williams	.10
266	Rich Harden	.10
267	Mike Scioscia	.10
268	Al Pedrique	.10
269	Bobby Cox	.10
270	Lee Mazzilli	.10
271	Terry Francona	.10
272	Dusty Baker	.10
273	Ozzie Guillen	.10
274	Dave Miley	.10
275	Eric Wedge	.10
276	Clint Hurdle	.10
277	Alan Trammell	.10
278	Jack McKeon	.10
279	Phil Garner	.10
280	Tony Pena	.10
281	Jim Tracy	.10
282	Ned Yost	.10
283	Ron Gardenhire	.10
284	Frank Robinson	.25
285	Art Howe	.10
286	Joe Torre	.25
287	Ken Macha	.10
288	Larry Bowa	.10
289	Lloyd McClendon	.10
290	Bruce Bochy	.10
291	Felipe Alou	.10
292	Bob Melvin	.10
293	Tony LaRussa	.10
294	Lou Piniella	.10
295	Buck Showalter	.10
296	Carlos Tosca	.10
297	Steven Doetsch RC	.10
298	Melky Cabrera RC	1.00
299	Luis Ramirez RC	.10
300	Chris Seddon RC	.10
301	Nate Schierholtz	1.00
302	Ian Kinsler RC	2.00
303	Brandon Moss RC	1.50
304	Chadd Blasko RC	.10
305	Jeremy West RC	1.00
306	Sean Marshall RC	.75
307	Matt DeSalvo RC	.50
308	Ryan Sweeney RC	1.50
309	Matt Lindstrom RC	.50
310	Ryan Goleski RC	.50
311	Brett Harper RC	.25
312	Chris Roberson RC	.10
313	Andre Ethier RC	1.50
314	Chris Denorfia RC	.10
315	Ian Bladergroen RC	.75
316	Darren Fenster RC	.10
317	Kevin West RC	.10
318	Chaz Lytle RC	.50
319	James Jurries RC	.10
320	Matt Rogelstad RC	.10
321	Wade Robinson RC	.10
322	Jake Dittler	.10
323	Edgar Huerta RC	.10
324	Kole Strayhorn	.10
325	Jose Vaquedano RC	.10
326	Elvys Quezada RC	.10
327	John Maine, Val Majewski	.10
328	Rickie Weeks, J.J. Hardy	.10
329	Gabe Gross, Guillermo Quiroz	.10
330	David Wright, Craig Brazell	1.50
331	Dallas McPherson, Jeff Mathis	.10
332	Randy Johnson	.10
333	Randy Johnson	.10
334	Ichiro Suzuki	.10
335	Ken Griffey Jr.	.10
336	Greg Maddux	.10
337	Ichiro Suzuki, Melvin Mora, Vladimir Guerrero	.10
338	Ichiro Suzuki, Michael Young, Vladimir Guerrero	.10
339	Manny Ramirez, Paul Konerko, David Ortiz	.10
340	Miguel Tejada, David Ortiz, Manny Ramirez	.10
341	Johan Santana, Curt Schilling, Jake Westbrook	.10
342	Johan Santana, Pedro J. Martinez, Curt Schilling	.10
343	Todd Helton, Mark Loretta, Adrian Beltre	.10
344	Juan Pierre, Mark Loretta, Jack Wilson	.10
345	Adrian Beltre, Adam Dunn, Albert Pujols	.10
346	Vinny Castilla, Scott Rolen, Albert Pujols	.10
347	Jake Peavy, Randy Johnson, Ben Sheets	.10
348	Randy Johnson, Ben Sheets, Jason Schmidt	.10
349	Postseason Highlight	.10
350	Postseason Highlight	.10
351	Postseason Highlight	.10
352	Postseason Highlight	.10
353	Postseason Highlight	.10
354	Postseason Highlight	.10
355	Postseason Highlight	.10
356	Paul Konerko	.10
357	Alfonso Soriano	.10
358	Miguel Tejada	.10
359	Melvin Mora	.10
360	Vladimir Guerrero	.10
361	Ichiro Suzuki	.10
362	Manny Ramirez	.25
363	Ivan Rodriguez	.10
364	Johan Santana	.10
365	Paul Konerko	.10
366	David Ortiz	.10
367	Bobby Crosby	.10
368	Sox Celebration WS4	1.50
369	Garret Anderson	.25
370	Randy Johnson	.75
371	Charles Thomas	.10
372	Rafael Palmeiro	.40
373	Kevin Youkilis	.10
374	Freddy Garcia	.10
375	Magglio Ordonez	.10
376	Aaron Harang	.10
377	Grady Sizemore	.25
378	Chin-Hui Tsao	.10
379	Eric Munson	.10
380	Juan Pierre	.10
381	Brad Lidge	.10
382	Brian Anderson	.10
383	Alex Cora	.10
384	Brady Clark	.10
385	Todd Helton	.40
386	Chad Cordero	.10
387	Kris Benson	.10
388	Brad Halsey	.10
389	Jermaine Dye	.10
390	Manny Ramirez	.50
391	Daryle Ward	.10
392	Adam Eaton	.10
393	Brett Tomko	.10
394	Bucky Jacobsen	.10
395	Dontrelle Willis	.40
396	B.J. Upton	.25
397	Rocco Baldelli	.10
398	Ted Lilly	.10
399	Ryan Drese	.10
400	Ichiro Suzuki	1.25
401	Brendan Donnelly	.10
402	Brandon Lyon	.10
403	Nick Green	.10
404	Jerry Hairston Jr.	.10
405	Mike Lowell	.10
406	Kerry Wood	.50
407	Carl Everett	.10
408	Hideki Matsui	1.25
409	Omar Vizquel	.25
410	Joe Kennedy	.10
411	Carlos Pena	.10
412	Armando Benitez	.10
413	Carlos Beltran	.50
414	Kevin Appier	.10
415	Jeff Weaver	.10
416	Chad Moeller	.10
417	Joe Mays	.10
418	Terrmel Sledge	.10
419	Richard Hidalgo	.10
420	Kenny Lofton	.10
421	Justin Duchscherer	.10
422	Eric Milton	.10
423	Jose Mesa	.10
424	Ramon Hernandez	.10
425	Jose Reyes	.25
426	Joel Pineiro	.10
427	Matt Morris	.10
428	John Halama	.10
429	Gary Matthews Jr.	.10
430	Ryan Madson	.10
431	Mark Kotsay	.10
432	Carlos Delgado	.10
433	Casey Kotchman	.10
434	Greg Aquino	.10
435	Eli Marrero	.10
436	David Newhan	.10
437	Mike Timlin	.10
438	LaTroy Hawkins	.10
439	Jose Contreras	.10
440	Ken Griffey Jr.	1.00
441	C.C. Sabathia	.10
442	Brandon Inge	.10
443	Peter Munro	.10
444	John Buck	.10
445	Hee Seop Choi	.10
446	Chris Capuano	.10
447	Jesse Crain	.10
448	Geoff Jenkins	.10
449	Brian Schneider	.10
450	Mike Piazza	1.00
451	Jorge Posada	.40
452	Nick Swisher	.10
453	Kevin Millwood	.25
454	Mike Gonzalez	.10
455	Jake Peavy	.25
456	Dustin Hermanson	.10
457	Jeremy Reed	.10
458	Julian Tavarez	.10
459	Geoff Blum	.10
460	Alfonso Soriano	.50
461	Alexis Rios	.10
462	David Eckstein	.10
463	Shea Hillenbrand	.10
464	Russ Ortiz	.10
465	Kurt Ainsworth	.10
466	Orlando Cabrera	.10
467	Carlos Silva	.10
468	Ross Gload	.10
469	Josh Phelps	.10
470	Marquis Grissom	.10
471	Mike Maroth	.10
472	Guillermo Mota	.10
473	Chris Burke	.10
474	David DeJesus	.10

475	Jose Lima	.10
476	Cristian Guzman	.10
477	Nick Johnson	.10
478	Victor Zambrano	.10
479	Rod Barajas	.10
480	Damian Miller	.10
481	Chase Utley	.25
482	Todd Pratt	.10
483	Sean Burnett	.10
484	David Wells	.10
485	Dustan Mohr	.10
486	Bobby Madritsch	.10
487	Ray King	.10
488	Reed Johnson	.10
489	R.A. Dickey	.10
490	Scott Kazmir	.25
491	Tony Womack	.10
492	Tomas Perez	.10
493	Esteban Loaiza	.10
494	Tomokazu Ohka	.10
495	Mike Lamb	.10
496	Ramon Ortiz	.10
497	Richie Sexson	.40
498	J.D. Drew	.25
499	David Segui	.10
500	Barry Bonds	2.00
501	Aramis Ramirez	.25
502	Wily Mo Pena	.10
503	Jeromy Burnitz	.10
504	Craig Monroe	.10
505	Nomar Garciaparra	1.00
506	Brandon Backe	.10
507	Marcus Thames	.10
508	Derek Lowe	.10
509	Doug Davis	.10
510	Joe Mauer	.25
511	Endy Chavez	.10
512	Bernie Williams	.25
513	Mark Redman	.10
514	Jason Michaels	.10
515	Craig Wilson	.10
516	Ryan Klesko	.10
517	Ray Durham	.10
518	Jose Lopez	.10
519	Jeff Suppan	.10
520	Julio Lugo	.10
521	Mike Wood	.10
522	David Bush	.10
523	Juan Rincon	.10
524	Paul Quantrill	.10
525	Marlon Byrd	.10
526	Roy Oswalt	.25
527	Rondell White	.10
528	Troy Glaus	.25
529	Scott Hairston	.10
530	Chipper Jones	.75
531	Daniel Cabrera	.10
532	Doug Mientkiewicz	.10
533	Glendon Rusch	.10
534	Jon Garland	.10
535	Austin Kearns	.10
536	Jake Westbrook	.10
537	Aaron Miles	.10
538	Omar Infante	.10
539	Paul LoDuca	.10
540	Morgan Ensberg	.10
541	Tony Graffanino	.10
542	Milton Bradley	.25
543	Keith Ginter	.10
544	Justin Morneau	.40
545	Tony Armas Jr.	.10
546	Mike Stanton	.10
547	Kevin Brown	.10
548	Marco Scutaro	.10
549	Tim Hudson	.10
550	Pat Burrell	.10
551	Ty Wigginton	.10
552	Jeff Cirillo	.10
553	Jim Brower	.10
554	Jamie Moyer	.10
555	Larry Walker	.10
556	Dewon Brazelton	.10
557	Brian Jordan	.10
558	Josh Towers	.10
559	Shigetoshi Hasegawa	.10
560	Octavio Dotel	.10
561	Travis Lee	.10
562	Michael Cuddyer	.10
563	Junior Spivey	.10
564	Zack Greinke	.10
565	Roger Clemens	1.50
566	Chris Shelton	.10
567	Ugueth Urbina	.10
568	Rafael Betancourt	.10
569	Willie Harris	.10
570	Todd Hollandsworth	.10
571	Keith Foulke	.10
572	Larry Bigbie	.10
573	Paul Byrd	.10
574	Troy Percival	.10
575	Pedro Martinez	.75
576	Matt Clement	.10
577	Ryan Wagner	.10
578	Jeff Francis	.10
579	Jeff Conine	.10
580	Wade Miller	.10
581	Matt Stairs	.10
582	Gavin Floyd	.10
583	Kazuhisa Ishii	.10
584	Victor Santos	.10
585	Jacque Jones	.10
586	Sunny Kim	.10
587	Dan Kolb	.10
588	Cory Lidle	.10
589	Jose Castillo	.10
590	Alex Gonzalez	.10
591	Kirk Rueter	.10
592	Jolbert Cabrera	.10
593	Erik Bedard	.10
594	Ben Grieve	.10
595	Ricky Ledee	.10
596	Mark Hendrickson	.10
597	Laynce Nix	.10
598	Jason Frasor	.10
599	Kevin Gregg	.10
600	Derek Jeter	1.50
601	Luis Terrero	.10
602	Jaret Wright	.10
603	Edwin Jackson	.10
604	Dave Roberts	.10
605	Moises Alou	.25
606	Aaron Rowand	.10
607	Kazuhito Tadano	.10
608	Luis Gonzalez	.10
609	A.J. Burnett	.25
610	Jeff Bagwell	.40
611	Brad Penny	.10
612	Craig Counsell	.10
613	Corey Koskie	.10
614	Mark Ellis	.10
615	Felix Rodriguez	.10
616	Jay Payton	.10
617	Hector Luna	.10
618	Miguel Olivo	.10
619	Rob Bell	.10
620	Scott Rolen	.50
621	Ricardo Rodriguez	.10
622	Eric Hinske	.10
623	Tim Salmon	.10
624	Adam LaRoche	.10
625	B.J. Ryan	.10
626	Roberto Alomar	.25
627	Steve Finley	.10
628	Joe Nathan	.10
629	Scott Linebrink	.10
630	Vicente Padilla	.10
631	Raul Mondesi	.10
632	Yadier Molina	.10
633	Tino Martinez	.10
634	Mark Teixeira	.25
635	Kelvim Escobar	.10
636	Pedro Felix	.10
637	Rich Aurilia	.10
638	Los Angeles Angels of Anaheim	.10
639	Arizona Diamondbacks	.10
640	Atlanta Braves	.10
641	Baltimore Orioles	.10
642	Boston Red Sox	.10
643	Chicago Cubs	.10
644	Chicago White Sox	.10
645	Cincinnati Reds	.10
646	Cleveland Indians	.10
647	Colorado Rockies	.10
648	Detroit Tigers	.10
649	Florida Marlins	.10
650	Houston Astros	.10
651	Kansas City Royals	.10
652	Los Angeles Dodgers	.10
653	Milwaukee Brewers	.10
654	Minnesota Twins	.10
655	Montreal Expos	.10
656	New York Mets	.10
657	New York Yankees	.10
658	Oakland Athletics	.10
659	Philadelphia Phillies	.10
660	Pittsburgh Pirates	.10
661	San Diego Padres	.10
662	San Francisco Giants	.10
663	Seattle Mariners	.10
664	St. Louis Cardinals	.10
665	Tampa Bay Devil Rays	.10
666	Texas Rangers	.10
667	Toronto Blue Jays	.10
668	Billy Butler RC	1.50
669	Wes Swackhamer RC	.25
670	Matt Campbell RC	.25
671	Ryan Webb RC	.50
672	Glen Perkins RC	.25
673	Michael Rogers RC	.25
674	Kevin Melillo RC	.25
675	Erik Cordier RC	.50
676	Landon Powell RC	.50
677	Justin Verlander RC	1.00
678	Eric Nielsen RC	.25
679	Alexander Smit RC	.25
680	Ryan Garko RC	.50
681	Bobby Livingston RC	.25
682	Jeff Niemann RC	.50
683	Wladimir Balentien RC	.50
684	Chip Cannon RC	.50
685	Yorman Bazardo RC	.50
686	Michael Bourn	.10
687	Andy LaRoche RC	2.00
688	Felix Hernandez, Justin Leone	.50
689	Ryan Howard, Cole Hamels	.75
690	Matt Cain, Merkin Valdez	.25
691	Andy Marte, Jeff Francoeur	.10
692	Chad Billingsley, Joel Guzman	.10
693	Jerry Hairston Jr., Scott Hairston	.10
694	Miguel Tejada, Lance Berkman	.25
695	Kenny Rogers	.10
696	Ivan Rodriguez	.25
697	Darin Erstad	.10
698	Bret Boone	.10
699	Eric Chavez	.10
700	Derek Jeter	1.00
701	Vernon Wells	.10
702	Ichiro Suzuki	.75
703	Torii Hunter	.10
704	Greg Maddux	.50
705	Mike Matheny	.10
706	Todd Helton	.25
707	Luis Castillo	.10
708	Scott Rolen	.40
709	Cesar Izturis	.10
710	Jim Edmonds	.25
711	Andruw Jones	.25
712	Steve Finley	.10
713	Johan Santana	.40
714	Roger Clemens	1.00
715	Vladimir Guerrero	.40
716	Barry Bonds	1.50
717	Bobby Crosby	.10
718	Jason Bay	.10
719	Albert Pujols	1.00
720	Mark Loretta	.10
721	Edgar Renteria	.10
722	Scott Rolen	.40
723	J.D. Drew	.10
724	Jim Edmonds	.25
725	Johnny Estrada	.10
726	Jason Schmidt	.10
727	Chris Carpenter	.10
728	Eric Gagne	.10
729	Jason Bay	.10
730	Bobby Cox	.10
731	Game 1	.50
732	Game 2	.50
733	Game 3	.50
734	Game 4	.50

Black

1st Edition:	20-50X

Production 54 Sets

Gold

Stars:	5-10X

Production 2,005 Sets

1st Edition

	NM/M
Stars:	3-5X
HTA Exclusive	
1st Edition Pack (10):	4.00
1st Edition Box (20):	65.00

All-Stars

	NM/M
Complete Set (15):	20.00
Common Player:	
Inserted 1:9	
TAS1	Todd Helton	.75
TAS2	Albert Pujols	3.00
TAS3	Vladimir Guerrero	1.00
TAS4	Ichiro Suzuki	2.00
TAS5	Randy Johnson	1.00
TAS6	Manny Ramirez	1.00
TAS7	Sammy Sosa	2.00
TAS8	Alfonso Soriano	1.00
TAS9	Jim Thome	1.00
TAS10	Barry Bonds	3.00
TAS11	Roger Clemens	3.00
TAS12	Mike Piazza	1.50
TAS13	Derek Jeter	3.00
TAS14	Alex Rodriguez	2.50
TAS15	Carlos Beltran	1.00

All-Star Stitches Relics

		NM/M
Common Player:		5.00
Inserted 1:96		
BA	Bobby Abreu	8.00
MA	Moises Alou	5.00
RB	Ronnie Belliard	5.00
CB	Carlos Beltran	10.00
LB	Lance Berkman	10.00
HB	Hank Blalock	10.00
MC	Miguel Cabrera	10.00
CC	Carl Crawford	5.00
JE	Johnny Estrada	8.00
EG	Eric Gagne	10.00
JG	Jason Giambi	10.00
TG	Tom Glavine	10.00
FG	Flash Gordon	5.00
VG	Vladimir Guerrero	10.00
KH	Ken Harvey	5.00
TH	Todd Helton	10.00
JK	Jeff Kent	8.00
DK	Danny Kolb	8.00
BL	Barry Larkin	10.00
MLA	Matt Lawton	5.00
TL	Ted Lilly	8.00
EL	Esteban Loaiza	5.00
PL	Paul LoDuca	5.00
MLO	Mark Loretta	5.00
ML	Mike Lowell	8.00
VM	Victor Martinez	10.00
MM	Mark Mulder	10.00
JN	Joe Nathan	8.00
DO	David Ortiz	20.00
CP	Carl Pavano	10.00
MP	Mike Piazza	12.00
AP	Albert Pujols	25.00
MR	Manny Ramirez	10.00
ER	Edgar Renteria	8.00
MRI	Mariano Rivera	10.00
FR	Francisco Rodriguez	10.00
IR	Ivan Rodriguez	10.00
SR	Scott Rolen	12.00
CS	C.C. Sabathia	8.00
BS	Ben Sheets	10.00
GS	Gary Sheffield	10.00
AS	Alfonso Soriano	10.00
SS	Sammy Sosa	15.00
MT	Miguel Tejada	10.00
JT	Jim Thome	12.00
JW	Jack Wilson	10.00
MY	Michael Young	15.00
CZ	Carlos Zambrano	10.00

All-Star Patches

No Pricing
Production 25 Sets

Autographs

		NM/M
Common Autograph:		
CB	Carlos Beltran	75.00
MC	Miguel Cabrera	40.00
JC	Jose Capellan	30.00
EC	Eric Chavez	25.00
DD	David DeJesus	20.00
ZG	Zack Greinke	20.00
CK	Casey Kotchman	20.00
JMA	John Maine	25.00
DM	Dallas McPherson	25.00
ARI	Alexis Rios	25.00
AR	Alex Rodriguez	160.00
CT	Chad Tracy	20.00
VW	Vernon Wells	25.00
DW	David Wright	80.00
Series 2		
JB	Jason Bay	25.00
CB	Carlos Beltran	60.00
BBO	Barry Bonds/25	
MB	Milton Bradley	25.00
BB	Billy Butler	25.00
MC	Matt Campbell	15.00
EC	Eric Chavez	20.00
ECO	Erik Cordier	10.00
CC	Carl Crawford	15.00
EG	Eric Gagne	50.00
FH	Felix Hernandez	25.00
SK	Scott Kazmir	25.00

ML	Mark Loretta	20.00
GP	Glen Perkins	15.00
LP	Landon Powell	20.00
AR2	Alex Rodriguez/50	250.00
IR	Ivan Rodriguez	50.00
MR	Michael Rogers	10.00
JS	Johan Santana	50.00
TS	Terrmel Sledge	15.00
CW	Craig Wilson	10.00

Barry Bonds Home Run Highlights

	NM/M
Complete Set (330):	
Common Bonds:	1.50
Inserted 1:4	

Bonds MVP

		NM/M
Production 25-500		
BBI2	Barry Bonds/50	40.00
BBI3	Barry Bonds/100	30.00
BBI4	Barry Bonds/200	25.00
BBI5	Barry Bonds/300	20.00
BBI6	Barry Bonds/400	15.00
BBI7	Barry Bonds/500	15.00

Bonds MVP Autographs

No Pricing

Bonds MVP Relics

		NM/M
Production 25-500		
BBR3	Barry Bonds/100	50.00
BBR4	Barry Bonds/200	40.00
BBR5	Barry Bonds/300	40.00
BBR6	Barry Bonds/400	25.00
BBR7	Barry Bonds/500	25.00

Celebrity Threads Relics

		NM/M
Common Player:		8.00
Inserted 1:562		
CC	Cesar Cedeno	8.00
CF	Cecil Fielder	15.00
RF	Rollie Fingers	12.00
GG	Rich "Goose" Gossage	10.00
HR	Harold Reynolds	8.00
MS	Mike Scott	8.00
OS	Ozzie Smith	25.00
DW	Dave Winfield	15.00

Dem Bums

RUSS MEYER

		NM/M
Complete Set (13):		40.00
Common Player:		4.00
Inserted 1:12		
WA	Walter Alston	4.00
BB	Bob Borkowski	4.00
RC	Roy Campanella	6.00
RCR	Roger Craig	4.00
CF	Carl Furillo	4.00
JG	Jim Gilliam	4.00
DH	Don Hoak	4.00
JH	Jim Hughes	4.00
RM	Russ Meyer	4.00
JR	Jackie Robinson	8.00
ER	Ed Roebuck	4.00
GS	George Shuba	4.00
KS	Karl Spooner	4.00

Dem Bums Autographs

	NM/M
Common Autograph:	30.00

CE	Carl Erskine	30.00
CL	Glen Labine	50.00
JP	Johnny Podres	30.00
DS	Duke Snider	50.00
DZ	Don Zimmer	50.00

Dem Bums Cuts

No Pricing
Production One Set

Derby Digs Relics

		NM/M
Common Player:		15.00
Production 100 Sets		
LB	Lance Berkman	15.00
HB	Hank Blalock	20.00
DO	David Ortiz	35.00
SS	Sammy Sosa	40.00
MT	Miguel Tejada	15.00
JT	Jim Thome	25.00

Series 2
Production 10 Sets

Factory Set Team Bonus

	NM/M
Complete Cubs Set (5):	15.00
Complete Yankees Set (5):	15.00
Complete Red Sox Set (5):	15.00
Complete Giants Set (5):	15.00
Complete Nationals Set (5):	15.00
Complete Tigers Set (5):	15.00

Issued in Team themed Factory Sets

Factory Set Draft Picks Bonus

		NM/M
Complete Set (5):		20.00
One set per Factory Set		
1	Beau Jones	4.00
2	Cliff Pennington	4.00
3	Chris Volstad	4.00
4	Ricky Romero	4.00
5	Jay Bruce	10.00

Factory Set First Year Draft Bonus

		NM/M
Complete Set (10):		50.00
One set per Green Factory Set		
1	Nick Webber	3.00
2	Aaron Thompson	4.00
3	Matt Garza	8.00
4	Tyler Greene	4.00
5	Ryan Braun	10.00
6	C.J. Henry	4.00
7	Ryan Zimmerman	20.00
8	John Mayberry Jr.	4.00
9	Cesar Carrillo	3.00
10	Mark McCormick	3.00

Factory Set First Year Player Bonus

		NM/M
Complete Set (5):		15.00
Issued in Red Factory Sets		
1	Bill McCarthy	4.00
2	John Hudgins	4.00
3	Kyle Nichols	4.00
4	Thomas Pauly	4.00
5	Philip Humber	4.00

Grudge Match

JORGE POSADA — PEDRO MARTINEZ — GRUDGE MATCH

		NM/M
Complete Set (10):		
Common Duo:		1.00
Inserted 1:24		
GM1	Jorge Posada, Pedro J. Martinez	2.00
GM2	Mike Piazza, Roger Clemens	3.00
GM3	Mariano Rivera, Luis Gonzalez	1.00
GM4	Carlos Zambrano, Jim Edmonds	1.00
GM5	Aaron Boone, Tim Wakefield	
GM6	Manny Ramirez, Roger Clemens	3.00
GM7	Michael Tucker, Eric Gagne	1.00
GM8	Ivan Rodriguez, J.T. Snow	1.00
GM9	Alex Rodriguez, Bronson Arroyo	3.00
GM10	Corky Miller, Sammy Sosa	2.50

Hit Parade

HIT PARADE RBI

		NM/M
Complete Set (30):		25.00
Common Player:		.50
Inserted 1:12		
HR1	Barry Bonds	4.00
HR2	Sammy Sosa	2.50
HR3	Rafael Palmeiro	1.00
HR4	Ken Griffey Jr.	2.00
HR5	Jeff Bagwell	1.00
HR6	Frank Thomas	1.00
HR7	Juan Gonzalez	.75
HR8	Jim Thome	1.00
HR9	Gary Sheffield	1.00
HR10	Manny Ramirez	1.50
RBI1	Barry Bonds	4.00
RBI2	Rafael Palmeiro	1.00
RBI3	Sammy Sosa	2.50
RBI4	Jeff Bagwell	1.00
RBI5	Ken Griffey Jr.	2.00
RBI6	Frank Thomas	1.00
RBI7	Juan Gonzalez	.75
RBI8	Gary Sheffield	1.00
RBI9	Ruben Sierra	.50
RBI10	Manny Ramirez	1.50
HIT1	Rafael Palmeiro	1.00
HIT2	Barry Bonds	4.00
HIT3	Roberto Alomar	.75
HIT4	Craig Biggio	.50
HIT5	Julio Franco	.50
HIT6	Steve Finley	.50
HIT7	Jeff Bagwell	.50
HIT8	B.J. Surhoff	.50
HIT9	Marquis Grissom	.50
HIT10	Sammy Sosa	2.50

Hobby Masters

NOMAR GARCIAPARRA — CHICAGO CUBS — HOBBY MASTERS

		NM/M
Complete Set (20):		25.00
Common Player:		.75
Inserted 1:18		
HM1	Alex Rodriguez	4.00
HM2	Sammy Sosa	2.50
HM3	Ichiro Suzuki	3.00
HM4	Albert Pujols	4.00
HM5	Derek Jeter	4.00
HM6	Jim Thome	1.50
HM7	Vladimir Guerrero	1.50
HM8	Nomar Garciaparra	2.00
HM9	Mike Piazza	2.00
HM10	Jason Giambi	.75
HM11	Ivan Rodriguez	1.00
HM12	Alfonso Soriano	1.50
HM13	Dontrelle Willis	.75
HM14	Chipper Jones	1.50
HM15	Mark Prior	1.50
HM16	Todd Helton	1.00
HM17	Randy Johnson	1.50
HM18	Hank Blalock	1.00
HM19	Ken Griffey Jr.	2.00
HM20	Roger Clemens	3.00

Midsummer Covers Relics

No Pricing
Production 10 Sets
Series 2
Production 10 Sets

On-Deck Relics

		NM/M
Inserted 1:1,493		
CB	Carlos Beltran	15.00
HB	Hank Blalock	12.00
TH	Todd Helton	12.00
AP	Albert Pujols	30.00
AR	Alex Rodriguez	25.00
IR	Ivan Rodriguez	15.00
SR	Scott Rolen	15.00
AS	Alfonso Soriano	15.00
SS	Sammy Sosa	25.00
JT	Jim Thome	15.00

Own The Game

DAVID ORTIZ — OWN THE GAME

		NM/M
Complete Set (30):		15.00
Common Player:		.50
Inserted 1:12		
OG1	Ichiro Suzuki	3.00
OG2	Todd Helton	1.00
OG3	Adrian Beltre	1.00
OG4	Albert Pujols	4.00
OG5	Adam Dunn	1.00
OG6	Jim Thome	1.50
OG7	Miguel Tejada	.75
OG8	David Ortiz	1.50
OG9	Manny Ramirez	1.50
OG10	Scott Rolen	1.50
OG11	Gary Sheffield	.75
OG12	Vladimir Guerrero	1.50
OG13	Jim Edmonds	.75
OG14	Ivan Rodriguez	1.00
OG15	Lance Berkman	.50
OG16	Michael Young	.50
OG17	Juan Pierre	.50
OG18	Craig Biggio	.75
OG19	Johnny Damon	.75
OG20	Jimmy Rollins	.50
OG21	Scott Podsednik	.50
OG22	Bobby Abreu	.50
OG23	Lyle Overbay	.50
OG24	Carl Crawford	.50
OG25	Mark Loretta	.50
OG26	Vinny Castilla	.50
OG27	Curt Schilling	1.00
OG28	Johan Santana	.75
OG29	Randy Johnson	1.50
OG30	Pedro J. Martinez	1.50

Power Brokers Cut Signatures

No Pricing

Spokesman

1998 DRAFT PICK — MARINER — Alex Rodriguez

	NM/M
Complete Set (4):	10.00
Common A-Rod:	3.00
Inserted 1:24	

Spokesman Autographs

NM/M

Production 1-200
ARA3 Alex Rodriguez/100 ... 200.00
ARA4 Alex Rodriguez/200 ... 180.00

Spokesman Relics

NM/M

Production 1-800
ARR2 Alex Rodriguez/50 ... 30.00
ARR3 Alex Rodriguez/300 ... 20.00
ARR4 Alex Rodriguez/800 ... 20.00

Spokesman Relic

NM/M

Inserted 1:5,627
AR Alex Rodriguez ... 50.00

Spokesman Relic Autographs

13 Sets

Touch'em All Relics

No Pricing

World Treasures

No Pricing
Production One Set

World Treasures - Dual

No Pricing
Production One Set

World Champion Red Sox Relics

NM/M

Common Player:		
OC	Orlando Cabrera	20.00
OC2	Orlando Cabrera	20.00
JD	Johnny Damon	25.00
JD2	Johnny Damon	25.00
DL	Derek Lowe	20.00
PM	Pedro Martinez	20.00
DMI	Doug Mientkiewicz	15.00
KM	Kevin Millar	20.00
BM	Bill Mueller	15.00
BM2	Bill Mueller	15.00
TN	Trot Nixon	20.00
DO	David Ortiz	20.00
DO2	David Ortiz	20.00
MR	Manny Ramirez	25.00
MR2	Manny Ramirez	25.00
MR3	Manny Ramirez	25.00
PR	Pokey Reese	15.00
DR	Dave Roberts	15.00
CS	Curt Schilling	25.00
KY	Kevin Youkilis	15.00

1955 World Series Cut Signatures

No Pricing

1955 World Series Dual Cut Signatures

Complete Set (3):
Common Player:
Production One Set

2005 Topps Update

	NM/M
Complete Set (330):	35.00
Complete Factory Set (330):	40.00
Common Player:	.10
Pack (10):	2.00

Box (36):		60.00
1	Sammy Sosa	1.00
2	Jeff Francoeur	.25
3	Tony Clark	.10
4	Michael Tucker	.10
5	Mike Matheny	.10
6	Eric Young	.10
7	Jose Valentin	.10
8	Matt Lawton	.10
9	Juan Rivera	.10
10	Shawn Green	.25
11	Aaron Boone	.10
12	Woody Williams	.10
13	Brad Wilkerson	.10
14	Anthony Reyes RC	1.50
15	Russ Adams	.10
16	Gustavo Chacin	.10
17	Mike Restovich	.10
18	Humberto Quintero	.10
19	Matt Ginter	.10
20	Scott Podsednik	.25
21	Byung-Hyun Kim	.10
22	Orlando Hernandez	.10
23	Mark Grudzielanek	.10
24	Jody Gerut	.10
25	Adrian Beltre	.25
26	Scott Schoeneweis	.10
27	Marlon Anderson	.10
28	Jason Vargas	.10
29	Claudio Vargas	.10
30	Jason Kendall	.10
31	Aaron Small	.10
32	Juan Cruz	.10
33	Placido Polanco	.10
34	Jorge Sosa	.10
35	John Olerud	.10
36	Ryan Langerhans	.10
37	Randy Winn	.10
38	Zachary Duke	.25
39	Garrett Atkins	.10
40	Al Leiter	.10
41	Shawn Chacon	.10
42	Mark DeRosa	.10
43	Miguel Ojeda	.10
44	A.J. Pierzynski	.10
45	Carlos Lee	.10
46	LaTroy Hawkins	.10
47	Nick Green	.10
48	Shawn Estes	.10
49	Eli Marrero	.10
50	Jeff Kent	.10
51	Joe Randa	.10
52	Jose Hernandez	.10
53	Joe Blanton	.10
54	Huston Street	.10
55	Marlon Byrd	.10
56	Alex Sanchez	.10
57	Livan Hernandez	.10
58	Chris Young	.10
59	Brad Eldred	.10
60	Terrence Long	.10
61	Phil Nevin	.10
62	Kyle Farnsworth	.10
63	Jon Lieber	.10
64	Antonio Alfonseca	.10
65	Tony Graffanino	.10
66	Tadahito Iguchi RC	1.00
67	Brad Thompson	.10
68	Jose Vidro	.10
69	Jason Phillips	.10
70	Carl Pavano	.10
71	Pokey Reese	.25
72	Jerome Williams	.10
73	Kazuhisa Ishii	.10
74	Zach Day	.10
75	Edgar Renteria	.25
76	Mike Myers	.10
77	Jeff Cirillo	.10
78	Endy Chavez	.10
79	Jose Guillen	.10
80	Ugueth Urbina	.10
81	Vinny Castilla	.10
82	Javier Vazquez	.10
83	Willy Taveras	.10
84	Mark Mulder	.25
85	Mike Hargrove	.10
86	Buddy Bell	.10
87	Charlie Manuel	.10
88	Willie Randolph	.10
89	Bob Melvin	.10
90	Chris Lambert	.10
91	Homer Bailey	.20
92	Ervin Santana	.10
93	Bill Bray	.10
94	Thomas Diamond	.10
95	Trevor Plouffe	.10
96	James Houser	.10
97	Jake Stevens	.10
98	Anthony Whittington	.10
99	Phillip Hughes	.10
100	Greg Golson	.10
101	Paul Maholm	.10
102	Carlos Quentin	.10
103	Dan Johnson	.10
104	Mark Rogers	.10
105	Neil Walker	.10
106	Omar Quintanilla	.10
107	Blake DeWitt	.10
108	Taylor Tankersley	.10
109	David Murphy	.10
110	Felix Hernandez	.50
111	Craig Biggio	.10
112	Greg Maddux	.50
113	Bobby Abreu	.10
114	Alex Rodriguez	.75
115	Trevor Hoffman	.10
116	A.J. Pierzynski, Tadahito Iguchi	.25
117	Reggie Sanders	.10
118	Bengie Molina, Ervin Santana	.10
119	Chris Burke, Lance Berkman, Adam LaRoche	.10
120	Garret Anderson	.25
121	A.J. Pierzynski	.10
122	Paul Konerko	.25
123	Joe Crede	.10
124	Mark Buehrle, Jon Garland	.10
125	Freddy Garcia, Jose Contreras	.10
126	Reggie Sanders	.10
127	Roy Oswalt	.10
128	Roger Clemens	.75
129	Albert Pujols	.75
130	Roy Oswalt	.25
131	Joe Crede, Bobby Jenks	.10
132	Paul Konerko, Scott Podsednik	.25
133	Geoff Blum	.10
134	White Sox Sweep	.10
135	Alex Rodriguez, David Ortiz, Manny Ramirez	.50
136	Michael Young, Alex Rodriguez, Vladimir Guerrero	.50
137	David Ortiz, Mark Teixeira, Manny Ramirez	.25
138	Bartolo Colon, Jon Garland, Cliff Lee	.10
139	Kevin Millwood, Johan Santana, Mark Buehrle	.10
140	Johan Santana, Randy Johnson, John Lackey	.25
141	Andruw Jones, Derrek Lee, Albert Pujols	.50
142	Derek Lee, Albert Pujols, Miguel Cabrera	.50
143	Andruw Jones, Albert Pujols, Pat Burrell	.50
144	Dontrelle Willis, Chris Carpenter, Roy Oswalt	.25
145	Roger Clemens, Andy Pettitte, Dontrelle Willis	.50
146	Jake Peavy, Chris Carpenter, Pedro Martinez	.25
147	Mark Teixeira	.25
148	Brian Roberts	.10
149	Michael Young	.10
150	Alex Rodriguez	1.00
151	Johnny Damon	.25
152	Vladimir Guerrero	.25
153	Manny Ramirez	.25
154	David Ortiz	.25
155	Mariano Rivera	.25
156	Joe Nathan	.10
157	Albert Pujols	1.00
158	Jeff Kent	.10
159	Felipe Lopez	.10
160	Morgan Ensberg	.10
161	Miguel Cabrera	.25
162	Ken Griffey Jr.	.50
163	Andruw Jones	.25
164	Paul LoDuca	.10
165	Chad Cordero	.10
166	Ken Griffey Jr.	.50
167	Jason Giambi	.10
168	Willy Taveras	.10
169	Huston Street	.10
170	Chris Carpenter	.10
171	Bartolo Colon	.10
172	Bobby Cox	.10
173	Ozzie Guillen	.10
174	Andruw Jones	.25
175	Johnny Damon	.25
176	Alex Rodriguez	1.00
177	David Ortiz	.25
178	Manny Ramirez	.25
179	Miguel Tejada	.25
180	Vladimir Guerrero	.25
181	Mark Teixeira	.25
182	Ivan Rodriguez	.25
183	Brian Roberts	.10
184	Mark Buehrle	.10
185	Bobby Abreu	.25
186	Carlos Beltran	.25
187	Albert Pujols	1.00
188	Derrek Lee	.25
189	Jim Edmonds	.25
190	Aramis Ramirez	.10
191	Mike Piazza	.50
192	Jeff Kent	.10
193	David Eckstein	.10
194	Chris Carpenter	.10
195	Bobby Abreu	.25
196	Ivan Rodriguez	.25
197	Carlos Lee	.10
198	David Ortiz	.25
199	Hee Seop Choi	.10
200	Andruw Jones	.25
201	Mark Teixeira	.25
202	Jason Bay	.10
203	Hanley Ramirez	.25
204	Shin-Soo Choo	.10
205	Justin Huber	.10
206	Nelson Cruz RC	.50
207	Edwin Encarnacion	.10
208	Miguel Montero RC	.50
209	William Bergolla	.10
210	Luis Montanez	.10
211	Francisco Liriano	.50
212	Kevin Thompson	.10
213	B.J. Upton	.10
214	Conor Jackson	.10
215	Delmon Young	.25
216	Andy LaRoche	.50
217	Ryan Garko	.10
218	Josh Barfield	.10
219	Chris Young	.10
220	Justin Verlander	.25
221	Drew Anderson RC	.25
222	Luis Hernandez RC	.25
223	Jim Burt RC	.25
224	Mike Morse RC	.25
225	Elliot Johnson RC	.50
226	C.J. Smith RC	.25
227	Casey McGehee RC	.25
228	Brian Miller RC	.15
229	Chris Vines RC	.40
230	D.J. Houlton RC	.25
231	Chuck Tiffany RC	.40
232	Humberto Sanchez RC	.75
233	Baltazar Lopez RC	.25
234	Russell Martin RC	1.00
235	Dana Eveland RC	.25
236	Johan Silva RC	.25
237	Adam Harben RC	1.00
238	Brian Bannister RC	.25
239	Adam Boeve RC	.25
240	Tom Oldham RC	.25
241	Cody Haerther RC	.25
242	Dan Santin RC	.25
243	Daniel Haigwood RC	.25
244	Craig Tatum RC	.25
245	Martin Prado RC	.40
246	Errol Simonitsch RC	.40
247	Lorenzo Scott RC	.25
248	Hayden Penn RC	.40
249	Heath Totten RC	.25
250	Nick Masset RC	.25
251	Pedro Lopez RC	.25
252	Benjamin Harrison	.15
253	Michael Spidale RC	.25
254	Jeremy Harts RC	.25
255	Danny Zell RC	.40
256	Kevin Collins RC	.15
257	Tony Arnerich RC	.15
258	Matt Albers RC	.50
259	Ricky Barrett RC	.25
260	Hernan Iribarren RC	.40
261	Sean Tracey RC	.25
262	Jerry Owens RC	.40
263	Steve Nelson RC	.25
264	Brandon McCarthy RC	1.00
265	David Shepard RC	.25
266	Steve Bondurant RC	.25
267	Billy Sadler	.15
268	Ryan Feierabend RC	.25
269	Stuart Pomeranz RC	.40
270	Shaun Marcum	.25
271	Erik Schindewolf RC	.25
272	Stefan Bailie RC	.15
273	Mike Esposito RC	.25
274	Buck Coats RC	.40
275	Andy Sides RC	.25
276	Micah Schnurstein RC	.25
277	Jesse Gutierrez RC	.25
278	Jake Postlewait RC	.25
279	Willy Mota RC	.50
280	Ryan Speier RC	.25
281	Frank Mata RC	.25
282	Jair Jurrjens RC	1.00
283	Nick Touchstone RC	.25

284	Matthew Kemp RC	1.50
285	Vinny Rottino RC	.40
286	J.B. Thurmond RC	.40
287	Kelvin Pichardo RC	.25
288	Scott Mitchinson RC	.25
289	Darwinson Salazar RC	.25
290	George Kottaras RC	.50
291	Ken Durost RC	.25
292	Jonathan Sanchez RC	.50
293	Brandon Moorhead RC	.25
294	Kennard Bibbs RC	.25
295	David Gassner RC	.40
296	Micah Furtado RC	.25
297	Ismael Ramirez RC	.25
298	Carlos Gonzalez RC	1.50
299	Brandon Sing RC	.50
300	Jason Motte RC	.25
301	Chuck James RC	1.00
302	Andy Santana RC	.25
303	Manny Parra RC	.40
304	Chris Young RC	1.00
305	Juan Senreiso RC	.25
306	Franklin Morales RC	1.00
307	Jared Gothreaux RC	.15
308	Jayce Tingler RC	.25
309	Matt Brown RC	.25
310	Frank Diaz RC	.40
311	Stephen Drew RC	2.00
312	Jered Weaver RC	4.00
313	Ryan Braun RC	4.00
314	John Mayberry Jr. RC	.75
315	Aaron Thompson RC	1.00
316	Cesar Carrillo RC	.50
317	Jacoby Ellsbury RC	6.00
318	Matt Garza RC	5.00
319	Cliff Pennington RC	.75
320	Colby Rasmus RC	2.00
321	Chris Volstad RC	1.00
322	Ricky Romero RC	.50
323	Ryan Zimmerman RC	3.00
324	C.J. Henry RC	.75
325	Jay Bruce RC	3.00
326	Beau Jones RC	.50
327	Mark McCormick RC	.50
328	Eli Iorg RC	.50
329	Andrew McCutchen RC	1.00
330	Mike Costanzo RC	.50

Blue
No Pricing
Production One Set

Gold
Gold Rookies:	2-4X
Gold Stars:	4-8X

Production 2,005 Sets

Printing Plates
No Pricing
Production one set per color.

All-Star Patches
NM/M

Common Player:		15.00
BA	Bobby Abreu/65	15.00
MA	Moises Alou/65	20.00
JB	Jason Bay/50	20.00
CB	Carlos Beltran/60	25.00
MB	Mark Buehrle/60	20.00
MC	Miguel Cabrera/70	30.00
CC	Chris Carpenter/70	20.00
LC	Luis Castillo/20	
MCL	Matt Clement/60	15.00
BC	Bartolo Colon/60	15.00
CCO	Chad Cordero/65	15.00
JD	Johnny Damon/60	25.00
DE	David Eckstein/50	20.00
JE	Jim Edmonds/50	20.00
ME	Morgan Ensberg/60	15.00
JG	Jon Garland/70	20.00
LG	Luis Gonzalez/70	15.00
LH	Livan Hernandez/70	15.00
JI	Jason Isringhausen/65	15.00
AJ	Andruw Jones/70	25.00
JK	Jeff Kent/65	20.00
PK	Paul Konerko/70	20.00
CL	Carlos Lee/65	20.00
DL	Derrek Lee/65	20.00
BL	Brad Lidge/65	15.00
FL	Felipe Lopez/35	20.00
MM	Melvin Mora/30	20.00
JN	Joe Nathan/65	15.00
DO	David Ortiz/70	25.00
RO	Roy Oswalt/60	20.00
JP	Jake Peavy/60	20.00
MP	Mike Piazza/50	30.00
SP	Scott Podsednik/65	20.00
AP	Albert Pujols/35	50.00
ARA	Aramis Ramirez/60	25.00
MR	Manny Ramirez/65	25.00
MRI	Mariano Rivera/65	30.00
BR	Brian Roberts/25	
AR	Alex Rodriguez/50	30.00
IR	Ivan Rodriguez/25	
KR	Kenny Rogers/50	15.00
JS	Johan Santana/60	30.00
GS	Gary Sheffield/50	20.00
JSM	John Smoltz/65	30.00
IS	Ichiro Suzuki/50	40.00
MTE	Mark Teixeira/60	20.00
MT	Miguel Tejada/60	20.00
BW	Billy Wagner/50	15.00
DW	Dontrelle Willis/60	20.00
MY	Michael Young/50	20.00

All-Star Stitches
NM/M

Common Player:		4.00
BA	Bobby Abreu/B	4.00
MA	Moises Alou/C	6.00
	Danys Baez	
JB	Jason Bay/C	4.00
CB	Carlos Beltran/D	6.00
MB	Mark Buehrle/B	4.00
MC	Miguel Cabrera/E	8.00
CC	Chris Carpenter/E	4.00
LC	Luis Castillo/B	4.00
	Hee Seop Choi	
MCL	Matt Clement/B	4.00
BC	Bartolo Colon/D	4.00
CCO	Chad Cordero/D	4.00
JD	Johnny Damon/B	8.00
	Justin Duchscherer	
DE	David Eckstein/B	4.00
JE	Jim Edmonds/A	6.00
ME	Morgan Ensberg/B	4.00
	Brian Fuentes	
JG	Jon Garland/E	4.00
LG	Luis Gonzalez/C	4.00
LH	Livan Hernandez	4.00
	Shea Hillenbrand	
JI	Jason Isringhausen/E	4.00
AJ	Andruw Jones/C	6.00
JK	Jeff Kent/C	4.00
PK	Paul Konerko/A	4.00
CL	Carlos Lee/E	4.00
DL	Derrek Lee/F	6.00
BL	Brad Lidge/D	4.00
	Paul LoDuca	
FL	Felipe Lopez/B	4.00
MM	Melvin Mora/B	4.00
JN	Joe Nathan/D	4.00
DO	David Ortiz/E	8.00
RO	Roy Oswalt/A	4.00
JP	Jake Peavy/D	4.00
MP	Mike Piazza/E	8.00
SP	Scott Podsednik/A	4.00
AP	Albert Pujols/E	20.00
ARA	Aramis Ramirez/E	4.00
MR	Manny Ramirez/E	8.00
MRI	Mariano Rivera	6.00
BR	Brian Roberts/C	4.00
AR	Alex Rodriguez/D	15.00
IR	Ivan Rodriguez/A	6.00
KR	Kenny Rogers/A	4.00
	B.J. Ryan	
JS	Johan Santana/C	6.00
GS	Gary Sheffield/D	6.00
JSM	John Smoltz/D	6.00
IS	Ichiro Suzuki/A	20.00
MTE	Mark Teixeira/C	6.00
MT	Miguel Tejada/D	6.00
BW	Billy Wagner/B	4.00
	Bob Wickman	
DW	Dontrelle Willis/F	6.00
MY	Michael Young/A	4.00

Derby Digs Jersey
NM/M
Production 100 Sets

BA	Bobby Abreu	25.00
JB	Jason Bay	15.00
AJ	Andruw Jones	25.00
CL	Carlos Lee	10.00
DO	David Ortiz	25.00
IR	Ivan Rodriguez	25.00
MT	Mark Teixeira	25.00

Hall of Fame Bat
NM/M
Complete Set (2):

WB	Wade Boggs/A	10.00
RS	Ryne Sandberg/B	15.00

Hall of Fame Dual Bat
NM/M
Production 200 Sets

BS	Wade Boggs, Ryne Sandberg	25.00

Legendary Sacks
NM/M
Production 300 Sets

JA	Jim Abbott	6.00
AD	Andre Dawson	6.00
MF	Mark Fidrych	4.00
RF	Rollie Fingers	4.00
BJ	Bo Jackson	8.00
HR	Harold Reynolds	4.00
OS	Ozzie Smith	8.00
LW	Lou Whitaker	4.00
DW	Dave Winfield	8.00

Midsummer Covers
NM/M
Production 150 Sets

CB	Carlos Beltran	15.00
RC	Roger Clemens	25.00
VG	Vladimir Guerrero	25.00
DL	Derrek Lee	15.00
AP	Albert Pujols	40.00
BR	Brian Roberts	10.00
AR	Alex Rodriguez	30.00
IS	Ichiro Suzuki	50.00
MT	Miguel Tejada	15.00
DW	Dontrelle Willis	10.00

Signature Moves
NM/M
Production 15-475 Sets
Red Foil: No Pricing
Production 25 Sets

MA	Matt Albers/475	15.00
TC	Travis Chick/475	8.00
TG	Troy Glaus/275	20.00
TH	Tim Hudson/275	25.00
KI	Kazuhisa Ishii/275	15.00
GK	George Kottaras/475	15.00
BL	Bobby Livingston/475	10.00
MM	Mark Mulder/275	20.00
GP	Glen Perkins/275	15.00
JP	Jake Postlewait/275	10.00
HS	Humberto Sanchez	30.00
BS	Benito Santiago	20.00
RS	Richie Sexson/275	25.00
CJS	C.J. Smith/475	10.00
JV	Justin Verlander/275	35.00
TW	Tony Womack	15.00

Touch Em All Base
NM/M
Production 1,000 Sets

VG	Vladimir Guerrero	10.00
DL	Derrek Lee	8.00
DO	David Ortiz	10.00
AP	Albert Pujols	20.00
MR	Manny Ramirez	10.00
AR	Alex Rodriguez	15.00
IR	Ivan Rodriguez	8.00
GS	Gary Sheffield	6.00
IS	Ichiro Suzuki	20.00
MT	Miguel Tejada	10.00

Washington Nationals Inaugural Lineup
NM/M
Inserted 1:10
Ball Relics: No Pricing
Production 5 Sets

VC	Vinny Castilla	.50
JG	Jose Guillen	1.00
CG	Cristian Guzman	.50
LH	Livan Hernandez	.50
NJ	Nick Johnson	.50
BS	Brian Schneider	.50
TS	Terrmel Sledge	.50
JV	Jose Vidro	.50
BW	Brad Wilkerson	.50
TEAM	Team Photo	1.00

2005 Topps All-Time Fan Favorites

	NM/M
Complete Set (142):	40.00

Common Player:		.25
Pack (6):		5.00
Box (24):		110.00
1	Andy Van Slyke	.25
2	Bill Freehan	.25
3	Bo Jackson	.75
4	Mark Grace	.50
5	Chuck Knoblauch	.25
6	Candy Maldonado	.25
7	David Cone	.25
8	Don Mattingly	1.50
9	Darryl Strawberry	.25
10	Dick Williams	.25
11	Frank Robinson	.75
12	Glenn Hubbard	.25
13	Jim Abbott	.25
14	Jeff Brantley	.25
15	John Elway	2.00
16	Jim Leyland	.25
17	Jesse Orosco	.25
18	Joe Pepitone	.25
19	J.R. Richard	.25
20	Jerome Walton	.25
21	Kevin Maas	.25
22	Lou Brock	.50
23	Lou Whitaker	.25
24	Carl Erskine	.25
25	John Candelaria	.25
26	Mike Norris	.25
27	Nolan Ryan	2.00
28	Pedro Guerrero	.25
29	Roger Craig	.25
30	Ron Gant	.25
31	Sid Bream	.25
32	Sid Fernandez	.25
33	Tony LaRussa	.25
34	Tom Seaver	.75
35	Yogi Berra	.75
36	Andre Dawson	.25
37	Al Kaline	.75
38	Brett Butler	.25
39	Bob Gibson	.75
40	Bill Mazeroski	.25
41	Matty Alou	.25
42	Chet Lemon	.25
43	Cal Ripken Jr.	2.00
44	Dusty Baker	.25
45	Dwight Gooden	.50
46	Dave Winfield	.50
47	Ernie Banks	1.00
48	Gary Carter	.50
49	Howard Johnson	.25
50	Mike Schmidt	1.50
51	Matt Williams	.25
52	Ozzie Smith	1.00
53	Atlee Hammaker	.25
54	Cleon Jones	.25
55	Dave Johnson	.25
56	Denny McLain	.25
57	Don Zimmer	.25
58	Gregg Jefferies	.25
59	Jay Buhner	.25
60	Johnny Bench	.75
61	George Brett	1.50
62	Dale Murphy	.50
63	Bob Welch	.25
64	Paul O'Neill	.25
65	Mark Lemke	.25
66	Kevin McReynolds	.25
67	Jesus Alou	.25
68	Joe Pignatano	.25
69	Jim Lonborg	.25
70	Jerry Grote	.25
71	Joaquin Andujar	.25
72	Gary Gaetti	.25
73	Edgar Martinez	.25
74	Ron Darling	.25
75	Duke Snider	.75
76	Dave Magadan	.25
77	Doug Drabek	.25
78	Carl Yastrzemski	1.00
79	Mitch Williams	.25
80	Marvin Miller	.25
81	Michael Kay	.25
82	Lonnie Smith	.25
83	John Wetteland	.25
84	Johnny Podres	.25
85	Joe Morgan	.50
86	Juan Marichal	.50
87	Jeffrey Leonard	.25
88	Bob Feller	.50
89	Brooks Robinson	.75
90	Clem Labine	.25
91	Barry Lyons	.25
92	Harmon Killebrew	.75
93	Jim Frey	.25
94	John Kruk	.25
95	Ed Kranepool	.25
96	Jose Oquendo	.25
97	Johnny Pesky	.25
98	John Tudor	.25
99	Keith Hernandez	.25
100	Monte Irvin	.25
101	Marty Barrett	.25

102	Oscar Gamble	.25
103	Hank Bauer	.25
104	Ron Blomberg	.25
105	Rod Carew	.50
106	Rick Dempsey	.25
107	Walt Jocketty	.25
108	Tom Kelly	.25
109	Steve Carlton	.50
110	Rick Monday	.25
111	Rob Dibble	.25
112	Shawon Dunston	.25
113	Tony Gwynn	.75
114	Tom Niedenfuer	.25
115	Bob Dernier	.25
116	Anthony Young	.25
117	Reggie Jackson	.75
118	Steve Garvey	.25
119	Tim Raines	.25
120	Whitey Ford	.75
121	Rafael Santana	.25
122	Scott Brosius	.25
123	Stan Musial	1.50
124	Ron Santo	.50
125	Wade Boggs	.75
126	Jose Canseco	.50
127	Brady Anderson	.25
128	Vida Blue	.25
129	Charlie Hough	.25
130	Jim Kaat	.25
131	Zane Smith	.25
132	Bob Boone	.25
133	Travis Fryman	.25
134	Harold Baines	.25
135	Orlando Cepeda	.25
136	Mike Cuellar	.25
137	Tito Fuentes	.25
138	Daryl Boston	.25
139	Jim Leyritz	.25
140	Bill "Moose" Skowron	.25
141	Theo Epstein	.25
142	Barry Bonds	3.00

Refractor

Stars (1-142): 3-5X
Production 299 Sets

Gold Refractor

No Pricing
Production 25 Sets

Printing Plates

No Pricing
Production one set per color.

Autographs

NM/M
Common Autograph: 15.00
Rainbow: No Pricing
Production 10 Sets

JA	Jim Abbott	30.00
JAN	Joaquin Andujar	20.00
DB	Dusty Baker	25.00
MB	Marty Barrett	15.00
JBE	Dr. Jim Beckett/SP/90	100.00
JB	Johnny Bench/SP/40	125.00
YB	Yogi Berra/SP/90	125.00
RB	Ron Blomberg	15.00
JBR	Jeff Brantley	20.00
SB	Sid Bream	20.00
GB	George Brett/SP/40	250.00
SBR	Scott Brosius/SP/40	85.00
JBU	Jay Buhner	20.00
BB	Brett Butler	20.00
SC	Steve Carlton/SP/90	60.00
GC	Gary Carter	25.00
DC	David Cone	25.00
RCR	Roger Craig	25.00
RD	Rick Dempsey	15.00
DD	Doug Drabek	20.00
SD	Shawon Dunston	20.00
JE	John Elway/SP/40	250.00
BFE	Bob Feller	85.00
SF	Sid Fernandez	15.00
WF	Whitey Ford/SP/90	150.00
BF	Bill Freehan	20.00
GG	Gary Gaetti	15.00
OG	Oscar Gamble	15.00
RG	Ron Gant/SP/90	50.00
SG	Steve Garvey	25.00
BG	Bob Gibson/SP/90	100.00
DG	Dwight Gooden	40.00
JG	Jerry Grote	30.00
TG	Tony Gwynn/SP/90	125.00
AH	Atlee Hammaker	15.00
GH	Glenn Hubbard	20.00
MI	Monte Irvin	50.00
BJ	Bo Jackson	70.00
RJ	Reggie Jackson/SP/40	100.00
GJ	Gregg Jefferies	40.00
WJ	Walt Jocketty/SP/90	60.00
DJ	Dave Johnson	20.00
HJ	Howard Johnson	20.00
CJ	Cleon Jones	35.00
AK	Al Kaline	60.00
TK	Tom Kelly	25.00
HK	Harmon Killebrew	85.00
CK	Chuck Knoblauch	25.00
JK	John Kruk	30.00
CL	Clem Labine	40.00
TL	Tony LaRussa	30.00
MLE	Mark Lemke	15.00
CLE	Chet Lemon	15.00
JLE	Jim Leyland	20.00
JLO	Jim Lonborg	15.00
BL	Barry Lyons	15.00
KM	Kevin Maas	15.00
DMA	Dave Magadan	20.00
CM	Candy Maldonado	15.00
JMA	Juan Marichal/SP/90	140.00
EM	Edgar Martinez	30.00
DM	Don Mattingly	140.00
BM	Bill Mazeroski	75.00
DMC	Denny McLain	30.00
KMC	Kevin McReynolds	15.00
MM	Marvin Miller/SP/90	80.00
RM	Rick Monday	25.00
DMU	Dale Murphy	25.00
SM	Stan Musial/SP/40	150.00
TN	Tom Niedenfuer	15.00
MNO	Mike Norris	15.00
PO	Paul O'Neill	60.00
JO	Jesse Orosco	25.00
JOQ	Jose Oquendo	15.00
JPE	Joe Pepitone	25.00
JPY	Johnny Pesky	65.00
JP	Joe Pignatano	30.00
TR	Tim Raines	25.00
JR	J.R. Richard	15.00
CR	Cal Ripken Jr./SP/90	200.00
BR	Brooks Robinson/SP/90	125.00
FR	Frank Robinson	100.00
NR	Nolan Ryan/SP/40	200.00
RS	Rafael Santana	20.00
RSA	Ron Santo/SP/90	75.00
MS	Mike Schmidt/SP/40	160.00
LS	Lonnie Smith	15.00
DSN	Duke Snider/SP/40	60.00
DS	Darryl Strawberry	25.00
JT	John Tudor	35.00
AV	Andy Van Slyke	25.00
JW	Jerome Walton	15.00
BW	Bob Welch	30.00
JWE	John Wetteland	15.00
LW	Lou Whitaker/SP/90	60.00
DWI	Dick Williams/SP/90	75.00
MW	Matt Williams	25.00
MWI	Mitch Williams	25.00
DW	Dave Winfield/SP/90	125.00
CY	Carl Yastrzemski/SP/90	125.00
AY	Anthony Young	15.00
DZ	Don Zimmer/SP/40	50.00

Best Seat in House

NM/M
Production 125 unless noted.
Rainbow: No Pricing
Production 25 Sets

MFBJ	Don Mattingly, Whitey Ford, Yogi Berra, Reggie Jackson/50	50.00
RR	Brooks Robinson, Cal Ripken Jr.	25.00
CR	Cal Ripken Jr., Frank Robinson	25.00
JD	Dave Johnson, Rick Dempsey	10.00
KMLW	Al Kaline, Lou Whitaker, Chet Lemon, Denny McLain	20.00

Fan Favorite Relics

NM/M
Inserted 1:Box
Rainbow: No Pricing
Production 25 Sets

WB	Wade Boggs/200	8.00
JCC	Jose Canseco/350	8.00
RC	Rod Carew/200	8.00
GC	Gary Carter/350	5.00
JC	Joe Carter/350	5.00
VC	Vince Coleman/200	5.00
ED	Eric Davis/200	5.00
AD	Andre Dawson/350	5.00
BD	Bucky Dent/200	5.00
LD	Lenny Dykstra/200	5.00
CF	Cecil Fielder/200	5.00
TG	Tony Gwynn/200	15.00
KH	Keith Hernandez/200	5.00
BJ	Bo Jackson/200	12.00
RJ	Reggie Jackson/200	10.00
WJ	Wally Joyner/200	5.00
WM	Willie McGee/350	5.00
DM	Dale Murphy/200	10.00
SM	Stan Musial/50	20.00
PO	Paul O'Neill/200	5.00
JR	Jim Rice/200	5.00
BR	Brooks Robinson/350	10.00
NR	Nolan Ryan/135	25.00
DS	Darryl Strawberry/350	5.00
BS	Bruce Sutter/350	7.50
MW	Mookie Wilson/135	5.00
CY	Carl Yastrzemski/50	25.00

League Leaders
Tr-Signers

Production 50 Sets

Originals Relics

NM/M
Production 50 Sets
Actual vintage cards used.

WB	Wade Boggs/Bat	15.00
RC	Rod Carew/Bat	20.00
GC	Gary Carter/Bat	10.00
AD	Andre Dawson/Bat	10.00
TG	Tony Gwynn/Jsy	20.00
BJ	Bo Jackson/Jsy	25.00
RJ	Reggie Jackson/Bat	20.00
DM	Dale Murphy/Bat	15.00
JR	Jim Rice/Bat	15.00
NR	Nolan Ryan/Jsy	35.00

Rookie Dual
Autograph

NM/M
Production 50 Sets

SC	Tom Seaver, Rod Carew	160.00
RB	Nolan Ryan, Johnny Bench	

2005 Topps Bazooka

ALEX RODRIGUEZ
NEW YORK YANKEES®

NM/M
Complete Set (220): 35.00
Common Player: .15
Common (191-220): .25
Pack (8): 2.50
Box (24): 50.00

1	Eric Gagne	.40
2	Aramis Ramirez	.40
3	Hank Blalock	.50
4	Jason Kendall	.15
5	Jeromy Burnitz	.15
6	Jose Guillen	.15
7	Tom Glavine	.40
8	Adrian Beltre	.25
9	Jason Bay	.25
10	Mark Teixeira	.40
11	Moises Alou	.25
12	Ronnie Belliard	.15
13	Aaron Guiel	.15
14	Vladimir Guerrero	.75
15	Scott Podsednik	.15
16	Alfonso Soriano	.75
17	Craig Wilson	.15
18	Jose Reyes	.25
19	Mark Prior	.75
20	Preston Wilson	.15
21	Shawn Green	.25
22	Troy Glaus	.25
23	Dmitri Young	.15
24	Garret Anderson	.25
25	Kazuo Matsui	.25
26	Kerry Wood	.75
27	Michael Young	.15
28	Oliver Perez	.15
29	Bartolo Colon	.15
30	Richie Sexson	.40
31	Brad Penny	.15
32	Carlos Guillen	.15
33	Carlos Zambrano	.25
34	David Wright	.50
35	Al Leiter	.25
36	Jack Wilson	.15
37	Ryan Drese	.15
38	Darin Erstad	.15
39	Derrek Lee	.25
40	Ivan Rodriguez	.50
41	Kenny Rogers	.15
42	Mike Piazza	1.00
43	Phil Nevin	.15
44	Geoff Jenkins	.15
45	Jorge Posada	.40
46	Khalil Greene	.40
47	Randy Johnson	.75
48	Rondell White	.15
49	Sammy Sosa	1.25
50	Vernon Wells	.15
51	Ben Sheets	.40
52	Brian Giles	.15
53	Carlos Delgado	.40
54	Derek Jeter	2.00
55	Jeremy Bonderman	.15
56	Magglio Ordonez	.25
57	Chad Tracy	.15
58	Kevin Brown	.15
59	Luis Castillo	.15
60	Lyle Overbay	.15
61	Mark Buehrle	.15
62	Mark Loretta	.15
63	Orlando Hudson	.15
64	Adam Dunn	.50
65	Frank Thomas	.50
66	Jake Peavy	.15
67	Jason Giambi	.40
68	Joe Mauer	.25
69	Marcus Giles	.15
70	Mike Lowell	.25
71	Roy Halladay	.15
72	Aaron Rowand	.15
73	Alex Rodriguez	1.50
74	Brian Lawrence	.15
75	Gabe Gross	.15
76	Johnny Estrada	.25
77	Justin Morneau	.40
78	Miguel Cabrera	.75
79	Alex Rios	.15
80	Gary Sheffield	.40
81	Jason Schmidt	.25
82	Juan Pierre	.15
83	Paul Konerko	.25
84	Jermaine Dye	.15
85	Rafael Furcal	.25
86	Torii Hunter	.25
87	A.J. Pierzynski	.15
88	Carl Pavano	.25
89	Carlos Lee	.25
90	J.D. Drew	.25
91	Javier Vazquez	.25
92	Lew Ford	.15
93	Ted Lilly	.15
94	Austin Kearns	.15
95	Chipper Jones	.75
96	Erubiel Durazo	.15
97	Johan Santana	.50
98	Josh Beckett	.25
99	Mariano Rivera	.25
100	Mark Mulder	.25
101	Andruw Jones	.25
102	Barry Zito	.25
103	Bret Boone	.15
104	Paul LoDuca	.15
105	Shannon Stewart	.15
106	Wily Mo Pena	.25
107	Dontrelle Willis	.25
108	Eric Chavez	.25
109	Jamie Moyer	.15
110	Joe Nathan	.15
111	Sidney Ponson	.15
112	John Smoltz	.25
113	Ichiro Suzuki	1.50
114	Javy Lopez	.25
115	Victor Martinez	.25
116	Ken Griffey Jr.	1.00
117	Lance Berkman	.25
118	Scott Hatteberg	.15
119	Jim Edmonds	.25
120	Kazuhisa Ishii	.15
121	Miguel Tejada	.40
122	Roger Clemens	2.00
123	Ryan Freel	.15
124	Albert Pujols	2.00
125	Hideo Nomo	.25

126	Mark Kotsay	.15
127	Melvin Mora	.15
128	Roy Oswalt	.25
129	Sean Casey	.25
130	Casey Blake	.15
131	Edgar Renteria	.25
132	Jeff Kent	.25
133	Rafael Palmeiro	.50
134	Tim Hudson	.25
135	Tony Batista	.15
136	Andy Pettitte	.25
137	Brian Roberts	.15
138	Jose Vidro	.15
139	Omar Vizquel	.15
140	Rich Harden	.25
141	Scott Rolen	.75
142	Carlos Beltran	.50
143	Chris Carpenter	.15
144	Manny Ramirez	.75
145	Nick Johnson	.15
146	Pat Burrell	.25
147	C.C. Sabathia	.15
148	Johnny Damon	.50
149	Juan Rivera	.15
150	Ken Harvey	.15
151	Kevin Millwood	.15
152	Larry Walker	.50
153	Aubrey Huff	.15
154	Curt Schilling	.75
155	Jake Westbrook	.15
156	Randy Wolf	.15
157	Zach Day	.15
158	Zack Greinke	.15
159	Brad Wilkerson	.15
160	Carl Crawford	.15
161	Jim Thome	.75
162	Mike Sweeney	.15
163	Pedro J. Martinez	.75
164	Travis Hafner	.15
165	Bobby Abreu	.25
166	Cliff Floyd	.15
167	David DeJesus	.15
168	David Ortiz	.75
169	Rocco Baldelli	.15
170	Todd Helton	.50
171	Dallas McPherson	.50
172	Kevin Youkilis	.25
173	Val Majewski	.15
174	Grady Sizemore	.25
175	Joey Gathright	.15
176	Rickie Weeks	.25
177	Jason Kubel	.25
178	Robinson Cano	.25
179	Nick Swisher	.25
180	Ryan Howard	.50
181	Tim Stauffer	.15
182	Merkin Valdez	.15
183	B.J. Upton	.40
184	Scott Kazmir	.40
185	Chris Burke	.25
186	Felix Hernandez	.50
187	Freddy Guzman	.15
188	Josh Labandeira	.15
189	Willy Taveras	.15
190	Casey Kotchman	.25
191	Steven Doetsch RC	.25
192	Melky Cabrera RC	.75
193	Luis Ramirez RC	.25
194	Chris Seddon RC	.40
195	Chad Orvella RC	.50
196	Ian Kinsler RC	1.50
197	Brandon Moss RC	1.00
198	Chadd Blasko RC	.50
199	Jeremy West RC	.75
200	Sean Marshall RC	.50
201	Matt DeSalvo RC	.50
202	Ryan Sweeney RC	1.50
203	Matt Lindstrom RC	.50
204	Ryan Goleski RC	.40
205	Brett Harper RC	.25
206	Chris Roberson RC	.25
207	Andre Ethier RC	1.00
208	Chris Denorfia RC	.25
209	Darren Fenster RC	.25
210	Elvys Quezada RC	.25
211	Kevin West RC	.50
212	Chaz Lytle RC	.50
213	James Jurries RC	.25
214	Matt Rogelstad RC	.25
215	Wade Robinson RC	.25
216	Ian Bladergroen RC	.75
217	Jake Dittler	.25

218	Nate McLouth RC	.40
219	Kole Strayhorn	.25
220	Jose Vaquedano RC	.25

Gold Chunks

ARAMIS RAMIREZ — CHICAGO CUBS™

Golds: 1-2X
Inserted 1:1

Minis

Mini: 1-2x
Inserted 1:1

Blasts

		NM/M
	Common Bat:	4.00
RA	Roberto Alomar	6.00
RB	Ron Belliard	4.00
AB	Angel Berroa	4.00
CB	Craig Biggio	8.00
HB	Hank Blalock	8.00
JB	Jeromy Burnitz	4.00
SB	Sean Burroughs	4.00
MC	Miguel Cabrera	10.00
VC	Vinny Castilla	4.00
TC	Tony Clark	4.00
JC	Jeff Conine	4.00
JCJ	Jose Cruz Jr.	4.00
AD	Adam Dunn	6.00
ME	Morgan Ensberg	4.00
DE	Darin Erstad	4.00
CE	Carl Everett	4.00
CF	Chone Figgins	4.00
JF	Julio Franco	4.00
NG	Nomar Garciaparra	8.00
AGO	Adrian Gonzalez	4.00
AG	Alex Gonzalez	4.00
LG	Luis Gonzalez	4.00
VG	Vladimir Guerrero	8.00
CGU	Carlos Guillen	4.00
CG	Cristian Guzman	4.00
TH	Todd Helton	6.00
LH	Livan Hernandez	4.00
RH	Richard Hidalgo	4.00
JK	Jeff Kent	4.00
PK	Paul Konerko	4.00
DL	Derrek Lee	4.00
ML	Mike Lowell	6.00
PM	Pedro Martinez	6.00
TM	Tino Martinez	6.00
VM	Victor Martinez	4.00
KM	Kazuo Matsui	8.00
MO	Magglio Ordonez	4.00
DO	David Ortiz	10.00
ARA	Aramis Ramirez	6.00
MR	Manny Ramirez	6.00
AR	Alex Rodriguez	20.00
CS	Curt Schilling	6.00
GS	Gary Sheffield	6.00
RS	Ruben Sierra	4.00
MT	Miguel Tejada	6.00
BU	B.J. Upton	10.00
JV	Jose Valentin	4.00
JVI	Jose Vidro	4.00
LW	Larry Walker	6.00
JW	Jayson Werth	4.00
PW	Preston Wilson	4.00
DW	David Wright	10.00
MY	Michael Young	4.00

Comics

	NM/M
Complete Set (24):	8.00

	Common Player:	.25
	Inserted 1:4	
1	Randy Johnson	.50
2	Gary Sheffield	.25
3	Ken Griffey Jr.	.75
4	Alex Rodriguez	.75
5	Vladimir Guerrero	.50
6	David Bell	.25
7	Carlos Pena	.25
8	Eric Gagne	.25
9	Jim Thome	.50
10	Cleveland Indians	.25
11	Greg Maddux	.50
12	Miguel Tejada	.25
13	Ichiro Suzuki	.75
14	Mariano Rivera	.25
15	Juan Pierre	.25
16	Carl Crawford	.25
17	Mike Mussina	.25
18	Vladimir Guerrero	.50
19	Oliver Perez	.25
20	Ichiro Suzuki	.75
21	Johan Santana	.25
22	Kevin Brown	.25
23	Mike Piazza	.50
24	Randy Johnson	.50

Fun Facts Relics

		NM/M
	Common Relic:	4.00
HB	Harold Baines	4.00
WB	Wade Boggs	6.00
GB	George Brett	12.00
JC	Jose Canseco	8.00
RC	Rod Carew	12.00
GC	Gary Carter	4.00
DD	Darren Daulton	4.00
DE	Darrell Evans	4.00
CF	Cecil Fielder	8.00
KG	Ken Griffey Sr.	4.00
WH	Willie Horton	4.00
WJ	Wally Joyner	4.00
DJ	David Justice	4.00
DJ2	David Justice	4.00
RK	Ron Kittle	4.00
JL	Jim Leyritz	4.00
DP	Dave Parker	4.00
HR	Harold Reynolds	4.00
MR	Mickey Rivers	4.00
MS	Mike Schmidt	10.00
OS	Ozzie Smith	20.00
CS	Cory Snyder	4.00
DS	Darryl Strawberry	4.00
WW	Walt Weiss	4.00

Moments Relics

		NM/M
	Common Relic:	6.00
MB	Matt Bush	8.00
RH	Ramon Hernandez	6.00
TL	Terrence Long	6.00
MM	Mark Mulder	6.00
MP	Mike Piazza	12.00
JP	Jorge Posada	8.00
AP	Albert Pujols	25.00
AR	Alex Rodriguez	12.00
IR	Ivan Rodriguez	8.00
KR	Kenny Rogers	6.00
AS	Alfonso Soriano	6.00
MT	Mark Teixeira	6.00
FT	Frank Thomas	6.00

Tatoos

		NM/M
	Common Player:	.25
	Inserted 1:4	
1	Alex Rodriguez	.50
2	Randy Johnson	.50
3	Jim Thome	.25
4	Pedro Martinez	.50
5	Roger Clemens	.50
6	Troy Glaus	.25
7	Todd Helton	.25
8	Albert Pujols	.50
9	Sammy Sosa	.50
10	David Wright	.50
11	Mike Piazza	.50
12	Gary Sheffield	.25
13	David Ortiz	.50
14	Hank Blalock	.25
15	Miguel Tejada	.25
16	Dontrelle Willis	.25

17	Ivan Rodriguez	.25
18	Nomar Garciaparra	.50
19	Alfonso Soriano	.25
20	Adrian Beltre	.25
21	Torii Hunter	.25
22	Brian Giles	.25
23	Chipper Jones	.50
24	Carlos Beltran	.25
25	Manny Ramirez	.50

4-on-1 Stickers

		NM/M
	Common Sticker:	.50
	Inserted 1:3 Hobby	
1	Alex Rodriguez, Hank Blalock, Scott Rolen, Mike Lowell	1.50
2	Jorge Posada, Ivan Rodriguez, Joe Mauer, Johnny Estrada	.75
3	Ichiro Suzuki, Carlos Beltran, Jim Edmonds, Brian Giles	1.50
4	Jim Thome, Mark Teixeira, Paul Konerko, Lyle Overbay	1.00
5	Jose Reyes, Mark Loretta, Jose Vidro, Luis Castillo	.50
6	Miguel Tejada, Derek Jeter, Michael Young, Edgar Renteria	2.00
7	Roy Oswalt, Rich Harden, Johan Santana, Mark Prior	1.00
8	Mariano Rivera, Eric Gagne, Joe Nathan, John Smoltz	.50
9	Larry Walker, Carl Crawford, Preston Wilson, Garret Anderson	.50
10	Wily Mo Pena, Mark Kotsay, Alex Rios, Geoff Jenkins	.50
11	Victor Martinez, David Wright, Justin Morneau, Jason Bay	.75
12	Carlos Lee, Andruw Jones, Ronnie Belliard, Eric Chavez	.50
13	Vladimir Guerrero, Vernon Wells, Miguel Cabrera, Adrian Beltre	1.00
14	David Ortiz, Marcus Giles, Jeff Kent, Bobby Abreu	1.00
15	Juan Pierre, Torii Hunter, J.D. Drew, Austin Kearns	.50
16	Bartolo Colon, Manny Ramirez, Ken Griffey Jr., Dontrelle Willis	1.50
17	Andy Pettitte, Tim Hudson, Curt Schilling, Randy Johnson	1.00
18	Jamie Moyer, Zach Day, Al Leiter, Oliver Perez	.50
19	Kazuo Matsui, Roger Clemens, Khalil Greene, Javier Vazquez	2.00
20	Pedro Martinez, Rocco Baldelli, Mike Piazza, Melvin Mora	1.50

21 Hideo Nomo, Kazuhisa Ishii, Ken Harvey, Mike Sweeney .50
22 Casey Blake, Ryan Freel, Bret Boone, Javy Lopez .50
23 Craig Wilson, Shawn Green, Aramis Ramirez, Darin Erstad .50
24 Troy Glaus, Lance Berkman, Scott Podsednik, Adam Dunn .50
25 Albert Pujols, Gary Sheffield, Chipper Jones, Magglio Ordonez 2.00
26 Johnny Damon, Carlos Zambrano, Jason Schmidt, Ted Lilly 1.00
27 Sidney Ponson, Chris Carpenter, C.C. Sabathia, Kevin Millwood .50
28 Carl Pavano, Mark Mulder, Rafael Furcal, Jack Wilson .50
29 Jeremy Bonderman, Jake Westbrook, Zack Greinke, Tom Glavine .50
30 Omar Vizquel, Carlos Guillen, Roy Halladay, Ben Sheets .50
31 Kerry Wood, Kevin Brown, Moises Alou, Travis Hafner .75
32 Nick Johnson, Erubiel Durazo, Alfonso Soriano, Jason Giambi .75
33 Chad Tracy, Richie Sexson, Aubrey Huff, Brian Roberts .50
34 Todd Helton, Dmitri Young, Jeromy Burnitz, Jose Guillen .75
35 Juan Rivera, Shannon Stewart, Sammy Sosa, Cliff Floyd 1.00
36 Pat Burrell, Gabe Gross, Aaron Guiel, Paul LoDuca .50
37 A.J. Pierzynski, Orlando Hudson, David DeJesus, Brian Lawrence .50
38 Josh Beckett, Barry Zito, Mark Buehrle, Randy Wolf .50
39 Brad Penny, Jake Peavy, Rondell White, Brad Wilkerson .50
40 Ryan Drese, Kenny Rogers, Jermaine Dye, Lew Ford .50
41 Aaron Rowand, Jason Kendall, Tony Batista, Derrek Lee .50
42 Phil Nevin, Sean Casey, Rafael Palmeiro, Frank Thomas .75
43 Scott Hatteberg, Josh Labandeira, Jason Kubel, Nick Swisher .50
44 Freddy Guzman, Tim Stauffer, Merkin Valdez, Felix Hernandez .50
45 Willy Taveras, Grady Sizemore, Joey Gathright, Carlos Delgado .50
46 Scott Kazmir, Rickie Weeks, Dallas McPherson, Kevin Youkilis 1.00
47 Val Majewski, Casey Kotchman, Ryan Howard, Chris Burke .50
48 Robinson Cano, B.J. Upton, Jake Dittler, Ian Bladergroen 1.00

49 Brett Harper, James Jurries, Jeremy West, Matt Rogelstad 1.00
50 Darren Fenster, Nate Schierholtz, Brandon Moss, Ryan Sweeney 2.00
51 Chris Roberson, Steven Doetsch, Andre Ethier, Kevin West .50
52 Melky Cabrera, Ryan Goleski, Chris Denorfia, Chaz Lytle 1.00
53 Luis Ramirez, Matt DeSalvo, Sean Marshall, Jose Vaquedano .50
54 Chris Seddon, Chadd Blasko, Elvys Quezada, Wade Robinson .50
55 Nate McLouth, Matt Lindstrom, Kole Strayhorn, Ian Kinsler 2.50

2005 Topps Chrome

	NM/M
Common Player:	.25
Common Rookie Auto. (221-252):	10.00
Inserted 1:20	
Series 1 Hobby Pack (4):	3.00
Series 1 Hobby Box (20):	50.00
Series 2 Hobby Pack (4):	5.00
Series 2 Hobby Box (20):	90.00

1 Alex Rodriguez 2.50
2 Placido Polanco .25
3 Torii Hunter .50
4 Lyle Overbay .25
5 Johnny Damon .75
6 Johnny Estrada .25
7 Rich Harden .25
8 Francisco Rodriguez .25
9 Jarrod Washburn .25
10 Sammy Sosa 1.00
11 Randy Wolf .25
12 Jason Bay .50
13 Tom Glavine .50
14 Michael Tucker .25
15 Brian Giles .50
16 Chad Tracy .25
17 Jim Edmonds .50
18 John Smoltz .50
19 Roy Halladay .25
20 Hank Blalock .75
21 Darin Erstad .50
22 Todd Walker .25
23 Mike Hampton .25
24 Mark Bellhorn .25
25 Jim Thome 1.00
26 Shingo Takatsu .25
27 Jody Gerut .25
28 Vinny Castilla .25
29 Luis Castillo .25
30 Ivan Rodriguez .75
31 Craig Biggio .50
32 Joe Randa .25
33 Adrian Beltre .50
34 Scott Podsednik .25
35 Cliff Floyd .25
36 Livan Hernandez .25
37 Eric Byrnes .25
38 Jose Acevedo .25
39 Jack Wilson .25
40 Gary Sheffield .75
41 Chan Ho Park .25
42 Carl Crawford .25
43 Shawn Estes .25

44 David Bell .25
45 Jeff DaVanon .25
46 Brandon Webb .25
47 Lance Berkman .50
48 Melvin Mora .25
49 David Ortiz 1.00
50 Andruw Jones .50
51 Chone Figgins .25
52 Danny Graves .25
53 Preston Wilson .25
54 Jeremy Bonderman .25
55 Carlos Guillen .25
56 Cesar Izturis .25
57 Kazuo Matsui .25
58 Jason Schmidt .50
59 Jason Marquis .25
60 Jose Vidro .25
61 Al Leiter .40
62 Javier Vazquez .25
63 Erubiel Durazo .25
64 Scott Spiezio .25
65 Scot Shields .25
66 Edgardo Alfonzo .25
67 Miguel Tejada .50
68 Francisco Cordero .25
69 Brett Myers .25
70 Curt Schilling 1.00
71 Matt Kata .25
72 Bartolo Colon .25
73 Rodrigo Lopez .25
74 Tim Wakefield .25
75 Frank Thomas .75
76 Jimmy Rollins .50
77 Barry Zito .50
78 Hideo Nomo .50
79 Brad Wilkerson .25
80 Adam Dunn .75
81 Derrek Lee .50
82 Joe Crede .25
83 Nate Robertson .25
84 John Thomson .25
85 Mike Sweeney .25
86 Kip Wells .25
87 Eric Gagne .25
88 David Wells .25
89 Alex Sanchez .25
90 Bret Boone .25
91 Mark Loretta .25
92 Miguel Cabrera 1.00
93 Randy Winn .25
94 Adam Everett .25
95 Aubrey Huff .25
96 Kevin Mench .25
97 Frank Catalanotto .25
98 Flash Gordon .25
99 Scott Hatteberg .25
100 Albert Pujols 3.00
101 Jose Molina, Bengie Molina .25
102 Jason Johnson .25
103 Jay Gibbons .25
104 Byung-Hyun Kim .25
105 Joe Borowski .25
106 Mark Grudzielanek .25
107 Mark Buehrle .25
108 Paul Wilson .25
109 Ronnie Belliard .25
110 Reggie Sanders .25
111 Tim Redding .25
112 Brian Lawrence .25
113 Travis Hafner .40
114 Jose Hernandez .25
115 Ben Sheets .50
116 Johan Santana .75
117 Billy Wagner .40
118 Mariano Rivera .50
119 Steve Trachsel .25
120 Akinori Otsuka .25
121 Jose Valentin .25
122 Orlando Hernandez .25
123 Raul Ibanez .25
124 Mike Matheny .25
125 Vernon Wells .25
126 Jason Isringhausen .25
127 Jose Guillen .25
128 Danny Bautista .25
129 Marcus Giles .25
130 Javy Lopez .40
131 Kevin Millar .25
132 Kyle Farnsworth .25
133 Carl Pavano .25
134 Rafael Furcal .25
135 Casey Blake .25
136 Matt Holliday .50
137 Bobby Higginson .25
138 Adam Kennedy .25
139 Alex Gonzalez .25
140 Jeff Kent .40
141 Aaron Guiel .25
142 Shawn Green .40
143 Bill Hall .25
144 Shannon Stewart .25
145 Juan Rivera .25
146 Coco Crisp .25

147 Mike Mussina .50
148 Eric Chavez .50
149 Jon Lieber .25
150 Vladimir Guerrero 1.00
151 Alex Cintron .25
152 Luis Matos .25
153 Sidney Ponson .25
154 Trot Nixon .25
155 Greg Maddux 2.00
156 Edgar Renteria .50
157 Ryan Freel .25
158 Matt Lawton .25
159 Mark Prior 1.00
160 Josh Beckett .50
161 Ken Harvey .25
162 Angel Berroa .25
163 Juan Encarnacion .25
164 Wes Helms .25
165 Brad Radke .25
166 Phil Nevin .25
167 Mike Cameron .25
168 Billy Koch .25
169 Bobby Crosby .50
170 Mike Lieberthal .25
171 Robert Mackowiak .25
172 Sean Burroughs .25
173 J.T. Snow Jr. .25
174 Paul Konerko .40
175 Luis Gonzalez .25
176 John Lackey .25
177 Oliver Perez .25
178 Brian Roberts .25
179 Bill Mueller .25
180 Carlos Lee .25
181 Corey Patterson .50
182 Sean Casey .40
183 Cliff Lee .25
184 Jason Jennings .25
185 Dmitri Young .25
186 Juan Uribe .25
187 Andy Pettitte .50
188 Juan Gonzalez .50
189 Orlando Hudson .50
190 Jason Phillips .25
191 Braden Looper .25
192 Lew Ford .25
193 Mark Mulder .40
194 Bobby Abreu .40
195 Jason Kendall .25
196 Khalil Greene .50
197 A.J. Pierzynski .25
198 Tim Worrell .25
199 So Taguchi .25
200 Jason Giambi .50
201 Tony Batista .25
202 Carlos Zambrano .50
203 Trevor Hoffman .25
204 Odalis Perez .25
205 Jose Cruz Jr. .25
206 Michael Barrett .25
207 Chris Carpenter .25
208 Michael Young .25
209 Toby Hall .25
210 Woody Williams .25
211 Chris Denorfia RC 1.00
212 Darren Fenster RC 1.00
213 Elvys Quezada RC 2.00
214 Ian Kinsler RC 4.00
215 Matt Lindstrom RC 2.00
216 Ryan Goleski RC 2.00
217 Ryan Sweeney RC 3.00
218 Sean Marshall RC 1.00
219 Steven Doetsch RC 2.00
220 Wade Robinson RC 3.00
221 Andre Ethier 40.00
222 Brandon Moss RC 20.00
223 Chadd Blasko RC 10.00
224 Chris Roberson RC 10.00
225 Chris Seddon RC 10.00
226 Ian Bladergroen RC 15.00
227 Jake Dittler 10.00
228 Jose Vaquedano RC 10.00
229 Jeremy West RC 15.00
230 Kole Strayhorn RC 10.00
231 Kevin West RC 10.00
232 Luis Ramirez RC 10.00
233 Melky Cabrera RC 40.00
234 Nate Schierholtz RC 15.00
235 Billy Butler RC 50.00
236 Brandon Szymanski RC 10.00
237 Chad Orvella RC 10.00
238 Chip Cannon RC 20.00
239 Eric Nielsen RC 10.00
240 Erik Cordier RC 10.00
241 Glen Perkins RC 15.00
242 Justin Verlander RC 60.00
243 Kevin Melillo RC 15.00
244 Landon Powell RC 20.00
245 Matt Campbell RC 10.00
246 Michael Rogers RC 20.00
247 Nate McLouth RC 20.00
248 Scott Mathieson RC 10.00
249 Shane Costa RC 10.00
250 Tony Giarratano RC 10.00

251 Tyler Pelland RC	10.00	
252 Wes Swackhamer RC	10.00	
253 Garret Anderson	.50	
254 Randy Johnson	1.00	
255 Charles Thomas	.25	
256 Rafael Palmeiro	.75	
257 Kevin Youkilis	.25	
258 Freddy Garcia	.25	
259 Magglio Ordonez	.25	
260 Aaron Harang	.25	
261 Grady Sizemore	.50	
262 Chin-Hui Tsao	.25	
263 Eric Munson	.25	
264 Juan Pierre	.25	
265 Brad Lidge	.25	
266 Brian Anderson	.25	
267 Todd Helton	.75	
268 Chad Cordero	.25	
269 Kris Benson	.25	
270 Brad Halsey	.25	
271 Jermaine Dye	.25	
272 Manny Ramirez	1.00	
273 Adam Eaton	.25	
274 Brett Tomko	.25	
275 Bucky Jacobsen	.25	
276 Dontrelle Willis	.50	
277 B.J. Upton	.25	
278 Rocco Baldelli	.25	
279 Ryan Drese	.25	
280 Ichiro Suzuki	2.50	
281 Brandon Lyon	.25	
282 Nick Green	.25	
283 Jerry Hairston	.25	
284 Mike Lowell	.25	
285 Kerry Wood	1.00	
286 Omar Vizquel	.25	
287 Carlos Beltran	.50	
288 Carlos Pena	.25	
289 Jeff Weaver	.25	
290 Chad Moeller	.25	
291 Joe Mays	.25	
292 Terrmel Sledge	.25	
293 Richard Hidalgo	.25	
294 Justin Duchscherer	.25	
295 Eric Milton	.25	
296 Ramon Hernandez	.25	
297 Jose Reyes	.50	
298 Joel Pineiro	.25	
299 Matt Morris	.25	
300 John Halama	.25	
301 Gary Matthews	.25	
302 Ryan Madson	.25	
303 Mark Kotsay	.25	
304 Carlos Delgado	.50	
305 Casey Kotchman	.25	
306 Greg Aquino	.25	
307 LaTroy Hawkins	.25	
308 Jose Contreras	.25	
309 Ken Griffey Jr.	2.00	
310 C.C. Sabathia	.25	
311 Brandon Inge	.25	
312 John Buck	.25	
313 Hee Seop Choi	.25	
314 Chris Capuano	.25	
315 Jesse Crain	.25	
316 Geoff Jenkins	.25	
317 Mike Piazza	2.00	
318 Jorge Posada	.50	
319 Nick Swisher	.25	
320 Kevin Millwood	.25	
321 Mike Gonzalez	.25	
322 Jake Peavy	.25	
323 Dustin Hermanson	.25	
324 Jeremy Reed	.25	
325 Alfonso Soriano	1.00	
326 Alexis Rios	.25	
327 David Eckstein	.25	
328 Shea Hillenbrand	.25	
329 Russ Ortiz	.25	
330 Kurt Ainsworth	.25	
331 Orlando Cabrera	.25	
332 Carlos Silva	.25	
333 Ross Gload	.25	
334 Josh Phelps	.25	
335 Mike Maroth	.25	
336 Guillermo Mota	.25	
337 Chris Burke	.25	
338 David DeJesus	.25	
339 Jose Lima	.25	
340 Cristian Guzman	.25	
341 Nick Johnson	.25	
342 Victor Zambrano	.25	
343 Rod Barajas	.25	
344 Damian Miller	.25	
345 Chase Utley	.50	
346 Sean Burnett	.25	
347 David Wells	.25	
348 Dustan Mohr	.25	
349 Bobby Madritsch	.25	
350 Reed Johnson	.25	
351 R.A. Dickey	.25	
352 Scott Kazmir	.25	
353 Tony Womack	.25	
354 Thomas Perez	.25	
355 Esteban Loaiza	.25	
356 Tomokazu Ohka	.25	
357 Ramon Ortiz	.25	
358 Richie Sexson	.50	
359 J.D. Drew	.40	
360 Barry Bonds	4.00	
361 Aramis Ramirez	.50	
362 Wily Mo Pena	.25	
363 Jeromy Burnitz	.25	
364 Nomar Garciaparra	2.00	
365 Brandon Backe	.25	
366 Derek Lowe	.25	
367 Doug Davis	.25	
368 Joe Mauer	.75	
369 Endy Chavez	.25	
370 Bernie Williams	.50	
371 Jason Michaels	.25	
372 Craig Wilson	.25	
373 Ryan Klesko	.25	
374 Ray Durham	.25	
375 Jose Lopez	.25	
376 Jeff Suppan	.25	
377 David Bush	.25	
378 Marlon Byrd	.25	
379 Roy Oswalt	.40	
380 Rondell White	.25	
381 Troy Glaus	.50	
382 Scott Hairston	.25	
383 Chipper Jones	1.00	
384 Daniel Cabrera	.25	
385 Jon Garland	.25	
386 Austin Kearns	.25	
387 Jake Westbrook	.25	
388 Aaron Miles	.25	
389 Omar Infante	.25	
390 Paul LoDuca	.25	
391 Morgan Ensberg	.25	
392 Tony Graffanino	.25	
393 Milton Bradley	.25	
394 Keith Ginter	.25	
395 Justin Morneau	.75	
396 Tony Armas Jr.	.25	
397 Kevin Brown	.25	
398 Marco Scutaro	.25	
399 Tim Hudson	.50	
400 Pat Burrell	.40	
401 Jeff Cirillo	.25	
402 Larry Walker	.50	
403 Dewon Brazelton	.25	
404 Shigetoshi Hasegawa	.25	
405 Octavio Dotel	.25	
406 Michael Cuddyer	.25	
407 Junior Spivey	.25	
408 Zack Greinke	.25	
409 Roger Clemens	3.00	
410 Chris Shelton	.25	
411 Ugueth Urbina	.25	
412 Rafael Betancourt	.25	
413 Willie Harris	.25	
414 Keith Foulke	.25	
415 Larry Bigbie	.25	
416 Paul Byrd	.25	
417 Troy Percival	.25	
418 Pedro J. Martinez	1.00	
419 Matt Clement	.25	
420 Ryan Wagner	.25	
421 Jeff Francis	.25	
422 Jeff Conine	.25	
423 Wade Miller	.25	
424 Gavin Floyd	.25	
425 Kazuhisa Ishii	.25	
426 Victor Santos	.25	
427 Jacque Jones	.25	
428 Hideki Matsui	2.00	
429 Cory Lidle	.25	
430 Jose Castillo	.25	
431 Alex Gonzalez	.25	
432 Kirk Rueter	.25	
433 Jolbert Cabrera	.25	
434 Erik Bedard	.25	
435 Ricky Ledee	.25	
436 Mark Hendrickson	.25	
437 Laynce Nix	.25	
438 Jason Frasor	.25	
439 Kevin Gregg	.25	
440 Derek Jeter	3.00	
441 Jaret Wright	.25	
442 Edwin Jackson	.25	
443 Moises Alou	.50	
444 Aaron Rowand	.25	
445 Kazuhito Tadano	.25	
446 Luis Gonzalez	.40	
447 A.J. Burnett	.40	
448 Jeff Bagwell	.50	
449 Brad Penny	.25	
450 Corey Koskie	.25	
451 Mark Ellis	.25	
452 Hector Luna	.25	
453 Miguel Olivo	.25	
454 Scott Rolen	1.00	
455 Ricardo Rodriguez	.25	
456 Eric Hinske	.25	
457 Tim Salmon	.25	
458 Adam LaRoche	.25	
459 B.J. Ryan	.25	
460 Steve Finley	.25	
461 Joe Nathan	.25	
462 Vicente Padilla	.25	
463 Yadier Molina	.25	
464 Tino Martinez	.25	
465 Mark Teixeira	.50	
466 Kelvim Escobar	.25	
467 Pedro Feliz	.25	
468 Ryan Garko RC	4.00	
469 Bobby Livingston RC	2.00	
470 Yorman Bazardo RC	3.00	
471 Michael Bourn	2.00	
472 Andy LaRoche RC	10.00	

Refractor

Refractor: 2-3X
Inserted 1:6
Rookie Auto. (221-252): 1-1.5X
Production 500

Black Refractor

Black Refractor: 3-5X
Production 225
Rookie Auto. (221-252): 1.5-3X
Production 200

X-Fractor

Cards (1-220): 5-10X
Rookie Auto.
(221-234): No Pricing
Production 25 Sets

Gold Refractor

No Pricing
Production One Set

Printing Plates

No Pricing
Production one set per color.

A-Rod Throwbacks

NM/M
Common A-Rod: 3.00

Chrome The Game Relics

	NM/M
Common Player:	5.00
Inserted 1:Box	
JB Jeff Bagwell	8.00
WB Wade Boggs	6.00
TH Torii Hunter	5.00
MPI Mike Piazza	8.00
JP Jorge Posada	6.00
MP Mark Prior	8.00
AR Alex Rodriguez	15.00
JS John Smoltz	8.00
AS Alfonso Soriano	8.00
SS Sammy Sosa	10.00
MY Michael Young	5.00

Chrome The Game Patch Relics

	NM/M
Common Player:	10.00
JB Jeff Bagwell	15.00
JBE Josh Beckett	10.00
LB Lance Berkman	10.00
BB Bret Boone	10.00
AD1 Adam Dunn	15.00
AD2 Adam Dunn	15.00
TG Troy Glaus	10.00
TH Todd Helton	15.00
KI Kazuhisa Ishii	10.00
CJ Chipper Jones	20.00
PL Paul LoDuca	10.00
ML Mike Lowell	10.00
PM Pedro Martinez	20.00
HN Hideo Nomo	20.00
MO Magglio Ordonez	10.00
MPI Mike Piazza	20.00
AP Albert Pujols	25.00
AR Alex Rodriguez	25.00
CS C.C. Sabathia	10.00
SS Sammy Sosa	20.00
MT Mark Teixeira	15.00
FT Frank Thomas	15.00
DW Dontrelle Willis	10.00
KW Kerry Wood	20.00

Dem Bums Autographs

	NM/M
Inserted 1:1,816	
CE Carl Erskine	50.00
DS Duke Snider	85.00

2005 Topps Chrome Update

	NM/M
Complete Set (237):	
Common Player:	.25
Common Rookie (106-215):	.50
Common Rk Auto.	
(221-237):	10.00
Pack (4):	4.00
Box (20):	70.00
UH1 Sammy Sosa	1.00
UH2 Jeff Francoeur	.50
UH3 Tony Clark	.25
UH4 Michael Tucker	.25
UH5 Mike Matheny	.25
UH6 Eric Young	.25
UH7 Jose Valentin	.25
UH8 Matt Lawton	.25
UH9 Juan Rivera	.25
UH10 Shawn Green	.50
UH11 Aaron Boone	.25
UH12 Woody Williams	.25
UH13 Brad Wilkerson	.25
UH14 Anthony Reyes RC	3.00
UH15 Gustavo Chacin	.25
UH16 Mike Restovich	.25
UH17 Humberto Quintero	.25
UH18 Matt Ginter	.25
UH19 Scott Podsednik	.50
UH20 Byung-Hyun Kim	.25
UH21 Orlando Hernandez	.25
UH22 Mark Grudzielanek	.25
UH23 Jody Gerut	.25
UH24 Adrian Beltre	.50
UH25 Scott Schoeneweis	.25
UH26 Marlon Anderson	.25

UH27	Jason Vargas	.25
UH28	Claudio Vargas	.25
UH29	Jason Kendall	.25
UH30	Aaron Small	.25
UH31	Juan Cruz	.25
UH32	Placido Polanco	.25
UH33	Jorge Sosa	.25
UH34	John Olerud	.25
UH35	Ryan Langerhans	.25
UH36	Randy Winn	.25
UH37	Zachary Duke	.50
UH38	Garrett Atkins	.25
UH39	Al Leiter	.25
UH40	Shawn Chacon	.25
UH41	Mark DeRosa	.25
UH42	Miguel Ojeda	.25
UH43	A.J. Pierzynski	.25
UH44	Carlos Lee	.25
UH45	LaTroy Hawkins	.25
UH46	Nick Green	.25
UH47	Shawn Estes	.25
UH48	Eli Marrero	.25
UH49	Jeff Kent	.25
UH50	Joe Randa	.25
UH51	Jose Hernandez	.25
UH52	Joe Blanton	.25
UH53	Huston Street	.25
UH54	Marlon Byrd	.25
UH55	Alex Sanchez	.25
UH56	Livan Hernandez	.25
UH57	Chris Young	.25
UH58	Brad Eldred	.25
UH59	Terrence Long	.25
UH60	Phil Nevin	.25
UH61	Kyle Farnsworth	.25
UH62	Jon Lieber	.25
UH63	Antonio Alfonseca	.25
UH64	Tony Graffanino	.25
UH65	Tadahito Iguchi	1.00
UH66	Brad Thompson	.25
UH67	Jose Vidro	.25
UH68	Jason Phillips	.25
UH69	Carl Pavano	.25
UH70	Pokey Reese	.25
UH71	Jerome Williams	.25
UH72	Kazuhisa Ishii	.25
UH73	Felix Hernandez	.50
UH74	Edgar Renteria	.50
UH75	Mike Myers	.25
UH76	Jeff Cirillo	.25
UH77	Endy Chavez	.25
UH78	Jose Guillen	.25
UH79	Ugueth Urbina	.25
UH80	Zach Day	.25
UH81	Javier Vazquez	.25
UH82	Willy Taveras	.25
UH83	Mark Mulder	.50
UH84	Vinny Castilla	.25
UH85	Russ Adams	.25
UH86	Homer Bailey	.25
UH87	Ervin Santana	.25
UH88	Bill Bray	.25
UH89	Thomas Diamond	.25
UH90	Trevor Plouffe	.25
UH91	James Houser	.25
UH92	Jake Stevens	.25
UH93	Anthony Whittington	.25
UH94	Phillip Hughes	.25
UH95	Greg Golson	.25
UH96	Paul Maholm	.25
UH97	Carlos Quentin	.25
UH98	Dan Johnson	.25
UH99	Mark Rogers	.25
UH100	Neil Walker	.25
UH101	Omar Quintanilla	.25
UH102	Blake DeWitt	.25
UH103	Taylor Tankersley	.25
UH104	David Murphy	.25
UH105	Chris Lambert	.25
UH106	Drew Anderson RC	.50
UH107	Luis Hernandez RC	.50
UH108	Jim Burt RC	.50
UH109	Mike Morse RC	.50
UH110	Elliot Johnson RC	2.00
UH111	C.J. Smith RC	.50
UH112	Casey McGehee RC	.50
UH113	Brian Miller RC	.50
UH114	Chris Vines RC	.50
UH115	D.J. Houlton RC	.50
UH116	Chuck Tiffany RC	2.00
UH117	Humberto Sanchez RC	3.00
UH118	Baltazar Lopez RC	.50
UH119	Russell Martin RC	4.00
UH120	Dana Eveland RC	1.00
UH121	Johan Silva RC	.50
UH122	Adam Harben RC	1.00
UH123	Brian Bannister RC	1.50
UH124	Adam Boeve RC	.75
UH125	Tom Oldham RC	.50
UH126	Cody Haerther RC	1.50
UH127	Dan Santin RC	.50
UH128	Daniel Haigwood RC	1.00
UH129	Craig Tatum RC	.50

UH130	Martin Prado RC	.75
UH131	Errol Simonitsch RC	.50
UH132	Lorenzo Scott RC	.50
UH133	Hayden Penn RC	1.00
UH134	Heath Totten RC	.50
UH135	Nick Masset RC	.50
UH136	Pedro Lopez RC	.75
UH137	Benjamin Harrison RC	.50
UH138	Michael Spidale RC	.50
UH139	Jeremy Harts RC	.50
UH140	Danny Zell RC	.50
UH141	Kevin Collins RC	.50
UH142	Tony Arnerich RC	.50
UH143	Matt Albers RC	2.50
UH144	Ricky Barrett RC	.50
UH145	Hernan Iribarren RC	.75
UH146	Sean Tracey RC	.50
UH147	Jerry Owens RC	1.00
UH148	Steve Nelson RC	.50
UH149	Brandon McCarthy RC	2.00
UH150	David Shepard RC	.75
UH151	Steve Bondurant RC	.50
UH152	Billy Sadler RC	.75
UH153	Ryan Feierabend RC	.50
UH154	Stuart Pomeranz RC	.50
UH155	Shawn Marcum RC	1.00
UH156	Erik Schindewolf RC	.50
UH157	Stefan Bailie RC	.50
UH158	Mike Esposito RC	.50
UH159	Buck Coats RC	.50
UH160	Andy Sides RC	.50
UH161	Micah Schnurstein RC	.75
UH162	Jesse Gutierrez RC	.50
UH163	Jake Postlewait RC	.50
UH164	Willy Mota RC	.50
UH165	Ryan Speier RC	.50
UH166	Frank Mata RC	.50
UH167	Jair Jurrjens RC	3.00
UH168	Nick Touchstone RC	.50
UH169	Matthew Kemp RC	6.00
UH170	Vinny Rottino RC	.50
UH171	J.B. Thurmond RC	.50
UH172	Kelvin Pichardo RC	.50
UH173	Scott Mitchinson RC	.50
UH174	Darwinson Salazar RC	.50
UH175	George Kottaras RC	1.50
UH176	Ken Durost RC	.75
UH177	Jonathan Sanchez RC	2.00
UH178	Brandon Moorhead RC	.75
UH179	Kennard Bibbs RC	.75
UH180	David Gassner RC	.50
UH181	Micah Furtado RC	.50
UH182	Ismael Ramirez RC	.50
UH183	Carlos Gonzalez RC	5.00
UH184	Brandon Sing RC	.75
UH185	Jason Motte RC	.50
UH186	Chuck James RC	3.00
UH187	Andy Santana RC	.50
UH188	Manny Parra RC	1.00
UH189	Chris Young RC	5.00
UH190	Juan Senreiso RC	.50
UH191	Franklin Morales RC	3.00
UH192	Jared Gothreaux RC	.50
UH193	Jayce Tingler RC	.50
UH194	Matt Brown RC	.50
UH195	Frank Diaz RC	1.50
UH196	Stephen Drew RC	8.00
UH197	Jered Weaver RC	10.00
UH198	Ryan Braun RC	25.00
UH199	John Mayberry Jr. RC	2.50
UH200	Aaron Thompson RC	2.00
UH201	Ben Copeland RC	4.00
UH202	Jacoby Ellsbury RC	25.00
UH203	Garrett Olson RC	1.50
UH204	Cliff Pennington RC	2.00
UH205	Colby Rasmus RC	8.00
UH206	Chris Volstad RC	3.00
UH207	Ricky Romero RC	2.00
UH208	Ryan Zimmerman RC	10.00
UH209	C.J. Henry RC	2.00
UH210	Nelson Cruz RC	1.00
UH211	Josh Wall RC	1.50
UH212	Nick Webber RC	.50
UH213	Paul Kelly RC	1.00
UH214	Kyle Winters RC	1.50
UH215	Mitch Boggs RC	.75
UH216	Craig Biggio RC	.50
UH217	Greg Maddux RC	1.00
UH218	Bobby Abreu RC	.25
UH219	Alex Rodriguez RC	2.00
UH220	Trevor Hoffman RC	.25
UH221	Trevor Bell RC	20.00
UH222	Jay Bruce RC	100.00
UH223	Travis Buck RC	20.00
UH224	Cesar Carrillo RC	15.00
UH225	Mike Costanzo RC	25.00
UH226	Brent Cox RC	10.00

UH227	Matt Garza RC	30.00
UH228	Josh Geer RC	10.00
UH229	Tyler Greene RC	10.00
UH230	Eli Iorg RC	10.00
UH231	Craig Italiano RC	15.00
UH232	Beau Jones RC	15.00
UH233	Mark McCormick RC	10.00
UH234	Andrew McCutchen RC	40.00
UH235	Micah Owings RC	25.00
UH236	Cesar Ramos RC	10.00
UH237	Chaz Roe RC	10.00

Refractor

Stars (1-105):	2-3X
Rookies (106-215):	1-2X
Inserted 1:5	
Refractor Auto. (221-237):1-1.5X	
Production 500	

Black Refractor

Black (1-105):	2-4X
Black (106-215):	2-3X
Production 250	
Black Auto. (221-237):	1-2.5X
Production 200	

Gold SuperFractor

No Pricing
Production One Set

Red X-Fractor

Red (1-105):	4-8X
Red (106-215):	6-12X
Production 65	
Red Auto. (221-237):	No Pricing
Production 25	

Printing Plates

No Pricing
Production one set per color.

Barry Bonds Home Run History

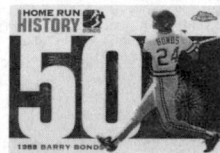

NM/M

Complete Set (15):	40.00
Common Bonds:	3.00
Inserted 1:12	
Refractor:	1-2X
Inserted 1:71	
Black Refractor:	2-3X
Production 200 Sets	
Red X-Fractor:	4-6X
Production 25 Sets	
Gold Super:	No Pricing
Production One Set	

2005 Topps Cracker Jack

CHRIS CARPENTER
St. Louis - National League

NM/M

Complete Set (240):	
Common Player:	.25
Common SP:	3.00
Inserted 1:3	
Pack (8):	
Box (20):	70.00

1	David Wright/SP	8.00
2	Rafael Furcal	.25
3	Alex Rodriguez	1.50

3	Alex Rodriguez/SP Fielding	5.00
4	Victor Martinez/SP	3.00
5	Ken Griffey Jr.	1.50
6	Bobby Crosby/SP	3.00
7	Ivan Rodriguez	.50
8	Darin Erstad	.25
9	Javy Lopez	.25
10	Brian Giles	.25
11	Aaron Rowand/SP	3.00
12	Joe Torre	.25
13	Zack Greinke/SP	3.00
14	Shannon Stewart	.25
15	Jack Wilson	.25
16	Jose Vidro	.25
17	Josh Beckett	.40
---	Josh Beckett (No number.)	4.00
18	Barry Zito	.40
19	Bret Boone	.25
20	Greg Maddux	1.00
21	Carl Crawford/SP	3.00
22	Mark Teixeira	.50
23	Jason Schmidt	.40
24	Kazuhisa Ishii	.25
25	Mike Piazza	1.00
26	Daniel Cabrera/SP	3.00
27	Mike Lieberthal	.25
28	Gil Meche	.25
29	Phil Nevin	.25
30	Adrian Beltre/SP	3.00
31	Chipper Jones/SP	4.00
32	Zach Day	.25
33	Ben Sheets	.40
34	Carlos Zambrano	.40
35	Melvin Mora	.25
36	Joe Mauer	.75
37	Ken Harvey	.25
38	Bernie Williams	.40
39	Mike Maroth	.25
40	Eric Chavez	.40
41	Matt Lawton/SP	3.00
42	Ray Durham	.25
43	Vernon Wells	.25
44	Mike Lowell	.25
45	Jim Thome	.50
46	Joel Pineiro	.25
47	Lance Berkman	.40
48	Ryan Klesko	.25
49	Adam Dunn	.50
50	Vladimir Guerrero	.75
51	Eric Gagne/SP	4.00
52	Richie Sexson	.40
53	Javier Vazquez	.25
54	Roy Oswalt	.40
55	Carlos Delgado	.50
56	John Buck/SP	3.00
57	Kenny Rogers	.25
58	Sidney Ponson	.25
59	Vicente Padilla	.25
60	Mark Prior/SP	.75
60	Mark Prior/SP Portrait	4.00
61	A.J. Pierzynski	.25
62	Aubrey Huff	.25
63	Shea Hillenbrand	.25
64	Carlos Guillen	.25
65	Lyle Overbay	.25
66	Al Leiter	.25
67	Eric Hinske	.25
68	Laynce Nix	.25
69	Scott Hairston	.25
70	Roger Clemens	2.00
71	Cesar Izturis/SP	3.00
72	Shawn Green	.25
73	Marcus Giles	.25
74	Rafael Palmeiro	.50
75	Melky Cabrera/SP	3.00
75	Gary Sheffield/SP	4.00
76	Juan Pierre	.25
77	Pat Burrell	.40
78	Sean Burroughs	.25
79	Frank Thomas	.50
80	Andruw Jones	.40
81	C.C. Sabathia	.25
82	Jeff Bagwell	.50
83	Tom Glavine	.40
84	Craig Wilson/SP	3.00
85	Johan Santana	.75
85	Johan Santana/SP Portrait	4.00
86	Raul Ibanez	.25
87	Sean Casey	.25
88	Bucky Jacobsen	.25
89	B.J. Upton	.40
90	Bobby Abreu	.40
91	Geoff Jenkins	.25
92	Troy Glaus	.40
93	Dontrelle Willis	.40
94	Jose Lima	.25
95	Rocco Baldelli	.25
96	Aramis Ramirez	.40
97	Paul LoDuca	.25
98	Torii Hunter	.40
99	Jay Payton	.25

100	Carlos Beltran	.50
101	Jaret Wright	.25
102	Jason Bay	.40
103	Cliff Floyd	.25
104	Mike Sweeney	.25
105	Sammy Sosa	1.50
106	Khalil Greene/SP	4.00
107	David DeJesus	.25
108	Jermaine Dye	.25
109	Miguel Cabrera	.75
110	Miguel Tejada/SP	5.00
111	Johnny Estrada/SP	3.00
112	Ronnie Belliard/SP	3.00
113	Austin Kearns	.25
114	Erubiel Durazo	.25
115	Preston Wilson	.25
116	Hideo Nomo	.40
117	Dmitri Young	.25
118	Jon Lieber	.25
119	Derrek Lee	.40
120	Todd Helton	.50
121	Omar Vizquel	.25
122	Wily Mo Pena	.40
123	J.D. Drew	.40
124	Matt Holliday	.25
125	Ichiro Suzuki	1.50
126	Mark Buehrle/SP	3.00
127	Eric Munson	.25
128	Jeff Kent	.25
129	Kerry Wood	.75
130	Mariano Rivera	.50
131	Nick Johnson	.25
132	Randy Winn	.25
133	Phil Garner	.25
134	Jose Reyes	.50
135	Michael Young/SP	3.00
135	Ian Kinsler/SP	6.00
136	Jose Contreras	.25
137	Oliver Perez	.25
138	Roy Halladay	.40
139	Kevin Millwood	.25
140	Jorge Posada	.40
141	Mike Cameron	.25
142	Edgardo Alfonzo	.25
143	Chris Shelton	.25
144	Luis Castillo	.25
145	Alfonso Soriano	.75
146	Ryan Drese/SP	3.00
147	Mark Mulder	.40
148	Jason Giambi	.25
149	Travis Hafner	.25
150	Randy Johnson	.75
151	Paul Konerko/SP	3.00
152	Mike Mussina	.50
153	Brad Wilkerson	.25
154	Tim Hudson	.40
155	Garret Anderson	.40
156	Chase Utley/SP	3.00
157	Jamie Moyer	.25
158	Scott Kazmir	.40
159	Brett Myers	.25
160	Kazuo Matsui	.25
161	Orlando Hudson	.25
162	Luis Gonzalez	.25
163	Kevin Youkilis	.25
164	Jason Kendall/SP	.25
164	Landon Powell/SP	3.00
165	Hank Blalock	.50
166	Mark Loretta/SP	3.00
167	Miguel Cairo	.25
168	Corey Patterson	.40
169	Carlos Zambrano	.25
170	Magglio Ordonez	.25
171	J.T. Snow	.25
172	Randy Wolf	.25
173	Rich Harden	.40
174	Bartolo Colon	.25
175	Derek Jeter	2.00
176	Casey Kotchman/SP	3.00
177	Val Majewski	.25
178	Grady Sizemore	.50
179	Rickie Weeks	.75
180	Robinson Cano	.75
181	Nick Swisher/SP	3.00
182	Ryan Howard	1.50
183	John Van Benschoten	.25
184	Delmon Young	.50
185	Aaron Hill	.25
186	Chris Burke/SP	3.00
187	Merkin Valdez	.25
188	Jeremy Reed	.25
189	Conor Jackson	.25
190	Melky Cabrera	.25
191	Joey Gathright/SP	3.00
192	Gavin Floyd	.25
193	Joe Blanton	.25
194	Jason Kubel	.25
195	Jeff Francis	.25
196	Angel Guzman/SP	3.00
197	Dallas McPherson	.25
198	Melky Cabrera RC	1.50
199	Jake Dittler	.25
200	Elvys Quezada RC	.50
201	Ian Kinsler/SP RC	6.00

202	Nate McLouth RC	.50
203	Chris Seddon RC	.75
204	Chad Orvella RC	.50
205	Ian Bladergroen RC	1.00
206	James Jurries SP RC	4.00
207	Landon Powell RC	.75
208	Eric Nielsen RC	.50
209	Chris Roberson RC	.50
210	Andre Ethier	2.00
211	Chris Denorfia/SP RC	4.00
212	Darren Fenster RC	.50
213	Jeremy West RC	1.00
214	Sean Marshall RC	.50
215	Ryan Sweeney	1.50
216	Steven Doetsch/	
	SP RC	3.00
217	Kevin Melillo RC	.50
218	Chip Cannon RC	1.00
219	Tony LaRussa	.25
220	Chris Carpenter	.25
221	Edgar Renteria/SP	
	Red Sox	3.00
221	Edgar Renteria/SP	
	Cardinals	3.00
222	Albert Pujols	2.00
223	Jim Edmonds	.40
224	Jason Marquis	.25
225	Scott Rolen/SP	4.00
226	Larry Walker/SP	4.00
227	Matt Morris	.25
228	Mike Matheny	3.00
228	Mike Matheny/SP	
	Cardinals	3.00
229	Jeromy Burnitz	.25
230	Terry Francona	.25
231	Johnny Damon	4.00
232	Keith Foulke	.25
233	Trot Nixon	.25
234	Manny Ramirez	.75
235	David Ortiz/SP	4.00
236	Pedro Martinez/SP	
	Mets	4.00
236	Pedro J. Martinez/SP	
	Red Sox	4.00
237	Curt Schilling	.75
238	Kevin Millar	.25
239	Bill Mueller	.25
240	Mark Bellhorn	.25
	Josh Beckett/SP	3.00

Mini Blue

Stars:		8-15X
SP's:		4-6X
Production 50 Sets		

Mini Grey

No Pricing		
Production 25 Sets		

Mini Red

Stars:		1-2X
Inserted 1:1		
SP's:		.75-1.5X
Inserted 1:20		

Mini White

No Pricing		
Production One Set		

Autographs

		NM/M
Production 50 Sets		
Bonds Production 25		
GA	Garret Anderson	30.00
CB	Carlos Beltran	80.00
BB	Barry Bonds	
EC	Eric Chavez	30.00
CC	Carl Crawford	50.00
EG	Eric Gagne	40.00
AR	Alex Rodriguez	250.00
CS	C.C. Sabathia	50.00
JS	Johan Santana	60.00
CW	Craig Wilson	
DW	David Wright	150.00

Mini Stickers

Stars:		1-2X
Inserted 1:1		
SP's:		.75-1.5X
Inserted 1:20		

Secret Surprise Autographs

		NM/M
Common Auto.:		8.00
GA	Garret Anderson	15.00
CB	Carlos Beltran	
EC	Eric Chavez	15.00
CC	Carl Crawford	
EG	Eric Gagne	20.00
AG	Angel Guzman	
SK	Scott Kazmir	25.00
MK	Mark Kotsay/100	15.00

ML	Mark Loretta/100	20.00
DM	Dallas	
	McPherson/100	15.00
KM	Kevin Millar	15.00
MM	Melvin Mora	15.00
CN	Chris Nelson	10.00
RR	Richie Robnett	10.00
AR	Alex Rodriguez	
CS	C.C. Sabathia	20.00
JS	Johan Santana	50.00
CT	Curtis Thigpen	15.00
CW	Craig Wilson	10.00
DW	David Wright	50.00

Take Me Out To/Ballgame Relics

		NM/M
Inserted 1:16		
JB	Jeff Bagwell	6.00
RB	Ronnie Belliard	4.00
CB	Carlos Beltran	8.00
AB	Adrian Beltre	6.00
LB1	Lance Berkman	6.00
LB2	Lance Berkman	6.00
AB1	Angel Berroa	4.00
AB2	Angel Berroa	4.00
CBI	Craig Biggio	6.00
HB1	Hank Blalock	8.00
HB2	Hank Blalock	8.00
HB3	Hank Blalock	8.00
SB	Sean Burroughs	4.00
MC	Miguel Cabrera	8.00
VC	Vinny Castilla	4.00
EC1	Eric Chavez	6.00
EC2	Eric Chavez	6.00
BC	Bobby Cox	4.00
CC	Coco Crisp	4.00
BCR	Bobby Crosby	6.00
AD	Adam Dunn	8.00
JE1	Jim Edmonds	6.00
JE2	Jim Edmonds	6.00
DE	Darin Erstad	4.00
JE	Johnny Estrada	4.00
RF	Rafael Furcal	6.00
JG	Jody Gerut	4.00
JGI	Jay Gibbons	4.00
MG	Marcus Giles	4.00
TG	Troy Glaus	6.00
LG	Luis Gonzalez	4.00
NG	Nick Green	4.00
SG	Shawn Green	4.00
VG	Vladimir Guerrero	10.00
JGU	Jose Guillen	6.00
CG	Cristian Guzman	4.00
TH	Todd Helton	8.00
THU	Torii Hunter	6.00
JJ	Jacque Jones	4.00
JK	Jason Kendall	4.00
BK	Bobby Kielty	4.00
RK	Ryan Klesko	4.00
PK	Paul Konerko	4.00
MK	Mark Kotsay	4.00
AL	Adam LaRoche	6.00
VM	Victor Martinez	6.00
KME	Kevin Mench	4.00
DM	Doug Mientkiewicz	4.00
KM	Kevin Millar	10.00
MM	Melvin Mora	6.00
PN	Phil Nevin	4.00
LN	Laynce Nix	4.00
MO	Magglio Ordonez	4.00
DO	David Ortiz	10.00
RP	Rafael Palmeiro	8.00
CP	Corey Patterson	6.00
MP	Mike Piazza	12.00
JP1	Jorge Posada	8.00
JP2	Jorge Posada	8.00
AP	Albert Pujols	20.00
MR	Manny Ramirez	10.00
JR	Jeremy Reed	8.00
MRE	Mike Restovich	4.00
AR	Alex Rodriguez	15.00
ARA	Aramis Ramirez	6.00
IR1	Ivan Rodriguez	8.00
IR2	Ivan Rodriguez	8.00
RS	Reggie Sanders	4.00
BS	Benito Santiago	4.00
GS	Gary Sheffield	8.00
AS	Alfonso Soriano	8.00
MT1	Mark Teixeira	8.00
MT2	Mark Teixeira	8.00

MT3	Mark Teixeira	8.00
MTE1	Miguel Tejada	8.00
MTE2	Miguel Tejada	8.00
CT	Charles Thomas	4.00
JT	Jim Thome	8.00
JTO	Joe Torre	10.00
OV	Omar Vizquel	6.00
BW	Bernie Williams	6.00
DW	Dontrelle Willis	8.00
MY	Michael Young	6.00

1,2,3 Strikes You're Out Relics

		NM/M
Inserted 1:204		
JB	Josh Beckett	8.00
RD	Ryan Drese	5.00
RO	Russ Ortiz	5.00
BR	Brad Radke	8.00
CS	Curt Schilling	15.00
JW	Jaret Wright	8.00

2005 Topps Gallery

		NM/M
Complete Set (195):		175.00
Common Player:		.25
Common SP (151-195):		1.00
Inserted 1:1		
Variations 1:40		
Pack (5):		6.00
Box (20):		100.00
1	Alex Rodriguez	2.50
1	Alex Rodriguez/SP/	
	Black Bat Glove	8.00
2	Eric Chavez	.50
3	Mike Piazza	1.50
4	Bret Boone	.25
5	Albert Pujols	3.00
6	Vernon Wells	.25
7	Andruw Jones	.50
8	Miguel Tejada	.50
9	Johnny Damon	.25
10	Nomar Garciaparra	2.00
11	Pat Burrell	.40
12	Bartolo Colon	.25
13	Johnny Estrada	.25
14	Luis Gonzalez	.40
15	Jay Gibbons	.25
16	Curt Schilling	1.00
17	Aramis Ramirez	.50
18	Frank Thomas	.75
19	Adam Dunn	.75
20	Sammy Sosa	2.00
21	Matt Lawton	.25
22	Preston Wilson	.25
23	Carlos Pena	.25
24	Josh Beckett	.50
25	Carlos Beltran	.75
26	Juan Gonzalez	.50
27	Adrian Beltre	.50
28	Lyle Overbay	.25
29	Justin Morneau	.50
30	Derek Jeter	3.00
31	Barry Zito	.50
32	Bobby Abreu	.40
33	Jason Bay	.25
34	Jose Reyes	.50
35	Nick Johnson	.25
36	Lew Ford	.25
37	Scott Podsednik	.25
38	Rocco Baldelli	.40
39	Eric Hinske	.25
40	Ichiro Suzuki	2.50
40	Ichiro Suzuki/SP/	
	Writing On Wall	8.00
41	Larry Walker	.50
42	Mark Teixeira	.50
43	Khalil Greene	.50
44	Edgardo Alfonzo	.25
45	Javier Vazquez	.25
46	Cliff Floyd	.25
47	Geoff Jenkins	.25

48	Ken Griffey Jr.	2.00
49	Vinny Castilla	.25
50	Mark Prior	1.00
51	Jose Guillen	.25
52	J.D. Drew	.50
53	Rafael Palmeiro	.75
54	Kevin Youkilis	.25
55	Derrek Lee	.50
56	Freddy Garcia	.25
57	Wily Mo Pena	.25
58	C.C. Sabathia	.25
59	Craig Biggio	.40
60	Ivan Rodriguez	.75
61	Angel Berroa	.25
62	Ben Sheets	.50
63	Johan Santana	.75
64	Al Leiter	.40
65	Bernie Williams	.50
66	Bobby Crosby	.50
67	Jack Wilson	.25
68	A.J. Pierzynski	.25
69	Jimmy Rollins	.50
70	Jason Giambi	.50
71	Tom Glavine	.50
72	Kevin Brown	.25
73	B.J. Upton	.50
74	Edgar Renteria	.50
75	Alfonso Soriano	1.00
76	Mike Lieberthal	.25
77	Kazuo Matsui	.25
78	Phil Nevin	.25
79	Shawn Green	.40
80	Miguel Cabrera	1.00
81	Todd Helton	.75
82	Magglio Ordonez	.40
83	Manny Ramirez	1.00
84	Bill Mueller	.25
85	Troy Glaus	.50
86	Richie Sexson	.50
87	Javy Lopez	.40
88	David Ortiz	1.00
89	Greg Maddux	1.50
90	Vladimir Guerrero	1.00
91	Jeromy Burnitz	.25
92	Jeff Kent	.40
93	Travis Hafner	.40
94	Mark Buehrle	.25
95	Paul LoDuca	.25
96	Roy Oswalt	.40
97	Torii Hunter	.40
98	Gary Sheffield	.75
99	Erubiel Durazo	.25
100	Jim Thome	1.00
100	Jim Thome/SP/ Kid's Shirt Is Red	6.00
101	Ken Harvey	.25
102	Shannon Stewart	.25
103	Dmitri Young	.25
104	Kevin Millar	.50
105	Kerry Wood	1.00
106	Paul Konerko	.40
107	Ronnie Belliard	.25
108	Mike Lowell	.40
109	Hee Seop Choi	.25
110	Joe Mauer	.50
111	David Wright	.50
112	Jorge Posada	.50
113	Tim Hudson	.50
114	Brian Giles	.25
115	Jason Schmidt	.50
116	Aubrey Huff	.25
117	Hank Blalock	.75
118	Jim Edmonds	.50
119	Raul Ibanez	.25
120	Carlos Delgado	.50
121	Craig Wilson	.40
122	Ryan Klesko	.50
123	Mark Mulder	.50
124	Jose Vidro	.25
125	Mike Sweeney	.25
126	Lance Berkman	.50
127	Juan Pierre	.25
128	Austin Kearns	.25
129	Moises Alou	.50
130	Garret Anderson	.50
131	Pedro J. Martinez	1.00
132	Melvin Mora	.25
133	Marcus Giles	.25
134	Corey Patterson	.50
135	Carlos Lee	.25
136	Sean Casey	.40
137	Jody Gerut	.25
138	Jose Valentin	.25
139	Aaron Miles	.25
140	Randy Johnson	1.00
141	Carlos Guillen	.25
142	Dontrelle Willis	.50
143	Jeff Bagwell	.75
144	Jason Kendall	.25
145	Mark Loretta	.25
146	Scott Rolen	1.00
147	Carl Crawford	.25
148	Michael Young	.25
149	Jermaine Dye	.25
150	Chipper Jones	1.00
151	Melky Cabrera RC	4.00
152	Chris Seddon RC	4.00
153	Nate Schierholtz RC	4.00
154	Ian Kinsler RC	8.00
154	Ian Kinsler/SP/ Gold Background	20.00
155	Brandon Moss RC	4.00
155	Brandon Moss/SP/ Red Hat	10.00
156	Chadd Blasko RC	2.00
157	Jeremy West RC	2.00
157	Jeremy West/SP/ Navy Blue Jersey	6.00
158	Sean Marshall RC	2.00
159	Ryan Sweeney RC	4.00
160	Matt Lindstrom RC	2.00
161	Ryan Goleski RC	4.00
162	Brett Harper RC	2.00
163	Chris Roberson RC	3.00
164	Andre Ethier	8.00
165	Ian Bladergroen RC	2.00
165	Ian Bladergroen/SP/ Swinging	6.00
166	James Jurries RC	2.00
167	Billy Butler RC	6.00
167	Billy Butler/SP/ Black Jsy	15.00
168	Michael Rogers RC	3.00
168	Michael Rogers/SP/ Baseball In Hand	8.00
169	Tyler Clippard RC	10.00
170	Luis Ramirez RC	3.00
171	Casey Kotchman	2.00
172	Chris Burke	2.00
173	Dallas McPherson	2.00
174	Edwin Jackson	1.00
175	Felix Hernandez	4.00
176	Gavin Floyd	1.00
177	Guillermo Quiroz	1.00
178	Jason Kubel	1.00
179	Jeff Mathis	1.00
180	Rickie Weeks	1.00
181	Ryan Howard	3.00
182	Franklin Gutierrez	1.00
183	Jeremy Reed	5.00
184	Carlos Quentin	5.00
185	Jeff Francis	5.00
186	Nolan Ryan	6.00
187	Hank Aaron	6.00
187	Hank Aaron/SP/ Red 755	15.00
188	Duke Snider	4.00
189	Mike Schmidt	5.00
190	Ernie Banks	4.00
191	Frank Robinson	3.00
192	Harmon Killebrew	4.00
193	Al Kaline	3.00
194	Rod Carew	3.00
195	Johnny Bench	4.00

Artist's Proof

Stars (1-150):	2-4X
SP's (151-195):	1-2X
Inserted 1:1	

Printing Plates

No Pricing
Production one for each color.

Cut Signatures

No Pricing

Gallo's Gallery Sketches

		NM/M
Complete Set (20):		50.00
Common Player:		1.50
Inserted 1:15		
HA	Hank Aaron	6.00
HB	Hank Blalock	1.50
NG	Nomar Garciaparra	4.00

GALLO'S GALLERY

HANK BLALOCK • TEXAS RANGERS

VG	Vladimir Guerrero	2.00
TH	Todd Helton	1.50
DJ	Derek Jeter	6.00
RJ	Randy Johnson	2.00
CJ	Chipper Jones	2.00
MPI	Mike Piazza	4.00
MP	Mark Prior	2.00
AP	Albert Pujols	6.00
AR	Alex Rodriguez	5.00
IR	Ivan Rodriguez	1.50
NR	Nolan Ryan	6.00
MS	Mike Schmidt	5.00
AS	Alfonso Soriano	2.00
SS	Sammy Sosa	4.00
IS	Ichiro Suzuki	4.00
MT	Miguel Tejada	1.50
JT	Jim Thome	2.00

Heritage Insert

JOHNNY BENCH — Catcher — REDS

		NM/M
Complete Set (25):		65.00
Common Player:		2.00
Inserted 1:15		
EB	Ernie Banks	4.00
CB	Carlos Beltran	3.00
JB	Johnny Bench	4.00
HB	Hank Blalock	2.00
GB	George Brett	6.00
JC	Jose Canseco	2.00
BG	Bob Gibson	3.00
AK	Al Kaline	3.00
DM	Don Mattingly	6.00
RP	Rafael Palmeiro	3.00
JP	Jim Palmer	2.00
AP	Albert Pujols	8.00
BR	Brooks Robinson	3.00
FR	Frank Robinson	2.00
RR	Frank Robinson, Brooks Robinson	3.00
RJ	Alex Rodriguez, Derek Jeter	8.00
IR	Ivan Rodriguez	3.00
NR	Nolan Ryan	8.00
CS	Curt Schilling	3.00
MS	Mike Schmidt	5.00
TS	Jim Thome, Mike Schmidt	5.00
OS	Ozzie Smith	3.00
DSN	Duke Snider	3.00
DS	Darryl Strawberry	2.00
DW	Dontrelle Willis	2.00

Heritage Relics

		NM/M
Common Player:		5.00
Inserted 1:40		
GB	George Brett	12.00
JC	Jose Canseco	8.00
DM	Don Mattingly	15.00
AP	Albert Pujols	15.00
AR	Alex Rodriguez	15.00

IR	Ivan Rodriguez	8.00
NR	Nolan Ryan	20.00
OS	Ozzie Smith	8.00
DS	Darryl Strawberry	5.00
DW	Dontrelle Willis	5.00

Heritage Relic Autographs

		NM/M
Production 25 Sets		
DM	Don Mattingly	75.00
AR	Alex Rodriguez	300.00
IR	Ivan Rodriguez	
NR	Nolan Ryan	150.00

Murray Olderman Sketches

No Pricing
Production One Set

Originals Relics

FRANK THOMAS CHICAGO WHITE SOX

		NM/M
Common Player:		4.00
Inserted 1:10		
JB	Jeff Bagwell	8.00
RB	Rocco Baldelli	4.00
JBE	Josh Beckett	4.00
LB	Lance Berkman	4.00
AB	Angel Berroa	4.00
HB	Hank Blalock	8.00
HBB	Hank Blalock	8.00
MC	Miguel Cabrera	8.00
JD	Johnny Damon	4.00
RD	Ryan Drese	4.00
JG	Jason Giambi	6.00
MG	Marcus Giles	4.00
VG	Vladimir Guerrero	8.00
RH	Rich Harden	4.00
TH	Todd Helton	8.00
CJ	Chipper Jones	8.00
JL	Javy Lopez	4.00
ML	Mike Lowell	4.00
PM	Pedro J. Martinez	8.00
KM	Kazuo Matsui	6.00
LN	Laynce Nix	4.00
DO	David Ortiz	8.00
MP	Mike Piazza	8.00
MPB	Mike Piazza	8.00
MPR	Mark Prior	8.00
AP	Albert Pujols	15.00
MR	Manny Ramirez	8.00
JR	Jose Reyes	4.00
AR	Alex Rodriguez	12.00
IR	Ivan Rodriguez	8.00
AS	Alfonso Soriano	8.00
SS	Sammy Sosa	10.00
MT	Mark Teixeira	4.00
MTE	Miguel Tejada	6.00
FT	Frank Thomas	8.00
BU	B.J. Upton	4.00
BW	Bernie Williams	6.00
DW	Dontrelle Willis	4.00
KW	Kerry Wood	8.00
MY	Michael Young	4.00

Penmanship Autographs

	NM/M
Common Autograph:	10.00

JB Jason Bartlett   10.00
TB Taylor Buchholz   10.00
EC Eric Chavez   15.00
FH Felix Hernandez   30.00
AH Aubrey Huff   15.00
JJ Justin Jones   15.00
ML Mike Lowell
DM Dallas McPherson   25.00
JP Jorge Posada
AR Alex Rodriguez   250.00
IR Ivan Rodriguez
VW Vernon Wells   10.00

2005 Topps Heritage

	NM/M
Complete Set (475):	400.00
Common Player:	.40
Common SP (398-475):	4.00
SP's & Variations Inserted 1:2	
Pack (8):	5.00
Box (24):	100.00

1   Will Harridge   .40
2   Warren Giles   .40
3   Alfonso Soriano   1.00
3   Alfonso Soriano/SP/
    Running   5.00
4   Mark Mulder   .75
5   Todd Helton/SP   5.00
6   Jason Bay   .40
6   Jason Bay/SP/
    1956 Pirates Uniform   5.00
7   Ichiro Suzuki   2.50
7   Ichiro Suzuki/SP/
    Squatting On-Deck   8.00
8   Jim Tracy   .40
9   Gavin Floyd   .40
10 John Smoltz   .75
11 Chicago Cubs   .50
12 Darin Erstad   .40
13 Chad Tracy   .40
14 Charles Thomas   .40
15 Miguel Tejada   .75
16 Andre Ethier   6.00
17 Jeff Francis   .40
18 Derrek Lee   .50
19 Juan Uribe   .40
20 Jim Edmonds/SP   5.00
21 Kenny Lofton   .40
22 Brad Ausmus   .40
23 Jon Garland   .40
24 Edwin Jackson   .40
25 Joe Mauer   .75
26 Wes Helms   .40
27 Brian Schneider   .40
28 Kazuo Matsui   .40
29 Tom Gordon   .40
30 Hideo Nomo/SP   .40
31 Albert Pujols/SP   15.00
31 Albert Pujols/SP/
    1956 Cards Uniform   15.00
32 Carl Crawford   .40
33 Vladimir Guerrero/SP   6.00
34 Nick Green   .40
35 Jay Gibbons   .40
36 Kevin Youkilis   .40
37 Billy Wagner   .40
38 Terrence Long   .40
39 Kevin Mench   .40
40 Garret Anderson   .50
41 Reed Johnson   .40
42 Reggie Sanders   .40
43 Kirk Rueter   .40
44 Jay Payton   .40
45 Tike Redman   .40
46 Mike Lieberthal   .40
47 Damian Miller   .40
48 Zach Day   .40
49 Juan Rincon   .40
50 Jim Thome   1.00
50 Jim Thome/SP/Fld   6.00
51 Jose Guillen   .40
52 Richie Sexson   .75
53 Juan Cruz   .40
54 Byung-Hyun Kim   .40
55 Carlos Zambrano   .50
56 Carlos Lee   .40
57 Adam Dunn   .75
58 David Riske   .40
59 Carlos Guillen   .40
60 Larry Bowa   .40
61 Barry Bonds   4.00
62 Chris Woodward   .40
63 Matt DeSalvo RC   2.50

64 Brian Stavisky RC   1.00
65 Scot Shields   .40
66 J.D. Drew   .50
67 Erik Bedard   .40
68 Scott Williamson   .40
69 Mark Prior   1.00
69 Mark Prior/SP/
    1956 Cubs Uniform   6.00
69 70Ken Griffey Jr.   2.00
71 Kazuhito Tadano   .40
72 Philadelphia Phillies   .40
73 Jeremy Reed   .40
74 Ricardo Rodriguez   .40
75 Carlos Delgado   .50
76 Eric Milton   .40
77 Miguel Olivo   .40
78 Edgardo Alfonzo   .40
78 Edgardo Alfonzo/SP/
    1956 Giants Uniform   4.00
79 Kazuhisa Ishii/SP   4.00
80 Jason Giambi   .75
81 Cliff Floyd   .40
82 Carl Pavano   .50
82 Torii Hunter/SP/1956
    Senators Uniform   4.00
83 Odalis Perez   .40
84 Scott Podsednik   .40
85 Cleveland Indians   .40
86 Jeff Suppan   .40
87 Ray Durham   .40
88 Tyler Clippard RC   10.00
89 Ryan Howard   2.00
90 Cincinnati Reds   .40
91 Bengie Molina   .40
92 Danny Bautista   .40
93 Eli Marrero   .40
94 Larry Bigbie   .40
95 Atlanta Braves   .40
96 Merkin Valdez   .40
97 Rocco Baldelli   .40
98 Woody Williams   .40
99 Jason Frasor   .40
100 Baltimore Orioles   .40
101 Ivan Rodriguez/SP   6.00
102 Joe Kennedy   .40
103 Mike Lowell   .50
104 Armando Benitez   .40
105 Craig Biggio   .50
106 David DeJesus   .40
107 Adrian Beltre   .75
108 Phil Nevin   .40
109 Cristian Guzman   .40
110 Jorge Posada/SP   6.00
111 Boston Red Sox   .75
112 Jeff Mathis   .40
113 Bartolo Colon   .40
114 Alex Cintron   .40
115 Russ Ortiz   .40
116 Doug Mientkiewicz   .40
117 Placido Polanco   .40
118 Magglio Ordonez   .40
118 Magglio Ordonez/SP/
    1956 White Sox Uni.   4.00
119 Chris Seddon RC   1.00
120 Bobby Abreu   .50
121 Pittsburgh Pirates   .40
122 Dallas McPherson   .75
123 Rodrigo Lopez   .40
124 Mark Bellhorn   .40
125 Nomar Garciaparra   2.00
125 Nomar Garciaparra/SP/
    1956 Cubs Uniform   8.00
126 Sean Casey   .40
127 Ronnie Belliard   .40
128 Tom Goodwin   .40
129 Preston Wilson   .40
130 Andruw Jones/SP   5.00
131 Roberto Alomar   .75
132 John Buck   .40
133 Jason LaRue   .40
134 St. Louis Cardinals   .75
135 Alex Rodriguez/SP   10.00
135 Alex Rodriguez/
    SP/Fld   10.00
136 Nate Robertson   .40
137 Juan Pierre   .40
138 Morgan Ensberg   .40
139 Vinny Castilla   .40
140 Jake Dittler   1.00
141 Chan Ho Park   .40
142 Felix Hernandez   2.50
143 Jason Isringhausen   .40
144 Dustan Mohr   .40
145 Khalil Greene   .75
146 Minnesota Twins   .40
147 Vicente Padilla   .40
148 Oliver Perez   .40
149 Brian Giles   .40
150 Shawn Green   .40
151 Matt Lawton   .40
152 Casey Blake   .40
153 Frank Thomas   .75
154 Orlando Hernandez   .40
155 Eric Chavez   .50

155 Eric Chavez/SP/1956
    Kansas City Uniform   4.00
156 Chase Utley   .75
157 John Olerud   .40
158 Adam Eaton   .40
159 Josh Fogg   .40
160 Michael Tucker   .40
161 Kevin Brown   .40
162 Bobby Crosby   .50
163 Jason Schmidt   .50
164 Shannon Stewart   .40
165 Tony Womack   .40
166 Los Angeles Dodgers   .40
167 Franklin Gutierrez   .40
168 Ted Lilly   .40
169 Mark Teixeira   .50
170 Matt Morris   .40
171 Bucky Jacobsen   .40
172 Steven Doetsch RC   1.00
173 Jeff Weaver   .40
174 Tony Graffanino   .40
175 Jeff Bagwell   .75
176 Carl Pavano   .50
177 Junior Spivey   .40
178 Carlos Silva   .40
179 Tim Redding   .40
180 Brett Myers   .40
181 Mike Mussina   .75
182 Richard Hidalgo   .40
183 Nick Johnson   .40
184 Lew Ford   .40
185 Barry Zito   .50
186 Jimmy Rollins   .50
187 Jack Wilson   .40
188 Chicago White Sox   .40
189 Guillermo Quiroz   .40
190 Mark Hendrickson   .40
191 Jeremy Bonderman   .40
192 Jason Jennings   .40
193 Paul LoDuca   .40
194 A.J. Burnett   .40
195 Ken Harvey   .40
196 Geoff Jenkins   .40
197 Joe Mays   .40
198 Jose Vidro   .40
199 David Wright   .75
200 Randy Johnson   1.00
201 Jeff DeVanon   .40
202 Paul Byrd   .40
203 David Ortiz   1.00
204 Kyle Farnsworth   .40
205 Keith Foulke   .40
206 Joe Crede   .40
207 Austin Kearns   .40
208 Jody Gerut   .40
209 Shawn Chacon   .40
210 Carlos Pena   .40
211 Luis Castillo   .40
212 Chris Denorfia RC   1.00
213 Detroit Tigers   .40
214 Aubrey Huff   .40
215 Brad Fullmer   .40
216 Frank Catalanotto   .40
217 Raul Ibanez   .40
218 Ryan Klesko   .40
219 Octavio Dotel   .40
220 Robert Mackowiak   .40
221 Scott Hatteberg   .40
222 Pat Burrell   .40
223 Bernie Williams   .50
224 Kris Benson   .40
225 Eric Gagne   .50
226 San Francisco Giants   .40
227 Roy Oswalt   .40
228 Josh Beckett   .50
229 Lee Mazzilli   .40
230 Rickie Weeks   .40
231 Troy Glaus   .50
232 Chone Figgins   .40
233 John Thomson   .40
234 Trot Nixon   .40
235 Brad Penny   .40
236 Oakland Athletics   .40
237 Miguel Batista   .40
238 Ryan Drese   .40
239 Aaron Miles   .40
240 Randy Wolf   .40
241 Brian Lawrence   .40
242 A.J. Pierzynski   .40
243 Jamie Moyer   .40
244 Chris Carpenter   .40
245 So Taguchi   .40
246 Rob Bell   .40
247 Francisco Cordero   .40
248 Tom Glavine   .50
249 Jermaine Dye   .40
250 Cliff Lee   .40
251 New York Yankees   .75
252 Vernon Wells   .40
253 R.A. Dickey   .40
254 Larry Walker   .50
255 Randy Winn   .40
256 Pedro Feliz   .40
257 Mark Loretta   .40

258 Tim Worrell   .40
259 Kip Wells   .40
260 Cesar Izturis/SP   4.00
261 Carlos Beltran   .75
261 Carlos Beltran/SP/Btg   6.00
262 Juan Encarnacion   .40
263 Luis Gonzalez   .40
264 Grady Sizemore   .75
265 Paul Wilson   .40
266 Mark Buehrle   .40
267 Todd Hollandsworth   .40
268 Orlando Cabrera   .50
269 Sidney Ponson   .40
270 Mike Hampton   .40
271 Luis Gonzalez   .50
272 Brendan Donnelly   .40
273 Chipper Jones   1.00
273 Chipper Jones/SP/
    Blue Background   6.00
274 Brandon Webb   .40
275 Marty Cordova   .40
276 Greg Maddux   2.00
277 Jose Contreras   .40
278 Aaron Harang   .40
279 Coco Crisp   .40
280 Bobby Higginson   .40
281 Guillermo Mota   .40
282 Andy Pettitte   .50
283 Jeremy West RC   3.00
284 Craig Brazell   .40
285 Eric Hinske   .40
286 Hank Blalock   .75
286 Hank Blalock/SP/Fld   6.00
287 B.J. Upton   .75
288 Jason Marquis   .40
289 Matt Herges   .40
290 Ramon Hernandez   .40
291 Marlon Byrd   .40
292 Ryan Sweeney/SP   8.00
293 Esteban Loaiza   .40
294 Al Leiter   .50
295 Alex Gonzalez   .40
296 Johan Santana   .75
296 Johan Santana/SP/1956
    Senators Uniform   6.00
297 Milton Bradley   .40
298 Mike Sweeney   .40
299 Wade Miller   .40
300 Sammy Sosa   2.00
300 Sammy Sosa/SP/
    Blue Jsy   8.00
301 Wily Mo Pena   .40
302 Tim Wakefield   .40
303 Rafael Palmeiro   .75
304 Rafael Furcal   .40
305 David Eckstein   .40
306 David Segui   .40
307 Kevin Millar   .40
308 Matt Clement   .40
309 Wade Robinson RC   1.00
310 Brad Radke   .40
311 Steve Finley   .40
312 Lance Berkman   .50
312 Lance Berkman/
    SP/Fld   5.00
313 Joe Randa   .40
314 Miguel Cabrera   1.00
315 Billy Koch   .40
316 Alex Sanchez   .40
317 Chin-Hui Tsao   .40
318 Omar Vizquel   .40
319 Ryan Freel   .40
320 LaTroy Hawkins   .40
321 Aaron Rowand   .40
322 Paul Konerko   .40
323 Joe Borowski   .40
324 Jarrod Washburn   .40
325 Jaret Wright   .40
326 Johnny Damon   .75
327 Corey Patterson   .50
328 Travis Hafner   .40
329 Shingo Takatsu   .40
330 Dmitri Young   .40
331 Matt Holliday   .50
332 Jeff Kent   .50
333 Desi Relaford   .40
334 Jose Hernandez   .40
335 Lyle Overbay   .40
336 Jacque Jones   .40
337 Terrmel Sledge   .40
338 Victor Zambrano   .40
339 Gary Sheffield   .75
340 Brad Wilkerson   .40
341 Ian Kinsler RC   5.00
342 Jesse Crain   .40
343 Orlando Hudson   .40
344 Laynce Nix   .40
345 Jose Cruz Jr.   .40
346 Edgar Renteria   .50
347 Eddie Guardado   .40
348 Jerome Williams   .40
349 Trevor Hoffman   .40
350 Mike Piazza   1.50
351 Jason Kendall   .40

352	Kevin Millwood	.40
353	Tim Hudson	.50
353	Tim Hudson/SP/ 1956 Braves Uniform	5.00
354	Paul Quantrill	.40
355	Jon Lieber	.40
356	Braden Looper	.40
357	Chad Cordero	.40
358	Joe Nathan	.40
359	Doug Davis	.40
360	Ian Bladergroen RC	1.00
361	Val Majewski	.40
362	Francisco Rodriguez	.40
363	Kelvim Escobar	.40
364	Marcus Giles	.40
365	Darren Fenster RC	1.00
366	David Bell	.40
367	Shea Hillenbrand	.40
368	Manny Ramirez	1.00
369	Ben Broussard	.40
370	Luis Ramirez RC	1.00
371	Dustin Hermanson	.40
372	Akinori Otsuka	.40
373	Chadd Blasko RC	1.00
374	Delmon Young	.75
375	Michael Young	.40
376	Bret Boone	.40
377	Jake Peavy	.40
378	Matt Lindstrom RC	1.00
379	Sean Burroughs	.40
380	Rich Harden	.40
381	Chris Roberson RC	1.00
382	John Lackey	.40
383	Johnny Estrada	.40
384	Matt Rogelstad RC	1.00
385	Toby Hall	.40
386	Adam LaRoche	.40
387	Bill Hall	.40
388	Tim Salmon	.50
389	Curt Schilling	1.00
389	Curt Schilling/SP/ Looking In	6.00
390	Michael Barrett	.40
391	Jose Acevedo	.40
392	Nate Schierholtz	1.00
393	J.T. Snow Jr.	.40
394	Mark Redman	.40
395	Ryan Madson	.40
396	Kevin West RC	1.00
397	Ramon Ortiz	.40
398	Derek Lowe	4.00
399	Kerry Wood	6.00
400	Derek Jeter	15.00
401	Livan Hernandez	4.00
402	Casey Kotchman	6.00
403	Chaz Lytle RC	6.00
404	Alexis Rios	5.00
405	Scott Spiezio	4.00
406	Craig Wilson	4.00
407	Felix Rodriguez	4.00
408	D'Angelo Jimenez	4.00
409	Rondell White	4.00
410	Shawn Estes	4.00
411	Troy Percival	4.00
412	Melvin Mora	4.00
413	Aramis Ramirez	6.00
414	Carl Everett	4.00
415	Elvys Quezada RC	6.00
416	Ben Sheets	5.00
417	Matt Stairs	4.00
418	Adam Everett	4.00
419	Jason Johnson	4.00
420	Billy Butler RC	15.00
421	Justin Morneau	6.00
422	Jose Reyes	6.00
423	Mariano Rivera	5.00
424	Jose Vaquedano RC	6.00
425	Gabe Gross	5.00
426	Scott Rolen	6.00
427	Ty Wigginton	4.00
428	James Jurries RC	6.00
429	Pedro J. Martinez	6.00
430	Mark Grudzielanek	4.00
431	Josh Phelps	4.00
432	Ryan Goleski RC	5.00
433	Mike Matheny	4.00
434	Bobby Kielty	4.00
435	Tony Batista	4.00
436	Corey Koskie	4.00
437	Brad Lidge	4.00
438	Dontrelle Willis	4.00
439	Angel Berroa	4.00
440	Jason Kubel	4.00
441	Roy Halladay	4.00
442	Brian Roberts	4.00
443	Bill Mueller	4.00
444	Adam Kennedy	4.00
445	Brandon Moss RC	5.00
446	Sean Burnett	4.00
447	Eric Byrnes	4.00
448	Matt Campbell RC	6.00
449	Ryan Webb RC	6.00
450	Jose Valentin	4.00
451	Jake Westbrook	4.00
452	Glen Perkins RC	6.00
453	Alex Gonzalez	4.00
454	Jeromy Burnitz	4.00
455	Zack Greinke	4.00
456	Sean Marshall RC	6.00
457	Erubiel Durazo	4.00
458	Michael Cuddyer	4.00
459	Hee Seop Choi	4.00
460	Melky Cabrera RC	10.00
461	Jerry Hairston Jr.	4.00
462	Moises Alou	5.00
463	Michael Rogers RC	6.00
464	Javy Lopez	4.00
465	Freddy Garcia	4.00
466	Brett Harper RC	5.00
467	Juan Gonzalez	5.00
468	Kevin Melillo RC	5.00
469	Todd Walker	5.00
470	C.C. Sabathia	4.00
471	Kole Strayhorn	5.00
472	Mark Kotsay	4.00
473	Javier Vazquez	4.00
474	Mike Cameron	4.00
475	Wes Swackhamer RC	6.00

Chrome Parallel

		NM/M
Complete Set (110):		
Common Player:		1.00
Production 1,956 Sets		
Refractors:		1.5-2X
Production 556 Sets		
Black Refractor:		3-5X
Production 56 Sets		
THC1	Will Harridge	2.00
THC2	Warren Giles	2.00
THC3	Alex Rodriguez	10.00
THC4	Alfonso Soriano	5.00
THC5	Barry Bonds	12.00
THC6	Todd Helton	3.00
THC7	Kazuo Matsui	2.00
THC8	Garret Anderson	1.50
THC9	Mark Prior	5.00
THC10	Jim Thome	4.00
THC11	Jason Giambi	2.00
THC12	Ivan Rodriguez	4.00
THC13	Mike Lowell	1.00
THC14	Vladimir Guerrero	5.00
THC15	Adrian Beltre	2.00
THC16	Andruw Jones	2.00
THC17	Jose Vidro	1.00
THC18	Josh Beckett	1.50
THC19	Mike Sweeney	1.00
THC20	Sammy Sosa	6.00
THC21	Scott Rolen	5.00
THC22	Javy Lopez	1.50
THC23	Albert Pujols	12.00
THC24	Adam Dunn	3.00
THC25	Ken Griffey Jr.	6.00
THC26	Torii Hunter	1.50
THC27	Jorge Posada	2.00
THC28	Magglio Ordonez	1.00
THC29	Shawn Green	1.50
THC30	Frank Thomas	3.00
THC31	Barry Zito	1.50
THC32	David Ortiz	5.00
THC33	Pat Burrell	1.50
THC34	Luis Gonzalez	1.50
THC35	Chipper Jones	5.00
THC36	Hank Blalock	3.00
THC37	Rafael Palmeiro	2.00
THC38	Lance Berkman	2.00
THC39	Miguel Cabrera	5.00
THC40	Paul Konerko	1.00
THC41	Jeff Kent	1.50
THC42	Gary Sheffield	3.00
THC43	Mike Piazza	6.00
THC44	Bret Boone	1.00
THC45	Kerry Wood	5.00
THC46	Derek Jeter	12.00
THC47	Pedro J. Martinez	5.00
THC48	Jason Bay	2.00
THC49	Ichiro Suzuki	8.00
THC50	Miguel Tejada	3.00
THC51	Richie Sexson	2.00
THC52	Jeff Bagwell	3.00
THC53	Lew Ford	1.00
THC54	Randy Johnson	5.00
THC55	Carlos Beltran	3.00
THC56	Greg Maddux	6.00
THC57	Lyle Overbay	1.00
THC58	Michael Young	1.00
THC59	Curt Schilling	5.00
THC60	Jose Reyes	3.00
THC61	Dontrelle Willis	1.50
THC62	Nomar Garciaparra	6.00
THC63	Paul LoDuca	1.00
THC64	Larry Walker	2.00
THC65	Andre Ethier	8.00
THC66	Matt DeSalvo	5.00
THC67	Brian Stavisky	2.00
THC68	Tyler Clippard	20.00
THC69	Chris Seddon	3.00
THC70	Steven Doetsch	3.00
THC71	Chris Denorfia	2.00
THC72	Jeremy West	3.00
THC73	Ryan Sweeney	5.00
THC74	Ian Kinsler	10.00
THC75	Ian Bladergroen	4.00
THC76	Darren Fenster	4.00
THC77	Luis Ramirez	2.00
THC78	Chadd Blasko	2.00
THC79	Matt Lindstrom	2.00
THC80	Chris Roberson	3.00
THC81	Matt Rogelstad	3.00
THC82	Nate Schierholtz	4.00
THC83	Kevin West	4.00
THC84	Chaz Lytle	4.00
THC85	Elvys Quezada	4.00
THC86	Billy Butler	15.00
THC87	Jose Vaquedano	4.00
THC88	James Jurries	4.00
THC89	Ryan Goleski	4.00
THC90	Brandon Moss	4.00
THC91	Matt Campbell	4.00
THC92	Ryan Webb	4.00
THC93	Glen Perkins	5.00
THC94	Sean Marshall	4.00
THC95	Melky Cabrera	8.00
THC96	Michael Rogers	4.00
THC97	Brett Harper	4.00
THC98	Kevin Melillo	4.00
THC99	Kole Strayhorn	4.00
THC100	Wes Swackhamer	4.00
THC101	Rickie Weeks	2.00
THC102	Delmon Young	4.00
THC103	Kazuhito Tadano	1.00
THC104	Kazuhisa Ishii	1.00
THC105	David Wright	4.00
THC106	Eric Gagne	3.00
THC107	So Taguchi	1.00
THC108	B.J. Upton	4.00
THC109	Shingo Takatsu	1.00
THC110	Akinori Otsuka	1.00

Clubhouse Collection
Relic Autograph

		NM/M
Production 25 Sets		
LA	Luis Aparicio	165.00
EB	Ernie Banks	200.00
AK	Al Kaline	200.00
HK	Harmon Killebrew	200.00
RS	Red Schoendienst	165.00

Clubhouse Collection
Relics

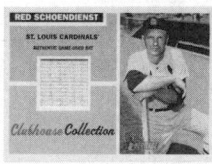

		NM/M
Common Player:		5.00
LA	Luis Aparicio	8.00
EB	Ernie Banks	15.00
LB	Lance Berkman	5.00
MC	Miguel Cabrera	8.00
AK	Al Kaline	15.00
HK	Harmon Killebrew	15.00
AP	Albert Pujols	20.00
MR	Manny Ramirez	8.00
AR	Alex Rodriguez	15.00
RS	Red Schoendienst	8.00
GS	Gary Sheffield	8.00
AS	Alfonso Soriano	8.00
MT	Miguel Tejada	8.00
BW	Bernie Williams	8.00
DW	Dontrelle Willis	5.00

Clubhouse Collection
Dual Relics

		NM/M
Production 56 Sets		
MP	Stan Musial, Albert Pujols	85.00
KR	Al Kaline, Ivan Rodriguez	65.00
BG	Ernie Banks, Nomar Garciaparra	85.00

Flashbacks

SEPTEMBER 30, 1956
HANK AARON WINS NL BATTING CROWN WITH .328 BATTING AVERAGE.

		NM/M
Complete Set (10):		8.00
Common Player:		.50
Inserted 1:12		
HA	Hank Aaron	4.00
LA	Luis Aparicio	.50
EB	Ernie Banks	2.00
BF	Bob Feller	.50
AK	Al Kaline	1.50
DL	Don Larsen	.50
SM	Stan Musial	2.00
FR	Frank Robinson	1.00
HS	Herb Score	.50
DS	Duke Snider	1.00

Flashbacks Autographs

		NM/M
Common Player:		
Production 25 Sets		
LA	Luis Aparicio	125.00
EB	Ernie Banks	200.00
BF	Bob Feller	165.00
AK	Al Kaline	165.00
DL	Don Larsen	175.00
SM	Stan Musial	200.00
FR	Frank Robinson	200.00
HS	Herb Score	150.00

Flashbacks Relic Autographs

YANKEE STADIUM BRONX, NY   AUTHENTIC STADIUM SEAT
OCTOBER 8, 1956
DON LARSEN PITCHES A PERFECT GAME IN THE WORLD SERIES

		NM/M
Production 25 Sets		
LA	Luis Aparicio	150.00
EB	Ernie Banks	200.00
BF	Bob Feller	175.00
AK	Al Kaline	175.00
DL	Don Larsen	175.00
SM	Stan Musial	200.00
FR	Frank Robinson	200.00
HS	Herb Score	150.00

Flashbacks Relics

	NM/M
Common Player:	8.00

SEPTEMBER 30, 1956
DUKE SNIDER'S 2 HOMERS LEAD DODGERS TO PENNANT ON LAST DAY OF SEASON.

AUTHENTIC STADIUM SEAT   EBBETS FIELD, BROOKLYN, NEW YORK

Inserted 1:96

		NM/M
HA	Hank Aaron	15.00
LA	Luis Aparicio	8.00
EB	Ernie Banks	15.00
BF	Bob Feller	10.00
AK	Al Kaline	15.00
DL	Don Larsen	8.00
SM	Stan Musial	15.00
FR	Frank Robinson	10.00
HS	Herb Score	8.00
DS	Duke Snider	10.00

New Age Performers

New Age PERFORMERS
DEREK JETER
shortstop NEW YORK YANKEES

		NM/M
Complete Set (15):		15.00
Common Player:		1.00
Inserted 1:15		
NAP1	Alfonso Soriano	1.50
NAP2	Alex Rodriguez	3.00
NAP3	Ichiro Suzuki	3.00
NAP4	Albert Pujols	4.00
NAP5	Vladimir Guerrero	1.50
NAP6	Jim Thome	1.50
NAP7	Derek Jeter	4.00
NAP8	Sammy Sosa	2.50
NAP9	Ivan Rodriguez	1.00
NAP10	Manny Ramirez	1.50
NAP11	Todd Helton	1.00
NAP12	David Ortiz	1.50
NAP13	Gary Sheffield	1.00
NAP14	Nomar Garciaparra	2.00
NAP15	Randy Johnson	1.50

Real One Autographs

		NM/M
Production 200 Sets		
Red Ink:		1.5-2X
Production 56 Sets		
HA	Hank Aaron	250.00
JA	Joe Astroth	50.00
EB	Ernie Banks	125.00
YB	Yogi Berra	100.00
JB	Jim Brady	50.00
CD	Chuck Diering	50.00
BF	Bob Feller	70.00
JG	Jim Greengrass	50.00
MI	Monte Irvin	60.00
SJ	Spook Jacobs	50.00
FM	Fred Marsh	50.00
JM	Jake Martin	50.00
RM	Rudy Minarcin	50.00
PM	Paul Minner	50.00
BN	Bob Nelson	50.00
LP	Laurin Pepper	40.00
LPO	Leroy Powell	60.00
JSA	Jose Santiago	50.00
JS	Johnny Schmitz	50.00
DS	Duke Snider	85.00
AS	Art Swanson	50.00
BT	Bill Tremel	50.00
WW	Wally Westlake	50.00

Then and Now

HANK AARON   ICHIRO
MILWAUKEE BRAVES   SEATTLE MARINERS

		NM/M
Complete Set (10):		8.00
Common Duo:		.50
Inserted 1:15		
TN1	Hank Aaron, Ichiro Suzuki	4.00
TN2	Don Newcombe, Curt Schilling	1.50
TN3	Robin Roberts, Livan Hernandez	.50
TN4	Bob Friend, Livan Hernandez	.50
TN5	Herb Score, Randy Johnson	1.50
TN6	Whitey Ford, Jake Peavy	1.00
TN7	Jimmy Piersall, Lyle Overbay	.50
TN8	Clem Labine, Mariano Rivera	.75
TN9	Bill Bruton, Carl Crawford	.50
TN10	Eddie Yost, Bobby Abreu	.50

1956 Cuts - Cut Signatures

No Pricing
Production One Set

2005 Topps Opening Day

		NM/M
Complete Set (165):		30.00
Common Player:		.15
Pack (6):		1.00
Box (36):		30.00
1	Alex Rodriguez	1.50
2	Placido Polanco	.15
3	Torii Hunter	.25
4	Lyle Overbay	.15
5	Johnny Damon	.50
6	Mike Cameron	.15
7	Ichiro Suzuki	1.50
8	Francisco Rodriguez	.15
9	Bobby Crosby	.25
10	Sammy Sosa	1.25
11	Randy Wolf	.15
12	Jason Bay	.25
13	Mike Lieberthal	.15
14	Paul Konerko	.15
15	Brian Giles	.15
16	Luis Gonzalez	.25
17	Jim Edmonds	.40
18	Carlos Lee	.25
19	Corey Patterson	.40
20	Hank Blalock	.50
21	Sean Casey	.25
22	Dmitri Young	.25
23	Mark Mulder	.25
24	Bobby Abreu	.25
25	Jim Thome	.50
26	Jason Kendall	.15
27	Jason Giambi	.25
28	Vinny Castilla	.15
29	Tony Batista	.15
30	Ivan Rodriguez	.50
31	Craig Biggio	.25
32	Chris Carpenter	.15
33	Adrian Beltre	.40
34	Scott Podsednik	.15
35	Cliff Floyd	.15
36	Chad Tracy	.15
37	John Smoltz	.25
38	Shingo Takatsu	.15
39	Jack Wilson	.15
40	Gary Sheffield	.50
41	Lance Berkman	.25
42	Carl Crawford	.25
43	Carlos Guillen	.15
44	David Bell	.15
45	Kazuo Matsui	.15
46	Jason Schmidt	.25
47	Jason Marquis	.15
48	Melvin Mora	.15
49	David Ortiz	.50
50	Andruw Jones	.40
51	Miguel Tejada	.50
52	Bartolo Colon	.15

53	Derek Lee	.25
54	Eric Gagne	.25
55	Miguel Cabrera	.75
56	Travis Hafner	.15
57	Jose Valentin	.15
58	Mark Prior	.75
59	Phil Nevin	.15
60	Jose Vidro	.15
61	Khalil Greene	.25
62	Carlos Zambrano	.40
63	Erubiel Durazo	.15
64	Michael Young	.15
65	Woody Williams	.15
66	Edgardo Alfonzo	.15
67	Troy Glaus	.40
68	Garret Anderson	.25
69	Richie Sexson	.40
70	Curt Schilling	.75
71	Randy Johnson	.75
72	Chipper Jones	.75
73	J.D. Drew	.25
74	Russ Ortiz	.15
75	Frank Thomas	.50
76	Jimmy Rollins	.25
77	Barry Zito	.25
78	Rafael Palmeiro	.50
79	Brad Wilkerson	.15
80	Adam Dunn	.50
81	Doug Mientkiewicz	.15
82	Manny Ramirez	.75
83	Pedro J. Martinez	.75
84	Moises Alou	.25
85	Mike Sweeney	.15
86	Boston Red Sox WC	1.00
87	Matt Clement	.15
88	Nomar Garciaparra	1.00
89	Magglio Ordonez	.15
90	Bret Boone	.15
91	Mark Loretta	.15
92	Jose Contreras	.15
93	Randy Winn	.15
94	Austin Kearns	.15
95	Ken Griffey Jr.	1.25
96	Jake Westbrook	.15
97	Kazuhito Tadano	.15
98	C.C. Sabathia	.15
99	Todd Helton	.50
100	Albert Pujols	2.00
101	Jose Molina	.15
102	Aaron Miles	.15
103	Mike Lowell	.25
104	Paul LoDuca	.15
105	Juan Pierre	.15
106	Dontrelle Willis	.40
107	Jeff Bagwell	.40
108	Carlos Beltran	.50
109	Ronnie Belliard	.15
110	Roy Oswalt	.25
111	Zack Greinke	.15
112	Steve Finley	.15
113	Kazuhisa Ishii	.15
114	Justin Morneau	.40
115	Ben Sheets	.25
116	Johan Santana	.50
117	Billy Wagner	.15
118	Mariano Rivera	.25
119	Corey Koskie	.15
120	Akinori Otsuka	.15
121	Joe Mauer	.40
122	Jacque Jones	.15
123	Joe Nathan	.15
124	Nick Johnson	.15
125	Vernon Wells	.15
126	Mike Piazza	1.00
127	Jose Guillen	.15
128	Jose Reyes	.25
129	Marcus Giles	.15
130	Javy Lopez	.25
131	Kevin Millar	.15
132	Jorge Posada	.40
133	Carl Pavano	.25
134	Bernie Williams	.40
135	Kerry Wood	.75
136	Matt Holiday	.15
137	Kevin Brown	.15
138	Derek Jeter	2.00
139	Barry Bonds	2.00
140	Jeff Kent	.25
141	Mark Kotsay	.15
142	Shawn Green	.25
143	Tim Hudson	.25
144	Shannon Stewart	.15
145	Pat Burrell	.25
146	Gavin Floyd	.15
147	Mike Mussina	.50
148	Eric Chavez	.25
149	Jon Lieber	.15
150	Vladimir Guerrero	.75
151	Vicente Padilla	.15
152	Ryan Klesko	.15
153	Jake Peavy	.25
154	Scott Rolen	.75
155	Greg Maddux	1.00
156	Edgar Renteria	.25

157	Larry Walker	.25
158	Scott Kazmir	.25
159	B.J. Upton	.25
160	Mark Teixeira	.50
161	Ken Harvey	.15
162	Alfonso Soriano	.75
163	Carlos Delgado	.40
164	Alexis Rios	.15
165	Checklist	.15

Autographs

		NM/M
Complete Set (6):		
Common Player:		
CC	Chad Cordero	10.00
FH	Felix Hernandez	25.00
AH	Aaron Hill	8.00
PM	Paul Maholm	8.00
OQ	Omar Quintanilla	15.00
AW	Anthony Whittington	8.00

MLB Game Worn Jersey Collection

		NM/M
Target Retail Exclusive		
37	Vladimir Guerrero	8.00
38	Albert Pujols	15.00
39	Torii Hunter	4.00
40	Alfonso Soriano	6.00
41	Bobby Abreu	6.00
42	Moises Alou	6.00
43	Sean Burroughs	4.00
44	Shannon Stewart	4.00
45	Troy Glaus	6.00
46	Fernando Vina	4.00
47	Dan Wilson	4.00
48	Paul Konerko	4.00
49	Jimmy Rollins	6.00
50	Livan Hernandez	4.00
51	Sean Casey	4.00
52	Paul LoDuca	4.00
53	Richie Sexson	6.00
54	Aubrey Huff	4.00

2005 Topps Pack Wars

SEAN BURROUGHS 114

PACK WARS

		NM/M
Complete Set (175):		40.00
Common Player:		.25
Pack (7):		20.00
Box (7):		120.00
1	Alex Rodriguez	3.00
2	Eric Chavez	.40
3	Jimmy Rollins	.40
4	Jason Bay	.50
5	Nomar Carciaparra	2.00
6	Melvin Mora	.25
7	Bobby Abreu	.50
8	Bartolo Colon	.25
9	Orlando Cabrera	1.00
10	Albert Pujols	3.00
11	Barry Zito	.40
12	Vernon Wells	.25
13	J.D. Drew	.40
14	Darin Erstad	.25
15	Manny Ramirez	1.00
16	Derek Lee	.40
17	Juan Uribe	.25
18	Wily Mo Pena	.25
19	Jeromy Burnitz	.25
20	Dontrelle Willis	.50
21	Craig Biggio	.40
22	Cesar Izturis	.25
23	Geoff Jenkins	.25
24	Joe Mauer	.50
25	Derek Jeter	3.00
26	David Wright	1.00
27	Jose Vidro	.25
28	Bobby Crosby	.25
29	Khalil Greene	.40
30	Ichiro Suzuki	2.00
31	Reggie Sanders	.25

32	A.J. Pierzynski	.25
33	Corey Patterson	.40
34	Frank Thomas	.75
35	Craig Wilson	.25
36	Carl Crawford	.25
37	Michael Young	.25
38	Mark Kotsay	.25
39	Javier Vazquez	.25
40	Kazuo Matsui	.25
41	Lew Ford	.25
42	Corey Koskie	.25
43	Larry Walker	.50
44	Mike Lowell	.40
45	Todd Helton	.75
46	Travis Hafner	.25
47	Sean Casey	.25
48	Ken Griffey Jr.	1.50
49	Milton Bradley	.25
50	Ivan Rodriguez	.75
51	Carlos Lee	.25
52	Aramis Ramirez	.50
53	Curt Schilling	1.00
54	Russ Ortiz	.25
55	Randy Johnson	1.00
56	Preston Wilson	.25
57	Jay Gibbons	.25
58	Mike Lieberthal	.25
59	Johnny Damon	.75
60	Mark Prior	1.00
61	Freddy Garcia	.25
62	Casey Blake	.25
63	Chipper Jones	1.00
64	Carlos Guillen	.25
65	Juan Pierre	.25
66	Tom Glavine	.50
67	Alex Sanchez	.25
68	Tony Batista	.25
69	Paul LoDuca	.25
70	Hank Blalock	.75
71	Pedro Feliz	.25
72	Jim Edmonds	.50
73	Phil Nevin	.25
74	Rocco Baldelli	.25
75	Alfonso Soriano	1.00
76	David Bell	.25
77	Eric Hinske	.25
78	Jose Guillen	.25
79	Marcus Giles	.25
80	Rafael Palmeiro	.75
81	Jeff Bagwell	.75
82	Kerry Wood	1.00
83	Johan Santana	.75
84	Troy Glaus	.40
85	Andruw Jones	.50
86	Barry Bonds	3.00
87	Jermaine Dye	.25
88	Carlos Zambrano	.50
89	Aaron Rowand	.25
90	Garret Anderson	.40
91	Ryan Klesko	.25
92	Paul Konerko	.25
93	Jeff Kent	.40
94	Richie Sexson	.50
95	Lyle Overbay	.25
96	Torii Hunter	.40
97	Mike Cameron	.25
98	Eric Byrnes	.25
99	Jason Kendall	.25
100	Vladimir Guerrero	1.00
101	Johnny Estrada	.25
102	Mark Bellhorn	.25
103	Moises Alou	.40
104	Ronnie Belliard	.25
105	Adam Dunn	.75
106	Dmitri Young	.25
107	Luis Castillo	.25
108	Carlos Beltran	.75
109	Steve Finley	.25
110	Shannon Stewart	.25
111	Al Leiter	.25
112	Bernie Williams	.50
113	Roy Oswalt	.40
114	Sean Burroughs	.25
115	Randy Winn	.25
116	Tony Womack	.25
117	Jim Thome	1.00
118	Aubrey Huff	.25
119	Bret Boone	.25
120	Carlos Delgado	.40
121	Jason Schmidt	.50
122	Rafael Furcal	.25
123	Miguel Tejada	.75
124	Bill Mueller	.25
125	Pedro Martinez	1.00
126	Michael Barrett	.25
127	Jody Gerut	.25
128	Vinny Castilla	.25
129	Rondell White	.25
130	Magglio Ordonez	.25
131	Lance Berkman	.25
132	Alex Gonzalez	.25
133	Mike Sweeney	.25
134	Ben Sheets	.50
135	Jacque Jones	.25
136	Brad Wilkerson	.25
137	Cliff Floyd	.25
138	Kevin Brown	.25
139	Scott Hatteberg	.25
140	Gary Sheffield	.50
141	Justin Morneau	.50
142	Scott Podsednik	.25
143	Shawn Green	.40
144	David Ortiz	1.00
145	Josh Beckett	.50
146	Tim Hudson	.50
147	Matt Lawton	.25
148	Mark Buehrle	.25
149	Todd Walker	.25
150	Jason Giambi	.50
151	Brian Giles	.25
152	Erubiel Durazo	.25
153	Jack Wilson	.25
154	Jose Reyes	.50
155	Scott Rolen	1.00
156	Raul Ibanez	.25
157	Mark Teixeira	.50
158	Luis Gonzalez	.25
159	Javy Lopez	.25
160	Greg Maddux	1.50
161	Kevin Millar	.25
162	Jose Valentin	.25
163	C.C. Sabathia	.25
164	Carlos Pena	.25
165	Miguel Cabrera	1.00
166	Adrian Beltre	.50
167	Sammy Sosa	2.00
168	Nick Johnson	.25
169	Jorge Posada	.50
170	Mike Piazza	1.50
171	Mark Mulder	.50
172	Mark Loretta	.25
173	Edgardo Alfonzo	.25
174	Edgar Renteria	.50
175	Pat Burrell	.25

Autographs

		NM/M
Common Autograph:		15.00
CB	Carlos Beltran	30.00
HB	Hank Blalock	20.00
BB	Barry Bonds	
AB	Aaron Boone	20.00
MC	Miguel Cabrera	25.00
EC	Eric Chavez	15.00
JE	Johnny Estrada	10.00
KG	Khalil Greene	
ZG	Zack Greinke	15.00
VM	Victor Martinez	15.00
AR	Alex Rodriguez	
CS	C.C. Sabathia	15.00
VW	Vernon Wells	10.00
MY	Michael Young	15.00

Collector Chips

		NM/M
Common Player:		8.00
Inserted 1:Box		
Blue:		No Pricing
Production 25 Sets		
Red:		No Pricing
Production 10 Sets		
1	Alex Rodriguez	
2	Ichiro Suzuki	30.00
3	Jim Thome	20.00
4	Albert Pujols	30.00
5	Vladimir Guerrero	15.00
6	Derek Jeter	30.00
7	Sammy Sosa	20.00
8	Barry Bonds	
9	Ivan Rodriguez	10.00
10	Alfonso Soriano	
11	Nomar Garciaparra	20.00
12	Ken Griffey Jr.	20.00
13	Mark Prior	10.00
14	Todd Helton	10.00
15	Mike Piazza	10.00
16	Jorge Posada	10.00
17	Chipper Jones	10.00
18	Randy Johnson	15.00
19	Gary Sheffield	8.00
20	Mike Schmidt	25.00
21	Ernie Banks	20.00
22	Frank Robinson	25.00
23	Reggie Jackson	10.00
24	George Brett	25.00
25	Nolan Ryan	30.00

Cut Signatures

No Pricing

Relics

		NM/M
Common Player:		8.00
RC	Roger Clemens	12.00
NG	Nomar Garciaparra	15.00
VG	Vladimir Guerrero	10.00
TH	Todd Helton	8.00
THB	Todd Helton	8.00
CJ	Chipper Jones	8.00
CJB	Chipper Jones	8.00
GM	Greg Maddux	10.00
PM	Pedro Martinez	8.00
RP	Rafael Palmeiro	8.00
MP	Mike Piazza	10.00
AP	Albert Pujols	15.00
MR	Manny Ramirez	10.00
MRB	Manny Ramirez	10.00
AR	Alex Rodriquez	15.00
IR	Ivan Rodriguez	8.00
SR	Scott Rolen	10.00
GS	Gary Sheffield	8.00
AS	Alfonso Soriano	10.00
SS	Sammy Sosa	10.00
FT	Frank Thomas	8.00
JT	Jim Thome	8.00

Relic Autographs

		NM/M
Common Autograph:		15.00
Production 200 Sets		
CB	Carlos Beltran	40.00
HB	Hank Blalock	25.00
MC	Miguel Cabrera	30.00
EC	Eric Chavez	20.00
JE	Johnny Estrada	15.00
VM	Victor Martinez	15.00
MY	Michael Young	20.00

2005 Topps Pristine

		NM/M
Common 1-100		.75
Common Rookie (101-130):		1.00
Common (131-180):		3.00
Production 500		
Common (181-205):		10.00
Production 100		
Common (206-210):		
Production 49		
Pack (8):		30.00
Box (5):		125.00
1	Alex Rodriguez	3.00
2	Jake Peavy	.75
3	Bobby Crosby	.75
4	J.D. Drew	.75
5	Scott Rolen	1.50
6	Bobby Abreu	.75
7	Ken Griffey Jr.	2.50
8	Jeremy Bonderman	.75
9	Mike Sweeney	.75
10	Mark Prior	1.50
11	Tim Hudson	.75
12	Clint Barmes	.75
13	Jeff Bagwell	1.00
14	Andruw Jones	1.50
15	Carlos Delgado	.75
16	Rocco Baldelli	.75
17	Adam Dunn	1.50
18	Greg Maddux	2.00
19	Torii Hunter	.75
20	Miguel Tejada	1.50
21	Lyle Overbay	.75
22	Craig Wilson	.75
23	Scott Kazmir	.75
24	Alex Rios	.75
25	Ichiro Suzuki	3.00
26	Jorge Posada	1.00
27	Jose Reyes	.75
28	Hank Blalock	.75
29	Troy Glaus	1.00
30	Todd Helton	1.50
31	Javy Lopez	.75
32	Barry Zito	1.00
33	Jimmy Rollins	1.00
34	Mark Loretta	.75
35	Richie Sexson	1.00
36	Nick Johnson	.75
37	Ivan Rodriguez	1.00
38	Jeff Kent	.75
39	Jake Westbrook	.75
40	Carlos Beltran	1.00
41	Rich Harden	.75
42	Joe Mauer	1.00
43	Luis Gonzalez	.75
44	Frank Thomas	1.00
45	Michael Young	.75
46	Jason Schmidt	.75
47	Eric Chavez	.75
48	Vinny Castilla	.75
49	John Smoltz	1.00
50	Barry Bonds	4.00
51	Jim Edmonds	1.00
52	Edgar Renteria	.75
53	Jose Vidro	.75
54	Chipper Jones	1.50
55	Curt Schilling	1.50
56	Victor Martinez	.75
57	Josh Beckett	.75
58	Derek Lee	1.50
59	Shawn Green	.75
60	Roger Clemens	4.00
61	Orlando Cabrera	.75
62	Mike Piazza	2.00
63	Gary Sheffield	1.00
64	Carl Crawford	.75
65	Johan Santana	1.50
66	Oliver Perez	.75
67	Manny Ramirez	1.50
68	Paul Konerko	1.00
69	Preston Wilson	.75
70	Sammy Sosa	2.00
71	Eric Gagne	.75
72	Geoff Jenkins	.75
73	Magglio Ordonez	.75
74	Kerry Wood	1.00
75	Albert Pujols	4.00
76	Roy Halladay	1.00
77	Aubrey Huff	.75
78	Nomar Garciaparra	1.50
79	Brian Roberts	.75
80	Randy Johnson	1.50
81	Pat Burrell	.75
82	Brian Giles	.75
83	Mike Mussina	1.00
84	Mark Teixeira	1.00
85	Pedro Martinez	1.50
86	Jason Bay	.75
87	Mark Buehrle	.75
88	Rafael Furcal	.75
89	Juan Pierre	.75
90	Jim Thome	1.00
91	Ben Sheets	1.00
92	Alfonso Soriano	1.50
93	Adrian Beltre	.75
94	Miguel Cabrera	1.50
95	Derek Jeter	4.00
96	Vernon Wells	.75
97	Lance Berkman	1.00
98	Hideki Matsui	2.50
99	David Ortiz	1.50
100	Vladimir Guerrero	1.50
101	Justin Verlander RC	3.00
102	Billy Butler RC	8.00
103	Wladimir Balentien RC	2.00
104	Jeremy West RC	2.00
105	Philip Humber RC	3.00
106	Tyler Pelland RC	1.00
107	Andy LaRoche RC	5.00
108	Hernan Iribarren RC	1.00
109	Luke Scott RC	1.00
110	Landon Powell RC	1.00
111	Alexander Smit RC	1.00
112	Ryan Garko RC	1.00
113	Bear Bay RC	1.00
114	Ian Bladergroen RC	1.00
115	Manny Parra RC	1.00
116	Andy Sides RC	1.00
117	Travis Chick RC	1.00
118	Stefan Bailie RC	1.00
119	Chuck Tiffany RC	2.00
120	Buck Coats RC	1.00
121	Jeff Niemann RC	2.00
122	Jake Postlewait RC	1.00
123	Matt Campbell RC	1.00
124	Kevin Melillo RC	2.00
125	Mike Morse RC	1.00
126	Anthony Reyes RC	6.00
127	Casey McGehee RC	1.00
128	Cody Haerther RC	1.00
129	Brandon McCarthy RC	4.00
130	Glen Perkins RC	2.00
131	Moises Alou	3.00
132	Nomar Garciaparra	6.00
133	Scott Rolen	6.00

134	Miguel Tejada	4.00
135	Alex Rodriguez	10.00
136	Michael Young	3.00
137	Tim Hudson	5.00
138	Troy Glaus	3.00
139	Eric Chavez	3.00
140	David Ortiz	10.00
141	Andruw Jones	5.00
142	Richie Sexson	5.00
143	Jim Thome	5.00
144	Javy Lopez	3.00
145	Lance Berkman	3.00
146	Gary Sheffield	5.00
147	Dontrelle Willis	4.00
148	Curt Schilling	5.00
149	Jorge Posada	5.00
150	Vladimir Guerrero	8.00
151	Adam Dunn	5.00
152	Ryan Drese	3.00
153	Hank Blalock	3.00
154	Kerry Wood	4.00
155	Alfonso Soriano	5.00
156	Aramis Ramirez	4.00
157	Mark Mulder	4.00
158	Paul Konerko	4.00
159	Jim Edmonds	6.00
160	Roger Clemens	10.00
161	Mariano Rivera	6.00
162	Rafael Palmeiro	6.00
163	Mark Teixeira	6.00
164	Eric Gagne	3.00
165	Sammy Sosa	8.00
166	Brett Myers	3.00
167	Kazuhisa Ishii	3.00
168	Ken Harvey	3.00
169	Johnny Estrada	3.00
170	Todd Helton	5.00
171	Rich Harden	3.00
172	Johnny Damon	6.00
173	Manny Ramirez	6.00
174	Benito Santiago	3.00
175	Albert Pujols	15.00
176	Chipper Jones	.75
177	Miguel Cabrera	8.00
178	Jeff Bagwell	5.00
179	Ivan Rodriguez	5.00
180	Mike Piazza	8.00
181	Chip Cannon RC	15.00
182	Erik Cordier RC	15.00
183	Billy Butler RC	40.00
184	C.J. Smith RC	10.00
185	Alfonso Soriano	25.00
186	Bobby Livingston RC	15.00
187	Wladimir Balentien RC	25.00
188	Mike Morse RC	15.00
189	Wes Swackhamer RC	15.00
190	Justin Verlander RC	50.00
191	Jake Postlewait RC	15.00
192	Michael Rogers RC	20.00
193	Matt Campbell RC	20.00
194	Eric Nielsen RC	15.00
195	Gary Sheffield	30.00
196	Glen Perkins RC	25.00
197	Kevin Melillo RC	20.00
198	Chad Orvella RC	10.00
199	Jeff Niemann RC	25.00
200	Alex Rodriguez	180.00
201	Brian Stavisky RC	15.00
202	Brian Miller RC	15.00
203	Landon Powell RC	20.00
204	Philip Humber RC	20.00
205	Mariano Rivera	100.00
206	Curt Schilling	50.00
207	Nolan Ryan	150.00
208	Albert Pujols	
209	Stan Musial	
210	Barry Bonds	

Red

Red (1-130): 2-4X
Production 66
Red (131-210): No Pricing
Production 3 Sets

Printing Plates

No Pricing
Production one set for each color.

Uncirculated Bronze

Bronze (1-130): 1.5-3X
Production 375
Bronze (131-180): 1-1.5X
Production 100
Bronze (181-205): No Pricing
Production 18
Bronze (206-210): No Pricing
Production 10

Doubles Act Autographs

No Pricing
Production 5 Sets

Fielder's Choice

No Pricing
Production 9 Sets

In The Name Patch

No Pricing
One card for each letter.

Personal Endorsements

NM/M

Common
Production 497 Sets
Uncirculated: No Pricing
Production 3 Sets

MB	Milton Bradley	10.00
BB	Billy Butler	25.00
LC	Lance Cormier	5.00
SE	Scott Elbert	8.00
JF	Josh Fields	5.00
LH	Livan Hernandez	12.00
JPH	J.P. Howell	8.00
PH	Philip Humber	10.00
ZJ	Zach Jackson	8.00
BJ	Blake Johnson	5.00
BL	Bobby Livingston	8.00
CO	Chad Orvella	5.00
GP	Glen Perkins	15.00
LP	Landon Powell	8.00
MR	Mike Rodriguez	5.00
MRO	Mark Rogers	8.00
TS	Terrmel Sledge	5.00
CJS	C.J. Smith	5.00
JS	Jeremy Sowers	10.00
JV	Justin Verlander	20.00

Uncommon
Production 247 Sets

JB	Jason Bay	25.00
AB	Aaron Boone	10.00
MB	Matt Bush	15.00
BB	Billy Butler	25.00
CC	Chip Cannon	8.00
CE	Carl Erskine	10.00
HK	Harmon Killebrew	25.00
BL	Bobby Livingston	8.00
ML	Mark Loretta	8.00
DO	David Ortiz	40.00
CW	Craig Wilson	10.00
DW	David Wright	60.00
DZ	Don Zimmer	15.00

Rare
Production 97 Sets

GA	Garret Anderson	15.00
EB	Ernie Banks	50.00
SM	Stan Musial	50.00
MR	Mariano Rivera	100.00
TS	Tom Seaver	30.00
AS	Alfonso Soriano	25.00

Scarce
Production 22 Sets

BB	Barry Bonds
AP	Albert Pujols

Personal Pieces

NM/M

Common
Production 425
Uncirculated: No Pricing
Production 3 Sets

JB	Jeff Bagwell	5.00
RB	Ronnie Belliard	3.00
AB	Adrian Beltre	3.00
LB	Lance Berkman	5.00
HB	Hank Blalock	5.00
EC	Eric Chavez	3.00
RC	Roger Clemens	12.00
BC	Bobby Crosby	5.00
JDD	J.D. Drew	3.00
AD	Adam Dunn	5.00
JE	Jim Edmonds	3.00
JES	Johnny Estrada	3.00
JG	Jason Giambi	5.00
JGI	Jay Gibbons	3.00
SG	Shawn Green	3.00
VG	Vladimir Guerrero	8.00
CG	Cristian Guzman	3.00
THA	Travis Hafner	3.00
TH	Todd Helton	5.00
THU	Tim Hudson	5.00
AJ	Andruw Jones	5.00
CJ	Chipper Jones	8.00
JL	Javy Lopez	3.00
ML	Mark Loretta	3.00
MLO	Mike Lowell	3.00
PM	Pedro Martinez	8.00
VM	Victor Martinez	3.00
KM	Kevin Millar	3.00
MM	Mark Mulder	5.00
BM	Brett Myers	3.00
LN	Laynce Nix	3.00
MP	Mike Piazza	8.00
MPR	Mark Prior	5.00
AP	Albert Pujols	15.00
BR	Brad Radke	3.00
MR	Manny Ramirez	8.00
ER	Edgar Renteria	3.00
MRI	Mariano Rivera	6.00
SR	Scott Rolen	3.00
CS	Curt Schilling	6.00
GS	Gary Sheffield	5.00
AS	Alfonso Soriano	5.00
MTE	Mark Teixeira	5.00
MT	Miguel Tejada	5.00
FT	Frank Thomas	8.00
JT	Jim Thome	5.00
BJU	B.J. Upton	3.00
BW	Bernie Williams	5.00
KW	Kerry Wood	5.00
BZ	Barry Zito	3.00

Uncommon
Production 200

CB	Carlos Beltran	5.00
AB	Adrian Beltre	3.00
MC	Miguel Cabrera	8.00
RC	Roger Clemens	12.00
JE	Jim Edmonds	5.00
EG	Eric Gagne	3.00
TG	Troy Glaus	3.00
TH	Torii Hunter	3.00
AJ	Andruw Jones	3.00
CJ	Chipper Jones	8.00
MM	Mark Mulder	5.00
MO	Magglio Ordonez	3.00
DO	David Ortiz	8.00
MP	Mike Piazza	8.00
JP	Jorge Posada	5.00
AP	Albert Pujols	15.00
MR	Manny Ramirez	8.00
MRI	Mariano Rivera	6.00
AR	Alex Rodriguez	15.00
IR	Ivan Rodriguez	5.00
SR	Scott Rolen	5.00
CS	Curt Schilling	6.00
AS	Alfonso Soriano	5.00
SS	Sammy Sosa	8.00
JT	Jim Thome	5.00

Rare

CB	Carlos Beltran	10.00
BB	Barry Bonds	40.00
RC	Roger Clemens	20.00
JD	Johnny Damon	12.00
EG	Eric Gagne	8.00
VG	Vladimir Guerrero	10.00
TH	Todd Helton	10.00
PM	Pedro Martinez	10.00
AP	Albert Pujols	25.00
AR	Alex Rodriguez	25.00

Scarce

BB	Barry Bonds
RC	Roger Clemens
VG	Vladimir Guerrero
AP	Albert Pujols
AR	Alex Rodriguez

Power Core

No Pricing
Production 3-10
Power Stick: No Pricing
Production One Set

Selective Swatch

No Pricing
Production One Set

2005 Topps Pristine Legends

NM/M

Complete Set (140):
Common Player: 1.00
Common SP (101-125): 2.00
Production 1,999
Common SP (126-135): 3.00
Production 999
Common SP (136-140): 4.00
Production 499
Pack (5): 30.00
Box (5): 120.00

1	Vida Blue	1.00
2	Bert Blyleven	1.00
3	Joe Carter	1.00
4	Bill Buckner	1.00
5	Luis Aparicio	1.00
6	Ernie Banks	2.50
7	Wade Boggs	2.00
8	George Brett	4.00
9	Lou Brock	2.00
10	Rod Carew	2.00
11	Gary Carter	1.00
12	Andre Dawson	1.00
13	Dennis Eckersley	1.00
14	Rollie Fingers	1.00
15	Steve Garvey	1.00
16	Dwight Gooden	1.00
17	Rich "Goose" Gossage	1.00
18	Ron Guidry	1.00
19	Keith Hernandez	1.00
20	Charlie Hough	1.00
21	Bo Jackson	2.50
22	Monte Irvin	2.00
23	Reggie Jackson	2.00
24	Ferguson Jenkins	1.00
25	Ralph Kiner	1.00
26	Juan Marichal	1.00
27	Stan Musial	4.00
28	Tony Oliva	1.00
29	Jim Palmer	1.50
30	Dave Parker	1.00
31	Gaylord Perry	1.00
32	Jimmy Piersall	1.00
33	Johnny Podres	1.00
34	Brooks Robinson	2.00
35	Frank Robinson	2.00
36	Nolan Ryan	5.00
37	Tom Seaver	2.00
38	Ozzie Smith	3.00
39	Duke Snider	2.00
40	Bobby Thomson	1.00
41	Carl Yastrzemski	3.00
42	Maury Wills	1.00
43	Robin Yount	3.00
44	Matt Williams	1.00
45	Orel Hershiser	1.00
46	Tim McCarver	1.00
47	Don Newcombe	1.00
48	Paul O'Neill	1.00
49	Al Kaline	2.00
50	Harmon Killebrew	2.00
51	Dave Kingman	1.00
52	Ken Griffey	1.00
53	George Foster	1.00
54	Mark Fidrych	1.00
55	Orlando Cepeda	1.00
56	Don Larsen	1.00
57	Bill Madlock	1.00
58	Dale Murphy	1.50
59	Graig Nettles	1.00
60	Phil Niekro	1.00
61	Al Oliver	1.00
62	Harold Reynolds	1.00
63	Bobby Richardson	1.00
64	Mike Scott	1.00
65	Dave Stewart	1.00
66	Rick Sutcliffe	1.00
67	Bruce Sutter	1.50
68	Luis Tiant	1.00
69	Bob Watson	1.00
70	Walt Weiss	1.00
71	Don Zimmer	1.00
72	Tommy John	1.00
73	Ray Knight	1.00
74	Jack Morris	1.00
75	Mickey Rivers	1.00
76	Lee Smith	1.00
77	Darryl Strawberry	1.00
78	David Justice	1.00
79	Wally Joyner	1.00
80	Jimmy Key	1.00
81	John Kruk	1.00
82	Greg Luzinski	1.00
83	Mookie Wilson	1.00
84	Wilbur Wood	1.00
85	Tim Raines	1.00
86	Jim Rice	1.00
87	Tony Armas	1.00
88	Harold Baines	1.00
89	Bucky Dent	1.00

90	Darrell Evans	1.00
91	Cecil Fielder	1.00
92	Jose Cruz	1.00
93	Dave Concepcion	1.00
94	Ron Cey	1.00
95	Davey Lopes	1.00
96	Boog Powell	1.00
97	Buddy Bell	1.00
98	George Bell	1.00
99	Bert Campaneris	1.00
100	Chet Lemon	1.00
101	Bo Jackson	4.00
102	Will Clark	2.00
103	Cecil Fielder	2.00
104	Ron Cey	2.00
105	Tony Gwynn	5.00
106	Orel Hershiser	2.00
107	Jimmy Key	2.00
108	Paul Molitor	3.00
109	Pete Incaviglia	2.00
110	Wally Joyner	2.00
111	Dave Kingman	2.00
112	Ron Guidry	2.00
113	Ron Darling	2.00
114	Mookie Wilson	2.00
115	Reggie Jackson	3.00
116	Walt Weiss	2.00
117	Joe Carter	2.00
118	Cory Snyder	2.00
119	Dave Winfield	3.00
120	Terry Steinbach	2.00
121	Matt Williams	2.00
122	Ozzie Smith	5.00
123	Jack McDowell	2.00
124	Bob Horner	2.00
125	Don Kessinger	2.00
126	Minnie Minoso	3.00
127	Cecil Kaiser	3.00
128	Buck O'Neil	3.00
129	Monte Irvin	4.00
130	Jim Gilliam	3.00
131	Josh Gibson	4.00
132	Ernie Banks	6.00
133	Don Newcombe	3.00
134	Red Moore	3.00
135	Willie Pope	3.00
136	Gary Carter	4.00
137	Bo Jackson	6.00
138	George Brett	8.00
139	Joe Carter	4.00
140	Nolan Ryan	8.00

Refractor

Refractor (1-100):	1-1.5X
Production 549	
Refractor (101-125):	1.5-2X
Production 199	
Refractor (126-135):	1.5-2.5X
Production 99	
Refractor (136-140):	No Pricing
Production 25	

Refractors Gold Die-Cut

Gold (1-100):	3-4X
Gold (101-135):	1-2.5X
Gold (136-140):	1-1.5X
Production 65 Sets	

Printing Plates

No Pricing
One set produced per color.

SuperFractor

No Pricing
Production One Set

Celebrity Threads

NM/M

Inserted 1:18
Refractor: No Pricing
Production 25 Sets

MM	Marilyn Monroe	75.00
EP	Elvis Presley	65.00

Leading Indicators

NM/M

Common Player: 4.00
Refractor: No Pricing
Production one or 25.

WB	Wade Boggs	10.00
LB	Lou Brock	
RC	Rod Carew	8.00
AD	Andre Dawson	6.00
BF	Bob Feller	10.00
CF	Cecil Fielder	8.00
GF	George Foster	
TG	Tony Gwynn	10.00
AK	Al Kaline	12.00
DK	Dave Kingman	6.00
RM	Roger Maris	35.00
DM	Don Mattingly	15.00
DBM	Dale Murphy	10.00

LEADING INDICATORS
TOTAL BASES LEADER – 1978
JIM RICE RED SOX

TO	Tony Oliva	6.00
PO	Paul O'Neill	10.00
DP	Dave Parker	4.00
GP	Gaylord Perry	4.00
TR	Tim Raines	6.00
TR2	Tim Raines	4.00
JR	Jim Rice	4.00
NR	Nolan Ryan	20.00
MS	Mike Scott	4.00
TS	Tom Seaver	10.00
DS	Darryl Strawberry	6.00
MW	Maury Wills	10.00
CY	Carl Yastrzemski	15.00

Personal Endorsements

NM/M

Common Autograph: 10.00
Gold: No Pricing
Production 25 Sets

JA	Jim Abbott	15.00
LA	Luis Aparicio	15.00
BB	Bert Blyleven	15.00
GB	George Brett	50.00
GC	Gary Carter	15.00
RD	Ron Darling	15.00
AD	Andre Dawson	15.00
DE	Dennis Eckersley	15.00
DWE	Darrell Evans	15.00
CF	Carlton Fisk	25.00
GF	George Foster	10.00
GG	Rich "Goose" Gossage	10.00
BG	Bobby Grich	10.00
KH	Keith Hernandez	12.00
BJ	Bo Jackson	60.00
RJ	Reggie Jackson	50.00
AK	Al Kaline	40.00
DL	Don Larsen	15.00
JM	Jack McDowell	10.00
SM	Stan Musial	50.00
GN	Graig Nettles	15.00
JO	Jesse Orosco	10.00
JP	Jim Palmer	15.00
JAP	Jimmy Piersall	15.00
CR	Cal Ripken Jr.	125.00
BR	Brooks Robinson	30.00
NR	Nolan Ryan	90.00
DS	Duke Snider	40.00
EW	Earl Weaver	15.00
CY	Carl Yastrzemski	50.00
RY	Robin Yount	50.00

Signature Marks

NM/M

No Pricing
Production One Set

RR	Sugar Ray Robinson (12/05 Auction)	1,000

Title Threads

NM/M

Common Player: 4.00
Refractors: No Pricing
Production 25 Sets

WB	Wade Boggs	10.00
GC	Gary Carter	6.00
JC	Joe Carter	6.00
OC	Orlando Cepeda	8.00
BD	Bucky Dent	6.00
LD	Lenny Dykstra	6.00
RF	Rollie Fingers	8.00
GF	George Foster	4.00
CS	Cesar Geronimo	6.00
GG	Rich "Goose" Gossage	6.00
KG	Ken Griffey Sr.	6.00
OH	Orel Hershiser	8.00
WH	Willie Horton	10.00
MI	Monte Irvin	12.00
DJ	David Justice	6.00
JK	Jimmy Key	6.00
EK	Ed Kranepool	6.00
TM	Tim McCarver	8.00
GN	Graig Nettles	8.00
PO	Paul O'Neill	10.00
JP	Jim Palmer	6.00
DS	Darryl Strawberry	6.00
MW	Mookie Wilson	4.00

Valuable Performances

NM/M

Common Player: 4.00
Refractor: No Pricing
Production one or 25.

YB	Yogi Berra	15.00
JC	Jose Canseco	10.00
RC	Roberto Clemente/9	
AD	Andre Dawson	6.00
DE	Dennis Eckersley	8.00
CF	Cecil Fielder	8.00
SG	Steve Garvey	6.00
KH	Keith Hernandez	4.00
RJ	Reggie Jackson	8.00
HK	Harmon Killebrew	12.00
DBM	Don Mattingly	15.00
JM	Joe Morgan	6.00
DM	Dale Murphy	10.00
SM	Stan Musial	15.00
DP	Dave Parker	4.00
JR	Jim Rice	8.00
CR	Cal Ripken Jr.	25.00
FR	Frank Robinson	8.00
MS	Mike Schmidt	15.00
CY	Carl Yastrzemski	15.00
RY	Robin Yount	8.00

2005 Topps Retired Signature Edition

NM/M

Complete Set (110):		150.00
Common Player:		1.00
Pack (5):		30.00
Box (5):		125.00
1	Josh Gibson	1.00
2	Andre Dawson	1.00
3	Al Kaline	2.00
4	Andy Van Slyke	1.00

GIBSON

5	Brett Butler	1.00
6	Bob Gibson	1.50
7	Bo Jackson	2.00
8	Carlton Fisk	1.00
9	Chuck Knoblauch	1.00
10	Cal Ripken Jr.	6.00
11	Carl Yastrzemski	3.00
12	Tom Niedenfuer	1.00
13	Dennis Eckersley	1.00
14	Darryl Strawberry	1.00
15	Dwight Gooden	1.00
16	Davey Johnson	1.00
17	Don Mattingly	3.00
18	Dave Winfield	1.50
19	Don Zimmer	1.00
20	Ernie Banks	2.00
21	George Brett	3.00
22	Gary Carter	1.00
23	Gregg Jefferies	1.00
24	Harold Baines	1.00
25	Ryne Sandberg	2.00
26	Howard Johnson	1.00
27	Jim Abbott	1.00
28	Johnny Bench	2.00
29	Jay Buhner	1.00
30	Johnny Podres	1.00
31	Jose Canseco	1.50
32	Keith Hernandez	1.00
33	Lou Brock	1.00
34	Lou Whitaker	1.00
35	Mark Fidrych	1.00
36	Orlando Cepeda	1.00
37	Ozzie Smith	2.00
38	Paul O'Neill	1.00
39	Reggie Jackson	1.50
40	Sid Fernandez	1.00
41	Tony Gwynn	2.00
42	Tim Raines	1.00
43	Tom Seaver	1.50
44	Vida Blue	1.00
45	Brady Anderson	1.00
46	Bob Brenly	1.00
47	Bob Feller	1.50
48	Bill Mazeroski	1.00
49	Brooks Robinson	1.50
50	Harmon Killebrew	1.50
51	Bob Welch	1.00
52	Carl Erskine	1.00
53	Dale Murphy	1.00
54	Denny McClain	1.00
55	Dave Magadan	1.00
56	Duke Snider	1.50
57	Ed Kranepool	1.00
58	Frank Robinson	1.50
59	Jesus Alou	1.00
60	Joe Girardi	1.00
61	John Kruk	1.00
62	Jim Leyland	1.00
63	Juan Marichal	1.00
64	Johnny Pesky	1.00
65	Jesse Orosco	1.00
66	Ken Singleton	1.00
67	Matty Alou	1.00
68	Monte Irvin	1.00
69	Matt Williams	1.00
70	Pedro Guerrero	1.00
71	Ron Blomberg	1.00
72	Rod Carew	1.50
73	Rafael Santana	1.00
74	Ralph Kiner	1.00
75	Wade Boggs	1.50
76	Roger Craig	1.00
77	Robin Yount	2.00
78	Steve Carlton	1.00
79	Shawon Dunston	1.00
80	Steve Garvey	1.00
81	Stan Musial	3.00
82	Travis Fryman	1.00
83	Tito Fuentes	1.00
84	Mike Cuellar	1.00
85	Roberto Clemente	4.00
86	Whitey Ford	1.50
87	Yogi Berra	2.00

88	Atlee Hammaker	1.00
89	Bill Freehan	1.00
90	Brian Cashman	1.00
91	Bobby Richardson	1.00
92	Bob Boone	1.00
93	Charlie Hough	1.00
94	Glenn Hubbard	1.00
95	Grady Little	1.00
96	Jimmy Piersall	1.00
97	Jim Frey	1.00
98	Jerry Grote	1.00
99	Jim Leyritz	1.00
100	Nolan Ryan	5.00
101	Jim Kaat	1.00
102	Joe Pepitone	1.00
103	J.R. Richard	1.00
104	John Candelaria	1.00
105	Bill "Moose" Skowron	1.00
106	Rick Cerone	1.00
107	Ron Santo	1.00
108	Rick Dempsey	1.00
109	Roy White	1.00
110	Tippy Martinez	1.00

Black

Black (1-110): 4-6X
Production 54 Sets

Gold

Gold (1-110): 2-4X
Production 500 Sets

Holographic

No Pricing
Production One Set

Autographs

		NM/M
	Common Autograph:	10.00
JAA	Jim Abbott	20.00
JA	Jesus Alou	15.00
MA	Matty Alou	15.00
BA	Brady Anderson	15.00
HB	Harold Baines	15.00
EB	Ernie Banks	150.00
JB	Johnny Bench	200.00
YB	Yogi Berra	200.00
RB	Ron Blomberg	15.00
VB	Vida Blue	25.00
WB	Wade Boggs	50.00
BRB	Bob Boone	20.00
DLB	Daryl Boston	15.00
BEB	Bob Brenly	10.00
GB	George Brett	150.00
LB	Lou Brock	25.00
JCB	Jay Buhner	25.00
BB	Brett Butler	20.00
JRC	John Candelaria	15.00
JC	Jose Canseco	50.00
RCC	Rod Carew	30.00
SC	Steve Carlton	35.00

GC	Gary Carter	20.00
BC	Brian Cashman	85.00
OC	Orlando Cepeda	15.00
RC	Rick Cerone	15.00
RLC	Roger Craig	15.00
MC	Mike Cuellar	15.00
RD	Ron Darling	15.00
AD	Andre Dawson	25.00
RRD	Rick Dempsey	15.00
BD	Bob Dernier	20.00
SD	Shawon Dunston	35.00
CE	Carl Erskine	30.00
BF	Bob Feller	30.00
SF	Sid Fernandez	20.00
CF	Carlton Fisk	30.00
BAF	Bill Freehan	10.00
JF	Jim Frey	15.00
TDF	Travis Fryman	15.00
TF	Tito Fuentes	15.00
REG	Ron Gant	25.00
SG	Steve Garvey	20.00
BG	Bob Gibson	150.00
DG	Dwight Gooden	20.00
JG	Jerry Grote	20.00
PG	Pedro Guerrero	15.00
TG	Tony Gwynn	100.00
AH	Atlee Hammaker	10.00
TH	Toby Harrah	15.00
KH	Keith Hernandez	20.00
CH	Charlie Hough	10.00
GH	Glenn Hubbard	10.00
MI	Monte Irvin	50.00
BJ	Bo Jackson	100.00
RJ	Reggie Jackson	150.00
GJ	Gregg Jefferies	20.00
HJ	Howard Johnson	25.00
JLK	Jim Kaat	15.00
AK	Al Kaline	40.00
HK	Harmon Killebrew	100.00
RK	Ralph Kiner	35.00
EK	Ed Kranepool	15.00
JK	John Kruk	20.00
TL	Tony LaRussa	20.00
JL	Jim Leyland	15.00
JJL	Jim Leyritz	15.00
GL	Grady Little	15.00
JRL	Jim Lonborg	15.00
DJM	Dave Magadan	15.00
JM	Juan Marichal	25.00
TM	Tippy Martinez	10.00
DM	Don Mattingly	140.00
BM	Bill Mazeroski	45.00
DDM	Denny McLain	20.00
DBM	Dale Murphy	30.00
TN	Tom Niedenfuer	15.00
PO	Paul O'Neill	40.00
JO	Jesse Orosco	15.00
JP	Joe Pepitone	15.00
JMP	Johnny Pesky	25.00
JAP	Jimmy Piersall	15.00
JJP	Johnny Podres	50.00
TR	Tim Raines	25.00
JR	J.R. Richard	20.00
BCR	Bobby Richardson	20.00
CR	Cal Ripken Jr.	180.00
BR	Brooks Robinson	80.00
FR	Frank Robinson	60.00
NR	Nolan Ryan	250.00
RS	Ryne Sandberg	90.00
RFS	Rafael Santana	10.00
RES	Ron Santo	30.00
TS	Tom Seaver	100.00
MS	Bill "Moose" Skowron	15.00
OS	Ozzie Smith	125.00
ZS	Zane Smith	10.00
DS	Duke Snider	60.00
DES	Darryl Strawberry	50.00
BW	Bob Welch	15.00
LW	Lou Whitaker	35.00
RW	Roy White	15.00
MW	Matt Williams	30.00
DW	Dave Winfield	50.00
CY	Carl Yastrzemski	120.00
AY	Anthony Young	10.00
RY	Robin Yount	125.00
DZ	Don Zimmer	30.00

Co-Signers

		NM/M
Some not priced.		
BS	Wade Boggs, Ryne Sandberg/49	140.00
BF	Johnny Bench, Carlton Fisk/49	125.00
GF	Bob Gibson, Whitey Ford/49	100.00

2005 Topps Total

		NM/M
Complete Set (770):		120.00
Common Player:		.15
Pack (10):		1.00
Box (36):		35.00
1	Rafael Furcal	.15
2	Tony Clark	.15
3	Hideki Matsui	1.25

Barry Bonds

4	Zach Day	.15
5	Garret Anderson	.40
6	B.J. Surhoff	.15
7	Trevor Hoffman	.15
8	Kenny Lofton	.15
9	Ross Gload	.15
10	Jorge Cantu	.15
11	Joel Pineiro	.15
12	Alex Cintron	.15
13	Mike Matheny	.15
14	Rod Barajas	.15
15	Ray Durham	.15
16	Danys Baez	.15
17	Brian Schneider	.15
18	Tike Redman	.15
19	Ricardo Rodriguez	.15
20	Mike Sweeney	.15
21	Greg Myers	.15
22	Chone Figgins	.15
23	Brian Lawrence	.15
24	Joe Nathan	.15
25	Placido Polanco	.15
26	Yadier Molina	.15
27	Gary Bennett	.15
28	Yorvit Torrealba	.15
29	Javier Valentin	.15
30	Jason Giambi	.25
31	Brandon Claussen	.15
32	Miguel Olivo	.15
33	Josh Bard	.15
34	Ramon Hernandez	.15
35	Geoff Jenkins	.15
36	Bobby Kielty	.15
37	Luis A. Gonzalez	.15
38	Benito Santiago	.15
39	Brandon Inge	.15
40	Mark Prior	.50
41	Mike Lieberthal	.15
42	Toby Hall	.15
43	Brad Ausmus	.15
44	Damian Miller	.15
45	Mark Kotsay	.15
46	John Buck	.15
47	Oliver Perez	.25
48	Matt Morris	.25
49	Raul Chavez	.15
50	Randy Johnson	.50
51	David Bush	.15
52	Jose Macias	.15
53	Paul Wilson	.15
54	Wilfredo Ledezma	.15
55	J.D. Drew	.25
56	Pedro Martinez	.50
57	Josh Towers	.15
58	Jamie Moyer	.15
59	Scott Elarton	.15
60	Ken Griffey Jr.	1.00
61	Steve Trachsel	.15
62	Bubba Crosby	.15
63	Michael Barrett	.15
64	Odalis Perez	.15
65	B.J. Upton	.25
66	Eric Bruntlett	.15
67	Carlos Zambrano	.15
68	Brandon League	.15
69	Carlos Silva	.15
70	Lyle Overbay	.25
71	Runelvys Hernandez	.15
72	Brad Penny	.15
73	Ty Wigginton	.15
74	Orlando Hudson	.15
75	Roy Oswalt	.25
76	Jason LaRue	.15
77	Ismael Valdez	.15
78	Calvin Pickering	.15
79	Bill Hall	.15
80	Carl Crawford	.15
81	Tomas Perez	.15
82	Joe Kennedy	.15
83	Chris Woodward	.15
84	Jason Lane	.15
85	Steve Finley	.15

86	Jeff Francis	.15
87	Felipe Lopez	.15
88	Chan Ho Park	.15
89	Joe Crede	.15
90	Jose Vidro	.15
91	Casey Kotchman	.25
92	Brandon Backe	.15
93	Mike Hampton	.15
94	Ryan Dempster	.15
95	Wily Mo Pena	.25
96	Matt Holliday	.25
97	A.J. Pierzynski	.15
98	Jason Jennings	.15
99	Eli Marrero	.15
100	Carlos Beltran	.40
101	Scott Kazmir	.25
102	Kenny Rogers	.15
103	Roy Halladay	.25
104	Alex Cora	.15
105	Richie Sexson	.25
106	Ben Sheets	.25
107	Bartolo Colon	.25
108	Eddie Perez	.15
109	Vicente Padilla	.15
110	Sammy Sosa	1.00
111	Mark Ellis	.15
112	Woody Williams	.15
113	Todd Greene	.15
114	Nook Logan	.15
115	Francisco Rodriguez	.15
116	Miguel Batista	.15
117	Livan Hernandez	.15
118	Chris Aguila	.15
119	Coco Crisp	.15
120	Jose Reyes	.25
121	Ricky Ledee	.15
122	Brad Radke	.15
123	Carlos Guillen	.15
124	Paul Bako	.15
125	Tom Glavine	.25
126	Chad Moeller	.15
127	Mark Buehrle	.25
128	Casey Blake	.15
129	Juan Rivera	.15
130	Preston Wilson	.15
131	Nate Robertson	.15
132	Julio Franco	.15
133	Derek Lowe	.15
134	Rob Bell	.15
135	Javy Lopez	.25
136	Javier Vazquez	.25
137	Desi Relaford	.15
138	Danny Graves	.15
139	Josh Fogg	.15
140	Bobby Crosby	.25
141	Ramon Castro	.15
142	Jerry Hairston Jr.	.15
143	Morgan Ensberg	.15
144	Brandon Webb	.25
145	Jack Wilson	.15
146	Bill Mueller	.15
147	Troy Glaus	.25
148	Armando Benitez	.15
149	Adam LaRoche	.15
150	Hank Blalock	.40
151	Ryan Franklin	.15
152	Kevin Millwood	.15
153	Jason Marquis	.15
154	Dewon Brazelton	.15
155	Al Leiter	.15
156	Garrett Atkins	.15
157	Todd Walker	.15
158	Kris Benson	.15
159	Eric Milton	.15
160	Bret Boone	.15
161	Matthew LeCroy	.15
162	Chris Widger	.15
163	Ruben Gotay	.15
164	Craig Monroe	.15
165	Travis Hafner	.25
166	Vance Wilson	.15
167	Jason Grabowski	.15
168	Tim Salmon	.25
169	Henry Blanco	.15
170	Josh Beckett	.25
171	Jake Westbrook	.15
172	Paul LoDuca	.15
173	Julio Lugo	.15
174	Juan Cruz	.15
175	Mark Mulder	.25
176	Juan Castro	.15
177	Damion Easley	.15
178	LaTroy Hawkins	.15
179	Jon Lieber	.25
180	Vernon Wells	.25
181	Jeff DaVanon	.15
182	Dustan Mohr	.15
183	Ryan Freel	.15
184	Doug Davis	.15
185	Sean Casey	.25
186	Robb Quinlan	.15
187	J.D. Closser	.15
188	Tim Wakefield	.15
189	Brian Jordan	.15

#	Player	Price
190	Adam Dunn	.40
191	Antonio Perez	.15
192	Brett Tomko	.15
193	John Flaherty	.15
194	Michael Cuddyer	.15
195	Ronnie Belliard	.15
196	Tony Womack	.15
197	Jason Johnson	.15
198	Victor Santos	.15
199	Dan Haren	.15
200	Derek Jeter	1.50
201	Brian Anderson	.15
202	Carlos Pena	.15
203	Jaret Wright	.15
204	Paul Byrd	.15
205	Shannon Stewart	.15
206	Chris Carpenter	.15
207	Matt Stairs	.15
208	Brad Hawpe	.15
209	Bobby Higginson	.15
210	Torii Hunter	.25
211	Shawn Green	.25
212	Todd Hollandsworth	.15
213	Scott Erickson	.15
214	C.C. Sabathia	.15
215	Mike Mussina	.40
216	Jason Kendall	.15
217	Todd Pratt	.15
218	Danny Kolb	.15
219	Tony Armas	.15
220	Edgar Renteria	.25
221	Dave Roberts	.15
222	Luis Rivas	.15
223	Adam Everett	.15
224	Jeff Cirillo	.15
225	Orlando Hernandez	.15
226	Ken Harvey	.15
227	Corey Patterson	.25
228	Humberto Cota	.15
229	A.J. Burnett	.25
230	Roger Clemens	1.50
231	Joe Randa	.15
232	David Dellucci	.15
233	Troy Percival	.15
234	Dustin Hermanson	.15
235	Eric Gagne	.25
236	Terry Tiffee	.15
237	Tony Graffanino	.15
238	Jayson Werth	.15
239	Michael Sweeney	.15
240	Chipper Jones	.75
241	Aramis Ramirez	.40
242	Frank Catalanotto	.15
243	Mike Maroth	.15
244	Kelvim Escobar	.15
245	Bobby Abreu	.25
246	Kyle Lohse	.15
247	Jason Isringhausen	.15
248	Jose Lima	.15
249	Adrian Gonzalez	.15
250	Alex Rodriguez	1.50
251	Ramon Ortiz	.15
252	Frank Menechino	.15
253	Keith Ginter	.15
254	Kip Wells	.15
255	Dmitri Young	.15
256	Craig Biggio	.25
257	Ramon E. Martinez	.15
258	Jason Bartlett	.15
259	Brad Lidge	.15
260	Brian Giles	.25
261	Luis Terrero	.15
262	Miguel Ojeda	.15
263	Rich Harden	.25
264	Jacque Jones	.15
265	Marcus Giles	.25
266	Carlos Zambrano	.25
267	Michael Tucker	.15
268	Wes Obermueller	.15
269	Peter Orr	.50
270	Jim Thome	.50
271	Omar Vizquel	.25
272	Jose Valentin	.15
273	Juan Uribe	.15
274	Doug Mirabelli	.15
275	Jeff Kent	.25
276	Brad Wilkerson	.15
277	Chris Burke	.25
278	Endy Chavez	.15
279	Richard Hidalgo	.15
280	John Smoltz	.25
281	Jarrod Washburn	.15
282	Larry Bigbie	.15
283	Edgardo Alfonzo	.15
284	Cliff Lee	.15
285	Carlos Lee	.25
286	Olmedo Saenz	.15
287	Tomokazu Ohka	.15
288	Ruben Sierra	.15
289	Nick Swisher	.15
290	Frank Thomas	.40
291	Aaron Cook	.15
292	Cody McKay	.15
293	Hee Seop Choi	.15
294	Carl Pavano	.25
295	Scott Rolen	.50
296	Matt Kata	.15
297	Terrence Long	.15
298	Jimmy Gobble	.15
299	Jason Repko	.15
300	Manny Ramirez	.50
301	Dan Wilson	.15
302	Jhonny Peralta	.15
303	Dan Mabry	.15
304	Adam Melhuse	.15
305	Kerry Wood	.50
306	Ryan Langerhans	.15
307	Antonio Alfonseca	.15
308	Marco Scutaro	.15
309	Jamey Carroll	.15
310	Lance Berkman	.25
311	Willie Harris	.15
312	Phil Nevin	.25
313	Gregg Zaun	.15
314	Michael Ryan	.15
315	Zack Greinke	.15
316	Ted Lilly	.15
317	David Eckstein	.15
318	Tony Torcato	.15
319	Robert Mackowiak	.15
320	Mark Teixeira	.40
321	Jason Phillips	.15
322	Jeremy Reed	.15
323	Bengie Molina	.15
324	Terrmel Sledge	.15
325	Justin Morneau	.40
326	Sandy Alomar Jr.	.15
327	Jon Garland	.25
328	Jay Payton	.15
329	Tino Martinez	.25
330	Jason Bay	.25
331	Jeff Conine	.15
332	Shawn Chacon	.15
333	Angel Berroa	.15
334	Reggie Sanders	.15
335	Kevin Brown	.15
336	Brady Clark	.15
337	Casey Fossum	.15
338	Raul Ibanez	.15
339	Derrek Lee	.40
340	Victor Martinez	.25
341	Kazuhisa Ishii	.15
342	Royce Clayton	.15
343	Trot Nixon	.25
344	Eric Young	.15
345	Aubrey Huff	.15
346	Brett Myers	.25
347	Joey Gathright	.15
348	Mark Grudzielanek	.15
349	Scott Spiezio	.15
350	Eric Chavez	.25
351	Einar Diaz	.15
352	Dallas McPherson	.15
353	John Thomson	.15
354	Neifi Perez	.15
355	Larry Walker	.25
356	Billy Wagner	.15
357	Mike Cameron	.15
358	Jimmy Rollins	.25
359	Kevin Mench	.15
360	Joe Mauer	.25
361	Jose Molina	.15
362	Joe Borchard	.15
363	Kevin Cash	.15
364	Jay Gibbons	.15
365	Khalil Greene	.25
366	Justin Leone	.15
367	Eddie Guardado	.15
368	Mike Lamb	.15
369	Matt Riley	.15
370	Luis Gonzalez	.25
371	Alfredo Amezaga	.15
372	J.J. Hardy	.15
373	Hector Luna	.15
374	Greg Aquino	.15
375	Jim Edmonds	.25
376	Joe Blanton	.15
377	Russell Branyan	.15
378	J.T. Snow	.15
379	Magglio Ordonez	.25
380	Rafael Palmeiro	.40
381	Andruw Jones	.25
382	David DeJesus	.15
383	Marquis Grissom	.15
384	Bobby Hill	.15
385	Kazuo Matsui	.15
386	Mark Loretta	.15
387	Chris Shelton	.15
388	Johnny Estrada	.15
389	Adam Hyzdu	.15
390	Nomar Garciaparra	1.00
391	Mark Teahen	.15
392	Chris Capuano	.15
393	Ben Broussard	.15
394	Daniel Cabrera	.15
395	Jeremy Bonderman	.25
396	Darin Erstad	.25
397	Alex S. Gonzalez	.15
398	Kevin Millar	.15
399	Freddy Garcia	.15
400	Alfonso Soriano	.50
401	Koyie Hill	.15
402	Omar Infante	.15
403	Alex Gonzalez	.15
404	Pat Burrell	.25
405	Wes Helms	.15
406	Junior Spivey	.15
407	Joe Mays	.15
408	Jason Stanford	.15
409	Gil Meche	.15
410	Tim Hudson	.25
411	Chase Utley	.25
412	Matt Clement	.25
413	Nick Green	.15
414	Jose Vizcaino	.15
415	Ryan Klesko	.15
416	Vinny Castilla	.15
417	Brian Roberts	.40
418	Geronimo Gil	.15
419	Gary Matthews	.15
420	Jeff Weaver	.15
421	Jerome Williams	.15
422	Andy Pettitte	.40
423	Randy Wolf	.15
424	D'Angelo Jimenez	.15
425	Moises Alou	.25
426	Eric Byrnes	.15
427	Mark Redman	.15
428	Jermaine Dye	.15
429	Cory Lidle	.15
430	Jason Schmidt	.25
431	Jason W. Smith	.15
432	Jose Castillo	.15
433	Pokey Reese	.15
434	Matt Lawton	.15
435	Jose Guillen	.25
436	Craig Counsell	.15
437	Jose Hernandez	.15
438	Braden Looper	.15
439	Scott Hatteberg	.15
440	Gary Sheffield	.40
441	Gabe Gross	.15
442	Chris Gomez	.15
443	Dontrelle Willis	.40
444	Jamey Wright	.15
445	Rocco Baldelli	.15
446	Bernie Williams	.25
447	Sean Burroughs	.15
448	Willie Bloomquist	.15
449	Luis Castillo	.15
450	Mike Piazza	1.00
451	Ryan Drese	.15
452	Pedro Feliz	.15
453	Horacio Ramirez	.15
454	Luis Matos	.15
455	Craig Wilson	.15
456	Russ Ortiz	.15
457	Xavier Nady	.15
458	Hideo Nomo	.25
459	Miguel Cairo	.15
460	Mike Lowell	.25
461	Corky Miller	.15
462	Bobby Madritsch	.15
463	Jose Contreras	.15
464	Johnny Damon	.25
465	Miguel Cabrera	.50
466	Eric Hinske	.15
467	Marlon Byrd	.15
468	Aaron Miles	.15
469	Ramon Vazquez	.15
470	Michael Young	.25
471	Alex Sanchez	.15
472	Shea Hillenbrand	.15
473	Jeff Bagwell	.40
474	Erik Bedard	.15
475	Jake Peavy	.40
476	Jody Gerut	.15
477	Randy Winn	.15
478	Kevin Youkilis	.15
479	Eric Dubose	.15
480	David Wright	.75
481	Wilson Valdez	.15
482	Cliff Floyd	.15
483	Jose Mesa	.25
484	Doug Mientkiewicz	.15
485	Jorge Posada	.40
486	Sidney Ponson	.15
487	David Krynzel	.15
488	Octavio Dotel	.15
489	Matt Treanor	.15
490	Johan Santana	.40
491	John Patterson	.15
492	So Taguchi	.15
493	Carl Everett	.15
494	Jason Dubois	.15
495	Albert Pujols	1.50
496	Kirk Rueter	.15
497	Geoff Blum	.15
498	Juan Encarnacion	.15
499	Mark Hendrickson	.15
500	Barry Bonds	2.00
501	Cesar Izturis	.15
502	David Wells	.15
503	Jorge Julio	.15
504	Cristian Guzman	.15
505	Juan Pierre	.15
506	Adam Eaton	.15
507	Nick Johnson	.25
508	Mike Redmond	.15
509	Daryle Ward	.15
510	Adrian Beltre	.25
511	Laynce Nix	.15
512	Reed Johnson	.15
513	Jeremy Affeldt	.15
514	R.A. Dickey	.15
515	Alex Rios	.15
516	Orlando Palmeiro	.15
517	Mark Belhorn	.15
518	Adam Kennedy	.15
519	Curtis Granderson	.15
520	Todd Helton	.40
521	Aaron Boone	.15
522	Milton Bradley	.25
523	Timoniel Perez	.15
524	Jeff Suppan	.15
525	Austin Kearns	.15
526	Charles Thomas	.15
527	Bronson Arroyo	.15
528	Roger Cedeno	.15
529	Russ Adams	.15
530	Barry Zito	.25
531	Bob Wickman	.15
532	Deivi Cruz	.15
533	Mariano Rivera	.40
534	J.J. Davis	.15
535	Greg Maddux	1.00
536	Ryan Vogelsong	.15
537	Josh Phelps	.15
538	Scott Hairston	.15
539	Vladimir Guerrero	.75
540	Ivan Rodriguez	.50
541	David Newhan	.15
542	David Bell	.15
543	Lew Ford	.15
544	Grady Sizemore	.25
545	David Ortiz	.75
546	Jose Cruz Jr.	.15
547	Aaron Rowand	.15
548	Marcus Thames	.15
549	Scott Podsednik	.25
550	Ichiro Suzuki	1.25
551	Eduardo Perez	.15
552	Chris Snyder	.15
553	Corey Koskie	.15
554	Miguel Tejada	.50
555	Orlando Cabrera	.25
556	Rondell White	.15
557	Wade Miller	.15
558	Rodrigo Lopez	.15
559	Chad Tracy	.15
560	Paul Konerko	.25
561	Wil Cordero	.15
562	John McDonald	.15
563	Jason Ellison	.15
564	Jason Michaels	.15
565	Melvin Mora	.25
566	Ryan Church	.15
567	Ryan Ludwick	.15
568	Erubiel Durazo	.15
569	Noah Lowry	.15
570	Curt Schilling	.50
571	Esteban Loaiza	.15
572	Freddy Sanchez	.15
573	Rich Aurilia	.15
574	Travis Lee	.15
575	Dennis Tankersley, Chris George	.15
576	Jason Christiansen, Kevin Correia	.15
577	Ryan Bukvich, Randy Williams	.15
578	Terry Adams, Gavin Floyd	.15
579	Seth Etherton, Dan Meyer	.15
580	Justin Lehr, Derrick Turnbow	.15
581	Mike Gosling, Brad Halsey	.15
582	Jim Mecir, Logan Kensing	.15
583	Brad Hennessey, Jeff Fassero	.15
584	Jason Grilli, John Adkins	.15
585	Jesse Crain, Juan Rincon	.15
586	Jaime Cerda, Nate Field	.15
587	Bartolome Fortunato, Jae Weong Seo	.15
588	Frank Brooks, Yhency Brazoban	.15
589	Jamie Walker, Ugueth Urbina	.15
590	Bret Prinz, Scott Proctor	.15

#	Players	Price
591	Bob Howry, Jason Davis	.15
592	Amauro Telemaco, Tim Worrell	.15
593	Jose Acevedo, Kent Mercker	.15
594	Chris Hammond, Scott Linebrink	.15
595	Fernando Nieve, John Franco	.15
596	Mike Lincoln, Randy Flores	.15
597	Joe Borowski, Kyle Farnsworth	.15
598	Jesus Colome, Lance Carter	.15
599	Abe Alvarez, Lenny DiNardo	.15
600	Chad Bradford, Kiko Calero	.15
601	David Aardsma, Jim Brower	.15
602	Geoff Geary, Ryan Madson	.15
603	Ben Howard, Nate Bump	.15
604	Chin-Hui Tsao, Jason Young	.15
605	Aaron Harang, Ryan Wagner	.15
606	Rick Bauer, Steve Kline	.15
607	Lance Cormier, Randy Choate	.15
608	Jon Leicester, Todd Wellemeyer	.15
609	Jason Frasor, Vinnie Chulk	.15
610	Brian Fuentes, Scott Dohmann	.15
611	Matt Ginter, Tyler Yates	.15
612	Cory Stewart, Salomon Torres	.15
613	Cal Eldred, Mike Myers	.15
614	Carlos Almanzar, Doug Brocail	.15
615	George Sherrill, J.J. Putz	.15
616	Bruce Chen, Matt Riley	.15
617	Ben Weber, David Weathers	.15
618	Dennys Reyes, Rudy Seanez	.15
619	Ricardo Rincon, Tim Harikkala	.15
620	D.J. Carrasco, Shawn Camp	.15
621	Allan Simpson, Javier Lopez	.15
622	Glendon Rusch, Mike Remlinger	.15
623	Kevin Gryboski, Roman Colon	.15
624	Chris Reitsma, Tom Martin	.15
625	Chad Qualls, Dan Wheeler	.15
626	Brooks Kieschnick, Matt Wise	.15
627	Justin Speier, Kerry Ligtenberg	.15
628	Francisco Cordero, Frank Francisco	.15
629	Matt Thornton, Rafael Soriano	.15
630	Mike Stanton, Steve Karsay	.15
631	Mike MacDougal, Scott Sullivan	.15
632	Brian Bruney, Oscar Villarreal	.15
633	Jeff Bennett, Mike Adams	.15
634	Dave Borkowski, Eddy Rodriguez	.15
635	David Riske, Rafael Betancourt	.15
636	Gary Glover, Jorge De La Rosa	.15
637	Justin Wayne, Matt Perisho	.15
638	Jeff Bajenaru, Luis Vizcaino	.15
639	Erasmo Ramirez, Ron Mahay	.15
640	John Grabow, Mike Gonzalez	.15
641	J.C. Romero, Matt Guerrier	.15
642	Brandon Duckworth, Tim Redding	.15
643	Franklin Nunez, Travis Harper	.15
644	Matt Herges, Tyler Walker	.15
645	Elmer Dessens, Wilson Alvarez	.15
646	Anastacio Martinez, Mark Malaska	.15
647	Gary Knotts, Roberto Novoa	.15
648	Jairo Garcia, Justin Duchscherer	.15
649	Aaron Rakers, Todd Williams	.15
650	Paul Quantrill, Tom Gordon	.15
651	Brandon Lyon, Shawn Estes	.15
652	Gustavo Chacin, Justin Miller	.15
653	John Lackey, Scot Shields	.15
654	Bobby Seay, Jorge Sosa	.15
655	Chad Cordero, Luis Ayala	.15
656	Julio Mateo, Ron Villone	.15
657	Byung-Hyun Kim, Matt Mantei	.15
658	Cliff Politte, Damaso Marte	.15
659	Joe Valentine, Luke Hudson	.15
660	John Riedling, Todd Jones	.15
661	Aaron Heilman, Heath Bell	.15
662	Akinori Otsuka, Blaine Neal	.15
663	Joe Horgan, Joey Eischen	.15
664	Grant Balfour, J.D. Durbin	.15
665	Alan Embree, Mike Timlin	.15
666	Keith Foulke, Aaron Fultz	.15
667	Rheal Cormier	.15
668	Kevin Gregg, Scott Dunn	.15
669	Franklyn German, Steve Coyler	.15
670	Scott Eyre, Wayne Franklin	.15
671	Brian Meadows, Mike Johnston	.15
672	Guillermo Mota, Tim Spooneybarger	.15
673	B.J. Ryan, Jason Grimsley	.15
674	Neal Cotts, Shingo Takatsu	.15
675	Felix Heredia, Mike DeJean	.15
676	Brian Shackelford, Josh Hancock	.15
677	Jon Rauch, T.J. Tucker	.15
678	Brian Shouse, Nick Regilio	.15
679	Julian Tavarez, Ray King	.15
680	Mike Wuertz, Stephen Randolph	.15
681	Gabe White, Jorge Vasquez	.15
682	Jose Valverde, Mike Koplove	.15
683	Arthur Rhodes, Scott Sauerbeck	.15
684	Felix Rodriguez, Tanyon Sturtze	.15
685	Duaner Sanchez, Giovanni Carrara	.15
686	Chad Harville, Mike Gallo	.15
687	Dave Williams, Sean Burnett	.15
688	Scott Atchison, Shigetoshi Hasegawa	.15
689	Claudio Vargas, Francis Beltran	.15
690	Brendan Donnelly, Esteban Yan	.15
691	Ervin Santana, Jeff Mathis	.15
692	Bill Bray, Clint Everts	.15
693	Jason Kubel, Trevor Plouffe	.15
694	Andy Marte, Jake Stevens	.15
695	Aaron Hill, Chad Gaudin	.15
696	Carlos Quentin, Jesus Cota	.15
697	Chris Young, Thomas Diamond	.15
698	Dan Johnson, Omar Quintanilla	.15
699	John Maine, Val Majewski	.15
700	James Houser, Jonny Gomes	.15
701	David Murphy, Hanley Ramirez	.25
702	Chris Lambert, Rick Ankiel	.15
703	Angel Guzman, Felix Pie	.15
704	Merkin Valdez, Nate Schierholtz	.15
705	Arnie Munoz, Gio Gonzalez	.15
706	Felix Hernandez, Travis Blackley	.15
707	Edwin Encarnacion, Tony Blanco	.15
708	Justin Germano, Tim Stauffer	.15
709	Jeremy Guthrie, Jeremy Sowers	.15
710	Jorge Cortes, Tom Gorzelanny	.15
711	Logan Kensing, Taylor Tankersley	.15
712	Neil Walker, Paul Maholm	.15
713	Carlos Hernandez, Willy Taveras	.50
714	Greg Golson, Ryan Howard	1.00
715	Blake DeWitt, Edwin Jackson	.15
716	Dan Putnam, Huston Street	.15
717	Mark Rogers, Rickie Weeks	.25
718	Phillip Hughes, Robinson Cano	.40
719	Jay Rainville, Kyle Waldrop	.15
720	Craig Brazell, Yusmeiro Petit	.15
721	Baltazar Lopez, Matt Brown RC	.25
722	Brett Price, Jerry Owens RC	.50
723	Dan Uggla, Kyle Nichols RC	2.00
724	Francisco Rosario, Jayce Tingler RC	.25
725	Eulogio de la Cruz, Tony Giarratano RC	.25
726	Matt Campbell, Shane Costa RC	.25
727	Bill McCarthy, Martin Prado RC	.25
728	Edinson Volquez, Ian Kinsler RC	3.00
729	Lorenzo Scott, Luis Ramirez RC	.25
730	Chris Seddon, Elliot Johnson RC	.75
731	Chris Dickerson, Thomas Pauly RC	.15
732	Jason Motte, Stuart Pomeranz RC	.25
733	Jose Vaquedano, Stefan Bailie RC	.25
734	D.J. Houlton, Wade Robinson RC	.25
735	Matt DeSalvo, Melky Cabrera RC	1.00
736	Brian Stavisky, Landon Powell RC	.25
737	Scott Mathieson, Scott Mitchinson RC	.50
738	Bear Bay, Sean Marshall RC	.50
739	Brandon McCarthy, Pedro Lopez RC	1.50
740	Alexander Smit, Jair Jurrjens RC	1.00
741	Matt Rogelstad, Ryan Feierabend RC	.25
742	Keith Ramsey, Nate McLouth RC	.25
743	Kevin Melillo, Michael Rogers RC	.25
744	Heath Totten, Matthew Kemp RC	2.00
745	Trevor Hutchinson, Yorman Bazardo RC	.15
746	Jesse Gutierrez, Tyler Pelland RC	.25
747	Jeremy West, Willy Mota RC	.25
748	Ryan Garko, Ryan Goleski RC	.50
749	Bryan Triplett, Jared Gothreaux RC	.25
750	Glen Perkins, Kevin West RC	.25
751	Michael Esposito, Zachary Parker RC	.25
752	Brian Miller, Ryan Sweeney	.25
753	Buck Coats, Casey McGehee RC	.25
754	Nate Cabrera, Zachary Cline RC	.15
755	Bobby Livingston, Mike Morse RC	.25
756	Brendan Ryan, Wes Swackhamer RC	.25
757	John Hudgins, Nick Masset RC	.25
758	George Kottaras, Peeter Ramos RC	.25
759	Elvys Quezada, T.J. Beam RC	.25
760	Dana Eveland, Travis Hinton RC	.25
761	Chris Vines, James Jurries RC	.25
762	Humberto Sanchez, Justin Verlander RC	2.00
763	Ian Bladergroen, Shawn Bowman RC	.50
764	J.B. Thurmond, Pat Misch RC	.25
765	Christian Colonel, Neil Wilson RC	.25
766	Checklist 1	.15
767	Checklist 2	.15
768	Checklist 3	.15
769	Checklist 4	.15
770	Checklist 5	.15

Press Plates

	NM/M
Common Card Front P. Plate:	25.00
Common Card Back P. Plate:	15.00

Stars not priced.
Production one set per color (4).

Silver

Stars:	1-3X

Inserted 1:1

Award Winners

DAVID ORTIZ

TOTAL AWARD WINNER

	NM/M
Complete Set (30):	15.00
Common Player:	.25

Inserted 1:10

AW1	Barry Bonds	2.00
AW2	Vladimir Guerrero	.75
AW3	Roger Clemens	2.00
AW4	Johan Santana	.75
AW5	Jason Bay	.25
AW6	Bobby Crosby	.25
AW7	Eric Gagne	.40
AW8	Mariano Rivera	.50
AW9	Albert Pujols	2.00
AW10	Mark Teixeira	.50
AW11	Mark Loretta	.25
AW12	Alfonso Soriano	.75
AW13	Jack Wilson	.25
AW14	Miguel Tejada	.50
AW15	Adrian Beltre	.40
AW16	Melvin Mora	.25
AW17	Barry Bonds	2.00
AW18	Jim Edmonds	.50
AW19	Bobby Abreu	.40
AW20	Manny Ramirez	.75
AW21	Gary Sheffield	.50
AW22	Vladimir Guerrero	.75
AW23	Johnny Estrada	.25
AW24	Victor Martinez	.25
AW25	Ivan Rodriguez	.50
AW26	Livan Hernandez	.25
AW27	David Ortiz	.75
AW28	Bobby Cox	.25

AW29 Buck Showalter .25
AW30 Barry Bonds 2.00

Domination

		NM/M
Complete Set (30):		15.00
Common Player:		.25
Inserted 1:10		
40	Mark Prior	.75
50	Randy Johnson	.75
56	Pedro Martinez	.75
60	Ken Griffey Jr.	1.00
100	Carlos Beltran	.50
110	Sammy Sosa	1.50
147	Troy Glaus	.50
150	Hank Blalock	.50
180	Vernon Wells	.25
190	Adam Dunn	.50
200	Derek Jeter	2.00
230	Roger Clemens	2.00
250	Alex Rodriguez	1.50
260	Brian Giles	.25
270	Jim Thome	.75
290	Frank Thomas	.50
300	Manny Ramirez	.75
345	Aubrey Huff	.25
350	Eric Chavez	.25
400	Alfonso Soriano	.75
465	Miguel Cabrera	.75
490	Johan Santana	.50
495	Albert Pujols	2.00
500	Barry Bonds	2.00
510	Adrian Beltre	.40
520	Todd Helton	.50
575	Vladimir Guerrero	.75
540	Ivan Rodriguez	.50
545	David Ortiz	.75
554	Miguel Tejada	.50

Domination Autograph

Production 10

Production

		NM/M
Complete Set (10):		8.00
Common Player:		.40
Inserted 1:15		
AB	Adrian Beltre	.40
BB	Barry Bonds	2.00
VG	Vladimir Guerrero	.75
TH	Todd Helton	.50
AP	Albert Pujols	2.00
MR	Manny Ramirez	.75
AR	Alex Rodriguez	1.50
AS	Alfonso Soriano	.75
MT	Miguel Tejada	.50
JT	Jim Thome	.75

Signatures

		NM/M
Common Autograph:		8.00
BB	Brian Bruney	8.00
RC	Robinson Cano	35.00
JG	Joey Gathright	10.00
ZG	Zack Greinke	12.00
BM	Brett Myers	12.00
TT	Terry Tiffee	15.00
DW	David Wright	50.00

Team Checklists

		NM/M
Complete Set (30):		8.00
Common Player:		.15
3	Miguel Tejada	.50
6	Frank Thomas	.50
8	Victor Martinez	.25
9	Todd Helton	.50
10	Ivan Rodriguez	.50
11	Miguel Cabrera	.50
12	Roger Clemens	1.00
13	Zack Greinke	.15
14	Vladimir Guerrero	.50

16	Ben Sheets	.25
17	Johan Santana	.50
18	Carlos Beltran	.50
19	Alex Rodriguez	1.00
20	Eric Chavez	.25
21	Jim Thome	.50
22	Jason Bay	.25
23	Brian Giles	.25
24	Barry Bonds	1.50
25	Ichiro Suzuki	1.00
26	Albert Pujols	1.00
27	Carl Crawford	.25
28	Alfonso Soriano	.50
29	Roy Halladay	.25
30	Jose Vidro	.15
7	Adam Dunn	.50
5	Kerry Wood	.50
1	Luis Gonzalez	.25
2	John Smoltz	.25
4	David Ortiz	.50
15	Eric Gagne	.25

Total Topps

		NM/M
Complete Set (20):		12.00
Common Player:		.25
Inserted 1:15		
CB	Carlos Beltran	.50
AB	Adrian Beltre	.40
BB	Barry Bonds	2.00
EC	Eric Chavez	.25
RC	Roger Clemens	2.00
VG	Vladimir Guerrero	.75
TH	Todd Helton	.50
DJ	Derek Jeter	2.00
RJ	Randy Johnson	.75
GM	Greg Maddux	1.00
MP	Mike Piazza	1.00
AP	Albert Pujols	2.00
MR	Manny Ramirez	.75
AR	Alex Rodriguez	1.50
IR	Ivan Rodriguez	.50
JS	Johan Santana	.50
AS	Alfonso Soriano	.75
SS	Sammy Sosa	1.50
MT	Miguel Tejada	.50
JT	Jim Thome	.50

2005 Topps Rookie Cup

		NM/M
Complete Set (160):		35.00
Common Player (1-150):		.15
Common Rookie Auto.		
(151-160):		8.00
Inserted 1:62		
Pack (7):		4.00
Box (24):		75.00
1	Pat Corrales	.15
2	Ron Santo	.25
3	Joe Torre	.40
4	Boog Powell	.15
5	Tom Tresh	.15
6	Jonny Gomes	.15
7	Rico Carty	.15
8	Bert Campaneris	.15
9	Tony Oliva	.25
10	Ron Swoboda	.15
11	Tony Perez	.40
12	Joe Morgan	.40
13	Davey Johnson	.15
14	Cleon Jones	.15
15	Tom Seaver	.75
16	Rod Carew	.50
17	Rick Monday	.15
18	Johnny Bench	.75
19	Bobby Cox	.15
20	Jerry Koosman	.15
21	Al Oliver	.25
22	Lou Piniella	.25
23	Larry Bowa	.25
24	Chris Chambliss	.15
25	Bill Buckner	.15
26	Don Baylor	.15
27	Buddy Bell	.15
28	Carlton Fisk	.50
29	Gary Mathews	.15
30	Davey Lopes	.15
31	Bob Boone	.15
32	Bill Madlock	.15
33	Claudell Washington	.15
34	Jim Rice	.25
35	Gary Carter	.15
36	Willie Randolph	.15
37	Chet Lemon	.15
38	Andre Dawson	.15
39	Eddie Murray	.50
40	Paul Molitor	.50
41	Ozzie Smith	1.00
42	Jeffrey Leonard	.15
43	Lonnie Smith	.15
44	Mookie Wilson	.15
45	Tim Wallach	.15
46	Tim Raines	.25
47	Fernando Valenzuela	.15
48	Cal Ripken Jr.	2.00
49	Ryne Sandberg	1.00
50	Willie McGee	.15
51	Darryl Strawberry	.15
52	Julio Franco	.15
53	Brook Jacoby	.15
54	Dwight Gooden	.15
55	Roger McDowell	.15
56	Ozzie Guillen	.15
57	Vince Coleman	.15
58	Pete Incaviglia	.15
59	Wally Joyner	.15
60	Jose Canseco	.50
61	Cory Snyder	.15
62	Devon White	.15
63	Walt Weiss	.15
64	Mark Grace	.40
65	Ron Gant	.15
66	Chris Sabo	.15
67	Jay Buhner	.15
68	Gary Sheffield	.40
69	Gregg Jefferies	.15
70	Ken Griffey Jr.	1.50
71	Tom Gordon	.15
72	Jim Abbott	.15
73	David Justice	.25
74	Larry Walker	.25
75	Sandy Alomar	.15
76	Chuck Knoblauch	.15
77	Jeff Bagwell	.50
78	Luis Gonzalez	.25
79	Ivan Rodriguez	.50
80	Eric Karros	.15
81	Jeff Kent	.15
82	Kenny Lofton	.15
83	Moises Alou	.25
84	Reggie Sanders	.15
85	Jeff Conine	.15
86	J.T. Snow	.15
87	Tim Salmon	.25
88	Mike Piazza	1.00
89	Manny Ramirez	.75
90	Ryan Klesko	.15
91	Javy Lopez	.15
92	Chipper Jones	.75
93	Ray Durham	.15
94	Garret Anderson	.25
95	Shawn Green	.15
96	Hideo Nomo	.25
97	Jermaine Dye	.15
98	Tony Clark	.15
99	Joe Randa	.15
100	Derek Jeter	2.00
101	Jason Kendall	.15
102	Billy Wagner	.15
103	Andruw Jones	.50
104	Dmitri Young	.15
105	Scott Rolen	.50
106	Nomar Garciaparra	.75
107	Jose Cruz Jr.	.15
108	Scott Hatteberg	.15
109	Mark Kotsay	.15
110	Todd Helton	.50
111	Miguel Cairo	.15
112	Magglio Ordonez	.25
113	Kerry Wood	.25
114	Preston Wilson	.15
115	Alex Gonzalez	.15
116	Carlos Beltran	.50
117	Rafael Furcal	.25
118	Pat Burrell	.15
119	Adam Kennedy	.15
120	Terrence Long	.15
121	Jay Payton	.15
122	Bengie Molina	.15
123	Albert Pujols	2.00
124	Craig Wilson	.15
125	Alfonso Soriano	.50
126	Jimmy Rollins	.25
127	Adam Dunn	.50
128	Ichiro Suzuki	1.50
129	Roy Oswalt	.25
130	C.C. Sabathia	.15
131	Brad Wilkerson	.15
132	Nick Johnson	.15
133	Eric Hinske	.15
134	Austin Kearns	.25
135	Dontrelle Willis	.40
136	Mark Teixeira	.50
137	Rocco Baldelli	.15
138	Scott Podsednik	.25
139	Brandon Webb	.15
140	Jason Bay	.25
141	Adam LaRoche	.15
142	Khalil Greene	.15
143	Joe Mauer	.50
144	Matt Holliday	.25
145	Chad Tracy	.15
146	Garrett Atkins	.15
147	Tadahito Iguchi	1.00
148	Russ Adams	.15
149	Huston Street	.15
150	Dan Johnson	.15
151	J. Brent Cox RC	15.00
152	John Drennen RC	20.00
153	Ryan Tucker RC	10.00
154	Yunel Escobar RC	25.00
155	Jacob Marceaux RC	10.00
156	Mark Pawelek RC	25.00
157	Brandon Snyder RC	25.00
158	Wade Townsend RC	15.00
159	Troy Tulowitzki RC	85.00
160	Kevin Whelan RC	12.00

Printing Plates

No Pricing
Production one set per color.

Blue

Blue (1-150):	3-6X
Blue (151-160):	1-2X
Production 50 Sets	

Gold

No Pricing
Production One Set

Green

Green (1-150):	2-4X
Production 199	
Green (151-160):	1-2X
Production 99	

Orange

Orange (1-150):	1.5-3X
Production 399	
Orange (151-160):	1X
Production 299	

Red

Red (1-150):	1-2X
Production 499	
Red (151-160):	1X
Production 399	

Silver

No Pricing
Production One Set

Yellow

Yellow (1-150):	2-3X
Production 299	
Yellow (151-160):	1X
Production 199	

Autographs

		NM/M
Common Autograph:		
Silver:	No Pricing	
Production Five Sets		
Gold:	No Pricing	
Production One Set		
JBA	Jason Bay	20.00
JB	Johnny Bench	65.00
AD	Andre Dawson	15.00
JD	Jermaine Dye	8.00
RF	Rafael Furcal	12.00
MG	Mark Grace	25.00
DRJ	Dan Johnson	15.00
DJ	Davey Johnson	8.00
AJ	Andruw Jones	40.00
CJ	Chipper Jones	35.00
DJ	David Justice	20.00
EK	Eric Karros	8.00
MK	Mark Kotsay	8.00
CK	Chuck Knoblauch	20.00
RM	Roger McDowell	10.00
PM	Paul Molitor	50.00
BP	Boog Powell	15.00
AP	Albert Pujols	
MR	Manny Ramirez	50.00
JR	Jim Rice	30.00
CR	Cal Ripken Jr.	
RSA	Ron Santo	25.00
TS	Tom Seaver	50.00
GS	Gary Sheffield	25.00
DS	Darryl Strawberry	15.00
RS	Ron Swoboda	10.00
JT	Joe Torre	25.00
BW	Brad Wilkerson	8.00
DW	Dontrelle Willis	20.00

Dual Autographs

		NM/M
Inserted 1:118		
GS	Mark Grace, Ron Santo	80.00
BW	Jason Bay, Dontrelle Willis	50.00
WD	Brad Wilkerson, Andre Dawson	50.00
CS	J. Brent Cox, Tom Seaver	40.00
RTW	Ryan Tucker, Dontrelle Willis	20.00
EF	Yunel Escobar, Rafael Furcal	20.00
MM	Jacob Marceaux, Roger McDowell	20.00
SP	Brandon Snyder, Boog Powell	25.00
TS	Wade Townsend, Tom Seaver	50.00
TW	Troy Tulowitzki, Walt Weiss	50.00
WM	Kevin Whelan, Roger McDowell	15.00

Original Relics

No Pricing
Production 1-10

Reprints

		NM/M
Complete Set (150):		60.00
Common Player:		.25
Reprints:		1-2X Base Card
2 Per Hobby Pack		
1 Per Retail Pack		
Chrome:	No Pricing	
Production 25 Sets		
Refractor:	No Pricing	
15 Sets		
Chrome Gold:	No Pricing	
Production One Set		
1	Pat Corrales/66	.25
2	Ron Santo/61	.50
3	Joe Torre/62	.75
4	Boog Powell/63	.25
5	Tom Tresh/63	.25
6	Jonny Gomes/06	.25
7	Rico Carty/65	.25
8	Bert Campaneris/65	.25
9	Tony Oliva/65	.50
10	Ron Swoboda/66	.25
11	Tony Perez/66	.75
12	Joe Morgan/66	.75
13	Davey Johnson/67	.25
14	Cleon Jones/67	.25
15	Tom Seaver/68	1.00
16	Rod Carew/68	.75
17	Rick Monday/68	.25
18	Johnny Bench/69	1.50
19	Bobby Cox/69	.25
20	Jerry Koosman/69	.25
21	Al Oliver/70	.50
22	Lou Piniella/70	.40
23	Larry Bowa/71	.40
24	Chris Chambliss/72	.25
25	Bill Buckner/72	.25
26	Don Baylor/73	.25
27	Buddy Bell/73	.25
28	Carlton Fisk/73	.75
29	Gary Mathews/74	.25
30	Davey Lopes/74	.25
31	Bob Boone/74	.25
32	Bill Madlock/75	.25
33	Claudell Washington/75	.25
34	Jim Rice/76	.40
35	Gary Carter/76	.25
36	Willie Randolph/77	.25
37	Chet Lemon/77	.25
38	Andre Dawson/78	.40
39	Eddie Murray/78	.75
40	Paul Molitor/79	.75
41	Ozzie Smith/79	1.50
42	Jeffrey Leonard/80	.25
43	Lonnie Smith/81	.25
44	Mookie Wilson/82	.25
45	Tim Wallach/82	.25
46	Tim Raines/82	.40
47	Fernando Valenzuela/82	.25
48	Cal Ripken Jr./83	3.00
49	Ryne Sandberg/84	1.50
50	Willie McGee/83	.25
51	Darryl Strawberry/84	.25
52	Julio Franco/84	.25
53	Brook Jacoby/85	.25
54	Dwight Gooden/85	.25
55	Roger McDowell/86	.25
56	Ozzie Guillen/86	.25
57	Vince Coleman/86	.25
58	Pete Incaviglia/87	.25
59	Wally Joyner/87	.25
60	Jose Canseco/87	.75
61	Cory Snyder/87	.25
62	Devon White/88	.25
63	Walt Weiss/88	.25
64	Mark Grace/89	.50
65	Ron Gant/89	.25
66	Chris Sabo/89	.25
67	Jay Buhner/89	.25
68	Gary Sheffield/90	.25
69	Gregg Jefferies/90	.25
70	Ken Griffey Jr./90	2.00
71	Tom Gordon/90	.25
72	Jim Abbott/90	.25
73	David Justice/91	.40
74	Larry Walker/91	.40
75	Sandy Alomar Jr./91	.25
76	Chuck Knoblauch/92	.25
77	Jeff Bagwell/92	.50
78	Luis Gonzalez/92	.25
79	Ivan Rodriguez/92	.50
80	Eric Karros/93	.25
81	Jeff Kent/93	.25
82	Kenny Lofton/93	.25
83	Moises Alou/93	.25
84	Reggie Sanders/93	.25
85	Jeff Conine/94	.25
86	J.T. Snow/94	.25
87	Tim Salmon/94	.25
88	Mike Piazza/94	1.50
89	Manny Ramirez/95	.75
90	Ryan Klesko/95	.25
91	Javy Lopez/95	.25
92	Chipper Jones/96	1.00
93	Ray Durham/96	.25
94	Garret Anderson/96	.25
95	Shawn Green/96	.25
96	Hideo Nomo/96	.40
97	Jermaine Dye/97	.25
98	Tony Clark/97	.25
99	Joe Randa/97	.25
100	Derek Jeter/97	3.00
101	Jason Kendall/97	.25
102	Billy Wagner/97	.25
103	Andruw Jones/98	.75
104	Dmitri Young/98	.25
105	Scott Rolen/98	.75
106	Nomar Garciaparra/98	.75
107	Jose Cruz Jr./98	.25
108	Scott Hatteberg/98	.25
109	Mark Kotsay/99	.25
110	Todd Helton/99	.50
111	Miguel Cairo/99	.25
112	Magglio Ordonez/99	.25
113	Kerry Wood/99	.40
114	Preston Wilson/00	.25
115	Alex Gonzalez/00	.25
116	Carlos Beltran/00	.50
117	Rafael Furcal/01	.25
118	Pat Burrell/01	.25
119	Adam Kennedy/01	.25
120	Terrence Long/01	.25
121	Jay Payton/01	.25
122	Bengie Molina/01	.25
123	Albert Pujols/02	3.00
124	Craig Wilson/02	.25
125	Alfonso Soriano/02	.50
126	Jimmy Rollins/02	.50
127	Adam Dunn/02	.75
128	Ichiro Suzuki/02	2.00
129	Roy Oswalt/02	.40
130	C.C. Sabathia/02	.25
131	Brad Wilkerson/03	.25
132	Nick Johnson/03	.25
133	Eric Hinske/03	.25
134	Austin Kearns/03	.25
135	Dontrelle Willis/04	.75
136	Mark Teixeira/04	.75
137	Rocco Baldelli/04	.25
138	Scott Podsednik/04	.25
139	Brandon Webb/04	.25
140	Jason Bay/04	.25
141	Adam LaRoche/05	.25
142	Khalil Greene/05	.25
143	Joe Mauer/05	.50
144	Matt Holliday/05	.25
145	Chad Tracy/05	.25
146	Garrett Atkins/06	.25
147	Tadahito Iguchi/06	1.50
148	Russ Adams/06	.25
149	Huston Street/06	.25
150	Dan Johnson/06	.25

2005 Topps Turkey Red

RUINS, CINCINNATI

	NM/M
Common Player:	.25
Common SP:	4.00
Inserted 1:4	
Pack (8):	5.00
Box (24):	100.00

1	Barry Bonds Grey Uniform/SP		15.00
1	Barry Bonds		4.00
2	Michael Young		.25
3	Jim Edmonds		.50
4	Cliff Floyd		.25
5	Roger Clemens Blue Sky/SP		12.00
5	Roger Clemens Yellow Sky/SP		12.00
6	Hal Chase		.25
7	Shannon Stewart		.25
8	Fred Clarke		.25
9	Travis Hafner		.50
10	Sammy Sosa w/Name/SP		6.00
10	Sammy Sosa w/o Name/SP		6.00
11	Jermaine Dye		.25
12	Lyle Overbay		.25
13	Oliver Perez		.25
14	Red Dooin		.25
15	Kid Elberfeld		.25
16	Mike Piazza Blue Uniform/SP		6.00
16	Mike Piazza Pinstripe		1.50
17	Bret Boone		.25
18	Hughie Jennings		.25
19	Jeff Francis		.25
20	Manny Ramirez/SP		6.00
21	Russ Ortiz		.25
22	Carlos Zambrano		.50
23	Luis Castillo		.25
24	David DeJesus		.25
25	Carlos Beltran/SP		5.00
26	Doug Davis		.25
27	Bobby Abreu		.50
28	Rich Harden/SP		4.00
29	Brian Giles		.25
30	Richie Sexson/SP		4.00
31	Nick Johnson		.25
32	Roy Halladay		.50
33	Andy Pettitte		.50
34	Miguel Cabrera		1.00
35	Jeff Kent		.25
36	Chone Figgins		.25
37	Carlos Lee		.50
38	Greg Maddux		2.00
39	Preston Wilson		.25
40	Chipper Jones		1.00
41	Coco Crisp		.25
42	Adam Dunn		.75
43	Miguel Tejada CL		.50
44	Gary Sheffield CL		.50
45	Javy Lopez CL		.25
46	Scott Rolen CL		.50
47	Todd Helton CL		.50
48	Roger Clemens CL		1.00
49	Jimmy Rollins CL		.40
50	Ichiro Suzuki CL		1.00
51	Cliff Floyd CL		.25
52	Johan Santana CL		.50
53	Mark Teixeira		.75
54	Chris Carpenter		.25
55	Roy Oswalt		4.00
56	Casey Kotchman		.25
57	Torii Hunter		.25
58	Jose Reyes		.50
59	Wily Mo Pena/SP		4.00
60	Magglio Ordonez/SP		4.00
61	Aaron Miles		.25
62	Dallas McPherson		.25
63	Javy Lopez		.25
64	Luis Gonzalez		.25
65	David Ortiz		1.00
66	Jorge Posada		.50
67	Xavier Nady		.25
68	Larry Walker		.50
69	Mark Loretta		.25
70	Jim Thome SP		5.00
71	Livan Hernandez		.25
72	Garrett Atkins		.25
73	Milton Bradley		.25
74	B.J. Upton		.25
75	Ichiro Suzuki w/Name/SP		8.00
75	Ichiro Suzuki w/o Name/SP		8.00
76	Aramis Ramirez		.25
77	Eric Milton		.25
78	Troy Glaus SP		4.00
79	David Newhan		.25
80	Delmon Young		.50
81	Justin Morneau		.40
82	Ramon Ortiz		.25
83	Eric Chavez Blue Sky		.25
83	Eric Chavez Purple Sky/SP		4.00
84	Sean Burroughs		.25
85	Scott Rolen/SP		6.00
86	Rocco Baldelli		.25
87	Joe Mauer/SP		5.00
88	Tony Womack		.25
89	Ken Griffey Jr.		2.00
90	Alfonso Soriano/SP		6.00
91	Paul Konerko		.25
92	Guillermo Mota		.25
93	Lance Berkman		.50
94	Mark Buehrle		.25
95	Matt Clement		.25
96	Melvin Mora		.25
97	Khalil Greene		.50
98	David Wright		1.50
99	Jack Wilson		.25
100	Alex Rodriguez w/Bat/SP		10.00
100	Alex Rodriguez w/Glove/SP		10.00
101	Joe Nathan		.25
102	Adrian Beltre Grey Uniform/SP		4.00
102	Adrian Beltre White Uniform		.25
103	Mike Sweeney		.25
104	Brad Lidge		.25
105	Shawn Green		.25
106	Miguel Tejada/SP		5.00
107	Derrek Lee		.75
108	Eric Hinske		.25
109	Eric Byrnes		.25
110	Hideki Matsui/SP		8.00
111	Tom Glavine		.50
112	Jimmy Rollins		.40
113	Ryan Drese		.25
114	Josh Beckett		.25
115	Curt Schilling/SP		6.00
116	Jeremy Bonderman		.25
117	Hideki Matsui		.25
118	Chase Utley		.50
119	Troy Percival		.25
120	Vladimir Guerrero w/Bat/SP		6.00

#	Player	Price
120	Vladimir Guerrero w/Glove/SP	6.00
121	Gary Sheffield	.50
122	Jeromy Burnitz	.25
123	Javier Vazquez	.25
124	Kevin Millar	.25
125	Randy Johnson Blue Sky	1.00
125	Randy Johnson Purple Sky/SP	5.00
126	Pat Burrell	.25
127	Jason Schmidt	.25
128	Jose Vidro	.25
129	Kip Wells	.25
130	Ivan Rodriguez w/Cap	.75
130	Ivan Rodriguez w/Helmet/SP	6.00
131	C.C. Sabathia	.25
132	Carlos Delgado/SP	4.00
133	Bartolo Colon	.25
134	Andruw Jones	.50
135	Kerry Wood	.50
136	Sidney Ponson	.25
137	Eric Gagne	.25
138	Rickie Weeks	.50
139	Mariano Rivera	.50
140	Bobby Crosby	.25
141	Jamie Moyer	.25
142	Corey Koskie	.25
143	John Smoltz	.50
144	Frank Thomas	.75
145	Cristian Guzman	.25
146	Paul LoDuca	.25
147	Geoff Jenkins	.25
148	Nick Swisher	.25
149	Jason Bay/SP	4.00
150	Albert Pujols/SP	10.00
151	Edwin Jackson	.25
152	Carl Crawford	.50
153	Mark Mulder	.50
154	Rafael Palmeiro	.75
155	Pedro Martinez/SP	6.00
156	Jake Westbrook	.25
157	Sean Casey	.25
158	Aaron Rowand	.25
159	J.D. Drew	.25
160	Johan Santana Glove on Knee/SP	5.00
160	Johan Santana Throwing/SP	5.00
161	Gavin Floyd	.25
162	Vernon Wells	.25
163	Aubrey Huff	.25
164	Jeff Bagwell	.50
165	David Wells	.25
166	Brad Penny	.25
167	Austin Kearns	.25
168	Mike Mussina	.50
169	Randy Wolf	.25
170	Tim Hudson/SP	4.00
171	Casey Blake	.25
172	Edgar Renteria	.50
173	Ben Sheets	.50
174	Kevin Brown	.25
175	Nomar Garciaparra/SP	8.00
176	Armando Benitez	.25
177	Jody Gerut	.25
178	Craig Biggio	.50
179	Omar Vizquel	.25
180	Jake Peavy	.50
181	Gustavo Chacin/SP	4.00
182	Johnny Damon	.75
183	Mike Lieberthal	.25
184	Felix Hernandez/SP	10.00
185	Zach Day/SP	4.00
186	Matt Cain	.25
187	Erubiel Durazo	.25
188	Zack Greinke	.25
189	Matt Morris	.25
190	Billy Wagner	.25
191	Al Leiter	.25
192	Miguel Olivo	.25
193	Jose Capellan/SP	4.00
194	Adam Eaton	.25
195	Steven White/SP	4.00
196	Joe Randa	.25
197	Richard Hidalgo	.25
198	Orlando Cabrera	.25
199	Joel Guzman/SP	6.00
200	Garret Anderson	.50
201	Endy Chavez	.25
202	Andy Marte	.25
203	Jose Guillen	.25
204	Victor Martinez	.25
205	Johnny Estrada	.25
206	Damian Miller	.25
207	Ken Harvey	.25
208	Ronnie Belliard	.25
209	Chan Ho Park	.25
210	Laynce Nix	.25
211	Lew Ford	.25
212	Moises Alou	.50
213	Kris Benson	.25
214	Mike Gonzalez/SP	4.00
215	Chris Burke	.25
216	Juan Pierre	.25
217	Phil Nevin	.25
218	Jerry Hairston Jr.	.25
219	Jeremy Reed	.25
220	Scott Kazmir SP	4.00
221	Mike Maroth	.25
222	Alex Rios	.25
223	Esteban Loaiza	.25
224	Terrmel Sledge	.25
225	Mark Prior	
225	Mark Prior Blue Sky/SP	5.00
225	Mark Prior Yellow Sky/SP	5.00
226	Hank Blalock	.50
227	Craig Wilson	.25
228	Cesar Izturis	.25
229	Dmitri Young	.25
230	Derek Jeter Blue Sky/SP	15.00
230	Derek Jeter Purple Sky/SP	15.00
231	Mark Kotsay	.25
232	Darin Erstad	.25
233	Brandon Backe/SP	4.00
234	Mike Lowell	.25
235	Scott Podsednik	.25
236	Michael Barrett	.25
237	Chad Tracy	.25
238	David Dellucci	.25
239	Brady Clark	.25
240	Jorge Cantu	.25
241	Wilfredo Ledezma	.25
242	Morgan Ensberg	.25
243	Omar Infante	.25
244	Corey Patterson	.25
245	Matt Holliday	.50
246	Vinny Castilla	.25
247	Jason Bartlett	.25
248	Noah Lowry	.25
249	Huston Street	.25
250	Russell Branyan	.25
251	Juan Uribe	.25
252	Larry Bigbie	.25
253	Grady Sizemore	.50
254	Pedro Feliz	.25
255	Brad Wilkerson	.25
256	Brandon Inge	.25
257	Dewon Brazelton	.25
258	Rodrigo Lopez	.25
259	Jacque Jones	.25
260	Jason Giambi	.50
261	Clint Barmes	.25
262	Willy Taveras	.25
263	Marcus Giles	.25
264	Joe Blanton	.25
265	John Thomson	.25
266	Steve Finley/SP	4.00
267	Kevin Millwood	.25
268	David Eckstein	.25
269	Barry Zito	.50
270	Todd Helton Purple Sky/SP	5.00
270	Todd Helton Yellow Sky/SP	5.00
271	Landon Powell RC	1.00
272	Justin Verlander RC	3.00
273	Wes Swackhamer RC	1.00
274	Wladimir Balentien RC	2.00
275	Philip Humber RC	1.00
276	Kevin Melillo RC	2.00
277	Billy Butler RC	5.00
278	Michael Rogers RC	1.00
279	Bobby Livingston RC	1.00
280	Glen Perkins RC	1.00
281	Michael Bourn RC	1.00
282	Tyler Pelland RC	1.00
283	Jeremy West RC	2.00
284	Brandon McCarthy RC	4.00
285	Ian Kinsler RC	3.00
286	Chris Roberson RC	1.00
287	Melky Cabrera RC	2.00
288	Ryan Sweeney RC	1.00
289	Chip Cannon RC	1.50
290	Andy LaRoche RC	5.00
291	Chuck Tiffany RC	1.00
292	Ian Bladergroen RC	1.00
293	Bear Bay RC	1.00
294	Hernan Iribarren RC	1.00
295	Stuart Pomeranz RC	1.00
296	Luke Scott RC	1.00
297	Chuck James RC	2.00
298	Kennard Bibbs RC	1.00
299	Steve Bondurant RC	1.50
300	Tom Oldham RC	1.00
301	Nolan Ryan	3.00
302	Reggie Jackson	1.00
303	Tom Seaver	1.00
304	Al Kaline	1.50
305	Cal Ripken Jr.	4.00
306	Josh Gibson	1.50
307	Frank Robinson	1.00
308	Duke Snider	1.00
309	Wade Boggs	1.50
310	Tony Gwynn	2.00
311	Carl Yastrzemski	2.00
312	Ryne Sandberg	2.00
313	Gary Carter	1.00
314	Brooks Robinson	1.50
315	Ernie Banks	1.50

Black

Stars (1-315):	3-5X
SP's:	1.5-2X
Inserted 1:20	

Gold

Stars (1-315):	5-10X
SP's:	3-5X
Production 50 Sets	

Red

Stars (1-315):	1-2X
SP's:	.5-1X

Suede

No Pricing
Production One Set

White

Stars (1-315):	2-3X
SP's:	1-1.5X
Inserted 1:4	

Autographs

		NM/M
	Common Auto.:	10.00
BB	Barry Bonds	
MB	Matt Bush	15.00
CC	Carl Crawford	20.00
SE	Scott Elbert	20.00
JF	Josh Fields	15.00
EG	Eric Gagne	20.00
JG	Jody Gerut	10.00
JPH	J.P. Howell	15.00
ZJ	Zach Jackson	12.00
JJ	Jason Jaramillo	12.00
BJ	Blake Johnson	15.00
CN	Chris Nelson	10.00
DO	David Ortiz	50.00
ZP	Zachary Parker	12.00
DP	Dustin Pedroia	40.00
MR	Mariano Rivera	60.00
MRO	Mike Rodriguez	10.00
GS	Gary Sheffield	40.00
AS	Alfonso Soriano	40.00
JS	Jeremy Sowers	20.00

B-18 Blanket Boxloaders

		NM/M
	Common Blanket	8.00
	Barry Bonds	20.00

	Roger Clemens	20.00
	Todd Helton	8.00
	Derek Jeter	20.00
	Alex Rodriguez	15.00
	Curt Schilling	12.00
	Alfonso Soriano	8.00
	Ichiro Suzuki	15.00

Cabinet Boxloaders

		NM/M
	Inserted 1:Box	
BB	Barry Bonds	25.00
GB	George W. Bush	10.00
RJ	Randy Johnson	12.00
MP	Mike Piazza	12.00
AP	Albert Pujols	20.00
MR	Manny Ramirez	12.00
AR	Alex Rodriguez	20.00
SR	Scott Rolen	10.00
JS	Johan Santana	12.00
SS	Sammy Sosa	15.00
WT	William H. Taft	15.00
MT	Miguel Tejada	10.00
JT	Jim Thome	10.00
GW	George Washington	25.00

Cabinet Autograph Relics

		NM/M
	Production 5-450	
MB	Matt Bush/450	25.00
CC	Carl Crawford/450	25.00
JG	Jody Gerut/450	20.00
MK	Mark Kotsay/450	30.00
BM	Brett Myers/150	40.00
DO	David Ortiz/75	100.00
MR	Mariano Rivera/25	90.00
AR	Alex Rodriguez/25	400.00
GS	Gary Sheffield/25	100.00
AS	Alfonso Soriano/75	75.00

Cut Signatures

Production One Set

Relics

		NM/M
	Common Player:	4.00
JB	Jeff Bagwell	6.00
CB	Carlos Beltran	6.00
AB	Adrian Beltre	6.00
HB	Hank Blalock	6.00
BB	Barry Bonds	20.00
MC	Miguel Cabrera	8.00
RC	Roger Clemens	15.00
RC2	Roger Clemens	15.00
JD	Johnny Damon	10.00
JD2	Johnny Damon	10.00
VG	Vladimir Guerrero	8.00
TH	Todd Helton	6.00
CJ	Chipper Jones	8.00
ML	Mike Lowell	4.00
MM	Mark Mulder	4.00
MO	Magglio Ordonez	4.00
DO	David Ortiz	8.00
RP	Rafael Palmeiro	6.00
MP	Mike Piazza	8.00
MPR	Mark Prior	6.00
AP	Albert Pujols	15.00
MR	Manny Ramirez	8.00
AR	Alex Rodriguez	12.00
AR2	Alex Rodriguez	12.00
CS	Curt Schilling	8.00
GS	Gary Sheffield	6.00
AS	Alfonso Soriano	8.00
SS	Sammy Sosa	10.00
MTE	Mark Teixeira	6.00
MT	Miguel Tejada	8.00
JT	Jim Thome	6.00
LW	Larry Walker	4.00

2006 Topps

	NM/M
Complete Set (659):	60.00
Complete Hobby Set (664):	75.00
Complete Holiday Set (659):	75.00
Complete Cardinals Set (664):	75.00
Complete Cubs Set (664):	75.00
Complete Pirates Set (664):	75.00

Complete Red Sox Set
(664): 75.00
Complete Yankees Set
(664): 75.00
Common Player: .10
Pack (10): 2.00
Box (36): 60.00
Jumbo Pack (35): 6.00
Jumbo Box (12): 60.00

1	Alex Rodriguez	1.50
2	Jose Valentin	.10
3	Garrett Atkins	.10
4	Scott Hatteberg	.10
5	Carl Crawford	.25
6	Armando Benitez	.10
7	Mickey Mantle	5.00
8	Mike Morse	.10
9	Damian Miller	.10
10	Clint Barmes	.10
11	Michael Barrett	.10
12	Coco Crisp	.10
13	Tadahito Iguchi	.25
14	Chris Snyder	.10
15	Brian Roberts	.10
16	David Wright	1.00
17	Victor Santos	.10
18	Trevor Hoffman	.10
19	Jeremy Reed	.10
20	Bobby Abreu	.25
21	Lance Berkman	.25
22	Zach Day	.10
23	Jonny Gomes	.10
24	Jason Marquis	.10
25	Chipper Jones	.50
26	Scott Hairston	.10
27	Ryan Dempster	.10
28	Brandon Inge	.10
29	Aaron Harang	.10
30	Jon Garland	.10
31	Pokey Reese	.10
32	Mike MacDougal	.10
33	Mike Lieberthal	.10
34	Cesar Izturis	.10
35	Brad Wilkerson	.10
36	Jeff Suppan	.10
37	Adam Everett	.10
38	Bengie Molina	.10
39	Rickie Weeks	.25
40	Jorge Posada	.25
41	Rheal Cormier	.10
42	Reed Johnson	.10
43	Laynce Nix	.10
44	Carl Everett	.10
45	Greg Maddux	1.00
46	Jeff Francis	.10
47	Felipe Lopez	.10
48	Dan Johnson	.10
49	Humberto Cota	.10
50	Manny Ramirez	.50
51	Juan Uribe	.10
52	Jaret Wright	.10
53	Tomokazu Ohka	.10
54	Mike Matheny	.10
55	Joe Mauer	.25
56	Jarrod Washburn	.10
57	Randy Winn	.10
58	Pedro Feliz	.10
59	Kenny Rogers	.10
60	Rocco Baldelli	.10
61	Eric Hinske	.10
62	Damaso Marte	.10
63	Desi Relaford	.10
64	Juan Encarnacion	.10
65	Nomar Garciaparra	.50
66	Shawn Estes	.10
67	Brian Jordan	.10
68	Steve Kline	.10
69	Braden Looper	.10
70	Carlos Lee	.10
71	Tom Glavine	.25
72	Craig Biggio	.25
73	Steve Finley	.10
74	David Newhan	.10
75	Eric Gagne	.20
76	Tony Graffanino	.10
77	Dallas McPherson	.10
78	Nick Punto	.10
79	Mark Kotsay	.10
80	Kerry Wood	.25
81	Kyle Farnsworth	.10
82	Huston Street	.20
83	Endy Chavez	.10
84	So Taguchi	.10
85	Hank Blalock	.25
86	Brad Radke	.10
87	Chien-Ming Wang	.50
88	B.J. Surhoff	.10
89	Glendon Rusch	.10
90	Mark Buehrle	.25
91	Rafael Betancourt	.10
92	Lance Cormier	.10
93	Alex Gonzalez	.10
94	Matt Stairs	.10
95	Andy Pettitte	.25
96	Jesse Crain	.10
97	Kenny Lofton	.10
98	Geoff Blum	.10
99	Mark Redman	.10
100	Barry Bonds	1.50
101	Chad Orvella	.10
102	Xavier Nady	.10
103	Junior Spivey	.10
104	Bernie Williams	.25
105	Victor Martinez	.25
106	Nook Logan	.10
107	Mark Teahen	.10
108	Mike Lamb	.10
109	Jayson Werth	.10
110	Mariano Rivera	.25
111	Erubiel Durazo	.10
112	Ryan Vogelsong	.10
113	Bobby Madritsch	.10
114	Travis Lee	.10
115	Adam Dunn	.40
116	David Riske	.10
117	Troy Percival	.10
118	Chad Tracy	.20
119	Andy Marte	.20
120	Edgar Renteria	.20
121	Jason Giambi	.25
122	Justin Morneau	.40
123	J.T. Snow	.10
124	Danys Baez	.10
125	Carlos Delgado	.25
126	John Buck	.10
127	Shannon Stewart	.10
128	Mike Cameron	.10
129	Joe McEwing	.10
130	Richie Sexson	.25
131	Rod Barajas	.10
132	Russ Adams	.10
133	J.D. Closser	.10
134	Ramon Ortiz	.10
135	Josh Beckett	.25
136	Ryan Freel	.10
137	Victor Zambrano	.10
138	Ronnie Belliard	.10
139	Jason Michaels	.10
140	Brian Giles	.20
141	Randy Wolf	.10
142	Robinson Cano	.40
143	Joe Blanton	.10
144	Esteban Loaiza	.10
145	Troy Glaus	.25
146	Matt Clement	.10
147	Geoff Jenkins	.10
148	John Thomson	.10
149	A.J. Pierzynski	.10
150	Pedro Martinez	.25
151	Roger Clemens	1.50
152	Jack Wilson	.10
153	Ray King	.10
154	Ryan Church	.10
155	Paul LoDuca	.10
156	Dan Wheeler	.10
157	Carlos Zambrano	.25
158	Mike Timlin	.10
159	Brandon Claussen	.10
160	Travis Hafner	.25
161	Chris Shelton	.10
162	Rafael Furcal	.25
163	Flash Gordon	.10
164	Noah Lowry	.10
165	Larry Walker	.25
166	Dave Roberts	.10
167	Scott Schoeneweis	.10
168	Julian Tavarez	.10
169	Jhonny Peralta	.25
170	Vernon Wells	.25
171	Jorge Cantu	.20
172	Todd Greene	.10
173	Willy Taveras	.10
174	Corey Patterson	.10
175	Ivan Rodriguez	.40
176	Bobby Kielty	.10
177	Jose Reyes	.25
178	Barry Zito	.25
179	Deivi Cruz	.10
180	Mark Teixeira	.50
181	Chone Figgins	.10
182	Aaron Rowand	.10
183	Tim Wakefield	.10
184	Mike Maroth	.10
185	Johnny Damon	.50
186	Vicente Padilla	.10
187	Ryan Klesko	.10
188	Gary Matthews	.10
189	Jose Mesa	.10
190	Nick Johnson	.10
191	Freddy Garcia	.10
192	Larry Bigbie	.10
193	Chris Ray	.10
194	Torii Hunter	.25
195	Mike Sweeney	.10
196	Brad Penny	.10
197	Jason Frasor	.10
198	Kevin Mench	.10
199	Adam Kennedy	.10
200	Albert Pujols	1.50
201	Jody Gerut	.10
202	Luis Gonzalez	.10
203	Zack Greinke	.10
204	Miguel Cairo	.10
205	Jimmy Rollins	.25
206	Edgardo Alfonzo	.10
207	Billy Wagner	.10
208	B.J. Ryan	.10
209	Orlando Hudson	.10
210	Preston Wilson	.10
211	Melvin Mora	.10
212	Bill Mueller	.10
213	Javy Lopez	.10
214	Wilson Betemit	.10
215	Garret Anderson	.10
216	Russell Branyan	.10
217	Jeff Weaver	.10
218	Doug Mientkiewicz	.10
219	Mark Ellis	.10
220	Jason Bay	.25
221	Adam LaRoche	.10
222	C.C. Sabathia	.10
223	Humberto Quintero	.10
224	Bartolo Colon	.10
225	Ichiro Suzuki	1.00
226	Brett Tomko	.10
227	Corey Koskie	.10
228	David Eckstein	.10
229	Cristian Guzman	.10
230	Jeff Kent	.25
231	Chris Capuano	.10
232	Rodrigo Lopez	.10
233	Jason Phillips	.10
234	Luis Rivas	.10
235	Cliff Floyd	.10
236	Gil Meche	.10
237	Adam Eaton	.10
238	Matt Morris	.25
239	Kyle Davies	.10
240	David Wells	.10
241	John Smoltz	.25
242	Felix Hernandez	.50
243	Kenny Rogers	.10
244	Mark Teixeira	.25
245	Orlando Hudson	.10
246	Derek Jeter	1.00
247	Eric Chavez	.20
248	Torii Hunter	.10
249	Vernon Wells	.10
250	Ichiro Suzuki	.50
251	Greg Maddux	.50
252	Mike Matheny	.10
253	Derrek Lee	.25
254	Luis Castillo	.10
255	Omar Vizquel	.10
256	Mike Lowell	.10
257	Andruw Jones	.25
258	Jim Edmonds	.20
259	Bobby Abreu	.20
260	Bartolo Colon	.10
261	Chris Carpenter	.10
262	Alex Rodriguez	1.00
263	Albert Pujols	1.00
264	Huston Street	.10
265	Ryan Howard	.50
266	Bob Melvin	.10
267	Bobby Cox	.10
268	Baltimore Orioles	.10
269	Boston Red Sox	.25
270	Chicago White Sox	.25
271	Dusty Baker	.10
272	Jerry Narron	.10
273	Cleveland Indians	.10
274	Clint Hurdle	.10
275	Detroit Tigers	.10
276	Jack McKeon	.10
277	Phil Garner	.10
278	Kansas City Royals	.10
279	Jim Tracy	.10
280	Angels	.10
281	Milwaukee Brewers	.10
282	Minnesota Twins	.10
283	Willie Randolph	.10
284	New York Yankees	.50
285	Oakland Athletics	.10
286	Charlie Manuel	.10
287	Pete Mackanin	.10
288	Bruce Bochy	.10
289	Felipe Alou	.10
290	Seattle Mariners	.10
291	Tony LaRussa	.10
292	Tampa Bay Devil Rays	.10
293	Texas Rangers	.10
294	Toronto Blue Jays	.10
295	Frank Robinson	.25
296	Anderson Hernandez (RC)	.10
297a	Alex Gordon (Complete card. Not officially issued.)	
297b	Alex Gordon (Cut-out card.)	80.00
298	Jason Botts (RC)	.10
299	Jeff Mathis (RC)	.10
300	Ryan Garko (RC)	.10
301	Charlton Jimerson (RC)	.10
302	Chris Denorfia (RC)	.10
303	Anthony Reyes (RC)	.10
304	Bryan Bullington (RC)	.10
305	Chuck James (RC)	.10
306	Danny Sandoval RC	.25
307	Walter Young (RC)	.10
308	Fausto Carmona (RC)	.10
309	Francisco Liriano (RC)	1.00
310	Hong-Chih Kuo (RC)	.10
311	Joe Saunders (RC)	.10
312	John Koronka (RC)	.10
313	Robert Andino RC	.25
314	Shaun Marcum (RC)	.10
315	Tom Gorzelanny (RC)	.10
316	Craig Breslow RC	.25
317	Chris Demaria RC	.50
318	Brayan Pena (RC)	.10
319	Rich Hill (RC)	.25
320	Rick Short RC	.25
321	C.J. Wilson (RC)	.10
322	Marshall McDougall (RC)	.10
323	Darrell Rasner (RC)	.10
324	Brandon Watson (RC)	.10
325	Paul McAnulty (RC)	.10
326	Derek Jeter, Alex Rodriguez	.50
327	Miguel Tejada, Melvin Mora	.25
328	Marcus Giles, Chipper Jones	.25
329	Manny Ramirez, David Ortiz	.25
330	Michael Barrett, Greg Maddux	.25
331	Matt Holliday	.25
332	Orlando Cabrera	.10
333	Ryan Langerhans	.10
334	Lew Ford	.10
335	Mark Prior	.40
336	Ted Lilly	.10
337	Michael Young	.25
338	Livan Hernandez	.10
339	Yadier Molina	.10
340	Eric Chavez	.25
341	Miguel Batista	.10
342	Bruce Chen	.10
343	Sean Casey	.10
344	Doug Davis	.10
345	Andruw Jones	.40
346	Hideki Matsui	1.00
347	Joe Randa	.10
348	Reggie Sanders	.10
349	Jason Jennings	.10
350	Joe Nathan	.10
351	Jose Lopez	.10
352	John Lackey	.10
353	Claudio Vargas	.10
354	Grady Sizemore	.25
355	Jonathan Papelbon (RC)	3.00
356	Luis Matos	.10
357	Orlando Hernandez	.10
358	Jamie Moyer	.10
359	Chase Utley	.25
360	Moises Alou	.25
361	Chad Cordero	.10
362	Brian McCann	.25
363	Jermaine Dye	.10
364	Ryan Madson	.10
365	Aramis Ramirez	.25
366	Matt Treanor	.10
367	Ray Durham	.10
368	Khalil Greene	.10
369	Mike Hampton	.10
370	Mike Mussina	.25
371	Brad Hawpe	.10
372	Marlon Byrd	.10
373	Woody Williams	.10
374	Victor Diaz	.10

#	Player	Value
375	Brady Clark	.10
376	Luis Gonzalez	.10
377	Raul Ibanez	.10
378	Tony Clark	.10
379	Shawn Chacon	.10
380	Marcus Giles	.10
381	Odalis Perez	.10
382	Steve Trachsel	.10
383	Russ Ortiz	.10
384	Toby Hall	.10
385	Bill Hall	.10
386	Luke Hudson	.10
387	Ken Griffey Jr.	1.00
388	Tim Hudson	.25
389	Brian Moehler	.10
390	Jake Peavy	.25
391	Casey Blake	.10
392	Sidney Ponson	.10
393	Brian Schneider	.10
394	J.J. Hardy	.10
395	Austin Kearns	.25
396	Pat Burrell	.25
397	Jason Vargas	.10
398	Ryan Howard	.75
399	Joe Crede	.10
400	Vladimir Guerrero	.50
401	Roy Halladay	.25
402	David Dellucci	.10
403	Brandon Webb	.10
404	Marlon Anderson	.10
405	Miguel Tejada	.25
406	Ryan Doumit	.10
407	Kevin Youkilis	.10
408	Jon Lieber	.10
409	Edwin Encarnacion	.10
410	Miguel Cabrera	.50
411	A.J. Burnett	.10
412	David Bell	.10
413	Gregg Zaun	.10
414	Lance Niekro	.10
415	Shawn Green	.10
416	Roberto Hernandez	.10
417	Jay Gibbons	.10
418	Johnny Estrada	.10
419	Omar Vizquel	.10
420	Gary Sheffield	.25
421	Brad Halsey	.10
422	Aaron Cook	.10
423	David Ortiz	.50
424	Tony Womack	.10
425	Joe Kennedy	.10
426	Dustin McGowan	.10
427	Carl Pavano	.10
428	Nick Green	.10
429	Francisco Cordero	.10
430	Octavio Dotel	.10
431	Julio Franco	.10
432	Brett Myers	.10
433	Casey Kotchman	.10
434	Frank Catalanotto	.10
435	Paul Konerko	.25
436	Keith Foulke	.10
437	Juan Rivera	.10
438	Todd Pratt	.10
439	Ben Broussard	.10
440	Scott Kazmir	.25
441	Rich Aurilia	.10
442	Craig Monroe	.10
443	Danny Kolb	.10
444	Curtis Granderson	.20
445	Jeff Francoeur	.20
446	Dustin Hermanson	.10
447	Jacque Jones	.10
448	Bobby Crosby	.10
449	Jason LaRue	.10
450	Derrek Lee	.40
451	Curt Schilling	.50
452	Jake Westbrook	.10
453	Daniel Cabrera	.10
454	Bobby Jenks	.10
455	Dontrelle Willis	.25
456	Brad Lidge	.10
457	Shea Hillenbrand	.10
458	Luis Castillo	.10
459	Mark Hendrickson	.10
460	Randy Johnson	.50
461	Placido Polanco	.10
462	Aaron Boone	.10
463	Todd Walker	.10
464	Nick Swisher	.10
465	Joel Pineiro	.10
466	Jay Payton	.10
467	Cliff Lee	.10
468	Johan Santana	.50
469	Josh Willingham (RC)	.10
470	Jeremy Bonderman	.10
471	Runelvys Hernandez	.10
472	Duaner Sanchez	.10
473	Jason Lane	.10
474	Trot Nixon	.10
475	Ramon Hernandez	.10
476	Mike Lowell	.10
477	Chan Ho Park	.10
478	Doug Waechter	.10
479	Carlos Silva	.10
480	Jose Contreras	.10
481	Vinny Castilla	.10
482	Chris Reitsma	.10
483	Jose Guillen	.10
484	Aaron Hill	.10
485	Kevin Millwood	.10
486	Wily Mo Pena	.10
487	Rich Harden	.10
488	Chris Carpenter	.25
489	Jason Bartlett	.10
490	Magglio Ordonez	.20
491	John Rodriguez	.10
492	Bob Wickman	.10
493	Eddie Guardado	.10
494	Kip Wells	.10
495	Adrian Beltre	.20
496	Jose Capellan (RC)	.10
497	Scott Podsednik	.20
498	Brad Thompson	.10
499	Aaron Heilman	.10
500	Derek Jeter	1.50
501	Emil Brown	.10
502	Morgan Ensberg	.20
503	Nate Bump	.10
504	Phil Nevin	.10
505	Jason Schmidt	.20
506	Michael Cuddyer	.10
507	John Patterson	.10
508	Danny Haren	.10
509	Freddy Sanchez	.10
510	J.D. Drew	.25
511	Dmitri Young	.10
512	Eric Milton	.10
513	Ervin Santana	.10
514	Mark Loretta	.10
515	Mark Grudzielanek	.10
516	Derrick Turnbow	.10
517	Danny Bautista	.10
518	Lyle Overbay	.10
519	Julio Lugo	.10
520	Carlos Beltran	.40
521	Jose Cruz Jr.	.10
522	Jason Isringhausen	.10
523	Bronson Arroyo	.10
524	Ben Sheets	.20
525	Zachary Duke	.10
526	Ryan Wagner	.10
527	Jose Vidro	.10
528	Doug Mirabelli	.10
529	Kris Benson	.10
530	Carlos Guillen	.10
531	Juan Pierre	.10
532	Scot Shields	.10
533	Scott Hatteberg	.10
534	Tim Stauffer	.10
535	Jim Edmonds	.25
536	Scott Eyre	.10
537	Ben Johnson (RC)	.10
538	Mark Mulder	.25
539	Juan Rincon	.10
540	Gustavo Chacin	.10
541	Oliver Perez	.10
542	Chris Young	.10
543	Edinson Volquez	.10
544	Mark Bellhorn	.10
545	Kelvim Escobar	.10
546	Andrew Sisco	.10
547	Derek Lowe	.10
548	Sean Burroughs	.10
549	Erik Bedard	.10
550	Alfonso Soriano	.40
551	Matt Murton	.10
552	Eric Byrnes	.10
553	Chris Duffy	.10
554	Kazuo Matsui	.10
555	Scott Rolen	.40
556	Robert Mackowiak	.10
557	Chris Burke	.10
558	Jeromy Burnitz	.10
559	Jerry Hairston Jr.	.10
560	Jim Thome	.40
561	Miguel Olivo	.10
562	Jose Castillo	.10
563	Brad Ausmus	.10
564	Yorvit Torrealba	.10
565	David DeJesus	.10
566	Paul Byrd	.10
567	Brandon Backe	.10
568	Aubrey Huff	.10
569	Mike Jacobs (RC)	.10
570	Todd Helton	.40
571	Angel Berroa	.10
572	Todd Jones	.10
573	Jeff Bagwell	.25
574	Darin Erstad	.10
575	Roy Oswalt	.25
576	Rondell White	.10
577	Alex Rios	.10
578	Wes Helms	.10
579	Javier Vazquez	.10
580	Frank Thomas	.40
581	Brian Fuentes	.10
582	Francisco Rodriguez	.10
583	Craig Counsell	.10
584	Jorge Sosa	.10
585	Mike Piazza	.50
586	Mike Scioscia	.10
587	Joe Torre	.25
588	Ken Macha	.10
589	John Gibbons	.10
590	Joe Maddon	.10
591	Eric Wedge	.10
592	Mike Hargrove	.10
593	Sam Perlozzo	.10
594	Buck Showalter	.10
595	Terry Francona	.10
596	Buddy Bell	.10
597	Jim Leyland	.10
598	Ron Gardenhire	.10
599	Ozzie Guillen	.10
600	Ned Yost	.10
601	Atlanta Braves	.10
602	Philadelphia Phillies	.10
603	New York Mets	.10
604	Washington Nationals	.10
605	Florida Marlins	.10
606	Houston Astros	.10
607	Chicago Cubs	.25
608	St. Louis Cardinals	.25
609	Pittsburgh Pirates	.10
610	Cincinnati Reds	.10
611	Colorado Rockies	.10
612	Los Angeles Dodgers	.25
613	San Francisco Giants	.10
614	San Diego Padres	.10
615	Arizona Diamondbacks	.10
616	Kenji Johjima RC	2.00
617	Ryan Zimmerman (RC)	2.00
618	Craig Hansen RC	1.50
619	Joey Devine RC	.25
620	Hanley Ramirez (RC)	.50
621	Scott Olsen (RC)	.25
622	Jason Bergmann RC	.25
623	Geovany Soto (RC)	.25
624	J.J. Furmaniak (RC)	.10
625	Jeremy Accardo RC	.10
626	Mark Woodyard (RC)	.10
627	Matt Capps (RC)	.10
628	Tim Corcoran RC	.25
629	Ryan Jorgensen RC	.25
630	Ronny Paulino (RC)	.10
631	Dan Uggla (RC)	.50
632	Ian Kinsler (RC)	.25
633	Josh Barfield (RC)	.25
634	Reggie Abercrombie (RC)	.10
635	Joel Zumaya (RC)	1.00
636	Matt Cain (RC)	.25
637	Conor Jackson (RC)	.25
638	Bryan Anderson (RC)	.10
639	Prince Fielder (RC)	1.00
640	Jeremy Hermida (RC)	.25
641	Justin Verlander (RC)	1.00
642	Brian Bannister (RC)	.10
643	Willie Eyre (RC)	.10
644	Ricky Nolasco (RC)	.10
645	Paul Maholm (RC)	.10
646	Johnny Damon, Jason Giambi	.25
647	Rondell White, Lew Ford	.10
648	Orlando Hernandez, Orlando Hudson	.10
649	Adam Dunn, Ken Griffey Jr.	.25
650	Pat Burrell, Mike Lieberthal	.10
651	Jose Reyes, Kazuo Matsui	.10
652	Hank Blalock, Michael Young	.10
653	Prince Fielder, Rickie Weeks	.50
654	Travis Lee, Rocco Baldelli	.10
655	Derrick Lee, Aramis Ramirez	.25
656	Grady Sizemore, Aaron Boone	.25
657	Luis Gonzalez, Shawn Green, Koyie Hill	.10
658	Ivan Rodriguez, Carlos Guillen	.10
659	Alex Rodriguez, Gary Sheffield	.25
660	Ervin Santana, Francisco Rodriguez	.10

Black

Stars:	15-25X
Production 55 Sets	
HTA Exclusive	

Gold

Stars:	5-10X
Production 2,006 Sets	

Platinum

No Pricing
Production One Set

Factory Set Rookie Bonus

		NM/M

1-5 issued in retail factory sets
6-10 issued in hobby factory sets
11-20 issued in holiday factory sets

1	Nicholas Markakis	5.00
2	Kelly Shoppach	3.00
3	Jordan Tata	3.00
4	Ruddy Lugo	3.00
5	Josh Wilson	3.00
6	Fernando Nieve	3.00
7	Sendy Rleal	3.00
8	Jason Kubel	3.00
9	James Loney	5.00
10	Fabio Castro	3.00
11	Jonathan Broxton	3.00
12	Eliezer Alfonzo	3.00
13	Jason Hirsh	3.00
14	Rajai Davis	3.00
15	Henry Owens	5.00
16	Kevin Frandsen	3.00
17	Matt Garza	5.00
18	Chris Duncan	3.00
19	Chris Coste	3.00
20	Jeff Karstens	5.00

Factory Set Team Bonus

		NM/M

Issued in specified factory team sets.

BRS1	Jonathan Papelbon	10.00
BRS2	Manny Ramirez	5.00
BRS3	David Ortiz	5.00
BRS4	Josh Beckett	3.00
BRS5	Curt Schilling	4.00
CC1	Sean Marshall	3.00
CC2	Freddie Bynum	3.00
CC3	Derrek Lee	4.00
CC4	Juan Pierre	3.00
CC5	Carlos Zambrano	3.00
NYY1	Wilbert Nieves	3.00
NYY2	Alex Rodriguez	6.00
NYY3	Derek Jeter	8.00
NYY4	Mariano Rivera	5.00
NYY5	Randy Johnson	5.00
PP1	Matt Capps	3.00
PP2	Paul Maholm	3.00
PP3	Nate McLouth	3.00
PP4	John Van Benschoten	3.00
PP5	Jason Bay	3.00
SLC1	Adam Wainwright	4.00
SLC2	Skip Schumaker	3.00
SLC3	Albert Pujols	10.00
SLC4	Jim Edmonds	3.00
SLC5	Scott Rolen	5.00

Autographs

		NM/M

Common Player:		
WB	Wade Boggs/250	50.00
JB	Jason Botts	10.00
MB	Milton Bradley	20.00
CB	Craig Breslow	10.00
FC	Fausto Carmona	15.00
BC	Brian Cashman/100	175.00
EC	Eric Chavez/200	60.00
LC	Lance Cormier	15.00
NC	Nelson Cruz	8.00
DD	Doug DeVore	8.00
TE	Theo Epstein/100	120.00
RG	Ryan Garko	20.00
AG	Alex Gordon	100.00
CG	Carlos Guillen	20.00
LH	Livan Hernandez	10.00
RH	Rich Hill	30.00
CJ	Chuck James	25.00
JJ	Josh Johnson	15.00
AL	Anthony Lerew	10.00
FL	Francisco Liriano	30.00
JM	Jeff Mathis	15.00
GN	Graig Nettles	25.00
SO	Scott Olsen	15.00
TO	Tim Olson	8.00
DO	David Ortiz/100	100.00
HR	Horacio Ramirez	10.00
DR	Darrell Rasner	10.00
ARE	Anthony Reyes	25.00
CR	Cal Ripken Jr./100	200.00
AR	Alex Rodriguez/100	450.00
RS	Ryne Sandberg/100	140.00
GS	Gary Sheffield/200	60.00
TS	Terrmel Sledge	15.00
BW	Brad Wilkerson	15.00
DW	Dave Winfield/100	150.00

MY Michael Young 25.00

Series 2

GA	Garrett Atkins	20.00
CB	Clint Barmes	15.00
JB	Jose Bautista	15.00
BB	Barry Bonds/120	400.00
RC	Robinson Cano	50.00
GC	Gary Carter/250	40.00
BC	Brandon Claussen	10.00
DD	Doug Drabek/250	20.00
JF	Jeff Francis	20.00
DJ	Dan Johnson	15.00
AJ	Andruw Jones/50	50.00
SK	Scott Kazmir	25.00
DL	Derrek Lee/250	50.00
BM	Brandon McCarthy	15.00
CO	Chad Orvella	10.00
JP	Jonathan Papelbon	60.00
WP	Wily Mo Pena/250	30.00
BR	Brian Roberts/250	40.00
DSN	Duke Snider/250	60.00
DS	Darryl Strawberry/250	25.00
CV	Claudio Vargas	15.00
RZ	Ryan Zimmerman	50.00

Hit Parade

GARY SHEFFIELD

		NM/M
Common Player:		.50
RB11	Barry Bonds	3.00
RB12	Ken Griffey Jr.	2.00
RB13	Jeff Bagwell	.75
RB14	Gary Sheffield	.75
RB15	Frank Thomas	.75
RB16	Manny Ramirez	1.00
RB17	Ruben Sierra	.50
RB18	Jeff Kent	.50
RB19	Luis Gonzalez	.75
RBl10	Alex Rodriguez	3.00
HR1	Barry Bonds	3.00
HR2	Ken Griffey Jr.	2.00
HR3	Jeff Bagwell	.75
HR4	Gary Sheffield	.75
HR5	Frank Thomas	.75
HR6	Manny Ramirez	1.00
HR7	Jim Thome	1.00
HR8	Alex Rodriguez	3.00
HR9	Mike Piazza	1.00
HR10	Carlos Delgado	.75
HT1	Craig Biggio	.50
HT2	Barry Bonds	3.00
HT3	Julio Franco	.50
HT4	Steve Finley	.50
HT5	Gary Sheffield	.75
HT6	Jeff Bagwell	.75
HT7	Ken Griffey Jr.	2.00
HT8	Omar Vizquel	.50
HT9	Marquis Grissom	.50
HT10	Bernie Williams	.50

Hobby Masters

		NM/M
Complete Set (20):		20.00
Common Player:		.75
Inserted 1:18		
HM1	Derrek Lee	1.00
HM2	Albert Pujols	4.00
HM3	Nomar Garciaparra	1.00
HM4	Alfonso Soriano	.75
HM5	Derek Jeter	4.00
HM6	Miguel Tejada	1.00
HM7	Alex Rodriguez	4.00
HM8	Jim Edmonds	1.00
HM9	Mark Prior	1.00
HM10	Roger Clemens	4.00
HM11	Randy Johnson	1.50
HM12	Manny Ramirez	1.50
HM13	Curt Schilling	1.50
HM14	Vladimir Guerrero	1.50
HM15	Barry Bonds	4.00
HM16	Ichiro Suzuki	2.50
HM17	Pedro Martinez	1.50
HM18	Carlos Beltran	1.50
HM19	David Ortiz	1.50
HM20	Andruw Jones	1.00

King of England Cut Signature

Production One

KGIII King George III

Mantle Homerun History

MICKEY MANTLE

NM/M

Inserted 1:4

Common Mantle: 2.00

Mantle Homerun History Relic

Inserted 1:4,540

Series 2

Production 7 Sets

Mantle Homerun History Cut Signature

Production One

Mickey Mantle

Opening Day

		NM/M
Common Team:		.50
WI	Chicago White Sox	2.00
MN	New York Mets	2.00
RR	Texas Rangers	1.00
BP	Milwaukee Brewers	.50
RC	Cincinnati Reds	1.00
PC	Philadelphia Phillies	1.00
OD	Baltimore Orioles	1.00
RD	Colorado Rockies	.50
DB	Los Angeles Dodgers	2.00
RT	Kansas City Royals	.50
MA	Seattle Mariners	1.00
AM	Houston Astros	1.00
PG	San Diego Padres	1.00
AY	Oakland Athletics	2.00
JT	Toronto Blue Jays	1.00

Own the Game

		NM/M
Complete Set (30):		20.00
Common Player:		.50
Inserted 1:12		
OG1	Derrek Lee	1.00
OG2	Michael Young	.75
OG3	Albert Pujols	3.00
OG4	Roger Clemens	3.00
OG5	Andy Pettitte	.75
OG6	Dontrelle Willis	.75
OG7	Michael Young	.75
OG8	Ichiro Suzuki	2.00
OG9	Derek Jeter	3.00
OG10	Andruw Jones	.75
OG11	Alex Rodriguez	3.00
OG12	David Ortiz	1.00
OG13	David Ortiz	1.00
OG14	Manny Ramirez	1.00
OG15	Mark Teixeira	1.00
OG16	Albert Pujols	3.00
OG17	Alex Rodriguez	3.00
OG18	Derek Jeter	3.00
OG19	Chad Cordero	.50
OG20	Francisco Rodriguez	.75
OG21	Mariano Rivera	.75
OG22	Chone Figgins	.50
OG23	Jose Reyes	.75
OG24	Scott Podsednik	.50
OG25	Jake Peavy	.75
OG26	Johan Santana	1.00
OG27	Pedro Martinez	1.00
OG28	Dontrelle Willis	.75
OG29	Chris Carpenter	.50
OG30	Bartolo Colon	.50

Signers of the Declaration of Independence

	NM/M
Complete Set (56):	80.00
Common Signer:	1.50
Inserted 1:4	
JA	John Adams	3.00
SA	Samuel Adams	3.00
JB	Josiah Bartlett	1.50
CB	Carter Braxton	1.50
CC	Charles Carroll	1.50
SC	Samuel Chase	1.50
AC	Abraham Clark	1.50
GC	George Clymer	1.50
WE	William Ellery	1.50
WF	William Floyd	1.50
BF	Benjamin Franklin	4.00
EG	Elbridge Gerry	1.50
BG	Button Gwinnett	1.50
LH	Lyman Hall	1.50
JH	John Hancock	3.00
BH	Benjamin Harrison	1.50
JHA	John Hart	1.50
JHE	Joseph Hewes	1.50
TH	Thomas Heyward Jr.	1.50
WH	William Hooper	1.50
SH	Stephen Hopkins	1.50
FH	Francis Hopkinson	1.50
SHU	Samuel Huntington	1.50
TJ	Thomas Jefferson	4.00
FLL	Francis Lightfoot Lee	1.50
RHL	Richard Henry Lee	1.50
FL	Francis Lewis	1.50
PL	Philip Livingston	1.50
TL	Thomas Lynch Jr.	1.50
TM	Thomas McKean	1.50
AM	Arthur Middleton	1.50
LM	Lewis Morris	1.50
RM	Robert Morris	1.50
JM	John Morton	1.50
TN	Thomas Nelson Jr.	1.50
WP	William Paca	1.50
RTP	Robert Treat Paine	1.50
JP	John Penn	1.50
GRE	George Read	1.50
CR	Caesar Rodney	1.50
GR	George Ross	1.50
BR	Benjamin Rush	1.50
ER	Edward Rutledge	1.50
RS	Roger Sherman	1.50
JS	James Smith	1.50
RST	Richard Stockton	1.50
TS	Thomas Stone	1.50
GT	George Taylor	1.50
MT	Matthew Thornton	1.50
GW	George Walton	1.50
WW	William Whipple	1.50
WWI	William Williams	1.50
JW	James Wilson	1.50
JWI	John Witherspoon	1.50
OW	Oliver Wolcott	1.50
GWY	George Wythe	1.50

Declaration of Independence Cuts

No Pricing

Production One Set

Signers of the Constitution

		NM/M
Common Signer:		1.50
Inserted 1:8		
AB	Abraham Baldwin	1.50
RB	Richard Bassett	1.50
GB	Gunning Bedford Jr.	1.50
JB	John Blair	1.50
WB	William Blount	1.50
DB	David Brearly	1.50
JBR	Jacob Broom	1.50
PB	Pierce Butler	1.50
DC	Daniel Carroll	1.50
GC	George Clymer	1.50
JD	Jonathan Dayton	1.50
JDI	John Dickinson	1.50
WF	William Few	1.50
TF	Thomas Fitzsimons	1.50
BF	Benjamin Franklin	4.00
NG	Nicholas Gilman	1.50
NGO	Nathaniel Gorham	1.50
AH	Alexander Hamilton	3.00
JI	Jared Ingersoll	1.50
DJ	Daniel of St. Thomas Jenifer	1.50
WJ	William Samuel Johnson	1.50
RK	Rufus King	1.50
JL	John Langdon	1.50
WL	William Livingston	1.50
JM	James Madison	2.00
JMC	James McHenry	1.50
TM	Thomas Mifflin	1.50
GM	Gouverneur Morris	1.50
RM	Robert Morris	1.50
WP	William Paterson	1.50
CCP	Charles Cotesworth Pinckney	1.50
CP	Charles Pinckney	1.50
GR	George Read	1.50
JR	John Rutledge	1.50
RS	Roger Sherman	1.50
RDS	Richard Dobbs Spaight	1.50
GW	George Washington	4.00
HW	Hugh Williamson	1.50
JW	James Wilson	1.50

Signers of the Constitution Cut Signatures

No Pricing

Stars

VLADIMIR GUERRERO

		NM/M
Common Player:		.75
BB	Barry Bonds	3.00
MC	Miguel Cabrera	1.00
RC	Roger Clemens	3.00
VG	Vladimir Guerrero	1.00
TH	Todd Helton	.75
DJ	Derek Jeter	3.00
PM	Pedro Martinez	1.00
HM	Hideki Matsui	2.00
DO	David Ortiz	1.00
AP	Albert Pujols	3.00
MR	Manny Ramirez	1.00
AR	Alex Rodriguez	3.00
AS	Alfonso Soriano	.75
IS	Ichiro Suzuki	2.00
MT	Miguel Tejada	.75

Trading Places

Troy Glaus

		NM/M
Common Player:		.50
MB	Milton Bradley	.50
CC	Coco Crisp	.50
JD	Johnny Damon	1.00
CD	Carlos Delgado	.75
JDN	Juan Encarnacion	.50
RF	Rafael Furcal	.50
NG	Nomar Garciaparra	1.00
TG	Troy Glaus	.50
RH	Ramon Hernandez	.50
KL	Kenny Lofton	.50
BM	Bill Mueller	.50
CP	Corey Patterson	.50
MJP	Mike Piazza	1.00
JP	Juan Pierre	.50
ER	Edgar Renteria	.50
AS	Alfonso Soriano	.75
FT	Frank Thomas	.75
JT	Jim Thome	1.00
BW	Brad Wilkerson	.50
PW	Preston Wilson	.50

Trading Places
Autographs

NM/M

Autographed Relics: No Pricing
Production 25 Sets

JE	Johnny Estrada	10.00
KJ	Kenji Johjima	140.00
PL	Paul LoDuca	20.00
ML	Mike Lowell	25.00
BR	B.J. Ryan	30.00
TS	Terrmel Sledge	10.00
BW	Billy Wagner	30.00

Trading Places
Autographed Relics

No Pricing
Production 25 Sets

Trading Places Relics

NM/M

Common Player:		4.00
MB	Milton Bradley	4.00
CC	Coco Crisp	6.00
JD	Johnny Damon	15.00
JE	Johnny Estrada	6.00
NG	Nomar Garciaparra	15.00
RH	Ramon Hernandez	4.00
KJ	Kenji Johjima	15.00
PL	Paul LoDuca	6.00
KL	Kenny Lofton	6.00
ML	Mike Lowell	10.00
BM	Bill Mueller	4.00
CP	Corey Patterson	8.00
JP	Juan Pierre	6.00
ER	Edgar Renteria	6.00
BR	B.J. Ryan	4.00
TS	Terrmel Sledge	4.00
AS	Alfonso Soriano	8.00
FT	Frank Thomas	8.00
JT	Jim Thome	10.00
BW	Billy Wagner	6.00
BW	Brad Wilkerson	4.00
PW	Preston Wilson	4.00

The Mantle Collection

NM/M

Complete Set (10): 65.00
Common Mantle: 8.00
Inserted 1:36
Black: No Pricing
Production 7 Sets

The Mantle Collection
Gold

NM/M

Varying quantities produced

MM2005	Mickey Mantle/ 977	30.00
MM2004	Mickey Mantle/ 877	30.00
MM2003	Mickey Mantle/ 777	40.00
MM2002	Mickey Mantle/ 677	40.00
MM2001	Mickey Mantle/ 577	50.00
MM2000	Mickey Mantle/ 477	50.00
MM1999	Mickey Mantle/ 377	50.00
MM1998	Mickey Mantle/ 277	60.00
MM1997	Mickey Mantle/ 177	100.00
MM1996	Mickey Mantle/ 77	150.00

The Mantle Collection
Relics

NM/M

Production 77-167
Gold:
Black: No Pricing
Production 7 Sets

MM2005	Mickey Mantle/ 167	160.00
MM2004	Mickey Mantle/ 157	160.00
MM2003	Mickey Mantle/ 147	160.00
MM2002	Mickey Mantle/ 137	160.00
MM2001	Mickey Mantle/ 127	200.00
MM2000	Mickey Mantle/ 117	200.00
MM1999	Mickey Mantle/ 107	200.00
MM1998	Mickey Mantle/ 97	200.00

MM1997	Mickey Mantle/ 87	200.00
MM1996	Mickey Mantle/ 77	200.00

Rookie of the Week

NM/M

Issued one per week via HTA shops.

1	Mickey Mantle	10.00
2	Barry Bonds	3.00
3	Roger Clemens	3.00
4	Ernie Banks	2.00
5	Nolan Ryan	5.00
6	Albert Pujols	4.00
7	Roberto Clemente	5.00
8	Frank Robinson	1.50
9	Brooks Robinson	1.50
10	Harmon Killebrew	1.50
11	Reggie Jackson	1.50
12	George Brett	3.00
13	Ichiro Suzuki	3.00
14	Cal Ripken Jr.	6.00
15	Tom Seaver	1.50
16	Johnny Bench	1.50
17	Mike Schmidt	2.00
18	Derek Jeter	5.00
19	Bob Gibson	1.50
20	Ozzie Smith	2.00
21	Rickey Henderson	1.50
22	Tony Gwynn	1.50
23	Wade Boggs	1.50
24	Ryne Sandberg	3.00
25	Mickey Mantle	10.00

Walmart Cards

NM/M

Complete Set (18):		25.00
Common Player:		.50
WM1	Stan Musial	2.00
WM2	Ted Williams	3.00
WM3	Yogi Berra	2.00
WM5	Mickey Mantle	10.00
WM6	Mickey Mantle	10.00
WM7	Alex Rodriguez	3.00
WM9	Gary Carter	.50
WM10	Roy Oswalt	.50
WM13	Carlos Lee	.50
WM14	Johan Santana	1.00
WM15	Roberto Clemente	3.00
WM16	Carl Yastrzemski	1.50
WM21	Chipper Jones	1.00
WM22	Ichiro Suzuki	2.00
WM23	Bobby Abreu	.50
WM24	Tom Seaver	1.00
WM25	Alfonso Soriano	.75
WM26	Andruw Jones	1.00
WM28	Adam Dunn	.75
WM30	Mark Teixeira	1.00
WM31	Albert Pujols	3.00
WM32	Cal Ripken Jr.	4.00
WM33	Ryne Sandberg	2.00
WM34	Don Mattingly	2.00
WM35	Roger Clemens	3.00
WM36	Jose Reyes	.50
WM38	Derek Lee	1.00
WM39	Miguel Cabrera	1.00
WM41	Barry Bonds	3.00
WM42	Barry Bonds	3.00
WM45	Livan Hernandez	.50
WM46	Derek Jeter	3.00
WM46	David Ortiz	1.00
WM48	Ivan Rodriguez	.75
WM52	Alex Rodriguez	3.00
WM53	Vladimir Guerrero	1.00

World Series Relics

NM/M

Common Player:		
MB	Mark Buehrle/ Glove/100	200.00
JC	Joe Crede	35.00
JD	Jermaine Dye	20.00
CEB	Carl Everett	15.00
CEU	Carl Everett/Uni./100	90.00
JG	Jon Garland	20.00
WH	Willie Harris	10.00
TI	Tadahito Iguchi	25.00
BJ	Bobby Jenks/ Glove/100	275.00
PKB	Paul Konerko	15.00
PKU	Paul Konerko	15.00

TP	Timoniel Perez	15.00
AP	A.J. Pierzynski	20.00
SP	Scott Podsednik	25.00
AR	Aaron Rowand	25.00
FT	Frank Thomas	20.00
JU	Juan Uribe	20.00

2006 Topps Updates & Highlights

NM/M

Complete Factory Set (333):		40.00
Complete Set (330):		30.00
Common Player:		.10
UH1	Austin Kearns	.10
UH2	Adam Eaton	.10
UH3	Juan Encarnacion	.10
UH4	Jarrod Washburn	.10
UH5	Alex Gonzalez	.10
UH6	Toby Hall	.10
UH7	Preston Wilson	.10
UH8	Ramon Ortiz	.10
UH9	Jason Michaels	.10
UH10	Jeff Weaver	.10
UH11	Russell Branyan	.10
UH12	Brett Tomko	.10
UH13	Doug Mientkiewicz	.10
UH14	David Wells	.10
UH15	Corey Koskie	.10
UH16	Russ Ortiz	.10
UH17	Carlos Pena	.10
UH18	Mark Hendrickson	.10
UH19	Julian Tavarez	.10
UH20	Jeff Conine	.20
UH21	Dioner Navarro	.10
UH22	Bob Wickman	.10
UH23	Felipe Lopez	.10
UH24	Eddie Guardado	.10
UH25	David Dellucci	.10
UH26	Ryan Wagner	.10
UH27	Nick Green	.10
UH28	Gary Majewski	.10
UH29	Shea Hillenbrand	.10
UH30	Jae Weong Seo	.10
UH31	Royce Clayton	.10
UH32	David Riske	.10
UH33	Joey Gathright	.10
UH34	Robinson Tejeda	.10
UH35	Edwin Jackson	.10
UH36	Aubrey Huff	.10
UH37	Akinori Otsuka	.10
UH38	Juan Castro	.10
UH39	Zach Day	.10
UH40	Jeremy Accardo	.10
UH41	Shawn Green	.10
UH42	Kazuo Matsui	.10
UH43	J.J. Putz	.10
UH44	David Ross	.10
UH45	Scott Williamson	.10
UH46	Joe Borchard	.10
UH47	Elmer Dessens	.10
UH48	Odalis Perez	.10
UH49	Kelly Shoppach	.10
UH50	Brandon Phillips	.10
UH51	Guillermo Mota	.10
UH52	Alex Cintron	.10
UH53	Denny Bautista	.10
UH54	Josh Bard	.10
UH55	Julio Lugo	.10
UH56	Doug Mirabelli	.10
UH57	Kip Wells	.10
UH58	Adrian Gonzalez	.10
UH59	Shawn Chacon	.10
UH60	Marcus Thames	.10
UH61	Craig Wilson	.10
UH62	Cory Sullivan	.10
UH63	Ben Broussard	.10
UH64	Todd Walker	.10
UH65	Greg Maddux	1.00
UH66	Xavier Nady	.10
UH67	Oliver Perez	.10
UH68	Sean Casey	.10

UH69	Kyle Lohse	.10
UH70	Carlos Lee	.20
UH71	Rheal Cormier	.10
UH72	Ronnie Belliard	.10
UH73	Cory Lidle	.10
UH74	David Bell	.10
UH75	Wilson Betemit	.10
UH76	Danys Baez	.10
UH77	Mike Stanton	.10
UH78	Kevin Mench	.10
UH79	Sandy Alomar	.10
UH80	Cesar Izturis	.10
UH81	Jeremy Affeldt	.10
UH82	Matt Stairs	.10
UH83	Hector Luna	.10
UH84	Tony Graffanino	.10
UH85	J.P. Howell	.10
UH86	Bengie Molina	.10
UH87	Maicer Izturis	.10
UH88	Marco Scutaro	.10
UH89	Daryle Ward	.10
UH90	Sal Fasano	.10
UH91	Oscar Villarreal	.10
UH92	Gabe Gross	.10
UH93	Phil Nevin	.10
UH94	Damon Hollins	.10
UH95	Juan Cruz	.10
UH96	Marlon Anderson	.10
UH97	Jason Davis	.10
UH98	Ryan Shealy	.10
UH99	Francisco Cordero	.10
UH100	Bobby Abreu	.25
UH101	Roberto Hernandez	.10
UH102	Gary Bennett	.10
UH103	Aaron Sele	.10
UH104	Nook Logan	.10
UH105	Alfredo Amezaga	.10
UH106	Chris Woodward	.10
UH107	Kevin Jarvis	.10
UH108	B.J. Upton	.10
UH109	Alan Embree	.10
UH110	Milton Bradley	.10
UH111	Peter Orr	.10
UH112	Jeff Cirillo	.10
UH113	Corey Patterson	.10
UH114	Josh Paul	.10
UH115	Fernando Rodney	.10
UH116	Jerry Hairston	.10
UH117	Scott Proctor	.10
UH118	Ambiorix Burgos	.10
UH119	Jose Bautista	.10
UH120	Livan Hernandez	.10
UH121	John McDonald	.10
UH122	Ronny Cedeno	.10
UH123	Nate Robertson	.10
UH124	Jamey Carroll	.10
UH125	Alex Escobar	.10
UH126	Endy Chavez	.10
UH127	Jorge Julio	.10
UH128	Kenny Lofton	.10
UH129	Matt Diaz	.10
UH130	David Bush	.10
UH131	Jose Molina	.10
UH132	Mike MacDougal	.10
UH133	Benjamin Zobrist (RC)	.50
UH134	Shane Komine RC	.25
UH135	Casey Janssen RC	.50
UH136	Kevin Frandsen (RC)	.25
UH137	John Rheinecker (RC)	.25
UH138	Matthew Kemp (RC)	.75
UH139	Scott Mathieson (RC)	.25
UH140	Jered Weaver (RC)	.75
UH141	Joel Guzman (RC)	.25
UH142	Anibal Sanchez (RC)	.50
UH143	Melky Cabrera (RC)	.50
UH144	Howie Kendrick (RC)	.50
UH145	Cole Hamels (RC)	1.00
UH146	Willy Aybar (RC)	.25
UH147	James Shields RC	.50
UH148	Kevin Thompson (RC)	.25
UH149	Jon Lester (RC)	1.00
UH150	Stephen Drew (RC)	.75
UH151	Andre Ethier (RC)	.50
UH152	Jordan Tata RC	.50
UH153	Michael Napoli RC	.50
UH154	Kason Gabbard (RC)	.25
UH155	Lastings Milledge (RC)	.50
UH156	Erick Aybar (RC)	.25
UH157	Fausto Carmona (RC)	.25
UH158	Russell Martin (RC)	.50
UH159	David Pauley (RC)	.25
UH160	Andy Marte (RC)	.25
UH161	Carlos Quentin (RC)	.25
UH162	Franklin Gutierrez (RC)	.25
UH163	Taylor Buchholz (RC)	.25
UH164	Josh Johnson (RC)	.25
UH165	Chad Billingsley (RC)	.50
UH166	Kendry Morales (RC)	.25
UH167	Adam Loewen (RC)	.25
UH168	Yusmeiro Petit (RC)	.25
UH169	Matt Albers (RC)	.25
UH170	John Maine (RC)	.25
UH171	Alex Rodriguez	.75

UH172	Mike Piazza	.40
UH173	Cory Sullivan	.10
UH174	Anibal Sanchez	.10
UH175	Trevor Hoffman	.10
UH176	Barry Bonds	.75
UH177	Derek Jeter	.75
UH178	Jose Reyes	.25
UH179	Manny Ramirez	.25
UH180	Vladimir Guerrero	.25
UH181	Mariano Rivera	.25
UH182	Postseason Highlights	.25
UH183	Postseason Highlights	.25
UH184	Postseason Highlights	.25
UH185	Postseason Highlights	.25
UH186	Postseason Highlights	.25
UH187	Postseason Highlights	.25
UH188	Postseason Highlights	.25
UH189	Postseason Highlights	.25
UH190	Postseason Highlights	.25
UH191	Postseason Highlights	.25
UH192	Postseason Highlights	.25
UH193	Postseason Highlights	.25
UH194	Postseason Highlights	.25
UH195	Postseason Highlights	.25
UH196	Postseason Highlights	.25
UH197	Postseason Highlights	.25
UH198	Postseason Highlights	.25
UH199	Postseason Highlights	.25
UH200	Postseason Highlights	.25
UH201	Postseason Highlights	.25
UH202	David Ortiz, Jermaine Dye, Travis Hafner	.25
UH203	Joe Mauer, Derek Jeter, Robinson Cano	.50
UH204	David Ortiz, Justin Morneau, Raul Ibanez	.25
UH205	Carl Crawford, Chone Figgins, Ichiro Suzuki	.50
UH206	Johan Santana, Chien-Ming Wang, Jon Garland	.50
UH207	Johan Santana, Roy Halladay, C.C. Sabathia	.25
UH208	Johan Santana, Jeremy Bonderman, John Lackey	.25
UH209	Francisco Rodriguez, Bobby Jenks, B.J. Ryan	.10
UH210	Ryan Howard, Albert Pujols, Alfonso Soriano	1.00
UH211	Freddy Sanchez, Miguel Cabrera, Albert Pujols	.50
UH212	Ryan Howard, Albert Pujols, Lance Berkman	1.00
UH213	Jose Reyes, Juan Pierre, Hanley Ramirez	.40
UH214	Derek Lowe, Brandon Webb, Carlos Zambrano	.10
UH215	Roy Oswalt, Chris Carpenter, Brandon Webb	.10
UH216	Aaron Harang, Jake Peavy, John Smoltz	.10
UH217	Trevor Hoffman, Billy Wagner, Joe Borowski	.10
UH218	Ichiro Suzuki	.50
UH219	Derek Jeter	.75
UH220	Alex Rodriguez	.75
UH221	David Ortiz	.25
UH222	Vladimir Guerrero	.25
UH223	Ivan Rodriguez	.25
UH224	Vernon Wells	.10
UH225	Mark Loretta	.10
UH226	Kenny Rogers	.10
UH227	Alfonso Soriano	.25

UH228	Carlos Beltran	.25
UH229	Albert Pujols	.75
UH230	Jason Bay	.25
UH231	Edgar Renteria	.10
UH232	David Wright	.50
UH233	Chase Utley	.25
UH234	Paul LoDuca	.10
UH235	Brad Penny	.10
UH236	Derrick Turnbow	.10
UH237	Mark Redman	.10
UH238	Francisco Liriano	.25
UH239	A.J. Pierzynski	.10
UH240	Grady Sizemore	.25
UH241	Jose Contreras	.10
UH242	Jermaine Dye	.10
UH243	Jason Schmidt	.10
UH244	Nomar Garciaparra	.25
UH245	Scott Kazmir	.10
UH246	Johan Santana	.25
UH247	Chris Capuano	.10
UH248	Magglio Ordonez	.10
UH249	Gary Matthews	.10
UH250	Carlos Lee	.10
UH251	David Eckstein	.10
UH252	Michael Young	.10
UH253	Matt Holliday	.25
UH254	Lance Berkman	.25
UH255	Scott Rolen	.25
UH256	Bronson Arroyo	.10
UH257	Barry Zito	.10
UH258	Brian McCann	.25
UH259	Jose Lopez	.10
UH260	Chris Carpenter	.25
UH261	Roy Halladay	.10
UH262	Jim Thome	.25
UH263	Dan Uggla	.10
UH264	Mariano Rivera	.25
UH265	Roy Oswalt	.20
UH266	Tom Gordon	.10
UH267	Troy Glaus	.10
UH268	Bobby Jenks	.10
UH269	Freddy Sanchez	.10
UH270	Paul Konerko	.10
UH271	Joe Mauer	.25
UH272	B.J. Ryan	.10
UH273	Ryan Howard	.75
UH274	Brian Fuentes	.10
UH275	Miguel Cabrera	.25
UH276	Brandon Webb	.10
UH277	Mark Buehrle	.10
UH278	Trevor Hoffman	.10
UH279	Jonathan Papelbon	.25
UH280	Andruw Jones	.25
UH281	Miguel Tejada	.20
UH282	Carlos Zambrano	.20
UH283	Ryan Howard	.75
UH284	David Wright	.50
UH285	Miguel Cabrera	.25
UH286	David Ortiz	.25
UH287	Jermaine Dye	.10
UH288	Miguel Tejada	.25
UH289	Lance Berkman	.25
UH290	Troy Glaus	.10
UH291	David Wright, Tom Glavine	.25
UH292	Ryan Howard, Tom Gordon	.50
UH293	Miguel Cabrera, Dontrelle Willis	.25
UH294	Andruw Jones, John Smoltz	.25
UH295	Alfonso Soriano	.25
UH296	Albert Pujols, Chris Carpenter	.50
UH297	Adam Dunn, Bronson Arroyo	.10
UH298	Lance Berkman, Roy Oswalt	.25
UH299	Chris Capuano, Prince Fielder	.50
UH300	Freddy Sanchez, Jason Bay	.10
UH301	Carlos Zambrano, Juan Pierre	.10
UH302	Adrian Gonzalez, Trevor Hoffman	.10
UH303	Derek Lowe, Rafael Furcal	.10
UH304	Omar Vizquel, Jason Schmidt	.10
UH305	Brandon Webb, Chad Tracy	.10
UH306	Matt Holliday, Garrett Atkins	.25
UH307	Alex Rodriguez, Chien-Ming Wang	.50
UH308	Curt Schilling, David Ortiz	.25
UH309	Roy Halladay, Vernon Wells	.10
UH310	Miguel Tejada, Erik Bedard	.10
UH311	Carl Crawford, Scott Kazmir	.10
UH312	Jeremy Bonderman, Magglio Ordonez	.10

UH313	Justin Morneau, Johan Santana	.25
UH314	Jon Garland, Jermaine Dye	.10
UH315	Travis Hafner, C.C. Sabathia	.10
UH316	Emil Brown, Mark Grudzielanek	.10
UH317	Frank Thomas, Barry Zito	.25
UH318	Jered Weaver, Vladimir Guerrero	.25
UH319	Michael Young, Gary Matthews	.10
UH320	Ichiro Suzuki, J.J. Putz	.50
UH321	Derek Jeter, Robinson Cano	.50
UH232	Mark Mulder, Chris Carpenter	.25
UH323	Trevpr Schmidt, Jason Schmidt	.10
UH324	David Wright, Paul LoDuca	.25
UH325	Lance Berkman, Roy Oswalt	.25
UH326	Derek Jeter, Jose Reyes	.50
UH327	David Wright, Cliff Floyd	.25
UH328	Johan Santana, Francisco Liriano	.25
UH329	Stephen Drew, J.D. Drew	.25
UH330	Jeff Weaver	.25

Black

Black: 15-25X
Production 55 Sets

First Edition

1st Edition: 4-6X
Inserted 1:Hobby Box

Gold

Gold: 5-10X
Production 2,006 Sets

Platinum

Production One Set

All-Star Autographs

No Pricing
Production 25 Sets

All-Star Stitches

NM/M
Common Player: 4.00
Inserted 1:43
Patch: No Pricing
Production 10 Sets
BA Bronson Arroyo 8.00

JB	Jason Bay	15.00
CB	Carlos Beltran	10.00
LB	Lance Berkman	10.00
MB	Mark Buehrle	8.00
MC	Miguel Cabrera	10.00
RC	Robinson Cano	10.00
CFC	Chris Capuano	4.00
CC	Chris Carpenter	10.00
JC	Jose Contreras	8.00
JD	Jermaine Dye	6.00
DE	David Eckstein	20.00
BF	Brian Fuentes	4.00
TEG	Troy Glaus	6.00
TMG	Tom Glavine	8.00
TG	Tom Gordon	4.00
VG	Vladimir Guerrero	8.00
RH	Roy Halladay	6.00
TH	Trevor Hoffman	6.00
MH	Matt Holliday	6.00
RJH	Ryan Howard	25.00
BJ	Bobby Jenks	4.00
AJ	Andruw Jones	10.00
SK	Scott Kazmir	6.00
PK	Paul Konerko	8.00
CL	Carlos Lee	8.00
PL	Paul LoDuca	6.00
JL	Jose Lopez	6.00
ML	Mark Loretta	6.00
GM	Gary Matthews	6.00
JM	Joe Mauer	10.00
BM	Brian McCann	15.00
MO	Magglio Ordonez	8.00
DO	David Ortiz	15.00
RO	Roy Oswalt	6.00
JP	Jonathan Papelbon	20.00
BP	Brad Penny	4.00
AJP	A.J. Pierzynski	6.00
AP	Albert Pujols	25.00
MAR	Mark Redman	4.00
ER	Edgar Renteria	6.00
JR	Jose Reyes	15.00
MR	Mariano Rivera	15.00
AR	Alex Rodriguez	15.00
IR	Ivan Rodriguez	8.00
KR	Kenny Rogers	8.00
SR	Scott Rolen	8.00
BR	B.J. Ryan	4.00
FS	Freddy Sanchez	6.00
JS	Johan Santana	10.00
JDS	Jason Schmidt	8.00
GS	Grady Sizemore	10.00
AS	Alfonso Soriano	8.00
MT	Miguel Tejada	8.00
JT	Jim Thome	10.00
DT	Derrick Turnbow	6.00
DU	Dan Uggla	10.00
CU	Chase Utley	10.00
BW	Brandon Webb	10.00
VW	Vernon Wells	8.00
DW	David Wright	20.00
MY	Michael Young	6.00
CZ	Carlos Zambrano	8.00

All-Star Patches

No Pricing
Production 10 Sets

Barry Bonds HR History

NM/M
Common Bonds HR History: 1.00
Inserted 1:6
Autographs: No Pricing
Production 5 Sets

Barry Bonds 715

NM/M
Inserted 1:36
715-BB Barry Bonds 3.00

Barry Bonds 715 Relic

NM/M

Production 715
Barry Bonds ... 35.00

Chrome RC Box Topper

NM/M

Production 599
Inserted one per box.
Refractors: ... 2-4X
Production 25 Sets

1	Aaron Zobrist	3.00
2	Shane Komine	3.00
3	Casey Janssen	3.00
4	Kevin Frandsen	5.00
5	John Rheinecker	3.00
6	Matthew Kemp	8.00
7	Scott Mathieson	5.00
8	Jered Weaver	8.00
9	Joel Guzman	5.00
10	Anibal Sanchez	5.00
11	Melky Cabrera	6.00
12	Howie Kendrick	6.00
13	Cole Hamels	8.00
14	Willy Aybar	3.00
15	James Shields	3.00
16	Kevin Thompson	5.00
17	Jon Lester	15.00
18	Stephen Drew	6.00
19	Andre Ethier	8.00
20	Jordan Tata	3.00
21	Michael Napoli	6.00
22	Kason Gabbard	5.00
23	Lastings Milledge	5.00
24	Erick Aybar	3.00
25	Fausto Carmona	3.00
26	Russell Martin	5.00
27	David Pauley	3.00
28	Andy Marte	5.00
29	Carlos Quentin	5.00
30	Franklin Gutierrez	5.00
31	Taylor Buchholz	5.00
32	Josh Johnson	5.00
33	Chad Billingsley	6.00
34	Kendry Morales	3.00
35	Adam Loewen	5.00
36	Yusmeiro Petit	5.00
37	Matt Albers	3.00
38	John Maine	5.00
39	Josh Willingham	5.00
40	Taylor Tankersley	5.00
41	Pat Neshek	30.00
42	Francisco Rosario	3.00
43	Matt Smith	5.00
44	Jonathan Sanchez	5.00
45	Chris Demaria	3.00
46	Manuel Corpas	5.00
47	Kevin Reese	3.00
48	Brent Clevlen	3.00
49	Anderson Hernandez	3.00
50	Chris Roberson	3.00

Derby Digs Relics

NM/M

Inserted 1:4,200
JD Jermaine Dye ... 25.00
TG Troy Glaus ... 25.00

Mantle HR History Relics

NM/M

Common Mantle: ... 140.00
Production 7 Sets

Mickey Mantle HR History

MICKEY MANTLE

Common Mantle (102-201): 2.00
Inserted 1:4

Midsummer Covers

No Pricing
Production 10 Sets

Rookie Debut

NM/M

Common Player: ... 1.00
Inserted 1:4
RD1 Joel Zumaya ... 2.00

07.20.06

ROOKIE DEBUT
Carlos Quentin
ARIZONA DIAMONDBACKS® | OUTFIELD

RD2	Ian Kinsler	2.00
RD3	Kenji Johjima	3.00
RD4	Josh Barfield	1.00
RD5	Nicholas Markakis	2.00
RD6	Dan Uggla	2.00
RD7	Eric Reed	1.00
RD8	Carlos Martinez	1.00
RD9	Angel Pagan	1.50
RD10	Jason Childers	1.00
RD11	Ruddy Lugo	1.00
RD12	James Loney	2.50
RD13	Fernando Nieve	1.00
RD14	Reggie Abercrombie	1.00
RD15	Boone Logan	1.00
RD16	Brian Bannister	1.00
RD17	Ricky Nolasco	1.50
RD18	Willie Eyre	1.00
RD19	Fabio Castro	1.00
RD20	Jordan Tata	1.00
RD21	Taylor Buchholz	1.50
RD22	Sean Marshall	1.00
RD23	John Rheinecker	1.00
RD24	Casey Janssen	1.00
RD25	Russell Martin	1.50
RD26	Yusmeiro Petit	1.50
RD27	Kendry Morales	1.50
RD28	Alay Soler	1.00
RD29	Jered Weaver	3.00
RD30	Matthew Kemp	2.00
RD31	Enrique Gonzalez	1.00
RD32	Lastings Milledge	2.00
RD33	James Shields	1.00
RD34	David Pauley	1.00
RD35	Zach Jackson	1.00
RD36	Zach Miner	1.00
RD37	Jon Lester	3.00
RD38	Chad Billingsley	2.00
RD39	Scott Thorman	1.00
RD40	Anibal Sanchez	2.00
RD41	Mike Thompson	1.00
RD42	T.J. Beam	1.00
RD43	Stephen Drew	3.00
RD44	Joe Saunders	1.00
RD45	Carlos Quentin	1.50

Rookie Debut Autographs

NM/M

Common Autograph: ... 15.00
RA Reggie Abercrombie ... 15.00
MA Matt Albers ... 20.00
FC Fausto Carmona ... 15.00
FF Emiliano Fruto ... 15.00
IK Ian Kinsler ... 20.00
JL Jon Lester ... 35.00
BL Bobby Livingston ... 15.00
AL Adam Loewen ... 40.00
MN Michael Napoli ... 30.00
RN Ricky Nolasco ... 15.00
YP Yusmeiro Petit ... 15.00
MP Martin Prado ... 20.00
JS Jeremy Sowers ... 15.00
ST Scott Thorman ... 20.00

Signature Moves

NM/M

Common Autograph:
AH Aubrey Huff ... 20.00
JL Julio Lugo ... 20.00
BP Brandon Phillips ... 20.00
BW Brad Wilkerson ... 10.00
CW Craig Wilson ... 10.00

Touch 'Em All Relics

NM/M

Inserted 1:610
CB Carlos Beltran ... 20.00
RH Ryan Howard ... 30.00
JM Joe Mauer ... 20.00
DO David Ortiz ... 20.00
AP Albert Pujols ... 30.00
AR Alex Rodriguez ... 25.00

IS	Ichiro Suzuki	25.00
MT	Miguel Tejada	10.00
DW	David Wright	25.00
MY	Michael Young	8.00

2006 Topps AFLAC

NM/M

Common Player: ... 15.00
BB	Blake Beavan	50.00
BK	Brett Krill	40.00
CC	Christian Colon	40.00
CR	Cameron Rupp	25.00
DB	Drake Britton	15.00
DD	Derek Dietrich	25.00
DM	D.J. LeMahieu	25.00
DR	Danny Rams	25.00
ED	Evan Danieli	30.00
EG	Erik Goeddel	30.00
FF	Freddie Freeman	75.00
GP	Greg Peavey	30.00
HM	Hunter Morris	40.00
JG	Jon Gilmore	25.00
JH	Jason Heyward	65.00
JL	Joe Leftridge	20.00
JS	Josh Smoker	40.00
JT	John Tolisano	25.00
JV	Josh Vitters	125.00
KB	Kyle Blair	15.00
KK	Kevin Keyes	15.00
MB	Madison Bumgarner	75.00
MH	Matt Harvey	60.00
MM	Michael Main	40.00
NN	Nick Noonan	15.00
NR	Neil Ramirez	25.00
PD	Paul Demny	15.00
RP	Rick Porcello	75.00
RS	Robert Stock	50.00
SB	Steven Brooks	25.00
SS	Sequoyah	
	Stonecipher	75.00
TA	Tim Alderson	25.00
YG	Yasmani Grandal	25.00

2006 Topps Allen & Ginter

JIM THORPE.
ALLEN & GINTER'S
BROOKLYN   NEW YORK

NM/M

Common Player: ... .25
Common SP: ... .50
SP's Inserted 1:2
Pack (7): ... 9.00
Box (24): ... 180.00
1	Albert Pujols	3.00
2	Aubrey Huff	.25
3	Mark Teixeira	.75
4	Vernon Wells	.50
5	Ken Griffey Jr./SP	4.00
6	Nick Swisher	.25
7	Jose Reyes	.50
8	David Wright	2.00
9	Vladimir Guerrero	1.00
10	Andruw Jones	.75
11	Ramon Hernandez	.25
12	Miguel Tejada	.75
13	Juan Pierre	.25
14	Jim Thome	.75
15	Austin Kearns/SP	.50
16	Jhonny Peralta	.25
17	Clint Barmes	.25
18	Angel Berroa	.25
19	Nomar Garciaparra	1.00
20	Joe Nathan	.25
21	Brandon Webb	.25
22	Chad Tracy	.25
23	Derek Jeter	3.00
24	Conor Jackson (RC)	.50
25	Jason Giambi/SP	1.00
26	Johnny Estrada	.25
27	Luis Gonzalez	.40
28	Javier Vazquez	.25
29	Orlando Hudson	.25
30	Shawn Green	.40
31	Mark Buehrle	.40

32	Wily Mo Pena	.25
33	C.C. Sabathia	.25
34	Ronnie Belliard	.25
35	Travis Hafner/SP	1.00
36	Mike Jacobs (RC)	.50
37	Roy Oswalt	.50
38	Zack Greinke	.25
39	J.D. Drew	.40
40	Jeff Kent	.40
41	Ben Sheets	.40
42	Luis Castillo	.25
43	Carlos Delgado	.75
44	Cliff Floyd	.25
45	Danny Haren/SP	.50
46	Bobby Abreu	.50
47	Jeromy Burnitz	.25
48	Khalil Greene	.25
49	Moises Alou	.50
50	Alex Rodriguez/SP	5.00
51	Ervin Santana/SP	.50
52	Bartolo Colon/SP	.50
53	John Smoltz/SP	1.00
54	David Ortiz/SP	2.00
55	Hideki Matsui/SP	3.00
56	Jermaine Dye/SP	.50
57	Victor Martinez/SP	.50
58	Willy Taveras/SP	.50
59	Brady Clark/SP	.50
60	Justin Morneau	.50
61	Xavier Nady	.25
62	Rich Harden	.25
63	Jack Wilson	.25
64	Brian Giles	.25
65	Jon Lieber/SP	.50
66	Dan Johnson	.25
67	Billy Wagner	.25
68	Rickie Weeks	.40
69	Chris Ray (RC)	.50
70	Chris Shelton	.25
71	Dmitri Young	.25
72	Ivan Rodriguez	.75
73	Jeremy Bonderman	.50
74	Justin Verlander (RC)	1.00
75	Randy Johnson	1.00
76	Magglio Ordonez	.25
77	Brandon Inge	.25
78	Placido Polanco	.25
79	Ryan Howard	1.00
80	Jason Bay	.50
81	Sean Casey	.25
82	Jeremy Hermida (RC)	.50
83	Mike Cameron	.25
84	Trevor Hoffman	.25
85	Mike Matheny/SP	.50
86	Steve Finley	.25
87	Adam Everett	.25
88	Jason Isringhausen	.25
89	Jonny Gomes	.25
90	Barry Zito	.50
91	Bobby Crosby	.25
92	Eric Chavez	.25
93	Frank Thomas	.75
94	Huston Street	.25
95	Jorge Posada	.50
96	Casey Kotchman	.25
97	Darin Erstad	.25
98	Chipper Jones	1.00
99	Jeff Francoeur	.40
100	Barry Bonds	3.00
101	Alfonso Soriano	1.00
102	Brandon Claussen	.25
103	Aaron Boone	.25
104	Roger Clemens	3.00
105	Andy Pettitte/SP	.75
106	Nick Johnson	.25
107	Tom Gordon	.25
108	Orlando Hernandez	.25
109	Francisco Rodriguez	.25
110	Orlando Cabrera	.25
111	Edgar Renteria	.40
112	Tim Hudson	.50
113	Coco Crisp	.25
114	Matt Clement	.25
115	Greg Maddux/SP	3.00
116	Paul Konerko	.50
117	Felipe Lopez	.25
118	Garrett Atkins	.25
119	Akinori Otsuka	.25
120	Craig Biggio	.50
121	Danys Baez	.25
122	Brad Penny	.25
123	Eric Gagne	.25
124	Lew Ford	.25
125	Mariano Rivera/SP	1.00
126	Carlos Beltran	.75
127	Pedro Martinez	1.00
128	Todd Helton	.75
129	Aaron Rowand	.25
130	Mike Lieberthal	.25
131	Oliver Perez	.25
132	Ryan Klesko	.25
133	Randy Winn	.25
134	Yuniesky Betancourt	.25
135	David Eckstein/SP	.50

#	Player	Value
136	Chad Orvella	.25
137	Toby Hall	.25
138	Hank Blalock	.50
139	B.J. Ryan	.25
140	Roy Halladay	.50
141	Livan Hernandez	.25
142	John Patterson	.25
143	Bengie Molina	.25
144	Brad Wilkerson	.25
145	Jorge Cantu SP	.50
146	Mark Mulder	.50
147	Felix Hernandez	.50
148	Paul LoDuca	.25
149	Prince Fielder (RC)	4.00
150	Johnny Damon/SP	2.00
151	Ryan Langerhans/SP	.50
152	Kris Benson/SP	.50
153	Curt Schilling/SP	2.00
154	Manny Ramirez/SP	2.00
155	Robinson Cano/SP	1.50
156	Derrek Lee/SP	1.50
157	A.J. Pierzynski/SP	.50
158	Adam Dunn/SP	1.00
159	Cliff Lee/SP	.50
160	Grady Sizemore	.50
161	Jeff Francis	.25
162	Dontrelle Willis	.50
163	Brad Ausmus	.25
164	Preston Wilson	.25
165	Derek Lowe/SP	.25
166	Chris Capuano	.25
167	Joe Mauer	.50
168	Torii Hunter	.40
169	Chase Utley	.75
170	Zachary Duke	.25
171	Jason Schmidt	.40
172	Adrian Beltre	.25
173	Eddie Guardado	.25
174	Richie Sexson	.50
175	Miguel Cabrera/SP	2.00
176	Julio Lugo	.25
177	Francisco Cordero	.25
178	Kevin Millwood	.25
179	A.J. Burnett	.25
180	Jose Guillen	.25
181	Larry Bigbie	.25
182	Raul Ibanez	.25
183	Jake Peavy	.50
184	Pat Burrell	.25
185	Tom Glavine/SP	.75
186	J.J. Hardy	.25
187	Emil Brown	.25
188	Lance Berkman	.50
189	Marcus Giles	.25
190	Scott Podsednik	.25
191	Chone Figgins	.25
192	Melvin Mora	.25
193	Mark Loretta	.25
194	Carlos Zambrano	.40
195	Chien-Ming Wang	.75
196	Mark Prior	.50
197	Bobby Jenks	.25
198	Brian Fuentes	.25
199	Garret Anderson	.25
200	Ichiro Suzuki	2.00
201	Brian Roberts	.25
202	Jason Kendall	.25
203	Milton Bradley	.25
204	Jimmy Rollins	.50
205	Brett Myers/SP	.50
206	Joe Randa	.25
207	Mike Piazza	1.00
208	Matt Morris	.25
209	Omar Vizquel	.25
210	Jeremy Reed	.25
211	Chris Carpenter	.50
212	Jim Edmonds	.50
213	Scott Kazmir	.50
214	Travis Lee	.25
215	Michael Young/SP	.75
216	Rod Barajas	.25
217	Gustavo Chacin	.25
218	Lyle Overbay	.25
219	Troy Glaus	.50
220	Chad Cordero	.25
221	Jose Vidro	.25
222	Scott Rolen	.75
223	Carl Crawford	.50
224	Rocco Baldelli	.50
225	Mike Mussina	.50
226	Kelvim Escobar	.25
227	Corey Patterson	.25
228	Javy Lopez	.25
229	Jonathan Papelbon/SP (RC)	5.00
230	Aramis Ramirez	.25
231	Tadahito Iguchi	.50
232	Morgan Ensberg	.25
233	Mark Grudzielanek	.25
234	Mike Sweeney	.25
235	Shawn Chacon/SP	.25
236	Nick Punto	.25
237	Geoff Jenkins	.25
238	Carlos Lee	.50
239	David DeJesus	.25
240	Brad Lidge	.25
241	Bob Wickman	.25
242	Jon Garland	.25
243	Kerry Wood	.25
244	Bronson Arroyo	.25
245	Matt Holliday/SP	.50
246	Josh Beckett	.50
247	Johan Santana	.75
248	Rafael Furcal	.25
249	Shannon Stewart	.25
250	Gary Sheffield	.50
251	Josh Barfield (RC)	.50
252	Kenji Johjima RC	2.00
253	Ian Kinsler (RC)	.50
254	Brian Anderson (RC)	.50
255	Matt Cain (RC)	1.00
256	Josh Willingham/SP (RC)	.50
257	John Koronka (RC)	.50
258	Chris Duffy (RC)	.50
259	Brian McCann (RC)	.50
260	Hanley Ramirez (RC)	1.00
261	Hong-Chih Kuo (RC)	.50
262	Francisco Liriano (RC)	5.00
263	Anderson Hernandez (RC)	.50
264	Ryan Zimmerman (RC)	4.00
265	Brian Bannister/SP (RC)	.50
266	Nolan Ryan	2.00
267	Frank Robinson	1.00
268	Roberto Clemente	3.00
269	Hank Greenberg	.50
270	Napoleon Lajoie	.50
271	Lloyd Waner	.25
272	Paul Waner	.25
273	Frankie Frisch	.25
274	Bill "Moose" Skowron	.25
275	Mickey Mantle	6.00
276	Brooks Robinson	1.00
277	Carl Yastrzemski	1.00
278	Johnny Pesky	.25
279	Stan Musial	1.50
280	Bill Mazeroski	.50
281	Harmon Killebrew	.75
282	Monte Irvin	.50
283	Bob Gibson	1.00
284	Ted Williams	2.00
285	Yogi Berra/SP	2.00
286	Ernie Banks	1.00
287	Bobby Doerr	.25
288	Josh Gibson	.50
289	Bob Feller	.25
290	Cal Ripken Jr.	3.00
291	Bobby Cox	.25
292	Terry Francona	.25
293	Dusty Baker	.25
294	Ozzie Guillen	.25
295	Jim Leyland	.50
296	Willie Randolph	.25
297	Joe Torre	.50
298	Felipe Alou	.25
299	Tony LaRussa	.25
300	Frank Robinson	.50
301	Mike Tyson	2.00
302	Duke Paoa Kahanamoku	.25
303	Jennie Finch	2.00
304	Brandi Chastain	.25
305	Danica Patrick/SP	10.00
306	Wendy Guey	.25
307	Hulk Hogan	.25
308	Carl Lewis	.25
309	John Wooden	.25
310	Randy Couture	.25
311	Andy Irons	.25
312	Takeru Kobayashi	.25
313	Leon Spinks	.25
314	Jim Thorpe	1.00
315	Jerry Bailey/SP	.50
316	Adrian C. Anson	.25
317	John M. Ward	.25
318	Mike Kelly	.25
319	Cpt. Jack Glasscock	.25
320	Aaron Hill	.25
321	Derrick Turnbow	.25
322	Nicholas Markakis	.25
323	Brad Hawpe	.25
324	Kevin Mench	.25
325	John Lackey/SP	.25
326	Chester A. Arthur	.25
327	Ulysses S. Grant	.50
328	Abraham Lincoln	1.00
329	Grover Cleveland	.25
330	Benjamin Harrison	.25
331	Theodore Roosevelt	.25
332	Rutherford B. Hayes	.25
333	Chancellor Otto Von Bismarck	.25
334	Kaiser Wilhelm II	.50
335	Queen Victoria/SP	.50
336	Pope Leo XIII	.25
337	Thomas Edison	.50
338	Orville Wright	.50
339	Wilbur Wright	.50
340	Nathaniel Hawthorne	.25
341	Herman Melville	.25
342	Stonewall Jackson	.50
343	Robert E. Lee	.50
344	Andrew Carnegie	.25
345	John Rockefeller/SP	.25
346	Bob Fitzsimmons	.25
347	Billy the Kid	.25
348	Buffalo Bill	.25
349	Jesse James	.25
350	Statue of Liberty	.25

Mini

BRONSON ARROYO.
ALLEN & GINTER'S
BROOKLYN NEW YORK

Mini:	2-4X
SP's:	1-2X
Mini SP's Inserted 1:13	
Mini (351-375):	No Pricing
#'s 351-375 Inserted In Rip Cards	
Allen & Ginter Back:	3-6X
Inserted 1:5	
A & G Back SP's:	2-3X
Inserted 1:65	
Bazooka Mini:	No Pricing
Production 25 Sets	
Black Mini:	5-10X
Inserted 1:10	
Black SP:	3-5X
Inserted 1:130	
Wood:	No Pricing
Production One Set	

Printing Plates

No Pricing
Production one set per color.

Autographs

NM/M
Cards are not serial numbered.

JB	Jerry Bailey/200	80.00
JBA	Josh Barfield	20.00
CB	Clint Barmes	15.00
BB	Barry Bonds/25	500.00
MC	Miguel Cabrera/100	150.00
RC	Robinson Cano	60.00
BC	Brandi Chastain/200	75.00
EC	Eric Chavez	15.00
RA	Randy Couture	80.00
BF	Bob Feller	75.00
PF	Prince Fielder	100.00
JF	Jennie Finch/200	140.00
LF	Lew Ford	10.00
JG	Jonny Gomes	15.00
VG	Vladimir Guerrero/50	200.00
WG	Wendy Guey	30.00
TG	Tony Gwynn/50	250.00
TH	Travis Hafner	30.00
HH	Hulk Hogan/200	200.00
RH	Ryan Howard	150.00
AI	Andy Irons/200	40.00
KJ	Kenji Johjima/50	275.00
SK	Scott Kazmir	30.00
TK	Takeru Kobayashi/200	125.00
DL	Derrek Lee	50.00
CL	Carl Lewis/200	120.00
FL	Francisco Liriano	50.00
VM	Victor Martinez	25.00
SM	Stan Musial/75	375.00
DP	Danica Patrick/100	500.00
WMP	Wily Mo Pena	20.00
CR	Cal Ripken Jr./50	300.00
AR	Alex Rodriguez/50	400.00
BJR	B.J. Ryan	15.00
NR	Nolan Ryan/50	350.00
ES	Ervin Santana	15.00
JS	Johan Santana/100	125.00
GS	Gary Sheffield/50	140.00
OS	Ozzie Smith/75	200.00
LS	Leon Spinks/200	75.00
HS	Huston Street	40.00
MT	Mike Tyson/200	275.00
CU	Chase Utley	75.00
BW	Billy Wagner	25.00
CMW	Chien-Ming Wang/100	400.00
DWI	Dontrelle Willis/100	40.00
JW	John Wooden/200	200.00
DW	David Wright	140.00
CY	Carl Yastrzemski/50	320.00
MY	Michael Young	35.00
RZ	Ryan Zimmerman	60.00

Allen & Ginter N43

NM/M
Inserted 1:2 Hobby Boxes

1	Alex Rodriguez	4.00
2	Barry Bonds	4.00
3	Albert Pujols	4.00
4	Josh Gibson	2.00
5	Nolan Ryan	4.00
6	Ichiro Suzuki	3.00
7	Mickey Mantle	10.00
8	Ted Williams	4.00
9	David Wright	3.00
10	Ken Griffey Jr.	3.00
11	Mark Teixeira	1.50
12	Adrian C. Anson	2.00
13	Mike Tyson	3.00
14	Kenji Johjima	2.00
15	Ryan Zimmerman	2.00

Allen & Ginter N43
Autographs

Production 10 Sets

Allen & Ginter N43
Relics

NM/M
Production 50 Sets

AP	Albert Pujols	100.00
JG	Josh Gibson	250.00

Dick Perez Sketches

TRAVIS HAFNER
THE DICK PEREZ COLLECTION

NM/M

Common Player	.25
Inserted 1:1	
Originals:	No Pricing
Production One Set	

ARI	Shawn Green	.25
ATL	Andruw Jones	.50
BAL	Miguel Tejada	.50
BOS	David Ortiz	1.00
CHC	Derrek Lee	.50
CHW	Paul Konerko	.50
CIN	Ken Griffey Jr.	1.00
CLE	Travis Hafner	.50
COL	Todd Helton	.50
DET	Ivan Rodriguez	.50
FLA	Miguel Cabrera	.75
HOU	Lance Berkman	.25
KC	Mike Sweeney	.25
LAA	Vladimir Guerrero	.75
LAD	Rafael Furcal	.25
MIL	Carlos Lee	.25
MIN	Johan Santana	.50
NYM	David Wright	1.00
NYY	Alex Rodriguez	2.00
OAK	Huston Street	.25
PHI	Bobby Abreu	.50
PIT	Jason Bay	.50
SDP	Jake Peavy	.50

SEA	Ichiro Suzuki	1.50
SFG	Barry Bonds	2.00
STL	Albert Pujols	2.00
TAM	Aubrey Huff	.25
TEX	Mark Teixeira	.50
TOR	Vernon Wells	.25
WAS	Alfonso Soriano	.75

Personalized Postcards

One Set Produced

Postcards

		NM/M
Inserted 1:2 Hobby Boxes		
BB	Barry Bonds	4.00
JG	Josh Gibson	2.00
KG	Ken Griffey Jr.	3.00
VG	Vladimir Guerrero	2.00
DJ	Derek Jeter	4.00
MM	Mickey Mantle	10.00
DO	David Ortiz	2.00
AP	Albert Pujols	4.00
MR	Manny Ramirez	2.00
CR	Cal Ripken Jr.	6.00
AR	Alex Rodriguez	4.00
I	Ichiro Suzuki	3.00
MT	Miguel Tejada	1.50
TW	Ted Williams	4.00
DW	David Wright	3.00

Relics

		NM/M
Common Player:		4.00
CBA	Clint Barmes	4.00
CB	Carlos Beltran	10.00
BB	Barry Bonds	20.00
MB	Mark Buehrle	8.00
GWB	George W. Bush	300.00
MC	Miguel Cabrera	10.00
RC	Robinson Cano	20.00
JC	Jorge Cantu	6.00
EC	Eric Chavez	6.00
BC	Bobby Crosby	4.00
JD	Johnny Damon	12.00
CD	Carlos Delgado	8.00
ZD	Zachary Duke	8.00
JDY	Jermaine Dye	8.00
JF	Jeff Francoeur	15.00
JG	Jonny Gomes	6.00
VG	Vladimir Guerrero	10.00
TH	Travis Hafner	10.00
FH	Felix Hernandez	8.00
MH	Matt Holliday	8.00
RH	Ryan Howard	30.00
JFK	John F. Kennedy	375.00
PK	Paul Konerko	10.00
HCK	Hong-Chih Kuo	20.00
RL	Ryan Langerhans	8.00
MM	Mickey Mantle	125.00

PM	Pedro Martinez	10.00
VM	Victor Martinez	8.00
HM	Hideki Matsui	15.00
BM	Brandon McCarthy	4.00
DO	David Ortiz	15.00
Ro	Roy Oswalt	6.00
JP	Jake Peavy	6.00
APE	Andy Pettitte	6.00
MPZ	Mike Piazza	10.00
MP	Mark Prior	8.00
AP	Albert Pujols	20.00
MR	Manny Ramirez	10.00
AR	Alex Rodriguez	20.00
JS	Johan Santana	10.00
CS	Curt Schilling	10.00
GS	Gary Sheffield	8.00
HS	Huston Street	6.00
NS	Nick Swisher	8.00
WT	Willy Taveras	6.00
MT	Miguel Tejada	10.00
FT	Frank Thomas	8.00
JT	Jim Thome	10.00
CU	Chase Utley	15.00
CMW	Chien-Ming Wang	50.00
DWI	Dontrelle Willis	8.00
DW	David Wright	15.00

Rip Card

	NM/M
All prices for unripped cards.	
1-4: Production 10 Sets	
5-9: Production 15 Sets	
10-19: Production 25 Sets	
20-50: Production 99 Sets	

RIP20	Kenji Johjima	100.00
RIP21	Cap Anson	100.00
RIP22	Ryan Zimmerman	100.00
RIP23	Andruw Jones	100.00
RIP24	Barry Bonds	100.00
RIP25	Cal Ripken Jr.	150.00
RIP26	David Ortiz	100.00
RIP27	Hideki Matsui	150.00
RIP28	Ken Griffey Jr.	150.00
RIP29	Manny Ramirez	100.00
RIP30	Mickey Mantle	200.00
RIP31	Alex Rodriguez	150.00
RIP32	Miguel Cabrera	100.00
RIP33	Miguel Tejada	100.00
RIP34	Pedro Martinez	100.00
RIP35	Albert Pujols	150.00
RIP36	Alex Rodriguez	150.00
RIP37	Alex Rodriguez, Derek Jeter	150.00
RIP38	Barry Bonds	150.00
RIP39	Derek Jeter	180.00
RIP40	Ichiro Suzuki	150.00
RIP41	Ichiro Suzuki, Hideki Matsui	150.00
RIP42	Josh Gibson	150.00
RIP43	Mickey Mantle	200.00
RIP44	Jonathan Papelbon	100.00
RIP45	Mickey Mantle, Ted Williams	200.00
RIP46	Albert Pujols	150.00
RIP47	Roberto Clemente	150.00
RIP48	Roger Clemens	150.00
RIP49	Ted Williams	150.00
RIP50	Vladimir Guerrero	100.00

2006 Topps Bazooka

JOHNNY DAMON

		NM/M
Complete Set (220):		30.00
Common Player:		.10
Pack (8):		2.50
Box (24):		50.00
1	Josh Gibson	.50
2	Scott Podsednik	.10
3	Sammy Sosa	.75
4	Ivan Rodriguez	.50
5	Derek Jeter	1.50
6	Manny Ramirez	.50

7	Nook Logan	.10
8	Adam Dunn	.40
9	Travis Hafner	.25
10	Felix Hernandez	.40
11	Larry Bigbie	.10
12	Magglio Ordonez	.10
13	Josh Beckett	.25
14	Mike Sweeney	.10
15	Mickey Mantle	2.00
16	Grady Sizemore	.25
17	Brian Fuentes	.10
18	Wily Mo Pena	.10
19	Morgan Ensberg	.10
20	Tim Hudson	.25
21	Justin Verlander (RC)	.25
22	Jermaine Dye	.10
23	Miguel Cabrera	.50
24	Greg Maddux	1.00
25	Jason Giambi	.25
26	Ben Sheets	.25
27	Brad Radke	.10
28	Torii Hunter	.25
29	Mike Piazza	.75
30	Jason Kendall	.10
31	Pat Burrell	.25
32	Khalil Greene	.10
33	Brian Roberts	.25
34	C.C. Sabathia	.10
35	Mike Mussina	.40
36	Bob Wickman	.10
37	Dmitri Young	.10
38	Dontrelle Willis	.25
39	David DeJesus	.10
40	J.D. Drew	.25
41	Chad Tracy	.10
42	Joe Mauer	.25
43	Melvin Mora	.10
44	Carlos Zambrano	.25
45	Mariano Rivera	.25
46	Coco Crisp	.10
47	Derrek Lee	.50
48	Cliff Floyd	.10
49	Willy Taveras	.10
50	Albert Pujols	1.50
51	Aaron Boone	.10
52	Mark Mulder	.25
53	Brad Wilkerson	.10
54	Hank Blalock	.25
55	Hideki Matsui	1.00
56	Victor Martinez	.10
57	Jeremy Bonderman	.10
58	Felipe Lopez	.10
59	Paul LoDuca	.10
60	Derek Lowe	.10
61	Luis Gonzalez	.10
62	Paul Konerko	.25
63	Miguel Tejada	.40
64	Jeromy Burnitz	.10
65	Orlando Hernandez	.10
66	Curt Schilling	.50
67	Joe Nathan	.10
68	Jose Reyes	.25
69	David Wright	.75
70	Eric Chavez	.25
71	Rich Harden	.25
72	A.J. Pierzynski	.10
73	Trevor Hoffman	.10
74	Adrian Beltre	.25
75	Alex Rodriguez	1.50
76	Larry Walker	.25
77	Jorge Cantu	.10
78	Mark Teixeira	.40
79	Jeff Bagwell	.40
80	Jeff Francoeur	.25
81	Ichiro Suzuki	1.00
82	Jhonny Peralta	.10
83	Todd Helton	.40
84	Brad Penny	.10
85	Shawn Chacon	.10
86	Billy Wagner	.10
87	Jason Schmidt	.10
88	Austin Kearns	.10
89	Chris Carpenter	.10
90	Chipper Jones	.50
91	Shawn Green	.25
92	A.J. Burnett	.10
93	Joe Crede	.10
94	Mark Prior	.40
95	Andy Pettitte	.25
96	Edgar Renteria	.10
97	Roy Halladay	.25
98	Eric Milton	.10
99	Craig Biggio	.25
100	Barry Bonds	1.50
101	Troy Glaus	.10
102	Aaron Rowand	.10
103	Aramis Ramirez	.25
104	Nomar Garciaparra	.50
105	Randy Johnson	.50
106	David Ortiz	.50
107	Vinny Castilla	.10
108	Carl Crawford	.25
109	Zachary Duke	.10
110	Barry Zito	.25

111	Darin Erstad	.10
112	Chris Capuano	.10
113	Javy Lopez	.10
114	Lew Ford	.10
115	Robinson Cano	.25
116	Ronnie Belliard	.10
117	Placido Polanco	.10
118	Rickie Weeks	.25
119	Brad Lidge	.10
120	Andruw Jones	.40
121	Nick Swisher	.10
122	Bartolo Colon	.10
123	Juan Pierre	.10
124	Johan Santana	.50
125	Jorge Posada	.25
126	Jeff Francis	.10
127	Matt Holliday	.25
128	Carlos Delgado	.25
129	Zack Greinke	.10
130	Lyle Overbay	.10
131	Conor Jackson (RC)	.10
132	Mark Buehrle	.25
133	Chone Figgins	.10
134	Pedro Martinez	.50
135	Roger Clemens	1.50
136	Raul Ibanez	.10
137	Jim Edmonds	.25
138	Michael Young	.10
139	Preston Wilson	.10
140	Rafael Furcal	.10
141	Bobby Abreu	.25
142	Tadahito Iguchi	.25
143	B.J. Ryan	.10
144	Francisco Rodriguez	.10
145	J.T. Snow	.10
146	Aubrey Huff	.10
147	Mike Morse	.10
148	Jason Bay	.25
149	Roy Oswalt	.25
150	Carlos Beltran	.40
151	Carlos Lee	.25
152	Emil Brown	.10
153	Craig Monroe	.10
154	Kris Benson	.10
155	Gary Sheffield	.40
156	Jake Peavy	.25
157	David Eckstein	.10
158	Tom Glavine	.25
159	Jeff Kent	.25
160	Livan Hernandez	.10
161	Orlando Hudson	.10
162	Randy Winn	.10
163	Jimmy Rollins	.20
164	Luis Castillo	.10
165	Nick Johnson	.10
166	Johnny Damon	.50
167	Eric Gagne	.10
168	Geoff Jenkins	.10
169	Mike Cameron	.10
170	Marcus Giles	.10
171	Huston Street	.25
172	Moises Alou	.25
173	Scott Rolen	.50
174	Jose Vidro	.10
175	Alfonso Soriano	.40
176	Toby Hall	.10
177	Orlando Cabrera	.10
178	Brian Giles	.10
179	Erubiel Durazo	.10
180	Matt Morris	.10
181	Jack Wilson	.10
182	Brady Clark	.10
183	Shannon Stewart	.10
184	Kerry Wood	.25
185	Carl Pavano	.10
186	Chase Utley	.25
187	Omar Vizquel	.10
188	Vladimir Guerrero	.50
189	Richie Sexson	.25
190	John Smoltz	.25
191	Garret Anderson	.10
192	Jon Garland	.10
193	Julio Lugo	.10
194	Rocco Baldelli	.10
195	Jaret Wright	.10
196	Matt Clement	.10
197	Vernon Wells	.10
198	Sean Casey	.10
199	Lance Berkman	.25
200	Justin Morneau	.25
201	Shaun Marcum (RC)	.20
202	Chuck James (RC)	.20
203	Hong-Chih Kuo (RC)	.20
204	Darrell Rasner (RC)	.20
205	Anthony Reyes (RC)	.25
206	Francisco Liriano (RC)	.50
207	Joe Saunders (RC)	.20
208	Fausto Carmona (RC)	.20
209	Charlton Jimerson (RC)	.20
210	Bryan Bullington (RC)	.20
211	Tom Gorzelanny (RC)	.20
212	Anderson Hernandez (RC)	.20
213	Ryan Garko (RC)	.20

214	John Koronka (RC)	.20
215	Chris Denorfia (RC)	.20
216	Jeff Mathis (RC)	.20
217	Jose Bautista (RC)	.20
218	Danny Sandoval RC	.20
219	Robert Andino RC	.20
220	Justin Huber (RC)	.20

Gold
Stars: 1-2X
Inserted 1:1

Autographs
		NM/M
BM	Brandon McCarthy	12.00
KM	Kevin Millar	20.00
MM	Mike Morse	15.00
AR	Alex Rodriguez/15	
VZ	Victor Zambrano	15.00

Bazooka Blasts

		NM/M
BA	Bobby Abreu	4.00
MA	Moises Alou	4.00
JB	Jason Bay	8.00
CB	Carlos Beltran	6.00
HB	Hank Blalock	4.00
BB	Barry Bonds	20.00
CC	Coco Crisp	4.00
JD	Johnny Damon	8.00
JD	J.D. Drew	4.00
AD	Adam Dunn	6.00
CF	Cliff Floyd	4.00
TG	Troy Glaus	4.00
VG	Vladimir Guerrero	6.00
GJ	Geoff Jenkins	4.00
AJ	Andruw Jones	6.00
CJ	Chipper Jones	8.00
PK	Paul Konerko	6.00
DL	Derrek Lee	6.00
PL	Paul LoDuca	4.00
ML	Mark Loretta	4.00
MM	Mickey Mantle/100	175.00
VM	Victor Martinez	4.00
TN	Trot Nixon	4.00
DO	David Ortiz	8.00
CP	Corey Patterson	4.00
MP	Mike Piazza	8.00
AR	Aramis Ramirez	6.00
AR	Alex Rodriguez	15.00
GS	Gary Sheffield	6.00
SS	Sammy Sosa	8.00
MT	Miguel Tejada	8.00
JT	Jim Thome	6.00
PW	Preston Wilson	4.00
DW	David Wright	10.00

Bazooka Basics
		NM/M
BA	Bobby Abreu	4.00
LB	Lance Berkman	6.00
CB	Craig Biggio	4.00
HB	Hank Blalock	4.00
SB	Sean Burroughs	4.00
MC	Miguel Cabrera	8.00
JD	Johnny Damon	8.00
CD	Carlos Delgado	4.00
EG	Eric Gagne	6.00
MG	Marcus Giles	4.00
MH	Matt Holliday	4.00
TH	Tim Hudson	6.00
AJ	Andruw Jones	6.00
CJ	Chipper Jones	8.00
ML	Mike Lowell	4.00
PM	Pedro Martinez	10.00
MM	Mark Mulder	4.00
MMU	Mike Mussina	6.00
AP	Albert Pujols	15.00
MR	Manny Ramirez	4.00
JR	Jose Reyes	4.00
BR	Brian Roberts	4.00
CS	Curt Schilling	8.00
MT	Mark Teixeira	6.00
BW	Bernie Williams	6.00
DW	Dontrelle Willis	6.00

Bazooka Rewind
		NM/M
CB	Clint Barmes	4.00
WB	William Bergolla	4.00
LB	Lance Berkman	4.00
CBI	Craig Biggio	6.00

JB	Jason Botts	4.00
PB	Pat Burrell	4.00
RC	Robinson Cano	15.00
SC	Shin-Soo Choo	4.00
CC	Carl Crawford	6.00
NC	Nelson Cruz	6.00
JDA	Johnny Damon	8.00
JD	Jermaine Dye	4.00
CE	Carl Everett	4.00
RG	Ryan Garko	4.00
JG	Jon Garland	4.00
MG	Mark Grudzielanek	4.00
JG	Jose Guillen	4.00
CG	Cristian Guzman	4.00
JH	Justin Huber	4.00
CJ	Conor Jackson/ SP/100	
MJ	Mike Jacobs	8.00
NJ	Nick Johnson	4.00
AJ	Andruw Jones	6.00
AK	Adam Kennedy	4.00
PK	Paul Konerko	6.00
AML	Adam LaRoche	4.00
CL	Carlos Lee	4.00
FL	Francisco Liriano	8.00
LM	Luis Montanez	4.00
MM	Miguel Montero	4.00
AP	A.J. Pierzynski	6.00
SP	Scott Podsednik	6.00
HR	Hanley Ramirez	8.00
MR	Manny Ramirez	8.00
ER	Edgar Renteria	4.00
BR	Brian Roberts	4.00
AR	Alex Rodriguez	15.00
JR	Jimmy Rollins	4.00
AR	Aaron Rowand	4.00
TS	Terrmel Sledge	4.00
WT	Willy Taveras	4.00
FT	Frank Thomas	6.00
KT	Kevin Thompson	4.00
BU	B.J. Upton/SP/100	
CU	Chase Utley	8.00
JV	Justin Verlander	6.00
RW	Rickie Weeks	6.00
DW	Dontrelle Willis	6.00
CY	Chris Young	4.00

Comics

		NM/M
Complete Set (24):		10.00
Common Player:		.25
Inserted 1:4		
1	Greg Maddux	1.00
2	Alex Rodriguez	1.00
3	Trevor Hoffman	.25
4	Rafael Palmeiro	.50
5	Roy Oswalt	.25
6	Bobby Abreu	.25
7	Miguel Tejada	.50
8	Vladimir Guerrero	.50
9	Mark Teixeira	.50
10	Zachary Duke	.25
11	Xavier Nady	.25
12	Alex Rodriguez	1.00
13	Jeremy Hermida	.25
14	Craig Biggio	.25
15	Manny Ramirez	.50
16	Texas Rangers	.25
17	Oakland A's	.25
18	Alex Rodriguez	1.00
19	Jason Giambi	.50
20	Aaron Small	.25
21	Jimmy Rollins	.25
22	Roger Clemens	1.00
23	White Sox/Mariners	.50
24	Andruw Jones	.50

Fortune
Stars: 1-2X
Inserted 1:1

Mickey Mantle Oversized Reprint
		NM/M
1952	Mickey Mantle	40.00
1953	Mickey Mantle	30.00
1956	Mickey Mantle	25.00
1957	Mickey Mantle	25.00
1958	Mickey Mantle	25.00
1959	Mickey Mantle	25.00
1960	Mickey Mantle	25.00
1961	Mickey Mantle	25.00
1962	Mickey Mantle	25.00
1963	Mickey Mantle	20.00
1964	Mickey Mantle	25.00
1965	Mickey Mantle	25.00
1966	Mickey Mantle	25.00
1967	Mickey Mantle	25.00
1968	Mickey Mantle	25.00
1969	Mickey Mantle	25.00

Stamps

		NM/M
Complete Set (30):		15.00
Common Player:		.50
Inserted 1:3 Hobby		
1	Bobby Abreu	.50
2	Lance Berkman	.50
3	Hank Blalock	.50
4	Barry Bonds	2.00
5	Mark Buehrle	.50
6	Miguel Cabrera	1.00
7	Jim Edmonds	.50
8	Morgan Ensberg	.50
9	Jeff Francoeur	.50
10	Roy Halladay	.50
11	Tim Hudson	.50
12	Derek Jeter	2.00
13	Andruw Jones	.75
14	Chipper Jones	1.00
15	Derrek Lee	.75
16	Mickey Mantle	3.00
17	Victor Martinez	.50
18	Justin Morneau	.50
19	Manny Ramirez	1.00
20	Brian Roberts	.50
21	Alex Rodriguez	2.00
22	Ivan Rodriguez	.50
23	Johan Santana	.50
24	Alfonso Soriano	.50
25	Huston Street	.50
26	Ichiro Suzuki	1.00
27	Mark Teixeira	.50
28	Miguel Tejada	.50
29	Rickie Weeks	.50
30	Dontrelle Willis	.50

4-on-1 Stickers
		NM/M
1	Josh Gibson, Mickey Mantle, Alex Rodriguez, Barry Bonds	2.00
2	Jason Giambi, David Ortiz, Carlos Delgado, Jeff Bagwell	.75
3	Vernon Wells, Shannon Stewart, Carl Crawford, Torii Hunter	.50
4	Jason Kendall, Javy Lopez, Joe Mauer, Jorge Posada	.50
5	Roger Clemens, Andy Pettitte, Mike Mussina, Orlando Hernandez	1.00
6	Ivan Rodriguez, Rafael Palmeiro, Alfonso Soriano, Hank Blalock	.50
7	Pedro Martinez, Curt Schilling, Matt Clement, Derek Lowe	.75
8	J.D. Drew, Andruw Jones, Gary Sheffield, Vladimir Guerrero	.50
9	Tim Hudson, Greg Maddux, Tom Glavine, John Smoltz	.75
10	Justin Morneau, Albert Pujols, Mark Teixeira, Derrek Lee	1.00
11	B.J. Ryan, Bob Wickman, Mariano Rivera, Trevor Hoffman	.50
12	Mike Morse, Mike Cameron, Mike Piazza, Mike Sweeney	.75
13	Michael Young, Jimmy Rollins, David Eckstein, Orlando Cabrera	.50
14	A.J. Burnett, A.J. Pierzynski, C.C. Sabathia, J.T. Snow	.50
15	Hideki Matsui, Ichiro Suzuki, Tadahito Iguchi, Chase Utley	1.00
16	Barry Zito, Zachary Duke, Zack Greinke, Jeff Francis	.50
17	Mark Buehrle, Mark Mulder, Mark Prior, Marcus Giles	.75
18	Sammy Sosa, Manny Ramirez, Bobby Abreu, Wily Mo Pena	.75
19	Scott Podsednik, Preston Wilson, Juan Pierre, Carlos Beltran	.50
20	Francisco Rodriguez, Billy Wagner, Huston Street, Joe Nathan	.50
21	Melvin Mora, Morgan Ensberg, Scott Rolen, Eric Chavez	.50
22	Garret Anderson, Jim Edmonds, Johnny Damon, Moises Alou	.50
23	Derek Jeter, Edgar Renteria, Miguel Tejada, Julio Lugo	1.00
24	Felix Hernandez, Dontrelle Willis, Rich Harden, Brian Fuentes	.50
25	Bartolo Colon, Jason Schmidt, Jeremy Bonderman, Carlos Zambrano	.50
26	Randy Johnson, Johan Santana, Roy Halladay, Chris Carpenter	.75
27	Roy Oswalt, Shawn Chacon, Kris Benson, Josh Beckett	.50
28	Jose Reyes, Felipe Lopez, Rafael Furcal, Jhonny Peralta	.50
29	Justin Verlander, Kerry Wood, Livan Hernandez, Matt Morris	.50
30	Khalil Greene, Nomar Garciaparra, Omar Vizquel, Jack Wilson	.50
31	Pat Burrell, Rocco Baldelli, Shawn Green, Jason Bay	.50

32	Brad Lidge, Brad Penny, Brad Radke, Brian Roberts .50
33	Jeff Francoeur, Willy Taveras, Rickie Weeks, Robinson Cano .50
34	Geoff Jenkins, Lance Berkman, Larry Bigbie, Matt Holliday .50
35	Paul LoDuca, Toby Hall, Victor Martinez, Carlos Lee .50
36	Aramis Ramirez, Chipper Jones, David Wright, Troy Glaus .75
37	Randy Winn, Brad Wilkerson, Craig Monroe, Aaron Rowand .50
38	Aaron Boone, Adrian Beltre, Vinny Castilla, Chone Figgins .50
39	Larry Walker, Cliff Floyd, Luis Gonzalez, Adam Dunn .50
40	Ronnie Belliard, Jeff Kent, Jorge Cantu, Placido Polanco .50
41	Craig Biggio, Jose Vidro, Luis Castillo, Orlando Hudson .50
42	Grady Sizemore, Lew Ford, Nick Swisher, Brian Giles .50
43	David DeJesus, Emil Brown, Coco Crisp, Jeromy Burnitz .50
44	Eric Gagne, Eric Milton, Jake Peavy, Jaret Wright .50
45	Aubrey Huff, Austin Kearns, Brady Clark, Nook Logan .50
46	Ben Sheets, Carl Pavano, Chris Capuano, Jon Garland .50
47	Darin Erstad, Dmitri Young, Erubiel Durazo, Travis Hafner .50
48	Magglio Ordonez, Miguel Cabrera, Jermaine Dye, Conor Jackson .50
49	Richie Sexson, Sean Casey, Chad Tracy, Lyle Overbay .50
50	Nick Johnson, Paul Konerko, Raul Ibanez, Todd Helton .50
51	Shaun Marcum, Chuck James, Hong-Chih Kuo, Darrell Rasner .50
52	Anthony Reyes, Francisco Liriano, Joe Saunders, Fausto Carmona .50
53	Charlton Jimerson, Bryan Bullington, Tom Gorzelanny, Anderson Hernandez .50
54	Ryan Garko, John Koronka, Chris Denorfia, Jeff Mathis .50
55	Jose Bautista, Danny Sandoval, Robert Andino, Alex Gordon .50

2006 Topps Chrome

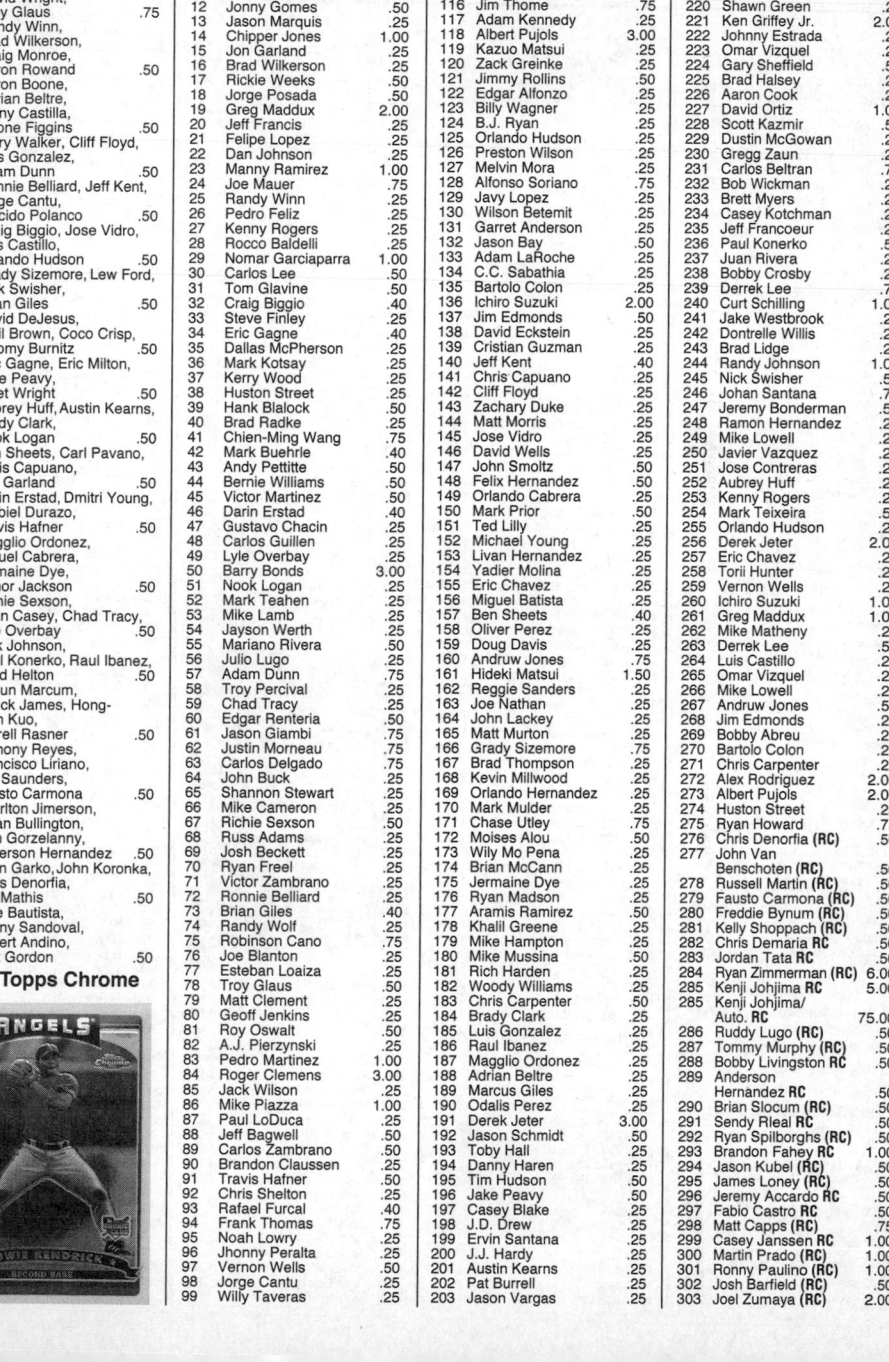

	NM/M
Common Player:	.25
Common Auto. (331-354):	10.00
Pack (4):	3.50
Box (24):	70.00
1 Alex Rodriguez	3.00
2 Garrett Atkins	.25
3 Carl Crawford	.50
4 Clint Barmes	.25
5 Tadahito Iguchi	.50
6 Brian Roberts	.40
7 Mickey Mantle	8.00
8 David Wright	2.00
9 Jeremy Reed	.25
10 Bobby Abreu	.50
11 Lance Berkman	.50
12 Jonny Gomes	.50
13 Jason Marquis	.25
14 Chipper Jones	1.00
15 Jon Garland	.25
16 Brad Wilkerson	.50
17 Rickie Weeks	.50
18 Jorge Posada	.50
19 Greg Maddux	2.00
20 Jeff Francis	.25
21 Felipe Lopez	.25
22 Dan Johnson	.25
23 Manny Ramirez	1.00
24 Joe Mauer	.75
25 Randy Winn	.25
26 Pedro Feliz	.25
27 Kenny Rogers	.25
28 Rocco Baldelli	.25
29 Nomar Garciaparra	1.00
30 Carlos Lee	.50
31 Tom Glavine	.50
32 Craig Biggio	.40
33 Steve Finley	.25
34 Eric Gagne	.40
35 Dallas McPherson	.25
36 Mark Kotsay	.25
37 Kerry Wood	.25
38 Huston Street	.25
39 Hank Blalock	.50
40 Brad Radke	.25
41 Chien-Ming Wang	.75
42 Mark Buehrle	.40
43 Andy Pettitte	.50
44 Bernie Williams	.50
45 Victor Martinez	.50
46 Darin Erstad	.40
47 Gustavo Chacin	.25
48 Carlos Guillen	.25
49 Lyle Overbay	.25
50 Barry Bonds	3.00
51 Nook Logan	.25
52 Mark Teahen	.25
53 Mike Lamb	.25
54 Jayson Werth	.25
55 Mariano Rivera	.50
56 Julio Lugo	.25
57 Adam Dunn	.75
58 Troy Percival	.25
59 Chad Tracy	.25
60 Edgar Renteria	.50
61 Jason Giambi	.75
62 Justin Morneau	.75
63 Carlos Delgado	.75
64 John Buck	.25
65 Shannon Stewart	.25
66 Mike Cameron	.25
67 Richie Sexson	.50
68 Russ Adams	.25
69 Josh Beckett	.25
70 Ryan Freel	.25
71 Victor Zambrano	.25
72 Ronnie Belliard	.25
73 Brian Giles	.40
74 Randy Wolf	.25
75 Robinson Cano	.75
76 Joe Blanton	.25
77 Esteban Loaiza	.25
78 Troy Glaus	.50
79 Matt Clement	.25
80 Geoff Jenkins	.25
81 Roy Oswalt	.50
82 A.J. Pierzynski	.25
83 Pedro Martinez	1.00
84 Roger Clemens	3.00
85 Jack Wilson	.25
86 Mike Piazza	1.00
87 Paul LoDuca	.25
88 Jeff Bagwell	.50
89 Carlos Zambrano	.50
90 Brandon Claussen	.25
91 Travis Hafner	.50
92 Chris Shelton	.25
93 Rafael Furcal	.40
94 Frank Thomas	.75
95 Noah Lowry	.25
96 Jhonny Peralta	.25
97 Vernon Wells	.50
98 Jorge Cantu	.25
99 Willy Taveras	.25

100 Ivan Rodriguez	.75
101 Jose Reyes	.75
102 Barry Zito	.50
103 Mark Teixeira	.75
104 Chone Figgins	.25
105 Todd Helton	.75
106 Tim Wakefield	.25
107 Mike Maroth	.25
108 Johnny Damon	1.00
109 David DeJesus	.25
110 Ryan Klesko	.25
111 Nick Johnson	.25
112 Freddy Garcia	.25
113 Torii Hunter	.50
114 Mike Sweeney	.25
115 Scott Rolen	1.00
116 Jim Thome	.75
117 Adam Kennedy	.25
118 Albert Pujols	3.00
119 Kazuo Matsui	.25
120 Zack Greinke	.25
121 Jimmy Rollins	.50
122 Edgar Alfonzo	.25
123 Billy Wagner	.25
124 B.J. Ryan	.25
125 Orlando Hudson	.25
126 Preston Wilson	.25
127 Melvin Mora	.25
128 Alfonso Soriano	.75
129 Javy Lopez	.25
130 Wilson Betemit	.25
131 Garret Anderson	.25
132 Jason Bay	.50
133 Adam LaRoche	.25
134 C.C. Sabathia	.25
135 Bartolo Colon	.25
136 Ichiro Suzuki	2.00
137 Jim Edmonds	.50
138 David Eckstein	.25
139 Cristian Guzman	.25
140 Jeff Kent	.40
141 Chris Capuano	.25
142 Cliff Floyd	.25
143 Zachary Duke	.25
144 Matt Morris	.25
145 Jose Vidro	.25
146 David Wells	.25
147 John Smoltz	.50
148 Felix Hernandez	.50
149 Orlando Cabrera	.25
150 Mark Prior	.50
151 Ted Lilly	.25
152 Michael Young	.25
153 Livan Hernandez	.25
154 Yadier Molina	.25
155 Eric Chavez	.25
156 Miguel Batista	.25
157 Ben Sheets	.40
158 Oliver Perez	.25
159 Doug Davis	.25
160 Andruw Jones	.50
161 Hideki Matsui	1.50
162 Reggie Sanders	.25
163 Joe Nathan	.25
164 John Lackey	.25
165 Matt Murton	.25
166 Grady Sizemore	.75
167 Brad Thompson	.25
168 Kevin Millwood	.25
169 Orlando Hernandez	.25
170 Mark Mulder	.25
171 Chase Utley	.75
172 Moises Alou	.50
173 Wily Mo Pena	.25
174 Brian McCann	.25
175 Jermaine Dye	.25
176 Ryan Madson	.25
177 Aramis Ramirez	.50
178 Khalil Greene	.25
179 Mike Hampton	.25
180 Mike Mussina	.50
181 Rich Harden	.25
182 Woody Williams	.25
183 Chris Carpenter	.50
184 Brady Clark	.25
185 Luis Gonzalez	.25
186 Raul Ibanez	.25
187 Magglio Ordonez	.25
188 Adrian Beltre	.25
189 Marcus Giles	.25
190 Odalis Perez	.25
191 Derek Jeter	3.00
192 Jason Schmidt	.50
193 Toby Hall	.25
194 Danny Haren	.25
195 Tim Hudson	.50
196 Jake Peavy	.50
197 Casey Blake	.25
198 J.D. Drew	.50
199 Ervin Santana	.25
200 J.J. Hardy	.25
201 Austin Kearns	.25
202 Pat Burrell	.25
203 Jason Vargas	.25

204 Ryan Howard	1.50
205 Joe Crede	.25
206 Vladimir Guerrero	1.00
207 Roy Halladay	.50
208 David Dellucci	.25
209 Brandon Webb	.25
210 Ryan Church	.25
211 Miguel Tejada	.75
212 Mark Loretta	.25
213 Kevin Youkilis	.50
214 Jon Lieber	.25
215 Miguel Cabrera	1.00
216 A.J. Burnett	.25
217 David Bell	.25
218 Eric Byrnes	.25
219 Lance Niekro	.25
220 Shawn Green	.25
221 Ken Griffey Jr.	2.00
222 Johnny Estrada	.25
223 Omar Vizquel	.25
224 Gary Sheffield	.50
225 Brad Halsey	.25
226 Aaron Cook	.25
227 David Ortiz	1.00
228 Scott Kazmir	.50
229 Dustin McGowan	.25
230 Gregg Zaun	.25
231 Carlos Beltran	.75
232 Bob Wickman	.25
233 Brett Myers	.25
234 Casey Kotchman	.25
235 Jeff Francoeur	.25
236 Paul Konerko	.50
237 Juan Rivera	.25
238 Bobby Crosby	.25
239 Derek Lee	.75
240 Curt Schilling	1.00
241 Jake Westbrook	.25
242 Dontrelle Willis	.25
243 Brad Lidge	.25
244 Randy Johnson	1.00
245 Nick Swisher	.50
246 Johan Santana	.75
247 Jeremy Bonderman	.50
248 Ramon Hernandez	.25
249 Mike Lowell	.25
250 Javier Vazquez	.25
251 Jose Contreras	.25
252 Aubrey Huff	.25
253 Kenny Rogers	.25
254 Mark Teixeira	.50
255 Orlando Hudson	.25
256 Derek Jeter	2.00
257 Eric Chavez	.25
258 Torii Hunter	.25
259 Vernon Wells	.25
260 Ichiro Suzuki	1.00
261 Greg Maddux	1.00
262 Mike Matheny	.25
263 Derek Lee	.50
264 Luis Castillo	.25
265 Omar Vizquel	.25
266 Mike Lowell	.25
267 Andruw Jones	.50
268 Jim Edmonds	.25
269 Bobby Abreu	.25
270 Bartolo Colon	.25
271 Chris Carpenter	.25
272 Alex Rodriguez	2.00
273 Albert Pujols	2.00
274 Huston Street	.25
275 Ryan Howard	.75
276 Chris Denorfia (RC)	.50
277 John Van Benschoten (RC)	.50
278 Russell Martin (RC)	.50
279 Fausto Carmona (RC)	.50
280 Freddie Bynum (RC)	.50
281 Kelly Shoppach (RC)	.50
282 Chris Demaria RC	.50
283 Jordan Tata RC	.50
284 Ryan Zimmerman (RC)	6.00
285 Kenji Johjima RC	5.00
285 Kenji Johjima/ Auto. RC	75.00
286 Ruddy Lugo (RC)	.50
287 Tommy Murphy (RC)	.50
288 Bobby Livingston RC	.50
289 Anderson Hernandez (RC)	.50
290 Brian Slocum (RC)	.50
291 Sendy Rleal RC	.50
292 Ryan Spilborghs (RC)	.50
293 Brandon Fahey RC	1.00
294 Jason Kubel (RC)	.50
295 James Loney (RC)	.50
296 Jeremy Accardo RC	.50
297 Fabio Castro (RC)	.50
298 Matt Capps (RC)	.75
299 Casey Janssen RC	1.00
300 Martin Prado (RC)	1.00
301 Ronny Paulino (RC)	1.00
302 Josh Barfield (RC)	.50
303 Joel Zumaya (RC)	2.00

304	Matt Cain (RC)	1.00
305	Conor Jackson (RC)	.50
306	Brian Anderson (RC)	.50
307	Prince Fielder (RC)	4.00
308	Jeremy Hermida (RC)	.75
309	Justin Verlander (RC)	4.00
310	Brian Bannister (RC)	.50
311	Josh Willingham (RC)	.50
312	John Rheinecker (RC)	.50
313	Nicholas Markakis (RC)	.75
314	Jonathan Papelbon (RC)	8.00
315	Mike Jacobs (RC)	.50
316	Jose Capellan (RC)	.50
317	Michael Napoli RC	4.00
318	Ricky Nolasco (RC)	.50
319	Ben Johnson (RC)	.50
320	Paul Maholm (RC)	.50
321	Drew Meyer (RC)	.50
322	Jeff Mathis (RC)	.50
323	Fernando Nieve (RC)	.50
324	John Koronka (RC)	.50
325	Wilbert Nieves (RC)	.50
326	Nate McLouth (RC)	1.00
327	Howard Kendrick (RC)	4.00
328	Sean Marshall (RC)	1.50
329	Brandon Watson (RC)	.50
330	Skip Schumaker (RC)	.50
331	Ryan Garko (RC)	15.00
332	Jason Bergmann RC	15.00
333	Chuck James (RC)	15.00
334	Adam Wainwright (RC)	20.00
335	Daniel Ortmeier (RC)	10.00
336	Francisco Liriano (RC)	30.00
337	Craig Breslow RC	10.00
338	Darrell Rasner (RC)	15.00
339	Jason Botts (RC)	10.00
340	Ian Kinsler (RC)	30.00
341	Joey Devine RC	10.00
342	Miguel Perez (RC)	10.00
343	Scott Olsen (RC)	15.00
344	Tyler Johnson (RC)	10.00
345	Anthony Lerew (RC)	10.00
346	Nelson Cruz (RC)	15.00
347	Willie Eyre (RC)	10.00
348	Josh Johnson (RC)	15.00
349	Shawn Marcum (RC)	15.00
350	Dustin Nippert (RC)	15.00
351	Josh Wilson (RC)	10.00
352	Hanley Ramirez (RC)	25.00
353	Reggie Abercrombie (RC)	15.00
354	Dan Uggla (RC)	30.00

Refractors

Cards (1-330): 2-3X
Inserted 1:4
Rookie Auto. (331-354): 1-1.5X
Production 500

Black Refractors

Cards (1-330): 3-5X
Production 549
Rookie Auto. (331-354): 1.5-2X
Production 200

Blue Refractors

Cards (1-330): 2-4X
Inserted 1:8

Gold Super-Fractor

No Pricing
Production One Set

Red Refractors

Cards (1-330): 4-8X
Production 90
Rookie Auto.
(331-354): No Pricing
Production 25

X-Fractor

Cards (1-330): 2-4X
Inserted 1:6 Retail

Printing Plates

No Pricing
Production One set per color.

Bonds Home Run History

HOME RUN HISTORY 7[0]0
2004 BARRY BONDS

	NM/M
Common Bonds:	2.00
Inserted 1:6	
Refractors:	2-4X
Production 500 Sets	
Black Refractor:	3-5X
Production 200 Sets	
Red Refractor:	10-20X
Production 25 Sets	

Mantle Home Run History

MICKEY MANTLE

	NM/M
Common Mantle:	3.00
Inserted 1:6	
Refractor:	2-4X
Production 500 Sets	
Black Refractor:	3-5X
Production 200 Sets	
Red Refractor:	15-20X
Production 25 Sets	

Signers of the Constitution

		NM/M
Common Signer:		1.50
Inserted 1:7		
Refractors:		1-2X
Inserted 1:11		
AB	Abraham Baldwin	1.50
RB	Richard Bassett	1.50
GB	Gunning Bedford Jr.	1.50
JB	John Blair	1.50
WB	William Blount	1.50
DB	David Brearly	1.50
JBR	Jacob Broom	1.50
PB	Pierce Butler	1.50
DC	Daniel Carroll	1.50
GC	George Clymer	1.50
JD	Jonathan Dayton	1.50
JDI	John Dickinson	1.50
WF	William Few	1.50
TF	Thomas Fitzsimons	1.50
BF	Benjamin Franklin	4.00
NG	Nicholas Gilman	1.50
NGO	Nathaniel Gorham	1.50
AH	Alexander Hamilton	3.00
JI	Jared Ingersoll	1.50
DJ	Daniel of St. Thomas Jenifer	1.50
WJ	William Samuel Johnson	1.50
RK	Rufus King	1.50
JL	John Langdon	1.50
WL	William Livingston	1.50
JM	James Madison	2.00
JMC	James McHenry	1.50
TM	Thomas Mifflin	1.50
GM	Gouverneur Morris	1.50
RM	Robert Morris	1.50
WP	William Paterson	1.50
CCP	Charles Cotesworth Pinckney	1.50
CP	Charles Pinckney	1.50
GR	George Read	1.50
JR	John Rutledge	1.50
RS	Roger Sherman	1.50
RDS	Richard Dobbs Spaight	1.50
GW	George Washington	4.00
HW	Hugh Williamson	1.50
JW	James Wilson	1.50

Signers of Declaration/ Independence

	NM/M
Common Signer:	1.50
Inserted 1:5	
Refractors:	1-2X

Inserted 1:9

JA	John Adams	2.00
SA	Samuel Adams	1.50
JB	Josiah Bartlett	1.50
CB	Carter Braxton	1.50
CC	Charles Carroll	1.50
SC	Samuel Chase	1.50
AC	Abraham Clark	1.50
GC	George Clymer	1.50
WE	William Ellery	1.50
WF	William Floyd	1.50
BF	Benjamin Franklin	4.00
EG	Elbridge Gerry	1.50
BG	Button Gwinnett	1.50
LH	Lyman Hall	1.50
JH	John Hancock	3.00
BH	Benjamin Harrison	1.50
JHA	John Hart	1.50
JHE	Joseph Hewes	1.50
TH	Thomas Heyward Jr.	1.50
WH	William Hooper	1.50
SH	Stephen Hopkins	1.50
FH	Francis Hopkinson	1.50
SHU	Samuel Huntington	1.50
TJ	Thomas Jefferson	4.00
FL	Francis Lewis	1.50
FLL	Francis Lightfoot Lee	1.50
RHL	Richard Henry Lee	1.50
PL	Philip Livingston	1.50
TL	Thomas Lynch Jr.	1.50
TM	Thomas McKean	1.50
AM	Arthur Middleton	1.50
LM	Lewis Morris	1.50
RM	Robert Morris	1.50
JM	John Morton	1.50
TN	Thomas Nelson Jr.	1.50
WP	William Paca	1.50
RTP	Robert Treat Paine	1.50
JP	John Penn	1.50
GRE	George Read	1.50
CR	Caesar Rodney	1.50
GR	George Ross	1.50
BR	Benjamin Rush	1.50
ER	Edward Rutledge	1.50
RS	Roger Sherman	1.50
JS	James Smith	1.50
RST	Richard Stockton	1.50
TS	Thomas Stone	1.50
GT	George Taylor	1.50
MT	Matthew Thornton	1.50
GW	George Walton	1.50
WW	William Whipple	1.50
WWI	William Williams	1.50
JW	James Wilson	1.50
JWI	John Witherspoon	1.50
OW	Oliver Wolcott	1.50
GWY	George Wythe	1.50

2006 Topps Co-Signers

		NM/M
Complete Set (120):		
Common Player (1-100):		.25
Common Auto. (101-120):		10.00
Pack (6):		12.00
Box (12):		130.00

Note: Each parallel has 3 versions.

1	Albert Pujols	3.00
2	Roger Clemens	3.00
3	Paul Konerko	.50
4	Jeff Francoeur	.25
5	Miguel Tejada	.75
6	Curt Schilling	1.00
7	Mickey Mantle	4.00
8	Miguel Cabrera	1.00
9	Derrek Lee	1.00
10	Jeff Kent	.50
11	Gary Sheffield	.50
12	Rich Harden	.25
13	Scott Rolen	.75
14	David Wright	1.50
15	Troy Glaus	.25
16	Torii Hunter	.25
17	Nolan Ryan	2.00
18	Alfonso Soriano	.75
19	Hank Blalock	.50
20	Chase Utley	.50
21	Ryan Howard	.75
22	Robinson Cano	1.00
23	Derek Jeter	3.00
24	Huston Street	.25
25	Jason Giambi	.50
26	Rafael Furcal	.25
27	Rickie Weeks	.25
28	Ivan Rodriguez	.50
29	Travis Hafner	.50
30	Greg Maddux	2.00
31	Andruw Jones	.75
32	Andy Pettitte	.50
33	Scott Podsednik	.25
34	Francisco Rodriguez	.25
35	Josh Beckett	.25
36	Lance Berkman	.50
37	Roy Oswalt	.50
38	Pedro Martinez	1.00
39	Jimmy Rollins	.50
40	Johan Santana	.75
41	Randy Johnson	1.00
42	Mariano Rivera	.50
43	Nick Johnson	.25
44	Josh Gibson	.50
45	Shawn Green	.25
46	Adrian Beltre	.25
47	Johnny Damon	1.00
48	Joe Mauer	.50
49	Todd Helton	.50
50	Alex Rodriguez	2.50
51	Jake Peavy	.50
52	David Ortiz	1.00
53	Mark Buehrle	.50
54	Eric Gagne	.50
55	Hideki Matsui	1.50
56	Bobby Abreu	.50
57	Victor Martinez	.50
58	Brian Roberts	.25
59	Chipper Jones	1.00
60	Carlos Beltran	.75
61	Tim Hudson	.50
62	Carlos Lee	.50
63	Barry Zito	.50
64	Moises Alou	.50
65	Mark Teixeira	.75
66	Lyle Overbay	.25
67	Kerry Wood	.50
68	B.J. Ryan	.25
69	Jim Edmonds	.50
70	Carlos Delgado	.50
71	Magglio Ordonez	.25
72	Juan Pierre	.25
73	Manny Ramirez	1.00
74	Dontrelle Willis	.50
75	Ichiro Suzuki	2.00
76	Nomar Garciaparra	1.00
77	Zachary Duke	.25
78	Chris Carpenter	.50
79	A.J. Burnett	.25
80	Scott Kazmir	.25
81	Carl Crawford	.25
82	Mark Prior	.50
83	Adam Dunn	.75
84	Justin Morneau	.50
85	Morgan Ensberg	.25
86	Pat Burrell	.25
87	Paul LoDuca	.25
88	Jason Bay	.50
89	Aubrey Huff	.25
90	Kevin Millwood	.25
91	Vernon Wells	.25
92	Javy Lopez	.25
93	Michael Young	.25
94	Felix Hernandez	.50
95	Ken Griffey Jr.	2.00
96	Bartolo Colon	.25
97	Billy Wagner	.25
98	Vladimir Guerrero	1.00
99	Jose Reyes	.75
100	Barry Bonds	3.00
101	Anthony LeRew (RC)	10.00
102	Ryan Zimmerman/ 440 (RC)	40.00
103	Craig Hansen/250 RC	25.00
104	Francisco Liriano (RC)	30.00
105	Jason Botts (RC)	10.00
106	Josh Johnson (RC)	10.00
107	Hanley Ramirez (RC)	30.00
108	Adam Wainwright (RC)	20.00
109	Kenji Johjima/200 RC	100.00
110	Daniel Ortmeier (RC)	10.00
111	Darrell Rasner (RC)	15.00
112	Chuck James (RC)	15.00
113	Nelson Cruz (RC)	15.00
114	Hong-Chih Kuo (RC)	25.00
115	Ryan Garko (RC)	15.00
116	R. Abercrombie (RC)	15.00

117	Ian Kinsler (RC)	25.00
118	Joel Zumaya (RC)	25.00
119	Willie Eyre (RC)	15.00
120	Dan Uggla (RC)	20.00

Bronze
Bronze (1-100): 2-3X
Production 150 Sets

Blue
Blue (1-100): 2-3X
Production 125 Sets

Gold
Gold (1-100): 2-3X
Production 115 Sets

Hyper Silver - Bronze
Hyper Silver/Bronze (1-100): 2-3X
Production 75 Sets

Hyper Silver - Blue
Hyper Silver/Blue: No Pricing
Production 10 Sets

Hyper Silver - Gold
Hyper Silver/Gold: No Pricing
Production 5 Sets

Hyper Silver - Red
Hyper Silver/Red: No Pricing
Production 25 Sets

Silver - Bronze
Silver/Bronze (1-100): 2-3X
Production 125 Sets

Silver - Blue
Silver/Blue (1-100): 2-3X
Production 75 Sets

Silver - Gold
Silver/Gold (1-100): 3-4X
Production 50 Sets

Silver - Red
Silver/Red (1-100): 2-3X
Production 100 Sets

Dual Autographs
NM/M

Cards are not serial #'d.

CS2	David Wright, Alex Rodriguez/25	275.00
CS3	Victor Martinez, Kenji Johjima/25	75.00
CS4	Kenji Johjima, Felix Hernandez/18	200.00
CS5	David Ortiz, Manny Ramirez/25	150.00
CS6	Nolan Ryan, Roger Clemens/25	350.00
CS7	David Ortiz, Albert Pujols/25	350.00
CS8	Chipper Jones, Dale Murphy/25	100.00
CS11	Stan Musial, Albert Pujols/20	500.00
CS15	Prince Fielder, Ryan Zimmerman/100	100.00
CS16	Cal Ripken Jr., Ozzie Smith/25	275.00
CS18	Don Larsen, Yogi Berra/25	200.00
CS19	Mike Schmidt, Brooks Robinson/25	125.00
CS20	Ryan Zimmerman, Wade Boggs/25	75.00
CS22	Ryan Howard, Derrek Lee/75	80.00
CS23	Jeff Mathis, Chris Snyder	15.00
CS25	Ray Knight, Keith Hernandez/100	25.00
CS26	Mike Schmidt, Chase Utley/25	100.00
CS27	Billy Wagner, Paul LoDuca/50	70.00
CS28	Tony Gwynn, Wade Boggs/25	140.00
CS30	Dwight Gooden, Darryl Strawberry/50	40.00
CS31	Ryan Howard, Huston Street	60.00
CS32	Mariano Rivera, Huston Street/25	140.00
CS33	Prince Fielder, Ryan Howard/50	80.00
CS34	Robinson Cano, Chase Utley/75	60.00
CS36	David Justice, Chipper Jones/25	80.00

CS37	Jose Reyes, David Wright/50	200.00
CS38	Jeff Mathis, Ryan Garko	15.00
CS39	Brandon McCarthy, Pedro Lopez	15.00
CS40	David Justice, Dale Murphy/100	50.00
CS42	Joe Mauer, Francisco Liriano	75.00
CS44	Ryan Zimmerman, David Wright/100	125.00
CS45	Rick Rhoden, Dave Parker/100	40.00
CS46	Jonathan Papelbon, Craig Breslow	50.00
CS48	Dan Johnson, Prince Fielder/100	40.00
CS49	Victor Martinez, Ryan Garko	20.00
CS50	Ben Hendrickson, Anthony Reyes	15.00
CS51	Nelson Cruz, Prince Fielder/100	40.00
CS52	Jonathan Papelbon, Anthony Reyes	50.00
CS53	Ben Hendrickson, Rich Hill	20.00
CS54	Shin-Soo Choo, Kenji Johjima/25	85.00
CS55	Francisco Liriano, Johan Santana/100	100.00
CS56	Brandon McCarthy, Zachary Duke	15.00
CS57	Josh Johnson, Scott Olsen	15.00
CS58	Tommy John, Bob Welch	15.00
CS59	Roy White, Joe Pepitone	25.00
CS60	Cecil Fielder, Prince Fielder	70.00
CS62	Conor Jackson, Ryan Howard	60.00
CS63	Dontrelle Willis, Zachary Duke/50	30.00
CS64	Mariano Rivera, Billy Wagner/25	150.00
CS65	Hong-Chih Kuo, Shin-Soo Choo	30.00
CS66	Jim Leyritz, Cecil Fielder	50.00
CS67	Scott Kazmir, Francisco Liriano	50.00
CS68	Scott Kazmir, Roy Oswalt/50	50.00
CS69	Chuck James, Anthony LeRew	15.00
CS70	Cecil Fielder, Ryan Howard	60.00
CS71	Chien-Ming Wang, Hong-Chih Kuo/25	200.00
CS72	Shin-Soo Choo, Chien-Ming Wang/50	160.00
CS73	Nelson Cruz, Jason Botts	15.00
CS74	Francisco Liriano, Ervin Santana	30.00
CS75	Adam Wainwright, Anthony Reyes	30.00
CS76	Ervin Santana, Scott Kazmir	30.00
CS77	Robinson Cano, Gary Sheffield	60.00
CS78	David Wright, Miguel Cabrera/50	120.00
CS79	Dan Johnson, Conor Jackson	15.00
CS80	Frank Tanana, Mickey Tettleton	15.00
CS81	Andruw Jones, Chipper Jones	75.00
CS82	Morgan Ensberg, Roy Oswalt	25.00
CS83	Michael Young, Ozzie Smith	50.00
CS84	Grady Sizemore, Nick Swisher	40.00
CS85	Garrett Atkins, Clint Barmes	20.00

Dual Cut Signatures
No Pricing

Solo Sigs
NM/M

Cards are not serial #'d.

CB	Clint Barmes	10.00
CBR	Craig Breslow	10.00
RC	Robinson Cano	50.00
GC	Gustavo Chacin	10.00
SSC	Shin-Soo Choo	15.00
JC	Jack Clark	10.00
AD	Andre Dawson	10.00
ZD	Zachary Duke	15.00
CF	Cecil Fielder	20.00
PF	Prince Fielder/250	50.00
RHI	Rich Hill	30.00
RH	Ryan Howard/100	75.00
DJ	Dan Johnson/250	10.00
CJ	Chipper Jones/25	80.00
AK	Al Kaline/100	50.00
SK	Scott Kazmir	20.00
DL	Don Larsen	20.00
DLE	Derrek Lee/50	40.00
VM	Victor Martinez/50	25.00
JM	Jeff Mathis	10.00
DM	Don Mattingly/50	120.00
CM	Craig Monroe	10.00
SO	Scott Olsen	15.00
DO	David Ortiz/25	60.00
JP	Jonathan Papelbon	60.00
ARE	Anthony Reyes	15.00
RR	Rick Rhoden	10.00
CR	Cal Ripken Jr./20	200.00
AR	Alex Rodriguez/20	200.00
NR	Nolan Ryan/20	125.00
ES	Ervin Santana/250	10.00
JS	Johan Santana/50	40.00
CS	Chris Snyder	8.00
DS	Darryl Strawberry	15.00
HS	Huston Street/250	20.00
DWI	Dontrelle Willis	20.00
DW	David Wright/75	80.00

2006 Topps Heritage

NM/M

Complete Set (485):		
Common Player:		.40
Common SP:		4.00
Pack (8):		5.00
Box (24):		100.00
1	David Ortiz/SP	8.00
2	Mike Piazza/SP	8.00
3	Daryle Ward	.40
4	Rafael Furcal	.40
5	Derek Lowe	.40
6	Eric Chavez	.75
7	Juan Uribe	.40
8	C.C. Sabathia	.40
9	Sean Casey	.40
10	Barry Bonds/SP	15.00
11	Gary Sheffield	.40
12	Ted Lilly	.40
13	Lew Ford	.40
14	Tom Gordon	.40
15	Curt Schilling	.40
16	Jason Kendall	.40
17	Frank Catalanotto	.40
18	Pedro Martinez/SP	8.00
19	David Dellucci	.40
20	Andruw Jones	1.00
20	Andruw Jones/ w/Seats/SP	6.00
21	Brad Halsey	.40
22	Vernon Wells	.40
23	Derek Jeter	4.00
23	Derek Jeter/ Blue Letter/SP	15.00
24	Todd Helton	1.00
25	Randy Johnson/SP	8.00
26	Jay Gibbons	.40
27	Joe Mays	.40
28	Paul Konerko	.75
29	Lyle Overbay	.40
30	Jorge Posada	.75
31	Brandon Webb	.40
32	Marcus Giles	.40
33	J.T. Snow	.40
34	Todd Walker	.40
35	Wily Mo Pena/SP	5.00
36	Carlos Delgado	.75

37	David Wright	2.00
38	Shea Hillenbrand	.40
39	Daniel Cabrera	.40
40	Trevor Hoffman	.40
41	Matt Morris	.40
42	Mariano Rivera	.75
43	Jeff Bagwell	1.00
44	J.D. Drew	.40
45	Carl Pavano	.40
46	Placido Polanco	.40
47	Adrian Beltre	.75
48	J.D. Closser	.40
49	Paul LoDuca	.40
50	Scott Rolen	1.00
51	Bernie Williams	.75
52	Jose Guillen	.40
53	Aubrey Huff	.40
54	Greg Maddux	2.50
55	Derrek Lee SP	8.00
56	Hideki Matsui	2.50
57	Jose Bautista	.40
58	Kyle Farnsworth	.40
59	Nate Robertson	.40
60	Sammy Sosa	1.50
61	Javier Vazquez	.40
62	Jeff Mathis (RC)	.40
63	Mark Buehrle	.75
64	Orlando Hernandez	.40
65	Brandon Claussen	.40
66	Miguel Batista	.40
67	Eddie Guardado	.40
68	Alex Gonzalez	.40
69	Kris Benson	.40
70	Bobby Abreu/SP	6.00
71	Vinny Castilla	.40
72	Ben Broussard	.40
73	Travis Hafner	1.00
74	Dmitri Young	.40
75	Alex S. Gonzalez	.40
76	Jason Bay/SP	6.00
77	Charlton Jimerson	.40
78	Ryan Garko (RC)	.50
79	Lance Berkman	.75
80	Tim Hudson	.75
80	Tim Hudson/ Blue Letter/SP	5.00
81	Guillermo Mota	.40
82	Chris Young	.40
83	Brad Lidge	.40
84	A.J. Pierzynski	.40
85	Maicer Izturis	.40
86	Vladimir Guerrero	1.50
87	J.J. Hardy	.40
88	Cesar Izturis	.40
89	Mark Ellis	.40
90	Chipper Jones	1.50
91	Chris Snelling/SP	4.00
92	Jose Reyes	.75
93	Mike Lieberthal	.40
94	Octavio Dotel	.40
95	Alex Rodriguez/ Fld/SP	10.00
95	Alex Rodriguez/ With Bat/SP	10.00
96	Brett Myers	.40
97	New York Yankees	1.00
98	Ryan Klesko	.40
99	Brian Jordan/SP	4.00
100	William Harridge, Warren Giles	.40
101	Adam Eaton	.40
102	Aaron Boone	.40
103	Alex Rios	.40
104	Andy Pettitte	.75
105	Barry Zito	.75
106	Bengie Molina/SP	4.00
107	Austin Kearns	.50
108	Adam Everett	.40
109	A.J. Burnett	.40
110	Mark Prior	1.00
111	Russ Ortiz	.40
112	Adam Dunn	1.00
113	Byung-Hyun Kim	.40
114	Atlanta Braves	.50
115	Carlos Silva	.40
116	Chad Cordero	.40
117	Chone Figgins	.40
118	Chris Reitsma	.40
119	Coco Crisp	.40
120	David DeJesus	.40
121	Chris Snyder	.40
122	Brad Eldred	.40
123	Humberto Cota/SP	5.00
124	Erubiel Durazo	.40
125	Josh Beckett	.75
126	Kenny Lofton	.40
127	Joe Nathan/SP	5.00
128	Bryan Bullington	.40
129	Jim Thome	1.00
130	Shawn Green	.75
131	LaTroy Hawkins	.40
132	Mark Kotsay	.40
133	Matt Lawton	.40
134	Luis Castillo	.40

#	Player	Price
135	Michael Barrett	.40
136	Preston Wilson	.40
137	Orlando Cabrera	.40
138	Chuck James (RC)	.40
139	Raul Ibanez	.40
140	Frank Thomas	1.00
141	Orlando Hudson	.40
142	Scott Kazmir	.40
143	Steve Finley	.40
144	Danny Sandoval RC	1.00
145	Javy Lopez	.40
146	Tony Giarratano	.40
147	Terrence Long	.40
148	Victor Martinez	.40
149	Toby Hall	.40
150	Fausto Carmona (RC)	.40
151	Tim Wakefield	.40
152	Troy Percival	.40
153	Chris Denorfia (RC)	.40
154	Junior Spivey	.40
155	Desi Relaford	.40
156	Francisco Liriano (RC)	.75
157	Corey Koskie	.40
158	Chris Carpenter	.40
159	Robert Andino RC	1.00
160	Cliff Floyd	.40
161	Pittsburgh Pirates	.40
162	Anderson Hernandez (RC)	.40
163	Mike Maroth	.40
164	Aaron Rowand	.40
165	Albert Pujols	4.00
165	Albert Pujols/ Red Shirt/SP	15.00
166	David Bell	.40
167	Angel Berroa	.40
168	B.J. Ryan	.40
169	Bartolo Colon	.40
170	Hong-Chih Kuo	.40
171	Cincinnati Reds	.40
172	Bill Mueller	.40
173	John Koronka (RC)	.40
174	Billy Wagner	.40
175	Zack Greinke	.40
176	Rick Short RC	1.00
177	Yadier Molina	.40
178	Willy Taveras	.40
179	Wes Helms	.40
180	Wade Miller	.40
181	Luis Gonzalez	.40
182	Carlos Zambrano	.40
183	Chicago Cubs	.50
184	Victor Santos	.40
185	Tyler Walker	.40
186	Bobby Crosby	.40
187	Trot Nixon	.40
188	Nick Johnson	.40
189	Nick Swisher	.40
190	Brian Roberts	.40
191	Nomar Garciaparra	1.50
192	Oliver Perez	.40
193	Ramon Hernandez	.40
194	Randy Winn	.40
195	Ryan Church	.40
196	Ryan Wagner	.40
197	Todd Hollandsworth	.40
198	Detroit Tigers	.40
199	Tino Martinez	.40
200	Roger Clemens	4.00
200	Roger Clemens/ Red Shirt/SP	12.00
201	Shawn Estes	.40
202	Justin Morneau	.75
203	Jeff Francis	.40
204	Oakland Athletics	.40
205	Jeff Francoeur	.40
206	C.J. Wilson	.40
207	Francisco Rodriguez	.40
208	Edgardo Alfonzo	.40
209	David Eckstein	.40
210	Cory Lidle	.40
211	Chase Utley	.75
212	Rocco Baldelli	.40
212	Rocco Baldelli/ Blue Letter/SP	5.00
213	So Taguchi	.40
214	Philadelphia Phillies	.40
215	Brad Hawpe	.40
216	Walter Young	.40
217	Tom Gorzelanny (RC)	.40
218	Shaun Marcum (RC)	.40
219	Ryan Howard	2.00
220	Damian Jackson	.40
221	Craig Counsell	.40
222	Damian Miller	.40
223	Derrick Turnbow	.40
224	Hank Blalock	.75
225	Brayan Pena	.40
226	Grady Sizemore	1.00
227	Ivan Rodriguez	1.00
228	Jason Isringhausen	.40
229	Brian Fuentes	.40
230	Jason Phillips	.40
231	Jason Schmidt	.75
232	Javier Valentin	.40
233	Jeff Kent	.75
234	John Buck	.40
235	Mike Matheny	.40
236	Jorge Cantu	.40
237	Jose Castillo	.40
238	Kenny Rogers	.40
239	Kerry Wood	.75
240	Kevin Mench	.40
241	Tim Stauffer	.40
242	Eric Milton	.40
243	St. Louis Cardinals	.75
244	Shawn Chacon	.40
245	Mike Jacobs (RC)	.40
246	Ryan Dempster	.40
247	Todd Jones	.40
248	Tom Glavine	.75
249	Tony Graffanino	.40
250	Ichiro Suzuki	2.50
251	Baltimore Orioles	.50
252	Brad Radke	.40
253	Brad Wilkerson	.40
254	Carlos Lee	.40
255	Alex Gordon Cut-Out	125.00
256	Gustavo Chacin	.40
257	Jermaine Dye	.40
258	Jose Mesa	.40
259	Julio Lugo	.40
260	Mark Redman	.40
261	Brandon Watson (RC)	.40
262	Pedro Feliz	.40
263	Esteban Loaiza	.40
264	Anthony Reyes	.40
265	Jose Contreras/SP	6.00
266	Tadahito Iguchi/SP	8.00
267	Mark Loretta/SP	6.00
268	Ray Durham/SP	4.00
269	Neifi Perez/SP	4.00
270	Washington Nationals	.40
271	Troy Glaus/SP	6.00
272	Matt Holliday/SP	6.00
273	Kevin Millwood/SP	5.00
274	Jon Lieber/SP	4.00
275	Cleveland Indians	.40
276	Jeremy Reed/SP	4.00
277	Garrett Atkins/SP	4.00
278	Geoff Jenkins/SP	4.00
279	Gary Gathright/SP	4.00
280	Ben Sheets/SP	6.00
281	Melvin Mora/SP	4.00
282	Jonathan Papelbon/ SP (RC)	10.00
283	John Smoltz/SP	5.00
284	Jake Peavy/SP	5.00
285	Felix Hernandez/SP	6.00
286	Alfonso Soriano/SP	6.00
287	Bronson Arroyo/SP	5.00
288	Dan LaRoche/SP	5.00
289	Aramis Ramirez/SP	5.00
290	Brad Hennessey/SP	4.00
291	Conor Jackson/ SP (RC)	4.00
292	Rod Barajas/SP	4.00
293	Chris Young/SP	4.00
294	Jeremy Bonderman/ SP	4.00
295	Jack Wilson/SP	4.00
296	Jay Payton/SP	4.00
297	Danys Baez/SP	4.00
298	Jose Lima/SP	4.00
299	Luis A. Gonzalez/SP	4.00
300	Mike Sweeney/SP	4.00
301	Nelson Cruz/SP (RC)	6.00
302	Eric Gagne/SP	5.00
303	Juan Castro/SP	4.00
304	Joe Mauer/SP	6.00
305	Richie Sexson/SP	5.00
306	Roy Oswalt/SP	5.00
307	Rickie Weeks/SP	4.00
308	Pat Borders/SP	4.00
309	Mike Morse/SP	4.00
310	Matt Stairs/SP	4.00
311	Chad Tracy/SP	4.00
312	Matt Cain/SP (RC)	6.00
313	Mark Mulder/SP	5.00
314	Mark Grudzielanek/SP	4.00
315	Johnny Damon/SP	8.00
316	Casey Kotchman/SP	4.00
317	San Francisco Giants	.40
318	Chris Burke/SP	4.00
319	Carl Crawford/SP	5.00
320	Edgar Renteria/SP	5.00
321	Chan Ho Park/SP	4.00
322	Boston Red Sox	6.00
323	Robinson Cano/SP	8.00
324	Los Angeles Dodgers	.40
325	Miguel Tejada/ w/Bat/SP	6.00
325	Miguel Tejada/ Hand Up/SP	6.00
326	Jimmy Rollins/SP	5.00
327	Juan Pierre/SP	4.00
328	Dan Johnson/SP	4.00
329	Chicago White Sox	.40
330	Pat Burrell/SP	5.00
331	Ramon Ortiz/SP	4.00
332	Rondell White/SP	4.00
333	David Wells/SP	4.00
334	Michael Young/SP	6.00
335	Mike Mussina/SP	6.00
336	Moises Alou/SP	5.00
337	Scott Podsednik/SP	5.00
338	Rich Harden/SP	6.00
339	Mark Teahen/SP	5.00
340	Jacque Jones/SP	4.00
341	Jason Giambi/SP	6.00
342	Bill Hall/SP	4.00
343	Jon Garland/SP	6.00
344	Dontrelle Willis/SP	6.00
345	Danny Haren/SP	4.00
346	Brian Giles/SP	4.00
347	Brad Penny/SP	4.00
348	Brandon McCarthy/SP	6.00
349	Chien-Ming Wang/SP	7.00
350	Torii Hunter/ Blue Letter/SP	5.00
350	Torii Hunter/ Red/Blue Letter/SP	5.00
351	Yhency Brazoban/SP	4.00
352	Rodrigo Lopez/SP	4.00
353	Paul McAnulty	.40
354	Francisco Cordero	.40
355	Brandon Inge	.40
356	Jason Lane	.40
357	Brian Schneider	.40
358	Dustin Hermanson	.40
359	Eric Hinske	.40
360	Jarrod Washburn	.40
361	Jayson Werth	.40
362	Craig Breslow RC	1.00
363	Jeff Weaver	.40
364	Jeromy Burnitz	.40
365	Jhonny Peralta	.75
366	Joe Crede	.40
367	Johan Santana	1.50
368	Jose Valentin	.40
369	Keith Foulke	.40
370	Larry Bigbie	.40
371	Manny Ramirez	1.50
372	Jim Edmonds	.75
373	Horacio Ramirez	.40
374	Garret Anderson	.75
375	Felipe Lopez	.75
376	Eric Byrnes	.40
377	Darin Erstad	.75
378	Carlos Zambrano	.75
379	Craig Biggio	.75
380	Darrell Rasner (RC)	.40
381	Dave Roberts	.40
382	Hanley Ramirez (RC)	.75
383	Geoff Blum	.40
384	Joel Pineiro	.40
385	Kip Wells	.40
386	Kelvim Escobar	.40
387	John Patterson	.40
388	Jody Gerut	.40
389	Marshall McDougall	.40
390	Mike MacDougal	.40
391	Orlando Palmeiro	.40
392	Rich Aurilia	.40
393	Ronnie Belliard	.40
394	Rich Hill	.50
395	Scott Hatteberg	.40
396	Ryan Langerhans	.40
397	Richard Hidalgo	.40
398	Omar Vizquel	.40
399	Mike Lowell	.40
400	Astros' Aces/SP	8.00
401	Mike Cameron	.40
402	Matt Clement	.40
403	Miguel Cabrera	1.50
404	Milton Bradley	.40
405	Laynce Nix	.40
406	Robert Mackowiak	.40
407	White Sox/ Power Hitters/SP	10.00
408	Mark Teixeira	1.00
409	Brady Clark	.40
410	Johnny Estrada	.40
411	Juan Encarnacion	.40
412	Morgan Ensberg	.40
413	Nook Logan	.40
414	Phil Nevin	.40
415	Reggie Sanders	.40
416	Roy Halladay	.75
417	Livan Hernandez	.40
418	Jose Vidro	.40
419	Shannon Stewart	.40
420	Brian Bruney	.40
421	Royce Clayton	.40
422	Chris Demaria RC	1.50
423	Eduardo Perez	.40
424	Jeff Suppan	.40
425	Jaret Wright	.40
426	Joe Randa	.40
427	Bobby Kielty	.40
428	Jason Ellison	.40
429	Gregg Zaun	.40
430	Runelvys Hernandez	.40
431	Joe McEwing	.40
432	Jason LaRue	.40
433	Aaron Miles	.40
434	Adam Kennedy	.40
435	Ambiorix Burgos	.40
436	Armando Benitez	.40
437	Brad Ausmus	.40
438	Brandon Backe	.40
439	Brian Anderson (RC)	.40
440	Bruce Chen	.40
441	Carlos Guillen	.40
442	Casey Blake	.40
443	Chris Capuano	.40
444	Chris Duffy	.40
445	Chris Ray	.40
446	Clint Barmes	.40
447	Andrew Sisco	.40
448	Dallas McPherson	.40
449	Tanyon Sturtze	.40
450	Carlos Beltran	1.50
451	Jason Vargas	.40
452	Ervin Santana	.40
453	Jason Marquis	.40
454	Juan Rivera	.40
455	Jake Westbrook	.40
456	Jason Johnson	.40
457	Joe Blanton	.40
458	Kevin Millar	.40
459	John Thomson	.40
460	J.P. Howell	.40
461	Justin Verlander (RC)	.40
462	Kelly Johnson	.40
463	Kyle Davies	.40
464	Lance Niekro	.40
465	Magglio Ordonez	.40
466	Melky Cabrera	.40
467	Nick Punto	.40
468	Paul Byrd	.40
469	Randy Wolf	.40
470	Ruben Gotay	.40
471	Ryan Madson	.40
472	Victor Diaz	.40
473	Xavier Nady	.40
474	Zachary Duke	.40
475	Huston Street	.75
475	Huston Street/ Blue Letter/SP	6.00
476	Brad Thompson	.40
477	Jonny Gomes	.40
478	B.J. Upton	.40
479	Jamey Carroll	.40
480	Mike Hampton	.40
481	Tony Clark	.40
482	Antonio Alfonseca	.40
483	Justin Duchscherer	.40
484	Mike Timlin	.40
485	Joe Saunders	.40

Chrome

		NM/M
Common Player:		2.00
Production 1,957 Sets		
Refractor:		1.5-2X
Production 557 Sets		
Black Refractor:		3-6X
Production 57 Sets		
1	Rafael Furcal	2.00
2	C.C. Sabathia	2.00
3	Sean Casey	2.00
4	Gary Sheffield	3.00
5	William Harridge, Warren Giles	2.00
6	Curt Schilling	3.00
7	Jay Gibbons	2.00
8	Paul Konerko	3.00
9	Lyle Overbay	2.00
10	Jorge Posada	3.00
11	Todd Walker	2.00
12	Carlos Delgado	3.00
13	David Wright	6.00

14	Matt Morris	2.00
15	Mariano Rivera	3.00
16	Jeff Bagwell	3.00
17	Carl Pavano	2.00
18	Adrian Beltre	3.00
19	Scott Rolen	4.00
20	Aubrey Huff	2.00
21	Hideki Matsui	6.00
22	Andruw Jones	3.00
23	Sammy Sosa	4.00
24	Mark Buehrle	3.00
25	Orlando Hernandez	2.00
26	Travis Hafner	3.00
27	Vladimir Guerrero	4.00
28	Chipper Jones	4.00
29	Jose Reyes	3.00
30	Roger Clemens	8.00
31	Aaron Boone	2.00
32	Andy Pettitte	3.00
33	David DeJesus	2.00
34	Shawn Green	2.00
35	Luis Castillo	2.00
36	Frank Thomas	3.00
37	Javy Lopez	2.00
38	Victor Martinez	2.00
39	Tim Wakefield	2.00
40	Cliff Floyd	2.00
41	Bartolo Colon	2.00
42	Billy Wagner	2.00
43	Dmitri Young	2.00
44	Mark Prior	3.00
45	Nick Johnson	2.00
46	Brian Roberts	2.00
47	Nomar Garciaparra	4.00
48	Jorge Cantu	2.00
49	Jeff Francoeur	3.00
50	Barry Bonds	10.00
51	Francisco Rodriguez	2.00
52	Rocco Baldelli	2.00
53	Ryan Howard	5.00
54	Hank Blalock	2.00
55	Ivan Rodriguez	3.00
56	Jason Schmidt	2.00
57	Jeff Kent	2.00
58	Jose Castillo	2.00
59	Kerry Wood	3.00
60	Chase Utley	2.00
61	Shawn Chacon	2.00
62	Tom Glavine	2.00
63	Ichiro Suzuki	6.00
64	Carlos Lee	2.00
65	Jeff Weaver	2.00
66	Jeromy Burnitz	2.00
67	Jhonny Peralta	2.00
68	Johan Santana	3.00
69	Keith Foulke	2.00
70	Manny Ramirez	4.00
71	Jim Edmonds	3.00
72	Garret Anderson	2.00
73	Felipe Lopez	2.00
74	Craig Biggio	2.00
75	Ryan Langerhans	2.00
76	Mike Cameron	2.00
77	Matt Clement	2.00
78	Miguel Cabrera	3.00
79	Mark Teixeira	3.00
80	Johnny Estrada	2.00
81	Nook Logan	2.00
82	Livan Hernandez	2.00
83	Roy Halladay	3.00
84	Jose Vidro	2.00
85	Shannon Stewart	2.00
86	Brian Bruney	2.00
87	Jaret Wright	2.00
88	Gregg Zaun	2.00
89	Jason LaRue	2.00
90	Adam Kennedy	2.00
91	Armando Benitez	2.00
92	Chris Ray	2.00
93	Clint Barmes	2.00
94	Ervin Santana	2.00
95	Justin Verlander	2.00
96	Magglio Ordonez	2.00
97	Todd Helton	3.00
98	Zachary Duke	2.00
99	Huston Street	2.00
100	Alex Rodriguez	8.00
101	Mike Hampton	2.00
102	Tony Clark	2.00
104	Barry Zito	2.00
105	Anderson Hernandez	2.00
106	B.J. Upton	2.00
107	Albert Pujols	10.00
108	Tim Hudson	3.00
109	Derek Jeter	10.00
110	Greg Maddux	6.00

Clubhouse Collection Relics

	NM/M
Common Player:	4.00

CB	Clint Barmes	6.00
BB	Barry Bonds	25.00
MC	Miguel Cabrera	8.00
RC	Robinson Cano	15.00
EC	Eric Chavez	4.00
SC	Shin-Soo Choo	4.00
CC	Carl Crawford	4.00
JD	Johnny Damon	6.00
JD2	Johnny Damon	6.00
AD	Adam Dunn	6.00
JE	Jim Edmonds	6.00
ME	Morgan Ensberg	4.00
JF	Jeff Francis	4.00
EG	Eric Gagne	4.00
KG	Khalil Greene	4.00
VG	Vladimir Guerrero	8.00
MH	Matt Holliday	8.00
TI	Tadahito Iguchi	10.00
CJ	Conor Jackson	4.00
AJ	Andruw Jones	6.00
AK	Al Kaline	20.00
DL	Derrek Lee	8.00
MM	Mickey Mantle	200.00
PM	Pedro Martinez	8.00
BM	Bill Mazeroski	30.00
MMU	Mark Mulder	4.00
SM	Stan Musial	35.00
DO	David Ortiz	10.00
JP	Jake Peavy	4.00
MP	Mike Piazza	8.00
AP	Albert Pujols	20.00
MR	Manny Ramirez	8.00
MR2	Manny Ramirez	8.00
BR	Brian Roberts	4.00
BR2	Brian Roberts	4.00
BRO	Brooks Robinson	30.00
FR	Frank Robinson	20.00
AR	Alex Rodriguez	20.00
AR2	Alex Rodriguez	20.00
JS	Johan Santana	6.00
CS	Curt Schilling	8.00
GS	Gary Sheffield	6.00
AS	Alfonso Soriano	6.00
MTE	Mark Teixeira	6.00
MT	Miguel Tejada	6.00
RW	Rickie Weeks	6.00
DWI	Dontrelle Willis	6.00
DW	David Wright	10.00

Clubhouse Collection Relic Autograph

	NM/M
Production 25 Sets	
CCA-3	Brooks Robinson	125.00
CCA-4	Al Kaline	200.00
CCA-5	Stan Musial	250.00

Clubhouse Collection Dual Relics

	NM/M
Production 57 Sets	
BR	Brooks Robinson, Brian Roberts	75.00
MR	Mickey Mantle, Alex Rodriguez	250.00
MP	Stan Musial, Albert Pujols	150.00

Clubhouse Collection Cut Signature Relic

Production One Set
CCCS-5 Mickey Mantle

Flashbacks

	NM/M
Complete Set (10):	10.00
Common Player:	.50
Inserted 1:12	
EB	Ernie Banks	1.50
YB	Yogi Berra	1.50
WF	Whitey Ford	1.00
AK	Al Kaline	1.50
MM	Mickey Mantle	5.00
BM	Bill Mazeroski	.50
SM	Stan Musial	1.50
BRI	Bobby Richardson	.50

BR	Brooks Robinson	1.00
FR	Frank Robinson	1.00

Flashbacks Autographs

No Pricing
Production 25 Sets

Flashbacks Relics

	NM/M
EB	Ernie Banks	15.00
YB	Yogi Berra	20.00
WF	Whitey Ford	20.00
AK	Al Kaline	15.00
MM	Mickey Mantle	40.00
BM	Bill Mazeroski	10.00
SM	Stan Musial	50.00
BRI	Bobby Richardson	15.00
BR	Brooks Robinson	10.00
FR	Frank Robinson	10.00

Flashbacks Relic Autographs

No Pricing
Production 25 Sets

New Age Performers

	NM/M
Complete Set (15):	20.00
Common Player:	1.00
Inserted 1:15	
BB	Barry Bonds	4.00
MC	Miguel Cabrera	1.50
RC	Roger Clemens	4.00
VG	Vladimir Guerrero	1.50
CL	Carlos Lee	1.00
DL	Derrek Lee	1.50
PM	Pedro Martinez	1.50
DO	David Ortiz	1.50
GM	Mark Prior	1.00
AP	Albert Pujols	4.00
MR	Manny Ramirez	1.50
AR	Alex Rodriguez	2.00
GS	Gary Sheffield	1.00
I	Ichiro Suzuki	2.50
MT	Mark Teixeira	1.50

Real One Autographs

	NM/M
Production 200 Sets	
Red Ink:	1.5-2X
Production 57 Sets	
EB	Ernie Banks	120.00
YB	Yogi Berra	120.00
TB	Tommy Byrne	60.00
BC	Bob Chakales	50.00
JAC	Jack Collum	40.00
JCR	Jack Crimian	50.00
JD	Jack Dittmer	60.00
WF	Whitey Ford	100.00
DK	Don Kaiser	40.00
NK	Nellie King	50.00
LK	Lou Kretlow	50.00
PL	Paul LaPalme	50.00
JM	Joe Margoneri	60.00
WM	Windy McCall	40.00
JRM	John (Red) Murff	50.00
SM	Stan Musial	150.00
RN	Ron Negray	40.00
EOB	Eddie O'Brien	50.00
KO	Karl Olson	50.00
EO	Ernie Oravetz	50.00
MP	Mel Parnell	60.00
JP	Jim Pyburn	50.00
DR	Dusty Rhodes	50.00
FR	Frank Robinson	100.00
JSM	Jim Small	50.00
DS	Duke Snider	140.00
JSN	Jerry Snyder	60.00
CT	Charles Thompson	50.00
BW	Bob Wiesler	60.00

Real One Cut Signatures

Production One Set

Then and Now

	NM/M
Complete Set (10):	20.00
Common Duo:	1.00
Inserted 1:15	
TN1	Mickey Mantle, Alex Rodriguez	6.00
TN2	Ted Williams, Michael Young	3.00
TN3	Mickey Mantle, Jason Giambi	6.00
TN4	Luis Aparicio, Chone Figgins	1.00
TN5	Ted Williams, Alex Rodriguez	4.00
TN6	Stan Musial, Derrek Lee	2.00
TN7	Stan Musial, Derrek Lee	2.00
TN8	Red Schoendienst, Derrek Lee	1.50
TN9	Johnny Podres, Roger Clemens	4.00
TN10	Clem Labine, Chad Cordero	1.00

2006 Topps Opening Day

	NM/M
Complete Set (165):	25.00
Common Player:	.10
Pack (6):	1.00
Box (36):	30.00
1	Alex Rodriguez	1.50
2	Jhonny Peralta	.20
3	Garrett Atkins	.10
4	Vernon Wells	.25
5	Carl Crawford	.25
6	Josh Beckett	.25
7	Mickey Mantle	3.00
8	Willy Taveras	.10
9	Ivan Rodriguez	.40
10	Clint Barmes	.10
11	Jose Reyes	.25
12	Travis Hafner	.40
13	Tadahito Iguchi	.25
14	Barry Zito	.25
15	Brian Roberts	.25
16	David Wright	1.00
17	Mark Teixeira	.50
18	Roy Halladay	.25
19	Scott Rolen	.40
20	Bobby Abreu	.25
21	Lance Berkman	.25
22	Moises Alou	.20
23	Chone Figgins	.10
24	Aaron Rowand	.10
25	Chipper Jones	.50
26	Johnny Damon	.50
27	Matt Clement	.10
28	Nick Johnson	.10
29	Freddy Garcia	.10
30	Jon Garland	.10
31	Torii Hunter	.20
32	Mike Sweeney	.10
33	Mike Lieberthal	.10
34	Rafael Furcal	.20
35	Brad Wilkerson	.10
36	Brad Penny	.10
37	Jorge Cantu	.10
38	Paul Konerko	.25
39	Rickie Weeks	.25
40	Jorge Posada	.25
41	Albert Pujols	1.50
42	Zack Greinke	.10
43	Jimmy Rollins	.25
44	Mark Prior	.40

45	Greg Maddux	1.00
46	Jeff Francis	.10
47	Felipe Lopez	.10
48	Dan Johnson	.10
49	B.J. Ryan	.10
50	Manny Ramirez	.50
51	Melvin Mora	.20
52	Javy Lopez	.10
53	Garret Anderson	.20
54	Jason Bay	.25
55	Joe Mauer	.20
56	C.C. Sabathia	.10
57	Bartolo Colon	.10
58	Ichiro Suzuki	1.00
59	Andruw Jones	.50
60	Rocco Baldelli	.10
61	Jeff Kent	.20
62	Cliff Floyd	.10
63	John Smoltz	.25
64	Shawn Green	.20
65	Nomar Garciaparra	.50
66	Miguel Cabrera	.50
67	Vladimir Guerrero	.50
68	Gary Sheffield	.25
69	Jake Peavy	.25
70	Carlos Lee	.20
71	Tom Glavine	.25
72	Craig Biggio	.25
73	Steve Finley	.10
74	Adrian Beltre	.10
75	Eric Gagne	.10
76	Aubrey Huff	.10
77	Livan Hernandez	.10
78	Scott Podsednik	.10
79	Todd Helton	.40
80	Kerry Wood	.25
81	Randy Johnson	.50
82	Huston Street	.20
83	Pedro Martinez	.50
84	Roger Clemens	1.50
85	Hank Blalock	.20
86	Carlos Beltran	.40
87	Chien-Ming Wang	.25
88	Rich Harden	.25
89	Mike Mussina	.25
90	Mark Buehrle	.25
91	Michael Young	.20
92	Mark Mulder	.20
93	Khalil Greene	.10
94	Johan Santana	.50
95	Andy Pettitte	.25
96	Derek Jeter	1.50
97	Jack Wilson	.10
98	Ben Sheets	.25
99	Miguel Tejada	.40
100	Barry Bonds	1.50
101	Dontrelle Willis	.20
102	Curt Schilling	.50
103	Jose Contreras	.10
104	Jeremy Bonderman	.10
105	David Ortiz	.50
106	Lyle Overbay	.10
107	Robinson Cano	.25
108	Tim Hudson	.25
109	Paul LoDuca	.10
110	Mariano Rivera	.25
111	Derrek Lee	.50
112	Morgan Ensberg	.20
113	Wily Mo Pena	.20
114	Roy Oswalt	.20
115	Adam Dunn	.40
116	Hideki Matsui	1.00
117	Pat Burrell	.25
118	Jason Schmidt	.25
119	Alfonso Soriano	.40
120	Aramis Ramirez	.25
121	Jason Giambi	.25
122	Orlando Hernandez	.10
123	Magglio Ordonez	.10
124	Troy Glaus	.20
125	Carlos Delgado	.25
126	Kevin Millwood	.20
127	Shannon Stewart	.10
128	Luis Castillo	.10
129	Jim Edmonds	.25
130	Richie Sexson	.10
131	Dmitri Young	.10
132	Russ Adams	.10
133	Nick Swisher	.10
134	Jermaine Dye	.10
135	Anderson Hernandez (RC)	.10
136	Justin Huber (RC)	.10
137	Jason Botts (RC)	.10
138	Jeff Mathis (RC)	.10
139	Ryan Garko (RC)	.10
140	Charlton Hernandez (RC)	.10
141	Chris Denorfia (RC)	.10
142	Anthony Reyes (RC)	.10
143	Bryan Bullington (RC)	.10
144	Chuck James (RC)	.10
145	Danny Sandoval RC	.25
146	Walter Young (RC)	.10
147	Fausto Carmona (RC)	.10
148	Francisco Liriano (RC)	.25
149	Hong-Chih Kuo (RC)	.10
150	Joe Saunders (RC)	.10
151	John Koronka (RC)	.10
152	Robert Andino RC	.25
153	Shaun Marcum (RC)	.10
154	Tom Gorzelanny (RC)	.10
155	Craig Breslow RC	.25
156	Chris Demaria RC	.50
157	Brayan Pena (RC)	.10
158	Rich Hill (RC)	.25
159	Rick Short RC	.25
160	Darrell Rasner (RC)	.10
161	C.J. Wilson (RC)	.10
162	Brandon Watson (RC)	.10
163	Paul McAnulty (RC)	.10
164	Marshall McDougall (RC)	.10
165	Checklist	.10

Red Foil

Red:	2-3X

Production 2,006 Sets

Printing Plates

No Pricing
Production one set per color.

Autographs

		NM/M
BE	Brad Eldred	15.00
JE	Johnny Estrada	20.00
TH	Toby Hall	10.00
MK	Mark Kotsay	10.00
EM	Eli Marrero	10.00
VZ	Victor Zambrano	10.00

Opening Day Relics

		NM/M
Common Team:		25.00
WI	Chicago White Sox	40.00
MN	New York Mets	40.00
RR	Texas Rangers	30.00
BP	Milwaukee Brewers	25.00
RC	Cincinnati Reds	30.00
PC	Philadelphia Phillies	40.00
OD	Baltimore Orioles	25.00
RD	Colorado Rockies	25.00
DB	Los Angeles Dodgers	40.00
RT	Kansas City Royals	25.00
MA	Seattle Mariners	30.00
AM	Houston Astros	30.00
PG	San Diego Padres	40.00
AY	Oakland Athletics	40.00
JT	Toronto Blue Jays	30.00

SI For Kids

		NM/M
1	Vladimir Guerrero	.50
2	Marcus Giles	.15
3	Michael Young	.15
4	Derek Jeter	1.50
5	Barry Bonds	1.50
6	Ivan Rodriguez	.40
7	Miguel Cabrera	.50
8	Jim Edmonds	.25
9	Jack Wilson	.15
10	Khalil Greene	.15
11	Miguel Tejada	.40
12	Eric Chavez	.25
13	Shannon Stewart	.15
14	Julio Lugo	.15
15	Andruw Jones	.50
16	Nick Johnson, Randy Johnson	.50
17	Tadahito Iguchi, Ivan Rodriguez	.25
18	Roy Oswalt, Jose Reyes	.25
19	Manny Ramirez, Ronnie Belliard	.50
20	Todd Helton, Khalil Greene	.25
21	David Ortiz, Dontrelle Willis	.50
22	Ichiro Suzuki, Johnny Damon	.75
23	Craig Biggio, Jack Wilson	.15
24	Brian Roberts, Richie Sexson	.25
25	Chipper Jones, Marcus Giles	.50

2006 Topps Sterling

		NM/M
Common Player:		10.00
Production 250 Sets		
Box (5 Cards):		300.00
1	All Barry Bond's	10.00
20	All Mickey Mantle's	25.00
40	All Josh Gibson's	30.00
44	All Rickey Henderson's	10.00
54	All Ted William's	15.00
63	All Roberto Clemente's	15.00
68	All Nolan Ryan's	25.00
78	All Cal Ripken Jr.'s	20.00
97	All Stan Musial's	20.00
102	All Reggie Jackson's	15.00
107	All Johnny Bench's	15.00
112	All George Brett's	15.00
122	All Don Mattingly's	15.00
132	All Roger Maris's	20.00
137	All Rod Carew's	10.00
147	All Yogi Berra's	15.00
152	All Mike Schmidt's	15.00
157	All Carl Yastrzemski's	15.00
176	All Tony Gwynn's	15.00
186	All Ryne Sandberg's	15.00
191	All Ozzie Smith's	15.00

Framed Burgundy

Burgundy (1-200):	3-5X

Production 10 Sets

Framed Silver

No Pricing
Production One Set

Framed White

White (1-200):	1-1.5X

Production 50 Sets

Baseball Cut Signatures

		NM/M
SA	Sparky Anderson	40.00
LA	Luis Aparicio	40.00
LB	Lou Brock	50.00
RC	Rod Carew	50.00
SC	Steve Carlton	50.00
GC	Gary Carter	50.00
OC	Orlando Cepeda	35.00
DE	Dennis Eckersley	40.00
BF	Bob Feller	40.00
RF	Rollie Fingers	45.00
CF	Carlton Fisk	60.00
BG	Bob Gibson	50.00
MI	Monte Irvin	45.00
AK	Al Kaline	60.00
GK	George Kell	40.00
HK	Harmon Killebrew	70.00
RK	Ralph Kiner	50.00
JM	Juan Marichal	40.00
JMO	Joe Morgan	50.00
PN	Phil Niekro	40.00
JP	Jim Palmer	40.00
TP	Tony Perez	40.00
GP	Gaylord Perry	40.00
RR	Robin Roberts	40.00
BR	Brooks Robinson	60.00
FR	Frank Robinson	60.00
RS	Ryne Sandberg	80.00
MS	Mike Schmidt	75.00
RSH	Red Schoendienst	60.00
DS	Duke Snider	75.00
EW	Earl Weaver	30.00
RY	Robin Yount	70.00

Career Stats Relics

No Pricing
Production 10 Sets
Prime: No Pricing
Production One Set
Sterling Silver: No Pricing
Production One Set

Career Stats Relics Autographs

Production 10 Sets
Prime: No Pricing
Production One Set
Sterling Silver: No Pricing
Production One Set

Cut from the Same Cloth Signatures

Production 1-5

Cut Signatures

46	Elmer Valo	80.00
53	Carl Furillo	100.00
61	Hal Newhouser	60.00
64	Dick Sisler	65.00
65	Frank Shea	75.00
66	Monty Stratton	80.00
67	Lloyd Waner	150.00
68	Sal Maglie	70.00
69	Waite Hoyt	80.00
70	Warren Spahn	100.00
72	A.B. Chandler	60.00
73	Al Barlick	75.00
74	Bill Dickey	100.00
75	Bill Terry	80.00
76	Billy Herman	75.00
77	Bob Lemon	60.00
78	Buck Leonard	80.00
79	Charles Gehringer	100.00
81	Earl Averill	60.00
82	Hoyt Wilhelm	80.00
83	Jim "Catfish" Hunter	100.00
84	Joe Sewell	80.00
85	Judy Johnson	80.00
86	Carl Hubbell	85.00
87	Lou Boudreau	65.00
88	Luke Appling	80.00
89	Ray Dandridge	75.00
90	Rick Ferrell	60.00
91	Stan Coveleski	75.00
92	Willie Stargell	120.00

Five Relics

NM/M
Production 10 Sets
Prime: No Pricing
Production 10 Sets
Sterling Silver: No Pricing
Production One Set

Five Relics Autographs

Production 10 Sets
Prime: No Pricing
Production 10 Sets
Sterling Silver: No Pricing
Production One Set

Josh Gibson Bat Barrel

Production One

Jumbo Jersey

Production 10 Sets
Prime: No Pricing
Production One Set
Patch: No Pricing
Production 10 Sets
Sterling Silver: No Pricing
Production One Set

Moments Relics

		NM/M
Production 10 Sets		
Prime:		No Pricing
Production One Set		
BB	All Barry Bond's	75.00
MM	All Mickey Mantle's	350.00
JG	All Josh Gibson's	500.00
RH	All Rickey Henderson's	60.00
TW	All Ted William's	150.00
RC	All Roberto Clemente's	200.00
NR	All Nolan Ryan's	100.00
CR	All Cal Ripken Jr.'s	100.00
SM	All Stan Musial's	75.00
RJ	All Reggie Jackson's	60.00
JB	All Johnny Bench's	65.00
GB	All George Brett's	60.00
RM	All Roger Maris's	125.00
YB	All Yogi Berra's	75.00
MS	All Mike Schmidt's	50.00
CY	All Carl Yastrzemski's	60.00
TG	All Tony Gwynn's	60.00
RS	All Ryne Sandberg's	70.00

Moments Relics Autographs

NM/M
Production 10 Sets
Prime: No Pricing

BB	Barry Bonds	
RH	All Rickey Henderson's	125.00
NR	All Nolan Ryan's	300.00
CR	All Cal Ripken Jr.'s	300.00
SM	All Stan Musial's	150.00
RJ	All Reggie Jackson's	150.00
JB	All Johnny Bench's	150.00
GB	All George Brett's	150.00
DM	All Don Mattingly's	140.00
RC	All Rod Carew's	80.00
YB	All Yogi Berra's	160.00
MS	All Mike Schmidt's	140.00
CY	All Carl Yastrzemski's	125.00
TG	All Tony Gwynn's	120.00
RS	All Ryne Sandberg's	150.00
OS	All Ozzie Smith's	100.00

Moments Relics Cut Signatures

Production 10 Sets	
Prime:	No Pricing
Production One Set	

Quad Relics

Production 10 Sets	
Prime:	No Pricing
Production 10 Sets	
Sterling Silver:	No Pricing
Production One Set	

Quad Relics Autographs

Production 10 Sets	
Prime:	No Pricing
Production 10 Sets	
Sterling Silver:	No Pricing
Production One Set	

Season Stats Relics

	NM/M
Production 10 Sets	
Prime:	No Pricing
Production One Set	
Sterling Silver:	No Pricing
Production One Set	

Season Stats Relics Autographs

Production 10 Sets	
Prime:	No Pricing
Production One Set	
Sterling Silver:	No Pricing
Production One Set	

Six Relics

Production 10 Sets	
Prime:	No Pricing
Production 10 Sets	
Sterling Silver:	No Pricing
Production One Set	

Six Relics Autographs

Production 10 Sets	
Prime:	No Pricing
Production 10 Sets	
Sterling Silver:	No Pricing
Production One Set	

Triple Relics Autographs

Production 10 Sets	
Prime:	No Pricing
Production 10 Sets	
Sterling Silver:	No Pricing
Production One Set	

2006 Topps Triple Threads

	NM/M
Complete Set (120):	
Common (1-100):	.50
Common (101-120):	
Production 225	
Pack (6):	140.00
Box (2):	270.00
1 Hideki Matsui	3.00
2 Josh Gibson	2.00
3 Roger Clemens	4.00
4 Paul Konerko	1.00
5 Brooks Robinson	1.00
6 Stan Musial	2.00
7 Dontrelle Willis	.75
8 Yogi Berra	1.50
9 John Smoltz	.75
10 Brian Roberts	.75
11 Gary Sheffield	.75
12 Wade Boggs	1.00

13	Alex Rodriguez	4.00
14	Ernie Banks	2.00
15	Ichiro Suzuki	3.00
16	Whitey Ford	1.00
17	Vladimir Guerrero	1.50
18	Tadahito Iguchi	.50
19	Robin Yount	1.50
20	Jason Schmidt	.50
21	Roberto Clemente	3.00
22	Andruw Jones	1.00
23	Don Mattingly	2.00
24	Joe Mauer	.50
25	Barry Bonds	4.00
26	Johnny Damon	1.50
27	Chris Carpenter	.75
28	Garret Anderson	.50
29	Scott Rolen	1.50
30	Tim Hudson	.75
31	Dave Winfield	.75
32	Steve Carlton	.75
33	Miguel Tejada	.75
34	Nolan Ryan	3.00
35	Mark Buehrle	.75
36	Travis Hafner	1.00
37	Rickie Weeks	.75
38	Sammy Sosa	1.50
39	Carlos Beltran	1.00
40	Todd Helton	1.00
41	Tom Seaver	1.00
42	Ted Williams	3.00
43	Alfonso Soriano	1.00
44	Reggie Jackson	1.00
45	Pedro Martinez	1.50
46	Randy Johnson	1.50
47	Ted Williams	3.00
48	Torii Hunter	.50
49	Manny Ramirez	1.50
50	George Brett	3.00
51	Chipper Jones	1.50
52	Nomar Garciaparra	1.50
53	Richie Sexson	.75
54	David Ortiz	1.50
55	Derek Jeter	4.00
56	Mickey Mantle	8.00
57	Michael Young	.75
58	Aramis Ramirez	.75
59	Bartolo Colon	.50
60	Troy Glaus	.75
61	Carlos Delgado	.75
62	Mike Sweeney	.50
63	Jorge Cantu	.50
64	Mike Mussina	.75
65	Hank Blalock	.75
66	Frank Robinson	1.50
67	Carl Yastrzemski	2.00
68	Adam Dunn	1.00
69	Eric Chavez	.75
70	Curt Schilling	1.50
71	Jeff Francoeur	.50
72	C.C. Sabathia	.50
73	Roy Oswalt	.75
74	Carlos Lee	.50
75	Barry Zito	.75
76	Derek Lee	1.00
77	Greg Maddux	3.00
78	Ivan Rodriguez	.75
79	Jeff Kent	.75
80	Gary Carter	.75
81	Jose Reyes	.75
82	Johan Santana	1.50
83	Magglio Ordonez	.50
84	Mark Prior	1.00
85	Johnny Bench	2.00
86	Vernon Wells	.75
87	Mark Mulder	.75
88	Cal Ripken Jr.	6.00
89	Mark Teixeira	1.00
90	Miguel Cabrera	1.50
91	Duke Snider	1.00
92	Jason Giambi	1.00
93	Albert Pujols	4.00
94	Carl Crawford	.75
95	Jim Edmonds	.75
96	Jose Contreras	.50
97	Victor Martinez	.75
98	Jeremy Bonderman	.50
99	Lance Berkman	.75
100	Rocco Baldelli	.50
101	Zachary Duke	20.00
102	Felix Hernandez	40.00
103	Dan Johnson	15.00
104	Brandon McCarthy	20.00
105	Huston Street	25.00
106	Robinson Cano	50.00
107	Jason Bay	25.00
108	Ryan Howard	100.00
109	Ervin Santana	15.00
110	Rich Harden	15.00
111	Aaron Hill	15.00
112	David Wright	75.00
113	Rich Hill (RC)	40.00
114	Nelson Cruz (RC)	20.00
115	Francisco Liriano (RC)	50.00

116	Hong-Chih Kuo (RC)	75.00
117	Ryan Garko (RC)	25.00
118	Craig Hansen RC	30.00
119	Shin-Soo Choo (RC)	20.00
120	Darrell Rasner (RC)	20.00

Sepia Tone

Sepia (1-100):	3-4X
Production 150	
Sepia (101-120):	1X
Production 125	

Emerald

Emerald (1-100):	4-6X
Production 99	
Emerald (101-120):	1X
Production 75	

Gold

Gold (1-100):	5-10X
Gold (101-120):	1-1.5X
Production 50 Sets	

Sapphire

Sapphire (1-100):	8-15X
Sapphire (101-120):	1-2X
Production 25 Sets	

Platinum

Platinum:	No Pricing
Production One Set	

Printing Plates

No Pricing
Production one set per color.

Heroes

	NM/M
Inserted 1:Pack	
Die-cut:	2-3X
Production 50 Sets	
Autograph:	No Pricing
Production 3 Sets	
MM1 All Mickey Mantle's	8.00
TW1 All Ted William's	5.00
FR1 All Frank Robinson's	4.00
CY1 All Carl Yastrzemski's	4.00

Heroes Co-Signer Autographs

No Pricing
Production 3 Sets

Heroes Quad Signers

Production One Card

Heroes Cut Signatures

Production One Set

Triple Signed Hides

Production One Set

Triple Relic

	NM/M
Production 18 Sets	
Gold:	No Pricing
Production 9 Sets	
Platinum:	No Pricing
Production 3 Sets	
1 Adam Dunn	30.00
2 Adam Dunn	30.00
3 Adrian Beltre	20.00
4 Adrian Beltre	20.00
5 Al Kaline	35.00
6 Al Kaline	35.00
7 Al Kaline	35.00
8 Joe Torre	25.00
9 Albert Pujols	90.00
10 Alex Rodriguez	100.00
11 Ichiro Suzuki	125.00
12 Alex Rodriguez	100.00
13 Alex Rodriguez	100.00
14 Alex Rodriguez	100.00
15 Alex Rodriguez	100.00
16 Alex Rodriguez	100.00
17 Alex Rodriguez	100.00
18 Alfonso Soriano	25.00
19 Dwight Gooden	25.00
20 Barry Bonds	100.00
21 Alfonso Soriano	25.00
22 Ozzie Smith	50.00
23 Andruw Jones	50.00
24 Andruw Jones	50.00
25 Andy Pettitte	30.00
26 Andy Pettitte	30.00
27 Aramis Ramirez	25.00
28 B.J. Upton	25.00
29 Barry Bonds	100.00
30 Vladimir Guerrero	35.00
31 Barry Bonds	100.00
32 Barry Bonds	100.00
33 Barry Bonds	100.00
34 Barry Bonds	100.00

35	Barry Bonds	100.00
36	Barry Bonds	100.00
37	Eric Chavez	25.00
38	Barry Zito	25.00
39	Ben Sheets	25.00
40	Bill Mazeroski	40.00
41	Bob Feller	30.00
42	Bobby Abreu	25.00
43	Bobby Cox	25.00
44	Bobby Doerr	20.00
45	Brad Lidge	20.00
46	Brian Giles	20.00
47	Brian Roberts	25.00
48	Michael Young	20.00
49	Cal Ripken Jr.	100.00
50	Cal Ripken Jr.	100.00
51	Carl Yastrzemski	50.00
52	Carl Yastrzemski	50.00
53	Carl Yastrzemski	50.00
54	Carlos Beltran	30.00
55	Carlos Beltran	30.00
56	Carlos Delgado	30.00
57	Carlton Fisk	40.00
58	Carlton Fisk	40.00
59	Carlton Fisk	40.00
60	Chipper Jones	50.00
61	Chipper Jones	50.00
62	Chipper Jones	50.00
63	Chris Carpenter	25.00
64	Craig Biggio	30.00
65	Craig Biggio	30.00
66	Curt Schilling	35.00
67	Curt Schilling	35.00
68	Curt Schilling	35.00
69	Curt Schilling	35.00
70	Sammy Sosa	50.00
71	Darryl Strawberry	25.00
72	Darryl Strawberry	25.00
73	Alex Rodriguez	100.00
74	Dave Winfield	30.00
75	Dave Winfield	30.00
76	Jorge Posada	30.00
77	David Ortiz	35.00
78	David Ortiz	35.00
79	Derrek Lee	35.00
80	Don Mattingly	40.00
81	Don Mattingly	40.00
82	Don Mattingly	40.00
83	Dontrelle Willis	25.00
84	Dontrelle Willis	25.00
85	Duke Snider	35.00
86	Dwight Gooden	25.00
87	Cal Ripken Jr.	100.00
88	David Ortiz	35.00
89	Ernie Banks	40.00
90	Ernie Banks	40.00
91	Ernie Banks	40.00
92	Frank Robinson	35.00
93	Frank Robinson	35.00
94	Frankie Frisch	30.00
95	Gary Carter	25.00
96	Mickey Mantle	200.00
97	Gary Sheffield	35.00
98	George Brett	50.00
99	George Brett	50.00
100	Greg Maddux	50.00
101	Hank Blalock	25.00
102	Hank Greenberg	65.00
103	Hank Greenberg	65.00
104	Hideki Matsui	80.00
105	Hideki Matsui	80.00
106	Hideki Matsui	80.00
107	Ichiro Suzuki	125.00
108	Johnny Bench	40.00
109	Ichiro Suzuki	125.00
110	Ivan Rodriguez	30.00
111	Ivan Rodriguez	30.00
112	Ivan Rodriguez	30.00
113	Ivan Rodriguez	30.00
114	Jake Peavy	20.00
115	Javy Lopez	20.00
116	Jeff Bagwell	35.00
117	Jim Edmonds	25.00
118	Jim Thome	30.00
119	Joe Mauer	20.00
120	Alex Rodriguez	100.00
121	Johan Santana	30.00
122	Johan Santana	30.00
123	Sean Burroughs	15.00
124	Johnny Bench	40.00
125	Johnny Damon	25.00
126	Jon Garland	20.00
127	Jon Garland	20.00
128	Jorge Posada	30.00
129	Manny Ramirez	25.00
130	Jose Canseco	25.00
131	Jose Reyes	25.00
132	Juan Marichal	25.00
133	Kerry Wood	25.00
134	Kerry Wood	25.00
135	Albert Pujols	90.00
136	Lance Berkman	30.00
137	Lloyd Waner	75.00
138	Lloyd Waner	75.00

139	Lou Brock	25.00
140	Miguel Tejada	25.00
141	Manny Ramirez	30.00
142	Mariano Rivera	35.00
143	Mariano Rivera	35.00
144	Mark Buehrle	30.00
145	Mark Mulder	25.00
146	Mark Mulder	25.00
147	Mark Prior	30.00
148	Mark Teixeira	30.00
149	Michael Young	20.00
150	Dale Murphy	35.00
151	Barry Zito	25.00
152	Mickey Mantle	200.00
153	Mickey Mantle	200.00
154	Mickey Mantle	200.00
155	Mickey Mantle	200.00
156	Miguel Cabrera	30.00
157	Miguel Tejada	25.00
158	Vladimir Guerrero	35.00
159	Miguel Tejada	25.00
160	Miguel Tejada	25.00
161	Mike Mussina	25.00
162	Mike Mussina	25.00
163	Mike Piazza	60.00
164	Gary Sheffield	35.00
165	Mike Piazza	60.00
166	Mike Schmidt	40.00
167	Mike Schmidt	40.00
168	Mike Schmidt	40.00
169	Monte Irvin	30.00
170	Morgan Ensberg	25.00
171	Lance Berkman	30.00
172	Nolan Ryan	65.00
173	Nolan Ryan	65.00
174	Nolan Ryan	65.00
175	Albert Pujols	90.00
176	Dave Winfield	30.00
177	Ozzie Smith	40.00
178	Pat Burrell	30.00
179	Paul Konerko	20.00
180	Paul Konerko	20.00
181	Paul Konerko	20.00
182	Paul Molitor	30.00
183	Pedro Martinez	35.00
184	Pedro Martinez	35.00
185	Pedro Martinez	35.00
186	Randy Johnson	35.00
187	Randy Johnson	35.00
188	Reggie Jackson	40.00
189	Reggie Jackson	40.00
190	Rickey Henderson	40.00
191	Rickey Henderson	40.00
192	Rickey Henderson	40.00
193	Rickey Henderson	40.00
194	Rickie Weeks	25.00
195	Rickie Weeks	25.00
196	Roberto Clemente	125.00
197	Roberto Clemente	125.00
198	Robin Yount	40.00
199	Rod Carew	30.00
200	Roger Clemens	60.00
201	Roger Clemens	60.00
202	Roger Clemens	60.00
203	Roger Clemens	60.00
204	Roger Clemens	60.00
205	Roger Clemens	60.00
206	Roy Halladay	25.00
207	Roy Oswalt	25.00
208	Roy Oswalt	25.00
209	Ryne Sandberg	60.00
210	Ryne Sandberg	60.00
211	Nolan Ryan	65.00
212	Sammy Sosa	60.00
213	Sammy Sosa	60.00
214	Sammy Sosa	60.00
215	Sammy Sosa	60.00
216	Scott Rolen	40.00
217	Scott Rolen	40.00
218	Orlando Cepeda	25.00
219	Stan Musial	50.00
220	Steve Carlton	25.00
221	Steve Carlton	25.00
222	Steve Carlton	25.00
223	Steve Garvey	20.00
224	Tadahito Iguchi	30.00
225	Ted Williams	80.00
226	Ted Williams	80.00
227	Tim Hudson	20.00
228	Tim Hudson	20.00
229	Todd Helton	25.00
230	Todd Helton	25.00
231	Todd Helton	25.00
232	Tom Seaver	40.00
233	Tony Gwynn	40.00
234	Tony Gwynn	40.00
235	Tony Gwynn	40.00
236	Torii Hunter	20.00
237	Torii Hunter	20.00
238	Travis Hafner	35.00
239	Mike Piazza	60.00
240	Albert Pujols	90.00
241	Wade Boggs	30.00
242	Willie Stargell	40.00
243	Willie Stargell	40.00
244	Willie Stargell	40.00
245	Willy Taveras	25.00

Triple Relic Combo

NM/M

Production 18 Sets
Gold: No Pricing
Production 9 Sets
Platinum: No Pricing
Production 3 Sets

1	Albert Pujols, Alex Rodriguez, Barry Bonds	100.00
2	Alex Rodriguez, Barry Bonds, Albert Pujols	100.00
3	Albert Pujols, Alex Rodriguez, Manny Ramirez	100.00
4	Albert Pujols, Barry Bonds, Ted Williams	125.00
5	Alex Rodriguez, Barry Bonds, Chipper Jones	75.00
6	Alex Rodriguez, Roberto Clemente, Barry Bonds	125.00
7	Alex Rodriguez, Vladimir Guerrero, Ichiro Suzuki	80.00
8	Alex Rodriguez, Stan Musial, Ted Williams	120.00
9	Andruw Jones, Alfonso Soriano, Vladimir Guerrero	40.00
10	Barry Bonds, Ichiro Suzuki, Roberto Clemente	150.00
11	Barry Bonds, Lloyd Waner, Roberto Clemente	160.00
12	Barry Bonds, Manny Ramirez, Andruw Jones	60.00
13	Barry Bonds, Manny Ramirez, Ted Williams	100.00
14	Barry Bonds, Roberto Clemente, Willie Stargell	125.00
15	Carl Yastrzemski, Paul Molitor, Manny Ramirez	40.00
16	Don Mattingly, Paul Molitor, Manny Ramirez	40.00
17	Don Mattingly, Rod Carew, Tony Gwynn	70.00
18	Gary Sheffield, Vladimir Guerrero, Ivan Rodriguez	30.00
19	Hank Greenberg, Stan Musial, Ted Williams	125.00
20	Ichiro Suzuki, Chipper Jones, Barry Bonds	80.00
21	Ichiro Suzuki, Ted Williams, Roberto Clemente	150.00
22	Joe Morgan, Paul Molitor, Gary Carter	35.00
23	Manny Ramirez, Vladimir Guerrero, Roberto Clemente	90.00
24	Mike Piazza, Paul Molitor, Rickey Henderson	40.00
25	Napoleon Lajoie, Stan Musial, Ted Williams	
26	Paul Molitor, Andruw Jones, Robin Yount	40.00
27	Paul Molitor, Andruw Jones, Alfonso Soriano	35.00
28	Reggie Jackson, Vladimir Guerrero, Andruw Jones	35.00
29	Rickey Henderson, Wade Boggs, Tony Gwynn	60.00
30	Roberto Clemente, Ted Williams, Tony Gwynn	
31	Stan Musial, Ted Williams, Tony Gwynn	70.00
32	Ted Williams, Ichiro Suzuki, Wade Boggs	140.00
33	Albert Pujols, Ted Williams, Mickey Mantle	250.00
34	Andruw Jones, George Brett, Chipper Jones	60.00
35	Greg Maddux, Nolan Ryan, Steve Carlton	60.00
36	Greg Maddux, Steve Carlton, Tom Seaver	50.00
37	Nolan Ryan, Steve Carlton, Tom Seaver	50.00
38	Nolan Ryan, Tom Seaver, Roger Clemens	60.00
39	Roger Clemens, Nolan Ryan, Tom Seaver	60.00
40	Barry Bonds, Rickey Henderson, Tony Gwynn	60.00
41	Cal Ripken Jr., Carl Yastrzemski, Paul Molitor	60.00
42	Cal Ripken Jr., George Brett, Roberto Clemente	100.00
43	Cal Ripken Jr., George Brett, Tony Gwynn	85.00
44	Cal Ripken Jr., Paul Molitor, Rickey Henderson	85.00
45	Cal Ripken Jr., Paul Molitor, Tony Gwynn	80.00
46	George Brett, Cal Ripken Jr., Rod Carew	80.00
47	George Brett, Cal Ripken Jr., Rod Carew	80.00
48	George Brett, Robin Yount, Rod Carew	50.00
49	George Brett, Tony Gwynn, Wade Boggs	60.00
50	George Brett, Tony Gwynn, Wade Boggs	60.00
51	Paul Molitor, Robin Yount, Wade Boggs	40.00
52	Paul Waner, Rickey Henderson, Stan Musial	60.00
53	Paul Waner, Rickey Henderson, Wade Boggs	50.00
54	Paul Waner, Rod Carew, Wade Boggs	50.00
55	Rickey Henderson, Stan Musial, Wade Boggs	50.00
56	Roberto Clemente, Robin Yount, Rod Carew	80.00
57	Roberto Clemente, Robin Yount, Rod Carew	90.00
58	Roberto Clemente, Robin Yount, Tony Gwynn	90.00
59	Rod Carew, Stan Musial, Tony Gwynn	50.00
60	Stan Musial, Tony Gwynn, Wade Boggs	50.00
61	Wade Boggs	30.00
62	Barry Bonds, Mickey Mantle, Frank Robinson	140.00
63	Barry Bonds, Ted Williams, Mickey Mantle	160.00
64	Barry Bonds, Frank Robinson, Reggie Jackson	70.00
65	Barry Bonds, Frank Robinson, Harmon Killebrew	60.00
66	Frank Robinson, Barry Bonds, Mike Schmidt	60.00
67	Frank Robinson, Harmon Killebrew, Mickey Mantle	150.00
68	Josh Gibson, Barry Bonds, Mickey Mantle	200.00
69	Josh Gibson, Barry Bonds, Ted Williams	150.00
70	Mike Schmidt, Harmon Killebrew, Reggie Jackson	75.00
71	Dave Winfield, Vladimir Guerrero, Reggie Jackson	50.00
72	Rod Carew, Reggie Jackson, Vladimir Guerrero	30.00
73	Andruw Jones, Chipper Jones, Jeff Francoeur	30.00
74	Bobby Cox, Andruw Jones, Chipper Jones	50.00
75	Chipper Jones, Greg Maddux, Andruw Jones	50.00
76	Brian Roberts, Sammy Sosa, Miguel Tejada	40.00
77	Brooks Robinson, Cal Ripken Jr., Jim Palmer	65.00
78	Brooks Robinson, Jim Palmer, Frank Robinson	40.00
79	Cal Ripken Jr., Brooks Robinson, Miguel Tejada	50.00
80	Cal Ripken Jr., Frank Robinson, Sammy Sosa	80.00
81	Frank Robinson, Reggie Jackson, Brooks Robinson	75.00
82	Jim Palmer, Frank Robinson, Reggie Jackson	60.00
83	Jim Palmer, Reggie Jackson, Sammy Sosa	50.00
84	Jim Palmer, Sammy Sosa, Miguel Tejada	40.00
85	Miguel Tejada, Brian Roberts, Cal Ripken Jr.	80.00
86	Reggie Jackson, Frank Robinson, Sammy Sosa	50.00
87	Bobby Doerr, Carl Yastrzemski, Ted Williams	80.00
88	Carl Yastrzemski, David Ortiz, Manny Ramirez	60.00
89	Carl Yastrzemski, Ted Williams, David Ortiz	80.00
90	Carl Yastrzemski, Ted Williams, Manny Ramirez	80.00
91	Curt Schilling, David Ortiz, Johnny Damon	40.00
92	Curt Schilling, David Ortiz, Manny Ramirez	40.00
93	Curt Schilling, Manny Ramirez, Johnny Damon	40.00
94	David Ortiz, Johnny Damon, Manny Ramirez	50.00
95	Johnny Damon, Manny Ramirez, Ted Williams	60.00
96	Manny Ramirez, David Ortiz, Pedro Martinez	40.00
97	Manny Ramirez, Ted Williams, David Ortiz	60.00
98	Pedro Martinez, Roger Clemens, Manny Ramirez	50.00
99	Greg Maddux, Randy Johnson, Roger Clemens	50.00
100	Johan Santana, Pedro Martinez, Roger Clemens	60.00
101	Roger Clemens	50.00
102	Roger Clemens	50.00
103	Randy Johnson, Curt Schilling, Roger Clemens	75.00
104	Derrek Lee, Aramis Ramirez, Mark Prior	35.00
105	Derrek Lee, Ryne Sandberg, Sammy Sosa	65.00
106	Ernie Banks, Ryne Sandberg, Derrek Lee	60.00
107	Ernie Banks, Ryne Sandberg, Sammy Sosa	60.00
108	Greg Maddux, Ryne Sandberg, Ernie Banks	75.00
109	Mark Prior, Kerry Wood, Greg Maddux	60.00
110	Sammy Sosa, Ernie Banks, Derrek Lee	60.00
111	Frank Robinson, Joe Morgan, Johnny Bench	40.00

112 Johnny Bench, Frank Robinson, Tom Seaver 50.00
113 Johnny Bench, Tom Seaver, Joe Morgan 50.00
114 Jermaine Dye, Scott Podsednik, Tadahito Iguchi 40.00
115 Jim Thome, Paul Konerko, Tadahito Iguchi 60.00
116 Jon Garland, Scott Podsednik, Mark Buehrle 25.00
117 Jon Garland, Tadahito Iguchi, Mark Buehrle 30.00
118 Paul Konerko, Sammy Sosa, Carlton Fisk 40.00
119 Paul Konerko, Tadahito Iguchi, Jermaine Dye 40.00
120 Al Kaline, Ivan Rodriguez, Hank Greenberg 60.00
121 Greg Maddux, Johan Santana, Roger Clemens 60.00
122 Juan Marichal, Nolan Ryan, Roger Clemens 80.00
123 Nolan Ryan, Randy Johnson, Whitey Ford 60.00
124 Cal Ripken Jr., Ozzie Smith, Mike Schmidt 60.00
125 Mike Schmidt, Cal Ripken Jr., Ozzie Smith 60.00
126 Al Kaline, Frank Robinson, Paul Waner 50.00
127 Al Kaline, Harmon Killebrew, Frank Robinson 75.00
128 Al Kaline, Mickey Mantle, Reggie Jackson 125.00
129 Al Kaline, Reggie Jackson, Stan Musial 60.00
130 Al Kaline, Robin Yount, Paul Waner 40.00
131 Barry Bonds, Chipper Jones, Manny Ramirez 65.00
132 Bob Feller, Juan Marichal, Nolan Ryan 60.00
133 Bob Feller, Whitey Ford, Steve Carlton 80.00
134 Bobby Doerr, Ted Williams, Wade Boggs 80.00
135 Brooks Robinson, Ozzie Smith, Ryne Sandberg 50.00
136 Carl Yastrzemski, George Brett, Paul Molitor 50.00
137 Carlton Fisk, Carl Yastrzemski, Wade Boggs 75.00
138 Joe Morgan, George Brett, Mike Schmidt 50.00
139 Yogi Berra, Carlton Fisk, Gary Carter 50.00
140 Andy Pettitte, Nolan Ryan, Brad Lidge 50.00
141 Andy Pettitte, Nolan Ryan, Randy Johnson 50.00
142 Andy Pettitte, Nolan Ryan, Roger Clemens 60.00
143 Andy Pettitte, Randy Johnson, Brad Lidge 30.00
144 Andy Pettitte, Roy Oswalt, Roger Clemens 50.00
145 Brad Lidge, Roy Oswalt, Andy Pettitte 35.00
146 Craig Biggio, Jeff Bagwell, Lance Berkman 40.00
147 Nolan Ryan, Roger Clemens, Randy Johnson 80.00
148 Roger Clemens, Brad Lidge, Andy Pettitte 50.00
149 Roger Clemens, Randy Johnson, Andy Pettitte 50.00
150 Ichiro Suzuki, Hideki Matsui 160.00
151 Ichiro Suzuki, Hideki Matsui, Kazuo Matsui 140.00
152 Ichiro Suzuki, Tadahito Iguchi, Hideki Matsui 150.00

153 Eric Gagne, Mike Piazza, Duke Snider 100.00
154 Gary Sheffield, Rickie Weeks, Paul Molitor 40.00
155 Paul Molitor, Gary Sheffield, Robin Yount 35.00
156 Robin Yount, Paul Molitor, Rickie Weeks 40.00
157 Harmon Killebrew, Rod Carew, Johan Santana 40.00
158 Harmon Killebrew, Torii Hunter, Rod Carew 40.00
159 Johan Santana, Joe Mauer, Torii Hunter 35.00
160 Paul Molitor, Rod Carew, Harmon Killebrew 40.00
161 Albert Pujols, Ichiro Suzuki, Barry Bonds 180.00
162 Alex Rodriguez, Barry Bonds, George Brett 60.00
163 Alex Rodriguez, Barry Bonds, Mickey Mantle 150.00
164 Alex Rodriguez, Ichiro Suzuki, Mickey Mantle 180.00
165 Alex Rodriguez, Reggie Jackson, Yogi Berra 50.00
166 Alex Rodriguez, Ted Williams, Mickey Mantle 200.00
167 Alex Rodriguez, Yogi Berra, Don Mattingly 60.00
168 Alex Rodriguez, Barry Bonds, Don Mattingly 70.00
169 Alex Rodriguez, Cal Ripken Jr., Miguel Tejada 60.00
170 Barry Bonds, Harmon Killebrew, Reggie Jackson 70.00
171 Barry Bonds, Roberto Clemente, Willie Stargell 120.00
172 Barry Bonds, Alex Rodriguez, Albert Pujols 100.00
173 Barry Bonds, Cal Ripken Jr., Mickey Mantle 200.00
174 Barry Bonds, Josh Gibson, Albert Pujols 120.00
175 Barry Bonds, Vladimir Guerrero, Ichiro Suzuki 75.00
176 Brooks Robinson, George Brett, Mike Schmidt 60.00
177 Cal Ripken Jr., Barry Bonds, Ichiro Suzuki 120.00
178 Cal Ripken Jr., Don Mattingly, George Brett 90.00
179 Cal Ripken Jr., George Brett, Don Mattingly 90.00
180 Cal Ripken Jr., Mike Schmidt, Don Mattingly 100.00
181 Cal Ripken Jr., Roger Clemens, Don Mattingly 125.00
182 Chipper Jones, Dale Murphy, Don Mattingly 75.00
183 Don Mattingly, Mickey Mantle, Reggie Jackson 150.00
184 George Brett, Johnny Bench, Mike Schmidt 60.00
185 George Brett, Johnny Bench, Mike Schmidt 60.00
186 Ichiro Suzuki, Barry Bonds, Mickey Mantle 180.00
187 Ivan Rodriguez, Vladimir Guerrero, Miguel Tejada 35.00
188 Ivan Rodriguez, Yogi Berra, Johnny Bench 50.00
189 Ivan Rodriguez, Yogi Berra, Johnny Bench 50.00
190 Johnny Bench, Mike Piazza, Yogi Berra 50.00

191 Mickey Mantle, Barry Bonds, Ted Williams 200.00
192 Mickey Mantle, Ichiro Suzuki, Roberto Clemente 200.00
193 Mickey Mantle, Roberto Clemente, Stan Musial 200.00
194 Mickey Mantle, Ted Williams, Roberto Clemente 220.00
195 Mickey Mantle, Vladimir Guerrero, Roberto Clemente 200.00
196 Miguel Tejada, Reggie Jackson, Rickey Henderson 40.00
197 Reggie Jackson, Alex Rodriguez, Yogi Berra 50.00
198 Roberto Clemente, Mickey Mantle, Barry Bonds 180.00
199 Buck O'Neil, Josh Gibson, Monte Irvin 100.00
200 Carlos Beltran, Carlos Delgado, David Wright 60.00
201 Carlos Beltran, Carlos Delgado, Jose Reyes 50.00
202 Carlos Beltran, David Wright, Pedro Martinez 60.00
203 Darryl Strawberry, Dwight Gooden, Gary Carter 30.00
204 David Wright, Carlos Beltran, Mike Piazza 60.00
205 David Wright, Mike Piazza, Jose Reyes 75.00
206 Jose Reyes, Kazuo Matsui, David Wright 40.00
207 Alex Rodriguez, Don Mattingly, Mickey Mantle 180.00
208 Alex Rodriguez, Hideki Matsui, Joe Torre 80.00
209 Alex Rodriguez, Hideki Matsui, Mickey Mantle 200.00
210 Don Mattingly, Mickey Mantle, Roger Clemens 200.00
211 Hideki Matsui, Gary Sheffield, Alex Rodriguez 50.00
212 Hideki Matsui, Gary Sheffield, Jorge Posada 50.00
213 Jorge Posada, Roger Clemens, Mike Mussina 75.00
214 Mickey Mantle, Whitey Ford, Yogi Berra 200.00
215 Mike Mussina, Whitey Ford, Roger Clemens 65.00
216 Roger Clemens, Mickey Mantle, Alex Rodriguez 200.00
217 Wade Boggs, Joe Torre, Alfonso Soriano 30.00
218 Barry Zito, Mark Mulder, Tim Hudson 25.00
219 Jose Canseco, Reggie Jackson, Rickey Henderson 40.00
220 Mark Mulder, Miguel Tejada, Tim Hudson 40.00
221 Bobby Abreu, Pat Burrell, Jim Thome 40.00
222 Curt Schilling, Mike Schmidt, Steve Carlton 50.00
223 Mike Schmidt, Pat Burrell, Scott Rolen 50.00
224 Barry Bonds, Roberto Clemente, Josh Gibson 150.00
225 Paul Waner, Roberto Clemente, Lloyd Waner 150.00
226 Willie Stargell, Bill Mazeroski, Roberto Clemente 140.00
227 Albert Pujols, Carlos Beltran, Dontrelle Willis 60.00

228 Albert Pujols, Dontrelle Willis, Ichiro Suzuki 90.00
229 Cal Ripken Jr., Albert Pujols, Orlando Cepeda 90.00
230 Cal Ripken Jr., Carlton Fisk, Tom Seaver 80.00
231 Cal Ripken Jr., Rod Carew, Carlton Fisk 75.00
232 Cal Ripken Jr., Rod Carew, Carlton Fisk 75.00
233 Jeff Bagwell, Albert Pujols, Mike Piazza 100.00
234 Mike Piazza, Jeff Bagwell, Scott Rolen 80.00
235 Rickey Henderson, Steve Garvey, Tony Gwynn 50.00
236 Adrian Beltre, Ichiro Suzuki, Alex Rodriguez 80.00
237 Ichiro Suzuki, Alex Rodriguez, Randy Johnson 100.00
238 Barry Bonds, Juan Marichal, Orlando Cepeda 75.00
239 Juan Marichal, Monte Irvin, Orlando Cepeda 40.00
240 Orlando Cepeda, Monte Irvin, Barry Bonds 60.00
241 Albert Pujols, Frankie Frisch, Stan Musial 120.00
242 Albert Pujols, Mark Mulder, Scott Rolen 65.00
243 Scott Rolen, Jim Edmonds, Albert Pujols 75.00
244 Stan Musial, Ozzie Smith, Albert Pujols 120.00
245 Alex Rodriguez, Ivan Rodriguez, Alfonso Soriano 50.00
246 Alex Rodriguez, Mark Teixeira, Alfonso Soriano 50.00
247 Alex Rodriguez, Nolan Ryan, Alfonso Soriano 60.00
248 Alex Rodriguez, Hank Blalock, Mark Teixeira 30.00
249 Hank Blalock, Michael Young 25.00
250 Mark Teixeira, Alfonso Soriano, Michael Young 30.00

Triple Relic Autograph

NM/M

Production 18 Sets
Gold: No Pricing
Production 9 Sets
Platinum: No Pricing
Production 3 Sets

#	Player	NM/M
1	Albert Pujols	475.00
2	Albert Pujols	475.00
3	Albert Pujols	475.00
4	Alex Rodriguez	275.00
5	Alex Rodriguez	275.00
6	Alex Rodriguez	275.00
7	Derrek Lee	60.00
8	Barry Bonds	400.00
9	Ben Sheets	400.00
10	Ben Sheets	400.00
11	Brad Lidge	35.00
12	Brad Lidge	35.00
13	Cal Ripken Jr.	220.00
14	Cal Ripken Jr.	220.00
15	Cal Ripken Jr.	220.00
16	Carl Yastrzemski	100.00
17	Carl Yastrzemski	100.00
18	Carl Yastrzemski	100.00
19	Chase Utley	65.00
20	Chase Utley	65.00
21	Chien-Ming Wang	750.00
22	Chien-Ming Wang	400.00
23	Chien-Ming Wang	400.00
24	Chien-Ming Wang	400.00
25	Chris Carpenter	100.00
26	Chris Carpenter	100.00
27	Clint Barmes	25.00
28	Clint Barmes	25.00
29	Conor Jackson	30.00
30	Conor Jackson	30.00
31	David Ortiz	125.00
32	Don Mattingly	140.00
33	Don Mattingly	140.00
34	Don Mattingly	140.00
35	Duke Snider	75.00
36	Duke Snider	75.00
37	Ernie Banks	120.00
38	Frank Robinson	65.00

#	Player	Price
39	Frank Robinson	65.00
40	Frank Robinson	65.00
41	Garrett Atkins	35.00
42	Garrett Atkins	35.00
43	Derrek Lee	60.00
44	Derrek Lee	60.00
45	Derrek Lee	60.00
46	J.J. Hardy	40.00
47	J.J. Hardy	40.00
48	Jake Peavy	40.00
49	Jake Peavy	40.00
50	Jeff Francis	30.00
51	Jeff Francis	30.00
52	Joe Mauer	50.00
53	Joe Mauer	50.00
54	Joey Devine	25.00
55	Joey Devine	25.00
56	Johan Santana	60.00
57	Johan Santana	60.00
58	Johan Santana	60.00
59	Johan Santana	60.00
60	Johnny Bench	80.00
61	Johnny Bench	80.00
62	Johnny Bench	80.00
63	Johnny Damon	80.00
64	Jonny Gomes	40.00
65	Jonny Gomes	40.00
66	Jose Reyes	50.00
67	Jose Reyes	50.00
68	Justin Morneau	40.00
69	Justin Morneau	40.00
70	Lou Brock	60.00
71	Lou Brock	60.00
72	Lou Brock	60.00
73	Lou Brock	60.00
74	Manny Ramirez	100.00
75	Mariano Rivera	150.00
76	Mark Prior	50.00
77	Miguel Cabrera	70.00
78	Miguel Cabrera	70.00
79	Miguel Cabrera	70.00
80	Miguel Cabrera	70.00
81	Mike Schmidt	100.00
82	Mike Schmidt	100.00
83	Mike Schmidt	100.00
84	Morgan Ensberg	35.00
85	Morgan Ensberg	35.00
86	Nick Swisher	60.00
87	Nick Swisher	60.00
88	Nolan Ryan	150.00
89	Nolan Ryan	150.00
90	Nolan Ryan	150.00
91	Zachary Duke	30.00
92	Zachary Duke	30.00
93	Ozzie Smith	80.00
94	Ozzie Smith	80.00
95	Ozzie Smith	80.00
96	Pedro Martinez	125.00
97	Robin Yount	75.00
98	Robin Yount	75.00
99	Robin Yount	75.00
100	Rod Carew	50.00
101	Rod Carew	50.00
102	Rod Carew	50.00
103	Rod Carew	50.00
104	Roger Clemens	180.00
105	Roger Clemens	180.00
106	Ryan Langerhans	40.00
107	Ryan Langerhans	40.00
108	Ryne Sandberg	100.00
109	Ryne Sandberg	100.00
110	Ryne Sandberg	100.00
111	Scott Kazmir	50.00
112	Scott Kazmir	50.00
113	Stan Musial	100.00
114	Stan Musial	100.00
115	Stan Musial	100.00
116	Steve Carlton	50.00
117	Steve Carlton	50.00
118	Steve Carlton	50.00
119	Steve Garvey	50.00
120	Steve Garvey	50.00
121	Tony Gwynn	100.00
122	Tony Gwynn	100.00
123	Tony Gwynn	100.00
124	Travis Hafner	50.00
125	Travis Hafner	50.00
126	Victor Martinez	50.00
127	Victor Martinez	50.00
128	Wade Boggs	60.00
129	Wade Boggs	60.00
130	Wade Boggs	60.00

Triple Relic Combos Autograph

NM/M

Production 18 Sets
Gold: No Pricing
Production 9 Sets
Platinum: No Pricing
Production 3 Sets

#	Players	Price
1	Albert Pujols, Barry Bonds, Alex Rodriguez	1,000
2	Felix Hernandez, Alex Rodriguez, Shin-Soo Choo	150.00
3	Nolan Ryan, Roger Clemens, Felix Hernandez	300.00
4	Johnny Damon, Alex Rodriguez, Robinson Cano	300.00
5	Manny Ramirez, Carl Yastrzemski, David Ortiz	250.00
6	Michael Young, Cal Ripken Jr., Ozzie Smith	300.00
7	Brian Roberts, Cal Ripken Jr., Frank Robinson	250.00
8	Stan Musial, Ozzie Smith, Lou Brock	180.00
9	Ozzie Smith, Stan Musial, Lou Brock	180.00
10	Tony Gwynn, Stan Musial, Rod Carew	180.00
11	Brooks Robinson, Cal Ripken Jr., Brian Roberts	200.00
12	Rod Carew, Robin Yount, Paul Molitor	120.00
13	Derrek Lee, Ryne Sandberg, Mark Prior	180.00
14	Chien-Ming Wang, Steve Carlton, Dontrelle Willis	275.00
15	Brad Lidge, Mariano Rivera, Huston Street	180.00
16	Morgan Ensberg, Wade Boggs, David Wright	120.00
17	Ben Sheets, Steve Carlton, Felix Hernandez	80.00
18	Victor Martinez, Johnny Bench, Joe Mauer	125.00
19	David Wright, Mike Schmidt, Aaron Hill	160.00
20	Chase Utley, Mike Schmidt, Ryan Howard	200.00
21	Felix Hernandez, Steve Carlton, Brandon McCarthy	75.00
22	David Wright, Miguel Cabrera, Jason Bay	140.00
23	Robinson Cano, Don Mattingly, Chien-Ming Wang	350.00
24	Justin Morneau, Don Mattingly, Travis Hafner	100.00
25	Steve Garvey, Don Mattingly, Dan Johnson	100.00
26	Travis Hafner, Miguel Cabrera, Jason Bay	100.00
27	Ben Sheets, Johan Santana, Jake Peavy	75.00
28	Ervin Santana, Johan Santana, Ben Sheets	70.00
29	Chris Carpenter, Johan Santana, Rich Harden	120.00
30	Zachary Duke, Johan Santana, Brandon McCarthy	75.00

2006 Topps Turkey Red

NM/M

Complete Set (316-630):

#	Player	Price
	Common Player:	.25
	Common SP:	4.00
	Inserted 1:4	
	Pack (8):	4.50
	Box (24):	90.00
316	Alex Rodriguez	3.00
316	Alex Rodriguez/ Rangers/SP	8.00
316	Alex Rodriguez/ M's/SP	8.00
317	Jeff Francoeur/SP	4.00
318	Shawn Green	.25
319	Daniel Cabrera	.25
320	Craig Biggio	.50
321	Jeremy Bonderman	.40
322	Mark Kotsay	.25
323	Cliff Floyd	.25
324	Jimmy Rollins	.40
325	Magglio Ordonez	.25
325	Magglio Ordonez/ W. Sox/SP	4.00
326	C.C. Sabathia	.25
327	Oliver Perez	.25
328	Orlando Hudson	.25
329	Chris Ray	.25
330	Manny Ramirez	1.00
331	Paul Konerko	.50
332	Joe Mauer/SP	5.00
333	Jorge Posada	.50
334	Mark Ellis	.25
335	A.J. Burnett	.25
336	Mike Sweeney	.25
337	Shannon Stewart	.25
338	Jake Peavy SP	4.00
339	Carlos Delgado/ Mets/SP	5.00
339	Carlos Delgado/ Blue Jays/SP	5.00
340	Brian Roberts	.25
341	Dontrelle Willis	.50
342	Aaron Rowand	.25
343	Richie Sexson	.50
343	Richie Sexson/ Brewers/SP	4.00
344	Chris Carpenter	.75
345	Carlos Zambrano	.40
346	Nomar Garciaparra	1.00
347	Carlos Lee	.40
348	Preston Wilson	.25
348	Preston Wilson/ Marlins/SP	4.00
349	Mariano Rivera	.50
350	Ichiro Suzuki/SP	8.00
351	Mike Piazza	1.00
351	Mike Piazza/Mets/SP	4.00
352	Jason Schmidt	.25
353	Jeff Weaver	.25
354	Rocco Baldelli	.25
355	Adam Dunn	.75
356	Jeromy Burnitz	.25
357	Chris Shelton/SP	4.00
358	Chone Figgins/SP	4.00
359	Javier Vazquez	.25
360	Chipper Jones	1.00
361	Frank Thomas	1.00
362	Mark Loretta	.25
363	Hideki Matsui	2.00
364	J.J. Hardy/SP	4.00
365	Todd Helton	.75
366	Reggie Sanders	.25
367	Jay Gibbons	.25
368	Johnny Estrada	.25
369	Grady Sizemore	.75
370	Jim Thome	1.00
371	Ivan Rodriguez	.75
372	Jason Bay	.75
373	Carl Crawford	.50
374	Adrian Beltre	.25
375	Derrek Lee/SP	6.00
376	Miguel Olivo	.25
377	Roy Oswalt	.50
378	Coco Crisp	.25
379	Moises Alou	.40
380	Kevin Millwood	.25
381	Mark Grudzielanek	.25
382	Justin Morneau	.75
383	Austin Kearns	.40
384	Brad Penny	.25
385	Troy Glaus	.50
386	Cliff Lee	.25
387	Armando Benitez	.25
388	Clint Barmes	.25
389	Orlando Cabrera	.25
390	Jim Edmonds/SP	4.00
391	Jermaine Dye	.25
392	Morgan Ensberg/SP	4.00
393	Paul LoDuca	.25
394	Eric Chavez	.25
395	Greg Maddux/SP	8.00
396	Jack Wilson	.25
397	Omar Vizquel	.25
398	Joe Nathan	.25
399	Bobby Abreu	.50
400	Barry Bonds/SP	8.00
401	Gary Sheffield	.50
402	John Patterson	.25
403	J.D. Drew	.25
404	Bruce Chen	.25
405	Johnny Damon	1.00
406	Aubrey Huff	.25
407	Mark Mulder	.40
408	Jamie Moyer	.25
409	Carlos Guillen	.25
410	Andruw Jones/SP	5.00
411	Jhonny Peralta/SP	4.00
412	Doug Davis	.25
413	Aaron Miles	.25
414	Jon Lieber	.25
415	Aaron Hill	.25
416	Josh Beckett SP	4.00
417	Bobby Crosby	.25
418	Noah Lowry SP	4.00
419	Sidney Ponson	.25
420	Luis Castillo	.25
421	Brad Wilkerson	.25
422	Felix Hernandez SP	4.00
423	Vinny Castilla	.25
424	Tom Glavine	.50
425	Vladimir Guerrero	1.00
426	Javy Lopez	.25
427	Ronnie Belliard	.25
428	Dmitri Young	.25
429	Johan Santana	1.00
430	David Ortiz/ Red Sox/SP	5.00
430	David Ortiz/Twins/SP	5.00
431	Ben Sheets	.50
432	Matt Holliday	.50
433	Brian McCann	.50
434	Joe Blanton	.25
435	Sean Casey	.25
436	Brad Lidge	.25
437	Chad Tracy	.25
438	Brett Myers	.25
439	Matt Morris	.25
440	Brian Giles	.25
441	Zachary Duke	.25
442	Jose Lopez	.25
443	Kris Benson	.25
444	Jose Reyes/SP	5.00
445	Travis Hafner	.75
446	Orlando Hernandez	.25
447	Edgar Renteria	.40
448	Scott Podsednik	.25
449	Nick Swisher/SP	4.00
450	Derek Jeter	8.00
451	Scott Kazmir	4.00
452	Hank Blalock	.50
453	Jake Westbrook	.25
454	Miguel Cabrera	1.00
455	Ken Griffey Jr.	2.00
455	Ken Griffey Jr./M's/SP	8.00
456	Rafael Furcal	.50
457	Lance Berkman	.50
458	Aramis Ramirez	.50
459	Xavier Nady	.25
459	Xavier Nady/ Padres/SP	4.00
460	Randy Johnson	1.00
460	Randy Johnson/ Astros/SP	6.00
461	Khalil Greene	.25
462	Bartolo Colon	.25
463	Mike Lowell	.25
464	David DeJesus	.25
465	Ryan Howard/SP	8.00
466	Tim Salmon/SP	4.00
467	Mark Buehrle/SP	4.00
468	Curtis Granderson	.25
469	Kerry Wood	.50
470	Miguel Tejada	.75
471	Geoff Jenkins	.25
472	Jeremy Reed	.25
473	David Eckstein	.25
474	Lyle Overbay	.25
475	Michael Young	.25
476	Nick Johnson/Nats/SP	4.00
476	Nick Johnson/ Yanks/SP	4.00
477	Carlos Beltran	1.00
478	Huston Street	.25
479	Brandon Webb	.25
480	Phil Nevin	.25
481	Ryan Madson/SP	4.00
482	Jason Giambi	1.00
483	Angel Berroa	.25
484	Casey Blake	.25
485	Pat Burrell	.50
486	B.J. Ryan	.25
487	Torii Hunter	.25
488	Garret Anderson	.25
489	Chase Utley/SP	6.00
490	Matt Murton	.25
491	Rich Harden	.25
492	Garrett Atkins	.25
493	Tadahito Iguchi/SP	5.00
494	Jarrod Washburn	.25
495	Carl Everett	.25
496	Kameron Loe	.25
497	Jorge Cantu/SP	4.00
498	Chris Young	.25
499	Marcus Giles	.25
500	Albert Pujols	3.00

501	Alfonso Soriano/Nats/SP	5.00
501	Alfonso Soriano/Yanks/SP	5.00
502	Randy Winn	.25
503	Roy Halladay	.50
504	Victor Martinez	.25
505	Pedro Martinez	1.00
506	Rickie Weeks	.40
507	Dan Johnson	.25
508	Tim Hudson	.50
508	Tim Hudson A's/SP	4.00
509	Mark Prior	.75
510	Melvin Mora	.25
511	Matt Clement	.25
512	Brandon Inge	.25
513	Mike Mussina	.75
514	Mike Cameron	.25
515	Barry Zito	.50
516	Luis Gonzalez	.25
517	Jose Castillo	.25
518	Andy Pettitte	.50
519	Wily Mo Pena	.25
520	Billy Wagner	.25
521	Ervin Santana/SP	4.00
522	Juan Pierre	.25
523	Danny Haren	.25
524	Adrian Gonzalez/SP	4.00
525	Robinson Cano	.75
526	Jeff Kent	.40
527	Cory Sullivan	.25
528	Joe Crede SP	4.00
529	John Smoltz	.50
530	David Wright	2.00
531	Chad Cordero	.25
532	Scott Rolen SP	5.00
533	Edwin Jackson	.25
534	Doug Mientkiewicz	.25
535	Mark Teixeira/SP	5.00
536	Kelvim Escobar	.25
537	Alex Rios	.25
538	Jose Vidro	.25
539	Alex Gonzalez	.25
540	Yadier Molina	.25
541	Ronny Cedeno/SP	4.00
542	Mark Hendrickson	.25
543	Russ Adams	.25
544	Chris Capuano	.25
545	Raul Ibanez	.25
546	Vicente Padilla	.25
547	Chris Duffy	.25
548	Bengie Molina	.25
549	Chien-Ming Wang	.75
550	Curt Schilling	.25
551	Craig Wilson	.25
552	Mike Lieberthal	.25
553	Kazuo Matsui	.25
554	Jeff Francis	.25
555	Brady Clark	.25
556	Willy Taveras	.25
557	Mike Maroth	.25
558	Bernie Williams	.50
559	Edwin Encarnacion	.25
560	Vernon Wells	.25
561	Livan Hernandez/Nats	.25
561	Livan Hernandez/Giants/SP	4.00
562	Kenny Rogers	.25
563	Steve Finley	.25
564	Trot Nixon	.25
565	Jonny Gomes/SP	4.00
566	Brandon Phillips	.25
567	Shawn Chacon	.25
568	David Bush	.25
569	Jose Guillen	.25
570	Gustavo Chacin	.25
571	A. Rod Safe at the Plate CL	1.00
572	Pujols At Bat CL	1.00
573	Bonds On Deck CL	1.00
574	Breaking Up Two CL	.25
575	Conference On The Mound CL	.25
576	Touch Em All CL	.50
577	Avoiding The Runner CL	.25
578	Bunting The Runner Over CL	.25
579	In The Hole CL	.50
580	Jeter Steals Third CL	1.00
581	Nolan Ryan	2.00
582	Cal Ripken Jr.	3.00
583	Carl Yastrzemski	1.00
584	Duke Snider	1.00
585	Tom Seaver	1.00
586	Mickey Mantle	5.00
587	Jim Palmer	.50
588	Gary Carter	.25
589	Stan Musial	1.50
590	Luis Aparicio	.25
591	Prince Fielder (RC)	4.00
592	Conor Jackson (RC)	.50
593	Jeremy Hermida (RC)	1.00
594	Jeff Mathis (RC)	.50
595	Alay Soler RC	1.00
596	Ryan Spilborghs (RC)	.50
597	Chuck James (RC)	1.00
598	Josh Barfield (RC)	1.00
599	Ian Kinsler (RC)	.50
600	Val Majewski (RC)	.50
601	Brian Slocum (RC)	.50
602	Matthew Kemp (RC)	2.00
603	Nate McLouth (RC)	.50
604	Sean Marshall (RC)	.50
605	Brian Bannister (RC)	.50
606	Ryan Zimmerman (RC)	4.00
607	Kendry Morales (RC)	1.00
608	Jonathan Papelbon (RC)	4.00
609	Matt Cain (RC)	1.00
610	Anderson Hernandez (RC)	.50
611	Jose Capellan (RC)	.50
612	Lastings Milledge (RC)	2.00
613	Francisco Liriano (RC)	4.00
614	Hanley Ramirez (RC)	2.00
615	Bryan Anderson (RC)	.50
616	Reggie Abercrombie (RC)	.50
617	Erick Aybar (RC)	.50
618	James Loney (RC)	1.00
619	Joel Zumaya (RC)	.50
620	Travis Ishikawa (RC)	.50
621	Jason Kubel (RC)	.50
622	Drew Meyer (RC)	.50
623	Kenji Johjima RC	4.00
624	Fausto Carmona (RC)	.50
625	Nicholas Markakis (RC)	.50
626	John Rheinecker (RC)	.50
627	Melky Cabrera (RC)	.50
628	Mike Pelfrey RC	5.00
629	Dan Uggla (RC)	1.00
630	Justin Verlander (RC)	4.00

Black

Stars (316-630):	3-5X
SP's:	1.5-2X
Inserted 1:20	

Gold

Stars (316-630):	5-10X
SP's:	3-5X
Inserted 1:60	

Red

Stars (316-630):	1-2X
SP's:	.5-1X

Suede

No Pricing
Production One Set

White

Stars (316-630):	2-3X
SP's:	1X
Inserted 1:4	

Autographs

		NM/M
Common Auto.:		8.00
Suede:		No Pricing
Production One Set		
GA	Garrett Atkins	15.00
JB	Josh Barfield	15.00
CB	Clint Barmes	10.00
MC	Miguel Cabrera	50.00
RC	Robinson Cano	60.00
JG	Jonny Gomes	25.00
RH	Ryan Howard	100.00
CJA	Conor Jackson	15.00
KJ	Kenji Johjima	90.00
DJ	Dan Johnson	15.00
CJ	Chipper Jones	60.00
DL	Derrek Lee	40.00
PL	Paul LoDuca	25.00
BM	Brian McCann	30.00
BMC	Brandon McCarthy/Exch.	15.00
MM	Mike Morse	10.00
RO	Roy Oswalt	25.00
AR	Alex Rodriguez	250.00
JS	Johan Santana/Exch.	65.00
HS	Huston Street/Exch.	25.00
NS	Nick Swisher/Exch.	20.00
CV	Claudio Vargas/Exch.	8.00
DW	David Wright	85.00

Autographs Black

		NM/M
Production 15 or 99		
GA	Garrett Atkins/99	15.00
JB	Josh Barfield/99	20.00
CB	Clint Barmes/99	15.00
CJA	Conor Jackson/99	20.00
DJ	Dan Johnson/99	15.00
BM	Brian McCann/99	40.00
BMC	Brandon McCarthy/99 Exch.	15.00
MM	Mike Morse/99	30.00
NS	Nick Swisher/99 Exch.	20.00
CV	Claudio Vargas/99 Exch.	15.00

Autographs Gold

		NM/M
Production 5 or 25		
JB	Josh Barfield/25	40.00
BM	Brian McCann/25	75.00
BMC	Brandon McCarthy/25 Exch.	
MM	Mike Morse/25	30.00
NS	Nick Swisher/25 Exch.	30.00

Autographs Red

		NM/M
Production 50 or 475		
GA	Garrett Atkins/475	15.00
JB	Josh Barfield/475	15.00
CB	Clint Barmes/475	15.00
MC	Miguel Cabrera/50	60.00
RC	Robinson Cano/50	100.00
JG	Jonny Gomes/50	30.00
RH	Ryan Howard/50	125.00
CJA	Conor Jackson/475	15.00
KJ	Kenji Johjima/50	100.00
DJ	Dan Johnson/475	15.00
CJ	Chipper Jones/50	100.00
DL	Derrek Lee/50	40.00
PL	Paul LoDuca/50	30.00
BM	Brian McCann/475	30.00
BMC	Brandon McCarthy/475 Exch.	15.00
MM	Mike Morse/50	10.00
RO	Roy Oswalt/50	30.00
AR	Alex Rodriguez/50	250.00
JS	Johan Santana/50 Exch.	75.00
HS	Huston Street/50 Exch.	30.00
NS	Nick Swisher/475 Exch.	20.00
CV	Claudio Vargas/475 Exch.	8.00
DW	David Wright/50	100.00

Autographs White

		NM/M
Production 25 or 100		
GA	Garrett Atkins/200	15.00
JB	Josh Barfield/200	20.00
CB	Clint Barmes/200	15.00
CJA	Conor Jackson/200	15.00
DJ	Dan Johnson/200	15.00
BM	Brandon McCarthy/200 Exch.	15.00
BMC	Brandon McCarthy/200 Exch.	15.00
MM	Mike Morse/200	10.00
NS	Nick Swisher/200 Exch.	20.00
CV	Claudio Vargas/200 Exch.	10.00

B-18 Blankets

		NM/M
Inserted 1:2 Boxes		
Original B-18 Blanket: No Pricing		
Inserted 1:159 Boxes		
BB1	Barry Bonds/White	15.00
BB2	Barry Bonds/Red	15.00
VG1	Vladimir Guerrero/White	10.00
VG2	Vladimir Guerrero/Green	10.00
KJ1	Kenji Johjima/White	10.00
KJ2	Kenji Johjima/Green	10.00
DL1	Derrek Lee/White	10.00
DL2	Derrek Lee/Red	10.00
MM1	Mickey Mantle/White	25.00
MM2	Mickey Mantle/Blue	25.00
HM1	Hideki Matsui/White	10.00
HM2	Hideki Matsui/Blue	10.00
DO1	David Ortiz/White	10.00
DO2	David Ortiz/Orange	10.00
MR1	Manny Ramirez/White	10.00
MR2	Manny Ramirez/Orange	10.00
AR1	Alex Rodriguez/White	15.00
AR2	Alex Rodriguez/Blue	15.00
IS1	Ichiro Suzuki/White	10.00
IS2	Ichiro Suzuki/Green	10.00

Cabinet

		NM/M
Common Player:		
Inserted 1:2 Boxes		
Cabinet Original:		No Pricing
Inserted 1:4,340 Boxes		
Suede:		No Pricing
Inserted 1:634 Boxes		
JB	Josh Barfield	10.00
JBE	Josh Beckett	10.00
BB	Barry Bonds	25.00
JC	Jorge Cantu	10.00
CCA	Chris Carpenter	10.00
GC	Gary Carter	10.00
CC	Carl Crawford	10.00
JD	Johnny Damon	20.00
CD	Carlos Delgado	10.00
PF	Prince Fielder	20.00
JF	Jeff Francoeur	15.00
NG	Nomar Garciaparra	15.00
TG	Troy Glaus	10.00
JG	Jonny Gomes	10.00
KG	Ken Griffey Jr.	20.00
RH	Ryan Howard	20.00
DJ	Derek Jeter	30.00
NJ	Nick Johnson	10.00
RJ	Randy Johnson	20.00
AJ	Andruw Jones	15.00
DL	Derrek Lee	10.00
FL	Francisco Liriano	10.00
MM	Mickey Mantle	50.00
NM	Nicholas Markakis	15.00
PM	Pedro Martinez	15.00
HM	Hideki Matsui	15.00
DO	David Ortiz	20.00
JPA	Jonathan Papelbon	25.00
JP	Jake Peavy	15.00
MP	Mike Piazza	15.00
AP	Albert Pujols	30.00
AR	Alex Rodriguez	25.00
IR	Ivan Rodriguez	10.00
JR	Jimmy Rollins	15.00
NR	Nolan Ryan	25.00
JS	Johan Santana	15.00
DS	Duke Snider	20.00
AS	Alfonso Soriano	20.00
IS	Ichiro Suzuki	20.00
JT	Jim Thome	15.00
DW	David Wright	15.00
CY	Carl Yastrzemski	25.00

Cabinet Auto. Relics

No Pricing
Inserted 1:86 Boxes
Suede: No Pricing
Production One Set

Cabinet Autograph Relics Dual

No Pricing
Inserted 1:1,368 Boxes
Suede: No Pricing
Production One Set

Relics

		NM/M
Common Player:		4.00
Red:		1-1.5X
Production 150 Sets		
White:		1.5-2X
Production 99 Sets		
Black:		2-3X
Production 50 Sets		
Gold:		2-4X
Production 25 Sets		
Suede:		No Pricing
Production One Set		
CBA	Clint Barmes	6.00
CB	Carlos Beltran	8.00
LB	Lance Berkman	6.00
HB	Hank Blalock	4.00
MC	Miguel Cabrera	8.00
RC	Robinson Cano	15.00
CC	Chris Carpenter	8.00
EC	Eric Chavez	6.00
JC	Jose Contreras	6.00
JD	Johnny Damon	15.00
CD	Carlos Delgado	6.00
JE	Jim Edmonds	6.00
ME	Morgan Ensberg	4.00

JF	Jeff Francoeur	8.00
JG	Jon Garland	4.00
VG	Vladimir Guerrero	8.00
RHA	Roy Halladay	6.00
RIH	Rich Harden	8.00
JH	Jeremy Hermida	6.00
RH	Ryan Howard	25.00
TH	Torii Hunter	6.00
CJ	Andruw Jones	6.00
CJ	Chipper Jones	10.00
PK	Paul Konerko	8.00
DL	Derrek Lee	8.00
BL	Brad Lidge	6.00
PL	Paul LoDuca	4.00
PM	Pedro Martinez	6.00
HM	Hideki Matsui	15.00
JM	Joe Mauer	10.00
MM	Mike Mussina	10.00
DO	David Ortiz	15.00
RO	Roy Oswalt	6.00
APE	Andy Pettitte	6.00
MP	Mike Piazza	10.00
AP	Albert Pujols	20.00
MR	Manny Ramirez	10.00
JR	Jose Reyes	8.00
MRI	Mariano Rivera	15.00
BR	Brian Roberts	6.00
AR	Alex Rodriguez	15.00
JS	Johan Santana	10.00
IS	Ichiro Suzuki	25.00
MT	Mark Teixeira	8.00
BW	Bernie Williams	8.00
DWI	Dontrelle Willis	6.00
DW	David Wright	15.00
MY	Michael Young	6.00

2006 Topps 1952 Edition

MICKEY MANTLE

NM/M

Complete Set (312):		
Common Player:		.25
Common SP (276-312):		5.00
Common 52 Logo Variation:		4.00
Inserted 1:5		
Pack (8):		4.50
Box (20):		80.00
1	Howie Kendrick (RC)	1.50
2	Enrique Gonzalez (RC)	.25
3	Chuck James (RC)	.75
4	Chris Britton RC	.50
5	David Pauley (RC)	.50
6	Angel Pagan (RC)	.25
7	Pat Neshek RC	6.00
8	Walter Young (RC)	.25
9	Chris Denorfia (RC)	.25
10	Rafael Perez RC	.50
11	Ryan Spilborghs (RC)	.25
12	Jon Huber RC	.50
13	Jordan Tata RC	.50
14	Eric Reed (RC)	.25
15	Norris Hopper RC	.75
16	Scott Olsen (RC)	.25
17	Fernando Nieve (RC)	.25
18	Chris Booker (RC)	.25
19	Chad Billingsley (RC)	.75
20	Carlos Villanueva RC	.75
21	Craig Hansen RC	2.00
22	David Gassner (RC)	.25
23	Mike Pelfrey (RC)	4.00
24	Matt Smith (RC)	1.00
25	Chris Roberson (RC)	.50
26	John Van Benschoten (RC)	.25
27	Kevin Frandsen (RC)	.25
28	Les Walrond (RC)	.50
29	James Shields RC	.50
30	Russell Martin (RC)	.50
31	Benjamin Zobrist (RC)	.25
32	John Rheinecker (RC)	.25
33	Francisco Rosario (RC)	.25
34	Santiago Ramirez (RC)	.25
35	Michael Napoli RC	1.50

36	Tony Pena (RC)	.25
37	Jeff Karstens RC	1.00
37	Jeff Karstens/ 52 logo/SP RC	5.00
38	Phil Stockman (RC)	.25
39	Kurt Birkins RC	1.00
40	Dustin Pedroia (RC)	.50
41	Buck Coats (RC)	.25
42	Jim Johnson RC	1.00
43	Angel Guzman (RC)	.25
44	Kelly Shoppach (RC)	.25
45	Josh Wilson (RC)	.25
46	Jack Hannahan RC	.75
47	Ricky Nolasco (RC)	.25
48	T.J. Bohn (RC)	.25
49	Joel Zumaya (RC)	1.00
50	Philip Barzilla RC	.75
51	Justin Huber (RC)	.25
52	Willy Aybar (RC)	.25
52	Willy Aybar 52 logo/ SP (RC)	4.00
53	Tony Gwynn Jr. (RC)	.50
54	Chris Barnwell (RC)	.50
55	Henry Owens RC	.75
56	Jeff Bajenaru (RC)	.25
57	Jonah Bayliss RC	.50
58	Joshua Sharpless RC	.50
59	Eliezer Alfonzo (RC)	.50
60	Bobby Livingston (RC)	.25
61	John Gall (RC)	.25
62	Ruddy Lugo (RC)	.25
63	Fabio Castro (RC)	.50
64	Casey Janssen RC	.75
65	Mike O'Connor RC	.50
66	Kendry Morales (RC)	.50
67	James Hoey RC	.75
68	Dustin Moseley (RC)	.25
69	Peter Moylan RC	.25
70	Manny Delcarmen (RC)	.50
71	Rich Hill (RC)	.40
72	Boone Logan RC	.50
73	Cody Ross (RC)	.25
74	Fausto Carmona (RC)	.25
75	Ramon Ramirez (RC)	.25
76	Zach Miner (RC)	.25
77	Hanley Ramirez (RC)	.50
78	Josh Johnson (RC)	.25
79	Taylor Buchholz (RC)	.25
80	Joe Nelson (RC)	.25
81	Hong-Chih Kuo (RC)	.50
82	Chris Mabeus (RC)	.25
83	Willie Eyre (RC)	.25
84	John Maine (RC)	.25
85	Yurendell DeCaster (RC)	.25
86	Mike Thompson RC	.50
87	Brian Wilson (RC)	.50
88	Matt Cain (RC)	.50
88	Matt Cain/ 52 logo/SP (RC)	8.00
89	Josh Rupe (RC)	.25
90	Tyler Johnson (RC)	.25
91	Jason Childers (RC)	.50
92	Wes Littleton (RC)	.50
93	Ty Taubenheim RC	.50
94	Saul Rivera (RC)	.25
95	Reggie Willits (RC)	1.50
96	Carlos Quentin (RC)	.50
97	Macay McBride (RC)	.25
98	Brandon Fahey (RC)	.50
99	Sean Marshall (RC)	.25
100	Sean Tracey (RC)	.25
101	Brian Slocum (RC)	.25
102	Choo Freeman (RC)	.25
103	Brent Clevlen (RC)	.25
104	Josh Willingham (RC)	.25
105	Chris Resop (RC)	.25
106	Chris Sampson RC	1.50
107	James Loney (RC)	.50
107	James Loney/ 52 logo/SP (RC)	8.00
108	Matthew Kemp (RC)	.50
109	Jason Kubel (RC)	.25
110	Brian Bannister (RC)	4.00
111	Kevin Thompson (RC)	.25
112	Jeremy Brown (RC)	.25
113	Brian Sanches (RC)	.25
114	Nate McLouth (RC)	.25
115	Ben Johnson (RC)	.25
116	Jonathan Sanchez (RC)	.25
117	Mark Lowe (RC)	.25
118	Skip Schumaker (RC)	.25
119	Jason Hammel (RC)	.25
120	Drew Meyer (RC)	.25
121	Melvin Dorta RC	.50
122	Jeff Mathis (RC)	.25
123	Davis Romero (RC)	.25
124	Joey Devine (RC)	.50
125	Sendy Rleal RC	.25
126	Freddie Bynum (RC)	.25
127	Bryan Anderson (RC)	.25
128	Jeremy Sowers (RC)	.25
129	Ryan Shealy (RC)	.25
130	Reggie Abercrombie (RC)	.25

131	Matt Albers (RC)	.25
132	Lastings Milledge (RC)	.50
133	Robert Andino (RC)	.50
134	Chris Demaria RC	.50
135	Boof Bonser (RC)	.25
136	Alay Soler RC	.50
137	Wilbert Nieves (RC)	.25
138	Mike Rouse (RC)	.25
139	Carlos Ruiz (RC)	.25
140	Matt Capps (RC)	.25
141	Travis Ishikawa (RC)	.25
142	Josh Kinney RC	1.50
143	Josh Rupe (RC)	.25
144	Shaun Marcum (RC)	.25
145	Jason Bergmann (RC)	.25
146	Tommy Murphy (RC)	.25
147	Martin Prado (RC)	.25
148	Val Majewski (RC)	.25
149	Ian Kinsler (RC)	.25
150	Joe Winkelsas (RC)	.25
151	Agustin Montero (RC)	.25
152	Joe Inglett (RC)	1.00
153	Manuel Corpas RC	.50
154	Yusmeiro Petit (RC)	.25
155	Mark Woodyard (RC)	.25
156	Jeff Fulchino (RC)	.50
157	Stephen Andrade (RC)	.25
158	Tim Hamulack (RC)	.25
159	Colter Bean (RC)	.25
160	Anderson Hernandez (RC)	.25
161	Kevin Reese (RC)	.25
162	Jason Windsor (RC)	.25
163	Paul Maholm (RC)	.25
163	Paul Maholm/ 52 logo/SP (RC)	4.00
164	Jeremy Accardo RC	.50
165	Joel Guzman (RC)	.25
166	Erick Aybar (RC)	.25
167	Scott Thorman (RC)	.25
168	Adam Loewen (RC)	.25
169	Carlos Marmol (RC)	.25
170	Bill Bray (RC)	.25
171	Edward Mujica (RC)	.50
172	Jeremy Hermida (RC)	.50
173	Taylor Tankersley (RC)	.25
174	Bobby Keppel (RC)	.25
175	Chris Young (RC)	.50
176	Josh Rabe RC	2.00
177	T.J. Beam (RC)	.25
178	Shane Komine RC	1.00
178	Shane Komine/ 52 logo/SP RC	6.00
179	Scott Mathieson (RC)	.25
180	Josh Barfield (RC)	.25
181	Justin Knoedler (RC)	.25
182	Emiliano Fruto RC	.50
183	Adam Wainwright (RC)	.25
184	Nick Masset (RC)	.25
185	Ryan Roberts RC	.50
186	Brandon Watson (RC)	.25
187	Chris Bootcheck (RC)	.25
188	Daniel Ortmeier (RC)	.25
189	Kevin Barry (RC)	.25
190	Cory Morris RC	.50
191	Kason Gabbard (RC)	.25
192	Tom Mastny (RC)	.25
193	David Aardsma (RC)	.25
194	Anthony Reyes (RC)	.25
195	Mike Jacobs (RC)	.25
196	Conor Jackson (RC)	.25
197	Kenji Johjima RC	3.00
198	Jack Taschner (RC)	.25
199	Renyel Pinto (RC)	.25
200	Chad Santos (RC)	.25
201	Aaron Rakers (RC)	.25
202	Franklin Gutierrez (RC)	.25
203	Chris Coste RC	2.00
204	Chris Iannetta (RC)	.50
205	Michael Vento (RC)	.25
206	Ryan O'Malley RC	1.00
207	Jason Botts (RC)	.25
208	John Hattig Jr. (RC)	.25
209	Brandon Harper (RC)	.50
210	Ryan Theriot (RC)	1.00
211	Travis Hughes (RC)	.25
212	Paul Hoover (RC)	.25
213	Brayan Pena (RC)	.25
214	Craig Breslow (RC)	.75
215	Eude Brito (RC)	.25
216	Melky Cabrera (RC)	.25
216	Melky Cabrera/ 52 logo/SP (RC)	8.00
217	Jonathan Broxton (RC)	5.00
217	Jonathan Broxton/ 52 logo/SP (RC)	8.00
218	Bryan Corey (RC)	.25
219	Ron Flores RC	.50
220	Andrew Brown (RC)	.25
221	Jaime Bubela (RC)	.25
222	Jason Bulger (RC)	.25
223	Alberto Callaspo (RC)	.25
224	Jose Capellan (RC)	.25
225	Cole Hamels (RC)	.50

225	Cole Hamels/ 52 logo/SP (RC)	6.00
226	Bernie Castro (RC)	.25
227	Shin-Soo Choo (RC)	.25
228	Doug Clark (RC)	.25
229	Roy Corcoran RC	.50
230	Tim Corcoran RC	.75
231	Nelson Cruz (RC)	.25
232	Rajai Davis (RC)	.25
233	Chris Duncan (RC)	.25
233	Chris Duncan/ 52 logo/SP (RC)	5.00
234	Scott Dunn (RC)	.25
235	Mike Esposito (RC)	.25
236	Scott Feldman RC	.50
237	Luis Figueroa RC	.50
238	Bartolome Fortunato (RC)	.25
239	Alejandro Freire RC	.50
240	J.J. Furmaniak (RC)	.25
241	Nicholas Markakis (RC)	.50
242	Matt Garza (RC)	1.00
243	Justin Germano (RC)	.25
244	Alexis Gomez (RC)	.25
245	Tom Gorzelanny (RC)	.25
246	Dan Uggla (RC)	.25
247	Jeremy Guthrie (RC)	.25
248	Stephen Drew (RC)	1.00
249	Brendan Harris (RC)	.25
250	Jeff Harris RC	.50
251	Corey Hart (RC)	.25
252	Chris Heintz (RC)	.25
253	Prince Fielder (RC)	1.00
254	Francisco Liriano (RC)	.50
255	Jason Hirsh (RC)	.25
256	J.R. House (RC)	.25
257	Zach Jackson (RC)	.25
258	Charlton Jimerson (RC)	.25
259	Greg Jones (RC)	.25
260	Mitch Jones (RC)	.25
261	Ryan Jorgensen RC	.50
262	Logan Kensing (RC)	.25
263	John Koronka (RC)	.25
264	Anthony Lerew (RC)	.25
265	Anibal Sanchez (RC)	.25
266	Juan Mateo (RC)	.50
267	Paul McAnulty (RC)	.25
268	Dustin McGowan (RC)	.25
269	Marty McLeary (RC)	.25
270	Ryan Zimmerman (RC)	2.00
271	Dustin Nippert (RC)	.25
272	Eric O'Flaherty RC	.50
273	Ronny Paulino (RC)	.25
274	Tony Pena (RC)	.25
275	Hayden Penn (RC)	.25
276	Miguel Perez (RC)	5.00
277	Paul Phillips (RC)	5.00
278	Omar Quintanilla (RC)	5.00
279	Guillermo Quiroz (RC)	5.00
280	Darrell Rasner (RC)	5.00
281	Kenny Ray (RC)	5.00
282	Royce Ring (RC)	5.00
283	Brian Rogers (RC)	5.00
284	Ed Rogers (RC)	5.00
285	Danny Sandoval (RC)	10.00
286	Joe Saunders (RC)	5.00
287	Chris Schroder RC	5.00
288	Nate Smith (RC)	5.00
289	Travis Smith (RC)	5.00
290	Geovany Soto (RC)	5.00
291	Brian Sweeney (RC)	5.00
292	Jon Switzer (RC)	5.00
293	Joe Thurston (RC)	5.00
294	Jermaine Van Buren (RC)	5.00
295	Ryan Garko (RC)	5.00
296	Cla Meredith (RC)	5.00
297	Luke Scott (RC)	5.00
298	Andy Marte (RC)	5.00
299	Jered Weaver (RC)	10.00
300	Freddy Guzman (RC)	5.00
301	Jonathan Papelbon (RC)	10.00
302	John-Ford Griffin (RC)	5.00
303	Jon Lester RC	15.00
304	Shawn Hill (RC)	5.00
305	Brian Myrow RC	10.00
306	Anderson Garcia RC	8.00
307	Andre Ethier (RC)	10.00
308	Ben Hendrickson (RC)	5.00
309	Alejandro Machado (RC)	8.00
310	Justin Verlander (RC)	15.00
311	Mickey Mantle/Blue	40.00
311	Mickey Mantle/Black	20.00
311	Mickey Mantle/Green	20.00
311	Mickey Mantle/ Orange	20.00
311	Mickey Mantle/Red	20.00
311	Mickey Mantle/ Yellow	20.00
312	Steve Stemle RC	5.00

Chrome

JEFF KARSTENS

	NM/M
Common Player:	1.50
Production 1,952 Sets	
Refractor:	2-3X
Production 552 Sets	
Gold Refractor:	4-6X
Production 52 Sets	
1 Howie Kendrick	4.00
2 David Pauley	1.50
3 Chris Denorfia	1.50
4 Jordan Tata	2.00
5 Fernando Nieve	1.50
6 Craig Hansen	4.00
7 Mickey Mantle	25.00
8 James Shields	2.00
9 Francisco Rosario	1.50
10 Jeff Karstens	3.00
11 Buck Coats	2.00
12 Josh Wilson	1.50
13 Joel Zumaya	4.00
14 Tony Gwynn Jr.	4.00
15 Jonah Bayliss	1.50
16 John Gall	1.50
17 Mike O'Connor	2.00
18 Peter Moylan	1.50
19 Cody Ross	1.50
20 Hanley Ramirez	3.00
21 Hong-Chih Kuo	3.00
22 Yurendell DeCaster	1.50
23 Sean Green	1.50
24 Ty Taubenheim	1.50
25 Macay McBride	1.50
26 Brian Slocum	1.50
27 Chris Resop	2.00
28 Jason Kubel	1.50
29 Brian Sanches	1.50
30 Mark Lowe	1.50
31 Melvin Dorta	1.50
32 Sendy Rleal	1.50
33 Ryan Shealy	1.50
34 Robert Andino	1.50
35 Wilbert Nieves	1.50
36 Travis Ishikawa	1.50
37 Jason Bergmann	1.50
38 Ian Kinsler	3.00
39 Manuel Corpas	1.50
40 Stephen Andrade	1.50
41 Kevin Reese	1.50
42 Joel Guzman	1.50
43 Carlos Marmol	2.00
44 Taylor Tankersley	1.50
45 T.J. Beam	1.50
46 Justin Knoedler	1.50
47 Ryan Roberts	1.50
48 Kevin Barry	1.50
49 David Aardsma	1.50
50 Kenji Johjima	5.00
51 Aaron Rakers	1.50
52 Michael Vento	1.50
53 Brandon Harper	1.50
54 Brayan Pena	1.50
55 Jonathan Broxton	2.00
56 Jaime Bubela	1.50
57 Cole Hamels	6.00
58 Roy Corcoran	1.50
59 Chris Duncan	4.00
60 Luis Figueroa	1.50
61 Kendry Morales	3.00
62 Tom Gorzelanny	1.50
63 Brendan Harris	1.50
64 Anibal Sanchez	3.00
65 Zach Jackson	1.50
66 Ryan Jorgensen	1.50
67 Josh Johnson	2.00
68 Marty McLeary	2.00
69 Ronny Paulino	1.50
70 Tyler Johnson	1.50
2 Reggie Abercrombie	1.50
72 Nicholas Markakis	6.00
73 J.J. Furmaniak	2.00

74 Prince Fielder	5.00
75 Enrique Gonzalez	1.50
76 Angel Pagan	1.50
77 Rafael Perez	2.00
78 Eric Reed	1.50
79 Chris Booker	1.50
80 David Gassner	1.50
81 John Van Benschoten	1.50
82 Russell Martin	2.00
83 Santiago Ramirez	1.50
84 Phil Stockman	1.50
85 Jim Johnson	3.00
86 Jack Hannahan	1.50
87 Philip Barzilla	1.50
88 Chris Barnwell	1.50
89 Joshua Sharpless	1.50
90 Chris Roberson	2.00

Autograph

BRIAN ANDERSON

	NM/M
Common Auto.:	10.00
Red Ink:	2-3X
Production 52 Sets	
RA Reggie Abercrombie	10.00
MA Matt Albers	10.00
BA Brian Anderson	10.00
EA Erick Aybar	10.00
BPB Brian Bannister	10.00
TJB T.J. Bohn	10.00
BB Boof Bonser	25.00
WB Bill Bray	15.00
MC Melky Cabrera	30.00
MTC Matt Cain	35.00
FC Fabio Castro	10.00
BC Buck Coats	10.00
YD Yurendell DeCaster	10.00
SD Stephen Drew	35.00
KF Kevin Frandsen	10.00
EF Emiliano Fruto	10.00
MG Matt Garza	25.00
EG Enrique Gonzalez	10.00
FG Franklin Gutierrez	10.00
AG Angel Guzman	10.00
JG Joel Guzman	10.00
CI Chris Iannetta	15.00
CHJ Chuck James	15.00
JWK Jeff Karstens	25.00
MK Matthew Kemp	20.00
HK Howie Kendrick	30.00
JK Josh Kinney	10.00
HCK Hong-Chih Kuo	40.00
AL Anthony Lerew	10.00
CM Chris Mabeus	10.00
TM Tom Mastny	15.00
SM Scott Mathieson	10.00
JM Jeff Mathis	10.00
KM Kendry Morales	15.00
EM Edward Mujica	10.00
MN Michael Napoli	15.00
RO Ryan O'Malley	15.00
AP Angel Pagan	10.00
JP Jonathan Papelbon	40.00
YP Yusmeiro Petit	15.00
AS Anibal Sanchez	15.00
JFS Joe Saunders	15.00
JS Joshua Sharpless	15.00
BS Brian Slocum	15.00
DU Dan Uggla	25.00
JVB John Van Benschoten	10.00
JV Justin Verlander	50.00
JW Jered Weaver	40.00
RZ Ryan Zimmerman	60.00
BZ Benjamin Zobrist	15.00
JZ Joel Zumaya	50.00

Debut Flashbacks

	NM/M
Common Player:	2.00
Chrome:	1.5-2X
Production 1,952 Sets	
Refractor:	2-3X

ALFONSO SORIANO

Production 552 Sets	
Gold Refractor:	4-6X
Production 52 Sets	
1 Dontrelle Willis	2.00
2 Carlos Beltran	3.00
3 Albert Pujols	8.00
4 Ichiro Suzuki	5.00
5 Mike Piazza	4.00
6 Nomar Garciaparra	3.00
7 Scott Rolen	3.00
8 Mariano Rivera	3.00
9 David Ortiz	4.00
10 Johnny Damon	4.00
11 Tom Glavine	3.00
12 David Wright	5.00
13 Greg Maddux	5.00
14 Manny Ramirez	4.00
15 Alex Rodriguez	6.00
16 Roger Clemens	6.00
17 Alfonso Soriano	3.00
18 Frank Thomas	3.00
19 Chipper Jones	4.00
20 Ivan Rodriguez	3.00

Dynamic Duos

DYNAMIC DUOS

ANDRE ETHIER   RUSSELL MARTIN

	NM/M
Common Duo:	1.00
Inserted 1:4	
1 Stephen Drew, Carlos Quentin	2.00
2 Jonathan Papelbon, Jon Lester	3.00
3 Joel Zumaya, Justin Verlander	4.00
4 Dan Uggla, Hanley Ramirez	1.50
5 Jonathan Broxton, Chad Billingsley	1.00
6 Francisco Liriano, Matt Garza	1.50
7 Lastings Milledge, John Maine	1.50
8 Chris Coste, Cole Hamels	2.00
9 Michael Napoli, Howie Kendrick	1.50
10 Joe Inglett, Andy Marte	1.00
11 Jeremy Hermida, Josh Willingham	1.00
12 Matthew Kemp, James Loney	1.50
13 Andre Ethier, Russell Martin	1.50
14 Melky Cabrera, Jeff Karstens	1.50
15 Ricky Nolasco, Scott Olsen, Josh Johnson, Anibal Sanchez	1.50

Ticket to Stardom Relics

No Pricing
Production 10 Sets

2007 Topps

	NM/M
Complete Set (661):	75.00
Common Player:	.10
Series 1 Hobby Pack (10):	3.00
Series 1 Hobby Box (36):	100.00
Series 1 Jumbo Pack (50):	15.00
Series 1 Jumbo Box (10):	140.00

Series 1 Rack Pack (22):	5.00
Series 1 Rack Box (24):	100.00
Series 2 Hobby Pack (10):	2.00
Series 2 Hobby Box (36):	60.00
Series 2 Jumbo Pack (50):	10.00
Series 2 Jumbo Box (10):	90.00
Series 2 Rack Pack (22):	4.00
Series 2 Rack Box (24):	85.00
Series 1 Variations:	No Pricing
Inserted 1:3700 Wal-Mart	
1 John Lackey	.10
2 Nick Swisher	.25
3 Brad Lidge	.10
4 Bengie Molina	.10
5 Bobby Abreu	.25
6 Edgar Renteria	.25
7 Mickey Mantle	5.00
8 Preston Wilson	.10
9 Ryan Dempster	.10
10 C.C. Sabathia	.10
11 Julio Lugo	.10
12 J.D. Drew	.25
13 Miguel Batista	.10
14 Eliezer Alfonzo	.10
15 Andrew Miller RC	3.00
15 Andrew Miller Posed RC	.10
16 Yuniesky Betancourt	.10
17 Saul Rivera	.10
18 Orlando Hernandez	.10
19 Alfredo Amezaga	.10
20 Delmon Young Face Right (RC)	.50
20 Delmon Young Face Left (RC)	.10
21 Javy Lopez	.10
22 Corey Patterson	.10
23 Josh Bard	.10
24 Tom Gordon	.10
25 Gary Matthews	.10
26 Jason Jennings	.10
27 Joey Gathright	.10
28 Brandon Inge	.10
29 Pat Neshek	.10
30 Bronson Arroyo	.10
31 Jay Payton	.10
32 Andy Pettitte	.25
33 Ervin Santana	.10
34 Paul Konerko	.25
35 Joel Zumaya	.25
36 Gregg Zaun	.10
37 Tony Gwynn	.50
38 Adam LaRoche	.10
39 Jim Edmonds	.25
40 Derek Jeter	15.00
41 Rich Hill	.25
42 Livan Hernandez	.10
43 Aubrey Huff	.10
44 Todd Greene	.10
45 Andre Ethier	.25
46 Jeremy Sowers	.10
47 Ben Broussard	.10
48 Darren Oliver	.10
49 Nook Logan	.10
50 Miguel Cabrera	.50
51 Carlos Lee	.25
52 Jose Castillo	.10
53 Mike Piazza	.75
54 Daniel Cabrera	.10
55 Cole Hamels	.40
56 Mark Loretta	.10
57 Brian Fuentes	.10
58 Todd Coffey	.10
59 Brent Clevlen	.10
60 John Smoltz	.25
61 Ross Gload	.10
62 Dan Wheeler	.10
63 Scott Proctor	.10
64 Bobby Kielty	.10
65 Dan Uggla	.25
66 Lyle Overbay	.10
67 Geoff Jenkins	.10
68 Michael Barrett	.10
69 Casey Fossum	.10
70 Ivan Rodriguez	.40
71 Jose Lopez	.10
72 Jake Westbrook	.10
73 Moises Alou	.25
74 Jose Valverde	.10
75 Jered Weaver	.25
76 Lastings Milledge	.25
77 Austin Kearns	.10
78 Adam Loewen	.10
79 Josh Barfield	.10

No.	Name	Val.	No.	Name	Val.	No.	Name	Val.	No.	Name	Val.
80	Johan Santana	.40	180	Roy Halladay	.25	282	Oswaldo Navarro RC	.50	381	Ronny Paulino	.10
81	Ian Kinsler	.10	181	Melvin Mora	.10	283	Drew Anderson (RC)	.25	382	Kevin Millwood	.10
82	Ian Snell	.10	182	Ramon Ortiz	.10	284	Jerry Owens (RC)	.25	383	Jon Lester	.10
83	Mike Lowell	.10	183	Jose Valentin	.10	285	Randy Johnson	.50	384	Alex Gonzalez	.10
84	Elizardo Ramirez	.10	184	Gil Meche	.10	286	Joaquin Arias (RC)	.25	385	Brad Hawpe	.10
85	Scott Rolen	.40	185	B.J. Upton	.25	287	Jose Garcia (RC)	.25	386	Placido Polanco	.10
86	Shannon Stewart	.10	186	Grady Sizemore	.40	288	Shane Youman RC	.50	387	Nate Robertson	.10
87	Alexis Gomez	.10	187	Matt Cain	.25	289	Brian Burres (RC)	.25	388	Torii Hunter	.25
88	Jimmy Gobble	.10	188	Eric Byrnes	.10	290	Matt Holliday	.25	389	Gavin Floyd	.10
89	Jamey Carroll	.10	189	Carl Crawford	.25	291	Ryan Feierabend (RC)	.25	390	Roy Oswalt	.40
90	Chipper Jones	.50	190	J.J. Putz	.10	292	Josh Fields (RC)	.25	391	Kelvim Escobar	.10
91	Carlos Silva	.10	191	Cla Meredith	.10	292	Josh Fields/ Running (RC)	.10	392	Craig Wilson	.10
92	Joe Crede	.25	192	Matt Capps	.10	293	Glen Perkins (RC)	.25	393	Milton Bradley	.10
93	Michael Napoli	.10	193	Rod Barajas	.10	294	Mike Rabelo RC	.50	394	Aaron Hill	.10
94	Willy Travis	.10	194	Edwin Encarnacion	.10	295	Jorge Posada	.25	395	Matt Diaz	.10
95	Rafael Furcal	.25	195	James Loney	.25	296	Ubaldo Jimenez (RC)	.25	396	Chris Capuano	.10
96	Phil Nevin	.10	196	Johnny Damon	.50	297	Brad Ausmus	.10	397	Juan Encarnacion	.10
97	David Bush	.10	197	Freddy Garcia	.10	298	Eric Chavez	.25	398	Jacque Jones	.10
98	Marcus Giles	.10	198	Mike Redmond	.10	299	Orlando Hudson	.10	399	James Shields	.10
99	Joe Blanton	.10	199	Ryan Shealy	.10	300	Vladimir Guerrero	.50	400	Ichiro Suzuki	.75
100	Dontrelle Willis	.25	200	Carlos Beltran	.40	301	Derek Jeter	1.00	401	Matthew Kemp	.10
101	Scott Kazmir	.25	201	Chuck James	.10	302	Scott Rolen	.25	402	Matt Morris	.10
102	Jeff Kent	.25	202	Mark Ellis	.10	303	Mark Grudzielanek	.10	403	Casey Blake	.10
103	Pedro Feliz	.10	203	Brad Ausmus	.10	304	Kenny Rogers	.10	404	Corey Hart	.10
104	Johnny Estrada	.10	204	Juan Rivera	.10	305	Frank Thomas	.50	405	Josh Willingham	.10
105	Travis Hafner	.25	205	Cory Sullivan	.10	306	Mike Cameron	.10	406	Ryan Madson	.10
106	Ryan Garko	.10	206	Ben Sheets	.25	307	Torii Hunter	.10	407	Nick Johnson	.10
107	Rafael Soriano	.10	207	Mark Mulder	.10	308	Albert Pujols	1.00	408	Kevin Millar	.10
108	Wes Helms	.10	208	Carlos Quentin	.10	309	Mark Teixeira	.25	409	Khalil Greene	.10
109	Billy Wagner	.10	209	Jonathan Broxton	.10	310	Jonathan Papelbon	.25	410	Tom Glavine	.25
110	Aaron Rowand	.10	210	Kazuo Matsui	.10	311	Greg Maddux	.50	411	Jason Bay	.25
111	Felipe Lopez	.10	211	Armando Benitez	.10	312	Carlos Beltran	.25	412	Gerald Laird	.10
112	Jeff Conine	.10	212	Richie Sexson	.40	313	Ichiro Suzuki	.75	413	Coco Crisp	.10
113	Nicholas Markakis	.25	213	Josh Johnson	.10	314	Andruw Jones	.25	414	Brandon Phillips	.25
114	John Koronka	.10	214	Brian Schneider	.10	315	Manny Ramirez	.50	415	Aaron Cook	.10
115	B.J. Ryan	.10	215	Craig Monroe	.10	316	Vernon Wells	.25	416	Mark Redman	.10
116	Tim Wakefield	.10	216	Chris Duffy	.10	317	Omar Vizquel	.10	417	Mike Maroth	.10
117	David Ross	.10	217	Chris Coste	.10	318	Ivan Rodriguez	.25	418	Boof Bonser	.10
118	Emil Brown	.10	218	Clay Hensley	.10	319	Brandon Webb	.25	419	Jorge Cantu	.10
119	Michael Cuddyer	.10	219	Chris Gomez	.10	320	Magglio Ordonez	.10	420	Jeff Weaver	.10
120	Jason Giambi	.40	220	Hideki Matsui	.75	321	Johan Santana	.25	421	Melky Cabrera	.25
121	Alex Cintron	.10	221	Robinson Tejeda	.10	322	Ryan Howard	1.00	422	Francisco Rodriguez	.10
122	Luke Scott	.10	222	Scott Hatteberg	.10	323	Justin Morneau	.25	423	Mike Lamb	.10
123	Chone Figgins	.10	223	Jeff Francis	.10	324	Hanley Ramirez	.40	424	Danny Haren	.25
124	Huston Street	.10	224	Matt Thornton	.10	325	Joe Mauer	.25	425	Tomokazu Ohka	.10
125	Carlos Delgado	.40	225	Robinson Cano	.40	326	Justin Verlander	.25	426	Jeff Francoeur	.25
126	Daryle Ward	.10	226	New York Yankees	1.00	327	Derek Jeter, Bobby Abreu	.50	427	Randy Wolf	.10
127	Chris Duncan	.10	227	Oakland A's	.25	328	Carlos Delgado, David Wright	.50	428	So Taguchi	.10
128	Damian Miller	.10	228	St. Louis Cardinals	.50	329	Yadier Molina, Albert Pujols	.50	429	Carlos Zambrano	.25
129	Aramis Ramirez	.25	229	Minnesota Twins	.25	330	Ryan Howard	.50	430	Justin Morneau	.50
130	Albert Pujols	1.50	230	Barry Zito	.25	331	Kelly Johnson	.10	431	Luis Gonzalez	.25
131	Chris Snyder	.10	231	Baltimore Orioles	.25	332	Chris Young	.25	432	Takashi Saito	.25
132	Ray Durham	.10	232	Seattle Mariners	.25	333	Mark Kotsay	.10	433	Brandon Morrow RC	.75
133	Franklin Gutierrez	.10	233	Houston Astros	.25	334	A.J. Burnett	.10	434	Victor Martinez	.25
134	Mike Jacobs	.10	234	Florida Marlins	.25	335	Brian McCann	.25	435	Felix Hernandez	.25
135	Troy Tulowitzki (RC)	.50	235	Reed Johnson	.10	336	Woody Williams	.10	436	Ricky Nolasco	.10
135	Troy Tulowitzki/ Throw (RC)	.10	236	Toronto Blue Jays	.25	337	Jason Isringhausen	.10	437	Paul LoDuca	.10
136	Jon Rauch	.10	237	Cincinnati Reds	.25	338	Juan Pierre	.10	438	Chad Cordero	.10
137	Jay Gibbons	.10	238	Philadelphia Phillies	.25	339	Jonny Gomes	.10	439	Miguel Tejada	.40
138	Adrian Gonzalez	.10	239	Anaheim Angels	.25	340	Roger Clemens	1.50	440	Mark Teixeira	.25
139	Randy Wolf	.10	240	Chris Carpenter	.25	341	Akinori Iwamura RC	1.50	441	Pat Burrell	.25
140	Freddy Sanchez	.10	241	Atlanta Braves	.25	342	Bengie Molina	.10	442	Paul Maholm	.10
141	Rich Aurilia	.10	242	Washington Nationals	.25	343	Shin-Soo Choo	.10	443	Mike Cameron	.10
142	Trot Nixon	.10	243	Joe Torre	.50	344	Kenji Johjima	.25	444	Josh Beckett	.25
143	Vicente Padilla	.10	244	Tampa Bay Devil Rays	.25	345	Joe Borowski	.10	445	Pablo Ozuna	.10
144	Jack Wilson	.10	245	Chad Tracey	.10	346	Shawn Green	.25	446	Jaret Wright	.10
145	Jake Peavy	.25	246	Mike Hargrove	.10	347	Chicago Cubs	.10	447	Angel Berroa	.10
146	Luke Hudson	.10	247	Mike Scioscia	.10	348	Rodrigo Lopez	.10	448	Fernando Rodney	.10
147	Javier Vazquez	.10	248	Ron Gardenhire	.10	349	Brian Giles	.25	449	Francisco Liriano	.25
148	Scott Podsednik	.10	249	Tony LaRussa	.10	350	Chase Utley	.50	450	Ken Griffey Jr.	1.00
149	Ivan Rodriguez, Magglio Ordonez	.25	250	Anibal Sanchez	.10	351	Mark DeRosa	.10	451	Bobby Jenks	.10
150	Todd Helton	.40	251	Charlie Manuel	.10	352	Carl Pavano	.10	452	Mike Mussina	.40
151	Kendry Morales	.10	252	John Gibbons	.10	353	Kyle Lohse	.10	453	Howie Kendrick	.25
152	Adam Everett	.10	253	Ken Macha	.10	354	Chris Iannetta	.25	454	Milwaukee Brewers	.10
153	Bob Wickman	.10	254	Jerry Narron	.10	355	Oliver Perez	.10	455	Dan Johnson	.10
154	Bill Hall	.25	255	Brad Penny	.10	356	Curtis Granderson	.25	456	Ted Lilly	.10
155	Jeremy Bonderman	.25	256	Bobby Cox	.10	357	Sean Casey	.10	457	Mike Hampton	.10
156	Ryan Theriot	.10	257	Bob Melvin	.10	358	Jason Tyner	.10	458	J.J. Hardy	.25
157	Rocco Baldelli	.25	258	Mike Hargrove	.10	359	Jon Garland	.10	459	Jeff Suppan	.10
158	Noah Lowry	.10	259	Phil Garner	.10	360	David Ortiz	.75	460	Jose Reyes	1.00
159	Jason Michaels	.10	260	David Wright	1.00	361	Adam Kennedy	.10	461	Jae Weong Seo	.10
160	Justin Verlander	.50	261	Vinny Rottino (RC)	.25	362	Chris Burke	.10	462	Edgar Gonzalez	.10
161	Eduardo Perez	.10	262	Ryan Braun (RC)	2.00	363	Bobby Crosby	.10	463	Russell Martin	.25
162	Chris Ray	.10	263	Kevin Kouzmanoff (RC)	.50	364	Conor Jackson	.10	464	Omar Vizquel	.10
163	Dave Roberts	.10	264	David Murphy (RC)	.25	365	Tim Hudson	.25	465	Jhonny Peralta	.25
164	Zachary Duke	.10	265	Jimmy Rollins	.25	366	Rickie Weeks	.25	466	Raul Ibanez	.10
165	Mark Buehrle	.10	266	Joe Maddon	.10	367	Cristian Guzman	.10	467	Hanley Ramirez	.50
166	Hank Blalock	.25	267	Grady Little	.10	368	Mark Prior	.25	468	Kerry Wood	.25
167	Royce Clayton	.10	268	Ryan Sweeney (RC)	.25	369	Benjamin Zobrist	.10	469	Ryan Church	.10
168	Mark Teahen	.10	269	Fred Lewis (RC)	.25	370	Troy Glaus	.25	470	Gary Sheffield	.40
169	Todd Jones	.10	270	Alfonso Soriano	.50	371	Kenny Lofton	.25	471	David Wells	.10
170	Chien-Ming Wang	.50	271	Delwyn Young (RC)	.25	372	Shane Victorino	.25	472	David Dellucci	.10
171	Nick Punto	.10	271	Delwyn Young Swing (RC)	.10	373	Cliff Lee	.10	473	Xavier Nady	.10
172	Morgan Ensberg	.10	272	Jeff Salazar (RC)	.25	374	Adrian Beltre	.25	474	Michael Young	.25
173	Robert Mackowiak	.10	273	Miguel Montero (RC)	.25	375	Miguel Olivo	.10	475	Kevin Youkilis	.40
174	Frank Catalanotto	.10	274	Shawn Riggans (RC)	.25	376	Endy Chavez	.10	476	Aaron Harang	.10
175	Matt Murton	.10	275	Greg Maddux	1.00	377	Zack Segovia (RC)	.25	477	Brian Lawrence	.10
176	Alfonso Soriano, Carlos Beltran	.40	276	Brian Stokes (RC)	.25	378	Ramon Hernandez	.10	478	Octavio Dotel	.10
177	Francisco Cordero	.10	277	Philip Humber (RC)	.25	379	Chris Young	.25	479	Chris Shelton	.10
178	Jason Marquis	.10	278	Scott Moore (RC)	.25	380	Jason Schmidt	.25	480	Matt Garza	.25
179	Joe Nathan	.10	279	Adam Lind (RC)	.25				481	Jim Thome	.40
			280	Curt Schilling	.50				482	Jose Contreras	.10
			281	Chris Narveson (RC)	.25				483	Kris Benson	.10
									484	John Maine	.25

485	Tadahito Iguchi	.10
486	Wandy Rodriguez	.10
487	Eric Chavez	.25
488	Vernon Wells	.25
489	Doug Davis	.10
490	Andruw Jones	.40
491	David Eckstein	.10
492	Michael Barrett	.10
493	Greg Norton	.10
494	Orlando Hudson	.10
495	Wilson Betemit	.10
496	Ryan Klesko	.10
497	Fausto Carmona	.10
498	Jarrod Washburn	.10
499	Aaron Boone	.10
500	Pedro Martinez	.50
501	Mike O'Connor	.10
502	Brian Roberts	.25
503	Jeff Cirillo	.10
504	Brett Myers	.25
505	Jose Bautista	.10
506	Akinori Otsuka	.10
507	Shea Hillenbrand	.10
508	Ryan Langerhans	.10
509	Josh Fogg	.10
510	Alex Rodriguez	1.50
511	Kenny Rogers	.10
512	Jason Kubel	.10
513	Jermaine Dye	.25
514	Mark Grudzielanek	.10
515	Josh Phelps	.10
516	Bartolo Colon	.25
517	Craig Biggio	.25
518	Esteban Loaiza	.10
519	Alex Rios	.25
520	Adam Dunn	.40
521	Derrick Turnbow	.10
522	Anthony Reyes	.10
523	Derrek Lee	.40
524	Ty Wigginton	.10
525	Jeremy Hermida	.10
526	Derek Lowe	.25
527	Randy Winn	.10
528	Paul Byrd	.10
529	Chris Snelling	.10
530	Brandon Webb	.25
531	Julio Franco	.10
532	Jose Vidro	.10
533	Erik Bedard	.25
534	Terrmel Sledge	.10
535	Jon Lieber	.10
536	Tom Gorzelanny	.10
537	Kip Wells	.10
538	Wily Mo Pena	.10
539	Eric Milton	.10
540	Chad Billingsley	.10
541	David DeJesus	.10
542	Omar Infante	.10
543	Rondell White	.10
544	Juan Uribe	.10
545	Miguel Cairo	.10
546	Orlando Cabrera	.25
547	Byung-Hyun Kim	.10
548	Jason Kendall	.10
549	Horacio Ramirez	.10
550	Trevor Hoffman	.25
551	Ronnie Belliard	.10
552	Chris Woodward	.10
553	Ramon Martinez	.10
554	Elizardo Ramirez	.10
555	Andy Marte	.10
556	John Patterson	.10
557	Scott Olsen	.10
558	Steve Trachsel	.10
559	Doug Mientkiewicz	.10
560	Randy Johnson	.50
561	Chan Ho Park	.10
562	Jamie Moyer	.10
563	Mike Gonzalez	.10
564	Nelson Cruz	.10
565	Alex Cora	.10
566	Ryan Freel	.10
567	Chris Stewart RC	.50
568	Carlos Guillen	.10
569	Jason Bartlett	.10
570	Mariano Rivera	.40
571	Norris Hopper	.10
572	Alex Escobar	.10
573	Gustavo Chacin	.10
574	Brandon McCarthy	.10
575	Seth McClung	.10
576	Yuniesky Betancourt	.10
577	Jason LaRue	.10
578	Dustin Pedroia	.25
579	Taylor Tankersley	.10
580	Garret Anderson	.10
581	Mike Sweeney	.10
582	Scott Thorman	.10
583	Joe Inglett	.10
584	Clint Barmes	.10
585	Willie Bloomquist	.10
586	Willy Aybar	.10
587	Brian Bannister	.10
588	Jose Guillen	.10

589	Brad Wilkerson	.10
590	Lance Berkman	.25
591	Toronto Blue Jays	.10
592	Florida Marlins	.10
593	Washington Nationals	.10
594	Los Angeles Angels	.10
595	Cleveland Indians	.10
596	Texas Rangers	.10
597	Detroit Tigers	.10
598	Arizona Diamondbacks	.10
599	Kansas City Royals	.10
600	Ryan Zimmerman	.40
601	Colorado Rockies	.10
602	Minnesota Twins	.10
603	Los Angeles Dodgers	.10
604	San Diego Padres	.10
605	Bruce Bochy	.10
606	Ron Washington	.10
607	Manny Acta	.10
608	Sam Perlozzo	.10
609	Terry Francona	.10
610	Jim Leyland	.10
611	Eric Wedge	.10
612	Ozzie Guillen	.10
613	Buddy Bell	.10
614	Bob Geren	.10
615	Lou Piniella	.10
616	Fredi Gonzalez	.10
617	Ned Yost	.10
618	Willie Randolph	.10
619	Bud Black	.10
620	Garrett Atkins	.10
621	Alexi Casilla RC	.25
622	Matt Chico (RC)	.25
623	Alejandro De Aza RC	.75
624	Jeremy Brown	.10
625	Josh Hamilton RC	.50
626	Doug Slaten RC	.50
627	Andy Cannizaro RC	.50
628	Juan Salas (RC)	.25
629	Levale Speigner RC	.50
630	Daisuke Matsuzaka RC	6.00
631	Elijah Dukes RC	1.00
632	Kevin Cameron RC	.50
633	Juan Perez RC	.50
634	Alex Gordon RC	4.00
635	Juan Lara RC	.50
636	Mike Rabelo RC	.50
637	Justin Hampson (RC)	.25
638	Cesar Jimenez RC	.50
639	Joe Smith RC	.50
640	Kei Igawa RC	1.00
641	Hideki Okajima RC	2.00
642	Sean Henn (RC)	.25
643	Jay Marshall RC	.50
644	Jared Burton RC	.50
645	Angel Sanchez RC	.50
646	Devern Hansack RC	1.00
647	Juan Morillo (RC)	.25
648	Hector Gimenez (RC)	.25
649	Brian Barden RC	.50
650	Alex Rodriguez, Jason Giambi	1.00
651	Jason Michaels, Travis Hafner	.25
652	J. Johnson, Miguel Olivo	.10
653	Sean Casey, Placido Polanco	.10
654	Ivan Rodriguez, Fernando Rodney	.25
655	Dan Uggla, H. Ramirez	.25
656	Carlos Beltran, Jose Reyes	.50
657	Alex Rodriguez, Derek Jeter	1.00
658	Aaron Rowand, Jimmy Rollins	.25
659	Angel Berroa, Andres Blanco	.10
660	Yadier Molina	.10
661	Barry Bonds	2.00

Copper

Copper: 25-50X
Production 56 Sets

Gold

Gold: 8-15X
Production 2,007 Sets

Platinum

No Pricing
Production One Set

1st Edition

1st Edition: 5-10X
Hobby Exclusive 1:36

Red Back

Red Back (1-330): 1-2.5X
Inserted 2:Hobby, 10:HTA

Printing Plates

Production one set per color.

All-Stars

		NM/M
Complete Set (12):		15.00
Common Player:		1.00
Inserted 1:Rack Pack		
1	Alfonso Soriano	2.00
2	Paul Konerko	1.50
3	Carlos Beltran	2.00
4	Troy Glaus	1.00
5	Jason Bay	1.50
6	Vladimir Guerrero	2.50
7	Chase Utley	3.00
8	Michael Young	1.00
9	David Wright	3.00
10	Gary Matthews	1.00
11	Brad Penny	1.00
12	Roy Halladay	1.00

All-Star Rookies

		NM/M
Complete Set (10):		12.00
Common Player:		1.50
Inserted 1:Rack Pack		
1	Prince Fielder	2.00
2	Dan Uggla	1.50
3	Ryan Zimmerman	2.00
4	Hanley Ramirez	2.00
5	Melky Cabrera	1.50
6	Andre Ethier	1.50
7	Nicholas Markakis	1.50
8	Justin Verlander	2.00
9	Francisco Liriano	2.00
10	Russell Martin	1.50

A-Rod Road to 500

	NM/M
Series 1 A-Rod (1-25):	3.00
Series 2 A-Rod (201-225):	3.00

A-Rod Road to 500 Autographs

Production One Set

Distinguished Service

		NM/M
Complete Set (20):		25.00
Common Player:		2.00
Inserted 1:12 Hobby, 1:12 HTA		
1	Duke Snider	3.00
2	Yogi Berra	3.00
3	Bob Feller	2.00
4	Bobby Doerr	2.00
5	Monte Irvin	2.00
6	Dwight D. Eisenhower	2.00
7	George Marshall	2.00
8	Franklin D. Roosevelt	2.00
9	Harry S. Truman	2.00
10	Douglas MacArthur	2.00
11	Ralph Kiner	2.00
12	Hank Sauer	2.00
13	Elmer Valo	2.00
14	Bob Lemon	2.00
15	Hoyt Wilhelm	2.00
16	James Doolittle	2.00
17	Curtis Lemay	2.00
18	Omar Bradley	2.00
19	Chester Nimitz	2.00
20	Mark Clark	2.00
21	Joe DiMaggio	4.00
22	Warren Spahn	3.00
23	Stan Musial	3.00
24	Red Schoendienst	2.00
25	Ted Williams	4.00
26	Winston Churchill	3.00
27	Charles de Gaulle	2.00
28	George Bush	2.00
29	John F. Kennedy	3.00
30	Richard Bong	2.00

Distinguished Service Autograph

		NM/M
Inserted 1:20,000 Hobby		
BD	Bobby Doerr	50.00
BF	Bob Feller	60.00
DS	Duke Snider	75.00
MI	Monte Irvin	50.00
RK	Ralph Kiner	75.00

Distinguished Service Cut Signatures

Production One Set

Generation Now

	NM/M
All Ryan Howard's:	2.00
All Chase Utley's:	1.00
All C. Ming Wang's:	3.00
All Mike Napoli's:	.50
All Justin Morneau's:	1.00
All David Wright's:	2.00
All Jered Weaver's:	1.00
All Andre Ethier's:	1.00
All Ryan Zimmerman's:	1.00
All Delmon Young's:	1.00
All Russell Martin's:	.75
All Justin Verlander's:	1.00
All Hanley Ramirez's:	1.00
All Nick Markakis's:	1.00
All Nick Swisher's:	.75

Generation Now Autographs

Production One Set

Highlights Autographs

		NM/M
Short prints are not serial #'d.		
JH	John Hattig Jr.	8.00
AM	Andrew Miller	10.00
AS	Anibal Sanchez	10.00
MN	Michael Napoli	10.00
JL	James Loney	20.00
MH	Matt Holliday	25.00
TT	Troy Tulowitzki	30.00
HR	Hanley Ramirez	20.00
JF	Josh Fields	15.00
CQ	Carlos Quentin	15.00
MG	Matt Garza	15.00
JM	John Maine	35.00
MP	Mike Piazza/450	120.00
TH	Travis Hafner	25.00
KM	Kevin Mench	10.00
CU	Chase Utley	50.00
DW	David Wright	75.00
JM	Justin Morneau	25.00
JS	Johan Santana/250	60.00
MC	Miguel Cabrera/250	35.00
DY	Delmon Young	30.00
DWW	Dontrelle Willis	20.00
CW	Chien-Ming Wang/100	250.00
JS	John Smoltz/250	50.00
AS	Alfonso Soriano/100	100.00
DO	David Ortiz/100	80.00
RH	Ryan Howard/100	100.00
AR	Alex Rodriguez/25	250.00
EF	Emiliano Fruto	10.00
RZ	Ryan Zimmerman	30.00
Series 2		
AB	Aaron Boone	10.00
AJ	Andruw Jones	35.00
AP	Albert Pujols	250.00
AR	Anthony Reyes	15.00
CG	Curtis Granderson	30.00
CW	Craig Wilson	15.00
DO	David Ortiz	80.00
DT	Derrick Turnbow	15.00
DU	Dan Uggla	20.00
DW	David Wright	50.00
DWW	Dontrelle Willis	20.00
EC	Endy Chavez	40.00
ES	Ervin Santana	15.00
JT	Jim Thome	40.00
JD	Johnny Damon	100.00
JG	Jon Garland	15.00
JV	Justin Verlander	50.00
JZ	Joel Zumaya	20.00

KE	Kelvim Escobar	20.00
KM	Kendry Morales	10.00
LM	Lastings Milledge	20.00
MC	Melky Cabrera	25.00
MTC	Matt Cain	20.00
PL	Paul LoDuca	40.00
RC	Robinson Cano	30.00
RH	Ryan Howard	100.00
RM	Russell Martin	20.00
RZ	Ryan Zimmerman	30.00
SC	Shawn Chacon	10.00
SP	Scott Podsednik	15.00
SR	Shawn Riggans	10.00
SSC	Shin-Soo Choo	20.00
ST	Steve Trachsel	25.00
TG	Tom Glavine	75.00
VG	Vladimir Guerrero	150.00

Highlights Relics

		NM/M
Common Player:		5.00
AP	Albert Pujols	25.00
AR	Alex Rodriguez	20.00
AS	Alfonso Soriano	15.00
BM	Brian McCann	15.00
CB	Carlos Beltran	10.00
CD	Carlos Delgado	8.00
CQ	Carlos Quentin	10.00
CB	Craig Biggio	10.00
CS	Curt Schilling	10.00
DO	David Ortiz	10.00
DW	Dontrelle Willis	8.00
ER	Edgar Renteria	5.00
FT	Frank Thomas	10.00
GS	Gary Sheffield	8.00
IS	Ichiro Suzuki	25.00
IR	Ivan Rodriguez	10.00
JB	Jason Bay	10.00
JPM	Joe Mauer	15.00
JAS	Johan Santana	20.00
JS	John Smoltz	10.00
JR	Jose Reyes	15.00
JM	Justin Morneau	15.00
MO	Magglio Ordonez	5.00
MAR	Manny Ramirez	10.00
MR	Mariano Rivera	15.00
MT	Miguel Tejada	8.00
PK	Paul Konerko	10.00
RC	Robinson Cano	15.00
RO	Roy Oswalt	8.00
RH	Ryan Howard	20.00
SK	Scott Kazmir	8.00
SR	Scott Rolen	10.00
TG	Tom Glavine	8.00
TG	Troy Glaus	5.00
VW	Vernon Wells	8.00
Series 2		
AB	Adrian Beltre	5.00
AER	Alex Rodriguez	20.00
AJ	Andruw Jones	8.00
ALR	Anthony Reyes	5.00
AP	Albert Pujols	25.00
AR	Aramis Ramirez	8.00
AS	Alfonso Soriano	10.00
CJ	Chipper Jones	10.00
DE	David Eckstein	20.00
DO	David Ortiz	15.00
DW	David Wright	15.00
DWW	Dontrelle Willis	8.00
GA	Garrett Atkins	5.00
GS	Grady Sizemore	10.00
JD	Jermaine Dye	5.00
JDD	Johnny Damon	15.00
JT	Jim Thome	10.00
JV	Justin Verlander	20.00
LB	Lance Berkman	8.00
MC	Matt Cain	8.00
MCT	Mark Teixeira	10.00
MEC	Melky Cabrera	10.00
MR	Manny Ramirez	10.00
MT	Miguel Tejada	8.00
NS	Nick Swisher	8.00
PK	Paul Konerko	8.00

PM	Pedro Martinez	8.00
RC	Robinson Cano	15.00
RH	Roy Halladay	10.00
RJH	Ryan Howard	20.00
SK	Scott Kazmir	8.00
TG	Tom Glavine	10.00
VG	Vladimir Guerrero	8.00
VW	Vernon Wells	8.00

Hit Parade

		NM/M
Inserted 1:9		
1	Barry Bonds	2.00
2	Ken Griffey Jr.	1.50
3	Frank Thomas	1.00
4	Jim Thome	.75
5	Manny Ramirez	1.00
6	Alex Rodriguez	2.00
7	Gary Sheffield	.75
8	Mike Piazza	1.00
9	Carlos Delgado	.75
10	Chipper Jones	1.00
11	Barry Bonds	2.00
12	Ken Griffey Jr.	1.50
13	Frank Thomas	1.00
14	Manny Ramirez	1.00
15	Gary Sheffield	.75
16	Jeff Kent	.50
17	Alex Rodriguez	2.00
18	Luis Gonzalez	.50
19	Jim Thome	.75
20	Mike Piazza	1.00
21	Craig Biggio	.50
22	Barry Bonds	2.00
23	Julio Franco	.50
24	Steve Finley	.50
25	Omar Vizquel	.50
26	Ken Griffey Jr.	1.50
27	Gary Sheffield	.75
28	Luis Gonzalez	.50
29	Ivan Rodriguez	.75
30	Bernie Williams	.50

Hobby Masters

		NM/M
Common Player:		.50
Inserted 1:6		
1	David Wright	3.00
2	Albert Pujols	4.00
3	David Ortiz	1.50
4	Ryan Howard	3.00
5	Alfonso Soriano	1.50
6	Delmon Young	1.50
7	Jered Weaver	1.50
8	Derek Jeter	4.00
9	Freddy Sanchez	.50
10	Alex Rodriguez	3.00
11	Johan Santana	1.50
12	Ichiro Suzuki	2.50
13	Andruw Jones	1.50
14	Vladimir Guerrero	1.50

15	Miguel Cabrera	1.50
16	Todd Helton	1.00
17	Manny Ramirez	1.50
18	Carlos Beltran	1.50
19	Justin Morneau	1.00
20	Francisco Liriano	1.00

Home Run Derby

		NM/M
Production 999 Sets		
DO	David Ortiz	4.00
RH	Ryan Howard	8.00
JD	Jermaine Dye	2.00
AP	Albert Pujols	10.00
TH	Travis Hafner	2.00
AS	Alfonso Soriano	4.00
JT	Jim Thome	3.00
LB	Lance Berkman	2.00
FT	Frank Thomas	4.00
CB	Carlos Beltran	4.00
TG	Troy Glaus	2.00
AJ	Andruw Jones	4.00
JG	Jason Giambi	3.00
AD	Adam Dunn	3.00
PK	Paul Konerko	2.00
CD	Carlos Delgado	3.00
MR	Manny Ramirez	4.00
AR	Aramis Ramirez	3.00
AER	Alex Rodriguez	10.00
JB	Jason Bay	2.00
NS	Nick Swisher	2.00
BH	Bill Hall	2.00
JM	Justin Morneau	4.00
MH	Matt Holliday	2.00
RS	Richie Sexson	2.00
AL	Adam LaRoche	2.00
VG	Vladimir Guerrero	4.00
CU	Chase Utley	4.00
RI	Raul Ibanez	2.00
GA	Garrett Atkins	2.00
MT	Mark Teixeira	4.00
PB	Pat Burrell	2.00
VW	Vernon Wells	2.00
PF	Prince Fielder	10.00
TKH	Torii Hunter	3.00
CL	Carlos Lee	2.00
CM	Craig Monroe	2.00
KG	Ken Griffey Jr.	10.00
JC	Joe Crede	2.00
DU	Dan Uggla	4.00
GS	Grady Sizemore	4.00
MC	Miguel Cabrera	4.00
MOT	Miguel Tejada	3.00
DW	David Wright	4.00
DY	Delmon Young	4.00
MMT	Marcus Thames	2.00
JDD	Johnny Damon	4.00
JF	Jeff Francoeur	3.00
AB	Adrian Beltre	2.00
MP	Mike Piazza	4.00

In The Name

Production One Set

Josh Gibson HR History

	NM/M
Common Gibson:	1.00
Inserted 1:9	

Mickey Mantle Home Run History

MICKEY MANTLE

	NM/M
Common Mantle HR History:	2.00
Inserted 1:9 Hobby	

Mickey Mantle Home Run History Relics

	NM/M
Common Mantle:	150.00
Production 7 Sets	

Opening Day

		NM/M
Inserted 1:12		
1	New York Mets, St. Louis Cardinals	2.00
2	Atlanta Braves, Philadelphia Phillies	1.00

3	Florida Marlins, Washington Nationals	1.00
4	Tampa Bay Devil Rays, New York Yankees	2.00
5	Toronto Blue Jays, Detroit Tigers	1.00
6	Cleveland Indians, Chicago White Sox	1.00
7	Los Angeles Dodgers, Milwaukee Brewers	1.00
8	Chicago Cubs, Cincinnati Reds	1.00
9	Arizona Diamondbacks, Colorado Rockies	1.00
10	Boston Red Sox, Kansas City Royals	2.00
11	Oakland Athletics, Seattle Mariners	1.00
12	Baltimore Orioles, Minnesota Twins	1.00
13	Pittsburgh Pirates, Houston Astros	1.00
14	Texas Rangers, Anaheim Angels	1.00
15	San Diego Padres, San Francisco Giants	1.00

Own The Game

CARLOS BELTRAN NEW YORK METS

		NM/M
Common Player:		.50
Inserted 1:6		
1	Ryan Howard	2.50
2	David Ortiz	1.00
3	Alfonso Soriano	1.00
4	Albert Pujols	3.00
5	Lance Berkman	.75
6	Jermaine Dye	.50
7	Travis Hafner	.75
8	Jim Thome	1.00
9	Carlos Beltran	1.00
10	Adam Dunn	.75
11	Ryan Howard	2.50
12	David Ortiz	1.00
13	Albert Pujols	3.00
14	Lance Berkman	.75
15	Justin Morneau	.75
16	Andruw Jones	1.00
17	Jermaine Dye	.50
18	Travis Hafner	.75
19	Alex Rodriguez	3.00
20	David Wright	2.00
21	Johan Santana	1.00
22	Chris Carpenter	.75
23	Brandon Webb	.50
24	Roy Oswalt	.75
25	Josh Johnson	.50

Ted Williams 406

	NM/M
Complete Set (18):	30.00
Common Williams:	2.50
Inserted 1:4 Target	

The Mickey Mantle Story

	NM/M
Complete Set (30):	40.00

Common Mantle: 3.00

The Streak

	NM/M
Common Joe DiMaggio (1-56):	1.50

Inserted 1:9

The Streak Before The Streak

	NM/M
Common Joe DiMaggio (1-61):	1.50

Inserted 1:9

Topps Stars

		NM/M
	Inserted 1:9	
1	Ryan Howard	1.50
2	Alfonso Soriano	1.00
3	Todd Helton	.75
4	Johan Santana	.75
5	David Wright	1.50
6	Albert Pujols	2.00
7	Daisuke Matsuzaka	3.00
8	Miguel Cabrera	1.00
9	David Ortiz	1.00
10	Alex Rodriguez	2.00
11	Vladimir Guerrero	1.00
12	Ichiro Suzuki	1.50
13	Derek Jeter	2.00
14	Lance Berkman	.50
15	Ryan Zimmerman	.50

Trading Places

		NM/M
	Inserted 1:9	
1	Jeff Weaver	.50
2	Frank Thomas	1.00
3	Mike Piazza	1.00
4	Alfonso Soriano	1.00
5	Freddy Garcia	.50
6	Jason Marquis	.50
7	Ted Lilly	.50
8	Mark Loretta	.50
9	Marcus Giles	.50
10	Barry Zito	.50
11	Andy Pettitte	.75
12	J.D. Drew	.50
13	Gary Matthews	.50
14	Jay Payton	.50
15	Aubrey Huff	.50
16	Brian Bannister	.50
17	Jeff Conine	.50
18	Gary Sheffield	.75
19	Shea Hillenbrand	.50
20	Wes Helms	.50
21	Frank Catalanotto	.50
22	Adam LaRoche	.50
23	Mike Gonzalez	.50
24	Greg Maddux	1.50
25	Jason Schmidt	.50

Trading Places Autographs

		NM/M
AL	Adam LaRoche	15.00
AS	Alfonso Soriano	
BB	Brian Bannister	20.00
FC	Frank Catalanotto	15.00
FG	Freddy Garcia	20.00
GS	Gary Sheffield	40.00
JS	Jason Schmidt	20.00
MG	Mike Gonzalez	10.00
SH	Shea Hillenbrand	15.00
WH	Wes Helms	15.00

Trading Places Relics

		NM/M
AP	Andy Pettitte	10.00
AS	Alfonso Soriano	10.00
BZ	Barry Zito	8.00
FT	Frank Thomas	10.00
GM	Greg Maddux	20.00
GS	Gary Sheffield	15.00
JW	Jeff Weaver	8.00
MG	Marcus Giles	5.00
ML	Mark Loretta	8.00
MP	Mike Piazza	20.00

Unlock the Mick

		NM/M
Complete Set (5):		
Common Mantle:		2.00
Inserted 1:18		

Wal-Mart

		NM/M
Complete Set (18):		40.00
Common Player:		1.50
3 per $9.99 Wal-Mart box.		
1	Frank Thomas	3.00
2	Mike Piazza	3.00
3	Ivan Rodriguez	2.00
4	David Ortiz	3.00
5	David Wright	4.00
6	Greg Maddux	4.00
7	Mickey Mantle	8.00
8	Jose Reyes	4.00
9	John Smoltz	1.50
10	Jim Edmonds	1.50
11	Ryan Howard	4.00
12	Miguel Cabrera	3.00
13	Carlos Delgado	2.00
14	Miguel Tejada	2.00
15	Ichiro Suzuki	4.00
16	Albert Pujols	5.00
17	Derek Jeter	5.00
18	Vladimir Guerrero	3.00

World Champion Relics

		NM/M
Production 100 Sets		
Cards are not serial #'d.		
1	Jeff Weaver	60.00
2	Chris Duncan	60.00
3	Chris Carpenter	75.00
4	Yadier Molina	40.00
5	Albert Pujols	160.00
6	Jim Edmonds	65.00
7	Ronnie Belliard	50.00
8	So Taguchi	80.00
9	Juan Encarnacion	50.00
10	Scott Rolen	75.00
11	Anthony Reyes	60.00
12	Preston Wilson	50.00
13	Jeff Suppan	60.00
14	Adam Wainwright	120.00
15	David Eckstein	100.00

1952 Mickey Mantle Reprint Relic

Production 52
52MM Mickey Mantle

1953 Mickey Mantle Reprint Relic

Production 53
53MM Mickey Mantle

2007 Topps Update

		NM/M
Complete Set (330):		40.00
Common player:		.10
Pack (10):		2.00
Box (36):		65.00
1	Tony Armas Jr.	.10
2	Shannon Stewart	.10
3	Jason Marquis	.10
4	Josh Wilson	.10
5	Steve Trachsel	.10
6	J.D. Drew	.25
7	Ronnie Belliard	.10
8	Trot Nixon	.10
9	Adam LaRoche	.25
10	Mark Loretta	.10
11	Matt Morris	.10
12	Marlon Anderson	.10
13	Jorge Julio	.10
14	Brady Clark	.10
15	David Wells	.10
16	Francisco Rosario	.10
17	Jason Ellison	.10
18	Adam Jones	.10
19	Russell Branyan	.10
20	Rob Bowen	.10
21	J.D. Durbin	.10
22	Jeff Salazar	.10
23	Tadahito Iguchi	.10
24	Brad Hennessey	.10
25	Mark Hendrickson	.10
26	Kameron Loe	.10
27	Yusmeiro Petit	.10
28	Olmedo Saenz	.10
29	Carlos Silva	.10
30	Kevin Frandsen	.10
31	Tony Pena	.10
32	Russ Ortiz	.10
33	Hong-Chih Kuo	.10
34	Paul McAnulty	.10
35	Hiram Bocachica	.10
36	Justin Germano	.10
37	Jason Simontacchi	.10
38	Jose Cruz	.10
39	Wilfredo Ledezma	.10
40	Chris Denorfia	.10
41	Ryan Langerhans	.10
42	Chris Snelling	.10
43	Ubaldo Jimenez	.10
44	Scott Spiezio	.10
45	Byung-Hyun Kim	.10
46	Brandon Lyon	.10
47	Scott Hairston	.10
48	Chad Durbin	.10
49	Sammy Sosa	.50
50	Jason Smith	.10
51	Zack Greinke	.10
52	Armando Benitez	.10
53	Randy Messenger	.10
54	Mark Teixeira	.50
55	Mike Maroth	.10
56	Jamie Burke	.10
57	Carlos Marmol	.10
58	David Weathers	.10
59	Ryan Doumit	.10
60	Michael Barrett	.10
61	Shawn Chacon	.10
62	Mike Fontenot	.10
63	Cesar Izturis	.10
64	Cliff Floyd	.10
65	Angel Pagan	.10
66	Aaron Miles	.10
67	Tony Graffanino	.10
68	Kevin Mench	.10
69	Claudio Vargas	.10
70	Jose Capellan	.10
71	A.J. Pierzynski	.10
72	Darin Erstad	.10
73	Boone Logan	.10
74	Luis Castillo	.10
75	Marcus Thames	.10
76	Neifi Perez	.10
77	Esteban German	.10
78	Tony Pena	.10
79	Adam Wainwright	.25
80	Reggie Sanders	.10
81	Kelly Shoppach	.10
82	Rafael Betancourt	.10
83	Tom Mastny	.10
84	Kyle Farnsworth	.10
85	Rick Ankiel	.25
86	Kevin Thompson	.10
87	Jeff Karstens	.10
88	Eric Hinske	.10
89	Doug Mirabelli	.10
90	Julian Tavarez	.10
91	Carlos Pena	.25
92	Brendan Harris	.10
93	Chris Sampson	.10
94	Al Reyes	.10
95	Dmitri Young	.10
96	Jason Bergmann	.10
97	Shawn Hill	.10
98	Greg Dobbs	.10
99	Carlos Ruiz	.10
100	Abraham Nunez	.10
100b	Jacoby Ellsbury (RC)	150.00
101	Jayson Werth	.10
102	Adam Eaton	.10
103	Antonio Alfonseca	.10
104	Jorge Sosa	.10
105	Ramon Castro	.10
106	Ruben Gotay	.10
107	Damion Easley	.10
108	David Newhan	.10
109	Jason Wood	.10
110	Reggie Abercrombie	.10
111	Kevin Gregg	.10
112	Henry Owens	.10
113	Willie Harris	.10
114	Peter Orr	.10
115	Casey Janssen	.10
116	Jason Frasor	.10
117	Jeremy Accardo	.10
118	John McDonald	.10
119	Matt Stairs	.10
120	Jason Phillips	.10
121	Justin Duchscherer	.10
122	Rich Harden	.10
123	Jack Cust	.10
124	Lenny DiNardo	.10
125	Joe Kennedy	.10
126	Chad Gaudin	.10
127	Marco Scutaro	.10
128	Brad Thompson	.10
129	Dustin Moseley	.10
130	Eric Gagne	.10
131	Marlon Byrd	.10
132	Scot Shields	.10
133	Victor Diaz	.10
134	Reggie Willits	.25
135	Jose Molina	.10
136	Ramon Vazquez	.10
137	Erick Aybar	.10
138	Sean Marshall	.10
139	Casey Kotchman	.25
140	Ryan Spilborghs	.10
141	Cameron Maybin RC	2.50
142	Jeremy Guthrie	.10
143	Jeff Baker	.10
144	Edwin Jackson	.10
145	Macay McBride	.10
146	Freddie Bynum	.10
147	Eric Patterson	.10
148	Dustin McGowan	.10
149	Homer Bailey (RC)	1.00
150	Ryan Braun (RC)	2.50
151	Tony Abreu RC	.50
152	Tyler Clippard (RC)	.50
153	Mark Reynolds (RC)	1.00
154	Jesse Litsch RC	.50
155	Carlos Gomez RC	2.00
156	Matt DeSalvo (RC)	.50
157	Andy LaRoche (RC)	1.00
158	Tim Lincecum RC	5.00
159	Jarrod Saltalamacchia (RC)	.50
160	Hunter Pence (RC)	2.00
161	Brandon Wood (RC)	.50
162	Phil Hughes (RC)	2.00
163	Rocky Cherry RC	.50
164	Chase Wright RC	.50
165	Dallas Braden RC	.50
166	Felix Pie (RC)	.50
167	Zach McClellan RC	.50
168	Rick Vanden Hurk RC	.50
169	Micah Owings (RC)	.50
170	Jon Coutlangus (RC)	.25
171	Andrew Sonnanstine RC	.25
172	Yunel Escobar (RC)	.25
173	Kevin Slowey (RC)	.50
174	Curtis Thigpen (RC)	.25
175	Masumi Kuwata RC	2.00
176	Kurt Suzuki (RC)	.50
177	Travis Buck (RC)	.25
178	Matt Lindstrom (RC)	.25
179	Jesus Flores RC	.50
180	Joakim Soria RC	.50
181	Nathan Haynes RC	.50
182	Matthew Brown RC	.50
183	Travis Metcalf RC	.50
184	Yovani Gallardo (RC)	1.00
185	Nate Schierholtz (RC)	.25
186	Kyle Kendrick RC	1.00

187	Kevin Melillo (RC)	.25
188	Ryan Rowland-Smith	.25
189	Lee Gronkiewicz RC	.50
190	Eulogio De La Cruz (RC)	.25
191	Brett Carroll RC	.50
192	Terry Evans RC	.50
193	Chase Headley (RC)	.25
194	Guillermo Rodriguez RC	.50
195	Marcus McBeth (RC)	.25
196	Brian Wolfe (RC)	.25
197	Troy Cate RC	.50
198	Mike Zagurski RC	.50
199	Yoel Hernandez	.25
200	Brad Salmon RC	.50
201	Alberto Arias RC	.50
202	Danny Putnam (RC)	.25
203	Jamie Vermilyea RC	.50
204	Kyle Lohse	.10
205	Sammy Sosa	.25
206	Tom Glavine	.25
207	Prince Fielder	.50
208	Mark Buehrle	.10
209	Troy Tulowitzki	1.00
210	Daisuke Matsuzaka RC	5.00
211	Randy Johnson	.50
212	Justin Verlander	.25
213	Trevor Hoffman	.10
214	Alex Rodriguez	1.00
215	Ivan Rodriguez	.25
216	David Ortiz	.50
217	Placido Polanco	.10
218	Derek Jeter	1.00
219	Alex Rodriguez	1.00
220	Vladimir Guerrero	.50
221	Magglio Ordonez	.25
222	Ichiro Suzuki	.75
223	Russell Martin	.25
224	Prince Fielder	.50
225	Chase Utley	.50
226	Jose Reyes	.50
227	David Wright	.50
228	Carlos Beltran	.25
229	Barry Bonds	1.00
230	Ken Griffey Jr.	.75
231	Torii Hunter	.25
232	Jonathan Papelbon	.25
233	J.J. Putz	.10
234	Francisco Rodriguez	.25
235	C.C. Sabathia	.25
236	Johan Santana	.50
237	Justin Verlander	.25
238	Francisco Cordero	.10
239	Mike Lowell	.25
240	Cole Hamels	.25
241	Trevor Hoffman	.10
242	Manny Ramirez	.50
243	Jake Peavy	.25
244	Brad Penny	.10
245	Takashi Saito	.10
246	Ben Sheets	.25
247	Hideki Okajima	.25
248	Roy Oswalt	.25
249	Billy Wagner	.10
250	Carl Crawford	.25
251	Chris Young	.10
252	Brian McCann	.10
253	Derrek Lee	.25
254	Albert Pujols	1.00
255	Dmitri Young	.10
256	Orlando Hudson	.10
257	J.J. Hardy	.25
258	Miguel Cabrera	.50
259	Freddy Sanchez	.10
260	Matt Holliday	.25
261	Carlos Lee	.25
262	Aaron Rowand	.10
263	Alfonso Soriano	.50
264	Victor Martinez	.25
265	Jorge Posada	.25
266	Justin Morneau	.25
267	Brian Roberts	.25
268	Carlos Guillen	.10
269	Grady Sizemore	.50
270	Josh Beckett	.25
271	Danny Haren	.10
272	Bobby Jenks	.10
273	John Lackey	.10
274	Gil Meche	.10
275	Mike Fontenot, Khalil Greene	.10
276	Alex Rodriguez, Russell Martin	.50
277	Troy Tulowitzki, Jose Reyes	.50
278	Jorge Posada, Derek Jeter, Alex Rodriguez	1.00
279	Chase Utley, Ichiro Suzuki	.50
280	Carl Crawford, Carlos Guillen	.10
281	Cole Hamels, Russell Martin	.25
282	Jonathan Papelbon, Jorge Posada	.25

283	Carl Crawford, Victor Martinez	.25
284	Alfonso Soriano, J.J. Hardy	.25
285	Justin Morneau	.25
286	Prince Fielder	.50
287	Alex Rios	.25
288	Vladimir Guerrero	.50
289	Albert Pujols	1.00
290	Ryan Howard	.75
291	Magglio Ordonez	.25
292	Matt Holliday	.25
293	Wilson Betemit	.10
294	Todd Wellemeyer	.10
295	Scott Baker	.10
296	Edgar Gonzalez	.10
297	J.P. Howell	.10
298	Shaun Marcum	.10
299	Edinson Volquez	.10
300	Kason Gabbard	.10
301	Bob Howry	.10
302	J.A. Happ	.10
303	Scott Feldman	.10
304	D'Angelo Jimenez	.10
305	Orlando Palmeiro	.10
306	Paul Bako	.10
307	Kyle Davies	.10
308	Gabe Gross	.10
309	John Wasdin	.10
310	Jon Knott	.10
311	Josh Phelps	.10
312	Joba Chamberlain RC	8.00
312	Joba Chamberlain Reverse Negative	200.00
313	Octavio Dotel	.10
314	Craig Monroe	.10
315	Edward Mujica	.10
316	Brandon Watson	.10
317	Chris Schroder	.10
318	Scott Proctor	.10
319	Ty Wigginton	.10
320	Troy Percival	.10
321	Scott Linebrink	.10
322	David Murphy	.10
323	Jorge Cantu	.10
324	Dan Wheeler	.10
325	Jason Kendall	.10
326	Milton Bradley	.10
327	Justin Upton RC	3.00
328	Kenny Lofton	.10
329	Roger Clemens	1.00
330	Brian Burres	.10
SQ1	Poley Walnuts	40.00

1st Edition

1st Edition:	5-10X
Hobby Exclusive 1:36	

Copper

Copper:	25-50X
Production 56 Sets	

Gold

Gold:	8-15X
Production 2,007 Sets	

Platinum

No Pricing
Production One Set

Red Back

Red Back (1-330):	1-2.5X
Inserted 2:Hobby, 10:HTA	

Printing Plates

Production one set per color.

All-Star Stitches

	NM/M
Common Player:	8.00
Inserted 1:45	
Patch:	No Pricing
Production 10 Sets	
AIR Alex Rios	10.00
AP Albert Pujols	25.00
AR Alex Rodriguez	25.00
ARR Aaron Rowand	10.00
BF Brian Fuentes	8.00
BJ Bobby Jenks	10.00
BM Brian McCann	15.00
BR Brian Roberts	8.00
BS Ben Sheets	10.00
BW Brandon Webb	15.00
CB Carlos Beltran	10.00
CC Carl Crawford	15.00
CH Cole Hamels	15.00
CL Carlos Lee	10.00
CS C.C. Sabathia	15.00
CU Chase Utley	15.00
CY Chris Young	8.00
DO David Ortiz	15.00
DW David Wright	25.00
DY Dmitri Young	8.00
FR Francisco Rodriguez	8.00

FC	Francisco Cordero	8.00
FS	Freddy Sanchez	10.00
GM	Gil Meche	8.00
GS	Grady Sizemore	15.00
HO	Hideki Okajima	20.00
IR	Ivan Rodriguez	10.00
IS	Ichiro Suzuki	30.00
JB	Josh Beckett	20.00
JEP	Jake Peavy	10.00
JH	J.J. Hardy	10.00
JL	John Lackey	10.00
JM	Justin Morneau	10.00
JP	J.J. Putz	8.00
JR	Jose Reyes	20.00
JRP	Jorge Posada	10.00
JRV	Jose Valverde	8.00
JS	Johan Santana	10.00
JV	Justin Verlander	10.00
MH	Matt Holliday	10.00
ML	Mike Lowell	10.00
MR	Manny Ramirez	15.00
OH	Orlando Hudson	8.00
PF	Prince Fielder	15.00
RH	Ryan Howard	20.00
RM	Russell Martin	15.00
RO	Roy Oswalt	10.00
TH	Torii Hunter	10.00
TS	Takashi Saito	15.00
TWH	Trevor Hoffman	8.00
VM	Victor Martinez	10.00

All-Star Dual Stitches

Production 25 Sets

All-Star Triple Stitches

Production 25 Sets

A-Rod Road to 500

	NM/M
A-Rod (376-400):	.50

A-Rod Road to 500 Autographs

Production One Set

Barry Bonds Home Run History

	NM/M
Common Bonds (735-756):	3.00
Inserted 1:12	

Barry Bonds Home Run King

	NM/M
Inserted 1:36	
HRK Barry Bonds	5.00

Barry Bonds Home Run King Relic

	NM/M
Production 756	
HRK Barry Bonds	50.00

Barry Bonds Home Run King Relic Autograph

Production 20

Chrome

		NM/M
Common Player:		5.00
Production 415 Sets		
1	Homer Bailey	10.00
2	Ryan Braun	25.00
3	Tony Abreu	5.00
4	Tyler Clippard	8.00
5	Mark Reynolds	10.00
6	Jesse Litsch	5.00
7	Carlos Gomez	15.00
8	Matt DeSalvo	5.00
9	Andy LaRoche	10.00
10	Tim Lincecum	20.00
11	Jarrod Saltalamacchia	15.00
12	Hunter Pence	20.00
13	Brandon Wood	10.00
14	Phil Hughes	15.00
15	Rocky Cherry	5.00
16	Chase Wright	5.00
17	Dallas Braden	5.00
18	Felix Pie	5.00
19	Zach McClellan	5.00
20	Rick Vanden Hurk	5.00
21	Micah Owings	8.00
22	Jon Coutlangus	5.00
23	Andrew Sonnanstine	5.00
24	Yunel Escobar	5.00
25	Kevin Slowey	10.00
26	Curtis Thigpen	5.00

27	Masumi Kuwata	15.00
28	Kurt Suzuki	5.00
29	Travis Buck	5.00
30	Matt Lindstrom	5.00
31	Jesus Flores	5.00
32	Joakim Soria	5.00
33	Nathan Haynes	5.00
34	Matthew Brown	5.00
35	Travis Metcalf	5.00
36	Yovani Gallardo	8.00
37	Nate Schierholtz	5.00
38	Kyle Kendrick	10.00
39	Kevin Melillo	5.00
40	Cameron Maybin	25.00
41	Lee Gronkiewicz	5.00
42	Eulogio De La Cruz	5.00
43	Brett Carroll	5.00
44	Terry Evans	5.00
45	Chase Headley	5.00
46	Guillermo Rodriguez	5.00
47	Marcus McBeth	5.00
48	Brian Wolfe	5.00
49	Troy Cate	5.00
50	Justin Upton	30.00
51	Joba Chamberlain	60.00
52	Brad Salmon	5.00
53	Alberto Arias	5.00
54	Danny Putnam	5.00
55	Jamie Vermilyea	5.00

Generation Now

	NM/M
All Ryan Zimmerman's:	1.00
All Justin Verlander's:	1.00
All Prince Fielder's:	2.00
All Ian Kinsler's:	1.00
All Kenji Johjima's:	1.00
All Jonathan Papelbon's:	1.00
All Jose Reyes':	2.00
All Curtis Granderson's:	1.00
All Josh Barfield's:	.50

Generation Now Autographs

Production One Set

Highlights Autographs

	NM/M
Some not priced due to scarcity.	
DW David Wright	75.00
RH Ryan Howard	60.00
AR Alex Rodriguez	200.00
JT Jim Thome	60.00
AP Albert Pujols	200.00
AJ Andruw Jones	30.00
AG Alex Gordon	35.00
GS Gary Sheffield	30.00
JS Jarrod Saltalamacchia	20.00
CJ Conor Jackson	15.00
RC Robinson Cano	30.00
PF Prince Fielder	40.00
AE Andre Ethier	15.00
JR Jimmy Rollins	40.00
AL Anthony Lerew	10.00
FC Francisco Cordero	15.00
BB Brian Bruney	20.00
AH Aaron Heilman	15.00
CS C.C. Sabathia	20.00
TT Troy Tulowitzki	25.00
RB Rod Barajas	10.00
RW Ron Washington	10.00
AC Asdrubal Cabrera	20.00
DE Damion Easley	15.00
MC Miguel Cairo	10.00

Mickey Mantle Home Run History

	NM/M
Common Mantle HR History:	2.00
Inserted 1:9 Hobby	

Mickey Mantle Home Run History Relics

	NM/M
Common Mantle:	125.00
Production 7 Sets	

Mickey Mantle Story

	NM/M
Complete Set (15):	30.00
Common Mantle:	3.00
Inserted 1:18	

Target

Common Mantle:	
Target Exclusive	

World Series Watch

	NM/M
Inserted 1:36	

1	New York Mets	1.00
2	Detroit Tigers	1.00
3	Boston Red Sox	5.00
4	Milwaukee Brewers	1.00
5	Cleveland Indians	1.00
6	Angels	1.00
7	San Diego Padres	1.00
8	Los Angeles Dodgers	1.00
9	Philadelphia Phillies	1.00
10	Chicago Cubs	1.00
11	St. Louis Cardinals	1.00
12	Arizona Diamondbacks	1.00
13	New York Yankees	1.00
14	Seattle Mariners	1.00
15	Atlanta Braves	1.00

1954 Mickey Mantle
Reprint Relic
Production 54
54MM Mickey Mantle

2007 Topps
Allen & Ginter

PRINCE FIELDER.
ALLEN & GINTER'S
BROOKLYN 2007 NEW YORK.

		NM/M
Complete Set (390):		
Common player:		.25
Mini Exclusives		
(351-390):		No Pricing
Inserted in Rip Cards		
Common SP:		2.00
Inserted 1:2		
Pack (8):		5.00
Box (24):		110.00
1	Ryan Howard	3.00
2	Mike Gonzalez	.25
3	Austin Kearns	.25
4	Josh Hamilton (RC)	.25
5	Stephen Drew/SP	2.00
6	Matt Murton	.25
7	Mickey Mantle	5.00
8	Howie Kendrick	.25
9	Alexander Graham Bell	.25
10	Jason Bay	.50
11	Hank Blalock	.50
12	Johan Santana	.75
13	Eleanor Roosevelt	.25
14	Kei Igawa	1.00
15	Jeff Francoeur	.50
16	Carl Crawford	.50
17	Jhonny Peralta	.25
18	Mariano Rivera	.50
19	Mario Andretti	.25
20	Vladimir Guerrero	.75
21	Adam Wainwright	.50
22	Huston Street	.25
23	Cael Sanderson	.25
24	Susan B. Anthony	.25
25	Jay Payton	.25
26	P.T. Barnum	.25
27	Scott Podsednik	.25
28	Willie Randolph	.25
29	Sean Casey	.25
30	Eiffel Tower	.25
31	Kenji Johjima	.25
32	Felix Hernandez	.50
33	Elijah Dukes RC	1.00
34	Mark Grudzielanek	.25
35	J.D. Drew	.25
36	Kevin Kouzmanoff (RC)	.50
37	Jonathan Papelbon	.50
38	Bobby Crosby	.25
39	Brooklyn Bridge	.25
40	Adam Dunn	.25
41	Lyle Overbay	.25
42	Brian Fuentes	.25
43	Scott Rolen/SP	3.00
44	Matt Lindstrom (RC)	.50
45	Carlos Zambrano	.50
46	Cole Hamels	.50
47	Matthew Kemp	.25
48	Gary Matthews/SP	2.00
49	J.J. Putz	.25

50	Albert Pujols	2.00
51	Danny Haren	.25
52	Aaron Harang	.25
53	Ferris Wheel	.25
54	Juan Rivera	.25
55	Ken Griffey Jr.	1.50
56	Chien-Ming Wang	1.00
57	Sean Henn (RC)	.50
58	Mike Mussina/SP	3.00
59	Ian Snell	.25
60	Josh Barfield	.25
61	Justin Morneau	.75
62	Dwight D. Eisenhower	.25
63	Bengie Molina/SP	2.00
64	Brett Myers	.25
65	Andy Marte	.25
66	Bill Hall	.25
67	Ryan Shealy	.25
68	Joe Scott	.25
69	Mike Rabelo RC	.50
70	Jermaine Dye	.50
71	Andre Ethier	.25
72	Bruce Lee	1.00
73	Nick Punto	.25
74	Ervin Santana	.25
75	Troy Tulowitzki (RC)	1.00
76	Garret Anderson	.25
77	Ryan Freel	.25
78	Carlos Guillen	.50
79	John Smoltz	.50
80	Chase Utley	.75
81	Mike Sweeney	.25
82	Joe Frazier	1.00
83	Brad Lidge	.25
84	Casey Blake	.25
85	Ivan Rodriguez	.50
86	Roy Oswalt	.50
87	Akinori Iwamura RC	2.00
88	Francisco Rodriguez	.25
89	John Lackey	.25
90	Miguel Cabrera	.75
91	Kevin Mench	.25
92	Victor Martinez	.50
93	Chad Tracy	.25
94	Charlie Manuel	.25
95	Hanley Ramirez	.50
96	Dontrelle Willis	.50
97	Doug Slaten RC	.25
98	Noah Lowry	.25
99	Shawn Green	.25
100	David Ortiz	1.00
101	Mark Reynolds RC	2.00
102	Preston Wilson	.25
103	Mohandas Gandhi	.25
104	Jeff Kent	.50
105	Lance Berkman	.50
106	C.C. Sabathia	.50
107	Jason Varitek/SP	3.00
108	Mark Twain	.25
109	Melvin Mora	.25
110	Michael Young/SP	2.00
111	Scott Hatteberg	.25
112	Erik Bedard	.50
113	Sitting Bull	.25
114	Homer Bailey (RC)	1.00
115	Mark Teahen	.25
116	Ryan Braun (RC)	3.00
117	John Miles	.25
118	Coco Crisp	.25
119	Hunter Pence/SP (RC)	6.00
120	Delmon Young (RC)	1.00
121	Aramis Ramirez	.50
122	Magglio Ordonez	.50
123	Tadahito Iguchi	.25
124	Mark Selby	.25
125	Gil Meche	.25
126	Curt Schilling	.75
127	Brandon Phillips	.25
128	Milton Bradley	.25
129	Craig Monroe	.25
130	Jason Schmidt/SP	2.00
131	Nick Markakis	.50
132	Paul Konerko	.50
133	Carlos Gomez RC	1.50
134	Garrett Atkins	.25
135	Jered Weaver	.50
136	Edgar Renteria	.50
137	Jason Isringhausen/SP	2.00
138	Ray Durham	.25
139	Bob Baffert	.25
140	Nick Swisher	.25
141	Brian McCann	.25
142	Orlando Hudson	.25
143	Brian Bannister	.25
144	Manny Acta	.25
145	Jose Vidro	.25
146	Carlos Quentin	.25
147	Billy Butler (RC)	1.00
148	Kenny Rogers	.25
149	Tom Gordon	.25
150	Derek Jeter	2.00
151	Bob Wickman	.25
152	Carlos Lee/SP	2.00

153	Willy Taveras	.25
154	Paul LoDuca	.25
155	Ben Sheets	.50
156	Brian Roberts	.50
157	Freddy Adu	.25
158	Jason Kendall	.25
159	Michael Barrett/SP	2.00
160	Frank Thomas	.75
161	Manny Ramirez	.75
162	Stanley Glenn	.25
163	Robinson Cano	.50
164	Phil Hughes (RC)	2.00
165	Joe Mauer	.50
166	Derrek Lee	.75
167	Jeff Weaver	.25
168	Joe Smith RC	.25
169	Louis Pasteur	.25
170	Gary Sheffield	.50
171	Luis Castillo	.25
172	Joe Torre	.50
173	Andy LaRoche (RC)	.50
174	Jamie Fischer	.25
175	Carlos Beltran	.50
176	Bronson Arroyo	.25
177	Rafael Furcal	.50
178	Juan Pierre SP	2.00
179	Matt Cain	.50
180	Alfonso Soriano	.75
181	Joe Borowski	.25
182	Conor Jackson	.25
183	Groundhog Day	.25
184	Pat Burrell	.25
185	Troy Glaus	.25
186	Joel Zumaya	.25
187	Russell Martin	.50
188	Josh Willingham	.25
189	Jarrod Saltalamacchia (RC)	.50
190	Scott Kazmir	.50
191	Jeremy Hermida	.25
192	Tower Bridge	.25
193	Rich Hill SP	2.00
194	Francisco Cordero/SP	2.00
195	Mike Piazza	1.00
196	Brad Ausmus	.25
197	Greg Louganis	.25
198	Frank Catalanotto	.25
199	Alejandro De Aza RC	1.00
200	David Wright	1.00
201	Freddy Sanchez	.25
202	Shea Hillenbrand	.25
203	Justin Verlander/SP	3.00
204	Alex Gordon RC	5.00
205	Jimmy Rollins	.50
206	Mike Napoli	.25
207	Chris Burke	.25
208	Chipper Jones	.75
209	Randy Johnson	.75
210	Daisuke Matsuzaka RC	5.00
211	Orlando Cabrera	.25
212	B.J. Upton	.50
213	Lou Piniella	.25
214	Mike Cameron	.25
215	Luis Gonzalez	.25
216	Rickie Weeks	.25
217	Hideki Okajima RC	2.00
218	Johnny Estrada	.25
219	Dan Uggla/SP	2.00
220	Ryan Zimmerman	.50
221	Tony Gwynn Jr.	.25
222	Rocco Baldelli/SP	2.00
223	Xavier Nady	.25
224	Josh Bard/SP	2.00
225	Raul Ibanez	.25
226	Chris Carpenter	.50
227	Matt DeSalvo (RC)	.50
228	Jack the Ripper	.25
229	Eric Chavez	.25
230	Jose Reyes	1.00
231	Glen Perkins (RC)	.50
232	Gregg Zaun	.25
233	Jim Thome	.75
234	Joe Crede	.25
235	Barry Zito	.50
236	Yoel Hernandez RC	1.00
237	Kelly Johnson	.25
238	Chris Young	.50
239	Fyodor Dostoevsky	.25
240	Miguel Tejada	.50
241	Doug Mientkiewicz	.25
242	Bobby Jenks	.25
243	Brad Hawpe/SP	2.00
244	Jay Marshall RC	.50
245	Brad Penny	.25
246	Johnny Damon	.75
247	Dave Roberts	.25
248	Ron Washington	.25
249	Mike Aponte	.25
250	Brandon Webb	.50
251	Andy Pettitte	.50
252	Bud Black	.25
253	Mike Cuddyer	.25
254	Chris Stewart RC	.50

255	Mark Teixeira	.75
256	Hideki Matsui	1.50
257	Curtis Granderson	.50
258	A.J. Pierzynski	.25
259	Tony LaRussa	.25
260	Andruw Jones	.75
261	Torii Hunter	.50
262	Mark Loretta	.25
263	Jim Edmonds/SP	2.00
264	Aaron Rowand	.25
265	Roy Halladay	.50
266	Freddy Garcia	.25
267	Reggie Sanders	.25
268	Washington Monument	.25
269	Franklin D. Roosevelt	.25
270	Alex Rodriguez	2.00
271	Wes Helms	.25
272	Mia Hamm	.50
273	Jorge Posada	.50
274	Tim Lincecum RC	5.00
275	Bobby Abreu	.50
276	Zachary Duke	.25
277	Carlos Delgado	.50
278	Julio Juarez	.25
279	Brandon Inge	.25
280	Todd Helton	.50
281	Marcus Giles	.25
282	Josh Johnson	.25
283	Chris Capuano	.25
284	B.J. Ryan	.25
285	Nick Johnson	.25
286	Khalil Greene	.25
287	Travis Hafner	.50
288	Ted Lilly	.25
289	Jim Leyland	.25
290	Prince Fielder	1.00
291	Trevor Hoffman	.25
292	Brian Giles	.25
293	Omar Vizquel	.25
294	Julio Lugo	.25
295	Jake Peavy	.50
296	Adrian Beltre	.25
297	Josh Beckett	.50
298	Harry S. Truman	.25
299	Mark Buehrle	.50
300	Ichiro Suzuki	1.50
301	Chris Duncan/SP	2.00
302	Augie Garrido/SP	2.00
303	Tyler Clippard/SP (RC)	2.00
304	Ramon Hernandez	.25
305	Jeremy Bonderman	.50
306	Morgan Ensberg/SP	2.00
307	J.J. Hardy/SP	2.00
308	Mark Zupan/SP	2.00
309	Laila Ali/SP	4.00
310	Greg Maddux/SP	4.00
311	David Ross	.25
312	Chris Duffy	.25
313	Moises Alou	.50
314	Yadier Molina	.25
315	Corey Patterson	.25
316	Dan O'Brien/SP	2.00
317	Michael Bourn/SP (RC)	2.00
318	Jonny Gomes/SP	2.00
319	Ken Jennings/SP	2.00
320	Barry Bonds/SP	5.00
321	Gary Hall Jr./SP	2.00
322	Kerri Walsh/SP	2.00
323	Craig Biggio	.50
324	Ian Kinsler	.25
325	Grady Sizemore/SP	3.00
326	Alex Rios/SP	3.00
327	Ted Toles/SP	2.00
328	Jason Jennings	.25
329	Vernon Wells	.50
330	Bob Geren/SP	2.00
331	Dennis Rodman/SP	2.00
332	Tom Glavine	.50
333	Pedro Martinez	.75
334	Gustavo Molina/SP RC	3.00
335	Bartolo Colon/SP	2.00
336	Misty May-Treanor/SP	2.00
337	Randy Winn	.25
338	Eric Byrnes	.50
339	Jason McElwain/SP	2.00
340	Placido Polanco/SP	2.00
341	Adrian Gonzalez	.50
342	Chad Coredo	.25
343	Jeff Francis	.25
344	Lastings Milledge	.25
345	Sammy Sosa/SP	3.00
346	Jacque Jones	.25
347	Anibal Sanchez	.25
348	Roger Clemens/SP	4.00
349	Jesse Litsch/SP RC	2.00
350	Adam LaRoche/SP	2.00

Mini

	NM/M
Mini:	2-3X
Mini (351-390):	No Pricing
#'s 351-390 Inserted in Rip Cards	
Allen & Ginter Back:	3-4X
Inserted 1:5	

Black Border: 4-6X
Inserted 1:10
No Number: 10-20X
Production 50 Sets
Bazooka Mini: No Pricing
Production 25 Sets
Wood: No Pricing
Production One Set

Printing Plates

Production one set per color.

Autographs

		NM/M

Short-prints are noted.
Red Ink: No pricing
Production 10 Sets

		NM/M
CS	Cael Sanderson/200	120.00
MS	Mark Selby/200	75.00
SJF	Joe Frazier/120	350.00
DR	Dennis Rodman/200	160.00
MZ	Mark Zupan/200	85.00
FA	Freddy Adu/200	125.00
BB	Bob Baffert/200	120.00
TT	Ted Toles/200	100.00
KJ	Ken Jennings/200	120.00
GH	Gary Hall Jr./200	80.00
DO	Dan O'Brien/200	75.00
JF	Jamie Fischer/200	80.00
GL	Greg Louganis/200	100.00
MA	Mike Aponte/200	60.00
JJ	Julio Juarez/200	60.00
KW	Kerri Walsh/200	100.00
LA	Laila Ali/200	200.00
TS	Tommie Smith/200	120.00
MGA	Mario Andretti/200	180.00
AG	Augie Garrido/200	100.00
JMC	Jason McElwain/200	100.00
SG	Stanley Glenn/200	125.00
JMM	John Miles/200	120.00
JBS	Joe Scott/200	120.00
MH	Mia Hamm/200	220.00
MMT	Misty May-Treanor/200	100.00
BC	Brian Cashman/100	250.00
AP	Albert Pujols/25	
CMW	Chien-Ming Wang/200	375.00
AI	Akinori Iwamura	50.00
RH	Ryan Howard/100	125.00
HR	Hanley Ramirez	50.00
HK	Howie Kendrick	25.00
AR	Alex Rodriguez/225	300.00
DW	David Wright/200	150.00
RM	Russell Martin	40.00
AE	Andre Ethier	40.00
JT	Jim Thome/100	80.00
JM	Justin Morneau	40.00
ES	Ervin Santana	20.00
BH	Bill Hall	30.00
CH	Cole Hamels	75.00
MEI	Maicer Izturis	20.00
CG	Curtis Granderson	50.00
AG2	Adrian Gonzalez	25.00
TT	Troy Tulowitzki	50.00
VW	Vernon Wells	30.00
JS	Johan Santana/100	150.00
JP	Jonathan Papelbon	50.00
MC	Miguel Cabrera/100	60.00
BPB	Brian Bannister	25.00
TH	Torii Hunter	30.00
RZ	Ryan Zimmerman	65.00
NM	Nicholas Markakis	50.00
JH	Jeremy Hermida	25.00
MN	Mike Napoli	25.00
NL	Nook Logan	20.00

Cut Signatures

Production One Set

Dick Perez Sketch Cards

		NM/M
Complete Set (30):		15.00
Common Player:		.50

Inserted 1:1
Dick Perez Originals: No Pricing
Production One Set

1	Brandon Webb	.50
2	Chipper Jones	1.00
3	Nick Markakis	.50
4	Daisuke Matsuzaka	2.00
5	Alfonso Soriano	1.00
6	Jermaine Dye	.50
7	Adam Dunn	.50
8	Grady Sizemore	1.00
9	Troy Tulowitzki	.50
10	Gary Sheffield	.75
11	Hanley Ramirez	.75
12	Carlos Lee	.50
13	Mark Teahen	.50
14	Gary Matthews	.50
15	Andre Ethier	.50
16	Prince Fielder	1.50
17	Joe Mauer	.75
18	Jose Reyes	1.00
19	Derek Jeter	2.00
20	Nick Swisher	.50
21	Ryan Howard	1.50
22	Freddy Sanchez	.50
23	Greg Maddux	1.50
24	Raul Ibanez	.50
25	Barry Zito	.50
26	Jim Edmonds	.50
27	Delmon Young	.50
28	Michael Young	.50
29	Roy Halladay	.50
30	Ryan Zimmerman	.75

Mini Flags

		NM/M
Common Card:		2.00
1	Angola	2.00
2	Argentina	2.00
3	Australia	2.00
4	Austria	2.00
5	Belgium	2.00
6	Brazil	2.00
7	Bulgaria	2.00
8	Canada	2.00
9	Chile	2.00
10	China	2.00
11	Colombia	2.00
12	Costa Rica	2.00

13	Denmark	2.00
14	Dominican Republic	2.00
15	Ecuador	2.00
16	Egypt	2.00
17	France	2.00
18	Germany	2.00
19	Greece	2.00
20	Greenland	2.00
21	Honduras	2.00
22	Iceland	2.00
23	India	2.00
24	Indonesia	2.00
25	Ireland	2.00
26	Israel	2.00
27	Italy	2.00
28	Ivory Coast	2.00
29	Jamaica	2.00
30	Japan	2.00
31	Kenya	2.00
32	Mexico	2.00
33	Morocco	2.00
34	Netherlands	2.00
35	Nigeria	2.00
36	Norway	2.00
37	Panama	2.00
38	Peru	2.00
39	Phillipines	2.00
40	Portugal	2.00
41	Puerto Rico	2.00
42	Russian Federation	2.00
43	Spain	2.00
44	Switzerland	2.00
45	Taiwan	2.00
46	Thailand	2.00
47	Turkey	2.00
48	United Arab Emirates	2.00
49	United Kingdom	2.00
50	United States	2.00

Mini Snakes

		NM/M
Common Mini Snake:		25.00
1	Arizona Coral Snake	25.00
2	Copperhead	25.00
3	Black Mamba	25.00
4	King Cobra	25.00
5	Cottonmouth	25.00
		25.00

Mini Emperors

		NM/M
Common Emperor:		5.00
1	Julius Caesar	5.00
2	Caesar Augustus	5.00
3	Tiberius	5.00
4	Caligula	5.00
5	Claudius	5.00
6	Nero	5.00
7	Titus	5.00
8	Hadrian	5.00
9	Marcus Aurelius	5.00
10	Septimus Severus	5.00

National Pride Box Loaders

		NM/M
Common Card:		5.00

Inserted 1:Box

1	Kei Igawa, Daisuke Matsuzaka, Hideki Matsui, Ichiro Suzuki	8.00
2	Hideki Okajima, Akinori Iwamura, Kenji Johjima, Tadahito Iguchi	6.00
3	Bobby Abreu, Miguel Cabrera, Felix Hernandez, Johan Santana	5.00
4	Shin-Soo Choo, Chan Ho Park, Byung-Hyun Kim, Jae-Kuk Ryu	5.00
5	Jason Bay, Russell Martin, Justin Morneau, Rich Harden	6.00
6	Hanley Ramirez, Manny Ramirez, Aramis Ramirez, Vladimir Guerrero	8.00
7	Jose Reyes, Pedro Martinez, David Ortiz, Albert Pujols	8.00
8	Carlos Beltran, Carlos Delgado, Ivan Rodriguez, Jorge Posada	6.00
9	Prince Fielder, Alex Rodriguez, Ryan Howard, David Wright	8.00

10	Brandon Webb, Justin Verlander, Greg Maddux, John Smoltz	5.00

N43 Box Loader

		NM/M
Common Player:		4.00

Inserted 1:Box

AR	Alex Rodriguez	8.00
RH	Ryan Howard	6.00
DW	David Wright	6.00
IS	Ichiro Suzuki	6.00
AP	Albert Pujols	8.00
DM	Daisuke Matsuzaka	10.00
VG	Vladimir Guerrero	4.00
BB	Barry Bonds	8.00
PF	Prince Fielder	6.00
RZ	Ryan Zimmerman	4.00
DJ	Ch Felicity's Diamond Jim	15.00
BL	Bruce Lee	10.00
MA	Mario Andretti	4.00
GL	Greg Louganis	4.00
JF	Joe Frazier	6.00

N43 Box Loader Autographs

Production 10 Sets

N43 Box Loader Relics

Production 25 Sets

Relics

		NM/M
Common Relic:		5.00
KJ	Ken Jennings/250	40.00
JF	Jamie Fischer/250	30.00
TS	Tommie Smith/250	50.00
KW	Kerri Walsh/250	60.00
LA	Laila Ali/250	50.00
JJ	Julio Juarez/250	25.00
MH	Mia Hamm/250	70.00
GW1	George Washington	
GW2	George Washington	
GW3	George Washington	
BL	Bruce Lee/250	300.00
DO	Dan O'Brien/250	20.00
SJF	Joe Frazier/250	50.00
GH	Gary Hall Jr./250	50.00
AL	Adam LaRoche	8.00
AP	Albert Pujols	30.00
AR	Aramis Ramirez	8.00
CB	Carlos Beltran	8.00
CC	Carl Crawford	8.00
CK	Casey Kotchman	5.00
EC	Eric Chavez	5.00
EG	Eric Gagne	8.00
HB	Hank Blalock	5.00
HR	Hanley Ramirez	8.00
JB	Jason Bay	5.00
JG	Jason Giambi	8.00
MC1	Miguel Cabrera	10.00
MC2	Miguel Cabrera	10.00
MG	Marcus Giles	5.00
MMU	Mark Mulder	5.00
MCM	Mike Mussina	8.00
MP	Mike Piazza	15.00
MR	Manny Ramirez	10.00
MT	Miguel Tejada	8.00
NS	Nick Swisher	5.00
PF	Prince Fielder	20.00
PK	Paul Konerko	8.00
RC	Robinson Cano	20.00
RH	Rich Harden	8.00
RW	Randy Winn	5.00
SD	Stephen Drew	8.00
SP	Scott Podsednik	8.00
SR1	Scott Rolen	8.00
SR2	Scott Rolen	8.00
TG	Troy Glaus	5.00

VG	Vladimir Guerrero	10.00
DAO	David Ortiz 250	20.00
AER	Alex Rodriguez/250	30.00
BB	Barry Bonds/250	35.00
MM	Mickey Mantle/250	150.00
BR	Brian Roberts	8.00
BZ	Barry Zito	5.00
CMS	Curt Schilling	10.00
DW	Dontrelle Willis	5.00
IR	Ivan Rodriguez	8.00
PL	Paul LoDuca	5.00
CLC	Coco Crisp	8.00
CP	Corey Patterson	5.00
CT	Chad Tracy	5.00
DL	Derrek Lee	8.00
RA	Rich Aurilia	5.00
SS	Sammy Sosa	10.00
TN	Trot Nixon	5.00
BC	Brian Cashman/250	35.00
AS	Arthur Shorin/50	150.00
KO	Keith Olbermann/100	150.00

Rip Cards

		NM/M
	Production 10-99	75.00
1	Grady Sizemore/90	125.00
2	Miguel Cabrera/99	125.00
3	Adam Dunn/99	100.00
4	Jose Reyes/99	150.00
5	Alfonso Soriano/90	125.00
6	Chase Utley/99	125.00
7	Frank Thomas/95	150.00
8	Andruw Jones/95	125.00
9	Nick Markakis/75	100.00
10	Felix Hernandez/99	125.00
11	Jered Weaver/99	125.00
12	Ivan Rodriguez/99	125.00
13	Joe Mauer/99	100.00
14	Derek Jeter/99	180.00
17	Miguel Tejada/95	100.00
18	Vladimir Guerrero/75	125.00
19	Greg Maddux/99	150.00
20	Michael Young/99	100.00
21	Barry Zito/99	100.00
22	Russell Martin/95	150.00
23	Daisuke Matsuzaka/99	180.00
24	Stephen Drew/95	100.00
25	Alex Rodriguez/99	150.00
26	J.D. Drew/99	100.00
27	Paul Konerko/99	100.00
28	Josh Hamilton/90	125.00
29	Mike Piazza/99	125.00
31	Carl Crawford/99	100.00
32	Adam LaRoche/99	100.00
33	Bill Hall/95	100.00
34	Scott Kazmir/95	100.00
35	Gary Matthews/99	100.00
36	Gary Sheffield/99	125.00
37	Francisco Rodriguez/95	100.00
38	Todd Helton/99	100.00
40	David Wright/99	150.00
42	Barry Bonds/99	180.00
43	Johan Santana/75	125.00
44	Albert Pujols/90	200.00
45	Carlos Lee/99	75.00
46	Cole Hamels/95	125.00
47	Prince Fielder/99	125.00
48	Hanley Ramirez/99	125.00
49	Ryan Zimmerman/90	125.00
50	Kei Igawa/75	100.00

2007 Topps Chrome

	NM/M
Complete Set (363):	
Common Player:	.25
Common RC Auto. (331-363):	10.00

	Pack (4):	3.00
	Box (24):	60.00
1	Nick Swisher	.50
2	Bobby Abreu	.50
3	Edgar Renteria	.50
4	Mickey Mantle	5.00
5	Preston Wilson	.25
6	C.C. Sabathia	.50
7	Julio Lugo	.25
8	J.D. Drew	.50
9	Jason Varitek	.50
10	Orlando Hernandez	.25
11	Corey Patterson	.25
12	Josh Bard	.25
13	Gary Matthews	.25
14	Jason Jennings	.25
15	Bronson Arroyo	.25
16	Andy Pettitte	.50
17	Ervin Santana	.50
18	Paul Konerko	.50
19	Adam LaRoche	.25
20	Jim Edmonds	.50
21	Derek Jeter	3.00
22	Aubrey Huff	.25
23	Andre Ethier	.25
24	Jeremy Sowers	.25
25	Miguel Cabrera	1.00
26	Carlos Lee	.50
27	Mike Piazza	1.00
28	Cole Hamels	.75
29	Mark Loretta	.25
30	John Smoltz	.50
31	Dan Uggla	.50
32	Lyle Overbay	.25
33	Michael Barrett	.25
34	Ivan Rodriguez	.75
35	Jake Westbrook	.25
36	Moises Alou	.50
37	Jered Weaver	.50
38	Lastings Milledge	.50
39	Austin Kearns	.25
40	Adam Loewen	.25
41	Josh Barfield	.25
42	Johan Santana	1.00
43	Ian Kinsler	.25
44	Mike Lowell	.50
45	Scott Rolen	.75
46	Chipper Jones	1.00
47	Joe Crede	.25
48	Rafael Furcal	.25
49	David Bush	.25
50	Marcus Giles	.25
51	Joe Blanton	.25
52	Dontrelle Willis	.25
53	Scott Kazmir	.50
54	Jeff Kent	.50
55	Travis Hafner	.50
56	Ryan Garko	.25
57	Nicholas Markakis	.50
58	Michael Cuddyer	.25
59	Jason Giambi	.75
60	Chone Figgins	.25
61	Carlos Delgado	.50
62	Aramis Ramirez	.50
63	Albert Pujols	3.00
64	Gary Sheffield	.75
65	Adrian Gonzalez	.50
66	Prince Fielder	1.50
67	Freddy Sanchez	.25
68	Jack Wilson	.25
69	Jake Peavy	.50
70	Javier Vazquez	.25
71	Todd Helton	.75
72	Bill Hall	.50
73	Jeremy Bonderman	.50
74	Rocco Baldelli	.25
75	Noah Lowry	.25
76	Justin Verlander	.75
77	Mark Buehrle	.50
78	Hank Blalock	.25
79	Mark Teahen	.25
80	Chien-Ming Wang	1.00
81	Roy Halladay	.50
82	Melvin Mora	.25
83	Grady Sizemore	.75
84	Matt Cain	.50
85	Carl Crawford	.50
86	Johnny Damon	.75
87	Freddy Garcia	.25
88	Ryan Shealy	.25
89	Carlos Beltran	.75
90	Chuck James	.25
91	Ben Sheets	.50
92	Mark Mulder	.25
93	Carlos Quentin	.50
94	Richie Sexson	.50
95	Brian Schneider	.25
96	Hideki Matsui	2.00
97	Robinson Tejada	.25
98	Scott Hatteberg	.25
99	Jeff Francis	.25
100	Robinson Cano	.50
101	Barry Zito	.50
102	Reed Johnson	.25
103	Chris Carpenter	.50
104	Chad Tracy	.25
105	Anibal Sanchez	.25
106	Brad Penny	.25
107	David Wright	2.00
108	Jimmy Rollins	.75
109	Alfonso Soriano	1.00
110	Greg Maddux	2.00
111	Curt Schilling	.75
112	Stephen Drew	.25
113	Matt Holliday	.50
114	Jorge Posada	.50
115	Vladimir Guerrero	1.00
116	Frank Thomas	.75
117	Jonathan Papelbon	.50
118	Manny Ramirez	1.00
119	Magglio Ordonez	.50
120	Joe Mauer	.50
121	Ryan Howard	2.00
122	Chris Young	.50
123	A.J. Burnett	.25
124	Brian McCann	.25
125	Juan Pierre	.25
126	Jonny Gomes	.25
127	Roger Clemens	2.50
128	Chad Billingsley	.25
129	Kenji Johjima	.25
130	Brian Giles	.25
131	Chase Utley	1.00
132	Carl Pavano	.25
133	Curtis Granderson	.50
134	Sean Casey	.25
135	Jon Garland	.25
136	David Ortiz	1.00
137	Bobby Crosby	.25
138	Conor Jackson	.25
139	Tim Hudson	.50
140	Rickie Weeks	.25
141	Mark Prior	.25
142	Benjamin Zobrist	.25
143	Troy Glaus	.50
144	Cliff Lee	.25
145	Adrian Beltre	.50
146	Endy Chavez	.25
147	Ramon Hernandez	.25
148	Chris Young	.50
149	Jason Schmidt	.25
150	Kevin Millwood	.25
151	Placido Polanco	.25
152	Torii Hunter	.50
153	Roy Oswalt	.50
154	Kelvim Escobar	.25
155	Milton Bradley	.25
156	Chris Capuano	.25
157	Juan Encarnacion	.25
158	Ichiro Suzuki	2.00
159	Matthew Kemp	.50
160	Matt Morris	.25
161	Casey Blake	.25
162	Josh Willingham	.25
163	Nick Johnson	.25
164	Khalil Greene	.25
165	Tom Glavine	.75
166	Jason Bay	.50
167	Brandon Phillips	.25
168	Jorge Cantu	.25
169	Jeff Weaver	.25
170	Melky Cabrera	.25
171	Danny Haren	.25
172	Jeff Francoeur	.50
173	Randy Wolf	.25
174	Carlos Zambrano	.50
175	Justin Morneau	.75
176	Takashi Saito	.25
177	Victor Martinez	.50
178	Felix Hernandez	.50
179	Paul LoDuca	.25
180	Miguel Tejada	.75
181	Mark Teixeira	.75
182	Pat Burrell	.25
183	Mike Cameron	.25
184	Josh Beckett	.50
185	Francisco Liriano	.50
186	Ken Griffey Jr.	2.00
187	Mike Mussina	.50
188	Howie Kendrick	.25
189	Ted Lilly	.25
190	Mike Hampton	.25
191	Jeff Suppan	.25
192	Jose Reyes	2.00
193	Russell Martin	.50
194	Jhonny Peralta	.50
195	Raul Ibanez	.25
196	Hanley Ramirez	1.00
197	Kerry Wood	.25
198	Gary Sheffield	.50
199	David Dellucci	.25
200	Xavier Nady	.25
201	Michael Young	.50
202	Kevin Youkilis	.50
203	Aaron Harang	.25
204	Mario Garza	.50
205	Jim Thome	.50
206	Jose Contreras	.25
207	Tadahito Iguchi	.25
208	Eric Chavez	.25
209	Vernon Wells	.50
210	Doug Davis	.25
211	Andruw Jones	.75
212	David Eckstein	.25
213	J.J. Hardy	.25
214	Orlando Hudson	.25
215	Pedro Martinez	1.00
216	Brian Roberts	.50
217	Brett Myers	.25
218	Alex Rodriguez	3.00
219	Kenny Rogers	.25
220	Jason Kubel	.25
221	Jermaine Dye	.25
222	Bartolo Colon	.25
223	Craig Biggio	.50
224	Alex Rios	.50
225	Adam Dunn	.75
226	Anthony Reyes	.25
227	Derrek Lee	.50
228	Jeremy Hermida	.25
229	Derek Lowe	.25
230	Randy Winn	.25
231	Brandon Webb	.50
232	Jose Vidro	.25
233	Erik Bedard	.50
234	Jon Lieber	.25
235	Wily Mo Pena	.25
236	Kelly Johnson	.25
237	David DeJesus	.25
238	Andy Marte	.25
239	Scott Olsen	.25
240	Randy Johnson	1.00
241	Nelson Cruz	.25
242	Carlos Guillen	.25
243	Brandon McCarthy	.25
244	Garret Anderson	.25
245	Mike Sweeney	.25
246	Brian Bannister	.25
247	Jose Guillen	.25
248	Brad Wilkerson	.25
249	Lance Berkman	.50
250	Ryan Zimmerman	.50
251	Garrett Atkins	.25
252	Johan Santana	1.00
253	Brandon Webb	.50
254	Justin Verlander	.75
255	Hanley Ramirez	1.00
256	Justin Morneau	.75
257	Ryan Howard	2.00
258	Eric Chavez	.25
259	Scott Rolen	.75
260	Derek Jeter	3.00
261	Omar Vizquel	.25
262	Mark Grudzielanek	.25
263	Orlando Hudson	.25
264	Mark Teixeira	.50
265	Albert Pujols	3.00
266	Ivan Rodriguez	.75
267	Brad Ausmus	.25
268	Torii Hunter	.50
269	Mike Cameron	.25
270	Ichiro Suzuki	2.00
271	Carlos Beltran	.75
272	Vernon Wells	.50
273	Andruw Jones	.50
274	Kenny Rogers	.25
275	Greg Maddux	2.00
276	Danny Putnam (RC)	1.00
277	Chase Wright RC	2.00
278	Zach McClellan RC	1.00
279	Jamie Vermilyea RC	1.00
280	Felix Pie (RC)	2.00
281	Phil Hughes (RC)	5.00
282	Jon Knott (RC)	1.00
283	Micah Owings (RC)	1.00
284	Devern Hansack RC	2.00
285	Andy Cannizaro RC	1.00
286	Lee Gardner (RC)	1.00
287	Josh Hamilton (RC)	1.00
288	Angel Sanchez/ Auto. RC	10.00
289	J.D. Durbin (RC)	1.00
290	Jamie Burke (RC)	1.00
291	Joseph Bisenius RC	1.00
292	Rick Vanden Hurk RC	2.00
293	Brian Barden RC	1.00
294	Levale Speigner RC	1.00
295	Kevin Cameron RC	1.00
296	Donald Kelly (RC)	1.00
297	Hideki Okajima (RC)	3.00
298	Andrew Miller RC	5.00
299	Delmon Young (RC)	1.00
300	Vinny Rottino (RC)	1.00
301	Philip Humber (RC)	1.00
302	Drew Anderson (RC)	1.00
303	Jerry Owens (RC)	1.00
304	Jose Garcia RC	1.00
305	Shane Youman RC	1.00
306	Ryan Feierabend (RC)	1.00
307	Mike Rabelo RC	1.00
308	Josh Fields (RC)	1.00
309	Jon Coutlangus (RC)	1.00

310	Travis Buck (RC)	1.00
311	Doug Slaten RC	1.00
312	Ryan Braun RC	1.00
313	Juan Salas (RC)	1.00
314	Matt Lindstrom (RC)	1.00
315	Cesar Jimenez RC	1.00
316	Jay Marshall RC	1.00
317	Jared Burton RC	1.00
318	Juan Perez RC	1.00
319	Elijah Dukes RC	2.00
320	Juan Lara RC	1.00
321	Justin Hampson (RC)	1.00
322	Kei Igawa RC	2.00
323	Zack Segovia (RC)	1.00
324	Alejandro De Aza RC	1.00
325	Brandon Morrow RC	2.00
326	Gustavo Molina RC	1.00
327	Joe Smith RC	1.00
328	Jesus Flores RC	2.00
329	Jeff Baker (RC)	1.00
330	Daisuke Matsuzaka RC	10.00
331	Troy Tulowitzki/Auto. (RC)	25.00
332	John Danks/Auto. RC	20.00
333	Kevin Kouzmanoff/Auto. (RC)	15.00
334	David Murphy/Auto. (RC)	15.00
335	Ryan Sweeney/Auto. (RC)	15.00
336	Fred Lewis/Auto. (RC)	15.00
337	Delwyn Young/Auto. (RC)	15.00
338	Matt Chico/Auto. (RC)	10.00
339	Miguel Montero/Auto. (RC)	10.00
340	Shawn Riggans/Auto. (RC)	10.00
341	Brian Stokes/Auto. (RC)	10.00
342	Scott Moore/Auto. (RC)	10.00
343	Adam Lind/Auto. (RC)	15.00
344	Chris Narveson/Auto. (RC)	10.00
345	Alex Gordon/Auto. RC	50.00
346	Joaquin Arias/Auto. (RC)	10.00
347	Brian Burres/Auto. (RC)	10.00
348	Glen Perkins/Auto. (RC)	10.00
349	Ubaldo Jimenez/Auto. (RC)	15.00
350	Chris Stewart/Auto. RC	10.00
351	Beltran Perez/Auto. (RC)	10.00
352	Dennis Sarfate/Auto. (RC)	10.00
353	Carlos Maldonado/Auto. (RC)	10.00
354	Mitch Maier/Auto. RC	10.00
355	Kory Casto/Auto. (RC)	10.00
356	Juan Morillo/Auto. (RC)	10.00
357	Hector Gimenez/Auto. (RC)	10.00
358	Alexi Casilla/Auto. RC	15.00
359	Michael Bourn/Auto. (RC)	15.00
360	Sean Henn/Auto. (RC)	10.00
361	Tim Gradoville/Auto. RC	10.00
362	Akinori Iwamura/Auto. RC	30.00
363	Oswaldo Navarro/Auto. (RC)	10.00

Refractor

Refractor (1-330):	2-3X
Ref. RC Auto. (288, 331-363):	1-1.5X
Auto. production 500	

Red Refractor

Red Ref. (1-330):	4-8X
Production 99	
Red Auto. (288, 331-363):	3-4X
Auto. Production 25	

White Refractor

White Ref. (1-330):	3-4X
Production 660	
White Auto. (288, 331-363):	1-1.5X
Auto. production 200	

Printing Plates

Production one set per color.

A-Rod Road to 500

	NM/M
Complete Set (226-250):	40.00
Common A-Rod:	2.00

A-Rod Road to 500 Autographs

	NM/M
Production One Set	40.00

Generation Now

	NM/M
Common Player:	.50
Refractor:	2-3X
Production 500 Sets	
White Refractor:	3-4X
Production 200 Sets	
Red Refractor:	3-5X
Production 99 Sets	
GN201	Ryan Howard	2.00
GN203	Ryan Howard	2.00
GN204	Ryan Howard	2.00
GN205	Ryan Howard	2.00
GN208	Ryan Howard	2.00
GN209	Chase Utley	2.00
GN210	Chien-Ming Wang	3.00
GN211	Mike Napoli	.50
GN213	Justin Morneau	2.00
GN214	Justin Morneau	2.00
GN215	Justin Morneau	2.00
GN216	Justin Morneau	2.00
GN217	Jered Weaver	1.00
GN218	Andre Ethier	1.00
GN219	Ryan Zimmerman	1.00
GN238	Ryan Zimmerman	1.00
GN264	Ryan Zimmerman	1.00
GN265	Delmon Young	1.00
GN269	Delmon Young	1.00
GN274	Delmon Young	1.00
GN278	Delmon Young	1.00
GN279	Russell Martin	1.00
GN280	Russell Martin	1.00
GN281	Russell Martin	1.00
GN282	Russell Martin	1.00
GN283	Justin Verlander	1.50
GN292	Justin Verlander	1.50
GN297	Justin Verlander	1.50
GN298	Justin Verlander	1.50
GN299	Hanley Ramirez	1.50
GN308	Hanley Ramirez	1.50
GN318	Hanley Ramirez	1.50
GN328	Hanley Ramirez	1.50
GN338	Hanley Ramirez	1.50
GN349	Hanley Ramirez	1.50
GN350	Nicholas Markakis	1.00
GN359	Nicholas Markakis	1.00
GN360	Nick Swisher	.50
GN364	Nick Swisher	.50
GN379	Nick Swisher	.50
GN394	Nick Swisher	.50

Mickey Mantle Home Run History

	NM/M
Common Mantle:	2.00
Refractor:	2-3X
Production 500 Sets	
White Refractor:	3-5X
Production 200 Sets	
Red Refractor:	4-8X
Production 99 Sets	

The Mickey Mantle Story

	NM/M
Complete Set (30):	50.00
Common Mantle:	2.00

Refractor:	2-3X
Production 500 Sets	
White Refractor:	3-4X
Production 200 Sets	
Red Refractor:	3-6X
Production 99 Sets	

2007 Topps Co-Signers

	NM/M
Complete Set (122):	
Common Player:	.25
Common RC Auto.:	10.00
Pack (6):	10.00
Box (12):	100.00
1	Ryan Howard	2.00
2	Jered Weaver	.50
3	Brian McCann	.25
4	Garrett Atkins	.25
5	Travis Hafner	.50
6	Jason Schmidt	.25
7	Curtis Granderson	.25
8	Ben Sheets	.50
9	Chien-Ming Wang	1.50
10	Francisco Liriano	.50
11	Freddy Sanchez	.25
12	Roy Oswalt	.75
13	Jim Edmonds	.50
14	Matt Cain	.50
15	Jake Peavy	.75
16	Ryan Zimmerman	.75
17	Troy Glaus	.50
18	Kenji Johjima	.50
19	Curt Schilling	1.00
20	Alfonso Soriano	1.00
21	Adam Dunn	.75
22	Hanley Ramirez	.75
23	Mark Teahen	.25
24	Todd Helton	.75
25	Alex Rodriguez	3.00
26	Mike Mussina	.75
27	Jason Bay	.50
28	Carl Crawford	.75
29	Vernon Wells	.50
30	Rich Harden	.25
31	Justin Morneau	1.00
32	Andre Ethier	.25
33	Ramon Hernandez	.25
34	Erik Bedard	.50
35	Vladimir Guerrero	1.00
36	Stephen Drew	.50
37	Felix Hernandez	.50
38	C.C. Sabathia	.50
39	Adrian Gonzalez	.50
40	Prince Fielder	1.00
41	Carlos Delgado	.75
42	Jimmy Rollins	.75
43	Raul Ibanez	.25
44	Jorge Cantu	.25
45	Michael Young	.50
46	Austin Kearns	.25
47	Ivan Rodriguez	.75
48	Chad Billingsley	.25
49	David Ortiz	1.00
50	David Wright	1.50
51	Justin Verlander	.75
52	Nicholas Markakis	.50
53	Miguel Cabrera	1.00
54	Lance Berkman	.50
55	Robinson Cano	.75
56	Jon Lieber	.25
57	Andruw Jones	.75
58	Danny Haren	.50
59	Grady Sizemore	.75
60	Gary Sheffield	.75
61	Paul LoDuca	.25
62	Cole Hamels	1.00
63	Richie Sexson	.50
64	David Eckstein	.25
65	Carlos Zambrano	.50
66	Scott Kazmir	.25
67	Anthony Reyes	.25
68	Mark Kotsay	.25
69	Miguel Tejada	.75
70	Pedro Martinez	1.00
71	Jack Wilson	.25
72	Joe Mauer	.75
73	Brian Giles	.25
74	Jonathan Papelbon	1.00
75	Albert Pujols	3.00
76	Nick Swisher	.25
77	Bill Hall	.50
78	Jose Contreras	.25
79	David DeJesus	.25
80	Bobby Abreu	.50
81	John Smoltz	.50
82	Chipper Jones	1.00
83	Mark Buehrle	.25
84	Josh Barfield	.25
85	Derrek Lee	.75
86	Jim Thome	.75
87	Kenny Rogers	.25
88	Jeremy Sowers	.25
89	Brandon Webb	.50
90	Roy Halladay	.50
91	Tadahito Iguchi	.25
92	Jeff Kent	.50
93	Johnny Damon	1.00
94	Daisuke Matsuzaka RC	5.00
95	Mark Teixeira	.75
96a	Delmon Young RC	2.00
96b	Delmon Young/Auto.	25.00
97a	Jeff Baker RC	1.00
97b	Jeff Baker/Auto.	10.00
98a	Michael Bourn (RC)	1.00
98b	Michael Bourn/Auto.	10.00
99a	Ubaldo Jimenez RC	1.00
99b	Ubaldo Jimenez/Auto.	10.00
100a	Andrew Miller (RC)	5.00
100b	Andrew Miller/Auto.	35.00
101	Angel Sanchez/Auto. (RC)	10.00
102	Troy Tulowitzki/Auto. (RC)	25.00
103	Joaquin Arias/Auto. RC	10.00
104	Beltran Perez/Auto. RC	10.00
105	Josh Fields/Auto. RC	10.00
106	Hector Gimenez/Auto. RC	10.00
107	Kevin Kouzmanoff/Auto. RC	15.00
108	Miguel Montero/Auto. RC	10.00
109	Philip Humber/Auto. RC	15.00
110	Jerry Owens/Auto. RC	15.00
111	Shawn Riggans/Auto. RC	10.00
112	Brian Stokes/Auto. RC	10.00
113	Scott Moore/Auto. RC	10.00
114	David Murphy/Auto. RC	10.00
115	Mitch Maier/Auto. RC	10.00
116	Adam Lind/Auto. RC	15.00
117	Adam Lind/Auto. RC	10.00
118	Dennis Sarfate/Auto. RC	10.00
119	Elijah Dukes/Auto. (RC)	15.00
120	Josh Hamilton/Auto. RC	20.00
121	Alex Gordon/Auto. RC	50.00
122	Barry Bonds	3.00

Bronze

Bronze Non-Auto.:	2-3X
Bronze RC Auto.:	1X
Production 250 Sets	

Blue

Blue Non-Auto.:	2-3X
Blue RC Auto.:	1X
Production 225 Sets	

Gold

Gold Non-Auto.:	2-3X
Gold RC Auto.:	1X
Production 200 Sets	

Red

Red Non-Auto.:	2-3X
Production 299 Sets	
Red RC Auto.:	1X
Production 275 Sets	

Silver-Red

Silver Red Non-Auto.:	2-3X
Silver Red RC Auto.:	1X
Production 175 Sets	

Silver-Bronze

Silver Bronze Non-Auto.:	2-4X
Silver Bronze RC Auto.:	1-1.5X
Production 150 Sets	

Silver-Blue

Silver Blue Non-Auto.:	2-4X
Silver Blue RC Auto.:	1-1.5X
Production 125 Sets	

Silver-Gold

Silver Gold Non-Auto.:	2-4X
Silver Gold RC Auto.:	1-1.5X
Production 100 Sets	

Hyper Silver-Red

Hyper Silver Red Non-Auto.:	2-4X
Hyper Silver Red RC Auto.:	1-1.5X
Production 75 Sets	

Hyper Silver-Bronze

Hyper Silver Bronze Non-Auto.:	3-4X
Hyper Silver Bronze Auto.:	1-2X
Production 50 Sets	

Hyper Silver Blue

No Pricing
Production 25 Sets

Hyper Silver Gold

No Pricing
Production 5 Sets

Hyper Plaid Silver

No Pricing
Production One Set

Printing Plates

No Pricing
Production one set per color.

A-Rod Road to 500

	NM/M
Common A-Rod:	3.00
2:Box	
Autograph:	No Pricing
Production One Set	

Cut Signatures Dual

Production One Set

Dual Autograph

		NM/M
Common Dual Auto.:		10.00
AH	Garrett Atkins, Matt Holliday	30.00
AI	Matt Albers, Chris Iannetta	10.00
AS	Matt Albers, Brian Slocum	10.00
BB	Brian Bannister, Floyd Bannister	20.00
BDE	Erik Bedard, Zachary Duke	20.00
BG	Jeremy Bonderman, Curtis Granderson	30.00
BS	Jeff Baker, Jeff Salazar	10.00
BV	Jeremy Bonderman, Justin Verlander	50.00
CC	Melky Cabrera, Robinson Cano	60.00
CJ	Chris Carpenter, Tyler Johnson	40.00
CK	Robinson Cano, Chuck Knoblauch	40.00
CM	Fabio Castro, Scott Mathieson	15.00
CW	Miguel Cabrera, Dontrelle Willis	30.00
CY	Alberto Callaspo, Chris Young	20.00
CZ	Alberto Callaspo, Benjamin Zobrist	15.00
GB	Garrett Atkins, Clint Barmes	15.00
GC	Curtis Granderson, Melky Cabrera	25.00
GM	Hector Gimenez, Miguel Montero	15.00
GS	Dwight Gooden, Darryl Strawberry	40.00
HH	Bill Hall, J.J. Hardy	30.00
HO	Ryan Howard, David Ortiz	100.00
IK	Chris Iannetta, Matthew Kemp	15.00
IM	Chris Iannetta, Miguel Montero	15.00
JJ	Andruw Jones, David Justice	50.00
JS	Ubaldo Jimenez, Dennis Sarfate	10.00
JY	Conor Jackson, Chris Young	25.00

KA	Howie Kendrick, Erick Aybar	25.00
KF	Kevin Kouzmanoff, Josh Fields	20.00
KG	Matthew Kemp, Franklin Gutierrez	15.00
KM	Josh Kinney, Tom Mastny	15.00
KMA	Jeff Karstens, Scott Mathieson	15.00
KZ	Austin Kearns, Ryan Zimmerman	25.00
LG	Adam LaRoche, Tom Gorzelanny	20.00
LK	Francisco Liriano, Jim Kaat	20.00
LL	Tony Larussa, Jim Leyland	50.00
LP	Francisco Liriano, Jonathan Papelbon	35.00
LV	Francisco Liriano, Justin Verlander	40.00
LY	Adam Lind, Delmon Young	20.00
MB	Nicholas Markakis, Brian Roberts	30.00
MC	Omar Minaya, Brian Cashman	60.00
MCA	Nicholas Markakis, Melky Cabrera	30.00
MG	Craig Monroe, Curtis Granderson	30.00
MH	John Maine, Philip Humber	30.00
MM	Lastings Milledge, John Maine	25.00
MMA	David Murphy, Mitch Maier	15.00
MP	Andrew Miller, Glen Perkins	30.00
MQ	Nicholas Markakis, Carlos Quentin	20.00
MS	Justin Morneau, Nick Swisher	30.00
MSL	Tom Mastny, Brian Slocum	10.00
MW	Lastings Milledge, David Wright	50.00
OB	Jerry Owens, Michael Bourn	15.00
PC	Angel Pagan, Buck Coats	15.00
PS	Yusmeiro Petit, Anibal Sanchez	15.00
PV	Jonathan Papelbon, Justin Verlander	50.00
SH	Jonathan Sanchez, Brad Hennessey	15.00
SM	Freddy Sanchez, Joe Mauer	30.00
SMA	Chris Stewart, Carlos Maldonado	15.00
SR	Brian Stokes, Shawn Riggans	15.00
VF	Justin Verlander, Mark Fidrych	50.00
VM	John Van Benschoten, Scott Mathieson	15.00
VP	Jason Varitek, Jorge Posada	80.00
WC	David Wright, Robinson Cano	80.00
WS	Dontrelle Willis, Anibal Sanchez	20.00
YL	Chris Young, Nook Logan	15.00
YU	Delmon Young, B.J. Upton	35.00
ZG	Benjamin Zobrist, Joel Guzman	15.00

Moon Shots Autographs

		NM/M
Common Auto.:		80.00
BA	Buzz Aldrin	200.00
WC	Walt Cunningham	80.00
WS	Wally Schirra	180.00
RC	Robert Crippen	80.00
CD	Charles Duke	80.00
AW	Alfred Worden	90.00
EM	Edgar Mitchell	80.00
FH	Fred Haise	100.00
RG	Richard Gordon	100.00
SC	Scott Carpenter	100.00

Moon Shots Autographs Dual

		NM/M
Common Dual Auto.:		100.00
AC	Garrett Atkins, Scott Carpenter	100.00

AD	Andre Dawson, Alfred Worden	140.00
DG	Jermaine Dye, Richard Gordon	100.00
HC	Ryan Howard, W. Cunningham	140.00
OS	David Ortiz, Wally Schirra	150.00
RA	Alex Rodriguez, Buzz Aldrin	375.00
SC	Alfonso Soriano, Robert Crippen	150.00
SH	Duke Snider, Fred Haise	160.00
WD	David Wright, Charles Duke	180.00
WM	Dave Winfield, Edgar Mitchell	125.00

Solo Sigs

		NM/M
Common Autograph:		10.00
AH	Aaron Hill	10.00
AL	Anthony Lerew	10.00
AS	Anibal Sanchez	10.00
BB	Boof Bonser	10.00
CB	Clint Barmes	10.00
CH	Cole Hamels	35.00
CJ	Chuck James	10.00
CQ	Carlos Quentin	15.00
DH	Dave Henderson	10.00
DU	Dan Uggla	15.00
ES	Ervin Santana	15.00
FL	Francisco Liriano	20.00
FS	Freddy Sanchez	15.00
GA	Garrett Atkins	10.00
HK	Howie Kendrick	20.00
HM	Hideki Matsui	250.00
HR	Hanley Ramirez	20.00
JM	Justin Morneau	30.00
JS	Jeremy Sowers	10.00
MC	Matt Cain	20.00
MH	Matt Holliday	35.00
NM	Nicholas Markakis	25.00
RC	Robinson Cano	30.00
RCE	Ronny Cedeno	10.00
RG	Ryan Garko	10.00
RH	Ryan Howard	60.00
RR	Rick Rhoden	10.00
VG	Vladimir Guerrero	50.00

Tri-Signers

		NM/M
Inserted 1:288		
ANS	Joaquin Arias, Oswaldo Navarro, Angel Sanchez	20.00
CPC	Melky Cabrera, Wily Mo Pena, Miguel Cabrera	40.00
HLC	Brad Hennessey, J. Sanchez, Matt Cain	40.00
JGK	Conor Jackson, Ryan Garko, Howie Kendrick	40.00
JHS	Chuck James, Cole Hamels, Jeremy Sowers	50.00
LNB	Francisco Liriano, Joe Nathan, Boof Bonser	50.00
MAR	Justin Morneau, Garrett Atkins, Brian Roberts	40.00
MLM	Justin Morneau, Francisco Liriano, Matt Garza	60.00
MLP	Justin Morneau, Francisco Liriano, Glen Perkins	50.00
MSG	Justin Morneau, Nick Swisher, Adrian Gonzalez	50.00
MYT	Andrew Miller, Delmon Young, Troy Tulowitzki	60.00
OPV	David Ortiz, Jonathan Papelbon, Jason Varitek	150.00
OWH	David Ortiz, David Wright, Ryan Howard	150.00
QJY	Carlos Quentin, Conor Jackson, Chris Young	40.00
RCC	Alex Rodriguez, Melky Cabrera, Robinson Cano	250.00
RWH	Alex Rodriguez, David Wright, Ryan Howard	250.00
SHH	Huston Street, Rich Harden, Danny Haren	50.00

TPW	Taylor Tankersley, Yusmeiro Petit, Dontrelle Willis	35.00
URW	Dan Uggla, Hanley Ramirez, Dontrelle Willis	50.00

Yankees Cut Signatures

Production One Set

2007 Topps Heritage

	NM/M
Complete Set (495):	325.00
Common Player:	.40
Common SP:	5.00
Inserted 1:2	
Common Variation:	5.00
Inserted 1:6	
Pack (8):	3.00
Box (24):	65.00
1 David Ortiz	1.50
2 Roger Clemens	15.00
3 David Wells	.40
4 Ronny Paulino/SP	5.00
5 Derek Jeter/SP	15.00
6 Felix Hernandez	2.00
7 Todd Helton	1.00
8 David Eckstein	5.00
9 Craig Wilson	.40
10 John Smoltz	.75
11 Robert Mackowiak	.40
12 Scott Hatteberg	.40
13 Wilfredo Ledezma/SP	5.00
13 Wilfredo Ledezma/Yellow Team Name/SP	5.00
14 Bobby Abreu/SP	8.00
15 Austin Kearns	.40
16 Wilson Betemit	.40
17 Darren Oliver	.40
18 Josh Beckett	.40
19 San Francisco Giants	.40
20 Robinson Cano	1.00
20 Robinson Cano/Yellow Team Name/SP	8.00
21 Matt Cain	1.00
22 Jason Kendall/SP	5.00
23 Mark Kotsay/SP	5.00
23 Mark Kotsay/Yellow Name/SP	5.00
24 Yadier Molina	.40
24 Yadier Molina/Yellow Name/SP	5.00
25 Brad Penny	.40
26 Adrian Gonzalez	.50
27 Danny Haren	.40
28 Brian Giles	.50
29 Jose Lopez	.40
30 Ichiro Suzuki	2.50
30 Ichiro Suzuki/Yellow Name/SP	10.00
31 Beltran Perez/SP (RC)	5.00
32 Brad Hawpe/SP	5.00
33 Jim Thome	1.50
33 Jim Thome/Yellow Team Name/SP	8.00
34 Mark DeRosa	.40
35 Woody Williams	.40
35 Woody Williams/Yellow Team Name/SP	5.00
36 Luis Gonzalez	.40
37 Billy Sadler (RC)	1.00
38 Dave Roberts	.40
39 Mitch Maier (RC)	1.00
40 Francisco Cordero/SP	5.00
41 Anthony Reyes/SP	8.00
42 Russell Martin	.40
43 Scott Proctor	.40
44 Washington Nationals	.40
45 Shane Victorino	.40
46 Joel Zumaya	1.00

Caption: Chase Utley — PHILADELPHIA PHILS. — 2nd B.

No.	Player	Price
46	Joel Zumaya/ Yellow Name/SP	5.00
47	Delmon Young (RC)	1.00
48	Alex Rios	.40
49	Willy Taveras/SP	5.00
50	Mark Buehrle/SP	5.00
50	Mark Buehrle/Yellow Team Name/SP	5.00
51	Livan Hernandez	.40
52	Jason Bay	1.00
52	Jason Bay/Yellow Team Name/SP	5.00
53	Jose Valentin	.40
53	Jose Valentin/Yellow Name/SP	5.00
54	Kevin Reese	.40
55	Felipe Lopez	.40
56	Ryan Sweeney (RC)	1.00
57	Kelvim Escobar	.40
57	Kelvim Escobar/ Yellow Name/SP	5.00
58	Nick Swisher/SP	5.00
58	Nick Swisher/Yellow Team Name/SP	8.00
59	Kevin Millwood/SP	5.00
60	Preston Wilson	.40
60	Preston Wilson/Yellow Name/SP	5.00
61	Mariano Rivera	.75
61	Mariano Rivera/Yellow Name/SP	8.00
62	Josh Barfield	.40
63	Ryan Freel	.40
64	Tim Hudson	.75
65	Chris Narveson (RC)	1.00
65	Chris Narveson/ Name/SP	5.00
66	Matt Murton	.40
67	Melvin Mora/SP	5.00
68	Jason Jennings/SP	5.00
69	Emil Brown	.40
70	Magglio Ordonez	.40
70	Magglio Ordonez/Yellow Name/SP	5.00
71	Los Angeles Dodgers	.40
72	Huston Street	.40
73	David Ross	.40
74	Juan Uribe	.40
75	Scott Podsednik	.40
76	Cole Hamels/SP	8.00
76	Cole Hamels/Yellow Team Name/SP	8.00
77	Rafael Furcal SP	5.00
77	Rafael Furcal/Yellow Team Name/SP	5.00
78	Ryan Theriot	.40
78	Ryan Theriot/ Yellow Name/SP	5.00
79	Corey Patterson	.40
79	Corey Patterson/Yellow Team Name/SP	5.00
80	Jered Weaver	.40
81	Stephen Drew	.75
81	Stephen Drew/Yellow Team Name/SP	8.00
82	Adam Kennedy	.40
83	Tony Gwynn Jr.	.40
84	Erik Bedard	.40
85	Omar Vizquel/SP	5.00
85	Omar Vizquel/Yellow Team Name/SP	5.00
86	Fred Lewis/SP (RC)	5.00
87	Brad Radke	.40
87	Shawn Chacon/Yellow Name/SP	5.00
88	Frank Catalanotto	.40
89	Orlando Hudson	.40
90	Pat Burrell	.40
91	David DeJesus	.40
92	David Wright	2.50
92	David Wright/Yellow Name/SP	10.00
93	Conor Jackson	.40
94	Xavier Nady/SP	5.00
95	Bill Hall/SP	8.00
96	Andre Ethier	.75
97	Jeff Suppan	.40
97	Jeff Suppan/Yellow Name/SP	5.00
98	Ryan Zimmerman	.75
98	Ryan Zimmerman/Yellow Name/SP	8.00
99	Yuniesky Betancourt	.40
100	Jose Contreras	.40
100	Jose Contreras/Yellow Team Name/SP	5.00
101	Miguel Cairo	.40
101	Miguel Cairo/Yellow Name/SP	5.00
102	Brian Roberts	.40
103	Carl Crawford/SP	8.00
104	Mike Lamb/SP	5.00
105	Mark Ellis	.40
106	Scott Rolen	1.50
107	Garrett Atkins	.40
108	Hanley Ramirez	.75
108	Hanley Ramirez/Yellow Team Name/SP	8.00
109	Trot Nixon	.40
110	Edgar Renteria	.40
111	Jeff Francis	.40
112	Marcus Thames/SP	5.00
113	Brian Burres/SP (RC)	5.00
114	Brian Schneider	.40
115	Jeremy Bonderman	.75
116	Ryan Madson	.40
117	Gerald Laird	.40
118	Roy Halladay	.75
119	Victor Martinez	.40
120	Greg Maddux	2.50
121	Jay Payton/SP	5.00
122	Jacque Jones/SP	5.00
123	Juan Lara RC	1.00
124	Derrick Turnbow	.40
125	Adam Everett	.40
126	Michael Cuddyer	.40
127	Gil Meche	.40
128	Willy Aybar	.40
129	Jerry Owens RC	1.00
130	Manny Ramirez/SP	10.00
131	Howie Kendrick/SP	8.00
132	Byung-Hyun Kim	.40
133	Kevin Kouzmanoff (RC)	1.00
134	Philadelphia Phillies	.40
135	Joe Blanton	.40
136	Ray Durham	.40
137	Luke Hudson	.40
138	Eric Byrnes	.40
139	Ryan Braun/SP (RC)	8.00
140	Johnny Damon/SP	10.00
141	Ambiorix Burgos	.40
142	Hideki Matsui	.40
143	Josh Johnson	.40
144	Miguel Cabrera	.40
146	Delwyn Young (RC)	1.00
147	Chuck James	.40
148	Morgan Ensberg	.40
149	Jose Vidro/SP	5.00
150	Alex Rodriguez/SP	15.00
151	Carlos Maldonado (RC)	1.00
152	Jason Schmidt	.40
153	Alex Escobar	.40
154	Chris Gomez	.40
155	Endy Chavez	.40
156	Kris Benson	.40
157	Bronson Arroyo	.40
158	Cleveland Indians/SP	8.00
159	Chris Ray SP	5.00
160	Richie Sexson	.40
161	Huston Street	.40
162	Kevin Youkilis	.40
163	Armando Benitez	.40
164	Vinny Rottino (RC)	1.00
165	Garret Anderson	.40
166	Todd Greene	.40
167	Brian Stokes/SP (RC)	5.00
168	Albert Pujols/SP	15.00
169	Todd Coffey	.40
170	Jason Michaels	.40
171	David Dellucci	.40
172	Eric Milton	.40
173	Austin Kearns	.40
174	Kansas City Royals	.40
175	Andy Cannizaro RC	2.00
176	David Weathers/SP	5.00
177	Jermaine Dye/SP	5.00
178	Wily Mo Pena	.40
179	Chris Burke	.40
180	Jeff Weaver	.40
181	Juan Encarnacion	.40
182	Jeremy Hermida	.40
183	Tim Wakefield	.40
184	Rich Hill	.50
185	Aaron Hill/SP	5.00
186	Scot Shields/SP	5.00
187	Randy Johnson	.40
188	Dan Johnson	.40
189	Sean Marshall	.40
190	Marcus Giles	.40
191	Jonathan Broxton	.40
192	Mike Piazza	.40
193	Carlos Quentin	.40
194	Derek Lowe/SP	5.00
195	Russell Branyan/SP	5.00
196	Jason Marquis	.40
197	Khalil Greene	.40
198	Ryan Dempster	.40
199	Ronnie Belliard	.40
200	Josh Fogg	.40
201	Carlos Lee	.40
202	Chris Denorfia	.40
203	Kendry Morales/SP	5.00
204	Rafael Soriano/SP	5.00
205	Brandon Phillips	.40
206	Andrew Miller RC	5.00
207	John Koronka	.40
208	Luis Castillo	.40
209	Angel Guzman	.40
210	Jim Edmonds	.40
211	Patrick Misch (RC)	1.00
212	Ty Wigginton/SP	5.00
213	Brandon Inge/SP	5.00
214	Royce Clayton	.40
215	Ben Broussard	.40
216	St. Louis Cardinals	.40
217	Mark Mulder	.40
218	Kenji Johjima	.40
219	Joe Crede	.40
220	Danny Haren	.40
221	Josh Fields/SP (RC)	8.00
222	Pat Neshek/SP	10.00
223	Reed Johnson	.40
224	Mike Mussina	.40
225	Randy Winn	.40
226	Brian Rogers (RC)	.40
227	Juan Rivera	.40
228	Shawn Green	.40
229	Mike Napoli	.40
230	Chase Utley/SP	10.00
231	John Nelson/SP (RC)	10.00
232	Casey Blake	.40
233	Lyle Overbay	.40
234	Adam LaRoche	.40
235	Jeff Weaver	.40
236	Johnny Estrada	.40
237	James Shields	.40
238	Jose Castillo	.40
239	Doug Davis/SP	5.00
240	Jason Giambi/SP	8.00
241	Mike Gonzalez	.40
242	Scott Downs	.40
243	Joe Inglett	.40
244	Matthew Kemp	.40
245	Ted Lilly	.40
246	New York Yankees	.40
247	Jamey Carroll	.40
248	Adam Wainwright/SP	8.00
249	Matt Thornton/SP	5.00
250	Alfonso Soriano	.40
251	Tom Gordon	.40
252	Dennis Sarfate (RC)	.40
253	Zachary Duke	.40
254	Hank Blalock	.40
255	Johan Santana	.40
256	Chicago White Sox	.40
257	Aaron Cook/SP	5.00
258	Cliff Lee/SP	5.00
259	Miguel Tejada	.40
260	Mike Lowell	.40
261	Ian Snell	.40
262	Jason Tyner	.40
263	Troy Tulowitzki (RC)	.75
264	Ervin Santana	.40
265	Jon Lester	.40
266	Andy Pettitte/SP	8.00
267	A.J. Pierzynski/SP	5.00
268	Rich Aurilia	.40
269	Phil Nevin	.40
270	Tom Glavine	.40
271	Chris Coste	.40
272	Moises Alou	.40
273	J.D. Drew	.40
274	Abraham Nunez	.40
275	Jorge Posada/SP	8.00
276	Jeff Conine/SP	5.00
277	Chad Cordero	.40
278	Nick Johnson	.40
279	Kevin Millar	.40
280	Mark Grudzielanek	.40
281	Chris Stewart RC	1.00
282	Nate Robertson	.40
283	Drew Anderson (RC)	1.00
284	Doug Mientkiewicz/SP	5.00
285	Ken Griffey Jr./SP	10.00
286	Cory Sullivan	.40
287	Chris Carpenter	.40
288	Gary Matthews	.40
289	Justin Verlander, Jeff Weaver	.40
290	Vicente Padilla	.40
291	Chris Roberson	.40
292	Chris Young	.40
293	Ryan Garko/SP	5.00
294	Miguel Batista/SP	5.00
295	B.J. Upton	.40
296	Justin Verlander	.40
297	Benjamin Zobrist	.40
298	Ben Sheets	.40
299	Eric Chavez	.40
300	William Harridge, Warren Giles	.40
301	Placido Polanco	.40
302	Angel Sanchez/SP RC	5.00
303	Freddy Sanchez/SP	5.00
304	Magglio Ordonez, Carlos Guillen	.40
305	A.J. Burnett	.40
306	Juan Perez RC	1.00
307	Chris Britton	.40
308	Jon Garland	.40
309	Pedro Feliz	.40
310	Ryan Howard	.40
311	Aaron Harang/SP	5.00
312	Boston Red Sox/SP	8.00
313	Chad Billingsley	.40
314	Bobby Cox, Chipper Jones	.40
315	Johan Santana	.40
316	Juan Pierre	.40
317	Luke Scott	.40
318	Javier Valentin	.40
319	Mark Loretta	.40
320	Kenny Lofton/SP	5.00
321	Vladimir Guerrero/SP, Ivan Rodriguez/SP	8.00
322	Josh Willingham	.40
323	Lance Berkman	.40
324	Anibal Sanchez	.40
325	Maicer Izturis	.40
326	Brett Myers	.40
327	Chicago Cubs	.40
328	Francisco Liriano	.40
329	Craig Monroe/SP	5.00
330	Paul LoDuca/SP	5.00
331	Steve Trachsel	.40
332	Bernie Williams	.40
333	Carlos Guillen	.40
334	Johan Santana, Francisco Liriano	.40
335	David Bush	.40
336	Carlos Beltran	.40
337	Jason Isringhausen	.40
338	Todd Walker/SP	5.00
339	Jarrod Washburn/SP	5.00
340	Brandon Webb	.40
341	Pittsburgh Pirates	.40
342	Derrick Turnbow	.40
343	Chad Santos	.40
344	Brad Lidge	.40
345	Brad Ausmus	.40
346	Carlos Delgado	.40
347	Boone Logan/SP	5.00
348	Jimmy Rollins/SP	8.00
349	Orlando Hernandez	.40
350	Gary Sheffield	.40
351	Albert Pujols, Yadier Molina, Jim Edmonds, Chris Duncan	.40
352	Jake Peavy	.40
353	Jason Varitek	.40
354	Freddy Garcia	.40
355	Matt Diaz	.40
356	Bernie Castro/SP	5.00
357	Eric Stults/SP RC	5.00
358	John Lackey	.40
359	Bobby Jenks	.40
360	Mark Teixeira	.40
361	Jonathan Papelbon	.40
362	Paul Konerko	.40
363	Erik Bedard	.40
364	Eliezer Alfonzo	.40
365	Fernando Rodney SP	5.00
366	Chris Duncan/SP	8.00
367	Jose Diaz RC	1.00
368	Travis Hafner	.40
369	Matt Capps	.40
370	Ivan Rodriguez	.40
371	David Murphy (RC)	1.00
372	Carlos Zambrano	.40
373	Chris Iannetta	.40
374	Jose Mesa/SP	5.00
375	Michael Young/SP	8.00
376	Bill Bray	.40
377	Milwaukee Brewers	.40
378	Robert Mackowiak	.40
379	Barry Zito	.40
380	Clay Hensley	.40
381	J.J. Putz	.40
382	C.C. Sabathia	.40
383	Eduardo Perez/SP	5.00
384	Scott Moore/SP (RC)	8.00
385	Scott Olsen	.40
386	Ryan Howard, Chase Utley	.40
387	Aaron Rowand	.40
388	Mike Rouse	.40
389	Alexis Gomez	.40
390	Brian McCann	.40
391	Ryan Shealy	.40
392	Shane Youman/ SP RC	8.00
393	Melky Cabrera/SP	8.00
394	Jeremy Sowers	.40
395	Casey Janssen	.40
396	Miguel Perez	.40
397	Detroit Tigers	.40
398	Reggie Abercrombie	.40
399	Ricky Nolasco	.40
400	Tadahito Iguchi	.40
401	Jose Reyes	10.00
402	Juan Encarnacion/SP	5.00
403	Brandon Harper	.40
404	Torii Hunter	.40
405	Dan Uggla	.40

406	Orlando Cabrera	.40
407	Jose Capellan	.40
408	Baltimore Orioles	.40
409	Frank Thomas	.40
410	Francisco Rodriguez/SP	5.00
411	Ian Kinsler/SP	5.00
412	Billy Wagner	.40
413	Andy Marte	.40
414	Mike Jacobs	.40
415	Raul Ibanez	.40
416	Jhonny Peralta	.40
417	Chris Young	.40
418	Albert Pujols, Craig Monroe	.40
419	Scott Kazmir/SP	5.00
420	Norris Hopper/SP	8.00
421	Chris Capuano	.40
422	Troy Glaus	.40
423	Roy Oswalt	.40
424	Grady Sizemore	.40
425	Chone Figgins	.40
426	Chad Tracy	.40
427	Brian Fuentes	.40
428	Cincinnati Reds/SP	8.00
429	Ramon Hernandez/SP	5.00
430	Mike Cameron	.40
431	Dontrelle Willis	.40
432	Joshua Sharpless	.40
433	Adrian Beltre	.40
434	Curtis Granderson	.40
435	B.J. Ryan	.40
436	Ryan Howard, David Wright	.40
437	Vernon Wells/SP	8.00
438	Vladimir Guerrero/SP	8.00
439	Jake Westbrook	.40
440	Chipper Jones	.40
441	James Loney	.40
442	St. Louis Cardinals	.40
443	Oswaldo Navarro	.40
444	Joe Mauer	.40
445	Miguel Montero	.40
446	Franklin Gutierrez/SP	5.00
447	Mark Redman/SP	5.00
448	Mike Rabelo **RC**	1.00
449	Philip Humber	.40
450	Justin Morneau	.40
451	Hector Gimenez	.40
452	Matt Holliday	.50
453	Akinori Otsuka	.40
454	Prince Fielder	.50
455	Chien-Ming Wang/SP	10.00
456	Shawn Riggans/SP	8.00
457	John Maine	.40
458	Adam Lind **(RC)**	1.00
459	Ubaldo Jimenez	.40
460	Drew Anderson	.40
461	Cla Meredith	.40
462	Joaquin Arias	.40
463	Kenny Rogers	.40
464	Jose Garcia/SP	5.00
465	Pedro Martinez/SP	8.00
466	Jeff Salazar	.40
467	Glen Perkins **(RC)**	.40
468	Travis Ishikawa	.40
469	Joe Borowski	.40
470	Jeremy Brown	.40
471	Andre Ethier	.40
472	Taylor Tankersley	.40
473	Lastings Milledge/SP	8.00
474	Brian Sanchez/SP	8.00
475	Ozzie Guillen, Phil Garner	.40
476	Albert Pujols	.40
477	David Ortiz	.40
478	Chase Utley	.40
479	Mark Loretta	.40
480	David Wright	.40
481	Alex Rodriguez	.40
482	Edgar Renteria/SP	5.00
483	Derek Jeter/SP	15.00
484	Alfonso Soriano	.40
485	Vladimir Guerrero	.40
486	Carlos Beltran	.40
487	Vernon Wells	.40
488	Jason Bay	.40
489	Ichiro Suzuki	.40
490	Paul LoDuca	.40
491	Ivan Rodriguez/SP	8.00
492	Brad Penny/SP	5.00
493	Roy Halladay	.40
494	Brian Fuentes	.40
495	Kenny Rogers	.40

Chrome

		NM/M
Common Player:		2.00
Production 1,958 Sets		
Refractors:		1.5-2X
Production 558 Sets		
Black Refractors:		3-6X
Production 58 Sets		
1	David Ortiz	6.00

Freddy Garcia
PITCHER — PHILA. PHILS.®

2	John Smoltz	3.00
4	Brian Giles	2.00
5	Billy Sadler	4.00
6	Joel Zumaya	4.00
7	Felipe Lopez	3.00
8	Tim Hudson	3.00
9	David Ross	2.00
10	Adam Kennedy	2.00
11	David DeJesus	2.00
12	Jose Contreras	2.00
13	Trot Nixon	2.00
14	Roy Halladay	2.00
15	Gil Meche	2.00
16	Ray Durham	2.00
17	Delwyn Young	2.00
18	Endy Chavez	2.00
19	Vinny Rottino	3.00
20	Austin Kearns	3.00
21	Jeremy Hermida	3.00
22	Jonathan Broxton	4.00
23	Josh Fogg	2.00
24	Angel Guzman	4.00
25	Kenji Johjima	4.00
26	Juan Rivera	2.00
27	Johnny Estrada	2.00
28	Ted Lilly	2.00
29	Hank Blalock	3.00
30	Troy Tulowitzki	5.00
31	Moises Alou	3.00
32	Chris Stewart	2.00
33	Vicente Padilla	2.00
34	Eric Chavez	3.00
35	Jon Garland	2.00
36	Luke Scott	3.00
37	Brett Myers	5.00
38	David Bush	2.00
39	Brad Lidge	2.00
40	Jason Varitek	5.00
41	Paul Konerko	4.00
42	David Murphy	2.00
43	Clay Hensley	2.00
44	Alexis Gomez	2.00
45	Reggie Abercrombie	2.00
46	Jose Capellan	2.00
47	Jhonny Peralta	3.00
48	Chone Figgins	3.00
49	Curtis Granderson	4.00
50	Oswaldo Navarro	3.00
51	Matt Holliday	4.00
52	Cla Meredith	2.00
53	Jeremy Brown	3.00
54	Mark Loretta	2.00
55	Jason Bay	4.00
56	Roger Clemens	8.00
57	Robert Mackowiak	2.00
58	Robinson Cano	6.00
59	Jason Lopez	3.00
60	Dave Roberts	2.00
61	Delmon Young	6.00
62	Ryan Sweeney	2.00
63	Chris Narveson	3.00
64	Juan Uribe	2.00
65	Tony Gwynn Jr.	2.00
66	David Wright	8.00
67	Miguel Cairo	2.00
68	Edgar Renteria	2.00
69	Victor Martinez	3.00
70	Willy Aybar	2.00
71	Luke Hudson	2.00
72	Chuck James	3.00
73	Kris Benson	2.00
74	Garret Anderson	2.00
75	Tim Wakefield	2.00
76	Mike Piazza	6.00
77	Carlos Lee	4.00
78	Jim Edmonds	4.00
79	Joe Crede	2.00
80	Shawn Green	3.00
81	James Shields	2.00
82	Johan Santana	8.00
83	Ervin Santana	3.00
85	J.D. Drew	4.00
86	Nate Robertson	3.00

88	Chris Roberson	3.00
90	Pedro Feliz	2.00
91	Javier Valentin	2.00
93	Carlos Beltran	5.00
94	Brad Ausmus	2.00
95	Freddy Garcia	2.00
96	Erik Bedard	4.00
97	Carlos Zambrano	4.00
98	J.J. Putz	4.00
99	Brian McCann	4.00
100	Ricky Nolasco	2.00
102	Chris Young	4.00
103	Chad Tracy	2.00
104	B.J. Ryan	2.00
105	Joe Mauer	5.00
106	Akinori Otsuka	2.00
107	Joaquin Arias	2.00
108	Andre Ethier	4.00
109	David Wright	10.00
110	Ichiro Suzuki	8.00

A-Rod Road to 500

	NM/M
Common A-Rod:	3.00
Inserted 1:24	
Autograph:	No Pricing
Production One Set	

Clubhouse Collection

Clubhouse Collection

		NM/M
Common Player:		8.00
SM	Stan Musial	30.00
DS	Duke Snider	20.00
FR	Frank Robinson	20.00
BR	Brooks Robinson	15.00
YB	Yogi Berra	25.00
AK	Al Kaline	20.00
AW	Adam Wainwright	15.00
AJP	Albert Pujols	20.00
AR	Alex Rodriguez	20.00
ALR	Anthony Reyes	10.00
BU	B.J. Upton	8.00
BZ	Barry Zito	10.00
BS	Ben Sheets	10.00
BW	Billy Wagner	8.00
BR	Brian Roberts	10.00
CU	Chase Utley	15.00
CJ	Chipper Jones	15.00
CC	Chris Carpenter	15.00
CD	Chris Duncan	10.00
CJ	Conor Jackson	10.00
DE	David Eckstein	20.00
DO	David Ortiz	15.00
DW	David Wright	30.00
DY	Delmon Young	10.00
DWW	Dontrelle Willis	8.00
DM	Doug Mientkiewicz	8.00
ER	Edgar Renteria	8.00
EC	Eric Chavez	8.00
ES	Ervin Santana	8.00
FL	Francisco Liriano	10.00
GS	Gary Sheffield	10.00
HB	Hank Blalock	8.00
IR	Ivan Rodriguez	10.00
JS	Jeff Suppan	10.00
JW	Jeff Weaver	8.00
JR	Jimmy Rollins	10.00
JD	Johnny Damon	15.00
JL	Jon Lester	10.00
JRP	Jorge Posada	10.00
JBR	Jose Reyes	20.00
JV	Jose Vidro	8.00
JP	Juan Pierre	8.00
JM	Justin Morneau	15.00
LB	Lance Berkman	10.00
LG	Luis Gonzalez	8.00
MO	Magglio Ordonez	8.00
MR	Manny Ramirez	10.00
MK	Mark Kotsay	8.00
MT	Mark Teixeira	10.00
MM	Melvin Mora	8.00

MC	Miguel Cabrera	10.00
MOT	Miguel Tejada	8.00
MP	Mike Piazza	15.00
MA	Moises Alou	8.00
NS	Nick Swisher	10.00
OV	Omar Vizquel	8.00
PB	Pat Burrell	10.00
PP	Placido Polanco	8.00
RF	Rafael Furcal	8.00
RS	Richie Sexson	10.00
RB	Ronnie Belliard	8.00
RH	Ryan Howard	30.00
TH	Todd Helton	10.00
TKH	Torii Hunter	10.00
VM	Victor Martinez	8.00
YM	Yadier Molina	15.00

Clubhouse Collection
Dual Relic

		NM/M
Production 58 Sets		
MP	Stan Musial, Albert Pujols	180.00
KR	Al Kaline, Ivan Rodriguez	80.00

Clubhouse Collection
Relic Autograph

Production 25 Sets

Felt Team Emblem

	NM/M
Inserted 1:Box	
Los Angeles Dodgers	3.00
Washington Senators	3.00
San Francisco Giants	3.00
Boston Red Sox	5.00
Cincinnati Redlegs	3.00
Pittsburgh Pirates	3.00
Milwaukee Braves	3.00
Chicago Cubs	5.00
Baltimore Orioles	3.00
New York Yankees	5.00
Cleveland Indians	3.00
St. Louis Cardinals	5.00
Kansas City Athletics	3.00
Detroit Tigers	3.00
Chicago White Sox	3.00
Philadelphia Phillies	3.00

Flashbacks

SPAHN BLAZES SOUTHPAW TRAIL
WARREN SPAHN
SEPTEMBER 17, 1950

		NM/M
Common Player:		1.00
Inserted 1:12		
SM	Stan Musial	2.00
AK	Al Kaline	2.00
BR	Brooks Robinson	2.00
RS	Red Schoendienst	1.00
LA	Luis Aparicio	1.00
WS	Warren Spahn	2.00
HS	Hank Sauer	1.00
LB	Lew Burdette	1.00
EY	Eddie Yost	1.00
JB	Jim Bunning	1.00

Flashback Autograph

No Pricing
Production 25 Sets

Flashbacks Relics

		NM/M
Common Player:		20.00
SM	Stan Musial	30.00
AK	Al Kaline	25.00
BR	Brooks Robinson	25.00
RS	Red Schoendienst	20.00
WS	Warren Spahn	25.00
LB	Lew Burdette	25.00
EY	Eddie Yost	20.00
JB	Jim Bunning	20.00

Flashbacks Relic Autograph
Production 25 Sets
Dual Flashbacks
Production 10 Sets
New Age Performers

DAVID ORTIZ
BOSTON RED SOX®

		NM/M
Common Player:		1.00
Inserted 1:15		
RH	Ryan Howard	3.00
AR	Alex Rodriguez	3.00
AS	Alfonso Soriano	2.00
DO	David Ortiz	2.00
TH	Trevor Hoffman	1.00
DJ	Derek Jeter	4.00
AAS	Anibal Sanchez	1.00
RC	Roger Clemens	3.00
JS	Johan Santana	2.00
AP	Albert Pujols	4.00
CJ	Chipper Jones	2.00
FT	Frank Thomas	2.00
IR	Ivan Rodriguez	1.50
IS	Ichiro Suzuki	3.00
CB	Craig Biggio	1.00

Real One Autographs

		NM/M
Common Autograph:		
Red Ink:		1.5-2X
Production 58 Sets		
AK	Al Kaline	150.00
BH	Bob Henrich	60.00
BM	Bobby Morgan	70.00
BP	Buddy Pritchard	65.00
BR	Brooks Robinson	100.00
BT	Bill Taylor	50.00
BW	Bill Wight	50.00
CH	Chuck Harmon	60.00
CJD	Jim Derrington	65.00
CR	Charley Rabe	60.00
DM	Dave Melton	60.00
DS	Duke Snider	100.00
DW	David Wright	140.00
DWW	Dontrelle Willis	50.00
DY	Delmon Young	60.00
DZ	Don Zimmer	50.00
EM	Ed Mayer	60.00
GK	George Kell	75.00
HP	Harding Peterson	60.00
JC	Joe Caffie	60.00
JD	Joe Durham	70.00
JL	Joe Lonnett	50.00
JM	Justin Morneau	60.00
JP	Johnny Podres	60.00
LA	Luis Aparicio	80.00
LM	Lloyd Merritt	60.00
LS	Lou Sleater	60.00
MB	Milt Bolling	60.00
MEB	Mack Burk	60.00
OH	Orlando Hudson	40.00
PS	Paul Smith	60.00
RC	Ray Crone	60.00
RH	Ryan Howard	250.00
RS	Red Schoendienst	85.00
SP	Stan Palys	50.00
TT	Tim Thompson	50.00

Then and Now

		NM/M
Common Player:		1.00
Inserted 1:15		
RH	Ryan Howard	3.00
DO	David Ortiz	2.00
JM	Joe Mauer	1.50
JR	Jose Reyes	2.00
JS	Johan Santana	2.00
AH	Aaron Harang	1.00
IS	Ichiro Suzuki	3.00

TH	Travis Hafner	1.50
FR	Francisco Rodriguez	1.00
CW	Chien-Ming Wang	2.00

1958 A.L. Home Run Champion

	NM/M
Common Mantle:	3.00
Inserted 1:6	

1958 Cut Signatures
Production One Set

2007 Topps Moments & Milestones

		NM/M
Complete Set (193):		
Common Player:		.50
Production 150 Sets		
Pack (6):		9.00
Box (18):		140.00
1	Albert Pujols (37/5,550)	4.00
2	Albert Pujols (130/19,500)	4.00
3	Albert Pujols (194/29,100)	4.00
4	Albert Pujols (112/16,800)	4.00
5	Albert Pujols (47/7,050)	4.00
6	Ichiro Suzuki (242/36,300)	2.50
7	Ichiro Suzuki (34/5,100)	2.50
8	Ichiro Suzuki (8/1,200)	2.50
9	Ichiro Suzuki (56/8,400)	2.50
10	Ichiro Suzuki (69/10,350)	2.50
11	Ichiro Suzuki (8/1,200)	2.50
12	Greg Maddux (20/3,000)	3.00
13	Greg Maddux (199/29,850)	3.00
14	Greg Maddux (20/3,000)	3.00
15	Greg Maddux (197/29,550)	3.00
16	Roger Clemens (24/3,600)	3.00
17	Roger Clemens (10/1,500)	3.00
18	Roger Clemens (238/35,700)	3.00
19	Roger Clemens (20/3,000)	3.00
20	Roger Clemens (256/38,400)	3.00
21	Chipper Jones (45/6,750)	1.50
22	Chipper Jones (110/16,500)	1.50
23	Chipper Jones (181/27,150)	1.50
24	Chipper Jones (116/17,400)	1.50
25	Chipper Jones (41/6,150)	1.50
26	Chipper Jones (25/3,750)	1.50
27	Alex Rodriguez (47/7,050)	4.00
28	Alex Rodriguez (118/17,700)	4.00
29	Alex Rodriguez (181/27,150)	4.00
30	Alex Rodriguez (124/18,600)	4.00
31	Alex Rodriguez (30/4,500)	4.00

32	Alex Rodriguez (17/2,550)	4.00
33	Alex Rodriguez (48/7,200)	4.00
34	Alex Rodriguez (130/19,500)	4.00
35	Alex Rodriguez (194/29,100)	4.00
36	Alex Rodriguez (124/18,600)	4.00
37	Alex Rodriguez (29/4,350)	4.00
38	Alex Rodriguez (21/3,150)	4.00
39	Vladimir Guerrero (39/5,850)	1.50
40	Vladimir Guerrero (126/18,900)	1.50
41	Vladimir Guerrero (206/30,900)	1.50
42	Vladimir Guerrero (124/18,600)	1.50
43	Vladimir Guerrero (39/5,850)	1.50
44	Vladimir Guerrero (13/1,950)	1.50
45	Ken Griffey Jr. (56/8,400)	3.00
46	Ken Griffey Jr. (147/22,050)	3.00
47	Ken Griffey Jr. (185/27,750)	3.00
48	Barry Zito (23/3,450)	.75
49	Barry Zito (182/27,300)	.75
50	Randy Johnson (18/2,700)	1.50
51	Randy Johnson (294/44,100)	1.50
52	Randy Johnson (6/900)	1.50
53	Randy Johnson (3/450)	1.50
54	Randy Johnson (17/2,550)	1.50
55	Randy Johnson (364/54,600)	1.50
56	Randy Johnson (12/1,800)	1.50
57	Randy Johnson (2/300)	1.50
58	Prince Fielder (35/5,250)	2.00
59	Prince Fielder (81/12,150)	2.00
60	Dan Uggla (26/3,900)	.50
61	Dan Uggla (27/4,050)	.50
62	Dan Uggla (172/25,800)	.50
63	Justin Verlander (17/2,550)	1.50
64	Justin Verlander (124/18,600)	1.50
65	Francisco Liriano (12/1,800)	1.50
66	Francisco Liriano (144/21,600)	1.50
67	Ryan Zimmerman (176/26,400)	1.00
68	Ryan Zimmerman (110/16,500)	1.00
69	Ryan Zimmerman (84/12,600)	1.00
70	Hanley Ramirez (51/7,650)	1.50
71	Hanley Ramirez (119/17,850)	1.50
72	Hanley Ramirez (185/27,750)	1.50
73	Russ Martin (65/9,750)	1.00
74	Russ Martin (26/3,900)	1.00
75	Mickey Mantle (173/25,950)	5.00
76	Mickey Mantle (121/18,150)	5.00
77	Mickey Mantle (146/21,900)	5.00
78	Mickey Mantle (94/14,100)	5.00
79	Mike Piazza (35/5,250)	1.50
80	Mike Piazza (112/16,800)	1.50
81	Derek Jeter (10/1,500)	4.00
82	Derek Jeter (78/1,700)	4.00
83	Derek Jeter (183/27,450)	4.00
84	Dontrelle Willis (14/2,100)	.75
85	Dontrelle Willis (142/21,300)	.75
86	Dontrelle Willis (2/300)	.75
87	Bobby Crosby (22/3,300)	.50
88	Bobby Crosby (64/9,600)	.50
89	Ryan Howard (22/3,300)	3.00

90	Ryan Howard (63/9,450)	3.00
91	Curt Schilling (21/3,150)	1.50
92	Curt Schilling (203/30,450)	1.50
93	Andruw Jones (52/7,800)	1.50
94	Andruw Jones (128/19,200)	1.50
95	Andruw Jones (11/1,650)	1.50
96	Hideki Matsui (23/3,450)	2.50
97	Hideki Matsui (116/17400)	2.50
98	Hideki Matsui (192/28,800)	2.50
99	David Wright (27/4,050)	2.50
100	David Wright (102/15,300)	2.50
101	David Wright (42/6,300)	2.50
102	David Wright (17/2,550)	2.50
103	David Ortiz (75/11,250)	2.00
104	David Wright (47/7,050)	2.00
105	David Ortiz (11/1,650)	2.00
106	Frank Thomas (38/5,700)	1.50
107	Frank Thomas (101/15,150)	1.50
108	Craig Biggio (40/6,000)	1.00
109	Miguel Cabrera (33/4,950)	2.00
110	Miguel Cabrera (116/17,400)	2.00
111	Vernon Wells (12/1,800)	1.00
112	Michael Young (24/3,600)	1.00
113	Michael Young (40/6,000)	1.00
114	Joe Mauer (144/21,600)	1.50
115	Gary Sheffield (34/5,100)	1.00
116	Jim Edmonds (42/6,300)	1.00
117	Jorge Posada (19/2,850)	1.00
118	Jorge Posada (23/3,450)	1.00
119	Pat Burrell (32/4,800)	.75
120	Adam Dunn (40/6,000)	1.00
121	Johnny Damon (35/5,250)	2.00
122	Scott Rolen (34/5,100)	1.50
123	Paul Konerko (6/900)	1.00
124	Roy Halladay (22/3,300)	1.00
125	Grady Sizemore (22/3,300)	1.50
126	Grady Sizemore (37/5,550)	1.50
127	John Smoltz (24/3,600)	1.00
128	Jeff Kent (29/4,350)	.75
129	Billy Wagner (38/5,700)	.50
130	Mark Prior (18/2,700)	.75
131	Eric Chavez (32/4,800)	.75
132	Jimmy Rollins (41/6,150)	1.50
133	Manny Ramirez (7/1,050)	1.50
134	Manny Ramirez (45/6,750)	1.50
135	Manny Ramirez (144/21,600)	1.50
136	Derrek Lee (46/6,900)	1.50
137	Derrek Lee (107/16,050)	1.50
138	Tom Glavine (14/2,100)	1.00
139	Tom Glavine (20/3,000)	1.00
140	Jose Reyes (17/2,550)	2.00
141	Pedro Martinez (15/2,250)	1.50
142	Pedro Martinez (208/31,200)	1.50
143	Mark Teixeira (43/6,450)	1.00
144	Jake Peavy (13/1,950)	1.00
145	Carlos Lee (32/4,800)	.75
146	Josh Beckett (16/2,400)	.75
147	Johan Santana (20/3,000)	2.00
148	Todd Helton (33/4,950)	1.50
149	Mariano Rivera (43/6,450)	1.50
150	Travis Hafner (33/4,950)	1.00
151	Jason Bay (24/3,600)	1.00
152	Bobby Abreu (30/4,500)	1.00

153	Mike Mussina (13/1,950)	1.00
154	Miguel Tejada (34/5,100)	1.00
155	Miguel Tejada (150/22,500)	1.00
156	Robinson Cano (14/2,100)	1.50
157	Robinson Cano (34/5,100)	1.50
158	Ryan Zimmerman (23/3,450)	1.00
159	Carlos Beltran (16/2,400)	1.50
160	Carlos Beltran (17/2,550)	1.50
161	Roger Clemens (18/2,700)	3.00
162	Roger Clemens (218/32,700)	3.00
163	Mickey Mantle (52/7,800)	5.00
164	Mickey Mantle (130/19,500)	5.00
165	Mickey Mantle (188/28,200)	5.00
166	Mickey Mantle (132/19,800)	5.00
167	Mickey Mantle (42/6,300)	5.00
168	Mickey Mantle (97/14,550)	5.00
169	Mickey Mantle (127/19,050)	5.00
170	Daisuke Matsuzaka RC	150.00
171	Daisuke Matsuzaka RC	150.00
172	Daisuke Matsuzaka RC	150.00
173	Delmon Young (RC)	5.00
174	Delmon Young (RC)	5.00
175	Delmon Young (RC)	5.00
176	Andrew Miller RC	30.00
177	Andrew Miller RC	30.00
178	Andrew Miller RC	25.00
179	Troy Tulowitzki (RC)	5.00
180	Troy Tulowitzki (RC)	5.00
181	Troy Tulowitzki (RC)	5.00
182	Josh Fields (RC)	5.00
183	Josh Fields (RC)	5.00
184	Josh Fields (RC)	5.00
185	Jeff Baker (RC)	5.00
186	Jeff Baker (RC)	5.00
187	Jeff Baker (RC)	5.00
188	Philip Humber (RC)	5.00
189	Philip Humber (RC)	5.00
190	Philip Humber (RC)	5.00
191	Kevin Kouzmanoff (RC)	5.00
192	Kevin Kouzmanoff (RC)	5.00
193	Kevin Kouzmanoff (RC)	5.00

Black

Stars: 2-3X
Production 29 Sets

Red

No Pricing
Production One Set

Printing Plates

No Pricing
Production one set per color.

A-Rod Road to 500

NM/M
Common A-Rod (101-125): 3.00
Inserted 2:Box

A-Rod Road to 500 Autograph

NM/M
Production One Set 3.00

Milestone Autographs

NM/M
Common Auto.: 15.00
Black: 1-1.5X
Production 40 Sets
Red: No Pricing
Production One Set

AJ	Andruw Jones/100	50.00
AR	Alex Rodriguez/100	180.00
BP	Brandon Phillips	15.00
BR	Brian Roberts	15.00
CJ	Conor Jackson	15.00
DO	David Ortiz	60.00
DW	David Wright	60.00
GA	Garrett Atkins	15.00
GS	Gary Sheffield/100	35.00
HS	Huston Street/200	20.00
JF	Jeff Francoeur	50.00
JG	Jason Giambi/100	50.00
JJG	Jonny Gomes	15.00
JL	Julio Lugo	15.00
JP	Jonathan Papelbon	40.00
JR	Jose Reyes/200	70.00
JS	Jeremy Sowers	15.00
KJ	Kenji Johjima	35.00
KM	Kendry Morales	15.00
LM	Lastings Milledge	20.00
MK	Matthew Kemp	15.00
MN	Mike Napoli	15.00
MP	Martin Prado	15.00
NS	Nick Swisher	15.00
RH	Ryan Howard/200	75.00
RP	Ronny Paulino	15.00
TH	Travis Hafner	20.00
VG	Vladimir Guerrero/100	50.00
WP	Wily Mo Pena/100	20.00

Rookie Autographs

NM/M
Common Auto.: 10.00
Black: 2-3X
Production 40 Sets
Red: No Pricing
Production One Set

AL	Adam Lind	15.00
AM	Andrew Miller	40.00
DM	David Murphy	10.00
HG	Hector Gimenez	10.00
JA	Joaquin Arias	10.00
KK	Kevin Kouzmanoff	15.00
MB	Michael Bourn	10.00
MM	Miguel Montero	10.00
SR	Shawn Riggans	10.00
TT	Troy Tulowitzki	30.00

2007 Topps Opening Day

		NM/M
	Complete Set (220):	35.00
	Common Player:	.15
	Pack (6):	1.25
	Box (36):	40.00
1	Bobby Abreu	.25
2	Mike Piazza	.75
3	Jake Westbrook	.15
4	Zachary Duke	.15
5	David Wright	1.00
6	Adrian Gonzalez	.25
7	Mickey Mantle	3.00
8	Bill Hall	.25
9	Robinson Cano	.25
10	Dontrelle Willis	.25
11	J.D. Drew	.25
12	Paul Konerko	.25
13	Austin Kearns	.15
14	Mike Lowell	.25
15	Magglio Ordonez	.25
16	Rafael Furcal	.25
17	Matt Cain	.25
18	Craig Monroe	.15
19	Matt Holliday	.25
20	Edgar Renteria	.25
21	Mark Buehrle	.15
22	Carlos Quentin	.15
23	C.C. Sabathia	.25
24	Nicholas Markakis	.25
25	Chipper Jones	.50
26	Jason Giambi	.40
27	Barry Zito	.25
28	Jake Peavy	.25
29	Hank Blalock	.25
30	Johnny Damon	.50
31	Chad Tracy	.15
32	Nick Swisher	.25
33	Willy Taveras	.15
34	Chuck James	.15
35	Carlos Delgado	.40
36	Livan Hernandez	.15
37	Freddy Garcia	.15
38	Bronson Arroyo	.15
39	Jack Wilson	.15
40	Dan Uggla	.15
41	Chris Carpenter	.50
42	Jorge Posada	.25
43	Joe Mauer	.40
44	Corey Patterson	.15
45	Chien-Ming Wang	.50
46	Derek Jeter	1.50
47	Carlos Beltran	.50
48	Jim Edmonds	.25
49	Jeremy Sowers	.15
50	Randy Johnson	.50
51	Jered Weaver	.25
52	Josh Barfield	.15
53	Scott Rolen	.40
54	Ryan Shealy	.15
55	Freddy Sanchez	.15
56	Javier Vazquez	.15
57	Jeremy Bonderman	.25
58	Miguel Cabrera	.50
59	Kazuo Matsui	.15
60	Curt Schilling	.25
61	Alfonso Soriano	.50
62	Orlando Hernandez	.15
63	Joe Blanton	.15
64	Aramis Ramirez	.25
65	Ben Sheets	.25
66	Jimmy Rollins	.25
67	Mark Loretta	.15
68	Cole Hamels	.25
69	Albert Pujols	1.50
70	Moises Alou	.25
71	Mark Teahen	.15
72	Roy Halladay	.25
73	Cory Sullivan	.15
74	Frank Thomas	.50
75	Ryan Howard	1.50
76	Rocco Baldelli	.25
77	Manny Ramirez	.50
78	Ray Durham	.15
79	Gary Sheffield	.40
80	Jay Gibbons	.15
81	Todd Helton	.40
82	Gary Matthews	.15
83	Brandon Inge	.15
84	Jonathan Papelbon	.40
85	John Smoltz	.25
86	Chone Figgins	.15
87	Hideki Matsui	.75
88	Carlos Lee	.25
89	Jose Reyes	.75
90	Lyle Overbay	.25
91	Johan Santana	.50
92	Ian Kinsler	.15
93	Scott Kazmir	.25
94	Hanley Ramirez	.40
95	Greg Maddux	1.00
96	Johnny Estrada	.15
97	B.J. Upton	.25
98	Francisco Liriano	.25
99	Chase Utley	.50
100	Preston Wilson	.15
101	Marcus Giles	.15
102	Jeff Kent	.25
103	Grady Sizemore	.50
104	Ken Griffey Jr.	1.00
105	Garret Anderson	.15
106	Brian McCann	.25
107	Jon Garland	.15
108	Troy Glaus	.25
109	Brandon Webb	.25
110	Jason Schmidt	.25
111	Ramon Hernandez	.15
112	Justin Morneau	.50
113	Mike Cameron	.15
114	Andruw Jones	.40
115	Russell Martin	.15
116	Vernon Wells	.25
117	Orlando Hudson	.15
118	Derek Lowe	.15
119	Alex Rodriguez	1.50
120	Chad Billingsley	.15
121	Kenji Johjima	.15
122	Nick Johnson	.15
123	Danny Haren	.15
124	Mark Teixeira	.40
125	Jeff Francoeur	.25
126	Ted Lilly	.15
127	Jhonny Peralta	.15
128	Aaron Harang	.15
129	Ryan Zimmerman	.25
130	Jermaine Dye	.25
131	Orlando Cabrera	.15
132	Juan Pierre	.15
133	Brian Giles	.25
134	Jason Bay	.25
135	David Ortiz	.50
136	Chris Capuano	.15
137	Carlos Zambrano	.25
138	Luis Gonzalez	.15
139	Jeff Weaver	.15
140	Lance Berkman	.25
141	Raul Ibanez	.15
142	Jim Thome	.40
143	Jose Contreras	.15
144	David Eckstein	.15
145	Adam Dunn	.40
146	Alex Rios	.25
147	Garrett Atkins	.25
148	A.J. Burnett	.25
149	Jeremy Hermida	.15
150	Conor Jackson	.15
151	Adrian Beltre	.25
152	Torii Hunter	.25
153	Andrew Miller RC	3.00
154	Ichiro Suzuki	1.00
155	Mark Redman	.15
156	Paul LoDuca	.15
157	Xavier Nady	.15
158	Stephen Drew	.25
159	Eric Chavez	.25
160	Pedro Martinez	.50
161	Derrek Lee	.40
162	David DeJesus	.15
163	Troy Tulowitzki (RC)	.50
164	Vinny Rottino (RC)	.25
165	Philip Humber (RC)	.25
166	Jerry Owens (RC)	.25
167	Ubaldo Jimenez (RC)	.25
168	Michael Young	.25
169	Ryan Braun (RC)	.25
170	Kevin Kouzmanoff (RC)	.25
171	Oswaldo Navarro RC	.25
172	Miguel Montero (RC)	.25
173	Roy Oswalt	.25
174	Shane Youman RC	.25
175	Josh Fields (RC)	.25
176	Adam Lind (RC)	.25
177	Miguel Tejada	.40
178	Delwyn Young (RC)	.25
179	Scott Moore (RC)	.25
180	Fred Lewis (RC)	.25
181	Glen Perkins (RC)	.25
182	Vladimir Guerrero	.50
183	Drew Anderson (RC)	.25
184	Jeff Salazar (RC)	.25
185	Tom Gordon	.15
186	The Bird	.15
187	Justin Verlander	.40
188	Delmon Young (RC)	.50
189	Homer	.15
190	Wally the Green Monster	.15
191	Southpaw	.15
192	Dinger	.15
193	Carl Crawford	.15
194	Slider	.15
195	Gapper	.15
196	Paws	.15
197	Billy the Marlin	.15
198	Ivan Rodriguez	.15
199	Slugger	.15
200	Junction Jack	.15
201	Bernie the Brewer	.15
202	Travis Hafner	.40
203	Stomper	.15
204	Mr. Met	.15
205	The Moose	.15
206	Phillie Phanatic	.15
207	Prince Fielder	.50
208	Julio Lugo	.15
209	Pirate Parrot	.15
210	Joel Zumaya	.25
211	Swinging Friar	.15
212	Jay Payton	.15
213	Lou Seal	.15
214	Fredbird	.15
215	Screech	.15
216	TC Bear	.15
217	Andre Ethier	.15
218	Ervin Santana	.15
219	Melvin Mora	.15
220	Checklist	.15

Autographs

NM/M
Common Auto.: 15.00

EF	Emiliano Fruto	20.00
HK	Howie Kendrick	40.00
JT	Jordan Tata	25.00
JM	Juan Morillo	15.00
MC	Matt Cain	20.00
MK	Matthew Kemp	25.00
MN	Mike Napoli	20.00
OH	Orlando Hudson	20.00
RM	Robert Mackowiak	15.00
SS	Shannon Stewart	15.00

A-Rod Road to 500

NM/M
Common A-Rod (76-100): 3.00

A-Rod Road to 500 Autograph

Production One Set

Diamond Stars

NM/M
Common Player: .25

1	Ryan Howard	1.50
2	Alfonso Soriano	.75
3	Alex Rodriguez	1.50
4	David Ortiz	.75
5	Raul Ibanez	.25
6	Matt Holliday	.50

7	Delmon Young	.50
8	Derrick Turnbow	.25
9	Freddy Sanchez	.25
10	Troy Glaus	.50
11	A.J. Pierzynski	.25
12	Dontrelle Willis	.50
13	Justin Morneau	.75
14	Jose Reyes	1.00
15	Derek Jeter	1.50
16	Ivan Rodriguez	.50
17	Jay Payton	.25
18	Adrian Gonzalez	.25
19	David Eckstein	.25
20	Chipper Jones	.75
21	Aramis Ramirez	.50
22	David Wright	1.00
23	Mark Teixeira	.50
24	Stephen Drew	.50
25	Ichiro Suzuki	1.00

Movie Gallery

	NM/M
Alex Rodriguez	1.00

Puzzle

	NM/M
Complete Puzzle:	10.00
Common Player:	.25

1	Adam Dunn	.25
2	Adam Dunn	.25
3	Miguel Tejada	.25
4	Miguel Tejada	.25
5	Hanley Ramirez	.25
6	Hanley Ramirez	.25
7	Johan Santana	.50
8	Johan Santana	.50
9	Brandon Webb	.25
10	Brandon Webb	.25
11	David Wright	.75
12	David Wright	.75
13	Alex Rodriguez	.75
14	Alex Rodriguez	.75
15	Ryan Howard	.75
16	Ryan Howard	.75
17	Albert Pujols	1.00
18	Albert Pujols	1.00
19	Andruw Jones	.50
20	Andruw Jones	.50
21	Alfonso Soriano	.50
22	Alfonso Soriano	.50
23	Vladimir Guerrero	.50
24	Vladimir Guerrero	.50
25	David Ortiz	.50
26	David Ortiz	.50
27	Ichiro Suzuki	.75
28	Ichiro Suzuki	.75

2007 Topps Triple Threads

	NM/M
Complete Set (189):	

Common Player (1-125):	1.00
Production 1,350	
Common Auto. (126-189):	10.00
Production 99	
Pack (6):	100.00
Box (2):	200.00

1	Alex Rodriguez	6.00
2	Barry Zito	1.50
3	Corey Patterson	1.00
4	Roberto Clemente	5.00
5	David Wright	3.00
6	Dontrelle Willis	1.50
7	Mickey Mantle	8.00
8	Adam Dunn	2.00
9	Richie Ashburn	2.00
10	Ryan Howard	5.00
11	Miguel Tejada	2.00
12	Ernie Banks	4.00
13	Ken Griffey Jr.	5.00
14	Johnny Bench	3.00
15	Ichiro Suzuki	4.00
16	Gil Meche	1.00
17	Kazuo Matsui	1.00
18	Matt Holliday	1.50
19	Juan Pierre	1.00
20	Yogi Berra	3.00
21	Bill Hall	1.00
22	Wade Boggs	2.00
23	Jason Bay	1.50
24	Troy Glaus	1.50
25	Paul Konerko	1.50
26	Rod Carew	2.00
27	Jay Gibbons	1.00
28	Frank Thomas	3.00
29	Joe Mauer	2.00
30	Carlos Beltran	2.00
31	Frank Robinson	3.00
32	Bobby Abreu	1.50
33	Roy Oswalt	1.50
34	Edgar Renteria	1.50
35	Magglio Ordonez	1.50
36	Mike Piazza	4.00
37	Trevor Hoffman	1.50
38	Eddie Mathews	3.00
39	Albert Pujols	6.00
40	Dennis Eckersley	1.50
41	Andruw Jones	2.00
42	Alfonso Soriano	2.00
43	Bob Feller	2.00
44	J.D. Drew	1.50
45	Jason Schmidt	1.00
46	Vladimir Guerrero	3.00
47	Reggie Jackson	3.00
48	Lance Berkman	1.50
49	Michael Young	1.50
50	Carlton Fisk	2.00
51	Brandon Webb	1.00
52	Adrian Beltre	1.00
53	Hideki Matsui	4.00
54	Bronson Arroyo	1.00
55	Tony Gwynn	3.00
56	Ray Durham	1.00
57	Garrett Atkins	1.50
58	Nolan Ryan	4.00
59	Daisuke Matsuzaka RC	25.00
60	Todd Helton	2.00
61	Carl Crawford	1.50
62	Jake Peavy	2.00
63	Rafael Furcal	1.50
64	Joe Morgan	2.00
65	Greg Maddux	4.00
66	Luis Aparicio	1.50
67	Derrek Lee	2.00
68	Johnny Damon	2.00
69	Mike Lowell	1.00
70	Roger Maris	4.00
71	Vernon Wells	1.50
72	Monte Irvin	2.00
73	Jermaine Dye	1.50
74	Miguel Cabrera	3.00
75	Barry Bonds	6.00
76	Stan Musial	3.00
77	Derek Lowe	1.00
78	Don Mattingly	5.00
79	Lyle Overbay	1.00
80	Chien-Ming Wang	5.00
81	Carlos Zambrano	1.50
82	Kei Igawa RC	5.00
83	Cole Hamels	2.00
84	Gary Sheffield	2.00
85	Nick Johnson	1.00
86	Brooks Robinson	3.00
87	Curt Schilling	3.00
88	Ryne Sandberg	3.00
89	Mike Cameron	1.00
90	Mike Schmidt	3.00
91	Chris Carpenter	2.00
92	Scott Rolen	2.00
93	Rocco Baldelli	1.50
94	C.C. Sabathia	1.50
95	Jeff Francis	1.00
96	Ozzie Smith	3.00
97	Aramis Ramirez	1.50
98	Aaron Harang	1.00
99	Duke Snider	3.00
100	David Ortiz	3.00
101	Raul Ibanez	1.00
102	Bruce Sutter	1.00
103	Gary Matthews	1.00
104	Chipper Jones	3.00
105	Craig Biggio	1.50
106	Roy Halladay	1.50
107	Hoyt Wilhelm	1.00
108	Manny Ramirez	3.00
109	Randy Johnson	3.00
110	Carl Yastrzemski	3.00
111	Mark Teixeira	2.00
112	Derek Jeter	6.00
113	Stephen Drew	1.50
114	Darryl Strawberry	1.50
115	Travis Hafner	1.50
116	Torii Hunter	1.50
117	Jim Edmonds	1.50
118	John Smoltz	1.50
119	Bo Jackson	3.00
120	Roger Clemens	5.00
121	Pedro Martinez	3.00
122	Rickey Henderson	2.00
123	Ivan Rodriguez	3.00
124	Robin Yount	3.00
125	Johan Santana	2.00
126a	Robinson Cano	40.00
126b	Robinson Cano	40.00
127a	Jose Reyes	75.00
127b	Jose Reyes	75.00
128a	Justin Morneau	35.00
128b	Justin Morneau	35.00
129a	Curtis Granderson	30.00
129b	Curtis Granderson	30.00
130a	Justin Verlander	50.00
130b	Justin Verlander	50.00
131	Prince Fielder	65.00
132a	Ryan Zimmerman	40.00
132b	Ryan Zimmerman	40.00
133	Mike Napoli	20.00
134	Melky Cabrera	30.00
135	Jonathan Papelbon	40.00
136a	Nicholas Markakis	30.00
136b	Nicholas Markakis	30.00
137	B.J. Upton	25.00
138a	Joel Zumaya	30.00
138b	Joel Zumaya	30.00
140	Nick Swisher	25.00
141	Andre Ethier	25.00
142a	Jered Weaver	30.00
142b	Jered Weaver	30.00
143	Matt Cain	25.00
144	Lastings Milledge	25.00
145	Brian McCann	35.00
146	Shin-Soo Choo	20.00
147a	Dan Uggla	25.00
147b	Dan Uggla	25.00
148	Hanley Ramirez	30.00
149	Russell Martin	40.00
150	Francisco Liriano	30.00
151	Anthony Reyes	10.00
152	Josh Barfield	20.00
153	Anibal Sanchez	20.00
154	Jeremy Hermida	15.00
155	Kendry Morales	15.00
156	Matthew Kemp	30.00
157	Freddy Sanchez	20.00
158	Howie Kendrick	20.00
159	Scott Thorman	20.00
160	Franklin Gutierrez	20.00
161	Jason Bartlett	15.00
162	Chris Duncan	50.00
163	Maicer Izturis	20.00
164	Jason Botts	20.00
165	Tony Gwynn Jr.	30.00
166	Jorge Cantu	20.00
167	Adam Jones	30.00
168	Edinson Volquez	15.00
169	Joey Gathright	20.00
170	Carlos Marmol	30.00
171	Benjamin Zobrist	15.00
172	Josh Willingham	20.00
173	Brad Thompson	20.00
174a	Chris Ray	20.00
174b	Ervin Santana	20.00
175	Ronny Paulino	15.00
176	Tyler Johnson	20.00
177	J.J. Hardy	40.00
178	Adrian Gonzalez	25.00
179	Scott Kazmir	30.00
180	Juan Morillo (RC)	10.00
181a	Shawn Riggans (RC)	15.00
181b	Shawn Riggans (RC)	15.00
182	Brian Stokes (RC)	20.00
183	Delmon Young (RC)	35.00
184a	Troy Tulowitzki (RC)	60.00
184b	Troy Tulowitzki (RC)	60.00
185	Adam Lind (RC)	20.00
186	David Murphy (RC)	20.00
187a	Philip Humber (RC)	25.00
187b	Philip Humber (RC)	25.00
188a	Andrew Miller RC	60.00
188b	Andrew Miller RC	60.00
189a	Glen Perkins (RC)	20.00
189b	Glen Perkins (RC)	20.00

Sepia

Sepia (1-125):	1-2X
Production 559 Sets	
Autos. (126-189):	1X
Production 75 Sets	

Emerald

Emerald (1-125):	2-3X
Production 239 Sets	
Autos. (126-189):	1-1.5X
Production 50 Sets	

Gold

Gold (1-125):	3-4X
Production 99 Sets	
Autos. (126-189):	1-2X
Production 25 Sets	

Sapphire

Sapphire (1-125):	4-8X
Production 25 Sets	
Autos. (126-189):	No Pricing
Production 10 Sets	

Platinum

Production One Set

Printing Plates

Production one set per color.

All-Star Triple Patches

No Pricing	
Production 9 Sets	
Platinum:	No Pricing
Production One Set	

Bat-Barrels

No Pricing

Logo Man

No Pricing
Production One Set

Relics

	NM/M
Common Player:	20.00
Production 36 Sets	
Sepia:	1X
Production 27 Sets	
Emerald:	1-1.5X
Production 18 Sets	
Gold:	No Pricing
Production 9 Sets	
Sapphire:	No Pricing
Production 3 Sets	
Platinum:	No Pricing
Production One Set	

1	Carl Yastrzemski	30.00
2	Carl Yastrzemski	30.00
3	Carl Yastrzemski	30.00
4	Roberto Clemente	100.00
5	Roberto Clemente	100.00
6	Roberto Clemente	100.00
7	Roberto Clemente	100.00
8	Roberto Clemente	100.00
9	Roberto Clemente	100.00
10	Alex Rodriguez	50.00
11	Alex Rodriguez	50.00
12	Alex Rodriguez	50.00
13	Alex Rodriguez	50.00
14	Alex Rodriguez	50.00
15	Alex Rodriguez	50.00
16	Ryan Howard	40.00
17	Ryan Howard	40.00
18	Ryan Howard	40.00
19	David Wright	40.00
20	David Wright	40.00
21	David Wright	40.00
22	Chien-Ming Wang	100.00
23	Chien-Ming Wang	100.00
24	Chien-Ming Wang	100.00
25	Ichiro Suzuki	80.00
26	Ichiro Suzuki	80.00
27	Ichiro Suzuki	80.00
28	Hideki Matsui	60.00
29	Hideki Matsui	60.00
30	Hideki Matsui	60.00
31	Luis Aparicio	20.00
32	Luis Aparicio	20.00
33	Luis Aparicio	20.00
34	Joe DiMaggio	100.00
35	Joe DiMaggio	100.00
36	Joe DiMaggio	100.00
37	Ted Williams	100.00
38	Ted Williams	100.00
39	Ted Williams	100.00
40	Mickey Mantle	150.00
41	Mickey Mantle	150.00
42	Mickey Mantle	150.00
43	Mickey Mantle	150.00

#	Player	Price
44	Mickey Mantle	150.00
45	Mickey Mantle	150.00
46	Mickey Mantle	120.00
47	Mickey Mantle	150.00
48	Mickey Mantle	150.00
49	David Ortiz	30.00
50	David Ortiz	30.00
51	David Ortiz	30.00
52	Albert Pujols	50.00
53	Albert Pujols	50.00
54	Albert Pujols	50.00
55	Justin Morneau	25.00
56	Justin Morneau	25.00
57	Justin Morneau	25.00
58	Nolan Ryan	50.00
59	Nolan Ryan	50.00
60	Nolan Ryan	50.00
61	Nolan Ryan	50.00
62	Nolan Ryan	50.00
63	Nolan Ryan	50.00
64	Manny Ramirez	20.00
65	Manny Ramirez	20.00
66	Manny Ramirez	20.00
67	Roger Maris	80.00
68	Roger Maris	80.00
69	Roger Maris	80.00
70	Daisuke Matsuzaka	100.00
71	Daisuke Matsuzaka	100.00
72	Daisuke Matsuzaka	100.00
73	Brian Cashman	25.00
74	Brian Cashman	25.00
75	Brian Cashman	25.00
76	Ernie Banks	40.00
77	Ernie Banks	40.00
78	Ernie Banks	40.00
79	Stan Musial	50.00
80	Stan Musial	50.00
81	Stan Musial	50.00
82	Duke Snider	30.00
83	Duke Snider	30.00
84	Duke Snider	30.00
85	Yogi Berra	50.00
86	Yogi Berra	50.00
87	Yogi Berra	50.00
88	Harmon Killebrew	40.00
89	Harmon Killebrew	40.00
90	Harmon Killebrew	40.00
91	Joe Mauer	25.00
92	Joe Mauer	25.00
93	Joe Mauer	25.00
94	Alfonso Soriano	25.00
95	Alfonso Soriano	25.00
96	Alfonso Soriano	25.00
97	Reggie Jackson	35.00
98	Reggie Jackson	35.00
99	Reggie Jackson	35.00
100	Reggie Jackson	35.00
101	Reggie Jackson	35.00
102	Reggie Jackson	35.00
103	Vladimir Guerrero	20.00
104	Vladimir Guerrero	20.00
105	Vladimir Guerrero	20.00
106	Pedro Martinez	30.00
107	Pedro Martinez	30.00
108	Pedro Martinez	30.00
109	Roger Clemens	40.00
110	Roger Clemens	40.00
111	Roger Clemens	40.00
112	Randy Johnson	25.00
113	Randy Johnson	25.00
114	Randy Johnson	25.00
115	Don Mattingly	50.00
116	Don Mattingly	50.00
117	Don Mattingly	50.00
118	Bill Dickey	50.00
119	Bill Dickey	50.00
120	Bill Dickey	50.00
121a	Barry Bonds	100.00
121b	Bruce Sutter	20.00
122a	Barry Bonds	100.00
122b	Bruce Sutter	20.00
123a	Barry Bonds	100.00
123b	Bruce Sutter	20.00
124	John F. Kennedy	200.00
125	John F. Kennedy	200.00
126	John F. Kennedy	200.00
127	Johnny Bench	35.00
128	Johnny Bench	35.00
129	Johnny Bench	35.00
130	Mark Teixeira	20.00
131	Mark Teixeira	20.00
132	Mark Teixeira	20.00
133	Johan Santana	30.00
134	Johan Santana	30.00
135	Johan Santana	30.00
136	Alex Rodriguez	50.00
137	Alex Rodriguez	50.00
138	Alex Rodriguez	50.00
139	Brooks Robinson	30.00
140	Brooks Robinson	30.00
141	Brooks Robinson	30.00
142	Rickey Henderson	30.00
143	Rickey Henderson	30.00
144	Rickey Henderson	30.00
145	Ozzie Smith	50.00
146	Ozzie Smith	50.00
147	Ozzie Smith	50.00
148	Chipper Jones	30.00
149	Chipper Jones	30.00
150	Chipper Jones	30.00

Relics Autographs

		NM/M
Production 18 Sets		
Gold:		No Pricing
Production 9 Sets		
Sapphire:		No Pricing
Production 3 Sets		
Platinum:		No Pricing
Production One Set		
1	Alex Rodriguez	275.00
2	Alex Rodriguez	275.00
3	Alex Rodriguez	275.00
4	Chien-Ming Wang	450.00
5	Chien-Ming Wang	450.00
6	Chien-Ming Wang	450.00
7	David Ortiz	100.00
8	David Ortiz	100.00
9	David Ortiz	100.00
10	Manny Ramirez	75.00
11	Manny Ramirez	75.00
12	Manny Ramirez	75.00
13	Johnny Damon	75.00
14	Johnny Damon	75.00
15	Johnny Damon	75.00
16	Miguel Tejada	50.00
17	Miguel Tejada	50.00
18	Miguel Tejada	50.00
19	Carl Crawford	40.00
20	Carl Crawford	40.00
21	Carl Crawford	40.00
22	Johan Santana	60.00
23	Johan Santana	60.00
24	Johan Santana	60.00
25	Francisco Liriano	30.00
26	Francisco Liriano	30.00
27	Francisco Liriano	30.00
28	Bob Feller	60.00
29	Bob Feller	60.00
30	Bob Feller	60.00
31	Vladimir Guerrero	75.00
32	Vladimir Guerrero	75.00
33	Vladimir Guerrero	75.00
34	Ernie Banks	150.00
35	Ernie Banks	150.00
36	Ernie Banks	150.00
37	Yogi Berra	100.00
38	Yogi Berra	100.00
39	Yogi Berra	100.00
40	Nolan Ryan	150.00
41	Nolan Ryan	150.00
42	Nolan Ryan	150.00
43	Ozzie Smith	100.00
44	Ozzie Smith	100.00
45	Ozzie Smith	100.00
46	David Wright	100.00
47	David Wright	100.00
48	David Wright	100.00
49	Albert Pujols	350.00
50	Albert Pujols	350.00
51	Albert Pujols	350.00
52	Ryan Howard	120.00
53	Ryan Howard	120.00
54	Ryan Howard	120.00
55	Don Mattingly	100.00
56	Don Mattingly	100.00
57	Don Mattingly	100.00
58	Brooks Robinson	60.00
59	Brooks Robinson	60.00
60	Brooks Robinson	60.00
61	Robin Yount	75.00
62	Robin Yount	75.00
63	Robin Yount	75.00
64	Mike Schmidt	100.00
65	Mike Schmidt	100.00
66	Mike Schmidt	100.00
67	Carl Yastrzemski	100.00
68	Carl Yastrzemski	100.00
69	Carl Yastrzemski	100.00
70	Wade Boggs	65.00
71	Wade Boggs	65.00
72	Wade Boggs	65.00
73	Andre Dawson	50.00
74	Andre Dawson	50.00
75	Andre Dawson	50.00
76	Reggie Jackson	75.00
77	Reggie Jackson	75.00
78	Reggie Jackson	75.00
79	Miguel Cabrera	60.00
80	Miguel Cabrera	60.00
81	Miguel Cabrera	60.00
82	Tom Seaver	75.00
83	Tom Seaver	75.00
84	Tom Seaver	75.00
85	Ralph Kiner	65.00
86	Ralph Kiner	65.00
87	Ralph Kiner	65.00
88	Chipper Jones	100.00
89	Chipper Jones	100.00
90	Chipper Jones	100.00
91	Andruw Jones	60.00
92	Andruw Jones	60.00
93	Andruw Jones	60.00
94	Dontrelle Willis	40.00
95	Dontrelle Willis	40.00
96	Dontrelle Willis	40.00
97	Bob Gibson	80.00
98	Bob Gibson	80.00
99	Bob Gibson	80.00
100	Johnny Bench	85.00
101	Johnny Bench	85.00
102	Johnny Bench	85.00
103	Joe Morgan	50.00
104	Joe Morgan	50.00
105	Joe Morgan	50.00
106	Ryne Sandberg	120.00
107	Ryne Sandberg	120.00
108	Ryne Sandberg	120.00
109	Dwight Gooden	40.00
110	Dwight Gooden	40.00
111	Dwight Gooden	40.00
112	Johnny Podres	60.00
113	Johnny Podres	60.00
114	Johnny Podres	60.00
115	Monte Irvin	50.00
116	Monte Irvin	50.00
117	Monte Irvin	50.00
118	Orlando Cepeda	50.00
119	Orlando Cepeda	50.00
120	Orlando Cepeda	50.00
121	Bo Jackson	140.00
122	Bo Jackson	140.00
123	Bo Jackson	140.00
124	Gary Sheffield	60.00
125	Gary Sheffield	60.00
126	Gary Sheffield	60.00
127	Tom Glavine	100.00
128	Tom Glavine	100.00
129	Tom Glavine	100.00
130	Tony LaRussa	40.00
131	Tony LaRussa	40.00
132	Tony LaRussa	40.00
133	Jim Leyland	50.00
134	Jim Leyland	50.00
135	Jim Leyland	50.00
136	Joe Torre	60.00
137	Joe Torre	60.00
138	Joe Torre	60.00
139	Gary Carter	75.00
140	Gary Carter	75.00
141	Gary Carter	75.00
142	Roy Oswalt	50.00
143	Roy Oswalt	50.00
144	Roy Oswalt	50.00
145	Carlos Delgado	50.00
146	Carlos Delgado	50.00
147	Carlos Delgado	50.00
148	Jason Varitek	75.00
149	Jason Varitek	75.00
150	Jason Varitek	75.00
151	Bobby Abreu	50.00
152	Bobby Abreu	50.00
153	Bobby Abreu	50.00
154	Juan Marichal	60.00
155	Juan Marichal	60.00
156	Juan Marichal	60.00
157	Frank Robinson	65.00
158	Frank Robinson	65.00
159	Frank Robinson	65.00
160	Jorge Posada	80.00
161	Jorge Posada	80.00
162	Jorge Posada	80.00
163	Luis Aparicio	50.00
164	Luis Aparicio	50.00
165	Luis Aparicio	50.00
166	Carlton Fisk	50.00
167	Carlton Fisk	50.00
168	Carlton Fisk	50.00
169	Dale Murphy	80.00
170	Dale Murphy	80.00
171	Dale Murphy	80.00
172	Mark Teixeira	60.00
173	Mark Teixeira	60.00
174	Mark Teixeira	60.00
175	Darryl Strawberry	50.00
176	Darryl Strawberry	50.00
177	Darryl Strawberry	50.00
178	Justin Morneau	50.00
179	Justin Morneau	50.00
180	Justin Morneau	50.00

Relics Combos Autographs

		NM/M
Production 36 Sets		
Sepia:		1X
Production 27 Sets		
Emerald:		1-1.5X
Production 18 Sets		
Gold:		No Pricing
Production 9 Sets		
Sapphire:		No Pricing
Production 3 Sets		
Platinum:		No Pricing
Production One Set		
1	Brooks Robinson, Robin Yount, Johnny Bench	125.00
2	Reggie Jackson, Joe Morgan, Ryne Sandberg	125.00
3	Tom Seaver, Bob Gibson, Nolan Ryan	180.00
4	Albert Pujols, Alex Rodriguez, Vladimir Guerrero	375.00
5	Tom Seaver, Roger Clemens, Dwight Gooden	160.00
6	Johan Santana, Tom Glavine, Roger Clemens	200.00
7	Alex Rodriguez, Chien-Ming Wang, Don Mattingly	300.00
8	Ryan Howard, Mike Schmidt, Bobby Abreu	150.00
9	Ryan Howard, David Ortiz, Albert Pujols	350.00
10	Alex Rodriguez, David Wright, Jose Reyes	300.00
11	Miguel Cabrera, Manny Ramirez, David Ortiz	125.00
12	Justin Verlander, Jered Weaver, Chien-Ming Wang	250.00
13	Ralph Kiner, Duke Snider, Yogi Berra	125.00
14	Ryan Howard, Alex Rodriguez, Andruw Jones	260.00
15	Adam Lind, Brian Stokes, David Murphy	30.00
16	Andrew Miller, Brian Stokes, Glen Perkins	50.00
17	Shawn Riggans, Troy Tulowitzki, Andrew Miller	80.00
18	Glen Perkins, Lastings Milledge, Troy Tulowitzki	50.00

Relics Combos

		NM/M
Production 36 Sets		
Sepia:		1X
Production 27 Sets		
Emerald:		1-1.5X
Production 18 Sets		
Gold:		No Pricing
Production 9 Sets		
Sapphire:		No Pricing
Production 3 Sets		
Platinum:		No Pricing
Production One Set		
1	Albert Pujols, Manny Ramirez, David Ortiz	40.00
2	Albert Pujols, Pedro Martinez, Vladimir Guerrero	40.00
3	Ivan Rodriguez, Carlos Delgado, Roberto Clemente	60.00
4	Roberto Clemente, Bernie Williams, Carlos Beltran	65.00
5	Jose Reyes, Alfonso Soriano, Miguel Tejada	30.00
6	Carl Crawford, Jose Reyes, Juan Pierre	25.00
7	Hideki Matsui, Ichiro Suzuki, So Taguchi	60.00
8	Miguel Cabrera, Johan Santana, Bobby Abreu	25.00
9	Alex Rodriguez, Mariano Rivera, Hideki Matsui	60.00
10	Reggie Jackson, Alex Rodriguez, Don Mattingly	50.00
11	Yogi Berra, Don Mattingly, Reggie Jackson	75.00
12	David Ortiz, Wade Boggs, Manny Ramirez	25.00
13	David Ortiz, Manny Ramirez, Pedro Martinez	30.00

14	Miguel Tejada, Eddie Murray, Brooks Robinson	30.00
15	Joe Mauer, Justin Morneau, Johan Santana	30.00
16	Harmon Killebrew, Joe Mauer, Justin Morneau	40.00
17	Justin Verlander, Ivan Rodriguez, Joel Zumaya	25.00
18	Barry Zito, Dennis Eckersley, Huston Street	20.00
19	Reggie Jackson, Rod Carew, Vladimir Guerrero	30.00
20	Vladimir Guerrero, Pedro Martinez, Moises Alou	30.00
21	Michael Young, Mark Teixeira, Alex Rodriguez	40.00
22	Edgar Martinez, Ichiro Suzuki, Alex Rodriguez	70.00
23	David Wright, Carlos Delgado, Jose Reyes	40.00
24	Jose Reyes, Pedro Martinez, David Wright	50.00
25	Jose Reyes, Carlos Beltran, David Wright	40.00
26	Ryan Howard, Chase Utley, Jimmy Rollins	50.00
27	Jeff Francoeur, Chipper Jones, Brian McCann	30.00
28	John Smoltz, Tom Glavine, Greg Maddux	40.00
29	Chipper Jones, Jeff Francoeur, Andruw Jones	40.00
30	Nolan Ryan, Pedro Martinez, Tom Seaver	50.00
31	Mike Schmidt, Jim Thome, Ryan Howard	40.00
32	Stan Musial, Albert Pujols, Ozzie Smith	60.00
33	Albert Pujols, David Eckstein, Jim Edmonds	50.00
34	Lance Berkman, Roy Oswalt, Craig Biggio	25.00
35	Roger Clemens, Roy Oswalt, Nolan Ryan	40.00
36	Frank Robinson, Joe Morgan, Johnny Bench	30.00
37	Paul Molitor, Prince Fielder, Robin Yount	40.00
38	Ernie Banks, Alfonso Soriano, Ryne Sandberg	50.00
39	Andre Ethier, Matthew Kemp, Jered Weaver	25.00
40	Chien-Ming Wang, Alex Rodriguez, Mariano Rivera	100.00
41	Albert Pujols, Ichiro Suzuki, Vladimir Guerrero	50.00
42	Albert Pujols, Alex Rodriguez, Ichiro Suzuki	75.00
43	Ryan Howard, Justin Morneau, Albert Pujols	50.00
44	Albert Pujols, Roberto Clemente, Ichiro Suzuki	100.00
45	Albert Pujols, Roberto Clemente, Mickey Mantle	150.00
46	Joe DiMaggio, Mickey Mantle, Alex Rodriguez	150.00
47	Ted Williams, Joe DiMaggio, Mickey Mantle	200.00
48	Roberto Clemente, Mickey Mantle, Reggie Jackson	125.00
49	Stan Musial, Roberto Clemente, Frank Robinson	100.00
50	Albert Pujols, Johnny Bench, Mickey Mantle	100.00
51	Carl Yastrzemski, Ted Williams, Mickey Mantle	140.00
52	Brandon Webb, Tom Seaver, Johan Santana	30.00
53	Roger Clemens, Dwight Gooden, Pedro Martinez	40.00
54	Johan Santana, Greg Maddux, Roger Clemens	35.00
55	Johan Santana, Pedro Martinez, Roger Clemens	30.00
56	Randy Johnson, Roger Clemens, Tom Glavine	30.00
57	Justin Verlander, Ryan Howard, Ichiro Suzuki	50.00
58	Dontrelle Willis, Carlos Beltran, Jason Bay	20.00
59	Albert Pujols, Scott Rolen, Ryan Howard	40.00
60	Roberto Clemente, Joe DiMaggio, Mickey Mantle	200.00
61	Stan Musial, Ernie Banks, Mickey Mantle	140.00
62	Mike Schmidt, Joe Morgan, Johnny Bench	35.00
63	George Brett, Robin Yount, Ozzie Smith	60.00
64	Albert Pujols, Ichiro Suzuki, Rod Carew	50.00
65	Alfonso Soriano, Mickey Mantle, Alex Rodriguez	100.00
66	Don Mattingly, Wade Boggs, Tony Gwynn	50.00
67	Rod Carew, Vladimir Guerrero, Garret Anderson	25.00
68	Tony Gwynn, Wade Boggs, George Brett	50.00
69	Vladimir Guerrero, Alfonso Soriano, Bobby Abreu	30.00
70	Darryl Strawberry, Carlos Beltran, Howard Johnson	30.00
71	Jim Thome, Manny Ramirez, Frank Thomas	30.00
72	Mickey Mantle, Mike Piazza, Mike Schmidt	120.00
73	Carl Yastrzemski, Alex Rodriguez, Dave Winfield	50.00
74	Johan Santana, Pedro Martinez, Roger Clemens	30.00
75	Greg Maddux, Nolan Ryan, Tom Seaver	60.00
76	Bob Gibson, Dwight Gooden, Greg Maddux	50.00
77	Roberto Clemente, Reggie Jackson, Manny Ramirez	75.00
78	Johnny Podres, Don Larsen, Lew Burdette	30.00
79	Ichiro Suzuki, Kenji Johjima, Tadahito Iguchi	70.00
80	Paul Molitor, Jimmy Rollins, Chase Utley	35.00
81	Gary Carter, Paul LoDuca, Mike Piazza	60.00
82	George Brett, Alex Rodriguez, David Wright	50.00
83	Hoyt Wilhelm, Phil Niekro, Tim Wakefield	35.00
84	Franklin D. Roosevelt, Harry S. Truman, Dwight D. Eisenhower	80.00
85	Ichiro Suzuki, Eric Chavez, Torii Hunter	50.00
86	Richard Nixon, Ronald Reagan, George W. Bush	100.00
87	John Smoltz, Carlos Delgado, Edgar Martinez	30.00
88	Manny Ramirez, Vladimir Guerrero, David Ortiz	30.00
89	Livan Hernandez, Orel Hershiser, Willie Stargell	20.00
90	David Ortiz, Ryan Howard, Albert Pujols	50.00
91	Chien-Ming Wang, Johan Santana, Jon Garland	80.00
92	Deion Sanders, Bo Jackson, Brian Jordan	60.00
93	Franklin D. Roosevelt, John F. Kennedy, Bill Clinton	125.00
94	Vladimir Guerrero, Ichiro Suzuki, Vernon Wells	50.00
95	Jim Thome, Jermaine Dye, Paul Konerko	25.00
96	A.J. Pierzynski, Kelvim Escobar, Josh Paul	20.00
97	Joe Carter, Rickey Henderson, Paul Molitor	50.00
98	Kirk Gibson, Dennis Eckersley	25.00
99	Luis Castillo, Moises Alou, Mark Prior	20.00
100	Mookie Wilson, Ray Knight, Bill Buckner	50.00

Relics Combos
Double

	NM/M
Production 36 Sets Sepia:	No Pricing
Production 27 Sets Emerald:	1-1.5X
Production 18 Sets Gold:	No Pricing
Production 9 Sets Sapphire:	No Pricing
Production 3 Sets Platinum:	No Pricing

Production One Set

1	Mickey Mantle, Joe DiMaggio	250.00
2	Alex Rodriguez, Chien-Ming Wang, Johnny Damon, Manny Ramirez, David Ortiz, Jason Varitek	100.00
3	David Wright, Carlos Beltran, Tom Glavine, Chipper Jones, Andruw Jones, John Smoltz	50.00
4	David Wright	50.00
5	Albert Pujols	70.00
6	Chien-Ming Wang	100.00
7	David Wright, Ryan Howard	60.00
8	Alex Rodriguez	70.00
9	Ryan Howard	60.00
10	Ichiro Suzuki	100.00
11	Albert Pujols, Pedro Martinez, David Ortiz, Vladimir Guerrero, Manny Ramirez, Alfonso Soriano	70.00
12	Ichiro Suzuki, So Taguchi, Hideki Matsui, Kazuo Matsui, Tadahito Iguchi, Kenji Johjima	140.00
13	Roberto Clemente, Ivan Rodriguez, Carlos Beltran, Bernie Williams, Carlos Delgado, Javy Lopez	125.00
14	Johan Santana, Miguel Cabrera, Bobby Abreu, Omar Vizquel, Ozzie Guillen, Luis Aparicio	50.00
15	Mickey Mantle, Joe DiMaggio, Ted Williams, Ernie Banks, Yogi Berra, Stan Musial	200.00
16	Mickey Mantle, Albert Pujols, Vladimir Guerrero, Ted Williams, Roberto Clemente, Joe DiMaggio	200.00
17	Mickey Mantle, Alex Rodriguez, Don Mattingly, Yogi Berra, Chien-Ming Wang, Reggie Jackson	200.00
18	Carl Yastrzemski, Manny Ramirez, David Ortiz, Pedro Martinez, Johnny Damon, Carlton Fisk	60.00
19	Justin Morneau, Torii Hunter, Joe Mauer, Johan Santana, Francisco Liriano, Harmon Killebrew	60.00
20	Justin Verlander, Joel Zumaya, Curtis Granderson, Magglio Ordonez, Ivan Rodriguez, Kenny Rogers	50.00
21	Nick Swisher, Huston Street, Reggie Jackson, Barry Zito, Jose Canseco, Dennis Eckersley	40.00
22	Vladimir Guerrero, Rod Carew, Jered Weaver, Reggie Jackson, Garret Anderson, Francisco Rodriguez	50.00
23	Vladimir Guerrero, Pedro Martinez, Moises Alou, Gary Carter, Andre Dawson, Randy Johnson	50.00
24	Nolan Ryan, Mark Teixeira, Michael Young, Alex Rodriguez, Ivan Rodriguez, Hank Blalock	65.00
25	Kenji Johjima, Ichiro Suzuki, Alex Rodriguez, Randy Johnson, Edgar Martinez, Richie Sexson	90.00
26	David Wright, Jose Reyes, Carlos Beltran, Pedro Martinez, Tom Glavine, Carlos Delgado	75.00
27	David Eckstein, Albert Pujols, Chris Carpenter, Stan Musial, Ozzie Smith, Jim Edmonds	75.00
28	Nolan Ryan, Andy Pettitte, Roger Clemens, Roy Oswalt, Lance Berkman, Craig Biggio	75.00
29	Ryan Howard, Chase Utley, Mike Schmidt, Jimmy Rollins, Richie Ashburn, Steve Carlton	100.00
30	Jeff Francoeur, Brian McCann, Chipper Jones, Andruw Jones, John Smoltz, Tim Hudson	70.00
31	Alfonso Soriano, Ernie Banks, Ryne Sandberg, Kerry Wood, Mark Prior, Andre Dawson	60.00
32	David Wright, Justin Morneau, Ryan Howard, Chien-Ming Wang, Chase Utley, Jose Reyes	75.00
33	David Ortiz	35.00
34	Roger Maris, Stan Musial, Roberto Clemente, Ernie Banks, Johnny Bench, Carl Yastrzemski	150.00
35	Albert Pujols, Jim Edmonds, Scott Rolen, Ivan Rodriguez, Kenny Rogers, Magglio Ordonez	50.00
36	Derrek Lee, Juan Pierre, Greg Maddux, Paul Konerko, Jermaine Dye, Jim Thome	60.00
37	David WC.C. Sabathia	50.00

42	Chien-Ming Wang, Johan Santana, Jon Garland, Randy Johnson, Kenny Rogers, Freddy Garcia	85.00
43	Johan Santana, Aaron Harang, Jake Peavy, John Smoltz, Carlos Zambrano, Jeremy Bonderman	50.00
44	Jeff Suppan, Roy Oswalt, Albert Pujols, Placido Polanco, Paul Konerko, David Ortiz	50.00
45	Orlando Cepeda, Monte Irvin, Bobby Thomson, Duke Snider, Johnny Podres, Don Zimmerman	75.00
46	Ryne Sandberg, Wade Boggs, Dennis Eckersley, Paul Molitor, Gary Carter, Eddie Murray	70.00
47	Jermaine Dye, Paul Konerko, A.J. Pierzynski, Craig Biggio, Lance Berkman, Morgan Ensberg	50.00
48	Roger Clemens, Randy Johnson, Greg Maddux, Curt Schilling, Pedro Martinez, John Smoltz	85.00
49	David Wright, Brooks Robinson, George Brett, Mike Schmidt, Alex Rodriguez, Eddie Murray	80.00
50	Alfonso Soriano, Bobby Abreu, Carlos Beltran, Vladimir Guerrero, Alex Rodriguez, Preston Wilson	70.00

Triple Signed Hide
Production One Set

2007 Topps Turkey Red

		NM/M
Complete Set (186):		
Common Player:		.25
Common SP:		4.00
Inserted 1:4		
Pack (8):		4.00
Box (24):		85.00
1	Ryan Howard	2.00
1	Ryan Howard/SP Ad Back	8.00
2	Dontrelle Willis	.25
3	Matt Cain	.50
4	John Maine	.50
5	Cole Hamels	.75
6	Corey Patterson	.25
7	Mickey Mantle/SP	25.00
8	Johan Santana/CL	.75
9	Josh Beckett	.75
10	Jimmy Rollins	1.00
11	Kenji Johjima	.50
12	Orlando Hernandez	.25
13	Jorge Posada/CL	.50
14	Ivan Rodriguez	.75
15	Ichiro Suzuki	2.00
15	Ichiro Suzuki/SP Ad Back	6.00
16	Ken Griffey Jr./CL	1.00
17	Stephen Drew	.25
18	B.J. Upton	.50
19	Mickey Mantle	3.00
20	Alex Rodriguez	3.00
20	Alex Rodriguez/SP Ad Back	8.00
21	Adam Dunn	.75
22	Adam Lind/SP (RC)	6.00
23	Adrian Gonzalez	.50
24	Akinori Iwamura RC	2.00
25	Albert Pujols	3.00
25	Albert Pujols/SP Ad Back	8.00
26	Frank Thomas	1.00
27	Roy Halladay	.50
28	Alejandro De Aza RC	.50
29	Alex Gordon RC	4.00
30	Barry Bonds	3.00
31	Andrew Miller RC	4.00
32	Andruw Jones	.75
33	Kurt Suzuki/SP (RC)	5.00
34	Mickey Mantle	3.00
35	Andy Pettitte	.50
36	Tadahito Iguchi	.25
37	Edgar Renteria	.50
38	Tim Hudson	.50
39	Micah Owings (RC)	.50
40	Chipper Jones	1.00
40	Chipper Jones/SP Ad Back	6.00
41	Barry Zito	.50
42	Daisuke Matsuzaka/CL	2.00
43	Jarrod Saltalamacchia/SP (RC)	6.00
44	Bill Hall	.25
45	Billy Butler (RC)	1.00
46	Billy Wagner	.25
47	Rich Harden/SP	.50
48	Albert Pujols/CL	1.00
49	Brandon Inge	.25
50	Jason Giambi	.50
51	Brandon Webb	.75
52	Brandon Wood (RC)	1.00
53	Carl Crawford/CL	.50
54	Brian Giles	.25
55	Josh Hamilton (RC)	1.00
56	Chase Utley	1.50
56	Chase Utley/SP Ad Back	6.00
57	Miguel Montero (RC)	.50
58	Carl Crawford	.50
59	Carlos Beltran	1.00
60	Mariano Rivera	.50
61	Carlos Delgado	.75
62	Carlos Lee/SP	5.00
63	Carlos Zambrano/SP	5.00
64	Miguel Tejada	.50
65	Mike Cameron	.25
66	Chase Utley/SP	8.00
67	Chase Wright/SP	1.00
68	Chien-Ming Wang	1.00
69	Nick Swisher	.50
70	David Wright	1.50
71	Mike Piazza/SP	1.00
72	Chris Carpenter	1.00
73	Mark Buehrle/SP	4.00
74	Torii Hunter/SP	5.00
75	Tyler Clippard (RC)	.50
76	Nicholas Markakis	.50
77	Mickey Mantle	3.00
78	Curt Schilling	1.00
79	Curtis Granderson	.75
80	Craig Biggio	.50
81	Juan Pierre	.50
82	Dallas Braden/SP RC	4.00
83	Dan Haren/SP	6.00
84	Dan Uggla	.50
85	Danny Putnam (RC)	.50
86	David DeJesus	.25
87	David Eckstein	.25
88	Tim Lincecum RC	6.00
89	Johnny Damon/SP	6.00
90	Justin Morneau	1.00
91	Delmon Young (RC)	1.00
92	Homer Bailey (RC)	1.00
93	Carlos Gomez RC	1.00
94	Josh Fields/SP (RC)	4.00
95	Derek Jeter	3.00
95	Derek Jeter/SP Ad Back	8.00
96	Derrek Lee	.75
97	Donald Kelly (RC)	.50
98	Doug Slaten RC	.50
99	Dustin Moseley	.25
100	Gary Sheffield	.75
101	Orlando Hudson/SP	4.00
102	Elijah Dukes RC	1.00
103	Eric Byrnes/SP	4.00
104	Eric Chavez	.50
105	Phil Hughes (RC)	1.00
105	Phil Hughes/SP Ad Back	6.00
106	Felix Hernandez/SP	4.00
106	Felix Hernandez/SP Ad Back	6.00
107	Mickey Mantle	3.00
108	Felix Pie (RC)	1.00
109	Derek Jeter CL	1.00
110	Daisuke Matsuzaka RC	5.00
110	Daisuke Matsuzaka/SP Ad Back RC	10.00
111	Francisco Rodriguez	.50
112	Ramon Hernandez	.25
113	Randy Johnson	1.00
114	Gary Matthews	.25
115	Prince Fielder	1.00
116	Vladimir Guerrero/CL	1.00
117	Mickey Mantle	3.00
118	Hideki Matsui	2.00
119	Hideki Okajima RC	1.00
120	Manny Ramirez	1.00
121	Hunter Pence/SP (RC)	10.00
122	Roy Oswalt	.50
123	Josh Willingham/SP	4.00
124	Tom Gordon/SP	.50
125	Michael Young	.50
126	J.D. Drew	.25
127	Ryan Zimmerman	.50
128	James Shields/SP	4.00
129	Jack Wilson	.25
130	David Ortiz	1.00
130	David Ortiz/SP Ad Back	6.00
131	Jose Reyes/CL	.50
132	Jamie Vermilyea RC	.50
133	Jason Bay	.50
134	Scott Kazmir/SP	4.00
135	Jason Isringhausen/SP	4.00
136	Jason Marquis/SP	4.00
137	Jason Schmidt	.50
138	Shawn Green	.25
139	Jeff Francoeur/SP	5.00
140	Alfonso Soriano	1.00
141	Kevin Kouzmanoff (RC)	.50
142	Jered Weaver	.75
143	Todd Helton/SP	5.00
144	Jermaine Dye	.50
145	Jim Thome	.75
146	Tom Glavine/SP	5.00
147	Joe Mauer	.75
148	Joe Nathan	.50
149	Joe Smith RC	.50
150	Ken Griffey Jr.	2.00
150	Ken Griffey Jr./SP Ad Back	6.00
151	Grady Sizemore	1.00
152	Sammy Sosa/SP	5.00
153	Andy LaRoche (RC)	1.00
154	Travis Buck (RC)	.50
155	Alex Rios	.50
156	Travis Hafner	.50
157	Jake Peavy	.50
158	Jeff Kent	.50
159	Johan Santana	1.00
159	Johan Santana/SP Ad Back	5.00
160	Ivan Rodriguez	.75
161	Trevor Hoffman	.50
162	Troy Glaus	.50
163	Troy Tulowitzki (RC)	1.00
164	Jorge Posada	.50
165	Kei Igawa/SP RC	1.00
166	Jose Reyes	1.00
167	Mickey Mantle	3.00
168	Chase Utley/CL	.50
169	Justin Verlander	.50
170	Hanley Ramirez	1.00
171	Kelly Johnson/SP	4.00
172	Kelvin Jimenez RC	.50
173	Roger Clemens	2.00
174	Khalil Greene/SP	5.00
175	Lance Berkman	.50
176	Hanley Ramirez/CL	.50
177	Kyle Kendrick RC	2.00
178	Magglio Ordonez	.50
179	Marcus Giles/SP	4.00
180	Miguel Cabrera	1.00
180	Miguel Cabrera/SP Ad Back	5.00
181	Mark Teahen	.25
182	Mark Teixeira/SP	5.00
183	Matt Chico/SP (RC)	4.00
184	Matt Holliday	.75
185	Vladimir Guerrero	1.00
185	Vladimir Guerrero/SP Ad Back	5.00
186	Yovani Gallardo (RC)	1.00

Chrome
Chrome: 2-3X
Chrome SP's: 1X
Production 1,999 Sets

Chrome Refractors
Refractors: 3-4X
Refractor SP's: 1-2X
Production 999 Sets

Chrome Black Refractors
Refractors: 5-10X
Refractor SP's: 2-4X
Production 99 Sets

A-Rod Road to 500
Common A-Rod (301-325): Inserted 2:Box

A-Rod Road to 500 Autographs
Production One Set

Cabinet

		NM/M
Common Player:		3.00
Inserted 1:Box		
JB	Jason Bay	5.00
LB	Lance Berkman	6.00
MC	Miguel Cabrera	6.00
CC	Chris Carpenter	8.00
SD	Stephen Drew	4.00
ED	Elijah Dukes	4.00
JD	Jermaine Dye	4.00
AD	Adam Dunn	4.00
PF	Prince Fielder	15.00
JF	Jeff Francoeur	10.00
AG	Alex Gordon	15.00
KG	Ken Griffey Jr.	15.00
VG	Vladimir Guerrero	8.00
FH	Felix Hernandez	5.00
RH	Ryan Howard	15.00
KI	Kei Igawa	4.00
AI	Akinori Iwamura	3.00
DJ	Derek Jeter	20.00
AJ	Andruw Jones	5.00
CL	Carlos Lee	4.00
MM	Mickey Mantle	25.00
NM	Nicholas Markakis	8.00
DM	Daisuke Matsuzaka	15.00
JM	Joe Mauer	5.00
JEM	Justin Morneau	5.00
HO	Hideki Okajima	8.00
DO	David Ortiz	15.00
MP	Mike Piazza	10.00
AP	Albert Pujols	20.00
HR	Hanley Ramirez	10.00
MR	Manny Ramirez	10.00
JR	Jose Reyes	15.00
AR	Alex Rodriguez	20.00
FR	Francisco Rodriguez	4.00
IR	Ivan Rodriguez	5.00
JS	Johan Santana	8.00
JDS	Jason Schmidt	3.00
GS	Grady Sizemore	10.00
AS	Alfonso Soriano	8.00
IS	Ichiro Suzuki	15.00
MT	Miguel Tejada	5.00
TT	Troy Tulowitzki	8.00
CU	Chase Utley	10.00
JV	Justin Verlander	5.00
CW	Chien-Ming Wang	8.00
BW	Brandon Webb	4.00
DW	David Wright	15.00
DY	Delmon Young	5.00
MY	Michael Young	5.00
RZ	Ryan Zimmerman	10.00
BZ	Barry Zito	3.00

Cabinet Dick Perez Autographs
NM/M
Production 25 Sets

JB	Jason Bay	30.00
LB	Lance Berkman	30.00
MC	Miguel Cabrera	30.00
CC	Chris Carpenter	30.00
SD	Stephen Drew	25.00
ED	Elijah Dukes	20.00
AD	Adam Dunn	25.00
JD	Jermaine Dye	30.00
PF	Prince Fielder	40.00
JF	Jeff Francoeur	30.00
AG	Alex Gordon	35.00
KG	Ken Griffey Jr.	50.00
VG	Vladimir Guerrero	30.00
FH	Felix Hernandez	30.00
RH	Ryan Howard	40.00
KI	Kei Igawa	25.00
AI	Akinori Iwamura	30.00
AJ	Andruw Jones	30.00
CL	Carlos Lee	30.00
MM	Mickey Mantle	100.00
NM	Nicholas Markakis	30.00
JM	Joe Mauer	30.00
JEM	Justin Morneau	30.00
HO	Hideki Okajima	30.00
DO	David Ortiz	50.00
MP	Mike Piazza	40.00
AP	Albert Pujols	80.00
HR	Hanley Ramirez	40.00
MR	Manny Ramirez	30.00
JR	Jose Reyes	40.00
AR	Alex Rodriguez	80.00
FR	Francisco Rodriguez	25.00
IR	Ivan Rodriguez	30.00
JS	Johan Santana	30.00
JDS	Jason Schmidt	25.00
GS	Grady Sizemore	40.00
AS	Alfonso Soriano	50.00
IS	Ichiro Suzuki	80.00
MT	Miguel Tejada	30.00
TT	Troy Tulowitzki	30.00
CU	Chase Utley	50.00
JV	Justin Verlander	30.00
CW	Chien-Ming Wang	50.00
BW	Brandon Webb	30.00
DW	David Wright	50.00
DY	Delmon Young	30.00
MY	Michael Young	30.00
RZ	Ryan Zimmerman	30.00
BZ	Barry Zito	30.00

Chromographs

		NM/M
	Common Autograph:	10.00
AG	Alex Gordon	50.00
AK	Austin Kearns	15.00
AR	Alex Rodriguez	250.00
BJ	Bobby Jenks	25.00
BW	Brad Wilkerson	10.00
CAH	Clay Hensley	10.00
CG	Curtis Granderson	75.00
CH	Cole Hamels	40.00
CJ	Chuck James	15.00
DE	Darin Erstad	15.00
DU	Dan Uggla	20.00
EC	Eric Chavez	20.00
FP	Felix Pie	20.00
GS	Gary Sheffield	40.00
HCK	Hong-Chih Kuo	25.00
HR	Hanley Ramirez	30.00
JB	Jason Bay	40.00
JD	Johnny Damon	40.00
JM	John Maine	25.00
JZ	Joel Zumaya	20.00
KE	Kelvim Escobar	15.00
LM	Lastings Milledge	20.00
MC	Melky Cabrera	30.00
MG	Mike Gonzalez	10.00
NM	Nicholas Markakis	25.00
NR	Nate Robertson	20.00
PL	Paul LoDuca	15.00
RC	Robinson Cano	40.00
RH	Ryan Howard	80.00
RJH	Rich Hill	20.00
RM	Robert Mackowiak	15.00
RNM	Russell Martin	25.00
SC	Sean Casey	25.00
SP	Scott Podsednik	15.00
SV	Shane Victorino	25.00
TG	Tony Gwynn Jr.	20.00
WN	Wilbert Nieves	10.00

Presidents

		NM/M
	Common President:	1.00
	Inserted 1:12	
1	George Washington	4.00
2	John Adams	2.00
3	Thomas Jefferson	3.00
4	James Madison	2.00
5	James Monroe	2.00
6	John Quincy Adams	2.00
7	Andrew Jackson	2.00
8	Martin Van Buren	1.00
9	William H. Harrison	1.00

10	John Tyler	1.00
11	James K. Polk	1.00
12	Zachary Taylor	1.00
13	Millard Fillmore	1.00
14	Franklin Pierce	1.00
15	James Buchanan	1.00
16	Abraham Lincoln	4.00
17	Andrew Johnson	1.00
18	Ulysses S. Grant	2.00
19	Rutherford B. Hayes	1.00
20	James Garfield	1.00
21	Chester A. Arthur	1.00
22	Grover Cleveland	1.00
23	Benjamin Harrison	1.00
24	Grover Cleveland	1.00
25	William McKinley	1.00
26	Theodore Roosevelt	3.00
27	William H. Taft	1.00
28	Woodrow Wilson	1.00
29	Warren G. Harding	1.00
30	Calvin Coolidge	1.00
31	Herbert Hoover	1.00
32	Franklin D. Roosevelt	3.00
33	Harry S. Truman	2.00
34	Dwight D. Eisenhower	3.00
35	John F. Kennedy	4.00
36	Lyndon B. Johnson	1.00
37	Richard Nixon	2.00
38	Gerald Ford	1.00
39	Jimmy Carter	2.00
40	Ronald Reagan	2.00
41	George H.W. Bush	2.00
42	Bill Clinton	2.00
43	George W. Bush	2.00

Relics

		NM/M
	Common Relic:	4.00
AB	Adrian Beltre	4.00
AD	Adam Dunn	6.00
AH	Aaron Harang	4.00
AJ1	Andruw Jones	6.00
AJ2	Andruw Jones	6.00
AM	Andrew Miller	8.00
ANB	Angel Berroa	4.00
AS	Alfonso Soriano	10.00
BB	Barry Bonds	30.00
BC	Bobby Crosby	4.00
BJR	B.J. Ryan	4.00
BR	Brian Roberts	6.00
BS	Brian Stokes	4.00
BT	Brad Thompson	4.00
BW	Brandon Webb	6.00
BZ	Benjamin Zobrist	6.00
CB1	Carlos Beltran	8.00
CB2	Carlos Beltran	8.00
CC	Coco Crisp	6.00
CD	Carlos Delgado	8.00
CH	Cole Hamels	10.00
CJ	Chipper Jones	10.00
CJC	Chris Carpenter	8.00
CL	Carlos Lee	6.00
CR	Chris Ray	4.00
CS	C.C. Sabathia	6.00
DN	Dioner Navarro	4.00
DO	David Ortiz	10.00
DR	Darrell Rasner	4.00
DU	Dan Uggla	6.00
DW	David Wright	15.00
DWA	Daryle Ward	4.00
DWW	Dontrelle Willis	6.00
DY	Delmon Young	6.00
ES	Ervin Santana	4.00
GP	Glen Perkins	4.00
HB	Hank Blalock	8.00
HR	Hanley Ramirez	10.00
IR	Ivan Rodriguez	8.00
IS	Ichiro Suzuki	20.00
JB	Josh Beckett	6.00
JC	Jorge Cantu	4.00
JD	Jermaine Dye	6.00
JE	Jim Edmonds	6.00
JF	Jeff Francoeur	15.00
JG	Jon Garland	4.00
JH	Josh Hamilton	8.00
JK	Jeff Kent	4.00
JM	Justin Morneau	8.00
JP	Josh Paul	4.00
JPM	Joe Mauer	8.00
JR	Jose Reyes	10.00
JRB	Jason Bay	6.00
JS	John Smoltz	8.00
JV2	Jason Varitek	10.00

JW	Jered Weaver	8.00
JZ	Joel Zumaya	8.00
KM	Kazuo Matsui	6.00
LB	Lance Berkman	6.00
LC	Luis Castillo	4.00
MC	Melky Cabrera	8.00
ME	Morgan Ensberg	4.00
MG	Marcus Giles	4.00
MJC	Miguel Cairo	4.00
MM	Mickey Mantle	125.00
MP	Mike Piazza	10.00
MR	Manny Ramirez	8.00
MT	Miguel Tejada	6.00
MY	Michael Young	6.00
NM	Nicholas Markakis	20.00
NP	Neifi Perez	4.00
NS	Nick Swisher	6.00
PM	Pedro Martinez	8.00
PP	Placido Polanco	6.00
RB1	Rocco Baldelli	4.00
RB2	Rocco Baldelli	4.00
RH	Ryan Howard	15.00
RJH	Rich Hill	6.00
RK	Ryan Klesko	4.00
RS	Reggie Sanders	4.00
RZ	Ryan Zimmerman	10.00
SR	Scott Rolen	8.00
SS	Sammy Sosa	8.00
ST	So Taguchi	4.00
TB	Travis Buck	4.00
TH	Travis Hafner	8.00
TI	Tadahito Iguchi	6.00
TJ	Tyler Johnson	8.00
VG	Vladimir Guerrero	8.00
VW	Vernon Wells	6.00

Silks

		NM/M
	Common Player:	15.00
	Production 99 Sets	
AD	Adam Dunn	15.00
AI	Akinori Iwamura	15.00
AIR	Alex Rios	15.00
AP	Albert Pujols	50.00
AR	Alex Rodriguez	50.00
AS	Alfonso Soriano	20.00
BB	Billy Butler	20.00
BLB	Barry Bonds	40.00
CH	Cole Hamels	25.00
CJ	Chipper Jones	25.00
CS	C.C. Sabathia	15.00
CY	Adrian Gonzalez	15.00
DH	Danny Haren	15.00
DJ	Derek Jeter	50.00
DM	Daisuke Matsuzaka	80.00
DO	David Ortiz	30.00
DU	Dan Uggla	15.00
DW	David Wright	30.00
DWW	Dontrelle Willis	20.00
EB	Erik Bedard	20.00
GS	Grady Sizemore	25.00
HP	Hunter Pence	30.00
HR	Hanley Ramirez	20.00
IS	Ichiro Suzuki	50.00
JAS	John Smoltz	20.00
JB	Josh Beckett	20.00
JBR	Jose Reyes	25.00
JD	Jermaine Dye	15.00
JH	J.J. Hardy	15.00
JL	John Lackey	15.00
JM	Justin Morneau	20.00
JP	Jake Peavy	20.00
JR	Jimmy Rollins	25.00
JRB	Jason Bay	15.00
JS	Johan Santana	25.00
JV	Justin Verlander	25.00
KG	Ken Griffey Jr.	40.00
MAR	Manny Ramirez	25.00
MH	Matt Holliday	25.00
MM	Mickey Mantle	80.00
MO	Magglio Ordonez	25.00
MR	Mark Reynolds	15.00

MT	Mark Teixeira	20.00
NS	Nick Swisher	20.00
PF	Prince Fielder	30.00
RH	Ryan Howard	40.00
RM	Russell Martin	20.00
RZ	Ryan Zimmerman	25.00
TH	Torii Hunter	15.00
VG	Vladimir Guerrero	15.00

U

1991 Ultra

		NM/M
Complete Set (400):		12.00
Common Player:		.05
Wax Pack (14):		.50
Wax Box (36):		9.00
1	Steve Avery	.05
2	Jeff Blauser	.05
3	Francisco Cabrera	.05
4	Ron Gant	.05
5	Tom Glavine	.25
6	Tommy Gregg	.05
7	Dave Justice	.05
8	Oddibe McDowell	.05
9	Greg Olson	.05
10	Terry Pendleton	.05
11	Lonnie Smith	.05
12	John Smoltz	.05
13	Jeff Treadway	.05
14	Glenn Davis	.05
15	Mike Devereaux	.05
16	Leo Gomez	.05
17	Chris Hoiles	.05
18	Dave Johnson	.05
19	Ben McDonald	.05
20	Randy Milligan	.05
21	Gregg Olson	.05
22	Joe Orsulak	.05
23	Bill Ripken	.05
24	Cal Ripken, Jr.	1.50
25	David Segui	.05
26	Craig Worthington	.05
27	Wade Boggs	.60
28	Tom Bolton	.05
29	Tom Brunansky	.05
30	Ellis Burks	.05
31	Roger Clemens	.65
32	Mike Greenwell	.05
33	Greg Harris	.05
34	Daryl Irvine	.05
35	Mike Marshall	.05
36	Tim Naehring	.05
37	Tony Pena	.05
38	Phil Plantier RC	.05
39	Carlos Quintana	.05
40	Jeff Reardon	.05
41	Jody Reed	.05
42	Luis Rivera	.05
43	Jim Abbott	.05
44	Chuck Finley	.05
45	Bryan Harvey	.05
46	Donnie Hill	.05
47	Jack Howell	.05
48	Wally Joyner	.05
49	Mark Langston	.05
50	Kirk McCaskill	.05
51	Lance Parrish	.05
52	Dick Schofield	.05
53	Lee Stevens	.05
54	Dave Winfield	.50
55	George Bell	.05
56	Damon Berryhill	.05
57	Mike Bielecki	.05
58	Andre Dawson	.25
59	Shawon Dunston	.05
60	Joe Girardi	.05
61	Mark Grace	.05
62	Mike Harkey	.05

63	Les Lancaster	.05	159	Tim Belcher	.05	263	Charlie Hayes	.05	367	John Olerud	.05

No.	Player	Price
63	Les Lancaster	.05
64	Greg Maddux	.60
65	Derrick May	.05
66	Ryne Sandberg	.60
67	Luis Salazar	.05
68	Dwight Smith	.05
69	Hector Villanueva	.05
70	Jerome Walton	.05
71	Mitch Williams	.05
72	Carlton Fisk	.50
73	Scott Fletcher	.05
74	Ozzie Guillen	.05
75	Greg Hibbard	.05
76	Lance Johnson	.05
77	Steve Lyons	.05
78	Jack McDowell	.05
79	Dan Pasqua	.05
80	Melido Perez	.05
81	Tim Raines	.05
82	Sammy Sosa	.60
83	Cory Snyder	.05
84	Bobby Thigpen	.05
85	Frank Thomas	.50
86	Robin Ventura	.05
87	Todd Benzinger	.05
88	Glenn Braggs	.05
89	Tom Browning	.05
90	Norm Charlton	.05
91	Eric Davis	.05
92	Rob Dibble	.05
93	Bill Doran	.05
94	Mariano Duncan	.05
95	Billy Hatcher	.05
96	Barry Larkin	.05
97	Randy Myers	.05
98	Hal Morris	.05
99	Joe Oliver	.05
100	Paul O'Neill	.05
101a	Jeff Reed	.05
101b	Beau Allred (Should be #104.)	.05
102	Jose Rijo	.05
103a	Chris Sabo	.05
103b	Carlos Baerga (Should be #106.)	.05
104	Not Issued (See #101b.)	
105	Sandy Alomar,Jr.	.05
106	Not Issued (See #103b.)	
107	Albert Belle	.05
108	Jerry Browne	.05
109	Tom Candiotti	.05
110	Alex Cole	.05
111a	John Farrell	.05
111b	Chris James (Should be #114.)	.05
112	Felix Fermin	.05
113	Brook Jacoby	.05
114	Not Issued (See #111b.)	
115	Doug Jones	.05
116a	Steve Olin	.05
116b	Mitch Webster (Should be #119.)	.05
117	Greg Swindell	.05
118	Turner Ward	.05
119	Not Issued (See #116b)	
120	Dave Bergman	.05
121	Cecil Fielder	.05
122	Travis Fryman	.05
123	Mike Henneman	.05
124	Lloyd Moseby	.05
125	Dan Petry	.05
126	Tony Phillips	.05
127	Mark Salas	.05
128	Frank Tanana	.05
129	Alan Trammell	.05
130	Lou Whitaker	.05
131	Eric Anthony	.05
132	Craig Biggio	.05
133	Ken Caminiti	.05
134	Casey Candaele	.05
135	Andujar Cedeno	.05
136	Mark Davidson	.05
137	Jim Deshaies	.05
138	Mark Portugal	.05
139	Rafael Ramirez	.05
140	Mike Scott	.05
141	Eric Yelding	.05
142	Gerald Young	.05
143	Kevin Appier	.05
144	George Brett	.65
145	Jeff Conine RC	.40
146	Jim Eisenreich	.05
147	Tom Gordon	.05
148	Mark Gubicza	.05
149	Bo Jackson	.10
150	Brent Mayne	.05
151	Mike Macfarlane	.05
152	Brian McRae RC	.10
153	Jeff Montgomery	.05
154	Bret Saberhagen	.05
155	Kevin Seitzer	.05
156	Terry Shumpert	.05
157	Kurt Stillwell	.05
158	Danny Tartabull	.05
159	Tim Belcher	.05
160	Kal Daniels	.05
161	Alfredo Griffin	.05
162	Lenny Harris	.05
163	Jay Howell	.05
164	Ramon Martinez	.05
165	Mike Morgan	.05
166	Eddie Murray	.50
167	Jose Offerman	.05
168	Juan Samuel	.05
169	Mike Scioscia	.05
170	Mike Sharperson	.05
171	Darryl Strawberry	.05
172	Greg Brock	.05
173	Chuck Crim	.05
174	Jim Gantner	.05
175	Ted Higuera	.05
176	Mark Knudson	.05
177	Tim McIntosh	.05
178	Paul Molitor	.50
179	Dan Plesac	.05
180	Gary Sheffield	.35
181	Bill Spiers	.05
182	B.J. Surhoff	.05
183	Greg Vaughn	.05
184	Robin Yount	.50
185	Rick Aguilera	.05
186	Greg Gagne	.05
187	Dan Gladden	.05
188	Brian Harper	.05
189	Kent Hrbek	.05
190	Gene Larkin	.05
191	Shane Mack	.05
192	Pedro Munoz	.05
193	Al Newman	.05
194	Junior Ortiz	.05
195	Kirby Puckett	.60
196	Kevin Tapani	.05
197	Dennis Boyd	.05
198	Tim Burke	.05
199	Ivan Calderon	.05
200	Delino DeShields	.05
201	Mike Fitzgerald	.05
202	Steve Frey	.05
203	Andres Galarraga	.05
204	Marquis Grissom	.05
205	Dave Martinez	.05
206	Dennis Martinez	.05
207	Junior Noboa	.05
208	Spike Owen	.05
209	Scott Ruskin	.05
210	Tim Wallach	.05
211	Daryl Boston	.05
212	Vince Coleman	.05
213	David Cone	.05
214	Ron Darling	.05
215	Kevin Elster	.05
216	Sid Fernandez	.05
217	John Franco	.05
218	Dwight Gooden	.05
219	Tom Herr	.05
220	Todd Hundley	.05
221	Gregg Jefferies	.05
222	Howard Johnson	.05
223	Dave Magadan	.05
224	Kevin McReynolds	.05
225	Keith Miller	.05
226	Mackey Sasser	.05
227	Frank Viola	.05
228	Jesse Barfield	.05
229	Greg Cadaret	.05
230	Alvaro Espinoza	.05
231	Bob Geren	.05
232	Lee Guetterman	.05
233	Mel Hall	.05
234	Andy Hawkins	.05
235	Roberto Kelly	.05
236	Tim Leary	.05
237	Jim Leyritz	.05
238	Kevin Maas	.05
239	Don Mattingly	.65
240	Hensley Meulens	.05
241	Eric Plunk	.05
242	Steve Sax	.05
243	Todd Burns	.05
244	Jose Canseco	.35
245	Dennis Eckersley	.40
246	Mike Gallego	.05
247	Dave Henderson	.05
248	Rickey Henderson	.50
249	Rick Honeycutt	.05
250	Carney Lansford	.05
251	Mark McGwire	1.00
252	Mike Moore	.05
253	Terry Steinbach	.05
254	Dave Stewart	.05
255	Walt Weiss	.05
256	Bob Welch	.05
257	Curt Young	.05
258	Wes Chamberlain	.05
259	Pat Combs	.05
260	Darren Daulton	.05
261	Jose DeJesus	.05
262	Len Dykstra	.05
263	Charlie Hayes	.05
264	Von Hayes	.05
265	Ken Howell	.05
266	John Kruk	.05
267	Roger McDowell	.05
268	Mickey Morandini	.05
269	Terry Mulholland	.05
270	Dale Murphy	.15
271	Randy Ready	.05
272	Dickie Thon	.05
273	Stan Belinda	.05
274	Jay Bell	.05
275	Barry Bonds	1.50
276	Bobby Bonilla	.05
277	Doug Drabek	.05
278	Carlos Garcia RC	.05
279	Neal Heaton	.05
280	Jeff King	.05
281	Bill Landrum	.05
282	Mike LaValliere	.05
283	Jose Lind	.05
284	Orlando Merced RC	.10
285	Gary Redus	.05
286	Don Slaught	.05
287	Andy Van Slyke	.05
288	Jose DeLeon	.05
289	Pedro Guerrero	.05
290	Ray Lankford	.05
291	Joe Magrane	.05
292	Jose Oquendo	.05
293	Tom Pagnozzi	.05
294	Bryn Smith	.05
295	Lee Smith	.05
296	Ozzie Smith	.60
297	Milt Thompson	.05
298	Craig Wilson RC	.05
299	Todd Zeile	.05
300	Shawn Abner	.05
301	Andy Benes	.05
302	Paul Faries	.05
303	Tony Gwynn	.60
304	Greg Harris	.05
305	Thomas Howard	.05
306	Bruce Hurst	.05
307	Craig Lefferts	.05
308	Fred McGriff	.05
309	Dennis Rasmussen	.05
310	Bip Roberts	.05
311	Benito Santiago	.05
312	Garry Templeton	.05
313	Ed Whitson	.05
314	Dave Anderson	.05
315	Kevin Bass	.05
316	Jeff Brantley	.05
317	John Burkett	.05
318	Will Clark	.05
319	Steve Decker	.05
320	Scott Garrelts	.05
321	Terry Kennedy	.05
322	Mark Leonard	.05
323	Darren Lewis	.05
324	Greg Litton	.05
325	Willie McGee	.05
326	Kevin Mitchell	.05
327	Don Robinson	.05
328	Andres Santana	.05
329	Robby Thompson	.05
330	Jose Uribe	.05
331	Matt Williams	.05
332	Scott Bradley	.05
333	Henry Cotto	.05
334	Alvin Davis	.05
335	Ken Griffey Sr.	.05
336	Ken Griffey Jr.	.75
337	Erik Hanson	.05
338	Brian Holman	.05
339	Randy Johnson	.50
340	Edgar Martinez	.05
341	Tino Martinez	.05
342	Pete O'Brien	.05
343	Harold Reynolds	.05
344	David Valle	.05
345	Omar Vizquel	.05
346	Brad Arnsberg	.05
347	Kevin Brown	.05
348	Julio Franco	.05
349	Jeff Huson	.05
350	Rafael Palmeiro	.40
351	Geno Petralli	.05
352	Gary Pettis	.05
353	Kenny Rogers	.05
354	Jeff Russell	.05
355	Nolan Ryan	1.50
356	Ruben Sierra	.05
357	Bobby Witt	.05
358	Roberto Alomar	.15
359	Pat Borders	.05
360	Joe Carter	.05
361	Kelly Gruber	.05
362	Tom Henke	.05
363	Glenallen Hill	.05
364	Jimmy Key	.05
365	Manny Lee	.05
366	Rance Mulliniks	.05
367	John Olerud	.05
368	Dave Stieb	.05
369	Duane Ward	.05
370	David Wells	.05
371	Mark Whiten	.05
372	Mookie Wilson	.05
373	Willie Banks	.05
374	Steve Carter	.05
375	Scott Chiamparino	.05
376	Steve Chitren	.05
377	Darrin Fletcher	.05
378	Rich Garces	.05
379	Reggie Jefferson	.05
380	Eric Karros RC	.50
381	Pat Kelly	.05
382	Chuck Knoblauch	.05
383	Denny Neagle	.05
384	Dan Opperman	.05
385	John Ramos	.05
386	Henry Rodriguez RC	.05
387	Mo Vaughn	.05
388	Gerald Williams	.05
389	Mike York	.05
390	Eddie Zosky	.05
391	Barry Bonds	.75
392	Cecil Fielder	.05
393	Rickey Henderson	.25
394	Dave Justice	.05
395	Nolan Ryan	.75
396	Bobby Thigpen	.05
397	Checklist	.05
398	Checklist	.05
399	Checklist	.05
400	Checklist	.05

Gold

BO JACKSON
KANSAS CITY ROYALS • OUTFIELD

		NM/M
Complete Set (10):		5.00
Common Player:		.15
1	Barry Bonds	2.50
2	Will Clark	.15
3	Doug Drabek	.15
4	Ken Griffey Jr.	1.50
5	Rickey Henderson	.75
6	Bo Jackson	.25
7	Ramon Martinez	.15
8	Kirby Puckett	1.00
9	Chris Sabo	.15
10	Ryne Sandberg	1.00

Update

RICK WILKINS CUBS CATCHER

		NM/M
Complete Set (120):		15.00
Common Player:		.05
1	Dwight Evans	.05
2	Chito Martinez	.05
3	Bob Melvin	.05
4	Mike Mussina RC	3.00
5	Jack Clark	.05
6	Dana Kiecker	.05
7	Steve Lyons	.05

8	Gary Gaetti	.05
9	Dave Gallagher	.05
10	Dave Parker	.05
11	Luis Polonia	.05
12	Luis Sojo	.05
13	Wilson Alvarez	.05
14	Alex Fernandez	.05
15	Craig Grebeck	.05
16	Ron Karkovice	.05
17	Warren Newson	.05
18	Scott Radinsky	.05
19	Glenallen Hill	.05
20	Charles Nagy	.05
21	Mark Whiten	.05
22	Milt Cuyler	.05
23	Paul Gibson	.05
24	Mickey Tettleton	.05
25	Todd Benzinger	.05
26	Storm Davis	.05
27	Kirk Gibson	.05
28	Bill Pecota	.05
29	Gary Thurman	.05
30	Darryl Hamilton	.05
31	Jaime Navarro	.05
32	Willie Randolph	.05
33	Bill Wegman	.05
34	Randy Bush	.05
35	Chili Davis	.05
36	Scott Erickson	.05
37	Chuck Knoblauch	.05
38	Scott Leius	.05
39	Jack Morris	.05
40	John Habyan	.05
41	Pat Kelly	.05
42	Matt Nokes	.05
43	Scott Sanderson	.05
44	Bernie Williams	.05
45	Harold Baines	.05
46	Brook Jacoby	.05
47	Ernest Riles	.05
48	Willie Wilson	.05
49	Jay Buhner	.05
50	Rich DeLucia	.05
51	Mike Jackson	.05
52	Bill Krueger	.05
53	Bill Swift	.05
54	Brian Downing	.05
55	Juan Gonzalez	.75
56	Dean Palmer	.05
57	Kevin Reimer	.05
58	Ivan Rodriguez RC	6.00
59	Tom Candiotti	.05
60	Juan Guzman	.05
61	Bob MacDonald	.05
62	Greg Myers	.05
63	Ed Sprague	.05
64	Devon White	.05
65	Rafael Belliard	.05
66	Juan Berenguer	.05
67	Brian Hunter	.05
68	Kent Mercker	.05
69	Otis Nixon	.05
70	Danny Jackson	.05
71	Chuck McElroy	.05
72	Gary Scott	.05
73	Heathcliff Slocumb	.05
74	Chico Walker	.05
75	Rick Wilkins	.05
76	Chris Hammond	.05
77	Luis Quinones	.05
78	Herm Winningham	.05
79	Jeff Bagwell RC	6.00
80	Jim Corsi	.05
81	Steve Finley	.05
82	Luis Gonzalez RC	1.00
83	Pete Harnisch	.05
84	Darryl Kile	.05
85	Brett Butler	.05
86	Gary Carter	1.00
87	Tim Crews	.05
88	Orel Hershiser	.05
89	Bob Ojeda	.05
90	Bret Barberie	.05
91	Barry Jones	.05
92	Gilberto Reyes	.05
93	Larry Walker	.05
94	Hubie Brooks	.05
95	Tim Burke	.05
96	Rick Cerone	.05
97	Jeff Innis	.05
98	Wally Backman	.05
99	Tommy Greene	.05
100	Ricky Jordan	.05
101	Mitch Williams	.05
102	John Smiley	.05
103	Randy Tomlin	.05
104	Gary Varsho	.05
105	Cris Carpenter	.05
106	Ken Hill	.05
107	Felix Jose	.05
108	Omar Oliveras RC	.05
109	Gerald Perry	.05
110	Jerald Clark	.05
111	Tony Fernandez	.05
112	Darrin Jackson	.05
113	Mike Maddux	.05
114	Tim Teufel	.05
115	Bud Black	.05
116	Kelly Downs	.05
117	Mike Felder	.05
118	Willie McGee	.05
119	Trevor Wilson	.05
120	Checklist	.05

1992 Ultra

		NM/M
Complete Set (600):		12.00
Common Player:		.05
Ser. 1 or 2 Pack (14):		.60
Ser. 1 or 2 Box (36):		12.50
Tony Gwynn Auto.		60.00
1	Glenn Davis	.05
2	Mike Devereaux	.05
3	Dwight Evans	.05
4	Leo Gomez	.05
5	Chris Hoiles	.05
6	Sam Horn	.05
7	Chito Martinez	.05
8	Randy Milligan	.05
9	Mike Mussina	.30
10	Billy Ripken	.05
11	Cal Ripken, Jr.	1.00
12	Tom Brunansky	.05
13	Ellis Burks	.05
14	Jack Clark	.05
15	Roger Clemens	.60
16	Mike Greenwell	.05
17	Joe Hesketh	.05
18	Tony Pena	.05
19	Carlos Quintana	.05
20	Jeff Reardon	.05
21	Jody Reed	.05
22	Luis Rivera	.05
23	Mo Vaughn	.05
24	Gary DiSarcina	.05
25	Chuck Finley	.05
26	Gary Gaetti	.05
27	Bryan Harvey	.05
28	Lance Parrish	.05
29	Luis Polonia	.05
30	Dick Schofield	.05
31	Luis Sojo	.05
32	Wilson Alvarez	.05
33	Carlton Fisk	.40
34	Craig Grebeck	.05
35	Ozzie Guillen	.05
36	Greg Hibbard	.05
37	Charlie Hough	.05
38	Lance Johnson	.05
39	Ron Karkovice	.05
40	Jack McDowell	.05
41	Donn Pall	.05
42	Melido Perez	.05
43	Tim Raines	.40
44	Frank Thomas	.40
45	Sandy Alomar, Jr.	.05
46	Carlos Baerga	.05
47	Albert Belle	.05
48	Jerry Browne	.05
49	Felix Fermin	.05
50	Reggie Jefferson	.05
51	Mark Lewis	.05
52	Carlos Martinez	.05
53	Steve Olin	.05
54	Jim Thome	.35
55	Mark Whiten	.05
56	Dave Bergman	.05
57	Milt Cuyler	.05
58	Rob Deer	.05
59	Cecil Fielder	.05
60	Travis Fryman	.05
61	Scott Livingstone	.05
62	Tony Phillips	.05
63	Mickey Tettleton	.05
64	Alan Trammell	.05
65	Lou Whitaker	.05
66	Kevin Appier	.05
67	Mike Boddicker	.05
68	George Brett	.60
69	Jim Eisenreich	.05
70	Mark Gubicza	.05
71	David Howard	.05
72	Joel Johnston	.05
73	Mike Macfarlane	.05
74	Brent Mayne	.05
75	Brian McRae	.05
76	Jeff Montgomery	.05
77	Terry Shumpert	.05
78	Don August	.05
79	Dante Bichette	.05
80	Ted Higuera	.05
81	Paul Molitor	.40
82	Jamie Navarro	.05
83	Gary Sheffield	.30
84	Bill Spiers	.05
85	B.J. Surhoff	.05
86	Greg Vaughn	.05
87	Robin Yount	.40
88	Rick Aguilera	.05
89	Chili Davis	.05
90	Scott Erickson	.05
91	Brian Harper	.05
92	Kent Hrbek	.05
93	Chuck Knoblauch	.05
94	Scott Leius	.05
95	Shane Mack	.05
96	Mike Pagliarulo	.05
97	Kirby Puckett	.50
98	Kevin Tapani	.05
99	Jesse Barfield	.05
100	Alvaro Espinoza	.05
101	Mel Hall	.05
102	Pat Kelly	.05
103	Roberto Kelly	.05
104	Kevin Maas	.05
105	Don Mattingly	.60
106	Hensley Meulens	.05
107	Matt Nokes	.05
108	Steve Sax	.05
109	Harold Baines	.05
110	Jose Canseco	.30
111	Ron Darling	.05
112	Mike Gallego	.05
113	Dave Henderson	.05
114	Rickey Henderson	.40
115	Mark McGwire	.75
116	Terry Steinbach	.05
117	Dave Stewart	.05
118	Todd Van Poppel	.05
119	Bob Welch	.05
120	Greg Briley	.05
121	Jay Buhner	.05
122	Rich DeLucia	.05
123	Ken Griffey Jr.	.65
124	Erik Hanson	.05
125	Randy Johnson	.40
126	Edgar Martinez	.05
127	Tino Martinez	.05
128	Pete O'Brien	.05
129	Harold Reynolds	.05
130	Dave Valle	.05
131	Julio Franco	.05
132	Juan Gonzalez	.20
133	Jeff Huson	.05
134	Mike Jeffcoat	.05
135	Terry Mathews	.05
136	Rafael Palmeiro	.35
137	Dean Palmer	.05
138	Geno Petralli	.05
139	Ivan Rodriguez	.35
140	Jeff Russell	.05
141	Nolan Ryan	1.00
142	Ruben Sierra	.05
143	Roberto Alomar	.15
144	Pat Borders	.05
145	Joe Carter	.05
146	Kelly Gruber	.05
147	Jimmy Key	.05
148	Manny Lee	.05
149	Rance Mulliniks	.05
150	Greg Myers	.05
151	John Olerud	.05
152	Dave Stieb	.05
153	Todd Stottlemyre	.05
154	Duane Ward	.05
155	Devon White	.05
156	Eddie Zosky	.05
157	Steve Avery	.05
158	Rafael Belliard	.05
159	Jeff Blauser	.05
160	Sid Bream	.05
161	Ron Gant	.05
162	Tom Glavine	.25
163	Brian Hunter	.05
164	Dave Justice	.05
165	Mark Lemke	.05
166	Greg Olson	.05
167	Terry Pendleton	.05
168	Lonnie Smith	.05
169	John Smoltz	.05
170	Mike Stanton	.05
171	Jeff Treadway	.05
172	Paul Assenmacher	.05
173	George Bell	.05
174	Shawon Dunston	.05
175	Mark Grace	.05
176	Danny Jackson	.05
177	Les Lancaster	.05
178	Greg Maddux	.50
179	Luis Salazar	.05
180	Rey Sanchez	.05
181	Ryne Sandberg	.50
182	Jose Vizcaino	.05
183	Chico Walker	.05
184	Jerome Walton	.05
185	Glenn Braggs	.05
186	Tom Browning	.05
187	Rob Dibble	.05
188	Bill Doran	.05
189	Chris Hammond	.05
190	Billy Hatcher	.05
191	Barry Larkin	.05
192	Hal Morris	.05
193	Joe Oliver	.05
194	Paul O'Neill	.05
195	Jeff Reed	.05
196	Jose Rijo	.05
197	Chris Sabo	.05
198	Jeff Bagwell	.40
199	Craig Biggio	.05
200	Ken Caminiti	.05
201	Andujar Cedeno	.05
202	Steve Finley	.05
203	Luis Gonzalez	.05
204	Pete Harnisch	.05
205	Xavier Hernandez	.05
206	Darryl Kile	.05
207	Al Osuna	.05
208	Curt Schilling	.25
209	Brett Butler	.05
210	Kal Daniels	.05
211	Lenny Harris	.05
212	Stan Javier	.05
213	Ramon Martinez	.05
214	Roger McDowell	.05
215	Jose Offerman	.05
216	Juan Samuel	.05
217	Mike Scioscia	.05
218	Mike Sharperson	.05
219	Darryl Strawberry	.05
220	Delino DeShields	.05
221	Tom Foley	.05
222	Steve Frey	.05
223	Dennis Martinez	.05
224	Spike Owen	.05
225	Gilberto Reyes	.05
226	Tim Wallach	.05
227	Daryl Boston	.05
228	Tim Burke	.05
229	Vince Coleman	.05
230	David Cone	.05
231	Kevin Elster	.05
232	Dwight Gooden	.05
233	Todd Hundley	.05
234	Jeff Innis	.05
235	Howard Johnson	.05
236	Dave Magadan	.05
237	Mackey Sasser	.05
238	Anthony Young	.05
239	Wes Chamberlain	.05
240	Darren Daulton	.05
241	Len Dykstra	.05
242	Tommy Greene	.05
243	Charlie Hayes	.05
244	Dave Hollins	.05
245	Ricky Jordan	.05
246	John Kruk	.05
247	Mickey Morandini	.05
248	Terry Mulholland	.05
249	Dale Murphy	.25
250	Jay Bell	.05
251	Barry Bonds	1.00
252	Steve Buechele	.05
253	Doug Drabek	.05
254	Mike LaValliere	.05
255	Jose Lind	.05
256	Lloyd McClendon	.05
257	Orlando Merced	.05
258	Don Slaught	.05
259	John Smiley	.05
260	Zane Smith	.05
261	Randy Tomlin	.05
262	Andy Van Slyke	.05
263	Pedro Guerrero	.05
264	Felix Jose	.05
265	Ray Lankford	.05
266	Omar Olivares	.05
267	Jose Oquendo	.05
268	Tom Pagnozzi	.05
269	Bryn Smith	.05
270	Lee Smith	.05
271	Ozzie Smith	.50
272	Milt Thompson	.05
273	Todd Zeile	.05

#	Player	Price	#	Player	Price	#	Player	Price	#	Player	Price
274	Andy Benes	.05	375	Keith Miller	.05	479	Tim Belcher	.05	583	Craig Shipley	.05
275	Jerald Clark	.05	376	Rico Rossy	.05	480	Freddie Benavides	.05	584	Kurt Stillwell	.05
276	Tony Fernandez	.05	377	Curtis Wilkerson	.05	481	Jacob Brumfield	.05	585	Tim Teufel	.05
277	Tony Gwynn	.50	378	Ricky Bones	.05	482	Norm Charlton	.05	586	Rod Beck RC	.05
278	Greg Harris	.05	379	Chris Bosio	.05	483	Dwayne Henry	.05	587	Dave Burba	.05
279	Thomas Howard	.05	380	Cal Eldred	.05	484	Dave Martinez	.05	588	Craig Colbert	.05
280	Bruce Hurst	.05	381	Scott Fletcher	.05	485	Bip Roberts	.05	589	Bryan Hickerson	.05
281	Mike Maddux	.05	382	Jim Gantner	.05	486	Reggie Sanders	.05	590	Mike Jackson	.05
282	Fred McGriff	.05	383	Darryl Hamilton	.05	487	Greg Swindell	.05	591	Mark Leonard	.05
283	Benito Santiago	.05	384	Doug Henry	.05	488	Ryan Bowen	.05	592	Jim McNamara	.05
284	Kevin Bass	.05	385	Pat Listach RC	.05	489	Casey Candaele	.05	593	John Patterson	.05
285	Jeff Brantley	.05	386	Tim McIntosh	.05	490	Juan Guerrero	.05	594	Dave Righetti	.05
286	John Burkett	.05	387	Edwin Nunez	.05	491	Pete Incaviglia	.05	595	Cory Snyder	.05
287	Will Clark	.05	388	Dan Plesac	.05	492	Jeff Juden	.05	596	Bill Swift	.05
288	Royce Clayton	.05	389	Kevin Seitzer	.05	493	Rob Murphy	.05	597	Ted Wood	.05
289	Steve Decker	.05	390	Franklin Stubbs	.05	494	Mark Portugal	.05	598	Scott Sanderson	
290	Kelly Downs	.05	391	William Suero	.05	495	Rafael Ramirez	.05		Checklist 301-403	.05
291	Mike Felder	.05	392	Bill Wegman	.05	496	Scott Servais	.05	599	Junior Ortiz	
292	Darren Lewis	.05	393	Willie Banks	.05	497	Ed Taubensee	.05		Checklist 404-498	.05
293	Kirt Manwaring	.05	394	Jarvis Brown	.05	498	Brian Williams	.05	600	Mike Morgan	
294	Willie McGee	.05	395	Greg Gagne	.05	499	Todd Benzinger	.05		Checklist 499-600	.05
295	Robby Thompson	.05	396	Mark Guthrie	.05	500	John Candelaria	.05			
296	Matt Williams	.05	397	Bill Krueger	.05	501	Tom Candiotti	.05			
297	Trevor Wilson	.05	398	Pat Mahomes RC	.05	502	Tim Crews	.05			
298	Sandy Alomar, Jr.		399	Pedro Munoz	.05	503	Eric Davis	.05			
	Checklist 1-108	.05	400	John Smiley	.05	504	Jim Gott	.05			
299	Rey Sanchez		401	Gary Wayne	.05	505	Dave Hansen	.05			
	Checklist 109-208	.05	402	Lenny Webster	.05	506	Carlos Hernandez	.05			
300	Nolan Ryan		403	Carl Willis	.05	507	Orel Hershiser	.05			
	Checklist 209-300	.25	404	Greg Cadaret	.05	508	Eric Karros	.05			
301	Brady Anderson	.05	405	Steve Farr	.05	509	Bob Ojeda	.05			
302	Todd Frohwirth	.05	406	Mike Gallego	.05	510	Steve Wilson	.05			
303	Ben McDonald	.05	407	Charlie Hayes	.05	511	Moises Alou	.05			
304	Mark McLemore	.05	408	Steve Howe	.05	512	Bret Barberie	.05			
305	Jose Mesa	.05	409	Dion James	.05	513	Ivan Calderon	.05			
306	Bob Milacki	.05	410	Jeff Johnson	.05	514	Gary Carter	.40			
307	Gregg Olson	.05	411	Tim Leary	.05	515	Archi Cianfrocco	.05			
308	David Segui	.05	412	Jim Leyritz	.05	516	Jeff Fassero	.05			
309	Rick Sutcliffe	.05	413	Melido Perez	.05	517	Darrin Fletcher	.05			
310	Jeff Tackett	.05	414	Scott Sanderson	.05	518	Marquis Grissom	.05			
311	Wade Boggs	.50	415	Andy Stankiewicz	.05	519	Chris Haney	.05			
312	Scott Cooper	.05	416	Mike Stanley	.05	520	Ken Hill	.05			
313	John Flaherty	.05	417	Danny Tartabull	.05	521	Chris Nabholz	.05			
314	Wayne Housie	.05	418	Lance Blankenship	.05	522	Bill Sampen	.05			
315	Peter Hoy	.05	419	Mike Bordick	.05	523	John VanderWal	.05			
316	Jim Marzano	.05	420	Scott Brosius RC	.05	524	David Wainhouse	.05			
317	Tim Naehring	.05	421	Dennis Eckersley	.35	525	Larry Walker	.05			
318	Phil Plantier	.05	422	Scott Hemond	.05	526	John Wetteland	.05			
319	Frank Viola	.05	423	Carney Lansford	.05	527	Bobby Bonilla	.05			
320	Matt Young	.05	424	Henry Mercedes	.05	528	Sid Fernandez	.05			
321	Jim Abbott	.05	425	Mike Moore	.05	529	Jim Franco	.05			
322	Hubie Brooks	.05	426	Gene Nelson	.05	530	Dave Gallagher	.05			
323	Chad Curtis RC	.25	427	Randy Ready	.05	531	Paul Gibson	.05			
324	Alvin Davis	.05	428	Bruce Walton	.05	532	Eddie Murray	.40			
325	Junior Felix	.05	429	Willie Wilson	.05	533	Junior Noboa	.05			
326	Von Hayes	.05	430	Rich Amaral	.05	534	Charlie O'Brien	.05			
327	Mark Langston	.05	431	Dave Cochrane	.05	535	Bill Pecota	.05			
328	Scott Lewis	.05	432	Henry Cotto	.05	536	Willie Randolph	.05			
329	Don Robinson	.05	433	Calvin Jones	.05	537	Bret Saberhagen	.05			
330	Bobby Rose	.05	434	Kevin Mitchell	.05	538	Dick Schofield	.05			
331	Lee Stevens	.05	435	Clay Parker	.05	539	Pete Schourek	.05			
332	George Bell	.05	436	Omar Vizquel	.05	540	Ruben Amaro	.05			
333	Esteban Beltre	.05	437	Floyd Bannister	.05	541	Andy Ashby	.05			
334	Joey Cora	.05	438	Kevin Brown	.05	542	Kim Batiste	.05			
335	Alex Fernandez	.05	439	John Cangelosi	.05	543	Cliff Brantley	.05			
336	Roberto Hernandez	.05	440	Brian Downing	.05	544	Mariano Duncan	.05			
337	Mike Huff	.05	441	Monty Fariss	.05	545	Jeff Grotewold	.05			
338	Kirk McCaskill	.05	442	Jose Guzman	.05	546	Barry Jones	.05			
339	Dan Pasqua	.05	443	Donald Harris	.05	547	Julio Peguero	.05			
340	Scott Radinsky	.05	444	Kevin Reimer	.05	548	Curt Schilling	.25			
341	Steve Sax	.05	445	Kenny Rogers	.05	549	Mitch Williams	.05			
342	Bobby Thigpen	.05	446	Wayne Rosenthal	.05	550	Stan Belinda	.05			
343	Robin Ventura	.05	447	Dickie Thon	.05	551	Scott Bullett	.05			
344	Jack Armstrong	.05	448	Derek Bell	.05	552	Cecil Espy	.05			
345	Alex Cole	.05	449	Juan Guzman	.05	553	Jeff King	.05			
346	Dennis Cook	.05	450	Tom Henke	.05	554	Roger Mason	.05			
347	Glenallen Hill	.05	451	Candy Maldonado	.05	555	Paul Miller	.05			
348	Thomas Howard	.05	452	Jack Morris	.05	556	Denny Neagle	.05			
349	Brook Jacoby	.05	453	David Wells	.05	557	Vocente Palacios	.05			
350	Kenny Lofton	.05	454	Dave Winfield	.40	558	Bob Patterson	.05			
351	Charles Nagy	.05	455	Juan Berenguer	.05	559	Tom Prince	.05			
352	Rod Nichols	.05	456	Damon Berryhill	.05	560	Gary Redus	.05			
353	Junior Ortiz	.05	457	Mike Bielecki	.05	561	Gary Varsho	.05			
354	Dave Otto	.05	458	Marvin Freeman	.05	562	Juan Agosto	.05			
355	Tony Perezchica	.05	459	Charlie Leibrandt	.05	563	Cris Carpenter	.05			
356	Scott Scudder	.05	460	Kent Mercker	.05	564	Mark Clark RC	.05			
357	Paul Sorrento	.05	461	Otis Nixon	.05	565	Jose DeLeon	.05			
358	Skeeter Barnes	.05	462	Alejandro Pena	.05	566	Rich Gedman	.05			
359	Mark Carreon	.05	463	Ben Rivera	.05	567	Bernard Gilkey	.05			
360	John Doherty	.10	464	Deion Sanders	.10	568	Rex Hudler	.05			
361	Dan Gladden	.05	465	Mark Wohlers	.05	569	Tim Jones	.05			
362	Bill Gullickson	.05	466	Shawn Boskie	.05	570	Donovan Osborne	.05			
363	Shawn Hare	.05	467	Frank Castillo	.05	571	Mike Perez	.05			
364	Mike Henneman	.05	468	Andre Dawson	.25	572	Gerald Perry	.05			
365	Chad Kreuter	.05	469	Joe Girardi	.05	573	Bob Tewksbury	.05			
366	Mark Leiter	.05	470	Chuck McElroy	.05	574	Todd Worrell	.05			
367	Mike Munoz	.05	471	Mike Morgan	.05	575	Dave Eiland	.05			
368	Kevin Ritz	.05	472	Ken Patterson	.05	576	Jeremy Hernandez	.05			
369	Mark Davis	.05	473	Bob Scanlan	.05	577	Craig Lefferts	.05			
370	Tom Gordon	.05	474	Gary Scott	.05	578	Jose Melendez	.05			
371	Chris Gwynn	.05	475	Dave Smith	.05	579	Randy Myers	.05			
372	Gregg Jefferies	.05	476	Sammy Sosa	.50	580	Gary Pettis	.05			
373	Wally Joyner	.05	477	Hector Villanueva	.05	581	Rich Rodriguez	.05			
374	Kevin McReynolds	.05	478	Scott Bankhead	.05	582	Gary Sheffield	.30			

All-Rookies

		NM/M
Complete Set (10):		2.00
Common Player:		.25
1	Eric Karros	.35
2	Andy Stankiewicz	.25
3	Gary DiSarcina	.25
4	Archi Cianfrocco	.25
5	Jim McNamara	.25
6	Chad Curtis	.25
7	Kenny Lofton	.35
8	Reggie Sanders	.25
9	Pat Mahomes	.25
10	Donovan Osborne	.25

All-Stars

		NM/M
Complete Set (20):		7.50
Common Player:		.15
1	Mark McGwire	1.25
2	Roberto Alomar	.30
3	Cal Ripken, Jr.	1.50
4	Wade Boggs	.75
5	Mickey Tettleton	.15
6	Ken Griffey Jr.	1.00
7	Roberto Kelly	.15
8	Kirby Puckett	.75
9	Frank Thomas	.65
10	Jack McDowell	.15
11	Will Clark	.75
12	Ryne Sandberg	.75
13	Barry Larkin	.35
14	Gary Sheffield	.35
15	Tom Pagnozzi	.15
16	Barry Bonds	1.50
17	Deion Sanders	.15
18	Darryl Strawberry	.15
19	David Cone	.15
20	Tom Glavine	.30

Award Winners

	NM/M
Complete Set (26):	10.00
Common Player:	.20
1 Jack Morris	.20
2 Chuck Knoblauch	.20
3 Jeff Bagwell	.75
4 Terry Pendleton	.20
5 Cal Ripken, Jr.	2.00
6 Roger Clemens	1.25
7 Tom Glavine	.35
8 Tom Pagnozzi	.20
9 Ozzie Smith	1.00
10 Andy Van Slyke	.20
11 Barry Bonds	2.00
12 Tony Gwynn	1.00
13 Matt Williams	.20
14 Will Clark	.20
15 Robin Ventura	.20
16 Mark Langston	.20
18 Devon White	.20
19 Don Mattingly	1.25
20 Roberto Alomar	.40
21a Cal Ripken, Jr.	
(Reversed negative.)	2.00
21b Cal Ripken, Jr.	
(Correct)	2.00
22 Ken Griffey Jr.	1.50
23 Kirby Puckett	1.00
24 Greg Maddux	1.00
25 Ryne Sandberg	1.00

Tony Gwynn

	NM/M
Complete Set (12):	9.00
Common Gwynn:	.75
Certified Autograph Card:	60.00
SEND-AWAY CARDS	
1 Tony Gwynn/Btg	2.00
2 Tony Gwynn/Fld	2.00
SPECIAL CARDS	
--- Tony Gwynn,	
Paul Mullan	3.00
--- Tony Gwynn	
(Casa de Amparo)	7.50

1993 Ultra

	NM/M
Complete Set (650):	15.00
Common Player:	.05
Series 1 or 2 Pack (14):	.75
Series 1 or 2 Wax	
Box (36):	15.00
1 Steve Avery	.05
2 Rafael Belliard	.05
3 Damon Berryhill	.05
4 Sid Bream	.05
5 Ron Gant	.05
6 Tom Glavine	.20
7 Ryan Klesko	.05

8	Mark Lemke	.05
9	Javier Lopez	.05
10	Greg Olson	.05
11	Terry Pendleton	.05
12	Deion Sanders	.05
13	Mike Stanton	.05
14	Paul Assenmacher	.05
15	Steve Buechele	.05
16	Frank Castillo	.05
17	Shawon Dunston	.05
18	Mark Grace	.05
19	Derrick May	.05
20	Chuck McElroy	.05
21	Mike Morgan	.05
22	Bob Scanlan	.05
23	Dwight Smith	.05
24	Sammy Sosa	.60
25	Rick Wilkins	.05
26	Tim Belcher	.05
27	Jeff Branson	.05
28	Bill Doran	.05
29	Chris Hammond	.05
30	Barry Larkin	.05
31	Hal Morris	.05
32	Joe Oliver	.05
33	Jose Rijo	.05
34	Bip Roberts	.05
35	Chris Sabo	.05
36	Reggie Sanders	.05
37	Craig Biggio	.05
38	Ken Caminiti	.05
39	Steve Finley	.05
40	Luis Gonzalez	.05
41	Juan Guerrero	.05
42	Pete Harnisch	.05
43	Xavier Hernandez	.05
44	Doug Jones	.05
45	Al Osuna	.05
46	Eddie Taubensee	.05
47	Scooter Tucker	.05
48	Brian Williams	.05
49	Pedro Astacio	.05
50	Rafael Bournigal	.05
51	Brett Butler	.05
52	Tom Candiotti	.05
53	Eric Davis	.05
54	Lenny Harris	.05
55	Orel Hershiser	.05
56	Eric Karros	.05
57	Pedro Martinez	.50
58	Roger McDowell	.05
59	Jose Offerman	.05
60	Mike Piazza	.75
61	Moises Alou	.05
62	Kent Bottenfield	.05
63	Archi Cianfrocco	.05
64	Greg Colbrunn	.05
65	Wil Cordero	.05
66	Delino DeShields	.05
67	Darrin Fletcher	.05
68	Ken Hill	.05
69	Chris Nabholz	.05
70	Mel Rojas	.05
71	Larry Walker	.05
72	Sid Fernandez	.05
73	John Franco	.05
74	Dave Gallagher	.05
75	Todd Hundley	.05
76	Howard Johnson	.05
77	Jeff Kent	.05
78	Eddie Murray	.50
79	Bret Saberhagen	.05
80	Chico Walker	.05
81	Anthony Young	.05
82	Kyle Abbott	.05
83	Ruben Amaro Jr.	.05
84	Juan Bell	.05
85	Wes Chamberlain	.05
86	Darren Daulton	.05
87	Mariano Duncan	.05
88	Dave Hollins	.05
89	Ricky Jordan	.05

90	John Kruk	.05
91	Mickey Morandini	.05
92	Terry Mulholland	.05
93	Ben Rivera	.05
94	Mike Williams	.05
95	Stan Belinda	.05
96	Jay Bell	.05
97	Jeff King	.05
98	Mike LaValliere	.05
99	Lloyd McClendon	.05
100	Orlando Merced	.05
101	Zane Smith	.05
102	Randy Tomlin	.05
103	Andy Van Slyke	.05
104	Tim Wakefield	.05
105	John Wehner	.05
106	Bernard Gilkey	.05
107	Brian Jordan	.05
108	Ray Lankford	.05
109	Donovan Osborne	.05
110	Tom Pagnozzi	.05
111	Mike Perez	.05
112	Lee Smith	.05
113	Ozzie Smith	.60
114	Bob Tewksbury	.05
115	Todd Zeile	.05
116	Andy Benes	.05
117	Greg Harris	.05
118	Darrin Jackson	.05
119	Fred McGriff	.05
120	Rich Rodriguez	.05
121	Frank Seminara	.05
122	Gary Sheffield	.35
123	Craig Shipley	.05
124	Kurt Stillwell	.05
125	Dan Walters	.05
126	Rod Beck	.05
127	Mike Benjamin	.05
128	Jeff Brantley	.05
129	John Burkett	.05
130	Will Clark	.05
131	Royce Clayton	.05
132	Steve Hosey	.05
133	Mike Jackson	.05
134	Darren Lewis	.05
135	Kirt Manwaring	.05
136	Bill Swift	.05
137	Robby Thompson	.05
138	Brady Anderson	.05
139	Glenn Davis	.05
140	Leo Gomez	.05
141	Chito Martinez	.05
142	Ben McDonald	.05
143	Alan Mills	.05
144	Mike Mussina	.30
145	Gregg Olson	.05
146	David Segui	.05
147	Jeff Tackett	.05
148	Jack Clark	.05
149	Scott Cooper	.05
150	Danny Darwin	.05
151	John Dopson	.05
152	Mike Greenwell	.05
153	Tim Naehring	.05
154	Tony Pena	.05
155	Paul Quantrill	.05
156	Mo Vaughn	.05
157	Frank Viola	.05
158	Bob Zupcic	.05
159	Chad Curtis	.05
160	Gary DiScarcina	.05
161	Damion Easley	.05
162	Chuck Finley	.05
163	Tim Fortugno	.05
164	Rene Gonzales	.05
165	Joe Grahe	.05
166	Mark Langston	.05
167	John Orton	.05
168	Luis Polonia	.05
169	Julio Valera	.05
170	Wilson Alvarez	.05
171	George Bell	.05
172	Joey Cora	.05
173	Alex Fernandez	.05
174	Lance Johnson	.05
175	Ron Karkovice	.05
176	Jack McDowell	.05
177	Scott Radinsky	.05
178	Tim Raines	.05
179	Steve Sax	.05
180	Bobby Thigpen	.05
181	Frank Thomas	.50
182	Sandy Alomar Jr.	.05
183	Carlos Baerga	.05
184	Felix Fermin	.05
185	Thomas Howard	.05
186	Mark Lewis	.05
187	Derek Lilliquist	.05
188	Carlos Martinez	.05
189	Charles Nagy	.05
190	Scott Scudder	.05
191	Paul Sorrento	.05
192	Jim Thome	.40
193	Mark Whiten	.05

194	Milt Cuyler	.05
195	Rob Deer	.05
196	John Doherty	.05
197	Travis Fryman	.05
198	Dan Gladden	.05
199	Mike Henneman	.05
200	John Kiely	.05
201	Chad Kreuter	.05
202	Scott Livingstone	.05
203	Tony Phillips	.05
204	Alan Trammell	.05
205	Mike Boddicker	.05
206	George Brett	.65
207	Tom Gordon	.05
208	Mark Gubicza	.05
209	Gregg Jefferies	.05
210	Wally Joyner	.05
211	Kevin Koslofski	.05
212	Brent Mayne	.05
213	Brian McRae	.05
214	Kevin McReynolds	.05
215	Rusty Meacham	.05
216	Steve Shifflett	.05
217	James Austin	.05
218	Cal Eldred	.05
219	Darryl Hamilton	.05
220	Doug Henry	.05
221	John Jaha	.05
222	Dave Nilsson	.05
223	Jesse Orosco	.05
224	B.J. Surhoff	.05
225	Greg Vaughn	.05
226	Bill Wegman	.05
227	Robin Yount	.50
228	Rick Aguilera	.05
229	J.T. Bruett	.05
230	Scott Erickson	.05
231	Kent Hrbek	.05
232	Terry Jorgensen	.05
233	Scott Leius	.05
234	Pat Mahomes	.05
235	Pedro Munoz	.05
236	Kirby Puckett	.60
237	Kevin Tapani	.05
238	Lenny Webster	.05
239	Carl Willis	.05
240	Mike Gallego	.05
241	John Habyan	.05
242	Pat Kelly	.05
243	Kevin Maas	.05
244	Don Mattingly	.65
245	Hensley Meulens	.05
246	Sam Militello	.05
247	Matt Nokes	.05
248	Melido Perez	.05
249	Andy Stankiewicz	.05
250	Randy Velarde	.05
251	Bob Wickman	.05
252	Bernie Williams	.05
253	Lance Blankenship	.05
254	Mike Bordick	.05
255	Jerry Browne	.05
256	Ron Darling	.05
257a	Dennis Eckersley	.40
257b	Dennis Eckersley	
	(Wt. 195; no "MLBPA"	
	on back - unmarked	
	sample card.)	1.50
257c	Dennis Eckersley	
	(Wt. 195; no "Printed in	
	USA" on back - unmarked	
	sample card.)	1.50
258	Rickey Henderson	.50
259	Vince Horsman	.05
260	Troy Neel	.05
261	Jeff Parrett	.05
262	Terry Steinbach	.05
263	Bob Welch	.05
264	Bobby Witt	.05
265	Rich Amaral	.05
266	Bret Boone	.05
267	Jay Buhner	.05
268	Dave Fleming	.05
269	Randy Johnson	.50
270	Edgar Martinez	.05
271	Mike Schooler	.05
272	Russ Swan	.05
273	Dave Valle	.05
274	Omar Vizquel	.05
275	Kerry Woodson	.05
276	Kevin Brown	.05
277	Julio Franco	.05
278	Jeff Frye	.05
279	Juan Gonzalez	.25
280	Jeff Huson	.05
281	Rafael Palmeiro	.40
282	Dean Palmer	.05
283	Roger Pavlik	.05
284	Ivan Rodriguez	.40
285	Kenny Rogers	.05
286	Derek Bell	.05
287	Pat Borders	.05
288	Joe Carter	.05
289	Bob MacDonald	.05

290 Jack Morris	.05	396 Scott Servais	.05
291 John Olerud	.05	397 Greg Swindell	.05
292 Ed Sprague	.05	398 Tom Goodwin	.05
293 Todd Stottlemyre	.05	399 Kevin Gross	.05
294 Mike Timlin	.05	400 Carlos Hernandez	.05
295 Duane Ward	.05	401 Ramon Martinez	.05
296 David Wells	.05	402 Raul Mondesi	.05
297 Devon White	.05	403 Jody Reed	.05
298 Ray Lankford Checklist	.05	404 Mike Sharperson	.05
299 Bobby Witt Checklist	.05	405 Cory Snyder	.05
300 Mike Piazza Checklist	.40	406 Darryl Strawberry	.05
301 Steve Bedrosian	.05	407 Rick Trlicek RC	.05
302 Jeff Blauser	.05	408 Tim Wallach	.05
303 Francisco Cabrera	.05	409 Todd Worrell	.05
304 Marvin Freeman	.05	410 Tavo Alvarez	.05
305 Brian Hunter	.05	411 Sean Berry RC	.05
306 Dave Justice	.05	412 Frank Bolick RC	.05
307 Greg Maddux	.60	413 Cliff Floyd	.05
308 Greg McMichael RC	.05	414 Mike Gardiner	.05
309 Kent Mercker	.05	415 Marquis Grissom	.05
310 Otis Nixon	.05	416 Tim Laker RC	.05
311 Pete Smith	.05	417 Mike Lansing RC	.10
312 John Smoltz	.05	418 Dennis Martinez	.05
313 Jose Guzman	.05	419 John Vander Wal	.05
314 Mike Harkey	.05	420 John Wetteland	.05
315 Greg Hibbard	.05	421 Rondell White	.05
316 Candy Maldonado	.05	422 Bobby Bonilla	.05
317 Randy Myers	.05	423 Jeromy Burnitz	.05
318 Dan Plesac	.05	424 Vince Burnitz RC	.05
319 Rey Sanchez	.05	425 Mike Draper RC	.05
320 Ryne Sandberg	.60	426 Tony Fernandez	.05
321 Tommy Shields RC	.05	427 Dwight Gooden	.05
322 Jose Vizcaino	.05	428 Jeff Innis	.05
323 Matt Walbeck RC	.05	429 Bobby Jones	.05
324 Willie Wilson	.05	430 Mike Maddux	.05
325 Tom Browning	.05	431 Charlie O'Brien	.05
326 Tim Costo	.05	432 Joe Orsulak	.05
327 Rob Dibble	.05	433 Pete Schourek	.05
328 Steve Foster	.05	434 Frank Tanana	.05
329 Roberto Kelly	.05	435 Ryan Thompson RC	.05
330 Randy Milligan	.05	436 Kim Batiste	.05
331 Kevin Mitchell	.05	437 Mark Davis	.05
332 Tim Pugh RC	.05	438 Jose DeLeon	.05
333 Jeff Reardon	.05	439 Len Dykstra	.05
334 John Roper RC	.05	440 Jim Eisenreich	.05
335 Juan Samuel	.05	441 Tommy Greene	.05
336 John Smiley	.05	442 Pete Incaviglia	.05
337 San Wilson	.05	443 Danny Jackson	.05
338 Scott Aldred	.05	444 Todd Pratt RC	.05
339 Andy Ashby	.05	445 Curt Schilling	.20
340 Freddie Benavides	.05	446 Milt Thompson	.05
341 Dante Bichette	.05	447 David West	.05
342 Willie Blair	.05	448 Mitch Williams	.05
343 Daryl Boston	.05	449 Steve Cooke	.05
344 Vinny Castilla	.05	450 Carlos Garcia	.05
345 Jerald Clark	.05	451 Al Martin	.05
346 Alex Cole	.05	452 Blas Minor RC	.05
347 Andres Galarraga	.05	453 Dennis Moeller	.05
348 Joe Girardi	.05	454 Denny Neagle	.05
349 Ryan Hawblitzel RC	.05	455 Don Slaught	.05
350 Charlie Hayes	.05	456 Lonnie Smith	.05
351 Butch Henry	.05	457 Paul Wagner	.05
352 Darren Holmes	.05	458 Bob Walk	.05
353 Dale Murphy	.20	459 Kevin Young	.05
354 David Nied	.05	460 Rene Arocha RC	.05
355 Jeff Parrett	.05	461 Brian Barber	.05
356 Steve Reed RC	.05	462 Rheal Cormier	.05
357 Bruce Ruffin	.05	463 Gregg Jefferies	.05
358 Danny Sheaffer RC	.05	464 Joe Magrane	.05
359 Bryn Smith	.05	465 Omar Olivares	.05
360 Jim Tatum RC	.05	466 Geronimo Pena	.05
361 Eric Young	.05	467 Allen Watson	.05
362 Gerald Young	.05	468 Mark Whiten	.05
363 Luis Aquino	.05	469 Derek Bell	.05
364 Alex Arias RC	.05	470 Phil Clark	.05
365 Jack Armstrong	.05	471 Pat Gomez RC	.05
366 Bret Barberie	.05	472 Tony Gwynn	.60
367 Ryan Bowen	.05	473 Jeremy Hernandez	.05
368 Greg Briley	.05	474 Bruce Hurst	.05
369 Cris Carpenter	.05	475 Phil Plantier	.05
370 Chuck Carr	.05	476 Scott Sanders RC	.05
371 Jeff Conine RC	.25	477 Tim Scott RC	.05
372 Steve Decker	.05	478 Darrell Sherman RC	.05
373 Orestes Destrade	.05	479 Guillermo Velasquez	.05
374 Monty Fariss	.05	480 Tim Worrell RC	.05
375 Junior Felix	.05	481 Todd Benzinger	.05
376 Chris Hammond	.05	482 Bud Black	.05
377 Bryan Harvey	.05	483 Barry Bonds	1.50
378 Trevor Hoffman RC	.25	484 Dave Burba	.05
379 Charlie Hough	.05	485 Bryan Hickerson	.05
380 Joe Klink	.05	486 Dave Martinez	.05
381 Richie Lewis RC	.05	487 Willie McGee	.05
382 Dave Magadan	.05	488 Jeff Reed	.05
383 Bob McClure	.05	489 Kevin Rogers	.05
384 Scott Pose RC	.05	490 Matt Williams	.05
385 Rich Renteria RC	.05	491 Trevor Wilson	.05
386 Benito Santiago	.05	492 Harold Baines	.05
387 Walt Weiss	.05	493 Mike Devereaux	.05
388 Nigel Wilson	.05	494 Todd Frohwirth	.05
389 Eric Anthony	.05	495 Chris Hoiles	.05
390 Jeff Bagwell	.50	496 Luis Mercedes	.05
391 Andujar Cedeno	.05	497 Sherman Obando RC	.05
392 Doug Drabek	.05	498 Brad Pennington RC	.05
393 Darryl Kile	.05	499 Harold Reynolds	.05
394 Mark Portugal	.05	500 Arthur Rhodes	.05
395 Karl Rhodes	.05	501 Cal Ripken, Jr.	1.50

502 Rick Sutcliffe	.05	608 Dave Henderson	.05
503 Fernando Valenzuela	.05	609 Mark McGwire	1.00
504 Mark Williamson	.05	610 Mike Mohler RC	.05
505 Scott Bankhead	.05	611 Edwin Nunez	.05
506 Greg Blosser	.05	612 Kevin Seitzer	.05
507 Ivan Calderon	.05	613 Ruben Sierra	.05
508 Roger Clemens	.65	614 Chris Bosio	.05
509 Andre Clemens	.05	615 Norm Charlton	.05
510 Scott Fletcher	.05	616 Jim Converse RC	.05
511 Greg Harris	.05	617 John Cummings RC	.05
512 Billy Hatcher	.05	618 Mike Felder	.05
513 Bob Melvin	.05	619 Ken Griffey Jr.	.75
514 Carlos Quintana	.05	620 Mike Hampton	.05
515 Luis Rivera	.05	621 Erik Hanson	.05
516 Jeff Russell	.05	622 Bill Haselman	.05
517 Ken Ryan RC	.05	623 Tino Martinez	.05
518 Chili Davis	.05	624 Lee Tinsley	.05
519 Jim Edmonds RC	1.50	625 Fernando Vina RC	.05
520 Gary Gaetti	.05	626 David Wainhouse RC	.05
521 Torey Lovullo	.05	627 Jose Canseco	.30
522 Tony Percival RC	.05	628 Benji Gil	.05
523 Tim Salmon	.05	629 Tom Henke	.05
524 Scott Sanderson	.05	630 David Hulse RC	.05
525 J.T. Snow RC	.75	631 Manuel Lee	.05
526 Jerome Walton	.05	632 Craig Lefferts	.05
527 Jason Bere	.05	633 Robb Nen RC	.05
528 Rod Bolton RC	.05	634 Gary Redus	.05
529 Ellis Burks	.05	635 Bill Ripken	.05
530 Carlton Fisk	.50	636 Nolan Ryan	1.50
531 Craig Grebeck	.05	637 Dan Smith	.05
532 Ozzie Guillen	.05	638 Matt Whiteside RC	.05
533 Roberto Hernandez	.05	639 Roberto Alomar	.25
534 Bo Jackson	.10	640 Juan Guzman	.05
535 Kirk McCaskill	.05	641 Pat Hentgen	.05
536 Dave Stieb	.05	642 Darrin Jackson	.05
537 Robin Ventura	.05	643 Randy Knorr	.05
538 Albert Belle	.05	644 Domingo Martinez RC	.05
539 Mike Bielecki	.05	645 Paul Molitor	.50
540 Glenallen Hill	.05	646 Dick Schofield	.05
541 Reggie Jefferson	.05	647 Dave Stewart	.05
542 Kenny Lofton	.05	648 Rey Sanchez Checklist	.05
543 Jeff Mutis RC	.05	649 Jeremy Hernandez Checklist	.05
544 Junior Ortiz	.05	650 Junior Ortiz Checklist	.05
545 Manny Ramirez	.50		
546 Jeff Treadway	.05		
547 Kevin Wickander	.05		
548 Cecil Fielder	.05		
549 Kirk Gibson	.05		
550 Greg Gohr RC	.05		
551 David Haas	.05		
552 Bill Krueger	.05		
553 Mike Moore	.05		
554 Mickey Tettleton	.05		
555 Lou Whitaker	.05		
556 Kevin Appier	.05		
557 Billy Brewer RC	.05		
558 David Cone	.05		
559 Greg Gagne	.05		
560 Mark Gardner	.05		
561 Phil Hiatt	.05		
562 Felix Jose	.05		
563 Jose Lind	.05		
564 Mike Macfarlane	.05		
565 Keith Miller	.05		
566 Jeff Montgomery	.05		
567 Hipolito Pechardo	.05		
568 Ricky Bones	.05		
569 Tom Brunansky	.05		
570 Joe Kmak RC	.05		
571 Pat Listach	.05		
572 Graeme Lloyd RC	.05		
573 Carlos Maldonado RC	.05		
574 Josias Manzanillo	.05		
575 Matt Mieske	.05		
576 Kevin Reimer	.05		
577 Bill Spiers	.05		
578 Dickie Thon	.05		
579 Willie Banks	.05		
580 Jim Deshaies	.05		
581 Mark Guthrie	.05		
582 Brian Harper	.05		
583 Chuck Knoblauch	.05		
584 Gene Larkin	.05		
585 Shane Mack	.05		
586 David McCarty	.05		
587 Mike Pagliarulo	.05		
588 Mike Trombley	.05		
589 Dave Winfield	.50		
590 Jim Abbott	.05		
591 Wade Boggs	.60		
592 Russ Davis RC	.05		
593 Steve Farr	.05		
594 Steve Howe	.05		
595 Mike Humphreys RC	.05		
596 Jimmy Key	.05		
597 Jim Leyritz	.05		
598 Bobby Munoz RC	.05		
599 Paul O'Neill	.05		
600 Spike Owen	.05		
601 Mike Stanley	.05		
602 Danny Tartabull	.05		
603 Scott Brosius	.05		
604 Storm Davis	.05		
605 Eric Fox	.05		
606 Goose Gossage	.05		
607 Scott Hammond	.05		

All-Rookies

		NM/M
Complete Set (10):		4.00
Common Player:		.25
1	Rene Arocha	.25
2	Jeff Conine	.25
3	Phil Hiatt	.25
4	Mike Lansing	.25
5	Al Martin	.25
6	David Nied	.25
7	Mike Piazza	3.00
8	Tim Salmon	.50
9	J.T. Snow	.45
10	Kevin Young	.25

All-Stars

	NM/M
Complete Set (20):	17.50
Common Player:	.25

1	Darren Daulton	.25
2	Will Clark	.35
3	Ryne Sandberg	1.50
4	Barry Larkin	.25
5	Gary Sheffield	.40
6	Barry Bonds	3.00
7	Ray Lankford	.25
8	Larry Walker	.25
9	Greg Maddux	1.50
10	Lee Smith	.25
11	Ivan Rodriguez	.75
12	Mark McGwire	2.50
13	Carlos Baerga	.25
14	Cal Ripken, Jr.	3.00
15	Edgar Martinez	.25
16	Juan Gonzalez	1.00
17	Ken Griffey Jr.	2.00
18	Kirby Puckett	1.50
19	Frank Thomas	1.25
20	Mike Mussina	.65

Award Winners

		NM/M
Complete Set (25):		12.00
Common Player:		.25
1	Greg Maddux	.75
2	Tom Pagnozzi	.25
3	Mark Grace	.25
4	Jose Lind	.25
5	Terry Pendleton	.25
6	Ozzie Smith	.75
7	Barry Bonds	2.00
8	Andy Van Slyke	.25
9	Larry Walker	.25
10	Mark Langston	.25
11	Ivan Rodriguez	.60
12	Don Mattingly	.75
13	Roberto Alomar	.35
14	Robin Ventura	.25
15	Cal Ripken, Jr.	2.00
16	Ken Griffey Jr.	1.00
17	Kirby Puckett	.75
18	Devon White	.25
19	Pat Listach	.25
20	Eric Karros	.25
21	Pat Borders	.25
22	Greg Maddux	.75
23	Dennis Eckersley	.60
24	Barry Bonds	2.00
25	Gary Sheffield	.45

Commemorative

	NM/M
Dennis Eckersley, Paul Mullan	5.00

Dennis Eckersley Career Highlights

	NM/M
Complete Set (12):	6.00
Common Card:	.50
Autographed Card:	35.00
1	"Perfection" (A's 1987-92)	.50
2	"The Kid" (Indians 1975-77)	.50
3	"The Warrior" (Indians 1975-77)	.50

4	"Beantown Blazer" (Red Sox 1978-84)	.50
5	"Eckspeak" (Red Sox 1978-84)	.50
6	"Down to Earth" (Red Sox 1978-84)	.50
7	"Wrigley Bound" (Cubs 1984-86)	.50
8	"No Relief" (A's 1987-92)	.50
9	"In Control" (A's 1987-92)	.50
10	"Simply the Best" (A's 1987-92)	.50
11	"Reign of Perfection" (A's 1987-92)	.50
12	"Leaving His Mark" (A's 1987-92)	.50

Home Run Kings

		NM/M
Complete Set (10):		8.00
Common Player:		.50
1	Juan Gonzalez	.65
2	Mark McGwire	2.50
3	Cecil Fielder	.50
4	Fred McGriff	.50
5	Albert Belle	.50
6	Barry Bonds	2.50
7	Joe Carter	.50
8	Gary Sheffield	.65
9	Darren Daulton	.50
10	Dave Hollins	.50

Performers

	NM/M
Complete Set (10):	5.00
Common Player:	.25

1	Barry Bonds	2.50
2	Juan Gonzalez	.30
3	Ken Griffey Jr.	1.00
4	Eric Karros	.25
5	Pat Listach	.25
6	Greg Maddux	.75
7	David Nied	.25
8	Gary Sheffield	.40
9	J.T. Snow	.25
10	Frank Thomas	.65

Strikeout Kings

		NM/M
Complete Set (5):		7.50
Common Player:		.25
1	Roger Clemens	2.50
2	Juan Guzman	.25
3	Randy Johnson	1.25
4	Nolan Ryan	5.00
5	John Smoltz	.50

1994 Ultra

		NM/M
Complete Set (600):		15.00
Common Player:		.05
Series 1 or 2 Pack (14):		.50
Series 1 or 2 Wax Box (36):		15.00
1	Jeffrey Hammonds	.05
2	Chris Hoiles	.05
3	Ben McDonald	.05
4	Mark McLemore	.05
5	Alan Mills	.05
6	Jamie Moyer	.05
7	Brad Pennington	.05
8	Jim Poole	.05
9	Cal Ripken, Jr.	1.50
10	Jack Voigt	.05
11	Roger Clemens	.65
12	Danny Darwin	.05
13	Andre Dawson	.25
14	Scott Fletcher	.05
15	Greg Harris	.05
16	Billy Hatcher	.05
17	Jeff Russell	.05
18	Aaron Sele	.05
19	Mo Vaughn	.25
20	Mike Butcher	.05
21	Rod Correia	.05
22	Steve Frey	.05
23	Phil Leftwich RC	.05
24	Torey Lovullo	.05
25	Ken Patterson	.05
26	Eduardo Perez	.05
27	Tim Salmon	.25
28	J.T. Snow	.05
29	Chris Turner	.05
30	Wilson Alvarez	.05
31	Jason Bere	.05
32	Joey Cora	.05
33	Alex Fernandez	.05
34	Roberto Hernandez	.05

35	Lance Johnson	.05
36	Ron Karkovice	.05
37	Kirk McCaskill	.05
38	Jeff Schwarz	.05
39	Frank Thomas	.50
40	Sandy Alomar Jr.	.05
41	Albert Belle	.05
42	Felix Fermin	.05
43	Wayne Kirby	.05
44	Tom Kramer	.05
45	Kenny Lofton	.05
46	Jose Mesa	.05
47	Eric Plunk	.05
48	Paul Sorrento	.05
49	Jim Thome	.35
50	Bill Wertz	.05
51	John Doherty	.05
52	Cecil Fielder	.05
53	Travis Fryman	.05
54	Chris Gomez	.05
55	Mike Henneman	.05
56	Chad Kreuter	.05
57	Bob MacDonald	.05
58	Mike Moore	.05
59	Tony Phillips	.05
60	Lou Whitaker	.05
61	Kevin Appier	.05
62	Greg Gagne	.05
63	Chris Gwynn	.05
64	Bob Hamelin	.05
65	Chris Haney	.05
66	Phil Hiatt	.05
67	Felix Jose	.05
68	Jose Lind	.05
69	Mike Macfarlane	.05
70	Jeff Montgomery	.05
71	Hipolito Pichardo	.05
72	Juan Bell	.05
73	Cal Eldred	.05
74	Darryl Hamilton	.05
75	Doug Henry	.05
76	Mike Ignasiak	.05
77	John Jaha	.05
78	Graeme Lloyd	.05
79	Angel Miranda	.05
80	Dave Nilsson	.05
81	Troy O'Leary	.05
82	Kevin Reimer	.05
83	Willie Banks	.05
84	Larry Casian	.05
85	Scott Erickson	.05
86	Eddie Guardado	.05
87	Kent Hrbek	.05
88	Terry Jorgensen	.05
89	Chuck Knoblauch	.05
90	Pat Meares	.05
91	Mike Trombley	.05
92	Dave Winfield	.50
93	Wade Boggs	.60
94	Scott Kamieniecki	.05
95	Pat Kelly	.05
96	Jimmy Key	.05
97	Jim Leyritz	.05
98	Bobby Munoz	.05
99	Paul O'Neill	.05
100	Melido Perez	.05
101	Mike Stanley	.05
102	Danny Tartabull	.05
103	Bernie Williams	.05
104	Kurt Abbott RC	.05
105	Mike Bordick	.05
106	Ron Darling	.05
107	Brent Gates	.05
108	Miguel Jimenez	.05
109	Steve Karsay	.05
110	Scott Lydy	.05
111	Mark McGwire	1.00
112	Troy Neel	.05
113	Craig Paquette	.05
114	Bob Welch	.05
115	Bobby Witt	.05
116	Rich Amaral	.05
117	Mike Blowers	.05
118	Jay Buhner	.05
119	Dave Fleming	.05
120	Ken Griffey Jr.	.75
121	Tino Martinez	.05
122	Marc Newfield	.05
123	Ted Power	.05
124	Mackey Sasser	.05
125	Omar Vizquel	.05
126	Kevin Brown	.05
127	Juan Gonzalez	.25
128	Tom Henke	.05
129	David Hulse	.05
130	Dean Palmer	.05
131	Roger Pavlik	.05
132	Ivan Rodriguez	.40
133	Kenny Rogers	.05
134	Doug Strange	.05
135	Pat Borders	.05
136	Joe Carter	.05
137	Darnell Coles	.05
138	Pat Hentgen	.05

#	Player	Price
139	Al Leiter	.05
140	Paul Molitor	.50
141	John Olerud	.05
142	Ed Sprague	.05
143	Dave Stewart	.05
144	Mike Timlin	.05
145	Duane Ward	.05
146	Devon White	.05
147	Steve Avery	.05
148	Steve Bedrosian	.05
149	Damon Berryhill	.05
150	Jeff Blauser	.05
151	Tom Glavine	.20
152	Chipper Jones	.60
153	Mark Lemke	.05
154	Fred McGriff	.05
155	Greg McMichael	.05
156	Deion Sanders	.05
157	John Smoltz	.05
158	Mark Wohlers	.05
159	Jose Bautista	.05
160	Steve Buechele	.05
161	Mike Harkey	.05
162	Greg Hibbard	.05
163	Chuck McElroy	.05
164	Mike Morgan	.05
165	Kevin Roberson	.05
166	Ryne Sandberg	.60
167	Jose Vizcaino	.05
168	Rick Wilkins	.05
169	Willie Wilson	.05
170	Willie Greene	.05
171	Roberto Kelly	.05
172	Larry Luebbers	.05
173	Kevin Mitchell	.05
174	Joe Oliver	.05
175	John Roper	.05
176	Johnny Ruffin	.05
177	Reggie Sanders	.05
178	John Smiley	.05
179	Jerry Spradlin	.05
180	Freddie Benavides	.05
181	Dante Bichette	.05
182	Willie Blair	.05
183	Kent Bottenfield	.05
184	Jerald Clark	.05
185	Joe Girardi	.05
186	Roberto Mejia	.05
187	Steve Reed	.05
188	Armando Reynoso	.05
189	Bruce Ruffin	.05
190	Eric Young	.05
191	Luis Aquino	.05
192	Bret Barberie	.05
193	Ryan Bowen	.05
194	Chuck Carr	.05
195	Orestes Destrade	.05
196	Richie Lewis	.05
197	Dave Magadan	.05
198	Bob Natal	.05
199	Gary Sheffield	.30
200	Matt Turner	.05
201	Darrell Whitmore	.05
202	Eric Anthony	.05
203	Jeff Bagwell	.50
204	Andujar Cedeno	.05
205	Luis Gonzalez	.05
206	Xavier Hernandez	.05
207	Doug Jones	.05
208	Darryl Kile	.05
209	Scott Servais	.05
210	Greg Swindell	.05
211	Brian Williams	.05
212	Pedro Astacio	.05
213	Brett Butler	.05
214	Omar Daal	.05
215	Jim Gott	.05
216	Raul Mondesi	.05
217	Jose Offerman	.05
218	Mike Piazza	.75
219	Cory Snyder	.05
220	Tim Wallach	.05
221	Todd Worrell	.05
222	Moises Alou	.05
223	Sean Berry	.05
224	Wil Cordero	.05
225	Jeff Fassero	.05
226	Darrin Fletcher	.05
227	Cliff Floyd	.05
228	Marquis Grissom	.05
229	Ken Hill	.05
230	Mike Lansing	.05
231	Kirk Rueter	.05
232	John Wetteland	.05
233	Rondell White	.05
234	Tim Bogar	.05
235	Jeromy Burnitz	.05
236	Dwight Gooden	.05
237	Todd Hundley	.05
238	Jeff Kent	.05
239	Josias Manzanillo	.05
240	Joe Orsulak	.05
241	Ryan Thompson	.05
242	Kim Batiste	.05
243	Darren Daulton	.05
243a	Darren Daulton (Promotional Sample)	1.00
244	Tommy Greene	.05
245	Dave Hollins	.05
246	Pete Incaviglia	.05
247	Danny Jackson	.05
248	Ricky Jordan	.05
249	John Kruk	.05
249a	John Kruk (Promotional Sample)	1.00
250	Mickey Morandini	.05
251	Terry Mulholland	.05
252	Ben Rivera	.05
253	Kevin Stocker	.05
254	Jay Bell	.05
255	Steve Cooke	.05
256	Jeff King	.05
257	Al Martin	.05
258	Danny Miceli	.05
259	Blas Minor	.05
260	Don Slaught	.05
261	Paul Wagner	.05
262	Tim Wakefield	.05
263	Kevin Young	.05
264	Rene Arocha	.05
265	Richard Batchelor RC	.05
266	Gregg Jefferies	.05
267	Brian Jordan	.05
268	Jose Oquendo	.05
269	Donovan Osborne	.05
270	Erik Pappas	.05
271	Mike Perez	.05
272	Bob Tewksbury	.05
273	Mark Whiten	.05
274	Todd Zeile	.05
275	Andy Ashby	.05
276	Brad Ausmus	.05
277	Phil Clark	.05
278	Jeff Gardner	.05
279	Ricky Gutierrez	.05
280	Tony Gwynn	.60
281	Tim Mauser	.05
282	Scott Sanders	.05
283	Frank Seminara	.05
284	Wally Whitehurst	.05
285	Rod Beck	.05
286	Barry Bonds	1.50
287	Dave Burba	.05
288	Mark Carreon	.05
289	Royce Clayton	.05
290	Mike Jackson	.05
291	Darren Lewis	.05
292	Kirt Manwaring	.05
293	Dave Martinez	.05
294	Billy Swift	.05
295	Salomon Torres	.05
296	Matt Williams	.05
297	Checklist 1-103 (Joe Orsulak)	.05
298	Checklist 104-201 (Pete Incaviglia)	.05
299	Checklist 202-300 (Todd Hundley)	.05
300	Checklist - Inserts (John Doherty)	.05
301	Brady Anderson	.05
302	Harold Baines	.05
303	Damon Buford	.05
304	Mike Devereaux	.05
305	Sid Fernandez	.05
306	Rick Krivda	.05
307	Mike Mussina	.30
308	Rafael Palmeiro	.40
309	Arthur Rhodes	.05
310	Chris Sabo	.05
311	Lee Smith	.05
312	Gregg Zaun RC	.05
313	Scott Cooper	.05
314	Mike Greenwell	.05
315	Tim Naehring	.05
316	Otis Nixon	.05
317	Paul Quantrill	.05
318	John Valentin	.05
319	Dave Valle	.05
320	Frank Viola	.05
321	Brian Anderson RC	.10
322	Garret Anderson RC	.05
323	Chad Curtis	.05
324	Chili Davis	.05
325	Gary DiSarcina	.05
326	Damion Easley	.05
327	Jim Edmonds	.05
328	Chuck Finley	.05
329	Joe Grahe	.05
330	Bo Jackson	.10
331	Mark Langston	.05
332	Harold Reynolds	.05
333	James Baldwin	.05
334	Ray Durham RC	.50
335	Julio Franco	.05
336	Craig Grebeck	.05
337	Ozzie Guillen	.05
338	Joe Hall	.05
339	Darrin Jackson	.05
340	Jack McDowell	.05
341	Tim Raines	.05
342	Robin Ventura	.05
343	Carlos Baerga	.05
344	Derek Lilliquist	.05
345	Dennis Martinez	.05
346	Jack Morris	.05
347	Eddie Murray	.50
348	Chris Nabholz	.05
349	Charles Nagy	.05
350	Chad Ogea	.05
351	Manny Ramirez	.50
352	Omar Vizquel	.05
353	Tim Belcher	.05
354	Eric Davis	.05
355	Kirk Gibson	.05
356	Rick Greene	.05
357	Mickey Tettleton	.05
358	Alan Trammell	.05
359	David Wells	.05
360	Stan Belinda	.05
361	Vince Coleman	.05
362	David Cone	.05
363	Gary Gaetti	.05
364	Tom Gordon	.05
365	Dave Henderson	.05
366	Wally Joyner	.05
367	Brent Mayne	.05
368	Brian McRae	.05
369	Michael Tucker	.05
370	Ricky Bones	.05
371	Brian Harper	.05
372	Tyrone Hill	.05
373	Mark Kiefer	.05
374	Pat Listach	.05
375	Mike Matheny RC	.10
376	Jose Mercedes RC	.05
377	Jody Reed	.05
378	Kevin Seitzer	.05
379	B.J. Surhoff	.05
380	Greg Vaughn	.05
381	Turner Ward	.05
382	Wes Weger RC	.05
383	Bill Wegman	.05
384	Rick Aguilera	.05
385	Rich Becker	.05
386	Alex Cole	.05
387	Steve Dunn	.05
388	Keith Garagozzo RC	.05
389	LaTroy Hawkins RC	.05
390	Shane Mack	.05
391	David McCarty	.05
392	Pedro Munoz	.05
393	Derek Parks RC	.05
394	Kirby Puckett	.60
395	Kevin Tapani	.05
396	Matt Walbeck	.05
397	Jim Abbott	.05
398	Mike Gallego	.05
399	Xavier Hernandez	.05
400	Don Mattingly	.65
401	Terry Mulholland	.05
402	Matt Nokes	.05
403	Luis Polonia	.05
404	Bob Wickman	.05
405	Mark Acre	.05
406	Fausto Cruz RC	.05
407	Dennis Eckersley	.45
408	Rickey Henderson	.50
409	Stan Javier	.05
410	Carlos Reyes RC	.05
411	Ruben Sierra	.05
412	Terry Steinbach	.05
413	Bill Taylor	.05
414	Todd Van Poppel	.05
415	Eric Anthony	.05
416	Bobby Ayala	.05
417	Chris Bosio	.05
418	Tim Davis	.05
419	Randy Johnson	.50
420	Kevin King	.05
421	Anthony Manahan RC	.05
422	Edgar Martinez	.05
423	Keith Mitchell	.05
424	Roger Salkeld	.05
425	Mac Suzuki RC	.05
426	Dan Wilson	.05
427	Duff Brumley RC	.05
428	Jose Canseco	.30
429	Will Clark	.05
430	Steve Dreyer	.05
431	Rick Helling	.05
432	Chris James	.05
433	Matt Whiteside	.05
434	Roberto Alomar	.20
435	Scott Brow	.05
436	Domingo Cedeno RC	.05
437	Carlos Delgado	.35
438	Juan Guzman	.05
439	Paul Spoljaric	.05
440	Todd Stottlemyre	.05
441	Woody Williams	.05
442	Dave Justice	.05
443	Mike Kelly	.05
444	Ryan Klesko	.05
445	Javier Lopez	.05
446	Greg Maddux	.60
447	Kent Mercker	.05
448	Charlie O'Brien	.05
449	Terry Pendleton	.05
450	Mike Stanton	.05
451	Tony Tarasco	.05
452	Terrell Wade RC	.05
453	Willie Banks	.05
454	Shawon Dunston	.05
455	Mark Grace	.05
456	Jose Guzman	.05
457	Jose Hernandez	.05
458	Glenallen Hill	.05
459	Blaise Ilsley	.05
460	Brooks Kieschnick RC	.05
461	Derrick May	.05
462	Randy Myers	.05
463	Karl Rhodes	.05
464	Sammy Sosa	.60
465	Steve Trachsel RC	.10
466	Anthony Young	.05
467	Eddie Zambrano RC	.05
468	Bret Boone	.05
469	Tom Browning	.05
470	Hector Carrasco RC	.05
471	Rob Dibble	.05
472	Erik Hanson	.05
473	Thomas Howard	.05
474	Barry Larkin	.05
475	Hal Morris	.05
476	Jose Rijo	.05
477	John Burke	.05
478	Ellis Burks	.05
479	Marvin Freeman	.05
480	Andres Galarraga	.05
481	Greg Harris	.05
482	Charlie Hayes	.05
483	Darren Holmes	.05
484	Howard Johnson	.05
485	Marcus Moore RC	.05
486	David Nied	.05
487	Mark Thompson	.05
488	Walt Weiss	.05
489	Kurt Abbott	.05
490	Matias Carrillo	.05
491	Jeff Conine	.05
492	Chris Hammond	.05
493	Bryan Harvey	.05
494	Charlie Hough	.05
495	Yorkis Perez RC	.05
496	Pat Rapp	.05
497	Benito Santiago	.05
498	David Weathers	.05
499	Craig Biggio	.05
500	Ken Caminiti	.05
501	Doug Drabek	.05
502	Tony Eusebio RC	.10
503	Steve Finley	.05
504	Pete Harnisch	.05
505	Brian Hunter	.05
506	Domingo Jean	.05
507	Todd Jones	.05
508	Orlando Miller	.05
509	James Mouton	.05
510	Roberto Petagine	.05
511	Shane Reynolds	.05
512	Mitch Williams	.05
513	Billy Ashley	.05
514	Tom Candiotti	.05
515	Delino DeShields	.05
516	Kevin Gross	.05
517	Orel Hershiser	.05
518	Eric Karros	.05
519	Ramon Martinez	.05
520	Chan Ho Park RC	.75
521	Henry Rodriguez	.05
522	Joey Eischen	.05
523	Rod Henderson	.05
524	Pedro Martinez	.50
525	Mel Rojas	.05
526	Larry Walker	.05
527	Gabe White RC	.10
528	Bobby Bonilla	.05
529	Jonathan Hurst	.05
530	Bobby Jones	.05
531	Kevin McReynolds	.05
532	Bill Pulsipher	.05
533	Bret Saberhagen	.05
534	David Segui	.05
535	Pete Smith	.05
536	Kelly Stinnett RC	.05
537	Dave Telgheder	.05
538	Quilvio Veras RC	.05
539	Jose Vizcaino	.05
540	Pete Walker	.05
541	Ricky Bottalico	.05
542	Wes Chamberlain	.05
543	Mariano Duncan	.05
544	Len Dykstra	.05
545	Jim Eisenreich	.05
546	Phil Geisler RC	.05

547	Wayne Gomes RC	.10
548	Doug Jones	.05
549	Jeff Juden	.05
550	Mike Lieberthal	.05
551	Tony Longmire RC	.05
552	Tom Marsh	.05
553	Bobby Munoz	.05
554	Curt Schilling	.15
555	Carlos Garcia	.05
556	Ravelo Manzanillo RC	.05
557	Orlando Merced	.05
558	Will Pennyfeather RC	.05
559	Zane Smith	.05
560	Andy Van Slyke	.05
561	Rick White	.05
562	Luis Alicea	.05
563	Brian Barber RC	.05
564	Clint Davis RC	.05
565	Bernard Gilkey	.05
566	Ray Lankford	.05
567	Tom Pagnozzi	.05
568	Ozzie Smith	.60
569	Rick Sutcliffe	.05
570	Allen Watson	.05
571	Dmitri Young	.05
572	Derek Bell	.05
573	Andy Benes	.05
574	Archi Cianfrocco	.05
575	Joey Hamilton	.05
576	Gene Harris	.05
577	Trevor Hoffman	.05
578	Tim Hyers RC	.05
579	Brian Johnson RC	.05
580	Keith Lockhart RC	.05
581	Pedro Martinez	.05
582	Ray McDavid	.05
583	Phil Plantier	.05
584	Bip Roberts	.05
585	Dave Staton	.05
586	Todd Benzinger	.05
587	John Burkett	.05
588	Bryan Hickerson	.05
589	Willie McGee	.05
590	John Patterson	.05
591	Mark Portugal	.05
592	Kevin Rogers	.05
593	Joe Rosselli RC	.05
594	Steve Soderstrom RC	.05
595	Robby Thompson	.05
596	125th Anniversary Card	.05
597	Checklist	.05
598	Checklist	.05
599	Checklist	.05
600	Checklist	.05

All-Rookie Team

		NM/M
Complete Set (10):		4.00
Common Player:		.35
1	Kurt Abbott	.35
2	Carlos Delgado	3.00
3	Cliff Floyd	.35
4	Jeffrey Hammonds	.35
5	Ryan Klesko	.35
6	Javier Lopez	.35
7	Raul Mondesi	.35
8	James Mouton	.35
9	Chan Ho Park	.50
10	Dave Staton	.35

All-Stars

		NM/M
Complete Set (20):		5.00
Common Player:		.15
1	Chris Hoiles	.15
2	Frank Thomas	.35
3	Roberto Alomar	.20
4	Cal Ripken, Jr.	1.00
5	Robin Ventura	.15
6	Albert Belle	.15
7	Juan Gonzalez	.20
8	Ken Griffey Jr.	.50

9	John Olerud	.15
10	Jack McDowell	.15
11	Mike Piazza	.50
12	Fred McGriff	.15
13	Ryne Sandberg	.40
14	Jay Bell	.15
15	Matt Williams	.15
16	Barry Bonds	1.00
17	Len Dykstra	.15
18	Dave Justice	.15
19	Tom Glavine	.20
20	Greg Maddux	.40

Award Winners

		NM/M
Complete Set (25):		5.00
Common Player:		.10
1	Ivan Rodriguez	.25
2	Don Mattingly	.45
3	Roberto Alomar	.20
4	Robin Ventura	.10
5	Omar Vizquel	.10
6	Ken Griffey Jr.	.50
7	Kenny Lofton	.25
8	Devon White	.10
9	Mark Langston	.10
10	Kirt Manwaring	.10
11	Mark Grace	.10
12	Robby Thompson	.10
13	Matt Williams	.10
14	Jay Bell	.10
15	Barry Bonds	.60
16	Marquis Grissom	.10
17	Larry Walker	.10
18	Greg Maddux	.40
19	Frank Thomas	.35
20	Barry Bonds	.60
21	Paul Molitor	.35
22	Jack McDowell	.10
23	Greg Maddux	.40
24	Tim Salmon	.10
25	Mike Piazza	.50

Career Achievement Awards

		NM/M
Complete Set (5):		4.00
Common Player:		.50
1	Joe Carter	.50
2	Paul Molitor	.75
3	Cal Ripken, Jr.	2.00
4	Ryne Sandberg	1.00
5	Dave Winfield	.75

Firemen

	NM/M
Complete Set (10):	2.00
Common Player:	.25

1	Jeff Montgomery	.25
2	Duane Ward	.25
3	Tom Henke	.25
4	Roberto Hernandez	.25
5	Dennis Eckersley	1.25
6	Randy Myers	.25
7	Rod Beck	.25
8	Bryan Harvey	.25
9	John Wetteland	.25
10	Mitch Williams	.25

Hitting Machines

		NM/M
Complete Set (10):		4.00
Common Player:		.15
1	Roberto Alomar	.25
2	Carlos Baerga	.15
3	Barry Bonds	2.00
4	Andres Galarraga	.15
5	Juan Gonzalez	.25
6	Tony Gwynn	.50
7	Paul Molitor	.40
8	John Olerud	.15
9	Mike Piazza	.75
10	Frank Thomas	.40

Home Run Kings

		NM/M
Complete Set (12):		15.00
Common Player:		.75
1	Juan Gonzalez	1.00
2	Ken Griffey Jr.	2.50
3	Frank Thomas	2.00
4	Albert Belle	.75
5	Rafael Palmeiro	1.50
6	Joe Carter	.75
7	Barry Bonds	4.00
8	Dave Justice	.75
9	Matt Williams	.75
10	Fred McGriff	.75
11	Ron Gant	.75
12	Mike Piazza	2.50

League Leaders

		NM/M
Complete Set (10):		3.00
Common Player:		.25
1	John Olerud	.25
2	Rafael Palmeiro	1.00

3	Kenny Lofton	.25
4	Jack McDowell	.25
5	Randy Johnson	1.50
6	Andres Galarraga	.25
7	Len Dykstra	.25
8	Chuck Carr	.25
9	Tom Glavine	.35
10	Jose Rijo	.25

On-Base Leaders

		NM/M
Complete Set (12):		25.00
Common Player:		1.50
1	Roberto Alomar	2.00
2	Barry Bonds	6.50
3	Len Dykstra	1.50
4	Andres Galarraga	1.50
5	Mark Grace	1.50
6	Ken Griffey Jr.	5.00
7	Gregg Jefferies	1.50
8	Orlando Merced	1.50
9	Paul Molitor	3.50
10	John Olerud	1.50
11	Tony Phillips	1.50
12	Frank Thomas	3.50

Phillies Finest

		NM/M
Complete Set (24):		4.00
Common Player:		.25
Autographed Daulton:		45.00
Autographed Kruk:		30.00
1-5	Darren Daulton	.25
6-10	John Kruk	.25
11-15	Darren Daulton	.25
16-20	John Kruk	.25
9a	John Kruk (Promotional Sample)	1.50

MAIL-IN CARDS

1M, 3M Darren Daulton .75
2M, 4M John Kruk .75

Rising Stars

		NM/M
Complete Set (12):		15.00
Common Player:		1.00
1	Carlos Baerga	1.00
2	Jeff Bagwell	5.00
3	Albert Belle	1.00
4	Cliff Floyd	1.00
5	Travis Fryman	1.00
6	Marquis Grissom	1.00
7	Kenny Lofton	1.00
8	John Olerud	1.00
9	Mike Piazza	7.50
10	Kirk Rueter	1.00
11	Tim Salmon	1.00
12	Aaron Sele	1.00

RBI Kings

		NM/M
Complete Set (12):		16.00
Common Player:		1.00
1	Albert Belle	1.00
2	Frank Thomas	2.50
3	Joe Carter	1.00
4	Juan Gonzalez	1.25
5	Cecil Fielder	1.00
6	Carlos Baerga	1.00
7	Barry Bonds	5.00
8	David Justice	1.00
9	Ron Gant	1.00
10	Mike Piazza	3.50
11	Matt Williams	1.00
12	Darren Daulton	1.00

Second Year Standouts

		NM/M
Complete Set (10):		5.00
Common Player:		.25
1	Jason Bere	.25
2	Brent Gates	.25
3	Jeffrey Hammonds	.25
4	Tim Salmon	.50
5	Aaron Sele	.25
6	Chuck Carr	.25

7	Jeff Conine	.25
8	Greg McMichael	.25
9	Mike Piazza	4.00
10	Kevin Stocker	.25

Strikeout Kings

		NM/M
Complete Set (5):		2.00
Common Player:		.25
1	Randy Johnson	.75
2	Mark Langston	.25
3	Greg Maddux	1.00
4	Jose Rijo	.25
5	John Smoltz	.25

1995 Ultra

		NM/M
Complete Set (450):		10.00
Common Player:		.05
Series 1 or 2 Pack (12):		.50
Series 1 or 2 Wax Box (36):		12.50
1	Brady Anderson	.05
2	Sid Fernandez	.05
3	Jeffrey Hammonds	.05
4	Chris Hoiles	.05
5	Ben McDonald	.05
6	Mike Mussina	.35
7	Rafael Palmeiro	.65
8	Jack Voigt	.05
9	Wes Chamberlain	.05
10	Roger Clemens	1.00
11	Chris Howard	.05
12	Tim Naehring	.05
13	Otis Nixon	.05
14	Rich Rowland	.05
15	Ken Ryan	.05
16	John Valentin	.05
17	Mo Vaughn	.05
18	Brian Anderson	.05
19	Chili Davis	.05
20	Damion Easley	.05
21	Jim Edmonds	.05
22	Mark Langston	.05
23	Tim Salmon	.05
24	J.T. Snow	.05
25	Chris Turner	.05
26	Wilson Alvarez	.05
27	Joey Cora	.05
28	Alex Fernandez	.05
29	Roberto Hernandez	.05
30	Lance Johnson	.05
31	Ron Karkovice	.05
32	Kirk McCaskill	.05
33	Tim Raines	.05
34	Frank Thomas	.75
35	Sammy Alomar	.05
36	Albert Belle	.05
37	Mark Clark	.05
38	Kenny Lofton	.05
39	Eddie Murray	.75

40	Eric Plunk	.05
41	Manny Ramirez	.75
42	Jim Thome	.60
43	Omar Vizquel	.05
44	Danny Bautista	.05
45	Junior Felix	.05
46	Cecil Fielder	.05
47	Chris Gomez	.05
48	Chad Kreuter	.05
49	Mike Moore	.05
50	Tony Phillips	.05
51	Alan Trammell	.05
52	David Wells	.05
53	Kevin Appier	.05
54	Billy Brewer	.05
55	David Cone	.05
56	Greg Gagne	.05
57	Bob Hamelin	.05
58	Jose Lind	.05
59	Brent Mayne	.05
60	Brian McRae	.05
61	Terry Shumpert	.05
62	Ricky Bones	.05
63	Mike Fetters	.05
64	Darryl Hamilton	.05
65	John Jaha	.05
66	Graeme Lloyd	.05
67	Matt Mieske	.05
68	Kevin Seitzer	.05
69	Jose Valentin	.05
70	Turner Ward	.05
71	Rick Aguilera	.05
72	Rich Becker	.05
73	Alex Cole	.05
74	Scott Leius	.05
75	Pat Meares	.05
76	Kirby Puckett	1.00
77	Dave Stevens	.05
78	Kevin Tapani	.05
79	Matt Walbeck	.05
80	Wade Boggs	1.00
81	Scott Kamieniecki	.05
82	Pat Kelly	.05
83	Jimmy Key	.05
84	Paul O'Neill	.05
85	Luis Polonia	.05
86	Mike Stanley	.05
87	Danny Tartabull	.05
88	Bob Wickman	.05
89	Mark Acre	.05
90	Geronimo Berroa	.05
91	Mike Bordick	.05
92	Ron Darling	.05
93	Stan Javier	.05
94	Mark McGwire	1.50
95	Troy Neel	.05
96	Ruben Sierra	.05
97	Terry Steinbach	.05
98	Eric Anthony	.05
99	Chris Bosio	.05
100	Dave Fleming	.05
101	Ken Griffey Jr.	1.25
102	Reggie Jefferson	.05
103	Randy Johnson	.75
104	Edgar Martinez	.05
105	Bill Risley	.05
106	Dan Wilson	.05
107	Cris Carpenter	.05
108	Will Clark	.05
109	Juan Gonzalez	.40
110	Rusty Greer	.05
111	David Hulse	.05
112	Roger Pavlik	.05
113	Ivan Rodriguez	.75
114	Doug Strange	.05
115	Matt Whiteside	.05
116	Roberto Alomar	.20
117	Brad Cornett	.05
118	Carlos Delgado	.45
119	Alex Gonzalez	.05
120	Darren Hall	.05
121	Pat Hentgen	.05
122	Paul Molitor	.75
123	Ed Sprague	.05
124	Devon White	.05
125	Tom Glavine	.25
126	Dave Justice	.05
127	Roberto Kelly	.05
128	Mark Lemke	.05
129	Greg Maddux	1.00
130	Charles Johnson	.05
131	Kent Mercker	.05
132	Charlie O'Brien	.05
133	John Smoltz	.05
134	Willie Banks	.05
135	Steve Buechele	.05
136	Kevin Foster	.05
137	Glenallen Hill	.05
138	Ray Sanchez	.05
139	Sammy Sosa	1.00
140	Steve Trachsel	.05
141	Rick Wilkins	.05
142	Jeff Brantley	.05
143	Hector Carrasco	.05

144	Kevin Jarvis	.05
145	Barry Larkin	.05
146	Chuck McElroy	.05
147	Jose Rijo	.05
148	Johnny Ruffin	.05
149	Deion Sanders	.05
150	Eddie Taubensee	.05
151	Dante Bichette	.05
152	Ellis Burks	.05
153	Joe Girardi	.05
154	Charlie Hayes	.05
155	Mike Kingery	.05
156	Steve Reed	.05
157	Kevin Ritz	.05
158	Bruce Ruffin	.05
159	Eric Young	.05
160	Kurt Abbott	.05
161	Chuck Carr	.05
162	Chris Hammond	.05
163	Bryan Harvey	.05
164	Terry Mathews	.05
165	Yorkis Perez	.05
166	Pat Rapp	.05
167	Gary Sheffield	.40
168	Dave Weathers	.05
169	Jeff Bagwell	.75
170	Ken Caminiti	.05
171	Doug Drabek	.05
172	Steve Finley	.05
173	John Hudek	.05
174	Todd Jones	.05
175	James Mouton	.05
176	Shane Reynolds	.05
177	Scott Servais	.05
178	Tom Candiotti	.05
179	Omar Daal	.05
180	Darren Dreifort	.05
181	Eric Karros	.05
182	Ramon Martinez	.05
183	Raul Mondesi	.05
184	Henry Rodriguez	.05
185	Todd Worrell	.05
186	Moises Alou	.05
187	Sean Berry	.05
188	Wil Cordero	.05
189	Jeff Fassero	.05
190	Darrin Fletcher	.05
191	Butch Henry	.05
192	Ken Hill	.05
193	Mel Rojas	.05
194	John Wetteland	.05
195	Bobby Bonilla	.05
196	Rico Brogna	.05
197	Bobby Jones	.05
198	Jeff Kent	.05
199	Josias Manzanillo	.05
200	Kelly Stinnett	.05
201	Ryan Thompson	.05
202	Jose Vizcaino	.05
203	Lenny Dykstra	.05
204	Jim Eisenreich	.05
205	Dave Hollins	.05
206	Mike Lieberthal	.05
207	Mickey Morandini	.05
208	Bobby Munoz	.05
209	Curt Schilling	.20
210	Heathcliff Slocumb	.05
211	David West	.05
212	Dave Clark	.05
213	Steve Cooke	.05
214	Midre Cummings	.05
215	Carlos Garcia	.05
216	Jeff King	.05
217	Jon Lieber	.05
218	Orlando Merced	.05
219	Don Slaught	.05
220	Rick White	.05
221	Rene Arocha	.05
222	Bernard Gilkey	.05
223	Brian Jordan	.05
224	Tom Pagnozzi	.05
225	Vicente Palacios	.05
226	Geronimo Pena	.05
227	Ozzie Smith	1.00
228	Allen Watson	.05
229	Mark Whiten	.05
230	Brad Ausmus	.05
231	Derek Bell	.05
232	Andy Benes	.05
233	Tony Gwynn	1.00
234	Joey Hamilton	.05
235	Luis Lopez	.05
236	Pedro A. Martinez	.05
237	Scott Sanders	.05
238	Eddie Williams	.05
239	Rod Beck	.05
240	Dave Burba	.05
241	Darren Lewis	.05
242	Kirt Manwaring	.05
243	Mark Portugal	.05
244	Darryl Strawberry	.05
245	Robby Thompson	.05
246	William Van Landingham	.05

247	Matt Williams	.05
248	Checklist	.05
249	Checklist	.05
250	Checklist	.05
251	Harold Baines	.05
252	Bret Barberie	.05
253	Armando Benitez	.05
254	Mike Devereaux	.05
255	Leo Gomez	.05
256	Jamie Moyer	.05
257	Arthur Rhodes	.05
258	Cal Ripken Jr.	2.00
259	Luis Alicea	.05
260	Jose Canseco	.45
261	Scott Cooper	.05
262	Andre Dawson	.25
263	Mike Greenwell	.05
264	Aaron Sele	.05
265	Garret Anderson	.05
266	Chad Curtis	.05
267	Gary DiSarcina	.05
268	Chuck Finley	.05
269	Rex Hudler	.05
270	Andrew Lorraine	.05
271	Spike Owen	.05
272	Lee Smith	.05
273	Jason Bere	.05
274	Ozzie Guillen	.05
275	Norberto Martin	.05
276	Scott Ruffcorn	.05
277	Robin Ventura	.05
278	Carlos Baerga	.05
279	Jason Grimsley	.05
280	Dennis Martinez	.05
281	Charles Nagy	.05
282	Paul Sorrento	.05
283	Dave Winfield	.75
284	John Doherty	.05
285	Travis Fryman	.05
286	Kirk Gibson	.05
287	Lou Whitaker	.05
288	Gary Gaetti	.05
289	Tom Gordon	.05
290	Mark Gubicza	.05
291	Wally Joyner	.05
292	Mike Macfarlane	.05
293	Jeff Montgomery	.05
294	Jeff Cirillo	.05
295	Cal Eldred	.05
296	Pat Listach	.05
297	Jose Mercedes	.05
298	Dave Nilsson	.05
299	Duane Singleton	.05
300	Greg Vaughn	.05
301	Scott Erickson	.05
302	Denny Hocking	.05
303	Chuck Knoblauch	.05
304	Pat Mahomes	.05
305	Pedro Munoz	.05
306	Erik Schullstrom	.05
307	Jim Abbott	.05
308	Tony Fernandez	.05
309	Sterling Hitchcock	.05
310	Jim Leyritz	.05
311	Don Mattingly	1.00
312	Jack McDowell	.05
313	Melido Perez	.05
314	Bernie Williams	.05
315	Scott Brosius	.05
316	Dennis Eckersley	.65
317	Brent Gates	.05
318	Rickey Henderson	.75
319	Steve Karsay	.05
320	Steve Ontiveros	.05
321	Bill Taylor	.05
322	Todd Van Poppel	.05
323	Bob Welch	.05
324	Bobby Ayala	.05
325	Mike Blowers	.05
326	Jay Buhner	.05
327	Felix Fermin	.05
328	Tino Martinez	.05
329	Marc Newfield	.05
330	Greg Pirkl	.05
331	Alex Rodriguez	1.50
332	Kevin Brown	.05
333	John Burkett	.05
334	Jeff Frye	.05
335	Kevin Gross	.05
336	Dean Palmer	.05
337	Joe Carter	.05
338	Shawn Green	.35
339	Juan Guzman	.05
340	Mike Huff	.05
341	Al Leiter	.05
342	John Olerud	.05
343	Dave Stewart	.05
344	Todd Stottlemyre	.05
345	Steve Avery	.05
346	Jeff Blauser	.05
347	Chipper Jones	1.00
348	Mike Kelly	.05
349	Ryan Klesko	.05
350	Javier Lopez	.05

351	Fred McGriff	.05
352	Jose Oliva	.05
353	Terry Pendleton	.05
354	Mike Stanton	.05
355	Tony Tarasco	.05
356	Mark Wohlers	.05
357	Jim Bullinger	.05
358	Shawon Dunston	.05
359	Mark Grace	.05
360	Derrick May	.05
361	Randy Myers	.05
362	Karl Rhodes	.05
363	Bret Boone	.05
364	Brian Dorsett	.05
365	Ron Gant	.05
366	Brian R. Hunter	.05
367	Hal Morris	.05
368	Jack Morris	.05
369	John Roper	.05
370	Reggie Sanders	.05
371	Pete Schourek	.05
372	John Smiley	.05
373	Marvin Freeman	.05
374	Andres Galarraga	.05
375	Mike Munoz	.05
376	David Nied	.05
377	Walt Weiss	.05
378	Greg Colbrunn	.05
379	Jeff Conine	.05
380	Charles Johnson	.05
381	Kurt Miller	.05
382	Robb Nen	.05
383	Benito Santiago	.05
384	Craig Biggio	.05
385	Tony Eusebio	.05
386	Luis Gonzalez	.05
387	Brian L. Hunter	.05
388	Darryl Kile	.05
389	Orlando Miller	.05
390	Phil Plantier	.05
391	Greg Swindell	.05
392	Billy Ashley	.05
393	Pedro Astacio	.05
394	Brett Butler	.05
395	Delino DeShields	.05
396	Orel Hershiser	.05
397	Garey Ingram	.05
398	Chan Ho Park	.05
399	Mike Piazza	1.25
400	Ismael Valdes	.05
401	Tim Wallach	.05
402	Cliff Floyd	.05
403	Marquis Grissom	.05
404	Mike Lansing	.05
405	Pedro Martinez	.75
406	Kirk Rueter	.05
407	Tim Scott	.05
408	Jeff Shaw	.05
409	Larry Walker	.05
410	Rondell White	.05
411	John Franco	.05
412	Todd Hundley	.05
413	Jason Jacome	.05
414	Joe Orsulak	.05
415	Bret Saberhagen	.05
416	David Segui	.05
417	Darren Daulton	.05
418	Mariano Duncan	.05
419	Tommy Greene	.05
420	Gregg Jefferies	.05
421	John Kruk	.05
422	Kevin Stocker	.05
423	Jay Bell	.05
424	Al Martin	.05
425	Denny Neagle	.05
426	Zane Smith	.05
427	Andy Van Slyke	.05
428	Paul Wagner	.05
429	Tom Henke	.05
430	Danny Jackson	.05
431	Ray Lankford	.05
432	John Mabry	.05
433	Bob Tewksbury	.05
434	Todd Zeile	.05
435	Andy Ashby	.05
436	Andujar Cedeno	.05
437	Donnie Elliott	.05
438	Bryce Florie	.05
439	Trevor Hoffman	.05
440	Melvin Nieves	.05
441	Bip Roberts	.05
442	Barry Bonds	2.00
443	Royce Clayton	.05
444	Mike Jackson	.05
445	John Patterson	.05
446	J.R. Phillips	.05
447	Bill Swift	.05
448	Checklist	.05
449	Checklist	.05
450	Checklist	.05

Gold Medallion

	NM/M
Complete Set (450):	60.00

Common Player:	.25
Stars/Rookies:	2X

(See 1995 Ultra for checklist and base card values.)

All-Rookies

		NM/M
Complete Set (10):		2.25
Common Player:		.15
Gold Medallion:		2X
1	Cliff Floyd	.15
2	Chris Gomez	.15
3	Rusty Greer	.15
4	Bob Hamelin	.15
5	Joey Hamilton	.15
6	John Hudek	.15
7	Ryan Klesko	.15
8	Raul Mondesi	.15
9	Manny Ramirez	2.00
10	Steve Trachsel	.15

All-Stars

		NM/M
Complete Set (20):		7.50
Common Player:		.15
Gold Medallion:		2X
1	Moises Alou	.15
2	Albert Belle	.15
3	Craig Biggio	.15
4	Wade Boggs	.60
5	Barry Bonds	1.50
6	David Cone	.15
7	Ken Griffey Jr.	.75
8	Tony Gwynn	.60
9	Chuck Knoblauch	.15
10	Barry Larkin	.15
11	Kenny Lofton	.15
12	Greg Maddux	.60
13	Fred McGriff	.15
14	Paul O'Neill	.15
15	Mike Piazza	.75
16	Kirby Puckett	.60
17	Cal Ripken Jr.	1.50
18	Ivan Rodriguez	.45
19	Frank Thomas	.50
20	Matt Williams	.15

Award Winners

		NM/M
Complete Set (25):		6.00
Common Player:		.10
Gold Medallion:		2X
1	Ivan Rodriguez	.30
2	Don Mattingly	.65
3	Roberto Alomar	.20
4	Wade Boggs	.60
5	Omar Vizquel	.10
6	Ken Griffey Jr.	.75
7	Kenny Lofton	.10
8	Devon White	.10
9	Mark Langston	.10
10	Tom Pagnozzi	.10
11	Jeff Bagwell	.45
12	Craig Biggio	.10
13	Matt Williams	.10
14	Barry Larkin	.10
15	Barry Bonds	1.00
16	Marquis Grissom	.10
17	Darren Lewis	.10
18	Greg Maddux	.60
19	Frank Thomas	.45
20	Jeff Bagwell	.45
21	David Cone	.10
22	Greg Maddux	.60
23	Bob Hamelin	.10
24	Raul Mondesi	.10
25	Moises Alou	.10

Golden Prospects

		NM/M
Complete Set (10):		5.00
Common Player:		.10
Gold Medallion:		2X
1	James Baldwin	.10
2	Alan Benes	.10
3	Armando Benitez	.10
4	Ray Durham	.10
5	LaTroy Hawkins	.10
6	Brian Hunter	.10
7	Derek Jeter	3.00
8	Charles Johnson	.10
9	Alex Rodriguez	2.00
10	Michael Tucker	.10

Hitting Machines

		NM/M
Complete Set (10):		6.00
Common Player:		.40
Gold Medallion:		2X
1	Jeff Bagwell	.65
2	Albert Belle	.25
3	Dante Bichette	.25
4	Barry Bonds	2.50
5	Jose Canseco	.50
6	Ken Griffey Jr.	1.00
7	Tony Gwynn	.75
8	Fred McGriff	.25
9	Mike Piazza	1.00
10	Frank Thomas	.65

Home Run Kings

		NM/M
Complete Set (10):		7.50
Common Player:		.25
Gold Medallion:		2X
1	Ken Griffey Jr.	2.00
2	Frank Thomas	.75
3	Albert Belle	.25
4	Jose Canseco	.50
5	Cecil Fielder	.25
6	Matt Williams	.25
7	Jeff Bagwell	.75
8	Barry Bonds	3.00
9	Fred McGriff	.25
10	Andres Galarraga	.25

League Leaders

		NM/M
Complete Set (10):		2.50
Common Player:		.15
Gold Medallion:		2X
1	Paul O'Neill	.15
2	Kenny Lofton	.15
3	Jimmy Key	.15
4	Randy Johnson	.50
5	Lee Smith	.15
6	Tony Gwynn	.75
7	Craig Biggio	.15
8	Greg Maddux	.75
9	Andy Benes	.15
10	John Franco	.15

On-Base Leaders

		NM/M
Complete Set (10):		15.00
Common Player:		1.00
Gold Medallion:		2X
1	Jeff Bagwell	2.00
2	Albert Belle	1.00
3	Craig Biggio	1.00
4	Wade Boggs	2.50
5	Barry Bonds	6.00
6	Will Clark	1.00
7	Tony Gwynn	2.50
8	Dave Justice	1.00
9	Paul O'Neill	1.00
10	Frank Thomas	2.00

Power Plus

		NM/M
Complete Set (6):		7.50
Common Player:		.50
Gold Medallion:		2X
1	Albert Belle	.50
2	Ken Griffey Jr.	2.00
3	Frank Thomas	1.00
4	Jeff Bagwell	1.00
5	Barry Bonds	4.00
6	Matt Williams	.50

Rising Stars

		NM/M
Complete Set (9):		7.00
Common Player:		.50
Gold Medallion:		2X
1	Moises Alou	.50
2	Jeff Bagwell	1.50
3	Albert Belle	.65
4	Juan Gonzalez	1.50
5	Chuck Knoblauch	.50
6	Kenny Lofton	.50
7	Raul Mondesi	.50
8	Mike Piazza	2.50
9	Frank Thomas	1.50

RBI Kings

		NM/M
Complete Set (10):		12.00
Common Player:		.50
Gold Medallion:		2X
1	Kirby Puckett	3.00
2	Joe Carter	.50
3	Albert Belle	.50
4	Frank Thomas	2.00
5	Julio Franco	.50
6	Jeff Bagwell	2.00
7	Matt Williams	.50
8	Dante Bichette	.50
9	Fred McGriff	.50
10	Mike Piazza	4.00

Second Year Standouts

		NM/M
Complete Set (15):		3.50
Common Player:		.15

Gold Medallion:		2X
1	Cliff Floyd	.15
2	Chris Gomez	.15
3	Rusty Greer	.15
4	Darren Hall	.15
5	Bob Hamelin	.15
6	Joey Hamilton	.15
7	Jeffrey Hammonds	.15
8	John Hudek	.15
9	Ryan Klesko	.15
10	Raul Mondesi	.15
11	Manny Ramirez	3.00
12	Bill Risley	.15
13	Steve Trachsel	.15
14	William Van Landingham	.15
15	Rondell White	.15

Strikeout Kings

		NM/M
Complete Set (6):		3.00
Common Player:		.10
Gold Medallion:		2X
1	Andy Benes	.10
2	Roger Clemens	1.50
3	Randy Johnson	.75
4	Greg Maddux	1.00
5	Pedro Martinez	.75
6	Jose Rijo	.10

1996 Ultra

		NM/M
Complete Set (600):		22.50
Common Player:		.05
Series 1 or 2 Pack (12):		1.25
Series 1 or 2 Wax Box (24):		20.00
1	Manny Alexander	.05
2	Brady Anderson	.05
3	Bobby Bonilla	.05
4	Scott Erickson	.05
5	Curtis Goodwin	.05
6	Chris Hoiles	.05
7	Doug Jones	.05
8	Jeff Manto	.05
9	Mike Mussina	.35
10	Rafael Palmeiro	.50
11	Cal Ripken Jr.	1.50
12	Rick Aguilera	.05
13	Luis Alicea	.05
14	Stan Belinda	.05
15	Jose Canseco	.40
16	Roger Clemens	.85
17	Mike Greenwell	.05
18	Mike Macfarlane	.05
19	Tim Naehring	.05
20	Troy O'Leary	.05
21	John Valentin	.05
22	Mo Vaughn	.05
23	Tim Wakefield	.05
24	Brian Anderson	.05
25	Garret Anderson	.05
26	Chili Davis	.05
27	Gary DiSarcina	.05
28	Jim Edmonds	.05
29	Jorge Fabregas	.05
30	Chuck Finley	.05
31	Mark Langston	.05
32	Troy Percival	.05
33	Tim Salmon	.05
34	Lee Smith	.05
35	Wilson Alvarez	.05
36	Ray Durham	.05
37	Alex Fernandez	.05
38	Ozzie Guillen	.05
39	Roberto Hernandez	.05
40	Lance Johnson	.05
41	Ron Karkovice	.05
42	Lyle Mouton	.05
43	Tim Raines	.05
44	Frank Thomas	.60
45	Carlos Baerga	.05
46	Albert Belle	.05
47	Orel Hershiser	.05
48	Kenny Lofton	.05
49	Dennis Martinez	.05
50	Jose Mesa	.05
51	Eddie Murray	.60
52	Chad Ogea	.05
53	Manny Ramirez	.60
54	Jim Thome	.50
55	Omar Vizquel	.05
56	Dave Winfield	.60
57	Chad Curtis	.05
58	Cecil Fielder	.05
59	John Flaherty	.05
60	Travis Fryman	.05
61	Chris Gomez	.05
62	Bob Higginson	.05
63	Felipe Lira	.05
64	Brian Maxcy	.05
65	Alan Trammell	.05
66	Lou Whitaker	.05
67	Kevin Appier	.05
68	Gary Gaetti	.05
69	Tom Goodwin	.05
70	Tom Gordon	.05
71	Jason Jacome	.05
72	Wally Joyner	.05
73	Brent Mayne	.05
74	Jeff Montgomery	.05
75	Jon Nunnally	.05
76	Joe Vitiello	.05
77	Ricky Bones	.05
78	Jeff Cirillo	.05
79	Mike Fetters	.05
80	Darryl Hamilton	.05
81	David Hulse	.05
82	Dave Nilsson	.05
83	Kevin Seitzer	.05
84	Steve Sparks	.05
85	B.J. Surhoff	.05
86	Jose Valentin	.05
87	Greg Vaughn	.05
88	Marty Cordova	.05
89	Chuck Knoblauch	.05
90	Pat Meares	.05
91	Pedro Munoz	.05
92	Kirby Puckett	.75
93	Brad Radke	.05
94	Scott Stahoviak	.05
95	Dave Stevens	.05
96	Mike Trombley	.05
97	Matt Walbeck	.05
98	Wade Boggs	.75
99	Russ Davis	.05
100	Jim Leyritz	.05
101	Don Mattingly	.85
102	Jack McDowell	.05
103	Paul O'Neill	.05
104	Andy Pettitte	.30
105	Mariano Rivera	.15
106	Ruben Sierra	.05
107	Darryl Strawberry	.05
108	John Wetteland	.05
109	Bernie Williams	.05
110	Geronimo Berroa	.05
111	Scott Brosius	.05
112	Dennis Eckersley	.50
113	Brent Gates	.05
114	Rickey Henderson	.60
115	Mark McGwire	1.25
116	Ariel Prieto	.05

117 Terry Steinbach	.05	221 Ramon Martinez	.05
118 Todd Stottlemyre	.05	222 Raul Mondesi	.05
119 Todd Van Poppel	.05	223 Hideo Nomo	.30
120 Steve Wojciechowski	.05	224 Mike Piazza	1.00
121 Rich Amaral	.05	225 Kevin Tapani	.05
122 Bobby Ayala	.05	226 Ismael Valdes	.05
123 Mike Blowers	.05	227 Todd Worrell	.05
124 Chris Bosio	.05	228 Moises Alou	.05
125 Joey Cora	.05	229 Wil Cordero	.05
126 Ken Griffey Jr.	1.00	230 Jeff Fassero	.05
127 Randy Johnson	.60	231 Darrin Fletcher	.05
128 Edgar Martinez	.05	232 Mike Lansing	.05
129 Tino Martinez	.05	233 Pedro Martinez	.60
130 Alex Rodriguez	1.25	234 Carlos Perez	.05
131 Dan Wilson	.05	235 Mel Rojas	.05
132 Will Clark	.05	236 David Segui	.05
133 Jeff Frye	.05	237 Tony Tarasco	.05
134 Benji Gil	.05	238 Rondell White	.05
135 Juan Gonzalez	.30	239 Edgardo Alfonzo	.05
136 Rusty Greer	.05	240 Rico Brogna	.05
137 Mark McLemore	.05	241 Carl Everett	.05
138 Roger Pavlik	.05	242 Todd Hundley	.05
139 Ivan Rodriguez	.50	243 Butch Huskey	.05
140 Kenny Rogers	.05	244 Jason Isringhausen	.05
141 Mickey Tettleton	.05	245 Bobby Jones	.05
142 Roberto Alomar	.20	246 Jeff Kent	.05
143 Joe Carter	.05	247 Bill Pulsipher	.05
144 Tony Castillo	.05	248 Jose Vizcaino	.05
145 Alex Gonzalez	.05	249 Ricky Bottalico	.05
146 Shawn Green	.35	250 Darren Daulton	.05
147 Pat Hentgen	.05	251 Jim Eisenreich	.05
148 Sandy Martinez RC	.05	252 Tyler Green	.05
149 Paul Molitor	.60	253 Charlie Hayes	.05
150 John Olerud	.05	254 Gregg Jefferies	.05
151 Ed Sprague	.05	255 Tony Longmire	.05
152 Jeff Blauser	.05	256 Michael Mimbs	.05
153 Brad Clontz	.05	257 Mickey Morandini	.05
154 Tom Glavine	.30	258 Paul Quantrill	.05
155 Marquis Grissom	.05	259 Heathcliff Slocumb	.05
156 Chipper Jones	.75	260 Jay Bell	.05
157 David Justice	.05	261 Jacob Brumfield	.05
158 Ryan Klesko	.05	262 Angelo Encarnacion RC	.05
159 Javier Lopez	.05	263 John Ericks	.05
160 Greg Maddux	.75	264 Mark Johnson	.05
161 John Smoltz	.05	265 Esteban Loaiza	.05
162 Mark Wohlers	.05	266 Al Martin	.05
163 Jim Bullinger	.05	267 Orlando Merced	.05
164 Frank Castillo	.05	268 Dan Miceli	.05
165 Shawon Dunston	.05	269 Denny Neagle	.05
166 Kevin Foster	.05	270 Brian Barber	.05
167 Luis Gonzalez	.05	271 Scott Cooper	.05
168 Mark Grace	.05	272 Tripp Cromer	.05
169 Rey Sanchez	.05	273 Bernard Gilkey	.05
170 Scott Servais	.05	274 Tom Henke	.05
171 Sammy Sosa	.75	275 Brian Jordan	.05
172 Ozzie Timmons	.05	276 John Mabry	.05
173 Steve Trachsel	.05	277 Tom Pagnozzi	.05
174 Bret Boone	.05	278 Mark Petkovsek RC	.05
175 Jeff Branson	.05	279 Ozzie Smith	.75
176 Jeff Brantley	.05	280 Andy Ashby	.05
177 Dave Burba	.05	281 Brad Ausmus	.05
178 Ron Gant	.05	282 Ken Caminiti	.05
179 Barry Larkin	.05	283 Glenn Dishman	.05
180 Darren Lewis	.05	284 Tony Gwynn	.75
181 Mark Portugal	.05	285 Joey Hamilton	.05
182 Reggie Sanders	.05	286 Trevor Hoffman	.05
183 Pete Schourek	.05	287 Phil Plantier	.05
184 John Smiley	.05	288 Jody Reed	.05
185 Jason Bates	.05	289 Eddie Williams	.05
186 Dante Bichette	.05	290 Barry Bonds	1.50
187 Ellis Burks	.05	291 Jamie Brewington	.05
188 Vinny Castilla	.05	292 Mark Carreon	.05
189 Andres Galarraga	.05	293 Royce Clayton	.05
190 Darren Holmes	.05	294 Glenallen Hill	.05
191 Armando Reynoso	.05	295 Mark Leiter	.05
192 Kevin Ritz	.05	296 Kirt Manwaring	.05
193 Bill Swift	.05	297 J.R. Phillips	.05
194 Larry Walker	.05	298 Deion Sanders	.05
195 Kurt Abbott	.05	299 William Van Landingham	.05
196 John Burkett	.05	300 Matt Williams	.05
197 Greg Colbrunn	.05	301 Roberto Alomar	.20
198 Jeff Conine	.05	302 Armando Benitez	.05
199 Andre Dawson	.25	303 Mike Devereaux	.05
200 Chris Hammond	.05	304 Jeffrey Hammonds	.05
201 Charles Johnson	.05	305 Jimmy Haynes	.05
202 Robb Nen	.05	306 Scott McClain RC	.05
203 Terry Pendleton	.05	307 Kent Mercker	.05
204 Quilvio Veras	.05	308 Randy Myers	.05
205 Jeff Bagwell	.60	309 B.J. Surhoff	.05
206 Derek Bell	.05	310 Tony Tarasco	.05
207 Doug Drabek	.05	311 David Wells	.05
208 Tony Eusebio	.05	312 Wil Cordero	.05
209 Mike Hampton	.05	313 Alex Delgado	.05
210 Brian Hunter	.05	314 Tom Gordon	.05
211 Todd Jones	.05	315 Dwayne Hosey	.05
212 Orlando Miller	.05	316 Jose Malave	.05
213 James Mouton	.05	317 Kevin Mitchell	.05
214 Shane Reynolds	.05	318 Jamie Moyer	.05
215 Dave Veres	.05	319 Aaron Sele	.05
216 Billy Ashley	.05	320 Heathcliff Slocumb	.05
217 Brett Butler	.05	321 Mike Stanley	.05
218 Chad Fonville	.05	322 Jeff Suppan	.05
219 Todd Hollandsworth	.05	323 Jim Abbott	.05
220 Eric Karros	.05		

324 George Arias	.05	428 Felipe Crespo	.05
325 Todd Greene	.05	429 Carlos Delgado	.40
326 Bryan Harvey	.05	430 Juan Guzman	.05
327 J.T. Snow	.05	431 Erik Hanson	.05
328 Randy Velarde	.05	432 Marty Janzen RC	.05
329 Tim Wallach	.05	433 Otis Nixon	.05
330 Harold Baines	.05	434 Robert Perez	.05
331 Jason Bere	.05	435 Paul Quantrill	.05
332 Darren Lewis	.05	436 Bill Risley	.05
333 Norberto Martin	.05	437 Steve Avery	.05
334 Tony Phillips	.05	438 Jermaine Dye	.05
335 Bill Simas	.05	439 Mark Lemke	.05
336 Chris Snopek	.05	440 Marty Malloy RC	.05
337 Kevin Tapani	.05	441 Fred McGriff	.05
338 Danny Tartabull	.05	442 Greg McMichael	.05
339 Robin Ventura	.05	443 Wonderful Monds	.05
340 Sandy Alomar	.05	444 Eddie Perez	.05
341 Julio Franco	.05	445 Jason Schmidt	.05
342 Jack McDowell	.05	446 Terrell Wade	.05
343 Charles Nagy	.05	447 Terry Adams	.05
344 Julian Tavarez	.05	448 Scott Bullett	.05
345 Kimera Bartee	.05	449 Robin Jennings RC	.05
346 Greg Keagle	.05	450 Doug Jones	.05
347 Mark Lewis	.05	451 Brooks Kieschnick	.05
348 Jose Lima	.05	452 Dave Magadan	.05
349 Melvin Nieves	.05	453 Jason Maxwell RC	.05
350 Mark Parent	.05	454 Brian McRae	.05
351 Eddie Williams	.05	455 Rodney Myers	.05
352 Johnny Damon	.30	456 Jaime Navarro	.05
353 Sal Fasano	.05	457 Ryne Sandberg	.75
354 Mark Gubicza	.05	458 Vince Coleman	.05
355 Bob Hamelin	.05	459 Eric Davis	.05
356 Chris Haney	.05	460 Steve Gibralter	.05
357 Keith Lockhart	.05	461 Thomas Howard	.05
358 Mike Macfarlane	.05	462 Mike Kelly	.05
359 Jose Offerman	.05	463 Hal Morris	.05
360 Bip Roberts	.05	464 Eric Owens	.05
361 Michael Tucker	.05	465 Jose Rijo	.05
362 Chuck Carr	.05	466 Chris Sabo	.05
363 Bobby Hughes	.05	467 Eddie Taubensee	.05
364 John Jaha	.05	468 Trenidad Hubbard	.05
365 Mark Loretta	.05	469 Curt Leskanic	.05
366 Mike Matheny	.05	470 Quinton McCracken	.05
367 Ben McDonald	.05	471 Jayhawk Owens	.05
368 Matt Mieske	.05	472 Steve Reed	.05
369 Angel Miranda	.05	473 Bryan Rekar	.05
370 Fernando Vina	.05	474 Bruce Ruffin	.05
371 Rick Aguilera	.05	475 Bret Saberhagen	.05
372 Rich Becker	.05	476 Walt Weiss	.05
373 LaTroy Hawkins	.05	477 Eric Young	.05
374 Dave Hollins	.05	478 Kevin Brown	.05
375 Roberto Kelly	.05	479 Al Leiter	.05
376 Matt Lawton RC	.25	480 Pat Rapp	.05
377 Paul Molitor	.60	481 Gary Sheffield	.35
378 Dan Naulty RC	.05	482 Devon White	.05
379 Rich Robertson	.05	483 Bob Abreu	.05
380 Frank Rodriguez	.05	484 Sean Berry	.05
381 David Cone	.05	485 Craig Biggio	.05
382 Mariano Duncan	.05	486 Jim Dougherty	.05
383 Andy Fox RC	.05	487 Richard Hidalgo	.05
384 Joe Girardi	.05	488 Darryl Kile	.05
385 Dwight Gooden	.05	489 Derrick May	.05
386 Derek Jeter	1.50	490 Greg Swindell	.05
387 Pat Kelly	.05	491 Rick Wilkins	.05
388 Jimmy Key	.05	492 Mike Blowers	.05
389 Matt Luke RC	.05	493 Tom Candiotti	.05
390 Tino Martinez	.05	494 Roger Cedeno	.05
391 Jeff Nelson	.05	495 Delino DeShields	.05
392 Melido Perez	.05	496 Greg Gagne	.05
393 Tim Raines	.05	497 Karim Garcia	.10
394 Ruben Rivera	.05	498 Wilton Guerrero RC	.05
395 Kenny Rogers	.05	499 Chan Ho Park	.05
396 Tony Batista RC	.25	500 Israel Alcantara	.05
397 Allen Battle	.05	501 Shane Andrews	.05
398 Mike Bordick	.05	502 Yamil Benitez	.05
399 Steve Cox	.05	503 Cliff Floyd	.05
400 Jason Giambi	.40	504 Mark Grudzielanek	.05
401 Doug Johns	.05	505 Ryan McGuire	.05
402 Pedro Munoz	.05	506 Sherman Obando	.05
403 Phil Plantier	.05	507 Jose Paniagua	.05
404 Scott Spiezio	.05	508 Henry Rodriguez	.05
405 George Williams	.05	509 Kirk Rueter	.05
406 Ernie Young	.05	510 Juan Acevedo	.05
407 Darren Bragg	.05	511 John Franco	.05
408 Jay Buhner	.05	512 Bernard Gilkey	.05
409 Norm Charlton	.05	513 Lance Johnson	.05
410 Russ Davis	.05	514 Rey Ordonez	.05
411 Sterling Hitchcock	.05	515 Robert Person	.05
412 Edwin Hurtado	.05	516 Paul Wilson	.05
413 Raul Ibanez RC	.05	517 Toby Borland	.05
414 Mike Jackson	.05	518 David Doster RC	.05
415 Luis Sojo	.05	519 Lenny Dykstra	.05
416 Paul Sorrento	.05	520 Sid Fernandez	.05
417 Bob Wolcott	.05	521 Mike Grace RC	.05
418 Damon Buford	.05	522 Rich Hunter RC	.05
419 Kevin Gross	.05	523 Benito Santiago	.05
420 Darryl Hamilton	.05	524 Gene Schall	.05
421 Mike Henneman	.05	525 Curt Schilling	.15
422 Ken Hill	.05	526 Kevin Sefcik RC	.05
423 Dean Palmer	.05	527 Lee Tinsley	.05
424 Bobby Witt	.05	528 David West	.05
425 Tilson Brito	.05	529 Mark Whiten	.05
426 Giovanni Carrara	.05	530 Todd Zeile	.05
427 Domingo Cedeno	.05	531 Carlos Garcia	.05

532	Charlie Hayes	.05
533	Jason Kendall	.05
534	Jeff King	.05
535	Mike Kingery	.05
536	Nelson Liriano	.05
537	Dan Plesac	.05
538	Paul Wagner	.05
539	Luis Alicea	.05
540	David Bell	.05
541	Alan Benes	.05
542	Andy Benes	.05
543	Mike Busby RC	.05
544	Royce Clayton	.05
545	Dennis Eckersley	.50
546	Gary Gaetti	.05
547	Ron Gant	.05
548	Aaron Holbert	.05
549	Ray Lankford	.05
550	T.J. Mathews	.05
551	Willie McGee	.05
552	Miguel Mejia RC	.05
553	Todd Stottlemyre	.05
554	Sean Bergman	.05
555	Willie Blair	.05
556	Andujar Cedeno	.05
557	Steve Finley	.05
558	Rickey Henderson	.60
559	Wally Joyner	.05
560	Scott Livingstone	.05
561	Marc Newfield	.05
562	Bob Tewksbury	.05
563	Fernando Valenzuela	.05
564	Rod Beck	.05
565	Doug Creek	.05
566	Shawon Dunston	.05
567	Osvaldo Fernandez RC	.20
568	Stan Javier	.05
569	Marcus Jensen	.05
570	Steve Scarsone	.05
571	Robby Thompson	.05
572	Allen Watson	.05
573	Roberto Alomar	.10
574	Jeff Bagwell	.30
575	Albert Belle	.05
576	Wade Boggs	.40
577	Barry Bonds	.75
578	Juan Gonzalez	.15
579	Ken Griffey Jr.	.50
580	Tony Gwynn	.40
581	Randy Johnson	.30
582	Chipper Jones	.40
583	Barry Larkin	.05
584	Kenny Lofton	.05
585	Greg Maddux	.40
586	Raul Mondesi	.05
587	Mike Piazza	.50
588	Cal Ripken Jr.	.75
589	Tim Salmon	.05
590	Frank Thomas	.35
591	Mo Vaughn	.05
592	Matt Williams	.05
593	Marty Cordova	.05
594	Jim Edmonds	.05
595	Cliff Floyd	.05
596	Chipper Jones	.40
597	Ryan Klesko	.05
598	Raul Mondesi	.05
599	Manny Ramirez	.30
600	Ruben Rivera	.05

Gold Medallion

	NM/M
Complete Set (600):	75.00
Common Player:	.25

(Star cards valued at 2X
regular edition Fleer Ultra.)

Call to the Hall

	NM/M
Complete Set (10):	10.00
Common Player:	1.00
Gold Medallion Edition:	2X

FRANK THOMAS

1	Barry Bonds	3.00
2	Ken Griffey Jr.	2.00
3	Tony Gwynn	1.25
4	Rickey Henderson	1.00
5	Greg Maddux	1.25
6	Eddie Murray	1.00
7	Cal Ripken Jr.	3.00
8	Ryne Sandberg	1.25
9	Ozzie Smith	1.25
10	Frank Thomas	1.00

Diamond Producers

	NM/M
Complete Set (12):	15.00
Common Player:	.50
Gold Medallions:	2X
1	Albert Belle	.50
2	Barry Bonds	3.00
3	Ken Griffey Jr.	2.00
4	Tony Gwynn	1.50
5	Greg Maddux	1.50
6	Hideo Nomo	.75
7	Mike Piazza	2.00
8	Kirby Puckett	1.50
9	Cal Ripken Jr.	3.00
10	Frank Thomas	1.25
11	Mo Vaughn	.50
12	Matt Williams	.50

Fresh Foundations

	NM/M
Complete Set (10):	2.00
Common Player:	.15
Gold Medallions:	2X
1	Garret Anderson	.15
2	Marty Cordova	.15
3	Jim Edmonds	.15
4	Brian Hunter	.15
5	Chipper Jones	.50
6	Ryan Klesko	.15
7	Raul Mondesi	.15
8	Hideo Nomo	.25
9	Manny Ramirez	.40
10	Rondell White	.15

Golden Prospects, Series 1

	NM/M
Complete Set (10):	7.00

Common Player:	.25
Gold Medallions:	2X
1	Yamil Benitez	.25
2	Alberto Castillo	.25
3	Roger Cedeno	.25
4	Johnny Damon	1.00
5	Micah Franklin	.25
6	Jason Giambi	1.00
7	Jose Herrera	.25
8	Derek Jeter	5.00
9	Kevin Jordan	.25
10	Ruben Rivera	.25

Golden Prospects, Series 2

WILTON GUERRERO

	NM/M
Complete Set (15):	10.00
Common Player:	1.00
Gold Medallions:	2X
1	Bob Abreu	1.50
2	Israel Alcantara	1.00
3	Tony Batista	1.00
4	Mike Cameron	1.00
5	Steve Cox	1.00
6	Jermaine Dye	1.00
7	Wilton Guerrero	1.00
8	Richard Hidalgo	1.00
9	Raul Ibanez	1.00
10	Marty Janzen	1.00
11	Robin Jennings	1.00
12	Jason Maxwell	1.00
13	Scott McClain	1.00
14	Wonderful Monds	1.00
15	Chris Singleton	1.00

Hitting Machines

	NM/M
Complete Set (10):	35.00
Common Player:	2.00
Gold Medallion:	2X
1	Albert Belle	2.00
2	Barry Bonds	12.00
3	Juan Gonzalez	2.50
4	Ken Griffey Jr.	6.00
5	Edgar Martinez	2.00
6	Rafael Palmeiro	3.00
7	Mike Piazza	6.00
8	Tim Salmon	2.00
9	Frank Thomas	4.00
10	Matt Williams	2.00

Home Run Kings

	NM/M
Complete Set (12):	50.00
Common Player:	2.50
Gold Medallions:	2X
1	Albert Belle	2.50
2	Dante Bichette	2.50

3	Barry Bonds	12.50
4	Jose Canseco	5.00
5	Juan Gonzalez	3.00
6	Ken Griffey Jr.	9.00
7	Mark McGwire	10.00
8	Manny Ramirez	6.50
9	Tim Salmon	2.50
10	Frank Thomas	6.50
11	Mo Vaughn	2.50
12	Matt Williams	2.50

On-Base Leaders

	NM/M
Complete Set (10):	4.50
Common Player:	.25
Gold Medallion:	2X
1	Wade Boggs	.75
2	Barry Bonds	2.00
3	Tony Gwynn	.75
4	Rickey Henderson	.60
5	Chuck Knoblauch	.25
6	Edgar Martinez	.25
7	Mike Piazza	1.00
8	Tim Salmon	.25
9	Frank Thomas	.60
10	Jim Thome	.50

Power Plus

	NM/M
Complete Set (12):	10.00
Common Player:	.40
Gold Medallions:	2X
1	Jeff Bagwell	1.25
2	Barry Bonds	3.00
3	Ken Griffey Jr.	2.00
4	Raul Mondesi	.40
5	Rafael Palmeiro	1.00
6	Mike Piazza	2.00
7	Manny Ramirez	1.25
8	Tim Salmon	.40
9	Reggie Sanders	.40
10	Frank Thomas	1.25
11	Larry Walker	.40
12	Matt Williams	.40

Prime Leather

	NM/M
Complete Set (18):	17.50
Common Player:	.50

Gold Medallions:		2X
1	Ivan Rodriguez	1.50
2	Will Clark	.50
3	Roberto Alomar	.65
4	Cal Ripken Jr.	4.00
5	Wade Boggs	2.00
6	Ken Griffey Jr.	2.50
7	Kenny Lofton	.50
8	Kirby Puckett	2.00
9	Tim Salmon	.65
10	Mike Piazza	2.50
11	Mark Grace	.50
12	Craig Biggio	.50
13	Barry Larkin	.50
14	Matt Williams	.50
15	Barry Bonds	4.00
16	Tony Gwynn	2.00
17	Brian McRae	.50
18	Raul Mondesi	.50

R-E-S-P-E-C-T

		NM/M
Complete Set (10):		20.00
Common Player:		.50
Gold Medallion:		2X
1	Joe Carter	.50
2	Ken Griffey Jr.	3.00
3	Tony Gwynn	2.50
4	Greg Maddux	2.50
5	Eddie Murray	2.00
6	Kirby Puckett	2.50
7	Cal Ripken Jr.	5.00
8	Ryne Sandberg	2.50
9	Frank Thomas	2.00
10	Mo Vaughn	.50

Rawhide

		NM/M
Complete Set (10):		10.00
Common Player:		.45
Gold Medallion:		2X
1	Roberto Alomar	.65
2	Barry Bonds	3.00
3	Mark Grace	.45
4	Ken Griffey Jr.	1.50
5	Kenny Lofton	.45
6	Greg Maddux	1.00
7	Raul Mondesi	.45
8	Mike Piazza	1.50
9	Cal Ripken Jr.	3.00
10	Matt Williams	.45

Rising Stars

		NM/M
Complete Set (10):		4.00
Common Player:		.20
Gold Medallion:		2X
1	Garret Anderson	.20
2	Marty Cordova	.20
3	Jim Edmonds	.35
4	Cliff Floyd	.20
5	Brian Hunter	.20
6	Chipper Jones	2.00
7	Ryan Klesko	.20
8	Hideo Nomo	.65
9	Manny Ramirez	1.25
10	Rondell White	.20

RBI Kings

		NM/M
Complete Set (10):		4.00
Common Player:		.10
Gold Medallions:		2X
1	Derek Bell	.10
2	Albert Belle	.10
3	Dante Bichette	.10
4	Barry Bonds	2.00
5	Jim Edmonds	.15
6	Manny Ramirez	1.00
7	Reggie Sanders	.10
8	Sammy Sosa	1.50
9	Frank Thomas	1.00
10	Mo Vaughn	.10

Season Crowns

		NM/M
Complete Set (10):		12.50
Common Player:		.75
Gold Medallions:		2X
1	Barry Bonds	4.00
2	Tony Gwynn	2.00
3	Randy Johnson	1.25
4	Kenny Lofton	.75
5	Greg Maddux	2.00
6	Edgar Martinez	.75
7	Hideo Nomo	1.00
8	Cal Ripken Jr.	4.00
9	Frank Thomas	1.25
10	Tim Wakefield	.75

Thunderclap

		NM/M
Complete Set (20):		45.00
Common Player:		1.00
Gold Medallion:		2X
1	Albert Belle	1.00
2	Barry Bonds	7.50
3	Bobby Bonilla	1.00
4	Jose Canseco	1.50
5	Joe Carter	1.00
6	Will Clark	1.00
7	Andre Dawson	1.50
8	Cecil Fielder	1.00
9	Andres Galarraga	1.00
10	Juan Gonzalez	1.50
11	Ken Griffey Jr.	5.00
12	Fred McGriff	1.00
13	Mark McGwire	6.00
14	Eddie Murray	2.50
15	Rafael Palmeiro	2.00
16	Kirby Puckett	4.00
17	Cal Ripken Jr.	7.50
18	Ryne Sandberg	4.00
19	Frank Thomas	2.50
20	Matt Williams	1.00

Diamond Dust

	NM/M
Cal Ripken Jr. (Numbered)	40.00
Cal Ripken Jr. (Unnumbered)	20.00

1997 Ultra

		NM/M
Complete Set (553):		80.00
Common Player:		.05
Series 1 Wax Pack (10):		1.25
Series 1 Wax Box (24):		20.00
Series 2 Wax Pack (10):		5.00
Series 2 Wax Box (24):		90.00
1	Roberto Alomar	.25
2	Brady Anderson	.05
3	Rocky Coppinger	.05
4	Jeffrey Hammonds	.05
5	Chris Hoiles	.05
6	Eddie Murray	.75
7	Mike Mussina	.45
8	Jimmy Myers	.05
9	Randy Myers	.05
10	Arthur Rhodes	.05
11	Cal Ripken Jr.	2.50
12	Jose Canseco	.50
13	Roger Clemens	1.25
14	Tom Gordon	.05
15	Jose Malave	.05
16	Tim Naehring	.05
17	Troy O'Leary	.05
18	Bill Selby	.05
19	Heathcliff Slocumb	.05
20	Mike Stanley	.05
21	Mo Vaughn	.05
22	Garret Anderson	.05
23	George Arias	.05
24	Chili Davis	.05
25	Jim Edmonds	.05
26	Darin Erstad	.25
27	Chuck Finley	.05
28	Todd Greene	.05
29	Troy Percival	.05
30	Tim Salmon	.05
31	Jeff Schmidt	.05
32	Randy Velarde	.05
33	Shad Williams	.05
34	Wilson Alvarez	.05
35	Harold Baines	.05
36	James Baldwin	.05
37	Mike Cameron	.05
38	Ray Durham	.05
39	Ozzie Guillen	.05
40	Roberto Hernandez	.05
41	Darren Lewis	.05
42	Jose Munoz	.05
43	Tony Phillips	.05
44	Frank Thomas	.75
45	Sandy Alomar Jr.	.05
46	Albert Belle	.05
47	Mark Carreon	.05
48	Julio Franco	.05
49	Orel Hershiser	.05
50	Kenny Lofton	.05
51	Jack McDowell	.05
52	Jose Mesa	.05
53	Charles Nagy	.05
54	Manny Ramirez	.75
55	Julian Tavarez	.05
56	Omar Vizquel	.05
57	Raul Casanova	.05
58	Tony Clark	.05
59	Travis Fryman	.05
60	Bob Higginson	.05
61	Melvin Nieves	.05
62	Curtis Pride	.05
63	Justin Thompson	.05
64	Alan Trammell	.05
65	Kevin Appier	.05
66	Johnny Damon	.35
67	Keith Lockhart	.05
68	Jeff Montgomery	.05
69	Jose Offerman	.05
70	Bip Roberts	.05
71	Jose Rosado	.05
72	Chris Stynes	.05
73	Mike Sweeney	.05
74	Jeff Cirillo	.05
75	Jeff D'Amico	.05
76	John Jaha	.05
77	Scott Karl	.05
78	Mike Matheny	.05
79	Ben McDonald	.05
80	Matt Mieske	.05
81	Marc Newfield	.05
82	Dave Nilsson	.05
83	Jose Valentin	.05
84	Fernando Vina	.05
85	Rick Aguilera	.05
86	Marty Cordova	.05
87	Chuck Knoblauch	.05
88	Matt Lawton	.05
89	Pat Meares	.05
90	Paul Molitor	.75
91	Greg Myers	.05
92	Dan Naulty	.05
93	Kirby Puckett	1.00
94	Frank Rodriguez	.05
95	Wade Boggs	1.00
96	Cecil Fielder	.05
97	Joe Girardi	.05
98	Dwight Gooden	.05
99	Derek Jeter	2.50
100	Tino Martinez	.05
101	Ramiro Mendoza RC	.05
102	Andy Pettitte	.20
103	Mariano Rivera	.15
104	Ruben Rivera	.05
105	Kenny Rogers	.05
106	Darryl Strawberry	.05
107	Bernie Williams	.05
108	Tony Batista	.05
109	Geronimo Berroa	.05
110	Bobby Chouinard	.05
111	Brent Gates	.05
112	Jason Giambi	.60

#	Player	Value
113	Damon Mashore RC	.05
114	Mark McGwire	2.00
115	Scott Spiezio	.05
116	John Wasdin	.05
117	Steve Wojciechowski	.05
118	Ernie Young	.05
119	Norm Charlton	.05
120	Joey Cora	.05
121	Ken Griffey Jr.	1.50
122	Sterling Hitchcock	.05
123	Raul Ibanez	.05
124	Randy Johnson	.75
125	Edgar Martinez	.05
126	Alex Rodriguez	2.00
127	Matt Wagner	.05
128	Bob Wells	.05
129	Dan Wilson	.05
130	Will Clark	.05
131	Kevin Elster	.05
132	Juan Gonzalez	.40
133	Rusty Greer	.05
134	Darryl Hamilton	.05
135	Mike Henneman	.05
136	Ken Hill	.05
137	Mark McLemore	.05
138	Dean Palmer	.05
139	Roger Pavlik	.05
140	Ivan Rodriguez	.65
141	Joe Carter	.05
142	Carlos Delgado	.50
143	Alex Gonzalez	.05
144	Juan Guzman	.05
145	Pat Hentgen	.05
146	Marty Janzen	.05
147	Otis Nixon	.05
148	Charlie O'Brien	.05
149	John Olerud	.05
150	Robert Perez	.05
151	Jermaine Dye	.05
152	Tom Glavine	.30
153	Andruw Jones	.75
154	Chipper Jones	1.00
155	Ryan Klesko	.05
156	Javier Lopez	.05
157	Greg Maddux	1.00
158	Fred McGriff	.05
159	Wonderful Monds	.05
160	John Smoltz	.05
161	Terrell Wade	.05
162	Mark Wohlers	.05
163	Brant Brown	.05
164	Mark Grace	.05
165	Tyler Houston	.05
166	Robin Jennings	.05
167	Jason Maxwell	.05
168	Ryne Sandberg	1.00
169	Sammy Sosa	1.00
170	Amaury Telemaco	.05
171	Steve Trachsel	.05
172	Pedro Valdes RC	.05
173	Tim Belk	.05
174	Bret Boone	.05
175	Jeff Brantley	.05
176	Eric Davis	.05
177	Barry Larkin	.05
178	Chad Mottola	.05
179	Mark Portugal	.05
180	Reggie Sanders	.05
181	John Smiley	.05
182	Eddie Taubensee	.05
183	Dante Bichette	.05
184	Ellis Burks	.05
185	Andres Galarraga	.05
186	Curt Leskanic	.05
187	Quinton McCracken	.05
188	Jeff Reed	.05
189	Kevin Ritz	.05
190	Walt Weiss	.05
191	Jamey Wright	.05
192	Eric Young	.05
193	Kevin Brown	.05
194	Luis Castillo	.05
195	Jeff Conine	.05
196	Andre Dawson	.25
197	Charles Johnson	.05
198	Al Leiter	.05
199	Ralph Milliard	.05
200	Robb Nen	.05
201	Edgar Renteria	.05
202	Gary Sheffield	.40
203	Bob Abreu	.10
204	Jeff Bagwell	.75
205	Derek Bell	.05
206	Sean Berry	.05
207	Richard Hidalgo	.05
208	Todd Jones	.05
209	Darryl Kile	.05
210	Orlando Miller	.05
211	Shane Reynolds	.05
212	Billy Wagner	.05
213	Donne Wall	.05
214	Roger Cedeno	.05
215	Greg Gagne	.05
216	Karim Garcia	.10
217	Wilton Guerrero	.05
218	Todd Hollandsworth	.05
219	Ramon Martinez	.05
220	Raul Mondesi	.05
221	Hideo Nomo	.40
222	Chan Ho Park	.05
223	Mike Piazza	1.50
224	Ismael Valdes	.05
225	Moises Alou	.05
226	Derek Aucoin	.05
227	Yamil Benitez	.05
228	Jeff Fassero	.05
229	Darrin Fletcher	.05
230	Mark Grudzielanek	.05
231	Barry Manuel	.05
232	Pedro Martinez	.75
233	Henry Rodriguez	.05
234	Ugueth Urbina	.05
235	Rondell White	.05
236	Carlos Baerga	.05
237	John Franco	.05
238	Bernard Gilkey	.05
239	Todd Hundley	.05
240	Butch Huskey	.05
241	Jason Isringhausen	.05
242	Lance Johnson	.05
243	Bobby Jones	.05
244	Alex Ochoa	.05
245	Rey Ordonez	.05
246	Paul Wilson	.05
247	Ron Blazier	.05
248	David Doster	.05
249	Jim Eisenreich	.05
250	Mike Grace	.05
251	Mike Lieberthal	.05
252	Wendell Magee	.05
253	Mickey Morandini	.05
254	Ricky Otero	.05
255	Scott Rolen	.60
256	Curt Schilling	.20
257	Todd Zeile	.05
258	Jermaine Allensworth	.05
259	Trey Beamon	.05
260	Carlos Garcia	.05
261	Mark Johnson	.05
262	Jason Kendall	.05
263	Jeff King	.05
264	Al Martin	.05
265	Denny Neagle	.05
266	Matt Ruebel	.05
267	Marc Wilkins RC	.05
268	Alan Benes	.05
269	Dennis Eckersley	.65
270	Ron Gant	.05
271	Aaron Holbert	.05
272	Brian Jordan	.05
273	Ray Lankford	.05
274	John Mabry	.05
275	T.J. Mathews	.05
276	Ozzie Smith	1.00
277	Todd Stottlemyre	.05
278	Mark Sweeney	.05
279	Andy Ashby	.05
280	Steve Finley	.05
281	John Flaherty	.05
282	Chris Gomez	.05
283	Tony Gwynn	1.00
284	Joey Hamilton	.05
285	Rickey Henderson	.75
286	Trevor Hoffman	.05
287	Jason Thompson	.05
288	Fernando Valenzuela	.05
289	Greg Vaughn	.05
290	Barry Bonds	2.50
291	Jay Canizaro	.05
292	Jacob Cruz	.05
293	Shawon Dunston	.05
294	Shawn Estes	.05
295	Mark Gardner	.05
296	Marcus Jensen	.05
297	Bill Mueller RC	.35
298	Chris Singleton	.05
299	Allen Watson	.05
300	Matt Williams	.05
301	Rod Beck	.05
302	Jay Bell	.05
303	Shawon Dunston	.05
304	Reggie Jefferson	.05
305	Darren Oliver	.05
306	Benito Santiago	.05
307	Gerald Williams	.05
308	Damon Buford	.05
309	Jeromy Burnitz	.05
310	Sterling Hitchcock	.05
311	Dave Hollins	.05
312	Mel Rojas	.05
313	Robin Ventura	.05
314	David Wells	.05
315	Cal Eldred	.05
316	Gary Gaetti	.05
317	John Hudek	.05
318	Brian Johnson	.05
319	Denny Neagle	.05
320	Larry Walker	.05
321	Russ Davis	.05
322	Delino DeShields	.05
323	Charlie Hayes	.05
324	Jermaine Dye	.05
325	John Ericks	.05
326	Jeff Fassero	.05
327	Nomar Garciaparra	1.00
328	Willie Greene	.05
329	Greg McMichael	.05
330	Damion Easley	.05
331	Ricky Bones	.05
332	John Burkett	.05
333	Royce Clayton	.05
334	Greg Colbrunn	.05
335	Tony Eusebio	.05
336	Gregg Jefferies	.05
337	Wally Joyner	.05
338	Jim Leyritz	.05
339	Paul O'Neill	.05
340	Bruce Ruffin	.05
341	Michael Tucker	.05
342	Andy Benes	.05
343	Craig Biggio	.05
344	Rex Hudler	.05
345	Brad Radke	.05
346	Deion Sanders	.05
347	Moises Alou	.05
348	Brad Ausmus	.05
349	Armando Benitez	.05
350	Mark Gubicza	.05
351	Terry Steinbach	.05
352	Mark Whiten	.05
353	Ricky Bottalico	.05
354	Brian Giles RC	.75
355	Eric Karros	.05
356	Jimmy Key	.05
357	Carlos Perez	.05
358	Alex Fernandez	.05
359	J.T. Snow	.05
360	Bobby Bonilla	.05
361	Scott Brosius	.05
362	Greg Swindell	.05
363	Jose Vizcaino	.05
364	Matt Williams	.05
365	Darren Daulton	.05
366	Shane Andrews	.05
367	Jim Eisenreich	.05
368	Ariel Prieto	.05
369	Bob Tewksbury	.05
370	Mike Bordick	.05
371	Rheal Cormier	.05
372	Cliff Floyd	.05
373	David Justice	.05
374	John Wetteland	.05
375	Mike Blowers	.05
376	Jose Canseco	.50
377	Roger Clemens	1.25
378	Kevin Mitchell	.05
379	Todd Zeile	.05
380	Jim Thome	.60
381	Turk Wendell	.05
382	Rico Brogna	.05
383	Eric Davis	.05
384	Mike Lansing	.05
385	Devon White	.05
386	Marquis Grissom	.05
387	Todd Worrell	.05
388	Jeff Kent	.05
389	Mickey Tettleton	.05
390	Steve Avery	.05
391	David Cone	.05
392	Scott Cooper	.05
393	Lee Stevens	.05
394	Kevin Elster	.05
395	Tom Goodwin	.05
396	Shawn Green	.25
397	Pete Harnisch	.05
398	Eddie Murray	.75
399	Joe Randa	.05
400	Scott Sanders	.05
401	John Valentin	.05
402	Todd Jones	.05
403	Terry Adams	.05
404	Brian Hunter	.05
405	Pat Listach	.05
406	Kenny Lofton	.05
407	Hal Morris	.05
408	Ed Sprague	.05
409	Rich Becker	.05
410	Edgardo Alfonzo	.05
411	Albert Belle	.05
412	Jeff King	.05
413	Kirt Manwaring	.05
414	Jason Schmidt	.05
415	Allen Watson	.05
416	Lee Tinsley	.05
417	Brett Butler	.05
418	Carlos Garcia	.05
419	Mark Lemke	.05
420	Jaime Navarro	.05
421	David Segui	.05
422	Ruben Sierra	.05
423	B.J. Surhoff	.05
424	Julian Tavarez	.05
425	Billy Taylor	.05
426	Ken Caminiti	.05
427	Chuck Carr	.05
428	Benji Gil	.05
429	Terry Mulholland	.05
430	Mike Stanton	.05
431	Wil Cordero	.05
432	Chili Davis	.05
433	Mariano Duncan	.05
434	Orlando Merced	.05
435	Kent Mercker	.05
436	John Olerud	.05
437	Quilvio Veras	.05
438	Mike Fetters	.05
439	Glenallen Hill	.05
440	Bill Swift	.05
441	Tim Wakefield	.05
442	Pedro Astacio	.05
443	Vinny Castilla	.05
444	Doug Drabek	.05
445	Alan Embree	.05
446	Lee Smith	.05
447	Darryl Hamilton	.05
448	Brian McRae	.05
449	Mike Timlin	.05
450	Bob Wickman	.05
451	Jason Dickson	.05
452	Chad Curtis	.05
453	Mark Leiter	.05
454	Damon Berryhill	.05
455	Kevin Orie	.05
456	Dave Burba	.05
457	Chris Holt	.05
458	Ricky Ledee	.10
459	Mike Devereaux	.05
460	Pokey Reese	.05
461	Tim Raines	.05
462	Ryan Jones	.05
463	Shane Mack	.05
464	Darren Dreifort	.05
465	Mark Parent	.05
466	Mark Portugal	.05
467	Dante Powell	.05
468	Craig Grebeck	.05
469	Ron Villone	.05
470	Dmitri Young	.05
471	Shannon Stewart	.05
472	Rick Helling	.05
473	Bill Haselman	.05
474	Albie Lopez	.05
475	Glendon Rusch	.05
476	Derrick May	.05
477	Chad Ogea	.05
478	Kirk Reuter	.05
479	Chris Hammond	.05
480	Russ Johnson	.05
481	James Mouton	.05
482	Mike Macfarlane	.05
483	Scott Ruffcorn	.05
484	Jeff Frye	.05
485	Richie Sexson	.05
486	Emil Brown RC	.05
487	Desi Wilson	.05
488	Brent Gates	.05
489	Tony Graffanino	.05
490	Dan Miceli	.05
491	Orlando Cabrera RC	.65
492	Tony Womack RC	.20
493	Jerome Walton	.05
494	Mark Thompson	.05
495	Jose Guillen	.05
496	Willie Blair	.05
497	T.J. Staton RC	.05
498	Scott Kamieniecki	.05
499	Vince Coleman	.05
500	Jeff Abbott	.05
501	Chris Widger	.05
502	Kevin Tapani	.05
503	Carlos Castillo RC	.05
504	Luis Gonzalez	.05
505	Tim Belcher	.05
506	Armando Reynoso	.05
507	Jamie Moyer	.05
508	Randall Simon RC	.05
509	Vladimir Guerrero	.75
510	Wady Almonte RC	.05
511	Dustin Hermanson	.05
512	Deivi Cruz RC	.25
513	Luis Alicea	.05
514	Felix Heredia RC	.15
515	Don Slaught	.05
516	Shigetosi Hasegawa	.05
517	Matt Walbeck	.05
518	David Arias RC (Last name actually Ortiz.)	40.00
519	Brady Raggio RC	.05
520	Rudy Pemberton	.05
521	Wayne Kirby	.05
522	Calvin Maduro	.05
523	Mark Lewis	.05
524	Mike Jackson	.05
525	Sid Fernandez	.05
526	Mike Bielecki	.05
527	Bubba Trammell RC	.05
528	Brent Brede RC	.05
529	Matt Morris	.05
530	Joe Borowski	.05
531	Orlando Miller	.05
532	Jim Bullinger	.05
533	Robert Person	.05
534	Doug Glanville	.05
535	Terry Pendleton	.05
536	Jorge Posada	.05
537	Marc Sagmoen RC	.05
538	Fernando Tatis RC	.20
539	Aaron Sele	.05

540	Brian Banks	.05
541	Derek Lee	.50
542	John Wasdin	.05
543	Justin Towle RC	.05
544	Pat Cline	.05
545	Dave Magadan	.05
546	Jeff Blauser	.05
547	Phil Nevin	.05
548	Todd Walker	.05
549	Elieser Marrero	.05
550	Bartolo Colon	.05
551	Jose Cruz Jr. RC	.50
552	Todd Dunwoody	.05
553	Hideki Irabu RC	.25

Gold Medallion Edition

	NM/M
Complete Set (553):	100.00
Common Player:	.25
Stars/Rookies:	3X

(See 1997 Ultra for checklist and base card values.)

Platinum Medallion Edition

	NM/M
Common Player:	2.00
Stars/Rookies:	25X

(See 1997 Ultra for checklist and base card values.)

Baseball Rules!

		NM/M
Complete Set (10):		45.00
Common Player:		.50
1	Barry Bonds	10.00
2	Ken Griffey Jr.	6.00
3	Derek Jeter	10.00
4	Chipper Jones	5.00
5	Greg Maddux	5.00
6	Mark McGwire	7.50
7	Troy Percival	.50
8	Mike Piazza	6.00
9	Cal Ripken Jr.	10.00
10	Frank Thomas	4.00

Diamond Producers

		NM/M
Complete Set (12):		110.00
Common Player:		2.50
1	Jeff Bagwell	7.00
2	Barry Bonds	20.00
3	Ken Griffey Jr.	12.50
4	Chipper Jones	10.00
5	Kenny Lofton	2.50
6	Greg Maddux	10.00
7	Mark McGwire	15.00
8	Mike Piazza	12.50
9	Cal Ripken Jr.	20.00
10	Alex Rodriguez	15.00
11	Frank Thomas	7.50
12	Matt Williams	2.50

Double Trouble

		NM/M
Complete Set (20):		10.00
Common Player:		.15
1	Roberto Alomar, Cal Ripken Jr.	1.50
2	Mo Vaughn, Jose Canseco	.40
3	Jim Edmonds, Tim Salmon	.15
4	Harold Baines, Frank Thomas	.50
5	Albert Belle, Kenny Lofton	.15
6	Chuck Knoblauch, Marty Cordova	.15
7	Andy Pettitte, Derek Jeter	1.50
8	Jason Giambi, Mark McGwire	1.00
9	Ken Griffey Jr., Alex Rodriguez	1.00
10	Juan Gonzalez, Will Clark	.30
11	Greg Maddux, Chipper Jones	.60
12	Mark Grace, Sammy Sosa	.60
13	Dante Bichette, Andres Galarraga	.15
14	Jeff Bagwell, Derek Bell	.50
15	Hideo Nomo, Mike Piazza	.75
16	Henry Rodriguez, Moises Alou	.15
17	Rey Ordonez, Alex Ochoa	.15
18	Ray Lankford, Ron Gant	.15
19	Tony Gwynn, Rickey Henderson	.60
20	Barry Bonds, Matt Williams	1.50

Fame Game

	NM/M
Complete Set (18):	20.00

Common Player:		.35
1	Ken Griffey Jr.	1.75
2	Frank Thomas	1.00
3	Alex Rodriguez	2.00
4	Cal Ripken Jr.	3.00
5	Mike Piazza	1.75
6	Greg Maddux	1.25
7	Derek Jeter	3.00
8	Jeff Bagwell	1.00
9	Juan Gonzalez	.50
10	Albert Belle	.35
11	Tony Gwynn	1.25
12	Mark McGwire	2.00
13	Andy Pettitte	.45
14	Kenny Lofton	.35
15	Roberto Alomar	.40
16	Ryne Sandberg	1.25
17	Barry Bonds	3.00
18	Eddie Murray	1.00

Fielder's Choice

		NM/M
Complete Set (18):		80.00
Common Player:		1.00
1	Roberto Alomar	1.50
2	Jeff Bagwell	6.00
3	Wade Boggs	7.50
4	Barry Bonds	15.00
5	Mark Grace	1.00
6	Ken Griffey Jr.	10.00
7	Marquis Grissom	1.00
8	Charles Johnson	1.00
9	Chuck Knoblauch	1.00
10	Barry Larkin	1.00
11	Kenny Lofton	1.00
12	Greg Maddux	7.50
13	Raul Mondesi	1.00
14	Rey Ordonez	1.00
15	Cal Ripken Jr.	15.00
16	Alex Rodriguez	12.50
17	Ivan Rodriguez	5.00
18	Matt Williams	1.00

Golden Prospects

		NM/M
Complete Set (10):		3.00
Common Player:		.25
1	Andruw Jones	1.50
2	Vladimir Guerrero	1.50
3	Todd Walker	.25
4	Karim Garcia	.25
5	Kevin Orie	.25
6	Brian Giles	.25
7	Jason Dickson	.25
8	Jose Guillen	.25
9	Ruben Rivera	.25
10	Derek Lee	1.00

Hitting Machines

		NM/M
Complete Set (18):		60.00
Common Player:		1.00
1	Andruw Jones	3.00
2	Ken Griffey Jr.	5.00
3	Frank Thomas	3.00
4	Alex Rodriguez	6.50
5	Cal Ripken Jr.	9.00
6	Mike Piazza	5.00
7	Derek Jeter	9.00
8	Albert Belle	1.00
9	Tony Gwynn	4.00
10	Jeff Bagwell	3.00
11	Mark McGwire	6.50
12	Kenny Lofton	1.00
13	Manny Ramirez	3.00
14	Roberto Alomar	1.25
15	Ryne Sandberg	4.00
16	Eddie Murray	3.00
17	Sammy Sosa	4.00
18	Ken Caminiti	1.00

HR Kings

		NM/M
Complete Set (12):		30.00
Common Player:		1.00
1	Albert Belle	1.00
2	Barry Bonds	7.50
3	Juan Gonzalez	1.50
4	Ken Griffey Jr.	4.50
5	Todd Hundley	1.00
6	Ryan Klesko	1.00
7	Mark McGwire	6.00
8	Mike Piazza	4.50
9	Sammy Sosa	3.50
10	Frank Thomas	2.50
11	Mo Vaughn	1.00
12	Matt Williams	1.00

Leather Shop

		NM/M
Complete Set (12):		9.00
Common Player:		.25
1	Ken Griffey Jr.	1.25
2	Alex Rodriguez	1.50
3	Cal Ripken Jr.	2.00
4	Derek Jeter	2.00
5	Juan Gonzalez	.45
6	Tony Gwynn	1.00
7	Jeff Bagwell	.75

8	Roberto Alomar	.40
9	Ryne Sandberg	1.00
10	Ken Caminiti	.25
11	Kenny Lofton	.25
12	John Smoltz	.25

Power Plus Series 2

		NM/M
Complete Set (12):		6.50
Common Player:		.25
1	Ken Griffey Jr.	.75
2	Frank Thomas	.50
3	Alex Rodriguez	1.00
4	Cal Ripken Jr.	1.50
5	Mike Piazza	.75
6	Chipper Jones	.65
7	Albert Belle	.25
8	Juan Gonzalez	.35
9	Jeff Bagwell	.50
10	Mark McGwire	1.00
11	Mo Vaughn	.25
12	Barry Bonds	1.50

Power Plus Series 1

		NM/M
Complete Set (12):		15.00
Common Player:		.50
1	Jeff Bagwell	.75
2	Barry Bonds	3.00
3	Juan Gonzalez	.60
4	Ken Griffey Jr.	1.50
5	Chipper Jones	1.00
6	Mark McGwire	2.00
7	Mike Piazza	1.50
8	Cal Ripken Jr.	3.00
9	Alex Rodriguez	2.00
10	Sammy Sosa	1.00
11	Frank Thomas	.75
12	Matt Williams	.50

Rookie Reflections

		NM/M
Complete Set (10):		3.50
Common Player:		.25
1	James Baldwin	.25
2	Jermaine Dye	.25
3	Darin Erstad	.40
4	Todd Hollandsworth	.25
5	Derek Jeter	3.00
6	Jason Kendall	.25
7	Alex Ochoa	.25
8	Rey Ordonez	.25
9	Edgar Renteria	.25
10	Scott Rolen	.50

RBI Kings

		NM/M
Complete Set (10):		12.50
Common Player:		.75
1	Jeff Bagwell	1.50
2	Albert Belle	.75
3	Dante Bichette	.75
4	Barry Bonds	4.00
5	Jay Buhner	.75
6	Juan Gonzalez	1.00
7	Ken Griffey Jr.	2.50
8	Sammy Sosa	2.00
9	Frank Thomas	1.50
10	Mo Vaughn	.75

Season Crowns

		NM/M
Complete Set (12):		10.00
Common Player:		.50
1	Albert Belle	.50
2	Dante Bichette	.50
3	Barry Bonds	3.00
4	Kenny Lofton	.50
5	Edgar Martinez	.50
6	Mark McGwire	2.00
7	Andy Pettitte	.50
8	Mike Piazza	1.50
9	Alex Rodriguez	2.00
10	John Smoltz	.50
11	Sammy Sosa	1.25
12	Frank Thomas	1.00

Starring Role

		NM/M
Complete Set (12):		175.00
Common Player:		7.50
1	Andruw Jones.	12.00
2	Ken Griffey Jr.	20.00
3	Frank Thomas.	12.00
4	Alex Rodriguez.	25.00
5	Cal Ripken Jr.	30.00
6	Mike Piazza.	20.00
7	Greg Maddux.	15.00
8	Chipper Jones.	15.00
9	Derek Jeter.	30.00
10	Juan Gonzalez.	9.00
11	Albert Belle.	7.50
12	Tony Gwynn.	15.00

Thunderclap

		NM/M
Complete Set (10):		20.00
Common Player:		.75
1	Barry Bonds	5.00
2	Mo Vaughn	.75
3	Mark McGwire	4.00
4	Jeff Bagwell	1.50
5	Juan Gonzalez	1.00
6	Alex Rodriguez	4.00
7	Chipper Jones	2.50
8	Ken Griffey Jr.	3.00
9	Mike Piazza	3.00
10	Frank Thomas	2.00

Top 30

		NM/M
Complete Set (30):		12.00
Common Player:		.20
Gold Medallions:		6X
1	Andruw Jones	.75
2	Ken Griffey Jr.	1.25
3	Frank Thomas	.75
4	Alex Rodriguez	1.50
5	Cal Ripken Jr.	2.00
6	Mike Piazza	1.25
7	Greg Maddux	1.00
8	Chipper Jones	1.00
9	Derek Jeter	2.00
10	Juan Gonzalez	.40
11	Albert Belle	.20
12	Tony Gwynn	1.00
13	Jeff Bagwell	.75
14	Mark McGwire	1.50
15	Andy Pettitte	.30
16	Mo Vaughn	.20
17	Kenny Lofton	.20
18	Manny Ramirez	.75
19	Roberto Alomar	.40
20	Ryne Sandberg	1.00
21	Hideo Nomo	.40
22	Barry Bonds	2.00
23	Eddie Murray	.75
24	Ken Caminiti	.20
25	John Smoltz	.20
26	Pat Hentgen	.20
27	Todd Hollandsworth	.20
28	Matt Williams	.20
29	Bernie Williams	.20
30	Brady Anderson	.20

1998 Ultra

		NM/M
Complete Set (501):		75.00
Common Player:		.05
Alex Rodriguez Autograph		
(750):		50.00
Pack (10):		1.25
Wax Box (24):		20.00
1	Ken Griffey Jr.	1.25
2	Matt Morris	.05
3	Roger Clemens	1.00
4	Matt Williams	.05
5	Roberto Hernandez	.05
6	Rondell White	.05
7	Tim Salmon	.05
8	Brad Radke	.05
9	Brett Butler	.05
10	Carl Everett	.05
11	Chili Davis	.05
12	Chuck Finley	.05
13	Darryl Kile	.05
14	Deivi Cruz	.05
15	Gary Gaetti	.05
16	Matt Stairs	.05
17	Pat Meares	.05
18	Will Cunnane	.05
19	Steve Woodard **RC**	.15
20	Andy Ashby	.05
21	Bobby Higginson	.05
22	Brian Jordan	.05
23	Craig Biggio	.05
24	Jim Edmonds	.05
25	Ryan McGuire	.05
26	Scott Hatteberg	.05
27	Willie Greene	.05
28	Albert Belle	.05
29	Ellis Burks	.05
30	Hideo Nomo	.40
31	Jeff Bagwell	.75
32	Kevin Brown	.05
33	Nomar Garciaparra	1.00
34	Pedro Martinez	.75
35	Raul Mondesi	.05
36	Ricky Bottalico	.05
37	Shawn Estes	.05
38	Shawon Dunston	.05
39	Terry Steinbach	.05

No.	Player	Price
40	Tom Glavine	.25
41	Todd Dunwoody	.05
42	Deion Sanders	.05
43	Gary Sheffield	.45
44	Mike Lansing	.05
45	Mike Lieberthal	.05
46	Paul Sorrento	.05
47	Paul O'Neill	.05
48	Tom Goodwin	.05
49	Andruw Jones	.75
50	Barry Bonds	2.00
51	Bernie Williams	.05
52	Jeremi Gonzalez	.05
53	Mike Piazza	1.25
54	Russ Davis	.05
55	Vinny Castilla	.05
56	Rod Beck	.05
57	Andres Galarraga	.05
58	Ben McDonald	.05
59	Billy Wagner	.05
60	Charles Johnson	.05
61	Fred McGriff	.05
62	Dean Palmer	.05
63	Frank Thomas	.75
64	Ismael Valdes	.05
65	Mark Bellhorn	.05
66	Jeff King	.05
67	John Wetteland	.05
68	Mark Grace	.05
69	Mark Kotsay	.05
70	Scott Rolen	.60
71	Todd Hundley	.05
72	Todd Worrell	.05
73	Wilson Alvarez	.05
74	Bobby Jones	.05
75	Jose Canseco	.50
76	Kevin Appier	.05
77	Neifi Perez	.05
78	Paul Molitor	.75
79	Quilvio Veras	.05
80	Randy Johnson	.75
81	Glendon Rusch	.05
82	Curt Schilling	.15
83	Alex Rodriguez	1.50
84	Rey Ordonez	.05
85	Jeff Juden	.05
86	Mike Cameron	.05
87	Ryan Klesko	.05
88	Trevor Hoffman	.05
89	Chuck Knoblauch	.05
90	Larry Walker	.05
91	Mark McLemore	.05
92	B.J. Surhoff	.05
93	Darren Daulton	.05
94	Ray Durham	.05
95	Sammy Sosa	1.00
96	Eric Young	.05
97	Gerald Williams	.05
98	Javy Lopez	.05
99	John Smiley	.05
100	Juan Gonzalez	.40
101	Shawn Green	.30
102	Charles Nagy	.05
103	David Justice	.05
104	Joey Hamilton	.05
105	Pat Hentgen	.05
106	Raul Casanova	.05
107	Tony Phillips	.05
108	Tony Gwynn	1.00
109	Will Clark	.05
110	Jason Giambi	.50
111	Jay Bell	.05
112	Johnny Damon	.30
113	Alan Benes	.05
114	Jeff Suppan	.05
115	Kevin Polcovich RC	.05
116	Shigetosi Hasegawa	.05
117	Steve Finley	.05
118	Tony Clark	.05
119	David Cone	.05
120	Jose Guillen	.05
121	Kevin Millwood RC	1.00
122	Greg Maddux	1.00
123	Dave Nilsson	.05
124	Hideki Irabu	.05
125	Jason Kendall	.05
126	Jim Thome	.60
127	Delino DeShields	.05
128	Edgar Renteria	.05
129	Edgardo Alfonzo	.05
130	J.T. Snow	.05
131	Jeff Abbott	.05
132	Jeffrey Hammonds	.05
133	Rich Loiselle	.05
134	Vladimir Guerrero	.75
135	Jay Buhner	.05
136	Jeff Cirillo	.05
137	Jeromy Burnitz	.05
138	Mickey Morandini	.05
139	Tino Martinez	.05
140	Jeff Shaw	.05
141	Rafael Palmeiro	.65
142	Bobby Bonilla	.05
143	Cal Ripken Jr.	2.00
144	Chad Fox RC	.05
145	Dante Bichette	.05
146	Dennis Eckersley	.65
147	Mariano Rivera	.15
148	Mo Vaughn	.05
149	Reggie Sanders	.05
150	Derek Jeter	2.00
151	Rusty Greer	.05
152	Brady Anderson	.05
153	Brett Tomko	.05
154	Jaime Navarro	.05
155	Kevin Orie	.05
156	Roberto Alomar	.20
157	Edgar Martinez	.05
158	John Olerud	.05
159	John Smoltz	.05
160	Ryne Sandberg	1.00
161	Billy Taylor	.05
162	Chris Holt	.05
163	Damion Easley	.05
164	Darin Erstad	.25
165	Joe Carter	.05
166	Kelvim Escobar	.05
167	Ken Caminiti	.05
168	Pokey Reese	.05
169	Ray Lankford	.05
170	Livan Hernandez	.05
171	Steve Kline	.05
172	Tom Gordon	.05
173	Travis Fryman	.05
174	Al Martin	.05
175	Andy Pettitte	.25
176	Jeff Kent	.05
177	Jimmy Key	.05
178	Mark Grudzielanek	.05
179	Tony Saunders	.05
180	Barry Larkin	.05
181	Bubba Trammell	.05
182	Carlos Delgado	.50
183	Carlos Baerga	.05
184	Derek Bell	.05
185	Henry Rodriguez	.05
186	Jason Dickson	.05
187	Ron Gant	.05
188	Tony Womack	.05
189	Justin Thompson	.05
190	Fernando Tatis	.05
191	Mark Wohlers	.05
192	Takashi Kashiwada	.05
193	Garret Anderson	.05
194	Jose Cruz, Jr.	.05
195	Ricardo Rincon	.05
196	Tim Naehring	.05
197	Moises Alou	.05
198	Eric Karros	.05
199	John Jaha	.05
200	Marty Cordova	.05
201	Travis Lee	.10
202	Mark Davis	.05
203	Vladimir Nunez	.05
204	Stanton Cameron	.05
205	Mike Stoner RC	.05
206	Rolando Arrojo RC	.40
207	Rick White	.05
208	Luis Polonia	.05
209	Greg Blosser	.05
210	Cesar Devarez	.05
211	Jeff Bagwell	1.00
212	Barry Bonds	3.00
213	Roger Clemens	1.75
214	Nomar Garciaparra	1.50
215	Ken Griffey Jr.	2.00
216	Tony Gwynn	1.50
217	Randy Johnson	1.00
218	Mark McGwire	3.00
219	Scott Rolen	.75
220	Frank Thomas	1.25
221	Matt Perisho	.25
222	Wes Helms	.25
223	David Dellucci RC	.25
224	Todd Helton	1.00
225	Brian Rose	.25
226	Aaron Boone	.25
227	Keith Foulke	.25
228	Homer Bush	.25
229	Shannon Stewart	.25
230	Richard Hidalgo	.25
231	Russ Johnson	.25
232	Henry Blanco RC	.25
233	Paul Konerko	.35
234	Antone Williamson	.25
235	Shane Bowers RC	.25
236	Jose Vidro	.25
237	Derek Wallace	.25
238	Ricky Ledee	.25
239	Ben Grieve	.65
240	Lou Collier	.25
241	Derrek Lee	.65
242	Ruben Rivera	.25
243	Jorge Velandia	.25
244	Andrew Vessel	.25
245	Chris Carpenter	.25
246	Ken Griffey Jr. Checklist	.65
247	Andruw Jones Checklist	.50
248	Alex Rodriguez Checklist	.75
249	Frank Thomas Checklist	.60
250	Cal Ripken Jr. Checklist	1.00
251	Carlos Perez	.05
252	Larry Sutton	.05
253	Brad Rigby	.05
254	Wally Joyner	.05
255	Todd Stottlemyre	.05
256	Nerio Rodriguez	.05
257	Jeff Frye	.05
258	Pedro Astacio	.05
259	Cal Eldred	.05
260	Chili Davis	.05
261	Freddy Garcia	.05
262	Bobby Witt	.05
263	Michael Coleman	.05
264	Mike Caruso	.05
265	Mike Lansing	.05
266	Dennis Reyes	.05
267	F.P. Santangelo	.05
268	Darryl Hamilton	.05
269	Mike Fetters	.05
270	Charlie Hayes	.05
271	Royce Clayton	.05
272	Doug Drabek	.05
273	James Baldwin	.05
274	Brian Hunter	.05
275	Chan Ho Park	.05
276	John Franco	.05
277	David Wells	.05
278	Eli Marrero	.05
279	Kerry Wood	.40
280	Donnie Sadler	.05
281	Scott Winchester RC	.05
282	Hal Morris	.05
283	Brad Fullmer	.05
284	Bernard Gilkey	.05
285	Ramiro Mendoza	.05
286	Kevin Brown	.05
287	David Segui	.05
288	Willie McGee	.05
289	Darren Oliver	.05
290	Antonio Alfonseca	.05
291	Eric Davis	.05
292	Mickey Morandini	.05
293	Frank Catalanotto RC	.20
294	Derrek Lee	.50
295	Todd Zeile	.05
296	Chuck Knoblauch	.05
297	Wilson Delgado	.05
298	Raul Ibanez	.05
299	Orel Hershiser	.05
300	Ozzie Guillen	.05
301	Aaron Sele	.05
302	Joe Carter	.05
303	Darryl Kile	.05
304	Shane Reynolds	.05
305	Todd Dunn	.05
306	Bob Abreu	.10
307	Doug Glanville	.05
308	Jose Canseco	.50
309	Lance Johnson	.05
310	Harold Baines	.05
311	Todd Pratt	.05
312	Greg Colbrunn	.05
313	Masato Yoshii RC	.25
314	Felix Heredia	.05
315	Dennis Martinez	.05
316	Geronimo Berroa	.05
317	Darren Lewis	.05
318	Billy Ripken	.05
319	Enrique Wilson	.05
320	Alex Ochoa	.05
321	Doug Glanville	.05
322	Mike Stanley	.05
323	Gerald Williams	.05
324	Pedro Martinez	.75
325	Jaret Wright	.05
326	Terry Pendleton	.05
327	LaTroy Hawkins	.05
328	Emil Brown	.05
329	Walt Weiss	.05
330	Omar Vizquel	.05
331	Carl Everett	.05
332	Fernando Vina	.05
333	Mike Blowers	.05
334	Dwight Gooden	.05
335	Mark Lewis	.05
336	Jim Leyritz	.05
337	Kenny Lofton	.05
338	John Halama RC	.05
339	Jose Valentin	.05
340	Desi Relaford	.05
341	Dante Powell	.05
342	Ed Sprague	.05
343	Reggie Jefferson	.05
344	Mike Hampton	.05
345	Marquis Grissom	.05
346	Heathcliff Slocumb	.05
347	Francisco Cordova	.05
348	Ken Cloude	.05
349	Benito Santiago	.05
350	Denny Neagle	.05
351	Sean Casey	.15
352	Robb Nen	.05
353	Orlando Merced	.05
354	Adrian Brown	.05
355	Gregg Jefferies	.05
356	Otis Nixon	.05
357	Michael Tucker	.05
358	Eric Milton	.05
359	Travis Fryman	.05
360	Gary DiSarcina	.05
361	Mario Valdez	.05
362	Craig Counsell	.05
363	Jose Offerman	.05
364	Tony Fernandez	.05
365	Jason McDonald	.05
366	Sterling Hitchcock	.05
367	Donovan Osborne	.05
368	Troy Percival	.05
369	Henry Rodriguez	.05
370	Dmitri Young	.05
371	Jay Powell	.05
372	Jeff Conine	.05
373	Orlando Cabrera	.10
374	Butch Huskey	.05
375	Mike Lowell RC	.50
376	Kevin Young	.05
377	Jamie Moyer	.05
378	Jeff D'Amico	.05
379	Scott Erickson	.05
380	Magglio Ordonez RC	2.50
381	Melvin Nieves	.05
382	Ramon Martinez	.05
383	A.J. Hinch	.05
384	Jeff Brantley	.05
385	Kevin Elster	.05
386	Allen Watson	.05
387	Moises Alou	.05
388	Jeff Blauser	.05
389	Pete Harnisch	.05
390	Shane Andrews	.05
391	Rico Brogna	.05
392	Stan Javier	.05
393	David Howard	.05
394	Darryl Strawberry	.05
395	Kent Mercker	.05
396	Juan Encarnacion	.05
397	Sandy Alomar	.05
398	Al Leiter	.05
399	Tony Graffanino	.05
400	Terry Adams	.05
401	Bruce Aven	.05
402	Derrick Gibson	.05
403	Jose Cabrera	.05
404	Rich Becker	.05
405	David Ortiz	.50
406	Brian McRae	.05
407	Bobby Estalella	.05
408	Bill Mueller	.05
409	Dennis Eckersley	.65
410	Sandy Martinez	.05
411	Jose Vizcaino	.05
412	Jermaine Allensworth	.05
413	Miguel Tejada	.20
414	Turner Ward	.05
415	Glenallen Hill	.05
416	Lee Stevens	.05
417	Cecil Fielder	.05
418	Ruben Sierra	.05
419	Jon Nunnally	.05
420	Rod Myers	.05
421	Dustin Hermanson	.05
422	James Mouton	.05
423	Dan Wilson	.05
424	Roberto Kelly	.05
425	Antonio Osuna	.05
426	Jacob Cruz	.05
427	Brent Mayne	.05
428	Matt Karchner	.05
429	Damian Jackson	.05
430	Roger Cedeno	.05
431	Rickey Henderson	.75
432	Joe Randa	.05
433	Greg Vaughn	.05
434	Andres Galarraga	.05
435	Rod Beck	.05
436	Curtis Goodwin	.05
437	Brad Ausmus	.05
438	Bob Hamelin	.05
439	Todd Walker	.05
440	Scott Brosius	.05
441	Lenny Dykstra	.05
442	Abraham Nunez	.05
443	Brian Johnson	.05
444	Randy Myers	.05
445	Bret Boone	.15
446	Oscar Henriquez	.05
447	Mike Sweeney	.05
448	Kenny Rogers	.05
449	Mark Langston	.05
450	Luis Gonzalez	.05
451	John Burkett	.05
452	Bip Roberts	.05
453	Travis Lee	.15
454	Felix Rodriguez	.05
455	Andy Benes	.05
456	Willie Blair	.05
457	Brian Anderson	.05
458	Jay Bell	.05

459	Matt Williams	.05
460	Devon White	.05
461	Karim Garcia	.10
462	Jorge Fabregas	.05
463	Wilson Alvarez	.05
464	Roberto Hernandez	.05
465	Tony Saunders	.05
466	Rolando Arrojo RC	.35
467	Wade Boggs	1.00
468	Fred McGriff	.05
469	Paul Sorrento	.05
470	Kevin Stocker	.05
471	Bubba Trammell	.05
472	Quinton McCracken	.05
473	Ken Griffey Jr. Checklist	.65
474	Cal Ripken Jr. Checklist	1.00
475	Frank Thomas Checklist	.60
476	Ken Griffey Jr.	1.75
477	Cal Ripken Jr.	3.00
478	Frank Thomas	1.25
479	Alex Rodriguez	2.00
480	Nomar Garciaparra	1.50
481	Derek Jeter	3.00
482	Andruw Jones	1.00
483	Chipper Jones	1.50
484	Greg Maddux	1.50
485	Mike Piazza	1.75
486	Juan Gonzalez	.60
487	Jose Cruz	.50
488	Jaret Wright	.50
489	Hideo Nomo	.60
490	Scott Rolen	.65
491	Tony Gwynn	1.50
492	Roger Clemens	1.60
493	Darin Erstad	.50
494	Mark McGwire	2.00
495	Jeff Bagwell	1.00
496	Mo Vaughn	.50
497	Albert Belle	.50
498	Kenny Lofton	.50
499	Ben Grieve	.50
500	Barry Bonds	2.50
501	Mike Piazza (Mets)	1.50

Gold Medallion

	NM/M
Common Player:	.25
Stars/RC's:	2X
Checklists:	2X
Season Crowns:	1X
Prospects:	1X
Pizzazz:	1X

(See 1998 Ultra for checklist and base card values.)

Platinum Medallion

	NM/M
Common Player:	5.00

Stars/RC's:		25X
Checklists:		25X
Season Crowns:		8X
Prospects:		8X
Pizzazz:		8X

(See 1998 Ultra for checklist and base card values.)

Masterpiece

	NM/M
Common Player:	50.00

(Individual players cannot be priced due to scarcity and fluctuating demand.)

Artistic Talents

	NM/M
Complete Set (18):	12.00
Common Player:	.40
Inserted 1:8	
1	Ken Griffey Jr.	1.00
2	Andruw Jones	.60
3	Alex Rodriguez	1.25
4	Frank Thomas	.60
5	Cal Ripken Jr.	1.50
6	Derek Jeter	1.50
7	Chipper Jones	.75
8	Greg Maddux	.75
9	Mike Piazza	1.00
10	Albert Belle	.40
11	Darin Erstad	.50
12	Juan Gonzalez	.50
13	Jeff Bagwell	.60
14	Tony Gwynn	.75
15	Mark McGwire	1.25
16	Scott Rolen	.50
17	Barry Bonds	1.50
18	Kenny Lofton	.40

Back to the Future

	NM/M
Complete Set (15):	4.00
Common Player:	.10
Inserted 1:6	
1	Andruw Jones	.50
2	Alex Rodriguez	1.00
3	Derek Jeter	1.50
4	Darin Erstad	.25
5	Mike Cameron	.10

6	Scott Rolen	.35
7	Nomar Garciaparra	.75
8	Hideki Irabu	.10
9	Jose Cruz, Jr.	.10
10	Vladimir Guerrero	.50
11	Mark Kotsay	.10
12	Tony Womack	.10
13	Jason Dickson	.10
14	Jose Guillen	.10
15	Tony Clark	.10

Big Shots

	NM/M
Complete Set (15):	4.00
Common Player:	.10
Inserted 1:4	
1	Ken Griffey Jr.	.75
2	Frank Thomas	.35
3	Chipper Jones	.50
4	Albert Belle	.10
5	Juan Gonzalez	.25
6	Jeff Bagwell	.35
7	Mark McGwire	1.00
8	Barry Bonds	1.50
9	Manny Ramirez	.35
10	Mo Vaughn	.10
11	Matt Williams	.10
12	Jim Thome	.30
13	Tino Martinez	.10
14	Mike Piazza	.75
15	Tony Clark	.10

Diamond Producers

	NM/M
Complete Set (15):	180.00
Common Player:	7.50
Inserted 1:288	
1	Ken Griffey Jr.	30.00
2	Andruw Jones	12.50
3	Alex Rodriguez	40.00
4	Frank Thomas	12.50
5	Cal Ripken Jr.	50.00
6	Derek Jeter	50.00
7	Chipper Jones	20.00
8	Greg Maddux	20.00
9	Mike Piazza	30.00
10	Juan Gonzalez	9.00
11	Jeff Bagwell	12.50
12	Tony Gwynn	20.00
13	Mark McGwire	40.00
14	Barry Bonds	50.00
15	Jose Cruz, Jr.	7.50

Diamond Immortals

	NM/M
Complete Set (15):	330.00
Common Player:	7.50
Inserted 1:288	
1	Ken Griffey Jr.	30.00
2	Frank Thomas	12.50

3	Alex Rodriguez	40.00
4	Cal Ripken Jr.	50.00
5	Mike Piazza	30.00
6	Mark McGwire	40.00
7	Greg Maddux	20.00
8	Andruw Jones	12.50
9	Chipper Jones	20.00
10	Derek Jeter	50.00
11	Tony Gwynn	20.00
12	Juan Gonzalez	9.00
13	Jose Cruz	7.50
14	Roger Clemens	25.00
15	Barry Bonds	50.00

Double Trouble

	NM/M
Complete Set (20):	12.00
Common Player:	.15
Inserted 1:4	
1	Ken Griffey Jr., Alex Rodriguez	1.25
2	Vladimir Guerrero, Pedro Martinez	.60
3	Andruw Jones, Kenny Lofton	.60
4	Chipper Jones, Greg Maddux	.65
5	Derek Jeter, Tino Martinez	1.50
6	Frank Thomas, Albert Belle	.60
7	Cal Ripken Jr., Roberto Alomar	1.50
8	Mike Piazza, Hideo Nomo	1.00
9	Darin Erstad, Jason Dickson	.15
10	Juan Gonzalez, Ivan Rodriguez	.25
11	Jeff Bagwell, Darryl Kile	.60
12	Tony Gwynn, Steve Finley	.65
13	Mark McGwire, Ray Lankford	1.00
14	Barry Bonds, Jeff Kent	1.50
15	Andy Pettitte, Bernie Williams	.25
16	Mo Vaughn, Nomar Garciaparra	.65
17	Matt Williams, Jim Thome	.15
18	Hideki Irabu, Mariano Rivera	.25
19	Roger Clemens, Jose Cruz, Jr.	.75
20	Manny Ramirez, David Justice	.60

Fall Classics

	NM/M
Complete Set (15):	35.00
Common Player:	1.00
Inserted 1:18	
1	Ken Griffey Jr.	3.00
2	Andruw Jones	1.50
3	Alex Rodriguez	4.00
4	Frank Thomas	1.50
5	Cal Ripken Jr.	5.00
6	Derek Jeter	5.00
7	Chipper Jones	2.00
8	Greg Maddux	2.00

9	Mike Piazza	4.00
10	Albert Belle	1.00
11	Juan Gonzalez	1.00
12	Jeff Bagwell	1.50
13	Tony Gwynn	2.00
14	Mark McGwire	3.00
15	Barry Bonds	5.00

Kid Gloves

		NM/M
Complete Set (12):		9.00
Common Player:		.25
Inserted 1:8		
1	Andruw Jones	.75
2	Alex Rodriguez	2.00
3	Derek Jeter	3.00
4	Chipper Jones	1.00
5	Darin Erstad	.35
6	Todd Walker	.25
7	Scott Rolen	.65
8	Nomar Garciaparra	1.00
9	Jose Cruz, Jr.	.25
10	Charles Johnson	.25
11	Rey Ordonez	.25
12	Vladimir Guerrero	.75

Millennium Men

		NM/M
Complete Set (15):		30.00
Common Player:		.75
Inserted 1:35		
1	Jose Cruz	.75
2	Ken Griffey Jr.	3.50
3	Cal Ripken Jr.	6.00
4	Derek Jeter	6.00
5	Andruw Jones	2.00
6	Alex Rodriguez	4.50
7	Chipper Jones	2.50
8	Scott Rolen	1.00

9	Nomar Garciaparra	2.50
10	Frank Thomas	2.00
11	Mike Piazza	3.50
12	Greg Maddux	2.50
13	Juan Gonzalez	1.00
14	Ben Grieve	.75
15	Jaret Wright	.75

Power Plus

		NM/M
Complete Set (10):		16.00
Common Player:		1.00
Inserted 1:36		
1	Ken Griffey Jr.	4.00
2	Andruw Jones	2.00
3	Alex Rodriguez	3.00
4	Frank Thomas	2.00
5	Mike Piazza	3.00
6	Albert Belle	1.00
7	Juan Gonzalez	1.25
8	Jeff Bagwell	2.00
9	Barry Bonds	5.00
10	Jose Cruz, Jr.	1.00

Prime Leather

		NM/M
Complete Set (18):		135.00
Common Player:		2.00
Inserted 1:144		
1	Ken Griffey Jr.	12.50
2	Andruw Jones	7.50
3	Alex Rodriguez	15.00
4	Frank Thomas	7.50
5	Cal Ripken Jr.	20.00
6	Derek Jeter	20.00
7	Chipper Jones	10.00
8	Greg Maddux	10.00
9	Mike Piazza	12.50
10	Albert Belle	2.00
11	Darin Erstad	3.00
12	Juan Gonzalez	3.00
13	Jeff Bagwell	7.50
14	Tony Gwynn	10.00
15	Roberto Alomar	2.50
16	Barry Bonds	20.00
17	Kenny Lofton	2.00
18	Jose Cruz, Jr.	2.00

Notables

		NM/M
Complete Set (20):		13.50
Common Player:		.20
Inserted 1:4		
1	Frank Thomas	.50
2	Ken Griffey Jr.	1.25
3	Edgar Renteria	.20
4	Albert Belle	.20
5	Juan Gonzalez	.30
6	Jeff Bagwell	.50
7	Mark McGwire	1.50

8	Barry Bonds	2.25
9	Scott Rolen	.40
10	Mo Vaughn	.20
11	Andruw Jones	.50
12	Chipper Jones	.75
13	Tino Martinez	.20
14	Mike Piazza	1.25
15	Tony Clark	.20
16	Jose Cruz	.20
17	Nomar Garciaparra	.75
18	Cal Ripken Jr.	2.25
19	Alex Rodriguez	1.50
20	Derek Jeter	2.25

Rocket to Stardom

		NM/M
Complete Set (15):		15.00
Common Player:		.75
Inserted 1:20		
1	Ben Grieve	.75
2	Magglio Ordonez	4.00
3	Travis Lee	1.00
4	Carl Pavano	.75
5	Brian Rose	.75
6	Brad Fullmer	.75
7	Michael Coleman	.75
8	Juan Encarnacion	.75
9	Karim Garcia	1.00
10	Todd Helton	7.50
11	Richard Hildalgo	.75
12	Paul Konerko	1.50
13	Rod Myers	.75
14	Jaret Wright	.75
15	Miguel Tejada	1.50

Win Now

		NM/M
Complete Set (20):		100.00
Common Player:		2.50

Inserted 1:72

1	Alex Rodriguez	10.00
2	Andruw Jones	4.00
3	Cal Ripken Jr.	12.50
4	Chipper Jones	5.00
5	Darin Erstad	3.00
6	Derek Jeter	12.50
7	Frank Thomas	4.00
8	Greg Maddux	5.00
9	Hideo Nomo	3.00
10	Jeff Bagwell	4.00
11	Jose Cruz	2.50
12	Juan Gonzalez	3.00
13	Ken Griffey Jr.	7.50
14	Mark McGwire	10.00
15	Mike Piazza	7.50
16	Mo Vaughn	2.50
17	Nomar Garciaparra	5.00
18	Roger Clemens	6.00
19	Scott Rolen	3.00
20	Tony Gwynn	5.00

Ticket Studs

		NM/M
Complete Set (15):		150.00
Common Player:		2.50
Inserted 1:144		
1	Travis Lee	3.00
2	Tony Gwynn	12.00
3	Scott Rolen	6.00
4	Nomar Garciaparra	12.00
5	Mike Piazza	15.00
6	Mark McGwire	17.50
7	Ken Griffey Jr.	15.00
8	Juan Gonzalez	5.00
9	Jose Cruz	2.50
10	Frank Thomas	9.00
11	Derek Jeter	20.00
12	Chipper Jones	12.00
13	Cal Ripken Jr.	20.00
14	Andruw Jones	9.00
15	Alex Rodriguez	17.50

Top 30

		NM/M
Complete Set (30):		20.00
Common Player:		.15
Inserted 1:1 R		
1	Barry Bonds	2.00
2	Ivan Rodriguez	.65
3	Kenny Lofton	.15
4	Albert Belle	.15
5	Mo Vaughn	.15
6	Jeff Bagwell	.75
7	Mark McGwire	1.50
8	Darin Erstad	.35
9	Roger Clemens	1.00
10	Tony Gwynn	1.00
11	Scott Rolen	.45
12	Hideo Nomo	.35
13	Juan Gonzalez	.35
14	Mike Piazza	1.25
15	Greg Maddux	1.00
16	Chipper Jones	1.00
17	Andruw Jones	.75
18	Derek Jeter	2.00
19	Nomar Garciaparra	1.00
20	Alex Rodriguez	1.50
21	Frank Thomas	.75
22	Cal Ripken Jr.	2.00
23	Ken Griffey Jr.	1.25
24	Jose Cruz Jr.	.15
25	Jaret Wright	.15
26	Travis Lee	.30
27	Wade Boggs	1.00
28	Chuck Knoblauch	.15
29	Joe Carter	.15
30	Ben Grieve	.15

1999 Ultra

	NM/M
Complete Set (250):	35.00

Common Player:	.05
Common Season Crown:	.25
Inserted 1:8	
Common Prospect:	.25
Inserted 1:4	
Pack (10):	1.50
Wax Box (24):	25.00

1	Greg Maddux	1.00
2	Greg Vaughn	.05
3	John Wetteland	.05
4	Tino Martinez	.05
5	Todd Walker	.05
6	Troy O'Leary	.05
7	Barry Larkin	.05
8	Mike Lansing	.05
9	Delino DeShields	.05
10	Brett Tomko	.05
11	Carlos Perez	.05
12	Mark Langston	.05
13	Jamie Moyer	.05
14	Jose Guillen	.05
15	Bartolo Colon	.05
16	Brady Anderson	.05
17	Walt Weiss	.05
18	Shane Reynolds	.05
19	David Segui	.05
20	Vladimir Guerrero	.75
21	Freddy Garcia	.05
22	Carl Everett	.05
23	Jose Cruz Jr.	.05
24	David Ortiz	.40
25	Andruw Jones	.75
26	Darren Lewis	.05
27	Ray Lankford	.05
28	Wally Joyner	.05
29	Charles Johnson	.05
30	Derek Jeter	2.00
31	Sean Casey	.10
32	Bobby Bonilla	.05
33	Todd Zelle	.05
34	Todd Helton	.65
35	David Wells	.05
36	Darin Erstad	.30
37	Ivan Rodriguez	.65
38	Antonio Osuna	.05
39	Mickey Morandini	.05
40	Rusty Greer	.05
41	Rod Beck	.05
42	Larry Sutton	.05
43	Edgar Renteria	.05
44	Otis Nixon	.05
45	Eli Milton	.05
46	Reggie Jefferson	.05
47	Trevor Hoffman	.05
48	Andres Galarraga	.05
49	Scott Brosius	.05
50	Vinny Castilla	.05
51	Bret Boone	.05
52	Masato Yoshii	.05
53	Matt Williams	.05
54	Robin Ventura	.05
55	Jay Powell	.05
56	Dean Palmer	.05
57	Eric Milton	.05
58	Willie McGee	.05
59	Tony Gwynn	1.00
60	Tom Gordon	.05
61	Dante Bichette	.05
62	Jaret Wright	.05
63	Devon White	.05
64	Frank Thomas	.75
65	Mike Piazza	1.25
66	Jose Offerman	.05
67	Pat Meares	.05
68	Brian Meadows	.05
69	Nomar Garciaparra	1.00
70	Mark McGwire	1.50
71	Tony Graffanino	.05
72	Ken Griffey Jr.	1.25
73	Ken Caminiti	.05
74	Todd Jones	.05
75	A.J. Hinch	.05
76	Marquis Grissom	.05
77	Jay Buhner	.05
78	Albert Belle	.05
79	Brian Anderson	.05
80	Quinton McCracken	.05
81	Omar Vizquel	.05
82	Todd Stottlemyre	.05
83	Cal Ripken Jr.	2.00
84	Magglio Ordonez	.30
85	John Olerud	.05
86	Hal Morris	.05
87	Derrek Lee	.40
88	Doug Glanville	.05
89	Marty Cordova	.05
90	Kevin Brown	.05
91	Kevin Young	.05
92	Rico Brogna	.05
93	Wilson Alvarez	.05
94	Bob Wickman	.05
95	Jim Thome	.50
96	Mike Mussina	.35
97	Al Leiter	.05
98	Travis Lee	.10
99	Jeff King	.05
100	Kerry Wood	.40
101	Cliff Floyd	.05
102	Jose Valentin	.05
103	Manny Ramirez	.75
104	Butch Huskey	.05
105	Scott Erickson	.05
106	Ray Durham	.05
107	Johnny Damon	.30
108	Craig Counsell	.05
109	Rolando Arrojo	.05
110	Bob Abreu	.05
111	Tony Womack	.05
112	Mike Stanley	.05
113	Kenny Lofton	.05
114	Eric Davis	.05
115	Jeff Conine	.05
116	Carlos Baerga	.05
117	Rondell White	.05
118	Billy Wagner	.05
119	Ed Sprague	.05
120	Jason Schmidt	.05
121	Edgar Martinez	.05
122	Travis Fryman	.05
123	Armando Benitez	.05
124	Matt Stairs	.05
125	Roberto Hernandez	.05
126	Jay Bell	.05
127	Justin Thompson	.05
128	John Jaha	.05
129	Mike Caruso	.05
130	Miguel Tejada	.20
131	Geoff Jenkins	.05
132	Wade Boggs	1.00
133	Andy Benes	.05
134	Aaron Sele	.05
135	Bret Saberhagen	.05
136	Mariano Rivera	.15
137	Neifi Perez	.05
138	Paul Konerko	.15
139	Barry Bonds	2.00
140	Garret Anderson	.05
141	Bernie Williams	.05
142	Gary Sheffield	.40
143	Rafael Palmeiro	.65
144	Orel Hershiser	.05
145	Craig Biggio	.05
146	Dmitri Young	.05
147	Damion Easley	.05
148	Henry Rodriguez	.05
149	Brad Radke	.05
150	Pedro Martinez	.75
151	Mike Lieberthal	.05
152	Jim Leyritz	.05
153	Chuck Knoblauch	.05
154	Darryl Kile	.05
155	Brian Jordan	.05
156	Chipper Jones	1.00
157	Pete Harnisch	.05
158	Moises Alou	.05
159	Ismael Valdes	.05
160	Stan Javier	.05
161	Mark Grace	.05
162	Jason Giambi	.40
163	Chuck Finley	.05
164	Juan Encarnacion	.05
165	Chan Ho Park	.05
166	Randy Johnson	.75
167	J.T. Snow	.05
168	Tim Salmon	.05
169	Brian Hunter	.05
170	Rickey Henderson	.75
171	Cal Eldred	.05
172	Curt Schilling	.05
173	Alex Rodriguez	1.50
174	Dustin Hermanson	.05
175	Mike Hampton	.05
176	Shawn Green	.30
177	Roberto Alomar	.20
178	Sandy Alomar Jr.	.05
179	Larry Walker	.05
180	Mo Vaughn	.05
181	Raul Mondesi	.05
182	Hideki Irabu	.05
183	Jim Edmonds	.05
184	Shawn Estes	.05
185	Tony Clark	.05
186	Dan Wilson	.05
187	Michael Tucker	.05
188	Jeff Shaw	.05
189	Mark Grudzielanek	.05
190	Roger Clemens	1.00
191	Juan Gonzalez	.40
192	Sammy Sosa	1.00
193	Troy Percival	.05
194	Robb Nen	.05
195	Bill Mueller	.05
196	Ben Grieve	.05
197	Luis Gonzalez	.05
198	Will Clark	.05
199	Jeff Cirillo	.05
200	Scott Rolen	.50
201	Reggie Sanders	.05
202	Fred McGriff	.05
203	Denny Neagle	.05
204	Brad Fullmer	.05
205	Royce Clayton	.05
206	Jose Canseco	.50
207	Jeff Bagwell	.75
208	Hideo Nomo	.40
209	Karim Garcia	.15
210	Kenny Rogers	.05
211	Kerry Wood Checklist	.25
212	Alex Rodriguez Checklist	.75
213	Cal Ripken Jr. Checklist	1.00
214	Frank Thomas Checklist	.50
215	Ken Griffey Jr. Checklist	.65
216	Alex Rodriguez (Season Crowns)	1.00
217	Greg Maddux (Season Crowns)	.50
218	Juan Gonzalez (Season Crowns)	.20
219	Ken Griffey Jr. (Season Crowns)	.75
220	Kerry Wood (Season Crowns)	.25
221	Mark McGwire (Season Crowns)	1.00
222	Mike Piazza (Season Crowns)	.75
223	Rickey Henderson (Season Crowns)	.40
224	Sammy Sosa (Season Crowns)	.50
225	Travis Lee (Season Crowns)	.25
226	Gabe Alvarez	.25
227	Matt Anderson	.25
228	Adrian Beltre	.35
229	Orlando Cabrera	.35
230	Orlando Hernandez	.25
231	Aramis Ramirez	.25
232	Troy Glaus	1.00
233	Gabe Kapler	.25
234	Jeremy Giambi	.25
235	Derrick Gibson	.25
236	Carlton Loewer	.25
237	Mike Frank	.25
238	Carlos Guillen	.25
239	Alex Gonzalez	.25
240	Enrique Wilson	.25
241	J.D. Drew	.75
242	Bruce Chen	.25
243	Ryan Minor	.25
244	Preston Wilson	.35
245	Josh Booty	.25
246	Luis Ordaz	.25
247	George Lombard	.25
248	Matt Clement	.25
249	Eric Chavez	.35
250	Corey Koskie	.30

Gold Medallion

	NM/M
Common Player (1-215):	.25
Stars/RC's:	2X
Season Crowns (216-225):	4X
Prospects (226-250):	3X
(See 1999 Ultra for checklist and base card values.)	

Platinum Medallion

	NM/M
Common Player (1-215):	5.00
Stars/RC's:	25X
Season Crowns (216-225):	20X
Prospects (226-250):	6X
(See 1999 Ultra for checklist and base card values.)	

Masterpiece

	NM/M
Common Player:	50.00
(Individual player cards cannot be valueddue to scarcity and fluctuating demand.)	

Book On

	NM/M
Complete Set (20):	13.50
Common Player:	.25
Inserted 1:6	
1	Kerry Wood	.35
2	Ken Griffey Jr.	1.00
3	Frank Thomas	.65
4	Albert Belle	.25
5	Juan Gonzalez	.35
6	Jeff Bagwell	.65
7	Mark McGwire	1.25
8	Barry Bonds	1.50
9	Andruw Jones	.65
10	Mo Vaughn	.25
11	Scott Rolen	.40
12	Travis Lee	.25
13	Tony Gwynn	.75
14	Greg Maddux	.75
15	Mike Piazza	1.00
16	Chipper Jones	.75
17	Nomar Garciaparra	.75
18	Cal Ripken Jr.	1.50
19	Derek Jeter	1.50
20	Alex Rodriguez	1.25

Damage Inc.

	NM/M
Complete Set (15):	50.00
Common Player:	1.00
Inserted 1:72	
1	Alex Rodriguez	5.00
2	Greg Maddux	3.50
3	Cal Ripken Jr.	7.50
4	Chipper Jones	3.50
5	Derek Jeter	7.50

6 Frank Thomas 2.50
7 Juan Gonzalez 1.50
8 Ken Griffey Jr. 4.00
9 Kerry Wood 1.25
10 Mark McGwire 5.00
11 Mike Piazza 4.00
12 Nomar Garciaparra 3.50
13 Scott Rolen 1.50
14 Tony Gwynn 3.50
15 Travis Lee 1.00

Diamond Producers

NM/M
Complete Set (10): 140.00
Common Player: 6.00
Inserted 1:288
1 Ken Griffey Jr. 17.50
2 Frank Thomas 12.00
3 Alex Rodriguez 20.00
4 Cal Ripken Jr. 25.00
5 Mike Piazza 17.50
6 Mark McGwire 20.00
7 Greg Maddux 15.00
8 Kerry Wood 6.00
9 Chipper Jones 15.00
10 Derek Jeter 25.00

RBI Kings

NM/M
Complete Set (30): 12.00
Common Player: .15
Inserted 1:1 R
1 Rafael Palmeiro .40
2 Mo Vaughn .15
3 Ivan Rodriguez .40
4 Barry Bonds 1.25
5 Albert Belle .15
6 Jeff Bagwell .45
7 Mark McGwire 1.00
8 Darin Erstad .25
9 Manny Ramirez .45
10 Chipper Jones .60
11 Jim Thome .40
12 Scott Rolen .35
13 Tony Gwynn .60
14 Juan Gonzalez .25
15 Mike Piazza .75
16 Sammy Sosa .60
17 Andruw Jones .45

18 Derek Jeter 1.25
19 Nomar Garciaparra .60
20 Alex Rodriguez 1.00
21 Frank Thomas .45
22 Cal Ripken Jr. 1.25
23 Ken Griffey Jr. .75
24 Travis Lee .25
25 Paul O'Neill .15
26 Greg Vaughn .15
27 Andres Galarraga .15
28 Tino Martinez .15
29 Jose Canseco .30
30 Ben Grieve .15

Thunderclap

NM/M
Complete Set (15): 35.00
Common Player: .75
Inserted 1:36
1 Alex Rodriguez 4.00
2 Andruw Jones 1.50
3 Cal Ripken Jr. 6.00
4 Chipper Jones 2.50
5 Darin Erstad .75
6 Derek Jeter 6.00
7 Frank Thomas 1.50
8 Jeff Bagwell 1.50
9 Juan Gonzalez .75
10 Ken Griffey Jr. 3.00
11 Mark McGwire 4.00
12 Mike Piazza 3.00
13 Travis Lee .75
14 Nomar Garciaparra 2.50
15 Scott Rolen 1.00

World Premiere

NM/M
Complete Set (15): 8.00
Common Player: .50
Inserted 1:18
1 Gabe Alvarez .50
2 Kerry Wood 1.50
3 Orlando Hernandez .60
4 Mike Caruso .50
5 Matt Anderson .50
6 Randall Simon .50
7 Adrian Beltre .65
8 Scott Elarton .50
9 Karim Garcia .60
10 Mike Frank .50
11 Richard Hidalgo .50
12 Paul Konerko .60
13 Travis Lee .65
14 J.D. Drew 1.50
15 Miguel Tejada .75

2000 Ultra

NM/M
Complete Set (300): 35.00
Common Player: .10

Common Player (251-300): .50
Inserted 1:4
Pack (10): 2.00
Wax Box (24): 35.00
1 Alex Rodriguez 1.50
2 Shawn Green .25
3 Magglio Ordonez .25
4 Tony Gwynn .75
5 Joe McEwing .10
6 Jose Rosado .10
7 Sammy Sosa 1.00
8 Gary Sheffield .25
9 Mickey Morandini .10
10 Mo Vaughn .15
11 Todd Hollandsworth .10
12 Tom Gordon .10
13 Charles Johnson .10
14 Derek Bell .10
15 Kevin Young .10
16 Jay Buhner .15
17 J.T. Snow .10
18 Jay Bell .10
19 John Rocker .10
20 Ivan Rodriguez .40
21 Pokey Reese .10
22 Paul O'Neill .20
23 Ronnie Belliard .10
24 Ryan Rupe .10
25 Travis Fryman .20
26 Trot Nixon .10
27 Wally Joyner .10
28 Andy Pettitte .25
29 Dan Wilson .10
30 Orlando Hernandez .20
31 Dmitri Young .10
32 Edgar Renteria .20
33 Eric Karros .20
34 Fernando Seguignol .10
35 Jason Kendall .20
36 Jeff Shaw .10
37 Matt Lawton .10
38 Robin Ventura .20
39 Scott Williamson .10
40 Ben Grieve .10
41 Billy Wagner .10
42 Javy Lopez .20
43 Joe Randa .10
44 Neifi Perez .10
45 David Justice .20
46 Ray Durham .10
47 Dustin Hermanson .10
48 Andres Galarraga .20
49 Brad Fullmer .10
50 Nomar Garciaparra 1.50
51 David Cone .15
52 David Nilsson .10
53 David Wells .10
54 Miguel Tejada .25
55 Ismael Valdes .10
56 Jose Lima .10
57 Juan Encarnacion .10
58 Fred McGriff .20
59 Kenny Rogers .10
60 Vladimir Guerrero .75
61 Benito Santiago .10
62 Chris Singleton .10
63 Carlos Lee .10
64 Sean Casey .20
65 Tom Goodwin .10
66 Todd Hundley .10
67 Ellis Burks .10
68 Tim Hudson .25
69 Matt Stairs .10
70 Chipper Jones 1.00
71 Craig Biggio .20
72 Brian Rose .10
73 Carlos Delgado .40
74 Eddie Taubensee .10
75 John Smoltz .20
76 Ken Caminiti .15
77 Rafael Palmeiro .40
78 Sidney Ponson .10
79 Todd Helton .50

80 Juan Gonzalez .50
81 Bruce Aven .10
82 Desi Relaford .10
83 Johnny Damon .20
84 Albert Belle .15
85 Mark McGwire 1.50
86 Rico Brogna .10
87 Tom Glavine .25
88 Harold Baines .10
89 Chad Allen .10
90 Barry Bonds 2.00
91 Mark Grace .25
92 Paul Byrd .10
93 Roberto Alomar .40
94 Roberto Hernandez .10
95 Steve Finley .10
96 Bret Boone .20
97 Charles Nagy .10
98 Eric Chavez .20
99 Jamie Moyer .10
100 Ken Griffey Jr. 1.00
101 J.D. Drew .20
102 Todd Stottlemyre .10
103 Tony Fernandez .10
104 Jeromy Burnitz .10
105 Jeremy Giambi .10
106 Livan Hernandez .10
107 Marlon Anderson .10
108 Troy Glaus .50
109 Troy O'Leary .10
110 Scott Rolen .50
111 Bernard Gilkey .10
112 Brady Anderson .15
113 Chuck Knoblauch .10
114 Jeff Weaver .10
115 B.J. Surhoff .10
116 Alex Gonzalez .10
117 Vinny Castilla .10
118 Tim Salmon .20
119 Brian Jordan .10
120 Corey Koskie .10
121 Dean Palmer .10
122 Gabe Kapler .15
123 Jim Edmonds .25
124 John Jaha .10
125 Mark Grudzielanek .10
126 Mike Bordick .10
127 Mike Lieberthal .10
128 Pete Harnisch .10
129 Russ Ortiz .10
130 Kevin Brown .20
131 Troy Percival .10
132 Alex Gonzalez .10
133 Bartolo Colon .10
134 John Valentin .10
135 Jose Hernandez .10
136 Marquis Grissom .10
137 Wade Boggs .25
138 Dante Bichette .10
139 Bobby Higginson .10
140 Frank Thomas .50
141 Geoff Jenkins .20
142 Jason Giambi .50
143 Jeff Cirillo .10
144 Sandy Alomar Jr. .10
145 Luis Gonzalez .20
146 Preston Wilson .10
147 Carlos Beltran .20
148 Greg Vaughn .10
149 Carlos Febles .10
150 Jose Canseco .40
151 Kris Benson .10
152 Chuck Finley .10
153 Michael Barrett .10
154 Rey Ordonez .10
155 Adrian Beltre .20
156 Andruw Jones .50
157 Barry Larkin .20
158 Brian Giles .20
159 Carl Everett .10
160 Manny Ramirez .50
161 Darryl Kile .10
162 Edgar Martinez .15
163 Jeff Kent .20
164 Matt Williams .20
165 Mike Piazza 1.00
166 Pedro J. Martinez .75
167 Ray Lankford .10
168 Roger Cedeno .10
169 Ron Coomer .10
170 Cal Ripken Jr. 2.00
171 Jose Offerman .10
172 Kenny Lofton .20
173 Kent Bottenfield .10
174 Kevin Millwood .20
175 Omar Daal .10
176 Orlando Cabrera .10
177 Pat Hentgen .10
178 Tino Martinez .20
179 Tony Clark .10
180 Roger Clemens 1.25
181 Brad Radke .10
182 Darin Erstad .20
183 Jose Jimenez .10

184	Jim Thome	.50
185	John Wetteland	.10
186	Justin Thompson	.10
187	John Hamala	.10
188	Lee Stevens	.10
189	Miguel Cairo	.10
190	Mike Mussina	.40
191	Raul Mondesi	.15
192	Armando Rios	.10
193	Trevor Hoffman	.10
194	Tony Batista	.10
195	Will Clark	.40
196	Brad Ausmus	.10
197	Chili Davis	.10
198	Cliff Floyd	.10
199	Curt Schilling	.25
200	Derek Jeter	2.00
201	Henry Rodriguez	.10
202	Jose Cruz Jr.	.10
203	Omar Vizquel	.20
204	Randy Johnson	.75
205	Reggie Sanders	.10
206	Al Leiter	.10
207	Damion Easley	.10
208	David Bell	.10
209	Fernando Tatis	.10
210	Kerry Wood	.25
211	Kevin Appier	.10
212	Mariano Rivera	.20
213	Mike Caruso	.10
214	Moises Alou	.20
215	Randy Winn	.10
216	Roy Halladay	.20
217	Shannon Stewart	.10
218	Todd Walker	.10
219	Jim Parque	.10
220	Travis Lee	.10
221	Andy Ashby	.10
222	Ed Sprague	.10
223	Larry Walker	.20
224	Rick Helling	.10
225	Rusty Greer	.10
226	Todd Zeile	.10
227	Freddy Garcia	.15
228	Hideo Nomo	.40
229	Marty Cordova	.10
230	Greg Maddux	1.00
231	Rondell White	.20
232	Paul Konerko	.15
233	Warren Morris	.10
234	Bernie Williams	.40
235	Bobby Abreu	.20
236	John Olerud	.25
237	Doug Glanville	.10
238	Eric Young	.10
239	Robb Nen	.10
240	Jeff Bagwell	.50
241	Sterling Hitchcock	.10
242	Todd Greene	.10
243	Bill Mueller	.10
244	Rickey Henderson	.25
245	Chan Ho Park	.10
246	Jason Schmidt	.10
247	Jeff Zimmerman	.10
248	Jermaine Dye	.10
249	Randall Simon	.10
250	Richie Sexson	.40
251	Micah Bowie	.50
252	Joe Nathan	.50
253	Chris Woodward	.50
254	Lance Berkman	.75
255	Ruben Mateo	.50
256	Russell Branyan	.50
257	Randy Wolf	.75
258	A.J. Burnett	.75
259	Mark Quinn	.50
260	Buddy Carlyle	.50
261	Ben Davis	.50
262	Yamid Haad	.50
263	Mike Colangelo	.50
264	Rick Ankiel	.75
265	Jacque Jones	.75
266	Kelly Dransfeldt	.50
267	Matt Riley	.50
268	Adam Kennedy	.50
269	Octavio Dotel	.50
270	Francisco Cordero	.50
271	Wilton Veras	.50
272	Calvin Pickering	.50
273	Alex Sanchez	.50
274	Tony Armas Jr.	.50
275	Pat Burrell	1.00
276	Chad Meyers	.50
277	Ben Petrick	.50
278	Ramon Hernandez	.50
279	Ed Yarnall	.50
280	Erubiel Durazo	.50
281	Vernon Wells	1.00
282	Gary Matthews	.50
283	Kip Wells	.50
284	Peter Bergeron	.50
285	Travis Dawkins	.50
286	Jorge Toca	.50
287	Cole Liniak	.50

288	Chad Hermansen	.50
289	Eric Gagne	.50
290	Chad Hutchinson	.50
291	Eric Munson	.50
292	Wiki Gonzalez	.50
293	Alfonso Soriano	1.50
294	Trent Durrington	.50
295	Ben Molina	.50
296	Aaron Myette	.50
297	Willi Mo Pena	.75
298	Kevin Barker	.50
299	Geoff Blum	.50
300	Josh Beckett	.75

Gold Medallion

	NM/M
Stars:	2X
Inserted 1:1	
Prospects (251-300):	2-4X
Inserted 1:24	

(See 2000 Ultra for checklist and base card values.)

Platinum Medallion

	NM/M
Stars:	15-30X
Production 50 Sets	
Prospects (251-300):	4-8X
Production 25 Sets	

(See 2000 Ultra for checklist and base card values.)

Masterpiece Edition

(Star card values undetermined because of unique status.)

Diamond Mine

	NM/M
Complete Set (15):	20.00
Common Player:	1.00

GREG MADDUX

	Inserted 1:6	
1	Greg Maddux	1.50
2	Mark McGwire	2.00
3	Ken Griffey Jr.	1.50
4	Cal Ripken Jr.	3.00
5	Nomar Garciaparra	2.50
6	Mike Piazza	2.00
7	Alex Rodriguez	2.50
8	Frank Thomas	1.00
9	Juan Gonzalez	1.00
10	Derek Jeter	2.50
11	Tony Gwynn	1.00
12	Chipper Jones	1.50
13	Sammy Sosa	2.00
14	Roger Clemens	1.50
15	Vladimir Guerrero	1.00

Club 3000

	NM/M
Common Player:	3.00
Inserted 1:24	
Wade Boggs	2.00
Tony Gwynn	3.00
Carl Yastrzemski	3.00

Club 3000 Memorabilia

	NM/M
Wade Boggs/ Bat/100	20.00
Wade Boggs/ Hat/100	40.00
Wade Boggs/Jsy/440	20.00
Wade Boggs/ Bat/Jsy/100	40.00
Wade Boggs/ Bat/Hat/Jsy/25	150.00
Tony Gwynn/Bat/260	40.00
Tony Gwynn/ Hat/115	60.00
Tony Gwynn/ Jsy/450	25.00
Tony Gwynn/ Bat/Jsy/100	65.00
Tony Gwynn/ Bat/Hat/Jsy/25	375.00
Carl Yastrzemski/ Bat/250	40.00
Carl Yastrzemski/ Hat/100	60.00
Carl Yastrzemski/ Jsy/440	25.00
Carl Yastrzemski/ Bat/100	75.00
Carl Yastrzemski/ Bat/Hat/Jsy/25	300.00

Crunch Time

	NM/M
Complete Set (15):	50.00

	NM/M
Common Player:	2.00
Inserted 1:72	
1	Nomar Garciaparra	8.00
2	Ken Griffey Jr.	5.00
3	Mark McGwire	8.00
4	Alex Rodriguez	8.00
5	Derek Jeter	8.00
6	Sammy Sosa	6.00
7	Mike Piazza	5.00
8	Cal Ripken Jr.	10.00
9	Frank Thomas	3.00
10	Juan Gonzalez	3.00
11	J.D. Drew	2.00
12	Greg Maddux	5.00
13	Tony Gwynn	3.00
14	Vladimir Guerrero	3.00
15	Ben Grieve	2.00

Feel the Game

	NM/M
Common Player:	5.00
Roberto Alomar	10.00
J.D. Drew	5.00
Tony Gwynn/SP	40.00
Randy Johnson	20.00
Greg Maddux	20.00
Edgar Martinez	10.00
Pedro Martinez	20.00
Kevin Millwood	10.00
Cal Ripken Jr.	40.00
Alex Rodriguez	25.00
Scott Rolen	10.00
Curt Schilling	10.00
Chipper Jones	20.00
Frank Thomas/SP	40.00
Robin Ventura	5.00

Fresh Ink

	NM/M
Common Player:	5.00
1	Bobby Abreu/400	10.00
2	Chad Allen/1,000	5.00
3	Marlon Anderson/ 1,000	5.00
4	Glen Barker/1,000	5.00
5	Michael Barrett/1,000	5.00
6	Carlos Beltran/1,000	15.00
7	Adrian Beltre/1,000	5.00
8	Wade Boggs/250	40.00
9	Barry Bonds/250	150.00
10	Peter Bergeron/1,000	5.00
11	Pat Burrell/500	20.00
12	Roger Cedeno/500	5.00
13	Eric Chavez/750	10.00
14	Bruce Chen/600	5.00
15	Johnny Damon/750	8.00
16	Ben Davis/1,000	5.00
17	Carlos Delgado/300	10.00
18	Einar Diaz/1,000	5.00

19	Octavio Dotel/1,000	6.00
20	J.D. Drew/600	8.00
21	Scott Elarton/1,000	5.00
22	Freddy Garcia/500	8.00
23	Jeremy Giambi/1,000	5.00
24	Troy Glaus/500	20.00
25	Shawn Green/350	30.00
26	Tony Gwynn/250	50.00
27	Richard Hidalgo/500	8.00
28	Bobby Higginson/1,000	6.00
29	Tim Hudson/1,000	10.00
30	Norm Hutchins/1,000	5.00
31	Derek Jeter/95	200.00
32	Randy Johnson/150	50.00
33	Gabe Kapler/750	8.00
34	Jason Kendall/800	8.00
35	Paul Konerko/500	8.00
36	Matt Lawton/1,000	6.00
37	Carlos Lee/1,000	8.00
38	Jose Macias/1,000	5.00
39	Greg Maddux/250	65.00
40	Ruben Mateo/250	8.00
41	Kevin Millwood/500	10.00
42	Warren Morris/1,000	5.00
43	Eric Munson/1,000	6.00
44	Heath Murray/1,000	5.00
45	Joe Nathan/1,000	5.00
46	Magglio Ordonez/350	10.00
47	Angel Pena/1,000	5.00
48	Cal Ripken Jr./350	125.00
49	Alex Rodriguez/350	80.00
50	Scott Rolen/250	35.00
51	Ryan Rupe/1,000	5.00
52	Curt Schilling/375	25.00
53	Randall Simon/1,000	5.00
54	Alfonso Soriano/1,000	60.00
55	Shannon Stewart/300	5.00
56	Miguel Tejada/1,000	25.00
57	Frank Thomas/150	60.00
58	Jeff Weaver/1,000	6.00
59	Randy Wolf/1,000	8.00
60	Ed Yarnall/1,000	5.00
61	Kevin Young/1,000	5.00
62	Tony Gwynn, Wade Boggs, Nolan Ryan/100	450.00
63	Rick Ankiel/500	5.00

Swing King

		NM/M
Complete Set (10):		20.00
Common Player:		1.00
Inserted 1:24		
1	Cal Ripken Jr.	4.00
2	Nomar Garciaparra	3.00
3	Frank Thomas	1.00
4	Tony Gwynn	1.50
5	Ken Griffey Jr.	2.00
6	Chipper Jones	2.00
7	Mark McGwire	3.00
8	Sammy Sosa	2.50
9	Derek Jeter	3.00
10	Alex Rodriguez	3.00

Ultra Talented

		NM/M
Common Player:		5.00
Production 100 Sets		
1	Sammy Sosa	15.00
2	Derek Jeter	20.00
3	Alex Rodriguez	20.00
4	Mike Piazza	15.00
5	Ken Griffey Jr.	15.00
6	Nomar Garciaparra	20.00
7	Mark McGwire	20.00
8	Cal Ripken Jr.	25.00

ULTRA TALENTED
MIKE PIAZZA

9	Frank Thomas	8.00
10	J.D. Drew	5.00

World Premiere

		NM/M
Complete Set (10):		5.00
Common Player:		.50
Inserted 1:12		
1	Ruben Mateo	.50
2	Lance Berkman	1.00
3	Octavio Dotel	.50
4	Ben Davis	.50
5	Warren Morris	.50
6	Carlos Beltran	.75
7	Rick Ankiel	.50
8	Adam Kennedy	.50
9	Tim Hudson	1.00
10	Jorge Toca	.50

2001 Ultra

		NM/M
Complete Set (275):		65.00
Common Player:		.15
Common Prospect (251-275):		1.00
Inserted 1:4		
Pack (10):		3.00
Box (24):		55.00
1	Pedro Martinez	.75
2	Derek Jeter	2.00
3	Cal Ripken Jr.	2.00
4	Alex Rodriguez	1.50
5	Vladimir Guerrero	.75
6	Troy Glaus	.40
7	Sammy Sosa	1.25
8	Mike Piazza	1.00
9	Tony Gwynn	.75
10	Tim Hudson	.25
11	John Flaherty	.15
12	Jeff Cirillo	.15
13	Ellis Burks	.15
14	Carlos Lee	.15
15	Carlos Beltran	.25
16	Ruben Rivera	.15
17	Richard Hidalgo	.15
18	Omar Vizquel	.25
19	Michael Barrett	.15
20	Jose Canseco	.40
21	Jason Giambi	.50
22	Greg Maddux	1.00
23	Charles Johnson	.15
24	Sandy Alomar	.15
25	Rick Ankiel	.15
26	Richie Sexson	.40
27	Matt Williams	.25
28	Joe Girardi	.15
29	Jason Kendall	.25
30	Brad Fullmer	.15
31	Alex Gonzalez	.15
32	Rick Helling	.15
33	Mike Mussina	.50
34	Joe Randa	.15
35	J.T. Snow	.15
36	Edgardo Alfonzo	.15
37	Dante Bichette	.15
38	Brad Ausmus	.15
39	Bobby Abreu	.25
40	Warren Morris	.15
41	Tony Womack	.15
42	Russell Branyan	.15
43	Mike Lowell	.15
44	Mark Grace	.40
45	Jeromy Burnitz	.15
46	J.D. Drew	.25
47	David Justice	.25
48	Alex Gonzalez	.15
49	Tino Martinez	.25
50	Raul Mondesi	.25
51	Rafael Furcal	.25
52	Marquis Grissom	.15
53	Kevin Young	.15
54	Jon Lieber	.15
55	Henry Rodriguez	.15
56	Dave Burba	.15
57	Shannon Stewart	.15
58	Preston Wilson	.15
59	Paul O'Neill	.25
60	Jimmy Haynes	.15
61	Darryl Kile	.15
62	Bret Boone	.25
63	Bartolo Colon	.25
64	Andres Galarraga	.25
65	Trot Nixon	.15
66	Steve Finley	.15
67	Shawn Green	.30
68	Robert Person	.15
69	Kenny Rogers	.15
70	Bobby Higginson	.15
71	Barry Larkin	.30
72	Al Martin	.15
73	Tom Glavine	.40
74	Rondell White	.15
75	Ray Lankford	.15
76	Moises Alou	.25
77	Matt Clement	.15
78	Geoff Jenkins	.25
79	David Wells	.15
80	Chuck Finley	.15
81	Andy Pettitte	.25
82	Travis Fryman	.25
83	Ron Coomer	.15
84	Mark McGwire	1.50
85	Kerry Wood	.50
86	Jorge Posada	.40
87	Jeff Bagwell	.50
88	Andruw Jones	.50
89	Ryan Klesko	.25
90	Mariano Rivera	.25
91	Lance Berkman	.25
92	Kenny Lofton	.25
93	Jacque Jones	.15
94	Eric Young	.15
95	Edgar Renteria	.15
96	Chipper Jones	1.00
97	Todd Helton	.50
98	Shawn Estes	.15
99	Mark Mulder	.25
100	Lee Stevens	.15
101	Jermaine Dye	.15
102	Greg Vaughn	.15
103	Chris Singleton	.15
104	Brady Anderson	.15
105	Terrence Long	.15
106	Quilvio Veras	.15
107	Magglio Ordonez	.40
108	Johnny Damon	.25
109	Jeffrey Hammonds	.15
110	Fred McGriff	.25
111	Carl Pavano	.15
112	Bobby Estalella	.15
113	Todd Hundley	.15
114	Scott Rolen	.75
115	Robin Ventura	.25
116	Pokey Reese	.15
117	Luis Gonzalez	.25
118	Jose Offerman	.15
119	Edgar Martinez	.25
120	Dean Palmer	.15
121	David Segui	.15
122	Troy O'Leary	.15
123	Tony Batista	.15
124	Todd Zeile	.15
125	Randy Johnson	.75
126	Luis Castillo	.15
127	Kris Benson	.15
128	John Olerud	.25
129	Eric Karros	.25
130	Eddie Taubensee	.15
131	Neifi Perez	.15
132	Matt Stairs	.15
133	Luis Alicea	.15
134	Jeff Kent	.25
135	Javier Vazquez	.15
136	Garret Anderson	.25
137	Frank Thomas	.50
138	Carlos Febles	.15
139	Albert Belle	.15
140	Tony Clark	.15
141	Pat Burrell	.50
142	Mike Sweeney	.15
143	Jay Buhner	.15
144	Gabe Kapler	.15
145	Derek Bell	.15
146	B.J. Surhoff	.15
147	Adam Kennedy	.15
148	Aaron Boone	.15
149	Todd Stottlemyre	.15
150	Roberto Alomar	.40
151	Orlando Hernandez	.25
152	Jason Varitek	.15
153	Gary Sheffield	.40
154	Cliff Floyd	.15
155	Chad Hermansen	.15
156	Carlos Delgado	.50
157	Aaron Sele	.15
158	Sean Casey	.15
159	Ruben Mateo	.15
160	Mike Bordick	.15
161	Mike Cameron	.15
162	Doug Glanville	.15
163	Damion Easley	.15
164	Carl Everett	.15
165	Bengie Molina	.15
166	Adrian Beltre	.25
167	Tom Goodwin	.15
168	Rickey Henderson	.40
169	Mo Vaughn	.25
170	Mike Lieberthal	.15
171	Ken Griffey Jr.	1.00
172	Juan Gonzalez	.50
173	Ivan Rodriguez	.50
174	Al Leiter	.25
175	Vinny Castilla	.15
176	Peter Bergeron	.15
177	Pedro Astacio	.15
178	Paul Konerko	.15
179	Mitch Meluskey	.15
180	Kevin Millwood	.25
181	Ben Grieve	.15
182	Barry Bonds	2.00
183	Rusty Greer	.15
184	Miguel Tejada	.40
185	Mark Quinn	.15
186	Larry Walker	.25
187	Jose Valentin	.15
188	Jose Vidro	.15
189	Delino DeShields	.15
190	Darin Erstad	.25
191	Bill Mueller	.15
192	Ray Durham	.15
193	Ken Caminiti	.15
194	Jim Thome	.75
195	Javy Lopez	.25
196	Fernando Vina	.15
197	Eric Chavez	.25
198	Eric Owens	.15
199	Brad Radke	.15
200	Travis Lee	.15
201	Tim Salmon	.25
202	Rafael Palmeiro	.50
203	Nomar Garciaparra	1.50
204	Mike Hampton	.15
205	Kevin Brown	.25
206	Juan Encarnacion	.15
207	Danny Graves	.15
208	Carlos Guillen	.15
209	Phil Nevin	.15
210	Matt Lawton	.15
211	Manny Ramirez	.50
212	James Baldwin	.15
213	Fernando Tatis	.15
214	Craig Biggio	.25
215	Brian Jordan	.15
216	Bernie Williams	.40
217	Ryan Dempster	.15
218	Roger Clemens	1.50
219	Jose Cruz Jr.	.15
220	John Valentin	.15
221	Dmitri Young	.15
222	Curt Schilling	.40
223	Jim Edmonds	.30

224	Chan Ho Park	.15
225	Brian Giles	.25
226	Jimmy Anderson	.15
227	Adam Piatt	.15
228	Kenny Kelly	.15
229	Randy Choate	.15
230	Eric Cammack	.15
231	Yovanny Lara	.15
232	Wayne Franklin	.15
233	Cameron Cairncross	.15
234	J.C. Romero	.15
235	Geraldo Guzman	.15
236	Morgan Burkhart	.15
237	Pascual Coco	.15
238	John Parrish	.15
239	Keith McDonald	.15
240	Carlos Casimiro	.15
241	Daniel Garibay	.15
242	Sang-Hoon Lee	.15
243	Hector Ortiz	.15
244	Jeff Sparks	.15
245	Jason Boyd	.15
246	Mark Buehrle	.15
247	Adam Melhuse	.15
248	Kane Davis	.15
249	Mike Darr	.15
250	Vicente Padilla	.15
251	Barry Zito	4.00
252	Tim Drew	1.00
253	Luis Matos	2.00
254	Alex Cabrera	1.00
255	Jon Garland	1.00
256	Milton Bradley	1.50
257	Juan Pierre	2.00
258	Ismael Villegas	1.00
259	Eric Munson	1.00
260	Tomas De La Rosa	1.00
261	Chris Richard	1.00
262	Jason Tyner	1.00
263	B.J. Waszgis	1.00
264	Jason Marquis	1.00
265	Dusty Allen	1.00
266	Corey Patterson	2.00
267	Eric Byrnes	2.00
268	Xavier Nady	2.00
269	George Lombard	1.00
270	Timoniel Perez	1.00
271	Gary Matthews Jr.	1.00
272	Chad Durbin	1.00
273	Tony Armas Jr.	2.00
274	Francisco Cordero	1.00
275	Alfonso Soriano	5.00

Gold Medallion

Stars (1-250): 1-2X
Inserted 1:1
Prospects (251-275): 1-2X
Inserted 1:24

Platinum Medallion

Stars (1-250): 15-25X
Production 50 Sets

Prospects (251-275): 5-10X
Production 25 Sets

Autographics

		NM/M
Common Player:		5.00
Inserted 1:48		
Silvers:		1-1.5X
Production 250 Sets		
1	Roberto Alomar	25.00
2	Jimmy Anderson	5.00
3	Lance Berkman	15.00
4	Barry Bonds	150.00
5	Roosevelt Brown	5.00
6	Jeromy Burnitz	5.00
7	Pat Burrell	10.00
8	Alex Cabrera	5.00
9	Eric Chavez	10.00
10	Joe Crede	5.00
11	Johnny Damon	30.00
12	Carlos Delgado	10.00
13	Adam Dunn	20.00
14	Jim Edmonds	15.00
15	Chad Green	5.00
16	Dustin Hermanson	5.00
17	Randy Johnson	50.00
18	Corey Lee	5.00
19	Derrek Lee	25.00
20	Terrence Long	5.00
21	Julio Lugo	5.00
22	Edgar Martinez	20.00
23	Justin Miller	5.00
24	Russ Ortiz	5.00
25	Pablo Ozuna	5.00
26	Adam Piatt	5.00
27	Mark Redman	5.00
28	Richie Sexson	15.00
29	Gary Sheffield	15.00
30	Alfonso Soriano	25.00
31	Jose Vidro	8.00
32	Vernon Wells	10.00
33	Preston Wilson	10.00
34	Jamey Wright	5.00
35	Julio Zuleta	5.00

Decade of Dominance

		NM/M
Complete Set (15):		15.00
Common Player:		.50
Inserted 1:8		
1	Barry Bonds	3.00
2	Mark McGwire	2.00
3	Sammy Sosa	2.00
4	Ken Griffey Jr.	1.50
5	Cal Ripken Jr.	3.00
6	Tony Gwynn	1.00
7	Albert Belle	.50
8	Frank Thomas	1.00
9	Randy Johnson	1.00
10	Juan Gonzalez	.75
11	Greg Maddux	1.50
12	Craig Biggio	.50
13	Edgar Martinez	.50
14	Roger Clemens	2.00
15	Andres Galarraga	.50

Fall Classics

		NM/M
Complete Set (37):		150.00
Common Player:		2.00
Inserted 1:20		

1	Jackie Robinson	8.00
2	Enos Slaughter	2.00
3	Mariano Rivera	2.00
4	Hank Bauer	2.00
5	Cal Ripken Jr.	12.00
6	Babe Ruth	15.00
7	Thurman Munson	5.00
8	Tom Glavine	3.00
9	Fred Lynn	2.00
10	Johnny Bench	6.00
11	Tony Lazzeri	2.00
12	Al Kaline	5.00
13	Reggie Jackson	5.00
14	Derek Jeter	10.00
15	Willie Stargell	3.00
16	Roy Campanella	4.00
17	Phil Rizzuto	4.00
18	Roberto Clemente	12.00
19	Carlton Fisk	4.00
20	Duke Snider	4.00
21	Ted Williams	12.00
22	Bill Skowron	2.00
23	Bucky Dent	2.00
24	Mike Schmidt	8.00
25	Lou Brock	3.00
26	Whitey Ford	5.00
27	Brooks Robinson	4.00
28	Roberto Alomar	3.00
29	Yogi Berra	5.00
30	Joe Carter	2.00
31	Bill Mazeroski	2.00
32	Bob Gibson	3.00
33	Hank Greenberg	4.00
34	Andruw Jones	4.00
35	Bernie Williams	3.00
36	Don Larsen	3.00
37	Billy Martin	3.00

Fall Classics Memorabilia

		NM/M
Common Player:		10.00
Inserted 1:288		
1	Jackie Robinson/Pants	80.00
2	Enos Slaughter/Bat	15.00
3	Mariano Rivera/Jsy	15.00
4	Hank Bauer/Bat	10.00
5	Cal Ripken Jr./Jsy	40.00
6	Thurman Munson/Bat	25.00
7	Tom Glavine/Jsy	15.00
8	Fred Lynn/Bat	10.00
9	Babe Ruth/Bat	200.00
10	Tony Lazzeri/Bat	10.00
11	Al Kaline/Jsy	20.00
12	Reggie Jackson/Jsy	20.00
13	Derek Jeter/Jersey	40.00
14	Willie Stargell/Bat	15.00
15	Roy Campanella/Bat	50.00
16	Phil Rizzuto/Bat	20.00
17	Roberto Clemente/Bat	120.00
18	Carlton Fisk/Jsy	20.00
19	Duke Snider/Bat	25.00
20	Ted Williams/Bat	120.00
21	Bill Skowron/Bat	10.00
22	Bucky Dent/Bat	10.00
23	Mike Schmidt/Jsy	40.00
24	Lou Brock/Jsy	15.00
25	Brooks Robinson/Bat	20.00
26	Johnny Bench/Jsy	25.00

Fall Classics Memorabilia Autographs

No pricing due to scarcity.

Feel the Game

		NM/M
Common Player:		5.00
Inserted 1:48		
Golds:		2X
Production 50 Sets		
1	Moises Alou	5.00
2	Brady Anderson	5.00
3	Adrian Beltre	5.00
4	Carlos Delgado	8.00
5	J.D. Drew	5.00
6	Jermaine Dye	5.00
7	Jason Giambi	8.00
8	Richard Hidalgo	5.00
9	Chipper Jones	10.00
10	Eric Karros	5.00
11	Raul Mondesi	5.00
12	Chan Ho Park	8.00
13	Ivan Rodriguez	8.00
14	Matt Stairs	5.00
15	Frank Thomas	8.00
16	Jose Vidro	5.00
17	Matt Williams	5.00
18	Preston Wilson	5.00

Power Plus

		NM/M
Complete Set (10):		15.00
Common Player:		1.00
Inserted 1:24		
1	Vladimir Guerrero	1.50
2	Mark McGwire	3.00
3	Mike Piazza	2.00
4	Derek Jeter	4.00
5	Chipper Jones	2.00
6	Carlos Delgado	1.00
7	Sammy Sosa	2.00
8	Ken Griffey Jr.	2.00
9	Nomar Garciaparra	2.50
10	Alex Rodriguez	3.00

Season Pass

No Pricing

The Greatest Hits of ...

		NM/M
Complete Set (10):		10.00
Common Player:		.50
Inserted 1:12		
1	Mark McGwire	2.00
2	Alex Rodriguez	2.00
3	Ken Griffey Jr.	1.50

4	Ivan Rodriguez	.75
5	Cal Ripken Jr.	3.00
6	Todd Helton	.75
7	Derek Jeter	3.00
8	Pedro Martinez	1.00
9	Tony Gwynn	1.00
10	Jim Edmonds	.50

Tomorrow's Legends

		NM/M
Complete Set (15):		10.00
Common Player:		.25
Inserted 1:4		
1	Rick Ankiel	.25
2	J.D. Drew	.40
3	Carlos Delgado	.75
4	Todd Helton	.75
5	Andruw Jones	.75
6	Troy Glaus	.75
7	Jermaine Dye	.25
8	Vladimir Guerrero	1.00
9	Brian Giles	.25
10	Scott Rolen	.75
11	Darin Erstad	.40
12	Derek Jeter	3.00
13	Alex Rodriguez	3.00
14	Pat Burrell	.50
15	Nomar Garciaparra	2.00

2002 Ultra

		NM/M
Complete Set (285):		100.00
Common Player:		.15
Common SP (201-285):		.50
Inserted 1:4		
Pack (10):		2.00
Box (24):		40.00
1	Jeff Bagwell	.50
2	Derek Jeter	2.00
3	Alex Rodriguez	1.50
4	Eric Chavez	.40
5	Tsuyoshi Shinjo	.15
6	Chris Stynes	.15
7	Ivan Rodriguez	.50
8	Cal Ripken Jr.	2.00
9	Freddy Garcia	.15
10	Chipper Jones	.75
11	Hideo Nomo	.40
12	Rafael Furcal	.25
13	Preston Wilson	.15

14	Jimmy Rollins	.25
15	Cristian Guzman	.15
16	Garret Anderson	.40
17	Todd Helton	.50
18	Moises Alou	.25
19	Tony Gwynn	.75
20	Jorge Posada	.40
21	Sean Casey	.25
22	Kazuhiro Sasaki	.15
23	Ray Lankford	.15
24	Manny Ramirez	.50
25	Barry Bonds	2.00
26	Fred McGriff	.25
27	Vladimir Guerrero	.75
28	Jermaine Dye	.15
29	Adrian Beltre	.25
30	Ken Griffey Jr.	1.00
31	Ramon Hernandez	.15
32	Kerry Wood	.75
33	Greg Maddux	1.00
34	Rondell White	.15
35	Mike Mussina	.50
36	Jim Edmonds	.40
37	Scott Rolen	.75
38	Mike Lowell	.25
39	Al Leiter	.25
40	Tony Clark	.15
41	Joe Mays	.15
42	Mo Vaughn	.25
43	Geoff Jenkins	.25
44	Curt Schilling	.50
45	Pedro Martinez	.75
46	Andy Pettitte	.40
47	Tim Salmon	.25
48	Carl Everett	.15
49	Lance Berkman	.25
50	Troy Glaus	.40
51	Ichiro Suzuki	1.00
52	Alfonso Soriano	.75
53	Tomo Ohka	.15
54	Dean Palmer	.15
55	Kevin Brown	.25
56	Albert Pujols	1.50
57	Homer Bush	.15
58	Tim Hudson	.40
59	Frank Thomas	.50
60	Joe Randa	.15
61	Chan Ho Park	.15
62	Bobby Higginson	.15
63	Bartolo Colon	.15
64	Aramis Ramirez	.15
65	Jeff Cirillo	.15
66	Roberto Alomar	.25
67	Mark Kotsay	.15
68	Mike Cameron	.15
69	Mike Hampton	.15
70	Trot Nixon	.15
71	Juan Gonzalez	.50
72	Damian Rolls	.15
73	Brad Fullmer	.15
74	David Ortiz	.25
75	Brandon Inge	.15
76	Orlando Hernandez	.15
77	Matt Stairs	.15
78	Jay Gibbons	.15
79	Greg Vaughn	.15
80	Brady Anderson	.15
81	Jim Thome	.75
82	Ben Sheets	.40
83	Rafael Palmeiro	.25
84	Edgar Renteria	.25
85	Doug Mientkiewicz	.15
86	Raul Mondesi	.15
87	Shane Reynolds	.15
88	Steve Finley	.15
89	Jose Cruz Jr.	.15
90	Edgardo Alfonzo	.15
91	Jose Valentin	.15
92	Mark McGwire	2.00
93	Mark Grace	.40
94	Mike Lieberthal	.15
95	Barry Larkin	.25
96	Chuck Knoblauch	.15
97	Deivi Cruz	.15
98	Jeromy Burnitz	.15
99	Shannon Stewart	.15
100	David Wells	.15
101	Brook Fordyce	.15
102	Rusty Greer	.15
103	Andruw Jones	.50
104	Jason Kendall	.15
105	Nomar Garciaparra	1.25
106	Shawn Green	.25
107	Craig Biggio	.25
108	Masato Yoshii	.15
109	Ben Petrick	.15
110	Gary Sheffield	.40
111	Travis Lee	.15
112	Matt Williams	.25
113	Billy Wagner	.15
114	Robin Ventura	.15
115	Jerry Hairston Jr.	.15
116	Paul LoDuca	.15
117	Darin Erstad	.25

118	Ruben Sierra	.15
119	Ricky Gutierrez	.15
120	Bret Boone	.25
121	John Rocker	.15
122	Roger Clemens	1.50
123	Eric Karros	.15
124	J.D. Drew	.25
125	Carlos Delgado	.40
126	Jeffrey Hammonds	.15
127	Jeff Kent	.25
128	David Justice	.25
129	Cliff Floyd	.15
130	Omar Vizquel	.25
131	Matt Morris	.25
132	Rich Aurilia	.15
133	Larry Walker	.25
134	Miguel Tejada	.25
135	Eric Young	.15
136	Aaron Sele	.15
137	Eric Milton	.15
138	Travis Fryman	.15
139	Magglio Ordonez	.25
140	Sammy Sosa	1.50
141	Pokey Reese	.15
142	Adam Eaton	.15
143	Adam Kennedy	.15
144	Mike Piazza	1.00
145	Larry Barnes	.15
146	Darryl Kile	.15
147	Tom Glavine	.25
148	Ryan Klesko	.15
149	Jose Vidro	.15
150	Joe Kennedy	.15
151	Bernie Williams	.40
152	C.C. Sabathia	.15
153	Alex Ochoa	.15
154	A.J. Pierzynski	.15
155	Johnny Damon	.25
156	Omar Daal	.15
157	A.J. Burnett	.15
158	Eric Munson	.15
159	Fernando Vina	.15
160	Chris Singleton	.15
161	Juan Pierre	.15
162	John Olerud	.25
163	Randy Johnson	.75
164	Paul Konerko	.25
165	Tino Martinez	.25
166	Richard Hidalgo	.15
167	Luis Gonzalez	.25
168	Ben Grieve	.15
169	Matt Lawton	.15
170	Gabe Kapler	.25
171	Mariano Rivera	.25
172	Kenny Lofton	.25
173	Brian Jordan	.15
174	Brian Giles	.25
175	Mark Quinn	.15
176	Neifi Perez	.15
177	Ellis Burks	.15
178	Bobby Abreu	.40
179	Jeff Weaver	.15
180	Andres Galarraga	.25
181	Javy Lopez	.25
182	Todd Walker	.15
183	Fernando Tatis	.15
184	Charles Johnson	.15
185	Pat Burrell	.40
186	Jay Bell	.15
187	Aaron Boone	.15
188	Jason Giambi	.50
189	Jay Payton	.15
190	Carlos Lee	.15
191	Phil Nevin	.15
192	Mike Sweeney	.15
193	J.T. Snow	.15
194	Dmitri Young	.15
195	Richie Sexson	.40
196	Derrek Lee	.25
197	Corey Koskie	.15
198	Edgar Martinez	.25
199	Wade Miller	.15
200	Tony Batista	.15
201	John Olerud	.50
202	Bret Boone	.50
203	Cal Ripken Jr.	3.00
204	Alex Rodriguez	2.50
205	Ichiro Suzuki	2.00
206	Manny Ramirez	.75
207	Juan Gonzalez	.75
208	Ivan Rodriguez	.75
209	Roger Clemens	2.00
210	Edgar Martinez	.50
211	Todd Helton	.75
212	Jeff Kent	.50
213	Chipper Jones	1.00
214	Rich Aurilia	.50
215	Barry Bonds	3.00
216	Sammy Sosa	2.00
217	Luis Gonzalez	.50
218	Mike Piazza	2.00
219	Randy Johnson	1.00
220	Larry Walker	.50

221	Todd Helton, Juan Uribe	.50
222	Pat Burrell, Eric Valent	.50
223	Edgar Martinez, Ichiro Suzuki	2.00
224	Ben Grieve, Jason Tyner	.50
225	Mark Quinn, Dee Brown	.50
226	Cal Ripken Jr., Brian Roberts	3.00
227	Cliff Floyd, Abraham Nunez	.50
228	Jeff Bagwell, Adam Everett	.75
229	Mark McGwire, Albert Pujols	3.00
230	Doug Mientkiewicz, Luis Rivas	.50
231	Juan Gonzalez, Danny Peoples	.75
232	Kevin Brown, Luke Prokopec	.50
233	Richie Sexson, Ben Sheets	.50
234	Jason Giambi, Jason Hart	.75
235	Barry Bonds, Carlos Valderrama	3.00
236	Tony Gwynn, Cesar Crespo	1.00
237	Ken Griffey Jr., Adam Dunn	1.50
238	Frank Thomas, Joe Crede	.75
239	Derek Jeter, Drew Henson	3.00
240	Chipper Jones, Wilson Betemit	1.00
241	Luis Gonzalez, Junior Spivey	.50
242	Bobby Higginson, Andres Torres	.50
243	Carlos Delgado, Vernon Wells	.50
244	Sammy Sosa, Corey Patterson	2.00
245	Nomar Garciaparra, Shea Hillenbrand	2.00
246	Alex Rodriguez, Jason Romano	2.50
247	Troy Glaus, David Eckstein	.75
248	Mike Piazza, Alex Escobar	2.00
249	Brian Giles, Jack Wilson	.50
250	Vladimir Guerrero, Scott Hodges	1.00
251	Bud Smith	1.00
252	Juan Diaz	1.00
253	Wilkin Ruan	1.00
254	Chris Spurling **RC**	1.00
255	Toby Hall	1.00
256	Jason Jennings	1.00
257	George Perez	1.00
258	D'Angelo Jimenez	1.00
259	Jose Acevedo	1.00
260	Josue Perez	1.00
261	Brian Rogers	1.00
262	Carlos Maldonado	1.00
263	Travis Phelps	1.00
264	Rob Mackowiak	1.50
265	Ryan Drese	1.00
266	Carlos Garcia	1.00
267	Alexis Gomez	1.00
268	Jeremy Affeldt	1.00
269	Scott Podsednik	3.00
270	Adam Johnson	1.00
271	Pedro Santana	1.00
272	Les Walrond	1.00
273	Jackson Melian	1.00
274	Carlos Hernandez	1.00
275	Mark Nussbeck **RC**	1.00
276	Cory Aldridge	1.00
277	Troy Mattes	1.00
278	Brent Abernathy	1.00
279	J.J. Davis	1.00
280	Brandon Duckworth	1.00
281	Kyle Lohse	1.00
282	Justin Kaye	1.00
283	Cody Ransom	1.00
284	Dave Williams	1.00
285	Luis Lopez	1.00

Gold Medallion

Stars (1-200):	2-3X
Inserted 1:1	
Stars (201-250):	2-4X
Inserted 1:24	

Prospects (251-285): 4-8X
Production 100

Fall Classic

		NM/M
Complete Set (39):		180.00
Common Player:		2.50
Inserted 1:20		
1FC	Ty Cobb	10.00
2FC	Lou Gehrig	10.00
3FC	Babe Ruth	15.00
4FC	Stan Musial	8.00
5FC	Ted Williams	12.00
6FC	Dizzy Dean	6.00
7FC	Mickey Cochrane	2.50
8FC	Jimmie Foxx	8.00
9FC	Mel Ott	5.00
10FC	Rogers Hornsby	6.00
11FC	Hank Aaron	10.00
12FC	Clete Boyer	2.50
13FC	George Brett	10.00
14FC	Bob Gibson	5.00
15FC	Carlton Fisk	4.00
16FC	Johnny Bench	8.00
17FC	Rusty Staub	2.50
18FC	Willie McCovey	2.50
19FC	Paul Molitor	5.00
20FC	Jim Palmer	4.00
21FC	Frank Robinson	5.00
22FC	Derek Jeter	10.00
23FC	Earl Weaver	2.50
24FC	Lefty Grove	2.50
25FC	Tony Perez	2.50
26FC	Reggie Jackson	5.00
27FC	Sparky Anderson	2.50
28FC	Casey Stengel	2.50
29FC	Roy Campanella	6.00
30FC	Roberto Clemente	10.00
31FC	Don Drysdale	6.00
32FC	Joe Morgan	4.00
33FC	Eddie Murray	5.00
34FC	Nolan Ryan	15.00
35FC	Tom Seaver	8.00
36FC	Bill Mazeroski	2.50
37FC	Jackie Robinson	8.00
38FC	Kirk Gibson	2.50
39FC	Robin Yount	8.00

Fall Classic Game-Used

	NM/M
Inserted 1:113	
Sparky Anderson/ Pants	5.00
Johnny Bench/Jsy	15.00
Johnny Bench/Pants	10.00
George Brett/Bat	15.00
George Brett/ Blue Jsy/65	45.00

George Brett/ White Jsy	15.00
Roy Campanella/ Bat/21	225.00
Carlton Fisk/Bat/42	35.00
Carlton Fisk/Jsy	8.00
Jimmie Foxx/Bat	35.00
Bob Gibson/Jsy	10.00
Kirk Gibson/Bat	5.00
Reggie Jackson/Bat	10.00
Reggie Jackson/ Jsy/73	20.00
Derek Jeter/Pants	30.00
Willie McCovey/Jersey	5.00
Paul Molitor/Bat	10.00
Paul Molitor/Jersey	10.00
Joe Morgan/Bat	8.00
Joe Morgan/Jersey	8.00
Eddie Murray/Bat	10.00
Eddie Murray/Jsy/91	35.00
Jim Palmer/ Gray Jsy/85	20.00
Jim Palmer/White Jsy	5.00
Tony Perez/Bat	8.00
Frank Robinson/ Bat/40	25.00
Jackie Robinson/Jsy	50.00
Babe Ruth/Bat/44	200.00
Nolan Ryan/Pants	30.00
Tom Seaver/Jsy	10.00
Earl Weaver/Jsy	5.00
Ted Williams/Bat/30	200.00
Ted Williams/Jsy	75.00
Robin Yount/Bat	10.00
Robin Yount/ Gray Jsy	10.00
Robin Yount/ White Jsy/30	30.00

Fall Classic Autographs

		NM/M
Common Autograph:		10.00
Inserted 1:240		
1	Sparky Anderson	15.00
2	Johnny Bench/SP	40.00
3	George Brett/SP	80.00
4	Carlton Fisk	25.00
5	Bob Gibson	25.00
6	Kirk Gibson	15.00
7	Reggie Jackson/SP	40.00
8	Derek Jeter/SP	
9	Bill Mazeroski	20.00
10	Willie McCovey/SP	30.00
11	Joe Morgan	15.00
12	Eddie Murray/SP	40.00
13	Stan Musial/SP	
14	Jim Palmer	15.00
15	Tony Perez	15.00
16	Frank Robinson	20.00
17	Nolan Ryan/SP	175.00
18	Tom Seaver/SP	30.00
19	Earl Weaver	10.00
20	Robin Yount/SP	50.00

Glove Works

		NM/M
Complete Set (15):		25.00
Common Player:		1.00
Inserted 1:20		
1GW	Andruw Jones	1.50
2GW	Derek Jeter	6.00
3GW	Cal Ripken Jr.	8.00
4GW	Larry Walker	1.00
5GW	Chipper Jones	2.00
6GW	Barry Bonds	6.00
7GW	Scott Rolen	2.00
8GW	Jim Edmonds	1.00
9GW	Robin Ventura	1.00
10GW	Darin Erstad	1.00
11GW	Barry Larkin	1.00
12GW	Raul Mondesi	1.00
13GW	Mark Grace	1.50
14GW	Bernie Williams	1.00
15GW	Ivan Rodriguez	1.50

Glove Works Game-Worn

	NM/M
Common Player:	10.00
Production 450 Sets	

Platinum (25 Sets) randomly inserted.	
Derek Jeter	35.00
Andruw Jones/SP/100	
Cal Ripken Jr.	50.00
Chipper Jones/SP/100	
Barry Bonds	40.00
Robin Ventura	10.00
Barry Larkin/SP	15.00
Raul Mondesi	10.00
Ivan Rodriguez	15.00

Hitting Machine

		NM/M
Complete Set (25):		60.00
Common Player:		1.00
Inserted 1:20		
1HM	Frank Thomas	2.00
2HM	Derek Jeter	8.00
3HM	Vladimir Guerrero	3.00
4HM	Jim Edmonds	1.50
5HM	Mike Piazza	5.00
6HM	Ivan Rodriguez	2.00
7HM	Chipper Jones	3.00
8HM	Tony Gwynn	3.00
9HM	Manny Ramirez	2.00
10HM	Andruw Jones	2.00
11HM	Carlos Delgado	1.50
12HM	Bernie Williams	1.50
13HM	Larry Walker	1.00
14HM	Juan Gonzalez	2.00
15HM	Ichiro Suzuki	5.00
16HM	Albert Pujols	6.00
17HM	Barry Bonds	8.00
18HM	Cal Ripken Jr.	8.00
19HM	Edgar Martinez	1.50
20HM	Luis Gonzalez	1.00
21HM	Moises Alou	1.50
22HM	Roberto Alomar	2.00
23HM	Todd Helton	2.00
24HM	Rafael Palmeiro	2.00
25HM	Bobby Abreu	1.50

Hitting Machine Game Worn

	NM/M
Common Player:	8.00
Inserted 1:81	
Platinum (25 Sets) randomly inserted.	
Frank Thomas	15.00
Derek Jeter	25.00
Jim Edmonds	10.00
Mike Piazza	15.00
Ivan Rodriguez	15.00
Chipper Jones	15.00
Tony Gwynn	15.00
Manny Ramirez	10.00
Andruw Jones	10.00
Carlos Delgado	10.00
Bernie Williams	10.00
Larry Walker	8.00
Juan Gonzalez	10.00
Albert Pujols	30.00
Barry Bonds	25.00
Cal Ripken Jr.	40.00
Edgar Martinez	10.00
Luis Gonzalez	8.00
Moises Alou	10.00
Roberto Alomar	15.00
Todd Helton	15.00
Rafael Palmeiro	10.00
Bobby Abreu	10.00

On the Road Game-Used

	NM/M
Common Player:	10.00
Inserted 1:93	
Platinum (25 Sets) randomly inserted.	

Derek Jeter	30.00
Ivan Rodriguez	10.00
Carlos Delgado	8.00
Larry Walker	8.00
Roberto Alomar	15.00
Tony Gwynn	15.00
Greg Maddux	20.00
Barry Bonds	30.00
Todd Helton	15.00
Kazuhiro Sasaki	10.00
Jeff Bagwell	15.00
Omar Vizquel	8.00
Chan Ho Park	10.00
Tom Glavine	10.00

Rising Stars

		NM/M
Complete Set (15):		15.00
Common Player:		.50
Inserted 1:12		
1RS	Ichiro Suzuki	2.50
2RS	Derek Jeter	4.00
3RS	Albert Pujols	3.00
4RS	Jimmy Rollins	1.00
5RS	Adam Dunn	1.00
6RS	Sean Casey	1.00
7RS	Kerry Wood	2.00
8RS	Tsuyoshi Shinjo	.50
9RS	Shea Hillenbrand	.50
10RS	Pat Burrell	1.00
11RS	Ben Sheets	1.00
12RS	Alfonso Soriano	1.50
13RS	J.D. Drew	1.00
14RS	Kazuhiro Sasaki	.50
15RS	Corey Patterson	.75

Rising Stars Game Worn

	NM/M
Common Player:	20.00
Production 100 Sets	
Platinum (25 Sets) randomly seeded.	
Derek Jeter	75.00
Albert Pujols	50.00
Tsuyoshi Shinjo	25.00
Alfonso Soriano	25.00
J.D. Drew	25.00
Kazuhiro Sasaki	20.00

2003 Ultra

		NM/M
Complete Set (250):		75.00
Common Player:		.15
Common SP (201-250):		.50
Inserted 1:4		
Hobby Pack (10):		2.00
Hobby Box (24):		35.00
1	Barry Bonds	2.00
2	Derek Jeter	2.50

3	Ichiro Suzuki	1.50
4	Mike Lowell	.15
5	Hideo Nomo	.50
6	Javier Vazquez	.15
7	Jeremy Giambi	.15
8	Jamie Moyer	.15
9	Rafael Palmeiro	.40
10	Magglio Ordonez	.25
11	Trot Nixon	.15
12	Luis Castillo	.15
13	Paul Byrd	.15
14	Adam Kennedy	.15
15	Trevor Hoffman	.15
16	Matt Morris	.15
17	Nomar Garciaparra	1.50
18	Matt Lawton	.15
19	Carlos Beltran	.15
20	Jason Giambi	1.25
21	Brian Giles	.25
22	Jim Edmonds	.25
23	Garret Anderson	.25
24	Tony Batista	.15
25	Aaron Boone	.15
26	Mike Hampton	.15
27	Billy Wagner	.15
28	Kazuhisa Ishii	.15
29	Al Leiter	.25
30	Pat Burrell	.40
31	Jeff Kent	.25
32	Randy Johnson	.75
33	Ray Durham	.15
34	Josh Beckett	.15
35	Cristian Guzman	.15
36	Roger Clemens	1.25
37	Freddy Garcia	.15
38	Roy Halladay	.15
39	David Eckstein	.15
40	Jerry Hairston Jr.	.15
41	Barry Larkin	.25
42	Larry Walker	.25
43	Craig Biggio	.25
44	Edgardo Alfonzo	.15
45	Marlon Byrd	.15
46	J.T. Snow	.15
47	Juan Gonzalez	.50
48	Ramon Ortiz	.15
49	Jay Gibbons	.15
50	Adam Dunn	.60
51	Juan Pierre	.15
52	Jeff Bagwell	.60
53	Kevin Brown	.15
54	Pedro Astacio	.15
55	Mike Lieberthal	.15
56	Johnny Damon	.15
57	Tim Salmon	.25
58	Mike Bordick	.15
59	Ken Griffey Jr.	1.50
60	Jason Jennings	.15
61	Lance Berkman	.50
62	Jeromy Burnitz	.15
63	Jimmy Rollins	.25
64	Tsuyoshi Shinjo	.15
65	Alex Rodriguez	2.00
66	Greg Maddux	1.25
67	Mark Prior	.40
68	Mike Maroth	.15
69	Geoff Jenkins	.15
70	Tony Armas Jr.	.15
71	Jermaine Dye	.15
72	Albert Pujols	.75
73	Shannon Stewart	.15
74	Troy Glaus	.60
75	Brook Fordyce	.15
76	Juan Encarnacion	.15
77	Todd Hollandsworth	.15
78	Roy Oswalt	.25
79	Paul LoDuca	.15
80	Mike Piazza	1.50
81	Bobby Abreu	.15
82	Sean Burroughs	.15
83	Randy Winn	.15
84	Curt Schilling	.50
85	Chris Singleton	.15
86	Sean Casey	.25
87	Todd Zeile	.15
88	Richard Hidalgo	.15
89	Roberto Alomar	.50
90	Tim Hudson	.25
91	Ryan Klesko	.15
92	Greg Vaughn	.15
93	Tony Womack	.15
94	Fred McGriff	.25
95	Tom Glavine	.40
96	Todd Walker	.15
97	Travis Fryman	.15
98	Shane Reynolds	.15
99	Shawn Green	.25
100	Mo Vaughn	.25
101	Adam Piatt	.15
102	Deivi Cruz	.15
103	Steve Cox	.15
104	Luis Gonzalez	.25
105	Russell Branyan	.15
106	Daryle Ward	.15

107	Mariano Rivera	.25
108	Phil Nevin	.15
109	Ben Grieve	.15
110	Moises Alou	.15
111	Omar Vizquel	.25
112	Joe Randa	.15
113	Jorge Posada	.40
114	Mark Kotsay	.15
115	Ryan Rupe	.15
116	Javy Lopez	.15
117	Corey Patterson	.15
118	Bobby Higginson	.15
119	Jose Vidro	.15
120	Barry Zito	.25
121	Matt Morris	.15
122	Gary Sheffield	.25
123	Kerry Wood	.15
124	Brandon Inge	.15
125	Jose Hernandez	.15
126	Michael Barrett	.15
127	Miguel Tejada	.40
128	Edgar Renteria	.15
129	Junior Spivey	.15
130	Jose Valentin	.15
131	Derrek Lee	.15
132	A.J. Pierzynski	.15
133	Mike Mussina	.50
134	Bret Boone	.15
135	Chan Ho Park	.15
136	Steve Finley	.15
137	Mark Buehrle	.15
138	A.J. Burnett	.15
139	Ben Sheets	.15
140	David Ortiz	.15
141	Nick Johnson	.15
142	Randall Simon	.15
143	Carlos Delgado	.40
144	Darin Erstad	.25
145	Shea Hillenbrand	.15
146	Todd Helton	.40
147	Preston Wilson	.15
148	Eric Gagne	.15
149	Vladimir Guerrero	.75
150	Brandon Duckworth	.15
151	Rich Aurilia	.15
152	Ivan Rodriguez	.50
153	Andruw Jones	.50
154	Carlos Lee	.15
155	Robert Fick	.15
156	Jacque Jones	.15
157	Bernie Williams	.50
158	John Olerud	.25
159	Eric Hinske	.15
160	Matt Clement	.15
161	Dmitri Young	.15
162	Torii Hunter	.15
163	Carlos Pena	.15
164	Mike Cameron	.15
165	Raul Mondesi	.15
166	Pedro J. Martinez	.75
167	Bob Wickman	.15
168	Mike Sweeney	.15
169	David Wells	.15
170	Jason Kendall	.15
171	Tino Martinez	.15
172	Matt Williams	.15
173	Frank Thomas	.60
174	Cliff Floyd	.15
175	Corey Koskie	.15
176	Orlando Hernandez	.15
177	Edgar Martinez	.15
178	Richie Sexson	.25
179	Manny Ramirez	.60
180	Jim Thome	.50
181	Andy Pettitte	.40
182	Aramis Ramirez	.15
183	J.D. Drew	.25
184	Brian Jordan	.15
185	Sammy Sosa	1.25
186	Jeff Weaver	.15
187	Jeffrey Hammonds	.15
188	Eric Milton	.15
189	Eric Chavez	.25
190	Kazuhiro Sasaki	.15
191	Jose Cruz Jr.	.15
192	Derek Lowe	.15
193	C.C. Sabathia	.15
194	Adrian Beltre	.15
195	Alfonso Soriano	1.00
196	Jack Wilson	.15
197	Fernando Vina	.15
198	Chipper Jones	1.25
199	Paul Konerko	.15
200	Rusty Greer	.15
201	Jason Giambi	2.00
202	Alfonso Soriano	2.00
203	Shea Hillenbrand	.50
204	Alex Rodriguez	3.00
205	Jorge Posada	.60
206	Ichiro Suzuki	3.00
207	Manny Ramirez	1.00
208	Torii Hunter	.50
209	Todd Helton	.75
210	Roberto Alomar	.75

211	Scott Rolen	.75
212	Jimmy Rollins	.50
213	Mike Piazza	3.00
214	Barry Bonds	3.00
215	Sammy Sosa	2.00
216	Vladimir Guerrero	1.50
217	Lance Berkman	.75
218	Derek Jeter	4.00
219	Nomar Garciaparra	3.00
220	Luis Gonzalez	.75
221	Kazuhisa Ishii	1.00
222	Satoru Komiyama	.50
223	So Taguchi	.50
224	Jorge Padilla	.50
225	Ben Howard	.50
226	Jason Simontacchi	.50
227	Barry Wesson	.50
228	Howie Clark	.50
229	Aaron Guiel	.50
230	Oliver Perez	.75
231	David Ross	.50
232	Julius Matos	.50
233	Chris Snelling	.50
234	Rodrigo Lopez	.50
235	Wilbert Nieves	.50
236	Brendan Donnelly	.50
237	Aaron Cook	.50
238	Anderson Machado	.50
239	Corey Thurman	.50
240	Tyler Yates	.50
241	Coco Crisp	4.00
242	Andy Van Hekken	1.50
243	Jim Rushford	2.00
244	Jeriome Robertson	1.00
245	Shane Nance	1.00
246	Kevin Cash	.50
247	Kirk Saarloos	1.50
248	Josh Bard	2.00
249	David Pember **RC**	1.00
250	Freddy Sanchez	1.50

Gold Medallion

Stars (1-200):	2-3X
Inserted 1:1	
Stars (201-220):	3-4X
Inserted 1:24	
Rookies (221-250):	1-3X
Inserted 1:24	

Back 2 Back

	NM/M
Complete Set (17):	60.00
Common Player:	2.00
Production 1,000 Sets	
1B2B Derek Jeter	10.00
2B2B Barry Bonds	8.00
3B2B Mike Piazza	6.00
4B2B Alex Rodriguez	8.00
5B2B Todd Helton	2.00
6B2B Edgar Martinez	2.00
7B2B Chipper Jones	5.00
8B2B Shawn Green	2.00
9B2B Chan Ho Park	2.00
10B2B Preston Wilson	2.00
11B2B Manny Ramirez	3.00
12B2B Aramis Ramirez	2.00
13B2B Pedro J. Martinez	4.00
14B2B Ivan Rodriguez	2.00
15B2B Ichiro Suzuki	5.00
16B2B Sammy Sosa	5.00
17B2B Jason Giambi	5.00

Back 2 Back Memorabilia

	NM/M
Common Player:	5.00
Production 500 Sets	
Golds:	1.5-3X
Production 50 Sets	
Derek Jeter	25.00
Barry Bonds/Bat	20.00

	Mike Piazza/Jsy	12.00
	Alex Rodriguez/Jsy	12.00
	Todd Helton/Jsy	8.00
	Edgar Martinez/Jsy	6.00
	Chipper Jones/Jsy	15.00
	Shawn Green/Jsy	6.00
	Chan Ho Park/Bat	6.00
	Preston Wilson/Jsy	5.00
	Manny Ramirez/Jsy	8.00
	Aramis Ramirez/Jsy	5.00
	Pedro Martinez/Jsy	10.00
	Ivan Rodriguez/Jsy	8.00
	Ichiro Suzuki/Base	15.00
	Sammy Sosa/Base	10.00
	Jason Giambi/Base	8.00

Double Up

	NM/M
Complete Set (16):	30.00
Common Card:	1.00
Inserted 1:8	
1DU Derek Jeter, Mike Piazza	4.00
2DU Alex Rodriguez, Rafael Palmeiro	3.00
3DU Chipper Jones, Andruw Jones	2.00
4DU Derek Jeter, Alex Rodriguez	4.00
5DU Nomar Garciaparra, Derek Jeter	4.00
6DU Barry Bonds, Jason Giambi	3.00
7DU Ichiro Suzuki, Hideo Nomo	3.00
8DU Randy Johnson, Curt Schilling	1.00
9DU Pedro J. Martinez, Nomar Garciaparra	2.50
10DU Roger Clemens, Kevin Brown	2.00
11DU Nomar Garciaparra, Manny Ramirez	2.50
12DU Kazuhiro Sasaki, Hideo Nomo	1.00
13DU Mike Piazza, Ivan Rodriguez	3.00
14DU Ichiro Suzuki, Ken Griffey Jr.	3.00
15DU Barry Bonds, Sammy Sosa	3.00
16DU Alfonso Soriano, Roberto Alomar	2.00

Double Up Memorabilia

	NM/M
Common Card:	15.00
Production 100 Sets	
Derek Jeter, Mike Piazza	50.00
Alex Rodriguez, Rafael Palmeiro	25.00
Chipper Jones, Andruw Jones	15.00
Derek Jeter, Alex Rodriguez	50.00
Nomar Garciaparra, Derek Jeter	50.00
Barry Bonds, Jason Giambi	30.00
Ichiro Suzuki, Hideo Nomo	80.00
Randy Johnson, Curt Schilling	20.00
Pedro J. Martinez, Nomar Garciaparra	30.00
Roger Clemens, Kevin Brown	25.00
Nomar Garciaparra, Manny Ramirez	25.00

Kazuhiro Sasaki, Hideo Nomo	50.00
Mike Piazza, Ivan Rodriguez	25.00
Ichiro Suzuki, Ken Griffey Jr.	50.00
Barry Bonds, Sammy Sosa	40.00
Alfonso Soriano, Roberto Alomar	25.00

Moonshots

	NM/M
Complete Set (20):	30.00
Common Player:	.75
Inserted 1:12	
1M	Mike Piazza	4.00
2M	Alex Rodriguez	4.00
3M	Manny Ramirez	1.50
4M	Ivan Rodriguez	1.00
5M	Luis Gonzalez	.75
6M	Shawn Green	.75
7M	Barry Bonds	5.00
8M	Jason Giambi	3.00
9M	Nomar Garciaparra	4.00
10M	Edgar Martinez	.75
11M	Mo Vaughn	.75
12M	Chipper Jones	3.00
13M	Todd Helton	1.00
14M	Raul Mondesi	.75
15M	Preston Wilson	.75
16M	Rafael Palmeiro	1.00
17M	Jim Edmonds	.75
18M	Bernie Williams	1.00
19M	Vladimir Guerrero	2.00
20M	Alfonso Soriano	2.00

Moonshots Memorabilia

	NM/M
Common Player:	4.00
Inserted 1:20	
Mike Piazza/Jsy	12.00
Alex Rodriguez/Jsy	12.00
Manny Ramirez/Jsy	5.00
Ivan Rodriguez/Jsy	5.00
Luis Gonzalez/Jsy	4.00
Shawn Green/Jsy	4.00
Barry Bonds/Jsy	12.00
Jason Giambi/Base	8.00
Nomar Garciaparra/Jsy	12.00
Edgar Martinez/Jsy	5.00
Mo Vaughn/Jsy	4.00
Chipper Jones/Jsy	8.00
Todd Helton/Jsy	6.00
Raul Mondesi/Jsy	5.00
Preston Wilson/Jsy	4.00
Rafael Palmeiro/Jsy	5.00
Jim Edmonds/Jsy	5.00

Bernie Williams/Jsy	6.00
Vladimir Guerrero/Base	5.00
Alfonso Soriano/Jsy	8.00

Photo Effex

Vladimir Guerrero
Montreal Expos™

◆ Photo Effex

	NM/M
Complete Set (20):	45.00
Common Player:	1.00
Inserted 1:12	
Golds:	6-12X
Production 25 Sets	
1PE	Derek Jeter	6.00
2PE	Barry Bonds	5.00
3PE	Sammy Sosa	3.00
4PE	Troy Glaus	1.50
5PE	Albert Pujols	2.00
6PE	Alex Rodriguez	5.00
7PE	Ichiro Suzuki	4.00
8PE	Greg Maddux	3.00
9PE	Nomar Garciaparra	4.00
10PE	Jeff Bagwell	1.50
11PE	Chipper Jones	3.00
12PE	Mike Piazza	4.00
13PE	Randy Johnson	2.00
14PE	Vladimir Guerrero	2.00
15PE	Alfonso Soriano	3.00
16PE	Lance Berkman	1.00
17PE	Todd Helton	1.00
18PE	Mike Lowell	1.00
19PE	Carlos Delgado	1.00
20PE	Jason Giambi	3.00

When it was a Game

	NM/M
Complete Set (40):	125.00
Common Player:	2.00
Inserted 1:20	
1WG	Derek Jeter	10.00
2WG	Barry Bonds	8.00
3WG	Luis Aparicio	2.00
4WG	Richie Ashburn	2.00
5WG	Ernie Banks	5.00
6WG	Enos Slaughter	3.00
7WG	Yogi Berra	5.00
8WG	Lou Boudreau	2.00
9WG	Lou Brock	4.00
10WG	Jim Bunning	2.00
11WG	Rod Carew	4.00
12WG	Orlando Cepeda	2.00
13WG	Larry Doby	4.00
14WG	Bobby Doerr	2.00
15WG	Bob Feller	3.00
16WG	Brooks Robinson	5.00
17WG	Rollie Fingers	2.00
18WG	Whitey Ford	3.00
19WG	Bob Gibson	4.00
20WG	Jim "Catfish" Hunter	3.00
21WG	Nolan Ryan	15.00
22WG	Reggie Jackson	5.00
23WG	Fergie Jenkins	3.00
24WG	Al Kaline	6.00
25WG	Mike Schmidt	8.00
26WG	Harmon Killebrew	8.00
27WG	Ralph Kiner	4.00
28WG	Willie Stargell	4.00
29WG	Billy Williams	2.00
30WG	Tom Seaver	5.00
31WG	Juan Marichal	3.00
32WG	Eddie Mathews	6.00
33WG	Willie McCovey	4.00

34WG	Joe Morgan	4.00
35WG	Stan Musial	8.00
36WG	Robin Roberts	4.00
37WG	Robin Yount	8.00
38WG	Jim Palmer	3.00
39WG	Phil Rizzuto	4.00
40WG	Pee Wee Reese	4.00

When it was a Game Memorabilia

	NM/M
Common Player:	
Varying quantities produced.	
Derek Jeter/Jsy/200	35.00
Barry Bonds/Bat/200	25.00
Yogi Berra/100	35.00
Larry Doby/Bat/150	20.00
Catfish Hunter/Jsy	8.00
Reggie Jackson/Bat	12.00
Tom Seaver/Jsy	15.00
Juan Marichal/Jsy	8.00
Eddie Mathews/Bat	25.00
Willie McCovey/Jsy/150	15.00
Joe Morgan/Jsy/200	10.00
Jim Palmer/Jsy/300	10.00

When it was a Game Autograph

No Pricing

2004 Ultra

	NM/M
Complete Set (220):	45.00
Common Player:	.15
Common All-Rookie (201-220):	.50
Common Player (221-295):	.25
Minor Stars (221-295):	.40
Unlisted Stars (221-295):	.60
Common Player (296-382):	2.00
Inserted 2:1	
Common Player (383-395):	15.00
Production 500 Sets	
Pack (8):	3.00
Box (24):	60.00
1	Magglio Ordonez	.40
2	Bobby Abreu	.25
3	Eric Munson	.15
4	Eric Byrnes	.15
5	Bartolo Colon	.25
6	Juan Encarnacion	.15
7	Jody Gerut	.15
8	Eddie Guardado	.15
9	Shea Hillenbrand	.15
10	Andruw Jones	.50
11	Carlos Lee	.15
12	Pedro J. Martinez	.75
13	Barry Larkin	.25
14	Angel Berroa	.15
15	Edgar Martinez	.25
16	Sidney Ponson	.15
17	Mariano Rivera	.25
18	Richie Sexson	.40
19	Frank Thomas	.50
20	Jerome Williams	.15
21	Barry Zito	.40
22	Roberto Alomar	.50
23	Rocky Biddle	.15
24	Orlando Cabrera	.25
25	Placido Polanco	.15
26	Morgan Ensberg	.15
27	Jason Giambi	.75
28	Jim Thome	.75
29	Vladimir Guerrero	.75
30	Tim Hudson	.40
31	Jacque Jones	.15
32	Derrek Lee	.25
33	Rafael Palmeiro	.40
34	Mike Mussina	.40

35	Corey Patterson	.15
36	Mike Cameron	.15
37	Ivan Rodriguez	.50
38	Ben Sheets	.15
39	Woody Williams	.15
40	Ichiro Suzuki	1.00
41	Moises Alou	.25
42	Craig Biggio	.25
43	Jorge Posada	.40
44	Craig Monroe	.15
45	Darin Erstad	.25
46	Jay Gibbons	.25
47	Aaron Guiel	.15
48	Travis Lee	.15
49	Jorge Julio	.15
50	Torii Hunter	.25
51	Luis Matos	.15
52	Brett Myers	.15
53	Sean Casey	.25
54	Mark Prior	1.50
55	Alex Rodriguez	1.50
56	Gary Sheffield	.40
57	Jason Varitek	.15
58	Dontrelle Willis	.40
59	Garret Anderson	.25
60	Casey Blake	.15
61	Jay Payton	.15
62	Carl Crawford	.15
63	Carl Everett	.15
64	Marcus Giles	.15
65	Jose Guillen	.15
66	Eric Karros	.15
67	Mike Lieberthal	.15
68	Hideki Matsui	3.00
69	Xavier Nady	.15
70	Hank Blalock	.40
71	Albert Pujols	1.50
72	Jose Cruz Jr.	.15
73	Randall Simon	.15
74	Javier Vazquez	.15
75	Preston Wilson	.15
76	Danys Baez	.15
77	Alex Cintron	.15
78	Jake Peavy	.15
79	Scott Rolen	.50
80	Robert Fick	.15
81	Brian Giles	.25
82	Roy Halladay	.25
83	Kazuhisa Ishii	.15
84	Austin Kearns	.40
85	Paul LoDuca	.15
86	Darrell May	.15
87	Phil Nevin	.15
88	Carlos Pena	.15
89	Manny Ramirez	.50
90	C.C. Sabathia	.15
91	John Smoltz	.25
92	Jose Vidro	.15
93	Randy Wolf	.15
94	Jeff Bagwell	.50
95	Barry Bonds	2.00
96	Frank Catalanotto	.15
97	Zach Day	.15
98	David Ortiz	.15
99	Troy Glaus	.40
100	Bo Hart	.15
101	Geoff Jenkins	.25
102	Jason Kendall	.15
103	Esteban Loiaza	.15
104	Doug Mientkiewicz	.15
105	Trot Nixon	.15
106	Troy Percival	.15
107	Aramis Ramirez	.15
108	Alex Sanchez	.15
109	Alfonso Soriano	.75
110	Omar Vizquel	.25
111	Kerry Wood	.50
112	Rocco Baldelli	.15
113	Bret Boone	.25
114	Shawn Chacon	.15
115	Carlos Delgado	.50
116	Shawn Green	.40
117	Tim Worrell	.15
118	Tom Glavine	.25
119	Shigetoshi Hasegawa	.15
120	Derek Jeter	2.00
121	Jeff Kent	.25
122	Braden Looper	.15
123	Kevin Millwood	.25
124	Hideo Nomo	.40
125	Jason Phillips	.15
126	Tim Redding	.15
127	Reggie Sanders	.15
128	Sammy Sosa	1.25
129	Billy Wagner	.25
130	Miguel Batista	.15
131	Milton Bradley	.15
132	Eric Chavez	.25
133	J.D. Drew	.25
134	Keith Foulke	.15
135	Luis Gonzalez	.25
136	LaTroy Hawkins	.15
137	Randy Johnson	.75
138	Byung-Hyun Kim	.15

139	Javy Lopez	.25	243	Carlos Guillen	.25
140	Melvin Mora	.15	244	Kenny Lofton	.25
141	Aubrey Huff	.15	245	Pokey Reese	.25
142	Mike Piazza	1.00	246	Rafael Palmeiro	.75
143	Mark Redman	.15	247	Nomar Garciaparra	2.50
144	Kazuhiro Sasaki	.15	248	Hee Seop Choi	.25
145	Shannon Stewart	.15	249	Juan Uribe	.25
146	Larry Walker	.25	250	Nick Johnson	.25
147	Dmitri Young	.15	251	Scott Podsednik	.25
148	Josh Beckett	.50	252	Richie Sexson	.60
149	Jae Weong Seo	.15	253	Keith Foulke	.25
150	Hee Seop Choi	.15	254	Jaret Wright	.25
151	Adam Dunn	.40	255	Johnny Estrada	.25
152	Rafael Furcal	.25	256	Michael Barrett	.25
153	Juan Gonzalez	.50	257	Bernie Williams	.60
154	Todd Helton	.50	258	Octavio Dotel	.25
155	Carlos Zambrano	.15	259	Jeromy Burnitz	.25
156	Ryan Klesko	.25	260	Kevin Youkilis	.25
157	Mike Lowell	.25	261	Derrek Lee	.40
158	Jamie Moyer	.15	262	Jack Wilson	.25
159	Russ Ortiz	.15	263	Craig Wilson	.25
160	Juan Pierre	.15	264	Richard Hidalgo	.25
161	Edgar Renteria	.15	265	Royce Clayton	.25
162	Curt Schilling	.40	266	Curt Schilling	.60
163	Mike Sweeney	.15	267	Joe Mauer	.75
164	Brandon Webb	.15	268	Bobby Crosby	.25
165	Michael Young	.15	269	Zack Greinke	.25
166	Carlos Beltran	.25	270	Victor Martinez	.25
167	Sean Burroughs	.15	271	Pedro Feliz	.25
168	Luis Castillo	.15	272	Tony Batista	.25
169	David Eckstein	.15	273	Casey Kotchman	.25
170	Eric Gagne	.25	274	Freddy Garcia	.25
171	Chipper Jones	1.00	275	Adam Everett	.25
172	Livan Hernandez	.15	276	Alexis Rios	.25
173	Nick Johnson	.15	277	Lew Ford	.25
174	Corey Koskie	.15	278	Adam LaRoche	.25
175	Jason Schmidt	.15	279	Lyle Overbay	.25
176	Bill Mueller	.15	280	Juan Gonzalez	.40
177	Steve Finley	.15	281	A.J. Pierzynski	.25
178	A.J. Pierzynski	.15	282	Scott Hairston	.25
179	Rene Reyes	.15	283	Danny Bautista	.25
180	Jason Johnson	.15	284	Brad Penny	.25
181	Mark Teixeira	.15	285	Paul Konerko	.25
182	Kip Wells	.15	286	Matt Lawton	.25
183	Mike MacDougal	.15	287	Carl Pavano	.25
184	Lance Berkman	.25	288	Pat Burrell	.40
185	Victor Zambrano	.15	289	Kenny Rogers	.25
186	Roger Clemens	1.50	290	Laynce Nix	.25
187	Jim Edmonds	.25	291	Johnny Damon	.40
188	Nomar Garciaparra	1.50	292	Paul Wilson	.25
189	Ken Griffey Jr.	1.00	293	Vinny Castilla	.25
190	Richard Hidalgo	.15	294	Aaron Miles	.25
191	Cliff Floyd	.15	295	Ken Harvey	.25
192	Greg Maddux	1.00	296	Onil Joseph RC	2.00
193	Mark Mulder	.25	297	Kazuhito Tadano RC	3.00
194	Roy Oswalt	.15	298	Jeff Bennett RC	2.00
195	Marlon Byrd	.15	299	Chad Bentz RC	3.00
196	Jose Reyes	.25	300	Akinori Otsuka RC	3.00
197	Kevin Brown	.25	301	Jon Knott RC	2.00
198	Miguel Tejada	.25	302	Ian Snell RC	3.00
199	Vernon Wells	.25	303	Fernando Nieve RC	2.00
200	Joel Pineiro	.15	304	Mike Rouse RC	2.00
201	Rickie Weeks	5.00	305	Dennis Sarfate RC	2.00
202	Chad Gaudin	1.50	306	Josh Labandeira RC	3.00
203	Ryan Wagner	1.50	307	Chris Oxspring RC	2.00
204	Chris Bootcheck	.50	308	Alfredo Simon RC	2.00
205	Koyie Hill	.50	309	Rusty Tucker RC	2.00
206	Jeff Duncan	1.00	310	Lincoln Holdzkom RC	2.00
207	Rich Harden	1.00	311	Justin Leone RC	2.00
208	Edwin Jackson	.50	312	Jorge Sequea RC	2.00
209	Robby Hammock	.50	313	Brian Dallimore RC	2.00
210	Khalil Greene	.50	314	Tim Bittner RC	2.00
211	Chien-Ming Wang	.50	315	Ronny Cedeno RC	2.00
212	Prentice Redman	.50	316	Justin Hampson RC	2.00
213	Todd Wellemeyer	.50	317	Ryan Wing RC	2.00
214	Clint Barmes	1.00	318	Mariano Gomez RC	2.00
215	Matt Kata	.50	319	Carlos Vasquez RC	2.00
216	Jon Leicester	.50	320	Casey Daigle RC	2.00
217	Jeremy Guthrie	.50	321	Renyel Pinto RC	2.00
218	Chin-Hui Tsao	1.50	322	Chris Shelton RC	4.00
219	Dan Haren	1.00	323	Mike Gosling RC	2.00
220	Delmon Young	5.00	324	Aarom Baldiris RC	2.00
221	Vladimir Guerrero	1.00	325	Ramon Ramirez RC	2.00
222	Andy Pettitte	.60	326	Roberto Novoa RC	2.00
223	Gary Sheffield	.60	327	Sean Henn RC	2.00
224	Javier Vazquez	.25	328	Nick Regilio RC	2.00
225	Alex Rodriguez	2.50	329	David Crouthers RC	2.00
226	Billy Wagner	.25	330	Greg Dobbs RC	2.00
227	Miguel Tejada	.60	331	Angel Chavez RC	2.00
228	Greg Maddux	1.50	332	Luis A. Gonzalez RC	2.00
229	Ivan Rodriguez	.60	333	Justin Knoedler RC	2.00
230	Roger Clemens	2.50	334	Jason Frasor RC	2.00
231	Alfonso Soriano	1.00	335	Jerry Gil RC	2.00
232	Miguel Cabrera	.75	336	Carlos Hines RC	2.00
233	Javy Lopez	.40	337	Ivan Ochoa RC	3.00
234	David Wells	.25	338	Jose Capellan RC	3.00
235	Eric Milton	.25	339	Hector Gimenez RC	2.00
236	Armando Benitez	.25	340	Shawn Hill RC	3.00
237	Mike Cameron	.25	341	Freddy Guzman RC	2.00
238	J.D. Drew	.40	342	Scott Proctor RC	2.00
239	Carlos Beltran	.60	343	Frank Francisco RC	2.00
240	Bartolo Colon	.25	344	Brandon Medders RC	2.00
241	Jose Guillen	.25	345	Andy Green RC	2.00
242	Kevin Brown	.40	346	Eddy Rodriguez RC	2.00

347	Tim Hamulack RC	2.00
348	Mike Wuertz RC	2.00
349	Arnie Munoz RC	2.00
350	Enemencio Pacheco RC	2.00
351	Dusty Bergman RC	2.00
352	Charles Thomas RC	5.00
353	William Bergolla RC	2.00
354	Ramon Castro RC	2.00
355	Justin Lehr RC	2.00
356	Lino Urdaneta RC	2.00
357	Donnie Kelly RC	2.00
358	Kevin Cave RC	2.00
359	Franklyn Gracesqui RC	2.00
360	Chris Aguila RC	2.00
361	Jorge Vasquez RC	2.00
362	Andres Blanco RC	2.00
363	Orlando Rodriguez RC	2.00
364	Colby Miller RC	2.00
365	Shawn Camp RC	2.00
366	Jake Woods RC	2.00
367	George Sherrill RC	2.00
368	Justin Huisman RC	2.00
369	Jimmy Serrano RC	3.00
370	Mike Johnston RC	3.00
371	Ryan Meaux RC	2.00
372	Scott Dohmann RC	2.00
373	Brad Halsey RC	5.00
374	Joey Gathright RC	3.00
375	Yadier Molina RC	2.00
376	Travis Blackley RC	2.00
377	Steve Andrade RC	2.00
378	Phil Stockman RC	2.00
379	Roman Colon RC	2.00
380	Jesse Crain RC	2.00
381	Edwardo Sierra RC	2.00
382	Justin Germano RC	2.00
383	Kazuo Matsui RC	30.00
384	Shingo Takatsu RC	20.00
385	John Gall RC	15.00
386	Chris Saenz RC	15.00
387	Merkin Valdez RC	20.00
388	Jamie Brown RC	15.00
389	Jason Bartlett RC	20.00
390	David Aardsma RC	20.00
391	Scott Kazmir RC	30.00
392	David Wright RC	40.00
393	Dioner Navarro RC	30.00
394	B.J. Upton RC	25.00
395	Gavin Floyd RC	30.00

Gold Medallion

Cards (1-200):	2-3X
Inserted 1:1	
All-Rookies (201-220):	3-4X
Inserted 1:8	
Cards (221-295):	.75-1.5X
Inserted 1:1	
Cards (296-382):	.75-1.25X
Cards (383-395):	.25-.75X
Inserted 1:4	

Platinum Medallion

Cards (1-200):	8-15X
All-Rookies (201-220):	5-10X
Production 66 Sets	
Cards (221-295):	4-8X
Cards (296-382):	2-4X
Production 100 Sets	
Cards (383-395):	No Pricing
Production 13 Sets	

Diamond Producers

	NM/M
Complete Set (10):	60.00
Common Player:	4.00
Inserted 1:144	
1DP	Greg Maddux	8.00
2DP	Dontrelle Willis	4.00
3DP	Jim Thome	5.00
4DP	Alfonso Soriano	6.00
5DP	Alex Rodriguez	10.00
6DP	Sammy Sosa	10.00
7DP	Nomar Garciaparra	10.00
8DP	Derek Jeter	15.00
9DP	Adam Dunn	4.00
10DP	Mark Prior	8.00

Diamond Producers Memorabilia

	NM/M
Production 1,000 Sets	
Dontrelle Willis	15.00
Alfonso Soriano	10.00
Alex Rodriguez	10.00
Sammy Sosa	10.00
Nomar Garciaparra	10.00
Derek Jeter	15.00
Mark Prior	10.00

Diamond Producers UltraSwatch

	NM/M
Numbered to Jersey #.	
Dontrelle Willis/35	25.00

Hitting Machines

	NM/M
Common Player:	3.00
Inserted 1:12	
Die-Cut:	1-2X
1HM	Albert Pujols	6.00
2HM	Ken Griffey Jr.	4.00
3HM	Vladimir Guerrero	3.50
4HM	Mike Piazza	4.00
5HM	Ichiro Suzuki	5.00
6HM	Miguel Cabrera	3.00
7HM	Hideki Matsui	6.00
8HM	Nomar Garciaparra	6.00
9HM	Derek Jeter	8.00
10HM	Chipper Jones	4.00

HR Kings

	NM/M
Complete Set (10):	35.00
Inserted 1:96	
Golds:	2-3X
Production 50 Sets	
1HK	Barry Bonds	8.00
2HK	Albert Pujols	6.00
3HK	Jason Giambi	3.00
4HK	Jeff Bagwell	2.00
5HK	Ken Griffey Jr.	4.00
6HK	Alex Rodriguez	5.00
7HK	Sammy Sosa	5.00
8HK	Alfonso Soriano	3.00
9HK	Chipper Jones	4.00
10HK	Mike Piazza	4.00

Legendary 13 Memorabilia

Numbered to 13 each. Each player's jersey swatch on each cardMasterpiece 1/1 auto. by named player.

Inserted 1:192 Series 2 Hobby
players on each card.

Legendary 13
Memorabilia
Autographs

NM/M

Numbered to 5 each
Masterpiece: 1/1
Numbered with "L13A-" prefix
Limited pricing due to scarcity.
TW Ted Williams 900.00

Legendary 13 Dual
Memorabilia
Autographs

Numbered to 3 each.
Masterpiece 1/1
No pricing due to scarcity.

Performers

		NM/M
Complete Set (15):		12.00
Common Player:		.50
Inserted 1:24		
1UP	Ichiro Suzuki	1.50
2UP	Albert Pujols	2.00
3UP	Barry Bonds	3.00
4UP	Hideki Matsui	2.00
5UP	Randy Johnson	1.00
6UP	Jason Giambi	1.00
7UP	Pedro J. Martinez	1.00
8UP	Hank Blalock	.50
9UP	Chipper Jones	1.50
10UP	Mike Piazza	1.50
11UP	Derek Jeter	3.00
12UP	Vladimir Guerrero	1.00
13UP	Barry Zito	.75
14UP	Rocco Baldelli	.50
15UP	Hideo Nomo	.75

Performers
Memorabilia

	NM/M
Common Player:	6.00
Production 500 Sets	
Albert Pujols	15.00
Barry Bonds/base	15.00
Randy Johnson	8.00
Jason Giambi	8.00
Pedro J. Martinez	10.00
Hank Blalock	6.00
Chipper Jones	10.00
Mike Piazza	10.00
Derek Jeter	15.00
Vladimir Guerrero	8.00

Rocco Baldelli	10.00
Hideo Nomo	15.00

Performers
UltraSwatch

	NM/M
Numbered to Jersey #.	
Randy Johnson/51	15.00
Pedro Martinez/45	20.00
Mike Piazza/31	25.00
Vladimir Guerrero/27	20.00

RBI Kings

		NM/M
Complete Set (10):		15.00
Inserted 1:32		
Golds:		3-4X
Production 50 Sets		
1RK	Hideki Matsui	4.00
2RK	Albert Pujols	4.00
3RK	Todd Helton	1.50
4RK	Jim Thome	1.50
5RK	Carlos Delgado	1.50
6RK	Alex Rodriguez	4.00
7RK	Barry Bonds	5.00
8RK	Manny Ramirez	1.50
9RK	Vladimir Guerrero	1.50
10RK	Nomar Garciaparra	4.00

Season Crowns
Memorabilia

	NM/M
Common Player:	4.00
Production 399 Sets	
Golds:	1-2X
Production 99 Sets	
Platinums:	No Pricing
Production 25 Sets	
Adam Dunn	6.00
Carlos Pena	4.00
Torii Hunter	8.00
Gary Sheffield	8.00
Sean Casey	4.00
Lance Berkman	6.00
Tom Glavine	6.00
Sean Burroughs	4.00
Shawn Green	6.00
Jason Kendall	4.00
Vladimir Guerrero	10.00
Todd Helton	8.00
Tim Hudson	6.00
Troy Glaus	6.00
Larry Walker	4.00
Carlos Beltran	6.00
Hideo Nomo	10.00
Kazuhiro Sasaki	4.00
Mike Piazza	10.00
Scott Rolen	8.00
Carlos Delgado	6.00
Andruw Jones	8.00
Alfonso Soriano	10.00
Angel Berroa	4.00
Brandon Webb	6.00
Jason Giambi	8.00
Pedro J. Martinez	10.00
Manny Ramirez	8.00
Alex Rodriguez	10.00
Derek Jeter	15.00
Mark Mulder	6.00

Greg Maddux	10.00
Sammy Sosa	15.00
Jim Thome	10.00
Hank Blalock	6.00
Roberto Alomar	8.00
Omar Vizquel	5.00
Austin Kearns	8.00
Jeff Bagwell	8.00
Frank Thomas	8.00
Randy Johnson	8.00
Rocco Baldelli	12.00
Albert Pujols	15.00
Jose Reyes	8.00
Dontrelle Willis	12.00
Hideki Matsui/Base	20.00
Barry Bonds/Base	15.00
Ichiro Suzuki/Base	15.00
Chipper Jones	10.00
Roger Clemens	15.00

Season Crowns
Autograph

	NM/M
Common Player:	15.00
Production 150 Sets	
Golds:	No Pricing
Production 25 Sets	
Rocco Baldelli	35.00
Hank Blalock	15.00
Bo Hart	30.00
Aubrey Huff	15.00
Chipper Jones	60.00
Austin Kearns	15.00
Mike Lowell	15.00
Corey Patterson	20.00
Carlos Pena	15.00
Jose Reyes	30.00
Scott Rolen	20.00
Miguel Tejada	25.00
Brandon Webb	15.00
Rickie Weeks	50.00
Dontrelle Willis	35.00

Strikeout Kings

		NM/M
Complete Set (10):		10.00
Common Player:		.75
Inserted 1:24		
Golds:		3-5X
Production 50 Sets		
1KK	Randy Johnson	1.50
2KK	Pedro J. Martinez	1.50
3KK	Curt Schilling	1.00
4KK	Roger Clemens	3.00
5KK	Mike Mussina	1.00
6KK	Roy Halladay	.75
7KK	Kerry Wood	1.00
8KK	Dontrelle Willis	1.00
9KK	Greg Maddux	2.00
10KK	Mark Prior	2.00

Turn Back the Clock

		NM/M
Common Player:		1.50
Inserted 1:6		
1	Roger Clemens	5.00
2	Alex Rodriguez	5.00
3	Randy Johnson	2.00
4	Pedro Martinez	2.00
5	Alfonso Soriano	2.00

6	Curt Schilling	1.50
7	Miguel Tejada	1.50
8	Scott Rolen	2.00
9	Jim Thome	2.00
10	Manny Ramirez	1.50
11	Vladimir Guerrero	2.00
12	Tom Glavine	1.50
13	Andy Pettitte	1.50
14	Ivan Rodriguez	1.50
15	Jason Giambi	2.00
16	Rafael Palmeiro	2.00
17	Greg Maddux	3.00
18	Hideo Nomo	1.50
19	Mike Mussina	1.50
20	Sammy Sosa	4.00

Turn Back the Clock
Game-Used Copper

		NM/M
Common Player:		8.00
Production 399 Sets		
Silver:		.75-1.5X
Production 199 Sets		
Gold:		1-2X
Production 99 Sets		
Platinum Patch:		2-5X
Production 29 Sets		
RC	Roger Clemens	12.00
JG	Jason Giambi	10.00
TG	Tom Glavine	8.00
VG	Vladimir Guerrero	10.00
RJ	Randy Johnson	10.00
GM	Greg Maddux	12.00
PR	Pedro Martinez	10.00
MM	Mike Mussina	8.00
HM	Hideo Nomo	8.00
RP	Rafael Palmeiro	10.00
AP	Andy Pettitte	8.00
MR	Manny Ramirez	10.00
IR	Ivan Rodriguez	8.00
SR	Scott Rolen	10.00
CS	Curt Schilling	8.00
AS	Alfonso Soriano	10.00
SS	Sammy Sosa	12.00
MT	Miguel Tejada	8.00
JT	Jim Thome	10.00

3 Kings

	NM/M
Production 33 Sets	
Mike Piazza, Roger Clemens, Alex Rodriguez	
Albert Pujols, Mark Prior, Todd Helton	50.00
Alfonso Soriano, Dontrelle Willis, Albert Pujols	60.00
P. Martinez, Sammy Sosa, Albert Pujols	70.00
Randy Johnson, Albert Pujols, Todd Helton	50.00
Dontrelle Willis, Chipper Jones, Albert Pujols	60.00
Dontrelle Willis, Jeff Bagwell, Jim Thome	40.00
Greg Maddux, Jason Giambi, Manny Ramirez	50.00

2005 Ultra

	NM/M
Common Player (1-200):	.15
Minor Stars (1-200):	.25
Unlisted Stars (1-200):	.50
Common Player (201-220):	2.00
Minor Stars (201-220):	3.00
Inserted 1:4	

Pack (8):		3.50
Box (24):		75.00
1	Andy Pettitte	.40
2	Jose Cruz	.15
3	Cliff Floyd	.25
4	Paul Konerko	.15
5	Joe Mauer	.75
6	Scott Spiezio	.15
7	Ben Sheets	.25
8	Kerry Wood	.50
9	Carl Pavano	.15
10	Matt Morris	.15
11	Kazuo Matsui	.75
12	Ivan Rodriguez	.40
13	Victor Martinez	.15
14	Justin Morneau	.25
15	Adam Everett	.15
16	Carl Crawford	.15
17	David Ortiz	.25
18	Jason Giambi	.75
19	Derrek Lee	.25
20	Magglio Ordonez	.25
21	Bobby Abreu	.25
22	Milton Bradley	.15
23	Jeff Bagwell	.50
24	Jim Edmonds	.25
25	Garret Anderson	.25
26	Jacque Jones	.15
27	Ted Lilly	.15
28	Greg Maddux	1.00
29	Jermaine Dye	.15
30	Bill Mueller	.15
31	Roy Oswalt	.25
32	Tony Womack	.15
33	Andruw Jones	.50
34	Tom Glavine	.25
35	Mariano Rivera	.25
36	Sean Casey	.15
37	Edgardo Alfonzo	.15
38	Brad Penny	.15
39	Johan Santana	.15
40	Mark Teixeira	.25
41	Manny Ramirez	.50
42	Gary Sheffield	.40
43	Matt Lawton	.15
44	Troy Percival	.15
45	Rocco Baldelli	.40
46	Doug Mientkiewicz	.15
47	Corey Patterson	.15
48	Austin Kearns	.15
49	Edgar Martinez	.25
50	Brad Radke	.15
51	Barry Larkin	.25
52	Chone Figgins	.15
53	Alexis Rios	.15
54	Alex Rodriguez	1.50
55	Vinny Castilla	.15
56	Javier Vazquez	.15
57	Javy Lopez	.25
58	Mike Cameron	.15
59	Brian Giles	.25
60	Dontrelle Willis	.25
61	Rafael Furcal	.15
62	Trot Nixon	.15
63	Mark Mulder	.25
64	Josh Beckett	.50
65	J.D. Drew	.25
66	Brandon Webb	.15
67	Wade Miller	.15
68	Lyle Overbay	.15
69	Pedro J. Martinez	.75
70	Rich Harden	.15
71	Al Leiter	.15
72	Adam Eaton	.15
73	Mike Sweeney	.15
74	Steve Finley	.15
75	Kris Benson	.15
76	Jim Thome	.75
77	Juan Pierre	.15
78	Bartolo Colon	.25
79	Carlos Delgado	.50
80	Jack Wilson	.15
81	Ken Harvey	.15
82	Nomar Garciaparra	1.50
83	Paul LoDuca	.15
84	Cesar Izturis	.15
85	Adrian Beltre	.25
86	Brian Roberts	.15
87	David Eckstein	.15
88	Jimmy Rollins	.25
89	Roger Clemens	1.00
90	Randy Johnson	.75
91	Orlando Hudson	.15
92	Tim Hudson	.25
93	Dmitri Young	.15
94	Chipper Jones	1.00
95	John Smoltz	.25
96	Billy Wagner	.15
97	Hideo Nomo	.25
98	Sammy Sosa	1.25
99	Darin Erstad	.25
100	Todd Helton	.50
101	Aubrey Huff	.15
102	Alfonso Soriano	.75

103	Jose Vidro	.15
104	Carlos Lee	.15
105	Corey Koskie	.15
106	Bret Boone	.25
107	Torii Hunter	.40
108	Aramis Ramirez	.15
109	Chase Utley	.15
110	Reggie Sanders	.15
111	Livan Hernandez	.15
112	Jeromy Burnitz	.15
113	Carlos Zambrano	.15
114	Hank Blalock	.40
115	Sidney Ponson	.15
116	Zack Greinke	.15
117	Trevor Hoffman	.15
118	Jeff Kent	.25
119	Richie Sexson	.40
120	Melvin Mora	.15
121	Eric Chavez	.25
122	Miguel Cabrera	.50
123	Ryan Freel	.15
124	Russ Ortiz	.15
125	Craig Wilson	.15
126	Craig Biggio	.25
127	Curt Schilling	.40
128	Kazuhisa Ishii	.15
129	Marquis Grissom	.15
130	Bernie Williams	.40
131	Travis Hafner	.15
132	Hee Seop Choi	.15
133	Scott Rolen	.15
134	Tony Batista	.75
135	Frank Thomas	.15
136	Jason Varitek	.15
137	Ichiro Suzuki	1.25
138	Junior Spivey	.15
139	Adam Dunn	.40
140	Jorge Posada	.40
141	Edgar Renteria	.15
142	Hideki Matsui	1.50
143	Carlos Guillen	.15
144	Jody Gerut	.15
145	Wily Mo Pena	.15
146	Derek Jeter	2.00
147	C.C. Sabathia	.15
148	Geoff Jenkins	.25
149	Albert Pujols	1.50
150	Eric Munson	.15
151	Moises Alou	.25
152	Jerry Hairston	.15
153	Ray Durham	.15
154	Mike Piazza	1.00
155	Omar Vizquel	.25
156	A.J. Pierzynski	.15
157	Michael Young	.15
158	Jason Bay	.15
159	Mark Loretta	.15
160	Shawn Green	.25
161	Luis Gonzalez	.25
162	Johnny Damon	.25
163	Eric Milton	.15
164	Mike Lowell	.15
165	Jose Guillen	.15
166	Eric Hinske	.15
167	Jason Kendall	.25
168	Carlos Beltran	.40
169	Johnny Estrada	.15
170	Scott Hatteberg	.15
171	Laynce Nix	.15
172	Eric Gagne	.25
173	Richard Hidalgo	.15
174	Bobby Crosby	.15
175	Woody Williams	.15
176	Justin Leone	.15
177	Orlando Cabrera	.15
178	Mark Prior	1.50
179	Jorge Julio	.15
180	Jamie Moyer	.15
181	Jose Reyes	.40
182	Ken Griffey Jr.	1.00
183	Mike Lieberthal	.15
184	Kenny Rogers	.15
185	Mike Mussina	.40
186	Preston Wilson	.15
187	Khalil Greene	.50
188	Angel Berroa	.15
189	Miguel Tejada	.40
190	Freddy Garcia	.15
191	Pat Burrell	.25
192	Luis Castillo	.15
193	Vladimir Guerrero	.75
194	Roy Halladay	.25
195	Barry Zito	.40
196	Lance Berkman	.25
197	Rafael Palmeiro	.50
198	Nate Robertson	.15
199	Jason Schmidt	.25
200	Scott Podsednik	.15
201	Casey Kotchman	3.00
202	Scott Kazmir	4.00
203	Bucky Jacobsen	4.00
204	Jeff Keppinger	3.00
205	David Bush	2.00
206	Gavin Floyd	5.00
207	David Wright	8.00

208	B.J. Upton	3.00
209	David Aardsma	2.00
210	Jason Bartlett	3.00
211	Dioner Navarro	3.00
212	Jason Kubel	3.00
213	Ryan Howard	3.00
214	Charles Thomas RC	2.00
215	Freddy Guzman	2.00
216	Brad Halsey	3.00
217	Joey Gathright	2.00
218	Jeff Francis	2.00
219	Terry Tiffee	2.00
220	Nick Swisher	5.00

Gold

Cards 1-200:	1-3X
Inserted 1:1	
Cards 201-220:	.5-1X
Inserted 1:8	

Platinum

Cards 1-200:	5-8X
Cards 201-220:	3-5X
Production 50 Sets	

Follow the Leader

	NM/M
Common Player:	1.50
Inserted 1:6	
Copper Game-Used:	3-5X
Inserted 1:72 (Hobby Only)	
Red Game-Used:	2-4X
Inserted 1:48 (Retail Only)	
Gold Game-Used:	4-6X
Production 250 Sets	
Platinum Game-Used:	5-8X
Production 99 Sets	
Ultra Game-Used:	
Numbered 26-51:	5-10X
Numbered 25 or less: No Pricing	
Production to player's jersey	
number.	

1	Roger Clemens	3.00
2	Albert Pujols	3.00
3	Sammy Sosa	2.50
4	Manny Ramirez	1.50
5	Vladimir Guerrero	2.00
6	Ivan Rodriguez	1.50
7	Mike Piazza	2.00
8	Scott Rolen	2.00
9	Ichiro Suzuki	2.50
10	Randy Johnson	2.00
11	Mark Prior	2.00
12	Jim Thome	2.00
13	Greg Maddux	2.00
14	Pedro J. Martinez	2.00
15	Miguel Cabrera	1.50

HR Kings

	NM/M
Common Player:	2.50
Inserted 1:96	
Ultra Kings Gold:	1-3X
Production 50 Sets	

1	Jim Thome	4.00
2	David Ortiz	3.00
3	Adam Dunn	3.00
4	Albert Pujols	8.00
5	Manny Ramirez	3.50
6	Vladimir Guerrero	4.00
7	Miguel Tejada	3.00
8	Rafael Palmeiro	3.50
9	Mark Teixeira	2.50
10	Sammy Sosa	6.00
11	Frank Thomas	3.50
12	Pat Burrell	2.50
13	Adrian Beltre	2.50
14	Miguel Cabrera	3.50
15	Gary Sheffield	3.00

RBI Kings

	NM/M
Common Player:	2.50
Inserted 1:32	
Ultra Kings Gold:	2-4X
Production 50 Sets	

1	Sean Casey	2.50
2	Ivan Rodriguez	2.50
3	Mike Piazza	4.00
4	Todd Helton	3.00
5	Scott Rolen	3.50
6	Hideki Matsui	6.00
7	Gary Sheffield	2.50
8	Alfonso Soriano	3.50
9	Bobby Abreu	2.50
10	Lance Berkman	2.50
11	Miguel Tejada	2.50
12	Travis Hafner	2.50
13	Hank Blalock	2.50
14	Jeff Bagwell	3.00
15	Chipper Jones	4.00

Season Crowns
Copper Game-Used

	NM/M
Common Player:	5.00
Production 399 Sets	
Gold:	.75-1.5X
Production 99 Sets	
Platinum:	No Pricing
Production 25 Sets	

1	Andy Pettitte/Jsy	8.00
3	Cliff Floyd/Jsy	5.00
7	Ben Sheets/Jsy	5.00
8	Kerry Wood/Jsy	8.00
11	Kazuo Matsui/Bat	15.00
13	Victor Martinez/Jsy	5.00
17	David Carr/Jsy	8.00
20	Magglio Ordonez/Bat	5.00
21	Bobby Abreu/Bat	5.00
24	Jim Edmonds/Jsy	5.00
31	Roy Oswalt/Jsy	5.00
33	Andruw Jones/Jsy	8.00
34	Tom Glavine/Bat	5.00
36	Sean Casey/Jsy	5.00
37	Edgardo Alfonzo/Bat	5.00
41	Manny Ramirez/Bat	8.00
42	Gary Sheffield/Bat	8.00
45	Rocco Baldelli/Jsy	5.00
48	Austin Kearns/Jsy	5.00
49	Edgar Martinez/Jsy	5.00
60	Dontrelle Willis/Jsy	5.00
65	J.D. Drew/Jsy	5.00
70	Rich Harden/Jsy	5.00
71	Al Leiter/Jsy	5.00
80	Jack Wilson/Bat	5.00
93	Dmitri Young/Bat	5.00
94	Chipper Jones/Bat	10.00
97	Hideo Nomo/Jsy	8.00
98	Sammy Sosa/Bat	12.00
100	Todd Helton/Bat	8.00
102	Alfonso Soriano/Bat	8.00
107	Torii Hunter/Bat	8.00
114	Hank Blalock/Bat	8.00
119	Richie Sexson/Jsy	8.00
121	Eric Chavez/Jersey	5.00
130	Bernie Williams/Bat	8.00
135	Frank Thomas/Bat	8.00
139	Adam Dunn/Bat	8.00
142	Hideki Matsui/Bat	15.00
144	Jody Gerut/Bat	8.00

154	Mike Piazza/Bat	10.00
158	Jason Bay/Bat	8.00
162	Johnny Damon/Jsy	10.00
168	Carlos Beltran/Bat	8.00
173	Richard Hidalgo/Jsy	5.00
181	Jose Reyes/Bat	6.00
187	Khalil Greene/Jsy	15.00
191	Pat Burrell/Bat	8.00
193	Vladimir Guerrero/Bat	8.00
197	Rafael Palmeiro/Jsy	8.00

Season Crown
Autographs Copper

	NM/M
Common Player:	20.00

Stated Production 199 Sets
All 199 cards not released
for some players.

31	Roy Oswalt/50	25.00
80	Jack Wilson/199	20.00
125	Craig Wilson/130	20.00
157	Michael Young/150	20.00
200	Scott Podsednik/22	

Season Crown
Autographs Gold

	NM/M
Common Player:	20.00

Stated Production 99 Sets
All 99 cards not released for
some players.

20	Magglio Ordonez/13	
21	Roy Oswalt/99	20.00
40	Mark Teixeira/25	
50	Brad Radke/89	20.00
51	Barry Larkin/99	25.00
62	Trot Nixon/37	25.00
70	Rich Harden/41	20.00
80	Jack Wilson/99	20.00
88	Jimmy Rollins/45	25.00
121	Eric Chavez/69	20.00
125	Craig Wilson/99	20.00
157	Michael Young/99	20.00
200	Scott Podsednik/99	20.00
201	Casey Kotchman/21	

Season Crown
Autographs Platinum

	NM/M
Common Player:	25.00

Stated Production 50 Sets
All 50 cards not released for
some players.

Masterpiece:		No Pricing

Production One Set

20	Magglio Ordonez/50	25.00
25	Garret Anderson/50	25.00
31	Roy Oswalt/50	25.00
40	Mark Teixeira/50	30.00
50	Brad Radke/50	25.00
51	Barry Larkin/50	30.00
62	Trot Nixon/50	25.00
70	Rich Harden/50	25.00
80	Jack Wilson/50	25.00
87	David Eckstein/45	25.00
88	Jimmy Rollins/50	25.00
96	Billy Wagner/50	30.00
116	Zack Greinke/49	25.00
121	Eric Chavez/50	25.00
125	Craig Wilson/50	25.00
157	Michael Young/50	25.00
161	Luis Gonzalez/50	25.00
185	Mike Mussina/50	30.00
195	Barry Zito/50	25.00
199	Jason Schmidt/50	25.00
200	Scott Podsednik/50	25.00
201	Casey Kotchman/50	25.00

Strikeout Kings

	NM/M
Common Player:	2.50

Inserted 1:24

Ultra Kings Gold:	2-4X

Production 50 Sets

1	Pedro J. Martinez	3.50
2	Randy Johnson	3.50
3	Mark Mulder	2.50
4	Barry Zito	2.50
5	Roger Clemens	6.00
6	Mark Prior	5.00

7	Ben Sheets	2.50
8	Curt Schilling	2.50
9	Billy Wagner	2.50
10	Eric Gagne	2.50
11	Josh Beckett	3.00
12	Kerry Wood	3.00
13	Jason Schmidt	2.50
14	Roy Halladay	2.50
15	Greg Maddux	4.00

Ultra Kings
Game-Used Gold

	NM/M
Common Player:	8.00

Production 150 Sets
Ultra Swatch

Numbered 51-75:	.75-1.5X
Numbered 26-50:	1-2X
Numbered 25 or less:	No Pricing

Production to player's jersey
number.

Platinum:	No Pricing

Production 25 Sets

1	Pedro J. Martinez	12.00
2	Randy Johnson	12.00
3	Mark Mulder	8.00
4	Barry Zito	8.00
5	Roger Clemens	25.00
6	Mark Prior	20.00
7	Ben Sheets	8.00
8	Curt Schilling	8.00
9	Billy Wagner	8.00
10	Eric Gagne	8.00
11	Josh Beckett	10.00
12	Kerry Wood	10.00
13	Jason Schmidt	8.00
14	Roy Halladay	8.00
15	Greg Maddux	15.00
16	Sean Casey	8.00
17	Ivan Rodriguez	8.00
18	Mike Piazza	15.00
19	Todd Helton	15.00
20	Scott Rolen	12.00
21	Hideki Matsui	30.00
22	Gary Sheffield	8.00
23	Alfonso Soriano	12.00
24	Bobby Abreu	8.00
25	Lance Berkman	8.00
26	Miguel Tejada	8.00
27	Travis Hafner	8.00
28	Hank Blalock	8.00
29	Jeff Bagwell	10.00
30	Chipper Jones	15.00
31	Jim Thome	12.00
32	David Ortiz	8.00
33	Adam Dunn	8.00
34	Albert Pujols	25.00
35	Manny Ramirez	10.00
36	Vladimir Guerrero	12.00
37	Miguel Tejada	8.00
38	Rafael Palmeiro	10.00
39	Mark Teixeira	8.00
40	Sammy Sosa	20.00
41	Frank Thomas	10.00
42	Pat Burrell	8.00
43	Adrian Beltre	8.00
44	Miguel Cabrera	10.00
45	Gary Sheffield	8.00

Ultra 3 Kings Triple
Swatch

	NM/M
Common Card:	40.00

Production 33 Sets

1	Greg Maddux, Mark Prior, Kerry Wood	75.00
2	Mark Teixeira, Hank Blalock, Alfonso Soriano	40.00
3	Jeff Bagwell, Roger Clemens, Lance Berkman	60.00
4	Jim Thome, Pat Burrell, Billy Wagner	40.00
5	Gary Sheffield, Hideki Matsui, Mike Piazza	75.00
6	Scott Rolen, Chipper Jones, Adrian Beltre	40.00

7	Albert Pujols, Adam Dunn, Miguel Cabrera	50.00
8	Curt Schilling, Pedro J. Martinez, Manny Ramirez	60.00
9	Randy Johnson, Greg Maddux, Pedro J. Martinez	50.00
10	Josh Beckett, Miguel Cabrera, Ivan Rodriguez	40.00

2006 Ultra

	NM/M
Complete Set (251):	60.00
Common Player:	.15
Common SP (201-250):	.50

Inserted 1:4

Pack (8):	3.00
Box (24):	65.00

1	Vladimir Guerrero	.75
2	Bartolo Colon	.15
3	Francisco Rodriguez	.15
4	Darin Erstad	.15
5	Chone Figgins	.15
6	Bengie Molina	.15
7	Roger Clemens	2.00
8	Lance Berkman	.25
9	Morgan Ensberg	.15
10	Roy Oswalt	.25
11	Andy Pettitte	.25
12	Craig Biggio	.25
13	Eric Chavez	.25
14	Barry Zito	.25
15	Huston Street	.15
16	Bobby Crosby	.15
17	Nick Swisher	.25
18	Rich Harden	.15
19	Vernon Wells	.25
20	Roy Halladay	.25
21	Alex Rios	.15
22	Orlando Hudson	.15
23	Shea Hillenbrand	.15
24	Gustavo Chacin	.15
25	Chipper Jones	.75
26	Andruw Jones	.50
27	Jeff Francoeur	.15
28	John Smoltz	.25
29	Tim Hudson	.25
30	Marcus Giles	.15
31	Carlos Lee	.25
32	Ben Sheets	.25
33	Rickie Weeks	.25
34	Chris Capuano	.15
35	Geoff Jenkins	.15
36	Brady Clark	.15
37	Albert Pujols	2.00
38	Jim Edmonds	.25
39	Chris Carpenter	.25
40	Mark Mulder	.25
41	Yadier Molina	.15
42	Scott Rolen	.75
43	Derrek Lee	.50
44	Mark Prior	.50
45	Aramis Ramirez	.25
46	Carlos Zambrano	.25
47	Greg Maddux	1.50
48	Nomar Garciaparra	.75
49	Jonny Gomes	.25
50	Carl Crawford	.25
51	Scott Kazmir	.25
52	Jorge Cantu	.15
53	Julio Lugo	.15
54	Aubrey Huff	.15
55	Luis Gonzalez	.25
56	Brandon Webb	.25
57	Troy Glaus	.25
58	Shawn Green	.15
59	Craig Counsell	.15
60	Conor Jackson (RC)	.15
61	Jeff Kent	.25
62	Eric Gagne	.15

63	J.D. Drew	.25
64	Milton Bradley	.15
65	Jeff Weaver	.15
66	Cesar Izturis	.15
67	Jason Schmidt	.25
68	Moises Alou	.25
69	Pedro Feliz	.15
70	Randy Winn	.15
71	Omar Vizquel	.15
72	Noah Lowry	.15
73	Travis Hafner	.40
74	Victor Martinez	.25
75	C.C. Sabathia	.15
76	Grady Sizemore	.40
77	Coco Crisp	.15
78	Cliff Lee	.15
79	Raul Ibanez	.15
80	Ichiro Suzuki	1.00
81	Richie Sexson	.25
82	Felix Hernandez	.25
83	Adrian Beltre	.15
84	Jamie Moyer	.15
85	Miguel Cabrera	.75
86	A.J. Burnett	.15
87	Juan Pierre	.15
88	Carlos Delgado	.50
89	Dontrelle Willis	.25
90	Juan Encarnacion	.15
91	Carlos Beltran	.50
92	Jose Reyes	.50
93	David Wright	.75
94	Tom Glavine	.25
95	Mike Piazza	.75
96	Pedro Martinez	.75
97	Ryan Zimmerman (RC)	.15
98	Nick Johnson	.15
99	Jose Vidro	.15
100	Jose Guillen	.15
101	Livan Hernandez	.15
102	John Patterson	.15
103	Miguel Tejada	.25
104	Melvin Mora	.15
105	Brian Roberts	.15
106	Erik Bedard	.15
107	Javy Lopez	.15
108	Rodrigo Lopez	.15
109	Jake Peavy	.25
110	Mike Cameron	.15
111	Mark Loretta	.15
112	Brian Giles	.25
113	Trevor Hoffman	.15
114	Ramon Hernandez	.15
115	Bobby Abreu	.25
116	Chase Utley	.40
117	Pat Burrell	.25
118	Jimmy Rollins	.40
119	Ryan Howard	.75
120	Billy Wagner	.15
121	Jason Bay	.40
122	Oliver Perez	.15
123	Jack Wilson	.15
124	Zachary Duke	.15
125	Robert Mackowiak	.15
126	Freddy Sanchez	.15
127	Mark Teixeira	.50
128	Michael Young	.25
129	Alfonso Soriano	.50
130	Hank Blalock	.25
131	Kenny Rogers	.15
132	Kevin Mench	.15
133	Manny Ramirez	.75
134	Josh Beckett	.25
135	David Ortiz	.75
136	Johnny Damon	.75
137	Edgar Renteria	.25
138	Curt Schilling	.75
139	Ken Griffey Jr.	1.50
140	Adam Dunn	.50
141	Felipe Lopez	.15
142	Wily Mo Pena	.15
143	Aaron Harang	.15
144	Sean Casey	.15
145	Todd Helton	.50
146	Garrett Atkins	.15
147	Matt Holliday	.25
148	Jeff Francis	.15
149	Clint Barmes	.15
150	Luis Gonzalez	.15
151	Mike Sweeney	.15
152	Zack Greinke	.15
153	Angel Berroa	.15
154	Emil Brown	.15
155	David DeJesus	.15
156	Ivan Rodriguez	.50
157	Jeremy Bonderman	.15
158	Brandon Inge	.15
159	Craig Monroe	.15
160	Chris Shelton	.15
161	Dmitri Young	.15
162	Johan Santana	.50
163	Joe Mauer	.50
164	Torii Hunter	.25
165	Shannon Stewart	.15
166	Scott Baker	.15

167	Brad Radke	.15
168	Jon Garland	.15
169	Tadahito Iguchi	.15
170	Paul Konerko	.25
171	Scott Podsednik	.15
172	Mark Buehrle	.25
173	Joe Crede	.15
174	Derek Jeter	2.00
175	Alex Rodriguez	1.50
176	Hideki Matsui	1.00
177	Randy Johnson	.75
178	Gary Sheffield	.40
179	Mariano Rivera	.40
180	Jason Giambi	.40
181	Joey Devine RC	.50
182	Alejandro Freire RC	.75
183	Craig Hansen RC	2.00
184	Robert Andino RC	.50
185	Ryan Jorgensen RC	.50
186	Chris Demaria RC	.50
187	Jonah Bayliss RC	.50
188	Ryan Theriot (RC)	.25
189	Steve Stemle RC	.50
190	Brian Myrow RC	.50
191	Chris Heintz RC	.50
192	Ron Flores RC	.50
193	Danny Sandoval RC	.50
194	Craig Breslow RC	1.00
195	Jeremy Accardo RC	.50
196	Jeff Harris RC	.50
197	Tim Corcoran RC	.50
198	Scott Feldman RC	1.00
199	Robinson Cano	.50
200	Jason Bergmann RC	3.00
201	Ken Griffey Jr.	4.00
202	Frank Thomas	1.00
203	Chipper Jones	2.00
204	Tony Clark	.50
205	Mike Lieberthal	.50
206	Manny Ramirez	2.00
207	Phil Nevin	.50
208	Derek Jeter	6.00
209	Preston Wilson	.50
210	Billy Wagner	.50
211	Alex Rodriguez	6.00
212	Trot Nixon	1.00
213	Jaret Wright	.50
214	Nomar Garciaparra	2.00
215	Paul Konerko	1.00
216	Paul Wilson	.50
217	Dustin Hermanson	.50
218	Todd Walker	.50
219	Matt Morris	.50
220	Darin Erstad	.50
221	Todd Helton	1.50
222	Geoff Jenkins	.50
223	Eric Chavez	1.00
224	Kris Benson	.50
225	Jon Garland	.50
226	Troy Glaus	1.00
227	Vernon Wells	1.00
228	Michael Cuddyer	.50
229	Justin Verlander (RC)	2.00
230	Pat Burrell	2.00
231	Mark Mulder	1.00
232	Corey Patterson	1.00
233	J.D. Drew	1.00
234	Austin Kearns	1.00
235	Felipe Lopez	.50
236	Sean Burroughs	.50
237	Ben Sheets	1.00
238	Brett Myers	.50
239	Josh Beckett	1.00
240	Barry Zito	1.00
241	Adrian Gonzalez	.50
242	Rocco Baldelli	.50
243	Chris Burke	.50
244	Joe Mauer	2.00
245	Mark Prior	1.00
246	Mark Teixeira	2.00
247	Khalil Greene	.50
248	Zack Greinke	.50
249	Prince Fielder (RC)	6.00
250	Rickie Weeks	1.00
251	Kenji Johjima RC	20.00

Gold

Gold (1-200):	2-3X
Inserted 1:1	
Gold (201-251):	2-3X
Inserted 1:13	

AUTOGRAPHics

No Pricing

Diamond Producers

		NM/M
Complete Set (25):		15.00
Common Player:		.50
DP1	Derek Jeter	3.00
DP2	Chipper Jones	1.00
DP3	Jim Edmonds	.75
DP4	Ken Griffey Jr.	2.00
DP5	David Ortiz	1.00

DP6	Manny Ramirez	1.00
DP7	Mark Teixeira	.75
DP8	Alex Rodriguez	3.00
DP9	Jeff Kent	.50
DP10	Albert Pujols	3.00
DP11	Todd Helton	.75
DP12	Miguel Cabrera	1.00
DP13	Hideki Matsui	.75
DP14	Derek Lee	.75
DP15	Vladimir Guerrero	1.00
DP16	Miguel Tejada	.75
DP17	Jorge Cantu	.75
DP18	Travis Hafner	.75
DP19	Pat Burrell	.50
DP20	Bobby Abreu	.75
DP21	David Wright	2.00
DP22	Jason Bay	.75
DP23	Adam Dunn	.75
DP24	Eric Chavez	.50
DP25	Paul Konerko	.50

Feel the Game

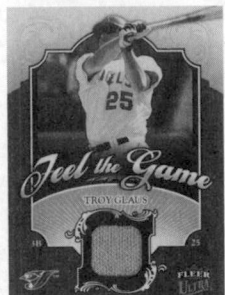

		NM/M
Common Player:		4.00
BA	Bobby Abreu	6.00
JB	Josh Beckett	6.00
CB	Carlos Beltran	8.00
AB	Adrian Beltre	6.00
EC	Eric Chavez	4.00
MC	Matt Clement/SP	8.00
CD	Carlos Delgado	6.00
BG	Brian Giles	4.00
TG	Troy Glaus	4.00
SG	Shawn Green	4.00
KG	Ken Griffey Jr.	20.00
VG	Vladimir Guerrero	8.00
FH	Felix Hernandez	8.00
DJ	Derek Jeter	20.00
RJ	Randy Johnson/SP	10.00
AJ	Andruw Jones	8.00
CJ	Chipper Jones	8.00
GM	Greg Maddux	10.00
MO	Magglio Ordonez	4.00
MP	Mike Piazza	10.00
AP	Albert Pujols	20.00
MR	Manny Ramirez	10.00
JR	Jose Reyes/SP	8.00
IR	Ivan Rodriguez	6.00
RS	Richie Sexson	6.00
AS	Alfonso Soriano	8.00
MT	Miguel Tejada	8.00
FT	Frank Thomas/SP	8.00
PW	Preston Wilson	4.00
DW	David Wright	15.00

Fine Fabrics

		NM/M
BA	Bobby Abreu	6.00
JB	Josh Beckett	6.00
CB	Carlos Beltran	8.00
AB	Adrian Beltre	6.00

HB	Hank Blalock	6.00
SB	Sean Burroughs	4.00
EC	Eric Chavez	4.00
RC	Roger Clemens/SP	15.00
MC	Matt Clement	4.00
BC	Bobby Crosby	4.00
CD	Carlos Delgado	6.00
JD	J.D. Drew	4.00
AD	Adam Dunn	8.00
SF	Steve Finley	4.00
JG	Jason Giambi	10.00
BG	Brian Giles	4.00
TG	Troy Glaus	6.00
SG	Shawn Green	4.00
KH	Khalil Greene/SP	8.00
KG	Ken Griffey Jr.	20.00
VG	Vladimir Guerrero	8.00
TH	Travis Hafner	8.00
FH	Felix Hernandez	8.00
RH	Ramon Hernandez	4.00
RY	Ryan Howard	15.00
DJ	Derek Jeter	20.00
RJ	Randy Johnson/SP	10.00
AJ	Andruw Jones	8.00
CJ	Chipper Jones	8.00
JK	Jeff Kent	4.00
RK	Ryan Klesko	4.00
DL	Derrek Lee	8.00
GM	Greg Maddux	10.00
MO	Magglio Ordonez	4.00
DO	David Ortiz	8.00
CP	Corey Patterson	4.00
MP	Mike Piazza	10.00
JP	Jorge Posada	8.00
AP	Albert Pujols	20.00
MR	Manny Ramirez	10.00
JR	Jose Reyes	8.00
BR	Brian Roberts	6.00
IR	Ivan Rodriguez	6.00
SR	Scott Rolen	10.00
RS	Richie Sexson	6.00
JS	John Smoltz	8.00
AS	Alfonso Soriano	8.00
SS	Sammy Sosa	10.00
HS	Huston Street	4.00
TX	Mark Teixeira	8.00
MT	Miguel Tejada	8.00
FT	Frank Thomas	8.00
CU	Chase Utley	15.00
VW	Vernon Wells	6.00
BW	Bernie Williams	6.00
WI	Dontrelle Willis	6.00
PW	Preston Wilson	4.00
KW	Kerry Wood	6.00
DW	David Wright	15.00
BZ	Barry Zito	6.00

Home Run Kings

		NM/M
Complete Set (15):		10.00
Common Player:		.50
HRK1	Albert Pujols	3.00
HRK2	Ken Griffey Jr.	2.00
HRK3	Andruw Jones	1.00
HRK4	Alex Rodriguez	3.00
HRK5	David Ortiz	1.00
HRK6	Manny Ramirez	1.00
HRK7	Derrek Lee	.75
HRK8	Mark Teixeira	.75
HRK9	Adam Dunn	.75
HRK10	Paul Konerko	.50
HRK11	Richie Sexson	.50
HRK12	Alfonso Soriano	.75
HRK13	Vladimir Guerrero	1.00
HRK14	Gary Sheffield	.75
HRK15	Mike Piazza	1.00

Midsummer Classic Kings

	NM/M
Complete Set (10):	10.00

Common Player (right column header)

Common Player:		.50
MCK1	Ken Griffey Jr.	2.00
MCK2	Mike Piazza	1.00
MCK3	Derek Jeter	3.00
MCK4	Roger Clemens	3.00
MCK5	Randy Johnson	1.00
MCK6	Miguel Tejada	.75
MCK7	Alfonso Soriano	.75
MCK8	Garret Anderson	.50
MCK9	Pedro Martinez	1.00
MCK10	Ivan Rodriguez	.75

Rising Stars

		NM/M
Complete Set (10):		10.00
Common Player:		.50
URS1	Ryan Howard	3.00
URS2	Huston Street	.50
URS3	Jeff Francoeur	.75
URS4	Felix Hernandez	1.50
URS5	Chase Utley	2.00
URS6	Robinson Cano	1.00
URS7	Zachary Duke	.75
URS8	Scott Kazmir	1.00
URS9	Willy Taveras	.50
URS10	Tadahito Iguchi	1.00

RBI Kings

		NM/M
Complete Set (20):		15.00
Common Player:		.50
RBI1	Ken Griffey Jr.	2.00
RBI2	David Ortiz	1.00
RBI3	Manny Ramirez	1.00
RBI4	Mark Teixeira	.75
RBI5	Alex Rodriguez	3.00
RBI6	Andruw Jones	1.00
RBI7	Jeff Bagwell	.75
RBI8	Gary Sheffield	.75
RBI9	Richie Sexson	.50
RBI10	Jeff Kent	.50
RBI11	Albert Pujols	3.00
RBI12	Todd Helton	.75
RBI13	Miguel Cabrera	1.00
RBI14	Hideki Matsui	2.00
RBI15	Carlos Delgado	.75
RBI16	Carlos Lee	.50
RBI17	Derrek Lee	.75
RBI18	Vladimir Guerrero	1.00
RBI19	Luis Gonzalez	.50
RBI20	Mike Piazza	1.00

Strikeout Kings

		NM/M
Complete Set (10):		8.00
Common Player:		.50
SOK1	Roger Clemens	3.00
SOK2	Johan Santana	1.00
SOK3	Jake Peavy	.50

SOK4	Randy Johnson	1.00
SOK5	Curt Schilling	1.00
SOK6	Chris Carpenter	.75
SOK7	Pedro Martinez	1.00
SOK8	Mark Prior	.75
SOK9	Carlos Zambrano	.50
SOK10	John Smoltz	.50

2007 Ultra

Verlander

		NM/M
Complete Set (250):		
Common Player (1-200):		.15
Common RC (201-250):		1.00
Hobby SE Pack (15):		12.00
Hobby SE Box (5):		55.00
1	Brandon Webb	.25
2	Randy Johnson	.75
3	Conor Jackson	.15
4	Stephen Drew	.25
5	Eric Byrnes	.25
6	Carlos Quentin	.15
7	Andruw Jones	.50
8	Chipper Jones	.75
9	Jeff Francoeur	.50
10	Tim Hudson	.25
11	John Smoltz	.50
12	Ed Renteria	.25
13	Erik Bedard	.25
14	Kris Benson	.15
15	Miguel Tejada	.50
16	Nicholas Markakis	.25
17	Brian Roberts	.25
18	Melvin Mora	.15
19	Aubrey Huff	.15
20	Curt Schilling	.75
21	Jonathan Papelbon	1.00
22	Josh Beckett	.50
23	Jason Varitek	.25
24	David Ortiz	1.00
25	Manny Ramirez	.75
26	J.D. Drew	.25
27	Carlos Zambrano	.25
28	Derrek Lee	.50
29	Aramis Ramirez	.50
30	Alfonso Soriano	.75
31	Rich Hill	.15
32	Jacque Jones	.15
33	A.J. Pierzynski	.15
34	Jermaine Dye	.25
35	Paul Konerko	.25
36	Bobby Jenks	.15
37	Jon Garland	.15
38	Mark Buehrle	.25
39	Tadahito Iguchi	.15
40	Adam Dunn	.50
41	Ken Griffey Jr.	1.50
42	Aaron Harang	.15
43	Bronson Arroyo	.15
44	Ryan Freel	.15
45	Brandon Phillips	.25
46	Grady Sizemore	1.00
47	Travis Hafner	.25
48	Victor Martinez	.25
49	Jhonny Peralta	.25
50	C.C. Sabathia	.25
51	Jeremy Sowers	.15
52	Ryan Garko	.15
53	Garrett Atkins	.25
54	Willy Taveras	.15
55	Todd Helton	.50
56	Jeff Francis	.15
57	Brad Hawpe	.15
58	Matt Holliday	.50
59	Justin Verlander	.75
60	Jeremy Bonderman	.50
61	Magglio Ordonez	.50
62	Ivan Rodriguez	.50
63	Gary Sheffield	.50
64	Kenny Rogers	.15
65	Brandon Inge	.15
66	Anibal Sanchez	.15
67	Scott Olsen	.15
68	Dontrelle Willis	.25
69	Dan Uggla	.15
70	Hanley Ramirez	1.00
71	Miguel Cabrera	1.00
72	Jeremy Hermida	.15
73	Roy Oswalt	.50
74	Brad Lidge	.15
75	Lance Berkman	.50
76	Carlos Lee	.50
77	Morgan Ensberg	.15
78	Craig Biggio	.50
79	Reggie Sanders	.15
80	Mike Sweeney	.15
81	Mark Teahen	.15
82	John Buck	.15
83	Mark Grudzielanek	.15
84	Gary Matthews	.25
85	Vladimir Guerrero	1.00
86	Garret Anderson	.25
87	Howie Kendrick	.25
88	Jered Weaver	.50
89	Chone Figgins	.25
90	Bartolo Colon	.15
91	Francisco Rodriguez	.25
92	Nomar Garciaparra	.75
93	Andre Ethier	.15
94	Rafael Furcal	.25
95	Jeff Kent	.50
96	Derek Lowe	.25
97	Jason Schmidt	.25
98	Takashi Saito	.15
99	Ben Sheets	.25
100	Prince Fielder	1.00
101	Bill Hall	.25
102	Rickie Weeks	.25
103	Francisco Cordero	.15
104	J.J. Hardy	.25
105	Johan Santana	.75
106	Justin Morneau	.50
107	Joe Mauer	.25
108	Joe Nathan	.15
109	Torii Hunter	.25
110	Michael Cuddyer	.15
111	Boof Bonser	.15
112	Tom Glavine	.50
113	Pedro Martinez	.75
114	Billy Wagner	.15
115	Jose Reyes	1.00
116	David Wright	1.00
117	Carlos Delgado	.50
118	Carlos Beltran	.50
119	Alex Rodriguez	2.00
120	Chien-Ming Wang	1.00
121	Mariano Rivera	.50
122	Bobby Abreu	.50
123	Hideki Matsui	1.50
124	Johnny Damon	.75
125	Robinson Cano	.75
126	Derek Jeter	2.00
127	Nick Swisher	.25
128	Eric Chavez	.15
129	Jason Kendall	.15
130	Bobby Crosby	.15
131	Huston Street	.15
132	Danny Haren	.15
133	Rich Harden	.15
134	Mike Piazza	.75
135	Chase Utley	1.00
136	Jimmy Rollins	.75
137	Aaron Rowand	.25
138	Jamie Moyer	.15
139	Cole Hamels	.50
140	Pat Burrell	.25
141	Ryan Howard	1.50
142	Freddy Sanchez	.25
143	Zachary Duke	.15
144	Ian Snell	.15
145	Jack Wilson	.15
146	Jason Bay	.25
147	Albert Pujols	2.00
148	Scott Rolen	.50
149	Jim Edmonds	.25
150	Chris Carpenter	.50
151	Yadier Molina	.15
152	Adam Wainwright	.25
153	David Eckstein	.15
154	Trevor Hoffman	.15
155	Brian Giles	.15
156	Adrian Gonzalez	.25
157	Jake Peavy	.50
158	Khalil Greene	.25
159	Chris Young	.25
160	Greg Maddux	1.00
161	Mike Cameron	.15
162	Matt Cain	.15
163	Matt Morris	.15
164	Pedro Feliz	.15
165	Omar Vizquel	.15
166	Randy Winn	.15
167	Barry Zito	.25
168	Adrian Beltre	.15
169	Yuniesky Betancourt	.15
170	Richie Sexson	.25
171	Raul Ibanez	.15
172	Kenji Johjima	.25
173	Ichiro Suzuki	1.50
174	Felix Hernandez	.50
175	Scott Kazmir	.25
176	Carl Crawford	.25
177	B.J. Upton	.25
178	James Shields	.15
179	Rocco Baldelli	.15
180	Jorge Cantu	.15
181	Ty Wigginton	.15
182	Mark Teixeira	.50
183	Hank Blalock	.25
184	Ian Kinsler	.25
185	Michael Young	.25
186	Vicente Padilla	.15
187	Akinori Otsuka	.15
188	Kenny Lofton	.15
189	A.J. Burnett	.15
190	Roy Halladay	.25
191	B.J. Ryan	.15
192	Vernon Wells	.25
193	Alex Rios	.50
194	Troy Glaus	.25
195	Frank Thomas	.75
196	Ryan Zimmerman	.50
197	Michael O'Connor	.15
198	Chad Cordero	.15
199	Nick Johnson	.15
200	Felipe Lopez	.15
201	Miguel Montero	1.00
202	Doug Slaten RC	1.00
203	Joseph Bisenius RC	1.00
204	Jared Burton RC	1.00
205	Kevin Cameron RC	1.00
206	Matt Chico (RC)	1.00
207	Chris Stewart RC	1.00
208	Joe Smith RC	2.00
209	Zack Segovia (RC)	1.00
210	John Danks RC	2.00
211	Lee Gardner (RC)	1.00
212	Jeff Baker (RC)	2.00
213	Jamie Burke (RC)	1.00
214	Phil Hughes (RC)	4.00
215	Mike Rabelo RC	1.00
216	Jose Garcia RC	1.00
217	Hector Gimenez (RC)	1.00
218	Jesus Flores RC	1.00
219	Brandon Morrow RC	3.00
220	Hideki Okajima RC	3.00
221	Jay Marshall RC	1.00
222	Matt Lindstrom (RC)	1.00
223	Juan Salas (RC)	1.00
224	Juan Perez RC	1.00
225	Sean Henn (RC)	1.00
226	Travis Buck (RC)	1.00
227	Gustavo Molina RC	1.00
228	Hunter Pence (RC)	6.00
229	Michael Bourn (RC)	1.00
230	Brian Barden RC	1.00
231	Donald Kelly (RC)	1.00
232	Joakim Soria RC	3.00
233	Cesar Jimenez RC	1.00
234	Levale Speigner RC	2.00
235	Micah Owings (RC)	1.00
236	Brian Stokes (RC)	1.00
237	Joaquin Arias (RC)	1.00
238	Josh Hamilton (RC)	2.00
239	Daisuke Matsuzaka RC	5.00
240	Alejandro De Aza RC	1.00
241	Kory Casto (RC)	1.00
242	Troy Tulowitzki (RC)	4.00
243	Akinori Iwamura RC	2.00
244	Angel Sanchez RC	1.00
245	Ryan Braun (RC)	8.00
246	Alex Gordon RC	5.00
247	Elijah Dukes RC	1.00
248	Kei Igawa RC	1.00
249	Kevin Kouzmanoff (RC)	1.00
250	Delmon Young (RC)	1.00

Gold

Gold (1-200):	2-3X
Gold RC (201-250):	1X
Inserted 1:10 Hobby	

Retail

Retail (1-200):	.5X
Retail RC (201-250):	.5X

Printing Plates

Production one set per color.

Autographics

		NM/M
Common Auto.:		
AG	Alex Gordon/499	40.00
AH	Aaron Harang/499	15.00
BA	Bronson Arroyo/49	
BM	Brandon McCarthy/499	
CC	Chad Cordero/499	
CH	Clay Hensley/499	10.00
CI	Cesar Izturis/499	
JA	Jason Bay/499	15.00
JB	Joe Blanton/499	10.00
JE	Johnny Estrada/132	10.00
JS	Johan Santana/173	30.00
KG	Khalil Greene/499	15.00
KI	Kei Igawa/199	25.00

Dual Materials

		NM/M
Common Player:		5.00
Production 160 unless noted.		
Gold:		1-1.5x
Production 20-75		
Patch:		No Pricing
Production 25 Sets		
AB	A.J. Burnett	5.00
AE	Andre Ethier	5.00
AJ	Andruw Jones	8.00
AK	Austin Kearns	5.00
AL	Adam LaRoche	5.00
AN	Garret Anderson	5.00
AP	Albert Pujols	20.00
AS	Anibal Sanchez	5.00
BA	Bobby Abreu	5.00
BC	Bobby Crosby	5.00
BE	Adrian Beltre	5.00
BG	Brian Giles	5.00
BI	Craig Biggio	8.00
BJ	Bobby Jenks	5.00
BL	Brad Lidge	5.00
BM	Brandon McCarthy	5.00
BR	Brian Roberts	8.00
BS	Ben Sheets	5.00
BW	Brandon Webb	5.00
CA	Carlos Beltran	10.00
CB	Chris Burke	5.00
CC	Carl Crawford	5.00
CF	Chone Figgins	5.00
CH	Chris Carpenter	8.00
CJ	Conor Jackson	5.00
CK	Casey Kotchman	5.00
CL	Carlos Lee	5.00
CP	Corey Patterson	5.00
CR	Coco Crisp	5.00
CS	C.C. Sabathia	8.00
CU	Curt Schilling	8.00
DJ	Derek Jeter	20.00
DL	Derek Lowe	5.00
DO	David Ortiz	10.00
DR	J.D. Drew	5.00
DU	Dan Uggla	5.00
DW	David Wells	5.00
ED	Jim Edmonds	5.00
ES	Ervin Santana	5.00
FG	Freddy Garcia	5.00
FH	Felix Hernandez	10.00
GA	Garrett Atkins	5.00
GJ	Geoff Jenkins	5.00
GM	Greg Maddux	15.00
GS	Gary Sheffield	5.00
HE	Todd Helton	10.00
HO	Trevor Hoffman	8.00
HR	Hanley Ramirez	10.00
HU	Torii Hunter	5.00
IS	Ian Snell	5.00
JB	Jeremy Bonderman	5.00
JC	Chipper Jones	10.00
JD	Jermaine Dye	5.00
JG	Jonny Gomes	5.00
JH	J.J. Hardy	5.00
JJ	Josh Johnson	5.00
JK	Jeff Kent	8.00
JM	Justin Morneau	10.00
JN	Joe Nathan	5.00
JO	Josh Beckett	15.00
JP	Jorge Posada	10.00
JS	James Shields	5.00
JV	Jason Varitek	10.00
JW	Josh Willingham	5.00
KG	Khalil Greene	8.00
KW	Kerry Wood	5.00
LB	Lance Berkman	8.00
LE	Derrek Lee	10.00
LG	Luis Gonzalez	5.00
LM	Lastings Milledge	5.00
LS	Luke Scott	5.00
MC	Matt Cain	8.00
ME	Melky Cabrera	10.00
MH	Matt Holliday	8.00
MI	Mike Mussina	10.00
MM	Melvin Mora	5.00
MO	Magglio Ordonez	8.00
MR	Manny Ramirez	10.00
MS	Mike Sweeney	5.00
MT	Miguel Tejada	5.00
MU	Mark Mulder	5.00
PE	Andy Pettitte	8.00
PF	Prince Fielder	15.00
PJ	Jhonny Peralta	5.00
RH	Rich Harden	8.00
SC	Jason Schmidt	5.00
SI	Grady Sizemore	20.00
SO	Scott Olsen	5.00
TE	Mark Teixeira	10.00
TH	Travis Hafner	8.00

TW	Tim Wakefield	5.00
VG	Vladimir Guerrero	10.00
VM	Victor Martinez	8.00
VW	Vernon Wells	5.00
WI	Dontrelle Willis	5.00
ZD	Zachary Duke	5.00

Faces of the Game

TOM GLAVINE
NEW YORK METS

		NM/M
Common Player:		.50
AB	Adrian Beltre	.50
AJ	Andruw Jones	.75
BS	Ben Sheets	.50
CJ	Chipper Jones	1.00
CS	C.C. Sabathia	.75
CU	Chase Utley	1.00
DJ	Derek Jeter	3.00
FR	Francisco Rodriguez	.50
GM	Greg Maddux	2.00
HO	Trevor Hoffman	.50
JB	Jason Bay	.75
JG	Jason Giambi	.75
KG	Ken Griffey Jr.	2.00
LG	Luis Gonzalez	.50
MC	Miguel Cabrera	1.00
MP	Mike Piazza	1.00
MR	Mariano Rivera	.75
OV	Omar Vizquel	.50
TG	Tom Glavine	.75
TH	Torii Hunter	.50

Faces of the Game Materials

		NM/M
Common Jersey:		5.00
AB	Adrian Beltre	5.00
AJ	Andruw Jones	8.00
BS	Ben Sheets	8.00
CJ	Chipper Jones	8.00
CS	C.C. Sabathia	8.00
CU	Chase Utley	10.00
DJ	Derek Jeter	20.00
FR	Francisco Rodriguez	5.00
GM	Greg Maddux	10.00
HU	Torii Hunter	5.00
JB	Jason Bay	5.00
JG	Jason Giambi	8.00
KG	Ken Griffey Jr.	15.00
LG	Luis Gonzalez	5.00
MC	Miguel Cabrera	8.00
MP	Mike Piazza	8.00
MR	Mariano Rivera	8.00
OV	Omar Vizquel	5.00
TG	Tom Glavine	8.00
TH	Trevor Hoffman	5.00

Feel the Game

		NM/M
Common Player:		.50
AP	Albert Pujols	3.00
BA	Bobby Abreu	.50
BR	Brian Roberts	.50
BW	Brandon Webb	.50
CC	Chris Carpenter	.75
CJ	Chipper Jones	1.00
CR	Carl Crawford	.50
CS	Curt Schilling	1.00
CZ	Carlos Zambrano	.50
DJ	Derek Jeter	3.00
DW	Dontrelle Willis	.50
EC	Eric Chavez	.50
GS	Grady Sizemore	1.00
HR	Hanley Ramirez	1.00
IR	Ivan Rodriguez	.75
JM	Justin Morneau	.75
JP	Jonathan Papelbon	.75
JR	Jose Reyes	2.00
JS	John Smoltz	.75
KG	Ken Griffey Jr.	2.00
KJ	Kenji Johjima	.50
LB	Lance Berkman	.50

LG	Luis Gonzalez	.50
MC	Miguel Cabrera	1.00
RC	Robinson Cano	1.00
RJ	Randy Johnson	1.00
SA	Johan Santana	1.00
SC	Jason Schmidt	.50
VG	Vladimir Guerrero	1.00

Feel the Game Materials

Bobby Abreu
Outfield

FEELTHEGAME

YANKEES

		NM/M
Common Jersey:		5.00
AP	Albert Pujols	20.00
BA	Bobby Abreu	5.00
BR	Brian Roberts	5.00
BW	Brandon Webb	5.00
CC	Chris Carpenter	8.00
CJ	Chipper Jones	8.00
CR	Carl Crawford	5.00
CS	Curt Schilling	8.00
CU	Chase Utley	10.00
CZ	Carlos Zambrano	8.00
DJ	Derek Jeter	20.00
DW	Dontrelle Willis	5.00
EC	Eric Chavez	5.00
GS	Grady Sizemore	10.00
HR	Hanley Ramirez	8.00
IR	Ivan Rodriguez	8.00
JM	Justin Morneau	8.00
JP	Jonathan Papelbon	10.00
JR	Jose Reyes	10.00
JS	John Smoltz	8.00
KJ	Ken Griffey Jr.	15.00
KJ	Kenji Johjima	8.00
LB	Lance Berkman	5.00
LG	Luis Gonzalez	5.00
MC	Miguel Cabrera	8.00
RC	Robinson Cano	10.00
RJ	Randy Johnson	8.00
SA	Johan Santana	8.00
SC	Jason Schmidt	5.00
VG	Vladimir Guerrero	8.00

Hitting Machines

		NM/M
Common Player:		.50
AR	Aramis Ramirez	.75
AS	Alfonso Soriano	1.00
BI	Craig Biggio	.50
CB	Carlos Beltran	1.00
DO	David Ortiz	1.00
FS	Freddy Sanchez	.50
FT	Frank Thomas	1.00
JK	Jeff Kent	.50
JM	Joe Mauer	.75
JT	Jim Thome	.75
MT	Mark Teixeira	1.00
NS	Nick Swisher	.50
TE	Miguel Tejada	.75
TG	Troy Glaus	.75
TH	Todd Helton	.75

Hitting Machines Materials

		NM/M
Common Jersey:		5.00
AR	Aramis Ramirez	8.00
AS	Alfonso Soriano	8.00
BI	Craig Biggio	8.00
CB	Carlos Beltran	8.00
DO	David Ortiz	8.00
FS	Freddy Sanchez	5.00
FT	Frank Thomas	10.00
JK	Jeff Kent	5.00
JM	Joe Mauer	8.00
JT	Jim Thome	8.00
MT	Mark Teixeira	8.00
NS	Nick Swisher	5.00
TE	Miguel Tejada	5.00
TG	Troy Glaus	5.00
TH	Todd Helton	8.00

Iron Man

Cal Ripken Jr. - Orioles

	NM/M
Common Ripken (1-50):	3.00
Autograph:	No Pricing
Production 10 Sets	

Lucky 13 Rookies Autograph

		NM/M
Quantity produced listed		10.00
Parallel:		1-1.5x
Production 99 or 199		
238	Josh Hamilton/499	30.00
241	Kory Casto/499	10.00
242	Troy Tulowitzki/499	40.00
245	Ryan Braun/499	100.00
246	Alex Gordon/499	40.00
248	Kei Igawa/299	40.00
249	Kevin Kouzmanoff/	
	499	15.00

Lucky 13 Rookies Auto-Retail

		NM/M
Common Autograph:		10.00
238	Josh Hamilton	30.00
241	Kory Casto	10.00
242	Troy Tulowitzki	40.00
243	Akinori Iwamura	
246	Alex Gordon/SP	30.00
248	Kei Igawa/SP	40.00
249	Kevin Kouzmanoff	15.00
250	Delmon Young	

Rookies Autograph

		NM/M
Production 299 unless noted.		
Parallel:		1x
Production 99-349		
201	Miguel Montero	10.00
202	Doug Slaten	10.00
203	Joseph Bisenius	10.00
204	Jared Burton	10.00
205	Kevin Cameron	10.00
206	Matt Chico	10.00
207	Chris Stewart	10.00
209	Zack Segovia	15.00
210	John Danks	15.00
213	Jamie Burke	15.00
215	Mike Rabelo	15.00
217	Hector Gimenez	10.00
219	Brandon Morrow	25.00
221	Jay Marshall	10.00
223	Juan Salas 23	
225	Sean Henn	10.00
226	Travis Buck	10.00
227	Gustavo Molina	10.00
229	Michael Bourn	15.00
232	Joakim Soria	25.00
233	Cesar Jimenez 38	
234	Levale Speigner	10.00
236	Brian Stokes	10.00
237	Joaquin Arias	10.00

Rookies Auto-Retail

		NM/M
Common Autograph:		10.00
201	Miguel Montero	10.00
202	Doug Slaten	10.00
204	Jared Burton/SP	10.00
205	Kevin Cameron/SP	10.00
206	Matt Chico	10.00
207	Chris Stewart	10.00
209	Zack Segovia	10.00
212	Jeff Baker	
215	Mike Rabelo	15.00
217	Hector Gimenez	10.00
223	Juan Salas	
225	Sean Henn	10.00
229	Michael Bourn/SP	15.00

234	Levale Speigner	10.00
236	Brian Stokes	10.00
237	Joaquin Arias	10.00

Stike Zone

		NM/M
Common Player:		.50
BZ	Barry Zito	.50
CC	C.C. Sabathia	.75
CZ	Carlos Zambrano	.75
DW	Dontrelle Willis	.50
JS	Johan Santana	1.00
JV	Justin Verlander	1.00
MM	Mike Mussina	.75
PM	Pedro Martinez	1.00
RH	Roy Halladay	.75
RO	Roy Oswalt	.75

Strike Zone Materials

		NM/M
Common Player:		5.00
BZ	Barry Zito	5.00
CC	C.C. Sabathia	5.00
CZ	Carlos Zambrano	8.00
DW	Dontrelle Willis	5.00
JS	Johan Santana	8.00
JV	Justin Verlander	8.00
MM	Mike Mussina	8.00
PM	Pedro Martinez	8.00
RH	Roy Halladay	8.00
RO	Roy Oswalt	8.00

Swing Kings

SWING KINGS

		NM/M
Common Player:		.50
AD	Adam Dunn	.75
AJ	Andruw Jones	1.00
AP	Albert Pujols	3.00
AR	Aramis Ramirez	.75
AS	Alfonso Soriano	1.00
CB	Carlos Beltran	.75
CL	Carlos Lee	.75
DJ	Derek Jeter	3.00
DO	David Ortiz	1.00
FT	Frank Thomas	1.00
GS	Gary Sheffield	.75
HE	Todd Helton	.75
JM	Joe Mauer	.75
JR	Jose Reyes	2.00
JT	Jim Thome	.75
KG	Ken Griffey Jr.	2.00
MC	Miguel Cabrera	1.00
MR	Manny Ramirez	1.00
MT	Miguel Tejada	1.00
NG	Nomar Garciaparra	1.00
PB	Pat Burrell	.75
TE	Mark Teixeira	.75
TH	Travis Hafner	.75
VG	Vladimir Guerrero	1.00
VW	Vernon Wells	.50

Swing Kings Materials

		NM/M
Common Player:		5.00
AD	Adam Dunn	8.00
AJ	Andruw Jones	8.00
AP	Albert Pujols	20.00
AR	Aramis Ramirez	8.00
AS	Alfonso Soriano	8.00
CB	Carlos Beltran	8.00
CL	Carlos Lee	5.00
DJ	Derek Jeter	20.00
DO	David Ortiz	8.00
FT	Frank Thomas	10.00
GS	Gary Sheffield	8.00
HE	Todd Helton	8.00
JM	Joe Mauer	8.00
JR	Jose Reyes	10.00
JT	Jim Thome	8.00
KG	Ken Griffey Jr.	15.00
MC	Miguel Cabrera	8.00
MR	Manny Ramirez	8.00

MT	Miguel Tejada	5.00
NG	Nomar Garciaparra	8.00
PB	Pat Burrell	5.00
TE	Mark Teixeira	8.00
TH	Travis Hafner	5.00
VG	Vladimir Guerrero	8.00
VW	Vernon Wells	5.00

Ultragraphs

		NM/M
	Common Auto.:	8.00
AI	Akinori Iwamura/49	
AK	Austin Kearns/499	10.00
AL	Adam LaRoche/499	8.00
AN	Garret Anderson/499	10.00
BB	Boof Bonser/499	10.00
GA	Garrett Atkins/499	10.00
JJ	Jorge Julio/499	8.00
JN	Joe Nathan/299	10.00
JW	Jered Weaver/499	10.00
MM	Mark Mulder/319	8.00
RW	Rickie Weeks/499	10.00
TH	Travis Hafner/499	10.00
ZG	Zack Greinke/199	8.00

1989 Upper Deck

Dale Murphy

	NM/M
Unopened Fact. Set (800):	80.00
Complete Set (800):	45.00
Complete Low Set (700):	40.00
Complete High Set (100):	5.00
Common Player:	.05
Low Foil Pack (15):	4.00
Low Foil Box (36):	100.00
High Foil Pack (15):	2.00
High Foil Box (36):	60.00

1	Ken Griffey Jr. RC	40.00
2	Luis Medina RC	.05
3	Tony Chance RC	.05
4	Dave Otto RC	.05
5	Sandy Alomar, Jr. RC	1.00
6	Rolando Roomes RC	.05
7	David West RC	.05
8	Cris Carpenter RC	.05
9	Gregg Jefferies	.25
10	Doug Dascenzo RC	.05
11	Ron Jones RC	.05
12	Luis de los Santos RC	.05
13a	Gary Sheffield RC ("SS" upside-down)	8.00
13b	Gary Sheffield RC ("SS" correct)	8.00
14	Mike Harkey RC	.05
15	Lance Blankenship RC	.05
16	William Brennan RC	.05
17	John Smoltz	3.00
18	Ramon Martinez RC	.25
19	Mark Lemke RC	.05
20	Juan Bell RC	.05
21	Rey Palacios RC	.05
22	Felix Jose RC	.05
23	Van Snider RC	.05
24	Dante Bichette RC	.75
25	Randy Johnson RC	15.00
26	Carlos Quintana RC	.05
27	Star Rookie Checklist 1-26	
28	Mike Schooler RC	.05
29	Randy St. Claire	.05
30	Jerald Clark RC	.05
31	Kevin Gross	.05
32	Dan Firova RC	.05
33	Jeff Calhoun	.05
34	Tommy Hinzo	.05
35	Ricky Jordan RC	.05
36	Larry Parrish	.05
37	Bret Saberhagen	.05
38	Mike Smithson	.05
39	Dave Dravecky	.05
40	Ed Romero	.05
41	Jeff Musselman	.05
42	Ed Hearn	.05
43	Rance Mulliniks	.05
44	Jim Eisenreich	.05
45	Sil Campusano RC	.05
46	Mike Krukow	.05
47	Paul Gibson RC	.05
48	Mike LaCoss	.05
49	Larry Herndon	.05
50	Scott Garrelts	.05
51	Dwayne Henry	.05
52	Jim Acker	.05
53	Steve Sax	.05
54	Pete O'Brien	.05
55	Paul Runge	.05
56	Rick Rhoden	.05
57	John Dopson RC	.05
58	Casey Candaele	.05
59	Dave Righetti	.05
60	Joe Hesketh	.05
61	Frank DiPino	.05
62	Tim Laudner	.05
63	Jamie Moyer	.05
64	Fred Toliver	.05
65	Mitch Webster	.05
66	John Tudor	.05
67	John Cangelosi	.05
68	Mike Devereaux	.05
69	Brian Fisher	.05
70	Mike Marshall	.05
71	Zane Smith	.05
72a	Brian Holton (Ball not visible on card front, photo a ctually Shawn Hillegas.)	.75
72b	Brian Holton (Ball visible, correct photo.)	.05
73	Jose Guzman	.05
74	Rick Mahler	.05
75	John Shelby	.05
76	Jim Deshaies	.05
77	Bobby Meacham	.05
78	Bryn Smith	.05
79	Joaquin Andujar	.05
80	Richard Dotson	.05
81	Charlie Lea	.05
82	Calvin Schiraldi	.05
83	Les Straker	.05
84	Les Lancaster	.05
85	Allan Anderson	.05
86	Junior Ortiz	.05
87	Jesse Orosco	.05
88	Felix Fermin	.05
89	Dave Anderson	.05
90	Rafael Belliard	.05
91	Franklin Stubbs	.05
92	Cecil Espy	.05
93	Albert Hall	.05
94	Tim Leary	.05
95	Mitch Williams	.05
96	Tracy Jones	.05
97	Danny Darwin	.05
98	Gary Ward	.05
99	Neal Heaton	.05
100	Jim Pankovits	.05
101	Bill Doran	.05
102	Tim Wallach	.05
103	Joe Magrane	.05
104	Ozzie Virgil	.05
105	Alvin Davis	.05
106	Tom Brookens	.05
107	Shawon Dunston	.05
108	Tracy Woodson	.05
109	Nelson Liriano	.05
110	Devon White	.05
111	Steve Balboni	.05
112	Buddy Bell	.05
113	German Jimenez RC	.05
114	Ken Dayley	.05
115	Andres Galarraga	.05
116	Mike Scioscia	.05
117	Gary Pettis	.05
118	Ernie Whitt	.05
119	Bob Boone	.05
120	Ryne Sandberg	1.50
121	Bruce Benedict	.05
122	Hubie Brooks	.05
123	Mike Moore	.05
124	Wallace Johnson	.05
125	Bob Horner	.05
126	Chili Davis	.05
127	Manny Trillo	.05
128	Chet Lemon	.05
129	John Cerutti	.05
130	Orel Hershiser	.05
131	Terry Pendleton	.05
132	Jeff Blauser	.05
133	Mike Fitzgerald	.05
134	Henry Cotto	.05
135	Gerald Young	.05
136	Luis Salazar	.05
137	Alejandro Pena	.05
138	Jack Howell	.05
139	Tony Fernandez	.05
140	Mark Grace	.50
141	Ken Caminiti	.05
142	Mike Jackson	.05
143	Larry McWilliams	.05
144	Andres Thomas	.05
145	Nolan Ryan	2.00
146	Mike Davis	.05
147	DeWayne Buice	.05
148	Jody Davis	.05
149	Jesse Barfield	.05
150	Matt Nokes	.05
151	Jerry Reuss	.05
152	Rick Cerone	.05
153	Storm Davis	.05
154	Marvell Wynne	.05
155	Will Clark	.05
156	Luis Aguayo	.05
157	Willie Upshaw	.05
158	Randy Bush	.05
159	Ron Darling	.05
160	Kal Daniels	.05
161	Spike Owen	.05
162	Luis Polonia	.05
163	Kevin Mitchell	.05
164	Dave Gallagher RC	.05
165	Benito Santiago	.05
166	Greg Gagne	.05
167	Ken Phelps	.05
168	Sid Fernandez	.05
169	Bo Diaz	.05
170	Cory Snyder	.05
171	Eric Show	.05
172	Robby Thompson	.05
173	Marty Barrett	.05
174	Dave Henderson	.05
175	Ozzie Guillen	.05
176	Barry Lyons	.05
177	Kelvin Torve RC	.05
178	Don Slaught	.05
179	Steve Lombardozzi	.05
180	Chris Sabo RC	.05
181	Jose Uribe	.05
182	Shane Mack	.05
183	Ron Karkovice	.05
184	Todd Benzinger	.05
185	Dave Stewart	.05
186	Julio Franco	.05
187	Ron Robinson	.05
188	Wally Backman	.05
189	Randy Velarde	.05
190	Joe Carter	.05
191	Bob Welch	.05
192	Kelly Paris	.05
193	Chris Brown	.05
194	Rick Reuschel	.05
195	Roger Clemens	1.60
196	Dave Concepcion	.05
197	Al Newman	.05
198	Brook Jacoby	.05
199	Mookie Wilson	.05
200	Don Mattingly	1.60
201	Dick Schofield	.05
202	Mark Gubicza	.05
203	Gary Gaetti	.05
204	Dan Pasqua	.05
205	Andre Dawson	.35
206	Chris Speier	.05
207	Kent Tekulve	.05
208	Rod Scurry	.05
209	Scott Bailes	.05
210	Rickey Henderson	1.00
211	Harold Baines	.05
212	Tony Armas	.05
213	Kent Hrbek	.05
214	Darrin Jackson	.05
215	George Brett	1.60
216	Rafael Santana	.05
217	Andy Allanson	.05
218	Brett Butler	.05
219	Steve Jeltz	.05
220	Jay Buhner	.05
221	Bo Jackson	.15
222	Angel Salazar	.05
223	Kirk McCaskill	.05
224	Steve Lyons	.05
225	Bert Blyleven	.05
226	Scott Bradley	.05
227	Bob Melvin	.05
228	Ron Kittle	.05
229	Phil Bradley	.05
230	Tommy John	.05
231	Greg Walker	.05
232	Juan Berenguer	.05
233	Pat Tabler	.05
234	Terry Clark RC	.05
235	Rafael Palmeiro	.75
236	Paul Zuvella	.05
237	Willie Randolph	.05
238	Bruce Fields	.05
239	Mike Aldrete	.05
240	Lance Parrish	.05
241	Greg Maddux	1.50
242	John Moses	.05
243	Melido Perez	.05
244	Willie Wilson	.05
245	Mark McLemore	.05
246	Von Hayes	.05
247	Matt Williams	.05
248	John Candelaria	.05
249	Harold Reynolds	.05
250	Greg Swindell	.05
251	Juan Agosto	.05
252	Mike Felder	.05
253	Vince Coleman	.05
254	Larry Sheets	.05
255	George Bell	.05
256	Terry Steinbach	.05
257	Jack Armstrong RC	.05
258	Dickie Thon	.05
259	Ray Knight	.05
260	Darryl Strawberry	.05
261	Doug Sisk	.05
262	Alex Trevino	.05
263	Jeff Leonard	.05
264	Tom Henke	.05
265	Ozzie Smith	1.50
266	Dave Bergman	.05
267	Tony Phillips	.05
268	Mark Davis	.05
269	Kevin Elster	.05
270	Barry Larkin	.05
271	Manny Lee	.05
272	Tom Brunansky	.05
273	Craig Biggio	.05
274	Jim Gantner	.05
275	Eddie Murray	1.00
276	Jeff Reed	.05
277	Tim Teufel	.05
278	Rick Honeycutt	.05
279	Guillermo Hernandez	.05
280	John Kruk	.05
281	Luis Alicea RC	.15
282	Jim Clancy	.05
283	Billy Ripken	.05
284	Craig Reynolds	.05
285	Robin Yount	1.00
286	Jimmy Jones	.05
287	Ron Oester	.05
288	Terry Leach	.05
289	Dennis Eckersley	.75
290	Alan Trammell	.05
291	Jimmy Key	.05
292	Chris Bosio	.05
293	Jose DeLeon	.05
294	Jim Traber	.05
295	Mike Scott	.05
296	Roger McDowell	.05
297	Garry Templeton	.05
298	Doyle Alexander	.05
299	Nick Esasky	.05
300	Mark McGwire	1.75
301	Darryl Hamilton RC	.05
302	Dave Smith	.05
303	Rick Sutcliffe	.05
304	Dave Stapleton	.05
305	Alan Ashby	.05
306	Pedro Guerrero	.05
307	Ron Guidry	.05
308	Steve Farr	.05
309	Curt Ford	.05
310	Claudell Washington	.05
311	Tom Prince	.05
312	Chad Kreuter RC	.15
313	Ken Oberkfell	.05
314	Jerry Browne	.05
315	R.J. Reynolds	.05
316	Scott Bankhead	.05
317	Milt Thompson	.05
318	Mario Diaz	.05
319	Bruce Ruffin	.05
320	Dave Valle	.05
321a	Gary Varsho RC (Batting righty on card back, photo actually Mike Bielecki.)	1.00
321b	Gary Varsho RC (Batting lefty on card back, correct photo.)	.05
322	Paul Mirabella	.05
323	Chuck Jackson	.05
324	Drew Hall	.05
325	Don August	.05
326	Israel Sanchez RC	.05
327	Denny Walling	.05
328	Joel Skinner	.05
329	Danny Tartabull	.05
330	Tony Pena	.05
331	Jim Sundberg	.05
332	Jeff Robinson	.05
333	Odibbe McDowell	.05
334	Jose Lind	.05
335	Paul Kilgus	.05
336	Juan Samuel	.05
337	Mike Campbell	.05
338	Mike Maddux	.05
339	Darnell Coles	.05
340	Bob Dernier	.05
341	Rafael Ramirez	.05
342	Scott Sanderson	.05
343	B.J. Surhoff	.05
344	Billy Hatcher	.05

#	Player	Value
345	Pat Perry	.05
346	Jack Clark	.05
347	Gary Thurman	.05
348	Timmy Jones RC	.05
349	Dave Winfield	1.00
350	Frank White	.05
351	Dave Collins	.05
352	Jack Morris	.05
353	Eric Plunk	.05
354	Leon Durham	.05
355	Ivan DeJesus	.05
356	Brian Holman RC	.05
357a	Dale Murphy (Reversed negative.)	20.00
357b	Dale Murphy (Corrected)	.25
358	Mark Portugal	.05
359	Andy McGaffigan	.05
360	Tom Glavine	.25
361	Keith Moreland	.05
362	Todd Stottlemyre	.05
363	Dave Leiper	.05
364	Cecil Fielder	.05
365	Carmelo Martinez	.05
366	Dwight Evans	.05
367	Kevin McReynolds	.05
368	Rich Gedman	.05
369	Len Dykstra	.05
370	Jody Reed	.05
371	Jose Canseco	.60
372	Rob Murphy	.05
373	Mike Henneman	.05
374	Walt Weiss	.05
375	Rob Dibble RC	.05
376	Kirby Puckett	1.50
377	Denny Martinez	.05
378	Ron Gant	.05
379	Brian Harper	.05
380	Nelson Santovenia RC	.05
381	Lloyd Moseby	.05
382	Lance McCullers	.05
383	Dave Stieb	.05
384	Tony Gwynn	1.50
385	Mike Flanagan	.05
386	Bob Ojeda	.05
387	Bruce Hurst	.05
388	Dave Magadan	.05
389	Wade Boggs	1.50
390	Gary Carter	1.00
391	Frank Tanana	.05
392	Curt Young	.05
393	Jeff Treadway	.05
394	Darrell Evans	.05
395	Glenn Hubbard	.05
396	Chuck Cary	.05
397	Frank Viola	.05
398	Jeff Parrett	.05
399	Terry Blocker RC	.05
400	Dan Gladden	.05
401	Louie Meadows RC	.05
402	Tim Raines	.05
403	Joey Meyer	.05
404	Larry Andersen	.05
405	Rex Hudler	.05
406	Mike Schmidt	1.60
407	John Franco	.05
408	Brady Anderson	.05
409	Don Carman	.05
410	Eric Davis	.05
411	Bob Stanley	.05
412	Pete Smith	.05
413	Jim Rice	.25
414	Bruce Sutter	.75
415	Oil Can Boyd	.05
416	Ruben Sierra	.05
417	Mike LaValliere	.05
418	Steve Buechele	.05
419	Gary Redus	.05
420	Scott Fletcher	.05
421	Dale Sveum	.05
422	Bob Knepper	.05
423	Luis Rivera	.05
424	Ted Higuera	.05
425	Kevin Bass	.05
426	Ken Gerhart	.05
427	Shane Rawley	.05
428	Paul O'Neill	.05
429	Joe Orsulak	.05
430	Jackie Gutierrez	.05
431	Gerald Perry	.05
432	Mike Greenwell	.05
433	Jerry Royster	.05
434	Ellis Burks	.05
435	Ed Olwine	.05
436	Dave Rucker	.05
437	Charlie Hough	.05
438	Bob Walk	.05
439	Bob Brower	.05
440	Barry Bonds	2.00
441	Tom Foley	.05
442	Rob Deer	.05
443	Glenn Davis	.05
444	Dave Martinez	.05
445	Bill Wegman	.05
446	Lloyd McClendon	.05
447	Dave Schmidt	.05
448	Darren Daulton	.05
449	Frank Williams	.05
450	Don Aase	.05
451	Lou Whitaker	.05
452	Goose Gossage	.05
453	Ed Whitson	.05
454	Jim Walewander	.05
455	Damon Berryhill	.05
456	Tim Burke	.05
457	Barry Jones	.05
458	Carney Lansford	.05
459	Floyd Youmans	.05
460	Mark Salas	.05
461	Jeff Russell	.05
462	Darrell Miller	.05
463	Jeff Kunkel	.05
464	Sherman Corbett RC	.05
465	Curtis Wilkerson	.05
466	Bud Black	.05
467	Cal Ripken, Jr.	2.00
468	John Farrell	.05
469	Terry Kennedy	.05
470	Tom Candiotti	.05
471	Roberto Alomar	.20
472	Jeff Robinson	.05
473	Vance Law	.05
474	Randy Ready	.05
475	Walt Terrell	.05
476	Kelly Downs	.05
477	Johnny Paredes RC	.05
478	Shawn Hillegas	.05
479	Bob Brenly	.05
480	Otis Nixon	.05
481	Johnny Ray	.05
482	Geno Petralli	.05
483	Stu Cliburn	.05
484	Pete Incaviglia	.05
485	Brian Downing	.05
486	Jeff Stone	.05
487	Carmen Castillo	.05
488	Tom Niedenfuer	.05
489	Jay Bell	.05
490	Rick Schu	.05
491	Jeff Pico RC	.05
492	Mark Parent RC	.05
493	Eric King	.05
494	Al Nipper	.05
495	Andy Hawkins	.05
496	Daryl Boston	.05
497	Ernie Riles	.05
498	Pascual Perez	.05
499	Bill Long	.05
500	Kirt Manwaring	.05
501	Chuck Crim	.05
502	Candy Maldonado	.05
503	Dennis Lamp	.05
504	Glenn Braggs	.05
505	Joe Price	.05
506	Ken Williams	.05
507	Bill Pecota	.05
508	Rey Quinones	.05
509	Jeff Bittiger RC	.05
510	Kevin Seitzer	.05
511	Steve Bedrosian	.05
512	Todd Worrell	.05
513	Chris James	.05
514	Jose Oquendo	.05
515	David Palmer	.05
516	John Smiley	.05
517	Dave Clark	.05
518	Mike Dunne	.05
519	Ron Washington	.05
520	Bob Kipper	.05
521	Lee Smith	.05
522	Juan Castillo	.05
523	Don Robinson	.05
524	Kevin Romine	.05
525	Paul Molitor	1.00
526	Mark Langston	.05
527	Donnie Hill	.05
528	Larry Owen	.05
529	Jerry Reed	.05
530	Jack McDowell	.05
531	Greg Mathews	.05
532	John Russell	.05
533	Dan Quisenberry	.05
534	Greg Gross	.05
535	Danny Cox	.05
536	Terry Francona	.05
537	Andy Van Slyke	.05
538	Mel Hall	.05
539	Jim Gott	.05
540	Doug Jones	.05
541	Criag Lefferts	.05
542	Mike Boddicker	.05
543	Greg Brock	.05
544	Atlee Hammaker	.05
545	Tom Bolton	.05
546	Mike Macfarlane RC	.25
547	Rich Renteria RC	.05
548	John Davis	.05
549	Floyd Bannister	.05
550	Mickey Brantley	.05
551	Duane Ward	.05
552	Dan Petry	.05
553	Mickey Tettleton	.05
554	Rick Leach	.05
555	Mike Witt	.05
556	Sid Bream	.05
557	Bobby Witt	.05
558	Tommy Herr	.05
559	Randy Milligan	.05
560	Jose Cecena RC	.05
561	Mackey Sasser	.05
562	Carney Lansford	.05
563	Rick Aguilera	.05
564	Ron Hassey	.05
565	Dwight Gooden	.05
566	Paul Assenmacher	.05
567	Neil Allen	.05
568	Jim Morrison	.05
569	Mike Pagliarulo	.05
570	Ted Simmons	.05
571	Mark Thurmond	.05
572	Fred McGriff	.05
573	Wally Joyner	.05
574	Jose Bautista RC	.05
575	Kelly Gruber	.05
576	Cecilio Guante	.05
577	Mark Davidson	.05
578	Bobby Bonilla	.05
579	Mike Stanley	.05
580	Gene Larkin	.05
581	Stan Javier	.05
582	Howard Johnson	.05
583a	Mike Gallego (Photo on card back reversed.)	.75
583b	Mike Gallego (Correct photo.)	.05
584	David Cone	.05
585	Doug Jennings RC	.05
586	Charlie Hudson	.05
587	Dion James	.05
588	Al Leiter	.05
589	Charlie Puleo	.05
590	Roberto Kelly	.05
591	Thad Bosley	.05
592	Pete Stanicek	.05
593	Pat Borders RC	.25
594	Bryan Harvey RC	.05
595	Jeff Ballard	.05
596	Jeff Reardon	.05
597	Doug Drabek	.05
598	Edwin Correa	.05
599	Keith Atherton	.05
600	Dave LaPoint	.05
601	Don Baylor	.05
602	Tom Pagnozzi	.05
603	Tim Flannery	.05
604	Gene Walter	.05
605	Dave Parker	.05
606	Mike Diaz	.05
607	Chris Gwynn	.05
608	Odell Jones	.05
609	Carlton Fisk	1.00
610	Jay Howell	.05
611	Tim Crews	.05
612	Keith Hernandez	.05
613	Willie Fraser	.05
614	Jim Eppard	.05
615	Jeff Hamilton	.05
616	Kurt Stillwell	.05
617	Tom Browning	.05
618	Jeff Montgomery	.05
619	Jose Rijo	.05
620	Jamie Quirk	.05
621	Willie McGee	.05
622	Mark Grant	.05
623	Bill Swift	.05
624	Orlando Mercado	.05
625	John Costello RC	.05
626	Jose Gonzalez	.05
627a	Bill Schroeder (Putting on shin guards on card back, photo actually Ronn Reynolds.)	.75
627b	Bill Schroeder (Arms crossed on card back, correct photo.)	.05
628a	Fred Manrique (Throwing on card back, photo actually Ozzie Guillen.)	.75
628b	Fred Manrique (Batting on card back, correct photo.)	.05
629	Ricky Horton	.05
630	Dan Plesac	.05
631	Alfredo Griffin	.05
632	Chuck Finley	.05
633	Kirk Gibson	.05
634	Randy Myers	.05
635	Greg Minton	.05
636	Herm Winningham	.05
637	Charlie Leibrandt	.05
638	Tim Birtsas	.05
639	Bill Buckner	.05
640	Danny Jackson	.05
641	Greg Booker	.05
642	Jim Presley	.05
643	Gene Nelson	.05
644	Rod Booker	.05
645	Dennis Rasmussen	.05
646	Juan Nieves	.05
647	Bobby Thigpen	.05
648	Tim Belcher	.05
649	Mike Young	.05
650	Ivan Calderon	.05
651	Oswaldo Peraza RC	.05
652a	Pat Sheridan (No position on front.)	8.00
652b	Pat Sheridan (Position on front.)	.05
653	Mike Morgan	.05
654	Mike Heath	.05
655	Jay Tibbs	.05
656	Fernando Valenzuela	.05
657	Lee Mazzilli	.05
658	Frank Viola	.05
659	Jose Canseco	.60
660	Walt Weiss	.05
661	Orel Hershiser	.05
662	Kirk Gibson	.05
663	Chris Sabo	.05
664	Dennis Eckersley	.75
665	Orel Hershiser	.05
666	Kirk Gibson	.05
667	Orel Hershiser	.05
668	Wally Joyner/TC	.05
669	Nolan Ryan/TC	1.00
670	Jose Canseco/TC	.30
671	Fred McGriff/TC	.05
672	Dale Murphy/TC	.20
673	Paul Molitor/TC	.50
674	Ozzie Smith/TC	.75
675	Ryne Sandberg/TC	.40
676	Kirk Gibson/TC	.05
677	Andres Galarraga/TC	.05
678	Will Clark/TC	.05
679	Cory Snyder/TC	.05
680	Alvin Davis/TC	.05
681	Darryl Strawberry/TC	.05
682	Cal Ripken, Jr./TC	1.00
683	Tony Gwynn/TC	.40
684	Mike Schmidt/TC	.85
685	Andy Van Slyke/TC	.05
686	Ruben Sierra/TC	.05
687	Wade Boggs/TC	.40
688	Eric Davis/TC	.05
689	George Brett/TC	.85
690	Alan Trammell/TC	.05
691	Frank Viola/TC	.05
692	Harold Baines/TC	.05
693	Don Mattingly/TC	.85
694	Checklist 1-100	.05
695	Checklist 101-200	.05
696	Checklist 201-300	.05
697	Checklist 301-400	.05
698	Checklist 401-500	.05
699	Checklist 501-600	.05
700	Checklist 601-700	.05
701	Checklist 701-800	.05
702	Jessie Barfield	.05
703	Walt Terrell	.05
704	Dickie Thon	.05
705	Al Leiter	.05
706	Dave LaPoint	.05
707	Charlie Hayes RC	.05
708	Andy Hawkins	.05
709	Mickey Hatcher	.05
710	Lance McCullers	.05
711	Ron Kittle	.05
712	Bert Blyleven	.05
713	Rick Dempsey	.05
714	Ken Williams	.05
715	Steve Rosenberg	.05
716	Joe Skalski	.05
717	Spike Owen	.05
718	Todd Burns	.05
719	Kevin Gross	.05
720	Tommy Herr	.05
721	Rob Ducey	.05
722	Gary Green	.05
723	Gregg Olson RC	.10
724	Greg Harris	.05
725	Craig Worthington	.05
726	Tom Howard	.05
727	Dale Mohorcic	.05
728	Rich Yett	.05
729	Mel Hall	.05
730	Floyd Youmans	.05
731	Lonnie Smith	.05
732	Wally Backman	.05
733	Trevor Wilson	.05
734	Jose Alvarez	.05
735	Bob Milacki	.05
736	Tom Gordon RC	.50
737	Wally Whitehurst	.05
738	Mike Aldrete	.05
739	Keith Miller	.05
740	Randy Milligan	.05

741	Jeff Parrett	.05
742	Steve Finley RC	.75
743	Junior Felix RC	.05
744	Pete Harnisch RC	.25
745	Bill Spiers	.05
746	Hensley Meulens	.05
747	Juan Bell	.05
748	Steve Sax	.05
749	Phil Bradley	.05
750	Rey Quinones	.05
751	Tommy Gregg	.05
752	Kevin Brown	.25
753	Derek Lilliquist	.05
754	Todd Zeile RC	.75
755	Jim Abbott	.05
756	Ozzie Canseco RC	.05
757	Nick Esasky	.05
758	Mike Moore	.05
759	Rob Murphy	.05
760	Rick Mahler	.05
761	Fred Lynn	.05
762	Kevin Blankenship RC	.05
763	Eddie Murray	1.00
764	Steve Searcy RC	.05
765	Jerome Walton RC	.05
766	Erik Hanson RC	.05
767	Bob Boone	.05
768	Edgar Martinez	.05
769	Jose DeJesus RC	.05
770	Greg Briley RC	.05
771	Steve Peters RC	.05
772	Rafael Palmeiro	.75
773	Jack Clark	.05
774	Nolan Ryan	2.00
775	Lance Parrish	.05
776	Joe Girardi RC	.30
777	Willie Randolph	.05
778	Mitch Williams	.05
779	Dennis Cook RC	.05
780	Dwight Smith RC	.05
781	Lenny Harris RC	.10
782	Torey Lovullo RC	.05
783	Norm Charlton RC	.15
784	Chris Brown	.05
785	Todd Benzinger	.05
786	Shane Rawley	.05
787	Omar Vizquel RC	2.00
788	LaVel Freeman RC	.05
789	Jeffrey Leonard	.05
790	Eddie Williams RC	.05
791	Jamie Moyer	.05
792	Bruce Hurst	.05
793	Julio Franco	.05
794	Claudell Washington	.05
795	Jody Davis	.05
796	Oddibe McDowell	.05
797	Paul Kilgus	.05
798	Tracy Jones	.05
799	Steve Wilson	.05
800	Pete O'Brien	.05

1990 Upper Deck

Tom Gordon

		NM/M
Unopened Factory Set (800):		20.00
Complete Set (800):		15.00
Complete Low Set (700):		12.00
Complete High Set (100):		5.00
Common Player:		.05
Low or High Foil Pack (15):		.50
Low or High Foil Box (36):		12.00
1	Star Rookie Checklist	.05
2	Randy Nosek RC	.05
3	Tom Drees RC	.05
4	Curt Young	.05
5	Devon White Angels Checklist	.05
6	Luis Salazar	.05
7	Von Hayes Phillies Checklist	.05
8	Jose Bautista	.05
9	Marquis Grissom RC	.50

10	Orel Hershiser Dodgers Checklist	.05
11	Rick Aguilera	.05
12	Benito Santiago Padres Checklist	.05
13	Deion Sanders	.10
14	Marvell Wynne	.05
15	David West	.05
16	Bobby Bonilla Pirates Checklist	.05
17	Sammy Sosa RC	5.00
18	Steve Sax Yankees Checklist	.05
19	Jack Howell	.05
20	Mike Schmidt Mike Schmidt Retires	.75
21	Robin Ventura	.05
22	Brian Meyer	.05
23	Blaine Beatty RC	.05
24	Ken Griffey Jr. Mariners Checklist	.50
25	Greg Vaughn	.05
26	Xavier Hernandez RC	.05
27	Jason Grimsley RC	.05
28	Eric Anthony RC	.05
29	Tim Raines Expos Checklist	.05
30	David Wells	.05
31	Hal Morris	.05
32	Bo Jackson Royals Checklist	.10
33	Kelly Mann RC	.05
34	Nolan Ryan Nolan Ryan 5000 Strikeouts	1.00
35	Scott Service RC	.05
36	Mark McGwire Athletics Checklist	.50
37	Tino Martinez	.05
38	Chili Davis	.05
39	Scott Sanderson	.05
40	Kevin Mitchell Giants Checklist	.05
41	Lou Whitaker Tigers Checklist	.05
42	Scott Coolbaugh RC	.05
43	Jose Cano RC	.05
44	Jose Vizcaino RC	.10
45	Bob Hamelin RC	.05
46	Jose Offerman RC	.15
47	Kevin Blankenship	.05
48	Kirby Puckett Twins Checklist	.40
49	Tommy Greene RC	.05
50	Will Clark N.L. Top Vote Getter	.05
51	Rob Nelson	.05
52	Chris Hammond RC	.15
53	Joe Carter Indians Checklist	.05
54a	Ben McDonald RC (Orioles Logo)	1.00
54b	Ben McDonald RC (Star Rookie logo)	.25
55	Andy Benes	.05
56	John Olerud RC	1.00
57	Roger Clemens Red Sox Checklist	.45
58	Tony Armas	.05
59	George Canale RC	.05
60a	Mickey Tettleton Orioles Checklist (#683 Jamie Weston)	1.00
60b	Mickey Tettleton Orioles Checklist (#683 Mickey Weston)	.05
61	Mike Stanton RC	.05
62	Dwight Gooden Mets Checklist	.05
63	Kent Mercker RC	.10
64	Francisco Cabrera RC	.05
65	Steve Avery	.05
66	Jose Canseco	.35
67	Matt Merullo RC	.05
68	Vince Coleman Cardinals Checklist	.05
69	Ron Karkovice	.05
70	Kevin Maas RC	.05
71	Dennis Cook	.05
72	Juan Gonzalez RC	2.00
73	Andre Dawson Cubs Checklist	.10
74	Dean Palmer RC	.25
75	Bo Jackson A.L. Top Vote Getter	.10
76	Ron Richie RC	.05
77	Bobby Rose RC	.05
78	Brian DuBois RC	.05
79	Ozzie Guillen White Sox Checklist	.05
80	Gene Nelson	.05
81	Bob McClure	.05
82	Julio Franco Rangers Checklist	.05
83	Greg Minton	.05

84	John Smoltz Braves Checklist	.05
85	Willie Fraser	.05
86	Neal Heaton	.05
87	Kevin Tapani RC	.05
88	Mike Scott Astros Checklist	.05
89a	Jim Gott (Incorrect photo.)	1.00
89b	Jim Gott (Correct photo.)	.05
90	Lance Johnson	.05
91	Robin Yount Brewers Checklist	.35
92	Jeff Parrett	.05
93	Julio Machado RC	.05
94	Ron Jones	.05
95	George Bell Blue Jays Checklist	.05
96	Jerry Reuss	.05
97	Brian Fisher	.05
98	Kevin Ritz RC	.05
99	Barry Larkin Reds Checklist	.05
100	Checklist 1-100	.05
101	Gerald Perry	.05
102	Kevin Appier	.05
103	Julio Franco	.05
104	Craig Biggio	.05
105	Bo Jackson	.10
106	Junior Felix RC	.05
107	Mike Harkey	.05
108	Fred McGriff	.05
109	Rick Sutcliffe	.05
110	Pete O'Brien	.05
111	Kelly Gruber	.05
112	Pat Borders	.05
113	Dwight Evans	.05
114	Dwight Gooden	.05
115	Kevin Batiste RC	.05
116	Eric Davis	.05
117	Kevin Mitchell	.05
118	Ron Oester	.05
119	Brett Butler	.05
120	Danny Jackson	.05
121	Tommy Gregg	.05
122	Ken Caminiti	.05
123	Kevin Brown	.05
124	George Brett	.85
125	Mike Scott	.05
126	Cory Snyder	.05
127	George Bell	.05
128	Mark Grace	.05
129	Devon White	.05
130	Tony Fernandez	.05
131	Don Aase	.05
132	Rance Mulliniks	.05
133	Marty Barrett	.05
134	Nelson Liriano	.05
135	Mark Carreon	.05
136	Candy Maldonado	.05
137	Tim Birtsas	.05
138	Tom Brookens	.05
139	John Franco	.05
140	Mike LaCoss	.05
141	Jeff Treadway	.05
142	Pat Tabler	.05
143	Darrell Evans	.05
144	Rafael Ramirez	.05
145	Oddibe McDowell	.05
146	Brian Downing	.05
147	Curtis Wilkerson	.05
148	Ernie Whitt	.05
149	Bill Schroeder	.05
150	Domingo Ramos	.05
151	Rick Honeycutt	.05
152	Don Slaught	.05
153	Mitch Webster	.05
154	Tony Phillips	.05
155	Paul Kilgus	.05
156	Ken Griffey Jr.	1.50
157	Gary Sheffield	.35
158	Wally Backman	.05
159	B.J. Surhoff	.05
160	Louie Meadows	.05
161	Paul O'Neill	.05
162	Jeff McKnight RC	.05
163	Alvaro Espinoza	.05
164	Scott Scudder RC	.05
165	Jeff Reed	.05
166	Gregg Jefferies	.05
167	Barry Larkin	.05
168	Gary Carter	.60
169	Robby Thompson	.05
170	Rolando Roomes	.05
171	Mark McGwire	1.50
172	Steve Sax	.05
173	Mark Williamson	.05
174	Mitch Williams	.05
175	Brian Holton	.05
176	Rob Deer	.05
177	Tim Raines	.05
178	Mike Felder	.05
179	Harold Reynolds	.05

180	Terry Francona	.05
181	Chris Sabo	.05
182	Darryl Strawberry	.05
183	Willie Randolph	.05
184	Billy Ripken	.05
185	Mackey Sasser	.05
186	Todd Benzinger	.05
187	Kevin Elster	.05
188	Jose Uribe	.05
189	Tom Browning	.05
190	Keith Miller	.05
191	Don Mattingly	.85
192	Dave Parker	.05
193	Roberto Kelly	.05
194	Phil Bradley	.05
195	Ron Hassey	.05
196	Gerald Young	.05
197	Hubie Brooks	.05
198	Bill Doran	.05
199	Al Newman	.05
200	Checklist 101-200	.05
201	Terry Puhl	.05
202	Frank DiPino	.05
203	Jim Clancy	.05
204	Bob Ojeda	.05
205	Alex Trevino	.05
206	Dave Henderson	.05
207	Henry Cotto	.05
208	Rafael Belliard	.05
209	Stan Javier	.05
210	Jerry Reed	.05
211	Doug Dascenzo	.05
212	Andres Thomas	.05
213	Greg Maddux	.75
214	Mike Schooler	.05
215	Lonnie Smith	.05
216	Jose Rijo	.05
217	Greg Gagne	.05
218	Jim Gantner	.05
219	Allan Anderson	.05
220	Rick Mahler	.05
221	Jim Deshaies	.05
222	Keith Hernandez	.05
223	Vince Coleman	.05
224	David Cone	.05
225	Ozzie Smith	.75
226	Matt Nokes	.05
227	Barry Bonds	2.00
228	Felix Jose	.05
229	Dennis Powell	.05
230	Mike Gallego	.05
231	Shawon Dunston	.05
232	Ron Gant	.05
233	Omar Vizquel	.05
234	Derek Lilliquist	.05
235	Erik Hanson	.05
236	Kirby Puckett	.75
237	Bill Spiers	.05
238	Dan Gladden	.05
239	Bryan Clutterbuck	.05
240	John Moses	.05
241	Ron Darling	.05
242	Joe Magrane	.05
243	Dave Magadan	.05
244	Pedro Guerrero	.05
245	Glenn Davis	.05
246	Terry Steinbach	.05
247	Fred Lynn	.05
248	Gary Redus	.05
249	Kenny Williams	.05
250	Sid Bream	.05
251	Bob Welch	.05
252	Bill Buckner	.05
253	Carney Lansford	.05
254	Paul Molitor	.60
255	Jose DeJesus	.05
256	Orel Hershiser	.05
257	Tom Brunansky	.05
258	Mike Davis	.05
259	Jeff Ballard	.05
260	Scott Terry	.05
261	Sid Fernandez	.05
262	Mike Marshall	.05
263	Howard Johnson	.05
264	Kirk Gibson	.05
265	Kevin McReynolds	.05
266	Cal Ripken, Jr.	2.00
267	Ozzie Guillen	.05
268	Jim Traber	.05
269	Bobby Thigpen	.05
270	Joe Orsulak	.05
271	Bob Boone	.05
272	Dave Stewart	.05
273	Tim Wallach	.05
274	Luis Aquino	.05
275	Mike Moore	.05
276	Tony Pena	.05
277	Eddie Murray	.60
278	Milt Thompson	.05
279	Alejandro Pena	.05
280	Ken Dayley	.05
281	Carmen Castillo	.05
282	Tom Henke	.05
283	Mickey Hatcher	.05

No.	Player	Price
284	Roy Smith (RC)	.05
285	Manny Lee	.05
286	Dan Pasqua	.05
287	Larry Sheets	.05
288	Garry Templeton	.05
289	Eddie Williams	.05
290	Brady Anderson	.05
291	Spike Owen	.05
292	Storm Davis	.05
293	Chris Bosio	.05
294	Jim Eisenreich	.05
295	Don August	.05
296	Jeff Hamilton	.05
297	Mickey Tettleton	.05
298	Mike Scioscia	.05
299	Kevin Hickey (RC)	.05
300	Checklist 201-300	.05
301	Shawn Abner	.05
302	Kevin Bass	.05
303	Bip Roberts (RC)	.05
304	Joe Girardi	.05
305	Danny Darwin	.05
306	Mike Heath	.05
307	Mike Macfarlane	.05
308	Ed Whitson	.05
309	Tracy Jones	.05
310	Scott Fletcher	.05
311	Darnell Coles	.05
312	Mike Brumley	.05
313	Bill Swift	.05
314	Charlie Hough	.05
315	Jim Presley	.05
316	Luis Polonia	.05
317	Mike Morgan	.05
318	Lee Guetterman	.05
319	Jose Oquendo	.05
320	Wayne Tolleson	.05
321	Jody Reed	.05
322	Damon Berryhill	.05
323	Roger Clemens	.85
324	Ryne Sandberg	.75
325	Benito Santiago	.05
326	Bret Saberhagen	.05
327	Lou Whitaker	.05
328	Dave Gallagher	.05
329	Mike Pagliarulo	.05
330	Doyle Alexander	.05
331	Jeffrey Leonard	.05
332	Torey Lovullo	.05
333	Pete Incaviglia	.05
334	Rickey Henderson	.60
335	Rafael Palmeiro	.50
336	Ken Hill (RC)	.05
337	Dave Winfield	.60
338	Alfredo Griffin	.05
339	Andy Hawkins	.05
340	Ted Power	.05
341	Steve Wilson	.05
342	Jack Clark	.05
343	Ellis Burks	.05
344	Tony Gwynn	.75
345	Jerome Walton	.05
346	Roberto Alomar	.20
347	Carlos Martinez RC	.05
348	Chet Lemon	.05
349	Willie Wilson	.05
350	Greg Walker	.05
351	Tom Bolton	.05
352	German Gonzalez	.05
353	Harold Baines	.05
354	Mike Greenwell	.05
355	Ruben Sierra	.05
356	Andres Galarraga	.05
357	Andre Dawson	.25
358	Jeff Brantley RC	.05
359	Mike Bielecki	.05
360	Ken Oberkfell	.05
361	Kurt Stillwell	.05
362	Brian Holman	.05
363	Kevin Seitzer	.05
364	Alvin Davis	.05
365	Tom Gordon	.05
366	Bobby Bonilla	.05
367	Carlton Fisk	.60
368	Steve Carter RC	.05
369	Joel Skinner	.05
370	John Cangelosi	.05
371	Cecil Espy	.05
372	Gary Wayne RC	.05
373	Jim Rice	.20
374	Mike Dyer RC	.05
375	Joe Carter	.05
376	Dwight Smith	.05
377	John Wetteland RC	.15
378	Ernie Riles	.05
379	Otis Nixon	.05
380	Vance Law	.05
381	Dave Bergman	.05
382	Frank White	.05
383	Scott Bradley	.05
384	Israel Sanchez	.05
385	Gary Pettis	.05
386	Donn Pall (RC)	.05
387	John Smiley	.05
388	Tom Candiotti	.05
389	Junior Ortiz	.05
390	Steve Lyons	.05
391	Brian Harper	.05
392	Fred Manrique	.05
393	Lee Smith	.05
394	Jeff Kunkel	.05
395	Claudell Washington	.05
396	John Tudor	.05
397	Terry Kennedy	.05
398	Lloyd McClendon	.05
399	Craig Lefferts	.05
400	Checklist 301-400	.05
401	Keith Moreland	.05
402	Rich Gedman	.05
403	Jeff Robinson	.05
404	Randy Ready	.05
405	Rick Cerone	.05
406	Jeff Blauser	.05
407	Larry Andersen	.05
408	Joe Boever	.05
409	Felix Fermin	.05
410	Glenn Wilson	.05
411	Rex Hudler	.05
412	Mark Grant	.05
413	Dennis Martinez	.05
414	Darrin Jackson	.05
415	Mike Aldrete	.05
416	Roger McDowell	.05
417	Jeff Reardon	.05
418	Darren Daulton	.05
419	Tim Laudner	.05
420	Don Carman	.05
421	Lloyd Moseby	.05
422	Doug Drabek	.05
423	Lenny Harris	.05
424	Jose Lind	.05
425	Dave Johnson RC	.05
426	Jerry Browne	.05
427	Eric Yelding RC	.05
428	Brad Komminsk	.05
429	Jody Davis	.05
430	Mariano Duncan	.05
431	Mark Davis	.05
432	Nelson Santovenia	.05
433	Bruce Hurst	.05
434	Jeff Huson RC	.05
435	Chris James	.05
436	Mark Guthrie RC	.05
437	Charlie Hayes	.05
438	Shane Rawley	.05
439	Dickie Thon	.05
440	Juan Berenguer	.05
441	Kevin Romine	.05
442	Bill Landrum	.05
443	Todd Frohwirth	.05
444	Craig Worthington	.05
445	Fernando Valenzuela	.05
446	Albert Belle	.05
447	Ed Whited RC	.05
448	Dave Smith	.05
449	Dave Clark	.05
450	Juan Agosto	.05
451	Dave Valle	.05
452	Kent Hrbek	.05
453	Gary Ward	.05
454	Gary Gaetti	.05
455	Greg Briley	.05
456	Glenn Braggs	.05
457	Kirt Manwaring	.05
458	Mel Hall	.05
459	Brook Jacoby	.05
460	Pat Sheridan	.05
461	Rob Murphy	.05
462	Jimmy Key	.05
463	Nick Esasky	.05
464	Rob Ducey	.05
465	Carlos Quintana	.05
466	Larry Walker RC	1.00
467	Todd Worrell	.05
468	Kevin Gross	.05
469	Terry Pendleton	.05
470	Dave Martinez	.05
471	Gene Larkin	.05
472	Len Dykstra	.05
473	Barry Lyons	.05
474	Terry Mulholland	.05
475	Chip Hale RC	.05
476	Jesse Barfield	.05
477	Dan Plesac	.05
478a	Scott Garrelts (Photo actually Bill Bathe.)	1.00
478b	Scott Garrelts (Correct photo.)	.05
479	Dave Righetti	.05
480	Gus Polidor	.05
481	Mookie Wilson	.05
482	Luis Rivera	.05
483	Mike Flanagan	.05
484	Dennis "Oil Can" Boyd	.05
485	John Cerutti	.05
486	John Costello	.05
487	Pascual Perez	.05
488	Tommy Herr	.05
489	Tom Foley	.05
490	Curt Ford	.05
491	Steve Lake	.05
492	Tim Teufel	.05
493	Randy Bush	.05
494	Mike Jackson	.05
495	Steve Jeltz	.05
496	Paul Gibson	.05
497	Steve Balboni	.05
498	Bud Black	.05
499	Dale Sveum	.05
500	Checklist 401-500	.05
501	Timmy Jones	.05
502	Mark Portugal	.05
503	Ivan Calderon	.05
504	Rick Rhoden	.05
505	Willie McGee	.05
506	Kirk McCaskill	.05
507	Dave LaPoint	.05
508	Jay Howell	.05
509	Johnny Ray	.05
510	Dave Anderson	.05
511	Chuck Crim	.05
512	Joe Hesketh	.05
513	Dennis Eckersley	.40
514	Greg Brock	.05
515	Tim Burke	.05
516	Frank Tanana	.05
517	Jay Bell	.05
518	Guillermo Hernandez	.05
519	Randy Kramer	.05
520	Charles Hudson	.05
521	Jim Corsi	.05
522	Steve Rosenberg	.05
523	Cris Carpenter	.05
524	Matt Winters RC	.05
525	Melido Perez	.05
526	Chris Gwynn	.05
527	Bert Blyleven	.05
528	Chuck Cary	.05
529	Daryl Boston	.05
530	Dale Mohorcic	.05
531	Geronimo Berroa	.05
532	Edgar Martinez	.05
533	Dale Murphy	.20
534	Jay Buhner	.05
535	John Smoltz	.05
536	Andy Van Slyke	.05
537	Mike Henneman	.05
538	Miguel Garcia	.05
539	Frank Williams	.05
540	R.J. Reynolds	.05
541	Shawn Hillegas	.05
542	Walt Weiss	.05
543	Greg Hibbard RC	.05
544	Nolan Ryan	2.00
545	Todd Zeile	.05
546	Hensley Meulens	.05
547	Tim Belcher	.05
548	Mike Witt	.05
549	Greg Cadaret	.05
550	Franklin Stubbs	.05
551	Tony Castillo RC	.05
552	Jeff Robinson	.05
553	Steve Olin RC	.05
554	Alan Trammell	.05
555	Wade Boggs	.75
556	Will Clark	.05
557	Jeff King	.05
558	Mike Fitzgerald	.05
559	Ken Howell	.05
560	Bob Kipper	.05
561	Scott Bankhead	.05
562a	Jeff Innis RC (Photo actually David West.)	1.00
562b	Jeff Innis RC (Correct photo.)	.05
563	Randy Johnson	.60
564	Wally Whithurst RC	.05
565	Gene Harris RC	.05
566	Norm Charlton	.05
567	Robin Yount	.60
568	Joe Oliver RC	.05
569	Mark Parent	.05
570	John Farrell	.05
571	Tom Glavine	.20
572	Rod Nichols	.05
573	Jack Morris	.05
574	Greg Swindell	.05
575	Steve Searcy	.05
576	Ricky Jordan	.05
577	Matt Williams	.05
578	Mike LaValliere	.05
579	Bryn Smith	.05
580	Bruce Ruffin	.05
581	Randy Myers	.05
582	Rick Wrona RC	.05
583	Juan Samuel	.05
584	Les Lancaster	.05
585	Jeff Musselman	.05
586	Rob Dibble	.05
587	Eric Show	.05
588	Jesse Orosco	.05
589	Herm Winningham	.05
590	Andy Allanson	.05
591	Dion James	.05
592	Carmelo Martinez	.05
593	Luis Quinones	.05
594	Dennis Rasmussen	.05
595	Rich Yett	.05
596	Bob Walk	.05
597a	Andy McGaffigan (Player #48, photo actually Rich Thompson.)	.75
597b	Andy McGaffigan (Player #27, correct photo.)	.05
598	Billy Hatcher	.05
599	Bob Knepper	.05
600	Checklist 501-600	.05
601	Joey Cora	.05
602	Steve Finley RC	.20
603	Kal Daniels	.05
604	Gregg Olson	.05
605	Dave Steib	.05
606	Kenny Rogers RC	.05
607	Zane Smith	.05
608	Bob Geren RC	.05
609	Chad Kreuter	.05
610	Mike Smithson	.05
611	Jeff Wetherby RC	.05
612	Gary Mielke RC	.05
613	Pete Smith	.05
614	Jack Daugherty RC	.05
615	Lance McCullers	.05
616	Don Robinson	.05
617	Jose Guzman	.05
618	Steve Bedrosian	.05
619	Jamie Moyer	.05
620	Atlee Hammaker	.05
621	Rick Luecken RC	.05
622	Greg W. Harris	.05
623	Pete Harnisch	.05
624	Jerald Clark (RC)	.05
625	Jack McDowell	.05
626	Frank Viola	.05
627	Ted Higuera	.05
628	Marty Pevey RC	.05
629	Bill Wegman	.05
630	Eric Plunk	.05
631	Drew Hall	.05
632	Doug Jones	.05
633	Geno Petralli	.05
634	Jose Alvarez	.05
635	Bob Milacki	.05
636	Bobby Witt	.05
637	Trevor Wilson	.05
638	Jeff Russell	.05
639	Mike Krukow	.05
640	Rick Leach	.05
641	Dave Schmidt	.05
642	Terry Leach	.05
643	Calvin Schiraldi	.05
644	Bob Melvin	.05
645	Jim Abbott	.05
646	Jaime Navarro RC	.05
647	Mark Langston	.05
648	Juan Nieves	.05
649	Damaso Garcia	.05
650	Charlie O'Brien	.05
651	Eric King	.05
652	Mike Boddicker	.05
653	Duane Ward	.05
654	Bob Stanley	.05
655	Sandy Alomar, Jr.	.05
656	Danny Tartabull	.05
657	Randy McCament	.05
658	Charlie Leibrandt	.05
659	Dan Quisenberry	.05
660	Paul Assenmacher	.05
661	Walt Terrell	.05
662	Tim Leary	.05
663	Randy Milligan	.05
664	Bo Diaz	.05
665	Mark Lemke	.05
666	Jose Gonzalez	.05
667	Chuck Finley	.05
668	John Kruk	.05
669	Dick Schofield	.05
670	Tim Crews	.05
671	John Dopson	.05
672	John Orton RC	.05
673	Eric Hetzel	.05
674	Lance Parrish	.05
675	Ramon Martinez	.05
676	Mark Gubicza	.05
677	Greg Litton	.05
678	Greg Mathews	.05
679	Dave Dravecky	.05
680	Steve Farr	.05
681	Mike Devereaux	.05
682	Ken Griffey Sr.	.05
683a	Jamie Weston RC (First name incorrect.)	1.00
683b	Mickey Weston RC (Corrected)	.05
684	Jack Armstrong	.05
685	Steve Buechele	.05
686	Bryan Harvey	.05

687	Lance Blankenship	.05
688	Dante Bichette	.05
689	Todd Burns	.05
690	Dan Petry	.05
691	Kent Anderson RC	.05
692	Todd Stottlemyre	.05
693	Wally Joyner	.05
694	Mike Rochford	.05
695	Floyd Bannister	.05
696	Rick Reuschel	.05
697	Jose DeLeon	.05
698	Jeff Montgomery	.05
699	Kelly Downs	.05
700a	Checklist 601-700 (#683 Jamie Weston)	.05
700b	Checklist 601-700 (# 683 Mickey Weston)	.05
701	Jim Gott	.05
702	Delino DeShields, Larry Walker, Marquis Grissom "Rookie Threats"	.25
703	Alejandro Pena	.05
704	Willie Randolph	.05
705	Tim Leary	.05
706	Chuck McElroy	.05
707	Gerald Perry	.05
708	Tom Brunansky	.05
709	John Franco	.05
710	Mark Davis	.05
711	Dave Justice RC	1.50
712	Storm Davis	.05
713	Scott Ruskin	.05
714	Glenn Braggs	.05
715	Kevin Bearse	.05
716	Jose Nunez	.05
717	Tim Layana	.05
718	Greg Myers	.05
719	Pete O'Brien	.05
720	John Candelaria	.05
721	Craig Grebeck	.05
722	Shawn Boskie	.05
723	Jim Leyritz	.10
724	Bill Sampen	.05
725	Scott Radinsky	.05
726	Todd Hundley RC	.25
727	Scott Hemond	.05
728	Lenny Webster	.05
729	Jeff Reardon	.05
730	Mitch Webster	.05
731	Brian Bohanon	.05
732	Rick Parker	.05
733	Terry Shumpert	.05
734a	Nolan Ryan (300-win stripe on front)	1.50
734b	Nolan Ryan (No stripe.)	4.00
735	John Burkett	.05
736	Derrick May RC	.05
737	Carlos Baerga RC	.05
738	Greg Smith	.05
739	Joe Kraemer	.05
740	Scott Sanderson	.05
741	Hector Villanueva	.05
742	Mike Fetters	.05
743	Mark Gardner	.05
744	Matt Nokes	.05
745	Dave Winfield	.60
746	Delino DeShields RC	.15
747	Dann Howitt	.05
748	Tony Pena	.05
749	Oil Can Boyd	.05
750	Mike Benjamin	.05
751	Alex Cole	.05
752	Eric Gunderson	.05
753	Howard Farmer	.05
754	Joe Carter	.05
755	Ray Lankford RC	.25
756	Sandy Alomar,Jr.	.05
757	Alex Sanchez	.05
758	Nick Esasky	.05
759	Stan Belinda	.05
760	Jim Presley	.05
761	Gary DiSarcina	.05
762	Wayne Edwards	.05
763	Pat Combs	.05
764	Mickey Pina	.05
765	Wilson Alvarez RC	.25
766	Dave Parker	.05
767	Mike Blowers	.05
768	Tony Phillips	.05
769	Pascual Perez	.05
770	Gary Pettis	.05
771	Fred Lynn	.05
772	Mel Rojas RC	.10
773	David Segui	.25
774	Gary Carter	.60
775	Rafael Valdez	.05
776	Glenallen Hill	.05
777	Keith Hernandez	.05
778	Billy Hatcher	.05
779	Marty Clary	.05
780	Candy Maldonado	.05
781	Mike Marshall	.05

782	Billy Jo Robidoux	.05
783	Mark Langston	.05
784	Paul Sorrento RC	.05
785	Dave Hollins RC	.05
786	Cecil Fielder	.05
787	Matt Young	.05
788	Jeff Huson	.05
789	Lloyd Moseby	.05
790	Ron Kittle	.05
791	Hubie Brooks	.05
792	Craig Lefferts	.05
793	Kevin Bass	.05
794	Bryn Smith	.05
795	Juan Samuel	.05
796	Sam Horn	.05
797	Randy Myers	.05
798	Chris James	.05
799	Bill Gullickson	.05
800	Checklist 701-800	.05

Baseball Heroes
Reggie Jackson

	NM/M
Complete Set (10):	5.00
Common Player:	.50
Autographed Card:	100.00
1 Reggie Jackson 1969 Emerging Superstar	.50
2 Reggie Jackson 1973 An MVP Year	.50
3 Reggie Jackson 1977 "Mr. October"	.50
4 Reggie Jackson 1978 Jackson vs. Welch	.50
5 Reggie Jackson 1982 Under the Halo	.50
6 Reggie Jackson 1984 500!	.50
7 Reggie Jackson 1986 Moving Up the List	.50
8 Reggie Jackson 1987 A Great Career Ends	.50
9 Reggie Jackson Heroes Checklist 1-9	.50
---- Header Card	.50

1991 Upper Deck

Shawn Abner

	NM/M
Unopened Factory Set (800):	15.00
Complete Set (800):	10.00
Complete Low Series (700):	9.00
Complete High Series (100):	1.00
Common Player:	.05
Low or High Wax Pack (15):	.60
Low or High Wax Box (36):	13.50
1 Star Rookie Checklist	.05
2 Phil Plantier RC	.05
3 D.J. Dozier RC	.05
4 Dave Hansen	.05

5	Mo Vaughn	.10
6	Leo Gomez RC	.05
7	Scott Aldred RC	.05
8	Scott Chiamparino RC	.05
9	Lance Dickson RC	.05
10	Sean Berry RC	.05
11	Bernie Williams	.25
12	Brian Barnes RC	.05
13	Narciso Elvira RC	.05
14	Mike Gardiner RC	.05
15	Greg Colbrunn RC	.05
16	Bernard Gilkey RC	.05
17	Mark Lewis	.05
18	Mickey Morandini RC	.05
19	Charles Nagy	.05
20	Geronimo Pena RC	.05
21	Henry Rodriguez RC	.05
22	Scott Cooper	.05
23	Andujar Cedeno RC	.05
24	Eric Karros RC	.25
25	Steve Decker RC	.05
26	Kevin Belcher RC	.05
27	Jeff Conine RC	.25
28	Dave Stewart Oakland Athletics Checklist	.05
29	Carlton Fisk Chicago White Sox Checklist	.20
30	Rafael Palmeiro Texas Rangers Checklist	.20
31	Chuck Finley California Angels Checklist	.05
32	Harold Reynolds Seattle Mariners Checklist	.05
33	Bret Saberhagen Kansas City Royals Checklist	.05
34	Gary Gaetti Minnesota Twins Checklist	.05
35	Scott Leius	.05
36	Neal Heaton	.05
37	Terry Lee RC	.05
38	Gary Redus	.05
39	Barry Jones	.05
40	Chuck Knoblauch	.05
41	Larry Andersen	.05
42	Darryl Hamilton	.05
43	Mike Greenwell Boston Red Sox checklist	.05
44	Kelly Gruber Toronto Blue Jays checklist	.05
45	Jack Morris Detroit Tigers checklist	.05
46	Sandy Alomar Jr. Cleveland Indians Checklist	.05
47	Gregg Olson Baltimore Orioles checklist	.05
48	Dave Parker Milwaukee Brewers checklist	.05
49	Roberto Kelly New York Yankees checklist	.05
50	Top Prospect '91 Checklist	.05
51	Kyle Abbott RC	.10
52	Jeff Juden	.05
53	Todd Van Poppel RC	.10
54	Steve Karsay RC	.10
55	Chipper Jones RC	3.00
56	Chris Johnson RC	.05
57	John Ericks RC	.05
58	Gary Scott RC	.05
59	Kiki Jones RC	.05
60	Wil Cordero RC	.05
61	Royce Clayton RC	.05
62	Tim Costo RC	.05
63	Roger Salkeld	.05
64	Brook Fordyce RC	.05
65	Mike Mussina RC	1.00
66	Dave Staton RC	.05
67	Mike Lieberthal RC	.50
68	Kurt Miller RC	.05
69	Dan Peltier RC	.05
70	Greg Blosser	.05
71	Reggie Sanders RC	.25
72	Brent Mayne	.05
73	Rico Brogna RC	.05
74	Willie Banks RC	.05
75	Len Brutcher RC	.05
76	Pat Kelly RC	.05
77	Chris Sabo Cincinnati Reds Checklist	.05
78	Ramon Martinez Los Angeles Dodgers Checklist	.05
79	Matt Williams San Francisco Giants Checklist	.05
80	Roberto Alomar San Diego Padres checklist	.05
81	Glenn Davis Houston Astros Checklist	.05
82	Ron Gant Atlanta Braves Checklist	.05
83	Cecil Fielder "Fielder's Feat"	.05

84	Orlando Merced RC	.10
85	Domingo Ramos	.05
86	Tom Bolton	.05
87	Andres Santana RC	.05
88	John Dopson	.05
89	Kenny Williams	.05
90	Marty Barrett	.05
91	Tom Pagnozzi	.05
92	Carmelo Martinez	.05
93	Bobby Thigpen "Save Master"	.05
94	Barry Bonds Pittsburgh Pirates Checklist	.50
95	Gregg Jefferies New York Mets Checklist	.05
96	Tim Wallach Montreal Expos Checklist	.05
97	Lenny Dykstra Philadelphia Phillies Checklist	.05
98	Pedro Guerrero St. Louis Cardinals checklist	.05
99	Mark Grace Chicago Cubs Checklist	.05
100	Checklist 1-100	.05
101	Kevin Elster	.05
102	Tom Brookens	.05
103	Mackey Sasser	.05
104	Felix Fermin	.05
105	Kevin McReynolds	.05
106	Dave Steib	.05
107	Jeffrey Leonard	.05
108	Dave Henderson	.05
109	Sid Bream	.05
110	Henry Cotto	.05
111	Shawon Dunston	.05
112	Mariano Duncan	.05
113	Joe Girardi	.05
114	Billy Hatcher	.05
115	Greg Maddux	.50
116	Jerry Browne	.05
117	Juan Samuel	.05
118	Steve Olin	.05
119	Alfredo Griffin	.05
120	Mitch Webster	.05
121	Joel Skinner	.05
122	Frank Viola	.05
123	Cory Snyder	.05
124	Howard Johnson	.05
125	Carlos Baerga	.05
126	Tony Fernandez	.05
127	Dave Stewart	.05
128	Jay Buhner	.05
129	Mike LaValliere	.05
130	Scott Bradley	.05
131	Tony Phillips	.05
132	Ryne Sandberg	.50
133	Paul O'Neil	.05
134	Mark Grace	.05
135	Chris Sabo	.05
136	Ramon Martinez	.05
137	Brook Jacoby	.05
138	Candy Maldonado	.05
139	Mike Scioscia	.05
140	Chris James	.05
141	Craig Worthington	.05
142	Manny Lee	.05
143	Tim Raines	.05
144	Sandy Alomar, Jr.	.05
145	John Olerud	.05
146	Ozzie Canseco RC	.05
147	Pat Borders	.05
148	Harold Reynolds	.05
149	Tom Henke	.05
150	R.J. Reynolds	.05
151	Mike Gallego	.05
152	Bobby Bonilla	.05
153	Terry Steinbach	.05
154	Barry Bonds	1.00
155	Jose Canseco	.30
156	Gregg Jefferies	.05
157	Matt Williams	.05
158	Craig Biggio	.05
159	Daryl Boston	.05
160	Ricky Jordan	.05
161	Stan Belinda	.05
162	Ozzie Smith	.50
163	Tom Brunansky	.05
164	Todd Zeile	.05
165	Mike Greenwell	.05
166	Kal Daniels	.05
167	Kent Hrbek	.05
168	Franklin Stubbs	.05
169	Dick Schofield	.05
170	Junior Ortiz	.05
171	Hector Villanueva RC	.05
172	Dennis Eckersley	.35
173	Mitch Williams	.05
174	Mark McGwire	.75
175	Fernando Valenzuela	.05
176	Gary Carter	.40
177	Dave Magadan	.05
178	Robby Thompson	.05
179	Bob Ojeda	.05
180	Ken Caminiti	.05

No.	Name	Price
181	Don Slaught	.05
182	Luis Rivera	.05
183	Jay Bell	.05
184	Jody Reed	.05
185	Wally Backman	.05
186	Dave Martinez	.05
187	Luis Polonia	.05
188	Shane Mack	.05
189	Spike Owen	.05
190	Scott Bailes	.05
191	John Russell	.05
192	Walt Weiss	.05
193	Jose Oquendo	.05
194	Carney Lansford	.05
195	Jeff Huson	.05
196	Keith Miller	.05
197	Eric Yelding	.05
198	Ron Darling	.05
199	John Kruk	.05
200	Checklist 101-200	.05
201	John Shelby	.05
202	Bob Geren	.05
203	Lance McCullers	.05
204	Alvaro Espinoza	.05
205	Mark Salas	.05
206	Mike Pagliarulo	.05
207	Jose Uribe	.05
208	Jim Deshaies	.05
209	Ron Karkovice	.05
210	Rafael Ramirez	.05
211	Donnie Hill	.05
212	Brian Harper	.05
213	Jack Howell	.05
214	Wes Gardner	.05
215	Tim Burke	.05
216	Doug Jones	.05
217	Hubie Brooks	.05
218	Tom Candiotti	.05
219	Gerald Perry	.05
220	Jose DeLeon	.05
221	Wally Whitehurst	.05
222	Alan Mills RC	.05
223	Alan Trammell	.05
224	Dwight Gooden	.05
225	Travis Fryman	.05
226	Joe Carter	.05
227	Julio Franco	.05
228	Craig Lefferts	.05
229	Gary Pettis	.05
230	Dennis Rasmussen	.05
231a	Brian Downing (No position on front.)	2.00
231b	Brian Downing (DH on front)	.05
232	Carlos Quintana	.05
233	Gary Gaetti	.05
234	Mark Langston	.05
235	Tim Wallach	.05
236	Greg Swindell	.05
237	Eddie Murray	.40
238	Jeff Manto	.05
239	Lenny Harris	.05
240	Jesse Orosco	.05
241	Scott Lusader	.05
242	Sid Fernandez	.05
243	Jim Leyritz	.05
244	Cecil Fielder	.05
245	Darryl Strawberry	.05
246	Frank Thomas	.50
247	Kevin Mitchell	.05
248	Lance Johnson	.05
249	Rick Rueschel	.05
250	Mark Portugal	.05
251	Derek Lilliquist	.05
252	Brian Holman	.05
253	Rafael Valdez	.05
254	B.J. Surhoff	.05
255	Tony Gwynn	.50
256	Andy Van Slyke	.05
257	Todd Stottlemyre	.05
258	Jose Lind	.05
259	Greg Myers	.05
260	Jeff Ballard	.05
261	Bobby Thigpen	.05
262	Jimmy Kremers RC	.05
263	Robin Ventura	.05
264	John Smoltz	.05
265	Sammy Sosa	.50
266	Gary Sheffield	.30
267	Len Dykstra	.05
268	Bill Spiers	.05
269	Charlie Hayes	.05
270	Brett Butler	.05
271	Bip Roberts	.05
272	Rob Deer	.05
273	Fred Lynn	.05
274	Dave Parker	.05
275	Andy Benes	.05
276	Glenallen Hill	.05
277	Steve Howard RC	.05
278	Doug Drabek	.05
279	Joe Oliver	.05
280	Todd Benzinger	.05
281	Eric King	.05
282	Jim Presley	.05
283	Ken Patterson	.05
284	Jack Daugherty	.05
285	Ivan Calderon	.05
286	Edgar Diaz RC	.05
287	Kevin Bass	.05
288	Don Carman	.05
289	Greg Brock	.05
290	John Franco	.05
291	Joey Cora	.05
292	Bill Wegman	.05
293	Eric Show	.05
294	Scott Bankhead	.05
295	Garry Templeton	.05
296	Mickey Tettleton	.05
297	Luis Sojo	.05
298	Jose Rijo	.05
299	Dave Johnson	.05
300	Checklist 201-300	.05
301	Mark Grant	.05
302	Pete Harnisch	.05
303	Greg Olson	.05
304	Anthony Telford RC	.05
305	Lonnie Smith	.05
306	Chris Hoiles	.05
307	Bryn Smith	.05
308	Mike Devereaux	.05
309a	Milt Thompson ("86" in stats obscured by "bull's eye.")	.50
309b	Milt Thompson ("86" visible)	.05
310	Bob Melvin	.05
311a	Luis Salazar (Circled dot over "i" in Luis on back.)	2.00
311b	Luis Salazar (Corrected)	.05
312	Ed Whitson	.05
313	Charlie Hough	.05
314	Dave Clark	.05
315	Eric Gunderson RC	.05
316	Dan Petry	.05
317	Dante Bichette	.05
318	Mike Heath	.05
319	Damon Berryhill	.05
320	Walt Terrell	.05
321	Scott Fletcher	.05
322	Dan Plesac	.05
323	Jack McDowell	.05
324	Paul Molitor	.40
325	Ozzie Guillen	.05
326	Gregg Olson	.05
327	Pedro Guerrero	.05
328	Bob Milacki	.05
329	John Tudor	.05
330	Steve Finley	.05
331	Jack Clark	.05
332	Jerome Walton	.05
333	Andy Hawkins	.05
334	Derrick May	.05
335	Roberto Alomar	.20
336	Jack Morris	.05
337	Dave Winfield	.40
338	Steve Searcy	.05
339	Chili Davis	.05
340	Larry Sheets	.05
341	Ted Higuera	.05
342	David Segui RC	.10
343	Greg Cadaret	.05
344	Robin Yount	.05
345	Nolan Ryan	1.00
346	Ray Lankford	.05
347	Cal Ripken, Jr.	1.00
348	Lee Smith	.05
349	Brady Anderson	.05
350	Frank DiPino	.05
351	Hal Morris	.05
352	Deion Sanders	.10
353	Barry Larkin	.05
354	Don Mattingly	.60
355	Eric Davis	.05
356	Jose Offerman	.05
357	Mel Rojas	.05
358	Rudy Seanez	.05
359	Oil Can Boyd	.05
360	Nelson Liriano	.05
361	Ron Gant	.05
362	Howard Farmer RC	.05
363	Dave Justice	.05
364	Delino DeShields	.05
365	Steve Avery	.05
366	David Cone	.05
367	Lou Whitaker	.05
368	Von Hayes	.05
369	Frank Tanana	.05
370	Tim Teufel	.05
371	Randy Myers	.05
372	Roberto Kelly	.05
373	Jack Armstrong	.05
374	Kelly Gruber	.05
375	Kevin Maas	.05
376	Randy Johnson	.40
377	David West	.05
378	Brent Knackert RC	.05
379	Rick Honeycutt	.05
380	Kevin Gross	.05
381	Tom Foley	.05
382	Jeff Blauser	.05
383	Scott Ruskin RC	.05
384	Andres Thomas	.05
385	Dennis Martinez	.05
386	Mike Henneman	.05
387	Felix Jose	.05
388	Alejandro Pena	.05
389	Chet Lemon	.05
390	Craig Wilson RC	.05
391	Chuck Crim	.05
392	Mel Hall	.05
393	Mark Knudson	.05
394	Norm Charlton	.05
395	Mike Felder	.05
396	Tim Layana RC	.05
397	Steve Frey	.05
398	Bill Doran	.05
399	Dion James	.05
400	Checklist 301-400	.05
401	Ron Hassey	.05
402	Don Robinson	.05
403	Gene Nelson	.05
404	Terry Kennedy	.05
405	Todd Burns	.05
406	Roger McDowell	.05
407	Bob Kipper	.05
408	Darren Daulton	.05
409	Chuck Cary	.05
410	Bruce Ruffin	.05
411	Juan Berenguer	.05
412	Gary Ward	.05
413	Al Newman	.05
414	Danny Jackson	.05
415	Greg Gagne	.05
416	Tom Herr	.05
417	Jeff Parrett	.05
418	Jeff Reardon	.05
419	Mark Lemke	.05
420	Charlie O'Brien	.05
421	Willie Randolph	.05
422	Steve Bedrosian	.05
423	Mike Moore	.05
424	Jeff Brantley	.05
425	Bob Welch	.05
426	Terry Mulholland	.05
427	Willie Blair RC	.05
428	Darrin Fletcher	.05
429	Mike Witt	.05
430	Joe Boever	.05
431	Tom Gordon	.05
432	Pedro Munoz RC	.05
433	Kevin Seitzer	.05
434	Kevin Tapani	.05
435	Bret Saberhagen	.05
436	Ellis Burks	.05
437	Chuck Finley	.05
438	Mike Boddicker	.05
439	Francisco Cabrera	.05
440	Todd Hundley	.05
441	Kelly Downs	.05
442	Dann Howitt RC	.05
443	Scott Garrelts	.05
444	Rickey Henderson	.40
445	Will Clark	.05
446	Ben McDonald	.05
447	Dale Murphy	.20
448	Dave Righetti	.05
449	Dickie Thon	.05
450	Ted Power	.05
451	Scott Coolbaugh	.05
452	Dwight Smith	.05
453	Pete Incaviglia	.05
454	Andre Dawson	.25
455	Ruben Sierra	.05
456	Andres Galarraga	.05
457	Alvin Davis	.05
458	Tony Castillo	.05
459	Pete O'Brien	.05
460	Charlie Leibrandt	.05
461	Vince Coleman	.05
462	Steve Sax	.05
463	Omar Oliveras RC	.05
464	Oscar Azocar RC	.05
465	Joe Magrane	.05
466	Karl Rhodes RC	.05
467	Benito Santiago	.05
468	Joe Klink RC	.05
469	Sil Campusano	.05
470	Mark Parent	.05
471	Shawn Boskie RC	.05
472	Kevin Brown	.05
473	Rick Sutcliffe	.05
474	Rafael Palmeiro	.35
475	Mike Harkey	.05
476	Jaime Navarro	.05
477	Marquis Grissom	.05
478	Marty Clary	.05
479	Greg Briley	.05
480	Tom Glavine	.25
481	Lee Guetterman	.05
482	Rex Hudler	.05
483	Dave LaPoint	.05
484	Terry Pendleton	.05
485	Jesse Barfield	.05
486	Jose DeJesus	.05
487	Paul Abbott RC	.05
488	Ken Howell	.05
489	Greg W. Harris	.05
490	Roy Smith	.05
491	Paul Assenmacher	.05
492	Geno Petralli	.05
493	Steve Wilson	.05
494	Kevin Reimer	.05
495	Bill Long	.05
496	Mike Jackson	.05
497	Oddibe McDowell	.05
498	Bill Swift	.05
499	Jeff Treadway	.05
500	Checklist 401-500	.05
501	Gene Larkin	.05
502	Bob Boone	.05
503	Allan Anderson	.05
504	Luis Aquino	.05
505	Mark Guthrie	.05
506	Joe Orsulak	.05
507	Dana Kiecker RC	.05
508	Dave Gallagher	.05
509	Greg A. Harris	.05
510	Mark Williamson	.05
511	Casey Candaele	.05
512	Mookie Wilson	.05
513	Dave Smith	.05
514	Chuck Carr RC	.05
515	Glenn Wilson	.05
516	Mike Fitzgerald	.05
517	Devon White	.05
518	Dave Hollins	.05
519	Mark Eichhorn	.05
520	Otis Nixon	.05
521	Terry Shumpert RC	.05
522	Scott Erickson RC	.15
523	Danny Tartabull	.05
524	Orel Hershiser	.05
525	George Brett	.60
526	Greg Vaughn	.05
527	Tim Naehring	.05
528	Curt Schilling	.25
529	Chris Bosio	.05
530	Sam Horn	.05
531	Mike Scott	.05
532	George Bell	.05
533	Eric Anthony	.05
534	Julio Valera RC	.05
535	Glenn Davis	.05
536	Larry Walker	.05
537	Pat Combs	.05
538	Chris Nabholz RC	.05
539	Kirk McCaskill	.05
540	Randy Ready	.05
541	Mark Gubicza	.05
542	Rick Aguilera	.05
543	Brian McRae RC	.05
544	Kirby Puckett	.50
545	Bo Jackson	.10
546	Wade Boggs	.50
547	Tim McIntosh	.05
548	Randy Milligan	.05
549	Dwight Evans	.05
550	Billy Ripken	.05
551	Erik Hanson	.05
552	Lance Parrish	.05
553	Tino Martinez	.05
554	Jim Abbott	.05
555	Ken Griffey Jr.	.65
556	Milt Cuyler	.05
557	Mark Leonard RC	.05
558	Jay Howell	.05
559	Lloyd Moseby	.05
560	Chris Gwynn	.05
561	Mark Whiten RC	.05
562	Harold Baines	.05
563	Junior Felix	.05
564	Darren Lewis	.05
565	Fred McGriff	.05
566	Kevin Appier	.05
567	Luis Gonzalez RC	1.00
568	Frank White	.05
569	Juan Agosto	.05
570	Mike Macfarlane	.05
571	Bert Blyleven	.05
572	Ken Griffey Sr.	.05
573	Lee Stevens	.05
574	Edgar Martinez	.05
575	Wally Joyner	.05
576	Tim Belcher	.05
577	John Burkett	.05
578	Mike Morgan	.05
579	Paul Gibson	.05
580	Jose Vizcaino	.05
581	Duane Ward	.05
582	Scott Sanderson	.05
583	David Wells	.05
584	Willie McGee	.05
585	John Cerutti	.05
586	Danny Darwin	.05
587	Kurt Stillwell	.05
588	Rich Gedman	.05
589	Mark Davis	.05
590	Bill Gullickson	.05
591	Matt Young	.05
592	Bryan Harvey	.05
593	Omar Vizquel	.05
594	Scott Lewis RC	.05

595 Dave Valle .05
596 Tim Crews .05
597 Mike Bielecki .05
598 Mike Sharperson .05
599 Dave Bergman .05
600 Checklist 501-600 .05
601 Steve Lyons .05
602 Bruce Hurst .05
603 Donn Pall .05
604 Jim Vatcher RC .05
605 Dan Pasqua .05
606 Kenny Rogers .05
607 Jeff Schulz RC .05
608 Brad Arnsberg .05
609 Willie Wilson .05
610 Jamie Moyer .05
611 Ron Oester .05
612 Dennis Cook .05
613 Rick Mahler .05
614 Bill Landrum .05
615 Scott Scudder .05
616 Tom Edens RC .05
617 "1917 Revisited" (Chicago White Sox team photo.) .05
618 Jim Gantner .05
619 Darrel Akerfelds .05
620 Ron Robinson .05
621 Scott Radinsky .05
622 Pete Smith .05
623 Melido Perez .05
624 Jerald Clark .05
625 Carlos Martinez .05
626 Wes Chamberlain RC .05
627 Bobby Witt .05
628 Ken Dayley .05
629 John Barfield RC .05
630 Bob Tewksbury .05
631 Glenn Braggs .05
632 Jim Neidlinger RC .05
633 Tom Browning .05
634 Kirk Gibson .05
635 Rob Dibble .05
636 Lou Brock, Rickey Henderson "Stolen Base Leaders" .15
637 Jeff Montgomery .05
638 Mike Schooler .05
639 Storm Davis .05
640 Rich Rodriguez RC .05
641 Phil Bradley .05
642 Kent Mercker .05
643 Carlton Fisk .40
644 Mike Bell .05
645 Alex Fernandez RC .05
646 Juan Gonzalez .30
647 Ken Hill .05
648 Jeff Russell .05
649 Chuck Malone RC .05
650 Steve Buechele .05
651 Mike Benjamin .05
652 Tony Pena .05
653 Trevor Wilson .05
654 Alex Cole .05
655 Roger Clemens .60
656 Mark McGwire "The Bashing Years" .50
657 Joe Grahe RC .05
658 Jim Eisenreich .05
659 Dan Gladden .05
660 Steve Farr .05
661 Bill Sampen RC .05
662 Dave Rohde RC .05
663 Mark Gardner .05
664 Mike Simms RC .05
665 Moises Alou .05
666 Mickey Hatcher .05
667 Jimmy Key .05
668 John Wetteland .05
669 John Smiley .05
670 Jim Acker .05
671 Pascual Perez .05
672 Reggie Harris RC .05
673 Matt Nokes .05
674 Rafael Novoa RC .05
675 Hensley Meulens .05
676 Jeff M. Robinson .05
677 "Ground Breaking" (New Comiskey Park) .15
678 Johnny Ray .05
679 Greg Hibbard .05
680 Paul Sorrento .05
681 Mike Marshall .05
682 Jim Clancy .05
683 Rob Murphy .05
684 Dave Schmidt .05
685 Jeff Gray RC .05
686 Mike Hartley .05
687 Jeff King .05
688 Stan Javier .05
689 Bob Walk .05
690 Jim Gott .05
691 Mike LaCoss .05
692 John Farrell .05
693 Tim Leary .05
694 Mike Walker RC .05

695 Eric Plunk .05
696 Mike Fetters .05
697 Wayne Edwards .05
698 Tim Drummond .05
699 Willie Fraser .05
700 Checklist 601-700 .05
701 Mike Heath .05
702 Luis Gonzalez, Karl Rhodes, Jeff Bagwell "Rookie Threats" .45
703 Jose Mesa .05
704 Dave Smith .05
705 Danny Darwin .05
706 Rafael Belliard .05
707 Rob Murphy .05
708 Terry Pendleton .05
709 Mike Pagliarulo .05
710 Sid Bream .05
711 Junior Felix .05
712 Dante Bichette .05
713 Kevin Gross .05
714 Luis Sojo .05
715 Bob Ojeda .05
716 Julio Machado .05
717 Steve Farr .05
718 Franklin Stubbs .05
719 Mike Boddicker .05
720 Willie Randolph .05
721 Willie McGee .05
722 Chili Davis .05
723 Danny Jackson .05
724 Cory Snyder .05
725 Andre Dawson, George Bell, Ryne Sandberg "MVP Lineup" .20
726 Rob Deer .05
727 Rich DeLucia .05
728 Mike Perez .05
729 Mickey Tettleton .05
730 Mike Blowers .05
731 Gary Gaetti .05
732 Brett Butler .05
733 Dave Parker .05
734 Eddie Zosky .05
735 Jack Clark .05
736 Jack Morris .05
737 Kirk Gibson .05
738 Steve Bedrosian .05
739 Candy Maldonado .05
740 Matt Young .05
741 Rich Garces .05
742 George Bell .05
743 Deion Sanders .10
744 Bo Jackson .10
745 Luis Mercedes .05
746 Reggie Jefferson .05
747 Pete Incaviglia .05
748 Chris Hammond .05
749 Mike Stanton .05
750 Scott Sanderson .05
751 Paul Faries .05
752 Al Osuna .05
753 Steve Chitren .05
754 Tony Fernandez .05
755 Jeff Bagwell RC 1.50
756 Kirk Dressendorfer .05
757 Glenn Davis .05
758 Gary Carter .40
759 Zane Smith .05
760 Vance Law .05
761 Denis Boucher .05
762 Turner Ward .05
763 Roberto Alomar .20
764 Albert Belle .05
765 Joe Carter .05
766 Pete Schourek .05
767 Heathcliff Slocumb .05
768 Vince Coleman .05
769 Mitch Williams .05
770 Brian Downing .05
771 Dana Allison .05
772 Pete Harnisch .05
773 Tim Raines .05
774 Darryl Kile .05
775 Fred McGriff .05
776 Dwight Evans .05
777 Joe Slusarski .05
778 Dave Righetti .05
779 Jeff Hamilton .05
780 Ernest Riles .05
781 Ken Dayley .05
782 Eric King .05
783 Devon White .05
784 Beau Allred .05
785 Mike Timlin .05
786 Ivan Calderon .05
787 Hubie Brooks .05
788 Juan Agosto .05
789 Barry Jones .05
790 Wally Backman .05
791 Jim Presley .05
792 Charlie Hough .05
793 Larry Andersen .05
794 Steve Finley .05

795 Shawn Abner .05
796 Jeff M. Robinson .05
797 Joe Bitker .05
798 Eric Show .05
799 Bud Black .05
800 Checklist 701-800 .05
SP1 Michael Jordan 3.00
SP2 Rickey Henderson, Nolan Ryan "A Day to Remember" 1.00
HH1 Hank Aaron (Hologram) 1.00

Final Edition

Oil Can Boyd

NM/M

Complete Set (100): 9.00
Common Player: .05
1 Ryan Klesko, Reggie Sanders (Minor League Diamond Skills Checklist) .10
2 Pedro Martinez RC 5.00
3 Lance Dickson .05
4 Royce Clayton .05
5 Scott Bryant .05
6 Dan Wilson .05
7 Dmitri Young RC .50
8 Ryan Klesko RC .50
9 Tom Goodwin .05
10 Rondell White RC .25
11 Reggie Sanders .05
12 Todd Van Poppel .05
13 Arthur Rhodes .05
14 Eddie Zosky .05
15 Gerald Williams .05
16 Robert Eenhoorn .05
17 Jim Thome RC 3.00
18 Marc Newfield RC .05
19 Kerwin Moore .05
20 Jeff McNeely .05
21 Frankie Rodriguez .05
22 Andy Mota .05
23 Chris Haney .05
24 Kenny Lofton RC .25
25 Dave Nilsson .05
26 Derek Bell .05
27 Frank Castillo .05
28 Candy Maldonado .05
29 Chuck McElroy .05
30 Chito Martinez .05
31 Steve Howe .05
32 Freddie Benavides .05
33 Scott Kamieniecki .05
34 Denny Neagle .05
35 Mike Humphreys .05
36 Mike Remlinger .05
37 Scott Coolbaugh .05
38 Darren Lewis .05
39 Thomas Howard .05
40 John Candelaria .05
41 Todd Benzinger .05
42 Wilson Alvarez .05
43 Patrick Lennon .05
44 Rusty Meacham .05
45 Ryan Bowen RC .05
46 Rick Wilkins RC .10
47 Ed Sprague RC .05
48 Bob Scanlan RC .05
49 Tom Candiotti .05
50 Dennis Martinez (Perfecto) .05
51 Oil Can Boyd .05
52 Glenallen Hill .05
53 Scott Livingstone RC .05
54 Brian Hunter RC .05
55 Ivan Rodriguez RC 1.50
56 Keith Mitchell RC .05
57 Roger McDowell .05
58 Otis Nixon .05
59 Juan Bell RC .05
60 Bill Krueger .05
61 Chris Donnels RC .05
62 Tommy Greene .05

63 Doug Simons .05
64 Andy Ashby RC .15
65 Anthony Young RC .05
66 Kevin Morton RC .05
67 Bret Barberie RC .05
68 Scott Servais RC .05
69 Ron Darling .05
70 Vicente Palacios .05
71 Tim Burke RC .05
72 Gerald Alexander RC .05
73 Reggie Jefferson .05
74 Dean Palmer .05
75 Mark Whiten .05
76 Randy Tomlin .05
77 Mark Wohlers RC .05
78 Brook Jacoby .05
79 Ken Griffey Jr., Ryne Sandberg (All-Star Checklist) .25
80 Jack Morris/AS .05
81 Sandy Alomar, Jr./AS .05
82 Cecil Fielder/AS .05
83 Roberto Alomar/AS .10
84 Wade Boggs/AS .25
85 Cal Ripken, Jr./AS .60
86 Rickey Henderson/AS .15
87 Ken Griffey Jr./AS .60
88 Dave Henderson/AS .05
89 Danny Tartabull/AS .05
90 Tom Glavine/AS .10
91 Benito Santiago/AS .05
92 Will Clark/AS .05
93 Ryne Sandberg/AS .50
94 Chris Sabo/AS .05
95 Ozzie Smith/AS .50
96 Ivan Calderon/AS .05
97 Tony Gwynn/AS .25
98 Andre Dawson/AS .05
99 Bobby Bonilla/AS .05
100 Checklist .05

Baseball Heroes Hank Aaron

NM/M

Complete Set (10): 4.00
Common Aaron: .50
Autographed Card: 180.00
Aaron Header: 1.00

Baseball Heroes Nolan Ryan

NM/M

Complete Set (10): 3.00
Common Ryan: .50
Ryan Header Card: 1.00
Autographed Card: 200.00
"Strike Out King" Auto.: 575.00

1991 Upper Deck Heroes of Baseball

		NM/M
Complete Set (4):		7.00
Common Card:		2.00
1	Harmon Killebrew	2.00
1a	Harmon Killebrew/Auto.	10.00
2	Gaylord Perry	2.00
2a	Gaylord Perry/Auto.	10.00
3	Ferguson Jenkins	2.00
3a	Ferguson Jenkins/Auto.	10.00
4	Gaylord Perry, Ferguson Jenkins, Harmon Killebrew	2.00

Silver Sluggers

Alan Trammell

		NM/M
Complete Set (18):		5.00
Common Player:		.15
1	Julio Franco	.15
2	Alan Trammell	.15
3	Rickey Henderson	.75
4	Jose Canseco	.50
5	Barry Bonds	2.00
6	Eddie Murray	.75
7	Kelly Gruber	.15
8	Ryne Sandberg	1.00
9	Darryl Strawberry	.15
10	Ellis Burks	.15
11	Lance Parrish	.15
12	Cecil Fielder	.15
13	Matt Williams	.15
14	Dave Parker	.15
15	Bobby Bonilla	.15
16	Don Robinson	.15
17	Benito Santiago	.15
18	Barry Larkin	.15

1992 Upper Deck

TONY GWYNN

		NM/M
Unopened Fact. Set (800):		20.00
Complete Set (800):		15.00
Common Player:		.05
Low or High Pack (15):		.50
Low or High Box (36):		12.50

Jumbo Pack (27):		1.00
Jumbo Box (20):		16.00
Bench/Morgan Auto.		75.00
Ted Williams Auto.		425.00
1	Ryan Klesko, Jim Thome Star Rookie Checklist	.25
2	Royce Clayton	.05
3	Brian Jordan RC	.30
4	Dave Fleming RC	.05
5	Jim Thome	.40
6	Jeff Juden	.05
7	Roberto Hernandez RC	.15
8	Kyle Abbott	.05
9	Chris George RC	.05
10	Rob Maurer RC	.05
11	Donald Harris RC	.05
12	Ted Wood RC	.05
13	Patrick Lennon RC	.05
14	Willie Banks	.05
15	Roger Salkeld	.05
16	Wil Cordero	.05
17	Arthur Rhodes RC	.05
18	Pedro Martinez	.40
19	Andy Ashby RC	.10
20	Tom Goodwin	.05
21	Braulio Castillo RC	.05
22	Todd Van Poppel	.05
23	Brian Williams RC	.05
24	Ryan Klesko	.05
25	Kenny Lofton	.05
26	Derek Bell	.05
27	Reggie Sanders	.05
28	Dave Winfield (Winfield's 400th)	.25
29	Dave Justice Atlanta Braves Checklist	.05
30	Rob Dibble Cincinnati Reds Checklist	.05
31	Craig Biggio (RC) Houston Astros Checklist	.05
32	Eddie Murray Los Angeles Dodgers Checklist	.20
33	Fred McGriff San Diego Padres Checklist	.05
34	Willie McGee San Francisco Giants Checklist	.05
35	Shawon Dunston Chicago Cubs Checklist	.05
36	Delino DeShields Montreal Expos Checklist	.05
37	Howard Johnson New York Mets Checklist	.05
38	John Kruk Philadelphia Phillies Checklist	.05
39	Doug Drabek Pittsburgh Pirates Checklist	.05
40	Todd Zeile St. Louis Cardinals Checklist	.05
41	Steve Avery (Playoff Perfection)	.05
42	Jeremy Hernandez RC	.05
43	Doug Henry RC	.05
44	Chris Donnels RC	.05
45	Mo Sanford RC	.05
46	Scott Kamieniecki RC	.10
47	Mark Lemke	.05
48	Steve Farr	.05
49	Francisco Oliveras	.05
50	Ced Landrum RC	.05
51	Rondell White, Marc Newfield Top Prospect Checklist	.05
52	Eduardo Perez RC	.10
53	Tom Nevers RC	.05
54	David Zancanaro RC	.05
55	Shawn Green RC	1.50
56	Mark Wohlers RC	.05
57	Dave Nilsson	.05
58	Dmitri Young	.05
59	Ryan Hawblitzel RC	.05
60	Raul Mondesi	.05
61	Rondell White	.05
62	Steve Hosey	.05
63	Manny Ramirez RC	2.00
64	Marc Newfield	.05
65	Jeromy Burnitz	.05
66	Mark Smith RC	.05
67	Joey Hamilton RC	.10
68	Tyler Green RC	.05
69	John Farrell RC	.05
70	Kurt Miller RC	.05
71	Jeff Plympton RC	.05
72	Dan Wilson	.05
73	Joe Vitiello RC	.05
74	Rico Brogna	.05
75	David McCarty RC	.05
76	Bob Wickman RC	.05
77	Carlos Rodriguez RC	.05
78	Jim Abbott (Stay in School)	.05
79	Pedro Martinez, Ramon Martinez Bloodlines	.25

80	Kevin Mitchell, Keith Mitchell Bloodlines	.05
81	Sandy Jr. & Roberto Alomar, Sandy Jr. & Roberto Alomar Bloodlines	.10
82	Cal Jr. & Billy Ripken, Cal Jr. & Billy Ripken Bloodlines	.40
83	Tony & Chris Gwynn, Tony & Chris Gwynn Bloodlines	.20
84	Dwight Gooden, Gary Sheffield Bloodlines	.15
85	Ken, Sr.; Ken, Jr.; & Craig Griffey, Ken, Sr.; Ken, Jr.; & Craig Griffey, Ken, Sr.; Ken, Jr.; & Craig Griffey Bloodlines	.30
86	Jim Abbott California Angels Checklist	.05
87	Frank Thomas Chicago White Sox Checklist	.25
88	Danny Tartabull Kansas City Royals Checklist	.05
89	Scott Erickson Minnesota Twins Checklist	.05
90	Rickey Henderson Oakland Athletics Checklist	.25
91	Edgar Martinez Seattle Mariners Checklist	.05
92	Nolan Ryan Texas Rangers Checklist	.50
93	Ben McDonald Baltimore Orioles Checklist	.05
94	Ellis Burks Boston Red Sox Checklist	.05
95	Greg Swindell Cleveland Indians Checklist	.05
96	Cecil Fielder Detroit Tigers Checklist	.05
97	Greg Vaughn Milwaukee Brewers Checklist	.05
98	Kevin Maas New York Yankees Checklist	.05
99	Dave Steib Toronto Blue Jays Checklist	.05
100	Checklist 1-100	.05
101	Joe Oliver	.05
102	Hector Villanueva	.05
103	Ed Whitson	.05
104	Danny Jackson	.05
105	Chris Hammond	.05
106	Ricky Jordan	.05
107	Kevin Bass	.05
108	Darrin Fletcher	.05
109	Junior Ortiz	.05
110	Tom Bolton	.05
111	Jeff King	.05
112	Dave Magadan	.05
113	Mike LaValliere	.05
114	Hubie Brooks	.05
115	Jay Bell	.05
116	David Wells	.05
117	Jim Leyritz	.05
118	Manuel Lee	.05
119	Alvaro Espinoza	.05
120	B.J. Surhoff	.05
121	Hal Morris	.05
122	Shawon Dunston	.05
123	Chris Sabo	.05
124	Andre Dawson	.25
125	Eric Davis	.05
126	Chili Davis	.05
127	Dale Murphy	.15
128	Kirk McCaskill	.05
129	Terry Mulholland	.05
130	Rick Aguilera	.05
131	Vince Coleman	.05
132	Andy Van Slyke	.05
133	Gregg Jefferies	.05
134	Barry Bonds	1.00
135	Dwight Gooden	.05
136	Dave Steib	.05
137	Albert Belle	.05
138	Teddy Higuera	.05
139	Jesse Barfield	.05
140	Pat Borders	.05
141	Bip Roberts	.05
142	Rob Dibble	.05
143	Mark Grace	.05
144	Barry Larkin	.05
145	Ryne Sandberg	.50
146	Scott Erickson	.05
147	Luis Polonia	.05
148	John Burkett	.05
149	Luis Sojo	.05
150	Dickie Thon	.05
151	Walt Weiss	.05
152	Mike Scioscia	.05
153	Mark McGwire	.75

154	Matt Williams	.05
155	Rickey Henderson	.40
156	Sandy Alomar, Jr.	.05
157	Brian McRae	.05
158	Harold Baines	.05
159	Kevin Appier	.05
160	Felix Fermin	.05
161	Leo Gomez	.05
162	Craig Biggio	.05
163	Ben McDonald	.05
164	Randy Johnson	.40
165	Cal Ripken, Jr.	1.00
166	Frank Thomas	.40
167	Delino DeShields	.05
168	Greg Gagne	.05
169	Ron Karkovice	.05
170	Charlie Leibrandt	.05
171	Dave Righetti	.05
172	Dave Henderson	.05
173	Steve Decker	.05
174	Darryl Strawberry	.05
175	Will Clark	.05
176	Ruben Sierra	.05
177	Ozzie Smith	.50
178	Charles Nagy	.05
179	Gary Pettis	.05
180	Kirk Gibson	.05
181	Randy Milligan	.05
182	Dave Valle	.05
183	Chris Hoiles	.05
184	Tony Phillips	.05
185	Brady Anderson	.05
186	Scott Fletcher	.05
187	Gene Larkin	.05
188	Lance Johnson	.05
189	Greg Olson	.05
190	Melido Perez	.05
191	Lenny Harris	.05
192	Terry Kennedy	.05
193	Mike Gallego	.05
194	Willie McGee	.05
195	Juan Samuel	.05
196	Jeff Huson	.05
197	Alex Cole	.05
198	Ron Robinson	.05
199	Joel Skinner	.05
200	Checklist 101-200	.05
201	Kevin Reimer	.05
202	Stan Belinda	.05
203	Pat Tabler	.05
204	Jose Guzman	.05
205	Jose Lind	.05
206	Spike Owen	.05
207	Joe Orsulak	.05
208	Charlie Hayes	.05
209	Mike Devereaux	.05
210	Mike Fitzgerald	.05
211	Willie Randolph	.05
212	Rod Nichols	.05
213	Mike Boddicker	.05
214	Bill Spiers	.05
215	Steve Olin	.05
216	David Howard RC	.05
217	Gary Varsho	.05
218	Mike Harkey	.05
219	Luis Aquino	.05
220	Chuck McElroy	.05
221	Doug Drabek	.05
222	Dave Winfield	.40
223	Rafael Palmeiro	.35
224	Joe Carter	.05
225	Bobby Bonilla	.05
226	Ivan Calderon	.05
227	Gregg Olson	.05
228	Tim Wallach	.05
229	Terry Pendleton	.05
230	Gilberto Reyes	.05
231	Carlos Baerga	.05
232	Greg Vaughn	.05
233	Bret Saberhagen	.05
234	Gary Sheffield	.30
235	Mark Lewis	.05
236	George Bell	.05
237	Danny Tartabull	.05
238	Willie Wilson	.05
239	Doug Dascenzo	.05
240	Bill Pecota	.05
241	Julio Franco	.05
242	Ed Sprague	.05
243	Juan Gonzalez	.20
244	Chuck Finley	.05
245	Ivan Rodriguez	.35
246	Len Dykstra	.05
247	Deion Sanders	.10
248	Dwight Evans	.05
249	Larry Walker	.05
250	Billy Ripken	.05
251	Mickey Tettleton	.05
252	Tony Pena	.05
253	Benito Santiago	.05
254	Kirby Puckett	.50
255	Cecil Fielder	.05
256	Howard Johnson	.05
257	Andujar Cedeno	.05

No	Player	Price
258	Jose Rijo	.05
259	Al Osuna	.05
260	Todd Hundley	.05
261	Orel Hershiser	.05
262	Ray Lankford	.05
263	Robin Ventura	.05
264	Felix Jose	.05
265	Eddie Murray	.40
266	Kevin Mitchell	.05
267	Gary Carter	.40
268	Mike Benjamin	.05
269	Dick Schofield	.05
270	Jose Uribe	.05
271	Pete Incaviglia	.05
272	Tony Fernandez	.05
273	Alan Trammell	.05
274	Tony Gwynn	.50
275	Mike Greenwell	.05
276	Jeff Bagwell	.40
277	Frank Viola	.05
278	Randy Myers	.05
279	Ken Caminiti	.05
280	Bill Doran	.05
281	Dan Pasqua	.05
282	Alfredo Griffin	.05
283	Jose Oquendo	.05
284	Kal Daniels	.05
285	Bobby Thigpen	.05
286	Robby Thompson	.05
287	Mark Eichhorn	.05
288	Mike Felder	.05
289	Dave Gallagher	.05
290	Dave Anderson	.05
291	Mel Hall	.05
292	Jerald Clark	.05
293	Al Newman	.05
294	Rob Deer	.05
295	Matt Nokes	.05
296	Jack Armstrong	.05
297	Jim Deshaies	.05
298	Jeff Innis	.05
299	Jeff Reed	.05
300	Checklist 201-300	.05
301	Lonnie Smith	.05
302	Jimmy Key	.05
303	Junior Felix	.05
304	Mike Heath	.05
305	Mark Langston	.05
306	Greg W. Harris	.05
307	Brett Butler	.05
308	Luis Rivera	.05
309	Bruce Ruffin	.05
310	Paul Faries	.05
311	Terry Leach	.05
312	Scott Brosius RC	.10
313	Scott Leius	.05
314	Harold Reynolds	.05
315	Jack Morris	.05
316	David Segui	.05
317	Bill Gullickson	.05
318	Todd Frohwirth	.05
319	Mark Leiter RC	.05
320	Jeff M. Robinson	.05
321	Gary Gaetti	.05
322	John Smoltz	.05
323	Andy Benes	.05
324	Kelly Gruber	.05
325	Jim Abbott	.05
326	John Kruk	.05
327	Kevin Seitzer	.05
328	Darrin Jackson	.05
329	Kurt Stillwell	.05
330	Mike Maddux	.05
331	Dennis Eckersley	.35
332	Dan Gladden	.05
333	Jose Canseco	.30
334	Kent Hrbek	.05
335	Ken Griffey Sr.	.05
336	Greg Swindell	.05
337	Trevor Wilson	.05
338	Sam Horn	.05
339	Mike Henneman	.05
340	Jerry Browne	.05
341	Glenn Braggs	.05
342	Tom Glavine	.20
343	Wally Joyner	.05
344	Fred McGriff	.05
345	Ron Gant	.05
346	Ramon Martinez	.05
347	Wes Chamberlain	.05
348	Terry Shumpert	.05
349	Tim Teufel	.05
350	Wally Backman	.05
351	Joe Girardi	.05
352	Devon White	.05
353	Greg Maddux	.50
354	Ryan Bowen RC	.05
355	Roberto Alomar	.20
356	Don Mattingly	.60
357	Pedro Guerrero	.05
358	Steve Sax	.05
359	Joey Cora	.05
360	Jim Gantner	.05
361	Brian Barnes (RC)	.05
362	Kevin McReynolds	.05
363	Bret Barberie RC	.05
364	David Cone	.05
365	Dennis Martinez	.05
366	Brian Hunter RC	.05
367	Edgar Martinez	.05
368	Steve Finley	.05
369	Greg Briley	.05
370	Jeff Blauser	.05
371	Todd Stottlemyre	.05
372	Luis Gonzalez	.05
373	Rick Wilkins	.05
374	Darryl Kile RC	.05
375	John Olerud	.05
376	Lee Smith	.05
377	Kevin Maas	.05
378	Dante Bichette	.05
379	Tom Pagnozzi	.05
380	Mike Flanagan	.05
381	Charlie O'Brien	.05
382	Zane Smith	.05
383	Keith Miller	.05
384	Scott Ruskin	.05
385	Kevin Elster	.05
386	Alvin Davis	.05
387	Casey Candaele	.05
388	Pete O'Brien	.05
389	Jeff Treadway	.05
390	Scott Bradley	.05
391	Mookie Wilson	.05
392	Jimmy Jones	.05
393	Candy Maldonado	.05
394	Eric Yelding	.05
395	Tom Henke	.05
396	Franklin Stubbs	.05
397	Milt Thompson	.05
398	Mark Carreon	.05
399	Randy Velarde	.05
400	Checklist 301-400	.05
401	Omar Vizquel	.05
402	Joe Boever	.05
403	Bill Krueger	.05
404	Jody Reed	.05
405	Mike Schooler	.05
406	Jason Grimsley	.05
407	Greg Myers	.05
408	Randy Ready	.05
409	Mike Timlin RC	.15
410	Mitch Williams	.05
411	Garry Templeton	.05
412	Greg Cadaret	.05
413	Donnie Hill	.05
414	Wally Whitehurst	.05
415	Scott Sanderson	.05
416	Thomas Howard	.05
417	Neal Heaton	.05
418	Charlie Hough	.05
419	Jack Howell	.05
420	Greg Hibbard	.05
421	Carlos Quintana	.05
422	Kim Batiste RC	.05
423	Paul Molitor	.40
424	Ken Griffey Jr.	.65
425	Phil Plantier	.05
426	Denny Neagle	.05
427	Von Hayes	.05
428	Shane Mack	.05
429	Darren Daulton	.05
430	Dwayne Henry	.05
431	Lance Parrish	.05
432	Mike Humphreys RC	.05
433	Tim Burke	.05
434	Bryan Harvey	.05
435	Pat Kelly	.05
436	Ozzie Guillen	.05
437	Bruce Hurst	.05
438	Sammy Sosa	.50
439	Dennis Rasmussen	.05
440	Ken Patterson	.05
441	Jay Buhner	.05
442	Pat Combs	.05
443	Wade Boggs	.50
444	George Brett	.60
445	Mo Vaughn	.05
446	Chuck Knoblauch	.50
447	Tom Candiotti	.05
448	Mark Portugal	.05
449	Mickey Morandini	.05
450	Duane Ward	.05
451	Otis Nixon	.05
452	Bob Welch	.05
453	Rusty Meacham	.05
454	Keith Mitchell	.05
455	Marquis Grissom	.05
456	Robin Yount	.40
457	Harvey Pulliam RC	.05
458	Jose DeLeon	.05
459	Mark Gubicza	.05
460	Darryl Hamilton	.05
461	Tom Browning	.05
462	Monty Fariss	.05
463	Jerome Walton	.05
464	Paul O'Neill	.05
465	Dean Palmer	.05
466	Travis Fryman	.05
467	John Smiley	.05
468	Lloyd Moseby	.05
469	John Wehner RC	.05
470	Skeeter Barnes	.05
471	Steve Chitren	.05
472	Kent Mercker	.05
473	Terry Steinbach	.05
474	Andres Galarraga	.05
475	Steve Avery	.05
476	Tom Gordon	.05
477	Cal Eldred	.05
478	Omar Olivares	.05
479	Julio Machado	.05
480	Bob Milacki	.05
481	Les Lancaster	.05
482	John Candelaria	.05
483	Brian Downing	.05
484	Roger McDowell	.05
485	Scott Scudder	.05
486	Zane Smith	.05
487	John Cerutti	.05
488	Steve Buechele	.05
489	Paul Gibson	.05
490	Curtis Wilkerson	.05
491	Marvin Freeman	.05
492	Tom Foley	.05
493	Juan Berenguer	.05
494	Ernest Riles	.05
495	Sid Bream	.05
496	Chuck Crim	.05
497	Mike Macfarlane	.05
498	Dale Sveum	.05
499	Storm Davis	.05
500	Checklist 401-500	.05
501	Jeff Reardon	.05
502	Shawn Abner	.05
503	Tony Fossas	.05
504	Cory Snyder	.05
505	Matt Young	.05
506	Allan Anderson	.05
507	Mark Lee	.05
508	Gene Nelson	.05
509	Mike Pagliarulo	.05
510	Rafael Belliard	.05
511	Jay Howell	.05
512	Bob Tewksbury	.05
513	Mike Morgan	.05
514	John Franco	.05
515	Kevin Gross	.05
516	Lou Whitaker	.05
517	Orlando Merced	.05
518	Todd Benzinger	.05
519	Gary Redus	.05
520	Walt Terrell	.05
521	Jack Clark	.05
522	Dave Parker	.05
523	Tim Naehring	.05
524	Mark Whiten	.05
525	Ellis Burks	.05
526	Frank Castillo RC	.05
527	Brian Harper	.05
528	Brook Jacoby	.05
529	Rick Sutcliffe	.05
530	Joe Klink	.05
531	Terry Bross	.05
532	Jose Offerman	.05
533	Todd Zeile	.05
534	Eric Karros	.05
535	Anthony Young RC	.05
536	Milt Cuyler	.05
537	Randy Tomlin	.05
538	Scott Livingstone RC	.05
539	Jim Eisenreich	.05
540	Don Slaught	.05
541	Scott Cooper	.05
542	Joe Grahe	.05
543	Tom Brunansky	.05
544	Eddie Zosky	.05
545	Roger Clemens	.60
546	Dave Justice	.05
547	Dave Stewart	.05
548	David West	.05
549	Dave Smith	.05
550	Dan Plesac	.05
551	Alex Fernandez	.05
552	Bernard Gilkey	.05
553	Jack McDowell	.05
554	Tino Martinez	.05
555	Bo Jackson	.10
556	Bernie Williams	.05
557	Mark Gardner	.05
558	Glenallen Hill	.05
559	Oil Can Boyd	.05
560	Chris James	.05
561	Scott Servais RC	.05
562	Rey Sanchez RC	.05
563	Paul McClellan RC	.05
564	Andy Mota RC	.05
565	Darren Lewis	.05
566	Jose Melendez RC	.05
567	Tommy Greene	.05
568	Rich Rodriguez	.05
569	Heathcliff Slocumb RC	.05
570	Joe Hesketh	.05
571	Carlton Fisk	.40
572	Erik Hanson	.05
573	Wilson Alvarez	.05
574	Rheal Cormier RC	.05
575	Tim Raines	.05
576	Bobby Witt	.05
577	Roberto Kelly	.05
578	Kevin Brown	.05
579	Chris Nabholz	.05
580	Jesse Orosco	.05
581	Jeff Brantley	.05
582	Rafael Ramirez	.05
583	Kelly Downs	.05
584	Mike Simms	.05
585	Mike Remlinger RC	.05
586	Dave Hollins	.05
587	Larry Andersen	.05
588	Mike Gardiner	.05
589	Craig Lefferts	.05
590	Paul Assenmacher	.05
591	Bryn Smith	.05
592	Donn Pall	.05
593	Mike Jackson	.05
594	Scott Radinsky	.05
595	Brian Holman	.05
596	Geronimo Pena	.05
597	Mike Jeffcoat	.05
598	Carlos Martinez	.05
599	Geno Petralli	.05
600	Checklist 501-600	.05
601	Jerry Don Gleaton	.05
602	Adam Peterson	.05
603	Craig Grebeck	.05
604	Mark Guthrie	.05
605	Frank Tanana	.05
606	Hensley Meulens	.05
607	Mark Davis	.05
608	Eric Plunk	.05
609	Mark Williamson	.05
610	Lee Guetterman	.05
611	Bobby Rose	.05
612	Bill Wegman	.05
613	Mike Hartley	.05
614	Chris Beasley RC	.05
615	Chris Bosio	.05
616	Henry Cotto	.05
617	Chico Walker RC	.05
618	Russ Swan	.05
619	Bob Walk	.05
620	Billy Swift	.05
621	Warren Newson RC	.05
622	Steve Bedrosian	.05
623	Ricky Bones RC	.05
624	Kevin Tapani	.05
625	Juan Guzman RC	.05
626	Jeff Johnson RC	.05
627	Jeff Montgomery	.05
628	Ken Hill	.05
629	Gary Thurman	.05
630	Steve Howe	.05
631	Jose DeJesus	.05
632	Bert Blyleven	.05
633	Jaime Navarro	.05
634	Lee Stevens	.05
635	Pete Harnisch	.05
636	Bill Landrum	.05
637	Rich DeLucia	.05
638	Luis Salazar	.05
639	Rob Murphy	.05
640	Rickey Henderson, Jose Canseco A.L. Diamond Skills Checklist	.05
641	Roger Clemens	.40
642	Jim Abbott	.05
643	Travis Fryman	.05
644	Jesse Barfield	.05
645	Cal Ripken, Jr.	.50
646	Wade Boggs	.35
647	Cecil Fielder	.05
648	Rickey Henderson	.20
649	Jose Canseco	.15
650	Ken Griffey Jr.	.45
651	Kenny Rogers	.05
652	Luis Mercedes RC	.05
653	Mike Stanton	.05
654	Glenn Davis	.05
655	Nolan Ryan	1.00
656	Reggie Jefferson	.05
657	Javier Ortiz RC	.05
658	Greg A. Harris	.05
659	Mariano Duncan	.05
660	Jeff Shaw	.05
661	Mike Moore	.05
662	Chris Haney RC	.05
663	Joe Slusarski RC	.05
664	Wayne Housie RC	.05
665	Carlos Garcia	.05
666	Bob Ojeda	.05
667	Bryan Hickerson RC	.05
668	Tim Belcher	.05
669	Ron Darling	.05
670	Rex Hudler	.05

671	Sid Fernandez	.05
672	Chito Martinez RC	.05
673	Pete Schourek RC	.05
674	Armando Renoso RC	.05
675	Mike Mussina	.30
676	Kevin Morton	.05
677	Norm Charlton	.05
678	Danny Darwin	.05
679	Eric King	.05
680	Ted Power	.05
681	Barry Jones	.05
682	Carney Lansford	.05
683	Mel Rojas	.05
684	Rick Honeycutt	.05
685	Jeff Fassero RC	.05
686	Cris Carpenter	.05
687	Tim Crews	.05
688	Scott Terry	.05
689	Chris Gwynn	.05
690	Gerald Perry	.05
691	John Barfield	.05
692	Bob Melvin	.05
693	Juan Agosto	.05
694	Alejandro Pena	.05
695	Jeff Russell	.05
696	Carmelo Martinez	.05
697	Bud Black	.05
698	Dave Otto	.05
699	Billy Hatcher	.05
700	Checklist 601-700	.05
701	Clemente Nunez	.05
702	Donovan Osborne, Brian Jordan, Mark Clark "Rookie Threats"	.05
703	Mike Morgan	.05
704	Keith Miller	.05
705	Kurt Stillwell	.05
706	Damon Berryhill	.05
707	Von Hayes	.05
708	Rick Sutcliffe	.05
709	Hubie Brooks	.05
710	Ryan Turner	.05
711	Barry Bonds, Andy Van Slyke N.L. Diamond Skills Checklist	.30
712	Jose Rijo	.05
713	Tom Glavine	.05
714	Shawon Dunston	.05
715	Andy Van Slyke	.05
716	Ozzie Smith	.35
717	Tony Gwynn	.35
718	Will Clark	.05
719	Marquis Grissom	.05
720	Howard Johnson	.05
721	Barry Bonds	.50
722	Kirk McCaskill	.05
723	Sammy Sosa	.50
724	George Bell	.05
725	Gregg Jefferies	.05
726	Gary DiSarcina	.05
727	Mike Bordick	.05
728	Eddie Murray (400 Home Run Club)	.20
729	Rene Gonzales	.05
730	Mike Bielecki	.05
731	Calvin Jones	.05
732	Jack Morris	.05
733	Frank Viola	.05
734	Dave Winfield	.40
735	Kevin Mitchell	.05
736	Billy Swift	.05
737	Dan Gladden	.05
738	Mike Jackson	.05
739	Mark Carreon	.05
740	Kirt Manwaring	.05
741	Randy Myers	.05
742	Kevin McReynolds	.05
743	Steve Sax	.05
744	Wally Joyner	.05
745	Gary Sheffield	.25
746	Danny Tartabull	.05
747	Julio Valera	.05
748	Denny Neagle	.05
749	Lance Blankenship	.05
750	Mike Gallego	.05
751	Bret Saberhagen	.05
752	Ruben Amaro	.05
753	Eddie Murray	.40
754	Kyle Abbott	.05
755	Bobby Bonilla	.05
756	Eric Davis	.05
757	Eddie Taubensee	.05
758	Andres Galarraga	.05
759	Pete Incaviglia	.05
760	Tom Candiotti	.05
761	Tim Belcher	.05
762	Ricky Bones	.05
763	Bip Roberts	.05
764	Pedro Munoz	.05
765	Greg Swindell	.05
766	Kenny Lofton	.40
767	Gary Carter	.40
768	Charlie Hayes	.05

769	Dickie Thon	.05
770	Donovan Osborne Diamond Debuts Checklist	.05
771	Bret Boone	.10
772	Archi Cianfrocco RC	.05
773	Mark Clark RC	.05
774	Chad Curtis RC	.20
775	Pat Listach RC	.05
776	Pat Mahomes RC	.05
777	Donovan Osborne RC	.05
778	John Patterson RC	.05
779	Andy Stankiewicz RC	.05
780	Turk Wendell RC	.10
781	Bill Krueger	.05
782	Rickey Henderson (Grand Theft)	.20
783	Kevin Seitzer	.05
784	Dave Martinez	.05
785	John Smiley	.05
786	Matt Stairs	.05
787	Scott Scudder	.05
788	John Wetteland	.05
789	Jack Armstrong	.05
790	Ken Hill	.05
791	Dick Schofield	.05
792	Mariano Duncan	.05
793	Bill Pecota	.05
794	Mike Kelly RC	.05
795	Willie Randolph	.05
796	Butch Henry RC	.05
797	Carlos Hernandez RC	.05
798	Doug Jones	.05
799	Melido Perez	.05
800	Checklist	.05
SP3	Deion Sanders "Prime Time's Two"	.25
SP4	Tom Selleck, Frank Thomas "Mr. Baseball"	2.00
HH2	Ted Williams (Hologram)	2.00

Baseball Heroes Bench/Morgan

		NM/M
Complete Set (10):		4.00
Common Card:		.50
Autographed Card:		65.00
---	Header Card	.75
37	Johnny Bench 1968 Rookie of the Year	.75
38	Johnny Bench 1968-77 Ten Straight Gold Gloves	.75
39	Johnny Bench 1970 & 1972 MVP	.75
40	Joe Morgan 1965 Rookie Year	.50
41	Joe Morgan 1975-76 Back-to-Back MVP	.50
42	Joe Morgan 1980-83 The Golden Years	.50
43	Johnny Bench, Joe Morgan 1972-79 Big Red Machine	.60
44	Johnny Bench, Joe Morgan 1989 & 1990 Hall of Fame	.60
45	Johnny Bench, Joe Morgan Checklist - Heroes 37-45	.60

Baseball Heroes Ted Williams

		NM/M
Complete Set (10):		3.00
Common Player:		.50
Autographed Card:		425.00
---	Header Card	.75
28	Ted Williams 1939 Rookie Year	.50
29	Ted Williams 1941 .406!	.50
30	Ted Williams 1942 Triple Crown Year	.50
31	Ted Williams 1946 & 1949 MVP	.50
32	Ted Williams 1947 Second Triple Crown	.50
33	Ted Williams 1950s Player of the Decade	.50

34	Ted Williams 1960 500 Home Run Club	.50
35	Ted Williams 1966 Hall of Fame	.50
36	Ted Williams Checklist - Heroes 28-36	.50

Hall of Fame Heroes

		NM/M
Complete Set (4):		2.50
Common Player:		.50
5	Vida Blue	.50
5a	Vida Blue/Auto.	20.00
6	Lou Brock	1.00
6a	Lou Brock/Auto.	35.00
7	Rollie Fingers	.50
7a	Rollie Fingers/Auto.	30.00
8	Vida Blue, Lou Brock, Rollie Fingers	1.00

Heroes Highlights

		NM/M
Complete Set (10):		4.00
Common Player:		.45
1	Bobby Bonds	.45
2	Lou Brock	.45
3	Rollie Fingers	.45
4	Bob Gibson	.45
5	Reggie Jackson	.75
6	Gaylord Perry	.45
7	Robin Roberts	.45
8	Brooks Robinson	.45
9	Billy Williams	.45
10	Ted Williams	2.00

Home Run Heroes

	NM/M
Complete Set (26):	5.00
Common Player:	.15

1	Jose Canseco	.45
2	Cecil Fielder	.15
3	Howard Johnson	.15
4	Cal Ripken, Jr.	1.50
5	Matt Williams	.15
6	Joe Carter	.15
7	Ron Gant	.15
8	Frank Thomas	.75
9	Andre Dawson	.40
10	Fred McGriff	.15
11	Danny Tartabull	.15
12	Chili Davis	.15
13	Albert Belle	.15
14	Jack Clark	.15
15	Paul O'Neill	.15
16	Darryl Strawberry	.15
17	Dave Winfield	.75
18	Jay Buhner	.15
19	Juan Gonzalez	.25
20	Greg Vaughn	.15
21	Barry Bonds	1.50
22	Matt Nokes	.15
23	John Kruk	.15
24	Ivan Calderon	.15
25	Jeff Bagwell	.75
26	Todd Zeile	.15

Scouting Report

		NM/M
Complete Set (25):		2.00
Common Player:		.25
1	Andy Ashby	.25
2	Willie Banks	.25
3	Kim Batiste	.25
4	Derek Bell	.25
5	Archi Cianfrocco	.25
6	Royce Clayton	.25
7	Gary DiSarcina	.25
8	Dave Fleming	.25
9	Butch Henry	.25
10	Todd Hundley	.25
11	Brian Jordan	.25
12	Eric Karros	.25
13	Pat Listach	.25
14	Scott Livingstone	.25
15	Kenny Lofton	.25
16	Pat Mahomes	.25
17	Denny Neagle	.25
18	Dave Nilsson	.25
19	Donovan Osborne	.25
20	Reggie Sanders	.25
21	Andy Stankiewicz	.25
22	Jim Thome	1.50
23	Julio Valera	.25
24	Mark Wohlers	.25
25	Anthony Young	.25

Ted Williams' Best Hitters/Future

	NM/M
Complete Set (20):	3.00

Common Player:		.12
1	Wade Boggs	.50
2	Barry Bonds	1.00
3	Jose Canseco	.25
4	Will Clark	.10
5	Cecil Fielder	.10
6	Tony Gwynn	.50
7	Rickey Henderson	.40
8	Fred McGriff	.10
9	Kirby Puckett	.50
10	Ruben Sierra	.10
11	Roberto Alomar	.20
12	Jeff Bagwell	.40
13	Albert Belle	.10
14	Juan Gonzalez	.20
15	Ken Griffey Jr.	.75
16	Chris Hoiles	.10
17	Dave Justice	.10
18	Phil Plantier	.10
19	Frank Thomas	.40
20	Robin Ventura	.10

1993 Upper Deck

		NM/M
Unopened Fact. Set (840):		30.00
Complete Set (840):		25.00
Common Player:		.05
Gold Hologram:		4X
Series 1 or 2 Pack (15):		.75
Series 1 or 2 Wax		
Box (36):		17.50
Jumbo Pack, USA (27):		1.50
Jumbo Box, USA (20):		17.50
Jumbo Pack, Canada (23):		2.00
Jumbo Box, Canada (20):		20.00
1	Tim Salmon (Checklist)	.05
2	Mike Piazza	1.25
3	Rene Arocha RC	.05
4	Willie Greene RC	.05
5	Manny Alexander RC	.05
6	Dan Wilson	.05
7	Dan Smith RC	.05
8	Kevin Rogers RC	.05
9	Nigel Wilson RC	.05
10	Joe Vitko RC	.05
11	Tim Costo	.05
12	Alan Embree	.05
13	Jim Tatum RC	.05
14	Cris Colon RC	.05
15	Steve Hosey	.05
16	Sterling Hitchcock RC	.15
17	Dave Mlicki RC	.05
18	Jessie Hollins RC	.05
19	Bobby J. Jones RC	.05
20	Kurt Miller RC	.05
21	Melvin Nieves RC	.05
22	Billy Ashley RC	.05
23	J.T. Snow RC	.50
24	Chipper Jones	.85
25	Tim Salmon	.75
26	Tim Pugh RC	.05

27	David Nied	.05
28	Mike Trombley RC	.05
29	Javier Lopez	.05
30	Jim Abbott Community Heroes Checklist	.05
31	Jim Abbott	.05
32	Dale Murphy	.10
33	Tony Pena	.05
34	Kirby Puckett	.40
35	Harold Reynolds	.05
36	Cal Ripken, Jr.	.65
37	Nolan Ryan	.65
38	Ryne Sandberg	.35
39	Dave Stewart	.05
40	Dave Winfield	.25
41	Joe Carter, Mark McGwire Teammates Checklist	.50
42	Joe Carter, Roberto Alomar Blockbuster Trade	.05
43	Pat Listach, Robin Yount, Paul Molitor Brew Crew	.15
44	Brady Anderson, Cal Ripken, Jr. Iron and Steal	.45
45	Albert Belle, Sandy Alomar Jr., Jim Thome, Carlos Baerga, Kenny Lofton Youthful Tribe	.25
46	Cecil Fielder, Mickey Tettleton Motown Mashers	.05
47	Roberto Kelly, Don Mattingly Yankee Pride	.45
48	Frank Viola, Roger Clemens Boston Cy Sox	.30
49	Ruben Sierra, Mark McGwire Bash Brothers	.50
50	Kent Hrbek, Kirby Puckett Twin Titles	.35
51	Robin Ventura, Frank Thomas Southside Sluggers	.35
52	Jose Canseco, Ivan Rodriguez, Rafael Palmeiro, Juan Gonzalez Latin Stars	.35
53	Mark Langston, Jim Abbott, Chuck Finley Lethal Lefties	.05
54	Gregg Jefferies, George Brett, Wally Joyner Royal Family	.35
55	Kevin Mitchell, Jay Buhner, Ken Griffey Jr. Pacific Sox Exchange	.40
56	George Brett	.85
57	Scott Cooper	.05
58	Mike Maddux	.05
59	Rusty Meacham RC	.05
60	Wil Cordero	.05
61	Tim Teufel	.05
62	Jeff Montgomery	.05
63	Scott Livingstone	.05
64	Doug Dascenzo	.05
65	Bret Boone	.05
66	Tim Wakefield RC	.10
67	Curt Schilling	.20
68	Frank Tanana	.05
69	Len Dykstra	.05
70	Derek Lilliquist	.05
71	Anthony Young	.05
72	Hipolito Pichardo RC	.05
73	Rod Beck	.05
74	Kent Hrbek	.05
75	Tom Glavine	.20
76	Kevin Brown	.05
77	Chuck Finley	.05
78	Bob Walk	.05
79	Rheal Cormier	.05
80	Rick Sutcliffe	.05
81	Harold Baines	.05
82	Lee Smith	.05
83	Geno Petralli	.05
84	Jose Oquendo	.05
85	Mark Gubicza	.05
86	Mickey Tettleton	.05
87	Bobby Witt	.05
88	Mark Lewis	.05
89	Kevin Appier	.05
90	Mike Stanton	.05
91	Rafael Belliard	.05
92	Kenny Rogers	.05
93	Randy Velarde	.05
94	Luis Sojo	.05
95	Mark Leiter	.05
96	Jody Reed	.05
97	Pete Harnisch	.05
98	Tom Candiotti	.05
99	Mark Portugal	.05

100	Dave Valle	.05
101	Shawon Dunston	.05
102	B.J. Surhoff	.05
103	Jay Bell	.05
104	Sid Bream	.05
105	Frank Thomas Checklist 1-105	.35
106	Mike Morgan	.05
107	Bill Doran	.05
108	Lance Blankenship	.05
109	Mark Lemke	.05
110	Brian Harper	.05
111	Brady Anderson	.05
112	Bip Roberts	.05
113	Mitch Williams	.05
114	Craig Biggio	.05
115	Eddie Murray	.65
116	Matt Nokes	.05
117	Lance Parrish	.05
118	Bill Swift	.05
119	Jeff Innis	.05
120	Mike LaValliere	.05
121	Hal Morris	.05
122	Walt Weiss	.05
123	Ivan Rodriguez	.60
124	Andy Van Slyke	.05
125	Roberto Alomar	.20
126	Robby Thompson	.05
127	Sammy Sosa	.75
128	Mark Langston	.05
129	Jerry Browne	.05
130	Chuck McElroy	.05
131	Frank Viola	.05
132	Leo Gomez	.05
133	Ramon Martinez	.05
134	Don Mattingly	.85
135	Roger Clemens	.85
136	Rickey Henderson	.65
137	Darren Daulton	.05
138	Ken Hill	.05
139	Ozzie Guillen	.05
140	Jerald Clark	.05
141	Dave Fleming	.05
142	Delino DeShields	.05
143	Matt Williams	.05
144	Larry Walker	.05
145	Ruben Sierra	.05
146	Ozzie Smith	.75
147	Chris Sabo	.05
148	Carlos Hernandez RC	.05
149	Pat Borders	.05
150	Orlando Merced	.05
151	Royce Clayton	.05
152	Kurt Stillwell	.05
153	Dave Hollins	.05
154	Mike Greenwell	.05
155	Nolan Ryan	1.50
156	Felix Jose	.05
157	Junior Felix	.05
158	Derek Bell	.05
159	Steve Buechele	.05
160	John Burkett	.05
161	Pat Howell RC	.05
162	Milt Cuyler	.05
163	Terry Pendleton	.05
164	Jack Morris	.05
165	Tony Gwynn	.75
166	Deion Sanders	.10
167	Mike Devereaux	.05
168	Ron Darling	.05
169	Orel Hershiser	.05
170	Mike Jackson	.05
171	Doug Jones	.05
172	Dan Walters RC	.05
173	Darren Lewis	.05
174	Carlos Baerga	.05
175	Ryne Sandberg	.75
176	Gregg Jefferies	.05
177	John Jaha	.05
178	Luis Polonia	.05
179	Kirt Manwaring	.05
180	Mike Magnante	.05
181	Billy Ripken	.05
182	Mike Moore	.05
183	Eric Anthony	.05
184	Lenny Harris	.05
185	Tony Pena	.05
186	Mike Felder	.05
187	Greg Olson	.05
188	Rene Gonzales	.05
189	Mike Bordick	.05
190	Mel Rojas	.05
191	Todd Frohwirth	.05
192	Darryl Hamilton	.05
193	Mike Fetters	.05
194	Omar Olivares	.05
195	Tony Phillips	.05
196	Paul Sorrento	.05
197	Trevor Wilson	.05
198	Kevin Gross	.05
199	Ron Karkovice	.05
200	Brook Jacoby	.05
201	Mariano Duncan	.05
202	Dennis Cook	.05

203	Daryl Boston	.05
204	Mike Perez	.05
205	Manuel Lee	.05
206	Steve Olin	.05
207	Charlie Hough	.05
208	Scott Scudder	.05
209	Charlie O'Brien	.05
210	Barry Bonds Checklist 106-210	.60
211	Jose Vizcaino	.05
212	Scott Leius	.05
213	Kevin Mitchell	.05
214	Brian Barnes	.05
215	Pat Kelly	.05
216	Chris Hammond	.05
217	Rob Deer	.05
218	Cory Snyder	.05
219	Gary Carter	.65
220	Danny Darwin	.05
221	Tom Gordon	.05
222	Gary Sheffield	.40
223	Joe Carter	.05
224	Jay Buhner	.05
225	Jose Offerman	.05
226	Jose Rijo	.05
227	Mark Whiten	.05
228	Randy Milligan	.05
229	Bud Black	.05
230	Gary DiSarcina	.05
231	Steve Finley	.05
232	Dennis Martinez	.05
233	Mike Mussina	.30
234	Joe Oliver	.05
235	Chad Curtis	.05
236	Shane Mack	.05
237	Jaime Navarro	.05
238	Brian McRae	.05
239	Chili Davis	.05
240	Jeff King	.05
241	Dean Palmer	.05
242	Danny Tartabull	.05
243	Charles Nagy	.05
244	Ray Lankford	.05
245	Barry Larkin	.05
246	Steve Avery	.05
247	John Kruk	.05
248	Derrick May	.05
249	Stan Javier	.05
250	Roger McDowell	.05
251	Dan Gladden	.05
252	Wally Joyner	.05
253	Pat Listach	.05
254	Chuck Knoblauch	.05
255	Sandy Alomar Jr.	.05
256	Jeff Bagwell	.65
257	Andy Stankiewicz	.05
258	Darrin Jackson	.05
259	Brett Butler	.05
260	Joe Orsulak	.05
261	Andy Benes	.05
262	Kenny Lofton	.05
263	Robin Ventura	.05
264	Ron Gant	.05
265	Ellis Burks	.05
266	Juan Guzman	.05
267	Wes Chamberlain	.05
268	John Smiley	.05
269	Franklin Stubbs	.05
270	Tom Browning	.05
271	Dennis Eckersley	.60
272	Carlton Fisk	.65
273	Lou Whitaker	.05
274	Phil Plantier	.05
275	Bobby Bonilla	.05
276	Ben McDonald	.05
277	Bob Zupcic	.05
278	Terry Steinbach	.05
279	Terry Mulholland	.05
280	Lance Johnson	.05
281	Willie McGee	.05
282	Bret Saberhagen	.05
283	Randy Myers	.05
284	Randy Tomlin	.05
285	Mickey Morandini	.05
286	Brian Williams	.05
287	Tino Martinez	.05
288	Jose Melendez	.05
289	Jeff Huson	.05
290	Joe Grahe	.05
291	Mel Hall	.05
292	Otis Nixon	.05
293	Todd Hundley	.05
294	Casey Candaele	.05
295	Kevin Seitzer	.05
296	Eddie Taubensee	.05
297	Moises Alou	.05
298	Scott Radinsky	.05
299	Thomas Howard	.05
300	Kyle Abbott	.05
301	Omar Vizquel	.05
302	Keith Miller	.05
303	Rick Aguilera	.05
304	Bruce Hurst	.05
305	Ken Caminiti	.05

No.	Player	Price
306	Mike Pagiarulo	.05
307	Frank Seminara	.05
308	Andre Dawson	.30
309	Jose Lind	.05
310	Joe Boever	.05
311	Jeff Parrett (RC)	.05
312	Alan Mills	.05
313	Kevin Tapani	.05
314	Darryl Kile	.05
315	Will Clark Checklist 211-315	.05
316	Mike Sharperson	.05
317	John Orton	.05
318	Bob Tewksbury	.05
319	Xavier Hernandez	.05
320	Paul Assenmacher	.05
321	John Franco	.05
322	Mike Timlin	.05
323	Jose Guzman	.05
324	Pedro Martinez	.65
325	Bill Spiers	.05
326	Melido Perez	.05
327	Mike Macfarlane	.05
328	Ricky Bones	.05
329	Scott Bankhead	.05
330	Rich Rodriguez	.05
331	Geronimo Pena	.05
332	Bernie Williams	.05
333	Paul Molitor	.65
334	Roger Mason	.05
335	David Cone	.05
336	Randy Johnson	.65
337	Pat Mahomes	.05
338	Erik Hanson	.05
339	Duane Ward	.05
340	Al Martin	.05
341	Pedro Munoz	.05
342	Greg Colbrunn	.05
343	Julio Valera	.05
344	John Olerud	.05
345	George Bell	.05
346	Devon White	.05
347	Donovan Osborne	.05
348	Mark Gardner	.05
349	Zane Smith	.05
350	Wilson Alvarez	.05
351	Kevin Koslofski RC	.05
352	Roberto Hernandez	.05
353	Glenn Davis	.05
354	Reggie Sanders	.05
355	Ken Griffey Jr.	1.00
355a	Ken Griffey Jr. (Promo, hologram-dated hologram on back.)	3.00
355b	Ken Griffey Jr. (8-1/2" x 11" limited edition of 1,000)	15.00
356	Marquis Grissom	.05
357	Jack McDowell	.05
358	Jimmy Key	.05
359	Stan Belinda	.05
360	Gerald Williams	.05
361	Sid Fernandez	.05
362	Alex Fernandez	.05
363	John Smoltz	.05
364	Travis Fryman	.05
365	Jose Canseco	.50
366	Dave Justice	.05
367	Pedro Astacio RC	.10
368	Tim Belcher	.05
369	Steve Sax	.05
370	Gary Gaetti	.05
371	Jeff Frye	.05
372	Bob Wickman	.05
373	Ryan Thompson RC	.05
374	David Hulse RC	.05
375	Cal Eldred	.05
376	Ryan Klesko	.05
377	Damion Easley RC	.10
378	John Kiely RC	.05
379	Jim Bullinger RC	.05
380	Brian Bohanon	.05
381	Rod Brewer	.05
382	Fernando Ramsey RC	.05
383	Sam Militello	.05
384	Arthur Rhodes	.05
385	Eric Karros	.05
386	Rico Brogna	.05
387	John Valentin RC	.10
388	Kerry Woodson RC	.05
389	Ben Rivera RC	.05
390	Matt Whiteside RC	.05
391	Henry Rodriguez	.05
392	John Wetteland	.05
393	Kent Mercker	.05
394	Bernard Gilkey	.05
395	Doug Henry	.05
396	Mo Vaughn	.05
397	Scott Erickson	.05
398	Bill Gullickson	.05
399	Mark Guthrie	.05
400	Dave Martinez	.05
401	Jeff Kent RC	.50
402	Chris Hoiles	.05
403	Mike Henneman	.05
404	Chris Nabholz	.05
405	Tom Pagnozzi	.05
406	Kelly Gruber	.05
407	Bob Welch	.05
408	Frank Castillo	.05
409	John Dopson	.05
410	Steve Farr	.05
411	Henry Cotto	.05
412	Bob Patterson	.05
413	Todd Stottlemyre	.05
414	Greg A. Harris	.05
415	Denny Neagle	.05
416	Bill Wegman	.05
417	Willie Wilson	.05
418	Terry Leach	.05
419	Willie Randolph	.05
420	Mark McGwire Checklist 316-420	.65
421	Calvin Murray (Top Prospects Checklist)	.05
422	Pete Janicki RC	.05
423	Todd Jones	.05
424	Mike Neill	.05
425	Carlos Delgado	.40
426	Jose Oliva	.05
427	Tyrone Hill	.05
428	Dmitri Young	.05
429	Derek Wallace RC	.05
430	Michael Moore RC	.05
431	Cliff Floyd	.05
432	Calvin Murray	.05
433	Manny Ramirez	.75
434	Marc Newfield	.05
435	Charles Johnson	.05
436	Butch Huskey	.05
437	Brad Pennington	.05
438	Ray McDavid RC	.05
439	Chad McConnell	.05
440	Midre Cummings RC	.05
441	Benji Gil	.05
442	Frank Rodriguez	.05
443	Chad Mottola RC	.05
444	John Burke RC	.05
445	Michael Tucker	.05
446	Rick Greene	.05
447	Rich Becker	.05
448	Mike Robertson	.05
449	Derek Jeter RC	10.00
450	David McCarty, Ivan Rodriguez Checklist 451-470 Inside the Numbers	.05
451	Jim Abbott	.05
452	Jeff Bagwell	.40
453	Jason Bere	.05
454	Charlie DeShields	.05
455	Travis Fryman	.05
456	Alex Gonzalez	.05
457	Phil Hiatt	.05
458	Dave Hollins	.05
459	Chipper Jones	.65
460	Dave Justice	.05
461	Ray Lankford	.05
462	David McCarty	.05
463	Mike Mussina	.15
464	Jose Offerman	.05
465	Dean Palmer	.05
466	Geronimo Pena	.05
467	Eduardo Perez	.05
468	Ivan Rodriguez	.25
469	Reggie Sanders	.05
470	Bernie Williams	.05
471	Barry Bonds, Matt Williams, Will Clark Checklist 472-485 Team Stars	.45
472	John Smoltz, Steve Avery, Greg Maddux, Tom Glavine Strike Force	.10
473	Jose Rijo, Rob Dibble, Roberto Kelly, Reggie Sanders, Barry Larkin Red October	.10
474	Gary Sheffield, Phil Plantier, Tony Gwynn, Fred McGriff Four Corners	.20
475	Doug Drabek, Craig Biggio, Jeff Bagwell Shooting Stars	.15
476	Will Clark, Barry Bonds, Matt Williams Giant Sticks	.40
477	Darryl Strawberry, Eric Davis Boyhood Friends	.05
478	Dante Bichette, David Nied, Andres Galarraga Rock Solid	.05
479	Dave Magadan, Orestes Destrade, Bret Barbarie, Jeff Conine Inaugural Catch	.05
480	Tim Wakefield, Andy Van Slyke, Jay Bell Steel City Champions	.05
481	Marquis Grissom, Delino DeShields, Dennis Martinez, Larry Walker "Les Grandes Etoiles"	.05
482	Geronimo Pena, Ray Lankford, Ozzie Smith, Bernard Gilkey Runnin' Redbirds	.10
483	Ryne Sandberg, Mark Grace, Randy Myers Ivy Leaguers	.15
484	Eddie Murray, Bobby Bonilla, Howard Johnson Big Apple Power Switch	.10
485	John Kruk, Dave Hollins, Darren Daulton, Len Dykstra Hammers & Nails	.05
486	Barry Bonds	.60
487	Dennis Eckersley	.30
488	Greg Maddux	.40
489	Dennis Eckersley	.30
490	Eric Karros	.05
491	Pat Listach	.05
492	Gary Sheffield	.10
493	Mark McGwire	.75
494	Gary Sheffield	.10
495	Edgar Martinez	.05
496	Fred McGriff	.05
497	Juan Gonzalez	.20
498	Darren Daulton	.05
499	Cecil Fielder	.05
500	Brent Gates Checklist 501-510 Diamond Debuts	.05
501	Tavo Alvarez	.05
502	Rod Bolton	.05
503	John Cummings RC	.05
504	Brent Gates	.05
505	Tyler Green	.05
506	Jose Martinez RC	.05
507	Troy Percival	.05
508	Kevin Stocker	.05
509	Matt Walbeck RC	.10
510	Rondell White	.05
511	Billy Ripken	.05
512	Mike Moore	.05
513	Jose Lind	.05
514	Chito Martinez	.05
515	Jose Guzman	.05
516	Kim Batiste	.05
517	Jeff Tackett	.05
518	Charlie Hough	.05
519	Marvin Freeman	.05
520	Carlos Martinez	.05
521	Eric Young	.05
522	Pete Incaviglia	.05
523	Scott Fletcher	.05
524	Orestes Destrade	.05
525	Ken Griffey Jr. Checklist 421-525	.40
526	Ellis Burks	.05
527	Juan Samuel	.05
528	Dave Magadan	.05
529	Jeff Parrett	.05
530	Jeff Krueger	.05
531	Frank Bolick	.05
532	Alan Trammell	.05
533	Walt Weiss	.05
534	David Cone	.05
535	Greg Maddux	.75
536	Kevin Young	.05
537	Dave Hansen	.05
538	Alex Cole	.05
539	Greg Hibbard	.05
540	Gene Larkin	.05
541	Jeff Reardon	.05
542	Felix Jose	.05
543	Jimmy Key	.05
544	Reggie Jefferson	.05
545	Gregg Jefferies	.05
546	Dave Stewart	.05
547	Tim Wallach	.05
548	Spike Owen	.05
549	Tommy Greene	.05
550	Fernando Valenzuela	.05
551	Rich Amaral	.05
552	Bret Barberie	.05
553	Edgar Martinez	.05
554	Jim Abbott	.05
555	Frank Thomas	.65
556	Wade Boggs	.75
557	Tom Henke	.05
558	Milt Thompson	.05
559	Lloyd McClendon	.05
560	Vinny Castilla	.05
561	Ricky Jordan	.05
562	Andujar Cedeno	.05
563	Greg Vaughn	.05
564	Cecil Fielder	.05
565	Kirby Puckett	.75
566	Mark McGwire	1.25
567	Barry Bonds	1.50
568	Jody Reed	.05
569	Todd Zeile	.05
570	Mark Carreon	.05
571	Joe Girardi	.05
572	Luis Gonzalez	.05
573	Mark Grace	.05
574	Rafael Palmeiro	.60
575	Darryl Strawberry	.05
576	Will Clark	.05
577	Fred McGriff	.05
578	Kevin Reimer	.05
579	Dave Righetti	.05
580	Juan Bell	.05
581	Jeff Brantley	.05
582	Brian Hunter	.05
583	Tim Naehring	.05
584	Glenallen Hill	.05
585	Cal Ripken, Jr.	1.50
586	Albert Belle	.05
587	Robin Yount	.65
588	Chris Bosio	.05
589	Pete Smith	.05
590	Chuck Carr	.05
591	Jeff Blauser	.05
592	Kevin McReynolds	.05
593	Andres Galarraga	.05
594	Kevin Maas	.05
595	Eric Davis	.05
596	Brian Jordan	.05
597	Tim Raines	.05
598	Rick Wilkins	.05
599	Steve Cooke	.05
600	Mike Gallego	.05
601	Mike Munoz	.05
602	Luis Rivera	.05
603	Junior Ortiz	.05
604	Brent Mayne	.05
605	Luis Alicea	.05
606	Damon Berryhill	.05
607	Dave Henderson	.05
608	Kirk McCaskill	.05
609	Jeff Fassero	.05
610	Mike Harkey	.05
611	Francisco Cabrera	.05
612	Rey Sanchez	.05
613	Scott Servais	.05
614	Darrin Fletcher	.05
615	Felix Fermin	.05
616	Kevin Seitzer	.05
617	Bob Scanlan	.05
618	Billy Hatcher	.05
619	John Vander Wal	.05
620	Joe Hesketh	.05
621	Hector Villanueva	.05
622	Randy Milligan	.05
623	Tony Tarasco RC	.05
624	Russ Swan	.05
625	Willie Wilson	.05
626	Frank Tanana	.05
627	Pete O'Brien	.05
628	Lenny Webster	.05
629	Mark Clark	.05
630	Roger Clemens Checklist 526-630	.40
631	Alex Arias	.05
632	Chris Gwynn	.05
633	Tom Bolton	.05
634	Greg Briley	.05
635	Kent Bottenfield	.05
636	Kelly Downs	.05
637	Manuel Lee	.05
638	Al Leiter	.05
639	Jeff Gardner	.05
640	Mike Gardiner	.05
641	Mark Gardner	.05
642	Jeff Branson	.05
643	Paul Wagner	.05
644	Sean Berry	.05
645	Phil Hiatt	.05
646	Kevin Mitchell	.05
647	Charlie Hayes	.05
648	Jim Deshaies	.05
649	Dan Pasqua	.05
650	Mike Maddux	.05
651	Domingo Martinez RC	.05
652	Greg McMichael RC	.05
653	Eric Wedge RC	.05
654	Mark Whiten	.05
655	Bobby Kelly	.05
656	Julio Franco	.05
657	Gene Harris	.05
658	Pete Schourek	.05
659	Mike Bielecki	.05
660	Ricky Gutierrez	.05
661	Chris Hammond	.05
662	Tim Scott	.05
663	Norm Charlton	.05
664	Doug Drabek	.05
665	Dwight Gooden	.05
666	Jim Gott	.05
667	Randy Myers	.05

668	Darren Holmes	.05
669	Tim Spehr	.05
670	Bruce Ruffin	.05
671	Bobby Thigpen	.05
672	Tony Fernandez	.05
673	Darrin Jackson	.05
674	Gregg Olson	.05
675	Rob Dibble	.05
676	Howard Johnson	.05
677	Mike Lansing RC	.15
678	Charlie Leibrandt	.05
679	Kevin Bass	.05
680	Hubie Brooks	.05
681	Scott Brosius	.05
682	Randy Knorr	.05
683	Dante Bichette	.05
684	Bryan Harvey	.05
685	Greg Gohr	.05
686	Willie Banks	.05
687	Robb Nen	.05
688	Mike Scioscia	.05
689	John Farrell	.05
690	John Candelaria	.05
691	Damon Buford	.05
692	Todd Worrell	.05
693	Pat Hentgen	.05
694	John Smiley	.05
695	Greg Swindell	.05
696	Derek Bell	.05
697	Terry Jorgensen	.05
698	Jimmy Jones	.05
699	David Wells	.05
700	Dave Martinez	.05
701	Steve Bedrosian	.05
702	Jeff Russell	.05
703	Joe Magrane	.05
704	Matt Mieske	.05
705	Paul Molitor	.65
706	Dale Murphy	.15
707	Steve Howe	.05
708	Greg Gagne	.05
709	Dave Eiland	.05
710	David West	.05
711	Luis Aquino	.05
712	Joe Orsulak	.05
713	Eric Plunk	.05
714	Mike Felder	.05
715	Joe Klink	.05
716	Lonnie Smith	.05
717	Monty Fariss	.05
718	Craig Lefferts	.05
719	John Habyan	.05
720	Willie Blair	.05
721	Darnell Coles	.05
722	Mark Williamson	.05
723	Bryn Smith	.05
724	Greg W. Harris	.05
725	Graeme Lloyd RC	.05
726	Cris Carpenter	.05
727	Chico Walker	.05
728	Tracy Woodson	.05
729	Jose Uribe	.05
730	Stan Javier	.05
731	Jay Howell	.05
732	Freddie Benavides	.05
733	Jeff Reboulet	.05
734	Scott Sanderson	.05
735	Ryne Sandberg Checklist 631-735	.20
736	Archi Cianfrocco	.05
737	Daryl Boston	.05
738	Craig Grebeck	.05
739	Doug Dascenzo	.05
740	Gerald Young	.05
741	Candy Maldonado	.05
742	Joey Cora	.05
743	Don Slaught	.05
744	Steve Decker	.05
745	Blas Minor	.05
746	Storm Davis	.05
747	Carlos Quintana	.05
748	Vince Coleman	.05
749	Todd Burns	.05
750	Steve Frey	.05
751	Ivan Calderon	.05
752	Steve Reed RC	.05
753	Danny Jackson	.05
754	Jeff Conine	.05
755	Juan Gonzalez	.35
756	Mike Kelly	.05
757	John Doherty	.05
758	Jack Armstrong	.05
759	John Wehner	.05
760	Scott Bankhead	.05
761	Jim Tatum	.05
762	Scott Pose RC	.05
763	Andy Ashby	.05
764	Ed Sprague	.05
765	Harold Baines	.05
766	Kirk Gibson	.05
767	Troy Neel	.05
768	Dick Schofield	.05
769	Dickie Thon	.05
770	Butch Henry	.05

771	Junior Felix	.05
772	Ken Ryan RC	.05
773	Trevor Hoffman	.05
774	Phil Plantier	.05
775	Bo Jackson	.10
776	Benito Santiago	.05
777	Andre Dawson	.25
778	Bryan Hickerson	.05
779	Dennis Moeller	.05
780	Ryan Bowen	.05
781	Eric Fox	.05
782	Joe Kmak	.05
783	Mike Hampton	.05
784	Darrell Sherman RC	.05
785	J.T. Snow	.05
786	Dave Winfield	.65
787	Jim Austin	.05
788	Craig Shipley	.05
789	Greg Myers	.05
790	Todd Benzinger	.05
791	Cory Snyder	.05
792	David Segui	.05
793	Armando Reynoso	.05
794	Chili Davis	.05
795	Dave Nilsson	.05
796	Paul O'Neill	.05
797	Jerald Clark	.05
798	Jose Mesa	.05
799	Brian Holman	.05
800	Jim Eisenreich	.05
801	Mark McLemore	.05
802	Luis Sojo	.05
803	Harold Reynolds	.05
804	Dan Plesac	.05
805	Dave Stieb	.05
806	Tom Brunansky	.05
807	Kelly Gruber	.05
808	Bob Ojeda	.05
809	Dave Burba	.05
810	Joe Boever	.05
811	Jeremy Hernandez	.05
812	Tim Salmon Angels Checklist	.05
813	Jeff Bagwell Astros Checklist	.35
814	Mark McGwire Athletics Checklist	.75
815	Roberto Alomar Blue Jays Checklist	.10
816	Steve Avery Braves Checklist	.05
817	Pat Listach Brewers Checklist	.05
818	Gregg Jefferies Cardinals Checklist	.05
819	Sammy Sosa Cubs Checklist	.40
820	Darryl Strawberry Dodgers Checklist	.05
821	Dennis Martinez Expos Checklist	.05
822	Robby Thompson Giants Checklist	.05
823	Albert Belle Indians Checklist	.05
824	Randy Johnson Mariners Checklist	.30
825	Nigel Wilson Marlins Checklist	.05
826	Bobby Bonilla Mets Checklist	.05
827	Glenn Davis Orioles Checklist	.05
828	Gary Sheffield Padres Checklist	.10
829	Darren Daulton Phillies Checklist	.05
830	Jay Bell Pirates Checklist	.05
831	Juan Gonzalez Rangers Checklist	.20
832	Andre Dawson Red Sox Checklist	.10
833	Hal Morris Reds Checklist	.05
834	David Nied Rockies Checklist	.05
835	Felix Jose Royals Checklist	.05
836	Travis Fryman Tigers Checklist	.05
837	Shane Mack Twins Checklist	.05
838	Robin Ventura White Sox Checklist	.05
839	Danny Tartabull Yankees Checklist	.05
840	Roberto Alomar Checklist 736-840	.10
SP5	Robin Yount, George Brett 3,000 Hits	.50
SP6	Nolan Ryan	1.50

1993 Upper Deck All-Time Heroes

		NM/M
Complete Set (165):		35.00
Common Player:		.10
Wax Pack (12):		2.00
Wax Box (24):		30.00
1	Hank Aaron	2.00
2	Tommie Agee	.10
3	Bob Allison	.10
4	Matty Alou	.10
5	Sal Bando	.10
6	Hank Bauer	.15
7	Don Baylor	.10
8	Glenn Beckert	.10
9	Yogi Berra	.50
10	Buddy Biancalana	.10
11	Jack Billingham	.10
12	Joe Black	.10
13	Paul Blair	.10
14	Steve Blass	.10
15	Ray Boone	.10
16	Lou Boudreau	.10
17	Ken Brett	.10
18	Nellie Briles	.10
19	Bobby Brown	.10
20	Bill Buckner	.10
21	Don Buford	.10
22	Al Bumbry	.10
23	Lew Burdette	.10
24	Jeff Burroughs	.10
25	Johnny Callison	.10
26	Bert Campaneris	.10
27	Rico Carty	.10
28	Dave Cash	.10
29	Cesar Cedeno	.10
30	Frank Chance	.25
31	Joe Charboneau	.15
32	Ty Cobb	2.00
33	Jerry Coleman	.10
34	Cecil Cooper	.10
35	Frankie Crossetti	.10
36	Alvin Dark	.10
37	Tommy Davis	.10
38	Dizzy Dean	.25
39	Doug DeCinces	.10
40	Bucky Dent	.10
41	Larry Dierker	.10
42	Larry Doby	.20
43	Moe Drabowsky	.10
44	Dave Dravecky	.10
45	Del Ennis	.10
46	Carl Erskine	.10
47	Johnny Evers	.25
48	Elroy Face	.10
49	Rick Ferrell	.10
50	Mark Fidrych	.15
51	Curt Flood	.10
52	Whitey Ford	.50
53	George Foster	.10
54	Jimmie Foxx	.25
55	Jim Fregosi	.10
56	Phil Garner	.10
57	Ralph Garr	.10
58	Lou Gehrig	2.00
59	Bobby Grich	.10
60	Jerry Grote	.10
61	Harvey Haddix	.10
62	Toby Harrah	.10
63	Bud Harrelson	.10
64	Jim Hegan	.10
65	Gil Hodges	.25
66	Ken Holtzman	.10
67	Bob Horner	.10
68	Rogers Hornsby	.25
69	Carl Hubbell	.25
70	Ron Hunt	.10
71	Monte Irvin	.10
72a	Reggie Jackson (Regular issue, black printing on back.)	.50
72b	Reggie Jackson (Dealer promo, red printing on back.)	6.00
73	Larry Jansen	.10
74	Ferguson Jenkins	.10
75	Tommy John	.10
76	Cliff Johnson	.10
77	Davey Johnson	.10
78	Walter Johnson	.45
79	George Kell	.10
80	Don Kessinger	.10
81	Vern Law	.10
82	Dennis Leonard	.10
83	Johnny Logan	.10

84	Mickey Lolich	.10
85	Jim Lonborg	.10
86	Bill Madlock	.10
87	Mickey Mantle	4.00
88	Billy Martin	.25
89	Christy Mathewson	.45
90	Lee May	.10
91	Willie Mays	2.00
92	Bill Mazeroski	.25
93	Gil McDougald	.15
94	Sam McDowell	.10
95	Minnie Minoso	.15
96	Johnny Mize	.25
97	Rick Monday	.10
98	Wally Moon	.10
99	Manny Mota	.10
100	Bobby Murcer	.10
101	Ron Necciai	.10
102	Al Oliver	.15
103	Mel Ott	.15
104	Mel Parnell	.10
105	Jimmy Piersall	.10
106	Johnny Podres	.15
107	Bobby Richardson	.15
108	Robin Roberts	.15
109	Al Rosen	.10
110	Babe Ruth	3.00
111	Joe Sambito	.10
112	Manny Sanguillen	.10
113	Ron Santo	.10
114	Bill Skowron	.15
115	Enos Slaughter	.15
116	Warren Spahn	.20
117	Tris Speaker	.20
118	Frank Thomas	.10
119	Bobby Thomson	.10
120	Andre Thornton	.10
121	Marv Throneberry	.10
122	Luis Tiant	.10
123	Joe Tinker	.25
124	Honus Wagner	.50
125	Bill White	.10
126	Ted Williams	1.00
127	Earl Wilson	.10
128	Joe Wood	.10
129	Cy Young	.40
130	Richie Zisk	.10
131	Babe Ruth, Lou Gehrig	2.00
132	Ted Williams, Rogers Hornsby	1.00
133	Lou Gehrig, Babe Ruth	2.00
134	Babe Ruth, Mickey Mantle	3.00
135	Mickey Mantle, Reggie Jackson	1.00
136	Mel Ott, Carl Hubbell	.15
137	Mickey Mantle, Willie Mays	2.00
138	Cy Young, Walter Johnson	.25
139	Honus Wagner, Rogers Hornsby	.25
140	Mickey Mantle, Whitey Ford	2.00
141	Mickey Mantle, Billy Martin	2.00
142	Cy Young, Walter Johnson	.25
143	Christy Mathewson, Walter Johnson	.25
144	Warren Spahn, Christy Mathewson	.15
145	Honus Wagner, Ty Cobb	.50
146	Babe Ruth, Ty Cobb	1.00
147	Joe Tinker, Johnny Evers	.15
148	Johnny Evers, Frank Chance	.15
149	Hank Aaron, Babe Ruth	1.00
150	Willie Mays, Hank Aaron	1.00
151	Babe Ruth, Willie Mays	1.00
152	Babe Ruth, Whitey Ford	1.00
153	Larry Doby, Minnie Minoso	.25
154	Joe Black, Monte Irvin	.10
155	Joe Wood, Christy Mathewson	.15
156	Christy Mathewson, Cy Young	.25
157	Cy Young, Joe Wood	.15
158	Cy Young, Whitey Ford	.20
159	Cy Young, Ferguson Jenkins	.15
160	Ty Cobb, Rogers Hornsby	.45
161	Tris Speaker, Ted Williams	1.00

162	Rogers Hornsby,	
	Ted Williams	1.00
163	Willie Mays, Monte Irvin	.50
164	Willie Mays,	
	Bobby Thomson	.50
165	Reggie Jackson,	
	Mickey Mantle	2.00

Baseball Heroes
Reggie Jackson
Supers

	NM/M
Complete Set (10):	25.00
Common Jackson:	3.00

Baseball Heroes
Willie Mays

	NM/M
Complete Set (10):	4.00
Common Mays:	.50
Header Card:	1.00

Clutch Performers

		NM/M
Complete Set (20):		8.00
Common Player:		.25
1	Roberto Alomar	.30
2	Wade Boggs	1.00
3	Barry Bonds	2.50
4	Jose Canseco	.40
5	Joe Carter	.25
6	Will Clark	.25
7	Roger Clemens	1.25
8	Dennis Eckersley	.60
9	Cecil Fielder	.25
10	Juan Gonzalez	.60
11	Ken Griffey Jr.	2.00
12	Rickey Henderson	.75
13	Barry Larkin	.25
14	Don Mattingly	1.25
15	Fred McGriff	.25
16	Terry Pendleton	.25
17	Kirby Puckett	1.00
18	Ryne Sandberg	1.00
19	John Smoltz	.25
20	Frank Thomas	.75

Diamond Gallery

		NM/M
Complete Set (36):		6.00
Common Player:		.10
1	Tim Salmon	.10
2	Jeff Bagwell	.30
3	Mark McGwire	.75
4	Roberto Alomar	.25
5	Terry Pendleton	.10
6	Robin Yount	.30
7	Ray Lankford	.10
8	Ryne Sandberg	.40
9	Darryl Strawberry	.10
10	Marquis Grissom	.10
11	Barry Bonds	1.00
12	Carlos Baerga	.10
13	Ken Griffey Jr.	.65
14	Benito Santiago	.10
15	Dwight Gooden	.10
16	Cal Ripken, Jr.	1.00
17	Tony Gwynn	.40
18	Dave Hollins	.10
19	Andy Van Slyke	.10
20	Juan Gonzalez	.25
21	Roger Clemens	.50
22	Barry Larkin	.10
23	Dave Nied	.10
24	George Brett	.50
25	Travis Fryman	.10
26	Kirby Puckett	.40
27	Frank Thomas	.30
28	Don Mattingly	.50
29	Rickey Henderson	.30
30	Nolan Ryan	1.00
31	Ozzie Smith	.40
32	Wil Cordero	.10
33	Phil Hiatt	.10
34	Mike Piazza	.65
35	J.T. Snow	.10
36	Kevin Young	.10

Future Heroes

		NM/M
Complete Set (10):		5.00
Common Player:		.50
Header Card:		.25
55	Roberto Alomar	.50
56	Barry Bonds	2.50
57	Roger Clemens	1.00
58	Juan Gonzalez	.50
59	Ken Griffey Jr.	1.50
60	Mark McGwire	2.00
61	Kirby Puckett	.85
62	Frank Thomas	.75
63	Checklist	.05

Highlights

		NM/M
Complete Set (20):		20.00
Common Player:		.25
1	Roberto Alomar	.50
2	Steve Avery	.25
3	Harold Baines	.25
4	Damon Berryhill	.25
5	Barry Bonds	7.50
6	Bret Boone	.25
7	George Brett	4.00
8	Francisco Cabrera	.25
9	Ken Griffey Jr.	5.00
10	Rickey Henderson	2.00

11	Kenny Lofton	.25
12	Mickey Morandini	.25
13	Eddie Murray	2.00
14	David Nied	.25
15	Jeff Reardon	.25
16	Bip Roberts	.25
17	Nolan Ryan	7.50
18	Ed Sprague	.25
19	Dave Winfield	2.00
20	Robin Yount	2.00

Home Run Heroes

		NM/M
Complete Set (28):		7.50
Common Player:		.15
1	Juan Gonzalez	.50
2	Mark McGwire	2.25
3	Cecil Fielder	.15
4	Fred McGriff	.15
5	Albert Belle	.15
6	Barry Bonds	2.50
7	Joe Carter	.15
8	Darren Daulton	.15
9	Ken Griffey Jr.	2.00
10	Dave Hollins	.15
11	Ryne Sandberg	1.00
12	George Bell	.15
13	Danny Tartabull	.15
14	Mike Devereaux	.15
15	Greg Vaughn	.15
16	Larry Walker	.15
17	Dave Justice	.15
18	Terry Pendleton	.15
19	Eric Karros	.15
20	Ray Lankford	.15
21	Matt Williams	.15
22	Eric Anthony	.15
23	Bobby Bonilla	.15
24	Kirby Puckett	1.00
25	Mike Macfarlane	.15
26	Tom Brunansky	.15
27	Paul O'Neill	.15
28	Gary Gaetti	.15

Iooss Collection

		NM/M
Complete Set (27):		10.00
Common Player:		.25
Header Card:		.25
1	Tim Salmon	.25
2	Jeff Bagwell	.75
3	Mark McGwire	1.50
4	Roberto Alomar	.35
5	Steve Avery	.25
6	Paul Molitor	.75
7	Ozzie Smith	1.00
8	Mark Grace	.25
9	Eric Karros	.25
10	Delino DeShields	.25
11	Will Clark	.25
12	Albert Belle	.35
13	Ken Griffey Jr.	1.50

14	Howard Johnson	.25
15	Cal Ripken, Jr.	2.00
16	Fred McGriff	.25
17	Darren Daulton	.25
18	Andy Van Slyke	.25
19	Nolan Ryan	2.00
20	Wade Boggs	1.00
21	Barry Larkin	.25
22	George Brett	1.25
23	Cecil Fielder	.25
24	Kirby Puckett	1.00
25	Frank Thomas	.75
26	Don Mattingly	1.25

Next Generation

		NM/M
Complete Set (18):		100.00
Common Player:		1.50
1	Roberto Alomar	2.50
2	Carlos Delgado	4.00
3	Cliff Floyd	1.50
4	Alex Gonzalez	1.50
5	Juan Gonzalez	3.00
6	Ken Griffey Jr.	10.00
7	Jeffrey Hammonds	1.50
8	Michael Jordan	30.00
9	Dave Justice	1.50
10	Ryan Klesko	1.50
11	Javier Lopez	1.50
12	Raul Mondesi	1.50
13	Mike Piazza	10.00
14	Kirby Puckett	7.50
15	Manny Ramirez	6.50
16	Alex Rodriguez	30.00
17	Tim Salmon	1.50
18	Gary Sheffield	4.00

On Deck

	NM/M
Complete Set (25):	10.00

	Common Player:	.15
1	Jim Abbott	.15
2	Roberto Alomar	.25
3	Carlos Baerga	.15
4	Albert Belle	.15
5	Wade Boggs	1.00
6	George Brett	1.25
7	Jose Canseco	.45
8	Will Clark	.15
9	Roger Clemens	1.25
10	Dennis Eckersley	.65
11	Cecil Fielder	.15
12	Juan Gonzalez	.40
13	Ken Griffey Jr.	1.50
14	Tony Gwynn	1.00
15	Bo Jackson	.20
16	Chipper Jones	1.00
17	Eric Karros	.15
18	Mark McGwire	2.00
19	Kirby Puckett	1.00
20	Nolan Ryan	2.50
21	Tim Salmon	.15
22	Ryne Sandberg	1.00
23	Darryl Strawberry	.15
24	Frank Thomas	.75
25	Andy Van Slyke	.15

Then And Now

		NM/M
	Complete Set (18):	30.00
	Common Player:	.75
1	Wade Boggs	2.00
2	George Brett	2.50
3	Rickey Henderson	1.25
4	Cal Ripken, Jr.	4.00
5	Nolan Ryan	4.00
6	Ryne Sandberg	2.00
7	Ozzie Smith	2.00
8	Darryl Strawberry	.75
9	Dave Winfield	1.25
10	Dennis Eckersley	1.00
11	Tony Gwynn	2.00
12	Howard Johnson	.75
13	Don Mattingly	2.50
14	Eddie Murray	1.25
15	Robin Yount	1.25
16	Reggie Jackson	2.00
17	Mickey Mantle	6.00
17a	Mickey Mantle (5" x 7")	13.50
18	Willie Mays	3.00

Triple Crown Contenders

		NM/M
	Complete Set (10):	6.00
	Common Player:	.25
1	Barry Bonds	1.50
2	Jose Canseco	.45
3	Will Clark	.25
4	Ken Griffey Jr.	1.25
5	Fred McGriff	.25
6	Kirby Puckett	.75
7	Cal Ripken, Jr.	1.50
8	Gary Sheffield	.35
9	Frank Thomas	.60
10	Larry Walker	.25

5th Anniversary

		NM/M
	Complete Set (15):	7.00

Chipper Jones

	Common Player:	.25
1	Ken Griffey Jr.	1.50
2	Gary Sheffield	.35
3	Roberto Alomar	.35
4	Jim Abbott	.25
5	Nolan Ryan	2.00
6	Juan Gonzalez	.35
7	Dave Justice	.25
8	Carlos Baerga	.25
9	Reggie Jackson	1.00
10	Eric Karros	.25
11	Chipper Jones	1.00
12	Ivan Rodriguez	.50
13	Pat Listach	.25
14	Frank Thomas	.90
15	Tim Salmon	.25

SP Insert

		NM/M
	Complete Set (15):	60.00
	Common Player:	.50
	EASTERN REGION	
1	Roberto Alomar	1.00
2	Cliff Floyd	.50
3	Javier Lopez	.50
4	Don Mattingly	6.00
5	Cal Ripken, Jr.	10.00
	CENTRAL REGION	
1	Jeff Bagwell	3.00
2	Michael Jordan	10.00
3	Kirby Puckett	6.00
4	Manny Ramirez	3.00
5	Frank Thomas	4.00
	WESTERN REGION	
1	Barry Bonds	10.00
2	Juan Gonzalez	1.50
3	Ken Griffey Jr.	5.00
4	Mike Piazza	5.00
5	Tim Salmon	.50

1994 Upper Deck

		NM/M
	Complete Set (550):	30.00
	Complete Series 1 (280):	25.00
	Complete Series 2 (270):	5.00
	Common Player:	.05
	Series 1 Hobby Pack (12):	2.50
	Series 1 Hobby Box (36):	65.00
	Series 1 Retail Pack (12):	2.00
	Series 1 Retail Box (36):	40.00
	Series 2 Hobby Pack (12):	.75
	Series 2 Hobby Box (36):	20.00
	Series 2 Retail Pack (12):	1.25
	Series 2 Retail Box (36):	25.00
1	Brian Anderson RC	.15
2	Shane Andrews	.05
3	James Baldwin	.05
4	Rich Becker	.05
5	Greg Blosser	.05
6	Ricky Bottalico RC	.05
7	Midre Cummings	.05
8	Carlos Delgado	.50
9	Steve Dreyer RC	.05
10	Joey Eischen RC	.05
11	Carl Everett	.05
12	Cliff Floyd	.05
13	Alex Gonzalez	.05
14	Jeff Granger	.05
15	Shawn Green	.35
16	Brian Hunter	.05
17	Butch Huskey	.05
18	Mark Hutton	.05
19	Michael Jordan RC	5.00
20	Steve Karsay	.05
21	Jeff McNeely	.05
22	Marc Newfield	.05
23	Manny Ramirez	.60
24	Alex Rodriguez RC	20.00
25	Scott Ruffcorn	.05
26	Paul Spoljaric	.05
27	Salomon Torres RC	.05
28	Steve Trachsel	.05
29	Chris Turner RC	.05
30	Gabe White	.05
31	Randy Johnson	.40
32	John Wetteland	.05
33	Mike Piazza	.65
34	Rafael Palmeiro	.35
35	Roberto Alomar	.10
36	Matt Williams	.05
37	Travis Fryman	.05
38	Barry Bonds	1.00
39	Marquis Grissom	.05
40	Albert Belle	.05
41	Steve Avery	.05
42	Jason Bere	.05
43	Alex Fernandez	.05
44	Mike Mussina	.15
45	Aaron Sele	.05
46	Rod Beck	.05
47	Mike Piazza	.65
48	John Olerud	.05
49	Carlos Baerga	.05
50	Gary Sheffield	.20
51	Travis Fryman	.20
52	Juan Gonzalez	.20
53	Ken Griffey Jr.	.65
54	Tim Salmon	.05
55	Frank Thomas	.45
56	Tony Phillips	.05
57	Julio Franco	.05
58	Kevin Mitchell	.05
59	Raul Mondesi	.05
60	Rickey Henderson	.75
61	Jay Buhner	.05
62	Bill Swift	.05
63	Brady Anderson	.05
64	Ryan Klesko	.05
65	Darren Daulton	.05
66	Damion Easley	.05
67	Mark McGwire	1.50
68	John Roper	.05
69	Dave Telgheder	.05
70	Dave Nied	.05
71	Mo Vaughn	.05
72	Tyler Green	.05
73	Dave Magadan	.05
74	Chili Davis	.05
75	Archi Cianfrocco	.05
76	Joe Girardi	.05
77	Chris Hoiles	.05
78	Ryan Bowen	.05
79	Greg Gagne	.05
80	Aaron Sele	.05
81	Dave Winfield	.75
82	Chad Curtis	.05
83	Andy Van Slyke	.05
84	Kevin Stocker	.05
85	Deion Sanders	.05
86	Bernie Williams	.05
87	John Smoltz	.05
88	Ruben Santana RC	.05
89	Dave Stewart	.05
90	Don Mattingly	1.00
91	Joe Carter	.05
92	Ryne Sandberg	.90
93	Chris Gomez	.05
94	Tino Martinez	.05
95	Terry Pendleton	.05
96	Andre Dawson	.25
97	Wil Cordero	.05
98	Kent Hrbek	.05
99	John Olerud	.05
100	Kirt Manwaring	.05
101	Tim Bogar	.05
102	Mike Mussina	.30
103	Nigel Wilson	.05
104	Ricky Gutierrez	.05
105	Roberto Mejia	.05
106	Tom Pagnozzi	.05
107	Mike Macfarlane	.05
108	Jose Bautista	.05
109	Luis Ortiz	.05
110	Brent Gates	.05
111	Tim Salmon	.05
112	Wade Boggs	.90
113	Tripp Cromer RC	.05
114	Denny Hocking	.05
115	Carlos Baerga	.05
116	J.R. Phillips RC	.05
117	Bo Jackson	.10
118	Lance Johnson	.05
119	Bobby Jones	.05
120	Bobby Witt	.05
121	Ron Karkovice	.05
122	Jose Vizcaino	.05
123	Danny Darwin	.05
124	Eduardo Perez	.05
125	Brian Looney	.05
126	Pat Hentgen	.05
127	Frank Viola	.05
128	Darren Holmes	.05
129	Wally Whitehurst	.05
130	Matt Walbeck	.05
131	Albert Belle	.05
132	Steve Cooke	.05
133	Kevin Appier	.05
134	Joe Oliver	.05
135	Benji Gil	.05
136	Steve Buechele	.05
137	Devon White	.05
138	Sterling Hitchcock	.05
139	Phil Leftwich RC	.05
140	Jose Canseco	.45
141	Rick Aguilera	.05
142	Rod Beck	.05
143	Jose Rijo	.05
144	Tom Glavine	.25
145	Phil Plantier	.05
146	Jason Bere	.05
147	Jamie Moyer	.05
148	Wes Chamberlain	.05
149	Glenallen Hill	.05
150	Mark Whiten	.05
151	Bret Barberie	.05
152	Chuck Knoblauch	.05
153	Trevor Hoffman	.05
154	Rick Wilkins	.05
155	Juan Gonzalez	.40
156	Ozzie Guillen	.05
157	Jim Eisenreich	.05
158	Pedro Astacio	.05
159	Joe Magrane	.05
160	Ryan Thompson	.05
161	Jose Lind	.05
162	Jeff Conine	.05
163	Todd Benzinger	.05
164	Roger Salkeld	.05
165	Gary DiSarcina	.05
166	Kevin Gross	.05
167	Charlie Hayes	.05
168	Tim Costo	.05
169	Wally Joyner	.05
170	Johnny Ruffin	.05
171	Kirk Rueter RC	.10
172	Len Dykstra	.05
173	Ken Hill	.05
174	Mike Bordick	.05
175	Billy Hall	.05
176	Rob Butler	.05
177	Jay Bell	.05
178	Jeff Kent	.05
179	David Wells	.05
180	Dean Palmer	.05
181	Mariano Duncan	.05
182	Orlando Merced	.05
183	Brett Butler	.05
184	Milt Thompson	.05
185	Chipper Jones	.90
186	Paul O'Neill	.05
187	Mike Greenwell	.05
188	Harold Baines	.05
189	Todd Stottlemyre	.05
190	Jeromy Burnitz	.05
191	Rene Arocha	.05
192	Jeff Fassero	.05
193	Robby Thompson	.05
194	Greg W. Harris	.05
195	Todd Van Poppel	.05

#	Player	Price
196	Jose Guzman	.05
197	Shane Mack	.05
198	Carlos Garcia	.05
199	Kevin Roberson	.05
200	David McCarty	.05
201	Alan Trammell	.05
202	Chuck Carr	.05
203	Tommy Greene	.05
204	Wilson Alvarez	.05
205	Dwight Gooden	.05
206	Tony Tarasco	.05
207	Darren Lewis	.05
208	Eric Karros	.05
209	Chris Hammond	.05
210	Jeffrey Hammonds	.05
211	Rich Amaral	.05
212	Danny Tartabull	.05
213	Jeff Russell	.05
214	Dave Staton	.05
215	Kenny Lofton	.05
216	Manuel Lee	.05
217	Brian Koelling	.05
218	Scott Lydy	.05
219	Tony Gwynn	.90
220	Cecil Fielder	.05
221	Royce Clayton	.05
222	Reggie Sanders	.05
223	Brian Jordan	.05
224	Ken Griffey Jr.	1.25
224a	Ken Griffey Jr./PC	3.00
225	Fred McGriff	.05
226	Felix Jose	.05
227	Brad Pennington	.05
228	Chris Bosio	.05
229	Mike Stanley	.05
230	Willie Greene	.05
231	Alex Fernandez	.05
232	Brad Ausmus	.05
233	Darrell Whitmore	.05
234	Marcus Moore	.05
235	Allen Watson	.05
236	Jose Offerman	.05
237	Rondell White	.05
238	Jeff King	.05
239	Luis Alicea	.05
240	Dan Wilson	.05
241	Ed Sprague	.05
242	Todd Hundley	.05
243	Al Martin	.05
244	Mike Lansing	.05
245	Ivan Rodriguez	.65
246	Dave Fleming	.05
247	John Doherty	.05
248	Mark McLemore	.05
249	Bob Hamelin	.05
250	Curtis Pride RC	.05
251	Zane Smith	.05
252	Eric Young	.05
253	Brian McRae	.05
254	Tim Raines	.05
255	Javier Lopez	.05
256	Melvin Nieves	.05
257	Randy Myers	.05
258	Willie McGee	.05
259	Jimmy Key	.05
260	Tom Candiotti	.05
261	Eric Davis	.05
262	Craig Paquette	.05
263	Robin Ventura	.05
264	Pat Kelly	.05
265	Gregg Jefferies	.05
266	Cory Snyder	.05
267	Dave Justice	.05
268	Sammy Sosa	.45
269	Barry Larkin	.05
270	Andres Galarraga	.05
271	Gary Sheffield	.20
272	Jeff Bagwell	.40
273	Mike Piazza	.65
274	Larry Walker	.05
275	Bobby Bonilla	.05
276	John Kruk	.05
277	Jay Bell	.05
278	Ozzie Smith	.45
279	Tony Gwynn	.45
280	Barry Bonds	1.00
281	Cal Ripken, Jr.	1.00
282	Mo Vaughn	.05
283	Tim Salmon	.05
284	Frank Thomas	.40
285	Albert Belle	.05
286	Cecil Fielder	.05
287	Wally Joyner	.05
288	Greg Vaughn	.05
289	Kirby Puckett	.45
290	Don Mattingly	.50
291	Terry Steinbach	.05
292	Ken Griffey Jr.	.90
293	Juan Gonzalez	.20
294	Paul Molitor	.40
295	Tavo Alvarez	.05
296	Matt Brunson	.05
297	Shawn Green	.20
298	Alex Rodriguez	2.00
299	Shannon Stewart	.05
300	Frank Thomas	.75
301	Mickey Tettleton	.05
302	Pedro Munoz	.05
303	Jose Valentin	.05
304	Orestes Destrade	.05
305	Pat Listach	.05
306	Scott Brosius	.05
307	Kurt Miller RC	.05
308	Rob Dibble	.05
309	Mike Blowers	.05
310	Jim Abbott	.05
311	Mike Jackson	.05
312	Craig Biggio	.05
313	Kurt Abbott RC	.05
314	Chuck Finley	.05
315	Andres Galarraga	.05
316	Mike Moore	.05
317	Doug Strange	.05
318	Pedro J. Martinez	.75
319	Kevin McReynolds	.05
320	Greg Maddux	.90
321	Mike Henneman	.05
322	Scott Leius	.05
323	John Franco	.05
324	Jeff Blauser	.05
325	Kirby Puckett	.90
326	Darryl Hamilton	.05
327	John Smiley	.05
328	Derrick May	.05
329	Jose Vizcaino	.05
330	Randy Johnson	.75
331	Jack Morris	.05
332	Graeme Lloyd	.05
333	Dave Valle	.05
334	Greg Myers	.05
335	John Wetteland	.05
336	Jim Gott	.05
337	Tim Naehring	.05
338	Mike Kelly	.05
339	Jeff Montgomery	.05
340	Rafael Palmeiro	.65
341	Eddie Murray	.75
342	Xavier Hernandez	.05
343	Bobby Munoz	.05
344	Bobby Bonilla	.05
345	Travis Fryman	.05
346	Steve Finley	.05
347	Chris Sabo	.05
348	Armando Reynoso	.05
349	Ramon Martinez	.05
350	Will Clark	.05
351	Moises Alou	.05
352	Jim Thome	.50
353	Bob Tewksbury	.05
354	Andujar Cedeno	.05
355	Orel Hershiser	.05
356	Mike Devereaux	.05
357	Mike Perez	.05
358	Dennis Martinez	.05
359	Dave Nilsson	.05
360	Ozzie Smith	.90
361	Eric Anthony	.05
362	Scott Sanders	.05
363	Paul Sorrento	.05
364	Tim Belcher	.05
365	Dennis Eckersley	.60
366	Mel Rojas	.05
367	Tom Henke	.05
368	Randy Tomlin	.05
369	B.J. Surhoff	.05
370	Larry Walker	.05
371	Joey Cora	.05
372	Mike Harkey	.05
373	John Valentin	.05
374	Doug Jones	.05
375	Dave Justice	.05
376	Vince Coleman	.05
377	David Hulse	.05
378	Kevin Seitzer	.05
379	Pete Harnisch	.05
380	Ruben Sierra	.05
381	Mark Lewis	.05
382	Bip Roberts	.05
383	Paul Wagner	.05
384	Stan Javier	.05
385	Barry Larkin	.05
386	Mark Portugal	.05
387	Roberto Kelly	.05
388	Andy Benes	.05
389	Felix Fermin	.05
390	Marquis Grissom	.05
391	Troy Neel	.05
392	Chad Kreuter	.05
393	Gregg Olson	.05
394	Charles Nagy	.05
395	Jack McDowell	.05
396	Luis Gonzalez	.05
397	Benito Santiago	.05
398	Chris James	.05
399	Terry Mulholland	.05
400	Barry Bonds	2.00
401	Joe Grahe	.05
402	Duane Ward	.05
403	John Burkett	.05
404	Scott Servais	.05
405	Bryan Harvey	.05
406	Bernard Gilkey	.05
407	Greg McMichael	.05
408	Tim Wallach	.05
409	Ken Caminiti	.05
410	John Kruk	.05
411	Darrin Jackson	.05
412	Mike Gallego	.05
413	David Cone	.05
414	Lou Whitaker	.05
415	Sandy Alomar Jr.	.05
416	Bill Wegman	.05
417	Pat Borders	.05
418	Roger Pavlik	.05
419	Pete Smith	.05
420	Steve Avery	.05
421	David Segui	.05
422	Rheal Cormier	.05
423	Harold Reynolds	.05
424	Edgar Martinez	.05
425	Cal Ripken, Jr.	2.00
426	Jaime Navarro	.05
427	Sean Berry	.05
428	Bret Saberhagen	.05
429	Bob Welch	.05
430	Juan Guzman	.05
431	Cal Eldred	.05
432	Dave Hollins	.05
433	Sid Fernandez	.05
434	Willie Banks	.05
435	Darryl Kile	.05
436	Henry Rodriguez	.05
437	Tony Fernandez	.05
438	Walt Weiss	.05
439	Kevin Tapani	.05
440	Mark Grace	.05
441	Brian Harper	.05
442	Kent Mercker	.05
443	Anthony Young	.05
444	Todd Zeile	.05
445	Greg Vaughn	.05
446	Ray Lankford	.05
447	David Weathers	.05
448	Bret Boone	.05
449	Charlie Hough	.05
450	Roger Clemens	1.00
451	Mike Morgan	.05
452	Doug Drabek	.05
453	Danny Jackson	.05
454	Dante Bichette	.05
455	Roberto Alomar	.20
456	Ben McDonald	.05
457	Kenny Rogers	.05
458	Bill Gullickson	.05
459	Darrin Fletcher	.05
460	Curt Schilling	.20
461	Billy Hatcher	.05
462	Howard Johnson	.05
463	Mickey Morandini	.05
464	Frank Castillo	.05
465	Delino DeShields	.05
466	Gary Gaetti	.05
467	Steve Farr	.05
468	Roberto Hernandez	.05
469	Jack Armstrong	.05
470	Paul Molitor	.75
471	Melido Perez	.05
472	Greg Hibbard	.05
473	Jody Reed	.05
474	Tom Gordon	.05
475	Gary Sheffield	.35
476	John Jaha	.05
477	Shawon Dunston	.05
478	Reggie Jefferson	.05
479	Don Slaught	.05
480	Jeff Bagwell	.75
481	Tim Pugh	.05
482	Kevin Young	.05
483	Ellis Burks	.05
484	Greg Swindell	.05
485	Mark Langston	.05
486	Omar Vizquel	.05
487	Kevin Brown	.05
488	Terry Steinbach	.05
489	Mark Lemke	.05
490	Matt Williams	.05
491	Pete Incaviglia	.05
492	Karl Rhodes	.05
493	Shawn Green	.30
494	Hal Morris	.05
495	Derek Bell	.05
496	Luis Polonia	.05
497	Otis Nixon	.05
498	Ron Darling	.05
499	Mitch Williams	.05
500	Mike Piazza	1.25
501	Pat Meares	.05
502	Scott Cooper	.05
503	Scott Erickson	.05
504	Jeff Juden	.05
505	Lee Smith	.05
506	Bobby Ayala	.05
507	Dave Henderson	.05
508	Erik Hanson	.05
509	Bob Wickman	.05
510	Sammy Sosa	.90
511	Hector Carrasco	.05
512	Tim Davis	.05
513	Joey Hamilton	.05
514	Robert Eenhoorn	.05
515	Jorge Fabregas	.05
516	Tim Hyers	.05
517	John Hudek	.05
518	James Mouton RC	.05
519	Herbert Perry	.05
520	Chan Ho Park RC	.75
521	Bill VanLandingham	.05
522	Paul Shuey	.05
523	Ryan Hancock RC	.05
524	Billy Wagner RC	.25
525	Jason Giambi	.50
526	Jose Silva RC	.05
527	Terrell Wade RC	.05
528	Todd Dunn	.05
529	Alan Benes RC	.05
530	Brooks Kieschnick RC	.05
531	Todd Hollandsworth	.05
532	Brad Fullmer RC	.15
533	Steve Soderstrom RC	.05
534	Daron Kirkreit	.05
535	Arquimedez Pozo RC	.05
536	Charles Johnson	.05
537	Preston Wilson	.10
538	Alex Ochoa	.05
539	Derek Lee RC	3.00
540	Wayne Gomes RC	.05
541	Jermaine Allensworth RC	.05
542	Mike Bell RC	.05
543	Trot Nixon RC	1.25
544	Pokey Reese	.05
545	Neifi Perez RC	.05
546	Johnny Damon	.30
547	Matt Brunson	.05
548	LaTroy Hawkins RC	.05
549	Eddie Pearson RC	.05
550	Derek Jeter	2.00

Electric Diamond

	NM/M
Complete Set (550):	75.00
Common Player:	.25
Stars:	1.5X

(See 1994 Upper Deck for checklist and base card values.)

Alex Rodriguez Autograph

	NM/M
A298 Alex Rodriguez/Auto. (Classic Alumni)	500.00

All-Stars

	NM/M
Complete Set (48):	9.00
Common Player:	.15
Gold:	4X
1	Ken Griffey Jr.	1.00
2	Ruben Sierra, Todd Van Poppel	.15
3	Bryan Harvey, Gary Sheffield	.35

KG1	Ken Griffey Jr., Mickey Mantle (Griffey Autograph)	250.00
MM1	Ken Griffey Jr., Mickey Mantle (Mantle Autograph)	650.00
GM1	Ken Griffey Jr., Mickey Mantle (Both Autographs)	1,150

Mickey Mantle's Long Shots

		NM/M
Complete Set (21):		20.00
Common Player:		.50
Electric Diamonds:		1X
(1)	Mickey Mantle Trade Card (Silver): (Redeemable for 21-card Mantle Long Shots set.)	4.00
(2)	Mickey Mantle Trade Card (Blue): (Redeemable for Electric Diamond version Mantle Long Shots set.)	4.00
1	Jeff Bagwell	1.50
2	Albert Belle	.50
3	Barry Bonds	4.00
4	Jose Canseco	.75
5	Joe Carter	.50
6	Carlos Delgado	.75
7	Cecil Fielder	.50
8	Cliff Floyd	.50
9	Juan Gonzalez	.75
10	Ken Griffey Jr.	2.50
11	David Justice	.50
12	Fred McGriff	.50
13	Mark McGwire	3.00
14	Dean Palmer	.50
15	Mike Piazza	2.50
16	Manny Ramirez	1.50
17	Tim Salmon	.50
18	Frank Thomas	1.50
19	Mo Vaughn	.50
20	Matt Williams	.50
21	Mickey Mantle Header	4.00

1995 Upper Deck

		NM/M
Complete Set (450):		20.00
Common Player:		.05
Electric Diamond Golds:		8X
Series 1 or 2 Pack (12):		.85
Series 1 or 2 Wax Box (36):		20.00
1	Ruben Rivera	.05
2	Bill Pulsipher	.05
3	Ben Grieve	.05
4	Curtis Goodwin	.05
5	Damon Hollins	.05
6	Todd Greene	.05
7	Glenn Williams	.05
8	Bret Wagner	.05
9	Karim Garcia RC	.50
10	Nomar Garciaparra	1.00
11	Raul Casanova RC	.10
12	Matt Smith	.05
13	Paul Wilson	.05
14	Jason Isringhausen	.05
15	Reid Ryan	.05
16	Lee Smith	.05
17	Chili Davis	.05
18	Brian Anderson	.05
19	Gary DiSarcina	.05
20	Bo Jackson	.10
21	Chuck Finley	.05
22	Darryl Kile	.05
23	Shane Reynolds	.05
24	Tony Eusebio	.05
25	Craig Biggio	.05
26	Doug Drabek	.05
27	Brian L. Hunter	.05
28	James Mouton	.05
29	Geronimo Berroa	.05
30	Rickey Henderson	.75
31	Steve Karsay	.05
32	Steve Ontiveros	.05
33	Ernie Young	.05
34	Dennis Eckersley	.65
35	Mark McGwire	1.50
36	Dave Stewart	.05
37	Pat Hentgen	.05
38	Carlos Delgado	.45
39	Joe Carter	.05
40	Roberto Alomar	.20
41	John Olerud	.05
42	Devon White	.05
43	Roberto Kelly	.05
44	Jeff Blauser	.05
45	Fred McGriff	.05
46	Tom Glavine	.25
47	Mike Kelly	.05
48	Javy Lopez	.05
49	Greg Maddux	1.00
50	Matt Mieske	.05
51	Troy O'Leary	.05
52	Jeff Cirillo	.05
53	Cal Eldred	.05
54	Pat Listach	.05
55	Jose Valentin	.05
56	John Mabry	.05
57	Bob Tewksbury	.05
58	Brian Jordan	.05
59	Gregg Jefferies	.05
60	Ozzie Smith	1.00
61	Geronimo Pena	.05
62	Mark Whiten	.05
63	Rey Sanchez	.05
64	Willie Banks	.05
65	Mark Grace	.05
66	Randy Myers	.05
67	Steve Trachsel	.05
68	Derrick May	.05
69	Brett Butler	.05
70	Eric Karros	.05
71	Tim Wallach	.05
72	Delino DeShields	.05
73	Darren Dreifort	.05
74	Orel Hershiser	.05
75	Billy Ashley	.05
76	Sean Berry	.05
77	Ken Hill	.05
78	John Wetteland	.05
79	Moises Alou	.05
80	Cliff Floyd	.05
81	Marquis Grissom	.05
82	Larry Walker	.05
83	Rondell White	.05
84	William Van Landingham	.05
85	Matt Williams	.05
86	Rod Beck	.05
87	Darren Lewis	.05
88	Robby Thompson	.05
89	Darryl Strawberry	.05
90	Kenny Lofton	.05
91	Charles Nagy	.05
92	Sandy Alomar Jr.	.05
93	Mark Clark	.05
94	Dennis Martinez	.05
95	Dave Winfield	.75
96	Jim Thome	.60
97	Manny Ramirez	.75
98	Goose Gossage	.05
99	Tim Naehring	.05
100	Ken Griffey Jr.	1.25
100a	Ken Griffey Jr./OPS	2.00
101	Greg Maddux	.50
102	Randy Johnson	.40
103	Barry Bonds	1.00
104	Juan Gonzalez	.20
105	Frank Thomas	.40

4	Gregg Jefferies, Brian Jordan	.15
5	Ryne Sandberg	.75
6	Matt Williams, John Burkett	.15
7	Darren Daulton, John Kruk	.15
8	Don Mattingly, Wade Boggs	.75
9	Pat Listach, Greg Vaughn	.15
10	Tim Salmon, Eduardo Perez	.25
11	Fred McGriff, Tom Glavine	.25
12	Mo Vaughn, Andre Dawson	.35
13	Brian McRae, Kevin Appier	.15
14	Kirby Puckett, Kent Hrbek	.75
15	Cal Ripken, Jr.	2.00
16	Roberto Alomar, Paul Molitor	.65
17	Tony Gwynn, Phil Plantier	.75
18	Greg Maddux, Steve Avery	.75
19	Mike Mussina, Chris Hoiles	.50
20	Randy Johnson	.65
21	Roger Clemens, Aaron Sele	.75
22	Will Clark, Dean Palmer	.25
23	Cecil Fielder, Travis Fryman	.15
24	John Olerud, Joe Carter	.15
25	Juan Gonzalez	.65
26	Jose Rijo, Barry Larkin	.15
27	Andy Van Slyke, Jeff King	.15
28	Larry Walker, Marquis Grissom	.15
29	Kenny Lofton, Albert Belle	.25
30	Mark Grace, Sammy Sosa	1.00
31	Mike Piazza	1.00
32	Ramon Martinez, Orel Hershiser	.15
33	Dave Justice, Terry Pendleton	.15
34	Ivan Rodriguez, Jose Canseco	.50
35	Barry Bonds	2.00
36	Jeff Bagwell, Craig Biggio	.65
37	Jay Bell, Orlando Merced	.15
38	Jeff Kent, Dwight Gooden	.15
39	Andres Galarraga, Charlie Hayes	.15
40	Frank Thomas	.70
41	Bobby Bonilla	.15
42	Jack McDowell, Tim Raines	.15
43	1869 Red Stockings	.15
44	Ty Cobb	.50
45	Babe Ruth	1.50
46	Mickey Mantle	2.50
47	Reggie Jackson	.50
48	Ken Griffey Jr.	1.00
48a	Ken Griffey Jr./PC	1.00

Baseball Heroes
Mickey Mantle

	NM/M
Complete Set (10):	25.00
Common Card:	3.00

64	Mickey Mantle 1951 - The Early Years	3.00
65	Mickey Mantle 1953 - Tape Measure Home Runs	3.00
66	Mickey Mantle 1956 - Triple Crown Season	3.00
67	Mickey Mantle 1957 - 2nd Consecutive MVP	3.00
68	Mickey Mantle 1961 - Chases The Babe	3.00
69	Mickey Mantle 1964 - Series Home Run Record	3.00
70	Mickey Mantle 1967 - 500th Home Run	3.00
71	Mickey Mantle 1974: Hall of Fame	3.00
72	Mickey Mantle/Portrait	3.00
----	Mickey Mantle Header Card	5.00

Diamond Collection

	NM/M
Complete Set (30):	40.00
Common Player:	.25
Complete Central (10):	18.00
1	Michael Jordan	10.00
2	Jeff Bagwell	2.00
3	Barry Larkin	.25
4	Kirby Puckett	2.50
5	Manny Ramirez	2.00
6	Ryne Sandberg	2.50
7	Ozzie Smith	2.50
8	Frank Thomas	2.00
9	Andy Van Slyke	.25
10	Robin Yount	2.00
Complete East (10):	11.00
1	Roberto Alomar	1.00
2	Roger Clemens	2.50
3	Len Dykstra	.25
4	Cecil Fielder	.25
5	Cliff Floyd	.25
6	Dwight Gooden	.25
7	Dave Justice	.25
8	Don Mattingly	2.50
9	Cal Ripken, Jr.	6.00
10	Gary Sheffield	.50
Complete West (10):	14.00
1	Barry Bonds	4.00
2	Andres Galarraga	.25
3	Juan Gonzalez	1.50
4	Ken Griffey Jr.	3.00
5	Tony Gwynn	2.00
6	Rickey Henderson	1.50
7	Bo Jackson	.50
8	Mark McGwire	4.00
9	Mike Piazza	4.00
10	Tim Salmon	.50

Ken Griffey Jr. 5th Anniversary Jumbo

	NM/M
Ken Griffey Jr.	20.00

Mantle-Griffey Autographed Inserts

| | NM/M |

#	Player	Value
106	Matt Williams	.05
107	Paul Molitor	.40
108	Fred McGriff	.05
109	Carlos Baerga	
	(Analysis: '90s	
	Midpoint)	.05
110	Ken Griffey Jr.	
	(Analysis: '90s	
	Midpoint)	.65
111	Reggie Jefferson	.05
112	Randy Johnson	.75
113	Marc Newfield	.05
114	Robb Nen	.05
115	Jeff Conine	.05
116	Kurt Abbott	.05
117	Charlie Hough	.05
118	Dave Weathers	.05
119	Juan Castillo	.05
120	Bret Saberhagen	.05
121	Rico Brogna	.05
122	John Franco	.05
123	Todd Hundley	.05
124	Jason Jacome	.05
125	Bobby Jones	.05
126	Bret Barberie	.05
127	Ben McDonald	.05
128	Harold Baines	.05
129	Jeffrey Hammonds	.05
130	Mike Mussina	.30
131	Chris Hoiles	.05
132	Brady Anderson	.05
133	Eddie Williams	.05
134	Andy Benes	.05
135	Tony Gwynn	1.00
136	Bip Roberts	.05
137	Joey Hamilton	.05
138	Luis Lopez	.05
139	Ray McDavid	.05
140	Lenny Dykstra	.05
141	Mariano Duncan	.05
142	Fernando Valenzuela	.05
143	Bobby Munoz	.05
144	Kevin Stocker	.05
145	John Kruk	.05
146	Jon Lieber	.05
147	Zane Smith	.05
148	Steve Cooke	.05
149	Andy Van Slyke	.05
150	Jay Bell	.05
151	Carlos Garcia	.05
152	John Dettmer	.05
153	Darren Oliver	.05
154	Dean Palmer	.05
155	Otis Nixon	.05
156	Rusty Greer	.05
157	Rick Helling	.05
158	Jose Canseco	.40
159	Roger Clemens	1.00
160	Andre Dawson	.25
161	Mo Vaughn	.05
162	Aaron Sele	.05
163	John Valentin	.05
164	Brian Hunter	.05
165	Bret Boone	.05
166	Hector Carrasco	.05
167	Pete Schourek	.05
168	Willie Greene	.05
169	Kevin Mitchell	.05
170	Deion Sanders	.05
171	John Roper	.05
172	Charlie Hayes	.05
173	David Nied	.05
174	Ellis Burks	.05
175	Dante Bichette	.05
176	Marvin Freeman	.05
177	Eric Young	.05
178	David Cone	.05
179	Greg Gagne	.05
180	Bob Hamelin	.05
181	Wally Joyner	.05
182	Jeff Montgomery	.05
183	Jose Lind	.05
184	Chris Gomez	.05
185	Travis Fryman	.05
186	Kirk Gibson	.05
187	Mike Moore	.05
188	Lou Whitaker	.05
189	Sean Bergman	.05
190	Shane Mack	.05
191	Rick Aguilera	.05
192	Denny Hocking	.05
193	Chuck Knoblauch	.05
194	Kevin Tapani	.05
195	Kent Hrbek	.05
196	Ozzie Guillen	.05
197	Wilson Alvarez	.05
198	Tim Raines	.05
199	Scott Ruffcorn	.05
200	Michael Jordan	2.00
201	Robin Ventura	.05
202	Jason Bere	.05
203	Darrin Jackson	.05
204	Russ Davis	.05
205	Jimmy Key	.05

#	Player	Value
206	Jack McDowell	.05
207	Jim Abbott	.05
208	Paul O'Neill	.05
209	Bernie Williams	.05
210	Don Mattingly	1.00
211	Orlando Miller/SR	.05
212	Alex Gonzalez/SR	.05
213	Terrell Wade/SR	.05
214	Jose Oliva/SR	.05
215	Alex Rodriguez/SR	1.50
216	Garret Anderson/SR	.05
217	Alan Benes/SR	.05
218	Armando Benitez/	
	SR	.05
219	Dustin Hermanson/	
	SR	.05
220	Charles Johnson/SR	.05
221	Julian Tavarez/SR	.05
222	Jason Giambi/SR	.50
223	LaTroy Hawkins/SR	.05
224	Todd	
	Hollandsworth/SR	.05
225	Derek Jeter/SR	2.00
226	Hideo Nomo/SR RC	2.00
227	Tony Clark/SR	.05
228	Roger Cedeno/SR	.05
229	Scott Stahoviak/SR	.05
230	Michael Tucker/SR	.05
231	Joe Rosselli/SR	.05
232	Antonio Osuna/SR	.05
233	Bobby Higginson/	
	SR RC	.25
234	Mark	
	Grudzielanek/SR RC	.25
235	Ray Durham/SR	.05
236	Frank Rodriguez/SR	.05
237	Quilvio Veras/SR	.05
238	Darren Bragg/SR	.05
239	Ugueth Urbina/SR	.05
240	Jason Bates/SR	.05
241	David Bell	.05
242	Ron Villone	.05
243	Joe Randa	.05
244	Carlos Perez RC	.05
245	Brad Clontz	.05
246	Steve Rodriguez	.05
247	Joe Vitiello	.05
248	Ozzie Timmons	.05
249	Rudy Pemberton	.05
250	Marty Cordova	.05
251	Tony Graffanino	.05
252	Mark Johnson RC	.05
253	Tomas Perez RC	.05
254	Jimmy Hurst	.05
255	Edgardo Alfonzo	.05
256	Jose Malave	.05
257	Brad Radke RC	.30
258	Jon Nunnally	.05
259	Dilson Torres	.05
260	Esteban Loaiza	.05
261	Freddy Garcia RC	.05
262	Don Wengert	.05
263	Robert Person RC	.05
264	Tim Unroe RC	.05
265	Juan Acevedo	.05
266	Eduardo Perez	.05
267	Tony Phillips	.05
268	Jim Edmonds	.05
269	Jorge Fabregas	.05
270	Tim Salmon	.05
271	Mark Langston	.05
272	J.T. Snow	.05
273	Phil Plantier	.05
274	Derek Bell	.05
275	Jeff Bagwell	.75
276	Luis Gonzalez	.05
277	John Hudek	.05
278	Todd Stottlemyre	.05
279	Mark Acre	.05
280	Ruben Sierra	.05
281	Mike Bordick	.05
282	Ron Darling	.05
283	Brent Gates	.05
284	Todd Van Poppel	.05
285	Paul Molitor	.75
286	Ed Sprague	.05
287	Juan Guzman	.05
288	David Cone	.05
289	Shawn Green	.30
290	Marquis Grissom	.05
291	Kent Mercker	.05
292	Steve Avery	.05
293	Chipper Jones	1.00
294	John Smoltz	.05
295	Dave Justice	.05
296	Ryan Klesko	.05
297	Joe Oliver	.05
298	Ricky Bones	.05
299	John Jaha	.05
300	Greg Vaughn	.05
301	Dave Nilsson	.05
302	Kevin Seitzer	.05
303	Bernard Gilkey	.05
304	Allen Battle	.05

#	Player	Value
305	Ray Lankford	.05
306	Tom Pagnozzi	.05
307	Allen Watson	.05
308	Danny Jackson	.05
309	Ken Hill	.05
310	Todd Zeile	.05
311	Kevin Roberson	.05
312	Steve Buechele	.05
313	Rick Wilkins	.05
314	Kevin Foster	.05
315	Sammy Sosa	1.00
316	Howard Johnson	.05
317	Greg Hansell	.05
318	Pedro Astacio	.05
319	Rafael Bournigal	.05
320	Mike Piazza	1.25
321	Ramon Martinez	.05
322	Raul Mondesi	.05
323	Ismael Valdes	.05
324	Wil Cordero	.05
325	Tony Tarasco	.05
326	Roberto Kelly	.05
327	Jeff Fassero	.05
328	Mike Lansing	.05
329	Pedro J. Martinez	.75
330	Kirk Rueter	.05
331	Glenallen Hill	.05
332	Kirt Manwaring	.05
333	Royce Clayton	.05
334	J.R. Phillips	.05
335	Barry Bonds	2.00
336	Mark Portugal	.05
337	Terry Mulholland	.05
338	Omar Vizquel	.05
339	Carlos Baerga	.05
340	Albert Belle	.05
341	Eddie Murray	.75
342	Wayne Kirby	.05
343	Chad Ogea	.05
344	Tim Davis	.05
345	Jay Buhner	.05
346	Bobby Ayala	.05
347	Mike Blowers	.05
348	Dave Fleming	.05
349	Edgar Martinez	.05
350	Andre Dawson	.30
351	Darrell Whitmore	.05
352	Chuck Carr	.05
353	John Burkett	.05
354	Chris Hammond	.05
355	Gary Sheffield	.40
356	Pat Rapp	.05
357	Greg Colbrunn	.05
358	David Segui	.05
359	Jeff Kent	.05
360	Bobby Bonilla	.05
361	Pete Harnisch	.05
362	Ryan Thompson	.05
363	Jose Vizcaino	.05
364	Brett Butler	.05
365	Cal Ripken Jr.	2.00
366	Rafael Palmeiro	.65
367	Leo Gomez	.05
368	Andy Van Slyke	.05
369	Arthur Rhodes	.05
370	Ken Caminiti	.05
371	Steve Finley	.05
372	Melvin Nieves	.05
373	Andujar Cedeno	.05
374	Trevor Hoffman	.05
375	Fernando Valenzuela	.05
376	Ricky Bottalico	.05
377	Dave Hollins	.05
378	Charlie Hayes	.05
379	Tommy Greene	.05
380	Darren Daulton	.05
381	Curt Schilling	.25
382	Midre Cummings	.05
383	Al Martin	.05
384	Jeff King	.05
385	Orlando Merced	.05
386	Denny Neagle	.05
387	Don Slaught	.05
388	Dave Clark	.05
389	Kevin Gross	.05
390	Will Clark	.05
391	Ivan Rodriguez	.65
392	Benji Gil	.05
393	Jeff Frye	.05
394	Kenny Rogers	.05
395	Juan Gonzalez	.40
396	Mike Macfarlane	.05
397	Lee Tinsley	.05
398	Tim Naehring	.05
399	Tim Vanegmond	.05
400	Mike Greenwell	.05
401	Ken Ryan	.05
402	John Smiley	.05
403	Tim Pugh	.05
404	Reggie Sanders	.05
405	Barry Larkin	.05
406	Hal Morris	.05
407	Jose Rijo	.05
408	Lance Painter	.05

#	Player	Value
409	Joe Girardi	.05
410	Andres Galarraga	.05
411	Mike Kingery	.05
412	Roberto Mejia	.05
413	Walt Weiss	.05
414	Bill Swift	.05
415	Larry Walker	.05
416	Billy Brewer	.05
417	Pat Borders	.05
418	Tom Gordon	.05
419	Kevin Appier	.05
420	Gary Gaetti	.05
421	Greg Gohr	.05
422	Felipe Lira	.05
423	John Doherty	.05
424	Chad Curtis	.05
425	Cecil Fielder	.05
426	Alan Trammell	.05
427	David McCarty	.05
428	Scott Erickson	.05
429	Pat Mahomes	.05
430	Kirby Puckett	1.00
431	Dave Stevens	.05
432	Pedro Munoz	.05
433	Chris Sabo	.05
434	Alex Fernandez	.05
435	Frank Thomas	.75
436	Roberto Hernandez	.05
437	Lance Johnson	.05
438	Jim Abbott	.05
439	John Wetteland	.05
440	Melido Perez	.05
441	Tony Fernandez	.05
442	Pat Kelly	.05
443	Mike Stanley	.05
444	Danny Tartabull	.05
445	Wade Boggs	1.00
446	Robin Yount	.75
447	Ryne Sandberg	1.00
448	Nolan Ryan	2.00
449	George Brett	1.00
450	Mike Schmidt	1.00

Electric Diamond

	NM/M
Complete Set (1-450):	60.00
Common Player:	.25
Stars/Rookies:	2X

(See 1995 Upper Deck for checklist and base card values.)

Autographed Jumbos

	NM/M
Complete Set (2):	100.00
(1) Roger Clemens	50.00
(2) Alex Rodriguez	75.00

Autograph Redemption Cards

	NM/M
Complete Set (5):	220.00
Common Player:	15.00
AC1 Reggie Jackson	20.00
AC2 Willie Mays	100.00
AC3 Frank Robinson	30.00

New York Yankees® - OF

| AC4 | Roger Clemens | 125.00 |
| AC5 | Raul Mondesi | 10.00 |

Baseball Heroes
Babe Ruth

NM/M

Complete Set (10):	45.00
Common Card:	6.00
73	Babe Ruth 1914-18	
	Pitching Career	6.00
74	Babe Ruth 1919 -	
	Move to Outfield	6.00
75	Babe Ruth 1920 -	
	Renaissance Man	6.00
76	Babe Ruth 1923 -	
	House That Ruth Built	6.00
77	Babe Ruth 1927 -	
	60-Homer Season	6.00
78	Babe Ruth 1928 -	
	Three-homer Game	6.00
79	Babe Ruth 1932 -	
	The Called Shot	6.00
80	Babe Ruth 1930-35 -	
	Milestones	6.00
81	Babe Ruth 1935 -	
	The Last Hurrah	6.00
---	Header Card	7.50

Cal Ripken
Commemorative
Jumbo

NM/M

| Cal Ripken Jr. (Silver edition of 5,000.) | 10.00 |
| Cal Ripken Jr. (Gold edition of 2,131.) | 13.50 |

Special Edition

NM/M

Complete Set (270):	60.00
Common Player:	.10
Gold:	3X
1	Cliff Floyd	.10
2	Wil Cordero	.10
3	Pedro Martinez	1.50
4	Larry Walker	.10
5	Derek Jeter	4.00
6	Mike Stanley	.10

7	Melido Perez	.10
8	Jim Leyritz	.10
9	Danny Tartabull	.10
10	Wade Boggs	2.00
11	Ryan Klesko	.10
12	Steve Avery	.10
13	Damon Hollins	.10
14	Chipper Jones	2.00
15	Dave Justice	.10
16	Glenn Williams	.10
17	Jose Oliva	.10
18	Terrell Wade	.10
19	Alex Fernandez	.10
20	Frank Thomas	1.50
21	Ozzie Guillen	.10
22	Roberto Hernandez	.10
23	Albie Lopez	.10
24	Eddie Murray	1.50
25	Albert Belle	.10
26	Omar Vizquel	.10
27	Carlos Baerga	.10
28	Jose Rijo	.10
29	Hal Morris	.10
30	Reggie Sanders	.10
31	Jack Morris	.10
32	Mark Mondesi	.10
33	Karim Garcia	.15
34	Todd Hollandsworth	.10
35	Mike Piazza	2.50
36	Chan Ho Park	.10
37	Ramon Martinez	.10
38	Kenny Rogers	.10
39	Will Clark	.10
40	Juan Gonzalez	.75
41	Ivan Rodriguez	1.25
42	Orlando Miller	.10
43	John Hudek	.10
44	Luis Gonzalez	.10
45	Jeff Bagwell	1.50
46	Cal Ripken Jr.	4.00
47	Mike Oquist	.10
48	Armando Benitez	.10
49	Ben McDonald	.10
50	Rafael Palmeiro	1.25
51	Curtis Goodwin	.10
52	Vince Coleman	.10
53	Tom Gordon	.10
54	Mike Macfarlane	.10
55	Brian McRae	.10
56	Matt Smith	.10
57	David Segui	.10
58	Paul Wilson	.10
59	Bill Pulsipher	.10
60	Bobby Bonilla	.10
61	Jeff Kent	.10
62	Ryan Thompson	.10
63	Jason Isringhausen	.10
64	Ed Sprague	.10
65	Paul Molitor	1.50
66	Juan Guzman	.10
67	Alex Gonzalez	.10
68	Shawn Green	.50
69	Mark Portugal	.10
70	Barry Bonds	4.00
71	Robby Thompson	.10
72	Royce Clayton	.10
73	Ricky Bottalico	.10
74	Doug Jones	.10
75	Darren Daulton	.10
76	Gregg Jefferies	.10
77	Scott Cooper	.10
78	Nomar Garciaparra	2.00
79	Ken Ryan	.10
80	Mike Greenwell	.10
81	LaTroy Hawkins	.10
82	Rich Becker	.10
83	Scott Erickson	.10
84	Pedro Munoz	.10
85	Kirby Puckett	2.00
86	Orlando Merced	.10
87	Jeff King	.10
88	Midre Cummings	.10
89	Bernard Gilkey	.10

90	Ray Lankford	.10
91	Todd Zeile	.10
92	Alan Benes	.10
93	Bret Wagner	.10
94	Rene Arocha	.10
95	Cecil Fielder	.10
96	Alan Trammell	.10
97	Tony Phillips	.10
98	Junior Felix	.10
99	Brian Harper	.10
100	Greg Vaughn	.10
101	Ricky Bones	.10
102	Walt Weiss	.10
103	Lance Painter	.10
104	Roberto Mejia	.10
105	Andres Galarraga	.10
106	Todd Van Poppel	.10
107	Ben Grieve	.10
108	Brent Gates	.10
109	Jason Giambi	1.00
110	Ruben Sierra	.10
111	Terry Steinbach	.10
112	Chris Hammond	.10
113	Charles Johnson	.10
114	Jesus Tavarez	.10
115	Gary Sheffield	.40
116	Chuck Carr	.10
117	Bobby Ayala	.10
118	Randy Johnson	1.50
119	Edgar Martinez	.10
120	Alex Rodriguez	3.00
121	Kevin Foster	.10
122	Kevin Roberson	.10
123	Sammy Sosa	2.00
124	Steve Trachsel	.10
125	Eduardo Perez	.10
126	Tim Salmon	.10
127	Todd Greene	.10
128	Jorge Fabregas	.10
129	Mark Langston	.10
130	Mitch Williams	.10
131	Raul Casanova	.10
132	Mel Nieves	.10
133	Andy Benes	.10
134	Dustin Hermanson	.10
135	Trevor Hoffman	.10
136	Mark Grudzielanek	.10
137	Ugueth Urbina	.10
138	Moises Alou	.10
139	Roberto Kelly	.10
140	Rondell White	.10
141	Paul O'Neill	.10
142	Jimmy Key	.10
143	Jack McDowell	.10
144	Ruben Rivera	.10
145	Don Mattingly	2.25
146	John Wetteland	.10
147	Tom Glavine	.25
148	Marquis Grissom	.10
149	Javy Lopez	.10
150	Fred McGriff	.10
151	Greg Maddux	2.00
152	Chris Sabo	.10
153	Ray Durham	.10
154	Robin Ventura	.10
155	Jim Abbott	.10
156	Jimmy Hurst	.10
157	Tim Raines	.10
158	Dennis Martinez	.10
159	Kenny Lofton	.10
160	Dave Winfield	1.50
161	Manny Ramirez	1.50
162	Jim Thome	1.00
163	Barry Larkin	.10
164	Bret Boone	.10
165	Deion Sanders	.10
166	Ron Gant	.10
167	Benito Santiago	.10
168	Hideo Nomo	.75
169	Billy Ashley	.10
170	Roger Cedeno	.10
171	Ismael Valdes	.10
172	Eric Karros	.10
173	Rusty Greer	.10
174	Rick Helling	.10
175	Nolan Ryan	4.00
176	Dean Palmer	.10
177	Phil Plantier	.10
178	Darryl Kile	.10
179	Derek Bell	.10
180	Doug Drabek	.10
181	Craig Biggio	.10
182	Kevin Brown	.10
183	Harold Baines	.10
184	Jeffrey Hammonds	.10
185	Chris Hoiles	.10
186	Mike Mussina	.50
187	Bob Hamelin	.10
188	Jeff Montgomery	.10
189	Michael Tucker	.10
190	George Brett	2.25
191	Edgardo Alfonzo	.10
192	Brett Butler	.10
193	Bobby Jones	.10

194	Todd Hundley	.10
195	Bret Saberhagen	.10
196	Pat Hentgen	.10
197	Roberto Alomar	.30
198	David Cone	.10
199	Carlos Delgado	1.00
200	Joe Carter	.10
201	William	
	Van Landingham	.10
202	Rod Beck	.10
203	J.R. Phillips	.10
204	Darren Lewis	.10
205	Matt Williams	.10
206	Lenny Dykstra	.10
207	Dave Hollins	.10
208	Mike Schmidt	2.25
209	Charlie Hayes	.10
210	Mo Vaughn	.10
211	Jose Malave	.10
212	Roger Clemens	2.25
213	Jose Canseco	.75
214	Mark Whiten	.10
215	Marty Cordova	.10
216	Rick Aguilera	.10
217	Kevin Tapani	.10
218	Chuck Knoblauch	.10
219	Al Martin	.10
220	Jay Bell	.10
221	Carlos Garcia	.10
222	Freddy Garcia	.10
223	Jon Lieber	.10
224	Danny Jackson	.10
225	Ozzie Smith	2.00
226	Brian Jordan	.10
227	Ken Hill	.10
228	Scott Cooper	.10
229	Chad Curtis	.10
230	Lou Whitaker	.10
231	Kirk Gibson	.10
232	Travis Fryman	.10
233	Jose Valentin	.10
234	Dave Nilsson	.10
235	Cal Eldred	.10
236	Matt Mieske	.10
237	Bill Swift	.10
238	Marvin Freeman	.10
239	Jason Bates	.10
240	Larry Walker	.10
241	David Nied	.10
242	Dante Bichette	.10
243	Dennis Eckersley	1.25
244	Todd Stottlemyre	.10
245	Rickey Henderson	1.50
246	Geronimo Berroa	.10
247	Mark McGwire	3.00
248	Quilvio Veras	.10
249	Terry Pendleton	.10
250	Andre Dawson	.30
251	Jeff Conine	.10
252	Kurt Abbott	.10
253	Jay Buhner	.10
254	Darren Bragg	.10
255	Ken Griffey Jr.	2.50
256	Tino Martinez	.10
257	Mark Grace	.10
258	Ryne Sandberg	2.00
259	Randy Myers	.10
260	Howard Johnson	.10
261	Lee Smith	.10
262	J.T. Snow	.10
263	Chili Davis	.10
264	Chuck Finley	.10
265	Eddie Williams	.10
266	Joey Hamilton	.10
267	Ken Caminiti	.10
268	Andujar Cedeno	.10
269	Steve Finley	.10
270	Tony Gwynn	2.00

Steal of a Deal

NM/M

Complete Set (15):	25.00
Common Player:	1.00
1	Mike Piazza	6.00
2	Fred McGriff	1.00
3	Kenny Lofton	1.00
4	Jose Oliva	1.00
5	Jeff Bagwell	3.00
6	Roberto Alomar,	
	Joe Carter	1.00
7	Steve Karsay	1.00
8	Ozzie Smith	4.00
9	Dennis Eckersley	2.00

10	Jose Canseco	1.50
11	Carlos Baerga	1.00
12	Cecil Fielder	1.00
13	Don Mattingly	5.00
14	Bret Boone	1.00
15	Michael Jordan	10.00

Update

OREL HERSHISER
Cleveland Indians - P

NM/M

Complete Set (45):		7.50
Common Player:		.25
451	Jim Abbott	.25
452	Danny Tartabull	.25
453	Ariel Prieto	.25
454	Scott Cooper	.25
455	Tom Henke	.25
456	Todd Zeile	.25
457	Brian McRae	.25
458	Luis Gonzalez	.25
459	Jaime Navarro	.25
460	Todd Worrell	.25
461	Roberto Kelly	.25
462	Chad Fonville	.25
463	Shane Andrews	.25
464	David Segui	.25
465	Deion Sanders	.50
466	Orel Hershiser	.25
467	Ken Hill	.25
468	Andy Benes	.25
469	Terry Pendleton	.25
470	Bobby Bonilla	.25
471	Scott Erickson	.25
472	Kevin Brown	.25
473	Glenn Dishman	.25
474	Phil Plantier	.25
475	Gregg Jefferies	.25
476	Tyler Green	.25
477	Heathcliff Slocumb	.25
478	Mark Whiten	.25
479	Mickey Tettleton	.25
480	Tim Wakefield	.25
481	Vaughn Eshelman	.25
482	Rick Aguilera	.25
483	Erik Hanson	.25
484	Willie McGee	.25
485	Troy O'Leary	.25
486	Benito Santiago	.25
487	Darren Lewis	.25
488	Dave Burba	.25
489	Ron Gant	.25
490	Bret Saberhagen	.25
491	Vinny Castilla	.25
492	Frank Rodriguez	.25
493	Andy Pettitte	5.00
494	Ruben Sierra	.25
495	David Cone	.25

1996 Upper Deck

RUBEN SIERRA
Yankees - of

NM/M

Unopened Wood Box		
Set (510):		40.00
Unopened Fact. Set (510):		35.00

Complete Set (480):		20.00
Common Player:		.05
Wax Pack (10):		.75
Wax Box (32):		17.50
1	Cal Ripken Jr. (Milestones)	1.00
2	Eddie Murray (Milestones)	.40
3	Mark Wohlers	.05
4	Dave Justice	.05
5	Chipper Jones	1.00
6	Javier Lopez	.05
7	Mark Lemke	.05
8	Marquis Grissom	.05
9	Tom Glavine	.25
10	Greg Maddux	1.00
11	Manny Alexander	.05
12	Curtis Goodwin	.05
13	Scott Erickson	.05
14	Chris Hoiles	.05
15	Rafael Palmeiro	.65
16	Rick Krivda	.05
17	Jeff Manto	.05
18	Mo Vaughn	.05
19	Tim Wakefield	.05
20	Roger Clemens	1.00
21	Tim Naehring	.05
22	Troy O'Leary	.05
23	Mike Greenwell	.05
24	Stan Belinda	.05
25	John Valentin	.05
26	J.T. Snow	.05
27	Gary DiSarcina	.05
28	Mark Langston	.05
29	Brian Anderson	.05
30	Jim Edmonds	.05
31	Garret Anderson	.05
32	Orlando Palmeiro	.05
33	Brian McRae	.05
34	Kevin Foster	.05
35	Sammy Sosa	1.00
36	Todd Zeile	.05
37	Jim Bullinger	.05
38	Luis Gonzalez	.05
39	Lyle Mouton	.05
40	Ray Durham	.05
41	Ozzie Guillen	.05
42	Alex Fernandez	.05
43	Brian Keyser	.05
44	Robin Ventura	.05
45	Reggie Sanders	.05
46	Pete Schourek	.05
47	John Smiley	.05
48	Jeff Brantley	.05
49	Thomas Howard	.05
50	Bret Boone	.05
51	Kevin Jarvis	.05
52	Jeff Branson	.05
53	Carlos Baerga	.05
54	Jim Thome	.50
55	Manny Ramirez	.75
56	Omar Vizquel	.05
57	Jose Mesa	.05
58	Julian Tavarez	.05
59	Orel Hershiser	.05
60	Larry Walker	.05
61	Bret Saberhagen	.05
62	Vinny Castilla	.05
63	Eric Young	.05
64	Bryan Rekar	.05
65	Andres Galarraga	.05
66	Steve Reed	.05
67	Chad Curtis	.05
68	Bobby Higginson	.05
69	Phil Nevin	.05
70	Cecil Fielder	.05
71	Felipe Lira	.05
72	Chris Gomez	.05
73	Charles Johnson	.05
74	Quilvio Veras	.05
75	Jeff Conine	.05
76	John Burkett	.05
77	Greg Colbrunn	.05
78	Terry Pendleton	.05
79	Shane Reynolds	.05
80	Jeff Bagwell	.75
81	Orlando Miller	.05
82	Mike Hampton	.05
83	James Mouton	.05
84	Brian L. Hunter	.05
85	Derek Bell	.05
86	Kevin Appier	.05
87	Joe Vitiello	.05
88	Wally Joyner	.05
89	Michael Tucker	.05
90	Johnny Damon	.20
91	Jon Nunnally	.05
92	Jason Jacome	.05
93	Chad Fonville	.05
94	Chan Ho Park	.05
95	Hideo Nomo	.40
96	Ismael Valdes	.05
97	Greg Gagne	.05
98	Diamondbacks-Devil Rays	.10

99	Raul Mondesi	.05
100	Dave Winfield	.75
101	Dennis Eckersley	.35
102	Andre Dawson	.15
103	Dennis Martinez	.05
104	Lance Parrish	.05
105	Eddie Murray	.40
106	Alan Trammell	.05
107	Lou Whitaker	.05
108	Ozzie Smith	.50
109	Paul Molitor	.40
110	Rickey Henderson	.40
111	Tim Raines	.05
112	Harold Baines	.05
113	Lee Smith	.05
114	Fernando Valenzuela	.05
115	Cal Ripken Jr.	1.00
116	Tony Gwynn	.50
117	Wade Boggs	.50
118	Todd Hollandsworth	.05
119	Dave Nilsson	.05
120	Jose Valentin **RC**	.05
121	Steve Sparks	.05
122	Chuck Carr	.05
123	John Jaha	.05
124	Scott Karl	.05
125	Chuck Knoblauch	.05
126	Brad Radke	.05
127	Pat Meares	.05
128	Ron Coomer	.05
129	Pedro Munoz	.05
130	Kirby Puckett	1.00
131	David Segui	.05
132	Mark Grudzielanek	.05
133	Mike Lansing	.05
134	Sean Berry	.05
135	Rondell White	.05
136	Pedro Martinez	.75
137	Carl Everett	.05
138	Dave Mlicki	.05
139	Bill Pulsipher	.05
140	Jason Isringhausen	.05
141	Rico Brogna	.05
142	Edgardo Alfonzo	.05
143	Jeff Kent	.05
144	Andy Pettitte	.25
145	Mike Piazza	.65
146	Cliff Floyd	.05
147	Jason Isringhausen	.05
148	Tim Wakefield	.05
149	Chipper Jones	.50
150	Hideo Nomo	.20
151	Mark McGwire	.75
152	Ron Gant	.05
153	Gary Gaetti	.05
154	Don Mattingly	1.00
155	Paul O'Neill	.05
156	Derek Jeter	2.00
157	Joe Girardi	.05
158	Ruben Sierra	.05
159	Jorge Posada	.05
160	Geronimo Berroa	.05
161	Steve Ontiveros	.05
162	George Williams	.05
163	Doug Johns	.05
164	Ariel Prieto	.05
165	Scott Brosius	.05
166	Mike Bordick	.05
167	Tyler Green	.05
168	Mickey Morandini	.05
169	Darren Daulton	.05
170	Gregg Jefferies	.05
171	Jim Eisenreich	.05
172	Heathcliff Slocumb	.05
173	Kevin Stocker	.05
174	Esteban Loaiza	.05
175	Jeff King	.05
176	Mark Johnson	.05
177	Denny Neagle	.05
178	Orlando Merced	.05
179	Carlos Garcia	.05
180	Brian Jordan	.05
181	Mike Morgan	.05
182	Mark Petkovsek	.05
183	Bernard Gilkey	.05
184	John Mabry	.05
185	Tom Henke	.05
186	Glenn Dishman	.05
187	Andy Ashby	.05
188	Bip Roberts	.05
189	Melvin Nieves	.05
190	Ken Caminiti	.05
191	Brad Ausmus	.05
192	Deion Sanders	.05
193	Jamie Brewington	.05
194	Glenallen Hill	.05
195	Barry Bonds	2.00
196	William Van Landingham	.05

197	Mark Carreon	.05
198	Royce Clayton	.05
199	Joey Cora	.05
200	Ken Griffey Jr.	1.25
201	Jay Buhner	.05
202	Alex Rodriguez	1.50
203	Norm Charlton	.05
204	Andy Benes	.05
205	Edgar Martinez	.05
206	Juan Gonzalez	.40
207	Will Clark	.05
208	Kevin Gross	.05
209	Roger Pavlik	.05
210	Ivan Rodriguez	.65
211	Rusty Greer	.05
212	Angel Martinez	.05
213	Tomas Perez	.05
214	Alex Gonzalez	.05
215	Joe Carter	.05
216	Shawn Green	.30
217	Edwin Hurtado	.05
218	Edgar Martinez, Tony Pena (Post Season Checklist)	.05
219	Chipper Jones, Barry Larkin	.05
220	Orel Hershiser	.05
221	Mike Devereaux	.05
222	Tom Glavine	.05
223	Karim Garcia	.10
224	Arquimedez Pozo	.05
225	Billy Wagner	.05
226	John Wasdin	.05
227	Jeff Suppan	.05
228	Steve Gibralter	.05
229	Jimmy Haynes	.05
230	Ruben Rivera	.05
231	Chris Snopek	.05
232	Alex Ochoa	.05
233	Shannon Stewart	.05
234	Quinton McCracken	.05
235	Trey Beamon	.05
236	Billy McMillon	.05
237	Steve Cox	.05
238	George Arias	.05
239	Yamil Benitez	.05
240	Todd Greene	.05
241	Jason Kendall	.05
242	Brooks Kieschnick	.05
243	Osvaldo Fernandez **RC**	.15
244	Livan Hernandez **RC**	.35
245	Rey Ordonez	.05
246	Mike Grace **RC**	.05
247	Jay Canizaro	.05
248	Bob Wolcott	.05
249	Jermaine Dye	.05
250	Jason Schmidt	.05
251	Mike Sweeney **RC**	1.00
252	Marcus Jensen	.05
253	Mendy Lopez	.05
254	Wilton Guerrero **RC**	.10
255	Paul Wilson	.05
256	Edgar Renteria	.05
257	Richard Hidalgo	.05
258	Bob Abreu	.10
259	Robert Smith **RC**	.05
260	Sal Fasano	.05
261	Enrique Wilson	.05
262	Rich Hunter **RC**	.05
263	Sergio Nunez	.05
264	Dan Serafini	.05
265	David Doster **RC**	.05
266	Ryan McGuire	.05
267	Scott Spiezio	.05
268	Rafael Orellano	.05
269	Steve Avery	.05
270	Fred McGriff	.05
271	John Smoltz	.05
272	Ryan Klesko	.05
273	Jeff Blauser	.05
274	Brad Clontz	.05
275	Roberto Alomar	.20
276	B.J. Surhoff	.05
277	Jeffrey Hammonds	.05
278	Brady Anderson	.05
279	Bobby Bonilla	.05
280	Cal Ripken Jr.	2.00
281	Mike Mussina	.30
282	Wil Cordero	.05
283	Mike Stanley	.05
284	Aaron Sele	.05
285	Jose Canseco	.40
286	Tom Gordon	.05
287	Heathcliff Slocumb	.05
288	Lee Smith	.05
289	Troy Percival	.05
290	Tim Salmon	.05
291	Chuck Finley	.05
292	Jim Abbott	.05
293	Chili Davis	.05
294	Steve Trachsel	.05
295	Mark Grace	.05
296	Rey Sanchez	.05
297	Scott Servais	.05
298	Jaime Navarro	.05
299	Frank Castillo	.05
300	Frank Thomas	.75

ABBREVIATIONS

AS - All-Star

301	Jason Bere	.05
302	Danny Tartabull	.05
303	Darren Lewis	.05
304	Roberto Hernandez	.05
305	Tony Phillips	.05
306	Wilson Alvarez	.05
307	Jose Rijo	.05
308	Hal Morris	.05
309	Mark Portugal	.05
310	Barry Larkin	.05
311	Dave Burba	.05
312	Eddie Taubensee	.05
313	Sandy Alomar Jr.	.05
314	Dennis Martinez	.05
315	Albert Belle	.15
316	Eddie Murray	.75
317	Charles Nagy	.05
318	Chad Ogea	.05
319	Kenny Lofton	.05
320	Dante Bichette	.05
321	Armando Reynoso	.05
322	Walt Weiss	.05
323	Ellis Burks	.05
324	Kevin Ritz	.05
325	Bill Swift	.05
326	Jason Bates	.05
327	Tony Clark	.05
328	Travis Fryman	.05
329	Mark Parent	.05
330	Alan Trammell	.05
331	C.J. Nitkowski	.05
332	Jose Lima	.05
333	Phil Plantier	.05
334	Kurt Abbott	.05
335	Andre Dawson	.25
336	Chris Hammond	.05
337	Robb Nen	.05
338	Pat Rapp	.05
339	Al Leiter	.05
340	Gary Sheffield	.35
341	Todd Jones	.05
342	Doug Drabek	.05
343	Greg Swindell	.05
344	Tony Eusebio	.05
345	Craig Biggio	.05
346	Darryl Kile	.05
347	Mike Macfarlane	.05
348	Jeff Montgomery	.05
349	Chris Haney	.05
350	Bip Roberts	.05
351	Tom Goodwin	.05
352	Mark Gubicza	.05
353	Joe Randa	.05
354	Ramon Martinez	.05
355	Eric Karros	.05
356	Delino DeShields	.05
357	Brett Butler	.05
358	Todd Worrell	.05
359	Mike Blowers	.05
360	Mike Piazza	1.25
361	Ben McDonald	.05
362	Ricky Bones	.05
363	Greg Vaughn	.05
364	Matt Mieske	.05
365	Kevin Seitzer	.05
366	Jeff Cirillo	.05
367	LaTroy Hawkins	.05
368	Frank Rodriguez	.05
369	Rick Aguilera	.05
370	Roberto Alomar	.15
371	Albert Belle	.05
372	Wade Boggs	.50
373	Barry Bonds	1.00
374	Roger Clemens	.65
375	Dennis Eckersley	.35
376	Ken Griffey Jr.	.65
377	Tony Gwynn	.50
378	Rickey Henderson	.40
379	Greg Maddux	.50
380	Fred McGriff	.05
381	Paul Molitor	.40
382	Eddie Murray	.40
383	Mike Piazza	.65
384	Kirby Puckett	.50
385	Cal Ripken Jr.	1.00
386	Ozzie Smith	.50
387	Frank Thomas	.45
388	Matt Walbeck	.05
389	Dave Stevens	.05
390	Marty Cordova	.05
391	Darrin Fletcher	.05
392	Cliff Floyd	.05
393	Mel Rojas	.05
394	Shane Andrews	.05
395	Moises Alou	.05
396	Carlos Perez	.05
397	Jeff Fassero	.05
398	Bobby Jones	.05
399	Todd Hundley	.05
400	John Franco	.05
401	Jose Vizcaino	.05
402	Bernard Gilkey	.05
403	Pete Harnisch	.05
404	Pat Kelly	.05
405	David Cone	.05
406	Bernie Williams	.05

407	John Wetteland	.05
408	Scott Kamieniecki	.05
409	Tim Raines	.05
410	Wade Boggs	1.00
411	Terry Steinbach	.05
412	Jason Giambi	.40
413	Todd Van Poppel	.05
414	Pedro Munoz	.05
415	Eddie Murray-1990	.40
416	Dennis Eckersley-1990	.35
417	Bip Roberts-1992	.05
418	Glenallen Hill-1992	.05
419	John Hudek-1994	.05
420	Derek Bell-1995	.05
421	Larry Walker-1995	.05
422	Greg Maddux-1995	.50
423	Ken Caminiti-1995	.05
424	Brent Gates	.05
425	Mark McGwire	1.50
426	Mark Whiten	.05
427	Sid Fernandez	.05
428	Ricky Bottalico	.05
429	Mike Mimbs	.05
430	Lenny Dykstra	.05
431	Todd Zeile	.05
432	Benito Santiago	.05
433	Danny Miceli	.05
434	Al Martin	.05
435	Jay Bell	.05
436	Charlie Hayes	.05
437	Mike Kingery	.05
438	Paul Wagner	.05
439	Tom Pagnozzi	.05
440	Ozzie Smith	1.00
441	Ray Lankford	.05
442	Dennis Eckersley	.65
443	Ron Gant	.05
444	Alan Benes	.05
445	Rickey Henderson	.75
446	Jody Reed	.05
447	Trevor Hoffman	.05
448	Andujar Cedeno	.05
449	Steve Finley	.05
450	Tony Gwynn	1.00
451	Joey Hamilton	.05
452	Mark Leiter	.05
453	Rod Beck	.05
454	Kirt Manwaring	.05
455	Matt Williams	.05
456	Robby Thompson	.05
457	Shawon Dunston	.05
458	Russ Davis	.05
459	Paul Sorrento	.05
460	Randy Johnson	.75
461	Chris Bosio	.05
462	Luis Sojo	.05
463	Sterling Hitchcock	.05
464	Benji Gil	.05
465	Mickey Tettleton	.05
466	Mark McLemore	.05
467	Darryl Hamilton	.05
468	Ken Hill	.05
469	Dean Palmer	.05
470	Carlos Delgado	.40
471	Ed Sprague	.05
472	Otis Nixon	.05
473	Pat Hentgen	.05
474	Juan Guzman	.05
475	John Olerud	.05
476	Buck Showalter Checklist	.05
477	Bobby Cox Checklist	.05
478	Tommy Lasorda Checklist	.05
479	Jim Leyland Checklist	.05
480	Sparky Anderson Checklist	.05

A Cut Above

(See 1996 Collector's Choice A Cut Above.)

Blue Chip Prospects

		NM/M
Complete Set (20):		50.00
Common Player:		1.00
1	Hideo Nomo	4.00
2	Johnny Damon	3.50
3	Jason Isringhausen	1.00
4	Bill Pulsipher	1.00
5	Marty Cordova	1.00
6	Michael Tucker	1.00
7	John Wasdin	1.00
8	Karim Garcia	1.50
9	Ruben Rivera	1.00
10	Chipper Jones	10.00
11	Billy Wagner	1.00
12	Brooks Kieschnick	1.00
13	Alex Ochoa	1.00
14	Roger Cedeno	1.00
15	Alex Rodriguez	15.00
16	Jason Schmidt	1.00
17	Derek Jeter	20.00
18	Brian L. Hunter	1.00
19	Garret Anderson	1.00
20	Manny Ramirez	7.50

Cal Ripken Collection

	NM/M
Complete Set (8):	12.50
Common Ripken:	2.00
Header:	2.00

Diamond Destiny

		NM/M
Complete Set (Bronze):		35.00
Common Player (Bronze):		.30
Silver:		6X
Gold:		12X
1	Chipper Jones	1.50
2	Fred McGriff	.30
3	Ryan Klesko	.30

4	John Smoltz	.30
5	Greg Maddux	1.50
6	Cal Ripken Jr.	3.00
7	Roberto Alomar	.45
8	Eddie Murray	1.25
9	Brady Anderson	.30
10	Mo Vaughn	.30
11	Roger Clemens	1.75
12	Darin Erstad	.60
13	Sammy Sosa	1.50
14	Frank Thomas	1.25
15	Barry Larkin	.30
16	Albert Belle	.30
17	Manny Ramirez	1.25
18	Kenny Lofton	.30
19	Dante Bichette	.30
20	Gary Sheffield	.75
21	Jeff Bagwell	1.25
22	Hideo Nomo	.65
23	Mike Piazza	2.00
24	Kirby Puckett	1.50
25	Paul Molitor	1.25
26	Chuck Knoblauch	.30
27	Wade Boggs	1.50
28	Derek Jeter	3.00
29	Rey Ordonez	.30
30	Mark McGwire	2.50
31	Ozzie Smith	1.50
32	Tony Gwynn	1.50
33	Barry Bonds	3.00
34	Matt Williams	.30
35	Ken Griffey Jr.	2.00
36	Jay Buhner	.30
37	Randy Johnson	1.25
38	Alex Rodriguez	2.00
39	Juan Gonzalez	.65
40	Joe Carter	.30

Gameface

		NM/M
Complete Set (10):		6.00
Common Player:		.15
1	Ken Griffey Jr.	1.00
2	Frank Thomas	.65
3	Barry Bonds	1.50
4	Albert Belle	.15
5	Cal Ripken Jr.	1.50
6	Mike Piazza	1.00
7	Chipper Jones	.75
8	Matt Williams	.15
9	Hideo Nomo	.40
10	Greg Maddux	.75

Future Stock

		NM/M
Complete Set (20):		4.00
Common Player:		.25
1	George Arias	.25
2	Brian Barnes	.25
3	Trey Beamon	.25
4	Yamil Benitez	.25
5	Jamie Brewington	.25

6	Tony Clark	.25
7	Steve Cox	.25
8	Carlos Delgado	.75
9	Chad Fonville	.25
10	Steve Gibralter	.25
11	Curtis Goodwin	.25
12	Todd Greene	.25
13	Jimmy Haynes	.25
14	Quinton McCracken	.25
15	Billy McMillon	.25
16	Chan Ho Park	.25
17	Arquimedez Pozo	.25
18	Chris Snopek	.25
19	Shannon Stewart	.25
20	Jeff Suppan	.25

Hideo Nomo R.O.Y.

	NM/M
Hideo Nomo	15.00

Hot Commodities

		NM/M
Complete Set (20):		30.00
Common Player:		.75
1	Ken Griffey Jr.	3.00
2	Hideo Nomo	1.50
3	Roberto Alomar	1.50
4	Paul Wilson	.75
5	Albert Belle	.75
6	Manny Ramirez	2.25
7	Kirby Puckett	2.50
8	Johnny Damon	2.00
9	Randy Johnson	2.25
10	Greg Maddux	2.50
11	Chipper Jones	2.50
12	Barry Bonds	5.00
13	Mo Vaughn	.75
14	Mike Piazza	3.00
15	Cal Ripken Jr.	5.00
16	Tim Salmon	.75
17	Sammy Sosa	2.50
18	Kenny Lofton	.75
19	Tony Gwynn	2.50
20	Frank Thomas	2.25

Lovero Collection

		NM/M
Complete Set (20):		17.50
Common Player:		.25
1	Rod Carew	1.00

2	Hideo Nomo	.50
3	Derek Jeter	3.00
4	Barry Bonds	3.00
5	Greg Maddux	1.50
6	Mark McGwire (W/Will Clark.)	2.50
7	Jose Canseco	.50
8	Ken Caminiti	.25
9	Raul Mondesi	.25
10	Ken Griffey Jr.	2.50
11	Jay Buhner	.25
12	Randy Johnson	1.00
13	Roger Clemens	2.00
14	Brady Anderson	.25
15	Frank Thomas	1.00
16	Angels Outfielders	.25
17	Mike Piazza	2.50
18	Dante Bichette	.25
19	Tony Gwynn	1.50
20	Jim Abbott	.25

National Heroes

	NM/M
Complete Set (2):	20.00
Complete Set, Autographed (2):	190.00
(1) Ken Griffey Jr.	7.50
(1a) Ken Griffey Jr./Auto.	90.00
(2) Cal Ripken Jr.	10.00
(2a) Cal Ripken Jr./Auto.	100.00

Nomo Highlights

	NM/M
Complete Set (5):	3.00
Common Nomo:	.75

Power Driven

	NM/M
Complete Set (20):	24.00
Common Player:	.30

1	Albert Belle	.30
2	Barry Bonds	5.00
3	Jay Buhner	.30
4	Jose Canseco	.75
5	Cecil Fielder	.30
6	Juan Gonzalez	.75
7	Ken Griffey Jr.	3.00
8	Eric Karros	.30
9	Fred McGriff	.30
10	Mark McGwire	4.00
11	Rafael Palmeiro	1.25
12	Mike Piazza	3.00
13	Manny Ramirez	1.50
14	Tim Salmon	.30
15	Reggie Sanders	.30
16	Sammy Sosa	2.50
17	Frank Thomas	1.50
18	Mo Vaughn	.30
19	Larry Walker	.30
20	Matt Williams	.30

Run Producers

		NM/M
Complete Set (20):		50.00
Common Player:		1.00
1	Albert Belle	1.00
2	Dante Bichette	1.00
3	Barry Bonds	10.00
4	Jay Buhner	1.00
5	Jose Canseco	2.00
6	Juan Gonzalez	1.50
7	Ken Griffey Jr.	6.00
8	Tony Gwynn	5.00
9	Kenny Lofton	1.00
10	Edgar Martinez	1.00
11	Fred McGriff	1.00
12	Mark McGwire	7.50
13	Rafael Palmeiro	2.50
14	Mike Piazza	6.00
15	Manny Ramirez	3.00
16	Tim Salmon	1.00
17	Sammy Sosa	5.00
18	Frank Thomas	3.00
19	Mo Vaughn	1.00
20	Matt Williams	1.00

1996 Upper Deck Update

		NM/M
Complete Set (30):		8.00
Common Player:		.25
481	Randy Myers	.25
482	Kent Mercker	.25
483	David Wells	.35
484	Kevin Mitchell	.25
485	Randy Velarde	.25
486	Ryne Sandberg	4.00
487	Doug Jones	.25
488	Terry Adams	.25
489	Kevin Tapani	.25
490	Harold Baines	.25
491	Eric Davis	.25
492	Julio Franco	.25
493	Jack McDowell	.25
494	Devon White	.25
495	Kevin Brown	.35
496	Rick Wilkins	.25
497	Sean Berry	.25
498	Keith Lockhart	.25
499	Mark Loretta	.25
500	Paul Molitor	2.50
501	Roberto Kelly	.25
502	Lance Johnson	.25
503	Tino Martinez	.25
504	Kenny Rogers	.25
505	Todd Stottlemyre	.25
506	Gary Gaetti	.25
507	Royce Clayton	.25
508	Andy Benes	.25
509	Wally Joyner	.25
510	Erik Hanson	.25

1997 Upper Deck

	NM/M
Complete Set (550):	75.00
Complete Series 1 Set (240):	35.00
Complete Update Set (241-270):	5.00
Complete Series 2 Set (271-520):	35.00
Complete Update Set (521-550):	7.50
Common Player:	.05
Series 1 or 2 Pack (12):	1.50
Series 1 or 2 Wax Box (28):	25.00

1	Jackie Robinson	.50
2	Jackie Robinson	.50
3	Jackie Robinson	.50
4	Jackie Robinson	.50
5	Jackie Robinson	.50
6	Jackie Robinson	.50
7	Jackie Robinson	.50
8	Jackie Robinson	.50
9	Jackie Robinson	.50
10	Chipper Jones	1.00
11	Marquis Grissom	.05
12	Jermaine Dye	.05
13	Mark Lemke	.05
14	Terrell Wade	.05
15	Fred McGriff	.05
16	Tom Glavine	.20
17	Mark Wohlers	.05
18	Randy Myers	.05
19	Roberto Alomar	.25
20	Cal Ripken Jr.	2.00
21	Rafael Palmeiro	.65
22	Mike Mussina	.30
23	Brady Anderson	.05
24	Jose Canseco	.50
25	Mo Vaughn	.50
26	Roger Clemens	1.00
27	Tim Naehring	.05
28	Jeff Suppan	.05
29	Troy Percival	.05
30	Sammy Sosa	1.00
31	Amaury Telemaco	.05
32	Rey Sanchez	.05
33	Scott Servais	.05
34	Steve Trachsel	.05
35	Mark Grace	.05
36	Wilson Alvarez	.05
37	Harold Baines	.05
38	Tony Phillips	.05
39	James Baldwin	.05
40	Frank Thomas (Wrong (Ken Griffey Jr.'s) vital data.)	.85
41	Lyle Mouton	.05
42	Chris Snopek	.05
43	Hal Morris	.05
44	Eric Davis	.05
45	Barry Larkin	.05
46	Reggie Sanders	.05
47	Pete Schourek	.05
48	Lee Smith	.05
49	Charles Nagy	.05
50	Albert Belle	.05
51	Julio Franco	.05
52	Kenny Lofton	.05
53	Orel Hershiser	.05
54	Omar Vizquel	.05
55	Eric Young	.05
56	Curtis Leskanic	.05
57	Quinton McCracken	.05
58	Kevin Ritz	.05
59	Walt Weiss	.05
60	Dante Bichette	.05
61	Marc Lewis	.05
62	Tony Clark	.05
63	Travis Fryman	.05
64	John Smoltz	.05
65	Greg Maddux	.50
66	Tom Glavine	.10

No.	Player	Value
67	Mike Mussina	.15
68	Andy Pettitte	.15
69	Mariano Rivera	.10
70	Hideo Nomo	.20
71	Kevin Brown	.05
72	Randy Johnson	.40
73	Felipe Lira	.05
74	Kimera Bartee	.05
75	Alan Trammell	.05
76	Kevin Brown	.05
77	Edgar Renteria	.05
78	Al Leiter	.05
79	Charles Johnson	.05
80	Andre Dawson	.25
81	Billy Wagner	.05
82	Donne Wall	.05
83	Jeff Bagwell	.75
84	Keith Lockhart	.05
85	Jeff Montgomery	.05
86	Tom Goodwin	.05
87	Tim Belcher	.05
88	Mike Macfarlane	.05
89	Joe Randa	.05
90	Brett Butler	.05
91	Todd Worrell	.05
92	Todd Hollandsworth	.05
93	Ismael Valdes	.05
94	Hideo Nomo	.40
95	Mike Piazza	1.25
96	Jeff Cirillo	.05
97	Ricky Bones	.05
98	Fernando Vina	.05
99	Ben McDonald	.05
100	John Jaha	.05
101	Mark Loretta	.05
102	Paul Molitor	.75
103	Rick Aguilera	.05
104	Marty Cordova	.05
105	Kirby Puckett	1.00
106	Dan Naulty	.05
107	Frank Rodriguez	.05
108	Shane Andrews	.05
109	Henry Rodriguez	.05
110	Mark Grudzielanek	.05
111	Pedro Martinez	.75
112	Ugueth Urbina	.05
113	David Segui	.05
114	Rey Ordonez	.05
115	Bernard Gilkey	.05
116	Butch Huskey	.05
117	Paul Wilson	.05
118	Alex Ochoa	.05
119	John Franco	.05
120	Dwight Gooden	.05
121	Ruben Rivera	.05
122	Andy Pettitte	.20
123	Tino Martinez	.05
124	Bernie Williams	.05
125	Wade Boggs	1.00
126	Paul O'Neill	.05
127	Scott Brosius	.05
128	Ernie Young	.05
129	Doug Johns	.05
130	Geronimo Berroa	.05
131	Jason Giambi	.50
132	John Wasdin	.05
133	Jim Eisenreich	.05
134	Ricky Otero	.05
135	Ricky Bottalico	.05
136	Mark Langston	.05
137	Greg Maddux	.50
138	Ivan Rodriguez	.35
139	Charles Johnson	.05
140	J.T. Snow	.05
141	Mark Grace	.05
142	Roberto Alomar	.15
143	Craig Biggio	.05
144	Ken Caminiti	.05
145	Matt Williams	.05
146	Omar Vizquel	.05
147	Cal Ripken Jr.	1.00
148	Ozzie Smith	.40
149	Rey Ordonez	.05
150	Ken Griffey Jr.	.65
151	Devon White	.05
152	Barry Bonds	1.00
153	Kenny Lofton	.05
154	Mickey Morandini	.05
155	Gregg Jefferies	.05
156	Curt Schilling	.20
157	Jason Kendall	.05
158	Francisco Cordova	.05
159	Dennis Eckersley	.65
160	Ron Gant	.05
161	Ozzie Smith	1.00
162	Brian Jordan	.05
163	John Mabry	.05
164	Andy Ashby	.05
165	Steve Finley	.05
166	Fernando Valenzuela	.05
167	Archi Cianfrocco	.05
168	Wally Joyner	.05
169	Greg Vaughn	.05
170	Barry Bonds	2.00
171	William Van Landingham	.05
172	Marvin Benard	.05
173	Rich Aurilia	.05
174	Jay Canizaro	.05
175	Ken Griffey Jr.	1.25
176	Bob Wells	.05
177	Jay Buhner	.05
178	Sterling Hitchcock	.05
179	Edgar Martinez	.05
180	Rusty Greer	.05
181	Dave Nilsson	.05
182	Larry Walker	.05
183	Edgar Renteria	.05
184	Rey Ordonez	.05
185	Rafael Palmeiro	.35
186	Osvaldo Fernandez	.05
187	Raul Mondesi	.05
188	Manny Ramirez	.40
189	Sammy Sosa	.50
190	Robert Eenhoorn	.05
191	Devon White	.05
192	Hideo Nomo	.20
193	Mac Suzuki	.05
194	Chan Ho Park	.05
195	Fernando Valenzuela	.05
196	Andruw Jones	.40
197	Vinny Castilla	.05
198	Dennis Martinez	.05
199	Ruben Rivera	.05
200	Juan Gonzalez	.20
201	Roberto Alomar	.30
202	Edgar Martinez	.05
203	Ivan Rodriguez	.35
204	Carlos Delgado	.20
205	Andres Galarraga	.05
206	Ozzie Guillen	.05
207	Andre Cummings	.05
208	Roger Pavlik	.05
209	Darren Oliver	.05
210	Dean Palmer	.05
211	Ivan Rodriguez	.65
212	Otis Nixon	.05
213	Pat Hentgen	.05
214	Ozzie Smith, Andre Dawson, Kirby Puckett CL	.10
215	Barry Bonds, Gary Sheffield, Brady Anderson	.25
216	Ken Caminiti	.05
217	John Smoltz	.05
218	Eric Young	.05
219	Juan Gonzalez	.10
220	Eddie Murray	.15
221	Tommy Lasorda	.05
222	Paul Molitor	.15
223	Luis Castillo	.05
224	Justin Thompson	.05
225	Rocky Coppinger	.05
226	Jermaine Allensworth	.05
227	Jeff D'Amico	.05
228	Jamey Wright	.05
229	Scott Rolen	.60
230	Darin Erstad	.25
231	Marty Janzen	.05
232	Jacob Cruz	.05
233	Raul Ibanez	.05
234	Nomar Garciaparra	1.00
235	Todd Walker	.05
236	Brian Giles RC	.75
237	Matt Beech	.05
238	Mike Cameron	.05
239	Jose Paniagua	.05
240	Andruw Jones	.75
241	Brant Brown	.25
242	Robin Jennings	.25
243	Willie Adams	.25
244	Ken Caminiti	.25
245	Brian Jordan	.25
246	Chipper Jones	2.50
247	Juan Gonzalez	1.00
248	Bernie Williams	.25
249	Roberto Alomar	.30
250	Bernie Williams	.25
251	David Wells	.25
252	Cecil Fielder	.25
253	Darryl Strawberry	.25
254	Andy Pettitte	.40
255	Javier Lopez	.25
256	Gary Gaetti	.25
257	Ron Gant	.25
258	Brian Jordan	.25
259	John Smoltz	.25
260	Greg Maddux	2.50
261	Tom Glavine	.45
262	Chipper Jones	2.50
263	Greg Maddux	2.50
264	David Cone	.25
265	Jim Leyritz	.25
266	Andy Pettitte	.40
267	John Wetteland	.25
268	Dario Veras RC	.25
269	Neifi Perez	.25
270	Bill Mueller	.25
271	Vladimir Guerrero	.75
272	Dmitri Young	.05
273	Nerio Rodriguez RC	.05
274	Kevin Orie	.05
275	Felipe Crespo	.05
276	Danny Graves	.05
277	Roderick Myers	.05
278	Felix Heredia RC	.25
279	Ralph Milliard	.05
280	Greg Norton	.05
281	Derek Wallace	.05
282	Trot Nixon	.10
283	Bobby Chouinard	.05
284	Jay Witasick	.05
285	Travis Miller	.05
286	Brian Bevil	.05
287	Bobby Estalella	.05
288	Steve Soderstrom	.05
289	Mark Langston	.05
290	Tim Salmon	.05
291	Jim Edmonds	.05
292	Garret Anderson	.05
293	George Arias	.05
294	Gary DiSarcina	.05
295	Chuck Finley	.05
296	Todd Greene	.05
297	Randy Velarde	.05
298	David Justice	.05
299	Ryan Klesko	.05
300	John Smoltz	.05
301	Javier Lopez	.05
302	Greg Maddux	1.00
303	Denny Neagle	.05
304	B.J. Surhoff	.05
305	Chris Hoiles	.05
306	Eric Davis	.05
307	Scott Erickson	.05
308	Mike Bordick	.05
309	John Valentin	.05
310	Heathcliff Slocumb	.05
311	Tom Gordon	.05
312	Mike Stanley	.05
313	Reggie Jefferson	.05
314	Darren Bragg	.05
315	Troy O'Leary	.05
316	John Mabry	.05
317	Mark Whiten	.05
318	Edgar Martinez	.05
319	Alex Rodriguez	.75
320	Mark McGwire	.75
321	Hideo Nomo	.20
322	Todd Hundley	.05
323	Barry Bonds	1.00
324	Andruw Jones	.40
325	Ryne Sandberg	1.00
326	Brian McRae	.05
327	Frank Castillo	.05
328	Shawon Dunston	.05
329	Ray Durham	.05
330	Robin Ventura	.05
331	Ozzie Guillen	.05
332	Roberto Hernandez	.05
333	Albert Belle	.25
334	Dave Martinez	.05
335	Willie Greene	.05
336	Jeff Brantley	.05
337	Kevin Jarvis	.05
338	John Smiley	.05
339	Eddie Taubensee	.05
340	Bret Boone	.05
341	Kevin Seitzer	.05
342	Jack McDowell	.05
343	Sandy Alomar Jr.	.05
344	Chad Curtis	.05
345	Manny Ramirez	.75
346	Chad Ogea	.05
347	Jim Thome	.05
348	Mark Thompson	.05
349	Ellis Burks	.05
350	Andres Galarraga	.05
351	Vinny Castilla	.05
352	Kirt Manwaring	.05
353	Larry Walker	.05
354	Omar Olivares	.05
355	Bobby Higginson	.05
356	Melvin Nieves	.05
357	Brian Johnson	.05
358	Devon White	.05
359	Jeff Conine	.05
360	Gary Sheffield	.35
361	Robb Nen	.05
362	Mike Hampton	.05
363	Bob Abreu	.10
364	Luis Gonzalez	.05
365	Derek Bell	.05
366	Sean Berry	.05
367	Craig Biggio	.05
368	Darryl Kile	.05
369	Shane Reynolds	.05
370	Jeff Bagwell	.40
371	Ron Gant	.05
372	Andy Benes	.05
373	Gary Gaetti	.05
374a	Ramon Martinez (Gold back.)	.05
374b	Ramon Martinez (White back.)	.05
375	Raul Mondesi	.05
376a	Steve Finley (Gold back.)	.05
376b	Steve Finley (White back.)	.05
377	Ken Caminiti	.05
378	Tony Gwynn	.40
379	Dario Veras	.05
380	Andy Pettitte	.10
381	Ruben Rivera	.05
382	David Cone	.05
383	Roberto Alomar	.20
384	Edgar Martinez	.05
385	Ken Griffey Jr.	.65
386	Mark McGwire	.75
387	Rusty Greer	.05
388	Jose Rosado	.05
389	Kevin Appier	.05
390	Johnny Damon	.25
391	Jose Offerman	.05
392	Michael Tucker	.05
393	Craig Paquette	.05
394	Bip Roberts	.05
395	Ramon Martinez	.05
396	Greg Gagne	.05
397	Chan Ho Park	.05
398	Karim Garcia	.10
399	Wilton Guerrero	.05
400	Eric Karros	.05
401	Raul Mondesi	.05
402	Matt Mieske	.05
403	Mike Fetters	.05
404	Dave Nilsson	.05
405	Jose Valentin	.05
406	Scott Karl	.05
407	Marc Newfield	.05
408	Cal Eldred	.05
409	Rich Becker	.05
410	Terry Steinbach	.05
411	Chuck Knoblauch	.05
412	Pat Meares	.05
413	Brad Radke	.05
414	Not Issued	
415a	Kirby Puckett (Should be #414.)	1.00
415b	Andruw Jones	1.50
416	Chipper Jones	2.00
417	Mo Vaughn	.50
418	Frank Thomas	1.50
419	Albert Belle	.50
420	Mark McGwire	3.00
421	Derek Jeter	4.50
422	Alex Rodriguez	3.00
423	Juan Gonzalez	.75
424	Ken Griffey Jr.	2.50
425	Rondell White	.05
426	Darrin Fletcher	.05
427	Cliff Floyd	.05
428	Mike Lansing	.05
429	F.P. Santangelo	.05
430	Todd Hundley	.05
431	Mark Clark	.05
432	Pete Harnisch	.05
433	Jason Isringhausen	.05
434	Bobby Jones	.05
435	Lance Johnson	.05
436	Carlos Baerga	.05
437	Mariano Duncan	.05
438	David Cone	.05
439	Mariano Rivera	.15
440	Derek Jeter	2.00
441	Joe Girardi	.05
442	Charlie Hayes	.05
443	Tim Raines	.05
444	Darryl Strawberry	.05
445	Cecil Fielder	.05
446	Ariel Prieto	.05
447	Tony Batista	.05
448	Brent Gates	.05
449	Scott Spiezio	.05
450	Mark McGwire	1.50
451	Don Wengert	.05
452	Mike Lieberthal	.05
453	Lenny Dykstra	.05
454	Rex Hudler	.05
455	Darren Daulton	.05
456	Kevin Stocker	.05
457	Trey Beamon	.05
458	Midre Cummings	.05
459	Mark Johnson	.05
460	Al Martin	.05
461	Kevin Elster	.05
462	Jon Lieber	.05
463	Jason Schmidt	.05
464	Paul Wagner	.05
465	Andy Benes	.05
466	Alan Benes	.05
467	Royce Clayton	.05
468	Gary Gaetti	.05
469	Curt Lyons	.05

470	Eugene Kingsale	.05
471	Damian Jackson	.05
472	Wendell Magee	.05
473	Kevin L. Brown	.05
474	Raul Casanova	.05
475	Ramiro Mendoza RC	.25
476	Todd Dunn	.05
477	Chad Mottola	.05
478	Andy Larkin	.05
479	Jaime Bluma	.05
480	Mac Suzuki	.05
481	Brian Banks	.05
482	Desi Wilson	.05
483	Einar Diaz	.05
484	Tom Pagnozzi	.05
485	Ray Lankford	.05
486	Todd Stottlemyre	.05
487	Donovan Osborne	.05
488	Trevor Hoffman	.05
489	Chris Gomez	.05
490	Ken Caminiti	.05
491	John Flaherty	.05
492	Tony Gwynn	1.00
493	Joey Hamilton	.05
494	Rickey Henderson	.75
495	Glenallen Hill	.05
496	Rod Beck	.05
497	Osvaldo Fernandez	.05
498	Rick Wilkins	.05
499	Joey Cora	.05
500	Alex Rodriguez	1.50
501	Randy Johnson	.75
502	Paul Sorrento	.05
503	Dan Wilson	.05
504	Jamie Moyer	.05
505	Will Clark	.05
506	Mickey Tettleton	.05
507	John Burkett	.05
508	Ken Hill	.05
509	Mark McLemore	.05
510	Juan Gonzalez	.40
511	Bobby Witt	.05
512	Carlos Delgado	.40
513	Alex Gonzalez	.25
514	Shawn Green	.25
515	Joe Carter	.05
516	Juan Guzman	.05
517	Charlie O'Brien	.05
518	Ed Sprague	.05
519	Mike Timlin	.05
520	Roger Clemens	1.00
521	Eddie Murray	2.00
522	Jason Dickson	.25
523	Jim Leyritz	.25
524	Michael Tucker	.25
525	Kenny Lofton	.25
526	Jimmy Key	.25
527	Mel Rojas	.25
528	Deion Sanders	.25
529	Bartolo Colon	.25
530	Matt Williams	.25
531	Marquis Grissom	.25
532	David Justice	.25
533	Bubba Trammell RC	.35
534	Moises Alou	.25
535	Bobby Bonilla	.25
536	Alex Fernandez	.25
537	Jay Bell	.25
538	Chili Davis	.25
539	Jeff King	.25
540	Todd Zeile	.25
541	John Olerud	.25
542	Jose Guillen	.25
543	Derrek Lee	1.00
544	Dante Powell	.25
545	J.T. Snow	.25
546	Jeff Kent	.25
547	Jose Cruz Jr. RC	.75
548	John Wetteland	.25
549	Orlando Merced	.25
550	Hideki Irabu RC	.50

Amazing Greats

		NM/M
Complete Set (20):		140.00
Common Player:		2.50
1	Ken Griffey Jr.	12.50
2	Roberto Alomar	3.00
3	Alex Rodriguez	15.00
4	Paul Molitor	7.50
5	Chipper Jones	10.00
6	Tony Gwynn	10.00
7	Kenny Lofton	2.50
8	Albert Belle	2.50
9	Matt Williams	2.50

10	Frank Thomas	7.50
11	Greg Maddux	10.00
12	Sammy Sosa	10.00
13	Kirby Puckett	10.00
14	Jeff Bagwell	7.50
15	Cal Ripken Jr.	20.00
16	Manny Ramirez	7.50
17	Barry Bonds	20.00
18	Mo Vaughn	2.50
19	Eddie Murray	7.50
20	Mike Piazza	12.50

Blue Chip Prospects

		NM/M
Common Player:		6.00
Production 500 Sets		
1	Andruw Jones	25.00
2	Derek Jeter	60.00
3	Scott Rolen	15.00
4	Manny Ramirez	25.00
5	Todd Walker	6.00
6	Rocky Coppinger	6.00
7	Nomar Garciaparra	30.00
8	Darin Erstad	7.50
9	Jermaine Dye	6.00
10	Vladimir Guerrero	25.00
11	Edgar Renteria	6.00
12	Bob Abreu	7.50
13	Karim Garcia	6.00
14	Jeff D'Amico	6.00
15	Chipper Jones	30.00
16	Todd Hollandsworth	6.00
17	Andy Pettitte	9.00
18	Ruben Rivera	6.00
19	Jason Kendall	6.00
20	Alex Rodriguez	40.00

Game Jersey

		NM/M
Complete Set (3):		160.00
Common Player:		15.00
GJ1	Ken Griffey Jr.	135.00
GJ2	Tony Gwynn	25.00
GJ3	Rey Ordonez	15.00

Home Team Heroes

		NM/M
Complete Set (12):		10.00
Common Player:		.50
1	Alex Rodriguez, Ken Griffey Jr.	2.00
2	Bernie Williams, Derek Jeter	2.50
3	Bernard Gilkey, Randy Hundley	.50
4	Hideo Nomo, Mike Piazza	1.50
5	Andruw Jones, Chipper Jones	1.00
6	John Smoltz, Greg Maddux	1.00

7	Mike Mussina, Cal Ripken Jr.	2.50
8	Andres Galarraga, Dante Bichette	.50
9	Juan Gonzalez, Ivan Rodriguez	.65
10	Albert Belle, Frank Thomas	.75
11	Jim Thome, Manny Ramirez	.75
12	Ken Caminiti, Tony Gwynn	1.00

Hot Commodities

		NM/M
Complete Set (20):		20.00
Common Player:		.30
1	Alex Rodriguez	2.00
2	Andruw Jones	1.00
3	Derek Jeter	2.50
4	Frank Thomas	1.00
5	Ken Griffey Jr.	1.50
6	Chipper Jones	1.25
7	Juan Gonzalez	.50
8	Cal Ripken Jr.	2.50
9	John Smoltz	.30
10	Mark McGwire	2.00
11	Barry Bonds	2.50
12	Albert Belle	.30
13	Mike Piazza	1.50
14	Manny Ramirez	1.00
15	Mo Vaughn	.30
16	Tony Gwynn	1.25
17	Vladimir Guerrero	1.00
18	Hideo Nomo	.50
19	Greg Maddux	1.25
20	Kirby Puckett	1.25

Jackie Robinson Tribute

		NM/M
Jackie Robinson		3.50

Long Distance Connec.

		NM/M
Complete Set (20):		32.50
Common Player:		.60
1	Mark McGwire	4.00
2	Brady Anderson	.60
3	Ken Griffey Jr.	3.00

Memorable Moments

Braves / P. Maddux wins four NL Cy Young Awards in a row (1992-95)

		NM/M
Complete Set (20):		20.00
Common Player:		.50
SERIES 1		
1	Andruw Jones	.75
2	Chipper Jones	1.00
3	Cal Ripken Jr.	2.50
4	Frank Thomas	.75
5	Manny Ramirez	.75
6	Mike Piazza	1.50
7	Mark McGwire	2.00
8	Barry Bonds	2.50
9	Ken Griffey Jr.	1.50
10	Alex Rodriguez	2.00
SERIES 2		
1	Ken Griffey Jr.	1.50
2	Albert Belle	.50
3	Derek Jeter	2.50
4	Greg Maddux	1.00
5	Tony Gwynn	1.00
6	Ryne Sandberg	1.00
7	Juan Gonzalez	.60
8	Roger Clemens	1.25
9	Jose Cruz Jr.	.50
10	Mo Vaughn	.50

(top portion of this column, Hot Commodities header)
HOT COMMODITIES
DEREK JETER NEW YORK YANKEES • SHORTSTOP

Power Package

		NM/M
Complete Set (20):		30.00
Common Player:		1.00
1	Ken Griffey Jr.	3.50
2	Joe Carter	1.00
3	Rafael Palmeiro	1.75
4	Jay Buhner	1.00
5	Sammy Sosa	3.00
6	Fred McGriff	1.00
7	Jeff Bagwell	2.00
8	Albert Belle	1.00
9	Matt Williams	1.00
10	Mark McGwire	4.00
11	Gary Sheffield	1.25
12	Tim Salmon	1.00

(fourth column top data, continuing list 4–20)

4	Albert Belle	.60
5	Juan Gonzalez	1.25
6	Andres Galarraga	.60
7	Jay Buhner	.60
8	Mo Vaughn	.60
9	Barry Bonds	5.00
10	Gary Sheffield	1.25
11	Todd Hundley	.60
12	Frank Thomas	2.00
13	Sammy Sosa	2.50
14	Rafael Palmeiro	1.75
15	Alex Rodriguez	4.00
16	Mike Piazza	3.00
17	Ken Caminiti	.60
18	Chipper Jones	2.50
19	Manny Ramirez	2.00
20	Andruw Jones	2.00

APRIL 15, 1947

13	Ryan Klesko	1.00
14	Manny Ramirez	2.00
15	Mike Piazza	3.50
16	Barry Bonds	5.00
17	Mo Vaughn	1.00
18	Jose Canseco	1.25
19	Juan Gonzalez	1.25
20	Frank Thomas	2.00

Rock Solid Foundation

		NM/M
Complete Set (20):		7.50
Common Player:		.15
1	Alex Rodriguez	1.50
2	Rey Ordonez	.15
3	Derek Jeter	2.00
4	Darin Erstad	.35
5	Chipper Jones	1.25
6	Johnny Damon	.35
7	Ryan Klesko	.15
8	Charles Johnson	.15
9	Andy Pettitte	.30
10	Manny Ramirez	.75
11	Ivan Rodriguez	.65
12	Jason Kendall	.15
13	Rondell White	.15
14	Alex Ochoa	.15
15	Javy Lopez	.15
16	Pedro Martinez	.75
17	Carlos Delgado	.50
18	Paul Wilson	.15
19	Alan Benes	.15
20	Raul Mondesi	.15

Run Producers

		NM/M
Complete Set (24):		45.00
Common Player:		.50
1	Ken Griffey Jr.	5.00
2	Barry Bonds	7.50
3	Albert Belle	.50
4	Mark McGwire	6.00
5	Frank Thomas	3.00
6	Juan Gonzalez	1.50
7	Brady Anderson	.50
8	Andres Galarraga	.50
9	Rafael Palmeiro	2.50
10	Alex Rodriguez	6.00
11	Jay Buhner	.50
12	Gary Sheffield	1.50
13	Sammy Sosa	4.00
14	Dante Bichette	.50
15	Mike Piazza	5.00
16	Manny Ramirez	3.00
17	Kenny Lofton	.50
18	Mo Vaughn	.50
19	Tim Salmon	.50
20	Chipper Jones	4.00
21	Jim Thome	2.00
22	Ken Caminiti	.50
23	Jeff Bagwell	3.00
24	Paul Molitor	3.00

Star Attractions

		NM/M
Complete Set (20):		30.00
Common Player:		.30
Gold:		1.5X
1	Ken Griffey Jr.	3.00
2	Barry Bonds	5.00
3	Jeff Bagwell	2.00
4	Nomar Garciaparra	2.50
5	Tony Gwynn	2.50
6	Roger Clemens	2.75
7	Chipper Jones	2.50
8	Tino Martinez	.30
9	Albert Belle	.30
10	Kenny Lofton	.30
11	Alex Rodriguez	4.00
12	Mark McGwire	4.00
13	Cal Ripken Jr.	5.00
14	Larry Walker	.30
15	Mike Piazza	3.00
16	Frank Thomas	2.00
17	Juan Gonzalez	.65
18	Greg Maddux	2.50
19	Jose Cruz Jr.	.30
20	Mo Vaughn	.30

Ticket to Stardom

		NM/M
Complete Set (20):		35.00
Common Player:		.75
1	Chipper Jones	5.00
2	Jermaine Dye	.75
3	Rey Ordonez	.75
4	Alex Ochoa	.75
5	Derek Jeter	7.50
6	Ruben Rivera	.75
7	Billy Wagner	.75
8	Jason Kendall	.75
9	Darin Erstad	1.00
10	Alex Rodriguez	6.00
11	Bob Abreu	.75
12	Richard Hidalgo	.75
13	Karim Garcia	1.00
14	Andruw Jones	4.00
15	Carlos Delgado	1.50
16	Rocky Coppinger	.75
17	Jeff D'Amico	.75
18	Johnny Damon	2.00
19	John Wasdin	.75
20	Manny Ramirez	4.00

Tony Gwynn Commemorative

		NM/M
	Tony Gwynn	7.50

1997 Upper Deck UD3

		NM/M
Complete Set (60):		30.00
Common Player:		.15
Pack (3):		1.50
Wax Box (24):		30.00
1	Mark McGwire	2.50
2	Brady Anderson	.15
3	Ken Griffey Jr.	2.00
4	Albert Belle	.15
5	Andres Galarraga	.15
6	Juan Gonzalez	.40
7	Jay Buhner	.15
8	Mo Vaughn	.15
9	Barry Bonds	3.00
10	Gary Sheffield	.40
11	Todd Hundley	.15
12	Ellis Burks	.15
13	Ken Caminiti	.15
14	Vinny Castilla	.15
15	Sammy Sosa	1.50
16	Frank Thomas	.75
17	Rafael Palmeiro	.65
18	Mike Piazza	2.00
19	Matt Williams	.15
20	Eddie Murray	.75
21	Roger Clemens	1.75
22	Tim Salmon	.15
23	Robin Ventura	.15
24	Ron Gant	.15
25	Cal Ripken Jr.	3.00
26	Bernie Williams	.15
27	Hideo Nomo	.40
28	Ivan Rodriguez	.65
29	John Smoltz	.15
30	Paul Molitor	.75
31	Greg Maddux	1.50
32	Raul Mondesi	.15
33	Roberto Alomar	.25
34	Barry Larkin	.15
35	Tony Gwynn	1.50
36	Jim Thome	.60
37	Kenny Lofton	.75
38	Jeff Bagwell	.75
39	Ozzie Smith	1.50
40	Kirby Puckett	1.50
41	Andruw Jones	.75
42	Vladimir Guerrero	.75
43	Edgar Renteria	.15
44	Luis Castillo	.15
45	Darin Erstad	.30
46	Nomar Garciaparra	1.50
47	Todd Greene	.15
48	Jason Kendall	.15
49	Rey Ordonez	.15
50	Alex Rodriguez	2.50
51	Manny Ramirez	.75
52	Todd Walker	.15
53	Ruben Rivera	.15
54	Andy Pettitte	.30
55	Derek Jeter	3.00
56	Todd Hollandsworth	.15
57	Rocky Coppinger	.15
58	Scott Rolen	.60
59	Jermaine Dye	.15
60	Chipper Jones	1.50

Generation Next

		NM/M
Complete Set (20):		35.00
Common Player:		1.00
1	Alex Rodriguez	5.00
2	Vladimir Guerrero	2.50
3	Luis Castillo	1.00
4	Rey Ordonez	1.00
5	Andruw Jones	2.50
6	Darin Erstad	1.25
7	Edgar Renteria	1.00
8	Jason Kendall	1.00
9	Jermaine Dye	1.00
10	Chipper Jones	3.00
11	Rocky Coppinger	1.00
12	Andy Pettitte	1.25
13	Todd Greene	1.00
14	Todd Hollandsworth	1.00
15	Derek Jeter	6.00
16	Ruben Rivera	1.00
17	Todd Walker	1.00
18	Nomar Garciaparra	2.00
19	Scott Rolen	2.00
20	Manny Ramirez	2.50

Marquee Attraction

		NM/M
Complete Set (10):		40.00
Common Player:		1.25
1	Ken Griffey Jr.	6.00
2	Mark McGwire	7.50
3	Juan Gonzalez	1.75
4	Barry Bonds	9.00
5	Frank Thomas	2.50
6	Albert Belle	1.25
7	Mike Piazza	6.00
8	Cal Ripken Jr.	9.00
9	Mo Vaughn	1.25
10	Alex Rodriguez	7.50

Superb Signatures

		NM/M
Complete Set (4):		450.00
Common Autograph:		15.00
1	Ken Caminiti	45.00
2	Ken Griffey Jr.	150.00
3	Vladimir Guerrero	50.00
4	Derek Jeter	225.00

1998 Upper Deck

		NM/M
Complete Set (750):		100.00
Complete Series 1 Set (270):		25.00
Complete Series 2 Set (270):		25.00
Complete Series 3 Set (210):		75.00
Common Eminent Prestige (601-630):		.25
Common Player:		.05
Series 1 or 2 Pack (12):		1.50
Series 3 Pack (10):		1.50
Series 1 or 2 Wax Box (24):		35.00
Series 3 Wax Box (24):		35.00
1	Tino Martinez	.05
2	Jimmy Key	.05
3	Jay Buhner	.05
4	Mark Gardner	.05

No.	Player	Price
5	Greg Maddux	.25
6	Pedro Martinez	.20
7	Hideo Nomo, Shigetoshi Hasegawa	.25
8	Sammy Sosa	.35
9	Mark McGwire	.50
10	Ken Griffey Jr.	.45
11	Larry Walker	.05
12	Tino Martinez	.05
13	Mike Piazza	.40
14	Jose Cruz, Jr.	.05
15	Tony Gwynn	.25
16	Greg Maddux	.25
17	Roger Clemens	.35
18	Alex Rodriguez	.50
19	Shigetoshi Hasegawa	.05
20	Eddie Murray	.50
21	Jason Dickson	.05
22	Darin Erstad	.25
23	Chuck Finley	.05
24	Dave Hollins	.05
25	Garret Anderson	.05
26	Michael Tucker	.05
27	Kenny Lofton	.05
28	Javier Lopez	.05
29	Fred McGriff	.05
30	Greg Maddux	.65
31	Jeff Blauser	.05
32	John Smoltz	.05
33	Mark Wohlers	.05
34	Scott Erickson	.05
35	Jimmy Key	.05
36	Harold Baines	.05
37	Randy Myers	.05
38	B.J. Surhoff	.05
39	Eric Davis	.05
40	Rafael Palmeiro	.35
41	Jeffrey Hammonds	.05
42	Mo Vaughn	.05
43	Tom Gordon	.05
44	Tim Naehring	.05
45	Darren Bragg	.05
46	Aaron Sele	.05
47	Troy O'Leary	.05
48	John Valentin	.05
49	Doug Glanville	.05
50	Ryne Sandberg	.65
51	Steve Trachsel	.05
52	Mark Grace	.05
53	Kevin Foster	.05
54	Kevin Tapani	.05
55	Kevin Orie	.05
56	Lyle Mouton	.05
57	Ray Durham	.05
58	Jaime Navarro	.05
59	Mike Cameron	.05
60	Albert Belle	.05
61	Doug Drabek	.05
62	Chris Snopek	.05
63	Eddie Taubensee	.05
64	Terry Pendleton	.05
65	Barry Larkin	.05
66	Willie Greene	.05
67	Deion Sanders	.05
68	Pokey Reese	.05
69	Jeff Shaw	.05
70	Jim Thome	.35
71	Orel Hershiser	.05
72	Omar Vizquel	.05
73	Brian Giles	.05
74	David Justice	.05
75	Bartolo Colon	.05
76	Sandy Alomar Jr.	.05
77	Neifi Perez	.05
78	Eric Young	.05
79	Vinny Castilla	.05
80	Dante Bichette	.05
81	Quinton McCracken	.05
82	Jamey Wright	.05
83	John Thomson	.05
84	Damion Easley	.05
85	Justin Thompson	.05
86	Willie Blair	.05
87	Raul Casanova	.05
88	Bobby Higginson	.05
89	Bubba Trammell	.05
90	Tony Clark	.05
91	Livan Hernandez	.05
92	Charles Johnson	.05
93	Edgar Renteria	.05
94	Alex Fernandez	.05
95	Gary Sheffield	.30
96	Moises Alou	.05
97	Tony Saunders	.05
98	Robb Nen	.05
99	Darryl Kile	.05
100	Craig Biggio	.05
101	Chris Holt	.05
102	Bob Abreu	.10
103	Luis Gonzalez	.05
104	Billy Wagner	.05
105	Brad Ausmus	.05
106	Chili Davis	.05
107	Tim Belcher	.05
108	Dean Palmer	.05
109	Jeff King	.05
110	Jose Rosado	.05
111	Mike Macfarlane	.05
112	Jay Bell	.05
113	Todd Worrell	.05
114	Chan Ho Park	.05
115	Raul Mondesi	.05
116	Brett Butler	.05
117	Greg Gagne	.05
118	Hideo Nomo	.25
119	Todd Zeile	.05
120	Eric Karros	.05
121	Cal Eldred	.05
122	Jeff D'Amico	.05
123	Antone Williamson	.05
124	Doug Jones	.05
125	Dave Nilsson	.05
126	Gerald Williams	.05
127	Fernando Vina	.05
128	Ron Coomer	.05
129	Matt Lawton	.05
130	Paul Molitor	.50
131	Todd Walker	.05
132	Rick Aguilera	.05
133	Brad Radke	.05
134	Bob Tewksbury	.05
135	Vladimir Guerrero	.50
136	Tony Gwynn	.25
137	Roger Clemens	.35
138	Dennis Eckersley	.15
139	Brady Anderson	.05
140	Ken Griffey Jr.	.40
141	Derek Jeter	.75
142	Ken Caminiti	.05
143	Frank Thomas	.20
144	Barry Bonds	.75
145	Cal Ripken Jr.	.75
146	Alex Rodriguez	.25
147	Greg Maddux	.25
148	Kenny Lofton	.05
149	Mike Piazza	.40
150	Mark McGwire	.45
151	Andruw Jones	.20
152	Rusty Greer	.05
153	F.P. Santangelo	.05
154	Mike Lansing	.05
155	Lee Smith	.05
156	Carlos Perez	.05
157	Pedro Martinez	.05
158	Ryan McGuire	.05
159	F.P. Santangelo	.05
160	Rondell White	.05
161	Takashi Kashiwada RC	.05
162	Butch Huskey	.05
163	Edgardo Alfonzo	.05
164	John Franco	.05
165	Todd Hundley	.05
166	Rey Ordonez	.05
167	Armando Reynoso	.05
168	John Olerud	.05
169	Bernie Williams	.05
170	Andy Pettitte	.15
171	Wade Boggs	.65
172	Paul O'Neill	.05
173	Cecil Fielder	.05
174	Charlie Hayes	.05
175	David Cone	.05
176	Hideki Irabu	.05
177	Mark Bellhorn	.05
178	Steve Karsay	.05
179	Damon Mashore	.05
180	Jason McDonald	.05
181	Scott Spiezio	.05
182	Ariel Prieto	.05
183	Jason Giambi	.30
184	Wendell Magee	.05
185	Rico Brogna	.05
186	Garrett Stephenson	.05
187	Wayne Gomes	.05
188	Ricky Bottalico	.05
189	Mickey Morandini	.05
190	Mike Lieberthal	.05
191	Kevin Polcovich RC	.05
192	Francisco Cordova	.05
193	Kevin Young	.05
194	Jon Lieber	.05
195	Kevin Elster	.05
196	Tony Womack	.05
197	Lou Collier	.05
198	Mike Defelice RC	.05
199	Gary Gaetti	.05
200	Dennis Eckersley	.40
201	Alan Benes	.05
202	Willie McGee	.05
203	Ron Gant	.05
204	Fernando Valenzuela	.05
205	Mark McGwire	1.00
206	Archi Cianfrocco	.05
207	Andy Ashby	.05
208	Steve Finley	.05
209	Quilvio Veras	.05
210	Ken Caminiti	.05
211	Rickey Henderson	.50
212	Joey Hamilton	.05
213	Derrek Lee	.30
214	Bill Mueller	.05
215	Shawn Estes	.05
216	J.T. Snow	.05
217	Mark Gardner	.05
218	Terry Mulholland	.05
219	Dante Powell	.05
220	Jeff Kent	.05
221	Jamie Moyer	.05
222	Joey Cora	.05
223	Jeff Fassero	.05
224	Dennis Martinez	.05
225	Ken Griffey Jr.	.75
226	Edgar Martinez	.05
227	Russ Davis	.05
228	Dan Wilson	.05
229	Will Clark	.05
230	Ivan Rodriguez	.40
231	Benji Gil	.05
232	Lee Stevens	.05
233	Mickey Tettleton	.05
234	Julio Santana	.05
235	Rusty Greer	.05
236	Bobby Witt	.05
237	Ed Sprague	.05
238	Pat Hentgen	.05
239	Kevin Escobar	.05
240	Joe Carter	.05
241	Carlos Delgado	.25
242	Shannon Stewart	.05
243	Benito Santiago	.05
244	Tino Martinez	.05
245	Ken Griffey Jr.	.40
246	Kevin Brown	.05
247	Ryne Sandberg	.35
248	Mo Vaughn	.05
249	Darryl Hamilton	.05
250	Randy Johnson	.20
251	Steve Finley	.05
252	Bobby Higginson	.05
253	Brett Tomko	.05
254	Mark Kotsay	.05
255	Jose Guillen	.05
256	Elieser Marrero	.05
257	Dennis Reyes	.05
258	Richie Sexson	.05
259	Pat Cline	.05
260	Todd Helton	.50
261	Juan Melo	.05
262	Matt Morris	.05
263	Jeremi Gonzalez	.05
264	Jeff Abbott	.05
265	Aaron Boone	.05
266	Todd Dunwoody	.05
267	Jaret Wright	.05
268	Derrick Gibson	.05
269	Mario Valdez	.05
270	Fernando Tatis	.05
271	Craig Counsell	.05
272	Brad Rigby	.05
273	Danny Clyburn	.05
274	Brian Rose	.05
275	Miguel Tejada	.15
276	Jason Varitek	.05
277	David Dellucci RC	.15
278	Michael Coleman	.05
279	Adam Riggs	.05
280	Ben Grieve	.05
281	Brad Fullmer	.05
282	Ken Cloude	.05
283	Tom Evans	.05
284	Kevin Millwood RC	.75
285	Paul Konerko	.15
286	Juan Encarnacion	.05
287	Chris Carpenter	.05
288	Tom Fordham	.05
289	Gary DiSarcina	.05
290	Tim Salmon	.05
291	Troy Percival	.05
292	Todd Greene	.05
293	Ken Hill	.05
294	Dennis Springer	.05
295	Jim Edmonds	.05
296	Allen Watson	.05
297	Brian Anderson	.05
298	Keith Lockhart	.05
299	Tom Glavine	.20
300	Chipper Jones	.65
301	Randall Simon	.05
302	Mark Lemke	.05
303	Ryan Klesko	.05
304	Denny Neagle	.05
305	Andruw Jones	.05
306	Mike Mussina	.30
307	Brady Anderson	.05
308	Chris Hoiles	.05
309	Mike Bordick	.05
310	Cal Ripken Jr.	1.50
311	Geronimo Berroa	.05
312	Armando Benitez	.05
313	Roberto Alomar	.25
314	Tim Wakefield	.05
315	Reggie Jefferson	.05
316	Jeff Frye	.05
317	Scott Hatteberg	.05
318	Steve Avery	.05
319	Robinson Checo	.05
320	Nomar Garciaparra	.65
321	Lance Johnson	.05
322	Tyler Houston	.05
323	Mark Clark	.05
324	Terry Adams	.05
325	Sammy Sosa	.65
326	Scott Servais	.05
327	Manny Alexander	.05
328	Norberto Martin	.05
329	Scott Eyre RC	.05
330	Frank Thomas	.50
331	Robin Ventura	.05
332	Matt Karchner	.05
333	Keith Foulke	.05
334	James Baldwin	.05
335	Chris Stynes	.05
336	Bret Boone	.05
337	Jon Nunnally	.05
338	Dave Burba	.05
339	Eduardo Perez	.05
340	Reggie Sanders	.05
341	Mike Remlinger	.05
342	Pat Watkins	.05
343	Chad Ogea	.05
344	John Smiley	.05
345	Kenny Lofton	.05
346	Jose Mesa	.05
347	Charles Nagy	.05
348	Bruce Aven	.05
349	Enrique Wilson	.05
350	Manny Ramirez	.50
351	Jerry DiPoto	.05
352	Ellis Burks	.05
353	Kirt Manwaring	.05
354	Vinny Castilla	.05
355	Larry Walker	.05
356	Kevin Ritz	.05
357	Pedro Astacio	.05
358	Scott Sanders	.05
359	Deivi Cruz	.05
360	Brian L. Hunter	.05
361	Pedro Martinez	.20
362	Tom Glavine	.05
363	Willie McGee	.05
364	J.T. Snow	.05
365	Rusty Greer	.05
366	Mike Grace	.05
367	Tony Clark	.05
368	Ben Grieve	.05
369	Gary Sheffield	.10
370	Joe Oliver	.05
371	Todd Jones	.05
372	Frank Catalanotto RC	.10
373	Brian Moehler	.05
374	Cliff Floyd	.05
375	Bobby Bonilla	.05
376	Al Leiter	.05
377	Josh Booty	.05
378	Darren Daulton	.05
379	Jay Powell	.05
380	Felix Heredia	.05
381	Jim Eisenreich	.05
382	Richard Hidalgo	.05
383	Mike Hampton	.05
384	Shane Reynolds	.05
385	Jeff Bagwell	.50
386	Derek Bell	.05
387	Ricky Gutierrez	.05
388	Bill Spiers	.05
389	Jose Offerman	.05
390	Johnny Damon	.25
391	Jermaine Dye	.05
392	Jeff Montgomery	.05
393	Glendon Rusch	.05
394	Mike Sweeney	.05
395	Kevin Appier	.05
396	Joe Vitiello	.05
397	Ramon Martinez	.05
398	Darren Dreifort	.05
399	Wilton Guerrero	.05
400	Mike Piazza	.75
401	Eddie Murray	.50
402	Ismael Valdes	.05
403	Todd Hollandsworth	.05
404	Mark Loretta	.05
405	Jeromy Burnitz	.05
406	Jeff Cirillo	.05
407	Scott Karl	.05
408	Mike Matheny	.05
409	Jose Valentin	.05
410	John Jaha	.05
411	Terry Steinbach	.05
412	Torii Hunter	.05
413	Pat Meares	.05
414	Marty Cordova	.05
415	Jaret Wright	.05
416	Mike Mussina	.10
417	John Smoltz	.05
418	Devon White	.05
419	Denny Neagle	.05

420	Livan Hernandez	.05	
421	Kevin Brown	.05	
422	Marquis Grissom	.05	
423	Mike Mussina	.10	
424	Eric Davis	.05	
425	Tony Fernandez	.05	
426	Moises Alou	.05	
427	Sandy Alomar Jr.	.05	
428	Gary Sheffield	.10	
429	Jaret Wright	.05	
430	Livan Hernandez	.05	
431	Chad Ogea	.05	
432	Edgar Renteria	.05	
433	LaTroy Hawkins	.05	
434	Rich Robertson	.05	
435	Chuck Knoblauch	.05	
436	Jose Vidro	.05	
437	Dustin Hermanson	.05	
438	Jim Bullinger	.05	
439	Orlando Cabrera	.10	
440	Vladimir Guerrero	.50	
441	Ugueth Urbina	.05	
442	Brian McRae	.05	
443	Matt Franco	.05	
444	Bobby Jones	.05	
445	Bernard Gilkey	.05	
446	Dave Mlicki	.05	
447	Brian Bohanon	.05	
448	Mel Rojas	.05	
449	Tim Raines	.05	
450	Derek Jeter	1.50	
451	Roger Clemens	.35	
452	Nomar Garciaparra	.35	
453	Mike Piazza	.40	
454	Mark McGwire	.50	
455	Ken Griffey Jr.	.40	
456	Larry Walker	.05	
457	Alex Rodriguez	.50	
458	Tony Gwynn	.25	
459	Frank Thomas	.20	
460	Tino Martinez	.05	
461	Chad Curtis	.05	
462	Ramiro Mendoza	.05	
463	Joe Girardi	.05	
464	David Wells	.05	
465	Mariano Rivera	.15	
466	Willie Adams	.05	
467	George Williams	.05	
468	Dave Telgheder	.05	
469	Dave Magadan	.05	
470	Matt Stairs	.05	
471	Billy Taylor	.05	
472	Jimmy Haynes	.05	
473	Gregg Jefferies	.05	
474	Midre Cummings	.05	
475	Curt Schilling	.15	
476	Mike Grace	.05	
477	Mark Leiter	.05	
478	Matt Beech	.05	
479	Scott Rolen	.35	
480	Jason Kendall	.05	
481	Esteban Loaiza	.05	
482	Jermaine Allensworth	.05	
483	Mark Smith	.05	
484	Jason Schmidt	.05	
485	Jose Guillen	.05	
486	Al Martin	.05	
487	Delino DeShields	.05	
488	Todd Stottlemyre	.05	
489	Brian Jordan	.05	
490	Ray Lankford	.05	
491	Matt Morris	.05	
492	Royce Clayton	.05	
493	John Mabry	.05	
494	Wally Joyner	.05	
495	Trevor Hoffman	.05	
496	Chris Gomez	.05	
497	Sterling Hitchcock	.05	
498	Pete Smith	.05	
499	Greg Vaughn	.05	
500	Tony Gwynn	.65	
501	Will Cunnane	.05	
502	Darryl Hamilton	.05	
503	Brian Johnson	.05	
504	Kirk Rueter	.05	
505	Barry Bonds	1.50	
506	Osvaldo Fernandez	.05	
507	Stan Javier	.05	
508	Julian Tavarez	.05	
509	Rich Aurilia	.05	
510	Alex Rodriguez	1.00	
511	David Segui	.05	
512	Rich Amaral	.05	
513	Raul Ibanez	.05	
514	Jay Buhner	.05	
515	Randy Johnson	.50	
516	Heathcliff Slocumb	.05	
517	Tony Saunders	.05	
518	Kevin Elster	.05	
519	John Burkett	.05	
520	Juan Gonzalez	.25	
521	John Wetteland	.05	
522	Domingo Cedeno	.05	
523	Darren Oliver	.05	
524	Roger Pavlik	.05	
525	Jose Cruz Jr.	.05	
526	Woody Williams	.05	
527	Alex Gonzalez	.05	
528	Robert Person	.05	
529	Juan Guzman	.05	
530	Roger Clemens	.70	
531	Shawn Green	.20	
532	Cordova, Ricon, Smith	.05	
533	Nomar Garciaparra	.35	
534	Roger Clemens	.35	
535	Mark McGwire	.50	
536	Larry Walker	.05	
537	Mike Piazza	.40	
538	Curt Schilling	.05	
539	Tony Gwynn	.25	
540	Ken Griffey Jr.	.40	
541	Carl Pavano	.05	
542	Shane Monahan	.05	
543	Gabe Kapler RC	.25	
544	Eric Milton	.05	
545	Gary Matthews Jr. RC	.05	
546	Mike Kinkade RC	.05	
547	Ryan Christenson RC	.10	
548	Corey Koskie RC	.25	
549	Norm Hutchins	.05	
550	Russell Branyan RC	.05	
551	Masato Yoshii RC	.25	
552	Jesus Sanchez RC	.05	
553	Anthony Sanders	.05	
554	Edwin Diaz	.05	
555	Gabe Alvarez	.05	
556	Carlos Lee RC	.25	
557	Kerry Darr	.05	
558	Kerry Wood	.20	
559	Carlos Guillen	.05	
560	Sean Casey	.15	
561	Manny Aybar RC	.05	
562	Octavio Dotel	.05	
563	Jarrod Washburn	.05	
564	Mark L. Johnson	.05	
565	Ramon Hernandez	.05	
566	Rich Butler RC	.05	
567	Mike Caruso	.05	
568	Cliff Politte	.05	
569	Scott Elarton	.05	
570	Magglio Ordonez RC	1.50	
571	Adam Butler RC	.05	
572	Marlon Anderson	.05	
573	Julio Ramirez RC	.05	
574	Darron Ingram RC	.05	
575	Bruce Chen	.05	
576	Steve Woodard RC	.05	
577	Hiram Bocachica	.05	
578	Kevin Witt	.05	
579	Javier Vazquez	.10	
580	Alex Gonzalez	.05	
581	Brian Powell	.05	
582	Wes Helms	.05	
583	Ron Wright	.05	
584	Rafael Medina	.05	
585	Daryle Ward	.05	
586	Geoff Jenkins	.05	
587	Preston Wilson	.10	
588	Jim Chamblee RC	.05	
589	Mike Lowell RC	.75	
590	A.J. Hinch	.05	
591	Francisco Cordero RC	.10	
592	Rolando Arrojo RC	.25	
593	Braden Looper	.05	
594	Sidney Ponson	.05	
595	Matt Clement	.05	
596	Carlton Loewer	.05	
597	Brian Meadows	.05	
598	Danny Klassen	.05	
599	Larry Sutton	.05	
600	Randy Johnson	.15	
601	Randy Johnson	1.50	
602	Greg Maddux	2.00	
603	Roger Clemens	2.25	
604	Jaret Wright	.25	
605	Mike Piazza	2.50	
606	Tino Martinez	.25	
607	Frank Thomas	1.50	
608	Mo Vaughn	.25	
609	Todd Helton	1.00	
610	Mark McGwire	3.00	
611	Jeff Bagwell	1.50	
612	Travis Lee	.40	
613	Scott Rolen	1.00	
614	Cal Ripken Jr.	4.00	
615	Chipper Jones	2.00	
616	Nomar Garciaparra	2.00	
617	Alex Rodriguez	3.00	
618	Derek Jeter	4.00	
619	Tony Gwynn	2.00	
620	Ken Griffey Jr.	2.50	
621	Kenny Lofton	.25	
622	Juan Gonzalez	.75	
623	Jose Cruz Jr.	.25	
624	Larry Walker	.25	
625	Barry Bonds	4.00	
626	Ben Grieve	.25	
627	Andruw Jones	1.50	
628	Vladimir Guerrero	1.50	
629	Paul Konerko	.50	
630	Paul Molitor	1.50	
631	Cecil Fielder	.05	
632	Jack McDowell	.05	
633	Mike James	.05	
634	Brian Anderson	.05	
635	Jay Bell	.05	
636	Devon White	.05	
637	Andy Stankiewicz	.05	
638	Tony Batista	.05	
639	Omar Daal	.05	
640	Matt Williams	.05	
641	Brent Brede	.05	
642	Jorge Fabregas	.05	
643	Karim Garcia	.10	
644	Felix Rodriguez	.05	
645	Andy Benes	.05	
646	Willie Blair	.05	
647	Jeff Suppan	.05	
648	Yamil Benitez	.05	
649	Walt Weiss	.05	
650	Andres Galarraga	.05	
651	Doug Drabek	.05	
652	Ozzie Guillen	.05	
653	Joe Carter	.05	
654	Dennis Eckersley	.40	
655	Pedro Martinez	.50	
656	Jim Leyritz	.05	
657	Henry Rodriguez	.05	
658	Rod Beck	.05	
659	Mickey Morandini	.05	
660	Jeff Blauser	.05	
661	Ruben Sierra	.05	
662	Mike Sirotka	.05	
663	Pete Harnisch	.05	
664	Damian Jackson	.05	
665	Dmitri Young	.05	
666	Steve Cooke	.05	
667	Geronimo Berroa	.05	
668	Shawon Dunston	.05	
669	Mike Jackson	.05	
670	Travis Fryman	.05	
671	Dwight Gooden	.05	
672	Paul Assenmacher	.05	
673	Eric Plunk	.05	
674	Mike Lansing	.05	
675	Darryl Kile	.05	
676	Luis Gonzalez	.05	
677	Frank Castillo	.05	
678	Joe Randa	.05	
679	Bip Roberts	.05	
680	Derrek Lee	.30	
681a	Mike Piazza/Marlins	2.00	
681b	Mike Piazza/Mets	1.00	
682	Sean Berry	.05	
683	Ramon Garcia	.05	
684	Carl Everett	.05	
685	Moises Alou	.05	
686	Hal Morris	.05	
687	Jeff Conine	.05	
688	Gary Sheffield	.25	
689	Jose Vizcaino	.05	
690	Charles Johnson	.05	
691	Bobby Bonilla	.05	
692	Marquis Grissom	.05	
693	Alex Ochoa	.05	
694	Mike Morgan	.05	
695	Orlando Merced	.05	
696	David Ortiz	.30	
697	Brent Gates	.05	
698	Otis Nixon	.05	
699	Trey Moore	.05	
700	Derrick May	.05	
701	Rich Becker	.05	
702	Al Leiter	.05	
703	Chili Davis	.05	
704	Scott Brosius	.05	
705	Chuck Knoblauch	.05	
706	Kenny Rogers	.05	
707	Mike Blowers	.05	
708	Mike Fetters	.05	
709	Tom Candiotti	.05	
710	Rickey Henderson	.50	
711	Bob Abreu	.05	
712	Mark Lewis	.05	
713	Doug Glanville	.05	
714	Desi Relaford	.05	
715	Kent Mercker	.05	
716	J. Kevin Brown	.05	
717	James Mouton	.05	
718	Mark Langston	.05	
719	Greg Myers	.05	
720	Orel Hershiser	.05	
721	Charlie Hayes	.05	
722	Robb Nen	.05	
723	Glenallen Hill	.05	
724	Tony Saunders	.05	
725	Wade Boggs	.65	
726	Kevin Stocker	.05	
727	Wilson Alvarez	.05	
728	Albie Lopez	.05	
729	Dave Martinez	.05	
730	Fred McGriff	.05	
731	Quinton McCracken	.05	
732	Bryan Rekar	.05	
733	Paul Sorrento	.05	
734	Roberto Hernandez	.05	
735	Bubba Trammell	.05	
736	Miguel Cairo	.05	
737	John Flaherty	.05	
738	Terrell Wade	.05	
739	Roberto Kelly	.05	
740	Mark Mclemore (McLemore)	.05	
741	Danny Patterson	.05	
742	Aaron Sele	.05	
743	Tony Fernandez	.05	
744	Randy Myers	.05	
745	Jose Canseco	.30	
746	Darrin Fletcher	.05	
747	Mike Stanley	.05	
748	Marquis Grissom	.05	
749	Fred McGriff	.05	
750	Travis Lee	.05	

Amazing Greats

		NM/M
Complete Set (30):		75.00
Common Player:		.60
Die-Cuts (250):		8X
1	Ken Griffey Jr.	5.00
2	Derek Jeter	7.50
3	Alex Rodriguez	6.00
4	Paul Molitor	3.00
5	Jeff Bagwell	3.00
6	Larry Walker	.60
7	Kenny Lofton	.60
8	Cal Ripken Jr.	7.50
9	Juan Gonzalez	1.50
10	Chipper Jones	4.00
11	Greg Maddux	4.00
12	Roberto Alomar	1.25
13	Mike Piazza	5.00
14	Andres Galarraga	.60
15	Barry Bonds	7.50
16	Andy Pettitte	1.25
17	Nomar Garciaparra	4.00
18	Hideki Irabu	.60
19	Tony Gwynn	4.00
20	Frank Thomas	3.00
21	Roger Clemens	4.50
22	Sammy Sosa	5.00
23	Jose Cruz, Jr.	.60
24	Manny Ramirez	3.00
25	Mark McGwire	6.00
26	Randy Johnson	3.00
27	Mo Vaughn	.60
28	Gary Sheffield	1.50
29	Andruw Jones	3.00
30	Albert Belle	.60

A Piece of the Action

	NM/M
Complete Set (14):	250.00

Common Player:		5.00
Inserted 1:2,500		
SERIES 1		
(1)	Jay Buhner/Bat	25.00
(2)	Tony Gwynn/Bat	25.00
(3)	Tony Gwynn/Jsy	25.00
(4)	Todd Hollandsworth/Bat	5.00
(5)	Todd Hollandsworth/Jsy	5.00
(6)	Greg Maddux/Jsy	40.00
(7)	Alex Rodriguez/Bat	40.00
(8)	Alex Rodriguez/Bat	40.00
(9)	Gary Sheffield/Bat	15.00
(10)	Gary Sheffield/Jsy	15.00
SERIES 2		
RA	Roberto Alomar	35.00
JB	Jay Buhner	10.00
AJ	Andruw Jones	40.00
GS	Gary Sheffield	15.00

Blue Chip Prospects

		NM/M
Complete Set (30):		75.00
Common Player:		2.00
1	Nomar Garciaparra	8.00
2	Scott Rolen	5.00
3	Jason Dickson	2.00
4	Darin Erstad	3.00
5	Brad Fullmer	2.00
6	Jaret Wright	2.00
7	Justin Thompson	2.00
8	Matt Morris	2.00
9	Fernando Tatis	2.00
10	Alex Rodriguez	12.00
11	Todd Helton	6.50
12	Andy Pettitte	2.50
13	Jose Cruz Jr.	2.00
14	Mark Kotsay	2.00
15	Derek Jeter	15.00
16	Paul Konerko	3.00
17	Todd Dunwoody	2.00
18	Vladimir Guerrero	6.00
19	Miguel Tejada	5.00
20	Chipper Jones	8.00
21	Kevin Orie	2.00
22	Juan Encarnacion	2.00
23	Brian Rose	2.00
24	Andruw Jones	6.00
25	Livan Hernandez	2.00
26	Brian Giles	2.00
27	Brett Tomko	2.00
28	Jose Guillen	2.00
29	Aaron Boone	2.00
30	Ben Grieve	2.00

Clearly Dominant

		NM/M
Complete Set (30):		300.00
Common Player:		3.00
Production 250 Sets		
1	Mark McGwire	25.00
2	Derek Jeter	30.00
3	Alex Rodriguez	25.00
4	Paul Molitor	12.00
5	Jeff Bagwell	12.00
6	Ivan Rodriguez	10.00
7	Kenny Lofton	3.00
8	Cal Ripken Jr.	30.00
9	Albert Belle	3.00
10	Chipper Jones	15.00
11	Gary Sheffield	5.00
12	Roberto Alomar	4.00
13	Mo Vaughn	3.00
14	Andres Galarraga	3.00
15	Nomar Garciaparra	15.00
16	Randy Johnson	12.00
17	Mike Mussina	6.00
18	Greg Maddux	15.00
19	Tony Gwynn	15.00
20	Frank Thomas	12.00

21	Roger Clemens	17.50
22	Dennis Eckersley	10.00
23	Juan Gonzalez	6.00
24	Tino Martinez	3.00
25	Andruw Jones	12.00
26	Larry Walker	3.00
27	Ken Caminiti	3.00
28	Mike Piazza	20.00
29	Barry Bonds	30.00
30	Ken Griffey Jr.	20.00

Ken Griffey Jr.'s HR Chronicles

		NM/M
Complete Set (56):		45.00
Common Card:		1.00
Inserted 1:9		
1-56	Ken Griffey Jr.	

Mark McGwire's Chase for 62

		NM/M
Complete Boxed Set:		7.50
Common Card:		.50
1-30	Mark McGwire	.50
---	Mark McGwire (3-1/2" x 5" HR #61/62)	3.00

National Pride

		NM/M
Complete Set (42):		65.00
Common Player:		.75
1	Dave Nilsson	.75
2	Larry Walker	.75
3	Edgar Renteria	.75
4	Jose Canseco	1.25
5	Rey Ordonez	.75
6	Rafael Palmeiro	2.50
7	Livan Hernandez	.75
8	Andruw Jones	3.00
9	Manny Ramirez	3.00
10	Sammy Sosa	4.00
11	Raul Mondesi	.75
12	Moises Alou	.75
13	Pedro Martinez	3.00
14	Vladimir Guerrero	3.00
15	Chili Davis	.75
16	Hideo Nomo	1.50

17	Hideki Irabu	.75
18	Shigetosi Hasegawa	.75
19	Takashi Kashiwada	.75
20	Chan Ho Park	.75
21	Fernando Valenzuela	.75
22	Vinny Castilla	.75
23	Armando Reynoso	.75
24	Karim Garcia	1.00
25	Marvin Benard	.75
26	Mariano Rivera	1.00
27	Juan Gonzalez	1.50
28	Roberto Alomar	1.00
29	Ivan Rodriguez	2.50
30	Carlos Delgado	1.00
31	Bernie Williams	.75
32	Edgar Martinez	.75
33	Frank Thomas	3.00
34	Barry Bonds	7.50
35	Mike Piazza	5.00
36	Chipper Jones	4.00
37	Cal Ripken Jr.	7.50
38	Alex Rodriguez	6.00
39	Ken Griffey Jr.	5.00
40	Andres Galarraga	.75
41	Omar Vizquel	.75
42	Ozzie Guillen	.75

Prime Nine

		NM/M
Complete Set (60):		50.00
Common Griffey:		1.00
Common Piazza:		1.25
Common Thomas:		.60
Common McGwire:		1.25
Common Ripken:		1.75
Common Gonzalez:		.50
Common Gwynn:		.70
Common Bonds:		1.75
Common Maddux:		.70
Inserted 1:5		
PN1	Ken Griffey Jr./1989-1992	1.00
PN2	Ken Griffey Jr./1993	1.00
PN3	Ken Griffey Jr./1994	1.00
PN4	Ken Griffey Jr./1995	1.00
PN5	Ken Griffey Jr./1996	1.00
PN6	Ken Griffey Jr./1997	1.00
PN7	Ken Griffey Jr./1997	1.00
PN8	Mike Piazza/1991	1.00
PN9	Mike Piazza/1992	1.00
PN10	Mike Piazza/1993	1.00
PN11	Mike Piazza/1994	1.00
PN12	Mike Piazza/1995	1.00
PN13	Mike Piazza/1996	1.00
PN14	Mike Piazza/1997	1.00
PN15	Frank Thomas/1991	.60
PN16	Frank Thomas/1992	.60
PN17	Frank Thomas/1993	.60
PN18	Frank Thomas/1994	.60
PN19	Frank Thomas/1995	.60
PN20	Frank Thomas/1996	.60
PN21	Frank Thomas/1997	.60
PN22	Mark McGwire/1987	1.25
PN23	Mark McGwire/1988-1990	1.25
PN24	Mark McGwire/1992	1.25
PN25	Mark McGwire/1995-1996	1.25
PN26	Mark McGwire/1997	1.25
PN27	Mark McGwire/1997	1.25
PN28	Mark McGwire/1997	1.25
PN29	Cal Ripken Jr./1982	1.75
PN30	Cal Ripken Jr./1983	1.75
PN31	Cal Ripken Jr./1989	1.75
PN32	Cal Ripken Jr./1991	1.75
PN33	Cal Ripken Jr./1995	1.75
PN34	Cal Ripken Jr./1996	1.75
PN35	Cal Ripken Jr./1997	1.75
PN36	Juan Gonzalez/1992	.50
PN37	Juan Gonzalez/1993	.50
PN38	Juan Gonzalez/1994	.50
PN39	Juan Gonzalez/1995	.50
PN40	Juan Gonzalez/1996	.50
PN41	Juan Gonzalez/1996	.50
PN42	Juan Gonzalez/1997	.50
PN43	Tony Gwynn/1984	.75
PN44	Tony Gwynn/1987-1989	.75
PN45	Tony Gwynn/1990-1993	.75
PN46	Tony Gwynn/1994	.75
PN47	Tony Gwynn/1996	.75
PN48	Tony Gwynn/1997	.75
PN49	Tony Gwynn/1997	.75
PN50	Barry Bonds/1986-1992	1.75
PN51	Barry Bonds/1990-1993	1.75
PN52	Barry Bonds/1993	1.75
PN53	Barry Bonds/1994	1.75
PN54	Barry Bonds/1996	1.75
PN55	Barry Bonds/1997	1.75
PN56	Greg Maddux/1992	.75
PN57	Greg Maddux/1993-1994	.75
PN58	Greg Maddux/1995	.75
PN59	Greg Maddux/1996	.75
PN60	Greg Maddux/1997	.75

Rookie Edition Preview

		NM/M
Complete Set (10):		5.00
Common Player:		.50
1	Nomar Garciaparra	2.00
2	Scott Rolen	1.00
3	Mark Kotsay	.50
4	Todd Helton	1.50
5	Paul Konerko	.60
6	Juan Encarnacion	.50
7	Brad Fullmer	.50
8	Miguel Tejada	.65
9	Richard Hidalgo	.50
10	Ben Grieve	.50

Superstar Xcitement

		NM/M
Complete Set (10):		275.00
Common Player:		10.00
Production 250 Sets		
PZ1	Jose Cruz Jr.	10.00
PZ2	Frank Thomas	25.00
PZ3	Juan Gonzalez	10.00
PZ4	Mike Piazza	40.00
PZ5	Mark McGwire	45.00
PZ6	Barry Bonds	50.00
PZ7	Greg Maddux	35.00
PZ8	Alex Rodriguez	45.00
PZ9	Nomar Garciaparra	35.00
PZ10	Ken Griffey Jr.	40.00

Tape Measure Titans

		NM/M
Complete Set (30):		45.00
Common Player:		.40
Inserted 1:23		
Gold:		1.5X
1	Mark McGwire	5.00
2	Andres Galarraga	.40
3	Jeff Bagwell	2.00
4	Larry Walker	.40
5	Frank Thomas	2.50
6	Rafael Palmeiro	1.50
7	Nomar Garciaparra	4.00
8	Mo Vaughn	.40
9	Albert Belle	.60
10	Ken Griffey Jr.	4.00
11	Manny Ramirez	2.00
12	Jim Thome	.40
13	Tony Clark	.40
14	Juan Gonzalez	2.00
15	Mike Piazza	4.00
16	Jose Canseco	1.00
17	Jay Buhner	.40
18	Alex Rodriguez	5.00
19	Jose Cruz Jr.	.40
20	Tino Martinez	.40
21	Carlos Delgado	.75
22	Andruw Jones	2.00
23	Chipper Jones	3.00
24	Fred McGriff	.40
25	Matt Williams	.40
26	Sammy Sosa	4.00
27	Vinny Castilla	.40
28	Tim Salmon	.60
29	Ken Caminiti	.40
30	Barry Bonds	6.00

10th Anniversary Preview

		NM/M
Complete Set (60):		45.00
Common Player:		.30
1	Greg Maddux	2.00
2	Mike Mussina	.50
3	Roger Clemens	2.25
4	Hideo Nomo	.75
5	David Cone	.30
6	Tom Glavine	.45
7	Andy Pettitte	.60
8	Jimmy Key	.30
9	Randy Johnson	1.50
10	Dennis Eckersley	1.00
11	Lee Smith	.30
12	John Franco	.30
13	Randy Myers	.30
14	Mike Piazza	2.50
15	Ivan Rodriguez	1.25
16	Todd Hundley	.30
17	Sandy Alomar Jr.	.30
18	Frank Thomas	1.50

19	Rafael Palmeiro	1.25
20	Mark McGwire	3.00
21	Mo Vaughn	.30
22	Fred McGriff	.30
23	Andres Galarraga	.30
24	Mark Grace	.30
25	Jeff Bagwell	1.50
26	Roberto Alomar	.45
27	Chuck Knoblauch	.30
28	Ryne Sandberg	2.00
29	Eric Young	.30
30	Craig Biggio	.30
31	Carlos Baerga	.30
32	Robin Ventura	.30
33	Matt Williams	.30
34	Wade Boggs	2.00
35	Dean Palmer	.30
36	Chipper Jones	2.00
37	Vinny Castilla	.30
38	Ken Caminiti	.30
39	Omar Vizquel	.30
40	Cal Ripken Jr.	3.50
41	Derek Jeter	3.50
42	Alex Rodriguez	3.00
43	Barry Larkin	.30
44	Mark Grudzielanek	.30
45	Albert Belle	.30
46	Manny Ramirez	1.50
47	Jose Canseco	.75
48	Ken Griffey Jr.	2.50
49	Juan Gonzalez	.75
50	Kenny Lofton	.30
51	Sammy Sosa	2.00
52	Larry Walker	.30
53	Gary Sheffield	.60
54	Rickey Henderson	1.50
55	Tony Gwynn	2.00
56	Barry Bonds	3.50
57	Paul Molitor	1.50
58	Edgar Martinez	.30
59	Chili Davis	.30
60	Eddie Murray	1.50

Rookie Edition A Piece of the Action

		NM/M
Common Card:		15.00
KG	Ken Griffey Jr./300	100.00
KGS	Ken Griffey Jr./ Auto./24	300.00
BG	Ben Grieve/200	15.00
JC	Jose Cruz Jr./200	15.00
TL	Travis Lee/200	15.00

Rookie Edition All-Star Credentials

		NM/M
Complete Set (30):		25.00
Common Player:		.25
Inserted 1:9		
AS1	Ken Griffey Jr.	1.50
AS2	Travis Lee	.40
AS3	Ben Grieve	.25
AS4	Jose Cruz Jr.	.25
AS5	Andruw Jones	.75
AS6	Craig Biggio	.25
AS7	Hideo Nomo	.40
AS8	Cal Ripken Jr.	2.50
AS9	Jaret Wright	.25

AS10	Mark McGwire	2.00
AS11	Derek Jeter	2.50
AS12	Scott Rolen	.60
AS13	Jeff Bagwell	.75
AS14	Manny Ramirez	.75
AS15	Alex Rodriguez	2.00
AS16	Chipper Jones	1.00
AS17	Larry Walker	.25
AS18	Barry Bonds	2.50
AS19	Tony Gwynn	1.00
AS20	Mike Piazza	1.50
AS21	Roger Clemens	1.25
AS22	Greg Maddux	1.00
AS23	Jim Thome	.60
AS24	Tino Martinez	.25
AS25	Nomar Garciaparra	1.00
AS26	Juan Gonzalez	.40
AS27	Kenny Lofton	.25
AS28	Randy Johnson	.75
AS29	Todd Helton	.65
AS30	Frank Thomas	.75

Rookie Edition Destination Stardom

		NM/M
Complete Set (60):		40.00
Common Player:		.50
Inserted 1:5		
1	Travis Lee	.75
2	Nomar Garciaparra	3.50
3	Alex Gonzalez	.50
4	Richard Hidalgo	.50
5	Jaret Wright	.50
6	Mike Kinkade	.50
7	Matt Morris	.50
8	Gary Mathews Jr.	.50
9	Brett Tomko	.50
10	Todd Helton	2.00
11	Scott Elarton	.50
12	Scott Rolen	1.50
13	Jose Cruz Jr.	.50
14	Jarrod Washburn	.50
15	Sean Casey	.50
16	Magglio Ordonez	2.00
17	Gabe Alvarez	.50
18	Todd Dunwoody	.50
19	Kevin Witt	.50
20	Ben Grieve	.50
21	Daryle Ward	.50
22	Matt Clement	.50
23	Carlton Loewer	.50
24	Javier Vazquez	.50
25	Paul Konerko	.75
26	Preston Wilson	.60
27	Wes Helms	.50
28	Derek Jeter	5.00
29	Corey Koskie	.50
30	Russell Branyan	.50
31	Vladimir Guerrero	2.50
32	Ryan Christenson	.50
33	Carlos Lee	.60
34	David Dellucci	.50
35	Bruce Chen	.50
36	Ricky Ledee	.50
37	Ron Wright	.50
38	Derrek Lee	1.50
39	Miguel Tejada	.75
40	Brad Fullmer	.50
41	Rich Butler	.50
42	Chris Carpenter	.50
43	Alex Rodriguez	4.00
44	Darron Ingram	.50
45	Kerry Wood	1.50
46	Jason Varitek	.50
47	Ramon Hernandez	.50
48	Aaron Boone	.50
49	Juan Encarnacion	.50
50	A.J. Hinch	.50
51	Mike Lowell	.60
52	Fernando Tatis	.50
53	Jose Guillen	.50
54	Mike Caruso	.50

55	Carl Pavano	.50
56	Chris Clemons	.50
57	Mark L. Johnson	.50
58	Ken Cloude	.50
59	Rolando Arrojo	.50
60	Mark Kotsay	.50

Rookie Edition Eminent Prestige 5x7

		NM/M
Complete Set (10):		25.00
Common Player:		2.00
605	Mike Piazza	3.50
607	Frank Thomas	2.50
610	Mark McGwire	4.00
611	Jeff Bagwell	2.50
612	Travis Lee	2.00
614	Cal Ripken Jr.	5.00
616	Nomar Garciaparra	3.00
617	Alex Rodriguez	4.00
619	Tony Gwynn	3.00
620	Ken Griffey Jr.	3.50

Rookie Edition Retrospectives

		NM/M
Complete Set (30):		55.00
Common Player:		.50
Inserted 1:24		
1	Dennis Eckersley	2.50
2	Rickey Henderson	3.00
3	Harold Baines	.50
4	Cal Ripken Jr.	7.50
5	Tony Gwynn	4.00
6	Wade Boggs	4.00
7	Orel Hershiser	.50
8	Joe Carter	.50
9	Roger Clemens	4.50
10	Barry Bonds	7.50
11	Mark McGwire	6.00
12	Greg Maddux	4.00
13	Fred McGriff	.50
14	Rafael Palmeiro	3.00
15	Craig Biggio	.50
16	Brady Anderson	.50
17	Randy Johnson	3.00
18	Gary Sheffield	1.00
19	Albert Belle	.50
20	Ken Griffey Jr.	5.00
21	Juan Gonzalez	1.50
22	Larry Walker	.50
23	Tino Martinez	.50
24	Frank Thomas	3.00
25	Jeff Bagwell	3.00
26	Kenny Lofton	.50
27	Mo Vaughn	.50
28	Mike Piazza	5.00
29	Alex Rodriguez	6.00
30	Chipper Jones	4.00

Rookie Edition Unparalleled

		NM/M
Complete Set (20):		75.00
Common Player:		1.00
Inserted 1:72		
1	Ken Griffey Jr.	6.00
2	Travis Lee	1.50

3	Ben Grieve	1.00
4	Jose Cruz Jr.	1.00
5	Nomar Garciaparra	5.00
6	Hideo Nomo	1.75
7	Kenny Lofton	1.00
8	Cal Ripken Jr.	10.00
9	Roger Clemens	5.50
10	Mike Piazza	6.00
11	Jeff Bagwell	3.50
12	Chipper Jones	5.00
13	Greg Maddux	5.00
14	Randy Johnson	3.50
15	Alex Rodriguez	7.50
16	Barry Bonds	10.00
17	Frank Thomas	3.50
18	Juan Gonzalez	1.75
19	Tony Gwynn	5.00
20	Mark McGwire	7.50

1998 Upper Deck Special F/X

		NM/M
Complete Set (150):		30.00
Common Player:		.05
1	Ken Griffey Jr.	1.00
2	Mark McGwire	1.25
3	Alex Rodriguez	2.50
4	Larry Walker	.05
5	Tino Martinez	.05
6	Mike Piazza	2.50
7	Jose Cruz Jr.	.05
8	Greg Maddux	.75
9	Tony Gwynn	.75
10	Roger Clemens	1.75
11	Jason Dickson	.05
12	Darin Erstad	.25
13	Chuck Finley	.05
14	Dave Hollins	.05
15	Garret Anderson	.05
16	Michael Tucker	.05
17	Javier Lopez	.05
18	John Smoltz	.05
19	Mark Wohlers	.05
20	Greg Maddux	1.50
21	Scott Erickson	.05
22	Jimmy Key	.05
23	B.J. Surhoff	.05
24	Eric Davis	.05
25	Rafael Palmeiro	.75
26	Tim Naehring	.05
27	Darren Bragg	.05
28	Troy O'Leary	.05
29	John Valentin	.05
30	Mo Vaughn	.05
31	Mark Grace	.05
32	Kevin Foster	.05
33	Kevin Tapani	.05
34	Kevin Orie	.05
35	Albert Belle	.05
36	Ray Durham	.05
37	Jaime Navarro	.05
38	Mike Cameron	.05
39	Eddie Taubensee	.05
40	Barry Larkin	.05
41	Willie Greene	.05
42	Jeff Shaw	.05
43	Omar Vizquel	.05
44	Brian Giles	.05
45	Jim Thome	.60
46	David Justice	.05

47	Sandy Alomar Jr.	.05
48	Neifi Perez	.05
49	Dante Bichette	.05
50	Vinny Castilla	.05
51	John Thomson	.05
52	Damion Easley	.05
53	Justin Thompson	.05
54	Bobby Higginson	.05
55	Tony Clark	.05
56	Charles Johnson	.05
57	Edgar Renteria	.05
58	Alex Fernandez	.05
59	Gary Sheffield	.50
60	Livan Hernandez	.05
61	Craig Biggio	.05
62	Chris Holt	.05
63	Billy Wagner	.05
64	Brad Ausmus	.05
65	Dean Palmer	.05
66	Tim Belcher	.05
67	Jeff King	.05
68	Jose Rosado	.05
69	Chan Ho Park	.05
70	Raul Mondesi	.05
71	Hideo Nomo	.50
72	Todd Zeile	.05
73	Eric Karros	.05
74	Cal Eldred	.05
75	Jeff D'Amico	.05
76	Doug Jones	.05
77	Dave Nilsson	.05
78	Todd Walker	.05
79	Rick Aguilera	.05
80	Paul Molitor	1.00
81	Brad Radke	.05
82	Vladimir Guerrero	1.00
83	Carlos Perez	.05
84	F.P. Santangelo	.05
85	Rondell White	.05
86	Butch Huskey	.05
87	Edgardo Alfonzo	.05
88	John Franco	.05
89	John Olerud	.05
90	Todd Hundley	.05
91	Bernie Williams	.05
92	Andy Pettitte	.30
93	Paul O'Neill	.05
94	David Cone	.05
95	Jason Giambi	.50
96	Damon Mashore	.05
97	Scott Spiezio	.05
98	Ariel Prieto	.05
99	Rico Brogna	.05
100	Mike Lieberthal	.05
101	Garrett Stephenson	.05
102	Ricky Bottalico	.05
103	Kevin Polcovich	.05
104	Jon Lieber	.05
105	Kevin Young	.05
106	Tony Womack	.05
107	Gary Gaetti	.05
108	Alan Benes	.05
109	Willie McGee	.05
110	Mark McGwire	2.50
111	Ron Gant	.05
112	Andy Ashby	.05
113	Steve Finley	.05
114	Quilvio Veras	.05
115	Ken Caminiti	.05
116	Joey Hamilton	.05
117	Bill Mueller	.05
118	Mark Gardner	.05
119	Shawn Estes	.05
120	J.T. Snow	.05
121	Dante Powell	.05
122	Jeff Kent	.05
123	Jamie Moyer	.05
124	Joey Cora	.05
125	Ken Griffey Jr.	2.00
126	Jeff Fassero	.05
127	Edgar Martinez	.05
128	Will Clark	.05
129	Lee Stevens	.05
130	Ivan Rodriguez	.75
131	Rusty Greer	.05
132	Ed Sprague	.05
133	Pat Hentgen	.05
134	Shannon Stewart	.05
135	Carlos Delgado	.40
136	Brett Tomko	.05
137	Jose Guillen	.05
138	Elieser Marrero	.05
139	Dennis Reyes	.05
140	Mark Kotsay	.05
141	Richie Sexson	.05
142	Todd Helton	.75
143	Jeremi Gonzalez	.05

ABBREVIATIONS

PC - Promo Card

144	Jeff Abbott	.05
145	Matt Morris	.05
146	Aaron Boone	.05
147	Todd Dunwoody	.05
148	Mario Valdez	.05
149	Fernando Tatis	.05
		.05
150	Jaret Wright	.05

OctoberBest

		NM/M
Complete Set (15):		40.00
Common Player:		1.00
Inserted 1:34		
PZ1	Frank Thomas	3.00
PZ2	Juan Gonzalez	1.50
PZ3	Mike Piazza	5.00
PZ4	Mark McGwire	6.00
PZ5	Jeff Bagwell	3.00
PZ6	Barry Bonds	7.50
PZ7	Ken Griffey Jr.	5.00
PZ8	John Smoltz	1.00
PZ9	Andruw Jones	3.00
PZ10	Greg Maddux	4.00
PZ11	Sandy Alomar Jr.	1.00
PZ12	Roberto Alomar	1.25
PZ13	Chipper Jones	4.00
PZ14	Kenny Lofton	1.00
PZ15	Tom Glavine	1.25

Power Driven

		NM/M
Complete Set (10):		40.00
Common Player:		1.50
Inserted 1:69		
PZ1	Frank Thomas	4.50
PZ2	Juan Gonzalez	2.50
PZ3	Mike Piazza	6.00
PZ4	Larry Walker	1.50
PZ5	Mark McGwire	7.50
PZ6	Jeff Bagwell	4.50
PZ7	Mo Vaughn	1.50
PZ8	Barry Bonds	10.00
PZ9	Tino Martinez	1.50
PZ10	Ken Griffey Jr.	6.00

Power Zone

		NM/M
Complete Set (20):		40.00
Common Player:		.50
Inserted 1:7		
PZ1	Jose Cruz Jr.	.50
PZ2	Frank Thomas	2.50
PZ3	Juan Gonzalez	1.25
PZ4	Mike Piazza	4.50
PZ5	Mark McGwire	4.50
PZ6	Barry Bonds	6.00
PZ7	Greg Maddux	3.00
PZ8	Alex Rodriguez	4.50
PZ9	Nomar Garciaparra	3.00

PZ10	Ken Griffey Jr.	3.50
PZ11	John Smoltz	.50
PZ12	Andruw Jones	2.50
PZ13	Sandy Alomar Jr.	.50
PZ14	Roberto Alomar	1.00
PZ15	Chipper Jones	3.00
PZ16	Kenny Lofton	.50
PZ17	Larry Walker	.50
PZ18	Jeff Bagwell	2.50
PZ19	Mo Vaughn	.50
PZ20	Tom Glavine	1.00

1998 Upper Deck UD 3

	NM/M
Complete Set (270):	200.00
Common Future Impact (1-30):	.50
Inserted 1:12	
Die-Cuts (2,000 Sets):	1X
Common Power Corps (31-60):	.25
Inserted 1:1	
Die-Cuts (2,000 Sets):	3X
Common Establishment (61-90):	.25
Inserted 1:6	
Die-Cuts (2,000 Sets):	2X
Common Future Impact Embossed (91-120):	.25
Inserted 1:6	
Die-Cuts (1,000 Sets):	3X
Common Power Corps Embossed (121-150):	.25
Inserted 1:4	
Die-Cuts (1,000 Sets):	6X
Common Establishment Embossed (151-180):	.25
Inserted 1:1	
Die-Cuts (1,000 Sets):	12X
Common Future Impact Rainbow (181-210):	.25
Inserted 1:1	
Die-Cuts (100 Sets):	15X
Common Power Corps Rainbow (211-240):	.50
Inserted 1:12	
Die-Cuts (100 Sets):	8X
Common Establishment Rainbow (241-270):	.75
Inserted 1:24	
Die-Cuts (100 Sets):	5X
Pack (3):	1.00
Wax Box (24):	20.00
LIGHT FX FUTURE IMPACT (1:12)	
1 Travis Lee	.50
2 A.J. Hinch	.50
3 Mike Caruso	.50
4 Miguel Tejada	.75
5 Brad Fullmer	.50
6 Eric Milton	.50
7 Mark Kotsay	.50
8 Darin Erstad	.75
9 Magglio Ordonez	1.00
10 Ben Grieve	.50
11 Brett Tomko	.50
12 Mike Kinkade RC	.75
13 Rolando Arrojo	.50
14 Todd Helton	1.00
15 Scott Rolen	1.00
16 Bruce Chen	.50

17	Daryle Ward	.50
18	Jaret Wright	.50
19	Sean Casey	.65
20	Paul Konerko	.65
21	Kerry Wood	1.00
22	Russell Branyan	.50
23	Gabe Alvarez	.50
24	Juan Encarnacion	.50
25	Andruw Jones	1.50
26	Vladimir Guerrero	1.50
27	Eli Marrero	.50
28	Matt Clement	.50
29	Gary Matthews Jr.	.50
30	Derrek Lee	1.50

LIGHT FX POWER CORPS (1:1)

31	Ken Caminiti	.25
32	Gary Sheffield	.50
33	Jay Buhner	.25
34	Ryan Klesko	.25
35	Nomar Garciaparra	.75
36	Vinny Castilla	.25
37	Tony Clark	.25
38	Sammy Sosa	.75
39	Tino Martinez	.25
40	Mike Piazza	1.00
41	Manny Ramirez	.65
42	Larry Walker	.25
43	Jose Cruz Jr.	.25
44	Matt Williams	.25
45	Frank Thomas	.65
46	Jim Edmonds	.25
47	Raul Mondesi	.25
48	Alex Rodriguez	1.50
49	Albert Belle	.25
50	Mark McGwire	1.50
51	Tim Salmon	.25
52	Andres Galarraga	.25
53	Jeff Bagwell	.65
54	Jim Thome	.50
55	Barry Bonds	2.50
56	Carlos Delgado	.40
57	Mo Vaughn	.25
58	Chipper Jones	.75
59	Juan Gonzalez	.40
60	Ken Griffey Jr.	1.00

LIGHT FX THE ESTABLISHMENT (1:6)

61	David Cone	.25
62	Hideo Nomo	.75
63	Edgar Martinez	.25
64	Fred McGriff	.25
65	Cal Ripken Jr.	4.00
66	Todd Hundley	.25
67	Barry Larkin	.25
68	Dennis Eckersley	1.00
69	Randy Johnson	1.50
70	Paul Molitor	1.50
71	Eric Karros	.25
72	Rafael Palmeiro	1.00
73	Chuck Knoblauch	.25
74	Ivan Rodriguez	1.25
75	Greg Maddux	2.00
76	Dante Bichette	.25
77	Brady Anderson	.25
78	Craig Biggio	.25
79	Derek Jeter	4.00
80	Roger Clemens	2.25
81	Roberto Alomar	.40
82	Wade Boggs	2.00
83	Charles Johnson	.25
84	Mark Grace	.25
85	Kenny Lofton	.25
86	Mike Mussina	1.00
87	Pedro Martinez	1.50
88	Curt Schilling	.50
89	Bernie Williams	.25
90	Tony Gwynn	2.00

EMBOSSED FUTURE IMPACT (1:6)

91	Travis Lee	.40
92	A.J. Hinch	.25
93	Mike Caruso	.25
94	Miguel Tejada	.40
95	Brad Fullmer	.25
96	Eric Milton	.25
97	Mark Kotsay	.25
98	Darin Erstad	1.00
99	Magglio Ordonez	1.00
100	Ben Grieve	.25
101	Brett Tomko	.25
102	Mike Kinkade RC	.40
103	Rolando Arrojo	.25
104	Todd Helton	1.00
105	Scott Rolen	1.00
106	Bruce Chen	.25
107	Daryle Ward	.25
108	Jaret Wright	.25
109	Sean Casey	.25
110	Paul Konerko	.40
111	Kerry Wood	1.00
112	Russell Branyan	.25
113	Gabe Alvarez	.25
114	Juan Encarnacion	.25
115	Andruw Jones	1.50

116	Vladimir Guerrero	1.50
117	Eli Marrero	.25
118	Matt Clement	.25
119	Gary Matthews Jr.	.25
120	Derrek Lee	1.00

EMBOSSED POWER CORPS (1:4)

121	Ken Caminiti	.25
122	Gary Sheffield	.50
123	Jay Buhner	.25
124	Ryan Klesko	.25
125	Nomar Garciaparra	1.50
126	Vinny Castilla	.25
127	Tony Clark	.25
128	Sammy Sosa	1.50
129	Tino Martinez	.25
130	Mike Piazza	2.00
131	Manny Ramirez	1.00
132	Larry Walker	.25
133	Jose Cruz Jr.	.25
134	Matt Williams	.25
135	Frank Thomas	1.00
136	Jim Edmonds	.25
137	Raul Mondesi	.25
138	Alex Rodriguez	3.00
139	Albert Belle	.25
140	Mark McGwire	3.00
141	Tim Salmon	.25
142	Andres Galarraga	.25
143	Jeff Bagwell	1.00
144	Jim Thome	.75
145	Barry Bonds	5.00
146	Carlos Delgado	.50
147	Mo Vaughn	.25
148	Chipper Jones	1.50
149	Juan Gonzalez	.50
150	Ken Griffey Jr.	2.00

EMBOSSED THE ESTABLISHMENT (1:1)

151	David Cone	.25
152	Hideo Nomo	.40
153	Edgar Martinez	.25
154	Fred McGriff	.25
155	Cal Ripken Jr.	2.00
156	Todd Hundley	.25
157	Barry Larkin	.25
158	Dennis Eckersley	.65
159	Randy Johnson	.75
160	Paul Molitor	.75
161	Eric Karros	.25
162	Rafael Palmeiro	.65
163	Chuck Knoblauch	.25
164	Ivan Rodriguez	.65
165	Greg Maddux	1.00
166	Dante Bichette	.25
167	Brady Anderson	.25
168	Craig Biggio	.25
169	Derek Jeter	2.00
170	Roger Clemens	1.25
171	Roberto Alomar	.30
172	Wade Boggs	1.00
173	Charles Johnson	.25
174	Mark Grace	.25
175	Kenny Lofton	.25
176	Mike Mussina	.40
177	Pedro Martinez	.75
178	Curt Schilling	.40
179	Bernie Williams	.25
180	Tony Gwynn	1.00

RAINBOW FUTURE IMPACT (1:1)

181	Travis Lee	.40
182	A.J. Hinch	.25
183	Mike Caruso	.25
184	Miguel Tejada	.40
185	Brad Fullmer	.25
186	Eric Milton	.25
187	Mark Kotsay	.25
188	Darin Erstad	.50
189	Magglio Ordonez	1.25
190	Ben Grieve	.25
191	Brett Tomko	.25
192	Mike Kinkade RC	.40
193	Rolando Arrojo	.25
194	Todd Helton	.65
195	Scott Rolen	.60
196	Bruce Chen	.25
197	Daryle Ward	.25
198	Jaret Wright	.25
199	Sean Casey	.40
200	Paul Konerko	.40
201	Kerry Wood	.60
202	Russell Branyan	.25
203	Gabe Alvarez	.25
204	Juan Encarnacion	.25
205	Andruw Jones	1.50
206	Vladimir Guerrero	1.50
207	Eli Marrero	.25
208	Matt Clement	.25
209	Gary Matthews Jr.	.25
210	Derrek Lee	1.00

RAINBOW POWER CORPS (1:12)

| 211 | Ken Caminiti | .50 |

212	Gary Sheffield	1.00
213	Jay Buhner	.50
214	Ryan Klesko	.50
215	Nomar Garciaparra	3.00
216	Vinny Castilla	.50
217	Tony Clark	.50
218	Sammy Sosa	3.00
219	Tino Martinez	.50
220	Mike Piazza	4.00
221	Manny Ramirez	2.00
222	Larry Walker	.50
223	Jose Cruz Jr.	.50
224	Matt Williams	.50
225	Frank Thomas	2.00
226	Jim Edmonds	.50
227	Raul Mondesi	.50
228	Alex Rodriguez	6.00
229	Albert Belle	.50
230	Mark McGwire	6.00
231	Tim Salmon	.50
232	Andres Galarraga	.50
233	Jeff Bagwell	2.00
234	Jim Thome	1.50
235	Barry Bonds	9.00
236	Carlos Delgado	.75
267	Mo Vaughn	.50
238	Chipper Jones	3.00
239	Juan Gonzalez	1.00
240	Ken Griffey Jr.	4.00

RAINBOW THE ESTABLISHMENT 1:24

241	David Cone	.75
242	Hideo Nomo	1.50
243	Edgar Martinez	.75
244	Fred McGriff	.75
245	Cal Ripken Jr.	12.00
246	Todd Hundley	.75
247	Barry Larkin	.75
248	Dennis Eckersley	3.00
249	Randy Johnson	4.50
250	Paul Molitor	4.50
251	Eric Karros	.75
252	Rafael Palmeiro	3.50
253	Chuck Knoblauch	.75
254	Ivan Rodriguez	4.00
255	Greg Maddux	6.00
256	Dante Bichette	.75
257	Brady Anderson	.75
258	Craig Biggio	.75
259	Derek Jeter	12.00
260	Roger Clemens	6.50
261	Roberto Alomar	1.25
262	Wade Boggs	6.00
263	Charles Johnson	.75
264	Mark Grace	.75
265	Kenny Lofton	.75
266	Mike Mussina	1.25
267	Pedro Martinez	4.50
268	Curt Schilling	1.50
269	Bernie Williams	.75
270	Tony Gwynn	6.00

1998 Upper Deck UD 3 Die-Cut

NM/M

Light FX Die-Cuts (2,000 Each)

Future Impact (1-30):	.75X
Power Corps (31-60):	3X
Establishment (61-90):	2X

Embossed Die-Cuts (1,000 Each)

Future Impact (91-120):	1X
Power Corps (121-150):	3X
Establishment (151-180):	6X

Rainbow Die-Cuts (100 Each)

Future Impact (181-210):	20X
Power Corps (211-240):	4X
Establishment (241-270):	12X

(See 1998 UD 3 for checklist and base card values.)

1998 UD Retro

NM/M

Complete Set (129):	15.00
Common Player:	.05
Pack (6):	2.25
Lunchbox (24):	40.00
1	Jim Edmonds	.05
2	Darin Erstad	.25
3	Tim Salmon	.05
4	Jay Bell	.05
5	Matt Williams	.05
6	Andres Galarraga	.05
7	Andruw Jones	.60
8	Chipper Jones	.75
9	Greg Maddux	.75
10	Rafael Palmeiro	.50
11	Cal Ripken Jr.	2.00
12	Brooks Robinson	.15
13	Nomar Garciaparra	.75
14	Pedro Martinez	.60
15	Mo Vaughn	.05
16	Ernie Banks	.50
17	Mark Grace	.05
18	Gary Matthews	.05
19	Sammy Sosa	.75
20	Albert Belle	.05
21	Carlton Fisk	.15
22	Frank Thomas	.60
23	Ken Griffey Sr.	.05
24	Paul Konerko	.15
25	Barry Larkin	.05
26	Sean Casey	.10
27	Tony Perez	.05
28	Bob Feller	.15
29	Kenny Lofton	.05
30	Manny Ramirez	.60
31	Jim Thome	.45
32	Omar Vizquel	.05
33	Dante Bichette	.05
34	Larry Walker	.05
35	Tony Clark	.05
36	Damion Easley	.05
37	Cliff Floyd	.05
38	Livan Hernandez	.05
39	Jeff Bagwell	.60
40	Craig Biggio	.05
41	Al Kaline	.15
42	Johnny Damon	.20
43	Dean Palmer	.05
44	Charles Johnson	.05
45	Eric Karros	.05
46	Gaylord Perry	.05
47	Raul Mondesi	.05
48	Gary Sheffield	.30
49	Eddie Mathews	.15
50	Warren Spahn	.15
51	Jeromy Burnitz	.05
52	Jeff Cirillo	.05
53	Marquis Grissom	.05
54	Paul Molitor	.60
55	Kirby Puckett	.75
56	Brad Radke	.05
57	Todd Walker	.05
58	Vladimir Guerrero	.60
59	Brad Fullmer	.05
60	Rondell White	.05
61	Bobby Jones	.05
62	Hideo Nomo	.30
63	Mike Piazza	1.00
64	Tom Seaver	.15
65	Frank J. Thomas	.05
66	Yogi Berra	.50
67	Derek Jeter	2.00
68	Tino Martinez	.05
69	Paul O'Neill	.05
70	Andy Pettitte	.20
71	Rollie Fingers	.05
72	Rickey Henderson	.60
73	Matt Stairs	.05
74	Scott Rolen	.50
75	Curt Schilling	.05
76	Jose Guillen	.05
77	Jason Kendall	.05
78	Lou Brock	.10
79	Bob Gibson	.10
80	Ray Lankford	.05
81	Mark McGwire	1.50
82	Not Issued	
83	Kevin Brown	
84	Ken Caminiti	.05
85	Tony Gwynn	.75
86	Greg Vaughn	.05
87	Barry Bonds	2.00
88	Willie Stargell	.10
89	Willie McCovey	.10

90	Ken Griffey Jr.	1.00
91	Randy Johnson	.60
92	Alex Rodriguez	1.50
93	Quinton McCracken	.05
94	Fred McGriff	.05
95	Juan Gonzalez	.30
96	Ivan Rodriguez	.50
97	Nolan Ryan	1.50
98	Jose Canseco	.45
99	Roger Clemens	.90
100	Jose Cruz Jr.	.05
101	Justin Baughman RC	.05
102	David Dellucci RC	.15
103	Travis Lee	.15
104	Troy Glaus RC	1.00
105	Kerry Wood	.40
106	Mike Caruso	.05
107	Jim Parque RC	.10
108	Brett Tomko	.05
109	Russell Branyan	.05
110	Jaret Wright	.05
111	Todd Helton	.60
112	Gabe Alvarez	.05
113	Matt Anderson RC	.10
114	Alex Gonzalez	.05
115	Mark Kotsay	.10
116	Derrek Lee	.50
117	Richard Hidalgo	.05
118	Adrian Beltre	.10
119	Geoff Jenkins	.05
120	Eric Milton	.05
121	Brad Fullmer	.05
122	Vladimir Guerrero	.60
123	Carl Pavano	.05
124	Orlando Hernandez RC	.25
125	Ben Grieve	.05
126	A.J. Hinch	.05
127	Matt Clement	.05
128	Gary Matthews Jr. RC	.05
129	Aramis Ramirez	.05
130	Rolando Arrojo	.05

Big Boppers

		NM/M
Complete Set (30):		80.00
Common Player:		1.00
Production 500 Sets		
B1	Darin Erstad	1.50
B2	Rafael Palmeiro	3.00
B3	Cal Ripken Jr.	10.00
B4	Nomar Garciaparra	5.00
B5	Mo Vaughn	1.00
B6	Frank Thomas	4.00
B7	Albert Belle	1.00
B8	Jim Thome	2.50
B9	Manny Ramirez	4.00
B10	Tony Clark	1.00
B11	Tino Martinez	1.00
B12	Ben Grieve	1.00
B13	Ken Griffey Jr.	6.00
B14	Alex Rodriguez	7.50
B15	Jay Buhner	1.00
B16	Juan Gonzalez	2.00
B17	Jose Cruz Jr.	1.00
B18	Jose Canseco	2.50
B19	Travis Lee	1.50
B20	Chipper Jones	5.00
B21	Andres Galarraga	1.00
B22	Andruw Jones	4.00
B23	Sammy Sosa	5.00
B24	Vinny Castilla	1.00

ABBREVIATIONS

OPS - Overprinted
"Promotional Sample"
PC - Promo Card
SR - Star Rookie

B25	Larry Walker	1.00
B26	Jeff Bagwell	4.00
B27	Gary Sheffield	2.00
B28	Mike Piazza	6.00
B29	Mark McGwire	7.50
B30	Barry Bonds	10.00

Groovy Kind of Glove

		NM/M
Complete Set (30):		50.00
Common Player:		.60
Inserted 1:7		
G1	Roberto Alomar	1.00
G2	Cal Ripken Jr.	7.50
G3	Nomar Garciaparra	3.50
G4	Frank Thomas	2.25
G5	Robin Ventura	.60
G6	Omar Vizquel	.60
G7	Kenny Lofton	.60
G8	Ben Grieve	.60
G9	Alex Rodriguez	6.00
G10	Ken Griffey Jr.	5.00
G11	Ivan Rodriguez	1.50
G12	Travis Lee	.75
G13	Matt Williams	.60
G14	Greg Maddux	3.50
G15	Andres Galarraga	.60
G16	Andruw Jones	2.25
G17	Kerry Wood	1.25
G18	Mark Grace	.60
G19	Craig Biggio	.60
G20	Charles Johnson	.60
G21	Raul Mondesi	.60
G22	Mike Piazza	5.00
G23	Rey Ordonez	.60
G24	Derek Jeter	7.50
G25	Scott Rolen	1.25
G26	Mark McGwire	6.00
G27	Ken Caminiti	.60
G28	Tony Gwynn	3.50
G29	J.T. Snow	.60
G30	Barry Bonds	7.50

Legendary Cut

		NM/M
LC	Babe Ruth (3 issued; 1/04 Auction)	9,500

Lunchbox

		NM/M
Complete Set (6):		40.00
Common Lunchbox:		4.00
	Nomar Garciaparra	6.00
	Ken Griffey Jr.	7.50
	Chipper Jones	6.00
	Travis Lee	4.00
	Mark McGwire	10.00
	Cal Ripken Jr.	12.00

New Frontier

		NM/M
Complete Set (30):		45.00
Common Player:		1.00
Production 1,000 Sets		
NF1	Justin Baughman	1.00
NF2	David Dellucci	1.00
NF3	Travis Lee	1.50

NF4	Troy Glaus	6.00
NF5	Mike Caruso	1.00
NF6	Jim Parque	1.00
NF7	Kerry Wood	2.00
NF8	Brett Tomko	1.00
NF9	Russell Branyan	1.00
NF10	Jaret Wright	1.00
NF11	Todd Helton	5.00
NF12	Gabe Alvarez	1.00
NF13	Matt Anderson	1.00
NF14	Alex Gonzalez	1.00
NF15	Mark Kotsay	1.00
NF16	Derrek Lee	3.00
NF17	Richard Hidalgo	1.00
NF18	Adrian Beltre	2.00
NF19	Geoff Jenkins	1.00
NF20	Eric Milton	1.00
NF21	Brad Fullmer	1.00
NF22	Vladimir Guerrero	6.00
NF23	Carl Pavano	1.00
NF24	Orlando Hernandez	1.25
NF25	Ben Grieve	1.00
NF26	A.J. Hinch	1.00
NF27	Matt Clement	1.00
NF28	Gary Matthews	1.00
NF29	Aramis Ramirez	1.00
NF30	Rolando Arrojo	1.00

Quantum Leap

		NM/M
Common Player:		15.00
Production 50 Sets		
Q1	Darin Erstad	20.00
Q2	Cal Ripken Jr.	100.00
Q3	Nomar Garciaparra	50.00
Q4	Frank Thomas	40.00
Q5	Kenny Lofton	15.00
Q6	Ben Grieve	15.00
Q7	Ken Griffey Jr.	60.00
Q8	Alex Rodriguez	75.00
Q9	Juan Gonzalez	20.00
Q10	Jose Cruz Jr.	15.00
Q11	Roger Clemens	55.00
Q12	Travis Lee	15.00
Q13	Chipper Jones	50.00
Q14	Greg Maddux	50.00
Q15	Kerry Wood	20.00
Q16	Jeff Bagwell	40.00
Q17	Mike Piazza	60.00
Q18	Scott Rolen	30.00
Q19	Mark McGwire	75.00
Q20	Tony Gwynn	50.00
Q21	Larry Walker	15.00
Q22	Derek Jeter	100.00
Q23	Sammy Sosa	50.00
Q24	Barry Bonds	100.00
Q25	Mo Vaughn	15.00
Q26	Roberto Alomar	20.00
Q27	Todd Helton	30.00
Q28	Ivan Rodriguez	30.00
Q29	Vladimir Guerrero	40.00
Q30	Albert Belle	15.00

Sign of the Times

		NM/M
Common Autograph:		5.00
Inserted 1:36		
EB	Ernie Banks/300	40.00
YB	Yogi Berra/150	60.00
RB	Russell Branyan/750	7.50
LB	Lou Brock/300	25.00
JC	Jose Cruz Jr./300	7.50
RF	Rollie Fingers/600	10.00
BF	Bob Feller/300	17.50
CF	Carlton Fisk/600	25.00
BGi	Bob Gibson/300	25.00
BGr	Ben Grieve/300	7.50
KGj	Ken Griffey Jr./100	185.00
KGs	Ken Griffey Sr./600	7.50
TG	Tony Gwynn/200	40.00
AK	Al Kaline/600	25.00
PK	Paul Konerko/750	20.00

TLe	Travis Lee/300	7.50
EM	Eddie Mathews/600	60.00
GMj	Gary Matthews Jr./ 750	7.50
GMs	Gary Matthews/600	7.50
WM	Willie McCovey/600	30.00
TP	Tony Perez/600	20.00
GP	Gaylord Perry/1,000	7.50
KP	Kirby Puckett/450	80.00
BR	Brooks Robinson/300	30.00
SR	Scott Rolen/300	20.00
NR	Nolan Ryan/500	100.00
TS	Tom Seaver/300	30.00
WS	Warren Spahn/600	40.00
WiS	Willie Stargell/600	50.00
FT	Frank Thomas/600	15.00
KW	Kerry Wood/200	25.00

Time Capsule

		NM/M
Complete Set (50):		35.00
Common Player:		.25
Inserted 1:2		
TC1	Mike Mussina	.50
TC2	Rafael Palmeiro	.65
TC3	Cal Ripken Jr.	3.00
TC4	Nomar Garciaparra	1.50
TC5	Pedro Martinez	1.00
TC6	Mo Vaughn	.25
TC7	Albert Belle	.25
TC8	Frank Thomas	1.00
TC9	David Justice	.25
TC10	Kenny Lofton	.25
TC11	Manny Ramirez	1.00
TC12	Jim Thome	.60
TC13	Derek Jeter	3.00
TC14	Tino Martinez	.25
TC15	Ben Grieve	.25
TC16	Rickey Henderson	1.00
TC17	Ken Griffey Jr.	2.00
TC18	Randy Johnson	1.00
TC19	Alex Rodriguez	2.50
TC20	Wade Boggs	1.50
TC21	Fred McGriff	.25
TC22	Juan Gonzalez	.50
TC23	Ivan Rodriguez	.75
TC24	Nolan Ryan	2.50
TC25	Jose Canseco	.50
TC26	Roger Clemens	1.75
TC27	Jose Cruz Jr.	.25
TC28	Travis Lee	.40
TC29	Matt Williams	.25
TC30	Andres Galarraga	.25
TC31	Andruw Jones	1.00
TC32	Chipper Jones	1.50
TC33	Greg Maddux	1.50
TC34	Kerry Wood	.50
TC35	Barry Larkin	.25
TC36	Dante Bichette	.25
TC37	Larry Walker	.25
TC38	Livan Hernandez	.25
TC39	Jeff Bagwell	1.00
TC40	Craig Biggio	.25
TC41	Charles Johnson	.25
TC42	Gary Sheffield	.50
TC43	Marquis Grissom	.25
TC44	Mike Piazza	2.00
TC45	Scott Rolen	.65
TC46	Curt Schilling	.40
TC47	Mark McGwire	2.50
TC48	Ken Caminiti	.25

TC49	Tony Gwynn	1.50
TC50	Barry Bonds	3.00

1999 Upper Deck

	NM/M
Complete Set (525):	45.00
Complete Series 1 (255):	25.00
Complete Series 2 (270):	20.00
Common Player:	.05
Exclusive Stars/RC's:	15X
Production 100 Each	
Pack (10):	1.50
Wax Box (24):	35.00

No.	Player	Price
1	Troy Glaus	.60
2	Adrian Beltre	.25
3	Matt Anderson	.05
4	Eric Chavez	.15
5	Jin Cho	.05
6	Robert Smith RC	.05
7	George Lombard	.05
8	Mike Kinkade	.05
9	Seth Greisinger	.05
10	J.D. Drew	.50
11	Aramis Ramirez	.05
12	Carlos Guillen	.05
13	Justin Baughman	.05
14	Jim Parque	.05
15	Ryan Jackson	.05
16	Ramon Martinez	.05
17	Orlando Hernandez	.05
18	Jeremy Giambi	.05
19	Gary DiSarcina	.05
20	Darin Erstad	.25
21	Troy Glaus	.50
22	Chuck Finley	.05
23	Dave Hollins	.05
24	Troy Percival	.05
25	Tim Salmon	.05
26	Brian Anderson	.05
27	Jay Bell	.05
28	Andy Benes	.05
29	Brent Brede	.05
30	David Dellucci	.05
31	Karim Garcia	.10
32	Travis Lee	.20
33	Andres Galarraga	.05
34	Ryan Klesko	.05
35	Keith Lockhart	.05
36	Kevin Millwood	.05
37	Denny Neagle	.05
38	John Smoltz	.05
39	Michael Tucker	.05
40	Walt Weiss	.05
41	Dennis Martinez	.05
42	Javy Lopez	.05
43	Brady Anderson	.05
44	Harold Baines	.05
45	Mike Bordick	.05
46	Roberto Alomar	.20
47	Scott Erickson	.05
48	Mike Mussina	.30
49	Cal Ripken Jr.	2.00
50	Darren Bragg	.05
51	Dennis Eckersley	.50
52	Nomar Garciaparra	.75
53	Scott Hatteberg	.05
54	Troy O'Leary	.05
55	Bret Saberhagen	.05
56	John Valentin	.05
57	Rod Beck	.05
58	Jeff Blauser	.05
59	Brant Brown	.05
60	Mark Clark	.05
61	Mark Grace	.05
62	Kevin Tapani	.05
63	Henry Rodriguez	.05
64	Mike Cameron	.05
65	Mike Caruso	.05
66	Ray Durham	.05
67	Jaime Navarro	.05
68	Magglio Ordonez	.30
69	Mike Sirotka	.05
70	Sean Casey	.15
71	Barry Larkin	.05
72	Jon Nunnally	.05
73	Paul Konerko	.15
74	Chris Stynes	.05
75	Brett Tomko	.05
76	Dmitri Young	.05
77	Sandy Alomar	.05
78	Bartolo Colon	.05
79	Travis Fryman	.05
80	Brian Giles	.05
81	David Justice	.05
82	Omar Vizquel	.05
83	Jaret Wright	.05
84	Jim Thome	.40
85	Charles Nagy	.05
86	Pedro Astacio	.05
87	Todd Helton	.50
88	Darryl Kile	.05
89	Mike Lansing	.05
90	Neifi Perez	.05
91	John Thomson	.05
92	Larry Walker	.05
93	Tony Clark	.05
94	Deivi Cruz	.05
95	Damion Easley	.05
96	Brian L. Hunter	.05
97	Todd Jones	.05
98	Brian Moehler	.05
99	Gabe Alvarez	.05
100	Craig Counsell	.05
101	Cliff Floyd	.05
102	Livan Hernandez	.05
103	Andy Larkin	.05
104	Derrek Lee	.35
105	Brian Meadows	.05
106	Moises Alou	.05
107	Sean Berry	.05
108	Craig Biggio	.05
109	Ricky Gutierrez	.05
110	Mike Hampton	.05
111	Jose Lima	.05
112	Billy Wagner	.05
113	Hal Morris	.05
114	Johnny Damon	.30
115	Jeff King	.05
116	Jeff Montgomery	.05
117	Glendon Rusch	.05
118	Larry Sutton	.05
119	Bobby Bonilla	.05
120	Jim Eisenreich	.05
121	Eric Karros	.05
122	Matt Luke	.05
123	Ramon Martinez	.05
124	Gary Sheffield	.40
125	Eric Young	.05
126	Charles Johnson	.05
127	Jeff Cirillo	.05
128	Marquis Grissom	.05
129	Jeromy Burnitz	.05
130	Bob Wickman	.05
131	Scott Karl	.05
132	Mark Loretta	.05
133	Fernando Vina	.05
134	Matt Lawton	.05
135	Pat Meares	.05
136	Eric Milton	.05
137	Paul Molitor	.60
138	David Ortiz	.35
139	Todd Walker	.05
140	Shane Andrews	.05
141	Brad Fullmer	.05
142	Vladimir Guerrero	.60
143	Dustin Hermanson	.05
144	Ryan McGuire	.05
145	Ugueth Urbina	.05
146	John Franco	.05
147	Butch Huskey	.05
148	Bobby Jones	.05
149	John Olerud	.05
150	Rey Ordonez	.05
151	Mike Piazza	1.25
152	Hideo Nomo	.30
153	Masato Yoshii	.05
154	Derek Jeter	2.00
155	Chuck Knoblauch	.05
156	Paul O'Neill	.05
157	Andy Pettitte	.20
158	Mariano Rivera	.15
159	Darryl Strawberry	.05
160	David Wells	.05
161	Jorge Posada	.05
162	Ramiro Mendoza	.05
163	Miguel Tejada	.15
164	Ryan Christenson	.05
165	Rickey Henderson	.60
166	A.J. Hinch	.05
167	Ben Grieve	.05
168	Kenny Rogers	.05
169	Matt Stairs	.05
170	Bob Abreu	.05
171	Rico Brogna	.05
172	Doug Glanville	.05
173	Mike Grace	.05
174	Desi Relaford	.05
175	Scott Rolen	.40
176	Jose Guillen	.05
177	Francisco Cordova	.05
178	Al Martin	.05
179	Jason Schmidt	.05
180	Turner Ward	.05
181	Kevin Young	.05
182	Mark McGwire	1.50
183	Delino DeShields	.05
184	Eli Marrero	.05
185	Tom Lampkin	.05
186	Ray Lankford	.05
187	Willie McGee	.05
188	Matt Morris	.05
189	Andy Ashby	.05
190	Kevin Brown	.05
191	Ken Caminiti	.05
192	Trevor Hoffman	.05
193	Wally Joyner	.05
194	Greg Vaughn	.05
195	Danny Darwin	.05
196	Shawn Estes	.05
197	Orel Hershiser	.05
198	Jeff Kent	.05
199	Bill Mueller	.05
200	Robb Nen	.05
201	J.T. Snow	.05
202	Ken Cloude	.05
203	Russ Davis	.05
204	Jeff Fassero	.05
205	Ken Griffey Jr.	1.00
206	Shane Monahan	.05
207	David Segui	.05
208	Dan Wilson	.05
209	Wilson Alvarez	.05
210	Wade Boggs	.75
211	Miguel Cairo	.05
212	Bubba Trammell	.05
213	Quinton McCracken	.05
214	Paul Sorrento	.05
215	Kevin Stocker	.05
216	Will Clark	.05
217	Rusty Greer	.05
218	Rick Helling	.05
219	Mike McLemore	.05
220	Ivan Rodriguez	.50
221	John Wetteland	.05
222	Jose Canseco	.40
223	Roger Clemens	.85
224	Carlos Delgado	.25
225	Darrin Fletcher	.05
226	Alex Gonzalez	.05
227	Jose Cruz Jr.	.05
228	Shannon Stewart	.05
229	Rolando Arrojo	.05
230	Livan Hernandez	.05
231	Orlando Hernandez	.05
232	Raul Mondesi	.05
233	Moises Alou	.05
234	Pedro Martinez	.30
235	Sammy Sosa	.50
236	Vladimir Guerrero	.40
237	Bartolo Colon	.05
238	Miguel Tejada	.05
239	Ismael Valdes	.05
240	Mariano Rivera	.05
241	Jose Cruz Jr.	.05
242	Juan Gonzalez	.20
243	Ivan Rodriguez	.15
244	Sandy Alomar	.05
245	Roberto Alomar	.10
246	Magglio Ordonez	.05
247	Kerry Wood	.10
248	Mark McGwire	.75
249	David Wells	.05
250	Rolando Arrojo	.05
251	Ken Griffey Jr.	.65
252	Trevor Hoffman	.05
253	Travis Lee	.05
254	Roberto Alomar	.10
255	Sammy Sosa	.50
256	Not Issued	
257	Not Issued	
258	Not Issued	
259	Not Issued	
260	Not Issued	
261	Not Issued	
262	Not Issued	
263	Not Issued	
264	Not Issued	
265	Not Issued	
266	Pat Burrell RC	2.00
267	Shea Hillenbrand RC	.65
268	Robert Fick	.05
269	Roy Halladay	.05
270	Ruben Mateo	.05
271	Bruce Chen	.05
272	Angel Pena	.05
273	Michael Barrett	.05
274	Kevin Witt	.05
275	Damon Minor	.05
276	Ryan Minor	.05
277	A.J. Pierzynski	.05
278	A.J. Burnett RC	.50
279	Dermal Brown	.05
280	Joe Lawrence	.05
281	Derrick Gibson	.05
282	Carlos Febles	.05
283	Chris Haas	.05
284	Cesar King	.05
285	Calvin Pickering	.05
286	Mitch Meluskey	.05
287	Carlos Beltran	.50
288	Ron Belliard	.05
289	Jerry Hairston Jr.	.05
290	Fernando Seguignol	.05
291	Kris Benson	.05
292	Chad Hutchinson RC	.05
293	Jarrod Washburn	.05
294	Jason Dickson	.05
295	Mo Vaughn	.05
296	Garrett Anderson	.05
297	Jim Edmonds	.05
298	Ken Hill	.05
299	Shigetosi Hasegawa	.05
300	Todd Stottlemyre	.05
301	Randy Johnson	.60
302	Omar Daal	.05
303	Steve Finley	.05
304	Matt Williams	.05
305	Danny Klassen	.05
306	Tony Batista	.05
307	Brian Jordan	.05
308	Greg Maddux	.75
309	Chipper Jones	.75
310	Bret Boone	.05
311	Ozzie Guillen	.05
312	John Rocker	.05
313	Tom Glavine	.25
314	Andruw Jones	.60
315	Albert Belle	.05
316	Charles Johnson	.05
317	Will Clark	.05
318	B.J. Surhoff	.05
319	Delino DeShields	.05
320	Heathcliff Slocumb	.05
321	Sidney Ponson	.05
322	Juan Guzman	.05
323	Reggie Jefferson	.05
324	Mark Portugal	.05
325	Tim Wakefield	.05
326	Jason Varitek	.05
327	Jose Offerman	.05
328	Pedro Martinez	.60
329	Trot Nixon	.05
330	Kerry Wood	.30
331	Sammy Sosa	.75
332	Glenallen Hill	.05
333	Gary Gaetti	.05
334	Mickey Morandini	.05
335	Benito Santiago	.05
336	Jeff Blauser	.05
337	Frank Thomas	.65
338	Paul Konerko	.15
339	Jaime Navarro	.05
340	Carlos Lee	.05
341	Brian Simmons	.05
342	Mark Johnson	.05
343	Jeff Abbot	.05
344	Steve Avery	.05
345	Mike Cameron	.05
346	Michael Tucker	.05
347	Greg Vaughn	.05
348	Hal Morris	.05
349	Pete Harnisch	.05
350	Denny Neagle	.05
351	Manny Ramirez	.60
352	Roberto Alomar	.20
353	Dwight Gooden	.05
354	Kenny Lofton	.05
355	Mike Jackson	.05
356	Charles Nagy	.05
357	Enrique Wilson	.05
358	Russ Branyan	.05
359	Richie Sexson	.05
360	Vinny Castilla	.05
361	Dante Bichette	.05
362	Kirt Manwaring	.05
363	Darryl Hamilton	.05
364	Jamey Wright	.05
365	Curt Leskanic	.05
366	Jeff Reed	.05
367	Bobby Higginson	.05
368	Justin Thompson	.05
369	Brad Ausmus	.05
370	Dean Palmer	.05
371	Gabe Kapler	.05
372	Juan Encarnacion	.05
373	Karim Garcia	.10
374	Alex Gonzalez	.05
375	Braden Looper	.05
376	Preston Wilson	.05
377	Todd Dunwoody	.05
378	Alex Fernandez	.05
379	Mark Kotsay	.05
380	Mark Mantei	.05
381	Ken Caminiti	.05
382	Scott Elarton	.05
383	Jeff Bagwell	.60
384	Derek Bell	.05
385	Ricky Gutierrez	.05

386	Richard Hildalgo	.05
387	Shane Reynolds	.05
388	Carl Everett	.05
389	Scott Service	.05
390	Jeff Suppan	.05
391	Joe Randa	.05
392	Kevin Appier	.05
393	Shane Halter	.05
394	Chad Kreuter	.05
395	Mike Sweeney	.05
396	Kevin Brown	.05
397	Devon White	.05
398	Todd Hollandsworth	.05
399	Todd Hundley	.05
400	Chan Ho Park	.05
401	Mark Grudzielanek	.05
402	Raul Mondesi	.05
403	Ismael Valdes	.05
404	Rafael Roque	.05
405	Sean Berry	.05
406	Kevin Barker	.05
407	Dave Nilsson	.05
408	Geoff Jenkins	.05
409	Jim Abbott	.05
410	Bobby Hughes	.05
411	Corey Koskie	.05
412	Rick Aguilera	.05
413	LaTroy Hawkins	.05
414	Ron Coomer	.05
415	Denny Hocking	.05
416	Marty Cordova	.05
417	Terry Steinbach	.05
418	Rondell White	.05
419	Wilton Guerrero	.05
420	Shane Andrews	.05
421	Orlando Cabrera	.05
422	Carl Pavano	.05
423	Jeff Vasquez	.05
424	Chris Widger	.05
425	Robin Ventura	.05
426	Rickey Henderson	.60
427	Al Leiter	.05
428	Bobby Jones	.05
429	Brian McRae	.05
430	Roger Cedeno	.05
431	Bobby Bonilla	.05
432	Edgardo Alfonzo	.05
433	Bernie Williams	.05
434	Ricky Ledee	.05
435	Chili Davis	.05
436	Tino Martinez	.05
437	Scott Brosius	.05
438	David Cone	.05
439	Joe Girardi	.05
440	Roger Clemens	.85
441	Chad Curtis	.05
442	Hideki Irabu	.05
443	Jason Giambi	.40
444	Scott Spezio	.05
445	Tony Phillips	.05
446	Ramon Hernandez	.05
447	Mike Macfarlane	.05
448	Tom Candiotti	.05
449	Billy Taylor	.05
450	Bobby Estella	.05
451	Curt Schilling	.25
452	Carlton Loewer	.05
453	Marlon Anderson	.05
454	Kevin Jordan	.05
455	Ron Gant	.05
456	Chad Ogea	.05
457	Abraham Nunez	.05
458	Jason Kendall	.05
459	Pat Meares	.05
460	Brant Brown	.05
461	Brian Giles	.05
462	Chad Hermansen	.05
463	Freddy Garcia	.05
464	Edgar Renteria	.05
465	Fernando Tatis	.05
466	Eric Davis	.05
467	Darren Bragg	.05
468	Donovan Osborne	.05
469	Manny Aybar	.05
470	Jose Jimenez	.05
471	Kent Mercker	.05
472	Reggie Sanders	.05
473	Ruben Rivera	.05
474	Tony Gwynn	.75
475	Jim Leyritz	.05
476	Chris Gomez	.05
477	Matt Clement	.05
478	Carlos Hernandez	.05
479	Sterling Hitchcock	.05
480	Ellis Burks	.05
481	Barry Bonds	2.00
482	Marvin Bernard	.05
483	Kirk Rueter	.05
484	F.P. Santangelo	.05
485	Stan Javier	.05
486	Jeff Kent	.05
487	Alex Rodriguez	1.50
488	Tom Lampkin	.05
489	Jose Mesa	.05
490	Jay Buhner	.05
491	Edgar Martinez	.05

492	Butch Huskey	.05
493	John Mabry	.05
494	Jamie Moyer	.05
495	Roberto Hernandez	.05
496	Tony Saunders	.05
497	Fred McGriff	.05
498	Dave Martinez	.05
499	Jose Canseco	.40
500	Rolando Arrojo	.05
501	Esteban Yan	.05
502	Juan Gonzalez	.30
503	Rafael Palmeiro	.50
504	Aaron Sele	.05
505	Royce Clayton	.05
506	Todd Zeile	.05
507	Tom Goodwin	.05
508	Lee Stevens	.05
509	Esteban Loaiza	.05
510	Joey Hamilton	.05
511	Homer Bush	.05
512	Willie Greene	.05
513	Shawn Green	.25
514	David Wells	.05
515	Kelvim Escobar	.05
516	Tony Fernandez	.05
517	Pat Hentgen	.05
518	Mark McGwire	.75
519	Ken Griffey Jr.	.65
520	Sammy Sosa	.50
521	Juan Gonzalez	.20
522	J.D. Drew	.10
523	Chipper Jones	.40
524	Alex Rodriguez	.75
525	Mike Piazza	.65
526	Nomar Garciaparra	.50
527	Mark McGwire Season Highlights Checklist	.75
528	Sammy Sosa Season Highlights Checklist	.50
529	Scott Brosius Season Highlights Checklist	.05
530	Cal Ripken Jr. Season Highlights Checklist	1.00
531	Barry Bonds Season Highlights Checklist	1.00
532	Roger Clemens Season Highlights Checklist	.40
533	Ken Griffey Jr. Season Highlights Checklist	.65
534	Alex Rodriguez Season Highlights Checklist	.75
535	Curt Schilling Season Highlights Checklist	.05

Exclusives

		NM/M
Common Player:		3.00
Stars/Rookies:		15X
Greens (1-255):		
	Values Undetermined	
Greens (266-535):		100X
(See 1999 Upper Deck for checklist and base card values.)		

Babe Ruth Piece of History Bat

		NM/M
PH	Babe Ruth/Bat	900.00
PHLC	Babe Ruth/Legendary Cut Auto.	25,000

Crowning Glory

	NM/M
Complete Set (3):	22.50
Common Player:	3.00
Inserted 1:23	
Doubles (1,000 Sets):	2X
Triples (25 Sets):	8X
Home Runs (One Set):	
Values Undetermined	

CG1	Roger Clemens, Kerry Wood	6.00
CG2	Mark McGwire, Barry Bonds	12.00
CG3	Ken Griffey Jr., Mark McGwire	7.50

Forte

		NM/M
Complete Set (30):		50.00
Common Player:		.50
Inserted 1:23		
Doubles (2,000 Sets):		3X
Triples (100):		15X
Quadruples (10):		40X
1	Darin Erstad	1.50
2	Troy Glaus	1.50
3	Mo Vaughn	.50
4	Greg Maddux	2.50
5	Andres Galarraga	.50
6	Chipper Jones	2.50
7	Cal Ripken Jr.	5.00
8	Albert Belle	.50
9	Nomar Garciaparra	2.50
10	Sammy Sosa	2.50
11	Kerry Wood	1.00
12	Frank Thomas	2.00
13	Jim Thome	1.50
14	Jeff Bagwell	2.00
15	Vladimir Guerrero	2.00
16	Mike Piazza	3.00
17	Derek Jeter	5.00
18	Ben Grieve	.50
19	Eric Chavez	.50
20	Scott Rolen	1.50
21	Mark McGwire	4.00
22	J.D. Drew	1.00
23	Tony Gwynn	2.50
24	Barry Bonds	5.00
25	Alex Rodriguez	4.00
26	Ken Griffey Jr.	3.00
27	Ivan Rodriguez	1.50
28	Juan Gonzalez	1.00
29	Roger Clemens	2.75
30	Andruw Jones	2.00

Game Jersey

		NM/M
Common Player:		6.00
AB	Adrian Beltre H1	10.00

		NM/M
EC	Eric Chavez H2	6.00
JD	J.D. Drew H2	10.00
JDs	J.D. Drew/ Auto./8 H2	150.00
DE	Darin Erstad H1	10.00
BF	Brad Fullmer H2	4.50
JG	Juan Gonzalez HR1	15.00
BG	Ben Grieve H1	6.00
KG	Ken Griffey Jr. H1	20.00
KGs	Ken Griffey Jr./ Auto./24 H1	150.00
JR	Ken Griffey Jr. HR2	20.00
JRs	Ken Griffey Jr./ Auto./24 HR2	150.00
TGw	Tony Gwynn H2	15.00
TH	Todd Helton H2	15.00
CJ	Charles Johnson HR1	6.00
CJ	Chipper Jones H2	15.00
TL	Travis Lee H1	6.00
GM	Greg Maddux HR2	15.00
MP	Mike Piazza HR1	20.00
MR	Manny Ramirez H2	10.00
AR	Alex Rodriguez HR1	25.00
IR	Ivan Rodriguez H1	7.50
NRa	Nolan Ryan/ Astros H2	25.00
NRas	Nolan Ryan/ H2 Auto./34	450.00
NRb	Nolan Ryan/ Rangers HR2	25.00
SS	Sammy Sosa H2	20.00
BT	Bubba Trammell H2	6.00
FT	Frank Thomas HR2	15.00
KW	Kerry Wood HR1	15.00
KWs	Kerry Wood/ Auto./34 HR1	150.00

Hitter.Net Ted Williams

		NM/M
9	Ted Williams	7.50

Homerun Heroes

		NM/M
Complete Set (10):		10.00
Common Player:		.50
Complete Set Cans (6):		10.00
Common Player Can:		2.00
H1	Ken Griffey Jr.	1.25
H2	Mark McGwire	2.00

H3	Sammy Sosa	1.00
H4	Troy Glaus	.75
H5	Mike Piazza	2.00
H6	Chipper Jones	1.00
H7	Vladimir Guerrero	.75
H8	Frank Thomas	.75
H9	Juan Gonzalez	.50
H10	Alex Rodriguez	2.00

SEALED CANS

1	Ken Griffey Jr.	2.50
2	Mark McGwire	2.50
3	Sammy Sosa	2.00
4	Troy Glaus	1.50
5	Mike Piazza	2.50
6	Chipper Jones	2.00

Immaculate Perception

	NM/M
Complete Set (27):	45.00
Common Player:	.25
Inserted 1:23	
Doubles (1,000 Sets):	1.5X
Triples (25):	8X
Home Runs (1):	
Values Undetermined	
I1 Jeff Bagwell	2.00
I2 Craig Biggio	.25
I3 Barry Bonds	5.00
I4 Roger Clemens	2.75
I5 Jose Cruz Jr.	.25
I6 Nomar Garciaparra	2.50
I7 Tony Clark	.25
I8 Ben Grieve	.25
I9 Ken Griffey Jr.	3.00
I10 Tony Gwynn	2.50
I11 Randy Johnson	2.00
I12 Chipper Jones	2.50
I13 Travis Lee	.40
I14 Kenny Lofton	.25
I15 Greg Maddux	2.50
I16 Mark McGwire	4.00
I17 Hideo Nomo	1.00
I18 Mike Piazza	3.00
I19 Manny Ramirez	2.00
I20 Cal Ripken Jr.	5.00
I21 Alex Rodriguez	4.00
I22 Scott Rolen	1.50
I23 Frank Thomas	2.00
I24 Kerry Wood	1.00
I25 Larry Walker	.25
I26 Vinny Castilla	.25
I27 Derek Jeter	5.00

Ken Griffey Jr. 1989 Buyback Autograph

	NM/M
Ken Griffey Jr./100	1,250

Piece of History 500 Club Babe Ruth

		NM/M
BR	Babe Ruth/50	4,000

Textbook Excellence

	NM/M
Complete Set (30):	12.50
Common Player:	.25
Inserted 1:4	

Doubles (2,000 Sets):	1.5X
Triples (100):	5X
Quadruples (10):	40X
T1 Mo Vaughn	.25
T2 Greg Maddux	.75
T3 Chipper Jones	.75
T4 Andruw Jones	.60
T5 Cal Ripken Jr.	2.00
T6 Albert Belle	.25
T7 Roberto Alomar	.30
T8 Nomar Garciaparra	.75
T9 Kerry Wood	.30
T10 Sammy Sosa	.75
T11 Greg Vaughn	.25
T12 Jeff Bagwell	.60
T13 Kevin Brown	.25
T14 Vladimir Guerrero	.60
T15 Mike Piazza	1.00
T16 Bernie Williams	.25
T17 Derek Jeter	2.00
T18 Ben Grieve	.25
T19 Eric Chavez	.25
T29 Scott Rolen	.50
T21 Mark McGwire	1.50
T22 David Wells	.25
T23 J.D. Drew	.50
T24 Tony Gwynn	.75
T25 Barry Bonds	2.00
T26 Alex Rodriguez	1.50
T27 Ken Griffey Jr.	1.00
T28 Juan Gonzalez	.30
T29 Ivan Rodriguez	.50
T30 Roger Clemens	.85

View to a Thrill

	NM/M
Complete Set (30):	25.00
Common Player:	.35
Inserted 1:7	
Doubles (2,000 Sets):	1.5X
Triples (100):	4X
Quadruples (10):	30X
V1 Mo Vaughn	.35
V2 Darin Erstad	.40
V3 Travis Lee	.40
V4 Chipper Jones	1.50
V5 Greg Maddux	1.50
V6 Gabe Kapler	.35
V7 Cal Ripken Jr.	3.00
V8 Nomar Garciaparra	1.50
V9 Kerry Wood	.40
V10 Frank Thomas	1.00
V11 Manny Ramirez	1.00
V12 Larry Walker	.35
V13 Tony Clark	.35
V14 Jeff Bagwell	1.00
V15 Craig Biggio	.35
V16 Vladimir Guerrero	1.00
V17 Mike Piazza	2.00
V18 Bernie Williams	.35
V19 Derek Jeter	3.00
V20 Ben Grieve	.35
V21 Eric Chavez	.35
V22 Scott Rolen	.65
V23 Mark McGwire	2.50
V24 Tony Gwynn	1.50
V25 Barry Bonds	3.00
V26 Ken Griffey Jr.	2.00
V27 Alex Rodriguez	2.50
V28 J.D. Drew	.65
V29 Juan Gonzalez	.50
V30 Roger Clemens	1.75

Wonder Years

	NM/M
Complete Set (30):	30.00
Common Player:	.50
Inserted 1:7	
Doubles (2,000):	2.5X
Triples (50):	10X
Home Runs (1):	
Values Undetermined	
WY1 Kerry Wood	.75
WY2 Travis Lee	.65
WY3 Jeff Bagwell	1.50
WY4 Barry Bonds	4.00
WY5 Roger Clemens	2.25
WY6 Jose Cruz Jr.	.50
WY7 Andres Galarraga	.50
WY8 Nomar Garciaparra	2.00
WY9 Juan Gonzalez	.75
WY10 Ken Griffey Jr.	2.50
WY11 Tony Gwynn	2.00
WY12 Derek Jeter	4.00
WY13 Randy Johnson	1.50
WY14 Andruw Jones	1.50
WY15 Chipper Jones	2.00
WY16 Kenny Lofton	.50
WY17 Greg Maddux	2.00
WY18 Tino Martinez	.50
WY19 Mark McGwire	3.00
WY20 Paul Molitor	1.50
WY21 Mike Piazza	2.50
WY22 Manny Ramirez	1.50
WY23 Cal Ripken Jr.	4.00
WY24 Alex Rodriguez	2.00
WY25 Sammy Sosa	2.00
WY26 Frank Thomas	1.50
WY27 Mo Vaughn	.50
WY28 Larry Walker	.50
WY29 Scott Rolen	1.00
WY30 Ben Grieve	.50

10th Anniversary Team

	NM/M
Complete Set (30):	20.00
Common Player:	.15
Inserted 1:4	
Doubles (4,000 Sets):	2X
Triples (100):	6X
Home Runs (1):	
Values Undetermined	
X1 Mike Piazza	1.50
X2 Mark McGwire	2.00
X3 Roberto Alomar	.30
X4 Chipper Jones	1.00
X5 Cal Ripken Jr.	3.00
X6 Ken Griffey Jr.	1.50
X7 Barry Bonds	3.00
X8 Tony Gwynn	1.00
X9 Nolan Ryan	3.00
X10 Randy Johnson	.75
X11 Dennis Eckersley	.65
X12 Ivan Rodriguez	.65
X13 Frank Thomas	.75
X14 Craig Biggio	.15
X15 Wade Boggs	1.00
X16 Alex Rodriguez	2.00
X17 Albert Belle	.15
X18 Juan Gonzalez	.40
X19 Rickey Henderson	.75
X20 Greg Maddux	1.00
X21 Tom Glavine	.35
X22 Randy Myers	.15
X23 Sandy Alomar	.15
X24 Jeff Bagwell	.75
X25 Derek Jeter	3.00
X26 Matt Williams	.15
X27 Kenny Lofton	.15
X28 Sammy Sosa	1.00
X29 Larry Walker	.15
X30 Roger Clemens	1.25

1999 Upper Deck Black Diamond

	NM/M
Complete Set (120):	30.00
Common Player:	.10
Common Diamond Debut (91-120):	.25
Inserted 1:4	
Double Diamonds (3,000 Each):	3X
Double Diamond Debuts (2,500):	2X
Triple Diamonds (1,500):	6X
Triple Diamond Debuts (1,000):	3X
Pack (6):	2.00
Wax Box (30):	40.00
1 Darin Erstad	.25
2 Tim Salmon	.10
3 Jim Edmonds	.10
4 Matt Williams	.10
5 David Dellucci	.10
6 Jay Bell	.10
7 Andres Galarraga	.10
8 Chipper Jones	1.00
9 Greg Maddux	1.00
10 Andruw Jones	.75
11 Cal Ripken Jr.	2.50
12 Rafael Palmeiro	.65
13 Brady Anderson	.10
14 Mike Mussina	.40
15 Nomar Garciaparra	1.00
16 Mo Vaughn	.10
17 Pedro Martinez	.75
18 Sammy Sosa	1.00
19 Henry Rodriguez	.10
20 Frank Thomas	.75
21 Magglio Ordonez	.40
22 Albert Belle	.10
23 Paul Konerko	.20
24 Sean Casey	.10
25 Jim Thome	.60
26 Kenny Lofton	.10
27 Sandy Alomar Jr.	.10
28 Jaret Wright	.10
29 Larry Walker	.10
30 Todd Helton	.65
31 Vinny Castilla	.10
32 Tony Clark	.10
33 Damion Easley	.10
34 Mark Kotsay	.10
35 Derrek Lee	.50
36 Moises Alou	.10

37	Jeff Bagwell	.75
38	Craig Biggio	.10
39	Randy Johnson	.75
40	Dean Palmer	.10
41	Johnny Damon	.35
42	Chan Ho Park	.10
43	Raul Mondesi	.10
44	Gary Sheffield	.40
45	Jeromy Burnitz	.10
46	Marquis Grissom	.10
47	Jeff Cirillo	.10
48	Paul Molitor	.75
49	Todd Walker	.10
50	Vladimir Guerrero	.75
51	Brad Fullmer	.10
52	Mike Piazza	1.50
53	Hideo Nomo	.40
54	Carlos Baerga	.10
55	John Olerud	.10
56	Derek Jeter	2.50
57	Hideki Irabu	.10
58	Tino Martinez	.10
59	Bernie Williams	.10
60	Miguel Tejada	.25
61	Ben Grieve	.10
62	Jason Giambi	.55
63	Scott Rolen	.60
64	Doug Glanville	.10
65	Desi Relaford	.10
66	Tony Womack	.10
67	Jason Kendall	.10
68	Jose Guillen	.10
69	Tony Gwynn	1.00
70	Ken Caminiti	.10
71	Greg Vaughn	.10
72	Kevin Brown	.10
73	Barry Bonds	2.50
74	J.T. Snow	.10
75	Jeff Kent	.10
76	Ken Griffey Jr.	1.50
77	Alex Rodriguez	2.00
78	Edgar Martinez	.10
79	Jay Buhner	.10
80	Mark McGwire	2.00
81	Delino DeShields	.10
82	Brian Jordan	.10
83	Quinton McCracken	.10
84	Fred McGriff	.10
85	Juan Gonzalez	.40
86	Ivan Rodriguez	.65
87	Will Clark	.10
88	Roger Clemens	1.25
89	Jose Cruz Jr.	.10
90	Babe Ruth	2.00
91	Troy Glaus	1.00
92	Jarrod Washburn	.25
93	Travis Lee	.75
94	Bruce Chen	.25
95	Mike Caruso	.25
96	Jim Parque	.25
97	Kerry Wood	.50
98	Jeremy Giambi	.25
99	Matt Anderson	.25
100	Seth Greisinger	.25
101	Gabe Alvarez	.25
102	Rafael Medina	.25
103	Daryle Ward	.25
104	Alex Cora	.25
105	Adrian Beltre	.50
106	Geoff Jenkins	.25
107	Eric Milton	.25
108	Carl Pavano	.25
109	Eric Chavez	.50
110	Orlando Hernandez	.25
111	A.J. Hinch	.25
112	Carlton Loewer	.25
113	Aramis Ramirez	.25
114	Cliff Politte	.25
115	Matt Clement	.25
116	Alex Gonzalez	.25
117	J.D. Drew	.75
118	Shane Monahan	.25
119	Rolando Arrojo	.25
120	George Lombard	.25

Double Diamond

	NM/M
Complete Set (120):	200.00
Common Player (1-90):	.25
Common Diamond Debut	
(91-120):	1.00
Stars (1-90):	3X
Diamond Debuts (91-120):	2X
(See 1999 Upper Deck Black Diamond for checklist and base card values.)	

Triple Diamond

	NM/M
Common Player (1-90):	1.00
Common Diamond Debut	
(91-120):	1.50
Stars (1-90):	6X
Diamond Debuts (91-120):	3X
(See 1999 Upper Deck Black Diamond for checklist and base card values.)	

Quadruple Diamond

	NM/M
Common Player (1-90):	4.00
Production 150 each.	
Common Diamond Debut	
(91-120):	6.00
Production 100 each.	
Stars (1-90):	25X
Diamond Debuts (91-120):	8X
18	Sammy Sosa/66	50.00
76	Ken Griffey Jr. /56	60.00
80	Mark McGwire/70	75.00
(See 1999 Upper Deck Black Diamond for checklist and base card values.)	

A Piece of History

	NM/M
Common Player:	5.00
JG	Juan Gonzalez	7.50
TG	Tony Gwynn	10.00
BW	Bernie Williams	5.00
MM	Mark McGwire	200.00
MV	Mo Vaughn	5.00
SS	Sammy Sosa	25.00

Diamond Dominance

	NM/M
Complete Set (30):	65.00
Common Player:	.50
Production 1,500 Sets	
D01	Kerry Wood	1.00
D02	Derek Jeter	6.00
D03	Alex Rodriguez	5.00
D04	Frank Thomas	2.00
D05	Jeff Bagwell	2.00
D06	Mo Vaughn	.50
D07	Ivan Rodriguez	1.50
D08	Cal Ripken Jr.	6.00
D09	Rolando Arrojo	.50
D10	Chipper Jones	3.00
D11	Kenny Lofton	.50
D12	Paul Konerko	.75
D13	Mike Piazza	4.00
D14	Ben Grieve	.50
D15	Nomar Garciaparra	3.00
D16	Travis Lee	.65
D17	Scott Rolen	1.00
D18	Juan Gonzalez	1.00
D19	Tony Gwynn	3.00
D20	Tony Clark	.50
D21	Roger Clemens	3.50
D22	Sammy Sosa	3.00
D23	Larry Walker	.50
D24	Ken Griffey Jr.	4.00
D25	Mark McGwire	5.00
D26	Barry Bonds	6.00
D27	Vladimir Guerrero	2.00
D28	Tino Martinez	.50
D29	Greg Maddux	3.00
D30	Babe Ruth	5.00

Mystery Numbers

	NM/M
Complete Set (30):	100.00
Common Player:	.75
M1	Babe Ruth/100	25.00
M2	Ken Griffey Jr./200	12.50
M3	Kerry Wood/300	4.00
M4	Mark McGwire/400	12.50
M5	Alex Rodriguez/500	12.50
M6	Chipper Jones/600	6.00
M7	Nomar Garciaparra/700	6.00
M8	Derek Jeter/800	10.00
M9	Mike Piazza/900	6.00
M10	Roger Clemens/1,000	4.50
M11	Greg Maddux/1,100	4.00
M12	Scott Rolen/1,200	1.25
M13	Cal Ripken Jr./1,300	7.50
M14	Ben Grieve/1,400	.75
M15	Troy Glaus/1,500	3.00
M16	Sammy Sosa/1,600	4.50
M17	Darin Erstad/1,700	1.25
M18	Juan Gonzalez/1,800	1.25
M19	Pedro Martinez/1,900	1.50
M20	Larry Walker/2,000	.75
M21	Vladimir Guerrero/2,100	1.50
M22	Jeff Bagwell/2,200	1.50
M23	Jaret Wright/2,300	.75
M24	Travis Lee/2,400	.75
M25	Barry Bonds/2,500	6.00
M26	Orlando Hernandez/2,600	.75
M27	Frank Thomas/2,700	1.50
M28	Tony Gwynn/2,800	2.00
M29	Andres Galarraga/2,900	.75
M30	Craig Biggio/3,000	.75

Piece of History 500 Club

	NM/M
Reggie Jackson	165.00
Reggie Jackson/Auto.	500.00

1999 Upper Deck Century Legends

	NM/M
Complete Set (131):	20.00
Common Player:	.10
Century Collection:	20X
Production 100 Sets	
Pack (5):	3.00
Wax Box (24):	60.00
1	Babe Ruth	2.00
1	Babe Ruth (SAMPLE overprint on back.)	2.00
2	Willie Mays	1.00
3	Ty Cobb	1.00
4	Walter Johnson	.40
5	Hank Aaron	1.00
6	Lou Gehrig	1.50
7	Christy Mathewson	.40
8	Ted Williams	1.25
9	Rogers Hornsby	.25
10	Stan Musial	.65
12	Grover Alexander	.25
13	Honus Wagner	.40
14	Cy Young	.40
15	Jimmie Foxx	.25
16	Johnny Bench	.50
17	Mickey Mantle	2.00
18	Josh Gibson	.25
19	Satchel Paige	.50
20	Roberto Clemente	1.50
21	Warren Spahn	.20
22	Frank Robinson	.20
23	Lefty Grove	.20
24	Eddie Collins	.10
27	Tris Speaker	.25
28	Mike Schmidt	.50
29	Napoleon LaJoie	.20
30	Steve Carlton	.25

31	Bob Gibson	.25
32	Tom Seaver	.25
33	George Sisler	.10
34	Barry Bonds	1.50
35	Joe Jackson	1.25
36	Bob Feller	.25
37	Hank Greenberg	.25
38	Ernie Banks	.40
39	Greg Maddux	.75
40	Yogi Berra	.40
41	Nolan Ryan	2.00
42	Mel Ott	.25
43	Al Simmons	.10
44	Jackie Robinson	1.25
45	Carl Hubbell	.25
46	Charley Gehringer	.10
47	Buck Leonard	.10
48	Reggie Jackson	.40
49	Tony Gwynn	.75
50	Roy Campanella	.40
51	Ken Griffey Jr.	1.00
52	Barry Bonds	1.50
53	Roger Clemens	.85
54	Tony Gwynn	.75
55	Cal Ripken Jr.	1.50
56	Greg Maddux	.75
57	Frank Thomas	.65
58	Mark McGwire	1.25
59	Mike Piazza	1.00
60	Wade Boggs	.75
61	Alex Rodriguez	1.25
62	Juan Gonzalez	.30
63	Mo Vaughn	.10
64	Albert Belle	.10
65	Sammy Sosa	.75
66	Nomar Garciaparra	.75
67	Derek Jeter	1.50
68	Kevin Brown	.10
69	Jose Canseco	.35
70	Randy Johnson	.60
71	Tom Glavine	.25
72	Barry Larkin	.10
73	Curt Schilling	.25
74	Moises Alou	.10
75	Fred McGriff	.10
76	Pedro Martinez	.65
77	Andres Galarraga	.10
78	Will Clark	.10
79	Larry Walker	.10
80	Ivan Rodriguez	.50
81	Chipper Jones	.75
82	Jeff Bagwell	.60
83	Craig Biggio	.10
84	Kerry Wood	.35
85	Roberto Alomar	.20
86	Vinny Castilla	.10
87	Kenny Lofton	.10
88	Rafael Palmeiro	.50
89	Manny Ramirez	.60
90	David Wells	.10
91	Mark Grace	.10
92	Bernie Williams	.10
93	David Cone	.10
94	John Olerud	.10
95	John Smoltz	.10
96	Tino Martinez	.10
97	Raul Mondesi	.10
98	Gary Sheffield	.35
99	Orel Hershiser	.10
100	Rickey Henderson	.65
101	J.D. Drew	.50
102	Troy Glaus	.50
103	Nomar Garciaparra	.75
104	Scott Rolen	.45
105	Ryan Minor	.10
106	Travis Lee	.20
107	Roy Halladay	.10
108	Carlos Beltran	.50
109	Alex Rodriguez	1.25
110	Eric Chavez	.20
111	Vladimir Guerrero	.60
112	Ben Grieve	.15
113	Kerry Wood	.30
114	Alex Gonzalez	.10
115	Darin Erstad	.30
116	Derek Jeter	1.50
117	Jaret Wright	.10
118	Jose Cruz Jr.	.10
119	Chipper Jones	.75
120	Gabe Kapler	.10
121	Satchel Paige	.25
122	Willie Mays	1.00
123	Roberto Clemente	1.50
124	Lou Gehrig	1.50
125	Mark McGwire	1.25
127	Bob Gibson	.25
128	Johnny Vander Meer	.10
129	Walter Johnson	.25
130	Ty Cobb	.75
131	Don Larsen	.20
132	Jackie Robinson	1.00
133	Tom Seaver	.25
134	Johnny Bench	.35
135	Frank Robinson	.25

Century Collection

	NM/M
Common Player:	2.00
Stars:	30X

(See 1999 Upper Deck Century Legends for checklist and base card values.)

All-Century Team

Lou Gehrig • Yankees • First Base

		NM/M
Complete Set (10):		30.00
Common Player:		2.50
Inserted 1:23		
1	Babe Ruth	7.50
2	Ty Cobb	3.50
3	Willie Mays	3.50
4	Lou Gehrig	6.00
5	Jackie Robinson	5.00
6	Mike Schmidt	2.50
7	Ernie Banks	2.50
8	Johnny Bench	2.50
9	Cy Young	2.50
10	Lineup Sheet	.25

Century Artifacts

1900s Framed Cut of Cobb
1910s Framed Cut of Ruth
1920s Framed Cut of Hornsby
1930s Framed Cut of Paige
1950s Auto. Balls: Aaron, Mays, Mantle
1960s Auto. Balls: Banks, Gibson, Bench
1970s Auto. Balls: Seaver, Schmidt, Carlton
1980s Auto. Balls: Ryan, Griffey Jr.
1990s Ken Griffey Autographed Jersey

Century Epic Signatures

		NM/M
Common Player:		20.00
Production 100 Sets		
EB	Ernie Banks	85.00
JB	Johnny Bench	90.00
YB	Yogi Berra	75.00
BB	Barry Bonds	240.00

SC	Steve Carlton	50.00
BD	Bucky Dent	20.00
BF	Bob Feller	50.00
CF	Carlton Fisk	40.00
BG	Bob Gibson	60.00
JG	Juan Gonzalez	60.00
Jr.	Ken Griffey Jr.	165.00
Sr.	Ken Griffey Sr.	20.00
VG	Vladimir Guerrero	70.00
TG	Tony Gwynn	90.00
RJ	Reggie Jackson	60.00
HK	Harmon Killebrew	75.00
DL	Don Larsen	30.00
GM	Greg Maddux	150.00
EMa	Eddie Mathews	90.00
WM	Willie Mays	300.00
BM	Bill Mazeroski	25.00
WMc	Willie McCovey	50.00
SM	Stan Musial	100.00
FR	Frank Robinson	50.00
AR	Alex Rodriguez	200.00
NR	Nolan Ryan	200.00
MS	Mike Schmidt	125.00
TS	Tom Seaver	75.00
WS	Warren Spahn	80.00
FT	Frank Thomas	80.00
BT	Bobby Thomson	20.00
TW	Ted Williams	750.00

Century MVPs

One Set Produced
Values Undetermined

Epic Milestones

HANK AARON Braves ... OF

		NM/M
Complete Set (9):		5.00
Common Player:		.25
Inserted 1:12		
2	Jackie Robinson	.75
3	Nolan Ryan	1.00
4	Mark McGwire	.75
5	Roger Clemens	.60
6	Sammy Sosa	.50
7	Cal Ripken Jr.	1.00
8	Rickey Henderson	.25
9	Hank Aaron	.75
10	Barry Bonds	1.00

Epic Signatures

		NM/M
Common Player:		10.00
Inserted 1:24		
EB	Ernie Banks	65.00
JB	Johnny Bench	40.00
YB	Yogi Berra	50.00
BB	Barry Bonds	180.00
SC	Steve Carlton	20.00
BD	Bucky Dent	10.00
BF	Bob Feller	15.00
CF	Carlton Fisk	25.00
BG	Bob Gibson	25.00
JG	Juan Gonzalez	20.00
Jr.	Ken Griffey Jr.	100.00
Sr.	Ken Griffey Sr.	10.00
VG	Vladimir Guerrero	30.00
TG	Tony Gwynn	40.00
RJ	Reggie Jackson	40.00
HK	Harmon Killebrew	30.00
DL	Don Larsen	15.00
GM	Greg Maddux	100.00
EMa	Eddie Mathews	80.00
BM	Bill Mazeroski	30.00
WMc	Willie McCovey	20.00
SM	Stan Musial	80.00
FR	Frank Robinson	30.00
AR	Alex Rodriguez	150.00
NR	Nolan Ryan	150.00
MS	Mike Schmidt	50.00
TS	Tom Seaver	40.00
WS	Warren Spahn	60.00
FT	Frank Thomas	50.00
BT	Bobby Thomson	10.00

Century Legends Hank Aaron Blowup

		NM/M
5	Hank Aaron	125.00

Jerseys of the Century

		NM/M
Common Player:		12.50
Inserted 1:418		
GB	George Brett	25.00
RC	Roger Clemens	25.00
TG	Tony Gwynn	20.00
GM	Greg Maddux	20.00
EM	Eddie Murray	15.00
NR	Nolan Ryan	90.00
MS	Mike Schmidt	25.00
OZ	Ozzie Smith	20.00
DW	Dave Winfield	15.00

Legendary Cuts

		NM/M
Values Undetermined		
CY	Cy Young	
	(11/00 Auction)	1,850

Memorable Shots

		NM/M
Complete Set (10):		15.00
Common Player:		.50
Inserted 1:12		
1	Babe Ruth	5.00
2	Bobby Thomson	1.00
3	Kirk Gibson	.50
4	Carlton Fisk	.50
5	Bill Mazeroski	1.00
6	Bucky Dent	.50
7	Mark McGwire	2.00
8	Mickey Mantle	5.00
9	Joe Carter	.50
10	Mark McGwire	2.00

500 Club Piece History

		NM/M
JF	Jimmie Foxx	125.00

1999 Upper Deck Challengers for 70

		NM/M
Complete Set (90):		15.00
Common Player:		.05
Challenger's Edition		
(600 Sets):		5X
Pack (5):		2.00
Wax Box (20):		25.00
1	Mark McGwire	1.50
2	Sammy Sosa	1.00
3	Ken Griffey Jr.	1.25
4	Alex Rodriguez	1.50
5	Albert Belle	.05
6	Mo Vaughn	.05
7	Mike Piazza	1.25
8	Frank Thomas	.75
9	Juan Gonzalez	.35
10	Barry Bonds	2.00
11	Rafael Palmeiro	.60
12	Jose Canseco	.50
13	Nomar Garciaparra	1.00
14	Carlos Delgado	.20
15	Brian Jordan	.05
16	Vladimir Guerrero	.65
17	Vinny Castilla	.05
18	Chipper Jones	1.00
19	Jeff Bagwell	.65
20	Moises Alou	.05
21	Tony Clark	.05
22	Jim Thome	.50
23	Tino Martinez	.05
24	Greg Vaughn	.05
25	Javy Lopez	.05
26	Jeromy Burnitz	.05
27	Cal Ripken Jr.	2.00
28	Manny Ramirez	.65
29	Darin Erstad	.25
30	Ken Caminiti	.05
31	Edgar Martinez	.05
32	Ivan Rodriguez	.60
33	Larry Walker	.05
34	Todd Helton	.60
35	Andruw Jones	.65
36	Ray Lankford	.05
37	Travis Lee	.10
38	Raul Mondesi	.05
39	Scott Rolen	.50
40	Ben Grieve	.05
41	J.D. Drew	.50
42	Troy Glaus	.60
43	Eric Chavez	.10
44	Gabe Kapler	.05
45	Michael Barrett	.05
46	Mark McGwire	.75
47	Jose Canseco	.25
48	Greg Vaughn	.05
49	Albert Belle	.05
50	Mark McGwire	.75
51	Vinny Castilla	.05
52	Vladimir Guerrero	.35
53	Andres Galarraga	.05
54	Rafael Palmeiro	.30
55	Juan Gonzalez	.20
56	Ken Griffey Jr.	.60
57	Barry Bonds	1.00
58	Mo Vaughn	.05
59	Nomar Garciaparra	.50
60	Tino Martinez	.05
61	Mark McGwire	.75
62	Mark McGwire	.75
63	Mark McGwire	.75
64	Mark McGwire	.75
65	Mark McGwire	.75
66	Sammy Sosa	.50
67	Mark McGwire	.75
68	Mark McGwire	.75
69	Mark McGwire	.75
70	Mark McGwire	.75
71	Mark McGwire	.75
72	Scott Brosius	.05
73	Tony Gwynn	.40
74	Chipper Jones	.50
75	Jeff Bagwell	.35
76	Moises Alou	.05
77	Manny Ramirez	.35
78	Carlos Delgado	.05
79	Kerry Wood	.20
80	Ken Griffey Jr.	.60
81	Cal Ripken Jr.	1.00
82	Alex Rodriguez	.75
83	Barry Bonds	1.00
84	Ken Griffey Jr.	.60
85	Travis Lee	.15
86	George Lombard	.05
87	Michael Barrett	.05
88	Jeremy Giambi	.05
89	Troy Glaus	.30
90	J.D. Drew	.25

Autographed Swinging

		NM/M
Complete Set (6):		200.00
Common Player:		5.00
JR	Ken Griffey Jr.	95.00
VG	Vladimir Guerrero	25.00
TH	Todd Helton	15.00
GK	Gabe Kapler	5.00
TL	Travis Lee	7.50
AR	Alex Rodriguez	90.00

Challengers Insert

		NM/M
Complete Set (30):		9.00
Common Player:		.15
Parallel Edition (70 Sets):		15X
1	Mark McGwire	1.00
2	Sammy Sosa	.65
3	Ken Griffey Jr.	.75
4	Alex Rodriguez	1.00
5	Albert Belle	.15
6	Mo Vaughn	.15
7	Mike Piazza	.75
8	Frank Thomas	.50
9	Juan Gonzalez	.25
10	Barry Bonds	1.50
11	Rafael Palmeiro	.35
12	Nomar Garciaparra	.65
13	Vladimir Guerrero	.45
14	Vinny Castilla	.15
15	Chipper Jones	.60
16	Jeff Bagwell	.45
17	Moises Alou	.15
18	Tony Clark	.15
19	Jim Thome	.35
20	Tino Martinez	.15
21	Greg Vaughn	.15
22	Manny Ramirez	.45
23	Darin Erstad	.25
24	Ken Caminiti	.15
25	Ivan Rodriguez	.35
26	Andruw Jones	.45
27	Travis Lee	.25
28	Scott Rolen	.35
29	Ben Grieve	.15
30	J.D. Drew	.35

Longball Legends

		NM/M
Complete Set (30):		20.00
Common Player:		.50
1	Ken Griffey Jr.	1.50
2	Mark McGwire	2.00
3	Sammy Sosa	1.00
4	Cal Ripken Jr.	2.50
5	Barry Bonds	2.50
6	Larry Walker	.50
7	Fred McGriff	.50
8	Alex Rodriguez	2.00
9	Frank Thomas	.75
10	Juan Gonzalez	.60
11	Jeff Bagwell	.75
12	Mo Vaughn	.50
13	Albert Belle	.50
14	Mike Piazza	1.50
15	Vladimir Guerrero	.75
16	Chipper Jones	1.00
17	Ken Caminiti	.50
18	Rafael Palmeiro	.65
19	Nomar Garciaparra	1.00
20	Jim Thome	.50
21	Edgar Martinez	.50
22	Ivan Rodriguez	.65
23	Andres Galarraga	.50
24	Scott Rolen	.60
25	Darin Erstad	.65
26	Moises Alou	.50
27	J.D. Drew	.65
28	Andruw Jones	.75
29	Manny Ramirez	.75
30	Tino Martinez	.50

Mark on History

		NM/M
Complete Set (25):		25.00
Common McGwire:		1.50
Parallel:		8X

Piece of History 500

	NM/M
Harmon Killebrew	120.00

	NM/M
Harmon Killebrew/ Auto.	450.00

Swinging/Fences

		NM/M
Complete Set (15):		15.00
Common Player:		.50
1	Ken Griffey Jr.	1.50
2	Mark McGwire	2.00
3	Sammy Sosa	1.25
4	Alex Rodriguez	2.00
5	Nomar Garciaparra	1.25
6	J.D. Drew	.75
7	Vladimir Guerrero	1.00
8	Ben Grieve	.50
9	Chipper Jones	1.25
10	Gabe Kapler	.50
11	Travis Lee	.60
12	Todd Helton	.75
13	Juan Gonzalez	.60
14	Mike Piazza	1.50
15	Mo Vaughn	.50

1999 Upper Deck Encore

		NM/M
Complete Set (180):		75.00
Common Player (1-90):		.05
Common Player (91-135):		.25
Inserted 1:4		
Common Player (136-165):		.35
Inserted 1:6		
Common Player (166-180):		.50
Inserted 1:8		
Gold (1-90):		10X
Gold (91-135):		1.5X
Gold (136-165):		3X
Gold (166-180):		4X
Production 125 Sets		
Pack (6):		1.50
Wax Box (24):		25.00
1	Darin Erstad	.25
2	Mo Vaughn	.05
3	Travis Lee	.15
4	Randy Johnson	.60
5	Matt Williams	.05
6	John Smoltz	.05
7	Greg Maddux	.75
8	Chipper Jones	.75
9	Tom Glavine	.25
10	Andruw Jones	.60
11	Cal Ripken Jr.	1.50
12	Mike Mussina	.30
13	Albert Belle	.05
14	Nomar Garciaparra	.75
15	Jose Offerman	.05
16	Pedro Martinez	.60
17	Trot Nixon	.10
18	Kerry Wood	.40
19	Sammy Sosa	.75

20	Frank Thomas	.60
21	Paul Konerko	.15
22	Sean Casey	.15
23	Barry Larkin	.05
24	Greg Vaughn	.05
25	Travis Fryman	.05
26	Jaret Wright	.05
27	Jim Thome	.45
28	Manny Ramirez	.60
29	Roberto Alomar	.20
30	Kenny Lofton	.05
31	Todd Helton	.60
32	Larry Walker	.05
33	Vinny Castilla	.05
34	Dante Bichette	.05
35	Tony Clark	.05
36	Dean Palmer	.05
37	Gabe Kapler	.05
38	Juan Encarnacion	.05
39	Alex Gonzalez	.05
40	Preston Wilson	.05
41	Mark Kotsay	.05
42	Moises Alou	.05
43	Craig Biggio	.05
44	Ken Caminiti	.05
45	Jeff Bagwell	.60
46	Johnny Damon	.30
47	Gary Sheffield	.25
48	Kevin Brown	.05
49	Raul Mondesi	.05
50	Jeff Cirillo	.05
51	Jeromy Burnitz	.05
52	Todd Walker	.05
53	Corey Koskie	.05
54	Brad Fullmer	.05
55	Vladimir Guerrero	.60
56	Mike Piazza	1.25
57	Robin Ventura	.05
58	Rickey Henderson	.60
59	Derek Jeter	1.50
60	Paul O'Neill	.05
61	Bernie Williams	.05
62	Tino Martinez	.05
63	Roger Clemens	.85
64	Ben Grieve	.05
65	Jason Giambi	.35
66	Bob Abreu	.10
67	Scott Rolen	.40
68	Curt Schilling	.25
69	Marlon Anderson	.05
70	Kevin Young	.05
71	Jason Kendall	.05
72	Brian Giles	.05
73	Mark McGwire	1.25
74	Fernando Tatis	.05
75	Eric Davis	.05
76	Trevor Hoffman	.05
77	Tony Gwynn	.75
78	Matt Clement	.05
79	Robb Nen	.05
80	Barry Bonds	1.50
81	Ken Griffey Jr.	1.00
82	Alex Rodriguez	1.25
83	Wade Boggs	.75
84	Fred McGriff	.05
85	Jose Canseco	.30
86	Ivan Rodriguez	.50
87	Juan Gonzalez	.30
88	Rafael Palmeiro	.50
89	Carlos Delgado	.25
90	David Wells	.05
91	Troy Glaus	1.00
92	Adrian Beltre	.50
93	Matt Anderson	.25
94	Eric Chavez	.40
95	Jeff Weaver RC	.50
96	Warren Morris	.25
97	George Lombard	.25
98	Mike Kinkade	.25
99	Kyle Farnsworth RC	.25
100	J.D. Drew	.50
101	Joe McEwing RC	.50
102	Carlos Guillen	.25
103	Kelly Dransfeldt RC	.25
104	Eric Munson RC	.50
105	Armando Rios	.25
106	Ramon Martinez	.25
107	Orlando Hernandez	.45
108	Jeremy Giambi	.25
109	Pat Burrell RC	2.50
110	Shea Hillenbrand RC	1.00
111	Billy Koch	.25
112	Roy Halladay	.35
113	Ruben Mateo	.25
114	Bruce Chen	.25
115	Angel Pena	.25
116	Michael Barrett	.25
117	Kevin Witt	.25
118	Damon Minor	.25
119	Ryan Minor	.25
120	A.J. Pierzynski	.25
121	A.J. Burnett RC	.50
122	Christian Guzman	.25
123	Joe Lawrence	.25
124	Derrick Gibson	.25
125	Carlos Febles	.25

126	Chris Haas	.25
127	Cesar King	.25
128	Calvin Pickering	.25
129	Mitch Meluskey	.25
130	Carlos Beltran	1.00
131	Ron Belliard	.25
132	Jerry Hairston Jr.	.25
133	Fernando Seguignol	.25
134	Kris Benson	.25
135	Chad Hutchinson RC	.25
136	Ken Griffey Jr.	1.50
137	Mark McGwire	2.00
138	Sammy Sosa	1.25
139	Albert Belle	.35
140	Mo Vaughn	.35
141	Alex Rodriguez	2.00
142	Manny Ramirez	.75
143	J.D. Drew	.50
144	Juan Gonzalez	.45
145	Vladimir Guerrero	.75
146	Fernando Tatis	.35
147	Mike Piazza	2.00
148	Barry Bonds	2.50
149	Ivan Rodriguez	.60
150	Jeff Bagwell	.75
151	Raul Mondesi	.35
152	Nomar Garciaparra	1.25
153	Jose Canseco	.50
154	Greg Vaughn	.35
155	Scott Rolen	.50
156	Vinny Castilla	.35
157	Troy Glaus	.65
158	Craig Biggio	.35
159	Tino Martinez	.35
160	Jim Thome	.60
161	Frank Thomas	1.00
162	Tony Clark	.35
163	Ben Grieve	.35
164	Matt Williams	.35
165	Derek Jeter	2.50
166	Ken Griffey Jr.	2.00
167	Tony Gwynn	1.50
168	Mike Piazza	2.00
169	Mark McGwire	2.50
170	Sammy Sosa	1.50
171	Juan Gonzalez	.60
172	Mo Vaughn	.50
173	Derek Jeter	3.00
174	Bernie Williams	.50
175	Ivan Rodriguez	.75
176	Barry Bonds	3.00
177	Scott Rolen	.75
178	Larry Walker	.50
179	Chipper Jones	1.50
180	Alex Rodriguez	2.50

FX Gold

		NM/M
Common Player:		1.00
Gold (1-90):		10X
Gold (91-135):		1.5X
Gold (136-165):		3X
Gold (166-180):		4X

(See 1999 Upper Deck Encore for checklist and base card values.)

Batting Practice Caps

	NM/M
Complete Set (15):	85.00
Common Player:	4.00
Inserted 1:750	

CB	Carlos Beltran	8.00
BB	Barry Bonds	30.00
VC	Vinny Castilla	4.00
EC	Eric Chavez	6.00
TC	Tony Clark	4.00
JD	J.D. Drew	6.00
VG	Vladimir Guerrero	8.00
TG	Tony Gwynn	15.00
TH	Todd Helton	8.00
GK	Gabe Kapler	4.00
JK	Jason Kendall	4.00
DP	Dean Palmer	4.00
BH	Frank Thomas	8.00
GV	Greg Vaughn	4.00
TW	Todd Walker	4.00

Driving Forces

		NM/M
Complete Set (15):		30.00
Common Player:		1.00
Inserted 1:23		
Gold (10 Sets):		30X
D1	Ken Griffey Jr.	3.00
D2	Mark McGwire	4.00
D3	Sammy Sosa	2.50
D4	Albert Belle	1.00
D5	Alex Rodriguez	4.00
D6	Mo Vaughn	1.00
D7	Juan Gonzalez	1.00
D8	Jeff Bagwell	2.00
D9	Mike Piazza	3.00
D10	Frank Thomas	2.00
D11	Barry Bonds	5.00
D12	Vladimir Guerrero	2.00
D13	Chipper Jones	2.50
D14	Tony Gwynn	2.50
D15	J.D. Drew	1.50

McGwired!

		NM/M
Complete Set (10):		12.50
Common Card:		1.50
Inserted 1:23		
Parallel:		2X
Production 500 Sets		
1	Mark McGwire, Carl Pavano	1.50
2	Mark McGwire, Michael Morgan	1.50
3	Mark McGwire, Steve Trachsel	1.50
4	Mark McGwire	2.50
5	Mark McGwire	2.50
6	Mark McGwire, Scott Elarton	1.50
7	Mark McGwire, Jim Parque	1.50
8	Mark McGwire	2.50
9	Mark McGwire, Rafael Roque	1.50
10	Mark McGwire, Jaret Wright	1.50

Pure Excitement

		NM/M
Complete Set (30):		35.00
Common Player:		.50
Inserted 1:7		
1	Mo Vaughn	.50
2	Darin Erstad	.75
3	Travis Lee	.65
4	Chipper Jones	1.50
5	Greg Maddux	1.50
6	Gabe Kapler	.50
7	Cal Ripken Jr.	4.00
8	Nomar Garciaparra	1.50
9	Kerry Wood	.75
10	Frank Thomas	1.00
11	Manny Ramirez	1.00
12	Larry Walker	.50
13	Tony Clark	.50
14	Jeff Bagwell	1.00
15	Craig Biggio	.50
16	Vladimir Guerrero	1.00
17	Mike Piazza	2.00
18	Bernie Williams	.60
19	Derek Jeter	4.00
20	Ben Grieve	.60
21	Eric Chavez	.60
22	Scott Rolen	.75
23	Mark McGwire	3.00
24	Tony Gwynn	1.50
25	Barry Bonds	4.00
26	Ken Griffey Jr.	2.00
27	Alex Rodriguez	3.00
28	J.D. Drew	.75
29	Juan Gonzalez	.60
30	Roger Clemens	1.75

Rookie Encore

		NM/M
Complete Set (10):		17.50
Common Player:		1.00
Inserted 1:23		
FX Gold:		2X
Production 500 Sets		
1	J.D. Drew	2.00
2	Eric Chavez	1.00
3	Gabe Kapler	1.00
4	Bruce Chen	1.00
5	Carlos Beltran	3.00
6	Troy Glaus	5.00
7	Roy Halladay	1.00
8	Adrian Beltre	2.00
9	Michael Barrett	1.00
10	Pat Burrell	5.00

Upper Realm

		NM/M
Complete Set (15):		13.00
Common Player:		.30
Inserted 1:11		
1	Ken Griffey Jr.	1.25

2	Mark McGwire	1.50
3	Sammy Sosa	.75
4	Tony Gwynn	.75
5	Alex Rodriguez	1.50
6	Juan Gonzalez	.40
7	J.D. Drew	.50
8	Roger Clemens	.85
9	Greg Maddux	.75
10	Randy Johnson	.60
11	Mo Vaughn	.30
12	Derek Jeter	2.00
13	Vladimir Guerrero	.60
14	Cal Ripken Jr.	2.00
15	Nomar Garciaparra	.75

UD Authentics

		NM/M
Complete Set (6):		130.00
Common Player:		5.00
Inserted 1:288		
MB	Michael Barrett	4.00
PB	Pat Burrell	10.00
JD	J.D. Drew	12.00
NG	Nomar Garciaparra	70.00
TG	Troy Glaus	12.00
JR	Ken Griffey Jr.	90.00

2K Countdown

		NM/M
Complete Set (10):		16.00
Common Player:		.75
Inserted 1:11		
1	Ken Griffey Jr.	2.00
2	Derek Jeter	3.00
3	Mike Piazza	2.00
4	J.D. Drew	.75
5	Vladimir Guerrero	1.00
6	Chipper Jones	1.50
7	Alex Rodriguez	2.50
8	Nomar Garciaparra	1.50
9	Mark McGwire	2.50
10	Sammy Sosa	1.50

1999 Upper Deck HoloGrFX

	NM/M
Complete Set (60):	12.00
Common Player:	.10

AUsome:		1.5X
Inserted 1:8		
Pack (3):		1.00
Wax Box (36):		20.00
1	Mo Vaughn	.10
2	Troy Glaus	.60
3	Tim Salmon	.10
4	Randy Johnson	.65
5	Travis Lee	.25
6	Chipper Jones	.75
7	Greg Maddux	.75
8	Andruw Jones	.65
9	Tom Glavine	.25
10	Cal Ripken Jr.	1.50
11	Albert Belle	.10
12	Nomar Garciaparra	.75
13	Pedro J. Martinez	.65
14	Sammy Sosa	.75
15	Frank Thomas	.65
16	Greg Vaughn	.10
17	Kenny Lofton	.10
18	Jim Thome	.50
19	Manny Ramirez	.65
20	Todd Helton	.60
21	Larry Walker	.10
22	Tony Clark	.10
23	Juan Encarnacion	.10
24	Mark Kotsay	.10
25	Jeff Bagwell	.65
26	Craig Biggio	.10
27	Ken Caminiti	.10
28	Carlos Beltran	.50
29	Jeremy Giambi	.10
30	Raul Mondesi	.10
31	Kevin Brown	.10
32	Jeromy Burnitz	.10
33	Corey Koskie	.10
34	Todd Walker	.10
35	Vladimir Guerrero	.65
36	Mike Piazza	1.00
37	Robin Ventura	.10
38	Derek Jeter	1.50
39	Roger Clemens	.85
40	Bernie Williams	.10
41	Orlando Hernandez	.10
42	Ben Grieve	.10
43	Eric Chavez	.15
44	Scott Rolen	.45
45	Pat Burrell RC	1.50
46	Warren Morris	.10
47	Jason Kendall	.10
48	Mark McGwire	1.25
49	J.D. Drew	.50
50	Tony Gwynn	.75
51	Trevor Hoffman	.10
52	Barry Bonds	1.50
53	Ken Griffey Jr.	1.00
54	Alex Rodriguez	1.25
55	Jose Canseco	.35
56	Juan Gonzalez	.30
57	Ivan Rodriguez	.60
58	Rafael Palmeiro	.60
59	David Wells	.10
60	Carlos Delgado	.25

Future Fame

	NM/M
Complete Set (6):	15.00
Common Player:	2.50
Inserted 1:34	
Gold:	2X

1	Tony Gwynn	2.50
2	Cal Ripken Jr.	5.00
3	Mark McGwire	4.00
4	Ken Griffey Jr.	3.50
5	Greg Maddux	2.50
6	Roger Clemens	3.00

Launchers

		NM/M
Complete Set (15):		20.00
Common Player:		.50
Inserted 1:3		
Gold:		2X
Inserted 1:105		
1	Mark McGwire	3.00
2	Ken Griffey Jr.	2.50
3	Sammy Sosa	2.00
4	J.D. Drew	.75
5	Mo Vaughn	.50
6	Juan Gonzalez	.50
7	Mike Piazza	2.50
8	Alex Rodriguez	3.00
9	Chipper Jones	2.00
10	Nomar Garciaparra	2.00
11	Vladimir Guerrero	1.00
12	Albert Belle	.50
13	Barry Bonds	4.00
14	Frank Thomas	1.00
15	Jeff Bagwell	1.00

StarView

		NM/M
Complete Set (9):		25.00
Common Player:		2.50
Inserted 1:17		
Gold:		2X
Inserted 1:210		
1	Mark McGwire	5.00
2	Ken Griffey Jr.	4.00
3	Sammy Sosa	2.50
4	Nomar Garciaparra	2.50
5	Roger Clemens	3.00
6	Greg Maddux	2.50
7	Mike Piazza	4.00
8	Alex Rodriguez	5.00
9	Chipper Jones	2.50

UD Authentics

	NM/M
Common Player:	4.00

Inserted 1:431		
CB	Carlos Beltran	25.00
BC	Bruce Chen	4.00
JD	J.D. Drew	12.00
AG	Alex Gonzalez	4.00
JR	Ken Griffey Jr.	80.00
CJ	Chipper Jones	50.00
GK	Gabe Kapler	6.00
MK	Mike Kinkade	4.00
CK	Corey Koskie	7.50
GL	George Lombard	4.00
RM	Ryan Minor	4.00
SM	Shane Monahan	4.00

500 Club Piece of History

	NM/M
Eddie Mathews/350	150.00
Eddie Mathews/ Auto./41	550.00
Willie McCovey/350	120.00
Willie McCovey/ Auto./44	650.00

1999 Upper Deck MVP

		NM/M
Complete Set (220):		10.00
Common Player:		.05
Silver Script:		1X
Inserted 1:2		
Gold Script:		10X
Production 100 Sets		
Super Script:		30X
Production 25 Sets		
Pack (10):		1.00
Wax Box (36):		20.00
1	Mo Vaughn	.05
2	Tim Belcher	.05
3	Jack McDowell	.05
4	Troy Glaus	.60
5	Darin Erstad	.40
6	Tim Salmon	.15
7	Jim Edmonds	.05
8	Randy Johnson	.60
9	Steve Finley	.05
10	Travis Lee	.15
11	Matt Williams	.05
12	Todd Stottlemyre	.05
13	Jay Bell	.05
14	David Dellucci	.05
15	Chipper Jones	.75
16	Andruw Jones	.60
17	Greg Maddux	.75
18	Tom Glavine	.25
19	Javy Lopez	.05
20	Brian Jordan	.05
21	George Lombard	.05
22	John Smoltz	.05
23	Cal Ripken Jr.	1.50
24	Charles Johnson	.05
25	Albert Belle	.15
26	Brady Anderson	.05
27	Mike Mussina	.35
28	Calvin Pickering	.05
29	Ryan Minor	.05
30	Jerry Hairston Jr.	.05
31	Nomar Garciaparra	1.00
32	Pedro Martinez	.60
33	Jason Varitek	.05

34	Troy O'Leary	.05
35	Donnie Sadler	.05
36	Mark Portugal	.05
37	John Valentin	.05
38	Kerry Wood	.35
39	Sammy Sosa	1.00
40	Mark Grace	.10
41	Henry Rodriguez	.05
42	Rod Beck	.05
43	Benito Santiago	.05
44	Kevin Tapani	.05
45	Frank Thomas	.60
46	Mike Caruso	.05
47	Magglio Ordonez	.40
48	Paul Konerko	.05
49	Ray Durham	.05
50	Jim Parque	.05
51	Carlos Lee	.05
52	Denny Neagle	.05
53	Pete Harnisch	.05
54	Michael Tucker	.05
55	Sean Casey	.15
56	Eddie Taubensee	.05
57	Barry Larkin	.05
58	Pokey Reese	.05
59	Sandy Alomar	.05
60	Roberto Alomar	.25
61	Bartolo Colon	.05
62	Kenny Lofton	.05
63	Omar Vizquel	.05
64	Travis Fryman	.05
65	Jim Thome	.05
66	Manny Ramirez	.60
67	Jaret Wright	.05
68	Darryl Kile	.05
69	Kirt Manwaring	.05
70	Vinny Castilla	.05
71	Todd Helton	.60
72	Dante Bichette	.05
73	Larry Walker	.05
74	Derrick Gibson	.05
75	Gabe Kapler	.05
76	Dean Palmer	.05
77	Matt Anderson	.05
78	Bobby Higginson	.05
79	Damion Easley	.05
80	Tony Clark	.05
81	Juan Encarnacion	.05
82	Livan Hernandez	.05
83	Alex Gonzalez	.05
84	Preston Wilson	.05
85	Derrek Lee	.05
86	Mark Kotsay	.05
87	Todd Dunwoody	.05
88	Cliff Floyd	.05
89	Ken Caminiti	.05
90	Jeff Bagwell	.60
91	Moises Alou	.05
92	Craig Biggio	.05
93	Billy Wagner	.05
94	Richard Hidalgo	.05
95	Derek Bell	.05
96	Hipolito Pichardo	.05
97	Jeff King	.05
98	Carlos Beltran	.40
99	Jeremy Giambi	.05
100	Larry Sutton	.05
101	Johnny Damon	.20
102	Dee Brown	.05
103	Kevin Brown	.10
104	Chan Ho Park	.05
105	Raul Mondesi	.05
106	Eric Karros	.05
107	Adrian Beltre	.15
108	Devon White	.05
109	Gary Sheffield	.35
110	Sean Berry	.05
111	Alex Ochoa	.05
112	Marquis Grissom	.05
113	Fernando Vina	.05
114	Jeff Cirillo	.05
115	Geoff Jenkins	.05
116	Jeromy Burnitz	.05
117	Brad Radke	.05
118	Eric Milton	.05
119	A.J. Pierzynski	.05
120	Todd Walker	.05
121	David Ortiz	.05
122	Corey Koskie	.05
123	Vladimir Guerrero	.60
124	Rondell White	.05
125	Brad Fullmer	.05
126	Ugueth Urbina	.05
127	Dustin Hermanson	.05
128	Michael Barrett	.05
129	Fernando Seguignol	.05
130	Mike Piazza	1.00
131	Rickey Henderson	.60
132	Rey Ordonez	.05
133	John Olerud	.05
134	Robin Ventura	.05
135	Hideo Nomo	.60

136	Mike Kinkade	.05
137	Al Leiter	.05
138	Brian McRae	.05
139	Derek Jeter	1.50
140	Bernie Williams	.15
141	Paul O'Neill	.05
142	Scott Brosius	.05
143	Tino Martinez	.05
144	Roger Clemens	.85
145	Orlando Hernandez	.10
146	Mariano Rivera	.10
147	Ricky Ledee	.05
148	A.J. Hinch	.05
149	Ben Grieve	.10
150	Eric Chavez	.15
151	Miguel Tejada	.15
152	Matt Stairs	.05
153	Ryan Christenson	.05
154	Jason Giambi	.35
155	Curt Schilling	.25
156	Scott Rolen	.45
157	Pat Burrell RC	1.50
158	Doug Glanville	.05
159	Bobby Abreu	.05
160	Rico Brogna	.05
161	Ron Gant	.05
162	Jason Kendall	.05
163	Aramis Ramirez	.05
164	Jose Guillen	.05
165	Emil Brown	.05
166	Pat Meares	.05
167	Kevin Young	.05
168	Brian Giles	.05
169	Mark McGwire	1.25
170	J.D. Drew	.40
171	Edgar Renteria	.05
172	Fernando Tatis	.05
173	Matt Morris	.05
174	Eli Marrero	.05
175	Ray Lankford	.05
176	Tony Gwynn	.75
177	Sterling Hitchcock	.05
178	Ruben Rivera	.05
179	Wally Joyner	.05
180	Trevor Hoffman	.05
181	Jim Leyritz	.05
182	Carlos Hernandez	.05
183	Barry Bonds	1.50
184	Ellis Burks	.05
185	F.P. Santangelo	.05
186	J.T. Snow	.05
187	Ramon Martinez	.05
188	Jeff Kent	.05
189	Robb Nen	.05
190	Ken Griffey Jr.	1.00
191	Alex Rodriguez	1.25
192	Shane Monahan	.05
193	Carlos Guillen	.05
194	Edgar Martinez	.05
195	David Segui	.05
196	Jose Mesa	.05
197	Jose Canseco	.35
198	Rolando Arrojo	.05
199	Wade Boggs	.75
200	Fred McGriff	.05
201	Quinton McCracken	.05
202	Bobby Smith	.05
203	Bubba Trammell	.05
204	Juan Gonzalez	.60
205	Ivan Rodriguez	.45
206	Rafael Palmeiro	.45
207	Royce Clayton	.05
208	Rick Helling	.05
209	Todd Zeile	.05
210	Rusty Greer	.05
211	David Wells	.05
212	Roy Halladay	.05
213	Carlos Delgado	.25
214	Darrin Fletcher	.05
215	Shawn Green	.15
216	Kevin Witt	.05
217	Jose Cruz Jr.	.05
218	Ken Griffey Jr. Checklist	.45
219	Sammy Sosa Checklist	.45
220	Mark McGwire Checklist	.50

Scripts/Super Scripts

Silver Script:	1X
Gold Script:	10X

Super Script: 30X
(See 1999 UD MVP for checklist and base card values.)

All-Star Game

		NM/M
Complete Set (30):		12.50
Common Player:		.25
1	Mo Vaughn	.25
2	Randy Johnson	.60
3	Chipper Jones	.75
4	Greg Maddux	.75
5	Cal Ripken Jr.	2.00
6	Albert Belle	.35
7	Nomar Garciaparra	1.00
8	Pedro Martinez	.60
9	Sammy Sosa	1.00
10	Frank Thomas	.60
11	Sean Casey	.35
12	Roberto Alomar	.30
13	Manny Ramirez	.60
14	Larry Walker	.25
15	Jeff Bagwell	.60
16	Craig Biggio	.25
17	Raul Mondesi	.25
18	Vladimir Guerrero	.60
19	Mike Piazza	1.00
20	Derek Jeter	2.00
21	Roger Clemens	.85
22	Scott Rolen	.40
23	Mark McGwire	1.50
24	Tony Gwynn	.75
25	Barry Bonds	2.00
26	Ken Griffey Jr.	1.00
27	Alex Rodriguez	1.50
28	Jose Canseco	.40
29	Juan Gonzalez	.60
30	Ivan Rodriguez	.50

Dynamics

		NM/M
Complete Set (15):		17.50
Common Player:		.60
Inserted 1:28		
1	Ken Griffey Jr.	2.00
2	Alex Rodriguez	2.50
3	Nomar Garciaparra	2.00
4	Mike Piazza	2.00
5	Mark McGwire	2.25
6	Sammy Sosa	2.00
7	Chipper Jones	1.50
8	Mo Vaughn	.60
9	Tony Gwynn	1.50
10	Vladimir Guerrero	1.25
11	Derek Jeter	3.00
12	Jeff Bagwell	1.25
13	Cal Ripken Jr.	3.00
14	Juan Gonzalez	1.25
15	J.D. Drew	.90

Game Used Souvenirs

		NM/M
Complete Set (9):		75.00
Common Player:		5.00
Inserted 1:144		
JB	Jeff Bagwell	8.00
BB	Barry Bonds	20.00
JD	J.D. Drew	8.00
KGj	Ken Griffey Jr.	15.00
CJ	Chipper Jones	10.00
MP	Mike Piazza	15.00
CR	Cal Ripken Jr.	20.00
SR	Scott Rolen	8.00
MV	Mo Vaughn	5.00

Power Surge

		NM/M
Complete Set (15):		12.50
Common Player:		.50
Inserted 1:9		
1	Mark McGwire	1.50
2	Sammy Sosa	1.25
3	Ken Griffey Jr.	1.25
4	Alex Rodriguez	1.50
5	Juan Gonzalez	.75
6	Nomar Garciaparra	1.25
7	Vladimir Guerrero	.75
8	Chipper Jones	1.00
9	Albert Belle	.50
10	Frank Thomas	.75
11	Mike Piazza	1.25
12	Jeff Bagwell	.75
13	Manny Ramirez	.75
14	Mo Vaughn	.50
15	Barry Bonds	2.00

ProSign

		NM/M
Common Autograph:		5.00
Inserted 1:216 R		
MA	Matt Anderson	5.00
CB	Carlos Beltran	15.00
RB	Russ Branyan	5.00
EC	Eric Chavez	10.00
BC	Bruce Chen	5.00
BF	Brad Fuller	5.00
NG	Nomar Garciaparra	80.00
JG	Jeremy Giambi	5.00
DG	Derrick Gibson	5.00
CG	Chris Gomez	5.00
AG	Alex Gonzalez	5.00
BG	Ben Grieve	5.00
JR.	Ken Griffey Jr.	80.00
RH	Richard Hidalgo	5.00
SH	Shea Hillenbrand	10.00

CJ	Chipper Jones/SP	50.00
GK	Gabe Kapler	6.00
SK	Scott Karl	5.00
CK	Corey Koskie	7.50
RL	Ricky Ledee	5.00
ML	Mike Lincoln	5.00
GL	George Lombard	5.00
MLo	Mike Lowell	7.50
RM	Ryan Minor	5.00
SM	Shane Monahan	5.00
AN	Abraham Nunez	5.00
JP	Jim Parque	5.00
CP	Calvin Pickering	5.00
JRa	Jason Rakers	5.00
RR	Ruben Rivera	5.00
IR	Ivan Rodriguez/SP	50.00
KW	Kevin Witt	5.00

Scout's Choice

		NM/M
Complete Set (15):		5.00
Common Player:		.25
Inserted 1:9		
1	J.D. Drew	.65
2	Ben Grieve	.35
3	Troy Glaus	1.50
4	Gabe Kapler	.25
5	Carlos Beltran	.45
6	Aramis Ramirez	.25
7	Pat Burrell	1.00
8	Kerry Wood	.65
9	Ryan Minor	.25
10	Todd Helton	1.00
11	Eric Chavez	.35
12	Russ Branyon	.35
13	Travis Lee	.35
14	Ruben Mateo	.25
15	Roy Halladay	.35

Signed Game Used Souvenirs

		NM/M
KGj	Ken Griffey Jr.	300.00
CJ	Chipper Jones	200.00

Super Tools

		NM/M
Complete Set (15):		25.00
Common Player:		.50
Inserted 1:14		
1	Ken Griffey Jr.	2.50
2	Alex Rodriguez	3.00
3	Sammy Sosa	2.00
4	Derek Jeter	4.00
5	Vladimir Guerrero	1.50
6	Ben Grieve	.50
7	Mike Piazza	2.50
8	Kenny Lofton	.50
9	Barry Bonds	4.00

10	Darin Erstad	1.00
11	Nomar Garciaparra	2.00
12	Cal Ripken Jr.	4.00
13	J.D. Drew	1.00
14	Larry Walker	.50
15	Chipper Jones	2.00

Swing Time

		NM/M
Complete Set (12):		5.00
Common Player:		.35
Inserted 1:6		
1	Ken Griffey Jr.	.75
2	Mark McGwire	1.00
3	Sammy Sosa	.60
4	Tony Gwynn	.60
5	Alex Rodriguez	1.00
6	Nomar Garciaparra	.60
7	Barry Bonds	1.50
8	Frank Thomas	.45
9	Chipper Jones	.60
10	Ivan Rodriguez	.35
11	Mike Piazza	.75
12	Derek Jeter	1.50

500 Club Piece of History

	NM/M
Mike Schmidt/350	160.00
Mike Schmidt/ Auto./20	1,250

1999 Upper Deck Ovation

		NM/M
Complete Set (90):		20.00
Common Player:		.05
Common World Premiere:		.15
Inserted 1:3.5		
Common Superstar Spotlight:		.60
Inserted 1:6		
Pack (5):		1.00
Box (20):		30.00
1	Ken Griffey Jr.	1.50
2	Rondell White	.05
3	Tony Clark	.05
4	Barry Bonds	2.50
5	Larry Walker	.05

6	Greg Vaughn	.05
7	Mark Grace	.05
8	John Olerud	.05
9	Matt Williams	.05
10	Craig Biggio	.05
11	Quinton McCracken	.05
12	Kerry Wood	.35
13	Derek Jeter	2.50
14	Frank Thomas	.75
15	Tino Martinez	.05
16	Albert Belle	.05
17	Ben Grieve	.05
18	Cal Ripken Jr.	2.50
19	Johnny Damon	.30
20	Jose Cruz Jr.	.05
21	Barry Larkin	.05
22	Jason Giambi	.45
23	Sean Casey	.10
24	Scott Rolen	.60
25	Jim Thome	.45
26	Curt Schilling	.25
27	Moises Alou	.05
28	Alex Rodriguez	2.00
29	Mark Kotsay	.05
30	Darin Erstad	.25
31	Mike Mussina	.30
32	Todd Walker	.05
33	Nomar Garciaparra	1.00
34	Vladimir Guerrero	.75
35	Jeff Bagwell	.75
36	Mark McGwire	2.00
37	Travis Lee	.15
38	Dean Palmer	.05
39	Fred McGriff	.05
40	Sammy Sosa	1.00
41	Mike Piazza	1.50
42	Andres Galarraga	.05
43	Pedro Martinez	.75
44	Juan Gonzalez	.40
45	Greg Maddux	1.00
46	Jeromy Burnitz	.05
47	Roger Clemens	1.25
48	Vinny Castilla	.05
49	Kevin Brown	.05
50	Mo Vaughn	.05
51	Raul Mondesi	.05
52	Randy Johnson	.75
53	Ray Lankford	.05
54	Jaret Wright	.05
55	Tony Gwynn	1.00
56	Chipper Jones	1.00
57	Gary Sheffield	.40
58	Ivan Rodriguez	.65
59	Kenny Lofton	.05
60	Jason Kendall	.05
61	J.D. Drew	.75
62	Gabe Kapler	.15
63	Adrian Beltre	.40
64	Carlos Beltran	.50
65	Eric Chavez	.35
66	Mike Lowell	.25
67	Troy Glaus	1.00
68	George Lombard	.15
69	Alex Gonzalez	.15
70	Mike Kinkade	.15
71	Jeremy Giambi	.15
72	Bruce Chen	.15
73	Preston Wilson	.25
74	Kevin Witt	.15
75	Carlos Guillen	.15
76	Ryan Minor	.15
77	Corey Koskie	.15
78	Robert Fick	.15
79	Michael Barrett	.15
80	Calvin Pickering	.15
81	Ken Griffey Jr.	1.00
82	Mark McGwire	1.50
83	Cal Ripken Jr.	2.00
84	Derek Jeter	2.00
85	Chipper Jones	.75
86	Nomar Garciaparra (Garciaparra)	.75
87	Sammy Sosa	.75
88	Juan Gonzalez	.30

89	Mike Piazza	1.00
90	Alex Rodriguez	1.50

Standing Ovation

Stars (1-60):	3X
World Premiere (61-80):	1.5X
Superstar Spotlight (81-90):	2X

Production 500 Sets
(See 1999 Upper Deck Ovation for checklist and base card values.)

Curtain Calls

		NM/M
Complete Set (20):		20.00
Common Player:		.25
Inserted 1:8		
R1	Mark McGwire	2.00
R2	Sammy Sosa	1.00
R3	Ken Griffey Jr.	1.50
R4	Alex Rodriguez	2.00
R5	Roger Clemens	1.25
R6	Cal Ripken Jr.	2.50
R7	Barry Bonds	2.50
R8	Kerry Wood	.40
R9	Nomar Garciaparra	1.00
R10	Derek Jeter	2.50
R11	Juan Gonzalez	.50
R12	Greg Maddux	1.00
R13	Pedro Martinez	1.00
R14	David Wells	.25
R15	Moises Alou	.25
R16	Tony Gwynn	1.00
R17	Albert Belle	.25
R18	Mike Piazza	1.50
R19	Ivan Rodriguez	.65
R20	Randy Johnson	.75

Major Production

	NM/M
Complete Set (20):	45.00

Common Player:	.75

Inserted 1:45

S1	Mike Piazza	4.00
S2	Mark McGwire	5.00
S3	Chipper Jones	3.00
S4	Cal Ripken Jr.	6.00
S5	Ken Griffey Jr.	4.00
S6	Barry Bonds	6.00
S7	Tony Gwynn	3.00
S8	Randy Johnson	2.50
S9	Ivan Rodriguez	2.00
S10	Frank Thomas	2.50
S11	Alex Rodriguez	5.00
S12	Albert Belle	.75
S13	Juan Gonzalez	1.25
S14	Greg Maddux	3.00
S15	Jeff Bagwell	2.50
S16	Derek Jeter	6.00
S17	Matt Williams	.75
S18	Kenny Lofton	.75
S19	Sammy Sosa	3.00
S20	Roger Clemens	3.50

Piece of History

	NM/M
Common Player:	5.00

Inserted 1:247

BB	Barry Bonds	25.00
CJ	Chipper Jones	15.00
BW	Bernie Williams	5.00
KGj	Ken Griffey Jr.	20.00
NG	Nomar Garciaparra	15.00
JG	Juan Gonzalez	5.00
DJ	Derek Jeter	25.00
SS	Sammy Sosa	15.00
TG	Tony Gwynn	15.00
AR	Alex Rodriguez	20.00
CR	Cal Ripken Jr.	25.00
BG	Ben Grieve	5.00
VG	Vladimir Guerrero	10.00
MP	Mike Piazza	20.00
BGAU	Ben Grieve/ Auto./25	30.00
KWAU	Kerry Wood/ Auto./25	50.00

ReMarkable

	NM/M
Complete Set (15):	20.00
Common #1-5:	1.50

Inserted 1:9

Common #6-10:	3.00

Inserted 1:25

Common # 11-15	5.00

Inserted 1:99

500 Club Piece of History

	NM/M
MIC-P	Mickey Mantle/ 350	600.00
	Mickey Mantle/ Bat Auto.	8,000

1999 Upper Deck PowerDeck

	NM/M
Complete Set (25):	20.00

Common Player:	.50
Pack (3):	1.50
Wax Box (24):	20.00
1	Ken Griffey Jr.	2.00
2	Mark McGwire	2.50
3	Cal Ripken Jr.	3.00
4	Sammy Sosa	1.50
5	Derek Jeter	3.00
6	Mike Piazza	2.00
7	Nomar Garciaparra	1.50
8	Greg Maddux	1.50
9	Tony Gwynn	1.50
10	Roger Clemens	1.75
11	Scott Rolen	1.00
12	Alex Rodriguez	2.50
13	Manny Ramirez	1.25
14	Chipper Jones	1.50
15	Juan Gonzalez	.65
16	Ivan Rodriguez	1.00
17	Frank Thomas	1.25
18	Mo Vaughn	.50
19	Barry Bonds	3.00
20	Vladimir Guerrero	1.25
21	Jose Canseco	.65
22	Jeff Bagwell	1.25
23	Pedro Martinez	1.25
24	Gabe Kapler	.50
25	J.D. Drew	.75
---	Checklist	.10

Auxiliary Power

	NM/M
Complete Set (25):	6.00
Common Player:	.10
1	Ken Griffey Jr.	.50
2	Mark McGwire	.60
3	Cal Ripken Jr.	.75
4	Sammy Sosa	.40
5	Derek Jeter	.75
6	Mike Piazza	.50
7	Nomar Garciaparra	.40
8	Greg Maddux	.40
9	Tony Gwynn	.40
10	Roger Clemens	.45
11	Scott Rolen	.25
12	Alex Rodriguez	.60
13	Manny Ramirez	.30
14	Chipper Jones	.40
15	Juan Gonzalez	.15
16	Ivan Rodriguez	.25
17	Frank Thomas	.30
18	Mo Vaughn	.10
19	Barry Bonds	.75
20	Vladimir Guerrero	.30
21	Jose Canseco	.20
22	Jeff Bagwell	.30
23	Pedro Martinez	.30
24	Gabe Kapler	.10
25	J.D. Drew	.25

A Season to Remember

	NM/M
Mark McGwire	3.00

Most Valuable Performances

	NM/M
Complete Set (7):	75.00
Common Player:	6.00

Inserted 1:287

1	Sammy Sosa	10.00
2	Barry Bonds	20.00
3	Cal Ripken Jr.	20.00
4	Juan Gonzalez	6.00
5	Ken Griffey Jr.	12.50
6	Roger Clemens	10.00
7	Mark McGwire, Sammy Sosa	12.50

MVP Auxiliary

	NM/M
Complete Set (7):	60.00
Common Player:	4.00

Inserted 1:287

1	Sammy Sosa	7.50
2	Barry Bonds	15.00
3	Cal Ripken Jr.	15.00
4	Juan Gonzalez	4.00
5	Ken Griffey Jr.	10.00
6	Roger Clemens	7.50
7	Mark McGwire, Sammy Sosa	12.50

Powerful Moments

	NM/M
Complete Set (6):	10.00
Common Player:	1.00

Inserted 1:7

1	Mark McGwire	2.00
2	Sammy Sosa	1.00
3	Cal Ripken Jr.	3.00
4	Ken Griffey Jr.	1.50
5	Derek Jeter	3.00
6	Alex Rodriguez	2.00

Powerful Moments Auxiliary

	NM/M
Complete Set (6):	10.00
Common Player:	1.00

Inserted 1:7

	Gold (one each):	Values Undetermined
1	Mark McGwire	2.00
2	Sammy Sosa	1.00
3	Cal Ripken Jr.	3.00
4	Ken Griffey Jr.	1.50
5	Derek Jeter	3.00
6	Alex Rodriguez	2.00

Time Capsule

	NM/M
Complete Set (6):	12.50
Common Player:	1.00

Inserted 1:23

1	Ken Griffey Jr.	2.50
2	Mike Piazza	2.50
3	Mark McGwire	3.00
4	Derek Jeter	4.00
5	Jose Canseco	1.00
6	Nomar Garciaparra	2.00

Time Capsule- Auxiliary Power

	NM/M
Complete Set (6):	15.00
Common Player:	1.00

Inserted 1:23

	Gold (One of each.):	Values Undetermined
1	Ken Griffey Jr.	2.50
2	Mike Piazza	2.50
3	Mark McGwire	3.00
4	Derek Jeter	4.00
5	Jose Canseco	1.00
6	Nomar Garciaparra	2.00

1999 Upper Deck Ultimate Victory

	NM/M
Complete Set (180):	125.00
Common Player:	.10
Common 99 Rookie (121-150):	.50
Common McGwire Magic (151-180):	1.00
Victory (1-120):	3.5X
Victory SP (121-180):	2X
Inserted 1:12	
Ultimate (1-120):	12X
Ultimate SP (121-180):	5X
Production 100 Sets	
Pack (5):	4.50
Wax Box (24):	75.00
1	Troy Glaus	.65
2	Tim Salmon	.10
3	Mo Vaughn	.10
4	Garret Anderson	.10
5	Darin Erstad	.30
6	Randy Johnson	.75
7	Matt Williams	.10
8	Travis Lee	.25
9	Jay Bell	.10
10	Steve Finley	.10
11	Luis Gonzalez	.10
12	Greg Maddux	1.00
13	Chipper Jones	1.00
14	Javy Lopez	.10
15	Tom Glavine	.35
16	John Smoltz	.10
17	Cal Ripken Jr.	3.00
18	Charles Johnson	.10
19	Albert Belle	.10
20	Mike Mussina	.40
21	Pedro Martinez	.75
22	Nomar Garciaparra	1.00
23	Jose Offerman	.10
24	Sammy Sosa	1.00
25	Mark Grace	.10
26	Kerry Wood	.35

27	Frank Thomas	.75
28	Ray Durham	.10
29	Paul Konerko	.20
30	Pete Harnisch	.10
31	Greg Vaughn	.10
32	Sean Casey	.20
33	Manny Ramirez	.75
34	Jim Thome	.65
35	Sandy Alomar	.10
36	Roberto Alomar	.30
37	Travis Fryman	.10
38	Kenny Lofton	.10
39	Omar Vizquel	.10
40	Larry Walker	.65
41	Todd Helton	.65
42	Vinny Castilla	.10
43	Tony Clark	.10
44	Juan Encarnacion	.10
45	Dean Palmer	.10
46	Damion Easley	.10
47	Mark Kotsay	.10
48	Cliff Floyd	.10
49	Jeff Bagwell	.75
50	Ken Caminiti	.10
51	Craig Biggio	.10
52	Moises Alou	.10
53	Johnny Damon	.35
54	Larry Sutton	.10
55	Kevin Brown	.10
56	Adrian Beltre	.25
57	Raul Mondesi	.10
58	Gary Sheffield	.50
59	Jeromy Burnitz	.10
60	Sean Berry	.10
61	Jeff Cirillo	.10
62	Brad Radke	.10
63	Todd Walker	.10
64	Matt Lawton	.10
65	Vladimir Guerrero	.75
66	Rondell White	.10
67	Dustin Hermanson	.10
68	Mike Piazza	2.00
69	Rickey Henderson	.75
70	Robin Ventura	.10
71	John Olerud	.10
72	Derek Jeter	3.00
73	Roger Clemens	1.25
74	Orlando Hernandez	.10
75	Paul O'Neill	.10
76	Bernie Williams	.10
77	Chuck Knoblauch	.10
78	Tino Martinez	.10
79	Jason Giambi	.50
80	Ben Grieve	.10
81	Matt Stairs	.10
82	Scott Rolen	.60
83	Ron Gant	.10
84	Bobby Abreu	.10
85	Curt Schilling	.35
86	Brian Giles	.10
87	Jason Kendall	.10
88	Kevin Young	.10
89	Mark McGwire	2.00
90	Fernando Tatis	.10
91	Ray Lankford	.10
92	Eric Davis	.10
93	Tony Gwynn	1.00
94	Reggie Sanders	.10
95	Wally Joyner	.10
96	Trevor Hoffman	.10
97	Robb Nen	.10
98	Barry Bonds	3.00
99	Jeff Kent	.10
100	J.T. Snow	.10
101	Ellis Burks	.10
102	Ken Griffey Jr.	1.50
103	Alex Rodriguez	2.00
104	Jay Buhner	.10
105	Edgar Martinez	.10
106	David Bell	.10
107	Bobby Smith	.10
108	Wade Boggs	1.00
109	Fred McGriff	.10
110	Rolando Arrojo	.10
111	Jose Canseco	.50
112	Ivan Rodriguez	.65
113	Juan Gonzalez	.40
114	Rafael Palmeiro	.65
115	Rusty Greer	.10
116	Todd Zeile	.10
117	Jose Cruz Jr.	.10
118	Carlos Delgado	.35
119	Shawn Green	.30
120	David Wells	.10
121	Eric Munson RC	2.50
122	Lance Berkman	2.00
123	Ed Yarnall	.50
124	Jacque Jones	1.00
125	Kyle Farnsworth	1.00
126	Ryan Rupe	1.00
127	Jeff Weaver RC	2.00
128	Gabe Kapler	.50
129	Alex Gonzalez	.50
130	Randy Wolf	1.00
131	Ben Davis	.50
132	Carlos Beltran	2.00

133	Jim Morris	2.00
134	Jeff Zimmerman	2.00
135	Bruce Aven	.50
136	Alfonso Soriano RC	50.00
137	Tim Hudson RC	15.00
138	Josh Beckett RC	50.00
139	Michael Barrett	.50
140	Eric Chavez	1.00
141	Pat Burrell RC	10.00
142	Kris Benson	1.00
143	J.D. Drew	2.00
144	Matt Clement	1.00
145	Rick Ankiel RC	15.00
146	Vernon Wells	1.00
147	Ruben Mateo	.50
148	Roy Halladay	1.00
149	Joe McEwing	.50
150	Freddy Garcia RC	8.00
151	Mark McGwire	1.00
152	Mark McGwire	1.00
153	Mark McGwire	1.00
154	Mark McGwire	1.00
155	Mark McGwire	1.00
156	Mark McGwire	1.00
157	Mark McGwire	1.00
158	Mark McGwire	1.00
159	Mark McGwire	1.00
160	Mark McGwire	1.00
161	Mark McGwire	1.00
162	Mark McGwire	1.00
163	Mark McGwire	1.00
164	Mark McGwire	1.00
165	Mark McGwire	1.00
166	Mark McGwire	1.00
167	Mark McGwire	1.00
168	Mark McGwire	1.00
169	Mark McGwire	1.00
170	Mark McGwire	1.00
171	Mark McGwire	1.00
172	Mark McGwire	1.00
173	Mark McGwire	1.00
174	Mark McGwire	1.00
175	Mark McGwire	1.00
176	Mark McGwire	1.00
177	Mark McGwire	1.00
178	Mark McGwire	1.00
179	Mark McGwire	1.00
180	Mark McGwire	1.00

Ultimate Collection

	NM/M
Common Player (1-120, 151-180):	2.00
Common Player (121-150):	12.00
Stars (1-120):	12X
Stars (121-150):	5X

(See 1999 Upper Deck Ultimate Victory for checklist and base card values.)

Victory Collection

STEVE FINLEY

	NM/M
Common Player (1-120, 151-180):	1.00
Common Player (121-150):	5.00
Stars (1-120):	3.5X
Stars (121-150):	2X

(See 1999 Ultimate Victory for checklist and base card values.)

Bleacher Reachers

		NM/M
Complete Set (11):		20.00
Common Player:		.75
Inserted 1:23		
1	Ken Griffey Jr.	2.50
2	Mark McGwire	3.00
3	Sammy Sosa	2.00
4	Barry Bonds	4.00
5	Nomar Garciaparra	2.00
6	Juan Gonzalez	.75
7	Jose Canseco	.75
8	Manny Ramirez	1.50
9	Mike Piazza	2.50
10	Jeff Bagwell	1.50
11	Alex Rodriguez	3.00

Fame-Used Combo

	NM/M
Edition of 99:	
HOF Nolan Ryan, George Brett, Robin Yount, Orlando Cepeda	250.00

Fame-Used Memorabilia

		NM/M
Complete Set (4):		50.00
Common Player:		7.50
Production 350 Cards		
GB	George Brett	20.00
OC	Orlando Cepeda	7.50
NR	Nolan Ryan	25.00
RY	Robin Yount	10.00

Frozen Ropes

		NM/M
Complete Set (10):		15.00
Common Player:		.50
Inserted 1:23		
1	Ken Griffey Jr.	2.00
2	Mark McGwire	2.50
3	Sammy Sosa	1.50
4	Derek Jeter	3.00
5	Tony Gwynn	1.50
6	Nomar Garciaparra	1.50
7	Alex Rodriguez	2.50
8	Mike Piazza	2.00
9	Mo Vaughn	.50
10	Craig Biggio	.50

STATure

		NM/M
Complete Set (15):		9.00
Common Player:		.30
Inserted 1:6		
1	Ken Griffey Jr.	.75

2	Mark McGwire	1.00
3	Sammy Sosa	.65
4	Nomar Garciaparra	.65
5	Roger Clemens	.65
6	Greg Maddux	.65
7	Alex Rodriguez	1.00
8	Derek Jeter	1.50
9	Juan Gonzalez	.30
10	Manny Ramirez	.50
11	Mike Piazza	.75
12	Tony Gwynn	.65
13	Chipper Jones	.65
14	Pedro Martinez	.50
15	Frank Thomas	.50

Tribute 1999

		NM/M
Complete Set (4):		5.00
Common Player:		1.00
Inserted 1:11		
1	Nolan Ryan	2.00
2	Robin Yount	1.50
3	George Brett	1.50
4	Orlando Cepeda	1.00

Ultimate Competitors

		NM/M
Complete Set (12):		20.00
Common Player:		.60
Inserted 1:23		
1	Ken Griffey Jr.	3.00
2	Roger Clemens	2.50
3	Scott Rolen	1.00
4	Greg Maddux	2.00
5	Mark McGwire	4.00
6	Derek Jeter	5.00
7	Randy Johnson	1.50
8	Cal Ripken Jr.	5.00
9	Craig Biggio	.50
10	Kevin Brown	.50
11	Chipper Jones	2.00
12	Vladimir Guerrero	1.50

Ultimate Hit Men

		NM/M
Complete Set (8):		15.00
Common Player:		1.00
Inserted 1:23		
1	Tony Gwynn	2.00

		NM/M
2	Cal Ripken Jr.	4.00
3	Wade Boggs	2.00
4	Larry Walker	1.00
5	Alex Rodriguez	3.00
6	Derek Jeter	4.00
7	Ivan Rodriguez	1.25
8	Ken Griffey Jr.	2.50

1999 Upper Deck Victory

![Carlos Delgado card](Blue Jays First Base)

CARLOS DELGADO
Blue Jays First Base

		NM/M
Complete Set (470):		30.00
Common Player:		.05
Pack (12):		.75
Wax Box (36):		20.00
1	Anaheim Angels (Team Checklist)	.05
2	Mark Harriger RC	.10
3	Mo Vaughn	.05
4	Darin Erstad	.10
5	Troy Glaus	.45
6	Tim Salmon	.05
7	Mo Vaughn	.05
8	Darin Erstad	.25
9	Garret Anderson	.05
10	Todd Greene	.05
11	Troy Percival	.05
12	Chuck Finley	.05
13	Jason Dickson	.05
14	Jim Edmonds	.05
15	Arizona Diamondbacks (Team Checklist)	.05
16	Randy Johnson	.50
17	Matt Williams	.05
18	Travis Lee	.15
19	Jay Bell	.05
20	Tony Womack	.05
21	Steve Finley	.05
22	Bernard Gilkey	.05
23	Tony Batista	.05
24	Todd Stottlemyre	.05
25	Omar Daal	.05
26	Atlanta Braves (Team Checklist)	.05
27	Bruce Chen	.05
28	George Lombard	.05
29	Chipper Jones	.35
30	Chipper Jones	.35
31	Greg Maddux	.65
32	Chipper Jones	.65
33	Javy Lopez	.05
34	Tom Glavine	.25
35	John Smoltz	.05
36	Andruw Jones	.50
37	Brian Jordan	.05
38	Walt Weiss	.05
39	Bret Boone	.05
40	Andres Galarraga	.05
41	Baltimore Orioles (Team Checklist)	.05
42	Ryan Minor	.05

43	Jerry Hairston Jr.	.05
44	Calvin Pickering	.05
45	Cal Ripken Jr.	.75
46	Cal Ripken Jr.	1.50
47	Charles Johnson	.05
48	Albert Belle	.05
49	Delino DeShields	.05
50	Mike Mussina	.30
51	Scott Erickson	.05
52	Brady Anderson	.05
53	B.J. Surhoff	.05
54	Harold Baines	.05
55	Will Clark	.05
56	Boston Red Sox (Team Checklist)	.05
57	Shea Hillenbrand RC	.50
58	Trot Nixon	.10
59	Jin Ho Cho	.05
60	Nomar Garciaparra	.35
61	Nomar Garciaparra	.35
62	Pedro Martinez	.50
63	Nomar Garciaparra	.65
64	Jose Offerman	.05
65	Jason Varitek	.05
66	Darren Lewis	.05
67	Troy O'Leary	.05
68	Donnie Sadler	.05
69	John Valentin	.05
70	Tim Wakefield	.05
71	Bret Saberhagen	.05
72	Chicago Cubs (Team Checklist)	.05
73	Kyle Farnsworth RC	.10
74	Sammy Sosa	.35
75	Sammy Sosa	.35
76	Sammy Sosa	.35
77	Kerry Wood	.10
78	Sammy Sosa	.65
79	Mark Grace	.05
80	Kerry Wood	.25
81	Kevin Tapani	.05
82	Benito Santiago	.05
83	Gary Gaetti	.05
84	Mickey Morandini	.05
85	Glenallen Hill	.05
86	Henry Rodriguez	.05
87	Rod Beck	.05
88	Chicago White Sox (Team Checklist)	.05
89	Carlos Lee	.10
90	Mark Johnson	.05
91	Frank Thomas	.30
92	Frank Thomas	.50
93	Jim Parque	.05
94	Mike Sirotka	.05
95	Mike Caruso	.05
96	Ray Durham	.05
97	Magglio Ordonez	.25
98	Paul Konerko	.15
99	Bob Howry	.05
100	Brian Simmons	.05
101	Jaime Navarro	.05
102	Cincinnati Reds (Team Checklist)	.05
103	Denny Neagle	.05
104	Pete Harnisch	.05
105	Greg Vaughn	.05
106	Brett Tomko	.05
107	Mike Cameron	.05
108	Sean Casey	.10
109	Aaron Boone	.05
110	Michael Tucker	.05
111	Dmitri Young	.05
112	Barry Larkin	.05
113	Cleveland Indians (Team Checklist)	.05
114	Russ Branyan	.05
115	Jim Thome	.20
116	Manny Ramirez	.25
117	Manny Ramirez	.50
118	Jim Thome	.40
119	David Justice	.05
120	Sandy Alomar	.05
121	Roberto Alomar	.20
122	Jaret Wright	.05
123	Bartolo Colon	.05
124	Travis Fryman	.05
125	Kenny Lofton	.05
126	Omar Vizquel	.05
127	Colorado Rockies (Team Checklist)	.05
128	Derrick Gibson	.05
129	Larry Walker	.05
130	Larry Walker	.05
131	Dante Bichette	.05
132	Todd Helton	.45
133	Neifi Perez	.05
134	Vinny Castilla	.05
135	Darryl Kile	.05
136	Pedro Astacio	.05
137	Darryl Hamilton	.05
138	Mike Lansing	.05
139	Kirt Manwaring	.05

140	Detroit Tigers (Team Checklist)	.05
141	Jeff Weaver RC	.50
142	Gabe Kapler	.05
143	Tony Clark	.05
144	Tony Clark	.05
145	Juan Encarnacion	.05
146	Dean Palmer	.05
147	Damion Easley	.05
148	Bobby Higginson	.05
149	Karim Garcia	.05
150	Justin Thompson	.05
151	Matt Anderson	.05
152	Willie Blair	.05
153	Brian Hunter	.05
154	Florida Marlins (Team Checklist)	.05
155	Alex Gonzalez	.05
156	Mark Kotsay	.05
157	Livan Hernandez	.05
158	Cliff Floyd	.05
159	Todd Dunwoody	.05
160	Alex Fernandez	.05
161	Mark Mantei	.05
162	Derrek Lee	.40
163	Kevin Orie	.05
164	Craig Counsell	.05
165	Rafael Medina	.05
166	Houston Astros (Team Checklist)	.05
167	Daryle Ward	.05
168	Mitch Meluskey	.05
169	Jeff Bagwell	.25
170	Jeff Bagwell	.50
171	Ken Caminiti	.05
172	Craig Biggio	.05
173	Derek Bell	.05
174	Moises Alou	.05
175	Billy Wagner	.05
176	Shane Reynolds	.05
177	Carl Everett	.05
178	Scott Elarton	.05
179	Richard Hidalgo	.05
180	Kansas City Royals (Team Checklist)	.05
181	Carlos Beltran	.60
182	Carlos Febles	.05
183	Jeremy Giambi	.05
184	Johnny Damon	.30
185	Joe Randa	.05
186	Jeff King	.05
187	Hipolito Pichardo	.05
188	Kevin Appier	.05
189	Chad Kreuter	.05
190	Rey Sanchez	.05
191	Larry Sutton	.05
192	Jeff Montgomery	.05
193	Jermaine Dye	.05
194	Los Angeles Dodgers (Team Checklist)	.05
195	Adam Riggs	.05
196	Angel Pena	.05
197	Todd Hundley	.05
198	Kevin Brown	.05
199	Ismael Valdes	.05
200	Chan Ho Park	.05
201	Adrian Beltre	.15
202	Mark Grudzielanek	.05
203	Raul Mondesi	.05
204	Gary Sheffield	.35
205	Eric Karros	.05
206	Devon White	.05
207	Milwaukee Brewers (Team Checklist)	.05
208	Ron Belliard	.05
209	Rafael Roque	.05
210	Jeromy Burnitz	.05
211	Fernando Vina	.05
212	Scott Karl	.05
213	Jim Abbott	.05
214	Sean Berry	.05
215	Marquis Grissom	.05
216	Geoff Jenkins	.05
217	Jeff Cirillo	.05
218	Dave Nilsson	.05
219	Jose Valentin	.05
220	Minnesota Twins (Team Checklist)	.05
221	Corey Koskie	.05
222	Christian Guzman	.05
223	A.J. Pierzynski	.05
224	David Ortiz	.05
225	Brad Radke	.05
226	Todd Walker	.05
227	Matt Lawton	.05
228	Rick Aguilera	.05
229	Eric Milton	.05
230	Marty Cordova	.05
231	Torii Hunter	.05
232	Ron Coomer	.05
233	LaTroy Hawkins	.05
234	Montreal Expos (Team Checklist)	.05
235	Fernando Seguignol	.05

236	Michael Barrett	.05
237	Vladimir Guerrero	.25
238	Vladimir Guerrero	.50
239	Brad Fullmer	.05
240	Rondell White	.05
241	Ugueth Urbina	.05
242	Dustin Hermanson	.05
243	Orlando Cabrerra	.05
244	Wilton Guerrero	.05
245	Carl Pavano	.05
246	Javier Vasquez	.05
247	Chris Widger	.05
248	New York Mets (Team Checklist)	.05
249	Mike Kinkade	.05
250	Octavio Dotel	.05
251	Mike Piazza	.40
252	Mike Piazza	.75
253	Rickey Henderson	.50
254	Edgardo Alfonzo	.05
255	Robin Ventura	.05
256	Al Leiter	.05
257	Brian McRae	.05
258	Rey Ordonez	.05
259	Bobby Bonilla	.05
260	Orel Hershiser	.05
261	John Olerud	.05
262	New York Yankees (Team Checklist)	.05
263	Ricky Ledee	.05
264	Bernie Williams	.05
265	Derek Jeter	.75
266	Scott Brosius	.05
267	Derek Jeter	1.50
268	Roger Clemens	.65
269	Orlando Hernandez	.05
270	Scott Brosius	.05
271	Paul O'Neill	.05
272	Bernie Williams	.05
273	Chuck Knoblauch	.05
274	Tino Martinez	.05
275	Mariano Rivera	.10
276	Jorge Posada	.05
277	Oakland Athletics (Team Checklist)	.05
278	Eric Chavez	.15
279	Ben Grieve	.05
280	Jason Giambi	.30
281	John Jaha	.05
282	Miguel Tejada	.15
283	Ben Grieve	.05
284	Matt Stairs	.05
285	Ryan Christenson	.05
286	A.J. Hinch	.05
287	Kenny Rogers	.05
288	Tom Candiotti	.05
289	Scott Spezio	.05
290	Philadelphia Phillies (Team Checklist)	.05
291	Pat Burrell RC	1.50
292	Marlon Anderson	.05
293	Scott Rolen	.20
294	Scott Rolen	.40
295	Doug Glanville	.05
296	Rico Brogna	.05
297	Ron Gant	.05
298	Bobby Abreu	.05
299	Desi Relaford	.05
300	Curt Schilling	.25
301	Chad Ogea	.05
302	Kevin Jordan	.05
303	Carlton Loewer	.05
304	Pittsburgh Pirates (Team Checklist)	.05
305	Kris Benson	.05
306	Brian Giles	.05
307	Jason Kendall	.05
308	Jose Guillen	.05
309	Pat Meares	.05
310	Brant Brown	.05
311	Kevin Young	.05
312	Ed Sprague	.05
313	Francisco Cordova	.05
314	Aramis Ramirez	.05
315	Freddy Garcia	.05
316	Saint Louis Cardinals (Team Checklist)	.05
317	J.D. Drew	.40
318	Chad Hutchinson RC	.05
319	Mark McGwire	.50
320	J.D. Drew	.20
321	Mark McGwire	.50
322	Mark McGwire	.50
323	Mark McGwire	1.00
324	Fernando Tatis	.05
325	Edgar Renteria	.05
326	Ray Lankford	.05
327	Willie McGee	.05
328	Ricky Bottalico	.05
329	Eli Marrero	.05
330	Matt Morris	.05
331	Eric Davis	.05
332	Darren Bragg	.05

333	Padres (Team Checklist)	.05
334	Matt Clement	.05
335	Ben Davis	.05
336	Gary Matthews Jr.	.05
337	Tony Gwynn	.35
338	Tony Gwynn	.35
339	Tony Gwynn	.65
340	Reggie Sanders	.05
341	Ruben Rivera	.05
342	Wally Joyner	.05
343	Sterling Hitchcock	.05
344	Carlos Hernandez	.05
345	Andy Ashby	.05
346	Trevor Hoffman	.05
347	Chris Gomez	.05
348	Jim Leyritz	.05
349	San Francisco Giants (Team Checklist)	.05
350	Armando Rios	.05
351	Barry Bonds	.75
352	Barry Bonds	.75
353	Barry Bonds	.75
354	Robb Nen	.05
355	Bill Mueller	.05
356	Barry Bonds	1.50
357	Jeff Kent	.05
358	J.T. Snow	.05
359	Ellis Burks	.05
360	F.P. Santangelo	.05
361	Marvin Benard	.05
362	Stan Javier	.05
363	Shawn Estes	.05
364	Seattle Mariners (Team Checklist)	.05
365	Carlos Guillen	.05
366	Ken Griffey Jr.	.40
367	Alex Rodriguez	.50
368	Ken Griffey Jr.	.40
369	Alex Rodriguez	.50
370	Ken Griffey Jr.	.40
371	Alex Rodriguez	.50
372	Ken Griffey Jr.	.75
373	Alex Rodriguez	1.00
374	Jay Buhner	.05
375	Edgar Martinez	.05
376	Jeff Fassero	.05
377	David Bell	.05
378	David Segui	.05
379	Russ Davis	.05
380	Dan Wilson	.05
381	Jamie Moyer	.05
382	Tampa Bay Devil Rays (Team Checklist)	.05
383	Roberto Hernandez	.05
384	Bobby Smith	.05
385	Wade Boggs	.65
386	Fred McGriff	.05
387	Rolando Arrojo	.05
388	Jose Canseco	.35
389	Wilson Alvarez	.05
390	Kevin Stocker	.05
391	Miguel Cairo	.05
392	Quinton McCracken	.05
393	Texas Rangers (Team Checklist)	.05
394	Ruben Mateo	.05
395	Cesar King	.05
396	Juan Gonzalez	.15
397	Juan Gonzalez	.15
398	Ivan Rodriguez	.40
399	Juan Gonzalez	.25
400	Rafael Palmeiro	.40
401	Rick Helling	.05
402	Aaron Sele	.05
403	John Wetteland	.05
404	Rusty Greer	.05
405	Todd Zeile	.05
406	Royce Clayton	.05
407	Tom Goodwin	.05
408	Toronto Blue Jays (Team Checklist)	.05
409	Kevin Witt	.05
410	Roy Halladay	.05
411	Jose Cruz Jr.	.05
412	Carlos Delgado	.30
413	Willie Greene	.05
414	Shawn Green	.25
415	Homer Bush	.05
416	Shannon Stewart	.05
417	David Wells	.05
418	Kelvim Escobar	.05
419	Joey Hamilton	.05
420	Alex Gonzalez	.05
421	Mark McGwire	.20
422	Mark McGwire	.20
423	Mark McGwire	.20
424	Mark McGwire	.20
425	Mark McGwire	.20
426	Mark McGwire	.20
427	Mark McGwire	.20
428	Mark McGwire	.20
429	Mark McGwire	.20
430	Mark McGwire	.20

431	Mark McGwire	.20
432	Mark McGwire	.20
433	Mark McGwire	.20
434	Mark McGwire	.20
435	Mark McGwire	.20
436	Mark McGwire	.20
437	Mark McGwire	.20
438	Mark McGwire	.20
439	Mark McGwire	.20
440	Mark McGwire	.20
441	Mark McGwire	.20
442	Mark McGwire	.20
443	Mark McGwire	.20
444	Mark McGwire	.20
445	Mark McGwire	.20
446	Mark McGwire	.20
447	Mark McGwire	.20
448	Mark McGwire	.20
449	Mark McGwire	.20
450	Mark McGwire	.20
451	Chipper Jones '93	.35
452	Cal Ripken Jr. '81	.75
453	Roger Clemens '84	.40
454	Wade Boggs '82	.35
455	Greg Maddux '86	.35
456	Frank Thomas '90	.30
457	Jeff Bagwell '91	.25
458	Mike Piazza '92	.45
459	Randy Johnson '88	.25
460	Mo Vaughn '91	.05
461	Mark McGwire '86	.50
462	Rickey Henderson '79	.25
463	Barry Bonds '86	.75
464	Tony Gwynn '82	.35
465	Ken Griffey Jr. '89	.45
466	Alex Rodriquez '94	.50
467	Sammy Sosa '89	.35
468	Juan Gonzalez '89	.15
469	Kevin Brown '86	.05
470	Fred McGriff '86	.05

1999 Upper Deck UD Choice

VLADIMIR guerrero OF 27 EXPOS

	NM/M
Complete Set (155):	7.50
Common Player:	.03
Prime Choice Reserve Stars:	10X
Production 100 Sets	
Pack (12):	.50
Wax Box (36):	10.00

1	Gabe Kapler/RC	.05
2	Jin Ho Cho/RC	.05
3	Matt Anderson/RC	.03
4	Ricky Ledee/RC	.05
5	Bruce Chen/RC	.05
6	Alex Gonzalez/RC	.05
7	Ryan Minor /RC	.05
8	Michael Barrett/RC	.05
9	Carlos Beltran/RC	.50
10	Ramon Martinez/RC	.05
11	Dermal Brown/RC	.05
12	Robert Fick/RC	.05
13	Preston Wilson/RC	.05
14	Orlando Hernandez/RC	.05
15	Troy Glaus/RC	.65
16	Calvin Pickering/RC	.05
17	Corey Koskie/RC	.05
18	Fernando Seguignol/RC	.05
19	Carlos Guillen/RC	.05
20	Kevin Witt/RC	.05
21	Mike Kinkade/RC	.05
22	Eric Chavez/RC	.15
23	Mike Lowell/RC	.10
24	Adrian Beltre/RC	.10
25	George Lombard/RC	.05
26	Jeremy Giambi/RC	.05
27	J.D. Drew/RC	.40
28	Mark McGwire	.60
29	Kerry Wood	.15
30	David Wells	.05
31	Juan Gonzalez	.15

32	Randy Johnson	.35
33	Derek Jeter	.75
34	Tony Gwynn	.45
35	Greg Maddux	.45
36	Cal Ripken Jr.	.75
37	Ken Griffey Jr.	.50
38	Bartolo Colon	.05
39	Troy Glaus	.30
40	Ben Grieve	.05
41	Roger Clemens	.50
42	Chipper Jones	.45
43	Scott Rolen	.25
44	Nomar Garciaparra	.45
45	Sammy Sosa	.45
46	Tim Salmon	.05
47	Darin Erstad	.25
48	Chuck Finley	.05
49	Garrett Anderson	.05
50	Matt Williams	.05
51	Jay Bell	.05
52	Travis Lee	.10
53	Andruw Jones	.65
54	Andres Galarraga	.05
55	Chipper Jones	.75
56	Greg Maddux	.75
57	Javy Lopez	.05
58	Cal Ripken Jr.	1.50
59	Brady Anderson	.05
60	Rafael Palmeiro	.50
61	B.J. Surhoff	.05
62	Nomar Garciaparra	.75
63	Troy O'Leary	.05
64	Pedro Martinez	.65
65	Jason Varitek	.05
66	Kerry Wood	.35
67	Sammy Sosa	.75
68	Mark Grace	.05
69	Mickey Morandini	.05
70	Albert Belle	.05
71	Mike Caruso	.05
72	Frank Thomas	.65
73	Sean Casey	.10
74	Pete Harnisch	.05
75	Dmitri Young	.05
76	Manny Ramirez	.65
77	Omar Vizquel	.05
78	Travis Fryman	.05
79	Jim Thome	.40
80	Kenny Lofton	.05
81	Todd Helton	.50
82	Larry Walker	.05
83	Vinny Castilla	.05
84	Gabe Alvarez	.05
85	Tony Clark	.05
86	Damion Easley	.05
87	Livan Hernandez	.05
88	Mark Kotsay	.05
89	Cliff Floyd	.05
90	Jeff Bagwell	.65
91	Moises Alou	.05
92	Randy Johnson	.65
93	Craig Biggio	.05
94	Larry Sutton	.05
95	Dean Palmer	.05
96	Johnny Damon	.20
97	Charles Johnson	.05
98	Gary Sheffield	.25
99	Raul Mondesi	.05
100	Mark Grudzielanek	.05
101	Jeromy Burnitz	.05
102	Jeff Cirillo	.05
103	Jose Valentin	.05
104	Mark Loretta	.05
105	Todd Walker	.05
106	David Ortiz	.35
107	Brad Radke	.05
108	Brad Fullmer	.05
109	Rondell White	.05
110	Vladimir Guerrero	.65
111	Mike Piazza	1.00
112	Brian McRae	.05
113	John Olerud	.05
114	Rey Ordonez	.05
115	Derek Jeter	1.50
116	Bernie Williams	.05
117	David Wells	.05
118	Paul O'Neill	.05
119	Tino Martinez	.05
120	A.J. Hinch	.05
121	Jason Giambi	.30
122	Miguel Tejada	.10
123	Ben Grieve	.05
124	Scott Rolen	.50
125	Desi Relaford	.05
126	Bobby Abreu	.10
127	Jose Guillen	.05
128	Jason Kendall	.05
129	Aramis Ramirez	.05
130	Mark McGwire	1.25
131	Ray Lankford	.05
132	Eli Marrero	.05
133	Wally Joyner	.05
134	Greg Vaughn	.05
135	Trevor Hoffman	.05

136	Kevin Brown	.05
137	Tony Gwynn	.75
138	Bill Mueller	.05
139	Ellis Burks	.05
140	Barry Bonds	1.50
141	Robb Nen	.05
142	Ken Griffey Jr.	1.00
143	Alex Rodriguez	1.25
144	Jay Buhner	.05
145	Edgar Martinez	.05
146	Rolando Arrojo	.05
147	Robert Smith	.05
148	Quinton McCracken	.05
149	Ivan Rodriguez	.50
150	Will Clark	.05
151	Mark McLemore	.05
152	Juan Gonzalez	.35
153	Jose Cruz Jr.	.05
154	Carlos Delgado	.25
155	Roger Clemens	.85

Prime Choice Reserve

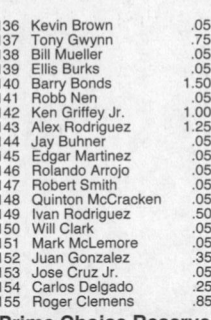

JUAN gonzalez OF 19 RANGERS

	NM/M
Common Player:	2.50
Stars:	10X
(See 1999 UD Choice for checklist and base card values.)	

All-Star Game '99

KENNY lofton OF 7 INDIANS

	NM/M
Complete Set (21):	12.50
Common Player:	.35

1	Kenny Lofton	.35
2	Pedro Martinez	.75
3	Nomar Garciaparra	1.00
4	Ken Griffey Jr.	1.25
5	Derek Jeter	2.00
6	Manny Ramirez	.75
7	Ivan Rodriguez	.65
8	Bernie Williams	.35
9	Cal Ripken Jr.	2.00
10	Jim Thome	.60
11	Mike Piazza	1.25
12	Jeff Bagwell	.75
13	Craig Biggio	.35
14	Mark McGwire	1.50
15	Matt Williams	.35
16	Chipper Jones	1.00
17	Tony Gwynn	1.00
18	Sammy Sosa	1.00
19	Raul Mondesi	.35
20	Larry Walker	.35
---	Header Card	.35

Mini Bobbing Head

	NM/M
Complete Set (30):	15.00
Common Player:	.25
Inserted 1:5	
B1	Randy Johnson	.50

B2	Troy Glaus	.50
B3	Chipper Jones	.65
B4	Cal Ripken Jr.	1.50
B5	Nomar Garciaparra	.65
B6	Pedro Martinez	.50
B7	Kerry Wood	.35
B8	Sammy Sosa	.65
B9	Frank Thomas	.50
B10	Paul Konerko	.35
B11	Omar Vizquel	.25
B12	Kenny Lofton	.25
B13	Gabe Kapler	.25
B14	Adrian Beltre	.35
B15	Orlando Hernandez	.25
B16	Derek Jeter	1.50
B17	Mike Piazza	.75
B18	Tino Martinez	.25
B19	Ben Grieve	.25
B20	Rickey Henderson	.50
B21	Scott Rolen	.40
B22	Aramis Ramirez	.25
B23	Greg Vaughn	.25
B24	Tony Gwynn	.65
B25	Barry Bonds	1.50
B26	Alex Rodriguez	1.00
B27	Ken Griffey Jr.	.75
B28	Mark McGwire	1.00
B29	J.D. Drew	.45
B30	Juan Gonzalez	.30

Piece of History
500 Club

		NM/M
EM	Eddie Murray/350	150.00

StarQuest

	NM/M
Complete Set (30):	7.50
Common Player:	.10
Inserted 1:1	
Green (1:8):	1.5X
Red (1:23):	3X
Gold (100 Sets):	50X

SQ1	Ken Griffey Jr.	.60
SQ2	Sammy Sosa	.50
SQ3	Alex Rodriguez	.75
SQ4	Derek Jeter	1.00
SQ5	Troy Glaus	.35
SQ6	Mike Piazza	.60
SQ7	Barry Bonds	1.00
SQ8	Tony Gwynn	.50
SQ9	Juan Gonzalez	.20
SQ10	Chipper Jones	.50
SQ11	Greg Maddux	.50
SQ12	Randy Johnson	.40
SQ13	Roger Clemens	.55
SQ14	Ben Grieve	.10
SQ15	Nomar Garciaparra	.50
SQ16	Travis Lee	.15
SQ17	Frank Thomas	.40
SQ18	Vladimir Guerrero	.40
SQ19	Scott Rolen	.30
SQ20	Ivan Rodriguez	.35
SQ21	Cal Ripken Jr.	1.00
SQ22	Mark McGwire	.75
SQ23	Jeff Bagwell	.40
SQ24	Tony Clark	.10
SQ25	Kerry Wood	.25
SQ26	Kenny Lofton	.10
SQ27	Adrian Beltre	.15
SQ28	Larry Walker	.10
SQ29	Curt Schilling	.25
SQ30	Jim Thome	.40

Yard Work

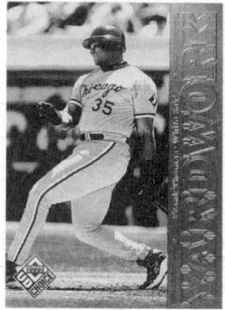

	NM/M
Complete Set (30):	20.00
Common Player:	.35
Inserted 1:13	

Y1	Andres Galarraga	.35
Y2	Chipper Jones	1.50
Y3	Rafael Palmeiro	.75
Y4	Nomar Garciaparra	1.50
Y5	Sammy Sosa	1.50
Y6	Frank Thomas	1.00
Y7	J.D. Drew	.75
Y8	Albert Belle	.35
Y9	Jim Thome	.60
Y10	Manny Ramirez	1.00
Y11	Larry Walker	.35
Y12	Vinny Castilla	.35
Y13	Tony Clark	.35
Y14	Jeff Bagwell	1.00
Y15	Moises Alou	.35
Y16	Dean Palmer	.35
Y17	Gary Sheffield	.50
Y18	Vladimir Guerrero	1.00
Y19	Mike Piazza	1.75
Y20	Tino Martinez	.35
Y21	Ben Grieve	.35
Y22	Greg Vaughn	.35
Y23	Ken Caminiti	.35
Y24	Barry Bonds	3.00
Y25	Ken Griffey Jr.	1.75
Y26	Alex Rodriguez	2.25
Y27	Mark McGwire	2.25
Y28	Juan Gonzalez	.50
Y29	Jose Canseco	.50
Y30	Jose Cruz Jr.	.35

1999 UD Ionix

	NM/M
Complete Set (90):	45.00
Common Player (1-60):	.25
Common Techno (61-90):	.50
Inserted 1:4	
Reciprocals (1-60):	3X
Production 750 Sets	
Techno Reciprocals (61-90):	1.5X
Production 100 Sets	
Pack (4):	2.00
Wax Box (20):	25.00

1	Troy Glaus	.60
2	Darin Erstad	.50
3	Travis Lee	.35
4	Matt Williams	.25
5	Chipper Jones	.75
6	Greg Maddux	.75
7	Andruw Jones	.65
8	Andres Galarraga	.25
9	Tom Glavine	.35
10	Cal Ripken Jr.	2.00
11	Ryan Minor	.25
12	Nomar Garciaparra	1.00
13	Mo Vaughn	.25
14	Pedro Martinez	.65
15	Sammy Sosa	.75
16	Kerry Wood	.50
17	Albert Belle	.25
18	Frank Thomas	.65
19	Sean Casey	.25
20	Kenny Lofton	.25
21	Manny Ramirez	.65
22	Jim Thome	.60
23	Bartolo Colon	.25
24	Jaret Wright	.25
25	Larry Walker	.25
26	Tony Clark	.25
27	Gabe Kapler	.25
28	Edgar Renteria	.25
29	Randy Johnson	.65
30	Craig Biggio	.25
31	Jeff Bagwell	.65
32	Moises Alou	.25
33	Johnny Damon	.50
34	Adrian Beltre	.35
35	Jeromy Burnitz	.25
36	Todd Walker	.25
37	Corey Koskie	.25
38	Vladimir Guerrero	.65
39	Mike Piazza	1.00
40	Hideo Nomo	.35
41	Derek Jeter	2.00
42	Tino Martinez	.25
43	Orlando Hernandez	.25
44	Ben Grieve	.25
45	Rickey Henderson	.65
46	Scott Rolen	.60
47	Curt Schilling	.35
48	Aramis Ramirez	.25
49	Tony Gwynn	.75
50	Kevin Brown	.25
51	Barry Bonds	2.00
52	Ken Griffey Jr.	1.00
53	Alex Rodriguez	1.50
54	Mark McGwire	1.50
55	J.D. Drew	.60
56	Rolando Arrojo	.25
57	Ivan Rodriguez	.60
58	Juan Gonzalez	.35
59	Roger Clemens	.85
60	Jose Cruz Jr.	.25
61	Travis Lee	.65
62	Andres Galarraga	.50
63	Andruw Jones	1.50
64	Chipper Jones	2.00
65	Greg Maddux	2.00
66	Cal Ripken Jr.	4.00
67	Nomar Garciaparra	2.00
68	Mo Vaughn	.50
69	Sammy Sosa	2.00
70	Frank Thomas	1.50
71	Kerry Wood	.75
72	Kenny Lofton	.50
73	Manny Ramirez	1.50
74	Larry Walker	.50
75	Jeff Bagwell	1.50
76	Randy Johnson	1.50
77	Paul Molitor	1.50
78	Derek Jeter	4.00
79	Tino Martinez	.50
80	Mike Piazza	2.50
81	Ben Grieve	.50
82	Scott Rolen	.75
83	Mark McGwire	3.00
84	Tony Gwynn	2.00
85	Barry Bonds	4.00
86	Ken Griffey Jr.	2.50
87	Alex Rodriguez	3.00
88	Juan Gonzalez	.75
89	Roger Clemens	2.25
90	J.D. Drew	1.00
100	Ken Griffey Jr. (SAMPLE)	2.50

Reciprocal

	NM/M
Stars (1-60):	3X
Stars (61-90):	1.5X

(See 1999 UD Ionix for checklist and base card values.)

Cyber

	NM/M
Complete Set (25):	125.00
Common Player:	2.00

C01	Ken Griffey Jr.	8.00
C02	Cal Ripken Jr.	12.50
C03	Frank Thomas	5.00
C04	Greg Maddux	6.50
C05	Mike Piazza	8.00
C06	Alex Rodriguez	10.00
C07	Chipper Jones	6.50
C08	Derek Jeter	12.50
C09	Mark McGwire	10.00
C10	Juan Gonzalez	2.50
C11	Kerry Wood	2.50
C12	Tony Gwynn	6.50
C13	Scott Rolen	4.00
C14	Nomar Garciaparra	6.50
C15	Roger Clemens	7.00
C16	Sammy Sosa	6.50
C17	Travis Lee	2.00
C18	Ben Grieve	2.00
C19	Jeff Bagwell	5.00
C20	Ivan Rodriguez	4.00
C21	Barry Bonds	12.50
C22	J.D. Drew	4.00
C23	Kenny Lofton	2.00
C24	Andruw Jones	5.00
C25	Vladimir Guerrero	5.00

HoloGrFX

	NM/M
Complete Set (10):	800.00

	NM/M
Common Player:	50.00
Inserted 1:1,500	
HG01 Ken Griffey Jr.	100.00
HG02 Cal Ripken Jr.	150.00
HG03 Frank Thomas	75.00
HG04 Greg Maddux	90.00
HG05 Mike Piazza	100.00
HG06 Alex Rodriguez	125.00
HG07 Chipper Jones	90.00
HG08 Derek Jeter	150.00
HG09 Mark McGwire	125.00
HG10 Juan Gonzalez	50.00

Hyper

	NM/M
Complete Set (20):	37.00
Common Player:	.75
Inserted 1:9	
H01 Ken Griffey Jr.	3.00
H02 Cal Ripken Jr.	4.50
H03 Frank Thomas	1.50
H04 Greg Maddux	2.25
H05 Mike Piazza	3.00
H06 Alex Rodriguez	3.75
H07 Chipper Jones	2.25
H08 Derek Jeter	4.50
H09 Mark McGwire	3.75
H10 Juan Gonzalez	.75
H11 Kerry Wood	1.00
H12 Tony Gwynn	2.25
H13 Scott Rolen	1.00
H14 Nomar Garciaparra	2.25
H15 Roger Clemens	2.75
H16 Sammy Sosa	2.25
H17 Travis Lee	1.00
H18 Ben Grieve	.75
H19 Jeff Bagwell	1.50
H20 J.D. Drew	1.00

Nitro

	NM/M
Complete Set (10):	18.00
Common Player:	1.00
Inserted 1:18	
N01 Ken Griffey Jr.	2.50
N02 Cal Ripken Jr.	4.00
N03 Frank Thomas	1.50
N04 Greg Maddux	2.00
N05 Mike Piazza	2.50
N06 Alex Rodriguez	3.00
N07 Chipper Jones	2.00
N08 Derek Jeter	4.00
N09 Mark McGwire	3.00
N10 J.D. Drew	1.00

Warp Zone

	NM/M
Complete Set (15):	195.00
Common Player:	6.00
Inserted 1:216	

WZ1 Ken Griffey Jr.	20.00
WZ2 Cal Ripken Jr.	30.00
WZ3 Frank Thomas	10.00
WZ4 Greg Maddux	15.00
WZ5 Mike Piazza	20.00
WZ6 Alex Rodriguez	25.00
WZ7 Chipper Jones	15.00
WZ8 Derek Jeter	30.00
WZ9 Mark McGwire	25.00
WZ10 Juan Gonzalez	6.00
WZ11 Kerry Wood	6.00
WZ12 Tony Gwynn	15.00
WZ13 Scott Rolen	6.00
WZ14 Nomar Garciaparra	15.00
WZ15 J.D. Drew	6.00

500 Club Piece of History

	NM/M
FR Frank Robinson/350	165.00
FRA Frank Robinson/Auto./20	650.00

1999 UD Retro

	NM/M
Complete Set (110):	15.00
Common Player:	.05
Gold:	12X
Production 250 Sets	
Platinum 1/1:Values Undetermined	
Wax Pack (6):	2.50
Lunchbox (24):	45.00
1 Mo Vaughn	.05
2 Troy Glaus	.65
3 Tim Salmon	.05
4 Randy Johnson	.75
5 Travis Lee	.15
6 Matt Williams	.05
7 Greg Maddux	.85
8 Chipper Jones	.85
9 Andruw Jones	.75
10 Tom Glavine	.25
11 Javy Lopez	.05
12 Albert Belle	.05
13 Cal Ripken Jr.	2.00
14 Brady Anderson	.05
15 Nomar Garciaparra	.85

16 Pedro J. Martinez	.75
17 Sammy Sosa	.85
18 Mark Grace	.05
19 Frank Thomas	.75
20 Ray Durham	.05
21 Sean Casey	.10
22 Greg Vaughn	.05
23 Barry Larkin	.05
24 Manny Ramirez	.75
25 Jim Thome	.50
26 Jaret Wright	.05
27 Kenny Lofton	.05
28 Larry Walker	.05
29 Todd Helton	.65
30 Vinny Castilla	.05
31 Tony Clark	.05
32 Juan Encarnacion	.05
33 Dean Palmer	.05
34 Mark Kotsay	.05
35 Alex Gonzalez	.05
36 Shane Reynolds	.05
37 Ken Caminiti	.05
38 Jeff Bagwell	.75
39 Craig Biggio	.05
40 Carlos Febles	.05
41 Carlos Beltran	.35
42 Jeremy Giambi	.05
43 Raul Mondesi	.05
44 Adrian Beltre	.10
45 Kevin Brown	.05
46 Jeromy Burnitz	.05
47 Jeff Cirillo	.05
48 Corey Koskie	.05
49 Todd Walker	.05
50 Vladimir Guerrero	.75
51 Michael Barrett	.05
52 Mike Piazza	1.00
53 Robin Ventura	.05
54 Edgardo Alfonzo	.05
55 Derek Jeter	2.00
56 Roger Clemens	.90
57 Tino Martinez	.05
58 Orlando Hernandez	.05
59 Chuck Knoblauch	.05
60 Bernie Williams	.05
61 Eric Chavez	.10
62 Ben Grieve	.05
63 Jason Giambi	.40
64 Scott Rolen	.60
65 Curt Schilling	.25
66 Bobby Abreu	.10
67 Jason Kendall	.05
68 Kevin Young	.05
69 Mark McGwire	1.50
70 J.D. Drew	.60
71 Eric Davis	.05
72 Tony Gwynn	.85
73 Trevor Hoffman	.05
74 Barry Bonds	2.00
75 Robb Nen	.05
76 Ken Griffey Jr.	1.00
77 Alex Rodriguez	1.50
78 Jay Buhner	.05
79 Carlos Guillen	.05
80 Jose Canseco	.40
81 Bobby Smith	.05
82 Juan Gonzalez	.40
83 Ivan Rodriguez	.65
84 Rafael Palmeiro	.65
85 Rick Helling	.05
86 Jose Cruz Jr.	.05
87 David Wells	.05
88 Carlos Delgado	.20
89 Nolan Ryan	1.50
90 George Brett	.90
91 Robin Yount	.50
92 Paul Molitor	.50
93 Dave Winfield	.50
94 Steve Garvey	.25
95 Ozzie Smith	.85
96 Ted Williams	1.50
97 Don Mattingly	.90
98 Mickey Mantle	2.50
99 Harmon Killebrew	.25
100 Rollie Fingers	.10
101 Kirk Gibson	.05
102 Bucky Dent	.05
103 Willie Mays	1.00
104 Babe Ruth	1.50
105 Gary Carter	.50
106 Reggie Jackson	.85
107 Frank Robinson	.25
108 Ernie Banks	.50
109 Eddie Murray	.50
110 Mike Schmidt	.90

Gold/Platinum

	NM/M
Common Gold:	1.00
Gold Stars:	15X

Platinum 1/1: Values Undetermined
(See 1999 UD Retro for checklist and base card values.)

Distant Replay

	NM/M
Complete Set (15):	30.00
Common Player:	1.00
Inserted 1:8	
Level 2:	6X
Production 100 Sets	
1 Ken Griffey Jr.	2.50
2 Mark McGwire	3.00
3 Cal Ripken Jr.	4.00
4 Greg Maddux	2.00
5 Nomar Garciaparra	2.00
6 Roger Clemens	2.25
7 Alex Rodriguez	3.00
8 Frank Thomas	1.50
9 Mike Piazza	2.50
10 Chipper Jones	2.00
11 Juan Gonzalez	1.00
12 Tony Gwynn	2.00
13 Barry Bonds	4.00
14 Ivan Rodriguez	1.00
15 Derek Jeter	4.00

INKredible

	NM/M
Common Player:	4.00
Inserted 1:23	
CBe Carlos Beltran	30.00
GB George Brett/SP	80.00
PB Pat Burrell	10.00
SC Sean Casey	10.00
TC Tony Clark	4.00
BD Bucky Dent	8.00
DE Darin Erstad	15.00
RF Rollie Fingers	8.00
SG Steve Garvey	10.00
KG Kirk Gibson	10.00
RG Rusty Greer	4.00
JR Ken Griffey Jr.	80.00
TG Tony Gwynn	30.00
CJ Chipper Jones	30.00
GK Gabe Kapler	5.00
HK Harmon Killebrew	30.00
FL Fred Lynn	10.00

DM	Don Mattingly	50.00
PM	Paul Molitor	20.00
EM	Eddie Murray/SP	50.00
PO	Paul O'Neill	15.00
AP	Angel Pena	4.00
MR	Manny Ramirez	30.00
IR	Ivan Rodriguez	25.00
NR	Nolan Ryan	150.00
OZ	Ozzie Smith	30.00
DWe	David Wells	15.00
BW	Bernie Williams	40.00
DW	Dave Winfield	20.00
RY	Robin Yount	35.00

INKredible Level 2

		NM/M
	Common Player:	10.00
Limited to player's jersey #.		
CBe	Carlos Beltran/36	60.00
GB	George Brett/5	
PB	Pat Burrell/76	50.00
SC	Sean Casey/21	40.00
TC	Tony Clark/17	20.00
BD	Bucky Dent/20	25.00
DE	Darin Erstad/17	50.00
RF	Rollie Fingers/34	25.00
SG	Steve Garvey/6	
KG	Kirk Gibson/23	30.00
RG	Rusty Greer/29	20.00
JR	Ken Griffey Jr./24	200.00
TG	Tony Gwynn/19	150.00
CJ	Chipper Jones/10	
GK	Gabe Kapler/23	40.00
HK	Harmon Killebrew/3	
FL	Fred Lynn/19	30.00
DM	Don Mattingly/23	200.00
PM	Paul Molitor/4	
EM	Eddie Murray/33	80.00
PO	Paul O'Neill/21	50.00
AP	Angel Pena/36	10.00
MR	Manny Ramirez /24	80.00
IR	Ivan Rodriguez/7	
NR	Nolan Ryan/34	400.00
OZ	Ozzie Smith/1	
DWe	David Wells/33	25.00
BW	Bernie Williams/51	60.00
DW	Dave Winfield/31	60.00
RY	Robin Yount/19	90.00

Lunchbox

	NM/M
Complete Set (17):	140.00
Common Lunchbox:	7.50
One dual-player per case.	
Roger Clemens	7.50
Ken Griffey Jr.	7.50
Mickey Mantle	10.00
Mark McGwire	10.00
Mike Piazza	7.50
Alex Rodriguez	7.50
Babe Ruth	10.00
Sammy Sosa	7.50
Ted Williams	10.00
Ken Griffey Jr., Mark McGwire	12.50
Ken Griffey Jr., Babe Ruth	12.50
Ken Griffey Jr., Ted Williams	12.50
Mickey Mantle, Babe Ruth	15.00
Mark McGwire, Mickey Mantle	15.00
Mark McGwire, Babe Ruth	15.00
Mark McGwire, Ted Williams	15.00

Old/New School

		NM/M
Complete Set (30):		35.00
Common Player:		.40
Production 1,000 Sets		
Level 2:		5X
Production 50 Sets		
1	Ken Griffey Jr.	2.50
2	Alex Rodriguez	3.00
3	Frank Thomas	1.50
4	Cal Ripken Jr.	4.00
5	Chipper Jones	2.00
6	Craig Biggio	.40
7	Greg Maddux	2.00
8	Jeff Bagwell	1.50
9	Juan Gonzalez	.75
10	Mark McGwire	3.00
11	Mike Piazza	2.50
12	Mo Vaughn	.40
13	Roger Clemens	2.25
14	Sammy Sosa	2.00
15	Tony Gwynn	2.00
16	Gabe Kapler	.40
17	J.D. Drew	1.00
18	Pat Burrell	1.00
19	Roy Halladay	.40
20	Jeff Weaver	.40
21	Troy Glaus	1.00
22	Vladimir Guerrero	1.50
23	Michael Barrett	.40
24	Carlos Beltran	.40
25	Scott Rolen	1.00
26	Nomar Garciaparra	2.00
27	Warren Morris	.40
28	Alex Gonzalez	.40
29	Kyle Farnsworth	.40
30	Derek Jeter	4.00

Piece of History 500 Club

		NM/M
TW	Ted Williams/350	250.00
TWA	Ted Williams/Auto./9	

Throwback Attack

	NM/M
Complete Set (15):	20.00
Common Player:	.50
Inserted 1:5	
Level 2:	3X

Production 500 Sets		
1	Ken Griffey Jr.	2.00
2	Mark McGwire	2.50
3	Sammy Sosa	1.25
4	Roger Clemens	1.50
5	J.D. Drew	.75
6	Alex Rodriguez	2.50
7	Greg Maddux	1.25
8	Mike Piazza	2.00
9	Juan Gonzalez	.50
10	Mo Vaughn	.50
11	Cal Ripken Jr.	3.00
12	Frank Thomas	1.00
13	Nomar Garciaparra	1.25
14	Vladimir Guerrero	1.00
15	Tony Gwynn	1.25

2000 Upper Deck

		NM/M
Complete Set (540):		40.00
Complete Series I (270):		20.00
Complete Series II (270):		20.00
Common Player:		.15
Silver Stars:		5-10X
Rookies:		2-4X
Hobby Pack (10):		3.00
Hobby Box (24):		55.00
1	Rick Ankiel	.20
2	Vernon Wells	.50
3	Ryan Anderson	.15
4	Ed Yarnall	.15
5	Brian McNichol	.15
6	Ben Petrick	.15
7	Kip Wells	.15
8	Eric Munson	.20
9	Matt Riley	.15
10	Peter Bergeron	.15
11	Eric Gagne	.25
12	Ramon Ortiz	.25
13	Josh Beckett	.50
14	Alfonso Soriano	1.50
15	Jorge Toca	.15
16	Buddy Carlyle	.15
17	Chad Hermansen	.15
18	Matt Perisho	.15
19	Tomokazu Ohka RC	.75
20	Jacque Jones	.15
21	Josh Paul	.15
22	Dermal Brown	.15
23	Adam Kennedy	.15
24	Chad Harville	.15
25	Calvin Murray	.15
26	Chad Meyers	.15
27	Brian Cooper	.15
28	Troy Glaus	.50
29	Ben Molina	.15
30	Troy Percival	.15
31	Ken Hill	.15
32	Chuck Finley	.15
33	Todd Greene	.15
34	Tim Salmon	.25
35	Gary DiSarcina	.15
36	Luis Gonzalez	.25
37	Tony Womack	.15
38	Omar Daal	.15
39	Randy Johnson	.50
40	Erubiel Durazo	.20
41	Jay Bell	.15
42	Steve Finley	.15
43	Travis Lee	.15
44	Greg Maddux	1.00
45	Bret Boone	.25
46	Brian Jordan	.15
47	Kevin Millwood	.25
48	Odalis Perez	.15
49	Javy Lopez	.25
50	John Smoltz	.25
51	Bruce Chen	.15
52	Albert Belle	.15
53	Jerry Hairston Jr.	.15
54	Will Clark	.40
55	Sidney Ponson	.15
56	Charles Johnson	.15
57	Cal Ripken Jr.	2.00
58	Ryan Minor	.15
59	Mike Mussina	.40
60	Tom Gordon	.15
61	Jose Offerman	.15
62	Trot Nixon	.15
63	Pedro Martinez	.75
64	John Valentin	.15
65	Jason Varitek	.15
66	Juan Pena	.15
67	Troy O'Leary	.15
68	Sammy Sosa	1.25
69	Henry Rodriguez	.15
70	Kyle Farnsworth	.15
71	Glenallen Hill	.15
72	Lance Johnson	.15
73	Mickey Morandini	.15
74	Jon Lieber	.15
75	Kevin Tapani	.15
76	Carlos Lee	.15
77	Ray Durham	.15
78	Jim Parque	.15
79	Bob Howry	.15
80	Magglio Ordonez	.25
81	Paul Konerko	.20
82	Mike Caruso	.15
83	Chris Singleton	.15
84	Sean Casey	.20
85	Barry Larkin	.25
86	Pokey Reese	.15
87	Eddie Taubensee	.15
88	Scott Williamson	.15
89	Jason LaRue	.15
90	Aaron Boone	.20
91	Jeffrey Hammonds	.15
92	Omar Vizquel	.20
93	Manny Ramirez	.50
94	Kenny Lofton	.20
95	Jaret Wright	.15
96	Einar Diaz	.15
97	Charles Nagy	.15
98	David Justice	.25
99	Richie Sexson	.15
100	Steve Karsay	.15
101	Todd Helton	.50
102	Dante Bichette	.15
103	Larry Walker	.25
104	Pedro Astacio	.15
105	Neifi Perez	.15
106	Brian Bohanon	.15
107	Edgard Clemente	.15
108	Dave Veres	.15
109	Gabe Kapler	.15
110	Juan Encarnacion	.15
111	Jeff Weaver	.15
112	Damion Easley	.15
113	Justin Thompson	.15
114	Brad Ausmus	.15
115	Frank Catalanotto	.15
116	Todd Jones	.15
117	Preston Wilson	.25
118	Cliff Floyd	.15
119	Mike Lowell	.15
120	Jorge Fabregas	.15
121	Alex Gonzalez	.15
122	Braden Looper	.15
123	Bruce Aven	.15
124	Richard Hidalgo	.15
125	Mitch Meluskey	.15
126	Jeff Bagwell	.50
127	Jose Lima	.15
128	Derek Bell	.15
129	Billy Wagner	.15
130	Shane Reynolds	.15
131	Moises Alou	.25
132	Carlos Beltran	.25
133	Carlos Febles	.15
134	Jermaine Dye	.15
135	Jeremy Giambi	.15
136	Joe Randa	.15
137	Jose Rosado	.15
138	Chad Kreuter	.15
139	Jose Vizcaino	.15
140	Adrian Beltre	.25
141	Kevin Brown	.25
142	Ismael Valdes	.15
143	Angel Pena	.15
144	Chan Ho Park	.15
145	Mark Grudzielanek	.15
146	Jeff Shaw	.15
147	Geoff Jenkins	.20
148	Jeromy Burnitz	.15
149	Hideo Nomo	.25
150	Ron Belliard	.15
151	Sean Berry	.15
152	Mark Loretta	.15
153	Steve Woodard	.15
154	Joe Mays	.15
155	Eric Milton	.15
156	Corey Koskie	.15
157	Ron Coomer	.15
158	Brad Radke	.15
159	Terry Steinbach	.15
160	Christian Guzman	.15

#	Player	Price
161	Vladimir Guerrero	.50
162	Wilton Guerrero	.15
163	Michael Barrett	.15
164	Chris Widger	.15
165	Fernando Seguignol	.15
166	Ugueth Urbina	.15
167	Dustin Hermanson	.15
168	Kenny Rogers	.15
169	Edgardo Alfonzo	.15
170	Orel Hershiser	.15
171	Robin Ventura	.20
172	Octavio Dotel	.15
173	Rickey Henderson	.25
174	Roger Cedeno	.15
175	John Olerud	.25
176	Derek Jeter	2.00
177	Tino Martinez	.25
178	Orlando Hernandez	.20
179	Chuck Knoblauch	.15
180	Bernie Williams	.40
181	Chili Davis	.15
182	David Cone	.20
183	Ricky Ledee	.15
184	Paul O'Neill	.25
185	Jason Giambi	.50
186	Eric Chavez	.25
187	Matt Stairs	.15
188	Miguel Tejada	.25
189	Olmedo Saenz	.15
190	Tim Hudson	.40
191	John Jaha	.15
192	Randy Velarde	.15
193	Rico Brogna	.15
194	Mike Lieberthal	.20
195	Marlon Anderson	.15
196	Bobby Abreu	.25
197	Ron Gant	.15
198	Randy Wolf	.15
199	Desi Relaford	.15
200	Doug Glanville	.15
201	Warren Morris	.15
202	Kris Benson	.15
203	Kevin Young	.15
204	Brian Giles	.25
205	Jason Schmidt	.15
206	Ed Sprague	.15
207	Francisco Cordova	.15
208	Mark McGwire	2.00
209	Jose Jimenez	.15
210	Fernando Tatis	.15
211	Kent Bottenfield	.15
212	Eli Marrero	.15
213	Edgar Renteria	.15
214	Joe McEwing	.15
215	J.D. Drew	.20
216	Tony Gwynn	.75
217	Gary Matthews Jr.	.15
218	Eric Owens	.15
219	Damian Jackson	.15
220	Reggie Sanders	.15
221	Trevor Hoffman	.15
222	Ben Davis	.15
223	Shawn Estes	.15
224	F.P. Santangelo	.15
225	Livan Hernandez	.15
226	Ellis Burks	.15
227	J.T. Snow	.15
228	Jeff Kent	.25
229	Robb Nen	.15
230	Marvin Benard	.15
231	Ken Griffey Jr.	1.00
232	John Halama	.15
233	Gil Meche	.15
234	David Bell	.15
235	Brian L. Hunter	.15
236	Jay Buhner	.25
237	Edgar Martinez	.25
238	Jose Mesa	.15
239	Wilson Alvarez	.15
240	Wade Boggs	.40
241	Fred McGriff	.25
242	Jose Canseco	.40
243	Kevin Stocker	.15
244	Roberto Hernandez	.15
245	Bubba Trammell	.15
246	John Flaherty	.15
247	Ivan Rodriguez	.40
248	Rusty Greer	.15
249	Rafael Palmeiro	.40
250	Jeff Zimmerman	.15
251	Royce Clayton	.15
252	Todd Zeile	.15
253	John Wetteland	.15
254	Ruben Mateo	.15
255	Kelvim Escobar	.15
256	David Wells	.15
257	Shawn Green	.40
258	Homer Bush	.15
259	Shannon Stewart	.15
260	Carlos Delgado	.50
261	Roy Halladay	.25
262	Fernando Tatis CL	.15
263	Jose Jimenez CL	.15
264	Tony Gwynn CL	.40
265	Wade Boggs CL	.25
266	Cal Ripken Jr. CL	1.00
267	David Cone CL	.15
268	Mark McGwire CL	.75
269	Pedro Martinez CL	.40
270	Nomar Garciaparra CL	.75
271	Nick Johnson	.40
272	Mark Quinn	.15
273	Roosevelt Brown	.15
274	Adam Everett	.15
275	Jason Marquis	.15
276	Kazuhiro Sasaki RC	1.50
277	Aaron Myette	.15
278	Danys Baez RC	.50
279	Travis Dawkins	.15
280	Mark Mulder	.25
281	Chris Haas	.15
282	Milton Bradley	.15
283	Brad Penny	.15
284	Rafael Furcal	.25
285	Luis Matos RC	1.00
286	Victor Santos	.15
287	Rico Washington RC	.15
288	Rob Bell	.15
289	Joe Crede	.15
290	Pablo Ozuna	.15
291	Wascar Serrano RC	.15
292	Sang-Hoon Lee RC	.25
293	Chris Wakeland	.15
294	Luis Rivera	.15
295	Mike Lamb RC	.20
296	Wily Pena	.20
297	Mike Meyers RC	.15
298	Mo Vaughn	.20
299	Darin Erstad	.25
300	Garret Anderson	.25
301	Tim Belcher	.15
302	Scott Spiezio	.15
303	Kent Bottenfield	.15
304	Orlando Palmeiro	.15
305	Jason Dickson	.15
306	Matt Williams	.20
307	Brian Anderson	.15
308	Hanley Frias	.15
309	Todd Stottlemyre	.15
310	Matt Mantei	.15
311	David Dellucci	.15
312	Armando Reynoso	.15
313	Bernard Gilkey	.15
314	Chipper Jones	1.00
315	Tom Glavine	.25
316	Quilvio Veras	.15
317	Andruw Jones	.50
318	Bobby Bonilla	.15
319	Reggie Sanders	.15
320	Andres Galarraga	.20
321	George Lombard	.15
322	John Rocker	.15
322	Wally Joyner	.15
324	B.J. Surhoff	.15
325	Scott Erickson	.15
326	Delino DeShields	.15
327	Jeff Conine	.15
328	Mike Timlin	.15
329	Brady Anderson	.15
330	Mike Bordick	.15
331	Harold Baines	.15
332	Nomar Garciaparra	1.50
333	Bret Saberhagen	.15
334	Ramon Martinez	.15
335	Donnie Sadler	.15
336	Wilton Veras	.15
337	Mike Stanley	.15
338	Brian Rose	.15
339	Carl Everett	.15
340	Tim Wakefield	.15
341	Mark Grace	.25
342	Kerry Wood	.30
343	Eric Young	.15
344	Jose Nieves	.15
345	Ismael Valdes	.15
346	Joe Girardi	.15
347	Damon Buford	.15
348	Ricky Gutierrez	.15
349	Frank Thomas	.50
350	Brian Simmons	.15
351	James Baldwin	.15
352	Brook Fordyce	.15
353	Jose Valentin	.15
354	Mike Sirotka	.15
355	Greg Norton	.15
356	Dante Bichette	.15
357	Deion Sanders	.25
358	Ken Griffey Jr.	1.00
359	Denny Neagle	.15
360	Dmitri Young	.15
361	Pete Harnisch	.15
362	Michael Tucker	.15
363	Roberto Alomar	.40
364	Dave Roberts	.15
365	Jim Thome	.50
366	Bartolo Colon	.15
367	Travis Fryman	.20
368	Chuck Finley	.15
369	Russell Branyan	.15
370	Alex Ramirez	.15
371	Jeff Cirillo	.15
372	Jeffrey Hammonds	.15
373	Scott Karl	.15
374	Brent Mayne	.15
375	Tom Goodwin	.15
376	Jose Jimenez	.15
377	Rolando Arrojo	.15
378	Terry Shumpert	.15
379	Juan Gonzalez	.50
380	Bobby Higginson	.15
381	Tony Clark	.15
382	Dave Mlicki	.15
383	Deivi Cruz	.15
384	Brian Moehler	.15
385	Dean Palmer	.15
386	Luis Castillo	.15
387	Mike Redmond	.15
388	Alex Fernandez	.15
389	Brant Brown	.15
390	Dave Berg	.15
391	A.J. Burnett	.15
392	Mark Kotsay	.15
393	Craig Biggio	.20
394	Daryle Ward	.15
395	Lance Berkman	.25
396	Roger Cedeno	.15
397	Scott Elarton	.15
398	Octavio Dotel	.15
399	Ken Caminiti	.15
400	Johnny Damon	.25
401	Mike Sweeney	.15
402	Jeff Suppan	.15
403	Rey Sanchez	.15
404	Blake Stein	.15
405	Ricky Bottalico	.15
406	Jay Witasick	.15
407	Shawn Green	.40
408	Orel Hershiser	.15
409	Gary Sheffield	.40
410	Todd Hollandsworth	.15
411	Terry Adams	.15
412	Todd Hundley	.15
413	Eric Karros	.15
414	F.P. Santangelo	.15
415	Alex Cora	.15
416	Marquis Grissom	.15
417	Henry Blanco	.15
418	Jose Hernandez	.15
419	Kyle Peterson	.15
420	John Snyder RC	.15
421	Bob Wickman	.15
422	Jamey Wright	.15
423	Chad Allen	.15
424	Todd Walker	.15
425	J.C. Romero RC	.15
426	Butch Huskey	.15
427	Jacque Jones	.15
428	Matt Lawton	.15
429	Rondell White	.25
430	Jose Vidro	.15
431	Hideki Irabu	.15
432	Javier Vazquez	.15
433	Lee Stevens	.15
434	Mike Thurman	.15
435	Geoff Blum	.15
436	Mike Hampton	.15
437	Mike Piazza	1.00
438	Al Leiter	.15
439	Derek Bell	.15
440	Armando Benitez	.15
441	Rey Ordonez	.15
442	Todd Zeile	.15
443	Roger Clemens	1.25
444	Ramiro Mendoza	.15
445	Andy Pettitte	.25
446	Scott Brosius	.15
447	Mariano Rivera	.25
448	Jim Leyritz	.15
449	Jorge Posada	.25
450	Omar Olivares	.15
451	Ben Grieve	.15
452	A.J. Hinch	.15
453	Gil Heredia	.15
454	Kevin Appier	.15
455	Ryan Christenson	.15
456	Ramon Hernandez	.15
457	Scott Rolen	.50
458	Alex Arias	.15
459	Andy Ashby	.15
460	(Not issued, see #474.)	
460		.15
461	Robert Person	.15
462	Paul Byrd	.15
463	Curt Schilling	.25
464	Mike Jackson	.15
465	Jason Kendall	.25
466	Pat Meares	.15
467	Bruce Aven	.15
468	Todd Ritchie	.15
469	Wil Cordero	.15
470	Aramis Ramirez	.15
471	Andy Benes	.15
472	Ray Lankford	.15
473	Fernando Vina	.15
474a	Jim Edmonds	.25
474b	Kevin Jordan (Should be #460.)	.15
475	Craig Paquette	.15
476	Pat Hentgen	.15
477	Darryl Kile	.15
478	Sterling Hitchcock	.15
479	Ruben Rivera	.15
480	Ryan Klesko	.15
481	Phil Nevin	.15
482	Woody Williams	.15
483	Carlos Hernandez	.15
484	Brian Meadows	.15
485	Bret Boone	.25
486	Barry Bonds	1.50
487	Russ Ortiz	.15
488	Bobby Estalella	.15
489	Rich Aurilia	.15
490	Bill Mueller	.15
491	Joe Nathan	.15
492	Russ Davis	.15
493	John Olerud	.25
494	Alex Rodriguez	1.50
495	Fred Garcia	.15
496	Carlos Guillen	.15
497	Aaron Sele	.15
498	Brett Tomko	.15
499	Jamie Moyer	.15
500	Mike Cameron	.15
501	Vinny Castilla	.15
502	Gerald Williams	.15
503	Mike DiFelice	.15
504	Ryan Rupe	.15
505	Greg Vaughn	.15
506	Miguel Cairo	.15
507	Juan Guzman RC	.15
508	Jose Guillen	.15
509	Gabe Kapler	.15
510	Rick Helling	.15
511	David Segui	.15
512	Doug Davis	.15
513	Justin Thompson	.15
514	Chad Curtis	.15
515	Tony Batista	.15
516	Billy Koch	.15
517	Raul Mondesi	.20
518	Joey Hamilton	.15
519	Darrin Fletcher	.15
520	Brad Fullmer	.15
521	Jose Cruz Jr.	.15
522	Kevin Witt	.15
523	Mark McGwire	1.00
524	Roberto Alomar	.25
525	Chipper Jones	.50
526	Derek Jeter	1.00
527	Ken Griffey Jr.	.50
528	Sammy Sosa	.75
529	Manny Ramirez	.40
530	Ivan Rodriguez	.25
531	Pedro J. Martinez	.40
532	Mariano Rivera	.15
533	Sammy Sosa	.75
534	Cal Ripken Jr.	1.00
535	Vladimir Guerrero	.40
536	Tony Gwynn	.25
537	Mark McGwire	1.00
538	Bernie Williams	.25
539	Pedro J. Martinez	.40
540	Ken Griffey Jr.	.50

Exclusives

NM/M

Common Silver Exclusive:	1.00
Silver Stars/Rookies:	8X

(See 2000 Upper Deck for
checklist and base card values.)

Cooperstown Calling

NM/M

Complete Set (15):	25.00
Common Player:	.75

Inserted 1:23

1	Roger Clemens	3.00
2	Cal Ripken Jr.	5.00
3	Ken Griffey Jr.	3.00
4	Mike Piazza	3.00
5	Tony Gwynn	2.00
6	Sammy Sosa	2.50
7	Jose Canseco	1.00
8	Larry Walker	.75

9	Barry Bonds	4.00
10	Greg Maddux	2.50
11	Derek Jeter	5.00
12	Mark McGwire	4.00
13	Randy Johnson	2.00
14	Frank Thomas	1.50
15	Jeff Bagwell	1.50

e-Card

		NM/M
Complete Set (6):		10.00
Common Player:		1.00
Inserted 1:12		
1	Ken Griffey Jr.	2.00
2	Alex Rodriguez	3.00
3	Cal Ripken Jr.	3.00
4	Jeff Bagwell	1.00
5	Barry Bonds	3.00
6	Manny Ramirez	1.00

eVolve Jersey

		NM/M
Common Player:		15.00
Production 300 Sets		
1	Ken Griffey Jr.	40.00
2	Alex Rodriguez	40.00
3	Cal Ripken Jr.	65.00
4	Jeff Bagwell	20.00
5	Barry Bonds	50.00
6	Manny Ramirez	20.00

eVolve Signature

		NM/M
Common Player:		40.00
Production 200 Sets		
1	Ken Griffey Jr.	85.00
2	Alex Rodriguez	85.00
3	Cal Ripken Jr.	150.00

4	Jeff Bagwell	40.00
5	Barry Bonds	120.00
6	Manny Ramirez	40.00

eVolve Signed Jersey

		NM/M
Common Player:		80.00
Production 50 Sets		
1	Ken Griffey Jr.	150.00
2	Alex Rodriguez	150.00
3	Cal Ripken Jr.	200.00
4	Jeff Bagwell	60.00
5	Barry Bonds	150.00
6	Manny Ramirez	60.00

Faces of the Game

		NM/M
Complete Set (20):		30.00
Common Player:		.75
Inserted 1:11		
Silver:		4-8X
Production 100 Sets		
1	Ken Griffey Jr.	2.50
2	Mark McGwire	3.00
3	Sammy Sosa	2.00
4	Alex Rodriguez	3.00
5	Manny Ramirez	1.00
6	Derek Jeter	4.00
7	Jeff Bagwell	1.00
8	Roger Clemens	2.00
9	Scott Rolen	.75
10	Tony Gwynn	1.50
11	Nomar Garciaparra	2.50
12	Randy Johnson	1.50
13	Greg Maddux	2.00
14	Mike Piazza	2.50
15	Frank Thomas	1.00
16	Cal Ripken Jr.	4.00
17	Ivan Rodriguez	.75
18	Mo Vaughn	.75
19	Chipper Jones	2.00
20	Sean Casey	.75

Five-Tool Talents

		NM/M
Complete Set (15):		15.00
Common Player:		.50
Inserted 1:11		
1	Vladimir Guerrero	1.50
2	Barry Bonds	3.00

3	Jason Kendall	.50
4	Derek Jeter	4.00
5	Ken Griffey Jr.	2.50
6	Andruw Jones	.75
7	Bernie Williams	.75
8	Jose Canseco	.75
9	Scott Rolen	.75
10	Shawn Green	.50
11	Nomar Garciaparra	2.50
12	Jeff Bagwell	1.00
13	Larry Walker	.75
14	Chipper Jones	2.00
15	Alex Rodriguez	3.00

Game Balls

		NM/M
Common Player:		10.00
JB	Jeff Bagwell	10.00
RC	Roger Clemens	30.00
KG	Ken Griffey Jr.	25.00
VG	Vladimir Guerrero	15.00
TG	Tony Gwynn	25.00
DJ	Derek Jeter	40.00
CJ	Chipper Jones	20.00
GM	Greg Maddux	20.00
MM	Mark McGwire	50.00
AR	Alex Rodriguez	30.00
BW	Bernie Williams	10.00

Game Jersey

		NM/M
Common Player:		10.00
Inserted 1:2,500		
JC	Jose Canseco	15.00
JG	Juan Gonzalez	15.00
VG	Vladimir Guerrero	20.00
TH	Todd Helton	15.00
CJ	Chipper Jones	25.00
GK	Gabe Kapler	10.00
GM	Greg Maddux	35.00
MR	Manny Ramirez	20.00
CR	Cal Ripken Jr.	60.00
GV	Greg Vaughn	10.00

Game Jersey Hobby

		NM/M
Common Player:		10.00
Inserted 1:288		
JB	Jeff Bagwell	15.00
TG	Troy Glaus	15.00
CY	Tom Glavine	10.00
Jr.	Ken Griffey Jr.	25.00
DJ	Derek Jeter	40.00
PM	Pedro J. Martinez	20.00
MP	Mike Piazza	30.00
AR	Alex Rodriguez	30.00
FT	Frank Thomas	15.00
LW	Larry Walker	10.00

Game Jersey Series 2

		NM/M
Common Player:		10.00
AR	Alex Rodriguez	30.00
TG	Tony Gwynn	20.00
FT	Frank Thomas	15.00
MW	Matt Williams	10.00
JT	Jim Thome	15.00
MV	Mo Vaughn	10.00
TGI	Tom Glavine	15.00
BG	Ben Grieve	10.00

TrG	Troy Glaus	15.00
RJ	Randy Johnson	20.00
KM	Kevin Millwood	10.00
KG	Ken Griffey Jr.	25.00
AB	Albert Belle	10.00
DC	David Cone	10.00
MH	Mike Hampton	10.00
EC	Eric Chavez	10.00
EM	Edgar Martinez	15.00
PW	Preston Wilson	10.00
RV	Robin Ventura	10.00

Game Jersey Patch

		NM/M
Common Player:		40.00
Inserted 1:10,000		
JB	Jeff Bagwell	60.00
JC	Jose Canseco	60.00
TG	Troy Glaus	50.00
CY	Tom Glavine	60.00
Jr.	Ken Griffey Jr.	100.00
VG	Vladimir Guerrero	100.00
TH	Todd Helton	60.00
DJ	Derek Jeter	150.00
CJ	Chipper Jones	75.00
GK	Gabe Kapler	40.00
GM	Greg Maddux	100.00
PM	Pedro J. Martinez	100.00
MP	Mike Piazza	100.00
MR	Manny Ramirez	80.00
CR	Cal Ripken Jr.	200.00
AR	Alex Rodriguez	125.00
FT	Frank Thomas	80.00
GV	Greg Vaughn	40.00
LW	Larry Walker	50.00

Game Jersey Patch Series 2

		NM/M
Common Player:		50.00
JB	Jeff Bagwell	75.00
BB	Barry Bonds	200.00
JC	Jose Canseco	75.00
TGI	Troy Glaus	75.00
KG	Ken Griffey Jr.	125.00
VG	Vladimir Guerrero	100.00
TG	Tony Gwynn	100.00
DJ	Derek Jeter	150.00
RJ	Randy Johnson	100.00
AJ	Andruw Jones	80.00
CJ	Chipper Jones	100.00
GM	Greg Maddux	100.00
PM	Pedro Martinez	100.00
MR	Manny Ramirez	100.00
CR	Cal Ripken Jr.	200.00
SR	Scott Rolen	75.00
AR	Alex Rodriguez	150.00
IR	Ivan Rodriguez	90.00
FT	Frank Thomas	100.00
MV	Mo Vaughn	50.00
MW	Matt Williams	50.00

Game Jersey Autograph Hobby Series 2

		NM/M
Common Player:		30.00
H-KG	Ken Griffey Jr.	100.00
H-CR	Cal Ripken Jr.	150.00

H-DJ	Derek Jeter	150.00
H-IR	Ivan Rodriguez	40.00
H-AR	Alex Rodriguez	100.00
H-MR	Manny Ramirez	50.00
H-JC	Jose Canseco	30.00
H-BB	Barry Bonds	180.00
H-SR	Scott Rolen	40.00
H-PO	Paul O'Neill	40.00
H-JK	Jason Kendall	30.00
H-VG	Vladimir Guerrero	50.00
H-JB	Jeff Bagwell	40.00

Hit Brigade

		NM/M
Complete Set (15):		15.00
Common Player:		.50
Inserted 1:8		
Silver:		5-10X
Production 100 Sets		
1	Ken Griffey Jr.	2.00
2	Tony Gwynn	1.00
3	Alex Rodriguez	2.50
4	Derek Jeter	3.00
5	Mike Piazza	2.00
6	Sammy Sosa	1.50
7	Juan Gonzalez	.75
8	Scott Rolen	.50
9	Nomar Garciaparra	2.00
10	Barry Bonds	2.50
11	Craig Biggio	.50
12	Chipper Jones	1.50
13	Frank Thomas	.75
14	Larry Walker	.50
15	Mark McGwire	2.50

Hot Properties

		NM/M
Complete Set (15):		10.00
Common Player:		.50
Inserted 1:11		
1	Carlos Beltran	1.00
2	Rick Ankiel	.50
3	Sean Casey	1.00
4	Preston Wilson	1.00
5	Vernon Wells	1.00
6	Pat Burrell	1.50
7	Eric Chavez	1.00
8	J.D. Drew	1.00
9	Alfonso Soriano	2.00
10	Gabe Kapler	.50
11	Rafael Furcal	1.00
12	Ruben Mateo	.50
13	Corey Koskie	.75
14	Kip Wells	.50
15	Ramon Ortiz	.75

Pennant Driven

	NM/M
Complete Set (10):	8.00
Common Player:	.50

Inserted 1:4		
1	Derek Jeter	2.00
2	Roberto Alomar	.50
3	Chipper Jones	1.50
4	Jeff Bagwell	.75
5	Roger Clemens	1.00
6	Nomar Garciaparra	1.50
7	Manny Ramirez	.75
8	Mike Piazza	1.50
9	Ivan Rodriguez	.75
10	Randy Johnson	.75

Piece of History-500 Club

		NM/M
755HR	Hank Aaron	275.00
HAAU	Hank Aaron/ Auto./44	900.00

Power Deck

		NM/M
Complete Set (11):		60.00
Common Player:		2.50
Inserted 1:23		
1	Ken Griffey Jr.	5.00
2	Cal Ripken Jr.	7.50
3	Mark McGwire	6.00
4	Tony Gwynn	3.50
5	Roger Clemens	3.50
6	Alex Rodriguez	6.00
7	Sammy Sosa	3.50
8	Derek Jeter	7.50
9	Ken Griffey Jr.	25.00
10	Mark McGwire	30.00
11	Reggie Jackson	15.00

Power MARK

	NM/M
Complete Set (10):	25.00
Common McGwire:	3.00
Inserted 1:23	
Silver:	5-10X
Production 100 Sets	

Power Rally

	NM/M
Complete Set (15):	20.00
Common Player:	.75
Inserted 1:11	

Silver:		4-8X
Production 100 Sets		
1	Ken Griffey Jr.	2.50
2	Mark McGwire	3.00
3	Sammy Sosa	2.00
4	Jose Canseco	.75
5	Juan Gonzalez	1.00
6	Bernie Williams	.75
7	Jeff Bagwell	1.00
8	Chipper Jones	2.00
9	Vladimir Guerrero	1.50
10	Mo Vaughn	.75
11	Derek Jeter	4.00
12	Mike Piazza	2.50
13	Barry Bonds	3.00
14	Alex Rodriguez	3.00
15	Nomar Garciaparra	2.50

Prime Performers

		NM/M
Complete Set (10):		10.00
Common Player:		.50
Inserted 1:8		
1	Manny Ramirez	.75
2	Pedro Martinez	1.00
3	Carlos Delgado	.50
4	Ken Griffey Jr.	2.00
5	Derek Jeter	3.00
6	Chipper Jones	1.50
7	Sean Casey	.50
8	Shawn Green	.50
9	Sammy Sosa	1.50
10	Alex Rodriguez	2.50

STATitude

		NM/M
Complete Set (30):		25.00
Common Player:		.40
Inserted 1:4		
Silver:		5-10X
Production 100 Sets		
1	Mo Vaughn	.40
2	Matt Williams	.40
3	Travis Lee	.40
4	Chipper Jones	1.50
5	Greg Maddux	1.50
6	Gabe Kapler	.40
7	Cal Ripken Jr.	3.00
8	Nomar Garciaparra	2.00
9	Sammy Sosa	1.50
10	Frank Thomas	.75
11	Manny Ramirez	.75
12	Larry Walker	.50
13	Ivan Rodriguez	.50
14	Jeff Bagwell	.75
15	Craig Biggio	.50
16	Vladimir Guerrero	1.00
17	Mike Piazza	2.00
18	Bernie Williams	.50
19	Derek Jeter	3.00
20	Jose Canseco	.50

21	Eric Chavez	.50
22	Scott Rolen	.50
23	Mark McGwire	2.50
24	Tony Gwynn	1.00
25	Barry Bonds	2.50
26	Ken Griffey Jr.	2.00
27	Alex Rodriguez	2.50
28	J.D. Drew	.50
29	Juan Gonzalez	.50
30	Roger Clemens	1.50

The People's Choice

		NM/M
Complete Set (15):		20.00
Common Player:		.75
Inserted 1:23		
1	Mark McGwire	3.00
2	Nomar Garciaparra	3.00
3	Derek Jeter	3.00
4	Shawn Green	.75
5	Manny Ramirez	1.00
6	Pedro Martinez	1.50
7	Ivan Rodriguez	.75
8	Alex Rodriguez	3.00
9	Juan Gonzalez	1.00
10	Ken Griffey Jr.	2.00
11	Sammy Sosa	2.50
12	Jeff Bagwell	1.00
13	Chipper Jones	2.00
14	Cal Ripken Jr.	4.00
15	Mike Piazza	2.00

2K Plus

		NM/M
Complete Set (12):		15.00
Common Player:		.50
Inserted 1:23		
Silver:		5-10X
Production 100 Sets		
1	Ken Griffey Jr.	2.00
2	J.D. Drew	.50
3	Derek Jeter	3.00
4	Nomar Garciaparra	3.00
5	Pat Burrell	.75
6	Ruben Mateo	.50
7	Carlos Beltran	.50
8	Vladimir Guerrero	1.00
9	Scott Rolen	1.00
10	Chipper Jones	2.00
11	Alex Rodriguez	3.00
12	Magglio Ordonez	.75

3,000 Hit Club Series 2

		NM/M
HA-B	Hank Aaron/ Bat/350	50.00
HA-JB	Hank Aaron/ Bat/Jsy/100	100.00

| HA-J | Hank Aaron/ Jsy/350 | 50.00 |
| HA-JBS | Hank Aaron/Auto. Bat/Jsy/44 | 700.00 |

3,000 Hit Club Series 1

		NM/M
CR-B	Cal Ripken Jr./ Bat/350	25.00
CR-J	Cal Ripken Jr./ Jsy/350	25.00
CR-JB	Cal Ripken Jr./ Jsy/Bat/100	150.00
CR-JBS	Cal Ripken Jr./ Jsy/Bat/Auto./8	
EM-B	Eddie Murray/ Bat/350	10.00
EM-J	Eddie Murray/ Jsy/350	8.00
EM-JB	Eddie Murray/ Jsy/Bat/100	60.00
EM-JBS	Eddie Murray/ Jsy/Bat/Auto./33	

2000 Upper Deck Black Diamond

		NM/M
Complete Set (120):		25.00
Common Player:		.15
Common Diamond Debut:		.50
Pack (6):		1.50
Wax Box (24):		30.00
1	Darin Erstad	.25
2	Tim Salmon	.25
3	Mo Vaughn	.20
4	Matt Williams	.25
5	Travis Lee	.15
6	Randy Johnson	.75
7	Tom Glavine	.40
8	Chipper Jones	1.50
9	Greg Maddux	1.50
10	Andruw Jones	.50
11	Brian Jordan	.15
12	Cal Ripken Jr.	2.50
13	Albert Belle	.20
14	Mike Mussina	.50
15	Nomar Garciaparra	2.00
16	Troy O'Leary	.15
17	Pedro J. Martinez	1.00
18	Sammy Sosa	1.50
19	Henry Rodriguez	.15
20	Frank Thomas	.75
21	Magglio Ordonez	.40
22	Greg Vaughn	.15
23	Barry Larkin	.25
24	Sean Casey	.25
25	Jim Thome	.75
26	Kenny Lofton	.25
27	Roberto Alomar	.50
28	Manny Ramirez	.75
29	Larry Walker	.25
30	Todd Helton	.75
31	Gabe Kapler	.15
32	Tony Clark	.15
33	Dean Palmer	.15
34	Cliff Floyd	.15
35	Alex Gonzalez	.15
36	Moises Alou	.25
37	Jeff Bagwell	.75
38	Craig Biggio	.25
39	Richard Hidalgo	.15
40	Carlos Beltran	.25
41	Johnny Damon	.25
42	Adrian Beltre	.25
43	Gary Sheffield	.40
44	Kevin Brown	.25
45	Jeromy Burnitz	.15
46	Jeff Cirillo	.15
47	Joe Mays	.15
48	Todd Walker	.15
49	Vladimir Guerrero	.75
50	Michael Barrett	.15
51	Rickey Henderson	.40
52	Mike Piazza	1.50
53	Robin Ventura	.25
54	John Olerud	.25
55	Edgardo Alfonzo	.15
56	Derek Jeter	2.00
57	Orlando Hernandez	.15
58	Tino Martinez	.25
59	Bernie Williams	.50
60	Roger Clemens	1.50
61	Eric Chavez	.25
62	Ben Grieve	.15
63	Jason Giambi	1.00
64	Scott Rolen	.50
65	Bobby Abreu	.25
66	Curt Schilling	.40
67	Mike Lieberthal	.15
68	Warren Morris	.15
69	Brian Giles	.25
70	Eric Owens	.15
71	Tony Gwynn	1.00
72	Reggie Sanders	.15
73	Barry Bonds	2.00
74	J.T. Snow	.15
75	Jeff Kent	.25
76	Ken Griffey Jr.	1.50
77	Alex Rodriguez	2.00
78	Edgar Martinez	.15
79	Jay Buhner	.15
80	Mark McGwire	2.00
81	J.D. Drew	.25
82	Eric Davis	.15
83	Fernando Tatis	.15
84	Wade Boggs	.50
85	Fred McGriff	.25
86	Juan Gonzalez	.75
87	Ivan Rodriguez	.50
88	Rafael Palmeiro	.50
89	Shawn Green	.40
90	Carlos Delgado	.60
91	Pat Burrell	1.00
92	Eric Munson	.50
93	Jorge Toca	.50
94	Rick Ankiel	.50
95	Tony Armas Jr.	.75
96	Byung-Hyun Kim	.75
97	Alfonso Soriano	3.00
98	Mark Quinn	.50
99	Ryan Rupe	.50
100	Adam Kennedy	.50
101	Jeff Weaver	.75
102	Ramon Ortiz	.75
103	Eugene Kingsale	.50
104	Josh Beckett	1.00
105	Eric Gagne	1.00
106	Peter Bergeron	.50
107	Erubiel Durazo	.75
108	Chad Meyers	.50
109	Kip Wells	.50
110	Chad Harville	.50
111	Matt Riley	.50
112	Ben Petrick	.50
113	Ed Yarnall	.50
114	Calvin Murray	.50
115	Vernon Wells	1.00
116	A.J. Burnett	.75
117	Jacque Jones	.75
118	Francisco Cordero	.50
119	Tomokazu Ohka **RC**	1.50
120	Julio Ramirez	.50

Final Cut

| Stars (1-90): | 5-10X |

| Diamond Debuts: | 2-4X |

Production 100 Sets
(See 2000 UD Black Diamond for checklist and base card values.)

Reciprocal Cut

| Stars (1-90): | 2-5X |
| Diamond Debuts: | 1-1.5X |

1-90 inserted 1:7
Diamond Debuts inserted 1:12
(See 2000 UD Black Diamond for checklist and base card values.)

A Piece of History Single

		NM/M
Common Player:		8.00
Inserted 1:179		
AB	Albert Belle	8.00
BB	Barry Bonds	40.00
JC	Jose Canseco	10.00
DE	Darin Erstad	8.00
JR	Ken Griffey Jr.	25.00
VG	Vladimir Guerrero	15.00
TG	Tony Gwynn	20.00
TH	Todd Helton	10.00
DJ	Derek Jeter	40.00
AJ	Andruw Jones	10.00
CJ	Chipper Jones	20.00
TL	Travis Lee	8.00
RM	Raul Mondesi	8.00
MP	Mike Piazza	25.00
CAL	Cal Ripken Jr.	50.00
AR	Alex Rodriguez	25.00
IR	Ivan Rodriguez	10.00
SR	Scott Rolen	10.00
MV	Mo Vaughn	8.00

A Piece of History Double

		NM/M
Common Player:		10.00
Inserted 1:1079		
AB	Albert Belle	10.00
BB	Barry Bonds	75.00
JC	Jose Canseco	20.00
DE	Darin Erstad	15.00
JR	Ken Griffey Jr.	50.00
VG	Vladimir Guerrero	30.00
TG	Tony Gwynn	40.00
TH	Todd Helton	15.00
DJ	Derek Jeter	75.00
AJ	Andruw Jones	15.00
CJ	Chipper Jones	40.00
TL	Travis Lee	10.00
RM	Raul Mondesi	10.00
MP	Mike Piazza	50.00
CAL	Cal Ripken Jr.	80.00
AR	Alex Rodriguez	50.00
IR	Ivan Rodriguez	15.00
SR	Scott Rolen	15.00
MV	Mo Vaughn	10.00

Barrage

	NM/M
Complete Set (10):	15.00
Common Player:	1.00

Inserted 1:29

1	Mark McGwire	3.00
2	Ken Griffey Jr.	2.00
3	Sammy Sosa	2.50
4	Jeff Bagwell	1.00
5	Juan Gonzalez	1.00
6	Alex Rodriguez	3.00
7	Manny Ramirez	1.00
8	Ivan Rodriguez	1.00
9	Chipper Jones	2.00
10	Mike Piazza	2.00

Constant Threat

	NM/M
Complete Set (10):	20.00
Common Player:	1.00

Inserted 1:29

1	Ken Griffey Jr.	2.00
2	Vladimir Guerrero	1.00
3	Alex Rodriguez	3.00
4	Sammy Sosa	2.50
5	Juan Gonzalez	1.00
6	Derek Jeter	3.00
7	Nomar Garciaparra	3.00
8	Barry Bonds	4.00
9	Chipper Jones	2.00
10	Mike Piazza	2.00

Diamonation

	NM/M
Complete Set (10):	6.00
Common Player:	.50

Inserted 1:4

1	Ken Griffey Jr.	1.00
2	Randy Johnson	1.00
3	Mark McGwire	1.50
4	Manny Ramirez	.75
5	Scott Rolen	.75
6	Bernie Williams	.75
7	Roger Clemens	1.50
8	Mo Vaughn	.50
9	Frank Thomas	.75
10	Sean Casey	.50

Diamond Gallery

	NM/M
Complete Set (10):	20.00
Common Player:	1.50

Inserted 1:14

		NM/M
1	Derek Jeter	3.00
2	Alex Rodriguez	3.00
3	Nomar Garciaparra	3.00
4	Cal Ripken Jr.	4.00
5	Sammy Sosa	2.50
6	Tony Gwynn	1.50
7	Mark McGwire	3.00
8	Roger Clemens	2.50
9	Greg Maddux	2.00
10	Pedro Martinez	1.50

Diamonds in the Rough

		NM/M
Complete Set (10):		8.00
Common Player:		.75
Inserted 1:9		
1	Pat Burrell	2.00
2	Eric Munson	.75
3	Alfonso Soriano	3.00
4	Ruben Mateo	.75
5	A.J. Burnett	1.00
6	Ben Davis	.75
7	Lance Berkman	1.50
8	Ed Yarnall	.75
9	Rick Ankiel	.75
10	Ryan Bradley	.75

DiamondMight

		NM/M
Complete Set (10):		15.00
Common Player:		1.00
Inserted 1:14		
1	Ken Griffey Jr.	2.00
2	Mark McGwire	3.00
3	Sammy Sosa	2.50
4	Manny Ramirez	1.00
5	Jeff Bagwell	1.00
6	Frank Thomas	1.00
7	Mike Piazza	2.00
8	Juan Gonzalez	1.00
9	Barry Bonds	4.00
10	Alex Rodriguez	3.00

500 Club Piece of History

	NM/M
Reggie Jackson	165.00

Reggie Jackson/ Auto./44		500.00

2000 Upper Deck Black Diamond Rookie Edition

		NM/M
Complete Set (154):		200.00
Common Player:		.15
Common Rookie Gem (91-120):		4.00
Production 1,000		
Rookie Jersey Gems (121-136):		
Inserted 1:24		
USA Authentics (137-154):		
Inserted 1:96		
Golds (1-90):		2-4X
Gold Gems (91-120):		1X
Gold Jerseys (121-136):		1-2X
Pack (6):		2.00
Box (24):		40.00
1	Troy Glaus	.75
2	Mo Vaughn	.40
3	Darin Erstad	.40
4	Jason Giambi	.40
5	Tim Hudson	.25
6	Ben Grieve	.25
7	Eric Chavez	.25
8	Tony Batista	.15
9	Carlos Delgado	.60
10	David Wells	.15
11	Greg Vaughn	.15
12	Fred McGriff	.25
13	Manny Ramirez	.75
14	Roberto Alomar	.60
15	Jim Thome	.40
16	Alex Rodriguez	2.50
17	Edgar Martinez	.15
18	John Olerud	.20
19	Albert Belle	.40
20	Mike Mussina	.40
21	Cal Ripken Jr.	2.50
22	Ivan Rodriguez	.75
23	Rafael Palmeiro	.40
24	Pedro J. Martinez	.75
25	Nomar Garciaparra	2.00
26	Carl Everett	.15
27	Jermaine Dye	.15
28	Mike Sweeney	.15
29	Juan Gonzalez	.75
30	Bobby Higginson	.15
31	Dean Palmer	.15
32	Jacque Jones	.15
33	Eric Milton	.15
34	Matt Lawton	.15
35	Magglio Ordonez	.25
36	Paul Konerko	.25
37	Frank Thomas	1.00
38	Ray Durham	.15
39	Roger Clemens	1.00
40	Derek Jeter	2.50
41	Bernie Williams	.50
42	Jose Canseco	.40
43	Craig Biggio	.25
44	Richard Hidalgo	.15
45	Jeff Bagwell	.75
46	Greg Maddux	1.50
47	Chipper Jones	1.50
48	Rafael Furcal	.25
49	Andruw Jones	.50
50	Geoff Jenkins	.25
51	Jeromy Burnitz	.15
52	Mark McGwire	3.00
53	Rick Ankiel	.50
54	Jim Edmonds	.25
55	Kerry Wood	.25
56	Sammy Sosa	2.00
57	Matt Williams	.25
58	Randy Johnson	.75
59	Steve Finley	.15
60	Curt Schilling	.15

61	Kevin Brown	.15
62	Gary Sheffield	.30
63	Shawn Green	.30
64	Jose Vidro	.15
65	Vladimir Guerrero	1.00
66	Jeff Kent	.15
67	Barry Bonds	1.00
68	Ryan Dempster	.15
69	Cliff Floyd	.15
70	Preston Wilson	.15
71	Mike Piazza	2.00
72	Al Leiter	.15
73	Edgardo Alfonzo	.25
74	Derek Bell	.15
75	Ryan Klesko	.15
76	Tony Gwynn	1.00
77	Bobby Abreu	.15
78	Pat Burrell	.50
79	Scott Rolen	.50
80	Mike Lieberthal	.15
81	Jason Kendall	.15
82	Brian Giles	.25
83	Ken Griffey Jr.	2.00
84	Pokey Reese	.15
85	Dmitri Young	.15
86	Sean Casey	.15
87	Jeff Cirillo	.15
88	Todd Helton	.75
89	Jeffrey Hammonds	.15
90	Larry Walker	.30
91	Barry Zito RC	15.00
92	Keith Ginter RC	6.00
93	Dane Sardinha RC	4.00
94	Kenny Kelly RC	4.00
95	Ryan Kohlmeier RC	4.00
96	Leo Estrella RC	4.00
97	Danys Baez RC	4.00
98	Paul Rigdon RC	4.00
99	Mike Lamb RC	4.00
100	Aaron McNeal RC	4.00
101	Juan Pierre RC	6.00
102	Rico Washington RC	4.00
103	Luis Matos RC	8.00
104	Adam Bernero RC	4.00
105	Wascar Serrano RC	4.00
106	Chris Richard RC	4.00
107	Justin Miller RC	4.00
108	Julio Zuleta RC	4.00
109	Alex Cabrera RC	4.00
110	Gene Stechschulte RC	4.00
111	Tony Mota RC	4.00
112	Tomokazu Ohka RC	4.00
113	Geraldo Guzman RC	4.00
114	Scott Downs RC	4.00
115	Timoniel Perez RC	4.00
116	Chad Durbin RC	4.00
117	Sun-Woo Kim RC	4.00
118	Tomas de la Rosa RC	4.00
119	Javier Cardona RC	4.00
120	Kazuhiro Sasaki RC	6.00
121	Brad Cresse RC	5.00
122	Matt Wheatland RC	5.00
123	Joe Torres RC	5.00
124	Dave Krynzel RC	5.00
125	Ben Diggins RC	5.00
126	Sean Burnett RC	8.00
127	David Espinosa RC	5.00
128	Scott Heard RC	5.00
129	Daylan Holt RC	5.00
130	Koyie Hill RC	5.00
131	Mark Buehrle RC	15.00
132	Xavier Nady RC	8.00
133	Mike Tonis RC	5.00
134	Matt Ginter RC	5.00
135	Lorenzo Barcelo RC	5.00
136	Cory Vance RC	5.00
137	Sean Burroughs RC	8.00
138	Todd Williams RC	5.00
139	Brad Wilkerson RC	5.00
140	Ben Sheets RC	20.00
141	Kurt Ainsworth RC	8.00
142	Anthony Sanders RC	5.00
143	Ryan Franklin RC	5.00
144	Shane Heams RC	5.00
145	Roy Oswalt RC	20.00
146	Jon Rauch RC	5.00
147	Brent Abernathy RC	5.00
148	Ernie Young RC	5.00
149	Chris George RC	5.00
150	Gookie Dawkins RC	5.00
151	Adam Everett RC	5.00
152	John Cotton RC	5.00
153	Pat Borders RC	5.00
154	Doug Mientkiewicz RC	5.00

Authentics

		NM/M
Jeter Authentic Pinstripes		
APJ	Derek Jeter/ Jsy/1,000	35.00
APB	Derek Jeter/ Bat/1,000	35.00
APC	Derek Jeter/Cap/200	70.00
APG	Derek Jeter/ Glove/200	80.00

Combos

		NM/M
Random game-used inserts.		
25 produced of each combo bat		
100 produced of combo jersey		
JDM	Derek Jeter, Joe DiMaggio, Mickey Mantle/ Bat	925.00
JWO	Derek Jeter, Bernie Williams, Paul O'Neill/Jsy	150.00

Diamonation

		NM/M
Complete Set (9):		10.00
Common Player:		.50
Inserted 1:12		
1	Pedro J. Martinez	1.00
2	Derek Jeter	2.50
3	Jason Giambi	1.00
4	Todd Helton	.75
5	Nomar Garciaparra	2.50
6	Randy Johnson	1.00
7	Jeff Bagwell	.75
8	Cal Ripken Jr.	3.00
9	Ivan Rodriguez	.50

Diamond Gallery

		NM/M
Complete Set (6):		10.00
Common Player:		1.00
Inserted 1:20		
1	Sammy Sosa	2.00
2	Barry Bonds	3.00
3	Vladimir Guerrero	1.00
4	Cal Ripken Jr.	3.00
5	Mike Piazza	1.50
6	Mark McGwire	1.50

Diamond Might

		NM/M
Complete Set (9):		10.00
Common Player:		.50
Inserted 1:12		
1	Mark McGwire	2.50
2	Mike Piazza	1.50
3	Frank Thomas	.75
4	Ken Griffey Jr.	1.50
5	Sammy Sosa	2.00
6	Alex Rodriguez	2.50

7	Carlos Delgado	.50
8	Vladimir Guerrero	1.00
9	Barry Bonds	3.00

Diamond Skills

		NM/M
Complete Set (6):		8.00
Common Player:		.75
Inserted 1:20		
1	Alex Rodriguez	2.50
2	Chipper Jones	1.50
3	Ken Griffey Jr.	1.50
4	Pedro J. Martinez	1.00
5	Ivan Rodriguez	.75
6	Derek Jeter	2.50

2000 Upper Deck Gold Reserve

		NM/M
Complete Set (300):		75.00
Common Player:		.15
Common 268-297:		3.00
Production 2,500 Sets		
Pack (10):		2.00
Box (24):		40.00
1	Mo Vaughn	.20
2	Darin Erstad	.25
3	Garret Anderson	.25
4	Troy Glaus	.50
5	Troy Percival	.15
6	Kent Bottenfield	.15
7	Orlando Palmeiro	.15
8	Tim Salmon	.25
9	Jason Giambi	.75
10	Eric Chavez	.25
11	Matt Stairs	.15
12	Miguel Tejada	.40
13	Tim Hudson	.25
14	John Jaha	.15
15	Ben Grieve	.15
16	Kevin Appier	.15
17	David Wells	.15
18	Jose Cruz Jr.	.15
19	Homer Bush	.15
20	Shannon Stewart	.15
21	Carlos Delgado	.50
22	Roy Halladay	.25
23	Tony Batista	.15
24	Raul Mondesi	.25
25	Fred McGriff	.25
26	Jose Canseco	.40
27	Roberto Hernandez	.15
28	Vinny Castilla	.15
29	Gerald Williams	.15
30	Ryan Rupe	.15
31	Greg Vaughn	.15
32	Miguel Cairo	.15
33	Roberto Alomar	.40
34	Jim Thome	.50
35	Bartolo Colon	.15
36	Omar Vizquel	.25
37	Manny Ramirez	.50
38	Chuck Finley	.15
39	Travis Fryman	.25
40	Kenny Lofton	.25
41	Richie Sexson	.40
42	Charles Nagy	.15
43	John Halama	.15
44	David Bell	.15
45	Jay Buhner	.15
46	Edgar Martinez	.15
47	Alex Rodriguez	1.50
48	Fred Garcia	.15
49	Aaron Sele	.15
50	Jamie Moyer	.15
51	Mike Cameron	.15
52	Albert Belle	.20
53	Jerry Hairston Jr.	.15
54	Sidney Ponson	.15
55	Cal Ripken Jr.	2.00
56	Mike Mussina	.40
57	B.J. Surhoff	.15
58	Brady Anderson	.15
59	Mike Bordick	.15
60	Ivan Rodriguez	.40
61	Rusty Greer	.15
62	Rafael Palmeiro	.40
63	John Wetteland	.15
64	Ruben Mateo	.15
65	Gabe Kapler	.15
66	David Segui	.15
67	Justin Thompson	.15
68	Rick Helling	.15
69	Jose Offerman	.15
70	Trot Nixon	.15
71	Pedro Martinez	.75
72	Jason Varitek	.15
73	Troy O'Leary	.15
74	Nomar Garciaparra	1.50
75	Carl Everett	.15
76	Wilton Veras	.15
77	Tim Wakefield	.15
78	Ramon Martinez	.15
79	Johnny Damon	.25
80	Mike Sweeney	.15
81	Rey Sanchez	.15
82	Carlos Beltran	.25
83	Carlos Febles	.15
84	Jermaine Dye	.15
85	Joe Randa	.15
86	Jose Rosado	.15
87	Jeff Suppan	.15
88	Juan Encarnacion	.15
89	Damion Easley	.15
90	Brad Ausmus	.15
91	Todd Jones	.15
92	Juan Gonzalez	.50
93	Bobby Higginson	.15
94	Tony Clark	.15
95	Brian Moehler	.15
96	Dean Palmer	.15
97	Joe Mays	.15
98	Eric Milton	.15
99	Corey Koskie	.15
100	Ron Coomer	.15
101	Brad Radke	.15
102	Todd Walker	.15
103	Butch Huskey	.15
104	Jacque Jones	.15
105	Frank Thomas	.50
106	Mike Sirotka	.15
107	Carlos Lee	.15
108	Ray Durham	.15
109	Bob Howry	.15
110	Magglio Ordonez	.25
111	Paul Konerko	.25
112	Chris Singleton	.15
113	James Baldwin	.15
114	Derek Jeter	2.00
115	Tino Martinez	.25
116	Orlando Hernandez	.25
117	Chuck Knoblauch	.15
118	Bernie Williams	.50
119	David Cone	.25
120	Paul O'Neill	.25
121	Roger Clemens	1.25
122	Mariano Rivera	.25
123	Ricky Ledee	.15
124	Richard Hidalgo	.25
125	Jeff Bagwell	.50
126	Jose Lima	.15
127	Billy Wagner	.15
128	Shane Reynolds	.15
129	Moises Alou	.25
130	Craig Biggio	.25
131	Roger Cedeno	.15
132	Octavio Dotel	.15
133	Greg Maddux	1.00
134	Brian Jordan	.15
135	Kevin Millwood	.25
136	Javy Lopez	.25
137	Bruce Chen	.15
138	Chipper Jones	1.00
139	Tom Glavine	.40
140	Andruw Jones	.40
141	Andres Galarraga	.25
142	Reggie Sanders	.15
143	Geoff Jenkins	.25
144	Jeromy Burnitz	.15
145	Ron Belliard	.15
146	Mark Loretta	.15
147	Steve Woodard	.15
148	Marquis Grissom	.15
149	Bob Wickman	.15
150	Mark McGwire	1.50
151	Fernando Tatis	.15
152	Edgar Renteria	.15
153	J.D. Drew	.20
154	Ray Lankford	.15
155	Fernando Vina	.15
156	Pat Hentgen	.15
157	Jim Edmonds	.25
158	Mark Grace	.25
159	Kerry Wood	.40
160	Eric Young	.15
161	Ismael Valdes	.15
162	Sammy Sosa	1.25
163	Henry Rodriguez	.15
164	Kyle Farnsworth	.15
165	Glenallen Hill	.15
166	Jon Lieber	.15
167	Luis Gonzalez	.25
168	Tony Womack	.15
169	Omar Daal	.15
170	Randy Johnson	.75
171	Erubiel Durazo	.15
172	Jay Bell	.15
173	Steve Finley	.15
174	Travis Lee	.15
175	Matt Williams	.25
176	Matt Mantei	.15
177	Adrian Beltre	.25
178	Kevin Brown	.25
179	Chan Ho Park	.25
180	Mark Grudzielanek	.15
181	Jeff Shaw	.15
182	Shawn Green	.25
183	Gary Sheffield	.40
184	Todd Hundley	.15
185	Eric Karros	.25
186	Kevin Elster	.15
187	Vladimir Guerrero	.75
188	Michael Barrett	.15
189	Chris Widger	.15
190	Ugueth Urbina	.15
191	Dustin Hermanson	.15
192	Rondell White	.15
193	Jose Vidro	.15
194	Hideki Irabu	.15
195	Lee Stevens	.15
196	Livan Hernandez	.15
197	Ellis Burks	.15
198	J.T. Snow	.15
199	Jeff Kent	.25
200	Robb Nen	.15
201	Marvin Benard	.15
202	Barry Bonds	1.50
203	Russ Ortiz	.15
204	Rich Aurilia	.15
205	Joe Nathan	.15
206	Preston Wilson	.25
207	Cliff Floyd	.15
208	Mike Lowell	.15
209	Ryan Dempster	.15
210	Luis Castillo	.15
211	Alex Fernandez	.15
212	Mark Kotsay	.15
213	Brant Brown	.15
214	Edgardo Alfonzo	.15
215	Robin Ventura	.25
216	Rickey Henderson	.25
217	Mike Hampton	.15
218	Mike Piazza	1.00
219	Al Leiter	.15
220	Derek Bell	.15
221	Armando Benitez	.15
222	Rey Ordonez	.15
223	Todd Zeile	.15
224	Tony Gwynn	.75
225	Eric Owens	.15
226	Damian Jackson	.15
227	Trevor Hoffman	.15
228	Ben Davis	.15
229	Sterling Hitchcock	.15
230	Ruben Rivera	.15
231	Ryan Klesko	.15
232	Phil Nevin	.15
233	Mike Lieberthal	.15
234	Bobby Abreu	.25
235	Doug Glanville	.15
236	Rico Brogna	.15
237	Scott Rolen	.50
238	Andy Ashby	.15
239	Robert Person	.15
240	Curt Schilling	.25
241	Mike Jackson	.15
242	Warren Morris	.15
243	Kris Benson	.15
244	Kevin Young	.15
245	Brian Giles	.25
246	Jason Schmidt	.15
247	Jason Kendall	.25
248	Todd Ritchie	.15
249	Wil Cordero	.15
250	Aramis Ramirez	.15
251	Sean Casey	.25
252	Barry Larkin	.25
253	Pokey Reese	.15
254	Scott Williamson	.15
255	Aaron Boone	.25
256	Dante Bichette	.15
257	Ken Griffey Jr.	1.00
258	Denny Neagle	.15
259	Dmitri Young	.15
260	Todd Helton	.50
261	Larry Walker	.25
262	Pedro Astacio	.15
263	Neifi Perez	.15
264	Jeff Cirillo	.15
265	Jeffrey Hammonds	.15
266	Tom Goodwin	.15
267	Rolando Arrojo	.15
268	Rick Ankiel	3.00
269	Pat Burrell	4.00
270	Eric Munson	3.00
271	Rafael Furcal	3.00
272	Brad Penny	3.00
273	Adam Kennedy	3.00
274	Mike Lamb RC	3.00
275	Matt Riley	3.00
276	Eric Gagne	5.00
277	Kazuhiro Sasaki RC	3.00
278	Julio Lugo	3.00
279	Kip Wells	3.00
280	Danys Baez RC	3.00
281	Josh Beckett	4.00
282	Alfonso Soriano	4.00
283	Vernon Wells	4.00
284	Nick Johnson	3.00
285	Ramon Ortiz	3.00
286	Peter Bergeron	3.00
287	Wascar Serrano RC	3.00
288	Josh Paul	3.00
289	Mark Quinn	3.00
290	Jason Marquis	3.00
291	Rob Bell	3.00
292	Pablo Ozuna	3.00
293	Milton Bradley	3.00
294	Roosevelt Brown	3.00
295	Terrence Long	3.00
296	Chad Durbin RC	3.00
297	Matt LeCroy	3.00
298	Ken Griffey Jr. (Checklist)	.50
299	Mark McGwire (Checklist)	.75
300	Derek Jeter (Checklist)	1.00

Game-Used Ball

		NM/M
Common Player:		10.00
Inserted 1:480		
JB	Jeff Bagwell	25.00
BB	Barry Bonds	70.00
SC	Sean Casey	10.00
RC	Roger Clemens	35.00
NG	Nomar Garciaparra	40.00
SG	Shawn Green	10.00

KG	Ken Griffey Jr.	30.00
TG	Tony Gwynn	25.00
DJ	Derek Jeter	60.00
AJ	Andruw Jones	15.00
CJ	Chipper Jones	30.00
GM	Greg Maddux	30.00
MM	Mark McGwire	60.00
MP	Mike Piazza	30.00
MR	Manny Ramirez	15.00
IR	Ivan Rodriguez	15.00
SR	Scott Rolen	10.00
GS	Gary Sheffield	10.00
SS	Sammy Sosa	30.00
BW	Bernie Williams	10.00

Setting the Standard

		NM/M
Complete Set (15):		25.00
Common Player:		.50
Inserted 1:11		
1	Tony Gwynn	1.50
2	Manny Ramirez	1.00
3	Derek Jeter	3.00
4	Cal Ripken Jr.	4.00
5	Mo Vaughn	.50
6	Jose Canseco	.75
7	Barry Bonds	4.00
8	Nomar Garciaparra	3.00
9	Juan Gonzalez	1.00
10	Mark McGwire	3.00
11	Alex Rodriguez	3.00
12	Jeff Bagwell	1.00
13	Ken Griffey Jr.	2.00
14	Frank Thomas	1.00
15	Sammy Sosa	2.50

Solid Gold Gallery

		NM/M
Complete Set (12):		20.00
Common Player:		1.00
Inserted 1:13		
1	Ken Griffey Jr.	2.00
2	Alex Rodriguez	3.00
3	Mike Piazza	2.00
4	Sammy Sosa	2.50
5	Derek Jeter	3.00
6	Jeff Bagwell	1.00
7	Mark McGwire	3.00
8	Cal Ripken Jr.	4.00
9	Pedro Martinez	1.50
10	Chipper Jones	2.00
11	Ivan Rodriguez	1.00
12	Vladimir Guerrero	1.00

UD Authentics

		NM/M
Inserted 1:480		
CB	Carlos Beltran	40.00
JC	Jose Canseco	35.00
SG	Shawn Green	20.00

KG	Ken Griffey Jr.	
TG	Tony Gwynn	30.00
CJ	Chipper Jones	60.00
MR	Manny Ramirez	25.00
CR	Cal Ripken Jr.	100.00
AR	Alex Rodriguez	80.00
IR	Ivan Rodriguez	20.00

UD Authentics Gold
Values Undetermined

3,000 Hit Club

		NM/M
AK-B	Al Kaline Bat/400	20.00
AK-BS	Al Kaline Bat/Auto./6	

24-Karat Gems

		NM/M
Complete Set (15):		12.00
Common Player:		.50
Inserted 1:7		
1	Pedro Martinez	1.50
2	Scott Rolen	1.00
3	Jason Giambi	1.50
4	Jeromy Burnitz	.50
5	Rafael Palmeiro	1.00
6	Rick Ankiel	.50
7	Carlos Beltran	.75
8	Derek Jeter	3.00
9	Jason Kendall	.50
10	Chipper Jones	2.00
11	Carlos Delgado	1.00
12	Alex Rodriguez	3.00
13	Randy Johnson	1.50
14	Tony Gwynn	1.50
15	Shawn Green	.75

2000 Upper Deck Hitter's Club

		NM/M
Complete Set (90):		20.00
Common Player:		.15
Pack (5):		1.50
Wax Box (24):		25.00
1	Mo Vaughn	.20
2	Troy Glaus	.40
3	Jeff Bagwell	.50
4	Craig Biggio	.25
5	Jason Giambi	.75
6	Eric Chavez	.25
7	Carlos Delgado	.50
8	Chipper Jones	1.00
9	Andruw Jones	.50
10	Andres Galarraga	.20
11	Jeromy Burnitz	.15
12	Mark McGwire	1.50
13	Mark Grace	.25
14	Sammy Sosa	1.25
15	Jose Canseco	.40
16	Vinny Castilla	.15
17	Matt Williams	.25
18	Gary Sheffield	.25
19	Shawn Green	.25
20	Vladimir Guerrero	.50
21	Barry Bonds	1.50
22	Manny Ramirez	.50
23	Roberto Alomar	.40
24	Jim Thome	.50
25	Ken Griffey Jr.	1.00
26	Alex Rodriguez	1.50
27	Edgar Martinez	.15
28	Preston Wilson	.25
29	Mike Piazza	1.00
30	Robin Ventura	.25
31	Albert Belle	.25
32	Cal Ripken Jr.	2.00
33	Tony Gwynn	.75
34	Scott Rolen	.50
35	Bob Abreu	.25
36	Brian Giles	.25
37	Ivan Rodriguez	.40
38	Rafael Palmeiro	.40
39	Nomar Garciaparra	1.50
40	Sean Casey	.20
41	Larry Walker	.25
42	Todd Helton	.50
43	Carlos Beltran	.25
44	Dean Palmer	.15
45	Juan Gonzalez	.50
46	Corey Koskie	.15
47	Frank Thomas	.50
48	Magglio Ordonez	.25
49	Derek Jeter	2.00
50	Bernie Williams	.40
51	Paul Waner	.25
52	Honus Wagner	.50
53	Tris Speaker	.25
54	Nap Lajoie	.25
55	Eddie Collins	.25
56	Roberto Clemente	1.00
57	Ty Cobb	1.50
58	Cap Anson	.50
59	Robin Yount	.50
60	Carl Yastrzemski	.50
61	Dave Winfield	.25
62	Stan Musial	1.00
63	Eddie Murray	.40
64	Paul Molitor	.50
65	Willie Mays	1.50
66	Al Kaline	.50
67	Tony Gwynn	.75
68	Rod Carew	.40
69	Lou Brock	.25
70	George Brett	1.00
71	Wade Boggs	.25
72	Hank Aaron	1.50
73	Jorge Luis Toca	.15
74	J.D. Drew	.15
75	Pat Burrell	.25
76	Vernon Wells	.25
77	Julio Ramirez	.15
78	Gabe Kapler	.15
79	Erubiel Durazo	.15
80	Lance Berkman	.25
81	Peter Bergeron	.15
82	Alfonso Soriano	.75
83	Jacque Jones	.15
84	Ben Petrick	.15
85	Jerry Hairston Jr.	.15
86	Kevin Witt	.15
87	Dermal Brown	.15
88	Chad Hermansen	.15
89	Ruben Mateo	.15
90	Ken Griffey Jr.	.50
	Checklist	.50

Accolades

		NM/M
Complete Set (10):		12.00
Common Player:		.75
Inserted 1:11		
1	Robin Yount	1.00
2	Tony Gwynn	1.00

3	Sammy Sosa	2.00
4	Mike Piazza	1.50
5	Cal Ripken Jr.	3.00
6	Mark McGwire	2.50
7	Barry Bonds	2.50
8	Wade Boggs	.75
9	Ken Griffey Jr.	1.50
10	Willie Mays	2.00

Autographs

		NM/M
Common Player:		15.00
Inserted 1:215		
HA	Hank Aaron #44	240.00
WB	Wade Boggs #12	30.00
GB	George Brett #5	80.00
Lou	Lou Brock #20	15.00
Rod	Rod Carew #29	15.00
TG	Tony Gwynn #19	40.00
Al	Al Kaline #6	30.00
WM	Willie Mays #24	150.00
PM	Paul Molitor #4	30.00
EM	Eddie Murray #33	30.00
Man	Stan Musial #6	75.00
Cal	Cal Ripken Jr. #8	150.00
DW	Dave Winfield #31	20.00
Yaz	Carl Yastrzemski #7	60.00
RY	Robin Yount #19	40.00

Epic Performances

		NM/M
Complete Set (10):		12.00
Common Player:		1.00
Inserted 1:3		
3	Mark McGwire	2.50
3	Sammy Sosa	2.00
4	Ken Griffey Jr.	1.50
5	Carl Yastrzemski	1.00
6	Tony Gwynn	1.00

7	Nomar Garciaparra	2.50
8	Cal Ripken Jr.	3.00
9	George Brett	1.50
10	Hank Aaron	2.00
11	Wade Boggs	1.00

Eternals

		NM/M
Complete Set (10):		20.00
Common Player:		1.00
Inserted 1:23		
1	Cal Ripken Jr.	4.00
2	Mark McGwire	3.00
3	Ken Griffey Jr.	2.00
4	Nomar Garciaparra	3.00
5	Tony Gwynn	1.50
6	Derek Jeter	3.00
7	Jose Canseco	1.00
8	Mike Piazza	2.00
9	Alex Rodriguez	3.00
10	Barry Bonds	4.00

Generations of Excellence

		NM/M
Complete Set (10):		15.00
Common Card:		1.00
Inserted 1:6		
1	Cal Ripken Jr., Eddie Murray	3.00
2	Vladimir Guerrero, Roberto Clemente	2.00
3	George Brett, Robin Yount	2.00
4	Barry Bonds, Willie Mays	3.00
5	Chipper Jones, Hank Aaron	2.00
6	Mark McGwire, Sammy Sosa	2.00
7	Tony Gwynn, Wade Boggs	1.00
8	Rickey Henderson, Lou Brock	1.00
9	Derek Jeter, Nomar Garciaparra	3.00
10	Alex Rodriguez, Ken Griffey Jr.	2.50

On Target

		NM/M
Complete Set (10):		12.00
Common Player:		.50
Inserted 1:23		
1	Nomar Garciaparra	3.00
2	Sean Casey	.50
3	Alex Rodriguez	3.00
4	Troy Glaus	1.00

5	Ivan Rodriguez	1.00
6	Chipper Jones	2.00
7	Manny Ramirez	1.00
8	Derek Jeter	3.00
9	Vladimir Guerrero	1.00
10	Scott Rolen	1.00

The Hitters' Club

		NM/M
Complete Set (10):		60.00
Common Player:		3.00
1	Rod Carew	5.00
2	Alex Rodriguez	15.00
3	Willie Mays	10.00
4	George Brett	10.00
5	Tony Gwynn	8.00
6	Stan Musial	8.00
7	Frank Thomas	5.00
8	Wade Boggs	3.00
9	Larry Walker	3.00
10	Nomar Garciaparra	15.00

3,000 Hit Club

		NM/M
Common Player:		25.00
WB	Wade Boggs/Bat/350	25.00
WB	Wade Boggs/Bat & Cap/50	65.00
TG	Tony Gwynn/Bat/350	25.00
TG	Tony Gwynn/Bat & Cap/50	100.00
TG	Tony Gwynn AU/19	550.00
GB	Tony Gwynn, Wade Boggs/Bat/99	85.00

2000 Upper Deck HoloGrFX

		NM/M
Complete Set (90):		20.00
Common Player:		.15
Pack (4):		1.50
Wax Box (32):		25.00
1	Mo Vaughn	.20
2	Troy Glaus	.50
3	Daryle Ward	.15
4	Jeff Bagwell	.50
5	Craig Biggio	.25
6	Jose Lima	.15
7	Jason Giambi	.75
8	Eric Chavez	.25
9	Tim Hudson	.25
10	Raul Mondesi	.25
11	Carlos Delgado	.50
12	David Wells	.15
13	Chipper Jones	1.00
14	Greg Maddux	1.00
15	Andruw Jones	.50
16	Brian Jordan	.15

17	Jeromy Burnitz	.15
18	Ron Belliard	.15
19	Mark McGwire	1.50
20	Fernando Tatis	.15
21	J.D. Drew	.25
22	Sammy Sosa	1.00
23	Mark Grace	.40
24	Greg Vaughn	.15
25	Jose Canseco	.40
26	Vinny Castilla	.15
27	Fred McGriff	.25
28	Matt Williams	.25
29	Randy Johnson	.75
30	Erubiel Durazo	.15
31	Shawn Green	.25
32	Gary Sheffield	.40
33	Kevin Brown	.25
34	Vladimir Guerrero	.50
35	Michael Barrett	.15
36	Russ Ortiz	.15
37	Barry Bonds	1.50
38	Jeff Kent	.25
39	Kenny Lofton	.25
40	Manny Ramirez	.50
41	Roberto Alomar	.40
42	Richie Sexson	.25
43	Edgar Martinez	.25
44	Alex Rodriguez	1.50
45	Fred Garcia	.15
46	Preston Wilson	.15
47	Alex Gonzalez	.15
48	Mike Hampton	.15
49	Mike Piazza	1.00
50	Robin Ventura	.25
51	Edgardo Alfonzo	.15
52	Albert Belle	.15
53	Cal Ripken Jr.	2.00
54	B.J. Surhoff	.15
55	Tony Gwynn	.75
56	Trevor Hoffman	.15
57	Mike Lieberthal	.15
58	Scott Rolen	.50
59	Bob Abreu	.25
60	Curt Schilling	.40
61	Jason Kendall	.25
62	Brian Giles	.25
63	Kris Benson	.15
64	Rafael Palmeiro	.40
65	Ivan Rodriguez	.50
66	Gabe Kapler	.40
67	Nomar Garciaparra	1.50
68	Pedro Martinez	.75
69	Troy O'Leary	.15
70	Barry Larkin	.25
71	Dante Bichette	.15
72	Sean Casey	.20
73	Ken Griffey Jr.	1.00
74	Jeff Cirillo	.15
75	Todd Helton	.50
76	Larry Walker	.25
77	Carlos Beltran	.25
78	Jermaine Dye	.15
79	Juan Gonzalez	.50
80	Juan Encarnacion	.15
81	Dean Palmer	.15
82	Corey Koskie	.15
83	Eric Milton	.15
84	Frank Thomas	.50
85	Magglio Ordonez	.25
86	Carlos Lee	.15
87	Derek Jeter	2.00
88	Tino Martinez	.25
89	Bernie Williams	.50
90	Roger Clemens	1.50

A Piece of the Series

		NM/M
Common Player:		5.00
Inserted 1:215		
1	Derek Jeter	40.00
2	Chipper Jones	20.00
3	Roger Clemens	30.00
4	Greg Maddux	30.00
5	Bernie Williams	10.00
6	Andruw Jones	10.00
7	Tino Martinez	8.00
8	Brian Jordan	5.00
9	Mariano Rivera	8.00
10	Paul O'Neill	8.00
11		
12	Tom Glavine	10.00

A Piece of Series Autograph

		NM/M
Common Player:		40.00
Production 25 Sets		
PSA1	Derek Jeter	300.00
PSA2	Chipper Jones	125.00
PSA3	Roger Clemens	220.00
PSA4	Greg Maddux	220.00
PSA6	Andruw Jones	85.00
PSA7	Tino Martinez	65.00
PSA8	Brian Jordan	40.00
PSA11	Paul O'Neill	75.00
PSA12	Tom Glavine	100.00

Bomb Squad

		NM/M
Complete Set (6):		15.00
Common Player:		2.00
Inserted 1:34		
1	Ken Griffey Jr.	2.00
2	Mark McGwire	3.00
3	Chipper Jones	2.00
4	Alex Rodriguez	3.00
5	Sammy Sosa	2.50
6	Barry Bonds	4.00

Future Fame

		NM/M
Complete Set (6):		10.00
Common Player:		2.00
Inserted 1:34		
1	Cal Ripken Jr.	4.00
2	Mark McGwire	3.00
3	Greg Maddux	2.00
4	Tony Gwynn	1.50
5	Ken Griffey Jr.	2.00
6	Roger Clemens	2.50

Longball Legacy

		NM/M
Complete Set (15):		15.00
Common Player:		.50
Inserted 1:6		
1	Mike Piazza	2.00
2	Ivan Rodriguez	.75
3	Jeff Bagwell	1.00
4	Alex Rodriguez	3.00
5	Jose Canseco	.75
6	Mark McGwire	3.00
7	Scott Rolen	.75
8	Carlos Delgado	.75
9	Mo Vaughn	.50
10	Manny Ramirez	1.00
11	Matt Williams	.50
12	Sammy Sosa	2.50
13	Ken Griffey Jr.	2.00

14 Nomar Garciaparra 3.00
15 Larry Walker .50

Stars of the System

	NM/M
Complete Set (10):	8.00
Common Player:	.75
Inserted 1:8	
1 Rick Ankiel	.75
2 Alfonso Soriano	2.00
3 Vernon Wells	1.00
4 Ben Petrick	.75
5 Francisco Cordero	.75
6 Matt Riley	.75
7 A.J. Burnett	1.00
8 Pat Burrell	1.50
9 Ed Yarnall	.75
10 Dermal Brown	.75

StarView

	NM/M
Complete Set (8):	15.00
Common Player:	2.00
Inserted 1:11	
1 Ken Griffey Jr.	2.00
2 Nomar Garciaparra	3.00
3 Chipper Jones	2.00
4 Mark McGwire	3.00
5 Sammy Sosa	2.50
6 Derek Jeter	4.00
7 Mike Piazza	2.00
8 Alex Rodriguez	3.00

3,000 Hit Club

	NM/M
Common Card:	20.00
RY Robin Yount/Bat/350	20.00
RYJ Robin Yount/Jsy/350	20.00
GB George Brett/Bat/350	35.00
GBJ George Brett/Jsy/350	35.00
BY George Brett, Robin Yount Bat/99	120.00
BYJ George Brett, Robin Yount/Jsy/99	120.00

2000 Upper Deck Legends

	NM/M
Complete Set (135):	80.00
Common Player:	.15
Common Y2K:	.75
Inserted 1:9	
Common 20th Century Legend	1.00
Inserted 1:5	
Pack (7):	5.00
Box (24):	90.00
1 Darin Erstad	.25
2 Troy Glaus	.75
3 Mo Vaughn	.20
4 Craig Biggio	.25
5 Jeff Bagwell	.75
6 Reggie Jackson	1.00
7 Tim Hudson	.25
8 Jason Giambi	1.00
9 Hank Aaron	2.00
10 Greg Maddux	1.50
11 Chipper Jones	1.50

12 Andres Galarraga	.25
13 Robin Yount	.50
14 Jeromy Burnitz	.15
15 Paul Molitor	.50
16 David Wells	.15
17 Carlos Delgado	.75
18 Ernie Banks	.75
19 Sammy Sosa	2.00
20 Kerry Wood	.40
21 Stan Musial	.75
22 Bob Gibson	.50
23 Mark McGwire	2.00
24 Fernando Tatis	.15
25 Randy Johnson	1.00
26 Matt Williams	.40
27 Jackie Robinson	2.00
28 Sandy Koufax	1.50
29 Shawn Green	.40
30 Kevin Brown	.25
31 Gary Sheffield	.40
32 Greg Vaughn	.15
33 Jose Canseco	.50
34 Gary Carter	.15
35 Vladimir Guerrero	.75
36 Willie Mays	2.00
37 Barry Bonds	2.00
38 Jeff Kent	.25
39 Bob Feller	.40
40 Roberto Alomar	.75
41 Jim Thome	.75
42 Manny Ramirez	.75
43 Alex Rodriguez	2.00
44 Preston Wilson	.15
45 Tom Seaver	.75
46 Robin Ventura	.15
47 Mike Piazza	1.50
48 Mike Hampton	.15
49 Brooks Robinson	.75
50 Frank Robinson	.75
51 Cal Ripken Jr.	2.50
52 Albert Belle	.20
53 Eddie Murray	.40
54 Tony Gwynn	1.00
55 Roberto Clemente	1.50
56 Willie Stargell	.25
57 Brian Giles	.25
58 Jason Kendall	.25
59 Mike Schmidt	1.00
60 Bob Abreu	.25
61 Scott Rolen	.50
62 Curt Schilling	.40
63 Johnny Bench	1.00
64 Sean Casey	.15
65 Barry Larkin	.25
66 Ken Griffey Jr.	1.50
67 George Brett	1.50
68 Carlos Beltran	.15
69 Nolan Ryan	3.00
70 Ivan Rodriguez	.75
71 Rafael Palmeiro	.40
72 Larry Walker	.25
73 Todd Helton	.75
74 Jeff Cirillo	.15
75 Carl Everett	.15
76 Nomar Garciaparra	2.00
77 Pedro Martinez	1.00
78 Harmon Killebrew	.50
79 Corey Koskie	.15
80 Ty Cobb	2.00
81 Dean Palmer	.15
82 Juan Gonzalez	.75
83 Carlton Fisk	.15
84 Frank Thomas	.75
85 Magglio Ordonez	.25
86 Lou Gehrig	2.00
87 Babe Ruth	3.00
88 Derek Jeter	2.50
89 Roger Clemens	1.50
90 Bernie Williams	.50
91 Rick Ankiel	.75
92 Kip Wells	.75
93 Pat Burrell	1.50

94 Mark Quinn	.75
95 Ruben Mateo	.75
96 Adam Kennedy	.75
97 Brad Penny	.75
98 Kazuhiro Sasaki RC	2.00
99 Peter Bergeron	.75
100 Rafael Furcal	1.00
101 Eric Munson	.75
102 Nick Johnson	1.00
103 Rob Bell	.75
104 Vernon Wells	1.00
105 Ben Petrick	.75
106 Babe Ruth	8.00
107 Mark McGwire	6.00
108 Nolan Ryan	8.00
109 Hank Aaron	5.00
110 Barry Bonds	6.00
111 Nomar Garciaparra	5.00
112 Roger Clemens	5.00
113 Johnny Bench	2.50
114 Alex Rodriguez	6.00
115 Cal Ripken Jr.	8.00
116 Willie Mays	6.00
117 Mike Piazza	4.00
118 Reggie Jackson	2.00
119 Tony Gwynn	3.00
120 Cy Young	2.00
121 George Brett	4.00
122 Greg Maddux	4.00
123 Yogi Berra	2.00
124 Sammy Sosa	5.00
125 Randy Johnson	2.50
126 Bob Gibson	2.00
127 Lou Gehrig	6.00
128 Ken Griffey Jr.	4.00
129 Derek Jeter	6.00
130 Mike Schmidt	3.00
131 Pedro Martinez	2.50
132 Jackie Robinson	5.00
133 Jose Canseco	1.00
134 Ty Cobb	5.00
135 Stan Musial	3.00

Commemorative Collection

Stars (1-90): 4-8X
Y2K: 1-2X
20th Century Legends: 2-3X
Production 100 Sets
(See 2000 Upper Deck Legends for checklist and base card values.)

Eternal Glory

	NM/M
Complete Set (7):	15.00
Common Player:	2.00
Inserted 1:24	
1 Nolan Ryan	4.00
2 Ken Griffey Jr.	2.00

4 Sammy Sosa	2.50
5 Derek Jeter	4.00
6 Willie Mays	3.00
7 Roger Clemens	3.00

Defining Moments

	NM/M
Complete Set (10):	20.00
Common Player:	1.00
Inserted 1:12	
1 Reggie Jackson	1.50
2 Hank Aaron	3.00
3 Babe Ruth	4.00
4 Cal Ripken Jr.	4.00
5 Carlton Fisk	1.00
6 Ken Griffey Jr.	2.00
7 Nolan Ryan	4.00
8 Roger Clemens	2.50
9 Willie Mays	3.00
10 Mark McGwire	3.00

Legendary Jerseys

		NM/M
Common Player:		8.00
Inserted 1:48		
HA	Hank Aaron	40.00
JB	Jeff Bagwell	10.00
JB	Johnny Bench	20.00
WB	Wade Boggs	10.00
BaB	Barry Bonds	40.00
BoB	Bobby Bonds	8.00
GB	George Brett	30.00
LB	Lou Brock	8.00
JC	Jose Canseco	10.00
RC	Roger Clemens	30.00
DC	Dave Concepcion	8.00
DD	Don Drysdale	25.00
RF	Rollie Fingers	8.00
LG	Lou Gehrig/Pants	250.00
BG	Bob Gibson/Pants	10.00
KG	Ken Griffey Jr.	35.00
TG	Tony Gwynn	20.00
RJ	Reggie Jackson	10.00
DJ	Derek Jeter	40.00
RaJ	Randy Johnson	20.00
CJ	Chipper Jones	20.00
SK	Sandy Koufax	250.00
SK	Sandy Koufax/ Auto./32	1,200
GM	Greg Maddux	30.00
MM	Mickey Mantle	150.00
RM	Roger Maris/Pants	60.00
EM	Eddie Mathews	20.00
WM	Willie Mays/SP/29	675.00
BM	Bill Mazeroski	8.00
WMc	Willie McCovey	10.00
TM	Thurman Munson	30.00
DM	Dale Murphy	10.00
SM	Stan Musial/SP/28	650.00
JP	Jim Palmer	8.00
GP	Gaylord Perry	8.00
MR	Manny Ramirez	10.00
CR	Cal Ripken Jr.	40.00
BR	Brooks Robinson	20.00
FR	Frank Robinson	10.00
AR	Alex Rodriguez	35.00
NR	Nolan Ryan	40.00
MS	Mike Schmidt	25.00
TS	Tom Seaver	20.00
OS	Ozzie Smith	20.00
WS	Willie Stargell	8.00

FT	Frank Thomas	10.00
JT	Joe Torre	8.00
EW	Earl Weaver	8.00
MW	Matt Williams	8.00
MW	Maury Wills	8.00
DW	Dave Winfield	10.00

Legendary Signatures

	NM/M
Common Player:	8.00
Inserted 1:23	
Golds:	1-2X
Production 50 Sets	
HA	Hank Aaron/SP/94	275.00
JB	Johnny Bench	30.00
BB	Bobby Bonds	8.00
LB	Lou Brock	8.00
GB	George Brett	60.00
JC	Jose Canseco	20.00
GC	Gary Carter	10.00
SC	Sean Casey	8.00
RC	Roger Clemens	80.00
DC	Dave Concepcion	8.00
AD	Andre Dawson	10.00
KG	Ken Griffey Jr.	85.00
VG	Vladimir Guerrero	30.00
TG	Tony Gwynn	40.00
RJ	Reggie Jackson	20.00
DJ	Derek Jeter/SP/61	400.00
RaJ	Randy Johnson	50.00
CJ	Chipper Jones	35.00
HK	Harmon Killebrew	25.00
FL	Fred Lynn	8.00
DM	Dale Murphy	15.00
SM	Stan Musial	50.00
PN	Phil Niekro	8.00
JP	Jim Palmer	10.00
MP	Mike Piazza	120.00
MR	Manny Ramirez/SP/141	60.00
CR	Cal Ripken Jr.	120.00
AR	Alex Rodriguez	85.00
IR	Ivan Rodriguez	25.00
NR	Nolan Ryan	85.00
MS	Mike Schmidt	50.00
TS	Tom Seaver	30.00
OS	Ozzie Smith	40.00
WS	Willie Stargell	60.00
FT	Frank Thomas	30.00
AT	Alan Trammell	10.00
BW	Matt Williams	8.00

Ones for the Ages

	NM/M
Complete Set (7):	15.00
Inserted 1:24	
01	Ty Cobb	2.50
02	Cal Ripken Jr.	4.00
03	Babe Ruth	4.00
04	Jackie Robinson	2.50
05	Mark McGwire	3.00
06	Alex Rodriguez	3.00
07	Mike Piazza	4.00

Reflections in Time

	NM/M
Complete Set (10):	25.00
Common Player:	2.00
Inserted 1:12	
1	Ken Griffey Jr., Hank Aaron	3.00
2	Sammy Sosa, Roberto Clemente	3.00
3	Roger Clemens, Nolan Ryan	4.00
4	Ivan Rodriguez, Johnny Bench	2.00
5	Alex Rodriguez, Ernie Banks	3.00
6	Tony Gwynn, Stan Musial	2.00
7	Barry Bonds, Willie Mays	4.00
8	Cal Ripken Jr., Lou Gehrig	4.00
9	Chipper Jones, Mike Schmidt	2.50
10	Mark McGwire, Babe Ruth	4.00

UD Millennium Team

	NM/M
Complete Set (10):	15.00
Common Player:	1.50
Inserted 1:4	
1	Mark McGwire	2.00
2	Jackie Robinson	2.00
3	Mike Schmidt	1.50
4	Cal Ripken Jr.	3.00
5	Babe Ruth	3.00
7	Willie Mays	2.00
8	Johnny Bench	1.50
9	Nolan Ryan	3.00
10	Ken Griffey Jr.	1.50

3,000 Hit Club

	NM/M
CY	Carl Yastrzemski/Bat/350	30.00
CY	Carl Yastrzemski/Jsy/350	30.00
CY	Carl Yastrzemski/Bat/Jsy/100	80.00
CY	Carl Yastrzemski/Auto./Bat/Jsy/8	

2000 Upper Deck MVP

	NM/M
Complete Set (220):	20.00
Common Player:	.10
Pack (10):	1.25
Wax Box (28):	25.00

1	Garret Anderson	.25
2	Mo Vaughn	.15
3	Tim Salmon	.20
4	Ramon Ortiz	.10
5	Darin Erstad	.25
6	Troy Glaus	.50
7	Troy Percival	.10
8	Jeff Bagwell	.50
9	Ken Caminiti	.10
10	Daryle Ward	.10
11	Craig Biggio	.25
12	Jose Lima	.10
13	Moises Alou	.20
14	Octavio Dotel	.10
15	Ben Grieve	.10
16	Jason Giambi	.50
17	Tim Hudson	.20
18	Eric Chavez	.20
19	Matt Stairs	.10
20	Miguel Tejada	.25
21	John Jaha	.10
22	Chipper Jones	1.00
23	Kevin Millwood	.20
24	Brian Jordan	.10
25	Andruw Jones	.25
26	Andres Galarraga	.20
27	Greg Maddux	1.00
28	Reggie Sanders	.10
29	Javy Lopez	.20
30	Jeromy Burnitz	.10
31	Kevin Barker	.10
32	Jose Hernandez	.10
33	Ron Belliard	.10
34	Henry Blanco	.10
35	Marquis Grissom	.10
36	Geoff Jenkins	.20
37	Carlos Delgado	.50
38	Raul Mondesi	.20
39	Roy Halladay	.20
40	Tony Batista	.10
41	David Wells	.10
42	Shannon Stewart	.10
43	Vernon Wells	.10
44	Sammy Sosa	1.00
45	Ismael Valdes	.10
46	Joe Girardi	.10
47	Mark Grace	.20
48	Henry Rodriguez	.10
49	Kerry Wood	.25
50	Eric Young	.10
51	Mark McGwire	2.00
52	Daryle Kile	.10
53	Fernando Vina	.10
54	Ray Lankford	.10
55	J.D. Drew	.20
56	Fernando Tatis	.10
57	Rick Ankiel	.10
58	Matt Williams	.20
59	Erubiel Durazo	.15
60	Tony Womack	.10
61	Jay Bell	.10
62	Randy Johnson	.75
63	Steve Finley	.10
64	Matt Mantei	.10
65	Luis Gonzalez	.20
66	Gary Sheffield	.25
67	Eric Gagne	.10
68	Adrian Beltre	.20
69	Mark Grudzielanek	.10
70	Kevin Brown	.20
71	Chan Ho Park	.10
72	Shawn Green	.40
73	Vinny Castilla	.15
74	Fred McGriff	.25
75	Wilson Alvarez	.10
76	Greg Vaughn	.10
77	Gerald Williams	.10
78	Ryan Rupe	.10
79	Jose Canseco	.25
80	Vladimir Guerrero	.50
81	Dustin Hermanson	.10
82	Michael Barrett	.10
83	Rondell White	.20
84	Tony Armas Jr.	.10
85	Wilton Guerrero	.10
86	Jose Vidro	.10
87	Barry Bonds	1.50
88	Russ Ortiz	.10
89	Ellis Burks	.10
90	Jeff Kent	.20
91	Russ Davis	.10
92	J.T. Snow	.10
93	Roberto Alomar	.40
94	Manny Ramirez	.50
95	Chuck Finley	.10
96	Kenny Lofton	.20
97	Jim Thome	.50
98	Bartolo Colon	.20
99	Omar Vizquel	.20
100	Richie Sexson	.25
101	Mike Cameron	.10
102	Brett Tomko	.10
103	Edgar Martinez	.20
104	Alex Rodriguez	1.50
105	John Olerud	.20
106	Fred Garcia	.10
107	Kazuhiro Sasaki **RC**	1.00
108	Preston Wilson	.20
109	Luis Castillo	.10
110	A.J. Burnett	.10
111	Mike Lowell	.10
112	Cliff Floyd	.10
113	Brad Penny	.10
114	Alex Gonzalez	.10
115	Mike Piazza	1.00
116	Derek Bell	.10
117	Edgardo Alfonzo	.10
118	Rickey Henderson	.20
119	Todd Zeile	.10
120	Mike Hampton	.10
121	Al Leiter	.20
122	Robin Ventura	.20
123	Cal Ripken Jr.	1.50
124	Mike Mussina	.40
125	B.J. Surhoff	.10
126	Jerry Hairston Jr.	.10
127	Brady Anderson	.10
128	Albert Belle	.10
129	Sidney Ponson	.10
130	Tony Gwynn	.75
131	Ryan Klesko	.10
132	Sterling Hitchcock	.10
133	Eric Owens	.10
134	Trevor Hoffman	.10
135	Al Martin	.10
136	Bret Boone	.25
137	Brian Giles	.25
138	Chad Hermansen	.10
139	Kevin Young	.10
140	Kris Benson	.10
141	Warren Morris	.10
142	Jason Kendall	.20
143	Wil Cordero	.10
144	Scott Rolen	.50
145	Curt Schilling	.40
146	Doug Glanville	.10
147	Mike Lieberthal	.10
148	Mike Jackson	.10
149	Rico Brogna	.10
150	Andy Ashby	.10
151	Bob Abreu	.20
152	Sean Casey	.20
153	Pete Harnisch	.10
154	Dante Bichette	.10
155	Pokey Reese	.10
156	Aaron Boone	.20
157	Ken Griffey Jr.	1.00
158	Barry Larkin	.25
159	Scott Williamson	.10
160	Carlos Beltran	.20
161	Jermaine Dye	.20
162	Jose Rosado	.10
163	Joe Randa	.10
164	Johnny Damon	.20
165	Mike Sweeney	.10
166	Mark Quinn	.10
167	Ivan Rodriguez	.40
168	Rusty Greer	.10
169	Ruben Mateo	.10
170	Doug Davis	.10
171	Gabe Kapler	.10
172	Justin Thompson	.10
173	Rafael Palmeiro	.40
174	Larry Walker	.20
175	Neifi Perez	.10
176	Rolando Arrojo	.10
177	Jeffrey Hammonds	.10
178	Todd Helton	.50
179	Pedro Astacio	.10
180	Jeff Cirillo	.10
181	Pedro Martinez	.75
182	Carl Everett	.10
183	Troy O'Leary	.10
184	Nomar Garciaparra	1.25
185	Jose Offerman	.10
186	Bret Saberhagen	.10
187	Trot Nixon	.10
188	Jason Varitek	.10
189	Todd Walker	.10
190	Eric Milton	.10
191	Chad Allen	.10

192	Jacque Jones	.10
193	Brad Radke	.10
194	Corey Koskie	.10
195	Joe Mays	.10
196	Juan Gonzalez	.50
197	Jeff Weaver	.10
198	Juan Encarnacion	.10
199	Deivi Cruz	.10
200	Damion Easley	.10
201	Tony Clark	.10
202	Dean Palmer	.10
203	Frank Thomas	.50
204	Carlos Lee	.10
205	Mike Sirotka	.10
206	Kip Wells	.10
207	Magglio Ordonez	.20
208	Paul Konerko	.20
209	Chris Singleton	.10
210	Derek Jeter	1.50
211	Tino Martinez	.25
212	Mariano Rivera	.20
213	Roger Clemens	.75
214	Nick Johnson	.25
215	Paul O'Neill	.20
216	Bernie Williams	.40
217	David Cone	.20
218	Ken Griffey Jr. Checklist	.50
219	Sammy Sosa Checklist	.50
220	Mark McGwire Checklist	.75

Silver

Stars:	1-2X
Inserted 1:2

Gold

Stars:	10-20X
Production 50 Sets

Super

Stars:	15-30X
Production 25 Sets

All-Star Game

		NM/M
	Complete Set (30):	25.00
	Common Player:	.25
AS1	Mo Vaughn	.25
AS2	Jeff Bagwell	.75
AS3	Jason Giambi	.75
AS4	Chipper Jones	1.50
AS5	Greg Maddux	1.00
AS6	Tony Batista	.25
AS7	Sammy Sosa	2.00
AS8	Mark McGwire	2.50
AS9	Randy Johnson	.75
AS10	Shawn Green	.50
AS11	Greg Vaughn	.25
AS12	Vladimir Guerrero	.75
AS13	Barry Bonds	2.50
AS14	Manny Ramirez	.75
AS15	Alex Rodriguez	2.50
AS16	Preston Wilson	.25
AS17	Mike Piazza	1.50
AS18	Cal Ripken Jr.	3.00
AS19	Tony Gwynn	1.00
AS20	Scott Rolen	.75
AS21	Ken Griffey Jr.	1.50
AS22	Carlos Beltran	.25
AS23	Ivan Rodriguez	.60
AS24	Larry Walker	.25
AS25	Nomar Garciaparra	2.00
AS26	Pedro Martinez	.75
AS27	Juan Gonzalez	.75
AS28	Frank Thomas	.75
AS29	Derek Jeter	2.50
AS30	Bernie Williams	.50

Drawing Power

		NM/M
	Complete Set (7):	12.00
	Common Player:	1.00
	Inserted 1:28	
1	Mark McGwire	3.00
2	Ken Griffey Jr.	2.00
3	Mike Piazza	2.00
4	Chipper Jones	2.00
5	Nomar Garciaparra	3.00
6	Sammy Sosa	2.50
7	Jose Canseco	1.00

Game-Used Souvenirs

		NM/M
	Common Glove:	8.00
	Inserted 1:130	
RA	Roberto Alomar	15.00
JB	Jeff Bagwell	20.00
AB	Albert Belle	8.00
BB	Barry Bonds	65.00
JC	Jose Canseco	15.00
WC	Will Clark	20.00
AF	Alex Fernandez	8.00
JG	Jason Giambi	15.00
TGl	Troy Glaus	15.00
AG	Alex Gonzalez	8.00
BG	Ben Grieve	8.00
KG	Ken Griffey Jr.	40.00
VG	Vladimir Guerrero	15.00
TG	Tony Gwynn	30.00
AJ	Andruw Jones	15.00
CJ	Chipper Jones	30.00
KL	Kenny Lofton	8.00
RM	Raul Mondesi	8.00
PO	Paul O'Neill	10.00
RP	Rafael Palmeiro	15.00
MR	Manny Ramirez	15.00
CR	Cal Ripken Jr.	65.00
AR	Alex Rodriguez	40.00
IR	Ivan Rodriguez	15.00
NR	Nolan Ryan	65.00
TS	Tim Salmon	8.00

LW	Larry Walker	8.00
BW	Bernie Williams	15.00
MW	Matt Williams	8.00

Game-Used Souvenirs - Bats

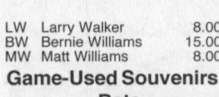

Game Used Souvenirs / Tony Gwynn

		NM/M
	Common Bat:	8.00
	Inserted 1:130	
BB	Barry Bonds	40.00
JC	Jose Canseco	8.00
KG	Ken Griffey Jr.	20.00
VG	Vladimir Guerrero	10.00
TG	Tony Gwynn	15.00
CJ	Chipper Jones	15.00
MR	Manny Ramirez	10.00
AR	Alex Rodriguez	20.00
IR	Ivan Rodriguez	8.00
BW	Bernie Williams	10.00

Pure Grit

		NM/M
	Complete Set (10):	10.00
	Common Player:	.50
	Inserted 1:6	
1	Derek Jeter	2.00
2	Kevin Brown	.50
3	Craig Biggio	.50
4	Ivan Rodriguez	.75
5	Scott Rolen	.75
6	Carlos Beltran	.50
7	Ken Griffey Jr.	1.50
8	Cal Ripken Jr.	2.50
9	Nomar Garciaparra	2.00
10	Randy Johnson	1.00

Prolifics

		NM/M
	Complete Set (7):	10.00
	Common Player:	.50
	Inserted 1:28	
1	Manny Ramirez	1.00
2	Vladimir Guerrero	1.00
3	Derek Jeter	3.00
4	Pedro Martinez	1.50
5	Shawn Green	.50
6	Alex Rodriguez	3.00
7	Cal Ripken Jr.	4.00

ProSign

		NM/M
	Common Player:	5.00
	Inserted 1:216 R	
RA	Rick Ankiel	5.00
MB	Michael Barrett	5.00
RB	Rob Bell	5.00
CB	Carlos Beltran	20.00
LB	Lance Berkman	15.00
RB	Rico Brogna	5.00
SC	Sean Casey	8.00
DD	Doug Davis	5.00
ED	Erubiel Durazo	8.00
RF	Robert Fick	8.00
NG	Nomar Garciaparra	65.00
AG	Alex Gonzalez	8.00
KG	Ken Griffey Jr.	60.00
TG	Tony Gwynn	40.00
TH	Tim Hudson	15.00
DJ	Derek Jeter	80.00
CJ	Chipper Jones	50.00
MM	Mike Meyers	5.00
EM	Eric Milton	8.00
JM	Jim Morris	5.00
WM	Warren Morris	5.00
TN	Trot Nixon	8.00
BP	Ben Petrick	5.00
AP	Adam Piatt	5.00
MP	Mike Piazza	60.00
MQ	Mark Quinn	5.00
MR	Manny Ramirez	25.00
RR	Rob Ramsay	5.00
MRe	Mike Redmond	5.00
MRi	Mariano Rivera	15.00
AR	Alex Rodriguez	65.00
MS	Mike Sweeney	8.00
BT	Bubba Trammell	5.00
JV	Jose Vidro	8.00
DW	Daryle Ward	5.00
KW	Kip Wells	8.00
SW	Scott Williamson	5.00
PW	Preston Wilson	8.00
KW	Kevin Witt	5.00
TW	Tony Womack	5.00
EY	Ed Yarnall	5.00
JZ	Jeff Zimmerman	5.00

Scout's Choice

		NM/M
	Complete Set (10):	8.00
	Common Player:	.50
	Inserted 1:14	
1	Rick Ankiel	.50
2	Vernon Wells	1.00
3	Pat Burrell	1.50
4	Travis Dawkins	.50
5	Eric Munson	.50
6	Nick Johnson	1.00
7	Dermal Brown	.50
8	Alfonso Soriano	2.00
9	Ben Petrick	.50
10	Adam Everett	.50

Second Season Standouts

		NM/M
	Complete Set (10):	6.00
	Common Player:	.25
	Inserted 1:6	

SECOND SEASON STANDOUTS

1	Pedro Martinez	1.00
2	Mariano Rivera	.40
3	Orlando Hernandez	.25
4	Ken Caminiti	.25
5	Bernie Williams	.50
6	Jim Thome	.75
7	Nomar Garciaparra	2.00
8	Edgardo Alfonzo	.25
9	Derek Jeter	2.50
10	Kevin Millwood	.40

3,000 Hit Club

		NM/M
	Common Player:	
SM	Stan Musial/Jsy-350	30.00
SM	Stan Musial Bat-350	30.00
SM	Stan Musial/	
	Jsy/Bat-100	80.00
SM	Stan Musial/J/B/Auto.-6	

2000 Upper Deck Ovation

		NM/M
Complete Set (90):		65.00
Common Player:		.25
Common World Prem. (61-80):		1.00
Inserted 1:3		
Common Super. Spot (81-90):		1.50
Inserted 1:6		
Pack (5):		2.00
Wax Box (20):		30.00
1	Mo Vaughn	.25
2	Troy Glaus	.75
3	Jeff Bagwell	.75
4	Craig Biggio	.40
5	Mike Hampton	.25
6	Jason Giambi	.75
7	Tim Hudson	.40
8	Chipper Jones	1.50
9	Greg Maddux	1.50
10	Kevin Millwood	.40
11	Brian Jordan	.25
12	Jeromy Burnitz	.25
13	David Wells	.25
14	Carlos Delgado	.75
15	Sammy Sosa	2.50
16	Mark McGwire	3.00
17	Matt Williams	.25
18	Randy Johnson	.75
19	Erubiel Durazo	.40
20	Kevin Brown	.40
21	Shawn Green	.75
22	Gary Sheffield	.50
23	Jose Canseco	.50
24	Vladimir Guerrero	1.00
25	Barry Bonds	3.00
26	Manny Ramirez	.75
27	Roberto Alomar	.75
28	Richie Sexson	.40
29	Jim Thome	.75
30	Alex Rodriguez	2.50
31	Ken Griffey Jr.	1.50
32	Preston Wilson	.25
33	Mike Piazza	1.50
34	Al Leiter	.25
35	Robin Ventura	.25
36	Cal Ripken Jr.	3.00
37	Albert Belle	.25
38	Tony Gwynn	1.00
39	Brian Giles	.40
40	Jason Kendall	.40
41	Scott Rolen	.75
42	Bob Abreu	.40
43	Ken Griffey Jr.	1.50
44	Sean Casey	.25
45	Carlos Beltran	.40
46	Gabe Kapler	.25
47	Ivan Rodriguez	.75
48	Rafael Palmeiro	.50
49	Larry Walker	.40
50	Nomar Garciaparra	2.00
51	Pedro J. Martinez	1.00
52	Eric Milton	.25
53	Juan Gonzalez	.75
54	Tony Clark	.25
55	Frank Thomas	.75
56	Magglio Ordonez	.40
57	Roger Clemens	1.50
58	Derek Jeter	2.50
59	Bernie Williams	.50
60	Orlando Hernandez	.40
61	Rick Ankiel	1.00
62	Josh Beckett	1.50
63	Vernon Wells	1.50
64	Alfonso Soriano	3.00
65	Pat Burrell	2.00
66	Eric Munson	1.00
67	Chad Hutchinson	1.00
68	Eric Gagne	1.00
69	Peter Bergeron	1.00
70	Ryan Anderson (Supposed to have been withdrawn, all known cards have embossed UD racing mark.)	300.00
71	A.J. Burnett	1.00
72	Jorge Luis Toca	1.00
73	Matt Riley	1.00
74	Chad Hermansen	1.00
75	Doug Davis	1.00
76	Jim Morris	1.00
77	Ben Petrick	1.00
78	Mark Quinn	1.00
79	Ed Yarnall	1.00
80	Ramon Ortiz	1.00
81	Ken Griffey Jr.	3.00
82	Mark McGwire	5.00
83	Derek Jeter	5.00
84	Jeff Bagwell	1.50
85	Nomar Garciaparra	5.00
86	Sammy Sosa	4.00
87	Mike Piazza	3.00
88	Alex Rodriguez	5.00
89	Cal Ripken Jr.	6.00
90	Pedro Martinez	2.00

Standing Ovation

	NM/M
Stars (1-60):	8-15X
World Prem. (61-80):	2-3X
Super. Spot. (81-90):	3-5X

A Piece of History

Production 50 Sets
(See 2000 UD Ovation for checklist and base card values.)

		NM/M
Common Player:		5.00
Production 400 Sets		
JB	Jeff Bagwell	10.00
CB	Carlos Beltran	10.00
SC	Sean Casey	5.00
KG	Ken Griffey Jr.	25.00
DJ	Derek Jeter	35.00
TG	Tony Gwynn	15.00
AJ	Andruw Jones	10.00
CJ	Chipper Jones	20.00
RP	Rafael Palmeiro	10.00
MP	Mike Piazza	20.00
MR	Manny Ramirez	10.00
CR	Cal Ripken Jr.	35.00
AR	Alex Rodriguez	25.00
SR	Scott Rolen	15.00
SS	Sammy Sosa	25.00
FT	Frank Thomas	10.00

Center Stage

		NM/M
Complete Set (10):		20.00
Common Player:		1.00
Inserted 1:9		
Gold:		2X
Inserted 1:39		
Rainbow:		3-4X
Inserted 1:99		
1	Jeff Bagwell	1.00
2	Ken Griffey Jr.	2.00
3	Nomar Garciaparra	3.00
4	Mike Piazza	2.00
5	Mark McGwire	3.00
6	Alex Rodriguez	3.00
7	Cal Ripken Jr.	4.00
8	Derek Jeter	3.00
9	Chipper Jones	2.00
10	Sammy Sosa	2.50

Curtain Calls

	NM/M
Complete Set (20):	15.00
Common Player:	.50

Inserted 1:3

1	David Cone	.50
2	Mark McGwire	2.00
3	Sammy Sosa	2.00
4	Eric Milton	.50
5	Bernie Williams	.75
6	Tony Gwynn	1.00
7	Nomar Garciaparra	2.00
8	Manny Ramirez	1.00
9	Wade Boggs	.50
10	Randy Johnson	1.00
11	Cal Ripken Jr.	3.00
12	Pedro J. Martinez	1.00
13	Alex Rodriguez	2.00
14	Fernando Tatis	.50
15	Vladimir Guerrero	1.00
16	Robin Ventura	.50
17	Larry Walker	.50
18	Carlos Beltran	.50
19	Jose Canseco	.75
20	Ken Griffey Jr.	1.50

Diamond Futures

		NM/M
Complete Set (10):		8.00
Common Player:		.50
Inserted 1:6		
1	J.D. Drew	.75
2	Alfonso Soriano	2.50
3	Preston Wilson	1.00
4	Erubiel Durazo	.75
5	Rick Ankiel	.50
6	Octavio Dotel	.50
7	A.J. Burnett	.50
8	Carlos Beltran	.75
9	Vernon Wells	1.00
10	Troy Glaus	2.00

Lead Performers

		NM/M
Complete Set (10):		20.00
Common Player:		1.00
Inserted 1:19		
1	Mark McGwire	3.00
2	Derek Jeter	3.00
3	Vladimir Guerrero	1.00
4	Mike Piazza	2.00
5	Cal Ripken Jr.	4.00
6	Sammy Sosa	2.50
7	Jeff Bagwell	1.00
8	Nomar Garciaparra	3.00
9	Chipper Jones	2.00
10	Ken Griffey Jr.	2.00

Superstar Theatre

		NM/M
Complete Set (20):		20.00
Common Player:		.50
Inserted 1:19		
1	Ivan Rodriguez	1.00
2	Brian Giles	.50
3	Bernie Williams	1.00

4	Greg Maddux	2.00
5	Frank Thomas	1.00
6	Sean Casey	.50
7	Mo Vaughn	.50
8	Carlos Delgado	1.00
9	Tony Gwynn	1.50
10	Pedro Martinez	1.50
11	Scott Rolen	1.00
12	Mark McGwire	3.00
13	Manny Ramirez	1.00
14	Rafael Palmeiro	.75
15	Jose Canseco	.75
16	Randy Johnson	1.50
17	Gary Sheffield	.75
18	Larry Walker	.50
19	Barry Bonds	4.00
20	Roger Clemens	3.00

Super Signatures

NM/M

Common Card:		
Jr	Ken Griffey/Rainbow/10	
KG	Ken Griffey/Gold/50	180.00
KG	Ken Griffey/Silver/100	100.00
MP	Mike Piazza/Rainbow/10	
MP	Mike Piazza/Gold/50	180.00
MP	Mike Piazza/Silver/100	150.00

3,000 Hit Club

NM/M

1	Willie Mays/Jsy/350	40.00
2	Willie Mays/Bat/300	40.00
3	Willie Mays/Jsy/Bat/50	180.00
4	Willie Mays/Jsy/Bat/Auto./24	675.00

2000 Upper Deck Pros and Prospects

NM/M

Complete Set (132):		300.00
Common Player (1-90):		.15
Common (91-120):		5.00
Production 1,350 Sets		
Common (121-132):		4.00
Production 1,000 Sets		

Pack (5):		2.50
Box (24):		40.00
1	Darin Erstad	.40
2	Troy Glaus	.75
3	Mo Vaughn	.20
4	Jason Giambi	.75
5	Tim Hudson	.25
6	Ben Grieve	.15
7	Eric Chavez	.25
8	Shannon Stewart	.15
9	Raul Mondesi	.25
10	Carlos Delgado	.75
11	Jose Canseco	.40
12	Fred McGriff	.25
13	Greg Vaughn	.15
14	Manny Ramirez	.75
15	Roberto Alomar	.50
16	Jim Thome	.75
17	Alex Rodriguez	2.50
18	Fred Garcia	.15
19	John Olerud	.25
20	Cal Ripken Jr.	2.50
21	Albert Belle	.20
22	Mike Mussina	.40
23	Ivan Rodriguez	.50
24	Rafael Palmeiro	.50
25	Ruben Mateo	.15
26	Gabe Kapler	.15
27	Pedro Martinez	1.00
28	Nomar Garciaparra	2.00
29	Carl Everett	.15
30	Carlos Beltran	.25
31	Jermaine Dye	.15
32	Johnny Damon	.25
33	Juan Gonzalez	.75
34	Juan Encarnacion	.15
35	Dean Palmer	.15
36	Jacque Jones	.15
37	Matt Lawton	.15
38	Frank Thomas	.75
39	Paul Konerko	.15
40	Magglio Ordonez	.25
41	Derek Jeter	2.00
42	Bernie Williams	.50
43	Mariano Rivera	.25
44	Roger Clemens	1.50
45	Jeff Bagwell	.75
46	Craig Biggio	.25
47	Richard Hidalgo	.25
48	Chipper Jones	1.50
49	Andres Galarraga	.25
50	Andruw Jones	.50
51	Greg Maddux	1.50
52	Jeromy Burnitz	.15
53	Geoff Jenkins	.25
54	Mark McGwire	2.00
55	Jim Edmonds	.25
56	Fernando Tatis	.15
57	J.D. Drew	.15
58	Sammy Sosa	2.00
59	Kerry Wood	.50
60	Randy Johnson	.75
61	Matt Williams	.25
62	Erubiel Durazo	.15
63	Shawn Green	.25
64	Kevin Brown	.25
65	Gary Sheffield	.25
66	Adrian Beltre	.25
67	Vladimir Guerrero	.75
68	Jose Vidro	.15
69	Barry Bonds	2.00
70	Jeff Kent	.25
71	Preston Wilson	.15
72	Ryan Dempster	.15
73	Mike Lowell	.15
74	Mike Piazza	1.50
75	Robin Ventura	.25
76	Edgardo Alfonzo	.15
77	Derek Bell	.15
78	Tony Gwynn	1.00
79	Matt Clement	.15
80	Scott Rolen	.75
81	Bobby Abreu	.25
82	Curt Schilling	.40
83	Brian Giles	.25
84	Jason Kendall	.25
85	Kris Benson	.15
86	Ken Griffey Jr.	1.50
87	Sean Casey	.25
88	Pokey Reese	.15
89	Larry Walker	.25
90	Todd Helton	.75
91	Rick Ankiel	5.00
92	Milton Bradley	5.00
93	Vernon Wells	6.00
94	Rafael Furcal	6.00
95	Kazuhiro Sasaki RC	8.00
96	Joe Torres RC	5.00
97	Adam Kennedy	5.00
98	Adam Piatt	5.00
99	Matt Wheatland RC	5.00
100	Alex Cabrera RC	5.00
101	Barry Zito RC	25.00
102	Mike Lamb RC	5.00
103	Scott Heard RC	5.00
104	Danys Baez RC	8.00

105	Matt Riley	5.00
106	Mark Mulder	6.00
107	Wilfredo Rodriguez RC	5.00
108	Luis Matos RC	10.00
109	Alfonso Soriano	8.00
110	Pat Burrell	6.00
111	Mike Tonis RC	5.00
112	Aaron McNeal RC	5.00
113	Dave Krynzel RC	8.00
114	Josh Beckett	5.00
115	Sean Burnett RC	8.00
116	Eric Munson	5.00
117	Scott Downs RC	5.00
118	Brian Tollberg RC	5.00
119	Nick Johnson	5.00
120	Leo Estrella RC	5.00
121	Ken Griffey Jr.	8.00
122	Frank Thomas	4.00
123	Cal Ripken Jr.	15.00
124	Ivan Rodriguez	4.00
125	Derek Jeter	12.00
126	Mark McGwire	12.00
127	Pedro Martinez	5.00
128	Chipper Jones	8.00
129	Sammy Sosa	10.00
130	Alex Rodriguez	10.00
131	Vladimir Guerrero	4.00
132	Jeff Bagwell	4.00

Future Forces

NM/M

Complete Set (10):		5.00
Common Player:		.50
Inserted 1:6		
1	Pat Burrell	2.00
2	Brad Penny	.50
3	Rick Ankiel	.50
4	Adam Kennedy	.50
5	Eric Munson	.50
6	Rafael Furcal	.75
7	Mark Mulder	.75
8	Vernon Wells	.75
9	Matt Riley	.50
10	Nick Johnson	.75

ProMotion

NM/M

Complete Set (10):		15.00
Common Player:		.75
Inserted 1:6		
1	Derek Jeter	3.00
2	Mike Piazza	1.50
3	Mark McGwire	2.50
4	Ivan Rodriguez	.75
5	Kerry Wood	.75
6	Nomar Garciaparra	2.00
7	Sammy Sosa	2.00
8	Alex Rodriguez	2.50
9	Ken Griffey Jr.	1.50
10	Vladimir Guerrero	1.00

Rare Breed

NM/M

Complete Set (12):		15.00
Common Player:		.50
Inserted 1:12		
1	Mark McGwire	3.00
2	Frank Thomas	1.00
3	Mike Piazza	2.00
4	Barry Bonds	4.00
5	Manny Ramirez	1.00
6	Ken Griffey Jr.	2.00
7	Nomar Garciaparra	3.00
8	Randy Johnson	1.50
9	Vladimir Guerrero	1.00
10	Jeff Bagwell	1.00
11	Rick Ankiel	.50
12	Alex Rodriguez	3.00

Signed Game-Worn Jerseys

NM/M

Common Player:		25.00
Inserted 1:96		
BB	Barry Bonds	200.00
JC	Jose Canseco	40.00
JD	J.D. Drew	25.00
TG	Tom Glavine	40.00
LG	Luis Gonzalez	25.00
KG	Ken Griffey Jr.	100.00
TG	Tony Gwynn	50.00
DJ	Derek Jeter/SP	350.00
RJ	Randy Johnson	80.00
CJ	Chipper Jones	50.00
KL	Kenny Lofton	25.00
CR	Cal Ripken Jr.	140.00
AR	Alex Rodriguez	120.00
IR	Ivan Rodriguez	40.00
SR	Scott Rolen	50.00
GS	Gary Sheffield	40.00
FT	Frank Thomas	40.00
MV	Mo Vaughn	25.00
RV	Robin Ventura	25.00
MW	Matt Williams	25.00
PW	Preston Wilson	25.00

The Best in the Bigs

NM/M

Complete Set (10):		15.00
Common Player:		1.00
Inserted 1:12		
1	Sammy Sosa	2.50
2	Tony Gwynn	1.50
3	Pedro Martinez	1.50
4	Mark McGwire	3.00
5	Chipper Jones	2.00
6	Derek Jeter	3.00
7	Ken Griffey Jr.	2.00

		NM/M
8	Cal Ripken Jr.	4.00
9	Greg Maddux	2.00
10	Ivan Rodriguez	1.00

3,000 Hit Club

	NM/M
Lou Brock/Bat/350	20.00
Lou Brock/Jsy/350	20.00
Lou Brock/Bat/Jsy/100	40.00
Rod Carew/Bat/350	20.00
Rod Carew/Jsy/350	20.00
Rod Carew/Bat/Jsy/100	40.00

2000 Upper Deck Rookie Update

		NM/M
Common Player:		.25
Common Rookie:		5.00
Pack (4):		4.50
Box (15):		50.00
SP Authentic Update		
(136-164) Production 1,700		
136	Barry Zito RC	25.00
137	Aaron McNeal RC	5.00
138	Teofilo Perez RC	5.00
139	Sun-Woo Kim RC	5.00
140	Xavier Nady RC	15.00
141	Matt Wheatland RC	5.00
142	Brent Abernathy RC	5.00
143	Cory Vance RC	5.00
144	Scott Heard RC	5.00
145	Mike Meyers RC	5.00
146	Ben Diggins RC	5.00
147	Luis Matos RC	5.00
148	Ben Sheets RC	15.00
149	Kurt Ainsworth RC	5.00
150	Dave Krynzel RC	5.00
151	Alex Cabrera RC	5.00
152	Mike Tonis RC	5.00
153	Dane Sardinha RC	5.00
154	Keith Ginter RC	5.00
155	David Espinosa RC	5.00
156	Joe Torres RC	5.00
157	Daylan Holt RC	5.00
158	Koyie Hill RC	5.00
159	Brad Wilkerson RC	8.00
160	Juan Pierre RC	10.00
161	Matt Ginter RC	5.00
162	Dane Artman RC	5.00
163	Jon Rauch RC	5.00
164	Sean Burnett RC	5.00
166	Darin Erstad	.50
167	Ben Grieve	.25
168	David Wells	.25
169	Fred McGriff	.40
170	Bob Wickman	.25
171	Al Martin	.25
172	Melvin Mora	.25

173	Ricky Ledee	.25
174	Dante Bichette	.25
175	Mike Sweeney	.25
176	Bobby Higginson	.25
177	Matt Lawton	.25
178	Charles Johnson	.25
179	David Justice	.50
180	Richard Hidalgo	.40
181	B.J. Surhoff	.25
182	Richie Sexson	.50
183	Jim Edmonds	.50
184	Rondell White	.25
185	Curt Schilling	.50
186	Tom Goodwin	.25
187	Jose Vidro	.25
188	Ellis Burks	.25
189	Henry Rodriguez	.25
190	Mike Bordick	.25
191	Eric Owens	.25
192	Travis Lee	.25
193	Kevin Young	.25
194	Aaron Boone	.40
195	Todd Hollandsworth	.25
SPx Update		
(121-135, 182-196) 1,600		
(136-151) Production 1,500		
Common Autograph		10.00
121	Brad Wilkerson RC	15.00
122	Roy Oswalt RC	125.00
123	Wascar Serrano RC	5.00
124	Sean Burnett RC	10.00
125	Alex Cabrera RC	5.00
126	Timoniel Perez RC	5.00
127	Juan Pierre RC	10.00
128	Daylan Holt RC	5.00
129	Tomokazu Ohka RC	5.00
130	Kazuhiro Sasaki RC	10.00
131	Kurt Ainsworth RC	10.00
132	Brent Abernathy RC	5.00
133	Danys Baez RC	5.00
134	Brad Cresse RC	5.00
135	Ryan Franklin RC	5.00
136	Mike Lamb RC	10.00
137	David Espinosa RC	5.00
138	Matt Wheatland RC	5.00
139	Xavier Nady RC	30.00
140	Scott Heard RC	5.00
141	Pascual Coco RC	5.00
142	Justin Miller RC	5.00
143	Dave Krynzel RC	10.00
144	Dane Sardinha RC	5.00
145	Ben Sheets RC	40.00
146	Leo Estrella RC	10.00
147	Ben Diggins RC	10.00
148	Barry Zito RC	40.00
149	Joe Torres RC	5.00
150	Mike Meyers RC	10.00
151	Kris Wilson RC	10.00
152	Darin Erstad	.50
153	Richard Hidalgo	.40
154	Eric Chavez	.50
155	B.J. Surhoff	.25
156	Richie Sexson	.75
157	Raul Mondesi	.50
158	Rondell White	.50
159	Jim Edmonds	.75
160	Curt Schilling	.75
161	Tom Goodwin	.25
162	Fred McGriff	.50
163	Jose Vidro	.25
164	Ellis Burks	.25
165	David Segui	.25
166	Aaron Sele	.25
167	Henry Rodriguez	.25
168	Mike Bordick	.25
169	Mike Mussina	1.00
170	Ryan Klesko	.25
171	Kevin Young	.25
172	Travis Lee	.25
173	Aaron Boone	.50
174	Jermaine Dye	.25
175	Ricky Ledee	.25
176	Jeffrey Hammonds	.25
177	Carl Everett	.25
178	Matt Lawton	.25
179	Bobby Higginson	.25
180	Charles Johnson	.25
181	David Justice	.75
182	Joey Nation RC	4.00
183	Rico Washington RC	4.00
184	Luis Matos RC	10.00
185	Chris Wakeland RC	4.00
186	Sun-Woo Kim RC	4.00
187	Keith Ginter RC	5.00
188	Geraldo Guzman RC	4.00
189	Jay Spurgeon RC	4.00
190	Jace Brewer RC	4.00
191	Juan Guzman RC	4.00
192	Ross Gload RC	4.00
193	Paxton Crawford RC	4.00
194	Ryan Kohlmeier RC	4.00
195	Julio Zuleta RC	4.00
196	Matt Ginter RC	4.00
UD Pros & Prospects Update		
(133-162) Production 1,600		

133	Dane Artman RC	5.00
134	Juan Pierre RC	8.00
135	Jace Brewer RC	5.00
136	Sun-Woo Kim RC	6.00
137	Jon Rauch RC	6.00
138	Juan Guzman RC	5.00
139	Daylan Holt RC	5.00
140	Rico Washington RC	5.00
141	Ben Diggins RC	8.00
142	Mike Meyers RC	5.00
143	Chris Wakeland RC	5.00
144	Cory Vance RC	5.00
145	Keith Ginter RC	8.00
146	Koyie Hill RC	8.00
147	Julio Zuleta RC	5.00
148	Geraldo Guzman RC	5.00
149	Jay Spurgeon RC	5.00
150	Ross Gload RC	5.00
151	Ben Sheets RC	15.00
152	Josh Kalinowski RC	5.00
153	Kurt Ainsworth RC	5.00
154	Paxton Crawford RC	5.00
155	Xavier Nady RC	8.00
156	Brad Wilkerson RC	10.00
157	Kris Wilson RC	5.00
158	Paul Rigdon RC	5.00
159	Ryan Kohlmeier RC	5.00
160	Dane Sardinha RC	5.00
161	Javier Cardona RC	5.00
162	Brad Cresse RC	5.00
163	Ron Gant	.25
164	Mark Mulder	.50
165	David Wells	.25
166	Jason Tyner	.25
167	David Segui	.25
168	Al Martin	.25
169	Melvin Mora	.25
170	Ricky Ledee	.25
171	Rolando Arrojo	.25
172	Mike Sweeney	.25
173	Bobby Higginson	.25
174	Eric Milton	.25
175	Charles Johnson	.25
176	David Justice	.50
177	Moises Alou	.50
178	Andy Ashby	.25
179	Richie Sexson	.75
180	Will Clark	.75
181	Rondell White	.40
182	Curt Schilling	.75
183	Tom Goodwin	.25
184	Lee Stevens	.25
185	Ellis Burks	.25
186	Henry Rodriguez	.25
187	Mike Bordick	.25
188	Ryan Klesko	.50
189	Travis Lee	.25
190	Kevin Young	.25
191	Barry Larkin	.75
192	Jeff Cirillo	.25

Winning Materials

		NM/M
Common Card:		10.00
Inserted 1:15		
NG-PM	Nomar Garciaparra, Pedro Martinez	40.00
DJ-AR	Derek Jeter, Alex Rodriguez	40.00
DJ-NG	Derek Jeter, Nomar Garciaparra	40.00
MM-KG	Mark McGwire, Ken Griffey Jr.	40.00
MM-SS	Mark McGwire, Sammy Sosa	40.00
MM-RA	Mark McGwire, Rick Ankiel	30.00
KG-SS	Ken Griffey Jr., Sammy Sosa	25.00
RC-PM	Roger Clemens, Pedro Martinez	30.00
CR-TG	Cal Ripken Jr., Tony Gwynn	40.00
JC-BB	Jose Canseco, Barry Bonds	30.00
FT-MO	Frank Thomas, Magglio Ordonez	10.00
JB-CB	Jeff Bagwell, Craig Biggio	10.00
MP-RV	Mike Piazza, Robin Ventura	25.00

IR-RP	Ivan Rodriguez, Rafael Palmeiro	10.00
J-G-R	Derek Jeter, Nomar Garciaparra, Alex Rodriguez	75.00
G-S-R	Ken Griffey Jr., Sammy Sosa, Alex Rodriguez	40.00

Winning Materials Gold

		NM/M
Common Player:		5.00
JC	John Cotton	5.00
BS	Ben Sheets	15.00
SB	Sean Burroughs	8.00
MN	Mike Neill	5.00
DM	Doug Mientkiewicz	8.00
EY	Ernie Young	5.00
GD	Travis Dawkins, Mike Kinkade	5.00
BS	Sean Burroughs, Ben Sheets	15.00
AE	Brent Abernathy, Adam Everett	5.00
EY	Brad Wilkerson, Ernie Young	8.00

2000 Upper Deck Ultimate Victory

		NM/M
Complete Set (120):		200.00
Common Player:		.15
Common Ultimate Rookie (91-120):		4.00
Varying Production Levels		
Pack (5):		1.50
Box (24):		25.00
1	Mo Vaughn	.20
2	Darin Erstad	.40
3	Troy Glaus	.75
4	Adam Kennedy	.15
5	Jason Giambi	.75
6	Ben Grieve	.15
7	Terrence Long	.15
8	Tim Hudson	.25
9	David Wells	.15
10	Carlos Delgado	.75
11	Shannon Stewart	.15
12	Greg Vaughn	.15
13	Gerald Williams	.15
14	Manny Ramirez	.75
15	Roberto Alomar	.60
16	Jim Thome	.75
17	Edgar Martinez	.25
18	Alex Rodriguez	2.50
19	Matt Riley	.15
20	Cal Ripken Jr.	2.50
21	Mike Mussina	.50
22	Albert Belle	.20
23	Ivan Rodriguez	.75
24	Rafael Palmeiro	.50
25	Nomar Garciaparra	2.00
26	Pedro Martinez	1.00
27	Carl Everett	.15
28	Tomokazu Ohka RC	.40
29	Jermaine Dye	.15
30	Johnny Damon	.25
31	Dean Palmer	.15
32	Juan Gonzalez	.75
33	Eric Milton	.15
34	Matt Lawton	.15
35	Frank Thomas	.75
36	Paul Konerko	.15
37	Magglio Ordonez	.25
38	Jon Garland	.15
39	Derek Jeter	2.50
40	Roger Clemens	1.50
41	Bernie Williams	.50
42	Nick Johnson	.15
43	Julio Lugo	.15

44 Jeff Bagwell .75
45 Richard Hidalgo .15
46 Chipper Jones 1.50
47 Greg Maddux 1.50
48 Andruw Jones .50
49 Andres Galarraga .25
50 Rafael Furcal .50
51 Jeromy Burnitz .15
52 Geoff Jenkins .25
53 Mark McGwire 2.00
54 Jim Edmonds .25
55 Rick Ankiel .15
56 Sammy Sosa 2.00
57 Julio Zuleta RC .25
58 Kerry Wood .40
59 Randy Johnson .75
60 Matt Williams .25
61 Steve Finley .15
62 Gary Sheffield .40
63 Kevin Brown .25
64 Shawn Green .25
65 Milton Bradley .15
66 Vladimir Guerrero .75
67 Jose Vidro .15
68 Barry Bonds 2.00
69 Jeff Kent .25
70 Preston Wilson .15
71 Mike Lowell .15
72 Mike Piazza 2.00
73 Robin Ventura .25
74 Edgardo Alfonzo .15
75 Jay Payton .15
76 Tony Gwynn 1.00
77 Adam Eaton .15
78 Phil Nevin .15
79 Scott Rolen .75
80 Bob Abreu .25
81 Pat Burrell .50
82 Brian Giles .25
83 Jason Kendall .25
84 Kris Benson .15
85 Gookie Dawkins .15
86 Ken Griffey Jr. 1.50
87 Barry Larkin .40
88 Larry Walker .25
89 Todd Helton .75
90 Ben Petrick .15
91 Alex Cabrera 3,500 RC 4.00
92 Matt Wheatland 1,000 RC 4.00
93 Joe Torres 1,000 RC 4.00
94 Xavier Nady 1,000 RC 12.00
95 Kenny Kelly 3,500 RC 4.00
96 Matt Ginter 3,500 RC 4.00
97 Ben Diggins 1,000 RC 8.00
98 Danys Baez 3,500 RC 6.00
99 Daylan Holt 2,500 RC 4.00
100 Kazuhiro Sasaki 3,500 RC 5.00
101 Dane Artman 2,500 RC 4.00
102 Mike Tonis 1,000 RC 4.00
103 Timoniel Perez 2,500 RC 4.00
104 Barry Zito 2,500 RC 20.00
105 Koyie Hill 2,500 RC 4.00
106 Brad Wilkerson 2,500 RC 8.00
107 Juan Pierre 3,500 RC 8.00
108 Aaron McNeal 3,500 RC 4.00
109 Jay Spurgeon 3,500 RC 4.00
110 Sean Burnett 1,000 RC 8.00
111 Luis Matos 3,500 RC 8.00
112 Dave Krynzel 1,000 RC 6.00
113 Scott Heard 1,000 RC 8.00
114 Ben Sheets 2,500 RC 15.00
115 Dane Sardinha 1,000 RC 4.00
116 David Espinosa 1,000 RC 4.00
117 Leo Estrella 3,500 RC 4.00
118 Kurt Ainsworth 2,500 RC 4.00
119 Jon Rauch 2,500 RC 4.00
120 Ryan Franklin 2,500 4.00

Collection

Parallel 25 Stars: 20-40X
Rookies (91-120): 2-4X
Production 25 Sets
Parallel 100 Stars: 4-8X
Rookies (91-120): 1-2X
Production 100 Sets
Parallel 250 Stars: 2-4X
Rookies (91-120): 1-2X
Production 250 Sets

Diamond Dignitaries

NM/M
Complete Set (10): 20.00
Common Player: 1.00
Inserted 1:23
1 Ken Griffey Jr. 2.00
2 Nomar Garciaparra 3.00
3 Chipper Jones 2.00

4 Ivan Rodriguez 1.00
5 Mark McGwire 3.00
6 Cal Ripken Jr. 4.00
7 Vladimir Guerrero 1.00
8 Alex Rodriguez 3.00
9 Sammy Sosa 2.50
10 Derek Jeter 3.00

HOF Game Jersey

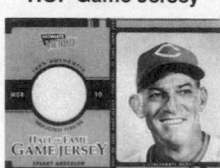

NM/M
Common Card: 8.00
SA Sparky Anderson 8.00
CF Carlton Fisk 10.00
TP Tony Perez 8.00

HOF Game Jersey Combo

NM/M
UV-C Sparky Anderson, Carlton Fisk, Tony Perez 40.00

Lasting Impressions

NM/M
Complete Set (10): 15.00
Common Player: 1.00
Inserted 1:11
1 Barry Bonds 3.00
2 Mike Piazza 2.00
3 Manny Ramirez 1.00
4 Pedro J. Martinez 1.50
5 Mark McGwire 2.00
6 Ken Griffey Jr. 2.00
7 Ivan Rodriguez 1.00
8 Jeff Bagwell 1.00
9 Randy Johnson 1.50
10 Alex Rodriguez 3.00

Starstruck

NM/M

ABBREVIATIONS

RC - Rookie Class

Complete Set (10): 20.00
Common Player: 1.00
Inserted 1:11
1 Alex Rodriguez 3.00
2 Frank Thomas 1.00
3 Derek Jeter 3.00
4 Mark McGwire 3.00
5 Nomar Garciaparra 3.00
6 Chipper Jones 2.00
7 Cal Ripken Jr. 4.00
8 Sammy Sosa 2.00
9 Vladimir Guerrero 1.00
10 Ken Griffey Jr. 2.00

2000 Upper Deck Victory

NM/M
Complete Set (440): 20.00
Complete Factory Set (466): 25.00
Common Player: .10
Common Griffey (391-440): .50
Common USA (441-466): .40
Pack (12): 1.00
Wax Box (36): 25.00
1 Mo Vaughn .15
2 Garret Anderson .20
3 Tim Salmon .20
4 Troy Percival .10
5 Orlando Palmeiro .10
6 Darin Erstad .20
7 Ramon Ortiz .10
8 Ben Molina .10
9 Troy Glaus .40
10 Jim Edmonds .20
11 Mo Vaughn, Troy Percival .15
12 Craig Biggio .25
13 Roger Cedeno .10
14 Shane Reynolds .10
15 Jeff Bagwell .50
16 Octavio Dotel .10
17 Moises Alou .20
18 Jose Lima .10
19 Ken Caminiti .15
20 Richard Hidalgo .10
21 Billy Wagner .10
22 Lance Berkman .20
23 Jeff Bagwell, Jose Lima .25
24 Jason Giambi .50
25 Randy Velarde .10
26 Miguel Tejada .25
27 Matt Stairs .10
28 A.J. Hinch .10
29 Olmedo Saenz .10
30 Ben Grieve .10
31 Ryan Christenson .10
32 Eric Chavez .20
33 Tim Hudson .20
34 John Jaha .10
35 Jason Giambi, Matt Stairs .25
36 Raul Mondesi .20
37 Tony Batista .10
38 David Wells .10
39 Homer Bush .10
40 Carlos Delgado .40
41 Billy Koch .10
42 Darrin Fletcher .10
43 Tony Fernandez .10
44 Shannon Stewart .10
45 Roy Halladay .20
46 Chris Carpenter .10
47 Carlos Delgado, David Wells .20
48 Chipper Jones 1.00
49 Greg Maddux 1.00
50 Andruw Jones .40
51 Andres Galarraga .20
52 Tom Glavine .20
53 Brian Jordan .10
54 John Smoltz .15

55 John Rocker .10
56 Javy Lopez .15
57 Eddie Perez .10
58 Kevin Millwood .20
59 Chipper Jones, Greg Maddux .50
60 Jeromy Burnitz .10
61 Steve Woodard .10
62 Ron Belliard .10
63 Geoff Jenkins .20
64 Bob Wickman .10
65 Marquis Grissom .10
66 Henry Blanco .10
67 Mark Loretta .10
68 Alex Ochoa .10
69 Marquis Grissom, Jeromy Burnitz .10
70 Mark McGwire 1.50
71 Edgar Renteria .10
72 Dave Veres .10
73 Eli Marrero .10
74 Fernando Tatis .10
75 J.D. Drew .20
76 Ray Lankford .10
77 Daryle Kile .10
78 Kent Bottenfield .10
79 Joe McEwing .10
80 Mark McGwire, Ray Lankford .75
81 Sammy Sosa 1.25
82 Jose Nieves .10
83 Jon Lieber .10
84 Henry Rodriguez .10
85 Mark Grace .20
86 Eric Young .10
87 Kerry Wood .25
88 Ismael Valdes .10
89 Glenallen Hill .10
90 Sammy Sosa, Mark Grace .60
91 Greg Vaughn .10
92 Fred McGriff .20
93 Ryan Rupe .10
94 Bubba Trammell .10
95 Miguel Cairo .10
96 Roberto Hernandez .10
97 Jose Canseco .40
98 Wilson Alvarez .10
99 John Flaherty .10
100 Vinny Castilla .15
101 Jose Canseco, Roberto Hernandez .25
102 Randy Johnson .50
103 Matt Williams .15
104 Matt Mantei .10
105 Steve Finley .10
106 Luis Gonzalez .20
107 Travis Lee .10
108 Omar Daal .10
109 Jay Bell .10
110 Erubiel Durazo .10
111 Tony Womack .10
112 Todd Stottlemyre .10
113 Randy Johnson, Matt Williams .25
114 Gary Sheffield .25
115 Adrian Beltre .10
116 Kevin Brown .20
117 Todd Hundley .10
118 Eric Karros .20
119 Shawn Green .40
120 Chan Ho Park .10
121 Mark Grudzielanek .10
122 Todd Hollandsworth .10
123 Jeff Shaw .10
124 Darren Dreifort .10
125 Gary Sheffield, Kevin Brown .15
126 Vladimir Guerrero .50
127 Michael Barrett .10
128 Dustin Hermanson .10
129 Jose Vidro .10
130 Chris Widger .10
131 Mike Thurman .10
132 Wilton Guerrero .10
133 Brad Fullmer .10
134 Rondell White .20
135 Ugueth Urbina .10
136 Vladimir Guerrero, Rondell White .40
137 Barry Bonds 1.50
138 Russ Ortiz .10
139 J.T. Snow .10
140 Joe Nathan .10
141 Rich Aurilia .10
142 Jeff Kent .20
143 Armando Rios .10
144 Ellis Burks .10
145 Robb Nen .10
146 Marvin Benard .10
147 Barry Bonds, Russ Ortiz .75
148 Manny Ramirez .50
149 Bartolo Colon .10

150	Kenny Lofton	.20
151	Sandy Alomar Jr.	.10
152	Travis Fryman	.15
153	Omar Vizquel	.15
154	Roberto Alomar	.40
155	Richie Sexson	.25
156	David Justice	.20
157	Jim Thome	.50
158	Manny Ramirez, Roberto Alomar	.25
159	Ken Griffey Jr.	1.00
160	Edgar Martinez	.15
161	Fred Garcia	.10
162	Alex Rodriguez	1.50
163	John Halama	.10
164	Russ Davis	.10
165	David Bell	.10
166	Gil Meche	.10
167	Jamie Moyer	.10
168	John Olerud	.20
169	Ken Griffey Jr., Fred Garcia	.50
170	Preston Wilson	.20
171	Antonio Alfonseca	.10
172	A.J. Burnett	.10
173	Luis Castillo	.10
174	Mike Lowell	.10
175	Alex Fernandez	.10
176	Mike Redmond	.10
177	Alex Gonzalez	.10
178	Vladimir Nunez	.10
179	Mark Kotsay	.10
180	Preston Wilson, Luis Castillo	.10
181	Mike Piazza	1.00
182	Darryl Hamilton	.10
183	Al Leiter	.20
184	Robin Ventura	.20
185	Rickey Henderson	.20
186	Rey Ordonez	.10
187	Edgardo Alfonzo	.10
188	Derek Bell	.10
189	Mike Hampton	.10
190	Armando Benitez	.10
191	Mike Piazza, Rickey Henderson	.50
192	Cal Ripken Jr.	1.50
193	B.J. Surhoff	.10
194	Mike Mussina	.40
195	Albert Belle	.15
196	Jerry Hairston Jr.	.10
197	Will Clark	.20
198	Sidney Ponson	.10
199	Brady Anderson	.10
200	Scott Erickson	.10
201	Ryan Minor	.10
202	Cal Ripken Jr., Albert Belle	.75
203	Tony Gwynn	.75
204	Bret Boone	.20
205	Ryan Klesko	.10
206	Ben Davis	.10
207	Matt Clement	.10
208	Eric Owens	.10
209	Trevor Hoffman	.10
210	Sterling Hitchcock	.10
211	Phil Nevin	.10
212	Tony Gwynn, Trevor Hoffman	.40
213	Scott Rolen	.50
214	Bob Abreu	.20
215	Curt Schilling	.25
216	Rico Brogna	.10
217	Robert Person	.10
218	Doug Glanville	.10
219	Mike Lieberthal	.10
220	Andy Ashby	.10
221	Randy Wolf	.10
222	Bob Abreu, Curt Schilling	.20
223	Brian Giles	.20
224	Jason Kendall	.20
225	Kris Benson	.10
226	Warren Morris	.10
227	Kevin Young	.10
228	Al Martin	.10
229	Wil Cordero	.10
230	Bruce Aven	.10
231	Todd Ritchie	.10
232	Jason Kendall, Brian Giles	.10
233	Ivan Rodriguez	.50
234	Rusty Greer	.10
235	Ruben Mateo	.10
236	Justin Thompson	.10
237	Rafael Palmeiro	.25
238	Chad Curtis	.10
239	Royce Clayton	.10
240	Gabe Kapler	.10
241	Jeff Zimmerman	.10
242	John Wetteland	.10
243	Ivan Rodriguez, Rafael Palmeiro	.25
244	Nomar Garciaparra	1.25

245	Pedro Martinez	.75
246	Jose Offerman	.10
247	Jason Varitek	.10
248	Troy O'Leary	.10
249	John Valentin	.10
250	Trot Nixon	.10
251	Carl Everett	.10
252	Wilton Veras	.10
253	Bret Saberhagen	.10
254	Nomar Garciaparra, Pedro J. Martinez	.60
255	Sean Casey	.10
256	Barry Larkin	.25
257	Pokey Reese	.10
258	Pete Harnisch	.10
259	Aaron Boone	.20
260	Dante Bichette	.10
261	Scott Williamson	.10
262	Steve Parris	.10
263	Dmitri Young	.10
264	Mike Cameron	.10
265	Sean Casey, Scott Williamson	.10
266	Larry Walker	.25
267	Rolando Arrojo	.10
268	Pedro Astacio	.10
269	Todd Helton	.50
270	Jeff Cirillo	.10
271	Neifi Perez	.10
272	Brian Bohanon	.10
273	Jeffrey Hammonds	.10
274	Tom Goodwin	.10
275	Larry Walker, Todd Helton	.25
276	Carlos Beltran	.15
277	Jermaine Dye	.10
278	Mike Sweeney	.10
279	Joe Randa	.10
280	Jose Rosado	.10
281	Carlos Febles	.10
282	Jeff Suppan	.10
283	Johnny Damon	.20
284	Jeremy Giambi	.10
285	Mike Sweeney, Carlos Beltran	.10
286	Tony Clark	.10
287	Damion Easley	.10
288	Jeff Weaver	.10
289	Dean Palmer	.10
290	Juan Gonzalez	.50
291	Juan Encarnacion	.10
292	Todd Jones	.10
293	Karim Garcia	.10
294	Deivi Cruz	.10
295	Dean Palmer, Juan Encarnacion	.10
296	Corey Koskie	.10
297	Brad Radke	.10
298	Doug Mientkiewicz	.10
299	Ron Coomer	.10
300	Joe Mays	.10
301	Eric Milton	.10
302	Jacque Jones	.10
303	Chad Allen	.10
304	Cristian Guzman	.10
305	Jason Ryan	.10
306	Todd Walker	.10
307	Corey Koskie, Eric Milton	.10
308	Frank Thomas	.50
309	Paul Konerko	.10
310	Mike Sirotka	.10
311	Jim Parque	.10
312	Magglio Ordonez	.25
313	Bob Howry	.10
314	Carlos Lee	.10
315	Ray Durham	.10
316	Chris Singleton	.10
317	Brook Fordyce	.10
318	Frank Thomas, Magglio Ordonez	.25
319	Derek Jeter	1.50
320	Roger Clemens	1.00
321	Paul O'Neill	.20
322	Bernie Williams	.40
323	Mariano Rivera	.20
324	Tino Martinez	.20
325	David Cone	.20
326	Chuck Knoblauch	.10
327	Darryl Strawberry	.20
328	Orlando Hernandez	.10
329	Ricky Ledee	.10
330	Derek Jeter, Bernie Williams	.75
331	Pat Burrell	.50
332	Alfonso Soriano	.75
333	Josh Beckett	.25
334	Matt Riley	.15
335	Brian Cooper	.10
336	Eric Munson	.20
337	Vernon Wells	.25
338	Juan Pena	.10
339	Mark DeRosa	.10
340	Kip Wells	.10

341	Roosevelt Brown	.10
342	Jason LaRue	.10
343	Ben Petrick	.10
344	Mark Quinn	.10
345	Julio Ramirez	.10
346	Rod Barajas	.10
347	Robert Fick	.10
348	David Newhan	.10
349	Eric Gagne	.15
350	Jorge Toca	.10
351	Mitch Meluskey	.10
352	Ed Yarnall	.10
353	Chad Hermansen	.10
354	Peter Bergeron	.10
355	Dermal Brown	.10
356	Adam Kennedy	.10
357	Kevin Barker	.10
358	Francisco Cordero	.10
359	Travis Dawkins	.10
360	Jeff Williams	.10
361	Chad Hutchinson	.10
362	D'Angelo Jimenez	.10
363	Derrick Gibson	.10
364	Calvin Murray	.10
365	Doug Davis	.10
366	Rob Ramsay RC	.20
367	Mark Redman	.10
368	Rick Ankiel	.10
369	Domingo Guzman	.10
370	Eugene Kingsale	.10
371	Nomar Garciaparra	.75
372	Ken Griffey Jr.	.50
373	Randy Johnson	.25
374	Jeff Bagwell	.25
375	Ivan Rodriguez	.25
376	Derek Jeter	.75
377	Carlos Beltran	.10
378	Vladimir Guerrero	.40
379	Sammy Sosa	.60
380	Barry Bonds	.75
381	Pedro Martinez	.40
382	Chipper Jones	.50
383	Mo Vaughn	.10
384	Mike Piazza	.50
385	Alex Rodriguez	.75
386	Manny Ramirez	.25
387	Mark McGwire	.75
388	Tony Gwynn	.40
389	Sean Casey	.10
390	Cal Ripken Jr.	.75
391	Ken Griffey Jr.	.40
392	Ken Griffey Jr.	.40
393	Ken Griffey Jr.	.40
394	Ken Griffey Jr.	.40
395	Ken Griffey Jr.	.40
396	Ken Griffey Jr.	.40
397	Ken Griffey Jr.	.40
398	Ken Griffey Jr.	.40
399	Ken Griffey Jr.	.40
400	Ken Griffey Jr.	.40
401	Ken Griffey Jr.	.40
402	Ken Griffey Jr.	.40
403	Ken Griffey Jr.	.40
404	Ken Griffey Jr.	.40
405	Ken Griffey Jr.	.40
406	Ken Griffey Jr.	.40
407	Ken Griffey Jr.	.40
408	Ken Griffey Jr.	.40
409	Ken Griffey Jr.	.40
410	Ken Griffey Jr.	.40
411	Ken Griffey Jr.	.40
412	Ken Griffey Jr.	.40
413	Ken Griffey Jr.	.40
414	Ken Griffey Jr.	.40
415	Ken Griffey Jr.	.40
416	Ken Griffey Jr.	.40
417	Ken Griffey Jr.	.40
418	Ken Griffey Jr.	.40
419	Ken Griffey Jr.	.40
420	Ken Griffey Jr.	.40
421	Ken Griffey Jr.	.40
422	Ken Griffey Jr.	.40
423	Ken Griffey Jr.	.40
424	Ken Griffey Jr.	.40
425	Ken Griffey Jr.	.40
426	Ken Griffey Jr.	.40
427	Ken Griffey Jr.	.40
428	Ken Griffey Jr.	.40
429	Ken Griffey Jr.	.40
430	Ken Griffey Jr.	.40
431	Ken Griffey Jr.	.40
432	Ken Griffey Jr.	.40
433	Ken Griffey Jr.	.40
434	Ken Griffey Jr.	.40
435	Ken Griffey Jr.	.40
436	Ken Griffey Jr.	.40
437	Ken Griffey Jr.	.40
438	Ken Griffey Jr.	.40
439	Ken Griffey Jr.	.40
440	Ken Griffey Jr.	.40
441	Tommy Lasorda	.50
442	Sean Burroughs	.75
443	Rick Krivda	.40
444	Ben Sheets RC	1.50

445	Pat Borders	.40
446	Brent Abernathy RC	.75
447	Tim Young	.40
448	Adam Everett	.50
449	Anthony Sanders	.40
450	Ernie Young	.40
451	Brad Wilkerson RC	1.50
452	Kurt Ainsworth	1.00
453	Ryan Franklin	.40
454	Todd Williams	.40
455	Jon Rauch RC	.50
456	Roy Oswalt RC	5.00
457	Shane Heams	.50
458	Chris George	.50
459	Bobby Seay	.40
460	Mike Kinkade	.40
461	Marcus Jensen	.40
462	Travis Dawkins	.50
463	Doug Mientkiewicz	.40
464	John Cotton	.40
465	Mike Neill	.40
466	Team Photo USA	2.50

2000 Upper Deck Yankees Legends

		NM/M
Complete Set (90):		20.00
Common Player:		.15
Pack (5):		6.00
Box (24):		100.00
1	Babe Ruth	2.00
2	Mickey Mantle	2.00
3	Lou Gehrig	2.00
4	Joe DiMaggio	2.00
5	Yogi Berra	.75
6	Don Mattingly	1.00
7	Reggie Jackson	.75
8	Dave Winfield	.40
9	Bill Skowron	.15
10	Willie Randolph	.15
11	Phil Rizzuto	.50
12	Tony Kubek	.15
13	Thurman Munson	1.00
14	Roger Maris	1.00
15	Billy Martin	.40
16	Elston Howard	.15
17	Graig Nettles	.15
18	Whitey Ford	.50
19	Earl Combes	.15
20	Tony Lazzeri	.15
21	Bob Meusel	.15
22	Joe Gordon	.15
23	Jerry Coleman	.15
24	Joe Torre	.50
25	Bucky Dent	.15
26	Don Larsen	.40
27	Bobby Richardson	.15
28	Ron Guidry	.15
29	Bobby Murcer	.15
30	Tommy Henrich	.15
31	Hank Bauer	.15
32	Joe Pepitone	.15
33	Clete Boyer	.15
34	Chris Chambliss	.15
35	Tommy John	.15
36	Goose Gossage	.15
37	Red Ruffing	.15
38	Charlie Keller	.15
39	Billy Gardner	.15
40	Hector Lopez	.15
41	Cliff Johnson	.15
42	Oscar Gamble	.15
43	Allie Reynolds	.15
44	Mickey Rivers	.15
45	Bill Dickey	.40
46	Dave Righetti	.15
47	Mel Stottlemyre	.15
48	Waite Hoyt	.15
49	Lefty Gomez	.15
50	Wade Boggs	.50
51	Billy Martin	.25
52	Babe Ruth	1.00

53	Lou Gehrig	1.00
54	Joe DiMaggio	1.00
55	Mickey Mantle	1.00
56	Yogi Berra	.40
57	Bill Dickey	.25
58	Roger Maris	.50
59	Phil Rizzuto	.25
60	Thurman Munson	.50
61	Whitey Ford	.25
62	Don Mattingly	.50
63	Elston Howard	.15
64	Casey Stengel	.15
65	Reggie Jackson	.50
66	Babe Ruth/1923	1.00
67	Lou Gehrig/1927	1.00
68	Tony Lazzeri/1928	.15
69	Babe Ruth/1932	1.00
70	Lou Gehrig/1936	1.00
71	Lefty Gomez/1937	.15
72	Bill Dickey/1938	.25
73	Tommy Henrich/1939	.15
74	Joe DiMaggio/1941	1.00
75	Spud Chandler/1943	.15
76	Tommy Henrich/1947	.15
77	Phil Rizzuto/1949	.25
78	Whitey Ford/1950	.25
79	Yogi Berra/1951	.40
80	Casey Stengel/1952	.15
81	Billy Martin/1953	.25
82	Don Larsen/1956	.25
83	Elston Howard/1958	.15
84	Roger Maris/1961	.50
85	Mickey Mantle/1962	1.00
86	Reggie Jackson/1977	.50
87	Bucky Dent/1978	.15
88	Wade Boggs/1996	.25
89	Joe Torre/1998	.25
90	Joe Torre/1999	.25

DiMaggio Memorabilia

		NM/M
YLB-JD	Joe DiMaggio/ Bat	125.00
YLG-JD	Joe DiMaggio/ Gold Bat/56	200.00
YLC-JD	Joe DiMaggio/ Bat, Cut Sig./5	650.00

Legendary Pinstripes

		NM/M
Common Player:		20.00
Inserted 1:144		
BD	Bucky Dent	20.00
WF	Whitey Ford	50.00
LG	Lou Gehrig	300.00
GG	Goose Gossage	20.00
RG	Ron Guidry	20.00
TH	Tommy Henrich	20.00
EH	Elston Howard	20.00
RJ	Reggie Jackson	40.00
HL	Hector Lopez	20.00
MM	Mickey Mantle	250.00
RM	Roger Maris	75.00
BM	Billy Martin	40.00

ABBREVIATIONS
SP - Short Print

DM	Don Mattingly	60.00
TM	Thurman Munson	75.00
JP	Joe Pepitone	20.00
AR	Allie Reynolds	20.00
BR	Bobby Richardson	20.00
PR	Phil Rizzuto	40.00
DW	Dave Winfield	40.00

Autograph Legendary Pinstripe

		NM/M
Common Player:		30.00
BD	Bucky Dent	30.00
WF	Whitey Ford	60.00
GG	Goose Gossage	30.00
RG	Ron Guidry	35.00
TH	Tommy Henrich	30.00
GM	Gil MacDougald	30.00
DM	Don Mattingly	150.00
JP	Joe Pepitone	30.00
PR	Phil Rizzuto	60.00
DW	Dave Winfield	35.00

Legendary Lumber

		NM/M
Common Player:		5.00
Inserted 1:23		
HB	Hank Bauer	8.00
YB	Yogi Berra	20.00
PB	Paul Blair	5.00
CB	Clete Boyer	5.00
CC	Chris Chambliss	8.00
JC	Joe Collins	5.00
BD	Bucky Dent	8.00
JD	Joe DiMaggio	140.00
OG	Oscar Gamble	5.00
BG	Billy Gardner	5.00
TH	Tommy Henrich	5.00
RH	Ralph Houk	8.00
EH	Elston Howard	8.00
RJ	Reggie Jackson	20.00
TJ	Tommy John	8.00
CJ	Cliff Johnson	5.00
CK	Charlie Keller	5.00
TK	Tony Kubek	8.00
HL	Hector Lopez	5.00
MM	Mickey Mantle	165.00
RM	Roger Maris	45.00
DM	Don Mattingly	35.00
TM	Thurman Munson	35.00
BM	Bobby Murcer	8.00
GN	Graig Nettles	10.00
JP	Joe Pepitone	6.00
WR	Willie Randolph	6.00
MR	Mickey Rivers	5.00
BR	Babe Ruth	185.00
MS	Moose Skowron	6.00
DW	Dave Winfield	15.00

Leg. Lumber/Sign. Cut

	NM/M
Complete Set (10):	20.00
Common Player:	1.50

		NM/M
MM-LC	Mickey Mantle/7	4,000

Monument Park

	NM/M
Complete Set (6):	20.00
Common Player:	1.50
Inserted 1:23	3.00
1 Lou Gehrig	6.00
2 Babe Ruth	6.00
3 Mickey Mantle	6.00
4 Joe DiMaggio	6.00
5 Thurman Munson	3.00
6 Elston Howard	1.50

Murderer's Row

	NM/M
Complete Set (10):	17.50
Common Player:	1.50
Inserted 1:11	
1 Tony Lazzeri	1.50
2 Babe Ruth	6.00
3 Bob Meusel	1.50
4 Lou Gehrig	6.00
5 Joe Dugan	1.50
6 Bill Dickey	1.50
7 Waite Hoyt	1.50
8 Red Ruffing	1.50
9 Earl Combes	1.50
10 Lefty Gomez	1.50

Pride of the Pinstripes

	NM/M
Complete Set (6):	17.50
Common Player:	2.50
Inserted 1:23	
1 Babe Ruth	6.00
2 Mickey Mantle	6.00
3 Joe DiMaggio	5.00
4 Lou Gehrig	5.00
5 Reggie Jackson	2.50
6 Yogi Berra	2.50

The Golden Years

		Inserted 1:11
1	Joe DiMaggio	6.00
2	Phil Rizzuto	2.50
3	Yogi Berra	3.00
4	Billy Martin	2.50
5	Whitey Ford	2.50
6	Roger Maris	5.00
7	Mickey Mantle	7.50
8	Elston Howard	1.50
9	Tommy Henrich	1.50
10	Joe Gordon	1.50

The New Dynasty

	NM/M
Complete Set (10):	15.00
Common Player:	1.50
Inserted 1:11	
1 Reggie Jackson	3.50
2 Graig Nettles	1.50
3 Don Mattingly	6.50
4 Goose Gossage	1.50
5 Dave Winfield	3.00
6 Chris Chambliss	1.50
7 Thurman Munson	4.00
8 Willie Randolph	1.50
9 Ron Guidry	2.50
10 Bucky Dent	2.50

2000 UD Ionix

	NM/M
Complete Set (90):	50.00
Common Player:	.15
Common Futuristic:	1.00
Inserted 1:4	
Reciprocal (1-60):	1.5-2X
Reciprocal (61-90):	1-1.5X
Inserted 1:4	
Future Recip. 1:11	
Pack (4):	2.00
Wax Box (24):	35.00
1 Mo Vaughn	.20
2 Troy Glaus	.75
3 Jeff Bagwell	.75
4 Craig Biggio	.40
5 Jose Lima	.15
6 Jason Giambi	1.00
7 Tim Hudson	.40
8 Shawn Green	.50
9 Carlos Delgado	.75
10 Chipper Jones	1.50
11 Andruw Jones	.75
12 Greg Maddux	1.50
13 Jeromy Burnitz	.15
14 Mark McGwire	2.00
15 J.D. Drew	.25
16 Sammy Sosa	2.00
17 Jose Canseco	.50
18 Fred McGriff	.40
19 Randy Johnson	.75
20 Matt Williams	.25
21 Kevin Brown	.40

22	Gary Sheffield	.40
23	Vladimir Guerrero	.75
24	Barry Bonds	2.50
25	Jim Thome	.75
26	Manny Ramirez	.75
27	Roberto Alomar	.50
28	Kenny Lofton	.25
29	Ken Griffey Jr.	1.50
30	Alex Rodriguez	2.50
31	Alex Gonzalez	.15
32	Preston Wilson	.15
33	Mike Piazza	1.50
34	Robin Ventura	.25
35	Cal Ripken Jr.	2.50
36	Albert Belle	.20
37	Tony Gwynn	1.00
38	Scott Rolen	.75
39	Curt Schilling	.50
40	Brian Giles	.25
41	Juan Gonzalez	.75
42	Ivan Rodriguez	.75
43	Rafael Palmeiro	.60
44	Pedro J. Martinez	1.00
45	Nomar Garciaparra	2.00
46	Sean Casey	.25
47	Aaron Boone	.25
48	Barry Larkin	.40
49	Larry Walker	.25
50	Vinny Castilla	.20
51	Carlos Beltran	.25
52	Gabe Kapler	.15
53	Dean Palmer	.15
54	Eric Milton	.15
55	Corey Koskie	.15
56	Frank Thomas	.75
57	Magglio Ordonez	.40
58	Roger Clemens	2.00
59	Bernie Williams	.75
60	Derek Jeter	2.50
61	Josh Beckett	1.50
62	Eric Munson	1.00
63	Rick Ankiel	1.00
64	Matt Riley	1.00
65	Robert Ramsay	1.00
66	Vernon Wells	2.00
67	Eric Gagne	1.50
68	Robert Fick	1.50
69	Mark Quinn	1.00
70	Kip Wells	1.00
71	Peter Bergeron	1.00
72	Ed Yarnall	1.00
73	Jorge Luis Toca	1.00
74	Alfonso Soriano	4.00
75	Calvin Murray	1.00
76	Ramon Ortiz	1.50
77	Chad Meyers	1.00
78	Jason LaRue	1.00
79	Pat Burrell	2.00
80	Chad Hermansen	1.00
81	Lance Berkman	1.50
82	Erubiel Durazo	1.50
83	Juan Pena	1.00
84	Adam Kennedy	1.00
85	Ben Petrick	1.00
86	Kevin Barker	1.00
87	Bruce Chen	1.00
88	Jerry Hairston Jr.	1.00
89	A.J. Burnett	1.00
90	Gary Matthews Jr.	1.00

Atomic

		NM/M
Complete Set (15):		25.00
Common Player:		1.00
Inserted 1:8		
1	Pedro J. Martinez	1.50
2	Mark McGwire	3.00
3	Ken Griffey Jr.	2.00
4	Jeff Bagwell	1.00
5	Greg Maddux	2.00
6	Derek Jeter	3.00
7	Cal Ripken Jr.	4.00
8	Manny Ramirez	1.00
9	Randy Johnson	1.50
10	Nomar Garciaparra	3.00
11	Tony Gwynn	1.50
12	Bernie Williams	1.00
13	Mike Piazza	2.00
14	Roger Clemens	3.00
15	Alex Rodriguez	3.00

Awesome Powers

		NM/M
Complete Set (15):		50.00
Common Player:		1.00
Inserted 1:23		
1	Ken Griffey Jr.	4.00
2	Mike Piazza	4.00
3	Carlos Delgado	2.00
4	Mark McGwire	6.00
5	Chipper Jones	4.00
6	Scott Rolen	2.00
7	Cal Ripken Jr.	8.00
8	Alex Rodriguez	6.00
9	Larry Walker	1.00
10	Sammy Sosa	5.00
11	Barry Bonds	6.00
12	Nomar Garciaparra	6.00
13	Jose Canseco	1.50
14	Manny Ramirez	2.00
15	Jeff Bagwell	2.00

BIOrhythm

		NM/M
Complete Set (15):		25.00
Common Player:		.50
Inserted 1:11		
1	Randy Johnson	1.50
2	Derek Jeter	3.00
3	Sammy Sosa	2.50
4	Jose Lima	.50
5	Chipper Jones	2.00
6	Barry Bonds	4.00
7	Ken Griffey Jr.	2.00
8	Nomar Garciaparra	3.00
9	Frank Thomas	1.00
10	Pedro Martinez	1.50
11	Larry Walker	.50
12	Greg Maddux	2.00
13	Alex Rodriguez	3.00
14	Mark McGwire	3.00
15	Cal Ripken Jr.	4.00

Pyrotechnics

		NM/M
Complete Set (15):		125.00
Common Player:		5.00
Inserted 1:72		
1	Roger Clemens	12.00
2	Chipper Jones	10.00
3	Alex Rodriguez	15.00
4	Jeff Bagwell	5.00
5	Mark McGwire	15.00
6	Pedro Martinez	6.00
7	Manny Ramirez	5.00
8	Cal Ripken Jr.	20.00
9	Mike Piazza	10.00
10	Derek Jeter	15.00
11	Ken Griffey Jr.	10.00
12	Frank Thomas	5.00
13	Sammy Sosa	12.00
14	Nomar Garciaparra	15.00
15	Greg Maddux	10.00

Shockwave

		NM/M
Complete Set (15):		15.00
Common Player:		.50
Inserted 1:4		
1	Mark McGwire	2.00
2	Sammy Sosa	2.00
3	Manny Ramirez	1.00
4	Ken Griffey Jr.	1.50
5	Vladimir Guerrero	1.00
6	Barry Bonds	2.50
7	Albert Belle	.50
8	Ivan Rodriguez	1.00
9	Chipper Jones	1.50
10	Mo Vaughn	.50
11	Jose Canseco	.75
12	Jeff Bagwell	1.00
13	Matt Williams	.50
14	Alex Rodriguez	2.50
15	Carlos Delgado	.75

UD Authentics

		NM/M
Common Player:		10.00
Inserted 1:144		
CBE	Carlos Beltran	30.00
AB	Adrian Beltre	15.00
PB	Pat Burrell	15.00
JC	Jose Canseco	25.00
SC	Sean Casey	15.00
BD	Ben Davis	10.00
SG	Shawn Green	20.00
JR	Ken Griffey Jr.	100.00
VG	Vladimir Guerrero	30.00
DJ	Derek Jeter	100.00
GK	Gabe Kapler	10.00
PM	Pedro Martinez	
RM	Ruben Mateo	10.00
RB	Joe McEwing	10.00
MR	Manny Ramirez	35.00
SR	Scott Rolen	30.00
MW	Matt Williams	15.00

Warp Zone

		NM/M
Complete Set (15):		250.00
Common Player:		8.00

| 14 | Nomar Garciaparra | 15.00 |
| 15 | Greg Maddux | 10.00 |

Inserted 1:288		
1	Cal Ripken Jr.	30.00
2	Barry Bonds	30.00
3	Ken Griffey Jr.	20.00
4	Nomar Garciaparra	25.00
5	Chipper Jones	20.00
6	Ivan Rodriguez	8.00
7	Greg Maddux	20.00
8	Derek Jeter	25.00
9	Mike Piazza	20.00
10	Sammy Sosa	20.00
11	Roger Clemens	20.00
12	Alex Rodriguez	25.00
13	Vladimir Guerrero	10.00
14	Pedro Martinez	10.00
15	Mark McGwire	25.00

3,000 Hit Club

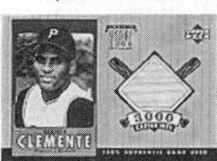

		NM/M
RC1	Roberto Clemente/ Bat/350	125.00

2001 Upper Deck

		NM/M
Complete Set (450):		125.00
Complete Series 1 (270):		25.00
Complete Series 2 (180):		100.00
Common Player:		.15
Series 1 Pack (10):		2.00
Series 1 Box (24):		35.00
Series 2 Pack (10):		6.00
Series 2 Box (24):		120.00
1	Jeff DaVanon	.25
2	Aubrey Huff	.25
3	Pascual Coco	.25
4	Barry Zito	.75
5	Augie Ojeda	.25
6	Chris Richard	.25
7	Josh Phelps	.25
8	Kevin Nicholson	.25
9	Juan Guzman	.25
10	Brandon Kolb	.25
11	Johan Santana	4.00
12	Josh Kalinowski	.25
13	Tike Redman	.25
14	Ivanon Coffie	.25
15	Chad Durbin	.25
16	Derrick Turnbow	.25
17	Scott Downs	.25

No.	Player	Val.	No.	Player	Val.	No.	Player	Val.	No.	Player	Val.
18	Jason Grilli	.25	122	Damion Easley	.15	226	Ryan Klesko	.25	330	Mike Bordick	.15
19	Mark Buehrle	.25	123	Juan Encarnacion	.15	227	Adam Eaton	.15	331	David Segui	.15
20	Paxton Crawford	.25	124	Tony Clark	.15	228	Eric Owens	.15	332	Pat Hentgen	.15
21	Bronson Arroyo	.25	125	Cristian Guzman	.15	229	Tony Gwynn	.75	333	Alex Rodriguez	1.50
22	Tomas de la Rosa	.25	126	Matt LeCroy	.15	230	Matt Clement	.15	334	Andres Galarraga	.25
23	Paul Rigdon	.25	127	Eric Milton	.15	231	Wiki Gonzalez	.15	335	Gabe Kapler	.15
24	Rob Ramsay	.25	128	Jay Canizaro	.15	232	Robert Person	.15	336	Ken Caminiti	.15
25	Damian Rolls	.25	129	David Ortiz	.15	233	Doug Glanville	.15	337	Rafael Palmeiro	.50
26	Jason Conti	.25	130	Brad Radke	.15	234	Scott Rolen	.50	338	Manny Ramirez	.50
27	John Parrish	.25	131	Jacque Jones	.15	235	Mike Lieberthal	.15	339	David Cone	.15
28	Geraldo Guzman	.25	132	Magglio Ordonez	.25	236	Randy Wolf	.15	340	Nomar Garciaparra	1.50
29	Tony Mota	.25	133	Carlos Lee	.15	237	Bobby Abreu	.25	341	Trot Nixon	.15
30	Luis Rivas	.25	134	Mike Sirotka	.15	238	Pat Burrell	.40	342	Derek Lowe	.15
31	Brian Tollberg	.25	135	Ray Durham	.15	239	Bruce Chen	.15	343	Roberto Hernandez	.15
32	Adam Bernero	.25	136	Paul Konerko	.15	240	Kevin Young	.15	344	Mike Sweeney	.15
33	Michael Cuddyer	.25	137	Charles Johnson	.15	241	Todd Ritchie	.15	345	Carlos Febles	.15
34	Josue Espada	.25	138	James Baldwin	.15	242	Adrian Brown	.15	346	Jeff Suppan	.15
35	Joe Lawrence	.25	139	Jeff Abbott	.15	243	Chad Hermansen	.15	347	Roger Cedeno	.15
36	Chad Moeller	.25	140	Roger Clemens	1.50	244	Warren Morris	.15	348	Bobby Higginson	.15
37	Nick Bierbrodt	.25	141	Derek Jeter	2.00	245	Kris Benson	.15	349	Deivi Cruz	.15
38	Dewayne Wise	.25	142	David Justice	.25	246	Jason Kendall	.25	350	Mitch Meluskey	.15
39	Javier Cardona	.25	143	Ramiro Mendoza	.15	247	Pokey Reese	.15	351	Matt Lawton	.15
40	Hiram Bocachica	.25	144	Chuck Knoblauch	.15	248	Rob Bell	.15	352	Mark Redman	.15
41	Giuseppe Chiaramonte	.25	145	Orlando Hernandez	.25	249	Ken Griffey Jr.	1.00	353	Jay Canizaro	.15
42	Alex Cabrera	.25	146	Alfonso Soriano	.75	250	Sean Casey	.15	354	Corey Koskie	.15
43	Jimmy Rollins	.40	147	Jeff Bagwell	.50	251	Aaron Boone	.15	355	Matt Kinney	.15
44	Pat Flury RC	.25	148	Julio Lugo	.15	252	Pete Harnisch	.15	356	Frank Thomas	.50
45	Leo Estrella	.25	149	Mitch Meluskey	.15	253	Barry Larkin	.40	357	Sandy Alomar Jr.	.15
46	Darin Erstad	.40	150	Jose Lima	.15	254	Dmitri Young	.15	358	David Wells	.15
47	Seth Etherton	.15	151	Richard Hidalgo	.15	255	Todd Hollandsworth	.15	359	Jim Parque	.15
48	Troy Glaus	.40	152	Moises Alou	.25	256	Pedro Astacio	.15	360	Chris Singleton	.15
49	Brian Cooper	.15	153	Scott Elarton	.15	257	Todd Helton	.50	361	Tino Martinez	.25
50	Tim Salmon	.25	154	Andruw Jones	.50	258	Terry Shumpert	.15	362	Paul O'Neill	.25
51	Adam Kennedy	.15	155	Quilvio Veras	.15	259	Neifi Perez	.15	363	Mike Mussina	.40
52	Bengie Molina	.15	156	Greg Maddux	1.00	260	Jeffrey Hammonds	.15	364	Bernie Williams	.50
53	Jason Giambi	.50	157	Brian Jordan	.15	261	Ben Petrick	.15	365	Andy Pettitte	.40
54	Miguel Tejada	.40	158	Andres Galarraga	.20	262	Mark McGwire	.75	366	Mariano Rivera	.25
55	Tim Hudson	.25	159	Kevin Millwood	.25	263	Derek Jeter	1.00	367	Brad Ausmus	.15
56	Eric Chavez	.25	160	Rafael Furcal	.25	264	Sammy Sosa	.75	368	Craig Biggio	.25
57	Terrence Long	.15	161	Jeromy Burnitz	.15	265	Cal Ripken Jr.	1.00	369	Lance Berkman	.25
58	Jason Isringhausen	.15	162	Jimmy Haynes	.15	266	Pedro J. Martinez	.40	370	Shane Reynolds	.15
59	Ramon Hernandez	.15	163	Mark Loretta	.15	267	Barry Bonds	1.00	371	Chipper Jones	1.00
60	Raul Mondesi	.25	164	Ron Belliard	.15	268	Fred McGriff	.20	372	Tom Glavine	.40
61	David Wells	.15	165	Richie Sexson	.15	269	Randy Johnson	.40	373	B.J. Surhoff	.15
62	Shannon Stewart	.15	166	Kevin Barker	.15	270	Darin Erstad	.25	374	John Smoltz	.25
63	Tony Batista	.15	167	Jeff D'Amico	.15	271	Ichiro Suzuki RC	15.00	375	Rico Brogna	.15
64	Brad Fullmer	.15	168	Rick Ankiel	.15	272	Wilson Betemit RC	.50	376	Geoff Jenkins	.25
65	Chris Carpenter	.15	169	Mark McGwire	1.50	273	Corey Patterson	.25	377	Jose Hernandez	.15
66	Homer Bush	.15	170	J.D. Drew	.25	274	Sean Douglass RC	.25	378	Tyler Houston	.15
67	Gerald Williams	.15	171	Eli Marrero	.15	275	Mike Penney RC	.25	379	Henry Blanco	.15
68	Miguel Cairo	.15	172	Darryl Kile	.15	276	Nate Teut RC	.25	380	Jeffrey Hammonds	.15
69	Ryan Rupe	.15	173	Edgar Renteria	.15	277	Ricardo Rodriguez RC	.25	381	Jim Edmonds	.25
70	Greg Vaughn	.15	174	Will Clark	.40	278	Brandon Duckworth RC	.50	382	Fernando Vina	.15
71	John Flaherty	.15	175	Eric Young	.15	279	Rafael Soriano RC	.75	383	Andy Benes	.15
72	Dan Wheeler	.15	176	Mark Grace	.40	280	Juan Diaz RC	.25	384	Ray Lankford	.15
73	Fred McGriff	.25	177	Jon Lieber	.15	281	Horacio Ramirez RC	.75	385	Dustin Hermanson	.15
74	Roberto Alomar	.40	178	Damon Buford	.15	282	Tsuyoshi Shinjo RC	.50	386	Todd Hundley	.15
75	Bartolo Colon	.25	179	Kerry Wood	.50	283	Keith Ginter RC	.25	387	Sammy Sosa	1.50
76	Kenny Lofton	.25	180	Rondell White	.15	284	Esix Snead RC	.25	388	Tom Gordon	.15
77	David Segui	.15	181	Joe Girardi	.15	285	Erick Almonte RC	.25	389	Bill Mueller	.15
78	Omar Vizquel	.15	182	Curt Schilling	.40	286	Travis Hafner RC	3.00	390	Ron Coomer	.15
79	Russ Branyan	.15	183	Randy Johnson	.75	287	Jason Smith RC	.25	391	Matt Stairs	.15
80	Chuck Finley	.15	184	Steve Finley	.15	288	Jackson Melian RC	.25	392	Mark Grace	.40
81	Manny Ramirez	.50	185	Kelly Stinnett	.15	289	Tyler Walker RC	.25	393	Matt Williams	.25
82	Alex Rodriguez	1.50	186	Jay Bell	.15	290	Jason Standridge RC	.25	394	Todd Stottlemyre	.15
83	John Halama	.15	187	Matt Mantei	.15	291	Juan Uribe RC	.50	395	Tony Womack	.15
84	Mike Cameron	.15	188	Luis Gonzalez	.25	292	Adrian Hernandez RC	.25	396	Erubiel Durazo	.15
85	David Bell	.15	189	Shawn Green	.25	293	Jason Michaels RC	.25	397	Reggie Sanders	.15
86	Jay Buhner	.15	190	Todd Hundley	.15	294	Jason Hart	.15	398	Andy Ashby	.15
87	Aaron Sele	.15	191	Chan Ho Park	.15	295	Albert Pujols RC	80.00	399	Eric Karros	.15
88	Rickey Henderson	.40	192	Adrian Beltre	.25	296	Morgan Ensberg RC	2.00	400	Kevin Brown	.25
89	Brook Fordyce	.15	193	Mark Grudzielanek	.15	297	Brandon Inge	.25	401	Darren Dreifort	.15
90	Cal Ripken Jr.	2.00	194	Gary Sheffield	.40	298	Jesus Colome	.25	402	Fernando Tatis	.15
91	Mike Mussina	.40	195	Tom Goodwin	.15	299	Kyle Kessel RC	.25	403	Jose Vidro	.15
92	Delino DeShields	.15	196	Lee Stevens	.15	300	Timo Perez	.25	404	Peter Bergeron	.15
93	Melvin Mora	.15	197	Javier Vazquez	.15	301	Mo Vaughn	.20	405	Geoff Blum	.15
94	Sidney Ponson	.15	198	Milton Bradley	.15	302	Ismael Valdes	.15	406	J.T. Snow	.15
95	Brady Anderson	.15	199	Vladimir Guerrero	.75	303	Glenallen Hill	.15	407	Livan Hernandez	.15
96	Ivan Rodriguez	.50	200	Carl Pavano	.15	304	Garret Anderson	.40	408	Robb Nen	.15
97	Ricky Ledee	.15	201	Orlando Cabrera	.15	305	Johnny Damon	.25	409	Bobby Estalella	.15
98	Rick Helling	.15	202	Tony Armas Jr.	.15	306	Jose Ortiz	.15	410	Rich Aurilia	.15
99	Ruben Mateo	.15	203	Jeff Kent	.25	307	Mark Mulder	.25	411	Eric Davis	.15
100	Luis Alicea	.15	204	Calvin Murray	.15	308	Adam Piatt	.15	412	Charles Johnson	.15
101	John Wetteland	.15	205	Ellis Burks	.15	309	Gil Heredia	.15	413	Alex Gonzalez	.15
102	Mike Lamb	.15	206	Barry Bonds	2.00	310	Mike Sirotka	.15	414	A.J. Burnett	.15
103	Carl Everett	.15	207	Russ Ortiz	.15	311	Carlos Delgado	.50	415	Antonio Alfonseca	.15
104	Troy O'Leary	.15	208	Marvin Benard	.15	312	Alex Gonzalez	.15	416	Derek Lee	.15
105	Wilton Veras	.15	209	Joe Nathan	.15	313	Jose Cruz Jr.	.15	417	Jay Payton	.15
106	Pedro Martinez	.75	210	Preston Wilson	.15	314	Darrin Fletcher	.15	418	Kevin Appier	.15
107	Rolando Arrojo	.15	211	Cliff Floyd	.15	315	Ben Grieve	.15	419	Steve Trachsel	.15
108	Scott Hatteberg	.15	212	Mike Lowell	.15	316	Vinny Castilla	.15	420	Rey Ordonez	.15
109	Jason Varitek	.15	213	Ryan Dempster	.15	317	Wilson Alvarez	.15	421	Darryl Hamilton	.15
110	Jose Offerman	.15	214	Brad Penny	.15	318	Brent Abernathy	.15	422	Ben Davis	.15
111	Carlos Beltran	.25	215	Mike Redmond	.15	319	Ellis Burks	.15	423	Damian Jackson	.15
112	Johnny Damon	.15	216	Luis Castillo	.15	320	Jim Thome	.75	424	Mark Kotsay	.15
113	Mark Quinn	.15	217	Derek Bell	.15	321	Juan Gonzalez	.50	425	Trevor Hoffman	.15
114	Rey Sanchez	.15	218	Mike Hampton	.25	322	Ed Taubensee	.15	426	Travis Lee	.15
115	Mac Suzuki	.15	219	Todd Zeile	.15	323	Travis Fryman	.15	427	Omar Daal	.15
116	Jermaine Dye	.15	220	Robin Ventura	.25	324	John Olerud	.15	428	Paul Byrd	.15
117	Chris Fussell	.15	221	Mike Piazza	1.00	325	Edgar Martinez	.25	429	Reggie Taylor	.15
118	Jeff Weaver	.15	222	Al Leiter	.25	326	Fred Garcia	.15	430	Brian Giles	.25
119	Dean Palmer	.15	223	Edgardo Alfonzo	.15	327	Bret Boone	.25	431	Derek Bell	.15
120	Robert Fick	.15	224	Mike Bordick	.15	328	Kazuhiro Sasaki	.25	432	Francisco Cordova	.15
121	Brian Moehler	.15	225	Phil Nevin	.15	329	Albert Belle	.15	433	Pat Meares	.15

434	Scott Williamson	.15
435	Jason LaRue	.15
436	Michael Tucker	.15
437	Wilton Guerrero	.15
438	Mike Hampton	.15
439	Ron Gant	.15
440	Jeff Cirillo	.15
441	Denny Neagle	.15
442	Larry Walker	.40
443	Juan Pierre	.15
444	Todd Walker	.15
445	Jason Giambi	.40
446	Jeff Kent	.15
447	Mariano Rivera	.15
448	Edgar Martinez	.15
449	Troy Glaus	.25
450	Alex Rodriguez	.75

Exclusives

Silver Stars:	8-15X
Production 100 Sets	
Gold Stars:	15-30X
Production 25 Sets	

All-Star Heroes Base Cards

		NM/M
Quantity produced listed		
DJ	Derek Jeter/2000	20.00
MP	Mike Piazza/1996	10.00

All-Star Heroes Jersey Cards

		NM/M
Common Player:		10.00
RC	Roger Clemens/1986	20.00
JD	Joe DiMaggio/36	300.00
TG	Tony Gwynn/1994	10.00
RJ	Randy Johnson/1993	10.00
ASH-MM	Mickey Mantle/54	400.00
ASH-SS	Sammy Sosa/2000	20.00

All-Star Heroes Bat Cards

		NM/M
Common Player:		10.00
RoC	Roberto Clemente/1961	75.00
KG	Ken Griffey Jr./1992	20.00
TP	Tony Perez/1967	10.00
CR	Cal Ripken Jr/1991	40.00
AR	Alex Rodriguez/1998	20.00
BR	Babe Ruth/1933	175.00

All-Star Salute

		NM/M
Common Player:		10.00
	Inserted 1:288	
HA	Hank Aaron/Bat	35.00
HA	Hank Aaron/Jsy	35.00
LA	Luis Aparicio/Jsy	10.00

JB	Johnny Bench/Bat	20.00
JB	Johnny Bench/Jsy	20.00
LB	Lou Brock/Bat	15.00
RC	Roberto Clemente/Jsy	125.00
RJ	Reggie Jackson/Jsy	20.00
TM	Thurman Munson/Jsy	35.00
BR	Brooks Robinson/Bat	20.00
FR	Frank Robinson/Jsy	15.00
TS	Tom Seaver/Jsy	20.00

Big League Beat

		NM/M
Complete Set (20):		15.00
Common Player:		.50
	Inserted 1:3	
1	Barry Bonds	2.00
2	Nomar Garciaparra	1.50
3	Mark McGwire	1.50
4	Roger Clemens	1.25
5	Chipper Jones	1.00
6	Jeff Bagwell	.50
7	Sammy Sosa	1.50
8	Cal Ripken Jr.	2.00
9	Randy Johnson	.75
10	Carlos Delgado	.50
11	Manny Ramirez	.50
12	Derek Jeter	2.00
13	Tony Gwynn	.75
14	Pedro J. Martinez	.75
15	Jose Canseco	.50
16	Frank Thomas	.75
17	Alex Rodriguez	1.50
18	Bernie Williams	.50
19	Greg Maddux	1.00
20	Rafael Palmeiro	.50

Big League Challenge Jerseys

		NM/M
Common Player:		5.00
	Inserted 1:288	
BB	Barry Bonds	40.00
JC	Jose Canseco	8.00
JE	Jim Edmonds	8.00
TF	Steve Finley	5.00
TG	Troy Glaus	8.00
TH	Todd Helton	10.00
RH	Richard Hidalgo	5.00
RP	Rafael Palmeiro	10.00
MP	Mike Piazza	20.00
GS	Gary Sheffield	8.00
FT	Frank Thomas	10.00

Classic Midsummer Moments

		NM/M
Complete Set (20):		25.00

Common Player:		.50
	Inserted 1:12	
CM1	Joe DiMaggio/1936	3.00
CM2	Joe DiMaggio/1951	3.00
CM3	Mickey Mantle/1952	4.00
CM4	Mickey Mantle/1968	4.00
CM5	Roger Clemens/1986	2.50
CM6	Mark McGwire/1987	2.50
CM7	Cal Ripken Jr./1991	3.00
CM8	Ken Griffey Jr./1992	1.50
CM9	Randy Johnson/1993	1.00
CM10	Tony Gwynn/1994	1.00
CM11	Fred McGriff/1994	.50
CM12	Hideo Nomo/1995	.75
CM13	Jeff Conine/1995	.50
CM14	Mike Piazza/1996	1.50
CM15	Sandy Alomar Jr./1997	.50
CM16	Alex Rodriguez/1998	2.50
CM17	Roberto Alomar/1998	.75
CM18	Pedro Martinez/1999	1.00
CM19	Andres Galarraga/2000	.50
CM20	Derek Jeter/2000	2.50

E-Card

		NM/M
Complete Set (6):		10.00
Common Player:		1.00
	Inserted 1:12	
1	Andruw Jones	1.00
2	Alex Rodriguez	3.00
3	Frank Thomas	1.50
4	Todd Helton	1.50
5	Troy Glaus	1.50
6	Barry Bonds	4.00

Evolve Jersey

		NM/M
Common Player:		10.00
BB	Barry Bonds	60.00
TG	Troy Glaus	10.00
TH	Todd Helton	15.00
AJ	Andruw Jones	15.00
AR	Alex Rodriguez	30.00
SS	Sammy Sosa	40.00
IS	Ichiro Suzuki	65.00
FT	Frank Thomas	15.00

Evolve Signature

		NM/M
Common Player:		35.00
BB	Barry Bonds	200.00
TG	Troy Glaus	35.00
TH	Todd Helton	35.00
AJ	Andruw Jones	35.00
AR	Alex Rodriguez	75.00

SS	Sammy Sosa	150.00
IS	Ichiro Suzuki	250.00
FT	Frank Thomas	40.00

Jersey Autograph

		NM/M
Common Player:		50.00
BB	Barry Bonds	180.00
TG	Troy Glaus	50.00
TH	Todd Helton	50.00
AJ	Andruw Jones	50.00
AR	Alex Rodriguez	120.00
SS	Sammy Sosa	180.00
IS	Ichiro Suzuki	300.00
FT	Frank Thomas	75.00

Game Jersey

		NM/M
Common Player:		8.00
	Inserted 1:288	
KG	Ken Griffey Jr.	30.00
TG	Tony Gwynn	20.00
TH	Todd Helton	12.00
TiH	Tim Hudson	10.00
DJ	Derek Jeter	50.00
AJ	Andruw Jones	10.00
SK	Sandy Koufax	100.00
PO	Paul O'Neill	10.00
MR	Manny Ramirez	10.00
CR	Cal Ripken Jr.	60.00
AR	Alex Rodriguez	40.00
IR	Ivan Rodriguez	10.00
NRa	Nolan Ryan	65.00
NRr	Nolan Ryan	65.00
FT	Fernando Tatis	8.00
RV	Robin Ventura	8.00
BW	Bernie Williams	10.00
MW	Matt Williams	8.00

Game Jersey Autograph

		NM/M
Print Runs Listed		
KG	Ken Griffey/30	250.00
RA	Rick Ankiel/66	25.00
SK	Sandy Koufax/32	900.00
PO	Paul O'Neill/21	
JP	Javy Lopez/8	110.00
NRa	Nolan Ryan/Mets/30	350.00
NRr	Nolan Ryan/Angels/30	350.00
RV	Robin Ventura/4	50.00
MW	Matt Williams/9	200.00

Game Jersey Auto. Series 2

		NM/M
Common Player:		30.00
	Inserted 1:288 H	
JB	Johnny Bench	50.00
BB	Barry Bonds	200.00
JC	Jose Canseco	40.00
RC	Roger Clemens	125.00
TG	Troy Glaus	30.00
KG	Ken Griffey Jr.	100.00
AJ	Andruw Jones	40.00

CJ	Chipper Jones	50.00
CR	Cal Ripken Jr./SP	200.00
AR	Alex Rodriguez	100.00
IR	Ivan Rodriguez/SP	75.00
NR	Nolan Ryan	150.00
GS	Gary Sheffield	30.00
SS	Sammy Sosa/SP	150.00

Game Jersey Hobby Autograph

		NM/M
Common Player:		15.00
Inserted 1:288		
RA	Rick Ankiel	15.00
JB	Jeff Bagwell	40.00
BB	Barry Bonds	180.00
JC	Jose Canseco	50.00
SC	Sean Casey	25.00
JD	J.D. Drew	30.00
JG	Jason Giambi	30.00
SG	Shawn Green	30.00
KG	Ken Griffey Jr.	100.00
MH	Mike Hampton	20.00
RJ	Randy Johnson	75.00
JL	Javy Lopez	20.00
GM	Greg Maddux	125.00
RP	Rafael Palmeiro	40.00
AR	Alex Rodriguez	125.00
NRm	Nolan Ryan	125.00
NRa	Nolan Ryan	125.00
FT	Frank Thomas	150.00

Game Jersey Combo

		NM/M
Production 50 Sets		
BB-KG	Barry Bonds, Ken Griffey Jr.	100.00
IR-RP	Ivan Rodriguez, Rafael Palmeiro	25.00
DJ-AR	Derek Jeter, Alex Rodriguez	100.00
MM-KG	Mickey Mantle, Ken Griffey Jr.	250.00
TG-CR	Tony Gwynn, Cal Ripken Jr.	100.00
NR-AR	Nolan Ryan/ Astros/Rangers	100.00
NR-MA	Nolan Ryan/ Mets/Astros	100.00
RJ-GM	Randy Johnson, Greg Maddux	50.00
VG-MR	Vladimir Guerrero, Manny Ramirez	40.00
BB-JC	Barry Bonds, Jose Canseco	80.00
FT-JB	Frank Thomas, Jeff Bagwell	40.00
AJ-KG	Andruw Jones, Ken Griffey Jr.	60.00

Game Jersey Combo Autograph

Production 10 Sets
Values Undetermined

Game Jersey Patch

	NM/M
Common Player:	40.00

Production 25 Sets		
RA	Rick Ankiel	40.00
JB	Jeff Bagwell	60.00
BB	Barry Bonds	150.00
JC	Jose Canseco	50.00
JG	Jason Giambi	50.00
KG	Ken Griffey Jr.	75.00
TG	Tony Gwynn	75.00
DJ	Derek Jeter	125.00
RP	Rafael Palmeiro	60.00
CR	Cal Ripken Jr.	150.00
AR	Alex Rodriguez	100.00
IR	Ivan Rodriguez	60.00
NRa	Nolan Ryan	150.00
NRr	Nolan Ryan	150.00
FT	Frank Thomas	60.00

Game Jersey Patch Gold

		NM/M
Production 25 Sets		
BB	Barry Bonds	200.00
JC	Jose Canseco	100.00
JG	Jason Giambi	100.00
KG	Ken Griffey Jr.	150.00
TG	Tony Gwynn	100.00
DJ	Derek Jeter	200.00
CR	Cal Ripken Jr.	200.00
NRa	Nolan Ryan	200.00
NRr	Nolan Ryan	200.00
FT	Frank Thomas	90.00

Game Jersey Patch Autograph

		NM/M
Print Runs Listed		
RA	Rick Ankiel/66	65.00
KG	Ken Griffey Jr. /30	600.00

Game-Used Ball

		NM/M
Common Player:		10.00
Production 100 Sets		
RA	Rick Ankiel	10.00
JB	Jeff Bagwell	15.00
BB	Barry Bonds	50.00
JG	Jason Giambi	15.00
SG	Shawn Green	10.00
KG	Ken Griffey Jr.	35.00
ToG	Tony Gwynn	25.00
DJ	Derek Jeter	60.00
RJ	Randy Johnson	25.00
AJ	Andruw Jones	15.00
MM	Mark McGwire	75.00
AR	Alex Rodriguez	40.00
IR	Ivan Rodriguez	15.00
SS	Sammy Sosa	40.00

Game-Used Ball Series 2

		NM/M
Common Player:		5.00
Inserted 1:288		
JB	Jeff Bagwell	10.00
BB	Barry Bonds	30.00
RC	Roger Clemens	20.00
NG	Nomar Garciaparra	30.00

KG	Ken Griffey Jr.	20.00
VG	Vladimir Guerrero	10.00
DJ	Derek Jeter	30.00
AJ	Andruw Jones	8.00
CJ	Chipper Jones	10.00
JK	Jeff Kent	5.00
MM	Mark McGwire	40.00
MP	Mike Piazza	20.00
CR	Cal Ripken Jr.	25.00
MR	Mariano Rivera	8.00
AR	Alex Rodriguez	20.00
GS	Gary Sheffield	8.00
SS	Sammy Sosa	20.00
BW	Bernie Williams	10.00

Game-Used Ball Autographs

		NM/M
Production 25 Sets		
RA	Rick Ankiel	40.00
JB	Jeff Bagwell	60.00
BB	Barry Bonds	150.00
JG	Jason Giambi	75.00
KG	Ken Griffey Jr.	90.00
SG	Shawn Green	60.00
TH	Todd Helton	60.00
RJ	Randy Johnson	90.00
AR	Alex Rodriguez	80.00

Home Run Derby Heroes

		NM/M
Complete Set (10):		25.00
Common Player:		1.00
Inserted 1:36		
HD1	Mark McGwire/1999	5.00
HD2	Sammy Sosa/2000	3.00
HD3	Frank Thomas/1996	2.00
HD4	Cal Ripken Jr./1991	5.00
HD5	Tino Martinez/1997	1.00
HD6	Ken Griffey Jr./1999	3.00
HD7	Barry Bonds/1996	5.00
HD8	Albert Belle/1995	1.00
HD9	Mark McGwire/1992	5.00
HD10	Juan Gonzalez/1993	2.00

Home Run Explosion

		NM/M
Complete Set (15):		20.00
Common Player:		.50
Inserted 1:12		
1	Mark McGwire	3.00
2	Chipper Jones	2.00
3	Jeff Bagwell	1.00
4	Carlos Delgado	1.00
5	Barry Bonds	4.00
6	Troy Glaus	1.00
7	Sammy Sosa	2.50
8	Alex Rodriguez	3.00

9	Mike Piazza	2.00
10	Vladimir Guerrero	1.50
11	Ken Griffey Jr.	2.00
12	Frank Thomas	1.00
13	Ivan Rodriguez	1.00
14	Jason Giambi	1.00
15	Carl Everett	.50

Midseason Superstar Summit

		NM/M
Complete Set (15):		25.00
Common Player:		.75
Inserted 1:24		
MS1	Derek Jeter	5.00
MS2	Sammy Sosa	3.00
MS3	Jeff Bagwell	1.50
MS4	Tony Gwynn	1.50
MS5	Alex Rodriguez	4.00
MS6	Greg Maddux	2.50
MS7	Jason Giambi	1.50
MS8	Mark McGwire	4.00
MS9	Barry Bonds	5.00
MS10	Ken Griffey Jr.	3.00
MS11	Carlos Delgado	1.50
MS12	Troy Glaus	1.00
MS13	Todd Helton	1.50
MS14	Manny Ramirez	1.50
MS15	Jeff Kent	.75

Most Wanted

		NM/M
Complete Set (15):		20.00
Common Player:		.75
Inserted 1:14 Series 1		
MW1	Mark McGwire	2.50
MW2	Cal Ripken Jr.	3.00
MW3	Ivan Rodriguez	.75
MW4	Pedro Martinez	1.00
MW5	Sammy Sosa	2.00
MW6	Tony Gwynn	1.00
MW7	Vladimir Guerrero	1.00
MW8	Derek Jeter	3.00
MW9	Mike Piazza	1.50
MW10	Chipper Jones	1.50
MW11	Alex Rodriguez	2.50
MW12	Barry Bonds	3.00
MW13	Jeff Bagwell	.75
MW14	Frank Thomas	.75
MW15	Nomar Garciaparra	2.00

Rookie Roundup

		NM/M
Complete Set (10):		5.00
Common Player:		.50
Inserted 1:6		
1	Rick Ankiel	.50
2	Adam Kennedy	.50

3 Mike Lamb .50
4 Adam Eaton .50
5 Rafael Furcal .75
6 Pat Burrell 1.50
7 Adam Piatt .50
8 Eric Munson .50
9 Brad Penny .50
10 Mark Mulder .75

Subway Series Jersey Cards

	NM/M
Common Player:	5.00
Inserted 1:144	
SS-EA Edgardo Alfonzo	5.00
SS-RC Roger Clemens	40.00
SS-JF John Franco	5.00
SS-OH Orlando Hernandez	8.00
SS-AL Al Leiter	5.00
SS-PO Paul O'Neill	10.00
SS-JP Jay Payton	5.00
SS-TP Timo Perez	5.00
SS-AP Andy Pettitte	15.00
SS-BW Bernie Williams	15.00

The Franchise

	NM/M
Complete Set (10):	25.00
Common Player:	1.50
Inserted 1:36	
F1 Frank Thomas	1.50
F2 Mark McGwire	5.00
F3 Ken Griffey Jr.	3.00
F4 Manny Ramirez	1.50
F5 Alex Rodriguez	5.00
F6 Greg Maddux	3.00
F7 Sammy Sosa	4.00
F8 Derek Jeter	6.00
F9 Mike Piazza	3.00
F10 Vladimir Guerrero	2.00

The People's Choice

	NM/M
Complete Set (15):	35.00
Common Player:	1.50
Inserted 1:24	
PC1 Alex Rodriguez	5.00
PC2 Ken Griffey Jr.	3.00
PC3 Mark McGwire	5.00
PC4 Todd Helton	1.50
PC5 Manny Ramirez	1.50
PC6 Mike Piazza	3.00
PC7 Vladimir Guerrero	2.00
PC8 Randy Johnson	2.00
PC9 Cal Ripken Jr.	6.00
PC10 Andruw Jones	1.50
PC11 Sammy Sosa	4.00
PC12 Derek Jeter	6.00
PC13 Pedro Martinez	2.00
PC14 Frank Thomas	1.50
PC15 Nomar Garciaparra	4.00

Superstar Summit

	NM/M
Complete Set (15):	25.00
Common Player:	1.00
Inserted 1:12	
1 Derek Jeter	4.00
2 Randy Johnson	1.50

3 Barry Bonds	4.00
4 Frank Thomas	1.00
5 Cal Ripken Jr.	4.00
6 Pedro J. Martinez	1.50
7 Ivan Rodriguez	1.00
8 Mike Piazza	2.00
9 Mark McGwire	3.00
10 Manny Ramirez	1.00
11 Ken Griffey Jr.	2.00
12 Sammy Sosa	2.50
13 Alex Rodriguez	3.00
14 Chipper Jones	2.00
15 Nomar Garciaparra	2.50

UD's Most Wanted

	NM/M
Complete Set (15):	25.00
Common Player:	1.00
Inserted 1:14	
1 Mark McGwire	3.00
2 Cal Ripken Jr.	4.00
3 Ivan Rodriguez	1.00
4 Pedro J. Martinez	1.50
5 Sammy Sosa	2.50
6 Tony Gwynn	1.50
7 Vladimir Guerrero	1.50
8 Derek Jeter	4.00
9 Mike Piazza	2.00
10 Chipper Jones	2.00
11 Alex Rodriguez	3.00
12 Barry Bonds	4.00
13 Jeff Bagwell	1.00
14 Frank Thomas	1.00
15 Nomar Garciaparra	3.00

UD Game-Worn Patch

	NM/M
Common Player:	40.00
P-JB Johnny Bench	120.00
P-BB Barry Bonds	150.00
P-KG Ken Griffey Jr.	100.00
P-CJ Chipper Jones	60.00
P-CR Cal Ripken Jr.	150.00
P-AR Alex Rodriguez	125.00
P-IR Ivan Rodriguez	60.00
P-NR Nolan Ryan	150.00
P-SS Sammy Sosa	100.00

2001 Upper Deck Decade

	NM/M
Complete Set (180):	25.00
Common Player:	.15
Pack (5):	1.50
Box (24):	30.00
1 Nolan Ryan	3.00
2 Don Baylor	.15
3 Bobby Grich	.15
4 Reggie Jackson	.50

5 Jim "Catfish" Hunter	.25
6 Gene Tenace	.15
7 Rollie Fingers	.25
8 Sal Bando	.15
9 Bert Campaneris	.15
10 John Mayberry	.15
11 Rico Carty	.15
12 Gaylord Perry	.25
13 Andre Thornton	.15
14 Buddy Bell	.15
15 Dennis Eckersley	.25
16 Ruppert Jones	.15
17 Brooks Robinson	.75
18 Tommy Davis	.15
19 Eddie Murray	.25
20 Boog Powell	.15
21 Al Oliver	.15
22 Jeff Burroughs	.15
23 Mike Hargrove	.15
24 Dwight Evans	.15
25 Fred Lynn	.15
26 Rico Petrocelli	.15
27 Carlton Fisk	.50
28 Luis Aparicio	.15
29 Amos Otis	.15
30 Hal McRae	.15
31 Jason Thompson	.15
32 Al Kaline	.75
33 Jim Perry	.15
34 Bert Blyleven	.15
35 Harmon Killebrew	1.00
36 Wilbur Wood	.15
37 Jim Kaat	.15
38 Ron Guidry	.15
39 Thurman Munson	1.00
40 Graig Nettles	.15
41 Bobby Murcer	.15
42 Chris Chambliss	.15
43 Roy White	.15
44 J.R. Richard	.15
45 Jose Cruz	.15
46 Hank Aaron	2.00
47 Phil Niekro	.15
48 Bob Horner	.15
49 Darrell Evans	.15
50 Gorman Thomas	.15
51 Don Money	.15
52 Robin Yount	.75
53 Joe Torre	.25
54 Tim McCarver	.15
55 Lou Brock	.40
56 Keith Hernandez	.15
57 Bill Madlock	.15
58 Ron Santo	.15
59 Billy Williams	.25
60 Ferguson Jenkins	.25
61 Steve Garvey	.15
62 Bill Russell	.15
63 Maury Wills	.25
64 Ron Cey	.15
65 Manny Mota	.15
66 Ron Fairly	.15
67 Steve Rogers	.15
68 Gary Carter	.15
69 Andre Dawson	.25
70 Bobby Bonds	.25
71 Jack Clark	.15
72 Willie McCovey	.15
73 Tom Seaver	1.00
74 Bud Harrelson	.15
75 Dave Kingman	.15
76 Jerry Koosman	.15
77 Jon Matlack	.15
78 Randy Jones	.15
79 Ozzie Smith	1.00
80 Garry Maddox	.15
81 Mike Schmidt	1.00
82 Greg Luzinski	.15
83 Tug McGraw	.15
84 Willie Stargell	.75
85 Dave Parker	.15
86 Roberto Clemente	2.00
87 Johnny Bench	1.50

88 Joe Morgan	.40
89 George Foster	.15
90 Ken Griffey Sr.	.15
91 Carlton Fisk/1972	.50
92 Andre Dawson/1977	.25
93 Fred Lynn/1975	.15
94 Eddie Murray/1977	.25
95 Bob Horner/1978	.15
96 Jon Matlack/1972	.15
97 Mike Hargrove/1974	.15
98 Robin Yount/1974	.50
99 Mike Schmidt/1972	.50
100 Gary Carter/1974	.15
101 Ozzie Smith/1978	.50
102 Paul Molitor/1978	.50
103 Dennis Eckersley/1975	.25
104 Dale Murphy/1976	.15
105 Bert Blyleven/1970	.15
106 Thurman Munson/1970	.75
107 Dave Parker/1973	.15
108 Jack Clark/1975	.15
109 Keith Hernandez/1974	.15
110 Ron Cey/1971	.15
111 Billy Williams/1970	.15
112 Tom Seaver/1970	.75
113 Reggie Jackson/1971	.75
114 Barry Bonds/1971	.15
115 Willie Stargell/1971	.40
116 Harmon Killebrew/1971	.50
117 Roberto Clemente/1972	1.00
118 Wilbur Wood/1972	.15
119 Billy Williams/1972	.15
120 Nolan Ryan/1973	1.50
121 Ron Blomberg/1973	.15
122 Hank Aaron/1974	1.00
123 Lou Brock/1974	.25
124 Al Kaline/1974	.40
125 Brooks Robinson/1975	.40
126 Bill Madlock/1975	.15
127 Rennie Stennett/1975	.15
128 Carlton Fisk/1975	.40
129 Chris Chambliss/1976	.15
130 Ruppert Jones/1977	.15
131 Ron Fairly/1977	.15
132 George Foster/1977	.15
133 Reggie Jackson/1977	.75
134 Ron Guidry/1978	.15
135 Gaylord Perry/1978	.15
136 Bucky Dent/1978	.15
137 Dave Kingman/1979	.15
138 Lou Brock/1979	.15
139 Thurman Munson/1979	.75
140 Willie Stargell/1979	.40
141 Johnny Bench/1970 NL MVP	.75
142 Boog Powell/1970 AL MVP	.15
143 Jim Perry/1970 AL CY	.15
144 Joe Torre/1971 NL MVP	.15
145 Chris Chambliss/1971 AL ROY	.15
146 Ferguson Jenkins/1971 NL CY	.15
147 Carlton Fisk/1972 AL ROY	.40
148 Gaylord Perry/1972 AL CY	.15
149 Johnny Bench/1972 NL MVP	.75
150 Reggie Jackson/1973 AL MVP	.75
151 Tom Seaver/1973 NL CY	.75
152 Thurman Munson/1973 AL GG	.75
153 Steve Garvey 1974/NL MVP	.15
154 Jim "Catfish" Hunter/1974 AL CY	.15
155 Mike Hargrove 1974/AL ROY	.15
156 Joe Morgan/1975 NL MVP	.15
157 Fred Lynn/1975 AL MVP & ROY	.15
158 Tom Seaver/1975 NL CY	.75
159 Thurman Munson/1976 AL MVP	.75
160 Randy Jones/1976 NL CY	.15
161 Joe Morgan/1976 NL ROY	.15
162 George Foster/1977 NL MVP	.15
163 Eddie Murray/1977 AL ROY	.25
164 Andre Dawson/1977 NL ROY	.25
165 Gaylord Perry/1978 NL CY	.15

166	Ron Guidry/ 1978 AL CY	.15
167	Dave Parker/ 1978 NL MVP	.15
168	Don Baylor/ 1979 AL MVP	.15
169	Bruce Sutter/ 1979 NL CY	.30
170	Willie Stargell/1979 NL co-MVP	.40
171	Brooks Robinson/1970	.50
172	Roberto Clemente/ 1971	1.00
173	Gene Tenace/1972	.15
174	Reggie Jackson/1973	.75
175	Rollie Fingers/1974	.15
176	Carlton Fisk/1975	.40
177	Johnny Bench/1976	.75
178	Reggie Jackson/1977	.75
179	Bucky Dent/1978	.15
180	Willie Stargell/1979	.40

Bellbottomed Bashers

WILLIE McCOVEY • Giants

		NM/M
Complete Set (10):		12.00
Common Player:		1.00
Inserted 1:14		
BB1	Reggie Jackson	2.00
BB2	Gorman Thomas	1.00
BB3	Willie McCovey	1.50
BB4	Willie Stargell	1.50
BB5	Mike Schmidt	3.00
BB6	George Foster	1.00
BB7	Johnny Bench	2.50
BB8	Dave Kingman	1.00
BB9	Graig Nettles	1.00
BB10	Steve Garvey	1.00

Decade Dynasties

		NM/M
Complete Set (10):		15.00
Common Player:		1.00
Inserted 1:14		
D1	Boog Powell	1.00
D2	Johnny Bench	3.00
D3	Willie Stargell	1.50
D4	Jim "Catfish" Hunter	1.00
D5	Steve Garvey	1.00
D6	Carlton Fisk	2.00
D7	Mike Schmidt	4.00
D8	Hal McRae	1.00
D9	Tom Seaver	3.00
D10	Reggie Jackson	2.50

Game-Used Bat

OZZIE SMITH • Padres

		NM/M
Common Player:		5.00
Inserted 1:24 H		
HA	Hank Aaron	40.00

DB	Don Baylor	5.00
BB	Bobby Bonds	5.00
GC	Gary Carter	8.00
JaC	Jack Clark	5.00
RC	Roberto Clemente/ 243	100.00
DC	Dave Concepcion	5.00
JoC	Jose Cruz	5.00
TD	Tommy Davis	5.00
AD	Andre Dawson	8.00
DaE	Darryl Evans	5.00
DwE	Dwight Evans	5.00
CF	Carlton Fisk	10.00
GF	George Foster	5.00
SG	Steve Garvey	5.00
BG	Bobby Grich	5.00
KG	Ken Griffey Sr.	5.00
BH	Bud Harrelson/290	5.00
KH	Keith Hernandez/243	20.00
RH	Ron Hunt	5.00
ReJ	Reggie Jackson	15.00
RaJ	Randy Jones	5.00
GL	Greg Luzinski	5.00
FL	Fred Lynn	5.00
GM	Garry Maddox	5.00
BiM	Bill Madlock	5.00
TiM	Tim McCarver	5.00
TuM	Tug McGraw/97	25.00
HM	Hal McRae	5.00
RM	Rick Monday	5.00
WM	Willie Montanez	5.00
JM	Joe Morgan	5.00
BoM	Bobby Murcer	20.00
EM	Eddie Murray	10.00
GN	Graig Nettles/219	15.00
AO	Al Oliver	5.00
DP	Dave Parker	5.00
BP	Boog Powell	5.00
WR	Willie Randolph	5.00
BR	Bill Russell	5.00
NR	Nolan Ryan	50.00
RS	Ron Santo	5.00
ToS	Tom Seaver/121	20.00
OS	Ozzie Smith	15.00
RW	Roy White	5.00
MW	Maury Wills	5.00
DW	Dave Winfield	8.00

Game-Used Bat Combo

		NM/M
Common Card:		20.00
Inserted 1:336		
NYY	Reggie Jackson, Graig Nettles, Chris Chambliss, Roy White	40.00
LA	Steve Garvey, Ron Cey, Bill Russell, Rick Monday	25.00
NYM	Tom Seaver, Bud Harrelson, Ron Hunt, Tug McGraw	50.00
CIN	Johnny Bench, George Foster, Ken Griffey Sr., Joe Morgan	50.00
ROY	Andre Dawson, Fred Lynn, Carlton Fisk, Eddie Murray	40.00
MVPN	Johnny Bench, Steve Garvey, Willie Stargell, George Foster	50.00
BAT	Keith Hernandez, Bill Madlock, Fred Lynn, Dave Parker	20.00
GGA	Carlton Fisk, Graig Nettles, Bobby Grich, Fred Lynn	25.00
GGN	Johnny Bench, Roberto Clemente, Dave Concepcion, Garry Maddox	100.00
WS72	Reggie Jackson, Bert Campaneris, Dave Concepcion, Johnny Bench/97	80.00

WS73	Reggie Jackson, Bert Campaneris, Tom Seaver, Bud Harrelson	40.00
WS74	Reggie Jackson, Bert Campaneris, Steve Garvey, Ron Cey	40.00
WS75	Carlton Fisk, Fred Lynn, George Foster, Joe Morgan	40.00
WS76	Chris Chambliss, Graig Nettles, Johnny Bench, Ken Griffey Sr./97	80.00
WS77	Reggie Jackson, Graig Nettles, Steve Garvey, Ron Cey	40.00
WS78	Graig Nettles, Chris Chambliss, Bill Russell, Ron Cey/238	50.00
ASMV	Bill Madlock, Joe Morgan, Steve Garvey, Dave Parker	40.00
RY	Chris Chambliss, Reggie Jackson, Roy White, Hal McRae/238	40.00
RD	George Foster, Joe Morgan, Ron Cey, Bill Russell	25.00

Game-Used Jersey

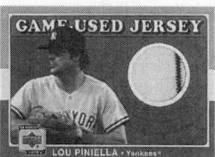

LOU PINIELLA • Yankees

		NM/M
Common Player:		8.00
Inserted 1:168		
HA	Hank Aaron	40.00
LA	Luis Aparicio	8.00
SB	Sal Bando/15	8.00
JB	Johnny Bench	15.00
RC	Roberto Clemente	100.00
WD	Willie Davis	8.00
RF	Rollie Fingers	8.00
CF	Carlton Fisk	10.00
KG	Ken Griffey Sr./15	8.00
RG	Ron Guidry	8.00
BH	Burt Hooton	8.00
CH	Jim "Catfish" Hunter	10.00
RJ	Reggie Jackson	15.00
JKa	Jim Kaat	8.00
JKo	Jerry Koosman	8.00
BM	Bill Madlock	8.00
JM	Jon Matlack	8.00
TM	Tug McGraw	8.00
BM	Bobby Murcer	15.00
JP	Jim Perry	8.00
RP	Rico Petrocelli/15	8.00
LP	Lou Piniella	10.00
WR	Willie Randolph	8.00
NR	Nolan Ryan/50	75.00
TS	Tom Seaver	20.00
WS	Willie Stargell	10.00
MW	Maury Wills	8.00

Game-Used Jersey Autograph

MAURY WILLS • Dodgers

		NM/M
Common Autograph:		20.00
Inserted 1:168 H		
HA	Hank Aaron/97	200.00
LA	Luis Aparicio	30.00
SB	Sal Bando	20.00
JB	Johnny Bench	70.00
RF	Rollie Fingers	25.00
CF	Carlton Fisk/243	40.00
KG	Ken Griffey Sr.	20.00
RG	Ron Guidry	30.00
BH	Burt Hooton	20.00
RJ	Reggie Jackson/291	65.00

JKa	Jim Kaat	25.00
JKo	Jerry Koosman	20.00
BM	Bill Madlock	20.00
TM	Tug McGraw	20.00
BM	Bobby Murcer	50.00
RP	Rico Petrocelli	25.00
NR	Nolan Ryan/291	125.00
MW	Maury Wills	20.00

The Arms Race

PHIL NIEKRO • Braves

		NM/M
Complete Set (10):		10.00
Common Player:		.50
Inserted 1:14		
AR1	Nolan Ryan	4.00
AR2	Ferguson Jenkins	1.00
AR3	Jim "Catfish" Hunter	1.00
AR4	Tom Seaver	2.00
AR5	Randy Jones	.50
AR6	J.R. Richard	.50
AR7	Rollie Fingers	1.00
AR8	Gaylord Perry	.75
AR9	Ron Guidry	.75
AR10	Phil Niekro	.75

70s Disco Era Dandies

mike schmidt / phillies

		NM/M
Complete Set (6):		5.00
Common Player:		.50
Inserted 1:23		
DE1	Mike Schmidt	2.00
DE2	Johnny Bench	1.00
DE3	Lou Brock	.50
DE4	Reggie Jackson	2.00
DE5	Willie Stargell	.50
DE6	Tom Seaver	1.00

70s Super Powers

	NM/M
Complete Set (6):	12.00

Common Player:		1.50
Inserted 1:24		
SP1	Reggie Jackson	3.00
SP2	Joe Morgan	1.50
SP3	Willie Stargell	2.00
SP4	Willie McCovey	1.50
SP5	Mike Schmidt	4.00
SP6	Nolan Ryan	5.00

2001 Upper Deck Evolution

		NM/M
Complete Set (120):		125.00
Common Player:		.15
Common SP (91-120):		3.00
Production 2,250		
Pack (5):		2.00
Box (24):		40.00
1	Darin Erstad	.25
2	Troy Glaus	.50
3	Jason Giambi	.50
4	Tim Hudson	.40
5	Jermaine Dye	.15
6	Barry Zito	.40
7	Carlos Delgado	.50
8	Shannon Stewart	.15
9	Jose Cruz Jr.	.15
10	Greg Vaughn	.15
11	Juan Gonzalez	.50
12	Roberto Alomar	.50
13	Omar Vizquel	.25
14	Jim Thome	.50
15	Edgar Martinez	.25
16	John Olerud	.25
17	Kazuhiro Sasaki	.15
18	Cal Ripken Jr.	2.00
19	Alex Rodriguez	1.50
20	Ivan Rodriguez	.50
21	Rafael Palmeiro	.50
22	Pedro Martinez	.50
23	Nomar Garciaparra	1.50
24	Manny Ramirez	.50
25	Carl Everett	.15
26	Mark Quinn	.15
27	Mike Sweeney	.15
28	Neifi Perez	.15
29	Tony Clark	.15
30	Eric Milton	.15
31	Doug Mientkiewicz	.15
32	Corey Koskie	.15
33	Frank Thomas	.50
34	David Wells	.15
35	Magglio Ordonez	.40
36	Derek Jeter	2.00
37	Mike Mussina	.40
38	Bernie Williams	.50
39	Roger Clemens	1.50
40	David Justice	.25
41	Jeff Bagwell	.50
42	Richard Hidalgo	.25
43	Wade Miller	.15
44	Chipper Jones	1.00
45	Greg Maddux	1.00
46	Andruw Jones	.50
47	Rafael Furcal	.25
48	Geoff Jenkins	.25
49	Jeromy Burnitz	.15
50	Ben Sheets	.25
51	Richie Sexson	.40
52	Mark McGwire	1.50
53	Jim Edmonds	.40
54	Darryl Kile	.15
55	J.D. Drew	.25
56	Sammy Sosa	1.50
57	Kerry Wood	.50
58	Randy Johnson	.75
59	Luis Gonzalez	.50
60	Matt Williams	.25
61	Kevin Brown	.25
62	Gary Sheffield	.40
63	Shawn Green	.40
64	Chan Ho Park	.15

65	Vladimir Guerrero	.75
66	Jose Vidro	.15
67	Fernando Tatis	.15
68	Barry Bonds	2.00
69	Jeff Kent	.25
70	Russ Ortiz	.15
71	Preston Wilson	.15
72	Ryan Dempster	.15
73	Charles Johnson	.15
74	Mike Piazza	1.00
75	Edgardo Alfonzo	.15
76	Robin Ventura	.25
77	Jay Payton	.15
78	Tony Gwynn	.75
79	Phil Nevin	.15
80	Pat Burrell	.40
81	Scott Rolen	.50
82	Bob Abreu	.25
83	Brian Giles	.25
84	Jason Kendall	.25
85	Ken Griffey Jr.	1.00
86	Barry Larkin	.40
87	Sean Casey	.25
88	Todd Helton	.50
89	Larry Walker	.25
90	Mike Hampton	.15
91	Ichiro Suzuki RC	20.00
92	Albert Pujols RC	40.00
93	Wilson Betemit RC	3.00
94	Jay Gibbons RC	8.00
95	Juan Uribe RC	5.00
96	Morgan Ensberg RC	8.00
97	Christian Parker RC	3.00
98	Tsuyoshi Shinjo RC	8.00
99	Jack Wilson RC	8.00
100	Donaldo Mendez RC	3.00
101	Ryan Freel RC	4.00
102	Juan Diaz RC	3.00
103	Horacio Ramirez RC	8.00
104	Ricardo Rodriguez RC	3.00
105	Erick Almonte RC	3.00
106	Josh Towers RC	3.00
107	Adrian Hernandez RC	3.00
108	Brandon Duckworth RC	4.00
109	Travis Hafner RC	10.00
110	Martin Vargas RC	3.00
111	Kris Keller RC	3.00
112	Brian Lawrence RC	3.00
113	Esix Snead RC	3.00
114	Wilken Ruan RC	3.00
115	Jose Mieses RC	3.00
116	Johnny Estrada RC	8.00
117	Elpidio Guzman RC	3.00
118	Sean Douglass RC	3.00
119	Billy Sylvester RC	3.00
120	Bret Prinz RC	3.00

UD Classics

		NM/M
Complete Set (15):		15.00
Common Player:		.50
Prices for unscratched cards.		
Winners Evolve Into Game Jersey.		
Inserted 1:4		
EC1	Ken Griffey Jr.	3.00
EC2	Gary Sheffield	.75
EC3	Randy Johnson	1.50
EC4	Sammy Sosa	3.00
EC5	Carlos Delgado	1.00
EC6	Ichiro Suzuki	3.00
EC7	Andruw Jones	1.00
EC8	Chipper Jones	2.00
EC9	Kazuhiro Sasaki	.50
EC10	Shawn Green	.75
EC11	Alex Rodriguez	3.00
EC12	Brian Giles	.75
EC13	J.D. Drew	.50
EC14	Pat Burrell	1.00
EC15	Ivan Rodriguez	1.00

Autographed Bat/Jersey

		NM/M
Common Player:		25.00
RB	Russell Branyan	25.00
PB	Pat Burrell	40.00
CD	Carlos Delgado	40.00
JD	J.D. Drew	25.00
JaG	Jason Giambi	65.00
SG	Shawn Green	40.00
KG	Ken Griffey Jr.	100.00
AJ	Andruw Jones	50.00
CJ	Chipper Jones	60.00
JK	Jason Kendall	30.00
CR	Cal Ripken Jr.	150.00
AR	Alex Rodriguez	150.00
GS	Gary Sheffield	50.00
SS	Sammy Sosa	200.00
IS	Ichiro Suzuki	300.00

Game-Used Bat Cards

		NM/M
Common Player:		5.00
Winners Evolve Into Bat/Jsy Auto.		
Inserted 1:120		
RB	Russell Branyan	5.00
PB	Pat Burrell	8.00
CD	Carlos Delgado	8.00
JD	J.D. Drew	5.00
JaG	Jason Giambi	8.00
KG	Ken Griffey Jr.	20.00
AJ	Andruw Jones	8.00
JK	Jason Kendall	5.00
AR	Alex Rodriguez	15.00
GS	Gary Sheffield	6.00

Game-Used Jersey Cards

		NM/M
Common Player:		5.00
Inserted 1:120		
RB	Russell Branyan	5.00
PB	Pat Burrell	8.00
JD	J.D. Drew	5.00
JaG	Jason Giambi	10.00
BG	Brian Giles	6.00
TG	Troy Glaus	8.00
SG	Shawn Green	6.00
KG	Ken Griffey Jr.	20.00
AJ	Andruw Jones	8.00
CJ	Chipper Jones	10.00
JK	Jason Kendall	5.00
CR	Cal Ripken Jr.	30.00
AR	Alex Rodriguez	15.00
GS	Gary Sheffield	8.00
SS	Sammy Sosa	15.00

Ichiro Suzuki All-Star Game

		NM/M
Random Inserts		
51B	Ichiro Suzuki/Bronze	8.00
51S	Ichiro Suzuki/ Silver/2001	20.00
51G	Ichiro Suzuki/ Gold/51	120.00

2001 Upper Deck Gold Glove

		NM/M
Common Player:		.25
Common SP (91-129):		4.00
Production 1,000		
Common SP (130-135):		8.00
Production 500		
Pack (4):		8.00
Box (20):		140.00
1	Troy Glaus	1.00
2	Darin Erstad	.50
3	Jason Giambi	1.00
4	Tim Hudson	.50
5	Jermaine Dye	.25
6	Raul Mondesi	.25
7	Carlos Delgado	1.00
8	Shannon Stewart	.25
9	Greg Vaughn	.25
10	Aubrey Huff	.25
11	Juan Gonzalez	1.00
12	Roberto Alomar	1.00
13	Omar Vizquel	.25
14	Jim Thome	1.00
15	John Olerud	.50
16	Edgar Martinez	.50
17	Kazuhiro Sasaki	.25
18	Aaron Sele	.25
19	Cal Ripken Jr.	4.00
20	Chris Richard	.25
21	Ivan Rodriguez	1.00
22	Rafael Palmeiro	.75
23	Alex Rodriguez	3.00
24	Pedro Martinez	1.50
25	Nomar Garciaparra	3.00
26	Manny Ramirez	1.00
27	Neifi Perez	.25
28	Mike Sweeney	.25
29	Bobby Higginson	.25
30	Dean Palmer	.25
31	Tony Clark	.25
32	Doug Mientkiewicz	.25
33	Brad Radke	.25
34	Joe Mays	.25
35	Frank Thomas	1.00
36	Magglio Ordonez	.50
37	Carlos Lee	.25
38	Bernie Williams	1.00
39	Mike Mussina	1.00
40	Derek Jeter	4.00
41	Roger Clemens	2.50
42	Craig Biggio	.40
43	Jeff Bagwell	1.00
44	Lance Berkman	.50
45	Andruw Jones	1.00
46	Greg Maddux	2.00
47	Chipper Jones	2.00
48	Geoff Jenkins	.40
49	Ben Sheets	.25
50	Jeromy Burnitz	.25
51	Jim Edmonds	.50
52	Mark McGwire	3.00
53	Mike Matheny	.25
54	J.D. Drew	.50
55	Sammy Sosa	2.50
56	Kerry Wood	.75
57	Fred McGriff	.40
58	Randy Johnson	1.50
59	Steve Finley	.25
60	Mark Grace	.75
61	Matt Williams	.40

62	Luis Gonzalez	.40
63	Shawn Green	.40
64	Kevin Brown	.40
65	Gary Sheffield	.50
66	Vladimir Guerrero	1.25
67	Tony Armas Jr.	.25
68	Barry Bonds	4.00
69	J.T. Snow	.25
70	Jeff Kent	.25
71	Charles Johnson	.25
72	Preston Wilson	.25
73	Cliff Floyd	.25
74	Robin Ventura	.25
75	Mike Piazza	2.00
76	Edgardo Alfonzo	.25
77	Tony Gwynn	1.50
78	Ryan Klesko	.50
79	Scott Rolen	1.00
80	Mike Lieberthal	.25
81	Pat Burrell	.75
82	Jason Kendall	.25
83	Brian Giles	.50
84	Ken Griffey Jr.	2.50
85	Barry Larkin	.50
86	Pokey Reese	.25
87	Larry Walker	.40
88	Mike Hampton	.25
89	Juan Pierre	.25
90	Todd Helton	1.00
91	Mike Penney RC	4.00
92	Wilkin Ruan RC	4.00
93	Greg Miller RC	4.00
94	Johnny Estrada RC	8.00
95	Tsuyoshi Shinjo RC	4.00
96	Josh Towers RC	4.00
97	Horacio Ramirez RC	6.00
98	Ryan Freel RC	4.00
99	Morgan Ensberg RC	8.00
100	Adrian Hernandez RC	8.00
101	Juan Uribe RC	6.00
102	Jose Mieses RC	4.00
103	Jack Wilson RC	8.00
104	Cesar Crespo RC	4.00
105	Bud Smith RC	4.00
106	Erick Almonte RC	4.00
107	Elpidio Guzman RC	4.00
108	Brandon Duckworth RC	4.00
109	Juan Diaz RC	4.00
110	Kris Keller RC	4.00
111	Jason Michaels RC	4.00
112	Bret Prinz RC	4.00
113	Henry Mateo RC	4.00
114	Ricardo Rodriguez RC	4.00
115	Travis Hafner RC	20.00
116	Nate Teut RC	4.00
117	Alexis Gomez RC	4.00
118	Billy Sylvester RC	4.00
119	Adam Pettyjohn RC	4.00
120	Josh Fogg RC	4.00
121	Juan Cruz RC	4.00
122	Carlos Valderrama RC	4.00
123	Jay Gibbons RC	8.00
124	Donaldo Mendez RC	4.00
125	William Ortega RC	4.00
126	Sean Douglass RC	4.00
127	Christian Parker RC	4.00
128	Grant Balfour RC	4.00
129	Joe Kennedy RC	4.00
130	Albert Pujols RC	140.00
131	Wilson Betemit RC	10.00
132	Mark Teixeira RC	50.00
133	Mark Prior RC	60.00
134	Dewon Brazelton RC	10.00
135	Ichiro Suzuki RC	60.00

Limited

NM/M
Stars (1-90): 4-8X
Rookies (91-135): .75-1.5X
Production 100 Sets
(See 2001 Upper Deck Gold Glove for checklist and base card values.)

Finite

NM/M
Common Player: 9.00
Stars (1-90): 15-25X
Rookies (91-135): 3-5X
Production 25 Sets
(See 2001 Upper Deck Gold Glove for checklist and base card values.)

Batting Gloves

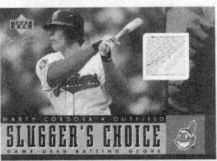

NM/M

Common Player:		5.00
Inserted 1:20		
BA	Bobby Abreu	8.00
BA	Brady Anderson	5.00
TB	Tony Batista	5.00
BB	Barry Bonds	30.00
MC	Marty Cordova	5.00
JC	Jose Cruz	5.00
RF	Rafael Furcal	8.00
AG	Andres Galarraga	5.00
JG	Juan Gonzalez	8.00
KGR	Ken Griffey Jr./Reds	20.00
KGM	Ken Griffey Jr.	20.00
CJ	Chipper Jones	10.00
EM	Edgar Martinez	8.00
PO	Paul O'Neill	8.00
RP	Rafael Palmeiro	10.00
NP	Neifi Perez	5.00
MR	Manny Ramirez	8.00
ARR	Alex Rodriguez/ Rangers	20.00
ARM	Alex Rodriguez/M's	20.00
HR	Henry Rodriguez	5.00
IR	Ivan Rodriguez	8.00
GS	Gary Sheffield	8.00
SS	Sammy Sosa	15.00
FT	Fernando Tatis	5.00
MT	Miguel Tejada	8.00

Fielder's Gloves

NM/M

Common Player:		6.00
Inserted 1:60		
GA	Garret Anderson/100	15.00
CB	Craig Biggio	15.00
JBi	Johnny Blanchard	10.00
BB	Barry Bonds	50.00
JBu	Jay Buhner/100	
KC	Ken Caminiti	10.00
RCa	Roy Campanella	60.00
GC	Gary Carter	10.00
RCe	Roger Cedeno	10.00
JD	Johnny Damon	15.00
LD	Leon Day/100	60.00
OD	Octavio Dotel	6.00
JE	Jim Edmonds	15.00
DE	Dock Ellis	10.00

AF	Alex Fernandez	6.00
CF	Cliff Floyd	10.00
NF	Nellie Fox	25.00
RF	Rafael Furcal	10.00
AG	Alex Gonzalez	6.00
BG	Ben Grieve	8.00
KG	Ken Griffey Jr.	30.00
MG	Marquis Grissom	8.00
LG	Lefty Grove	100.00
THe	Todd Helton	20.00
OH	Orlando Hernandez	8.00
THo	Todd Hollandsworth	8.00
HI	Hideki Irabu	8.00
JI	Jason Isringhausen	10.00
RJ	Reggie Jackson	20.00
CJ	Chipper Jones	25.00
JKa	Jim Kaat	10.00
JKe	Jason Kendall	10.00
RK	Ryan Klesko	8.00
HK	Harvey Kuenn	15.00
CL	Carlos Lee	8.00
KL	Kenny Lofton	10.00
JL	Javy Lopez	10.00
GL	Greg Luzinski	10.00
EM	Edgar Martinez	15.00
PM	Pedro Martinez	25.00
JM	Jose Mesa	10.00
JO	John Olerud	10.00
PO	Paul O'Neill	15.00
RP	Rafael Palmeiro	15.00
CP	Chan Ho Park	10.00
MP	Mike Piazza	30.00
MR	Manny Ramirez	25.00
FR	Frank Robinson	15.00
AR	Alex Rodriguez	30.00
IR	Ivan Rodriguez	15.00
TS	Tim Salmon	8.00
AS	Aaron Sele	6.00
GS	Gary Sheffield	10.00
OS	Ozzie Smith	40.00
SS	Sammy Sosa	30.00
I	Ichiro Suzuki	250.00
FT	Frank Thomas	20.00
OV	Omar Vizquel	15.00
DW	Dave Winfield	20.00
MY	Masato Yoshii	10.00

Fielder's Gloves Autograph

NM/M

Inserted 1:240		
JD	Johnny Damon	50.00
CF	Cliff Floyd	20.00
RF	Rafael Furcal	25.00
RP	Ken Griffey Jr./49	150.00
RJ	Reggie Jackson/68	60.00
JK	Jim Kaat	25.00
JK	Jason Kendall	20.00
RK	Ryan Klesko	20.00
KL	Kenny Lofton	20.00
JL	Javy Lopez	20.00
GL	Greg Luzinski	20.00
EM	Edgar Martinez	50.00
JO	John Olerud	25.00
PO	Paul O'Neill	50.00
FR	Frank Robinson	50.00
IR	Ivan Rodriguez	60.00
OS	Ozzie Smith	85.00
FT	Frank Thomas	60.00
DW	Dave Winfield	50.00

Game-Used Ball

NM/M

Common Player:		5.00
Inserted 1:20		
GC	Ken Griffey Jr., Sean Casey	20.00
RR	Alex Rodriguez, Ivan Rodriguez	20.00

SW	Sammy Sosa, Rondell White	15.00
MP	Mark McGwire, Albert Pujols	75.00
RE	Manny Ramirez, Carl Everett	15.00
GE	Troy Glaus, Darin Erstad	8.00
GT	Jason Giambi, Miguel Tejada	10.00
IO	Ichiro Suzuki, John Olerud	40.00
RP	Ivan Rodriguez, Rafael Palmeiro	10.00
GV	Vladimir Guerrero, Jose Vidro	10.00
PS	Mike Piazza, Tsuyoshi Shinjo	20.00
JJ	Chipper Jones, Andruw Jones	15.00
RB	Scott Rolen, Pat Burrell	10.00
WF	Preston Wilson, Cliff Floyd	5.00
JF	Andruw Jones, Rafael Furcal	10.00
BB	Jeff Bagwell, Lance Berkman	15.00
PE	Albert Pujols, Jim Edmonds	35.00
JB	Geoff Jenkins, Jeromy Burnitz	5.00
KG	Jason Kendall, Brian Giles	5.00
BK	Barry Bonds, Jeff Kent	25.00
NK	Phil Nevin, Ryan Klesko	5.00
SG	Gary Sheffield, Shawn Green	8.00
GG	Luis Gonzalez, Mark Grace	10.00
HW	Todd Helton, Larry Walker	10.00
WP	Larry Walker, Juan Pierre	5.00
AG	Roberto Alomar, Juan Gonzalez	10.00
VM	Greg Vaughn, Fred McGriff	5.00
RB	Cal Ripken Jr., Tony Batista	30.00
DM	Carlos Delgado, Raul Mondesi	8.00
MG	Doug Mientkiewicz, Cristian Guzman	5.00
TO	Frank Thomas, Magglio Ordonez	10.00
HC	Bobby Higginson, Tony Clark	5.00
SB	Mike Sweeney, Carlos Beltran	5.00
MO	Edgar Martinez, John Olerud	8.00
EA	Darin Erstad, Garret Anderson	8.00
TC	Miguel Tejada, Eric Chavez	8.00
PR	Rafael Palmeiro, Alex Rodriguez	20.00
BA	Pat Burrell, Bobby Abreu	8.00
FJ	Cliff Floyd, Charles Johnson	5.00
VP	Robin Ventura, Mike Piazza	15.00
WS	Kerry Wood, Sammy Sosa	20.00
DP	J.D. Drew, Albert Pujols	40.00
BH	Lance Berkman, Richard Hidalgo	8.00
BS	Jeromy Burnitz, Richie Sexson	5.00
LG	Barry Larkin, Ken Griffey Jr.	20.00
GR	Brian Giles, Aramis Ramirez	5.00
JG	Randy Johnson, Luis Gonzalez	15.00
GB	Shawn Green, Adrian Beltre	8.00
KA	Jeff Kent, Rich Aurilia	5.00
GK	Tony Gwynn, Ryan Klesko	15.00
MJ	Greg Maddux, Chipper Jones	20.00
HH	Mike Hampton, Todd Helton	10.00
SV	Tsuyoshi Shinjo, Robin Ventura	5.00
GJ	Cristian Guzman, Jacque Jones	5.00
CJ	Roger Clemens, Derek Jeter	125.00

Jerseys

		NM/M
Common Player:		5.00
Inserted 1:20		
LA	Luis Aparicio	5.00
JB	Jeff Bagwell	8.00
BB	Barry Bonds	25.00
GC	Gary Carter	5.00
CC	Cesar Cedeno	5.00
DE	Darin Erstad	6.00
CF	Carlton Fisk	8.00
MG	Mark Grace	8.00
SG	Shawn Green	5.00
KG	Ken Griffey Jr.	20.00
RG	Ron Guidry	5.00
AJ	Andruw Jones	8.00
JK	Jim Kaat	5.00
GM	Greg Maddux	15.00
MM	Mickey Mantle	175.00
RM	Roger Maris	75.00
DM	Don Mattingly	30.00
TM	Thurman Munson	60.00
MM	Mike Mussina	10.00
RP	Rafael Palmeiro	10.00
BR	Bobby Richardson	8.00
CR	Cal Ripken Jr.	35.00
IR	Ivan Rodriguez	10.00
OS	Ozzie Smith	15.00
IS	Ichiro Suzuki	65.00
OV	Omar Vizquel	8.00
BW	Bernie Williams	8.00

2001 Upper Deck Hall of Famers

		NM/M
Complete Set (90):		25.00
Common Player:		.15
Hobby Pack (5):		4.00
Box (24):		80.00
1	Reggie Jackson	.75
2	Hank Aaron	1.50
3	Eddie Mathews	.75
4	Warren Spahn	.40
5	Robin Yount	.40
6	Lou Brock	.25
7	Dizzy Dean	.15
8	Bob Gibson	.40
9	Stan Musial	.75
10	Enos Slaughter	.15
11	Rogers Hornsby	.40
12	Ernie Banks	.50
13	Ferguson Jenkins	.15
14	Roy Campanella	.75
15	Pee Wee Reese	.40
16	Jackie Robinson	1.50
17	Juan Marichal	.15
18	Christy Mathewson	.15
19	Willie Mays	1.50
20	Hoyt Wilhelm	.15
21	Buck Leonard	.15
22	Bob Feller	.40
23	Cy Young	.40
24	Satchel Paige	.40
25	Tom Seaver	.50
26	Brooks Robinson	.40
27	Mike Schmidt	.75
28	Roberto Clemente	1.50
29	Ralph Kiner	.15
30	Willie Stargell	.50
31	Honus Wagner	.75
32	Josh Gibson	.40
33	Nolan Ryan	1.50
34	Carlton Fisk	.15
35	Jimmie Foxx	.75
36	Johnny Bench	.75
37	Joe Morgan	.40
38	George Brett	.75
39	Walter Johnson	.40
40	Cool Papa Bell	.15
41	Ty Cobb	1.00
42	Al Kaline	.15
43	Harmon Killebrew	.15
44	Luis Aparicio	.15
45	Yogi Berra	.75
46	Joe DiMaggio	1.50
47	Whitey Ford	.25
48	Lou Gehrig	2.00
49	Mickey Mantle	2.00
50	Babe Ruth	2.00
51	Josh Gibson	.15
52	Honus Wagner	.20
53	Hoyt Wilhelm	.15
54	Cy Young	.20
55	Walter Johnson	.20
56	Satchel Paige	.25
57	Rogers Hornsby	.20
58	Christy Mathewson	.15
59	Tris Speaker	.20
60	Nap Lajoie	.15
61	Mickey Mantle	1.00
62	Jackie Robinson	.75
63	Nolan Ryan	.75
64	Josh Gibson	.20
65	Yogi Berra	.40
66	Brooks Robinson	.20
67	Stan Musial	.40
68	Mike Schmidt	.40
69	Joe DiMaggio	1.00
70	Ernie Banks	.25
71	Willie Stargell	.25
72	Johnny Bench	.40
73	Willie Mays	.75
74	Satchel Paige	.25
75	Bob Gibson	.20
76	Harmon Killebrew	.15
77	Al Kaline	.15
78	Carlton Fisk	.15
79	Tom Seaver	.25
80	Reggie Jackson	.40
81	Bob Gibson	.20
82	Nolan Ryan	.75
83	Walter Johnson	.20
84	Stan Musial	.40
85	Josh Gibson	.20
86	Cy Young	.20
87	Joe DiMaggio	1.00
88	Hoyt Wilhelm	.15
89	Lou Brock	.15
90	Mickey Mantle	1.00

Hall of Fame Gallery

		NM/M
Complete Set (15):		25.00
Common Player:		1.00
Inserted 1:6		
1	Reggie Jackson	1.50
2	Tom Seaver	1.50
3	Bob Gibson	1.50
4	Jackie Robinson	3.00
5	Joe DiMaggio	3.00
6	Ernie Banks	1.50
7	Mickey Mantle	4.00
8	Willie Mays	3.00

9	Cy Young	1.50
10	Nolan Ryan	4.00
11	Johnny Bench	1.50
12	Yogi Berra	1.50
13	Satchel Paige	1.00
14	George Brett	2.00
15	Stan Musial	2.00

The Endless Summer

		NM/M
Complete Set (11):		15.00
Common Player:		1.00
Inserted 1:8		
1	Mickey Mantle	3.00
2	Yogi Berra	1.00
3	Mike Schmidt	2.50
4	Jackie Robinson	2.50
5	Johnny Bench	1.50
6	Tom Seaver	1.50
7	Ernie Banks	1.50
8	Harmon Killebrew	1.00
9	Joe DiMaggio	3.00
10	Willie Mays	3.00
11	Brooks Robinson	1.00

20th Century Showcase

		NM/M
Complete Set (11):		15.00
Common Player:		1.00
Inserted 1:8		
1	Cy Young	1.00
2	Joe DiMaggio	3.00
3	Harmon Killebrew	1.00
4	Stan Musial	2.00
5	Mickey Mantle	4.00
6	Satchel Paige	1.00
7	Nolan Ryan	4.00
8	Bob Gibson	1.00
9	Ernie Banks	1.50
10	Mike Schmidt	2.00
11	Willie Mays	3.00

The Class of '36

		NM/M
Complete Set (5):		8.00
Common Player:		1.50
Inserted 1:17		

1	Ty Cobb	2.00
2	Babe Ruth	5.00
3	Christy Mathewson	1.50
4	Walter Johnson	1.50
5	Honus Wagner	1.50

Coop. Coll. Game Bat

		NM/M
Common Player:		5.00
Inserted 1:24		
HA	Hank Aaron	30.00
LA	Luis Aparicio	5.00
EB	Ernie Banks	15.00
JB	Johnny Bench	15.00
YB	Yogi Berra	10.00
JBo	Jim Bottomley	5.00
GB	George Brett	20.00
RC	Roy Campanella	30.00
OC	Orlando Cepeda	5.00
RC	Roberto Clemente/SP/409	120.00
JD	Joe DiMaggio	100.00
CF	Carlton Fisk	10.00
RF	Rollie Fingers	5.00
JF	Jimmie Foxx	50.00
HG	Hank Greenberg	40.00
RH	Rogers Hornsby	100.00
RJ	Reggie Jackson	15.00
GK	George Kell	5.00
RK	Ralph Kiner	10.00
MM	Mickey Mantle	125.00
WM	Willie Mays	30.00
JM	Johnny Mize	10.00
JMo	Joe Morgan	5.00
MO	Mel Ott	50.00
JP	Jim Palmer/SP/372	50.00
TP	Tony Perez	5.00
BR	Brooks Robinson	10.00
FR	Frank Robinson	10.00
JR	Jackie Robinson/SP/371	175.00
BR	Babe Ruth	200.00
NR	Nolan Ryan	50.00
RS	Red Schoendienst	5.00
ES	Enos Slaughter	5.00
DS	Duke Snider	10.00
WS	Willie Stargell	5.00
BW	Billy Williams	5.00
EW	Early Wynn	5.00
RY	Robin Yount	15.00

Coop. Coll. Game Jersey

		NM/M
Common Player:		10.00
Inserted 1:168		
LA	Luis Aparicio	10.00
OC	Orlando Cepeda	10.00
RC	Roberto Clemente	100.00
JD	Joe DiMaggio	100.00
DD	Don Drysdale/SP/49	200.00
LG	Lou Gehrig/SP/194	250.00
MM	Mickey Mantle/SP/216	250.00
WM	Willie Mays	80.00
JM	Joe Morgan	10.00
TP	Tony Perez	10.00
PW	Pee Wee Reese	15.00
BR	Brooks Robinson	20.00
FR	Frank Robinson	10.00
NR	Nolan Ryan	30.00
TS	Tom Seaver	15.00
DS	Duke Snider/SP/267	50.00
WS	Willie Stargell	15.00
DSu	Don Sutton	10.00

Coop. Coll. Jersey Autograph

	NM/M
Common Autograph:	40.00

Inserted 1:504

		NM/M
LA	Luis Aparicio	40.00
OC	Orlando Cepeda	40.00
RJ	Reggie Jackson	75.00
EB	Ernie Banks	90.00
JM	Joe Morgan	40.00
TP	Tony Perez	40.00
GB	George Brett	125.00
BR	Brooks Robinson	80.00
FR	Frank Robinson	60.00
NR	Nolan Ryan	175.00
TS	Tom Seaver	75.00
DS	Duke Snider	65.00
WS	Willie Stargell	75.00
DSu	Don Sutton	40.00

Mantle Pinstripes Exclusive

	NM/M
Complete Set (56):	75.00
Common Mantle:	2.00
One Pack/Box	

Mantle Pinstripe Memorabilia

		NM/M
Print Runs Listed		
MMB	Mickey Mantle/ Bat/100	100.00
MMCJ	Mickey Mantle, Joe DiMaggio/ Jsy/50	300.00
MMJ	Mickey Mantle/ Jsy/100	125.00

2001 Upper Deck Legends

		NM/M
	Complete Set (90):	20.00
	Common Player:	.20
	Pack (5):	4.00
	Box (24):	80.00
1	Darin Erstad	.40
2	Troy Glaus	.75
3	Nolan Ryan	3.00
4	Reggie Jackson	.50
5	Jim "Catfish" Hunter	.50
6	Jason Giambi	.50
7	Tim Hudson	.30
8	Miguel Tejada	.30
9	Carlos Delgado	.50
10	Shannon Stewart	.20
11	Greg Vaughn	.20
12	Larry Doby	.20
13	Jim Thome	.40
14	Juan Gonzalez	.75
15	Roberto Alomar	.50
16	Edgar Martinez	.20
17	John Olerud	.40
18	Eddie Murray	.40
19	Cal Ripken Jr.	2.50
20	Alex Rodriguez	2.00
21	Ivan Rodriguez	.75
22	Rafael Palmeiro	.40
23	Jimmie Foxx	.50
24	Cy Young	.50
25	Manny Ramirez	.75
26	Pedro Martinez	1.00
27	Nomar Garciaparra	2.00
28	George Brett	1.00
29	Mike Sweeney	.20
30	Jermaine Dye	.20
31	Ty Cobb	1.50
32	Dean Palmer	.20
33	Harmon Killebrew	.50
34	Matt Lawton	.20
35	Luis Aparicio	.20
36	Frank Thomas	.75
37	Magglio Ordonez	.20
38	David Wells	.20
39	Mickey Mantle	3.00
40	Joe DiMaggio	3.00
41	Roger Maris	.75
42	Babe Ruth	3.00
43	Derek Jeter	2.50
44	Roger Clemens	1.00
45	Bernie Williams	.50
46	Jeff Bagwell	.75
47	Richard Hidalgo	.40
48	Warren Spahn	.40
49	Greg Maddux	1.50
50	Chipper Jones	1.50
51	Andruw Jones	.50
52	Robin Yount	.50
53	Jeromy Burnitz	.20
54	Jeffrey Hammonds	.20
55	Ozzie Smith	.50
56	Stan Musial	1.00
57	Mark McGwire	2.50
58	Jim Edmonds	.30
59	Sammy Sosa	1.50
60	Ernie Banks	.50
61	Kerry Wood	.20
62	Randy Johnson	.75
63	Luis Gonzalez	.40
64	Don Drysdale	.50
65	Jackie Robinson	2.00
66	Gary Sheffield	.20
67	Kevin Brown	.20
68	Vladimir Guerrero	1.00
69	Willie Mays	1.50
70	Mel Ott	.20
71	Jeff Kent	.20
72	Barry Bonds	1.00
73	Preston Wilson	.20
74	Ryan Dempster	.20
75	Tom Seaver	.40
76	Mike Piazza	2.00
77	Robin Ventura	.20
78	Dave Winfield	.40
79	Tony Gwynn	1.00
80	Bob Abreu	.20
81	Scott Rolen	.40
82	Mike Schmidt	.75
83	Roberto Clemente	1.50
84	Brian Giles	.20
85	Ken Griffey Jr.	2.00
86	Frank Robinson	.40
87	Johnny Bench	.75
88	Todd Helton	.75
89	Larry Walker	.40
90	Mike Hampton	.20

Legendary Cuts

NM/M

Most not priced due to scarcity.

C-TC	Ty Cobb/3	3,150
C-BRu	Babe Ruth/7	6,000

Fiorentino Collection

		NM/M
	Complete Set (14):	40.00
	Common Player:	1.50
	Inserted 1:12	
F1	Babe Ruth	6.00
F2	Satchel Paige	1.50
F3	Joe DiMaggio	5.00
F4	Willie Mays	4.00
F5	Ty Cobb	3.00
F6	Nolan Ryan	5.00
F7	Lou Gehrig	5.00
F8	Jackie Robinson	4.00
F9	Hank Aaron	4.00
F10	Roberto Clemente	4.00
F11	Stan Musial	3.00
F12	Johnny Bench	2.00
F13	Honus Wagner	1.50
F14	Reggie Jackson	1.50

Reflections

		NM/M
	Complete Set (10):	25.00
	Common Card:	1.00
	Inserted 1:18	
R1	Bernie Williams, Mickey Mantle	6.00
R2	Pedro Martinez, Cy Young	2.00
R3	Barry Bonds, Willie Mays	5.00
R4	Scott Rolen, Mike Schmidt	3.00
R5	Mark McGwire, Stan Musial	4.00
R6	Ken Griffey Jr., Frank Robinson	3.00
R7	Sammy Sosa, Andre Dawson	3.00
R8	Kevin Brown, Don Drysdale	1.50
R9	Jason Giambi, Reggie Jackson	1.50
R10	Tim Hudson, Jim "Catfish" Hunter	1.00

Legendary Game Jerseys

		NM/M
	Common Player:	5.00
	Inserted 1:24	
HA	Hank Aaron	40.00
JB	Jeff Bagwell	8.00
EB	Ernie Banks	15.00
YB	Yogi Berra	10.00
BB	Barry Bonds	25.00

		NM/M
JC	Jose Canseco	10.00
RCl	Roger Clemens	20.00
RoC	Roberto Clemente/ 195	170.00
JD	Joe DiMaggio/245	175.00
KG	Ken Griffey Jr.	15.00
TG	Tony Gwynn	10.00
RJa	Reggie Jackson	10.00
RJo	Randy Johnson	10.00
CJ	Chipper Jones	10.00
GM	Greg Maddux	15.00
MM	Mickey Mantle/245	200.00
RM	Roger Maris/343	65.00
PM	Pedro Martinez	10.00
WM	Willie Mays	30.00
SM	Stan Musial/490	30.00
MP	Mike Piazza	20.00
MR	Manny Ramirez	8.00
CR	Cal Ripken Jr.	30.00
AR	Alex Rodriguez	20.00
IR	Ivan Rodriguez	8.00
NR	Nolan Ryan	50.00
KS	Kazuhiro Sasaki	5.00
TS	Tom Seaver	15.00
GS	Gary Sheffield	5.00
OS	Ozzie Smith	15.00
SS	Sammy Sosa	15.00
DW	Dave Winfield	5.00
RY	Robin Yount	12.00

Legendary Jerseys Gold

		NM/M
	Common Player:	30.00
	Production 25 Sets	
RCl	Roger Clemens	75.00
RoC	Roberto Clemente	180.00
KG	Ken Griffey Jr.	75.00
RJ	Reggie Jackson	40.00
WM	Willie Mays	120.00
AR	Alex Rodriguez	75.00
NR	Nolan Ryan	100.00
SS	Sammy Sosa	75.00
DW	Dave Winfield	30.00

Legendary Jerseys Autograph

Inserted 1:288

		NM/M
EB	Ernie Banks	75.00
RC	Roger Clemens/211	100.00
KG	Ken Griffey Jr.	80.00
RJ	Reggie Jackson/224	60.00
SM	Stan Musial/266	100.00
AR	Alex Rodriguez	85.00
NR	Nolan Ryan	125.00
TS	Tom Seaver	60.00
OS	Ozzie Smith	60.00
SS	Sammy Sosa/91	175.00

Legendary Jerseys Gold Autograph

No pricing due to scarcity.
Production 25 Sets

Legendary Lumber

		NM/M
Common Player:		5.00
Inserted 1:24		
HA	Hank Aaron	30.00
LA	Luis Aparicio	5.00
EB	Ernie Banks/80	50.00
JB	Johnny Bench	15.00
BB	Barry Bonds	25.00
RCa	Roy Campanella/335	40.00
JC	Jose Canseco	8.00
RCl	Roger Clemens	20.00
RoC	Roberto Clemente/170	120.00
JD	Joe DiMaggio	85.00
JF	Jimmie Foxx/351	50.00
KG	Ken Griffey Jr.	15.00
TG	Tony Gwynn	10.00
RJ	Reggie Jackson	10.00
RJ	Randy Johnson	10.00
AJ	Andruw Jones	8.00
CJ	Chipper Jones	10.00
MM	Mickey Mantle	150.00
RM	Roger Maris	40.00
WM	Willie Mays	30.00
EM	Eddie Murray	8.00
MO	Mel Ott/355	40.00
MP	Mike Piazza	15.00
AP	Albert Pujols	45.00
MR	Manny Ramirez	8.00
FR	Frank Robinson	8.00
CR	Cal Ripken Jr.	40.00
AR	Alex Rodriguez	15.00
IR	Ivan Rodriguez	8.00
GS	Gary Sheffield	5.00
OS	Ozzie Smith	10.00
SS	Sammy Sosa	15.00

Legendary Lumber Gold

		NM/M
Common Player:		25.00
Production 25 Sets		
RC	Roger Clemens	75.00
RC	Roberto Clemente	180.00
KG	Ken Griffey Jr.	75.00
RJ	Reggie Jackson	40.00
WM	Willie Mays	120.00
AR	Alex Rodriguez	75.00
GS	Gary Sheffield	25.00
SS	Sammy Sosa	75.00

Legendary Lumber Autograph

		NM/M
Common Player:		25.00
Inserted 1:288		
LA	Luis Aparicio	25.00
EB	Ernie Banks	65.00
RC	Roger Clemens/227	100.00
KG	Ken Griffey Jr.	80.00
TG	Tony Gwynn	60.00
RJ	Reggie Jackson/211	65.00
EM	Eddie Murray	40.00
AR	Alex Rodriguez	100.00
SS	Sammy Sosa/66	240.00

2001 Upper Deck Legends of New York

		NM/M
Complete Set (200):		40.00
Common Player:		.20
Pack (5):		2.50
Box (24):		50.00
1	Billy Herman	.20
2	Carl Erskine	.20
3	Burleigh Grimes	.20
4	Don Newcombe	.20
5	Gil Hodges	.75
6	Pee Wee Reese	.75
7	Jackie Robinson	2.00
8	Duke Snider	1.00
9	Jim Gilliam	.20
10	Roy Campanella	1.50
11	Carl Furillo	.20
12	Casey Stengel	.75
13	Casey Stengel	.40
14	Billy Herman	.20
15	Jackie Robinson	1.00
16	Jackie Robinson	1.00
17	Gil Hodges	.40
18	Carl Furillo	.20
19	Roy Campanella	.50
20	Don Newcombe	.40
21	Duke Snider	.75
22	Casey Stengel	.40
23	Burleigh Grimes	.20
24	Pee Wee Reese	.50
25	Jackie Robinson	1.00
26	Jackie Robinson	1.00
27	Carl Erskine	.20
28	Roy Campanella	.75
29	Duke Snider	.75
30	Rube Marquard	.20
31	Ross Youngs	.20
32	Bobby Thomson	.20
33	Christy Mathewson	1.00
34	Carl Hubbell	.20
35	Hoyt Wilhelm	.20
36	Johnny Mize	.40
37	John McGraw	.20
38	Monte Irvin	.50
39	Travis Jackson	.20
40	Mel Ott	1.00
41	Dusty Rhodes	.20
42	Leo Durocher	.50
43	John McGraw	.20
44	Christy Mathewson	.50
45	The Polo Grounds	.20
46	Travis Jackson	.20
47	Mel Ott	.50
48	Johnny Mize	.20
49	Leo Durocher	.30
50	Bobby Thomson	.20
51	Monte Irvin	.30
52	Bobby Thomson	.20
53	Christy Mathewson	.50
54	Christy Mathewson	.50
55	Christy Mathewson	.50
56	John McGraw	.20
57	John McGraw	.20
58	John McGraw	.20
59	Travis Jackson	.20
60	Mel Ott	.50
61	Mel Ott	.50
62	Carl Hubbell	.20
63	Bobby Thomson	.20
64	Monte Irvin	.20
65	Al Weis	.20
66	Donn Clendenon	.20
67	Ed Kranepool	.20
68	Gary Carter	.20
69	Tommie Agee	.20
70	Jon Matlack	.20
71	Ken Boswell	.20
72	Len Dykstra	.20
73	Nolan Ryan	3.00
74	Ray Sadecki	.20
75	Ron Darling	.20
76	Ron Swoboda	.20
77	Dwight Gooden	.20
78	Tom Seaver	1.00
79	Wayne Garrett	.20
80	Casey Stengel	.50
81	Tom Seaver	.50
82	Tommie Agee	.20
83	Tom Seaver	.50
84	Yogi Berra	.50
85	Yogi Berra	.50
86	Tom Seaver	.50
87	Dwight Gooden	.20
88	Gary Carter	.20
89	Ron Darling	.20
90	Tommie Agee	.20
91	Tom Seaver	.50
92	Gary Carter	.20
93	Len Dykstra	.20
94	Babe Ruth	3.00
95	Bill Dickey	.50
96	Rich "Goose" Gossage	.20
97	Casey Stengel	.50
98	Jim "Catfish" Hunter	.75
99	Charlie Keller	.20
100	Chris Chambliss	.20
101	Don Larsen	.40
102	Dave Winfield	.75
103	Don Mattingly	2.00
104	Elston Howard	.20
105	Frankie Crosetti	.20
106	Hank Bauer	.20
107	Joe DiMaggio	3.00
108	Graig Nettles	.20
109	Lefty Gomez	.20
110	Phil Rizzuto	1.00
111	Lou Gehrig	2.00
112	Lou Piniella	.20
113	Mickey Mantle	3.00
114	Red Rolfe	.20
115	Reggie Jackson	1.00
116	Roger Maris	1.50
117	Ray White	.20
118	Thurman Munson	1.50
119	Tom Tresh	.20
120	Tommy Henrich	.20
121	Waite Hoyt	.20
122	Willie Randolph	.20
123	Whitey Ford	.75
124	Yogi Berra	1.00
125	Babe Ruth	1.50
126	Babe Ruth	1.50
127	Lou Gehrig	1.25
128	Babe Ruth	1.50
129	Joe DiMaggio	1.50
130	Joe DiMaggio	1.50
131	Mickey Mantle	1.50
132	Roger Marris	.75
133	Mickey Mantle	1.50
134	Reggie Jackson	.75
135	Babe Ruth	1.50
136	Babe Ruth	1.50
137	Babe Ruth	1.50
138	Lefty Gomez	.20
139	Lou Gehrig	1.25
140	Lou Gehrig	1.25
141	Joe DiMaggio	1.50
142	Joe DiMaggio	1.50
143	Casey Stengel	.40
144	Mickey Mantle	1.50
145	Yogi Berra	.50
146	Mickey Mantle	1.50
147	Elston Howard	.40
148	Whitey Ford	.50
149	Reggie Jackson	.50
150	Reggie Jackson	.50
151	John McGraw, Babe Ruth	1.00
152	Babe Ruth, John McGraw	1.00
153	Lou Gehrig, Mel Ott	.75
154	Joe DiMaggio, Mel Ott	1.00
155	Joe DiMaggio, Billy Herman	1.00
156	Joe DiMaggio, Jackie Robinson	1.50
157	Mickey Mantle, Bobby Thomson	1.00
158	Yogi Berra, Pee Wee Reese	.75
159	Roy Campanella, Mickey Mantle	1.00
160	Don Larsen, Duke Snider	.50
161	Christy Mathewson	.75
162	Christy Mathewson	.50
163	Rube Marquard	.20
164	Christy Mathewson	.50
165	John McGraw	.20
166	Burleigh Grimes	.20
167	Babe Ruth	1.50
168	Burleigh Grimes	.20
169	Babe Ruth	1.50
170	John McGraw	.40
171	Lou Gehrig	1.25
172	Babe Ruth	1.50
173	Babe Ruth	1.50
174	Carl Hubbell	.20
175	Joe DiMaggio	1.50
176	Lou Gehrig	1.25
177	Leo Durocher	.40
178	Mel Ott	.50
179	Joe DiMaggio	1.50
180	Jackie Robinson	1.00
181	Babe Ruth	1.50
182	Bobby Thomson	.20
183	Joe DiMaggio	1.50
184	Mickey Mantle	1.50
185	Monte Irvin	.20
186	Roy Campanella	.50
187	Duke Snider	.50
188	Dusty Rhodes	.20
189	Yogi Berra	.50
190	Mickey Mantle	1.50
191	Mickey Mantle	1.50
192	Casey Stengel	.40
193	Tom Seaver	.50
194	Mickey Mantle	1.50
195	Tommie Agee	.20
196	Tom Seaver	.50
197	Chris Chambliss	.20
198	Reggie Jackson	.50
199	Reggie Jackson	.50
200	Gary Carter	.20

Bat Cards

		NM/M
Common Player:		5.00
Inserted 1:24		
DODGERS		
JG	Jim Gilliam	10.00
BH	Billy Herman	8.00
DN	Don Newcombe/67	40.00
GIANTS		
BTh	Bobby Thomson	25.00
METS		
KB	Ken Boswell	5.00
GC	Gary Carter	15.00
DC	Donn Clendenon/60	
LD	Len Dykstra	5.00
WG	Wayne Garrett	8.00
EK	Ed Kranepool	10.00
JM	J.C. Martin	8.00
NR	Nolan Ryan	40.00
TS	Tom Seaver	20.00
RSw	Ron Swoboda	8.00
AW	Al Weis	5.00
YANKEES		
HB	Hank Bauer	10.00

YB	Yogi Berra	15.00
CC	Chris Chambliss/130	15.00
BD	Bill Dickey	15.00
TH	Tommy Henrich	8.00
EH	Elston Howard	10.00
RJ	Reggie Jackson	15.00
CK	Charlie Keller	8.00
MM	Mickey Mantle/134	200.00
RM	Roger Maris/60	85.00
DM	Don Mattingly	30.00
TM	Thurman Munson	20.00
LP	Lou Piniella	8.00
MR	Mickey Rivers	5.00
BR	Babe Ruth/107	250.00
TT	Tom Tresh	10.00
DW	Dave Winfield	10.00

Bat Autographs

NM/M

Common Autograph:		
DODGERS		
DN	Don Newcombe	30.00
METS		
GC	Gary Carter	40.00
DC	Donn Clendenon	30.00
NR	Nolan Ryan/129	200.00
TS	Tom Seaver/89	100.00
YANKEES		
YB	Yogi Berra	75.00
CC	Chris Chambliss	30.00
RJ	Reggie Jackson/123	75.00
DM	Don Mattingly	100.00
MR	Mickey Rivers	25.00
RW	Roy White	25.00

Combination Signatures

NM/M

Common Card:		75.00
NP	Don Newcombe, Johnny Podres	85.00
WM	Dave Winfield, Don Mattingly	200.00
RS	Nolan Ryan, Tom Seaver	400.00
LB	Don Larsen, Yogi Berra	150.00
GJ	Ron Guidry, Tommy John	60.00
CN	Chris Chambliss, Graig Nettles	60.00
RD	Willie Randolph, Bucky Dent	60.00
RW	Mickey Rivers, Roy White	60.00
WJ	Dave Winfield, Reggie Jackson	150.00

Cut Signatures

NM/M

Most not priced due to scarcity.

LC-JD	Joe DiMaggio (38 Issued)	1,000

Dodgers Game Jersey

NM/M

Common Player:	5.00
Gold Edition of 400:	1.25X

HB	Hank Behrman	5.00
CD	Chuck Dressen	5.00
CE	Carl Erskine	10.00
SJ	Spider Jurgenson	5.00
JR	Jackie Robinson/126	120.00

Giants Game Jersey

NM/M

Complete Set (1):		
CM	Christy Mathewson/63	350.00

Mets Game Jersey

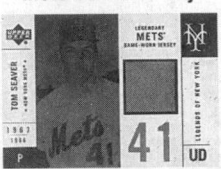

NM/M

Common Player:		5.00
Gold Edition of 400:		1.25X
RD	Ron Darling	5.00
JM	Jon Matlack	5.00
RS	Ray Sadecki	5.00
TS	Tom Seaver	15.00
CS	Casey Stengel	8.00
JT	Joe Torre	5.00

Yankees Game Jersey

NM/M

Common Player:		5.00
Gold Edition of 400:		1.25X
HB	Hank Bauer	8.00
FC	Frank Crosetti	10.00
TH	Tommy Henrich	10.00
EH	Elston Howard	10.00
CH	Jim "Catfish" Hunter	10.00
DM	Duke Maas	5.00
MM	Mickey Mantle/63	250.00
LM	Lindy McDaniel	5.00
TM	Thurman Munson	30.00
GN	Graig Nettles	10.00
PN	Phil Niekro	10.00
JP	Joe Pepitone	5.00
WR	Willie Randolph	8.00
RR	Red Rolfe	5.00
BT	Bob Turley	8.00
DW	Dave Winfield	15.00

Signed Game Jersey

NM/M

Common Autograph:	15.00

DODGERS		
CE	Carl Erskine	50.00
JP	Johnny Podres/193	50.00
METS		
GF	George Foster/196	30.00
NR	Nolan Ryan/47	200.00
CS	Craig Swan	30.00
YANKEES		
YG	Yogi Berra/73	125.00
BD	Bucky Dent	30.00
RG	Rich Gossage/145	30.00
RG	Ron Guidry	50.00
TJ	Tommy John	30.00
DL	Don Larsen	60.00
HL	Hector Lopez/195	15.00
SL	Sparky Lyle	30.00
DM	Don Mattingly/72	125.00
PN	Phil Niekro/195	40.00
GN	Graig Nettles	30.00
JP	Joe Pepitone	30.00
WR	Willie Randolph	30.00
DR	Dave Righetti	30.00

Ebbets Field Seat

NM/M

Complete Set (1):		
JR	Jackie Robinson	50.00

Ebbets Field G-U Base

NM/M

Complete Set (1):		
JR	Jackie Robinson/100	50.00
JR	Jackie Robinson/Silver/50	60.00
JR	Jackie Robinson/Gold/25	75.00

Shea Stadium G-U Base

NM/M

Quantity produced listed

TS	Tom Seaver/100	25.00
TS	Tom Seaver/Silver/50	40.00
TS	Tom Seaver/Gold/25	50.00

United We Stand

NM/M

Complete Set (15):	10.00
Common United We Stand:	1.00
Inserted 1:12	

Yankee Stadium Seat

No Pricing

2001 Upper Deck MVP

NM/M

Complete Set (330):		35.00
Common Player:		.10
Pack (8):		1.50
Box (24):		30.00
1	Mo Vaughn	.10
2	Troy Percival	.10
3	Adam Kennedy	.10
4	Darin Erstad	.25
5	Tim Salmon	.10
6	Bengie Molina	.10
7	Troy Glaus	.40
8	Garret Anderson	.25
9	Ismael Valdes	.10
10	Glenallen Hill	.10
11	Tim Hudson	.25
12	Eric Chavez	.20
13	Johnny Damon	.20
14	Barry Zito	.40
15	Jason Giambi	.40
16	Terrence Long	.10
17	Jason Hart	.10
18	Jose Ortiz	.10
19	Miguel Tejada	.25
20	Jason Isringhausen	.10
21	Adam Piatt	.10
22	Jeremy Giambi	.10
23	Tony Batista	.10
24	Darrin Fletcher	.10
25	Mike Sirotka	.10
26	Carlos Delgado	.40
27	Billy Koch	.10
28	Shannon Stewart	.10
29	Raul Mondesi	.15
30	Brad Fullmer	.10
31	Jose Cruz Jr.	.10
32	Kelvim Escobar	.10
33	Greg Vaughn	.10
34	Aubrey Huff	.10
35	Albie Lopez	.10
36	Gerald Williams	.10
37	Ben Grieve	.10
38	John Flaherty	.10
39	Fred McGriff	.15
40	Ryan Rupe	.10
41	Travis Harper	.10
42	Steve Cox	.10
43	Roberto Alomar	.40
44	Jim Thome	.50
45	Russell Branyan	.10
46	Bartolo Colon	.20
47	Omar Vizquel	.15
48	Travis Fryman	.15
49	Kenny Lofton	.15
50	Chuck Finley	.10
51	Ellis Burks	.10
52	Eddie Taubensee	.10
53	Juan Gonzalez	.40
54	Edgar Martinez	.20
55	Aaron Sele	.10
56	John Olerud	.20
57	Jay Buhner	.10
58	Mike Cameron	.10
59	John Halama	.10
60	Ichiro Suzuki RC	8.00
61	David Bell	.10
62	Freddy Garcia	.10
63	Carlos Guillen	.10
64	Bret Boone	.20
65	Al Martin	.10
66	Cal Ripken Jr.	1.50
67	Delino DeShields	.10
68	Chris Richard	.10
69	Sean Douglass RC	.25
70	Melvin Mora	.10
71	Luis Matos	.10
72	Sidney Ponson	.10
73	Mike Bordick	.10

No.	Player	Price
74	Brady Anderson	.10
75	David Segui	.10
76	Jeff Conine	.10
77	Alex Rodriguez	1.25
78	Gabe Kapler	.10
79	Ivan Rodriguez	.40
80	Rick Helling	.10
81	Kenny Rogers	.10
82	Andres Galarraga	.15
83	Rusty Greer	.10
84	Justin Thompson	.10
85	Ken Caminiti	.10
86	Rafael Palmeiro	.40
87	Ruben Mateo	.10
88	Travis Hafner RC	1.00
89	Manny Ramirez	.40
90	Pedro Martinez	.50
91	Carl Everett	.10
92	Dante Bichette	.10
93	Derek Lowe	.10
94	Jason Varitek	.10
95	Nomar Garciaparra	1.25
96	David Cone	.10
97	Tomokazu Ohka	.10
98	Troy O'Leary	.10
99	Trot Nixon	.10
100	Jermaine Dye	.10
101	Joe Randa	.10
102	Jeff Suppan	.10
103	Roberto Hernandez	.10
104	Mike Sweeney	.10
105	Mac Suzuki	.10
106	Carlos Febles	.10
107	Jose Rosado	.10
108	Mark Quinn	.10
109	Carlos Beltran	.20
110	Dean Palmer	.10
111	Mitch Meluskey	.10
112	Bobby Higginson	.10
113	Brandon Inge	.10
114	Tony Clark	.10
115	Brian Moehler	.10
116	Juan Encarnacion	.10
117	Damion Easley	.10
118	Roger Cedeno	.10
119	Jeff Weaver	.10
120	Matt Lawton	.10
121	Jay Canizaro	.10
122	Eric Milton	.10
123	Corey Koskie	.10
124	Mark Redman	.10
125	Jacque Jones	.10
126	Brad Radke	.10
127	Cristian Guzman	.10
128	Joe Mays	.10
129	Denny Hocking	.10
130	Frank Thomas	.40
131	David Wells	.10
132	Ray Durham	.10
133	Paul Konerko	.10
134	Joe Crede	.10
135	Jim Parque	.10
136	Carlos Lee	.10
137	Magglio Ordonez	.25
138	Sandy Alomar Jr.	.10
139	Chris Singleton	.10
140	Jose Valentin	.10
141	Roger Clemens	1.00
142	Derek Jeter	1.50
143	Orlando Hernandez	.15
144	Tino Martinez	.10
145	Bernie Williams	.40
146	Jorge Posada	.25
147	Mariano Rivera	.20
148	David Justice	.20
149	Paul O'Neill	.15
150	Mike Mussina	.25
151	Christian Parker RC	.10
152	Andy Pettitte	.25
153	Alfonso Soriano	.50
154	Jeff Bagwell	.40
155	Morgan Ensberg RC	.50
156	Daryle Ward	.10
157	Craig Biggio	.20
158	Richard Hidalgo	.10
159	Shane Reynolds	.10
160	Scott Elarton	.10
161	Julio Lugo	.10
162	Moises Alou	.20
163	Lance Berkman	.20
164	Chipper Jones	.75
165	Greg Maddux	1.00
166	Javy Lopez	.15
167	Andruw Jones	.40
168	Rafael Furcal	.25
169	Brian Jordan	.10
170	Wes Helms	.10
171	Tom Glavine	.25
172	B.J. Surhoff	.10
173	John Smoltz	.10
174	Quilvio Veras	.10
175	Rico Brogna	.10
176	Jeromy Burnitz	.10
177	Jeff D'Amico	.10
178	Geoff Jenkins	.20
179	Henry Blanco	.10
180	Mark Loretta	.10
181	Richie Sexson	.25
182	Jimmy Haynes	.10
183	Jeffrey Hammonds	.10
184	Ron Belliard	.10
185	Tyler Houston	.10
186	Mark McGwire	1.00
187	Rick Ankiel	.10
188	Darryl Kile	.10
189	Jim Edmonds	.25
190	Mike Matheny	.10
191	Edgar Renteria	.10
192	Ray Lankford	.10
193	Garrett Stephenson	.10
194	J.D. Drew	.20
195	Fernando Vina	.10
196	Dustin Hermanson	.10
197	Sammy Sosa	1.00
198	Corey Patterson	.25
199	Jon Lieber	.10
200	Kerry Wood	.40
201	Todd Hundley	.10
202	Kevin Tapani	.10
203	Rondell White	.10
204	Eric Young	.10
205	Matt Stairs	.10
206	Bill Mueller	.10
207	Randy Johnson	.50
208	Mark Grace	.25
209	Jay Bell	.10
210	Curt Schilling	.25
211	Erubiel Durazo	.10
212	Luis Gonzalez	.20
213	Steve Finley	.10
214	Matt Williams	.20
215	Reggie Sanders	.10
216	Tony Womack	.10
217	Gary Sheffield	.25
218	Kevin Brown	.15
219	Adrian Beltre	.20
220	Shawn Green	.20
221	Darren Dreifort	.10
222	Chan Ho Park	.10
223	Eric Karros	.15
224	Alex Cora	.10
225	Mark Grudzielanek	.10
226	Andy Ashby	.10
227	Vladimir Guerrero	.75
228	Tony Armas Jr.	.10
229	Fernando Tatis	.10
230	Jose Vidro	.10
231	Javier Vazquez	.10
232	Lee Stevens	.10
233	Milton Bradley	.10
234	Carl Pavano	.10
235	Peter Bergeron	.10
236	Wilton Guerrero	.10
237	Ugueth Urbina	.10
238	Barry Bonds	1.50
239	Livan Hernandez	.10
240	Jeff Kent	.15
241	Pedro Feliz	.10
242	Bobby Estalella	.10
243	J.T. Snow	.10
244	Shawn Estes	.10
245	Robb Nen	.10
246	Rich Aurilia	.10
247	Russ Ortiz	.10
248	Preston Wilson	.10
249	Brad Penny	.10
250	Cliff Floyd	.10
251	A.J. Burnett	.10
252	Mike Lowell	.10
253	Luis Castillo	.10
254	Ryan Dempster	.10
255	Derrek Lee	.10
256	Charles Johnson	.10
257	Pablo Ozuna	.10
258	Antonio Alfonseca	.10
259	Mike Piazza	1.00
260	Robin Ventura	.15
261	Al Leiter	.15
262	Timoniel Perez	.10
263	Edgardo Alfonzo	.10
264	Jay Payton	.10
265	Tsuyoshi Shinjo RC	.75
266	Todd Zeile	.10
267	Armando Benitez	.10
268	Glendon Rusch	.10
269	Rey Ordonez	.10
270	Kevin Appier	.10
271	Tony Gwynn	.50
272	Phil Nevin	.10
273	Mark Kotsay	.10
274	Ryan Klesko	.20
275	Adam Eaton	.10
276	Mike Darr	.10
277	Damian Jackson	.10
278	Woody Williams	.10
279	Chris Gomez	.10
280	Trevor Hoffman	.10
281	Xavier Nady	.15
282	Scott Rolen	.40
283	Bruce Chen	.10
284	Pat Burrell	.30
285	Mike Lieberthal	.10
286	Brandon Duckworth RC	.40
287	Travis Lee	.10
288	Bobby Abreu	.10
289	Jimmy Rollins	.25
290	Robert Person	.10
291	Randy Wolf	.10
292	Jason Kendall	.10
293	Derek Bell	.10
294	Brian Giles	.25
295	Kris Benson	.10
296	John Vander Wal	.10
297	Todd Ritchie	.10
298	Warren Morris	.10
299	Kevin Young	.10
300	Francisco Cordova	.10
301	Aramis Ramirez	.10
302	Ken Griffey Jr.	1.00
303	Pete Harnisch	.10
304	Aaron Boone	.10
305	Sean Casey	.20
306	Jackson Melian RC	.40
307	Rob Bell	.10
308	Barry Larkin	.25
309	Dmitri Young	.10
310	Danny Graves	.10
311	Pokey Reese	.10
312	Leo Estrella	.10
313	Todd Helton	.40
314	Mike Hampton	.15
315	Juan Pierre	.10
316	Brent Mayne	.10
317	Larry Walker	.25
318	Denny Neagle	.10
319	Jeff Cirillo	.10
320	Pedro Astacio	.10
321	Todd Hollandsworth	.10
322	Neifi Perez	.10
323	Ron Gant	.10
324	Todd Walker	.10
325	Alex Rodriguez CL	.50
326	Ken Griffey Jr. CL	.50
327	Mark McGwire CL	.50
328	Pedro Martinez CL	.30
329	Derek Jeter CL	.75
330	Mike Piazza CL	.40

Authentic Griffey

NM/M

Inserted 1:288

AGS	Ken Griffey Jr./ Auto.	125.00
AGJ	Ken Griffey Jr./Jsy	15.00
AGC	Ken Griffey Jr./Cap	40.00
AGB	Ken Griffey Jr./Bat	15.00
AGU	Ken Griffey Jr./Unif.	15.00
AGGS	Ken Griffey Jr./ Gold Auto./30	250.00
AGGJ	Ken Griffey Jr./ Gold Jsy/30	75.00
AGGC	Ken Griffey Jr./ Gold Cap/30	75.00
AGGB	Ken Griffey Jr./ Gold Bat/30	75.00
CGR	Ken Griffey Jr., Alex Rodriguez/100	35.00
CGS	Ken Griffey Jr., Sammy Sosa/100	35.00
CGT	Ken Griffey Jr., Frank Thomas/100	25.00

Drawing Power

NM/M

Complete Set (10):		10.00
Common Player:		.75
Inserted 1:12		
DP1	Mark McGwire	2.00
DP2	Vladimir Guerrero	1.00
DP3	Manny Ramirez	.75
DP4	Frank Thomas	.75
DP5	Ken Griffey Jr.	1.50
DP6	Alex Rodriguez	2.50
DP7	Mike Piazza	1.50
DP8	Derek Jeter	3.00
DP9	Sammy Sosa	2.00
DP10	Todd Helton	.75

Mantle Pinstripes Exclusive

NM/M

Complete Set (56):	75.00
Common Mantle:	2.00
One Pack/Box	

Mantle Pinstripes Excl. Memorabilia

NM/M

Print runs listed.

MMCJ3	Mickey Mantle, Ken Griffey Jr./50	200.00
MMJ3	Mickey Mantle/ Jsy/100	125.00

Souvenirs Batting Gloves

NM/M

Common Player:		8.00
Inserted 1:96 H		
BB	Barry Bonds	20.00
TrG	Troy Glaus	40.00
JG	Juan Gonzalez	10.00
KG	Ken Griffey Jr.	20.00
ToG	Tony Gwynn/200	30.00
CJ	Chipper Jones	15.00
JL	Javy Lopez	8.00
GM	Greg Maddux/95	60.00
EM	Edgar Martinez	8.00
FM	Fred McGriff	8.00
RP	Rafael Palmeiro	15.00
CR	Cal Ripken Jr.	50.00
AR	Alex Rodriguez	20.00
IR	Ivan Rodriguez	10.00
SS	Sammy Sosa	20.00
MT	Miguel Tejada	8.00
FT	Frank Thomas	10.00
MV	Mo Vaughn	8.00

Souvenirs Batting Gloves Autographs

NM/M

Production 25 Sets

TrG	Troy Glaus	
KG	Ken Griffey Jr.	150.00
ToG	Tony Gwynn	80.00

CJ	Chipper Jones	
CR	Cal Ripken Jr.	250.00
AR	Alex Rodriguez	150.00
IR	Ivan Rodriguez	80.00
SS	Sammy Sosa	250.00
FT	Frank Thomas	80.00

Souvenirs Two-Player Bat Combo

		NM/M
Common Combo:		10.00
Inserted 1:144		
TS	Frank Thomas, Sammy Sosa	25.00
RR	Alex Rodriguez, Ivan Rodriguez	25.00
TG	Jim Thome, Ken Griffey Jr.	25.00
GS	Ken Griffey Jr., Sammy Sosa	30.00
WA	Kerry Wood, Rick Ankiel	10.00
3K	Tony Gwynn, Cal Ripken Jr.	40.00
DV	Carlos Delgado, Jose Vidro	10.00
JJ	Andruw Jones, Chipper Jones	20.00
HR	Jose Canseco, Ken Griffey Jr.	20.00
JF	Chipper Jones, Rafael Furcal	15.00
OW	Paul O'Neill, Bernie Williams	10.00
TO	Frank Thomas, Magglio Ordonez	15.00
RM	Alex Rodriguez, Edgar Martinez	20.00
RP	Ivan Rodriguez, Rafael Palmeiro	15.00

Souvenirs Three Player Bat Combo

No pricing due to scarcity.
Production 25 Sets

Souvenirs Two-Player Bat Autograph

		NM/M
Production 25 Sets		
RG	Alex Rodriguez, Ken Griffey Jr.	250.00
SG	Sammy Sosa, Ken Griffey Jr.	300.00
RR	Alex Rodriguez, Ivan Rodriguez	200.00
JG	Chipper Jones, Troy Glaus	125.00
TS	Frank Thomas, Sammy Sosa	275.00
GD	Jason Giambi, Carlos Delgado	75.00
3K	Cal Ripken Jr., Tony Gwynn	300.00
TG	Frank Thomas, Jason Giambi	85.00
HH	Todd Helton, Mike Hampton	60.00

Super Tools

		NM/M
Complete Set (20):		20.00
Common Player:		.50
Inserted 1:6		
ST1	Ken Griffey Jr.	1.50
ST2	Carlos Delgado.	.75
ST3	Alex Rodriguez.	2.50
ST4	Troy Glaus.	.75
ST5	Jeff Bagwell.	.75
ST6	Ichiro Suzuki.	3.00
ST7	Derek Jeter.	3.00
ST8	Jim Edmonds.	.50
ST9	Vladimir Guerrero.	1.00
ST10	Jason Giambi.	.75
ST11	Todd Helton.	.75
ST12	Cal Ripken Jr.	3.00
ST13	Barry Bonds.	3.00
ST14	Nomar Garciaparra.	2.00
ST15	Randy Johnson.	1.00
ST16	Jermaine Dye.	.50
ST17	Andruw Jones.	.75
ST18	Ivan Rodriguez.	.75
ST19	Sammy Sosa.	2.00
ST20	Pedro Martinez.	1.00

2001 Upper Deck Ovation

Pedro Martinez • P

		NM/M
Complete Set (90):		100.00
Common Player:		.20
Common WP (61-90):		3.00
WP Production 2,000		
Pack (5):		5.00
Box (20):		80.00
1	Troy Glaus	.50
2	Darin Erstad	.40
3	Jason Giambi	.50
4	Tim Hudson	.40
5	Eric Chavez	.30
6	Carlos Delgado	.50
7	David Wells	.20
8	Greg Vaughn	.20
9	Omar Vizquel	.20
10	Jim Thome	.50
11	Roberto Alomar	.40
12	John Olerud	.30
13	Edgar Martinez	.20
14	Cal Ripken Jr.	2.00
15	Alex Rodriguez	1.50
16	Ivan Rodriguez	.50
17	Manny Ramirez	.50
18	Nomar Garciaparra	1.50
19	Pedro Martinez	.75
20	Jermaine Dye	.20
21	Juan Gonzalez	.50
22	Matt Lawton	.20
23	Frank Thomas	.50
24	Magglio Ordonez	.40
25	Bernie Williams	.40

26	Derek Jeter	2.00
27	Roger Clemens	1.50
28	Jeff Bagwell	.50
29	Richard Hidalgo	.20
30	Chipper Jones	1.00
31	Greg Maddux	1.00
32	Andruw Jones	.50
33	Jeromy Burnitz	.20
34	Mark McGwire	1.50
35	Jim Edmonds	.40
36	Sammy Sosa	1.50
37	Kerry Wood	.50
38	Randy Johnson	.75
39	Steve Finley	.20
40	Gary Sheffield	.40
41	Kevin Brown	.40
42	Shawn Green	.40
43	Vladimir Guerrero	.75
44	Jose Vidro	.20
45	Barry Bonds	2.00
46	Jeff Kent	.30
47	Preston Wilson	.20
48	Luis Castillo	.20
49	Mike Piazza	1.00
50	Edgardo Alfonzo	.20
51	Tony Gwynn	.75
52	Ryan Klesko	.30
53	Scott Rolen	.50
54	Bob Abreu	.30
55	Jason Kendall	.20
56	Brian Giles	.30
57	Ken Griffey Jr.	1.00
58	Barry Larkin	.40
59	Todd Helton	.50
60	Mike Hampton	.20
61	Corey Patterson	3.00
62	Timoniel Perez	3.00
63	Toby Hall	3.00
64	Brandon Inge	3.00
65	Joe Crede	3.00
66	Xavier Nady	3.00
67	Adam Pettyjohn RC	3.00
68	Keith Ginter	3.00
69	Brian Cole	3.00
70	Tyler Walker RC	3.00
71	Juan Uribe RC	5.00
72	Alex Hernandez	3.00
73	Leo Estrella	3.00
74	Joey Nation	3.00
75	Aubrey Huff	3.00
76	Ichiro Suzuki RC	75.00
77	Jay Spurgeon	3.00
78	Sun-Woo Kim	3.00
79	Pedro Feliz	3.00
80	Pablo Ozuna	3.00
81	Hiram Bocachica	3.00
82	Brad Wilkerson	3.00
83	Rocky Biddle	3.00
84	Aaron McNeal	3.00
85	Adam Bernero	3.00
86	Danys Baez	3.00
87	Dee Brown	3.00
88	Jimmy Rollins	4.00
89	Jason Hart	3.00
90	Ross Gload	3.00

A Piece of History

		NM/M
Common Player:		5.00
Inserted 1:40		
RA	Rick Ankiel	5.00
JB	Johnny Bench	15.00
BB	Barry Bonds	30.00
KB	Kevin Brown	5.00
JC	Jose Canseco	8.00
RC	Roger Clemens	15.00
DC	David Cone	5.00
CD	Carlos Delgado	8.00
JD	Joe DiMaggio	100.00
DD	Don Drysdale/SP	25.00
DE	Darin Erstad	5.00
RF	Rollie Fingers/SP	8.00
CF	Carlton Fisk	10.00
RF	Rafael Furcal	5.00
TrG	Troy Glaus	8.00
TG	Tom Glavine	8.00
SG	Shawn Green	5.00
KG	Ken Griffey Jr.	15.00
KGs	Ken Griffey Sr.	5.00
MH	Mike Hampton	5.00
RJ	Randy Johnson	10.00
AJ	Andruw Jones	8.00
CJ	Chipper Jones	10.00
GM	Greg Maddux	15.00

MM	Mickey Mantle	125.00
JP	Jim Palmer	10.00
CR	Cal Ripken Jr.	30.00
BR	Brooks Robinson	15.00
AR	Alex Rodriguez	15.00
IR	Ivan Rodriguez	8.00
NR	Nolan Ryan/SP	120.00
TS	Tom Seaver	10.00
GS	Gary Sheffield	5.00
OS	Ozzie Smith SP	20.00
SS	Sammy Sosa	15.00
FT	Frank Thomas	8.00
BW	Bernie Williams	8.00
MW	Matt Williams	5.00
EW	Early Wynn	5.00

A Piece of History Autograph

No Pricing
Values Undetermined

Curtain Calls

		NM/M
Complete Set (10):		10.00
Common Player:		.50
Inserted 1:7		
1	Sammy Sosa	2.00
2	Darin Erstad	.50
3	Barry Bonds	2.50
4	Todd Helton	.75
5	Mike Piazza	1.50
6	Ken Griffey Jr.	1.50
7	Nomar Garciaparra	2.00
8	Carlos Delgado	.75
9	Jason Giambi	.75
10	Alex Rodriguez	2.00

DiMaggio Pinstripes Exclusive

	NM/M
Complete Set (56):	60.00
Common DiMaggio:	1.50
One Pack/Box	

DiMaggio Pinstripes Memorabilia

	NM/M
Print Runs Listed:	150.00

		NM/M
JDB	Joe DiMaggio/Bat/100	75.00
JDBC	Joe DiMaggio/Bat/Cut/5	
JDCJ	Joe DiMaggio, Mickey Mantle/Jsy/50	300.00
JDJ	Joe DiMaggio/Jsy/100	100.00

Lead Performers

		NM/M
Complete Set (11):		15.00
Common Player:		1.00
Inserted 1:12		
1	Mark McGwire	3.00
2	Derek Jeter	4.00
3	Alex Rodriguez	3.00
4	Frank Thomas	1.00
5	Sammy Sosa	2.50
6	Mike Piazza	2.00
7	Vladimir Guerrero	1.50
8	Pedro Martinez	1.50
9	Carlos Delgado	1.00
10	Ken Griffey Jr.	2.00
11	Jeff Bagwell	1.00

POH Combo Cards

Production 25 Sets
Values Undetermined

Superstar Theatre

		NM/M
Complete Set (11):		20.00
Common Player:		1.00
Inserted 1:12		
1	Nomar Garciaparra	2.50
2	Ken Griffey Jr.	2.00
3	Frank Thomas	1.00
4	Derek Jeter	4.00
5	Mike Piazza	2.00
6	Sammy Sosa	2.50
7	Barry Bonds	4.00
8	Alex Rodriguez	3.00
9	Todd Helton	1.00
10	Mark McGwire	3.00
11	Jason Giambi	1.00

2001 Upper Deck Prospect Premieres

		NM/M
Complete Set (90):		100.00
Common Player:		.25
Common Auto. SP (91-102):		10.00
Auto. Production 1,000		
Pack (4):		8.00
Box (18):		125.00
1	Jeff Mathis RC	1.00
2	Jake Woods RC	.25
3	Dallas McPherson RC	1.00
4	Steven Shell RC	.25
5	Ryan Budde RC	.25
6	Kirk Saarloos RC	.40
7	Ryan Stegall RC	.25
8	Bobby Crosby RC	2.00
9	J.T. Stotts RC	.25
10	Neal Cotts RC	.75
11	Jeremy Bonderman RC	3.00
12	Brandon League RC	.40
13	Tyrell Godwin RC	.25
14	Gabe Gross RC	1.00
15	Chris Neylan RC	.25
16	Michael Rouse RC	.25
17	Macay McBride RC	.25
18	Josh Burrus RC	.25
19	Adam Stern RC	.25
20	Richard Lewis RC	.40
21	Cole Barthel RC	.50
22	Mike Jones RC	.25
23	J.J. Hardy RC	3.00
24	Brad Nelson RC	1.00
25	Justin Pope RC	.25
26	Dan Haren RC	2.00
27	Andy Sisco RC	.50
28	Ryan Theriot RC	2.50
29	Ricky Nolasco RC	1.00
30	Jon Switzer RC	.25
31	Justin Wechsler RC	.25
32	Mike Gosling RC	.25
33	Scott Hairston RC	1.00
34	Brian Pilkington RC	.25
35	Kole Strayhorn RC	.25
36	David Taylor RC	.25
37	Donald Levinski RC	.25
38	Mike Hinckley RC	.50
39	Nick Long RC	.25
40	Brad Hennessey RC	.25
41	Noah Lowry RC	2.00
42	Josh Cram RC	.25
43	Jesse Foppert RC	.50
44	Julian Benavidez RC	.25
45	Daniel Denham RC	.25
46	Travis Foley RC	.40
47	Mike Conroy RC	.25
48	Jake Dittler RC	.25
49	Rene Rivera RC	.25
50	John Cole RC	.25
51	Lazaro Abreu RC	.25
52	David Wright RC	30.00
53	Aaron Heilman RC	.40
54	Lenny DiNardo RC	.25
55	Alhaji Turay RC	.40
56	Chris Smith RC	.25
57	Rommie Lewis RC	.25
58	Bryan Bass RC	.25
59	David Crouthers RC	.25
60	Josh Barfield RC	2.00
61	Jake Peavy RC	4.00
62	Ryan Howard RC	50.00
63	Gavin Floyd RC	1.50
64	Mike Floyd RC	.25
65	Stefan Bailie RC	.25
66	Jon DeVries RC	.25
67	Steve Kelly RC	.25
68	Alan Moye RC	.25
69	Justin Gillman RC	.25
70	Jayson Nix RC	1.00
71	John Draper RC	.25
72	Kenny Baugh RC	.25
73	Michael Woods RC	.25
74	Preston Larrison RC	.25
75	Matt Coenen RC	.25
76	Scott Tyler RC	.50
77	Jose Morales RC	.25
78	Corwin Malone RC	.50
79	Dennis Ulacia RC	.40
80	Andy Gonzalez RC	.25
81	Kris Honel RC	1.00
82	Wyatt Allen RC	.25
83	Ryan Wing RC	.25
84	Sean Henn RC	.40
85	John-Ford Griffin RC	.50
86	Bronson Sardinha RC	.50
87	Jon Skaggs RC	.25
88	Shelley Duncan RC	.25
89	Jason Arnold RC	.75
90	Aaron Rifkin RC	.50
91	Colt Griffin RC	10.00
92	J.D. Martin RC	10.00
93	Justin Wayne RC	10.00
94	John VanBenschotten RC	15.00
95	Chris Burke RC	25.00
96	Casey Kotchman RC	40.00
97	Michael Garciaparra RC	10.00
98	Jake Gautreau RC	10.00
99	Jerome Williams RC	10.00
100	Greg Nash RC	10.00
101	Joe Borchard RC	15.00
102	Mark Prior RC	80.00

Heroes of Baseball Bat

		NM/M
Common Player:		4.00
Inserted 1:18		
DB	Don Baylor	4.00
WB	Wade Boggs	8.00
BB	Bill Buckner	4.00
GC	Gary Carter	8.00
DE	Dwight Evans	4.00
SG	Steve Garvey	4.00
KiG	Kirk Gibson	4.00
KeG	Ken Griffey Sr.	4.00
RJ	Reggie Jackson	10.00
DL	Davey Lopes	4.00
FL	Fred Lynn	4.00
BM	Bill Madlock	4.00
TM	Tim McCarver	4.00
JM	Joe Morgan	4.00
MM	Manny Mota	4.00
EM	Eddie Murray	8.00
AO	Al Oliver	4.00
DP	Dave Parker	4.00
TP	Tony Perez	4.00
KP	Kirby Puckett	15.00
OS	Ozzie Smith	10.00
DW	Dave Winfield	8.00

MJ Grandslam Bat

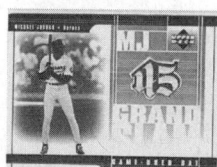

		NM/M
Common MJ:		25.00
MJ1	Michael Jordan	25.00
MJ2	Michael Jordan	25.00
MJ3	Michael Jordan	25.00
MJ4	Michael Jordan	25.00
MJ5	Michael Jordan/White Sox	40.00

HOB Bat Autograph

Production 25 Sets
Values Undetermined

HOB Dual Combo Jersey

		NM/M
Common Duo:		8.00
Inserted 1:144		
BH	Bryan Bass, J.J. Hardy	10.00
DG	Shelley Duncan, Tyrell Godwin	8.00
GS	Steve Garvey, Reggie Smith	10.00
HB	Aaron Heilman, Jeremy Bonderman	10.00
JJ	Michael Jordan, Michael Jordan	100.00
SG	Jon Switzer, Mike Gosling	8.00
WP	Dave Winfield, Kirby Puckett	20.00

HOB Dual Combo Jersey Autograph

Values Undetermined

HOB Triple Combo Jersey

		NM/M
Common Card:		
Inserted 1:144		
BKH	Bobby Crosby, Michael Garciaparra, Bronson Sardinha	15.00
BBC	Chris Burke, Bryan Bass, Bubba Crosby	10.00
GGH	Jake Gautreau, Tyrell Godwin, Aaron Heilman	8.00
GMS	Colt Griffin, J.D. Martin, Jon Switzer	8.00
GKB	Gabe Gross, Casey Kotchman, Kenny Baugh	10.00
JMD	Michael Jordan, Mickey Mantle, Joe DiMaggio	350.00
JPW	Michael Jordan, Kirby Puckett, Dave Winfield	40.00
MMD	Roger Maris, Mickey Mantle, Joe DiMaggio	700.00
VPJ	John VanBenschotten, Mark Prior, Mike Jones	25.00

HOB Triple Combo Jersey Autograph

Values Undetermined

Tribute to 42

		NM/M
Inserted 1:750		
42-B	Jackie Robinson/Bat	40.00

42-J	Jackie Robinson/ Jsy	60.00
42-C	Jackie Robinson/ Cut	500.00
42-B	Jackie Robinson/ Bat/42	100.00
42-J	Jackie Robinson/ Jsy/42	100.00

2001 Upper Deck Pros & Prospects

		NM/M
Complete Set (141):		
Common Player:		.15
Common (91-135):		4.00
Production 1,250		
Common (136-141):		8.00
Production 500		
Pack (5):		6.00
Box (24):		120.00
1	Troy Glaus	.50
2	Darin Erstad	.25
3	Tim Hudson	.40
4	Jason Giambi	.50
5	Jermaine Dye	.15
6	Barry Zito	.40
7	Carlos Delgado	.50
8	Shannon Stewart	.15
9	Raul Mondesi	.15
10	Greg Vaughn	.15
11	Ben Grieve	.15
12	Roberto Alomar	.40
13	Juan Gonzalez	.50
14	Jim Thome	.50
15	C.C. Sabathia	.15
16	Edgar Martinez	.25
17	Kazuhiro Sasaki	.15
18	Aaron Sele	.15
19	John Olerud	.25
20	Cal Ripken Jr.	2.00
21	Rafael Palmeiro	.50
22	Ivan Rodriguez	.50
23	Alex Rodriguez	1.50
24	Manny Ramirez	.50
25	Pedro Martinez	.75
26	Carl Everett	.15
27	Nomar Garciaparra	1.50
28	Neifi Perez	.15
29	Mike Sweeney	.15
30	Bobby Higginson	.15
31	Tony Clark	.15
32	Doug Mientkiewicz	.15
33	Cristian Guzman	.15
34	Brad Radke	.15
35	Magglio Ordonez	.40
36	Carlos Lee	.15
37	Frank Thomas	.50
38	Roger Clemens	1.50
39	Bernie Williams	.50
40	Derek Jeter	2.00
41	Tino Martinez	.25
42	Wade Miller	.15
43	Jeff Bagwell	.50
44	Lance Berkman	.25
45	Richard Hidalgo	.15
46	Greg Maddux	1.00
47	Andruw Jones	.50
48	Chipper Jones	1.00
49	Rafael Furcal	.25
50	Jeromy Burnitz	.15
51	Geoff Jenkins	.15
52	Ben Sheets	.25
53	Mark McGwire	1.50
54	Jim Edmonds	.40
55	J.D. Drew	.25
56	Fred McGriff	.25
57	Sammy Sosa	1.50
58	Kerry Wood	.50
59	Randy Johnson	.75
60	Luis Gonzalez	.25
61	Curt Schilling	.40
62	Kevin Brown	.25
63	Shawn Green	.25
64	Gary Sheffield	.40
65	Vladimir Guerrero	.75
66	Jose Vidro	.15
67	Barry Bonds	2.00
68	Jeff Kent	.25
69	Rich Aurilia	.15
70	Preston Wilson	.15
71	Charles Johnson	.15
72	Cliff Floyd	.15
73	Mike Piazza	1.00
74	Al Leiter	.25
75	Matt Lawton	.15
76	Tony Gwynn	.75
77	Ryan Klesko	.25
78	Phil Nevin	.15
79	Scott Rolen	.50
80	Pat Burrell	.40
81	Jimmy Rollins	.25
82	Jason Kendall	.25
83	Brian Giles	.25
84	Aramis Ramirez	.15
85	Ken Griffey Jr.	1.00
86	Barry Larkin	.40
87	Sean Casey	.25
88	Larry Walker	.25
89	Todd Helton	.50
90	Mike Hampton	.15
91	Juan Cruz RC	4.00
92	Brian Lawrence RC	4.00
93	Brandon Lyon RC	4.00
94	Adrian Hernandez RC	4.00
95	Jose Mieses RC	4.00
96	Juan Uribe RC	4.00
97	Morgan Ensberg RC	8.00
98	Wilson Betemit RC	8.00
99	Ryan Freel RC	4.00
100	Jack Wilson RC	8.00
101	Cesar Crespo RC	4.00
102	Bret Prinz RC	4.00
103	Horacio Ramirez RC	8.00
104	Elpidio Guzman RC	4.00
105	Josh Towers RC	4.00
106	Brandon Duckworth RC	4.00
107	Esix Snead RC	4.00
108	Billy Sylvester RC	4.00
109	Alexis Gomez RC	4.00
110	Johnny Estrada RC	8.00
111	Joe Kennedy RC	4.00
112	Travis Hafner RC	25.00
113	Martin Vargas RC	4.00
114	Jay Gibbons RC	8.00
115	Andres Torres RC	4.00
116	Sean Douglass RC	4.00
117	Juan Diaz RC	4.00
118	Greg Miller RC	4.00
119	Carlos Valderrama RC	4.00
120	William Ortega RC	4.00
121	Josh Fogg RC	4.00
122	Wilken Ruan RC	4.00
123	Kris Keller RC	4.00
124	Erick Almonte RC	4.00
125	Ricardo Rodriguez RC	4.00
126	Grant Balfour RC	4.00
127	Nick Maness RC	4.00
128	Jeremy Owens RC	4.00
129	Doug Nickle RC	4.00
130	Bert Snow RC	4.00
131	Jason Smith RC	4.00
132	Henry Mateo RC	4.00
133	Mike Penney RC	4.00
134	Bud Smith RC	4.00
135	Junior Spivey RC	6.00
136	Ichiro Suzuki RC	90.00
137	Albert Pujols RC	180.00
138	Mark Teixeira RC	100.00
139	Dewon Brazelton RC	8.00
140	Mark Prior RC	25.00
141	Tsuyoshi Shinjo RC	8.00

Bats

		NM/M
Common Card:		4.00
Inserted 1:24		
Golds:		3-5X
Production 25 Sets		
WI	Bernie Williams, Ichiro Suzuki	35.00
RG	Manny Ramirez, Juan Gonzalez	8.00
RP	Ivan Rodriguez, Mike Piazza	15.00
BT	Jeff Bagwell, Frank Thomas	8.00
GBo	Ken Griffey Jr., Barry Bonds	35.00
SG	Sammy Sosa, Luis Gonzalez	15.00
KA	Jeff Kent, Roberto Alomar	4.00
RF	Alex Rodriguez, Rafael Furcal	15.00
PT	Rafael Palmeiro, Jim Thome	10.00
JP	Chipper Jones, Albert Pujols	40.00
GBu	Shawn Green, Jeromy Burnitz	4.00
JL	Andruw Jones, Kenny Lofton	6.00
MJ	Greg Maddux, Randy Johnson	15.00

Ichiro World Tour

	NM/M
Complete Set (15):	25.00
Common Ichiro:	2.00
Inserted 1:12	

Legends Bats

		NM/M
Common Card:		15.00
Inserted 1:216		
Gold:		3-5X
Production 25 Sets		
RF	Manny Ramirez, Carlton Fisk	15.00
BY	Jeromy Burnitz, Robin Yount	15.00
WJ	Bernie Williams, Reggie Jackson	15.00
RG	Cal Ripken Jr., Tony Gwynn	50.00

Specialty Jersey

		NM/M
Common Player:		4.00
Inserted 1:24		
Golds:		3-5X
Production 25 Sets		
RA	Roberto Alomar	6.00
BB	Barry Bonds	25.00
JE	Jim Edmonds	4.00
JG	Juan Gonzalez	6.00
SG	Shawn Green	4.00
TG	Tony Gwynn	10.00
RJ	Randy Johnson	10.00
CR	Cal Ripken Jr.	30.00
AR	Alex Rodriguez	15.00
SR	Scott Rolen	8.00
SS	Sammy Sosa	15.00
I	Ichiro	60.00
JT	Jim Thome	8.00
LW	Larry Walker	4.00

Then & Now Jersey

		NM/M
Common Player:		4.00
Inserted 1:24		
Golds:		3-5X
Production 25 Sets		

RA	Rick Ankiel	4.00
BB	Barry Bonds	30.00
KB	Kevin Brown	6.00
RC	Roger Clemens	20.00
JE	Jim Edmonds	6.00
FG	Freddy Garcia	4.00
JGi	Jason Giambi	8.00
JGo	Juan Gonzalez	8.00
KG	Ken Griffey Jr.	20.00
RJ	Randy Johnson	10.00
GM	Greg Maddux	20.00
PM	Pedro Martinez	10.00
XN	Xavier Nady	4.00
PN	Phil Nevin	4.00
MP	Mike Piazza	15.00
MR	Manny Ramirez	8.00
AR	Alex Rodriguez	15.00
CS	Curt Schilling	6.00
GS	Gary Sheffield	4.00
RV	Robin Ventura	4.00

2001 Upper Deck Rookie Update

		NM/M
Common Player:		.25
Common Rookie:		
Pack (4):		17.00
Box (18):		260.00
Sweet Spot		
Common SP (121-150):		3.00
Production 1,500		
91	Garret Anderson	.50
92	Jermaine Dye	.25
93	Shannon Stewart	.25
94	Ben Grieve	.25
95	Juan Gonzalez	.75
96	Bret Boone	.50
97	Tony Batista	.25
98	Rafael Palmeiro	1.00
99	Carl Everett	.25
100	Mike Sweeney	.25
101	Tony Clark	.25
102	Doug Mientkiewicz	.25
103	Jose Canseco	.50
104	Mike Mussina	.75
105	Lance Berkman	.50
106	Andruw Jones	.75
107	Geoff Jenkins	.40
108	Matt Morris	.25
109	Fred McGriff	.40
110	Luis Gonzalez	.50
111	Kevin Brown	.25
112	Tony Armas Jr.	.25
113	John Vander Wal	.25
114	Cliff Floyd	.25
115	Matt Lawton	.25
116	Phil Nevin	.25
117	Pat Burrell	.50
118	Aramis Ramirez	.25
119	Sean Casey	.40
120	Larry Walker	.40
121	Albert Pujols RC	200.00
122	Johnny Estrada RC	8.00
123	Wilson Betemit RC	3.00
124	Adrian Hernandez RC	3.00
125	Morgan Ensberg RC	15.00
126	Horacio Ramirez RC	6.00
127	Josh Towers RC	6.00
128	Juan Uribe RC	5.00
129	Wilken Ruan RC	3.00

130	Andres Torres **RC**	3.00
131	Brian Lawrence **RC**	4.00
132	Ryan Freel **RC**	4.00
133	Brandon Duckworth **RC**	4.00
134	Juan Diaz **RC**	3.00
135	Rafael Soriano **RC**	6.00
136	Ricardo Rodriguez **RC**	3.00
137	Bud Smith **RC**	3.00
138	Mark Teixeira **RC**	70.00
139	Mark Prior **RC**	25.00
140	Jackson Melian **RC**	3.00
141	Dewon Brazelton **RC**	3.00
142	Greg Miller **RC**	3.00
143	Billy Sylvester **RC**	3.00
144	Elpidio Guzman **RC**	8.00
145	Jack Wilson **RC**	8.00
146	Jose Mieses **RC**	3.00
147	Brandon Lyon **RC**	3.00
148	Tsuyoshi Shinjo **RC**	4.00
149	Juan Cruz **RC**	3.00
150	Jay Gibbons **RC**	8.00

SPx
Common (181-205) 3.00
Production 1,500
Cards (206-210) Autographed

151	Garret Anderson	.50
152	Jermaine Dye	.25
153	Shannon Stewart	.25
154	Toby Hall	.25
155	C.C. Sabathia	.25
156	Bret Boone	.50
157	Tony Batista	.25
158	Gabe Kapler	.25
159	Carl Everett	.25
160	Mike Sweeney	.25
161	Dean Palmer	.25
162	Doug Mientkiewicz	.25
163	Carlos Lee	.25
164	Mike Mussina	.75
165	Lance Berkman	.50
166	Ken Caminiti	.25
167	Ben Sheets	.40
168	Matt Morris	.25
169	Fred McGriff	.40
170	Curt Schilling	.50
171	Paul LoDuca	.25
172	Javier Vazquez	.25
173	Rich Aurilia	.25
174	A.J. Burnett	.25
175	Al Leiter	.40
176	Mark Kotsay	.25
177	Jimmy Rollins	.40
178	Aramis Ramirez	.25
179	Aaron Boone	.25
180	Jeff Cirillo	.25
181	Johnny Estrada **RC**	10.00
182	Dave Williams **RC**	3.00
183	Donaldo Mendez **RC**	3.00
184	Junior Spivey **RC**	8.00
185	Jay Gibbons **RC**	10.00
186	Kyle Lohse **RC**	8.00
187	Willie Harris **RC**	3.00
188	Juan Cruz **RC**	5.00
189	Joe Kennedy **RC**	3.00
190	Duaner Sanchez **RC**	3.00
191	Jorge Julio **RC**	5.00
192	Cesar Crespo **RC**	3.00
193	Casey Fossum **RC**	5.00
194	Brian Roberts **RC**	15.00
195	Troy Mattes **RC**	3.00
196	Rob Mackowiak **RC**	3.00
197	Tsuyoshi Shinjo **RC**	8.00
198	Nick Punto **RC**	3.00
199	Wilmy Caceres **RC**	3.00
200	Jeremy Affeldt **RC**	3.00
201	Bret Prinz **RC**	3.00
202	Delvin James **RC**	3.00
203	Luis Pineda **RC**	3.00
204	Matt White **RC**	3.00
205	Brandon Knight **RC**	3.00
206	Albert Pujols **RC**	900.00
207	Mark Teixeira **RC**	240.00
208	Mark Prior **RC**	125.00
209	Dewon Brazelton **RC**	10.00
210	Bud Smith **RC**	8.00

SP Authentic
Common (211-240): 4.00
Production 1,500

181	Garrett Anderson	.50
182	Jermaine Dye	.25
183	Shannon Stewart	.25
184	Ben Grieve	.25
185	Ellis Burks	.25
186	John Olerud	.50
187	Tony Batista	.25
188	Ruben Sierra	.25
189	Carl Everett	.25
190	Neifi Perez	.25
191	Tony Clark	.25
192	Doug Mientkiewicz	.25
193	Carlos Lee	.25
194	Jorge Posada	.50
195	Lance Berkman	.50
196	Ken Caminiti	.25
197	Ben Sheets	.50
198	Matt Morris	.25
199	Fred McGriff	.40
200	Mark Grace	.50
201	Paul LoDuca	.25
202	Tony Armas, Jr.	.25
203	Andres Galarraga	.40
204	Cliff Floyd	.25
205	Matt Lawton	.25
206	Ryan Klesko	.40
207	Jimmy Rollins	.25
208	Aramis Ramirez	.25
209	Aaron Boone	.25
210	Jose Ortiz	.25
211	Mark Prior **RC**	60.00
212	Mark Teixeira **RC**	125.00
213	Bud Smith **RC**	4.00
214	Wilmy Caceres **RC**	4.00
215	Dave Williams **RC**	4.00
216	Delvin James **RC**	4.00
217	Endy Chavez **RC**	4.00
218	Doug Nickle **RC**	4.00
219	Bret Prinz **RC**	4.00
220	Troy Mattes **RC**	4.00
221	Duaner Sanchez **RC**	4.00
222	Dewon Brazelton **RC**	4.00
223	Brian Bowles **RC**	4.00
224	Donaldo Mendez **RC**	4.00
225	Jorge Julio **RC**	6.00
226	Matt White **RC**	4.00
227	Casey Fossum **RC**	6.00
228	Mike Rivera **RC**	4.00
229	Joe Kennedy **RC**	6.00
230	Kyle Lohse **RC**	6.00
231	Juan Cruz **RC**	4.00
232	Jeremy Affeldt **RC**	4.00
233	Brandon Lyon **RC**	4.00
234	Brian Roberts **RC**	15.00
235	Willie Harris **RC**	4.00
236	Pedro Santana **RC**	4.00
237	Rafael Soriano **RC**	6.00
238	Steve Green **RC**	4.00
239	Junior Spivey **RC**	6.00
240	Rob Mackowiak **RC**	4.00

Ichiro ROY

NM/M
Complete Set (51): 35.00
Common Ichiro: 1.00

Ichiro ROY Game Jersey

NM/M
Numbers 1-12 Production 100 50.00
Numbers 13-17 Production 50 75.00
Numbers 18-19 Production 25 150.00

Ichiro ROY Game-Used Bat

NM/M
Numbers 1-12 Production 100 50.00
Numbers 13-17 Production 50 75.00
Numbers 18-19 Production 25 150.00

SP Chirography

NM/M
Common Autograph: 15.00
Production 250
Silver: .75-1.5X
Production 100
Gold: No Pricing
Production 25 Sets

LB	Lance Berkman/100	10.00
KG	Ken Griffey Jr./250	90.00
TG	Tony Gwynn/250	30.00
TG	Tony Gwynn/100	40.00
MS	Doug Mientkiewicz/100	15.00
JP	Jorge Posada/250	25.00
JP	Jorge Posada/100	30.00
CR	Cal Ripken Jr.	100.00
MS	Mike Sweeney/100	15.00

SP Chirography - Ichiro

NM/M
Ichiro (Unnumbered) 300.00
Ichiro/Silver/100 500.00

USA Touch of Gold

NM/M
Common Autograph: 8.00
Production 500 Sets

BA	Brent Abernathy	8.00
KU	Kurt Ainsworth	10.00
PB	Pat Borders	8.00
SB	Sean Burroughs	12.00
JC	John Cotton	8.00
TD	Gookie Dawkins	8.00
AE	Adam Everett	8.00
RF	Ryan Franklin	8.00
CG	Chris George	8.00
SH	Shane Heams	8.00
MJ	Marcus Jensen	8.00
MK	Mike Kinkade	8.00
RK	Rick Krivda	8.00
DM	Doug Mientkiewicz	12.00
MN	Mike Neill	8.00
RO	Roy Oswalt	20.00
JR	Jon Rauch	8.00
AS	Anthony Sanders	8.00
BSe	Bobby Seay	8.00
BSh	Ben Sheets	12.00
BW	Brad Wilkerson	8.00
TW	Todd Williams	8.00
EY	Ernie Young	8.00
TY	Tim Young	8.00

Materials 2-Player

NM/M
Common Card: 10.00
Inserted 1:15

BB-LG	Barry Bonds, Luis Gonzalez	25.00
JG-BB	Jason Giambi, Barry Bonds	25.00
IR-AR	Ivan Rodriguez, Alex Rodriguez	25.00
AP-JE	Albert Pujols, Jim Edmonds	35.00
GS-SG	Gary Sheffield, Shawn Green	15.00
MP-EA	Mike Piazza, Edgardo Alfonzo	20.00
LW-TH	Larry Walker, Todd Helton	15.00
MR-JG	Manny Ramirez, Juan Gonzalez	15.00
TG-CR	Tony Gwynn, Cal Ripken Jr.	40.00
SR-BA	Scott Rolen, Bobby Abreu	15.00
EM-IS	Edgar Martinez, Ichiro Suzuki	
JB-CB	Jeff Bagwell, Craig Biggio	20.00
KG-SC	Ken Griffey Jr., Sean Casey	25.00
EM-JM	Eric Milton, Joe Mays	10.00
HN-MY	Hideo Nomo, Masato Yoshii	20.00
TS-HN	Tsuyoshi Shinjo, Hideo Nomo	15.00
CS-RJ	Curt Schilling, Randy Johnson	20.00
AS-KS	Aaron Sele, Kazuhiro Sasaki	10.00
PM-RJ	Pedro Martinez, Randy Johnson	15.00
BW-MR	Bernie Williams, Mariano Rivera	15.00
TG-X2	Tony Gwynn	15.00
CR-X2	Cal Ripken Jr.	40.00
JB-RY	Jeromy Burnitz, Robin Yount	15.00
CR-EM	Cal Ripken Jr., Eddie Murray	30.00
TG-DW	Tony Gwynn, Dave Winfield	15.00
FT-MO	Frank Thomas, Magglio Ordonez	15.00
PM-GM	Pedro Martinez, Greg Maddux	20.00
BW-RJ	Bernie Williams, Reggie Jackson	20.00
SS-EB	Sammy Sosa, Ernie Banks	30.00
CP-FV	Chan Ho Park, Fernando Valenzuela	10.00

Materials 3-Player Jsy

NM/M
Common Card: 10.00
Inserted 1:15

KBA	Jeff Kent, Barry Bonds, Rich Aurilia	25.00
JAF	Chipper Jones, Andruw Jones, Rafael Furcal	15.00
GZH	Jason Giambi, Barry Zito, Tim Hudson	15.00
SKB	Gary Sheffield, Eric Karros, Kevin Brown	15.00
SSM	Aaron Sele, Ichiro Suzuki, Edgar Martinez	40.00
HDG	Todd Helton, Carlos Delgado, Jason Giambi	15.00
VRF	Omar Vizquel, Alex Rodriguez, Rafael Furcal	25.00
SYN	Kazuhiro Sasaki, Masato Yoshii, Hideo Nomo	20.00
BTD	Jeff Bagwell, Frank Thomas, Carlos Delgado	15.00
BGG	Barry Bonds, Luis Gonzalez, Ken Griffey Jr.	30.00
RPK	Ivan Rodriguez, Mike Piazza, Jason Kendall	20.00
PPV	Jay Payton, Mike Piazza, Robin Ventura	15.00
CHN	Roger Clemens, Tim Hudson, Hideo Nomo	20.00
PWO	Andy Pettitte, Bernie Williams, Paul O'Neill	20.00
TDK	Frank Thomas, Ray Durham, Paul Konerko	15.00

SJC	Curt Schilling, Randy Johnson, Roger Clemens	20.00
DEA	J.D. Drew, Jim Edmonds, Bobby Abreu	15.00
DOP	Carlos Delgado, Magglio Ordonez, Albert Pujols	35.00
TGA	Jim Thome, Juan Gonzalez, Roberto Alomar	15.00
GWS	Luis Gonzalez, Matt Williams, Curt Schilling	20.00
MGJ	Greg Maddux, Tom Glavine, Andruw Jones	20.00

2001 Upper Deck Sweet Spot

		NM/M
Complete Set (90):		200.00
Common Player:		.25
Common Sweet Beginnings:		5.00
(61-90) Production 1,000		
Pack (4):		15.00
Box (18):		250.00
1	Troy Glaus	.75
2	Darin Erstad	.50
3	Jason Giambi	.75
4	Tim Hudson	.50
5	Ben Grieve	.25
6	Carlos Delgado	.75
7	David Wells	.25
8	Greg Vaughn	.25
9	Roberto Alomar	.75
10	Jim Thome	.75
11	John Olerud	.50
12	Edgar Martinez	.40
13	Cal Ripken Jr.	3.00
14	Albert Belle	.25
15	Ivan Rodriguez	.75
16	Alex Rodriguez	2.50
17	Pedro Martinez	1.00
18	Nomar Garciaparra	2.00
19	Manny Ramirez	.75
20	Jermaine Dye	.25
21	Juan Gonzalez	.75
22	Dean Palmer	.25
23	Matt Lawton	.25
24	Eric Milton	.25
25	Frank Thomas	.75
26	Magglio Ordonez	.50
27	Derek Jeter	3.00
28	Bernie Williams	.75
29	Roger Clemens	2.00
30	Jeff Bagwell	.75
31	Richard Hidalgo	.25
32	Chipper Jones	1.50
33	Greg Maddux	1.50
34	Richie Sexson	.50
35	Jeromy Burnitz	.25
36	Mark McGwire	2.50
37	Jim Edmonds	.50
38	Sammy Sosa	2.00
39	Randy Johnson	1.00
40	Steve Finley	.25
41	Gary Sheffield	.50
42	Shawn Green	.50
43	Vladimir Guerrero	1.00
44	Jose Vidro	.25
45	Barry Bonds	3.00
46	Jeff Kent	.40
47	Preston Wilson	.25
48	Luis Castillo	.25
49	Mike Piazza	1.50
50	Edgardo Alfonzo	.25
51	Tony Gwynn	1.00
52	Ryan Klesko	.40
53	Scott Rolen	.75
54	Bob Abreu	.40
55	Jason Kendall	.40
56	Brian Giles	.40

57	Ken Griffey Jr.	1.50
58	Barry Larkin	.50
59	Todd Helton	.75
60	Mike Hampton	.25
61	Corey Patterson	5.00
62	Ichiro Suzuki RC	160.00
63	Jason Grilli	5.00
64	Brian Cole	5.00
65	Juan Pierre	5.00
66	Matt Ginter	5.00
67	Jimmy Rollins	8.00
68	Jason Smith RC	5.00
69	Israel Alcantara	5.00
70	Adam Pettyjohn RC	5.00
71	Luke Prokopec	5.00
72	Barry Zito	5.00
73	Keith Ginter	5.00
74	Sun-Woo Kim	5.00
75	Ross Gload	5.00
76	Matt Wise	5.00
77	Aubrey Huff	5.00
78	Ryan Franklin	5.00
79	Brandon Inge	5.00
80	Wes Helms	5.00
81	Junior Spivey RC	8.00
82	Ryan Vogelsong	5.00
83	John Parrish	5.00
84	Joe Crede	5.00
85	Damian Rolls	5.00
86	Esix Snead RC	5.00
87	Rocky Biddle	5.00
88	Brady Clark	5.00
89	Timoniel Perez	5.00
90	Jay Spurgeon	5.00

Big League Challenge

		NM/M
Complete Set (20):		20.00
Common Player:		.50
Inserted 1:6		
1	Mark McGwire	2.50
2	Richard Hidalgo	.50
3	Alex Rodriguez	2.50
4	Shawn Green	.75
5	Frank Thomas	1.00
6	Chipper Jones	1.50
7	Rafael Palmeiro	1.00
8	Troy Glaus	1.00
9	Mike Piazza	1.50
10	Andruw Jones	1.00
11	Todd Helton	1.00
12	Jason Giambi	1.00
13	Sammy Sosa	2.00
14	Carlos Delgado	1.00
15	Barry Bonds	3.00
16	Jose Canseco	.75
17	Jim Edmonds	.75
18	Manny Ramirez	1.00
19	Gary Sheffield	.75
20	Nomar Garciaparra	2.00

DiMaggio Pinstripes Exclusive

	NM/M
Complete Set (56):	60.00
Common DiMaggio:	1.50
One Pack/Box	

DiMaggio Pinstripes Memorabilia

		NM/M
Print Runs Listed:		150.00
JDB	Joe DiMaggio/ Bat/100	80.00
JDCJ	Joe DiMaggio, Lou Gehrig/Jsy/50	600.00
JDJ	Joe DiMaggio/ Jsy/100	100.00

Game-Used Bat

		NM/M
Common Player:		5.00
Inserted 1:18		
HA	Hank Aaron	60.00
RA	Rick Ankiel	5.00
BB	Barry Bonds	25.00
JC	Jose Canseco	8.00
TC	Ty Cobb	175.00
JD	Joe DiMaggio	80.00
KG	Ken Griffey Jr.	15.00
RJ	Reggie Jackson	10.00
AJ	Andruw Jones	10.00
MM	Mickey Mantle	140.00
WM	Willie Mays	75.00
SM	Stan Musial	50.00
CR	Cal Ripken Jr.	40.00
AR	Alex Rodriguez	20.00
IR	Ivan Rodriguez	8.00
NR	Nolan Ryan	65.00
GS	Gary Sheffield	8.00
SS	Sammy Sosa	20.00
FT	Frank Thomas	10.00

Game Jerseys

		NM/M
Common Player:		8.00
Inserted 1:18		
BB	Barry Bonds	25.00
JC	Jose Canseco	8.00
RC	Roger Clemens	20.00
RC	Roberto Clemente	125.00
JD	Joe DiMaggio	80.00
KG	Ken Griffey Jr.	20.00
RJ	Randy Johnson	10.00
AJ	Andruw Jones	8.00
CJ	Chipper Jones	10.00
MM	Mickey Mantle	150.00
WM	Willie Mays	100.00
SM	Stan Musial	65.00
CR	Cal Ripken Jr.	40.00
AR	Alex Rodriguez	20.00
IR	Ivan Rodriguez	8.00
NR	Nolan Ryan	65.00
DS	Duke Snider	10.00
SS	Sammy Sosa	20.00
IS	Ichiro Suzuki	100.00
FT	Frank Thomas	10.00

S.S. Game-Used Bases Tier 1

		NM/M
Common Card:		5.00
BH	Barry Bonds, Todd Helton	25.00
MG	Mark McGwire, Ken Griffey Jr.	60.00
JG	Chipper Jones, Nomar Garciaparra	20.00
GD	Vladimir Guerrero, Carlos Delgado	8.00
ST	Sammy Sosa, Frank Thomas	20.00
SR	Gary Sheffield, Alex Rodriguez	15.00
GR	Tony Gwynn, Ivan Rodriguez	10.00
PJ	Mike Piazza, Derek Jeter	30.00
HG	Jeffrey Hammonds, Troy Glaus	5.00
JGi	Randy Johnson, Jason Giambi	8.00
BD	Jeff Bagwell, Jermaine Dye	8.00
RR	Scott Rolen, Cal Ripken Jr.	25.00
GR	Ken Griffey Jr., Manny Ramirez	15.00
RJ	Alex Rodriguez, Derek Jeter	40.00
MP	Mark McGwire, Timoniel Perez	35.00
CP	Roger Clemens, Mike Piazza	20.00

S.S. Game-Used Bases Tier 2

		NM/M
Common Card:		20.00
Production 50 Sets		
BHK	Barry Bonds, Todd Helton, Jeff Kent	75.00
MGE	Mark McGwire, Ken Griffey Jr., Bobby Edmonds	120.00
JGJ	Chipper Jones, Nomar Garciaparra, Andruw Jones	60.00
GDM	Vladimir Guerrero, Carlos Delgado, Raul Mondesi	20.00
STO	Sammy Sosa, Frank Thomas, Magglio Ordonez	50.00
SRM	Gary Sheffield, Alex Rodriguez, Edgar Martinez	50.00
GRP	Tony Gwynn, Ivan Rodriguez, Rafael Palmeiro	40.00
PJW	Mike Piazza, Derek Jeter, Bernie Williams	75.00
HGH	Jeffrey Hammonds, Troy Glaus, Todd Helton	20.00
JGC	Randy Johnson, Jason Giambi, Eric Chavez	25.00
BDH	Jeff Bagwell, Jermaine Dye, Richard Hidalgo	20.00
RRB	Scott Rolen, Cal Ripken Jr., Albert Belle	75.00
GRT	Ken Griffey Jr., Manny Ramirez, Jim Thome	50.00

Players Party

		NM/M
Complete Set (10):		10.00
Common Player:		.75
Inserted 1:12		
1	Derek Jeter	3.00
2	Randy Johnson	1.00
3	Frank Thomas	1.00
4	Nomar Garciaparra	2.00
5	Ken Griffey Jr.	1.50
6	Carlos Delgado	.75
7	Mike Piazza	1.50

8	Barry Bonds	3.00
9	Sammy Sosa	2.00
10	Pedro Martinez	1.00

2001 Upper Deck Ultimate Collection

	NM/M
Common Player:	1.00
Common SP (91-100):	5.00
Production 1,000	
Common SP (101-110):	5.00
Production 750	
Common (111-120):	20.00
Production 250	
Pack (4):	160.00
Box (4):	575.00

1	Troy Glaus	2.50
2	Darin Erstad	1.50
3	Jason Giambi	3.00
4	Barry Zito	2.00
5	Tim Hudson	2.00
6	Miguel Tejada	1.50
7	Carlos Delgado	2.50
8	Shannon Stewart	1.00
9	Greg Vaughn	1.00
10	Toby Hall	1.00
11	Roberto Alomar	2.00
12	Juan Gonzalez	2.50
13	Jim Thome	3.00
14	Edgar Martinez	1.50
15	Freddy Garcia	1.00
16	Bret Boone	1.50
17	Kazuhiro Sasaki	1.00
18	Cal Ripken Jr.	10.00
19	Tim Raines Jr.	1.00
20	Alex Rodriguez	8.00
21	Ivan Rodriguez	2.50
22	Rafael Palmeiro	2.50
23	Pedro Martinez	3.00
24	Nomar Garciaparra	6.00
25	Manny Ramirez	2.50
26	Hideo Nomo	2.00
27	Mike Sweeney	1.00
28	Carlos Beltran	1.50
29	Tony Clark	1.00
30	Dean Palmer	1.00
31	Doug Mientkiewicz	1.00
32	Cristian Guzman	1.00
33	Corey Koskie	1.00
34	Frank Thomas	3.00
35	Magglio Ordonez	1.50
36	Jose Canseco	2.00
37	Roger Clemens	6.00
38	Derek Jeter	10.00
39	Bernie Williams	2.00
40	Mike Mussina	2.00
41	Tino Martinez	1.00
42	Jeff Bagwell	2.50
43	Lance Berkman	2.00
44	Roy Oswalt	1.50

45	Chipper Jones	5.00
46	Greg Maddux	5.00
47	Andruw Jones	2.50
48	Tom Glavine	2.00
49	Richie Sexson	2.00
50	Jeromy Burnitz	1.00
51	Ben Sheets	1.00
52	Mark McGwire	8.00
53	Matt Morris	1.00
54	Jim Edmonds	2.00
55	J.D. Drew	1.50
56	Sammy Sosa	6.00
57	Fred McGriff	1.00
58	Kerry Wood	2.50
59	Randy Johnson	3.00
60	Luis Gonzalez	2.00
61	Curt Schilling	2.00
62	Shawn Green	1.50
63	Kevin Brown	1.50
64	Gary Sheffield	2.00
65	Vladimir Guerrero	3.00
66	Barry Bonds	10.00
67	Jeff Kent	1.50
68	Rich Aurilia	1.00
69	Cliff Floyd	1.00
70	Charles Johnson	1.00
71	Josh Beckett	2.00
72	Mike Piazza	5.00
73	Edgardo Alfonzo	1.00
74	Robin Ventura	1.00
75	Tony Gwynn	2.50
76	Ryan Klesko	1.50
77	Phil Nevin	1.00
78	Scott Rolen	2.50
79	Bobby Abreu	1.00
80	Jimmy Rollins	1.50
81	Brian Giles	1.50
82	Jason Kendall	1.00
83	Aramis Ramirez	1.00
84	Ken Griffey Jr.	6.00
85	Adam Dunn	2.00
86	Sean Casey	1.50
87	Barry Larkin	2.00
88	Larry Walker	1.50
89	Mike Hampton	1.00
90	Todd Helton	2.50
91	Ken Harvey	5.00
92	William Ortega **RC**	5.00
93	Juan Diaz **RC**	5.00
94	Greg Miller **RC**	5.00
95	Brandon Berger **RC**	5.00
96	Brandon Lyon **RC**	5.00
97	Jay Gibbons **RC**	20.00
98	Rob Mackowiak **RC**	5.00
99	Erick Almonte **RC**	5.00
100	Jason Middlebrook **RC**	5.00
101	Johnny Estrada **RC**	10.00
102	Juan Uribe **RC**	10.00
103	Travis Hafner **RC**	30.00
104	Morgan Ensberg **RC**	20.00
105	Mike Rivera **RC**	5.00
106	Josh Towers **RC**	5.00
107	Adrian Hernandez **RC**	5.00
108	Rafael Soriano **RC**	10.00
109	Jackson Melian **RC**	5.00
110	Wilken Ruan **RC**	5.00
111	Albert Pujols **RC**	600.00
112	Tsuyoshi Shinjo **RC**	15.00
113	Brandon Duckworth **RC**	20.00
114	Juan Cruz **RC**	20.00
115	Dewon Brazelton **RC**	20.00
116	Mark Prior/Auto. **RC**	200.00
117	Mark Teixeira/ Auto. **RC**	300.00
118	Wilson Betemit/ Auto. **RC**	25.00
119	Bud Smith/Auto. **RC**	20.00
120	Ichiro Suzuki/ Auto. **RC**	1,500

Game Jersey

	NM/M
Common Player:	10.00
Inserted 1:2	

RA	Roberto Alomar	20.00
JB	Jeff Bagwell	20.00
BB	Barry Bonds	50.00
JC	Jose Canseco	10.00
RC	Roger Clemens	40.00
CD	Carlos Delgado	10.00
DE	Darin Erstad	10.00
JaG	Jason Giambi	20.00

JG	Juan Gonzalez	20.00
LG	Luis Gonzalez	10.00
SG	Shawn Green	10.00
KG	Ken Griffey Jr.	40.00
TG	Tony Gwynn	20.00
TH	Todd Helton	15.00
RJ	Randy Johnson	15.00
AJ	Andruw Jones	10.00
CJ	Chipper Jones	15.00
GM	Greg Maddux	40.00
MO	Magglio Ordonez	10.00
MP	Mike Piazza	30.00
AP	Albert Pujols	75.00
CR	Cal Ripken Jr.	75.00
AR	Alex Rodriguez	40.00
IR	Ivan Rodriguez	15.00
SR	Scott Rolen	15.00
GS	Gary Sheffield	10.00
SS	Sammy Sosa	40.00
FT	Frank Thomas	15.00
LW	Larry Walker	10.00
BW	Bernie Williams	10.00

Ichiro

		NM/M
Pricing not available for all Ichiro's.		
B-IA	Ichiro Suzuki/ Bat Away	65.00
B-IH	Ichiro Suzuki/ Bat Home	65.00
B-IS	Ichiro Suzuki/ Bat/250	80.00
B-IG	Ichiro Suzuki/ Bat/200	90.00
SB-I	Ichiro Suzuki/ Bat/Auto./50	675.00
J-IA	Ichiro Suzuki/ Jsy/Away	50.00
J-IH	Ichiro Suzuki/ Jsy/Home	50.00
J-IS	Ichiro Suzuki/ Jsy/250	75.00
J-IG	Ichiro Suzuki/ Jsy/200	85.00
SJ-I	Ichiro Suzuki/ Jsy/Auto./50	675.00
UB-I	Ichiro Suzuki/Base	25.00
UB-IC	Ichiro Suzuki/ Base/150	80.00
UB-IS	Ichiro Suzuki/ Base/50	100.00
BB-I	Ichiro Suzuki/Ball	60.00
BB-IC	Ichiro Suzuki/ Ball/150	85.00
BB-IS	Ichiro Suzuki/ Ball/50	100.00
SBB-I	Ichiro Suzuki/ Ball/Auto./25	675.00
C-I	Ichiro Suzuki/ Glove/75	180.00
BG-I	Ichiro Suzuki/ Bat/Glove/75	180.00
BG-IG	Ichiro Suzuki/ Bat/Glove/25	

Magic Numbers

		NM/M
Common Player:		10.00
Production 150		
Coppers #'d to 24 not priced.		
Silvers #'d to 20 not priced.		
Golds #'d to 15 not priced.		
RA	Roberto Alomar	20.00
JB	Jeff Bagwell	20.00
BB	Barry Bonds	50.00
JC	Jose Canseco	15.00
RC	Roger Clemens	50.00
CD	Carlos Delgado	15.00
DE	Darin Erstad	10.00
JaG	Jason Giambi	20.00
JG	Juan Gonzalez	15.00

LG	Luis Gonzalez	10.00
SG	Shawn Green	10.00
KG	Ken Griffey Jr.	40.00
TG	Tony Gwynn	20.00
TH	Todd Helton	15.00
RJ	Randy Johnson	15.00
AJ	Andruw Jones	10.00
CJ	Chipper Jones	15.00
GM	Greg Maddux	40.00
MO	Magglio Ordonez	10.00
MP	Mike Piazza	30.00
AP	Albert Pujols	75.00
CR	Cal Ripken Jr.	90.00
AR	Alex Rodriguez	40.00
IR	Ivan Rodriguez	15.00
SR	Scott Rolen	15.00
GS	Gary Sheffield	10.00
SS	Sammy Sosa	40.00
FT	Frank Thomas	15.00
LW	Larry Walker	10.00
BW	Bernie Williams	10.00

Ultimate Signatures

		NM/M
Common Autograph:		20.00
Inserted 1:4		
Silvers #'d to 24 not priced.		
Golds #'d to 15 not priced.		
RA	Roberto Alomar	40.00
EB	Ernie Banks	50.00
BaB	Barry Bonds	200.00
RC	Roger Clemens	100.00
CD	Carlos Delgado	25.00
CF	Carlton Fisk	40.00
JaG	Jason Giambi	25.00
TGl	Tom Glavine	40.00
LG	Luis Gonzalez	25.00
KG	Ken Griffey Jr.	100.00
TG	Tony Gwynn	60.00
RK	Ryan Klesko	20.00
SK	Sandy Koufax	275.00
EM	Edgar Martinez	30.00
HN	Hideo Nomo	
TP	Tony Perez	20.00
KP	Kirby Puckett	50.00
CR	Cal Ripken Jr.	125.00
AR	Alex Rodriguez	80.00
IR	Ivan Rodriguez	50.00
TS	Tom Seaver	40.00
GS	Gary Sheffield	30.00
DS	Duke Snider	35.00
SS	Sammy Sosa	120.00
FT	Frank Thomas	40.00
JT	Jim Thome	50.00
RY	Robin Yount	60.00

2001 Upper Deck Victory

	NM/M
Complete Set (660):	50.00
Common Player:	.15

1	Troy Glaus	.50
2	Scott Spiezio	.15
3	Gary DiSarcina	.15
4	Darin Erstad	.20
5	Tim Salmon	.20
6	Troy Percival	.15
7	Ramon Ortiz	.15
8	Orlando Palmeiro	.15
9	Tim Belcher	.15

No.	Player	Value
10	Mo Vaughn	.15
11	Bengie Molina	.15
12	Benji Gil	.15
13	Scott Schoeneweis	.15
14	Garret Anderson	.15
15	Matt Wise	.15
16	Adam Kennedy	.15
17	Jarrod Washburn	.15
18	Darin Erstad, Troy Percival	.15
19	Jason Giambi	.20
20	Tim Hudson	.20
21	Ramon Hernandez	.15
22	Eric Chavez	.15
23	Gil Heredia	.15
24	Jason Isringhausen	.15
25	Jeremy Giambi	.15
26	Miguel Tejada	.15
27	Barry Zito	.50
28	Terrence Long	.15
29	Ryan Christenson	.15
30	Mark Mulder	.15
31	Olmedo Saenz	.15
32	Adam Piatt	.15
33	Ben Grieve	.20
34	Omar Olivares	.15
35	John Jaha	.15
36	Jason Giambi, Tim Hudson	.15
37	Carlos Delgado	.40
38	Esteban Loaiza	.15
39	Brad Fullmer	.15
40	David Wells	.15
41	Chris Woodward	.15
42	Billy Koch	.15
43	Shannon Stewart	.15
44	Chris Carpenter	.15
45	Steve Parris	.15
46	Darrin Fletcher	.15
47	Joey Hamilton	.15
48	Jose Cruz Jr.	.15
49	Vernon Wells	.15
50	Raul Mondesi	.15
51	Kelvim Escobar	.15
52	Tony Batista	.15
53	Alex Gonzalez	.15
54	Carlos Delgado, David Wells	.20
55	Greg Vaughn	.15
56	Albie Lopez	.15
57	Randy Winn	.15
58	Ryan Rupe	.15
59	Steve Cox	.15
60	Vinny Castilla	.15
61	Jose Guillen	.15
62	Wilson Alvarez	.15
63	Bryan Rekar	.15
64	Gerald Williams	.15
65	Esteban Yan	.15
66	Felix Martinez	.15
67	Fred McGriff	.20
68	John Flaherty	.15
69	Jason Tyner	.15
70	Russ Johnson	.15
71	Roberto Hernandez	.15
72	Greg Vaughn, Albie Lopez	.15
73	Eddie Taubensee	.15
74	Bob Wickman	.15
75	Ellis Burks	.15
76	Kenny Lofton	.20
77	Einar Diaz	.15
78	Travis Fryman	.15
79	Omar Vizquel	.15
80	Jason Bere	.15
81	Bartolo Colon	.15
82	Jim Thome	.20
83	Roberto Alomar	.40
84	Chuck Finley	.15
85	Steve Woodard	.15
86	Russ Branyan	.15
87	Dave Burba	.15
88	Jaret Wright	.15
89	Jacob Cruz	.15
90	Steve Karsay	.15
91	Manny Ramirez, Bartolo Colon	.20
92	Raul Ibanez	.15
93	Freddy Garcia	.15
94	Edgar Martinez	.15
95	Jay Buhner	.15
96	Jamie Moyer	.15
97	John Olerud	.20
98	Aaron Sele	.15
99	Kazuhiro Sasaki	.20
100	Mike Cameron	.15
101	John Halama	.15
102	David Bell	.15
103	Gil Meche	.15
104	Carlos Guillen	.15
105	Mark McLemore	.15
106	Stan Javier	.15
107	Al Martin	.15
108	Dan Wilson	.15
109	Alex Rodriguez, Kazuhiro Sasaki	.50
110	Cal Ripken Jr.	1.50
111	Delino DeShields	.15
112	Sidney Ponson	.15
113	Albert Belle	.15
114	Jose Mercedes	.15
115	Scott Erickson	.15
116	Jerry Hairston Jr.	.15
117	Brook Fordyce	.15
118	Luis Matos	.15
119	Eugene Kingsale	.15
120	Jeff Conine	.15
121	Chris Richard	.15
122	Fernando Lunar	.15
123	John Parrish	.15
124	Brady Anderson	.15
125	Ryan Kohlmeier	.15
126	Melvin Mora	.15
127	Albert Belle, Jose Mercedes	.15
128	Ivan Rodriguez	.50
129	Justin Thompson	.15
130	Kenny Rogers	.15
131	Rafael Palmeiro	.30
132	Rusty Greer	.15
133	Gabe Kapler	.15
134	John Wetteland	.15
135	Mike Lamb	.15
136	Doug Davis	.15
137	Ruben Mateo	.15
138	Alex Rodriguez	1.25
139	Chad Curtis	.15
140	Rick Helling	.15
141	Ryan Glynn	.15
142	Andres Galarraga	.25
143	Ricky Ledee	.15
144	Frank Catalanotto	.15
145	Rafael Palmeiro, Rick Helling	.20
146	Pedro Martinez	.60
147	Wilton Veras	.15
148	Manny Ramirez	.50
149	Rolando Arrojo	.15
150	Nomar Garciaparra	1.00
151	Darren Lewis	.15
152	Troy O'Leary	.15
153	Tomokazu Ohka	.15
154	Carl Everett	.15
155	Jason Varitek	.15
156	Frank Castillo	.15
157	Pete Schourek	.15
158	Jose Offerman	.15
159	Derek Lowe	.15
160	John Valentin	.15
161	Dante Bichette	.15
162	Trot Nixon	.15
163	Nomar Garciaparra, Pedro Martinez	.25
164	Jermaine Dye	.15
165	Dave McCarty	.15
166	Jose Rosado	.15
167	Mike Sweeney	.15
168	Rey Sanchez	.15
169	Jeff Suppan	.15
170	Chad Durbin	.15
171	Carlos Beltran	.15
172	Brian Meadows	.15
173	Todd Dunwoody	.15
174	Johnny Damon	.15
175	Blake Stein	.15
176	Carlos Febles	.15
177	Joe Randa	.15
178	Makoto Suzuki	.15
179	Mark Quinn	.15
180	Gregg Zaun	.15
181	Mike Sweeney, Jeff Suppan	.15
182	Juan Gonzalez	.50
183	Dean Palmer	.15
184	Wendell Magee	.15
185	Todd Jones	.15
186	Bobby Higginson	.15
187	Brian Moehler	.15
188	Juan Encarnacion	.15
189	Tony Clark	.15
190	Rich Becker	.15
191	Roger Cedeno	.15
192	Mitch Meluskey	.15
193	Shane Halter	.15
194	Jeff Weaver	.15
195	Deivi Cruz	.15
196	Damion Easley	.15
197	Robert Fick	.15
198	Matt Anderson	.15
199	Bobby Higginson, Brian Moehler	.15
200	Brad Radke	.15
201	Mark Redman	.15
202	Corey Koskie	.15
203	Matt Lawton	.15
204	Eric Milton	.15
205	Chad Moeller	.15
206	Jacque Jones	.15
207	Matt Kinney	.15
208	Jay Canizaro	.15
209	Torii Hunter	.15
210	Ron Coomer	.15
211	Chad Allen	.15
212	Denny Hocking	.15
213	Cristian Guzman	.15
214	LaTroy Hawkins	.15
215	Joe Mays	.15
216	David Ortiz	.15
217	Matt Lawton, Eric Milton	.15
218	Frank Thomas	.60
219	Jose Valentin	.15
220	Mike Sirotka	.15
221	Kip Wells	.15
222	Magglio Ordonez	.25
223	Herbert Perry	.15
224	James Baldwin	.15
225	Jon Garland	.15
226	Sandy Alomar	.15
227	Chris Singleton	.15
228	Keith Foulke	.15
229	Paul Konerko	.15
230	Jim Parque	.15
231	Greg Norton	.15
232	Carlos Lee	.15
233	Cal Eldred	.15
234	Ray Durham	.15
235	Jeff Abbott	.15
236	Frank Thomas, Mike Sirotka	.20
237	Derek Jeter	1.50
238	Glenallen Hill	.15
239	Roger Clemens	1.00
240	Bernie Williams	.40
241	David Justice	.25
242	Luis Sojo	.15
243	Orlando Hernandez	.20
244	Mike Mussina	.25
245	Jorge Posada	.20
246	Andy Pettitte	.20
247	Paul O'Neill	.20
248	Scott Brosius	.15
249	Alfonso Soriano	.50
250	Mariano Rivera	.20
251	Chuck Knoblauch	.20
252	Ramiro Mendoza	.15
253	Tino Martinez	.15
254	David Cone	.15
255	Derek Jeter, Andy Pettitte	.40
256	Jeff Bagwell	.50
257	Lance Berkman	.15
258	Craig Biggio	.20
259	Scott Elarton	.15
260	Bill Spiers	.15
261	Moises Alou	.15
262	Billy Wagner	.15
263	Shane Reynolds	.15
264	Tony Eusebio	.15
265	Julio Lugo	.15
266	Jose Lima	.15
267	Octavio Dotel	.15
268	Brad Ausmus	.15
269	Daryle Ward	.15
270	Glen Barker	.15
271	Wade Miller	.15
272	Richard Hidalgo	.25
273	Chris Truby	.15
274	Jeff Bagwell, Scott Elarton	.25
275	Greg Maddux	.75
276	Chipper Jones	.75
277	Tom Glavine	.25
278	Brian Jordan	.15
279	Andruw Jones	.40
280	Kevin Millwood	.15
281	Rico Brogna	.15
282	George Lombard	.15
283	Reggie Sanders	.15
284	John Rocker	.15
285	Rafael Furcal	.25
286	John Smoltz	.15
287	Javy Lopez	.15
288	Walt Weiss	.15
289	Quilvio Veras	.15
290	Eddie Perez	.15
291	B.J. Surhoff	.15
292	Chipper Jones, Tom Glavine	.25
293	Jeromy Burnitz	.15
294	Charlie Hayes	.15
295	Jeff D'Amico	.15
296	Jose Hernandez	.15
297	Richie Sexson	.15
298	Tyler Houston	.15
299	Paul Rigdon	.15
300	Jamey Wright	.15
301	Mark Loretta	.15
302	Geoff Jenkins	.20
303	Luis Lopez	.15
304	John Snyder	.15
305	Henry Blanco	.15
306	Curtis Leskanic	.15
307	Ron Belliard	.15
308	Jimmy Haynes	.15
309	Marquis Grissom	.15
310	Geoff Jenkins, Jeff D'Amico	.15
311	Mark McGwire	1.00
312	Rick Ankiel	.20
313	Dave Veres	.15
314	Carlos Hernandez	.15
315	Jim Edmonds	.20
316	Andy Benes	.15
317	Garrett Stephenson	.15
318	Ray Lankford	.15
319	Dustin Hermanson	.15
320	Steve Kline	.15
321	Mike Matheny	.15
322	Edgar Renteria	.15
323	J.D. Drew	.15
324	Craig Paquette	.15
325	Darryl Kile	.15
326	Fernando Vina	.15
327	Eric Davis	.15
328	Placido Polanco	.15
329	Jim Edmonds, Darryl Kile	.15
330	Sammy Sosa	1.00
331	Rick Aguilera	.15
332	Willie Greene	.15
333	Kerry Wood	.20
334	Todd Hundley	.15
335	Rondell White	.20
336	Julio Zuleta	.15
337	Jon Lieber	.15
338	Joe Girardi	.15
339	Damon Buford	.15
340	Kevin Tapani	.15
341	Ricky Gutierrez	.15
342	Bill Mueller	.15
343	Ruben Quevedo	.15
344	Eric Young	.15
345	Gary Matthews Jr.	.15
346	Daniel Garibay	.15
347	Sammy Sosa, Jon Lieber	.30
348	Randy Johnson	.50
349	Matt Williams	.20
350	Kelly Stinnett	.15
351	Brian Anderson	.15
352	Steve Finley	.15
353	Curt Schilling	.20
354	Erubiel Durazo	.15
355	Todd Stottlemyre	.15
356	Mark Grace	.20
357	Luis Gonzalez	.20
358	Danny Bautista	.15
359	Matt Mantei	.15
360	Tony Womack	.15
361	Armando Reynoso	.15
362	Greg Colbrunn	.15
363	Jay Bell	.15
364	Byung-Hyun Kim	.15
365	Luis Gonzalez, Randy Johnson	.20
366	Gary Sheffield	.20
367	Eric Karros	.15
368	Jeff Shaw	.15
369	Jim Leyritz	.15
370	Kevin Brown	.20
371	Alex Cora	.15
372	Andy Ashby	.15
373	Eric Gagne	.15
374	Chan Ho Park	.15
375	Shawn Green	.20
376	Kevin Elster	.15
377	Mark Grudzielanek	.15
378	Darren Dreifort	.15
379	Dave Hansen	.15
380	Bruce Aven	.15
381	Adrian Beltre	.20
382	Tom Goodwin	.15
383	Gary Sheffield, Chan Ho Park	.15
384	Vladimir Guerrero	.60
385	Ugueth Urbina	.15
386	Michael Barrett	.15
387	Geoff Blum	.15
388	Fernando Tatis	.15
389	Carl Pavano	.15
390	Jose Vidro	.15
391	Orlando Cabrera	.15
392	Terry Jones	.15
393	Mike Thurman	.15
394	Lee Stevens	.15
395	Tony Armas Jr.	.15
396	Wilton Guerrero	.15
397	Peter Bergeron	.15
398	Milton Bradley	.15
399	Javier Vazquez	.15
400	Fernando Seguignol	.15
401	Vladimir Guerrero, Dustin Hermanson	.25
402	Barry Bonds	.60
403	Russ Ortiz	.15
404	Calvin Murray	.15

405	Armando Rios	.15
406	Livan Hernandez	.15
407	Jeff Kent	.20
408	Bobby Estalella	.15
409	Felipe Crespo	.15
410	Shawn Estes	.15
411	J.T. Snow	.15
412	Marvin Benard	.15
413	Joe Nathan	.15
414	Robb Nen	.15
415	Shawon Dunston	.15
416	Mark Gardner	.15
417	Kirk Rueter	.15
418	Rich Aurilia	.15
419	Doug Mirabelli	.15
420	Russ Davis	.15
421	Barry Bonds, Livan Hernandez	.30
422	Cliff Floyd	.15
423	Luis Castillo	.15
424	Antonio Alfonseca	.15
425	Preston Wilson	.15
426	Ryan Dempster	.15
427	Jesus Sanchez	.15
428	Derrek Lee	.15
429	Brad Penny	.15
430	Mark Kotsay	.15
431	Alex Fernandez	.15
432	Mike Lowell	.15
433	Chuck Smith	.15
434	Alex Gonzalez	.15
435	Dave Berg	.15
436	A.J. Burnett	.15
437	Charles Johnson	.15
438	Reid Cornelius	.15
439	Mike Redmond	.15
440	Preston Wilson, Ryan Dempster	.15
441	Mike Piazza	.75
442	Kevin Appier	.15
443	Jay Payton	.15
444	Steve Trachsel	.15
445	Al Leiter	.20
446	Joe McEwing	.15
447	Armando Benitez	.15
448	Edgardo Alfonzo	.15
449	Glendon Rusch	.15
450	Mike Bordick	.15
451	Lenny Harris	.15
452	Matt Franco	.15
453	Darryl Hamilton	.15
454	Bobby J. Jones	.15
455	Robin Ventura	.15
456	Todd Zeile	.15
457	John Franco	.15
458	Mike Piazza, Al Leiter	.40
459	Tony Gwynn	.75
460	John Mabry	.15
461	Trevor Hoffman	.15
462	Phil Nevin	.15
463	Ryan Klesko	.15
464	Wiki Gonzalez	.15
465	Matt Clement	.15
466	Alex Arias	.15
467	Woody Williams	.15
468	Ruben Rivera	.15
469	Sterling Hitchcock	.15
470	Ben Davis	.15
471	Bubba Trammell	.15
472	Jay Witasick	.15
473	Eric Owens	.15
474	Damian Jackson	.15
475	Adam Eaton	.15
476	Mike Darr	.15
477	Phil Nevin, Trevor Hoffman	.15
478	Scott Rolen	.25
479	Robert Person	.15
480	Mike Lieberthal	.15
481	Reggie Taylor	.15
482	Paul Byrd	.15
483	Bruce Chen	.15
484	Pat Burrell	.25
485	Kevin Jordan	.15
486	Bobby Abreu	.15
487	Randy Wolf	.15
488	Kevin Sefcik	.15
489	Brian Hunter	.15
490	Doug Glanville	.15
491	Kent Bottenfield	.15
492	Travis Lee	.15
493	Jeff Brantley	.15
494	Omar Daal	.15
495	Bobby Abreu, Randy Wolf	.15
496	Jason Kendall	.15
497	Adrian Brown	.15
498	Warren Morris	.15
499	Brian Giles	.20
500	Jimmy Anderson	.15
501	John Vander Wal	.15
502	Mike Williams	.15
503	Aramis Ramirez	.15
504	Pat Meares	.15
505	Jason Schmidt	.15
506	Todd Ritchie	.15
507	Abraham Nunez	.15
508	Jose Silva	.15
509	Francisco Cordova	.15
510	Kevin Young	.15
511	Derek Bell	.15
512	Kris Benson	.15
513	Brian Giles, Jose Silva	.15
514	Ken Griffey Jr.	1.00
515	Scott Williamson	.15
516	Dmitri Young	.15
517	Sean Casey	.20
518	Barry Larkin	.25
519	Juan Castro	.15
520	Danny Graves	.15
521	Aaron Boone	.15
522	Pokey Reese	.15
523	Elmer Dessens	.15
524	Michael Tucker	.15
525	Benito Santiago	.15
526	Pete Harnisch	.15
527	Alex Ochoa	.15
528	Gookie Dawkins	.15
529	Seth Etherton	.15
530	Rob Bell	.15
531	Ken Griffey Jr., Steve Parris	.50
532	Todd Helton	.50
533	Jose Jimenez	.15
534	Todd Walker	.15
535	Ron Gant	.15
536	Neifi Perez	.15
537	Butch Huskey	.15
538	Pedro Astacio	.15
539	Juan Pierre	.15
540	Jeff Cirillo	.15
541	Ben Petrick	.15
542	Brian Bohanon	.15
543	Larry Walker	.25
544	Masato Yoshii	.15
545	Denny Neagle	.15
546	Brent Mayne	.15
547	Mike Hampton	.20
548	Todd Hollandsworth	.15
549	Brian Rose	.15
550	Todd Helton, Pedro Astacio	.20
551	Jason Hart	.15
552	Joe Crede	.15
553	Timoniel Perez	.15
554	Brady Clark	.15
555	Adam Pettyjohn RC	.15
556	Jason Grilli	.15
557	Paxton Crawford	.15
558	Jay Spurgeon	.15
559	Hector Ortiz	.15
560	Vernon Wells	.15
561	Aubrey Huff	.15
562	Xavier Nady	.25
563	Billy McMillon	.15
564	Ichiro Suzuki RC	8.00
565	Tomas de la Rosa	.15
566	Matt Ginter	.15
567	Sun-Woo Kim	.15
568	Nick Johnson	.15
569	Pablo Ozuna	.15
570	Tike Redman	.15
571	Brian Cole	.15
572	Ross Gload	.15
573	Dee Brown	.15
574	Tony McKnight	.15
575	Allen Levrault	.15
576	Lesli Brea	.15
577	Adam Bernero	.15
578	Tom Davey	.15
579	Morgan Burkhart	.15
580	Britt Reames	.15
581	Dave Coggin	.15
582	Trey Moore	.15
583	Matt Kinney	.15
584	Pedro Feliz	.15
585	Brandon Inge	.15
586	Alex Hernandez	.15
587	Toby Hall	.15
588	Grant Roberts	.15
589	Brian Sikorski	.15
590	Aaron Myette	.15
591	Derek Jeter	1.00
592	Ivan Rodriguez	.40
593	Alex Rodriguez	.75
594	Carlos Delgado	.30
595	Mark McGwire	.75
596	Troy Glaus	.40
597	Sammy Sosa	.75
598	Vladimir Guerrero	.50
599	Manny Ramirez	.40
600	Pedro J. Martinez	.50
601	Chipper Jones	.75
602	Jason Giambi	.20
603	Frank Thomas	.50
604	Ken Griffey Jr.	.75
605	Nomar Garciaparra	.75
606	Randy Johnson	.40
607	Mike Piazza	.75
608	Barry Bonds	.50
609	Todd Helton	.40
610	Jeff Bagwell	.40
611	Ken Griffey Jr.	.75
612	Carlos Delgado	.40
613	Jeff Bagwell	.40
614	Jason Giambi	.20
615	Cal Ripken Jr.	1.00
616	Brian Giles	.15
617	Bernie Williams	.30
618	Greg Maddux	.75
619	Troy Glaus	.40
620	Greg Vaughn	.15
621	Sammy Sosa	.75
622	Pat Burrell	.20
623	Ivan Rodriguez	.40
624	Chipper Jones	.75
625	Barry Bonds	.50
626	Roger Clemens	.50
627	Jim Edmonds	.15
628	Nomar Garciaparra	.75
629	Frank Thomas	.50
630	Mike Piazza	.75
631	Randy Johnson	.40
632	Andruw Jones	.30
633	David Wells	.15
634	Manny Ramirez	.40
635	Preston Wilson	.15
636	Todd Helton	.40
637	Kerry Wood	.15
638	Albert Belle	.15
639	Juan Gonzalez	.40
640	Vladimir Guerrero	.50
641	Gary Sheffield	.15
642	Larry Walker	.15
643	Magglio Ordonez	.15
644	Jermaine Dye	.15
645	Scott Rolen	.20
646	Tony Gwynn	.50
647	Shawn Green	.15
648	Roberto Alomar	.30
649	Eric Milton	.15
650	Mark McGwire	.75
651	Tim Hudson	.15
652	Jose Canseco	.20
653	Tom Glavine	.20
654	Derek Jeter	1.00
655	Alex Rodriguez	.75
656	Darin Erstad	.15
657	Jason Kendall	.15
658	Pedro Martinez	.50
659	Richie Sexson	.15
660	Rafael Palmeiro	.20

2001 Upper Deck Vintage

IVAN RODRIGUEZ
TEXAS RANGERS C

		NM/M
Complete Set (400):		30.00
Common Player:		.10
Pack (10):		2.00
Box (24):		40.00
1	Darin Erstad	.25
2	Seth Etherton	.10
3	Troy Glaus	.50
4	Bengie Molina	.10
5	Mo Vaughn	.20
6	Tim Salmon	.25
7	Ramon Ortiz	.10
8	Adam Kennedy	.10
9	Garret Anderson	.25
10	Troy Percival	.10
11	2000 Angels Lineup	.10
12	Jason Giambi	.50
13	Tim Hudson	.25
14	Adam Piatt	.10
15	Miguel Tejada	.25
16	Mark Mulder	.25
17	Eric Chavez	.25
18	Ramon Hernandez	.10
19	Terrence Long	.10
20	Jason Isringhausen	.10
21	Barry Zito	.50
22	Ben Grieve	.10
23	2000 Athletics Lineup	.10
24	David Wells	.10
25	Raul Mondesi	.20
26	Darrin Fletcher	.10
27	Shannon Stewart	.10
28	Kelvim Escobar	.10
29	Tony Batista	.10
30	Carlos Delgado	.50
31	Brad Fullmer	.10
32	Billy Koch	.10
33	Jose Cruz Jr.	.10
34	2000 Blue Jays Lineup	.10
35	Greg Vaughn	.10
36	Roberto Hernandez	.10
37	Vinny Castilla	.10
38	Gerald Williams	.10
39	Aubrey Huff	.10
40	Bryan Rekar	.10
41	Albie Lopez	.10
42	Fred McGriff	.25
43	Miguel Cairo	.10
44	Ryan Rupe	.10
45	2000 Devil Rays Lineup	.10
46	Jim Thome	.50
47	Roberto Alomar	.50
48	Bartolo Colon	.25
49	Omar Vizquel	.20
50	Travis Fryman	.20
51	Manny Ramirez	.50
52	Dave Burba	.10
53	Chuck Finley	.10
54	Russ Branyan	.10
55	Kenny Lofton	.25
56	2000 Indians Lineup	.10
57	Alex Rodriguez	1.50
58	Jay Buhner	.10
59	Aaron Sele	.10
60	Kazuhiro Sasaki	.20
61	Edgar Martinez	.20
62	John Halama	.10
63	Mike Cameron	.10
64	Fred Garcia	.10
65	John Olerud	.20
66	Jamie Moyer	.10
67	Gil Meche	.10
68	2000 Mariners Lineup	.10
69	Cal Ripken Jr.	2.00
70	Sidney Ponson	.10
71	Chris Richard	.10
72	Jose Mercedes	.10
73	Albert Belle	.15
74	Mike Mussina	.50
75	Brady Anderson	.15
76	Delino DeShields	.10
77	Melvin Mora	.10
78	Luis Matos	.10
79	Brook Fordyce	.10
80	2000 Orioles Lineup	.10
81	Rafael Palmeiro	.50
82	Rick Helling	.10
83	Ruben Mateo	.10
84	Rusty Greer	.10
85	Ivan Rodriguez	.50
86	Doug Davis	.10
87	Gabe Kapler	.15
88	Mike Lamb	.10
89	Alex Rodriguez	1.50
90	Kenny Rogers	.10
91	2000 Rangers Lineup	.10
92	Nomar Garciaparra	1.50
93	Trot Nixon	.10
94	Tomokazu Ohka	.10
95	Pedro Martinez	.75
96	Dante Bichette	.10
97	Jason Varitek	.10
98	Rolando Arrojo	.10
99	Carl Everett	.10
100	Derek Lowe	.10
101	Troy O'Leary	.10
102	Tim Wakefield	.10
103	2000 Red Sox Lineup	.10
104	Mike Sweeney	.10
105	Carlos Febles	.10
106	Joe Randa	.10
107	Jeff Suppan	.10
108	Mac Suzuki	.10
109	Jermaine Dye	.10
110	Carlos Beltran	.25
111	Mark Quinn	.10
112	Johnny Damon	.20
113	2000 Royals Lineup	.10
114	Tony Clark	.10
115	Dean Palmer	.10
116	Brian Moehler	.10
117	Brad Ausmus	.10
118	Juan Gonzalez	.50
119	Juan Encarnacion	.10
120	Jeff Weaver	.10
121	Bobby Higginson	.10
122	Todd Jones	.10
123	Deivi Cruz	.10
124	2000 Tigers Lineup	.10
125	Corey Koskie	.10
126	Matt Lawton	.10
127	Mark Redman	.10
128	David Ortiz	.10
129	Jay Canizaro	.10

130	Eric Milton	.10
131	Jacque Jones	.10
132	J.C. Romero	.10
133	Ron Coomer	.10
134	Brad Radke	.10
135	2000 Twins Lineup	.10
136	Carlos Lee	.10
137	Frank Thomas	.75
138	Mike Sirotka	.10
139	Charles Johnson	.10
140	James Baldwin	.10
141	Magglio Ordonez	.25
142	Jon Garland	.10
143	Paul Konerko	.10
144	Ray Durham	.10
145	Keith Foulke	.10
146	Chris Singleton	.10
147	2000 White Sox Lineup	.10
148	Bernie Williams	.50
149	Orlando Hernandez	.15
150	David Justice	.25
151	Andy Pettitte	.25
152	Mariano Rivera	.25
153	Derek Jeter	2.00
154	Jorge Posada	.25
155	Jose Canseco	.50
156	Glenallen Hill	.10
157	Paul O'Neill	.25
158	Denny Neagle	.10
159	Chuck Knoblauch	.10
160	Roger Clemens	1.50
161	2000 Yankees Lineup	.10
162	Jeff Bagwell	.50
163	Moises Alou	.20
164	Lance Berkman	.40
165	Shane Reynolds	.10
166	Ken Caminiti	.10
167	Craig Biggio	.25
168	Jose Lima	.10
169	Octavio Dotel	.10
170	Richard Hidalgo	.20
171	Scott Elarton	.10
172	2000 Astros Lineup	.10
173	Rafael Furcal	.25
174	Greg Maddux	1.00
175	Quilvio Veras	.10
176	Chipper Jones	1.00
177	Andres Galarraga	.25
178	Brian Jordan	.10
179	Tom Glavine	.25
180	Kevin Millwood	.25
181	Javier Lopez	.25
182	B.J. Surhoff	.10
183	Andruw Jones	.50
184	Andy Ashby	.10
185	2000 Braves Lineup	.10
186	Richie Sexson	.40
187	Jeff D'Amico	.10
188	Ron Belliard	.10
189	Jeromy Burnitz	.10
190	Jimmy Haynes	.10
191	Marquis Grissom	.10
192	Jose Hernandez	.10
193	Geoff Jenkins	.20
194	Jamey Wright	.10
195	Mark Loretta	.10
196	2000 Brewers Lineup	.10
197	Rick Ankiel	.10
198	Mark McGwire	1.50
199	Fernando Vina	.10
200	David Renteria	.10
201	Darryl Kile	.10
202	Jim Edmonds	.25
203	Ray Lankford	.10
204	Garrett Stephenson	.10
205	Fernando Tatis	.10
206	Will Clark	.40
207	J.D. Drew	.15
208	2000 Cardinals Lineup	.10
209	Mark Grace	.25
210	Eric Young	.10
211	Sammy Sosa	1.50
212	Jon Lieber	.10
213	Joe Girardi	.10
214	Kevin Tapani	.10
215	Ricky Gutierrez	.10
216	Kerry Wood	.50
217	Rondell White	.10
218	Damon Buford	.10
219	2000 Cubs Lineup	.10
220	Luis Gonzalez	.25
221	Randy Johnson	.75
222	Jay Bell	.10
223	Erubiel Durazo	.10
224	Matt Williams	.25
225	Steve Finley	.10
226	Curt Schilling	.40
227	Todd Stottlemyre	.10
228	Tony Womack	.10
229	Brian Anderson	.10
230	2000 Diamondbacks Lineup	.10
231	Gary Sheffield	.40
232	Adrian Beltre	.25

233	Todd Hundley	.10
234	Chan Ho Park	.10
235	Shawn Green	.25
236	Kevin Brown	.25
237	Tom Goodwin	.10
238	Mark Grudzielanek	.10
239	Ismael Valdes	.10
240	Eric Karros	.10
241	2000 Dodgers Lineup	.10
242	Jose Vidro	.10
243	Javier Vazquez	.20
244	Orlando Cabrera	.10
245	Peter Bergeron	.10
246	Vladimir Guerrero	.75
247	Dustin Hermanson	.10
248	Tony Armas Jr.	.10
249	Lee Stevens	.10
250	Milton Bradley	.10
251	Carl Pavano	.10
252	2000 Expos Lineup	.10
253	Ellis Burks	.10
254	Robb Nen	.10
255	J.T. Snow	.10
256	Barry Bonds	2.00
257	Shawn Estes	.10
258	Jeff Kent	.20
259	Kirk Rueter	.10
260	Bill Mueller	.10
261	Livan Hernandez	.10
262	Rich Aurilia	.10
263	2000 Giants Lineup	.10
264	Ryan Dempster	.10
265	Cliff Floyd	.10
266	Mike Lowell	.10
267	A.J. Burnett	.10
268	Preston Wilson	.10
269	Luis Castillo	.10
270	Henry Rodriguez	.10
271	Antonio Alfonseca	.10
272	Derek Lee	.10
273	Mark Kotsay	.10
274	Brad Penny	.10
275	2000 Marlins Lineup	.10
276	Mike Piazza	1.00
277	Jay Payton	.10
278	Al Leiter	.15
279	Mike Bordick	.10
280	Armando Benitez	.10
281	Todd Zeile	.10
282	Mike Hampton	.20
283	Edgardo Alfonzo	.10
284	Derek Bell	.10
285	Robin Ventura	.20
286	2000 Mets Lineup	.10
287	Tony Gwynn	.75
288	Trevor Hoffman	.10
289	Ryan Klesko	.20
290	Phil Nevin	.10
291	Matt Clement	.10
292	Ben Davis	.10
293	Ruben Rivera	.10
294	Bret Boone	.25
295	Adam Eaton	.10
296	Eric Owens	.10
297	2000 Padres Lineup	.10
298	Bob Abreu	.20
299	Mike Lieberthal	.10
300	Robert Person	.10
301	Scott Rolen	.50
302	Randy Wolf	.10
303	Bruce Chen	.10
304	Travis Lee	.10
305	Kent Bottenfield	.10
306	Pat Burrell	.50
307	Doug Glanville	.10
308	2000 Phillies Lineup	.10
309	Brian Giles	.25
310	Todd Ritchie	.10
311	Warren Morris	.10
312	John Vander Wal	.10
313	Kris Benson	.10
314	Jason Kendall	.10
315	Kevin Young	.10
316	Francisco Cordova	.10
317	Jimmy Anderson	.10
318	2000 Pirates Lineup	.10
319	Ken Griffey Jr.	1.00
320	Pokey Reese	.10
321	Chris Stynes	.10
322	Barry Larkin	.40
323	Steve Parris	.10
324	Michael Tucker	.10
325	Dmitri Young	.10
326	Pete Harnisch	.10
327	Adam Graves	.10
328	Aaron Boone	.10
329	Sean Casey	.10
330	2000 Reds Lineup	.10
331	Todd Helton	.50
332	Pedro Astacio	.10
333	Larry Walker	.25
334	Ben Petrick	.10
335	Brian Bohanon	.10
336	Juan Pierre	.10

337	Jeffrey Hammonds	.10
338	Jeff Cirillo	.10
339	Todd Hollandsworth	.10
340	2000 Rockies Lineup	.10
341	Matt Wise, Keith Luuloa, Derrick Turnbow	.10
342	Jason Hart, Jose Ortiz, Mario Encarnacion	.10
343	Vernon Wells, Pascual Coco, Josh Phelps	.25
344	Travis Harper, Kenny Kelley, Toby Hall	.10
345	Danys Baez, Tim Drew, Martin Vargas RC	.10
346	Ichiro Suzuki, Ryan Franklin, Ryan Christianson	10.00
347	Jay Spurgeon, Lesli Brea, Carlos Casimiro	.10
348	B.J. Waszgis, Brian Sikorski, Joaquin Benoit	.10
349	Sun-Woo Kim, Paxton Crawford, Steve Lomasney	.10
350	Kris Wilson, Orber Moreno, Dee Brown	.10
351	Mark Johnson, Brandon Inge, Adam Bernero	.10
352	Danny Ardoin, Matt Kinney, Jason Ryan	.10
353	Rocky Biddle, Joe Crede, Aaron Myette	.10
354	Nick Johnson, D'Angelo Jimenez, Willi Mo Pena	.10
355	Tony McKnight, Aaron McNeal, Keith Ginter	.10
356	Mark DeRosa, Jason Marquis, Wes Helms	.10
357	Allen Levrault, Horacio Estrada, Santiago Perez	.10
358	Luis Saturria, Gene Stechschulte, Britt Reames	.10
359	Joey Nation, Corey Patterson, Cole Liniak	.25
360	Alex Cabrera, Geraldo Guzman, Nelson Figueroa	.10
361	Hiram Bocachica, Mike Judd, Luke Prokopec	.10
362	Tomas de la Rosa, Yohanny Valera, Talmadge Nunnari	.10
363	Ryan Vogelsong, Juan Melo, Chad Zerbe	.10
364	Jason Grilli, Pablo Ozuna, Ramon Castro	.10
365	Timoniel Perez, Grant Roberts, Brian Cole	.10
366	Tom Davey, Xavier Nady, Dave Maurer	.50
367	Jimmy Rollins, Mark Brownson, Reggie Taylor	.25
368	Alex Hernandez, Adam Hyzdu, Tike Redman	.10
369	Brady Clark, John Riedling, Mike Bell	.10
370	Giovanni Carrara, Josh Kalinowski, Elvis Pena	.10
371	Jim Edmonds	.10
372	Edgar Martinez	.10
373	Rickey Henderson	.10
374	Barry Zito	.25
375	Tino Martinez	.10
376	J.T. Snow	.10
377	Bobby Jones	.10
378	Alex Rodriguez	1.00
379	Mike Hampton	.10
380	Roger Clemens	.50
381	Jay Payton	.10
382	John Olerud	.10
383	David Justice	.25
384	Mike Hampton	.10
385	Yankees Celebrate	.75
386	Jose Vizcaino	.10
387	Roger Clemens	.75
388	Todd Zeile	.10
389	Derek Jeter	1.25
390	Yankees Celebrate	.50
391	Nomar Garciaparra - AL Batting	.75

392	Todd Helton - NL Batting	.25
393	Troy Glaus - AL HR	.25
394	Sammy Sosa - NL HR	.50
395	Edgar Martinez - AL RBI	.10
396	Todd Helton - NL RBI	.25
397	Pedro Martinez - AL ERA	.40
398	Kevin Brown - NL ERA	.10
399	David Wells, Tim Hudson - AL Wins	.10
400	Tom Glavine - NL Wins	.10

All-Star Tributes

		NM/M
Complete Set (10):		20.00
Common Player:		1.00
Inserted 1:23		
1	Derek Jeter	4.00
2	Mike Piazza	2.00
3	Carlos Delgado	1.00
4	Pedro Martinez	1.50
5	Vladimir Guerrero	1.50
6	Mark McGwire	3.00
7	Alex Rodriguez	3.00
8	Barry Bonds	4.00
9	Chipper Jones	2.00
10	Sammy Sosa	2.50

Fantasy Outfield Combo Jersey

		NM/M
Production 25 Cards		
FO-CJ	Joe DiMaggio, Mickey Mantle, Ken Griffey Jr.	1,000

Glory Days

		NM/M
Complete Set (15):		15.00
Common Player:		.50
Inserted 1:15		
1	Jermaine Dye	.50
2	Chipper Jones	2.00
3	Todd Helton	1.00
4	Magglio Ordonez	.75
5	Tony Gwynn	1.50
6	Jim Edmonds	.75
7	Rafael Palmeiro	1.00
8	Barry Bonds	4.00
9	Carl Everett	.50
10	Mike Piazza	2.00
11	Brian Giles	.50
12	Tony Batista	.50
13	Jeff Bagwell	1.00
14	Ken Griffey Jr.	2.00
15	Troy Glaus	1.00

Mantle Pinstripes Exclusive

	NM/M
Complete Set (56):	75.00
Common Mantle:	2.00
One Pack/Box	

Mantle Pinstripes Memorabilia

		NM/M
Print runs listed:		
MMB	Mickey Mantle/Bat/100	100.00
MMCJ	Mickey Mantle, Roger Maris/Jsy/50	300.00
MMJ	Mickey Mantle/Jsy/100	125.00

Matinee Idols

	NM/M
Complete Set (20):	10.00
Common Player:	.50
Inserted 1:4	
1 Ken Griffey Jr.	1.00
2 Derek Jeter	2.00
3 Barry Bonds	2.00
4 Chipper Jones	1.00
5 Mike Piazza	1.00
6 Todd Helton	.50
7 Randy Johnson	.75
8 Alex Rodriguez	1.50
9 Sammy Sosa	1.50
10 Cal Ripken Jr.	2.00
11 Nomar Garciaparra	1.50
12 Carlos Delgado	.50
13 Jason Giambi	.50
14 Ivan Rodriguez	.50
15 Vladimir Guerrero	.75
16 Gary Sheffield	.50
17 Frank Thomas	.50
18 Jeff Bagwell	.50
19 Pedro Martinez	.75
20 Mark McGwire	1.50

Retro Rules

	NM/M
Complete Set (15):	20.00
Common Player:	.50
Inserted 1:15	
1 Nomar Garciaparra	3.00
2 Frank Thomas	1.00
3 Jeff Bagwell	1.00
4 Sammy Sosa	2.50
5 Derek Jeter	4.00
6 David Wells	.50
7 Vladimir Guerrero	1.50
8 Jim Thome	1.00

9	Mark McGwire	3.00
10	Todd Helton	1.00
11	Tony Gwynn	1.50
12	Bernie Williams	.75
13	Cal Ripken Jr.	4.00
14	Brian Giles	.75
15	Jason Giambi	1.50

Timeless Teams Bat

	NM/M
Common Player:	8.00
Inserted 1:72	
NYY-JD Joe DiMaggio	150.00
NYY-TH Tommy Henrich	8.00
NYY-CK Charlie Keller	8.00
NYY-BD Bill Dickey	20.00
BK-JR Jackie Robinson	90.00
BK-RC Roy Campanella	50.00
BK-GH Gil Hodges	25.00
BK-DN Don Newcombe	8.00
LA-SG Steve Garvey	8.00
LA-RC Ron Cey	8.00
LA-BR Bill Russell	8.00
LA-DB Dusty Baker	8.00
BA-BP Boog Powell	8.00
BA-BR Brooks Robinson	25.00
BA-FR Frank Robinson	20.00
BA-MB Mark Belanger	8.00
PI-RC Roberto Clemente	100.00
PI-WS Willie Stargell	8.00
PI-MS Manny Sanguillen	8.00
PI-AO Al Oliver	8.00
OA-RJ Reggie Jackson	20.00
OA-SB Sal Bando	8.00
OA-GT Gene Tenace	8.00
OA-JR Joe Rudi	8.00
CI2-JB Johnny Bench	25.00
CI2-TP Tony Perez	15.00
CI2-JM Joe Morgan	8.00
CI2-KG Ken Griffey Sr.	8.00
NYM-NR Nolan Ryan	40.00
NYM-RS Ron Swoboda	8.00
NYM-EK Ed Kranepool	8.00
NYM-TA Tommie Agee	8.00

Timeless Teams Jersey

	NM/M
Common Player:	15.00
Inserted 1:288	
NYY-MM Mickey Mantle	160.00
NYY-RM Roger Maris	50.00
NYY-BR Bobby Richardson	15.00
CI-DC Dave Concepcion	15.00
CI-TP Tony Perez	20.00
CI-KG Ken Griffey Sr.	15.00
CI-JM Joe Morgan	20.00

Timeless Teams Combo Bat

	NM/M
Common Card:	75.00
Production 100 Sets	

NYY41	Joe DiMaggio, Tommy Henrich, Bill Dickey, Charlie Keller	200.00
BKN55	Jackie Robinson, Roy Campanella, Gil Hodges, Don Newcombe	175.00
BAL70	Frank Robinson, Brooks Robinson, Mark Belanger, Boog Powell	120.00
LA81	Steve Garvey, Ron Cey, Dusty Baker, Bill Russell	75.00
PIT71	Roberto Clemente, Willie Stargell, Bill Mazeroski, Al Oliver	200.00
OAK72	Reggie Jackson, Sal Bando, Gene Tenace, Joe Rudi	80.00
CIN75	Johnny Bench, Tony Perez, Joe Morgan, Ken Griffey Sr.	120.00
NYM69	Nolan Ryan, Ron Swoboda, Ed Kranepool, Tommie Agee	200.00

Timeless Teams Combo Jersey

	NM/M
Production 100 Sets	
NYY61 Mickey Mantle, Roger Maris, Bobby Richardson	250.00
CIN75 Dave Concepcion, Tony Perez, Ken Griffey Sr.	120.00

2001 UD Reserve

	NM/M
Common Player:	.15
Common SP (181-210):	3.00
Production 2,500	
Pack (5):	3.00
Box (24):	60.00
1 Darin Erstad	.25
2 Tim Salmon	.25
3 Bengie Molina	.15
4 Troy Glaus	.50
5 Glenallen Hill	.15
6 Garret Anderson	.25
7 Jason Giambi	.50
8 Johnny Damon	.25
9 Eric Chavez	.25
10 Tim Hudson	.25
11 Miguel Tejada	.25
12 Barry Zito	.25
13 Jose Ortiz	.15
14 Tony Batista	.15
15 Carlos Delgado	.50
16 Shannon Stewart	.15
17 Raul Mondesi	.15
18 Ben Grieve	.15
19 Aubrey Huff	.15
20 Greg Vaughn	.15

21	Fred McGriff	.25
22	Gerald Williams	.15
23	Bartolo Colon	.25
24	Roberto Alomar	.40
25	Jim Thome	.50
26	Omar Vizquel	.25
27	Juan Gonzalez	.50
28	Ellis Burks	.15
29	Edgar Martinez	.25
30	Aaron Sele	.15
31	Jay Buhner	.15
32	Mike Cameron	.15
33	Kazuhiro Sasaki	.15
34	John Olerud	.25
35	Cal Ripken Jr.	2.00
36	Brady Anderson	.15
37	Pat Hentgen	.15
38	Chris Richard	.15
39	Jerry Hairston Jr.	.15
40	Mike Bordick	.15
41	Ivan Rodriguez	.50
42	Rick Helling	.15
43	Rafael Palmeiro	.25
44	Alex Rodriguez	1.50
45	Andres Galarraga	.25
46	Rusty Greer	.15
47	Ruben Mateo	.15
48	Ken Caminiti	.15
49	Nomar Garciaparra	1.50
50	Pedro Martinez	.75
51	Manny Ramirez	.50
52	Carl Everett	.15
53	Dante Bichette	.15
54	Hideo Nomo	.40
55	Mike Sweeney	.15
56	Carlos Beltran	.25
57	Jeff Suppan	.15
58	Jermaine Dye	.15
59	Mark Quinn	.15
60	Joe Randa	.15
61	Bobby Higginson	.15
62	Tony Clark	.15
63	Brian Moehler	.15
64	Dean Palmer	.15
65	Brandon Inge	.15
66	Damion Easley	.15
67	Brad Radke	.15
68	Corey Koskie	.15
69	Cristian Guzman	.15
70	Eric Milton	.15
71	Jacque Jones	.15
72	Matt Lawton	.15
73	Frank Thomas	.50
74	David Wells	.15
75	Magglio Ordonez	.25
76	Paul Konerko	.15
77	Sandy Alomar Jr.	.15
78	Ray Durham	.15
79	Roger Clemens	1.50
80	Bernie Williams	.50
81	Derek Jeter	2.00
82	David Justice	.25
83	Paul O'Neill	.25
84	Mike Mussina	.40
85	Jorge Posada	.40
86	Jeff Bagwell	.50
87	Richard Hidalgo	.15
88	Craig Biggio	.25
89	Scott Elarton	.15
90	Moises Alou	.25
91	Greg Maddux	1.00
92	Rafael Furcal	.25
93	Andruw Jones	.50
94	Tom Glavine	.25
95	Chipper Jones	1.00
96	Javy Lopez	.25
97	Richie Sexson	.40
98	Jeromy Burnitz	.15
99	Jeff D'Amico	.15
100	Jeffrey Hammonds	.15
101	Geoff Jenkins	.25
102	Ben Sheets	.25
103	Mark McGwire	1.50
104	Rick Ankiel	.15
105	Darryl Kile	.15
106	Edgar Renteria	.15
107	Jim Edmonds	.25
108	J.D. Drew	.25
109	Sammy Sosa	1.50
110	Corey Patterson	.25
111	Kerry Wood	.50
112	Todd Hundley	.15
113	Rondell White	.15
114	Matt Stairs	.15
115	Randy Johnson	.75
116	Mark Grace	.40
117	Steve Finley	.15
118	Luis Gonzalez	.25
119	Matt Williams	.25
120	Curt Schilling	.40
121	Gary Sheffield	.40
122	Kevin Brown	.25
123	Shawn Green	.25
124	Eric Karros	.15

125	Chan Ho Park	.15
126	Adrian Beltre	.25
127	Vladimir Guerrero	.75
128	Fernando Tatis	.15
129	Lee Stevens	.15
130	Jose Vidro	.15
131	Peter Bergeron	.15
132	Michael Barrett	.15
133	Jeff Kent	.25
134	Russ Ortiz	.15
135	Barry Bonds	2.00
136	J.T. Snow	.15
137	Livan Hernandez	.15
138	Rich Aurilia	.15
139	Preston Wilson	.15
140	Mike Lowell	.15
141	Ryan Dempster	.15
142	Charles Johnson	.15
143	Matt Clement	.15
144	Luis Castillo	.15
145	Mike Piazza	1.00
146	Al Leiter	.15
147	Robin Ventura	.25
148	Jay Payton	.15
149	Todd Zeile	.15
150	Edgardo Alfonzo	.15
151	Tony Gwynn	.75
152	Ryan Klesko	.25
153	Phil Nevin	.15
154	Mark Kotsay	.15
155	Trevor Hoffman	.15
156	Damian Jackson	.15
157	Scott Rolen	.50
158	Mike Lieberthal	.15
159	Bruce Chen	.15
160	Bobby Abreu	.25
161	Pat Burrell	.40
162	Travis Lee	.15
163	Jason Kendall	.15
164	Derek Bell	.15
165	Kris Benson	.15
166	Kevin Young	.15
167	Brian Giles	.25
168	Pat Meares	.15
169	Sean Casey	.25
170	Pokey Reese	.15
171	Pete Harnisch	.15
172	Barry Larkin	.25
173	Ken Griffey Jr.	1.00
174	Dmitri Young	.15
175	Mike Hampton	.15
176	Todd Helton	.50
177	Jeff Cirillo	.15
178	Denny Neagle	.15
179	Larry Walker	.25
180	Todd Hollandsworth	.15
181	Ichiro Suzuki RC	35.00
182	Wilson Betemit RC	6.00
183	Adrian Hernandez RC	3.00
184	Travis Hafner RC	15.00
185	Sean Douglass RC	3.00
186	Juan Diaz RC	3.00
187	Horacio Ramirez RC	5.00
188	Morgan Ensberg RC	10.00
189	Brandon Duckworth RC	3.00
190	Jack Wilson RC	8.00
191	Erick Almonte RC	3.00
192	Ricardo Rodriguez RC	3.00
193	Elpidio Guzman RC	3.00
194	Juan Uribe RC	5.00
195	Ryan Freel RC	4.00
196	Christian Parker RC	3.00
197	Jackson Melian RC	3.00
198	Jose Mieses RC	3.00
199	Andres Torres RC	3.00
200	Jason Smith RC	3.00
201	Johnny Estrada RC	6.00
202	Cesar Crespo RC	3.00
203	Carlos Valderrama RC	3.00
204	Albert Pujols RC	100.00
205	Wilken Ruan RC	3.00
206	Josh Fogg RC	4.00
207	Bert Snow RC	3.00
208	Brian Lawrence RC	5.00
209	Esix Snead RC	3.00
210	Tsuyoshi Shinjo RC	4.00

Big Game Reserve

		NM/M
Complete Set (10):		15.00
Common Player:		1.00
Inserted 1:24		
BG1	Alex Rodriguez	3.00
BG2	Derek Jeter	2.00
BG3	Mark McGwire	3.00
BG4	Derek Jeter	4.00
BG5	Sammy Sosa	2.50
BG6	Pedro Martinez	1.50
BG7	Jason Giambi	1.00
BG8	Todd Helton	1.00

Ken Griffey Jr. OF

BG9	Carlos Delgado	1.00
BG10	Mike Piazza	2.00

G-U Reserve Base/ Ball Duo

		NM/M
Inserted 1:240		
JR	Derek Jeter, Alex Rodriguez	50.00
JP	Derek Jeter, Mike Piazza	60.00
MP	Mark McGwire, Mike Piazza	100.00
MJ	Mark McGwire, Derek Jeter	100.00
RM	Alex Rodriguez, Mark McGwire	100.00
CR	Roger Clemens, Alex Rodriguez	40.00
ST	Sammy Sosa, Frank Thomas	40.00
GD	Vladimir Guerrero, Carlos Delgado	20.00
BH	Barry Bonds, Todd Helton	35.00
MG	Mark McGwire, Ken Griffey Jr.	40.00
GS	Ken Griffey Jr., Sammy Sosa	20.00
GJ	Ken Griffey Jr., Derek Jeter	35.00
JN	Chipper Jones, Nomar Garciaparra	20.00
NJ	Nomar Garciaparra, Derek Jeter	35.00
GR	Nomar Garciaparra, Alex Rodriguez	30.00

G-U Reserve Base/ Ball Trio

		NM/M
Inserted 1:480		
JRG	Derek Jeter, Alex Rodriguez, Nomar Garciaparra	50.00
SGM	Sammy Sosa, Ken Griffey Jr., Mark McGwire	65.00
PRS	Mike Piazza, Alex Rodriguez, Sammy Sosa	40.00
GSG	Ken Griffey Jr., Sammy Sosa, Vladimir Guerrero	30.00
THM	Frank Thomas, Todd Helton, Mark McGwire	65.00

CMJ	Roger Clemens, Pedro Martinez, Derek Jeter	45.00
BSH	Barry Bonds, Gary Sheffield, Todd Helton	40.00
GPJ	Vladimir Guerrero, Mike Piazza, Chipper Jones	30.00
MJR	Mark McGwire, Derek Jeter, Alex Rodriguez	75.00
JGS	Derek Jeter, Ken Griffey Jr., Sammy Sosa	45.00

G-U Reserve Base/ Ball Quad

		NM/M
Production 50 Sets		
SGRM	Sammy Sosa, Ken Griffey Jr., Alex Rodriguez, Mark McGwire	175.00
GPJG	Vladimir Guerrero, Mike Piazza, Chipper Jones, Nomar Garciaparra	65.00
THMJ	Frank Thomas, Todd Helton, Mark McGwire, Derek Jeter	90.00
GBJE	Ken Griffey Jr., Barry Bonds, Andruw Jones, Jim Edmonds	75.00
PMJR	Mike Piazza, Mark McGwire, Derek Jeter, Alex Rodriguez	150.00

Jerseys Duo

		NM/M
Common Duo:		15.00
Inserted 1:240		
HG	Tim Hudson, Jason Giambi	25.00
BK	Barry Bonds, Jeff Kent	40.00
JJ	Andruw Jones, Chipper Jones	25.00
GE	Troy Glaus, Darin Erstad	15.00
WO	David Wells, Magglio Ordonez	15.00
WE	Bernie Williams, Jim Edmonds	15.00
DG	Carlos Delgado, Jason Giambi	20.00
GK	Jason Giambi, Jeff Kent	20.00
JW	Randy Johnson, David Wells	25.00
JG	Chipper Jones, Troy Glaus	25.00
SB	Gary Sheffield, Barry Bonds	40.00
HE	Todd Helton, Darin Erstad	20.00
RB	Alex Rodriguez, Tony Batista	25.00
GW	Brian Giles, Bernie Williams	15.00
SG	Sammy Sosa, Troy Glaus	30.00

Jerseys Trio

		NM/M
Common Trio:		25.00
Inserted 1:480		
GHD	Jason Giambi, Todd Helton, Carlos Delgado	30.00
RSS	Alex Rodriguez, Sammy Sosa, Gary Sheffield	50.00
WEJ	Bernie Williams, Jim Edmonds, Andruw Jones	25.00

HJW	Tim Hudson, Randy Johnson, David Wells	30.00
SOD	Sammy Sosa, Magglio Ordonez, Carlos Delgado	40.00
GGR	Jason Giambi, Troy Glaus, Alex Rodriguez	40.00
BWD	Tony Batista, Bernie Williams, Carlos Delgado	25.00
BSH	Barry Bonds, Gary Sheffield, Todd Helton	50.00
WSH	David Wells, Sammy Sosa, Todd Helton	40.00
EKE	Darin Erstad, Jeff Kent, Jim Edmonds	25.00

Jerseys Quad

		NM/M
Common Quad:		25.00
Production 50 Sets		
DRGS	Carlos Delgado, Alex Rodriguez, Troy Glaus, Sammy Sosa	40.00
GWBG	Jason Giambi, Bernie Williams, Barry Bonds, Brian Giles	75.00
HKEJ	Todd Helton, Jeff Kent, Jim Edmonds, Chipper Jones	40.00
HKEJ	Gary Sheffield, Magglio Ordonez, Darin Erstad, Tony Batista	25.00
JRSB	Andruw Jones, Alex Rodriguez, Sammy Sosa, Barry Bonds	100.00

The New Order

		NM/M
Complete Set (10):		15.00
Common Player:		.75
Inserted 1:24		
NO1	Vladimir Guerrero	1.50
NO2	Andruw Jones	1.00
NO3	Corey Patterson	.75
NO4	Derek Jeter	4.00
NO5	Alex Rodriguez	3.00
NO6	Pat Burrell	.75
NO7	Ichiro Suzuki	5.00
NO8	Barry Zito	.75
NO9	Rafael Furcal	.75
NO10	Troy Glaus	1.00

UD Royalty

		NM/M
Complete Set (10):		15.00
Common Player:		1.00
Inserted 1:24		
R1	Ken Griffey Jr.	2.00
R2	Derek Jeter	4.00
R3	Alex Rodriguez	3.00
R4	Sammy Sosa	2.50
R5	Mark McGwire	3.00

R6	Mike Piazza	2.00
R7	Vladimir Guerrero	1.50
R8	Chipper Jones	2.00
R9	Frank Thomas	1.00
R10	Nomar Garciaparra	3.00

2002 Upper Deck

		NM/M
Complete Set (745):		150.00
Complete Series I (500):		100.00
Complete Series II (245):		50.00
Common Player:		.15
Series 1 Hobby Pack (8):		4.00
Series 1 Hobby Box (24):		75.00
Series 2 Hobby Pack (8):		1.25
Series 2 Hobby Box (24):		25.00
1	Mark Prior	4.00
2	Mark Teixeira	1.50
3	Brian Roberts	.25
4	Jason Romano	.25
5	Dennis Stark RC	.50
6	Oscar Salazar	.50
7	John Patterson	.25
8	Shane Loux	.25
9	Marcus Giles	.40
10	Juan Cruz	.25
11	Jorge Julio	.25
12	Adam Dunn	.50
13	Delvin James	.25
14	Jeremy Affeldt	.25
15	Tim Raines Jr.	.25
16	Luke Hudson	.25
17	Todd Sears	.25
18	George Perez	.25
19	Wilmy Caceres	.25
20	Abraham Nunez	.25
21	Mike Amrhein	.25
22	Carlos Hernandez	.25
23	Scott Hodges	.25
24	Brandon Knight	.25
25	Geoff Goetz	.25
26	Carlos Garcia	.25
27	Luis Pineda	.25
28	Chris Gissell	.25
29	Jae Weong	.25
30	Paul Phillips	.25
31	Cory Aldridge	.25
32	Aaron Cook RC	.50
33	Rendy Espina	.25
34	Jason Phillips	.25
35	Carlos Silva	.25
36	Ryan Mills	.25
37	Pedro Santana	.25
38	John Grabow	.25
39	Cody Ransom	.15
40	Orlando Woodlands	.25
41	Bud Smith	.25
42	Junior Guerrero	.25
43	David Brous	.25
44	Steve Green	.25
45	Brian Rogers	.25

46	Juan Figueroa	.25
47	Nick Punto	.25
48	Junior Herndon	.25
49	Justin Kaye	.25
50	Jason Karnuth	.25
51	Troy Glaus	.40
52	Bengie Molina	.15
53	Ramon Ortiz	.15
54	Adam Kennedy	.15
55	Jarrod Washburn	.15
56	Troy Percival	.15
57	David Eckstein	.15
58	Ben Weber	.15
59	Larry Barnes	.15
60	Ismael Valdes	.15
61	Benji Gil	.15
62	Scott Schoeneweis	.15
63	Pat Rapp	.15
64	Jason Giambi	.50
65	Mark Mulder	.25
66	Ron Gant	.15
67	Johnny Damon	.25
68	Adam Piatt	.15
69	Jermaine Dye	.25
70	Jason Hart	.15
71	Eric Chavez	.40
72	Jim Mecir	.15
73	Barry Zito	.40
74	Jason Isringhausen	.15
75	Jeremy Giambi	.15
76	Olmedo Saenz	.15
77	Terrence Long	.15
78	Ramon Hernandez	.15
79	Chris Carpenter	.15
80	Raul Mondesi	.15
81	Carlos Delgado	.50
82	Billy Koch	.15
83	Vernon Wells	.25
84	Darrin Fletcher	.15
85	Homer Bush	.15
86	Pasqual Coco	.15
87	Shannon Stewart	.15
88	Chris Woodward	.15
89	Joe Lawrence	.15
90	Esteban Loaiza	.15
91	Cesar Izturis	.15
92	Kelvim Escobar	.15
93	Greg Vaughn	.15
94	Brent Abernathy	.15
95	Tanyon Sturtze	.15
96	Steve Cox	.15
97	Aubrey Huff	.15
98	Jesus Colome	.15
99	Ben Grieve	.15
100	Esteban Yan	.15
101	Joe Kennedy	.15
102	Felix Martinez	.15
103	Nick Bierbrodt	.15
104	Damian Rolls	.15
105	Russ Johnson	.15
106	Toby Hall	.15
107	Roberto Alomar	.40
108	Bartolo Colon	.25
109	John Rocker	.15
110	Juan Gonzalez	.50
111	Einar Diaz	.15
112	Chuck Finley	.15
113	Kenny Lofton	.25
114	Danys Baez	.15
115	Travis Fryman	.25
116	C.C. Sabathia	.25
117	Paul Shuey	.15
118	Marty Cordova	.15
119	Ellis Burks	.15
120	Bob Wickman	.15
121	Edgar Martinez	.25
122	Freddy Garcia	.15
123	Ichiro Suzuki	1.50
124	John Olerud	.25
125	Gil Meche	.15
126	Dan Wilson	.15
127	Aaron Sele	.15
128	Kazuhiro Sasaki	.15
129	Mark McLemore	.15
130	Carlos Guillen	.15
131	Al Martin	.15
132	David Bell	.15
133	Jay Buhner	.15
134	Stan Javier	.15
135	Tony Batista	.15
136	Jason Johnson	.15
137	Brook Fordyce	.15
138	Mike Kinkade	.15
139	Willis Roberts	.15
140	David Segui	.15
141	Josh Towers	.15
142	Jeff Conine	.15
143	Chris Richard	.15
144	Pat Hentgen	.15
145	Melvin Mora	.15
146	Jerry Hairston Jr.	.15
147	Calvin Maduro	.15
148	Brady Anderson	.15
149	Alex Rodriguez	1.50

150	Kenny Rogers	.15
151	Chad Curtis	.15
152	Ricky Ledee	.15
153	Rafael Palmeiro	.50
154	Rob Bell	.15
155	Rick Helling	.15
156	Doug Davis	.15
157	Mike Lamb	.15
158	Gabe Kapler	.15
159	Jeff Zimmerman	.15
160	Bill Haselman	.15
161	Tim Crabtree	.15
162	Carlos Pena	.15
163	Nomar Garciaparra	1.00
164	Shea Hillenbrand	.15
165	Hideo Nomo	.40
166	Manny Ramirez	.50
167	Jose Offerman	.15
168	Scott Hatteberg	.15
169	Trot Nixon	.25
170	Darren Lewis	.15
171	Derek Lowe	.25
172	Troy O'Leary	.15
173	Tim Wakefield	.15
174	Chris Stynes	.15
175	John Valentin	.15
176	David Cone	.15
177	Neifi Perez	.15
178	Brent Mayne	.15
179	Dan Reichert	.15
180	A.J. Hinch	.15
181	Chris George	.15
182	Mike Sweeney	.15
183	Jeff Suppan	.15
184	Roberto Hernandez	.15
185	Joe Randa	.15
186	Paul Byrd	.15
187	Luis Ordaz	.15
188	Kris Wilson	.15
189	Dee Brown	.15
190	Tony Clark	.15
191	Matt Anderson	.15
192	Robert Fick	.15
193	Juan Encarnacion	.15
194	Dean Palmer	.15
195	Victor Santos	.15
196	Damion Easley	.15
197	Jose Lima	.15
198	Deivi Cruz	.15
199	Roger Cedeno	.15
200	Jose Macias	.15
201	Jeff Weaver	.15
202	Brandon Inge	.15
203	Brian Moehler	.15
204	Brad Radke	.15
205	Doug Mientkiewicz	.15
206	Cristian Guzman	.15
207	Corey Koskie	.15
208	LaTroy Hawkins	.15
209	J.C. Romero	.15
210	Chad Allen	.15
211	Torii Hunter	.25
212	Travis Miller	.15
213	Joe Mays	.15
214	Todd Jones	.15
215	David Ortiz	.40
216	Brian Buchanan	.15
217	A.J. Pierzynski	.15
218	Carlos Lee	.15
219	Gary Glover	.15
220	Jose Valentin	.15
221	Aaron Rowand	.15
222	Sandy Alomar Jr.	.15
223	Herbert Perry	.15
224	Jon Garland	.15
225	Mark Buehrle	.15
226	Chris Singleton	.15
227	Kip Wells	.15
228	Ray Durham	.15
229	Joe Crede	.15
230	Keith Foulke	.15
231	Royce Clayton	.15
232	Andy Pettitte	.40
233	Derek Jeter	2.00
234	Jorge Posada	.40
235	Roger Clemens	1.50
236	Paul O'Neill	.25
237	Nick Johnson	.15
238	Gerald Williams	.15
239	Mariano Rivera	.25
240	Alfonso Soriano	.50
241	Ramiro Mendoza	.15
242	Mike Mussina	.50
243	Luis Sojo	.15
244	Scott Brosius	.15
245	David Justice	.25
246	Wade Miller	.15
247	Brad Ausmus	.15
248	Jeff Bagwell	.50
249	Daryle Ward	.15
250	Shane Reynolds	.15
251	Chris Truby	.15
252	Billy Wagner	.15
253	Craig Biggio	.25

254	Moises Alou	.25
255	Vinny Castilla	.15
256	Tim Redding	.15
257	Roy Oswalt	.40
258	Julio Lugo	.15
259	Chipper Jones	.75
260	Greg Maddux	1.00
261	Ken Caminiti	.15
262	Kevin Millwood	.25
263	Keith Lockhart	.15
264	Rey Sanchez	.15
265	Jason Marquis	.15
266	Brian Jordan	.15
267	Steve Karsay	.15
268	Wes Helms	.15
269	B.J. Surhoff	.15
270	Wilson Betemit	.15
271	John Smoltz	.25
272	Rafael Furcal	.25
273	Jeromy Burnitz	.15
274	Jimmy Haynes	.15
275	Mark Loretta	.15
276	Jose Hernandez	.15
277	Paul Rigdon	.15
278	Alex Sanchez	.15
279	Chad Fox	.15
280	Devon White	.15
281	Tyler Houston	.15
282	Ronnie Belliard	.15
283	Luis Lopez	.15
284	Ben Sheets	.40
285	Curtis Leskanic	.15
286	Henry Blanco	.15
287	Mark McGwire	2.00
288	Edgar Renteria	.25
289	Matt Morris	.25
290	Gene Stechschulte	.15
291	Dustin Hermanson	.15
292	Eli Marrero	.15
293	Albert Pujols	1.50
294	Luis Saturria	.15
295	Bobby Bonilla	.15
296	Garrett Stephenson	.15
297	Jim Edmonds	.40
298	Rick Ankiel	.15
299	Placido Polanco	.15
300	Dave Veres	.15
301	Sammy Sosa	1.50
302	Eric Young	.15
303	Kerry Wood	.75
304	Jon Lieber	.15
305	Joe Girardi	.15
306	Fred McGriff	.25
307	Jeff Fassero	.15
308	Julio Zuleta	.15
309	Kevin Tapani	.15
310	Rondell White	.15
311	Julian Tavarez	.15
312	Tom Gordon	.15
313	Corey Patterson	.25
314	Bill Mueller	.15
315	Randy Johnson	.75
316	Chad Moeller	.15
317	Tony Womack	.15
318	Erubiel Durazo	.15
319	Luis Gonzalez	.25
320	Brian Anderson	.15
321	Reggie Sanders	.15
322	Greg Colbrunn	.15
323	Robert Ellis	.15
324	Jack Cust	.15
325	Bret Prinz	.15
326	Steve Finley	.15
327	Byung-Hyun Kim	.15
328	Albie Lopez	.15
329	Gary Sheffield	.40
330	Mark Grudzielanek	.15
331	Paul LoDuca	.15
332	Tom Goodwin	.15
333	Andy Ashby	.15
334	Hiram Bocachica	.15
335	Dave Hansen	.15
336	Kevin Brown	.25
337	Marquis Grissom	.15
338	Terry Adams	.15
339	Chan Ho Park	.15
340	Adrian Beltre	.25
341	Luke Prokopec	.15
342	Jeff Shaw	.15
343	Vladimir Guerrero	.75
344	Orlando Cabrera	.15
345	Tony Armas Jr.	.15
346	Michael Barrett	.15
347	Geoff Blum	.15
348	Ryan Minor	.15
349	Peter Bergeron	.15
350	Graeme Lloyd	.15
351	Jose Vidro	.15
352	Javier Vazquez	.15
353	Matt Blank	.15
354	Masato Yoshii	.15
355	Carl Pavano	.15
356	Barry Bonds	2.00
357	Shawon Dunston	.15

#	Player	Price
358	Livan Hernandez	.15
359	Felix Rodriguez	.15
360	Pedro Feliz	.15
361	Calvin Murray	.15
362	Robb Nen	.15
363	Marvin Benard	.15
364	Russ Ortiz	.15
365	Jason Schmidt	.25
366	Rich Aurilia	.15
367	John Vander Wal	.15
368	Benito Santiago	.15
369	Ryan Dempster	.15
370	Charles Johnson	.15
371	Alex Gonzalez	.15
372	Luis Castillo	.15
373	Mike Lowell	.25
374	Antonio Alfonseca	.15
375	A.J. Burnett	.15
376	Brad Penny	.15
377	Jason Grilli	.15
378	Derrek Lee	.25
379	Matt Clement	.15
380	Eric Owens	.15
381	Vladimir Nunez	.15
382	Cliff Floyd	.15
383	Mike Piazza	1.25
384	Lenny Harris	.15
385	Glendon Rusch	.15
386	Todd Zeile	.15
387	Al Leiter	.25
388	Armando Benitez	.15
389	Alex Escobar	.15
390	Kevin Appier	.15
391	Matt Lawton	.15
392	Bruce Chen	.15
393	John Franco	.15
394	Tsuyoshi Shinjo	.15
395	Rey Ordonez	.15
396	Joe McEwing	.15
397	Ryan Klesko	.15
398	Brian Lawrence	.15
399	Kevin Walker	.15
400	Phil Nevin	.15
401	Bubba Trammell	.15
402	Wiki Gonzalez	.15
403	D'Angelo Jimenez	.15
404	Rickey Henderson	.40
405	Mike Darr	.15
406	Trevor Hoffman	.15
407	Damian Jackson	.15
408	Santiago Perez	.15
409	Cesar Crespo	.15
410	Robert Person	.15
411	Travis Lee	.15
412	Scott Rolen	.75
413	Turk Wendell	.15
414	Randy Wolf	.15
415	Kevin Jordan	.15
416	Jose Mesa	.15
417	Mike Lieberthal	.15
418	Bobby Abreu	.25
419	Tomas Perez	.15
420	Doug Glanville	.15
421	Reggie Taylor	.15
422	Jimmy Rollins	.40
423	Brian Giles	.25
424	Rob Mackowiak	.15
425	Bronson Arroyo	.15
426	Kevin Young	.15
427	Jack Wilson	.15
428	Adam Brown	.15
429	Chad Hermansen	.15
430	Jimmy Anderson	.15
431	Aramis Ramirez	.25
432	Todd Ritchie	.15
433	Pat Meares	.15
434	Warren Morris	.15
435	Derek Bell	.15
436	Ken Griffey Jr.	1.00
437	Elmer Dessens	.15
438	Ruben Rivera	.15
439	Jason LaRue	.15
440	Sean Casey	.25
441	Pete Harnisch	.15
442	Danny Graves	.15
443	Aaron Boone	.15
444	Dmitri Young	.15
445	Brandon Larson	.15
446	Pokey Reese	.15
447	Todd Walker	.15
448	Juan Castro	.15
449	Todd Helton	.50
450	Ben Petrick	.15
451	Juan Pierre	.15
452	Jeff Cirillo	.15
453	Juan Uribe	.15
454	Brian Bohanon	.15
455	Terry Shumpert	.15
456	Mike Hampton	.15
457	Shawn Chacon	.15
458	Adam Melhuse	.15
459	Greg Norton	.15
460	Gabe White	.15
461	Ichiro Suzuki	1.50
462	Carlos Delgado	.40
463	Manny Ramirez	.50
464	Miguel Tejada	.25
465	Tsuyoshi Shinjo	.15
466	Bernie Williams	.40
467	Omar Gonzalez	.50
468	Andruw Jones	.40
469	Ivan Rodriguez	.50
470	Larry Walker	.25
471	Hideo Nomo	.15
472	Albert Pujols	1.00
473	Pedro Martinez	.75
474	Vladimir Guerrero	.75
475	Tony Batista	.15
476	Kazuhiro Sasaki	.15
477	Richard Hidalgo	.15
478	Carlos Lee	.15
479	Roberto Alomar	.40
480	Rafael Palmeiro	.50
481	Ken Griffey Jr.	.50
482	Ken Griffey Jr.	.50
483	Ken Griffey Jr.	.50
484	Ken Griffey Jr.	.50
485	Ken Griffey Jr.	.50
486	Ken Griffey Jr.	.50
487	Ken Griffey Jr.	.50
488	Ken Griffey Jr.	.50
489	Ken Griffey Jr.	.50
490	Ken Griffey Jr.	.50
491	Barry Bonds	.75
492	Hideo Nomo	.15
493	Ichiro Suzuki	.50
494	Cal Ripken Jr.	.75
495	Tony Gwynn	.40
496	Randy Johnson	.40
497	A.J. Burnett	.15
498	Rickey Henderson	.15
499	Albert Pujols	.75
500	Luis Gonzalez	.25
501	Brandon Puffer RC	.50
502	Rodrigo Rosario RC	.50
503	Tom Shearn RC	.50
504	Reed Johnson RC	.50
505	Chris Baker RC	.50
506	John Ennis RC	.50
507	Luis Martinez RC	.50
508	So Taguchi RC	.75
509	Scotty Layfield RC	.50
510	Francis Beltran RC	.50
511	Brandon Backe RC	.50
512	Doug DeVore RC	.50
513	Jeremy Ward RC	.50
514	Jose Vaverde RC	.50
515	P.J. Bevis RC	.50
516	Victor Alvarez RC	.50
517	Kazuhisa Ishii RC	2.00
518	Jorge Nunez RC	.50
519	Eric Good RC	.50
520	Ron Calloway RC	.50
521	Valentino Pasucci	.25
522	Nelson Castro RC	.25
523	Deivis Santos	.25
524	Luis Ugueto RC	.50
525	Matt Thornton	.25
526	Hansel Izquierdo RC	.75
527	Tyler Yates RC	.50
528	Mark Corey RC	.50
529	Jaime Cerda RC	.50
530	Satoru Komiyama RC	.50
531	Steve Bechler RC	.50
532	Ben Howard RC	.50
533	Anderson Machado RC	.50
534	Jorge Padilla RC	.50
535	Eric Junge RC	.50
536	Adrian Burnside RC	.50
537	Mike Gonzalez RC	.50
538	Josh Hancock RC	.50
539	Colin Young RC	.50
540	Rene Reyes RC	.50
541	Cam Esslinger RC	.50
542	Tim Kalita RC	.50
543	Kevin Frederick RC	.50
544	Kyle Kane RC	.50
545	Edwin Almonte RC	.50
546	Aaron Sele	.15
547	Garret Anderson	.40
548	Darin Erstad	.25
549	Brad Fullmer	.15
550	Kevin Appier	.15
551	Tim Salmon	.25
552	David Justice	.25
553	Billy Koch	.15
554	Scott Hatteberg	.15
555	Tim Hudson	.25
556	Miguel Tejada	.25
557	Carlos Pena	.15
558	Mike Sirotka	.15
559	Jose Cruz Jr.	.15
560	Josh Phelps	.15
561	Brandon Lyon	.15
562	Luke Prokopec	.15
563	Felipe Lopez	.15
564	Jason Standridge	.15
565	Chris Gomez	.15
566	John Flaherty	.15
567	Jason Tyner	.15
568	Bobby Smith	.15
569	Wilson Alvarez	.15
570	Matt Lawton	.15
571	Omar Vizquel	.25
572	Jim Thome	.75
573	Brady Anderson	.15
574	Alex Escobar	.15
575	Russell Branyan	.15
576	Bret Boone	.25
577	Ben Davis	.15
578	Mike Cameron	.15
579	Jamie Moyer	.15
580	Ruben Sierra	.15
581	Jeff Cirillo	.15
582	Marty Cordova	.15
583	Mike Bordick	.15
584	Brian Roberts	.15
585	Luis Matos	.15
586	Geronimo Gil	.15
587	Jay Gibbons	.15
588	Carl Everett	.15
589	Ivan Rodriguez	.50
590	Chan Ho Park	.15
591	Juan Gonzalez	.50
592	Hank Blalock	.40
593	Todd Van Poppel	.15
594	Pedro J. Martinez	.75
595	Jason Varitek	.15
596	Tony Clark	.15
597	Johnny Damon	.25
598	Dustin Hermanson	.15
599	John Burkett	.15
600	Carlos Beltran	.40
601	Mark Quinn	.15
602	Chuck Knoblauch	.15
603	Michael Tucker	.15
604	Carlos Febles	.15
605	Jose Rosado	.15
606	Dmitri Young	.15
607	Bobby Higginson	.15
608	Craig Paquette	.15
609	Mitch Meluskey	.15
610	Wendell Magee	.15
611	Mike Rivera	.15
612	Jacque Jones	.15
613	Luis Rivas	.15
614	Eric Milton	.15
615	Eddie Guardado	.15
616	Matt LeCroy	.15
617	Mike Jackson	.15
618	Magglio Ordonez	.25
619	Frank Thomas	.50
620	Rocky Biddle	.15
621	Paul Konerko	.25
622	Todd Ritchie	.15
623	Jon Rauch	.15
624	John Vander Wal	.15
625	Rondell White	.15
626	Jason Giambi	.50
627	Robin Ventura	.25
628	David Wells	.15
629	Bernie Williams	.50
630	Lance Berkman	.25
631	Richard Hidalgo	.15
632	Gregg Zaun	.15
633	Jose Vizcaino	.15
634	Octavio Dotel	.15
635	Morgan Ensberg	.15
636	Andruw Jones	.50
637	Tom Glavine	.40
638	Gary Sheffield	.40
639	Vinny Castilla	.15
640	Javy Lopez	.25
641	Albie Lopez	.15
642	Geoff Jenkins	.25
643	Jeffrey Hammonds	.15
644	Alex Ochoa	.15
645	Richie Sexson	.40
646	Eric Young	.15
647	Glendon Rusch	.15
648	Tino Martinez	.25
649	Fernando Vina	.15
650	J.D. Drew	.25
651	Woody Williams	.15
652	Darryl Kile	.15
653	Jason Isringhausen	.15
654	Moises Alou	.25
655	Alex Gonzalez	.15
656	Delino DeShields	.15
657	Todd Hundley	.15
658	Chris Stynes	.15
659	Jason Bere	.15
660	Curt Schilling	.40
661	Craig Counsell	.15
662	Mark Grace	.40
663	Matt Williams	.25
664	Jay Bell	.15
665	Rick Helling	.15
666	Shawn Green	.40
667	Eric Karros	.15
668	Hideo Nomo	.40
669	Omar Daal	.15
670	Brian Jordan	.15
671	Cesar Izturis	.15
672	Fernando Tatis	.15
673	Lee Stevens	.15
674	Tomokazu Ohka	.15
675	Brian Schneider	.15
676	Brad Wilkerson	.15
677	Bruce Chen	.15
678	Tsuyoshi Shinjo	.15
679	Jeff Kent	.25
680	Kirk Rueter	.15
681	J.T. Snow	.15
682	David Bell	.15
683	Reggie Sanders	.15
684	Preston Wilson	.15
685	Vic Darensbourg	.15
686	Josh Beckett	.40
687	Pablo Ozuna	.15
688	Mike Redmond	.15
689	Scott Strickland	.15
690	Mo Vaughn	.25
691	Roberto Alomar	.50
692	Edgardo Alfonzo	.15
693	Shawn Estes	.15
694	Roger Cedeno	.15
695	Jeromy Burnitz	.15
696	Ray Lankford	.15
697	Mark Kotsay	.15
698	Kevin Jarvis	.15
699	Bobby Jones	.15
700	Sean Burroughs	.15
701	Ramon Vazquez	.15
702	Pat Burrell	.40
703	Marlon Byrd	.15
704	Brandon Duckworth	.15
705	Marlon Anderson	.15
706	Vicente Padilla	.15
707	Kip Wells	.15
708	Jason Kendall	.15
709	Pokey Reese	.15
710	Pat Meares	.15
711	Kris Benson	.15
712	Armando Rios	.15
713	Mike Williams	.15
714	Barry Larkin	.40
715	Adam Dunn	.50
716	Juan Encarnacion	.15
717	Scott Williamson	.15
718	Wilton Guerrero	.15
719	Chris Reitsma	.15
720	Larry Walker	.25
721	Denny Neagle	.15
722	Todd Zeile	.15
723	Jose Ortiz	.15
724	Jason Jennings	.15
725	Tony Eusebio	.15
726	Ichiro Suzuki	1.00
727	Barry Bonds	1.50
728	Randy Johnson	.50
729	Albert Pujols	1.00
730	Roger Clemens	.50
731	Sammy Sosa	.50
732	Alex Rodriguez	.50
733	Chipper Jones	.40
734	Rickey Henderson	.25
735	Marioners Team Photo	.15
736	Luis Gonzalez	.25
737	Derek Jeter	1.50
738	Ichiro Suzuki	1.00
739	Barry Bonds	1.50
740	Curt Schilling	.25
741	Shawn Green	.25
742	Jason Giambi	.50
743	Roberto Alomar	.25
744	Larry Walker	.15
745	Mark McGwire	.75

2001's Greatest Hits

	NM/M
Complete Set (10):	20.00
Common Player:	1.00
Inserted 1:14	
GH1 Barry Bonds	4.00
GH2 Ichiro Suzuki	3.00
GH3 Albert Pujols	3.00
GH4 Mike Piazza	2.50
GH5 Alex Rodriguez	3.00
GH6 Mark McGwire	3.00
GH7 Manny Ramirez	1.00
GH8 Ken Griffey Jr.	2.00
GH9 Sammy Sosa	3.00
GH10 Derek Jeter	4.00

AL Centennial G-U Jerseys Autograph

No Pricing
Production 25 Sets

AL Centennial Bats

		NM/M
JD	Joe DiMaggio	125.00
MM	Mickey Mantle	150.00
BR	Babe Ruth	150.00

AL Centennial Jerseys

		NM/M
Common Player:		10.00
Inserted 1:144		
PM	Pedro Martinez	10.00
CR	Cal Ripken Jr.	40.00
AR	Alex Rodriguez	15.00
IR	Ivan Rodriguez	10.00
NR	Nolan Ryan	40.00
FT	Frank Thomas	10.00

All-Star Salute Game Jerseys

		NM/M
Common Player:		10.00
Inserted 1:288		
SA	Sparky Anderson	10.00
LB	Lou Boudreau	10.00
DE	Dennis Eckersley	10.00
NF	Nellie Fox	15.00
KG	Ken Griffey Jr.	25.00
AR	Alex Rodriguez	25.00
DS	Don Sutton	10.00
IS	Ichiro Suzuki	40.00

Big Fly Zone

		NM/M
Complete Set (10):		15.00
Common Player:		.50
Inserted 1:14		
Z1	Mark McGwire	4.00
Z2	Ken Griffey Jr.	3.00
Z3	Manny Ramirez	1.00
Z4	Sammy Sosa	3.00
Z5	Todd Helton	1.00
Z6	Barry Bonds	4.00
Z7	Luis Gonzalez	.50
Z8	Alex Rodriguez	4.00
Z9	Carlos Delgado	1.00
Z10	Chipper Jones	1.50

Breakout Performers

		NM/M
Complete Set (10):		10.00
Common Player:		.50
Inserted 1:14		
BP1	Ichiro Suzuki	3.00
BP2	Albert Pujols	4.00
BP3	Doug Mientkiewicz	.50
BP4	Lance Berkman	1.00
BP5	Tsuyoshi Shinjo	.50
BP6	Ben Sheets	1.00
BP7	Jimmy Rollins	.75
BP8	J.D. Drew	.75
BP9	Bret Boone	.50
BP10	Alfonso Soriano	1.00

Championship Caliber

		NM/M
Complete Set (6):		10.00
Common Player:		1.00
Inserted 1:23		
CC1	Derek Jeter	5.00
CC2	Roberto Alomar	1.00
CC3	Chipper Jones	2.00
CC4	Gary Sheffield	1.00
CC5	Roger Clemens	3.00
CC6	Greg Maddux	2.50

Championship Caliber Swatches

		NM/M
Common Player:		8.00
Inserted 1:288		
RA	Roberto Alomar/SP	20.00
KB	Kevin Brown/SP	10.00
CF	Cliff Floyd	10.00
ChJ	Charles Johnson	8.00
RJ	Randy Johnson	10.00
CJo	Chipper Jones/SP	25.00
BL	Barry Larkin	10.00
GM	Greg Maddux/SP	40.00
TM	Tino Martinez	8.00
JO	John Olerud	8.00
AP	Andy Pettitte	10.00
JP	Jorge Posada	10.00
CS	Curt Schilling	10.00
BW	Bernie Williams	10.00

Chasing History

		NM/M
Complete Set (15):		12.00
Common Player:		.50
Inserted 1:11		
CH1	Sammy Sosa	2.00
CH2	Ken Griffey Jr.	1.50
CH3	Roger Clemens	2.00
CH4	Barry Bonds	3.00
CH5	Rafael Palmeiro	1.00
CH6	Andres Galarraga	.50
CH7	Juan Gonzalez	1.00
CH8	Roberto Alomar	1.00
CH9	Randy Johnson	1.00
CH10	Jeff Bagwell	1.00
CH11	Fred McGriff	.50
CH12	Matt Williams	.50
CH13	Greg Maddux	1.50
CH14	Robb Nen	.50
CH15	Kenny Lofton	.50

Combo Bat

		NM/M
Inserted 1:288		
CB-RG	Alex Rodriguez, Ken Griffey Jr.	30.00
CB-DM	Joe DiMaggio, Mickey Mantle	200.00

Combo Jersey

		NM/M
Common Duo:		10.00
Inserted 1:288		
RS	Alex Rodriguez, Sammy Sosa	30.00
RM	Nolan Ryan, Pedro Martinez	40.00
RC	Nolan Ryan, Roger Clemens	50.00
BS	Barry Bonds, Sammy Sosa	40.00
HK	Shigetoshi Hasegawa, Byung-Hun Kim	10.00

Double Game-Worn Gems

		NM/M
Common Card:		8.00
Production 450 Sets		
Golds:		1-2X
Production 100 Sets		
NK	Phil Nevin, Ryan Klesko	8.00
VB	Omar Vizquel, Russell Branyan	10.00
DH	Jermaine Dye, Tim Hudson	10.00
TO	Frank Thomas, Magglio Ordonez	15.00
MI	Edgar Martinez, Ichiro Suzuki/150	80.00
GS	Luis Gonzalez, Curt Schilling	15.00
AP	Roberto Alomar, Mike Piazza	20.00
PL	Robert Person, Mike Lieberthal	8.00
MM	Kevin Millwood, Greg Maddux	20.00
KG	Jason Kendall, Brian Giles	10.00
DF	Carlos Delgado, Shannon Stewart	10.00
PN	Chan Ho Park, Hideo Nomo	30.00

First Timers Jerseys

		NM/M
Common Player:		8.00
Inserted 1:288		
RB	Russell Branyan	8.00
OD	Omar Daal	8.00
FG	Freddy Garcia	8.00
ML	Matt Lawton	8.00
JM	Joe Mays	8.00
EM	Eric Milton	8.00
CP	Corey Patterson	10.00
AP	Albert Pujols	50.00
SS	Shannon Stewart	8.00

First Timers Jerseys Autograph

No Pricing
Production 25 Sets

Game Jerseys

		NM/M
Common Player:		8.00
Production 350 Sets		
Golds:		.75-1.5X
Production 100		
TB	Tony Batista	8.00
AB	Adrian Beltre	8.00
JC	Jeff Cirillo	8.00
KG	Ken Griffey Jr.	20.00
TH	Tim Hudson	10.00
MP	Mike Piazza	15.00
SR	Scott Rolen	15.00
CS	Curt Schilling	15.00
SS	Sammy Sosa	25.00
FT	Frank Thomas	12.00
PW	Preston Wilson	8.00

Game Jersey Autograph

		NM/M
Common Player:		20.00
Production 200 Sets		
BB	Barry Bonds	200.00
CD	Carlos Delgado	25.00
RF	Rafael Furcal	20.00
JGi	Jason Giambi	35.00
KG	Ken Griffey Jr.	125.00
AJ	Andruw Jones	35.00
AP	Albert Pujols	125.00
CR	Cal Ripken Jr.	200.00
NR	Nolan Ryan	140.00
GS	Gary Sheffield	20.00
IS	Ichiro Suzuki	300.00
PW	Preston Wilson	20.00

Game-Used Base

		NM/M
Common Player:		5.00

Inserted 1:288
BB	Barry Bonds	20.00
RC	Roger Clemens	20.00
CD	Carlos Delgado	5.00
JG	Jason Giambi	10.00
TG	Troy Glaus	8.00
JG	Juan Gonzalez	10.00
LG	Luis Gonzalez	5.00
SG	Shawn Green	5.00
KG	Ken Griffey Jr.	15.00
DJ	Derek Jeter	25.00
AJ	Andruw Jones	8.00
CJ	Chipper Jones	5.00
MM	Mark McGwire	40.00
MP	Mike Piazza	15.00
CR	Cal Ripken Jr.	40.00
AR	Alex Rodriguez	15.00
IR	Ivan Rodriguez	8.00
KS	Kazuhiro Sasaki	5.00
SS	Sammy Sosa	20.00
IS	Ichiro Suzuki	50.00

Game-Used Base Combo

		NM/M
Common Combo:		40.00
Inserted 1:288		
RG	Alex Rodriguez, Ken Griffey Jr.	40.00
MJ	Mark McGwire, Derek Jeter	60.00

Game-Used Base Autograph

Complete Set (1):
Production 25

Game-Worn Gems

		NM/M
Common Player:		5.00
Inserted 1:48		
Golds:		1-2X
Production 100 Sets		
RA	Roberto Alomar	8.00
EC	Eric Chavez	6.00
CD	Carlos Delgado	8.00
DE	Darin Erstad/SP	10.00
FG	Freddy Garcia/SP	8.00
TG	Tom Glavine	8.00
JG	Juan Gonzalez	8.00
LG	Luis Gonzalez/SP	10.00
MH	Mike Hampton/SP	8.00
CJ	Chipper Jones	10.00
JK	Jason Kendall	5.00
RK	Ryan Klesko/SP	8.00
GM	Greg Maddux	15.00
EM	Edgar Martinez	8.00
PM	Pedro Martinez/SP	15.00
TM	Tino Martinez	8.00
JM	Joe Mays	5.00
EM	Eric Milton	5.00
PN	Phil Nevin	5.00
HN	Hideo Nomo/SP	30.00
JO	John Olerud/SP	8.00
RP	Robert Person	5.00
CR	Cal Ripken Jr.	40.00
IR	Ivan Rodriguez	10.00
SR	Scott Rolen	15.00
CS	Curt Schilling	10.00
AS	Aaron Sele	5.00
GS	Gary Sheffield/SP	8.00
FT	Frank Thomas	10.00
OV	Omar Vizquel/SP	10.00
RY	Robin Yount	15.00

Global Swatch Jerseys

		NM/M
Common Player:		5.00
Inserted 1:144		
CD	Carlos Delgado	8.00
SH	Shigetoshi Hasegawa	5.00
BK	Byung-Hun Kim	5.00
HN	Hideo Nomo	35.00
CP	Chan Ho Park	5.00
MR	Manny Ramirez	10.00
KS	Kazuhiro Sasaki	5.00
TS	Tsuyoshi Shinjo	5.00
IS	Ichiro Suzuki	50.00
MY	Masato Yoshii	5.00

Global Swatch Jerseys Autograph

No Pricing
Production 25 Sets

McGwire Memorabilia

		NM/M
Common Card:		
AM-J	Mark McGwire/Jsy/70	75.00

AM-B	Mark McGwire/ Bat/70	75.00
MMc	Mark McGwire/ 500 HR Club Bat/350	300.00
MM-SS	Mark McGwire, Sammy Sosa/25 (Combo Jersey)	200.00
MM-KG	Mark McGwire, Ken Griffey Jr./25 (Combo Jersey)	250.00
MM-JG	Mark McGwire, Jason Giambi/25 (Combo Jersey)	200.00

Patch Stripes Autograph

No Pricing

Patch Numbers

No Pricing

Return of the Ace

		NM/M
Complete Set (15):		15.00
Common Player:		1.00
Inserted 1:11		
RA1	Randy Johnson	2.00
RA2	Greg Maddux	3.00
RA3	Pedro Martinez	2.00
RA4	Freddy Garcia	1.00
RA5	Matt Morris	1.00
RA6	Mark Mulder	1.00
RA7	Wade Miller	1.00
RA8	Kevin Brown	1.00
RA9	Roger Clemens	4.00
RA10	Jon Lieber	1.00
RA11	C.C. Sabathia	1.00
RA12	Tim Hudson	1.50
RA13	Curt Schilling	2.00
RA14	Al Leiter	1.00
RA15	Mike Mussina	1.50

Sons of Summer Game Jerseys

		NM/M
Common Player:		10.00
Inserted 1:288		
RA	Roberto Alomar	10.00
JB	Jeff Bagwell	10.00
RC	Roger Clemens	15.00
JG	Juan Gonzalez	10.00
GM	Greg Maddux	15.00
PM	Pedro Martinez/SP	15.00
MP	Mike Piazza	15.00
AR	Alex Rodriguez	15.00

Superstar Summit

		NM/M
Complete Set (6):		15.00
Common Player:		1.50
Inserted 1:23		
SS1	Sammy Sosa	3.00
SS2	Alex Rodriguez	4.00
SS3	Mark McGwire	4.00
SS4	Barry Bonds	4.00
SS5	Mike Piazza	3.00
SS6	Ken Griffey Jr.	2.50

Superstar Summit II

		NM/M
Complete Set (15):		25.00
Common Player:		1.00
Inserted 1:11		
SS1	Alex Rodriguez	4.00
SS2	Jason Giambi	1.00
SS3	Vladimir Guerrero	1.50
SS4	Randy Johnson	1.50
SS5	Chipper Jones	1.50
SS6	Ichiro Suzuki	3.00
SS7	Sammy Sosa	2.50
SS8	Greg Maddux	2.00
SS9	Ken Griffey Jr.	2.50
SS10	Todd Helton	1.00
SS11	Barry Bonds	4.00
SS12	Derek Jeter	4.00
SS13	Mike Piazza	3.00
SS14	Ivan Rodriguez	1.00
SS15	Frank Thomas	1.00

The People's Choice Game Jerseys

		NM/M
Common Player:		5.00
Inserted 1:24		
Golds:		1-2X
Production 100 Sets		
JBa	Jeff Bagwell	10.00
EB	Ellis Burks/SP	10.00
JBu	Jeromy Burnitz	5.00
OD	Omar Daal	5.00
CD	Carlos Delgado	8.00
RF	Rafael Furcal	6.00
AG	Andres Galarraga/SP	10.00
BG	Brian Giles	5.00
JG	Juan Gonzalez	10.00
KG	Ken Griffey Jr.	20.00
TG	Tony Gwynn	12.00
SH	Sterling Hitchcock	5.00
HI	Hideki Irabu	5.00
CJ	Charles Johnson	5.00
DL	Derek Lowe	8.00
GM	Greg Maddux	15.00
TM	Tino Martinez	10.00
JN	Jeff Nelson	5.00
RO	Rey Ordonez	5.00
RP	Rafael Palmeiro/SP	15.00
RP	Robert Person/SP	10.00
AP	Andy Pettitte	10.00
MP	Mike Piazza	15.00
TR	Tim Raines	5.00
MRa	Manny Ramirez	10.00
MRi	Mariano Rivera	8.00
AR	Alex Rodriguez	15.00
TS	Tim Salmon	6.00
CS	Curt Schilling	10.00
TSh	Tsuyoshi Shinjo	5.00
JS	J.T. Snow	5.00
SS	Sammy Sosa	20.00
MS	Mike Stanton	5.00
FT	Frank Thomas	10.00
RV	Robin Ventura	6.00
OV	Omar Vizquel	6.00
DW	David Wells	6.00
BW	Bernie Williams	8.00
MW	Matt Williams/SP	10.00

UD Patch Logo

	NM/M
Common Player:	60.00

Inserted 1:2,500
Prices for Stripes & Numbers identical.

BB	Barry Bonds	125.00
JG	Jason Giambi	60.00
KG	Ken Griffey Jr.	100.00
PM	Pedro Martinez	80.00
CR	Cal Ripken Jr.	150.00
AR	Alex Rodriguez	125.00
SS	Sammy Sosa	100.00

UD-Plus

		NM/M
Common Player:		2.00
Production 1,125 Sets		

One two-card pack per Series 2 H pack.
Comp. Set can be exchanged for Jsy cards.
Redemption deadline 5-16-03.

UD1	Darin Erstad	3.00
UD2	Troy Glaus	3.00
UD3	Tim Hudson	3.00
UD4	Jermaine Dye	2.00
UD5	Barry Zito	2.00
UD6	Carlos Delgado	3.00
UD7	Shannon Stewart	2.00
UD8	Greg Vaughn	2.00
UD9	Jim Thome	5.00
UD10	C.C. Sabathia	2.00
UD11	Ichiro Suzuki	10.00
UD12	Edgar Martinez	2.00
UD13	Bret Boone	2.00
UD14	Freddy Garcia	2.00
UD15	Matt Thornton	2.00
UD16	Jeff Conine	2.00
UD17	Steve Bechler	2.00
UD18	Rafael Palmeiro	4.00
UD19	Juan Gonzalez	4.00
UD20	Alex Rodriguez	10.00
UD21	Ivan Rodriguez	4.00
UD22	Carl Everett	2.00
UD23	Manny Ramirez	4.00
UD24	Nomar Garciaparra	10.00
UD25	Pedro J. Martinez	4.00
UD26	Mike Sweeney	2.00
UD27	Chuck Knoblauch	2.00
UD28	Dmitri Young	2.00
UD29	Bobby Higginson	2.00
UD30	Dean Palmer	2.00
UD31	Doug Mientkiewicz	2.00
UD32	Corey Koskie	2.00
UD33	Brad Radke	2.00
UD34	Cristian Guzman	2.00
UD35	Frank Thomas	4.00
UD36	Magglio Ordonez	3.00
UD37	Carlos Lee	2.00
UD38	Roger Clemens	10.00
UD39	Bernie Williams	3.00
UD40	Derek Jeter	15.00
UD41	Jason Giambi	4.00
UD42	Mike Mussina	3.00
UD43	Jeff Bagwell	4.00
UD44	Lance Berkman	3.00
UD45	Wade Miller	2.00
UD46	Greg Maddux	8.00
UD47	Chipper Jones	5.00
UD48	Andruw Jones	4.00
UD49	Gary Sheffield	3.00
UD50	Richie Sexson	3.00
UD51	Albert Pujols	10.00
UD52	J.D. Drew	3.00
UD53	Matt Morris	2.00
UD54	Jim Edmonds	3.00
UD55	So Taguchi	2.00
UD56	Sammy Sosa	10.00
UD57	Fred McGriff	3.00
UD58	Kerry Wood	5.00
UD59	Moises Alou	3.00
UD60	Randy Johnson	5.00
UD61	Luis Gonzalez	3.00
UD62	Mark Grace	3.00
UD63	Curt Schilling	4.00
UD64	Matt Williams	2.00
UD65	Kevin Brown	3.00
UD66	Brian Jordan	2.00
UD67	Shawn Green	3.00
UD68	Hideo Nomo	3.00
UD69	Kazuhisa Ishii	4.00
UD70	Vladimir Guerrero	4.00
UD71	Jose Vidro	2.00
UD72	Eric Good	2.00
UD73	Barry Bonds	15.00
UD74	Jeff Kent	3.00
UD75	Rich Aurilia	2.00
UD76	Deivis Santos	2.00
UD77	Preston Wilson	2.00
UD78	Cliff Floyd	2.00
UD79	Josh Beckett	4.00
UD80	Hansel Izquierdo	2.00
UD81	Mike Piazza	10.00
UD82	Roberto Alomar	3.00
UD83	Mo Vaughn	3.00
UD84	Jeromy Burnitz	2.00
UD85	Phil Nevin	2.00
UD86	Ryan Klesko	2.00
UD87	Bobby Abreu	3.00
UD88	Scott Rolen	5.00
UD89	Jimmy Rollins	2.50
UD90	Jason Kendall	2.00
UD91	Brian Giles	3.00
UD92	Aramis Ramirez	2.00
UD93	Ken Griffey Jr.	10.00
UD94	Sean Casey	2.00
UD95	Barry Larkin	3.00
UD96	Adam Dunn	4.00
UD97	Todd Helton	4.00
UD98	Larry Walker	3.00
UD99	Mike Hampton	2.00
UD100	Rene Reyes	2.00

UD-Plus Memorabila Moments Jerseys

		NM/M
Common DiMaggio (1-5):		125.00
Common Mantle: (1-5):		200.00
MM-JD1	Joe DiMaggio	125.00
MM-JD2	Joe DiMaggio	125.00
MM-JD3	Joe DiMaggio	125.00
MM-JD4	Joe DiMaggio	125.00
MM-JD5	Joe DiMaggio	125.00
MM-MM1	Mickey Mantle/25/ Pants	200.00
MM-MM2	Mickey Mantle 200.00	
MM-MM3	Mickey Mantle 200.00	
MM-MM4	Mickey Mantle 200.00	
MM-MM5	Mickey Mantle 200.00	

UD-Plus Pinstripe Immortals

No Pricing

Yankees Dynasty Jerseys

		NM/M
Common Combo:		20.00
Inserted 1:288		
PR	Andy Pettitte, Mariano Rivera	25.00
BT	Wade Boggs, Joe Torre	25.00
CP	Roger Clemens, Jorge Posada	50.00
DM	Joe DiMaggio, Mickey Mantle	300.00
RK	Willie Randolph, Chuck Knoblauch	20.00
BJ	Scott Brosius, David Justice	20.00

		NM/M
OM	Paul O'Neill, Tino Martinez	25.00
WO	Bernie Williams, Paul O'Neill	25.00
WG	David Wells, Dwight Gooden	25.00
GC	Joe Girardi, David Cone	25.00
KR	Chuck Knoblauch, Tim Raines	25.00

Yankees Dynasty Combo Base

		NM/M
	Common Combo:	50.00
JW	Derek Jeter, Bernie Williams	60.00
CJ	Roger Clemens, Derek Jeter	75.00

2001 All-Star HR Derby Jerseys

		NM/M
	Common Player:	10.00
	Inserted 1:288	
BrB	Bret Boone	10.00
JG	Jason Giambi	15.00
TH	Todd Helton	15.00
AR	Alex Rodriguez	20.00
SS	Sammy Sosa	25.00

2002 Upper Deck Ballpark Idols

		NM/M
	Complete Set (245):	125.00
	Common Player:	.15
	Common (201-245):	3.00
	Production 1,750	
	Pack (5):	2.00
	Box (24 + Bobber):	50.00
1	Troy Glaus	.40
2	Kevin Appier	.15
3	Darin Erstad	.25
4	Garret Anderson	.25
5	Brad Fullmer	.15
6	Tim Salmon	.25
7	Eric Chavez	.25
8	Tim Hudson	.25
9	David Justice	.25
10	Barry Zito	.25
11	Miguel Tejada	.40
12	Mark Mulder	.40
13	Jermaine Dye	.15
14	Carlos Delgado	.40
15	Jose Cruz Jr.	.15
16	Brandon Lyon	.15
17	Shannon Stewart	.15
18	Eric Hinske	.25
19	Chris Carpenter	.15
20	Greg Vaughn	.15
21	Tanyon Sturtze	.15
22	Jason Tyner	.15
23	Toby Hall	.15
24	Ben Grieve	.15
25	Jim Thome	.75
26	Omar Vizquel	.25
27	Ricky Gutierrez	.15
28	C.C. Sabathia	.25
29	Ellis Burks	.15
30	Matt Lawton	.15
31	Milton Bradley	.15
32	Edgar Martinez	.25
33	Ichiro Suzuki	1.50
34	Bret Boone	.25
35	Freddy Garcia	.25
36	Mike Cameron	.15
37	John Olerud	.25
38	Kazuhisa Sasaki	.15
39	Jeff Cirillo	.15
40	Jeff Conine	.15
41	Marty Cordova	.15
42	Tony Batista	.15
43	Jerry Hairston Jr.	.15
44	Jason Johnson	.15
45	David Segui	.15
46	Alex Rodriguez	2.00
47	Rafael Palmeiro	.50
48	Carl Everett	.15
49	Chan Ho Park	.15
50	Ivan Rodriguez	.50
51	Juan Gonzalez	.50
52	Hank Blalock	.50
53	Manny Ramirez	.50
54	Pedro J. Martinez	.75
55	Tony Clark	.15
56	Nomar Garciaparra	1.25
57	Johnny Damon	.25
58	Trot Nixon	.25
59	Rickey Henderson	.50
60	Mike Sweeney	.15
61	Neifi Perez	.15
62	Joe Randa	.15
63	Carlos Beltran	.25
64	Chuck Knoblauch	.15
65	Michael Tucker	.15
66	Dean Palmer	.15
67	Bobby Higginson	.15
68	Dmitri Young	.15
69	Randall Simon	.15
70	Mitch Meluskey	.15
71	Damion Easley	.15
72	Joe Mays	.15
73	Doug Mientkiewicz	.15
74	Corey Koskie	.15
75	Brad Radke	.15
76	Cristian Guzman	.15
77	Torii Hunter	.25
78	Eric Milton	.15
79	Frank Thomas	.50
80	Paul Konerko	.25
81	Mark Buehrle	.15
82	Magglio Ordonez	.25
83	Carlos Lee	.15
84	Joe Crede	.15
85	Derek Jeter	2.00
86	Bernie Williams	.50
87	Mike Mussina	.50
88	Jorge Posada	.40
89	Roger Clemens	1.50
90	Jason Giambi	.50
91	Alfonso Soriano	.75
92	Rondell White	.15
93	Jeff Bagwell	.50
94	Lance Berkman	.40
95	Roy Oswalt	.25
96	Richard Hidalgo	.15
97	Wade Miller	.15
98	Craig Biggio	.25
99	Greg Maddux	1.00
100	Chipper Jones	.75
101	Gary Sheffield	.40
102	Rafael Furcal	.15
103	Andruw Jones	.50
104	Vinny Castilla	.15
105	Marcus Giles	.15
106	Tom Glavine	.40
107	Richie Sexson	.40
108	Geoff Jenkins	.15
109	Glendon Rusch	.15
110	Eric Young	.15
111	Ben Sheets	.25
112	Alex Sanchez	.15
113	Albert Pujols	1.50
114	J.D. Drew	.25
115	Matt Morris	.25
116	Jim Edmonds	.40
117	Tino Martinez	.15
118	Scott Rolen	.75
119	Edgar Renteria	.25
120	Sammy Sosa	1.50
121	Kerry Wood	.75
122	Moises Alou	.25
123	Jon Lieber	.15
124	Fred McGriff	.25
125	Juan Cruz	.15
126	Alex Gonzalez	.15
127	Corey Patterson	.25
128	Randy Johnson	.75
129	Luis Gonzalez	.25
130	Steve Finley	.15
131	Matt Williams	.25
132	Curt Schilling	.50
133	Mark Grace	.40
134	Craig Counsell	.15
135	Shawn Green	.25
136	Kevin Brown	.25
137	Hideo Nomo	.40
138	Paul LoDuca	.15
139	Brian Jordan	.15
140	Eric Karros	.15
141	Adrian Beltre	.25
142	Vladimir Guerrero	.75
143	Fernando Tatis	.15
144	Javier Vazquez	.15
145	Orlando Cabrera	.15
146	Tony Armas Jr.	.15
147	Jose Vidro	.15
148	Barry Bonds	2.00
149	Rich Aurilia	.15
150	Tsuyoshi Shinjo	.15
151	Jeff Kent	.25
152	Russ Ortiz	.15
153	Jason Schmidt	.25
154	Reggie Sanders	.15
155	Preston Wilson	.15
156	Luis Castillo	.15
157	Charles Johnson	.15
158	Josh Beckett	.40
159	Derrek Lee	.25
160	Mike Lowell	.25
161	Mike Piazza	1.00
162	Roberto Alomar	.40
163	Al Leiter	.25
164	Mo Vaughn	.25
165	Jeromy Burnitz	.15
166	Edgardo Alfonzo	.15
167	Roger Cedeno	.15
168	Ryan Klesko	.25
169	Brian Lawrence	.15
170	Sean Burroughs	.15
171	Phil Nevin	.15
172	Ramon Vazquez	.15
173	Mark Kotsay	.15
174	Marlon Anderson	.15
175	Mike Lieberthal	.15
176	Bobby Abreu	.25
177	Pat Burrell	.40
178	Robert Person	.15
179	Brandon Duckworth	.15
180	Jimmy Rollins	.25
181	Brian Giles	.25
182	Pokey Reese	.15
183	Kris Benson	.15
184	Aramis Ramirez	.25
185	Jason Kendall	.15
186	Kip Wells	.15
187	Ken Griffey Jr.	1.00
188	Adam Dunn	.50
189	Barry Larkin	.40
190	Sean Casey	.25
191	Austin Kearns	.25
192	Aaron Boone	.15
193	Todd Helton	.50
194	Juan Pierre	.15
195	Mike Hampton	.15
196	Jose Ortiz	.15
197	Larry Walker	.25
198	Juan Uribe	.15
199	Ichiro Suzuki (Checklist)	.75
200	Jason Giambi (Checklist)	.25
201	Franklyn German RC	3.00
202	Rodrigo Rosario RC	3.00
203	Brandon Puffer RC	3.00
204	Kirk Saarloos RC	3.00
205	Chris Baker RC	3.00
206	John Ennis RC	3.00
207	Luis Martinez RC	3.00
208	So Taguchi RC	6.00
209	Michael Crudale RC	3.00
210	Francis Beltran RC	3.00
211	Brandon Backe RC	3.00
212	Felix Escalona RC	3.00
213	Jose Valverde RC	4.00
214	Doug DeVore RC	3.00
215	Kazuhisa Ishii RC	6.00
216	Victor Alvarez RC	3.00
217	Ron Calloway RC	3.00
218	Eric Good RC	3.00
219	Jorge Nunez RC	3.00
220	Deivis Santos RC	3.00
221	Nelson Castro RC	3.00
222	Matt Thornton RC	3.00
223	Jason Simontacchi RC	3.00
224	Hansel Izquierdo RC	3.00
225	Tyler Yates RC	4.00
226	Jaime Cerda RC	3.00
227	Satoru Komiyama RC	3.00
228	Steve Bechler RC	3.00
229	Ben Howard RC	3.00
230	Todd Donovan RC	3.00
231	Jorge Padilla RC	3.00
232	Eric Junge RC	3.00
233	Anderson Machado RC	3.00
234	Adrian Burnside RC	3.00
235	Mike Gonzalez RC	3.00
236	Josh Hancock RC	3.00
237	Anastacio Martinez RC	3.00
238	Chris Booker RC	3.00
239	Rene Reyes RC	3.00
240	Cam Esslinger RC	3.00
241	Oliver Perez RC	10.00
242	Tim Kalita RC	3.00
243	Kevin Frederick RC	3.00
244	Mitch Wylie RC	3.00
245	Edwin Almonte RC	3.00

Bronze

Stars (1-200):	5-10X
SP's (201-245):	.75-1.5X
Production 100 Sets	

Gold

No pricing due to scarcity.
Production 25 Sets

Bobbers

	NM/M
Inserted 1:Box	
Roberto Alomar	10.00
Jeff Bagwell	15.00
Josh Beckett	10.00
Barry Bonds	30.00
Sean Burroughs	8.00
Roger Clemens	20.00
Joe DiMaggio/ 555/Away	40.00
Joe DiMaggio/ 361/Home	50.00
Nomar Garciaparra	20.00
Jason Giambi	10.00
Luis Gonzalez	8.00
Ken Griffey Jr.	15.00
Vladimir Guerrero	15.00
Kazuhisa Ishii	10.00
Derek Jeter/SP/Away	40.00
Randy Johnson/ D'backs	15.00
Randy Johnson/ Expos	15.00
Chipper Jones	15.00
Greg Maddux	20.00
Mickey Mantle/ 777/Away	50.00
Mickey Mantle/ 536/Home	60.00
Mark McGwire/ Cards	35.00
Mike Piazza/Mets	20.00
Mark Prior	15.00
Albert Pujols	25.00
Alex Rodriguez	20.00
Ivan Rodriguez	10.00
Curt Schilling/ D'backs	10.00
Sammy Sosa/ Cubs/Away	25.00
Ichiro Suzuki/ SP/Away	30.00
Frank Thomas	10.00
Jim Thome	15.00

Bobbers Gold

	NM/M
Amount produced listed.	
Joe DiMaggio/ 56/Away	100.00
Joe DiMaggio/ 41/Home	125.00
Mickey Mantle/ 77/Away	140.00
Mickey Mantle/ 61/Home	125.00

Field Garb Jerseys

		NM/M
	Common Player:	4.00
	Inserted 1:72	
TB	Tony Batista	4.00
BG	Brian Giles	4.00
RJ	Randy Johnson	10.00
JK	Jeff Kent	4.00
TM	Tino Martinez	4.00
JO	John Olerud	4.00
AR	Alex Rodriguez	12.00
IR	Ivan Rodriguez	6.00
MS	Mike Sweeney	4.00
RV	Robin Ventura	4.00
LW	Larry Walker	4.00
BZ	Barry Zito	6.00

Figure Heads

		NM/M
	Complete Set (10):	20.00
	Common Player:	1.00
	Inserted 1:12	
F1	Ichiro Suzuki	3.00
F2	Sammy Sosa	2.50
F3	Alex Rodriguez	4.00

F4	Jason Giambi	1.00
F5	Barry Bonds	4.00
F6	Chipper Jones	1.50
F7	Mike Piazza	2.00
F8	Derek Jeter	4.00
F9	Nomar Garciaparra	2.50
F10	Ken Griffey Jr.	2.00

Player's Club Jerseys

NM/M

Common Player:		6.00
Inserted 1:72		
KB	Kevin Brown	6.00
DE	Darin Erstad	8.00
RF	Rafael Furcal	6.00
TH	Tim Hudson	6.00
AJ	Andruw Jones	8.00
JK	Jason Kendall	6.00
MM	Mark McGwire/SP	70.00
PN	Phil Nevin	6.00
HN	Hideo Nomo	20.00
MO	Magglio Ordonez	6.00
CS	Curt Schilling	8.00
IS	Ichiro Suzuki/SP	40.00
JT	Jim Thome	12.00

Playmakers 2002

NM/M

Complete Set (20):		25.00
Common Player:		.75
Inserted 1:6		
P1	Ken Griffey Jr.	2.00
P2	Alex Rodriguez	4.00
P3	Sammy Sosa	2.50
P4	Derek Jeter	4.00
P5	Mike Piazza	2.00
P6	Jason Giambi	1.00
P7	Barry Bonds	4.00
P8	Frank Thomas	1.00
P9	Randy Johnson	1.50
P10	Chipper Jones	1.50
P11	Jeff Bagwell	1.00
P12	Vladimir Guerrero	1.50
P13	Albert Pujols	3.00
P14	Nomar Garciaparra	2.50
P15	Ichiro Suzuki	3.00
P16	Troy Glaus	1.00
P17	Ivan Rodriguez	1.00
P18	Carlos Delgado	.75
P19	Greg Maddux	2.00
P20	Todd Helton	1.50

Uniform Sluggers

NM/M

Common Player:		5.00
Inserted 1:72		
JB	Jeff Bagwell	8.00
JGi	Jason Giambi	8.00
JGo	Juan Gonzalez	8.00
SG	Shawn Green	5.00
KG	Ken Griffey Jr./SP	25.00
TH	Todd Helton	8.00
CJ	Chipper Jones	10.00
MM	Mickey Mantle/SP	100.00
MP	Mike Piazza	15.00
AR	Alex Rodriguez	12.00
SS	Sammy Sosa/95	
BW	Bernie Williams	8.00

2002 Upper Deck Diamond Connection

		NM/M
Complete Set (550):		
Common Player:		.15
Common Rk (91-200):		4.00
Production 1,500		
Common Jersey (201-270):		4.00
Production 775		
Common Jersey (271-320):		5.00
Production 200		
Common Jersey (321-353):		5.00
Production 150		
Common Jersey (354-368):		6.00
Production 100		
Common Bat (369-438):		5.00
Production 775		
Common Bat (439-488):		5.00
Production 200		
Common Bat (489-521):		5.00
Production 150		
Common Bat (522-536):		10.00
Production 100		
Pack (5):		4.00
Box (14):		50.00
1	Troy Glaus	.50
2	Darin Erstad	.40
3	Barry Zito	.40
4	Eric Chavez	.40
5	Tim Hudson	.40
6	Miguel Tejada	.40
7	Carlos Delgado	.40
8	Shannon Stewart	.15
9	Greg Vaughn	.15
10	Jim Thome	.75
11	C.C. Sabathia	.15
12	Ichiro Suzuki	1.50
13	Edgar Martinez	.25
14	Bret Boone	.25
15	Freddy Garcia	.15
16	Jeff Conine	.15
17	Alex Rodriguez	2.00
18	Rafael Palmeiro	.50
19	Ivan Rodriguez	.50
20	Juan Gonzalez	.50
21	Pedro J. Martinez	.75
22	Nomar Garciaparra	1.50
23	Manny Ramirez	.50
24	Carlos Beltran	.25
25	Mike Sweeney	.15
26	Dmitri Young	.15
27	Bobby Higginson	.15
28	Corey Koskie	.15
29	Cristian Guzman	.15
30	Doug Mientkiewicz	.15
31	Torii Hunter	.25
32	Frank Thomas	.50
33	Mark Buehrle	.15
34	Carlos Lee	.15
35	Magglio Ordonez	.40
36	Roger Clemens	1.50
37	Bernie Williams	.50
38	Jason Giambi	.75
39	Derek Jeter	2.00
40	Mike Mussina	.50
41	Jeff Bagwell	.50
42	Richard Hidalgo	.15
43	Lance Berkman	.40
44	Roy Oswalt	.40
45	Chipper Jones	.75
46	Gary Sheffield	.40
47	Andruw Jones	.50
48	Greg Maddux	1.00
49	Geoff Jenkins	.15
50	Ben Sheets	.25
51	Richie Sexson	.40
52	Albert Pujols	1.50
53	Matt Morris	.15
54	J.D. Drew	.40
55	Tino Martinez	.25
56	Sammy Sosa	1.50
57	Kerry Wood	.75
58	Moises Alou	.25
59	Fred McGriff	.25
60	Randy Johnson	.75
61	Luis Gonzalez	.25
62	Curt Schilling	.50
63	Kevin Brown	.25
64	Shawn Green	.40
65	Paul LoDuca	.15
66	Vladimir Guerrero	.75
67	Jose Vidro	.15
68	Barry Bonds	2.00
69	Jeff Kent	.25
70	Rich Aurilia	.15
71	Preston Wilson	.15
72	Josh Beckett	.40
73	Cliff Floyd	.25
74	Mike Piazza	1.00
75	Mo Vaughn	.25
76	Roberto Alomar	.40
77	Jeromy Burnitz	.15
78	Phil Nevin	.15
79	Sean Burroughs	.15
80	Scott Rolen	.75
81	Bobby Abreu	.25
82	Pat Burrell	.40
83	Brian Giles	.40
84	Jason Kendall	.15
85	Ken Griffey Jr.	1.00
86	Adam Dunn	.50
87	Aaron Boone	.15
88	Larry Walker	.25
89	Todd Helton	.50
90	Mike Hampton	.15
91	Brandon Puffer RC	4.00
92	Rodrigo Rosario RC	4.00
93	Tom Shearn RC	4.00
94	Morgan Ensberg	4.00
95	Jason Lane	4.00
96	Franklyn German RC	4.00
97	Carlos Pena	4.00
98	Joe Orloski RC	4.00
99	Reed Johnson RC	6.00
100	Chris Baker RC	4.00
101	Corey Thurman RC	4.00
102	Gustavo Chacin RC	4.00
103	Eric Hinske	4.00
104	John Foster RC	4.00
105	John Ennis RC	4.00
106	Kevin Gryboski RC	4.00
107	Jung Bong	4.00
108	Travis Wilson	4.00
109	Luis Martinez RC	4.00
110	Brian Mallette RC	4.00
111	Takahito Nomura RC	4.00
112	Bill Hall	4.00
113	Jeff Deardorff RC	4.00
114	Cristian Guerrero	4.00
115	Scotty Layfield RC	4.00
116	Michael Crudale RC	4.00
117	So Taguchi RC	6.00
118	Jeremy Lambert RC	4.00
119	Jimmy Journell	4.00
120	Francis Beltran RC	4.00
121	Mark Prior	6.00
122	Ben Christensen	4.00
123	Jorge Sosa RC	4.00
124	Brandon Backe RC	4.00
125	Steve Kent RC	4.00
126	Felix Escalona RC	4.00
127	P.J. Bevis RC	4.00
128	Jose Valverde RC	4.00
129	Doug DeVore RC	4.00
130	Jeremy Ward RC	4.00
131	Mike Koplove	4.00
132	Luis Terrero	4.00
133	John Patterson	4.00
134	Victor Alvarez RC	4.00
135	Kirk Saarloos	4.00
136	Kazuhisa Ishii RC	8.00
137	Steve Colyer	4.00
138	Cesar Izturis	4.00
139	Ron Calloway RC	4.00
140	Eric Good RC	4.00
141	Jorge Nunez RC	4.00
142	Ron Chiavacci RC	4.00
143	Donnie Bridges	4.00
144	Nelson Castro RC	4.00
145	Deivis Santos	4.00
146	Kurt Ainsworth	4.00
147	Arturo McDowell	4.00
148	Allan Simpson RC	4.00
149	Matt Thornton	4.00
150	Luis Ugueto RC	4.00
151	J.J. Putz RC	4.00
152	Hansel Izquierdo RC	4.00
153	Oliver Perez RC	4.00
154	Jaime Cerda RC	4.00
155	Mark Corey RC	4.00
156	Tyler Yates RC	6.00
157	Satoru Komiyama RC	4.00
158	Adam Walker RC	4.00
159	Steve Bechler RC	6.00
160	Erik Bedard RC	4.00
161	Todd Donovan RC	4.00
162	Clifford Bartosh RC	4.00
163	Ben Howard RC	8.00
164	Andy Shibilo RC	4.00
165	Dennis Tankersley	4.00
166	Mike Bynum	4.00
167	Anderson Machado RC	4.00
168	Peter Zamora RC	5.00
169	Eric Junge RC	4.00
170	Elio Serrano RC	4.00
171	Jorge Padilla RC	4.00
172	Marlon Byrd RC	4.00
173	Adrian Burnside RC	4.00
174	Mike Gonzalez RC	4.00
175	J.R. House	4.00
176	Hank Blalock	6.00
177	Travis Hughes RC	4.00
178	Mark Teixeira	6.00
179	Josh Hancock RC	4.00
180	Anastacio Martinez RC	4.00
181	Jorge de la Rosa RC	4.00
182	Ben Broussard	4.00
183	Austin Kearns	4.00
184	Corky Miller	4.00
185	Colin Young RC	4.00
186	Cam Esslinger RC	4.00
187	Rene Reyes RC	4.00
188	Aaron Cook RC	4.00
189	Alexis Gomez	4.00
190	Nate Field RC	4.00
191	Miguel Asencio RC	4.00
192	Brandon Berger	4.00
193	Fernando Rodney	4.00
194	Andy Van Hekken	4.00
195	Kevin Frederick RC	4.00
196	Todd Sears	4.00
197	Edwin Almonte RC	4.00
198	Kyle Kane RC	4.00
199	Mitch Wylie RC	4.00
200	Mike Porzio	4.00
201	Darin Erstad	6.00
202	Tim Salmon	6.00
203	Jeff Bagwell	10.00
204	Lance Berkman	6.00
205	Eric Chavez	6.00
206	Tim Hudson	6.00
207	Carlos Delgado	6.00
208	Chipper Jones	10.00
209	Gary Sheffield	6.00
210	Greg Maddux	15.00
211	Tom Glavine	6.00
212	Mike Mussina	10.00
213	J.D. Drew	6.00
214	Rick Ankiel	4.00
215	Sammy Sosa	15.00
216	Mike Lieberthal	6.00
217	Fred McGriff	8.00
218	David Wells	4.00
219	Curt Schilling	10.00
220	Luis Gonzalez	6.00
221	Mark Grace	10.00
222	Kevin Brown	4.00
223	Hideo Nomo	20.00
224	Jose Vidro	4.00
225	Jeff Kent	4.00
226	Rich Aurilia	4.00
227	Kenny Lofton	4.00
228	C.C. Sabathia	4.00
229	Edgar Martinez	8.00
230	Freddy Garcia	4.00
231	Cliff Floyd	4.00
232	Preston Wilson	4.00
233	Mike Piazza	10.00
234	Roberto Alomar	8.00
235	Trevor Hoffman	4.00
236	Ryan Klesko	5.00
237	Sean Burroughs	4.00
238	Scott Rolen	10.00
239	Pat Burrell	4.00
240	Edgardo Alfonzo	4.00
241	Brian Giles	8.00
242	Jason Kendall	5.00
243	Alex Rodriguez	15.00
244	Juan Gonzalez	8.00
245	Ivan Rodriguez	8.00
246	Rafael Palmeiro	8.00
247	Ken Griffey Jr.	12.00
248	Adam Dunn	15.00
249	Barry Larkin	5.00
250	Manny Ramirez	10.00
251	Pedro Martinez	10.00
252	Todd Helton	8.00
253	Larry Walker	6.00
254	Randy Johnson	10.00
255	Mike Sweeney	4.00
256	Carlos Beltran	8.00
257	Dmitri Young	4.00
258	Joe Mays	4.00
259	Doug Mientkiewicz	4.00
260	Corey Koskie	4.00
261	Magglio Ordonez	8.00
262	Frank Thomas	8.00
263	Ray Durham	4.00
264	Jason Giambi	10.00
265	Bernie Williams	8.00
266	Roger Clemens	15.00
267	Mariano Rivera	8.00
268	Robin Ventura	4.00
269	Andy Pettitte	10.00
270	Jorge Posada	8.00
271	Mike Piazza	15.00
272	Alex Rodriguez	15.00
273	Ken Griffey Jr.	15.00
274	Jason Giambi	10.00
275	Frank Thomas	15.00
276	Greg Maddux	15.00
277	Sammy Sosa	15.00
278	Roger Clemens	15.00
279	Jeff Bagwell	10.00
280	Todd Helton	8.00
281	Ichiro Suzuki	40.00
282	Randy Johnson	10.00
283	Jim Thome	15.00
284	Ivan Rodriguez	8.00
285	Darin Erstad	6.00
286	Eric Chavez	8.00
287	Barry Zito	10.00
288	Carlos Delgado	8.00
289	Omar Vizquel	6.00

#	Player	Price
290	Edgar Martinez	8.00
291	Manny Ramirez	10.00
292	Mike Sweeney	6.00
293	Tom Glavine	8.00
294	Joe Mays	6.00
295	Eric Milton	6.00
296	Magglio Ordonez	8.00
297	Bernie Williams	8.00
298	Trevor Hoffman	6.00
299	Andruw Jones	8.00
300	Aubrey Huff	5.00
301	Jim Edmonds	8.00
302	Kerry Wood	10.00
303	Luis Gonzalez	8.00
304	Shawn Green	6.00
305	Jose Vidro	5.00
306	Jeff Kent	5.00
307	Edgardo Alfonzo	5.00
308	Preston Wilson	5.00
309	Roberto Alomar	10.00
310	Jeromy Burnitz	5.00
311	Phil Nevin	5.00
312	Ryan Klesko	5.00
313	Bobby Abreu	6.00
314	Scott Rolen	12.00
315	Kazuhiro Sasaki	5.00
316	Jason Kendall	5.00
317	Sean Casey	5.00
318	Larry Walker	5.00
319	Mike Hampton	5.00
320	Juan Gonzalez	8.00
321	Darin Erstad	8.00
322	Tim Hudson	8.00
323	Carlos Delgado	8.00
324	Greg Vaughn	5.00
325	Jim Thome	15.00
326	Ichiro Suzuki	40.00
327	Rafael Palmeiro	8.00
328	Alex Rodriguez	15.00
329	Juan Gonzalez	8.00
330	Manny Ramirez	10.00
331	Carlos Beltran	6.00
332	Eric Milton	5.00
333	Frank Thomas	8.00
334	Roger Clemens	15.00
335	Jason Giambi	10.00
336	Lance Berkman	8.00
337	Greg Maddux	15.00
338	Chipper Jones	10.00
339	Sean Casey	8.00
340	Jim Edmonds	8.00
341	Kerry Wood	10.00
342	Sammy Sosa	15.00
343	Luis Gonzalez	8.00
344	Shawn Green	6.00
345	Jeff Kent	6.00
346	Preston Wilson	5.00
347	Roberto Alomar	10.00
348	Phil Nevin	5.00
349	Scott Rolen	12.00
350	Mike Sweeney	5.00
351	Ken Griffey Jr.	15.00
352	Todd Helton	8.00
353	Larry Walker	5.00
354	Alex Rodriguez	15.00
355	Pedro J. Martinez	10.00
356	Frank Thomas	10.00
357	Jason Giambi	10.00
358	Bernie Williams	10.00
359	Jeff Bagwell	10.00
360	Chipper Jones	10.00
361	Sammy Sosa	20.00
362	Randy Johnson	10.00
363	Shawn Green	6.00
364	Mike Piazza	15.00
365	Ichiro Suzuki	50.00
366	Ken Griffey Jr.	15.00
367	Larry Walker	8.00
368	Jim Edmonds	8.00
369	Darin Erstad	8.00
370	Tim Salmon	8.00
371	Mark Kotsay	5.00
372	Craig Biggio	8.00
373	Eric Chavez	10.00
374	David Justice	8.00
375	Carlos Delgado	8.00
376	Chipper Jones	15.00
377	Gary Sheffield	6.00
378	Greg Maddux	15.00
379	Eric Karros	5.00
380	Fred McGriff	8.00
381	J.D. Drew	8.00
382	Rick Ankiel	5.00
383	Sammy Sosa	15.00
384	Moises Alou	5.00
385	Ben Grieve	5.00
386	Greg Vaughn	5.00
387	Jay Payton	5.00
388	Luis Gonzalez	6.00
389	Ray Durham	5.00
390	Shawn Green	8.00
391	Hideo Nomo	20.00
392	Jose Vidro	5.00
393	Jeff Kent	5.00
394	Adrian Beltre	5.00
395	Jim Thome	15.00
396	Bobby Abreu	5.00
397	Edgar Martinez	10.00
398	Carl Everett	5.00
399	Luis Castillo	5.00
400	Preston Wilson	5.00
401	Jermaine Dye	8.00
402	Roberto Alomar	8.00
403	Todd Hundley	5.00
404	Ryan Klesko	5.00
405	Phil Nevin	5.00
406	Scott Rolen	10.00
407	Rafael Furcal	5.00
408	Miguel Tejada	8.00
409	Brian Giles	6.00
410	Jason Kendall	5.00
411	Alex Rodriguez	15.00
412	Juan Gonzalez	8.00
413	Ivan Rodriguez	8.00
414	Rafael Palmeiro	8.00
415	Ken Griffey Jr.	15.00
416	Edgardo Alfonzo	5.00
417	Barry Larkin	8.00
418	Manny Ramirez	8.00
419	Pedro J. Martinez	12.00
420	Todd Helton	8.00
421	Larry Walker	8.00
422	Garret Anderson	6.00
423	Mike Sweeney	5.00
424	Carlos Beltran	5.00
425	Javier Lopez	5.00
426	J.T. Snow	5.00
427	Doug Mientkiewicz	5.00
428	John Olerud	5.00
429	Magglio Ordonez	6.00
430	Frank Thomas	10.00
431	Kenny Lofton	5.00
432	Al Leiter	5.00
433	Bernie Williams	8.00
434	Roger Clemens	15.00
435	Tom Glavine	8.00
436	Robin Ventura	6.00
437	Chan Ho Park	5.00
438	Jorge Posada	8.00
439	Charles Johnson	5.00
440	Alex Rodriguez	20.00
441	Ken Griffey Jr.	15.00
442	Mark Kotsay	5.00
443	Frank Thomas	10.00
444	Greg Maddux	20.00
445	Sammy Sosa	20.00
446	Tom Glavine	10.00
447	Chipper Jones	15.00
448	Todd Helton	10.00
449	Jeff Cirillo	5.00
450	Steve Finley	8.00
451	Jim Thome	15.00
452	Ivan Rodriguez	8.00
453	Darin Erstad	8.00
454	Eric Chavez	8.00
455	Miguel Tejada	8.00
456	Carlos Delgado	8.00
457	Omar Vizquel	5.00
458	Edgar Martinez	10.00
459	Johnny Damon	8.00
460	Russell Branyan	5.00
461	Kenny Lofton	5.00
462	Jermaine Dye	5.00
463	Ellis Burks	5.00
464	Magglio Ordonez	8.00
465	Bernie Williams	10.00
466	Tim Salmon	5.00
467	Andruw Jones	8.00
468	Jeffrey Hammonds	5.00
469	Jim Edmonds	10.00
470	Kerry Wood	15.00
471	Luis Gonzalez	8.00
472	Shawn Green	8.00
473	Jose Vidro	5.00
474	Jeff Kent	6.00
475	Javier Lopez	5.00
476	Preston Wilson	5.00
477	Roberto Alomar	10.00
478	Robin Ventura	6.00
479	Phil Nevin	5.00
480	Ryan Klesko	8.00
481	Bobby Abreu	6.00
482	Scott Rolen	10.00
483	Brian Giles	8.00
484	Jason Kendall	5.00
485	Tsuyoshi Shinjo	5.00
486	Larry Walker	6.00
487	Mike Lieberthal	5.00
488	Juan Gonzalez	8.00
489	Darin Erstad	6.00
490	Tom Glavine	10.00
491	Carlos Delgado	6.00
492	Greg Vaughn	5.00
493	Jim Thome	15.00
494	Mark Grace	15.00
495	Rafael Palmeiro	8.00
496	Alex Rodriguez	20.00
497	Juan Gonzalez	10.00
498	Miguel Tejada	8.00
499	Carlos Beltran	5.00
500	Andruw Jones	8.00
501	Frank Thomas	10.00
502	Andres Galarraga	5.00
503	Gary Sheffield	8.00
504	Craig Biggio	8.00
505	Greg Maddux	20.00
506	Chipper Jones	20.00
507	Pat Burrell	10.00
508	Jim Edmonds	10.00
509	Kerry Wood	15.00
510	Sammy Sosa	20.00
511	Luis Gonzalez	8.00
512	Shawn Green	8.00
513	Edgardo Alfonzo	5.00
514	Preston Wilson	5.00
515	Roberto Alomar	10.00
516	Phil Nevin	5.00
517	Scott Rolen	15.00
518	Brian Giles	8.00
519	Jorge Posada	10.00
520	Todd Helton	12.00
521	Larry Walker	8.00
522	Alex Rodriguez	25.00
523	Pedro J. Martinez	20.00
524	Frank Thomas	12.00
525	Jason Giambi	15.00
526	Bernie Williams	10.00
527	J.D. Drew	10.00
528	Chipper Jones	20.00
529	Sammy Sosa	25.00
530	Randy Johnson	15.00
531	Shawn Green	10.00
532	Kevin Brown	10.00
533	Brian Giles	10.00
534	Ken Griffey Jr.	20.00
535	Larry Walker	10.00
536	Jim Edmonds	10.00
537	Sean Casey/Jsy/775	8.00
538	Ichiro Suzuki/Jsy/775	40.00
539	Pat Burrell/Jsy/200	10.00
540	Adam Dunn/Jsy/200	20.00
541	Lance Berkman/ Jsy/200	10.00
542	Cliff Floyd/Jsy/150	8.00
543	Roger Clemens/ Jsy/100	20.00
544	Kerry Wood/Bat/775	15.00
545	Andruw Jones/ Bat/775	8.00
546	Manny Ramirez/ Bat/200	10.00
547	Jorge Posada/ Bat/200	10.00
548	Fred McGriff/Bat/200	8.00
549	Mike Sweeney/ Bat/150	6.00
550	Todd Helton/Bat/100	12.00

Great Connections

		NM/M
Production 50 Sets		
GC-GR	Jason Giambi, Babe Ruth	350.00
GC-MD	Mickey Mantle, Joe DiMaggio	350.00
GC-MR	Mark McGwire, Babe Ruth	350.00
GC-MS	Mark McGwire, Sammy Sosa	200.00
GC-RR	Alex Rodriguez, Nolan Ryan	150.00
GC-IG	Ichiro Suzuki, Ken Griffey Jr.	150.00

Mem. Signatures Bat

		NM/M
Varying quantities produced		
JD	Joe DiMaggio/20	600.00
JG	Jason Giambi/49	60.00
KG	Ken Griffey Jr./49	150.00

MMc	Mark McGwire/49	300.00
JM	Joe Morgan/99	35.00
KP	Kirby Puckett/145	75.00
CR	Cal Ripken Jr/145	150.00
AR	Alex Rodriguez/145	100.00
NR	Nolan Ryan/99	150.00
SS	Sammy Sosa/99	150.00
IS	Ichiro Suzuki/99	250.00

Mem. Signatures Jsy

		NM/M
Varying quantities produced		
Gold:		.75-1X
Production 150		
EB	Ernie Banks/150	80.00
JD	Joe DiMaggio/20	550.00
KG	Ken Griffey Jr./49	150.00
SK	Sandy Koufax/150	300.00
MMc	Mark McGwire/49	300.00
JM	Joe Morgan/99	35.00
CR	Cal Ripken Jr/145	150.00
AR	Alex Rodriguez/145	100.00
NR	Nolan Ryan/99	150.00
SS	Sammy Sosa/99	200.00
IS	Ichiro Suzuki/99	250.00

2002 Upper Deck Honor Roll

		NM/M
Complete Set (100):		25.00
Common Player:		.15
Pack (5):		2.00
Box (24):		30.00
1	Randy Johnson	.50
2	Mike Piazza	.75
3	Albert Pujols	1.00
4	Roberto Alomar	.25
5	Chipper Jones	.50
6	Rich Aurilia	.15
7	Barry Bonds	1.00
8	Ken Griffey Jr.	.75
9	Sammy Sosa	.75
10	Roger Clemens	.75
11	Ivan Rodriguez	.40
12	Jason Giambi	.40
13	Bret Boone	.15
14	Troy Glaus	.25
15	Alex Rodriguez	.75
16	Manny Ramirez	.40
17	Bernie Williams	.40
18	Ichiro Suzuki	.75
19	Matt Thornton	.25
20	Chris Baker RC	.25
21	Tyler Yates RC	.50
22	Jorge Nunez RC	.50
23	Rene Reyes RC	.50
24	Ben Howard RC	.50
25	Ron Calloway RC	.40

26	Danny Wright	.15
27	Reed Johnson RC	.50
28	Randy Johnson	.25
29	Randy Johnson	.25
30	Randy Johnson	.25
31	Randy Johnson	.25
32	Mike Piazza	.50
33	Mike Piazza	.50
34	Mike Piazza	.50
35	Mike Piazza	.50
36	Albert Pujols	.75
37	Albert Pujols	.75
38	Albert Pujols	.75
39	Albert Pujols	.75
40	Roberto Alomar	.20
41	Roberto Alomar	.20
42	Roberto Alomar	.20
43	Roberto Alomar	.20
44	Chipper Jones	.50
45	Chipper Jones	.50
46	Chipper Jones	.50
47	Chipper Jones	.50
48	Rich Aurilia	.15
49	Rich Aurilia	.15
50	Rich Aurilia	.15
51	Rich Aurilia	.15
52	Barry Bonds	1.00
53	Barry Bonds	1.00
54	Barry Bonds	1.00
55	Barry Bonds	1.00
56	Ken Griffey Jr.	.75
57	Ken Griffey Jr.	.75
58	Ken Griffey Jr.	.75
59	Ken Griffey Jr.	.75
60	Sammy Sosa	.50
61	Sammy Sosa	.50
62	Sammy Sosa	.50
63	Sammy Sosa	.50
64	Roger Clemens	.75
65	Roger Clemens	.75
66	Roger Clemens	.75
67	Roger Clemens	.75
68	Ivan Rodriguez	.25
69	Ivan Rodriguez	.25
70	Ivan Rodriguez	.25
71	Ivan Rodriguez	.25
72	Jason Giambi	.25
73	Jason Giambi	.25
74	Jason Giambi	.25
75	Jason Giambi	.25
76	Bret Boone	.15
77	Bret Boone	.15
78	Bret Boone	.15
79	Bret Boone	.15
80	Troy Glaus	.20
81	Troy Glaus	.20
82	Troy Glaus	.20
83	Troy Glaus	.20
84	Alex Rodriguez	.75
85	Alex Rodriguez	.75
86	Alex Rodriguez	.75
87	Alex Rodriguez	.75
88	Manny Ramirez	.25
89	Manny Ramirez	.25
90	Manny Ramirez	.25
91	Manny Ramirez	.25
92	Bernie Williams	.20
93	Bernie Williams	.20
94	Bernie Williams	.20
95	Bernie Williams	.20
96	Ichiro Suzuki	1.00
97	Ichiro Suzuki	1.00
98	Ichiro Suzuki	1.00
99	Ichiro Suzuki	1.00
100	Checklist	
	(Original nine players.)	
	(Nine team names.)	.25

Silver

Stars: 4-8X
Production 100 Sets

Gold

Gold Stars (1-100): 15-25X
Production 25 Sets

Batting Glove

		NM/M
Numbered to 250		
BB	Bret Boone/89	20.00
JG	Jason Giambi	20.00
KG	Ken Griffey Jr.	40.00
AR	Alex Rodriguez	25.00
IR1	Ivan Rodriguez	20.00
IR2	Ivan Rodriguez	20.00
SS	Sammy Sosa	30.00
I	Ichiro Suzuki/46	150.00

Game Jersey

	NM/M
Common Player:	10.00
Inserted 1:90	
Golds:	2-3X
Production 99 Sets	

SAMMY SOSA

HONOR ROLL GAME JERSEY

Each player has multiple versions.

BB	Bret Boone/SP/45	10.00
RC	Roger Clemens	20.00
JG	Jason Giambi/SP	15.00
KG	Ken Griffey Jr.	25.00
CJ	Chipper Jones	15.00
AR	Alex Rodriguez	15.00
IR	Ivan Rodriguez	10.00
SS	Sammy Sosa/SP	25.00
I	Ichiro Suzuki/SP	40.00

Game-Used Bat

JASON GIAMBI

	NM/M
Common Player:	10.00

Numbered to 99
Each player has multiple versions.

BB	Bret Boone	10.00
RC	Roger Clemens	30.00
JG	Jason Giambi	15.00
KG	Ken Griffey Jr.	40.00
CJ	Chipper Jones	20.00
AR	Alex Rodriguez	20.00
IR	Ivan Rodriguez	15.00
SS	Sammy Sosa	30.00
I	Ichiro Suzuki	40.00

Star Swatches Game Jersey

STAR SWATCHES ICHIRO

	NM/M
Common Player:	10.00
Inserted 1:90	
Golds:	2-5X
Production 24	
BB	Bret Boone/45	10.00
RC	Roger Clemens/29	40.00
JG	Jason Giambi	15.00
KG	Ken Griffey Jr./SP	25.00
CJ	Chipper Jones	15.00

AR	Alex Rodriguez	15.00
IR	Ivan Rodriguez	10.00
SS	Sammy Sosa	20.00
I	Ichiro Suzuki/SP	40.00

Stitch of Nine Game Jersey

ALEX RODRIGUEZ

	NM/M
Common Player:	10.00
Inserted 1:90	
Golds:	2-5X
Production 24 Sets	
BB	Bret Boone/45	10.00
RC	Roger Clemens	20.00
JG	Jason Giambi/SP	10.00
KG	Ken Griffey Jr.	15.00
CJ	Chipper Jones	10.00
AR	Alex Rodriguez	15.00
IR	Ivan Rodriguez	10.00
SS	Sammy Sosa	20.00
I	Ichiro Suzuki/85	40.00

Time Capsule Game Jersey

TIME CAPSULE

	NM/M
Common Player:	8.00
Inserted 1:90	
Golds:	2-3X
Production 99 Sets	
BB	Bret Boone	8.00
RC	Roger Clemens	20.00
JG	Jason Giambi/52	15.00
CJ	Chipper Jones	10.00
AR	Alex Rodriguez	15.00
IR	Ivan Rodriguez/SP	15.00
SS	Sammy Sosa	20.00
I	Ichiro Suzuki	40.00

2002 Upper Deck MVP

SAMMY SOSA

	NM/M
Complete Set (300):	20.00
Common Player:	.10
Pack (8):	1.50
Box (24):	25.00
1	Darin Erstad	.20
2	Ramon Ortiz	.10
3	Garret Anderson	.20
4	Jarrod Washburn	.10
5	Troy Glaus	.20
6	Brendan Donnelly RC	.10
7	Troy Percival	.10
8	Tim Salmon	.15
9	Aaron Sele	.10
10	Brad Fullmer	.10
11	Scott Hatteberg	.10
12	Barry Zito	.20
13	Tim Hudson	.20
14	Miguel Tejada	.25

15	Jermaine Dye	.10
16	Mark Mulder	.20
17	Eric Chavez	.15
18	Terrence Long	.10
19	Carlos Pena	.20
20	David Justice	.20
21	Jeremy Giambi	.10
22	Shannon Stewart	.10
23	Raul Mondesi	.15
24	Chris Carpenter	.10
25	Carlos Delgado	.20
26	Mike Sirotka	.10
27	Reed Johnson RC	.15
28	Darrin Fletcher	.10
29	Jose Cruz Jr.	.10
30	Vernon Wells	.10
31	Tanyon Sturtze	.10
32	Toby Hall	.10
33	Brent Abernathy	.10
34	Ben Grieve	.10
35	Joe Kennedy	.10
36	Dewon Brazelton	.10
37	Aubrey Huff	.10
38	Steve Cox	.10
39	Greg Vaughn	.10
40	Brady Anderson	.10
41	Chuck Finley	.10
42	Jim Thome	.40
43	Russell Branyan	.10
44	C.C. Sabathia	.10
45	Matt Lawton	.10
46	Omar Vizquel	.10
47	Bartolo Colon	.15
48	Alex Escobar	.10
49	Ellis Burks	.10
50	Bret Boone	.10
51	John Olerud	.20
52	Jeff Cirillo	.10
53	Ichiro Suzuki	1.00
54	Kazuhiro Sasaki	.10
55	Freddy Garcia	.10
56	Edgar Martinez	.15
57	Matt Thornton	.10
58	Mike Cameron	.10
59	Carlos Guillen	.10
60	Jeff Conine	.10
61	Tony Batista	.10
62	Jason Johnson	.10
63	Melvin Mora	.10
64	Brian Roberts	.10
65	Josh Towers	.10
66	Steve Bechler RC	.10
67	Jerry Hairston Jr.	.10
68	Chris Richard	.10
69	Alex Rodriguez	1.00
70	Chan Ho Park	.10
71	Ivan Rodriguez	.25
72	Jeff Zimmerman	.10
73	Mark Teixeira	.20
74	Gabe Kapler	.10
75	Frank Catalanotto	.10
76	Rafael Palmeiro	.25
77	Doug Davis	.10
78	Carl Everett	.10
79	Pedro J. Martinez	.10
80	Nomar Garciaparra	.75
81	Tony Clark	.10
82	Trot Nixon	.10
83	Manny Ramirez	.25
84	Josh Hancock RC	.10
85	Johnny Damon	.20
86	Jose Offerman	.10
87	Rich Garces	.10
88	Shea Hillenbrand	.10
89	Carlos Beltran	.20
90	Mike Sweeney	.10
91	Jeff Suppan	.10
92	Joe Randa	.10
93	Chuck Knoblauch	.10
94	Mark Quinn	.10
95	Neifi Perez	.10
96	Carlos Febles	.10
97	Miguel Asencio RC	.10
98	Michael Tucker	.10
99	Dean Palmer	.10
100	Jose Lima	.10
101	Craig Paquette	.10
102	Dmitri Young	.10
103	Bobby Higginson	.10
104	Jeff Weaver	.10
105	Matt Anderson	.10
106	Damion Easley	.10
107	Eric Milton	.10
108	Doug Mientkiewicz	.10
109	Cristian Guzman	.10
110	Brad Radke	.10
111	Torii Hunter	.20
112	Corey Koskie	.10
113	Joe Mays	.10
114	Jacque Jones	.10
115	David Ortiz	.20
116	Kevin Frederick RC	.20

117	Magglio Ordonez	.20
118	Ray Durham	.10
119	Mark Buehrle	.10
120	Jon Garland	.10
121	Paul Konerko	.10
122	Todd Ritchie	.10
123	Frank Thomas	.25
124	Edwin Almonte RC	.10
125	Carlos Lee	.10
126	Kenny Lofton	.15
127	Roger Clemens	.75
128	Derek Jeter	1.00
129	Jorge Posada	.20
130	Bernie Williams	.25
131	Mike Mussina	.25
132	Alfonso Soriano	.40
133	Robin Ventura	.15
134	John Vander Wal	.10
135	Jason Giambi	.25
136	Mariano Rivera	.20
137	Rondell White	.10
138	Jeff Bagwell	.25
139	Wade Miller	.10
140	Richard Hidalgo	.10
141	Julio Lugo	.10
142	Roy Oswalt	.20
143	Rodrigo Rosario RC	.10
144	Lance Berkman	.20
145	Craig Biggio	.20
146	Shane Reynolds	.10
147	John Smoltz	.20
148	Chipper Jones	.40
149	Gary Sheffield	.20
150	Rafael Furcal	.10
151	Greg Maddux	.50
152	Tom Glavine	.20
153	Andruw Jones	.25
154	John Ennis RC	.20
155	Vinny Castilla	.10
156	Marcus Giles	.10
157	Javy Lopez	.10
158	Richie Sexson	.20
159	Geoff Jenkins	.10
160	Jeffrey Hammonds	.10
161	Alex Ochoa	.10
162	Ben Sheets	.20
163	Jose Hernandez	.10
164	Eric Young	.10
165	Luis Montanez	.10
166	Albert Pujols	.75
167	Darryl Kile	.10
168	So Taguchi RC	.50
169	Jim Edmonds	.20
170	Fernando Vina	.10
171	Matt Morris	.10
172	J.D. Drew	.10
173	Bud Smith	.10
174	Edgar Renteria	.20
175	Placido Polanco	.10
176	Tino Martinez	.10
177	Sammy Sosa	.75
178	Moises Alou	.20
179	Kerry Wood	.20
180	Delino DeShields	.10
181	Alex Gonzalez	.10
182	Jon Lieber	.10
183	Fred McGriff	.15
184	Corey Patterson	.15
185	Mark Prior	.50
186	Tom Gordon	.10
187	Francis Beltran RC	.10
188	Randy Johnson	.40
189	Luis Gonzalez	.20
190	Matt Williams	.15
191	Mark Grace	.25
192	Curt Schilling	.25
193	Doug DeVore RC	.20
194	Erubiel Durazo	.15
195	Steve Finley	.15
196	Craig Counsell	.10
197	Shawn Green	.25
198	Kevin Brown	.20
199	Paul LoDuca	.10
200	Brian Jordan	.15
201	Andy Ashby	.10
202	Darren Dreifort	.10
203	Adrian Beltre	.15
204	Victor Alvarez RC	.10
205	Eric Karros	.10
206	Hideo Nomo	.25
207	Vladimir Guerrero	.40
208	Javier Vazquez	.10
209	Michael Barrett	.10
210	Jose Vidro	.10
211	Brad Wilkerson	.10
212	Tony Armas Jr.	.10
213	Eric Good RC	.10
214	Orlando Cabrera	.10
215	Lee Stevens	.10
216	Jeff Kent	.10
217	Rich Aurilia	.10
218	Robb Nen	.10

219	Calvin Murray	.10
220	Russ Ortiz	.10
221	Deivis Santos	.10
222	Marvin Benard	.10
223	Jason Schmidt	.10
224	Reggie Sanders	.10
225	Barry Bonds	1.00
226	Brad Penny	.10
227	Cliff Floyd	.10
228	Mike Lowell	.20
229	Derrek Lee	.10
230	Ryan Dempster	.10
231	Josh Beckett	.20
232	Hansel Izquierdo RC	.10
233	Preston Wilson	.10
234	A.J. Burnett	.10
235	Charles Johnson	.10
236	Mike Piazza	.50
237	Al Leiter	.20
238	Jay Payton	.10
239	Roger Cedeno	.10
240	Jeromy Burnitz	.10
241	Roberto Alomar	.20
242	Mo Vaughn	.20
243	Shawn Estes	.10
244	Armando Benitez	.10
245	Tyler Yates RC	.10
246	Phil Nevin	.10
247	D'Angelo Jimenez	.10
248	Ramon Vazquez	.10
249	Bubba Trammell	.10
250	Trevor Hoffman	.10
251	Ben Howard RC	.20
252	Mark Kotsay	.10
253	Ray Lankford	.10
254	Ryan Klesko	.10
255	Scott Rolen	.40
256	Robert Person	.10
257	Jimmy Rollins	.25
258	Pat Burrell	.20
259	Anderson Machado RC	.10
260	Randy Wolf	.10
261	Travis Lee	.10
262	Mike Lieberthal	.10
263	Doug Glanville	.10
264	Bobby Abreu	.10
265	Brian Giles	.15
266	Kris Benson	.10
267	Aramis Ramirez	.10
268	Kevin Young	.10
269	Jack Wilson	.10
270	Mike Williams	.10
271	Jimmy Anderson	.10
272	Jason Kendall	.10
273	Pokey Reese	.10
274	Robert Mackowiak	.10
275	Sean Casey	.20
276	Juan Encarnacion	.10
277	Austin Kearns	.20
278	Danny Graves	.10
279	Ken Griffey Jr.	.50
280	Barry Larkin	.20
281	Todd Walker	.10
282	Elmer Dessens	.10
283	Aaron Boone	.10
284	Adam Dunn	.40
285	Larry Walker	.15
286	Rene Reyes RC	.20
287	Juan Uribe	.10
288	Mike Hampton	.10
289	Todd Helton	.40
290	Juan Pierre	.10
291	Denny Neagle	.10
292	Jose Ortiz	.10
293	Todd Zeile	.10
294	Ben Petrick	.10
295	Ken Griffey Jr.	
	Checklist 1-50	.25
296	Derek Jeter	
	Checklist 51-100	.50
297	Sammy Sosa	
	Checklist 101-150	.30
298	Ichiro Suzuki	
	Checklist 151-200	.50
299	Barry Bonds	
	Checklist 201-250	.50
300	Alex Rodriguez	
	Checklist 251-300	.40

Silver

Stars:	5-10X
Production 100 Sets	

Gold

No Pricing
Production 25 Sets

Ichiro - A Season to Remember

	NM/M
Complete Set (10):	15.00
Ichiro's (1-10):	2.00
Inserted 1:10	

- A Season to Remember Jersey

Complete Set (1):	

Ichiro - A Season to Remember Bat

No Pricing
Production 25

Souvenirs Jerseys

		NM/M
Common Player:		5.00
Inserted 1:48		
RA	Roberto Alomar	10.00
GA	Garret Anderson	10.00
JB	Jeff Bagwell	10.00
AB	Adrian Beltre	8.00
JB	Jeromy Burnitz	5.00
RC	Roger Clemens	15.00
CD	Carlos Delgado	8.00
DE	Darin Erstad	8.00
RF	Rafael Furcal	8.00
JG	Juan Gonzalez	10.00
THo	Trevor Hoffman	5.00
THu	Tim Hudson	8.00
JK	Jeff Kent	8.00
PK	Paul Konerko/SP	10.00
MK	Mark Kotsay	5.00
KL	Kenny Lofton	8.00
EM	Edgar Martinez	10.00
JP	Jay Payton/SP	10.00
MP	Mike Piazza	15.00
AR	Alex Rodriguez	15.00
IR	Ivan Rodriguez	10.00
SR	Scott Rolen	10.00
TS	Tim Salmon	10.00
FT	Frank Thomas	15.00
JT	Jim Thome/SP	15.00
RV	Robin Ventura	5.00
OV	Omar Vizquel	8.00
PW	Preston Wilson	5.00
TZ	Todd Zeile	5.00

Souvenirs Bat/Jersey Combos

		NM/M
Common Card:		10.00
Inserted 1:144		
Gold:		No Pricing
Production 25 Sets		
EA	Edgardo Alfonzo	10.00
RA	Roberto Alomar	15.00
JB	Jeff Bagwell	20.00
AB	Adrian Beltre	15.00
CD	Carlos Delgado	15.00
DE	Darin Erstad	20.00
JG	Jason Giambi	20.00
BG	Brian Giles	15.00
LG	Luis Gonzalez	15.00
SG	Shawn Green	15.00
KG	Ken Griffey Jr.	40.00
TH	Todd Helton	20.00
RJ	Randy Johnson	25.00
CJ	Chipper Jones	20.00
JK	Jeff Kent	15.00
MO	Magglio Ordonez	15.00
RP	Rafael Palmeiro	20.00
MP	Mike Piazza	15.00
AR	Alex Rodriguez	25.00
IR	Ivan Rodriguez	15.00
SR	Scott Rolen	15.00
SS	Sammy Sosa	15.00

JT	Jim Thome	25.00
RV	Robin Ventura	10.00
OV	Omar Vizquel/97	20.00
BW	Bernie Williams/97	25.00
TZ	Todd Zeile	10.00

Souvenirs Bats

		NM/M
Common Player:		8.00
Inserted 1:144		
RA	Roberto Alomar	20.00
CD	Carlos Delgado	8.00
BG	Brian Giles	8.00
LG	Luis Gonzalez	8.00
SG	Shawn Green	8.00
KG	Ken Griffey Jr.	25.00
TH	Todd Helton	15.00
DJ	David Justice	8.00
JK	Jeff Kent	8.00
RK	Ryan Klesko	8.00
GM	Greg Maddux	20.00
EM	Edgar Martinez	10.00
DM	Doug Mientkiewicz	8.00
MO	Magglio Ordonez	8.00
RP	Rafael Palmeiro/97	18.00
MP	Mike Piazza/97	25.00
AR	Alex Rodriguez	15.00
IR	Ivan Rodriguez	8.00
SR	Scott Rolen	10.00
GS	Gary Sheffield	8.00
SS	Sammy Sosa	20.00
MS	Mike Sweeney	8.00
FT	Frank Thomas/97	25.00
JT	Jim Thome	10.00
GV	Greg Vaughn	8.00
LW	Larry Walker	8.00
BW	Bernie Williams	10.00

2002 Upper Deck Piece of History

	NM/M
Complete Set (132):	200.00
Common Player:	.15
Common SP (91-132):	5.00
Production 625	
Pack (5):	2.00
Box (24):	40.00

1	Troy Glaus	.40
2	Darin Erstad	.25
3	Reggie Jackson	.50
4	Miguel Tejada	.40
5	Tim Hudson	.25
6	Jim "Catfish" Hunter	.25
7	Joe Carter	.15
8	Carlos Delgado	.40
9	Greg Vaughn	.15
10	Early Wynn	.15
11	Omar Vizquel	.15
12	Jim Thome	.75
13	Ichiro Suzuki	1.50
14	Edgar Martinez	.25
15	Freddy Garcia	.15
16	Cal Ripken Jr/SP	15.00
17	Jeff Conine	.15
18	Juan Gonzalez	.50
19	Nolan Ryan/SP	15.00
20	Alex Rodriguez/SP	10.00
21	Rafael Palmeiro	.50
22	Ivan Rodriguez	.50
23	Carlton Fisk	.25
24	Wade Boggs	.30
25	Pedro J. Martinez	.75
26	Nomar Garciaparra	1.50
27	Manny Ramirez	.50
28	Mike Sweeney	.15
29	Bobby Higginson	.15
30	Kirby Puckett	.75
31	Doug Mientkiewicz	.15
32	Corey Koskie	.15
33	Joe Mays	.15
34	Frank Thomas	.50
35	Magglio Ordonez	.25
36	Jason Giambi/SP	5.00
37	Derek Jeter/SP	10.00
38	Mickey Mantle/SP	15.00
39	Joe DiMaggio	2.00
40	Roger Maris	1.00
41	Roger Clemens	1.50
42	Bernie Williams	.50
43	Jeff Bagwell	.50
44	Lance Berkman	.25
45	Eddie Mathews	.50

46	Andruw Jones	.40
47	Phil Niekro	.15
48	Gary Sheffield	.25
49	Chipper Jones	.75
50	Greg Maddux	1.00
51	Robin Yount	.50
52	Richie Sexson	.25
53	Jim Edmonds	.25
54	J.D. Drew	.25
55	Albert Pujols	1.50
56	Andre Dawson	.25
57	Billy Williams	.15
58	Ernie Banks	.50
59	Sammy Sosa/SP	10.00
60	Randy Johnson	.75
61	Curt Schilling	.50
62	Luis Gonzalez	.25
63	Kirk Gibson	.15
64	Steve Garvey	.15
65	Sandy Koufax/SP	15.00
66	Shawn Green	.25
67	Hideo Nomo	.25
68	Kevin Brown	.15
69	Vladimir Guerrero	.75
70	Tim Raines	.15
71	Gaylord Perry	.15
72	Mel Ott	.25
73	Willie McCovey	.15
74	Barry Bonds/SP	10.00
75	Jeff Kent	.15
76	Cliff Floyd	.15
77	Dwight Gooden	.15
78	Tom Seaver	.50
79	Mike Piazza	1.00
80	Roberto Alomar	.50
81	Dave Winfield	.25
82	Tony Gwynn	.75
83	Scott Rolen	.75
84	Bill Mazeroski	.15
85	Willie Stargell	.25
86	Brian Giles	.25
87	Ken Griffey Jr./SP	10.00
88	Sean Casey	.25
89	Todd Helton	.50
90	Larry Walker	.25
91	Brendan Donnelly RC	5.00
92	Tom Shearn RC	5.00
93	Brandon Puffer RC	5.00
94	Corey Thurman RC	5.00
95	Reed Johnson RC	8.00
96	Gustavo Chacin RC	5.00
97	Chris Baker RC	5.00
98	John Ennis RC	5.00
99	So Taguchi RC	8.00
100	Michael Crudale RC	5.00
101	Francis Beltran RC	5.00
102	Jose Valverde RC	8.00
103	Doug DeVore RC	5.00
104	Jeremy Ward RC	5.00
105	P.J. Bevis RC	5.00
106	Steve Kent RC	5.00
107	Brandon Backe RC	5.00
108	Jorge Nunez RC	5.00
109	Kazuhisa Ishii RC	10.00
110	Ron Calloway RC	5.00
111	Valentino Pasucci RC	5.00
112	J.J. Putz RC	5.00
113	Matt Thornton RC	5.00
114	Allan Simpson RC	5.00
115	Jaime Cerda RC	5.00
116	Mark Corey RC	5.00
117	Tyler Yates RC	8.00
118	Steve Bechler RC	5.00
119	Ben Howard RC	5.00
120	Clifford Bartosh RC	5.00
121	Todd Donovan RC	5.00
122	Eric Junge RC	5.00
123	Adrian Burnside RC	5.00
124	Andy Pratt RC	5.00
125	Josh Hancock RC	5.00
126	Rene Reyes RC	5.00
127	Cam Esslinger RC	5.00
128	Colin Young RC	5.00
129	Kevin Frederick RC	5.00
130	Kyle Kane RC	5.00
131	Mitch Wylie RC	5.00
132	Danny Wright	5.00

Batting Champs

Complete Set (10): 18.00
Common Player: 1.50
Inserted 1:30

B1	Tony Gwynn	2.00
B2	Frank Thomas	2.00
B3	Billy Williams	1.50
B4	Edgar Martinez	1.50
B5	Bernie Williams	1.50
B6	Mickey Mantle	6.00
B7	Larry Walker	1.50
B8	Gary Sheffield	1.50
B9	Wade Boggs	1.50
B10	Alex Rodriguez	4.00

Batting Champ Jerseys

NM/M

Common Player: 8.00
Inserted 1:96

WB	Wade Boggs	10.00
AG	Andres Galarraga	5.00
TG	Tony Gwynn	15.00
MM	Mickey Mantle/50	200.00
EM	Edgar Martinez	10.00
JO	John Olerud	8.00
PO	Paul O'Neil	10.00
TR	Tim Raines	8.00
AR	Alex Rodriguez	15.00
GS	Gary Sheffield/SP	8.00
FT	Frank Thomas	10.00
LW	Larry Walker/SP	10.00
BeW	Bernie Williams	10.00

Batting Champ Jerseys Autograph

Complete Set (5):
Common Player:

ERA Leaders

NM/M

Complete Set (10): 18.00
Common Player: 1.00
Inserted 1:30

E1	Greg Maddux	3.00
E2	Pedro J. Martinez	2.00
E3	Freddy Garcia	1.00
E4	Randy Johnson	2.00
E5	Tom Seaver	2.00
E6	Early Wynn	1.00
E7	Dwight Gooden	1.00
E8	Kevin Brown	1.00
E9	Roger Clemens	3.00
E10	Nolan Ryan	6.00

ERA Leaders Jerseys Autographs

NM/M

Production 24 Sets

RC	Roger Clemens	200.00
FG	Freddy Garcia	
SK	Sandy Koufax	750.00

ERA Leaders Jerseys

NM/M

Common Player: 8.00
Inserted 1:96

KB	Kevin Brown	8.00
RC	Roger Clemens	15.00
FG	Freddy Garcia	8.00
DG	Dwight Gooden	8.00
CH	"Catfish" Hunter/SP	15.00
RJ	Randy Johnson	15.00
SK	Sandy Koufax/SP	100.00
GM	Greg Maddux	15.00
PM	Pedro Martinez	15.00
PN	Phil Niekro	8.00
NR	Nolan Ryan/SP	50.00
TS	Tom Seaver	15.00

Hitting for the Cycle

NM/M

Complete Set (20): 35.00

Common Player:		1.00

Inserted 1:15

H1	Alex Rodriguez	4.00
H2	Andre Dawson	1.00
H3	Cal Ripken Jr.	6.00
H4	Carlton Fisk	1.50
H5	Dante Bichette	1.00
H6	Dave Winfield	1.50
H7	Eric Chavez	1.00
H8	Robin Yount	2.00
H9	Jason Kendall	1.00
H10	Jay Buhner	1.00
H11	Jeff Kent	1.00
H12	Joe DiMaggio	6.00
H13	John Olerud	1.00
H14	Kirby Puckett	3.00
H15	Luis Gonzalez	1.50
H16	Mark Grace	1.50
H17	Mickey Mantle	6.00
H18	Miguel Tejada	1.00
H19	Rondell White	1.00
H20	Todd Helton	2.00

Hitting for the Cycle Bats

NM/M

Inserted 1:576

DB	Dante Bichette	10.00
JB	Jay Buhner	10.00
EC	Eric Chavez	10.00
AD	Andre Dawson	10.00
CF	Carlton Fisk	25.00
LG	Luis Gonzalez	10.00
MM	Mickey Mantle/50	200.00
CR	Cal Ripken Jr/SP	75.00
AR	Alex Rodriguez	25.00
DW	Dave Winfield	15.00

Hitting for the Cycle Bats Autograhs

No Pricing
Production 10 Sets

The MVP Club

NM/M

Complete Set (14): 30.00
Common Player: 1.00
Inserted 1:22

M1	Jason Giambi	2.00
M2	Sammy Sosa	3.00
M3	Cal Ripken Jr.	6.00
M4	Robin Yount	2.00
M5	Ken Griffey Jr.	5.00
M6	Kirk Gibson	1.00
M7	Mickey Mantle	6.00
M8	Barry Bonds	2.00
M9	Frank Thomas	2.00
M10	Reggie Jackson	2.00
M11	Jeff Bagwell	2.00
M12	Roger Clemens	1.00
M13	Steve Garvey	1.00
M14	Chipper Jones	3.00

MVP Club Jerseys

NM/M

Common Player: 8.00
Inserted 1:96

JB	Jeff Bagwell	10.00
RC	Roger Clemens	15.00
SG	Steve Garvey	8.00
JGi	Jason Giambi	10.00
KGi	Kirk Gibson	10.00
JGo	Juan Gonzalez	10.00
KGr	Ken Griffey Jr.	15.00
RJ	Reggie Jackson	15.00
CJ	Chipper Jones	15.00
JK	Jeff Kent	8.00
BL	Barry Larkin/SP	25.00
MM	Mickey Mantle/50	200.00

RM	Roger Maris/50	100.00
CR	Cal Ripken Jr.	35.00
IR	Ivan Rodriguez	10.00
SS	Sammy Sosa	15.00
FT	Frank Thomas	10.00
RY	Robin Yount/SP	25.00

MVP Club Jerseys Autographs

No Pricing
Production 10 Sets

Tape Measure Heroes

NM/M

Complete Set (30): 50.00
Common Player: 1.00
Inserted 1:10

TM1	Joe Carter	1.00
TM2	Cal Ripken Jr.	6.00
TM3	Mike Piazza	4.00
TM4	Shawn Green	1.25
TM5	Mark McGwire	5.00
TM6	Reggie Jackson	1.50
TM7	Mickey Mantle	6.00
TM8	Manny Ramirez	2.00
TM9	Mo Vaughn	1.00
TM10	Jeff Bagwell	2.00
TM11	Sammy Sosa	3.00
TM12	Tony Gwynn	2.00
TM13	Bill Mazeroski	1.00
TM14	Jose Canseco	1.50
TM15	Brian Giles	1.00
TM16	Kirk Gibson	1.00
TM17	Kirby Puckett	3.00
TM18	Wade Boggs	1.50
TM19	Albert Pujols	3.00
TM20	David Justice	1.00
TM21	Steve Garvey	1.00
TM22	Luis Gonzalez	1.50
TM23	Derek Jeter	6.00
TM24	Robin Yount	2.00
TM25	Barry Bonds	3.00
TM26	Alex Rodriguez	4.00
TM27	Willie Stargell	1.50
TM28	Carlton Fisk	1.50
TM29	Carlos Delgado	1.50
TM30	Ken Griffey Jr.	5.00

Tape Measure Heroes Jerseys

NM/M

Common Player: 5.00
Inserted 1:96

JB	Jeff Bagwell	12.00
WB	Wade Boggs	15.00
JCa	Jose Canseco	10.00
JoC	Joe Carter	5.00
CD	Carlos Delgado	8.00
CF	Carlton Fisk	10.00
SGa	Steve Garvey	5.00
KGi	Kirk Gibson	8.00
BG	Brian Giles	5.00
SGr	Shawn Green	8.00
KGr	Ken Griffey Jr./90	40.00
MMa	Mickey Mantle/50	200.00
RM	Roger Maris/50	100.00
BM	Bill Mazeroski	10.00
MP	Mike Piazza	15.00
MR	Manny Ramirez	10.00
CR	Cal Ripken Jr.	30.00
AR	Alex Rodriguez	15.00
SS	Sammy Sosa	15.00
WS	Willie Stargell	15.00
RY	Robin Yount/SP	25.00

300 Game Winners

NM/M

Complete Set (6): 12.00
Common Player: 1.00
Inserted 1:50

GW1	Nolan Ryan	6.00
GW2	Tom Seaver	3.00
GW3	Cy Young	3.00
GW4	Gaylord Perry	1.00
GW5	Early Wynn	1.00
GW6	Phil Niekro	1.00

300 Game Winners Jerseys

		NM/M
Common Player:		15.00
Inserted 1:576		
PN	Phil Niekro	10.00
GP	Gaylord Perry	10.00
NR	Nolan Ryan/SP	50.00
TS	Tom Seaver/SP	20.00

The 500 Home Run Club

		NM/M
Complete Set (9):		25.00
Common Player:		1.50
Inserted 1:9		
HR1	Harmon Killebrew	3.00
HR2	Jimmie Foxx	3.00
HR3	Reggie Jackson	3.00
HR4	Mickey Mantle	8.00
HR5	Ernie Banks	3.00
HR6	Eddie Mathews	3.00
HR7	Mark McGwire	6.00
HR8	Willie McCovey	1.50
HR9	Mel Ott	3.00

500 HR Club Jerseys

		NM/M
Inserted 1:336		
HA	Hank Aaron	40.00
EB	Ernie Banks/SP	40.00
JF	Jimmie Foxx	40.00
RJ	Reggie Jackson	25.00
MM	Mickey Mantle/50	200.00
EM	Eddie Mathews	30.00
WM	Willie McCovey	20.00
MO	Mel Ott	40.00

500 HR Club Jerseys Autographs

No Pricing
Production 10 Sets

2002 Upper Deck Prospect Premieres

		NM/M
Complete Set (109):		
Common Player (1-60):		.40
Common (61-85):		5.00
Inserted 1:18		
Common (86-97):		10.00
Inserted 1:18		
Pack (4):		8.00
Box (18):		120.00
1	Josh Rupe RC	.40
2	Blair Johnson RC	.40

3	Jason Pridie RC	.75
4	Tim Gilhooly RC	.40
5	Kennard Jones RC	.40
6	Darrell Rasner RC	.40
7	Adam Donachie RC	.75
8	Josh Murray RC	.40
9	Brian Dopirak RC	1.00
10	Jason Cooper RC	.50
11	Zach Hammes RC	.40
12	Jon Lester RC	15.00
13	Kevin Jepsen RC	.40
14	Curtis Granderson RC	4.00
15	David Bush RC	.75
16	Joel Guzman RC	.50
17a	Matt Pender RC (Black, photo is Curtis Granderson.)	.40
17b	Matt Pender RC (White, correct photo.)	2.00
18	Derick Grigsby RC	.40
19	Jeremy Reed RC	3.00
20	Jonathan Broxton RC	1.00
21	Jesse Crain RC	.40
22	Justin Jones RC	1.00
23	Brian Slocum RC	.50
24	Brian McCann RC	5.00
25	Francisco Liriano RC	8.00
26	Fred Lewis RC	1.00
27	Steve Stanley RC	.40
28	Chris Snyder RC	.40
29	Daniel Cevette RC	.40
30	Kiel Fisher RC	.40
31	Brandon Wheeder RC	.40
32	Pat Osborn RC	.40
33	Taber Lee RC	.40
34	Dan Ortmeyer RC	.75
35	Josh Johnson RC	2.00
36	Val Majewski RC	.75
37	Larry Broadway RC	.50
38	Joey Gomes RC	1.00
39	Eric Thomas RC	.40
40	James Loney RC	4.00
41	Charlie Morton RC	.40
42	Mark McLemore RC	.40
43	Matt Craig RC	.40
44	Ryan Rodriguez RC	.40
45	Rich Hill RC	2.00
46	Bob Malek RC	.40
47	Justin Maureau RC	.40
48	Randy Braun RC	.40
49	Brian Grant RC	.50
50	Tyler Davidson RC	.50
51	Travis Hanson RC	.50
52	Kyle Boyer RC	.40
53	James Holcomb RC	.40
54	Ryan Williams RC	.40
55	Ben Crockett RC	.40
56	Adam Greenberg RC	.75
57	John Baker RC	.40
58	Matt Carson RC	.40
59	Jonathan George RC	.40
60	David Jensen RC	.40
61	Nick Swisher RC	15.00
62	Brent Cleven RC	8.00
63	Royce Ring RC	8.00
64	Mike Nixon RC	5.00
65	Ricky Barrett RC	5.00
66	Russ Adams RC	8.00
67	Joe Mauer RC	30.00
68	Jeff Francoeur RC	40.00
69	Joseph Blanton RC	10.00
70	Micah Schilling RC	8.00
71	John McCurdy RC	5.00
72	Sergio Santos RC	8.00
73	Josh Womack RC	5.00
74	Jared Doyle RC	5.00
75	Ben Fritz RC	5.00
76	Greg Miller RC	10.00
77	Luke Hagerty RC	8.00
78	Matt Whitney RC	10.00
79	Dan Meyer RC	5.00
80	Bill Murphy RC	5.00
81	Zach Segovia RC	8.00
82	Steve Obenchain RC	8.00
83	Matt Clanton RC	8.00
84	Mark Teahen RC	10.00
85	Kyle Pawelczyk RC	8.00
86	Khalil Greene/ Auto. RC	50.00
87	Joe Saunders/ Auto. RC	10.00
88	Jeremy Hermida/ Auto. RC	40.00
89	Drew Meyer/Auto. RC	10.00
90	Jeff Francis/Auto. RC	30.00
91	Scott Moore/Auto. RC	10.00
92	Prince Fielder/ Auto. RC	250.00
93	Zack Greinke/ Auto. RC	40.00
94	Chris Gruler/Auto. RC	10.00
95	Scott Kazmir/ Auto. RC	80.00
96	B.J. Upton/Auto. RC	75.00

97	Clint Everts/Auto. RC	15.00
98	Cal Ripken Jr.	1.00
99	Cal Ripken Jr.	1.00
100	Mark McGwire	1.00
101	Mark McGwire	1.00
102	Mark McGwire	1.00
103	Mark McGwire	1.00
104	Mark McGwire	1.00
105	Joe DiMaggio	1.00
106	Joe DiMaggio	1.00
107	Joe DiMaggio	1.00
108	Joe DiMaggio	1.00
109	Joe DiMaggio	1.00

Heroes of Baseball Quads

		NM/M
Common Quad:		10.00
Production 85 Sets		
1	Joe DiMaggio, Tony Gwynn	15.00
2	Joe DiMaggio, Tony Gwynn, Cal Ripken Jr.	20.00
3	Joe DiMaggio, Mickey Mantle, Willie Stargell	20.00
4	Tony Gwynn, Ozzie Smith, Willie Stargell	10.00
5	Tony Gwynn, Willie Stargell, Joe DiMaggio, Joe Morgan	15.00
6	Tony Gwynn, Willie Stargell, Cal Ripken Jr., Ozzie Smith	15.00
7	Mickey Mantle, Mark McGwire, Joe Morgan, Tom Seaver	20.00
8	Mickey Mantle, Tom Seaver	20.00
9	Mark McGwire, Joe Morgan	20.00
10	Mark McGwire, Cal Ripken Jr., Tony Gwynn, Joe DiMaggio	25.00
11	Mark McGwire, Tom Seaver, Joe Morgan, Ozzie Smith	15.00
12	Joe Morgan, Tony Gwynn	10.00
13	Joe Morgan, Joe DiMaggio, Mickey Mantle, Cal Ripken Jr.	25.00
14	Joe Morgan, Joe DiMaggio, Willie Stargell, Tony Gwynn	15.00
15	Ozzie Smith, Joe DiMaggio, Ozzie Smith, Willie Stargell	15.00
16	Ozzie Smith, Mark McGwire, Willie Stargell, Tony Gwynn	15.00
17	Ozzie Smith, Tom Seaver, Mark McGwire	15.00
18	Cal Ripken Jr., Mickey Mantle, Joe DiMaggio, Joe Morgan	20.00
19	Cal Ripken Jr., Mark McGwire, Cal Ripken Jr.	20.00
20	Tom Seaver, Joe DiMaggio, Tom Seaver, Joe DiMaggio	15.00
21	Tom Seaver, Joe Morgan, Ozzie Smith, Willie Stargell	10.00
22	Tom Seaver, Cal Ripken Jr., Mark McGwire, Mickey Mantle	20.00
23	Willie Stargell, Ozzie Smith	10.00
24	Willie Stargell, Ozzie Smith, Tom Seaver, Joe Morgan	10.00

Future Gems Quads

		NM/M
Common Card:		4.00
Inserted 1:Box		
1	David Bush, Matt Craig, Blair Johnson, Brian McCann	4.00
2	Jason Cooper, Jonathan George, Larry Broadway, Joel Guzman	4.00
3	Matt Craig, Josh Murray, Brian McCann, Jason Pridie	4.00
4	Jesse Crain, Brian Grant, Curtis Granderson, Joey Gomes	4.00
5	Tyler Davidson, Val Majewski, Kennard Jones, Daniel Cevette	4.00
6	Joe DiMaggio, Jon Lester, Mac, Mark McLemore	4.00
7	Jonathan George, Jeremy Reed, Adam Donachie, Matt Carson	4.00
8	Jonathan George, Eric Thomas, Joel Guzman, Kiel Fisher	4.00
9	Tim Gilhooly, Brandon Wheeder, Brian Slocum, Brian Dopirak	4.00
10	Brian Grant, Rich Hill, Joey Gomes, Joe DiMaggio	4.00
11	Derick Grigsby, Bob Malek, James Loney, Fred Lewis	4.00
12	Zach Hammes, James Holcomb, Cal Ripken Jr., Kennard Jones	4.00
13	Rich Hill, Mark McGwire, Brian Grant, Matt Carson	4.00
14	James Holcomb, David Jensen, Kennard Jones, Ryan Williams	4.00
15	David Jensen, Francisco Liriano, Ryan Williams, Travis Hanson	4.00
16	Blair Johnson, Jesse Crain, Adam Greenberg, Curtis Granderson	4.00
17	Jon Lester, Jonathan George, Adam Donachie, Mark McLemore	4.00
18	Francisco Liriano, Mark McGwire, Travis Hanson, Taber Lee	4.00

19 Val Majewski, Charlie Morton, Daniel Cevette, Joey Gomes 4.00
20 Bob Malek, Zach Hammes, Fred Lewis, Cal Ripken Jr. 4.00
21 Justin Maureau, Joe DiMaggio, Chris Snyder, Mark McGwire 4.00
22 Mark McGwire, Bob Malek, Joe DiMaggio, Kyle Boyer 4.00
23 Charlie Morton, David Bush, Joey Gomes, Blair Johnson 4.00
24 Josh Murray, Mark McGwire, Jason Pridie, Joe DiMaggio 4.00
25 Matt Pender, Mark McGwire, Mark McLemore, Ryan Rodriguez 4.00
26 Jason Pridie, Josh Murray, Matt Craig, Brian McCann 4.00
27 Jeremy Reed, Blair Johnson, Matt Carson, Adam Greenberg 4.00
28 Cal Ripken Jr., Jason Cooper, Matt Carson, Larry Broadway 4.00
29 Ryan Rodriguez, Eric Thomas, Pat Osborn, Randy Braun 4.00
30 Josh Rupe, Tyler Davidson, John Baker, Kennard Jones 4.00
31 Eric Thomas, Derick Grigsby, Randy Braun, James Loney 4.00
32 Eric Thomas, Matt Pender, Kiel Fisher, Mark McLemore 4.00
33 Brandon Wheeder, Rich Hill, Brian Dopirak, Brian Grant 4.00

Heroes of Baseball

Cal Ripken Jr.
Ripkens caps off 1981 season by winning MVP

	NM/M
Complete Ripken Set (10):	15.00
Common Ripken:	2.00
Complete Morgan Set (10):	4.00
Common Morgan:	.50
Complete Stargell Set (10):	5.00
Common Stargell:	.50
Complete Seaver Set (10):	10.00
Common Seaver:	1.25
Complete Mantle Set (10):	15.00
Common Mantle:	2.00
Complete DiMaggio Set (10):	12.00
Common DiMaggio:	1.50
Complete Gwynn Set (10):	10.00
Common Gwynn:	1.25
Complete McGwire Set (10):	12.00
Common McGwire:	1.50
Complete Ozzie Smith (10):	8.00
Common Ozzie:	1.00

Sets include Headers
Inserted 1:1

2002 Upper Deck Rookie Debut

	NM/M
Common Player:	.10

Pack (5):	1.50
Box (24):	30.00

Honor Roll
Common Honor Roll Rk (131-190): .25
Golds (131-190): 5-10X
Production 50

101 Curt Schilling .40
102 Geronimo Gil .10
103 Cliff Floyd .10
104 Derek Lowe .10
105 Hee Seop Choi .10
106 Mark Prior .50
107 Joe Borchard .10
108 Austin Kearns .40
109 Adam Dunn .50
110 Brandon Phillips .10
111 Carlos Pena .10
112 Andy Van Hekken .10
113 Juan Encarnacion .10
114 Lance Berkman .25
115 Torii Hunter .25
116 Bartolo Colon .10
117 Raul Mondesi .20
118 Alfonso Soriano .75
119 Miguel Tejada .40
120 Ray Durham .10
121 Eric Chavez .20
122 Brett Myers .10
123 Marlon Byrd .10
124 Sean Burroughs .10
125 Kenny Lofton .10
126 Scott Rolen .50
127 Carl Crawford .10
128 Josh Phelps .10
129 Eric Hinske .10
130 Orlando Hudson .10
131 Barry Wesson .40
132 Jose Valverde RC .25
133 Jason Grybowski RC .25
134 Trey Hodges RC .25
135 Howie Clark RC .25
136 Josh Hancock RC .25
137 Freddy Sanchez RC .25
138 Francis Beltran RC .10
139 Mike Mahoney .10
140 Brian Tallet .10
141 Jason Davis RC .50
142 Carl Sadler RC .25
143 Jason Beverlin RC .25
144 Josh Bard RC .25
145 Aaron Cook RC .25
146 Eric Eckenstahler RC .25
147 Tim Kalita RC .25
148 Franklyn German RC .25
149 Hansel Izquierdo RC .25
150 Brandon Puffer RC .25
151 Rodrigo Rosario RC .25
152 Kirk Saarloos RC .25
153 Jeriome Robertson RC .25
154 Jeremy Hill RC .25
155 Wes Obermueller RC .25
156 Aaron Guiel RC .25
157 Kazuhisa Ishii RC 1.00
158 David Ross .10
159 Jayson Durocher RC .25
160 Luis Martinez RC .25
161 Shane Nance RC .25
162 Eric Good RC .25
163 Jamey Carroll RC .25
164 Jaime Cerda RC .25
165 Satoru Komiyama RC .25
166 Adam Walker RC .25
167 Nate Field RC .25
168 Cody McKay RC .25
169 Jose Flores RC .25
170 Eric Junge RC .25
171 Oliver Perez RC 1.00
172 Oliver Perez RC 1.00
173 Julius Matos RC .25
174 Wilbert Nieves RC .25
175 Clay Condrey RC .25
176 Mike Crudale RC .25
177 Jason Simontacchi RC .50
178 So Taguchi RC .50
179 Jose Rodriguez .10
180 Jorge Sosa RC .25
181 Felix Escalona RC .25
182 Lance Carter RC .25
183 Travis Hughes .10
184 Reynaldo Garcia RC .25
185 Mike Smith .10
186 Corey Thurman RC .25
187 Ken Huckaby RC .25
188 Reed Johnson RC .50
189 Kevin Cash RC .25
190 Scott Wiggins RC .25

Ovation
Common SP (151-180): 3.00
Production 2,002
Golds (151-180): 2-4X
Production 50

121 Curt Schilling .50
122 Cliff Floyd .15
123 Derek Lowe .15
124 Hee Seop Choi .25
125 Mark Prior .75
126 Joe Borchard .15
127 Austin Kearns .50
128 Adam Dunn .75
129 Jay Payton .15
130 Carlos Pena .15
131 Andy Van Hekken .15
132 Andres Torres .15
133 Ben Diggins .15
134 Torii Hunter .40
135 Bartolo Colon .25
136 Raul Mondesi .15
137 Alfonso Soriano 1.00
138 Miguel Tejada .75
139 Ray Durham .15
140 Eric Chavez .40
141 Marlon Byrd .15
142 Brett Myers .15
143 Sean Burroughs .15
144 Kenny Lofton .15
145 Scott Rolen .75
146 Carl Crawford .15
147 Jayson Werth .15
148 Josh Phelps .15
149 Eric Hinske .15
150 Orlando Hudson .15
151 Jose Valverde RC 5.00
152 Trey Hodges RC 3.00
153 Joey Dawley RC 3.00
154 Travis Driskill RC 3.00
155 Howie Clark RC 3.00
156 Jorge De La Rosa RC 3.00
157 Freddy Sanchez RC 3.00
158 Earl Snyder RC 5.00
159 Cliff Lee RC 8.00
160 Josh Bard RC 3.00
161 Aaron Cook RC 3.00
162 Franklyn German RC 3.00
163 Brandon Puffer RC 3.00
164 Kirk Saarloos RC 3.00
165 Jeriome Robertson RC 3.00
166 Miguel Asencio RC 3.00
167 Shawn Sedlacek RC 3.00
168 Jayson Durocher RC 3.00
169 Shane Nance RC 3.00
170 Jamey Carroll RC 8.00
171 Oliver Perez RC 10.00
172 Wilbert Nieves RC 3.00
173 Clay Condrey RC 3.00
174 Chris Snelling RC 5.00
175 Mike Crudale RC 3.00
176 Jason Simontacchi RC 3.00
177 Felix Escalona RC 3.00
178 Lance Carter RC 3.00
179 Scott Wiggins RC 3.00
180 Kevin Cash RC 3.00

Victory
Common Rk (606-660): .20

551 John Lackey .25
552 Francisco Rodriguez .50
553 Cliff Floyd .10
554 Derek Lowe .10
555 Mark Bellhorn .10
556 Matt Clement .10
557 Hee Seop Choi .25
558 Joe Borchard .10
559 Ryan Dempster .10
560 Russell Branyan .10
561 Brandon Larson .10
562 Coco Crisp .10
563 Karim Garcia .10
564 Brandon Phillips .10
565 Jay Payton .10
566 Gabe Kapler .10
567 Carlos Pena .10
568 George Lombard .10
569 Andy Van Hekken .10
570 Andres Torres .10
571 Justin Wayne .10
572 Juan Encarnacion .10
573 Abraham Nunez .10
574 Peter Munro .10
575 Jason Lane .10
576 Dave Roberts .10
577 Eric Gagne .10
578 Alex Sanchez .10
579 Jim Rushford RC .10
580 Ben Diggins .10
581 Eddie Guardado .10
582 Bartolo Colon .20
583 Endy Chavez .10
584 Raul Mondesi .20
585 Jeff Weaver .10
586 Marcus Thames .10
587 Ted Lilly .10
588 Ray Durham .10
589 Jeremy Giambi .10
590 Vicente Padilla .10
591 Brett Myers .10
592 Josh Fogg .10
593 Tony Alvarez .10
594 Jake Peavy .10
595 Dennis Tankersley .10
596 Sean Burroughs .10
597 Kenny Lofton .10
598 Scott Rolen .50
599 Chuck Finley .10
600 Carl Crawford .10
601 Kevin Mench .10
602 Juan Gonzalez .50
603 Jayson Werth .10
604 Eric Hinske .10
605 Josh Phelps .10
606 Jose Valverde RC .20
607 John Ennis RC .20
608 Trey Hodges RC .20
609 Kevin Gryboski RC .20
610 Travis Driskill RC .20
611 Howie Clark RC .20
612 Freddy Sanchez RC .20
613 Josh Hancock RC .20
614 Jorge De La Rosa RC .20
615 Mike Mahoney .10
616 Jason Davis RC .20
617 Josh Bard RC .20
618 Jason Beverlin RC .20
619 Carl Sadler RC .20
620 Earl Snyder RC .50
621 Aaron Cook RC .20
622 Eric Eckenstahler RC .20
623 Franklyn German RC .20
624 Kirk Saarloos RC .50
625 Rodrigo Rosario RC .20
626 Jeriome Robertson RC .20
627 Brandon Puffer RC .20
628 Miguel Asencio RC .20
629 Aaron Guiel RC .30
630 Ryan Bukvich RC .20
631 Jeremy Hill RC .20
632 Kazuhisa Ishii RC .75
633 Jayson Durocher RC .20
634 Shane Nance RC .20
635 Eric Good RC .20
636 Jamey Carroll RC .50
637 Jaime Cerda RC .20
638 Nate Field RC .20
639 Cody McKay RC .20
640 Jose Flores RC .20
641 Jorge Padilla RC .20
642 Anderson Machado RC .20
643 Eric Junge RC .20
644 Oliver Perez RC .75
645 Julius Matos RC .20
646 Ben Howard RC .20
647 Julio Mateo RC .20
648 Matt Thornton .10
649 Chris Snelling RC .50
650 Jason Simontacchi RC .50
651 So Taguchi RC .40
652 Mike Crudale RC .20
653 Mike Coolbaugh .10
654 Felix Escalona RC .20
655 Jorge Sosa RC .20
656 Lance Carter RC .20
657 Reynaldo Garcia RC .20
658 Kevin Cash RC .40
659 Ken Huckaby RC .20
660 Scott Wiggins RC .20

Climbing the Ladder

Common Player:
Production 25 Sets, Not Priced

Elite Company

Common Player:
Production 25, Not Priced

Making Their Marks

Common Player:
Production 25 Sets, Not Priced

Solid Contact

	NM/M
Common Player:	4.00

Inserted 1:24

BA	Bobby Abreu	4.00
EA	Edgardo Alfonzo	4.00
RA	Roberto Alomar	10.00
MA	Moises Alou	6.00
JC	Jose Cruz Jr.	6.00
CD	Carlos Delgado/SP	8.00
JE	Jim Edmonds	6.00
CE	Carl Everett	4.00
JG	Jason Giambi/50	15.00
BG	Brian Giles	6.00
KG	Ken Griffey Jr.	15.00
TH	Todd Helton	8.00
JK	Jason Kendall	4.00
BL	Barry Larkin	10.00
EM	Edgar Martinez	8.00
FM	Fred McGriff	8.00
DM	Doug Mientkiewicz	6.00
JO	John Olerud	6.00
MO	Magglio Ordonez	6.00
JP	Jorge Posada	10.00
AR	Alex Rodriguez	15.00
IR	Ivan Rodriguez	6.00
GS	Gary Sheffield	6.00
SS	Sammy Sosa	15.00
TA	Fernando Tatis	4.00
FT	Frank Thomas	8.00
JT	Jim Thome	12.00
OV	Omar Vizquel	6.00
BW	Bernie Williams	8.00
MW	Matt Williams	8.00

2002 Upper Deck Rookie Update

		NM/M
Common Player:		.25
Pack (5):		3.00
Box (15):		35.00
SP Authentic		
Common SP (201-230):		5.00
Production 1,999		
171	Erubiel Durazo	.25
172	Junior Spivey	.25
173	Geronimo Gil	.25
174	Cliff Floyd	.25
175	Brandon Larsen	.25
176	Aaron Boone	.25
177	Shawn Estes	.25
178	Austin Kearns	.75
179	Joe Borchard	.25
180	Russell Branyan	.25
181	Jay Payton	.25
182	Andres Torres	.25
183	Andy Van Hekken	.25
184	Alex Sanchez	.25
185	Endy Chavez	.25
186	Bartolo Colon	.25
187	Raul Mondesi	.40
188	Robin Ventura	.25
189	Mike Mussina	.75
190	Jorge Posada	.75
191	Ted Lilly	.25
192	Ray Durham	.25
193	Brett Myers	.25
194	Marlon Byrd	.25
195	Vicente Padilla	.25
196	Josh Fogg	.25
197	Kenny Lofton	.25
198	Scott Rolen	1.00
199	Jason Lane	.25
200	Josh Phelps	.25
201	Travis Driskill RC	5.00
202	Howie Clark RC	5.00
203	Mike Mahoney	5.00
204	Brian Tallet	5.00
205	Kirk Saarloos	5.00
206	Barry Wesson	5.00
207	Aaron Guiel RC	5.00
208	Shawn Sedlacek	5.00
209	Jose Diaz	5.00
210	Jorge Nunez	5.00
211	Danny Mota	5.00
212	David Ross	5.00
213	Jayson Durocher RC	5.00
214	Shane Nance RC	5.00
215	Wilbert Nieves RC	5.00
216	Freddy Sanchez RC	5.00
217	Alex Pelaez	5.00
218	Jamey Carroll RC	5.00
219	J.J. Trujillo	5.00
220	Kevin Pickford	5.00
221	Clay Condrey RC	5.00
222	Chris Snelling RC	5.00
223	Cliff Lee RC	8.00
224	Jeremy Hill RC	5.00
225	Jose Rodriguez	5.00
226	Lance Carter RC	5.00
227	Ken Huckaby RC	5.00
228	Scott Wiggins RC	5.00
229	Corey Thurman RC	5.00
230	Kevin Cash RC	5.00
SPx		
Common SPx Auto.		
(221-250):		10.00
Production 825		
191	Tom Glavine	.75
192	Cliff Floyd	.25
193	Mark Prior	1.50
194	Corey Patterson	.50
195	Paul Konerko	.50
196	Adam Dunn	1.00
197	Joe Borchard	.25
198	Carlos Pena	.25
199	Juan Encarnacion	.25
200	Luis Castillo	.25
201	Torii Hunter	.50
202	Hee Seop Choi	.50
203	Bartolo Colon	.40
204	Raul Mondesi	.40
205	Jeff Weaver	.25
206	Eric Munson	.25
207	Alfonso Soriano	1.00
208	Ray Durham	.25
209	Eric Chavez	.50
210	Brett Myers	.25
211	Jeremy Giambi	.25
212	Vicente Padilla	.25
213	Felipe Lopez	.25
214	Sean Burroughs	.25
215	Kenny Lofton	.25
216	Scott Rolen	1.00
217	Carl Crawford	.25
218	Juan Gonzalez	.75
219	Orlando Hudson	.25
220	Eric Hinske	.25
221	Adam Walker RC	10.00
222	Aaron Cook RC	10.00
223	Cam Esslinger RC	10.00
224	Kirk Saarloos	10.00
225	Jose Diaz	10.00
226	David Ross	10.00
227	Jayson Durocher RC	10.00
228	Brian Mallette	10.00
229	Aaron Guiel RC	10.00
230	Jorge Nunez	10.00
231	Satoru Komiyama RC	15.00
232	Tyler Yates RC	15.00
233	Peter Zamora RC	10.00
234	Mike Gonzalez RC	10.00
235	Oliver Perez RC	30.00
236	Julius Matos RC	10.00
237	Andy Shibilo	10.00
238	Jason Simontacchi RC	10.00
239	Ron Chiavacci	10.00
240	Deivis Santos	10.00
241	Travis Driskill RC	10.00
242	Jorge De La Rosa RC	10.00
243	Anastacio Martinez RC	10.00
244	Earl Snyder RC	10.00
245	Freddy Sanchez RC	10.00
246	Miguel Asencio RC	10.00
247	Juan Brito	10.00
248	Franklyn German RC	10.00
249	Chris Snelling RC	10.00
250	Ken Huckaby RC	10.00
Diamond Connection		
Common SP (601-630):		4.00
Production 1,999		
571	Erubiel Durazo	.25
572	Geronimo Gil	.25
573	Shea Hillenbrand	.50
574	Cliff Floyd	.25
575	Corey Patterson	.50
576	Joe Borchard	.25
577	Austin Kearns	.75
578	Ryan Dempster	.25
579	Brandon Larsen	.25
580	Luis Castillo	.25
581	Juan Encarnacion	.25
582	Chin-Feng Chen	.25
583	Hideo Nomo	.75
584	Bartolo Colon	.40
585	Raul Mondesi	.40
586	Eric Munson	.25
587	Alfonso Soriano	1.00
588	Ted Lilly	.25
589	Ray Durham	.25
590	Brett Myers	.25
591	Brandon Phillips	.25
592	Kenny Lofton	.25
593	Scott Rolen	1.00
594	Jim Edmonds	.50
595	Carl Crawford	.25
596	Hank Blalock	.50
597	Kevin Mench	.25
598	Josh Phelps	.25
599	Orlando Hudson	.25
600	Eric Hinske	.25
601	Mike Mahoney	4.00
602	Jason Davis RC	8.00
603	Trey Hodges RC	4.00
604	Josh Bard RC	4.00
605	Jeriome Robertson RC	4.00
606	Jose Diaz	4.00
607	Jorge Nunez	4.00
608	Danny Mota	4.00
609	David Ross	4.00
610	Jayson Durocher RC	4.00
611	Freddy Sanchez RC	4.00
612	Julius Matos RC	4.00
613	Wilbert Nieves RC	4.00
614	Brian Kozlowski	4.00
615	Jason Simontacchi RC	4.00
616	Mike Coolbaugh	4.00
617	Travis Driskill RC	4.00
618	Howie Clark RC	4.00
619	Earl Snyder RC	6.00
620	Carl Sadler RC	4.00
621	Jason Beverlin RC	4.00
622	Terry Pearson	4.00
623	Eric Eckenstahler RC	4.00
624	Shawn Sedlacek	4.00
625	Aaron Guiel RC	5.00
626	Ryan Bukvich RC	4.00
627	Julio Mateo RC	4.00
628	Chris Snelling RC	6.00
629	Lance Carter RC	4.00
630	Scott Wiggins RC	4.00

Star Tributes

		NM/M
Common Player:		5.00
Inserted 1:15		
JB	Josh Beckett	8.00
LB	Lance Berkman	6.00
RC	Roger Clemens	15.00
CD	Carlos Delgado	5.00
JD	Joe DiMaggio/SP	75.00
AD	Adam Dunn	8.00
JG	Jason Giambi	10.00
TG	Tom Glavine	8.00
LG	Luis Gonzalez/SP	8.00
SG	Shawn Green	5.00
KG	Ken Griffey Jr.	12.00
KI	Kazuhisa Ishii	8.00
RJ	Randy Johnson	10.00
CJ	Chipper Jones	10.00
PM	Pedro J. Martinez	8.00
MM	Mark McGwire/SP	50.00
RP	Rafael Palmeiro	8.00
MPi	Mike Piazza	10.00
MPr	Mark Prior	5.00
AR	Alex Rodriguez	10.00
IR	Ivan Rodriguez	8.00
KS	Kazuhiro Sasaki	5.00
CS	Curt Schilling	8.00
TS	Tsuyoshi Shinjo	5.00
AS	Alfonso Soriano	10.00
SS	Sammy Sosa	12.00
IS	Ichiro Suzuki/19	
MS	Mike Sweeney	5.00
FT	Frank Thomas	8.00

Signed Star Tributes

	NM/M
Production 50 Sets	

Copper & Silver:		No Pricing
Production 25		
Gold:		No Pricing
Production 5		
SS-MM	Mark McGwire	350.00

USA Future Watch Swatches

		NM/M
Common Player:		5.00
Inserted 1:15		
Red:		1.5-2X
Production 50		
Copper:		No Pricing
Production 25		
Gold:		No Pricing
Production 5		
AA	Abe Alvarez	5.00
MA	Michael Aubrey	10.00
KB	Kyle Bakker	8.00
CC	Chad Cordero	5.00
SC	Shane Costa	5.00
SF	Sam Fuld	8.00
AH	Aaron Hill	8.00
PH	Philip Humber	8.00
CJ	Conor Jackson	5.00
GJ	Grant Johnson	5.00
MJ	Mark Jurich	5.00
WL	Wes Littleton	8.00
EP	Eric Patterson	5.00
DP	Dustin Pedroia	8.00
LP	Landon Powell	5.00
CQ	Carlos Quentin	8.00
CS	Clint Sammons	5.00
KS	Kyle Sleeth	10.00
HS	Huston Street	5.00
BS	Brad Sullivan	8.00
RW	Rickie Weeks	15.00
BZ	Bob Zimmermann	5.00

2002 Upper Deck Sweet Spot

		NM/M
Complete Set (175):		
Common Player:		.25
Common (91-130):		4.00
Production 1,300		
Common Auto. (131-145):		15.00
Production 750 or 100		
Common Game Faces		
(146-175):		3.00
Inserted 1:24		
Parallel (146-175):		1.5-3X
Production 100		
Pack (4):		8.00
Box (12):		90.00
1	Troy Glaus	.50
2	Darin Erstad	.50
3	Tim Hudson	.50
4	Eric Chavez	.50
5	Barry Zito	.50
6	Miguel Tejada	.50
7	Carlos Delgado	.50
8	Eric Hinske	.25
9	Ben Grieve	.25
10	Jim Thome	1.00
11	C.C. Sabathia	.25
12	Omar Vizquel	.40
13	Ichiro Suzuki	2.00
14	Edgar Martinez	.40

15	Bret Boone	.40
16	Freddy Garcia	.25
17	Tony Batista	.25
18	Geronimo Gil	.25
19	Alex Rodriguez	2.50
20	Rafael Palmeiro	.75
21	Ivan Rodriguez	.75
22	Hank Blalock	.50
23	Juan Gonzalez	.75
24	Nomar Garciaparra	2.00
25	Pedro J. Martinez	1.00
26	Manny Ramirez	1.00
27	Mike Sweeney	.25
28	Carlos Beltran	.50
29	Dmitri Young	.25
30	Torii Hunter	.50
31	Eric Milton	.25
32	Corey Koskie	.25
33	Frank Thomas	.75
34	Mark Buehrle	.25
35	Magglio Ordonez	.50
36	Roger Clemens	2.00
37	Derek Jeter	3.00
38	Jason Giambi	.75
39	Alfonso Soriano	1.00
40	Bernie Williams	.50
41	Jeff Bagwell	.75
42	Roy Oswalt	.50
43	Lance Berkman	.50
44	Greg Maddux	1.50
45	Chipper Jones	1.00
46	Gary Sheffield	.50
47	Andruw Jones	.75
48	Richie Sexson	.50
49	Ben Sheets	.50
50	Albert Pujols	2.00
51	Matt Morris	.40
52	J.D. Drew	.50
53	Sammy Sosa	2.00
54	Kerry Wood	1.00
55	Mark Prior	1.00
56	Moises Alou	.50
57	Corey Patterson	.50
58	Randy Johnson	1.00
59	Luis Gonzalez	.40
60	Curt Schilling	.75
61	Shawn Green	.50
62	Kevin Brown	.40
63	Paul LoDuca	.25
64	Adrian Beltre	.50
65	Vladimir Guerrero	1.00
66	Jose Vidro	.25
67	Javier Vazquez	.25
68	Barry Bonds	3.00
69	Jeff Kent	.40
70	Rich Aurilia	.25
71	Mike Lowell	.40
72	Josh Beckett	.50
73	Brad Penny	.25
74	Roberto Alomar	.50
75	Mike Piazza	1.50
76	Jeromy Burnitz	.25
77	Mo Vaughn	.25
78	Phil Nevin	.25
79	Sean Burroughs	.25
80	Jeremy Giambi	.25
81	Bobby Abreu	.50
82	Jimmy Rollins	.50
83	Pat Burrell	.50
84	Brian Giles	.50
85	Aramis Ramirez	.50
86	Ken Griffey Jr.	1.50
87	Adam Dunn	.75
88	Austin Kearns	.50
89	Todd Helton	.75
90	Larry Walker	.50
91	Earl Snyder RC	6.00
92	Jorge Padilla RC	4.00
93	Felix Escalona RC	4.00
94	John Foster RC	4.00
95	Brandon Puffer RC	4.00
96	Steve Bechler RC	4.00
97	Hansel Izquierdo RC	4.00
98	Chris Baker RC	4.00
99	Jeremy Ward RC	4.00
100	Kevin Frederick RC	4.00
101	Josh Hancock RC	4.00
102	Allan Simpson RC	4.00
103	Mitch Wylie RC	4.00
104	Mark Corey RC	4.00
105	Victor Alvarez RC	4.00
106	Todd Donovan RC	4.00
107	Nelson Castro RC	4.00
108	Chris Booker RC	4.00
109	Corey Thurman RC	4.00
110	Kirk Saarloos RC	4.00
111	Michael Crudale RC	4.00
112	Jason Simontacchi RC	4.00
113	Ron Calloway RC	4.00
114	Brandon Backe RC	4.00
115	Tom Shearn RC	4.00
116	Oliver Perez RC	6.00
117	Kyle Kane RC	4.00

118	Francis Beltran RC	4.00
119	So Taguchi RC	8.00
120	Doug DeVore RC	4.00
121	Juan Brito RC	4.00
122	Clifford Bartosh RC	4.00
123	Eric Junge RC	4.00
124	Joe Orloski RC	4.00
125	Scotty Layfield RC	4.00
126	Jorge Sosa RC	4.00
127	Satoru Komiyama RC	4.00
128	Edwin Almonte RC	4.00
129	Takahito Nomura RC	4.00
130	John Ennis RC	4.00
131	Kazuhisa Ishii/ Auto./100 RC	90.00
132	Ben Howard/ Auto./100 RC	20.00
133	Aaron Cook/ Auto./750 RC	15.00
134	Anderson Machado/ Auto./750 RC	15.00
135	Luis Ugueto/ Auto./750 RC	15.00
136	Tyler Yates/ Auto./750 RC	20.00
137	Rodrigo Rosario/ Auto./750 RC	15.00
138	Jaime Cerda/ Auto./750 RC	15.00
139	Luis Martinez/ Auto./750 RC	15.00
140	Rene Reyes/ Auto./750 RC	15.00
141	Eric Good/ Auto./750 RC	15.00
142	Matt Thornton/ Auto./100	25.00
143	Steve Kent/ Auto./750 RC	15.00
144	Jose Valverde/ Auto./750 RC	15.00
145	Adrian Burnside/ Auto./750 RC	15.00
146	Barry Bonds	15.00
147	Ken Griffey Jr.	10.00
148	Alex Rodriguez	12.00
149	Jason Giambi	4.00
150	Chipper Jones	5.00
151	Nomar Garciaparra	10.00
152	Mike Piazza	10.00
153	Sammy Sosa	10.00
154	Derek Jeter	15.00
155	Jeff Bagwell	4.00
156	Albert Pujols	10.00
157	Ichiro Suzuki	10.00
158	Randy Johnson	5.00
159	Frank Thomas	4.00
160	Greg Maddux	8.00
161	Jim Thome	5.00
162	Scott Rolen	6.00
163	Shawn Green	3.00
164	Vladimir Guerrero	6.00
165	Troy Glaus	3.00
166	Carlos Delgado	4.00
167	Luis Gonzalez	3.00
168	Roger Clemens	10.00
169	Todd Helton	4.00
170	Eric Chavez	3.00
171	Rafael Palmeiro	4.00
172	Pedro J. Martinez	5.00
173	Lance Berkman	3.00
174	Josh Beckett	4.00
175	Sean Burroughs	3.00

Bat Barrels

Common Player: 100 Total Produced

Legendary Signatures

		NM/M
Common Autograph: Inserted 1:72		20.00
LA	Luis Aparicio/485	25.00
JD	Joe DiMaggio/50	
RF	Rollie Fingers/866	20.00
SG	Steve Garvey/871	20.00
KH	Keith Hernandez/906	20.00
FJ	Ferguson Jenkins/857	20.00
AK	Al Kaline/835	40.00
SK	Sandy Koufax/485	200.00
FL	Fred Lynn/853	20.00
MM	Mark McGwire/90	575.00

PM	Paul Molitor/852	30.00
GP	Gaylord Perry/921	25.00
BP	Boog Powell/944	20.00
CR	Cal Ripken Jr./194	175.00
BR	Brooks Robinson	35.00
AT	Alan Trammell/843	25.00

Gwire Priority Signing Redemption

		NM/M
100 Produced		
MM	Mark McGwire	500.00

Signatures

		NM/M
Common Autograph: Inserted 1:72		25.00
LB	Lance Berkman/291	35.00
HB	Hank Blalock/291	40.00
BB	Barry Bonds/380	200.00
JB	Jeromy Burnitz/291	20.00
SB	Sean Burroughs/291	20.00
RC	Roger Clemens/194	150.00
CD	Carlos Delgado/291	20.00
AD	Adam Dunn/291	40.00
FG	Freddy Garcia/145	25.00
JG	Jason Giambi/291	40.00
BG	Brian Giles/291	25.00
TG	Tom Glavine/291	40.00
LG	Luis Gonzalez/291	20.00
KG	Ken Griffey Jr./291	125.00
AJ	Andruw Jones/291	20.00
RO	Roy Oswalt/291	20.00
MPr	Mark Prior/291	60.00
AR	Alex Rodriguez/291	160.00
SR	Scott Rolen/291	40.00
SS	Sammy Sosa/145	200.00
MS	Mike Sweeney/291	20.00
IS	Ichiro Suzuki/145	400.00
FT	Frank Thomas/291	60.00
JT	Jim Thome/291	50.00
BZ	Barry Zito/291	30.00

Sweet Swatches

		NM/M
Common Player: Inserted 1:12		5.00
JBa	Jeff Bagwell	8.00

JBe	Josh Beckett	6.00
SB	Sean Burroughs	5.00
EC	Eric Chavez	6.00
JE	Jim Edmonds	8.00
DE	Darin Erstad	5.00
JGi	Jason Giambi	8.00
BG	Brian Giles	5.00
JGo	Juan Gonzalez	6.00
LG	Luis Gonzalez	5.00
SG	Shawn Green	5.00
KG	Ken Griffey Jr.	15.00
KI	Kazuhisa Ishii	10.00
CJ	Chipper Jones	10.00
GM	Greg Maddux	12.00
PM	Pedro J. Martinez	10.00
MP	Mike Piazza	15.00
AR	Alex Rodriguez	15.00
IR	Ivan Rodriguez	8.00
SR	Scott Rolen	8.00
SS	Sammy Sosa	15.00
IS	Ichiro Suzuki	40.00
FT	Frank Thomas	8.00
OV	Omar Vizquel	5.00
BW	Bernie Williams	8.00

USA Jerseys

		NM/M
Common Player: Inserted 1:12		5.00
BA	Brent Abernathy	5.00
TB	Taggert Bozied	8.00
DB	Dewon Brazelton	5.00
AE	Adam Everett	5.00
DG	Danny Graves	5.00
JG	Jake Gautreau	5.00
JK	Josh Karp	5.00
AK	Adam Kennedy	8.00
JM	Joe Mauer	20.00
DM	Doug Mientkiewicz	6.00
EM	Eric Munson	5.00
XN	Xavier Nady	5.00
RO	Roy Oswalt	8.00
MP	Mark Prior	10.00
JR	Jon Rauch	5.00
MT	Mark Teixeira	8.00
JW	Justin Wayne	5.00

2002 Upper Deck Sweet Spot Classics

		NM/M
Complete Set (90):		40.00
Common Player:		.40
Pack (4):		20.00
Box (12):		200.00
1	Mickey Mantle	4.00
2	Joe DiMaggio	3.00
3	Babe Ruth	3.00
4	Ty Cobb	1.50
5	Nolan Ryan	3.00
6	Sandy Koufax	2.00

7	Cy Young	1.00
8	Roberto Clemente	2.00
9	Lefty Grove	.50
10	Lou Gehrig	2.50
11	Walter Johnson	1.00
12	Honus Wagner	1.00
13	Christy Mathewson	.75
14	Jackie Robinson	1.50
15	Joe Morgan	.50
16	Reggie Jackson	.75
17	Eddie Collins	.40
18	Cal Ripken Jr.	3.00
19	Hank Greenberg	.40
20	Harmon Killebrew	.75
21	Johnny Bench	1.00
22	Ernie Banks	1.00
23	Willie McCovey	.40
24	Mel Ott	.40
25	Tom Seaver	1.00
26	Tony Gwynn	.75
27	Dave Winfield	.50
28	Willie Stargell	.40
29	Mark McGwire	2.00
30	Al Kaline	.75
31	Jimmie Foxx	.75
32	Satchel Paige	1.50
33	Eddie Murray	.40
34	Lou Boudreau	.40
35	"Shoeless" Joe Jackson	1.50
36	Luke Appling	.40
37	Ralph Kiner	.40
38	Robin Yount	.75
39	Paul Molitor	.75
40	Juan Marichal	.40
41	Brooks Robinson	.75
42	Wade Boggs	.50
43	Kirby Puckett	1.00
44	Yogi Berra	1.00
45	George Sisler	.40
46	Buck Leonard	.40
47	Billy Williams	.40
48	Duke Snider	.75
49	Don Drysdale	.60
50	Bill Mazeroski	.40
51	Tony Oliva	.40
52	Luis Aparicio	.40
53	Carlton Fisk	.40
54	Kirk Gibson	.40
55	Jim "Catfish" Hunter	.40
56	Joe Carter	.40
57	Gaylord Perry	.40
58	Don Mattingly	2.00
59	Eddie Mathews	1.25
60	Ferguson Jenkins	.40
61	Roy Campanella	1.00
62	Orlando Cepeda	.40
63	Tony Perez	.40
64	Dave Parker	.40
65	Richie Ashburn	.40
66	Andre Dawson	.40
67	Dwight Evans	.40
68	Rollie Fingers	.40
69	Dale Murphy	.40
70	Ron Santo	.40
71	Steve Garvey	.40
72	Monte Irvin	.40
73	Alan Trammell	.40
74	Ryne Sandberg	1.00
75	Gary Carter	.40
76	Fred Lynn	.40
77	Maury Wills	.40
78	Ozzie Smith	1.00
79	Bobby Bonds	.40
80	Mickey Cochrane	.60
81	Dizzy Dean	.60
82	Graig Nettles	.40
83	Keith Hernandez	.40
84	Boog Powell	.40
85	Jack Clark	.40
86	Dave Stewart	.40
87	Tommy Lasorda	.40
88	Dennis Eckersley	.40
89	Ken Griffey Sr.	.40
90	Bucky Dent	.40

Bat Barrels

Values undetermined due to scarcity.

Game Jersey

	NM/M
Common Player:	5.00

Inserted 1:8

WB	Wade Boggs	12.00
GC	Gary Carter	10.00
JC	Joe Carter	5.00
JD	Joe DiMaggio/53	180.00
RF	Rollie Fingers	5.00
SG	Steve Garvey	5.00
TG	Tony Gwynn	15.00
RJ	Reggie Jackson	15.00
SK	Sandy Koufax/SP	125.00
BM	Bill Madlock	5.00
MM	Mickey Mantle/53	250.00
JMa	Juan Marichal	10.00
DM	Don Mattingly	25.00
PM	Paul Molitor	15.00
EM	Eddie Murray	10.00
GN	Graig Nettles	8.00
DP	Dave Parker	5.00
CR	Cal Ripken Jr.	25.00
NR	Nolan Ryan	40.00
RS	Ryne Sandberg	15.00
TS	Tom Seaver	15.00
OS	Ozzie Smith	15.00
DSn	Duke Snider/53	80.00
WS	Willie Stargell	10.00
DSt	Dave Stewart	5.00
BW	Billy Williams	8.00
RY	Robin Yount	15.00

Game Jersey Gold

No Pricing
Production 25 Sets

Game-Used Bats

		NM/M
Common Player:		5.00
Inserted 1:8		
JB	Johnny Bench	15.00
YB	Yogi Berra	15.00
WB	Wade Boggs	12.00
BBo	Bob Boone	5.00
BBu	Bill Buckner	5.00
GC	Gary Carter	10.00
RC	Roberto Clemente	50.00
BD	Bucky Dent	8.00
JD	Joe DiMaggio/40	180.00
DE	Dwight Evans	8.00
SG	Steve Garvey	8.00
HG	Hank Greenberg/SP	50.00
KG	Ken Griffey Sr.	5.00
TG	Tony Gwynn	15.00
RJ	Reggie Jackson	10.00
FJ	Ferguson Jenkins	10.00
AK	Al Kaline	15.00
FL	Fred Lynn	5.00
BM	Bill Madlock	5.00
DM	Don Mattingly	25.00
PM	Paul Molitor	15.00
TM	Thurman Munson	35.00
GN	Graig Nettles	8.00
DP	Dave Parker	5.00
KP	Kirby Puckett	15.00
CR	Cal Ripken Jr.	25.00
BR	Brooks Robinson	15.00
NR	Nolan Ryan	40.00
BW	Billy Williams	8.00
DW	Dave Winfield	10.00

Game-Used Bats Gold

	NM/M
Common Player:	25.00

JB	Johnny Bench	100.00
YB	Yogi Berra	125.00
WB	Wade Boggs	100.00
BBo	Bob Boone	40.00
BBu	Bill Buckner	35.00
GC	Gary Carter	40.00
RC	Roberto Clemente	250.00
BD	Bucky Dent	25.00
JD	Joe DiMaggio	250.00
DE	Dwight Evans	25.00
SG	Steve Garvey	35.00
HG	Hank Greenberg	125.00
KG	Ken Griffey Sr.	25.00
TG	Tony Gwynn	150.00
RJ	Reggie Jackson	150.00
FJ	Ferguson Jenkins	45.00
AK	Al Kaline	75.00
FL	Fred Lynn	25.00
BM	Bill Madlock	25.00
DM	Don Mattingly	125.00
PM	Paul Molitor	40.00
TM	Thurman Munson	150.00
GN	Graig Nettles	25.00
DP	Dave Parker	25.00
KP	Kirby Puckett	125.00
CR	Cal Ripken Jr.	225.00
BR	Brooks Robinson	75.00
NR	Nolan Ryan	175.00
BW	Billy Williams	45.00
DW	Dave Winfield	45.00

Sweet Spot Signatures

		NM/M
Common Autograph:		20.00
Inserted 1:24		
EB	Ernie Banks	60.00
JB	Johnny Bench	60.00
YB	Yogi Berra	150.00
AD	Andre Dawson/100	100.00
BD	Bucky Dent	20.00
DeE	Dennis Eckersley	40.00
RF	Rollie Fingers	25.00
CF	Carlton Fisk/100	125.00
SG	Steve Garvey	25.00
KG	Kirk Gibson/SP	50.00
KH	Keith Hernandez	30.00
RJ	Reggie Jackson/SP	100.00
FJ	Ferguson Jenkins	25.00
AK	Al Kaline	40.00
SK	Sandy Koufax/SP	250.00
TL	Tommy Lasorda	35.00
FL	Fred Lynn	25.00
DoM	Don Mattingly	100.00
BM	Bill Mazeroski	40.00
WM	Willie McCovey/SP	75.00
PM	Paul Molitor	40.00
JM	Joe Morgan	25.00
DaM	Dale Murphy	50.00
GP	Gaylord Perry	25.00
BP	Boog Powell	25.00
KP	Kirby Puckett	180.00
CR	Cal Ripken Jr.	180.00
BR	Brooks Robinson	50.00
NR	Nolan Ryan/74	300.00
TS	Tom Seaver	50.00
OS	Ozzie Smith/137	200.00
DaS	Dave Stewart	25.00
AT	Alan Trammell	30.00
DW	Dave Winfield/70	125.00

Sweet Spot Signatures Gold

No Pricing

Production 25 Sets

2002 Upper Deck Ultimate Collection

	NM/M
Complete Set (120):	
Common Player (1-60):	2.00
Production 799	
Common Player (61-110, 114-120):	10.00
Production 550	
Common (111-113):	25.00
Production 330	
Pack (4):	100.00
Box (4):	350.00
1	Troy Glaus	2.50
2	Luis Gonzalez	2.00
3	Curt Schilling	2.50
4	Randy Johnson	4.00
5	Andruw Jones	2.50
6	Greg Maddux	6.00
7	Chipper Jones	5.00
8	Gary Sheffield	2.00
9	Cal Ripken Jr.	12.00
10	Manny Ramirez	3.00
11	Pedro J. Martinez	4.00
12	Nomar Garciaparra	8.00
13	Sammy Sosa	6.00
14	Kerry Wood	4.00
15	Mark Prior	4.00
16	Magglio Ordonez	2.00
17	Frank Thomas	3.00
18	Adam Dunn	3.00
19	Ken Griffey Jr.	8.00
20	Jim Thome	4.00
21	Larry Walker	2.00
22	Todd Helton	3.00
23	Nolan Ryan	12.00
24	Jeff Bagwell	3.00
25	Roy Oswalt	2.00
26	Lance Berkman	2.00
27	Mike Sweeney	2.00
28	Shawn Green	2.00
29	Hideo Nomo	2.00
30	Torii Hunter	2.00
31	Vladimir Guerrero	5.00
32	Tom Seaver	4.00
33	Mike Piazza	8.00
34	Roberto Alomar	2.00
35	Derek Jeter	12.00
36	Alfonso Soriano	5.00
37	Jason Giambi	4.00
38	Roger Clemens	8.00
39	Mike Mussina	2.50
40	Bernie Williams	2.50
41	Joe DiMaggio	10.00
42	Mickey Mantle	15.00
43	Miguel Tejada	3.00
44	Eric Chavez	2.00
45	Barry Zito	2.00
46	Pat Burrell	2.50
47	Jason Kendall	2.00
48	Brian Giles	2.00
49	Barry Bonds	15.00
50	Ichiro Suzuki	8.00
51	Stan Musial	8.00
52	J.D. Drew	2.00
53	Scott Rolen	5.00
54	Albert Pujols	10.00
55	Mark McGwire	10.00
56	Alex Rodriguez	10.00

#	Player	Price
57	Ivan Rodriguez	3.00
58	Juan Gonzalez	2.50
59	Rafael Palmeiro	3.00
60	Carlos Delgado	2.50
61	Jose Valverde RC	10.00
62	Doug DeVore RC	10.00
63	John Ennis RC	10.00
64	Joey Dawley	10.00
65	Trey Hodges RC	10.00
66	Mike Mahoney	10.00
67	Aaron Cook RC	10.00
68	Rene Reyes RC	10.00
69	Mark Corey	10.00
70	Hansel Izquierdo RC	10.00
71	Brandon Puffer RC	10.00
72	Jeriome Robertson RC	10.00
73	Jose Diaz	10.00
74	David Ross	10.00
75	Jayson Durocher RC	10.00
76	Eric Good RC	10.00
77	Satoru Komiyama RC	10.00
78	Tyler Yates RC	10.00
79	Eric Junge RC	10.00
80	Anderson Machado RC	10.00
81	Adrian Burnside RC	10.00
82	Ben Howard RC	10.00
83	Clay Condrey RC	10.00
84	Nelson Castro RC	10.00
85	So Taguchi RC	15.00
86	Mike Crudale RC	10.00
87	Scotty Layfield RC	10.00
88	Steve Bechler RC	10.00
89	Travis Driskill RC	10.00
90	Howie Clark RC	10.00
91	Josh Hancock RC	10.00
92	Jorge De La Rosa RC	10.00
93	Anastacio Martinez RC	10.00
94	Brian Tallet RC	10.00
95	Carl Sadler RC	10.00
96	Cliff Lee RC	15.00
97	Josh Bard RC	10.00
98	Wes Obermueller RC	10.00
99	Juan Brito	10.00
100	Aaron Guiel RC	10.00
101	Jeremy Hill RC	10.00
102	Kevin Frederick RC	10.00
103	Nate Field RC	10.00
104	Julio Mateo RC	10.00
105	Chris Snelling RC	15.00
106	Felix Escalona RC	10.00
107	Reynaldo Garcia RC	10.00
108	Mike Smith RC	10.00
109	Ken Huckaby RC	10.00
110	Kevin Cash RC	10.00
111	Kazuhisa Ishii/Auto. RC	40.00
112	Freddy Sanchez/Auto. RC	25.00
113	Jason Simontacchi/Auto. RC	25.00
114	Jorge Padilla/Auto. RC	15.00
115	Kirk Saarloos/Auto.	15.00
116	Rodrigo Rosario/Auto. RC	15.00
117	Oliver Perez/Auto. RC	50.00
118	Miguel Asencio/Auto. RC	15.00
119	Franklyn German/Auto. RC	15.00
120	Jaime Cerda/Auto. RC	15.00

Double Barrel

NM/M

Quantity produced listed
DB-RI	Ivan Rodriguez, Alex Rodriguez/5	2,225
DB-RR	Cal Ripken Jr., Alex Rodriguez/9	1,625
DB-TO	Magglio Ordonez, Frank Thomas/4	950.00

Double Patches

NM/M

Production 100 Sets
Golds: .75-1.5X
Production 50 Sets

Code	Player	Price
DE	J.D. Drew, Jim Edmonds	60.00
GC	Jason Giambi, Roger Clemens	80.00
IG	Ken Griffey Jr., Ichiro Suzuki	125.00
JS	Randy Johnson, Curt Schilling	60.00
MG	Tom Glavine, Greg Maddux	75.00
MS	Sammy Sosa, Mark McGwire	150.00
PA	Mike Piazza, Roberto Alomar	80.00
RG	Alex Rodriguez, Juan Gonzalez	80.00
RM	Manny Ramirez, Pedro J. Martinez	50.00

Jerseys Tier 1

NM/M

Common Player: 10.00
Production 99 Sets
Golds: .75-1.5X
Production 50 Sets
Code	Player	Price
RC	Roger Clemens	20.00
JD	Joe DiMaggio	100.00
AD	Adam Dunn	15.00
JG	Jason Giambi	15.00
KG	Ken Griffey Jr.	20.00
KI	Kazuhisa Ishii	10.00
RJ	Randy Johnson	10.00
AJ	Andruw Jones	10.00
CJ	Chipper Jones	15.00
MM	Mickey Mantle	125.00
PM	Pedro J. Martinez	15.00
MC	Mark McGwire	60.00
MP	Mike Piazza	15.00
PR	Mark Prior	15.00
MR	Manny Ramirez	10.00
CR	Cal Ripken Jr.	40.00
AR	Alex Rodriguez	25.00
IR	Ivan Rodriguez	15.00
AS	Alfonso Soriano	20.00
SS	Sammy Sosa	25.00
IS	Ichiro Suzuki	45.00

Jerseys Tier 2

NM/M

Same price as Tier 1.
Production 99 Sets
Golds: 1.5-2X
Production 25 Sets
Code	Player	Price
JF-RC	Roger Clemens	20.00
JF-JD	Joe DiMaggio	100.00
JF-AD	Adam Dunn	15.00
JF-JG	Jason Giambi	15.00
JF-KG	Ken Griffey Jr.	20.00
JF-KI	Kazuhisa Ishii	10.00
JF-RJ	Randy Johnson	15.00
JF-AJ	Andruw Jones	10.00
JF-CJ	Chipper Jones	15.00
JF-MM	Mickey Mantle	125.00
JF-PM	Pedro J. Martinez	15.00
JF-MC	Mark McGwire	60.00
JF-MP	Mike Piazza	15.00
JF-PR	Mark Prior	20.00
JF-MR	Manny Ramirez	10.00
JF-CR	Cal Ripken Jr.	40.00
JF-AR	Alex Rodriguez	25.00
JF-IR	Ivan Rodriguez	15.00
JF-AS	Alfonso Soriano	20.00
JF-SS	Sammy Sosa	25.00
JF-IS	Ichiro Suzuki	45.00

Jerseys Tier 3

NM/M

Common Player: 8.00
Stars: .4-.6X Tier 1 Price
Production 199 Sets
Code	Player	Price
JP-RC	Roger Clemens	15.00
JP-AD	Adam Dunn	10.00
JP-JG	Jason Giambi	8.00
JP-KG	Ken Griffey Jr.	15.00
JP-KI	Kazuhisa Ishii	8.00
JP-RJ	Randy Johnson	12.00
JP-AJ	Andruw Jones	8.00
JP-CJ	Chipper Jones	12.00
JP-MM	Mickey Mantle	75.00
JP-PM	Pedro J. Martinez	10.00
JP-MC	Mark McGwire	40.00
JP-MP	Mike Piazza	15.00
JP-PR	Mark Prior	10.00
JP-MR	Manny Ramirez	8.00
JP-CR	Cal Ripken Jr.	30.00
JP-AR	Alex Rodriguez	15.00
JP-IR	Ivan Rodriguez	8.00
JP-AS	Alfonso Soriano	12.00
JP-SS	Sammy Sosa	20.00
JP-IS	Ichiro Suzuki	30.00
JP-BW	Bernie Williams	8.00

Jerseys Tier 4

NM/M

Common Player: 8.00
Stars: .4-.6X Tier 1 price
Production 199 Sets
Code	Player	Price
JR-RC	Roger Clemens	15.00
JR-AD	Adam Dunn	10.00
JR-JG	Jason Giambi	10.00
JR-KG	Ken Griffey Jr.	15.00
JR-KI	Kazuhisa Ishii	8.00
JR-RJ	Randy Johnson	10.00
JR-AJ	Andruw Jones	8.00
JR-CJ	Chipper Jones	10.00
JR-MM	Mickey Mantle	75.00
JR-PM	Pedro J. Martinez	10.00
JR-MC	Mark McGwire	40.00
JR-MP	Mike Piazza	15.00
JR-PR	Mark Prior	10.00
JR-MR	Manny Ramirez	8.00
JR-CR	Cal Ripken Jr.	25.00
JR-AR	Alex Rodriguez	15.00
JR-IR	Ivan Rodriguez	8.00
JR-AS	Alfonso Soriano	15.00
JR-SS	Sammy Sosa	20.00
JR-IS	Ichiro Suzuki	30.00
JR-BW	Bernie Williams	8.00

Mark McGwire Signing Redemption

NM/M

Exchange Card 1:500 Packs:
1-MM	Mark McGwire	500.00

Patch

NM/M

Common Player: 25.00
Production 100 Sets
Code	Player	Price
LG	Luis Gonzalez	25.00
SG	Shawn Green	25.00

Code	Player	Price
TH	Todd Helton	40.00
KI	Kazuhisa Ishii	40.00
CJ	Chipper Jones	40.00
MM	Mark McGwire	125.00
MP	Mark Prior	30.00
IR	Ivan Rodriguez	40.00
SS	Sammy Sosa	65.00
IS	Ichiro Suzuki	150.00

Signed Excellence

NM/M

Quantity produced listed
Golds: No Pricing
Production One Set
Code	Player	Price
I1	Ichiro Suzuki/56	375.00
I2	Ichiro Suzuki/51	375.00
I5	Ichiro Suzuki/Btg	250.00
I6	Ichiro Suzuki/Throwing	250.00
MM1	Mark McGwire/70	275.00
MM2	Mark McGwire/65	275.00
MM3	Mark McGwire/49	300.00
MM5	Mark McGwire/Standing	220.00
MM6	Mark McGwire/Waving	220.00
MM7	Mark McGwire/Fld	220.00
SS1	Sammy Sosa/66	175.00
SS2	Sammy Sosa/64	175.00
SS3	Sammy Sosa/54	175.00
SS5	Sammy Sosa/Running	150.00
SS6	Sammy Sosa/Holding Bat	150.00
SS7	Sammy Sosa/150	150.00

Signatures Tier 1

NM/M

Common Autograph: 20.00
Quantity produced listed
Golds: No Pricing
Production 25 Sets
Code	Player	Price
RA1	Roberto Alomar/155	45.00
LB1	Lance Berkman/179	25.00
PB1	Pat Burrell/95	25.00
RC1	Roger Clemens/320	80.00
CD1	Carlos Delgado/95	25.00
JD1	J.D. Drew/220	25.00
AD1	Adam Dunn/125	45.00
JG1	Jason Giambi/295	25.00
BG1	Brian Giles/220	20.00
LG1	Luis Gonzalez/199	20.00
KG1	Ken Griffey Jr./195	100.00
JK1	Jason Kendall/220	20.00
MP1	Mark Prior/160	40.00
CR1	Cal Ripken Jr./75	165.00
AR1	Alex Rodriguez/329	100.00
SR1	Scott Rolen/160	20.00
GS1	Gary Sheffield/95	20.00
JT1	Jim Thome/95	60.00
BZ1	Barry Zito/199	25.00

Signatures Tier 2

NM/M

Quantity produced listed
Golds: No Pricing
Production 10 Sets
Code	Player	Price
JB2	Jeff Bagwell/51	55.00
LB2	Lance Berkman/85	40.00

JG2	Jason Giambi/50	60.00
LG2	Luis Gonzalez/70	25.00
KG2	Ken Griffey Jr./30	150.00
TG2	Tony Gwynn/51	75.00
TH2	Todd Helton/51	60.00
AJ2	Andruw Jones/51	50.00
MP2	Mark Prior/60	60.00
KP2	Kirby Puckett/75	60.00
AR2	Alex Rodriguez/75	100.00
SR2	Scott Rolen/60	50.00
DS2	Duke Snider/51	60.00
FT2	Frank Thomas/51	65.00
KW2	Kerry Wood/51	75.00
BZ2	Barry Zito/70	40.00

2002 Upper Deck Victory

VLADIMIR GUERRERO

	NM/M
Complete Set (550):	40.00
Common Player:	.10
Pack (10):	1.00
Box (36):	25.00

1	Troy Glaus	.30
2	Tim Salmon	.20
3	Troy Percival	.10
4	Darin Erstad	.25
5	Adam Kennedy	.10
6	Scott Spiezio	.10
7	Ramon Ortiz	.10
8	Ismael Valdes	.10
9	Jarrod Washburn	.10
10	Garret Anderson	.10
11	David Eckstein	.10
12	Mo Vaughn	.25
13	Benji Gil	.10
14	Bengie Molina	.10
15	Scott Schoeneweis	.10
16	Troy Glaus,	
	Ramon Ortiz	.20
17	David Justice	.25
18	Jermaine Dye	.10
19	Eric Chavez	.25
20	Jeremy Giambi	.10
21	Terrence Long	.10
22	Miguel Tejada	.20
23	Johnny Damon	.10
24	Jason Hart	.10
25	Adam Piatt	.10
26	Billy Koch	.10
27	Ramon Hernandez	.10
28	Eric Byrnes	.10
29	Olmedo Saenz	.10
30	Barry Zito	.20
31	Tim Hudson	.25
32	Mark Mulder	.20
33	Jason Giambi,	
	Mark Mulder	.25
34	Carlos Delgado	.40
35	Shannon Stewart	.10
36	Vernon Wells	.10
37	Homer Bush	.10
38	Brad Fullmer	.10
39	Jose Cruz	.10
40	Felipe Lopez	.10
41	Raul Mondesi	.20
42	Esteban Loaiza	.10
43	Darrin Fletcher	.10
44	Mike Sirotka	.10
45	Luke Prokopec	.10
46	Chris Carpenter	.10
47	Roy Halladay	.10
48	Kelvim Escobar	.10
49	Carlos Delgado,	
	Billy Koch	.20
50	Nick Bierbrodt	.10
51	Greg Vaughn	.10
52	Ben Grieve	.10
53	Damian Rolls	.10
54	Russ Johnson	.10
55	Brent Abernathy	.10
56	Steve Cox	.10
57	Aubrey Huff	.10

58	Randy Winn	.10
59	Jason Tyner	.10
60	Tanyon Sturtze	.10
61	Joe Kennedy	.10
62	Jared Sandberg	.10
63	Esteban Yan	.10
64	Ryan Rupe	.10
65	Toby Hall	.10
66	Greg Vaughn,	
	Tanyon Sturtze	.10
67	Matt Lawton	.10
68	Juan Gonzalez	.40
69	Jim Thome	.25
70	Einar Diaz	.10
71	Ellis Burks	.10
72	Kenny Lofton	.10
73	Omar Vizquel	.10
74	Russell Branyan	.10
75	Brady Anderson	.10
76	John Rocker	.10
77	Travis Fryman	.10
78	Wil Cordero	.10
79	Chuck Finley	.10
80	C.C. Sabathia	.10
81	Bartolo Colon	.10
82	Bob Wickman	.10
83	Roberto Alomar,	
	C.C. Sabathia	.20
84	Ichiro Suzuki	1.50
85	Edgar Martinez	.10
86	Aaron Sele	.10
87	Carlos Guillen	.10
88	Bret Boone	.10
89	John Olerud	.20
90	Jamie Moyer	.10
91	Ben Davis	.10
92	Dan Wilson	.10
93	Jeff Cirillo	.10
94	John Halama	.10
95	Freddy Garcia	.10
96	Kazuhiro Sasaki	.10
97	Mike Cameron	.10
98	Paul Abbott	.10
99	Mark McLemore	.10
100	Ichiro Suzuki,	
	Freddy Garcia	.50
101	Jeff Conine	.10
102	David Segui	.10
103	Marty Cordova	.10
104	Tony Batista	.10
105	Chris Richard	.10
106	Willis Roberts	.10
107	Melvin Mora	.10
108	Mike Bordick	.10
109	Jay Gibbons	.10
110	Mike Kinkade	.10
111	Brian Roberts	.10
112	Jerry Hairston Jr.	.10
113	Jason Johnson	.10
114	Josh Towers	.10
115	Calvin Maduro	.10
116	Sidney Ponson	.10
117	Jeff Conine,	
	Jason Johnson	.10
118	Alex Rodriguez	1.00
119	Ivan Rodriguez	.40
120	Frank Catalanotto	.10
121	Mike Lamb	.10
122	Ruben Sierra	.10
123	Rusty Greer	.10
124	Rafael Palmeiro	.20
125	Gabe Kapler	.15
126	Aaron Myette	.10
127	Kenny Rogers	.10
128	Carl Everett	.10
129	Rick Helling	.10
130	Ricky Ledee	.10
131	Michael Young	.10
132	Doug Davis	.10
133	Jeff Zimmerman	.10
134	Alex Rodriguez,	
	Rick Helling	.40
135	Manny Ramirez	.40
136	Nomar Garciaparra	1.00
137	Jason Varitek	.10
138	Dante Bichette	.10
139	Tony Clark	.10
140	Scott Hatteberg	.10
141	Trot Nixon	.10
142	Hideo Nomo	.25
143	Dustin Hermanson	.10
144	Chris Stynes	.10
145	Jose Offerman	.10
146	Pedro Martinez	.50
147	Shea Hillenbrand	.10
148	Tim Wakefield	.10
149	Troy O'Leary	.10
150	Ugueth Urbina	.10
151	Manny Ramirez,	
	Hideo Nomo	.25
152	Carlos Beltran	.10
153	Dee Brown	.10
154	Mike Sweeney	.10
155	Luis Alicea	.10

156	Raul Ibanez	.10
157	Mark Quinn	.10
158	Joe Randa	.10
159	Roberto Hernandez	.10
160	Neifi Perez	.10
161	Carlos Febles	.10
162	Jeff Suppan	.10
163	Dave McCarty	.10
164	Blake Stein	.10
165	Chad Durbin	.10
166	Paul Byrd	.10
167	Carlos Beltran,	
	Jeff Suppan	.10
168	Craig Paquette	.10
169	Dean Palmer	.10
170	Shane Halter	.10
171	Bobby Higginson	.10
172	Robert Fick	.10
173	Jose Macias	.10
174	Deivi Cruz	.10
175	Damion Easley	.10
176	Brandon Inge	.10
177	Mark Redman	.10
178	Dmitri Young	.10
179	Steve Sparks	.10
180	Jeff Weaver	.10
181	Victor Santos	.10
182	Jose Lima	.10
183	Matt Anderson	.10
184	Roger Cedeno,	
	Steve Sparks	.10
185	Doug Mientkiewicz	.10
186	Cristian Guzman	.10
187	Torii Hunter	.10
188	Matt LeCroy	.10
189	Corey Koskie	.10
190	Jacque Jones	.10
191	Luis Rivas	.10
192	David Ortiz	.10
193	A.J. Pierzynski	.10
194	Brian Buchanan	.10
195	Joe Mays	.10
196	Brad Radke	.10
197	Denny Hocking	.10
198	Eric Milton	.10
199	LaTroy Hawkins	.10
200	Doug Mientkiewicz,	
	Joe Mays	.10
201	Magglio Ordonez	.20
202	Jose Valentin	.10
203	Chris Singleton	.10
204	Aaron Rowand	.10
205	Paul Konerko	.10
206	Carlos Lee	.10
207	Ray Durham	.10
208	Keith Foulke	.10
209	Todd Ritchie	.10
210	Royce Clayton	.10
211	Jose Canseco	.20
212	Frank Thomas	.40
213	David Wells	.10
214	Mark Buehrle	.10
215	Jon Garland	.10
216	Magglio Ordonez,	
	Mark Buehrle	.15
217	Derek Jeter	1.50
218	Bernie Williams	.30
219	Rondell White	.10
220	Jorge Posada	.20
221	Alfonso Soriano	.50
222	Ramiro Mendoza	.10
223	Jason Giambi	.75
224	John Vander Wal	.10
225	Steve Karsay	.10
226	Nick Johnson	.10
227	Mariano Rivera	.20
228	Orlando Hernandez	.10
229	Andy Pettitte	.20
230	Robin Ventura	.10
231	Roger Clemens	.60
232	Mike Mussina	.40
233	Derek Jeter,	
	Roger Clemens	.50
234	Moises Alou	.20
235	Lance Berkman	.20
236	Craig Biggio	.20
237	Octavio Dotel	.10
238	Jeff Bagwell	.40
239	Richard Hidalgo	.10
240	Morgan Ensberg	.10
241	Julio Lugo	.10
242	Daryle Ward	.10
243	Roy Oswalt	.20
244	Billy Wagner	.10
245	Brad Ausmus	.10
246	Jose Vizcaino	.10
247	Wade Miller	.10
248	Shane Reynolds	.10
249	Jeff Bagwell,	
	Wade Miller	.20
250	Chipper Jones	.75
251	Brian Jordan	.10
252	B.J. Surhoff	.10
253	Rafael Furcal	.10

254	Julio Franco	.10
255	Javy Lopez	.10
256	John Burkett	.10
257	Andruw Jones	.20
258	Marcus Giles	.10
259	Wes Helms	.10
260	Greg Maddux	.75
261	John Smoltz	.10
262	Tom Glavine	.20
263	Vinny Castilla	.10
264	Kevin Millwood	.10
265	Jason Marquis	.10
266	Chipper Jones,	
	Greg Maddux	.40
267	Tyler Houston	.10
268	Mark Loretta	.10
269	Richie Sexson	.20
270	Jeromy Burnitz	.10
271	Jimmy Haynes	.10
272	Geoff Jenkins	.20
273	Ron Belliard	.10
274	Jose Hernandez	.10
275	Jeffrey Hammonds	.10
276	Curtis Leskanic	.10
277	Devon White	.10
278	Ben Sheets	.20
279	Henry Blanco	.10
280	Jamey Wright	.10
281	Allen Levrault	.10
282	Jeff D'Amico	.10
283	Richie Sexson,	
	Jimmy Haynes	.10
284	Albert Pujols	.75
285	Jason Isringhausen	.10
286	J.D. Drew	.25
287	Placido Polanco	.10
288	Jim Edmonds	.20
289	Fernando Vina	.10
290	Edgar Renteria	.10
291	Mike Matheny	.10
292	Bud Smith	.10
293	Mike Defelice	.10
294	Woody Williams	.10
295	Eli Marrero	.10
296	Matt Morris	.10
297	Darryl Kile	.10
298	Kerry Robinson	.10
299	Luis Saturnia	.10
300	Albert Pujols,	
	Matt Morris	.40
301	Sammy Sosa	.75
302	Michael Tucker	.10
303	Bill Mueller	.10
304	Ricky Gutierrez	.10
305	Fred McGriff	.20
306	Eric Young	.10
307	Corey Patterson	.10
308	Alex Gonzalez	.10
309	Ron Coomer	.10
310	Kerry Wood	.20
311	Delino DeShields	.10
312	Jon Lieber	.10
313	Tom Gordon	.10
314	Todd Hundley	.10
315	Jason Bere	.10
316	Kevin Tapani	.10
317	Sammy Sosa,	
	Jon Lieber	.40
318	Steve Finley	.10
319	Luis Gonzalez	.25
320	Mark Grace	.25
321	Craig Counsell	.10
322	Matt Williams	.20
323	Tony Womack	.10
324	Junior Spivey	.10
325	David Dellucci	.10
326	Jay Bell	.10
327	Curt Schilling	.25
328	Randy Johnson	.40
329	Danny Bautista	.10
330	Miguel Batista	.10
331	Erubiel Durazo	.10
332	Brian Anderson	.10
333	Byung-Hyun Kim	.10
334	Luis Gonzalez,	
	Curt Schilling	.20
335	Paul LoDuca	.10
336	Gary Sheffield	.10
337	Shawn Green	.25
338	Adrian Beltre	.20
339	Darren Dreifort	.10
340	Mark Grudzielanek	.10
341	Eric Karros	.10
342	Cesar Izturis	.10
343	Tom Goodwin	.10
344	Marquis Grissom	.10
345	Kevin Brown	.20
346	James Baldwin	.10
347	Terry Adams	.10
348	Alex Cora	.10
349	Andy Ashby	.10
350	Chan Ho Park	.20
351	Shawn Green,	
	Chan Ho Park	.20

352	Jose Vidro	.10
353	Vladimir Guerrero	.40
354	Orlando Cabrera	.10
355	Fernando Tatis	.10
356	Michael Barrett	.10
357	Lee Stevens	.10
358	Geoff Blum	.10
359	Brad Wilkerson	.10
360	Peter Bergeron	.10
361	Javier Vazquez	.10
362	Tony Armas Jr.	.10
363	Tomokazu Ohka	.10
364	Scott Strickland	.10
365	Vladimir Guerrero, Javier Vazquez	.20
366	Barry Bonds	.75
367	Rich Aurilia	.10
368	Jeff Kent	.10
369	Andres Galarraga	.20
370	Desi Relaford	.10
371	Shawon Dunston	.10
372	Benito Santiago	.10
373	Tsuyoshi Shinjo	.10
374	Calvin Murray	.10
375	Marvin Benard	.10
376	J.T. Snow	.10
377	Livan Hernandez	.10
378	Russ Ortiz	.10
379	Robb Nen	.10
380	Jason Schmidt	.10
381	Barry Bonds, Russ Ortiz	.30
382	Cliff Floyd	.10
383	Antonio Alfonseca	.10
384	Mike Redmond	.10
385	Mike Lowell	.10
386	Derrek Lee	.10
387	Preston Wilson	.10
388	Luis Castillo	.10
389	Charles Johnson	.10
390	Eric Owens	.10
391	Alex Gonzalez	.10
392	Josh Beckett	.10
393	Brad Penny	.10
394	Ryan Dempster	.10
395	Matt Clement	.10
396	A.J. Burnett	.10
397	Cliff Floyd, Ryan Dempster	.10
398	Mike Piazza	1.00
399	Joe McEwing	.10
400	Todd Zeile	.10
401	Jay Payton	.10
402	Roger Cedeno	.10
403	Rey Ordonez	.10
404	Edgardo Alfonzo	.10
405	Roberto Alomar	.30
406	Glendon Rusch	.10
407	Timo Perez	.10
408	Al Leiter	.15
409	Lenny Harris	.10
410	Shawn Estes	.10
411	Armando Benitez	.10
412	Kevin Appier	.10
413	Bruce Chen	.10
414	Mike Piazza, Al Leiter	.40
415	Phil Nevin	.10
416	Ryan Klesko	.10
417	Mark Kotsay	.10
418	Ray Lankford	.10
419	Mike Darr	.10
420	D'Angelo Jimenez	.10
421	Bubba Trammell	.10
422	Adam Eaton	.10
423	Ramon Vazquez	.10
424	Cesar Crespo	.10
425	Trevor Hoffman	.10
426	Kevin Jarvis	.10
427	Wiki Gonzalez	.10
428	Damian Jackson	.10
429	Brian Lawrence	.10
430	Phil Nevin, Trevor Hoffman	.10
431	Scott Rolen	.25
432	Marlon Anderson	.10
433	Bobby Abreu	.10
434	Jimmy Rollins	.20
435	Doug Glanville	.10
436	Travis Lee	.10
437	Brandon Duckworth	.10
438	Pat Burrell	.25
439	Kevin Jordan	.10
440	Robert Person	.10
441	Johnny Estrada	.10
442	Randy Wolf	.10
443	Jose Mesa	.10
444	Mike Lieberthal	.10
445	Bobby Abreu, Robert Person	.10
446	Brian Giles	.20
447	Jason Kendall	.10
448	Aramis Ramirez	.10
449	Rob Mackowiak	.10
450	Abraham Nunez	.10
451	Pat Meares	.10
452	Craig Wilson	.10
453	Jack Wilson	.10
454	Gary Matthews Jr.	.10
455	Kevin Young	.10
456	Derek Bell	.10
457	Kip Wells	.10
458	Jimmy Anderson	.10
459	Kris Benson	.10
460	Brian Giles, Todd Ritchie	.10
461	Sean Casey	.20
462	Wilton Guerrero	.10
463	Jason LaRue	.10
464	Juan Encarnacion	.10
465	Todd Walker	.10
466	Aaron Boone	.10
467	Pete Harnisch	.10
468	Ken Griffey Jr.	1.00
469	Adam Dunn	.40
470	Barry Larkin	.20
471	Kelly Stinnett	.10
472	Pokey Reese	.10
473	Brady Clark	.10
474	Scott Williamson	.10
475	Danny Graves	.10
476	Ken Griffey Jr., Elmer Dessens	.10
477	Larry Walker	.25
478	Todd Helton	.40
479	Juan Pierre	.10
480	Juan Uribe	.10
481	Mario Encarnacion	.10
482	Jose Ortiz	.10
483	Todd Hollandsworth	.10
484	Alex Ochoa	.10
485	Mike Hampton	.10
486	Terry Shumpert	.10
487	Denny Neagle	.10
488	Jose Jimenez	.10
489	Jason Jennings	.10
490	Todd Helton, Mike Hampton	.20
491	Tim Redding	.10
492	Mark Teixeira	2.00
493	Alex Cintron	.10
494	Tim Raines Jr.	.10
495	Juan Cruz	.20
496	Joe Crede	.10
497	Steve Green	.10
498	Mike Rivera	.10
499	Mark Prior	1.00
500	Ken Harvey	.10
501	Tim Spooneybarger	.10
502	Adam Everett	.10
503	Jason Standridge	.10
504	Nick Neugebauer	.10
505	Adam Johnson	.10
506	Sean Douglass	.10
507	Brandon Berger	.10
508	Alex Escobar	.10
509	Doug Nickle	.10
510	Jason Middlebrook	.10
511	Dewon Brazelton	.10
512	Yorvit Torrealba	.10
513	Henry Mateo	.10
514	Dennis Tankersley	.10
515	Marlon Byrd	.75
516	Andy Barkett	.10
517	Orlando Hudson	.10
518	Josh Fogg	.10
519	Ryan Drese	.10
520	Mike MacDougal	.10
521	Luis Pineda	.10
522	Jack Cust	.10
523	Kurt Ainsworth	.10
524	Raul Miadich	.10
525	Dernell Stenson	.10
526	Carlos Zambrano	.10
527	Austin Kearns	.50
528	Larry Barnes	.10
529	Mike Cuddyer	.10
530	Carlos Pena	.75
531	Derek Jeter	1.00
532	Ken Griffey Jr.	.75
533	Manny Ramirez	.25
534	Luis Gonzalez	.20
535	Sammy Sosa	.50
536	Roger Clemens	.40
537	Phil Nevin	.10
538	Mike Piazza	.75
539	Alex Rodriguez	.75
540	Jason Giambi	.50
541	Randy Johnson	.25
542	Albert Pujols	.50
543	Jeff Bagwell	.25
544	Shawn Green	.15
545	Carlos Delgado	.15
546	Pedro Martinez	.25
547	Todd Helton	.25
548	Roberto Alomar	.20
549	Barry Bonds	.40
550	Ichiro Suzuki	1.00

Gold

Stars: 3-6X
Inserted 1:2

2002 Upper Deck Vintage

RED SOX
manny ramirez • outfield

		NM/M
Complete Set (300):		30.00
Common Player:		.10
Pack (10):		2.00
Box (24):		35.00
1	Darin Erstad	.20
2	Mo Vaughn	.20
3	Ramon Ortiz	.10
4	Garret Anderson	.25
5	Troy Glaus	.40
6	Troy Percival	.10
7	Tim Salmon	.20
8	Wilmy Caceres, Elpidio Guzman	.10
9	2001 Anaheim Angels	.10
10	Jason Giambi	.50
11	Mark Mulder	.25
12	Jermaine Dye	.10
13	Miguel Tejada	.40
14	Tim Hudson	.25
15	Eric Chavez	.25
16	Barry Zito	.25
17	Oscar Salazar, Juan Pena	.10
18	2001 Oakland Athletics	.10
19	Carlos Delgado	.40
20	Raul Mondesi	.15
21	Chris Carpenter	.10
22	Jose Cruz Jr.	.10
23	Alex Gonzalez	.10
24	Brad Fullmer	.10
25	Shannon Stewart	.10
26	Brandon Lyon, Vernon Wells	.10
27	2001 Toronto Blue Jays	.10
28	Greg Vaughn	.10
29	Toby Hall	.10
30	Ben Grieve	.10
31	Aubrey Huff	.10
32	Tanyon Sturtze	.10
33	Brent Abernathy	.10
34	Dewon Brazelton, Delvin James	.10
35	2001 Tampa Bay Devil Rays	.10
36	Roberto Alomar	.40
37	Juan Gonzalez	.50
38	Bartolo Colon	.25
39	C.C. Sabathia	.10
40	Jim Thome	.75
41	Omar Vizquel	.20
42	Russell Branyan	.10
43	Ryan Drese, Roy Smith	.10
44	2001 Cleveland Indians	.10
45	Edgar Martinez	.20
46	Bret Boone	.20
47	Freddy Garcia	.10
48	John Olerud	.25
49	Kazuhiro Sasaki	.10
50	Ichiro Suzuki	1.50
51	Mike Cameron	.10
52	Rafael Soriano, Dennis Stark	.10
53	2001 Seattle Mariners	.10
54	Tony Batista	.10
55	Jeff Conine	.10
56	Jason Johnson	.10
57	Jay Gibbons	.10
58	Chris Richard	.10
59	Josh Towers	.10
60	Jerry Hairston Jr.	.10
61	Sean Douglass, Tim Raines Jr.	.10
62	2001 Baltimore Orioles	.10
63	Alex Rodriguez	1.50
64	Ruben Sierra	.10
65	Ivan Rodriguez	.50
66	Gabe Kapler	.20
67	Rafael Palmeiro	.50
68	Frank Catalanotto	.10
69	Mark Teixeira, Carlos Pena	.40
70	2001 Texas Rangers	.10
71	Nomar Garciaparra	1.00
72	Pedro Martinez	.75
73	Trot Nixon	.10
74	Dante Bichette	.10
75	Manny Ramirez	.50
76	Carl Everett	.10
77	Hideo Nomo	.40
78	Dernell Stenson, Juan Diaz	.10
79	2001 Boston Red Sox	.10
80	Mike Sweeney	.10
81	Carlos Febles	.10
82	Dee Brown	.10
83	Neifi Perez	.10
84	Mark Quinn	.10
85	Carlos Beltran	.25
86	Joe Randa	.10
87	Ken Harvey, Mike MacDougal	.10
88	2001 Kansas City Royals	.10
89	Dean Palmer	.10
90	Jeff Weaver	.10
91	Jose Lima	.10
92	Tony Clark	.10
93	Damion Easley	.10
94	Bobby Higginson	.10
95	Robert Fick	.10
96	Pedro Santana, Mike Rivera	.10
97	2001 Detroit Tigers	.10
98	Doug Mientkiewicz	.10
99	David Ortiz	.25
100	Joe Mays	.10
101	Corey Koskie	.10
102	Eric Milton	.10
103	Cristian Guzman	.10
104	Brad Radke	.10
105	Adam Johnson, Juan Rincon	.10
106	2001 Minnesota Twins	.10
107	Frank Thomas	.50
108	Carlos Lee	.10
109	Mark Buehrle	.10
110	Jose Canseco	.25
111	Magglio Ordonez	.25
112	Jon Garland	.10
113	Ray Durham	.10
114	Joe Crede, Josh Fogg	.10
115	2001 Chicago White Sox	.10
116	Derek Jeter	2.00
117	Roger Clemens	1.50
118	Alfonso Soriano	.75
119	Paul O'Neill	.25
120	Jorge Posada	.25
121	Bernie Williams	.40
122	Mariano Rivera	.25
123	Tino Martinez	.20
124	Mike Mussina	.50
125	Nick Johnson, Erick Almonte	.10
126	2001 New York Yankees	.10
127	Jeff Bagwell	.50
128	Wade Miller	.10
129	Lance Berkman	.25
130	Moises Alou	.25
131	Craig Biggio	.20
132	Roy Oswalt	.10
133	Richard Hidalgo	.15
134	Morgan Ensberg, Tim Redding	.10
135	2001 Houston Astros	.10

136	Greg Maddux	1.00
137	Chipper Jones	.75
138	Brian Jordan	.10
139	Marcus Giles	.10
140	Andruw Jones	.40
141	Tom Glavine	.40
142	Rafael Furcal	.25
143	Wilson Betemit, Horacio Ramirez	.10
144	2001 Atlanta Braves	.10
145	Jeromy Burnitz	.10
146	Ben Sheets	.25
147	Geoff Jenkins	.20
148	Devon White	.10
149	Jimmy Haynes	.10
150	Richie Sexson	.40
151	Jose Hernandez	.10
152	Jose Mieses, Alex Sanchez	.10
153	2001 Milwaukee Brewers	.10
154	Mark McGwire	2.00
155	Albert Pujols	1.50
156	Matt Morris	.20
157	J.D. Drew	.25
158	Jim Edmonds	.25
159	Bud Smith	.10
160	Darryl Kile	.10
161	William Ortega, Luis Saturria	.10
162	2001 St. Louis Cardinals	.10
163	Sammy Sosa	1.00
164	Jon Lieber	.10
165	Eric Young	.10
166	Kerry Wood	.75
167	Fred McGriff	.25
168	Corey Patterson	.25
169	Rondell White	.15
170	Juan Cruz, Mark Prior	1.00
171	2001 Chicago Cubs	.10
172	Luis Gonzalez	.25
173	Randy Johnson	.75
174	Matt Williams	.20
175	Mark Grace	.10
176	Steve Finley	.10
177	Reggie Sanders	.10
178	Curt Schilling	.40
179	Alex Cintron, Jack Cust	.10
180	2001 Arizona Diamondbacks	.10
181	Gary Sheffield	.25
182	Paul LoDuca	.10
183	Chan Ho Park	.10
184	Shawn Green	.25
185	Eric Karros	.15
186	Adrian Beltre	.10
187	Kevin Brown	.25
188	Ricardo Rodriguez, Carlos Garcia	.10
189	2001 Los Angeles Dodgers	.10
190	Vladimir Guerrero	.75
191	Javier Vazquez	.10
192	Jose Vidro	.10
193	Fernando Tatis	.10
194	Orlando Cabrera	.10
195	Lee Stevens	.10
196	Tony Armas Jr.	.10
197	Donnie Bridges, Henry Mateo	.10
198	2001 Montreal Expos	.10
199	Barry Bonds	2.00
200	Rich Aurilia	.10
201	Russ Ortiz	.10
202	Jeff Kent	.20
203	Jason Schmidt	.25
204	John Vander Wal	.10
205	Robb Nen	.10
206	Yorvit Torrealba, Kurt Ainsworth	.10
207	2001 San Francisco Giants	.10
208	Preston Wilson	.10
209	Brad Penny	.10
210	Cliff Floyd	.10
211	Luis Castillo	.10
212	Ryan Dempster	.10
213	Charles Johnson	.10
214	A.J. Burnett	.10
215	Abraham Nunez, Josh Beckett	.20
216	2001 Florida Marlins	.10
217	Mike Piazza	1.00
218	Al Leiter	.20
219	Edgardo Alfonzo	.10
220	Tsuyoshi Shinjo	.10
221	Matt Lawton	.10
222	Robin Ventura	.15
223	Jay Payton	.10
224	Alex Escobar, Jae Weong Seo	.10
225	2001 New York Mets	.10
226	Ryan Klesko	.20

227	D'Angelo Jimenez	.10
228	Trevor Hoffman	.10
229	Phil Nevin	.10
230	Mark Kotsay	.10
231	Brian Lawrence	.10
232	Bubba Trammell	.10
233	Jason Middlebrook, Xavier Nady	.10
234	2001 San Diego Padres	.10
235	Scott Rolen	.75
236	Jimmy Rollins	.25
237	Mike Lieberthal	.10
238	Bobby Abreu	.25
239	Brandon Duckworth	.10
240	Robert Person	.10
241	Pat Burrell	.20
242	Nick Punto, Carlos Silva	.10
243	2001 Philadelphia Phillies	.10
244	Brian Giles	.20
245	Jack Wilson	.10
246	Kris Benson	.10
247	Jason Kendall	.20
248	Aramis Ramirez	.25
249	Todd Ritchie	.10
250	Robert Mackowiak	.10
251	John Grabow, Humberto Cota	.10
252	2001 Pittsburgh Pirates	.10
253	Ken Griffey Jr.	1.00
254	Barry Larkin	.25
255	Sean Casey	.25
256	Aaron Boone	.10
257	Dmitri Young	.10
258	Pokey Reese	.10
259	Adam Dunn	.50
260	David Espinosa, Dane Sardinha	.10
261	2001 Cincinnati Reds	.10
262	Todd Helton	.50
263	Mike Hampton	.20
264	Juan Pierre	.10
265	Larry Walker	.25
266	Juan Uribe	.10
267	Jose Ortiz	.10
268	Jeff Cirillo	.10
269	Jason Jennings, Luke Hudson	.10
270	2001 Colorado Rockies	.10
271	Ichiro Suzuki, Jason Giambi, Roberto Alomar	.75
272	Larry Walker, Todd Helton, Moises Alou	.10
273	Alex Rodriguez, Jim Thome, Rafael Palmeiro	.75
274a	Barry Bonds, Sammy Sosa, Juan Gonzalez (No player names.)	1.00
274b	Barry Bonds, Sammy Sosa, Juan Gonzalez (Player names added.)	3.00
275	Roger Clemens, Mark Mulder, Jamie Moyer	.50
276	Curt Schilling, Matt Morris, Randy Johnson	.10
277	Freddy Garcia, Mike Mussina, Joe Mays	.10
278	Randy Johnson, Curt Schilling, John Burkett	.10
279	Mariano Rivera, Kazuhiro Sasaki, Keith Foulke	.10
280	Robb Nen, Armando Benitez, Trevor Hoffman	.10
281	Jason Giambi	.25
282	Jorge Posada	.15
283	Jim Thome	.25
284	Edgar Martinez	.10
285	Andruw Jones	.10
286	Chipper Jones	.50
287	Matt Williams	.20
288	Curt Schilling	.20
289	Derek Jeter	1.00
290	Mike Mussina	.25
291	Bret Boone	.10
292	Alfonso Soriano	.40
293	Randy Johnson	.25
294	Tom Glavine	.20
295	Curt Schilling	.25
296	Randy Johnson	.40
297	Derek Jeter	1.00
298	Tino Martinez	.10
299	Curt Schilling	.20
300	Luis Gonzalez	.20

Day at the Park

DAY AT THE PARK — DEREK JETER • YANKEES

Complete Set (6): 15.00
Inserted 1:23

		NM/M
DP1	Ichiro Suzuki	3.00
DP2	Derek Jeter	5.00
DP3	Alex Rodriguez	4.00
DP4	Mark McGwire	4.00
DP5	Barry Bonds	5.00
DP6	Sammy Sosa	3.00

Night-Gamers

38 • troy • GLAUS • 25

		NM/M
Complete Set (12):		10.00
Common Player:		.50
Inserted 1:11		
NG1	Todd Helton	.75
NG2	Manny Ramirez	.75
NG3	Ivan Rodriguez	.50
NG4	Albert Pujols	2.50
NG5	Greg Maddux	1.50
NG6	Carlos Delgado	.50
NG7	Frank Thomas	.75
NG8	Derek Jeter	3.00
NG9	Troy Glaus	.50
NG10	Jeff Bagwell	.75
NG11	Juan Gonzalez	.75
NG12	Randy Johnson	.50

Sandlot Stars

SANDLOT STARS

		NM/M
Complete Set (12):		15.00
Common Player:		.75
Inserted 1:11		
SS1	Ken Griffey Jr.	1.50
SS2	Derek Jeter	3.00
SS3	Ichiro Suzuki	2.00
SS4	Nomar Garciaparra	2.00
SS5	Sammy Sosa	2.00
SS6	Chipper Jones	1.00
SS7	Jason Giambi	.75
SS8	Alex Rodriguez	2.50
SS9	Mark McGwire	2.50
SS10	Barry Bonds	3.00
SS11	Mike Piazza	2.00
SS12	Vladimir Guerrero	1.00

Special Collection Jerseys

		NM/M
Common Player:		8.00
Inserted 1:144		
StB	Stan Bahnsen	8.00
SaB	Sal Bando	10.00
BC	Bert Campaneris	10.00
AD	Andre Dawson	15.00
RF	Rollie Fingers	15.00

MG	Mark Grace
MH	Mike Hegan
CH	"Catfish" Hunter
RJ	Reggie Jackson
FJ	Ferguson Jenkins
PL	Paul Linblad
JR	Joe Rudi
RS	Ryne Sandberg
SS	Sammy Sosa
BW	Billy Williams

Timeless Team Jerseys

Common Player:		
Inserted 1:144		
JB	Johnny Bench	2...
DE	Dwight Evans	
RF	Rollie Fingers	1...
CH	"Catfish" Hunter	15...
RJ	Reggie Jackson	15...
AJ	Andruw Jones	15...
CJ	Chipper Jones	15...
FL	Fred Lynn	15...
GM	Greg Maddux/SP	
EMa	Edgar Martinez	15.00
WM	Willie McCovey	15.00
EMu	Eddie Murray	15.00
KS	Kazuhiro Sasaki	10.00
IS	Ichiro Suzuki/SP	

Timeless Teams Combos

TIMELESS TEAMS PANTS CARD — 1936 HALL OF FAME

		NM/M
Inserted 1:288		
NYY00	Roger Clemens, Mariano Rivera, Bernie Williams	40.00
ATL96	Greg Maddux, Chipper Jones, Andruw Jones	40.00
OAK74	Rollie Fingers, Jim "Catfish" Hunter, Reggie Jackson	40.00
HOF36	Ty Cobb, Babe Ruth, Honus Wagner/ Pants	1,500

Timeless Teams Bat

		NM/M
Inserted 1:288		
SEA	Ichiro Suzuki, Edgar Martinez, John Olerud, Bret Boone	75.00
NYY	Mariano Rivera, Bernie Williams, Paul O'Neill, Jorge Posada	40.00
ATL	Tom Glavine, Greg Maddux, Chipper Jones, Andruw Jones	40.00
CLE	Juan Gonzalez, Jim Thome, Roberto Alomar, Kenny Lofton	30.00
OAK	Jose Canseco, Ricky Henderson, Dave Parker, Don Baylor	30.00
OF	Mickey Mantle, Joe DiMaggio, Reggie Jackson, Babe Ruth	300.00
1B	Willie McCovey, Frank Thomas, Hank Greenberg, Eddie Murray	30.00

(left column — partially obscured)

	NM/M
...ys	
	8.00
	50.00
	25.00
	10.00
	10.00
	10.00
	20.00
	25.00
	15.00
	8.00
	20.00
	25.00
	20.00
	100.00
	20.00
	8.00

...gnature ...os

	NM/M
...nch	100.00
...Covey	80.00
...Dawson	100.00
...ndo, Joe Rudi	40.00
...Lynn	60.00
...erto Alomar, ...n Thome	75.00
...ohnny Bench	100.00
Ken Griffey Jr., Alex Rodriguez	300.00
Edgar Martinez, John Olerud	60.00

2002 Upper Deck World Series Heroes

	NM/M
Complete Set (180):	20.00
Common Player:	.15
Common RC (91-135):	1.50
Common (136-180):	1.00
Inserted 1:10	
Pack (5):	2.00
Box (24):	40.00
1 Jim "Catfish" Hunter	.15
2 Jimmie Foxx	.50
3 Mark McGwire	2.00
4 Rollie Fingers	.25
5 Rickey Henderson	.40
6 Joe Carter	.15
7 John Olerud	.15
8 Roberto Alomar	.50
9 Pat Hentgen	.15
10 Devon White	.15
11 Eddie Mathews	.50
12 Greg Maddux	1.00
13 Chipper Jones	.75
14 Tom Glavine	.25
15 Andruw Jones	.50
16 David Justice	.25
17 Fred McGriff	.15
18 Ryan Klesko	.15
19 John Smoltz	.25
20 Javy Lopez	.25
21 Marquis Grissom	.15
22 Robin Yount	.75
23 Ozzie Smith	.75
24 Frankie Frisch	.15
25 Stan Musial	1.00
26 Randy Johnson	.75
27 Luis Gonzalez	.25
28 Matt Williams	.15
29 Steve Finley	.15
30 Sandy Koufax	1.50
31 Duke Snider	.50
32 Kirk Gibson	.15
33 Steve Garvey	.15
34 Jackie Robinson	1.50
35 Don Drysdale	.50
36 Juan Marichal	.50
37 Mel Ott	.50
38 Orlando Cepeda	.15
39 Jim Thome	.75
40 Manny Ramirez	.50
41 Omar Vizquel	.15
42 Lou Boudreau	.15
43 Gary Sheffield	.25
44 Moises Alou	.25
45 Livan Hernandez	.15
46 Edgar Renteria	.25
47 Al Leiter	.15
48 Tom Seaver	.75
49 Gary Carter	.15
50 Mike Piazza	1.00
51 Nolan Ryan	2.00
52 Robin Ventura	.15
53 Mike Hampton	.15
54 Jesse Orosco	.15
55 Cal Ripken Jr.	2.00
56 Brooks Robinson	.75
57 Tony Gwynn	.75
58 Kevin Brown	.15
59 Curt Schilling	.50
60 Cy Young	.50
61 Honus Wagner	.75
62 Willie Stargell	.40
63 Wade Boggs	.40
64 Carlton Fisk	.40
65 Ken Griffey Sr.	.15
66 Joe Morgan	.15
67 Johnny Bench	1.00
68 Barry Larkin	.40
69 Jose Rijo	.15
70 Ty Cobb	1.50
71 Kirby Puckett	1.00
72 Chuck Knoblauch	.15
73 Harmon Killebrew	.50
74 Mickey Mantle	2.50
75 Joe DiMaggio	2.00
76 Don Larsen	.40
77 Thurman Munson	.75
78 Roger Maris	1.50
79 Phil Rizzuto	.50
80 Babe Ruth	2.50
81 Lou Gehrig	2.00
82 Billy Martin	.40
83 Derek Jeter	2.00
84 Roger Clemens	1.50
85 Tino Martinez	.15
86 Bernie Williams	.50
87 Mariano Rivera	.25
88 Andy Pettitte	.40
89 David Wells	.15
90 Jorge Posada	.25
91 Rodrigo Rosario RC	1.50
92 Brandon Puffer RC	1.50
93 Franklyn German RC	1.50
94 Reed Johnson RC	1.50
95 Chris Baker RC	1.50
96 John Ennis RC	1.50
97 Luis Martinez RC	1.50
98 Takaki Nomura RC	1.50
99 So Taguchi RC	4.00
100 Michael Crudale RC	1.50
101 Francis Beltran RC	1.50
102 Steve Kent RC	1.50
103 Jorge Sosa RC	1.50
104 Felix Escalona RC	1.50
105 Jose Valverde RC	1.50
106 Doug DeVore RC	1.50
107 Kazuhisa Ishii RC	4.00
108 Victor Alvarez RC	1.50
109 Eric Good RC	1.50
110 Jorge Nunez RC	1.50
111 Ron Calloway RC	1.50
112 Nelson Castro RC	1.50
113 Matt Thornton RC	1.50
114 Luis Ugueto RC	1.50
115 Hansel Izquierdo RC	1.50
116 Jaime Cerda RC	1.50
117 Mark Corey RC	1.50
118 Tyler Yates RC	2.50
119 Satoru Komiyama RC	1.50
120 Steve Bechler RC	1.50
121 Ben Howard RC	1.50
122 Anderson Machado RC	1.50
123 Jorge Padilla RC	1.50
124 Eric Junge RC	1.50
125 Adrian Burnside RC	1.50
126 Mike Gonzalez RC	1.50
127 Anastacio Martinez RC	1.50
128 Josh Hancock RC	1.50
129 Rene Reyes RC	1.50
130 Aaron Cook RC	1.50
131 Cam Esslinger RC	1.50
132 Juan Brito RC	1.50
133 Miguel Ascencio RC	1.50
134 Kevin Frederick RC	1.50
135 Edwin Almonte RC	1.50
136 Troy Glaus	1.00
137 Darin Erstad	1.00
138 Jeff Bagwell	1.50
139 Lance Berkman	1.50
140 Tim Hudson	1.25
141 Eric Chavez	1.25
142 Barry Zito	1.50
143 Carlos Delgado	1.00
144 Richie Sexson	1.50
145 Albert Pujols	4.00
146 Sammy Sosa	4.00
147 Kerry Wood	2.00
148 Greg Vaughn	1.00
149 Shawn Green	1.00
150 Vladimir Guerrero	2.50
151 Barry Bonds	6.00
152 C.C. Sabathia	1.00
153 Ichiro Suzuki	5.00
154 Freddy Garcia	1.00
155 Edgar Martinez	1.00
156 Josh Beckett	1.00
157 Cliff Floyd	1.00
158 Mo Vaughn	1.00
159 Jeromy Burnitz	1.00
160 Sean Burroughs	1.00
161 Phil Nevin	1.00
162 Scott Rolen	2.00
163 Brian Giles	1.25
164 Alex Rodriguez	5.00
165 Ivan Rodriguez	1.50
166 Juan Gonzalez	1.25
167 Rafael Palmeiro	1.50
168 Nomar Garciaparra	4.00
169 Pedro J. Martinez	2.00
170 Ken Griffey Jr.	4.00
171 Adam Dunn	1.50
172 Todd Helton	1.50
173 Mike Sweeney	1.00
174 Carlos Beltran	1.00
175 Dmitri Young	1.00
176 Doug Mientkiewicz	1.00
177 Torii Hunter	1.00
178 Frank Thomas	1.50
179 Magglio Ordonez	1.00
180 Jason Giambi	1.50

World Series Heroes Bats

	NM/M
Common Player:	15.00
Inserted 1:288	
JD Joe DiMaggio/SP	100.00
MM Mickey Mantle	125.00
KP Kirby Puckett	25.00
ES Enos Slaughter	15.00

World Series Heroes Base

	NM/M
Complete Set (1):	
DJ Derek Jeter	35.00

World Series Heroes Jerseys

	NM/M
Common Player:	10.00
Inserted 1:288	
JC Joe Carter	10.00
CF Carlton Fisk	15.00
DL Don Larsen	20.00
BM Bill Mazeroski	15.00

World Series Heroes Jerseys Autograph

No Pricing
Production 25 Sets

Match-ups Memorabilia

	NM/M
Common Card:	8.00
Inserted 1:24	
MU00 Mike Piazza, Roger Clemens	15.00
MU00a Andy Pettitte, Mike Piazza	15.00
MU00b Al Leiter, Derek Jeter	10.00
MU00d Edgardo Alfonzo, Mariano Rivera	8.00
MU00e John Franco, Derek Jeter	10.00
MU00c Robin Ventura, Roger Clemens	8.00
MU01 Mariano Rivera, Luis Gonzalez	8.00
MU01a Paul O'Neill, Curt Schilling	8.00
MU01b Bernie Williams, Randy Johnson	8.00
MU01c David Justice, Curt Schilling	8.00
MU01d Randy Johnson, Bernie Williams	8.00
MU01e Curt Schilling, Tino Martinez	8.00
MU01f Roger Clemens, Luis Gonzalez	15.00
MU01g Paul O'Neill, Byung-Hyun Kim	10.00
MU01h Luis Gonzalez, Mariano Rivera/97	12.00
MU03 Honus Wagner, Cy Young	100.00
MU09 Ty Cobb, Honus Wagner/SP	125.00
MU30 Jimmie Foxx	25.00
MU36 Joe DiMaggio, Mel Ott/SP	80.00
MU49 Duke Snider, Joe DiMaggio	25.00
MU53 Jackie Robinson, Billy Martin	25.00
MU55 Mickey Mantle, Jackie Robinson	110.00
MU56 Don Larsen, Duke Snider	25.00
MU56a Don Larsen, Jackie Robinson	20.00
MU57 Eddie Mathews, Yogi Berra	15.00
MU58 Yogi Berra, Eddie Mathews	15.00
MU62 Roger Maris, Juan Marichal	40.00
MU63 Sandy Koufax, Mickey Mantle	100.00
MU66 Don Drysdale, Brooks Robinson/SP	40.00
MU69 Nolan Ryan, Brooks Robinson	50.00
MU72 Joe Morgan, Jim "Catfish" Hunter	8.00
MU72a Rollie Fingers, Johnny Bench	10.00
MU73 Tom Seaver, "Catfish" Hunter	15.00
MU74 Jim "Catfish" Hunter, Steve Garvey	8.00
MU74a Davey Lopes, Jim "Catfish" Hunter	8.00
MU76 Ken Griffey Sr., Thurman Munson	12.00
MU76a Thurman Munson, Johnny Bench	20.00
MU78 Thurman Munson, Steve Garvey	15.00
MU78a Bill Russell, Thurman Munson	12.00
MU81 Steve Garvey, Dave Winfield	8.00
MU82 Robin Yount, Ozzie Smith	15.00
MU83 Cal Ripken Jr., Joe Morgan	25.00
MU84 Jack Morris, Tony Gwynn	12.00
MU86 Jesse Orosco, Roger Clemens	15.00
MU87 Ozzie Smith, Kirby Puckett	15.00
MU88 Mark McGwire, Kirk Gibson/SP	60.00
MU90 Barry Larkin, Mark McGwire/SP	20.00
MU91 Tom Glavine, Kirby Puckett	15.00
MU93 Joe Carter, Curt Schilling	8.00
MU95 Dennis Martinez, David Justice	8.00
MU96 Andruw Jones, Andy Pettitte	8.00
MU96a Tim Raines, Tom Glavine	10.00
MU96b Kenny Rogers, Chipper Jones	8.00

MU95a Kenny Lofton,
John Smoltz 8.00
MU97 Jim Thome,
Kevin Brown 10.00
MU98 Tony Gwynn,
Bernie Williams 10.00
MU98a Trevor Hoffman,
Bernie Williams/SP 8.00
MU99 Jorge Posada,
Greg Maddux 15.00
MU99a Greg Maddux,
Derek Jeter 15.00
MU99b Paul O'Neill,
John Smoltz 8.00
MU99c Chipper Jones,
Mariano Rivera 15.00

Patch Collection

	NM/M
Common Patch:	15.00

Inserted 1:Hobby Box

WS03	1903 World Series	25.00
WS05	1905 World Series	25.00
WS06	1906 World Series	20.00
WS07	1907 World Series	20.00
WS08	1908 World Series	25.00
WS09	1909 World Series	20.00
WS10	1910 World Series	20.00
WS11	1911 World Series	20.00
WS12	1912 World Series	30.00
WS13	1913 World Series	20.00
WS14	1914 World Series	25.00
WS15	1915 World Series	20.00
WS16	1916 World Series	25.00
WS17	1917 World Series	20.00
WS18	1918 World Series	30.00
WS19	1919 World Series	25.00
WS20	1920 World Series	20.00
WS21	1921 World Series	15.00
WS22	1922 World Series	20.00
WS23	1923 World Series	20.00
WS24	1924 World Series	20.00
WS25	1925 World Series	25.00
WS26	1926 World Series	20.00
WS27	1927 World Series	30.00
WS28	1928 World Series	25.00
WS29	1929 World Series	20.00
WS30	1930 World Series	20.00
WS31	1931 World Series	25.00
WS32	1932 World Series	30.00
WS33	1933 World Series	20.00
WS34	1934 World Series	20.00
WS35	1935 World Series	20.00
WS36	1936 World Series	20.00
WS37	1937 World Series	25.00
WS38	1938 World Series	25.00
WS39	1939 World Series	20.00
WS40	1940 World Series	20.00
WS41	1941 World Series	20.00
WS42	1942 World Series	20.00
WS43	1943 World Series	20.00
WS44	1944 World Series	30.00
WS45	1945 World Series	20.00
WS46	1946 World Series	25.00
WS47	1947 World Series	20.00
WS48	1948 World Series	30.00
WS49	1949 World Series	25.00
WS50	1950 World Series	25.00
WS51	1951 World Series	20.00
WS52	1952 World Series	20.00
WS53	1953 World Series	25.00
WS54	1954 World Series	15.00
WS55	1955 World Series	25.00
WS56	1956 World Series	25.00
WS57	1957 World Series	25.00
WS58	1958 World Series	20.00
WS59	1959 World Series	20.00
WS60	1960 World Series	20.00
WS61	1961 World Series	35.00
WS62	1962 World Series	20.00
WS63	1963 World Series	20.00
WS64	1964 World Series	20.00
WS65	1965 World Series	20.00
WS66	1966 World Series	20.00
WS67	1967 World Series	20.00
WS68	1968 World Series	20.00
WS69	1969 World Series	35.00
WS70	1970 World Series	20.00
WS71	1971 World Series	20.00
WS72	1972 World Series	20.00
WS73	1973 World Series	20.00
WS74	1974 World Series	20.00
WS75	1975 World Series	30.00
WS76	1976 World Series	30.00
WS77	1977 World Series	20.00
WS78	1978 World Series	20.00
WS79	1979 World Series	20.00
WS80	1980 World Series	20.00
WS81	1981 World Series	20.00
WS82	1982 World Series	25.00
WS83	1983 World Series	25.00
WS84	1984 World Series	20.00
WS85	1985 World Series	20.00
WS86	1986 World Series	20.00
WS87	1987 World Series	20.00
WS88	1988 World Series	20.00
WS89	1989 World Series	20.00
WS90	1990 World Series	20.00
WS91	1991 World Series	20.00
WS92	1992 World Series	20.00
WS93	1993 World Series	20.00
WS95	1995 World Series	20.00
WS96	1996 World Series	20.00
WS97	1997 World Series	20.00
WS98	1998 World Series	15.00
WS99	1999 World Series	20.00
WS00	2000 World Series	
WS01	2001 World Series	20.00

Patch Collection Autographs

	NM/M

Inserted 1:336

WS93	Joe Carter	40.00
WS99	Roger Clemens	100.00
WS74	Rollie Fingers	30.00
WS75	Carlton Fisk	60.00
WS81	Steve Garvey	35.00
WS65	Sandy Koufax	250.00
WS56	Don Larsen	60.00
WS89	Mark McGwire	275.00
WS76	Joe Morgan	40.00
WS91	Kirby Puckett	60.00
WS83	Cal Ripken Jr.	175.00
WS70	Brooks Robinson	80.00
WS69	Nolan Ryan	200.00
WS73	Tom Seaver	60.00
WS55	Duke Snider	75.00
WS82	Ozzie Smith	90.00

2002 Upper Deck 40-Man

	NM/M
Complete Set (1182):	200.00
Common Player:	.15
Silvers:	1-3X
Inserted 1:4	
Rainbows:	5-10X
Production 40 Sets	
Hobby Pack (10):	1.75
Hobby Box (24):	30.00

1	Darin Erstad	.40
2	Kevin Appier	.15
3	Scott Schoeneweis	.15
4	Bengie Molina	.15
5	Troy Glaus	.50
6	Adam Kennedy	.15
7	Aaron Sele	.15
8	Garret Anderson	.25
9	Ramon Ortiz	.15
10	Dennis Cook	.15
11	Scott Spiezio	.15
12	Orlando Palmeiro	.15
13	Troy Percival	.15
14	David Eckstein	.15
15	Jarrod Washburn	.40
16	Nathan Haynes	.15
17	Benji Gil	.15
18	Alfredo Amezaga	.15
19	Ben Weber	.15
20	Al Levine	.15
21	Brad Fullmer	.15
22	Elpidio Guzman	.15
23	Tim Salmon	.25
24	Jose Nieves	.15
25	Shawn Wooten	.15
26	Lou Pote	.15
27	Mickey Callaway	.15
28	Steve Green	.15
29	John Lackey	.15
30	Mark Lukasiewicz	.15
31	Jorge Fabregas	.15
32	Jeff Da Vanon	.15
33	Elvin Nina	.15
34	Donne Wall	.15
35	Eric Chavez	.50
36	Jermaine Dye	.15
37	Scott Hatteberg	.15
38	Mark Mulder	.50
39	Ramon Hernandez	.15
40	Jim Mecir	.15
41	Barry Zito	.50
42	Greg Myers	.15
43	David Justice	.50
44	Mike Magnante	.15
45	Terrence Long	.15
46	Tim Hudson	.50
47	Olmedo Saenz	.15
48	Billy Koch	.15
49	Carlos Pena	.50
50	Mike Venafro	.15
51	Mark Ellis	.15
52	Randy Velarde	.15
53	Jeremy Giambi	.15
54	Mike Colagelo	.15
55	Mike Holtz	.15
56	Chad Bradford	.15
57	Miguel Tejada	.50
58	Mike Fyhrie	.15
59	Eric Hiljus	.15
60	Juan Pena	.15
61	Mario Valdez	.15
62	Franklyn German RC	.50
63	Carlos Delgado	.50
64	Orlando Hudson	.15
65	Chris Carpenter	.15
66	Kelvim Escobar	.15
67	Felipe Lopez	.15
68	Brandon Lyon	.15
69	Jose Cruz Jr.	.15
70	Luke Prokopec	.15
71	Darrin Fletcher	.15
72	Bob File	.15
73	Felix Heredia	.15
74	Mike Sirotka	.15
75	Shannon Stewart	.15
76	Joe Lawrence	.15
77	Chris Woodward	.15
78	Dan Plesac	.15
79	Pedro Borbon	.15
80	Roy Halladay	.40
81	Raul Mondesi	.40
82	Steve Parris	.15
83	Homer Bush	.15
84	Esteban Loaiza	.15
85	Vernon Wells	.15
86	Justin Miller	.15
87	Scott Eyre	.15
88	Dave Berg	.15
89	Gustavo Chacin RC	.15
90	Joe Orloski RC	.40
91	Corey Thurman RC	.15
92	Tom Wilson	.15
93	Eric Hinske	.50
94	Chris Baker RC	.40
95	Reed Johnson RC	.40
96	Greg Vaughn	.15
97	Toby Hall	.15
98	Brent Abernathy	.15
99	Bobby Smith	.15
100	Tanyon Sturtze	.15
101	Chris Gomez	.15
102	Joe Kennedy	.15
103	Ben Grieve	.15
104	Aubrey Huff	.15
105	Jesus Colome	.15
106	Felix Escalona RC	.40
107	Paul Wilson	.15
108	Ryan Rupe	.15
109	Jason Tyner	.15
110	Esteban Yan	.15
111	Russ Johnson	.15
112	Randy Winn	.15
113	Wilson Alvarez	.15
114	Wilmy Caceres	.15
115	Steve Cox	.15
116	Dewon Brazelton	.15
117	Doug Creek	.15
118	Jason Conti	.15
119	John Flaherty	.15
120	Delvin James	.15
121	Steve Kent RC	.15
122	Kevin McGlinchy	.15
123	Travis Phelps	.15
124	Bobby Seay	.15
125	Travis Harper	.15
126	Victor Zambrano	.15
127	Jace Brewer	.15
128	Jason Smith	.15
129	Ramon Soler	.15
130	Brandon Backe RC	.50
131	Jorge Sosa RC	.25
132	Jim Thome	.75
133	Brady Anderson	.15
134	C.C. Sabathia	.15
135	Einar Diaz	.15
136	Ricky Gutierrez	.15
137	Danys Baez	.15
138	Bob Wickman	.15
139	Milton Bradley	.15
140	Bartolo Colon	.40
141	Jolbert Cabrera	.15
142	Eddie Taubensee	.15
143	Ellis Burks	.15
144	Omar Vizquel	.40
145	Eddie Perez	.15
146	Jaret Wright	.15
147	Chuck Finley	.15
148	Paul Shuey	.15
149	Travis Fryman	.15
150	Wil Cordero	.15
151	Ricardo Rincon	.15
152	Victor Martinez	.15
153	Charles Nagy	.15
154	Alex Escobar	.15
155	Russell Branyan	.15
156	Matt Lawton	.15
157	Ryan Drese	.15
158	Jerrod Riggan	.15
159	David Riske	.15
160	Jake Westbrook	.15
161	Mark Wohlers	.15
162	John McDonald	.15
163	Ichiro Suzuki	1.50
164	Freddy Garcia	.15
165	Edgar Martinez	.15
166	Ben Davis	.15
167	Shigetoshi Hasegawa	.15
168	Carlos Guillen	.15
169	Ruben Sierra	.15
170	Joel Pineiro	.15
171	Norm Charlton	.15
172	Bret Boone	.15
173	Jamie Moyer	.15
174	Jeff Nelson	.15
175	Kazuhiro Sasaki	.50
176	Jeff Cirillo	.15
177	Mark McLemore	.15
178	Paul Abbott	.15
179	Mike Cameron	.15
180	Dan Wilson	.15
181	John Olerud	.50
182	Arthur Rhodes	.15
183	Desi Relaford	.15
184	John Halama	.15
185	Antonio Perez	.15
186	Ryan Anderson	.15
187	James Baldwin	.15
188	Ryan Franklin	.15
189	Justin Kaye	.15
190	J.J. Putz RC	.40
191	Allan Simpson RC	.40
192	Matt Thornton	.15
193	Luis Ugueto RC	.40
194	Chris Richard	.15
195	Sidney Ponson	.15
196	Brook Fordyce	.15
197	Luis Matos	.15
198	Josh Towers	.15
199	David Segui	.15
200	Chris Brock	.15
201	Tony Batista	.15
202	Erik Bedard	.15
203	Marty Cordova	.15
204	Jerry Hairston Jr.	.15
205	Jason Johnson	.15
206	Buddy Groom	.15
207	Mike Bordick	.15
208	Melvin Mora	.15
209	Calvin Maduro	.15
210	Jeff Conine	.15
211	Luis Rivera	.15
212	Jay Gibbons	.15
213	B.J. Ryan	.15
214	Sean Douglass	.15
215	Rodrigo Lopez	.15
216	Rick Bauer	.15
217	Scott Erickson	.15
218	Jorge Julio	.15
219	Willis Roberts	.15
220	John Stephens	.15

#	Player	Price
221	Geronimo Gil	.15
222	Chris Singleton	.15
223	Mike Paradis	.15
224	John Parrish	.15
225	Steve Bechler RC	.50
226	Mike Moriarty RC	.15
227	Luis Garcia	.15
228	Alex Rodriguez	1.50
229	Mark Teixeira	.50
230	Chan Ho Park	.15
231	Todd Van Poppel	.15
232	Mike Young	.15
233	Kenny Rogers	.15
234	Rusty Greer	.15
235	Rafael Palmeiro	.50
236	Francisco Cordero	.15
237	John Rocker	.15
238	Dave Burba	.15
239	Travis Hafner	.15
240	Kevin Mench	.15
241	Carl Everett	.15
242	Ivan Rodriguez	.50
243	Jeff Zimmerman	.15
244	Juan Gonzalez	.50
245	Herbert Perry	.15
246	Rob Bell	.15
247	Doug Davis	.15
248	Frank Catalanotto	.15
249	Jay Powell	.15
250	Gabe Kapler	.15
251	Joaquin Benoit	.15
252	Jovanny Cedeno	.15
253	Hideki Irabu	.15
254	Dan Miceli	.15
255	Danny Kolb	.15
256	Colby Lewis	.15
257	Rich Rodriguez	.15
258	Ismael Valdes	.15
259	Bill Haselman	.15
260	Jason Hart	.15
261	Rudy Seanez	.15
262	Travis Hughes RC	.40
263	Hank Blalock	.50
264	Steve Woodard	.15
265	Nomar Garciaparra	1.50
266	Pedro J. Martinez	.75
267	Frank Castillo	.15
268	Johnny Damon	.15
269	Doug Mirabelli	.15
270	Derek Lowe	.40
271	Shea Hillenbrand	.50
272	Paxton Crawford	.15
273	Tony Clark	.15
274	Dustin Hermanson	.15
275	Trot Nixon	.15
276	John Burkett	.15
277	Rich Garces	.15
278	Josh Hancock RC	.15
279	Michael Coleman	.15
280	Darren Oliver	.15
281	Jason Varitek	.15
282	Jose Offerman	.15
283	Tim Wakefield	.15
284	Rolando Arrojo	.15
285	Rickey Henderson	.50
286	Ugueth Urbina	.15
287	Casey Fossum	.15
288	Manny Ramirez	.50
289	Sun-Woo Kim	.15
290	Juan Diaz	.15
291	Willie Banks	.15
292	Jorge De La Rosa RC	.50
293	Juan Pena	.15
294	Jeff Wallace	.15
295	Calvin Pickering	.15
296	Anastacio Martinez RC	.40
297	Carlos Baerga	.15
298	Rey Sanchez	.15
299	Mike Sweeney	.15
300	Jeff Suppan	.15
301	Brent Mayne	.15
302	Chad Durbin	.15
303	Dan Reichert	.15
304	Raul Ibanez	.15
305	Joe Randa	.15
306	Chris George	.15
307	Michael Tucker	.15
308	Paul Byrd	.15
309	Kris Wilson	.15
310	Luis Alicea	.15
311	Neifi Perez	.15
312	Brian Shouse	.15
313	Chuck Knoblauch	.15
314	Dave McCarty	.15
315	Blake Stein	.15
316	Alexis Gomez	.15
317	Mark Quinn	.15
318	A.J. Hinch	.15
319	Carlos Febles	.15
320	Roberto Hernandez	.15
321	Brandon Berger	.15
322	Jeff Austin RC	.40
323	Corey Bailey	.15
324	Tony Cogan	.15
325	Nate Field RC	.40
326	Jason Grimsley	.15
327	Darrell May	.15
328	Donnie Sadler	.15
329	Carlos Beltran	.15
330	Miguel Asencio RC	.40
331	Jeff Weaver	.15
332	Bobby Higginson	.15
333	Mike Rivera	.15
334	Matt Anderson	.15
335	Craig Paquette	.15
336	Jose Lima	.15
337	Juan Acevedo	.15
338	Danny Patterson	.15
339	Andres Torres	.15
340	Dean Palmer	.15
341	Randall Simon	.15
342	Craig Monroe	.15
343	Damion Easley	.15
344	Robert Fick	.15
345	Steve Sparks	.15
346	Dmitri Young	.15
347	Nate Cornejo	.15
348	Matt Miller	.15
349	Wendell Magee	.15
350	Shane Halter	.15
351	Brian Moehler	.15
352	Mitch Meluskey	.15
353	Jose Macias	.15
354	Mark Redman	.15
355	Jeff Farnsworth	.15
356	Kris Keller	.15
357	Adam Pettyjohn	.15
358	Fernando Rodney	.15
359	Andy Van Hekken	.15
360	Damian Jackson	.15
361	Jose Paniagua	.15
362	Jacob Cruz	.15
363	Doug Mientkiewicz	.15
364	Torii Hunter	.15
365	Brad Radke	.15
366	Denny Hocking	.15
367	Mike Jackson	.15
368	Eddie Guardado	.15
369	Jacque Jones	.15
370	Joe Mays	.15
371	Matt Kinney	.15
372	Kyle Lohse	.15
373	David Ortiz	.15
374	Luis Rivas	.15
375	Jay Canizaro	.15
376	Dustan Mohr	.15
377	LaTroy Hawkins	.15
378	Warren Morris	.15
379	A.J. Pierzynski	.15
380	Eric Milton	.15
381	Bob Wells	.15
382	Cristian Guzman	.15
383	Brian Buchanan	.15
384	Bobby Kielty	.15
385	Corey Koskie	.15
386	J.C. Romero	.15
387	Jack Cressend	.15
388	Mike Duvall	.15
389	Tony Fiore	.15
390	Tom Prince	.15
391	Todd Sears	.15
392	Kevin Frederick RC	.40
393	Frank Thomas	.50
394	Mark Buehrle	.15
395	Jon Garland	.15
396	Jeff Liefer	.15
397	Magglio Ordonez	.50
398	Rocky Biddle	.15
399	Lorenzo Barcelo	.15
400	Ray Durham	.15
401	Bob Howry	.15
402	Aaron Rowand	.15
403	Keith Foulke	.15
404	Paul Konerko	.50
405	Sandy Alomar Jr.	.15
406	Mark Johnson	.15
407	Carlos Lee	.15
408	Jose Valentin	.15
409	Jon Rauch	.15
410	Royce Clayton	.15
411	Kenny Lofton	.40
412	Tony Graffanino	.15
413	Todd Ritchie	.15
414	Antonio Osuna	.15
415	Gary Glover	.15
416	Mike Porzio	.15
417	Danny Wright	.15
418	Kelly Wunsch	.15
419	Miguel Olivo	.15
420	Edwin Almonte RC	.15
421	Kyle Kane RC	.50
422	Mitch Wylie RC	.15
423	Derek Jeter	2.00
424	Jason Giambi	.50
425	Roger Clemens	1.50
426	Enrique Wilson	.15
427	David Wells	.15
428	Mike Mussina	.50
429	Bernie Williams	.50
430	Mike Stanton	.15
431	Sterling Hitchcock	.15
432	Alex Graman	.15
433	Robin Ventura	.50
434	Mariano Rivera	.50
435	Jay Tessmer	.15
436	Andy Pettitte	.50
437	John Vander Wal	.15
438	Adrian Hernandez	.15
439	Alberto Castillo	.15
440	Steve Karsay	.15
441	Alfonso Soriano	.75
442	Rondell White	.15
443	Nick Johnson	.50
444	Jorge Posada	.50
445	Ramiro Mendoza	.15
446	Gerald Williams	.15
447	Orlando Hernandez	.15
448	Randy Choate	.15
449	Randy Keisler	.15
450	Ted Lilly	.15
451	Christian Parker	.15
452	Ron Coomer	.15
453	Marcus Thames	.15
454	Drew Henson	.50
455	Jeff Bagwell	.50
456	Wade Miller	.15
457	Lance Berkman	.50
458	Julio Lugo	.15
459	Roy Oswalt	.40
460	Nelson Cruz	.15
461	Morgan Ensberg	.15
462	Geoff Blum	.15
463	Ryan Jamison RC	.50
464	Billy Wagner	.15
465	Dave Mlicki	.15
466	Brad Ausmus	.15
467	Jose Vizcaino	.15
468	Craig Biggio	.50
469	Shane Reynolds	.15
470	Gregg Zaun	.15
471	Octavio Dotel	.15
472	Carlos Hernandez	.15
473	Richard Hidalgo	.15
474	Daryle Ward	.15
475	Orlando Merced	.15
476	John Buck	.15
477	Adam Everett	.15
478	Doug Brocail	.15
479	Brad Lidge	.15
480	Scott Linebrink	.15
481	T.J. Mathews	.15
482	Greg Miller	.15
483	Hipolito Pichardo	.15
484	Brandon Puffer RC	.15
485	Ricky Stone	.15
486	Jason Lane	.15
487	Brian L. Hunter	.15
488	Rodrigo Rosario RC	.50
489	Tom Shearn RC	.50
490	Gary Sheffield	.40
491	Tom Glavine	.40
492	Mike Remlinger	.15
493	Henry Blanco	.15
494	Vinny Castilla	.15
495	Chris Hammond	.15
496	Kevin Millwood	.50
497	Darren Holmes	.15
498	Cory Aldridge	.15
499	Tim Spooneybarger	.15
500	Rafael Furcal	.50
501	Albie Lopez	.15
502	Javy Lopez	.40
503	Greg Maddux	1.00
504	Andruw Jones	.50
505	Steve Torrealba	.15
506	George Lombard	.15
507	B.J. Surhoff	.15
508	Marcus Giles	.15
509	Derrick Lewis	.15
510	Wes Helms	.15
511	John Smoltz	.50
512	Chipper Jones	.75
513	Jason Marquis	.15
514	Mark DeRosa	.15
515	Jung Bong	.15
516	Kevin Gryboski RC	.15
517	Damian Moss	.15
518	Horacio Ramirez	.15
519	Scott Sobkowiak	.15
520	Billy Sylvester	.15
521	Nick Green	.15
522	Travis Wilson	.15
523	Ryan Langerhans	.15
524	John Ennis RC	.50
525	John Foster RC	.15
526	Keith Lockhart	.15
527	Julio Franco	.15
528	Richie Sexson	.50
529	Jeffrey Hammonds	.15
530	Ben Sheets	.50
531	Mike DeJean	.15
532	Mark Loretta	.15
533	Alex Ochoa	.15
534	Jamey Wright	.15
535	Jose Hernandez	.15
536	Glendon Rusch	.15
537	Geoff Jenkins	.50
538	Luis S. Lopez	.15
539	Curtis Leskanic	.15
540	Chad Fox	.15
541	Tyler Houston	.15
542	Nick Neugebauer	.15
543	Matt Stairs	.15
544	Paul Rigdon	.15
545	Bill Hall	.15
546	Luis Vizcaino	.15
547	Lenny Harris	.15
548	Alex Sanchez	.15
549	Raul Casanova	.15
550	Eric Young	.15
551	Jeff Deardorff RC	.15
552	Nelson Figueroa	.15
553	Ron Belliard	.15
554	Mike Buddie	.15
555	Jose Cabrera	.15
556	J.M. Gold	.15
557	Ray King	.15
558	Jose Mieses	.15
559	Takahito Nomura RC	.50
560	Ruben Quevedo	.15
561	Jackson Melian	.15
562	Cristian Guerrero	.15
563	Paul Bako	.15
564	Luis Martinez RC	.50
565	Brian Mallette RC	.15
566	Matt Morris	.50
567	Tino Martinez	.40
568	Fernando Vina	.15
569	Gene Stechschulte	.15
570	Andy Benes	.15
571	Placido Polanco	.15
572	Luis Garcia	.15
573	Jim Edmonds	.50
574	Bud Smith	.15
575	Mike Matheny	.15
576	Garrett Stephenson	.15
577	Miguel Cairo	.15
578	Darryl Kile	.15
579	Mike Timlin	.15
580	Rick Ankiel	.15
581	Jason Isringhausen	.15
582	Albert Pujols	1.50
583	Eli Marrero	.15
584	Steve Kline	.15
585	J.D. Drew	.50
586	Mike DiFelice	.15
587	Dave Veres	.15
588	Kerry Robinson	.15
589	Edgar Renteria	.15
590	Woody Williams	.15
591	Chance Caple	.15
592	Michael Crudale RC	.15
593	Luther Hackman	.15
594	Josh Pearce	.15
595	Kevin Joseph	.15
596	Jimmy Journell	.15
597	Jeremy Lambert RC	.40
598	Mike Matthews	.15
599	Les Walrond	.15
600	Keith McDonald	.15
601	William Ortega	.15
602	Scotty Layfield RC	.15
603	So Taguchi RC	1.00
604	Eduardo Perez	.15
605	Sammy Sosa	1.50
606	Kerry Wood	.75
607	Kyle Farnsworth	.15
608	Alex Gonzalez	.15
609	Tom Gordon	.15
610	Carlos Zambrano	.15
611	Roosevelt Brown	.15
612	Bill Mueller	.15
613	Mark Prior	1.50
614	Darren Lewis	.15
615	Joe Girardi	.15
616	Fred McGriff	.50
617	Jon Lieber	.15
618	Robert Machado	.15
619	Corey Patterson	.50
620	Joe Borowski	.15
621	Todd Hundley	.15
622	Jason Bere	.15
623	Moises Alou	.40
624	Jeff Fassero	.15
625	Jesus Sanchez	.15
626	Chris Stynes	.15
627	Delino DeShields	.15
628	Augie Ojeda	.15
629	Juan Cruz	.15
630	Ben Christensen	.15
631	Mike Meyers	.15
632	Will Ohman	.15
633	Steve Smyth	.15
634	Mark Bellhorn	.15
635	Nate Frese	.15
636	David Kelton	.15

#	Player	Value	#	Player	Value	#	Player	Value	#	Player	Value
637	Francis Beltran RC	.40	741	Henry Rodriguez	.15	845	Sean Burroughs	.40	949	Corky Miller	.15
638	Antonio Alfonseca	.15	742	Jeff Kent	.15	846	Alan Embree	.15	950	Elmer Dessens	.15
639	Donovan Osborne	.15	743	Russ Ortiz	.15	847	Dennis Tankersley	.15	951	Aaron Boone	.15
640	Shawn Sonnier	.15	744	Felix Rodriguez	.15	848	D'Angelo Jimenez	.15	952	Juan Encarnacion	.15
641	Matt Clement	.15	745	Benito Santiago	.15	849	Kevin Jarvis	.15	953	Chris Reitsma	.15
642	Luis Gonzalez	.25	746	Tsuyoshi Shinjo	.50	850	Mark Kotsay	.15	954	Wilton Guerrero	.15
643	Brian Anderson	.15	747	Tim Worrell	.15	851	Phil Nevin	.25	955	Danny Graves	.15
644	Randy Johnson	.75	748	Marvin Benard	.15	852	Jeremy Fikac	.15	956	Jim Brower	.15
645	Mark Grace	.50	749	Kurt Ainsworth	.15	853	Brett Tomko	.15	957	Barry Larkin	.50
646	Danny Bautista	.15	750	Edwards Guzman	.15	854	Brian Lawrence	.15	958	Todd Walker	.15
647	Junior Spivey	.15	751	J.T. Snow	.15	855	Steve Reed	.15	959	Gabe White	.15
648	Jay Bell	.15	752	Jason Christiansen	.15	856	Bubba Trammell	.15	960	Adam Dunn	.50
649	Miguel Batista	.15	753	Robb Nen	.15	857	Tom Davey	.15	961	Jason LaRue	.15
650	Tony Womack	.15	754	Barry Bonds	2.00	858	Ramon Vazquez	.15	962	Reggie Taylor	.15
651	Byung-Hyun Kim	.15	755	Shawon Dunston	.15	859	Tom Lampkin	.15	963	Sean Casey	.40
652	Steve Finley	.40	756	Chad Zerbe	.15	860	Bobby Jones	.15	964	Scott Williamson	.15
653	Rick Helling	.15	757	Ramon E. Martinez	.15	861	Ray Lankford	.15	965	Austin Kearns	.50
654	Curt Schilling	.50	758	Calvin Murray	.15	862	Mark Sweeney	.15	966	Kelly Stinnett	.15
655	Erubiel Durazo	.15	759	Pedro Feliz	.15	863	Adam Eaton	.15	967	Jose Acevedo	.15
656	Chris Donnels	.15	760	Jason Schmidt	.15	864	Trenidad Hubbard	.15	968	Gookie Dawkins	.15
657	Greg Colbrunn	.15	761	Damon Minor	.15	865	Jason Boyd	.15	969	Brady Clark	.15
658	Mike Morgan	.15	762	Reggie Sanders	.15	866	Javier Cardona	.15	970	Scott Sullivan	.15
659	Jose Guillen	.15	763	Rich Aurilia	.15	867	Clifford Bartosh RC	.50	971	Ricardo Aramboles	.15
660	Matt Williams	.50	764	Kirk Rueter	.15	868	Mike Bynum	.15	972	Lance Davis	.15
661	Craig Counsell	.15	765	David Bell	.15	869	Eric Cyr RC	.50	973	Seth Etherton	.15
662	Greg Swindell	.15	766	Yorvit Torrealba	.15	870	Jose Nunez	.15	974	Luke Hudson	.15
663	Rod Barajas	.15	767	Livan Hernandez	.15	871	Ron Gant	.15	975	Joey Hamilton	.15
664	David Dellucci	.15	768	Felix Diaz	.15	872	Deivi Cruz	.15	976	Luis Pineda	.15
665	Todd Stottlemyre	.15	769	Aaron Fultz	.15	873	Ben Howard RC	.50	977	John Riedling	.15
666	P.J. Bevis RC	.15	770	Ryan Jensen	.15	874	Todd Donovan RC	.25	978	Jose Silva	.15
667	Mike Koplove	.15	771	Arturo McDowell	.15	875	Andy Shibilo RC	.15	979	Dane Sardinha	.15
668	Mike Myers	.15	772	Carlos Valderrama	.15	876	Scott Rolen	.75	980	Ben Broussard	.15
669	John Patterson	.15	773	Nelson Castro RC	.50	877	Jose Mesa	.15	981	David Espinosa	.15
670	Bret Prinz	.15	774	Jay Witasick	.15	878	Rheal Cormier	.15	982	Ruben Mateo	.15
671	Jeremy Ward RC	.50	775	Deivis Santos	.15	879	Travis Lee	.15	983	Larry Walker	.50
672	Danny Klassen	.15	776	Josh Beckett	.15	880	Mike Lieberthal	.15	984	Juan Uribe	.15
673	Luis Terrero	.15	777	Charles Johnson	.15	881	Brandon Duckworth	.15	985	Mike Hampton	.15
674	Jose Valverde RC	.50	778	Derrek Lee	.15	882	David Coggin	.15	986	Aaron Cook RC	.15
675	Doug DeVore RC	.50	779	A.J. Burnett	.15	883	Bobby Abreu	.50	987	Jose Ortiz	.15
676	Quinton McCracken	.15	780	Vic Darensbourg	.15	884	Turk Wendell	.15	988	Todd Jones	.15
677	Paul LoDuca	.15	781	Cliff Floyd	.50	885	Marlon Byrd	.15	989	Todd Helton	.50
678	Mark Grudzielanek	.15	782	Jose Cueto	.15	886	Jason Michaels	.15	990	Shawn Chacon	.15
679	Kevin Brown	.50	783	Nate Teut	.15	887	Robert Person	.15	991	Jason Jennings	.15
680	Paul Quantrill	.15	784	Alex Gonzalez	.15	888	Tomas Perez	.15	992	Todd Zeile	.15
681	Shawn Green	.50	785	Brad Penny	.15	889	Jimmy Rollins	.50	993	Ben Petrick	.15
682	Hideo Nomo	.50	786	Kevin Olsen	.15	890	Vicente Padilla	.15	994	Denny Neagle	.15
683	Eric Gagne	.15	787	Mike Lowell	.15	891	Pat Burrell	.50	995	Jose Jimenez	.15
684	Giovanni Carrara	.15	788	Mike Redmond	.15	892	Dave Hollins	.15	996	Juan Pierre	.15
685	Marquis Grissom	.15	789	Braden Looper	.15	893	Randy Wolf	.15	997	Todd Hollandsworth	.15
686	Hiram Bocachica	.15	790	Eric Owens	.15	894	Jose Santiago	.15	998	Kent Mercker	.15
687	Guillermo Mota	.15	791	Andy Fox	.15	895	Doug Glanville	.15	999	Greg Norton	.15
688	Alex Cora	.15	792	Vladimir Nunez	.15	896	Cliff Politte	.15	1000	Terry Shumpert	.15
689	Odalis Perez	.15	793	Luis Castillo	.15	897	Marlon Anderson	.15	1001	Mark Little	.15
690	Brian Jordan	.15	794	Ryan Dempster	.15	898	Ricky Bottalico	.15	1002	Gary Bennett	.15
691	Andy Ashby	.15	795	Armando Almanza	.15	899	Terry Adams	.15	1003	Dennys Reyes	.15
692	Eric Karros	.40	796	Preston Wilson	.15	900	Brad Baisley	.15	1004	Justin Speier	.15
693	Chad Krueter	.15	797	Pablo Ozuna	.15	901	Hector Mercado	.15	1005	John Thomson	.15
694	Dave Roberts	.15	798	Gary Knotts	.15	902	Elio Serrano RC	.50	1006	Rick White	.15
695	Omar Daal	.15	799	Ramon Castro	.15	903	Todd Pratt	.15	1007	Colin Young RC	.40
696	Dave Hansen	.15	800	Benito Baez	.15	904	Peter Zamora RC	.50	1008	Cam Esslinger RC	.50
697	Adrian Beltre	.50	801	Michael Tejera	.15	905	Nick Punto	.15	1009	Rene Reyes RC	.50
698	Terry Mulholland	.15	802	Claudio Vargas	.15	906	Ricky Ledee	.15	1010	Mike James	.15
699	Cesar Izturis	.15	803	Chip Ambres	.15	907	Eric Junge RC	.15	1011	Morgan Ensberg	.15
700	Steve Colyer	.15	804	Hansel Izquierdo RC	.50	908	Anderson Machado RC	.50	1012	Adam Everett	.15
701	Carlos Garcia	.15	805	Tim Raines	.15	909	Jorge Padilla RC	.50	1013	Rodrigo Rosario	.15
702	Ricardo Rodriguez	.15	806	Marty Malloy	.15	910	John Mabry	.15	1014	Carlos Pena	.15
703	Darren Dreifort	.15	807	Julian Tavarez	.15	911	Brian Giles	.15	1015	Eric Hinske	.50
704	Jeff Reboulet	.15	808	Roberto Alomar	.50	912	Jason Kendall	.40	1016	Orlando Hudson	.15
705	Victor Alvarez RC	.50	809	Al Leiter	.50	913	Jack Wilson	.15	1017	Reed Johnson	.15
706	Kazuhisa Ishii RC	2.00	810	Jeromy Burnitz	.15	914	Kris Benson	.15	1018	Jung Bong	.15
707	Jose Vidro	.15	811	John Franco	.15	915	Aramis Ramirez	.15	1019	Bill Hall	.15
708	Henry Mateo	.15	812	Edgardo Alfonzo	.15	916	Mike Fetters	.15	1020	Mark Prior	1.50
709	Tony Armas Jr.	.15	813	Mike Piazza	1.00	917	Adrian Brown	.15	1021	Francis Beltran	.15
710	Carl Pavano	.15	814	Shawn Estes	.15	918	Pokey Reese	.15	1022	David Kelton	.15
711	Peter Bergeron	.15	815	Joe McEwing	.15	919	Dave Williams	.15	1023	Felix Escalona	.15
712	Bruce Chen	.15	816	David Weathers	.15	920	Mike Benjamin	.15	1024	Jorge Sosa	.15
713	Orlando Cabrera	.15	817	Pedro Astacio	.15	921	Kip Wells	.15	1025	Dewon Brazelton	.15
714	Britt Reames	.15	818	Timoniel Perez	.15	922	Mike Williams	.15	1026	Jose Valverde	.15
715	Masato Yoshii	.15	819	Grant Roberts	.15	923	Pat Meares	.15	1027	Luis Terrero	.15
716	Fernando Tatis	.15	820	Rey Ordonez	.15	924	Ron Villone	.15	1028	Kazuhisa Ishii	1.00
717	Graeme Lloyd	.15	821	Steve Trachsel	.15	925	Armando Rios	.15	1029	Cesar Izturis	.15
718	Scott Stewart	.15	822	Roger Cedeno	.15	926	Jimmy Anderson	.15	1030	Ryan Jensen	.15
719	Lou Collier	.15	823	Mark Johnson	.15	927	Robert Mackowiak	.15	1031	Matt Thornton	.15
720	Michael Barrett	.15	824	Armando Benitez	.15	928	Kevin Young	.15	1032	Hansel Izquierdo	.15
721	Vladimir Guerrero	.75	825	Vance Wilson	.15	929	Brian Boehringer	.15	1033	Jaime Cerda	.15
722	Troy Mattes	.15	826	Jay Payton	.15	930	Joe Beimel	.15	1034	Erik Bedard	.15
723	Brian Schneider	.15	827	Mo Vaughn	.50	931	Chad Hermansen	.15	1035	Sean Burroughs	.15
724	Lee Stevens	.15	828	Scott Strickland	.15	932	Scott Sauerbeck	.15	1036	Ben Howard	.15
725	Javier Vazquez	.15	829	Mark Guthrie	.15	933	Josh Fogg	.15	1037	Ramon Vazquez	.15
726	Brad Wilkerson	.15	830	Jeff D'Amico	.15	934	Mike Gonzalez RC	.15	1038	Marlon Byrd	.15
727	Zach Day	.15	831	Mark Corey RC	.50	935	Mike Lincoln	.15	1039	Josh Fogg	.15
728	Ed Vosberg	.15	832	Kane Davis	.15	936	Sean Lowe	.15	1040	Hank Blalock	.50
729	Tomokazu Ohka	.15	833	Jae Weong Seo	.15	937	Matt Guerrier	.15	1041	Mark Teixeira	.50
730	Mike Mordecai	.15	834	Pat Strange	.15	938	Ryan Vogelsong	.15	1042	Kevin Mench	.15
731	Donnie Bridges	.15	835	Adam Walker RC	.15	939	J.R. House	.15	1043	Dane Sardinha	.15
732	Ron Chiavacci	.15	836	Tyler Walker	.15	940	Craig Wilson	.15	1044	Austin Kearns	.50
733	T.J. Tucker	.15	837	Gary Matthews Jr.	.15	941	Tony Alvarez	.15	1045	Anastacio Martinez	.15
734	Scott Hodges	.15	838	Jaime Cerda RC	.25	942	J.J. Davis	.15	1046	Eric Munson	.15
735	Valentino Pascucci	.15	839	Satoru Komiyama RC	.50	943	Abraham Nunez	.15	1047	Jon Rauch	.15
736	Andres Galarraga	.15	840	Tyler Yates RC	.50	944	Adrian Burnside RC	.50	1048	Nick Johnson	.50
737	Scott Downs	.15	841	John Valentin	.15	945	Ken Griffey Jr.	1.00	1049	Alex Graman	.15
738	Eric Good RC	.15	842	Ryan Klesko	.40	946	Jimmy Haynes	.15	1050	Drew Henson	.50
739	Ron Calloway RC	.50	843	Wiki Gonzalez	.15	947	Juan Castro	.15	1051	Darin Erstad	.50
740	Jorge Nunez RC	.15	844	Trevor Hoffman	.15	948	Jose Rijo	.15	1052	Garret Anderson	.15

1053	Craig Biggio	.50
1054	Lance Berkman	.50
1055	Jeff Bagwell	.50
1056	Shannon Stewart	.15
1057	Chipper Jones	.75
1058	J.D. Drew	.50
1059	Moises Alou	.15
1060	Mark Grace	.50
1061	Jose Vidro Expos	.15
1062	Vladimir Guerrero	.75
1063	Matt Lawton	.15
1064	Ichiro Suzuki	1.50
1065	Edgar Martinez	.15
1066	John Olerud	.50
1067	Jeff Cirillo	.15
1068	Mike Lowell	.15
1069	Mike Piazza	1.00
1070	Roberto Alomar	.50
1071	Bobby Abreu	.15
1072	Jason Kendall	.15
1073	Brian Giles	.50
1074	Rafael Palmeiro	.50
1075	Ivan Rodriguez	.50
1076	Alex Rodriguez	1.50
1077	Juan Gonzalez	.50
1078	Nomar Garciaparra	1.50
1079	Manny Ramirez	.50
1080	Sean Casey	.25
1081	Barry Larkin	.25
1082	Larry Walker	.40
1083	Carlos Beltran	.15
1084	Corey Koskie	.15
1085	Magglio Ordonez	.25
1086	Frank Thomas	.50
1087	Kenny Lofton	.25
1088	Derek Jeter	2.00
1089	Bernie Williams	.50
1090	Jason Giambi	.50
1091	Troy Glaus	.50
1092	Jeff Bagwell	.50
1093	Lance Berkman	.50
1094	David Justice	.25
1095	Eric Chavez	.25
1096	Carlos Delgado	.40
1097	Gary Sheffield	.40
1098	Chipper Jones	.75
1099	Andruw Jones	.50
1100	Richie Sexson	.40
1101	Albert Pujols	1.50
1102	Sammy Sosa	1.50
1103	Fred McGriff	.40
1104	Greg Vaughn	.15
1105	Matt Williams	.25
1106	Luis Gonzalez	.40
1107	Shawn Green	.40
1108	Andres Galarraga	.15
1109	Vladimir Guerrero	.75
1110	Barry Bonds	2.00
1111	Rich Aurilia	.15
1112	Ellis Burks	.15
1113	Jim Thome	.50
1114	Bret Boone	.15
1115	Cliff Floyd	.15
1116	Mike Piazza	1.00
1117	Jeromy Burnitz	.15
1118	Phil Nevin	.15
1119	Brian Giles	.50
1120	Rafael Palmeiro	.50
1121	Juan Gonzalez	.50
1122	Alex Rodriguez	1.50
1123	Manny Ramirez	.50
1124	Ken Griffey Jr.	1.00
1125	Larry Walker	.40
1126	Todd Helton	.50
1127	Mike Sweeney	.15
1128	Frank Thomas	.50
1129	Paul Konerko	.40
1130	Jason Giambi	.50
1131	Aaron Sele	.15
1132	Roy Oswalt	.40
1133	Wade Miller	.15
1134	Tim Hudson	.50
1135	Barry Zito	.40
1136	Mark Mulder	.25
1137	Greg Maddux	1.00
1138	Tom Glavine	.40
1139	Ben Sheets	.40
1140	Darryl Kile	.15
1141	Matt Morris	.15
1142	Kerry Wood	.40
1143	Jon Lieber	.15
1144	Juan Cruz	.15
1145	Randy Johnson	.75
1146	Curt Schilling	.50
1147	Kevin Brown	.15
1148	Javier Vazquez	.15
1149	Russ Ortiz	.15
1150	C.C. Sabathia	.15
1151	Bartolo Colon	.15
1152	Freddy Garcia	.15
1153	Jamie Moyer	.15
1154	Josh Beckett	.50
1155	Brad Penny	.15
1156	Al Leiter	.40

1157	Brandon Duckworth	.15
1158	Robert Person	.15
1159	Kris Benson	.15
1160	Chan Ho Park	.15
1161	Pedro J. Martinez	.75
1162	Mike Hampton	.15
1163	Jeff Weaver	.15
1164	Joe Mays	.15
1165	Brad Radke	.15
1166	Eric Milton	.15
1167	Roger Clemens	1.00
1168	Mike Mussina	.50
1169	Andy Pettitte	.50
1170	David Wells	.15
1171	Ken Griffey Jr.	1.00
1172	Ichiro Suzuki	1.00
1173	Jason Giambi	.50
1174	Alex Rodriguez	1.00
1175	Sammy Sosa	.75
1176	Nomar Garciaparra	1.00
1177	Barry Bonds	1.00
1178	Mike Piazza	.75
1179	Derek Jeter	1.50
1180	Randy Johnson	.40
1181	Jeff Bagwell	.40
1182	Albert Pujols	1.00

Gargantuan Gear

		NM/M
Common Player:		3.00
Gold:		2X
Production 100 Sets		
G-JB	James Baldwin	3.00
G-BC	Bruce Chen	3.00
G-JD	Jermaine Dye/SP	5.00
G-JG	Juan Gonzalez	6.00
G-BG	Ben Grieve	3.00
G-KG	Ken Griffey Jr.	10.00
G-TH	Tim Hudson	6.00
G-AJ	Andruw Jones	6.00
G-JK	Jeff Kent	3.00
G-ML	Mike Lieberthal	3.00
G-TM	Tino Martinez	3.00
G-JO	John Olerud	3.00
G-MO	Magglio Ordonez	5.00
G-MP	Mike Piazza	15.00
G-JP	Jorge Posada	8.00
G-AP	Andy Pettitte	6.00
G-BR	Brad Radke	3.00
G-AR	Alex Rodriguez	10.00
G-SR	Scott Rolen	10.00
G-CS	Curt Schilling	8.00
G-AS	Aaron Sele	3.00
G-IS	Ichiro Suzuki/SP	30.00
G-BW	Bernie Williams	8.00
G-DY	Dmitri Young	3.00
G-TZ	Todd Zeile	3.00

Looming Large Jerseys

		NM/M
Common Player:		8.00
Production 250 Sets		
Gold:		2X
Production 40 Sets		
LBa	Jeff Bagwell	10.00
LB	Lance Berkman	10.00
JBu	John Burkett	8.00
SC	Sean Casey	10.00
TC	Tony Clark	8.00
RC	Roger Clemens	20.00
JC	Jeff Cirillo	8.00
JD	J.D. Drew	10.00
CE	Carl Everett	8.00
CF	Chuck Finley	8.00
TF	Travis Fryman	8.00
JGi	Jason Giambi	10.00
BG	Brian Giles	10.00
TG	Tom Glavine	10.00
JGo	Juan Gonzalez	10.00
KG	Ken Griffey Jr.	20.00
TH	Todd Helton	15.00
RJ	Randy Johnson	15.00
DK	Darryl Kile	8.00
AL	Al Leiter	8.00
ML	Mike Lieberthal	8.00
KL	Kenny Lofton	8.00
GM	Greg Maddux	15.00
EM	Edgar Martinez	8.00
FM	Fred McGriff	10.00
MO	Magglio Ordonez	8.00
HN	Hideo Nomo	50.00

RP	Rafael Palmeiro	10.00
JP	Jorge Posada	10.00
SR	Shane Reynolds	8.00
AR	Alex Rodriguez	15.00
JR	Jimmy Rollins	8.00
KS	Kazuhiro Sasaki	8.00
CS	Curt Schilling	10.00
JS	J.T. Snow	8.00
SS	Sammy Sosa	20.00
FT	Frank Thomas	10.00
IV	Ismael Valdes	8.00
RV	Randy Velarde	8.00
RV	Ron Villone	8.00
BZ	Barry Zito	10.00

Lumber Yard

		NM/M
Common Player:		10.00
Inserted 1:168		
LY1	Chipper Jones	15.00
LY2	Joe DiMaggio	40.00
LY3	Albert Pujols	20.00
LY4	Mark McGwire	30.00
LY5	Sammy Sosa	15.00
LY6	Vladimir Guerrero	15.00
LY7	Barry Bonds	25.00
LY8	Mickey Mantle	50.00
LY9	Mike Piazza	15.00
LY10	Alex Rodriguez	15.00
LY11	Nomar Garciaparra	15.00
LY12	Ken Griffey Jr.	20.00
LY13	Frank Thomas	10.00
LY14	Jason Giambi	15.00
LY15	Derek Jeter	25.00
LY16	Luis Gonzalez	10.00
LY17	Jeff Bagwell	10.00
LY18	Todd Helton	10.00

Mark McGwire Flashbacks

Mark McGwire Flashbacks

	NM/M
Complete Set (40):	120.00
Common McGwire:	4.00
Inserted 1:24	

Super Swatches

		NM/M
Common Player:		5.00
Production 250 Sets		
Gold:		1-2X
Production 40 Sets		
EA	Edgardo Alfonzo	5.00
RA	Rich Aurilia	5.00
JB	Jeff Bagwell	15.00
SC	Sean Casey	8.00
CD	Carlos Delgado	8.00
RD	Ray Durham	5.00
DE	Darin Erstad	8.00
JG	Juan Gonzalez	8.00
MG	Mark Grace	8.00
SG	Shawn Green	8.00
KG	Ken Griffey Jr.	20.00
TG	Tony Gwynn	15.00
MH	Mike Hampton	5.00
TH	Trevor Hoffman	5.00
CJ	Chipper Jones	10.00
DJ	David Justice	8.00
KL	Kenny Lofton	5.00
JM	Joe Mays	5.00
EM	Eric Milton	5.00
MM	Matt Morris	5.00
HN	Hideo Nomo	50.00
JP	Jorge Posada	10.00
MR	Manny Ramirez	12.00
MR	Mariano Rivera	10.00
AR	Alex Rodriguez	15.00
IR	Ivan Rodriguez	10.00
KS	Kazuhiro Sasaki	5.00
CS	Curt Schilling	10.00
BS	Ben Sheets	8.00
SS	Sammy Sosa	20.00
IS	Ichiro Suzuki	40.00

MS	Mike Sweeney	5.00
FT	Frank Thomas	10.00
GV	Greg Vaughn	5.00
JV	Jose Vidro	5.00
DW	David Wells	5.00
MY	Masato Yoshii	5.00

2002 UD Authentics

Kazuhisa Ishii

	NM/M
Complete Set (200):	50.00
Common Player:	.25
Reversed Negatives:	1-2.5X
Inserted 1:9	
Pack (5):	2.50
Box (18):	35.00

1	Brad Fullmer	.25
2	Garret Anderson	.40
3	Darin Erstad	.40
4	Jarrod Washburn	.25
5	Troy Glaus	.50
6	Barry Zito	.40
7	David Justice	.40
8	Eric Chavez	.40
9	Tim Hudson	.40
10	Miguel Tejada	.40
11	Jermaine Dye	.40
12	Mark Mulder	.40
13	Carlos Delgado	.50
14	Jose Cruz Jr.	.25
16	Shannon Stewart	.25
17	Raul Mondesi	.25
18	Tanyon Sturtze	.25
19	Toby Hall	.25
20	Greg Vaughn	.25
21	Aubrey Huff	.25
22	Ben Grieve	.25
23	Brent Abernathy	.25
24	Jim Thome	.75
25	C.C. Sabathia	.25
26	Matt Lawton	.25
27	Omar Vizquel	.25
28	Ellis Burks	.25
29	Russ Branyan	.25
30	Bartolo Colon	.40
31	Ichiro Suzuki	1.50
32	John Olerud	.40
33	Freddy Garcia	.25
34	Mike Cameron	.25
35	Jeff Cirillo	.25
36	Kazuhiro Sasaki	.25
37	Edgar Martinez	.40
38	Bret Boone	.25
39	Jeff Conine	.25
40	Melvin Mora	.25
41	Jason Johnson	.25
42	Chris Richard	.25
43	Tony Batista	.25
44	Ivan Rodriguez	.50
45	Gabe Kapler	.25
46	Rafael Palmeiro	.50
47	Alex Rodriguez	1.50
48	Juan Gonzalez	.50
49	Carl Everett	.25
50	Nomar Garciaparra	1.50
51	Trot Nixon	.25
52	Manny Ramirez	.50
53	Pedro J. Martinez	.75
54	Johnny Damon	.40
55	Shea Hillenbrand	.25
56	Mike Sweeney	.25
57	Mark Quinn	.25
58	Joe Randa	.25
59	Carlos Beltran	.40
60	Chuck Knoblauch	.25
61	Robert Fick	.25
62	Jeff Weaver	.25
63	Bobby Higginson	.25
64	Dean Palmer	.25
65	Dmitri Young	.25
66	Corey Koskie	.25
67	Doug Mientkiewicz	.25
68	Joe Mays	.25
69	Torii Hunter	.40

70	Cristian Guzman	.25
71	Jacque Jones	.25
72	Magglio Ordonez	.40
73	Paul Konerko	.25
74	Carlos Lee	.25
75	Mark Buehrle	.25
76	Jose Canseco	.50
77	Frank Thomas	.50
78	Roger Clemens	1.50
79	Derek Jeter	2.00
80	Jason Giambi	.50
81	Rondell White	.25
82	Bernie Williams	.50
83	Jorge Posada	.50
84	Mike Mussina	.50
85	Alfonso Soriano	.75
86	Wade Miller	.25
87	Jeff Bagwell	.50
88	Craig Biggio	.40
89	Roy Oswalt	.40
90	Lance Berkman	.40
91	Daryle Ward	.25
92	Chipper Jones	.75
93	Greg Maddux	1.00
94	Marcus Giles	.25
95	Gary Sheffield	.50
96	Tom Glavine	.50
97	Andruw Jones	.50
98	Rafael Furcal	.25
99	Richie Sexson	.40
100	Ben Sheets	.40
101	Jose Hernandez	.25
102	Geoff Jenkins	.40
103	Jeffrey Hammonds	.25
104	Edgar Renteria	.40
105	Matt Morris	.40
106	Tino Martinez	.25
107	Jim Edmonds	.40
108	Albert Pujols	1.50
109	J.D. Drew	.40
110	Fernando Vina	.25
111	Darryl Kile	.25
112	Sammy Sosa	1.50
113	Fred McGriff	.40
114	Kerry Wood	.75
115	Moises Alou	.40
116	Jon Lieber	.25
117	Mark Grace	.50
118	Randy Johnson	.75
119	Curt Schilling	.50
120	Luis Gonzalez	.40
121	Steve Finley	.25
122	Matt Williams	.40
123	Shawn Green	.40
124	Kevin Brown	.40
125	Adrian Beltre	.40
126	Paul LoDuca	.25
127	Hideo Nomo	.50
128	Brian Jordan	.25
129	Vladimir Guerrero	.75
130	Javier Vazquez	.25
131	Jose Vidro	.25
132	Orlando Cabrera	.25
133	Jeff Kent	.25
134	Rich Aurilia	.25
135	Russ Ortiz	.25
136	Barry Bonds	2.00
137	Preston Wilson	.25
138	Ryan Dempster	.25
139	Cliff Floyd	.25
140	Josh Beckett	.40
141	Mike Lowell	.40
142	Mike Piazza	1.00
143	Roberto Alomar	.50
144	Al Leiter	.40
145	Edgardo Alfonzo	.25
146	Roger Cedeno	.25
147	Jeromy Burnitz	.25
148	Phil Nevin	.25
149	Mark Kotsay	.25
150	Ryan Klesko	.25
151	Trevor Hoffman	.25
152	Bobby Abreu	.40
153	Scott Rolen	.75
154	Jimmy Rollins	.40
155	Robert Person	.25
156	Pat Burrell	.40
157	Randy Wolf	.25
158	Brian Giles	.40
159	Aramis Ramirez	.50
160	Kris Benson	.25
161	Jason Kendall	.25
162	Ken Griffey Jr.	1.00
163	Sean Casey	.40
164	Adam Dunn	.50
165	Barry Larkin	.50
166	Todd Helton	.50
167	Mike Hampton	.25
168	Larry Walker	.40
169	Juan Pierre	.25
170	Juan Uribe	.25
171	So Taguchi RC	2.00
172	Brendan Donnelly RC	.75
173	Chris Baker RC	.50
174	John Ennis RC	.75
175	Francis Beltran RC	.75
176	Danny Wright RC	.50
177	Brandon Backe RC	.75
178	Mark Corey RC	.75
179	Kazuhisa Ishii RC	3.00
180	Ron Calloway RC	.50
181	Kevin Frederick RC	.75
182	Jaime Cerda RC	.75
183	Doug DeVore RC	.50
184	Brandon Puffer RC	.75
185	Andy Pratt RC	.50
186	Adrian Burnside RC	.50
187	Josh Hancock RC	.75
188	Jorge Nunez RC	.50
189	Tyler Yates RC	1.00
190	Kyle Kane RC	.75
191	Jose Valverde RC	1.00
192	Matt Thornton RC	.50
193	Ben Howard RC	.50
194	Reed Johnson RC	1.50
195	Rene Reyes RC	.50
196	Jeremy Ward RC	.50
197	Steve Bechler RC	.50
198	Cam Esslinger RC	.50
199	Michael Crudale RC	.50
200	Todd Donovan RC	.50

Retro UD Jerseys

		NM/M
Common Player:		5.00
Inserted 1:16		
Golds:		1-2X
Production 275 Sets		
Reverse Neg.:		1-2X
Production 350 Sets		
JB	Jeff Bagwell	15.00
KB	Kevin Brown	8.00
EC	Eric Chavez	5.00
RC	Roger Clemens/SP	25.00
CD	Carlos Delgado	8.00
JD	J.D. Drew	10.00
JE	Jim Edmonds	8.00
DE	Darin Erstad	5.00
RF	Rafael Furcal	5.00
JG	Jason Giambi	10.00
TG	Tom Glavine	10.00
LG	Luis Gonzalez	5.00
KG	Ken Griffey Jr.	20.00
TH	Todd Helton	12.00
RJ	Randy Johnson	12.00
AJ	Andruw Jones	8.00
CJ	Chipper Jones	15.00
GM	Greg Maddux	15.00
TM	Tino Martinez/SP/25	
MP	Mike Piazza	15.00
MR	Manny Ramirez	10.00
AR	Alex Rodriguez	15.00
IR	Ivan Rodriguez	10.00
SR	Scott Rolen/SP/25	
SS	Sammy Sosa/SP	20.00
MS	Mike Sweeney	5.00
FT	Frank Thomas	10.00
BW	Bernie Williams	10.00
BZ	Barry Zito	5.00

Retro UD Star Rookie Jerseys

		NM/M
Common Player:		5.00
Inserted 1:16		
Golds:		1-2X
Production 275 Sets		
CB	Craig Biggio	8.00
PB	Pat Burrell	8.00
BG	Brian Giles	5.00
JG	Juan Gonzalez	8.00
LG	Luis Gonzalez	8.00
SG	Shawn Green	8.00
KG	Ken Griffey Jr.	20.00
RJ	Randy Johnson	10.00
CJ	Chipper Jones	10.00
DJ	David Justice	5.00
RK	Ryan Klesko	5.00
KL	Kenny Lofton	5.00
PM	Pedro J. Martinez	15.00
HN	Hideo Nomo	15.00
JO	John Olerud	5.00
MO	Magglio Ordonez	8.00
RP	Robert Person	5.00
AP	Albert Pujols	20.00
MR	Manny Ramirez/SP	15.00
AR	Alex Rodriguez	20.00
IR	Ivan Rodriguez	10.00
KS	Kazuhiro Sasaki	5.00
GS	Gary Sheffield	8.00
SS	Sammy Sosa/SP	20.00
I	Ichiro Suzuki	40.00
JT	Jim Thome	12.00
LW	Larry Walker	5.00

Signed UD Heroes of Baseball

		NM/M
Random Inserts:		
G	Ken Griffey Jr./185	125.00
R	Alex Rodriguez/185	90.00
I	Ichiro Suzuki/125	400.00

Signed Retro UD Star Rookie Jerseys

		NM/M
Production 40 Sets		
KG	Ken Griffey Jr.	100.00
AR	Alex Rodriguez	150.00
JT	Jim Thome	75.00

Stars of '89 Jerseys

		NM/M
Common Player:		5.00
Inserted 1:16		
RA	Roberto Alomar	8.00
KB	Kevin Brown	8.00
EB	Ellis Burks	5.00
JC	Jose Canseco	8.00
RC	Roger Clemens	15.00
DC	David Cone	5.00
AG	Andres Galarraga	5.00
TG	Tom Glavine	10.00
JG	Juan Gonzalez	10.00
MG	Mark Grace	8.00
KG	Ken Griffey Jr.	20.00
RH	Rickey Henderson	10.00
RJ	Randy Johnson	10.00
DJ	David Justice	5.00
BL	Barry Larkin/SP	15.00
AL	Al Leiter	5.00
GM	Greg Maddux	15.00
EM	Edgar Martinez	5.00
FM	Fred McGriff	5.00
JO	John Olerud	5.00
PO	Paul O'Neill	8.00
RP	Rafael Palmeiro	5.00
CS	Curt Schilling	8.00
GS	Gary Sheffield	5.00
SS	Sammy Sosa	15.00
RV	Robin Ventura	5.00
LW	Larry Walker	5.00
MW	Matt Williams	5.00

UD Heroes of Baseball

	NM/M
Complete Set (30):	150.00
Ichiro:	8.00
Griffey Jr.:	6.00
Alex Rodriguez:	8.00
Production 1,989 Sets	
HB-I1	Ichiro Suzuki	8.00
HB-I2	Ichiro Suzuki	8.00
HB-I3	Ichiro Suzuki	8.00
HB-I4	Ichiro Suzuki	8.00
HB-I5	Ichiro Suzuki	8.00
HB-I6	Ichiro Suzuki	8.00
HB-I7	Ichiro Suzuki	8.00
HB-I8	Ichiro Suzuki	8.00
HB-I9	Ichiro Suzuki	8.00
HB-I10	Ichiro Suzuki	8.00
HB-G1	Ken Griffey Jr.	6.00
HB-G2	Ken Griffey Jr.	6.00
HB-G3	Ken Griffey Jr.	6.00
HB-G4	Ken Griffey Jr.	6.00
HB-G5	Ken Griffey Jr.	6.00
HB-G6	Ken Griffey Jr.	6.00
HB-G7	Ken Griffey Jr.	6.00
HB-G8	Ken Griffey Jr.	6.00
HB-G9	Ken Griffey Jr.	6.00
HB-G10	Ken Griffey Jr.	6.00
HB-R1	Alex Rodriguez	8.00
HB-R2	Alex Rodriguez	8.00
HB-R3	Alex Rodriguez	8.00
HB-R4	Alex Rodriguez	8.00
HB-R5	Alex Rodriguez	8.00
HB-R6	Alex Rodriguez	8.00
HB-R7	Alex Rodriguez	8.00
HB-R8	Alex Rodriguez	8.00
HB-R9	Alex Rodriguez	8.00
HB-R10	Alex Rodriguez	8.00

1989 Flashbacks

		NM/M
Complete Set (12):		30.00
Common Player:		1.50
Production 4,225 Sets		
F1	Ken Griffey Jr.	8.00
F2	Gary Sheffield	1.50
F3	Randy Johnson	3.00
F4	Roger Clemens	4.00
F5	Greg Maddux	5.00
F6	Mark Grace	2.00
F7	Barry Bonds	5.00
F8	Roberto Alomar	2.00
F9	Sammy Sosa	5.00
F10	Rafael Palmeiro	2.00
F11	Edgar Martinez	1.50
F12	Jose Canseco	2.00

2003 Upper Deck

		NM/M
Complete Set (540):		75.00
Common Player:		.15
Common RC (501-529):		.50
Series 1 or 2 Pack (8):		2.50
Series 1 or 2 Box (24):		45.00
1	John Lackey	.15
2	Alex Cintron	.15
3	Jose Leon	.15
4	Bobby Hill	.15
5	Brandon Larson	.15
6	Raul Gonzalez	.15
7	Ben Broussard	.15
8	Earl Snyder	.15

#	Player		#	Player		#	Player		#	Player	
9	Ramon Santiago	.15	114	David Ortiz	.50	218	Rey Ordonez	.15	322	Marty Cordova	.15
10	Jason Lane	.15	115	Eric Milton	.15	219	Al Leiter	.15	323	Hank Blalock	.50
11	Keith Ginter	.15	116	Eddie Guardado	.15	220	Roger Cedeno	.15	324	Herbert Perry	.15
12	Kirk Saarloos	.15	117	Cristian Guzman	.15	221	Timoniel Perez	.15	325	Alex Rodriguez	2.00
13	Juan Brito	.15	118	Corey Koskie	.15	222	Jeromy Burnitz	.15	326	Carl Everett	.15
14	Runelvys Hernandez	.15	119	Magglio Ordonez	.25	223	Pedro Astacio	.15	327	Einar Diaz	.15
15	Shawn Sedlacek	.15	120	Mark Buehrle	.15	224	Joe McEwing	.15	328	Ugueth Urbina	.15
16	Jayson Durocher	.15	121	Todd Ritchie	.15	225	Ryan Klesko	.15	329	Mark Teixeira	.40
17	Kevin Frederick	.15	122	Jose Valentin	.15	226	Ramon Vazquez	.15	330	Manny Ramirez	.75
18	Zach Day	.15	123	Paul Konerko	.25	227	Mark Kotsay	.15	331	Johnny Damon	.50
20	Marcus Thames	.15	124	Carlos Lee	.15	228	Bubba Trammell	.15	332	Trot Nixon	.15
21	Esteban German	.15	125	Jon Garland	.15	229	Wiki Gonzalez	.15	333	Tim Wakefield	.15
22	Brett Myers	.15	126	Jason Giambi	.40	230	Trevor Hoffman	.15	334	Casey Fossum	.15
23	Oliver Perez	.25	127	Derek Jeter	2.00	231	Ron Gant	.15	335	Todd Walker	.15
24	Dennis Tankersley	.15	128	Roger Clemens	1.50	232	Bobby Abreu	.25	336	Jeremy Giambi	.15
25	Julius Matos	.15	129	Raul Mondesi	.15	233	Marlon Anderson	.15	337	Bill Mueller	.15
26	Jake Peavy	.15	130	Jorge Posada	.25	234	Jeremy Giambi	.15	338	Ramiro Mendoza	.15
27	Eric Cyr	.15	131	Rondell White	.15	235	Jimmy Rollins	.25	339	Carlos Beltran	.50
28	Mike Crudale	.15	132	Robin Ventura	.25	236	Mike Lieberthal	.15	340	Jason Grimsley	.15
29	Josh Pearce	.15	133	Mike Mussina	.50	237	Vicente Padilla	.15	341	Brent Mayne	.15
30	Carl Crawford	.15	134	Jeff Bagwell	.25	238	Randy Wolf	.15	342	Angel Berroa	.15
31	Tim Salmon	.25	135	Craig Biggio	.25	239	Pokey Reese	.15	343	Albie Lopez	.15
32	Troy Glaus	.50	136	Morgan Ensberg	.15	240	Brian Giles	.25	344	Michael Tucker	.15
33	Adam Kennedy	.15	137	Richard Hidalgo	.15	241	Jack Wilson	.15	345	Bobby Higginson	.15
34	David Eckstein	.15	138	Brad Ausmus	.15	242	Mike Williams	.15	346	Shane Halter	.15
35	Bengie Molina	.15	139	Roy Oswalt	.25	243	Kip Wells	.15	347	Jeremy Bonderman	2.00
36	Jarrod Washburn	.15	140	Carlos Hernandez	.15	244	Robert Mackowiak	.15	348	Eric Munson	.15
37	Ramon Ortiz	.15	141	Shane Reynolds	.15	245	Craig Wilson	.15	349	Andy Van Hekken	.15
38	Eric Chavez	.40	142	Gary Sheffield	.25	246	Adam Dunn	.60	350	Matt Anderson	.15
39	Miguel Tejada	.50	143	Andruw Jones	.50	247	Sean Casey	.25	351	Jacque Jones	.15
40	Adam Piatt	.15	144	Tom Glavine	.40	248	Todd Walker	.15	352	A.J. Pierzynski	.15
41	Jermaine Dye	.15	145	Rafael Furcal	.25	249	Corky Miller	.15	353	Joe Mays	.15
42	Olmedo Saenz	.15	146	Javy Lopez	.25	250	Ryan Dempster	.15	354	Brad Radke	.15
43	Tim Hudson	.25	147	Vinny Castilla	.15	251	Reggie Taylor	.15	355	Dustan Mohr	.15
44	Barry Zito	.25	148	Marcus Giles	.15	252	Aaron Boone	.15	356	Bobby Kielty	.15
45	Billy Koch	.15	149	Kevin Millwood	.25	253	Larry Walker	.30	357	Michael Cuddyer	.15
46	Shannon Stewart	.15	150	Jason Marquis	.15	254	Jose Ortiz	.15	358	Luis Rivas	.15
47	Kelvim Escobar	.15	151	Ruben Quevedo	.15	255	Todd Zeile	.15	359	Frank Thomas	.75
48	Jose Cruz Jr.	.15	152	Ben Sheets	.25	256	Bobby Estalella	.15	360	Joe Borchard	.15
49	Vernon Wells	.15	153	Geoff Jenkins	.15	257	Juan Pierre	.15	361	D'Angelo Jimenez	.15
50	Roy Halladay	.15	154	Jose Hernandez	.15	258	Terry Shumpert	.15	362	Bartolo Colon	.25
51	Esteban Loaiza	.15	155	Glendon Rusch	.15	259	Mike Hampton	.15	363	Joe Crede	.15
52	Eric Hinske	.15	156	Jeffrey Hammonds	.15	260	Denny Stark	.15	364	Miguel Olivo	.15
53	Steve Cox	.15	157	Alex Sanchez	.15	261	Shawn Green	.25	365	Billy Koch	.15
54	Brent Abernathy	.15	158	Jim Edmonds	.25	262	Derek Lowe	.15	366	Bernie Williams	.50
55	Ben Grieve	.15	159	Tino Martinez	.25	263	Barry Bonds	1.00	367	Nick Johnson	.15
56	Aubrey Huff	.15	160	Albert Pujols	1.50	264	Mike Cameron	.15	368	Andy Pettitte	.40
57	Jared Sandberg	.15	161	Eli Marrero	.15	265	Luis Castillo	.15	369	Mariano Rivera	.25
58	Paul Wilson	.15	162	Woody Williams	.15	266	Vladimir Guerrero	.40	370	Alfonso Soriano	.75
59	Tanyon Sturtze	.15	163	Fernando Vina	.15	267	Jason Giambi	.25	371	David Wells	.15
60	Jim Thome	.60	164	Jason Isringhausen	.15	268	Eric Gagne	.25	372	Drew Henson	.15
61	Omar Vizquel	.25	165	Jason Simontacchi	.15	269	Magglio Ordonez	.20	373	Juan Rivera	.15
62	C.C. Sabathia	.15	166	Kerry Robinson	.15	270	Jim Thome	.40	374	Steve Karsay	.15
63	Chris Magruder	.15	167	Sammy Sosa	1.25	271	Garret Anderson	.40	375	Jeff Kent	.25
64	Ricky Gutierrez	.15	168	Juan Cruz	.15	272	Tony Perez	.15	376	Lance Berkman	.50
65	Einar Diaz	.15	169	Fred McGriff	.25	273	Brad Fullmer	.15	377	Octavio Dotel	.15
66	Danys Baez	.15	170	Antonio Alfonseca	.15	274	Scott Spezio	.15	378	Julio Lugo	.15
67	Ichiro Suzuki	2.00	171	Jon Lieber	.15	275	Darin Erstad	.40	379	Jason Lane	.15
68	Ruben Sierra	.15	172	Mark Prior	.50	276	Francisco Rodriguez	.15	380	Wade Miller	.15
69	Carlos Guillen	.15	173	Moises Alou	.25	277	Kevin Appier	.15	381	Billy Wagner	.15
70	Mark McLemore	.15	174	Matt Clement	.15	278	Shawn Wooten	.15	382	Brad Ausmus	.15
71	Dan Wilson	.15	175	Mark Bellhorn	.15	279	Eric Owens	.15	383	Mike Hampton	.15
72	Jamie Moyer	.15	176	Randy Johnson	.75	280	Scott Hatteberg	.15	384	Chipper Jones	.75
73	Joel Pineiro	.15	177	Luis Gonzalez	.25	281	Terrence Long	.15	385	John Smoltz	.15
74	Edgar Martinez	.25	178	Tony Womack	.15	282	Mark Mulder	.25	386	Greg Maddux	1.25
75	Tony Batista	.15	179	Mark Grace	.30	283	Ramon Hernandez	.15	387	Javy Lopez	.25
76	Jay Gibbons	.15	180	Junior Spivey	.15	284	Ted Lilly	.15	388	Robert Fick	.15
77	Chris Singleton	.15	181	Byung-Hyun Kim	.15	285	Erubiel Durazo	.15	389	Mark DeRosa	.15
78	Melvin Mora	.15	182	Danny Bautista	.15	286	Mark Ellis	.15	390	Russ Ortiz	.15
79	Geronimo Gil	.15	183	Brian Anderson	.15	287	Carlos Delgado	.50	391	Julio Franco	.15
80	Rodrigo Lopez	.15	184	Shawn Green	.25	288	Orlando Hudson	.15	392	Richie Sexson	.50
81	Jorge Julio	.15	185	Brian Jordan	.15	289	Chris Woodward	.15	393	Eric Young	.15
82	Rafael Palmeiro	.50	186	Eric Karros	.15	290	Mark Hendrickson	.15	394	Robert Machado	.15
83	Juan Gonzalez	.50	187	Andy Ashby	.15	291	Josh Phelps	.15	395	Mike DeJean	.15
84	Mike Young	.15	188	Cesar Izturis	.15	292	Ken Huckaby	.15	396	Todd Ritchie	.15
85	Hideki Irabu	.15	189	Dave Roberts	.15	293	Justin Miller	.15	397	Royce Clayton	.15
86	Chan Ho Park	.15	190	Eric Gagne	.40	294	Travis Lee	.15	398	Nick Neugebauer	.15
87	Kevin Mench	.15	191	Kazuhisa Ishii	.15	295	Jorge Sosa	.15	399	J.D. Drew	.25
88	Doug Davis	.15	192	Adrian Beltre	.25	296	Joe Kennedy	.15	400	Edgar Renteria	.25
89	Pedro Martinez	.75	193	Vladimir Guerrero	.75	297	Carl Crawford	.15	401	Scott Rolen	.75
90	Shea Hillenbrand	.15	194	Tony Armas Jr.	.15	298	Toby Hall	.15	402	Matt Morris	.25
91	Derek Lowe	.15	195	Bartolo Colon	.15	299	Rey Ordonez	.15	403	Garrett Stephenson	.15
92	Jason Varitek	.25	196	Troy O'Leary	.15	300	Brandon Phillips	.15	404	Eduardo Perez	.15
93	Tony Clark	.15	197	Tomokazu Ohka	.15	301	Matt Lawton	.15	405	Mike Matheny	.15
94	John Burkett	.15	198	Brad Wilkerson	.15	302	Ellis Burks	.15	406	Miguel Cairo	.15
95	Frank Castillo	.15	199	Orlando Cabrera	.15	303	Bill Selby	.15	407	Brett Tomko	.15
96	Nomar Garciaparra	2.00	200	Barry Bonds	2.00	304	Travis Hafner	.15	408	Bobby Hill	.15
97	Rickey Henderson	.40	201	David Bell	.15	305	Milton Bradley	.15	409	Troy O'Leary	.15
98	Mike Sweeney	.15	202	Tsuyoshi Shinjo	.15	306	Karim Garcia	.15	410	Corey Patterson	.40
99	Carlos Febles	.15	203	Benito Santiago	.15	307	Cliff Lee	.15	411	Kerry Wood	.75
100	Mark Quinn	.15	204	Livan Hernandez	.15	308	Jeff Cirillo	.15	412	Eric Karros	.15
101	Raul Ibanez	.15	205	Jason Schmidt	.40	309	John Olerud	.25	413	Hee Seop Choi	.15
102	A.J. Hinch	.15	206	Kirk Reuter	.15	310	Kazuhiro Sasaki	.15	414	Alex Gonzalez	.15
103	Paul Byrd	.15	207	Ramon E. Martinez	.15	311	Freddy Garcia	.15	415	Matt Clement	.15
104	Chuck Knoblauch	.15	208	Mike Lowell	.25	312	Bret Boone	.25	416	Mark Grudzielanek	.15
105	Dmitri Young	.15	209	Luis Castillo	.15	313	Mike Cameron	.15	417	Curt Schilling	.50
106	Randall Simon	.15	210	Derrek Lee	.25	314	Ben Davis	.15	418	Steve Finley	.15
107	Brandon Inge	.15	211	Andy Fox	.15	315	Randy Winn	.15	419	Craig Counsell	.15
108	Damion Easley	.15	212	Eric Owens	.15	316	Gary Matthews Jr.	.15	420	Matt Williams	.15
109	Carlos Pena	.15	213	Charles Johnson	.15	317	Jeff Conine	.15	421	Quinton McCracken	.15
110	George Lombard	.15	214	Brad Penny	.15	318	Sidney Ponson	.15	422	Chad Moeller	.15
111	Juan Acevedo	.15	215	A.J. Burnett	.15	319	Jerry Hairston	.15	423	Lyle Overbay	.15
112	Torii Hunter	.25	216	Edgardo Alfonzo	.15	320	David Segui	.15	424	Miguel Batista	.15
113	Doug Mientkiewicz	.15	217	Roberto Alomar	.50	321	Scott Erickson	.15	425	Paul LoDuca	.15

426	Kevin Brown	.25
427	Hideo Nomo	.40
428	Fred McGriff	.25
429	Joe Thurston	.15
430	Odalis Perez	.15
431	Darren Dreifort	.15
432	Todd Hundley	.15
433	Dave Roberts	.15
434	Jose Vidro	.15
435	Javier Vazquez	.15
436	Michael Barrett	.15
437	Fernando Tatis	.15
438	Peter Bergeron	.15
439	Endy Chavez	.15
440	Orlando Hernandez	.15
441	Marvin Bernard	.15
442	Rich Aurilia	.15
443	Pedro Feliz	.15
444	Robb Nen	.15
445	Ray Durham	.15
446	Marquis Grissom	.15
447	Damian Moss	.15
448	Edgardo Alfonzo	.15
449	Juan Pierre	.15
450	Braden Looper	.15
451	Alex Gonzalez	.15
452	Justin Wayne	.15
453	Josh Beckett	.25
454	Juan Encarnacion	.15
455	Ivan Rodriguez	.50
456	Todd Hollandsworth	.15
457	Cliff Floyd	.15
458	Rey Sanchez	.15
459	Mike Piazza	1.50
460	Mo Vaughn	.15
461	Armando Benitez	.15
462	Tsuyoshi Shinjo	.15
463	Tom Glavine	.40
464	David Cone	.15
465	Phil Nevin	.15
466	Sean Burroughs	.15
467	Jake Peavy	.15
468	Brian Lawrence	.15
469	Mark Loretta	.15
470	Dennis Tankersley	.15
471	Jesse Orosco	.15
472	Jim Thome	.75
473	Kevin Millwood	.40
474	David Bell	.15
475	Pat Burrell	.40
476	Brandon Duckworth	.15
477	Jose Mesa	.15
478	Marlon Byrd	.15
479	Reggie Sanders	.15
480	Jason Kendall	.25
481	Aramis Ramirez	.40
482	Kris Benson	.15
483	Matt Stairs	.15
484	Kevin Young	.15
485	Kenny Lofton	.25
486	Austin Kearns	.40
487	Barry Larkin	.25
488	Jason LaRue	.15
489	Ken Griffey Jr.	1.25
490	Danny Graves	.15
491	Russell Branyan	.15
492	Reggie Taylor	.15
493	Jimmy Haynes	.15
494	Charles Johnson	.15
495	Todd Helton	.75
496	Juan Uribe	.15
497	Preston Wilson	.15
498	Chris Stynes	.15
499	Jason Jennings	.15
500	Jay Payton	.15
501	Hideki Matsui RC	5.00
502	Jose Contreras RC	2.00
503	Brandon Webb RC	2.00
504	Robby Hammock RC	.50
505	Matt Kata RC	.50
506	Tim Olson RC	.50
507	Michael Hessman RC	.50
508	Jon Leicester RC	.50
509	Todd Wellemeyer RC	.50
510	David Sanders RC	.50
511	Josh Stewart RC	.50
512	Luis Ayala RC	.50
513	Clint Barmes RC	2.00
514	Josh Willingham RC	.50
515	Alejandro Machado RC	.50
516	Felix Sanchez RC	.50
517	Willie Eyre RC	.50
518	Brent Hoard RC	.50
519	Lew Ford RC	1.50
520	Terrmel Sledge RC	.50
521	Jeremy Griffiths	.15
522	Phil Seibel RC	.50
523	Craig Brazell RC	.50
524	Prentice Redman RC	.50
525	Jeff Duncan RC	.50
526	Shane Bazzell RC	.75
527	Bernie Castro RC	.50
528	Rett Johnson RC	.50
529	Bobby Madritsch RC	3.00
530	Rocco Baldelli	.40
531	Alex Rodriguez	1.00
532	Eric Chavez	.25
533	Miguel Tejada	.25
534	Ichiro Suzuki	.75
535	Sammy Sosa	.75
536	Barry Zito	.25
537	Darin Erstad	.25
538	Alfonso Soriano	.50
539	Troy Glaus	.25
540	Nomar Garciaparra	.75

Gold

Gold (541-600): 2-3X
One gold set per hobby case.

AL All-Star Swatch

		NM/M
	Common Player:	5.00
	Inserted 1:144 Retail	
MC	Mike Cameron	5.00
RD	Ray Durham	5.00
CE	Carl Everett	5.00
CF	Chuck Finley	5.00
TF	Travis Fryman	6.00
JG	Juan Gonzalez	8.00
JM	Joe Mays	5.00
MO	Magglio Ordonez	8.00
AP	Andy Pettitte	8.00
JP	Jorge Posada	8.00
MR	Mariano Rivera	10.00
AS	Aaron Sele	5.00
MS	Mike Sweeney	5.00

Big League Breakdown

		NM/M
	Complete Set (15):	20.00
	Common Player:	.50
	Inserted 1:8	
BL1	Troy Glaus	.75
BL2	Miguel Tejada	.75
BL3	Chipper Jones	1.50
BL4	Torii Hunter	.50
BL5	Nomar Garciaparra	3.00
BL6	Sammy Sosa	2.50
BL7	Todd Helton	1.00
BL8	Lance Berkman	.75
BL9	Shawn Green	.50
BL10	Vladimir Guerrero	1.50
BL11	Jason Giambi	.60
BL12	Derek Jeter	4.00
BL13	Barry Bonds	4.00
BL14	Ichiro Suzuki	3.00
BL15	Alex Rodriguez	4.00

Game Swatches Hobby

		NM/M
	Common Player:	5.00
	Inserted 1:72	
SB	Sean Burroughs/SP	8.00
CD	Carlos Delgado/SP	8.00
GM	Greg Maddux	15.00
MM	Mike Mussina	10.00
MO	Magglio Ordonez	5.00
CP	Carlos Pena	5.00
MP	Mike Piazza/SP	15.00
AR	Alex Rodriguez	15.00
CC	C.C. Sabathia	5.00
CS	Curt Schilling/100	10.00
SS	Sammy Sosa	8.00
BW	Bernie Williams	10.00

Game Swatches Retail

		NM/M
	Common Player:	5.00
	Inserted 1:72	
RC	Roger Clemens	15.00
JD	J.D. Drew	5.00
AD	Adam Dunn	8.00
JE	Jim Edmonds	8.00
DE	Darin Erstad	8.00
JG	Jason Giambi	8.00
KG	Ken Griffey Jr.	12.00
TH	Tim Hudson	6.00
RJ	Randy Johnson	8.00
JK	Jeff Kent	5.00
EM	Edgar Martinez	6.00
IR	Ivan Rodriguez	6.00
FT	Frank Thomas	8.00

Game Jersey Autograph

		NM/M
	Golds:	1.5-2X
	Production 25 or 75	
RC	Roger Clemens/350	100.00
JG	Jason Giambi/350	40.00
KG	Ken Griffey Jr./350	110.00
MM	Mark McGwire/150	350.00
CR	Cal Ripken Jr/350	140.00
AR	Alex Rodriguez/350	120.00
SS	Sammy Sosa/150	140.00

Leading Swatches

		NM/M
	Common Player:	4.00
	Inserted 1:24	
	Golds:	1-2X
	Production 100 Sets	
BA	Bobby Abreu	6.00
GA	Garret Anderson	6.00
JB	Jeff Bagwell	6.00
JB1	Jeff Bagwell	6.00
TB	Tony Batista	4.00
AB	Adrian Beltre	6.00
PB	Pat Burrell	6.00
PB1	Pat Burrell	6.00
EC	Eric Chavez	6.00
RC	Roger Clemens	10.00
RC1	Roger Clemens	10.00
CD	Carlos Delgado	8.00
JD	J.D. Drew	4.00
AD	Adam Dunn	8.00
AD1	Adam Dunn	8.00
JE	Jim Edmonds	4.00
JG	Jason Giambi	6.00
JG1	Jason Giambi	6.00
BG	Brian Giles	4.00
TG	Troy Glaus	4.00
GO	Juan Gonzalez	6.00
LG	Luis Gonzalez	4.00
SG	Shawn Green	4.00
SG1	Shawn Green	4.00
KG	Ken Griffey Jr.	12.00
KG1	Ken Griffey Jr.	12.00
VG	Vladimir Guerrero	8.00
THe	Todd Helton	6.00
THu	Tim Hudson	4.00
TH1	Tim Hudson	4.00
KI	Kazuhisa Ishii	4.00
RJ	Randy Johnson	8.00
RJ1	Randy Johnson	8.00
AJ	Andruw Jones	6.00
AJ1	Andruw Jones	6.00
CJ	Chipper Jones	8.00
KE	Jason Kendall	4.00
JL	Javy Lopez	4.00
GM	Greg Maddux	10.00
GM1	Greg Maddux	10.00
PM	Pedro J. Martinez	8.00
HM	Hideki Matsui	40.00
HM1	Hideki Matsui	50.00
HN	Hideo Nomo	8.00
RO	Roy Oswalt	4.00
RO1	Roy Oswalt	4.00
RP	Rafael Palmeiro	6.00
RP1	Rafael Palmeiro	6.00
CP	Corey Patterson	6.00
JP	Jay Payton	4.00
TP	Troy Percival	4.00
AP	Andy Pettitte	4.00
MP	Mike Piazza	10.00
MP1	Mike Piazza	10.00
MR	Manny Ramirez	8.00
AR	Alex Rodriguez	10.00
AR1	Alex Rodriguez	10.00
IR	Ivan Rodriguez	6.00
SR	Scott Rolen	4.00
KS	Kazuhiro Sasaki	4.00
CS	Curt Schilling	4.00
AS	Aaron Sele	4.00
JS	J.T. Snow	4.00
AS	Alfonso Soriano	8.00
AS1	Alfonso Soriano	8.00
SS	Sammy Sosa	12.00
SS1	Sammy Sosa	12.00
MS	Mike Stanton	4.00
IS	Ichiro Suzuki	25.00
IS1	Ichiro Suzuki	25.00
MS	Mike Sweeney	4.00
MT	Miguel Tejada	6.00
MT1	Miguel Tejada	6.00
JT	Jim Thome	8.00
JT1	Jim Thome	8.00
OV	Omar Vizquel	4.00
LW	Larry Walker	4.00
BW	Bernie Williams	6.00
BW1	Bernie Williams	6.00
KW	Kerry Wood	8.00
BZ	Barry Zito	6.00

Lineup Time Jerseys

		NM/M
	Common Player:	6.00
	Inserted 1:96	
RC	Roger Clemens/SP	20.00
CD	Carlos Delgado	8.00
JD	J.D. Drew	6.00
SG	Shawn Green	8.00
TH	Todd Helton	8.00
RJ	Randy Johnson/SP	15.00
GM	Greg Maddux	10.00
IS	Ichiro Suzuki	40.00
JT	Jim Thome	10.00
BW	Bernie Williams	10.00

Magical Performances

		NM/M
	Common Player:	8.00
	Inserted 1:96	
	Golds:	1-2X
	Production 50 Sets	
MP1	Hideki Matsui	20.00
MP2	Ken Griffey Jr.	15.00
MP3	Ichiro Suzuki	15.00
MP4	Ken Griffey Jr.	15.00
MP5	Hideo Nomo	8.00
MP6	Mickey Mantle	40.00
MP7	Ken Griffey Jr.	15.00
MP8	Barry Bonds	20.00
MP9	Mickey Mantle	40.00
MP10	Tom Seaver	8.00
MP11	Mike Piazza	15.00
MP12	Roger Clemens	12.00
MP13	Nolan Ryan	30.00
MP14	Nomar Garciaparra	15.00
MP15	Ernie Banks	15.00
MP16	Stan Musial	25.00
MP17	Mickey Mantle	40.00
MP18	Nolan Ryan	30.00
MP19	Nolan Ryan	30.00
MP20	Mickey Mantle	40.00
MP21	Ichiro Suzuki	15.00
MP22	Nolan Ryan	30.00
MP23	Tom Seaver	8.00
MP24	Ken Griffey Jr.	15.00
MP25	Hideo Nomo	8.00
MP26	Ken Griffey Jr.	15.00
MP27	Mark McGwire	30.00
MP28	Barry Bonds	20.00
MP29	Alex Rodriguez	20.00
MP30	Nolan Ryan	30.00
MP31	Mark McGwire	30.00
MP32	Nolan Ryan	30.00
MP33	Sammy Sosa	15.00
MP34	Ichiro Suzuki	15.00
MP35	Barry Bonds	20.00
MP36	Derek Jeter	20.00
MP37	Roger Clemens	15.00
MP38	Jason Giambi	8.00
MP39	Mickey Mantle	40.00
MP40	Ted Williams	40.00
MP41	Ted Williams	40.00
MP42	Ted Williams	40.00

Mark of Greatness

		NM/M
	400 total cards produced.	
MoG	Mark McGwire	350.00
MoG	Mark McGwire/Silver/70	400.00

Masters with the Leather

		NM/M
Complete Set (12):		20.00
Common Player:		.75
Inserted 1:12		
L1	Darin Erstad	.75
L2	Andruw Jones	1.50
L3	Greg Maddux	3.00
L4	Nomar Garciaparra	3.00
L5	Torii Hunter	1.00
L6	Roberto Alomar	1.00
L7	Derek Jeter	5.00
L8	Eric Chavez	1.00
L9	Ichiro Suzuki	3.00
L10	Jim Edmonds	1.00
L11	Scott Rolen	1.50
L12	Alex Rodriguez	4.00

Mid-Summer Stars

		NM/M
Common Player:		5.00
Inserted 1:72		
RC	Roger Clemens	12.00
CD	Carlos Delgado	8.00
JE	Jim Edmonds	8.00
DE	Darin Erstad	8.00
FG	Freddy Garcia	5.00
TG	Tom Glavine	8.00
JG	Juan Gonzalez	8.00
SG	Shawn Green/SP	8.00
RJ	Randy Johnson	10.00
AJ	Andruw Jones	6.00
EM	Edgar Martinez	10.00
HN	Hideo Nomo	20.00
MP	Mike Piazza	15.00
MR	Manny Ramirez	8.00
AR	Alex Rodriguez	15.00
KS	Kazuhiro Sasaki	8.00
CS	Curt Schilling	10.00
SS	Sammy Sosa	15.00
IS	Ichiro Suzuki/SP	40.00
FT	Frank Thomas	8.00
RV	Robin Ventura	8.00
DW	David Wells	5.00
BZ	Barry Zito	5.00

National Pride

		NM/M
Common Player:		3.00
Inserted 1:24		
AA	Abe Alvarez	3.00
MA	Michael Aubrey	15.00
KB	Kyle Bakker	3.00
SB	Sean Burroughs	5.00
CC	Chad Cordero	3.00
SC	Shane Costa	3.00
RF	Robert Fick	3.00
SF	Sam Fuld	3.00
AH	Aaron Hill	8.00
BH	Bobby Hill	3.00
BH1	Bobby Hill	3.00
AJ	A.J. Hinch	3.00
PH	Philip Humber	5.00
CJ	Conor Jackson	3.00
JJe	Jason Jennings	3.00
GJ	Grant Johnson	3.00
JJ	Jacque Jones	8.00
JJ1	Jacque Jones	8.00
MJ	Mark Jurich	3.00
AK	Austin Kearns	12.00
AK1	Austin Kearns	12.00
WL	Wes Littleton	3.00
EM	Eric Milton	5.00
EM1	Eric Milton	5.00
RO	Roy Oswalt	6.00
RO1	Roy Oswalt	6.00
EP	Eric Patterson	3.00
DP	Dustin Pedroia	3.00
LP	Landon Powell	3.00
MP	Mark Prior	15.00
MP1	Mark Prior	15.00
CQ	Carlos Quentin	3.00
KSa	Kirk Saarloos	3.00
KSa1	Kirk Saarloos	3.00
CS	Clint Sammons	5.00
KSl	Kyle Sleeth	5.00
HS	Huston Street	3.00
BS	Brad Sullivan	3.00
BS1	Brad Sullivan	3.00
RW	Rickie Weeks	15.00

RW1	Rickie Weeks	15.00
BZ	Bob Zimmermann	3.00

NL All-Star Swatch

		NM/M
Common Player:		5.00
Inserted 1:72		
SC	Sean Casey	5.00
CF	Cliff Floyd	5.00
TGl	Tom Glavine	8.00
TGw	Tony Gwynn	12.00
MH	Mike Hampton	5.00
TH	Trevor Hoffman	5.00
RK	Ryan Klesko	5.00
AL	Al Leiter	5.00
FM	Fred McGriff	5.00
MM	Matt Morris	8.00
CS	Curt Schilling	8.00
JV	Jose Vidro	5.00

Patch Logo

		NM/M
Quantity produced listed		
JB	Jeff Bagwell/41	60.00
KG	Ken Griffey Jr./50	100.00
TH	Todd Helton/41	50.00
KI	Kazuhisa Ishii/54	40.00
RJ	Randy Johnson/50	75.00
CJ	Chipper Jones/52	80.00
GM	Greg Maddux/50	100.00
MP	Mike Piazza/61	120.00
SS	Sammy Sosa/60	100.00
FT	Frank Thomas/52	60.00
BW	Bernie Williams/42	40.00

Patch Number

		NM/M
Quantity produced listed		
JG	Jason Giambi/68	40.00
KG	Ken Griffey Jr./97	70.00
KI	Kazuhisa Ishii/63	40.00
RJ	Randy Johnson/90	75.00
MG	Mark McGwire/60	180.00
AR	Alex Rodriguez/56	90.00
SS	Sammy Sosa/100	80.00
FT	Frank Thomas/91	60.00
BW	Bernie Williams/66	50.00

Patch Stripes

		NM/M
Quantity produced listed		
JB	Jeff Bagwell/73	60.00
JG	Jason Giambi/66	40.00
KG	Ken Griffey Jr./63	75.00
KI	Kazuhisa Ishii/58	40.00
RJ	Randy Johnson/58	65.00
CJ	Chipper Jones/58	60.00
MG	Mark McGwire/63	180.00
AR	Alex Rodriguez/63	80.00
SS	Sammy Sosa/63	100.00
IS	Ichiro Suzuki/63	180.00
FT	Frank Thomas/58	60.00
BW	Bernie Williams/58	50.00

Piece of the Action

		NM/M
Common Player:		5.00
Inserted 1:288		
Cards are not serial numbered.		
Print runs provided by Upper Deck.		
BA	Bobby Abreu/125	5.00
GA	Garret Anderson/150	5.00
AB	Adrian Beltre/100	5.00
BB	Barry Bonds/125	30.00
KB	Kevin Brown/100	5.00
PB	Pat Burrell/150	8.00
DE	Darin Erstad/125	5.00
FG	Freddy Garcia/100	5.00
BG	Brian Giles/100	5.00
TG	Troy Glaus/150	6.00
JG	Juan Gonzalez/100	8.00
LG	Luis Gonzalez/100	5.00
SG	Shawn Green/175	5.00
VG	Vladimir Guerrero/50	15.00
THe	Todd Helton/100	10.00
THo	Trevor Hoffman/150	5.00
DJ	Derek Jeter/65	40.00
RJ	Randy Johnson/100	10.00
CJ	Chipper Jones/62	15.00
JK	Jason Kendall/100	5.00
KE	Jeff Kent/150	5.00
RK	Ryan Klesko/75	6.00
EM	Edgar Martinez/125	5.00
PM	Pedro Martinez/100	10.00
PN	Phil Nevin/75	5.00
HN	Hideo Nomo/100	20.00
RP	Rafael Palmeiro/150	10.00
Ara	Aramis Ramirez/100	8.00
MP	Mike Piazza/150	15.00
ARo	Alex Rodriguez/100	15.00
KS	Kazuhiro Sasaki/100	5.00
CS	Curt Schilling/100	10.00

RS	Richie Sexson/160	8.00
GS	Gary Sheffield/100	6.00
SS	Sammy Sosa/85	20.00
FT	Frank Thomas/150	8.00
JT	Jim Thome/125	10.00
JV	Jose Vidro/100	5.00
LW	Larry Walker/150	5.00
BW	Bernie Williams/125	6.00

Roger Clemens 300 Wins

		NM/M
Complete Set (6):		15.00
Common Card:		3.00
1	Roger Clemens (1999 post-season wins)	3.00
2	Roger Clemens (2000 post-season wins)	3.00
3	Roger Clemens (Sixth Cy Young)	3.00
4	Roger Clemens (4,000 Ks)	3.00
5	Roger Clemens (300th win)	3.00
--	Header Card	3.00

Slammin' Sammy Tribute Jersey

		NM/M
384 total produced.		
SST	Sammy Sosa	175.00
SST	Sammy Sosa/Gold/25	290.00
SST	Sammy Sosa/Silver/66	240.00

Star-Spangled Swatches

		NM/M
Common Player:		4.00
Inserted 1:72		
MA	Michael Aubrey	8.00
KB	Kyle Bakker	4.00
CC	Chad Cordero	4.00
SC	Shane Costa	6.00
AH	Aaron Hill	4.00
PH	Philip Humber	6.00
CJ	Conor Jackson	8.00
GJ	Grant Johnson	4.00
EP	Eric Patterson	8.00
DP	Dustin Pedroia	10.00
LP	Landon Powell	6.00
CQ	Carlos Quentin	8.00
KS	Kyle Sleeth	6.00
HS	Huston Street	10.00
BS	Brad Sullivan	4.00
RW	Rickie Weeks	15.00

Superstar Slam Jerseys

		NM/M
Common Player:		4.00
Inserted 1:48		
JB	Jeff Bagwell	8.00
JG	Jason Giambi	6.00
JGo	Juan Gonzalez	6.00
LG	Luis Gonzalez	4.00

UD Superstar Slam

KG	Ken Griffey Jr.	15.00
CJ	Chipper Jones	10.00
MP	Mike Piazza	10.00
AR	Alex Rodriguez	15.00
SS	Sammy Sosa	15.00
FT	Frank Thomas	8.00

The Chase for 755

		NM/M
Complete Set (15):		15.00
Common Player:		.75
Inserted 1:8		
C1	Troy Glaus	.75
C2	Andruw Jones	1.00
C3	Manny Ramirez	1.25
C4	Sammy Sosa	2.50
C5	Ken Griffey Jr.	3.00
C6	Adam Dunn	1.25
C7	Todd Helton	1.00
C8	Lance Berkman	.75
C9	Jeff Bagwell	1.00
C10	Shawn Green	.75
C11	Vladimir Guerrero	1.50
C12	Barry Bonds	4.00
C13	Alex Rodriguez	3.00
C14	Juan Gonzalez	.75
C15	Carlos Delgado	.75

Triple Game Jersey

		NM/M
Quantity produced listed		
Golds:		1.5-2X
Production 50, 25 or 10		
ARZ	Randy Johnson, Curt Schilling, Luis Gonzalez/150	40.00
CIN	Ken Griffey Jr., Sean Casey, Adam Dunn/150	40.00
HOU	Jeff Bagwell, Lance Berkman, Craig Biggio/150	40.00
TEX	Rafael Palmeiro, Alex Rodriguez, Juan Gonzalez/150	40.00
ATL	Chipper Jones, Greg Maddux, Gary Sheffield/75	65.00
CHC	Sammy Sosa, Moises Alou, Kerry Wood/75	50.00
NYM	Mike Piazza, Roberto Alomar, Mo Vaughn/75	40.00
SEA	Ichiro Suzuki, Freddy Garcia, Bret Boone/75	80.00

Superior Sluggers

		NM/M
Complete Set (18):		30.00
Common Player:		1.00
Inserted 1:8		
S1	Troy Glaus	1.00
S2	Chipper Jones	1.50
S3	Manny Ramirez	1.50
S4	Ken Griffey Jr.	2.50
S5	Jim Thome	1.50
S6	Todd Helton	1.00
S7	Lance Berkman	1.00
S8	Derek Jeter	4.00

S9	Vladimir Guerrero	1.50
S10	Mike Piazza	2.50
S11	Hideki Matsui	3.00
S12	Barry Bonds	4.00
S13	Mickey Mantle	5.00
S14	Alex Rodriguez	3.00
S15	Ted Williams	3.00
S16	Carlos Delgado	1.00
S17	Frank Thomas	1.00
S18	Adam Dunn	1.50

Super Patch Logos
Common Player:
Inserted 1:7,500
No Pricing

Super Patch Numbers
Common Player:
Inserted 1:7,500
No Pricing

Super Patch Stripes
Common Player:
Inserted 1:7,500
No Pricing

500 HR Club
NM/M
Production 350 Cards

SS	Sammy Sosa/350	150.00
SS	Sammy Sosa/ Auto./21	2,300

2003 UD Authentics

TED WILLIAMS

NM/M
Complete Set (130):
Common Player: .25
Common Rk Hype (101-130): 4.00
Production 999
Pack (4): 10.00
Box (10 + Framed Auto.): 170.00

1	Pee Wee Reese	.25
2	Richie Ashburn	.25
3	Derek Jeter	2.50
4	Alex Rodriguez	2.00
5	Jose Vidro	.25
6	Miguel Tejada	.50
7	Nomar Garciaparra	2.00
8	Pat Burrell	.50
9	Albert Pujols	2.00
10	Jeff Bagwell	.75
11	Stan Musial	1.00
12	Mickey Mantle	3.00
13	J.D. Drew	.75
14	Ivan Rodriguez	.75
15	Joe Morgan	.25
16	Ted Williams	2.00
17	Travis Hafner	.25
18	Chipper Jones	1.50
19	Hideo Nomo	.50
20	Gary Sheffield	.50
21	Jacque Jones	.25
22	Alfonso Soriano	1.50
23	Roberto Alomar	.50
24	Jeff Kent	.40
25	Omar Vizquel	.40
26	Ernie Banks	1.00
27	Shawn Green	.50
28	Tim Hudson	.50
29	Jim Edmonds	.50
30	Brandon Larson	.25
31	Doug Mientkiewicz	.25
32	Darin Erstad	.50
33	Bobby Hill	.25
34	Todd Helton	.75
35	Kazuhisa Ishii	.25
36	Lance Berkman	.50
37	Eric Hinske	.25
38	Jason Kendall	.25
39	Bob Feller	.50
40	Luis Gonzalez	.40
41	Sammy Sosa	2.00
42	Mike Piazza	1.50
43	Roger Clemens	2.00
44	Jose Cruz Jr.	.25
45	Mark Prior	1.50
46	Mark Teixeira	.40
47	Phil Nevin	.25
48	Lyle Overbay	.25
49	Manny Ramirez	.75
50	Brian Giles	.40
51	Preston Wilson	.25
52	Jermaine Dye	.25
53	Troy Glaus	.50
54	Frank Thomas	.75
55	Jim Thome	.75
56	Barry Bonds	2.50
57	Carlos Delgado	.75
58	Jason Giambi	1.00
59	Joe Mays	.25
60	Andruw Jones	.75
61	Billy Williams	.25
62	Vladimir Guerrero	.75
63	Scott Rolen	.75
64	Juan Marichal	.25
65	Austin Kearns	.50
66	Kerry Wood	.75
67	Bret Boone	.25
68	Shea Hillenbrand	.25
69	Mike Sweeney	.25
70	Rocco Baldelli	.25
71	Ken Griffey Jr.	1.50
72	Cliff Floyd	.25
73	Greg Maddux	1.50
74	Mike Hampton	.25
75	Larry Walker	.40
76	Nolan Ryan	3.00
77	Rollie Fingers	.25
78	Mike Mussina	.75
79	Matt Morris	.25
80	Robin Roberts	.25
81	Barry Zito	.50
82	Curt Schilling	.50
83	Ken Harvey	.25
84	Troy Percival	.25
85	Tom Seaver	1.00
86	Mariano Rivera	.40
87	Raul Mondesi	.25
88	Adam Dunn	.50
89	Roy Oswalt	.25
90	Pedro J. Martinez	1.00
91	Andy Pettitte	.50
92	Tom Glavine	.50
93	Torii Hunter	.50
94	Joe Thurston	.25
95	Runelvys Hernandez	.25
96	Randy Johnson	1.00
97	Bernie Williams	.75
98	Ichiro Suzuki	1.50
99	C.C. Sabathia	.25
100	Bobby Abreu	.40
101	Jose Contreras RC	6.00
102	Hideki Matsui RC	15.00
103	Chris Capuano RC	6.00
104	Willie Eyre RC	4.00
105	Lew Ford RC	6.00
106	Shane Bazzell RC	6.00
107	Guillermo Quiroz RC	6.00
108	Fernando Cabrera RC	4.00
109	Francisco Cruceta RC	4.00
110	Jhonny Peralta RC	4.00
111	Bobby Madritsch RC	6.00
112	Diegomar Markwell RC	4.00
113	Matt Bruback RC	4.00
114	Matt Kata RC	6.00
115	Rob Hammock RC	4.00
116	Brandon Webb RC	10.00
117	Jon Leicester RC	4.00
118	Josh Willingham RC	6.00
119	Prentice Redman RC	4.00
120	Jeff Duncan RC	4.00
121	Craig Brazell RC	6.00
122	Jeremy Griffiths RC	4.00
123	Phil Seibel RC	4.00
124	Luis Ayala RC	6.00
125	Miguel Ojeda RC	6.00
126	Jeremy Wedel RC	4.00
127	Josh Hall RC	6.00
128	Oscar Villarreal RC	4.00
129	Clint Barmes RC	8.00
130	Nook Logan RC	4.00

Threads of Time
NM/M
Common Player: 4.00
Production 350, unless noted.
Golds: 1-2X
Production 50, 25 or 10
No Pricing for #'d to 25 or less.

JB	Johnny Bench	10.00
GC	Gary Carter	4.00
RC	Roger Clemens	15.00
TC	Ty Cobb	100.00
DD	Don Drysdale	15.00
DE	Dennis Eckersley	4.00
RF	Rollie Fingers	4.00
LG	Lou Gehrig/250	140.00
JG	Jason Giambi/250	6.00
JU	Juan Gonzalez	5.00
KG	Ken Griffey Jr./250	12.00
VG	Vladimir Guerrero	6.00
RJ	Randy Johnson	8.00
CJ	Chipper Jones	8.00
HK	Harmon Killebrew	12.00
GM	Greg Maddux	8.00
MM	Mickey Mantle/250	100.00
RM	Roger Maris	40.00
PM	Pedro J. Martinez	8.00
DM	Don Mattingly	20.00
HN	Hideo Nomo	8.00
AP	Andy Pettitte	6.00
MP	Mike Piazza	10.00
AP	Albert Pujols	20.00
CR	Cal Ripken Jr.	25.00
FR	Frank Robinson	8.00
AR	Alex Rodriguez	12.00
IR	Ivan Rodriguez	5.00
NR	Nolan Ryan	30.00
RS	Ryne Sandberg	12.00
TS	Tom Seaver	8.00
OS	Ozzie Smith	10.00
SS	Sammy Sosa/250	12.00
IS	Ichiro Suzuki/250	30.00
FT	Frank Thomas	6.00
JT	Jim Thome	8.00
HW	Honus Wagner	75.00
TW	Ted Williams/250	65.00
MW	Maury Wills	4.00
DW	Dave Winfield/250	6.00

Star Quality

NM/M
Common Player: 4.00
Production 350 unless noted.
Golds: 1-2X
Production 50, 25 or 10
No Pricing for #'d to 25 or less.

RA	Roberto Alomar	6.00
JB	Jeff Bagwell	8.00
JO	Josh Beckett	4.00
LB	Lance Berkman	5.00
RC	Roger Clemens	15.00
RC1	Roger Clemens	15.00
CD	Carlos Delgado	5.00
JD	J.D. Drew	4.00
AD	Adam Dunn	6.00
JG	Jason Giambi	4.00
TR	Troy Glaus	5.00
TG	Tom Seaver	4.00
SG	Shawn Green	4.00
KG	Ken Griffey Jr./250	12.00
VG	Vladimir Guerrero	6.00
TH	Todd Helton	6.00
EH	Eric Hinske	4.00
CJ	Chipper Jones	8.00
AK	Austin Kearns	4.00
JK	Jeff Kent	4.00
MM	Mickey Mantle/250	100.00
HM	Hideki Matsui/250	25.00
PM	Paul Molitor/250	8.00
MU	Mike Mussina	8.00
HN	Hideo Nomo	8.00
RO	Roy Oswalt	6.00
RP	Rafael Palmeiro	6.00
MP	Mark Prior	10.00
AP	Albert Pujols	20.00
AP1	Albert Pujols	20.00
CR	Cal Ripken Jr./250	25.00
NR	Nolan Ryan/130	50.00
TS	Tom Seaver	8.00
GS	Gary Sheffield	4.00
AS	Alfonso Soriano	10.00
SS	Sammy Sosa/250	12.00
CS	Casey Stengel	15.00
JT	Jim Thome	8.00
BW	Bernie Williams	8.00
TW	Ted Williams/250	65.00
KW	Kerry Wood	8.00

Framed Autograph
NM/M
Common Framed Autograph: 40.00
Inserted 1:Box

Lance Berkman/150	40.00
Lance Berkman/60	60.00
Hank Blalock/325	45.00
Hank Blalock/300	45.00
Hank Blalock/200	45.00
Hank Blalock/175	45.00
Pat Burrell/330	40.00
Pat Burrell/240	40.00
Pat Burrell/150	40.00
Gary Carter/225	50.00
Gary Carter/75	60.00
Jose Contreras/350	50.00
Jose Contreras/120	50.00
Carlton Fisk/250	50.00
Carlton Fisk/125	75.00
Carlton Fisk/70	80.00
Nomar Garciaparra/250	100.00
Nomar Garciaparra/150	100.00
Nomar Garciaparra/75	120.00
Jason Giambi/350	40.00
Jason Giambi/300	40.00
Jason Giambi/200	40.00
Jason Giambi/150	40.00
Jason Giambi/100	40.00
Jason Giambi/75	40.00
Bob Gibson/200	60.00
Bob Gibson/50	120.00
Bob Gibson/45	120.00
Troy Glaus/350	40.00
Troy Glaus/200	40.00
Troy Glaus/100	50.00
Tom Glavine/275	50.00
Tom Glavine/150	50.00
Tom Glavine/47	75.00
Ken Griffey Jr./325	90.00
Ken Griffey Jr./200	90.00
Ken Griffey Jr/75	100.00
Ken Griffey Jr./30	120.00
Vladimir Guerrero/150	60.00
Vladimir Guerrero/27	125.00
Drew Henson/350	40.00
Drew Henson/300	40.00
Drew Henson/200	40.00
Drew Henson/100	40.00
Chipper Jones/350	70.00
Chipper Jones/200	70.00
Chipper Jones/100	85.00
Austin Kearns/325	40.00
Austin Kearns/300	40.00
Austin Kearns/200	40.00
Austin Kearns/175	40.00
Austin Kearns/28	80.00
Hideki Matsui/75	300.00
Hideki Matsui/55	300.00
Mark Prior/300	60.00
Mark Prior/250	60.00
Mark Prior/175	60.00
Mark Prior/100	60.00
Cal Ripken Jr/125	175.00
Cal Ripken Jr./50	200.00
Phil Rizzuto/350	50.00
Phil Rizzuto/200	60.00
Phil Rizzuto/100	75.00
Scott Rolen/300	50.00
Scott Rolen/100	65.00
Scott Rolen/27	120.00
Nolan Ryan/150	125.00
Nolan Ryan/100	180.00
Nolan Ryan/50	200.00
Nolan Ryan/30	240.00
Tom Seaver/100	75.00
Tom Seaver/50	100.00
Tom Seaver/41	100.00
Ozzie Smith/50	85.00
Ozzie Smith/50	120.00
Duke Snider/150	60.00
Duke Snider/50	100.00
Ichiro Suzuki/300	300.00
Ichiro Suzuki/51	350.00
Mark Teixeira/325	60.00
Mark Teixeira/200	60.00
Mark Teixeira/175	60.00
Mark Teixeira/150	60.00

Cut Signatures
Mickey Mantle/7
Ted Williams/9

Rookie Hype Gold
Cards (101-130): 1-2X
Production 50

2003 Upper Deck Classic Portraits

		NM/M
Complete Set (232):		
Common Player:		.15
Common SP (101-145):		2.00
Inserted 1:4		
Common SP (145-190):		3.00
Production 2,003		
Common Royalty (191-232):		2.00
Production 1,200		
Pack (5):		3.00
Box (18 + Bust):		75.00
1	Ken Griffey Jr.	1.50
2	Randy Johnson	1.00
3	Rafael Furcal	.25
4	Omar Vizquel	.25
5	Shawn Green	.40
6	Roy Oswalt	.40
7	Hideo Nomo	.40
8	Jason Giambi	.40
9	Barry Bonds	2.50
10	Mike Piazza	1.50
11	Ichiro Suzuki	2.00
12	Carlos Delgado	.40
13	Preston Wilson	.15
14	Lance Berkman	.25
15	Magglio Ordonez	.25
16	Kerry Wood	.75
17	Ivan Rodriguez	.75
18	Chipper Jones	1.00
19	Adam Dunn	.75
20	C.C. Sabathia	.15
21	Mike MacDougal	.15
22	Torii Hunter	.40
23	Jim Thome	.75
24	Hank Blalock	.40
25	Johnny Damon	.50
26	Troy Glaus	.40
27	Manny Ramirez	.75
28	Mark Prior	1.00
29	Brent Mayne	.15
30	Derek Jeter	2.50
31	Tim Hudson	.40
32	Mike Cameron	.15
33	Mark Teixeira	.40
34	Shannon Stewart	.15
35	Tim Salmon	.25
36	Luis Gonzalez	.25
37	Jason Johnson	.15
38	Shea Hillenbrand	.25
39	Bartolo Colon	.25
40	Austin Kearns	.40
41	Vladimir Guerrero	1.00
42	Tom Glavine	.40
43	Andres Galarraga	.25
44	Kazuhiro Sasaki	.15
45	Juan Gonzalez	.25
46	Vernon Wells	.25
47	Jeff Bagwell	.75
48	Mike Sweeney	.15
49	Carlos Beltran	.50
50	Dave Roberts	.15
51	Todd Helton	.75
52	Carlos Pena	.15
53	Darin Erstad	.25
54	Gary Sheffield	.40
55	Lyle Overbay	.15
56	Sammy Sosa	1.50
57	Mike Mussina	.50
58	Matt Morris	.25
59	Roberto Alomar	.50
60	Larry Walker	.25
61	Jacque Jones	.15
62	Josh Beckett	.40
63	Richie Sexson	.50
64	Derek Lowe	.15
65	Pedro J. Martinez	1.00
66	Moises Alou	.25
67	Craig Biggio	.25
68	Curt Schilling	.75
69	Jesse Foppert	.15
70	Nomar Garciaparra	1.50
71	Barry Zito	.40
72	Alfonso Soriano	.75
73	Miguel Tejada	.50
74	Rafael Palmeiro	.50
75	Albert Pujols	2.00
76	Mariano Rivera	.25
77	Bobby Abreu	.25
78	Alex Rodriguez	2.00
79	Andruw Jones	.50
80	Frank Thomas	.75
81	Greg Maddux	1.50
82	Jim Edmonds	.40
83	Bernie Williams	.50
84	Roger Clemens	2.00
85	Eric Chavez	.25
86	Scott Rolen	1.00
87	Jorge Posada	.50
88	Bret Boone	.25
89	Ben Sheets	.25
90	John Olerud	.15
91	J.D. Drew	.25
92	Aaron Boone	.15
93	Corey Koskie	.15
94	Sean Casey	.25
95	Jose Cruz Jr.	.15
96	Pat Burrell	.40
97	Jose Guillen	.15
98	Mark Mulder	.25
99	Garret Anderson	.25
100	Kazuhisa Ishii	.15
101	Dave Matranga RC	2.00
102	Colin Porter RC	2.00
103	Jason Gilfillan RC	2.00
104	Carlos Mendez RC	2.00
105	Jason Shiell RC	2.00
106	Kevin Tolar RC	2.00
107	Terrmel Sledge RC	3.00
108	Craig Brazell RC	4.00
109	Bernie Castro RC	2.00
110	Tim Olson RC	3.00
111	Kevin Ohme RC	2.00
112	Pedro Liriano RC	2.00
113	Joe Borowski	2.00
114	Edgar Gonzalez RC	3.00
115	Joe Thurston	2.00
116	Bobby Hill	2.00
117	Michel Hernandez RC	2.00
118	Arnie Munoz RC	2.00
119	David Sanders RC	2.00
120	Willie Eyre RC	3.00
121	Brent Hoard RC	2.00
122	Lew Ford RC	4.00
123	Beau Kemp RC	2.00
124	Jonathan Pridie RC	2.00
125	Mike Ryan RC	4.00
126	Richard Fischer RC	2.00
127	Luis Ayala RC	2.00
128	Mike Neu RC	2.00
129	Joe Valentine RC	2.00
130	Nate Bland RC	2.00
131	Shane Bazzell RC	2.00
132	Jason Roach RC	2.00
133	Diegomar Markwell RC	2.00
134	Francisco Rosario RC	2.00
135	Guillermo Quiroz RC	4.00
136	Jerome Williams	2.00
137	Fernando Cabrera RC	2.00
138	Francisco Cruceta RC	2.00
139	Jhonny Peralta	4.00
140	Rett Johnson RC	2.00
141	Aaron Looper RC	2.00
142	Bobby Madritsch RC	2.00
143	Dan Haren	3.00
144	Jose Castillo	2.00
145	Chris Waters RC	3.00
146	Hideki Matsui RC	10.00
147	Jose Contreras RC	4.00
148	Felix Sanchez RC	3.00
149	Jon Leicester RC	3.00
150	Todd Wellemeyer RC	3.00
151	Matt Bruback RC	3.00
152	Chris Capuano RC	5.00
153	Oscar Villarreal RC	3.00
154	Matt Kata RC	3.00
155	Robby Hammock RC	3.00
156	Gerald Laird	3.00
157	Brandon Webb RC	6.00
158	Tommy Whiteman RC	3.00
159	Andrew Brown RC	3.00
160	Alfredo Gonzalez RC	3.00
161	Carlos Rivera RC	3.00
162	Rick Roberts RC	3.00
163	Dontrelle Willis	3.00
164	Josh Willingham RC	4.00
165	Prentice Redman RC	3.00
166	Jeff Duncan RC	4.00
167	Jose Reyes	3.00
168	Jeremy Griffiths	3.00
169	Phil Seibel RC	3.00
170	Heath Bell RC	3.00
171	Anthony Ferrari RC	3.00
172	Mike Nicolas RC	3.00
173	Cory Stewart RC	3.00
174	Miguel Ojeda RC	5.00
175	Rickie Weeks RC	10.00
176	Delmon Young RC	10.00
177	Tommy Phelps RC	3.00
178	Josh Hall RC	4.00
179	Ryan Cameron RC	3.00
180	Garrett Atkins RC	3.00
181	Clint Barmes RC	6.00
182	Michael Hessman RC	3.00
183	Chin-Hui Tsao	3.00
184	Rocco Baldelli	3.00
185	Bo Hart RC	3.00
186	Wilfredo Ledezma RC	3.00
187	Miguel Cabrera	5.00
188	Ian Ferguson RC	3.00
189	Micheal Nakamura RC	3.00
190	Alejandro Machado RC	3.00
191	Mickey Mantle	12.00
192	Ted Williams	10.00
193	Mark Prior	6.00
194	Stan Musial	6.00
195	Phil Rizzuto	4.00
196	Nolan Ryan	12.00
197	Tom Seaver	4.00
198	Robin Yount	5.00
199	Yogi Berra	3.00
200	Ernie Banks	8.00
201	Willie McCovey	3.00
202	Ralph Kiner	3.00
203	Ken Griffey Jr.	4.00
204	Sammy Sosa	5.00
205	Derek Jeter	8.00
206	Nomar Garciaparra	6.00
207	Alex Rodriguez	6.00
208	Ichiro Suzuki	4.00
209	Mike Piazza	4.00
210	Jackie Robinson	6.00
211	Roberto Clemente	8.00
212	Babe Ruth	12.00
213	Duke Snider	3.00
214	Greg Maddux	4.00
215	Juan Marichal	3.00
216	Joe Morgan	2.00
217	Rollie Fingers	2.00
218	Warren Spahn	4.00
219	Pee Wee Reese	2.00
220	Troy Glaus	2.00
221	Jason Giambi	2.00
222	Roger Clemens	6.00
223	Pedro J. Martinez	3.00
224	Chipper Jones	4.00
225	Randy Johnson	3.00
226	Jim Thome	3.00
227	Barry Bonds	8.00
228	Hideo Nomo	2.00
229	Whitey Ford	3.00
230	Bob Gibson	4.00
231	Alfonso Soriano	4.00
232	Richie Ashburn	3.00

Gold

No pricing due to scarcity.
Production 25 Sets

Bronze Bust

		NM/M
Common Player:		
YB	Yogi Berra	25.00
RC	Roberto Clemente	60.00
NG	Nomar Garciaparra	40.00
JG	Jason Giambi	25.00
BG	Bob Gibson	25.00
KG	Ken Griffey Jr./300	40.00
MM	Mickey Mantle	70.00
HM	Hideki Matsui	30.00
SM	Stan Musial	40.00
BRS	Babe Ruth/Sox/300	60.00
BRY	Babe Ruth/Yanks	60.00
NRA	Nolan Ryan/ Astros	50.00
NRA	Nolan Ryan/ Astros/300	50.00
NRM	Nolan Ryan/Mets	50.00
TSM	Tom Seaver/Mets	25.00
TSR	Tom Seaver/ Reds/300	25.00
TSR	Tom Seaver/Reds	25.00
DS	Duke Snider	25.00
SS	Sammy Sosa/300	40.00
IS	Ichiro Suzuki/300	40.00
TW	Ted Williams	50.00

Bronze Bust Autograph

		NM/M
Some not priced due to scarcity.		
YB	Yogi Berra	100.00
NG	Nomar Garciaparra/106	125.00
BG	Bob Gibson	60.00
KG	Ken Griffey Jr.	100.00
HM	Hideki Matsui	250.00
SM	Stan Musial/62	120.00
DS	Duke Snider	90.00
IS	Ichiro Suzuki/62	275.00

Bust Signature

		NM/M
Complete Set (17):		
Common Player:		
NG	Nomar Garciaparra	80.00
HM	Hideki Matsui	180.00

Stitches Jersey

		NM/M
Common Player:		4.00
Production 299 Sets		
Golds:		No Pricing
Production 25 Sets		
JB	Jeff Bagwell	6.00
RB	Rocco Baldelli	4.00
HB	Hank Blalock	6.00
HC	Hee Seop Choi	4.00
RC	Roger Clemens	15.00
JD	J.D. Drew	4.00
AD	Adam Dunn	8.00
JE	Jim Edmonds	6.00
RF	Rafael Furcal	4.00
JG	Jason Giambi	6.00
TG	Troy Glaus	6.00
SG	Shawn Green	4.00
KG	Ken Griffey Jr.	10.00
VG	Vladimir Guerrero	8.00
TH	Torii Hunter	6.00
RJ	Randy Johnson	8.00
AJ	Andruw Jones	6.00
CJ	Chipper Jones	8.00
JK	Jeff Kent	4.00
ML	Mike Lowell	4.00
GM	Greg Maddux	10.00
PM	Pedro J. Martinez	8.00
HM	Hideki Matsui	40.00
MM	Matt Morris	6.00
HN	Hideo Nomo	8.00
MO	Magglio Ordonez	6.00
RO	Roy Oswalt	4.00
CP	Corey Patterson	6.00
AP	Andy Pettitte	6.00
MI	Mike Piazza	8.00
MP	Mark Prior	8.00
AL	Albert Pujols	15.00
AR	Alex Rodriguez	10.00
IR	Ivan Rodriguez	6.00
CS	Curt Schilling	6.00
GS	Gary Sheffield	6.00
AS	Alfonso Soriano	6.00
SS	Sammy Sosa	15.00
IS	Ichiro Suzuki	25.00
JT	Jim Thome	8.00
DW	Dontrelle Willis	8.00
KW	Kerry Wood	8.00

Stitches Patch

		NM/M
Common Player:		15.00
Production 99 Sets		
Golds:		No Pricing
Production 10 Sets		
JB	Jeff Bagwell	25.00
RB	Rocco Baldelli	15.00
HB	Hank Blalock	25.00
HC	Hee Seop Choi	15.00
RC	Roger Clemens	40.00
JD	J.D. Drew	15.00
AD	Adam Dunn	15.00
JE	Jim Edmonds	20.00
RF	Rafael Furcal	15.00
JG	Jason Giambi	15.00
TG	Troy Glaus	15.00
SG	Shawn Green	15.00
KG	Ken Griffey Jr.	50.00
VG	Vladimir Guerrero	25.00
TH	Torii Hunter	15.00
RJ	Randy Johnson	30.00
AJ	Andruw Jones	15.00
CJ	Chipper Jones	25.00
JK	Jeff Kent	15.00
ML	Mike Lowell	15.00
GM	Greg Maddux	35.00
PM	Pedro J. Martinez	25.00
HM	Hideki Matsui	85.00
MM	Matt Morris	15.00
HN	Hideo Nomo	40.00
MO	Magglio Ordonez	15.00
RO	Roy Oswalt	15.00
CP	Corey Patterson	20.00
AP	Andy Pettitte	20.00
MI	Mike Piazza	40.00
MP	Mark Prior	15.00
AL	Albert Pujols	40.00
AR	Alex Rodriguez	50.00
IR	Ivan Rodriguez	20.00
CS	Curt Schilling	20.00
GS	Gary Sheffield	15.00
AS	Alfonso Soriano	20.00
SS	Sammy Sosa	35.00
IS	Ichiro Suzuki	120.00
JT	Jim Thome	20.00
DW	Dontrelle Willis	20.00
KW	Kerry Wood	25.00

Marble Bust

		NM/M
Common Player:		
YB	Yogi Berra/125	40.00
YB	Yogi Berra/250	25.00
RC	Roberto Clemente/250	70.00
NG	Nomar Garciaparra/250	40.00
JG	Jason Giambi	25.00
BG	Bob Gibson/125	30.00
BG	Bob Gibson/250	25.00
KG	Ken Griffey Jr./250	40.00
MM	Mickey Mantle/80	80.00
MM	Mickey Mantle/250	80.00
HM	Hideki Matsui/250	60.00
SM	Stan Musial/250	50.00
BRS	Babe Ruth/Sox/250	60.00
BRY	Babe Ruth/Yanks/125	75.00
BRY	Babe Ruth/Yanks/250	65.00
NRA	Nolan Ryan/Astros/125	60.00
NRA	Nolan Ryan/Astros/250	50.00
NRM	Nolan Ryan/Mets/125	60.00
NRM	Nolan Ryan/Mets/250	50.00
TSM	Tom Seaver/Mets/125	40.00
TSM	Tom Seaver/Mets/250	30.00
TSR	Tom Seaver/Reds/125	40.00
TSR	Tom Seaver/Reds/250	30.00
DS	Duke Snider/100	40.00
DS	Duke Snider/250	40.00
SS	Sammy Sosa/250	40.00
IS	Ichiro Suzuki/250	50.00
TW	Ted Williams/125	65.00
TW	Ted Williams/250	50.00

Marble Autograph

No pricing due to scarcity.

Pewter Bust

		NM/M
Common Player:		
YB	Yogi Berra/75	40.00
YB	Yogi Berra/100	40.00
RC	Roberto Clemente/100	100.00
NG	Nomar Garciaparra/100	60.00
JG	Jason Giambi/100	40.00
BG	Bob Gibson/75	40.00
BG	Bob Gibson/100	40.00
KG	Ken Griffey Jr./100	70.00
MM	Mickey Mantle/75	125.00
MM	Mickey Mantle/100	125.00
HM	Hideki Matsui/100	50.00
SM	Stan Musial/100	60.00
BRS	Babe Ruth/Sox/100	80.00
BRY	Babe Ruth/Yanks/75	90.00
BRY	Babe Ruth/Yanks/100	90.00
NRA	Nolan Ryan/Astros/75	80.00
NRA	Nolan Ryan/Astros/100	80.00
NRM	Nolan Ryan/Mets/75	80.00
NRM	Nolan Ryan/Mets/100	80.00
TSM	Tom Seaver/Mets/75	40.00
TSM	Tom Seaver/Mets/100	40.00
TSR	Tom Seaver/Reds/100	40.00
TSR	Tom Seaver/Reds/75	40.00
DS	Duke Snider/75	40.00
DS	Duke Snider/100	40.00
SS	Sammy Sosa/100	60.00
IS	Ichiro Suzuki/100	65.00
TW	Ted Williams/75	100.00
TW	Ted Williams/100	100.00

Pewter Autograph Bust

No pricing due to scarcity.

Signs of Success

		NM/M
Common Player:		6.00
MI	Milton Bradley/220	10.00
DB	Dewon Brazelton/299	6.00
JB	John Buck/98	8.00
MB	Mark Buehrle/220	10.00
BR	Brandon Claussen/121	6.00
BC	Brad Cresse/121	10.00
JD	Johnny Damon/297	30.00
BD	Ben Diggins/299	6.00
AG	Alex Graman/215	10.00
KG	Ken Griffey Jr./299	90.00
TG	Tony Gwynn/49	80.00
DH	Drew Henson/246	15.00
BH	Ben Howard/299	6.00
HI	Hansel Izquierdo/299	8.00
JJ	Jimmy Journell/98	8.00
DK	David Kelton/102	8.00
KL	Kenny Lofton/296	15.00
CM	Corwin Malone/103	8.00
BP	Brandon Phillips/131	10.00
SR	Scott Rolen/100	20.00
CC	C.C. Sabathia/106	15.00
MT	Mark Teixeira/280	25.00
TH	Matt Thornton/298	6.00
AH	Andy Van Hekken/299	8.00
JU	Justin Wayne/299	8.00
JW	Jayson Werth/299	8.00
JE	Jerome Williams/103	15.00

2003 Upper Deck Finite

		NM/M
Complete Set (380):		
Common Player (1-100):		1.00
Production 1,999		
Common (101-150):		1.00
Production 1,599		
Common (151-180):		2.00
Production 499		
Common (181-200):		2.50
Production 299		
Common (201-300):		1.50
Production 1,299		
Common (301-330):		3.00
Production 599		
Common (331-360):		3.00
Production 299		
Common (361-380):		5.00
Production 150		
Pack (3):		9.00
Box (10):		80.00
1	Darin Erstad	1.00
2	Garret Anderson	1.50
3	Tim Salmon	1.00
4	Troy Glaus	1.50
5	Luis Gonzalez	1.00
6	Randy Johnson	2.00
7	Curt Schilling	1.50
8	Andruw Jones	1.50
9	Gary Sheffield	1.50
10	Rafael Furcal	1.00
11	Greg Maddux	3.00
12	Chipper Jones	2.50
13	Tony Batista	1.00
14	Jay Gibbons	1.00
15	Johnny Damon	1.00
16	Derek Lowe	1.00
17	Nomar Garciaparra	3.00
18	Pedro J. Martinez	2.00
19	Manny Ramirez	1.50
20	Mark Prior	2.00
21	Kerry Wood	1.50
22	Corey Patterson	1.00
23	Sammy Sosa	3.00
24	Moises Alou	1.00
25	Magglio Ordonez	1.00
26	Frank Thomas	1.50
27	Paul Konerko	1.00
28	Bartolo Colon	1.00
29	Adam Dunn	1.00
30	Austin Kearns	1.00
31	Aaron Boone	1.00
32	Ken Griffey Jr.	2.50
33	Omar Vizquel	1.00
34	C.C. Sabathia	1.00
35	Brandon Phillips	1.00
36	Larry Walker	1.00
37	Preston Wilson	1.00
38	Todd Helton	1.50
39	Eric Munson	1.00
40	Ivan Rodriguez	1.50
41	Josh Beckett	1.50
42	Roy Oswalt	1.00
43	Craig Biggio	1.00
44	Jeff Bagwell	1.50
45	Dontrelle Willis	1.00
46	Carlos Beltran	1.00
47	Brent Mayne	1.00
48	Hideo Nomo	1.00
49	Rickey Henderson	1.00
50	Adrian Beltre	1.00
51	Miguel Cabrera	2.00
52	Kazuhisa Ishii	1.00
53	Richie Sexson	1.00
54	Torii Hunter	1.00
55	Jacque Jones	1.00
56	A.J. Pierzynski	1.00
57	Jose Vidro	1.00
58	Vladimir Guerrero	2.00
59	Tom Glavine	1.00
60	Jose Reyes	1.00
61	Mike Piazza	2.50
62	Jorge Posada	1.50
63	Mike Mussina	1.50
64	Robin Ventura	1.00
65	Mariano Rivera	1.00
66	Roger Clemens	3.00
67	Jason Giambi	2.00
68	Bernie Williams	1.50
69	Alfonso Soriano	2.00
70	Derek Jeter	5.00
71	Miguel Tejada	1.50
72	Eric Chavez	1.00
73	Tim Hudson	1.00
74	Barry Zito	1.50
75	Pat Burrell	1.00
76	Jim Thome	2.00
77	Bobby Abreu	1.00
78	Brian Giles	1.00
79	Reggie Sanders	1.00
80	Ryan Klesko	1.00
81	Edgardo Alfonzo	1.00
82	Rich Aurilia	1.00
83	Barry Bonds	5.00
84	Mike Cameron	1.00
85	Kazuhiro Sasaki	1.00
86	Bret Boone	1.00
87	Ichiro Suzuki	3.00
88	J.D. Drew	1.00
89	Jim Edmonds	1.50
90	Scott Rolen	2.00
91	Matt Morris	1.00
92	Tino Martinez	1.00
93	Albert Pujols	3.00
94	Rocco Baldelli	1.00
95	Hank Blalock	1.50
96	Alex Rodriguez	3.00
97	Rafael Palmeiro	1.50
98	Eric Hinske	1.00
99	Orlando Hudson	1.00
100	Carlos Delgado	1.50
101	Albert Pujols	3.00
102	Alex Rodriguez	3.00
103	Alfonso Soriano	2.00
104	Andruw Jones	1.50
105	Barry Zito	1.50
106	Bernie Williams	1.50
107	Carlos Delgado	1.50
108	Chipper Jones	2.50
109	Curt Schilling	1.50
110	Doug Mientkiewicz	1.00
111	Frank Thomas	1.50
112	Garret Anderson	1.50
113	Gary Sheffield	1.50
114	Greg Maddux	3.00
115	Hank Blalock	4.00
116	Hideki Matsui	4.00
117	Hideo Nomo	1.50
118	Ichiro Suzuki	3.00
119	Ivan Rodriguez	1.50
120	Jason Giambi	2.00
121	Jeff Bagwell	1.50
122	Jeff Kent	1.00
123	Jerome Williams	1.00
124	Jeromy Burnitz	1.00
125	Jim Thome	2.00
126	Jose Cruz Jr.	1.00
127	Ken Griffey Jr.	2.50
128	Kerry Wood	1.50
129	Lance Berkman	1.50
130	Luis Gonzalez	1.00
131	Manny Ramirez	1.50
132	Mark Prior	2.00
133	Miguel Cabrera	2.00
134	Miguel Tejada	1.50
135	Mike Piazza	2.50
136	Pat Burrell	1.00
137	Pedro J. Martinez	2.00
138	Rafael Furcal	2.00
139	Randy Johnson	2.00
140	Rich Harden	2.00
141	Rickey Henderson	1.50
142	Roberto Alomar	1.50
143	Roger Clemens	3.00

144	Sammy Sosa	3.00
145	Shawn Green	1.00
146	Todd Helton	1.50
147	Tom Glavine	1.00
148	Torii Hunter	1.00
149	Troy Glaus	1.00
150	Vladimir Guerrero	2.00
151	Adam Dunn	2.00
152	Albert Pujols	6.00
153	Alex Rodriguez	6.00
154	Alfonso Soriano	3.00
155	Andruw Jones	2.50
156	Barry Bonds	8.00
157	Carlos Delgado	2.50
158	Chipper Jones	3.00
159	Derek Jeter	8.00
160	Gary Sheffield	2.50
161	Hank Blalock	2.50
162	Hideki Matsui	6.00
163	Ichiro Suzuki	4.00
164	J.D. Drew	2.00
165	Jason Giambi	3.00
166	Jeff Bagwell	3.00
167	Jeff Kent	2.00
168	Jim Edmonds	2.00
169	Jim Thome	3.00
170	Ken Griffey Jr.	5.00
171	Luis Gonzalez	2.00
172	Magglio Ordonez	2.00
173	Manny Ramírez	2.50
174	Mike Lowell	2.00
175	Mike Piazza	4.00
176	Nomar Garciaparra	6.00
177	Rafael Palmeiro	2.50
178	Shawn Green	2.00
179	Troy Glaus	2.00
180	Vladimir Guerrero	3.00
181	Albert Pujols	8.00
182	Alex Rodriguez	8.00
183	Alfonso Soriano	4.00
184	Bernie Williams	2.50
185	Chipper Jones	4.00
186	Derek Jeter	10.00
187	Hideki Matsui	8.00
188	Ichiro Suzuki	6.00
189	Jim Thome	3.00
190	Joe DiMaggio	8.00
191	Ken Griffey Jr.	6.00
192	Mickey Mantle	12.00
193	Mike Piazza	5.00
194	Pedro J. Martinez	4.00
195	Randy Johnson	4.00
196	Roger Clemens	6.00
197	Sammy Sosa	6.00
198	Ted Williams	8.00
199	Troy Glaus	2.50
200	Vladimir Guerrero	3.00
201	Aaron Looper RC	2.00
202	Alejandro Machado	1.50
203	Alfredo Gonzalez RC	2.00
204	Andrew Brown RC	1.50
205	Anthony Ferrari	1.50
206	Aquilino Lopez RC	2.00
207	Beau Kemp RC	2.00
208	Bernie Castro	1.50
209	Bobby Madritsch RC	8.00
210	Brandon Villafuerte	1.50
211	Brent Hoard RC	2.00
212	Brian Stokes	1.50
213	Carlos Mendez	1.50
214	Chris Capuano RC	4.00
215	Chris Waters	1.50
216	Clint Barmes RC	5.00
217	Colin Porter RC	1.50
218	Cory Stewart	1.50
219	Craig Brazell RC	3.00
220	D.J. Carrasco RC	1.50
221	Daniel Cabrera RC	1.50
222	Dave Matranga RC	2.00
223	David Sanders	1.50
224	Diegomar Markwell	1.50
225	Edgar Gonzalez RC	2.00
226	Felix Sanchez	1.50
227	Fernando Cabrera RC	2.00
228	Francisco Cruceta RC	2.00
229	Francisco Rosario RC	2.00
230	Garrett Atkins	1.50
231	Gerald Laird	1.50
232	Guillermo Quiroz RC	4.00
233	Heath Bell RC	2.00
234	Delmon Young RC	10.00
235	Jason Shiell RC	2.00
236	Jeremy Bonderman	10.00
237	Jeremy Griffiths	1.50
238	Jeremy Guthrie	1.50
239	Jeremy Wedel RC	2.00
240	Carlos Rivera	1.50
241	Joe Valentine	1.50
242	Jon Leicester	1.50
243	Jonathan Pridie	1.50
244	Jorge Cordova	1.50
245	Jose Castillo	1.50
246	Josh Hall RC	2.00
247	Josh Stewart RC	1.50
248	Josh Willingham RC	3.00
249	Julio Manon RC	1.50
250	Kevin Correia RC	1.50
251	Kevin Ohme RC	2.00
252	Kevin Tolar	1.50
253	Luis De Los Santos	1.50
254	Jermaine Clark	1.50
255	Mark Malaska RC	2.00
256	Juan Dominguez	1.50
257	Michael Hessman RC	1.50
258	Micheal Nakamura RC	2.00
259	Miguel Ojeda RC	1.50
260	Mike Gallo	1.50
261	Edwin Jackson RC	6.00
262	Mike Ryan RC	1.50
263	Nate Bland RC	1.50
264	Nate Robertson	3.00
265	Nook Logan RC	2.00
266	Phil Seibel RC	1.50
267	Prentice Redman RC	2.00
268	Rafael Betancourt	1.50
269	Rett Johnson RC	2.00
270	Richard Fischer	1.50
271	Rick Roberts RC	2.00
272	Roger Deago	1.50
273	Ryan Cameron RC	1.50
274	Shane Bazzell	2.00
275	Erasmo Ramirez	1.50
276	Terrmel Sledge RC	2.00
277	Tim Olson RC	3.00
278	Tommy Phelps	1.50
279	Tommy Whiteman	1.50
280	Willie Eyre RC	2.00
281	Alex Prieto RC	2.00
282	Michel Hernandez RC	1.50
283	Greg Jones RC	1.50
284	Victor Martinez	1.50
285	Tom Gregorio RC	2.00
286	Marcus Thames	1.50
287	Jorge DePaula RC	1.50
288	Aaron Miles RC	3.00
289	Reynaldo Garcia	1.50
290	Brian Sweeney RC	1.50
291	Pete LaForest RC	2.00
292	Pete Zoccolilo RC	1.50
293	Danny Garcia RC	1.50
294	Jonny Gomes	1.50
295	Rosman Garcia RC	1.50
296	Mike Edwards	1.50
297	Marlon Byrd	1.50
298	Khalil Greene	4.00
299	Jose Valverde	1.50
300	Drew Henson	1.50
301	Chris Bootcheck	3.00
302	Matt Belisle	3.00
303	Kevin Gregg	3.00
304	Bobby Jenks	3.00
305	Jason Young	3.00
306	Laynce Nix	3.00
307	Robb Quinlan	3.00
308	Chase Utley	3.00
309	Humberto Quintero RC	4.00
310	Tim Raines Jr.	3.00
311	Stephen Smitherman	3.00
312	Jason Anderson	3.00
313	Joe Dawley	3.00
314	Chad Cordero RC	3.00
315	Victor Alvarez	3.00
316	Jimmy Gobble	3.00
317	Jared Fernandez	3.00
318	Eric Bruntlett	3.00
319	Neal Cotts	3.00
320	Ryan Madson	3.00
321	Rocco Baldelli	3.00
322	Graham Koonce RC	3.00
323	Bobby Crosby	3.00
324	Mike Wood	3.00
325	Jesse Garcia	3.00
326	Noah Lowry	6.00
327	Edwin Almonte	3.00
328	Justin Morneau	3.00
329	Steve Colyer	3.00
330	Vinnie Chulk	3.00
331	Brian Schmack	3.00
332	Stephen Randolph RC	3.00
333	Pedro Feliciano	3.00
334	Koyie Hill	3.00
335	Geoff Geary RC	3.00
336	Jon Switzer	3.00
337	Xavier Nady	3.00
338	Rich Harden	4.00
339	Dontrelle Willis	4.00
340	Angel Berroa	3.00
341	Jerome Williams	3.00
342	Brandon Claussen	3.00
343	Kurt Ainsworth	3.00
344	Horacio Ramirez	3.00
345	Hee Seop Choi	3.00
346	Billy Traber	3.00
347	Brandon Phillips	3.00
348	Jody Gerut	3.00
349	Mark Teixeira	4.00

350	Javier Lopez	3.00
351	Miguel Cabrera	5.00
352	Brad Lidge	3.00
353	Mike MacDougal	3.00
354	Ken Harvey	3.00
355	Chien-Ming Wang RC	40.00
356	Aaron Heilman	3.00
357	Jason Phillips	3.00
358	Jason Bay	3.00
359	Arnie Munoz	3.00
360	Ian Ferguson	3.00
361	Ryan Wagner RC	8.00
362	Rickie Weeks RC	30.00
363	Chad Gaudin RC	8.00
364	Jason Gilfillan RC	5.00
365	Jason Roach	5.00
366	Jhonny Peralta	6.00
367	Mike Neu RC	5.00
368	Jose Contreras RC	10.00
369	Wilfredo Ledezma RC	5.00
370	Lew Ford RC	8.00
371	Luis Ayala RC	5.00
372	Bo Hart RC	5.00
373	Brandon Webb RC	15.00
374	Dan Haren	15.00
375	Hideki Matsui	50.00
376	Jeff Duncan RC	8.00
377	Matt Kata RC	5.00
378	Oscar Villarreal RC	5.00
379	Rob Hammock RC	5.00
380	Todd Wellemeyer RC	5.00

Game Face (193-217):
Common Rookie 5.00
Production 299

193	Aaron Looper RC	5.00
194	Alex Prieto RC	5.00
195	Bo Hart RC	5.00
196	Chad Gaudin RC	8.00
197	Colin Porter RC	5.00
198	D.J. Carrasco RC	5.00
199	Dan Haren	10.00
200	Delmon Young RC	25.00
201	Dontrelle Willis	5.00
202	Jon Switzer	5.00
203	Edwin Jackson RC	8.00
204	Fernando Cabrera RC	5.00
205	Garrett Atkins	8.00
206	Jeremy Bonderman	12.00
207	Kevin Ohme RC	5.00
208	Khalil Greene	10.00
209	Luis Ayala RC	5.00
210	Matt Kata RC	5.00
211	Noah Lowry	10.00
212	Rich Harden	5.00
213	Rickie Weeks RC	15.00
214	Rosman Garcia RC	5.00
215	Ryan Wagner RC	5.00
216	Tom Gregorio RC	5.00
217	Wilfredo Ledezma RC	5.00

SP Authentic (190-239):
Common SP Authentic Rookie: 4.00
Production 699

190	Aaron Looper	4.00
191	Alex Prieto	4.00
192	Alfredo Gonzalez RC	4.00
193	Andrew Brown RC	4.00
194	Anthony Ferrari	4.00
195	Aquilino Lopez RC	4.00
196	Beau Kemp RC	4.00
197	Bo Hart RC	4.00
198	Chad Gaudin RC	10.00
199	Colin Porter RC	4.00
200	D.J. Carrasco RC	20.00
201	Dan Haren	4.00
202	Danny Garcia RC	4.00
203	Jon Switzer	4.00
204	Edwin Jackson RC	4.00
205	Fernando Cabrera RC	4.00
206	Garrett Atkins	6.00
207	Gerald Laird	4.00
208	Greg Jones RC	4.00
209	Ian Ferguson RC	4.00
210	Jason Roach	4.00
211	Jason Shiell RC	4.00
212	Jeremy Bonderman	15.00
213	Jeremy Wedel RC	4.00
214	Jhonny Peralta	4.00
215	Delmon Young RC	35.00
216	Jorge DePaula RC	4.00
217	Josh Hall RC	4.00
218	Julio Manon RC	4.00
219	Kevin Correia RC	4.00
220	Kevin Ohme RC	4.00
221	Kevin Tolar	4.00
222	Luis Ayala RC	4.00
223	Luis De Los Santos	4.00
224	Chad Cordero RC	4.00
225	Mark Malaska RC	4.00
226	Khalil Greene	10.00
227	Micheal Nakamura RC	4.00
228	Michel Hernandez RC	4.00

229	Miguel Ojeda RC	4.00
230	Mike Neu RC	4.00
231	Nate Bland RC	4.00
232	Pete LaForest RC	4.00
233	Rickie Weeks RC	20.00
234	Rosman Garcia RC	4.00
235	Ryan Wagner RC	4.00
236	Lance Niekro	4.00
237	Tom Gregorio RC	4.00
238	Tommy Phelps	4.00
239	Wilfredo Ledezma RC	4.00

SPX (179-193, 381-387):

179	Chad Gaudin/150 RC	15.00
180	Chris Capuano/150 RC	15.00
181	Danny Garcia/150 RC	8.00
182	Delmon Young/150 RC	50.00
183	Edwin Jackson/150 RC	20.00
184	Greg Jones/150 RC	8.00
185	Jeremy Bonderman/150	25.00
186	Jorge DePaula/150 RC	8.00
187	Khalil Greene/150	25.00
188	Chad Cordero/150 RC	8.00
189	Miguel Cabrera/150	10.00
190	Rich Harden/150	10.00
191	Rickie Weeks/150 RC	30.00
192	Rosman Garcia/150 RC	8.00
193	Tom Gregorio/150 RC	8.00
381	Andrew Brown/Jsy/Auto./355 RC	15.00
382	Delmon Young/Jsy/Auto/355 RC	400.00
383	Colin Porter/Jsy/Auto./355 RC	15.00
385	Rickie Weeks/Jsy/Auto./355 RC	200.00
386	Dave Matranga/Jsy/Auto./355 RC	15.00
387	Bo Hart/Jsy/Auto./355 RC	15.00

UD Authentics (131-140):
Common Authentics: 5.00
Production 150

131	Dan Haren	10.00
132	Delmon Young RC	25.00
133	Dontrelle Willis	6.00
134	Edwin Jackson RC	15.00
135	Jeremy Bonderman	15.00
136	Khalil Greene	10.00
137	Rich Harden	5.00
138	Rickie Weeks RC	20.00
139	Rosman Garcia RC	5.00
140	Ryan Wagner RC	5.00

Gold

Gold (1-150):	1-2X
Gold (151-180):	1X
Production 199	
Gold (181-200):	1-2X
Production 99	

Elements Jersey

		NM/M
	Common Player:	4.00
JB	Jeff Bagwell	8.00
RB	Rocco Baldelli	6.00
HB	Hank Blalock	6.00
HC	Hee Seop Choi	4.00
JD	J.D. Drew	5.00
AD	Adam Dunn	6.00
JE	Jim Edmonds	5.00
SG	Shawn Green	5.00
KG	Ken Griffey Jr./SP	15.00
TH	Torii Hunter	6.00

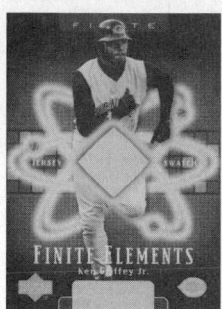

CJ	Chipper Jones	6.00
JK	Jeff Kent	4.00
ML	Mike Lowell	4.00
GM	Greg Maddux	8.00
HM	Hideki Matsui	25.00
MM	Matt Morris	5.00
RO	Roy Oswalt	5.00
CP	Corey Patterson	5.00
AP	Andy Pettitte	6.00
MI	Mike Piazza	8.00
MP	Mark Prior	10.00
AL	Albert Pujols	15.00
AR	Alex Rodriguez	10.00
AS	Alfonso Soriano	6.00
IS	Ichiro Suzuki	15.00
JT	Jim Thome	10.00
RW	Rickie Weeks/SP	15.00
DW	Dontrelle Willis	6.00
KW	Kerry Wood	8.00
DY	Delmon Young/SP	20.00

Elements Patch

No pricing due to scarcity.
Production 25 Sets
Patch Gold: No Pricing
Production 10 Sets

First Class Jersey

		NM/M
	Common Player:	4.00
RC	Roger Clemens	10.00
JD	Joe DiMaggio/SP	80.00
TG	Troy Glaus	5.00
LG	Luis Gonzalez	4.00
KG	Ken Griffey Jr.	12.00
VG	Vladimir Guerrero	8.00
RJ	Randy Johnson	8.00
CJ	Chipper Jones	6.00
MM	Mickey Mantle/SP	100.00
PM	Pedro J. Martinez	8.00
HM	Hideki Matsui	25.00
MP	Mike Piazza	8.00
AP	Albert Pujols	20.00
AR	Alex Rodriguez	10.00
AS	Alfonso Soriano	6.00
SS	Sammy Sosa	10.00
IS	Ichiro Suzuki	15.00
JT	Jim Thome	10.00
BW	Bernie Williams	6.00
TW	Ted Williams/SP	75.00

Signatures

		NM/M
	Common Auto.:	6.00
	Varying quantities produced	
EA	Erick Almonte/355	6.00
SZ	Shane Bazzell/250	6.00
MC	Miguel Cabrera/100	50.00
RC	Roger Clemens/50	150.00
WE	Willie Eyre/200	6.00
NG	Nomar Garciaparra/50	80.00
RK	Rob Hammock/200	6.00
RN	Rich Harden/150	25.00
BH	Bo Hart/15	8.00
HM	Hideki Matsui/99	250.00
MP	Mark Prior/75	40.00
JR	Jose Reyes/100	40.00
SR	Scott Rolen/100	40.00
CS	C.C. Sabathia/50	15.00
DS	David Sanders/150	6.00
PS	Phil Seibel/200	6.00
IS	Ichiro Suzuki/25	350.00
MT	Mark Teixeira/200	25.00
BW	Brandon Webb/150	25.00
RW	Rickie Weeks/25	
JW	Jerome Williams/150	15.00
DW	Dontrelle Willis/50	40.00
DY	Delmon Young/50	80.00

Stars and Stripes

		NM/M
	Common Player:	2.00
	Production 299 Sets	
USA-1	Justin Orenduff	2.00
USA-2	Micah Owings	2.00
USA-3	Steven Register	2.00
USA-4	Huston Street	6.00
USA-5	Justin Verlander	8.00
USA-6	Jered Weaver	8.00
USA-7	Matt Campbell	4.00
USA-8	Stephen Head	2.00
USA-9	Mark Romanczuk	2.00
USA-10	Jeff Clement	10.00
USA-11	Mike Nickeas	2.00
USA-12	Tyler Greene	2.00
USA-13	Paul Janish	2.00
USA-14	Jeff Larish	2.00
USA-15	Eric Patterson	2.00
USA-16	Dustin Pedroia	6.00
USA-17	Michael Griffin	2.00
USA-18	Brent Lillibridge	2.00
USA-19	Danny Putnam	5.00
USA-20	Seth Smith	5.00

Stars and Stripes Jersey

		NM/M
	Common Player:	4.00
J1	Justin Orenduff	4.00
J2	Micah Owings	4.00
J3	Steven Register	4.00
J4	Huston Street	8.00
J5	Justin Verlander	8.00
J6	Jered Weaver	8.00
J7	Matt Campbell	6.00
J8	Stephen Head	4.00
J9	Mark Romanczuk	4.00
J10	Jeff Clement	10.00
J11	Mike Nickeas	4.00
J12	Tyler Greene	4.00
J13	Paul Janish	4.00
J14	Jeff Larish	4.00
J15	Eric Patterson	4.00
J16	Dustin Pedroia	8.00
J17	Michael Griffin	4.00
J18	Brent Lillibridge	4.00
J19	Danny Putnam	6.00
J20	Seth Smith	6.00

SPX Jersey Autograph

		NM/M
	Production 355	
DW	Dontrelle Willis	40.00
KG	Khalil Greene	60.00
RH	Rich Harden	35.00

2003 Upper Deck First Pitch

		NM/M
Complete Set (300):		50.00
Common Player:		.10
Common SP (271-300):		1.00
Inserted 1:4		
Pack (5):		1.00
Box (36):		25.00
1	John Lackey	.10
2	Alex Cintron	.10
3	Jose Leon	.10
4	Bobby Hill	.10
5	Brandon Larson	.10
6	Raul Gonzalez	.10
7	Ben Broussard	.10
8	Earl Snyder	.10
9	Ramon Santiago	.10
10	Jason Lane	.10
11	Rob Hammock **RC**	.50
12	Kirk Saarloos	.10
13	Juan Brito	.10
14	Runelvys Hernandez	.10
15	Shawn Sedlacek	.10
16	Jayson Durocher	.10
17	Kevin Frederick	.10
18	Zach Day	.10
19	Marco Scutaro	.10
20	Marcus Thames	.10
21	Esteban German	.10
22	Brett Myers	.10
23	Oliver Perez	.10
24	Dennis Tankersley	.10
25	Julius Matos	.10
26	Jake Peavy	.10
27	Eric Cyr	.10
28	Mike Crudale	.10
29	Josh Pearce	.10
30	Carl Crawford	.10
31	Tim Salmon	.25
32	Troy Glaus	.50
33	Adam Kennedy	.10
34	David Eckstein	.10
35	Bengie Molina	.10
36	Jarrod Washburn	.10
37	Ramon Ortiz	.10
38	Eric Chavez	.25
39	Miguel Tejada	.25
40	Adam Piatt	.10
41	Jermaine Dye	.10
42	Olmedo Saenz	.10
43	Tim Hudson	.20
44	Barry Zito	.25
45	Billy Koch	.10
46	Shannon Stewart	.10
47	Kelvim Escobar	.10
48	Jose Cruz Jr.	.10
49	Vernon Wells	.10
50	Roy Halladay	.10
51	Esteban Loaiza	.10
52	Eric Hinske	.10
53	Steve Cox	.10
54	Brent Abernathy	.10
55	Ben Grieve	.10
56	Aubrey Huff	.10
57	Jared Sandberg	.10
58	Paul Wilson	.10
59	Tanyon Sturtze	.10
60	Jim Thome	.50
61	Omar Vizquel	.20
62	C.C. Sabathia	.10
63	Chris Magruder	.10
64	Ricky Gutierrez	.10
65	Einar Diaz	.10
66	Danys Baez	.10
67	Ichiro Suzuki	.75
68	Ruben Sierra	.10
69	Carlos Guillen	.10
70	Mark McLemore	.10
71	Dan Wilson	.10
72	Jamie Moyer	.10
73	Joel Pineiro	.10
74	Edgar Martinez	.10
75	Tony Batista	.10
76	Jay Gibbons	.10
77	Chris Singleton	.10
78	Melvin Mora	.10
79	Geronimo Gil	.10
80	Rodrigo Lopez	.10
81	Jorge Julio	.10
82	Rafael Palmeiro	.40
83	Juan Gonzalez	.40
84	Mike Young	.10
85	Hideki Irabu	.10
86	Chan Ho Park	.10
87	Kevin Mench	.10
88	Doug Davis	.10
89	Pedro J. Martinez	.75
90	Shea Hillenbrand	.10
91	Derek Lowe	.10
92	Jason Varitek	.10
93	Tony Clark	.10
94	John Burkett	.10
95	Frank Castillo	.10
96	Nomar Garciaparra	1.00
97	Rickey Henderson	.25
98	Mike Sweeney	.10
99	Carlos Febles	.10
100	Mark Quinn	.10
101	Raul Ibanez	.10
102	A.J. Hinch	.10
103	Paul Byrd	.10
104	Chuck Knoblauch	.10
105	Dmitri Young	.10
106	Randall Simon	.10
107	Brandon Inge	.10
108	Damion Easley	.10
109	Carlos Pena	.10
110	George Lombard	.10
111	Juan Acevedo	.10
112	Torii Hunter	.25
113	Doug Mientkiewicz	.10
114	David Ortiz	.10
115	Eric Milton	.10
116	Eddie Guardado	.10
117	Cristian Guzman	.10
118	Corey Koskie	.10
119	Magglio Ordonez	.25
120	Mark Buehrle	.10
121	Todd Ritchie	.10
122	Jose Valentin	.10
123	Paul Konerko	.10
124	Carlos Lee	.10
125	Jon Garland	.10
126	Jason Giambi	.25
127	Derek Jeter	1.50
128	Roger Clemens	1.00
129	Raul Mondesi	.25
130	Jorge Posada	.25
131	Rondell White	.10
132	Robin Ventura	.20
133	Mike Mussina	.40
134	Jeff Bagwell	.50
135	Craig Biggio	.20
136	Morgan Ensberg	.10
137	Richard Hidalgo	.10
138	Brad Ausmus	.10
139	Roy Oswalt	.20
140	Carlos Hernandez	.10
141	Shane Reynolds	.10
142	Gary Sheffield	.25
143	Andruw Jones	.25
144	Tom Glavine	.25
145	Rafael Furcal	.20
146	Javy Lopez	.10
147	Vinny Castilla	.10
148	Marcus Giles	.10
149	Kevin Millwood	.20
150	Jason Marquis	.10
151	Ruben Quevedo	.10
152	Ben Sheets	.10
153	Geoff Jenkins	.10
154	Jose Hernandez	.10
155	Glendon Rusch	.10
156	Jeffrey Hammonds	.10
157	Alex Sanchez	.10
158	Jim Edmonds	.25
159	Tino Martinez	.10
160	Albert Pujols	.75

161	Eli Marrero	.10
162	Woody Williams	.10
163	Fernando Vina	.10
164	Jason Isringhausen	.10
165	Jason Simontacchi	.10
166	Kerry Robinson	.10
167	Sammy Sosa	.75
168	Juan Cruz	.10
169	Fred McGriff	.20
170	Antonio Alfonseca	.10
171	Jon Lieber	.10
172	Mark Prior	.50
173	Moises Alou	.20
174	Matt Clement	.10
175	Mark Bellhorn	.10
176	Randy Johnson	.50
177	Luis Gonzalez	.20
178	Tony Womack	.10
179	Mark Grace	.25
180	Junior Spivey	.10
181	Byung-Hyun Kim	.10
182	Danny Bautista	.10
183	Brian Anderson	.10
184	Shawn Green	.25
185	Brian Jordan	.10
186	Eric Karros	.10
187	Andy Ashby	.10
188	Cesar Izturis	.10
189	Dave Roberts	.10
190	Eric Gagne	.10
191	Kazuhisa Ishii	.10
192	Adrian Beltre	.10
193	Vladimir Guerrero	.50
194	Tony Armas Jr.	.10
195	Bartolo Colon	.10
196	Troy O'Leary	.10
197	Tomokazu Ohka	.10
198	Brad Wilkerson	.10
199	Orlando Cabrera	.10
200	Barry Bonds	1.50
201	David Bell	.10
202	Tsuyoshi Shinjo	.10
203	Benito Santiago	.10
204	Livan Hernandez	.10
205	Jason Schmidt	.10
206	Kirk Rueter	.10
207	Ramon E. Martinez	.10
208	Mike Lowell	.10
209	Luis Castillo	.10
210	Derek Lee	.10
211	Andy Fox	.10
212	Eric Owens	.10
213	Charles Johnson	.10
214	Brad Penny	.10
215	A.J. Burnett	.10
216	Edgardo Alfonzo	.10
217	Roberto Alomar	.40
218	Rey Ordonez	.10
219	Al Leiter	.10
220	Roger Cedeno	.10
221	Timoniel Perez	.10
222	Jeromy Burnitz	.10
223	Pedro Astacio	.10
224	Joe McEwing	.10
225	Ryan Klesko	.20
226	Ramon Vazquez	.10
227	Mark Kotsay	.10
228	Bubba Trammell	.10
229	Wiki Gonzalez	.10
230	Trevor Hoffman	.10
231	Ron Gant	.10
232	Bobby Abreu	.20
233	Marlon Anderson	.10
234	Jeremy Giambi	.10
235	Jimmy Rollins	.20
236	Mike Lieberthal	.10
237	Vicente Padilla	.10
238	Randy Wolf	.10
239	Pokey Reese	.10
240	Brian Giles	.25
241	Jack Wilson	.10
242	Mike Williams	.10
243	Kip Wells	.10
244	Robert Mackowiak	.10
245	Craig Wilson	.10
246	Adam Dunn	.50
247	Sean Casey	.10
248	Todd Walker	.10
249	Corky Miller	.10
250	Ryan Dempster	.10
251	Reggie Taylor	.10
252	Aaron Boone	.10
253	Larry Walker	.10
254	Jose Ortiz	.10
255	Todd Zeile	.10
256	Bobby Estalella	.10
257	Juan Pierre	.10
258	Terry Shumpert	.10
259	Mike Hampton	.10
260	Denny Stark	.10
261	Shawn Green	.20
262	Derek Lowe	.10
263	Barry Bonds	.50
264	Mike Cameron	.10

265	Luis Castillo	.10
266	Vladimir Guerrero	.40
267	Jason Giambi	.40
268	Eric Gagne	.10
269	Magglio Ordonez	.20
270	Jim Thome	.25
271	Hideki Matsui RC	20.00
272	Jose Contreras RC	4.00
273	Robert Madritsch	1.00
274	Shane Bazzell RC	1.50
275	Felix Sanchez RC	2.00
276	Todd Wellemeyer RC	2.00
277	Lew Ford RC	2.00
278	Jeremy Griffiths	1.00
279	Oscar Villarreal RC	1.00
280	Brandon Webb RC	3.00
281	Delvis Lantigua	1.00
282	Josh Willingham RC	1.00
283	Mike Nicolas RC	1.00
284	Mike Hampton	1.00
285	Jim Thome	2.00
286	Bartolo Colon	1.00
287	Orlando Hernandez	1.00
288	Jeremy Giambi	1.00
289	Jeff Kent	1.50
290	Tom Glavine	1.50
291	Cliff Floyd	1.00
292	Tsuyoshi Shinjo	1.00
293	Jose Cruz Jr.	1.00
294	Edgardo Alfonzo	1.00
295	Andres Galarraga	1.00
296	Troy O'Leary	1.00
297	Eric Karros	1.00
298	Ivan Rodriguez	1.50
299	Fred McGriff	1.50
300	Preston Wilson	1.00

Signature Stars

NM/M

Print runs listed:

NM	Nomar Garciaparra/100	100.00
JG	Jason Giambi/100	30.00
KG	Ken Griffey Jr./100	75.00
KGS	Ken Griffey Sr./800	6.00
SS	Sammy Sosa/50	175.00
IS	Ichiro Suzuki/50	375.00

2003 Upper Deck Game Face

NM/M

Complete Set (192):		
Common Player:		.25
Common Base SP:		1.00
Inserted 1:4		
Common SP (121-150):		2.00
Inserted 1:8		
Common SP (151-192):		3.00
Inserted 1:16		
Pack (5):		4.00
Box (24):		75.00
1	Darin Erstad	.50
2	Garret Anderson	.50
3	Tim Salmon	.50
4	Jarrod Washburn	.25
5	Troy Glaus/SP	1.50
6	Luis Gonzalez	.50
7	Junior Spivey	.25
8	Randy Johnson/SP	2.00
9	Curt Schilling/SP	1.50

10	Andruw Jones	.75
11	Gary Sheffield	.50
12	Rafael Furcal	.25
13	Greg Maddux/SP	3.00
14	Chipper Jones/SP	3.00
15	Tony Batista	.25
16	Rodrigo Lopez	.25
17	Jay Gibbons	.25
18	Shea Hillenbrand	.25
19	Johnny Damon	.25
20	Derek Lowe	.25
21	Nomar Garciaparra	2.50
22	Pedro J. Martinez/SP	2.00
23	Manny Ramirez/SP	1.50
24	Mark Prior	1.00
25	Kerry Wood	.75
26	Corey Patterson	.25
27	Sammy Sosa	2.00
28	Magglio Ordonez	.50
29	Frank Thomas	1.00
30	Paul Konerko	.25
31	Adam Dunn	1.00
32	Austin Kearns	1.00
33	Aaron Boone	.25
34	Ken Griffey Jr./SP	3.00
35	Omar Vizquel	.40
36	C.C. Sabathia	.25
37	Karim Garcia/SP	1.00
38	Larry Walker	.40
39	Preston Wilson	.25
40	Jay Payton	.25
41	Todd Helton/SP	1.50
42	Carlos Pena	.25
43	Eric Munson	.25
44	Mike Lowell	.25
45	Josh Beckett	.25
46	A.J. Burnett	.25
47	Roy Oswalt	.25
48	Craig Biggio	.50
49	Jeff Bagwell	1.50
50	Lance Berkman/SP	1.25
51	Mike Sweeney	.25
52	Carlos Beltran	.25
53	Hideo Nomo	.75
54	Odalis Perez	.25
55	Adrian Beltre	.25
56	Shawn Green/SP	1.00
57	Kazuhisa Ishii/SP	1.00
58	Ben Sheets	.50
59	Richie Sexson	.50
60	Torii Hunter	.50
61	Jacque Jones	.25
62	Eric Milton	.25
63	Corey Koskie	.25
64	A.J. Pierzynski	.25
65	Jose Vidro	.25
66	Bartolo Colon	.25
67	Vladimir Guerrero/SP	1.50
68	Tom Glavine	.50
69	Mike Piazza/SP	3.00
70	Roberto Alomar/SP	1.50
71	Jorge Posada	.75
72	Mike Mussina	.75
73	Robin Ventura	.25
74	Raul Mondesi	.50
75	Roger Clemens/SP	3.00
76	Jason Giambi/SP	2.00
77	Bernie Williams/SP	1.50
78	Alfonso Soriano/SP	2.00
79	Derek Jeter/SP	6.00
80	Miguel Tejada	.75
81	Eric Chavez	.50
82	Tim Hudson	.50
83	Barry Zito	.50
84	Mark Mulder	.50
85	Pat Burrell	1.00
86	Jim Thome	1.00
87	Bobby Abreu	.50
88	Brian Giles	.50
89	Jason Kendall	.40
90	Aramis Ramirez	.25
91	Ryan Klesko	.25
92	Phil Nevin	.25
93	Sean Burroughs	.25
94	J.T. Snow	.25
95	Rich Aurilia	.25
96	Benito Santiago	.25
97	Barry Bonds/SP	6.00
98	Edgar Martinez	.25
99	John Olerud	.25
100	Bret Boone	.25
101	Ichiro Suzuki/SP	3.00
102	J.D. Drew	.50
103	Jim Edmonds	.50
104	Scott Rolen	1.00
105	Matt Morris	.50
106	Tino Martinez	.25
107	Albert Pujols/SP	2.00
108	Aubrey Huff	.25
109	Carl Crawford	.25
110	Rafael Palmeiro	.75
111	Hank Blalock	.25
112	Alex Rodriguez/SP	5.00
113	Kevin Mench/SP	1.00

114	Juan Gonzalez/SP	1.50
115	Shannon Stewart	.25
116	Vernon Wells	.25
117	Josh Phelps	.25
118	Eric Hinske	.25
119	Orlando Hudson	.25
120	Carlos Delgado/SP	1.00
121	David Sanders RC	2.00
122	Rob Hammock RC	2.00
123	Rett Johnson RC	2.00
124	Mike Nicolas RC	2.00
125	Terrmel Sledge RC	3.00
126	Ryan Cameron RC	4.00
127	Prentice Redman RC	2.00
128	Clint Barmes RC	6.00
129	Brent Hoard RC	2.00
130	Willie Eyre RC	2.00
131	Phil Seibel RC	2.00
132	Chris Capuano RC	5.00
133	Bobby Madritsch RC	8.00
134	Shane Bazzell RC	2.00
135	Jeremy Griffiths	3.00
136	Jon Leicester RC	3.00
137	Brandon Webb RC	5.00
138	Todd Wellemeyer RC	2.00
139	Jose Contreras RC	5.00
140	Felix Sanchez RC	2.00
141	Arnie Munoz RC	2.00
142	Delvis Lantigua RC	2.00
143	Francisco Cruceta RC	2.00
144	Josh Willingham RC	3.00
145	Oscar Villarreal RC	2.00
146	Ian Ferguson RC	2.00
147	Pedro Liriano	2.00
148	Lew Ford RC	5.00
149	Jeff Duncan RC	2.00
150	Richard Fischer RC	2.00
151	Troy Glaus	3.00
152	Randy Johnson	5.00
153	Hideki Matsui RC	15.00
154	Chipper Jones	6.00
155	Nomar Garciaparra	10.00
156	Pedro J. Martinez	5.00
157	Ted Williams	15.00
158	Sammy Sosa	8.00
159	Ken Griffey Jr.	8.00
160	Vladimir Guerrero	5.00
161	Mike Piazza	8.00
162	Mickey Mantle	30.00
163	Alfonso Soriano	6.00
164	Derek Jeter	15.00
165	Roger Clemens	15.00
166	Jason Giambi	4.00
167	Barry Bonds	15.00
168	Ichiro Suzuki	8.00
169	Albert Pujols	8.00
170	Mark McGwire	15.00
171	Alex Rodriguez	10.00
172	Ken Griffey Jr., Roy Oswalt	6.00
173	Barry Zito, Troy Glaus	3.00
174	Tim Hudson, Ichiro Suzuki	8.00
175	Alex Rodriguez, Mark Mulder	10.00
176	Tom Glavine, Vladimir Guerrero	4.00
177	Mike Piazza, Greg Maddux	6.00
178	Mark McGwire, Sammy Sosa	10.00
179	Lance Berkman, Mark Prior	4.00
180	Albert Pujols, Kerry Wood	6.00
181	Randy Johnson, Jeff Bagwell	4.00
182	Derek Jeter, Curt Schilling	10.00
183	Barry Bonds, Hideo Nomo	10.00
184	Todd Helton, Kazuhisa Ishii	4.00
185	Freddy Garcia, Eric Chavez	3.00
186	Al Leiter, Chipper Jones	6.00
187	Ted Williams, Nomar Garciaparra	10.00
188	Pedro J. Martinez, Hideki Matsui	15.00
189	Derek Lowe, Bernie Williams	3.00
190	Roger Clemens, Mike Piazza	10.00
191	Mike Mussina, Manny Ramirez	4.00
192	Jason Giambi, Mickey Mantle	20.00

Autograph

NM/M

Common Player:	
Inserted 1:576	

Golds:

		Not Priced
Production 25		
LB	Lance Berkman/SP	50.00
JG	Jason Giambi	40.00
KG	Ken Griffey Jr.	125.00
TH	Todd Helton/SP	45.00
HM	Hideki Matsui/SP	250.00
MM	Mark McGwire/SP	350.00
MP	Mark Prior/SP	40.00
SS	Sammy Sosa	120.00
IS	Ichiro Suzuki/SP	300.00
BZ	Barry Zito	40.00

Gear

		NM/M
Common Player:		4.00
Inserted 1:8		
Patches:		3-5X
Production 100 Sets		
BA	Bobby Abreu	4.00
EA	Edgardo Alfonzo	4.00
JB	Jeff Bagwell	8.00
CB	Carlos Beltran	6.00
LB	Lance Berkman	6.00
AB	Aaron Boone/SP	8.00
PB	Pat Burrell	6.00
EC	Eric Chavez	4.00
RC	Roger Clemens	15.00
CD	Carlos Delgado	4.00
DR	J.D. Drew	4.00
DR2	J.D. Drew	4.00
AD	Adam Dunn	8.00
JE	Jim Edmonds	6.00
DE	Darin Erstad	4.00
DE2	Darin Erstad	4.00
JG	Jason Giambi	6.00
BG	Brian Giles	4.00
TG	Tom Glavine	6.00
GO	Juan Gonzalez	6.00
LG	Luis Gonzalez	4.00
LG2	Luis Gonzalez	4.00
SG	Shawn Green	4.00
TH	Todd Helton/SP	8.00
TI	Tim Hudson	4.00
HU	Torii Hunter	4.00
KI	Kazuhisa Ishii	4.00
RJ	Randy Johnson	8.00
AJ	Andruw Jones	6.00
CJ	Chipper Jones	8.00
JJ	Jacque Jones	4.00
AK	Austin Kearns	4.00
JK	Jason Kendall	4.00
KE	Jeff Kent	6.00
RK	Ryan Klesko	4.00
ML	Mike Lowell	4.00
GM	Greg Maddux	10.00
GM2	Greg Maddux	10.00
EM	Edgar Martinez	6.00
PM	Pedro J. Martinez	8.00
MM	Mike Mussina	8.00
HN	Hideo Nomo	8.00
MO	Magglio Ordonez	4.00
RO	Roy Oswalt	4.00
RP	Rafael Palmeiro	8.00
MiP	Mike Piazza	10.00
JP	Jorge Posada	8.00
MaP	Mark Prior	8.00
MR	Manny Ramirez	8.00
AR	Alex Rodriguez	10.00
AR2	Alex Rodriguez	10.00
IR	Ivan Rodriguez	8.00
SR	Scott Rolen	8.00
CS	Curt Schilling	6.00
RS	Richie Sexson	6.00
AS	Alfonso Soriano	8.00
SS	Sammy Sosa	10.00
IS	Ichiro Suzuki/SP	50.00
MS	Mike Sweeney	4.00
MT	Miguel Tejada	6.00
FT	Frank Thomas	8.00
JT	Jim Thome	8.00
JV	Jose Vidro	4.00
OV	Omar Vizquel	4.00
LW	Larry Walker	4.00
BW	Bernie Williams	6.00
PW	Preston Wilson	4.00
KW	Kerry Wood	8.00
BZ	Barry Zito	4.00
BZ2	Barry Zito	4.00

Patch

Common Player:
Production 100 Sets

2003 Upper Deck Honor Roll

		NM/M
Complete Set (161):		
Common Player:		.20
Common Even # SP (2-60):		1.00
Inserted 1:6		
Common SP (131-161):		3.00
Production 2,500		
Pack (5):		1.50
Box (24):		30.00
1	Derek Jeter	2.00
2	Derek Jeter/SP	5.00
3	Alex Rodriguez	1.50
4	Alex Rodriguez/SP	5.00
5	Roger Clemens	1.50
6	Roger Clemens/SP	4.00
7	Mike Piazza	1.00
8	Mike Piazza/SP	3.00
9	Jeff Bagwell	.50
10	Jeff Bagwell/SP	1.50
11	Vladimir Guerrero	.75
12	Vladimir Guerrero/SP	2.00
13	Ken Griffey Jr.	1.00
14	Ken Griffey Jr./SP	3.00
15	Greg Maddux	1.00
16	Greg Maddux/SP	3.00
17	Chipper Jones	.75
18	Chipper Jones/SP	2.00
19	Randy Johnson	.75
20	Randy Johnson/SP	2.00
21	Miguel Tejada	.50
22	Miguel Tejada/SP	1.50
23	Nomar Garciaparra	1.50
24	Nomar Garciaparra/SP	4.00
25	Ichiro Suzuki	1.50
26	Ichiro Suzuki/SP	4.00
27	Sammy Sosa	1.00
28	Sammy Sosa/SP	3.00
29	Albert Pujols	2.00
30	Albert Pujols/SP	5.00
31	Alfonso Soriano	.75
32	Alfonso Soriano/SP	2.00
33	Barry Bonds	2.00
34	Barry Bonds/SP	6.00
35	Jeff Kent	.30
36	Jeff Kent/SP	1.00
37	Jim Thome	.50
38	Jim Thome/SP	1.50
39	Pedro J. Martinez	.75
40	Pedro J. Martinez/SP	2.00
41	Todd Helton	.50
42	Todd Helton/SP	1.50
43	Troy Glaus	.50
44	Troy Glaus/SP	1.50
45	Mark Prior	.75
46	Mark Prior/SP	2.00
47	Tom Glavine	.40
48	Tom Glavine/SP	1.00
49	Pat Burrell	.40
50	Pat Burrell/SP	1.00
51	Barry Zito	.40
52	Barry Zito/SP	1.00
53	Bernie Williams	.50
54	Bernie Williams/SP	1.50
55	Curt Schilling	.50
56	Curt Schilling/SP	1.50
57	Darin Erstad	.30
58	Darin Erstad/SP	1.00
59	Carlos Delgado	.50
60	Carlos Delgado/SP	1.50
61	Gary Sheffield	.40
62	Gary Sheffield	.40
63	Frank Thomas	.50
64	Frank Thomas	.50
65	Lance Berkman	.40
66	Lance Berkman	.40
67	Shawn Green	.40
68	Shawn Green	.40
69	Hideo Nomo	.40
70	Hideo Nomo	.40
71	Torii Hunter	.40
72	Torii Hunter	.40
73	Roberto Alomar	.50
74	Roberto Alomar	.50
75	Andruw Jones	.50
76	Andruw Jones	.50
77	Scott Rolen	.75
78	Scott Rolen	.75
79	Eric Chavez	.40
80	Eric Chavez	.40
81	Rafael Palmeiro	.50
82	Rafael Palmeiro	.50
83	Bobby Abreu	.20
84	Bobby Abreu	.20
85	Craig Biggio	.20
86	Craig Biggio	.20
87	Rafael Furcal	.20
88	Rafael Furcal	.20
89	Jose Vidro	.20
90	Jose Vidro	.20
91	Luis Gonzalez	.20
92	Luis Gonzalez	.20
93	Roy Oswalt	.20
94	Roy Oswalt	.20
95	Cliff Floyd	.20
96	Cliff Floyd	.20
97	Larry Walker	.20
98	Larry Walker	.20
99	Jim Edmonds	.30
100	Jim Edmonds	.30
101	Adam Dunn	.40
102	Adam Dunn	.40
103	J.D. Drew	.20
104	J.D. Drew	.20
105	Josh Beckett	.20
106	Josh Beckett	.20
107	Brian Giles	.20
108	Brian Giles	.20
109	Magglio Ordonez	.40
110	Magglio Ordonez	.40
111	Edgardo Alfonzo	.20
112	Edgardo Alfonzo	.20
113	Bartolo Colon	.20
114	Bartolo Colon	.20
115	Roy Halladay	.20
116	Roy Halladay	.20
117	Joe Thurston	.20
118	Joe Thurston	.20
119	Brandon Phillips	.20
120	Brandon Phillips	.20
121	Kazuhisa Ishii	.20
122	Kazuhisa Ishii	.20
123	Mike Mussina	.40
124	Mike Mussina	.40
125	Tim Hudson	.40
126	Tim Hudson	.40
127	Mariano Rivera	.20
128	Mariano Rivera	.20
129	Travis Hafner	.20
130	Travis Hafner	.20
131	Hideki Matsui RC	20.00
132	Jose Contreras RC	5.00
133	Jason Anderson RC	3.00
134	Willie Eyre RC	3.00
135	Shane Bazzell RC	3.00
136	Guillermo Quiroz RC	3.00
137	Francisco Cruceta RC	3.00
138	Jhonny Peralta	4.00
139	Aaron Looper RC	3.00
140	Bobby Madritsch RC	6.00
141	Michael Hessman RC	3.00
142	Todd Wellemeyer RC	3.00
143	Matt Bruback RC	3.00
144	Chris Capuano RC	5.00
145	Oscar Villarreal RC	3.00
146	Prentice Redman RC	3.00
147	Jeff Duncan RC	5.00
148	Phil Seibel RC	3.00
149	Arnaldo Munoz	3.00
150	David Sanders RC	3.00
151	Rick Roberts RC	3.00
152	Terrmel Sledge RC	4.00
153	Franklin Perez	3.00
154	Jeremy Wedel RC	3.00
155	Ian Ferguson RC	3.00
156	Josh Hall RC	4.00
157	Rocco Baldelli	3.00
158	Alejandro Machado RC	3.00
159	Jorge Cordova RC	3.00
160	Wilfredo Ledezma RC	3.00
161	Luis Ayala RC	3.00

Gold

Production 25 Sets:
No pricing due to scarcity.

Silver

Even # SP's (2-60):	1-2X
Non-SP's (1-130):	4-8X
SP's (132-161):	.5-1X
Production 150 Sets	

Dean's List

		NM/M
Common Player:		4.00
Inserted 1:24		
RC	Roger Clemens	10.00
RC1	Roger Clemens	10.00
JG1	Jason Giambi	4.00
JG1	Jason Giambi	4.00
TG	Troy Glaus	4.00
TG1	Troy Glaus	4.00
NG	Shawn Green	4.00
NG1	Shawn Green	4.00
VG	Vladimir Guerrero	6.00
VG	Vladimir Guerrero	6.00
KG	Ken Griffey Jr.	10.00
KG1	Ken Griffey Jr.	10.00
CJ	Chipper Jones	8.00
CJ1	Chipper Jones	8.00
HM	Hideki Matsui	20.00
HM1	Hideki Matsui	20.00
HN	Hideo Nomo	10.00
HN1	Hideo Nomo	10.00
MP	Mike Piazza	10.00
MP1	Mike Piazza	10.00
MA	Mark Prior	8.00
MA1	Mark Prior	8.00
AP	Albert Pujols	15.00
AP1	Albert Pujols	15.00
AR	Alex Rodriguez	10.00
AR1	Alex Rodriguez	10.00
SS	Sammy Sosa	10.00
IS	Ichiro Suzuki	20.00
IS1	Ichiro Suzuki	20.00

Grade A Batting Gloves

		NM/M
Most not priced due to scarcity.		
Inserted 1:960		
RA	Roberto Alomar/65	20.00
CD	Carlos Delgado/65	15.00
TG	Troy Glaus/60	15.00
JG	Juan Gonzalez/65	15.00
RM	Raul Mondesi/65	10.00
RP	Rafael Palmeiro/65	20.00
MR	Manny Ramirez/69	15.00
AR	Alex Rodriguez/67	25.00
IR	Ivan Rodriguez/70	20.00
MT	Miguel Tejada/70	10.00
FT	Frank Thomas/70	20.00

Leather of Distinction

		NM/M
Most not priced due to scarcity		
Inserted 1:960		
KG	Ken Griffey Jr./70	30.00
RP	Rafael Palmeiro/70	20.00
MP	Mike Piazza/50	40.00
MR	Manny Ramirez/70	20.00
AR	Alex Rodriguez/70	25.00
IR	Ivan Rodriguez/69	20.00
TS	Tim Salmon/70	10.00
GS	Gary Sheffield/70	10.00
FT	Frank Thomas/70	20.00
OV	Omar Vizquel/65	10.00

2003 Upper Deck MVP

	NM/M
Complete Set (220):	20.00
Complete Factory Set (330):	30.00
Common Player:	.10
Pack (8):	1.50
Box (24):	25.00

1	Troy Glaus	.40
2	Darin Erstad	.25
3	Jarrod Washburn	.10
4	Francisco Rodriguez	.10
5	Garret Anderson	.20
6	Tim Salmon	.20
7	Adam Kennedy	.10
8	Randy Johnson	.50
9	Luis Gonzalez	.20
10	Curt Schilling	.50
11	Junior Spivey	.10
12	Craig Counsell	.10
13	Mark Grace	.25
14	Steve Finley	.10
15	Javy Lopez	.10
16	Rafael Furcal	.10
17	John Smoltz	.15
18	Greg Maddux	.75
19	Chipper Jones	.50
20	Gary Sheffield	.20
21	Andruw Jones	.20
22	Tony Batista	.10
23	Geronimo Gil	.10
24	Jay Gibbons	.10
25	Rodrigo Lopez	.10
26	Chris Singleton	.10
27	Melvin Mora	.10
28	Jeff Conine	.10
29	Nomar Garciaparra	1.00
30	Pedro J. Martinez	.50
31	Manny Ramirez	.50
32	Shea Hillenbrand	.10
33	Johnny Damon	.40
34	Jason Varitek	.25
35	Derek Lowe	.10
36	Trot Nixon	.10
37	Sammy Sosa	.75
38	Kerry Wood	.50
39	Mark Prior	.50
40	Moises Alou	.20
41	Corey Patterson	.25
42	Hee Seop Choi	.10
43	Mark Bellhorn	.10
44	Frank Thomas	.40
45	Mark Buehrle	.20
46	Magglio Ordonez	.20
47	Carlos Lee	.20
48	Paul Konerko	.20
49	Joe Borchard	.10
50	Joe Crede	.10
51	Ken Griffey Jr.	.75
52	Adam Dunn	.40
53	Austin Kearns	.40
54	Aaron Boone	.10
55	Sean Casey	.10
56	Danny Graves	.10
57	Russell Branyan	.10
58	Matt Lawton	.10
59	C.C. Sabathia	.10
60	Omar Vizquel	.20
61	Brandon Phillips	.10
62	Karim Garcia	.10
63	Ellis Burks	.10
64	Cliff Lee	.10
65	Todd Helton	.40
66	Larry Walker	.20
67	Jay Payton	.10
68	Brent Butler	.10
69	Juan Uribe	.10
70	Jason Jennings	.10
71	Denny Stark	.10
72	Dmitri Young	.10
73	Carlos Pena	.10
74	Andres Torres	.10
75	Andy Van Hekken	.10
76	George Lombard	.10
77	Eric Munson	.10
78	Bobby Higginson	.10
79	Luis Castillo	.10
80	A.J. Burnett	.10
81	Juan Encarnacion	.10
82	Ivan Rodriguez	.40
83	Mike Lowell	.10
84	Josh Beckett	.25
85	Brad Penny	.10
86	Craig Biggio	.25
87	Jeff Kent	.20
88	Morgan Ensberg	.10
89	Daryle Ward	.10
90	Jeff Bagwell	.40
91	Roy Oswalt	.20
92	Lance Berkman	.25
93	Mike Sweeney	.10
94	Carlos Beltran	.40
95	Raul Ibanez	.10
96	Carlos Febles	.10
97	Joe Randa	.10
98	Shawn Green	.25
99	Kevin Brown	.15
100	Paul LoDuca	.10
101	Adrian Beltre	.25
102	Eric Gagne	.20
103	Kazuhisa Ishii	.10
104	Odalis Perez	.10
105	Brian Jordan	.10
106	Geoff Jenkins	.10
107	Richie Sexson	.25
108	Ben Sheets	.10
109	Alex Sanchez	.10
110	Eric Young	.10
111	Jose Hernandez	.10
112	Torii Hunter	.25
113	Eric Milton	.10
114	Corey Koskie	.10
115	Doug Mientkiewicz	.10
116	A.J. Pierzynski	.10
117	Jacque Jones	.10
118	Cristian Guzman	.10
119	Bartolo Colon	.10
120	Brad Wilkerson	.10
121	Michael Barrett	.10
122	Vladimir Guerrero	.50
123	Jose Vidro	.10
124	Javier Vazquez	.10
125	Endy Chavez	.10
126	Roberto Alomar	.25
127	Mike Piazza	1.00
128	Jeromy Burnitz	.10
129	Mo Vaughn	.15
130	Tom Glavine	.25
131	Al Leiter	.15
132	Armando Benitez	.10
133	Timoniel Perez	.10
134	Roger Clemens	1.00
135	Derek Jeter	1.50
136	Jason Giambi	.25
137	Alfonso Soriano	.50
138	Bernie Williams	.25
139	Mike Mussina	.25
140	Jorge Posada	.20
141	Hideki Matsui RC	4.00
142	Robin Ventura	.10
143	David Wells	.10
144	Nick Johnson	.10
145	Tim Hudson	.20
146	Eric Chavez	.20
147	Barry Zito	.25
148	Miguel Tejada	.40
149	Jermaine Dye	.20
150	Mark Mulder	.20
151	Terrence Long	.10
152	Scott Hatteberg	.10
153	Marlon Byrd	.10
154	Jim Thome	.40
155	Marlon Anderson	.10
156	Vicente Padilla	.10
157	Bobby Abreu	.25
158	Jimmy Rollins	.25
159	Pat Burrell	.40
160	Brian Giles	.20
161	Aramis Ramirez	.20
162	Jason Kendall	.20
163	Josh Fogg	.10
164	Kip Wells	.10
165	Pokey Reese	.10
166	Kris Benson	.10
167	Ryan Klesko	.20
168	Brian Lawrence	.10
169	Mark Kotsay	.10
170	Jake Peavy	.10
171	Phil Nevin	.10
172	Sean Burroughs	.10
173	Trevor Hoffman	.10
174	Jason Schmidt	.20
175	Kirk Rueter	.10
176	Barry Bonds	1.50
177	Pedro Feliz	.10
178	Rich Aurilia	.10
179	Benito Santiago	.10
180	J.T. Snow	.10
181	Robb Nen	.10
182	Ichiro Suzuki	1.00
183	Edgar Martinez	.10
184	Bret Boone	.10
185	Freddy Garcia	.10
186	John Olerud	.20
187	Mike Cameron	.10
188	Joel Pineiro	.10
189	Albert Pujols	1.25
190	Matt Morris	.20
191	J.D. Drew	.20
192	Scott Rolen	.50
193	Tino Martinez	.20
194	Jim Edmonds	.20
195	Edgar Renteria	.20
196	Fernando Vina	.10
197	Jason Isringhausen	.10
198	Ben Grieve	.10
199	Carl Crawford	.10
200	Dewon Brazelton	.10
201	Aubrey Huff	.10
202	Jared Sandberg	.10
203	Steve Cox	.10
204	Carl Everett	.10
205	Kevin Mench	.10
206	Alex Rodriguez	1.00
207	Rafael Palmeiro	.40
208	Michael Young	.10
209	Hank Blalock	.40
210	Juan Gonzalez	.25
211	Carlos Delgado	.20
212	Eric Hinske	.20
213	Josh Phelps	.10
214	Mark Hendrickson	.10
215	Roy Halladay	.10
216	Orlando Hudson	.10
217	Shannon Stewart	.10
218	Vernon Wells	.10
219	Ichiro Suzuki	.40
220	Jason Giambi	.25
221	Scott Spiezio	.10
222	Rich Fischer	.10
223	Bengie Molina	.10
224	David Eckstein	.10
225	Brandon Webb RC	1.50
226	Oscar Villarreal	.10
227	Rob Hammock RC	.40
228	Matt Kata RC	.40
229	Lyle Overbay	.10
230	Chris Capuano RC	.50
231	Horacio Ramirez	.10
232	Shane Reynolds	.10
233	Russ Ortiz	.10
234	Mike Hampton	.10
235	Mike Hessman	.10
236	Byung-Hyun Kim	.10
237	Freddy Sanchez	.10
238	Jason Shiell	.10
239	Ryan Cameron	.10
240	Todd Wellemeyer RC	.40
241	Joe Borowski	.10
242	Alex Gonzalez	.10
243	Jon Leicester	.10
244	David Sanders	.10
245	Roberto Alomar	.25
246	Barry Larkin	.25
247	Jhonny Peralta	.10
248	Zach Sorensen	.10
249	Jason Davis	.10
250	Coco Crisp	.10
251	Greg Vaughn	.10
252	Preston Wilson	.10
253	Denny Neagle	.10
254	Clint Barmes RC	1.00
255	Jeremy Bonderman	.10
256	Wilfredo Ledezma RC	.10
257	Dontrelle Willis	.25
258	Alex Gonzalez	.10
259	Tommy Phelps	.10
260	Kirk Saarloos	.10
261	Colin Porter RC	.10
262	Nate Bland	.10
263	Jason Gilfillan	.10
264	Mike MacDougal	.10
265	Ken Harvey	.10
266	Brent Mayne	.10
267	Miguel Cabrera	.40
268	Hideo Nomo	.25
269	Dave Roberts	.10
270	Fred McGriff	.20
271	Joe Thurston	.10
272	Royce Clayton	.10
273	Micheal Nakamura	.10
274	Brad Radke	.10
275	Joe Mays	.10
276	Lew Ford RC	1.00
277	Michael Cuddyer	.10
278	Luis Ayala	.10
279	Julio Manon	.10
280	Anthony Ferrari	.10
281	Livan Hernandez	.10
282	Jae Weong Seo	.10
283	Jose Reyes	.40
284	Tony Clark	.10
285	Ty Wigginton	.10
286	Cliff Floyd	.10
287	Jeremy Griffiths	.10
288	Jason Roach	.10
289	Jeff Duncan	.10
290	Phil Seibel	.10
291	Prentice Redman RC	.25
292	Jose Contreras RC	1.00
293	Ruben Sierra	.10
294	Andy Pettitte	.25
295	Aaron Boone	.10
296	Mariano Rivera	.20
297	Michel Hernandez	.10
298	Mike Neu	.10
299	Erubiel Durazo	.10
300	Billy McMillon	.10
301	Rich Harden	.10
302	David Bell	.10
303	Kevin Millwood	.20
304	Mike Lieberthal	.10
305	Jeremy Wedel	.10
306	Kenny Lofton	.10
307	Reggie Sanders	.10
308	Randall Simon	.10
309	Xavier Nady	.10
310	Rod Beck	.10
311	Miguel Ojeda	.10
312	Mark Loretta	.10
313	Edgardo Alfonzo	.10
314	Andres Galarraga	.10
315	Jose Cruz Jr.	.10
316	Jesse Foppert	.10
317	Kurt Ainsworth	.10
318	Dan Wilson	.10
319	Ben Davis	.10
320	Rocco Baldelli	.25
321	Al Martin	.10
322	Runelvys Hernandez	.10
323	Dan Haren	.50
324	Bo Hart RC	.25
325	Einar Diaz	.10
326	Mike Lamb	.10
327	Aquilino Lopez	.10
328	Reed Johnson	.10
329	Diegomar Markwell	.10
330	Hideki Matsui	.75

Gold

Stars (1-220):	6-12X
Production 150 Sets	
Black Stars:	10-20X
Production 50 Sets	
Silver Stars:	1-2X
Inserted 1:2	

Base-to-Base

		NM/M
Inserted 1:488		
CP	Roger Clemens, Mike Piazza	25.00
IG	Ichiro Suzuki, Ken Griffey Jr.	40.00
IJ	Ichiro Suzuki, Derek Jeter	45.00
JW	Derek Jeter, Bernie Williams	25.00
MB	Mark McGwire, Barry Bonds	60.00
RJ	Alex Rodriguez, Derek Jeter	40.00

Covering the Bases

		NM/M
Common Player:		4.00
Inserted 1:125		
BB	Barry Bonds	15.00
CD	Carlos Delgado	4.00
JD	J.D. Drew	4.00
DE	Darin Erstad	6.00
TG	Troy Glaus	6.00

LG	Luis Gonzalez	4.00
SG	Shawn Green	6.00
DJ	Derek Jeter	15.00
MP	Mike Piazza	12.00
AR	Alex Rodriguez	12.00
IR	Ivan Rodriguez	4.00
IS	Ichiro Suzuki	15.00
MT	Miguel Tejada	6.00
FT	Frank Thomas	8.00
JT	Jim Thome	10.00

Covering the Plate Bat

		NM/M
Common Player:		6.00
Inserted 1:160		
RA	Roberto Alomar	15.00
RF	Rafael Furcal	8.00
VG	Vladimir Guerrero	8.00
FM	Fred McGriff	6.00
MM	Mark McGwire	60.00
JT	Jim Thome	12.00

Dual Aces

		NM/M
Common Card:		8.00
Inserted 1:488		
BS	Kevin Brown, Curt Schilling	10.00
CJ	Roger Clemens, Randy Johnson	20.00
CL	Roger Clemens, Al Leiter	15.00
ML	Matt Morris, Al Leiter	8.00
SJ	Curt Schilling, Randy Johnson	12.00
SM	Curt Schilling, Andy Pettitte	10.00

Express Delivery

		NM/M
Complete Set (15):		10.00
Common Player:		.50
Inserted 1:12		
ED1	Randy Johnson	2.00
ED2	Curt Schilling	1.00
ED3	Pedro J. Martinez	2.00
ED4	Kerry Wood	1.00
ED5	Mark Prior	1.50
ED6	A.J. Burnett	.50
ED7	Josh Beckett	.50
ED8	Roy Oswalt	.75
ED9	Hideo Nomo	.75
ED10	Ben Sheets	.50
ED11	Bartolo Colon	.50
ED12	Roger Clemens	2.50
ED13	Mike Mussina	.75
ED14	Tim Hudson	.75
ED15	Matt Morris	.50

MVP Celebration

		NM/M
Common Player:		1.50
#'d to yr. MVP was won		
MVP1	Yogi Berra	4.00
MVP2	Mickey Mantle	15.00
MVP3	Mickey Mantle	15.00
MVP4	Mickey Mantle	15.00
MVP5	Roger Clemens	5.00
MVP6	Rickey Henderson	4.00
MVP7	Frank Thomas	4.00
MVP8	Mo Vaughn	1.50
MVP9	Juan Gonzalez	3.00
MVP10	Ken Griffey Jr.	6.00
MVP11	Juan Gonzalez	3.00
MVP12	Ivan Rodriguez	2.00
MVP13	Jason Giambi	4.00
MVP14	Ichiro Suzuki	6.00
MVP15	Miguel Tejada	2.00
MVP16	Barry Bonds	8.00
MVP17	Barry Bonds	8.00
MVP18	Barry Bonds	8.00
MVP19	Jeff Bagwell	4.00
MVP20	Barry Larkin	1.50
MVP21	Larry Walker	1.50
MVP22	Sammy Sosa	6.00
MVP23	Chipper Jones	5.00
MVP24	Jeff Kent	1.50
MVP25	Barry Bonds	8.00
MVP26	Barry Bonds	8.00
MVP27	Ken Griffey Sr.	1.50
MVP28	Roger Clemens	5.00
MVP29	Ken Griffey Jr.	6.00
MVP30	Fred McGriff	1.50
MVP31	Jeff Conine	1.50
MVP32	Mike Piazza	6.00
MVP33	Sandy Alomar Jr.	1.50
MVP34	Roberto Alomar	2.50
MVP35	Pedro J. Martinez	4.00
MVP36	Derek Jeter	8.00
MVP37	Rickey Henderson	4.00
MVP38	Roberto Alomar	2.50
MVP39	Bernie Williams	3.00
MVP40	Marquis Grissom	1.50
MVP41	David Wells	1.50
MVP42	Orlando Hernandez	1.50
MVP43	David Justice	1.50
MVP44	Andy Pettitte	2.00
MVP45	Adam Kennedy	1.50
MVP46	John Smoltz	1.50
MVP47	Curt Schilling	2.00
MVP48	Javy Lopez	1.50
MVP49	Livan Hernandez	1.50
MVP50	Sterling Hitchcock	1.50
MVP51	Mike Hampton	1.50
MVP52	Craig Counsell	1.50
MVP53	Benito Santiago	1.50
MVP54	Tom Glavine	2.00
MVP55	Livan Hernandez	1.50
MVP56	Mariano Rivera	1.50
MVP57	Derek Jeter	8.00
MVP58	Randy Johnson	4.00
MVP59	Curt Schilling	2.50
MVP60	Troy Glaus	3.00
MVP61	Yogi Berra	4.00
MVP62	Yogi Berra	4.00
MVP63	Mickey Mantle	15.00
MVP64	Mickey Mantle	15.00
MVP65	Ken Griffey Sr.	1.50
MVP66	Rickey Henderson	4.00
MVP67	Roberto Alomar	2.50
MVP68	Bernie Williams	3.00
MVP69	Livan Hernandez	1.50
MVP70	Sammy Sosa	6.00
MVP71	Sterling Hitchcock	1.50
MVP72	David Wells	1.50
MVP73	Mariano Rivera	1.50
MVP74	Chipper Jones	5.00
MVP75	Ivan Rodriguez	2.00
MVP76	Derek Jeter	8.00
MVP77	Jason Giambi	4.00
MVP78	Jeff Kent	1.50
MVP79	Mike Hampton	1.50
MVP80	Randy Johnson	4.00
MVP81	Curt Schilling	2.50
MVP82	Barry Bonds	8.00
MVP83	Ichiro Suzuki	6.00
MVP84	Ichiro Suzuki	6.00
MVP85	Adam Kennedy	1.50
MVP86	Benito Santiago	1.50
MVP87	Troy Glaus	3.00
MVP88	Troy Glaus	3.00
MVP89	Miguel Tejada	2.00
MVP90	Barry Bonds	8.00

Prosign

Production 25 Sets
No Pricing

Pro View

	NM/M
Complete Set (45):	65.00
Common Player:	.75
Inserted 2:Box	
Golds:	2-3X

PV1	Troy Glaus	1.50
PV2	Darin Erstad	1.00
PV3	Randy Johnson	2.00
PV4	Curt Schilling	1.50
PV5	Luis Gonzalez	.75
PV6	Chipper Jones	2.00
PV7	Andruw Jones	1.00
PV8	Greg Maddux	3.00
PV9	Pedro J. Martinez	2.00
PV10	Manny Ramirez	2.00
PV11	Sammy Sosa	3.00
PV12	Mark Prior	1.50
PV13	Magglio Ordonez	1.00
PV14	Frank Thomas	1.50
PV15	Ken Griffey Jr.	3.00
PV16	Adam Dunn	1.50
PV17	Jim Thome	1.50
PV18	Todd Helton	1.00
PV19	Jeff Bagwell	1.50
PV20	Lance Berkman	1.00
PV21	Shawn Green	.75
PV22	Hideo Nomo	1.00
PV23	Vladimir Guerrero	2.00
PV24	Roberto Alomar	1.00
PV25	Mike Piazza	4.00
PV26	Jason Giambi	1.00
PV27	Roger Clemens	3.00
PV28	Alfonso Soriano	2.00
PV29	Derek Jeter	6.00
PV30	Miguel Tejada	1.50
PV31	Eric Chavez	.75
PV32	Barry Zito	1.00
PV33	Pat Burrell	1.50
PV34	Brian Giles	.75
PV35	Barry Bonds	6.00
PV36	Ichiro Suzuki	4.00
PV37	Albert Pujols	5.00
PV38	Scott Rolen	1.50
PV39	J.D. Drew	.75
PV40	Mark McGwire	5.00
PV41	Alex Rodriguez	5.00
PV42	Rafael Palmeiro	1.00
PV43	Juan Gonzalez	1.00
PV44	Eric Hinske	.75
PV45	Carlos Delgado	.75

SportsNut Fantasy

		NM/M
Complete Set (90):		45.00
Common Player:		.40
Inserted 1:3		
Prices for unscratched cards.		
SN1	Troy Glaus	1.00
SN2	Darin Erstad	.50
SN3	Luis Gonzalez	.50
SN4	Andruw Jones	.75
SN5	Chipper Jones	2.00
SN6	Gary Sheffield	.50
SN7	Jay Gibbons	.40
SN8	Manny Ramirez	1.00
SN9	Shea Hillenbrand	.40
SN10	Johnny Damon	.40
SN11	Nomar Garciaparra	2.50
SN12	Sammy Sosa	2.00
SN13	Magglio Ordonez	.75
SN14	Frank Thomas	.75
SN15	Ken Griffey Jr.	1.50
SN16	Adam Dunn	1.00
SN17	Matt Lawton	.40
SN18	Larry Walker	.40
SN19	Todd Helton	.75
SN20	Carlos Pena	.40
SN21	Mike Lowell	.40
SN22	Jeff Bagwell	1.00
SN23	Lance Berkman	.75
SN24	Mike Sweeney	.50
SN25	Carlos Beltran	.40
SN26	Shawn Green	.75
SN27	Richie Sexson	.50
SN28	Torii Hunter	.40
SN29	Jacque Jones	.40
SN30	Vladimir Guerrero	1.50
SN31	Jose Vidro	.40
SN32	Roberto Alomar	.50
SN33	Mike Piazza	2.00
SN34	Alfonso Soriano	1.50
SN35	Derek Jeter	3.00
SN36	Jason Giambi	2.00
SN37	Bernie Williams	.75
SN38	Eric Chavez	.75
SN39	Miguel Tejada	.75
SN40	Jim Thome	1.00
SN41	Pat Burrell	1.00
SN42	Bobby Abreu	.50
SN43	Brian Giles	.50
SN44	Jason Kendall	.40
SN45	Ryan Klesko	.40
SN46	Phil Nevin	.40
SN47	Barry Bonds	4.00
SN48	Rich Aurilia	.40
SN49	Ichiro Suzuki	2.00
SN50	Bret Boone	.40
SN51	J.D. Drew	.40
SN52	Jim Edmonds	.75
SN53	Albert Pujols	1.50
SN54	Scott Rolen	1.00
SN55	Ben Grieve	.40
SN56	Alex Rodriguez	3.00
SN57	Rafael Palmeiro	.75
SN58	Juan Gonzalez	.50
SN59	Carlos Delgado	.40
SN60	Josh Phelps	.40
SN61	Jarrod Washburn	.40
SN62	Randy Johnson	1.00
SN63	Curt Schilling	.75
SN64	Greg Maddux	1.50
SN65	Mike Hampton	.40
SN66	Rodrigo Lopez	.40
SN67	Pedro J. Martinez	1.50
SN68	Derek Lowe	.40
SN69	Mark Prior	1.00
SN70	Kerry Wood	.75
SN71	Mark Buehrle	.40
SN72	Roy Oswalt	.50
SN73	Wade Miller	.40
SN74	Odalis Perez	.40
SN75	Hideo Nomo	.50
SN76	Ben Sheets	.40
SN77	Eric Milton	.40
SN78	Bartolo Colon	.40
SN79	Tom Glavine	.40
SN80	Al Leiter	.40
SN81	Roger Clemens	2.00
SN82	Mike Mussina	.75
SN83	Tim Hudson	.75
SN84	Barry Zito	.50
SN85	Mark Mulder	.50
SN86	Vicente Padilla	.40
SN87	Jason Schmidt	.40
SN88	Freddy Garcia	.40
SN89	Matt Morris	.40
SN90	Roy Halladay	.40

Talk of the Town

		NM/M
Complete Set (15):		20.00
Common Player:		.75
Inserted 1:12		
TT1	Hideki Matsui	3.00
TT2	Chipper Jones	1.00
TT3	Manny Ramirez	1.50
TT4	Sammy Sosa	2.00
TT5	Ken Griffey Jr.	2.00
TT6	Lance Berkman	.75

TT7	Shawn Green	.75
TT8	Vladimir Guerrero	1.50
TT9	Mike Piazza	2.50
TT10	Jason Giambi	.75
TT11	Alfonso Soriano	1.50
TT12	Ichiro Suzuki	2.50
TT13	Albert Pujols	3.00
TT14	Alex Rodriguez	3.00
TT15	Eric Hinske	.75

Three Bagger

		NM/M
	Inserted 1:488	
BMP	Barry Bonds, Mark McGwire, Mike Piazza	80.00
GIB	Ken Griffey Jr., Ichiro Suzuki, Barry Bonds	60.00
GTD	Troy Glaus, Frank Thomas, Carlos Delgado	10.00
IBJ	Ichiro Suzuki, Barry Bonds, Derek Jeter	80.00
JWP	Derek Jeter, Bernie Williams, Jorge Posada	35.00
SCB	Curt Schilling, Roger Clemens, Kevin Brown	20.00

Total Bases

		NM/M
	Production 150 Sets	
BB	Barry Bonds	20.00
RC	Roger Clemens	20.00
TG	Troy Glaus	8.00
KG	Ken Griffey Jr.	15.00
DJ	Derek Jeter	20.00
MM	Mark McGwire	25.00
MP	Mike Piazza	15.00
AR	Alex Rodriguez	15.00
IS	Ichiro Suzuki	30.00

2003 Upper Deck Patch Collection

		NM/M
Complete Set (161):		
Common Player:		.25
Common SP Patch (121-161):		4.00
All-Star & HOF Patches (121-150):		
Inserted 1:40		
Rookie Patches (151-161):		
Inserted 1:20		
Pack (5):		4.75
Box (20):		80.00
1	Darin Erstad	.40
2	Troy Glaus	.75
3	Robby Hammock RC	.40
4	Luis Gonzalez	.50
5	Randy Johnson/SP	3.00
6	Curt Schilling/SP	2.50
7	Oscar Villarreal RC	.40
8	Gary Sheffield	.50
9	Mike Hampton	.25
10	Greg Maddux	1.50
11	Chipper Jones	1.50
12	Tony Batista	.25
13	Rodrigo Lopez	.25
14	Jay Gibbons	.25
15	Shea Hillenbrand	.25
16	Johnny Damon	.25
17	Derek Lowe	.25
18	Nomar Garciaparra	2.00
19	Pedro J. Martinez	1.00
20	Manny Ramirez	.75
21	Mark Prior	.75
22	Kerry Wood	.50
23	Corey Patterson	.25
24	Sammy Sosa	1.50

25	Troy O'Leary	.25
26	Frank Thomas	.75
27	Magglio Ordonez	.40
28	Bartolo Colon	.25
29	Austin Kearns	.75
30	Aaron Boone	.25
31	Ken Griffey Jr.	1.50
32	Adam Dunn	.75
33	C.C. Sabathia	.25
34	Karim Garcia	.25
35	Larry Walker	.40
36	Preston Wilson	.40
37	Jason Jennings	.25
38	Todd Helton	.75
39	Carlos Pena	.25
40	Eric Munson	.25
41	Ivan Rodriguez	.50
42	Josh Beckett	.25
43	A.J. Burnett	.25
44	Roy Oswalt	.25
45	Craig Biggio	.40
46	Jeff Bagwell	.75
47	Lance Berkman	.50
48	Jeff Kent	.40
49	Carlos Beltran	.25
50	Mike Sweeney	.25
51	Hideo Nomo	.50
52	Adrian Beltre	.25
53	Shawn Green	.50
54	Kazuhisa Ishii	.25
55	Ben Sheets	.25
56	Richie Sexson	.50
57	Torii Hunter	.50
58	Doug Mientkiewicz	.25
59	Eric Milton	.25
60	Corey Koskie	.25
61	Joe Mays	.25
62	Jose Vidro	.25
63	Vladimir Guerrero	.75
64	Luis Ayala RC	.25
65	Cliff Floyd	.25
66	Tom Glavine	.50
67	Mike Piazza	2.00
68	Roberto Alomar	.50
69	Al Leiter	.25
70	Mike Mussina	.50
71	Mariano Rivera	.40
72	Drew Henson	.25
73	Roger Clemens	1.50
74	Jason Giambi	1.00
75	Bernie Williams	.50
76	Alfonso Soriano	1.50
77	Derek Jeter	3.00
78	Miguel Tejada	.50
79	Jermaine Dye	.25
80	Tim Hudson	.50
81	Barry Zito	.50
82	Mark Mulder	.40
83	Pat Burrell	.50
84	Jim Thome	.75
85	Bobby Abreu	.40
86	Kevin Millwood	.40
87	Jason Kendall	.40
88	Brian Giles	.40
89	Phil Nevin	.25
90	Sean Burroughs	.25
91	Oliver Perez	.25
92	Jose Cruz Jr.	.25
93	Rich Aurilia	.25
94	Edgardo Alfonzo	.25
95	Barry Bonds	3.00
96	J.T. Snow	.25
97	Mike Cameron	.25
98	John Olerud	.50
99	Bret Boone	.25
100	Ichiro Suzuki	1.50
101	J.D. Drew	.40
102	Jim Edmonds	.50
103	Scott Rolen	.75
104	Matt Morris	.40
105	Tino Martinez	.40
106	Albert Pujols	1.50
107	Rocco Baldelli	.25
108	Carl Crawford	.25
109	Mark Teixeira	.50
110	Rafael Palmeiro	.50
111	Hank Blalock	.50
112	Alex Rodriguez	2.50
113	Kevin Mench	.25
114	Juan Gonzalez	.75
115	Shannon Stewart	.25
116	Vernon Wells	.40
117	Josh Phelps	.25
118	Eric Hinske	.25
119	Orlando Hudson	.25
120	Carlos Delgado	.50
121	Alex Rodriguez	10.00
122	Nomar Garciaparra	10.00
123	Miguel Tejada	4.00
124	Jim Thome	8.00
125	Alfonso Soriano	6.00
126	Vladimir Guerrero	6.00
127	Derek Jeter	15.00
128	Mike Piazza	8.00

129	Ichiro Suzuki	12.00
130	Pedro J. Martinez	8.00
131	Luis Gonzalez	4.00
132	Adam Dunn	6.00
133	Shawn Green	4.00
134	Barry Zito	4.00
135	Torii Hunter	5.00
136	Ted Williams	20.00
137	Mickey Mantle	25.00
138	Ernie Banks	10.00
139	Yogi Berra	8.00
140	Rollie Fingers	4.00
141	Jim "Catfish" Hunter	4.00
142	Juan Marichal	8.00
143	Eddie Mathews	10.00
144	Willie McCovey	10.00
145	Joe Morgan	5.00
146	Stan Musial	12.00
147	Pee Wee Reese	10.00
148	Phil Rizzuto	6.00
149	Nolan Ryan	20.00
150	Tom Seaver	8.00
151	Hideki Matsui RC	15.00
152	Jose Contreras RC	5.00
153	Lew Ford RC	5.00
154	Jeremy Griffiths	4.00
155	Guillermo Quiroz RC	4.00
156	Ryan Cameron RC	4.00
157	Jon Leicester RC	4.00
158	Josh Willingham RC	4.00
159	Shane Bazzell RC	4.00
160	Willie Eyre RC	4.00
161	Prentice Redman RC	4.00

All-Star Game History Patches

		NM/M
Common Patch:		8.00
Inserted 2:Box		
1	1933 All-Star Game	12.00
2	1934 All-Star Game	15.00
3	1935 All-Star Game	15.00
4	1936 All-Star Game	10.00
5	1937 All-Star Game	10.00
6	1938 All-Star Game	10.00
7	1939 All-Star Game	15.00
8	1940 All-Star Game	15.00
9	1941 All-Star Game	10.00
10	1942 All-Star Game	15.00
11	1943 All-Star Game	12.00
12	1944 All-Star Game	15.00
13	1946 All-Star Game	15.00
14	1947 All-Star Game	15.00
15	1948 All-Star Game	15.00
16	1949 All-Star Game	15.00
17	1950 All-Star Game	12.00
18	1951 All-Star Game	15.00
19	1952 All-Star Game	15.00
20	1953 All-Star Game	12.00
21	1954 All-Star Game	12.00
22	1955 All-Star Game	10.00
23	1956 All-Star Game	15.00
24	1957 All-Star Game	15.00
25	1958 All-Star Game	12.00
26	1959 All-Star Game	15.00
27	1959 All-Star Game	15.00
28	1960 All-Star Game	10.00
29	1960 All-Star Game	15.00
30	1961 All-Star Game	10.00
31	1961 All-Star Game	15.00
32	1962 All-Star Game	8.00
33	1962 All-Star Game	12.00
34	1963 All-Star Game	15.00
35	1964 All-Star Game	10.00
36	1965 All-Star Game	15.00
37	1966 All-Star Game	15.00
38	1967 All-Star Game	12.00
39	1968 All-Star Game	8.00
40	1969 All-Star Game	15.00
41	1970 All-Star Game	15.00
42	1971 All-Star Game	15.00
43	1972 All-Star Game	10.00

44	1973 All-Star Game	10.00
45	1974 All-Star Game	10.00
46	1975 All-Star Game	10.00
47	1976 All-Star Game	15.00
48	1977 All-Star Game	10.00
49	1978 All-Star Game	10.00
50	1979 All-Star Game	8.00
51	1980 All-Star Game	8.00
52	1981 All-Star Game	10.00
53	1982 All-Star Game	8.00
54	1983 All-Star Game	10.00
55	1984 All-Star Game	10.00
56	1985 All-Star Game	10.00
57	1986 All-Star Game	10.00
58	1987 All-Star Game	8.00
59	1988 All-Star Game	10.00
60	1989 All-Star Game	10.00
61	1990 All-Star Game	15.00
62	1991 All-Star Game	8.00
63	1992 All-Star Game	8.00
64	1993 All-Star Game	10.00
65	1994 All-Star Game	15.00
66	1995 All-Star Game	10.00
67	1996 All-Star Game	12.00
68	1997 All-Star Game	10.00
69	1998 All-Star Game	8.00
70	1999 All-Star Game	15.00
71	2000 All-Star Game	10.00
72	2001 All-Star Game	8.00
73	2002 All-Star Game	12.00

MVPs Patches

		NM/M
Common Player:		5.00
Inserted 1:20		
1	Derek Jeter	15.00
2	Randy Johnson	8.00
3	Curt Schilling	6.00
4	Troy Glaus	5.00
5	Ted Williams	15.00
6	Ted Williams	15.00
7	Mickey Mantle	20.00
8	Mickey Mantle	20.00
9	Phil Rizzuto	5.00
10	Roger Clemens	10.00
11	Ken Griffey Jr.	10.00
12	Jason Giambi	5.00
13	Ichiro Suzuki	15.00
14	Roger Clemens	10.00
15	Yogi Berra	6.00
16	Sammy Sosa	10.00
17	Derek Jeter	15.00
18	Mike Piazza	10.00
19	Barry Bonds	15.00
20	Stan Musial	12.00
21	Joe Morgan	5.00

Signature Patches

		NM/M
Common Autograph:		25.00
Inserted 1:320		
JB	Jeff Bagwell	50.00
LB	Lance Berkman	50.00
RC	Roger Clemens	160.00
AD	Adam Dunn	60.00
FG	Freddy Garcia	30.00
JG	Jason Giambi	40.00
LG	Luis Gonzalez	40.00
KG	Ken Griffey Jr.	100.00
DH	Drew Henson	40.00
EH	Eric Hinske	25.00
HM	Hideki Matsui	
TP	Troy Percival	25.00
SR	Scott Rolen	50.00
CS	Curt Schilling	50.00
GS	Gary Sheffield	50.00
SS	Sammy Sosa	
IS	Ichiro Suzuki	300.00
MT	Miguel Tejada	50.00
BZ	Barry Zito	40.00

2003 Upper Deck Play Ball

		NM/M
Complete Set (104):		
Common Player:		.25
Common Summer of '41 (74-88):		4.00
Inserted 1:24		
Common Ted Williams (89-103):		10.00
Inserted 1:24		
Pack (5):		2.50
Box (24):		40.00
1	Troy Glaus	.40
2	Darin Erstad	.25
3	Randy Johnson	.75
4	Luis Gonzalez	.40
5	Curt Schilling	.75
6	Tom Glavine	.40
7	Chipper Jones	.75
8	Greg Maddux	1.00
9	Andruw Jones	.40

ROBIN YOUNT

10	Pedro J. Martinez	.75
11	Manny Ramirez	.75
12	Nomar Garciaparra	1.00
13	Billy Williams	.25
14	Sammy Sosa	1.00
15	Kerry Wood	.75
16	Mark Prior	.75
17	Ernie Banks	1.00
18	Frank Thomas	.75
19	Joe Morgan	.25
20	Ken Griffey Jr.	1.25
21	Adam Dunn	.50
22	Jim Thome	.75
23	Todd Helton	.50
24	Larry Walker	.40
25	Lance Berkman	.40
26	Roy Oswalt	.40
27	Jeff Bagwell	.50
28	Nolan Ryan	2.00
29	Mike Sweeney	.25
30	Shawn Green	.40
31	Hideo Nomo	.40
32	Kazuhisa Ishii	.25
33	Richie Sexson	.40
34	Robin Yount	.75
35	Harmon Killebrew	.75
36	Torii Hunter	.50
37	Vladimir Guerrero	.75
38	Roberto Alomar	.50
39	Mike Piazza	1.00
40	Tom Seaver	.75
41	Phil Rizzuto	.50
42	Yogi Berra	.75
43	Mike Mussina	.50
44	Roger Clemens	1.50
45	Derek Jeter	2.00
46	Jason Giambi	.25
47	Bernie Williams	.50
48	Alfonso Soriano	.50
49	Jim "Catfish" Hunter	.25
50	Barry Zito	.40
51	Eric Chavez	.40
52	Tim Hudson	.40
53	Rollie Fingers	.25
54	Miguel Tejada	.50
55	Pat Burrell	.40
56	Brian Giles	.40
57	Willie Stargell	.50
58	Phil Nevin	.25
59	Orlando Cepeda	.25
60	Barry Bonds	2.00
61	Jeff Kent	.40
62	Willie McCovey	.25
63	Ichiro Suzuki	1.50
64	Stan Musial	1.50
65	Albert Pujols	2.00
66	J.D. Drew	.40
67	Scott Rolen	.75
68	Mark McGwire	1.00
69	Alex Rodriguez	1.00
70	Juan Gonzalez	.40
71	Ivan Rodriguez	.50
72	Rafael Palmeiro	.50
73	Carlos Delgado	.40
74	Ted Williams	15.00
75	Hank Greenberg	6.00
76	Joe DiMaggio	15.00
77	Lefty Gomez	6.00
78	Tommy Henrich	4.00
79	Pee Wee Reese	5.00
80	Mel Ott	6.00
81	Carl Hubbell	6.00
82	Jimmie Foxx	8.00
83	Joe Cronin	4.00
84	Charlie Gehringer	5.00
85	Frank Hayes	5.00
86	Babe Dahlgren	4.00
87	Dolph Camilli	4.00
88	Johnny Vander Meer	4.00
89	Ted Williams	10.00
90	Ted Williams	10.00
91	Ted Williams	10.00
92	Ted Williams	10.00

93	Ted Williams	10.00
94	Ted Williams	10.00
95	Ted Williams	10.00
96	Ted Williams	10.00
97	Ted Williams	10.00
98	Ted Williams	10.00
99	Ted Williams	10.00
100	Ted Williams	10.00
101	Ted Williams	10.00
102	Ted Williams	10.00
103	Ted Williams	10.00
104	Hideki Matsui RC	5.00

Red Back

	NM/M
Stars (1-73):	1.5-2X
SP's (74-103):	1-1.5X
Matsui Red #104:	10.00
Inserted 1:2	

BuyBacks
No Pricing

Game-Used
Memorabilia Tier 1

SAMMY SOSA

	NM/M
Common Player:	5.00
Inserted 1:82	
Golds:	Not Priced
Production 25 Sets	

RC1	Roger Clemens	20.00
CD1	Carlos Delgado	5.00
DR1	J.D. Drew	5.00
AD1	Adam Dunn	10.00
JG1	Jason Giambi	5.00
LG1	Luis Gonzalez	5.00
KG1	Ken Griffey Jr.	15.00
TH1	Tommy Henrich	5.00
KI1	Kazuhisa Ishii	5.00
CJ1	Chipper Jones	10.00
MM1	Mark McGwire	50.00
RP1	Rafael Palmeiro	8.00
MP1	Mike Piazza	10.00
PR1	Mark Prior	8.00
IR1	Ivan Rodriguez	8.00
CS1	Curt Schilling	8.00
AS1	Alfonso Soriano	8.00
SS1	Sammy Sosa	10.00
IS1	Ichiro Suzuki	30.00
MS1	Mike Sweeney	5.00
BW1	Bernie Williams	5.00

Game-Used
Memorabilia Tier 2

	NM/M
Common Player:	5.00
Production 150 Sets	

JB2	Jeff Bagwell	10.00
LB2	Lance Berkman	5.00
JD2	Joe DiMaggio	100.00
DE2	Darin Erstad	5.00
JG2	Jason Giambi	5.00
SG2	Shawn Green	5.00
KG2	Ken Griffey Jr.	15.00
RJ2	Randy Johnson	8.00
AJ2	Andruw Jones	8.00
CJ2	Chipper Jones	10.00
GM2	Greg Maddux	15.00
PM2	Pedro J. Martinez	10.00
MM2	Mark McGwire	60.00
MP2	Mike Piazza	10.00
MR2	Manny Ramirez	10.00
AR2	Alex Rodriguez	15.00
CS2	Curt Schilling	10.00
SS2	Sammy Sosa	15.00
IS2	Ichiro Suzuki	50.00
JT2	Jim Thome	10.00
KW2	Kerry Wood	10.00

Game-Used
Memorabilia Autograph

MARK McGWIRE

	NM/M
Production 50 except A-Rod	

JB2	Jeff Bagwell	75.00
LB2	Lance Berkman	75.00
JG2	Jason Giambi	50.00
KG2	Ken Griffey Jr.	125.00
AJ2	Andruw Jones	50.00
MM2	Mark McGwire	350.00
AR2	Alex Rodriguez/ 285	100.00
CS2	Curt Schilling	75.00
SS2	Sammy Sosa	180.00
IS2	Ichiro Suzuki	375.00
JT2	Jim Thome	75.00
KW2	Kerry Wood	75.00

Mini

RICHIE SEXSON

	NM/M
Complete Set (73):	40.00
Common Player:	.50
Inserted 1:2	

1	Troy Glaus	.50
2	Darin Erstad	.50
3	Randy Johnson	1.00
4	Luis Gonzalez	.50
5	Curt Schilling	.75
6	Tom Glavine	.50
7	Chipper Jones	1.00
8	Greg Maddux	1.50
9	Andruw Jones	.75
10	Pedro J. Martinez	1.00
11	Manny Ramirez	1.00
12	Nomar Garciaparra	2.00
13	Billy Williams	.50
14	Sammy Sosa	2.00
15	Kerry Wood	1.00
16	Mark Prior	1.00
17	Ernie Banks	1.50
18	Frank Thomas	1.00
19	Joe Morgan	.50
20	Ken Griffey Jr.	2.00
21	Adam Dunn	1.00
22	Jim Thome	1.00
23	Todd Helton	.75
24	Larry Walker	.50
25	Lance Berkman	.75
26	Roy Oswalt	.50
27	Jeff Bagwell	1.00
28	Nolan Ryan	3.00
29	Mike Sweeney	.50
30	Shawn Green	.50
31	Hideo Nomo	.75
32	Kazuhisa Ishii	.50
33	Richie Sexson	.50
34	Robin Yount	1.00
35	Harmon Killebrew	1.00
36	Torii Hunter	.75
37	Vladimir Guerrero	1.00
38	Roberto Alomar	.75
39	Mike Piazza	2.00

40	Tom Seaver	1.00
41	Phil Rizzuto	.75
42	Yogi Berra	1.50
43	Mike Mussina	.75
44	Roger Clemens	2.00
45	Derek Jeter	3.00
46	Jason Giambi	.50
47	Bernie Williams	.75
48	Alfonso Soriano	1.00
49	Jim "Catfish" Hunter	.50
50	Barry Zito	.50
51	Eric Chavez	.50
52	Tim Hudson	.50
53	Rollie Fingers	.50
54	Miguel Tejada	1.00
55	Pat Burrell	1.00
56	Brian Giles	.50
57	Willie Stargell	.75
58	Phil Nevin	.50
59	Orlando Cepeda	.50
60	Barry Bonds	3.00
61	Jeff Kent	.50
62	Willie McCovey	.50
63	Ichiro Suzuki	2.50
64	Stan Musial	2.00
65	Albert Pujols	3.00
66	J.D. Drew	.50
67	Scott Rolen	1.00
68	Mark McGwire	2.00
69	Alex Rodriguez	2.50
70	Juan Gonzalez	1.00
71	Ivan Rodriguez	1.00
72	Rafael Palmeiro	.75
73	Carlos Delgado	.50

Original Artwork
Redemption
89 Total Redemption cards

Reprint Series
Original 1941

	NM/M
Complete Set (25):	15.00
Common Player:	.75
Inserted 1:2	

R1	Ted Williams	2.50
R2	Hank Greenberg	.75
R3	Joe DiMaggio	2.50
R4	Lefty Gomez	.75
R5	Tommy Henrich	.75
R6	Pee Wee Reese	.75
R7	Mel Ott	1.00
R8	Carl Hubbell	.75
R9	Jimmie Foxx	1.00
R10	Joe Cronin	.75
R11	Charley Gehringer	.75
R12	Frank Hayes	.75
R13	Babe Dahlgren	.75
R14	Dolph Camilli	.75
R15	Johnny Vander Meer	.75
R16	Bucky Walters	.75
R17	Red Ruffing	.75
R18	Charlie Keller	.75
R19	Bob Johnson	.75
R20	Emil "Dutch" Leonard	.75
R21	Barney McCosky	.75
R22	Soupy Campbell	.75
R23	Roy Weatherly	.75
R24	Bobby Doerr	.75
R25	Bill Dickey	.75

Yankee Clipper: 1941
Streak

THE YANKEE CLIPPER: 1941 STREAK

	NM/M
Complete Set (56):	250.00
Common DiMaggio (1-41):	5.00
Inserted 1:12	
Common DiMaggio (42-56):	8.00
Inserted 1:24	

2003 Upper Deck
Prospect Premieres

	NM/M
Complete Set (90):	30.00
Common Player:	.25
Pack (4):	7.00
Box (18):	100.00

1	Bryan Opdyke RC	.25
2	Gabriel Sosa RC	.25
3	Tila Reynolds RC	.25

4	Aaron Hill RC	1.00
5	Aaron Marsden RC	.25
6	Abe Alvarez RC	.75
7	Adam Jones RC	3.00
8	Adam Miller RC	2.50
9	Andre Ethier RC	3.00
10	Tony Gwynn Jr. RC	.75
11	Brad Snyder RC	1.00
12	Brad Sullivan RC	.75
13	Brian Anderson RC	1.50
14	Brian Buscher RC	.25
15	Brian Snyder RC	.75
16	Carlos Quentin RC	3.00
17	Chad Billingsley RC	3.00
18	Fraser Dizard RC	.50
19	Chris Durbin RC	.50
20	Chris Ray RC	.50
21	Conor Jackson RC	2.00
22	Kory Casto RC	.50
23	Craig Whitaker RC	.75
24	Daniel Moore RC	.25
25	Daric Barton RC	2.00
26	Darin Downs RC	.75
27	David Murphy RC	.50
28	Dustin Majewski RC	.50
29	Edgardo Baez RC	.25
30	Jake Fox RC	.75
31	Jake Stevens RC	.75
32	Jamie D'Antona RC	1.00
33	James Houser RC	.50
34	Jarrod Saltalamacchia RC	2.00
35	Jason Hirsh RC	2.00
36	Javi Herrera RC	1.00
37	Jeff Allison RC	.75
38	John Hudgins RC	.50
39	Jo Jo Reyes RC	.50
40	Justin James RC	.50
41	Kurt Isenberg RC	.50
42	Kyle Boyer RC	.75
43	Lastings Milledge RC	5.00
44	Luis Atilano RC	.50
45	Matt Murton RC	1.50
46	Matt Moses RC	1.00
47	Matt Harrison RC	.50
48	Michael Bourn RC	.50
49	Miguel Vega RC	.50
50	Mitch Maier RC	1.00
51	Omar Quintanilla RC	.50
52	Ryan Sweeney RC	1.50
53	Scott Baker RC	.75
54	Sean Rodriguez RC	.75
55	Steve Lerud RC	.25
56	Thomas Pauly RC	.25
57	Tom Gorzelanny RC	1.00
58	Tim Moss RC	.25
59	Robbie Wooley RC	.50
60	Trey Webb RC	.50
61	Wes Littleton RC	.50
62	Beau Vaughan RC	.50
63	Willy Jo Ronda RC	.50
64	Chris Lubanski RC	1.50
65	Ian Stewart RC	4.00
66	John Danks RC	1.00
67	Kyle Sleeth RC	1.00
68	Michael Aubrey RC	1.50
69	Kevin Kouzmanoff RC	3.00
70	Ryan Harvey RC	1.50
71	Tim Stauffer RC	1.00
72	Tony Richie RC	.25
73	Brandon Wood RC	8.00
74	David Aardsma RC	.75
75	David Shinskie RC	.50
76	Dennis Dove RC	.50
77	Eric Sultemeier RC	.25
78	Jay Sborz RC	.25
79	Jimmy Barthmaier RC	.25
80	Josh Whitesell RC	.25
81	Josh Anderson RC	.50
82	Kenny Lewis RC	.50
83	Mateo Miramontes RC	.25
84	Nicholas Markakis RC	4.00
85	Paul Bacot RC	.50

86	Peter Stonard RC	.25
87	Reggie Willits RC	3.00
88	Shane Costa RC	.50
89	Billy Sadler RC	.25
90	Delmon Young RC	8.00

Star Rookie Jersey

		NM/M
Common Player:		4.00
Inserted 1:18		
P72	Tony Richie	4.00
P73	Brandon Wood	15.00
P74	David Aardsma	5.00
P75	David Shinskie	4.00
P76	Dennis Dove	6.00
P77	Eric Sultemeier	4.00
P78	Jay Sborz	4.00
P79	Jimmy Barthmaier	4.00
P80	Josh Whitesell	4.00
P81	Josh Anderson	8.00
P82	Kenny Lewis	8.00
P83	Mateo Miramontes	8.00
P84	Nicholas Markakis	25.00
P85	Paul Bacot	4.00
P86	Peter Stonard	4.00
P87	Reggie Willits	30.00
P88	Shane Costa	4.00
P89	Billy Sadler	4.00
P91	Kyle Sleeth	8.00
P92	Ian Stewart	25.00
P93	Fraser Dizard	6.00
P94	Abe Alvarez	6.00
P95	Adam Jones	15.00
P96	Brian Anderson	8.00
P97	Chris Durbin	4.00
P98	Craig Whitaker	8.00
P99	Jake Fox	4.00
P100	Kurt Isenberg	4.00
P101	Luis Atilano	4.00
P102	Miguel Vega	4.00
P103	Mitch Maier	8.00
P104	Ryan Sweeney	10.00
P105	Scott Baker	4.00
P106	Sean Rodriguez	8.00
P107	Trey Webb	4.00
P108	Willy Jo Ronda	6.00
P109	John Danks	8.00
P111	Michael Aubrey	10.00
P112	Lastings Milledge	30.00
P113	Chris Lubanski	10.00

Star Rookie Signature

		NM/M
Common Autograph:		5.00
Inserted 1:9		
P1	Bryan Opdyke	10.00
P2	Gabriel Sosa	8.00
P3	Tila Reynolds	5.00
P4	Aaron Hill	15.00
P5	Aaron Marsden	10.00

P6	Abe Alvarez	15.00
P7	Adam Jones	90.00
P8	Adam Miller	75.00
P9	Andre Ethier	60.00
P10	Tony Gwynn Jr.	20.00
P11	Brad Snyder	25.00
P12	Brad Sullivan	15.00
P13	Brian Anderson	20.00
P14	Brian Buscher	8.00
P15	Brian Snyder	10.00
P16	Carlos Quentin	40.00
P17	Chad Billingsley	40.00
P19	Chris Durbin	10.00
P20	Chris Ray	8.00
P21	Conor Jackson	30.00
P22	Kory Casto	8.00
P23	Craig Whitaker	10.00
P24	Daniel Moore	10.00
P25	Daric Barton	60.00
P26	Darin Downs	15.00
P27	David Murphy	15.00
P29	Edgardo Baez	12.00
P30	Jake Fox	15.00
P31	Jake Stevens	20.00
P32	Jamie D'Antona	25.00
P33	James Houser	15.00
P34	Jarrod Saltalamacchia	60.00
P35	Jason Hirsh	35.00
P36	Javi Herrera	10.00
P37	Jeff Allison	25.00
P38	John Hudgins	10.00
P39	Jo Jo Reyes	10.00
P40	Justin James	10.00
P41	Kurt Isenberg	10.00
P42	Kyle Boyer	12.00
P43	Lastings Milledge	60.00
P44	Luis Atilano	8.00
P45	Matt Murton	25.00
P46	Matt Moses	35.00
P48	Michael Bourn	15.00
P49	Miguel Vega	15.00
P50	Mitch Maier	25.00
P51	Omar Quintanilla	15.00
P52	Ryan Sweeney	40.00
P53	Scott Baker	15.00
P55	Steve Lerud	15.00
P56	Thomas Pauly	10.00
P57	Tom Gorzelanny	30.00
P58	Tim Moss	10.00
P60	Trey Webb	10.00
P61	Wes Littleton	15.00
P62	Beau Vaughan	10.00
P63	Willy Jo Ronda	15.00
P64	Chris Lubanski	25.00
P65	Ian Stewart	80.00
P66	John Danks	50.00
P67	Kyle Sleeth	20.00
P68	Michael Aubrey	40.00
P70	Ryan Harvey	30.00
P71	Tim Stauffer	30.00

2003 Upper Deck Sweet Spot

		NM/M
Complete Set (232):		
Common Player:		.25
Common SP:		1.00
Inserted 1:4		
Common SP (131-190):		3.00
Production 2,003		
Common SP (191-232):		4.00
Production 1,430 unless noted.		
Pack (4):		9.00
Box (12):		90.00
1	Darin Erstad	.50
2	Garret Anderson	.50
3	Tim Salmon	.50
4	Troy Glaus	.75
5	Luis Gonzalez	.50
6	Randy Johnson	1.00
7	Curt Schilling	.50

8	Lyle Overbay	.25
9	Andruw Jones/SP	2.00
10	Gary Sheffield/SP	1.50
11	Rafael Furcal/SP	1.00
12	Greg Maddux/SP	4.00
13	Chipper Jones/SP	4.00
14	Tony Batista	.25
15	Rodrigo Lopez	.25
16	Jay Gibbons	.25
17	Jason Johnson	.25
18	Byung-Hyun Kim/SP	1.00
19	Johnny Damon/SP	2.50
20	Derek Lowe/SP	1.00
21	Nomar Garciaparra/SP	5.00
22	Pedro Martinez/SP	3.00
23	Manny Ramirez/SP	2.50
24	Mark Prior	1.00
25	Kerry Wood	1.00
26	Corey Patterson	.50
27	Sammy Sosa	2.00
28	Moises Alou	.40
29	Magglio Ordonez	.40
30	Frank Thomas	.75
31	Paul Konerko	.25
32	Roberto Alomar	.50
33	Adam Dunn	.75
34	Austin Kearns	.50
35	Ryan Wagner RC	.25
36	Ken Griffey Jr.	1.50
37	Sean Casey	.25
38	Omar Vizquel	.40
39	C.C. Sabathia	.25
40	Jason Davis	.25
41	Travis Hafner	.25
42	Brandon Phillips	.25
43	Larry Walker	.40
44	Preston Wilson	.25
45	Jay Payton	.25
46	Todd Helton	.75
47	Carlos Pena	.25
48	Eric Munson	.25
49	Ivan Rodriguez	.75
50	Josh Beckett	.50
51	Alex Gonzalez	.25
52	Roy Oswalt	.40
53	Craig Biggio	.40
54	Jeff Bagwell	.75
55	Lance Berkman	.50
56	Mike Sweeney	.25
57	Carlos Beltran	.75
58	Brent Mayne	.25
59	Mike MacDougal	.25
60	Hideo Nomo	.50
61	Dave Roberts	.25
62	Adrian Beltre	.50
63	Shawn Green	.50
64	Kazuhisa Ishii	.25
65	Rickey Henderson	.50
66	Richie Sexson	.50
67	Torii Hunter	.50
68	Jacque Jones	.25
69	Joe Mays	.25
70	Corey Koskie	.25
71	A.J. Pierzynski	.25
72	Jose Vidro	.25
73	Vladimir Guerrero	.75
74	Tom Glavine	.25
75	Mike Piazza	1.50
76	Jose Reyes	.50
77	Jae Weong Seo	.25
78	Jorge Posada/SP	2.00
79	Mike Mussina/SP	2.00
80	Robin Ventura/SP	1.00
81	Mariano Rivera/SP	1.50
82	Roger Clemens/SP	6.00
83	Jason Giambi/SP	1.50
84	Bernie Williams/SP	2.00
85	Alfonso Soriano/SP	3.00
86	Derek Jeter	2.50
87	Miguel Tejada	.75
88	Eric Chavez	.50
89	Tim Hudson	.50
90	Barry Zito	.50
91	Mark Mulder	.50
92	Erubiel Durazo	.25
93	Pat Burrell	.50
94	Jim Thome	.75
95	Bobby Abreu	.50
96	Brian Giles	.40
97	Reggie Sanders	.25
98	Jose Hernandez	.25
99	Ryan Klesko	.25
100	Sean Burroughs	.25
101	Edgardo Alfonzo/SP	1.00
102	Rich Aurilia/SP	1.00
103	Jose Cruz Jr./SP	1.00
104	Barry Bonds/SP	6.00
105	Andres Galarraga/SP	1.00
106	Mike Cameron	.25
107	Kazuhiro Sasaki	.25
108	Bret Boone	.40
109	Ichiro Suzuki	2.00
110	John Olerud	.40

111	J.D. Drew/SP	1.50
112	Jim Edmonds/SP	2.00
113	Scott Rolen/SP	3.00
114	Matt Morris/SP	1.00
115	Tino Martinez/SP	1.00
116	Albert Pujols/SP	6.00
117	Jared Sandberg	.25
118	Carl Crawford	.25
119	Rafael Palmeiro	.50
120	Hank Blalock	.50
121	Alex Rodriguez	2.50
122	Kevin Mench	.25
123	Juan Gonzalez	.75
124	Mark Teixeira	.50
125	Shannon Stewart	.25
126	Vernon Wells	.50
127	Josh Phelps	.25
128	Eric Hinske	.25
129	Orlando Hudson	.25
130	Carlos Delgado	.75
131	Jason Shiell **RC**	3.00
132	Kevin Tolar **RC**	3.00
133	Nate Bland **RC**	3.00
134	Brent Hoard **RC**	3.00
135	Jonathan Pridie **RC**	3.00
136	Mike Ryan **RC**	4.00
137	Francisco Rosario **RC**	3.00
138	Runelvys Hernandez	3.00
139	Guillermo Quiroz **RC**	3.00
140	Chin-Hui Tsao	3.00
141	Rett Johnson **RC**	3.00
142	Colin Porter **RC**	3.00
143	Jose Castillo	3.00
144	Chris Waters **RC**	3.00
145	Jeremy Guthrie	3.00
146	Pedro Liriano	3.00
147	Joe Borowski	3.00
148	Felix Sanchez **RC**	3.00
149	Todd Wellemeyer **RC**	3.00
150	Gerald Laird	3.00
151	Brandon Webb **RC**	8.00
152	Tommy Whiteman **RC**	3.00
153	Carlos Rivera	3.00
154	Rick Roberts **RC**	3.00
155	Terrmel Sledge **RC**	3.00
156	Jeff Duncan **RC**	3.00
157	Craig Brazell **RC**	3.00
158	Bernie Castro **RC**	3.00
159	Cory Stewart **RC**	3.00
160	Brandon Villafuerte **RC**	3.00
161	Tommy Phelps **RC**	3.00
162	Josh Hall **RC**	3.00
163	Ryan Cameron **RC**	3.00
164	Garrett Atkins	3.00
165	Brian Stokes **RC**	3.00
166	Rafael Betancourt **RC**	3.00
167	Jaime Cerda	3.00
168	Danny Carrasco **RC**	3.00
169	Ian Ferguson **RC**	3.00
170	Jorge Cordova **RC**	3.00
171	Eric Munson	3.00
172	Nook Logan **RC**	3.00
173	Jeremy Bonderman	10.00
174	Kyle Snyder	3.00
175	Rich Harden	5.00
176	Kevin Ohme **RC**	3.00
177	Roger Deago **RC**	3.00
178	Marlon Byrd	3.00
179	Dontrelle Willis	5.00
180	Bobby Hill	3.00
181	Jesse Foppert	3.00
182	Andrew Good	3.00
183	Chase Utley	3.00
184	Bo Hart **RC**	3.00
185	Dan Haren	4.00
186	Tim Olson **RC**	3.00
187	Joe Thurston	3.00
188	Jason Anderson	3.00
189	Jason Gilfillan **RC**	3.00
190	Rickie Weeks **RC**	12.00
191	Hideki Matsui/500 **RC**	25.00
192	Jose Contreras **RC**	8.00
193	Willie Eyre **RC**	4.00
194	Matt Bruback **RC**	4.00
195	Heath Bell **RC**	4.00
196	Lew Ford **RC**	8.00
197	Jeremy Griffiths	5.00
198	Oscar Villarreal/500 **RC**	5.00
199	Francisco Cruceta **RC**	5.00
200	Fernando Cabrera **RC**	5.00
201	Jhonny Peralta	4.00
202	Shane Bazzell **RC**	4.00
203	Bobby Madritsch/500 **RC**	15.00
204	Phil Seibel **RC**	4.00
205	Josh Willingham **RC**	6.00
206	Robby Hammock/500 **RC**	5.00
207	Alejandro Machado **RC**	5.00
208	David Sanders **RC**	4.00
209	Mike Neu/500 **RC**	5.00
210	Andrew Brown **RC**	4.00
211	Nathan Robertson **RC**	6.00
212	Miguel Ojeda **RC**	4.00
213	Beau Kemp **RC**	4.00
214	Aaron Looper **RC**	4.00
215	Alfredo Gonzalez **RC**	4.00
216	Richard Fischer/500 **RC**	5.00
218	Jeremy Wedel **RC**	6.00
219	Prentice Redman **RC**	4.00
220	Michel Hernandez **RC**	6.00
221	Rocco Baldelli/500	5.00
222	Luis Ayala **RC**	5.00
223	Arnie Munoz **RC**	4.00
224	Wilfredo Ledezma **RC**	4.00
225	Chris Capuano **RC**	8.00
226	Aquilino Lopez **RC**	4.00
227	Joe Valentine/500 **RC**	5.00
228	Matt Kata/1,200 **RC**	5.00
229	Diegomar Markwell/1,200 **RC**	4.00
230	Clint Barnes/1,200 **RC**	15.00
231	Mike Nicolas/500 **RC**	5.00
232	Jon Leicester/1,200 **RC**	5.00

Autographs Black Ink

NM/M

Common Player:
Red & Blue Ink variations exist.
Reds not priced due to scarcity.
Mirror Parallel: No Pricing
Production 25

HB	Hank Blalock	30.00
HB	Hank Blalock/Blue/40	40.00
PB	Pat Burrell	30.00
PB	Pat Burrell/Blue/40	40.00
RC	Roger Clemens/73	125.00
RC	Roger Clemens/Blue/40	150.00
JC	Jose Contreras	40.00
JC	Jose Contreras/Blue/40	50.00
AD	Adam Dunn	30.00
AD	Adam Dunn/Blue/40	50.00
NG	Nomar Garciaparra	75.00
NG	Nomar Garciaparra/Blue/40	100.00
JG	Jason Giambi	20.00
JG	Jason Giambi/Blue/40	30.00
TR	Troy Glaus	35.00
TR	Troy Glaus/Blue/40	50.00
GL	Tom Glavine	30.00
GL	Tom Glavine/Blue/40	50.00
KG	Ken Griffey Jr.	75.00
KG	Ken Griffey Jr./Blue/40	100.00
KGs	Ken Griffey Sr.	15.00
KGs	Ken Griffey Sr./Blue/40	20.00
VG	Vladimir Guerrero	50.00
VG	Vladimir Guerrero/Blue/40	65.00
TG	Tony Gwynn	40.00
HA	Travis Hafner	15.00
HA	Travis Hafner/Blue/40	25.00
BH	Bo Hart	10.00
BH	Bo Hart/Blue/40	15.00
TH	Todd Helton/45	75.00
TH	Todd Helton/Blue/40	75.00
DH	Drew Henson	25.00
DH	Drew Henson/Blue/40	40.00
KI	Kazuhisa Ishii	35.00
KI	Kazuhisa Ishii/Blue/40	50.00
AK	Austin Kearns	20.00
AK	Austin Kearns/Blue/40	25.00
MM	Mickey Mantle/7	300.00
HM	Hideki Matsui	300.00
HM	Hideki Matsui/Blue/40	375.00
RO	Roy Oswalt	25.00
RO	Roy Oswalt/Blue/40	35.00
LO	Lyle Overbay	15.00
LO	Lyle Overbay/Blue/40	20.00
BP	Brandon Phillips	10.00
BP	Brandon Phillips/Blue/40	15.00
MP	Mark Prior	30.00
MP	Mark Prior/Blue/40	40.00
JR	Jose Reyes	40.00
JR	Jose Reyes/Blue/40	60.00
CR	Cal Ripken Jr.	165.00
CR	Cal Ripken Jr./Blue/40	220.00
NR	Nolan Ryan	120.00
NR	Nolan Ryan/Blue/40	165.00
TS	Tim Salmon	25.00
TS	Tim Salmon/Blue/40	35.00
CS	Curt Schilling	40.00
CS	Curt Schilling/Blue/40	75.00
GS	Gary Sheffield	30.00
GS	Gary Sheffield/Blue/40	40.00
SS	Sammy Sosa/7	
SS	Sammy Sosa/Blue/40	150.00
IS	Ichiro Suzuki/Blue/40	400.00
IS	Ichiro Suzuki/Red/35	400.00
MT	Mark Teixeira	40.00
MT	Mark Teixeira/Blue/40	50.00
JT	Jim Thome	40.00
JT	Jim Thome/Blue/40	60.00
BW	Brandon Webb	40.00
BW	Brandon Webb/Blue/40	60.00
RW	Rickie Weeks	70.00
JW	Jerome Williams	25.00
JW	Jerome Williams/Blue/40	35.00
TW	Ted Williams/9	
DW	Dontrelle Willis	45.00
DW	Dontrelle Willis/Blue/40	75.00

Barrel Autographs

NM/M

Quantity produced listed

HB	Hank Blalock/420	35.00
PB	Pat Burrell/345	35.00
RC	Roger Clemens/49	220.00
AD	Adam Dunn/345	40.00
TR	Troy Glaus/345	40.00
TG	Tom Glavine/345	45.00
KG	Ken Griffey Jr./295	125.00
HM	Hideki Matsui/124	400.00
CR	Cal Ripken Jr./149	180.00
NR	Nolan Ryan/445	150.00
JT	Jim Thome/345	65.00

Game-Used Barrel

Quantity produced listed
No Pricing due to scarcity.
KW-BB Kerry Wood/2 (2/04 Auction) 1,000

Game-Used Patch

Production 25 or 10
No pricing due to scarcity.

Patch

NM/M

Common Player: 4.00
Inserted 1:6
Logo Patch Parallel: 1-2X
Production 75 Sets

JB1	Jeff Bagwell	6.00
LB1	Lance Berkman	5.00
BB1	Barry Bonds	15.00
PB1	Pat Burrell	5.00
RC1	Roger Clemens	12.00
CD1	Carlos Delgado	4.00
AD1	Adam Dunn	5.00

SWEET SPOT PATCHES

JE1	Jim Edmonds	4.00
DE1	Darin Erstad	4.00
NG1	Nomar Garciaparra	10.00
JG1	Jason Giambi	4.00
TG1	Troy Glaus	5.00
TO1	Tom Glavine	5.00
LG1	Luis Gonzalez	4.00
SG1	Shawn Green	5.00
KG1	Ken Griffey Jr.	8.00
VG1	Vladimir Guerrero	5.00
TH1	Torii Hunter	5.00
KI1	Kazuhisa Ishii	4.00
DJ1	Derek Jeter	15.00
RJ1	Randy Johnson	6.00
AJ1	Andruw Jones	5.00
CJ1	Chipper Jones	10.00
JK1	Jeff Kent	5.00
GM1	Greg Maddux	10.00
PM1	Pedro J. Martinez	6.00
HN1	Hideo Nomo	5.00
MO1	Magglio Ordonez	4.00
CP1	Corey Patterson	6.00
MP1	Mike Piazza	10.00
MA1	Mark Prior	8.00
AP1	Albert Pujols	15.00
AR1	Alex Rodriguez	10.00
CS1	Curt Schilling	6.00
GS1	Gary Sheffield	6.00
AS1	Alfonso Soriano	8.00
SS1	Sammy Sosa	10.00
IS1	Ichiro Suzuki	10.00
MT1	Miguel Tejada	6.00
JT1	Jim Thome	6.00
BW1	Bernie Williams	5.00
BZ1	Barry Zito	4.00

Swatches

SWEET SPOT SWATCHES
GAME-USED JERSEY

NM/M

Common Player: 4.00
Inserted 1:24
Tier 2: 1-2X
Production 75

RA	Roberto Alomar	4.00
PB	Pat Burrell	6.00
RC	Roger Clemens	10.00
NM	Nomar Garciaparra	15.00
NG1	Nomar Garciaparra	4.00
JG	Jason Giambi	8.00
TG	Troy Glaus	4.00
TG1	Troy Glaus	5.00
TO	Tom Glavine	4.00
LG	Luis Gonzalez	4.00
KG	Ken Griffey Jr.	10.00
VG	Vladimir Guerrero	6.00
TH	Torii Hunter	5.00
RJ	Randy Johnson	6.00
AJ	Andruw Jones	5.00
CJ	Chipper Jones	8.00
AK	Austin Kearns	4.00
GM	Greg Maddux	10.00
MM	Mickey Mantle	120.00

HM	Hideki Matsui	45.00
HM1	Hideki Matsui	4.00
RO	Roy Oswalt	4.00
RO1	Roy Oswalt	4.00
MP	Mike Piazza	10.00
MA	Mark Prior	3.00
AP	Albert Pujols	15.00
AR	Alex Rodriguez	10.00
CS	Curt Schilling	5.00
GS	Gary Sheffield	4.00
AS	Alfonso Soriano	10.00
AS1	Alfonso Soriano	4.00
SS	Sammy Sosa	12.00
IS	Ichiro Suzuki	20.00
MT	Miguel Tejada	4.00
FT	Frank Thomas	6.00
JT	Jim Thome	8.00
BW	Bernie Williams	4.00
TW	Ted Williams	60.00
BZ	Barry Zito	4.00

2003 Upper Deck Sweet Spot Classic

		NM/M
Complete Set (150):		
Common Player:		.40
Common Ted Williams		
(91-120):		5.00
Production 1,941		
Common Yankee Heritage		
(121-150):		2.00
Production 1,500		
Pack (4):		12.00
Box (12):		120.00
1	Al Hrabosky	.40
2	Al Lopez	.40
3	Andre Dawson	.75
4	Bill Buckner	.40
5	Billy Williams	.50
6	Bob Feller	.75
7	Bob Lemon	.40
8	Bobby Doerr	.40
9	Cecil Cooper	.40
10	Cal Ripken Jr.	2.50
11	Carlton Fisk	.60
12	Jim "Catfish" Hunter	.40
13	Chris Chambliss	.40
14	Dale Murphy	.75
15	Gaylord Perry	.40
16	Dave Kingman	.40
17	Dave Parker	.40
18	Dave Stewart	.40
19	David Cone	.40
20	Dennis Eckersley	.60
21	Don Baylor	.40
22	Don Sutton	.40
23	Duke Snider	1.00
24	Dwight Evans	.40
25	Dwight Gooden	.40
26	Earl Weaver	.40
27	Early Wynn	.40
28	Eddie Mathews	1.50
29	Enos Slaughter	.40
30	Ernie Banks	1.50
31	Fred Lynn	.40
32	Fred Stanley	.40
33	Gary Carter	.75
34	George Foster	.40
35	Hal Newhouser	.40
36	George Kell	.40
37	Harmon Killebrew	1.50
38	Hoyt Wilhelm	.40
39	Jack Morris	.40
40	Jim Bunning	.40
41	Jim Gilliam	.40
42	Jim Leyritz	.40
43	Jimmy Key	.40
44	Joe Carter	.40
45	Joe Morgan	.40
46	John Montefusco	.40
47	Johnny Bench	2.00
48	Johnny Podres	.40

49	Jose Canseco	.75
50	Juan Marichal	.40
51	Keith Hernandez	.40
52	Ken Griffey Sr.	.40
53	Kirby Puckett	1.50
54	Kirk Gibson	.40
55	Larry Doby	.40
56	Lee May	.40
57	Lee Mazzilli	.40
58	Lou Boudreau	.40
59	Mark McGwire	3.00
60	Maury Wills	.40
61	Mike Pagliarulo	.40
62	Monte Irvin	.75
63	Nolan Ryan	3.00
64	Orlando Cepeda	.40
65	Ozzie Smith	1.50
66	Paul O'Neill	.40
67	Pee Wee Reese	.40
68	Phil Niekro	.40
69	Ralph Kiner	.40
70	Red Schoendienst	.40
71	Richie Ashburn	.40
72	Rick Ferrell	.40
73	Robin Roberts	.40
74	Robin Yount	1.50
75	Hideki Matsui/1,999 **RC**	20.00
75	Hideki Matsui/Red/500	25.00
75	Hideki Matsui/Blue/250	30.00
75	Hideki Matsui/Silver/25	200.00
76	Rollie Fingers	.40
77	Ron Cey	.40
78	Tom Seaver	1.00
79	Sparky Anderson	.40
80	Stan Musial	2.00
81	Steve Garvey	.40
82	Ted Williams	3.00
83	Tommy Lasorda	.40
84	Tony Gwynn	1.00
85	Tony Perez	.40
86	Vida Blue	.40
87	Warren Spahn	.75
88	Bob Gibson	1.00
89	Willie McCovey	.40
90	Willie Stargell	.75
91	Ted Williams	5.00
92	Ted Williams	5.00
93	Ted Williams	5.00
94	Ted Williams	5.00
95	Ted Williams	5.00
96	Ted Williams	5.00
97	Ted Williams	5.00
98	Ted Williams	5.00
99	Ted Williams	5.00
100	Ted Williams	5.00
101	Ted Williams	5.00
102	Ted Williams	5.00
103	Ted Williams	5.00
104	Ted Williams	5.00
105	Ted Williams	5.00
106	Ted Williams	5.00
107	Ted Williams	5.00
108	Ted Williams	5.00
109	Ted Williams	5.00
110	Ted Williams	5.00
111	Ted Williams	5.00
112	Ted Williams	5.00
113	Ted Williams	5.00
114	Ted Williams	5.00
115	Ted Williams	5.00
116	Ted Williams	5.00
117	Ted Williams	5.00
118	Ted Williams	5.00
119	Ted Williams	5.00
120	Ted Williams	5.00
121	Babe Ruth	8.00
122	Bucky Dent	2.00
123	Casey Stengel	3.00
124	Dave Righetti	2.00
125	Dave Winfield	3.00
126	Dick Tidrow	2.00
127	Dock Ellis	2.00
128	Don Mattingly	8.00
129	Hank Bauer	2.00
130	Jim Bouton	2.00
131	Jim Kaat	2.00
132	Joe DiMaggio	6.00
133	Joe Torre	3.00
134	Lou Piniella	2.00
135	Mel Stottlemyre	2.00
136	Mickey Mantle	15.00
137	Mickey Rivers	2.00
138	Phil Rizzuto	4.00
139	Ralph Branca	2.00
140	Ralph Houk	2.00
141	Roger Maris	6.00
142	Ron Guidry	2.00
143	Ruben Amaro Jr.	2.00
144	Sparky Lyle	2.00
145	Thurman Munson	5.00

146	Tommy Henrich	2.00
147	Tommy John	2.00
148	Tony Kubek	2.00
149	Whitey Ford	4.00
150	Yogi Berra	4.00

Game Jersey

		NM/M
Common Player:		5.00
Inserted 1:16		
EB	Ernie Banks	15.00
JB	Johnny Bench	15.00
JC	Jose Canseco	6.00
GC	Gary Carter	6.00
RC	Ron Cey	5.00
CC	Cecil Cooper	6.00
AD	Andre Dawson	6.00
RF	Rollie Fingers	5.00
CF	Carlton Fisk	8.00
GF	George Foster	5.00
SG	Steve Garvey	5.00
JG	Jim Gilliam	6.00
TG	Tony Gwynn	8.00
HK	Harmon Killebrew	12.00
FL	Fred Lynn	5.00
LM	Lee May	5.00
MM	Mark McGwire	30.00
JM	Joe Morgan	6.00
DM	Dale Murphy	10.00
SM	Stan Musial	25.00
DP	Dave Parker	5.00
JP	Johnny Podres	5.00
KP	Kirby Puckett	12.00
CR	Cal Ripken Jr.	20.00
NR	Nolan Ryan	30.00
OS	Ozzie Smith	10.00
DS	Duke Snider	12.00
WS	Willie Stargell/SP	15.00
TW	Ted Williams/SP	100.00
RY	Robin Yount	10.00

Greats Autograph

		NM/M
Common Autograph:		
Blue, Black and Red ink variations		
exist.		
Listings without notations are blue		
ink.		
EB	Ernie Banks/Black/73	80.00
DB	Don Baylor	20.00
DB	Don Baylor/Black/50	35.00
JB	Johnny Bench/Black/73	100.00
BB	Bill Buckner	20.00
BB	Bill Buckner/Black/85	25.00
GC	Gary Carter/Black/173	40.00
JC	Joe Carter/Black/173	35.00
OC	Orlando Cepeda	20.00
OC	Orlando Cepeda/Black/34	35.00
AD	Andre Dawson	20.00
AD	Andre Dawson/Black/75	30.00
DEc	Dennis Eckersley	25.00
DE	Dwight Evans	20.00
DE	Dwight Evans/Black/100	30.00
RF	Rollie Fingers/Black/73	30.00
RF	Rollie Fingers/Red/25	90.00

CF	Carlton Fisk	50.00
GF	George Foster/Black/173	35.00
SG	Steve Garvey/Black/174	30.00
GI	Kirk Gibson/Black/173	30.00
KG	Ken Griffey Sr.	20.00
KG	Ken Griffey Sr./Black/100	25.00
TG	Tony Gwynn	45.00
TG	Tony Gwynn/Black/101	60.00
KH	Keith Hernandez/Black/173	40.00
KH	Keith Hernandez/Red/25	110.00
AH	Al Hrabosky	25.00
AH	Al Hrabosky/Black/100	35.00
HK	Harmon Killebrew/Black/73	80.00
FL	Fred Lynn	30.00
MM	Mark McGwire/Black/73	425.00
JoM	Joe Morgan/Black/169	40.00
JMo	Jack Morris/Black/123	40.00
DM	Dale Murphy	30.00
PN	Phil Niekro/Black/173	30.00
PN	Phil Niekro/Red/25	75.00
DP	Dave Parker/Black/113	30.00
TP	Tony Perez/Black/51	65.00
JP	Johnny Podres/Black/173	30.00
JP	Johnny Podres/Red/25	80.00
KP	Kirby Puckett	45.00
KP	Kirby Puckett/Black/174	60.00
CR	Cal Ripken Jr.	150.00
CR	Cal Ripken Jr/Black/38	250.00
RR	Robin Roberts/Black/173	40.00
TS	Tom Seaver/Black/74	80.00
TS	Tom Seaver/Red/25	135.00
SN	Duke Snider	40.00
SN	Duke Snider/Black/100	50.00
DSt	Dave Stewart	15.00
DSu	Don Sutton/Black/123	30.00
AT	Alan Trammell/Black/173	35.00
BW	Billy Williams/Black/173	35.00
TW	Ted Williams/9	3,650
MW	Maury Wills/Black/173	30.00
RY	Robin Yount/Black/73	100.00
RY	Robin Yount/Red/25	200.00

Patch Logo

		NM/M
Common Player:		5.00
Note: are actual game-used patches.		
EB1	Ernie Banks	12.00
JB1	Johnny Bench	12.00
JB2	Johnny Bench/50	50.00
JB3	Johnny Bench/150	35.00
YB1	Yogi Berra	12.00
YB2	Yogi Berra/350	25.00
YB3	Yogi Berra/150	35.00
JD1	Joe DiMaggio	20.00
JD2	Joe DiMaggio/50	85.00
JD3	Joe DiMaggio/350	30.00
JD4	Joe DiMaggio/150	40.00
CF1	Carlton Fisk	8.00
CF2	Carlton Fisk/150	15.00
GF1	George Foster/350	10.00
GF2	George Foster	5.00
SG1	Steve Garvey	5.00
SG2	Steve Garvey/350	10.00
SG3	Steve Garvey/150	25.00
SG4	Steve Garvey/50	30.00
SG5	Steve Garvey/50	25.00
KG1	Kirk Gibson	5.00
KG2	Kirk Gibson/350	12.00

TG1	Tony Gwynn	8.00
TG2	Tony Gwynn/150	50.00
TG3	Tony Gwynn/350	25.00
CH1	Catfish Hunter/350	10.00
CH2	Catfish Hunter	5.00
CH3	Catfish Hunter/39	30.00
CH4	Catfish Hunter/50	30.00
FL1	Fred Lynn	5.00
FL2	Fred Lynn/350	10.00
FL3	Fred Lynn/150	15.00
FL4	Fred Lynn/50	20.00
MM1	Mickey Mantle	35.00
MM2	Mickey Mantle/150	85.00
MM3	Mickey Mantle/150	85.00
MM4	Mickey Mantle/150	75.00
RM1	Roger Maris	15.00
RM2	Roger Maris/350	25.00
RM3	Roger Maris/150	40.00
RM4	Roger Maris/50	60.00
HM1	Hideki Matsui	25.00
MC1	Mark McGwire	20.00
MC2	Mark McGwire/350	50.00
MC3	Mark McGwire/9	
JM1	Joe Morgan	6.00
JM2	Joe Morgan/350	8.00
JM3	Joe Morgan/150	15.00
JM4	Joe Morgan/150	30.00
JM5	Joe Morgan/100	15.00
KP1	Kirby Puckett	10.00
KP2	Kirby Puckett/40	100.00
CR1	Cal Ripken Jr.	25.00
CR2	Cal Ripken Jr/75	100.00
CR3	Cal Ripken Jr./150	50.00
BR1	Babe Ruth/350	40.00
BR2	Babe Ruth	30.00
BR3	Babe Ruth/150	50.00
NR1	Nolan Ryan	25.00
NR2	Nolan Ryan/350	40.00
NR3	Nolan Ryan/150	50.00
NR4	Nolan Ryan/105	100.00
OS1	Ozzie Smith	10.00
OS2	Ozzie Smith/350	20.00
OS3	Ozzie Smith/150	60.00
OS4	Ozzie Smith/100	40.00
OS5	Ozzie Smith/150	35.00
DS1	Duke Snider	8.00
DS2	Duke Snider/150	25.00
DS3	Duke Snider/350	15.00
DS4	Duke Snider/25	
DS5	Duke Snider/150	20.00
DS6	Duke Snider/150	20.00
WS1	Willie Stargell	5.00
WS2	Willie Stargell/137	50.00
WS3	Willie Stargell/150	25.00
WS4	Willie Stargell/50	40.00
BW1	Billy Williams	6.00
TW1	Ted Williams	20.00
TW2	Ted Williams/350	40.00
RY1	Robin Yount	8.00
RY2	Robin Yount/150	40.00
RY3	Robin Yount/350	20.00

Pinstripes

NM/M

Common Player:		5.00
Inserted 1:40		
YB	Yogi Berra	15.00
JB	Jim Bouton	5.00
DE	Dave Righetti	8.00
JD	Joe DiMaggio	100.00
DG	Dwight Gooden	5.00
MM	Mickey Mantle	140.00
DM	Don Mattingly	25.00
TM	Thurman Munson	30.00
DR	Dave Righetti	5.00
PR	Phil Rizzuto	15.00
BR	Babe Ruth	250.00
CS	Casey Stengel	12.00

Yankee Greats Autograph

NM/M

Common Autograph:

RA	Ruben Amaro Sr.	25.00
RA	Ruben Amaro Sr./Black/100	30.00
RA	Ruben Amaro Sr./Red/25	60.00
HB	Hank Bauer	30.00
HB	Hank Bauer/Black/75	40.00
YB	Yogi Berra/Black/73	100.00
JB	Jim Bouton	25.00
JB	Jim Bouton/Black/100	30.00
RB	Ralph Branca	25.00
RB	Ralph Branca/Black/100	30.00
JC	Jose Canseco/Black/73	90.00
JC	Jose Canseco/Red/25	150.00
CC	Chris Chambliss	30.00
CC	Chris Chambliss/Black/101	35.00
CC	Chris Chambliss/Red/25	75.00
DC	David Cone/Black/74	75.00
DC	David Cone/Red/25	110.00
BD	Bucky Dent	20.00
JD	Joe DiMaggio/5	2,325
DE	Dock Ellis/Black/174	25.00
DE	Dock Ellis/Red/25	65.00
DG	Dwight Gooden/Black/74	70.00
GU	Ron Guidry	35.00
GU	Ron Guidry/Black/100	45.00
TH	Tommy Henrich	35.00
TH	Tommy Henrich/Black/100	40.00
TH	Tommy Henrich/Red/25	125.00
RH	Ralph Houk	25.00
RH	Ralph Houk/Black/100	30.00
TJ	Tommy John	30.00
TJ	Tommy John/Black/100	35.00
JKa	Jim Kaat	20.00
JKa	Jim Kaat/Black/25	25.00
JKe	Jimmy Key	40.00
JKe	Jimmy Key/Black/100	50.00
DK	Dave Kingman	25.00
DK	Dave Kingman/Black/100	30.00
TK	Tony Kubek/Black/123	15.00
JL	Jim Leyritz	25.00
JL	Jim Leyritz/Black/100	35.00
JL	Jim Leyritz/Red/25	65.00
SL	Sparky Lyle	30.00
SL	Sparky Lyle/Black/100	40.00
MM	Mickey Mantle/Blue/7	2,850
DM	Don Mattingly/Black/74	100.00
DM	Don Mattingly/Red/25	340.00
LM	Lee Mazzilli	30.00
JM	John Montefusco	20.00
JM	John Montefusco/Black/100	25.00
JM	John Montefusco/Red/25	50.00
PO	Paul O'Neill	50.00
PO	Paul O'Neill/Black/100	65.00
PO	Paul O'Neill/Red/25	100.00
MP	Mike Pagliarulo	20.00
MP	Mike Pagliarulo/Black/99	25.00
MP	Mike Pagliarulo/Red/25	60.00
LP	Lou Piniella	40.00
LP	Lou Piniella/Black/100	45.00
DR	Dave Righetti/Black/173	40.00
DR	Dave Righetti/Red/25	85.00
MR	Mickey Rivers/Black/73	40.00
PR	Phil Rizzuto/Black/173	55.00
FS	Fred Stanley	25.00
FS	Fred Stanley/Black/101	25.00
MS	Mel Stottlemyre/Black/73	85.00
MS	Mel Stottlemyre/Red/25	25.00
DT	Dick Tidrow	20.00
DT	Dick Tidrow/Black/101	25.00
DT	Dick Tidrow/Red/25	70.00
JT	Joe Torre/Black/73	60.00
JT	Joe Torre/Red/25	140.00
DW	Dave Winfield/Black/25	165.00

2003 Upper Deck Ultimate Collection

NM/M

Complete Set (181):	
Common Player (1-84):	2.00
Production 850	
Common (85-117):	3.00
Production 625	
Common (118-140):	3.00
Production 399	
Common (141-158):	4.00
Production 250	
Common (159-168):	6.00
Production 100	
Common (169-174):	25.00
Common (175-180):	10.00
169-180 Production 250	
Pack (4):	90.00
Box (4):	300.00

1	Ichiro Suzuki	8.00
2	Ken Griffey Jr.	6.00
3	Sammy Sosa	6.00
4	Jason Giambi	2.00
5	Mike Piazza	5.00
6	Derek Jeter	10.00
7	Randy Johnson	4.00
8	Barry Bonds	10.00
9	Carlos Delgado	3.00
10	Mark Prior	3.00
11	Vladimir Guerrero	4.00
12	Alfonso Soriano	4.00
13	Jim Thome	4.00
14	Pedro J. Martinez	4.00
15	Nomar Garciaparra	5.00
16	Chipper Jones	4.00
17	Rocco Baldelli	2.00
18	Dontrelle Willis	2.00
19	Garret Anderson	2.00
20	Jeff Bagwell	2.00
21	Jim Edmonds	2.50
22	Rickey Henderson	3.00
23	Torii Hunter	2.50
24	Tom Glavine	2.50
25	Hideo Nomo	2.50
26	Luis Gonzalez	2.50
27	Alex Rodriguez	8.00
28	Albert Pujols	10.00
29	Manny Ramirez	4.00
30	Rafael Palmeiro	3.00
31	Bernie Williams	3.00
32	Curt Schilling	3.00
33	Roger Clemens	8.00
34	Andruw Jones	2.00
35	J.D. Drew	2.00
36	Kerry Wood	3.00
37	Scott Rolen	3.00
38	Darin Erstad	2.00
39	Joe DiMaggio	8.00
40	Magglio Ordonez	3.00
41	Todd Helton	3.00
42	Barry Zito	3.00
43	Mickey Mantle	10.00
44	Miguel Tejada	3.00
45	Troy Glaus	2.00
46	Kazuhisa Ishii	2.00
47	Adam Dunn	3.00
48	Ted Williams	8.00
49	Mike Mussina	3.00
50	Ivan Rodriguez	3.00
51	Jacque Jones	2.00
52	Stan Musial	6.00
53	Mariano Rivera	2.50
54	Larry Walker	2.50
55	Aaron Boone	2.50
56	Hank Blalock	2.50
57	Rich Harden	2.00
58	Lance Berkman	2.00
59	Eric Chavez	2.00
60	Carlos Beltran	3.00
61	Roy Oswalt	2.00
62	Moises Alou	2.00
63	Nolan Ryan	10.00
64	Jeff Kent	2.00
65	Roberto Alomar	2.00
66	Runelvys Hernandez	2.00
67	Roy Halladay	3.00
68	Tim Hudson	2.50
69	Tom Seaver	4.00
70	Edgardo Alfonzo	2.00
71	Andy Pettitte	2.00
72	Preston Wilson	2.00
73	Frank Thomas	3.00
74	Jerome Williams	2.00
75	Shawn Green	2.50
76	David Wells	2.00
77	John Smoltz	2.00
78	Jorge Posada	2.00
79	Marlon Byrd	2.00
80	Austin Kearns	2.00
81	Bret Boone	2.00
82	Rafael Furcal	2.00
83	Jay Gibbons	2.00
84	Shane Reynolds	2.00
85	Nate Bland RC	3.00
86	Willie Eyre RC	3.00
87	Jeremy Guthrie RC	3.00
88	Jeremy Wedel RC	3.00
89	Jhonny Peralta RC	6.00
90	Luis Ayala RC	3.00
91	Michael Hessman RC	3.00
92	Micheal Nakamura RC	3.00
93	Nook Logan RC	3.00
94	Rett Johnson RC	3.00
95	Josh Hall RC	4.00
96	Julio Manon RC	3.00
97	Heath Bell RC	3.00
98	Ian Ferguson RC	3.00
99	Jason Gilfillan RC	3.00
100	Jason Roach RC	3.00
101	Jason Shiell RC	3.00
102	Terrmel Sledge RC	5.00
103	Phil Seibel RC	3.00
104	Jeff Duncan RC	6.00
105	Mike Neu RC	3.00
106	Colin Porter RC	3.00
107	Dave Matranga RC	3.00
108	Aaron Looper RC	3.00
109	Jeremy Bonderman RC	20.00
110	Miguel Ojeda RC	3.00
111	Chad Cordero RC	3.00
112	Shane Bazell RC	4.00
113	Tim Olson RC	5.00
114	Michel Hernandez RC	3.00
115	Chien-Ming Wang RC	50.00
116	Josh Stewart RC	3.00
117	Clint Barmes RC	10.00
118	Craig Brazell RC	5.00
119	Josh Willingham RC	8.00
120	Brent Hoard RC	3.00
121	Francisco Rosario RC	3.00
122	Rick Roberts RC	3.00
123	Geoff Geary RC	3.00
124	Edgar Gonzalez RC	3.00
125	Kevin Correia RC	3.00
126	Ryan Cameron RC	3.00
127	Beau Kemp RC	3.00
128	Tommy Phelps RC	3.00
129	Mark Malaska RC	3.00
130	Kevin Ohme RC	3.00
131	Humberto Quintero RC	3.00
132	Aquilino Lopez RC	3.00
133	Andrew Brown RC	3.00
134	Wilfredo Ledezma RC	3.00
135	Luis De Los Santos RC	3.00
136	Garrett Atkins RC	3.00
137	Fernando Cabrera RC	3.00
138	D.J. Carrasco RC	3.00
139	Alfredo Gonzalez RC	3.00
140	Alex Prieto RC	3.00
141	Matt Kata RC	5.00
142	Chris Capuano RC	15.00
143	Bobby Madritsch RC	20.00
144	Greg Jones RC	4.00
145	Pete Zoccolillo RC	4.00
146	Chad Gaudin RC	10.00
147	Rosman Garcia RC	4.00
148	Gerald Laird RC	4.00
149	Danny Garcia RC	4.00
150	Stephen Randolph RC	4.00
151	Pete LaForest RC	8.00
152	Brian Sweeney RC	4.00
153	Aaron Miles RC	4.00
154	Jorge DePaula RC	4.00
155	Graham Koonce RC	10.00
156	Tom Gregorio RC	4.00
157	Javier Lopez RC	4.00
158	Oscar Villarreal RC	4.00
159	Prentice Redman RC	6.00
160	Francisco Cruceta RC	6.00
161	Guillermo Quiroz RC	20.00

162	Jeremy Griffiths	10.00
163	Lew Ford RC	20.00
164	Rob Hammock RC	10.00
165	Todd Wellemeyer RC	10.00
166	Ryan Wagner RC	10.00
167	Edwin Jackson RC	20.00
168	Dan Haren	20.00
169	Hideki Matsui/ Auto. RC	275.00
170	Jose Contreras/Auto.	30.00
171	Delmon Young/ Auto. RC	275.00
172	Rickie Weeks/ Auto. RC	100.00
173	Brandon Webb/ Auto. RC	120.00
174	Bo Hart/Auto. RC	10.00
175	Rocco Baldelli/Auto.	25.00
176	Jose Reyes/Auto.	30.00
177	Dontrelle Willis/Auto.	40.00
178	Bobby Hill/Auto.	10.00
179	Jae Weong Seo/ Auto.	20.00
180	Jesse Foppert/Auto.	20.00
CL	Checklist	2.00

Gold

Stars (1-184):	1.5-3X
(85-117):	1-2X
Production 50	
(118-140):	1-2X
Production 35	
(141-158):	1-2X
Production 25	
(159-168):	No Pricing
Production 10	
(169-180):	No Pricing
Production 25	

Buybacks

	NM/M
Production 1-75	
Hank Blalock/35	40.00
Hank Blalock 03 40M/25	40.00
Hank Blalock 03 GF/25	40.00
Hank Blalock 03 Patch/25	40.00
Hank Blalock 03 SPA/20	40.00
Hank Blalock 03 SPA/25	40.00
Hank Blalock 03 VIN/25	40.00
Luis Gonzalez 03 40M HR/25	40.00
Luis Gonzalez 03 SPA/25	40.00
Luis Gonzalez 03 VIN/25	40.00
Ken Griffey Jr. 02-3 SUP/75	80.00
Ken Griffey Jr. 02-3 SUP Spok/50	80.00
Ken Griffey Jr. 03 40M/50	80.00
Ken Griffey Jr. 03 40M/50	80.00
Ken Griffey Jr. 03 40M/50	80.00
Ken Griffey Jr. 03 40M/50	80.00
Ken Griffey Jr. 03 40M T40/50	80.00
Ken Griffey Jr. 03 GF/50	80.00
Ken Griffey Jr. 03 HON/50	80.00
Ken Griffey Jr. 03 HON SP/30	100.00
Ken Griffey Jr. 03 Patch/75	80.00
Ken Griffey Jr. 03 PB/75	80.00
Ken Griffey Jr. 03 SPA/50	80.00
Ken Griffey Jr. 03 SPA/75	80.00
Ken Griffey Jr. 03 SPx/75	80.00
Ken Griffey Jr. 03 SWS/75	80.00
Ken Griffey Jr. 03 UDA/75	80.00
Ken Griffey Jr. 03 VIN/50	80.00
Torii Hunter 03 Patch/25	40.00
Torii Hunter 03 VIN/25	40.00
Austin Kearns 03 40M/33	30.00

	Hideki Matsui 03 40M/20	250.00
	Hideki Matsui 03 40M Flag/20	250.00
	Hideki Matsui 03 GF/18	250.00
	Hideki Matsui 03 PB/17	250.00
	Hideki Matsui 03 UD/25	250.00
	Hideki Matsui 03 VIN/25	250.00
	Stan Musial 02 SPLC/30	75.00
	Stan Musial 02 WSH/25	75.00
	Stan Musial 03 PB/50	60.00
	Stan Musial 03 SWSC/37	75.00
	Stan Musial 03 VIN/50	60.00
	Sammy Sosa 02-3 SUP/25	120.00
	Sammy Sosa 03 PB/25	120.00
	Sammy Sosa 03 SPA/25	120.00
	Sammy Sosa 03 VIN/25	120.00
	Mark Teixeira 03 40M/50	40.00
	Mark Teixeira 03 Patch/50	40.00
	Mark Teixeira 03 SPA RA/25	50.00
	Mark Teixeira 03 SWS/23	50.00
	Mark Teixeira 03 UD/25	50.00
	Mark Teixeira 03 VIN/25	50.00

Double Barrel

	NM/M
No pricing due to scarcity.	
DB-AE Darin Erstad, Garret Anderson/3 (3/04 Auction)	645.00
DB-GS Tom Seaver, Tom Glavine/2 (3/04 Auction)	700.00

Dual Jersey

	NM/M
Common Duo:	10.00
Production 50 Sets	
Gold:	1-1.25X
Production 25 Sets	
AH	Alfonso Soriano, Hideki Matsui	40.00
AI	Albert Pujols, Ichiro Suzuki	50.00
BK	Jeff Kent, Jeff Bagwell	15.00
CA	Chipper Jones, Andruw Jones	15.00
CJ	Carlos Delgado, Jason Giambi	15.00
DE	Jim Edmonds, J.D. Drew	10.00
DG	Carlos Delgado, Vladimir Guerrero	15.00
DM	Mickey Mantle, Joe DiMaggio	250.00
DP	Carlos Delgado, Rafael Palmeiro	15.00
DW	Joe DiMaggio, Ted Williams	150.00
GB	Shawn Green, Kevin Brown	10.00

GD	Adam Dunn, Ken Griffey Jr.	25.00
GE	Darin Erstad, Troy Glaus	10.00
GP	Rafael Palmeiro, Ken Griffey Jr.	25.00
GR	Alex Rodriguez, Nomar Garciaparra	25.00
GS	Vladimir Guerrero, Sammy Sosa	25.00
HJ	Torii Hunter, Jacque Jones	10.00
HZ	Roy Halladay, Barry Zito	10.00
IG	Ken Griffey Jr., Ichiro Suzuki	50.00
IN	Ichiro Suzuki, Hideo Nomo	50.00
IS	Sammy Sosa, Ichiro Suzuki	45.00
JF	Andruw Jones, Rafael Furcal	15.00
JM	Mike Piazza, Jorge Posada	20.00
MC	Greg Maddux, Roger Clemens	30.00
MW	Ted Williams, Mickey Mantle	250.00
NI	Hideo Nomo, Kazuhisa Ishii	30.00
NM	Hideki Matsui, Hideo Nomo	60.00
PC	Roger Clemens, Pedro J. Martinez	25.00
PM	Mike Mussina, Andy Pettitte	15.00
PS	Sammy Sosa, Mark Prior	30.00
RM	Pedro J. Martinez, Manny Ramirez	15.00
RP	Rafael Palmeiro, Alex Rodriguez	20.00
SA	Albert Pujols, Scott Rolen	40.00
SB	Alfonso Soriano, Bernie Williams	15.00
SJ	Randy Johnson, Curt Schilling	20.00
SM	Greg Maddux, John Smoltz	25.00
TB	Mark Teixeira, Hank Blalock	15.00
TH	Todd Helton, Jim Thome	15.00
TR	Alex Rodriguez, Miguel Tejada	20.00
WL	Mike Lowell, Dontrelle Willis	15.00
YW	Delmon Young, Rickie Weeks	35.00

Dual Patch

	NM/M
Common Duo:	20.00
Production 99 unless noted.	
Gold:	.75-1.25X
Production 35	
AI	Ichiro Suzuki, Albert Pujols	100.00
AM	Andy Pettitte, Mike Mussina	25.00
BK	Jeff Bagwell, Jeff Kent	25.00
CA	Andruw Jones, Chipper Jones	30.00
CV	Carlos Delgado, Vladimir Guerrero	35.00
DE	Jim Edmonds, J.D. Drew	25.00
DG	Carlos Delgado, Jason Giambi	25.00
DP	Carlos Delgado, Rafael Palmeiro/35	40.00
GB	Shawn Green, Kevin Brown	20.00
GD	Adam Dunn, Ken Griffey Jr.	45.00
GE	Darin Erstad, Troy Glaus	30.00
GP	Ken Griffey Jr., Rafael Palmeiro/35	50.00
GR	Alex Rodriguez, Nomar Garciaparra	75.00

GS	Vladimir Guerrero, Sammy Sosa	40.00
HJ	Torii Hunter, Jacque Jones/83	20.00
HZ	Roy Halladay, Barry Zito	35.00
IG	Ken Griffey Jr., Ichiro Suzuki	90.00
IN	Ichiro Suzuki, Hideo Nomo	140.00
IS	Sammy Sosa, Ichiro Suzuki	90.00
JF	Rafael Furcal, Andruw Jones	25.00
JG	John Smoltz, Greg Maddux	40.00
MC	Greg Maddux, Roger Clemens/75	60.00
NI	Hideo Nomo, Kazuhisa Ishii/63	65.00
NM	Hideki Matsui, Hideo Nomo/35	180.00
PM	Mike Piazza, Jorge Posada/73	35.00
PR	Roger Clemens, Pedro Martinez/35	60.00
PS	Sammy Sosa, Mark Prior	40.00
RM	Pedro J. Martinez, Manny Ramirez	40.00
RP	Rafael Palmeiro, Alex Rodriguez/35	40.00
SA	Albert Pujols, Scott Rolen	75.00
SJ	Randy Johnson, Curt Schilling	40.00
SM	Alfonso Soriano, Hideki Matsui	80.00
TB	Mark Teixeira, Hank Blalock	40.00
TH	Jim Thome, Todd Helton	35.00
TR	Alex Rodriguez, Miguel Tejada	50.00
WL	Mike Lowell, Dontrelle Willis/85	35.00
YW	Delmon Young, Rickie Weeks/28	75.00

Game Jersey Tier 1

	NM/M
Common Player:	8.00
Production 99 Sets	
Copper:	No Pricing
Production 10 Sets	
Gold:	.75-2X
No pricing production of 20 or less.	
RB	Rocco Baldelli	8.00
PB	Pat Burrell	8.00
RC	Roger Clemens	20.00
CD	Carlos Delgado	10.00
AD	Adam Dunn	10.00
JE	Jim Edmonds	8.00
RF	Rafael Furcal	8.00
JG	Jason Giambi	8.00
TR	Troy Glaus	10.00
TG	Tom Glavine	10.00
SG	Shawn Green	8.00
KG	Ken Griffey Jr.	20.00
VG	Vladimir Guerrero	10.00
TH	Torii Hunter	8.00
KI	Kazuhisa Ishii	8.00
RJ	Randy Johnson	12.00
AJ	Andruw Jones	10.00
CJ	Chipper Jones	15.00
GM	Greg Maddux	15.00
HM	Hideki Matsui	50.00
MM	Mike Mussina	8.00
HN	Hideo Nomo	15.00
MI	Mike Piazza	15.00
MP	Mark Prior	15.00
AP	Albert Pujols	25.00
MR	Manny Ramirez	12.00
JR	Jose Reyes	10.00
AR	Alex Rodriguez	15.00
CS	Curt Schilling	10.00
GS	Gary Sheffield	8.00
AS	Alfonso Soriano	10.00
SS	Sammy Sosa	25.00
IS	Ichiro Suzuki	50.00
MT	Miguel Tejada	10.00
FT	Frank Thomas	10.00
JT	Jim Thome	10.00
RW	Rickie Weeks	15.00
BW	Bernie Williams	10.00
DW	Dontrelle Willis	10.00
KW	Kerry Wood	10.00
DY	Delmon Young	15.00
BZ	Barry Zito	10.00

Game Jersey Tier 2

Tier 2:	1X Tier 1 Price
Production 75 Sets	

Game-Used Patch

ULTIMATE COLLECTION

		NM/M
Common Player:		15.00
Production 99 Sets		
Copper:		1-1.5X
Production 35 Sets		
Gold:		1-1.5X
Production 25 Sets		
RB	Rocco Baldelli	20.00
PB	Pat Burrell	20.00
RC	Roger Clemens	50.00
CD	Carlos Delgado	15.00
AD	Adam Dunn	20.00
JE	Jim Edmonds	20.00
RF	Rafael Furcal	15.00
JG	Jason Giambi	20.00
TR	Troy Glaus	25.00
TG	Tom Glavine	25.00
SG	Shawn Green	15.00
KG	Ken Griffey Jr.	45.00
VG	Vladimir Guerrero	30.00
RH	Roy Halladay	20.00
TH	Torii Hunter	20.00
KI	Kazuhisa Ishii	20.00
RJ	Randy Johnson	25.00
AJ	Andruw Jones	25.00
CJ	Chipper Jones	30.00
GM	Greg Maddux	40.00
HM	Hideki Matsui	85.00
MM	Mike Mussina	25.00
HN	Hideo Nomo	40.00
MI	Mike Piazza	35.00
MP	Mark Prior	30.00
AP	Albert Pujols	50.00
MR	Manny Ramirez	30.00
JR	Jose Reyes	30.00
AR	Alex Rodriguez	50.00
CS	Curt Schilling	25.00
AS	Alfonso Soriano/42	25.00
SS	Sammy Sosa	35.00
IS	Ichiro Suzuki	75.00
MT	Miguel Tejada	25.00
FT	Frank Thomas	25.00
JT	Jim Thome	30.00
RW	Rickie Weeks	25.00
BW	Bernie Williams	20.00
DW	Dontrelle Willis	30.00
KW	Kerry Wood	40.00
DY	Delmon Young	35.00
BZ	Barry Zito	20.00

2003 Upper Deck Victory

		NM/M
Complete Set (200):		40.00
Common Player (1-100):		.10
Common (101-200):		.40
Cards (101-128):	Inserted 1:4	
(129-168):		1:5
(169-188):		1:10
(189-200):		1:20
Pack (6):		.75
Box (36):		20.00
1	Troy Glaus	.40
2	Garret Anderson	.20
3	Tim Salmon	.20
4	Darin Erstad	.20
5	Luis Gonzalez	.20
6	Curt Schilling	.25
7	Randy Johnson	.50
8	Junior Spivey	.10
9	Andruw Jones	.25
10	Greg Maddux	.75
11	Chipper Jones	.75
12	Gary Sheffield	.20
13	John Smoltz	.10
14	Geronimo Gil	.10
15	Tony Batista	.10
16	Trot Nixon	.10
17	Manny Ramirez	.40
18	Pedro J. Martinez	.50
19	Nomar Garciaparra	1.00
20	Derek Lowe	.10
21	Shea Hillenbrand	.10
22	Sammy Sosa	.75
23	Kerry Wood	.25
24	Mark Prior	.40
25	Magglio Ordonez	.20
26	Frank Thomas	.40
27	Mark Buehrle	.10
28	Paul Konerko	.10
29	Adam Dunn	.40
30	Ken Griffey Jr.	.75
31	Austin Kearns	.25
32	Matt Lawton	.10
33	Larry Walker	.20
34	Todd Helton	.25
35	Jeff Bagwell	.40
36	Roy Oswalt	.20
37	Lance Berkman	.25
38	Mike Sweeney	.10
39	Carlos Beltran	.10
40	Kazuhisa Ishii	.10
41	Shawn Green	.20
42	Hideo Nomo	.25
43	Adrian Beltre	.20
44	Richie Sexson	.25
45	Ben Sheets	.20
46	Torii Hunter	.25
47	Jacque Jones	.10
48	Corey Koskie	.10
49	Vladimir Guerrero	.50
50	Jose Vidro	.10
51	Mo Vaughn	.20
52	Mike Piazza	1.00
53	Roberto Alomar	.25
54	Derek Jeter	1.50
55	Alfonso Soriano	.75
56	Jason Giambi	.75
57	Roger Clemens	.75
58	Mike Mussina	.25
59	Bernie Williams	.25
60	Jorge Posada	.20
61	Nick Johnson	.10
62	Hideki Matsui RC	4.00
63	Eric Chavez	.20
64	Barry Zito	.20
65	Miguel Tejada	.25
66	Tim Hudson	.20
67	Pat Burrell	.40
68	Bobby Abreu	.20
69	Jimmy Rollins	.20
70	Brett Myers	.10
71	Jim Thome	.40
72	Jason Kendall	.20
73	Brian Giles	.20
74	Aramis Ramirez	.10
75	Sean Burroughs	.10
76	Ryan Klesko	.20
77	Phil Nevin	.10
78	Barry Bonds	1.50
79	J.T. Snow	.10
80	Rich Aurilia	.10
81	Ichiro Suzuki	1.00
82	Edgar Martinez	.10
83	Freddy Garcia	.10
84	Jim Edmonds	.20
85	J.D. Drew	.10
86	Scott Rolen	.40
87	Albert Pujols	.75
88	Mark McGwire	1.25
89	Matt Morris	.20
90	Ben Grieve	.10
91	Carl Crawford	.10
92	Alex Rodriguez	1.25
93	Carl Everett	.10
94	Juan Gonzalez	.25
95	Rafael Palmeiro	.20
96	Hank Blalock	.20
97	Carlos Delgado	.20
98	Josh Phelps	.10
99	Eric Hinske	.10
100	Shannon Stewart	.10
101	Albert Pujols	1.00
102	Alex Rodriguez	2.50
103	Alfonso Soriano	1.00
104	Barry Bonds	3.00
105	Bernie Williams	.50
106	Brian Giles	.50
107	Chipper Jones	.75
108	Darin Erstad	.50
109	Derek Jeter	3.00
110	Eric Chavez	.50
111	Miguel Tejada	.50
112	Ichiro Suzuki	1.50
113	Rafael Palmeiro	.40
114	Jason Giambi	1.50
115	Jeff Bagwell	.75
116	Jim Thome	.75
117	Ken Griffey Jr.	1.50
118	Lance Berkman	.50
119	Luis Gonzalez	.40
120	Manny Ramirez	.75
121	Mike Piazza	2.00
122	J.D. Drew	.40
123	Sammy Sosa	1.50
124	Scott Rolen	.75
125	Shawn Green	.50
126	Todd Helton	.50
127	Troy Glaus	.75
128	Vladimir Guerrero	1.00
129	Albert Pujols	1.00
130	Brian Giles	.50
131	Carlos Delgado	.50
132	Curt Schilling	.50
133	Derek Jeter	3.00
134	Frank Thomas	.75
135	Greg Maddux	1.50
136	Jeff Bagwell	.75
137	Jim Thome	.75
138	Jorge Posada	.50
139	Kazuhisa Ishii	.40
140	Larry Walker	.40
141	Luis Gonzalez	.40
142	Miguel Tejada	.50
143	Pat Burrell	.75
144	Pedro J. Martinez	1.00
145	Rafael Palmeiro	.50
146	Roger Clemens	1.50
147	Tim Hudson	.50
148	Troy Glaus	.75
149	Alfonso Soriano	1.00
150	Andruw Jones	.50
151	Barry Zito	.50
152	Darin Erstad	.50
153	Eric Chavez	.50
154	Alex Rodriguez	2.50
155	J.D. Drew	.40
156	Jason Giambi	1.50
157	Jason Kendall	.40
158	Ken Griffey Jr.	1.50
159	Lance Berkman	.50
160	Mike Mussina	.50
161	Mike Piazza	2.00
162	Nomar Garciaparra	2.00
163	Randy Johnson	1.00
164	Roberto Alomar	.50
165	Scott Rolen	.75
166	Shawn Green	.50
167	Torii Hunter	.50
168	Vladimir Guerrero	1.00
169	Alex Rodriguez	2.50
170	Andruw Jones	.50
171	Bernie Williams	.50
172	Ichiro Suzuki	1.50
173	Miguel Tejada	.50
174	Nomar Garciaparra	2.00
175	Pedro J. Martinez	1.00
176	Randy Johnson	1.00
177	Todd Helton	.50
178	Vladimir Guerrero	1.00
179	Barry Bonds	3.00
180	Carlos Delgado	.50
181	Chipper Jones	1.50
182	Frank Thomas	.75
183	Lance Berkman	.50
184	Larry Walker	.40
185	Manny Ramirez	.75
186	Mike Piazza	2.00
187	Sammy Sosa	1.50
188	Shawn Green	.50
189	Chipper Jones	1.50
190	Curt Schilling	.50
191	Derek Jeter	3.00
192	Ken Griffey Jr.	1.50
193	Sammy Sosa	1.50
194	Vladimir Guerrero	1.00
195	Alex Rodriguez	2.50
196	Barry Bonds	3.00
197	Greg Maddux	1.50
198	Ichiro Suzuki	1.50
199	Jason Giambi	1.50
200	Mike Piazza	2.00

Parallels

Tier 1 Green:	1-2X
Inserted 1:1	
Tier 2 Orange:	2-4X
Inserted 1:8	
Tier 3 Blue:	3-6X
Production 650	
Tier 4 Purple:	10-25X
Production 50 Sets	
Tier 5 Red:	No Pricing
Production 25 Sets	

2003 Upper Deck Vintage

MINNESOTA TWINS

OUTFIELD
TORII HUNTER

		NM/M
Complete Set (280):		
Common Player:		.15
Common SP (223-232):		1.50
Inserted 1:7		
Common SP (233-247):		.50
Inserted 1:5		
Common 3D SP (248-277):		6.00
Inserted 1:48		
Pack (8):		2.00
Box (24):		45.00
1	Troy Glaus	.25
2	Darin Erstad	.25
3	Garret Anderson	.25
4	Jarrod Washburn	.15
5	Nolan Ryan	2.00
6	Tim Salmon	.25
7	Troy Percival	.15
8	Alex Ochoa/SP	4.00
9	Daryle Ward	.15
10	Jeff Bagwell	.50
11	Roy Oswalt	.25
12	Lance Berkman	.40
13	Craig Biggio	.25
14	Richard Hidalgo	.15
15	Tim Hudson	.25
16	Eric Chavez	.25
17	Barry Zito	.25
18	Miguel Tejada	.50
19	Mark Mulder	.25
20	Rollie Fingers	.15
21	Jim "Catfish" Hunter	.25
22	Jermaine Dye	.15
23	Ray Durham/SP	4.00
24	Carlos Delgado	.25
25	Eric Hinske	.15
26	Josh Phelps	.15
27	Shannon Stewart	.15
28	Vernon Wells	.15
29	John Smoltz	.25
30	Greg Maddux	1.00
31	Chipper Jones	.75
32	Gary Sheffield	.25
33	Andruw Jones	.40
34	Tom Glavine	.25
35	Rafael Furcal	.15
36	Phil Niekro	.15
37	Eddie Mathews	.50
38	Robin Yount	.75
39	Richie Sexson	.25
40	Ben Sheets	.15
41	Geoff Jenkins	.15
42	Alex Sanchez	.15
43	Jason Isringhausen	.15
44	Albert Pujols	1.50
45	Matt Morris	.15
46	J.D. Drew	.25
47	Jim Edmonds	.25
48	Stan Musial	1.00
49	Red Schoendienst	.15
50	Edgar Renteria	.25
51	Mark McGwire/SP	10.00
52	Scott Rolen/SP	5.00
53	Mark Bellhorn	.15
54	Kerry Wood	.50
55	Mark Prior	.50
56	Moises Alou	.25
57	Corey Patterson	.25
58	Ernie Banks	.75
59	Hee Seop Choi	.15
60	Billy Williams	.15
61	Sammy Sosa/SP	8.00
62	Ben Grieve	.15
63	Jared Sandberg	.15
64	Carl Crawford	.15
65	Randy Johnson	.75
66	Luis Gonzalez	.25
67	Steve Finley	.15
68	Junior Spivey	.15

#	Player	Price
69	Erubiel Durazo	.15
70	Curt Schilling/SP	8.00
71	Al Lopez	.15
72	Pee Wee Reese	.15
73	Eric Gagne	.25
74	Shawn Green	.25
75	Kevin Brown	.15
76	Paul LoDuca	.15
77	Adrian Beltre	.25
78	Hideo Nomo	.40
79	Eric Karros	.15
80	Odalis Perez	.15
81	Kazuhisa Ishii/SP	5.00
82	Tommy Lasorda	.15
83	Fernando Tatis	.15
84	Vladimir Guerrero	.75
85	Jose Vidro	.15
86	Javier Vazquez	.15
87	Brad Wilkerson	.15
88	Bartolo Colon/SP	4.00
89	Monte Irvin	.15
90	Robb Nen	.15
91	Reggie Sanders	.15
92	Jeff Kent	.25
93	Rich Aurilia	.15
94	Orlando Cepeda	.15
95	Juan Marichal	.25
96	Willie McCovey	.25
97	David Bell	.15
98	Barry Bonds/SP	10.00
99	Kenny Lofton/SP	4.00
100	Jim Thome	.50
101	C.C. Sabathia	.15
102	Omar Vizquel	.25
103	Lou Boudreau	.15
104	Larry Doby	.25
105	Bob Lemon	.15
106	John Olerud	.25
107	Edgar Martinez	.15
108	Bret Boone	.15
109	Freddy Garcia	.15
110	Mike Cameron	.15
111	Kazuhiro Sasaki	.15
112	Ichiro Suzuki/SP	8.00
113	Mike Lowell	.15
114	Josh Beckett	.25
115	A.J. Burnett	.15
116	Juan Pierre	.15
117	Derrek Lee	.25
118	Luis Castillo	.15
119	Juan Encarnacion/SP	4.00
120	Roberto Alomar	.40
121	Edgardo Alfonzo	.15
122	Jeromy Burnitz	.15
123	Mo Vaughn	.25
124	Tom Seaver	.50
125	Al Leiter	.15
126	Mike Piazza/SP	8.00
127	Tony Batista	.15
128	Geronimo Gil	.15
129	Chris Singleton	.15
130	Rodrigo Lopez	.15
131	Jay Gibbons	.15
132	Melvin Mora	.15
133	Earl Weaver	.15
134	Trevor Hoffman	.15
135	Phil Nevin	.15
136	Sean Burroughs	.15
137	Ryan Klesko	.15
138	Mark Kotsay	.15
139	Mike Lieberthal	.15
140	Bobby Abreu	.25
141	Jimmy Rollins	.25
142	Pat Burrell	.40
143	Vicente Padilla	.15
144	Richie Ashburn	.15
145	Jeremy Giambi/SP	4.00
146	Josh Fogg	.15
147	Brian Giles	.25
148	Aramis Ramirez	.25
149	Jason Kendall	.15
150	Ralph Kiner	.15
151	Willie Stargell	.25
152	Kevin Mench	.15
153	Rafael Palmeiro	.25
154	Ivan Rodriguez	.40
155	Hank Blalock	.25
156	Juan Gonzalez	.40
157	Carl Everett	.15
158	Alex Rodriguez/SP	10.00
159	Nomar Garciaparra	1.25
160	Derek Lowe	.15
161	Manny Ramirez	.50
162	Shea Hillenbrand	.25
163	Bobby Doerr	.15
164	Johnny Damon	.40
165	Jason Varitek	.25
166	Pedro Martinez/SP	8.00
167	Cliff Floyd/SP	4.00
168	Ken Griffey Jr.	1.25
169	Adam Dunn	.50
170	Austin Kearns	.25
171	Aaron Boone	.15
172	Joe Morgan	.25
173	Sean Casey	.15
174	Todd Walker	.15
175	Ryan Dempster/SP	4.00
176	Shawn Estes/SP	4.00
177	Gabe Kapler/SP	4.00
178	Jason Jennings	.15
179	Todd Helton	.40
180	Larry Walker	.25
181	Preston Wilson	.15
182	Jay Payton/SP	4.00
183	Mike Sweeney	.15
184	Carlos Beltran	.50
185	Paul Byrd	.15
186	Raul Ibanez	.15
187	Rick Ferrell	.15
188	Early Wynn	.15
189	Dmitri Young	.15
190	Jim Bunning	.15
191	George Kell	.15
192	Hal Newhouser	.15
193	Bobby Higginson	.15
194	Carlos Pena/SP	4.00
195	Sparky Anderson	.15
196	Torii Hunter	.25
197	Eric Milton	.15
198	Corey Koskie	.15
199	Jacque Jones	.15
200	Harmon Killebrew	.50
201	Doug Mientkiewicz	.15
202	Frank Thomas	.50
203	Mark Buehrle	.15
204	Magglio Ordonez	.25
205	Paul Konerko	.25
206	Joe Borchard	.15
207	Hoyt Wilhelm	.15
208	Carlos Lee	.15
209	Roger Clemens	1.50
210	Nick Johnson	.15
211	Jason Giambi	.25
212	Alfonso Soriano	.75
213	Bernie Williams	.40
214	Robin Ventura	.15
215	Jorge Posada	.25
216	Mike Mussina	.40
217	Yogi Berra	.75
218	Phil Rizzuto	.40
219	Mariano Rivera	.25
220	Derek Jeter/SP	12.00
221	Jeff Weaver/SP	4.00
222	Raul Mondesi/SP	4.00
223	Freddy Sanchez, Josh Hancock	2.00
224	Joe Borchard, Miguel Olivo	2.00
225	Brandon Phillips, Josh Bard	1.50
226	Andy Van Hekken, Andres Torres	1.50
227	Jason Lane, Jeriome Robertson	1.50
228	Chin-Feng Chen, Joe Thurston	1.50
229	Endy Chavez, Jamey Carroll	1.50
230	Drew Henson, Alex Graman	2.50
231	Dewon Brazelton, Lance Carter	1.50
232	Jayson Werth, Kevin Cash	1.50
233	Randy Johnson, Curt Schilling, Barry Zito	1.00
234	Pedro J. Martinez, Randy Johnson, Derek Lowe	1.00
235	Randy Johnson, Curt Schilling, Pedro J. Martinez	1.00
236	John Smoltz, Eric Gagne, Mike Williams	.50
237	Randy Johnson, Bartolo Colon, A.J. Burnett	1.00
238	Alfonso Soriano, Ichiro Suzuki, Vladimir Guerrero	1.50
239	Alex Rodriguez, Jim Thome, Sammy Sosa	2.00
240	Barry Bonds, Manny Ramirez, Mike Sweeney	2.00
241	Alfonso Soriano, Alex Rodriguez, Derek Jeter	2.00
242	Alex Rodriguez, Magglio Ordonez, Miguel Tejada	2.00
243	Luis Castillo, Juan Pierre, Dave Roberts	.50
244	Nomar Garciaparra, Garret Anderson, Alfonso Soriano	1.00
245	Johnny Damon, Jimmy Rollins, Kenny Lofton	.50
246	Barry Bonds, Jim Thome, Manny Ramirez	2.00
247	Barry Bonds, Brian Giles, Manny Ramirez	2.00
248	Troy Glaus	10.00
249	Luis Gonzalez	6.00
250	Chipper Jones	15.00
251	Nomar Garciaparra	15.00
252	Manny Ramirez	10.00
253	Sammy Sosa	15.00
254	Frank Thomas	10.00
255	Magglio Ordonez	6.00
256	Adam Dunn	10.00
257	Ken Griffey Jr.	15.00
258	Jim Thome	10.00
259	Todd Helton	8.00
260	Larry Walker	6.00
261	Lance Berkman	6.00
262	Jeff Bagwell	10.00
263	Mike Sweeney	6.00
264	Shawn Green	6.00
265	Vladimir Guerrero	12.00
266	Mike Piazza	15.00
267	Jason Giambi	15.00
268	Pat Burrell	20.00
269	Barry Bonds	15.00
270	Mark McGwire	20.00
271	Alex Rodriguez	15.00
272	Carlos Delgado	6.00
273	Richie Sexson	6.00
274	Andruw Jones	8.00
275	Derek Jeter	20.00
276	Juan Gonzalez	8.00
277	Albert Pujols	12.00
278	Jason Giambi/CL	.75
279	Sammy Sosa/CL	.75
280	Ichiro Suzuki/CL	.75

All Caps

		NM/M
Common Player:		8.00
Production 250 Sets		
JB	Jeff Bagwell	15.00
LB	Lance Berkman	8.00
DE	Darin Erstad	8.00
RF	Rafael Furcal	8.00
JG	Juan Gonzalez	10.00
LG	Luis Gonzalez	8.00
TG	Tony Gwynn	25.00
TH	Tim Hudson	10.00
GM	Greg Maddux	30.00
RP	Rafael Palmeiro	10.00
CP	Chan Ho Park	8.00
MP	Mike Piazza	35.00
KS	Kazuhiro Sasaki	8.00
MV	Mo Vaughn	8.00
RV	Robin Ventura	8.00

Capping the Action

		NM/M
Common Player:		10.00
Quantity produced listed		
RA	Roberto Alomar/101	20.00
CD	Carlos Delgado/91	10.00
JG	Juan Gonzalez/99	20.00
SG	Shawn Green/125	20.00
KG	Ken Griffey Jr./102	40.00
TH	Todd Helton/99	20.00
PM	Pedro Martinez/125	25.00
MM	Mike Mussina/109	40.00
HM	Hideo Nomo/117	45.00
RP	Rafael Palmeiro/125	20.00
AR	Alex Rodriguez/110	25.00
IR	Ivan Rodriguez/125	15.00
SR	Scott Rolen/109	25.00
AS	Alfonso Soriano/109	20.00
SS	Sammy Sosa/125	40.00

Crackin the Lumber

		NM/M
Production 25		
Golds:		No Pricing
Production 5		
JG	Jason Giambi	25.00
IS	Ichiro Suzuki	125.00

Crowning Glory

No pricing due to scarcity.
Production 25 Sets

Dropping the Hammer

		NM/M
Common Player:		6.00
Inserted 1:130		
Golds:		1.5-2X
Production 100 Sets		
BA	Bobby Abreu	8.00
RA	Roberto Alomar	10.00
LB	Lance Berkman	8.00
RF	Rafael Furcal	6.00
JG	Jason Giambi	6.00
SG	Shawn Green	6.00
KG	Ken Griffey Jr.	15.00
TH	Todd Helton	8.00
AJ	Andruw Jones	8.00
DJ	David Justice	8.00
KL	Kenny Lofton	8.00
FM	Fred McGriff	8.00
MO	Magglio Ordonez	8.00
RP	Rafael Palmeiro	8.00
MP	Mike Piazza	15.00
AR	Alex Rodriguez	15.00
SS	Sammy Sosa	20.00
TA	Fernando Tatis	8.00
MT	Miguel Tejada	8.00
FT	Frank Thomas	10.00
JT	Jim Thome	10.00
RV	Robin Ventura	6.00
OV	Omar Vizquel	6.00
LW	Larry Walker	6.00
PW	Preston Wilson	6.00

Men with Hats

		NM/M
Common Player:		8.00
Inserted 1:285		
VC	Vinny Castilla	8.00
EC	Eric Chavez	10.00
JD	Johnny Damon	15.00
AD	Adam Dunn	15.00
JG	Jason Giambi	8.00
TH	Todd Helton	10.00
HU	Tim Hudson	10.00
AJ	Andruw Jones	10.00
JK	Jason Kendall	8.00
KL	Kenny Lofton	8.00
AR	Alex Rodriguez	20.00
MT	Miguel Tejada	12.00
FT	Frank Thomas	12.00
TW	Todd Walker	8.00
BW	Bernie Williams	10.00

Slugfest

		NM/M
Common Player:		8.00
Production 200 Sets		
Golds:		1.5-2.5X
Production 50 Sets		
CD	Carlos Delgado	8.00
SG	Shawn Green	8.00
AJ	Andruw Jones	8.00
RP	Rafael Palmeiro	8.00
MP	Mike Piazza	20.00
AR	Alex Rodriguez	15.00
FT	Frank Thomas	10.00
JT	Jim Thome	10.00

		NM/M
LW	Larry Walker	8.00
BW	Bernie Williams	10.00

Timeless Teams Bat

		NM/M
Common Card:		20.00
Production 175 Sets		
BLAR	Pat Burrell, Mike Lieberthal, Bobby Abreu, Jimmy Rollins	25.00
CTDJ	Eric Chavez, Miguel Tejada, Jermaine Dye, David Justice	25.00
DEMR	J.D. Drew, Jim Edmonds, Tino Martinez, Scott Rolen	40.00
DGCL	Adam Dunn, Ken Griffey Jr., Sean Casey, Barry Larkin	40.00
GNBL	Shawn Green, Hideo Nomo, Adrian Beltre, Paul LoDuca	40.00
GPMS	Jason Giambi, Jorge Posada, Raul Mondesi, Alfonso Soriano	30.00
GWVS	Jason Giambi, Bernie Williams, Robin Ventura, Alfonso Soriano	40.00
HWPZ	Todd Helton, Larry Walker, Juan Pierre, Todd Zeile	25.00
IMBC	Ichiro Suzuki, Edgar Martinez, Bret Boone, Mike Cameron	90.00
JGSW	Randy Johnson, Luis Gonzalez, Curt Schilling, Matt Williams	40.00
JJSF	Chipper Jones, Andruw Jones, Gary Sheffield, Rafael Furcal	40.00
KNKB	Ryan Klesko, Phil Nevin, Mark Kotsay, Sean Burroughs	20.00
MGLJ	Greg Maddux, Tom Glavine, Javy Lopez, Chipper Jones	40.00
OTLK	Magglio Ordonez, Frank Thomas, Carlos Lee, Paul Konerko	30.00
PVAA	Mike Piazza, Mo Vaughn, Roberto Alomar, Edgardo Alfonzo	40.00
RGRP	Alex Rodriguez, Juan Gonzalez, Ivan Rodriguez, Rafael Palmeiro	40.00
RMHN	Manny Ramirez, Pedro J. Martinez, Shea Hillenbrand, Trot Nixon	30.00
SMAP	Sammy Sosa, Fred McGriff, Moises Alou, Corey Patterson	40.00

UD Giants

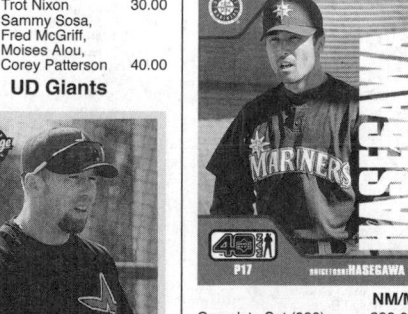

		NM/M
Complete Set (42):		45.00
Common Player:		.75
Inserted 1:Box		
RA	Roberto Alomar	1.00
JB	Jeff Bagwell	1.00
LB	Lance Berkman	1.00
BB	Barry Bonds	4.00
PB	Pat Burrell	1.00
RC	Roger Clemens	4.00
CD	Carlos Delgado	.75
JD	J.D. Drew	.75
AD	Adam Dunn	.75
NG	Nomar Garciaparra	3.00
JG	Jason Giambi	.75
BG	Brian Giles	.75
GO	Juan Gonzalez	1.00
LG	Luis Gonzalez	.75
SG	Shawn Green	.75
KG	Ken Griffey Jr.	3.00
VG	Vladimir Guerrero	1.50
TH	Todd Helton	1.00
KI	Kazuhisa Ishii	.75
RJ	Randy Johnson	1.50
AJ	Andruw Jones	1.00
CJ	Chipper Jones	2.50
GM	Greg Maddux	2.50
PM	Pedro J. Martinez	1.50
MM	Mike Mussina	1.00
HN	Hideo Nomo	1.00
MO	Magglio Ordonez	.75
RP	Rafael Palmeiro	1.00
MP	Mike Piazza	3.00
PR	Mark Prior	1.00
AP	Albert Pujols	4.00
MR	Manny Ramirez	1.50
AR	Alex Rodriguez	4.00
IR	Ivan Rodriguez	1.50
SR	Scott Rolen	1.50
CS	Curt Schilling	1.50
SS	Sammy Sosa	2.50
IS	Ichiro Suzuki	3.00
FT	Frank Thomas	1.00
JT	Jim Thome	1.50
BW	Bernie Williams	1.00
KW	Kerry Wood	1.50

Vintage Hitmen

		NM/M
Production 150 Sets		
Golds:		Not Priced
Production 10 Sets		
JG	Jason Giambi	10.00
KG	Ken Griffey Jr.	30.00
MM	Mark McGwire	60.00
IS	Ichiro Suzuki	60.00

Vintage Hitmen
Double Signed

		NM/M
Production 75		
Gold:		Not Priced
Production 5		
MS	Mark McGwire, Sammy Sosa	600.00

2003 Upper Deck 40-Man

		NM/M
Complete Set (990):		200.00
Common Player:		.25
Common Rk (877-960):		.40
Pack (10):		2.00
Box (24):		35.00
1	Troy Glaus	.50
2	Darin Erstad	.40
3	Garret Anderson	.50
4	Aaron Sele	.25
5	Adam Kennedy	.25
6	Scott Spiezio	.25
7	Troy Percival	.25
8	David Eckstein	.25
9	Ramon Ortiz	.25
10	Bengie Molina	.25
11	Tim Salmon	.50
12	John Lackey	.25
13	Brad Fullmer	.25
14	Jarrod Washburn	.25
15	Shawn Wooten	.25
16	Kevin Appier	.25
17	Ben Weber	.25
18	Eric Owens	.25
19	Matt Wise	.25
20	Francisco Rodriguez	.25
21	Scot Shields	.25
22	Jose Molina	.25
23	Scott Schoeneweis	.25
24	Derrick Turnbow	.25
25	Benji Gil	.25
26	Julio Ramirez	.25
27	Mickey Callaway	.25
28	Barry Zito	.50
29	Tim Hudson	.50
30	Mark Mulder	.40
31	Eric Chavez	.40
32	Miguel Tejada	.50
33	Terrence Long	.25
34	Jermaine Dye	.25
35	Erubiel Durazo	.25
36	Scott Hatteberg	.25
37	Chris Singleton	.25
38	Keith Foulke	.25
39	John Halama	.25
40	Mark Ellis	.25
41	Ted Lilly	.25
42	Jim Mecir	.25
43	Adam Piatt	.25
44	Freddie Bynum	.25
45	Adam Morrissey	.25
46	Jeremy Fikac	.25
47	Ricardo Rincon	.25
48	Ramon Hernandez	.25
49	Micah Bowie	.25
50	Chad Bradford	.25
51	Eric Byrnes	.25
52	Ron Gant	.25
53	Jose Flores	.25
54	Mark Johnson	.25
55	Carlos Delgado	.75
56	Orlando Hudson	.25
57	Kelvim Escobar	.25
58	Eric Hinske	.25
59	Doug Creek	.25
60	Josh Phelps	.25
61	Shannon Stewart	.25
62	Roy Halladay	.40
63	Vernon Wells	.40
64	Mark Henrickson	.25
65	Mike Bordick	.25
66	Jayson Werth	.25
67	Chris Woodward	.25
68	Ken Huckaby	.25
69	Frank Catalanotto	.25
70	Jason Kershner	.25
71	Greg Myers	.25
72	Tanyon Sturtze	.25
73	Trever Miller	.25
74	Pete Walker	.25
75	Alexis Rios	.25
76	Tom Wilson	.25
77	Dave Berg	.25
78	Doug Linton	.25
79	Cliff Politte	.25
80	Damion Easley	.25
81	Toby Hall	.25
82	George Lombard	.25
83	Ben Grieve	.25
84	Aubrey Huff	.25
85	Jesus Colome	.25
86	Dewon Brazelton	.25
87	Rey Ordonez	.25
88	Al Martin	.25
89	Carl Crawford	.25
90	Travis Lee	.25
91	Marlon Anderson	.25
92	Javier Valentin	.25
93	Joe Kennedy	.25
94	Jorge Sosa	.25
95	Travis Harper	.25
96	Bobby Seay	.25
97	Seth McClung	.25
98	Delvin James	.25
99	Victor Zambrano	.25
100	Terry Shumpert	.25
101	Josh Hamilton	.50
102	Jared Sandberg	.25
103	Steve Parris	.25
104	C.C. Sabathia	.25
105	Omar Vizquel	.40
106	Milton Bradley	.25
107	Ellis Burks	.25
108	Danys Baez	.25
109	Jason Davis	.25
110	Terry Mulholland	.25
111	Matt Lawton	.25
112	Alex Escobar	.25
113	Mark Wohlers	.25
114	Josh Bard	.25
115	Bill Selby	.25
116	Brandon Phillips	.25
117	Jason Bere	.25
118	Casey Blake	.25
119	Travis Hafner	.25
120	Brian Anderson	.25
121	David Riske	.25
122	Karim Garcia	.25
123	Ricardo Rodriguez	.25
124	Carl Sadler	.25
125	Jose Santiago	.25
126	Tim Laker	.25
127	John McDonald	.25
128	Jake Westbrook	.25
129	Ichiro Suzuki	1.00
130	Freddy Garcia	.25
131	Edgar Martinez	.40
132	Ben Davis	.25
133	Shigetoshi Hasegawa	.25
134	Carlos Guillen	.25
135	Randy Winn	.25
136	John Mabry	.25
137	Matt Thornton	.25
138	Bret Boone	.40
139	Jamie Moyer	.25
140	Giovanni Carrara	.25
141	Kazuhiro Sasaki	.25
142	Jeff Cirillo	.25
143	Mark McLemore	.25
144	Pat Borders	.25
145	Mike Cameron	.25
146	Dan Wilson	.25
147	John Olerud	.40
148	Arthur Rhodes	.25
149	Rafael Soriano	.25
150	Greg Colbrunn	.25
151	Ryan Franklin	.25
152	Joel Pineiro	.25
153	Jeff Nelson	.25
154	Jerry Hairston	.25
155	Rick Helling	.25
156	Gary Matthews Jr.	.25
157	Jeff Conine	.25
158	Sidney Ponson	.25
159	Tony Batista	.25
160	Jay Gibbons	.40
161	Marty Cordova	.25
162	Geronimo Gil	.25
163	Deivi Cruz	.25
164	B.J. Ryan	.25
165	Jason Johnson	.25
166	Buddy Groom	.25
167	Pat Hentgen	.25
168	Omar Daal	.25
169	Willis Roberts	.25
170	Scott Erickson	.25
171	David Segui	.25
172	Brook Fordyce	.25
173	Rodrigo Lopez	.25
174	Jose Leon	.25
175	Jose Morban	.25
176	Melvin Mora	.25
177	B.J. Surhoff	.25
178	Jorge Julio	.25
179	Alex Rodriguez	2.00
180	Mark Teixeira	.40
181	Chan Ho Park	.25
182	Todd Van Poppel	.25
183	Todd Greene	.25
184	Ismael Valdes	.25
185	Rusty Greer	.25
186	Rafael Palmeiro	.50
187	Francisco Cordero	.25
188	Einar Diaz	.25
189	Doug Glanville	.25
190	Michael Young	.25
191	Kevin Mench	.25
192	Carl Everett	.25
193	Herbert Perry	.25
194	Jeff Zimmerman	.25
195	Juan Gonzalez	.50
196	Ugueth Urbina	.25
197	Jermaine Clark	.25
198	John Thomson	.25
199	Hank Blalock	.50
200	Jay Powell	.25
201	Mike Lamb	.25
202	Aaron Fultz	.25
203	Esteban Yan	.25
204	Nomar Garciaparra	2.00
205	Pedro J. Martinez	.75
206	John Burkett	.25
207	Johnny Damon	.40
208	Doug Mirabelli	.25
209	Derek Lowe	.25
210	Shea Hillenbrand	.25
211	Brandon Lyon	.25
212	Trot Nixon	.25
213	Jason Varitek	.25
214	Tim Wakefield	.25

No.	Player		No.	Player		No.	Player		No.	Player	
215	Manny Ramirez	.75	319	Miguel Olivo	.25	423	John Foster	.25	527	Fred McGriff	.40
216	Todd Walker	.25	320	Rick White	.25	424	Curtis Leskanic	.25	528	Adrian Beltre	.40
217	Jeremy Giambi	.25	321	Billy Koch	.25	425	Todd Ritchie	.25	529	Daryle Ward	.25
218	Ramiro Mendoza	.25	322	Tom Gordon	.25	426	Enrique Cruz	.25	530	Todd Hundley	.25
219	Bill Mueller	.25	323	Bartolo Colon	.40	427	Wayne Franklin	.25	531	David Ross	.25
220	David Ortiz	.25	324	Josh Paul	.25	428	Matt Ford	.25	532	Paul Shuey	.25
221	Mike Timlin	.25	325	Joe Borchard	.25	429	Matt Kinney	.25	533	Paul LoDuca	.25
222	Alan Embree	.25	326	Damaso Marte	.25	430	Scott Podsednik	2.00	534	Dave Roberts	.25
223	Bob Howry	.25	327	Derek Jeter	2.00	431	Luis Vizcaino	.25	535	Mike Kinkade	.25
224	Chad Fox	.25	328	Jason Giambi	.75	432	Shane Nance	.25	536	Cesar Izturis	.25
225	Damian Jackson	.25	329	Roger Clemens	2.00	433	Alex Sanchez	.25	537	Ron Coomer	.25
226	Casey Fossum	.25	330	Enrique Wilson	.25	434	John Vander Wal	.25	538	Jose Vidro	.25
227	Steve Woodard	.25	331	Dave Wells	.25	435	Eric Young	.25	539	Henry Mateo	.25
228	Freddy Sanchez	.25	332	Mike Mussina	.50	436	Eddie Perez	.25	540	Tony Armas Jr.	.25
229	Mike Sweeney	.25	333	Bernie Williams	.50	437	Jason Conti	.25	541	Joey Eischen	.25
230	Desi Relaford	.25	334	Todd Zeile	.25	438	Matt Morris	.25	542	Orlando Cabrera	.25
231	Brent Mayne	.25	335	Sterling Hitchcock	.25	439	Tino Martinez	.25	543	Jose Macias	.25
232	Angel Berroa	.25	336	Juan Acevedo	.25	440	Fernando Vina	.25	544	Fernando Tatis	.25
233	Albie Lopez	.25	337	Robin Ventura	.25	441	Kiko Calero	.25	545	Jeff Liefer	.25
234	Raul Ibanez	.25	338	Mariano Rivera	.40	442	Cal Eldred	.25	546	Michael Barrett	.25
235	Joe Randa	.25	339	John Flaherty	.25	443	Jimmy Journell	.25	547	Vladimir Guerrero	.75
236	Chris George	.25	340	Andy Pettitte	.50	444	Jim Edmonds	.40	548	Javier Vazquez	.25
237	Michael Tucker	.25	341	Antonio Osuna	.25	445	Jeff Fassero	.25	549	Brad Wilkerson	.25
238	Mendy Lopez	.25	342	Erick Almonte	.25	446	Mike Matheny	.25	550	Zach Day	.25
239	Kris Wilson	.25	343	Chris Hammond	.25	447	Garrett Stephenson	.25	551	Tomokazu Ohka	.25
240	Jason Grimsley	.25	344	Steve Karsay	.25	448	Brett Tomko	.25	552	Livan Hernandez	.25
241	Carlos Febles	.25	345	Alfonso Soriano	1.00	449	So Taguchi	.25	553	Endy Chavez	.25
242	Runelvys Hernandez	.25	346	Bubba Trammell	.25	450	Eduardo Perez	.25	554	Dan Smith	.25
243	Mike MacDougal	.25	347	Nick Johnson	.25	451	Lance Painter	.25	555	Scott Stewart	.25
244	Carlos Beltran	.40	348	Jorge Posada	.50	452	Jason Isringhausen	.25	556	T.J. Tucker	.25
245	Brandon Berger	.25	349	Jeff Weaver	.25	453	Albert Pujols	2.00	557	Jamey Carroll	.25
246	Darrell May	.25	350	Raul Mondesi	.25	454	Eli Marrero	.25	558	Ron Calloway	.25
247	Miguel Asencio	.25	351	Randy Choate	.25	455	Jason Simontacchi	.25	559	Brian Schneider	.25
248	Ryan Bukvich	.25	352	Drew Henson	.25	456	J.D. Drew	.25	560	Orlando Hernandez	.25
249	Dee Brown	.25	353	Jeff Bagwell	.75	457	Scott Rolen	.75	561	Wil Cordero	.25
250	Jeremy Hill	.25	354	Wade Miller	.25	458	Orlando Palmeiro	.25	562	Rocky Biddle	.25
251	Jeremy Affeldt	.25	355	Lance Berkman	.40	459	Dustin Hermanson	.25	563	Edgardo Alfonzo	.25
252	Ken Harvey	.25	356	Julio Lugo	.25	460	Edgar Renteria	.25	564	Andres Galarraga	.25
253	Bobby Higginson	.25	357	Roy Oswalt	.40	461	Woody Williams	.25	565	Felix Rodriguez	.25
254	Matt Anderson	.25	358	Bruce Chen	.25	462	Chris Carpenter	.25	566	Benito Santiago	.25
255	Dmitri Young	.25	359	Morgan Ensberg	.25	463	Sammy Sosa	1.50	567	Jose Cruz	.25
256	Gene Kingsdale	.25	360	Geoff Blum	.25	464	Kerry Wood	.75	568	Tim Worrell	.25
257	Craig Paquette	.25	361	Brian Moehler	.25	465	Kyle Farnsworth	.25	569	Marvin Benard	.25
258	Adam Bernero	.25	362	Billy Wagner	.40	466	Alex Gonzalez	.25	570	Kurt Ainsworth	.25
259	Andres Torres	.25	363	Peter Munro	.25	467	Eric Karros	.25	571	Jim Brower	.25
260	Carlos Pena	.25	364	Brad Ausmus	.25	468	Troy O'Leary	.25	572	J.T. Snow	.25
261	Dean Palmer	.25	365	Jose Vizcaino	.25	469	Mark Grudzielanek	.25	573	Scott Eyre	.25
262	Eric Munson	.25	366	Craig Biggio	.40	470	Alan Benes	.25	574	Robb Nen	.25
263	Omar Infante	.25	367	Tim Redding	.25	471	Mark Prior	1.50	575	Barry Bonds	2.50
264	Shane Halter	.25	368	Gregg Zaun	.25	472	Paul Bako	.25	576	Ray Durham	.25
265	Jeremy Bonderman	2.00	369	Octavio Dotel	.25	473	Shawn Estes	.25	577	Marquis Grissom	.25
266	Steve Sparks	.25	370	Carlos Hernandez	.25	474	Matt Clement	.25	578	Pedro Feliz	.25
267	Gary Knotts	.25	371	Richard Hidalgo	.25	475	Ramon Martinez	.25	579	Jason Schmidt	.25
268	Mike Maroth	.25	372	Jeriome Robertson	.25	476	Tom Goodwin	.25	580	Rich Aurilia	.25
269	Nate Cornejo	.25	373	Orlando Merced	.25	477	Corey Patterson	.25	581	Kirk Rueter	.25
270	Matt Roney	.25	374	John Buck	.25	478	Moises Alou	.40	582	Chad Zerbe	.25
271	Franklyn German	.25	375	Adam Everett	.25	479	Juan Cruz	.25	583	Damian Moss	.25
272	Matt Walbeck	.25	376	Raul Chavez	.25	480	Bobby Hill	.25	584	Neifi Perez	.25
273	Brandon Inge	.25	377	Brad Lidge	.25	481	Mark Bellhorn	.25	585	Joe Nathan	.25
274	Hiram Bocachica	.25	378	Jeff Kent	.40	482	Mark Guthrie	.25	586	Ruben Rivera	.25
275	Chris Spurling	.25	379	Scott Linebrink	.25	483	Mike Remlinger	.25	587	Yorvit Torrealba	.25
276	Craig Monroe	.25	380	Greg Miller	.25	484	Lenny Harris	.25	588	Josh Beckett	.50
277	Ramon Santiago	.25	381	Kirk Saarloos	.25	485	Antonio Alfonseca	.25	589	Todd Hollandsworth	.25
278	Doug Mientkiewicz	.25	382	Brandon Puffer	.25	486	Dave Veres	.25	590	Derrek Lee	.25
279	Torii Hunter	.50	383	Ricky Stone	.25	487	Hee Seop Choi	.25	591	A.J. Burnett	.25
280	Brad Radke	.25	384	Jason Lane	.25	488	Luis Gonzalez	.40	592	Juan Pierre	.25
281	Denny Hocking	.25	385	Brian L. Hunter	.25	489	Lyle Overbay	.25	593	Mark Redman	.25
282	Tom Prince	.25	386	Rodrigo Rosario	.25	490	Randy Johnson	.75	594	Blaine Neal	.25
283	Eddie Guardado	.25	387	Horacio Ramirez	.25	491	Mark Grace	.50	595	Mike Mordecai	.25
284	Jacque Jones	.25	388	Gary Sheffield	.50	492	Danny Bautista	.25	596	Alex Gonzalez	.25
285	Joe Mays	.25	389	Mike Hampton	.25	493	Junior Spivey	.25	597	Brad Penny	.25
286	Mike Fetters	.25	390	Robert Fick	.25	494	Matt Williams	.25	598	Tim Spooneybarger	.25
287	LaTroy Hawkins	.25	391	Henry Blanco	.25	495	Miguel Batista	.25	599	Mike Lowell	.25
288	A.J. Pierzynski	.25	392	Vinny Castilla	.25	496	Tony Womack	.25	600	Mike Redmond	.25
289	Eric Milton	.25	393	Joe Dawley	.25	497	Byung-Hyun Kim	.25	601	Braden Looper	.25
290	Cristian Guzman	.25	394	Jung Bong	.25	498	Steve Finley	.25	602	Ivan Rodriguez	.50
291	Bobby Kielty	.25	395	Rafael Furcal	.40	499	Craig Counsell	.25	603	Andy Fox	.25
292	Corey Koskie	.25	396	Javy Lopez	.25	500	Curt Schilling	.50	604	Vladimir Nunez	.25
293	J.C. Romero	.25	397	Greg Maddux	1.25	501	Elmer Dessens	.25	605	Luis Castillo	.25
294	Mike Cuddyer	.25	398	Andruw Jones	.50	502	Rod Barajas	.25	606	Juan Encarnacion	.25
295	Luis Rivas	.25	399	John Smoltz	.40	503	David Dellucci	.25	607	Armando Almanza	.25
296	Matt LeCroy	.25	400	Chipper Jones	1.00	504	Mike Koplove	.25	608	Gerald Williams	.25
297	Tony Fiore	.25	401	Mark DeRosa	.25	505	Mike Myers	.25	609	Carl Pavano	.25
298	Dustan Mohr	.25	402	Shane Reynolds	.25	506	Matt Mantei	.25	610	Michael Tejera	.25
299	Chris Gomez	.25	403	Kevin Gryboski	.25	507	Stephen Randolph RC	.40	611	Ramon Castro	.25
300	Johan Santana	.25	404	Russ Ortiz	.25	508	Chad Moeller	.25	612	Brian Banks	.25
301	Kyle Lohse	.25	405	Roberto Hernandez	.25	509	Carlos Baerga	.25	613	Roberto Alomar	.50
302	Frank Thomas	.75	406	Ray King	.25	510	Andrew Good	.25	614	Al Leiter	.25
303	Mark Buehrle	.25	407	Matt Franco	.25	511	Quinton McCracken	.25	615	Jeromy Burnitz	.25
304	Jon Garland	.25	408	Marcus Giles	.25	512	Jason Romano	.25	616	John Franco	.25
305	Magglio Ordonez	.50	409	Trey Hodges	.25	513	Jolbert Cabrera	.25	617	Tom Glavine	.40
306	Paul Konerko	.25	410	Darren Holmes	.25	514	Darren Dreifort	.25	618	Mike Piazza	1.00
307	Sandy Alomar Jr.	.25	411	Julio Franco	.25	515	Kevin Brown	.40	619	Cliff Floyd	.25
308	Carlos Lee	.25	412	Darren Bragg	.25	516	Paul Quantrill	.25	620	Joe McEwing	.25
309	Jon Rauch	.25	413	Richie Sexson	.50	517	Shawn Green	.40	621	David Weathers	.25
310	Esteban Loaiza	.25	414	Jeffrey Hammonds	.25	518	Hideo Nomo	.40	622	Pedro Astacio	.25
311	Gary Glover	.25	415	Ben Sheets	.25	519	Eric Gagne	.25	623	Timoniel Perez	.25
312	Kelly Wunsch	.25	416	Mike DeJean	.25	520	Troy Brohawn	.25	624	Jason Phillips	.25
313	Tony Graffanino	.25	417	Royce Clayton	.25	521	Kazuhisa Ishii	.25	625	Ty Wigginton	.25
314	Aaron Rowand	.25	418	Wes Helms	.25	522	Guillermo Mota	.25	626	Steve Trachsel	.25
315	Armando Rios	.25	419	Valerio de los Santos	.25	523	Alex Cora	.25	627	Roger Cedeno	.25
316	Jose Valentin	.25	420	Brady Clark	.25	524	Odalis Perez	.25	628	Tsuyoshi Shinjo	.25
317	D'Angelo Jimenez	.25	421	Glendon Rusch	.25	525	Brian Jordan	.25	629	Armando Benitez	.25
318	Joe Crede	.25	422	Geoff Jenkins	.40	526	Andy Ashby	.25	630	Vance Wilson	.25

#	Player	Price
631	Mike Stanton	.25
632	Mo Vaughn	.25
633	Scott Strickland	.25
634	Rey Sanchez	.25
635	Jay Bell	.25
636	David Cone	.25
637	Jae Weong So	.25
638	Ryan Klesko	.40
639	Wiki Gonzalez	.25
640	Trevor Hoffman	.25
641	Sean Burroughs	.25
642	Mike Bynum	.25
643	Clay Condrey	.25
644	Gary Bennett	.25
645	Kevin Jarvis	.25
646	Mark Kotsay	.25
647	Phil Nevin	.25
648	Dave Hansen	.25
649	Keith Lockhart	.25
650	Brian Lawrence	.25
651	Jay Witasick	.25
652	Rondell White	.25
653	Jaret Wright	.25
654	Luther Hackman	.25
655	Jake Peavy	.25
656	Brian Buchanan	.25
657	Mark Loretta	.25
658	Oliver Perez	.25
659	Adam Eaton	.25
660	Xavier Nady	.25
661	Jesse Orosco	.25
662	Ramon Vazquez	.25
663	Jim Thome	.75
664	Jose Mesa	.25
665	Rheal Cormier	.25
666	David Bell	.25
667	Mike Lieberthal	.25
668	Brandon Duckworth	.25
669	David Coggin	.25
670	Bobby Abreu	.40
671	Turk Wendell	.25
672	Marlon Byrd	.25
673	Jason Michaels	.25
674	Kevin Millwood	.40
675	Tomas Perez	.25
676	Jimmy Rollins	.50
677	Vicente Padilla	.25
678	Pat Burrell	.50
679	Tyler Houston	.25
680	Hector Mercado	.25
681	Carlos Silva	.25
682	Nick Punto	.25
683	Ricky Ledee	.25
684	Randy Wolf	.25
685	Todd Pratt	.25
686	Placido Polanco	.25
687	Chase Utley	.25
688	Brian Giles	.25
689	Jason Kendall	.40
690	Matt Stairs	.25
691	Kris Benson	.25
692	Julian Tavarez	.25
693	Reggie Sanders	.25
694	Jeff D'Amico	.25
695	Pokey Reese	.25
696	Kenny Lofton	.25
697	Mike Williams	.25
698	David Williams	.25
699	Kevin Young	.25
700	Brian Boehringer	.25
701	Scott Sauerbeck	.25
702	Josh Fogg	.25
703	Joe Beimel	.25
704	Dennys Reyes	.25
705	Jeff Suppan	.25
706	Solomon Torres	.25
707	Kip Wells	.25
708	Craig Wilson	.25
709	Jack Wilson	.25
710	Robert Mackowiak	.25
711	Abraham Nunez	.25
712	Randall Simon	.25
713	Josias Manzanillo	.25
714	Ken Griffey Jr.	1.00
715	Jimmy Haynes	.25
716	Felipe Lopez	.25
717	Jimmy Anderson	.25
718	Ryan Dempster	.25
719	Russell Branyan	.25
720	Aaron Boone	.25
721	Luke Prokopec	.25
722	Felix Heredia	.25
723	Scott Sullivan	.25
724	Danny Graves	.25
725	Kent Mercker	.25
726	Barry Larkin	.40
727	Jason LaRue	.25
728	Gabe White	.25
729	Adam Dunn	.50
730	Brandon Larson	.25
731	Reggie Taylor	.25
732	Sean Casey	.25
733	Scott Williamson	.25
734	Austin Kearns	.50

#	Player	Price
735	Kelly Stinnett	.25
736	Ruben Mateo	.25
737	Wily Mo Pena	.25
738	Larry Walker	.40
439	Juan Uribe	.25
740	Denny Neagle	.25
741	Darren Oliver	.25
742	Charles Johnson	.25
743	Todd Jones	.25
744	Todd Helton	.75
745	Shawn Chacon	.25
746	Jason Jennings	.25
747	Preston Wilson	.25
748	Chris Richard	.25
749	Chris Stynes	.25
750	Jose Jimenez	.25
751	Gabe Kapler	.25
752	Jay Payton	.25
753	Aaron Cook	.25
754	Greg Norton	.25
755	Scott Elarton	.25
756	Brian Fuentes	.25
757	Jose Hernandez	.25
758	Nelson Cruz	.25
759	Justin Speier	.25
760	Javier Lopez	.40
761	Garret Anderson	.40
762	Tony Batista	.25
763	Mark Buehrle	.25
764	Johnny Damon	.40
765	Freddy Garcia	.25
766	Nomar Garciaparra	.75
767	Jason Giambi	.50
768	Roy Halladay	.25
769	Shea Hillenbrand	.25
770	Torii Hunter	.40
771	Derek Jeter	1.00
772	Paul Konerko	.25
773	Derek Lowe	.25
774	Pedro J. Martinez	.50
775	A.J. Pierzynski	.25
776	Jorge Posada	.40
777	Manny Ramirez	.40
778	Mariano Rivera	.25
779	Alex Rodriguez	1.00
780	Kazuhiro Sasaki	.25
781	Alfonso Soriano	.50
782	Ichiro Suzuki	.50
783	Mike Sweeney	.25
784	Miguel Tejada	.40
785	Ugueth Urbina	.25
786	Robin Ventura	.25
787	Omar Vizquel	.25
788	Randy Winn	.25
789	Barry Zito	.25
790	Lance Berkman	.25
791	Barry Bonds	1.00
792	Adam Dunn	.40
793	Tom Glavine	.25
794	Luis Gonzalez	.25
795	Shawn Green	.25
796	Vladimir Guerrero	.40
797	Todd Helton	.40
798	Trevor Hoffman	.25
799	Randy Johnson	.50
800	Andruw Jones	.40
801	Byung-Hyun Kim	.25
802	Mike Lowell	.25
803	Eric Gagne	.25
804	Matt Morris	.25
805	Robb Nen	.25
806	Vicente Padilla	.25
807	Odalis Perez	.25
808	Mike Piazza	.50
809	Mike Remlinger	.25
810	Scott Rolen	.40
811	Jimmy Rollins	.50
812	Benito Santiago	.25
813	Curt Schilling	.40
814	Richie Sexson	.40
815	John Smoltz	.25
816	Sammy Sosa	.75
817	Junior Spivey	.25
818	Jose Vidro	.25
819	Mike Williams	.25
820	Luis Castillo	.25
821	Jason Giambi	.40
822	Luis Gonzalez	.25
823	Sammy Sosa	.75
824	Ken Griffey Jr.	.75
825	Ken Griffey Jr.	.75
826	Tino Martinez	.25
827	Barry Bonds	1.00
828	Frank Thomas	.40
829	Ken Griffey Jr.	.75
830	Barry Bonds	1.00
831	Tim Salmon	.25
832	Troy Glaus	.25
833	Robb Nen	.25
834	Jeff Kent	.25
835	Scott Spiezio	.25
836	Darin Erstad	.25
837	Randy Johnson	.50
838	Chipper Jones	.50

#	Player	Price
839	Greg Maddux	.75
840	Nomar Garciaparra	.75
841	Manny Ramirez	.40
842	Pedro J. Martinez	.50
843	Sammy Sosa	.75
844	Ken Griffey Jr.	.75
845	Jim Thome	.40
846	Vladimir Guerrero	.50
847	Mike Piazza	.50
848	Derek Jeter	1.00
849	Jason Giambi	.40
850	Roger Clemens	1.00
851	Alfonso Soriano	.50
852	Hideki Matsui	4.00
853	Barry Bonds	1.00
854	Ichiro Suzuki	.50
855	Albert Pujols	.75
856	Alex Rodriguez	.75
857	Darin Erstad	.25
858	Troy Glaus	.25
859	Curt Schilling	.25
860	Luis Gonzalez	.25
861	Tom Glavine	.25
862	Andruw Jones	.40
863	Gary Sheffield	.25
864	Frank Thomas	.40
865	Mark Prior	1.00
866	Ivan Rodriguez	.40
867	Jeff Bagwell	.40
868	Lance Berkman	.25
869	Shawn Green	.25
870	Hideo Nomo	.40
871	Torii Hunter	.25
872	Bernie Williams	.25
873	Barry Zito	.25
874	Pat Burrell	.25
875	Carlos Delgado	.25
876	Miguel Tejada	.25
877	Hideki Matsui RC	4.00
878	Jose Contreras RC	2.00
879	Jason Anderson	.40
880	Jason Shiell RC	.40
881	Kevin Tolar RC	.40
882	Michel Hernandez RC	.40
883	Arnie Munoz RC	.40
884	David Sanders RC	.40
885	Willie Eyre RC	.40
886	Brent Hoard RC	.40
887	Lew Ford RC	2.00
888	Beau Kemp RC	.75
889	Jonathan Pridie RC	.40
890	Mike Ryan RC	.40
891	Richard Fischer RC	.40
892	Luis Ayala RC	.40
893	Mike Neu RC	.40
894	Joe Valentine RC	.40
895	Nate Bland RC	.40
896	Shane Bazzell RC	.75
897	Aquilino Lopez RC	.40
898	Diegomar Markwell RC	.40
899	Francisco Rosario RC	.40
900	Guillermo Quiroz RC	.75
901	Luis De Los Santos	.40
902	Fernando Cabrera RC	.40
903	Francisco Cruceta RC	.40
904	Jhonny Peralta	.50
905	Rett Johnson RC	.50
906	Aaron Looper RC	.40
907	Bobby Madritsch RC	.40
908	Luis Matos	.40
909	Jose Castillo	.25
910	Chris Waters RC	.40
911	Jeremy Guthrie	.25
912	Pedro Liriano	.25
913	Joe Borowski	.25
914	Felix Sanchez RC	.40
915	Jon Leicester RC	.40
916	Todd Wellemeyer RC	.75
917	Matt Bruback RC	.25
918	Chris Capuano RC	1.50
919	Oscar Villarreal RC	.25
920	Matt Kata RC	.75
921	Robby Hammock RC	.75
922	Gerald Laird	.25
923	Brandon Webb RC	3.00
924	Tommy Whiteman RC	.40
925	Andrew Brown RC	.40
926	Alfredo Gonzalez RC	.40
927	Carlos Rivera	.25
928	Rick Roberts RC	.40
929	Terrmel Sledge RC	.40
930	Josh Willingham RC	.40
931	Prentice Redman RC	.50
932	Jeff Duncan RC	1.50
933	Craig Brazell RC	1.00
934	Jeremy Griffiths	.25
935	Phil Seibel RC	.40
936	Heath Bell RC	.40
937	Bernie Castro RC	.40
938	Mike Nicolas RC	.40
939	Cory Stewart RC	.40
940	Shane Victorino RC	.40
941	Brandon Villafuerte RC	.40
942	Jeremy Wedel RC	.40

#	Player	Price
943	Tommy Phelps	.25
944	Josh Hall RC	.75
945	Ryan Cameron RC	.40
946	Garrett Atkins	.25
947	Clint Barmes RC	.75
948	Michael Hessman RC	.40
949	Brian Stokes RC	.40
950	Rocco Baldelli	1.00
951	Hector Luna	.25
952	Jaime Cerda	.25
953	D.J. Carrasco RC	.40
954	Ian Ferguson RC	.40
955	Tim Olson RC	.75
956	Alejandro Machado RC	.40
957	Jorge Cordova RC	.40
958	Wilfredo Ledezma RC	.40
959	Nathan Robertson RC	.40
960	Nook Logan RC	.25
961	Anaheim Angels	.25
962	Baltimore Orioles	.25
963	Boston Red Sox	.25
964	Chicago White Sox	.25
965	Cleveland Indians	.25
966	Detroit Tigers	.25
967	Kansas City Royals	.25
968	Minnesota Twins	.25
969	New York Yankees	.25
970	Oakland Athletics	.25
971	Seattle Mariners	.25
972	Tampa Bay Devil Rays	.25
973	Texas Rangers	.25
974	Toronto Blue Jays	.25
975	Arizona Diamondbacks	.25
976	Atlanta Braves	.25
977	Chicago Cubs	.25
978	Cincinnati Reds	.25
979	Colorado Rockies	.25
980	Florida Marlins	.25
981	Houston Astros	.25
982	Los Angeles Dodgers	.25
983	Milwaukee Brewers	.25
984	Montreal Expos	.25
985	New York Mets	.25
986	Philadelphia Phillies	.25
987	Pittsburgh Pirates	.25
988	San Diego Padres	.25
989	San Francisco Giants	.25
990	St. Louis Cardinals	.25

Rainbow

Stars (1-990):	10-20X
Rookies:	4-8X
Production 40 Sets	

Red, White & Blue

Stars (1-990):	1-3X
Rookies:	1-2X
#'s 1-752 Inserted 1:6	
#'s 877-960 1:36	

Endorsements

	NM/M
Inserted 1:500	
Some not priced due to scarcity.	
RA	Rick Ankiel	20.00
DB	Dewon Brazelton/50	15.00
BD	Ben Diggins	15.00
AG	Alex Graman/50	15.00
KGS	Ken Griffey Sr.	15.00
HI	Hansel Izquierdo/50	15.00
JL	Jon Lieber	15.00
CM	Corwin Malone/50	15.00
TO	Tomokazu Ohka	20.00

Vintage Update

	NM/M
Complete Set (61):	15.00
Common Player:	.40
Inserted 1:Pack	
281	Tom Glavine	1.00
282	Josh Stewart	.40
283	Aquilino Lopez	.40
284	Horacio Ramirez	.40
285	Brandon Phillips	.40
286	Kirk Saarloos	.40
287	Runelvys Hernandez	.40
288	Hideki Matsui	5.00
289	Jeremy Bonderman	3.00
290	Russ Ortiz	.40
291	Ken Harvey	.40
292	Edgardo Alfonzo	.40
293	Oscar Villarreal	.40
294	Marlon Byrd	.40
295	Josh Bard	.40
296	David Cone	.40
297	Mike Neu	.40
298	Cliff Floyd	.40
299	Travis Lee	.40
300	Jeff Kent	.50
301	Ron Calloway	.40
302	Bartolo Colon	.40
303	Jose Contreras	1.50
304	Mark Teixeira	1.00
305	Ivan Rodriguez	1.00

306	Jim Thome	1.00
307	Shane Reynolds	.40
308	Luis Ayala	.40
309	Lyle Overbay	.40
310	Travis Hafner	.40
311	Wilfredo Ledezma	.40
312	Rocco Baldelli	1.50
313	Jason Anderson	.40
314	Kenny Lofton	.75
315	Brandon Larson	.40
316	Ty Wigginton	.40
317	Fred McGriff	.40
318	Antonio Osuna	.40
319	Corey Patterson	.40
320	Erubiel Durazo	.40
321	Mike MacDougal	.40
322	Sammy Sosa	2.00
323	Mike Hampton	.40
324	Ramiro Mendoza	.40
325	Kevin Millwood	.75
326	Dave Roberts	.40
327	Todd Zeile	.40
328	Reggie Sanders	.40
329	Billy Koch	.40
330	Mike Stanton	.40
331	Orlando Hernandez	.40
332	Tony Clark	.40
333	Chris Hammond	.40
334	Michael Cuddyer	.40
335	Sandy Alomar	.40
336	Jose Cruz Jr.	.40
337	Omar Daal	.40
338	Robert Fick	.40
339	Daryle Ward	.40
340	David Bell	.40
341	Checklist	.40

2003 UD Yankees Signature Series

Bill Virdon · Manager

		NM/M
Complete Set (90):		65.00
Common Player:		.50
Pack (3):		17.00
Box (10):		140.00
1	Al Downing	.50
2	Allen Gettel	.50
3	Art Ditmar	.50
4	Babe Ruth	6.00
5	Bill Virdon	.50
6	Billy Martin	2.00
7	Bob Cerv	.50
8	Bob Turley	.50
9	Bobby Cox	.75
10	Bobby Richardson	1.00
11	Bobby Shantz	.50
12	Bucky Dent	.75
13	Bud Metheny	.50
14	Casey Stengel	2.00
15	Charlie Hayes	.50
16	Charlie Silvera	.50
17	Chris Chambliss	.50
18	Danny Cater	.50
19	Dave Kingman	.75
20	Dave Righetti	.75
21	Dave Winfield	2.00
22	David Cone	.75
23	Dick Tidrow	.50
24	Doc Medich	.50
25	Dock Ellis	.50
26	Don Gullett	.50
27	Don Mattingly	5.00
28	Dwight Gooden	.75
29	Eddie Robinson	.50
30	Felipe Alou	.50
31	Fred Sanford	.50
32	Fred Stanley	.50
33	Gene Michael	.50
34	Hank Bauer	.50
35	Hector Lopez	.50
36	Horace Clarke	.50
37	Jake Gibbs	.50
38	Jerry Coleman	.50
39	Jerry Lumpe	.50
40	Jim Bouton	.50
41	Jim Kaat	1.00
42	Jim Mason	.50
43	Jimmy Key	.50
44	Joe DiMaggio	5.00
45	Joe Torre	1.00
46	John Montefusco	.50
47	Johnny Blanchard	.50
48	Johnny Callison	.50
49	Lew Burdette	.50
50	Johnny Kucks	.50
51	Steve Balboni	.50
52	Ken Singleton	.50
53	Lee Mazzilli	.50
54	Lou Gehrig	5.00
55	Lou Piniella	1.00
56	Luis Tiant	.50
57	Marius Russo	.50
58	Mel Stottlemyre	.75
59	Mickey Mantle	6.00
60	Mike Pagliarulo	.50
61	Mike Torrez	.50
62	Miller Huggins	.50
63	Norm Siebern	.50
64	Paul O'Neill	.75
65	Phil Niekro	.50
66	Phil Rizzuto	3.00
67	Ralph Branca	.50
68	Ralph Houk	.50
69	Ralph Terry	.50
70	Randy Gumpert	.50
71	Roger Maris	5.00
72	Ron Blomberg	.50
73	Ron Guidry	1.00
74	Ruben Amaro	.50
75	Ryne Duren	.50
76	Sam McDowell	.50
77	Sparky Lyle	.50
78	Thurman Munson	3.00
79	Tom Sturdivant	.50
80	Tom Tresh	.50
81	Tommy Byrne	.50
82	Tommy Henrich	.50
83	Tommy John	.75
84	Tony Kubek	.75
85	Tony Lazzeri	.50
86	Virgil Trucks	.50
87	Wade Boggs	1.00
88	Whitey Ford	3.00
89	Willie Randolph	.75
90	Yogi Berra	3.00

Monumental Cuts

		NM/M
30 total cards produced:		
MC-LG	Lou Gehrig/1	
	(6/03 Auction)	17,600
MC-MM	Mickey Mantle/1	
	(1/04 Auction)	10,000
MC-RM	Roger Maris/6	
MC-BM	Billy Martin/9	825.00
MC-TM	Thurman Munson/1	
	(3/04 Auction)	2,605
MC-BR	Babe Ruth/1	
	(4/04 Auction)	12,600

Pinstripe Excellence Dual

		NM/M
Common Dual Autograph:		20.00
Some not priced yet.		
Production 125 Sets		
AA	Felipe Alou, Ruben Amaro	50.00
BA	Hank Bauer, Felipe Alou	50.00
BP	Wade Boggs, Mike Pagliarulo	60.00
BT	Jim Bouton, Ralph Terry	50.00
CK	Chris Chambliss, Dave Kingman	60.00
DC	Bucky Dent, Chris Chambliss	50.00
DR	Bucky Dent, Willie Randolph	80.00
DS	Ryne Duren, Tom Sturdivant	35.00
FB	Whitey Ford, Yogi Berra	150.00
GB	Jake Gibbs, Johnny Blanchard	40.00
GM	Ron Guidry, John Montefusco	80.00
GR	Ron Guidry, Willie Randolph	80.00
JK	Tommy John, Jim Kaat	60.00
LG	Sparky Lyle, Ron Guidry	75.00
LM	Jerry Lumpe, Jim Mason	25.00
MC	John Montefusco, Chris Chambliss	60.00
MK	Gene Michael, Tony Kubek	60.00
ML	Sam McDowell, Sparky Lyle	50.00
MR	Don Mattingly, Dave Righetti	150.00
NT	Phil Niekro, Luis Tiant	50.00
RB	Bobby Richardson, Hank Bauer	75.00
RC	Bobby Richardson, Jerry Coleman	50.00
SC	Ken Singleton, Jerry Coleman	60.00
ST	Tom Sturdivant, Bob Turley	40.00
TK	Luis Tiant, Jim Kaat	60.00
TM	Mike Torrez, Lee Mazzilli	50.00
BRi	Hank Bauer, Phil Rizzuto	75.00
BRu	Tommy Byrne, Marius Russo	30.00

Pride of New York Autograph

Ralph Houk · Manager

		NM/M
Common Autograph:		8.00
Inserted 1:1		
JA	Jason Alexander/SP	600.00
FA	Felipe Alou	15.00
RA	Ruben Amaro	8.00
SB	Steve Balboni	8.00
HB	Hank Bauer	10.00
YB	Yogi Berra	85.00
BL	Johnny Blanchard	15.00
RBI	Ron Blomberg	10.00
WB	Wade Boggs	40.00
JB	Jim Bouton	10.00
RBr	Ralph Branca	8.00
LB	Lew Burdette	10.00
TB	Tommy Byrne	10.00
CAS	Johnny Callison	8.00
TC	Tom Carroll	8.00
CAL	Brian Cashman/SP	250.00
DC	Danny Cater	8.00
CE	Bob Cerv	8.00
CC	Chris Chambliss	12.00
HC	Horace Clarke	10.00
JC	Jerry Coleman	10.00
CO	David Cone	25.00
CX	Bobby Cox	12.00
DE	Bucky Dent	12.00
DI	Art Ditmar	10.00
AD	Al Downing	8.00
BD	Brian Doyle	8.00
RD	Ryne Duren	10.00
EL	Dock Ellis	10.00
WF	Whitey Ford	50.00
AG	Allen Gettel	8.00
JG	Jake Gibbs	8.00
GO	Dwight Gooden	15.00
JO	John Goodman	300.00
RaG	Ron Guidry	15.00
DG	Don Gullett	8.00
RoG	Randy Gumpert	8.00
CH	Charlie Hayes	10.00
TH	Tommy Henrich	30.00
RH	Ralph Houk	12.00
TJ	Tommy John	10.00
JK	Jim Kaat	15.00
KE	Jimmy Key	15.00
DK	Dave Kingman	15.00
TK	Tony Kubek	25.00
KU	Johnny Kucks	10.00
HL	Hector Lopez	10.00
JL	Jerry Lumpe	8.00
SL	Sparky Lyle	10.00
JM	Jim Mason	8.00
MA	Don Mattingly	80.00
LM	Lee Mazzilli	10.00
SM	Sam McDowell	8.00
DM	Doc Medich	8.00
BM	Bud Metheny	
GM	Gene Michael	10.00
MO	John Montefusco	8.00
PN	Phil Niekro	15.00
PO	Paul O'Neill/SP	25.00
MP	Mike Pagliarulo	8.00
LP	Lou Piniella/SP	20.00
WR	Willie Randolph/SP	15.00
HR	Hal Reniff	8.00
BR	Bobby Richardson	15.00
DR	Dave Righetti	15.00
PR	Phil Rizzuto	40.00
ER	Eddie Robinson	8.00
MR	Marius Russo	10.00
FS	Fred Sanford	8.00
BS	Bobby Shantz	10.00
NS	Norm Siebern	8.00
CS	Charlie Silvera	10.00
KS	Ken Singleton	10.00
ST	Fred Stanley	8.00
MS	Mel Stottlemyre	15.00
TS	Tom Sturdivant	8.00
RT	Ralph Terry	10.00
LT	Luis Tiant	10.00
DT	Dick Tidrow	10.00
JT	Joe Torre	35.00
MT	Mike Torrez	8.00
TT	Tom Tresh	15.00
VT	Virgil Trucks	10.00
BT	Bob Turley	12.00
BV	Bill Virdon	8.00
DW	Dave Winfield/SP	75.00
JW	Jim Wynn	8.00
DZ	Don Zimmer	40.00

Yankees Forever Triple

		NM/M
Common Triple Auto.:		
Production 50 Sets		
ALB	Felipe Alou, Hector Lopez, Hank Bauer	120.00
AOM	Felipe Alou, Paul O'Neill, Lee Mazzilli	150.00
BSB	Yogi Berra, Bobby Shantz, Hank Bauer	200.00
DFB	Al Downing, Whitey Ford, Yogi Berra	240.00
DRC	Bucky Dent, Willie Randolph, Chris Chambliss	125.00
EMG	Dock Ellis, Doc Medich, Don Gullett	125.00
FKB	Whitey Ford, Johnny Kucks, Jim Bouton	150.00
GCK	Dwight Gooden, David Cone, Jimmy Key	150.00
GRJ	Ron Guidry, Dave Righetti, Tommy John	150.00
HMC	Ralph Houk, Gene Michael, Bobby Cox	120.00
HRB	Tommy Henrich, Phil Rizzuto, Ralph Branca	150.00
JKL	Tommy John, Jim Kaat, Sparky Lyle	120.00
KCC	Dave Kingman, Chris Chambliss, Danny Cater	120.00
KGT	Jim Kaat, Don Gullett, Mike Torrez	120.00
KJB	Jim Kaat, Tommy John, Jim Bouton	120.00
MTT	John Montefusco, Mike Torrez, Dick Tidrow	120.00
OBK	Paul O'Neill, Wade Boggs, Jimmy Key	175.00
PTV	Lou Piniella, Joe Torre, Bill Virdon	150.00
RBC	Phil Rizzuto, Yogi Berra, Jerry Coleman	220.00
RKD	Phil Rizzuto, Tony Kubek, Bucky Dent	150.00

RRC	Bobby Richardson, Willie Randolph, Jerry Coleman	150.00
RSB	Marius Russo, Tom Sturdivant, Tommy Byrne	120.00
SSB	Fred Stanley, Charlie Silvera, Johnny Blanchard	120.00
STE	Mel Stottlemyre, Luis Tiant, Dock Ellis	120.00
TCO	Joe Torre, David Cone, Paul O'Neill	175.00
TLN	Luis Tiant, Sparky Lyle, Phil Niekro	120.00
TMT	Luis Tiant, Sam McDowell, Ralph Terry	120.00
WHM	Dave Winfield, Tommy Henrich, Lee Mazzilli	160.00
WMG	Dave Winfield, Don Mattingly, Ron Guidry	300.00
WPC	Dave Winfield, Lou Piniella, Chris Chambliss	100.00

2003 Upper Deck Yankees 100th Anniversary

	NM/M
Complete Set (30):	15.00
Common Player:	.50
1 Babe Ruth	2.00
2 Tony Lazzeri	.50
3 Lou Gehrig	1.50
4 Lou Gehrig	1.50
5 Red Rolfe	.50
6 Lou Gehrig	1.50
7 Bill Dickey	.50
8 Joe DiMaggio	1.50
9 Charlie Keller	.50
10 Frank Crosetti	.50
11 Phil Rizzuto	.50
12 Joe DiMaggio	1.50
13 Joe DiMaggio	1.50
14 Phil Rizzuto	.50
15 Mickey Mantle	2.00
16 Yogi Berra	.75
17 Yogi Berra	.75
18 Mickey Mantle	2.00
19 Whitey Ford	.50
20 Mickey Mantle	2.00
21 Thurman Munson	.75
22 Thurman Munson	.75
23 Bernie Williams	.50
24 Jorge Posada	.50
25 Mariano Rivera	.50
26 Derek Jeter	1.50
27 Hideki Matsui	1.00
28 Hideki Matsui	1.00
29 Roger Clemens	1.50
30 Yankee Stadium	.50

2004 Upper Deck

	NM/M
Complete Set (540):	75.00
Common Player:	.15
Hobby Pack (8):	2.00
Hobby Box (24):	40.00
1 Dontrelle Willis	.40
2 Edgar Gonzalez	.15
3 Jose Reyes	.50
4 Jae Weong Seo	.15
5 Miguel Cabrera	.25
6 Jesse Foppert	.15
7 Mike Neu	.15
8 Micheal Nakamura	.15
9 Luis Ayala	.15
10 Jared Sandberg	.15

11 Jhonny Peralta	.15
12 Wilfredo Ledezma	.15
13 Jason Roach	.15
14 Kirk Saarloos	.15
15 Cliff Lee	.15
16 Bobby Hill	.15
17 Lyle Overbay	.15
18 Josh Hall	.15
19 Joe Thurston	.15
20 Matt Kata	.15
21 Jeremy Bonderman	.15
22 Julio Manon	.15
23 Rodrigo Rosario	.15
24 Robby Hammock	.15
25 David Sanders	.15
26 Miguel Ojeda	.15
27 Mark Teixeira	.25
28 Franklyn German	.15
29 Ken Harvey	.15
30 Xavier Nady	.15
31 Tim Salmon	.25
32 Troy Glaus	.40
33 Adam Kennedy	.15
34 David Eckstein	.15
35 Bengie Molina	.15
36 Jarrod Washburn	.15
37 Ramon Ortiz	.15
38 Eric Chavez	.25
39 Miguel Tejada	.25
40 Chris Singleton	.15
41 Jermaine Dye	.15
42 John Halama	.15
43 Tim Hudson	.40
44 Barry Zito	.40
45 Ted Lilly	.15
46 Bobby Kielty	.15
47 Kelvim Escobar	.15
48 Josh Phelps	.15
49 Vernon Wells	.25
50 Roy Halladay	.25
51 Orlando Hudson	.15
52 Eric Hinske	.15
53 Brandon Backe	.15
54 Dewon Brazelton	.15
55 Ben Grieve	.15
56 Aubrey Huff	.15
57 Toby Hall	.15
58 Rocco Baldelli	.40
59 Al Martin	.15
60 Brandon Phillips	.15
61 Omar Vizquel	.25
62 C.C. Sabathia	.15
63 Milton Bradley	.15
64 Ricky Gutierrez	.15
65 Matt Lawton	.15
66 Danys Baez	.15
67 Ichiro Suzuki	1.00
68 Randy Winn	.15
69 Carlos Guillen	.15
70 Mark McLemore	.15
71 Dan Wilson	.15
72 Jamie Moyer	.15
73 Joel Pineiro	.15
74 Edgar Martinez	.25
75 Tony Batista	.15
76 Jay Gibbons	.15
77 Jeff Conine	.15
78 Melvin Mora	.15
79 Geronimo Gil	.15
80 Rodrigo Lopez	.15
81 Jorge Julio	.15
82 Rafael Palmeiro	.50
83 Juan Gonzalez	.40
84 Mike Young	.15
85 Alex Rodriguez	1.50
86 Einar Diaz	.15
87 Kevin Mench	.15
88 Hank Blalock	.40
89 Pedro J. Martinez	.75
90 Byung-Hyun Kim	.15
91 Derek Lowe	.25
92 Jason Varitek	.15
93 Manny Ramirez	.50
94 John Burkett	.15
95 Todd Walker	.15
96 Nomar Garciaparra	1.50
97 Trot Nixon	.15
98 Mike Sweeney	.15
99 Carlos Febles	.15
100 Mike MacDougal	.15
101 Raul Ibanez	.15
102 Jason Grimsley	.15
103 Chris George	.15
104 Brent Mayne	.15
105 Dmitri Young	.15
106 Eric Munson	.15
107 A.J. Hinch	.15
108 Andres Torres	.15
109 Bobby Higginson	.15
110 Shane Halter	.15
111 Matt Walbeck	.15
112 Torii Hunter	.40
113 Doug Mientkiewicz	.15
114 Lew Ford	.15

115 Eric Milton	.15
116 Eddie Guardado	.15
117 Cristian Guzman	.15
118 Corey Koskie	.15
119 Magglio Ordonez	.40
120 Mark Buehrle	.15
121 Billy Koch	.15
122 Jose Valentin	.15
123 Paul Konerko	.15
124 Carlos Lee	.15
125 Jon Garland	.15
126 Jason Giambi	.75
127 Derek Jeter	1.50
128 Roger Clemens	1.50
129 Andy Pettitte	.40
130 Jorge Posada	.40
131 David Wells	.15
132 Hideki Matsui	1.50
133 Mike Mussina	.50
134 Jeff Bagwell	.50
135 Craig Biggio	.25
136 Morgan Ensberg	.15
137 Richard Hidalgo	.15
138 Brad Ausmus	.15
139 Roy Oswalt	.25
140 Billy Wagner	.25
141 Octavio Dotel	.15
142 Gary Sheffield	.40
143 Andruw Jones	.40
144 John Smoltz	.25
145 Rafael Furcal	.25
146 Javy Lopez	.25
147 Shane Reynolds	.15
148 Horacio Ramirez	.15
149 Mike Hampton	.15
150 Jung Bong	.15
151 Ruben Quevedo	.15
152 Ben Sheets	.15
153 Geoff Jenkins	.25
154 Royce Clayton	.15
155 Glendon Rusch	.15
156 John Vander Wal	.15
157 Scott Podsednik	.40
158 Jim Edmonds	.40
159 Tino Martinez	.15
160 Albert Pujols	1.50
161 Matt Morris	.15
162 Woody Williams	.15
163 Edgar Renteria	.15
164 Jason Isringhausen	.15
165 Jason Simontacchi	.15
166 Kerry Robinson	.15
167 Sammy Sosa	1.25
168 Joe Borowski	.15
169 Tony Womack	.15
170 Antonio Alfonseca	.15
171 Corey Patterson	.15
172 Mark Prior	1.00
173 Moises Alou	.25
174 Matt Clement	.15
175 Randall Simon	.15
176 Randy Johnson	.75
177 Luis Gonzalez	.25
178 Craig Counsell	.15
179 Miguel Batista	.15
180 Steve Finley	.15
181 Brandon Webb	.15
182 Danny Bautista	.15
183 Oscar Villarreal	.15
184 Shawn Green	.25
185 Brian Jordan	.15
186 Fred McGriff	.25
187 Andy Ashby	.15
188 Rickey Henderson	.50
189 Dave Roberts	.15
190 Eric Gagne	.15
191 Kazuhisa Ishii	.15
192 Adrian Beltre	.15
193 Vladimir Guerrero	.75
194 Livan Hernandez	.15
195 Ron Calloway	.15
196 Sun-Woo Kim	.15
197 Wil Cordero	.15
198 Brad Wilkerson	.15
199 Orlando Cabrera	.15
200 Barry Bonds	2.00
201 Ray Durham	.15
202 Andres Galarraga	.15
203 Benito Santiago	.15
204 Jose Cruz Jr.	.15
205 Jason Schmidt	.15
206 Kirk Rueter	.15
207 Felix Rodriguez	.15
208 Mike Lowell	.15
209 Luis Castillo	.15
210 Derrek Lee	.25
211 Andy Fox	.15
212 Tommy Phelps	.15
213 Todd Hollandsworth	.15
214 Brad Penny	.15
215 Juan Pierre	.15
216 Mike Piazza	1.00
217 Jae Weong Seo	.15
218 Ty Wigginton	.15

219 Al Leiter	.15
220 Roger Cedeno	.15
221 Timoniel Perez	.15
222 Aaron Heilman	.15
223 Pedro Astacio	.15
224 Joe McEwing	.15
225 Ryan Klesko	.15
226 Brian Giles	.25
227 Mark Kotsay	.15
228 Brian Lawrence	.15
229 Rod Beck	.15
230 Trevor Hoffman	.15
231 Sean Burroughs	.15
232 Bobby Abreu	.25
233 Jim Thome	.50
234 David Bell	.15
235 Jimmy Rollins	.25
236 Mike Lieberthal	.15
237 Vicente Padilla	.15
238 Randy Wolf	.15
239 Reggie Sanders	.15
240 Jason Kendall	.15
241 Jack Wilson	.15
242 Jose Hernandez	.15
243 Kip Wells	.15
244 Carlos Rivera	.15
245 Craig Wilson	.15
246 Adam Dunn	.40
247 Sean Casey	.15
248 Danny Graves	.15
249 Ryan Dempster	.15
250 Barry Larkin	.40
251 Reggie Taylor	.15
252 Wily Mo Pena	.15
253 Larry Walker	.25
254 Mark Sweeney	.15
255 Preston Wilson	.15
256 Jason Jennings	.15
257 Charles Johnson	.15
258 Jay Payton	.15
259 Chris Stynes	.15
260 Juan Uribe	.15
261 Hideki Matsui	1.00
262 Barry Bonds	1.00
263 Dontrelle Willis	.25
264 Kevin Millwood	.15
265 Billy Wagner	.15
266 Rocco Baldelli	.25
267 Roger Clemens	.75
268 Rafael Palmeiro	.25
269 Miguel Cabrera	.25
270 Jose Contreras	.15
271 Aaron Sele	.15
272 Bartolo Colon	.25
273 Darin Erstad	.25
274 Francisco Rodriguez	.15
275 Garret Anderson	.40
276 Jose Guillen	.15
277 Troy Percival	.15
278 Alex Cintron	.15
279 Casey Fossum	.15
280 Elmer Dessens	.15
281 Jose Valverde	.15
282 Matt Mantei	.15
283 Richie Sexson	.40
284 Roberto Alomar	.40
285 Shea Hillenbrand	.15
286 Chipper Jones	.75
287 Greg Maddux	1.00
288 J.D. Drew	.25
289 Marcus Giles	.15
290 Mike Hessman	.15
291 John Thomson	.15
292 Russ Ortiz	.15
293 Adam Loewen	.15
294 Jack Cust	.15
295 Jerry Hairston	.15
296 Kurt Ainsworth	.15
297 Luis Matos	.15
298 Marty Cordova	.15
299 Sidney Ponson	.15
300 Bill Mueller	.15
301 Curt Schilling	.50
302 David Ortiz	.50
303 Johnny Damon	.25
304 Keith Foulke	.15
305 Pokey Reese	.15
306 Scott Williamson	.15
307 Tim Wakefield	.15
308 Alex Gonzalez	.15
309 Aramis Ramirez	.40
310 Carlos Zambrano	.40
311 Juan Cruz	.15
312 Kerry Wood	.75
313 Kyle Farnsworth	.15
314 Aaron Rowand	.15
315 Esteban Loaiza	.15
316 Frank Thomas	.50
317 Joe Borchard	.15
318 Joe Crede	.15
319 Miguel Olivo	.15
320 Willie Harris	.15
321 Aaron Harang	.15
322 Austin Kearns	.25

323 Brandon Claussen .15	427 Oliver Perez .15	531 Akinori Otsuka .75	161 Fernando Nieve 2.00
324 Brandon Larson .15	428 Tike Redman .15	532 Rusty Tucker .25	162 Mike Wuertz 2.00
325 Ryan Freel .15	429 Adam Eaton .15	533 Justin Knoedler .25	163 Jerry Gil 2.00
326 Ken Griffey Jr. 1.00	430 Ismael Valdez .15	534 Merkin Valdez 1.00	164 Jorge Vasquez 2.00
327 Ryan Wagner .15	431 Jake Peavy .15	535 Greg Dobbs .25	165 Chad Bentz 4.00
328 Alex Escobar .15	432 Khalil Greene .15	536 Justin Leone .25	166 Luis Gonzalez 2.00
329 Coco Crisp .15	433 Mark Loretta .15	537 Shawn Camp .25	167 Ivan Ochoa 2.00
330 David Riske .15	434 Phil Nevin .15	538 Edwin Moreno .25	168 Onil Joseph 2.00
331 Jody Gerut .15	435 Ramon Hernandez .15	539 Angel Chavez .25	169 Enemencio Pacheco 2.00
332 Josh Bard .15	436 A.J. Pierzynski .15	540 Jesse Harper .25	170 Kazuo Matsui RC 8.00
333 Travis Hafner .25	437 Edgardo Alfonzo .15	**Reflections Update**	**Play Ball Update Set (50):** 20.00
334 Chin-Hui Tsao .15	438 J.T. Snow .15	**Set (50):** 30.00	183 Kazuo Matsui RC 3.00
335 Denny Stark .15	439 Jerome Williams .15	341 Shingo Takatsu 3.00	184 Jerry Gil .50
336 Jeromy Burnitz .15	440 Marquis Grissom .15	342 Franklyn Gracesqui .75	185 Jose Capellan RC 2.00
337 Shawn Chacon .15	441 Robb Nen .15	343 Angel Chavez .75	186 Tim Hamulack .50
338 Todd Helton .50	442 Bret Boone .25	344 Jorge Sequea .75	187 Renyel Pinto .50
339 Vinny Castilla .15	443 Freddy Garcia .15	345 David Aardsma .75	188 Carlos Vasquez .50
340 Alex Sanchez .15	444 Gil Meche .15	346 Ramon Ramirez RC .75	189 Enemencio Pacheco .50
341 Carlos Pena .15	445 John Olerud .25	347 Lino Urdaneta .75	190 Ronny Cedeno .50
342 Fernando Vina .15	446 Rich Aurilia .15	348 Orlando Rodriguez .75	191 Mariano Gomez .50
343 Jason Johnson .15	447 Shigetoshi Hasegawa .15	349 Jason Szuminski .75	192 Carlos Hines .50
344 Matt Anderson .15	448 Bo Hart .15	350 Luis Gonzalez .75	193 Michael Vento .50
345 Mike Maroth .15	449 Dan Haren .15	351 Jon Gall 1.00	194 David Aardsma .50
346 Rondell White .15	450 Jason Marquis .15	352 Kevin Cave .75	195 Hector Gimenez .50
347 A.J. Burnett .15	451 Marlon Anderson .15	353 Chris Oxspring .75	196 Fernando Nieve .50
348 Alex Gonzalez .15	452 Scott Rolen .75	354 Freddy Guzman .75	197 Chris Saenz .50
349 Armando Benitez .15	453 So Taguchi .15	355 Jeff Bennett .75	198 Shawn Hill .50
350 Carl Pavano .15	454 Carl Crawford .15	356 Jorge Vasquez .75	199 Angel Chavez .50
351 Hee Seop Choi .15	455 Delmon Young .25	357 Merkin Valdez 2.00	200 Scott Proctor .50
352 Ivan Rodriguez .50	456 Geoff Blum .15	358 Tim Hamulack .75	201 William Bergolla .50
353 Josh Beckett .50	457 Jesus Colome .15	359 Hector Gimenez .75	202 Justin Germano .50
354 Josh Willingham .15	458 Jonny Gomes .15	360 Jerry Gil .75	203 Onil Joseph .50
355 Adam Everett .15	459 Lance Carter .15	361 Ryan Wing .75	204 Rusty Tucker .50
356 Brandon Duckworth .15	460 Robert Fick .15	362 Shawn Hill .75	205 Justin Knoedler .50
357 Jason Lane .15	461 Chan Ho Park .15	363 Jason Bartlett .75	206 Casey Daigle .50
358 Jeff Kent .25	462 Francisco Cordero .15	364 Renyel Pinto .75	207 Edwin Moreno .50
359 Jeriome Robertson .15	463 Jeff Nelson .15	365 Carlos Vasquez .75	208 Chad Bentz .50
360 Lance Berkman .25	464 Jeff Zimmerman .15	366 Mike Vento 1.50	209 Ryan Wing .50
361 Wade Miller .15	465 Kenny Rogers .15	367 Casey Daigle .75	210 Shawn Camp .50
362 Aaron Guiel .15	466 Aquilino Lopez .15	368 Chad Bentz 1.00	211 Eddy Rodriguez .50
363 Angel Berroa .15	467 Carlos Delgado .50	369 Chris Saenz .75	212 Roman Colon .50
364 Carlos Beltran .50	468 Frank Catalanotto .15	370 Shawn Camp .75	213 Jason Bartlett .50
365 David DeJesus .15	469 Reed Johnson .15	371 Carlos Hines .75	214 Jorge Vasquez .50
366 Desi Relaford .15	470 Pat Hentgen .15	372 Edwin Moreno .75	215 Ivan Ochoa .50
367 Joe Randa .15	471 Curt Schilling .25	373 Mike Wuertz .75	216 Akinori Otsuka .50
368 Runelvys Hernandez .15	472 Gary Sheffield .25	374 Aarom Baldiris RC 1.50	217 Merkin Valdez RC 2.00
369 Edwin Jackson .15	473 Javier Vazquez .15	375 Ronny Cedeno .75	218 Shingo Takatsu RC 2.00
370 Hideo Nomo .40	474 Kazuo Matsui 1.00	376 Akinori Otsuka 1.50	219 Chris Oxspring .50
371 Jeff Weaver .15	475 Kevin Brown .25	377 Jose Capellan 2.00	220 Kevin Cave .50
372 Juan Encarnacion .15	476 Rafael Palmeiro .25	378 Justin Germano .75	221 Ramon Ramirez .50
373 Odalis Perez .15	477 Richie Sexson .25	379 Justin Knoedler .75	222 Orlando Rodriguez .50
374 Paul LoDuca .15	478 Roger Clemens .75	380 Mariano Gomez .75	223 Lino Urdaneta .50
375 Robin Ventura .15	479 Vladimir Guerrero .50	381 Fernando Nieve 1.50	224 Franklyn Gracesqui .50
376 Bill Hall .15	480 Alex Rodriguez 1.00	382 Scott Proctor .75	225 Mike Wuertz .50
377 Chad Moeller .15	481 Jake Woods .25	383 Roman Colon .75	226 Jorge Sequea .50
378 Chris Capuano .15	482 Tim Bittner .25	384 Onil Joseph .75	227 Luis Gonzalez .50
379 Junior Spivey .15	483 Brandon Medders .50	385 Eddy Rodriguez .75	228 Jason Szuminski .50
380 Rickie Weeks .25	484 Casey Daigle .25	386 Enemencio Pacheco .75	229 John Gall .50
381 Wes Helms .15	485 Jerry Gil .25	387 William Bergolla .75	230 Freddy Guzman .50
382 Brad Radke .15	486 Mike Gosling .25	388 Ivan Ochoa .75	231 Jeff Bennett .50
383 Jacque Jones .15	487 Jose Capellan 1.00	389 Rusty Tucker .75	232 Roberto Novoa .50
384 Joe Mays .15	488 Onil Joseph .25	390 Roberto Novoa .75	**Vintage Update Set (50):** 10.00
385 Joe Nathan .15	489 Roman Colon .25	**SPGU Patch Edition**	451 Alex Rodriguez 1.50
386 Johan Santana .15	490 David Crouthers .25	**Update Set (50):** 85.00	452 Javy Lopez .40
387 Nick Punto .15	491 Eddy Rodriguez .25	121 Richie Sexson 3.00	453 Alfonso Soriano .50
388 Shannon Stewart .15	492 Franklyn Gracesqui .50	122 Javier Vazquez 2.00	454 Vladimir Guerrero .50
389 Carl Everett .15	493 Jamie Brown .25	123 Alex Rodriguez 8.00	455 Rafael Palmeiro .50
390 Claudio Vargas .15	494 Jerome Gamble .25	124 Javy Lopez 3.00	456 Gary Sheffield .50
391 Jose Vidro .15	495 Tim Hamulack .25	125 Miguel Tejada 3.00	457 Curt Schilling .50
392 Nick Johnson .15	496 Carlos Vasquez .25	126 Bartolo Colon 2.00	458 Miguel Tejada .50
393 Rocky Biddle .15	497 Renyel Pinto .50	127 Ivan Rodriguez 4.00	459 Kevin Brown .40
394 Tony Armas .15	498 Ronny Cedeno .25	128 Rafael Palmeiro 3.00	460 Richie Sexson .50
395 Braden Looper .15	499 Enemencio Pacheco .25	129 Kevin Brown 3.00	461 Roger Clemens 1.50
396 Cliff Floyd .15	500 Ryan Meaux .25	130 Gary Sheffield 3.00	462 Javier Vazquez .25
397 Jason Phillips .15	501 Ryan Wing .25	131 Greg Maddux 5.00	463 Bartolo Colon .25
398 Mike Cameron .15	502 Shingo Takatsu 1.00	132 Curt Schilling 4.00	464 Ivan Rodriguez .50
399 Tom Glavine .40	503 William Bergolla .25	133 Roger Clemens 8.00	465 Greg Maddux 1.00
400 Kenny Lofton .25	504 Ivan Ochoa .25	134 Alfonso Soriano 3.00	466 Jamie Brown .25
401 Alfonso Soriano .50	505 Mariano Gomez .25	135 Vladimir Guerrero 4.00	467 David Crouthers .25
402 Bernie Williams .40	506 Justin Hampson .25	136 Carlos Vasquez 2.00	468 Jason Frasor .25
403 Javier Vazquez .15	507 Justin Huisman .25	137 Roman Colon 2.00	469 Greg Dobbs .25
404 Jon Lieber .15	508 Scott Dohmann .25	138 William Bergolla 2.00	470 Jesse Harper .25
405 Jose Contreras .15	509 Donnie Kelly .50	139 Jason Bartlett 2.00	471 Nick Regilio RC .25
406 Kevin Brown .25	510 Chris Aguila .25	140 Casey Daigle 2.00	472 Ryan Wing .25
407 Mariano Rivera .25	511 Lincoln Holdzkom RC .25	141 Ryan Wing 2.00	473 Akinori Otsuka RC 1.00
408 Arthur Rhodes .15	512 Freddy Guzman .25	142 Chris Saenz 2.00	474 Shingo Takatsu RC 1.50
409 Eric Byrnes .15	513 Hector Gimenez .25	143 Edwin Moreno 2.00	475 Kazuo Matsui RC 3.00
410 Erubiel Durazo .15	514 Jorge Vasquez .25	144 Shawn Hill 2.00	476 Michael Vento RC 1.00
411 Graham Koonce .15	515 Jason Frasor .25	145 Eddy Rodriguez 2.00	477 Mike Gosling .25
412 Marco Scutaro .15	516 Chris Saenz .50	146 Justin Knoedler 2.00	478 Justin Huisman .25
413 Mark Mulder .15	517 Dennis Sarfate .25	147 Renyel Pinto 2.00	479 Justin Hampson .25
414 Mark Redman .15	518 Colby Miller .25	148 Kevin Cave 2.00	480 Dennis Sarfate .25
415 Rich Harden .15	519 Jason Bartlett .25	149 Carlos Hines 2.00	481 Ian Snell RC 1.50
416 Brett Myers .15	520 Chad Bentz .25	150 Merkin Valdez RC 4.00	482 Tim Bausher RC .25
417 Chase Utley .15	521 Josh Labandeira .25	151 Tim Hamulack RC 2.00	483 Donnie Kelly .25
418 Kevin Millwood .25	522 Shawn Hill .25	152 Hector Gimenez RC 2.00	484 Jerome Gamble .25
419 Marlon Byrd .15	523 Kazuo Matsui RC 3.00	153 Mike Vento RC 5.00	485 Mike Rouse .25
420 Pat Burrell .25	524 Carlos Hines .25	154 Scott Proctor RC 3.00	486 Merkin Valdez RC .75
421 Placido Polanco .15	525 Michael Vento 2.00	155 Rusty Tucker RC 2.00	487 Lincoln Holdzkom RC .25
422 Tim Worrell .15	526 Scott Proctor .50	156 Akinori Otsuka RC 4.00	488 Justin Leone .25
423 Jason Bay .15	527 Sean Henn .50	157 Ronny Cedeno RC 2.00	489 Sean Henn .25
424 Josh Fogg .15	528 David Aardsma .25	158 Jose Capellan RC 6.00	490 Brandon Medders RC .25
425 Kris Benson .15	529 Ian Snell .50	159 Justin Germano RC 2.00	491 Mike Johnston RC .25
426 Mike Gonzalez .15	530 Mike Johnson .25	160 Shingo Takatsu RC 5.00	492 Tim Bittner .25

493	Mike Wuertz	.25
494	Chad Bentz	.50
495	Ryan Meaux RC	.25
496	Chris Aguila RC	.25
497	Jake Woods RC	.25
498	Scott Dohmann RC	.25
499	Colby Miller	.25
500	Josh Labandeira	.25

Glossy

NM/M

Complete Factory Set (590): 85.00
Glossy: 1-2X
Issued only in factory sets.

Authentic Stars Jersey

Mark Teixeira / First Base

NM/M

Common Player: 4.00
Inserted 1:48
Golds: 1-2X
Production 100 Sets

BA	Bobby Abreu	6.00
RO	Roberto Alomar	6.00
JB	Jeff Bagwell	6.00
RB	Rocco Baldelli	10.00
JH	Josh Beckett	5.00
HB	Hank Blalock	5.00
EC	Eric Chavez	4.00
RC	Roger Clemens	15.00
CD	Carlos Delgado	5.00
JD	J.D. Drew	4.00
DE	Darin Erstad	4.00
JG	Jason Giambi	8.00
TG	Troy Glaus	5.00
TL	Tom Glavine	6.00
VG	Vladimir Guerrero	8.00
SG	Shawn Green	5.00
KG	Ken Griffey Jr.	15.00
TH	Todd Helton	8.00
TO	Torii Hunter	6.00
RJ	Randy Johnson	8.00
AJ	Andruw Jones	6.00
CJ	Chipper Jones	8.00
JK	Jeff Kent	4.00
GM	Greg Maddux	10.00
PM	Pedro J. Martinez	8.00
TM	Tino Martinez	4.00
HM	Hideki Matsui	35.00
PN	Phil Nevin	4.00
MI	Mike Piazza	10.00
MP	Mark Prior	10.00
AP	Albert Pujols	15.00
AR	Alex Rodriguez	12.00
IR	Ivan Rodriguez	8.00
CS	Curt Schilling	5.00
AS	Alfonso Soriano	10.00
SS	Sammy Sosa	12.00
IS	Ichiro Suzuki	30.00
MT	Mark Teixeira	8.00
FT	Frank Thomas	8.00
LW	Larry Walker	4.00
BW	Bernie Williams	6.00
BZ	Barry Zito	6.00

Awesome Honors

NM/M

Complete Set (10): 15.00

1	Albert Pujols	5.00
2	Alex Rodriguez	5.00
3	Angel Berroa	5.00
4	Dontrelle Willis	1.00
5	Eric Gagne	1.50
6	Garret Anderson	1.00
7	Ivan Rodriguez	1.50
8	Josh Beckett	1.50
9	Mariano Rivera	1.00
10	Roy Halladay	.75

Awesome Honors Jersey

NM/M

Golds: 1.5-2X

JAMIE MOYER pitcher

Production 165

GA	Garret Anderson	5.00
JB	Josh Beckett	6.00
BB	Bret Boone	5.00
MC	Mike Cameron	4.00
LC	Luis Castillo	4.00
EC	Eric Chavez	5.00
JE	Jim Edmonds	5.00
EG	Eric Gagne	12.00
EG1	Eric Gagne	12.00
JG	Jason Giambi	8.00
VG	Vladimir Guerrero	8.00
RH	Roy Halladay	6.00
MH	Mike Hampton	4.00
TH	Todd Helton	6.00
HU	Torii Hunter	5.00
AJ	Andruw Jones	6.00
DL	Derrek Lee	5.00
EM	Edgar Martinez	5.00
BM	Bengie Molina	4.00
JM	Jamie Moyer	4.00
MU	Mike Mussina	8.00
JO	John Olerud	5.00
MO	Magglio Ordonez	5.00
AP	Albert Pujols	10.00
AP1	Albert Pujols	
AP2	Albert Pujols	10.00
MR	Mariano Rivera	5.00
AR	Alex Rodriguez	10.00
AR1	Alex Rodriguez	
AR2	Alex Rodriguez	
AR3	Alex Rodriguez	10.00
IR	Ivan Rodriguez	8.00
SR	Scott Rolen	8.00
JS	John Smoltz	8.00
AS	Alfonso Soriano	8.00
IS	Ichiro Suzuki	20.00
JT	Jim Thome	8.00
DW	Dontrelle Willis	6.00

Famous Quotes

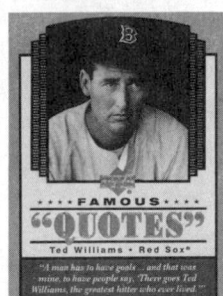

FAMOUS "QUOTES"
Ted Williams • Red Sox®

"A man has to have goals ... and that was mine, to have people say, 'There goes Ted Williams, the greatest hitter who ever lived.'"

NM/M

Complete Set (20): 30.00

Q-1	Al Lopez	.75
Q-2	Bob Feller	1.00
Q-3	Bob Gibson	1.50
Q-4	Brooks Robinson	1.50
Q-5	Cal Ripken Jr.	5.00
Q-6	Carl Yastrzemski	2.00
Q-7	Earl Weaver	.75
Q-8	Eddie Mathews	2.00
Q-9	Ernie Banks	2.00
Q-10	Greg Maddux	2.00
Q-11	Joe DiMaggio	4.00
Q-12	Mickey Mantle	6.00
Q-13	Nolan Ryan	6.00
Q-14	Stan Musial	4.00
Q-15	Ted Williams	5.00
Q-16	Tom Seaver	2.00
Q-17	Tommy Lasorda	.75
Q-18	Warren Spahn	2.00
Q-19	Whitey Ford	1.50
Q-20	Yogi Berra	2.00

First Pitch

NM/M

Common Player: 5.00
Inserted 1:72

SP7	LeBron James	20.00
SP8	Mr. Hockey	10.00
SP10	Ernie Banks	10.00
SP11	General Tommy Franks	5.00
SP12	Ben Affleck	10.00
SP13	Halle Berry	10.00
SP14	George H.W. Bush	5.00
SP15	George W. Bush	5.00

Game Winners

NM/M

Common Player: 5.00
Golds: 1-1.5X
Production 50 Sets

GW-BA	Bobby Abreu	8.00
GW-JB	Jeff Bagwell	8.00
GW-HB	Hank Blalock	8.00
GW-MC	Miguel Cabrera	8.00
GW-JE	Jim Edmonds	5.00
GW-DE	Darin Erstad	5.00
GW-RF	Rafael Furcal (Gold parallel only.)	5.00
GW-JG	Jason Giambi	8.00
GW-TG	Troy Glaus	5.00
GW-AG	Alex Gonzalez	5.00
GW-SG	Shawn Green	5.00
GW-VG	Vladimir Guerrero	10.00
GW-TH	Todd Helton	8.00
GW-RH	Ramon Hernandez	5.00
GW-HU	Torii Hunter	5.00
GW-DJ	Derek Jeter	25.00
GW-AJ	Andruw Jones	8.00
GW-CJ	Chipper Jones	8.00
GW-RK	Ryan Klesko	5.00
GW-ML	Mike Lowell	5.00
GW-HM	Hideki Matsui	25.00
GW-TN	Trot Nixon (Gold parallel only.)	10.00
GW-MO	Magglio Ordonez	5.00
GW-CP	Corey Patterson	5.00
GW-MP	Mike Piazza	10.00
GW-JP	Jorge Posada	8.00
GW-AP	Albert Pujols	15.00
GW-IR	Ivan Rodriguez	8.00
GW-SR	Scott Rolen	10.00
GW-GS	Gary Sheffield	5.00
GW-AS	Alfonso Soriano	8.00
GW-MT	Mark Teixeira	5.00
GW-TE	Miguel Tejada	5.00
GW-JT	Jim Thome	10.00
GW-BW	Bernie Williams	8.00

Going Deep Bat

NM/M

Common Player: 6.00
Inserted 1:288
Some not priced yet due to scarcity.
Golds: 1-2X
Production 50 Sets

BA	Bobby Abreu/SP/110	6.00
RO	Roberto Alomar	8.00
SC	Sandy Alomar Jr./ SP/95	6.00
GA	Garret Anderson	8.00
RA	Rich Aurilia/SP/102	6.00
JB	Jeff Bagwell/SP/92	10.00
RB	Rocco Baldelli/SP	15.00
CB	Craig Biggio/SP/89	6.00
JE	Jim Edmonds/SP	8.00
DE	Darin Erstad	6.00
RF	Rafael Furcal/SP	6.00
TG	Troy Glaus/SP/113	8.00
SG	Shawn Green/SP/100	8.00
KG	Ken Griffey Jr./SP	30.00
RH	Rickey Henderson/ SP/77	10.00
TH	Torii Hunter/SP/115	8.00
CJ	Chipper Jones/SP/69	15.00
JL	Javy Lopez/SP/77	8.00
HM	Hideki Matsui/SP/70	45.00
DM	Doug Mientkiewicz/ SP/123	6.00
HN	Hideo Nomo	15.00
MO	Magglio Ordonez	6.00
PO	Jay Payton/SP/100	6.00
MP	Mike Piazza	15.00
JP	Jorge Posada	8.00
AP	Albert Pujols	20.00
SR	Scott Rolen/SP/77	10.00
CS	Curt Schilling/SP/57	10.00
AS	Alfonso Soriano/ SP/53	10.00
JT	Jim Thome	10.00
OV	Omar Vizquel/SP/115	6.00
BW	Bernie Williams/ SP/56	8.00
KW	Kerry Wood/SP/108	8.00

Headliners Jersey

HEADLINERS
Lance Berkman • Houston Astros® • Outfield

NM/M

Common Player: 4.00
Inserted 1:48
Golds: 1-2X
Production 100 Sets

TB	Tony Batista	4.00
JB	Josh Beckett	8.00
LB	Lance Berkman	4.00
MB	Mark Buehrle	4.00
LC	Luis Castillo	4.00
JD	Joe DiMaggio/ SP/153	90.00
AD	Adam Dunn	6.00
JE	Jim Edmonds	6.00
RF	Robert Fick	4.00
TG	Tom Glavine	6.00
LG	Luis Gonzalez	4.00
SG	Shawn Green	4.00
KG	Ken Griffey Jr.	15.00
VG	Vladimir Guerrero/ SP/153	10.00
RH	Roy Halladay	4.00
JH	Jose Hernandez	4.00
TH	Trevor Hoffman	4.00
BK	Byung-Hyun Kim	4.00
RK	Ryan Klesko	4.00
PK	Paul Konerko	4.00
ML	Mike Lowell	4.00
GM	Greg Maddux	12.00
MM	Mickey Mantle/ SP/97	125.00
PM	Pedro J. Martinez	8.00
HM	Hideki Matsui	35.00
MY	Matt Morris	4.00
MU	Mike Mussina	8.00
MO	Magglio Ordonez	4.00
RO	Roy Oswalt	4.00
MR	Manny Ramirez	6.00
MA	Mariano Rivera	6.00
JR	Jimmy Rollins	6.00
BS	Benito Santiago	4.00
CS	Curt Schilling	6.00
JS	Junior Spivey	4.00
IS	Ichiro Suzuki/SP/153	30.00
MS	Mike Sweeney	4.00
MT	Miguel Tejada	6.00
JT	Jim Thome	8.00
JV	Jose Vidro	4.00
TW	Ted Williams/SP/153	75.00

Magical Performances

Magical Performances

NM/M

Common Player: 6.00
Inserted 1:96
Golds: 1-1.5X
Production 50 Sets

MP1	Mickey Mantle	35.00
MP2	Mickey Mantle	35.00
MP3	Joe DiMaggio	25.00
MP4	Joe DiMaggio	25.00
MP5	Derek Jeter	25.00
MP6	Derek Jeter	25.00

MP7	Roger Clemens	20.00
MP8	Roger Clemens	20.00
MP9	Alfonso Soriano	10.00
MP10	Andy Pettitte	8.00
MP11	Hideki Matsui	30.00
MP12	Mike Mussina	10.00
MP13	Jorge Posada	10.00
MP14	Jason Giambi	10.00
MP15	David Wells	6.00
MP16	Mariano Rivera	10.00
MP17	Yogi Berra	15.00
MP18	Phil Rizzuto	10.00
MP19	Whitey Ford	10.00
MP20	Jose Contreras	8.00
MP21	Jim "Catfish" Hunter	6.00
MP22	Mickey Mantle	35.00
MP23	Mickey Mantle	35.00
MP24	Joe DiMaggio	25.00
MP25	Joe DiMaggio	25.00
MP26	Derek Jeter	25.00
MP27	Derek Jeter	25.00
MP28	Roger Clemens	20.00
MP29	Roger Clemens	20.00
MP30	Alfonso Soriano	10.00
MP31	Andy Pettitte	8.00
MP32	Hideki Matsui	30.00
MP33	Mike Mussina	10.00
MP34	Jorge Posada	10.00
MP35	Jason Giambi	10.00
MP36	David Wells	6.00
MP37	Mariano Rivera	10.00
MP38	Yogi Berra	15.00
MP39	Phil Rizzuto	10.00
MP40	Whitey Ford	10.00
MP41	Jose Contreras	10.00
MP42	Jim "Catfish" Hunter	6.00

Matsui Chronicles

	NM/M
Complete Set (60):	35.00
Common Matsui:	1.00

National Pride

	NM/M
Complete Set (20):	25.00
Common Player:	1.00
Inserted 1:6	
USA1	Justin Orenduff	1.00
USA2	Micah Owings	2.00
USA3	Steven Register	2.00
USA4	Huston Street	1.00
USA5	Justin Verlander	2.00
USA6	Jered Weaver	1.00
USA7	Matt Campbell	1.00
USA8	Stephen Head	1.00
USA9	Mark Romanczuk	1.00
USA10	Jeff Clement	6.00
USA11	Mike Nickeas	2.00
USA12	Tyler Greene	1.00
USA13	Paul Janish	2.00
USA14	Jeff Larish	1.00
USA15	Eric Patterson	1.00
USA16	Dustin Pedroia	1.00
USA17	Michael Griffin	1.00
USA18	Brent Lillibridge	1.00
USA19	Danny Putnam	1.00
USA20	Seth Smith	1.00

National Pride Pants

	NM/M
CB	Chris Burke	9.00
JC	Jesse Crain	4.00
DU	Justin Duchscherer	6.00
GK	Graham Koonce	4.00
JL	Justin Leone	8.00
RM	Ryan Madson	6.00
JM	Joe Mauer	15.00
HR	Horacio Ramirez	8.00
RR	Royce Ring	6.00
ER	Eddie Rodriguez	5.00
MR	Mike Rouse	4.00
GS	Grady Sizemore	10.00
JS	Jason Stanford	6.00
JB	John Van Benschoten	8.00

National Pride Jersey

	NM/M
Common Player:	4.00
Inserted 1:24	
USA1	Justin Orenduff	4.00
USA2	Micah Owings	4.00
USA3	Steven Register	4.00
USA4	Huston Street	4.00
USA5	Justin Verlander	10.00

USA6	Jered Weaver	6.00
USA7	Matt Campbell	8.00
USA8	Stephen Head	4.00
USA9	Mark Romanczuk	4.00
USA10	Jeff Clement	15.00
USA11	Mike Nickeas	4.00
USA12	Tyler Greene	4.00
USA13	Paul Janish	4.00
USA14	Jeff Larish	6.00
USA15	Eric Patterson	4.00
USA16	Dustin Pedroia	10.00
USA17	Michael Griffin	4.00
USA18	Brent Lillibridge	6.00
USA19	Danny Putnam	4.00
USA20	Seth Smith	6.00
USA21	Justin Orenduff	4.00
USA22	Micah Owings	4.00
USA23	Steven Register	4.00
USA24	Huston Street	4.00
USA25	Justin Verlander	10.00
USA26	Jered Weaver	6.00
USA27	Matt Campbell	4.00
USA28	Stephen Head	4.00
USA29	Mark Romanczuk	4.00
USA30	Jeff Clement	15.00
USA31	Mike Nickeas	4.00
USA32	Tyler Greene	4.00
USA33	Paul Janish	4.00
USA34	Jeff Larish	6.00
USA35	Eric Patterson	4.00
USA36	Dustin Pedroia	10.00
USA37	Michael Griffin	4.00
USA38	Brent Lillibridge	6.00
USA39	Danny Putnam	4.00
USA40	Seth Smith	6.00
USA41	Delmon Young	35.00
USA42	Rickie Weeks	12.00

Series 2

TB	Thad Bosley	4.00
BB	Brian Bruney	6.00
CB	Chris Burke	9.00
JC	Jesse Crain	8.00
DU	Justin Duchscherer	6.00
JD	J.D. Durbin	4.00
JG	John Grabow	6.00
GG	Gabe Gross	4.00
JH	J.J. Hardy	6.00
GK	Graham Koonce	6.00
GL	Gerald Laird	6.00
ML	Mike Lamb	4.00
JL	Justin Leone	6.00
JM	Joe Mauer	15.00
HR	Horacio Ramirez	8.00
JR	Jeremy Reed	10.00
RR	Royce Ring	6.00
ER	Eddie Rodriguez	5.00
MR	Mike Rouse	4.00
GS	Grady Sizemore	10.00
JS	Jason Stanford	6.00
JB	John Van Benschoten	8.00
TW	Todd Williams	4.00
EY	Ernie Young	4.00

Peak Performers

		NM/M
Golds:		1.5-2X
Production 165		
PP-JB	Jeff Bagwell	8.00
PP-BE	Josh Beckett	6.00

PP-LB	Lance Berkman	5.00
PP-CB	Craig Biggio	5.00
PP-HB	Hank Blalock	8.00
PP-PB	Pat Burrell	6.00
PP-LC	Luis Castillo	4.00
PP-CD	Carlos Delgado	6.00
PP-RF	Rafael Furcal	4.00
PP-EG	Eric Gagne	12.00
PP-SG	Shawn Green	5.00
PP-KG	Ken Griffey Jr.	15.00
PP-VG	Vladimir Guerrero	8.00
PP-TH	Todd Helton	8.00
PP-PL	Paul LoDuca	4.00
PP-PM	Pedro J. Martinez	8.00
PP-HM	Hideki Matsui	25.00
PP-MM	Mike Mussina	8.00
PP-HN	Hideo Nomo	8.00
PP-MO	Magglio Ordonez	6.00
PP-RP	Rafael Palmeiro	6.00
PP-PE	Andy Pettitte	6.00
PP-BP	Brandon Phillips	4.00
PP-MP	Mark Prior	10.00
PP-AP	Albert Pujols	10.00
PP-JR	Jose Reyes	5.00
PP-IR	Ivan Rodriguez	8.00
PP-SR	Scott Rolen	8.00
PP-SA	C.C. Sabathia	4.00
PP-CS	Curt Schilling	8.00
PP-AS	Alfonso Soriano	8.00
PP-IS	Ichiro Suzuki	20.00
PP-MT	Miguel Tejada	5.00
PP-FT	Frank Thomas	8.00
PP-JT	Jim Thome	8.00
PP-DV	Omar Vizquel	4.00
PP-VW	Vernon Wells	4.00
PP-KW	Kerry Wood	10.00

Signature Stars
Black Ink

	NM/M
Some not priced due to lack of info.	
Inserted 1:288	
RA	Rich Aurilia/479	8.00
RC	Roger Clemens/19	
AG	Andres Galarraga/248	10.00
NG	Nomar Garciaparra/69	75.00
VG	Vladimir Guerrero/68	40.00
RH	Rich Harden/163	8.00
AH	Aaron Heilman/49	15.00
TH	Torii Hunter/374	8.00
KI	Kazuhisa Ishii/58	15.00
BK	Billy Koch/429	8.00
HM	Hideki Matsui/25	325.00
MU	Mike Mussina/68	50.00
MO	Magglio Ordonez/377	20.00
JRa	Joe Randa/271	10.00
CR	Cal Ripken Jr./69	200.00
DR	Dave Roberts/278	8.00
NR	Nolan Ryan/69	120.00

Series 2

BB	Bret Boone/43	15.00
DB	Dewon Brazelton/96	5.00
JC	Jose Canseco/160	25.00
EC	Eric Chavez/60	15.00
EG	Eric Gagne/160	20.00
KG	Ken Griffey Jr./450	90.00
RH	Rich Harden/65	15.00
DR	Dave Roberts/450	5.00
NR	Nolan Ryan/95	100.00
DS	Darryl Strawberry/160	10.00
MT	Mark Teixeira/200	25.00
JV	Javier Vazquez/60	15.00
BW	Brandon Webb/60	15.00
RW	Rickie Weeks/65	15.00
DW	Dontrelle Willis/160	15.00

Signature Stars
Blue Ink

	NM/M
No Pricing	
Production 25 Sets	
Matsui #'d to 324.	
HM	Hideki Matsui/324	180.00

Signature Stars
Red Ink

No Pricing
Production 10 Sets

Signature Stars
Gold Ink

Gold Ink:	1-2X Black Ink
Production 99 Sets	

Super Patches Logos

No pricing due to scarcity.
Inserted 1:7,500

Super Patches
Numbers

No pricing due to scarcity.
Inserted 1:7,500

Super Patches Stripes

No pricing due to scarcity.
Inserted 1:7,500

Super Sluggers

	NM/M
Complete Set (30):	15.00
Common Player:	.50
Inserted 1:1 Retail	
SL-1	Albert Pujols	2.00
SL-2	Alex Rodriguez	2.00
SL-3	Alfonso Soriano	.75
SL-4	Andruw Jones	.75
SL-5	Bret Boone	.50
SL-6	Carlos Delgado	.50
SL-7	Edgar Renteria	.50
SL-8	Eric Chavez	.50
SL-9	Frank Thomas	.75
SL-10	Garret Anderson	.50
SL-11	Gary Sheffield	.50
SL-12	Jason Giambi	.75
SL-13	Javy Lopez	.50
SL-14	Jeff Bagwell	.75
SL-15	Jim Edmonds	.50
SL-16	Jim Thome	1.00
SL-17	Jorge Posada	.50
SL-18	Lance Berkman	.50
SL-19	Magglio Ordonez	.50
SL-20	Manny Ramirez	.75
SL-21	Mike Lowell	.50
SL-22	Nomar Garciaparra	1.50
SL-23	Preston Wilson	.50
SL-24	Rafael Palmeiro	.75
SL-25	Richie Sexson	.50
SL-26	Sammy Sosa	2.00
SL-27	Shawn Green	.50
SL-28	Todd Helton	.75
SL-29	Vernon Wells	.50
SL-30	Vladimir Guerrero	1.00

500 HR Club

	NM/M
Production 350	
RP	Rafael Palmeiro	180.00
RPAU	Rafael Palmeiro/Auto./25	

Twenty-Five Salute

	NM/M
Common Player:	6.00
Inserted 1:12	
S1	Barry Bonds	3.00
S2	Troy Glaus	.75
S3	Andruw Jones	.75
S4	Jay Gibbons	.75
S5	Jeremy Giambi	.75
S6	Jason Giambi	1.00
S7	Jim Thome	1.00
S8	Rafael Palmeiro	1.00
S9	Carlos Delgado	1.00
S10	Dmitri Young	.75

2003 Update

	NM/M
Complete Set (60):	18.00
Common Player:	.15
One set per hobby box.	
541	Bo Hart	1.50
542	Dan Haren	.50
543	Ryan Wagner	1.00
544	Rich Harden	.50
545	Dontrelle Willis	.75
546	Jerome Williams	.25
547	Bobby Crosby	1.00
548	Greg Jones	.25
549	Todd Linden	.25
550	Byung-Hyun Kim	.25
551	Rickie Weeks	4.00
552	Jason Roach	.25
553	Oscar Villarreal	.25
554	Justin Duchscherer	.15
555	Chris Capuano	.15
556	Josh Hall	.50
557	Luis Matos	.15

558	Miguel Ojeda	.15
559	Kevin Ohme	.15
560	Julio Manon	.15
561	Kevin Correia	.15
562	Delmon Young	5.00
563	Aaron Boone	.15
564	Aaron Looper	.15
565	Mike Neu	.15
566	Aquilino Lopez	.15
567	Jhonny Peralta	.15
568	Duaner Sanchez	.15
569	Stephen Randolph	.15
570	Nate Bland	.15
571	Chin-Hui Tsao	.15
572	Michel Hernandez	.15
573	Rocco Baldelli	1.00
574	Robb Quinlan	.15
575	Aaron Heilman	.15
576	Jae Weong Seo	.15
577	Joe Borowski	.15
578	Chris Bootcheck	.15
579	Michael Ryan	.15
580	Mark Malaska	.15
581	Jose Guillen	.15
582	Josh Towers	.15
583	Tom Gregorio	.15
584	Edwin Jackson	.15
585	Jason Anderson	.15
586	Jose Reyes	.50
587	Miguel Cabrera	1.00
588	Nate Bump	.15
589	Jeromy Burnitz	.15
590	David Ross	.15
591	Chase Utley	1.00
592	Brandon Webb	1.00
593	Masao Kida	.15
594	Jimmy Journell	.15
595	Eric Young	.15
596	Tony Womack	.15
597	Amaury Telemaco	.15
598	Rickey Henderson	.50
599	Esteban Loaiza	.15
600	Sidney Ponson	.15

SPGU Patch Edition
Update Patch

NM/M

Production 20 unless noted.

BA	Bobby Abreu	40.00
GA	Garret Anderson	40.00
RB	Rocco Baldelli	30.00
LB	Lance Berkman	40.00
HB	Hank Blalock	40.00
BB	Bret Boone	30.00
BC	Bartolo Colon	25.00
JE	Jim Edmonds	35.00
EG	Eric Gagne	75.00
TG	Troy Glaus	35.00
VG	Vladimir Guerrero	50.00
TH	Torii Hunter	25.00
JJ	Jacque Jones	25.00
AK	Austin Kearns	30.00
JK	Jeff Kent	25.00
RK	Ryan Klesko	25.00
EM	Edgar Martinez	50.00
KM	Kevin Millwood	30.00
MM	Mark Mulder	40.00
HN	Hideo Nomo	40.00
RO	Roy Oswalt	35.00
CP	Corey Patterson	30.00
JR	Jose Reyes	30.00
RS	Richie Sexson	40.00
MS	Mike Sweeney	25.00
BW	Brandon Webb	25.00
VW	Vernon Wells/21	25.00
KW	Kerry Wood	50.00

2004 Upper Deck
Diamond Collection

NM/M

Complete Set (120):	70.00
Common Player:	.15

Common (91-120):		2.00
Inserted 1:6		
Pack (6):		2.00
Box (24):		40.00
1	Garret Anderson	.25
2	Darin Erstad	.25
3	Troy Glaus	.40
4	Curt Schilling	.50
5	Brandon Webb	.15
6	Randy Johnson	.75
7	Andruw Jones	.50
8	Chipper Jones	.75
9	Gary Sheffield	.40
10	Jay Gibbons	.25
11	Miguel Tejada	.40
12	Tony Batista	.15
13	Nomar Garciaparra	1.25
14	Manny Ramirez	.50
15	Pedro J. Martinez	.75
16	Mark Prior	1.00
17	Kerry Wood	.75
18	Sammy Sosa	1.25
19	Bartolo Colon	.25
20	Magglio Ordonez	.25
21	Frank Thomas	.50
22	Adam Dunn	.40
23	Austin Kearns	.25
24	Ken Griffey Jr.	1.00
25	Brandon Phillips	.15
26	Milton Bradley	.15
27	Jody Gerut	.15
28	Todd Helton	.50
29	Larry Walker	.25
30	Preston Wilson	.15
31	Jeremy Bonderman	.15
32	Carlos Pena	.15
33	Dmitri Young	.15
34	Dontrelle Willis	.50
35	Miguel Cabrera	.50
36	Mike Lowell	.25
37	Jeff Bagwell	.50
38	Roy Oswalt	.25
39	Lance Berkman	.25
40	Carlos Beltran	.40
41	Mike Sweeney	.25
42	Rondell White	.25
43	Hideo Nomo	.40
44	Kevin Brown	.25
45	Shawn Green	.25
46	Ben Sheets	.25
47	Geoff Jenkins	.25
48	Richie Sexson	.40
49	Jacque Jones	.15
50	Johan Santana	.15
51	Torii Hunter	.25
52	Javier Vazquez	.15
53	Jose Vidro	.15
54	Vladimir Guerrero	.75
55	Cliff Floyd	.15
56	Mike Piazza	1.00
57	Jose Reyes	.50
58	Derek Jeter	2.00
59	Jason Giambi	.50
60	Alfonso Soriano	.50
61	Eric Chavez	.25
62	Barry Zito	.25
63	Tim Hudson	.25
64	Bobby Abreu	.25
65	Jim Thome	.75
66	Kevin Millwood	.25
67	Roger Clemens	1.50
68	Jason Kendall	.15
69	Reggie Sanders	.15
70	Phil Nevin	.15
71	Ryan Klesko	.25
72	Brian Giles	.25
73	A.J. Pierzynski	.15
74	Jason Schmidt	.25
75	Sidney Ponson	.15
76	Edgar Martinez	.25
77	Ichiro Suzuki	1.00
78	Bret Boone	.25
79	Albert Pujols	1.50

80	Scott Rolen	.75
81	Jim Edmonds	.25
82	Aubrey Huff	.15
83	Delmon Young	.40
84	Rocco Baldelli	.40
85	Alex Rodriguez	1.50
86	Mark Teixeira	.25
87	Rafael Palmeiro	.50
88	Carlos Delgado	.50
89	Vernon Wells	.25
90	Roy Halladay	.25
91	Brandon Medders **RC**	2.00
92	Colby Miller **RC**	2.00
93	David Crouthers	2.00
94	Dennis Sarfate **RC**	3.00
95	Donald Kelly **RC**	2.00
96	Alec Zumwalt **RC**	2.00
97	Frank Brooks **RC**	2.00
98	Greg Dobbs **RC**	2.00
99	Ian Snell **RC**	3.00
100	Jake Woods	2.00
101	Jamie Brown **RC**	2.00
102	Jason Frasor **RC**	2.00
103	Jerome Gamble **RC**	2.00
104	Jesse Harper **RC**	2.00
105	Josh Labandeira **RC**	2.00
106	Justin Hampson **RC**	2.00
107	Justin Huisman **RC**	2.00
108	Justin Leone **RC**	2.00
109	Chris Aguila **RC**	2.00
110	Lincoln Holzdkom **RC**	2.00
111	Mike Bumatay **RC**	2.00
112	Mike Gosling **RC**	2.00
113	Mike Johnston **RC**	2.00
114	Mike Rouse	2.00
115	Nick Regilio **RC**	2.00
116	Ryan Meaux **RC**	2.00
117	Scott Dohmann **RC**	2.00
118	Sean Henn	2.00
119	Tim Bausher **RC**	2.00
120	Tim Bittner **RC**	2.00

Gold Honors

Gold (1-90):	5-10X
Gold (91-120):	1-2X
Production 50 Sets	

Silver Honors

Silver (1-90):	2-4X
Silver (91-120):	.75-1X
1-90 inserted 1:6	
91-120 inserted 1:48	

Class of 2004
Autograph

NM/M

Quantity produced listed

MC	Miguel Cabrera/50	40.00
KG	Ken Griffey Jr./100	75.00
VG	Vladimir Guerrero/100	40.00
RH	Rich Harden/100	15.00
HM	Hideki Matsui/100	250.00
MP	Mark Prior/100	40.00
JR	Jose Reyes/100	30.00
DW	Dontrelle Willis/100	40.00
BZ	Barry Zito/100	25.00

Dean's List Jersey

NM/M

Common Player:	4.00
Inserted 1:72	

BA	Jeff Bagwell	8.00
HB	Hank Blalock	6.00
JG	Jason Giambi	6.00
GL	Troy Glaus	6.00
LG	Luis Gonzalez	4.00
SG	Shawn Green	4.00
KG	Ken Griffey Jr.	10.00
VG	Vladimir Guerrero	8.00
GM	Greg Maddux	10.00

HM	Hideki Matsui	20.00
HN	Hideo Nomo	8.00
PI	Mike Piazza	8.00
MP	Mark Prior	8.00
AP	Albert Pujols	15.00
AR	Alex Rodriguez	10.00
AS	Alfonso Soriano	8.00
SS	Sammy Sosa	10.00
IS	Ichiro Suzuki	20.00
JT	Jim Thome	8.00
DW	Dontrelle Willis	6.00

Future Gems Jersey

NM/M

Common Player:	4.00
Inserted 1:72	

BA	Josh Bard	4.00
JB	Josh Beckett	8.00
SB	Sean Burroughs	6.00
MC	Mike Cameron	4.00
AE	Adam Eaton	4.00
WE	Willie Eyre	4.00
LF	Lew Ford	4.00
GU	Jeremy Guthrie	4.00
TH	Travis Hafner	6.00
RH	Roy Halladay	4.00
AH	Aaron Heilman	4.00
IS	Kazuhisa Ishii	4.00
JJ	Jason Jennings	4.00
KA	Matt Kata	4.00
MK	Mark Kotsay	4.00
JL	Jon Leicester	4.00
EM	Eric Milton	4.00
JR	Jose Reyes	8.00
RR	Rick Roberts	4.00
PS	Phil Seibel	4.00
BS	Ben Sheets	6.00
MT	Mark Teixeira	6.00
TW	Todd Wellemeyer	6.00
WI	Josh Willingham	4.00

Pick the All Star MVP

NM/M

Common Player:		.50
Inserted 1:1		
BA	Bobby Abreu	.50
GA	Garret Anderson	.50
JB	Jeff Bagwell	.50
BE	Josh Beckett	.50
CB	Carlos Beltran	.50
HB	Hank Blalock	.50
BO	Bret Boone	.50
OC	Orlando Cabrera	.50
EC	Eric Chavez	.50
BC	Bartolo Colon	.50
JD	Johnny Damon	.50
CD	Carlos Delgado	.50
AD	Adam Dunn	.50
JE	Jim Edmonds	.50
RF	Rafael Furcal	.50
NG	Nomar Garciaparra	1.50
JG	Jason Giambi	.75
MG	Marcus Giles	.50
TG	Troy Glaus	.50
SG	Shawn Green	.50
KG	Ken Griffey Jr.	1.00
VG	Vladimir Guerrero	.75
RH	Roy Halladay	.50
TH	Todd Helton	.75
HU	Tim Hudson	.50
TH	Torii Hunter	.50
DJ	Derek Jeter	2.50
RJ	Randy Johnson	.75
AJ	Andruw Jones	.50
CJ	Chipper Jones	.75
JJ	Jacque Jones	.50
AK	Austin Kearns	.50
JK	Jeff Kent	.50
JL	Javy Lopez	.50
ML	Mike Lowell	.50
PM	Pedro J. Martinez	.75
HM	Hideki Matsui	1.50
MM	Mark Mulder	.75
MU	Mike Mussina	.75
MO	Magglio Ordonez	.50
RP	Rafael Palmeiro	.75
PI	Mike Piazza	1.00
JP	Jorge Posada	.50
MP	Mark Prior	1.00
AP	Albert Pujols	2.00
MR	Manny Ramirez	.75
ER	Edgar Renteria	.50
AR	Alex Rodriguez	2.00
IR	Ivan Rodriguez	.75

SR	Scott Rolen	.75
CS	Curt Schilling	.75
JS	Jason Schmidt	.50
RS	Richie Sexson	.50
GS	Gary Sheffield	.50
AS	Alfonso Soriano	.75
SS	Sammy Sosa	1.50
IS	Ichiro Suzuki	1.50
MS	Mike Sweeney	.50
MT	Mark Teixeira	.50
TE	Miguel Tejada	.50
FT	Frank Thomas	.75
JT	Jim Thome	.75
JV	Jason Varitek	.50
VI	Jose Vidro	.50
VW	Vernon Wells	.50
DW	Dontrelle Willis	.50
PW	Preston Wilson	.50
KW	Kerry Wood	1.00
BZ	Barry Zito	.50

2004 UD Diamond Collection Pro Sigs

NM/M

Complete Set (1-240):
Common Player (1-90): .15
Common SP (91-150): 2.00
Inserted 1:6
Common Auto. (151-240): 5.00
Inserted 1:24
Pack (6): 2.00
Box (24): 40.00

1	Alfonso Soriano	.50
2	Josh Beckett	.50
3	Kerry Wood	.75
4	Brandon Webb	.15
5	Shannon Stewart	.15
6	Larry Walker	.25
7	Tim Hudson	.25
8	Carlos Lee	.25
9	Austin Kearns	.25
10	Vernon Wells	.25
11	Jeff Bagwell	.50
12	Hideo Nomo	.40
13	Jerome Williams	.15
14	Kevin Brown	.25
15	Jose Vidro	.15
16	Rocco Baldelli	.25
17	Frank Thomas	.75
18	Albert Pujols	1.50
19	Bartolo Colon	.25
20	C.C. Sabathia	.15
21	Andruw Jones	.50
22	Reggie Sanders	.15
23	Carlos Beltran	.40
24	Curt Schilling	.50
25	Miguel Tejada	.40
26	Barry Zito	.40
27	Pedro Martinez	.75
28	Sean Burroughs	.15
29	Sammy Sosa	1.50
30	Eric Chavez	.25
31	Roy Halladay	.25
32	Todd Helton	.50
33	Mark Prior	1.00
34	Mike Mussina	.50
35	Alex Rodriguez	2.00
36	Ivan Rodriguez	.50
37	Mike Piazza	1.00
38	Angel Berroa	.15
39	Orlando Cabrera	.25
40	Jim Thome	.75
41	Brian Giles	.25
42	Ichiro Suzuki	1.00
43	Edgar Renteria	.25
44	Eric Gagne	.25
45	Gary Sheffield	.40
46	Torii Hunter	.25
47	Roger Clemens	1.50
48	Scott Rolen	.75
49	Johan Santana	.15
50	Jacque Jones	.15
51	Hank Blalock	.40

52	Rafael Palmeiro	.50
53	Dmitri Young	.15
54	Ryan Klesko	.25
55	Mark Teixeira	.25
56	Nomar Garciaparra	1.50
57	Jose Reyes	.25
58	Vladimir Guerrero	.75
59	Mike Sweeney	.15
60	Jorge Posada	.40
61	Derek Jeter	2.00
62	Milton Bradley	.15
63	Bobby Abreu	.25
64	Greg Maddux	1.00
65	Adam Dunn	.50
66	Troy Glaus	.40
67	Luis Gonzalez	.25
68	Shawn Green	.25
69	Bret Boone	.25
70	Mark Mulder	.25
71	Lance Berkman	.25
72	Preston Wilson	.15
73	Phil Nevin	.15
74	Chipper Jones	.75
75	Garret Anderson	.40
76	Jason Giambi	.75
77	Magglio Ordonez	.25
78	Jeff Kent	.25
79	Richie Sexson	.40
80	Mike Lowell	.25
81	Ben Sheets	.25
82	Randy Johnson	.75
83	Dontrelle Willis	.25
84	Javier Vazquez	.25
85	Geoff Jenkins	.25
86	Manny Ramirez	.50
87	Jim Edmonds	.40
88	Roy Oswalt	.25
89	Edgar Martinez	.25
90	Carlos Delgado	.40
91	Chris Saenz RC	5.00
92	Justin Leone RC	2.00
93	Shawn Hill RC	4.00
94	Chad Bentz RC	4.00
95	Jesse Harper RC	2.00
96	David Crouthers RC	2.00
97	Justin Germano RC	2.00
98	Tim Bausher RC	2.00
99	Greg Dobbs RC	5.00
100	Enemencio Pacheco RC	8.00
101	Dennis Sarfate RC	2.00
102	Edwin Moreno RC	4.00
103	Colby Miller RC	2.00
104	Mike Rouse RC	2.00
105	Fernando Nieve RC	2.00
106	Tim Hamulack RC	6.00
107	Jason Frasor RC	2.00
108	Jose Capellan RC	5.00
109	Jamie Brown RC	3.00
110	Mariano Gomez RC	2.00
111	Mike Vento RC	8.00
112	Josh Labandeira RC	3.00
113	Mike Gosling RC	2.00
114	Shingo Takatsu RC	8.00
115	Justin Hampson RC	2.00
116	Tim Bittner RC	2.00
117	Jerry Gil RC	2.00
118	Carlos Vasquez RC	5.00
119	Lincoln Holdzkom RC	2.00
120	Mike Johnston RC	4.00
121	William Bergolla RC	2.00
122	Luis Gonzalez RC	2.00
123	Ivan Ochoa RC	4.00
124	Roman Colon RC	2.00
125	Renyel Pinto RC	6.00
126	Donnie Kelly RC	4.00
127	Chris Oxspring RC	2.00
128	Sean Henn RC	5.00
129	Ryan Meaux RC	2.00
130	Shawn Camp RC	2.00
131	Brandon Medders RC	2.00
132	Rusty Tucker RC	2.00
133	Kazuo Matsui RC	10.00
134	Jorge Sequea RC	2.00
135	Hector Gimenez RC	4.00
136	Casey Daigle RC	2.00
137	Ian Snell RC	3.00
138	Scott Dohmann RC	2.00
139	Ronny Cedeno RC	2.00
140	Jorge Vasquez RC	2.00
141	David Aardsma RC	4.00
142	Carlos Hines RC	2.00
143	Scott Proctor RC	3.00
144	Jerome Gamble RC	5.00
145	Jason Bartlett RC	6.00
146	Akinori Otsuka RC	8.00
147	Merkin Valdez RC	2.00
148	Jake Woods RC	4.00
149	Chris Aguila RC	2.00
150	John Gall RC	2.00
151	Aaron Miles RC	10.00
152	Aquilino Lopez RC	10.00
153	Bill Hall RC	10.00
154	Billy Traber RC	15.00
155	Brad Lidge RC	12.00
156	Brady Clark RC	10.00

157	Brandon Duckworth	8.00
158	Brett Tomko	6.00
159	Brian Fuentes	6.00
161	Brooks Kieschnick	8.00
162	Carlos Rivera	6.00
163	Chad Cordero	6.00
164	Chad Tracy	10.00
165	Claudio Vargas	5.00
166	D.J. Carrasco	5.00
167	Damian Rolls	5.00
168	David Sanders	5.00
170	Derrick Turnbow	5.00
171	Desi Relaford	5.00
172	Doug Davis	5.00
173	Dustan Mohr	6.00
176	Frank Catalanotto	8.00
178	Franklyn German	5.00
179	Ron Belliard	5.00
180	Geoff Geary	15.00
181	Greg Colbrunn	5.00
182	Henry Mateo	5.00
183	Brent Mayne	5.00
184	Horacio Ramirez	15.00
185	J.C. Romero	5.00
186	J.J. Putz	8.00
187	Ferdin Tejeda	5.00
188	Jaime Cerda	5.00
189	Jason Michaels	10.00
190	Jason Simontacchi	8.00
191	Jay Witasick	5.00
192	Joe Valentine	8.00
193	Joey Eischen	8.00
194	Johnny Estrada	8.00
195	Jon Garland	5.00
196	Jon Switzer	5.00
197	Jorge Julio	5.00
198	Jorge Sosa	5.00
199	Jose Castillo	.40
200	Jose Macias	8.00
201	Juan Bard	5.00
202	Juan Cruz	5.00
203	Juan Rivera	5.00
204	Ken Griffey Jr.	150.00
205	Kevin Hooper	5.00
206	Kiko Calero	15.00
207	Chad Gaudin	5.00
208	Luis Rivas	5.00
209	Mark Corey	5.00
210	Matt Ford	8.00
211	Matt Herges	5.00
212	Miguel Cairo	15.00
213	Fernando Cabrera	5.00
214	Mike MacDougal	5.00
215	Mike Neu	8.00
216	Lew Ford	15.00
217	Mike Wood	8.00
218	Nate Robertson	5.00
219	Nick Punto	5.00
221	Oscar Villarreal	5.00
222	Ramon Vazquez	10.00
223	Randall Simon	5.00
225	Ricky Stone	5.00
229	Ryan Drese	5.00
230	Ryan Ludwick	8.00
231	Scot Shields	5.00
232	Shane Nance	5.00
233	Steve Colyer	5.00
234	Tony Armas	5.00
235	Robby Hammock	5.00
236	Travis Hafner	5.00
237	Victor Martinez	8.00
238	Wilfredo Ledezma	5.00
239	Willie Bloomquist	5.00
240	Yorvit Torrealba	8.00

Gold

Gold (1-90): 3-6X
Overall odds for parallel 1:6.

Silver

Silver (1-90): 2-3X
Overall odds for parallel 1:6.

Blue Ink Autograph

No Pricing
Production 25 Sets

Red Signature

No Pricing
Production 10 Sets

Hall of Famers

No Pricing

2004 Upper Deck Etchings

NM/M

Complete Set (150):
Common Player: .15
Common SP (91-120): 4.00
Production 2,004
Common SP Black Auto.
(121-150): 8.00
Production 700
Blue Auto. (121-150): .75-1.5X
Production 200
Red Auto. (121-150): No Pricing
Production 25
Pack (5): 12.00
Box (12): 120.00

1	Albert Pujols	1.50
2	Torii Hunter	.40
3	Jim Edmonds	.40
4	Alex Rodriguez	1.50
5	Rafael Palmeiro	.50
6	Ken Griffey Jr.	1.00
7	Adam Dunn	.50
8	Andruw Jones	.50
9	Carlos Lee	.25
10	Mike Piazza	1.00
11	Jeff Bagwell	.50
12	Hideki Matsui	1.50
13	Gary Sheffield	.40
14	Edgar Renteria	.40
15	Shawn Green	.25
16	Kerry Wood	.75
17	Ivan Rodriguez	.50
18	Josh Beckett	.40
19	Scott Rolen	.75
20	Brian Giles	.25
21	Derrek Lee	.25
22	Mike Lowell	.25
23	Mike Mussina	.40
24	Sammy Sosa	1.50
25	Brandon Webb	.15
26	Jacque Jones	.15
27	Randy Johnson	1.00
28	Luis Gonzalez	.25
29	Eric Chavez	.25
30	Carlos Delgado	.25
31	Phil Nevin	.15
32	Ichiro Suzuki	1.50
33	Roy Oswalt	.25
34	Tim Hudson	.25
35	Juan Gonzalez	.50
36	Frank Thomas	.50
37	Mark Mulder	.40
38	Mark Teixeira	.40
39	Miguel Tejada	.40
40	Jeff Kent	.25
41	Andy Pettitte	.50
42	Barry Zito	.40
43	Roy Halladay	.25
44	Rocco Baldelli	.25
45	Derek Jeter	2.00
46	Corey Patterson	.40
47	Javy Lopez	.40
48	A.J. Burnett	.15
49	Chipper Jones	.75
50	Curt Schilling	.50
51	Todd Helton	.50
52	Pedro J. Martinez	.75
53	Hideo Nomo	.25
54	Jose Reyes	.50

#	Player	Price
55	Vernon Wells	.15
56	Geoff Jenkins	.15
57	Troy Glaus	.25
58	Greg Maddux	1.00
59	Jason Schmidt	.40
60	Preston Wilson	.15
61	Miguel Cabrera	.75
62	Hank Blalock	.50
63	Rafael Furcal	.15
64	Vladimir Guerrero	.75
65	Lance Berkman	.15
66	Javier Vazquez	.15
67	Bret Boone	.15
68	Mark Prior	1.00
69	Magglio Ordonez	.15
70	Dontrelle Willis	.25
71	Richie Sexson	.25
72	Alfonso Soriano	.75
73	Edwin Jackson	.15
74	Jose Vidro	.15
75	Jason Giambi	.50
76	Kevin Brown	.25
77	Orlando Cabrera	.15
78	Nomar Garciaparra	1.00
79	Bobby Abreu	.25
80	Manny Ramirez	.50
81	J.D. Drew	.15
82	Roger Clemens	1.50
83	Pat Burrell	.15
84	Ryan Klesko	.15
85	Garret Anderson	.40
86	Johan Santana	.15
87	Kevin Millwood	.25
88	Austin Kearns	.25
89	Jim Thome	.75
90	Carlos Beltran	.40
91	Kazuo Matsui RC	15.00
92	Jamie Brown RC	4.00
93	Brandon Medders RC	4.00
94	Carlos Vasquez RC	4.00
95	Chris Aguila RC	4.00
96	David Aardsma RC	4.00
97	Justin Leone RC	4.00
98	Mike Johnston RC	4.00
99	Tim Bittner RC	4.00
100	Mike Rouse RC	4.00
101	Dennis Sarfate RC	4.00
102	Jason Frasor RC	4.00
103	Jorge Vasquez RC	4.00
104	Mike Gosling RC	4.00
105	Jake Woods RC	4.00
106	Akinori Otsuka RC	8.00
107	Lincoln Holdzkom RC	4.00
108	Jesse Harper RC	4.00
109	Edwin Moreno RC	4.00
110	Shingo Takatsu RC	6.00
111	Ryan Meaux RC	4.00
112	Donnie Kelly RC	4.00
113	Jerome Gamble RC	4.00
114	Josh Labandeira RC	4.00
115	Ian Snell RC	8.00
116	Mike Wuertz RC	4.00
117	Greg Dobbs RC	4.00
118	Sean Henn RC	4.00
119	David Crouthers RC	4.00
120	Hector Gimenez RC	4.00
121	Renyel Pinto RC	10.00
122	Tim Hamulack RC	8.00
123	Chris Saenz RC	8.00
124	Carlos Hines RC	8.00
125	Justin Knoedler RC	10.00
126	Onil Joseph RC	10.00
127	Ryan Wing RC	8.00
128	Scott Proctor RC	10.00
129	Rusty Tucker RC	8.00
130	Fernando Nieve RC	8.00
131	Chad Bentz RC	10.00
132	Jerry Gil RC	8.00
133	Mariano Gomez RC	10.00
134	Justin Germano RC	10.00
135	Jason Bartlett RC	10.00
136	Ronald Belisario RC	8.00
137	Enemencio Pacheco	8.00
138	Justin Hampson RC	8.00
139	Michael Vento	8.00
140	Merkin Valdez RC	10.00
141	Casey Daigle RC	8.00
142	Eddy Rodriguez RC	8.00
143	William Bergolla RC	15.00
144	Jose Capellan RC	8.00
145	Ronny Cedeno RC	8.00
146	Franklyn Gracesqui RC	8.00
147	Roman Colon RC	10.00
148	Roberto Novoa RC	8.00
149	Ivan Ochoa RC	10.00
150	Shawn Hill RC	8.00

Combo Etchings
NM/M

Production 5-115
Gold Foil: .75-1.5X
Production 1-50
Silver Foil: .75-1X
Production 4-50

No Pricing 15 or less.

JB	Josh Beckett/25	60.00
MC	Miguel Cabrera/23	50.00
KG	Ken Griffey Jr./100	90.00
KG1	Ken Griffey Jr./90	90.00
KG2	Ken Griffey Jr./90	90.00
VG	Vladimir Guerrero/60	65.00
DJ1	Derek Jeter/25	200.00
MR	Manny Ramirez/60	65.00
MR1	Manny Ramirez/60	65.00
CR	Cal Ripken Jr./15	250.00
CR1	Cal Ripken Jr./15	250.00
AR	Alex Rodriguez/15	200.00
AR1	Alex Rodriguez/15	200.00
AR2	Alex Rodriguez/115	150.00
KW	Kerry Wood/20	65.00
KW1	Kerry Wood/20	65.00
KW2	Kerry Wood/30	50.00

Dual Etchings
NM/M

Production 150 Sets

RJ	Alex Rodriguez, Derek Jeter	60.00
WP	Kerry Wood, Mark Prior	25.00
RP	Jose Reyes, Mike Piazza	30.00
PG	Albert Pujols, Vladimir Guerrero	30.00
MM	Hideki Matsui, Kazuo Matsui	40.00
MW	Mickey Mantle, Ted Williams	180.00

Etched in Time
Black Ink
NM/M

Quantity produced listed
Common Autograph: 6.00

AA	Alfredo Amezaga/375	6.00
SA	Sparky Anderson/375	15.00
TA	Tony Armas/325	6.00
BA	Dusty Baker/150	15.00
JB	Jason Bay/375	15.00
BE	Carlos Beltran/150	30.00
AB	Angel Berroa/1,325	6.00
HB	Hank Blalock/375	15.00
GB	Geoff Blum/375	6.00
BB	Bert Blyleven/375	8.00
CB	Chris Bootcheck/375	8.00
DB	Dewon Brazelton/375	8.00
MB	Marlon Byrd/1,025	8.00
EB	Eric Byrnes/Redemp.	8.00
MC	Miguel Cabrera/1,025	15.00
CA	Chris Capuano/375	8.00
EC	Eric Chavez/375	15.00
AC	Alex Cintron/375	8.00
WC	Will Clark/150	20.00
CL	Brandon Claussen/375	8.00
CC	Chad Cordero/375	6.00
BC	Bobby Crosby/1,325	10.00
AD	Andre Dawson/375	10.00
BD	Brandon Duckworth/375	8.00
ME	Morgan Ensberg/1,325	8.00
DE	Dwight Evans/375	15.00
AE	Adam Everett/325	6.00
WE	Willie Eyre/375	6.00
KF	Kyle Farnsworth/1,325	8.00
PF	Pedro Feliz/325	8.00
RF	Rollie Fingers/375	10.00
JF	Josh Fogg/325	8.00
LF	Lew Ford/375	10.00
NG	Nomar Garciaparra/100	50.00
CG	Chad Gaudin/375	6.00
BG	Brian Giles/375	10.00
MG	Marcus Giles/325	10.00
GO	Jonny Gomes/325	6.00
AG	Adrian Gonzalez/325	8.00
DG	Dwight Gooden/375	10.00
KG	Ken Griffey Jr./1,625	60.00
GR	Ken Griffey Sr./375	8.00
VG	Vladimir Guerrero	
TG	Tony Gwynn/150	40.00
SH	Scott Hairston/375	8.00
RH	Rob Hammock/325	8.00
AH	Aaron Harang/325	12.00
HA	Rich Harden/325	10.00
HE	Ramon Hernandez/325	8.00
RI	Raul Ibanez/325	8.00
EJ	Edwin Jackson/325	8.00
DJ	Derek Jeter	100.00
JJ	Jacque Jones/375	10.00
KA	Al Kaline/375	25.00
MK	Matt Kata/325	8.00
AK	Adam Kennedy/375	6.00
BK	Bobby Kielty/1,325	6.00
HK	Harmon Killebrew/Redemp.	35.00
DK	Dave Kingman/375	8.00
GK	Graham Koonce/375	8.00
LA	Adam LaRoche/1,325	8.00
CS	Carlos Lee/325	10.00
LE	Cliff Lee/1,325	8.00
TL	Ted Lilly/325	8.00
AL	Adam Loewen/375	6.00
ML	Mike Lowell/375	10.00
LM	Luis Matos/325	8.00
DM	Don Mattingly/150	50.00
MA	Joe Mauer/375	25.00
JM	Justin Miller/325	8.00
MO	Jack Morris/375	10.00
MM	Mark Mulder/375	10.00
MU	Dale Murphy/375	20.00
MN	Mike Neu/325	6.00
LN	Laynce Nix/Redemp.	10.00
RO	Roy Oswalt/375	12.00
LO	Lyle Overbay/1,325	8.00
PA	Jim Palmer/375	15.00
CP	Corey Patterson/375	10.00
BP	Brad Penny/375	8.00
JP	Jason Phillips/375	8.00
PO	Boog Powell/375	15.00
MP	Mark Prior/150	30.00
JR	Jose Reyes/325	25.00
JI	Jim Rice/375	10.00
CR	Cal Ripken Jr./100	120.00
BR	Brooks Robinson/375	25.00
RS	Ryne Sandberg/150	50.00
SO	Ron Santo/375	25.00
SS	Steve Sax/375	10.00
MS	Mike Scioscia/375	15.00
BS	Ben Sheets/375	15.00
TS	Terrmel Sledge/325	6.00
DS	Darryl Strawberry/150	15.00
MT	Mark Teixeira/325	20.00
LT	Luis Tiant/375	10.00
AT	Alan Trammell/375	15.00
CU	Chase Utley/375	25.00
RW	Ryan Wagner/1,325	8.00
WK	Rickie Weeks/Redemp.	15.00
JW	Jerome Williams/1,325	8.00
WI	Josh Willingham/1,325	6.00
RA	Randy Winn/375	8.00
KW	Kerry Wood/150	15.00
DY	Delmon Young/375	20.00
MY	Michael Young/1,325	15.00
CZ	Carlos Zambrano/375	25.00

Etched in Time
Blue Ink

NM/M

Quantity produced listed
Common Autograph: 6.00

AA	Alfredo Amezaga/100	8.00
SA	Sparky Anderson/250	15.00
TA	Tony Armas/150	6.00
BA	Dusty Baker	
JB	Jason Bay/250	15.00
BE	Carlos Beltran	
AB	Angel Berroa/150	8.00
HB	Hank Blalock/250	15.00
GB	Geoff Blum/250	6.00
BB	Bert Blyleven/250	8.00
CB	Chris Bootcheck/250	8.00
DB	Dewon Brazelton/250	8.00
MB	Marlon Byrd/150	8.00
EB	Eric Byrnes/Redemp.	8.00
MC	Miguel Cabrera/25	25.00
CA	Chris Capuano/100	8.00
EC	Eric Chavez/250	15.00
AC	Alex Cintron/100	10.00
WC	Will Clark/50	20.00
CL	Brandon Claussen/100	8.00
CC	Chad Cordero/100	6.00
BC	Bobby Crosby/150	10.00
AD	Andre Dawson/250	10.00
BD	Brandon Duckworth/100	8.00
ME	Morgan Ensberg/150	8.00
DE	Dwight Evans/250	15.00
AE	Adam Everett/150	8.00
WE	Willie Eyre/100	8.00
KF	Kyle Farnsworth/150	8.00
PF	Pedro Feliz/150	8.00
RF	Rollie Fingers/250	10.00
JF	Josh Fogg/150	8.00
LF	Lew Ford/250	8.00
NG	Nomar Garciaparra/50	85.00
CG	Chad Gaudin/100	6.00
BG	Brian Giles/250	10.00
MG	Marcus Giles/150	8.00
GO	Jonny Gomes/150	6.00
AG	Adrian Gonzalez/150	6.00
DG	Dwight Gooden/250	10.00
KG	Ken Griffey Jr./150	75.00
GR	Ken Griffey Sr./250	8.00
VG	Vladimir Guerrero/50	50.00
TG	Tony Gwynn/50	50.00
SH	Scott Hairston/100	8.00
RH	Rob Hammock/150	8.00
AH	Aaron Harang/100	15.00
HA	Rich Harden/150	8.00
HE	Ramon Hernandez/150	8.00
RI	Raul Ibanez/150	8.00
EJ	Edwin Jackson/100	8.00
DJ	Derek Jeter/50	120.00
JJ	Jacque Jones/250	10.00
KA	Al Kaline/250	25.00
MK	Matt Kata/150	8.00
AK	Adam Kennedy/100	8.00
BK	Bobby Kielty/150	8.00
HK	Harmon Killebrew	
DK	Dave Kingman/250	8.00
GK	Graham Koonce/250	8.00
LA	Adam LaRoche/150	10.00
CS	Carlos Lee/325	
LE	Cliff Lee/150	10.00
TL	Ted Lilly/150	8.00
AL	Adam Loewen	
ML	Mike Lowell/250	10.00
LM	Luis Matos/150	8.00
DM	Don Mattingly/50	60.00
MA	Joe Mauer/250	25.00
JM	Justin Miller/150	8.00
MO	Jack Morris/250	10.00
MM	Mark Mulder/250	25.00
MU	Dale Murphy/250	25.00
MN	Mike Neu/150	6.00
RO	Roy Oswalt/250	15.00
LO	Lyle Overbay/150	10.00
PA	Jim Palmer/250	15.00
CP	Corey Patterson/250	15.00
BP	Brad Penny/100	8.00
JP	Jason Phillips/250	8.00
LP	Lou Piniella/50	15.00
PO	Boog Powell/250	15.00
MP	Mark Prior/50	20.00
JR	Jose Reyes/150	30.00
JI	Jim Rice/250	10.00
CR	Cal Ripken Jr./50	150.00
BR	Brooks Robinson/250	25.00
RS	Ryne Sandberg/50	60.00
SO	Ron Santo/250	25.00
SS	Steve Sax/250	10.00
MS	Mike Scioscia/250	10.00
BS	Ben Sheets/250	15.00
TS	Terrmel Sledge/150	6.00
DS	Darryl Strawberry	
MT	Mark Teixeira/150	25.00
LT	Luis Tiant/250	10.00
AT	Alan Trammell/250	15.00
CU	Chase Utley/250	25.00
RW	Ryan Wagner/150	10.00
JW	Jerome Williams/150	10.00
WI	Josh Willingham/150	6.00
RA	Randy Winn/100	10.00
KW	Kerry Wood/50	20.00
DY	Delmon Young/250	20.00
MY	Michael Young/150	15.00
CZ	Carlos Zambrano/250	25.00

Etched in Time
Red Ink

No Pricing
Production 25 Sets

Game Bat Blue

FRANK THOMAS

		NM/M
Common Player:		
Purple:		1X
Production 250		
Red:		1X
Production 150		
Green:		1-2X
Production 50		
BA	Bobby Abreu	6.00
RA	Roberto Alomar	6.00
GA	Garret Anderson	6.00
CB	Carlos Beltran	6.00
AB	Adrian Beltre	6.00
LB	Lance Berkman	4.00
HB	Hank Blalock	6.00
BB	Bret Boone	4.00
SC	Sean Casey	4.00
EC	Eric Chavez	6.00
JC	Jose Cruz Jr.	4.00
CD	Carlos Delgado	6.00
JD	J.D. Drew	4.00
AD	Adam Dunn	8.00
JE	Jim Edmonds	6.00
CF	Cliff Floyd	4.00
RF	Rafael Furcal	4.00
NG	Nomar Garciaparra	10.00
JG	Jason Giambi	6.00
BG	Brian Giles	4.00
TG	Troy Glaus	6.00
LG	Luis Gonzalez	4.00
SG	Shawn Green	6.00
KG	Ken Griffey Jr.	12.00
VG	Vladimir Guerrero	10.00
TH	Todd Helton	8.00
HU	Torii Hunter	6.00
GJ	Geoff Jenkins	4.00
DJ	Derek Jeter	20.00
RJ	Randy Johnson	8.00
AJ	Andruw Jones	8.00
CJ	Chipper Jones	8.00
JL	Javy Lopez	6.00
ML	Mike Lowell	6.00
KM	Kazuo Matsui	10.00
MO	Magglio Ordonez	4.00
RP	Rafael Palmeiro	8.00
JP	Jay Payton	4.00
PI	Mike Piazza	10.00
AP	Albert Pujols	15.00
MR	Manny Ramirez	8.00
JR	Jose Reyes	6.00
AR	Alex Rodriguez	15.00
IR	Ivan Rodriguez	8.00
SR	Scott Rolen	15.00
TS	Tim Salmon	6.00
CS	Curt Schilling	6.00
GS	Gary Sheffield	8.00
AS	Alfonso Soriano	8.00
SS	Sammy Sosa	10.00
IS	Ichiro Suzuki	15.00
MT	Mark Teixeira	6.00
TE	Miguel Tejada	6.00
FT	Frank Thomas	8.00
JT	Jim Thome	8.00
OV	Omar Vizquel	4.00
LW	Larry Walker	4.00
VW	Vernon Wells	4.00
BW	Bernie Williams	8.00
KW	Kerry Wood	8.00

Master Etchings

No Pricing
Production One Set

Star Etchings

		NM/M
Quantity produced listed		
BA	Bobby Abreu/50	20.00
GA	Garret Anderson/50	15.00
JB	Josh Beckett/50	25.00
CB	Carlos Beltran/50	40.00

LB	Lance Berkman/15	
HB	Hank Blalock/50	15.00
BB	Bret Boone/50	10.00
MC	Miguel Cabrera/50	30.00
EC	Eric Chavez/50	15.00
JD	J.D. Drew/50	15.00
AD	Adam Dunn/50	25.00
NG	Nomar Garciaparra/15	60.00
KG	Ken Griffey Jr./50	85.00
KG1	Ken Griffey Jr./50	85.00
VG	Vladimir Guerrero/15	80.00
RH	Roy Halladay/50	15.00
TH	Tim Hudson/50	25.00
GJ	Geoff Jenkins/50	10.00
DL	Derrek Lee/50	25.00
JL	Javy Lopez/50	10.00
ML	Mike Lowell/50	15.00
MU	Mark Mulder/50	15.00
MO	Magglio Ordonez/50	15.00
RO	Roy Oswalt/50	25.00
PR	Mark Prior/50	25.00
JS	Jason Schmidt/50	15.00
MT	Mark Teixeira/50	30.00
TE	Miguel Tejada/50	25.00
FT	Frank Thomas/15	
BW	Brandon Webb/50	15.00
VW	Vernon Wells/50	15.00
DW	Dontrelle Willis/50	15.00
KW	Kerry Wood/50	20.00

Triple Etchings

		NM/M
Production 50 Sets		
RJM	Alex Rodriguez, Derek Jeter, Hideki Matsui	125.00
PER	Albert Pujols, Jim Edmonds, Scott Rolen	90.00
SRG	Curt Schilling, Manny Ramirez, Nomar Garciaparra	40.00
SBT	Alfonso Soriano, Hank Blalock, Mark Teixeira	40.00
WPS	Kerry Wood, Mark Prior, Sammy Sosa	50.00
DMW	Joe DiMaggio, Mickey Mantle, Ted Williams	400.00

2004 Upper Deck First Pitch

		NM/M
Complete Set (300):		40.00
Common Player:		.10
Common SP (271-300):		1.00
Inserted 1:4		
Pack (5):		1.00
Box (36):		25.00
1	Dontrelle Willis	.50
2	Edgar Gonzalez	.25
3	Jose Reyes	.50
4	Jae Weong Seo	.25
5	Miguel Cabrera	.75
6	Jesse Foppert	.25
7	Mike Neu	.25
8	Micheal Nakamura	.25
9	Luis Ayala	.25
10	Jared Sandberg	.25
11	Jhonny Peralta	.25
12	Wilfredo Ledezma	.25
13	Jason Roach	.25
14	Kirk Saarloos	.25
15	Cliff Lee	.25
16	Bobby Hill	.25
17	Lyle Overbay	.25
18	Josh Hall	.25
19	Joe Thurston	.25
20	Matt Kata	.25
21	Jeremy Bonderman	.25

22	Julio Manon	.25
23	Rodrigo Rosario	.25
24	Robby Hammock	.25
25	David Sanders	.25
26	Miguel Ojeda	.25
27	Mark Teixeira	.50
28	Franklyn German	.25
29	Ken Harvey	.25
30	Xavier Nady	.25
31	Tim Salmon	.25
32	Troy Glaus	.25
33	Adam Kennedy	.10
34	David Eckstein	.10
35	Bengie Molina	.10
36	Jarrod Washburn	.10
37	Ramon Ortiz	.10
38	Eric Chavez	.25
39	Miguel Tejada	.25
40	Chris Singleton	.10
41	Jermaine Dye	.10
42	John Halama	.10
43	Tim Hudson	.25
44	Barry Zito	.25
45	Ted Lilly	.10
46	Bobby Kielty	.10
47	Kelvim Escobar	.10
48	Josh Phelps	.10
49	Vernon Wells	.20
50	Roy Halladay	.20
51	Orlando Hudson	.10
52	Eric Hinske	.10
53	Brandon Backe	.10
54	Dewon Brazelton	.10
55	Ben Grieve	.10
56	Aubrey Huff	.10
57	Toby Hall	.10
58	Rocco Baldelli	.50
59	Al Martin	.10
60	Brandon Phillips	.10
61	Omar Vizquel	.10
62	C.C. Sabathia	.10
63	Milton Bradley	.10
64	Ricky Gutierrez	.10
65	Matt Lawton	.10
66	Danys Baez	.10
67	Ichiro Suzuki	1.00
68	Randy Winn	.10
69	Carlos Guillen	.10
70	Mark McLemore	.10
71	Dan Wilson	.10
72	Jamie Moyer	.10
73	Joel Pineiro	.10
74	Edgar Martinez	.20
75	Tony Batista	.10
76	Jay Gibbons	.10
77	Jeff Conine	.10
78	Melvin Mora	.10
79	Geronimo Gil	.10
80	Rodrigo Lopez	.10
81	Jorge Julio	.10
82	Rafael Palmeiro	.40
83	Juan Gonzalez	.40
84	Mike Young	.10
85	Alex Rodriguez	1.00
86	Einar Diaz	.10
87	Kevin Mench	.10
88	Hank Blalock	.25
89	Pedro J. Martinez	.50
90	Byung-Hyun Kim	.10
91	Derek Lowe	.20
92	Jason Varitek	.10
93	Manny Ramirez	.40
94	John Burkett	.10
95	Todd Walker	.10
96	Nomar Garciaparra	1.00
97	Trot Nixon	.10
98	Mike Sweeney	.10
99	Carlos Febles	.10
100	Mike MacDougal	.10
101	Raul Ibanez	.10
102	Jason Grimsley	.10
103	Chris George	.10
104	Brent Mayne	.10
105	Dmitri Young	.10
106	Eric Munson	.10
107	A.J. Hinch	.10
108	Andres Torres	.10
109	Bobby Higginson	.10
110	Shane Halter	.10
111	Matt Walbeck	.10
112	Torii Hunter	.25
113	Doug Mientkiewicz	.10
114	Lew Ford	.10
115	Eric Milton	.10
116	Eddie Guardado	.10
117	Cristian Guzman	.10
118	Corey Koskie	.10
119	Magglio Ordonez	.25
120	Mark Buehrle	.10
121	Billy Koch	.10
122	Jose Valentin	.10
123	Paul Konerko	.10
124	Carlos Lee	.10
125	Jon Garland	.10

126	Jason Giambi	.50
127	Derek Jeter	1.50
128	Roger Clemens	1.00
129	Andy Pettitte	.25
130	Jorge Posada	.25
131	David Wells	.10
132	Hideki Matsui	1.25
133	Mike Mussina	.40
134	Jeff Bagwell	.40
135	Craig Biggio	.20
136	Morgan Ensberg	.10
137	Richard Hidalgo	.10
138	Brad Ausmus	.10
139	Roy Oswalt	.25
140	Billy Wagner	.20
141	Octavio Dotel	.10
142	Gary Sheffield	.25
143	Andruw Jones	.40
144	John Smoltz	.20
145	Rafael Furcal	.20
146	Javy Lopez	.25
147	Shane Reynolds	.10
148	Horacio Ramirez	.10
149	Mike Hampton	.10
150	Jung Bong	.10
151	Ruben Quevedo	.10
152	Ben Sheets	.20
153	Geoff Jenkins	.10
154	Royce Clayton	.10
155	Glendon Rusch	.10
156	John Vander Wal	.10
157	Scott Podsednik	.25
158	Jim Edmonds	.25
159	Tino Martinez	.20
160	Albert Pujols	1.00
161	Matt Morris	.10
162	Woody Williams	.10
163	Edgar Renteria	.10
164	Jason Isringhausen	.10
165	Jason Simontacchi	.10
166	Kerry Robinson	.10
167	Sammy Sosa	1.00
168	Joe Borowski	.10
169	Tony Womack	.10
170	Antonio Alfonseca	.10
171	Corey Patterson	.10
172	Mark Prior	.75
173	Moises Alou	.20
174	Matt Clement	.10
175	Randall Simon	.10
176	Randy Johnson	.50
177	Luis Gonzalez	.20
178	Craig Counsell	.10
179	Miguel Batista	.10
180	Steve Finley	.10
181	Brandon Webb	.10
182	Danny Bautista	.10
183	Oscar Villarreal	.10
184	Shawn Green	.25
185	Brian Jordan	.10
186	Fred McGriff	.20
187	Andy Ashby	.10
188	Rickey Henderson	.25
189	Dave Roberts	.10
190	Eric Gagne	.20
191	Kazuhisa Ishii	.10
192	Adrian Beltre	.10
193	Vladimir Guerrero	.50
194	Livan Hernandez	.10
195	Ron Calloway	.10
196	Sun-Woo Kim	.10
197	Wil Cordero	.10
198	Brad Wilkerson	.10
199	Orlando Cabrera	.10
200	Sidney Ponson	.10
201	Ray Durham	.10
202	Andres Galarraga	.10
203	Benito Santiago	.10
204	Jose Cruz Jr.	.10
205	Jason Schmidt	.10
206	Kirk Rueter	.10
207	Felix Rodriguez	.10
208	Mike Lowell	.10
209	Luis Castillo	.10
210	Derrek Lee	.10
211	Andy Fox	.10
212	Tommy Phelps	.10
213	Todd Hollandsworth	.10
214	Brad Penny	.10
215	Juan Pierre	.10
216	Mike Piazza	.75
217	Jae Weong Seo	.10
218	Ty Wigginton	.10
219	Al Leiter	.10
220	Roger Cedeno	.10
221	Timoniel Perez	.10
222	Aaron Heilman	.10
223	Pedro Astacio	.10
224	Joe McEwing	.10
225	Ryan Klesko	.20
226	Brian Giles	.20
227	Mark Kotsay	.10
228	Brian Lawrence	.10
229	Rod Beck	.10

230	Trevor Hoffman	.10
231	Sean Burroughs	.10
232	Bobby Abreu	.20
233	Jim Thome	.50
234	David Bell	.10
235	Jimmy Rollins	.10
236	Mike Lieberthal	.10
237	Vicente Padilla	.10
238	Randy Wolf	.10
239	Reggie Sanders	.10
240	Jason Kendall	.10
241	Jack Wilson	.10
242	Jose Hernandez	.10
243	Kip Wells	.10
244	Carlos Rivera	.10
245	Craig Wilson	.10
246	Adam Dunn	.25
247	Sean Casey	.10
248	Danny Graves	.10
249	Ryan Dempster	.10
250	Barry Larkin	.25
251	Reggie Taylor	.10
252	Wily Mo Pena	.10
253	Larry Walker	.20
254	Mark Sweeney	.10
255	Preston Wilson	.10
256	Jason Jennings	.10
257	Charles Johnson	.10
258	Jay Payton	.10
259	Chris Stynes	.10
260	Juan Uribe	.10
261	Hideki Matsui/CL	.50
262	Josh Beckett/CL	.20
263	Dontrelle Willis/CL	.20
264	Kevin Millwood/CL	.20
265	Billy Wagner/CL	.10
266	Rocco Baldelli/CL	.25
267	Roger Clemens/CL	.50
268	Rafael Palmeiro/CL	.20
269	Miguel Cabrera/CL	.25
270	Jose Contreras/CL	.10
271	Rickie Weeks	3.00
272	Delmon Young	4.00
273	Chien-Ming Wang	1.00
274	Rich Harden	1.00
275	Edwin Jackson	1.50
276	Dan Haren	1.00
277	Todd Wellemeyer	1.00
278	Prentice Redman	1.00
279	Ryan Wagner	1.50
280	Aaron Looper	1.00
281	Rick Roberts	1.00
282	Josh Willingham	1.00
283	David Crouthers	1.00
284	Chris Capuano	1.00
285	Mike Gosling	1.00
286	Brian Sweeney	1.00
287	Donald Kelly RC	1.00
288	Ryan Meaux RC	1.50
289	Colin Porter	1.00
290	Jerome Gamble	1.50
291	Colby Miller RC	1.50
292	Ian Ferguson	1.00
293	Tim Bittner RC	1.00
294	Jason Frasor RC	1.00
295	Brandon Medders RC	1.00
296	Mike Johnston RC	1.00
297	Tim Bausher RC	1.00
298	Justin Leone RC	1.00
299	Sean Henn	1.00
300	Michel Hernandez	1.00

First and Foremost

NM/M

Complete Set (14):		40.00
Common Player:		3.00
Inserted 1:Blaster Box		
EB	Ernie Banks	5.00
GH	George H.W. Bush	5.00
GW	George W. Bush	5.00
JC	Jose Contreras	3.00
WF	Whitey Ford	4.00
RH	Rich Harden	3.00
DH	Dan Haren	3.00
HR	Horacio Ramirez	3.00
MS	Mike Schmidt	5.00
LT	Luis Tiant	3.00
RW	Ryan Wagner	3.00
BW	Brandon Webb	3.00
JW	Jerome Williams	3.00
DW	Dontrelle Willis	3.00

2004 Upper Deck Play Ball

NM/M

Complete Set (183):	
Common Player:	.15
Common SP (133-162):	3.00
Production 2,004	
Common Classic Combo (163-183):	2.00
Production 1,999	
Pack (5):	3.00

DEREK JETER

Box (24):		65.00
1	Hideo Nomo	.25
2	Curt Schilling	.50
3	Barry Zito	.40
4	Nomar Garciaparra	1.50
5	Yogi Berra	.50
6	Randy Johnson	.75
7	Jason Giambi	.75
8	Sammy Sosa	1.25
9	David Ortiz	.40
10	Derek Jeter	2.00
11	Warren Spahn	.50
12	Mark Prior	1.00
13	Roger Clemens	1.50
14	Mike Piazza	1.00
15	Nolan Ryan	2.00
16	Joe DiMaggio	1.50
17	Alfonso Soriano	.75
18	Brandon Webb	.25
19	Shawn Green	.25
20	Bob Feller	.25
21	Mike Schmidt	.75
22	Mark Teixeira	.50
23	Pedro J. Martinez	.75
24	Vladimir Guerrero	.75
25	Rafael Furcal	.25
26	Derek Lee	.25
27	Carlos Delgado	.50
28	Mickey Mantle	3.00
29	Dontrelle Willis	.25
30	Ted Williams	1.50
31	Vernon Wells	.25
32	Alex Rodriguez	1.50
33	Brooks Robinson	.50
34	Tom Seaver	.50
35	Ernie Banks	.50
36	Bob Gibson	.50
37	Jim Thome	.75
38	Mike Mussina	.50
39	Eric Chavez	.25
40	Roy Halladay	.25
41	Eric Gagne	.40
42	Jose Reyes	.40
43	Jeff Bagwell	.50
44	Rich Harden	.15
45	Jeff Kent	.25
46	Lance Berkman	.25
47	Adam Dunn	.40
48	Richie Sexson	.40
49	Andruw Jones	.50
50	Ichiro Suzuki	1.25
51	Edgar Renteria	.25
52	Rocco Baldelli	.25
53	Jim Edmonds	.25
54	Magglio Ordonez	.25
55	Austin Kearns	.25
56	Garret Anderson	.40
57	Manny Ramirez	.50
58	Roy Oswalt	.25
59	Gary Sheffield	.40
60	Mark Mulder	.25
61	Ben Sheets	.25
62	Scott Rolen	.75
63	Greg Maddux	1.00
64	Jose Contreras	.15
65	Miguel Cabrera	.50
66	Hank Blalock	.40
67	Miguel Tejada	.40
68	Albert Pujols	1.50
69	Hideki Matsui	1.50
70	Mike Lowell	.25
71	Tim Hudson	.25
72	Bret Boone	.25
73	Ivan Rodriguez	.50
74	Josh Beckett	.50
75	Todd Helton	.50
76	Brian Giles	.25
77	Orlando Cabrera	.15
78	Carlos Beltran	.40
79	Jason Schmidt	.25
80	Kerry Wood	.75
81	Preston Wilson	.15
82	Troy Glaus	.40

83	Kevin Brown	.25
84	Rafael Palmeiro	.50
85	Chipper Jones	1.00
86	Reggie Sanders	.15
87	Cliff Floyd	.15
88	Corey Patterson	.25
89	Kevin Millwood	.25
90	Aaron Boone	.15
91	Darin Erstad	.25
92	Richard Hidalgo	.15
93	Dmitri Young	.15
94	Jeremy Bonderman	.15
95	Larry Walker	.25
96	Edgar Martinez	.25
97	Jerome Williams	.15
98	Luis Gonzalez	.25
99	Roberto Alomar	.40
100	Jerry Hairston Jr.	.15
101	Luis Matos	.15
102	Andy Pettitte	.40
103	Frank Thomas	.50
104	Rondell White	.25
105	Jody Gerut	.15
106	Bartolo Colon	.25
107	Johnny Damon	.25
108	Ryan Klesko	.25
109	Geoff Jenkins	.25
110	Jorge Posada	.40
111	Melvin Mora	.15
112	Bernie Williams	.40
113	Shannon Stewart	.15
114	Bobby Abreu	.25
115	Jose Guillen	.15
116	Brandon Phillips	.15
117	Jose Vidro	.15
118	Mike Sweeney	.15
119	Jacque Jones	.15
120	Josh Phelps	.15
121	Milton Bradley	.15
122	Torii Hunter	.25
123	Carl Crawford	.15
124	Javier Vazquez	.25
125	Juan Gonzalez	.50
126	Travis Hafner	.15
127	Ken Griffey Jr.	1.00
128	Phil Nevin	.15
129	Trot Nixon	.15
130	Carlos Lee	.15
131	Javy Lopez	.25
132	Jay Gibbons	.15
133	Brandon Medders RC	3.00
134	Colby Miller RC	3.00
135	David Crouthers RC	3.00
136	Dennis Sarfate RC	5.00
137	Donald Kelly RC	3.00
138	Frank Brooks RC	5.00
139	Chris Aguila RC	3.00
140	Greg Dobbs RC	3.00
141	Ian Snell RC	5.00
142	Jake Woods RC	3.00
143	Jamie Brown RC	3.00
144	Jason Frasor RC	4.00
145	Jerome Gamble RC	4.00
146	Jesse Harper RC	5.00
147	Josh Labandeira RC	4.00
148	Justin Hampson RC	4.00
149	Justin Huisman RC	4.00
150	Justin Leone RC	5.00
151	Lincoln Holdzkom RC	3.00
152	Mike Bumatay RC	5.00
153	Mike Gosling RC	3.00
154	Mike Johnston RC	3.00
155	Mike Rouse RC	3.00
156	Nick Regilio RC	3.00
157	Ryan Meaux RC	3.00
158	Scott Dohmann RC	3.00
159	Sean Henn RC	6.00
160	Tim Bausher RC	3.00
161	Tim Bittner RC	3.00
162	Alec Zumwalt RC	3.00
163	Aaron Boone, Bret Boone, Geoff Jenkins, Mark Prior, Barry Zito	3.00
164	Albert Pujols, Edgar Renteria, Alex Rodriguez	5.00
165	Alfonso Soriano, Sammy Sosa	4.00
166	Bobby Abreu, Jim Thome	2.00
167	Bret Boone, John Olerud, Ichiro Suzuki	4.00
168	Derek Jeter, Alfonso Soriano	6.00
169	Eric Chavez, Miguel Tejada	2.00
170	Garret Anderson, Jim Edmonds, Troy Glaus	2.00
171	Hank Blalock, Alex Rodriguez	5.00

172	Alex Rodriguez, Mark Teixeira, Michael Young, Rafael Palmeiro	5.00
173	Ivan Rodriguez, Dontrelle Willis	2.00
174	Jason Giambi, Derek Jeter	6.00
175	Joe DiMaggio, Mickey Mantle	8.00
176	Joe DiMaggio, Mickey Mantle, Ted Williams	8.00
177	Joe DiMaggio, Ted Williams	6.00
178	Nomar Garciaparra, Alfonso Soriano	4.00
179	Nomar Garciaparra, Jason Giambi	4.00
180	Paul LoDuca, Hideo Nomo	2.00
181	Rafael Palmeiro, Alex Rodriguez, Michael Young	4.00
182	Ralph Kiner, Ted Williams	5.00
183	Aaron Boone, Derek Jeter	6.00

Blue

Blue (1-132):	2-3X
Inserted 1:6	

Green

No Pricing
Production 15 Sets

Purple

No Pricing
Production One Set

Die-Cut

Die-Cut (1-132):	3-6X
Production 175	

Apparel Collection

NM/M

Common Player:		4.00
Inserted 1:24		
JB	Jeff Bagwell	6.00
RB	Rocco Baldelli	8.00
BE	Josh Beckett	6.00
LB	Lance Berkman	4.00
CD	Carlos Delgado	5.00
JD	Joe DiMaggio/SP/150	75.00
AD	Adam Dunn	6.00
RF	Rafael Furcal	6.00
JG	Jason Giambi	6.00
TG	Troy Glaus	4.00
KG	Ken Griffey Jr.	15.00
HA	Roy Halladay	5.00
RH	Rich Harden/SP	8.00
BH	Bo Hart	4.00
TH	Torii Hunter	4.00
DJ	Derek Jeter	15.00
RJ	Randy Johnson	8.00
CJ	Chipper Jones	8.00
ML	Mike Lowell	5.00
MM	Mickey Mantle/SP/150	100.00
PM	Pedro J. Martinez	8.00
HM	Hideki Matsui	20.00
MU	Mike Mussina	6.00
HN	Hideo Nomo	6.00
RO	Roy Oswalt	4.00
RP	Rafael Palmeiro	10.00
PI	Mike Piazza	10.00
JP	Jorge Posada	8.00
MP	Mark Prior	8.00
AP	Albert Pujols	10.00
MR	Manny Ramirez	6.00
AR	Alex Rodriguez	6.00
CS	Curt Schilling	6.00
AS	Alfonso Soriano	6.00
SS	Sammy Sosa	10.00
IS	Ichiro Suzuki	15.00
JT	Jim Thome	8.00
BW	Bernie Williams	5.00
TW	Ted Williams/SP/150	70.00
DW	Dontrelle Willis	5.00
KW	Kerry Wood	8.00
BZ	Barry Zito	5.00

Artist's Touch

		NM/M
Common Player:		4.00
Production 250		
Parallel:		1-2X
Production 50		
RB	Rocco Baldelli	8.00
JB	Josh Beckett	8.00
LB	Lance Berkman	5.00
CD	Carlos Delgado	6.00
RF	Rafael Furcal	5.00
JG	Jason Giambi	8.00
TG	Troy Glaus	8.00
KG	Ken Griffey Jr.	15.00
HA	Roy Halladay	5.00
BH	Bo Hart	4.00
TH	Torii Hunter	5.00
DJ	Derek Jeter	15.00
RJ	Randy Johnson	8.00
CJ	Chipper Jones	8.00
PM	Pedro J. Martinez	8.00
HM	Hideki Matsui	20.00
MM	Mike Mussina	8.00
HN	Hideo Nomo	8.00
RO	Roy Oswalt	4.00
RP	Rafael Palmeiro	5.00
PI	Mike Piazza	10.00
JP	Jorge Posada	8.00
MP	Mark Prior	10.00
AP	Albert Pujols	10.00
MR	Manny Ramirez/50	10.00
AR	Alex Rodriguez	10.00
AS	Alfonso Soriano	15.00
SS	Sammy Sosa	15.00
IS	Ichiro Suzuki	20.00
JT	Jim Thome	10.00
BW	Bernie Williams	6.00
DW	Dontrelle Willis	5.00
KW	Kerry Wood	8.00
BZ	Barry Zito	6.00

Home Run Heroics

		NM/M
Common Player:		2.00
Inserted 1:24		
EB	Ernie Banks	4.00
HB	Hank Blalock	3.00
AB	Aaron Boone	2.00
MC	Miguel Cabrera	4.00
CD	Carlos Delgado	3.00
JD	Joe DiMaggio	8.00
JD1	Joe DiMaggio	8.00
JG	Jason Giambi	3.00
SG	Shawn Green	2.00
KG	Ken Griffey Jr.	6.00
KG1	Ken Griffey Jr.	6.00
RH	Rickey Henderson	2.00
RJ	Randy Johnson	3.00
HK	Harmon Killebrew	4.00
MM	Mickey Mantle	15.00
MM1	Mickey Mantle	15.00
MM2	Mickey Mantle	15.00
EM	Eddie Mathews	4.00
HM	Hideki Matsui	6.00
HM1	Hideki Matsui	6.00
WM	Willie McCovey	2.00
BM	Bill Mueller	2.00
SM	Stan Musial	5.00
RP	Rafael Palmeiro	3.00
CR	Cal Ripken Jr.	10.00
CR1	Cal Ripken Jr.	10.00
AR	Alex Rodriguez	6.00
AR1	Alex Rodriguez	6.00
FR	Frank Robinson	3.00
MS	Mike Schmidt	5.00
RS	Red Schoendienst	2.00
AS	Alfonso Soriano	4.00
SS	Sammy Sosa	6.00
SS1	Sammy Sosa	6.00
SS2	Sammy Sosa	6.00
SS3	Sammy Sosa	6.00
TW	Ted Williams	10.00
TW1	Ted Williams	10.00
TW2	Ted Williams	10.00
TW3	Ted Williams	10.00

Rookie Signature Portfolio

	NM/M
Common Player:	5.00
Inserted 1:30	

CA	Chris Aguila	6.00
TB	Tim Bausher	8.00
BI	Tim Bittner	8.00
FB	Frank Brooks	8.00
JB	Jamie Brown	5.00
MB	Mike Bumatay	8.00
DC	David Crouthers	8.00
GD	Greg Dobbs	6.00
SD	Scott Dohmann	8.00
JF	Jason Frasor	8.00
JG	Jerome Gamble	8.00
MG	Mike Gosling	6.00
HA	Justin Hampson	8.00
JH	Jesse Harper	8.00
SH	Sean Henn	15.00
LH	Lincoln Holdzkom	5.00
HU	Justin Huisman	5.00
MJ	Mike Johnston	10.00
DK	Donald Kelly	5.00
JL	Josh Labandeira	8.00
LE	Justin Leone	10.00
RM	Ryan Meaux	5.00
BM	Brandon Medders	5.00
CM	Colby Miller	5.00
NR	Nick Regilio	5.00
MR	Mike Rouse	6.00
DS	Dennis Sarfate	8.00
IS	Ian Snell	20.00
JW	Jake Woods	5.00
AZ	Alec Zumwalt	8.00

Signature Portfolio

		NM/M
Production 100		
Parallel:		No Pricing
Production 25 or 10		
KG	Ken Griffey Jr.	100.00
HM	Hideki Matsui	250.00
CR	Cal Ripken Jr.	120.00
TS	Tom Seaver	40.00
CY	Carl Yastrzemski	50.00
BZ	Barry Zito	30.00

Tools of the Stars

		NM/M
Common Player:		6.00
Inserted 1:48		
Level 1 Parallel:		1-1.5X
Production 250		
Level 2 Parallel:		No Pricing
Production 25		
JB	Josh Beckett	6.00
CD	Carlos Delgado	6.00
KG	Ken Griffey Jr./SP	15.00
DJ	Derek Jeter	15.00
CJ	Chipper Jones	8.00
HM	Hideki Matsui	15.00
HN	Hideo Nomo	6.00
PI	Mike Piazza	10.00
AP	Albert Pujols	15.00
AR	Alex Rodriguez	10.00
AS	Alfonso Soriano	15.00
IS	Ichiro Suzuki	15.00
JT	Jim Thome	8.00
KW	Kerry Wood	8.00

2004 Upper Deck Power Up

	NM/M
Complete Set (100):	20.00
Common Player:	.15
Pack (9):	1.50
Box (24):	25.00
1 Austin Kearns	.25
2 Rafael Furcal	.25
3 Larry Walker	.25
4 Jeremy Bonderman	.15
5 Scott Rolen	.50
6 Nomar Garciaparra	1.00
7 Jody Gerut	.15

KEN GRIFFEY JR. • OF   10

8	Troy Glaus	.25
9	Roy Halladay	.25
10	Barry Zito	.40
11	Gary Sheffield	.40
12	Ichiro Suzuki	1.00
13	Juan Gonzalez	.25
14	Jim Edmonds	.25
15	Hank Blalock	.40
16	Roy Oswalt	.25
17	Magglio Ordonez	.25
18	Garret Anderson	.40
19	Mark Teixeira	.25
20	Mike Sweeney	.15
21	Reggie Sanders	.15
22	Rafael Palmeiro	.40
23	Orlando Cabrera	.15
24	Edgar Renteria	.25
25	Ryan Klesko	.25
26	Torii Hunter	.25
27	Bret Boone	.25
28	Roberto Alomar	.25
29	Frank Thomas	.50
30	Chipper Jones	.50
31	Eric Chavez	.25
32	Miguel Tejada	.40
33	Carlos Beltran	.40
34	Geoff Jenkins	.25
35	Hideki Matsui	1.00
36	Jason Kendall	.15
37	Adam Dunn	.40
38	Jay Gibbons	.15
39	Ivan Rodriguez	.50
40	Sidney Ponson	.15
41	Albert Pujols	1.00
42	Bartolo Colon	.25
43	Lance Berkman	.25
44	Brandon Webb	.15
45	Shannon Stewart	.15
46	Josh Beckett	.50
47	Jason Schmidt	.25
48	Luis Gonzalez	.25
49	Jacque Jones	.15
50	Andruw Jones	.40
51	Todd Helton	.50
52	Javier Vazquez	.25
53	Alfonso Soriano	.50
54	Manny Ramirez	.50
55	Bobby Abreu	.25
56	Rocco Baldelli	.25
57	Kerry Wood	.50
58	Derek Jeter	1.50
59	Phil Nevin	.15
60	Jeff Bagwell	.40
61	Sammy Sosa	1.00
62	Tom Glavine	.25
63	Miguel Cabrera	.50
64	Shawn Green	.25
65	Mark Prior	1.00
66	Jose Reyes	.25
67	Curt Schilling	.40
68	Hideo Nomo	.25
69	Mike Lowell	.25
70	Randy Johnson	.50
71	Edgar Martinez	.25
72	Dontrelle Willis	.25
73	Milton Bradley	.15
74	Preston Wilson	.15
75	Mike Piazza	.75
76	Mike Mussina	.40
77	Darin Erstad	.25
78	Greg Maddux	.75
79	Tim Hudson	.25
80	Kevin Millwood	.25
81	Dmitri Young	.15
82	Ben Sheets	.25
83	Alex Rodriguez	1.00
84	Johan Santana	.15
85	Jeff Kent	.25
86	Pedro Martinez	.50
87	Carlos Delgado	.40
88	Jim Thome	.50
89	Aubrey Huff	.15
90	Ken Griffey Jr.	1.00

91	Kevin Brown	.25
92	Tony Batista	.15
93	Richie Sexson	.25
94	Cliff Floyd	.15
95	Jose Vidro	.15
96	Brian Giles	.25
97	Jorge Posada	.40
98	Vernon Wells	.25
99	Vladimir Guerrero	.50
100	Jason Giambi	.50

Mega Rare
No Pricing
Inserted 1:240

Super Rare
Stars: 5-10X
Inserted 1:96

Rare
Stars: 3-4X
Inserted 1:6

Ultra Rare
Stars: 4-6X
Inserted 1:24

Shining Through

DONTRELLE WILLIS - P   50

		NM/M
1	Hideo Nomo	.25
2	Mark Prior	1.00
3	Scott Rolen	.75
4	Luis Gonzalez	.25
5	Miguel Tejada	.40
6	Richie Sexson	.40
7	Jim Edmonds	.40
8	Carlos Beltran	.40
9	Manny Ramirez	.50
10	Torii Hunter	.40
11	Garret Anderson	.40
12	Eric Chavez	.40
13	Juan Gonzalez	.40
14	Albert Pujols	1.50
15	Tim Hudson	.40
16	Roy Halladay	.40
17	Roy Oswalt	.25
18	Andruw Jones	.50
19	Gary Sheffield	.40
20	Magglio Ordonez	.40
21	Jason Giambi	.75
22	Brian Giles	.40
23	Barry Zito	.40
24	Todd Helton	.50
25	Randy Johnson	.75
26	Pedro Martinez	.75
27	Vernon Wells	.25
28	Lance Berkman	.40
29	Mike Mussina	.50
30	Carlos Delgado	.40
31	Ivan Rodriguez	.50
32	Kevin Brown	.40
33	Kerry Wood	.75
34	Mark Teixeira	.40
35	Hideki Matsui	1.50
36	Troy Glaus	.40
37	Mike Piazza	1.00
38	Nomar Garciaparra	1.50
39	Vladimir Guerrero	.75
40	Derek Jeter	2.00
41	Jason Schmidt	.40
42	Alex Rodriguez/Yanks	1.50
43	Jeff Bagwell	.50
44	Shawn Green	.40
45	Sammy Sosa	1.50
46	Josh Beckett	.75
47	Bret Boone	.40
48	Ichiro Suzuki	1.00
49	Jeff Kent	.40
50	Rafael Palmeiro	.50
51	Curt Schilling	.40
52	Greg Maddux	1.00
53	Mike Lowell	.40

54	Dontrelle Willis	.40
55	Alfonso Soriano	.50
56	Preston Wilson	.25
57	Jorge Posada	.40
58	Frank Thomas	.50
59	Jim Thome	.75
60	Ken Griffey Jr.	1.00
61	Rocco Baldelli	.40
62	Jose Vidro	.25
63	Austin Kearns	.25
64	Cliff Floyd	.25
65	Phil Nevin	.25
66	Darin Erstad	.25
67	Johan Santana	.25
68	Chipper Jones	.75
69	Brandon Webb	.25
70	Hank Blalock	.40
71	Adam Dunn	.40
72	Javier Vazquez	.25
73	Jacque Jones	.25
74	Bobby Abreu	.40
75	Edgar Renteria	.40
76	Roger Clemens	1.50
77	Rafael Furcal	.40
78	Mike Sweeney	.25
79	Geoff Jenkins	.25
80	Orlando Cabrera	.25
81	Ben Sheets	.40
82	Shannon Stewart	.25
83	Ryan Klesko	.40
84	Edgar Martinez	.40
85	Kevin Millwood	.40
86	Bartolo Colon	.40
87	Larry Walker	.25
88	Tom Glavine	.40
89	Miguel Cabrera	.75
90	Jose Reyes	.40

Stickers

POWER UP YOUR POINTS!

SCRATCH OFF

		NM/M
1	Hideo Nomo	.50
2	Mark Prior	2.00
3	Scott Rolen	1.50
4	Luis Gonzalez	.50
5	Miguel Tejada	.75
6	Richie Sexson	.75
7	Jim Edmonds	.75
8	Carlos Beltran	.75
9	Manny Ramirez	1.00
10	Torii Hunter	.75
11	Garret Anderson	.75
12	Eric Chavez	.75
13	Juan Gonzalez	.75
14	Albert Pujols	3.00
15	Tim Hudson	.75
16	Roy Halladay	.75
17	Roy Oswalt	.50
18	Andruw Jones	1.00
19	Gary Sheffield	.75
20	Magglio Ordonez	.75
21	Jason Giambi	1.50
22	Brian Giles	.75
23	Barry Zito	.75
24	Todd Helton	1.00
25	Randy Johnson	1.50
26	Pedro Martinez	1.50
27	Vernon Wells	.50
28	Lance Berkman	.75
29	Mike Mussina	.75
30	Carlos Delgado	.75
31	Ivan Rodriguez	1.00
32	Kevin Brown	.75
33	Kerry Wood	1.50
34	Mark Teixeira	.75
35	Hideki Matsui	2.50
36	Troy Glaus	.75
37	Mike Piazza	2.00
38	Nomar Garciaparra	3.00
39	Vladimir Guerrero	1.50
40	Derek Jeter	4.00
41	Jason Schmidt	.50
42	Alex Rodriguez	3.00
43	Jeff Bagwell	1.00
44	Shawn Green	.75
45	Sammy Sosa	2.50
46	Josh Beckett	1.00
47	Bret Boone	.50
48	Ichiro Suzuki	2.00
49	Jeff Kent	.75
50	Rafael Palmeiro	1.00
51	Curt Schilling	1.00
52	Greg Maddux	2.00
53	Mike Lowell	.75
54	Dontrelle Willis	.75
55	Alfonso Soriano	1.00
56	Preston Wilson	.50
57	Jorge Posada	.75
58	Frank Thomas	1.00
59	Jim Thome	1.50
60	Ken Griffey Jr.	2.00
61	Rocco Baldelli	.75
62	Jose Vidro	.50
63	Austin Kearns	.50
64	Phil Nevin	.50
65	Darin Erstad	.50
66	Johan Santana	.50
67	Chipper Jones	1.50
68	Brandon Webb	.50
69	Hank Blalock	.75
70	Adam Dunn	.75
71	Javier Vazquez	.75
72	Jacque Jones	.50
73	Bobby Abreu	.75
74	Edgar Renteria	.75
75	Rafael Furcal	.75
76	Mike Sweeney	.50
77	Geoff Jenkins	.50
78	Shannon Stewart	.50
79	Ryan Klesko	.75
80	Edgar Martinez	.75
81	Kevin Millwood	.75
82	Bartolo Colon	.75
83	Tom Glavine	.75
84	Miguel Cabrera	1.50
85	Jose Reyes	.75
86	Padres/Astros/A's/Angels/Cubs/D-Rays	.50
87	Pirates/M's/Expos/Twins/Reds/Phils	.50
88	Royals/O's/W.Sox/Dodgers/Marlins/Yanks	.50
89	Giants/Mets/Cards/Indians/Braves/Rangers	.50
90	Tigers/R.Sox/Rockies/D-Backs/Brewers/Jay	.50

2004 Upper Deck Reflections

		NM/M
Complete Set (340):		
Common (1-100):		.50
Common SP (101-130):		4.00
Production 1,250		
Common Jersey (131-214):		4.00
Common Jersey (215-298):		4.00
Production 100 (215-298):		
Common Auto. (299-340):		15.00
Production 35		
Pack (4):		8.00
Box (8):		50.00
1	Adam Dunn	1.00
2	Albert Pujols	3.00
3	Alex Rodriguez	3.00
4	Alfonso Soriano	1.00
5	Andruw Jones	1.00
6	Austin Kearns	.50
7	Rafael Furcal	.50
8	Barry Zito	.75
9	Bartolo Colon	.50
10	Ben Sheets	.50
11	Bernie Williams	.75
12	Bobby Abreu	.50
13	Brandon Webb	.50
14	Bret Boone	.50
15	Brian Giles	.50
16	Carlos Beltran	.50
17	Carlos Delgado	.75
18	Carlos Lee	.50
19	Chipper Jones	1.50
20	Corey Patterson	.50
21	Curt Schilling	.75
22	Delmon Young	.50
23	Derek Jeter	4.00
24	Dmitri Young	.50
25	Dontrelle Willis	.50
26	Edgar Martinez	.50
27	Edgar Renteria	.50
28	Eric Chavez	.50
29	Eric Gagne	.75
30	Frank Thomas	1.50
31	Garret Anderson	.50
32	Gary Sheffield	.50
33	Geoff Jenkins	.50
34	Greg Maddux	2.00
35	Hank Blalock	.75
36	Hideki Matsui	3.00
37	Hideo Nomo	.75
38	Ichiro Suzuki	2.50
39	Ivan Rodriguez	1.00
40	Jacque Jones	.50
41	Jason Giambi	1.50
42	Jason Schmidt	.75
43	Javy Lopez	.75
44	Jay Gibbons	.50
45	Jeff Bagwell	1.00
46	Jeff Kent	.50
47	Jeremy Bonderman	.50
48	Jim Edmonds	.75
49	Jim Thome	1.50
50	Johnny Damon	.50
51	Jorge Posada	.75
52	Jose Contreras	.50
53	Jose Reyes	.75
54	Jose Vidro	.50
55	Josh Beckett	1.00
56	Juan Gonzalez	1.00
57	Ken Griffey Jr.	2.50
58	Kerry Wood	1.50
59	Kevin Brown	.50
60	Kevin Millwood	.50
61	Lance Berkman	.50
62	Larry Walker	.50
63	Luis Gonzalez	.50
64	Magglio Ordonez	.50
65	Manny Ramirez	1.00
66	Mark Mulder	.50
67	Mark Prior	2.00
68	Mark Teixeira	.50
69	Miguel Cabrera	1.50
70	Miguel Tejada	.75
71	Mike Lowell	.75
72	Mike Mussina	.75
73	Mike Piazza	2.00
74	Mike Sweeney	.50
75	Milton Bradley	.50
76	Nomar Garciaparra	2.00
77	Orlando Cabrera	.50
78	Pedro Martinez	1.50
79	Phil Nevin	.50
80	Preston Wilson	.50
81	Rafael Palmeiro	1.00
82	Randy Johnson	1.50
83	Rich Harden	.50
84	Richie Sexson	.75
85	Rickie Weeks	.50
86	Rocco Baldelli	.75
87	Roy Halladay	.75
88	Roy Oswalt	.75
89	Ryan Klesko	.50
90	Sammy Sosa	2.50
91	Scott Rolen	1.50
92	Shannon Stewart	.50
93	Shawn Green	.50
94	Tim Hudson	.75
95	Todd Helton	1.00
96	Torii Hunter	.75
97	Trot Nixon	.50
98	Troy Glaus	.75
99	Vernon Wells	.50
100	Vladimir Guerrero	1.50
101	Brandon Medders RC	4.00
102	Colby Miller RC	4.00
103	David Crouthers	4.00
104	Dennis Sarfate RC	4.00
105	Donnie Kelly RC	4.00
106	Alec Zumwalt RC	4.00
107	Chris Aguila RC	4.00
108	Greg Dobbs RC	4.00
109	Ian Snell RC	8.00
110	Jake Woods	4.00
111	Jamie Brown RC	4.00
112	Jason Frasor RC	4.00
113	Jerome Gamble RC	4.00
114	Jesse Harper RC	4.00
115	Josh Labandeira RC	5.00
116	Justin Hampson RC	4.00
117	Justin Huisman RC	4.00
118	Justin Leone RC	8.00
119	Kazuo Matsui RC	15.00
120	Lincoln Holdzkom RC	4.00
121	Mike Bumatay RC	4.00
123	Mike Gosling	4.00
123	Mike Johnston RC	4.00
124	Mike Rouse	4.00
125	Nick Regilio RC	4.00
126	Ryan Meaux RC	4.00
127	Scott Dohmann RC	4.00
128	Sean Henn	6.00
129	Tim Bausher RC	4.00
130	Tim Bittner RC	4.00
131	Adam Dunn	4.00
132	Andruw Jones	6.00
133	Austin Kearns	4.00
134	Bartolo Colon	4.00
135	Ben Sheets	4.00
136	Bernie Williams	5.00
137	Bobby Abreu	4.00
138	Brian Giles	4.00
139	Carlos Lee	4.00
140	Chipper Jones	8.00
141	Corey Patterson	4.00
142	Darin Erstad	4.00
143	Edgar Martinez	4.00
144	Vladimir Guerrero	8.00
145	Eric Gagne	4.00
146	Frank Thomas	8.00
147	Garret Anderson	4.00
148	Roger Clemens	12.00
149	Greg Maddux	8.00
150	Jacque Jones	4.00
151	Randy Johnson	8.00
152	Javy Lopez	4.00
153	Mike Piazza	8.00
154	Albert Pujols	15.00
155	Jim Edmonds	4.00
156	Eric Milton	4.00
157	Jorge Posada	6.00
158	J.D. Drew	4.00
159	Jose Vidro	4.00
160	Kevin Millwood	4.00
161	Larry Walker	4.00
162	Luis Gonzalez	4.00
163	Mike Sweeney	4.00
164	Kerry Wood	4.00
165	Mike Cameron	4.00
166	Phil Nevin	4.00
167	Rocco Baldelli	4.00
168	Ryan Klesko	4.00
169	Shannon Stewart	4.00
170	Torii Hunter	6.00
171	Trot Nixon	4.00
172	Vernon Wells	4.00
173	Alfonso Soriano	6.00
174	Andruw Jones	6.00
175	Barry Zito	4.00
176	Brandon Webb	4.00
177	Bret Boone	4.00
178	Scott Rolen	6.00
179	Carlos Delgado	4.00
180	Curt Schilling	8.00
181	Dontrelle Willis	8.00
182	Eric Chavez	4.00
183	Frank Thomas	8.00
184	Gary Sheffield	6.00
185	Greg Maddux	8.00
186	Hank Blalock	4.00
187	Hideki Matsui	15.00
188	Hideo Nomo	8.00
189	Ichiro Suzuki	15.00
190	Ivan Rodriguez	6.00
191	Jason Giambi	6.00
192	Rafael Furcal	4.00
193	Jeff Bagwell	6.00
194	Jeff Kent	4.00
195	Jim Thome	6.00
196	Jose Reyes	6.00
197	Josh Beckett	6.00
198	Juan Gonzalez	6.00
199	Ken Griffey Jr.	15.00
200	Kevin Brown	4.00
201	Lance Berkman	5.00
202	Magglio Ordonez	6.00
203	Mark Mulder	4.00
204	Mark Teixeira	6.00
205	Miguel Tejada	6.00
206	Mike Mussina	6.00
207	Preston Wilson	4.00
208	Rafael Palmeiro	6.00
209	Alex Rodriguez	15.00
210	Richie Sexson	6.00
211	Roy Halladay	6.00
212	Roy Oswalt	5.00
213	Tim Hudson	6.00
214	Troy Glaus	4.00
215	Adam Dunn	8.00
216	Austin Kearns	4.00
217	Bartolo Colon	4.00
218	Ben Sheets	5.00
219	Bernie Williams	6.00
220	Bobby Abreu	5.00
221	Bret Boone	4.00

222	Todd Helton	6.00
223	Chipper Jones	8.00
224	Corey Patterson	4.00
225	Darin Erstad	4.00
226	Dontrelle Willis	4.00
227	Edgar Martinez	4.00
228	Eric Gagne	4.00
229	Garret Anderson	4.00
230	Roger Clemens	20.00
231	Hank Blalock	4.00
232	Jacque Jones	4.00
233	Jeff Bagwell	8.00
234	Jeff Kent	4.00
235	Jeremy Bonderman	4.00
236	Jim Edmonds	4.00
237	Jorge Posada	8.00
238	J.D. Drew	4.00
239	Jose Reyes	10.00
240	Jose Vidro	4.00
241	Kevin Millwood	4.00
242	Luis Gonzalez	4.00
243	Mike Sweeney	4.00
244	Jason Giambi	6.00
245	Manny Ramirez	8.00
246	Phil Nevin	4.00
247	Preston Wilson	4.00
248	Alex Rodriguez	20.00
249	Richie Sexson	4.00
250	Rocco Baldelli	4.00
251	Ryan Klesko	4.00
252	Sammy Sosa	8.00
253	Torii Hunter	4.00
254	Mike Lowell	6.00
255	Troy Glaus	4.00
256	Vernon Wells	6.00
257	Albert Pujols	20.00
258	Alex Rodriguez	20.00
259	Alfonso Soriano	8.00
260	Roger Clemens	20.00
261	Barry Zito	4.00
262	Brandon Webb	6.00
263	Carlos Delgado	6.00
264	Curt Schilling	8.00
265	Derek Jeter	25.00
266	Eric Chavez	4.00
267	Gary Sheffield	8.00
268	Hideki Matsui	25.00
269	Hideo Nomo	10.00
270	Ichiro Suzuki	25.00
271	Ivan Rodriguez	8.00
272	Jason Giambi	6.00
273	Jim Thome	8.00
274	Josh Beckett	10.00
275	Juan Gonzalez	8.00
276	Ken Griffey Jr.	20.00
277	Kerry Wood	4.00
278	Kevin Brown	4.00
279	Lance Berkman	6.00
280	Magglio Ordonez	8.00
281	Manny Ramirez	8.00
282	Mark Mulder	4.00
283	Mark Prior	6.00
284	Mark Teixeira	6.00
285	Miguel Tejada	6.00
286	Mike Mussina	8.00
287	Mike Piazza	10.00
288	Pedro Martinez	10.00
289	Rafael Palmeiro	8.00
290	Randy Johnson	10.00
291	Roy Halladay	6.00
292	Roy Oswalt	6.00
293	Sammy Sosa	10.00
294	Scott Rolen	8.00
295	Shawn Green	6.00
296	Tim Hudson	6.00
297	Todd Helton	6.00
298	Vladimir Guerrero	10.00
299	Bret Boone	10.00
300	Alex Rodriguez	200.00
301	Dontrelle Willis	30.00
302	Barry Larkin	30.00
303	Barry Zito	25.00
304	Eric Chavez	20.00
305	Bernie Williams	85.00
306	Brandon Webb	20.00
307	Cal Ripken Jr.	175.00
308	Carl Yastrzemski	65.00
309	Carlos Delgado	25.00
310	Shawn Green	25.00
311	Eric Gagne	15.00
312	Frank Thomas	40.00
313	Carlos Lee	20.00
314	Garret Anderson	20.00
315	Hideki Matsui	300.00
316	Jim Edmonds	40.00
317	Jeff Bagwell	40.00
318	Luis Gonzalez	20.00
319	Mike Mussina	40.00
320	John Smoltz	60.00
321	Jose Reyes	40.00
322	Josh Beckett	50.00
323	Juan Gonzalez	25.00
324	Ken Griffey Jr.	140.00
325	Rich Harden	20.00

326	Pat Burrell	25.00
327	Mark Teixeira	25.00
328	Roy Oswalt	30.00
329	Miguel Tejada	40.00
330	Mike Hampton	15.00
331	Mike Piazza	175.00
332	Nolan Ryan	120.00
333	Orlando Hernandez	25.00
334	Paul Lo Duca	25.00
335	Roberto Alomar	40.00
336	Rocco Baldelli	20.00
337	Trevor Hoffman	25.00
338	Tom Glavine	50.00
339	Tom Seaver	60.00
340	Mark Prior	25.00

Blue

Blue (1-100):	2-4X
Production 250	
Blue (215-256):	1-2X
Production 15	

Red

Red (1-100):	4-6X
Production 50	
Red Jersey (131-214):	1.5-2X
Production 50	
Red Jersey (215-256):	1-1.5X
Production 50	

Gold

Gold (1-100):	5-10X
Production 15	
Gold Auto. (101-130):	2X
Production 250	
Gold Auto. Parallel (101-130):	2X
Production 125	
Gold Jersey (131-172):	1.5-3X
Production 15	
Gold Jersey (257-298):	No Pricing
Production 5	
Gold Jsy Auto. (299-340):	1X
Production 15	

Black

Black (1-100):	No Pricing
Production One Set	
Black Auto. (101-130):	No Pricing
Production One Set	
Black Jersey (173-214):	No Pricing
Production One Set	
Black Jersey (257-298):	No Pricing
Production One Set	
Black Jersey Auto. (299-340):	No Pricing
Production One Set	

2004 Upper Deck R Class

	NM/M
Complete Set (180):	50.00
Common Player:	.10
Pack (6):	2.50
Box (24):	50.00
1 Adam Dunn	.50
2 Jose Vidro	.10
3 Vladimir Guerrero	.75
4 Hideo Nomo	.25
5 Eric Chavez	.25
6 Carlos Delgado	.40
7 Javy Lopez	.25
8 Javier Vazquez	.25
9 Miguel Cabrera	.75
10 Manny Ramirez	.50
11 Scott Rolen	.75
12 Rafael Furcal	.10
13 Jim Thome	.75
14 Edgar Renteria	.25
15 Jason Kendall	.10
16 Alfonso Soriano	.75
17 Troy Glaus	.40
18 Vernon Wells	.10
19 Todd Helton	.50
20 Mark Mulder	.25
21 Albert Pujols	2.00
22 Andy Pettitte	.25
23 Kevin Millwood	.10
24 Bret Boone	.10
25 Ken Griffey Jr.	1.00
26 Kevin Brown	.20
27 J.D. Drew	.25
28 Corey Patterson	.40
29 Jason Giambi	.40
30 Jason Schmidt	.25
31 Jose Reyes	.25
32 Torii Hunter	.25
33 Brian Giles	.25
34 Garret Anderson	.25
35 Mark Teixeira	.25
36 Rocco Baldelli	.25
37 Sammy Sosa	1.50
38 Jeff Bagwell	.50
39 Rafael Palmeiro	.50
40 Derek Lee	.25
41 Randy Johnson	.75
42 Roger Clemens	1.50
43 Austin Kearns	.25
44 Dontrelle Willis	.10
45 Lance Berkman	.25
46 Juan Gonzalez	.40
47 Ichiro Suzuki	1.50
48 Pat Burrell	.25
49 Miguel Tejada	.40
50 Mike Piazza	1.00
51 Mark Prior	.75
52 C.C. Sabathia	.10
53 Jacque Jones	.10
54 Carlos Beltran	.75
55 Mike Mussina	.40
56 Mike Lowell	.25
57 Phil Nevin	.10
58 Andruw Jones	.40
59 Barry Zito	.25
60 Magglio Ordonez	.25
61 Carlos Lee	.20
62 Nomar Garciaparra	1.00
63 Kerry Wood	.75
64 Luis Gonzalez	.20
65 Derek Jeter	2.00
66 Preston Wilson	.10
67 Greg Maddux	1.00
68 Pedro J. Martinez	.75
69 Richie Sexson	.25
70 Hank Blalock	.50
71 Chipper Jones	.75
72 Ivan Rodriguez	.50
73 Roy Halladay	.25
74 Tim Hudson	.25

75	Ryan Klesko	.10
76	Hideki Matsui	1.50
77	Josh Beckett	.40
78	Brandon Webb	.10
79	Alex Rodriguez	2.00
80	Jim Edmonds	.40
81	Jeff Kent	.10
82	Bobby Abreu	.25
83	Curt Schilling	.75
84	Roy Oswalt	.25
85	Orlando Cabrera	.75
86	Johan Santana	.50
87	Geoff Jenkins	.10
88	Gary Sheffield	.40
89	Shawn Green	.25
90	Frank Thomas	.50
91	Tim Hamulack RC	.25
92	Shingo Takatsu RC	.50
93	Justin Huisman	.25
94	Sean Henn	.50
95	Jamie Brown	.25
96	Dennis Sarfate RC	.25
97	Lincoln Holdzkom RC	.25
98	Roman Colon RC	.25
99	Scott Dohmann RC	.25
100	Ivan Ochoa	.25
101	Akinori Otsuka RC	.50
102	Fernando Nieve RC	.25
103	Mike Johnston RC	.25
104	Mariano Gomez RC	.25
105	Justin Leone RC	.25
106	Evan Rust RC	.25
107	Mike Rouse	.25
108	Ian Snell RC	.50
109	Jason Bartlett	.25
110	Ryan Wing	.25
111	Nick Regilio RC	.25
112	Merkin Valdez RC	.50
113	Josh Labandeira RC	.25
114	David Aardsma	.75
115	Justin Knoedler RC	.25
116	Shawn Hill RC	.25
117	Casey Daigle RC	.25
118	Donnie Kelly RC	.25
119	Justin Germano RC	.25
120	Eddy Rodriguez	.25
121	Onil Joseph RC	.25
122	Mike Wuertz	.50
123	Roberto Novoa RC	.25
124	Jerome Gamble RC	.50
125	Justin Hampson RC	.25
126	Ronald Belisario RC	.25
127	Tim Bausher RC	.25
128	Chris Saenz RC	.25
129	Hector Gimenez RC	.25
130	Ronny Cedeno RC	.25
131	Jason Frasor RC	.25
132	Kazuo Matsui RC	2.00
133	Mike Gosling	.25
134	Jerry Gil RC	.25
135	Orlando Rodriguez RC	.25
136	Jorge Vasquez RC	.50
137	Chris Aguila RC	.25
138	Tim Bittner RC	.25
139	Jake Woods	.25
140	Enemencio Pacheco	.25
141	David Crouthers	.25
142	Jose Capellan RC	1.00
143	Chad Bentz RC	.25
144	Michael Vento	.75
145	Scott Proctor RC	.50
146	Edwin Moreno RC	.25
147	Brandon Medders RC	.25
148	Renyel Pinto RC	.25
149	Rusty Tucker RC	.25
150	Ryan Meaux RC	.25
151	William Bergolla	.25
152	Angel Chavez	.25
153	Colby Miller RC	.25
154	John Gall RC	.25
155	Carlos Hines RC	.25
156	Carlos Vasquez RC	.50
157	Justin Lehr RC	.25
158	Kevin Cave RC	.25
159	Jeff Bennett RC	.25
160	Greg Dobbs RC	.25
161	Jorge Sequea RC	.25
162	Chris Oxspring RC	.25
163	Franklyn Gracesqui RC	.25
164	Shawn Camp RC	.25
165	Lino Urdaneta	.25
166	Luis Gonzalez	.25
167	Ramon Ramirez RC	.50
168	Freddy Guzman RC	.25
169	Chris Shelton RC	1.50
170	Andres Blanco	.25
171	Aarom Baldiris RC	.25
172	Kazuhito Tadano RC	.50
173	Brian Dallimore RC	.25
174	Eduardo Villacis	.25
175	Frank Francisco RC	.25
176	Edwin Jackson RC	.25
177	Bobby Crosby	.50
178	Joe Mauer	.50

179	Rickie Weeks	.50
180	Delmon Young	.50

First Class Black Ink Autograph

		NM/M
	Inserted 1:2,880	
SA	Sandy Alomar	20.00
PB	Pat Burrell	30.00
MC	Miguel Cabrera	40.00
CD	Carlos Delgado	30.00
EG	Eric Gagne	50.00
KG	Ken Griffey Jr.	80.00
TH	Trevor Hoffman	30.00
BL	Barry Larkin	40.00
PL	Paul LoDuca	30.00
EM	Edgar Martinez	40.00
MP	Mark Prior	40.00
HR	Horacio Ramirez	20.00
DW	Dontrelle Willis	30.00

First Class Blue Ink Autograph

No Pricing
Production 3 Sets

Jersey

		NM/M
	Common Player:	4.00
	Inserted 1:12	
RA	Roberto Alomar	6.00
BA	Jeff Bagwell	8.00
RB	Rocco Baldelli	4.00
JB	Josh Beckett	4.00
HB	Hank Blalock	8.00
BB	Bret Boone	4.00
KB	Kevin Brown	4.00
EC	Eric Chavez	4.00
RC	Roger Clemens	12.00
CD	Carlos Delgado	4.00
JG	Jason Giambi	6.00
GL	Troy Glaus	4.00
TG	Tom Glavine	6.00
KG	Ken Griffey Jr.	12.00
VG	Vladimir Guerrero	8.00
TH	Todd Helton	8.00
HU	Torii Hunter	4.00
DJ	Derek Jeter	15.00
RJ	Randy Johnson	8.00
AJ	Andruw Jones	6.00
CJ	Chipper Jones	8.00
EM	Edgar Martinez	4.00
PM	Pedro J. Martinez	8.00
HM	Hideki Matsui	20.00
KM	Kazuo Matsui	10.00
HN	Hideo Nomo	8.00
PI	Mike Piazza	10.00
MP	Mark Prior	6.00
AP	Albert Pujols	15.00
MR	Manny Ramirez	8.00
RI	Mariano Rivera	8.00
IR	Ivan Rodriguez	8.00
SR	Scott Rolen	8.00
CS	Curt Schilling	8.00
GS	Gary Sheffield	6.00
AS	Alfonso Soriano	8.00
SS	Sammy Sosa	10.00
IS	Ichiro Suzuki	25.00
MT	Miguel Tejada	6.00
BW	Bernie Williams	6.00
DW	Dontrelle Willis	4.00
KW	Kerry Wood	8.00

Taking Over!

		NM/M
	Common Player:	3.00
	1-20 Production 650	
	21-30 Production 150	
TO-1	Richie Sexson, Lyle Overbay	3.00
TO-2	Jason Phillips, Mike Piazza	6.00
TO-3	Barry Larkin, William Bergolla	4.00
TO-4	Jason Dubois, Moises Alou	3.00
TO-5	Nook Logan, Alex Sanchez	3.00
TO-6	Merkin Valdez, Robb Nen	4.00
TO-7	Troy Percival, Francisco Rodriguez	3.00
TO-8	Carlos Beltran, David DeJesus	4.00
TO-9	Alex Rodriguez, Michael Young	6.00
TO-10	Alexis Rios, Vernon Wells	3.00
TO-11	Matt Lawton, Grady Sizemore	3.00
TO-12	Danny Graves, Ryan Wagner	3.00
TO-13	Miguel Cabrera, Jeff Conine	4.00
TO-14	Josh Willingham, Ramon Castro	3.00
TO-15	Junior Spivey, Rickie Weeks	3.00
TO-16	Guillermo Quiroz, Greg Myers	3.00
TO-17	Scott Hatteberg, Graham Koonce	3.00
TO-18	Rene Reyes, Larry Walker	4.00
TO-19	Khalil Greene, Ramon Vazquez	4.00
TO-20	Billy Wagner, Octavio Dotel	3.00
TO-21	Joe Mauer, A.J. Pierzynski	8.00
TO-22	Javier Vazquez, Roger Clemens	10.00
TO-23	Curt Schilling, Brandon Webb	3.00
TO-24	Delmon Young, Cirilo Cruz Jr.	8.00
TO-25	Vladimir Guerrero, Tim Salmon	8.00
TO-26	Gary Sheffield, J.D. Drew	3.00
TO-27	Miguel Tejada, Bobby Crosby	8.00
TO-28	Edwin Jackson, Kevin Brown	3.00
TO-29	Kazuo Matsui, Jose Reyes	10.00
TO-30	Wily Mo Pena, Ken Griffey Jr.	10.00

2004 Upper Deck Rivals: Yankees vs Red Sox

		NM/M
	Complete Sealed Set (32):	25.00
	Common Player (1-30):	.50
1	Alex Rodriguez	2.00
2	Bobby Doerr	.75
3	Don Mattingly	1.50
4	Dwight Evans	.50
5	Fred Lynn	.50
6	Jason Giambi	.50
7	Jim Rice	.50
8	Lou Gehrig	2.00
9	Luis Tiant	.50
10	Manny Ramirez	1.00
11	Mike Mussina	.75
12	Pedro Martinez	1.00
13	Phil Rizzuto	.75
14	Whitey Ford	.75
15	Yogi Berra	1.00
16	Tim Wakefield	.50
17	Billy Martin	.75
18	Bill Torrez, Bucky Dent	.50
19	Nomar Garciaparra, Derek Jeter	2.00
20	Gary Sheffield, Curt Schilling	1.00
21	Joe DiMaggio, Dick Newsome	1.50
22	Joe DiMaggio, Lefty Grove	1.50
23	Joe DiMaggio, Ted Williams	1.50
24	Jorge Posada, Jason Varitek	.50
25	Mickey Mantle, Carl Yastrzemski	2.00
26	Tracy Stallard, Roger Maris	1.00
27	Carlton Fisk, Thurman Munson	1.00
28	Babe Ruth	2.00
29	Roger Clemens	1.50
30	Wade Boggs	.50

Commemorative

		NM/M
	Complete Set (5):	10.00
	One oversized card per set.	
	Babe Ruth	4.00
	Ted Williams	3.00
	Derek Jeter	3.00
	Nomar Garciaparra	2.00
	Mickey Mantle	5.00

"What If"

		NM/M
	Common Player:	4.00
	Production 2,150 Sets	
1	Aaron Boone	4.00
2	Alex Rodriguez	10.00
3	Babe Ruth	10.00
4	Babe Ruth	10.00
5	Billy Martin	4.00
6	Bucky Dent	4.00
7	Carl Yastrzemski	8.00
8	Carlton Fisk	5.00
9	Derek Jeter	10.00
10	Hideki Matsui	8.00
11	Joe DiMaggio	8.00
12	Joe Torre	4.00
13	Mickey Mantle	15.00
14	Pedro Martinez	6.00
15	Pee Wee Reese	4.00
16	Roger Clemens	8.00
17	Roger Maris	8.00
18	Ted Williams	8.00
19	Ted Williams	8.00
20	Carl Yastrzemski	8.00

What If Autograph

No Pricing

2004 Upper Deck Sweet Spot

		NM/M
	Complete Set (262):	
	Common Player:	.25
	Common (91-170):	3.00
	Production 799	
	Common SP (171-230):	1.50
	Production 399	
	Common SP (231-250):	1.50
	Production 299	
	Common SP (251-260):	3.00
	Production 199	
	Pack (4):	35.00
	Box (12):	100.00
1	Albert Pujols	3.00
2	Alex Rodriguez	3.00
3	Alfonso Soriano	1.00
4	Andruw Jones	.50
5	Andy Pettitte	.50
6	Aubrey Huff	.25
7	Austin Kearns	.50
8	Barry Zito	.50
9	Bobby Abreu	.50
10	Brandon Webb	.25
11	Bret Boone	.25
12	Brian Giles	.25
13	C.C. Sabathia	.25
14	Carlos Beltran	1.00
15	Carlos Delgado	.50
16	Chipper Jones	1.00
17	Cliff Floyd	.25
18	Curt Schilling	1.00
19	Delmon Young	.50
20	Derek Jeter	3.00
21	Dontrelle Willis	.25
22	Edgar Martinez	.50
23	Edgar Renteria	.50
24	Eric Chavez	.50
25	Eric Gagne	.50
26	Frank Thomas	.75
27	Garret Anderson	.50
28	Gary Sheffield	.75
29	Geoff Jenkins	.25
30	Greg Maddux	1.50
31	Hank Blalock	.75
32	Hideo Nomo	.50
33	Ichiro Suzuki	2.00
34	Ivan Rodriguez	.75
35	Jacque Jones	.25
36	Jason Giambi	.50
37	Jason Schmidt	.50
38	Javier Vazquez	.25
39	Javy Lopez	.50
40	Jeff Bagwell	.75
41	Jim Edmonds	.50
42	Jim Thome	.75
43	Joe Mauer	.50
44	John Smoltz	.50
45	Jose Cruz Jr.	.25
46	Jose Reyes	.50
47	Jose Vidro	.25
48	Josh Beckett	.50
49	Ken Griffey Jr.	1.50
50	Kerry Wood	1.00
51	Kevin Brown	.25
52	Larry Walker	.50
53	Magglio Ordonez	.25
54	Manny Ramirez	.75
55	Mark Mulder	.50
56	Mark Prior	1.00
57	Mark Teixeira	.50
58	Miguel Cabrera	1.00
59	Miguel Tejada	.50
60	Mike Lowell	.40
61	Mike Mussina	.75
62	Mike Piazza	1.50
63	Nomar Garciaparra	1.50
64	Orlando Cabrera	.40
65	Pat Burrell	.25
66	Pedro J. Martinez	1.00
67	Phil Nevin	.25
68	Preston Wilson	.25
69	Rafael Furcal	.25
70	Rafael Palmeiro	.75
71	Randy Johnson	1.00
72	Craig Wilson	.25
73	Rich Harden	.25
74	Richie Sexson	.50
75	Rickie Weeks	.50
76	Rocco Baldelli	.50
77	Roger Clemens	2.50
78	Roy Halladay	.25
79	Roy Oswalt	.50
80	Ryan Klesko	.25
81	Sammy Sosa	2.00
82	Scott Podsednik	.25
83	Scott Rolen	1.00
84	Shawn Green	.40
85	Tim Hudson	.40
86	Todd Helton	.75
87	Torii Hunter	.40
88	Troy Glaus	.25
89	Vernon Wells	.25
90	Vladimir Guerrero	1.00
91	Aarom Baldiris RC	3.00
92	Akinori Otsuka RC	8.00
93	Andres Blanco RC	5.00
94	Angel Chavez RC	3.00
95	Brian Dallimore RC	8.00
96	Carlos Hines RC	5.00
97	Carlos Vasquez RC	5.00
98	Casey Daigle RC	3.00
99	Chad Bentz RC	3.00
100	Chris Aguila RC	5.00
101	Chris Oxspring RC	5.00
102	Chris Saenz RC	5.00
103	Chris Shelton RC	10.00
104	Colby Miller RC	5.00
105	David Crouthers RC	3.00
106	David Aardsma RC	5.00
107	Dennis Sarfate RC	5.00
108	Donnie Kelly RC	3.00
109	Eddy Rodriguez RC	3.00
110	Eduardo Villacis RC	3.00
111	Edwin Moreno RC	5.00
112	Enemencio Pacheco RC	5.00
113	Fernando Nieve RC	3.00
114	Franklyn Gracesqui RC	3.00
115	Freddy Guzman RC	3.00
116	Greg Dobbs RC	3.00
117	Hector Gimenez RC	3.00

118	Ian Snell RC	5.00
119	Ivan Ochoa RC	5.00
120	Jake Woods RC	5.00
121	Jamie Brown RC	5.00
122	Jason Bartlett RC	3.00
123	Jason Frasor RC	3.00
124	Jeff Bennett RC	3.00
125	Jerome Gamble RC	5.00
126	Jerry Gil RC	3.00
127	Brandon Medders RC	3.00
128	Ryan Meaux RC	3.00
129	John Gall RC	3.00
130	Jorge Sequea RC	3.00
131	Jorge Vasquez RC	3.00
132	Jose Capellan RC	8.00
133	Josh Labandeira RC	3.00
134	Justin Germano RC	8.00
135	Justin Hampson RC	5.00
136	Justin Huisman RC	5.00
137	Justin Knoedler RC	5.00
138	Justin Leone RC	5.00
139	Kazuhito Tadano RC	5.00
140	Kazuo Matsui RC	10.00
141	Kevin Cave RC	5.00
142	Lincoln Holdzkom RC	3.00
143	Lino Urdaneta RC	3.00
144	Luis A. Gonzalez RC	5.00
145	Mariano Gomez RC	5.00
146	Merkin Valdez RC	5.00
147	Michael Vento RC	8.00
148	Mike Wuertz RC	5.00
149	Mike Gosling RC	5.00
150	Mike Johnston RC	3.00
151	Mike Rouse RC	5.00
152	Nick Regilio RC	5.00
153	Onil Joseph RC	3.00
154	Orlando Rodriguez RC	5.00
155	Ramon Ramirez RC	5.00
156	Renyel Pinto RC	5.00
157	Roberto Novoa RC	5.00
158	Roman Colon RC	3.00
159	Ronald Belisario RC	5.00
160	Ronny Cedeno RC	8.00
161	Rusty Tucker RC	5.00
162	Ryan Wing	3.00
163	Scott Dohmann RC	3.00
164	Scott Proctor RC	5.00
165	Sean Henn	5.00
166	Shawn Camp RC	5.00
167	Shawn Hill RC	3.00
168	Shingo Takatsu RC	8.00
169	Tim Hamulack RC	3.00
170	William Bergolla RC	3.00
171	Adam Dunn	2.00
172	Albert Pujols	8.00
173	Alex Rodriguez	8.00
174	Alfonso Soriano	3.00
175	Andruw Jones	2.00
176	Bret Boone	1.50
177	Brian Giles	1.50
178	Carlos Delgado	2.00
179	Derrek Lee	2.00
180	Eric Chavez	1.50
181	Frank Thomas	2.00
182	Garret Anderson	1.50
183	Gary Sheffield	2.00
184	Hank Blalock	2.00
185	Jason Giambi	1.50
186	Javy Lopez	1.50
187	Jeff Bagwell	2.00
188	Jim Edmonds	2.00
189	Jim Thome	2.00
190	Ken Griffey Jr.	4.00
191	Lance Berkman	1.50
192	Magglio Ordonez	1.50
193	Manny Ramirez	3.00
194	Mike Lowell	1.50
195	Mike Piazza	5.00
196	Preston Wilson	1.50
197	Rafael Palmeiro	2.00
198	Richie Sexson	1.50
199	Sammy Sosa	5.00
200	Scott Rolen	4.00
201	Shawn Green	1.50
202	Todd Helton	2.00
203	Troy Glaus	1.50
204	Vernon Wells	1.50
205	Vladimir Guerrero	3.00
206	Garret Anderson, Vladimir Guerrero	3.00
207	Luis Gonzalez, Richie Sexson	2.00
208	Andruw Jones, Chipper Jones	3.00
209	Javy Lopez, Miguel Tejada	2.00
210	Manny Ramirez, David Ortiz	5.00
211	Derrek Lee, Sammy Sosa	5.00
212	Frank Thomas, Magglio Ordonez	2.00
213	Austin Kearns, Ken Griffey Jr.	4.00
214	Preston Wilson, Todd Helton	2.00
215	Delmon Young, Ivan Rodriguez	2.00
216	Miguel Cabrera, Mike Lowell	3.00
217	Jeff Bagwell, Lance Berkman	2.00
218	Lyle Overbay, Geoff Jenkins	1.50
219	Adrian Beltre, Shawn Green	2.00
220	Jacque Jones, Torii Hunter	1.50
221	Jose Vidro, N. Johnson	1.50
222	Kazuo Matsui, Mike Piazza	5.00
223	Alex Rodriguez, Jason Giambi	6.00
224	Eric Chavez, Jermaine Dye	1.50
225	Jim Thome, Pat Burrell	2.50
226	Brian Giles, Phil Nevin	1.50
227	Bret Boone, Ichiro Suzuki	6.00
228	Albert Pujols, Scott Rolen	8.00
229	Hank Blalock, Mark Teixeira	3.00
230	Carlos Delgado, Vernon Wells	2.00
231	Albert Pujols	8.00
232	Alex Rodriguez	3.00
233	Chipper Jones	3.00
234	Craig Biggio	1.50
235	Curt Schilling	2.00
236	Derek Jeter	8.00
237	Ivan Rodriguez	2.00
238	Jeff Bagwell	2.00
239	Jim Edmonds	2.00
240	Jim Thome	2.00
241	Josh Beckett	2.00
242	Kerry Wood	3.00
243	Kevin Brown	1.50
244	Mark Prior	2.00
245	Miguel Tejada	2.00
246	Mike Mussina	2.00
247	Nomar Garciaparra	4.00
248	Pedro J. Martinez	3.00
249	Randy Johnson	3.00
250	Roger Clemens	6.00
251	Alex Rodriguez, Derek Jeter	12.00
252	Jason Soriano, Hank Blalock	4.00
253	Bobby Abreu, Pat Burrell	3.00
254	Edgar Renteria, Scott Rolen	4.00
255	Garret Anderson, Vladimir Guerrero	4.00
256	Jeff Bagwell, Jeff Kent	3.00
257	Jose Reyes, Kazuo Matsui	4.00
258	K. Greene, S. Burroughs	4.00
259	Marcus Giles, Rafael Furcal	3.00
260	Manny Ramirez, Johnny Damon	6.00
261	Tim Bausher RC	3.00
262	Tim Bittner RC	5.00

Wood

Stars (1-90):	3-6X
SP's (91-262):	.75-1.5X

Production 99 Sets

Limited

No Pricing
Production 10 Sets

Printing Plates

One of each color (black, cyan, magenta and yellow) issued for front and back.
(No values due to scarcity.)

Diamond Champs
Jersey

		NM/M
Common Player:		5.00

Production 150 Sets

GA	Garret Anderson	5.00
JB	Josh Beckett	8.00
RC	Roger Clemens	12.00
EG	Eric Gagne	8.00
KG	Ken Griffey Jr.	12.00
RH	Roy Halladay	5.00
DJ	Derek Jeter	20.00
RJ	Randy Johnson	10.00
CJ	Chipper Jones	8.00
GM	Greg Maddux	10.00
PM	Pedro J. Martinez	8.00
PE	Andy Pettitte	5.00
MP	Mike Piazza	10.00
AP	Albert Pujols	20.00
AR	Alex Rodriguez/ Yanks	15.00
IR	Ivan Rodriguez	8.00
CS	Curt Schilling	8.00
IS	Ichiro Suzuki	30.00
MT	Miguel Tejada	6.00
BZ	Barry Zito	5.00

Home Run Heroes
Jersey

		NM/M
Common Player:		5.00

Production 199 Sets

GA	Garret Anderson	5.00
JB	Jeff Bagwell	8.00
CB	Carlos Beltran	8.00
AB	Adrian Beltre	8.00
LB	Lance Berkman	5.00
HB	Hank Blalock	8.00
BB	Bret Boone	5.00
PB	Pat Burrell	5.00
MC	Miguel Cabrera	10.00
EC	Eric Chavez	5.00
CD	Carlos Delgado	5.00
JD	J.D. Drew	8.00
AD	Adam Dunn	8.00
JE	Jim Edmonds	5.00
JG	Jason Giambi	5.00
BG	Brian Giles	5.00
TG	Troy Glaus	5.00
LG	Luis Gonzalez	5.00
SG	Shawn Green	5.00
KG	Ken Griffey Jr./ Bat Up	12.00
KG1	Ken Griffey Jr./Swing	12.00
VG	Vladimir Guerrero	10.00
HA	Travis Hafner	5.00
TH	Todd Helton	8.00
DJ	Derek Jeter	20.00
AJ	Andruw Jones	6.00
CJ	Chipper Jones	8.00
JK	Jeff Kent	5.00
DL	Derrek Lee	5.00
ML	Mike Lowell	5.00
HM	Hideki Matsui	25.00
JM	Joe Mauer	8.00
FM	Fred McGriff	5.00
MO	Magglio Ordonez	5.00
DO	David Ortiz	15.00
RP	Rafael Palmeiro	8.00
MP	Mike Piazza	10.00
JP	Jorge Posada	5.00
AP	Albert Pujols	20.00
MR	Manny Ramirez	8.00
AR	Alex Rodriguez/ Yanks Bat Up	15.00
AR1	Alex Rodriguez/ Yanks Swing	15.00
IR	Ivan Rodriguez	8.00
SR	Scott Rolen	10.00
RS	Richie Sexson	5.00
GS	Gary Sheffield	8.00
AS	Alfonso Soriano	8.00
SS	Sammy Sosa	12.00
MT	Mark Teixeira	6.00
TE	Miguel Tejada	6.00
FT	Frank Thomas	8.00
JT	Jim Thome	10.00
VW	Vernon Wells	5.00
BW	Bernie Williams	5.00
PW	Preston Wilson	5.00

Marquee Attractions
Jersey

		NM/M
Common Player:		5.00

Production 199 Sets

HB	Hank Blalock	8.00
MC	Miguel Cabrera	10.00
EC	Eric Chavez	5.00
RC	Roger Clemens	12.00
CD	Carlos Delgado	5.00
EG	Eric Gagne	8.00
BG	Brian Giles	5.00
KG	Ken Griffey Jr.	12.00
VG	Vladimir Guerrero	10.00
TH	Todd Helton	8.00
HU	Torii Hunter	5.00
DJ	Derek Jeter	20.00
RJ	Randy Johnson	10.00
AJ	Andruw Jones	5.00
PI	Mike Piazza	10.00
MP	Mark Prior	8.00
AP	Albert Pujols	20.00
AR	Alex Rodriguez	15.00
IR	Ivan Rodriguez	8.00
CS	Curt Schilling	8.00
JS	Jason Schmidt	8.00
BS	Ben Sheets	8.00
IS	Ichiro Suzuki	30.00
MS	Mike Sweeney	5.00
MT	Miguel Tejada	8.00
FT	Frank Thomas	8.00
JT	Jim Thome	10.00

Signatures

		NM/M
Common Player:		10.00
Black Stitch:		No Pricing

Production One Set

GA	Garret Anderson	20.00
RB	Rocco Baldelli	20.00
BE	Josh Beckett	40.00
CB	Carlos Beltran	25.00
AB	Angel Berroa	10.00
HB	Hank Blalock	15.00
BB	Bret Boone	10.00
PB	Pat Burrell	15.00
SB	Sean Burroughs	10.00
MC	Miguel Cabrera	40.00
EC	Eric Chavez	20.00
WC	Will Clark	25.00
RC	Roger Clemens	150.00
JD	J.D. Drew	20.00
AD	Adam Dunn	20.00
NG	Nomar Garciaparra	50.00
BG	Brian Giles	20.00
MG	Marcus Giles	10.00
GL	Tom Glavine	40.00
JG	Juan Gonzalez	20.00
LG	Luis Gonzalez	15.00
KG	Ken Griffey Jr.	75.00
VG	Vladimir Guerrero	50.00
TG	Tony Gwynn	40.00
HA	Roy Halladay	20.00
RH	Rich Harden	15.00
TH	Todd Helton	40.00
HI	Richard Hidalgo	10.00
HO	Trevor Hoffman	20.00
TI	Tim Hudson	20.00
HU	Torii Hunter	20.00
GJ	Geoff Jenkins	10.00
DJ	Derek Jeter	160.00
JJ	Jacque Jones	10.00
AK	Austin Kearns	15.00
RK	Ryan Klesko	10.00
CL	Carlos Lee	15.00
DL	Derrek Lee	20.00
ML	Mike Lieberthal	10.00
EL	Esteban Loaiza	10.00
LO	Mike Lowell	10.00
MA	Mike Marshall/SP/34	40.00
EM	Edgar Martinez	50.00
DM	Don Mattingly	60.00
JM	Joe Mauer	25.00
MU	Mark Mulder	20.00
MM	Mike Mussina	40.00
RO	Roy Oswalt	20.00
CP	Corey Patterson	15.00
OP	Odalis Perez	10.00
PI	Mike Piazza	150.00
SP	Scott Podsednik	15.00
MP	Mark Prior	20.00
AP	Albert Pujols	220.00
MR	Manny Ramirez	60.00
JR	Jose Reyes	40.00
CR	Cal Ripken Jr.	180.00
AR	Alex Rodriguez/27	
IR	Ivan Rodriguez	50.00
SR	Scott Rolen	30.00
NR	Nolan Ryan	150.00

RS	Ryne Sandberg	75.00
SA	Johan Santana	40.00
JS	Jason Schmidt	15.00
TS	Tom Seaver	50.00
BS	Ben Sheets	20.00
GS	Gary Sheffield	35.00
SM	John Smoltz	50.00
IS	Ichiro Suzuki	250.00
MT	Mark Teixeira	25.00
TE	Miguel Tejada	25.00
FT	Frank Thomas	50.00
JV	Javier Vazquez	15.00
WA	Billy Wagner	15.00
BW	Brandon Webb	15.00
WE	Rickie Weeks	15.00
VW	Vernon Wells/30	25.00
DW	Dontrelle Willis	20.00
RW	Randy Wolf	15.00
KW	Kerry Wood	20.00
DY	Delmon Young	20.00
CZ	Carlos Zambrano	20.00

Signatures Red-Blue Stitch

NM/M

Quantity produced listed

GA	Garret Anderson/45	25.00
RB	Rocco Baldelli/45	25.00
BE	Josh Beckett/45	40.00
CB	Carlos Beltran/45	40.00
AB	Angel Berroa/45	20.00
HB	Hank Blalock/45	25.00
BB	Bret Boone/45	20.00
PB	Pat Burrell/35	25.00
SB	Sean Burroughs/45	15.00
MC	Miguel Cabrera/45	40.00
EC	Eric Chavez/45	25.00
WC	Will Clark/45	25.00
RC	Roger Clemens/30	175.00
JD	J.D. Drew/40	25.00
AD	Adam Dunn/45	25.00
NG	Nomar Garciaparra/45	60.00
BG	Brian Giles/45	15.00
MG	Marcus Giles/45	20.00
GL	Tom Glavine/45	60.00
JG	Juan Gonzalez/45	25.00
LG	Luis Gonzalez/45	25.00
KG	Ken Griffey Jr./44	100.00
VG	Vladimir Guerrero/45	75.00
TG	Tony Gwynn/45	60.00
HA	Roy Halladay/35	25.00
RH	Rich Harden/45	25.00
TH	Todd Helton/45	50.00
HI	Richard Hidalgo/45	15.00
HO	Trevor Hoffman/45	25.00
TI	Tim Hudson/45	25.00
HU	Torii Hunter/45	25.00
EJ	Edwin Jackson/45	15.00
GJ	Geoff Jenkins/45	15.00
DJ	Derek Jeter/35	275.00
JJ	Jacque Jones/45	20.00
AK	Austin Kearns/45	25.00
RK	Ryan Klesko/45	15.00
CL	Carlos Lee/45	20.00
DL	Derek Lee/45	35.00
ML	Mike Lieberthal/45	25.00
EL	Esteban Loaiza/45	15.00
LO	Mike Lowell/35	30.00
EM	Edgar Martinez/30	50.00
DM	Don Mattingly/45	85.00
JM	Joe Mauer/45	35.00
MU	Mark Mulder/45	20.00
RO	Roy Oswalt/45	25.00
CP	Corey Patterson/45	25.00
OP	Odalis Perez/45	20.00
PI	Mike Piazza/20	
SP	Scott Podsednik/45	20.00
MP	Mark Prior/45	25.00
AP	Albert Pujols/45	250.00
MR	Manny Ramirez/40	80.00
JR	Jose Reyes/45	50.00
CR	Cal Ripken Jr./35	250.00
IR	Ivan Rodriguez/45	50.00
NR	Nolan Ryan/45	170.00
RS	Ryne Sandberg/40	80.00
SA	Johan Santana/45	65.00
JS	Jason Schmidt/45	25.00
TS	Tom Seaver/35	75.00
BS	Ben Sheets/55	25.00
GS	Gary Sheffield/45	50.00
SM	John Smoltz/40	80.00
IS	Ichiro Suzuki/45	500.00
MT	Mark Teixeira/45	40.00
TE	Miguel Tejada/45	50.00
FT	Frank Thomas/25	75.00
JV	Javier Vazquez/45	20.00
WA	Billy Wagner/45	15.00
BW	Brandon Webb/45	25.00
WE	Rickie Weeks/45	25.00
VW	Vernon Wells/29	25.00
DW	Dontrelle Willis/45	25.00
RW	Randy Wolf/45	20.00
KW	Kerry Wood/45	25.00

DY	Delmon Young/45	25.00
CZ	Carlos Zambrano/30	50.00

Signatures Barrel

NM/M

Cards not serial numbered, quantity produced provided by Upper Deck.

GA	Garret Anderson/74	20.00
RB	Rocco Baldelli/19	25.00
BE	Josh Beckett/65	50.00
CB	Carlos Beltran/55	40.00
AB	Angel Berroa/45	15.00
HB	Hank Blalock/74	25.00
BB	Bret Boone/64	15.00
SB	Sean Burroughs/64	15.00
MC	Miguel Cabrera/64	40.00
EC	Eric Chavez/74	25.00
AD	Adam Dunn/74	30.00
NG	Nomar Garciaparra/38	75.00
BG	Brian Giles/64	15.00
MG	Marcus Giles/64	15.00
GL	Tom Glavine/64	50.00
KG	Ken Griffey Jr./64	125.00
VG	Vladimir Guerrero/38	60.00
HA	Roy Halladay/64	30.00
RH	Rich Harden/64	15.00
TH	Todd Helton/64	60.00
HI	Richard Hidalgo/64	15.00
HO	Trevor Hoffman/68	25.00
TI	Tim Hudson/64	30.00
HU	Torii Hunter/64	30.00
EJ	Edwin Jackson/ 64 Exch	15.00
GJ	Geoff Jenkins/64	15.00
DJ	Derek Jeter/53	275.00
JJ	Jacque Jones/64	15.00
AK	Austin Kearns/64	20.00
RK	Ryan Klesko/64	15.00
CL	Carlos Lee/64	25.00
DL	Derek Lee/64	50.00
ML	Mike Lieberthal/64	15.00
EL	Esteban Loaiza/64	15.00
LO	Mike Lowell/64	30.00
MA	Mike Marshall/13	
EM	Edgar Martinez/64	40.00
DM	Don Mattingly/38	125.00
JM	Joe Mauer/72	50.00
MU	Mark Mulder/64	20.00
MM	Mike Mussina/64	50.00
RO	Roy Oswalt/64	40.00
CP	Corey Patterson/ 74 Exch	25.00
OP	Odalis Perez/64	15.00
PI	Mike Piazza/38	150.00
SP	Scott Podsednik/64	25.00
MP	Mark Prior/64	25.00
AP	Albert Pujols/64	250.00
MR	Manny Ramirez/63	75.00
JR	Jose Reyes/49	50.00
CR	Cal Ripken Jr./38	220.00
AR	Alex Rodriguez/28	300.00
IR	Ivan Rodriguez/50	50.00
NR	Nolan Ryan/38	180.00
RS	Ryne Sandberg/14	
SA	Johan Santana/64	60.00
JS	Jason Schmidt/64	25.00
TS	Tom Seaver/38	75.00
BS	Ben Sheets/64	25.00
GS	Gary Sheffield/38	60.00
SM	John Smoltz/13	
IS	Ichiro Suzuki/64	500.00
MT	Mark Teixeira/64	25.00
TE	Miguel Tejada/64	50.00
FT	Frank Thomas/13	
JV	Javier Vazquez/64	20.00
WA	Billy Wagner/64	20.00
BW	Brandon Webb/64	30.00
WE	Rickie Weeks/64	25.00
VW	Vernon Wells/33	20.00
DW	Dontrelle Willis/64	25.00
RW	Randy Wolf/64	15.00
KW	Kerry Wood/64	25.00
DY	Delmon Young/74	50.00
CZ	Carlos Zambrano/38	40.00

Signatures Dual

No Pricing
Production 10 Sets

Signatures Glove

NM/M

Production 5-25

GA	Garret Anderson/25	40.00
RB	Rocco Baldelli/25	40.00
BE	Josh Beckett/25	75.00
CB	Carlos Beltran/25	50.00
AB	Angel Berroa/25	40.00
HB	Hank Blalock/25	40.00
BB	Bret Boone/25	40.00
PB	Pat Burrell/15	40.00
SB	Sean Burroughs/25	40.00
MC	Miguel Cabrera/25	100.00
EC	Eric Chavez/25	50.00

WC	Will Clark/25	100.00
AD	Adam Dunn/25	60.00
NG	Nomar Garciaparra/25	100.00
BG	Brian Giles/25.	35.00
MG	Marcus Giles/25	30.00
GL	Tom Glavine/25.	65.00
JG	Juan Gonzalez/25	50.00
LG	Luis Gonzalez/25	40.00
KG	Ken Griffey Jr./25	200.00
VG	Vladimir Guerrero/25	100.00
TG	Tony Gwynn/25	100.00
HA	Roy Halladay/25	50.00
RH	Rich Harden/25	40.00
TH	Todd Helton/25	40.00
HI	Richard Hidalgo/15	25.00
HO	Trevor Hoffman/15	50.00
TI	Tim Hudson/25	65.00
HU	Torii Hunter/25	40.00
EJ	Edwin Jackson/25	20.00
GJ	Geoff Jenkins/25	30.00
JJ	Jacque Jones/25	20.00
AK	Austin Kearns/25	40.00
CL	Carlos Lee/25	50.00
DL	Derek Lee/25	60.00
ML	Mike Lieberthal/25	30.00
EL	Esteban Loaiza/25	30.00
MA	Mike Marshall/25	50.00
EM	Edgar Martinez/25	75.00
DM	Don Mattingly/25	180.00
JM	Joe Mauer/25	50.00
MU	Mark Mulder/25	40.00
MM	Mike Mussina/25	75.00
RO	Roy Oswalt/25	65.00
CP	Corey Patterson/25	40.00
OP	Odalis Perez/25	40.00
SP	Scott Podsednik/25	40.00
MP	Mark Prior/25	50.00
AP	Albert Pujols/25	300.00
MR	Manny Ramirez/25	120.00
JR	Jose Reyes/25	75.00
CR	Cal Ripken Jr./25	275.00
IR	Ivan Rodriguez/25	75.00
NR	Nolan Ryan/25	250.00
RS	Ryne Sandberg/20	125.00
SA	Johan Santana/25	75.00
JS	Jason Schmidt/25	40.00
BS	Ben Sheets/25	50.00
GS	Gary Sheffield/20	50.00
MT	Mark Teixeira/25	75.00
TE	Miguel Tejada/25.	40.00
JV	Javier Vazquez/25	40.00
WA	Billy Wagner/25.	40.00
BW	Brandon Webb/25.	40.00
WE	Rickie Weeks/25	30.00
DW	Dontrelle Willis/25	50.00
KW	Kerry Wood/25	50.00
DY	Delmon Young/25	50.00

Signatures Historical Ball

No Pricing
Production One Set

Sweet Impressions Plates

No Pricing
Production One Set

Sweet Sticks

NM/M

Common Player: 4.00
Production 199 Sets

BA	Bobby Abreu	6.00
MA	Moises Alou	6.00
GA	Garret Anderson	4.00
JB	Jeff Bagwell	8.00
BE	Carlos Beltran	8.00
AB	Adrian Beltre	4.00
LB	Lance Berkman	4.00
CB	Craig Biggio	4.00

HB	Hank Blalock	8.00
BB	Bret Boone	4.00
PB	Pat Burrell	4.00
MC	Miguel Cabrera	8.00
EC	Eric Chavez	6.00
RC	Roger Clemens	15.00
CD	Carlos Delgado	6.00
JD	J.D. Drew	6.00
AD	Adam Dunn	8.00
JE	Jim Edmonds	6.00
RF	Rafael Furcal	4.00
NG	Nomar Garciaparra	12.00
JG	Jason Giambi	6.00
BG	Brian Giles	4.00
MG	Marcus Giles	4.00
TG	Troy Glaus	4.00
GL	Tom Glavine	6.00
LG	Luis Gonzalez	4.00
SG	Shawn Green	4.00
KG	Ken Griffey Jr.	15.00
VG	Vladimir Guerrero	8.00
TH	Todd Helton	8.00
DJ	Derek Jeter	25.00
RJ	Randy Johnson	8.00
CJ	Chipper Jones	10.00
AJ	Andruw Jones	6.00
JK	Jeff Kent	4.00
DL	Derek Lee	4.00
ML	Mike Lowell	4.00
GM	Greg Maddux	10.00
HM	Hideki Matsui	35.00
KM	Kazuo Matsui	15.00
MO	Magglio Ordonez	4.00
RP	Rafael Palmeiro	8.00
MP	Mike Piazza	10.00
PR	Mark Prior	6.00
AP	Albert Pujols	20.00
MR	Manny Ramirez	8.00
ER	Edgar Renteria	4.00
JR	Jose Reyes	6.00
CR	Cal Ripken Jr.	30.00
AR	Alex Rodriguez	15.00
IR	Ivan Rodriguez	8.00
SR	Scott Rolen	10.00
CS	Curt Schilling	6.00
RS	Richie Sexson	6.00
GS	Gary Sheffield	8.00
AS	Alfonso Soriano	8.00
SS	Sammy Sosa	10.00
IS	Ichiro Suzuki	40.00
MT	Mark Teixeira	6.00
TE	Miguel Tejada	6.00
FT	Frank Thomas	8.00
JT	Jim Thome	8.00
LW	Larry Walker	6.00
TW	Ted Williams	60.00
PW	Preston Wilson	4.00

Sweet Sticks Dual

NM/M

Common Duo: 10.00
Production 100 Sets

BT	Hank Blalock, Mark Teixeira	10.00
CL	Miguel Cabrera, Mike Lowell	10.00
JC	Randy Johnson, Roger Clemens	25.00
JG	Derek Jeter, Nomar Garciaparra	25.00
JM	Jose Reyes, Kazuo Matsui	25.00
MM	Hideki Matsui, Kazuo Matsui	40.00
PR	Albert Pujols, Scott Rolen	40.00
RG	Manny Ramirez, Nomar Garciaparra	15.00
RJ	Alex Rodriguez, Derek Jeter	50.00
RP	Ivan Rodriguez, Mike Piazza	15.00
TB	Jim Thome, Pat Burrell	20.00
WP	Kerry Wood, Mark Prior	12.00

Sweet Sticks Triple

NM/M

Production 50 Sets

GPS	Ken Griffey Jr., Rafael Palmeiro, Sammy Sosa	40.00
JJD	Andruw Jones, Chipper Jones, J.D. Drew	25.00
JSG	Derek Jeter, Ichiro Suzuki, Ken Griffey Jr.	120.00
MWP	Greg Maddux, Kerry Wood, Mark Prior	35.00
RJG	Alex Rodriguez, Derek Jeter, Jason Giambi	65.00

Sweet Sticks Quad

		NM/M
Production 25 Sets		
PRSG	Albert Pujols, Alex Rodriguez, Ichiro Suzuki, Ken Griffey Jr.	125.00
RGDM	Babe Ruth, Lou Gehrig, Joe DiMaggio, Mickey Mantle	1,200

Sweet Threads

		NM/M
Common Player:		4.00
Patch:		1.5-2.5X
Production 85 Sets		
JB	Jeff Bagwell	8.00
CB	Carlos Beltran	8.00
LB	Lance Berkman	4.00
HB	Hank Blalock	8.00
BB	Bret Boone	4.00
MC	Miguel Cabrera	8.00
EC	Eric Chavez	4.00
BC	Bartolo Colon	4.00
CD	Carlos Delgado	4.00
JG	Jason Giambi	6.00
BG	Brian Giles	4.00
TG	Troy Glaus	4.00
SG	Shawn Green	4.00
VG	Vladimir Guerrero	8.00
RH	Rich Harden	4.00
HE	Todd Helton	8.00
TH	Tim Hudson	4.00
ML	Mike Lowell	4.00
EM	Edgar Martinez	4.00
KM	Kazuo Matsui/SP	15.00
JM	Joe Mauer	8.00
MM	Mark Mulder	4.00
HN	Hideo Nomo	8.00
MO	Magglio Ordonez	4.00
RO	Roy Oswalt	4.00
MP	Mark Prior	6.00
MR	Manny Ramirez	8.00
JR	Jose Reyes	4.00
SS	Sammy Sosa	10.00
JS	Jason Schmidt	6.00
RS	Richie Sexson	4.00
GS	Gary Sheffield	6.00
AS	Alfonso Soriano	8.00
MT	Mark Teixeira	6.00
FT	Frank Thomas	8.00
JT	Jim Thome	8.00
RW	Rickie Weeks	4.00
VW	Vernon Wells	4.00
DW	Dontrelle Willis	4.00
PW	Preston Wilson	4.00
KW	Kerry Wood	8.00
DY	Delmon Young	8.00

Sweet Threads Dual

		NM/M
Common Duo:		5.00
Production 150 Sets		
Patch:		1.5-2X
Production 60 Sets		
BP	Angel Berroa, Scott Podsednik	4.00
BT	Hank Blalock, Mark Teixeira	10.00
CK	Curt Schilling, Kevin Brown	10.00
CS	Roger Clemens, Sammy Sosa	20.00
DT	Carlos Delgado, Jim Thome	8.00
GH	Eric Gagne, Roy Halladay	8.00
HG	Tim Hudson, Vladimir Guerrero	10.00
JC	Randy Johnson, Roger Clemens	25.00

JH	Andruw Jones, Torii Hunter	8.00
JJ	Andruw Jones, Chipper Jones	10.00
MM	Hideki Matsui, Kazuo Matsui	50.00
MP	Joe Mauer, Mark Prior	10.00
PC	Andy Pettitte, Roger Clemens	20.00
PP	Jorge Posada, Mike Piazza	15.00
PS	Albert Pujols, Ichiro Suzuki	50.00
PW	Albert Pujols, Kerry Wood	15.00
RJ	Alex Rodriguez, Derek Jeter	50.00
RM	Jose Reyes, Kazuo Matsui	15.00
SB	Alfonso Soriano, Bret Boone	8.00
SM	Gary Sheffield, Pedro J. Martinez	12.00
WP	Kerry Wood, Mark Prior	10.00
YW	Delmon Young, Rickie Weeks	10.00

Sweet Threads Triple

		NM/M
Common Trio:		10.00
Production 99 Sets		
Triple Patch:		2X
No pricing 15 or less.		
AGG	Garret Anderson, Troy Glaus, Vladimir Guerrero	20.00
BKE	Jeff Bagwell, Jeff Kent, Morgan Ensberg	15.00
BLR	Adrian Beltre, Mike Lowell, Scott Rolen	20.00
BMS	Bret Boone, Edgar Martinez, Ichiro Suzuki	50.00
BWC	Josh Beckett, Kerry Wood, Roger Clemens	30.00
CMM	Bobby Crosby, Joe Mauer, Kazuo Matsui	30.00
DHW	Carlos Delgado, Roy Halladay, Vernon Wells	15.00
DKG	Adam Dunn, Austin Kearns, Ken Griffey Jr.	20.00
DMJ	Joe DiMaggio, Mickey Mantle, Derek Jeter	220.00
DMW	Joe DiMaggio, Mickey Mantle, Ted Williams	250.00
DRN	Johnny Damon, Manny Ramirez, Trot Nixon	40.00
FRP	Keith Foulke, Mariano Rivera, Troy Percival	25.00
GPS	Ken Griffey Jr., Rafael Palmeiro, Sammy Sosa	35.00
JJD	Andruw Jones, Chipper Jones, J.D. Drew	20.00
JTG	Derek Jeter, Miguel Tejada, Nomar Garciaparra	40.00
JWH	Edwin Jackson, Jerome Williams, Rich Harden	10.00
KVG	Jeff Kent, Jose Vidro, Marcus Giles	10.00
LTO	Carlos Lee, Frank Thomas, Magglio Ordonez	20.00
LTP	Javy Lopez, Miguel Tejada, Rafael Palmeiro	20.00
MCF	Kazuo Matsui, Miguel Cabrera, Rafael Furcal	20.00
MMH	Mike Mussina, Pedro J. Martinez, Tim Hudson	25.00

MSH	Joe Mauer, Johan Santana, Torii Hunter	35.00
MWP	Greg Maddux, Kerry Wood, Mark Prior	25.00
PAS	Corey Patterson, Moises Alou, Sammy Sosa	30.00
PCO	Andy Pettitte, Roger Clemens, Roy Oswalt	25.00
PRR	Albert Pujols, Edgar Renteria, Scott Rolen	40.00
PTH	Albert Pujols, Jim Thome, Todd Helton	30.00
RCB	Alex Rodriguez, Eric Chavez, Hank Blalock	30.00
RGJ	Alex Rodriguez, Ken Griffey Jr., Randy Johnson	35.00
RGW	Jose Reyes, Khalil Greene, Rickie Weeks	30.00
RJG	Alex Rodriguez, Derek Jeter, Jason Giambi	60.00
RMP	Jose Reyes, Kazuo Matsui, Mike Piazza	25.00
SBK	Alfonso Soriano, Bret Boone, Jeff Kent	20.00
SBP	Jason Schmidt, Josh Beckett, Mark Prior	15.00
SBT	Alfonso Soriano, Hank Blalock, Mark Teixeira	20.00
SLM	Curt Schilling, Derek Lowe, Pedro J. Martinez	40.00
VBM	Javier Vazquez, Kevin Brown, Mike Mussina	20.00
WBP	Brandon Webb, Josh Beckett, Mark Prior	15.00
WGS	Billy Wagner, Eric Gagne, John Smoltz	20.00
WRC	Kerry Wood, Nolan Ryan, Roger Clemens	60.00
YCW	Delmon Young, Miguel Cabrera, Rickie Weeks	20.00
ZMH	Barry Zito, Mark Mulder, Tim Hudson	10.00

Sweet Threads Quad

		NM/M
Common Quad:		20.00
Production 99 Sets		
Quad Patch:		No Pricing
Production 1-15		
BADH	Carlos Beltran, Garret Anderson, Johnny Damon, Torii Hunter	30.00
BBGS	Angel Berroa, Carlos Beltran, Alex Gonzalez, Mike Sweeney	20.00
BPJC	Josh Beckett, Mark Prior, Randy Johnson, Roger Clemens	30.00
BWRC	Josh Beckett, Kerry Wood, Nolan Ryan, Roger Clemens	50.00
CAGG	Bartolo Colon, Garret Anderson, Troy Glaus, Vladimir Guerrero	25.00
DHHW	Carlos Delgado, Eric Hinske, Roy Halladay, Vernon Wells	20.00
DOGP	Carlos Delgado, David Ortiz, Jason Giambi, Rafael Palmeiro	25.00
GNKB	Brian Giles, Phil Nevin, Ryan Klesko, Sean Burroughs	25.00
GNLG	Eric Gagne, Hideo Nomo, Paul LoDuca, Shawn Green	30.00
JBGB	Chipper Jones, Lance Berkman, Luis Gonzalez, Pat Burrell	25.00

JEGW	Andruw Jones, Jim Edmonds, Ken Griffey Jr., Preston Wilson	35.00
JJDF	Andruw Jones, Chipper Jones, J.D. Drew, Rafael Furcal	25.00
JMSH	Jacque Jones, Joe Mauer, Shannon Stewart, Torii Hunter	35.00
JRMT	Derek Jeter, Edgar Renteria, Kazuo Matsui, Miguel Tejada	40.00
KGCS	Austin Kearns, Brian Giles, Miguel Cabrera, Sammy Sosa	25.00
LMRS	Carlos Lee, Hideki Matsui, Manny Ramirez, Shannon Stewart	75.00
LTOK	Carlos Lee, Frank Thomas, Magglio Ordonez, Paul Konerko	25.00
LTPP	Javy Lopez, Miguel Tejada, Raffy, Sidney Ponson	25.00
MMMH	Mark Mulder, Mike Mussina, Pedro J. Martinez, Roy Halladay	25.00
MTTS	Edgar Martinez, Jim Thome, Mark Teixeira, Mike Sweeney	20.00
NSGH	Phil Nevin, Richie Sexson, Shawn Green, Todd Helton	20.00
PBBC	Andy Pettitte, Craig Biggio, Jeff Bagwell, Roger Clemens	40.00
PLBT	Albert Pujols, Lee, Jeff Bagwell, Jim Thome	40.00
PRER	Albert Pujols, Edgar Renteria, Jim Edmonds, Scott Rolen	70.00
PWPS	Corey Patterson, Kerry Wood, Mark Prior, Sammy Sosa	40.00
RCBG	Alex Rodriguez, Eric Chavez, Hank Blalock, Troy Glaus	30.00
RJDM	Alex Rodriguez, Derek Jeter, Joe DiMaggio, Mickey Mantle	275.00
RLPM	Ivan Rodriguez, Javy Lopez, Jorge Posada, Joe Mauer	40.00
RMPG	Jose Reyes, Kazuo Matsui, Mike Piazza, Tom Glavine	30.00
SBKV	Alfonso Soriano, Bret Boone, Jeff Kent, Jose Vidro	20.00
SBMM	Curt Schilling, Kevin Brown, Mike Mussina, Pedro J. Martinez	40.00
SDRM	Curt Schilling, Johnny Damon, Manny Ramirez, Pedro J. Martinez	60.00
SSOG	Gary Sheffield, Ichiro Suzuki, Magglio Ordonez, Vladimir Guerrero	50.00
VCBM	Javier Vazquez, Jose Contreras, Kevin Brown, Mike Mussina	25.00
WATM	Billy Wagner, Bobby Abreu, Jim Thome, Kevin Millwood	30.00
WBCL	Dontrelle Willis, Josh Beckett, Miguel Cabrera, Mike Lowell	20.00
WGJS	Brandon Webb, Luis Gonzalez, Randy Johnson, Richie Sexson	25.00

ZMHH Barry Zito, Mark Mulder, Rich Harden, Tim Hudson ... 35.00

2004 Upper Deck Sweet Spot Classic

		NM/M
Complete Set (161):		
Common Player (1-90):		.40
Common (91-161):		2.00
Production 1,910-1,999		
Pack (4):		15.00
Box (12):		150.00
1	Al Kaline	1.00
2	Andre Dawson	.40
3	Bert Blyleven	.40
4	Bill Dickey	.40
5	Bill Mazeroski	.40
6	Billy Martin	.40
7	Bob Feller	.50
8	Bob Gibson	1.00
9	Bob Lemon	.40
10	George Kell	.40
11	Bobby Doerr	.40
12	Brooks Robinson	1.00
13	Cal Ripken Jr.	4.00
14	Carl Hubbell	.40
15	Carl Yastrzemski	1.50
16	Charlie Keller	.40
17	Chuck Dressen	.40
18	Cy Young	1.00
19	Dave Winfield	.75
20	Dizzy Dean	.75
21	Don Drysdale	.75
22	Don Larsen	.75
23	Don Mattingly	2.50
24	Don Newcombe	.75
25	Duke Snider	.75
26	Early Wynn	.40
27	Eddie Mathews	1.00
28	Elston Howard	.40
29	Frank Robinson	.75
30	Gary Carter	.40
31	Gil Hodges	.40
32	Gil McDougald	.40
33	Hank Greenberg	.75
34	Harmon Killebrew	1.50
35	Harry Caray	.40
36	Honus Wagner	1.00
37	Hoyt Wilhelm	.40
38	Jackie Robinson	2.00
39	Jim Bunning	.40
40	Jim Palmer	.75
41	Jimmie Foxx	1.00
42	Jimmy Wynn	.40
43	Joe DiMaggio	3.00
44	Joe Torre	.40
45	Johnny Mize	.40
46	Juan Marichal	.75
47	Larry Doby	.40
48	Lefty Gomez	.40
49	Lefty Grove	.40
50	Leo Durocher	.40
51	Lou Boudreau	.40
52	Lou Brock	.50
53	Lou Gehrig	3.00
54	Luis Aparicio	.40
55	Maury Wills	.40
56	Mel Allen	.40
57	Mel Ott	.40
58	Mickey Cochrane	.40
59	Mickey Mantle	4.00
60	Mike Schmidt	2.00
61	Monte Irvin	.40
62	Nolan Ryan	4.00
63	Pee Wee Reese	.40
64	Phil Rizzuto	.50
65	Ralph Kiner	.40
66	Richie Ashburn	.40
67	Rick Ferrell	.40
68	Roberto Clemente	2.50
69	Robin Roberts	.40
70	Robin Yount	1.00
71	Rogers Hornsby	.75
72	Rollie Fingers	.40
73	Roy Campanella	.75
74	Ryne Sandberg	1.50
75	Tony Gwynn	1.00
76	Satchel Paige	.75
77	Shoeless Joe Jackson	2.00
78	Stan Musial	2.00
79	Ted Williams	3.00
80	Thurman Munson	.75
81	Tom Seaver	1.50
82	Tommy Henrich	.40
83	Tony Perez	.40
84	Tris Speaker	.40
85	Vida Blue	.40
86	Wade Boggs	.50
87	Walter Johnson	.75
88	Warren Spahn	1.00
89	Whitey Ford	.75
90	Willie McCovey	.40
91	Andre Dawson	2.50
92	Andre Dawson	2.50
93	Ernie Banks	4.00
94	Bob Lemon	2.00
95	Cal Ripken Jr.	8.00
96	Cal Ripken Jr.	8.00
97	Carl Yastrzemski	3.00
98	Carlton Fisk	2.50
99	Cy Young	4.00
100	Don Larsen	2.50
101	Don Newcombe	2.00
102	Don Newcombe	2.00
103	Dwight Evans	2.00
104	Elston Howard	2.50
105	Frank Robinson	3.00
106	Frank Robinson	3.00
107	Frank Robinson	3.00
108	Gil McDougald	2.00
109	Hank Greenberg	4.00
110	Harmon Killebrew	4.00
111	Hoyt Wilhelm	2.00
112	Hoyt Wilhelm	2.00
113	Jackie Robinson	5.00
114	Jackie Robinson	5.00
115	Jackie Robinson	5.00
116	Jackie Robinson	5.00
117	Jim Bunning	2.00
118	Joe DiMaggio	6.00
119	Joe Morgan	2.00
120	Johnny Mize	2.50
121	Johnny Mize	2.50
122	Juan Marichal	3.00
123	Ken Griffey Sr.	2.00
124	Larry Doby	2.50
125	Lefty Gomez	2.00
126	Lou Boudreau	2.00
127	Lou Gehrig	6.00
128	Lou Gehrig	6.00
129	Mark McGwire	6.00
130	Mark McGwire	6.00
131	Maury Wills	2.00
132	Mel Ott	3.00
133	Mike Schmidt	5.00
134	Nolan Ryan	8.00
135	Pee Wee Reese	2.00
136	Pee Wee Reese	2.00
137	Nolan Ryan	8.00
138	Richie Ashburn	2.50
139	Roberto Clemente	8.00
140	Roberto Clemente	8.00
141	Robin Roberts	2.00
142	Robin Yount	3.00
143	Roger Clemens	2.00
144	Rollie Fingers	2.00
145	Rollie Fingers	2.00
146	Roy Campanella	3.00
147	Ryne Sandberg	4.00
148	Satchel Paige	4.00
149	Satchel Paige	4.00
150	Stan Musial	5.00
151	Stan Musial	5.00
152	Stan Musial	5.00
153	Ted Williams	6.00
154	Ted Williams	6.00
155	Tom Seaver	3.00
156	Tom Seaver	3.00
157	Wade Boggs	2.50
158	Warren Spahn	3.00
159	Warren Spahn	3.00
160	Joe DiMaggio	6.00
161	Yogi Berra	6.00

Game Used Patch

	NM/M
Some not priced due to scarcity.	
Holofoil:	No Pricing
Production 10	
BB Bert Blyleven/113	25.00
WB Wade Boggs/90	30.00
AD Andre Dawson/100	20.00
TG Tony Gwynn/100	35.00
CK Charlie Keller/55	30.00
ML Mickey Lolich/115	15.00
DM Don Mattingly/176	40.00
GM Gil McDougald/31	25.00
TM Thurman Munson/100	30.00
CR Cal Ripken Jr./17	
FR Frank Robinson/50	30.00
NR Nolan Ryan/96	65.00
TS Tom Seaver/94	30.00
MW Maury Wills/78	25.00
CY Carl Yastrzemski/20	65.00
RY Robin Yount/100	30.00

Jersey

		NM/M
Common Player:		5.00
Production 275 Sets		
Holofoils:		1.5-2X
Production 50		
SA	Sparky Anderson	6.00
SB	Sal Bando	5.00
RB	Ron Blomberg	5.00
BB	Bert Blyleven	5.00
WB	Wade Boggs	8.00
WB1	Wade Boggs	8.00
JB	Jim Bunning	5.00
GC	Gary Carter	6.00
RC	Roberto Clemente	65.00
AD	Andre Dawson	5.00
AD1	Andre Dawson	5.00
JD	Joe DiMaggio	70.00
CD	Chuck Dressen	5.00
KG	Ken Griffey Sr.	5.00
TG	Tony Gwynn	10.00
EH	Elston Howard	8.00
CK	Charlie Keller	15.00
ML	Mickey Lolich	6.00
MM	Mickey Mantle	125.00
JM	Juan Marichal	8.00
RM	Roger Maris	45.00
BM	Billy Martin	8.00
EM	Eddie Mathews	10.00
DM	Don Mattingly	20.00
GM	Gil McDougald	8.00
JO	Johnny Mize	10.00
TM	Thurman Munson	20.00
SM	Stan Musial	25.00
JP	Jim Palmer	8.00
CR	Cal Ripken Jr.	20.00
PR	Phil Rizzuto	15.00
FR	Frank Robinson	8.00
JR	Jackie Robinson	40.00
NR	Nolan Ryan	25.00
TS	Tom Seaver	15.00
OS	Ozzie Smith	10.00
JT	Joe Torre	5.00
TW	Ted Williams	70.00
MW	Maury Wills	5.00
CY	Carl Yastrzemski	15.00
RY	Robin Yount	10.00

Logo Patch

	NM/M
Common Level 1:	5.00
Production 300	
Level 2:	1X
Production 230	
Level 3:	1X
Production 200	
Level 4:	1-1.5X
Production 150	
Level 5:	1-1.5X
Production 125	
Level 6:	1-2X
Production 75	
Level 7:	1.5-2.5X
Production 50	
Level 8:	No Pricing
Production 25	
AL Mel Allen	5.00
LA Luis Aparicio	5.00
RA Richie Ashburn	6.00
WB Wade Boggs	8.00
LB Lou Boudreau	5.00
BR Lou Brock	8.00
JB Jim Bunning	5.00
CA Roy Campanella	8.00
GC Gary Carter	5.00
HC Harry Caray	10.00
RC Roberto Clemente	25.00
TC Ty Cobb	12.00
CO Mickey Cochrane	5.00
AD Andre Dawson	8.00
DD Dizzy Dean	8.00
BD Bill Dickey	5.00
JD Joe DiMaggio	15.00
LD Larry Doby	6.00
DO Bobby Doerr	6.00
DR Don Drysdale	6.00
DU Leo Durocher	5.00
BF Bob Feller	8.00
FI Rick Ferrell	5.00
FI Rollie Fingers	6.00
WF Whitey Ford	6.00
JF Jimmie Foxx	8.00
FF Frankie Frisch	5.00
GE Lou Gehrig	15.00
CG Charlie Gehringer	8.00
BG Bob Gibson	8.00
LG Lefty Gomez	5.00
HG Hank Greenberg	10.00
GR Lefty Grove	6.00
TH Tommy Henrich	5.00
GH Gil Hodges	8.00
RH Rogers Hornsby	5.00
CH Carl Hubbell	5.00
IR Monte Irvin	5.00
JJ Shoeless Joe Jackson	20.00
FJ Ferguson Jenkins	6.00
WJ Walter Johnson	8.00
AK Al Kaline	15.00
HK Harmon Killebrew	15.00
RK Ralph Kiner	8.00
DL Don Larsen	5.00
TL Tommy Lasorda	5.00
BL Bob Lemon	5.00
ML Mickey Lolich	5.00
MI Mickey Mantle	40.00
MA Juan Marichal	6.00
BM Billy Martin	8.00
EM Eddie Mathews	8.00
CM Christy Mathewson	10.00
DM Don Mattingly	20.00
WM Willie McCovey	8.00
JM Johnny Mize	6.00
TM Thurman Munson	10.00
SM Stan Musial	10.00
DN Don Newcombe	5.00
MO Mel Ott	5.00
SP Satchel Paige	10.00
JP Jim Palmer	8.00
TP Tony Perez	5.00
GP Gaylord Perry	5.00
PR Pee Wee Reese	5.00
CR Cal Ripken Jr.	30.00
RI Phil Rizzuto	8.00
RR Robin Roberts	6.00
RO Brooks Robinson	12.00
FR Frank Robinson	8.00
JR Jackie Robinson	12.00
RU Babe Ruth	20.00
NR Nolan Ryan	25.00
RS Ryne Sandberg	20.00
MS Mike Schmidt	20.00
TS Tom Seaver	10.00
SK Bill "Moose" Skowron	5.00
ES Enos Slaughter	5.00
DS Duke Snider	8.00
WS Warren Spahn	10.00
TR Tris Speaker	8.00
JT Joe Torre	5.00
HW Honus Wagner	10.00
WI Hoyt Wilhelm	5.00
TW Ted Williams	20.00
MW Maury Wills	5.00
DW Dave Winfield	6.00
EW Early Wynn	5.00

Signature Black Ink

NM/M

Common Autograph:		15.00
2	Preacher Roe/225	25.00
4	Bob Feller/65	45.00
5	Bob Gibson/50	50.00
6	Harry Kalas/100	45.00
7	Bobby Doerr/100	25.00
8	Cal Ripken Jr./50	165.00
9	Carl Yastrzemski/35	110.00
10	Carlton Fisk/100	45.00
11	Chuck Tanner/150	15.00
12	Cito Gaston/150	15.00
13	Danny Ozark/150	15.00
14	Dave Winfield/80	50.00
15	Davey Johnson/175	15.00
16	Ernie Harwell/100	50.00
17	Dick Williams/150	15.00
18	Don Mattingly/40	100.00
19	Don Newcombe/40	35.00
20	Duke Snider/35	60.00
21	Steve Carlton/150	35.00
22	Felipe Alou/175	20.00
23	Frank Robinson/65	40.00
24	Gary Carter/100	35.00
25	Gene Mauch/225	15.00
26	George Bamberger/225	15.00
28	Gus Suhr/100	30.00
30	Harmon Killebrew/50	70.00
31	Jack McKeon/225	20.00
32	Jim Bunning/100	25.00
33	Jimmy Piersall/212	20.00
35	Johnny Bench/50	75.00
36	Juan Marichal/50	40.00
37	Lou Brock/50	50.00
38	George Kell/40	50.00
39	Maury Wills/40	30.00
41	Mike Schmidt/40	100.00
42	Nolan Ryan/50	135.00
43	Ozzie Smith/65	75.00
44	Eddie Mayo/140	15.00
45	Phil Rizzuto/50	50.00
46	Ralph Kiner/40	45.00
47	Lonny Frey/114	15.00
48	Bill Mazeroski/50	40.00
49	Robin Roberts/40	40.00
50	Robin Yount/40	75.00
52	Roger Craig/150	15.00
55	Tony Perez/40	70.00
56	Sparky Anderson/175	20.00
57	Stan Musial/40	100.00
58	Ted Radcliffe/225	25.00
59	Ted Williams	
60	Tom Seaver/25	70.00
61	Tony Gwynn/65	75.00
62	Tony LaRussa/275	15.00
63	Tony Oliva/150	20.00
64	Tony Pena/150	15.00
66	Whitey Ford/45	65.00
67	Yogi Berra/50	75.00

Signature Blue Ink

NM/M

Common Autograph:		15.00
Some not priced due to scarcity.		
2	Preacher Roe/150	25.00
4	Bob Feller/50	45.00
5	Bob Gibson/50	60.00
6	Harry Kalas/50	50.00
7	Bobby Doerr/50	30.00
8	Cal Ripken Jr./25	200.00
10	Carlton Fisk/50	50.00
11	Chuck Tanner/125	15.00
12	Cito Gaston/125	15.00
13	Danny Ozark/125	15.00
14	Dave Winfield/35	60.00
15	Davey Johnson/150	15.00
16	Ernie Harwell/50	50.00
17	Dick Williams/125	15.00
21	Steve Carlton/100	35.00
22	Felipe Alou/150	20.00
23	Frank Robinson/40	40.00
24	Gary Carter/75	35.00
25	Gene Mauch/150	15.00
26	George Bamberger/150	15.00
28	Gus Suhr/85	30.00
31	Jack McKeon/150	25.00
32	Jim Bunning/60	60.00
33	Jimmy Piersall/150	25.00
35	Johnny Bench/20	90.00
38	George Kell/50	50.00
39	Maury Wills/25	40.00
41	Mike Schmidt/25	80.00
42	Nolan Ryan/50	175.00
43	Ozzie Smith/50	75.00
44	Eddie Mayo/50	20.00
45	Phil Rizzuto/25	60.00

YA	Carl Yastrzemski	12.00
CY	Cy Young	10.00
47	Lonny Frey/75	15.00
48	Bill Mazeroski/25	40.00
49	Robin Roberts/25	40.00
50	Robin Yount/25	75.00
52	Roger Craig/150	15.00
56	Sparky Anderson/150	25.00
57	Stan Musial/25	120.00
58	Ted Radcliffe/150	50.00
62	Tony LaRussa/145	15.00
63	Tony Oliva/125	25.00
64	Tony Pena/115	15.00
67	Yogi Berra/50	70.00

Signature Holofoil

NM/M

Many not priced due to scarcity.

SSA-4	Bob Feller/25	70.00
SSA-5	Bob Gibson/25	60.00
SSA-11	Chuck Tanner/25	15.00
SSA-12	Cito Gaston/100	15.00
SSA-13	Danny Ozark/100	15.00
SSA-15	Davey Johnson/50	20.00
SSA-17	Dick Williams/100	15.00
SSA-22	Felipe Alou/50	30.00
SSA-24	Gary Carter/50	45.00
SSA-45	Phil Rizzuto/25	60.00
SSA-49	Robin Roberts/25	40.00
SSA-50	Robin Yount/25	75.00
SSA-52	Roger Craig/50	20.00
SSA-56	Sparky Anderson/50	30.00
SSA-57	Stan Musial/25	120.00
SSA-62	Tony LaRussa/20	20.00
SSA-63	Tony Oliva/100	25.00
SSA-64	Tony Pena/100	25.00

Signature Red Ink

NM/M

Many not priced due to scarcity.

SSA-14	Dave Winfield/25	65.00
SSA-25	Gene Mauch/25	25.00
SSA-26	George Bamberger/25	30.00

Wood Barrel Autograph

NM/M

Varying quantities produced
Some not priced due to scarcity.

HB	Harold Baines/200	35.00
JB	Johnny Bench/25	120.00
WB	Wade Boggs/200	60.00
SM	Stan Musial/25	185.00
CR	Cal Ripken Jr./25	300.00
NR	Nolan Ryan/25	200.00
RS	Ron Santo/203	45.00
TS	Tom Seaver/25	140.00
BW	Billy Williams/200	35.00

2004 Upper Deck Ultimate Collection

NM/M

Complete Set (222):	
Common Player (1-126):	2.00
Production 675	
Common (127-168):	4.00
Production 525	
Common (169-194):	6.00
Production 299	
Common (195-209, 222):	8.00
Production 199	
Common (210-221):	15.00
Production 75	
Pack (4):	80.00
Box (4):	275.00
1 Al Kaline	4.00
2 Billy Williams	2.00
3 Bob Feller	2.00
4 Bob Gibson	4.00
5 Bob Lemon	2.00
6 Bobby Doerr	2.00
7 Brooks Robinson	3.00
8 Cal Ripken Jr.	10.00
9 Jim "Catfish" Hunter	2.00
10 Eddie Mathews	4.00
11 Enos Slaughter	2.00
12 Ernie Banks	4.00
13 Fergie Jenkins	2.00
14 Gaylord Perry	2.00
15 Harmon Killebrew	4.00
16 Jim Bunning	2.00
17 Joe DiMaggio	6.00
18 Joe Morgan	2.00
19 Juan Marichal	2.00
20 Lou Brock	2.00
21 Luis Aparicio	2.00
22 Mickey Mantle	12.00
23 Mike Schmidt	6.00
24 Monte Irvin	2.00
25 Nolan Ryan	8.00
26 Pee Wee Reese	2.00
27 Phil Niekro	2.00
28 Phil Rizzuto	3.00
29 Ralph Kiner	3.00
30 Richie Ashburn	2.00
31 Robin Roberts	3.00
32 Robin Yount	5.00
33 Rod Carew	2.00
34 Rollie Fingers	2.00
35 Stan Musial	6.00
36 Ted Williams	8.00
37 Tom Seaver	4.00
38 Warren Spahn	4.00
39 Whitey Ford	3.00
40 Willie McCovey	3.00
41 Willie Stargell	3.00
42 Yogi Berra	4.00
43 Adrian Beltre	2.00
44 Albert Pujols	8.00
45 Alex Rodriguez	6.00
46 Alfonso Soriano	3.00
47 Andruw Jones	2.00
48 Andy Pettitte	2.00
49 Aubrey Huff	2.00
50 Barry Larkin	2.00
51 Ben Sheets	2.00
52 Bernie Williams	2.00
53 Bobby Abreu	2.00
54 Brad Penny	2.00
55 Bret Boone	2.00
56 Brian Giles	2.00
57 Carlos Beltran	3.00
58 Carlos Delgado	2.00
59 Carlos Guillen	2.00
60 Carlos Lee	2.00
61 Carlos Zambrano	2.00
62 Chipper Jones	4.00
63 Craig Biggio	2.00
64 Craig Wilson	2.00
65 Curt Schilling	4.00
66 David Ortiz	4.00
67 Derek Jeter	10.00
68 Eric Chavez	2.00
69 Eric Gagne	3.00
70 Frank Thomas	3.00
71 Garret Anderson	2.00
72 Gary Sheffield	3.00
73 Greg Maddux	5.00
74 Hank Blalock	3.00
75 Hideki Matsui	6.00
76 Ichiro Suzuki	6.00
77 Ivan Rodriguez	3.00
78 J.D. Drew	2.00
79 Jake Peavy	2.00
80 Jason Schmidt	2.00
81 Jeff Bagwell	3.00
82 Jeff Kent	2.00
83 Jim Thome	4.00
84 Joe Mauer	2.00
85 Johan Santana	3.00
86 Jose Reyes	3.00
87 Jose Vidro	2.00
88 Ken Griffey Jr.	5.00
89 Kerry Wood	4.00
90 Larry Walker	2.00
91 Luis Gonzalez	2.00
92 Lyle Overbay	2.00
93 Magglio Ordonez	2.00
94 Manny Ramirez	4.00
95 Mark Mulder	2.00
96 Mark Prior	3.00
97 Mark Teixeira	4.00
98 Melvin Mora	2.00
99 Michael Young	2.00
100 Miguel Cabrera	4.00
101 Miguel Tejada	3.00
102 Mike Lowell	2.00
103 Mike Piazza	6.00
104 Mike Sweeney	2.00
105 Nomar Garciaparra	6.00
106 Oliver Perez	2.00
107 Pedro J. Martinez	4.00

108 Preston Wilson	2.00
109 Rafael Palmeiro	4.00
110 Randy Johnson	4.00
111 Roger Clemens	10.00
112 Roy Halladay	2.00
113 Roy Oswalt	2.00
114 Sammy Sosa	6.00
115 Scott Podsednik	2.00
116 Scott Rolen	4.00
117 Shawn Green	2.00
118 Tim Hudson	2.00
119 Todd Helton	3.00
120 Tom Glavine	3.00
121 Torii Hunter	2.00
122 Travis Hafner	2.00
123 Troy Glaus	2.00
124 Vernon Wells	2.00
125 Victor Martinez	2.00
126 Vladimir Guerrero	4.00
127 Aarom Baldiris RC	8.00
128 Alfredo Simon RC	4.00
129 Andres Blanco RC	4.00
130 Jeff Bajenaru RC	4.00
131 Bartolome Fortunato RC	4.00
132 Brandon Medders RC	4.00
133 Brian Dallimore RC	4.00
134 Carlos Hines RC	4.00
135 Carlos Vasquez RC	8.00
136 Casey Daigle RC	4.00
137 Chad Bentz RC	4.00
138 Chris Aguila RC	4.00
139 Chris Saenz RC	4.00
140 Chris Shelton RC	10.00
141 Colby Miller RC	4.00
142 David Crouthers RC	4.00
143 David Aardsma RC	4.00
144 Dennis Sarfate RC	4.00
145 Donnie Kelly RC	4.00
146 Eddy Rodriguez RC	8.00
147 Eduardo Villacis RC	4.00
148 Edwardo Sierra RC	6.00
149 Edwin Moreno RC	4.00
150 Kyle Denney RC	4.00
151 Evan Rust RC	4.00
152 Fernando Nieve RC	4.00
153 Frank Francisco RC	4.00
154 Franklyn Gracesqui RC	4.00
155 Freddy Guzman RC	4.00
156 Greg Dobbs RC	4.00
157 Hector Gimenez RC	4.00
158 Jason Alfaro RC	4.00
159 Jake Woods RC	4.00
160 Andy Green RC	4.00
161 Jason Bartlett RC	8.00
162 Jason Frasor RC	4.00
163 Jeff Bennett RC	4.00
164 Jerome Gamble RC	4.00
165 Jerry Gil RC	4.00
166 Joe Hietpas RC	4.00
167 Jorge Sequea RC	4.00
168 Jorge Vasquez RC	6.00
169 Josh Labandeira RC	6.00
170 Justin Germano RC	6.00
171 Justin Hampson RC	6.00
172 Chris Young RC	30.00
173 Justin Knoedler RC	6.00
174 Justin Lehr RC	6.00
175 Justin Leone RC	10.00
176 Kazuhito Tadano RC	8.00
177 Kevin Cave RC	6.00
178 Lincoln Holdzkom RC	6.00
179 Mike Rose RC	6.00
180 Luis Gonzalez RC	6.00
181 Mariano Gomez RC	6.00
182 Rene Rivera RC	6.00
183 Mike Wuertz RC	8.00
184 Mike Gosling RC	6.00
185 Mike Johnston RC	6.00
186 Mike Rouse RC	6.00
187 Nick Regilio RC	6.00
188 Onil Joseph RC	6.00
189 Orlando Rodriguez RC	6.00
190 Phil Stockman RC	6.00
191 Renyel Pinto RC	10.00
192 Roberto Novoa RC	12.00
193 Roman Colon RC	6.00
194 Ronald Belisario RC	6.00
195 Ronny Cedeno RC	8.00
196 Ryan Meaux RC	8.00
197 Ryan Wing RC	8.00
198 Scott Dohmann RC	8.00
199 Joey Gathright RC	10.00
200 Shawn Camp RC	8.00
201 Shawn Hill RC	8.00
202 Steve Andrade RC	8.00
203 Tim Bausher RC	8.00
204 Tim Bittner RC	8.00
205 Brad Halsey RC	10.00
206 William Bergolla RC	8.00
207 Kameron Loe RC	8.00
208 Jesse Crain RC	10.00
209 Scott Kazmir	25.00

210	Akinori Otsuka/ Auto. RC	60.00
211	Chris Oxspring/ Auto. RC	15.00
212	Ian Snell/Auto. RC	30.00
213	John Gall/Auto. RC	20.00
214	Jose Capellan/ Auto. RC	20.00
215	Yadier Molina/ Auto. RC	40.00
216	Merkin Valdez/ Auto. RC	25.00
217	Ramon Ramirez/ Auto. RC	15.00
218	Rusty Tucker/ Auto. RC	20.00
219	Scott Proctor/ Auto. RC	25.00
220	Sean Henn/Auto.	15.00
221	Shingo Takatsu/ Auto. RC	75.00
222	Kazuo Matsui RC	30.00

Gold

Gold (1-194): 1-2X
Production 50
Gold (195-222): No Pricing
Production 25
Gold 210-221 Production 15

Platinum

Platinum (1-126): No Pricing
Production 10
Platinum (210-221): No Pricing
Production One

Rainbow

Rainbows: No Pricing
Production One Set

Achievement Material
NM/M

	Common Player:	
EB	Ernie Banks/58	25.00
JB	Johnny Bench/68	15.00
YB	Yogi Berra/51	20.00
GB	George Brett/80	25.00
CA	Roy Campanella/51	25.00
RO	Rod Carew/77	15.00
SC	Steve Carlton/72	10.00
OC	Orlando Cepeda/58	10.00
CL	Roger Clemens/86	25.00
RC	Roberto Clemente/66	100.00
JD	Joe DiMaggio/39	100.00
DD	Don Drysdale/62	15.00
BG	Bob Gibson/68	15.00
KG	Ken Griffey Jr./97	25.00
DJ	Derek Jeter/96	40.00
RJ	Randy Johnson/99	15.00
HK	Harmon Killebrew/69	15.00
GM	Greg Maddux/92	20.00
MA	Mickey Mantle/56	200.00
RM	Roger Maris/61	80.00
PM	Pedro J. Martinez/99	15.00
DM	Don Mattingly/85	20.00
MC	Willie McCovey/59	15.00
TM	Thurman Munson/70	15.00
EM	Eddie Murray/77	15.00
JP	Jim Palmer/73	10.00
MP	Mike Piazza/93	20.00
CR	Cal Ripken Jr./82	50.00
BR	Brooks Robinson/64	15.00
FR	Frank Robinson/66	10.00
JR	Jackie Robinson/47	65.00
RS	Ryne Sandberg/84	40.00
MS	Mike Schmidt/80	25.00
TS	Tom Seaver/69	15.00
SS	Sammy Sosa/98	20.00
TW	Ted Williams/42	100.00
CY	Carl Yastrzemski/57	25.00
RY	Robin Yount/82	25.00

All-Stars Signatures
NM/M

Most not priced.

RC	Rod Carew/18	40.00
SM	Stan Musial/24	75.00
BR	Brooks Robinson/15	60.00
CY	Carl Yastrzemski/18	80.00

Bat Barrel Signatures

No Pricing
Production 1-5

Stat Patch
NM/M

Quantity produced listed

5+ Color Patch:		1.5X
JB	Jeff Bagwell/47	25.00
CB	Carlos Beltran/35	35.00
CB1	Carlos Beltran/41	30.00
BE	Johnny Bench/45	50.00

HB	Hank Blalock/29	20.00
GB	George Brett/20	80.00
GB1	George Brett/30	75.00
WC	Will Clark/35	50.00
CL1	Roger Clemens/24	50.00
DD	Don Drysdale/25	50.00
EG	Eric Gagne/55	25.00
VG	Vladimir Guerrero/44	25.00
VG1	Vladimir Guerrero/40	25.00
TG	Tony Gwynn/56	40.00
TG1	Tony Gwynn/25	50.00
DJ	Derek Jeter/32	60.00
DJ1	Derek Jeter/24	60.00
RJ	Randy Johnson/20	40.00
CJ	Chipper Jones/45	25.00
HK	Harmon Killebrew/49	50.00
GM1	Greg Maddux/20	40.00
GM2	Greg Maddux/17	40.00
JM	Juan Marichal/26	30.00
MA	Pedro Martinez/23	35.00
HM	Hideki Matsui/31	120.00
DM	Don Mattingly/35	75.00
PM	Paul Molitor/39	40.00
TM	Thurman Munson/20	75.00
PN	Phil Niekro/23	30.00
PN1	Phil Niekro/23	30.00
RP	Rafael Palmeiro/47	25.00
JP1	Jim Palmer/23	30.00
PI	Mike Piazza/40	40.00
AP	Albert Pujols/43	60.00
AP1	Albert Pujols/51	50.00
MR	Manny Ramirez/45	25.00
JR1	Jim Rice/46	25.00
CR	Cal Ripken Jr./34	100.00
CR1	Cal Ripken Jr./47	75.00
IR	Ivan Rodriguez/35	30.00
IR1	Ivan Rodriguez/25	30.00
SR	Scott Rolen/31	35.00
RS	Ryne Sandberg/40	65.00
RS1	Ryne Sandberg/19	100.00
MS	Mike Schmidt/48	65.00
TS	Tom Seaver/25	50.00
JS	John Smoltz/24	30.00
JS1	John Smoltz/55	25.00
AS	Alfonso Soriano/39	20.00
AS1	Alfonso Soriano/43	20.00
SS1	Sammy Sosa/66	30.00
WS	Willie Stargell/48	50.00
IS	Ichiro Suzuki/56	120.00
MT	Miguel Tejada/34	25.00
JT	Jim Thome/52	25.00
CY	Carl Yastrzemski/44	50.00
RY	Robin Yount/49	50.00
DW	Dave Winfield/37	25.00

Dual Game Patch
NM/M

Production 25 Sets

BB	Carlos Beltran, Jeff Bagwell	40.00
BC	Josh Beckett, Miguel Cabrera	40.00
BG	Lou Brock, Tony Gwynn	75.00
BS	Mike Schmidt, George Brett	100.00
BT	Hank Blalock, Mark Teixeira	40.00
CG	Rod Carew, Tony Gwynn	50.00
CP	Mike Piazza, Gary Carter	50.00
CR	Eric Chavez, Scott Rolen	50.00
FB	Johnny Bench, Carlton Fisk	50.00
FR	Nolan Ryan, Bob Feller	100.00
GC	Will Clark, Mark Grace	40.00
GG	Ken Griffey Sr., Ken Griffey Jr.	75.00
GM	Stan Musial, Bob Gibson	60.00
GS	Mark Grace, Ryne Sandberg	100.00
HF	Rollie Fingers, Jim "Catfish" Hunter	30.00
JC	Roger Clemens, Randy Johnson	75.00
JJ	Chipper Jones, Andruw Jones	40.00
JM	Derek Jeter, Hideki Matsui	125.00
KC	Rod Carew, Harmon Killebrew	60.00
KM	Willie McCovey, Harmon Killebrew	50.00
KS	Sammy Sosa, Ken Griffey Jr.	75.00
LS	Fred Lynn, Ichiro Suzuki	100.00
MG	Greg Maddux, Tom Glavine	50.00

MJ	Chipper Jones, Eddie Mathews	75.00
MM	Kazuo Matsui, Hideki Matsui	120.00
MY	Robin Yount, Paul Molitor	60.00
PC	Will Clark, Rafael Palmeiro	40.00
PR	Scott Rolen, Albert Pujols	100.00
RC	Nolan Ryan, Roger Clemens	100.00
RM	Cal Ripken Jr., Eddie Murray	150.00
RP	Cal Ripken Jr., Jim Palmer	125.00
RR	Jackie Robinson, Pee Wee Reese	150.00
RS	Nolan Ryan, Tom Seaver	100.00
RT	Cal Ripken Jr., Miguel Tejada	75.00
SB	Jim Bunning, Mike Schmidt	75.00
SM	Pedro J. Martinez, Curt Schilling	60.00
ST	Mike Schmidt, Jim Thome	75.00
WM	Don Mattingly, Dave Winfield	75.00
WP	Mark Prior, Kerry Wood	50.00
WS	Billy Williams, Sammy Sosa	60.00
YR	Carl Yastrzemski, Jim Rice	75.00

Dual Legendary Materials
NM/M

Common Player:
Production 50 Sets

BM	Willie McCovey, Ernie Banks	40.00
BR	Roger Maris, Babe Ruth	300.00
CB	Yogi Berra, Roy Campanella	35.00
CM	Roberto Clemente, Thurman Munson	100.00
CS	Duke Snider, Roy Campanella	40.00
DM	Mickey Mantle, Joe DiMaggio	200.00
DW	Joe DiMaggio, Ted Williams	150.00
FD	Don Drysdale, Bob Feller	25.00
MB	Yogi Berra, Thurman Munson	50.00
MC	Mickey Mantle, Roberto Clemente	180.00
MM	Mickey Mantle, Roger Maris	220.00
MW	Mickey Mantle, Ted Williams	200.00
RB	Ernie Banks, Jackie Robinson	75.00
RC	Jackie Robinson, Roy Campanella	75.00
RD	Joe DiMaggio, Babe Ruth	275.00
RM	Babe Ruth, Mickey Mantle	400.00
RP	Jackie Robinson, Satchel Paige	100.00
RW	Roberto Clemente, Willie McCovey	100.00
WM	Eddie Mathews, Ted Williams	125.00

Dual Materials
NM/M

Common Player:
Production 60 Sets

BC	Brooks Robinson, Cal Ripken Jr.	50.00
BM	Yogi Berra, Thurman Munson	40.00
BP	Johnny Bench, Mike Piazza	25.00
BS	Mike Schmidt, George Brett	40.00
CK	Harmon Killebrew, Rod Carew	30.00
CM	Willie McCovey, Will Clark	30.00
ER	Ryne Sandberg, Ernie Banks	60.00
GS	Sammy Sosa, Ken Griffey Jr.	40.00
JC	Randy Johnson, Roger Clemens	40.00

JM	Derek Jeter, Don Mattingly	60.00
MB	Johnny Bench, Thurman Munson	40.00
MC	Don Mattingly, Will Clark	40.00
MP	Mark Prior, Joe Mauer	25.00
MR	Bill Mazeroski, Jackie Robinson	60.00
MT	Kazuo Matsui, Shingo Takatsu	30.00
MY	Robin Yount, Paul Molitor	40.00
PR	Manny Ramirez, Albert Pujols	50.00
RC	Nolan Ryan, Roger Clemens	60.00
RP	Mike Piazza, Ivan Rodriguez	20.00
RR	Brooks Robinson, Frank Robinson	25.00
RT	Thurman Munson, Roy Campanella	30.00
SG	Ken Griffey Jr., Ichiro Suzuki	60.00
SP	Mark Prior, Ben Sheets	10.00
SR	Duke Snider, Pee Wee Reese	30.00
SS	Sammy Sosa, Ryne Sandberg	50.00
TS	Jim Thome, Mike Schmidt	35.00
WM	Don Mattingly, Dave Winfield	40.00
WP	Mark Prior, Kerry Wood	20.00
WR	Kerry Wood, Nolan Ryan	50.00
YR	Manny Ramirez, Carl Yastrzemski	35.00

Dual Materials Signature
NM/M

Production 25 Sets

AB	Luis Aparicio, Ernie Banks	100.00
BB	Wade Boggs, Hank Blalock	80.00
BC	Brooks Robinson, Cal Ripken Jr.	250.00
BF	Carlton Fisk, Johnny Bench	100.00
BG	Carlos Beltran, Ken Griffey Jr.	150.00
BJ	Derek Jeter, Yogi Berra	200.00
BM	Brian Giles, Marcus Giles	35.00
BP	Johnny Bench, Mike Piazza	160.00
BR	Jim Bunning, Robin Roberts	40.00
BS	Brooks Robinson, Scott Rolen	
BT	Hank Blalock, Mark Teixeira	60.00
CB	Hank Blalock, Eric Chavez	50.00
CC	Steve Carlton, Roger Clemens	150.00
CJ	Roger Clemens, Randy Johnson	300.00
CK	Harmon Killebrew, Rod Carew	80.00
CL	Miguel Cabrera, Mike Lowell	75.00
CM	Miguel Cabrera, Carlos Beltran	125.00
DD	Derek Jeter, Don Mattingly	300.00
DG	Gaylord Perry, Don Sutton	50.00
DJ	Jim Rice, Dave Parker	80.00
DS	Ryne Sandberg, Andre Dawson	125.00
DW	Andre Dawson, Billy Williams	50.00
ER	Ryne Sandberg, Ernie Banks	160.00
FC	Bob Feller, Rocky Colavito	75.00
FR	Bob Feller, Nolan Ryan	180.00
GB	Brooks Robinson, George Brett	140.00
GC	Ron Guidry, Steve Carlton	50.00
GG	Ken Griffey Sr., Ken Griffey Jr.	150.00

GM	Mike Schmidt, George Brett	150.00
GP	Rafael Palmeiro, Ken Griffey Jr.	150.00
GR	Greg Maddux, Roger Clemens	300.00
GS	John Smoltz, Eric Gagne	75.00
IV	Ivan Rodriguez, Victor Martinez	65.00
JB	Ernie Banks, Fergie Jenkins	100.00
JC	Randy Johnson, Steve Carlton	125.00
JD	Johnny Podres, Don Sutton	50.00
JG	Randy Johnson, Ken Griffey Jr.	200.00
JM	Chipper Jones, Dale Murphy	150.00
JP	Jim Palmer, Fergie Jenkins	50.00
JR	Cal Ripken Jr., Derek Jeter	500.00
KG	Ken Griffey Jr., Harmon Killebrew	150.00
KN	Kerry Wood, Nolan Ryan	175.00
KT	Scott Kazmir, Shingo Takatsu	75.00
LB	Yogi Berra, Don Larsen	180.00
MB	Johnny Bench, Joe Morgan	80.00
MC	Don Mattingly, Will Clark	125.00
MH	Mark Mulder, Tim Hudson	50.00
MP	Mark Prior, Joe Mauer	80.00
MS	Bill Mazeroski, Ryne Sandberg	150.00
MW	Will Clark, Mark Grace	75.00
MY	Robin Yount, Paul Molitor	150.00
NR	Roger Clemens, Nolan Ryan	300.00
OR	Manny Ramirez, David Ortiz	200.00
OS	Stan Musial, Ozzie Smith	150.00
PC	Will Clark, Rafael Palmeiro	100.00
PN	Phil Niekro, Gaylord Perry	50.00
PS	Johnny Podres, Duke Snider	60.00
RB	Rod Carew, Bill Mazeroski	75.00
RC	Eric Chavez, Brooks Robinson	60.00
RM	Eddie Murray, Cal Ripken Jr.	275.00
RP	Brooks Robinson, Jim Palmer	65.00
RR	Brooks Robinson, Frank Robinson	75.00
RS	Robin Roberts, Steve Carlton	60.00
RT	Miguel Tejada, Cal Ripken Jr.	200.00
SC	Mike Schmidt, Steve Carlton	150.00
SF	Ben Sheets, Bob Feller	50.00
SG	Eric Gagne, Bruce Sutter	75.00
SO	Ben Sheets, Roy Oswalt	50.00
SP	Mark Prior, Ben Sheets	80.00
SR	Brooks Robinson, Mike Schmidt	150.00
SS	Tom Seaver, Ben Sheets	75.00
TB	Tony Gwynn, Brian Giles	75.00
TC	Mark Teixeira, Miguel Cabrera	75.00
WM	Dave Winfield, Don Mattingly	150.00
WO	Orlando Cepeda, Willie McCovey	75.00
WW	Will Clark, Willie McCovey	75.00
YR	Carl Yastrzemski, Manny Ramirez	160.00

Game Materials
NM/M
Common Player: 8.00
Production 99 Sets
EB	Ernie Banks	15.00

JB	Johnny Bench	10.00
WB	Wade Boggs	8.00
GB	George Brett	20.00
LB	Lou Brock	8.00
RC	Rod Carew	8.00
SC	Steve Carlton	8.00
WC	Will Clark	8.00
CL	Roger Clemens	20.00
TC	Ty Cobb	100.00
DD	Don Drysdale	8.00
BF	Bob Feller	8.00
CF	Carlton Fisk	10.00
BG	Bob Gibson	10.00
KG	Ken Griffey Jr.	20.00
TG	Tony Gwynn	10.00
DJ	Derek Jeter	30.00
RJ	Randy Johnson	15.00
AK	Al Kaline	15.00
HK	Harmon Killebrew	10.00
MA	Juan Marichal	8.00
RM	Roger Maris	50.00
ED	Eddie Mathews	15.00
DM	Don Mattingly	25.00
BM	Bill Mazeroski	8.00
WM	Willie McCovey	8.00
PM	Paul Molitor	10.00
TM	Thurman Munson	15.00
EM	Eddie Murray	15.00
SM	Stan Musial	25.00
JP	Jim Palmer	8.00
PI	Mike Piazza	15.00
MP	Mark Prior	10.00
AP	Albert Pujols	25.00
CR	Cal Ripken Jr.	40.00
BR	Brooks Robinson	10.00
FR	Frank Robinson	8.00
JR	Jackie Robinson	40.00
RS	Ryne Sandberg	25.00
MS	Mike Schmidt	15.00
TS	Tom Seaver	10.00
OS	Ozzie Smith	15.00
DS	Duke Snider	10.00
WS	Warren Spahn	15.00
WSt	Willie Stargell	8.00
IS	Ichiro Suzuki	60.00
DW	Dave Winfield	8.00
KW	Kerry Wood	10.00
CY	Carl Yastrzemski	20.00
RY	Robin Yount	20.00

Game Patch
NM/M
Common Player:
Production 75 unless noted.
5 Color +:		1.5X
BA	Jeff Bagwell	25.00
BE	Josh Beckett	15.00
CB	Carlos Beltran	25.00
JB	Johnny Bench	50.00
YB	Yogi Berra	50.00
HB	Hank Blalock	15.00
WB	Wade Boggs	20.00
GB	George Brett	50.00
BU	Jim Bunning/66	30.00
CA	Miguel Cabrera	30.00
RC	Rod Carew	30.00
RO	Rod Carew	30.00
GC	Gary Carter	30.00
EC	Eric Chavez	15.00
WC	Will Clark	30.00
WC1	Will Clark	30.00
RC	Roger Clemens	40.00
RB	Roberto Clemente	200.00
CO1	Rocky Colavito	80.00
JD	Joe DiMaggio	180.00
BF	Bob Feller	40.00
NF	Nellie Fox/55	125.00
GL	Troy Glaus	20.00
KG	Ken Griffey Jr.	50.00
VG	Vladimir Guerrero	30.00
RG	Ron Guidry	30.00
TG	Tony Gwynn	30.00
TH	Todd Helton	25.00
CH	Jim "Catfish" Hunter	30.00
DJ	Derek Jeter	25.00
RJ	Randy Johnson	25.00
RJ1	Randy Johnson	25.00
CJ	Chipper Jones	25.00
HK	Harmon Killebrew	40.00
GM	Greg Maddux	35.00
GM1	Greg Maddux	35.00
MA	Juan Marichal	25.00
PE	Pedro J. Martinez	25.00
HM	Hideki Matsui/44	100.00
KM	Kazuo Matsui	50.00
DM	Don Mattingly	40.00
JM	Joe Mauer	30.00
BM	Bill Mazeroski/55	60.00
WM	Willie McCovey	35.00
PM	Paul Molitor	30.00
MO	Joe Morgan	20.00
TM	Thurman Munson	40.00
MU	Eddie Murray	40.00

SM	Stan Musial	75.00
RP	Rafael Palmeiro	25.00
JP	Jim Palmer	25.00
PI	Mike Piazza	30.00
PO	Johnny Podres	30.00
MP	Mark Prior	20.00
AP	Albert Pujols	50.00
MR	Manny Ramirez	25.00
CR	Cal Ripken Jr.	60.00
BR	Brooks Robinson	40.00
IR	Ivan Rodriguez	40.00
SR	Scott Rolen	25.00
NR	Nolan Ryan/51	50.00
NR1	Nolan Ryan	50.00
NR2	Nolan Ryan	50.00
RS	Ryne Sandberg	50.00
CS	Curt Schilling	25.00
MS	Mike Schmidt	40.00
TS	Tom Seaver	20.00
BS	Ben Sheets	25.00
GS	Gary Sheffield	20.00
OS	Ozzie Smith	40.00
AS	Alfonso Soriano	25.00
SS	Sammy Sosa	35.00
SP	Warren Spahn/62	60.00
WS	Willie Stargell	30.00
IS	Ichiro Suzuki	120.00
MT	Mark Teixeira	15.00
TE	Miguel Tejada	25.00
JT	Jim Thome	35.00
BW	Bernie Williams	20.00
WI	Billy Williams	20.00
DW	Dave Winfield	35.00
KW	Kerry Wood	25.00
CY	Carl Yastrzemski	50.00
RY	Robin Yount	40.00

Gold Glove Signature Materials
No Pricing
Production 1-16

Game Patch Signatures
NM/M
Common Player:
Production 30 Sets
EB	Ernie Banks	75.00
CB	Carlos Beltran	65.00
JB	Johnny Bench	65.00
HB	Hank Blalock	50.00
WB	Wade Boggs	65.00
GB	George Brett	100.00
MC	Miguel Cabrera	65.00
RC	Rod Carew	50.00
EC	Eric Chavez	40.00
WC	Will Clark	60.00
AD	Andre Dawson	40.00
BG	Bob Gibson	50.00
KG	Ken Griffey Jr.	125.00
TG	Tony Gwynn	65.00
DJ	Derek Jeter	200.00
RJ	Randy Johnson	125.00
AK	Al Kaline	75.00
HK	Harmon Killebrew	75.00
GM	Greg Maddux	150.00
MA	Juan Marichal	50.00
DM	Don Mattingly	100.00
JM	Joe Mauer	60.00
WM	Willie McCovey	60.00
PM	Paul Molitor	60.00
MU	Mark Mulder	40.00
EM	Eddie Murray	80.00
SM	Stan Musial	120.00
RO	Roy Oswalt	50.00
JP	Jim Palmer	50.00
PI	Mike Piazza	125.00
MP	Mark Prior	60.00
JR	Jim Rice	50.00
CR	Cal Ripken Jr.	200.00
BR	Brooks Robinson	60.00
FR	Frank Robinson	50.00
NR	Nolan Ryan	150.00
RS	Ryne Sandberg	150.00
MS	Mike Schmidt	125.00
SC	Red Schoendienst	40.00
TS	Tom Seaver	75.00
BS	Ben Sheets	50.00
OS	Ozzie Smith	75.00
MT	Mark Teixeira	50.00
KW	Kerry Wood	75.00
CY	Carl Yastrzemski	100.00
RY	Robin Yount	80.00

Legendary Materials
NM/M
Common Player: 10.00
Production 50 Sets
EB	Ernie Banks	20.00
YB	Yogi Berra	20.00
CA	Roy Campanella	15.00
RC	Roberto Clemente	100.00

TC	Ty Cobb	100.00
JD	Joe DiMaggio	100.00
DD	Don Drysdale	15.00
BF	Bob Feller	10.00
MM	Mickey Mantle	200.00
RM	Roger Maris	60.00
EM	Eddie Mathews	20.00
WM	Willie McCovey	15.00
TM	Thurman Munson	25.00
SM	Stan Musial	40.00
SP	Satchel Paige	50.00
JR	Jackie Robinson	60.00
BR	Babe Ruth	250.00
DS	Duke Snider	15.00
TW	Ted Williams	75.00

Logo Patch Signatures
No Pricing
Production One Set

Game Jersey Signature
NM/M
Quantity produced listed
EB	Ernie Banks/19	85.00
GB	George Brett/21	100.00
TG	Tony Gwynn/20	70.00
HK	Harmon Killebrew/21	75.00
CR	Cal Ripken Jr./21	200.00
BR	Brooks Robinson/23	50.00
MS	Mike Schmidt/18	100.00
CY	Carl Yastrzemski/23	85.00
RY	Robin Yount/20	85.00

Materials Signatures
NM/M
Production 50 Sets
BA	Bobby Abreu	25.00
JE	Jeff Bagwell	50.00
EB	Ernie Banks	75.00
BE	Josh Beckett	25.00
CB	Carlos Beltran	60.00
JB	Johnny Bench	60.00
HB	Hank Blalock	30.00
WB	Wade Boggs	50.00
WB1	Wade Boggs	50.00
GB	George Brett	80.00
LB	Lou Brock	40.00
LB1	Lou Brock	40.00
BU	Jim Bunning	30.00
CA	Miguel Cabrera	40.00
RC	Rod Carew	40.00
RC1	Rod Carew	40.00
SC	Steve Carlton	35.00
SC1	Steve Carlton	35.00
GC	Gary Carter	30.00
GC1	Gary Carter	30.00
JC	Joe Carter	30.00
OC	Orlando Cepeda	35.00
OC1	Orlando Cepeda	35.00
EC	Eric Chavez	30.00
WC	Will Clark	40.00
WC1	Will Clark	40.00
WC2	Will Clark	40.00
WC3	Will Clark	40.00
CL	Roger Clemens	125.00
CL1	Roger Clemens	125.00
CL2	Roger Clemens	125.00
CO	Rocky Colavito	75.00
CO1	Rocky Colavito	75.00
AD	Andre Dawson	30.00
AD1	Andre Dawson	30.00
DE	Dennis Eckersley	30.00
DE1	Dennis Eckersley	30.00
BF	Bob Feller	30.00
RF	Rollie Fingers	30.00
RF1	Rollie Fingers	30.00
CF	Carlton Fisk	40.00
CF1	Carlton Fisk	40.00
EG	Eric Gagne	50.00
NG	Nomar Garciaparra	125.00
NG1	Nomar Garciaparra	125.00
BG	Bob Gibson	50.00
MG	Mark Grace	40.00
KG	Ken Griffey Jr.	100.00
KG1	Ken Griffey Jr.	100.00
VG	Vladimir Guerrero	65.00
RG	Ron Guidry	40.00
TG	Tony Gwynn	50.00
HE	Todd Helton	40.00
TH	Tim Hudson	30.00
FJ	Fergie Jenkins	30.00
DJ	Derek Jeter	150.00
RJ	Randy Johnson	100.00
RJ1	Randy Johnson	100.00
CJ	Chipper Jones	50.00
AK	Al Kaline	50.00
HK	Harmon Killebrew	60.00
DL	Don Larsen	50.00
ML	Mike Lowell	20.00
GM	Greg Maddux	100.00
GM1	Greg Maddux	100.00
JU	Juan Marichal	30.00

DO	Don Mattingly	80.00
JM	Joe Mauer	40.00
JM1	Joe Mauer	40.00
BM	Bill Mazeroski	40.00
MC	Willie McCovey	40.00
PM	Paul Molitor	50.00
PM1	Paul Molitor	50.00
PM2	Paul Molitor	50.00
MO	Joe Morgan	30.00
MU	Mark Mulder	30.00
DM	Dale Murphy	40.00
EM	Eddie Murray	80.00
EM1	Eddie Murray	80.00
RO	Roy Oswalt	25.00
RP	Rafael Palmeiro	50.00
JP	Jim Palmer	30.00
TP	Tony Perez	30.00
GP	Gaylord Perry	25.00
GP1	Gaylord Perry	25.00
PI	Mike Piazza	100.00
PI1	Mike Piazza	100.00
PO	Johnny Podres	30.00
MP	Mark Prior	60.00
MP1	Mark Prior	60.00
MR	Manny Ramirez	75.00
JR	Jim Rice	30.00
CR	Cal Ripken Jr.	180.00
RR	Robin Roberts	30.00
BR	Brooks Robinson	40.00
FR	Frank Robinson	35.00
FR1	Frank Robinson	35.00
IR	Ivan Rodriguez	50.00
SR	Scott Rolen	50.00
NR	Nolan Ryan	120.00
NR1	Nolan Ryan	120.00
NR2	Nolan Ryan	120.00
NR3	Nolan Ryan	120.00
SA	Ryne Sandberg	100.00
MS	Mike Schmidt	75.00
RS	Red Schoendienst	50.00
TS	Tom Seaver	50.00
TS1	Tom Seaver	50.00
BS	Ben Sheets	30.00
BS1	Ben Sheets	30.00
OS	Ozzie Smith	60.00
JS	John Smoltz	50.00
SN	Duke Snider	40.00
SN1	Duke Snider	40.00
AS	Alfonso Soriano	30.00
DS	Don Sutton	30.00
MT	Mark Teixeira	40.00
TE	Miguel Tejada	40.00
TE1	Miguel Tejada/34	40.00
FT	Frank Thomas	60.00
RW	Rickie Weeks	30.00
RW1	Rickie Weeks	30.00
BW	Billy Williams	30.00
DW	Dave Winfield	40.00
DW1	Dave Winfield	40.00
KW	Kerry Wood	50.00
CY	Carl Yastrzemski	75.00
DY	Delmon Young	40.00
DY1	Delmon Young	40.00
RY	Robin Yount	60.00

Quadruple Materials

No Pricing
Production 15 Sets

Super Patch

No Pricing
Production 4-20

Signatures

NM/M

Common Player: 20.00
Production 25 unless noted.
Gold: 1-1.5X
Production 10-25
No pricing 20 or less.
Platinum: No Pricing
Production One Set

LA1	Luis Aparicio	20.00
BE	Johnny Bench	50.00
YB	Yogi Berra	50.00
WB	Wade Boggs	50.00
MC1	Miguel Cabrera	50.00
CW	Rod Carew	40.00
CA1	Steve Carlton	30.00
CL	Roger Clemens	125.00
BF1	Bob Feller	35.00
RF1	Rollie Fingers	25.00
WF	Whitey Ford	50.00
NG	Nomar Garciaparra	100.00
GI	Bob Gibson	40.00
VG	Vladimir Guerrero	50.00
RJ	Randy Johnson	100.00
AK1	Al Kaline	50.00
HK1	Harmon Killebrew	60.00
RK1	Ralph Kiner	40.00
GM	Greg Maddux	80.00
WI	Willie McCovey	40.00
MO	Joe Morgan	25.00
EM	Eddie Murray	75.00
MU	Stan Musial	75.00
JP1	Jim Palmer	30.00
PI	Mike Piazza	100.00
MP	Mark Prior	40.00
KP	Kirby Puckett	65.00
CR	Cal Ripken Jr.	160.00
RR1	Robin Roberts	30.00
BR1	Brooks Robinson	50.00
RY	Ryne Sandberg	75.00
TS	Tom Seaver	50.00
OS	Ozzie Smith	60.00
SN	Duke Snider	40.00
DW	Dave Winfield	35.00
CY	Carl Yastrzemski	75.00

Signatures Tier B

NM/M

Common Player:

BA	Bobby Abreu/25	30.00
LA	Luis Aparicio/25	25.00
CB	Carlos Beltran/25	50.00
BI	Craig Biggio/25	40.00
HB	Hank Blalock/25	35.00
BL	Bert Blyleven/99	20.00
JB	Jim Bunning/99	20.00
MC	Miguel Cabrera/99	30.00
SC	Sean Casey/99	20.00
OC	Orlando Cepeda/25	20.00
EC	Eric Chavez/25	30.00
WC	Will Clark/25	40.00
RC	Rocky Colavito/99	50.00
DC	David Cone/99	20.00
CC	Carl Crawford/99	10.00
AD	Andre Dawson/25	25.00
BD	Bobby Doerr/25	25.00
DE	Dennis Eckersley/25	35.00
BF	Bob Feller/25	30.00
RF	Rollie Fingers/25	25.00
GF	George Foster/25	25.00
EG	Eric Gagne/25	50.00
BG	Brian Giles/99	10.00
MG	Marcus Giles/99	10.00
DG	Dwight Gooden/99	20.00
GG	Rich "Goose" Gossage/99	10.00
GR	Mark Grace/99	30.00
KG	Ken Griffey Sr./69	15.00
RG	Ron Guidry/25	40.00
TH	Travis Hafner/99	20.00
KH	Keith Hernandez/99	15.00
FH	Frank Howard/99	15.00
MI	Monte Irvin/25	25.00
JK	Jim Kaat/99	20.00
AK	Al Kaline/25	60.00
GK	George Kell/99	20.00
HK	Harmon Killebrew/25	60.00
RK	Ralph Kiner/25	40.00
ML	Mike Lowell/99	10.00
SL	Sparky Lyle/25	10.00
FL	Fred Lynn/25	20.00
VM	Victor Martinez/99	20.00
JM	Joe Mauer/99	25.00
BM	Bill Mazeroski/25	50.00
MM	Mark Mulder/99	20.00
DM	Dale Murphy/99	30.00
GN	Graig Nettles/99	15.00
DN	Don Newcombe/25	20.00
RO	Roy Oswalt/99	20.00
AO	Akinori Otsuka/99	20.00
JP	Jim Palmer/99	20.00
DP	Dave Parker/25	25.00
CP	Corey Patterson/99	20.00
TP	Tony Perez/25	35.00
GP	Gaylord Perry/25	25.00
PO	Johnny Podres/25	25.00
RR	Robin Roberts/25	30.00
BR	Brooks Robinson/25	50.00
AR	Al Rosen/99	20.00
SA	Ron Santo/99	25.00
JS	Jason Schmidt/99	20.00
RS	Red Schoendienst/25	30.00
BS	Ben Sheets/99	25.00
SM	John Smoltz/99	25.00
SU	Bruce Sutter/99	25.00
ST	Shingo Takatsu/99	40.00
MT	Mark Teixeira/25	40.00
LT	Luis Tiant/99	10.00
RW	Rickie Weeks/99	20.00
BW	Billy Williams/25	30.00
MW	Maury Wills/25	20.00
DY	Delmon Young/99	25.00
CZ	Carlos Zambrano/99	

Signatures Duals

NM/M

Production 25 Sets

BB	Wade Boggs, Hank Blalock	80.00
BC	Miguel Cabrera, Carlos Beltran	120.00
BG	Carlos Beltran, Ken Griffey Jr.	175.00
BR	Jim Bunning, Robin Roberts	75.00
BS	George Brett, Mike Schmidt	150.00
BT	Hank Blalock, Mark Teixeira	70.00
CB	Hank Blalock, Eric Chavez	50.00
CJ	Roger Clemens, Randy Johnson	300.00
CL	Mike Lowell, Miguel Cabrera	50.00
CR	Eric Chavez, Brooks Robinson	65.00
DW	Billy Williams, Andre Dawson	40.00
EF	Rollie Fingers, Dennis Eckersley	50.00
FR	Bob Feller, Nolan Ryan	160.00
GC	Will Clark, Mark Grace	65.00
GG	Marcus Giles, Brian Giles	40.00
GK	Ken Griffey Jr., Harmon Killebrew	150.00
GS	John Smoltz, Eric Gagne	85.00
IC	Monte Irvin, Orlando Cepeda	50.00
JC	Steve Carlton, Randy Johnson	125.00
JM	Derek Jeter, Don Mattingly	300.00
JP	Jim Palmer, Fergie Jenkins	50.00
JT	Fergie Jenkins, Luis Tiant	50.00
KG	Ken Griffey Sr., Ken Griffey Jr.	175.00
KK	Al Kaline, Harmon Killebrew	80.00
MC	Don Mattingly, Will Clark	125.00
MH	Mark Mulder, Tim Hudson	40.00
MP	Joe Mauer, Mark Prior	60.00
NR	Roger Clemens, Nolan Ryan	400.00
NS	Don Sutton, Don Newcombe	40.00
PC	Rafael Palmeiro, Will Clark	120.00
PN	Phil Niekro, Gaylord Perry	40.00
PR	Jim Rice, Dave Parker	60.00
PS	Ben Sheets, Mark Prior	60.00
RC	Steve Carlton, Robin Roberts	40.00
RJ	Derek Jeter, Cal Ripken Jr.	500.00
RP	Brooks Robinson, Jim Palmer	75.00
SF	Ben Sheets, Bob Feller	40.00
SG	Eric Gagne, Bruce Sutter	60.00
SO	Ben Sheets, Roy Oswalt	40.00
SP	Don Sutton, Gaylord Perry	40.00
TC	Mark Teixeira, Miguel Cabrera	80.00
VM	Miguel Cabrera, Vladimir Guerrero	100.00
WS	Billy Williams, Ron Santo	60.00

Signatures Triple

No Pricing
Production 20 Sets

Signatures Quadruple

No Pricing
Production 10 Sets

Signatures Six

No Pricing
Production 5 Sets

Signatures Eight

No Pricing
Production One Set

Signature Numbers Patch

NM/M

Quantity produced listed

WB	Wade Boggs/26	65.00
LB	Lou Brock/20	50.00
MC	Miguel Cabrera/24	60.00
BF	Bob Feller/19	50.00
EG	Eric Gagne/38	50.00
KG	Ken Griffey Jr./30	120.00
VG	Vladimir Guerrero/27	80.00
DM	Don Mattingly/23	100.00
WM	Willie McCovey/44	60.00
RO	Roy Oswalt/44	30.00
PI	Mike Piazza/31	120.00
MP	Mark Prior/22	60.00
RS	Ryne Sandberg/23	125.00
MS	Mike Schmidt/20	100.00
MT	Mark Teixeira/23	40.00
BW	Billy Williams/26	40.00
DW	Dave Winfield/31	50.00
RY	Robin Yount/19	100.00

2004 Upper Deck USA

NM/M

Complete Factory Set (204): 50.00
Complete Set (200): 25.00
Common Player: .15

1	Jim Abbott	.25
2	Brent Abernathy	.15
3	Kurt Ainsworth	.15
4	Abe Alvarez	.15
5	Matt Anderson	.15
6	Jeff Austin	.15
7	Justin Wayne	.15
8	Scott Bankhead	.15
9	Josh Bard	.15
10	Michael Barrett	.15
11	Mark Bellhorn	.25
12	Buddy Bell	.15
13	Andy Benes	.25
14	Kris Benson	.25
15	Peter Bergeron	.15
16	Rocky Biddle	.15
17	Casey Blake	.15
18	Willie Bloomquist	.15
19	Jeremy Bonderman	.25
20	Jeff Weaver	.15
21	Joe Borchard	.15
22	Rickie Weeks	.50
23	Rob Bowen	.15
24	Milton Bradley	.25
25	Dan Wheeler	.15
26	Ben Broussard	.15
27	Brian Bruney	.15
28	Mark Budzinski	.15
29	Kirk Bullinger	.15
30	Chris Burke	.25
31	Sean Burnett	.15
32	Jeromy Burnitz	.15
33	Pat Burrell	.50
34	Sean Burroughs	.50
35	Paul Byrd	.25
36	Chris Capuano	.25
37	Scott Cassidy	.15
38	Will Clark	.75
39	Chad Cordero	.15
40	Carl Crawford	.25
41	Bobby Crosby	.75
42	Brad Wilkerson	.15
43	Michael Cuddyer	.25
44	Ben Davis	.15
45	Gookie Dawkins	.15
46	Rod Dedeaux	.15
47	R.A. Dickey	.15
48	Ben Diggins	.15
49	Lenny DiNardo	.15
50	Ryan Drese	.15
51	Tim Drew	.15
52	Todd Williams	.15
53	Justin Duchscherer	.15
54	J.D. Durbin	.15
55	Scott Elarton	.15
56	Adam Everett	.15
57	Dan Wilson	.15
58	Steve Finley	.25
59	Casey Fossum	.15
60	Terry Francona	.15
61	Ryan Franklin	.15
62	Ryan Freel	.15
63	John Van Benschoten	.15
64	Nomar Garciaparra	1.00
65	Chris George	.15
66	Jody Gerut	.15
67	Jason Giambi	.40
68	Matt Ginter	.15
69	Troy Glaus	.50
70	Tom Goodwin	.15
71	Mike Gosling	.15
72	Danny Graves	.15
73	Shawn Green	.50
74	Khalil Greene	.75
75	Todd Greene	.15
76	Seth Greisinger	.15
77	Gabe Gross	.15
78	Jeffrey Hammonds	.25
79	Aaron Heilman	.15
80	Paul Wilson	.15
81	Todd Helton	.75

82	Dustin Hermanson	.15
83	Bobby Hill	.15
84	Koyie Hill	.15
85	A.J. Hinch	.15
86	Matt Holliday	.50
87	Ted Wood	.15
88	Ken Huckaby	.15
89	Orlando Hudson	.15
90	Ernie Young	.15
91	Jason Jennings	.25
92	Charles Johnson	.25
93	Jacque Jones	.15
94	Matt Kata	.15
95	Austin Kearns	.25
96	Adam Kennedy	.25
97	Brooks Kieschnick	.25
98	Jesse Crain	.15
99	Scott Kazmir	1.50
100	Billy Koch	.25
101	Paul Konerko	.25
102	Graham Koonce	.15
103	Casey Kotchman	.50
104	Chris Snyder	.15
105	Nick Swisher	.50
106	Gerald Laird	.15
107	Barry Larkin	.50
108	Mike Lamb	.15
109	Tommy Lasorda	.25
110	Matt LeCroy	.15
111	Travis Lee	.25
112	Justin Leone	.15
113	John Vander Wal	.15
114	Braden Looper	.15
115	Shane Loux	.15
116	Ryan Ludwick	.25
117	Jason Varitek	.40
118	Ryan Madson	.15
119	Dave Magadan	.15
120	Tino Martinez	.50
121	Joe Mauer	.50
122	David McCarty	.15
123	Robin Ventura	.25
124	Jack McDowell	.25
125	Todd Walker	.25
126	Mark McGwire	1.50
127	Gil Meche	.15
128	Doug Mientkiewicz	.25
129	Matt Morris	.15
130	Warren Morris	.15
131	Mark Mulder	.50
132	Calvin Murray	.15
133	Eric Munson	.15
134	Mike Mussina	.50
135	Xavier Nady	.15
136	Shane Nance	.15
137	Mike Neill	.15
138	Augie Ojeda	.15
139	John Olerud	.25
140	Gregg Olson	.15
141	Roy Oswalt	.50
142	Jim Parque	.15
143	John Patterson	.15
144	Brad Penny	.15
145	Jay Powell	.75
146	Mark Prior	.15
147	Horacio Ramirez	.15
148	Jon Rauch	.15
149	Jeremy Reed	.25
150	Bob Watson	.15
151	Matt Riley	.15
152	Brian Roberts	.15
153	Dave Roberts	.15
154	Frank Robinson	.15
155	J.C. Romero	.15
156	David Ross	.15
157	Cory Vance	.15
158	Kirk Saarloos	.15
159	Anthony Sanders	.15
160	Dane Sardinha	.15
161	Bobby Seay	.15
162	Phil Seibel	.15
163	Aaron Sele	.15
164	Ben Sheets	.50
165	Paul Shuey	.15
166	Grady Sizemore	.50
167	Reggie Smith	.15
168	John Smoltz	.50
169	Zach Sorensen	.15
170	Scott Spezio	.25
171	Ed Sprague	.15
172	Jason Stanford	.15
173	Dave Stewart	.15
174	Scott Stewart	.15
175	B.J. Surhoff	.15
176	Bill Swift	.15
177	Mike Tonis	.15
178	Jason Tyner	.15
179	Michael Tucker	.15
180	B.J. Upton	.75
181	Eric Valent	.15
182	Ron Villone	.15
183	2000: Team USA Shocks Cuba	.15
184	1984: Abbott halts Japan	.15
185	1996: Berman's Boys Take Third	.15
186	1984: Team USA Takes Second	.15
187	2000: Home Run Heroics	.15
188	1999: Neill's Hit Boosts Team USA	.15
189	1996: High Five for Team USA	.15
190	1992: Garciaparra Makes the Roster	.50
191	2003: USA Rolls to Record	.15
192	1995: Juniors Are Golden In Boston	.15
193	1999: The Streak Goes On	.15
194	1998: Perfect Finish in St. Louis	.15
195	1999: McGwire's Number Retired	1.00
196	2000: Filled with Firsts	.15
197	Red, White and Blue Cardinal	.15
198	2000: Quick Start for Neill	.15
199	1999: Jensen Goes Deep vs. Cuba	.15
200	2000: Mauer on the Mark	.25

Team USA Jersey

		NM/M
Common Player:		4.00
Inserted 1:Factory Set		
KA	Kurt Ainsworth	4.00
BB	Brian Bruney	4.00
CB	Chris Burke	4.00
SB	Sean Burroughs	4.00
JD	Justin Duchscherer	4.00
AE	Adam Everett	4.00
JG	Jason Giambi	6.00
GG	Gabe Gross	4.00
DH	Dustin Hermanson	4.00
MH	Matt Holliday	15.00
GK	Graham Koonce	4.00
GL	Gerald Laird	4.00
JL	Justin Leone	6.00
JM	Joe Mauer	10.00
DM	Doug Mientkiewicz	8.00
EM	Eric Munson	4.00
XN	Xavier Nady	4.00
RO	Roy Oswalt	6.00
MP	Mark Prior	8.00
HR	Horacio Ramirez	4.00
JR	Jon Rauch	4.00
RE	Jeremy Reed	5.00
FR	Frank Robinson	8.00
MR	Mike Rouse	4.00
BS	Ben Sheets	8.00
GS	Grady Sizemore	10.00
DS	Dave Stewart	6.00
JV	John Van Benschoten	4.00
JW	Jeff Weaver	4.00
BW	Brad Wilkerson	4.00

Team USA Signature Black Ink

		NM/M
Common Autograph:		5.00
Signatures Inserted 3:Factory Set		
ABB	Jim Abbott/180	20.00
ABE	Brent Abernathy/120	8.00
AIN	Kurt Ainsworth/360	8.00
ALV	Abe Alvarez/360	10.00
AND	Matt Anderson/360	5.00
AUS	Jeff Austin/360	5.00
BANK	Scott Bankhead/360	5.00
BARD	Josh Bard/350	5.00
BARR	Michael Barrett/360	10.00
BELL	Buddy Bell/81	25.00
BEN	Andy Benes/360	5.00
BENS	Kris Benson/180	15.00
BERG	Peter Bergeron/360	5.00
BLA	Casey Blake/180	10.00
BLO	Willie Bloomquist/175	15.00
BON	Jeremy Bonderman/150	10.00
BOR	Joe Borchard/350	10.00
BRAD	Milton Bradley/360	5.00
BRO	Ben Broussard/210	5.00
BRU	Brian Bruney/360	5.00
BUD	Mark Budzinski/360	5.00
BULL	Kirk Bullinger/360	5.00
BURK	Chris Burke/350	8.00
BU	Sean Burnett/180	5.00
BURN	Jeromy Burnitz/360	15.00
BUR	Pat Burrell/360	15.00
BURR	Sean Burroughs/360	10.00
BYRD	Paul Byrd/360	10.00
CAP	Chris Capuano/150	8.00
CASS	Scott Cassidy/360	5.00
CLA	Will Clark/60	75.00
COR	Chad Cordero/360	5.00
CR	Jesse Crain/180	10.00
CRA	Carl Crawford/60	35.00
CUD	Michael Cuddyer/370	5.00
DAV	Ben Davis/344	5.00
DED	Rod Dedeaux/29	40.00
DIC	R.A. Dickey/180	5.00
DIG	Ben Diggins/180	8.00
DIN	Lenny DiNardo/150	8.00
DRE	Ryan Drese/180	8.00
DREW	Tim Drew/360	5.00
DUCH	Justin Duchscherer/210	8.00
DUR	J.D. Durbin/180	5.00
ELAR	Scott Elarton/180	8.00
EVER	Adam Everett/360	8.00
FIN	Steve Finley/360	10.00
FOSS	Casey Fossum/320	8.00
FRAN	Terry Francona/150	40.00
FRA	Ryan Franklin/360	5.00
FRE	Ryan Freel/360	5.00
GEO	Chris George/360	5.00
GER	Jody Gerut/350	5.00
GIAM	Jason Giambi/60	50.00
GIN	Matt Ginter/179	8.00
GLA	Troy Glaus/120	35.00
GOS	Mike Gosling/150	8.00
DRA	Danny Graves/360	8.00
GR	Shawn Green/150	40.00
GRE	Khalil Greene/180	40.00
GREE	Todd Greene/120	10.00
GREI	Seth Greisinger/360	5.00
GRO	Gabe Gross/150	5.00
HAM	Jeffrey Hammonds/150	10.00
HEIL	Aaron Heilman/350	5.00
HELT	Todd Helton/71	50.00
HERM	Dustin Hermanson/150	5.00
HI	Bobby Hill/360	5.00
HILL	Koyie Hill/150	5.00
HIN	A.J. Hinch/360	5.00
HUCK	Ken Huckaby/360	5.00
HUD	Orlando Hudson/360	10.00
JENN	Jason Jennings/350	8.00
JON	Jacque Jones/150	10.00
KATA	Matt Kata/350	8.00
KAZ	Scott Kazmir/360	30.00
KENN	Adam Kennedy/150	8.00
KIES	Brooks Kieschnick/360	8.00
KOCH	Billy Koch/71	20.00
KON	Paul Konerko/179	15.00
KOO	Graham Koonce/360	8.00
KOTC	Casey Kotchman/150	20.00
LAMB	Mike Lamb/360	5.00
LAR	Barry Larkin/75	75.00
LEC	Matt LeCroy/360	5.00
LEE	Travis Lee/360	8.00
LEO	Justin Leone/150	10.00
LOO	Braden Looper/360	5.00
LOUX	Shane Loux/360	5.00
MAD	Ryan Madson/360	8.00
MAG	Dave Magadan/360	8.00
MART	Tino Martinez/360	20.00
MAU	Joe Mauer/360	35.00
MCC	David McCarty/360	5.00
MCDO	Jack McDowell/60	20.00
MC	Mark McGwire/20	
MEC	Gil Meche/360	5.00
MIE	Doug Mientkiewicz/300	10.00
MOR	Matt Morris/150	5.00
MORR	Warren Morris/360	5.00
MUL	Mark Mulder/180	10.00
MUN	Eric Munson/510	5.00
MURR	Calvin Murray/360	5.00
MUSS	Mike Mussina/360	50.00
NADY	Xavier Nady/360	5.00
NAN	Shane Nance/150	5.00
NEI	Mike Neill/360	5.00
OJE	Augie Ojeda/360	5.00
OLE	John Olerud/360	20.00
OLS	Gregg Olson/180	5.00
OSW	Roy Oswalt/350	15.00
PARQ	Jim Parque/360	5.00
PATT	John Patterson/210	5.00
PEN	Brad Penny/360	5.00
POW	Jay Powell/160	5.00
PRI	Mark Prior/350	40.00
RAM	Horacio Ramirez/150	10.00
RAU	Jon Rauch/359	5.00
REED	Jeremy Reed/180	10.00
RIL	Matt Riley/60	15.00
ROB	Brian Roberts/60	20.00
ROBE	Dave Roberts/360	10.00
ROM	J.C. Romero/360	5.00
ROSS	David Ross/360	5.00
SAAR	Kirk Saarloos/360	5.00
SAND	Anthony Sanders/360	5.00
SAR	Dane Sardinha/360	5.00
SEAY	Bobby Seay/360	5.00
SEI	Phil Seibel/150	8.00
SELE	Aaron Sele/360	10.00
SHE	Ben Sheets/143	25.00
SHU	Paul Shuey/360	5.00
SIZE	Grady Sizemore/160	35.00
SMI	Reggie Smith/360	10.00
SMO	John Smoltz/360	35.00
SNY	Chris Snyder/360	5.00
SPI	Scott Spiezio/360	5.00
SPR	Ed Sprague/360	5.00
STE	Dave Stewart/180	15.00
STEW	Scott Stewart/360	5.00
SUR	B.J. Surhoff/60	30.00
SWIF	Bill Swift/360	5.00
SWI	Nick Swisher/360	5.00
TON	Mike Tonis/350	5.00
TUCK	Michael Tucker/150	10.00
TYN	Jason Tyner/360	8.00
VAL	Eric Valent/360	8.00
VANB	John Van Benschoten/180	10.00
VAN	Cory Vance/360	5.00
VAND	John Vander Wal/360	10.00
VAR	Jason Varitek/360	40.00
VENT	Robin Ventura/360	15.00
VILL	Ron Villone/359	5.00
WALK	Todd Walker/60	20.00
WAT	Bob Watson/150	8.00
WAY	Justin Wayne/150	8.00
WEA	Jeff Weaver/360	10.00
WEEK	Rickie Weeks/360	15.00
WHEE	Dan Wheeler/360	5.00
WILL	Todd Williams/360	5.00
WI	Dan Wilson/360	10.00
WIL	Paul Wilson/360	5.00
WOOD	Ted Wood/330	5.00
YOUN	Ernie Young/360	5.00

Team USA Signature Blue Ink

		NM/M
Common Autograph:		8.00
ABB	Jim Abbott/60	30.00
ABE	Brent Abernathy/120	8.00
AIN	Kurt Ainsworth/120	8.00
ALV	Abe Alvarez/120	8.00
AND	Matt Anderson/110	8.00
AUS	Jeff Austin/120	8.00
BANK	Scott Bankhead/120	8.00
BARD	Josh Bard/100	8.00
BARR	Michael Barrett/120	8.00
BELL	Buddy Bell/29	25.00
BEN	Andy Benes/100	10.00
BENS	Kris Benson/60	25.00
BERG	Peter Bergeron/120	8.00
BLA	Casey Blake/60	20.00
BLO	Willie Bloomquist/51	20.00
BON	Jeremy Bonderman/90	10.00
BOR	Joe Borchard/100	8.00
BOW	Rob Bowen/510	8.00
BRAD	Milton Bradley/120	15.00
BRO	Ben Broussard/150	8.00
BRU	Brian Bruney/60	5.00
BUD	Mark Budzinski/120	8.00
BULL	Kirk Bullinger/120	8.00
BURK	Chris Burke/110	8.00
BU	Sean Burnett/60	10.00
BURN	Jeromy Burnitz/120	15.00
BUR	Pat Burrell/60	15.00
BURR	Sean Burroughs/142	8.00
BYRD	Paul Byrd/120	8.00
CAP	Chris Capuano/90	8.00
CASS	Scott Cassidy/120	8.00
CLA	Will Clark/30	80.00
COR	Chad Cordero/120	8.00
CR	Jesse Crain/60	15.00
CUD	Michael Cuddyer/89	8.00
DAV	Ben Davis/100	8.00
DED	Rod Dedeaux/25	30.00
DIC	R.A. Dickey/60	8.00
DIG	Ben Diggins/35	15.00
DIN	Lenny DiNardo/110	10.00
DRE	Ryan Drese/60	10.00

DREW Tim Drew/120 8.00
DUCH Justin Duchscherer/110 8.00
DUR J.D. Durbin/60 10.00
ELAR Scott Elarton/60 10.00
EVER Adam Everett/120 8.00
FIN Steve Finley/115 15.00
FOSS Casey Fossum/100 8.00
FRAN Terry Francona/40 40.00
FRA Ryan Franklin/120 8.00
FRE Ryan Freel/110 8.00
GAR Nomar Garciaparra/60 75.00
GEO Chris George/120 8.00
GER Jody Gerut/100 8.00
GIAM Jason Giambi/30 50.00
GIN Matt Ginter/42 10.00
GLA Troy Glaus/60 30.00
GOS Mike Gosling/60 10.00
DRA Danny Graves/120 8.00
GR Shawn Green/90 50.00
GRE Khalil Greene/60 10.00
GREE Todd Greene/60 10.00
GREI Seth Greisinger/120 8.00
GRO Gabe Gross/90 8.00
HAM Jeffrey Hammonds/90 10.00
HEIL Aaron Heilman/100 8.00
HELT Todd Helton/65 65.00
HERM Dustin Hermanson/90 10.00
HI Bobby Hill/120 8.00
HILL Koyie Hill/90 8.00
HIN A.J. Hinch/120 8.00
HUCK Ken Huckaby/120 8.00
HUD Orlando Hudson/110 15.00
JENN Jason Jennings/100 8.00
JON Jacque Jones/60 20.00
KATA Matt Kata/100 8.00
KAZ Scott Kazmir/110 35.00
KEAR Austin Kearns/110 20.00
KENN Adam Kennedy/90 8.00
KIES Brooks Kieschnick/120 8.00
KOCH Billy Koch/18 25.00
KON Paul Konerko/52 20.00
KOO Graham Koonce/120 8.00
KOTC Casey Kotchman/60 30.00
LAMB Mike Lamb/120 8.00
LAR Barry Larkin/20 80.00
LAS Tommy Lasorda/30 60.00
LEC Matt LeCroy/120 8.00
LEE Travis Lee/120 8.00
LEO Justin Leone/60 15.00
LOO Braden Looper/120 8.00
LOUX Shane Loux/110 8.00
LUD Ryan Ludwick/450 8.00
MAD Ryan Madson/110 8.00
MAG Dave Magadan/120 8.00
MART Tino Martinez/20 20.00
MAU Joe Mauer/120 35.00
MCC David McCarty/120 10.00
MCDO Jack McDowell/30 20.00
MC Mark McGwire/6
MEC Gil Meche/120 8.00
MIE Doug Mientkiewicz/120 10.00
MOR Matt Morris/90 15.00
MORR Warren Morris/120 8.00
MUL Jack Mulder/110 15.00
MURR Calvin Murray/120 8.00
MUSS Mike Mussina/30 50.00
NADY Xavier Nady/120 8.00
NAN Shane Nance/110 8.00
NEI Mike Neill/110 8.00
OJE Augie Ojeda/119 8.00
OLE John Olerud/120 20.00
OLS Gregg Olson/90 10.00
OSW Roy Oswalt/100 15.00
PARQ Jim Parque/120 8.00
PATT John Patterson/120 8.00
PEN Brad Penny/120 8.00
POW Jay Powell/60 10.00
PRI Mark Prior/108 40.00
RAM Horacio Ramirez/90 8.00
RAU Jon Rauch/100 8.00
REED Jeremy Reed/45 20.00
ROBE Dave Roberts/120 10.00
ROBI Frank Robinson/90 90.00
ROM J.C. Romero/120 8.00
ROSS Dave Ross/120 8.00
SAAR Kirk Saarloos/120 8.00
SAND Anthony Sanders/120 8.00
SAR Dane Sardinha/110 8.00

SEAY Bobby Seay/120 8.00
SEI Phil Seibel/90 8.00
SELE Aaron Sele/120 10.00
SHU Paul Shuey/115 8.00
SIZE Grady Sizemore/60 35.00
SMI Reggie Smith/120 10.00
SMO John Smoltz/120 8.00
SNY Chris Snyder/120 8.00
SOR Zach Sorensen/450 8.00
SPI Scott Spiezio/120 8.00
SPR Ed Sprague/120 8.00
STAN Jason Stanford/450 8.00
STE Dave Stewart/90 10.00
STEW Scott Stewart/119 8.00
SWIF Bill Swift/120 8.00
SWI Nick Swisher/120 20.00
TON Mike Tonis/100 8.00
TUCK Michael Tucker/90 10.00
TYN Jason Tyner/120 8.00
UPT B.J. Upton/120 30.00
VAL Eric Valent/120 8.00
VANB John Van Benschoten/60 20.00
VAN Cory Vance/120 8.00
VAND John Vander Wal/120 8.00
VAR Jason Varitek/100 40.00
VENT Robin Ventura/120 15.00
VILL Ron Villone/120 8.00
WAT Bob Watson/60 10.00
WAY Justin Wayne/120 10.00
WEA Jeff Weaver/120 8.00
WEEK Rickie Weeks/120 15.00
WHEE Dan Wheeler/120 8.00
WILL Todd Williams/90 8.00
WI Dan Wilson/120 10.00
WIL Paul Wilson/110 8.00
WOOD Ted Wood/120 8.00
YOUN Ernie Young/130 10.00

Team USA Signature Red Ink

NM/M
Common Autograph: 10.00
Some not priced due to scarcity.
ABB Jim Abbott/10
ABE Brent Abernathy/20 15.00
AIN Kurt Ainsworth/20 15.00
AND Matt Anderson/30 15.00
AUS Jeff Austin/20 15.00
BARD Josh Bard/50 10.00
BARR Michael Barrett/20 20.00
BEN Andy Benes/15 15.00
BLO Willie Bloomquist/25 25.00
BOR Joe Borchard/50 10.00
BRAD Milton Bradley/20 25.00
BRO Ben Broussard/40 25.00
BRU Brian Bruney/30 15.00
BURK Chris Burke/50 10.00
BURN Jeromy Burnitz/20 25.00
BUR Pat Burrell/29 25.00
BYRD Paul Byrd/20 20.00
CRO Bobby Crosby/60 50.00
CUD Michael Cuddyer/40 10.00
DAV Ben Davis/50 10.00
DIN Lenny DiNardo/40 10.00
EVER Adam Everett/20 15.00
FIN Steve Finley/25 25.00
FOSS Casey Fossum/42 10.00
FRE Ryan Freel/30 15.00
GAR Nomar Garciaparra/30 125.00
GER Jody Gerut/10 10.00
GLA Troy Glaus/20 60.00
GOS Mike Gosling/40 10.00
HEIL Aaron Heilman/50 10.00
HIN A.J. Hinch/15 15.00
HUD Orlando Hudson/25 10.00
JENN Jason Jennings/50 15.00
JON Jacque Jones/40 20.00
KATA Matt Kata/15 15.00
KAZ Scott Kazmir/20 75.00
KEAR Austin Kearns/30 35.00
KON Paul Konerko/23 25.00
KOO Graham Koonce/20 15.00
KOTC Casey Kotchman/40 35.00
LEC Matt LeCroy/20 15.00
LEE Travis Lee/20 15.00
LEO Justin Leone/40 20.00
LOUX Shane Loux/30 15.00
LUD Ryan Ludwick/30 10.00
MAD Ryan Madson/30 10.00
MART Tino Martinez/40 40.00
MAU Joe Mauer/65 65.00
MCC David McCarty/25 25.00
MIE Doug Mientkiewicz/20 25.00

NADY Xavier Nady/20 15.00
NAN Shane Nance/40 10.00
NEI Mike Neill/30 15.00
OSW Roy Oswalt/50 20.00
PARQ Jim Parque/20 15.00
PATT John Patterson/20 15.00
PEN Brad Penny/30 15.00
PRI Mark Prior/48 60.00
RAU Jon Rauch/53 10.00
REED Jeremy Reed/25 25.00
ROM J.C. Romero/20 15.00
SAR Dane Sardinha/30 15.00
SIZE Grady Sizemore/30 40.00
SMO John Smoltz/20 65.00
SOR Zach Sorensen/50 10.00
SPR Ed Sprague/20 15.00
STAN Jason Stanford/50 10.00
STE Dave Stewart/30 25.00
SWI Nick Swisher/30 40.00
TON Mike Tonis/50 25.00
UPT B.J. Upton/30 40.00
VAR Jason Varitek/30 70.00
VENT Robin Ventura/20 25.00
WAT Bob Watson/30 15.00
WAY Justin Wayne/40 10.00
WEA Jeff Weaver/20 25.00
WEEK Rickie Weeks/20 25.00
WILL Todd Williams/50 10.00
WIL Paul Wilson/30 15.00
WOOD Ted Wood/30 15.00
YOUN Ernie Young/50 10.00

Team USA Signature Green Ink

No Pricing
Production 1-3

2004 Upper Deck Vintage

ROGER CLEMENS
HOUSTON ASTROS • PITCHER

NM/M
Complete Set (450):
Common Player: .15
Common SP (301-315): .50
Inserted 1:5
Common SP (316-325): .40
Inserted 1:7
Common SP (326-350): .40
Inserted 1:5
Common 3D SP (351-440): 2.00
Inserted 1:12
Old Judge (441-450) found in bonus packs.
Pack (8): 2.50
Box (24 + 1 bonus pack): 50.00
1 Albert Pujols 1.50
2 Carlos Delgado .50
3 Todd Helton .50
4 Nomar Garciaparra 1.50
5 Vladimir Guerrero .75
6 Alfonso Soriano .75
7 Alex Rodriguez 1.50
8 Jason Giambi .75
9 Derek Jeter 2.00
10 Pedro J. Martinez .75
11 Ivan Rodriguez .50
12 Mark Prior 1.00
13 Marquis Grissom .15
14 Barry Zito .25
15 Alex Cintron .15
16 Wade Miller .15
17 Eric Chavez .25
18 Matt Clement .15
19 Orlando Cabrera .15
20 Odalis Perez .15
21 Lance Berkman .25
22 Keith Foulke .15
23 Shawn Green .25
24 Byung-Hyun Kim .15
25 Geoff Jenkins .25
26 Torii Hunter .40
27 Richard Hidalgo .15

28 Edgar Martinez .25
29 Placido Polanco .15
30 Brad Lidge .15
31 Alex Escobar .15
32 Garret Anderson .25
33 Larry Walker .25
34 Ken Griffey Jr. 1.00
35 Junior Spivey .15
36 Carlos Beltran .25
37 Bartolo Colon .15
38 Ichiro Suzuki 1.00
39 Ramon Ortiz .15
40 Roy Oswalt .25
41 Mike Piazza 1.00
42 Benito Santiago .15
43 Mike Mussina .50
44 Jeff Kent .25
45 Curt Schilling .50
46 Adam Dunn .40
47 Mike Sweeney .15
48 Chipper Jones 1.00
49 Frank Thomas .50
50 Kerry Wood .50
51 Rod Beck .15
52 Brian Giles .25
53 Hank Blalock .25
54 Andruw Jones .50
55 Dmitri Young .15
56 Juan Pierre .15
57 Jacque Jones .15
58 Phil Nevin .15
59 Rocco Baldelli .25
60 Greg Maddux 1.00
61 Eric Gagne .25
62 Tim Hudson .25
63 Brian Lawrence .15
64 Sammy Sosa 1.00
65 Corey Koskie .15
66 Bobby Abreu .25
67 Preston Wilson .15
68 Jay Gibbons .15
69 Dontrelle Willis .25
70 Richie Sexson .40
71 Kevin Millwood .25
72 Randy Johnson .75
73 Jack Cust .15
74 Randy Wolf .15
75 Johan Santana .15
76 Magglio Ordonez .25
77 Sean Casey .15
78 Billy Wagner .25
79 Javier Vazquez .15
80 Jorge Posada .40
81 Jason Schmidt .15
82 Bret Boone .25
83 Jeff Bagwell .50
84 Rickie Weeks .25
85 Troy Percival .15
86 Jose Vidro .15
87 Freddy Garcia .15
88 Manny Ramirez .50
89 John Smoltz .25
90 Moises Alou .25
91 Ugueth Urbina .15
92 Bobby Hill .15
93 Marcus Giles .25
94 Aramis Ramirez .25
95 Brad Wilkerson .15
96 Ray Durham .15
97 David Wells .15
98 Paul LoDuca .15
99 Danny Graves .15
100 Jason Kendall .25
101 Carlos Lee .25
102 Rafael Furcal .25
103 Mike Lowell .15
104 Kevin Brown .25
105 Vicente Padilla .15
106 Miguel Tejada .40
107 Bernie Williams .40
108 Octavio Dotel .15
109 Steve Finley .15
110 Lyle Overbay .15
111 Delmon Young .25
112 Bo Hart .15
113 Jason Lane .15
114 Matt Roney .15
115 Brian Roberts .15
116 Tom Glavine .25
117 Rich Aurilia .15
118 Adam Kennedy .15
119 Hee Seop Choi .15
120 Trot Nixon .15
121 Gary Sheffield .40
122 Jay Payton .15
123 Brad Penny .25
124 Garrett Atkins .25
125 Aubrey Huff .15
126 Juan Gonzalez .40
127 Jason Jennings .15
128 Luis Gonzalez .25
129 Vinny Castilla .15
130 Esteban Loaiza .15
131 Erubiel Durazo .15

132	Eric Hinske	.15
133	Scott Rolen	.75
134	Craig Biggio	.25
135	Tim Wakefield	.15
136	Darin Erstad	.25
137	Denny Stark	.15
138	Ben Sheets	.25
139	Hideo Nomo	.40
140	Derrek Lee	.25
141	Matt Mantei	.15
142	Reggie Sanders	.15
143	Jose Guillen	.15
144	Joe Mays	.15
145	Jimmy Rollins	.25
146	Juan Encarnacion	.15
147	Joe Crede	.15
148	Aaron Guiel	.15
149	Mark Mulder	.25
150	Travis Lee	.15
151	Josh Phelps	.15
152	Michael Young	.15
153	Paul Konerko	.15
154	John Lackey	.15
155	Damian Moss	.15
156	Javy Lopez	.25
157	Joe Borowski	.15
158	Jose Cruz Jr.	.15
159	Ramon Hernandez	.15
160	Raul Ibanez	.15
161	Adrian Beltre	.15
162	Bobby Higginson	.15
163	Jorge Julio	.15
164	Miguel Batista	.15
165	Luis Castillo	.15
166	Aaron Harang	.15
167	Ken Harvey	.15
168	Rocky Biddle	.15
169	Mariano Rivera	.25
170	Matt Morris	.15
171	Laynce Nix	.15
172	Mike Maroth	.15
173	Francisco Rodriguez	.15
174	Livan Hernandez	.15
175	Aaron Heilman	.15
176	Nick Johnson	.15
177	Woody Williams	.15
178	Joe Kennedy	.15
179	Jesse Foppert	.15
180	Ryan Franklin	.15
181	Endy Chavez	.15
182	Chin-Hui Tsao	.15
183	Todd Walker	.15
184	Edgardo Alfonzo	.15
185	Edgar Renteria	.15
186	Matt LeCroy	.15
187	Carl Everett	.15
188	Jeff Conine	.15
189	Jason Varitek	.15
190	Russ Ortiz	.15
191	Melvin Mora	.15
192	Mark Buehrle	.15
193	Bill Mueller	.15
194	Miguel Cabrera	.25
195	Carlos Zambrano	.15
196	Jose Valverde	.15
197	Danys Baez	.15
198	Mike MacDougal	.15
199	Zach Day	.15
200	Roy Halladay	.25
201	Jerome Williams	.15
202	Josh Fogg	.15
203	Mark Kotsay	.15
204	Pat Burrell	.40
205	A.J. Pierzynski	.15
206	Fred McGriff	.25
207	Brandon Larson	.15
208	Robb Quinlan	.15
209	David Ortiz	.15
210	A.J. Burnett	.15
211	John Vander Wal	.15
212	Jim Thome	.75
213	Matt Kata	.15
214	Kip Wells	.15
215	Scott Podsednik	.40
216	Rickey Henderson	.25
217	Travis Hafner	.15
218	Tony Batista	.15
219	Robert Fick	.15
220	Derek Lowe	.25
221	Ryan Klesko	.25
222	Joe Beimel	.15
223	Doug Mientkiewicz	.15
224	Angel Berroa	.15
225	Adam Eaton	.15
226	C.C. Sabathia	.15
227	Wilfredo Ledezma	.15
228	Jason Johnson	.15
229	Ryan Wagner	.15
230	Al Leiter	.15
231	Joel Pineiro	.15
232	Jason Isringhausen	.15
233	John Olerud	.25
234	Ron Calloway	.15
235	Jose Reyes	.40

236	J.D. Drew	.15
237	Jared Sandberg	.15
238	Gil Meche	.15
239	Jose Contreras	.15
240	Eric Milton	.15
241	Jason L. Phillips	.15
242	Luis Ayala	.15
243	Bobby Kielty	.15
244	Jose Lima	.15
245	Brooks Kieschnick	.15
246	Xavier Nady	.15
247	Dan Haren	.15
248	Victor Zambrano	.15
249	Kelvim Escobar	.15
250	Oliver Perez	.15
251	Jamie Moyer	.15
252	Orlando Hudson	.15
253	Danny Kolb	.15
254	Jake Peavy	.15
255	Kris Benson	.15
256	Roger Clemens	1.50
257	Jim Edmonds	.40
258	Rafael Palmeiro	.50
259	Jae Weong Seo	.15
260	Chase Utley	.15
261	Rich Harden	.15
262	Mark Teixeira	.25
263	Johnny Damon	.25
264	Luis Matos	.15
265	Shigetoshi Hasegawa	.15
266	Alfredo Amezaga	.15
267	Tim Worrell	.15
268	Kazuhisa Ishii	.15
269	Miguel Ojeda	.15
270	Kazuhiro Sasaki	.15
271	Hideki Matsui	2.00
272	Troy Glaus	.40
273	Michael Tucker	.15
274	Lew Ford	.15
275	Brian Jordan	.15
276	David Eckstein	.15
277	Robby Hammock	.15
278	Corey Patterson	.25
279	Wes Helms	.15
280	Jermaine Dye	.15
281	Cliff Floyd	.15
282	Dustan Mohr	.15
283	Kevin Mench	.15
284	Ellis Burks	.15
285	Jerry Hairston Jr.	.15
286	Tim Salmon	.25
287	Omar Vizquel	.25
288	Andy Pettitte	.40
289	Guillermo Mota	.15
290	Tino Martinez	.15
291	Lance Carter	.15
292	Francisco Cordero	.15
293	Robb Nen	.15
294	Mike Cameron	.15
295	Jhonny Peralta	.15
296	Braden Looper	.15
297	Jarrod Washburn	.15
298	Mark Prior	.50
299	Alfonso Soriano	.25
300	Rocco Baldelli	.25
301	Pedro J. Martinez	1.50
302	Mark Prior	2.00
303	Barry Zito	.75
304	Roger Clemens	2.50
305	Randy Johnson	1.50
306	Roy Halladay	.50
307	Hideo Nomo	.75
308	Roy Oswalt	.50
309	Kerry Wood	1.00
310	Dontrelle Willis	.75
311	Mark Mulder	.50
312	Brandon Webb	.50
313	Mike Mussina	.75
314	Curt Schilling	.75
315	Tim Hudson	.75
316	Dontrelle Willis	.75
317	Juan Pierre	.40
318	Hideki Matsui	4.00
319	Andy Pettitte	.75
320	Mike Mussina	.75
321	Roger Clemens	2.50
322	Alex Gonzalez	.40
323	Brad Penny	.40
324	Ivan Rodriguez	.75
325	Josh Beckett	1.00
326	Aaron Boone	.40
327	Jeff Suppan	.40
328	Shea Hillenbrand	.40
329	Jeromy Burnitz	.40
330	Sidney Ponson	.40
331	Rondell White	.50
332	Shannon Stewart	.40
333	Armando Benitez	.40
334	Roberto Alomar	1.00
335	Raul Mondesi	.50
336	Morgan Ensberg	.40
337	Milton Bradley	.40
338	Brandon Webb	.50
339	Marlon Byrd	.40

340	Carlos Pena	.40
341	Brandon Phillips	.40
342	Josh Beckett	1.00
343	Eric Munson	.40
344	Brett Myers	.40
345	Austin Kearns	1.00
346	Jody Gerut	.40
347	Vernon Wells	.50
348	Jeff Duncan	.40
349	Sean Burroughs	.40
350	Jeremy Bonderman	.40
351	Hideki Matsui	15.00
352	Jason Giambi	8.00
353	Alfonso Soriano	6.00
354	Derek Jeter	15.00
355	Aaron Boone	3.00
356	Jorge Posada	5.00
357	Bernie Williams	5.00
358	Manny Ramirez	5.00
359	Nomar Garciaparra	12.00
360	Johnny Damon	3.00
361	Jason Varitek	2.50
362	Carlos Delgado	5.00
363	Vernon Wells	4.00
364	Jay Gibbons	4.00
365	Tony Batista	2.00
366	Rocco Baldelli	5.00
367	Aubrey Huff	2.00
368	Carlos Beltran	4.00
369	Mike Sweeney	3.00
370	Magglio Ordonez	4.00
371	Frank Thomas	6.00
372	Carlos Lee	2.00
373	Roberto Alomar	4.00
374	Jacque Jones	2.00
375	Torii Hunter	4.00
376	Milton Bradley	2.00
377	Travis Hafner	2.00
378	Jody Gerut	2.00
379	Dmitri Young	2.00
380	Carlos Pena	2.00
381	Ichiro Suzuki	10.00
382	Bret Boone	3.00
383	Edgar Martinez	3.00
384	Eric Chavez	3.00
385	Miguel Tejada	3.00
386	Erubiel Durazo	2.00
387	Jose Guillen	2.00
388	Garret Anderson	3.00
389	Troy Glaus	4.00
390	Alex Rodriguez	10.00
391	Rafael Palmeiro	5.00
392	Hank Blalock	4.00
393	Mark Teixeira	4.00
394	Gary Sheffield	4.00
395	Andruw Jones	5.00
396	Chipper Jones	8.00
397	Javy Lopez	3.00
398	Marcus Giles	2.00
399	Rafael Furcal	3.00
400	Jim Thome	5.00
401	Bobby Abreu	3.00
402	Pat Burrell	4.00
403	Mike Lowell	3.00
404	Ivan Rodriguez	5.00
405	Derrek Lee	3.00
406	Miguel Cabrera	5.00
407	Vladimir Guerrero	6.00
408	Orlando Cabrera	2.00
409	Jose Vidro	2.00
410	Mike Piazza	8.00
411	Cliff Floyd	3.00
412	Albert Pujols	15.00
413	Scott Rolen	6.00
414	Jim Edmonds	4.00
415	Edgar Renteria	3.00
416	Lance Berkman	3.00
417	Jeff Bagwell	5.00
418	Jeff Kent	3.00
419	Richard Hidalgo	2.00
420	Morgan Ensberg	2.00
421	Sammy Sosa	10.00
422	Moises Alou	3.00
423	Ken Griffey Jr.	10.00
424	Adam Dunn	4.00
425	Austin Kearns	4.00
426	Richie Sexson	4.00
427	Geoff Jenkins	3.00
428	Brian Giles	3.00
429	Reggie Sanders	2.00
430	Rich Aurilia	2.00
431	Jose Cruz Jr.	2.00
432	Shawn Green	3.00
433	Jeromy Burnitz	2.00
434	Luis Gonzalez	3.00
435	Todd Helton	5.00
436	Preston Wilson	2.00
437	Larry Walker	3.00
438	Ryan Klesko	3.00
439	Phil Nevin	2.00
440	Sean Burroughs	2.00
441	Sammy Sosa	3.00
442	Albert Pujols	4.00
443	Magglio Ordonez	.50
444	Vladimir Guerrero	1.50
445	Todd Helton	1.00
446	Jason Giambi	1.50
447	Ichiro Suzuki	3.00
448	Alex Rodriguez	3.00
449	Carlos Delgado	.75
450	Manny Ramirez	1.00

Black & White

Cards (1-300):	1-2X
Inserted 1:6	
SP's (301-325):	1-2X
Inserted 1:24	
SP's (326-350):	1-2X
Inserted 1:20	
B/W Color Variations:	6-10X
Inserted 1:48	

Old Judge

HIDEKI MATSUI, OF
NEW YORK YANKEES
THE UPPER DECK COMPANY, LLC

	NM/M
Complete Set (20):	15.00
Common Player:	.40
Inserted 3:bonus pack.	
Blue Back:	1-2X
Inserted 1:4 bonus packs.	
Red Back:	2-3X
Inserted 1:12 bonus packs.	

11	Randy Johnson	1.50
12	Pedro J. Martinez	1.50
13	Mark Prior	2.00
14	Barry Zito	.50
15	Roy Oswalt	.40
16	Roy Halladay	.50
17	Curt Schilling	.75
18	Mike Mussina	.75
19	Kevin Brown	.40
20	Roger Clemens	2.50
21	Eric Gagne	.50
22	Mariano Rivera	.50
23	Mike Piazza	2.00
24	Jorge Posada	.75
25	Jeff Kent	.50
26	Alfonso Soriano	1.00
27	Scott Rolen	1.00
28	Eric Chavez	.50
29	Edgar Renteria	.40
30	Hideki Matsui	4.00

Stellar Signatures

		NM/M
Inserted 1:600		
HM	Hideki Matsui	300.00
MP	Mike Piazza	150.00
AR	Alex Rodriguez	100.00
TS	Tom Seaver	50.00
IS	Ichiro Suzuki	200.00
CY	C. Yastrzemski/125	75.00
BZ	Barry Zito	40.00

Stellar Stat Men

		NM/M
Common Player:		4.00
Inserted 1:24		
1	Jose Reyes	6.00
2	Bo Hart	8.00
3	Hideki Matsui	30.00
4	Dontrelle Willis	6.00
5	Rocco Baldelli	6.00
6	Ichiro Suzuki	20.00
7	Mike Lowell	6.00
8	Derek Jeter	20.00

9	Ken Griffey Jr.	15.00
10	Sammy Sosa	12.00
11	Kerry Wood	10.00
12	Chipper Jones	6.00
13	Alfonso Soriano	8.00
14	Khalil Greene	6.00
15	Jim Thome	8.00
16	Rafael Furcal	5.00
17	Andrew Brown	4.00
18	Mark Prior	10.00
19	Barry Zito	6.00
20	Al Leiter	4.00
21	Carlos Delgado	6.00
22	Pedro J. Martinez	8.00
23	Alex Rodriguez	10.00
24	Lance Berkman	5.00
25	Jeff Bagwell	6.00
26	Bernie Williams	6.00
27	Hideo Nomo	8.00
28	Randy Johnson	8.00
29	Curt Schilling	8.00
30	Mike Piazza	10.00
31	Albert Pujols	12.00
32	Joe DiMaggio	100.00
33	Ted Williams	60.00
34	Mickey Mantle	100.00
35	Mike Mussina	8.00
36	Rich Harden	5.00
37	Roy Oswalt	4.00
38	Torii Hunter	8.00
39	Jorge Posada	6.00
40	Troy Glaus	6.00
41	Manny Ramirez	6.00
42	Roy Halladay	5.00

Timeless Teams

NM/M

Common Quad: 15.00
Inserted 1:400
Production 175 Sets

1	Derek Jeter, Jason Giambi, Alfonso Soriano, Hideki Matsui	90.00
2	Randy Johnson, Luis Gonzalez, Steve Finley, Curt Schilling	20.00
4	Johnny Damon, Manny Ramirez, Nomar Garciaparra, Trot Nixon	35.00
5	Alex Rodriguez, Rafael Palmeiro, Mark Teixeira, Hank Blalock	35.00
6	Roberto Alomar, Frank Thomas, Magglio Ordonez, Carl Everett	20.00
7	Shannon Stewart, Torii Hunter, Jacque Jones, Doug Mientkiewicz	15.00
8	Jim Edmonds, Scott Rolen, J.D. Drew, Albert Pujols	40.00
9	Bret Boone, John Olerud, Mike Cameron, Ichiro Suzuki	45.00
10	Jeff Bagwell, Craig Biggio, Jeff Kent, Lance Berkman	20.00
11	Tim Salmon, Garret Anderson, Darin Erstad, Troy Glaus	15.00
12	Bernie Williams, Alfonso Soriano, Jorge Posada, Hideki Matsui	85.00
13	Carlos Beltran, Michael Tucker, Mike Sweeney, Brent Mayne	15.00
14	Jim Thome, Mike Lieberthal, Bobby Abreu, Marlon Byrd	30.00
15	Ivan Rodriguez, Juan Encarnacion, Mike Lowell, Miguel Cabrera	25.00
16	Sammy Sosa, Kerry Wood, Moises Alou, Corey Patterson	50.00
17	Andres Galarraga, Edgardo Alfonzo, Jose Cruz Jr., Rich Aurilia	15.00
18	Derek Jeter, Bernie Williams, Alfonso Soriano, Hideki Matsui	90.00

2004 Upper Deck Yankees Classics

NM/M

Complete Set (90):		20.00
Common Player:		.25
Pack (5):		6.00
Box (24):		120.00
1	Bill "Moose" Skowron	.50
2	Bob Cerv	.25
3	Bobby Murcer	.50
4	Bobby Richardson	.25
5	Brian Doyle	.25
6	Bucky Dent	.25
7	Chris Chambliss	.25
8	Clete Boyer	.25
9	Dave Kingman	.25
10	Dave Righetti	.25
11	Dave Winfield	.50
12	David Cone	.25
13	Red Ruffing	.25
14	Dock Ellis	.25
15	Don Baylor	.25
16	Don Larsen	.75
17	Don Mattingly	1.50
18	Dwight Gooden	.40
19	Ed Figueroa	.25
20	Joe Torre	.50
21	Darryl Strawberry	.40
22	Horace Clarke	.25
23	Gaylord Perry	.25
24	Phil Linz	.25
25	Gil McDougald	.25
26	Rich "Goose" Gossage	.25
27	Graig Nettles	.25
28	Hank Bauer	.25
29	Jack Clark	.25
30	Don Gullett	.25
31	Jim Abbott	.25
32	Jim Bouton	.25
33	Jim Kaat	.40
34	Jim Leyritz	.25
35	Jim Wynn	.25
36	Jimmy Key	.25
37	Joe Niekro	.25
38	Joe Pepitone	.25
39	John Wetteland	.25
40	Ken Griffey Sr.	.25
41	Felipe Alou	.25
42	Kevin Maas	.25
43	Lindy McDaniel	.25
44	Lou Piniella	.50
45	Luis Tiant	.25
46	Mel Stottlemyre	.25
47	Mickey Rivers	.25
48	Oscar Gamble	.25
49	Pat Dobson	.25
50	Paul O'Neill	.50
51	Phil Niekro	.25
52	Phil Rizzuto	.75
53	Doc Medich	.25
54	Rick Cerone	.25
55	Ron Blomberg	.25
56	Ron Guidry	.50
57	Roy White	.25
58	Rudy May	.25
59	Sam McDowell	.25
60	Sparky Lyle	.25
61	Steve Balboni	.25
62	Steve Sax	.25
63	Jerry Coleman	.25
64	Tom Tresh	.25
65	Tommy John	.25
66	Tony Kubek	.50
67	Wade Boggs	.50
68	Whitey Ford	.75
69	Willie Randolph	.25
70	Yogi Berra	1.00
71	Babe Ruth	3.00
72	Bill Dickey	.50
73	Billy Martin	.50
74	Bob Meusel	.25
75	Casey Stengel	.50
76	Elston Howard	.25
77	Jim "Catfish" Hunter	.50
78	Joe DiMaggio	2.00
79	Lefty Gomez	.50
80	Lou Gehrig	2.00
81	Mickey Mantle	3.00
82	Miller Huggins	.25
83	Roger Maris	1.50
84	Thurman Munson	.75
85	Tony Lazzeri	.50
86	Yankee Stadium	.75
87	Times Square	.50
88	Central Park	.50
89	Empire State Building	.50
90	Statue of Liberty	.50

Bronze

Bronze: 4-8X
Production 99 Sets

Gold

Gold: 8-15X
Production 30 Sets

Silver

Silver: No Pricing

Scripts Single Autogtraph

NM/M

Common Autograph: 10.00
Inserted 1:8

AU-1	Bill "Moose" Skowron	15.00
AU-2	Bob Cerv	10.00
AU-3	Bobby Murcer/SP	60.00
AU-4	Bobby Richardson	15.00
AU-5	Brian Doyle	10.00
AU-6	Bucky Dent	10.00
AU-7	Chris Chambliss	12.00
AU-8	Clete Boyer	15.00
AU-9	Dave Kingman	10.00
AU-10	Dave Righetti	10.00
AU-11	Dave Winfield/SP	60.00
AU-12	David Cone	10.00
AU-14	Dock Ellis	10.00
AU-15	Don Baylor/SP	25.00
AU-16	Don Larsen/SP	40.00
AU-17	Don Mattingly/SP	85.00
AU-18	Dwight Gooden	15.00
AU-19	Ed Figueroa	10.00
AU-20	Joe Torre/SP	125.00
AU-21	Darryl Strawberry	20.00
AU-23	Gaylord Perry	20.00
AU-24	Phil Linz	10.00
AU-25	Gil McDougald	15.00
AU-26	Rich "Goose" Gossage	20.00
AU-27	Graig Nettles	15.00
AU-28	Hank Bauer	15.00
AU-29	Jack Clark	15.00
AU-31	Jim Abbott	15.00
AU-32	Jim Bouton	15.00
AU-33	Jim Kaat	15.00
AU-34	Jim Leyritz/SP	25.00
AU-35	Jim Wynn	10.00
AU-36	Jimmy Key	10.00
AU-37	Joe Niekro	15.00
AU-38	Joe Pepitone	15.00
AU-39	John Wetteland/SP	20.00
AU-40	Ken Griffey Sr.	12.00
AU-42	Kevin Maas	10.00
AU-43	Lindy McDaniel	10.00
AU-44	Lou Piniella/SP	35.00
AU-45	Luis Tiant	20.00
AU-46	Mel Stottlemyre	15.00
AU-47	Mickey Rivers	10.00
AU-48	Oscar Gamble	15.00
AU-49	Pat Dobson	15.00
AU-50	Paul O'Neill/SP	40.00
AU-51	Phil Niekro	15.00
AU-52	Phil Rizzuto/SP	75.00
AU-53	Doc Medich	10.00
AU-54	Rick Cerone	15.00
AU-55	Ron Blomberg	10.00
AU-56	Ron Guidry	25.00
AU-57	Roy White	12.00
AU-58	Rudy May	10.00
AU-59	Sam McDowell	10.00
AU-60	Sparky Lyle	12.00
AU-61	Steve Balboni	10.00
AU-62	Steve Sax	10.00
AU-63	Jerry Coleman	15.00
AU-64	Tom Tresh	15.00
AU-65	Tommy John	15.00
AU-66	Tony Kubek/SP	400.00
AU-67	Wade Boggs/SP	60.00
AU-68	Whitey Ford/SP	60.00
AU-69	Willie Randolph/SP	25.00
AU-70	Yogi Berra/SP	75.00

Scripts Dual Autograph

NM/M

Production 100 Sets

SC	Bill "Moose" Skowron, Bob Cerv	50.00
MP	Bobby Murcer, Lou Piniella	65.00
CB	Chris Chambliss, Ron Blomberg	50.00
BN	Clete Boyer, Graig Nettles	50.00
RC	Dave Righetti, Rick Cerone	60.00
ED	Dock Ellis, Pat Dobson	70.00
BG	Don Baylor, Ken Griffey Sr.	65.00
MW	Don Mattingly, Dave Winfield	150.00
FG	Ed Figueroa, Ron Guidry	60.00
MB	Bobby Murcer, Hank Bauer	75.00
GL	Rich "Goose" Gossage, Sparky Lyle	50.00
NB	Graig Nettles, Wade Boggs	80.00
KJ	Jim Kaat, Tommy John	60.00
KA	Jimmy Key, Jim Abbott	50.00
PS	Joe Pepitone, Bill "Moose" Skowron	50.00
MM	Kevin Maas, Don Mattingly	100.00
RW	Mickey Rivers, Roy White	50.00
OL	Paul O'Neil, Jim Leyritz	75.00
RM	Phil Rizzuto, Gil McDougald	100.00
SD	Steve Sax, Brian Doyle	40.00
KR	Tony Kubek, Bobby Richardson	100.00
FL	Whitey Ford, Don Larsen	125.00
BL	Yogi Berra, Don Larsen	150.00
BH	Yogi Berra, Joe Torre	100.00
BF	Yogi Berra, Whitey Ford	150.00
WM	Bobby Murcer, Roy White	75.00
DN	Bucky Dent, Graig Nettles	50.00
CN	Chris Chambliss, Graig Nettles	50.00

CL	David Cone, Don Larsen	100.00
MC	Don Mattingly, Jack Clark	85.00
BM	Don Mattingly, Wade Boggs	150.00
SG	Darryl Strawberry, Dwight Gooden	75.00
CG	David Cone, Dwight Gooden	70.00

Scripts Triple Autograph

No Pricing
Production 20 Sets

Scripts Quad Autograph

No Pricing
Production 10 Sets

Classic Cuts

No Pricing
Production One Set

Mitchell & Ness Pennant

NM/M

Inserted 1:Box

Cards:		.3X
P2	1927 World Series/96	
P3	1928 World Series/96	25.00
P4	1932 World Series/96	25.00
P6	1937 World Series/96	25.00
P8	1939 World Series/96	25.00
P10	1943 World Series/97	25.00
P11	1947 World Series/97	25.00
P13	1950 World Series/97	25.00
P15	1952 World Series/97	25.00
P17	1956 World Series/97	25.00
P18	1958 World Series/97	25.00
P23	1996 World Series/99	25.00
P24	1998 World Series/99	25.00
P25	1999 World Series/99	25.00
P26	2000 World Series/100	25.00
MM57	Mickey Mantle/1957 MVP/97	30.00
MM62	Mickey Mantle 1962 MVP/98	30.00

Mitchell & Ness Pennant Card

NM/M

Inserted 1:Box

P2	1927 World Series/1927	5.00
P3	1928 World Series/1,928	5.00
P4	1932 World Series/1,932	5.00
P5	1936 World Series/36	10.00
P6	1937 World Series/1,937	5.00
P7	1938 World Series/38	10.00
P8	1939 World Series/1,939	5.00
P9	1941 World Series/41	10.00
P10	1943 World Series/1,943	5.00
P11	1947 World Series/1,947	5.00
P12	1949 World Series/49	10.00
P13	1950 World Series/1,950	5.00
P14	1951 World Series/51	10.00
P15	1952 World Series/1,952	5.00
P16	1953 World Series/53	10.00
P17	1956 World Series/1,956	5.00
P18	1958 World Series/1,958	5.00
P19	1961 World Series/61	10.00
P20	1962 World Series/62	10.00
P21	1977 World Series/77	8.00
P22	1978 World Series/78	8.00
P23	1996 World Series/1,996	5.00
P24	1998 World Series/1,998	5.00
P25	1999 World Series/1,999	5.00
P26	2000 World Series/2,000	5.00

MM57	Mickey Mantle/1957 MVP/1,957	8.00
MM62	Mickey Mantle/1962 MVP/1,962	8.00
MM56	Mickey Mantle/1956 MVP/7	

Mitchell & Ness Jersey Redempt

NM/M

Inserted 1:384
Production 40-99

MNJ1	Babe Ruth/40	350.00
MNJ2	Bill Dickey/75	120.00
MNJ3	Billy Martin/99	150.00
MNJ4	Bobby Murcer/99	100.00
MNJ5	Bucky Dent/92	100.00
MNJ6	Casey Stengel/65	120.00
MNJ7	"Catfish" Hunter/92	120.00
MNJ8	Chris Chambliss/99	80.00
MNJ9	Don Larsen/75	120.00
MNJ10	Don Mattingly/92	150.00
MNJ11	Elston Howard/88	100.00
MNJ12	Rich "Goose" Gossage/92	100.00
MNJ13	Graig Nettles/92	100.00
MNJ14	Joe DiMaggio/55	200.00
MNJ15	Lefty Gomez/81	120.00
MNJ16	Lou Gehrig/40	200.00
MNJ17	Lou Piniella/92	100.00
MNJ18	Mickey Mantle/50	275.00
MNJ19	Bill "Moose" Skowron/85	125.00
MNJ20	Phil Rizzuto/40	150.00
MNJ21	Roy White/50	100.00
MNJ22	Roger Maris/92	200.00
MNJ23	Ron Guidry/99	100.00
MNJ24	Sparky Lyle/99	100.00
MNJ25	Thurman Munson/91	200.00
MNJ26	Tony Kubek/75	150.00
MNJ27	Tony Lazzeri/79	120.00
MNJ28	Whitey Ford/43	180.00
MNJ29	Willie Randolph/92	100.00
MNJ30	Yogi Berra/50	200.00

2004 UD Legends Timeless Teams

NM/M

Complete Set (300):		40.00
Common Player:		.15
Pack (5):		5.00
Box (18):		75.00
1	Bob Gibson	.50
2	Lou Brock	.50
3	Ray Washburn	.15
4	Tim McCarver	.15
5	Harmon Killebrew	1.00
6	Jim Kaat	.25
7	Jim Perry	.15
8	Jim "Mudcat" Grant	.15
9	Boog Powell	.15
10	Brooks Robinson	.50
11	Frank Robinson	.50
12	Jim Palmer	.25
13	Carl Yastrzemski	1.00
14	Jim Lonborg	.15
15	George Scott	.15
16	Sparky Lyle	.15
17	Rico Petrocelli	.15
18	Bob Gibson	.50
19	Julian Javier	.15
20	Lou Brock	.50
21	Orlando Cepeda	.15
22	Ray Washburn	.15
23	Steve Carlton	.50
24	Tim McCarver	.15
25	Al Kaline	.50
26	Bill Freehan	.15
27	Denny McLain	.15
28	Dick McAuliffe	.15
29	Jim Northrup	.15
30	John Hiller	.15
31	Mickey Lolich	.15
32	Mickey Stanley	.15
33	Willie Horton	.15
34	Bob Gibson	.50
35	Julian Javier	.15
36	Lou Brock	.50
37	Orlando Cepeda	.25
38	Steve Carlton	.50
39	Boog Powell	.15
40	Brooks Robinson	.50
41	Davey Johnson	.15
42	Merv Rettenmund	.15
43	Eddie Watt	.15
44	Frank Robinson	.50
45	Jim Palmer	.25
46	Mike Cuellar	.15
47	Paul Blair	.15
48	Pete Richert	.15
49	Ellie Hendricks	.15
50	Billy Williams	.25
51	Randy Hundley	.15
52	Ernie Banks	1.00
53	Fergie Jenkins	.25
54	Jim Hickman	.15
55	Ken Holtzman	.15
56	Ron Santo	.25
57	Ed Kranepool	.15
58	Jerry Koosman	.15
59	Nolan Ryan	2.00
60	Tom Seaver	.50
61	Boog Powell	.15
62	Brooks Robinson	.50
63	Davey Johnson	.15
64	Merv Rettenmund	.15
65	Eddie Watt	.15
66	Frank Robinson	.50
67	Jim Palmer	.25
68	Mike Cuellar	.15
69	Paul Blair	.15
70	Pete Richert	.15
71	Ellie Hendricks	.15
72	Al Kaline	.50
73	Bill Freehan	.15
74	Dick McAuliffe	.15
75	Jim Northrup	.15
76	John Hiller	.15
77	Mickey Lolich	.15
78	Mickey Stanley	.15
79	Willie Horton	.15
80	Bert Campaneris	.15
81	Blue Moon Odom	.15
82	Sal Bando	.15
83	Joe Rudi	.15
84	Ken Holtzman	.15
85	Bill North	.15
86	Blue Moon Odom	.15
87	Gene Tenace	.15
88	Manny Trillo	.15
89	Dick Green	.15
90	Rollie Fingers	.25
91	Sal Bando	.15
92	Vida Blue	.15
93	Bill Buckner	.15
94	Davey Lopes	.15
95	Don Sutton	.25
96	Al Downing	.15
97	Ron Cey	.15
98	Steve Garvey	.15
99	Tommy John	.15
100	Bert Campaneris	.15
101	Bill North	.15
102	Joe Rudi	.15
103	Sal Bando	.15
104	Vida Blue	.15
105	Carl Yastrzemski	.75
106	Carlton Fisk	.25
107	Cecil Cooper	.15
108	Dwight Evans	.15
109	Fred Lynn	.15
110	Jim Rice	.25
111	Luis Tiant	.15
112	Rick Burleson	.15
113	Rico Petrocelli	.15
114	Pedro Borbon	.15
115	Dave Concepcion	.15
116	Don Gullett	.15
117	George Foster	.15
118	Joe Morgan	.25
119	Johnny Bench	.50
120	Rawly Eastwick	.15
121	Sparky Anderson	.15
122	Tony Perez	.25
123	Billy Williams	.25
124	Gene Tenace	.15
125	Jim Perry	.15
126	Vida Blue	.15
127	Pedro Borbon	.15
128	Dave Concepcion	.15
129	Don Gullett	.15
130	George Foster	.15
131	Joe Morgan	.25
132	Johnny Bench	.50
133	Ken Griffey Sr.	.15
134	Rawly Eastwick	.15
135	Tony Perez	.25
136	Bill Russell	.15
137	Burt Hooton	.15
138	Davey Lopes	.15
139	Don Sutton	.25
140	Dusty Baker	.15
141	Steve Yeager	.15
142	Ron Cey	.15
143	Steve Garvey	.15
144	Tommy John	.15
145	Bucky Dent	.15
146	Chris Chambliss	.15
147	Ed Figueroa	.15
148	Graig Nettles	.15
149	Lou Piniella	.25
150	Roy White	.15
151	Don Gullett	.15
152	Sparky Lyle	.15
153	Brian Doyle	.15
154	Bucky Dent	.15
155	Chris Chambliss	.15
156	Ed Figueroa	.15
157	Graig Nettles	.15
158	Lou Piniella	.25
159	Roy White	.15
160	Rich "Goose" Gossage	.15
161	Sparky Lyle	.15
162	Bobby Grich	.15
163	Brian Downing	.15
164	Dan Ford	.15
165	Nolan Ryan	2.00
166	Dave Concepcion	.15
167	George Foster	.15
168	Johnny Bench	.50
169	Ray Knight	.15
170	Tom Seaver	.50
171	Bert Blyleven	.15
172	Bill Madlock	.25
173	Dave Parker	.25
174	Phil Garner	.15
175	Bill Russell	.15
176	Steve Yeager	.15
177	Don Sutton	.25
178	Dusty Baker	.25
179	Jerry Reuss	.15
180	Mickey Hatcher	.15
181	Pedro Guerrero	.15
182	Ron Cey	.15
183	Steve Garvey	.15
184	Rudy May	.15
185	Brian Doyle	.15
186	Bucky Dent	.15
187	Jim Kaat	.15
188	Lou Piniella	.15
189	Luis Tiant	.15
190	Tommy John	.15
191	Bake McBride	.15
192	Bob Boone	.15
193	Dickie Noles	.15
194	Manny Trillo	.15
195	Mike Schmidt	1.00
196	Sparky Lyle	.15
197	Steve Carlton	.50
198	Steve Yeager	.15
199	Burt Hooton	.15
200	Dusty Baker	.15
201	Jerry Reuss	.15
202	Mike Scioscia	.15
203	Pedro Guerrero	.15
204	Ron Cey	.15
205	Steve Garvey	.15
206	Alejandro Pena	.15
207	Steve Sax	.15
208	Cecil Cooper	.15
209	Gorman Thomas	.15
210	Paul Molitor	.15
211	Robin Yount	1.00
212	Rollie Fingers	.25
213	Don Money	.15
214	Rudy May	.15
215	Bucky Dent	.15
216	Dave Winfield	.50
217	Lou Piniella	.25
218	Rich "Goose" Gossage	.15
219	Tommy John	.15
220	Cecil Cooper	.15
221	Gorman Thomas	.50
222	Paul Molitor	.50
223	Robin Yount	1.00
224	Don Money	.15
225	Cal Ripken Jr.	2.00
226	Dan Ford	.15
227	Jim Palmer	.25
228	John Shelby	.15
229	Alan Trammell	.25
230	Chet Lemon	.15
231	Howard Johnson	.15
232	Jack Morris	.25
233	Kirk Gibson	.25

234	Lou Whitaker	.15
235	Sparky Anderson	.15
236	Dave Winfield	.50
237	Don Mattingly	1.00
238	Ken Griffey Sr.	.15
239	Phil Niekro	.15
240	Yogi Berra	.75
241	Bill Buckner	.15
242	Bruce Hurst	.15
243	Dave Henderson	.15
244	Dwight Evans	.15
245	Jim Rice	.50
246	Tom Seaver	.50
247	Wade Boggs	.50
248	Bob Boone	.15
249	Bobby Grich	.15
250	Brian Downing	.15
251	Don Sutton	.25
252	Terry Forster	.15
253	Rick Burleson	.15
254	Wally Joyner	.15
255	Darryl Strawberry	.15
256	Dwight Gooden	.15
257	Gary Carter	.15
258	Jesse Orosco	.15
259	Keith Hernandez	.15
260	Lenny Dykstra	.15
261	Mookie Wilson	.15
262	Ray Knight	.15
263	Wally Backman	.15
264	Sid Fernandez	.15
265	Alan Trammell	.25
266	Dan Petry	.15
267	Chet Lemon	.15
268	Sparky Anderson	.15
269	Jack Morris	.15
270	Kirk Gibson	.15
271	Lou Whitaker	.15
272	Bert Blyleven	.15
273	Kent Hrbek	.15
274	Kirby Puckett	.75
275	Alejandro Pena	.15
276	Jesse Orosco	.15
277	John Shelby	.15
278	Kirk Gibson	.15
279	Mickey Hatcher	.15
280	Mike Scioscia	.15
281	Steve Sax	.15
282	Darryl Strawberry	.15
283	Dwight Gooden	.15
284	Gary Carter	.15
285	Howard Johnson	.15
286	Keith Hernandez	.15
287	Lenny Dykstra	.15
288	Mookie Wilson	.15
289	Wally Backman	.15
290	Sid Fernandez	.15
291	Jack Morris	.15
292	Kent Hrbek	.15
293	Kirby Puckett	.75
294	Dave Winfield	.50
295	Jack Morris	.15
296	Joe Carter	.15
297	Don Mattingly	1.00
298	Paul O'Neill	.15
299	Jack McDowell	.15
300	Wade Boggs	.50

Gold

No Pricing
Production 5 Sets

Autographs

Common Autograph:		10.00
Golds:		No Pricing
Production 5 Sets		
Platinum:		No Pricing
Production One Set		
2	Lou Brock MM/SP/75	20.00
3	Ray Washburn	10.00
4	Tim McCarver	15.00

5	Harmon Killebrew	40.00
6	Jim Kaat	10.00
7	Jim Perry	12.00
9	Boog Powell	10.00
10	Brooks Robinson	35.00
12	Jim Palmer/SP/50	20.00
13	Carl Yastrzemski/SP/25	80.00
14	Jim Lonborg	10.00
15	George Scott	10.00
16	Sparky Lyle	10.00
17	Rico Petrocelli	10.00
18	Bob Gibson/SP/35	40.00
19	Julian Javier	10.00
20	Lou Brock/SP/60	20.00
21	Orlando Cepeda/SP/50	20.00
22	Ray Washburn	10.00
24	Tim McCarver	12.00
25	Al Kaline	25.00
26	Bill Freehan	10.00
27	Denny McLain	20.00
28	Dick McAuliffe	10.00
29	Jim Northrup	15.00
30	John Hiller	10.00
31	Mickey Lolich	15.00
32	Mickey Stanley	10.00
33	Willie Horton	10.00
35	Julian Javier	10.00
36	Lou Brock/SP/50	20.00
38	Steve Carlton/SP/35	30.00
39	Boog Powell	10.00
40	Brooks Robinson/SP/100	40.00
41	Davey Johnson	10.00
42	Merv Rettenmund	10.00
43	Eddie Watt	10.00
46	Mike Cuellar	10.00
47	Paul Blair	10.00
48	Pete Richert	10.00
49	Ellie Hendricks	10.00
50	Billy Williams/SP/75	25.00
51	Randy Hundley	10.00
52	Ernie Banks/SP/50	
53	Fergie Jenkins	15.00
54	Jim Hickman	20.00
55	Ken Holtzman	15.00
56	Ron Santo	25.00
57	Ed Kranepool	10.00
58	Jerry Koosman	15.00
59	Nolan Ryan/SP/50	175.00
60	Tom Seaver/SP/50	50.00
61	Boog Powell	12.00
62	Brooks Robinson/SP/35	50.00
63	Davey Johnson	10.00
64	Merv Rettenmund	10.00
65	Eddie Watt	10.00
66	Frank Robinson/SP/50	30.00
67	Jim Palmer/SP/75	20.00
68	Mike Cuellar	12.00
69	Paul Blair	10.00
70	Pete Richert	10.00
71	Ellie Hendricks	10.00
72	Al Kaline	25.00
73	Bill Freehan	10.00
74	Dick McAuliffe	15.00
75	Jim Northrup	15.00
76	John Hiller	10.00
77	Mickey Lolich	15.00
78	Mickey Stanley	10.00
79	Willie Horton	12.00
80	Bert Campaneris	10.00
81	Blue Moon Odom	15.00
82	Sal Bando Exch	10.00
83	Joe Rudi	10.00
84	Ken Holtzman	10.00
85	Bill North	10.00
86	Blue Moon Odom	15.00
87	Gene Tenace	10.00
88	Manny Trillo	15.00
89	Dick Green	10.00
90	Rollie Fingers	15.00
91	Sal Bando	10.00
92	Vida Blue	15.00
93	Bill Buckner	10.00
94	Davey Lopes	10.00
95	Don Sutton	15.00
96	Al Downing MM	10.00
100	Bert Campaneris	10.00
101	Bill North	10.00
102	Joe Rudi	10.00
103	Sal Bando	10.00
104	Vida Blue/SP/100	15.00
105	Carl Yastrzemski/SP/50	60.00
106	Carlton Fisk/SP/100	30.00
107	Cecil Cooper/SP/75	15.00
108	Dwight Evans/SP/75	10.00
109	Fred Lynn	10.00
110	Jim Rice/SP/100 Exch	20.00
111	Luis Tiant Exch	10.00

112	Rick Burleson	10.00
113	Rico Petrocelli	10.00
114	Pedro Borbon	10.00
115	Dave Concepcion/Exch.	10.00
116	Don Gullett	15.00
117	George Foster/SP/50	15.00
119	Johnny Bench/SP/85	50.00
120	Rawly Eastwick	10.00
121	Sparky Anderson	10.00
122	Tony Perez	30.00
123	Billy Williams/SP/50	20.00
124	Gene Tenace	10.00
125	Jim Perry	10.00
126	Vida Blue/SP/75	20.00
127	Pedro Borbon	10.00
128	Dave Concepcion/Exch.	10.00
129	Don Gullett	15.00
133	Ken Griffey Sr.	10.00
134	Rawly Eastwick	10.00
135	Tony Perez	30.00
136	Bill Russell	10.00
137	Burt Hooton	10.00
138	Davey Lopes	10.00
139	Don Sutton	10.00
140	Dusty Baker/Exch.	15.00
141	Steve Yeager/SP/75 Exch.	10.00
144	Tommy John/SP/35	15.00
145	Bucky Dent/SP/75	10.00
146	Chris Chambliss	15.00
147	Ed Figueroa	10.00
148	Graig Nettles	15.00
150	Roy White	10.00
151	Don Gullett	15.00
152	Sparky Lyle	10.00
153	Brian Doyle	10.00
155	Chris Chambliss	15.00
156	Ed Figueroa	10.00
157	Graig Nettles	10.00
159	Roy White	10.00
160	Rich "Goose" Gossage	15.00
161	Sparky Lyle	10.00
162	Bobby Grich	10.00
163	Brian Downing	10.00
164	Dan Ford	10.00
166	Dave Concepcion/SP/75 Exch.	10.00
169	Ray Knight	10.00
171	Bert Blyleven	15.00
172	Bill Madlock	10.00
173	Dave Parker	12.00
174	Phil Garner	10.00
175	Bill Russell	10.00
176	Steve Yeager	10.00
177	Don Sutton/SP/50	20.00
178	Dusty Baker	15.00
179	Jerry Reuss	10.00
180	Mickey Hatcher	10.00
181	Pedro Guerrero	15.00
182	Ron Cey/SP/50	15.00
183	Steve Garvey/SP/50	15.00
184	Rudy May	10.00
185	Brian Doyle	10.00
186	Bucky Dent/SP/60	15.00
187	Jim Kaat	10.00
188	Lou Piniella/SP/50	15.00
189	Luis Tiant	10.00
190	Tommy John/SP/50	15.00
191	Bake McBride	15.00
192	Bob Boone	10.00
193	Dickie Noles	10.00
194	Manny Trillo	15.00
195	Mike Schmidt/SP/50	75.00
196	Sparky Lyle	10.00
197	Steve Carlton/SP/50	20.00
198	Steve Yeager	10.00
199	Burt Hooton	10.00
200	Dusty Baker/Exch.	15.00
201	Jerry Reuss	10.00
202	Mike Scioscia	10.00
203	Pedro Guerrero	10.00
204	Ron Cey/SP/75	15.00
205	Steve Garvey/SP/75	15.00
206	Alejandro Pena	10.00
207	Steve Sax/SP/100	10.00
208	Cecil Cooper/SP/85	15.00
209	Gorman Thomas/Exch.	10.00
212	Rollie Fingers	15.00
213	Don Money	10.00
214	Rudy May	10.00
216	Dave Winfield/SP/50	30.00
217	Lou Piniella/SP/75	15.00
218	Rich "Goose" Gossage	15.00
219	Tommy John/SP/75	10.00
220	Cecil Cooper	15.00
221	Gorman Thomas/Exch.	10.00
222	Paul Molitor/SP/50	45.00
223	Robin Yount/SP/50	75.00

224	Don Money	10.00
225	Cal Ripken Jr./SP/50	180.00
226	Dan Ford	10.00
228	John Shelby	10.00
229	Alan Trammell	15.00
230	Chet Lemon	15.00
231	Howard Johnson	15.00
232	Jack Morris/SP/35	15.00
233	Kirk Gibson	15.00
234	Lou Whitaker/SP/100	15.00
235	Sparky Anderson	15.00
237	Don Mattingly/SP/50	60.00
238	Ken Griffey Sr.	10.00
239	Phil Niekro	15.00
240	Yogi Berra/SP/47	50.00
241	Bill Buckner	15.00
242	Bruce Hurst	15.00
243	Dave Henderson	10.00
245	Jim Rice/SP/75 Exch.	20.00
247	Wade Boggs/SP/50	30.00
248	Bob Boone	10.00
249	Bobby Grich	10.00
250	Brian Downing	10.00
251	Don Sutton/SP/75	15.00
252	Terry Forster	10.00
253	Rick Burleson	10.00
254	Wally Joyner	15.00
255	Darryl Strawberry	15.00
256	Dwight Gooden	15.00
257	Gary Carter/SP/75	20.00
258	Jesse Orosco	10.00
259	Keith Hernandez	15.00
260	Lenny Dykstra	10.00
261	Mookie Wilson	10.00
262	Ray Knight	10.00
263	Wally Backman	10.00
264	Sid Fernandez/Exch.	10.00
265	Alan Trammell	15.00
266	Dan Petry	10.00
267	Chet Lemon	10.00
268	Sparky Anderson	10.00
270	Kirk Gibson	15.00
271	Lou Whitaker/SP/50	20.00
272	Bert Blyleven	10.00
273	Kent Hrbek	15.00
275	Alejandro Pena	10.00
276	Jesse Orosco	10.00
277	John Shelby	10.00
278	Kirk Gibson/SP/50	20.00
279	Mickey Hatcher	10.00
280	Mike Scioscia	10.00
281	Steve Sax	10.00
282	Darryl Strawberry	15.00
283	Dwight Gooden	15.00
284	Gary Carter/SP/50	20.00
285	Howard Johnson	10.00
286	Keith Hernandez	15.00
287	Lenny Dykstra	10.00
288	Mookie Wilson	10.00
289	Wally Backman	10.00
290	Sid Fernandez/Exch.	10.00
291	Jack Morris/SP/50	15.00
292	Kent Hrbek	15.00
293	Kirby Puckett/SP/50	50.00
294	Dave Winfield/SP/35	35.00
295	Jack Morris/SP/75	15.00
298	Paul O'Neill	40.00
299	Jack McDowell	10.00
300	Wade Boggs/SP/75	25.00

Legendary Signature Dual

NM/M

Quantity produced listed

BC	Lou Brock, Orlando Cepeda/75	40.00
BJ	Lou Brock, Julian Javier/150	25.00
BM	Wade Boggs, Don Mattingly/50	140.00
BO	Vida Blue, Blue Moon Odom/150	25.00
BW	Ernie Banks, Billy Williams/25	100.00
CB	Steve Carlton, Bret Boone/150	50.00
CG	Ron Cey, Steve Garvey/150	40.00
CH	Gary Carter, Keith Hernandez/150	30.00
CM	Dave Concepcion, Joe Morgan/75 Exch.	35.00
DD	Bucky Dent, Brian Doyle/150	25.00
FR	Fred Lynn, Jim Rice/150	40.00
GA	Kirk Gibson, Sparky Anderson/150	40.00

GB Bob Gibson, Lou Brock/50 — 75.00
GC Dwight Gooden, Gary Carter/150 — 30.00
GL Rich "Goose" Gossage, Sparky Lyle/150 Exch. — 25.00
HJ Ken Holtzman, Fergie Jenkins/150 — 40.00
HK Keith Hernandez, Ray Knight/150 — 30.00
JH Fergie Jenkins, Randy Hundley/150 — 40.00
JS Tommy John, Don Sutton/150 — 25.00
KH Al Kaline, Willie Horton/150 — 40.00
KK Harmon Killebrew, Jim Kaat/150 — 50.00
LM Mickey Lolich, Denny McLain/75 — 60.00
MB Joe Morgan, Johnny Bench/25 — 80.00
MF Denny McLain, Bill Freehan/150 — 40.00
NC Graig Nettles, Chris Chambliss/150 — 30.00
OM Paul O'Neill, Don Mattingly/75 — 140.00
PC Jim Palmer, Mike Cuellar/150 — 30.00
PF Tony Perez, George Foster/150 — 40.00
PH Kirby Puckett, Kent Hrbek/50 — 65.00
PN Lou Piniella, Graig Nettles/150 — 30.00
PR Jim Palmer, Merv Rettenmund/150 — 35.00
RL Bill Russell, Davey Lopes/150 — 30.00
RR Brooks Robinson, Frank Robinson/50 — 70.00
RS Nolan Ryan, Tom Seaver/25 — 250.00
SD Steve Garvey, Davey Lopes/150 — 25.00
SG Darryl Strawberry, Dwight Gooden/150 — 40.00
SY Don Sutton, Steve Yeager/150 — 30.00
TF Luis Tiant, Carlton Fisk/50 — 45.00
TM Gorman Thomas, Paul Molitor/150 Exch. — 35.00
WB Mookie Wilson, Bill Buckner/150 — 30.00
WT Lou Whitaker, Alan Trammell/75 — 75.00
YM Robin Yount, Paul Molitor/120 — 120.00
YP Carl Yastrzemski, Rico Petrocelli/50 — 75.00

Legendary Signature Triple

NM/M
Quantity produced listed
BCM Johnny Bench, Dave Concepcion, Joe Morgan/25 Exch. — 100.00
BOM Wade Boggs, Paul O'Neill, Don Mattingly/150 — 150.00
BRB Sal Bando, Joe Rudi, Vida Blue/75 — 50.00
BSW Ernie Banks, Ron Santo, Billy Williams/25 — 140.00
CDK Gary Carter, Lenny Dykstra, Ray Knight/50 — 75.00
CND Chris Chambliss, Graig Nettles, Bucky Dent/50 — 50.00
ERL Dwight Evans, Jim Rice, Fred Lynn/50 — 125.00
GBC Steve Garvey, Dusty Baker, Ron Cey/50 — 75.00
GBM Bob Gibson, Lou Brock, Tim McCarver/25 — 100.00
GDR Bobby Grich, Al Downing, Nolan Ryan/25 — 175.00
GHS Kirk Gibson, Mickey Hatcher, Mike Scioscia/75 — 85.00
GMP Phil Garner, Bill Madlock, Dave Parker/50 — 75.00
HHS Jim Hickman, Ken Holtzman, Ron Santo/75 — 60.00
HSJ Burt Hooton, Don Sutton, Tommy John/50 — 50.00
JHH Fergie Jenkins, Randy Hundley, Ken Holtzman/75 — 50.00

KKP Harmon Killebrew, Jim Kaat, Jim Perry/50 — 65.00
KPG Jim Kaat, Jim Perry, Jim "Mudcat" Grant/75 Exch. — 40.00
KSR Jerry Koosman, Tom Seaver, Nolan Ryan/25 — 250.00
MHP Jack Morris, Kent Hrbek, Kirby Puckett/50 — 100.00
MLF Denny McLain, Mickey Lolich, Bill Freehan/50 — 60.00
NKH Jim Northrup, Al Kaline, Willie Horton/75 — 65.00
PBH Kirby Puckett, Bert Blyleven, Kent Hrbek/50 — 90.00
PCR Jim Palmer, Mike Cuellar, Pete Richert/75 — 45.00
PPW Jim Palmer, Boog Powell, Earl Weaver/75 — 60.00
RPR Frank Robinson, Boog Powell, Brooks Robinson/50 — 80.00
RWP Cal Ripken Jr., Earl Weaver, Jim Palmer/25 — 250.00
SCB Mike Schmidt, Steve Carlton, Bob Boone/50 — 125.00
SGS Steve Sax, Pedro Guerrero, Mike Scioscia/75 — 60.00
TWA Alan Trammell, Lou Whitaker, Sparky Anderson/50 — 75.00
YCT Robin Yount, Cecil Cooper, Gorman Thomas/50 Exch. — 120.00
YFT Carl Yastrzemski, Carlton Fisk, Luis Tiant/25 — 140.00
YMT Robin Yount, Paul Molitor, Gorman Thomas/75 Exch. — 140.00

Legendary Combo Signatures

No Pricing

Legendary Combo Cuts

No Pricing

Team Terrific GU Team Logo

NM/M
Quantity produced listed
BO Baltimore Orioles/85 — 60.00
BR Boston Red Sox/85 — 50.00
CR Cincinnati Reds/85 — 75.00
LD Los Angeles Dodgers/85 — 50.00
MB Milwaukee Brewers/100 — 30.00
NM New York Mets/85 — 30.00
OA Oakland A's/100 — 30.00
SC St. Louis Cardinals/100 — 50.00

Team Terrific GU League

No Pricing
Production 15 Sets

Team Terrific GU Stats

No Pricing
Production 1-5

Team Terrific GU Hat Logo

NM/M
Quantity produced listed
BO Baltimore Orioles/50 — 90.00
BR Boston Red Sox/50 — 80.00
CR Cincinnati Reds/50 — 80.00
LD Los Angeles Dodgers/50 — 60.00
MB Milwaukee Brewers/82 — 40.00
NM New York Mets/50 — 50.00
OA Oakland A's/50 — 40.00
SC St. Louis Cardinals/50 — 75.00

Team Terrific GU Brand Logo

NM/M
Quantity produced listed

BO Baltimore Orioles/35 — 90.00
BR Boston Red Sox/35 — 80.00
CR Cincinnati Reds/35 — 80.00
LD Los Angeles Dodgers/35 — 60.00
MB Milwaukee Brewers/41 — 50.00
NM New York Mets/35 — 50.00
OA Oakland A's/39 — 40.00
SC St. Louis Cardinals/35 — 75.00

2005 Upper Deck

CARLOS BELTRAN OF

NM/M
Complete Set (500): — 75.00
Common Player: — .15
Common (211-250): — .50
Hobby Pack (8): — 3.00
Hobby Box (24): — 65.00
1 Casey Kotchman .15
2 Chone Figgins .15
3 David Eckstein .15
4 Jarrod Washburn .15
5 Robb Quinlan .15
6 Troy Glaus .25
7 Vladimir Guerrero .75
8 Brandon Webb .15
9 Danny Bautista .15
10 Luis Gonzalez .15
11 Matt Kata .15
12 Randy Johnson .75
13 Robby Hammock .15
14 Shea Hillenbrand .15
15 Adam LaRoche .15
16 Andruw Jones .25
17 Horacio Ramirez .15
18 John Smoltz .25
19 Johnny Estrada .15
20 Mike Hampton .15
21 Rafael Furcal .15
22 Brian Roberts .15
23 Javy Lopez .25
24 Jay Gibbons .15
25 Jorge Julio .15
26 Melvin Mora .15
27 Miguel Tejada .25
28 Rafael Palmeiro .50
29 Derek Lowe .25
30 Jason Varitek .25
31 Kevin Youkilis .15
32 Manny Ramirez .75
33 Curt Schilling .75
34 Pedro Martinez .75
35 Trot Nixon .15
36 Corey Patterson .25
37 Derrek Lee .25
38 LaTroy Hawkins .15
39 Mark Prior .75
40 Matt Clement .15
41 Moises Alou .25
42 Sammy Sosa 1.50
43 Aaron Rowand .15
44 Carlos Lee .15
45 Jose Valentin .15
46 Juan Uribe .15
47 Magglio Ordonez .25
48 Mark Buehrle .15
49 Paul Konerko .25
50 Adam Dunn .50
51 Barry Larkin .25
52 D'Angelo Jimenez .15
53 Danny Graves .15
54 Paul Wilson .15
55 Sean Casey .25
56 Wily Mo Pena .25
57 Ben Broussard .15
58 C.C. Sabathia .15
59 Casey Blake .15
60 Cliff Lee .15
61 Matt Lawton .15
62 Omar Vizquel .15
63 Victor Martinez .15

64 Charles Johnson .15
65 Joe Kennedy .15
66 Jeromy Burnitz .15
67 Matt Holliday .50
68 Preston Wilson .15
69 Royce Clayton .15
70 Shawn Estes .15
71 Bobby Higginson .15
72 Brandon Inge .15
73 Carlos Guillen .15
74 Dmitri Young .15
75 Eric Munson .15
76 Jeremy Bonderman .15
77 Ugueth Urbina .15
78 Josh Beckett .40
79 Dontrelle Willis .15
80 Jeff Conine .15
81 Juan Pierre .15
82 Luis Castillo .15
83 Miguel Cabrera .75
84 Mike Lowell .25
85 Andy Pettitte .15
86 Brad Lidge .15
87 Carlos Beltran .50
88 Craig Biggio .25
89 Jeff Bagwell .50
90 Roger Clemens 1.50
91 Roy Oswalt .25
92 Benito Santiago .15
93 Jeremy Affeldt .15
94 Juan Gonzalez .25
95 Ken Harvey .15
96 Mike MacDougal .15
97 Mike Sweeney .15
98 Zack Greinke .15
99 Adrian Beltre .40
100 Alex Cora .15
101 Cesar Izturis .15
102 Eric Gagne .40
103 Kazuhisa Ishii .15
104 Milton Bradley .15
105 Shawn Green .25
106 Danny Kolb .15
107 Ben Sheets .25
108 Brooks Kieschnick .15
109 Craig Counsell .15
110 Geoff Jenkins .15
111 Lyle Overbay .15
112 Scott Podsednik .15
113 Corey Koskie .15
114 Johan Santana .40
115 Joe Mauer .25
116 Justin Morneau .25
117 Lew Ford .15
118 Matt LeCroy .15
119 Torii Hunter .25
120 Brad Wilkerson .15
121 Chad Cordero .15
122 Livan Hernandez .15
123 Jose Vidro .15
124 Terrmel Sledge .15
125 Tony Batista .15
126 Zach Day .15
127 Al Leiter .25
128 Jae Weong Seo .15
129 Jose Reyes .40
130 Kazuo Matsui .15
131 Mike Piazza 1.00
132 Todd Zeile .15
133 Cliff Floyd .15
134 Alex Rodriguez 2.00
135 Derek Jeter 2.00
136 Gary Sheffield .40
137 Hideki Matsui 1.50
138 Jason Giambi .25
139 Jorge Posada .25
140 Mike Mussina .40
141 Barry Zito .25
142 Bobby Crosby .25
143 Octavio Dotel .15
144 Eric Chavez .25
145 Jermaine Dye .15
146 Mark Kotsay .15
147 Tim Hudson .25
148 Billy Wagner .15
149 Bobby Abreu .25
150 David Bell .15
151 Jim Thome .50
152 Jimmy Rollins .25
153 Mike Lieberthal .15
154 Randy Wolf .15
155 Craig Wilson .15
156 Daryle Ward .15
157 Jack Wilson .15
158 Jason Kendall .15
159 Kip Wells .15
160 Oliver Perez .15
161 Robert Mackowiak .15
162 Brian Giles .25
163 Brian Lawrence .15
164 David Wells .15
165 Jay Payton .15
166 Ryan Klesko .15
167 Sean Burroughs .15

#	Player	Price
168	Trevor Hoffman	.15
169	Brett Tomko	.15
170	J.T. Snow	.15
171	Jason Schmidt	.25
172	Kirk Rueter	.15
173	A.J. Pierzynski	.15
174	Pedro Feliz	.15
175	Ray Durham	.15
176	Eddie Guardado	.15
177	Edgar Martinez	.15
178	Ichiro Suzuki	1.50
179	Jamie Moyer	.15
180	Joel Pineiro	.15
181	Randy Winn	.15
182	Raul Ibanez	.15
183	Albert Pujols	2.00
184	Edgar Renteria	.25
185	Jason Isringhausen	.15
186	Jim Edmonds	.40
187	Matt Morris	.15
188	Reggie Sanders	.15
189	Tony Womack	.15
190	Aubrey Huff	.15
191	Danys Baez	.15
192	Carl Crawford	.15
193	Jose Cruz Jr.	.15
194	Rocco Baldelli	.15
195	Tino Martinez	.15
196	Dewon Brazelton	.15
197	Alfonso Soriano	.75
198	Brad Fullmer	.15
199	Gerald Laird	.15
200	Hank Blalock	.50
201	Laynce Nix	.15
202	Mark Teixeira	.25
203	Mike Young	.15
204	Alexis Rios	.15
205	Eric Hinske	.15
206	Miguel Batista	.15
207	Orlando Hudson	.15
208	Roy Halladay	.15
209	Ted Lilly	.15
210	Vernon Wells	.15
211	Aarom Baldiris	.50
212	B.J. Upton	1.00
213	Dallas McPherson	.50
214	Brian Dallimore	.50
215	Chris Oxspring	.50
216	Chris Shelton	.50
217	David Wright	1.50
218	Edwardo Sierra	.50
219	Fernando Nieve	.50
220	Frank Francisco	.50
221	Jeff Bennett	.50
222	Justin Lehr	.50
223	John Gall	.50
224	Jorge Sequea	.50
225	Justin Germano	.50
226	Kazuhito Tadano	.50
227	Kevin Cave	.50
228	Joe Blanton	.50
229	Luis Gonzalez	.50
230	Mike Wuertz	.50
231	Mike Rouse	.50
232	Nick Regilio	.50
233	Orlando Rodriguez	.50
234	Phil Stockman	.50
235	Ramon Ramirez	.50
236	Roberto Novoa	.50
237	Dioner Navarro	.50
238	Tim Bausher	.50
239	Logan Kensing	.50
240	Andy Green	.50
241	Brad Halsey	.50
242	Charles Thomas	.50
243	George Sherrill	.50
244	Jesse Crain	.50
245	Jimmy Serrano	.50
246	Joe Horgan	.50
247	Chris Young RC	1.50
248	Joey Gathright	.50
249	Gavin Floyd	.50
250	Ryan Howard	1.00
251	Lance Cormier	.15
252	Matt Treanor	.15
253	Jeff Francis	.15
254	Nick Swisher	.15
255	Scott Atchison	.15
256	Travis Blackley	.15
257	Travis Smith	.15
258	Yadier Molina	.15
259	Jeff Keppinger	.15
260	Scott Kazmir	1.00
261	Garret Anderson, Vladimir Guerrero	.40
262	Luis Gonzalez, Randy Johnson	.40
263	Andruw Jones, Chipper Jones	.40
264	Miguel Tejada, Rafael Palmeiro	.40
265	Curt Schilling, Manny Ramirez	.50
266	Mark Prior, Sammy Sosa	.75
267	Frank Thomas, Magglio Ordonez	.25
268	Barry Larkin, Ken Griffey Jr.	.75
269	C.C. Sabathia, Victor Martinez	.15
270	Jeromy Burnitz, Todd Helton	.25
271	Dmitri Young, Ivan Rodriguez	.40
272	Josh Beckett, Miguel Cabrera	.25
273	Jeff Bagwell, Roger Clemens	.75
274	Ken Harvey, Mike Sweeney	.15
275	Adrian Beltre, Eric Gagne	.25
276	Ben Sheets, Geoff Jenkins	.15
277	Joe Mauer, Torii Hunter	.15
278	Jose Vidro, Livan Hernandez	.15
279	Kazuo Matsui, Mike Piazza	.50
280	Alex Rodriguez, Derek Jeter	1.00
281	Eric Chavez, Tim Hudson	.15
282	Bobby Abreu, Jim Thome	.40
283	Craig Wilson, Jason Kendall	.15
284	Brian Giles, Phil Nevin	.15
285	A.J. Pierzynski, Jason Schmidt	.15
286	Bret Boone, Ichiro Suzuki	.75
287	Albert Pujols, Scott Rolen	.75
288	Aubrey Huff, Tino Martinez	.15
289	Hank Blalock, Mark Teixeira	.15
290	Carlos Delgado, Roy Halladay	.15
291	Vladimir Guerrero	.40
292	Curt Schilling	.25
293	Mark Prior	.40
294	Josh Beckett	.15
295	Roger Clemens	.75
296	Derek Jeter	.75
297	Eric Chavez	.15
298	Jim Thome	.25
299	Albert Pujols	.75
300	Hank Blalock	.25
301	Bartolo Colon	.25
302	Darin Erstad	.15
303	Garret Anderson	.25
304	Orlando Cabrera	.15
305	Steve Finley	.15
306	Javier Vazquez	.15
307	Russ Ortiz	.15
308	Chipper Jones	.75
309	Marcus Giles	.15
310	Raul Mondesi	.15
311	B.J. Ryan	.15
312	Luis Matos	.15
313	Sidney Ponson	.15
314	Bill Mueller	.15
315	David Ortiz	.75
316	Johnny Damon	.75
317	Keith Foulke	.15
318	Mark Bellhorn	.15
319	Wade Miller	.15
320	Aramis Ramirez	.40
321	Carlos Zambrano	.40
322	Greg Maddux	1.25
323	Kerry Wood	.50
324	Nomar Garciaparra	1.00
325	Todd Walker	.15
326	Frank Thomas	.50
327	Freddy Garcia	.15
328	Joe Crede	.15
329	Jose Contreras	.15
330	Orlando Hernandez	.15
331	Shingo Takatsu	.15
332	Austin Kearns	.15
333	Eric Milton	.15
334	Ken Griffey Jr.	1.00
335	Aaron Boone	.15
336	David Riske	.15
337	Jake Westbrook	.15
338	Kevin Millwood	.15
339	Travis Hafner	.25
340	Aaron Miles	.15
341	Jeff Baker	.15
342	Todd Helton	.50
343	Garrett Atkins	.15
344	Carlos Pena	.15
345	Ivan Rodriguez	.50
346	Rondell White	.15
347	Troy Percival	.15
348	A.J. Burnett	.25
349	Carlos Delgado	.40
350	Guillermo Mota	.15
351	Paul LoDuca	.15
352	Jason Lane	.15
353	Lance Berkman	.25
354	Angel Berroa	.15
355	David DeJesus	.15
356	Ruben Gotay	.15
357	Jose Lima	.15
358	Brad Penny	.15
359	J.D. Drew	.25
360	Jayson Werth	.15
361	Jeff Kent	.25
362	Odalis Perez	.15
363	Brady Clark	.15
364	Junior Spivey	.15
365	Rickie Weeks	.25
366	Jacque Jones	.15
367	Joe Nathan	.15
368	Nick Punto	.15
369	Shannon Stewart	.15
370	Doug Mientkiewicz	.15
371	Kris Benson	.15
372	Tom Glavine	.25
373	Victor Zambrano	.15
374	Bernie Williams	.40
375	Carl Pavano	.15
376	Jaret Wright	.15
377	Kevin Brown	.25
378	Mariano Rivera	.25
379	Dan Haren	.15
380	Eric Byrnes	.15
381	Erubiel Durazo	.15
382	Rich Harden	.25
383	Brett Myers	.15
384	Chase Utley	.25
385	Marlon Byrd	.15
386	Pat Burrell	.25
387	Placido Polanco	.15
388	Freddy Sanchez	.15
389	Jason Bay	.25
390	Josh Fogg	.15
391	Adam Eaton	.15
392	Jake Peavy	.40
393	Khalil Greene	.40
394	Mark Loretta	.15
395	Phil Nevin	.15
396	Ramon Hernandez	.15
397	Woody Williams	.15
398	Armando Benitez	.15
399	Edgardo Alfonzo	.15
400	Marquis Grissom	.15
401	Mike Matheny	.15
402	Richie Sexson	.40
403	Bret Boone	.15
404	Gil Meche	.15
405	Chris Carpenter	.40
406	Jeff Suppan	.15
407	Larry Walker	.40
408	Mark Grudzielanek	.15
409	Mark Mulder	.25
410	Scott Rolen	.75
411	Josh Phelps	.15
412	Jonny Gomes	.15
413	Francisco Cordero	.15
414	Kenny Rogers	.15
415	Richard Hidalgo	.15
416	David Bush	.15
417	Frank Catalanotto	.15
418	Gabe Gross	.15
419	Guillermo Quiroz	.15
420	Reed Johnson	.15
421	Cristian Guzman	.15
422	Esteban Loaiza	.15
423	Jose Guillen	.25
424	Nick Johnson	.15
425	Vinny Castilla	.15
426	Peter Orr RC	.50
427	Tadahito Iguchi RC	4.00
428	Jeff Baker	.15
429	Marcos Carvajal RC	.15
430	Justin Verlander RC	3.00
431	Luke Scott RC	1.00
432	Willy Taveras	.15
433	Ambiorix Burgos RC	.50
434	Andy Sisco	.15
435	Denny Bautista	.15
436	Mark Teahen	.15
437	Ervin Santana	.15
438	Dennis Houlton RC	.50
439	Philip Humber RC	1.00
440	Steve Schmoll RC	.50
441	J.J. Hardy	.25
442	Ambiorix Concepcion RC	.50
443	Dae-Sung Koo RC	.50
444	Andy Phillips	.15
445	Dan Meyer	.15
446	Huston Street	.25
447	Keiichi Yabu RC	.50
448	Jeff Niemann RC	1.00
449	Jeremy Reed	.15
450	Tony Blanco	.15
451	Albert Pujols	.75
452	Alex Rodriguez	.75
453	Curt Schilling	.40
454	Derek Jeter	.75
455	Greg Maddux	.50
456	Ichiro Suzuki	.50
457	Ivan Rodriguez	.25
458	Jeff Bagwell	.25
459	Jim Thome	.25
460	Ken Griffey Jr.	.50
461	Manny Ramirez	.40
462	Mike Mussina	.25
463	Mike Piazza	.40
464	Pedro Martinez	.40
465	Rafael Palmeiro	.25
466	Randy Johnson	.40
467	Roger Clemens	.75
468	Sammy Sosa	.50
469	Todd Helton	.25
470	Vladimir Guerrero	.40
471	Vladimir Guerrero	.25
472	Shawn Green	.15
473	John Smoltz	.15
474	Miguel Tejada	.25
475	Curt Schilling	.25
476	Mark Prior	.40
477	Frank Thomas	.25
478	Ken Griffey Jr.	.50
479	C.C. Sabathia	.15
480	Todd Helton	.25
481	Ivan Rodriguez	.25
482	Miguel Cabrera	.40
483	Roger Clemens	.50
484	Mike Sweeney	.15
485	Eric Gagne	.15
486	Ben Sheets	.15
487	Johan Santana	.25
488	Mike Piazza	.40
489	Derek Jeter	.50
490	Eric Chavez	.15
491	Jim Thome	.25
492	Craig Wilson	.15
493	Jake Peavy	.15
494	Jason Schmidt	.15
495	Ichiro Suzuki	.50
496	Albert Pujols	.50
497	Carl Crawford	.15
498	Mark Teixeira	.25
499	Vernon Wells	.15
500	Jose Vidro	.15

Blue

Stars (301-500): 4-6X
Production 150 Sets
Exclusive to Series 2.

Gold

Stars (301-500): 4-8X
Production 99 Sets
Exclusive to Series 2.

Emerald

Stars (301-500): 10-20X
Production 25 Sets
Exclusive to Series 2.

Platinum

No Pricing
Production 5 Sets
Exclusive to Series 2.

Retro

Retro: 2-3X
One retro box per hobby case.

Plates

No Pricing
Production one set per color.

American Flag

No Pricing
Production 15 Sets

Diamond Images - Wingfield Collection

	NM/M
Complete Set (20):	45.00
Common Player:	2.00
Inserted 1:9	
DI-1 Eddie Mathews	3.00
DI-2 Ernie Banks	4.00
DI-3 Joe DiMaggio	6.00
DI-4 Mickey Mantle	8.00
DI-5 Pee Wee Reese	2.00
DI-6 Phil Rizzuto	2.00
DI-7 Stan Musial	4.00
DI-8 Ted Williams	6.00
DI-9 Bob Feller	2.00
DI-10 Whitey Ford	2.00
DI-11 Willie Stargell	2.00
DI-12 Yogi Berra	2.00
DI-13 Roy Campanella	2.00

New York Yankees
DIAMOND IMAGES
The Wingfield Collection
MICKEY MANTLE

Mantle tripped the AL in home runs four times.

DI-14	Franklin D. Roosevelt	2.00
DI-15	Harry S. Truman	2.00
DI-16	Dwight D. Eisenhower	2.00
DI-17	John F. Kennedy	2.00
DI-18	Lyndon B. Johnson	2.00
DI-19	Richard Nixon	2.00
DI-20	Thurman Munson	3.00

Game Jersey

		NM/M
Common Jersey:		5.00
Inserted 1:8		
JB	Jeff Bagwell/SP	8.00
CB	Carlos Beltran/SP	8.00
AB	Adrian Beltre	5.00
LB	Lance Berkman	5.00
HB	Hank Blalock	5.00
MC	Miguel Cabrera	8.00
EC	Eric Chavez	5.00
EG	Eric Gagne	5.00
TG	Troy Glaus	5.00
KG	Ken Griffey Jr./SP	15.00
VG	Vladimir Guerrero	8.00
HE	Todd Helton	8.00
TH	Tim Hudson	5.00
HU	Torii Hunter	5.00
DJ	Derek Jeter	25.00
RJ	Randy Johnson/SP	10.00
CJ	Chipper Jones	8.00
JK	Jeff Kent	5.00
GM	Greg Maddux/SP	10.00
PM	Pedro Martinez	8.00
MM	Mark Mulder	5.00
DO	David Ortiz/SP	10.00
PI	Mike Piazza	8.00
MP	Mark Prior	8.00
AP	Albert Pujols	20.00
MR	Manny Ramirez/SP	10.00
IR	Ivan Rodriguez	8.00
SR	Scott Rolen	8.00
JS	Johan Santana/SP	10.00
CS	Curt Schilling	8.00
SM	John Smoltz	8.00
AS	Alfonso Soriano	8.00
SS	Sammy Sosa	10.00
MT	Mark Teixeira/SP	8.00
TE	Miguel Tejada	8.00
FT	Frank Thomas	8.00
JT	Jim Thome/SP	8.00
KW	Kerry Wood	8.00
DW	David Wright	10.00

Game Patch

		NM/M
Inserted 1:288		
DJ	Derek Jeter	75.00
CR	Cal Ripken Jr.	75.00

Hall of Fame Plaques

LYNN NOLAN RYAN JR.

NOLAN RYAN

		NM/M
Complete Set (10):		40.00
Common Player:		3.00
Inserted 1:36		
SP-16	Ernie Banks	4.00
SP-17	Yogi Berra	4.00
SP-18	Whitey Ford	3.00
SP-19	Bob Gibson	3.00
SP-20	Willie McCovey	3.00
SP-21	Stan Musial	6.00
SP-22	Nolan Ryan	12.00
SP-23	Mike Schmidt	8.00
SP-24	Tom Seaver	4.00
SP-25	Robin Yount	4.00

Lasting Impressions

No Pricing
Production One Set
One press plate per color.

Marquee Attractions

HIDEO NOMO • P
MARQUEE ATTRACTIONS
DODGERS

		NM/M
Common Player:		4.00
Inserted 1:12		
GA	Garret Anderson	4.00
JB	Jeff Bagwell	8.00
BE	Josh Beckett	4.00
KB	Kevin Brown	4.00
MC	Miguel Cabrera	8.00
RC	Roger Clemens	15.00
CD	Carlos Delgado	4.00
AD	Adam Dunn	8.00
EG	Eric Gagne	6.00
JG	Jason Giambi	4.00
BG	Brian Giles	4.00
SG	Shawn Green	4.00
KG	Ken Griffey Jr.	12.00
VG	Vladimir Guerrero	8.00
TH	Todd Helton	8.00
HO	Trevor Hoffman	4.00
DJ	Derek Jeter	20.00
RJ	Randy Johnson	10.00
AJ	Andruw Jones	6.00
CJ	Chipper Jones	8.00
GM	Greg Maddux	10.00
PM	Pedro Martinez	10.00
HM	Hideki Matsui	30.00
KM	Kazuo Matsui	8.00
JM	Joe Mauer	8.00
HN	Hideo Nomo	10.00
RO	Roy Oswalt	4.00
PE	Andy Pettitte	6.00
PI	Mike Piazza	10.00
MP	Mark Prior	6.00
AP	Albert Pujols	15.00
IR	Ivan Rodriguez	8.00
CS	Curt Schilling	8.00
JS	Jason Schmidt	6.00
SS	Sammy Sosa	12.00
IS	Ichiro Suzuki	25.00
MT	Miguel Tejada	6.00
JT	Jim Thome	8.00
BW	Billy Wagner	4.00
DW	Dontrelle Willis	4.00
PW	Preston Wilson	4.00
KW	Kerry Wood	8.00

Matinee Idols

MIKE PIAZZA
MATINEE Idols
MI
5 • METS

		NM/M
Common Player:		4.00
Inserted 1:12 Hobby		

JB	Jeff Bagwell	8.00
RB	Rocco Baldelli	4.00
BE	Josh Beckett	6.00
HB	Hank Blalock	8.00
BB	Bret Boone/SP	6.00
PB	Pat Burrell	6.00
SB	Sean Burroughs	4.00
EC	Eric Chavez	6.00
RC	Roger Clemens	15.00
CD	Carlos Delgado	4.00
JE	Jim Edmonds	6.00
JG	Jason Giambi	4.00
TG	Troy Glaus	4.00
KG	Ken Griffey Jr.	12.00
VG	Vladimir Guerrero	8.00
RH	Roy Halladay	4.00
TH	Todd Helton	8.00
HU	Torii Hunter	4.00
DJ	Derek Jeter	20.00
RJ	Randy Johnson	8.00
CJ	Chipper Jones	8.00
ML	Mike Lowell	4.00
MM	Mike Mussina	6.00
PI	Mike Piazza	10.00
MP	Mark Prior	6.00
CR	Cal Ripken Jr.	25.00
SR	Scott Rolen	8.00
NR	Nolan Ryan	25.00
CS	Curt Schilling	8.00
TS	Tom Seaver	8.00
GS	Gary Sheffield	6.00
SS	Sammy Sosa	12.00
MT	Mark Teixeira	6.00
JT	Jim Thome	8.00
BW	Billy Wagner	4.00
RW	Rickie Weeks	4.00
VW	Vernon Wells	4.00
DW	Dontrelle Willis	4.00
KW	Kerry Wood	8.00
BZ	Barry Zito	4.00

Milestone Materials

ERIC GAGNE • P
MILESTONE MATERIALS

		NM/M
Common Jersey:		5.00
BA	Jeff Bagwell	8.00
JB	Jason Bay	5.00
CB	Carlos Beltran	8.00
BC	Bobby Crosby	5.00
EG	Eric Gagne	5.00
KG	Ken Griffey Jr.	15.00
VG	Vladimir Guerrero	8.00
RJ	Randy Johnson	8.00
GM	Greg Maddux	10.00
DO	David Ortiz	8.00
RP	Rafael Palmeiro	8.00
JP	Jake Peavy	8.00
AP	Albert Pujols	20.00
MR	Manny Ramirez	8.00
JS	Johan Santana	8.00
CS	Curt Schilling	8.00
MT	Mark Teixeira	5.00
JT	Jim Thome	8.00

Origins

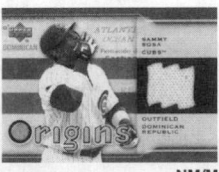

ATLANTA SAMMY
SOSA
Origins CUBS
OUTFIELD
DOMINICAN REPUBLIC

		NM/M
Common Player:		4.00
Inserted 1:12 Hobby		
Inserted 1:24 Retail		
GA	Garret Anderson	4.00
CB	Carlos Beltran	10.00
AB	Adrian Beltre	6.00

LB	Lance Berkman	4.00
MC	Miguel Cabrera	8.00
RF	Rafael Furcal	4.00
EG	Eric Gagne	6.00
BG	Brian Giles	4.00
JG	Juan Gonzalez	8.00
LG	Luis Gonzalez	4.00
VG	Vladimir Guerrero	8.00
TH	Tim Hudson	6.00
AJ	Andruw Jones	6.00
JK	Jeff Kent	4.00
JL	Javy Lopez	4.00
GM	Greg Maddux	10.00
PM	Pedro Martinez	10.00
HM	Hideki Matsui	30.00
KM	Kazuo Matsui	8.00
MM	Mark Mulder	4.00
HN	Hideo Nomo	10.00
MO	Magglio Ordonez	4.00
RP	Rafael Palmeiro	8.00
PE	Jake Peavy	4.00
JP	Jorge Posada	4.00
AP	Albert Pujols	15.00
MR	Manny Ramirez	8.00
JR	Jose Reyes	4.00
IR	Ivan Rodriguez	8.00
JS	Jason Schmidt	4.00
RS	Richie Sexson	4.00
AS	Alfonso Soriano	8.00
SS	Sammy Sosa	12.00
IS	Ichiro Suzuki	25.00
MT	Miguel Tejada	6.00
BU	B.J. Upton	8.00
JV	Javier Vazquez	4.00
PW	Preston Wilson	4.00

Rewind to 1997 Jersey

		NM/M
Common Jersey:		
Inserted 1:288		
JB	Jeff Bagwell	25.00
WC	Will Clark	20.00
KG	Ken Griffey Jr.	40.00
VG	Vladimir Guerrero	25.00
TG	Tony Gwynn	30.00
DJ	Derek Jeter	40.00
RJ	Randy Johnson	25.00
AJ	Andruw Jones	20.00
CJ	Chipper Jones	30.00
GM	Greg Maddux	40.00
PM	Pedro Martinez	25.00
MP	Mike Piazza	30.00
MR	Manny Ramirez	25.00
CR	Cal Ripken Jr.	40.00
IR	Ivan Rodriguez	20.00
SR	Scott Rolen	25.00
CS	Curt Schilling	20.00
JS	John Smoltz	25.00
FT	Frank Thomas	25.00
JT	Jim Thome	25.00

Signature Sensations

No Pricing
Production 15 Sets
Die-Cut: No Pricing
Production 10 Sets

Signature Stars

SIGNATURE STARS
MARK PRIOR • P

		NM/M
Common Player:		
Inserted 1:288 Hobby		
CB	Carlos Beltran/SP	40.00
HB	Hank Blalock	25.00
MC	Miguel Cabrera	35.00
BC	Bobby Crosby	30.00
LF	Lew Ford	10.00
KG	Ken Griffey Jr.	80.00
JL	Javy Lopez	15.00
JM	Joe Mauer	20.00
OP	Odalis Perez	20.00
CR	Cal Ripken Jr./SP	180.00
BS	Ben Sheets	15.00

DW	Dontrelle Willis	20.00
KW	Kerry Wood	25.00
DY	Delmon Young	25.00

Signature Stars Retail
Inserted 1:480 Retail

Super Patch - Names
No Pricing
Cards are not serial numbered.

Super Patch - Numbers
No Pricing
Cards are not serial numbered.

Super Patch - Logos
No Pricing
Cards are not serial numbered.

World Series Heroes

		NM/M
Complete Set (45):		20.00
Common Player:		.25
Inserted 1:1 Retail		
WS-1	Garret Anderson	.50
WS-2	Troy Glaus	.50
WS-3	Vladimir Guerrero	1.00
WS-4	Andruw Jones	.50
WS-5	Chipper Jones	1.00
WS-6	Curt Schilling	1.00
WS-7	Keith Foulke	.25
WS-8	Manny Ramirez	.75
WS-9	Nomar Garciaparra	1.50
WS-10	Pedro Martinez	1.00
WS-11	Kerry Wood	1.00
WS-12	Mark Prior	1.00
WS-13	Sammy Sosa	2.00
WS-14	Frank Thomas	.75
WS-15	Magglio Ordonez	.25
WS-16	Dontrelle Willis	.25
WS-17	Josh Beckett	.50
WS-18	Miguel Cabrera	.75
WS-19	Jeff Bagwell	.75
WS-20	Lance Berkman	.25
WS-21	Roger Clemens	2.00
WS-22	Eric Gagne	.50
WS-23	Torii Hunter	.50
WS-24	Mike Piazza	1.50
WS-25	Alex Rodriguez	2.00
WS-26	Derek Jeter	2.00
WS-27	Gary Sheffield	.50
WS-28	Hideki Matsui	1.50
WS-29	Jason Giambi	.50
WS-30	Jorge Posada	.50
WS-31	Kevin Brown	.25
WS-32	Mariano Rivera	.50
WS-33	Mike Mussina	.50
WS-34	Eric Chavez	.25
WS-35	Mark Mulder	.25
WS-36	Tim Hudson	.25
WS-37	Billy Wagner	.25
WS-38	Jim Thome	.75
WS-39	Brian Giles	.25
WS-40	Jason Schmidt	.25
WS-41	Albert Pujols	2.00
WS-42	Scott Rolen	.75
WS-43	Alfonso Soriano	.75
WS-44	Hank Blalock	.75
WS-45	Mark Teixeira	.50

4,000-Strikeout Commemorative

	NM/M
Production 4,000	
Steve Carlton, Nolan Ryan, Roger Clemens, Randy Johnson	12.00

4,000 Strikeout Autographs
Production 50 Sets
Quad Signature: No Pricing
Production 10

2004 Update Set

		NM/M
Complete Set (50):		10.00
Common Player:		.15
Inserted 1:Hobby Box		
541	Alex Rodriguez	1.50
542	Roger Clemens	1.50
543	Andy Pettitte	.25
544	Vladimir Guerrero	.75
545	David Wells	.15
546	Derek Lee	.25
547	Carlos Beltran	.50
548	Orlando Cabrera	.25
549	Paul LoDuca	.15
550	Dave Roberts	.15
551	Guillermo Mota	.15
552	Steve Finley	.15

553	Juan Encarnacion	.15
554	Larry Walker	.50
555	Ty Wigginton	.15
556	Doug Mientkiewicz	.15
557	Roberto Alomar	.40
558	B.J. Upton	.50
559	Brad Penny	.15
560	Hee Seop Choi	.15
561	David Wright	1.00
562	Nomar Garciaparra	1.00
563	Felix Rodriguez	.15
564	Victor Zambrano	.15
565	Kris Benson	.15
566	Aarom Baldiris	.15
567	Joey Gathright	.15
568	Charles Thomas	.15
569	Brian Dallimore	.15
570	Chris Oxspring	.15
571	Chris Shelton	.15
572	Dioner Navarro	.25
573	Edwardo Sierra	.15
574	Fernando Nieve	.15
575	Frank Francisco	.15
576	Jeff Bennett	.15
577	Justin Lehr	.15
578	John Gall	.15
579	Jorge Sequea	.15
580	Justin Germano	.15
581	Kazuhito Tadano	.15
582	Kevin Cave	.15
583	Jesse Crain	.15
584	Luis Gonzalez	.15
585	Mike Wuertz	.15
586	Orlando Rodriguez	.15
587	Phil Stockman	.15
588	Ramon Ramirez	.15
589	Roberto Novoa	.15
590	Scott Kazmir	1.50

2004 Update - Awesome Honors

		NM/M
Common Player:		8.00
1:12 '04 Update Set		
Production 75 Sets		
BE	Adrian Beltre	10.00
AB	Angel Berroa	8.00
KB	Kevin Brown	8.00
MC	Miguel Cabrera	15.00
RC	Roger Clemens	20.00
EG	Eric Gagne	12.00
BG	Brian Giles	8.00
DL	Derrek Lee	8.00
KM	Kazuo Matsui	20.00
JM	Joe Mauer	10.00
PE	Andy Pettitte	10.00
SP	Scott Podsednik	8.00
AP	Albert Pujols	25.00
IR	Ivan Rodriguez	12.00
SC	Curt Schilling	12.00
RS	Richie Sexson	8.00
GS	Gary Sheffield	8.00
AS	Alfonso Soriano	15.00
VA	Javier Vazquez	8.00

2004 Update - Authentic Stars

		NM/M
Common Player:		8.00
1:12 '04 Update Sets		
Production 75 Sets		
CB	Carlos Beltran	15.00
LB	Lance Berkman	8.00
JE	Jim Edmonds	8.00
RF	Rafael Furcal	8.00
HA	Roy Halladay	8.00
RH	Rich Harden	8.00
HU	Tim Hudson	8.00
DJ	Derek Jeter	35.00
AK	Austin Kearns	8.00
HN	Hideo Nomo	20.00

MO	Magglio Ordonez	8.00
OS	Roy Oswalt	8.00
RP	Rafael Palmeiro	12.00
MR	Manny Ramirez	15.00
JR	Jose Reyes	8.00
SR	Scott Rolen	15.00
TE	Miguel Tejada	8.00
JT	Jim Thome	12.00
WE	Brandon Webb	8.00
VW	Vernon Wells	8.00
PW	Preston Wilson	8.00
KW	Kerry Wood	8.00

2005 UD All-Star Classics

		NM/M
Complete Set (100):		25.00
Common Player:		.15
Pack (8):		3.00
Box (24):		60.00
1	Albert Pujols	2.00
2	Alex Rodriguez	1.50
3	Alfonso Soriano	.75
4	Barry Zito	.25
5	Bobby Abreu	.40
6	Carlos Beltran	.50
7	Carlos Delgado	.40
8	Chipper Jones	.75
9	Curt Schilling	.75
10	David Ortiz	.75
11	Derek Jeter	2.00
12	Edgar Renteria	.25
13	Eric Gagne	.25
14	Frank Thomas	.50
15	Gary Sheffield	.40
16	Greg Maddux	1.00
17	Hank Blalock	.40
18	Hideki Matsui	1.50
19	Ichiro Suzuki	1.50
20	Ivan Rodriguez	.50
21	Jason Schmidt	.25
22	Jason Varitek	.25
23	Jeff Kent	.25
24	Jim Thome	.75
25	Jorge Posada	.25
26	Ken Griffey Jr.	1.00
27	Kerry Wood	.75
28	Lance Berkman	.25
29	Manny Ramirez	.75
30	Mariano Rivera	.40
31	Mark Mulder	.25
32	Mark Prior	.75
33	Miguel Cabrera	.75
34	Miguel Tejada	.25
35	Mike Piazza	1.00
36	Nomar Garciaparra	1.00
37	Pedro Martinez	.75
38	Randy Johnson	.75
39	Richie Sexson	.25
40	Roger Clemens	2.00
41	Roy Halladay	.25
42	Sammy Sosa	1.50
43	Scott Rolen	.75
44	Sean Casey	.25
45	Tim Hudson	.25
46	Todd Helton	.50
47	Tom Glavine	.40
48	Torii Hunter	.25
49	Troy Glaus	.25
50	Vladimir Guerrero	.75
51	Adrian Beltre	.25
52	Alexis Rios	.15
53	Aubrey Huff	.15
54	Brandon Webb	.25
55	Dallas McPherson	.25
56	David Wright	.75
57	Edwin Jackson	.15
58	Grady Sizemore	.40
59	Tadahito Iguchi RC	3.00
60	Jake Peavy	.40
61	Jake Westbrook	.15
62	Jason Bay	.25

63	Jeff Francis	.15
64	Jeremy Reed	.15
65	Joe Mauer	.40
66	Johan Santana	.50
67	Jose Capellan	.15
68	Jose Reyes	.25
69	Justin Morneau	.40
70	Mark Teixeira	.40
71	Oliver Perez	.25
72	Rich Harden	.25
73	Rickie Weeks	.25
74	Ryan Howard	.75
75	Scott Kazmir	.15
76	Al Kaline	.75
77	Bill Mazeroski	.25
78	Bob Feller	.50
79	Bob Gibson	.50
80	Brooks Robinson	.75
81	Cal Ripken Jr.	3.00
82	Carlton Fisk	.25
83	Eddie Murray	.50
84	Gaylord Perry	.25
85	Harmon Killebrew	.75
86	Jim Palmer	.50
87	Joe DiMaggio	1.50
88	Joe Morgan	.25
89	Johnny Bench	.75
90	Juan Marichal	.25
91	Lou Brock	.25
92	Mike Schmidt	1.00
93	Nolan Ryan	2.00
94	Ozzie Smith	.75
95	Phil Niekro	.25
96	Robin Yount	.50
97	Rollie Fingers	.25
98	Tom Seaver	.50
99	Willie McCovey	.50
100	Yogi Berra	.75

Gold

Stars (1-100):	4-8X
Production 499 Sets	

Box Scores

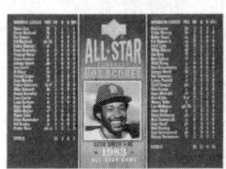

		NM/M
Complete Set (20):		50.00
Common Player:		1.50
Inserted 1:24		
1	Juan Marichal	2.00
2	Brooks Robinson	3.00
3	Tony Perez	1.50
4	Willie McCovey	2.00
5	Harmon Killebrew	3.00
6	Johnny Bench	3.00
7	Joe Morgan	1.50
8	Lou Brock	1.50
9	Jim Palmer	1.50
10	Mike Schmidt	5.00
11	Ozzie Smith	4.00
12	Roger Clemens	6.00
13	Cal Ripken Jr.	8.00
14	Ken Griffey Jr.	4.00
15	Greg Maddux	4.00
16	Alex Rodriguez	5.00
17	Derek Jeter	6.00
18	Johnny Damon	3.00
19	Garret Anderson	1.50
20	Alfonso Soriano	2.00

Matchups

		NM/M
Complete Set (20):		40.00
Common Player:		1.50
Inserted 1:24		
1	Hank Blalock	2.00
2	Curt Schilling	3.00
3	Manny Ramirez	3.00
4	Ken Griffey Jr.	4.00
5	Brooks Robinson	3.00
6	Harmon Killebrew	3.00
7	Carl Yastrzemski	4.00

8	Cal Ripken Jr.	8.00
9	Trevor Hoffman	1.50
10	Eric Gagne	2.00
11	Alfonso Soriano	2.00
12	David Ortiz	3.00
13	Andruw Jones	1.50
14	Garret Anderson	1.50
15	Magglio Ordonez	1.50
16	Derek Jeter	6.00
17	Chipper Jones	3.00
18	Roberto Alomar	2.00
19	Mike Piazza	3.00
20	Alex Rodriguez	5.00

Midsummer Classics

	NM/M
Complete Set (20):	40.00
Common Player:	1.50
Inserted 1:24	

1	Derek Jeter	6.00
2	Pedro Martinez	2.00
3	Mike Piazza	3.00
4	Randy Johnson	2.00
5	Gary Sheffield	2.00
6	Albert Pujols	6.00
7	David Ortiz	3.00
8	Manny Ramirez	3.00
9	Garret Anderson	1.50
10	Andruw Jones	1.50
11	Todd Helton	2.00
12	Paul Konerko	1.50
13	Alfonso Soriano	2.00
14	Magglio Ordonez	1.50
15	Cal Ripken Jr.	8.00
16	Ken Griffey Jr.	3.00
17	Harmon Killebrew	3.00
18	Mike Schmidt	5.00
19	Frank Thomas	2.00
20	Alex Rodriguez	5.00

Midsummer Swatches

	NM/M
Common Player:	4.00
Inserted 1:12	
Patches:	No Pricing
Production 25 Sets	

MA	Moises Alou/Jsy	6.00
JB	Jeff Bagwell/Jsy	6.00
CB	Carlos Beltran/Jsy	8.00
CI	Craig Biggio/Jsy	6.00
BB	Bret Boone/Jsy	4.00
CD	Carlos Delgado/Jsy	6.00
JE	Jim Edmonds/Jsy	6.00
KF	Keith Foulke/Jsy	6.00
RF	Rafael Furcal/Jsy	4.00
EG	Eric Gagne/Jsy	8.00
SG	Shawn Green/Jsy	4.00
KG	Ken Griffey Jr./Jsy	25.00
TH	Todd Helton/Jsy	8.00
TI	Torii Hunter/Jsy	6.00
AJ	Andruw Jones/Pants	6.00
CJ	Chipper Jones/Jsy	8.00
JK	Jeff Kent/Jsy	4.00
RK	Ryan Klesko	4.00
ML	Matt Lawton/Jsy	4.00
PL	Paul LoDuca/Jsy	4.00
JL	Javy Lopez/Jsy	4.00
PM	Pedro Martinez/Jsy	8.00
VM	Victor Martinez/Jsy	4.00
DO	David Ortiz/Pants	8.00
RP	Rafael Palmeiro/Jsy	8.00
MP	Mike Piazza/Jsy	15.00
ER	Edgar Renteria/Jsy	6.00
CR	Cal Ripken Jr./Pants	35.00
CC	C.C. Sabathia/Jsy	4.00
SC	Jason Schmidt/Jsy	4.00
BS	Ben Sheets/Jsy	6.00
GS	Gary Sheffield/Jsy	8.00
JS	John Smoltz/Jsy	10.00
SS	Sammy Sosa/Jsy	10.00
IS	Ichiro Suzuki/Jsy	30.00
MS	Mike Sweeney/Jsy	4.00
MT	Miguel Tejada/Jsy	8.00
FT	Frank Thomas/Jsy	8.00
JT	Jim Thome/Jsy	8.00
OM	Omar Vizquel/Jsy	6.00
WE	David Wells/Jsy	4.00
DW	Dontrelle Willis/Jsy	8.00

MVP's

	NM/M
Complete Set (20):	45.00
Common Player:	1.00
Inserted 1:24	

1	Alfonso Soriano	2.00
2	Ken Griffey Sr.	4.00
3	Brooks Robinson	3.00
4	Cal Ripken Jr.	8.00
5	Cal Ripken Jr.	8.00
6	Derek Jeter	6.00
7	Carl Yastrzemski	4.00
8	Garret Anderson	1.50
9	Jeff Conine	1.00
10	Joe Morgan	1.50
11	Juan Marichal	2.00
12	Julio Franco	1.00
13	Ken Griffey Jr.	4.00
14	Mike Piazza	3.00
15	Pedro Martinez	3.00
16	Roberto Alomar	2.00
17	Roger Clemens	6.00
18	Sandy Alomar Jr.	1.00
19	Tony Perez	1.50
20	Willie McCovey	2.00

Perennial All-Stars

	NM/M
Complete Set (20):	40.00
Common Player:	2.00
Inserted 1:24	

1	Albert Pujols	6.00
2	Alex Rodriguez	5.00
3	Alfonso Soriano	2.00
4	Curt Schilling	3.00
5	Derek Jeter	6.00
6	Eric Gagne	2.00
7	Greg Maddux	4.00
8	Ichiro Suzuki	5.00
9	Ivan Rodriguez	2.00
10	Jim Thome	2.00
11	Ken Griffey Jr.	4.00
12	Mariano Rivera	2.00
13	Miguel Tejada	2.00
14	Mike Piazza	3.00
15	Randy Johnson	2.00
16	Roger Clemens	6.00
17	Sammy Sosa	4.00
18	Scott Rolen	3.00
19	Todd Helton	2.00
20	Vladimir Guerrero	2.00

2005 Upper Deck Artifacts

	NM/M
Complete Set (200):	
Common Player (1-100):	.25
Common (101-150):	2.00
Production 1,350	
Common (151-200):	2.00
Production 1,999	
Pack (4):	10.00
Box (10):	90.00

1	Adam Dunn	.75
2	Adrian Beltre	.75
3	Albert Pujols	3.00
4	Alex Rodriguez	2.50
5	Alfonso Soriano	1.00
6	Andruw Jones	.50
7	Andy Pettitte	.50
8	Aramis Ramirez	.50
9	Aubrey Huff	.25
10	Barry Larkin	.50
11	Ben Sheets	.50
12	Bernie Williams	.50
13	Bobby Abreu	.50
14	Brad Penny	.25
15	Bret Boone	.25
16	Brian Giles	.25
17	Carl Crawford	.25
18	Carl Pavano	.50
19	Carlos Beltran	.75
20	Carlos Delgado	.75
21	Carlos Guillen	.25
22	Carlos Lee	.50
23	Carlos Zambrano	.50
24	Chipper Jones	1.00
25	Craig Biggio	.50
26	Craig Wilson	.25
27	Curt Schilling	1.00
28	David Ortiz	1.00
29	Derek Jeter	3.00
30	Eric Chavez	.50
31	Eric Gagne	.50
32	Frank Thomas	.75
33	Garret Anderson	.50
34	Gary Sheffield	.50
35	Greg Maddux	1.50
36	Hank Blalock	.75
37	Hideki Matsui	2.00
38	Ichiro Suzuki	2.50
39	Ivan Rodriguez	.75
40	J.D. Drew	.50
41	Jake Peavy	.50
42	Jason Kendall	.25
43	Jason Schmidt	.50
44	Jeff Bagwell	.75
45	Jeff Kent	.50
46	Jim Edmonds	.50
47	Jim Thome	1.00
48	Joe Mauer	.75
49	Johan Santana	.75
50	John Smoltz	.50
51	Jose Reyes	.50
52	Jose Vidro	.25
53	Josh Beckett	.50
54	Ken Griffey Jr.	1.50
55	Kerry Wood	1.00
56	Kevin Brown	.25
57	Lance Berkman	.50
58	Larry Walker	.50
59	Livan Hernandez	.25
60	Luis Gonzalez	.25
61	Lyle Overbay	.25
62	Magglio Ordonez	.50
63	Manny Ramirez	1.00
64	Mark Mulder	.50
65	Mark Prior	1.00
66	Mark Teixeira	.50
67	Melvin Mora	.25
68	Michael Young	.50
69	Miguel Cabrera	1.00
70	Miguel Tejada	.75
71	Mike Lowell	.25
72	Mike Mussina	.50
73	Mike Piazza	1.50
74	Mike Sweeney	.25
75	Nomar Garciaparra	2.00
76	Oliver Perez	.25
77	Paul Konerko	.25
78	Pedro Martinez	1.00
79	Preston Wilson	.25
80	Rafael Furcal	.25
81	Rafael Palmeiro	.25
82	Randy Johnson	1.00
83	Richie Sexson	.50
84	Roger Clemens	3.00
85	Roy Halladay	.50
86	Roy Oswalt	.50
87	Sammy Sosa	2.00
88	Scott Podsednik	.25
89	Scott Rolen	1.00
90	Shawn Green	.25
91	Steve Finley	.25
92	Tim Hudson	.50
93	Todd Helton	.75
94	Tom Glavine	.50
95	Torii Hunter	.25
96	Travis Hafner	.50
97	Troy Glaus	.50
98	Vernon Wells	.25
99	Victor Martinez	.50
100	Vladimir Guerrero	1.00
101	Aaron Rowand	2.00
102	Adam LaRoche	2.00
103	Adrian Gonzalez	2.00
104	Alexis Rios	2.00
105	Angel Guzman	2.00
106	B.J. Upton	3.00
107	Bobby Crosby	3.00
108	Bobby Madritsch	2.00
109	Brandon Claussen	2.00
110	Bucky Jacobsen	2.00
111	Casey Kotchman	2.00
112	Chad Cordero	2.00
113	Chase Utley	2.00
114	Chris Burke	2.00
115	Dallas McPherson	4.00
116	Daniel Cabrera	2.00
117	David DeJesus	2.00
118	David Wright	6.00
119	Eddy Rodriguez	2.00
120	Edwin Jackson	2.00
121	Gabe Gross	2.00
122	Garrett Atkins	2.00
123	Gavin Floyd	2.00
124	Gerald Laird	2.00
125	Guillermo Quiroz	2.00
126	J.D. Closser	2.00
127	Jason Bay	4.00
128	Jason Dubois	2.00
129	Jason Lane	2.00
130	Jayson Werth	2.00
131	Jeff Francis	2.00
132	Jesse Crain	2.00
133	Joe Blanton	2.00
134	Joe Mauer	4.00
135	Jose Capellan	2.00
136	Kevin Youkilis	2.00
137	Khalil Greene	3.00
138	Laynce Nix	2.00
139	Nick Swisher	2.00
140	Oliver Perez	2.00
141	Rickie Weeks	2.00
142	Robb Quinlan	2.00
143	Roman Colon	2.00
144	Ryan Howard	4.00
145	Ryan Wagner	2.00
146	Scott Kazmir	4.00
147	Scott Proctor	2.00
148	Wily Mo Pena	2.00
149	Yhency Brazoban	2.00
150	Zack Greinke	2.00
151	Al Kaline	5.00
152	Babe Ruth	8.00
153	Billy Williams	2.00
154	Bob Feller	3.00
155	Bob Gibson	4.00
156	Bob Lemon	2.00
157	Bobby Doerr	2.00
158	Brooks Robinson	4.00
159	Cal Ripken Jr.	10.00
160	Christy Mathewson	4.00
161	Cy Young	5.00
162	Dizzy Dean	5.00
163	Don Drysdale	2.00
164	Eddie Mathews	4.00
165	Enos Slaughter	2.00
166	Ernie Banks	5.00
167	Fergie Jenkins	2.00
168	George Sisler	2.00
169	Harmon Killebrew	4.00
170	Honus Wagner	5.00
171	Jackie Robinson	5.00
172	Jimmie Foxx	4.00
173	Joe DiMaggio	6.00
174	Joe Morgan	2.00

175	Juan Marichal	2.00
176	Lou Brock	2.00
177	Lou Gehrig	6.00
178	Luis Aparicio	2.00
179	Mel Ott	4.00
180	Mickey Cochrane	2.00
181	Mickey Mantle	10.00
182	Mike Schmidt	6.00
183	Nolan Ryan	8.00
184	Pee Wee Reese	2.00
185	Phil Rizzuto	2.00
186	Ralph Kiner	2.00
187	Rogers Hornsby	3.00
188	Roy Campanella	3.00
189	Satchel Paige	4.00
190	Stan Musial	5.00
191	Rick Ferrell	2.00
192	Thurman Munson	5.00
193	Tom Seaver	4.00
194	Ty Cobb	6.00
195	Walter Johnson	5.00
196	Warren Spahn	4.00
197	Whitey Ford	4.00
198	Willie McCovey	3.00
199	Willie Stargell	3.00
200	Yogi Berra	4.00

Rainbow Blue

Blue (1-100):	3-5X
Blue (101-200):	1-2X
Production 100 Sets	

Rainbow Gold

Gold (1-100):	6-10X
Gold (101-200):	2-3X
Production 25 Sets	

Rainbow Platinum

No Pricing
Production One Set

Rainbow Red

Red (1-100):	4-8X
Red (101-200):	1.5-3X
Production 50 Sets	

AL/NL Artifacts

	NM/M
Common Player:	4.00
Production 325 unless noted.	
Rainbow:	.75-1.5X
Production 99 Sets	
BA	Bobby Abreu/Jsy	6.00
JB	Jason Bay/Jsy	6.00
CB	Carlos Beltran/Jsy	8.00
AB	Adrian Beltre/Jsy	6.00
BE	Johnny Bench/Jsy	10.00
YB	Yogi Berra/Pants	15.00
HB	Hank Blalock/Jsy	8.00
BB	Bert Blyleven/Jsy	6.00
WB	Wade Boggs/Jsy	8.00
GB	George Brett/Jsy	15.00
MC	Miguel Cabrera/Jsy	10.00
RCA	Rod Carew/Jsy	8.00
CA	Steve Carlton/Jsy	6.00
SC	Sean Casey/Jsy	4.00
OC	Orlando Cepeda/ Jsy/185	8.00
EC	Eric Chavez/Jsy	4.00
WC	Will Clark/Jsy/100	10.00
CN	Roger Clemens/Jsy	15.00
BC	Bobby Crosby/Jsy	6.00
AD	Andre Dawson/Jsy	6.00
BD	Bobby Doerr/Bat	6.00
BF	Bob Feller/Pants	10.00
EG	Eric Gagne/Jsy	8.00
BG	Bob Gibson/Pants	10.00
GI	Brian Giles/Jsy	4.00
MG	Marcus Giles/Jsy	4.00
DG	Dwight Gooden/Pants	6.00
MK	Mark Grace/Jsy/175	8.00
KG	Ken Griffey Jr./Jsy	15.00
GR	Ken Griffey Sr./Jsy	4.00
TG	Tony Gwynn/Jsy	10.00
TH	Travis Hafner/Jsy	4.00
RH	Rich Harden/Jsy	8.00
KHN	Keith Hernandez/Bat	4.00
KHA	Kent Hrbek/Jsy	4.00
AH	Aubrey Huff/Jsy	4.00
DJ	Derek Jeter/Jsy	20.00
RJ	Randy Johnson/Jsy	10.00
JK	Jim Kaat/Jsy	6.00
AK	Al Kaline/Jsy	10.00

GK	George Kell/Bat	6.00
HK	Harmon Killebrew/ Jsy	10.00
RK	Ralph Kiner/Bat	6.00
DK	Dave Kingman/Bat	4.00
CK	Casey Kotchman/Jsy	4.00
DL	Derrek Lee/Jsy	6.00
ML	Mike Lowell/Jsy	4.00
SL	Sparky Lyle/Pants	4.00
FL	Fred Lynn/Bat	4.00
GM	Greg Maddux/Jsy/ 275	12.00
VM	Victor Martinez/Jsy	6.00
MA	Don Mattingly/Jsy	20.00
JM	Joe Mauer/Jsy	10.00
WM	Willie McCovey/Jsy	8.00
DMA	Dallas McPherson/Jsy	8.00
PM	Paul Molitor/Jsy	8.00
MM	Mark Mulder/Jsy	6.00
DMN	Dale Murphy/Jsy/150	8.00
GN	Graig Nettles/Jsy	4.00
PN	Phil Niekro/Jsy	4.00
LN	Laynce Nix/Jsy	4.00
DO	David Ortiz/Jsy	10.00
RO	Roy Oswalt/Jsy	4.00
AO	Akinori Otsuka/Jsy	4.00
JPA	Jim Palmer/Jsy	8.00
CP	Corey Patterson/Jsy	6.00
JPN	Jake Peavy/Jsy	6.00
BPN	Brad Penny/Jsy	4.00
RP	Rico Petrocelli/Pants	8.00
SP	Scott Podsednik/Jsy	4.00
BPA	Boog Powell/Jsy	6.00
MP	Mark Prior/Jsy	8.00
AP	Albert Pujols/Jsy	25.00
JRN	Jose Reyes/Jsy/250	8.00
JRA	Jim Rice/Jsy	8.00
CR	Cal Ripken Jr./Jsy	25.00
BR	Brooks Robinson/Jsy	8.00
FR	Frank Robinson/Jsy	8.00
SR	Scott Rolen/Jsy	10.00
NR	Nolan Ryan/Jsy	25.00
JSA	Johan Santana/Jsy	10.00
JSN	Jason Schmidt/Jsy	6.00
MS	Mike Schmidt/Jsy	15.00
TS	Tom Seaver/Jsy	8.00
BS	Ben Sheets/Jsy	6.00
SM	John Smoltz/Jsy	6.00
SU	Bruce Sutter/Jsy	6.00
ST	Shingo Takatsu/Jsy	4.00
MT	Mark Teixeira/Jsy	8.00
BU	B.J. Upton/Jsy	6.00
RW	Rickie Weeks/Jsy	6.00
MW	Maury Wills/Jsy	6.00
KW	Kerry Wood/Jsy	8.00
DW	David Wright/Jsy	10.00
CY	Carl Yastrzemski/Jsy	15.00
MY	Michael Young/Jsy	6.00
RY	Robin Yount/Jsy	15.00
CZ	Carlos Zambrano/Jsy	6.00

AL/NL Artifacts
Signatures

	NM/M
Production 30 Sets	
Rare Artifacts:	No Pricing
Production One Set	
BA	Bobby Abreu/Jsy/ Redemp.	20.00
JB	Jason Bay/Jsy	30.00
CB	Carlos Beltran/Jsy/ Redemp.	25.00
AB	Adrian Beltre/Jsy	30.00
BE	Johnny Bench/Jsy	65.00
YB	Yogi Berra/Pants	60.00
HB	Hank Blalock/Jsy	25.00
BB	Bert Blyleven/Jsy	30.00
WB	Wade Boggs/Jsy	50.00
GB	George Brett/Jsy	120.00
MC	Miguel Cabrera/Jsy	40.00
RCA	Rod Carew/Jsy	40.00
SC	Sean Casey/Jsy	30.00
CA	Steve Carlton/Jsy	40.00
OC	Orlando Cepeda/Jsy	35.00
EC	Eric Chavez/Jsy	30.00
WC	Will Clark/Jsy	50.00
RCN	Roger Clemens/ Jsy/Redemp.	100.00
BC	Bobby Crosby/ Jsy/Redemp.	20.00
AD	Andre Dawson/Jsy	30.00
BD	Bobby Doerr/Bat	45.00
BF	Bob Feller/Pants	40.00
EG	Eric Gagne/ Jsy/Redemp.	50.00
BG	Bob Gibson/Pants	50.00
GI	Brian Giles/Jsy	20.00
MG	Marcus Giles/Jsy	20.00
DG	Dwight Gooden/ Pants	30.00
MK	Mark Grace/Jsy	50.00
KL	Khalil Greene/Jsy	50.00
KG	Ken Griffey Jr./Jsy	120.00

GR	Ken Griffey Sr./Jsy	25.00
TG	Tony Gwynn/Jsy	90.00
TH	Travis Hafner/Jsy	50.00
RH	Rich Harden/Jsy	40.00
KHN	Keith Hernandez/Bat	20.00
KHA	Kent Hrbek/Jsy	50.00
AH	Aubrey Huff/Jsy	25.00
DJ	Derek Jeter/Jsy	200.00
RJ	Randy Johnson/ Jsy/Redemp.	
JK	Jim Kaat/Jsy	25.00
AK	Al Kaline/Jsy	50.00
GK	George Kell/Bat	30.00
HK	Harmon Killebrew/Jsy	60.00
RK	Ralph Kiner/Bat	50.00
DK	Dave Kingman/Bat	25.00
CK	Casey Kotchman/Jsy	25.00
DL	Derrek Lee/Jsy	40.00
ML	Mike Lowell/Jsy	20.00
SL	Sparky Lyle/Pants	25.00
FL	Fred Lynn/Bat	25.00
GM	Greg Maddux/ Jsy/Redemp.	150.00
VM	Victor Martinez/Jsy	25.00
MA	Don Mattingly/Jsy	100.00
JM	Joe Mauer/ Jsy/Redemp.	35.00
BM	Bill Mazeroski/ Jsy/Redemp.	30.00
WM	Willie McCovey/Jsy	50.00
DMA	Dallas McPherson/ Jsy/Redemp.	30.00
PM	Paul Molitor/Jsy	40.00
MM	Mark Mulder/Jsy	25.00
DMN	Dale Murphy/Jsy	35.00
GN	Graig Nettles/Jsy	35.00
PN	Phil Niekro/Jsy	25.00
LN	Laynce Nix/Jsy	20.00
DO	David Ortiz/Jsy	50.00
RO	Roy Oswalt/Jsy	25.00
AO	Akinori Otsuka/Jsy	40.00
JPA	Jim Palmer/Jsy	40.00
CP	Corey Patterson/Jsy/ Redemp.	30.00
JPN	Jake Peavy/Jsy	50.00
BPN	Brad Penny/Jsy	20.00
RP	Rico Petrocelli/Pants	25.00
SP	Scott Podsednik/Jsy	25.00
MP	Mark Prior/Jsy	50.00
AP	Albert Pujols/Jsy/ Redemp.	220.00
JRN	Jose Reyes/Jsy/ Redemp.	40.00
JRA	Jim Rice/Jsy	40.00
CR	Cal Ripken Jr./Jsy	200.00
BR	Brooks Robinson/Jsy	50.00
FR	Frank Robinson/Jsy	40.00
SR	Scott Rolen/ Jsy/Redemp.	75.00
NR	Nolan Ryan/Jsy	125.00
JSA	Johan Santana/Jsy/ Redemp.	65.00
JSN	Jason Schmidt/Jsy	60.00
MS	Mike Schmidt/Jsy	50.00
TS	Tom Seaver/Jsy	50.00
BS	Ben Sheets/Jsy/ Redemp.	30.00
SM	John Smoltz/Jsy/ Redemp.	75.00
SU	Bruce Sutter/Jsy	20.00
ST	Shingo Takatsu/Jsy	50.00
MT	Mark Teixeira/Jsy	45.00
BU	B.J. Upton/Jsy	25.00
RW	Rickie Weeks/Jsy	25.00
MW	Maury Wills/Jsy	50.00
KW	Kerry Wood/Jsy	50.00
DW	David Wright/Jsy	65.00
CY	Carl Yastrzemski/Jsy	85.00
MY	Michael Young/ Jsy/Redemp.	25.00
RY	Robin Yount/Jsy	75.00
CZ	Carlos Zambrano/Jsy	35.00

Autofacts

	NM/M
Production 15-699	
Rainbow:	No Pricing
Production One Set	
JB	Jason Bay/599	15.00
AB	Adrian Beltre/ 75 Redemp.	25.00
BE	Johnny Bench/15	75.00
HB	Hank Blalock/25	35.00
GB	George Brett/15	140.00
MI	Miguel Cabrera/25	40.00
OC	Orlando Cepeda/25	35.00
EC	Eric Chavez/25	30.00
RC	Rocky Colavito/75	75.00
BC	Bobby Crosby/ 350 Redemp.	15.00
AD	Andre Dawson/25	30.00
BF	Bob Feller/25	40.00
SF	Sid Fernandez/599	10.00

LD1	Lenny Dykstra/ Mets/599	10.00
LD2	Lenny Dykstra/ Phils/599	10.00
FR	Bill Freehan/ 599 Redemp.	10.00
GI	Marcus Giles/350	12.00
DG1	Dwight Gooden/ Mets/350	15.00
DG2	Dwight Gooden/ Yanks/350	15.00
MG	Mark Grace/25	
GR	Khalil Greene/599	25.00
JR	Ken Griffey Jr./699	75.00
KG1	Ken Griffey Sr./ Reds/699	10.00
KG2	Ken Griffey Sr./ Yanks/699	10.00
TH	Travis Hafner/599	12.00
RH	Rich Harden/599	20.00
KH1	Keith Hernandez/ Mets/350	15.00
KH2	Keith Hernandez/ Cards/350	15.00
HO	Ken Holtzman/599	10.00
BH	Burt Hooton/599	8.00
HR	Kent Hrbek/599	15.00
AH	Aubrey Huff/350	8.00
DJ	Derek Jeter/350	150.00
JK1	Jim Kaat Cards/458	15.00
JK2	Jim Kaat Twins/458	15.00
AK	Al Kaline/15	80.00
DK	Dave Kingman/75	25.00
CK	Casey Kotchman/599	10.00
EK	Ed Kranepool	12.00
JL	Jim Lonborg/599	15.00
ML	Mike Lowell/75	15.00
SL1	Sparky Lyle/Sox/599	8.00
SL2	Sparky Lyle/ Yanks/599	8.00
FL	Fred Lynn/25	25.00
VM	Victor Martinez/599	15.00
JM	Joe Mauer/ 25 Redemp.	30.00
MC	Dallas McPherson/ 599 Redemp.	20.00
DM	Dale Murphy/75	25.00
GN	Graig Nettles/75	25.00
PN1	Phil Niekro/ Braves/75	20.00
PN2	Phil Niekro/ Yanks/75	20.00
LN	Laynce Nix/599	10.00
RO	Roy Oswalt/350	15.00
AO	Akinori Otsuka/599	25.00
JP	Jim Palmer/25	35.00
CP	Corey Patterson/ 75 Redemp.	25.00
JA	Jake Peavy/75	30.00
BP	Brad Penny/599	15.00
OP	Oliver Perez/350	20.00
PE	Jim Perry/599	10.00
RP	Rico Petrocelli/599	15.00
SP	Scott Podsednik/75	15.00
PO	Boog Powell/350	15.00
MP	Mark Prior/15	50.00
CR	Cal Ripken Jr./15	250.00
BR	Brooks Robinson/25	50.00
NR	Nolan Ryan/15	175.00
JS	Johan Santana/ 350 Redemp.	40.00
BS	Ben Sheets/ 75 Redemp.	20.00
SU	Bruce Sutter/350	12.00
ST	Shingo Takatsu/599	20.00
MT	Mark Teixeira/25	40.00
LT	Luis Tiant/75	20.00
BU	B.J. Upton/599	15.00
RW	Rickie Weeks/75	15.00
KW	Kerry Wood/15	50.00
DW	David Wright/599	50.00
MY	Michael Young/ 599 Redemp.	12.00

Dual Artifacts

	NM/M
Production 99 Sets	
Rainbow:	1-2X
Production 25 Sets	
AB	Bobby Abreu/Jsy, Carlos Beltran/Jsy	15.00

AD	Adrian Beltre/Jsy, Dallas McPherson/Jsy	15.00
AG	Bobby Abreu/Jsy, Ken Griffey Jr./Jsy	15.00
BB	George Brett/Jsy, Wade Boggs/Jsy	20.00
BC	Adrian Beltre/Jsy, Eric Chavez/Jsy	8.00
BD	Bob Gibson/Pants, Dwight Gooden/Pants	8.00
BE	Bobby Crosby/Jsy, Eric Chavez/Jsy	10.00
BJ	Brooks Robinson/Jsy, Jim Palmer/Jsy	20.00
BK	Jason Bay/Jsy, Ralph Kiner/Bat	10.00
BM	Brian Giles/Jsy, Marcus Giles/Jsy	8.00
BN	Hank Blalock/Jsy, Laynce Nix/Jsy	8.00
BP	Carlos Beltran/Jsy, Corey Patterson/Jsy	12.00
BR	Ernie Banks/Pants, Frank Robinson/Jsy	20.00
BS	Ben Sheets/Jsy, Scott Podsednik/Jsy	8.00
BY	Hank Blalock/Jsy, Michael Young/Jsy	8.00
CB	Jason Bay/Jsy, Bobby Crosby/Jsy	8.00
CC	Miguel Cabrera/Jsy, Orlando Cepeda/Jsy	12.00
CG	Dwight Gooden/Pants, Gary Carter/Jsy	10.00
CH	Sean Casey/Jsy, Travis Hafner/Jsy	8.00
CK	Harmon Killebrew/Jsy, Rod Carew/Jsy	25.00
CL	Miguel Cabrera/Jsy, Mike Lowell/Jsy	10.00
CM	Will Clark/Jsy, Willie McCovey/Jsy/56	25.00
CN	Eric Chavez/Jsy, Graig Nettles/Jsy	8.00
CO	Roger Clemens/Jsy, Roy Oswalt/Jsy	15.00
CR	Bobby Crosby/Jsy, Cal Ripken Jr./Jsy	40.00
DC	Andre Dawson/Jsy, Orlando Cepeda/Jsy	10.00
DK	Bobby Doerr/Bat, George Kell/Bat	10.00
FB	Carlton Fisk/Jsy, Johnny Bench/Jsy	20.00
FW	Bob Feller/Pants, Kerry Wood/Jsy	15.00
GB	Brian Giles/Jsy, Jason Bay/Jsy	8.00
GC	Ken Griffey Jr./Jsy, Sean Casey/Jsy	15.00
GG	Ken Griffey Sr./Jsy, Ken Griffey Jr./Jsy	15.00
GK	Ken Griffey Jr./Jsy, Ralph Kiner/Bat	20.00
GL	Eric Gagne/Jsy, Sparky Lyle/Pants	10.00
GS	Dwight Gooden/Pants, Tom Seaver/Jsy	15.00
HC	Bobby Crosby/Jsy, Rich Harden/Jsy	8.00
HG	Keith Hernandez/Bat, Mark Grace/Jsy	10.00
HH	Aubrey Huff/Jsy, Travis Hafner/Jsy	8.00
HM	Travis Hafner/Jsy, Victor Martinez/Jsy	8.00
HU	Aubrey Huff/Jsy, B.J. Upton/Jsy	10.00
HW	Harmon Killebrew/Jsy, Willie McCovey/Jsy/44	25.00
JG	Derek Jeter/Jsy, Khalil Greene/Jsy	35.00
JJ	Joe Mauer/Jsy, Johan Santana/Jsy	15.00
JR	Jim Rice/Jsy, Rico Petrocelli/Pants	8.00
JW	Derek Jeter/Jsy, Maury Wills/Jsy	35.00
JY	Johnny Bench/Jsy, Yogi Berra/Pants	25.00
KB	Jim Kaat/Jsy, Bert Blyleven/Jsy	10.00
KC	Jim Kaat/Jsy, Steve Carlton/Jsy	10.00
KD	Keith Hernandez/Bat, Don Mattingly/Jsy	20.00
KK	Al Kaline/Jsy, Ralph Kiner/Bat	15.00
KM	Al Kaline/Jsy, Dale Murphy/Jsy	15.00
KN	Jim Kaat/Jsy, Phil Niekro/Jsy	10.00
LC	Derrek Lee/Jsy, Sean Casey/Jsy	10.00
LG	Derrek Lee/Jsy, Mark Grace/Jsy	10.00
LP	Fred Lynn/Bat, Rico Petrocelli/Pants	10.00
LR	Fred Lynn/Bat, Jim Rice/Jsy	10.00
MC	Don Mattingly/Jsy, Will Clark/Jsy	20.00
MD	Bill Mazeroski/Jsy, Bobby Doerr/Bat	10.00
MH	Mark Mulder/Jsy, Rich Harden/Jsy	10.00
MK	Bill Mazeroski/Jsy, Ralph Kiner/Bat	20.00
MM	Joe Mauer/Jsy, Victor Martinez/Jsy	8.00
MS	Dale Murphy/Jsy, Mike Schmidt/Jsy	20.00
MW	Paul Molitor/Jsy, Rickie Weeks/Jsy	15.00
NL	Graig Nettles/Jsy, Sparky Lyle/Pants	15.00
NT	Laynce Nix/Jsy, Mark Teixeira/Jsy	10.00
NY	Laynce Nix/Jsy, Michael Young/Jsy	10.00
OF	David Ortiz/Jsy, Carlton Fisk/Jsy	20.00
OG	Akinori Otsuka/Jsy, Khalil Greene/Jsy	15.00
OP	Akinori Otsuka/Jsy, Jake Peavy/Jsy	15.00
OT	Akinori Otsuka/Jsy, Shingo Takatsu/Jsy	20.00
PD	Andre Dawson/Jsy, Corey Patterson/Jsy	15.00
PG	Brad Penny/Jsy, Eric Gagne/Jsy	10.00
PH	Jake Peavy/Jsy, Rich Harden/Jsy	12.00
PP	Boog Powell/Jsy, Jim Palmer/Jsy	15.00
PR	Boog Powell/Jsy, Brooks Robinson/Jsy	20.00
PS	Brad Penny/Jsy, Jason Schmidt/Jsy	8.00
RB	Ernie Banks/Pants, Cal Ripken Jr./Jsy	40.00
RC	Nolan Ryan/Jsy, Steve Carlton/Jsy	30.00
RJ	Jose Reyes/Jsy, Rickie Weeks/Jsy	10.00
RP	Frank Robinson/Jsy, Boog Powell/Jsy	25.00
RR	Frank Robinson/Jsy, Brooks Robinson/Jsy	25.00
RW	David Wright/Jsy, Scott Rolen/Jsy	15.00
SB	Bert Blyleven/Jsy, Johan Santana/Jsy	15.00
SC	Johan Santana/Jsy, Roger Clemens/Jsy	20.00
SF	Ben Sheets/Jsy, Bob Feller/Pants	15.00
SG	Bruce Sutter/Jsy, Eric Gagne/Jsy	15.00
SM	Jason Schmidt/Jsy, Mark Mulder/Jsy	10.00
SO	Ben Sheets/Jsy, Roy Oswalt/Jsy	10.00
SP	Ben Sheets/Jsy, Brad Penny/Jsy	10.00
TH	Mark Teixeira/Jsy, Travis Hafner/Jsy	10.00
TL	Shingo Takatsu/Jsy, Sparky Lyle/Pants	
TY	Mark Teixeira/Jsy, Michael Young/Jsy	10.00
UJ	B.J. Upton/Jsy, Derek Jeter/Jsy	30.00
WL	David Wright/Jsy, Mike Lowell/Jsy	10.00
WR	David Wright/Jsy, Jose Reyes/Jsy	10.00
YM	Robin Yount/Jsy, Paul Molitor/Jsy	25.00
YP	Carl Yastrzemski/Jsy, Rico Petrocelli/Pants	15.00
ZM	Carlos Zambrano/Jsy, Greg Maddux/Jsy	15.00
ZP	Carlos Zambrano/Jsy, Mark Prior/Jsy	10.00
ZW	Carlos Zambrano/Jsy, Kerry Wood/Jsy	20.00

ABBREVIATIONS

SP - Short Print

Dual Artifacts Bat

NM/M

Production 25 Sets

BC	Josh Beckett, Miguel Cabrera	20.00
BW	Josh Beckett, Kerry Wood	20.00
DR	Carlos Delgado, Manny Ramirez	20.00
GC	Ken Griffey Jr., Miguel Cabrera	30.00
GS	Ken Griffey Sr., Ichiro Suzuki	80.00
JP	Derek Jeter, Mike Piazza	50.00
JR	Derek Jeter, Manny Ramirez	50.00
RG	Manny Ramirez, Vladimir Guerrero	20.00
RJ	Cal Ripken Jr., Derek Jeter	100.00
RT	Cal Ripken Jr., Miguel Tejada	60.00
SG	Ichiro Suzuki, Vladimir Guerrero	60.00
WP	Kerry Wood, Mark Prior	25.00

Dual Artifacts Signatures

No Pricing
Production 10 Sets

MLB Apparel

NM/M

Production 325 unless noted.

Rainbow:	1-2X

Production 99 Sets

BA	Bobby Abreu/Jsy	6.00
GA	Garret Anderson/Jsy	6.00
JB	Jason Bay/Jsy	6.00
CB	Carlos Beltran/Jsy	8.00
AB	Adrian Beltre/Jsy	6.00
BE	Johnny Bench/Jsy	10.00
YB	Yogi Berra/Pants	15.00
HB	Hank Blalock/Jsy	8.00
BB	Bert Blyleven/Jsy/150	8.00
WB	Wade Boggs/Jsy	8.00
BO	Bret Boone/Jsy	4.00
GB	George Brett/Jsy	15.00
MI	Miguel Cabrera/Jsy	10.00
RC	Rod Carew/Jsy	8.00
CA	Steve Carlton/Jsy	6.00
GC	Gary Carter/Jsy	8.00
SC	Sean Casey/Jsy	4.00
OC	Orlando Cepeda/Jsy	8.00
EC	Eric Chavez/Jsy	4.00
WC	Will Clark/Jsy/100	10.00
CL	Roger Clemens/Jsy	15.00
BC	Bobby Crosby/Jsy	6.00
AD	Andre Dawson/Jsy	6.00
BF	Bob Feller/Pants	10.00
CF	Carlton Fisk R. Sox/Jsy/175	10.00
CF1	Carlton Fisk W. Sox/Jsy/175	10.00
EG	Eric Gagne/Jsy	8.00
BG	Bob Gibson/Pants	10.00
GI	Brian Giles/Jsy	4.00
GS	Marcus Giles/Jsy	4.00
DG	Dwight Gooden/Pants	6.00
MK	Mark Grace/Jsy/175	8.00
KL	Khalil Greene/Jsy	8.00
KG	Ken Griffey Jr./Jsy	15.00
GR	Ken Griffey Sr./Jsy	8.00
TG	Tony Gwynn/Jsy	10.00
TH	Travis Hafner/Jsy	4.00
RH	Rich Harden/Jsy	8.00
KH	Kent Hrbek/Jsy	4.00
HU	Tim Hudson/Jsy	6.00
AH	Aubrey Huff/Jsy	4.00
TO	Torii Hunter/Jsy	4.00
DJ	Derek Jeter/Jsy	20.00
JJ	Jacque Jones/Jsy	4.00
JK	Jim Kaat/Jsy	6.00
AK	Al Kaline/Jsy	10.00
HK	Harmon Killebrew/Jsy	10.00
CK	Casey Kotchman/Jsy	4.00
DL	Derrek Lee/Jsy	6.00
ML	Mike Lowell/Jsy	4.00
SL	Sparky Lyle/Pants	4.00
VM	Victor Martinez/Jsy	6.00
MA	Don Mattingly/Jsy	20.00
JM	Joe Mauer/Jsy	10.00
BM	Bill Mazeroski/Jsy/100	12.00
WM	Willie McCovey/Jsy	8.00
MC	Dallas McPherson/Jsy	8.00
PM	Paul Molitor/Jsy	8.00
MM	Mark Mulder/Jsy	6.00
DM	Dale Murphy/Jsy/150	8.00
GN	Graig Nettles/Jsy	4.00
PN	Phil Niekro/Jsy	4.00
LN	Laynce Nix/Jsy	4.00
DO	David Ortiz/Jsy	10.00
RO	Roy Oswalt/Jsy	4.00
AO	Akinori Otsuka/Jsy	4.00
PA	Jim Palmer/Jsy	8.00
CP	Corey Patterson/Jsy	6.00
JP	Jake Peavy/Jsy	6.00
PE	Brad Penny/Jsy	4.00
RP	Rico Petrocelli/Pants	8.00
SP	Scott Podsednik/Jsy	4.00
BP	Boog Powell/Jsy	6.00
MP	Mark Prior/Jsy	8.00
RE	Jose Reyes/Jsy	6.00
JR	Jim Rice/Jsy	8.00
CR	Cal Ripken Jr./Jsy	25.00
BR	Brooks Robinson/Jsy	8.00
FR	Frank Robinson/Jsy	8.00
SR	Scott Rolen/Jsy	10.00
NR	Nolan Ryan/Jsy	25.00
SA	Johan Santana/Jsy	10.00
JS	Jason Schmidt/Jsy	6.00
MS	Mike Schmidt/Jsy	15.00
TS	Tom Seaver/Jsy/300	8.00
BS	Ben Sheets/Jsy	6.00
SM	John Smoltz/Jsy	8.00
SU	Bruce Sutter/Jsy	6.00
ST	Shingo Takatsu/Jsy	6.00
MT	Mark Teixeira/Jsy	8.00
BU	B.J. Upton/Jsy	6.00
JV	Jose Vidro/Jsy	4.00
RW	Rickie Weeks/Jsy	6.00
MW	Maury Wills/Jsy	8.00
KW	Kerry Wood/Jsy	8.00
DW	David Wright/Jsy	10.00
CY	Carl Yastrzemski/Jsy	15.00
MY	Michael Young/Jsy	6.00
RY	Robin Yount/Jsy	15.00
CZ	Carlos Zambrano/Jsy	6.00

MLB Apparel Autographs

NM/M

Production 30 Sets

Rare:	No Pricing

Production One Set

BA	Bobby Abreu/Jsy/Redemp.	25.00
GA	Garret Anderson/Jsy	20.00
JB	Jason Bay/Jsy	30.00
CB	Carlos Beltran/Jsy/Redemp.	25.00
AB	Adrian Beltre/Jsy	25.00
BE	Johnny Bench/Jsy	65.00
YB	Yogi Berra/Pants	60.00
HB	Hank Blalock/Jsy	25.00
BB	Bert Blyleven/Jsy	35.00
WB	Wade Boggs/Jsy	50.00
BO	Bret Boone/Jsy	20.00
GB	George Brett/Jsy	100.00
MI	Miguel Cabrera/Jsy	40.00
RC	Rod Carew/Jsy	40.00
CA	Steve Carlton/Jsy	30.00
GC	Gary Carter/Jsy	30.00
SC	Sean Casey/Jsy	30.00
OC	Orlando Cepeda/Jsy	35.00
EC	Eric Chavez/Jsy/Redemp.	30.00
WC	Will Clark/Jsy	50.00
CL	Roger Clemens/Jsy/Redemp.	120.00
BC	Bobby Crosby/Jsy/Redemp.	20.00
AD	Andre Dawson/Jsy	30.00
BF	Bob Feller/Pants	40.00
CF	Carlton Fisk R. Sox/Jsy	40.00
CF1	Carlton Fisk/W. Sox/Jsy	40.00
EG	Eric Gagne/Jsy	30.00
BG	Bob Gibson/Pants	50.00
GI	Brian Giles/Jsy	20.00

GS	Marcus Giles/Jsy	20.00
DG	Dwight Gooden/Pants	30.00
MK	Mark Grace/Jsy	40.00
KL	Khalil Greene/Jsy	30.00
KG	Ken Griffey Jr./Jsy	120.00
GR	Ken Griffey Sr./Jsy	25.00
TG	Tony Gwynn/Jsy	80.00
TH	Travis Hafner/Jsy	25.00
RH	Rich Harden/Jsy	30.00
KH	Kent Hrbek/Jsy	50.00
HU	Tim Hudson/Jsy	40.00
AH	Aubrey Huff/Jsy	25.00
TO	Torii Hunter/Jsy	25.00
DJ	Derek Jeter/Jsy	200.00
JJ	Jacque Jones/Jsy	20.00
JK	Jim Kaat/Jsy	25.00
AK	Al Kaline/Jsy	50.00
HK	Harmon Killebrew/Jsy	60.00
CK	Casey Kotchman/Jsy	25.00
DL	Derrek Lee/Jsy	40.00
ML	Mike Lowell/Jsy	20.00
SL	Sparky Lyle/Pants	20.00
VM	Victor Martinez/Jsy	25.00
MA	Don Mattingly/Jsy	100.00
JM	Joe Mauer/Jsy/Redemp.	35.00
BM	Bill Mazeroski/Jsy	30.00
WM	Willie McCovey/Jsy	50.00
MC	Dallas McPherson/Jsy/Redemp.	20.00
PM	Paul Molitor/Jsy	40.00
MM	Mark Mulder/Jsy	20.00
DM	Dale Murphy/Jsy	35.00
GN	Graig Nettles/Jsy	35.00
PN	Phil Niekro/Jsy	25.00
LN	Laynce Nix/Jsy	20.00
DO	David Ortiz/Jsy	50.00
RO	Roy Oswalt/Jsy	25.00
AO	Akinori Otsuka/Jsy	40.00
PA	Jim Palmer/Jsy	40.00
CP	Corey Patterson/Jsy/Redemp.	30.00
JP	Jake Peavy/Jsy	40.00
PE	Brad Penny/Jsy	20.00
RP	Rico Petrocelli/Pants	25.00
SP	Scott Podsednik/Jsy	25.00
BP	Boog Powell/Jsy	25.00
MP	Mark Prior/Jsy	35.00
RE	Jose Reyes/Jsy/Redemp.	40.00
JR	Jim Rice/Jsy	30.00
CR	Cal Ripken Jr./Jsy	200.00
BR	Brooks Robinson/Jsy	50.00
FR	Frank Robinson/Jsy	40.00
SR	Scott Rolen/Jsy/Redemp.	75.00
NR	Nolan Ryan/Jsy	125.00
SA	Johan Santana/Jsy/Redemp.	50.00
JS	Jason Schmidt/Jsy	30.00
MS	Mike Schmidt/Jsy	60.00
TS	Tom Seaver/Jsy	50.00
BS	Ben Sheets/Jsy/Redemp.	25.00
SM	John Smoltz/Jsy/Redemp.	75.00
SU	Bruce Sutter/Jsy	20.00
ST	Shingo Takatsu/Jsy	25.00
MT	Mark Teixeira/Jsy	40.00
BU	B.J. Upton/Jsy	25.00
JV	Jose Vidro/Jsy	20.00
RW	Rickie Weeks/Jsy	25.00
MW	Maury Wills/Jsy	25.00
KW	Kerry Wood/Jsy	30.00
DW	David Wright/Jsy	80.00
CY	Carl Yastrzemski/Jsy	85.00
MY	Michael Young/Jsy/Redemp.	25.00
RY	Robin Yount/Jsy	75.00
CZ	Carlos Zambrano/Jsy	35.00

Patches

NM/M

Production 50 unless noted.

BA	Bobby Abreu	15.00
GA	Garret Anderson	15.00
JB	Jason Bay	20.00
CB	Carlos Beltran	20.00
AB	Adrian Beltre	20.00
BE	Johnny Bench	25.00
HB	Hank Blalock	20.00
BB	Bert Blyleven	20.00
WB	Wade Boggs	20.00
BO	Bret Boone	12.00
GB	George Brett	40.00
MI	Miguel Cabrera	25.00
RC	Rod Carew	25.00
CA	Steve Carlton/30	25.00
GC	Gary Carter	30.00
SC	Sean Casey	12.00
EC	Eric Chavez	15.00
WC	Will Clark/20	50.00
CL	Roger Clemens	30.00

BC	Bobby Crosby	20.00
AD	Andre Dawson	20.00
EG	Eric Gagne	20.00
BG	Bob Gibson/10	
GI	Brian Giles	12.00
GS	Marcus Giles	12.00
DG	Dwight Gooden	20.00
MK	Mark Grace	35.00
KL	Khalil Greene	25.00
KG	Ken Griffey Jr.	40.00
GR	Ken Griffey Sr.	12.00
TG	Tony Gwynn	25.00
TH	Travis Hafner	15.00
RH	Rich Harden	20.00
KH	Kent Hrbek	35.00
HU	Tim Hudson	20.00
AH	Aubrey Huff	12.00
TO	Torii Hunter	15.00
DJ	Derek Jeter	65.00
RJ	Randy Johnson	25.00
JJ	Jacque Jones	15.00
JK	Jim Kaat	20.00
HK	Harmon Killebrew	40.00
CK	Casey Kotchman	20.00
DL	Derrek Lee	15.00
ML	Mike Lowell	12.00
GM	Greg Maddux	35.00
VM	Victor Martinez	15.00
MA	Don Mattingly	40.00
JM	Joe Mauer	30.00
WM	Willie McCovey	25.00
MC	Dallas McPherson	20.00
MM	Mark Mulder	20.00
DM	Dale Murphy	25.00
GN	Graig Nettles	20.00
PN	Phil Niekro	20.00
LN	Laynce Nix	12.00
DO	David Ortiz	20.00
RO	Roy Oswalt	15.00
AO	Akinori Otsuka	25.00
PA	Jim Palmer	20.00
CP	Corey Patterson	25.00
JP	Jake Peavy	20.00
PE	Brad Penny	12.00
SP	Scott Podsednik	12.00
BP	Boog Powell	20.00
MP	Mark Prior	20.00
RE	Jose Reyes	20.00
JR	Jim Rice/3	
CR	Cal Ripken Jr.	60.00
BR	Brooks Robinson/35	40.00
FR	Frank Robinson	20.00
SR	Scott Rolen	25.00
NR	Nolan Ryan	50.00
SA	Johan Santana	25.00
JS	Jason Schmidt	25.00
MS	Mike Schmidt	30.00
TS	Tom Seaver/11	
BS	Ben Sheets	20.00
SM	John Smoltz	30.00
SU	Bruce Sutter	15.00
ST	Shingo Takatsu	20.00
MT	Mark Teixeira	20.00
BU	B.J. Upton	20.00
JV	Jose Vidro	12.00
RW	Rickie Weeks	20.00
MW	Maury Wills/20	20.00
KW	Kerry Wood	20.00
DW	David Wright	35.00
CY	Carl Yastrzemski	40.00
MY	Michael Young	15.00
RY	Robin Yount	30.00
CZ	Carlos Zambrano	25.00

Signature Patches

No Pricing

Production 10 unless noted.

2005 Upper Deck Baseball Heroes

NM/M

Complete Set (200):		
Common (1-100):		2.00
Common (101-200):		2.00
Production 575		
Tin (8):		50.00
1	Bob Feller	3.00
2	Bob Feller	3.00
3	Bob Feller	3.00
4	Bob Feller	3.00
5	Bob Feller	3.00
6	Brooks Robinson	3.00

7	Brooks Robinson	3.00
8	Brooks Robinson	3.00
9	Brooks Robinson	3.00
10	Brooks Robinson	3.00
11	Cal Ripken Jr.	8.00
12	Cal Ripken Jr.	8.00
13	Cal Ripken Jr.	8.00
14	Cal Ripken Jr.	8.00
15	Cal Ripken Jr.	8.00
16	Carl Yastrzemski	5.00
17	Carl Yastrzemski	5.00
18	Carl Yastrzemski	5.00
19	Carl Yastrzemski	5.00
20	Carl Yastrzemski	5.00
21	Don Mattingly	6.00
22	Don Mattingly	6.00
23	Don Mattingly	6.00
24	Don Mattingly	6.00
25	Don Mattingly	6.00
26	Tom Seaver	3.00
27	Tom Seaver	3.00
28	Tom Seaver	3.00
29	Tom Seaver	3.00
30	Tom Seaver	3.00
31	Harmon Killebrew	3.00
32	Harmon Killebrew	3.00
33	Harmon Killebrew	3.00
34	Harmon Killebrew	3.00
35	Harmon Killebrew	3.00
36	Jim Palmer	2.00
37	Jim Palmer	2.00
38	Jim Palmer	2.00
39	Jim Palmer	2.00
40	Jim Palmer	2.00
41	Mike Schmidt	6.00
42	Mike Schmidt	6.00
43	Mike Schmidt	6.00
44	Mike Schmidt	6.00
45	Mike Schmidt	6.00
46	Ozzie Smith	4.00
47	Ozzie Smith	4.00
48	Ozzie Smith	4.00
49	Ozzie Smith	4.00
50	Ozzie Smith	4.00
51	Paul Molitor	3.00
52	Paul Molitor	3.00
53	Paul Molitor	3.00
54	Paul Molitor	3.00
55	Paul Molitor	3.00
56	Al Kaline	3.00
57	Al Kaline	3.00
58	Al Kaline	3.00
59	Al Kaline	3.00
60	Al Kaline	3.00
61	Robin Yount	4.00
62	Robin Yount	4.00
63	Robin Yount	4.00
64	Robin Yount	4.00
65	Robin Yount	4.00
66	Ryne Sandberg	4.00
67	Ryne Sandberg	4.00
68	Ryne Sandberg	4.00
69	Ryne Sandberg	4.00
70	Ryne Sandberg	4.00
71	Stan Musial	5.00
72	Stan Musial	5.00
73	Stan Musial	5.00
74	Stan Musial	5.00
75	Stan Musial	5.00
76	Steve Carlton	2.00
77	Steve Carlton	2.00
78	Steve Carlton	2.00
79	Steve Carlton	2.00
80	Steve Carlton	2.00
81	Tony Gwynn	3.00
82	Tony Gwynn	3.00
83	Tony Gwynn	3.00
84	Tony Gwynn	3.00
85	Tony Gwynn	3.00
86	Wade Boggs	3.00
87	Wade Boggs	3.00
88	Wade Boggs	3.00
89	Wade Boggs	3.00

90	Wade Boggs	3.00
91	Will Clark	3.00
92	Will Clark	3.00
93	Will Clark	3.00
94	Will Clark	3.00
95	Will Clark	3.00
96	Yogi Berra	4.00
97	Yogi Berra	4.00
98	Yogi Berra	4.00
99	Yogi Berra	4.00
100	Yogi Berra	4.00
101	Babe Ruth	8.00
102	Babe Ruth	8.00
103	Babe Ruth	8.00
104	Babe Ruth	8.00
105	Babe Ruth	8.00
106	Roger Maris	6.00
107	Roger Maris	6.00
108	Roger Maris	6.00
109	Roger Maris	6.00
110	Roger Maris	6.00
111	Don Drysdale	2.00
112	Don Drysdale	2.00
113	Don Drysdale	2.00
114	Don Drysdale	2.00
115	Don Drysdale	2.00
116	Eddie Mathews	4.00
117	Eddie Mathews	4.00
118	Eddie Mathews	4.00
119	Eddie Mathews	4.00
120	Eddie Mathews	4.00
121	Honus Wagner	6.00
122	Honus Wagner	6.00
123	Honus Wagner	6.00
124	Honus Wagner	6.00
125	Honus Wagner	6.00
126	Jackie Robinson	5.00
127	Jackie Robinson	5.00
128	Jackie Robinson	5.00
129	Jackie Robinson	5.00
130	Jackie Robinson	5.00
131	Jimmie Foxx	5.00
132	Jimmie Foxx	5.00
133	Jimmie Foxx	5.00
134	Jimmie Foxx	5.00
135	Jimmie Foxx	5.00
136	Joe DiMaggio	6.00
137	Joe DiMaggio	6.00
138	Joe DiMaggio	6.00
139	Joe DiMaggio	6.00
140	Joe DiMaggio	6.00
141	Johnny Mize	4.00
142	Johnny Mize	4.00
143	Johnny Mize	4.00
144	Johnny Mize	4.00
145	Johnny Mize	4.00
146	Lefty Grove	3.00
147	Lefty Grove	3.00
148	Lefty Grove	3.00
149	Lefty Grove	3.00
150	Lefty Grove	3.00
151	Lou Gehrig	6.00
152	Lou Gehrig	6.00
153	Lou Gehrig	6.00
154	Lou Gehrig	6.00
155	Lou Gehrig	6.00
156	Mel Ott	4.00
157	Mel Ott	4.00
158	Mel Ott	4.00
159	Mel Ott	4.00
160	Mel Ott	4.00
161	Mickey Mantle	12.00
162	Mickey Mantle	12.00
163	Mickey Mantle	12.00
164	Mickey Mantle	12.00
165	Mickey Mantle	12.00
166	Roberto Clemente	8.00
167	Roberto Clemente	8.00
168	Roberto Clemente	8.00
169	Roberto Clemente	8.00
170	Roberto Clemente	8.00
171	Rogers Hornsby	6.00
172	Rogers Hornsby	6.00
173	Rogers Hornsby	6.00
174	Rogers Hornsby	6.00
175	Rogers Hornsby	6.00
176	Roy Campanella	3.00
177	Roy Campanella	3.00
178	Roy Campanella	3.00
179	Roy Campanella	3.00
180	Roy Campanella	3.00
181	Satchel Paige	6.00
182	Satchel Paige	6.00
183	Satchel Paige	6.00
184	Satchel Paige	6.00
185	Satchel Paige	6.00
186	Ted Williams	8.00
187	Ted Williams	8.00
188	Ted Williams	8.00
189	Ted Williams	8.00
190	Ted Williams	8.00
191	Thurman Munson	5.00
192	Thurman Munson	5.00
193	Thurman Munson	5.00

194	Thurman Munson	5.00
195	Thurman Munson	5.00
196	Ty Cobb	5.00
197	Ty Cobb	5.00
198	Ty Cobb	5.00
199	Ty Cobb	5.00
200	Ty Cobb	5.00

Blue
No Pricing
Production 10 Sets

Emerald
Emerald (1-100):	1-1.5X
Emerald (101-200):	1-1.5X
Production 199 Sets

Gold
No Pricing
Production One Set

Red
Red (1-200):	1-2X
Production 75 Sets

Baseball Heroes Jeter
	NM/M
Complete Set (9):	25.00
Common Jeter:	3.00
Inserted 1:6

Baseball Heroes Jeter Jersey
Common Jeter:
Production 75 Sets

Baseball Heroes Jeter Signature
No Pricing
Production 2 Sets

Memorabilia
No Pricing
Production 10 Sets

Memorabilia Emerald
	NM/M
Production 99 Sets	
Blue:	1X
Production 99 Sets	
Bronze:	1-1.5X
Production 50 Sets	
Gold:	No Pricing
Production One Set	
Red:	1X
Production 99 Sets	
Silver:	No Pricing
Production 15 Sets	

1	Bob Feller	10.00
2	Bob Feller	10.00
3	Bob Feller	10.00
4	Bob Feller	10.00
5	Bob Feller	10.00
6	Brooks Robinson	10.00
7	Brooks Robinson	10.00
8	Brooks Robinson	10.00
9	Brooks Robinson	10.00
10	Brooks Robinson	10.00
11	Cal Ripken Jr.	25.00
12	Cal Ripken Jr.	25.00
13	Cal Ripken Jr.	25.00
14	Cal Ripken Jr.	25.00
15	Cal Ripken Jr.	25.00
16	Carl Yastrzemski	15.00
17	Carl Yastrzemski	15.00
18	Carl Yastrzemski	15.00
19	Carl Yastrzemski	15.00
20	Carl Yastrzemski	15.00
21	Don Mattingly	20.00
22	Don Mattingly	20.00
23	Don Mattingly	20.00
24	Don Mattingly	20.00
25	Don Mattingly	20.00
26	Tom Seaver	10.00
27	Tom Seaver	10.00
28	Tom Seaver	10.00
29	Tom Seaver	10.00
30	Tom Seaver	10.00
31	Harmon Killebrew	10.00
32	Harmon Killebrew	10.00
33	Harmon Killebrew	10.00
34	Harmon Killebrew	10.00
35	Harmon Killebrew	10.00
36	Jim Palmer	8.00
37	Jim Palmer	8.00
38	Jim Palmer	8.00
39	Jim Palmer	8.00
40	Jim Palmer	8.00
41	Mike Schmidt	20.00
42	Mike Schmidt	20.00
43	Mike Schmidt	20.00
44	Mike Schmidt	20.00
45	Mike Schmidt	20.00
46	Ozzie Smith	20.00
47	Ozzie Smith	20.00
48	Ozzie Smith	20.00
49	Ozzie Smith	20.00
50	Ozzie Smith	20.00
51	Paul Molitor	10.00
52	Paul Molitor	10.00
53	Paul Molitor	10.00
54	Paul Molitor	10.00
55	Paul Molitor	10.00
56	Al Kaline	12.00
57	Al Kaline	12.00
58	Al Kaline	12.00
59	Al Kaline	12.00
60	Al Kaline	12.00
61	Robin Yount	15.00
62	Robin Yount	15.00
63	Robin Yount	15.00
64	Robin Yount	15.00
65	Robin Yount	15.00
66	Ryne Sandberg	15.00
67	Ryne Sandberg	15.00
68	Ryne Sandberg	15.00
69	Ryne Sandberg	15.00
70	Ryne Sandberg	15.00
71	Stan Musial	20.00
72	Stan Musial	20.00
73	Stan Musial	20.00
74	Stan Musial	20.00
75	Stan Musial	20.00
76	Steve Carlton	10.00
77	Steve Carlton	10.00
78	Steve Carlton	10.00
79	Steve Carlton	10.00
80	Steve Carlton	10.00
81	Tony Gwynn	20.00
82	Tony Gwynn	20.00
83	Tony Gwynn	20.00
84	Tony Gwynn	20.00
85	Tony Gwynn	20.00
86	Wade Boggs	10.00
87	Wade Boggs	10.00
88	Wade Boggs	10.00
89	Wade Boggs	10.00
90	Wade Boggs	10.00
91	Will Clark	10.00
92	Will Clark	10.00
93	Will Clark	10.00
94	Will Clark	10.00
95	Will Clark	10.00
96	Yogi Berra	15.00
97	Yogi Berra	15.00
98	Yogi Berra	15.00
99	Yogi Berra	15.00
100	Yogi Berra	15.00

Signature Cuts
No Pricing
Production 1-10

Signature Emerald
	NM/M
Production 99 Sets	
Blue:	1-1.5X
Production 20 Sets	
Red:	1X
Production 49 Sets	
Gold:	No Pricing
Production One Set	
Patches:	No Pricing
Production 5 Sets	

1	Bob Feller	35.00
2	Bob Feller	35.00
3	Bob Feller	35.00
4	Bob Feller	35.00
5	Bob Feller	35.00
6	Brooks Robinson	35.00
7	Brooks Robinson	35.00
8	Brooks Robinson	35.00
9	Brooks Robinson	35.00
10	Brooks Robinson	35.00
11	Cal Ripken Jr.	125.00
12	Cal Ripken Jr.	125.00
13	Cal Ripken Jr.	125.00
14	Cal Ripken Jr.	125.00
15	Cal Ripken Jr.	125.00
16	Carl Yastrzemski	65.00
17	Carl Yastrzemski	65.00
18	Carl Yastrzemski	65.00
19	Carl Yastrzemski	65.00
20	Carl Yastrzemski	65.00
21	Don Mattingly	60.00
22	Don Mattingly	60.00
23	Don Mattingly	60.00
24	Don Mattingly	60.00
25	Don Mattingly	60.00
26	Tom Seaver	50.00
27	Tom Seaver	50.00
28	Tom Seaver	50.00
29	Tom Seaver	50.00
30	Tom Seaver	50.00
31	Harmon Killebrew	40.00
32	Harmon Killebrew	40.00
33	Harmon Killebrew	40.00
34	Harmon Killebrew	40.00
35	Harmon Killebrew	40.00
36	Jim Palmer	25.00
37	Jim Palmer	25.00
38	Jim Palmer	25.00
39	Jim Palmer	25.00
40	Jim Palmer	25.00
41	Mike Schmidt	50.00
42	Mike Schmidt	50.00
43	Mike Schmidt	50.00
44	Mike Schmidt	50.00
45	Mike Schmidt	50.00
46	Ozzie Smith	50.00
47	Ozzie Smith	50.00
48	Ozzie Smith	50.00
49	Ozzie Smith	50.00
50	Ozzie Smith	50.00
51	Paul Molitor	30.00
52	Paul Molitor	30.00
53	Paul Molitor	30.00
54	Paul Molitor	30.00
55	Paul Molitor	30.00
56	Al Kaline	40.00
57	Al Kaline	40.00
58	Al Kaline	40.00
59	Al Kaline	40.00
60	Al Kaline	40.00
61	Robin Yount	40.00
62	Robin Yount	40.00
63	Robin Yount	40.00
64	Robin Yount	40.00
65	Robin Yount	40.00
66	Ryne Sandberg	50.00
67	Ryne Sandberg	50.00
68	Ryne Sandberg	50.00
69	Ryne Sandberg	50.00
70	Ryne Sandberg	50.00
71	Stan Musial	75.00
72	Stan Musial	75.00
73	Stan Musial	75.00
74	Stan Musial	75.00
75	Stan Musial	75.00
76	Steve Carlton	25.00
77	Steve Carlton	25.00
78	Steve Carlton	25.00
79	Steve Carlton	25.00
80	Steve Carlton	25.00
81	Tony Gwynn	40.00
82	Tony Gwynn	40.00
83	Tony Gwynn	40.00
84	Tony Gwynn	40.00
85	Tony Gwynn	40.00
86	Wade Boggs	35.00
87	Wade Boggs	35.00
88	Wade Boggs	35.00
89	Wade Boggs	35.00
90	Wade Boggs	35.00
91	Will Clark	30.00
92	Will Clark	30.00
93	Will Clark	30.00
94	Will Clark	30.00
95	Will Clark	30.00
96	Yogi Berra	60.00
97	Yogi Berra	60.00
98	Yogi Berra	60.00
99	Yogi Berra	60.00
100	Yogi Berra	60.00

Signature Memorabilia
No Pricing
Production 15 Sets

2005 Upper Deck Classics

WARREN SPAHN

	NM/M
Complete Set (130):	50.00
Common Player:	.15
Common SP (101-130):	1.00
Inserted 1:4	
Pack (8):	3.00
Hobby Box (28):	60.00

1	Al Kaline	.50
2	Al Lopez	.15
3	Allie Reynolds	.15
4	Babe Herman	.15
5	Bill Mazeroski	.15
6	Bill Russell	.15
7	Billy Herman	.15
8	Billy Williams	.25
9	Bob Feller	.50
10	Bob Gibson	.75
11	Bob Lemon	.15
12	Bobby Doerr	.15
13	Boog Powell	.15
14	Ken Hubbs	.15
15	Brooks Robinson	.75
16	Buck Leonard	.15
17	Cal Ripken Jr.	2.00
18	Carl Hubbell	.15
19	Jim "Catfish" Hunter	.25
20	Johnny Hopp	.15
21	Charlie Gehringer	.15
22	Curt Flood	.15
23	Jimmie Foxx	.75
24	Dave McNally	.15
25	Davey Lopes	.15
26	Don Drysdale	.50
27	Don Sutton	.15
28	Earl Weaver	.15
29	Early Wynn	.15
30	Edd Roush	.15
31	Eddie Mathews	.75
32	Enos Slaughter	.15
33	Fergie Jenkins	.50
34	Frank Howard	.15
35	Leon Wagner	.15
36	Frank Crosetti	.15
37	Gaylord Perry	.15
38	George Bell	.15
39	George Kell	.15
40	Graig Nettles	.15
41	Hal Newhouser	.15
42	Harmon Killebrew	.75
43	Harvey Kuenn	.15
44	Howard Johnson	.15
45	Hoyt Wilhelm	.15
46	Jack Clark	.15
47	Jack Morris	.15
48	Jim Bunning	.15
49	Jim Palmer	.50
50	Joe Adcock	.15
51	Joe Carter	.15
52	Casey Stengel	.50
53	Joe Morgan	.50
54	Joe Sewell	.15
55	"Smoky" Joe Wood	.15
56	Johnny Bench	.75
57	Johnny Mize	.15
58	Jose Canseco	.50
59	Juan Marichal	.50
60	Keith Hernandez	.15
61	Ken Griffey Sr.	.15
62	Kent Hrbek	.15
63	Kevin Mitchell	.15
64	Kirk Gibson	.25
65	Larry Doby	.15
66	Lou Boudreau	.15
67	Lou Brock	.50
68	Luis Aparicio	.15
69	Luke Appling	.15
70	Monte Irvin	.50
71	Nellie Fox	.15
72	Norm Cash	.15
73	Orlando Cepeda	.25
74	Pedro Guerrero	.15
75	Pee Wee Reese	.15
76	Phil Niekro	.15
77	Phil Rizzuto	.50
78	Ralph Kiner	.15
79	Ray Dandridge	.15
80	Red Schoendienst	.15
81	Richie Ashburn	.15
82	Rick Ferrell	.15
83	Robin Roberts	.50
84	Rollie Fingers	.15
85	Ron Cey	.15
86	Sparky Anderson	.15
87	Stan Coveleski	.15
88	Ted Kluszewski	.15
89	Ted Lyons	.15
90	Tom Seaver	.50
91	Tommie Agee	.15
92	Tommy Lasorda	.15
93	Tony Perez	.25
94	Vada Pinson	.15
95	Waite Hoyt	.15
96	Warren Spahn	.75
97	Willie McCovey	.50
98	Lyman Bostock	.15
99	Willie Stargell	.50
100	Yogi Berra	1.00
101	Andre Dawson	1.00
102	Andy Van Slyke	1.00
103	Bret Saberhagen	1.00
104	Carl Yastrzemski	2.50

105	Carlton Fisk	1.50
106	Dale Murphy	1.50
107	Darryl Strawberry	1.00
108	David Cone	1.00
109	Dennis Eckersley	1.50
110	Don Mattingly	2.50
111	Dwight Gooden	1.00
112	Eddie Murray	1.50
113	Eric Davis	1.00
114	Fred Lynn	1.00
115	George Brett	3.00
116	Jim Rice	1.00
117	John Kruk	1.50
118	Lenny Dykstra	1.00
119	Mickey Mantle	4.00
120	Mike Schmidt	3.00
121	Nolan Ryan	3.00
122	Ozzie Smith	2.00
123	Paul Molitor	2.00
124	Robin Yount	2.00
125	Ryne Sandberg	2.00
126	Steve Carlton	1.50
127	Ted Williams	3.00
128	Tony Gwynn	2.00
129	Wade Boggs	2.00
130	Will Clark	2.00

Gold

Gold (1-100):	2-4X
Gold (101-130):	1-2X
Production 199 Sets	

Platinum

Platinum (1-100):	5-10X
Platinum (101-130):	3-5X
Production 25 Sets	

Silver

Silver (1-100):	2-3X
Silver (101-130):	1-2X
Production 399 Sets	

Classic Counterparts

		NM/M
Common Duo:		2.00
Production 1,999 Sets		
CC	Will Clark, Jack Clark	2.00
CG	David Cone, Dwight Gooden	2.00
DS	Darryl Strawberry, Lenny Dykstra	2.00
GB	Wade Boggs, Tony Gwynn	4.00
GP	Ken Griffey Sr., Tony Perez	2.00
KD	John Kruk, Lenny Dykstra	2.00
KH	John Kruk, Kent Hrbek	2.00
LR	Jim Rice, Fred Lynn	2.00
MC	Kevin Mitchell, Will Clark	2.00
MH	Don Mattingly, Keith Hernandez	6.00
MY	Robin Yount, Paul Molitor	5.00
NC	Ron Cey, Graig Nettles	2.00
PH	Boog Powell, Frank Howard	2.00
RC	Steve Carlton, Nolan Ryan	8.00
RL	Bill Russell, Davey Lopes	2.00
RS	Tom Seaver, Nolan Ryan	8.00
SD	Darryl Strawberry, Eric Davis	2.00
SG	Dwight Gooden, Darryl Strawberry	2.00
SR	Cal Ripken Jr., Mike Schmidt	10.00
VC	Andy Van Slyke, Jack Clark	2.00

Classic Counterparts Materials

		NM/M
CC	Jack Clark, Will Clark	8.00
CG	David Cone, Dwight Gooden	8.00
DS	Darryl Strawberry, Lenny Dykstra	8.00
GB	Wade Boggs, Tony Gwynn	20.00
GP	Ken Griffey Sr., Tony Perez	8.00
KD	John Kruk, Lenny Dykstra	15.00
KH	John Kruk, Kent Hrbek	8.00
LR	Jim Rice, Fred Lynn	8.00
MC	Kevin Mitchell, Will Clark	8.00
MH	Don Mattingly, Keith Hernandez	15.00
MY	Robin Yount, Paul Molitor	15.00
NC	Graig Nettles, Ron Cey	8.00
PH	Boog Powell, Frank Howard	10.00
RC	Steve Carlton, Nolan Ryan	40.00
RL	Bill Russell, Davey Lopes	8.00
RS	Tom Seaver, Nolan Ryan	50.00
SD	Darryl Strawberry, Eric Davis	10.00
SG	Dwight Gooden, Darryl Strawberry	8.00
SR	Cal Ripken Jr., Mike Schmidt	50.00
VC	Andy Van Slyke, Jack Clark	10.00

Classic Counterparts Signature

		NM/M
DS	Darryl Strawberry, Lenny Dykstra	20.00
GP	Ken Griffey Sr., Tony Perez	30.00
KD	John Kruk, Lenny Dykstra	40.00
KH	John Kruk, Kent Hrbek	40.00
LR	Jim Rice, Fred Lynn	40.00
NC	Graig Nettles, Ron Cey	35.00
RL	Bill Russell, Davey Lopes	25.00

Classic Cuts

	NM/M
Quantity produced listed	
FC	Frankie Crosetti/84	100.00
BH	Babe Herman/50	150.00
CH	Carl Hubbell/25	150.00
TL	Ted Lyons/83	120.00

Classic Materials

BILL RUSSELL

		NM/M
Common Player:		5.00
WB	Wade Boggs	10.00
GB	George Brett	10.00
CA	Jose Canseco	10.00
JO	Joe Carter	5.00
RC	Ron Cey	5.00
JC	Jack Clark	5.00
WC	Will Clark	8.00
DC	David Cone	8.00
ED	Eric Davis	10.00
AD	Andre Dawson	8.00
AD1	Andre Dawson	8.00
LD	Lenny Dykstra	5.00
DE	Dennis Eckersley	8.00
FI	Carlton Fisk	8.00
GI	Kirk Gibson	5.00
DG	Dwight Gooden	5.00
GG	Rich "Goose" Gossage	5.00
KG	Ken Griffey Jr.	5.00
PG	Pedro Guerrero	5.00
TG	Tony Gwynn	10.00
KH	Keith Hernandez	5.00
FH	Frank Howard	8.00
HR	Kent Hrbek	8.00
DL	Davey Lopes	5.00
FL	Fred Lynn	5.00
MA	Don Mattingly	15.00
PM	Paul Molitor	10.00
PM1	Paul Molitor/SP	10.00
JM	Jack Morris	5.00
DM	Dale Murphy	8.00
GN	Graig Nettles	10.00
BP	Boog Powell/SP	8.00
JR	Jim Rice	5.00
CR	Cal Ripken Jr.	25.00
BR	Bill Russell	5.00
NR	Nolan Ryan	20.00
RS	Ryne Sandberg	15.00
MS	Mike Schmidt	15.00
DS	Darryl Strawberry	5.00
AV	Andy Van Slyke	20.00
CY	Carl Yastrzemski	20.00
RY	Robin Yount	10.00

Classic Moments

CAL RIPKEN JR.

		NM/M
Common Player:		2.00
Production 1,999 Sets		
WB	Wade Boggs	4.00
SC	Steve Carlton	2.00
CA	Joe Carter	2.00
JC	Jack Clark	2.00
LD	Lenny Dykstra	2.00
FI	Carlton Fisk	3.00
KG	Kirk Gibson	2.00
TG	Tony Gwynn	4.00
WJ	Wally Joyner	2.00
KM	Kevin Mitchell	2.00
PM	Paul Molitor	4.00
JM	Jack Morris	2.00
GP	Gaylord Perry	2.00
CR	Cal Ripken Jr.	10.00
NR	Nolan Ryan	8.00
BS	Bret Saberhagen	2.00
RS	Ryne Sandberg	5.00
MS	Mike Schmidt	6.00
DS	Don Sutton	2.00
RY	Robin Yount	5.00

Classic Moments Materials

		NM/M
Common Player:		5.00
WB	Wade Boggs	10.00
SC	Steve Carlton	8.00
CA	Joe Carter	5.00
JC	Jack Clark	5.00
LD	Lenny Dykstra	5.00
FI	Carlton Fisk	8.00
KG	Kirk Gibson	5.00
TG	Tony Gwynn	10.00
WJ	Wally Joyner	5.00
KM	Kevin Mitchell	5.00
PM	Paul Molitor	10.00
JM	Jack Morris	5.00
GP	Gaylord Perry	5.00
CR	Cal Ripken Jr.	25.00
NR	Nolan Ryan	20.00
RS	Ryne Sandberg	15.00
MS	Mike Schmidt	15.00
DS	Don Sutton	5.00
RY	Robin Yount	12.00

Classic Moments Signatures

	NM/M
Common Autograph:	10.00
SC	Steve Carlton	20.00
JC	Jack Clark	15.00
LD	Lenny Dykstra	15.00
FI	Carlton Fisk	40.00
KG	Kirk Gibson	25.00
TG	Tony Gwynn	40.00
WJ	Wally Joyner	20.00
KM	Kevin Mitchell	10.00
PM	Paul Molitor	25.00
JM	Jack Morris	20.00
GP	Gaylord Perry	15.00
BS	Bret Saberhagen	15.00
MS	Mike Schmidt	60.00
DS	Don Sutton	15.00
RY	Robin Yount	40.00

Classic Seasons

ANDRE DAWSON

		NM/M
Common Player:		2.00
Production 1,999 Sets		
BE	George Bell	2.00
JC	Jose Canseco	3.00
CL	Jack Clark	2.00
WC	Will Clark	3.00
DC	David Cone	2.00
ED	Eric Davis	2.00
AD	Andre Dawson	2.00
KG	Kirk Gibson	2.00
DG	Dwight Gooden	2.00
FL	Fred Lynn	2.00
MA	Don Mattingly	6.00
KM	Kevin Mitchell	5.00
DM	Dale Murphy	3.00
JR	Jim Rice	2.00
CR	Cal Ripken Jr.	10.00
NR	Nolan Ryan	8.00
BS	Bret Saberhagen	2.00
RS	Ryne Sandberg	5.00
MS	Mike Schmidt	5.00
CY	Carl Yastrzemski	6.00

Classic Seasons Materials

		NM/M
Common Player:		5.00
BE	George Bell	5.00
JC	Jose Canseco	10.00
CL	Jack Clark	5.00
WC	Will Clark	8.00
DC	David Cone	5.00
ED	Eric Davis SP	8.00
AD	Andre Dawson	8.00
KG	Kirk Gibson	5.00
DG	Dwight Gooden	5.00
FL	Fred Lynn	5.00
MA	Don Mattingly	15.00
KM	Kevin Mitchell	5.00
DM	Dale Murphy	8.00
JR	Jim Rice	5.00
CR	Cal Ripken Jr.	25.00
NR	Nolan Ryan	20.00
RS	Ryne Sandberg	15.00
MS	Mike Schmidt	15.00
CY	Carl Yastrzemski	20.00

Classic Seasons Signatures

		NM/M
Common Auto.:		10.00
BE	George Bell	15.00
JC	Jose Canseco	40.00
CL	Jack Clark	15.00
WC	Will Clark	40.00
DC	David Cone	15.00
ED	Eric Davis	20.00
AD	Andre Dawson	20.00
KG	Kirk Gibson	25.00
DG	Dwight Gooden	12.00
FL	Fred Lynn	15.00
MA	Don Mattingly	60.00
KM	Kevin Mitchell	10.00

DM	Dale Murphy	20.00
BS	Bret Saberhagen	15.00
MS	Mike Schmidt	60.00

League Leaders

		NM/M
Common Player:		2.00
Production 999 Sets		
GB	George Bell	2.00
WB	Wade Boggs	4.00
JC	Jack Clark	2.00
WC	Will Clark	3.00
AD	Andre Dawson	3.00
LD	Lenny Dykstra	3.00
DE	Dennis Eckersley	3.00
DG	Dwight Gooden	2.00
GG	Rich "Goose" Gossage	2.00
PG	Pedro Guerrero	2.00
TG	Tony Gwynn	4.00
KH	Keith Hernandez	2.00
FH	Frank Howard	2.00
HJ	Howard Johnson	2.00
MA	Don Mattingly	8.00
KM	Kevin Mitchell	2.00
PM	Paul Molitor	4.00
DM	Dale Murphy	3.00
JR	Jim Rice	2.00
AV	Andy Van Slyke	2.00

League Leaders Materials

		NM/M
Common Player:		5.00
GB	George Bell	5.00
WB	Wade Boggs	10.00
JC	Jack Clark	5.00
WC	Will Clark	8.00
AD	Andre Dawson	8.00
LD	Lenny Dykstra	8.00
DE	Dennis Eckersley	8.00
DG	Dwight Gooden	5.00
GG	Rich "Goose" Gossage	5.00
PG	Pedro Guerrero	5.00
TG	Tony Gwynn/SP	10.00
KH	Keith Hernandez	5.00
FH	Frank Howard	8.00
HJ	Howard Johnson	5.00
MA	Don Mattingly	15.00
KM	Kevin Mitchell	5.00
PM	Paul Molitor	10.00
DM	Dale Murphy	8.00
JR	Jim Rice	5.00
AV	Andy Van Slyke	20.00

League Leaders Signatures

		NM/M
Common Auto.:		10.00
GB	George Bell	10.00
JC	Jack Clark	15.00
WC	Will Clark	40.00
AD	Andre Dawson	20.00
LD	Lenny Dykstra	15.00
DE	Dennis Eckersley	15.00
DG	Dwight Gooden	15.00
GG	Rich "Goose" Gossage	15.00
PG	Pedro Guerrero	10.00
KH	Keith Hernandez	15.00
FH	Frank Howard	15.00
HJ	Howard Johnson	15.00
MA	Don Mattingly	60.00
KM	Kevin Mitchell	10.00
PM	Paul Molitor	25.00
DM	Dale Murphy	20.00
JR	Jim Rice	15.00

Pirates All-Stars

	NM/M
Complete Set (7):	20.00

Common Player:		2.00
PP1	Ralph Kiner	4.00
PP2	Bill Mazeroski	5.00
PP3	Roberto Clemente	7.50
PP4	Willie Stargell	4.00
PP5	Tony Pena	2.00
PP6	Andy Van Slyke	2.00
PP7	Jason Bay	2.00

Post Season Performers

		NM/M
Common Player:		2.00
Production 999 Sets		
JO	Jose Canseco	3.00
CA	Joe Carter	2.00
JC	Jack Clark	2.00
WC	Will Clark	3.00
DC	David Cone	2.00
ED	Eric Davis	2.00
LD	Lenny Dykstra	2.00
CF	Carlton Fisk	3.00
DG	Dwight Gooden	2.00
PG	Pedro Guerrero	2.00
KH	Kent Hrbek	2.00
JK	John Kruk	3.00
KM	Kevin Mitchell	2.00
PM	Paul Molitor	4.00
JM	Jack Morris	2.00
CR	Cal Ripken Jr.	10.00
BR	Brooks Robinson	4.00
BS	Bret Saberhagen	2.00
MS	Mike Schmidt	6.00
DS	Darryl Strawberry	2.00

Post Season Performers Materials

		NM/M
Common Player:		5.00
JO	Jose Canseco	10.00
CA	Joe Carter	5.00
JC	Jack Clark/SP	5.00
WC	Will Clark	8.00
DC	David Cone	8.00
ED	Eric Davis/SP	10.00
LD	Lenny Dykstra/SP	5.00
CF	Carlton Fisk	8.00
DG	Dwight Gooden	5.00
PG	Pedro Guerrero	5.00
KH	Kent Hrbek	8.00
JK	John Kruk/SP	15.00
KM	Kevin Mitchell	5.00
PM	Paul Molitor/SP	10.00
JM	Jack Morris	5.00
CR	Cal Ripken Jr./SP	25.00
BR	Brooks Robinson	10.00
MS	Mike Schmidt	15.00
DS	Darryl Strawberry	5.00

Post Season Performers Signatures

		NM/M
Common Auto.:		10.00
JO	Jose Canseco	40.00
JC	Jack Clark	15.00
WC	Will Clark	40.00
DC	David Cone	15.00
ED	Eric Davis	20.00
LD	Lenny Dykstra	15.00
CF	Carlton Fisk	40.00
DG	Dwight Gooden	12.00
PG	Pedro Guerrero	10.00
KH	Kent Hrbek	20.00
JK	John Kruk	30.00
KM	Kevin Mitchell	10.00
PM	Paul Molitor	25.00
JM	Jack Morris	20.00
BR	Brooks Robinson	25.00
BS	Bret Saberhagen	15.00
MS	Mike Schmidt	60.00
SS	Darryl Strawberry	20.00

2005 Upper Deck ESPN

		NM/M
Complete Set (90):		20.00
Common Player:		.15
Pack (9):		3.00
Box (24):		60.00
1	Garret Anderson	.25
2	Troy Glaus	.25
3	Vladimir Guerrero	.75
4	Luis Gonzalez	.25
5	Randy Johnson	.75
6	Andruw Jones	.40
7	Chipper Jones	.75
8	J.D. Drew	.25
9	John Smoltz	.25
10	Miguel Tejada	.50
11	Rafael Palmeiro	.50
12	Curt Schilling	.75
13	David Ortiz	.75
14	Manny Ramirez	.75
15	Pedro J. Martinez	.75
16	Carlos Zambrano	.25
17	Greg Maddux	1.00
18	Kerry Wood	.75
19	Mark Prior	.75
20	Nomar Garciaparra	1.50
21	Sammy Sosa	1.50
22	Carlos Lee	.25
23	Frank Thomas	.50
24	Magglio Ordonez	.25
25	Paul Konerko	.25
26	Adam Dunn	.50
27	Ken Griffey Jr.	1.00
28	Travis Hafner	.15
29	Victor Martinez	.25
30	Todd Helton	.50
31	Ivan Rodriguez	.50
32	Carl Pavano	.15
33	Josh Beckett	.25
34	Miguel Cabrera	.75
35	Mike Lowell	.15
36	Carlos Beltran	.50
37	Craig Biggio	.25
38	Jeff Bagwell	.50
39	Lance Berkman	.25
40	Roger Clemens	2.00
41	Roy Oswalt	.25
42	Mike Sweeney	.15
43	Adrian Beltre	.25
44	Brad Penny	.15
45	Eric Gagne	.40
46	Shawn Green	.25
47	Steve Finley	.15
48	Ben Sheets	.25
49	Scott Podsednik	.15
50	Joe Mauer	.25
51	Johan Santana	.50
52	Torii Hunter	.25
53	Jose Vidro	.15
54	Livan Hernandez	.15
55	Jose Reyes	.25
56	Mike Piazza	1.00
57	Tom Glavine	.25
58	Alex Rodriguez	1.50
59	Bernie Williams	.25
60	Derek Jeter	2.00
61	Gary Sheffield	.50
62	Hideki Matsui	1.50
63	Kevin Brown	.15
64	Mike Mussina	.25
65	Eric Chavez	.25
66	Mark Mulder	.25
67	Tim Hudson	.25
68	Bobby Abreu	.25
69	Jim Thome	.75
70	Craig Wilson	.15
71	Jason Kendall	.15
72	Oliver Perez	.15
73	Brian Giles	.15
74	Jake Peavy	.15
75	Jason Schmidt	.25
76	Bret Boone	.15
77	Ichiro Suzuki	1.50
78	Albert Pujols	2.00
79	Jim Edmonds	.25
80	Larry Walker	.40
81	Scott Rolen	.75
82	Aubrey Huff	.15
83	Carl Crawford	.15
84	Alfonso Soriano	.75
85	Hank Blalock	.50
86	Mark Teixeira	.50
87	Michael Young	.25
88	Carlos Delgado	.40
89	Roy Halladay	.25
90	Vernon Wells	.25

Award Winners

		NM/M
Inserted 1:5		
25th Anniv.:		4-8X
Production 25 Sets		
AW-1	Gary Sheffield	1.00
AW-2	Greg Maddux	2.00
AW-3	Mike Piazza	2.00
AW-4	Jeff Bagwell	1.00
AW-5	Kenny Rogers	.50
AW-6	Cal Ripken Jr.	4.00
AW-7	Greg Maddux	2.00
AW-8	Hideo Nomo	.75
AW-9	Javier Lopez	.50
AW-10	Jim Edmonds	.50
AW-11	Ken Griffey Jr.	2.00
AW-12	Larry Walker	.75
AW-13	Nomar Garciaparra	2.50
AW-14	Roger Clemens	4.00
AW-15	David Wells	.50
AW-16	Sammy Sosa	2.50
AW-17	Pedro J. Martinez	1.50
AW-18	Andres Galarraga	.50
AW-19	Derek Jeter	4.00
AW-20	Alfonso Soriano	1.50

Ink

No Pricing

Sports Center Swatches

	NM/M
Common Player:	4.00

Inserted 1:12

GA	Garret Anderson	4.00
RB	Rocco Baldelli	4.00
CB	Carlos Beltran	8.00
AB	Adrian Beltre	8.00
LB	Lance Berkman	4.00
BI	Craig Biggio	4.00
HB	Hank Blalock	8.00
BB	Bret Boone	4.00
MG	Miguel Cabrera	8.00
EC	Eric Chavez	4.00
BC	Bartolo Colon	4.00
CC	Carl Crawford	4.00
JD	J.D. Drew	4.00
AD	Adam Dunn	8.00
JE	Jim Edmonds	6.00
EG	Eric Gagne	6.00
TG	Troy Glaus	6.00
KG	Ken Griffey Jr.	15.00
TH	Tim Hudson	4.00
AH	Aubrey Huff	4.00
DJ	Derek Jeter	20.00
JK	Jeff Kent	4.00
PK	Paul Konerko	4.00
DL	Derrek Lee	4.00
LO	Derek Lowe	4.00
MM	Mark Mulder	4.00
CP	Corey Patterson	6.00
AP	Albert Pujols	20.00
IR	Ivan Rodriguez	8.00
SA	Johan Santana	8.00
JS	Jason Schmidt	6.00
BS	Ben Sheets	4.00
AS	Alfonso Soriano	8.00
IS	Ichiro Suzuki	25.00
MS	Mike Sweeney	4.00
MT	Mark Teixeira	6.00
JT	Jim Thome	10.00
BU	B.J. Upton	6.00
VW	Vernon Wells	4.00
DW	David Wright/SP	15.00
MY	Mike Young/SP	10.00

Sports Century

		NM/M
Inserted 1:5		
25th Anniv.:		4-8X
Production 25 Sets		
SC-1	Babe Ruth	4.00
SC-2	Jackie Robinson	2.00
SC-4	Ty Cobb	2.00
SC-5	Joe DiMaggio	3.00
SC-6	Lou Gehrig	3.00
SC-7	Mickey Mantle	5.00
SC-8	Walter Johnson	1.00
SC-9	Stan Musial	2.00
SC-10	Satchel Paige	1.00
SC-11	Bob Gibson	1.00
SC-12	Roberto Clemente	3.00
SC-13	Cy Young	1.00
SC-14	Honus Wagner	2.00
SC-15	Rogers Hornsby	1.00

Sports Century Signatures

No Pricing

The Magazine Covers

		NM/M
Inserted 1:5		
25th Anniv.:		4-8X
Production 25 Sets		
MC-1	Roger Clemens	4.00
MC-2	Derek Jeter	4.00
MC-3	Randy Johnson, Pedro J. Martinez	1.50
MC-4	Nomar Garciaparra	2.50
MC-5	Manny Ramirez	1.50
MC-6	Ken Griffey Jr.	2.00
MC-7	Mike Piazza	2.00
MC-8	Ichiro Suzuki	3.00

MC-9	Vladimir Guerrero	1.50
MC-10	Randy Johnson	1.50
MC-11	A.J. Pierzynski, Doug Mientkiewicz, Jacque Jones, Torii Hunter	.50
MC-12	Jason Giambi	.50
MC-13	Jeff Kent	.50
MC-14	Albert Pujols	4.00
MC-15	Kazuo Matsui	.50
MC-16	Miguel Cabrera	1.50
MC-17	Alex Rodriguez	3.00
MC-18	Ivan Rodriguez	1.00
MC-19	Eric Gagne	1.00
MC-20	Jim Edmonds, Albert Pujols, Scott Rolen	.75

This Day in Baseball History

		NM/M
Inserted 1:5		
25th Anniv.:		4-8X
Production 25 Sets		
BH-1	Cal Ripken Jr.	4.00
BH-2	Nolan Ryan	4.00
BH-3	Nolan Ryan	4.00
BH-4	Roger Clemens	4.00
BH-5	Thurman Munson	2.00
BH-6	Mickey Mantle	5.00
BH-7	Ernie Banks	2.00
BH-8	Roy Campanella	1.00
BH-9	Yogi Berra	2.00
BH-10	Mickey Mantle	5.00
BH-11	Jackie Robinson	3.00
BH-12	Joe DiMaggio	3.00
BH-13	Bob Feller	1.00
BH-14	Lou Gehrig	3.00
BH-15	Ty Cobb	2.00
BH-16	Babe Ruth	4.00
BH-17	Walter Johnson	1.00
BH-18	Rogers Hornsby	1.00
BH-19	George Sisler	1.00
BH-20	Cy Young	1.00

Web Gems

		NM/M
Inserted 1:5		
25th Anniv.:		4-8X

Production 25 Sets

WG-1	Adrian Beltre	.75
WG-2	Alex Rodriguez	3.00
WG-3	Andruw Jones	.75
WG-4	Bernie Williams	.75
WG-5	Bret Boone	.50
WG-6	Cesar Izturis	.50
WG-7	Darin Erstad	.50
WG-8	Derek Jeter	4.00
WG-9	Derrek Lee	.75
WG-10	Eric Chavez	.75
WG-11	Greg Maddux	2.00
WG-12	Ichiro Suzuki	3.00
WG-13	Ivan Rodriguez	1.00
WG-14	Jim Edmonds	.75
WG-15	Ken Griffey Jr.	2.00
WG-16	Larry Walker	.75
WG-17	Miguel Tejada	.75
WG-18	Mike Mussina	.75
WG-19	Nomar Garciaparra	2.50
WG-20	Scott Rolen	1.50
WG-21	Steve Finley	.50
WG-22	Todd Helton	1.00
WG-23	Torii Hunter	.50
WG-24	Vernon Wells	.50
WG-25	Vladimir Guerrero	1.50

2005 Upper Deck First Pitch

	NM/M
Complete Set (330):	
Common (1-330):	.10
Common (301-330):	1.00
Inserted 1:4	
Common (321-330):	2.00
Inserted 1:36	
Pack (5):	1.00
Box (36):	30.00
1	Casey Kotchman	.10
2	Chone Figgins	.10
3	David Eckstein	.10
4	Jarrod Washburn	.10
5	Robb Quinlan	.10
6	Troy Glaus	.25
7	Vladimir Guerrero	.50
8	Brandon Webb	.10
9	Danny Bautista	.10
10	Luis Gonzalez	.25
11	Matt Kata	.10
12	Randy Johnson	.50
13	Robby Hammock	.10
14	Shea Hillenbrand	.10
15	Adam LaRoche	.10
16	Andruw Jones	.40
17	Horacio Ramirez	.10
18	John Smoltz	.25
19	Johnny Estrada	.10
20	Mike Hampton	.10
21	Rafael Furcal	.10
22	Brian Roberts	.10
23	Javy Lopez	.25
24	Jay Gibbons	.10
25	Jorge Julio	.10
26	Melvin Mora	.10
27	Miguel Tejada	.40
28	Rafael Palmeiro	.40
29	Derek Lowe	.10
30	Jason Varitek	.25
31	Kevin Youkilis	.10
32	Manny Ramirez	.50
33	Curt Schilling	.50
34	Pedro J. Martinez	.50
35	Trot Nixon	.10
36	Corey Patterson	.25
37	Derrek Lee	.25
38	LaTroy Hawkins	.10
39	Mark Prior	.50
40	Matt Clement	.10
41	Moises Alou	.25
42	Sammy Sosa	1.00
43	Aaron Rowand	.10
44	Carlos Lee	.10
45	Jose Valentin	.10
46	Juan Uribe	.10
47	Magglio Ordonez	.10
48	Mark Buehrle	.10
49	Paul Konerko	.10
50	Adam Dunn	.40
51	Barry Larkin	.25
52	D'Angelo Jimenez	.10
53	Danny Graves	.10
54	Paul Wilson	.10
55	Sean Casey	.10
56	Wily Mo Pena	.10
57	Ben Broussard	.10
58	C.C. Sabathia	.10
59	Casey Blake	.10
60	Cliff Lee	.10
61	Matt Lawton	.10
62	Omar Vizquel	.10
63	Victor Martinez	.25
64	Charles Johnson	.10
65	Joe Kennedy	.10
66	Jeromy Burnitz	.10
67	Matt Holliday	.25
68	Preston Wilson	.10
69	Royce Clayton	.10
70	Shawn Estes	.10
71	Bobby Higginson	.10
72	Brandon Inge	.10
73	Carlos Guillen	.10
74	Dmitri Young	.10
75	Eric Munson	.10
76	Jeremy Bonderman	.10
77	Ugueth Urbina	.10
78	Josh Beckett	.25
79	Dontrelle Willis	.25
80	Jeff Conine	.10
81	Juan Pierre	.10
82	Luis Castillo	.10
83	Miguel Cabrera	.50
84	Mike Lowell	.10
85	Andy Pettitte	.25
86	Brad Lidge	.10
87	Carlos Beltran	.40
88	Craig Biggio	.25
89	Jeff Bagwell	.40
90	Roger Clemens	1.50
91	Roy Oswalt	.25
92	Benito Santiago	.10
93	Jeremy Affeldt	.10
94	Juan Gonzalez	.25
95	Ken Harvey	.10
96	Mike MacDougal	.10
97	Mike Sweeney	.10
98	Zack Greinke	.10
99	Adrian Beltre	.25
100	Alex Cora	.10
101	Cesar Izturis	.10
102	Eric Gagne	.25
103	Kazuhisa Ishii	.10
104	Milton Bradley	.10
105	Shawn Green	.25
106	Danny Kolb	.10
107	Ben Sheets	.25
108	Brooks Kieschnick	.10
109	Craig Counsell	.10
110	Geoff Jenkins	.10
111	Lyle Overbay	.10
112	Scott Podsednik	.10
113	Corey Koskie	.10
114	Johan Santana	.50
115	Joe Mauer	.25
116	Justin Morneau	.25
117	Lew Ford	.10
118	Matt LeCroy	.10
119	Torii Hunter	.10
120	Brad Wilkerson	.10
121	Chad Cordero	.10
122	Livan Hernandez	.10
123	Jose Vidro	.10
124	Terrmel Sledge	.10
125	Tony Batista	.10
126	Zach Day	.10
127	Al Leiter	.10
128	Jae Weong Seo	.10
129	Jose Reyes	.25
130	Kazuo Matsui	.10
131	Mike Piazza	.75
132	Todd Zeile	.10
133	Cliff Floyd	.10
134	Alex Rodriguez	1.50
135	Derek Jeter	1.50
136	Gary Sheffield	.40
137	Hideki Matsui	1.00
138	Jason Giambi	.25
139	Jorge Posada	.25
140	Mike Mussina	.25
141	Barry Zito	.25
142	Bobby Crosby	.25
143	Octavio Dotel	.10
144	Eric Chavez	.25
145	Jermaine Dye	.10
146	Mark Kotsay	.10
147	Tim Hudson	.25
148	Billy Wagner	.10

149	Bobby Abreu	.25
150	David Bell	.10
151	Jim Thome	.50
152	Jimmy Rollins	.20
153	Mike Lieberthal	.10
154	Randy Wolf	.10
155	Craig Wilson	.10
156	Daryle Ward	.10
157	Jack Wilson	.10
158	Jason Kendall	.10
159	Kip Wells	.10
160	Oliver Perez	.25
161	Robert Mackowiak	.10
162	Brian Giles	.10
163	Brian Lawrence	.10
164	David Wells	.10
165	Jay Payton	.10
166	Ryan Klesko	.10
167	Sean Burroughs	.10
168	Trevor Hoffman	.10
169	Brett Tomko	.10
170	J.T. Snow	.10
171	Jason Schmidt	.25
172	Kirk Rueter	.10
173	A.J. Pierzynski	.10
174	Pedro Feliz	.10
175	Ray Durham	.10
176	Eddie Guardado	.10
177	Edgar Martinez	.10
178	Ichiro Suzuki	1.00
179	Jamie Moyer	.10
180	Joel Pineiro	.10
181	Randy Winn	.10
182	Raul Ibanez	.10
183	Albert Pujols	1.50
184	Edgar Renteria	.25
185	Jason Isringhausen	.10
186	Jim Edmonds	.25
187	Matt Morris	.10
188	Reggie Sanders	.10
189	Tony Womack	.10
190	Aubrey Huff	.10
191	Danys Baez	.10
192	Carl Crawford	.10
193	Jose Cruz Jr.	.10
194	Rocco Baldelli	.10
195	Tino Martinez	.10
196	Dewon Brazelton	.10
197	Alfonso Soriano	.50
198	Brad Fullmer	.10
199	Gerald Laird	.10
200	Hank Blalock	.50
201	Laynce Nix	.10
202	Mark Teixeira	.40
203	Mike Young	.25
204	Alexis Rios	.10
205	Eric Hinske	.10
206	Miguel Batista	.10
207	Orlando Hudson	.10
208	Roy Halladay	.10
209	Ted Lilly	.10
210	Vernon Wells	.10
211	Aarom Baldiris	.10
212	B.J. Upton	.25
213	Dallas McPherson	.25
214	Brian Dallimore	.10
215	Chris Oxspring	.10
216	Chris Shelton	.10
217	David Wright	.75
218	Edwardo Sierra	.10
219	Fernando Nieve	.10
220	Frank Francisco	.10
221	Jeff Bennett	.10
222	Justin Lehr	.10
223	John Gall	.10
224	Jorge Sequea	.10
225	Justin Germano	.10
226	Kazuhito Tadano	.10
227	Kevin Cave	.10
228	Joe Blanton	.10
229	Luis Gonzalez	.10
230	Mike Wuertz	.10
231	Mike Rouse	.10
232	Nick Regilio	.10
233	Orlando Rodriguez	.10
235	Ramon Ramirez	.10
236	Roberto Novoa	.10
237	Dioner Navarro	.10
238	Tim Bausher	.10
239	Logan Kensing	.10
240	Andy Green	.10
241	Brad Halsey	.10
242	Charles Thomas	.10
243	George Sherrill	.10
244	Jesse Crain	.10
245	Jimmy Serrano	.10
246	Joe Horgan	.10
247	Chris Young	.10
248	Joey Gathright	.10
249	Gavin Floyd	.10
250	Ryan Howard	.50
251	Lance Cormier	.10
252	Matt Treanor	.10
253	Jeff Francis	.10
254	Nick Swisher	.10
255	Scott Atchison	.10
256	Travis Blackley	.10
257	Travis Smith	.10
258	Yadier Molina	.10
259	Jeff Keppinger	.10
260	Scott Kazmir	.50
261	Garret Anderson, Vladimir Guerrero	.25
262	Luis Gonzalez, Randy Johnson	.25
263	Chipper Jones, Andruw Jones	.25
264	Miguel Tejada, Rafael Palmeiro	.25
265	Manny Ramirez, Curt Schilling	.25
266	Mark Prior, Sammy Sosa	.50
267	Frank Thomas, Magglio Ordonez	.25
268	Barry Larkin, Ken Griffey Jr.	.50
269	C.C. Sabathia, Victor Martinez	.10
270	Jeromy Burnitz, Todd Helton	.25
271	Ivan Rodriguez, Dmitri Young	.25
272	Josh Beckett, Miguel Cabrera	.25
273	Jeff Bagwell, Roger Clemens	.50
274	Mike Sweeney, Ken Harvey	.10
275	Eric Gagne, Adrian Beltre	.25
276	Ben Sheets, Geoff Jenkins	.10
277	Torii Hunter, Joe Mauer	.10
278	Jose Vidro, Livan Hernandez	.10
279	Mike Piazza, Kazuo Matsui	.25
280	Alex Rodriguez, Derek Jeter	.75
281	Eric Chavez, Tim Hudson	.10
282	Bobby Abreu, Jim Thome	.25
283	Jason Kendall, Craig Wilson	.10
284	Phil Nevin, Brian Giles	.10
285	Jason Schmidt, A.J. Pierzynski	.10
286	Bret Boone, Ichiro Suzuki	.50
287	Albert Pujols, Scott Rolen	.75
288	Aubrey Huff, Tino Martinez	.10
289	Hank Blalock, Mark Teixeira	.25
290	Roy Halladay, Carlos Delgado	.10
291	Vladimir Guerrero	.50
292	Curt Schilling	.50
293	Mark Prior	.50
294	Josh Beckett	.25
295	Roger Clemens	1.00
296	Derek Jeter	1.00
297	Eric Chavez	.10
298	Jim Thome	.50
299	Albert Pujols	1.00
300	Hank Blalock	.25
301	Guillermo Quiroz	1.00
302	Jeff Bajenaru	1.00
303	Bartolome Fortunato	1.00
304	Jason Alfaro	1.00
305	Mike Rose	1.00
306	Joe Hietpas	1.00
307	Kyle Denney	1.00
308	Rene Rivera	1.00
309	Kameron Loe	1.00
310	Rickie Weeks	1.50
311	Gustavo Chacin	1.00
312	Chris Burke	1.00
313	Yhency Brazoban	1.00
314	Brandon League	1.00
315	Jose Capellan	1.00
316	Russ Adams	1.00
317	Adrian Gonzalez	1.00
318	Jason Dubois	1.00
319	Abe Alvarez	1.00
320	Eric Crozier	1.00
321	Bengie Molina, Bartolo Colon	2.00
322	C.C. Sabathia, Victor Martinez	2.00
323	Jake Peavy, Ramon Hernandez	2.00
324	A.J. Pierzynski, Jason Schmidt	3.00
325	Joe Mauer, Johan Santana	3.00
326	Mark Prior, Michael Barrett	3.00
327	Jorge Posada, Mike Mussina	3.00
328	Roger Clemens, Brad Ausmus	4.00
329	Roy Halladay, Guillermo Quiroz	2.00
330	Mike Piazza, Tom Glavine	3.00

Fabric

NM/M

Common Player:
Inserted 1:180

JB	Jeff Bagwell	8.00
BE	Josh Beckett	5.00
BB	Bret Boone	5.00
EC	Eric Chavez	5.00
JE	Jim Edmonds	5.00
EG	Eric Gagne	8.00
TG	Troy Glaus	5.00
KG	Ken Griffey Jr./SP	20.00
TH	Torii Hunter	5.00
DJ	Derek Jeter	20.00
AJ	Andruw Jones	5.00
CJ	Chipper Jones	8.00
MM	Mark Mulder	5.00
MO	Magglio Ordonez	5.00
SR	Scott Rolen	8.00
CS	Curt Schilling	8.00
GS	Gary Sheffield/SP	8.00
AS	Alfonso Soriano	8.00
SS	Sammy Sosa	10.00
IS	Ichiro Suzuki/SP	25.00

Signature Stars

No Pricing

2005 Upper Deck MVP

NM/M

Complete Set (90):		20.00
Common Player:		.10
Pack (6):		1.50
Box (24):		30.00
1	Adam Dunn	.40
2	Adrian Beltre	.40
3	Albert Pujols	1.50
4	Alex Rodriguez	1.50
5	Alfonso Soriano	.50
6	Andruw Jones	.40
7	Aubrey Huff	.10
8	Barry Zito	.25
9	Ben Sheets	.25
10	Bobby Abreu	.25
11	Bobby Crosby	.25
12	Bret Boone	.10
13	Brian Giles	.10
14	Carlos Beltran	.40
15	Carlos Delgado	.25
16	Carlos Lee	.25
17	Chipper Jones	.50
18	Craig Biggio	.25
19	Curt Schilling	.40
20	Dallas McPherson	.10
21	David Ortiz	.50
22	David Wright	.50
23	Derek Jeter	1.50
24	Derek Lowe	.10
25	Eric Chavez	.25
26	Eric Gagne	.25
27	Frank Thomas	.40
28	Garret Anderson	.25
29	Gary Sheffield	.40
30	Greg Maddux	1.00
31	Hank Blalock	.25
32	Hideki Matsui	1.00
33	Ichiro Suzuki	1.00
34	Ivan Rodriguez	.40
35	J.D. Drew	.10
36	Jake Peavy	.25
37	Jason Bay	.10
38	Jason Giambi	.25
39	Jason Schmidt	.25
40	Jeff Bagwell	.40
41	Jeff Kent	.25
42	Jim Edmonds	.25
43	Jim Thome	.40
44	Joe Mauer	.25
45	Johan Santana	.50
46	John Smoltz	.25
47	Johnny Damon	.50
48	Jorge Posada	.25
49	Jose Vidro	.10
50	Josh Beckett	.25
51	Kazuo Matsui	.25
52	Ken Griffey Jr.	1.00
53	Kerry Wood	.25
54	Khalil Greene	.25
55	Lance Berkman	.25
56	Livan Hernandez	.10
57	Luis Gonzalez	.10
58	Magglio Ordonez	.10
59	Manny Ramirez	.50
60	Mark Mulder	.25
61	Mark Prior	.50
62	Mark Teixeira	.40
63	Miguel Cabrera	.50
64	Miguel Tejada	.40
65	Mike Mussina	.25
66	Mike Piazza	1.00
67	Mike Sweeney	.10
68	Moises Alou	.25
69	Nomar Garciaparra	.75
70	Oliver Perez	.10
71	Paul Konerko	.25
72	Pedro Martinez	.50
73	Rafael Palmeiro	.25
74	Randy Johnson	.50
75	Richie Sexson	.25
76	Roger Clemens	1.50
77	Roy Halladay	.25
78	Roy Oswalt	.25
79	Sammy Sosa	.75
80	Scott Rolen	.50
81	Shawn Green	.10
82	Steve Finley	.10
83	Tim Hudson	.25
84	Todd Helton	.40
85	Tom Glavine	.25
86	Torii Hunter	.25
87	Travis Hafner	.10
88	Troy Glaus	.25
89	Victor Martinez	.25
90	Vladimir Guerrero	.50

Batter Up!

NM/M

Common Player: .25
Inserted 1:1

BU-1	Al Kaline	.50
BU-2	Bill Mazeroski	.25
BU-3	Billy Williams	.25
BU-4	Bob Feller	.50
BU-5	Bob Gibson	.50
BU-6	Bob Lemon	.25
BU-7	Brooks Robinson	.50
BU-8	Carlton Fisk	.50
BU-9	Jim "Catfish" Hunter	.25
BU-10	Dennis Eckersley	.25
BU-11	Eddie Mathews	.75
BU-12	Eddie Murray	.50
BU-13	Fergie Jenkins	.25
BU-14	Gaylord Perry	.25
BU-15	Harmon Killebrew	.75
BU-16	Jim Bunning	.25
BU-17	Jim Palmer	.50
BU-18	Joe DiMaggio	1.50
BU-19	Joe Morgan	.25
BU-20	Johnny Bench	.75
BU-21	Juan Marichal	.50
BU-22	Lou Brock	.50
BU-23	Luis Aparicio	.25
BU-24	Mike Schmidt	1.50
BU-25	Monte Irvin	.25
BU-26	Nolan Ryan	2.00
BU-27	Orlando Cepeda	.25
BU-28	Ozzie Smith	.75
BU-29	Pee Wee Reese	.25
BU-30	Phil Niekro	.25
BU-31	Phil Rizzuto	.50
BU-32	Ralph Kiner	.25
BU-33	Richie Ashburn	.50
BU-34	Robin Roberts	.25
BU-35	Robin Yount	.75
BU-36	Rollie Fingers	.25
BU-37	Tom Seaver	.75
BU-38	Tony Perez	.25
BU-39	Warren Spahn	.75
BU-40	Willie McCovey	.50
BU-41	Willie Stargell	.50
BU-42	Yogi Berra	.75

All-Star Signatures

No Pricing
Inserted 1:480

Jersey

NM/M

Common Jersey: 4.00
Inserted 1:24

CB	Carlos Beltran	6.00
AB	Adrian Beltre	4.00
HB	Hank Blalock	4.00
SB	Sean Burroughs	4.00
MC	Miguel Cabrera	6.00
EC	Eric Chavez	4.00
EG	Eric Gagne	4.00
KG	Ken Griffey Jr.	10.00
VG	Vladimir Guerrero	6.00
TH	Todd Helton	6.00
DJ	Derek Jeter	15.00
RJ	Randy Johnson	6.00
CJ	Chipper Jones	6.00
GM	Greg Maddux	8.00
PI	Mike Piazza	8.00

MP	Mark Prior	6.00
AP	Albert Pujols	15.00
MR	Manny Ramirez	6.00
IR	Ivan Rodriguez	6.00
SR	Scott Rolen	6.00
JS	Johan Santana	6.00
CS	Curt Schilling	6.00
AS	Alfonso Soriano	6.00
SS	Sammy Sosa	8.00
MT	Mark Teixeira	6.00
TE	Miguel Tejada	6.00
JT	Jim Thome	6.00
KW	Kerry Wood	4.00

2005 Upper Deck Portraits

	NM/M
Complete Set (100):	25.00
Common Player:	.25
Box (7 Cards + 8x10):	100.00

#	Player	Price
1	Dallas McPherson	.25
2	Steve Finley	.25
3	Vladimir Guerrero	.75
4	Troy Glaus	.25
5	Andruw Jones	.50
6	Chipper Jones	.75
7	John Smoltz	.50
8	Marcus Giles	.25
9	Tim Hudson	.50
10	Cal Ripken Jr.	3.00
11	Miguel Tejada	.50
12	Curt Schilling	.75
13	David Ortiz	.75
14	Edgar Renteria	.25
15	Jason Varitek	.50
16	Jim Rice	.50
17	Johnny Damon	.75
18	Matt Clement	.25
19	Wade Boggs	.75
20	Aramis Ramirez	.50
21	Carlos Zambrano	.50
22	Corey Patterson	.25
23	Fergie Jenkins	.25
24	Greg Maddux	1.50
25	Kerry Wood	.50
26	Mark Prior	.75
27	Nomar Garciaparra	.75
28	Ryne Sandberg	1.50
29	Frank Thomas	.50
30	Adam Dunn	.50
31	Barry Larkin	.50
32	Ken Griffey Jr.	1.50
33	Sean Casey	.25
34	Travis Hafner	.25
35	Victor Martinez	.25
36	Todd Helton	.50
37	Ivan Rodriguez	.50
38	Magglio Ordonez	.25
39	Josh Beckett	.25
40	Miguel Cabrera	.75
41	Mike Lowell	.25
42	Craig Biggio	.50
43	Jeff Bagwell	.50
44	Roger Clemens	2.00
45	Roy Oswalt	.25
46	Bo Jackson	.50
47	Prince Fielder	5.00
48	Eric Gagne	.25
49	J.D. Drew	.25
50	Ben Sheets	.50
51	Robin Yount	.75
52	Jacque Jones	.25
53	Joe Mauer	.50
54	Johan Santana	.75
55	Justin Morneau	.25
56	Torii Hunter	.25
57	Dontrelle Willis	.50
58	David Wright	1.00
59	Gary Carter	.25
60	Jose Reyes	.40
61	Keith Hernandez	.25
62	Mike Piazza	1.00
63	Pedro Martinez	.75
64	Tom Glavine	.50
65	Carl Pavano	.25
66	Derek Jeter	2.00
67	Don Mattingly	1.00
68	Mike Mussina	.50
69	Randy Johnson	.75
70	Bobby Crosby	.25
71	Eric Chavez	.25
72	Rich Harden	.25
73	Bobby Abreu	.50
74	Mike Schmidt	1.00
75	Jason Bay	.25
76	Oliver Perez	.25
77	Brian Giles	.25
78	Jake Peavy	.50
79	Khalil Greene	.25
80	Tony Gwynn	.75
81	Jason Schmidt	.25
82	Will Clark	.50
83	Adrian Beltre	.25
84	Justin Verlander	2.00
85	Albert Pujols	2.00
86	Jim Edmonds	.50
87	Mark Mulder	.50
88	Scott Rolen	.75
89	Aubrey Huff	.25
90	B.J. Upton	.25
91	Carl Crawford	.25
92	Tadahito Iguchi	4.00
93	Scott Kazmir	.25
94	Alfonso Soriano	.75
95	Hank Blalock	.25
96	Mark Teixeira	.50
97	Michael Young	.25
98	Nolan Ryan	2.00
99	Roy Halladay	.50
100	Jose Vidro	.25

Emerald Jersey

	NM/M
Common Player:	4.00
Production 99 Sets	
Blue:	1-1.5X
Production 25 Sets	
Gold:	1-2X
Production 15 Sets	

#	Player	Price
1	Dallas McPherson	4.00
2	Steve Finley	4.00
3	Vladimir Guerrero	8.00
4	Troy Glaus	4.00
5	Andruw Jones	6.00
6	Chipper Jones	8.00
7	John Smoltz	6.00
8	Marcus Giles	6.00
9	Tim Hudson	6.00
10	Cal Ripken Jr.	25.00
11	Miguel Tejada	8.00
12	Curt Schilling	8.00
13	David Ortiz	8.00
14	Edgar Renteria	4.00
15	Jason Varitek	8.00
16	Jim Rice	6.00
17	Johnny Damon	8.00
18	Matt Clement	4.00
19	Wade Boggs	8.00
20	Aramis Ramirez	6.00
21	Carlos Zambrano	6.00
22	Corey Patterson	4.00
23	Fergie Jenkins	6.00
24	Greg Maddux	10.00
25	Kerry Wood	6.00
26	Mark Prior	8.00
27	Nomar Garciaparra	8.00
28	Ryne Sandberg	12.00
29	Frank Thomas	8.00
30	Adam Dunn	6.00
31	Barry Larkin	6.00
32	Ken Griffey Jr.	15.00
33	Sean Casey	4.00
34	Travis Hafner	4.00
35	Victor Martinez	4.00
36	Todd Helton	6.00
37	Ivan Rodriguez	6.00
38	Magglio Ordonez	4.00
39	Josh Beckett	4.00
40	Miguel Cabrera	8.00
41	Mike Lowell	4.00
42	Craig Biggio	6.00
43	Jeff Bagwell	8.00
44	Roger Clemens	15.00
45	Roy Oswalt	4.00
46	Bo Jackson	10.00
48	Eric Gagne	4.00
49	J.D. Drew	4.00
50	Ben Sheets	4.00
51	Robin Yount	15.00
52	Jacque Jones	4.00
53	Joe Mauer	6.00
54	Johan Santana	6.00
55	Justin Morneau	4.00
56	Torii Hunter	4.00
57	Dontrelle Willis	6.00
58	David Wright	10.00
59	Gary Carter	6.00
60	Jose Reyes	6.00
61	Keith Hernandez	4.00
62	Mike Piazza	8.00
63	Pedro Martinez	6.00
64	Tom Glavine	4.00
65	Carl Pavano	4.00
66	Derek Jeter	15.00
67	Don Mattingly	15.00
68	Mike Mussina	4.00
69	Randy Johnson	8.00
70	Bobby Crosby	4.00
71	Eric Chavez	4.00
72	Rich Harden	4.00
73	Bobby Abreu	6.00
74	Mike Schmidt	10.00
75	Jason Bay	4.00
76	Oliver Perez	4.00
77	Brian Giles	4.00
78	Jake Peavy	6.00
79	Khalil Greene	4.00
80	Tony Gwynn	8.00
81	Jason Schmidt	4.00
82	Will Clark	8.00
83	Adrian Beltre	4.00
85	Albert Pujols	15.00
86	Jim Edmonds	6.00
87	Mark Mulder	6.00
88	Scott Rolen	6.00
89	Aubrey Huff	4.00
90	B.J. Upton	4.00
91	Carl Crawford	4.00
92	Tadahito Iguchi	15.00
93	Scott Kazmir	4.00
94	Alfonso Soriano	6.00
95	Hank Blalock	6.00
96	Mark Teixeira	6.00
97	Michael Young	6.00
98	Nolan Ryan	15.00
99	Roy Halladay	6.00
100	Jose Vidro	4.00

Jersey Autograph Platinum

No Pricing
Production 10 Sets

Scrapbook Materials

	NM/M
Complete Set (59):	
Common Player:	

BA	Bobby Abreu	4.00
JB	Jeff Bagwell	6.00
BE	Josh Beckett	4.00
AB	Adrian Beltre	4.00
BI	Craig Biggio	6.00
CA	Miguel Cabrera	8.00
WC	Will Clark	6.00
CL	Matt Clement	4.00
BC	Bobby Crosby	4.00
JE	Jim Edmonds	6.00
PF	Prince Fielder	6.00
SF	Steve Finley	4.00
BG	Brian Giles	4.00
GR	Khalil Greene	4.00
KG	Ken Griffey Jr.	15.00
TG	Tony Gwynn	8.00
RH	Roy Halladay	4.00
TH	Todd Helton	6.00
KH	Keith Hernandez	4.00
BJ	Bo Jackson	10.00
DJ	Derek Jeter	20.00
AJ	Andruw Jones	6.00
CJ	Chipper Jones	8.00
JJ	Jacque Jones	4.00
SK	Scott Kazmir	4.00
BL	Barry Larkin	4.00
ML	Mike Lowell	4.00
VM	Victor Martinez	4.00
MA	Don Mattingly	15.00
JM	Joe Mauer	6.00
MC	Dallas McPherson	4.00
MO	Justin Morneau	4.00
DM	Dale Murphy	6.00
MM	Mike Mussina	6.00
OR	Magglio Ordonez	4.00
DO	David Ortiz	8.00
PA	Corey Patterson	4.00
CP	Carl Pavano	4.00
JP	Jake Peavy	6.00
OP	Oliver Perez	4.00
MP	Mark Prior	6.00
AP	Albert Pujols	15.00
JR	Jim Rice	6.00
CR	Cal Ripken Jr.	20.00
NR	Nolan Ryan	15.00
RS	Ryne Sandberg	10.00
SA	Johan Santana	6.00
JS	Jason Schmidt	4.00
MS	Mike Schmidt	10.00
SM	John Smoltz	6.00
MT	Mark Teixeira	6.00
FT	Frank Thomas	6.00
BU	B.J. Upton	4.00
JV	Jose Vidro	4.00
WI	Dontrelle Willis	6.00
DW	David Wright	10.00
CZ	Carlos Zambrano	6.00

Scrapbook Moments

	NM/M
Common Player:	1.00
Production 250 Sets	

BA	Bobby Abreu	1.50
JB	Jeff Bagwell	1.50
BE	Josh Beckett	1.50
AB	Adrian Beltre	1.50
BI	Craig Biggio	1.50
CA	Miguel Cabrera	2.00
WC	Will Clark	1.50
RC	Roger Clemens	6.00
CL	Matt Clement	1.00
BC	Bobby Crosby	1.00
JE	Jim Edmonds	1.50
PF	Prince Fielder	6.00
SF	Steve Finley	1.00
BG	Brian Giles	1.00
GR	Khalil Greene	1.50
KG	Ken Griffey Jr.	4.00
TG	Tony Gwynn	2.00
RH	Roy Halladay	1.00
TH	Todd Helton	1.50
KH	Keith Hernandez	1.00
HU	Torii Hunter	1.00
BJ	Bo Jackson	2.00
DJ	Derek Jeter	6.00
AJ	Andruw Jones	1.50
CJ	Chipper Jones	2.00
JJ	Jacque Jones	1.00
SK	Scott Kazmir	1.00
BL	Barry Larkin	1.50
ML	Mike Lowell	1.00
VM	Victor Martinez	1.00
MA	Don Mattingly	4.00
JM	Joe Mauer	1.50
MC	Dallas McPherson	1.00
MO	Justin Morneau	1.00
DM	Dale Murphy	2.00
MM	Mike Mussina	1.50
OR	Magglio Ordonez	1.00
DO	David Ortiz	2.00
PA	Corey Patterson	1.00
CP	Carl Pavano	1.00
JP	Jake Peavy	1.50
OP	Oliver Perez	1.00
MP	Mark Prior	2.00
AP	Albert Pujols	6.00
JR	Jim Rice	1.50
CR	Cal Ripken Jr.	8.00
NR	Nolan Ryan	6.00
RS	Ryne Sandberg	2.00
SA	Johan Santana	2.00
JS	Jason Schmidt	1.00
MS	Mike Schmidt	4.00

SM	John Smoltz	1.50
MT	Mark Teixeira	1.50
FT	Frank Thomas	1.50
BU	B.J. Upton	1.00
VE	Justin Verlander	2.00
JV	Jose Vidro	1.00
WI	Dontrelle Willis	1.50
DW	David Wright	3.00
CZ	Carlos Zambrano	1.50

Scrapbook Signatures

No Pricing
Production 20 Sets

Signature Portraits
8x10

		NM/M
Common Player:		
DB	Dusty Baker/100	25.00
JB	Jason Bay	25.00
HB	Hank Blalock	25.00
WB	Wade Boggs/40	50.00
CA	Miguel Cabrera	40.00
JD	Johnny Damon/99	50.00
NG	Nomar Garciaparra/25	
GR	Khalil Greene	35.00
VG	Vladimir Guerrero/40	75.00
KH	Keith Hernandez	20.00
DJ	Derek Jeter/150	200.00
SK	Scott Kazmir	25.00
VM	Victor Martinez	25.00
MA	Don Mattingly	65.00
JM	Joe Mauer	30.00
DM	Dale Murphy	30.00
SM	Stan Musial/40	80.00
JN	Jeff Niemann	25.00
RO	Roy Oswalt	30.00
PI	Mike Piazza/35	125.00
MP	Mark Prior/50	40.00
CR	Cal Ripken Jr./50	160.00
BR	Brooks Robinson	50.00
NR	Nolan Ryan/25	140.00
RS	Ryne Sandberg/99	100.00
MS	Mike Schmidt	50.00
BS	Ben Sheets	25.00
OS	Ozzie Smith	50.00
DS	Duke Snider/150	60.00
MT	Mark Teixeira	35.00
BU	B.J. Upton	20.00
VE	Justin Verlander	40.00
DW	David Wright	80.00

Signature Portraits
Cuts 8x10 Card

No Pricing
Production 1-25

Signature Portraits
Dual 8x10

		NM/M
Production 25-99		
BT	Mark Teixeira, Hank Blalock/99	50.00
CO	Roy Oswalt, Roger Clemens/25	
GC	Ken Griffey Jr., Miguel Cabrera/25	
HS	Rich Harden, Ben Sheets/99	40.00
JJ	Randy Johnson, Derek Jeter/25	
NV	Justin Verlander, Jeff Niemann/99	50.00
SB	Mike Schmidt, Pat Burrell/50	
SH	Tim Hudson, John Smoltz/75	75.00
WP	Kerry Wood, Mark Prior/99	85.00
WR	David Wright, Jose Reyes/99	140.00

Signature Portraits
Dual Cuts 8x10

No Pricing
Production 1-2

Signature Portraits
Quad 8x10

No Pricing
Production 5 Sets

Signature Portraits
Triple 8x10

No Pricing
Production 15 Sets

2005 Upper Deck
Pro Signatures

MANNY RAMIREZ

		NM/M
Complete Set (132):		25.00
Common Player:		.10
Common Rookie (91-132):		.25
Inserted 1:1		
Pack (6):		2.00
Box (24):		40.00
1	Dallas McPherson	.10
2	Garret Anderson	.25
3	Steve Finley	.10
4	Vladimir Guerrero	.50
5	Luis Gonzalez	.10
6	Shawn Green	.10
7	Troy Glaus	.25
8	Andruw Jones	.40
9	Chipper Jones	.50
10	John Smoltz	.25
11	Tim Hudson	.40
12	Miguel Tejada	.25
13	Rafael Palmeiro	.25
14	Sammy Sosa	.75
15	Curt Schilling	.50
16	David Ortiz	.50
17	Johnny Damon	.50
18	Manny Ramirez	.50
19	Greg Maddux	1.00
20	Kerry Wood	.25
21	Mark Prior	.50
22	Nomar Garciaparra	.50
23	Frank Thomas	.40
24	Paul Konerko	.25
25	Adam Dunn	.40
26	Ken Griffey Jr.	1.00
27	Travis Hafner	.10
28	Victor Martinez	.10
29	Todd Helton	.40
30	Ivan Rodriguez	.40
31	Magglio Ordonez	.10
32	Carlos Delgado	.25
33	Josh Beckett	.25
34	Miguel Cabrera	.50
35	Craig Biggio	.25
36	Jeff Bagwell	.40
37	Lance Berkman	.25
38	Roger Clemens	1.50
39	Roy Oswalt	.25
40	Mike Sweeney	.10
41	Derek Lowe	.10
42	Eric Gagne	.25
43	J.D. Drew	.10
44	Jeff Kent	.25
45	Ben Sheets	.25
46	Carlos Lee	.25
47	Joe Mauer	.25
48	Johan Santana	.50
49	Torii Hunter	.25
50	Carlos Beltran	.40
51	David Wright	1.00
52	Kazuo Matsui	.10
53	Mike Piazza	.75
54	Pedro Martinez	.50
55	Tom Glavine	.25
56	Alex Rodriguez	1.50
57	Derek Jeter	1.50
58	Gary Sheffield	.40
59	Hideki Matsui	1.00
60	Jason Giambi	.25
61	Jorge Posada	.25
62	Mike Mussina	.25
63	Randy Johnson	.50
64	Barry Zito	.25
65	Bobby Crosby	.25
66	Eric Chavez	.25
67	Bobby Abreu	.25
68	Jim Thome	.40
69	Jason Bay	.25
70	Oliver Perez	.10
71	Brian Giles	.10
72	Jake Peavy	.25

73	Khalil Greene	.25
74	Jason Schmidt	.10
75	Moises Alou	.25
76	Adrian Beltre	.25
77	Bret Boone	.10
78	Ichiro Suzuki	1.00
79	Richie Sexson	.25
80	Albert Pujols	1.50
81	Jim Edmonds	.25
82	Mark Mulder	.25
83	Scott Rolen	.50
84	Aubrey Huff	.10
85	Alfonso Soriano	.50
86	Hank Blalock	.25
87	Mark Teixeira	.25
88	Roy Halladay	.25
89	Jose Vidro	.10
90	Livan Hernandez	.10
91	Tony Pena RC	.25
92	Luis Hernandez RC	.25
93	Peter Orr RC	.25
94	Anibal Sanchez RC	.75
95	Luis Mendoza RC	.25
96	Stephen Drew RC	6.00
97	Russel Rohlicek RC	.25
98	Casey Rogowski RC	.25
99	Pedro Lopez RC	.25
100	Tadahito Iguchi RC	2.00
101	Daylan Childress RC	.25
102	Juan Morillo RC	.50
103	Marcos Carvajal RC	.25
104	Ubaldo Jimenez RC	.25
105	Justin Verlander RC	2.00
106	Chris Resop RC	.25
107	Yorman Bazardo RC	.25
108	Jared Gothreaux RC	.25
109	Luke Scott RC	1.00
110	Ambiorix Burgos RC	.50
111	Prince Fielder RC	4.00
112	Dennis Houlton RC	.25
113	Franquelis Osoria RC	.25
114	Norihiro Nakamura RC	1.00
115	Oscar Robles RC	.25
116	Steve Schmoll RC	.25
117	Luis Pena RC	.25
118	David Gassner RC	.25
119	Ambiorix Concepcion RC	.50
120	Dae-Sung Koo RC	.25
121	Matt Lindstrom RC	.25
122	Colter Bean RC	.25
123	Keiichi Yabu RC	.25
124	Philip Humber RC	1.00
125	Wladimir Balentien RC	1.00
126	Tony Giarratano RC	.25
127	Shane Costa RC	.25
128	Jeff Niemann RC	1.00
129	Nick Masset RC	.25
130	Ismael Ramirez RC	.25
131	John Hattig Jr. RC	.25
132	Brandon McCarthy RC	1.50

Gold

Gold:	2-4X
Production 350 Sets	

Silver

Silver:	1-3X
Inserted 1:5	

Signature Sensations

		NM/M
Inserted 1:24		
Silver:		1-2X
Production 50 Sets		
Gold:		No Pricing
Production 5 Sets		
AA	Abe Alvarez	10.00
BA	Bronson Arroyo	25.00
GA	Garrett Atkins	8.00
DB	Denny Bautista	5.00
RB	Russell Branyan	5.00
MC	Miguel Cabrera	35.00
KC	Kiko Calero	5.00
CC	Chad Cordero	10.00
JC	Juan Cruz	5.00
BD	Brandon Duckworth	5.00
JE	Johnny Estrada	5.00
LF	Lew Ford/SP	10.00
TH	Travis Hafner	15.00
KH	Keith Hernandez/SP	20.00
OH	Orlando Hernandez	75.00

OI	Omar Infante	5.00
DJ	Derek Jeter/SP	150.00
JJ	Jorge Julio	5.00
AM	Aaron Miles	5.00
YM	Yadier Molina	15.00
RN	Roberto Novoa	5.00
NP	Nick Punto	5.00
HR	Horacio Ramirez/SP	10.00
AR	Aaron Rowand	25.00
CS	Cory Sullivan	8.00
JS	Jeff Suppan	10.00
BT	Brett Tomko	5.00
CT	Chad Tracy/SP	
MV	Merkin Valdez	5.00
DW	David Wright	70.00

2005 Upper Deck
Pros & Prospects

		NM/M
Complete Set (200):		
Common Player (1-100):		.15
Common SP (101-150):		3.00
Production 999		
Common SP (151-175):		4.00
Production 499		
Common SP (176-200):		5.00
Production 199		
Pack (6):		2.75
Box (24):		60.00
1	Adam Dunn	.40
2	Aramis Ramirez	.40
3	Bobby Abreu	.25
4	Mike Lowell	.15
5	Josh Beckett	.25
6	Derek Jeter	1.50
7	Alex Rodriguez	1.25
8	Andruw Jones	.25
9	Brian Giles	.15
10	Ivan Rodriguez	.40
11	Aubrey Huff	.15
12	Jake Peavy	.25
13	Hank Blalock	.25
14	Curt Schilling	.50
15	Carlos Zambrano	.40
16	Mike Mussina	.40
17	Travis Hafner	.15
18	Scott Rolen	.50
19	Luis Gonzalez	.25
20	Torii Hunter	.25
21	Greg Maddux	1.00
22	J.D. Drew	.25
23	Kevin Brown	.15
24	Carl Pavano	.25
25	David Ortiz	.50
26	Jose Reyes	.40
27	Johan Santana	.50
28	Todd Helton	.40
29	Jason Kendall	.15
30	Pedro Martinez	.50
31	Chipper Jones	.50
32	Ben Sheets	.25
33	Garret Anderson	.25
34	Carl Crawford	.15
35	Jason Schmidt	.25
36	Johnny Damon	.50
37	Richie Sexson	.25
38	Brad Penny	.15
39	Carlos Delgado	.40
40	Gary Sheffield	.40
41	John Smoltz	.25
42	Eric Chavez	.25
43	Carlos Guillen	.15
44	Jeff Kent	.25
45	Miguel Tejada	.40
46	Shawn Green	.25
47	Vernon Wells	.25
48	Albert Pujols	1.50
49	Alfonso Soriano	.50
50	Eric Gagne	.40
51	Mark Prior	.50
52	Rafael Furcal	.25
53	Preston Wilson	.15

54	Barry Larkin	.25
55	Randy Johnson	.50
56	Craig Wilson	.15
57	Victor Martinez	.15
58	Jim Thome	.50
59	Paul Konerko	.15
60	Jeff Bagwell	.40
61	Lyle Overbay	.15
62	Miguel Cabrera	.50
63	Melvin Mora	.15
64	Scott Podsednik	.25
65	Mark Mulder	.25
66	Mark Teixeira	.40
67	Tom Glavine	.25
68	Frank Thomas	.40
69	Livan Hernandez	.15
70	Kazuo Matsui	.15
71	Jose Vidro	.15
72	Ichiro Suzuki	1.25
73	Roger Clemens	1.50
74	Manny Ramirez	.50
75	Michael Young	.15
76	Rafael Palmeiro	.40
77	Steve Finley	.15
78	Andy Pettitte	.25
79	Lance Berkman	.25
80	Adrian Beltre	.25
81	Carlos Lee	.25
82	Bret Boone	.15
83	Magglio Ordonez	.15
84	Sammy Sosa	1.00
85	Tim Hudson	.25
86	Vladimir Guerrero	.50
87	Carlos Beltran	.40
88	Kerry Wood	.50
89	Jim Edmonds	.25
90	Mike Sweeney	.15
91	Nomar Garciaparra	1.00
92	Mike Piazza	1.00
93	Roy Halladay	.25
94	Troy Glaus	.25
95	Bernie Williams	.25
96	Larry Walker	.25
97	Craig Biggio	.25
98	Roy Oswalt	.25
99	Ken Griffey Jr.	1.00
100	Hideki Matsui	1.00
101	Bucky Jacobsen	3.00
102	J.D. Closser	3.00
103	Antonio Perez	3.00
104	Chris Shelton	3.00
105	David Aardsma	3.00
106	Jake Woods	3.00
107	Jung Bong	3.00
108	Kazuhito Tadano	3.00
109	John Van Benschoten	3.00
110	Jesse Foppert	3.00
111	Joe Borchard	3.00
112	Brandon Phillips	3.00
113	J.D. Durbin	3.00
114	Brandon Claussen	3.00
115	Robb Quinlan	3.00
116	Aaron Harang	3.00
117	Chris Burke	3.00
118	Sergio Mitre	3.00
119	David DeJesus	3.00
120	Gustavo Chacin	3.00
121	Xavier Nady	3.00
122	Garrett Atkins	3.00
123	Jimmy Gobble	3.00
124	Yhency Brazoban	3.00
125	David Kelton	3.00
126	Dewon Brazelton	3.00
127	Koyie Hill	3.00
128	Roman Colon	3.00
129	Daniel Cabrera	3.00
130	Chris Bootcheck	3.00
131	Brad Halsey	3.00
132	Bobby Madritsch	3.00
133	Grady Sizemore	3.00
134	Akinori Otsuka	3.00
135	Wilfredo Ledezma	3.00
136	Russ Adams	3.00
137	Joe Crede	3.00
138	Chad Cordero	3.00
139	Willie Harris	3.00
140	Joey Gathright	3.00
141	Logan Kensing	3.00
142	Jon Leicester	3.00
143	Freddy Guzman	3.00
144	Jonny Gomes	3.00
145	Jeff Bajenaru	3.00
146	Andres Blanco	3.00
147	Jhonny Peralta	3.00
148	Jayson Werth	3.00
149	Bill Hall	3.00
150	Jason Davis	3.00
151	Gabe Gross	4.00
152	Abe Alvarez	4.00
153	Josh Willingham	4.00
154	Merkin Valdez	4.00
155	Jeff Niemann RC	8.00
156	Yadier Molina	4.00
157	Guillermo Quiroz	4.00
158	Ian Snell	4.00

159	Dan Meyer	4.00
160	Jason Lane	4.00
161	Adrian Gonzalez	4.00
162	Eddy Rodriguez	4.00
163	Jason Dubois	4.00
164	Juan Rincon	4.00
165	Ryan Wagner	4.00
166	Nick Swisher	4.00
167	Chad Tracy	4.00
168	Dioner Navarro	4.00
169	Gerald Laird	4.00
170	Alexis Rios	4.00
171	Aaron Rowand	4.00
172	Adam LaRoche	4.00
173	Kevin Youkilis	4.00
174	Philip Humber RC	6.00
175	Chin-Hui Tsao	4.00
176	Jeff Francis	5.00
177	Chase Utley	5.00
178	Gavin Floyd	5.00
179	David Wright	10.00
180	B.J. Upton	5.00
181	Laynce Nix	5.00
182	Joe Mauer	8.00
183	Justin Morneau	5.00
184	Zack Greinke	5.00
185	Jose Capellan	5.00
186	Khalil Greene	5.00
187	Oliver Perez	5.00
188	Joe Blanton	5.00
189	Wily Mo Pena	5.00
190	Dallas McPherson	6.00
191	Edwin Jackson	5.00
192	Casey Kotchman	5.00
193	Jesse Crain	5.00
194	Ryan Howard	6.00
195	Bobby Crosby	5.00
196	Jason Bay	5.00
197	Rickie Weeks	5.00
198	Scott Proctor	5.00
199	Dan Haren	5.00
200	Scott Kazmir	5.00

Gold

Gold (1-100):	4-8X
Production 125	
Gold (101-150):	1X
Production 150	
Gold (151-175):	1X
Production 99	
Gold (176-200):	No Pricing
Production 25	

Future Fabrics

		NM/M
Common Player:		4.00
Gold:		1-2X
Production 75 Sets		
MC	Miguel Cabrera	8.00
BC	Bobby Crosby	6.00
KG	Khalil Greene	6.00
RH	Rich Harden	4.00
EH	Eric Hinske	4.00
JJ	Jacque Jones	4.00
KE	Austin Kearns	4.00
AK	Adam Kennedy	4.00
CK	Casey Kotchman	4.00
VM	Victor Martinez	4.00
KM	Kazuo Matsui	4.00
JM	Joe Mauer	8.00
DM	Dallas McPherson	6.00
TN	Trot Nixon	4.00
SP	Sidney Ponson	4.00
JR	Jose Reyes	4.00
CS	C.C. Sabathia	4.00
SS	Shannon Stewart	4.00
BU	B.J. Upton	4.00
JW	Jayson Werth	4.00
DW	David Wright	15.00

Pro Material

		NM/M
Common Player:		6.00
Gold:		1-2X
Production 50 Sets		
JB	Jeff Bagwell	6.00
CB	Carlos Beltran	8.00
AB	Adrian Beltre	6.00
HB	Hank Blalock	6.00
EC	Eric Chavez	6.00
KG	Ken Griffey Jr.	10.00
VG	Vladimir Guerrero	8.00

TH	Todd Helton	8.00
DJ	Derek Jeter	20.00
RJ	Randy Johnson	8.00
CJ	Chipper Jones	8.00
PI	Mike Piazza	8.00
MP	Mark Prior	6.00
AP	Albert Pujols	15.00
MR	Manny Ramirez	8.00
SR	Scott Rolen	8.00
CS	Curt Schilling	8.00
SS	Sammy Sosa	8.00
IS	Ichiro Suzuki	25.00
MT	Miguel Tejada	8.00
JT	Jim Thome	8.00

Signs of Stardom

		NM/M
Common Autograph:		8.00
RB	Rocco Baldelli	15.00
JB	Josh Beckett	15.00
AB	Angel Berroa	8.00
HB	Hank Blalock	20.00
SB	Sean Burroughs	8.00
MC	Miguel Cabrera	30.00
CC	Chad Cordero	8.00
BC	Bobby Crosby	15.00
AE	Adam Eaton	12.00
FF	Frank Francisco	8.00
JF	Jason Frasor	8.00
GA	John Gall	8.00
MG	Marcus Giles	15.00
GR	Khalil Greene	25.00
RH	Rich Harden	20.00
MJ	Mike Johnston	8.00
SK	Scott Kazmir	20.00
JK	Jeff Keppinger	8.00
CK	Casey Kotchman	15.00
CL	Cliff Lee	8.00
JL	Justin Leone	8.00
MA	Joe Mauer	25.00
AO	Akinori Otsuka	10.00
LO	Lyle Overbay	10.00
CP	Corey Patterson	8.00
PE	Jake Peavy	30.00
OP	Oliver Perez	8.00
SP	Scott Podsednik	15.00
HR	Horacio Ramirez	8.00
JR	Jose Reyes	30.00
MR	Mike Rouse	8.00
BS	Ben Sheets	15.00
TS	Terrmel Sledge	8.00
KT	Kazuhito Tadano	20.00
ST	Shingo Takatsu	25.00
MT	Mark Teixeira	30.00
WA	Ryan Wagner	10.00
WE	Brandon Webb	10.00
RW	Rickie Weeks	15.00
JW	Jerome Williams	8.00
DW	Dontrelle Willis	25.00

Stardom Signatures

		NM/M
EB	Ernie Banks/240	50.00
BE	Josh Beckett/50	20.00
BL	Hank Blalock/50	20.00
JG	Jason Giambi/100	15.00
KG	Ken Griffey Jr./198	75.00
AK	Al Kaline/99	40.00
JM	Joe Morgan/194	25.00
KP	Kirby Puckett/156	50.00

2005 Upper Deck Reflections

		NM/M
Complete Set (200):		
Common (1-100):		.50
Common SP (101-150):		1.00
Inserted 1:2		
Common SP (151-200):		2.00
Inserted 1:2		
Pack (4):		8.00
Box (12):		80.00
1	Corey Patterson	.50
2	Curt Schilling	1.00
3	Todd Helton	.75
4	Johnny Damon	1.00
5	Alex Rodriguez	2.50
6	Vladimir Guerrero	1.00
7	John Smoltz	.50
8	Ivan Rodriguez	.75
9	Roy Halladay	.50
10	Carlos Beltran	.75
11	Ichiro Suzuki	2.00
12	Jim Edmonds	.50
13	Andruw Jones	.50
14	Scott Podsednik	.50
15	Troy Glaus	.50
16	Miguel Cabrera	1.00
17	Adrian Beltre	.50
18	Ben Sheets	.50
19	Alfonso Soriano	1.00
20	Brian Giles	.50
21	Carl Crawford	.50
22	Frank Thomas	.75
23	Jeff Kent	.50
24	Eric Gagne	.50
25	Shawn Green	.50
26	Sammy Sosa	2.00
27	Carlos Lee	.50
28	Ken Griffey Jr.	2.00
29	Mike Lowell	.50
30	Magglio Ordonez	.50
31	Aubrey Huff	.50
32	Travis Hafner	.50
33	Albert Pujols	3.00
34	Vernon Wells	.50
35	Roy Oswalt	.50
36	Jose Guillen	.50
37	Jim Thome	.75
38	Bobby Abreu	.50
39	Bret Boone	.50
40	Mark Teixeira	.50
41	Garret Anderson	.50
42	Jose Reyes	.75
43	Bernie Williams	.50
44	Greg Maddux	1.50
45	Gary Sheffield	.50
46	Josh Beckett	.50
47	Chipper Jones	1.00
48	Hank Blalock	.50
49	C.C. Sabathia	.50
50	Manny Ramirez	1.00
51	Pedro Martinez	1.00
52	Michael Young	.50
53	Jacque Jones	.50
54	Marcus Giles	.50
55	Steve Finley	.50
56	Miguel Tejada	.75
57	Mike Sweeney	.50
58	Lance Berkman	.50
59	J.D. Drew	.50
60	Jeromy Burnitz	.50
61	Johan Santana	.75
62	Victor Martinez	.50
63	Carl Pavano	.50
64	Roger Clemens	3.00
65	Richie Sexson	.50
66	Tim Hudson	.50
67	Melvin Mora	.50
68	Angel Berroa	.50
69	Rafael Palmeiro	.75
70	Randy Johnson	1.00
71	Torii Hunter	.50
72	Luis Gonzalez	.50
73	Kazuo Matsui	.50
74	Hideki Matsui	2.00
75	Mark Prior	1.00
76	Jeff Bagwell	.75
77	Eric Chavez	.50
78	Mark Loretta	.50
79	Adam Dunn	.75
80	Kerry Wood	1.00
81	Jose Vidro	.50
82	Jason Schmidt	.50
83	Carlos Delgado	.50
84	Scott Rolen	1.00
85	David Ortiz	1.00
86	Edgar Renteria	.50
87	Nomar Garciaparra	1.50
88	Mike Piazza	1.50
89	Mark Mulder	.50
90	Tom Glavine	.50
91	Paul Konerko	.50
92	Larry Walker	.50

93	Derek Jeter	3.00
94	Jake Peavy	.50
95	Carlos Zambrano	.50
96	Russ Ortiz	.50
97	Barry Zito	.50
98	Austin Kearns	.50
99	Pedro Feliz	.50
100	Rich Harden	.50
101	Adam LaRoche	1.00
102	Brandon Claussen	1.00
103	Gavin Floyd	1.00
104	Daniel Cabrera	1.00
105	Joe Mauer	2.00
106	Khalil Greene	2.00
107	David Wright	3.00
108	Rickie Weeks	2.00
109	Robb Quinlan	1.00
110	Bucky Jacobsen	1.00
111	Ryan Howard	2.00
112	Jeff Francis	1.00
113	Jason Lane	1.00
114	Alexis Rios	1.00
115	Bobby Madritsch	1.00
116	Jesse Crain	1.00
117	Oliver Perez	1.00
118	Garrett Atkins	1.00
119	Casey Kotchman	2.00
120	B.J. Upton	1.00
121	Laynce Nix	1.00
122	Adrian Gonzalez	1.00
123	Joe Blanton	1.00
124	Gabe Gross	1.00
125	Scott Kazmir	2.00
126	Zack Greinke	1.00
127	Edwin Jackson	1.00
128	Jason Bay	1.00
129	J.D. Closser	1.00
130	Jason Dubois	1.00
131	Dallas McPherson	2.00
132	Chad Cordero	1.00
133	Angel Guzman	1.00
134	Jayson Werth	1.00
135	Ryan Wagner	1.00
136	Guillermo Quiroz	1.00
137	Scott Proctor	1.00
138	Chris Burke	1.00
139	Nick Swisher	1.00
140	David DeJesus	1.00
141	Yhency Brazoban	1.00
142	Bobby Crosby	1.00
143	Chase Utley	1.00
144	Wily Mo Pena	1.00
145	Roman Colon	1.00
146	Eddy Rodriguez	1.00
147	Gerald Laird	1.00
148	Jose Capellan	1.00
149	Aaron Rowand	1.00
150	Kevin Youkilis	1.00
151	Bob Feller	2.00
152	Robin Yount	4.00
153	Willie Stargell	2.00
154	Cal Ripken Jr.	8.00
155	Monte Irvin	2.00
156	Nolan Ryan	6.00
157	Bob Lemon	2.00
158	Richie Ashburn	2.00
159	Billy Williams	2.00
160	Luis Aparicio	2.00
161	Phil Niekro	2.00
162	Bobby Doerr	2.00
163	Mike Schmidt	6.00
164	Stan Musial	4.00
165	George Kell	2.00
166	Joe Morgan	2.00
167	Whitey Ford	3.00
168	Rick Ferrell	2.00
169	Jim "Catfish" Hunter	2.00
170	Red Schoendienst	2.00
171	Tom Seaver	4.00
172	Pee Wee Reese	2.00
173	Lou Boudreau	2.00
174	Hal Newhouser	2.00
175	Harmon Killebrew	3.00
176	Jim Bunning	2.00
177	Willie McCovey	3.00
178	Bob Gibson	3.00
179	Juan Marichal	2.00
180	Robin Roberts	2.00
181	Gaylord Perry	2.00
182	Brooks Robinson	4.00
183	Al Lopez	2.00
184	Joe DiMaggio	6.00
185	Al Kaline	3.00
186	Rollie Fingers	2.00
187	Mickey Mantle	10.00
188	Enos Slaughter	2.00
189	Ernie Banks	4.00
190	Eddie Mathews	3.00
191	Tommy Lasorda	2.00
192	Fergie Jenkins	2.00
193	Lou Brock	2.00
194	Larry Doby	2.00
195	Phil Rizzuto	3.00
196	Warren Spahn	4.00
197	Ralph Kiner	2.00
198	Hoyt Wilhelm	2.00
199	Early Wynn	2.00
200	Yogi Berra	4.00

Red

Red (1-100):	2-4X
Red (101-200):	1-2.5X
Production 99 Sets	

Purple

Purple (1-100):	2-4X
Purple (101-200):	1-2.5X
Production 99 Sets	

Blue

Blue (1-100):	2-4X
Blue (101-200):	1-2.5X
Production 75 Sets	

Turquoise

Turquoise (1-100):	3-5X
Turquoise (101-200):	1.5-3X
Production 50 Sets	

Emerald

Emerald (1-100):	4-8X
Emerald (101-200):	3-5X
Production 25 Sets	

Platinum

Platinum (1-200):	No Pricing
Production One Set	

Cut From the Same Cloth

NM/M

Common Duo:		8.00
Production 225 Sets		
Red:		1-1.5X
Production 99 Sets		
Blue:		1-2X
Production 50 Sets		
Platinum:		No Pricing
Production One Set		
AA	Albert Pujols, Adrian Beltre	20.00
AB	Carlos Beltran, Bobby Abreu	10.00
AG	Garret Anderson, Vladimir Guerrero	10.00
AH	Alfonso Soriano, Hank Blalock	10.00
AJ	Albert Pujols, Jim Thome	20.00
AM	Adrian Beltre, Miguel Cabrera	10.00
AT	Jim Thome, Bobby Abreu	10.00
AW	Albert Pujols, Will Clark	20.00
BB	Jeff Bagwell, Craig Biggio	10.00
BG	Carlos Beltran, Ken Griffey Jr.	15.00
BM	Paul Molitor, George Brett	20.00
BO	Josh Beckett, Roy Oswalt	8.00
BP	Johnny Bench, Mike Piazza	15.00
BR	Adrian Beltre, Scott Rolen	10.00
BS	George Brett, Mike Schmidt	25.00
BT	Mark Teixeira, Hank Blalock	10.00
BW	Hank Blalock, David Wright	15.00
CB	Bobby Crosby, Jason Bay	8.00
CC	Bobby Crosby, Eric Chavez	8.00
CG	Bobby Crosby, Khalil Greene	8.00
CL	Miguel Cabrera, Mike Lowell	10.00
CP	Carl Crawford, Scott Podsednik	8.00
CR	Scott Rolen, Eric Chavez	10.00
CT	Miguel Tejada, Bobby Crosby	10.00
DM	Mike Schmidt, Dale Murphy	15.00
DR	Manny Ramirez, Johnny Damon	15.00
GI	Brian Giles, Marcus Giles	8.00
GS	Sammy Sosa, Ken Griffey Jr.	20.00
GV	Jose Guillen, Jose Vidro	8.00
HH	Tim Hudson, Rich Harden	8.00
HK	Kent Hrbek, Harmon Killebrew	20.00
JD	J.D. Drew, Chipper Jones	10.00
JH	Torii Hunter, Jacque Jones	8.00
JJ	Chipper Jones, Andruw Jones	10.00
JM	Don Mattingly, Derek Jeter	30.00
JR	Randy Johnson, Nolan Ryan	30.00
JS	Steve Carlton, Johan Santana	10.00
JT	Miguel Tejada, Derek Jeter	25.00
KH	Jason Kendall, Tim Hudson	8.00
KM	Dallas McPherson, Casey Kotchman	10.00
MB	Wade Boggs, Don Mattingly	20.00
MC	Don Mattingly, Will Clark	20.00
MH	Mark Mulder, Tim Hudson	8.00
MJ	Dale Murphy, Chipper Jones	15.00
MK	Harmon Killebrew, Justin Morneau	15.00
MM	Kazuo Matsui, Hideki Matsui	30.00
MS	Johan Santana, Joe Mauer	12.00
MW	Dallas McPherson, David Wright	20.00
MY	Robin Yount, Paul Molitor	20.00
OD	Johnny Damon, David Ortiz	15.00
OT	Shingo Takatsu, Akinori Otsuka	15.00
PB	Jim Bunning, Jim Palmer	10.00
PC	Miguel Cabrera, Albert Pujols	20.00
PG	Albert Pujols, Vladimir Guerrero	25.00
PP	Mike Piazza, Jorge Posada	15.00
PR	Albert Pujols, Scott Rolen	25.00
PS	Tom Seaver, Mark Prior	10.00
PT	Mark Teixeira, Albert Pujols	20.00
RJ	Cal Ripken Jr., Derek Jeter	40.00
RM	Ivan Rodriguez, Victor Martinez	8.00
RO	Manny Ramirez, David Ortiz	20.00
RP	Ivan Rodriguez, Mike Piazza	15.00
RR	Cal Ripken Jr., Brooks Robinson	35.00
RT	Miguel Tejada, Cal Ripken Jr.	30.00
RW	Scott Rolen, David Wright	15.00
SB	Ryne Sandberg, Wade Boggs	25.00
SM	Pedro J. Martinez, Curt Schilling	15.00
SO	Curt Schilling, David Ortiz	15.00
SP	Ben Sheets, Mark Prior	10.00
SR	Scott Rolen, Mike Schmidt	15.00
ST	Alfonso Soriano, Mark Teixeira	15.00
TC	Mark Teixeira, Miguel Cabrera	15.00
TH	Todd Helton, Jim Thome	10.00
TP	Rafael Palmeiro, Miguel Tejada	10.00
TR	Manny Ramirez, Jim Thome	12.00
TS	Jim Thome, Mike Schmidt	15.00
UJ	Derek Jeter, B.J. Upton	25.00
UK	B.J. Upton, Scott Kazmir	8.00
UW	B.J. Upton, David Wright	15.00
VJ	Jose Vidro, Nick Johnson	8.00
WB	Bernie Williams, Carlos Beltran	10.00
WJ	Bernie Williams, Derek Jeter	25.00
WM	Bernie Williams, Hideki Matsui	30.00
WP	Mark Prior, Kerry Wood	10.00
WR	Kerry Wood, Nolan Ryan	30.00
YR	Manny Ramirez, Carl Yastrzemski	20.00
ZM	Mark Mulder, Barry Zito	8.00
BD1	Carlos Beltran, Johnny Damon	10.00
BD2	Johnny Damon, Carlos Beltran	10.00
GG1	Ken Griffey Jr., Ken Griffey Sr.	15.00
GG2	Ken Griffey Sr., Ken Griffey Jr.	15.00

Cut From the Same Cloth Autograph Patch

NM/M

Production 25 Sets

BT	Mark Teixeira, Hank Blalock	120.00
DG	Ken Griffey Jr., Adam Dunn	240.00
GC	Miguel Cabrera, Ken Griffey Jr.	240.00
JR	Derek Jeter, Cal Ripken Jr.	500.00
MJ	Chipper Jones, Dale Murphy	140.00
PC	Albert Pujols, Miguel Cabrera	350.00
RP	Mike Piazza, Ivan Rodriguez	140.00
SB	Ryne Sandberg, Wade Boggs	160.00
TO	Mark Teixeira, David Ortiz	100.00
WB	David Wright, Hank Blalock	100.00
WR	David Wright, Scott Rolen	100.00

Cut From Same Cloth Patch

NM/M

Production 99 Sets

AM	Adrian Beltre, Miguel Cabrera	25.00
BR	Adrian Beltre, Scott Rolen	25.00
BS	George Brett, Mike Schmidt	40.00
BT	Mark Teixeira, Hank Blalock	20.00
CB	Jason Bay, Bobby Crosby	20.00
CG	Bobby Crosby, Khalil Greene	20.00
CP	Gary Carter, Mike Piazza	35.00
CR	Eric Chavez, Scott Rolen	25.00
DG	Ken Griffey Jr., Adam Dunn	40.00
GC	Miguel Cabrera, Ken Griffey Jr.	40.00
GI	Brian Giles, Marcus Giles	15.00
JM	Derek Jeter, Don Mattingly	60.00
JR	Cal Ripken Jr., Derek Jeter	80.00
KM	Dallas McPherson, Casey Kotchman	25.00
MJ	Chipper Jones, Dale Murphy	30.00
MP	Mike Piazza, Joe Mauer	30.00
MW	Dallas McPherson, David Wright	30.00
MY	Robin Yount, Paul Molitor	40.00
OB	Wade Boggs, David Ortiz	30.00
OT	Shingo Takatsu, Akinori Otsuka	30.00
PB	Albert Pujols, Adrian Beltre	40.00
PC	Albert Pujols, Miguel Cabrera	40.00
PR	Albert Pujols, Scott Rolen	40.00
RJ	Randy Johnson, Nolan Ryan	40.00
RP	Ivan Rodriguez, Mike Piazza	30.00

RR	Cal Ripken Jr., Brooks Robinson	50.00
RW	Nolan Ryan, Kerry Wood	40.00
SB	Ryne Sandberg, Wade Boggs	50.00
SP	Ben Sheets, Mark Prior	20.00
TC	Mark Teixeira, Miguel Cabrera	30.00
TO	Mark Teixeira, David Ortiz	25.00
UJ	Derek Jeter, B.J. Upton	40.00
UW	B.J. Upton, David Wright	25.00
WB	David Wright, Hank Blalock	30.00
WP	Mark Prior, Kerry Wood	30.00
WR	David Wright, Scott Rolen	30.00
YO	David Ortiz, Carl Yastrzemski	50.00
GG1	Ken Griffey Sr., Ken Griffey Jr.	40.00
GG2	Ken Griffey Jr., Ken Griffey Sr.	40.00

Dual Signature

		NM/M
Red:		1-1.5X
Production 99 Sets		
Blue:		1.5-2X
Production 35 Sets		
Platinum:		No Pricing
Production One Set		
ABAR	Al Rosen, Adrian Beltre	30.00
ABDM	Adrian Beltre, Dallas McPherson	30.00
ABDW	David Wright, Adrian Beltre	40.00
ABEC	Adrian Beltre, Eric Chavez	30.00
ABJL	Adrian Beltre, Justin Leone	30.00
ABSR	Adrian Beltre, Scott Rolen	30.00
AHBU	Aubrey Huff, B.J. Upton	25.00
AHCC	Carl Crawford, Aubrey Huff	25.00
AKDM	Al Kaline, Dale Murphy	50.00
AOST	Akinori Otsuka, Shingo Takatsu	40.00
ARCC	Alexis Rios, Carl Crawford	20.00
ARKG	Alexis Rios, Ken Griffey Jr.	65.00
ARTH	Al Rosen, Travis Hafner	25.00
BAKY	Kevin Youkilis, Bronson Arroyo	50.00
BCCR	Bobby Crosby, Cal Ripken Jr.	160.00
BCDJ	Derek Jeter, Bobby Crosby	125.00
BCEC	Bobby Crosby, Eric Chavez	25.00
BCJB	Bobby Crosby, Jason Bay	35.00
BCKG	Khalil Greene, Bobby Crosby	35.00
BDWB	Bobby Doerr, Wade Boggs	50.00
BGMG	Brian Giles, Marcus Giles	25.00
BPFH	Frank Howard, Boog Powell	30.00
BRRS	Brooks Robinson, Ron Santo	40.00
BSJC	Ben Sheets, Jose Capellan	20.00
BSRW	Rickie Weeks, Ben Sheets	35.00
BSSK	Ben Sheets, Scott Kazmir	20.00
BUDJ	B.J. Upton, Derek Jeter	125.00
BURW	B.J. Upton, Rickie Weeks	30.00
BUSK	B.J. Upton, Scott Kazmir	25.00
BWKG	Billy Williams, Ken Griffey Jr.	80.00
CCNJ	Nick Johnson, Chad Cordero	25.00
CKDM	Casey Kotchman, Dallas McPherson	35.00
CKKH	Keith Hernandez, Casey Kotchman	20.00

CKMT	Casey Kotchman, Mark Teixeira	35.00
CTDM	Charles Thomas, Dale Murphy	30.00
CTJC	Charles Thomas, Jose Capellan	15.00
CTRH	Charles Thomas, Ryan Howard	50.00
CZJS	Johan Santana, Carlos Zambrano	60.00
CZLT	Carlos Zambrano, Luis Tiant	20.00
DGDB	Dwight Gooden, Dewon Brazelton	20.00
DGJB	Jim Bouton, Dwight Gooden	20.00
DGJS	Dwight Gooden, Johan Santana	50.00
DJDM	Derek Jeter, Don Mattingly	200.00
DJKG	Derek Jeter, Khalil Greene	140.00
DKFH	Frank Howard, Dave Kingman	25.00
DMDW	David Wright, Dallas McPherson	50.00
DMJB	Dale Murphy, Jason Bay	40.00
DMJL	Justin Leone, Dallas McPherson	20.00
DMKY	Dallas McPherson, Kevin Youkilis	20.00
DMMS	Dallas McPherson, Mike Schmidt	75.00
DMRH	Dallas McPherson, Ryan Howard	50.00
DMSR	Dallas McPherson, Scott Rolen	
DOKY	David Ortiz, Kevin Youkilis	60.00
DWJL	Justin Leone, David Wright	40.00
DWKH	David Wright, Keith Hernandez	65.00
DWKY	David Wright, Kevin Youkilis	40.00
DWMS	David Wright, Mike Schmidt	100.00
DWSR	David Wright, Scott Rolen	65.00
ECSR	Scott Rolen, Eric Chavez	50.00
FHMT	Mark Teixeira, Frank Howard	40.00
FHNJ	Frank Howard, Nick Johnson	25.00
GPJP	Gaylord Perry, Jake Peavy	30.00
ISJC	Jose Capellan, Ian Snell	15.00
ISMV	Ian Snell, Merkin Valdez	15.00
ISSK	Ian Snell, Scott Kazmir	20.00
JBIS	Ian Snell, Joe Blanton	20.00
JBJP	Jim Bunning, Jim Palmer	30.00
JBMV	Merkin Valdez, Joe Blanton	15.00
JBRH	Joe Blanton, Rich Harden	20.00
JBSK	Scott Kazmir, Joe Blanton	20.00
JCMV	Merkin Valdez, Jose Capellan	15.00
JLRH	Justin Leone, Ryan Howard	50.00
JPJB	Jake Peavy, Joe Blanton	25.00
JPKG	Jake Peavy, Khalil Greene	50.00
JPRH	Jake Peavy, Rich Harden	40.00
JPSK	Jake Peavy, Scott Kazmir	30.00
JRDW	Jose Reyes, David Wright	75.00
JSMP	Johan Santana, Mark Prior	100.00
JSSC	Johan Santana, Steve Carlton	50.00
JSSK	Johan Santana, Scott Kazmir	40.00
JVMG	Marcus Giles, Jose Vidro	20.00
KGKG	Ken Griffey Sr., Ken Griffey Jr.	100.00
KGMC	Ken Griffey Jr., Miguel Cabrera	100.00
KYWB	Kevin Youkilis, Wade Boggs	50.00
MCRH	Ryan Howard, Miguel Cabrera	80.00

MGRW	Rickie Weeks, Marcus Giles	35.00
MTHB	Hank Blalock, Mark Teixeira	50.00
MTMC	Miguel Cabrera, Mark Teixeira	60.00
MTRH	Mark Teixeira, Ryan Howard	80.00
MVRH	Merkin Valdez, Rich Harden	20.00
PBKG	Pat Burrell, Ken Griffey Jr.	85.00
PBMC	Pat Burrell, Miguel Cabrera	40.00
RHDO	Ryan Howard, David Ortiz	80.00
RHRO	Roy Oswalt, Rich Harden	30.00
RHSK	Rich Harden, Scott Kazmir	25.00
THVM	Victor Martinez, Travis Hafner	20.00
TOKH	Kent Hrbek, Tony Oliva	30.00
VMYM	Victor Martinez, Yadier Molina	20.00

Fabric Jersey

		NM/M
Common Player:		
Inserted 1:12		
CB	Carlos Beltran	8.00
AB	Adrian Beltre	6.00
HB	Hank Blalock	6.00
WB	Wade Boggs/SP	10.00
GB	George Brett/SP	15.00
MC	Miguel Cabrera	8.00
EC	Eric Chavez	4.00
WC	Will Clark/SP	10.00
JD	Johnny Damon	10.00
KG	Ken Griffey Jr.	15.00
VG	Vladimir Guerrero	8.00
TH	Todd Helton	6.00
DJ	Derek Jeter/SP	20.00
RJ	Randy Johnson	8.00
CJ	Chipper Jones	8.00
GM	Greg Maddux	10.00
HM	Hideki Matsui	20.00
DM	Don Mattingly/SP	20.00
PM	Paul Molitor/SP	8.00
DO	David Ortiz	10.00
PI	Mike Piazza	10.00
MP	Mark Prior	6.00
AP	Albert Pujols	15.00
MR	Manny Ramirez	8.00
CR	Cal Ripken Jr./SP	25.00
IR	Ivan Rodriguez	8.00
SR	Scott Rolen	8.00
NR	Nolan Ryan/SP	25.00
JS	Johan Santana	8.00
CS	Curt Schilling	8.00
MS	Mike Schmidt/SP	15.00
AS	Alfonso Soriano	8.00
MT	Mark Teixeira	6.00
TE	Miguel Tejada	8.00
JT	Jim Thome	8.00
BW	Bernie Williams	6.00
KW	Kerry Wood	8.00
DW	David Wright	10.00
CY	Carl Yastrzemsk/SP	25.00
RY	Robin Yount/SP	10.00

Reflections Autograph Patch

		NM/M
Production 50 Sets		
JB	Jason Bay	50.00
AB	Adrian Beltre	30.00
HB	Hank Blalock	40.00
WB	Wade Boggs	60.00
PB	Pat Burrell	35.00
CA	Miguel Cabrera	40.00
EC	Eric Chavez	30.00
BC	Bobby Crosby	30.00
DG	Dwight Gooden	40.00
GR	Khalil Greene	50.00
KG	Ken Griffey Jr.	125.00
RH	Rich Harden	35.00
DJ	Derek Jeter	275.00
RJ	Randy Johnson	100.00
AJ	Andruw Jones	75.00
SK	Scott Kazmir	40.00
MA	Don Mattingly	125.00
MC	Dallas McPherson	60.00
PM	Paul Molitor	50.00
DM	Dale Murphy	50.00
DO	David Ortiz	75.00
RO	Roy Oswalt	50.00
JP	Jake Peavy	40.00
GP	Gaylord Perry	30.00
PI	Mike Piazza	120.00
MP	Mark Prior	50.00
AP	Albert Pujols	300.00

CR	Cal Ripken Jr.	225.00
SR	Scott Rolen	50.00
NR	Nolan Ryan	150.00
JS	Johan Santana	50.00
MS	Mike Schmidt	100.00
BS	Ben Sheets	30.00
ST	Shingo Takatsu	40.00
MT	Mark Teixeira	50.00
BU	B.J. Upton	35.00
DW	David Wright	100.00
RY	Robin Yount	75.00
CZ	Carlos Zambrano	40.00

Fabric Reflections Patch

		NM/M
Production 99 Sets		
JB	Jason Bay	15.00
AB	Adrian Beltre	10.00
HB	Hank Blalock	15.00
WB	Wade Boggs	20.00
GB	George Brett	50.00
PB	Pat Burrell	15.00
CA	Miguel Cabrera	20.00
EC	Eric Chavez	10.00
BC	Bobby Crosby	10.00
MG	Marcus Giles	10.00
DG	Dwight Gooden	15.00
GR	Khalil Greene	15.00
KG	Ken Griffey Jr.	40.00
RH	Rich Harden	15.00
DJ	Derek Jeter	15.00
RJ	Randy Johnson	20.00
AJ	Andruw Jones	15.00
SK	Scott Kazmir	10.00
MA	Don Mattingly	30.00
MC	Dallas McPherson	15.00
PM	Paul Molitor	20.00
DM	Dale Murphy	15.00
DO	David Ortiz	20.00
RO	Roy Oswalt	10.00
JP	Jake Peavy	15.00
GP	Gaylord Perry	10.00
PI	Mike Piazza	20.00
MP	Mark Prior	15.00
AP	Albert Pujols	50.00
CR	Cal Ripken Jr.	60.00
SR	Scott Rolen	20.00
NR	Nolan Ryan	40.00
JS	Johan Santana	20.00
MS	Mike Schmidt	25.00
BS	Ben Sheets	15.00
ST	Shingo Takatsu	15.00
MT	Mark Teixeira	15.00
BU	B.J. Upton	10.00
DW	David Wright	20.00
RY	Robin Yount	30.00
CZ	Carlos Zambrano	15.00

Super Swatch

		NM/M
Production 50 Sets		
Red:		1-1.5X
Production 25 Sets		
Blue:		No Pricing
Production 10 Sets		
BO	Bobby Abreu	15.00
RA	Roberto Alomar	15.00
MA	Moises Alou	10.00
GA	Garret Anderson	15.00
BA	Jeff Bagwell	15.00
RB	Rocco Baldelli	10.00
JB	Jason Bay	15.00
BE	Josh Beckett	10.00
CB	Carlos Beltran	15.00
AB	Adrian Beltre	8.00
LB	Lance Berkman	10.00
BI	Craig Biggio	10.00
HB	Hank Blalock	10.00
BB	Bret Boone	8.00
KB	Kevin Brown	8.00
MC	Miguel Cabrera	15.00
EC	Eric Chavez	10.00
CC	Carl Crawford	10.00
BC	Bobby Crosby	10.00
DA	Johnny Damon	20.00
CD	Carlos Delgado	15.00
JD	J.D. Drew	15.00
AD	Adam Dunn	15.00
JE	Jim Edmonds	15.00
KF	Keith Foulke	10.00
EG	Eric Gagne	10.00
JG	Jason Giambi	10.00
BG	Brian Giles	8.00
MG	Marcus Giles	8.00
TG	Tom Glavine	15.00
LG	Luis Gonzalez	10.00
SG	Shawn Green	10.00
GR	Khalil Greene	12.00
KG	Ken Griffey Jr.	40.00
VG	Vladimir Guerrero	15.00
HA	Roy Halladay	10.00
RH	Rich Harden	10.00

HE	Todd Helton	10.00
HO	Trevor Hoffman	10.00
TH	Tim Hudson	12.00
AH	Aubrey Huff	8.00
HU	Torii Hunter	10.00
DJ	Derek Jeter	40.00
RJ	Randy Johnson	15.00
AJ	Andruw Jones	15.00
CJ	Chipper Jones	15.00
JJ	Jacque Jones	8.00
SK	Scott Kazmir	8.00
JK	Jason Kendall	8.00
ML	Mike Lowell	8.00
GM	Greg Maddux	30.00
PM	Pedro Martinez	15.00
VM	Victor Martinez	8.00
HM	Hideki Matsui	50.00
KM	Kazuo Matsui	15.00
DM	Dallas McPherson	12.00
JM	Justin Morneau	20.00
MM	Mark Mulder	10.00
MU	Mike Mussina	15.00
HN	Hideo Nomo	40.00
MO	Magglio Ordonez	8.00
DO	David Ortiz	15.00
RO	Roy Oswalt	10.00
AO	Akinori Otsuka	15.00
RP	Rafael Palmeiro	15.00
CP	Corey Patterson	10.00
PI	Mike Piazza	20.00
SP	Scott Podsednik	10.00
JP	Jorge Posada	15.00
MP	Mark Prior	15.00
AP	Albert Pujols	40.00
MR	Manny Ramirez	20.00
ER	Edgar Renteria	10.00
JR	Jose Reyes	12.00
IR	Ivan Rodriguez	12.00
SR	Scott Rolen	15.00
CS	C.C. Sabathia	8.00
SA	Johan Santana	15.00
SC	Curt Schilling	15.00
JS	Jason Schmidt	12.00
RS	Richie Sexson	10.00
BS	Ben Sheets	10.00
GS	Gary Sheffield	15.00
AS	Alfonso Soriano	15.00
SS	Sammy Sosa	20.00
MS	Mike Sweeney	8.00
ST	Shingo Takatsu	15.00
MT	Mark Teixeira	15.00
TE	Miguel Tejada	15.00
JT	Jim Thome	15.00
JV	Jose Vidro	8.00
WA	Billy Wagner	10.00
VW	Vernon Wells	8.00
BW	Bernie Williams	10.00
KW	Kerry Wood	15.00
DW	David Wright	25.00
BZ	Barry Zito	10.00

2005 Upper Deck Sweet Spot

		NM/M
	Complete Set (90):	20.00
	Common Player:	.25
	Pack (5):	12.00
	Box (12):	120.00
1	Magglio Ordonez	.25
2	Craig Biggio	.50
3	Hank Blalock	.40
4	Nomar Garciaparra	.75
5	Ken Griffey Jr.	1.50
6	Khalil Greene	.40
7	Andruw Jones	.50
8	Ichiro Suzuki	1.50
9	Philip Humber RC	1.50
10	Vladimir Guerrero	.75
11	Carlos Delgado	.40
12	Jeff Niemann RC	1.50
13	Chipper Jones	.75
14	Jose Vidro	.25
15	Miguel Cabrera	.75
16	Albert Pujols	2.00
17	Tadahito Iguchi RC	2.50
18	Norihiro Nakamura RC	1.50
19	Jeff Bagwell	.50
20	Troy Glaus	.40
21	Scott Rolen	.75
22	Derek Lowe	.25
23	Mark Prior	.75
24	Bobby Abreu	.40
25	David Wright	1.00
26	Barry Zito	.40
27	Livan Hernandez	.25
28	Mark Teixeira	.50
29	Manny Ramirez	.75
30	Paul Konerko	.40
31	Victor Martinez	.25
32	Greg Maddux	1.50
33	Jim Thome	.50
34	Miguel Tejada	.50
35	Ivan Rodriguez	.50
36	Carlos Beltran	.50
37	Steve Finley	.25
38	Torii Hunter	.25
39	Bobby Crosby	.25
40	Jorge Posada	.40
41	Ben Sheets	.40
42	Mike Piazza	1.00
43	Luis Gonzalez	.25
44	Joe Mauer	.50
45	Shawn Green	.25
46	Eric Gagne	.40
47	Kerry Wood	.40
48	Derek Jeter	2.00
49	Josh Beckett	.25
50	Alex Rodriguez	1.50
51	Aubrey Huff	.25
52	Eric Chavez	.40
53	Sammy Sosa	1.00
54	Roger Clemens	2.00
55	Mike Mussina	.50
56	Mike Sweeney	.25
57	Oliver Perez	.25
58	Tim Hudson	.25
59	Justin Verlander RC	2.00
60	Johan Santana	.50
61	Hideki Matsui	1.50
62	Mark Mulder	.40
63	Jake Peavy	.40
64	Adam Dunn	.50
65	Dallas McPherson	.25
66	Jeff Kent	.25
67	Pedro Martinez	.75
68	J.D. Drew	.25
69	Frank Thomas	.50
70	Kazuo Matsui	.25
71	Travis Hafner	.40
72	John Smoltz	.40
73	Jason Schmidt	.25
74	Carlos Lee	.25
75	Todd Helton	.50
76	David Ortiz	.75
77	Roy Oswalt	.40
78	Brian Giles	.25
79	Gary Sheffield	.50
80	Jason Bay	.40
81	Alfonso Soriano	.75
82	Randy Johnson	.75
83	Tom Glavine	.40
84	Richie Sexson	.40
85	Curt Schilling	.75
86	Adrian Beltre	.40
87	Jim Edmonds	.40
88	Roy Halladay	.40
89	Johnny Damon	.75
90	Lance Berkman	.40

Gold

Gold (1-90): 1-2X
Production 599 Sets

Platinum

Platinum (1-90): 2-4X
Production 99 Sets

Plutonium

No Pricing
Production One Set

Majestic Materials

		NM/M
	Common Player:	
	Gold:	1-1.5X
	Production 75 Sets	
	Platinum:	No Pricing
	Production 10 Sets	
	Plutonium:	No Pricing
	Production One Set	
	Patch:	2-3X
	Production 35 Sets	
BA	Bobby Abreu	4.00
MA	Moises Alou	6.00
JB	Jason Bay	4.00
BE	Josh Beckett	4.00

LB	Lance Berkman	4.00
CB	Craig Biggio	6.00
BB	Bret Boone	4.00
BC	Bobby Crosby	4.00
CD	Carlos Delgado	4.00
JD	J.D. Drew	4.00
AD	Adam Dunn	6.00
JE	Jim Edmonds	6.00
JG	Jason Giambi	6.00
BG	Brian Giles	4.00
TG	Troy Glaus	4.00
LG	Luis Gonzalez	4.00
SG	Shawn Green	4.00
KG	Khalil Greene	6.00
HA	Travis Hafner	4.00
RH	Roy Halladay	4.00
TH	Tim Hudson	4.00
HU	Torii Hunter	4.00
TI	Tadahito Iguchi	5.00
AJ	Andruw Jones	6.00
SK	Scott Kazmir	4.00
JK	Jeff Kent	4.00
VM	Victor Martinez	4.00
KM	Kazuo Matsui	4.00
JM	Joe Mauer	6.00
DM	Dallas McPherson	4.00
MM	Mark Mulder	4.00
MU	Mike Mussina	6.00
MO	Magglio Ordonez	4.00
RO	Roy Oswalt	4.00
JP	Jake Peavy	6.00
OP	Oliver Perez	4.00
AP	Andy Pettitte	6.00
PO	Jorge Posada	6.00
ER	Edgar Renteria	4.00
JR	Jose Reyes	4.00
JS	Jason Schmidt	4.00
RS	Richie Sexson	6.00
BS	Ben Sheets	4.00
GS	Gary Sheffield	6.00
ST	Shingo Takatsu	4.00
BU	B.J. Upton	4.00
JV	Jose Vidro	4.00
VW	Vernon Wells	4.00
DW	David Wright	10.00
BZ	Barry Zito	4.00

Majestic Materials Dual

		NM/M
	Production 25 Sets	
	Gold:	No Pricing
	Production 5 Sets	
	Plutonium:	No Pricing
	Production One Set	
	Patch:	No Pricing
	Production 5 Sets	
BB	Craig Biggio, Jeff Bagwell	15.00
BP	Jason Bay, Oliver Perez	10.00
BS	Adrian Beltre, Richie Sexson	10.00
BT	Hank Blalock, Mark Teixeira	12.00
CC	Bobby Crosby, Eric Chavez	10.00
DG	Adam Dunn, Ken Griffey Jr.	25.00
DK	J.D. Drew, Jeff Kent	10.00
DR	Johnny Damon, Manny Ramirez	15.00
GG	Shawn Green, Troy Glaus	10.00
GR	Eric Gagne, Mariano Rivera	15.00
HM	Travis Hafner, Victor Martinez	10.00
JJ	Andruw Jones, Chipper Jones	15.00
MC	Don Mattingly, Will Clark	25.00
MW	Dallas McPherson, David Wright	15.00
PC	Albert Pujols, Miguel Cabrera	25.00
PG	Jake Peavy, Khalil Greene	12.00
PL	Albert Pujols, Derek Lee	25.00
RM	Jose Reyes, Kazuo Matsui	10.00
RO	Ivan Rodriguez, Magglio Ordonez	10.00
RT	Brian Roberts, Miguel Tejada	15.00
SH	John Smoltz, Tim Hudson	12.00
SM	Joe Mauer, Johan Santana	15.00
TI	Shingo Takatsu, Tadahito Iguchi	20.00
UK	B.J. Upton, Scott Kazmir	10.00
WC	David Wright, Miguel Cabrera	15.00

Majestic Materials Quad

		NM/M
	Production 25 Sets	
	Gold:	No Pricing
	Production 5 Sets	
	Plutonium:	No Pricing
	Production One Set	
	Patch:	No Pricing
	Production 5 Sets	
JJSH	Andruw Jones, Chipper Jones, John Smoltz, Tim Hudson	25.00
JSJP	Derek Jeter, Gary Sheffield, Randy Johnson, Jorge Posada	60.00
OVDR	David Ortiz, Jason Varitek, Johnny Damon, Manny Ramirez	40.00
PEWR	Albert Pujols, Jim Edmonds, Larry Walker, Scott Rolen	50.00
ZMWP	Carlos Zambrano, Greg Maddux, Kerry Wood, Mark Prior	30.00

Majestic Materials Triple

		NM/M
	Production 25 Sets	
	Gold:	No Pricing
	Production 5 Sets	
	Plutonium:	No Pricing
	Production One Set	
	Patch:	No Pricing
	Production 5 Sets	
BPO	Josh Beckett, Mark Prior, Roy Oswalt	15.00
BSB	George Brett, Mike Schmidt, Wade Boggs	30.00
BTH	Jeff Bagwell, Jim Thome, Todd Helton	20.00
HRG	Torii Hunter, Manny Ramirez, Vladimir Guerrero	20.00
JCG	Andruw Jones, Miguel Cabrera, Vladimir Guerrero	15.00
JRT	Derek Jeter, Edgar Renteria, Miguel Tejada	25.00
MMP	Greg Maddux, Pedro Martinez, Jake Peavy	25.00
MSG	Greg Maddux, John Smoltz, Tom Glavine	40.00
OGP	David Ortiz, Jason Giambi, Rafael Palmeiro	20.00
PBC	Albert Pujols, Carlos Beltran, Miguel Cabrera	40.00
RBW	Nolan Ryan, Josh Beckett, Kerry Wood	40.00
RGB	Cal Ripken Jr., Tony Gwynn, Wade Boggs	50.00

		NM/M
SSJ	Curt Schilling, Johan Santana, Randy Johnson	25.00
VPP	Jason Varitek, Jorge Posada, Mike Piazza	20.00
WRG	David Wright, Scott Rolen, Troy Glaus	25.00

Signatures Barrel Black Ink

NM/M
Production 25-50

JB	Jason Bay/50	20.00
HB	Hank Blalock/25	25.00
CA	Miguel Cabrera/25	70.00
SC	Steve Carlton/25	25.00
SE	Sean Casey/50	20.00
WC	Will Clark/25	25.00
CC	Carl Crawford/50	15.00
BC	Bobby Crosby/50	30.00
DA	Andre Dawson/25	25.00
AD	Adam Dunn/25	40.00
GF	Gavin Floyd/50	20.00
NG	Nomar Garciaparra/25	80.00
MG	Marcus Giles/50	15.00
GL	Tom Glavine/50	30.00
GR	Khalil Greene/50	35.00
KG	Ken Griffey Jr./25	85.00
HA	Travis Hafner/50	25.00
RH	Rich Harden/50	20.00
KH	Keith Hernandez/50	20.00
HO	Ryan Howard/50	90.00
AH	Aubrey Huff/50	15.00
PH	Philip Humber/50	25.00
BJ	Bo Jackson/25	75.00
DJ	Derek Jeter/25	250.00
RJ	Randy Johnson/25	125.00
AJ	Andruw Jones/50	50.00
SK	Scott Kazmir/50	20.00
BL	Barry Larkin/25	40.00
EM	Edgar Martinez/25	40.00
MA	Don Mattingly/25	85.00
PM	Paul Molitor/25	40.00
MO	Justin Morneau/50	25.00
MM	Mark Mulder/50	25.00
JN	Jeff Niemann/50	20.00
RO	Roy Oswalt/50	35.00
LO	Lyle Overbay/50	15.00
JP	Jake Peavy/50	25.00
PI	Mike Piazza/25	100.00
MP	Mark Prior/25	50.00
AP	Albert Pujols/25	220.00
AR	Aramis Ramirez/50	30.00
CR	Cal Ripken Jr./25	180.00
NR	Nolan Ryan/25	100.00
RS	Ryne Sandberg/25	75.00
MS	Mike Schmidt/25	70.00
MT	Mark Teixeira/25	40.00
BU	B.J. Upton/50	20.00
JV	Justin Verlander/50	40.00
DW	David Wright/50	100.00
RY	Robin Yount/25	90.00
CZ	Carlos Zambrano/50	30.00

Signatures Barrel Blue Ink

NM/M
Production 15-30

JB	Jason Bay/30	25.00
SE	Sean Casey/30	25.00
CC	Carl Crawford/30	20.00
BC	Bobby Crosby/30	35.00
AD	Adam Dunn/15	60.00
GF	Gavin Floyd/30	25.00
MG	Marcus Giles/30	15.00
GL	Tom Glavine/30	40.00
GR	Khalil Greene/30	40.00
HA	Travis Hafner/30	30.00
RH	Rich Harden/30	25.00
KH	Keith Hernandez/30	25.00
HO	Ryan Howard/30	90.00
AH	Aubrey Huff/30	20.00
PH	Philip Humber/30	30.00
SK	Scott Kazmir/30	20.00
MO	Justin Morneau/30	30.00
MM	Mark Mulder/30	30.00
JN	Jeff Niemann/30	25.00
RO	Roy Oswalt/30	40.00
LO	Lyle Overbay/30	15.00
CP	Corey Patterson/30	20.00
JP	Jake Peavy/30	30.00
AP	Albert Pujols/15	250.00
AR	Aramis Ramirez/30	40.00
BU	B.J. Upton/30	25.00
JV	Justin Verlander/30	50.00
DW	David Wright/30	100.00
CZ	Carlos Zambrano/30	35.00

Signatures Barrel Red Ink

No Pricing
Production 5-10

Signatures Glove Blue Ink

NM/M
No Pricing
Production 5-10
Red Ink: No Pricing
Production 2-5

Signature Black Stitch Black Ink

No Pricing
Production One Set
Blue Ink: No Pricing
Production One Set
Red Ink: No Pricing
Production One Set

Signatures Dual Barrel

No Pricing
Production 15 Sets

Signatures Dual Glove

No Pricing
Production 10 Sets

Signatures Dual Red Stitch

NM/M
Production 25 Sets

BJ	Bobby Crosby, Jason Bay	40.00
BW	Adrian Beltre, David Wright	90.00
CG	Bobby Crosby, Khalil Greene	50.00
DC	Adam Dunn, Sean Casey	50.00
FH	Gavin Floyd, Ryan Howard	120.00
GC	Ken Griffey Jr., Miguel Cabrera	120.00
GL	Khalil Greene, Mark Loretta	60.00
JC	Randy Johnson, Roger Clemens	240.00
JG	Andruw Jones, Ken Griffey Jr.	150.00
JM	Derek Jeter, Don Mattingly	300.00
LG	Barry Larkin, Ken Griffey Jr.	120.00
LR	Barry Larkin, Cal Ripken Jr.	160.00
MG	Greg Maddux, Tom Glavine	150.00
MJ	Pedro Martinez, Randy Johnson	125.00
NH	Jeff Niemann, Philip Humber	50.00
PB	Jason Bay, Oliver Perez	40.00
PC	Albert Pujols, Miguel Cabrera	300.00
PO	Jake Peavy, Roy Oswalt	75.00
RJ	Cal Ripken Jr., Derek Jeter	300.00
SB	Ryne Sandberg, Wade Boggs	125.00
SG	Nomar Garciaparra, Ryne Sandberg	150.00
SP	Ben Sheets, Jake Peavy	50.00
WC	David Wright, Miguel Cabrera	120.00
WR	David Wright, Jose Reyes	180.00

Signatures Game-Used Ball

No Pricing
Production One Set

Signature Game-Used Barrel

No Pricing
Production 1-10

Signatures Game Used Glove

No Pricing
Production 9-10

Signatures Glove Black Ink

NM/M
Production 15-30

JB	Jason Bay/30	40.00
SE	Sean Casey/30	35.00
CC	Carl Crawford/30	30.00
BC	Bobby Crosby/30	40.00
GF	Gavin Floyd/30	30.00
MG	Marcus Giles/30	25.00
GL	Tom Glavine/30	50.00
GR	Khalil Greene/30	50.00
HA	Travis Hafner/30	40.00
RH	Rich Harden/30	35.00
KH	Keith Hernandez/30	30.00
HO	Ryan Howard/30	100.00
AH	Aubrey Huff/30	25.00
PH	Philip Humber/30	40.00
SK	Scott Kazmir/30	30.00
MO	Justin Morneau/30	40.00
MM	Mark Mulder/30	40.00
JN	Jeff Niemann/30	30.00
RO	Roy Oswalt/30	50.00
LO	Lyle Overbay/30	20.00
CP	Corey Patterson/30	25.00
JP	Jake Peavy/30	40.00
AR	Aramis Ramirez/30	50.00
BU	B.J. Upton/30	35.00
JV	Justin Verlander/30	50.00
DW	David Wright/30	100.00
CZ	Carlos Zambrano/30	40.00

Signature Red Stitch Black Ink

NM/M
Production 58-350

JB	Jason Bay/350	20.00
HB	Hank Blalock/175	20.00
WB	Wade Boggs/175	40.00
CA	Miguel Cabrera/175	40.00
SC	Steve Carlton/58	25.00
SE	Sean Casey/350	15.00
WC	Will Clark/175	25.00
RC	Roger Clemens/175	120.00
CC	Carl Crawford/350	15.00
DA	Andre Dawson/175	20.00
AD	Adam Dunn/175	20.00
GF	Gavin Floyd/350	15.00
NG	Nomar Garciaparra/175	60.00
MG	Marcus Giles/350	15.00
GR	Khalil Greene/350	20.00
KG	Ken Griffey Jr./175	75.00
RH	Rich Harden/350	15.00
KH	Keith Hernandez/350	15.00
HO	Ryan Howard/350	75.00
AH	Aubrey Huff/350	15.00
PH	Philip Humber/350	15.00
BJ	Bo Jackson/175	70.00
DJ	Derek Jeter/175	150.00
RJ	Randy Johnson/175	75.00
AJ	Andruw Jones/175	40.00
SK	Scott Kazmir/350	15.00
BL	Barry Larkin/175	25.00
EM	Edgar Martinez/175	30.00
MA	Don Mattingly/175	60.00
PM	Paul Molitor/175	50.00
MO	Justin Morneau/350	25.00
MM	Mark Mulder/350	20.00
JN	Jeff Niemann/350	15.00
RO	Roy Oswalt/350	25.00
LO	Lyle Overbay/350	12.00
JP	Jake Peavy/350	20.00
PI	Mike Piazza/175	80.00
MP	Mark Prior/175	40.00
AP	Albert Pujols/175	160.00
AR	Aramis Ramirez/350	25.00
RE	Jose Reyes/350	35.00
CR	Cal Ripken Jr./175	120.00
NR	Nolan Ryan/350	80.00
RS	Ryne Sandberg/175	65.00
MS	Mike Schmidt/175	50.00
MT	Mark Teixeira/175	40.00
BU	B.J. Upton/350	15.00
JV	Justin Verlander/350	35.00
DW	David Wright/175	60.00
RY	Robin Yount/175	50.00
CZ	Carlos Zambrano/350	20.00

Signature Red Stitch Blue Ink

NM/M
Production 75-135

JB	Jason Bay	25.00
HB	Hank Blalock/75	20.00
WB	Wade Boggs/75	40.00
CA	Miguel Cabrera/75	40.00
SE	Sean Casey/135	15.00
WC	Will Clark/75	25.00
RC	Roger Clemens/75	120.00
CC	Carl Crawford/135	15.00
BC	Bobby Crosby/135	20.00
DA	Andre Dawson/75	20.00
AD	Adam Dunn/75	30.00
GF	Gavin Floyd/75	15.00
NG	Nomar Garciaparra/75	65.00
MG	Marcus Giles/135	15.00
GL	Tom Glavine/135	25.00
GR	Khalil Greene/135	25.00
KG	Ken Griffey Jr./75	80.00
HA	Travis Hafner/135	20.00
RH	Rich Harden/135	15.00
KH	Keith Hernandez/135	15.00
HO	Ryan Howard/135	75.00
AH	Aubrey Huff/135	15.00
PH	Philip Humber/135	15.00
BJ	Bo Jackson/75	75.00
DJ	Derek Jeter/75	150.00
RJ	Randy Johnson/75	85.00
AJ	Andruw Jones/75	40.00
SK	Scott Kazmir/75	15.00
BL	Barry Larkin/75	30.00
EM	Edgar Martinez/75	35.00
MA	Don Mattingly/75	70.00
PM	Paul Molitor/75	50.00
MO	Justin Morneau/135	30.00
MM	Mark Mulder/135	25.00
JN	Jeff Niemann/135	15.00
RO	Roy Oswalt/135	25.00
LO	Lyle Overbay/135	12.00
CP	Corey Patterson/135	15.00
JP	Jake Peavy/135	25.00
PI	Mike Piazza/75	80.00
MP	Mark Prior/75	50.00
AP	Albert Pujols/75	160.00
AR	Aramis Ramirez/135	25.00
RE	Jose Reyes/135	35.00
CR	Cal Ripken Jr./75	120.00
NR	Nolan Ryan/75	80.00
RS	Ryne Sandberg/75	65.00
MS	Mike Schmidt/75	40.00
MT	Mark Teixeira/75	40.00
BU	B.J. Upton/135	15.00
JV	Justin Verlander/135	35.00
DW	David Wright/135	60.00
RY	Robin Yount/75	50.00
CZ	Carlos Zambrano/135	20.00

Signature Red Stitch Red Ink

NM/M
Production 15-35

JB	Jason Bay/35	25.00
SE	Sean Casey/35	25.00
CC	Carl Crawford/35	20.00
AD	Adam Dunn/15	60.00
GF	Gavin Floyd/35	25.00
MG	Marcus Giles/35	15.00
GL	Tom Glavine/35	40.00
GR	Khalil Greene/35	40.00
HA	Travis Hafner/35	30.00
RH	Rich Harden/35	25.00
KH	Keith Hernandez/35	25.00
HO	Ryan Howard/35	90.00
AH	Aubrey Huff/35	30.00
PH	Philip Humber/35	30.00
SK	Scott Kazmir/35	20.00
MO	Justin Morneau/35	30.00
MM	Mark Mulder/35	30.00
JN	Jeff Niemann/35	25.00
RO	Roy Oswalt/35	40.00
LO	Lyle Overbay/35	15.00
CP	Corey Patterson/35	30.00
JP	Jake Peavy/35	30.00
AP	Albert Pujols/15	250.00
AR	Aramis Ramirez/35	40.00
RE	Jose Reyes/35	40.00
BU	B.J. Upton/35	25.00
JV	Justin Verlander/35	50.00
DW	David Wright/35	100.00
CZ	Carlos Zambrano/35	35.00

Signature Red-Blue Stitch Black Ink

NM/M
Production 25-50

JB	Jason Bay/50	25.00
HB	Hank Blalock/25	25.00
WB	Wade Boggs/25	50.00
CA	Miguel Cabrera/25	65.00
SC	Steve Carlton/25	25.00
SE	Sean Casey/50	20.00
WC	Will Clark/25	35.00
RC	Roger Clemens/25	160.00
CC	Carl Crawford/50	15.00
BC	Bobby Crosby/25	35.00
DA	Andre Dawson/25	25.00
AD	Adam Dunn/25	40.00

GF	Gavin Floyd/50	15.00
NG	Nomar Garciaparra/25	65.00
MG	Marcus Giles/50	15.00
GR	Khalil Greene/50	30.00
KG	Ken Griffey Jr./25	120.00
RH	Rich Harden/50	20.00
KG	Keith Hernandez/50	20.00
HO	Ryan Howard/50	85.00
AH	Aubrey Huff/50	20.00
PH	Philip Humber/50	20.00
BJ	Bo Jackson/25	90.00
DJ	Derek Jeter/25	250.00
RJ	Randy Johnson/25	120.00
AJ	Andruw Jones/25	50.00
SK	Scott Kazmir/25	20.00
BL	Barry Larkin/25	40.00
EM	Edgar Martinez/25	40.00
MA	Don Mattingly/25	90.00
PM	Paul Molitor/25	40.00
MO	Justin Morneau/25	25.00
MM	Mark Mulder/50	25.00
JN	Jeff Niemann/50	20.00
RO	Roy Oswalt/50	35.00
LO	Lyle Overbay/50	12.00
JP	Jake Peavy/25	25.00
PI	Mike Piazza/25	100.00
MP	Mark Prior/25	60.00
AP	Albert Pujols/25	220.00
RE	Jose Reyes/50	40.00
CR	Cal Ripken Jr./25	165.00
NR	Nolan Ryan/25	100.00
RS	Ryne Sandberg/25	80.00
JS	Johan Santana/25	50.00
MS	Mike Schmidt/25	75.00
MT	Mark Teixeira/25	50.00
BU	B.J. Upton/50	20.00
JV	Justin Verlander/25	40.00
DW	David Wright/25	120.00
RY	Robin Yount/25	65.00
CZ	Carlos Zambrano/50	30.00

Signature Red-Blue Stitch Blue Ink

NM/M

Production 15-30
Red Ink: No Pricing
Production 5-10

JB	Jason Bay/30	25.00
SE	Sean Casey/30	25.00
CC	Carl Crawford/30	20.00
BC	Bobby Crosby/30	35.00
GF	Gavin Floyd/30	25.00
MG	Marcus Giles/30	15.00
GL	Tom Glavine/30	40.00
GR	Khalil Greene/30	40.00
HA	Travis Hafner/30	30.00
RH	Rich Harden/30	25.00
KH	Keith Hernandez/30	25.00
HO	Ryan Howard/30	90.00
PH	Philip Humber/30	30.00
SK	Scott Kazmir/30	20.00
MO	Justin Morneau/30	30.00
MM	Mark Mulder/30	30.00
JN	Jeff Niemann/30	25.00
RO	Roy Oswalt/30	40.00
LO	Lyle Overbay/30	15.00
CP	Corey Patterson/30	20.00
JP	Jake Peavy/30	30.00
AR	Aramis Ramirez/30	40.00
RE	Jose Reyes/30	45.00
BU	B.J. Upton/30	25.00
JV	Justin Verlander/30	50.00
DW	David Wright/30	120.00
CZ	Carlos Zambrano/30	35.00

Sweet Threads

		NM/M
Common Player:		4.00
Gold:		1-1.5X
Production 75 Sets		
Platinum:		No Pricing

Production 10 Sets
Plutonium: No Pricing
Production One Set
Patch: 2-4X
Production 35 Sets

JB	Jeff Bagwell	6.00
CB	Carlos Beltran	6.00
AB	Adrian Beltre	4.00
HB	Hank Blalock	4.00
WB	Wade Boggs	8.00
GB	George Brett	10.00
MC	Miguel Cabrera	8.00
EC	Eric Chavez	4.00
WC	Will Clark	6.00
BC	Bartolo Colon	4.00
JD	Johnny Damon	6.00
EG	Eric Gagne	4.00
TG	Tom Glavine	6.00
KG	Ken Griffey Jr.	12.00
VG	Vladimir Guerrero	8.00
GW	Tony Gwynn	8.00
TH	Todd Helton	6.00
HO	Trevor Hoffman	4.00
BJ	Bo Jackson	8.00
DJ	Derek Jeter	20.00
RJ	Randy Johnson	8.00
CJ	Chipper Jones	8.00
CL	Carlos Lee	4.00
GM	Greg Maddux	10.00
PM	Pedro Martinez	8.00
DM	Don Mattingly	10.00
DO	David Ortiz	8.00
RP	Rafael Palmeiro	6.00
PI	Mike Piazza	8.00
MP	Mark Prior	6.00
AP	Albert Pujols	15.00
MR	Manny Ramirez	8.00
CR	Cal Ripken Jr.	20.00
IR	Ivan Rodriguez	6.00
SR	Scott Rolen	6.00
NR	Nolan Ryan	12.00
RS	Ryne Sandberg	8.00
JS	Johan Santana	6.00
CS	Curt Schilling	6.00
MS	Mike Schmidt	10.00
SM	John Smoltz	6.00
AS	Alfonso Soriano	6.00
SS	Sammy Sosa	8.00
MT	Mark Teixeira	6.00
TE	Miguel Tejada	6.00
FT	Frank Thomas	6.00
JT	Jim Thome	6.00
JV	Jason Varitek	10.00
BW	Bernie Williams	6.00
KW	Kerry Wood	4.00

Sweet Threads Dual

NM/M

Production 25 Sets
Gold: No Pricing
Production 5 Sets
Patch: No Pricing
Production 5 Sets
Plutonium: No Pricing
Production One Set

BG	Carlos Beltran, Ken Griffey Jr.	25.00
BM	Carlos Beltran, Pedro Martinez	15.00
DC	Carlos Delgado, Miguel Cabrera	15.00
GC	Ken Griffey Jr., Miguel Cabrera	25.00
GM	Dallas McPherson, Vladimir Guerrero	15.00
JB	Bo Jackson, George Brett	25.00
JJ	Randy Johnson, Derek Jeter	40.00
JM	Derek Jeter, Don Mattingly	50.00
JS	Jim Thome, Mike Schmidt	30.00
MG	Greg Maddux, Tom Glavine	25.00
MJ	Mike Mussina, Randy Johnson	20.00
MP	Greg Maddux, Mark Prior	25.00
OR	David Ortiz, Manny Ramirez	20.00
PO	Andy Pettitte, Roy Oswalt	10.00
PR	Pedro Martinez, Randy Johnson	20.00
PS	Rafael Palmeiro, Sammy Sosa	20.00
PW	David Wright, Mike Piazza	30.00
RJ	Cal Ripken Jr., Derek Jeter	70.00
RP	Albert Pujols, Scott Rolen	30.00

RT	Cal Ripken Jr., Miguel Tejada	40.00
SB	Ryne Sandberg, Wade Boggs	30.00
SJ	Curt Schilling, Randy Johnson	20.00
SV	Curt Schilling, Jason Varitek	20.00
WP	Kerry Wood, Mark Prior	15.00

Sweet Threads Quad

NM/M

Production 25 Sets
Gold: No Pricing
Production 5 Sets
Plutonium: No Pricing
Production One Set
Patch: No Pricing
Production 5 Sets

BMCB	Adrian Beltre, Dallas McPherson, Eric Chavez, Hank Blalock	25.00
BRGG	Carlos Beltran, Manny Ramirez, Ken Griffey Jr., Vladimir Guerrero	40.00
POTH	Albert Pujols, David Ortiz, Jim Thome, Todd Helton	40.00
RBGB	Cal Ripken Jr., Brett George, Tony Gwynn, Wade Boggs	90.00
RVMP	Ivan Rodriguez, Jason Varitek, Joe Mauer, Jorge Posada	30.00

Sweet Threads Triple

NM/M

Production 25 Sets
Gold: No Pricing
Production 5 Sets
Plutonium: No Pricing
Production One Set
Patch: No Pricing
Production 5 Sets

BBB	Craig Biggio, Jeff Bagwell, Lance Berkman	20.00
BWP	Carlos Beltran, David Wright, Mike Piazza	25.00
GGG	Luis Gonzalez, Shawn Green, Troy Glaus	10.00
JMB	Randy Johnson, Mike Mussina, Kevin Brown	25.00
JWS	Derek Jeter, Bernie Williams, Gary Sheffield	50.00
KGD	Austin Kearns, Ken Griffey Jr., Adam Dunn	30.00
LOP	Brad Lidge, Roy Oswalt, Andy Pettitte	15.00
ODR	David Ortiz, Johnny Damon, Manny Ramirez	25.00
PER	Albert Pujols, Jim Edmonds, Scott Rolen	40.00
PWM	Mark Prior, Kerry Wood, Greg Maddux	30.00
RDN	Manny Ramirez, Johnny Damon, Trot Nixon	30.00
SBT	Alfonso Soriano, Hank Blalock, Mark Teixeira	20.00
SMJ	Curt Schilling, Pedro Martinez, Randy Johnson	25.00
TPS	Miguel Tejada, Rafael Palmeiro, Sammy Sosa	20.00

2005 Upper Deck Sweet Spot Classic

NM/M

Complete Set (100):		30.00
Common Player:		.40
Pack (4):		12.00
Box (12):		120.00
1	Al Kaline	1.00
2	Al Rosen	.40
3	Babe Ruth	4.00
4	Bill Mazeroski	.40
5	Billy Williams	.40
6	Bob Feller	.75
7	Bob Gibson	1.00

8	Bobby Doerr	.40
9	Brooks Robinson	1.00
10	Cal Ripken Jr.	4.00
11	Carl Yastrzemski	2.00
12	Carlton Fisk	.40
13	Casey Stengel	.40
14	Christy Mathewson	2.00
15	Cy Young	1.50
16	Dale Murphy	.75
17	Dave Winfield	.75
18	Dennis Eckersley	.40
19	Dizzy Dean	1.00
20	Don Drysdale	.75
21	Don Mattingly	3.00
22	Don Newcombe	.40
23	Don Sutton	.40
24	Duke Snider	1.00
25	Dwight Evans	.40
26	Eddie Mathews	1.50
27	Eddie Murray	1.00
28	Enos Slaughter	.40
29	Ernie Banks	2.00
30	Frank Howard	.40
31	Frank Robinson	.75
32	Gary Carter	.40
33	Gaylord Perry	.40
34	George Brett	3.00
35	George Kell	.40
36	George Sisler	.40
37	Larry Doby	.40
38	Harmon Killebrew	1.50
39	Honus Wagner	2.00
40	Jackie Robinson	2.00
41	Jim Bunning	.40
42	Jim Palmer	.75
43	Jim Rice	.40
44	Jimmie Foxx	1.50
45	Joe DiMaggio	3.00
46	Joe Morgan	.40
47	Johnny Bench	2.00
48	Johnny Mize	.40
49	Johnny Podres	.40
50	Juan Marichal	.40
51	Keith Hernandez	.40
52	Kirby Puckett	1.00
53	Lefty Grove	.40
54	Lou Brock	.75
55	Lou Gehrig	4.00
56	Luis Aparicio	.40
57	Fergie Jenkins	.40
58	Maury Wills	.40
59	Mel Ott	1.50
60	Mickey Cochrane	1.00
61	Mickey Mantle	4.00
62	Mike Schmidt	3.00
63	Monte Irvin	.75
64	Nolan Ryan	4.00
65	Orlando Cepeda	.40
66	Ozzie Smith	1.50
67	Paul Molitor	1.00
68	Pee Wee Reese	.40
69	Phil Niekro	.40
70	Phil Rizzuto	1.00
71	Ralph Kiner	.40
72	Richie Ashburn	.40
73	Roberto Clemente	4.00
74	Robin Roberts	.40
75	Robin Yount	2.00
76	Rocky Colavito	1.00
77	Rod Carew	.75
78	Rogers Hornsby	1.00
79	Rollie Fingers	.40
80	Roy Campanella	1.00
81	Bob Lemon	.40
82	Red Schoendienst	.40
83	Satchel Paige	2.00
84	Stan Musial	2.50
85	Steve Carlton	.75
86	Ted Williams	3.00
87	Thurman Munson	1.50
88	Tom Seaver	1.00
89	Tony Gwynn	1.50
90	Tony Perez	.40

91	Ty Cobb	2.00
92	Wade Boggs	1.00
93	Walter Johnson	1.00
94	Warren Spahn	1.50
95	Whitey Ford	1.00
96	Will Clark	.75
97	Jim "Catfish" Hunter	.40
98	Willie McCovey	.75
99	Willie Stargell	1.00
100	Yogi Berra	1.50

Gold

Cards (1-100):	4-8X
Production 50 Sets	

Silver

Cards (1-100):	2-4X
Production 100 Sets	

Classic Materials

		NM/M
	Common Player:	6.00
BE	Johnny Bench	15.00
YB	Yogi Berra	20.00
WB	Wade Boggs	10.00
GB	George Brett	10.00
GB1	George Brett	10.00
LB	Lou Brock	8.00
JB	Jim Bunning	10.00
CP	Roy Campanella	12.00
CA	Rod Carew	8.00
SC	Steve Carlton	8.00
GC	Gary Carter	6.00
OC	Orlando Cepeda	8.00
WC	Will Clark	10.00
WC1	Will Clark	10.00
RC	Roberto Clemente	60.00
TC	Ty Cobb SP	100.00
CO	Rocky Colavito	25.00
DC	David Cone	6.00
AD	Andre Dawson	6.00
JD	Joe DiMaggio	80.00
DD	Don Drysdale	10.00
BF	Bob Feller	12.00
CF	Carlton Fisk	8.00
LG	Lou Gehrig/SP	160.00
BG	Bob Gibson	10.00
MG	Mark Grace	8.00
RG	Ron Guidry	8.00
TG	Tony Gwynn	12.00
CH	Jim "Catfish" Hunter	8.00
FJ	Fergie Jenkins	8.00
AK	Al Kaline	10.00
HK	Harmon Killebrew	12.00
MM	Mickey Mantle/SP	120.00
MA	Juan Marichal	8.00
EM	Eddie Mathews	10.00
DM	Don Mattingly	15.00
DM1	Don Mattingly	15.00
BM	Bill Mazeroski	10.00
WI	Willie McCovey	10.00

PM	Paul Molitor	10.00
JM	Joe Morgan	6.00
JM1	Joe Morgan	6.00
TM	Thurman Munson/SP	25.00
MU	Dale Murphy	10.00
ED	Eddie Murray	8.00
ED1	Eddie Murray	8.00
SM	Stan Musial/SP	20.00
PN	Phil Niekro	6.00
SP	Satchel Paige/SP	50.00
JP	Jim Palmer	8.00
TP	Tony Perez	8.00
GP	Gaylord Perry	6.00
RE	Pee Wee Reese/SP	15.00
RI	Jim Rice	8.00
CR	Cal Ripken Jr.	20.00
CR1	Cal Ripken Jr.	20.00
PR	Phil Rizzuto	15.00
RR	Robin Roberts	10.00
RO	Brooks Robinson	10.00
FR	Frank Robinson	8.00
JR	Jackie Robinson	50.00
BR	Babe Ruth SP	275.00
NR	Nolan Ryan	25.00
NR1	Nolan Ryan	25.00
MS	Mike Schmidt	15.00
MS1	Mike Schmidt	15.00
SD	Red Schoendienst	8.00
TS	Tom Seaver	10.00
OS	Ozzie Smith/SP	15.00
SN	Duke Snider	10.00
WS	Warren Spahn	15.00
ST	Willie Stargell/SP	
DS	Don Sutton	6.00
DS1	Don Sutton	6.00
FV	Fernando Valenzuela	6.00
TW	Ted Williams/SP	75.00
MW	Maury Wills	6.00
MW1	Maury Wills	6.00
DW	Dave Winfield	6.00
DW1	Dave Winfield	6.00
EW	Early Wynn	10.00
CY	Carl Yastrzemski	15.00
RY	Robin Yount	12.00

Dual Signatures

No Pricing
Production 15 Sets

Leather Signatures

No Pricing
Production 25 Sets

Patch

NM/M
Some not priced due to scarcity.

LA	Luis Aparicio/19	150.00
BE	Johnny Bench/32	100.00
WB	Wade Boggs/25	60.00
WB1	Wade Boggs/34	60.00
GB	George Brett/38	80.00
GB1	George Brett/50	80.00
LB	Lou Brock/34	90.00
SC	Steve Carlton/50	60.00
GC	Gary Carter/47	50.00
GC1	Gary Carter/34	50.00
OC	Orlando Cepeda/40	50.00
DC	David Cone/39	50.00
JD	Joe DiMaggio/38	250.00
CF1	Carlton Fisk/50	70.00
RG	Ron Guidry/30	40.00
TG	Tony Gwynn/34	80.00
TG1	Tony Gwynn/30	80.00
FH	Frank Howard/34	85.00
FJ	Fergie Jenkins/34	60.00
WI	Willie McCovey/50	60.00
JM	Joe Morgan/34	60.00
MU	Dale Murphy/34	80.00
ED	Eddie Murray/34	70.00
ED1	Eddie Murray/50	70.00
PN	Phil Niekro/44	50.00
TP	Tony Perez/34	75.00
GP	Gaylord Perry/34	50.00
PO	Johnny Podres/50	60.00
RI	Jim Rice/34	50.00
CR	Cal Ripken Jr./34	150.00
CR1	Cal Ripken Jr./34	150.00
RO	Brooks Robinson/50	85.00
RO1	Brooks Robinson/43	85.00
FR	Frank Robinson/34	80.00
JR	Jackie Robinson/12	250.00
SD	Red Schoendienst/42	60.00
TS	Tom Seaver/50	50.00
TS1	Tom Seaver/50	50.00
OS	Ozzie Smith/34	100.00
ST	Willie Stargell/50	65.00
BS	Bruce Sutter/50	50.00
DS	Don Sutton/34	40.00
DS1	Don Sutton/50	40.00
MW	Maury Wills/50	60.00
MW1	Maury Wills/47	50.00
DW1	Dave Winfield/50	75.00
CY	Carl Yastrzemski/35	100.00

RY	Robin Yount/34	75.00
RY1	Robin Yount/19	

Sweet Spot Signatures

		NM/M
Common Autograph:		20.00
Inserted 1:12		
Blue/Red Stitch:		1.5-2X
Production 40 Sets		
Black Stitch:		No Pricing
Production One Set		
LA	Luis Aparicio	25.00
HB	Harold Baines	20.00
EB	Ernie Banks	75.00
BE	Johnny Bench	60.00
YB	Yogi Berra/SP	60.00
WB	Wade Boggs	50.00
GB	George Brett	85.00
JB	Jim Bunning	20.00
JC	Jose Canseco	40.00
CA	Rod Carew	50.00
SC	Steve Carlton	40.00
GC	Gary Carter	25.00
OC	Orlando Cepeda	25.00
WC	Will Clark	30.00
RC	Rocky Colavito/SP	85.00
DC	David Cone	20.00
AD	Andre Dawson	20.00
JD	Joe DiMaggio/25	
BD	Bobby Doerr	25.00
DE	Dennis Eckersley	25.00
EV	Dwight Evans	25.00
BF	Bob Feller	40.00
RF	Rollie Fingers	20.00
CF	Carlton Fisk	40.00
WF	Whitey Ford	60.00
BG	Bob Gibson	40.00
MG	Mark Grace	40.00
TG	Tony Gwynn	50.00
EH	Ernie Harwell/SP	40.00
KH	Keith Hernandez	20.00
MI	Monte Irvin	25.00
BJ	Bo Jackson	75.00
DJ	David Justice	20.00
KA	Harry Kalas	25.00
AK	Al Kaline	40.00
GK	George Kell	25.00
HK	Harmon Killebrew	50.00
RK	Ralph Kiner/SP	50.00
MA	Juan Marichal	25.00
DM	Don Mattingly	80.00
BM	Bill Mazeroski	40.00
MC	Willie McCovey/SP	50.00
PM	Paul Molitor	40.00
JM	Joe Morgan SP	35.00
MU	Dale Murphy	25.00
SM	Stan Musial	100.00
DN	Don Newcombe	25.00
PN	Phil Niekro	25.00
JP	Jim Palmer	25.00
TP	Tony Perez	25.00
GP	Gaylord Perry	25.00
PO	Johnny Podres	20.00
KP	Kirby Puckett/SP	50.00
JR	Jim Rice	25.00
CR	Cal Ripken Jr.	160.00
PR	Phil Rizzuto	75.00
RR	Robin Roberts	30.00
BR	Brooks Robinson	40.00
FR	Frank Robinson	40.00
AR	Al Rosen	20.00
NR	Nolan Ryan	125.00
RS	Ron Santo	35.00
MS	Mike Schmidt	80.00
RE	Red Schoendienst	30.00
TS	Tom Seaver	60.00
OS	Ozzie Smith	60.00
SN	Duke Snider	40.00
ST	Rusty Staub	20.00
SU	Bruce Sutter	20.00
DS	Don Sutton	20.00
LT	Luis Tiant	20.00
FV	Fernando Valenzuela	30.00
BW	Billy Williams	25.00
MW	Matt Williams	20.00
WI	Maury Wills	20.00
CY	Carl Yastrzemski	100.00
RY	Robin Yount/SP	85.00

Sweet Sticks Signatures

NM/M
Production 35 Sets

LA	Luis Aparicio	50.00
HB	Harold Baines	40.00
EB	Ernie Banks	125.00
BE	Johnny Bench	75.00
YB	Yogi Berra	80.00
WB	Wade Boggs	75.00
GB	George Brett	140.00
JB	Jim Bunning	40.00
JC	Jose Canseco	75.00
CA	Rod Carew	75.00
SC	Steve Carlton	50.00
GC	Gary Carter	40.00
OC	Orlando Cepeda	50.00
WC	Will Clark	65.00
RC	Rocky Colavito	120.00
DC	David Cone	50.00
AD	Andre Dawson	50.00
BD	Bobby Doerr	50.00
DE	Dennis Eckersley	50.00
EV	Dwight Evans	60.00
BF	Bob Feller	75.00
RF	Rollie Fingers	45.00
CF	Carlton Fisk	75.00
WF	Whitey Ford	85.00
BG	Bob Gibson	65.00
MG	Mark Grace	75.00
TG	Tony Gwynn	85.00
EH	Ernie Harwell	50.00
KH	Keith Hernandez	40.00
FH	Frank Howard	50.00
MI	Monte Irvin	50.00
BJ	Bo Jackson	140.00
DJ	David Justice	40.00
AK	Al Kaline	80.00
GK	George Kell	50.00
HK	Harmon Killebrew	80.00
RK	Ralph Kiner	75.00
MA	Juan Marichal	50.00
DM	Don Mattingly	125.00
BM	Bill Mazeroski	90.00
MC	Willie McCovey	85.00
PM	Paul Molitor	60.00
JM	Joe Morgan	50.00
MU	Dale Murphy	50.00
SM	Stan Musial	140.00
DN	Don Newcombe	50.00
PN	Phil Niekro	40.00
JP	Jim Palmer	50.00
TP	Tony Perez	50.00
GP	Gaylord Perry	40.00
PO	Johnny Podres	40.00
KP	Kirby Puckett	100.00
JR	Jim Rice	50.00
CR	Cal Ripken Jr.	240.00
PR	Phil Rizzuto	75.00
RR	Robin Roberts	50.00
BR	Brooks Robinson	65.00
FR	Frank Robinson	60.00
AR	Al Rosen	50.00
NR	Nolan Ryan	150.00
RS	Ron Santo	65.00
MS	Mike Schmidt	125.00
RE	Red Schoendienst	85.00
TS	Tom Seaver	85.00
OS	Ozzie Smith	90.00
SN	Duke Snider	75.00
ST	Rusty Staub	40.00
SU	Bruce Sutter	30.00
DS	Don Sutton	40.00
LT	Luis Tiant	40.00
BW	Billy Williams	50.00
MW	Matt Williams	50.00
WI	Maury Wills	40.00
CY	Carl Yastrzemski	120.00
RY	Robin Yount	100.00

Wingfield Classic Collection

NM/M

Common Player:		4.00
Inserted 1:Box		
1	Al Kaline	4.00
2	Pee Wee Reese	4.00
3	Stan Musial, Ted Williams	6.00
4	Bill Dickey	4.00
5	Frank Robinson	5.00
6	Billy Martin	4.00
7	Casey Stengel, Joe DiMaggio	6.00
8	Bob Feller, Dwight D. Eisenhower	4.00
9	Duke Snider	5.00
10	Carl Yastrzemski	8.00
11	Honus Wagner	6.00
12	Dwight D. Eisenhower, Clark Griffith	4.00

13	Mickey Mantle, Joe DiMaggio	15.00
14	Don Drysdale	4.00
15	Ted Williams	8.00
16	Al Kaline, Mickey Mantle	15.00
17	Ernie Banks	6.00
18	Lou Boudreau	4.00
19	George Sisler, Harmon Killebrew	6.00
20	Gil Hodges	4.00
21	Rogers Hornsby	6.00
22	Luis Aparicio	4.00
23	Jackie Robinson	10.00
24	Joe Morgan	4.00
25	Enos Slaughter	4.00
26	Joe DiMaggio	8.00
27	Mickey Mantle, Ted Kluszewski	15.00
28	John F. Kennedy	6.00
29	Johnny Bench	8.00
30	Juan Marichal	4.00
31	Larry Doby	4.00
32	Don Newcombe, Elston Howard	4.00
33	Harmon Killebrew, Dwight D. Eisenhower	6.00
34	Roger Maris, Mickey Mantle	20.00
35	Mickey Mantle, Stan Musial	15.00
36	Ted Williams, Mickey Mantle, Yogi Berra	15.00
37	Nellie Fox	6.00
38	Richie Asburn	4.00
39	Roberto Clemente	15.00
40	Stan Musial, Robin Roberts	8.00
41	Tommy Heinrich, Joe DiMaggio	8.00
42	Roy Campanella	6.00
43	Rocky Colavito, Harmon Killebrew	6.00
44	Steve Carlton	4.00
45	Thurman Munson	6.00
46	Luis Aparicio, Ernie Banks	6.00
47	Gil Hodges, Yogi Berra, Dwight D. Eisenhower	6.00
48	Whitey Ford	6.00
49	Mickey Mantle, Yogi Berra, Joe DiMaggio	15.00
50	Yogi Berra	8.00

2005 Upper Deck Trilogy

		NM/M
Complete Set (100):		40.00
Common Player:		.50
Pack (5):		20.00
Box (9):		170.00
1	A.J. Burnett	.50
2	Adam Dunn	1.00
3	Adrian Beltre	.50
4	Albert Pujols	4.00
5	Alex Rodriguez	3.00
6	Alfonso Soriano	1.00
7	Andruw Jones	1.00
8	Aramis Ramirez	.50
9	Ben Sheets	.75
10	Bobby Abreu	.75
11	Bobby Crosby	.50
12	Ryan Zimmerman RC	15.00
13	Brian Giles	.50
14	Brian Roberts	.50
15	Carl Crawford	.50
16	Carlos Beltran	1.00
17	Carlos Delgado	.75
18	Carlos Zambrano	.75
19	Chipper Jones	1.00
20	Corey Patterson	.50

21	Craig Biggio	.50
22	Curt Schilling	1.50
23	Dallas McPherson	.50
24	David Ortiz	1.50
25	David Wright	1.50
26	Delmon Young	1.00
27	Derek Jeter	4.00
28	Derrek Lee	1.00
29	Dontrelle Willis	1.00
30	Eric Chavez	.50
31	Eric Gagne	.50
32	Francisco Rodriguez	.50
33	Gary Sheffield	1.00
34	Greg Maddux	2.00
35	Hank Blalock	.50
36	Hideki Matsui	2.50
37	Ichiro Suzuki	3.00
38	Ivan Rodriguez	1.00
39	J.D. Drew	.50
40	Jake Peavy	.75
41	Jason Bay	.50
42	Jason Schmidt	.50
43	Jeff Bagwell	1.00
44	Jeff Kent	.50
45	Jeff Niemann RC	2.00
46	Jeremy Bonderman	.50
47	Jim Edmonds	.75
48	Jim Thome	1.00
49	Joe Mauer	.75
50	Johan Santana	1.00
51	John Smoltz	.75
52	Johnny Damon	1.00
53	Jose Reyes	.75
54	Jose Vidro	.50
55	Josh Beckett	.50
56	Justin Morneau	.50
57	Justin Verlander RC	4.00
58	Ken Griffey Jr.	3.00
59	Kendry Morales RC	6.00
60	Kerry Wood	.75
61	Khalil Greene	.75
62	Lance Berkman	.75
63	Luis Gonzalez	.50
64	Manny Ramirez	1.50
65	Mark Buehrle	.75
66	Mark Mulder	.50
67	Mark Prior	1.00
68	Mark Teixeira	1.00
69	Michael Young	.50
70	Miguel Cabrera	1.50
71	Miguel Tejada	1.00
72	Mike Mussina	1.50
73	Mike Piazza	1.50
74	Nomar Garciaparra	1.00
75	Pat Burrell	.50
76	Paul Konerko	.75
77	Pedro Martinez	1.50
78	Philip Humber RC	2.00
79	Prince Fielder	8.00
80	Randy Johnson	1.50
81	Richie Sexson	.75
82	Rickie Weeks	.75
83	Roger Clemens	4.00
84	Roy Halladay	.75
85	Roy Oswalt	.75
86	Sammy Sosa	1.50
87	Scott Kazmir	.50
88	Scott Rolen	1.00
89	Stephen Drew RC	8.00
90	Tadahito Iguchi RC	4.00
91	Tim Hudson	.75
92	Todd Helton	1.00
93	Tom Glavine	.75
94	Torii Hunter	.75
95	Travis Hafner	.75
96	Troy Glaus	.75
97	Vernon Wells	.50
98	Victor Martinez	.50
99	Vladimir Guerrero	1.50
100	Zack Greinke	.50

Generations

	NM/M
Complete Set (6):	
Common Player:	

Generations Future Lumber Silver

		NM/M
Production 100 Sets		
Gold:		1X
Production 60 Sets		
RC	Robinson Cano	20.00
CA	Jorge Cantu	6.00
GF	Gavin Floyd	4.00
BH	Brad Halsey	4.00
JJ	J.J. Hardy	4.00
RH	Ryan Howard	50.00
LN	Laynce Nix	4.00
JP	Jhonny Peralta	6.00
JR	Jeremy Reed	4.00
AR	Alexis Rios	6.00
RI	Juan Rivera	4.00
BJ	B.J. Upton	6.00
JW	Jayson Werth	4.00
YO	Kevin Youkilis	6.00

Generations Future Materials Silver

		NM/M
Common Player:		4.00
Production 120 Sets		
Gold:		1X
Production 75 Sets		
BA	Bronson Arroyo	6.00
GA	Garrett Atkins	4.00
JE	Jeff Baker	4.00
CL	Clint Barmes	4.00
JB	Jason Bartlett	4.00
BL	Joe Blanton	4.00
DB	Dewon Brazelton	4.00
YB	Yhency Brazoban	4.00
CB	Chris Burke	6.00
DC	Daniel Cabrera	4.00
RC	Robinson Cano	20.00
CA	Jorge Cantu	6.00
GC	Gustavo Chacin	4.00
JD	J.D. Closser	4.00
DD	David DeJesus	4.00
DU	Jason Dubois	4.00
GF	Gavin Floyd	4.00
JF	Jeff Francis	4.00
AG	Adrian Gonzalez	4.00
BH	Brad Halsey	4.00
JJ	J.J. Hardy	4.00
DH	Danny Haren	4.00
AH	Aaron Hill	4.00
HO	Dennis Houlton	4.00
RH	Ryan Howard	20.00
TI	Tadahito Iguchi	15.00
EJ	Edwin Jackson	4.00
DK	Dae-Sung Koo	4.00
KO	Casey Kotchman	4.00
JL	Jason Lane	4.00
DM	Dallas McPherson	6.00
AM	Aaron Miles	4.00
YM	Yadier Molina	4.00
MY	Brett Myers	4.00
XN	Xavier Nady	4.00
LN	Laynce Nix	4.00
JP	Jhonny Peralta	6.00
RQ	Robb Quinlan	4.00
JR	Jeremy Reed	4.00
AR	Alexis Rios	6.00
RI	Juan Rivera	4.00
ES	Ervin Santana	6.00
SS	Steve Schmoll	4.00
LS	Luke Scott	4.00
SI	Grady Sizemore	10.00
HS	Huston Street	10.00
NS	Nick Swisher	8.00
WT	Willy Taveras	4.00
MT	Mark Teahen	4.00
TH	Charles Thomas	4.00
CT	Chad Tracy	4.00
BJ	B.J. Upton	4.00
CU	Chase Utley	10.00
WA	Ryan Wagner	4.00
RW	Rickie Weeks	8.00
JW	Jayson Werth	4.00
KY	Keiichi Yabu	4.00
YO	Kevin Youkilis	6.00

Generations Future Signature Silver

		NM/M
Common Player:		8.00
Production 50-199		
Bronze:		1-1.5X
Production 35 Sets		
Gold:		No Pricing
Production 15 Sets		
GA	Garrett Atkins/199	10.00
JB	Jason Bartlett/199	8.00
BE	Colter Bean/199	8.00
BL	Joe Blanton/199	10.00
YB	Yhency Brazoban/199	10.00

AB	Ambiorix Burgos/199	8.00
CB	Chris Burke/199	15.00
DC	Daniel Cabrera/199	15.00
JO	Jose Capellan/199	10.00
JD	J.D. Closser/99	10.00
AC	Ambiorix Concepcion/199	8.00
DD	David DeJesus/99	12.00
SD	Stephen Drew/75	100.00
DU	Jason Dubois/99	10.00
PF	Prince Fielder/75	100.00
GF	Gavin Floyd/99	10.00
JF	Jeff Francis/99	10.00
AG	Adrian Gonzalez/99	15.00
JG	Jared Gothreaux/199	8.00
GG	Gabe Gross/99	10.00
JJ	J.J. Hardy/99	25.00
JH	John Hattig Jr./199	10.00
FH	Felix Hernandez/99	80.00
HO	Dennis Houlton/199	10.00
RH	Ryan Howard/99	40.00
PH	Philip Humber/99	20.00
TI	Tadahito Iguchi/75	150.00
EJ	Edwin Jackson/99	10.00
KO	Casey Kotchman/99	10.00
JL	Jason Lane/99	10.00
ML	Matt Lindstrom/199	8.00
PL	Pedro Lopez/189	10.00
RM	Russell Martin/199	20.00
KM	Kendry Morales/199	30.00
JN	Jeff Niemann/75	40.00
PO	Peter Orr/199	15.00
TP	Tony Pena/199	8.00
RQ	Robb Quinlan/199	8.00
AR	Alexis Rios/99	15.00
CR	Casey Rogowski/199	10.00
RR	Russel Rohlicek/199	8.00
SS	Steve Schmoll/199	8.00
LS	Luke Scott/199	10.00
TS	Tim Stauffer/199	8.00
NS	Nick Swisher/99	15.00
MT	Mark Teahen/199	8.00
TH	Charles Thomas/199	12.00
BJ	B.J. Upton/50	20.00
CU	Chase Utley/50	20.00
JV	Justin Verlander/75	60.00
RW	Rickie Weeks/50	25.00
JW	Jayson Werth/99	15.00
KY	Keiichi Yabu/199	25.00
YO	Kevin Youkilis/99	25.00
DY	Delmon Young/50	40.00
RZ	Ryan Zimmerman/150	125.00

Generations of Lumber Triple

		NM/M
Production 85 Sets		10.00
ARU	B.J. Upton, Jimmy Rollins, Luis Aparicio	15.00
BCU	Wade Boggs, B.J. Upton, Carl Crawford	15.00
BHH	Travis Hafner, Ryan Howard, Harold Baines	15.00
BMY	Bill Mueller, Wade Boggs, Kevin Youkilis	15.00
CCC	Will Clark, Jack Clark, Orlando Cepeda	12.00
DAR	Bobby Abreu, Eric Davis, Alex Rios	10.00
EDY	Kevin Youkilis, Dwight Evans, Johnny Damon	20.00
GDP	Ken Griffey Jr., Wily Mo Pena, Adam Dunn	25.00
GGC	Miguel Cabrera, Ken Griffey Jr., Tony Gwynn	25.00
HDH	Ryan Howard, Adam Dunn, Frank Howard	15.00
HOH	Frank Howard, Ryan Howard, David Ortiz	20.00
JGU	Bo Jackson, Ken Griffey Jr., B.J. Upton	25.00
JHR	Alex Rios, Bo Jackson, Torii Hunter	15.00
JSP	Bo Jackson, Gary Sheffield, Wily Mo Pena	15.00
KBH	Pat Burrell, John Kruk, Ryan Howard	15.00
LJU	Barry Larkin, Derek Jeter, B.J. Upton	30.00
LYU	B.J. Upton, Barry Larkin, Michael Young	12.00
MDW	Jayson Werth, Dale Murphy, Adam Dunn	15.00

MMJ Don Mattingly, Derek Jeter, Bobby Murcer 50.00
MOH Ryan Howard, David Ortiz, Eddie Murray 20.00
NBW Adrian Beltre, David Wright, Graig Nettles 15.00
OAR Bobby Abreu, Tony Oliva, Alex Rios 10.00
PDP Wily Mo Pena, Eric Davis, Tony Perez 10.00
PGP Tony Perez, Ken Griffey Jr., Wily Mo Pena 25.00
RJC Cal Ripken Jr., Derek Jeter, Bobby Crosby 50.00
ROY David Ortiz, Jim Rice, Kevin Youkilis 20.00
RRT Brooks Robinson, Cal Ripken Jr., Miguel Tejada 40.00
SBW Mike Schmidt, Adrian Beltre, David Wright 20.00
SDW Duke Snider, Jayson Werth, J.D. Drew 20.00
SMR Aramis Ramirez, Bill Madlock, Ron Santo 20.00
SSP Ron Santo, Ryne Sandberg, Corey Patterson 35.00

Generations of Materials Triple

NM/M
Common Trio: 10.00
Production 50 Sets
AAD Aramis Ramirez, Al Rosen, Dallas McPherson 15.00
AFB Luis Aparicio, Rafael Furcal, Jason Bartlett 15.00
API Tadahito Iguchi, Scott Podsednik, Luis Aparicio 25.00
ARU Jimmy Rollins, Luis Aparicio, B.J. Upton 15.00
BCU B.J. Upton, Carl Crawford, Wade Boggs 15.00
BHH Ryan Howard, Harold Baines, Travis Hafner 15.00
BLS Craig Biggio, Jason Lane, Luke Scott 15.00
BMY Kevin Youkilis, Wade Boggs, Bill Mueller 15.00
CCC Will Clark, Jack Clark, Orlando Cepeda 15.00
CCK Sean Casey, Will Clark, Casey Kotchman 15.00
CMG Justin Morneau, Adrian Gonzalez, Will Clark 15.00
CTG Will Clark, Adrian Gonzalez, Mark Teixeira 15.00
DAR Alex Rios, Eric Davis, Bobby Abreu 10.00
DBS Lenny Dykstra, Jason Bay, Nick Swisher 15.00
DGL Jason Lane, Ken Griffey Jr., Andre Dawson 25.00
DHL Lenny Dykstra, Torii Hunter, Jason Lane 10.00

DPD Jason Dubois, Corey Patterson, Andre Dawson 10.00
DPT Lenny Dykstra, Scott Podsednik, Willy Taveras 15.00
EDY Kevin Youkilis, Johnny Damon, Dwight Evans 20.00
GAS Bobby Abreu, Tony Gwynn, Nick Swisher 25.00
GDP Wily Mo Pena, Adam Dunn, Ken Griffey Jr. 25.00
GGC Ken Griffey Jr., Tony Gwynn, Miguel Cabrera 25.00
GMY Kevin Youkilis, Mike Greenwell, Bill Mueller 15.00
GWJ Dwight Gooden, Dontrelle Willis, Edwin Jackson 15.00
HDH Frank Howard, Adam Dunn, Ryan Howard 15.00
HOH Ryan Howard, David Ortiz, Frank Howard 20.00
JGU B.J. Upton, Bo Jackson, Ken Griffey Jr. 25.00
JHR Bo Jackson, Torii Hunter, Alex Rios 20.00
JMK Casey Kotchman, Wally Joyner, Dallas McPherson 10.00
JSP Bo Jackson, Gary Sheffield, Wily Mo Pena 15.00
KBH Pat Burrell, John Kruk, Ryan Howard 15.00
KBU John Kruk, Pat Burrell, Chase Utley 25.00
LJU B.J. Upton, Barry Larkin, Derek Jeter 35.00
LYU Barry Larkin, Michael Young, B.J. Upton 35.00
MBS Nick Swisher, Pat Burrell, Dale Murphy 20.00
MCG Don Mattingly, Sean Casey, Adrian Gonzalez 30.00
MDW Adam Dunn, Jayson Werth, Dale Murphy 20.00
MMJ Don Mattingly, Derek Jeter, Bobby Murcer 60.00
MOH David Ortiz, Ryan Howard, Eddie Murray 20.00
NBW Adrian Beltre, David Wright, Graig Nettles 20.00
OAR Bobby Abreu, Tony Oliva, Alex Rios 10.00
PDP Wily Mo Pena, Eric Davis, Tony Perez 10.00
PGD Tony Perez, Brian Giles, Jason Dubois 10.00
PGP Wily Mo Pena, Ken Griffey Jr., Tony Perez 30.00
RBT Brooks Robinson, Adrian Beltre, Mark Teahen 20.00
RCD Carl Crawford, David DeJesus, Tim Raines 15.00
RJC Derek Jeter, Cal Ripken Jr., Bobby Crosby 50.00
ROY Jim Rice, David Ortiz, Kevin Youkilis 25.00
RRM Brooks Robinson, Cal Ripken Jr., Melvin Mora 50.00
RRT Miguel Tejada, Cal Ripken Jr., Brooks Robinson 50.00
SBM Dallas McPherson, Adrian Beltre, Mike Schmidt 20.00
SBW Mike Schmidt, Adrian Beltre, David Wright 20.00
SDW Duke Snider, Jayson Werth, J.D. Drew 20.00
SGU Ryne Sandberg, Chase Utley, Marcus Giles 35.00
SRU Chase Utley, Mike Schmidt, Jimmy Rollins 40.00

SRW Ryne Sandberg, Brian Roberts, Rickie Weeks 25.00
VGB Jason Bay, Brian Giles, Andy Van Slyke 10.00
VPD Andy Van Slyke, Corey Patterson, David DeJesus 10.00
WBI Tadahito Iguchi, Frank White, Craig Biggio 20.00
WCT Willie Wilson, Willy Taveras, Carl Crawford 15.00

Generations of Signatures

NM/M
Production 35 Sets
AYU B.J. Upton, Luis Aparicio, Michael Young 40.00
BPN Jake Peavy, Jeff Niemann, Jim Bunning 50.00
COS Tim Stauffer, Roy Oswalt, David Cone
CTG Will Clark, Mark Teixeira, Adrian Gonzalez 60.00
DBU Chase Utley, Craig Biggio, Bobby Doerr 50.00
DGL Ken Griffey Jr., Andre Dawson, Jason Lane 100.00
DGU Marcus Giles, Chase Utley, Bobby Doerr 50.00
DLB Bobby Doerr, Mark Loretta, Chris Burke 30.00
FPH Rich Harden, Mark Prior, Bob Feller 50.00
GDP Ken Griffey Jr., Adam Dunn, Wily Mo Pena 100.00
HDG Adam Dunn, Frank Howard, Gabe Gross 40.00
JHR Torii Hunter, Bo Jackson, Alex Rios 85.00
JKM Casey Kotchman, Kendry Morales, Wally Joyner 50.00
LJU Barry Larkin, Derek Jeter, B.J. Upton 250.00
MBV Justin Verlander, Jack Morris, Jeremy Bonderman 90.00
MMJ Derek Jeter, Don Mattingly, Bobby Murcer 260.00
NBW David Wright, Graig Nettles, Adrian Beltre 75.00
OHM Tony Oliva, Kent Hrbek, Justin Morneau 50.00
PBF Gaylord Perry, Jeremy Bonderman, Gavin Floyd 35.00
PGP Tony Perez, Ken Griffey Jr., Wily Mo Pena 100.00
PPH Philip Humber, Jim Palmer, Jake Peavy 50.00
PPS Jake Peavy, Tim Stauffer, Gaylord Perry 40.00
RCD Tim Raines, David DeJesus, Carl Crawford 40.00
RCY Miguel Cabrera, Delmon Young, Jim Rice
RJC Bobby Crosby, Cal Ripken Jr., Derek Jeter 400.00
RRM Cal Ripken Jr., Melvin Mora, Brooks Robinson 180.00
RSH Nolan Ryan, John Smoltz, Philip Humber 165.00
SBT Mark Teahen, Adrian Beltre, Ron Santo 50.00
SBW Adrian Beltre, Mike Schmidt, David Wright 100.00
SGH J.J. Hardy, Ozzie Smith, Khalil Greene 70.00
SMR Ron Santo, Bill Madlock, Aramis Ramirez 50.00
SRW Brian Roberts, Ryne Sandberg, Rickie Weeks 85.00
VGB Jason Bay, Brian Giles, Andy Van Slyke 65.00

Generations Past Lumber

NM/M
Common Player: 4.00

Production 115 unless noted.
Gold: 1-1.5X
Production 25-75
LA Luis Aparicio 8.00
HB Harold Baines 4.00
DB Dusty Baker 6.00
JB Johnny Bench 10.00
WB Wade Boggs 8.00
BB Bill Buckner 6.00
CA Rod Carew 8.00
SC Steve Carlton 6.00
GC Gary Carter 6.00
OC Orlando Cepeda 6.00
CY Ron Cey 4.00
JC Jack Clark 4.00
WC Will Clark 8.00
TC Ty Cobb/99 100.00
MC Mickey Cochrane/99 25.00
ED Eric Davis 8.00
AD Andre Dawson 6.00
JD Joe DiMaggio/99 65.00
BD Bobby Doerr 8.00
LD Lenny Dykstra 4.00
DE Dwight Evans 6.00
CF Carlton Fisk 6.00
GF George Foster 4.00
JF Jimmie Foxx/99 50.00
FR Bill Freehan 4.00
LG Lou Gehrig/99 140.00
DG Dwight Gooden 4.00
GR Lefty Grove/99 40.00
TG Tony Gwynn 10.00
KH Keith Hernandez 4.00
RH Rogers Hornsby/99 40.00
FH Frank Howard 4.00
BJ Bo Jackson 10.00
RJ Reggie Jackson 10.00
JO Wally Joyner 4.00
GK George Kell 8.00
JK John Kruk 4.00
BL Barry Larkin 4.00
DL Davey Lopes 4.00
BM Bill Madlock 4.00
MA Don Mattingly 25.00
FM Fred McGriff 6.00
JM Johnny Mize 4.00
TM Thurman Munson 20.00
MU Bobby Murcer 4.00
DM Dale Murphy 8.00
MY Eddie Murray 8.00
SM Stan Musial 20.00
GN Graig Nettles 6.00
TO Tony Oliva 6.00
MO Mel Ott 25.00
TP Tony Perez 6.00
GP Gaylord Perry 6.00
RP Rico Petrocelli 4.00
BP Boog Powell 4.00
TR Tim Raines 4.00
RI Jim Rice 4.00
CR Cal Ripken Jr. 25.00
RO Brooks Robinson 8.00
JR Jackie Robinson 4.00
AR Al Rosen 10.00
BR Babe Ruth/99 140.00
NR Nolan Ryan 25.00
SA Ryne Sandberg 15.00
RS Ron Santo 10.00
MS Mike Schmidt 15.00
SI George Sisler 20.00
SK Bill "Moose" Skowron 6.00
OS Ozzie Smith 20.00
SN Duke Snider 10.00
DS Darryl Strawberry 8.00
AT Alan Trammell 8.00
AV Andy Van Slyke 4.00
FW Frank White 4.00
WW Willie Wilson 4.00
YA Carl Yastrzemski 25.00

Generation Past Material Silver

NM/M
Common Player: 4.00
Production 99 unless noted.
Gold: 1-1.5X
Production 25 Sets
LA Luis Aparicio 8.00
HB Harold Baines 4.00
DB Dusty Baker 6.00
JB Johnny Bench 10.00
WB Wade Boggs 8.00
BU Jim Bunning 6.00
RC Roy Campanella 20.00
CA Rod Carew 8.00
SC Steve Carlton 8.00
GC Gary Carter 6.00
OC Orlando Cepeda 6.00
CY Ron Cey 4.00
JC Jack Clark 4.00
WC Will Clark 8.00
DC David Cone 4.00
ED Eric Davis 8.00
AD Andre Dawson 6.00

DD	Dizzy Dean/75	40.00
JD	Joe DiMaggio/75	85.00
DR	Don Drysdale	10.00
LD	Lenny Dykstra	4.00
BF	Bob Feller	10.00
CF	Carlton Fisk	8.00
LG	Lou Gehrig/75	150.00
DG	Dwight Gooden	4.00
RG	Ron Guidry	8.00
TG	Tony Gwynn	10.00
KH	Keith Hernandez	6.00
RH	Rogers Hornsby/75	65.00
FH	Frank Howard	6.00
HR	Kent Hrbek	8.00
BJ	Bo Jackson	10.00
RJ	Reggie Jackson	10.00
JO	Wally Joyner	6.00
JK	John Kruk	8.00
BL	Barry Larkin	6.00
DL	Davey Lopes	4.00
BM	Bill Madlock	4.00
EM	Eddie Mathews/75	20.00
CM	Christy Mathewson/75	80.00
MA	Don Mattingly	25.00
JM	Johnny Mize	15.00
JA	Jack Morris	4.00
TM	Thurman Munson	20.00
MU	Bobby Murcer	8.00
DM	Dale Murphy	8.00
MY	Eddie Murray	8.00
SM	Stan Musial	20.00
GN	Graig Nettles	6.00
TO	Tony Oliva	6.00
MO	Mel Ott/75	30.00
SP	Satchel Paige/75	50.00
JP	Jim Palmer	6.00
TP	Tony Perez	6.00
GP	Gaylord Perry	6.00
RP	Rico Petrocelli	6.00
BP	Boog Powell	4.00
TR	Tim Raines	4.00
RI	Jim Rice	6.00
CR	Cal Ripken Jr.	25.00
RO	Brooks Robinson	10.00
AR	Al Rosen	10.00
NR	Nolan Ryan	25.00
SA	Ryne Sandberg	15.00
MS	Mike Schmidt	15.00
AV	Andy Van Slyke	8.00
OS	Ozzie Smith	15.00
SN	Duke Snider	10.00
DS	Darryl Strawberry	6.00
FW	Frank White	4.00
WW	Willie Wilson	4.00
YA	Carl Yastrzemski	15.00

Generations Past Autograph Silver

NM/M
Common Player: 10.00
Production 24-99.
Bronze: 1-1.5X
Production 10 or 35.
No pricing for prod. of 10.
Gold: No Pricing
Production 5-15

LA	Luis Aparicio/50	20.00
HB	Harold Baines/199	15.00
DB	Dusty Baker/25	20.00
WB	Wade Boggs/50	35.00
BB	Bill Buckner/25	15.00
BU	Jim Bunning/99	20.00
CA	Rod Carew/25	35.00
SC	Steve Carlton/25	20.00
CY	Ron Cey/199	15.00
JC	Jack Clark/199	10.00
WC	Will Clark/25	45.00
DC	David Cone/99	15.00
ED	Eric Davis/199	15.00
AD	Andre Dawson/99	20.00
BD	Bobby Doerr/199	15.00
LD	Lenny Dykstra/199	15.00
DE	Dwight Evans/50	20.00
BF	Bob Feller/99	25.00
GF	George Foster/199	10.00
FR	Bill Freehan/199	15.00
RG	Ron Guidry/199	15.00
KH	Keith Hernandez/199	15.00
FH	Frank Howard/199	15.00
HR	Kent Hrbek/199	15.00
BJ	Bo Jackson/50	50.00
RJ	Reggie Jackson/25	50.00
JO	Wally Joyner/199	15.00
GK	George Kell/199	15.00
JK	John Kruk/199	20.00
BL	Barry Larkin/99	25.00
DL	Davey Lopes/199	10.00
BM	Bill Madlock/199	15.00
MA	Don Mattingly/25	75.00
FM	Fred McGriff/199	25.00
JA	Jack Morris/199	15.00
MU	Bobby Murcer/199	25.00
DM	Dale Murphy/99	25.00
SM	Stan Musial/25	30.00
GN	Graig Nettles/199	15.00
TO	Tony Oliva/199	15.00
JP	Jim Palmer/50	20.00
TP	Tony Perez/25	30.00
GP	Gaylord Perry/199	15.00
BP	Boog Powell/199	15.00
TR	Tim Raines/199	15.00
RI	Jim Rice/99	15.00
CR	Cal Ripken Jr./24	
RO	Brooks Robinson/50	30.00
AR	Al Rosen/199	15.00
NR	Nolan Ryan/25	100.00
SA	Ryne Sandberg/50	60.00
RS	Ron Santo/199	30.00
MS	Mike Schmidt/25	60.00
SK	Bill Skowron/199	15.00
OS	Ozzie Smith/25	50.00
DS	Darryl Strawberry/99	15.00
AT	Alan Trammell/50	20.00
AV	Andy Van Slyke/199	20.00
FW	Frank White/199	15.00
WW	Willie Wilson/199	15.00

Generation Present Lumber Silver

NM/M
Common Player: 4.00
Production 115 Sets
Gold: 1X
Production 75 Sets

BA	Bobby Abreu	4.00
GA	Garret Anderson	4.00
JE	Jeff Bagwell	6.00
CB	Carlos Beltran	6.00
AB	Adrian Beltre	4.00
LB	Lance Berkman	4.00
BI	Craig Biggio	6.00
HB	Hank Blalock	4.00
BO	Jeremy Bonderman	4.00
PB	Pat Burrell	4.00
AJ	A.J. Burnett	4.00
MC	Miguel Cabrera	8.00
SC	Sean Casey	4.00
EC	Eric Chavez	4.00
RC	Roger Clemens	12.00
CC	Carl Crawford	4.00
BC	Bobby Crosby	4.00
DA	Johnny Damon	8.00
CD	Carlos Delgado	4.00
JD	J.D. Drew	4.00
AD	Adam Dunn	6.00
RF	Rafael Furcal	4.00
JG	Jason Giambi	6.00
BG	Brian Giles	4.00
MG	Marcus Giles	4.00
TG	Troy Glaus	4.00
GR	Khalil Greene	6.00
KG1	Ken Griffey Jr.	20.00
KG2	Ken Griffey Jr.	20.00
KG3	Ken Griffey Jr.	20.00
VG	Vladimir Guerrero	8.00
HA	Travis Hafner	4.00
TH	Todd Helton	6.00
AH	Aubrey Huff	4.00
HU	Torii Hunter	4.00
DJ	Derek Jeter	20.00
RJ	Randy Johnson	8.00
JO	Andruw Jones	6.00
CJ	Chipper Jones	8.00
JK	Jeff Kent	4.00
DL	Derrek Lee	8.00
ML	Mark Loretta	4.00
GM	Greg Maddux	15.00
PM	Pedro Martinez	8.00
VM	Victor Martinez	4.00
JM	Joe Mauer	6.00
ME	Melvin Mora	4.00
MO	Justin Morneau	4.00
BM	Bill Mueller	4.00
MM	Mark Mulder	4.00
DO	David Ortiz	8.00
RO	Roy Oswalt	4.00
PA	Corey Patterson	4.00
JP	Jake Peavy	4.00
WM	Wily Mo Pena	4.00
PI	Mike Piazza	8.00
SP	Scott Podsednik	4.00
MP	Mark Prior	6.00
AP	Albert Pujols	20.00
AR	Aramis Ramirez	8.00
MR	Manny Ramirez	8.00
RE	Jose Reyes	6.00
BR	Brian Roberts	4.00
IR	Ivan Rodriguez	6.00
SR	Scott Rolen	6.00
JR	Jimmy Rollins	4.00
CS	Curt Schilling	8.00
GS	Gary Sheffield	6.00
SM	John Smoltz	6.00
AS	Alfonso Soriano	8.00
SS	Sammy Sosa	8.00
MT	Mark Teixeira	6.00
TE	Miguel Tejada	6.00
FT	Frank Thomas	6.00
JT	Jim Thome	6.00
JV	Jason Varitek	8.00
VI	Jose Vidro	4.00
BW	Bernie Williams	6.00
WI	Dontrelle Willis	6.00
KW	Kerry Wood	4.00
DW	David Wright	20.00
MY	Michael Young	4.00
CZ	Carlos Zambrano	4.00

Generations Present Materials Silver

NM/M
Common Player: 4.00
Production 99 Sets
Gold: 1-1.5X
Production 25 Sets

BA	Bobby Abreu	4.00
GA	Garret Anderson	4.00
JE	Jeff Bagwell	6.00
JB	Jason Bay	4.00
CB	Carlos Beltran	4.00
AB	Adrian Beltre	4.00
LB	Lance Berkman	4.00
BI	Craig Biggio	6.00
HB	Hank Blalock	4.00
BO	Jeremy Bonderman	4.00
PB	Pat Burrell	4.00
AJ	A.J. Burnett	4.00
MC	Miguel Cabrera	8.00
SC	Sean Casey	4.00
EC	Eric Chavez	4.00
RC	Roger Clemens	12.00
CC	Carl Crawford	4.00
BC	Bobby Crosby	4.00
DA	Johnny Damon	8.00
CD	Carlos Delgado	4.00
JD	J.D. Drew	4.00
AD	Adam Dunn	6.00
RF	Rafael Furcal	4.00
JG	Jason Giambi	6.00
BG	Brian Giles	4.00
MG	Marcus Giles	4.00
TG	Troy Glaus	4.00
GR	Khalil Greene	4.00
ZG	Zack Greinke	4.00
KG1	Ken Griffey Jr.	20.00
KG2	Ken Griffey Jr.	20.00
KG3	Ken Griffey Jr.	20.00
VG	Vladimir Guerrero	8.00
HA	Travis Hafner	4.00
RH	Rich Harden	4.00
TH	Todd Helton	6.00
AH	Aubrey Huff	4.00
HU	Torii Hunter	4.00
DJ	Derek Jeter	20.00
RJ	Randy Johnson	8.00
JO	Andruw Jones	6.00
CJ	Chipper Jones	8.00
SK	Scott Kazmir	4.00
JK	Jeff Kent	4.00
DL	Derrek Lee	8.00
BL	Brad Lidge	4.00
ML	Mark Loretta	4.00
GM	Greg Maddux	15.00
PM	Pedro Martinez	8.00
VM	Victor Martinez	4.00
JM	Joe Mauer	6.00
ME	Melvin Mora	4.00
MO	Justin Morneau	4.00
BM	Bill Mueller	4.00
MM	Mark Mulder	4.00
DO	David Ortiz	8.00
RO	Roy Oswalt	4.00
PA	Corey Patterson	4.00
WM	Wily Mo Pena	4.00
PI	Mike Piazza	8.00
SP	Scott Podsednik	4.00
MP	Mark Prior	6.00
AR	Aramis Ramirez	8.00
MR	Manny Ramirez	8.00
RE	Jose Reyes	4.00
BR	Brian Roberts	4.00
IR	Ivan Rodriguez	4.00
SR	Scott Rolen	6.00
JR	Jimmy Rollins	4.00
JS	Johan Santana	6.00
CS	Curt Schilling	8.00
BS	Ben Sheets	4.00
GS	Gary Sheffield	6.00
SM	John Smoltz	6.00
SS	Sammy Sosa	8.00
MT	Mark Teixeira	6.00
TE	Miguel Tejada	6.00
FT	Frank Thomas	6.00
JT	Jim Thome	6.00
VI	Jose Vidro	6.00
BW	Bernie Williams	6.00
WI	Dontrelle Willis	4.00
KW	Kerry Wood	4.00
DW	David Wright	20.00
MY	Michael Young	4.00
CZ	Carlos Zambrano	4.00

Generations Present Signatures

NM/M
Common Player: 10.00
Production 25-199.
Bronze: 1-1.5X
Production 10 or 35.
No pricing for prod. of 10.
Gold: No Pricing
Production 5-15.

GA	Garret Anderson/25	20.00
JB	Jason Bay/199	15.00
BI	Craig Biggio/25	35.00
BO	Jeremy Bonderman/199	15.00
MC	Miguel Cabrera/25	40.00
SC	Sean Casey/50	15.00
CC	Carl Crawford/99	15.00
BC	Bobby Crosby/99	15.00
AD	Adam Dunn/95	25.00
RF	Rafael Furcal/99	15.00
BG	Brian Giles/99	12.00
MG	Marcus Giles/199	10.00
GR	Khalil Greene/135	25.00
ZG	Zack Greinke/199	15.00
KG1	Ken Griffey Jr./199	75.00
KG2	Ken Griffey Jr./199	75.00
KG3	Ken Griffey Jr./199	75.00
HA	Travis Hafner/99	15.00
RH	Rich Harden/199	15.00
AH	Aubrey Huff/199	15.00
HU	Torii Hunter/25	25.00
DJ	Derek Jeter/99	150.00
DL	Derrek Lee/25	40.00
BL	Brad Lidge/99	25.00
ML	Mark Loretta/99	15.00
VM	Victor Martinez/99	15.00
JM	Joe Mauer/25	25.00
ME	Melvin Mora/199	10.00
MO	Justin Morneau/99	20.00
MM	Mark Mulder/99	15.00
DO	David Ortiz/25	50.00
RO	Roy Oswalt/25	30.00
JP	Jake Peavy/99	15.00
WM	Wily Mo Pena/199	15.00
SP	Scott Podsednik/99	20.00
MP	Mark Prior/25	40.00
AR	Aramis Ramirez/99	15.00
BR	Brian Roberts/99	15.00
BS	Ben Sheets/99	15.00
GS	Gary Sheffield/25	35.00
SM	John Smoltz/25	50.00
MT	Mark Teixeira/25	50.00
TE	Miguel Tejada/25	40.00
FT	Frank Thomas/25	50.00
VI	Jose Vidro/99	10.00
WI	Dontrelle Willis/25	50.00
DW	David Wright/135	50.00
MY	Michael Young/199	15.00

Signature Dual Material

NM/M
Common Player: 20.00
Production 75 Sets

HB	Harold Baines	25.00
AB	Adrian Beltre	25.00
BI	Craig Biggio	40.00
WB	Wade Boggs	50.00
MC	Miguel Cabrera	50.00
SC	Sean Casey	25.00
OC	Orlando Cepeda	40.00
CL	Jack Clark	20.00
WC	Will Clark	50.00
CC	Carl Crawford	20.00
BC	Bobby Crosby	30.00
ED	Eric Davis	35.00
AD	Andre Dawson	30.00
DU	Adam Dunn	40.00
LD	Lenny Dykstra	20.00
BG	Brian Giles	20.00
GI	Marcus Giles	20.00
KG	Ken Griffey Jr.	150.00
TG	Tony Gwynn	60.00
TH	Travis Hafner	30.00
FH	Frank Howard	30.00
RH	Ryan Howard	75.00
AH	Aubrey Huff	20.00
HU	Torii Hunter	30.00
DJ	Derek Jeter	300.00
WJ	Wally Joyner	40.00
BL	Barry Larkin	20.00
MA	Bill Madlock	25.00
VM	Victor Martinez	25.00
DM	Don Mattingly	90.00
BM	Bobby Murcer	35.00
GN	Graig Nettles	30.00
TO	Tony Oliva	25.00
DO	David Ortiz	75.00

CP	Corey Patterson	20.00
WP	Wily Mo Pena	25.00
TP	Tony Perez	40.00
SP	Scott Podsednik	50.00
AP	Albert Pujols	250.00
TR	Tim Raines	30.00
RA	Aramis Ramirez	35.00
RE	Jose Reyes	40.00
RI	Jim Rice	35.00
CR	Cal Ripken Jr.	150.00
BR	Brooks Robinson	50.00
RS	Ryne Sandberg	80.00
MS	Mike Schmidt	75.00
MT	Mark Teixeira	60.00
MI	Miguel Tejada	50.00
BU	B.J. Upton	25.00
AV	Andy Van Slyke	30.00
JV	Jose Vidro	20.00
JW	Jayson Werth	20.00
DW	David Wright	80.00
KY	Kevin Youkilis	20.00

2005 Upper Deck Update

NM/M

Complete Update Set (186):
Common Player (1-100): .15
Common Rookie (101-177): 3.00
Production 599
Common Rk Auto.
(178-186): 10.00
Production 75
Pack (5): 5.00
Box (24): 110.00

1	A.J. Burnett	.15
2	Adam Dunn	.50
3	Adrian Beltre	.25
4	Albert Pujols	2.00
5	Alex Rodriguez	2.00
6	Alfonso Soriano	.50
7	Andruw Jones	.50
8	Aramis Ramirez	.25
9	Barry Zito	.25
10	Bartolo Colon	.25
11	Ben Sheets	.25
12	Bobby Abreu	.25
13	Bobby Crosby	.25
14	Michael Cuddyer	.15
15	Brian Giles	.15
16	Brian Roberts	.15
17	Carl Crawford	.15
18	Carlos Beltran	.50
19	Carlos Delgado	.40
20	Carlos Lee	.15
21	Carlos Zambrano	.25
22	Chase Utley	.25
23	Chipper Jones	.75
24	Chris Carpenter	.25
25	Craig Biggio	.75
26	Curt Schilling	.75
27	David Ortiz	.75
28	David Wright	1.00
29	Derek Jeter	2.00
30	Derrek Lee	.50
31	Dontrelle Willis	.25
32	Eric Chavez	.25
33	Eric Gagne	.25
34	Francisco Rodriguez	.15
35	Gary Sheffield	.40
36	Greg Maddux	1.00
37	Hank Blalock	.25
38	Hideki Matsui	1.50
39	Ichiro Suzuki	1.50
40	Ivan Rodriguez	.50
41	J.D. Drew	.15
42	Jake Peavy	.25
43	Jason Bay	.25
44	Jason Schmidt	.15
45	Jeff Bagwell	.40
46	Jeff Kent	.25
47	Jeremy Bonderman	.25
48	Jim Edmonds	.40
49	Jim Thome	.50
50	Joe Mauer	.50
51	Johan Santana	.50
52	John Smoltz	.25
53	Johnny Damon	.75
54	Jose Reyes	.25
55	Jose Vidro	.15
56	Josh Beckett	.25
57	Justin Morneau	.15
58	Ken Griffey Jr.	1.50
59	Kenny Rogers	.15
60	Kerry Wood	.25
61	Khalil Greene	.25
62	Lance Berkman	.25
63	Livan Hernandez	.15
64	Luis Gonzalez	.15
65	Manny Ramirez	.75
66	Mark Buehrle	.25
67	Mark Mulder	.25
68	Mark Prior	.50
69	Mark Teixeira	.50
70	Michael Young	.25
71	Miguel Cabrera	.75
72	Miguel Tejada	.50
73	Mike Mussina	.40
74	Mike Piazza	.75
75	Moises Alou	.25
76	Morgan Ensberg	.25
77	Nomar Garciaparra	.50
78	Pat Burrell	.25
79	Paul Konerko	.75
80	Pedro Martinez	.75
81	Randy Johnson	.75
82	Rich Harden	.25
83	Richie Sexson	.25
84	Rickie Weeks	.25
85	Robinson Cano	.25
86	Roger Clemens	2.00
87	Roy Halladay	.25
88	Roy Oswalt	.25
89	Sammy Sosa	.25
90	Scott Kazmir	.15
91	Scott Rolen	.75
92	Shawn Green	.25
93	Tim Hudson	.25
94	Todd Helton	.50
95	Tom Glavine	.25
96	Torii Hunter	.25
.25	Travis Hafner	.15
.25	Troy Glaus	.15
99	Vernon Wells	.15
100	Vladimir Guerrero	.75
101	Adam Shabala RC	3.00
102	Ambiorix Burgos RC	3.00
103	Anibal Sanchez RC	10.00
104	Bill McCarthy RC	3.00
105	Brandon McCarthy RC	6.00
106	Brian Burres RC	3.00
107	Carlos Ruiz RC	4.00
108	Casey Rogowski RC	3.00
109	Chad Orvella RC	3.00
110	Chris Resop RC	5.00
111	Chris Roberson RC	3.00
112	Chris Seddon RC	3.00
113	Colter Bean RC	3.00
114	Dae-Sung Koo RC	3.00
115	David Gassner RC	3.00
116	Brian Anderson RC	5.00
117	D.J. Houlton RC	3.00
118	Derek Wathan RC	3.00
119	Devon Lowery RC	3.00
120	Enrique Gonzalez RC	3.00
121	Eude Brito RC	3.00
122	Francisco Butto RC	3.00
123	Franquelis Osoria RC	5.00
124	Garrett Jones RC	3.00
125	Geovany Soto RC	4.00
126	Hayden Penn RC	5.00
127	Ismael Ramirez RC	3.00
128	Jared Gothreaux RC	3.00
129	Jason Hammel RC	3.00
130	Jeff Miller RC	3.00
131	Joel Peralta RC	3.00
132	John Hattig Jr. RC	3.00
133	Jorge Campillo RC	3.00
134	Juan Morillo RC	3.00
135	Ryan Garko RC	6.00
136	Keiichi Yabu RC	6.00
137	Luis Hernandez RC	5.00
138	Luis Pena RC	3.00
139	Luis Rodriguez RC	3.00
140	Luke Scott RC	5.00
141	Marcos Carvajal RC	3.00
142	Mark Woodyard RC	3.00
143	Matt Smith RC	3.00
144	Matt Lindstrom RC	5.00
145	Miguel Negron RC	3.00
146	Mike Morse RC	5.00
147	Nate McLouth RC	3.00
148	Nelson Cruz RC	5.00
149	Nick Masset RC	3.00
150	Oscar Robles RC	3.00
151	Paulino Reynoso RC	3.00
152	Pedro Lopez RC	3.00
153	Peter Orr RC	3.00
154	Randy Messenger RC	3.00
155	Randy Williams RC	3.00
156	Raul Tablado RC	3.00
157	Ronny Paulino RC	4.00
158	Russel Rohlicek RC	3.00
159	Russell Martin RC	12.00
160	Scott Baker RC	5.00
161	Scott Munter RC	4.00
162	Sean Thompson RC	4.00
163	Sean Tracey RC	3.00
164	Shane Costa RC	5.00
165	Steve Schmoll RC	3.00
166	Tony Giarratano RC	3.00
167	Tony Pena RC	3.00
168	Travis Bowyer RC	3.00
169	Ubaldo Jimenez RC	3.00
170	Wladimir Balentien RC	8.00
171	Yorman Bazardo RC	3.00
172	Yuniesky Betancourt RC	5.00
173	Chris Denorfia RC	5.00
174	Dana Eveland RC	5.00
175	Jermaine Van Buren RC	3.00
176	Mark McLemore RC	3.00
177	Ryan Spilborghs RC	3.00
178	Ambiorix Concepcion RC	10.00
179	Jeff Niemann RC	25.00
180	Justin Verlander RC	80.00
181	Kendry Morales RC	30.00
182	Philip Humber RC	25.00
183	Prince Fielder	275.00
184	Stephen Drew RC	75.00
185	Tadahito Iguchi RC	80.00
186	Ryan Zimmerman RC	140.00

**Common Artifacts RC
(201-285):** 3.00
Production 799

201	Adam Shabala RC	3.00
202	Ambiorix Burgos RC	3.00
203	Ambiorix Concepcion RC	3.00
204	Anibal Sanchez RC	10.00
205	Bill McCarthy RC	3.00
206	Brandon McCarthy RC	5.00
207	Brian Burres RC	3.00
208	Carlos Ruiz RC	4.00
209	Casey Rogowski RC	3.00
210	Chad Orvella RC	3.00
211	Chris Resop RC	3.00
212	Chris Roberson RC	3.00
213	Chris Seddon RC	3.00
214	Colter Bean RC	3.00
215	Dae-Sung Koo RC	3.00
216	David Gassner RC	3.00
217	Brian Anderson RC	4.00
218	D.J. Houlton RC	3.00
219	Derek Wathan RC	3.00
220	Devon Lowery RC	3.00
221	Enrique Gonzalez RC	3.00
222	Eude Brito RC	3.00
223	Francisco Butto RC	3.00
224	Franquelis Osoria RC	5.00
225	Garrett Jones RC	3.00
226	Geovany Soto RC	4.00
227	Hayden Penn RC	3.00
228	Ismael Ramirez RC	3.00
229	Jared Gothreaux RC	3.00
230	Jason Hammel RC	3.00
231	Jeff Miller RC	3.00
232	Jeff Niemann RC	5.00
233	Joel Peralta RC	3.00
234	John Hattig Jr. RC	3.00
235	Jorge Campillo RC	3.00
236	Juan Morillo RC	3.00
237	Justin Verlander RC	15.00
238	Ryan Garko RC	5.00
239	Keiichi Yabu RC	3.00
240	Kendry Morales RC	5.00
241	Luis Hernandez RC	3.00
242	Luis Pena RC	3.00
243	Luis Rodriguez RC	3.00
244	Luke Scott RC	5.00
245	Marcos Carvajal RC	3.00
246	Mark Woodyard RC	3.00
247	Matt Smith RC	3.00
248	Matt Lindstrom RC	3.00
249	Miguel Negron RC	3.00
250	Mike Morse RC	3.00
251	Nate McLouth RC	4.00
252	Nelson Cruz RC	5.00
253	Nick Masset RC	3.00
254	Oscar Robles RC	3.00
255	Paulino Reynoso RC	3.00
256	Pedro Lopez RC	3.00
257	Peter Orr RC	3.00
258	Philip Humber RC	5.00
259	Prince Fielder	20.00
260	Randy Messenger RC	3.00
261	Randy Williams RC	3.00
262	Raul Tablado RC	3.00
263	Ronny Paulino RC	4.00
264	Russel Rohlicek RC	3.00
265	Russell Martin RC	8.00
266	Scott Baker RC	5.00
267	Scott Munter RC	3.00
268	Sean Thompson RC	3.00
269	Sean Tracey RC	3.00
270	Shane Costa RC	3.00
271	Stephen Drew RC	10.00
272	Steve Schmoll RC	5.00
273	Tadahito Iguchi RC	6.00
274	Tony Giarratano RC	4.00
275	Tony Pena RC	5.00
276	Travis Bowyer RC	5.00
277	Ubaldo Jimenez RC	5.00
278	Wladimir Balentien RC	5.00
279	Yorman Bazardo RC	4.00
280	Yuniesky Betancourt RC	5.00
281	Ryan Zimmerman RC	15.00
282	Chris Denorfia RC	5.00
283	Dana Eveland RC	5.00
284	Jermaine Van Buren RC	3.00
285	Mark McLemore RC	3.00

**Common Reflections RC
(201-286):** 1.00

201	Adam Shabala RC	1.00
202	Ambiorix Burgos RC	1.00
203	Ambiorix Concepcion RC	1.00
204	Anibal Sanchez RC	3.00
205	Bill McCarthy RC	1.00
206	Brandon McCarthy RC	2.00
207	Brian Burres RC	1.00
208	Carlos Ruiz RC	1.00
209	Casey Rogowski RC	1.00
210	Chad Orvella RC	1.00
211	Chris Resop RC	1.50
212	Chris Roberson RC	1.00
213	Chris Seddon RC	1.00
214	Colter Bean RC	1.00
215	Dae-Sung Koo RC	1.00
216	Yuniesky Betancourt RC	2.00
217	David Gassner RC	1.00
218	Brian Anderson RC	1.50
219	Dennis Houlton RC	1.00
220	Derek Wathan RC	1.00
221	Devon Lowery RC	1.00
222	Enrique Gonzalez RC	1.00
223	Ryan Zimmerman RC	8.00
224	Eude Brito RC	1.00
225	Francisco Butto RC	1.00
226	Franquelis Osoria RC	1.00
227	Garrett Jones RC	1.00
228	Geovany Soto RC	1.50
229	Hayden Penn RC	1.50
230	Ismael Ramirez RC	1.50
231	Jared Gothreaux RC	1.00
232	Jason Hammel RC	1.00
233	Chris Denorfia RC	1.50
234	Jeff Miller RC	1.00
235	Jeff Niemann RC	2.00
236	Dana Eveland RC	2.00
237	Joel Peralta RC	1.00
238	John Hattig Jr. RC	1.00
239	Jorge Campillo RC	1.00
240	Juan Morillo RC	1.00
241	Justin Verlander RC	5.00
242	Ryan Garko RC	2.50
243	Keiichi Yabu RC	1.00
244	Kendry Morales RC	2.00
245	Luis Hernandez RC	1.00
246	Jermaine Van Buren RC	1.00
247	Luis Pena RC	1.00
248	Luis Rodriguez RC	1.00
249	Luke Scott RC	1.50
250	Marcos Carvajal RC	1.00
251	Mark Woodyard RC	1.00
252	Matt Smith RC	1.00
253	Matt Lindstrom RC	1.00
254	Miguel Negron RC	1.00
255	Mike Morse RC	1.00
256	Nate McLouth RC	2.00
257	Nelson Cruz RC	1.00
258	Nick Masset RC	1.00
259	Mark McLemore RC	1.00
260	Oscar Robles RC	1.00
261	Paulino Reynoso RC	1.00
262	Pedro Lopez RC	1.00
263	Peter Orr RC	1.00
264	Philip Humber RC	2.00
265	Prince Fielder	10.00
266	Randy Messenger RC	1.00
267	Randy Williams RC	1.00
268	Raul Tablado RC	1.00
269	Ronny Paulino RC	1.50
270	Russel Rohlicek RC	1.00
271	Russell Martin RC	2.00
272	Scott Baker RC	1.00
273	Scott Munter RC	1.00
274	Sean Thompson RC	1.00
275	Sean Tracey RC	1.00
276	Shane Costa RC	1.00
277	Stephen Drew RC	5.00
278	Steve Schmoll RC	1.00
279	Ryan Spilborghs RC	1.50
280	Tadahito Iguchi RC	2.00
281	Tony Giarratano RC	1.00
282	Tony Pena RC	1.00
283	Travis Bowyer RC	1.50
284	Ubaldo Jimenez RC	1.00
285	Wladimir Balentien RC	2.50
286	Yorman Bazardo RC	1.00

**Common Origins
RC (201-286):** .75

201	Adam Shabala RC	.75
202	Ambiorix Burgos RC	.75
203	Ambiorix Concepcion RC	.75
204	Anibal Sanchez RC	2.00
205	Bill McCarthy RC	.75
206	Brandon McCarthy RC	2.00
207	Brian Burres RC	.75

#	Player	Price
208	Carlos Ruiz RC	1.00
209	Casey Rogowski RC	1.00
210	Chad Orvella RC	.75
211	Chris Resop RC	1.00
212	Chris Roberson RC	1.00
213	Chris Seddon RC	.75
214	Colter Bean RC	1.00
215	Dae-Sung Koo RC	.75
216	Yuniesky Betancourt RC	1.50
217	David Gassner RC	.75
218	Brian Anderson RC	1.00
219	Dennis Houlton RC	.75
220	Derek Wathan RC	.75
221	Devon Lowery RC	.75
222	Enrique Gonzalez RC	.75
223	Ryan Zimmerman RC	5.00
224	Eude Brito RC	.75
225	Francisco Butto RC	1.00
226	Franquelis Osoria RC	1.00
227	Garrett Jones RC	1.00
228	Geovany Soto RC	1.00
229	Hayden Penn RC	1.00
230	Ismael Ramirez RC	1.00
231	Jared Gothreaux RC	.75
232	Jason Hammel RC	.75
233	Chris Denorfia RC	1.00
234	Jeff Miller RC	.75
235	Jeff Niemann RC	1.50
236	Dana Eveland RC	1.00
237	Joel Peralta RC	.75
238	John Hattig Jr. RC	1.00
239	Jorge Campillo RC	1.00
240	Juan Morillo RC	1.00
241	Justin Verlander RC	5.00
242	Ryan Garko RC	2.00
243	Keiichi Yabu RC	1.00
244	Kendry Morales RC	2.00
245	Luis Hernandez RC	.75
246	Jermaine Van Buren RC	.75
247	Luis Pena RC	.75
248	Luis Rodriguez RC	.75
249	Luke Scott RC	1.50
250	Marcos Carvajal RC	1.00
251	Mark Woodyard RC	1.00
252	Matt Smith RC	1.00
253	Matt Lindstrom RC	1.00
254	Miguel Negron RC	1.50
255	Mike Morse RC	1.50
256	Nate McLouth RC	1.00
257	Nelson Cruz RC	1.50
258	Nick Masset RC	.75
259	Mark McLemore RC	1.00
260	Oscar Robles RC	.75
261	Paulino Reynoso RC	.75
262	Pedro Lopez RC	1.00
263	Peter Orr RC	1.00
264	Philip Humber RC	1.50
265	Prince Fielder RC	8.00
266	Randy Messenger RC	.75
267	Randy Williams RC	1.00
268	Raul Tablado RC	.75
269	Ronny Paulino RC	1.50
270	Russel Rohlicek RC	.75
271	Russell Martin RC	1.50
272	Scott Baker RC	1.50
273	Ryan Spilborghs RC	1.00
274	Scott Munter RC	.75
275	Sean Thompson RC	1.00
276	Sean Tracey RC	1.00
277	Shane Costa RC	1.00
278	Stephen Drew RC	4.00
279	Steve Schmoll RC	1.00
280	Tadahito Iguchi RC	2.00
281	Tony Giarratano RC	.75
282	Tony Pena RC	.75
283	Travis Bowyer RC	1.00
284	Ubaldo Jimenez RC	.75
285	Wladimir Balentien RC	2.00
286	Yorman Bazardo RC	1.00

Common SP Authentic Auto. (101-186): 8.00
Production 185

#	Player	Price
101	Adam Shabala RC	10.00
102	Ambiorix Burgos RC	10.00
103	Ambiorix Concepcion RC	10.00
104	Anibal Sanchez RC	25.00
106	Brandon McCarthy RC	25.00
107	Brian Burres RC	10.00
108	Carlos Ruiz RC	15.00
109	Casey Rogowski RC	10.00
110	Chad Orvella RC	10.00
111	Chris Resop RC	12.00
112	Chris Roberson RC	10.00
113	Chris Seddon RC	10.00
114	Colter Bean RC	15.00
116	David Gassner RC	10.00
117	Brian Anderson	25.00
120	Devon Lowery RC	10.00
121	Enrique Gonzalez RC	10.00
122	Eude Brito RC	8.00
123	Francisco Butto RC	10.00
124	Franquelis Osoria RC	15.00
125	Garrett Jones RC	10.00
126	Geovany Soto RC	30.00
127	Hayden Penn RC	15.00
128	Ismael Ramirez RC	8.00
129	Jared Gothreaux RC	15.00
130	Jason Hammel RC	10.00
131	Jeff Miller RC	8.00
132	Jeff Niemann RC	40.00
133	Joel Peralta RC	10.00
134	John Hattig Jr. RC	15.00
135	Jorge Campillo RC	8.00
136	Juan Morillo RC	10.00
137	Justin Verlander RC	185.00
138	Ryan Garko RC	50.00
139	Keiichi Yabu RC	15.00
140	Kendry Morales RC	60.00
141	Luis Hernandez RC	10.00
143	Luis Rodriguez RC	10.00
144	Luke Scott RC	50.00
145	Marcos Carvajal RC	10.00
146	Mark Woodyard RC	10.00
147	Matt Smith RC	8.00
148	Matt Lindstrom RC	10.00
149	Miguel Negron RC	10.00
150	Mike Morse RC	20.00
151	Nate McLouth RC	15.00
152	Nelson Cruz RC	30.00
153	Nick Masset RC	8.00
155	Paulino Reynoso RC	10.00
156	Pedro Lopez RC	15.00
157	Peter Orr RC	10.00
158	Philip Humber RC	20.00
159	Prince Fielder RC	250.00
160	Randy Messenger RC	8.00
162	Raul Tablado RC	10.00
163	Ronny Paulino RC	10.00
164	Russel Rohlicek RC	10.00
165	Russell Martin RC	125.00
166	Scott Baker RC	20.00
167	Scott Munter RC	10.00
168	Sean Thompson RC	10.00
169	Sean Tracey RC	15.00
170	Shane Costa RC	10.00
171	Stephen Drew RC	80.00
172	Steve Schmoll RC	10.00
173	Tadahito Iguchi RC	75.00
174	Tony Giarratano RC	15.00
175	Tony Pena RC	8.00
176	Travis Bowyer RC	10.00
177	Ubaldo Jimenez RC	15.00
178	Wladimir Balentien RC	75.00
179	Yorman Bazardo RC	15.00
181	Ryan Zimmerman RC	180.00
182	Chris Denorfia RC	15.00
184	Jermaine Van Buren RC	10.00
185	Mark McLemore RC	10.00

Common SPx Auto. (101-179): 8.00
Production 185

#	Player	Price
101	Adam Shabala RC	10.00
102	Ambiorix Burgos RC	10.00
103	Ambiorix Concepcion RC	10.00
104	Anibal Sanchez RC	25.00
106	Brandon McCarthy RC	25.00
107	Brian Burres RC	10.00
108	Carlos Ruiz RC	15.00
109	Casey Rogowski RC	15.00
110	Chad Orvella RC	15.00
111	Chris Resop RC	15.00
112	Chris Roberson RC	10.00
113	Chris Seddon RC	10.00
114	Colter Bean RC	15.00
115	David Gassner RC	10.00
116	Brian Anderson RC	10.00
118	Devon Lowery RC	8.00
119	Enrique Gonzalez RC	10.00
120	Eude Brito RC	10.00
121	Francisco Butto RC	10.00
122	Franquelis Osoria RC	10.00
123	Garrett Jones RC	10.00
124	Geovany Soto RC	30.00
125	Hayden Penn RC	15.00
126	Ismael Ramirez RC	8.00
127	Jared Gothreaux RC	10.00
128	Jason Hammel RC	10.00
129	Jeff Miller RC	8.00
130	Jeff Niemann RC	30.00
131	Joel Peralta RC	10.00
132	Jorge Campillo RC	8.00
134	Juan Morillo RC	10.00
135	Justin Verlander RC	160.00
136	Ryan Garko RC	40.00
137	Kendry Morales RC	50.00
138	Luis Hernandez RC	10.00
140	Luis Rodriguez RC	10.00
141	Mark Woodyard RC	10.00
142	Matt Smith RC	8.00
143	Matt Lindstrom RC	10.00
144	Miguel Negron RC	15.00
145	Mike Morse RC	20.00
146	Nate McLouth RC	15.00
147	Nelson Cruz RC	25.00
148	Nick Masset RC	8.00
150	Paulino Reynoso RC	10.00
151	Pedro Lopez RC	15.00
152	Philip Humber RC	20.00
153	Prince Fielder RC	250.00
154	Randy Messenger RC	8.00
156	Raul Tablado RC	10.00
157	Ronny Paulino RC	15.00
158	Russel Rohlicek RC	10.00
159	Russell Martin RC	125.00
160	Scott Baker RC	20.00
161	Scott Munter RC	10.00
162	Sean Thompson RC	10.00
163	Sean Tracey RC	10.00
164	Shane Costa RC	10.00
165	Stephen Drew RC	75.00
166	Tony Giarratano RC	15.00
167	Tony Pena RC	8.00
168	Travis Bowyer RC	10.00
169	Ubaldo Jimenez RC	15.00
170	Wladimir Balentien RC	75.00
171	Yorman Bazardo RC	10.00
173	Ryan Zimmerman RC	120.00
174	Chris Denorfia RC	15.00
176	Jermaine Van Buren RC	10.00
177	Mark McLemore RC	8.00
179	Ryan Speier RC	10.00

Common Sweet Spot RC (91-174): .75

#	Player	Price
91	Adam Shabala RC	.75
92	Ambiorix Burgos RC	.75
93	Ambiorix Concepcion RC	1.00
94	Anibal Sanchez RC	2.00
95	Bill McCarthy RC	.75
96	Brandon McCarthy RC	2.00
97	Brian Burres RC	.75
98	Carlos Ruiz RC	1.00
99	Casey Rogowski RC	1.00
100	Chad Orvella RC	.75
101	Chris Resop RC	1.00
102	Chris Roberson RC	1.00
103	Chris Seddon RC	.75
104	Colter Bean RC	1.00
105	Dae-Sung Koo RC	.75
106	Ryan Zimmerman RC	6.00
107	David Gassner RC	.75
108	Brian Anderson	1.50
109	D.J. Houlton RC	1.00
110	Derek Wathan RC	.75
111	Devon Lowery RC	.75
112	Enrique Gonzalez RC	.75
113	Chris Denorfia RC	.75
114	Eude Brito RC	.75
115	Francisco Butto RC	1.00
116	Franquelis Osoria RC	1.00
117	Garrett Jones RC	1.00
118	Geovany Soto RC	1.00
119	Hayden Penn RC	1.00
120	Ismael Ramirez RC	.75
121	Jared Gothreaux RC	.75
122	Jason Hammel RC	.75
123	Dana Eveland RC	1.50
124	Jeff Miller RC	.75
125	Jermaine Van Buren RC	1.00
126	Joel Peralta RC	.75
127	John Hattig Jr. RC	.75
128	Jorge Campillo RC	.75
129	Juan Morillo RC	.75
130	Ryan Garko RC	2.00
131	Keiichi Yabu RC	1.00
132	Kendry Morales RC	2.00
133	Luis Hernandez RC	1.00
134	Mark McLemore RC	1.00
135	Luis Pena RC	.75
136	Luis Rodriguez RC	.75
137	Luke Scott RC	1.50
138	Marcos Carvajal RC	1.00
139	Mark Woodyard RC	.75
140	Matt Smith RC	.75
141	Matt Lindstrom RC	1.00
142	Miguel Negron RC	1.00
143	Mike Morse RC	1.00
144	Nate McLouth RC	1.00
145	Nelson Cruz RC	1.50
146	Nick Masset RC	.75
147	Ryan Spilborghs RC	1.00
148	Oscar Robles RC	.75
149	Paulino Reynoso RC	.75
150	Pedro Lopez RC	.75
151	Peter Orr RC	.75
152	Prince Fielder RC	6.00
153	Randy Messenger RC	.75
154	Randy Williams RC	1.00
155	Raul Tablado RC	.75
156	Ronny Paulino RC	1.50
157	Russel Rohlicek RC	.75
158	Russell Martin RC	2.50
159	Scott Baker RC	1.50
160	Scott Munter RC	.75
161	Sean Thompson RC	1.00
162	Sean Tracey RC	1.00
163	Shane Costa RC	1.00
164	Stephen Drew RC	4.00
165	Steve Schmoll RC	.75
166	Ryan Speier RC	.75
167	Tadahito Iguchi RC	2.00
168	Tony Giarratano RC	1.00
169	Tony Pena RC	.75
170	Travis Bowyer RC	.75
171	Ubaldo Jimenez RC	.75
172	Wladimir Balentien RC	1.50
173	Yorman Bazardo RC	.75
174	Yuniesky Betancourt RC	1.50

Common Ultimate Signature Ed.(111-193): 8.00
Production 125

#	Player	Price
111	Adam Shabala RC	10.00
112	Anibal Sanchez RC	25.00
114	Brandon McCarthy RC	25.00
115	Brian Burres RC	10.00
116	Carlos Ruiz RC	15.00
117	Casey Rogowski RC	10.00
118	Chad Orvella RC	10.00
119	Chris Resop RC	12.00
120	Chris Roberson RC	12.00
121	Chris Seddon RC	12.00
122	Colter Bean RC	15.00
124	David Gassner RC	10.00
125	Brian Anderson	15.00
128	Devon Lowery RC	15.00
129	Enrique Gonzalez RC	15.00
130	Eude Brito RC	8.00
131	Francisco Butto RC	10.00
132	Franquelis Osoria RC	10.00
133	Garrett Jones RC	10.00
134	Geovany Soto RC	30.00
135	Hayden Penn RC	15.00
136	Ismael Ramirez RC	8.00
137	Jared Gothreaux RC	10.00
138	Jason Hammel RC	10.00
139	Jeff Miller RC	10.00
140	Jeff Niemann RC	30.00
141	Joel Peralta RC	10.00
142	John Hattig Jr. RC	15.00
143	Jorge Campillo RC	10.00
144	Juan Morillo RC	10.00
145	Justin Verlander RC	125.00
146	Ryan Garko RC	40.00
147	Keiichi Yabu RC	15.00
148	Kendry Morales RC	20.00
149	Luis Hernandez RC	10.00
151	Luis Rodriguez RC	10.00
152	Luke Scott RC	30.00
153	Marcos Carvajal RC	10.00
154	Mark Woodyard RC	10.00
155	Matt Smith RC	10.00
156	Matt Lindstrom RC	10.00
157	Miguel Negron RC	15.00
158	Mike Morse RC	15.00
159	Nate McLouth RC	15.00
160	Nelson Cruz RC	20.00
161	Nick Masset RC	8.00
162	Mark McLemore RC	10.00
163	Paulino Reynoso RC	10.00
165	Pedro Lopez RC	10.00
166	Peter Orr RC	10.00
167	Philip Humber RC	20.00
168	Prince Fielder RC	200.00
169	Randy Messenger RC	10.00
171	Raul Tablado RC	10.00
172	Ronny Paulino RC	15.00
173	Russel Rohlicek RC	8.00
174	Russell Martin RC	75.00
175	Scott Baker RC	20.00
176	Scott Munter RC	10.00
177	Sean Thompson RC	10.00
178	Sean Tracey RC	10.00
179	Shane Costa RC	10.00
180	Stephen Drew RC	60.00
181	Steve Schmoll RC	10.00
182	Tadahito Iguchi RC	50.00
183	Tony Giarratano RC	10.00
184	Tony Pena RC	10.00
185	Travis Bowyer RC	10.00
186	Ubaldo Jimenez RC	15.00
187	Wladimir Balentien RC	50.00
188	Yorman Bazardo RC	10.00
190	Ryan Zimmerman RC	100.00
191	Chris Denorfia RC	10.00
192	Ryan Speier RC	10.00
193	Jermaine Van Buren RC	10.00

Gold

Gold (101-177): 1-1.5X

Production 150
Gold (178-186): No Pricing
Production 10 Sets

Silver
Silver (101-177): 1X
Production 450
Silver (178-186): No Pricing
Production 25 Sets

Platinum
Platinum (101-177): No Pricing
Production 25
Platinum (178-186): No Pricing
Production One Set

Artifacts Blue
Blue (201-285): 1-1.5X
Production 100

Artifacts Gold
Gold (201-285): No Pricing
Production 25 Sets

Artifacts Red
Red (201-285): 1-2X
Production 50

Artifacts Platinum
No Pricing
Production One Set

Reflections Blue
Blue (201-286): 2-4X
Production 75 Sets

Reflections Emerald
Emerald (201-286): 3-6X
Production 25 Sets

Reflections Purple
Purple (201-286): 1.5-3X
Production 99 Sets

Reflections Platinum
No Pricing
Production One Set

Reflections Red
Red (201-286): 1.5-3X
Production 99 Sets

Reflections Turquoise
Turquoise (201-286): 2-4X
Production 50 Sets

Origins Blue
Blue (201-286): 2-4X
Production 50 Sets

Origins Gold
Gold (201-286): No Pricing
Production 20 Sets

Origins Black
No Pricing
Production One Set

Origins Red
Red (201-286): 2-3X
Production 99 Sets

Origins Old Judge
Old Judge (201-286): 1X
Inserted 1:2
Blue: 2-3X
Production 50 Sets
Red: 1-2X
Production 99 Sets
Gold: No Pricing
Production 20 Sets
Black: No Pricing
Production One Set

SP Authentic Gold
Gold (101-186): No Pricing
Production 10

SPx Silver
Silver (101-179): No Pricing
Production 10

Sweet Spot Gold
Gold (91-174): 1.5-2X
Production 399

Sweet Spot Platinum
Platinum (91-174): 2-3X
Production 99

Sweet Spot Plutonium
No Pricing
Production One Set

Ultimate Signature Edition Platinum

No Pricing
Production One Set

Quad Signatures
No Pricing
Production 5 Sets

Draft Generations Triple Signatures
No Pricing
Production 10 Sets

Link to Future Dual Autographs

		NM/M
Common Duo:		15.00
Production 35 Sets		
BR	Wladimir Balentien, Jeremy Reed	20.00
BW	Dontrelle Willis, Yorman Bazardo	40.00
CD	David DeJesus, Shane Costa	15.00
DD	J.D. Drew, Stephen Drew	125.00
DJ	Stephen Drew, Derek Jeter	275.00
FO	Prince Fielder, Lyle Overbay	75.00
FT	Prince Fielder, Mark Teixeira	100.00
FW	Prince Fielder, Rickie Weeks	100.00
GO	Roy Oswalt, Jared Gothreaux	25.00
HF	Luis Hernandez, Rafael Furcal	20.00
HG	Tom Glavine, Philip Humber	50.00
MB	Jason Bay, Nate McLouth	30.00
MK	Casey Kotchman, Kendry Morales	40.00
NK	Scott Kazmir, Jeff Niemann	40.00
NW	Vernon Wells, Miguel Negron	25.00
OB	Yhency Brazoban, Franquelis Osoria	20.00
OG	Peter Orr, Marcus Giles	25.00
PV	Javier Vazquez, Tony Pena	15.00
RH	Roy Halladay, Ismael Ramirez	30.00
SK	Chris Seddon, Scott Kazmir	30.00
SL	Jason Lane, Luke Scott	40.00
VB	Justin Verlander, Jeremy Bonderman	100.00
VC	Roger Clemens, Justin Verlander	175.00
ZC	Ryan Zimmerman, Chad Cordero	100.00

Link to the Past Dual Autographs

		NM/M
Common Duo:		20.00
Production 25 Sets		
BC	Steve Carlton, Eude Brito	30.00
BM	Juan Marichal, Brian Burres	30.00
CS	Darryl Strawberry, Ambiorix Concepcion	25.00

GT	Alan Trammell, Tony Giarratano	30.00
HG	Dwight Gooden, Philip Humber	40.00
HS	Philip Humber, Tom Seaver	50.00
IA	Luis Aparicio, Tadahito Iguchi	125.00
IC	Tadahito Iguchi, Rod Carew	125.00
JH	Kent Hrbek, Garrett Jones	40.00
JJ	Jack Morris, Justin Verlander	75.00
MC	Rod Carew, Kendry Morales	40.00
MJ	Kendry Morales, Wally Joyner	40.00
MV	Andy Van Slyke, Nate McLouth	40.00
NB	Miguel Negron, George Bell	40.00
NR	Nolan Ryan, Jeff Niemann	150.00
PP	Jim Palmer, Hayden Penn	40.00
RD	Lenny Dykstra, Chris Roberson	30.00
TP	Gaylord Perry, Sean Thompson	20.00
VM	Justin Verlander, Denny McLain	75.00

2005 UD Hall of Fame

	NM/M
Complete Set (100):	
Common Player:	3.00
Production 550 Sets	
Tin (4):	125.00
1 Al Kaline	4.00
2 Al Lopez	3.00
3 Bill Mazeroski	3.00
4 Billy Williams	3.00
5 Bob Feller	4.00
6 Bob Gibson	4.00
7 Bob Lemon	3.00
8 Bobby Doerr	3.00
9 Brooks Robinson	5.00
10 Buck Leonard	3.00
11 Carl Yastrzemski	5.00
12 Carlton Fisk	4.00
13 Casey Stengel	4.00
14 Jim "Catfish" Hunter	3.00
15 Dave Winfield	4.00
16 Dennis Eckersley	3.00
17 Dizzy Dean	4.00
18 Don Drysdale	3.00
19 Don Sutton	3.00
20 Duke Snider	4.00
21 Early Wynn	3.00
22 Eddie Mathews	5.00
23 Eddie Murray	4.00
24 Enos Slaughter	3.00
25 Ernie Banks	5.00
26 Fergie Jenkins	3.00
27 Frank Robinson	4.00
28 Gary Carter	3.00
29 Gaylord Perry	3.00
30 George Brett	8.00
31 George Kell	3.00
32 George Sisler	3.00
33 Hal Newhouser	3.00
34 Harmon Killebrew	5.00
35 Hoyt Wilhelm	3.00
36 Jackie Robinson	5.00
37 Jim Bunning	3.00
38 Jim Palmer	3.00
39 Jimmie Foxx	5.00
40 Joe Morgan	3.00
41 Johnny Bench	5.00
42 Johnny Mize	3.00
43 Juan Marichal	3.00

44	Kirby Puckett	4.00
45	Larry Doby	3.00
46	Lefty Grove	3.00
47	Lou Boudreau	3.00
48	Lou Brock	4.00
49	Luis Aparicio	3.00
50	Mel Ott	4.00
51	Mickey Cochrane	4.00
52	Monte Irvin	3.00
53	Orlando Cepeda	3.00
54	Ozzie Smith	5.00
55	Paul Molitor	4.00
56	Pee Wee Reese	3.00
57	Phil Niekro	3.00
58	Phil Rizzuto	3.00
59	Pie Traynor	3.00
60	Ralph Kiner	3.00
61	Red Schoendienst	3.00
62	Richie Ashburn	3.00
63	Rick Ferrell	3.00
64	Robin Roberts	3.00
65	Robin Yount	5.00
66	Rod Carew	3.00
67	Rogers Hornsby	4.00
68	Rollie Fingers	3.00
69	Roy Campanella	4.00
70	Steve Carlton	4.00
71	Tony Perez	3.00
72	Warren Spahn	5.00
73	Whitey Ford	4.00
74	Willie McCovey	4.00
75	Willie Stargell	4.00
76	Yogi Berra	5.00
77	Babe Ruth	8.00
78	Honus Wagner	4.00
79	Lou Gehrig	4.00
80	Mickey Mantle	15.00
81	Ty Cobb	6.00
82	Ryne Sandberg	5.00
83	Satchel Paige	5.00
84	Wade Boggs	4.00
85	Reggie Jackson	5.00
86	Babe Ruth	8.00
87	Christy Mathewson	4.00
88	Cy Young	4.00
89	Honus Wagner	5.00
90	Joe DiMaggio	6.00
91	Lou Gehrig	6.00
92	Mickey Mantle	15.00
93	Mike Schmidt	6.00
94	Nolan Ryan	8.00
95	Satchel Paige	5.00
96	Stan Musial	5.00
97	Ted Williams	6.00
98	Tom Seaver	4.00
99	Ty Cobb	6.00
100	Walter Johnson	4.00

Gold
Gold (1-100): 1.5-2X
Production 25 Sets

Green
Green (1-100): 1X
Production 200 Sets

Rainbow
No Pricing
Production One Set

Silver
Silver (1-100): 1-1.5X
Production 99 Sets

Class of Cooperstown

	NM/M
Production 50 Sets	
Gold:	No Pricing
Production 5 Sets	
Silver:	No Pricing
Production 15 Sets	
Rainbow:	No Pricing
Production One Set	
LA1 Luis Aparicio	4.00
LA2 Luis Aparicio	4.00
EB1 Ernie Banks	6.00
EB2 Ernie Banks	6.00
BE1 Johnny Bench	6.00
BE2 Johnny Bench	6.00
YB1 Yogi Berra	5.00
YB2 Yogi Berra	5.00
GB1 George Brett	10.00
GB2 George Brett	10.00
GB3 George Brett	10.00

LB1	Lou Brock	4.00
JB1	Jim Bunning	4.00
JB2	Jim Bunning	4.00
RC1	Rod Carew	4.00
RC2	Rod Carew	4.00
SC1	Steve Carlton	4.00
SC2	Steve Carlton	4.00
SC3	Steve Carlton	4.00
SC4	Steve Carlton	4.00
GC1	Gary Carter	4.00
GC2	Gary Carter	4.00
OC1	Orlando Cepeda	4.00
BD1	Bobby Doerr	4.00
BD2	Bobby Doerr	4.00
DE1	Dennis Eckersley	4.00
BF1	Bob Feller	4.00
BF2	Bob Feller	4.00
RF1	Rollie Fingers	4.00
CF1	Carlton Fisk	4.00
CF2	Carlton Fisk	4.00
WF1	Whitey Ford	5.00
WF2	Whitey Ford	5.00
BG1	Bob Gibson	5.00
BG2	Bob Gibson	5.00
MI1	Monte Irvin	4.00
MI2	Monte Irvin	4.00
RJ1	Reggie Jackson	5.00
RJ2	Reggie Jackson	5.00
RJ3	Reggie Jackson	5.00
FJ1	Fergie Jenkins	4.00
AK1	Al Kaline	6.00
AK2	Al Kaline	6.00
AK3	Al Kaline	6.00
GK1	George Kell	6.00
HK1	Harmon Killebrew	6.00
HK2	Harmon Killebrew	6.00
HK3	Harmon Killebrew	6.00
HK4	Harmon Killebrew	6.00
RK1	Ralph Kiner	4.00
RK2	Ralph Kiner	4.00
MA1	Juan Marichal	4.00
MA2	Juan Marichal	4.00
BM1	Bill Mazeroski	4.00
WM1	Willie McCovey	5.00
WM2	Willie McCovey	5.00
PM1	Paul Molitor	5.00
PM2	Paul Molitor	5.00
PM3	Paul Molitor	5.00
JM1	Joe Morgan	4.00
JM2	Joe Morgan	4.00
EM1	Eddie Murray	6.00
SM1	Stan Musial	6.00
SM2	Stan Musial	6.00
PN1	Phil Niekro	4.00
JP1	Jim Palmer	4.00
JP2	Jim Palmer	4.00
TP1	Tony Perez	4.00
GP1	Gaylord Perry	4.00
GP2	Gaylord Perry	4.00
KP1	Kirby Puckett	5.00
RR1	Robin Roberts	4.00
BR1	Brooks Robinson	5.00
BR2	Brooks Robinson	5.00
BR3	Brooks Robinson	5.00
FR1	Frank Robinson	5.00
FR2	Frank Robinson	5.00
NR1	Nolan Ryan	10.00
NR2	Nolan Ryan	10.00
NR3	Nolan Ryan	10.00
NR4	Nolan Ryan	10.00
MS1	Mike Schmidt	6.00
MS2	Mike Schmidt	6.00
MS3	Mike Schmidt	6.00
RS1	Red Schoendienst	4.00
TS1	Tom Seaver	5.00
TS2	Tom Seaver	5.00
OS1	Ozzie Smith	6.00
OS2	Ozzie Smith	6.00
SN1	Duke Snider	5.00
DS1	Don Sutton	4.00
BW1	Billy Williams	4.00
BW2	Billy Williams	4.00
BW3	Billy Williams	4.00
DW1	Dave Winfield	4.00
DW2	Dave Winfield	4.00
CY1	Carl Yastrzemski	6.00
CY2	Carl Yastrzemski	6.00
RY1	Robin Yount	6.00
RY2	Robin Yount	6.00

Class of Cooperstown Autograph

		NM/M
Production 25 Sets		
Gold:		No Pricing
Production 5 Sets		
Silver:		No Pricing
Production 15 Sets		
Rainbow:		No Pricing
Material Gold:		No Pricing
Production 5 Sets		
Material Silver:		No Pricing
Production 15 Sets		
Patch Gold:		No Pricing
Production 5 Sets		
Patch Silver:		No Pricing
Production 10 Sets		
LA1	Luis Aparicio	20.00
LA2	Luis Aparicio	20.00
EB1	Ernie Banks	50.00
EB2	Ernie Banks	50.00
BE1	Johnny Bench	40.00
BE2	Johnny Bench	40.00
YB1	Yogi Berra	60.00
YB2	Yogi Berra	60.00
GB1	George Brett	60.00
GB2	George Brett	60.00
GB3	George Brett	60.00
LB1	Lou Brock	35.00
JB1	Jim Bunning	25.00
JB2	Jim Bunning	25.00
RC1	Rod Carew	30.00
RC2	Rod Carew	30.00
SC1	Steve Carlton	20.00
SC2	Steve Carlton	20.00
SC3	Steve Carlton	20.00
SC4	Steve Carlton	20.00
GC1	Gary Carter	25.00
GC2	Gary Carter	25.00
OC1	Orlando Cepeda	25.00
BD1	Bobby Doerr	15.00
BD2	Bobby Doerr	15.00
DE1	Dennis Eckersley	20.00
BF1	Bob Feller	30.00
BF2	Bob Feller	30.00
RF1	Rollie Fingers	30.00
CF1	Carlton Fisk	30.00
CF2	Carlton Fisk	30.00
WF1	Whitey Ford	50.00
WF2	Whitey Ford	50.00
BG1	Bob Gibson	35.00
BG2	Bob Gibson	35.00
MI1	Monte Irvin	25.00
MI2	Monte Irvin	25.00
RJ1	Reggie Jackson	40.00
RJ2	Reggie Jackson	40.00
RJ3	Reggie Jackson	40.00
AK1	Al Kaline	40.00
AK2	Al Kaline	40.00
AK3	Al Kaline	40.00
GK1	George Kell	20.00
HK1	Harmon Killebrew	40.00
HK2	Harmon Killebrew	40.00
HK3	Harmon Killebrew	40.00
HK4	Harmon Killebrew	40.00
RK1	Ralph Kiner	40.00
RK2	Ralph Kiner	40.00
MA1	Juan Marichal	25.00
MA2	Juan Marichal	25.00
BM1	Bill Mazeroski	40.00
WM1	Willie McCovey	40.00
WM2	Willie McCovey	40.00
PM1	Paul Molitor	30.00
PM2	Paul Molitor	30.00
PM3	Paul Molitor	30.00
JM1	Joe Morgan	25.00
JM2	Joe Morgan	25.00
EM1	Eddie Murray	50.00
SM1	Stan Musial	60.00
SM2	Stan Musial	60.00
PN1	Phil Niekro	20.00
JP1	Jim Palmer	20.00
JP2	Jim Palmer	20.00
TP1	Tony Perez	20.00
GP1	Gaylord Perry	20.00
GP2	Gaylord Perry	20.00
KP1	Kirby Puckett	40.00
RR1	Robin Roberts	25.00
BR1	Brooks Robinson	30.00
BR2	Brooks Robinson	30.00
BR3	Brooks Robinson	30.00
FR1	Frank Robinson	20.00
FR2	Frank Robinson	20.00
NR1	Nolan Ryan	90.00
NR2	Nolan Ryan	90.00
NR3	Nolan Ryan	90.00
NR4	Nolan Ryan	90.00
MS1	Mike Schmidt	50.00
MS2	Mike Schmidt	50.00
MS3	Mike Schmidt	50.00
RS1	Red Schoendienst	35.00
TS1	Tom Seaver	40.00
TS2	Tom Seaver	40.00
OS1	Ozzie Smith	40.00
OS2	Ozzie Smith	40.00

SN1	Duke Snider	40.00
DS1	Don Sutton	20.00
BW1	Billy Williams	20.00
BW2	Billy Williams	20.00
BW3	Billy Williams	20.00
DW1	Dave Winfield	30.00
DW2	Dave Winfield	30.00
CY1	Carl Yastrzemski	50.00
CY2	Carl Yastrzemski	50.00
RY1	Robin Yount	40.00
RY2	Robin Yount	40.00

Class of Cooperstown Calling

		NM/M
Production 50 Sets		
Gold:		No Pricing
Production 5 Sets		
Green:		.75-1.5X
Production 25 Sets		
Silver:		No Pricing
Production 15 Sets		
Rainbow:		No Pricing
Production One Set		
LA1	Luis Aparicio	4.00
LA2	Luis Aparicio	4.00
EB1	Ernie Banks	6.00
BE1	Johnny Bench	6.00
YB1	Yogi Berra	5.00
WB1	Wade Boggs	5.00
WB2	Wade Boggs	5.00
WB3	Wade Boggs	5.00
GB1	George Brett	10.00
GB2	George Brett	10.00
LB1	Lou Brock	4.00
LB2	Lou Brock	4.00
JB1	Jim Bunning	4.00
RC1	Rod Carew	4.00
RC2	Rod Carew	4.00
SC1	Steve Carlton	4.00
SC2	Steve Carlton	4.00
GC1	Gary Carter	4.00
GC2	Gary Carter	4.00
GC3	Gary Carter	4.00
OC1	Orlando Cepeda	4.00
OC2	Orlando Cepeda	4.00
BD1	Bobby Doerr	4.00
BD2	Bobby Doerr	4.00
DE1	Dennis Eckersley	4.00
DE2	Dennis Eckersley	4.00
BF1	Bob Feller	4.00
BF2	Bob Feller	4.00
RF1	Rollie Fingers	4.00
RF2	Rollie Fingers	4.00
CF1	Carlton Fisk	4.00
CF2	Carlton Fisk	4.00
WF1	Whitey Ford	5.00
BG1	Bob Gibson	5.00
MI1	Monte Irvin	4.00
RJ1	Reggie Jackson	5.00
RJ2	Reggie Jackson	5.00
RJ3	Reggie Jackson	5.00
FJ1	Fergie Jenkins	4.00
FJ2	Fergie Jenkins	4.00
AK1	Al Kaline	6.00
AK2	Al Kaline	6.00
GK1	George Kell	4.00
HK1	Harmon Killebrew	6.00
HK2	Harmon Killebrew	6.00
RK1	Ralph Kiner	4.00
JM1	Juan Marichal	4.00
BM1	Bill Mazeroski	4.00
WM1	Willie McCovey	5.00
PM1	Paul Molitor	5.00
PM2	Paul Molitor	5.00
PM3	Paul Molitor	5.00
MO1	Joe Morgan	4.00
MO2	Joe Morgan	4.00
EM1	Eddie Murray	4.00
EM2	Eddie Murray	4.00
SM1	Stan Musial	6.00
SM2	Stan Musial	6.00
PN1	Phil Niekro	4.00
PN2	Phil Niekro	4.00
JP1	Jim Palmer	4.00
JP2	Jim Palmer	4.00
TP1	Tony Perez	4.00
TP2	Tony Perez	4.00
GP1	Gaylord Perry	4.00
GP2	Gaylord Perry	4.00
KP1	Kirby Puckett	5.00
KP2	Kirby Puckett	5.00
RR1	Robin Roberts	4.00
BR1	Brooks Robinson	5.00
BR2	Brooks Robinson	5.00
BR3	Brooks Robinson	5.00
FR1	Frank Robinson	5.00
NR1	Nolan Ryan	10.00
NR2	Nolan Ryan	10.00
NR3	Nolan Ryan	10.00
NR4	Nolan Ryan	10.00
SA1	Ryne Sandberg	6.00
SA2	Ryne Sandberg	6.00

SA3	Ryne Sandberg	6.00
MS1	Mike Schmidt	6.00
MS2	Mike Schmidt	6.00
MS3	Mike Schmidt	6.00
RS1	Red Schoendienst	4.00
TS1	Tom Seaver	5.00
OS1	Ozzie Smith	6.00
OS2	Ozzie Smith	6.00
OS3	Ozzie Smith	6.00
SN1	Duke Snider	5.00
DS1	Don Sutton	4.00
DS2	Don Sutton	4.00
DS3	Don Sutton	4.00
BW1	Billy Williams	4.00
BW2	Billy Williams	4.00
DW1	Dave Winfield	6.00
CY1	Carl Yastrzemski	6.00
CY2	Carl Yastrzemski	6.00
RY1	Robin Yount	6.00
RY2	Robin Yount	6.00
RY3	Robin Yount	6.00

Class of Cooperstown Calling Autograph

		NM/M
Production 25 Sets		
Gold:		No Pricing
Silver:		No Pricing
Production 15 Sets		
Rainbow:		No Pricing
Production One Set		
Material Gold:		No Pricing
Production 5 Sets		
Material Silver:		No Pricing
Production 15 Sets		
Patch Gold:		No Pricing
Production 2 Sets		
Patch Silver:		No Pricing
Production 10 Sets		
LA1	Luis Aparicio	20.00
LA2	Luis Aparicio	20.00
EB1	Ernie Banks	50.00
BE1	Johnny Bench	40.00
YB1	Yogi Berra	60.00
WB1	Wade Boggs	35.00
WB2	Wade Boggs	35.00
WB3	Wade Boggs	35.00
GB1	George Brett	60.00
GB2	George Brett	60.00
LB1	Lou Brock	35.00
LB2	Lou Brock	35.00
JB1	Jim Bunning	25.00
RC1	Rod Carew	30.00
RC2	Rod Carew	30.00
SC1	Steve Carlton	20.00
SC2	Steve Carlton	20.00
GC1	Gary Carter	25.00
GC2	Gary Carter	25.00
GC3	Gary Carter	25.00
OC1	Orlando Cepeda	25.00
OC2	Orlando Cepeda	25.00
BD1	Bobby Doerr	15.00
BD2	Bobby Doerr	15.00
DE1	Dennis Eckersley	20.00
DE2	Dennis Eckersley	20.00
BF1	Bob Feller	30.00
BF2	Bob Feller	30.00
RF1	Rollie Fingers	20.00
RF2	Rollie Fingers	20.00
CF1	Carlton Fisk	30.00
CF2	Carlton Fisk	30.00
WF1	Whitey Ford	50.00
BG1	Bob Gibson	35.00
MI1	Monte Irvin	25.00
RJ1	Reggie Jackson	40.00
RJ2	Reggie Jackson	40.00
RJ3	Reggie Jackson	40.00
FJ1	Fergie Jenkins	20.00
FJ2	Fergie Jenkins	20.00
AK1	Al Kaline	40.00
AK2	Al Kaline	40.00
GK1	George Kell	20.00
HK1	Harmon Killebrew	40.00
HK2	Harmon Killebrew	40.00
RK1	Ralph Kiner	40.00
JM1	Juan Marichal	25.00
BM1	Bill Mazeroski	40.00
WM1	Willie McCovey	40.00
PM1	Paul Molitor	30.00
PM2	Paul Molitor	30.00
PM3	Paul Molitor	30.00
MO1	Joe Morgan	25.00
MO2	Joe Morgan	25.00
EM1	Eddie Murray	50.00
EM2	Eddie Murray	50.00
SM1	Stan Musial	60.00
SM2	Stan Musial	60.00
PN1	Phil Niekro	20.00
PN2	Phil Niekro	20.00
JP1	Jim Palmer	20.00
JP2	Jim Palmer	20.00
TP1	Tony Perez	20.00

Card	Player	Price
TP2	Tony Perez	20.00
GP1	Gaylord Perry	20.00
GP2	Gaylord Perry	20.00
KP1	Kirby Puckett	40.00
KP2	Kirby Puckett	40.00
RR1	Robin Roberts	40.00
BR1	Brooks Robinson	30.00
BR2	Brooks Robinson	30.00
BR3	Brooks Robinson	30.00
FR1	Frank Robinson	20.00
NR1	Nolan Ryan	90.00
NR2	Nolan Ryan	90.00
NR3	Nolan Ryan	90.00
NR4	Nolan Ryan	90.00
SA1	Ryne Sandberg	60.00
SA2	Ryne Sandberg	60.00
SA3	Ryne Sandberg	60.00
MS1	Mike Schmidt	50.00
MS2	Mike Schmidt	50.00
MS3	Mike Schmidt	50.00
RS1	Red Schoendienst	35.00
TS1	Tom Seaver	40.00
OS1	Ozzie Smith	40.00
OS2	Ozzie Smith	40.00
OS3	Ozzie Smith	40.00
SN1	Duke Snider	40.00
DS1	Don Sutton	20.00
DS2	Don Sutton	20.00
DS3	Don Sutton	20.00
BW1	Billy Williams	20.00
BW2	Billy Williams	20.00
DW1	Dave Winfield	30.00
CY1	Carl Yastrzemski	50.00
CY2	Carl Yastrzemski	50.00
RY1	Robin Yount	40.00
RY2	Robin Yount	40.00
RY3	Robin Yount	40.00

Cooperstown Cuts

NM/M

Production 1-20
Card	Player	Price
MC	Mickey Cochrane/9	
DD	Dizzy Dean/10	
GR	Lefty Grove/10	
RH	Rogers Hornsby/1	
WJ	Walter Johnson/1	
CM	Christy Mathewson/1	
JM	Johnny Mize/20	180.00
GS	George Sisler/1	
PT	Pie Traynor/10	
HW1	Honus Wagner/1	
CY	Cy Young/1	

Cooperstown Cuts Memorabilia

No Pricing
Production 1-20
RC   Roy Campanella/1

Essential Enshrinement

NM/M

Production 50 Sets
Gold: No Pricing
Production 5 Sets
Silver: No Pricing
Production 15 Sets
Rainbow: No Pricing
Production One Set
Card	Player	Price
LA1	Luis Aparicio	4.00
EB1	Ernie Banks	6.00
BE1	Johnny Bench	6.00
BE2	Johnny Bench	6.00
YB1	Yogi Berra	5.00
YB2	Yogi Berra	5.00
WB1	Wade Boggs	5.00
WB2	Wade Boggs	5.00
WB3	Wade Boggs	5.00
GB1	George Brett	10.00
GB2	George Brett	10.00
GB3	George Brett	10.00
LB1	Lou Brock	4.00
LB2	Lou Brock	4.00
JB1	Jim Bunning	4.00
RC1	Rod Carew	4.00
RC2	Rod Carew	4.00
SC1	Steve Carlton	4.00
SC2	Steve Carlton	4.00
GC1	Gary Carter	4.00
GC2	Gary Carter	4.00
OC1	Orlando Cepeda	4.00

Card	Player	Price
BD1	Bobby Doerr	4.00
BD2	Bobby Doerr	4.00
DE1	Dennis Eckersley	4.00
BF1	Bob Feller	4.00
BF2	Bob Feller	4.00
RF1	Rollie Fingers	4.00
CF1	Carlton Fisk	4.00
CF2	Carlton Fisk	4.00
WF1	Whitey Ford	5.00
WF2	Whitey Ford	5.00
BG1	Bob Gibson	5.00
BG2	Bob Gibson	5.00
MI1	Monte Irvin	4.00
RJ1	Reggie Jackson	5.00
RJ2	Reggie Jackson	5.00
RJ3	Reggie Jackson	5.00
FJ1	Fergie Jenkins	4.00
FJ2	Fergie Jenkins	4.00
AK1	Al Kaline	6.00
AK2	Al Kaline	6.00
GK1	George Kell	4.00
HK1	Harmon Killebrew	6.00
HK2	Harmon Killebrew	6.00
RK1	Ralph Kiner	4.00
JM1	Juan Marichal	4.00
BM1	Bill Mazeroski	4.00
WM1	Willie McCovey	5.00
PM1	Paul Molitor	5.00
PM2	Paul Molitor	5.00
PM3	Paul Molitor	5.00
MO1	Joe Morgan	4.00
MO2	Joe Morgan	4.00
MO3	Joe Morgan	4.00
EM1	Eddie Murray	4.00
EM2	Eddie Murray	4.00
SM1	Stan Musial	6.00
SM2	Stan Musial	6.00
PN1	Phil Niekro	4.00
PN2	Phil Niekro	4.00
JP1	Jim Palmer	4.00
JP2	Jim Palmer	4.00
TP1	Tony Perez	4.00
GP1	Gaylord Perry	4.00
GP2	Gaylord Perry	4.00
KP1	Kirby Puckett	5.00
KP2	Kirby Puckett	5.00
RR1	Robin Roberts	4.00
BR1	Brooks Robinson	5.00
BR2	Brooks Robinson	5.00
BR3	Brooks Robinson	5.00
FR1	Frank Robinson	5.00
FR2	Frank Robinson	5.00
NR1	Nolan Ryan	10.00
NR2	Nolan Ryan	10.00
NR3	Nolan Ryan	10.00
NR4	Nolan Ryan	10.00
SA1	Ryne Sandberg	6.00
SA2	Ryne Sandberg	6.00
SA3	Ryne Sandberg	6.00
MS1	Mike Schmidt	6.00
MS2	Mike Schmidt	6.00
RS1	Red Schoendienst	4.00
TS1	Tom Seaver	5.00
OS1	Ozzie Smith	6.00
OS2	Ozzie Smith	6.00
SN1	Duke Snider	5.00
SN2	Duke Snider	5.00
DS1	Don Sutton	4.00
DS2	Don Sutton	4.00
BW1	Billy Williams	4.00
BW2	Billy Williams	4.00
DW1	Dave Winfield	4.00
CY1	Carl Yastrzemski	6.00
CY2	Carl Yastrzemski	6.00
CY3	Carl Yastrzemski	6.00
RY1	Robin Yount	6.00
RY2	Robin Yount	6.00
RY3	Robin Yount	6.00

Essential Enshrinement Autograph

NM/M

Production 25 Sets
Gold: No Pricing
Production 5 Sets
Silver: No Pricing
Production 15 Sets
Rainbow: No Pricing
Production One Set
Material Gold: No Pricing
Production 5 Sets
Material Silver: No Pricing
Production 15 Sets
Patch Gold: No Pricing
Production 5 Sets
Patch Silver: No Pricing
Production 10 Sets
Card	Player	Price
LA1	Luis Aparicio	20.00
EB1	Ernie Banks	50.00
BE1	Johnny Bench	40.00
BE2	Johnny Bench	40.00
YB1	Yogi Berra	60.00
YB2	Yogi Berra	60.00

Card	Player	Price
WB1	Wade Boggs	35.00
WB2	Wade Boggs	35.00
WB3	Wade Boggs	35.00
GB1	George Brett	60.00
GB2	George Brett	60.00
GB3	George Brett	60.00
LB1	Lou Brock	35.00
LB2	Lou Brock	35.00
JB1	Jim Bunning	25.00
RC1	Rod Carew	30.00
RC2	Rod Carew	30.00
SC1	Steve Carlton	20.00
SC2	Steve Carlton	20.00
GC1	Gary Carter	25.00
GC2	Gary Carter	25.00
OC1	Orlando Cepeda	20.00
BD1	Bobby Doerr	15.00
BD2	Bobby Doerr	15.00
DE1	Dennis Eckersley	20.00
BF1	Bob Feller	30.00
BF2	Bob Feller	30.00
RF1	Rollie Fingers	20.00
CF1	Carlton Fisk	30.00
CF2	Carlton Fisk	30.00
WF1	Whitey Ford	50.00
WF2	Whitey Ford	50.00
BG1	Bob Gibson	35.00
BG2	Bob Gibson	35.00
MI1	Monte Irvin	25.00
RJ1	Reggie Jackson	40.00
RJ2	Reggie Jackson	40.00
RJ3	Reggie Jackson	40.00
FJ1	Fergie Jenkins	20.00
FJ2	Fergie Jenkins	20.00
AK1	Al Kaline	40.00
AK2	Al Kaline	40.00
GK1	George Kell	20.00
HK1	Harmon Killebrew	40.00
HK2	Harmon Killebrew	40.00
RK1	Ralph Kiner	40.00
JM1	Juan Marichal	25.00
BM1	Bill Mazeroski	40.00
WM1	Willie McCovey	40.00
PM1	Paul Molitor	30.00
PM2	Paul Molitor	30.00
PM3	Paul Molitor	30.00
MO1	Joe Morgan	25.00
MO2	Joe Morgan	25.00
MO3	Joe Morgan	25.00
EM1	Eddie Murray	50.00
EM2	Eddie Murray	50.00
SM1	Stan Musial	60.00
SM2	Stan Musial	60.00
PN1	Phil Niekro	20.00
PN2	Phil Niekro	20.00
JP1	Jim Palmer	20.00
JP2	Jim Palmer	20.00
TP1	Tony Perez	20.00
GP1	Gaylord Perry	20.00
GP2	Gaylord Perry	20.00
KP1	Kirby Puckett	40.00
KP2	Kirby Puckett	40.00
RR1	Robin Roberts	25.00
BR1	Brooks Robinson	30.00
BR2	Brooks Robinson	30.00
BR3	Brooks Robinson	30.00
FR1	Frank Robinson	20.00
FR2	Frank Robinson	20.00
NR1	Nolan Ryan	90.00
NR2	Nolan Ryan	90.00
NR3	Nolan Ryan	90.00
NR4	Nolan Ryan	90.00
SA1	Ryne Sandberg	60.00
SA2	Ryne Sandberg	60.00
SA3	Ryne Sandberg	60.00
MS1	Mike Schmidt	50.00
MS2	Mike Schmidt	50.00
RS1	Red Schoendienst	35.00
TS1	Tom Seaver	40.00
OS1	Ozzie Smith	40.00
OS2	Ozzie Smith	40.00
SN1	Duke Snider	40.00
SN2	Duke Snider	40.00
DS1	Don Sutton	20.00
DS2	Don Sutton	20.00
BW1	Billy Williams	20.00
BW2	Billy Williams	20.00
DW1	Dave Winfield	30.00
CY1	Carl Yastrzemski	50.00
CY2	Carl Yastrzemski	50.00
CY3	Carl Yastrzemski	50.00
RY1	Robin Yount	40.00
RY2	Robin Yount	40.00
RY3	Robin Yount	40.00

Hall of Fame Materials

NM/M

Production 25 Sets
Gold: No Pricing
Production 5 Sets
Silver: No Pricing
Production 15 Sets
Rainbow: No Pricing
Production One Set

Green: No Pricing
Production 10 Sets
Card	Player	Price
RC1	Roberto Clemente	120.00
RC2	Roberto Clemente	120.00
RC3	Roberto Clemente	120.00
TC1	Ty Cobb	100.00
TC2	Ty Cobb	100.00
TC3	Ty Cobb	100.00
MC1	Mickey Cochrane	40.00
DD1	Dizzy Dean	80.00
DD2	Dizzy Dean	80.00
JD1	Joe DiMaggio	90.00
JD2	Joe DiMaggio	90.00
JD3	Joe DiMaggio	90.00
JF1	Jimmie Foxx	60.00
JF2	Jimmie Foxx	60.00
LG1	Lou Gehrig	180.00
LG2	Lou Gehrig	180.00
LG3	Lou Gehrig	180.00
RH1	Rogers Hornsby	80.00
MM1	Mickey Mantle	250.00
MM2	Mickey Mantle	250.00
MM3	Mickey Mantle	250.00
JM1	Johnny Mize	30.00
JM2	Johnny Mize	30.00
JM3	Johnny Mize	30.00
MO1	Mel Ott	40.00
MO2	Mel Ott	40.00
SP1	Satchel Paige	50.00
SP2	Satchel Paige	50.00
SP3	Satchel Paige	50.00
JR1	Jackie Robinson	60.00
JR2	Jackie Robinson	60.00
JR3	Jackie Robinson	60.00
BR1	Babe Ruth	250.00
BR2	Babe Ruth	250.00
BR3	Babe Ruth	250.00
GS1	George Sisler	40.00
GS2	George Sisler	40.00
TW1	Ted Williams	85.00
TW2	Ted Williams	85.00
TW3	Ted Williams	85.00

Hall of Fame Seasons

NM/M

Production 50 Sets
Gold: No Pricing
Production 5 Sets
Silver: No Pricing
Production 15 Sets
Rainbow: No Pricing
Production One Set
Card	Player	Price
LA1	Luis Aparicio	4.00
EB1	Ernie Banks	6.00
BE1	Johnny Bench	6.00
BE2	Johnny Bench	6.00
YB1	Yogi Berra	5.00
YB2	Yogi Berra	5.00
WB1	Wade Boggs	5.00
WB2	Wade Boggs	5.00
WB3	Wade Boggs	5.00
GB1	George Brett	10.00
GB2	George Brett	10.00
LB1	Lou Brock	4.00
LB2	Lou Brock	4.00
JB1	Jim Bunning	4.00
RC1	Rod Carew	4.00
RC2	Rod Carew	4.00
GC1	Gary Carter	4.00
SC1	Steve Carlton	4.00
SC2	Steve Carlton	4.00
SC3	Steve Carlton	4.00
OC1	Orlando Cepeda	4.00
BD1	Bobby Doerr	4.00
DE1	Dennis Eckersley	4.00
DE2	Dennis Eckersley	4.00
DE3	Dennis Eckersley	4.00
BF1	Bob Feller	4.00
BF2	Bob Feller	4.00
RF1	Rollie Fingers	4.00
CF1	Carlton Fisk	4.00
CF2	Carlton Fisk	4.00
WF1	Whitey Ford	5.00
WF2	Whitey Ford	5.00
BG1	Bob Gibson	5.00
BG2	Bob Gibson	5.00
MI1	Monte Irvin	4.00
RJ1	Reggie Jackson	5.00
RJ2	Reggie Jackson	5.00
RJ3	Reggie Jackson	5.00
FJ1	Fergie Jenkins	4.00
FJ2	Fergie Jenkins	4.00
AK1	Al Kaline	6.00
AK2	Al Kaline	6.00
AK3	Al Kaline	6.00
GK1	George Kell	4.00
HK1	Harmon Killebrew	6.00
HK2	Harmon Killebrew	6.00
HK3	Harmon Killebrew	6.00
RK1	Ralph Kiner	4.00
JM1	Juan Marichal	4.00
BM1	Bill Mazeroski	4.00
WM1	Willie McCovey	5.00
PM1	Paul Molitor	5.00

PM2	Paul Molitor	5.00
PM3	Paul Molitor	5.00
MO1	Joe Morgan	4.00
MO2	Joe Morgan	4.00
EM1	Eddie Murray	4.00
EM2	Eddie Murray	4.00
SM1	Stan Musial	6.00
SM2	Stan Musial	6.00
PN1	Phil Niekro	4.00
PN2	Phil Niekro	4.00
JP1	Jim Palmer	4.00
JP2	Jim Palmer	4.00
JP3	Jim Palmer	4.00
TP1	Tony Perez	4.00
GP1	Gaylord Perry	4.00
GP2	Gaylord Perry	4.00
KP1	Kirby Puckett	5.00
KP2	Kirby Puckett	5.00
RR1	Robin Roberts	4.00
BR1	Brooks Robinson	5.00
BR2	Brooks Robinson	5.00
BR3	Brooks Robinson	5.00
FR1	Frank Robinson	5.00
FR2	Frank Robinson	5.00
NR1	Nolan Ryan	10.00
NR2	Nolan Ryan	10.00
NR3	Nolan Ryan	10.00
NR4	Nolan Ryan	10.00
SA1	Ryne Sandberg	6.00
SA2	Ryne Sandberg	6.00
MS1	Mike Schmidt	6.00
MS2	Mike Schmidt	6.00
MS3	Mike Schmidt	6.00
RS1	Red Schoendienst	4.00
TS1	Tom Seaver	5.00
TS2	Tom Seaver	5.00
OS1	Ozzie Smith	6.00
OS2	Ozzie Smith	6.00
SN1	Duke Snider	5.00
DS1	Don Sutton	4.00
DS2	Don Sutton	4.00
BW1	Billy Williams	4.00
BW2	Billy Williams	4.00
DW1	Dave Winfield	6.00
CY1	Carl Yastrzemski	6.00
CY2	Carl Yastrzemski	6.00
RY1	Robin Yount	6.00
RY2	Robin Yount	6.00

Hall of Fame Seasons Autograph

	NM/M
Production 25 Sets	
Gold:	No Pricing
Production 5 Sets	
Silver:	No Pricing
Production 15 Sets	
Rainbow:	No Pricing
Production One Set	
Material Gold:	No Pricing
Production 5 Sets	
Material Silver:	No Pricing
Production 15 Sets	
Patch Gold:	No Pricing
Production 5 Sets	
Patch Silver:	No Pricing
Production 10 Sets	
LA1	Luis Aparicio	20.00
EB1	Ernie Banks	50.00
BE1	Johnny Bench	40.00
BE2	Johnny Bench	40.00
YB1	Yogi Berra	60.00
YB2	Yogi Berra	60.00
WB1	Wade Boggs	35.00
WB2	Wade Boggs	35.00
WB3	Wade Boggs	35.00
GB1	George Brett	60.00
GB2	George Brett	60.00
LB1	Lou Brock	35.00
LB2	Lou Brock	35.00
JB1	Jim Bunning	25.00
RC1	Rod Carew	30.00
RC2	Rod Carew	30.00
GC1	Gary Carter	25.00
SC1	Steve Carlton	20.00
SC2	Steve Carlton	20.00
SC3	Steve Carlton	20.00
OC1	Orlando Cepeda	25.00
BD1	Bobby Doerr	15.00
DE1	Dennis Eckersley	20.00
DE2	Dennis Eckersley	20.00
DE3	Dennis Eckersley	20.00
BF1	Bob Feller	30.00
BF2	Bob Feller	30.00
RF1	Rollie Fingers	20.00
CF1	Carlton Fisk	30.00
CF2	Carlton Fisk	30.00
WF1	Whitey Ford	50.00
WF2	Whitey Ford	50.00
BG1	Bob Gibson	35.00
BG2	Bob Gibson	35.00
MI1	Monte Irvin	25.00
RJ1	Reggie Jackson	40.00

RJ2	Reggie Jackson	40.00
RJ3	Reggie Jackson	40.00
FJ1	Fergie Jenkins	20.00
FJ2	Fergie Jenkins	20.00
AK1	Al Kaline	40.00
AK2	Al Kaline	40.00
AK3	Al Kaline	40.00
GK1	George Kell	40.00
HK1	Harmon Killebrew	40.00
HK2	Harmon Killebrew	40.00
HK3	Harmon Killebrew	40.00
RK1	Ralph Kiner	40.00
JM1	Juan Marichal	25.00
BM1	Bill Mazeroski	40.00
WM1	Willie McCovey	40.00
PM1	Paul Molitor	30.00
PM2	Paul Molitor	30.00
PM3	Paul Molitor	30.00
MO1	Joe Morgan	25.00
MO2	Joe Morgan	25.00
EM1	Eddie Murray	50.00
EM2	Eddie Murray	50.00
SM1	Stan Musial	60.00
SM2	Stan Musial	60.00
PN1	Phil Niekro	20.00
PN2	Phil Niekro	20.00
JP1	Jim Palmer	20.00
JP2	Jim Palmer	20.00
JP3	Jim Palmer	20.00
TP1	Tony Perez	20.00
GP1	Gaylord Perry	20.00
GP2	Gaylord Perry	20.00
KP1	Kirby Puckett	40.00
KP2	Kirby Puckett	40.00
RR1	Robin Roberts	25.00
BR1	Brooks Robinson	30.00
BR2	Brooks Robinson	30.00
BR3	Brooks Robinson	30.00
FR1	Frank Robinson	20.00
FR2	Frank Robinson	20.00
NR1	Nolan Ryan	90.00
NR2	Nolan Ryan	90.00
NR3	Nolan Ryan	90.00
NR4	Nolan Ryan	90.00
SA1	Ryne Sandberg	60.00
SA2	Ryne Sandberg	60.00
MS1	Mike Schmidt	50.00
MS2	Mike Schmidt	50.00
MS3	Mike Schmidt	50.00
RS1	Red Schoendienst	35.00
TS1	Tom Seaver	40.00
TS2	Tom Seaver	40.00
OS1	Ozzie Smith	40.00
OS2	Ozzie Smith	40.00
SN1	Duke Snider	40.00
DS1	Don Sutton	20.00
DS2	Don Sutton	20.00
BW1	Billy Williams	20.00
BW2	Billy Williams	20.00
DW1	Dave Winfield	30.00
CY1	Carl Yastrzemski	50.00
CY2	Carl Yastrzemski	50.00
RY1	Robin Yount	40.00
RY2	Robin Yount	40.00

Hall Worthy

	NM/M
Production 50 Sets	
Gold:	No Pricing
Production 5 Sets	
Silver:	No Pricing
Production 15 Sets	
Rainbow:	No Pricing
Production One Set	
LA1	Luis Aparicio	4.00
EB1	Ernie Banks	6.00
BE1	Johnny Bench	6.00
BE2	Johnny Bench	6.00
YB1	Yogi Berra	5.00
WB1	Wade Boggs	5.00
WB2	Wade Boggs	5.00
WB3	Wade Boggs	5.00
GB1	George Brett	10.00
GB2	George Brett	10.00
GB3	George Brett	10.00
LB1	Lou Brock	4.00
LB2	Lou Brock	4.00
JB1	Jim Bunning	4.00
RC1	Rod Carew	4.00
RC2	Rod Carew	4.00
SC1	Steve Carlton	4.00
SC2	Steve Carlton	4.00
GC1	Gary Carter	4.00
GC2	Gary Carter	4.00
OC1	Orlando Cepeda	4.00
OC2	Orlando Cepeda	4.00
BD1	Bobby Doerr	4.00
DE1	Dennis Eckersley	4.00
DE2	Dennis Eckersley	4.00
DE3	Dennis Eckersley	4.00
DE4	Dennis Eckersley	4.00
BF1	Bob Feller	4.00
BF2	Bob Feller	4.00
RF1	Rollie Fingers	4.00

RF2	Rollie Fingers	4.00
CF1	Carlton Fisk	4.00
CF2	Carlton Fisk	4.00
WF1	Whitey Ford	5.00
BG1	Bob Gibson	5.00
MI1	Monte Irvin	4.00
RJ1	Reggie Jackson	5.00
RJ2	Reggie Jackson	5.00
RJ3	Reggie Jackson	5.00
RJ4	Reggie Jackson	5.00
FJ1	Fergie Jenkins	4.00
FJ2	Fergie Jenkins	4.00
FJ3	Fergie Jenkins	4.00
AK1	Al Kaline	4.00
AK2	Al Kaline	4.00
GK1	George Kell	4.00
HK1	Harmon Killebrew	6.00
HK2	Harmon Killebrew	6.00
RK1	Ralph Kiner	4.00
JM1	Juan Marichal	4.00
BM1	Bill Mazeroski	4.00
WM1	Willie McCovey	5.00
PM1	Paul Molitor	5.00
PM2	Paul Molitor	5.00
MO1	Joe Morgan	4.00
MO2	Joe Morgan	4.00
EM1	Eddie Murray	4.00
EM2	Eddie Murray	4.00
EM3	Eddie Murray	4.00
SM1	Stan Musial	6.00
PN1	Phil Niekro	4.00
PN2	Phil Niekro	4.00
JP1	Jim Palmer	4.00
JP2	Jim Palmer	4.00
TP1	Tony Perez	4.00
TP2	Tony Perez	4.00
GP1	Gaylord Perry	4.00
GP2	Gaylord Perry	4.00
KP1	Kirby Puckett	5.00
RR1	Robin Roberts	4.00
BR1	Brooks Robinson	5.00
BR2	Brooks Robinson	5.00
FR1	Frank Robinson	5.00
FR2	Frank Robinson	5.00
NR1	Nolan Ryan	10.00
NR2	Nolan Ryan	10.00
NR3	Nolan Ryan	10.00
NR4	Nolan Ryan	10.00
SA1	Ryne Sandberg	6.00
SA2	Ryne Sandberg	6.00
SA3	Ryne Sandberg	6.00
MS1	Mike Schmidt	6.00
MS2	Mike Schmidt	6.00
MS3	Mike Schmidt	6.00
RS1	Red Schoendienst	4.00
TS1	Tom Seaver	5.00
TS2	Tom Seaver	5.00
OS1	Ozzie Smith	6.00
OS2	Ozzie Smith	6.00
SN1	Duke Snider	5.00
SN2	Duke Snider	5.00
DS1	Don Sutton	4.00
DS2	Don Sutton	4.00
DS3	Don Sutton	4.00
BW1	Billy Williams	4.00
DW1	Dave Winfield	4.00
CY1	Carl Yastrzemski	6.00
CY2	Carl Yastrzemski	6.00
RY1	Robin Yount	6.00
RY2	Robin Yount	6.00

Hall Worthy Autograph

	NM/M
Production 25 Sets	
Gold:	No Pricing
Production 5 Sets	
Silver:	No Pricing
Production 15 Sets	
Rainbow:	No Pricing
Production One Set	
Material Gold:	No Pricing
Production 5 Sets	
Material Silver:	No Pricing
Production 15 Sets	
Patch Gold:	No Pricing
Production 5 Sets	
Patch Silver:	No Pricing
Production 10 Sets	
LA1	Luis Aparicio	20.00
EB1	Ernie Banks	50.00
BE1	Johnny Bench	40.00
BE2	Johnny Bench	40.00
YB1	Yogi Berra	60.00
WB1	Wade Boggs	35.00
WB2	Wade Boggs	35.00
WB3	Wade Boggs	35.00
GB1	George Brett	60.00
GB2	George Brett	60.00
GB3	George Brett	60.00
LB1	Lou Brock	35.00
LB2	Lou Brock	35.00
JB1	Jim Bunning	25.00
RC1	Rod Carew	30.00
RC2	Rod Carew	30.00

SC1	Steve Carlton	20.00
SC2	Steve Carlton	20.00
GC1	Gary Carter	25.00
GC2	Gary Carter	25.00
OC1	Orlando Cepeda	25.00
OC2	Orlando Cepeda	25.00
BD1	Bobby Doerr	15.00
DE1	Dennis Eckersley	20.00
DE2	Dennis Eckersley	20.00
DE3	Dennis Eckersley	20.00
DE4	Dennis Eckersley	20.00
BF1	Bob Feller	30.00
BF2	Bob Feller	30.00
RF1	Rollie Fingers	20.00
RF2	Rollie Fingers	20.00
CF1	Carlton Fisk	30.00
CF2	Carlton Fisk	30.00
WF1	Whitey Ford	50.00
BG1	Bob Gibson	35.00
MI1	Monte Irvin	25.00
RJ1	Reggie Jackson	40.00
RJ2	Reggie Jackson	40.00
RJ3	Reggie Jackson	40.00
RJ4	Reggie Jackson	40.00
FJ1	Fergie Jenkins	20.00
FJ2	Fergie Jenkins	20.00
FJ3	Fergie Jenkins	20.00
AK1	Al Kaline	40.00
AK2	Al Kaline	40.00
GK1	George Kell	20.00
HK1	Harmon Killebrew	40.00
HK2	Harmon Killebrew	40.00
RK1	Ralph Kiner	40.00
JM1	Juan Marichal	25.00
BM1	Bill Mazeroski	40.00
WM1	Willie McCovey	40.00
PM1	Paul Molitor	30.00
PM2	Paul Molitor	30.00
MO1	Joe Morgan	25.00
MO2	Joe Morgan	25.00
EM1	Eddie Murray	50.00
EM2	Eddie Murray	50.00
EM3	Eddie Murray	50.00
SM1	Stan Musial	60.00
PN1	Phil Niekro	20.00
PN2	Phil Niekro	20.00
JP1	Jim Palmer	20.00
JP2	Jim Palmer	20.00
TP1	Tony Perez	20.00
TP2	Tony Perez	20.00
GP1	Gaylord Perry	20.00
GP2	Gaylord Perry	20.00
KP1	Kirby Puckett	40.00
RR1	Robin Roberts	25.00
BR1	Brooks Robinson	30.00
BR2	Brooks Robinson	30.00
FR1	Frank Robinson	20.00
FR2	Frank Robinson	20.00
NR1	Nolan Ryan	90.00
NR2	Nolan Ryan	90.00
NR3	Nolan Ryan	90.00
NR4	Nolan Ryan	90.00
SA1	Ryne Sandberg	60.00
SA2	Ryne Sandberg	60.00
SA3	Ryne Sandberg	60.00
MS1	Mike Schmidt	50.00
MS2	Mike Schmidt	50.00
MS3	Mike Schmidt	50.00
RS1	Red Schoendienst	35.00
TS1	Tom Seaver	40.00
TS2	Tom Seaver	40.00
OS1	Ozzie Smith	40.00
OS2	Ozzie Smith	40.00
SN1	Duke Snider	40.00
SN2	Duke Snider	40.00
DS1	Don Sutton	20.00
DS2	Don Sutton	20.00
DS3	Don Sutton	20.00
BW1	Billy Williams	20.00
DW1	Dave Winfield	30.00
CY1	Carl Yastrzemski	50.00
CY2	Carl Yastrzemski	50.00
RY1	Robin Yount	40.00
RY2	Robin Yount	40.00

Signs of Cooperstown Duals

	NM/M
Production 50 Sets	
Gold:	No Pricing
Production 5 Sets	
Silver:	No Pricing
Production 15 Sets	
Rainbow:	No Pricing
Production One Set	
AB	Ernie Banks, Luis Aparicio	6.00
AS	Luis Aparicio, Ozzie Smith	8.00
BC	Steve Carlton, Jim Bunning	4.00
BF	Frank Robinson, Brooks Robinson	5.00

BG	George Brett, Brooks Robinson	10.00
BM	Lou Brock, Stan Musial	8.00
BR	Jim Bunning, Robin Roberts	4.00
BS	Ernie Banks, Ryne Sandberg	10.00
CM	Orlando Cepeda, Willie McCovey	4.00
CS	Tom Seaver, Gary Carter	4.00
DB	Wade Boggs, Bobby Doerr	4.00
EF	Dennis Eckersley, Rollie Fingers	4.00
FB	Johnny Bench, Carlton Fisk	6.00
FC	Bob Feller, Steve Carlton	4.00
FP	Bob Feller, Gaylord Perry	4.00
GC	Bob Gibson, Steve Carlton	5.00
GF	Bob Gibson, Whitey Ford	5.00
IM	Monte Irvin, Willie McCovey	5.00
JJ	Joe Morgan, Johnny Bench	6.00
JM	Reggie Jackson, Willie McCovey	5.00
JW	Reggie Jackson, Dave Winfield	5.00
JY	Yogi Berra, Johnny Bench	6.00
KK	Al Kaline, George Kell	6.00
KP	Kirby Puckett, Harmon Killebrew	6.00
LO	Lou Brock, Ozzie Smith	8.00
MK	Bill Mazeroski, Ralph Kiner	5.00
MP	Joe Morgan, Tony Perez	4.00
MY	Robin Yount, Paul Molitor	6.00
NS	Steve Carlton, Nolan Ryan	10.00
PM	Gaylord Perry, Juan Marichal	4.00
PN	Gaylord Perry, Phil Niekro	4.00
PR	Rod Carew, Paul Molitor	5.00
RC	Rod Carew, Nolan Ryan	10.00
RP	Jim Palmer, Brooks Robinson	5.00
RS	Tom Seaver, Nolan Ryan	10.00
RW	Ryne Sandberg, Wade Boggs	10.00
SB	George Brett, Mike Schmidt	10.00
SC	Mike Schmidt, Steve Carlton	10.00
SK	Ralph Kiner, Duke Snider	5.00
SM	Ozzie Smith, Stan Musial	8.00
SP	Gaylord Perry, Don Sutton	4.00
SR	Mike Schmidt, Brooks Robinson	10.00
SS	Red Schoendienst, Ozzie Smith	8.00
SW	Billy Williams, Ryne Sandberg	10.00
WB	Billy Williams, Ernie Banks	6.00
WJ	Billy Williams, Fergie Jenkins	4.00
WS	Ozzie Smith, Dave Winfield	6.00
WY	Yogi Berra, Whitey Ford	6.00
YF	Carlton Fisk, Carl Yastrzemski	6.00
YJ	Reggie Jackson, Carl Yastrzemski	6.00

Signs of Cooperstown Duals Autographs

NM/M

Production 20 Sets	
Gold:	No Pricing
Production 5 Sets	
Silver:	No Pricing
Production 10 Sets	
Rainbow:	No Pricing
Production One Set	

AB	Ernie Banks, Luis Aparicio	80.00
AS	Luis Aparicio, Ozzie Smith	60.00
BC	Steve Carlton, Jim Bunning	35.00
BF	Frank Robinson, Brooks Robinson	60.00
BG	George Brett, Brooks Robinson	90.00
BM	Lou Brock, Stan Musial	100.00
BR	Jim Bunning, Robin Roberts	60.00
BS	Ernie Banks, Ryne Sandberg	120.00
CM	Orlando Cepeda, Willie McCovey	50.00
CS	Tom Seaver, Gary Carter	80.00
DB	Wade Boggs, Bobby Doerr	50.00
EF	Dennis Eckersley, Rollie Fingers	35.00
FB	Johnny Bench, Carlton Fisk	75.00
FC	Bob Feller, Steve Carlton	40.00
FP	Bob Feller, Gaylord Perry	40.00
GC	Bob Gibson, Steve Carlton	60.00
GF	Bob Gibson, Whitey Ford	75.00
IM	Monte Irvin, Willie McCovey	60.00
JJ	Joe Morgan, Johnny Bench	80.00
JM	Reggie Jackson, Willie McCovey	100.00
JW	Reggie Jackson, Dave Winfield	80.00
JY	Yogi Berra, Johnny Bench	150.00
KK	Al Kaline, George Kell	85.00
KP	Kirby Puckett, Harmon Killebrew	80.00
LO	Lou Brock, Ozzie Smith	65.00
MK	Bill Mazeroski, Ralph Kiner	75.00
MP	Joe Morgan, Tony Perez	50.00
MY	Robin Yount, Paul Molitor	85.00
NS	Steve Carlton, Nolan Ryan	150.00
PM	Gaylord Perry, Juan Marichal	40.00
PN	Gaylord Perry, Phil Niekro	40.00
PR	Rod Carew, Paul Molitor	50.00
RC	Rod Carew, Nolan Ryan	150.00
RP	Jim Palmer, Brooks Robinson	50.00
RS	Tom Seaver, Nolan Ryan	180.00
RW	Ryne Sandberg, Wade Boggs	100.00
SB	George Brett, Mike Schmidt	140.00
SC	Mike Schmidt, Steve Carlton	85.00
SK	Ralph Kiner, Duke Snider	65.00
SM	Ozzie Smith, Stan Musial	120.00
SP	Gaylord Perry, Don Sutton	40.00
SR	Mike Schmidt, Brooks Robinson	75.00
SS	Red Schoendienst, Ozzie Smith	65.00
SW	Billy Williams, Ryne Sandberg	90.00
WB	Billy Williams, Ernie Banks	90.00
WJ	Billy Williams, Fergie Jenkins	50.00
WS	Ozzie Smith, Dave Winfield	75.00
WY	Yogi Berra, Whitey Ford	100.00
YF	Carlton Fisk, Carl Yastrzemski	100.00
YJ	Reggie Jackson, Carl Yastrzemski	100.00

Signs of Cooperstown Quads

NM/M

Production 50 Sets

Gold:	No Pricing
Production 5 Sets	
Silver:	No Pricing
Production 15 Sets	
Rainbow:	No Pricing
Production One Set	

BMYC	George Brett, Rod Carew, Robin Yount, Paul Molitor	10.00
BSAY	Ernie Banks, Robin Yount, Luis Aparicio, Ozzie Smith	8.00
FCBB	Yogi Berra, Johnny Bench, Carlton Fisk, Gary Carter	6.00
FGRC	Bob Feller, Bob Gibson, Steve Carlton, Nolan Ryan	10.00
KCPM	Tony Perez, Orlando Cepeda, Harmon Killebrew, Willie McCovey	6.00
KYBM	Al Kaline, Lou Brock, Carl Yastrzemski, Stan Musial	8.00
MBKM	Ernie Banks, Eddie Murray, Harmon Killebrew, Willie McCovey	8.00
MDMC	Bill Mazeroski, Rod Carew, Joe Morgan, Bobby Doerr	5.00
MRKS	Eddie Murray, Mike Schmidt, Frank Robinson, Harmon Killebrew	10.00
RBKS	George Brett, Mike Schmidt, Brooks Robinson, George Kell	10.00
SPNS	Tom Seaver, Phil Niekro, Don Sutton, Gaylord Perry	6.00
SPSF	Tom Seaver, Jim Palmer, Whitey Ford, Don Sutton	6.00
SRCS	Tom Seaver, Steve Carlton, Don Sutton, Nolan Ryan	10.00
WYKM	Billy Williams, Ralph Kiner, Carl Yastrzemski, Stan Musial	8.00
YWMM	Eddie Murray, Carl Yastrzemski, Stan Musial, Dave Winfield	8.00

Signs of Cooperstown Triple Autographs

NM/M

Production 20 Sets	75.00
Gold:	No Pricing
Production 5 Sets	
Silver:	No Pricing
Production 10 Sets	
Rainbow:	No Pricing
Production One Set	
Production 20 Sets	75.00
Gold:	No Pricing
Production 5 Sets	
Silver:	No Pricing
Production 10 Sets	
Rainbow:	No Pricing
Production One Set	

ASY	Robin Yount, Luis Aparicio, Ozzie Smith	140.00
BFJ	Jim Palmer, Frank Robinson, Brooks Robinson	80.00
BSB	George Brett, Mike Schmidt, Wade Boggs	185.00
BSY	Ernie Banks, Robin Yount, Ozzie Smith	150.00
CMI	Monte Irvin, Orlando Cepeda, Willie McCovey	75.00
DFY	Carlton Fisk, Carl Yastrzemski, Bobby Doerr	125.00
DYB	Carl Yastrzemski, Wade Boggs, Bobby Doerr	125.00
FRC	Bob Feller, Steve Carlton, Nolan Ryan	200.00

GSM	Bob Gibson, Ozzie Smith, Stan Musial	185.00
JFB	Yogi Berra, Reggie Jackson, Whitey Ford	185.00
JPR	Nolan Ryan, Gaylord Perry, Fergie Jenkins	150.00
KPC	Rod Carew, Kirby Puckett, Harmon Killebrew	120.00
KSR	Ralph Kiner, Duke Snider, Frank Robinson	120.00
MBP	Joe Morgan, Tony Perez, Johnny Bench	160.00
MCM	Orlando Cepeda, Willie McCovey, Juan Marichal	100.00
MSC	Joe Morgan, Rod Carew, Ryne Sandberg	125.00
MYF	Robin Yount, Paul Molitor, Rollie Fingers	125.00
PMC	Rod Carew, Kirby Puckett, Paul Molitor	100.00
RAP	Jim Palmer, Luis Aparicio, Brooks Robinson	80.00
RBC	Steve Carlton, Jim Bunning, Robin Roberts	85.00
RBS	George Brett, Mike Schmidt, Brooks Robinson	200.00
SRC	Mike Schmidt, Steve Carlton, Robin Roberts	150.00
WJB	Reggie Jackson, Wade Boggs, Dave Winfield	120.00
WSP	Dave Winfield, Ozzie Smith, Gaylord Perry	120.00
YKM	Ralph Kiner, Carl Yastrzemski, Stan Musial	140.00

Signs of Cooperstown Triples

NM/M

Production 50 Sets	
Gold:	No Pricing
Production 5 Sets	
Silver:	No Pricing
Production 15 Sets	
Rainbow:	No Pricing
Production One Set	

ASY	Robin Yount, Luis Aparicio, Ozzie Smith	8.00
BFJ	Jim Palmer, Frank Robinson, Brooks Robinson	5.00
BSB	George Brett, Mike Schmidt, Wade Boggs	10.00
BSY	Ernie Banks, Robin Yount, Ozzie Smith	8.00
CMI	Monte Irvin, Orlando Cepeda, Willie McCovey	5.00
DFY	Carlton Fisk, Carl Yastrzemski, Bobby Doerr	8.00
DYB	Carl Yastrzemski, Wade Boggs, Bobby Doerr	8.00
FPE	Bob Feller, Dennis Eckersley, Gaylord Perry	4.00
FRC	Bob Feller, Steve Carlton, Nolan Ryan	10.00
FSE	Dennis Eckersley, Rollie Fingers, Don Sutton	4.00
GCE	Bob Gibson, Dennis Eckersley, Steve Carlton	4.00
GSM	Bob Gibson, Stan Musial, Ozzie Smith	8.00
JFB	Yogi Berra, Reggie Jackson, Whitey Ford	8.00
JPR	Nolan Ryan, Gaylord Perry, Fergie Jenkins	10.00
KKB	Al Kaline, George Kell, Jim Bunning	6.00
KPC	Rod Carew, Kirby Puckett, Harmon Killebrew	6.00
KSR	Ralph Kiner, Duke Snider, Frank Robinson	5.00
KWR	Al Kaline, Frank Robinson, Dave Winfield	6.00
MBP	Johnny Bench, Tony Perez, Joe Morgan	6.00

MCM	Orlando Cepeda, Willie McCovey, Juan Marichal	5.00
MMS	Joe Morgan, Red Schoendienst, Bill Mazeroski	4.00
MRJ	Eddie Murray, Reggie Jackson, Frank Robinson	5.00
MSC	Rod Carew, Joe Morgan, Ryne Sandberg	6.00
MYF	Robin Yount, Paul Molitor, Rollie Fingers	6.00
PMC	Rod Carew, Kirby Puckett, Paul Molitor	6.00
RAP	Jim Palmer, Luis Aparicio, Brooks Robinson	5.00
RBC	Steve Carlton, Jim Bunning, Robin Roberts	4.00
RBS	George Brett, Mike Schmidt, Brooks Robinson	10.00
RSR	Robin Roberts, Don Sutton, Nolan Ryan	10.00
SRC	Mike Schmidt, Steve Carlton, Robin Roberts	8.00
WBI	Billy Williams, Monte Irvin, Lou Brock	4.00
WBJ	Billy Williams, Ernie Banks, Fergie Jenkins	6.00
WJB	Reggie Jackson, Wade Boggs, Dave Winfield	6.00
WSP	Dave Winfield, Ozzie Smith, Gaylord Perry	6.00
YKM	Ralph Kiner, Carl Yastrzemski, Stan Musial	8.00

Signs of Cooperstown Quads Autographs

No Pricing
Production 10 Sets
Gold: No Pricing
Production 5 Sets
Rainbow: No Pricing
Production One Set

2005 UD Mini Jersey Collection

	NM/M
Complete Set (100):	15.00
Common Player:	.15

Pack (3 + Mini Jersey):		6.00
Box (18):		90.00
1	Garret Anderson	.25
2	Vladimir Guerrero	.75
3	Luis Gonzalez	.15
4	Shawn Green	.25
5	Troy Glaus	.25
6	Andruw Jones	.50
7	Chipper Jones	.75
8	John Smoltz	.40
9	Tim Hudson	.40
10	Miguel Tejada	.50
11	Sammy Sosa	1.00
12	Curt Schilling	.75
13	David Ortiz	.75
14	Johnny Damon	.75
15	Manny Ramirez	.75
16	Greg Maddux	1.00
17	Kerry Wood	.50
18	Mark Prior	.75
19	Nomar Garciaparra	1.00
20	Frank Thomas	.50
21	Adam Dunn	.50
22	Ken Griffey Jr.	1.50
23	Travis Hafner	.25
24	Victor Martinez	.15
25	Todd Helton	.50
26	Ivan Rodriguez	.50
27	Magglio Ordonez	.15
28	Carlos Delgado	.40
29	Miguel Cabrera	.75
30	Jeff Bagwell	.50
31	Lance Berkman	.25
32	Roger Clemens	2.00
33	Roy Oswalt	.25
34	Mike Sweeney	.15
35	Eric Gagne	.15
36	J.D. Drew	.15
37	Ben Sheets	.40
38	Johan Santana	.50
39	Torii Hunter	.15
40	Carlos Beltran	.50
41	Mike Piazza	1.00
42	Pedro Martinez	.75
43	Alex Rodriguez	1.50
44	Derek Jeter	2.00
45	Hideki Matsui	1.50
46	Mike Mussina	.40
47	Randy Johnson	.75
48	Bobby Crosby	.40
49	Eric Chavez	.40
50	Bobby Abreu	.40
51	Jim Thome	.50
52	Jason Bay	.15
53	Oliver Perez	.40
54	Jake Peavy	.40
55	Khalil Greene	.40
56	Jason Schmidt	.15
57	Moises Alou	.40
58	Adrian Beltre	.40
59	Ichiro Suzuki	1.50
60	Albert Pujols	2.00
61	Jim Edmonds	.40
62	Mark Mulder	.40
63	Scott Rolen	.75
64	Aubrey Huff	.15
65	Alfonso Soriano	.50
66	Hank Blalock	.40
67	Mark Teixeira	.50
68	Roy Halladay	.40
69	Jose Vidro	.15
70	Livan Hernandez	.15
71	Atlanta Braves	.15
72	Chicago Cubs	.15
73	Chicago White Sox	.15
74	Cincinnati Reds	.15
75	Cleveland Indians	.15
76	Houston Astros	.15
77	L.A. Angels of Anaheim	.15
78	Los Angeles Dodgers	.15
79	New York Yankees	.15
80	Oakland Athletics	.15
81	Philadelphia Phillies	.15
82	Pittsburgh Pirates	.15
83	San Diego Padres	.15
84	San Francisco Giants	.15
85	Texas Rangers	.15
86	Cal Ripken Jr.	2.00
87	Derek Jeter	2.00
88	Hank Blalock	.40
89	Hideo Nomo	.40
90	Joe DiMaggio	1.00
91	Joe Morgan	.50
92	Ken Griffey Jr.	1.50
93	Larry Doby	.50
94	Pedro J. Martinez	.75
95	Randy Johnson	.75
96	Rick Ferrell	.15
97	Roger Clemens	2.00
98	Stan Musial	1.00
99	Ted Williams	1.50
100	Torii Hunter	.15

Replica Flannel Jerseys

		NM/M
Inserted 1:18		
1	Ted Williams	20.00
2	Jackie Robinson	15.00
3	Satchel Paige	15.00
4	Ty Cobb	15.00
5	Babe Ruth	30.00
6	Joe DiMaggio	20.00
7	Lou Gehrig	25.00
8	Mickey Mantle	30.00
9	Roberto Clemente	20.00

Mini Jerseys

		NM/M
1	Vladimir Guerrero	5.00
2	Chipper Jones	5.00
3	Curt Schilling	5.00
4	Johnny Damon	5.00
5	Manny Ramirez	5.00
6	Kerry Wood	5.00
7	Nomar Garciaparra	5.00
8	Ken Griffey Jr.	5.00
9	Miguel Cabrera	5.00
10	Roger Clemens	10.00
11	Eric Gagne	5.00
12	Johan Santana	5.00
13	Carlos Beltran	5.00
14	Mike Piazza	5.00
15	Pedro Martinez	5.00
16	Alex Rodriguez	5.00
17	Derek Jeter	15.00
18	Hideki Matsui	8.00
19	Randy Johnson	5.00
20	Jim Thome	5.00
21	Ichiro Suzuki	8.00
22	Albert Pujols	10.00

Mini Jersey Autograph

		NM/M
Inserted 1:480		
1	Ken Griffey Jr.	150.00
2	David Wright	50.00
5	Adrian Beltre	50.00

2005 UD Origins

	NM/M
Complete Set (200):	
Common Player:	.50
Tin (20):	50.00

1	Jim Edmonds	.75
2	Jason Schmidt	.75
3	J.D. Drew	.75
4	Luis Gonzalez	.50
5	Nomar Garciaparra	2.00
6	Jake Peavy	.75
7	Rafael Furcal	.50
8	Craig Biggio	.75
9	Ken Griffey Jr.	3.00
10	Mike Piazza	2.00
11	Jose Vidro	.50
12	Ivan Rodriguez	1.00
13	Carl Crawford	.50
14	Roger Clemens	4.00
15	Kerry Wood	1.00
16	Vernon Wells	.50
17	Carlos Guillen	.50
18	Tim Hudson	.75
19	Carl Pavano	.50
20	Carlos Beltran	1.00
21	Pedro Martinez	1.50
22	Hideki Matsui	3.00
23	Frank Thomas	1.00
24	Curt Schilling	1.50
25	Manny Ramirez	1.50
26	Alex Rodriguez	4.00
27	Aubrey Huff	.50
28	David Ortiz	1.50
29	Mark Prior	1.50
30	Albert Pujols	4.00
31	Miguel Cabrera	1.50

32	Brad Penny	.50
33	Carlos Delgado	.75
34	Aramis Ramirez	1.00
35	Josh Beckett	1.00
36	Rafael Palmeiro	1.00
37	Bret Boone	.50
38	Lance Berkman	.75
39	Carlos Zambrano	.75
40	Adam Dunn	1.00
41	Livan Hernandez	.50
42	Mike Mussina	.75
43	Ben Sheets	.75
44	Derek Jeter	4.00
45	Kazuo Matsui	.50
46	Bobby Abreu	.75
47	Jeff Bagwell	1.00
48	Travis Hafner	.50
49	Torii Hunter	.75
50	Kevin Brown	.50
51	Alfonso Soriano	1.50
52	Jim Thome	1.00
53	John Smoltz	.75
54	Mike Sweeney	.50
55	Andy Pettitte	.75
56	Chipper Jones	1.50
57	Randy Johnson	1.50
58	Steve Finley	.50
59	Larry Walker	.75
60	Troy Glaus	.75
61	Greg Maddux	2.50
62	Shawn Green	.50
63	Roy Halladay	.75
64	Jeff Kent	.50
65	Scott Podsednik	.50
66	Miguel Tejada	1.00
67	Lyle Overbay	.50
68	Bernie Williams	.75
69	Todd Helton	1.00
70	Melvin Mora	.50
71	Magglio Ordonez	.50
72	Carlos Lee	.75
73	Roy Oswalt	.75
74	Victor Martinez	.75
75	Scott Rolen	1.50
76	Eric Chavez	.75
77	Paul Konerko	.75
78	Jose Reyes	.50
79	Barry Larkin	.75
80	Johnny Damon	1.00
81	Eric Gagne	.75
82	Andruw Jones	1.00
83	Gary Sheffield	1.00
84	Richie Sexson	.75
85	Sammy Sosa	2.50
86	Mark Teixeira	1.00
87	Vladimir Guerrero	1.50
88	Michael Young	.50
89	Johan Santana	1.00
90	Adrian Beltre	.75
91	Tom Glavine	.75
92	Hank Blalock	.75
93	Preston Wilson	.50
94	Jason Kendall	.50
95	Mike Lowell	.50
96	Craig Wilson	.50
97	Ichiro Suzuki	3.00
98	Mark Mulder	.75
99	Garret Anderson	.75
100	Brian Giles	.50
101	Robin Yount	3.00
102	Ernie Banks	3.00
103	Mike Schmidt	5.00
104	Enos Slaughter	1.00
105	Red Schoendienst	1.00
106	Hoyt Wilhelm	1.00
107	Lou Brock	2.00
108	Rollie Fingers	1.00
109	Gaylord Perry	1.00
110	Bobby Doerr	1.00
111	Larry Doby	1.00
112	Al Lopez	1.00
113	Joe Morgan	1.50
114	Luis Aparicio	1.50
115	Willie McCovey	2.00
116	Bob Lemon	1.00
117	Early Wynn	1.00
118	Bob Feller	2.00
119	Cal Ripken Jr.	8.00
120	George Kell	1.00
121	Juan Marichal	1.50
122	Monte Irvin	1.50
123	Harmon Killebrew	3.00
124	Lou Boudreau	1.00
125	Mickey Mantle	8.00
126	Richie Ashburn	1.00
127	Pee Wee Reese	1.50
128	Whitey Ford	2.00
129	Tom Seaver	2.00
130	Phil Rizzuto	2.00
131	Yogi Berra	3.00
132	Warren Spahn	2.00
133	Billy Williams	1.50
134	Jim Bunning	1.00
135	Ralph Kiner	1.00
136	Ted Williams	6.00
137	Rick Ferrell	1.00

138	Robin Roberts	1.00
139	Brooks Robinson	3.00
140	Hal Newhouser	1.00
141	Jim "Catfish" Hunter	1.00
142	Phil Niekro	1.00
143	Fergie Jenkins	1.00
144	Al Kaline	3.00
145	Stan Musial	4.00
146	Joe DiMaggio	6.00
147	Willie Stargell	2.00
148	Nolan Ryan	6.00
149	Babe Ruth	6.00
150	Bob Gibson	2.00
151	David DeJesus	.50
152	Chris Burke	.50
153	Chad Cordero	.50
154	Kevin Youkilis	.50
155	Bucky Jacobsen	.50
156	B.J. Upton	.50
157	Aaron Rowand	.50
158	Jose Capellan	.50
159	David Wright	2.00
160	Jason Bay	.50
161	Edwin Jackson	.50
162	Scott Kazmir	.50
163	J.D. Closser	.50
164	Chase Utley	1.00
165	Nick Swisher	.50
166	Casey Kotchman	.50
167	Bobby Crosby	.50
168	Zack Greinke	.50
169	Gavin Floyd	.50
170	Jeff Francis	.50
171	Dallas McPherson	.50
172	Gabe Gross	.50
173	Brandon Claussen	.50
174	Wily Mo Pena	.50
175	Robb Quinlan	.50
176	Oliver Perez	.50
177	Guillermo Quiroz	.50
178	Ryan Howard	1.00
179	Gerald Laird	.50
180	Jayson Werth	.50
181	Bobby Madritsch	.50
182	Laynce Nix	.50
183	Eddy Rodriguez	.50
184	Rickie Weeks	1.00
185	Scott Proctor	.50
186	Adam LaRoche	.50
187	Yhency Brazoban	.50
188	Adrian Gonzalez	.50
189	Jason Lane	.50
190	Ryan Wagner	.50
191	Roman Colon	.50
192	Alexis Rios	.50
193	Joe Mauer	1.00
194	Garrett Atkins	.50
195	Daniel Cabrera	.50
196	Khalil Greene	2.00
197	Joe Blanton	.50
198	Jason Dubois	.50
199	Angel Guzman	.50
200	Jesse Crain	.50

Black

No Pricing
Production One Set

Blue

Stars (1-200):	2-4X
Production 50 Sets	

Gold

No Pricing
Production 20 Sets

Red

Stars (1-200):	2-3X
Production 99 Sets	

Origins Materials
Jersey

		NM/M
Inserted 2:Tin		
Old Judge:		1X
JB	Jeff Bagwell	8.00
CB	Carlos Beltran	8.00
AB	Adrian Beltre	5.00
LB	Lance Berkman	5.00
HB	Hank Blalock	5.00
MC	Miguel Cabrera	8.00
EC	Eric Chavez	5.00
JD	J.D. Drew	5.00
GL	Troy Glaus	5.00
KG	Ken Griffey Jr.	10.00
VG	Vladimir Guerrero	8.00
TG	Tony Gwynn SP	10.00
HE	Todd Helton	5.00
TH	Tim Hudson	5.00
HU	Torii Hunter	5.00
DJ	Derek Jeter	15.00
RJ	Randy Johnson	8.00
AJ	Andruw Jones	5.00
CJ	Chipper Jones	8.00
GM	Greg Maddux	10.00
HM	Hideki Matsui	15.00
KM	Hideki Matsui	5.00
DO	David Ortiz	8.00
PI	Mike Piazza	8.00
MP	Mark Prior	8.00
AP	Albert Pujols	15.00
MR	Manny Ramirez	8.00
CR	Cal Ripken Jr. SP	25.00
IR	Ivan Rodriguez	8.00
SR	Scott Rolen	5.00
NR	Nolan Ryan SP	30.00
CS	Curt Schilling	8.00
BS	Ben Sheets	5.00
GS	Gary Sheffield	5.00
AS	Alfonso Soriano	8.00
SS	Sammy Sosa	8.00
IS	Ichiro Suzuki	20.00
MT	Mark Teixeira	5.00
TE	Miguel Tejada	8.00
FT	Frank Thomas	8.00
JT	Jim Thome	8.00
KW	Kerry Wood	8.00

Origins Nostalgic
Signs

		NM/M
One sign per tin.		
CB	Carlos Beltran	8.00
AB	Adrian Beltre	5.00
HB	Hank Blalock	5.00
MC	Miguel Cabrera	8.00
EC	Eric Chavez	5.00
RC	Roger Clemens	15.00
TC	Ty Cobb	20.00
JD	Joe DiMaggio	20.00
LG	Lou Gehrig	15.00
KG	Ken Griffey Jr.	12.00
VG	Vladimir Guerrero	8.00
TH	Todd Helton	5.00
DJ	Derek Jeter	15.00
RJ	Randy Johnson	8.00
WJ	Walter Johnson	15.00
CJ	Chipper Jones	8.00
PM	Pedro Martinez	8.00
HM	Hideki Matsui	20.00
DO	David Ortiz	8.00
SP	Satchel Paige	12.00
MP	Mike Piazza	10.00
MPR	Mark Prior	8.00
AP	Albert Pujols	20.00
MR	Manny Ramirez	8.00
CR	Cal Ripken Jr.	25.00
JR	Jackie Robinson	12.00
AR	Alex Rodriguez	12.00
IR	Ivan Rodriguez	8.00
SR	Scott Rolen	5.00
BR	Babe Ruth	20.00
NR	Nolan Ryan	20.00
JS	Johan Santana	8.00
CS	Curt Schilling	10.00
AS	Alfonso Soriano	10.00
SS	Sammy Sosa	10.00
IS	Ichiro Suzuki	12.00
MT	Miguel Tejada	8.00
FT	Frank Thomas	8.00
JT	Jim Thome	8.00
HW	Honus Wagner	10.00
TW	Ted Williams	25.00

Origins Old Judge

		NM/M
Common Player:		.50
Blue:		2-3X
Red:		1-2X
Gold:		No Pricing
1	Jake Peavy	1.00
2	Derek Jeter	5.00
3	Adrian Beltre	1.00
4	Hank Blalock	1.00
5	Preston Wilson	.50

6	Randy Johnson	2.00
7	Pedro Martinez	2.00
8	Michael Young	1.00
9	Steve Finley	.50
10	Shawn Green	.75
11	Carlos Beltran	1.50
12	Bernie Williams	1.00
13	Brian Giles	.50
14	Kevin Brown	.50
15	Barry Larkin	1.00
16	Troy Glaus	1.00
17	Bret Boone	.50
18	Jason Kendall	.50
19	Johnny Damon	1.50
20	Josh Beckett	1.00
21	Carl Pavano	.50
22	Chipper Jones	2.00
23	Ivan Rodriguez	1.50
24	Kerry Wood	1.50
25	Ken Griffey Jr.	3.00
26	Greg Maddux	3.00
27	Kazuo Matsui	.50
28	Albert Pujols	5.00
29	Victor Martinez	.50
30	Johan Santana	1.50
31	Bobby Abreu	.75
32	Paul Konerko	.75
33	Gary Sheffield	1.00
34	Jose Vidro	.50
35	Alex Rodriguez	4.00
36	Alfonso Soriano	1.50
37	Mark Teixeira	1.50
38	Nomar Garciaparra	2.50
39	Sammy Sosa	3.00
40	Garret Anderson	1.00
41	Eric Chavez	1.00
42	Magglio Ordonez	.50
43	Larry Walker	1.00
44	Brad Penny	.50
45	Jeff Bagwell	1.50
46	Craig Biggio	.75
47	Torii Hunter	.75
48	Mike Lowell	.50
49	Ben Sheets	1.00
50	Miguel Tejada	1.50
51	Jim Edmonds	1.00
52	Mark Mulder	1.00
53	Curt Schilling	1.50
54	Roger Clemens	5.00
55	Jason Schmidt	.50
56	Rafael Furcal	.50
57	Scott Rolen	2.00
58	Carlos Zambrano	.75
59	Mike Sweeney	.50
60	Vladimir Guerrero	2.00
61	Miguel Cabrera	2.00
62	Lance Berkman	.50
63	Lyle Overbay	.50
64	Livan Hernandez	.50
65	Aramis Ramirez	1.00
66	Ichiro Suzuki	4.00
67	Roy Oswalt	.50
68	Carl Crawford	.50
69	Craig Wilson	.50
70	Carlos Lee	.75
71	J.D. Drew	.50
72	Rafael Palmeiro	1.50
73	Jeff Kent	.50
74	Adam Dunn	1.50
75	Andy Pettitte	1.00
76	Luis Gonzalez	.50
77	Frank Thomas	1.50
78	John Smoltz	1.00
79	Hideki Matsui	3.00
80	Tom Glavine	.50
81	Jose Reyes	.50
82	Jim Thome	1.50
83	Mark Prior	2.00
84	Roy Halladay	.75
85	Carlos Delgado	1.00
86	Melvin Mora	.50
87	David Ortiz	2.00
88	Travis Hafner	.50
89	Carlos Guillen	.50
90	Tim Hudson	.50
91	Vernon Wells	.50
92	Andruw Jones	1.50
93	Mike Mussina	1.00
94	Mike Piazza	3.00
95	Richie Sexson	1.00
96	Aubrey Huff	.50
97	Scott Podsednik	.50
98	Eric Gagne	.50
99	Manny Ramirez	2.00
100	Todd Helton	1.50
101	Joe Morgan	1.00
102	Billy Williams	1.00
103	Pee Wee Reese	1.00
104	Lou Boudreau	1.00
105	Richie Ashburn	1.00
106	Jim Bunning	1.00
107	Hal Newhouser	1.00
108	Rick Ferrell	1.00
109	Ted Williams	5.00

110	Ralph Kiner	1.00
111	Warren Spahn	2.50
112	George Kell	.50
113	Willie Stargell	2.00
114	Jim "Catfish" Hunter	.50
115	Tom Seaver	2.00
116	Cal Ripken Jr.	8.00
117	Al Lopez	.50
118	Ernie Banks	3.00
119	Lou Brock	2.00
120	Robin Yount	3.00
121	Nolan Ryan	6.00
122	Larry Doby	1.00
123	Al Kaline	2.00
124	Willie McCovey	2.00
125	Stan Musial	3.00
126	Phil Niekro	1.00
127	Babe Ruth	6.00
128	Rollie Fingers	1.00
129	Juan Marichal	1.00
130	Early Wynn	1.00
131	Luis Aparicio	1.00
132	Brooks Robinson	3.00
133	Mike Schmidt	5.00
134	Gaylord Perry	1.00
135	Bob Lemon	1.00
136	Monte Irvin	1.50
137	Mickey Mantle	8.00
138	Phil Rizzuto	1.50
139	Robin Roberts	1.50
140	Bobby Doerr	1.00
141	Bob Gibson	2.00
142	Enos Slaughter	1.00
143	Yogi Berra	2.00
144	Whitey Ford	2.00
145	Red Schoendienst	1.00
146	Joe DiMaggio	5.00
147	Harmon Killebrew	2.00
148	Hoyt Wilhelm	1.00
149	Fergie Jenkins	1.00
150	Bob Feller	1.50
151	Scott Proctor	.50
152	Adam LaRoche	.50
153	Ryan Howard	1.00
154	Laynce Nix	.50
155	Garrett Atkins	.50
156	Chris Burke	.50
157	Oliver Perez	.50
158	Wily Mo Pena	.50
159	B.J. Upton	.50
160	Gavin Floyd	.50
161	Jesse Crain	.50
162	Khalil Greene	3.00
163	Eddy Rodriguez	.50
164	Edwin Jackson	.50
165	Scott Kazmir	.50
166	Ryan Wagner	.50
167	Nick Swisher	.50
168	Joe Blanton	.50
169	Alexis Rios	.50
170	Chad Cordero	.50
171	Jason Dubois	.50
172	Chase Utley	1.00
173	David DeJesus	.50
174	Zack Greinke	.50
175	Bobby Crosby	1.00
176	Angel Guzman	.50
177	Adrian Gonzalez	.50
178	Guillermo Quiroz	.50
179	Gerald Laird	.50
180	Rickie Weeks	1.00
181	Jayson Werth	.50
182	Buck Jacobsen	.50
183	J.D. Closser	.50
184	Jason Bay	.50
185	Roman Colon	.50
186	Casey Kotchman	.50
187	Yhency Brazoban	.50
188	Bobby Madritsch	.50
189	Gabe Gross	.50
190	Brandon Claussen	.50
191	Aaron Rowand	.50
192	Jeff Francis	.50
193	David Wright	2.00
194	Jose Capellan	.50
195	Jason Lane	.50
196	Daniel Cabrera	.50
197	Joe Mauer	1.00
198	Kevin Youkilis	.50
199	Dallas McPherson	.50
200	Robb Quinlan	.50

Origins Old Judge
Autographs

		NM/M
Common Auto.:		12.00
Bronze:		No Pricing
JB	Jason Bay	15.00
CB	Carlos Beltran/15	
AB	Adrian Beltre	12.00
MC	Miguel Cabrera	25.00
CC	Carl Crawford/Exch.	12.00
BC	Bobby Crosby/Exch.	15.00

BD	Bobby Doerr	15.00
BF	Bob Feller	25.00
MG	Marcus Giles/Exch.	15.00
DG	Dwight Gooden	15.00
GR	Khalil Greene	20.00
KG	Ken Griffey Jr.	75.00
RG	Ron Guidry	15.00
TG	Tony Gwynn	50.00
TH	Travis Hafner	15.00
RH	Rich Harden	15.00
KH	Keith Hernandez	15.00
FH	Frank Howard	20.00
HO	Ryan Howard	75.00
AH	Aubrey Huff	8.00
DJ	Derek Jeter	150.00
SK	Scott Kazmir	20.00
DK	Dave Kingman	15.00
CK	Casey Kotchman	15.00
SL	Sparky Lyle	12.00
VM	Victor Martinez	15.00
MA	Don Mattingly	65.00
DM	Dallas McPherson	12.00
PM	Paul Molitor	40.00
OS	Roy Oswalt	15.00
AO	Akinori Otsuka	15.00
JP	Jim Palmer	15.00
PE	Jake Peavy	25.00
OP	Oliver Perez	15.00
CR	Cal Ripken Jr./25	180.00
BR	Brooks Robinson	30.00
RO	Al Rosen	15.00
JS	Johan Santana/Exch.	35.00
RS	Ron Santo	25.00
MS	Mike Schmidt	75.00
BS	Ben Sheets	12.00
ST	Shingo Takatsu	15.00
MT	Mark Teixeira	25.00
BU	B.J. Upton	15.00
CU	Chase Utley	25.00
RW	Rickie Weeks	15.00
DW	David Wright	60.00
RY	Robin Yount	50.00
CZ	Carlos Zambrano	20.00

Origins Old Judge Materials Jersey

FRANK THOMAS

		NM/M
Common Jersey:		5.00
JB	Jeff Bagwell	8.00
CB	Carlos Beltran	8.00
AB	Adrian Beltre	5.00
LB	Lance Berkman	5.00
HB	Hank Blalock	5.00
MC	Miguel Cabrera	8.00
EC	Eric Chavez	5.00
JD	J.D. Drew	5.00
GL	Troy Glaus	5.00
KG	Ken Griffey Jr.	10.00
VG	Vladimir Guerrero	8.00
TG	Tony Gwynn/SP	10.00
HE	Todd Helton	5.00
TH	Tim Hudson	5.00
HU	Torii Hunter	5.00
DJ	Derek Jeter	15.00
RJ	Randy Johnson	8.00
AJ	Andruw Jones	5.00
CJ	Chipper Jones	8.00
GM	Greg Maddux	10.00
HM	Hideki Matsui	15.00
KM	Kazuo Matsui	5.00
DO	David Ortiz	8.00
PI	Mike Piazza	8.00
MP	Mark Prior	8.00
AP	Albert Pujols	15.00
MR	Manny Ramirez	8.00
CR	Cal Ripken Jr./SP	25.00
SR	Scott Rolen	8.00
NR	Nolan Ryan/SP	30.00
CS	Curt Schilling	8.00
BS	Ben Sheets	5.00
GS	Gary Sheffield	8.00
AS	Alfonso Soriano	8.00

SS	Sammy Sosa	8.00
IS	Ichiro Suzuki	20.00
MT	Mark Teixeira	5.00
TE	Miguel Tejada	8.00
FT	Frank Thomas	8.00
JT	Jim Thome	8.00
KW	Kerry Wood	8.00

Origins Signatures

		NM/M
Common Auto.:		12.00
Bronze:		No Pricing
Production 5 Sets		
JB1	Jason Bay	15.00
AB1	Adrian Beltre	12.00
MC1	Miguel Cabrera	25.00
CC1	Carl Crawford/Exch.	12.00
BC1	Bobby Crosby/Exch.	15.00
BD1	Bobby Doerr	15.00
BF1	Bob Feller	25.00
MG1	Marcus Giles	15.00
DG1	Dwight Gooden	15.00
GR1	Khalil Greene	20.00
KG1	Ken Griffey Jr.	75.00
RG1	Ron Guidry	15.00
TG1	Tony Gwynn	50.00
TH1	Travis Hafner	15.00
RH1	Rich Harden	15.00
KH1	Keith Hernandez	15.00
FH1	Frank Howard	20.00
HO1	Ryan Howard	75.00
AH1	Aubrey Huff	8.00
DJ1	Derek Jeter	150.00
SK1	Scott Kazmir	20.00
DK1	Dave Kingman	15.00
CK1	Casey Kotchman	15.00
SL1	Sparky Lyle	12.00
VM1	Victor Martinez	15.00
MA1	Don Mattingly	65.00
DM1	Dallas McPherson	12.00
PM1	Paul Molitor	40.00
OS1	Roy Oswalt	15.00
AO1	Akinori Otsuka	15.00
JP1	Jim Palmer	15.00
PE1	Jake Peavy	25.00
OP1	Oliver Perez	15.00
CR1	Cal Ripken Jr./25	180.00
BR1	Brooks Robinson	30.00
RO1	Al Rosen	15.00
JS1	Johan Santana/Exch.	35.00
RS1	Ron Santo	25.00
MS1	Mike Schmidt	75.00
BS1	Ben Sheets	12.00
ST1	Shingo Takatsu	15.00
MT1	Mark Teixeira	25.00
BU1	B.J. Upton	15.00
CU1	Chase Utley	25.00
RW1	Rickie Weeks	15.00
DW1	David Wright	60.00
RY1	Robin Yount	50.00
CZ1	Carlos Zambrano	20.00

Origins Tins

		NM/M
Common Tin:		5.00
TC	Ty Cobb	5.00
DJ	Derek Jeter	10.00
WJ	Walter Johnson	5.00
HW	Honus Wagner	5.00

2005 UD Past Time Pennants

PAUL MOLITOR

		NM/M
Complete Set (90):		20.00
Common Player:		.20
Pack (5):		4.00
Box (20):		70.00
1	Al Kaline	.50
2	Al Rosen	.20
3	Bert Blyleven	.20

4	Bill Mazeroski	.20
5	Billy Williams	.20
6	Bob Feller	.50
7	Bob Gibson	.75
8	Bob Lemon	.20
9	Bobby Doerr	.40
10	Brooks Robinson	.75
11	Bruce Sutter	.30
12	Bucky Dent	.20
13	Cal Ripken Jr.	2.00
14	Carl Yastrzemski	.75
15	Carlton Fisk	.40
16	Jim "Catfish" Hunter	.20
17	Dale Murphy	.40
18	Dave Parker	.20
19	Don Larsen	.50
20	Don Mattingly	1.00
21	Don Newcombe	.20
22	Duke Snider	.50
23	Early Wynn	.20
24	Eddie Matthews	.75
25	Eddie Murray	.50
26	Enos Slaughter	.20
27	Ernie Banks	.75
28	Fergie Jenkins	.20
29	Frank Howard	.20
30	Frank Robinson	.50
31	Fred Lynn	.20
32	Gary Carter	.20
33	Gaylord Perry	.20
34	George Brett	1.50
35	George Kell	.20
36	Rich "Goose" Gossage	.20
37	Graig Nettles	.20
38	Harmon Killebrew	.75
39	Jack Morris	.20
40	Jim Bunning	.20
41	Felipe Alou	.20
42	Jim Palmer	.40
43	Jim Rice	.20
44	Joe DiMaggio	1.50
45	Joe Morgan	.20
46	Johnny Bench	.75
47	Johnny Podres	.20
48	Juan Marichal	.20
49	Keith Hernandez	.20
50	Kirby Puckett	.75
51	Larry Doby	.20
52	Lou Brock	.40
53	Luis Aparicio	.20
54	Luis Tiant	.20
55	Maury 4illis	.20
56	Mickey Mantle	2.00
57	Mike Schmidt	1.50
58	Monte Irvin	.20
59	Nolan Ryan	1.50
60	Orlando Cepeda	.20
61	Ozzie Smith	.75
62	Paul Molitor	.50
63	Pee Wee Reese	.20
64	Phil Niekro	.20
65	Phil Rizzuto	.50
66	Ralph Kiner	.20
67	Richie Ashburn	.20
68	Rico Petrocelli	.20
69	Robin Roberts	.20
70	Robin Yount	.75
71	Rocky Colavito	.20
72	Rod Carew	.40
73	Rollie Fingers	.20
74	Ron Guidry	.20
75	Ron Santo	.20
76	Tony Gwynn	.75
77	Sparky Lyle	.20
78	Stan Musial	1.00
79	Steve Carlton	.40
80	Rick Ferrell	.20
81	Tom Seaver	.75
82	Tommy John	.20
83	Tony Perez	.20
84	Wade Boggs	.50
85	Warren Spahn	.75
86	Whitey Ford	.40
87	Will Clark	.50
88	Willie McCovey	.50
89	Willie Stargell	.40
90	Yogi Berra	.75

Gold

Gold:		4-8X
Production 50 Sets		

Silver

Gold:		3-5X
Production 100 Sets		

Mitchell & Ness Jersey Redemption

No Pricing

Mitchell & Ness Pennants

		NM/M
Common Pennant:		15.00

Inserted 1:Hobby Box				
1903	1903 Boston Americans/100			20.00
1905	1095 New York Giants/100			20.00
1906	1906 Chicago White Sox/100			20.00
1907	1907 Detroit Tigers/100			20.00
1908	1908 Chicago Cubs/105			25.00
1909	1909 Pittsburgh Pirates/125			20.00
1910	1910 Philadelphia A's/125			20.00
1912	1912 Boston Red Sox/125			20.00
1914	1914 Boston Braves/125			20.00
1915	1915 Philadelphia Phillies/125			20.00
1916	1916 Brooklyn Robins/200			20.00
1917	1917 New York Giants/200			20.00
1918	1918 Boston Red Sox/200			20.00
1919	1919 Chicago White Sox/200			20.00
1920	1920 Cleveland Indians/200			15.00
1921	1921 New York Yankees/200			25.00
1922	1922 New York Giants/200			20.00
1924	1924 Washington Senators/200			20.00
1925	1925 Pittsburgh Pirates/200			15.00
1926	1926 Saint Louis Cardinals/200			20.00
1927	1927 New York Yankees/500			20.00
1928	1928 New York Yankees/500			25.00
1929	1929 Chicago Cubs/337			20.00
1930	1930 Philadelphia A's/337			15.00
1931	1931 Saint Louis Cardinals/337			20.00
1932	1932 Chicago Cubs/337			20.00
1934	1934 Detroit Tigers/337			15.00
1935	1935 Chicago Cubs/337			20.00
1936	1936 New York Yankees/337			25.00
1937	1937 New York Giants/337			20.00
1938	1938 New York Yankees/337			25.00
1939	1939 Cincinnati Reds/337			15.00
1940	1940 Cincinnati Reds/337			15.00
1941	1941 Brooklyn Dodgers/337			25.00
1942	1942 Saint Louis Cardinals/337			20.00
1943	1943 New York Yankees/337			25.00
1944	1944 Saint Louis Browns/337			15.00
1945	1945 Chicago Cubs/337			20.00
1946	1946 Boston Red Sox/337			20.00
1947	1947 Brooklyn Dodgers/337			25.00
1948	1948 Boston Braves/337			15.00
1949	1949 New York Yankees/337			25.00
1950	1950 Philadelphia Phillies/337			15.00
1951	1951 New York Giants/337			15.00
1952	1952 Brooklyn Dodgers/500			20.00
1953	1953 New York Yankees/337			25.00
1954	1954 Cleveland Indians/337			15.00
1955	1955 Brooklyn Dodgers/337			25.00
1956	1956 Brooklyn Dodgers/500			25.00
1957	1957 Milwaukee Braves/337			20.00
1958	1958 New York Yankees/500			25.00

1959	1959 Los Angeles Dodgers/337	20.00
1960	1960 Pittsburgh Pirates/337	15.00
1961	1961 Cincinnati Reds/337	15.00
1962	1962 San Francisco Giants/337	20.00
1963	1963 Los Angeles Dodgers/337	20.00
1964	1964 Saint Louis Cardinals/337	20.00
1965	1965 Minnesota Twins/337	15.00
1966	1966 Baltimore Orioles/337	20.00
1967	1967 Boston Red Sox/337	20.00
1968	1968 Detroit Tigers/337	15.00
1969	1969 New York Mets/337	20.00
1970	1970 Baltimore Orioles/337	20.00
1971	1971 Pittsburgh Pirates/337	15.00
1972	1972 Oakland A's/337	20.00
1973	1973 Oakland A's/337	20.00
1974	1974 Los Angeles Dodgers/337	20.00
1977	1977 New York Yankees/337	25.00
1978	1978 Los Angeles Dodgers/337	20.00
1979	1979 Pittsburgh Pirates/337	15.00
1980	1980 Philadelphia Phillies/337	20.00
1981	1981 Los Angeles Dodgers/337	20.00
1982	1982 Milwaukee Brewers/337	20.00
1983	1983 Baltimore Orioles/337	20.00
1984	1984 San Diego Padres/337	15.00
1985	1985 Kansas City Royals/337	15.00
1986	1986 Boston Red Sox/337	25.00
1988	1988 Los Angeles Dodgers/337	20.00
1975B	1975 Boston Red Sox/337	25.00
1975C	1975 Cincinnati Reds/337	20.00

Mitchell & Ness Penn Autograph
NM/M

Production 86-87

JB	Johnny Bench/87	80.00
SC	Steve Carlton/87	60.00
RF	Rollie Fingers/87	40.00
CF	Carlton Fisk/87	60.00
SG	Steve Garvey/40	40.00
AK	Al Kaline/87	75.00
PM	Paul Molitor/87	75.00
GN	Graig Nettles/87	50.00
DN	Don Newcombe/87	40.00
BR	Brooks Robinson/87	75.00
TS	Tom Seaver/87	80.00
CY	Carl Yastrzemski/86	80.00

Signatures Bronze
NM/M

SP's Production 3-25

RB	Rick Burleson	10.00
DC	David Cone	15.00
LD	Lenny Dykstra	12.00
SF	Sid Fernandez	10.00
BF	Bill Freehan	10.00
DG	Dwight Gooden	15.00
KG	Ken Griffey Sr.	10.00
GU	Don Gullett	8.00
PG	Pedro Guerrero	10.00
HO	Ken Holtzman	10.00
BH	Burt Hooton	10.00
WH	Willie Horton/EXCH.	12.00
FH	Frank Howard	15.00
HR	Kent Hrbek	10.00
RH	Randy Hundley	10.00
TJ	Tommy John	15.00
WJ	Wally Joyner	15.00
DK	Dave Kingman	10.00
KN	Ray Knight	10.00
SL	Sparky Lyle	10.00
BM	Bill Madlock	10.00
BO	Bobby Murcer	15.00
RP	Rico Petrocelli	12.00
BP	Boog Powell	25.00

AR	Al Rosen	15.00
SS	Steve Sax	10.00
SC	Mike Scioscia/EXCH.	15.00
WI	Mookie Wilson	15.00

Signatures Dual

Production 15-24

Signatures Gold
NM/M

Many not priced due to scarcity.

FA	Felipe Alou	20.00
RB	Rick Burleson	15.00
LD	Lenny Dykstra	20.00
SF	Sid Fernandez	15.00
BF	Bill Freehan	15.00
KG	Ken Griffey Sr.	15.00
PG	Pedro Guerrero	15.00
GU	Don Gullett	10.00
HO	Ken Holtzman	15.00
BH	Burt Hooton	15.00
WH	Willie Horton EXCH	15.00
HR	Kent Hrbek	20.00
RH	Randy Hundley	10.00
DK	Dave Kingman	15.00
KN	Ray Knight	15.00
SL	Sparky Lyle	15.00
BM	Bill Madlock	15.00
BO	Bobby Murcer	25.00
RP	Rico Petrocelli	15.00

Signatures Silver
NM/M

FA	Felipe Alou	10.00
LA	Luis Aparicio	20.00
BB	Bert Blyleven	15.00
BR	Lou Brock	30.00
JB	Jim Bunning/EXCH.	15.00
RB	Rick Burleson	10.00
ST	Steve Carlton	35.00
GC	Gary Carter	20.00
OC	Orlando Cepeda	20.00
CC	Chris Chambliss	15.00
WC	Will Clark	40.00
RC	Rocky Colavito	65.00
DC	David Cone	15.00
DE	Bucky Dent	12.00
BD	Bobby Doerr	15.00
LD	Lenny Dykstra	10.00
CE	Carl Erskine/EXCH.	12.00
EV	Dwight Evans	30.00
FE	Bob Feller	30.00
SF	Sid Fernandez	10.00
RF	Rollie Fingers	20.00
BF	Bill Freehan	10.00
DG	Dwight Gooden	15.00
GG	Rich "Goose" Gossage	15.00
KG	Ken Griffey Sr.	10.00
GU	Don Gullett	8.00
PG	Pedro Guerrero	15.00
KH	Keith Hernandez	15.00
HO	Ken Holtzman	10.00
BH	Burt Hooton	10.00
WH	Willie Horton/EXCH.	10.00
FH	Frank Howard	15.00
HR	Kent Hrbek	10.00
RH	Randy Hundley	10.00
MI	Monte Irvin	25.00
FJ	Fergie Jenkins	20.00
TJ	Tommy Jones	15.00
WJ	Wally Joyner	15.00
AK	Al Kaline	50.00
GK	George Kell	15.00
HK	Harmon Killebrew	50.00
RK	Ralph Kiner	40.00
DK	Dave Kingman	10.00
KN	Ray Knight	10.00
DL	Don Larsen/EXCH.	30.00
SL	Sparky Lyle	10.00
FL	Fred Lynn	15.00

BM	Bill Madlock	10.00
JU	Juan Marichal/EXCH.	20.00
MA	Bill Mazeroski	30.00
PM	Paul Molitor	40.00
MO	Joe Morgan	20.00
JM	Jack Morris	15.00
BO	Bobby Murcer	20.00
MU	Dale Murphy	25.00
GN	Graig Nettles	20.00
DN	Don Newcombe	15.00
JP	Jim Palmer	30.00
DP	Dave Parker	15.00
TP	Tony Perez/EXCH.	40.00
GP	Gaylord Perry	15.00
RP	Rico Petrocelli	15.00
PO	Johnny Podres	25.00
BP	Boog Powell	20.00
JR	Jim Rice	20.00
RO	Brooks Robinson	60.00
AR	Al Rosen	15.00
RS	Ron Santo	25.00
SS	Steve Sax	10.00
SC	Mike Scioscia/EXCH.	20.00
BS	Bill "Moose" Skowron	15.00
SU	Bruce Sutter	15.00
LT	Luis Tiant	15.00
BW	Billy Williams/EXCH.	15.00
MW	Maury Wills	20.00

2005 UD Ultimate Collection
NM/M

Common (1-100):	1.50
Production 475	
Common (101-237):	3.00
Production 275	
Common (238-242):	50.00
Production 99	
Pack (4):	85.00
Box (4):	300.00
1	A.J. Burnett	1.50
2	Adam Dunn	2.00
3	Adrian Beltre	2.00
4	Albert Pujols	8.00
5	Alex Rodriguez	8.00
6	Alfonso Soriano	3.00
7	Andruw Jones	3.00
8	Andy Pettitte	2.00
9	Aramis Ramirez	2.00
10	Aubrey Huff	1.50
11	Ben Sheets	2.00
12	Bobby Abreu	2.00
13	Bobby Crosby	1.50
14	Chris Carpenter	2.00
15	Brian Giles	1.50
16	Brian Roberts	1.50
17	Carl Crawford	2.00
18	Carlos Beltran	3.00
19	Carlos Delgado	2.00
20	Carlos Zambrano	2.00
21	Chipper Jones	3.00
22	Corey Patterson	1.50
23	Craig Biggio	1.50
24	Curt Schilling	3.00
25	Dallas McPherson	1.50
26	David Ortiz	3.00
27	David Wright	5.00
28	Delmon Young	2.00
29	Derek Jeter	8.00
30	Derrek Lee	3.00
31	Dontrelle Willis	2.00
32	Eric Chavez	2.00
33	Eric Gagne	2.00
34	Francisco Rodriguez	1.50
35	Gary Sheffield	2.00
36	Greg Maddux	5.00
37	Hank Blalock	1.50
38	Hideki Matsui	5.00
39	Ichiro Suzuki	5.00
40	Ivan Rodriguez	3.00
41	J.D. Drew	1.50
42	Jake Peavy	2.00
43	Jason Bay	2.00
44	Jason Schmidt	2.00
45	Jeff Bagwell	2.00
46	Jeff Kent	2.00
47	Jeremy Bonderman	2.00
48	Jim Edmonds	2.00
49	Jim Thome	2.00
50	Joe Mauer	2.00
51	Johan Santana	3.00
52	John Smoltz	2.00
53	Johnny Damon	3.00
54	Jose Reyes	3.00
55	Jose Vidro	1.50
56	Josh Beckett	1.50
57	Justin Morneau	2.00
58	Ken Griffey Jr.	5.00
59	Kerry Wood	2.00
60	Khalil Greene	1.50
61	Lance Berkman	2.00
62	Larry Walker	2.00
63	Luis Gonzalez	1.50
64	Manny Ramirez	3.00
65	Mark Buehrle	2.00
66	Mark Mulder	2.00
67	Mark Prior	3.00
68	Mark Teixeira	3.00
69	Michael Young	2.00
70	Miguel Cabrera	3.00
71	Miguel Tejada	3.00
72	Mike Mussina	2.00
73	Mike Piazza	4.00
74	Moises Alou	2.00
75	Nomar Garciaparra	3.00
76	Oliver Perez	1.50
77	Pat Burrell	2.00
78	Paul Konerko	2.00
79	Pedro Feliz	1.50
80	Pedro Martinez	3.00
81	Randy Johnson	3.00
82	Richie Sexson	2.00
83	Rickie Weeks	2.00
84	Roger Clemens	8.00
85	Roy Halladay	2.00
86	Roy Oswalt	2.00
87	Sammy Sosa	3.00
88	Scott Kazmir	1.50
89	Scott Rolen	3.00
90	Shawn Green	2.00
91	Tim Hudson	2.00
92	Todd Helton	2.00
93	Tom Glavine	2.00
94	Torii Hunter	2.00
95	Travis Hafner	2.00
96	Troy Glaus	1.50
97	Vernon Wells	1.50
98	Victor Martinez	1.50
99	Vladimir Guerrero	3.00
100	Zack Greinke	1.50
101	Al Kaline	4.00
102	Babe Ruth	10.00
103	Bo Jackson	4.00
104	Bob Gibson	5.00
105	Brooks Robinson	5.00
106	Cal Ripken Jr.	12.00
107	Carl Yastrzemski	5.00
108	Carlton Fisk	3.00
109	Jim "Catfish" Hunter	3.00
110	Christy Mathewson	5.00
111	Cy Young	6.00
112	Don Mattingly	5.00
113	Eddie Mathews	5.00
114	Eddie Murray	4.00
115	Gary Carter	3.00
116	Harmon Killebrew	4.00
117	Jim Palmer	3.00
118	Jimmie Foxx	4.00
119	Joe DiMaggio	8.00
120	Johnny Bench	4.00
121	Lefty Grove	3.00
122	Lou Gehrig	8.00
123	Mel Ott	3.00
124	Reggie Jackson	4.00
125	Mike Schmidt	4.00
126	Nolan Ryan	8.00
127	Ozzie Smith	4.00
128	Paul Molitor	4.00
129	Pee Wee Reese	3.00
130	Robin Yount	4.00
131	Ryne Sandberg	6.00
132	Ted Williams	8.00
133	Thurman Munson	4.00
134	Tom Seaver	4.00
135	Tony Gwynn	4.00
136	Wade Boggs	3.00
137	Walter Johnson	4.00
138	Warren Spahn	4.00
139	Will Clark	3.00
140	Willie McCovey	4.00
141	Willie Stargell	4.00
142	Yogi Berra	5.00
143	Ambiorix Burgos RC	4.00
144	Ambiorix Concepcion RC	4.00
145	Anibal Sanchez RC	15.00
146	Bill McCarthy RC	4.00
147	Brian Burres RC	4.00
148	Carlos Ruiz RC	4.00
149	Casey Rogowski RC	6.00
150	Chris Resop RC	4.00
151	Chris Roberson RC	4.00
152	Chris Seddon RC	4.00
153	Colter Bean RC	4.00
154	Dae-Sung Koo RC	4.00
155	Danny Rueckel RC	4.00
156	David Gassner RC	4.00
157	Ryan Howard	8.00
158	D.J. Houlton RC	4.00
159	Derek Wathan RC	4.00
160	Devon Lowery RC	4.00
161	Enrique Gonzalez RC	4.00
162	Erick Threets RC	4.00
163	Eude Brito RC	4.00
164	Francisco Butto RC	4.00
165	Franquelis Osoria RC	4.00
166	Garrett Jones RC	4.00

167	Geovany Soto RC	6.00
168	Ismael Ramirez RC	4.00
169	Jared Gothreaux RC	4.00
170	Jason Hammel RC	4.00
171	Jeff Housman RC	4.00
172	Jeff Miller RC	4.00
173	Jeff Francoeur RC	10.00
174	John Hattig Jr. RC	4.00
175	Jorge Campillo RC	4.00
176	Juan Morillo RC	4.00
177	Justin Wechsler RC	4.00
178	Keiichi Yabu RC	4.00
179	Kendry Morales RC	15.00
180	Luis Hernandez RC	4.00
181	Luis Mendoza RC	4.00
182	Luis Pena RC	4.00
183	Luis Rodriguez RC	4.00
184	Luke Scott RC	10.00
185	Marcos Carvajal RC	4.00
186	Mark Woodyard RC	4.00
187	Matt Smith RC	4.00
188	Matt Lindstrom RC	4.00
189	Mike Negron RC	6.00
190	Mike Morse RC	4.00
191	Nate McLouth RC	4.00
192	Nick Masset RC	4.00
193	Paulino Reynoso RC	4.00
194	Pedro Lopez RC	4.00
195	Peter Orr RC	4.00
196	Randy Messenger RC	4.00
197	Randy Williams RC	4.00
198	Raul Tablado RC	4.00
199	Ronny Paulino RC	8.00
200	Russel Rohlicek RC	4.00
201	Russell Martin RC	15.00
202	Scott Baker RC	6.00
203	Scott Munter RC	4.00
204	Sean Thompson RC	4.00
205	Sean Tracey RC	4.00
206	Steve Schmoll RC	4.00
207	Tony Pena RC	4.00
208	Travis Bowyer RC	4.00
209	Ubaldo Jimenez RC	4.00
210	Wladimir Balentien RC	10.00
211	Yorman Bazardo RC	4.00
212	Yuniesky Betancourt RC	8.00
213	Adam Shabala RC	4.00
214	Brandon McCarthy RC	10.00
215	Chad Orvella RC	4.00
216	Jermaine Van Buren RC	4.00
217	Anthony Reyes RC	30.00
218	Dana Eveland RC	8.00
219	Brian Anderson RC	10.00
220	Hayden Penn RC	8.00
221	Chris Denorfia RC	6.00
222	Joel Peralta RC	4.00
223	Ryan Garko RC	10.00
224	Felix Hernandez RC	15.00
225	Mark McLemore RC	4.00
226	Melky Cabrera RC	15.00
227	Nelson Cruz RC	8.00
228	Norihiro Nakamura RC	8.00
229	Oscar Robles RC	4.00
230	Rick Short RC	4.00
231	Ryan Zimmerman RC	35.00
232	Ryan Speier RC	4.00
233	Ryan Spilborghs RC	6.00
234	Shana Costa RC	4.00
235	Zachary Duke RC	6.00
236	Tony Giarratano RC	4.00
237	Jeff Niemann RC	10.00
238	Stephen Drew/ Auto. RC	180.00
239	Justin Verlander/ Auto. RC	250.00
240	Prince Fielder/Auto.	500.00
241	Philip Humber/ Auto. RC	85.00
242	Tadahito Iguchi/ Auto. RC	100.00

Silver

Silver (101-237): 1-2X
Production 50 Sets

Baseball Star Signatures

NM/M
Production 5-25

JB	Jason Bay/25	25.00
AB	Adrian Beltre/15	25.00
CB	Craig Biggio/15	40.00
HB	Hank Blalock/15	25.00
BO	Jeremy Bonderman/25	25.00
MC	Miguel Cabrera/15	50.00
EC	Eric Chavez/15	25.00
WC	Will Clark/15	40.00
CC	Carl Crawford/25	20.00
CO	Coco Crisp/25	40.00
BC	Bobby Crosby/15	25.00
DA	Andre Dawson/15	25.00
RF	Rafael Furcal/20	25.00
BG	Brian Giles/15	20.00
DG	Dwight Gooden/25	25.00
GR	Khalil Greene/15	40.00
ZG	Zack Greinke/25	15.00
KG	Ken Griffey Jr./25	90.00
TR	Travis Hafner/25	25.00
RH	Rich Harden/25	20.00
KH	Keith Hernandez/15	25.00
TH	Tim Hudson/15	35.00
HU	Torii Hunter/15	25.00
SK	Scott Kazmir/25	25.00
BL	Barry Larkin/15	50.00
VM	Victor Martinez/25	20.00
JO	Joe Mauer/15	50.00
PM	Paul Molitor/15	25.00
JM	Justin Morneau/25	30.00
MM	Mark Mulder/15	25.00
RO	Roy Oswalt/15	30.00
JP	Jake Peavy/20	30.00
WP	Wily Mo Pena/25	20.00
SP	Scott Podsednik/25	30.00
AR	Aramis Ramirez/20	25.00
JR	Jose Reyes/20	30.00
BR	Brian Roberts/25	20.00
BS	Ben Sheets/15	25.00
SM	John Smoltz/15	75.00
MT	Mark Teixeira/15	40.00
BU	B.J. Upton/25	25.00
JV	Jose Vidro/20	10.00
RW	Rickie Weeks/15	30.00
DW	Dontrelle Willis/15	40.00
WR	David Wright/15	100.00
MY	Michael Young/20	25.00
CZ	Carlos Zambrano/20	30.00

Dual Materials

NM/M
Production 15 Sets
Patch: No Pricing
Production 10 Sets

AC	Andruw Jones, Chipper Jones	25.00
AE	Adrian Beltre, Eric Chavez	10.00
AH	Adrian Beltre, Hank Blalock	10.00
AJ	Josh Beckett, A.J. Burnett	10.00
AM	Albert Pujols, Miguel Cabrera	40.00
AP	Bobby Abreu, Corey Patterson	10.00
AU	Bobby Abreu, Chase Utley	30.00
BC	Josh Beckett, Miguel Cabrera	20.00
BG	Vladimir Guerrero, Jason Bay	25.00
BH	Adrian Beltre, Felix Hernandez	40.00
BJ	Ben Sheets, Jake Peavy	15.00
BK	Bobby Crosby, Khalil Greene	20.00
BM	Jeremy Bonderman, Matt Cain	40.00
BS	Ryne Sandberg, Wade Boggs	40.00
BT	Mark Teixeira, Hank Blalock	25.00
BY	Michael Young, Hank Blalock	10.00
CB	Bobby Crosby, Jason Bay	10.00
CC	Eric Chavez, Bobby Crosby	10.00
CG	Vladimir Guerrero, Miguel Cabrera	25.00
CJ	Jeff Bagwell, Craig Biggio	25.00
CO	Roger Clemens, Roy Oswalt	40.00
CP	Carl Crawford, Scott Podsednik	20.00
CR	Scott Rolen, Eric Chavez	20.00
CT	Tony Gwynn, Cal Ripken Jr.	80.00
CW	Eric Chavez, David Wright	10.00
DG	Ken Griffey Jr., Adam Dunn	30.00
DJ	David Wright, Jose Reyes	30.00
DP	Adam Dunn, Wily Mo Pena	10.00
DR	Randy Johnson, Derek Jeter	50.00
FW	Rickie Weeks, Prince Fielder	40.00
GC	Ken Griffey Jr., Miguel Cabrera	35.00
GF	Rafael Furcal, Marcus Giles	10.00
GG	Brian Giles, Marcus Giles	10.00
GH	Ken Griffey Jr., Torii Hunter	30.00
GJ	Ken Griffey Jr., Derek Jeter	50.00
GL	Mark Loretta, Khalil Greene	20.00
GP	Ken Griffey Jr., Wily Mo Pena	30.00
GR	Eric Gagne, Francisco Rodriguez	10.00
HC	Felix Hernandez, Matt Cain	60.00
HH	Rich Harden, Danny Haren	10.00
HM	Travis Hafner, Victor Martinez	10.00
HO	Roy Oswalt, Rich Harden	10.00
HS	Ben Sheets, Rich Harden	15.00
JC	Randy Johnson, Roger Clemens	40.00
JF	Johan Santana, Felix Hernandez	35.00
JG	Ken Griffey Jr., Andruw Jones	30.00
JH	Andruw Jones, Torii Hunter	20.00
JJ	Derek Jeter, Reggie Jackson	50.00
JL	Barry Larkin, Derek Jeter	50.00
JO	Johan Santana, Oliver Perez	20.00
JR	Derek Jeter, Jose Reyes	50.00
JV	Victor Martinez, Joe Mauer	10.00
LG	Eric Gagne, Brad Lidge	10.00
LO	Roy Oswalt, Brad Lidge	10.00
LR	Brad Lidge, Francisco Rodriguez	10.00
ME	Johnny Estrada, Joe Mauer	10.00
MG	Greg Maddux, Mark Prior	30.00
MH	Mark Mulder, Tim Hudson	15.00
MJ	Randy Johnson, Pedro Martinez	25.00
MM	Justin Morneau, Joe Mauer	10.00
MP	Mark Prior, Joe Mauer	20.00
MR	Mike Mussina, Randy Johnson	25.00
NR	Randy Johnson, Nolan Ryan	50.00
OF	David Ortiz, Prince Fielder	30.00
PC	Roger Clemens, Mark Prior	40.00
PD	Pedro Martinez, Dwight Gooden	20.00
PG	Ken Griffey Jr., Albert Pujols	50.00
PH	Jake Peavy, Rich Harden	15.00
PJ	Derek Jeter, Albert Pujols	60.00
PL	Derrek Lee, Albert Pujols	40.00
PM	Mike Piazza, Pedro Martinez	25.00
PS	Ben Sheets, Mark Prior	20.00
RB	Aramis Ramirez, Hank Blalock	10.00
RC	Roger Clemens, Nolan Ryan	50.00
RE	Eric Chavez, Aramis Ramirez	10.00
RF	Rafael Furcal, Jose Reyes	10.00
RG	Brian Roberts, Marcus Giles	10.00
RJ	Cal Ripken Jr., Derek Jeter	85.00
RL	Derrek Lee, Aramis Ramirez	20.00
RP	Aaron Rowand, Scott Podsednik	20.00
RR	Aaron Rowand, Jeremy Reed	10.00
RS	Cal Ripken Jr., Mike Schmidt	75.00
RT	Cal Ripken Jr., Miguel Tejada	60.00
RU	B.J. Upton, Jose Reyes	10.00
RW	Aramis Ramirez, David Wright	30.00
SB	Wade Boggs, Mike Schmidt	40.00
SC	Roger Clemens, Johan Santana	30.00
SH	John Smoltz, Tim Hudson	25.00
SJ	Randy Johnson, Curt Schilling	25.00
SM	Johan Santana, Joe Mauer	20.00
SO	Curt Schilling, David Ortiz	25.00
SP	Mark Prior, Johan Santana	20.00
SR	Mike Schmidt, Scott Rolen	40.00
TC	Mark Teixeira, Miguel Cabrera	20.00
UJ	Derek Jeter, B.J. Upton	50.00
WR	Scott Rolen, David Wright	35.00
ZH	Carlos Zambrano, Rich Harden	10.00
ZO	Roy Oswalt, Carlos Zambrano	10.00
ZP	Carlos Zambrano, Oliver Perez	10.00

Dual Material Signatures

NM/M
No Pricing
Production 10 Sets
Patch: No Pricing
Production 5 Sets

Dual Signatures

NM/M
Production 25 Sets

RW	Aramis Ramirez, David Wright	90.00
RP	Aaron Rowand, Scott Podsednik	50.00
BB	Jeff Bagwell, Craig Biggio	100.00
BC	Adrian Beltre, Eric Chavez	35.00
BH	Adrian Beltre, Felix Hernandez	125.00
BJ	Bobby Crosby, Jason Bay	35.00
BT	Mark Teixeira, Hank Blalock	50.00
BY	Michael Young, Hank Blalock	30.00
CC	Eric Chavez, Bobby Crosby	30.00
CG	Bobby Crosby, Khalil Greene	40.00
CP	Carl Crawford, Scott Podsednik	50.00
CT	Tony Gwynn, Cal Ripken Jr.	180.00
CY	Carl Crawford, Delmon Young	50.00
DG	Ken Griffey Jr., Adam Dunn	100.00
DJ	Derek Jeter, Jose Reyes	150.00
DK	Ken Griffey Jr., Derek Jeter	220.00
DM	Mike Schmidt, David Wright	100.00
DP	Andre Dawson, Corey Patterson	35.00
FF	Gavin Floyd, Jeff Francis	20.00
FW	Rickie Weeks, Prince Fielder	
GC	Ken Griffey Jr., Miguel Cabrera	120.00
GH	Ken Griffey Jr., Torii Hunter	100.00
GJ	Ken Griffey Jr., Andruw Jones	120.00
GL	Mark Loretta, Khalil Greene	40.00
GP	Ken Griffey Jr., Wily Mo Pena	100.00
GR	Eric Gagne, Francisco Rodriguez	50.00
HH	Rich Harden, Danny Haren	35.00
HM	Travis Hafner, Victor Martinez	40.00
HO	Roy Oswalt, Rich Harden	40.00

HS	Ben Sheets, Rich Harden	40.00
JB	Ben Sheets, Jake Peavy	35.00
JG	Derek Jeter, Nomar Garciaparra	180.00
JH	Andruw Jones, Torii Hunter	40.00
JJ	Andruw Jones, Chipper Jones	120.00
JM	Don Mattingly, Derek Jeter	250.00
JV	Victor Martinez, Joe Mauer	35.00
KH	Scott Kazmir, Felix Hernandez	125.00
LO	Roy Oswalt, Brad Lidge	50.00
LR	Brad Lidge, Francisco Rodriguez	50.00
MC	Don Mattingly, Will Clark	100.00
MG	Greg Maddux, Tom Glavine	150.00
MH	Travis Hafner, Justin Morneau	35.00
MM	Justin Morneau, Joe Mauer	40.00
MP	Mark Prior, Joe Mauer	60.00
MT	Mark Mulder, Tim Hudson	50.00
NH	Philip Humber, Jeff Niemann	50.00
NK	Scott Kazmir, Jeff Niemann	40.00
NV	Justin Verlander, Jeff Niemann	65.00
PH	Jake Peavy, Rich Harden	30.00
PJ	Derek Jeter, Albert Pujols	500.00
PP	Gaylord Perry, Jake Peavy	30.00
RB	Aramis Ramirez, Hank Blalock	30.00
RC	Roger Clemens, Nolan Ryan	220.00
RE	Eric Chavez, Aramis Ramirez	40.00
RF	Rafael Furcal, Jose Reyes	35.00
RJ	Cal Ripken Jr., Derek Jeter	300.00
RL	Derrek Lee, Aramis Ramirez	60.00
RP	Aaron Rowand, Corey Patterson	30.00
RR	Aaron Rowand, Jeremy Reed	30.00
RW	Ryne Sandberg, Wade Boggs	100.00
SH	John Smoltz, Tim Hudson	65.00
SJ	Randy Johnson, Curt Schilling	80.00
SO	Curt Schilling, David Ortiz	90.00
SP	Ben Sheets, Mark Prior	50.00
SW	Ben Sheets, Rickie Weeks	35.00
TC	Mark Teixeira, Miguel Cabrera	75.00
UJ	Derek Jeter, B.J. Upton	140.00
UW	Rickie Weeks, B.J. Upton	30.00
WR	David Wright, Jose Reyes	100.00
YU	B.J. Upton, Delmon Young	50.00
YW	Rickie Weeks, Delmon Young	50.00
ZH	Carlos Zambrano, Rich Harden	35.00
ZO	Roy Oswalt, Carlos Zambrano	35.00

Eight Star Signatures

No Pricing
Production 5 Sets

Four Star Signatures

No Pricing
Production 15 Sets

Game Materials

NM/M

Production 25 Sets
Patch: 1-2X
Production 5-25
No patch pricing 15 or less.

BA	Bobby Abreu	10.00
JB	Jeff Bagwell	10.00
JA	Jason Bay	10.00
BE	Josh Beckett	8.00
AB	Adrian Beltre	8.00
CB	Craig Biggio	10.00
HB	Hank Blalock	8.00
BO	Jeremy Bonderman	8.00
BU	A.J. Burnett	8.00
CA	Miguel Cabrera	15.00
MA	Matt Cain	25.00
CW	Rod Carew	15.00
SC	Sean Casey	8.00
EC	Eric Chavez	10.00
RC	Roger Clemens	25.00
MC	Matt Clement	8.00
CR	Carl Crawford	8.00
CO	Coco Crisp	8.00
BC	Bobby Crosby	8.00
JD	J.D. Drew	8.00
AD	Adam Dunn	8.00
ES	Johnny Estrada	8.00
PF	Prince Fielder	40.00
GF	Gavin Floyd	8.00
KF	Keith Foulke	8.00
JF	Jeff Francis	8.00
RF	Rafael Furcal	8.00
EG	Eric Gagne	10.00
BG	Brian Giles	8.00
MG	Marcus Giles	8.00
GR	Khalil Greene	10.00
ZG	Zack Greinke	8.00
KG	Ken Griffey Jr.	25.00
VG	Vladimir Guerrero	20.00
TR	Travis Hafner	10.00
HA	Roy Halladay	8.00
RH	Rich Harden	8.00
FH	Felix Hernandez	25.00
HO	Trevor Hoffman	8.00
TH	Tim Hudson	10.00
AH	Aubrey Huff	8.00
HU	Torii Hunter	8.00
TI	Tadahito Iguchi	20.00
DJ	Derek Jeter	30.00
RJ	Randy Johnson	15.00
AJ	Andruw Jones	10.00
SK	Scott Kazmir	8.00
JK	Jeff Kent	8.00
LE	Derrek Lee	15.00
BL	Brad Lidge	8.00
ML	Mark Loretta	8.00
DL	Derek Lowe	8.00
GM	Greg Maddux	20.00
PM	Pedro Martinez	15.00
VM	Victor Martinez	8.00
JM	Joe Mauer	8.00
MO	Justin Morneau	8.00
MM	Mark Mulder	8.00
DO	David Ortiz	15.00
OS	Roy Oswalt	8.00
RP	Rafael Palmeiro	10.00
PA	Corey Patterson	8.00
CP	Carl Pavano	8.00
JP	Jake Peavy	10.00
WP	Wily Mo Pena	8.00
OP	Oliver Perez	8.00
SP	Scott Podsednik	10.00
MP	Mark Prior	8.00
AP	Albert Pujols	30.00
RA	Aramis Ramirez	10.00
JR	Jeremy Reed	8.00
ER	Edgar Renteria	8.00
RE	Jose Reyes	10.00
RI	Cal Ripken Jr.	50.00
BR	Brian Roberts	8.00
FR	Francisco Rodriguez	8.00
SR	Scott Rolen	12.00
AR	Aaron Rowand	8.00
NR	Nolan Ryan	30.00
CC	C.C. Sabathia	8.00
RS	Ryne Sandberg	30.00
SA	Johan Santana	15.00
CS	Curt Schilling	10.00
MS	Mike Schmidt	30.00
BS	Ben Sheets	10.00
GS	Gary Sheffield	10.00
SM	John Smoltz	10.00
MT	Mark Teixeira	15.00
TE	Miguel Tejada	10.00
BJ	B.J. Upton	8.00
CU	Chase Utley	15.00
JV	Jose Vidro	8.00
TW	Tim Wakefield	25.00
RW	Rickie Weeks	10.00
JW	Jake Westbrook	8.00
DW	Dontrelle Willis	8.00
WR	David Wright	30.00
MY	Michael Young	8.00
CZ	Carlos Zambrano	10.00

Material Signatures

NM/M

Production 25 Sets
Patch: No Pricing
Production 10 Sets

JB	Jeff Bagwell	75.00
JA	Jason Bay	30.00
BE	Josh Beckett	35.00
AB	Adrian Beltre	20.00
CB	Craig Biggio	40.00
HB	Hank Blalock	20.00
BO	Jeremy Bonderman	20.00
CA	Miguel Cabrera	40.00
CW	Rod Carew	30.00
MC	Matt Clement	25.00
CR	Carl Crawford	25.00
BC	Bobby Crosby	20.00
JD	J.D. Drew	20.00
AD	Adam Dunn	25.00
ES	Johnny Estrada	15.00
GF	Gavin Floyd	15.00
JF	Jeff Francis	15.00
RF	Rafael Furcal	20.00
EG	Eric Gagne	25.00
BG	Brian Giles	20.00
GR	Khalil Greene	30.00
ZG	Zack Greinke	15.00
KG	Ken Griffey Jr.	120.00
VG	Vladimir Guerrero	50.00
TR	Travis Hafner	25.00
HA	Roy Halladay	25.00
FH	Felix Hernandez	100.00
TH	Tim Hudson	35.00
AH	Aubrey Huff	15.00
HU	Torii Hunter	25.00
TI	Tadahito Iguchi	100.00
DJ	Derek Jeter	220.00
AJ	Andruw Jones	40.00
SK	Scott Kazmir	25.00
LA	Barry Larkin	40.00
LE	Derrek Lee	40.00
BL	Brad Lidge	25.00
ML	Mark Loretta	20.00
VM	Victor Martinez	25.00
JM	Joe Mauer	30.00
MO	Justin Morneau	30.00
MM	Mark Mulder	25.00
DO	David Ortiz	50.00
OS	Roy Oswalt	25.00
RP	Rafael Palmeiro	35.00
JP	Jake Peavy	25.00
WP	Wily Mo Pena	20.00
SP	Scott Podsednik	30.00
MP	Mark Prior	40.00
RA	Aramis Ramirez	25.00
JR	Jeremy Reed	15.00
RE	Jose Reyes	35.00
RI	Cal Ripken Jr.	180.00
BR	Brian Roberts	20.00
FR	Francisco Rodriguez	25.00
NR	Nolan Ryan	100.00
RS	Ryne Sandberg	75.00
MS	Mike Schmidt	60.00
BS	Ben Sheets	25.00
GS	Gary Sheffield	35.00
SM	John Smoltz	50.00
MT	Mark Teixeira	50.00
TE	Miguel Tejada	40.00
BJ	B.J. Upton	20.00
CU	Chase Utley	40.00
JV	Jose Vidro	15.00
TW	Tim Wakefield	75.00
RW	Rickie Weeks	25.00
JW	Jake Westbrook	25.00
DW	Dontrelle Willis	35.00
WR	David Wright	90.00
MY	Michael Young	25.00
CZ	Carlos Zambrano	25.00

Hurler Materials

NM/M

Production 20 Sets
Patch: 1-2X
Production 2-25
No patch pricing 15 or less.

BE	Josh Beckett	8.00
JB	Joe Blanton	8.00
BO	Jeremy Bonderman	8.00
AB	A.J. Burnett	8.00
MA	Matt Cain	30.00
CA	Chris Carpenter	15.00
RC	Roger Clemens	25.00
MC	Matt Clement	8.00
GF	Gavin Floyd	8.00
KF	Keith Foulke	8.00
JF	Jeff Francis	8.00
EG	Eric Gagne	10.00
TG	Tom Glavine	8.00
DG	Dwight Gooden	8.00
HA	Roy Halladay	8.00
RH	Rich Harden	10.00
DH	Danny Haren	8.00
FH	Felix Hernandez	30.00
LH	Livan Hernandez	8.00
HO	Trevor Hoffman	8.00
TH	Tim Hudson	10.00
RJ	Randy Johnson	15.00
SK	Scott Kazmir	8.00
BL	Brad Lidge	8.00
DL	Derek Lowe	8.00
GM	Greg Maddux	20.00
PM	Pedro Martinez	15.00
MM	Mark Mulder	10.00
MU	Mike Mussina	10.00
BM	Brett Myers	8.00
RO	Roy Oswalt	10.00
CP	Carl Pavano	8.00
JP	Jake Peavy	8.00
OP	Odalis Perez	8.00
PE	Oliver Perez	8.00
GP	Gaylord Perry	8.00
MP	Mark Prior	15.00
FR	Francisco Rodriguez	8.00
NR1	Nolan Ryan	30.00
NR2	Nolan Ryan	30.00
CC	C.C. Sabathia	8.00
JS	Johan Santana	15.00
BS	Ben Sheets	10.00
CS	Curt Schilling	15.00
SM	John Smoltz	10.00
TW	Tim Wakefield	25.00
JW	Jake Westbrook	8.00
DW	Dontrelle Willis	8.00
KW	Kerry Wood	10.00
CZ	Carlos Zambrano	10.00

Hurler Material Signatures

NM/M

No Pricing
Production 20 Sets
Patch: No Pricing
Production 10 Sets

BE	Josh Beckett	25.00
JB	Joe Blanton	15.00
BO	Jeremy Bonderman	25.00
CA	Chris Carpenter	40.00
MC	Matt Clement	25.00
GF	Gavin Floyd	15.00
JF	Jeff Francis	15.00
EG	Eric Gagne	25.00
DG	Dwight Gooden	25.00
HA	Roy Halladay	25.00
DH	Danny Haren	20.00
FH	Felix Hernandez	100.00
LH	Livan Hernandez	25.00
TH	Tim Hudson	35.00
SK	Scott Kazmir	25.00
BL	Brad Lidge	30.00
MM	Mark Mulder	25.00
MU	Mike Mussina	50.00
BM	Brett Myers	15.00
RO	Roy Oswalt	25.00
JP	Jake Peavy	25.00
GP	Gaylord Perry	25.00
MP	Mark Prior	30.00
FR	Francisco Rodriguez	25.00
NR1	Nolan Ryan	100.00
NR2	Nolan Ryan	100.00
BS	Ben Sheets	25.00
SM	John Smoltz	50.00
TW	Tim Wakefield	75.00
JW	Jake Westbrook	15.00
DW	Dontrelle Willis	40.00
KW	Kerry Wood	30.00
CZ	Carlos Zambrano	25.00

Quad Materials

Production 10 Sets
Patch: No Pricing
Production 5 Sets

Signatures

NM/M

Production 10-99
Platinum: No Pricing
Production 5 Sets

JE	Jeff Bagwell/15	60.00
BA	Jason Bay/69	25.00
BE	Josh Beckett/35	30.00
AB	Adrian Beltre/69	20.00
JB	Johnny Bench/15	50.00
CB	Craig Biggio	40.00
HB	Hank Blalock/69	20.00
WB	Wade Boggs/15	50.00
MC	Miguel Cabrera/69	40.00
CW	Rod Carew/69	30.00
GC	Gary Carter/35	30.00
EC	Eric Chavez/52	25.00
WC	Will Clark/69	35.00
CO	Coco Crisp/69	25.00
BC	Bobby Crosby/69	25.00
JD	J.D. Drew/29	25.00
SD	Stephen Drew/69	180.00
AD	Adam Dunn/35	25.00
PF	Prince Fielder/35	150.00
CF	Carlton Fisk/15	40.00
EG	Eric Gagne/35	25.00
GR	Khalil Greene/69	30.00
ZG	Zack Greinke/69	15.00
KG	Ken Griffey Jr./69	80.00
GW	Tony Gwynn/25	50.00

TR	Travis Hafner/69	20.00
HA	Roy Halladay/35	25.00
RH	Rich Harden/69	20.00
FH	Felix Hernandez/69	80.00
TH	Tim Hudson/69	30.00
PH	Philip Humber/69	15.00
HU	Torii Hunter/69	20.00
TI	Tadahito Iguchi/85	85.00
BJ	Bo Jackson/35	50.00
JO	Andruw Jones/35	40.00
SK	Scott Kazmir/69	25.00
BL	Barry Larkin/69	50.00
VM	Victor Martinez/69	20.00
MA	Don Mattingly/25	90.00
JM	Joe Mauer/69	25.00
PM	Paul Molitor/49	30.00
KM	Kendry Morales/69	60.00
MM	Mark Mulder/69	20.00
MU	Mike Mussina/15	50.00
JN	Jeff Niemann/69	25.00
DO	David Ortiz/35	50.00
RO	Roy Oswalt/69	20.00
RP	Rafael Palmeiro/35	25.00
JP	Jake Peavy/69	25.00
MP	Mark Prior/15	25.00
AR	Aramis Ramirez/69	25.00
JR	Jose Reyes/69	35.00
BR	Brian Roberts/35	20.00
RS	Ryne Sandberg/69	90.00
MS	Mike Schmidt/25	60.00
BS	Ben Sheets/69	20.00
GS	Gary Sheffield/25	35.00
OS	Ozzie Smith/35	50.00
SM	John Smoltz/49	50.00
MT	Mark Teixeira/99	35.00
BU	B.J. Upton/69	20.00
JV	Justin Verlander/69	80.00
RW	Rickie Weeks/30	25.00
DW	Dontrelle Willis/35	35.00
KW	Kerry Wood/15	40.00
WR	David Wright/69	75.00
MY	Michael Young/69	20.00
RY	Robin Yount/15	50.00
CZ	Carlos Zambrano/69	30.00

Six Star Signatures
No Pricing
Production 10 Sets

Slugger Material
NM/M
Production 20 Sets
Patch: 1-2X
Production 19-25

BA	Bobby Abreu	8.00
JB	Jeff Bagwell	10.00
JA	Jason Bay	10.00
AB	Adrian Beltre	8.00
CB	Craig Biggio	10.00
HB	Hank Blalock	8.00
MC	Miguel Cabrera	15.00
CA	Rod Carew	15.00
SC	Sean Casey	8.00
EC	Eric Chavez	8.00
CC	Carl Crawford	10.00
CO	Coco Crisp	10.00
BC	Bobby Crosby	8.00
JD	J.D. Drew	8.00
AD	Adam Dunn	10.00
ES	Johnny Estrada	8.00
RF	Rafael Furcal	8.00
BG	Brian Giles	8.00
MG	Marcus Giles	8.00
GR	Khalil Greene	10.00
KG	Ken Griffey Jr.	25.00
VG	Vladimir Guerrero	15.00
HA	Travis Hafner	8.00
RH	Ryan Howard	20.00
AH	Aubrey Huff	8.00
TH	Torii Hunter	8.00
CJ	Derek Jeter	30.00
CJ	Chipper Jones	15.00
JK	Jeff Kent	8.00
DL	Derrek Lee	15.00
ML	Mark Loretta	8.00
VM	Victor Martinez	8.00
MA	Joe Mauer	8.00
JM	Justin Morneau	8.00
DO	David Ortiz	20.00
RP	Rafael Palmeiro	10.00
CP	Corey Patterson	8.00
WP	Wily Mo Pena	8.00
AP	Albert Pujols	30.00
AR	Aramis Ramirez	10.00
ER	Edgar Renteria	8.00
JR	Jose Reyes	10.00
BR	Brian Roberts	8.00
SR	Scott Rolen	12.00
GS	Gary Sheffield	10.00
MT	Mark Teixeira	15.00
JV	Jose Vidro	8.00
DW	David Wright	30.00
MY	Michael Young	10.00

Slugger Material Signatures
NM/M
Production 20 Sets
Patch: No Pricing
Production 3-10

JB	Jeff Bagwell	75.00
JA	Jason Bay	30.00
AB	Adrian Beltre	20.00
CB	Craig Biggio	40.00
HB	Hank Blalock	20.00
MC	Miguel Cabrera	40.00
CA	Rod Carew	30.00
EC	Eric Chavez	25.00
BC	Bobby Crosby	20.00
JD	J.D. Drew	20.00
AD	Adam Dunn	25.00
ES	Johnny Estrada	20.00
RF	Rafael Furcal	20.00
BG	Brian Giles	20.00
GR	Khalil Greene	30.00
KG	Ken Griffey Jr.	120.00
HA	Travis Hafner	25.00
RH	Ryan Howard	90.00
AH	Aubrey Huff	15.00
TH	Torii Hunter	25.00
CJ	Derek Jeter	220.00
CJ	Chipper Jones	50.00
DL	Derrek Lee	40.00
ML	Mark Loretta	20.00
VM	Victor Martinez	20.00
MA	Joe Mauer	30.00
JM	Justin Morneau	25.00
DO	David Ortiz	50.00
RP	Rafael Palmeiro	35.00
WP	Wily Mo Pena	20.00
AR	Aramis Ramirez	25.00
JR	Jose Reyes	25.00
BR	Brian Roberts	20.00
GS	Gary Sheffield	35.00
MT	Mark Teixeira	50.00
JV	Jose Vidro	15.00
DW	David Wright	90.00
MY	Michael Young	25.00

Three Star Signatures
No Pricing
Production 20 Sets

Triple Materials
No Pricing
Production 15 Sets
Patch: No Pricing
Production 10 Sets

Veteran Materials
NM/M
Production 20 Sets
Patch: 1-2X
Production 7-30
No patch pricing 15 or less.

BA	Bobby Abreu	10.00
JB	Jeff Bagwell	12.00
BE	Josh Beckett	8.00
AB	Adrian Beltre	8.00
CB	Craig Biggio	10.00
HB	Hank Blalock	8.00
CA	Rod Carew	15.00
SC	Sean Casey	8.00
EC	Eric Chavez	10.00
RC	Roger Clemens	25.00
MC	Matt Clement	8.00
JD	J.D. Drew	8.00
AD	Adam Dunn	10.00
KF	Keith Foulke	8.00
EG	Eric Gagne	10.00
BG	Brian Giles	8.00
KG	Ken Griffey Jr.	25.00
VG	Vladimir Guerrero	20.00
RH	Roy Halladay	10.00
LH	Livan Hernandez	8.00
HO	Trevor Hoffman	8.00
TH	Tim Hudson	10.00
AH	Aubrey Huff	8.00
HU	Torii Hunter	8.00
DJ	Derek Jeter	30.00
RJ	Randy Johnson	15.00
AJ	Andruw Jones	12.00
JK	Jeff Kent	8.00
LE	Derrek Lee	15.00
ML	Mark Loretta	8.00
DL	Derek Lowe	8.00
GM	Greg Maddux	20.00
MM	Mark Mulder	8.00
BM	Brett Myers	8.00
DO	David Ortiz	15.00
RO	Roy Oswalt	10.00
OP	Odalis Perez	8.00
MP	Mark Prior	10.00
AR	Aramis Ramirez	10.00
ER	Edgar Renteria	8.00
CR	Cal Ripken Jr.	50.00
SR	Scott Rolen	12.00
NR	Nolan Ryan	30.00
CS	C.C. Sabathia	8.00
AS	Alfonso Soriano	10.00
SM	John Smoltz	15.00
MT	Miguel Tejada	10.00
JV	Jose Vidro	8.00
TW	Tim Wakefield	25.00
DW	Dontrelle Willis	10.00

Veteran Material Signatures
NM/M
Production 20 Sets
Patch: No Pricing
Production 10 Sets

JB	Jeff Bagwell	75.00
BE	Josh Beckett	35.00
AB	Adrian Beltre	20.00
CB	Craig Biggio	40.00
HB	Hank Blalock	20.00
CA	Rod Carew	35.00
EC	Eric Chavez	25.00
MC	Matt Clement	25.00
JD	J.D. Drew	20.00
AD	Adam Dunn	20.00
EG	Eric Gagne	25.00
BG	Brian Giles	25.00
KG	Ken Griffey Jr.	120.00
VG	Vladimir Guerrero	50.00
RH	Roy Halladay	30.00
LH	Livan Hernandez	20.00
TH	Tim Hudson	35.00
AH	Aubrey Huff	15.00
HU	Torii Hunter	25.00
DJ	Derek Jeter	220.00
AJ	Andruw Jones	40.00
LE	Derrek Lee	40.00
ML	Mark Loretta	20.00
MM	Mark Mulder	25.00
BM	Brett Myers	15.00
DO	David Ortiz	50.00
RO	Roy Oswalt	25.00
MP	Mark Prior	40.00
AR	Aramis Ramirez	25.00
CR	Cal Ripken Jr.	180.00
NR	Nolan Ryan	100.00
SM	John Smoltz	50.00
MT	Miguel Tejada	40.00
JV	Jose Vidro	15.00
TW	Tim Wakefield	75.00
DW	Dontrelle Willis	35.00

Young Star Materials
NM/M
Production 20 Sets
Patch: 1-2X
Production 6-30
No patch pricing 15 or less.

BA	Jason Bay	12.00
JB	Joe Blanton	8.00
BO	Jeremy Bonderman	8.00
AB	A.J. Burnett	8.00
MC	Miguel Cabrera	15.00
MA	Matt Cain	30.00
CC	Carl Crawford	10.00
CO	Coco Crisp	8.00
BC	Bobby Crosby	8.00
JE	Johnny Estrada	8.00
PF	Prince Fielder	40.00
GF	Gavin Floyd	8.00
JF	Jeff Francis	8.00
RF	Rafael Furcal	8.00
MG	Marcus Giles	8.00
KG	Khalil Greene	12.00
ZG	Zack Greinke	8.00
TH	Travis Hafner	10.00
RH	Rich Harden	10.00
DH	Danny Haren	8.00
FH	Felix Hernandez	35.00
HO	Ryan Howard	25.00
TI	Tadahito Iguchi	25.00
SK	Scott Kazmir	8.00
BL	Brad Lidge	8.00
VM	Victor Martinez	10.00
JM	Joe Mauer	10.00
MO	Justin Morneau	8.00
PA	Corey Patterson	8.00
CP	Carl Pavano	8.00
JP	Jake Peavy	10.00
WP	Wily Mo Pena	10.00
OP	Oliver Perez	8.00
SP	Scott Podsednik	10.00
JR	Jeremy Reed	8.00
RE	Jose Reyes	10.00
BR	Brian Roberts	10.00
FR	Francisco Rodriguez	10.00
AR	Aaron Rowand	8.00
JS	Juan Santana	15.00
BS	Ben Sheets	10.00
MT	Mark Teixeira	15.00
BU	B.J. Upton	10.00
CU	Chase Utley	25.00
RW	Rickie Weeks	10.00
JW	Jake Westbrook	8.00
DW	David Wright	30.00
MY	Michael Young	10.00
CZ	Carlos Zambrano	10.00

Young Star Material Signature
NM/M
Production 20 Sets
Patch: No Pricing
Production 10 Sets

BA	Jason Bay	30.00
JB	Joe Blanton	20.00
BO	Jeremy Bonderman	20.00
MA	Matt Cain	125.00
CC	Carl Crawford	25.00
BC	Bobby Crosby	25.00
JE	Johnny Estrada	15.00
GF	Gavin Floyd	20.00
JF	Jeff Francis	15.00
RF	Rafael Furcal	20.00
KG	Khalil Greene	35.00
ZG	Zack Greinke	15.00
TH	Travis Hafner	20.00
DH	Danny Haren	15.00
TI	Tadahito Iguchi	140.00
SK	Scott Kazmir	20.00
BL	Brad Lidge	40.00
VM	Victor Martinez	25.00
JM	Joe Mauer	25.00
JP	Jake Peavy	25.00
WP	Wily Mo Pena	25.00
SP	Scott Podsednik	30.00
JR	Jeremy Reed	15.00
RE	Jose Reyes	25.00
BR	Brian Roberts	25.00
FR	Francisco Rodriguez	25.00
AR	Aaron Rowand	25.00
BS	Ben Sheets	25.00
MT	Mark Teixeira	50.00
BU	B.J. Upton	20.00
RW	Rickie Weeks	20.00
JW	Jake Westbrook	15.00
DW	David Wright	90.00
MY	Michael Young	20.00
CZ	Carlos Zambrano	30.00

2005 UD Ultimate Signature Edition

NM/M
Complete Set (110):
Common (1-100): 2.00
Production 825
Common (101-110): 8.00
Production 225
Tin (3): 85.00

1	Al Kaline	4.00
2	Babe Ruth	10.00
3	Billy Williams	2.00
4	Bob Feller	2.00
5	Bob Gibson	3.00
6	Brooks Robinson	3.00
7	Carlton Fisk	2.00
8	Cy Young	3.00
9	Dizzy Dean	3.00
10	Don Drysdale	2.00
11	Eddie Mathews	4.00
12	Enos Slaughter	2.00
13	Ernie Banks	5.00
14	Fergie Jenkins	2.00
15	Eddie Murray	3.00
16	Harmon Killebrew	4.00
17	Honus Wagner	5.00
18	Jackie Robinson	5.00
19	Jimmie Foxx	4.00
20	Joe DiMaggio	6.00
21	Joe Morgan	2.00
22	Juan Marichal	2.00
23	Larry Doby	2.00
24	Jim Palmer	2.00

25	Johnny Bench	4.00
26	Lou Brock	2.00
27	Lou Gehrig	6.00
28	Mel Ott	3.00
29	Mickey Cochrane	2.00
30	Mickey Mantle	12.00
31	Mike Schmidt	5.00
32	Nolan Ryan	8.00
33	Pee Wee Reese	2.00
34	Phil Rizzuto	3.00
35	Ralph Kiner	2.00
36	Robin Yount	3.00
37	Ozzie Smith	4.00
38	Roy Campanella	3.00
39	Satchel Paige	4.00
40	Stan Musial	5.00
41	Ted Williams	8.00
42	Thurman Munson	4.00
43	Tom Seaver	3.00
44	Ty Cobb	4.00
45	Walter Johnson	3.00
46	Warren Spahn	4.00
47	Whitey Ford	3.00
48	Willie McCovey	3.00
49	Willie Stargell	3.00
50	Yogi Berra	4.00
51	Adrian Beltre	8.00
52	Albert Pujols	6.00
53	Alex Rodriguez	3.00
54	Alfonso Soriano	2.00
55	Andruw Jones	2.00
56	B.J. Upton	2.00
57	Ben Sheets	2.00
58	Bret Boone	2.00
59	Brian Giles	2.00
60	Carlos Beltran	3.00
61	Carlos Delgado	2.00
62	Chipper Jones	4.00
63	Curt Schilling	4.00
64	David Ortiz	4.00
65	Derek Jeter	8.00
66	Eric Chavez	2.00
67	Frank Thomas	3.00
68	Gary Sheffield	2.00
69	Greg Maddux	5.00
70	Hank Blalock	2.00
71	Hideki Matsui	6.00
72	Ichiro Suzuki	6.00
73	Ivan Rodriguez	3.00
74	Jason Schmidt	2.00
75	Jeff Bagwell	2.00
76	Jim Thome	3.00
77	Johnny Damon	4.00
78	Jose Vidro	2.00
79	Ken Griffey Jr.	5.00
80	Kerry Wood	3.00
81	Manny Ramirez	4.00
82	Mark Prior	2.00
83	Mark Teixeira	2.00
84	Miguel Cabrera	3.00
85	Miguel Tejada	3.00
86	Mike Mussina	2.00
87	Mike Piazza	4.00
88	Mike Sweeney	2.00
89	Oliver Perez	2.00
90	Pedro Martinez	4.00
91	Rafael Palmeiro	3.00
92	Randy Johnson	4.00
93	Roger Clemens	8.00
94	Sammy Sosa	5.00
95	Scott Rolen	3.00
96	Tim Hudson	2.00
97	Todd Helton	2.00
98	Torii Hunter	2.00
99	Victor Martinez	2.00
100	Vladimir Guerrero	4.00
101	Adrian Gonzalez	8.00
102	Ambiorix Burgos RC	25.00
103	Ambiorix Concepcion RC	20.00
104	Dan Meyer	15.00
105	Ervin Santana	25.00
106	Gavin Floyd	20.00
107	Joe Blanton	20.00
108	Eric Crozier	10.00
109	Mark Teahen	25.00
110	Ryan Howard	50.00

Platinum

Cards (101-110):
Production One Set

Immortal Inscriptions

NM/M
Production 10-99
Platinum: No Pricing
Production One Set

WB	Wade Boggs/75	80.00
JB	Jim Bunning/99	60.00
SC	Steve Carlton/99	40.00
WC	Will Clark/99	60.00
EG	Eric Gagne/99	80.00
KG	Ken Griffey Jr./99	200.00
TG	Tony Gwynn/50	140.00

DM	Don Mattingly/75	150.00
BR	Brooks Robinson/99	50.00
TS	Tom Seaver/25	90.00
OS	Ozzie Smith/75	80.00
FT	Frank Thomas/50	100.00

Signature Cuts

Production One Set

Signature Cy Young

NM/M
Production 1-250

CM	David Cone, Greg Maddux/35	150.00
EG	Eric Gagne, Dennis Eckersley/200	50.00
ES	Dennis Eckersley, Bruce Sutter/250	30.00
GF	Ron Guidry, Whitey Ford/250	65.00
GM	Bob Gibson, Denny McLain/175	40.00
LC	Sparky Lyle, Steve Carlton/250	30.00
MS	Tom Seaver, Denny McLain	50.00
NF	Don Newcombe, Whitey Ford	60.00
PC	Gaylord Perry, Steve Carlton/250	40.00
PS	Jim Palmer, Tom Seaver/100	75.00

Signature Decades

NM/M
Some not priced due to scarcity.
Platinum: No Pricing
Production One Set

LA	Luis Aparicio	20.00
LA1	Luis Aparicio	20.00
CB	Carlos Beltran/99	35.00
YB	Yogi Berra/25	80.00
WB	Wade Boggs/25	65.00
WB1	Wade Boggs/25	65.00
LB	Lou Brock/50	35.00
JB	Jim Bunning	20.00
MC	Miguel Cabrera	30.00
JC	Jose Canseco/99	40.00
SC	Steve Carlton	20.00
SC1	Steve Carlton	20.00
GC	Gary Carter/50	25.00
OC	Orlando Cepeda	15.00
WC	Will Clark/99	50.00
RC	Rocky Colavito	40.00
RC1	Rocky Colavito	50.00
AD	Andre Dawson	15.00
BD	Bobby Doerr	15.00
DE	Dennis Eckersley	25.00
BF	Bob Feller	25.00
RF	Rollie Fingers	25.00
KG	Ken Griffey Jr.	65.00
RG	Ron Guidry	25.00
KH	Keith Hernandez	10.00
KH1	Keith Hernandez	10.00
MI	Monte Irvin	20.00
BJ	Bo Jackson/50	60.00
FJ	Fergie Jenkins/50	20.00
DJ	Derek Jeter/99	160.00
AK	Al Kaline/99	30.00
GK	George Kell	20.00
HK	Harmon Killebrew/99	40.00
RK	Ralph Kiner/99	30.00
DL	Don Larsen/99	25.00
FL	Fred Lynn/99	15.00
JM	Juan Marichal/99	25.00
DM	Don Mattingly/25	85.00
BM	Bill Mazeroski/99	40.00
PM	Paul Molitor/99	25.00
MO	Joe Morgan/50	25.00
MU	Dale Murphy	25.00
DN	Don Newcombe/99	20.00
PN	Phil Niekro	20.00
DO	David Ortiz	40.00
RO	Roy Oswalt	15.00
JP	Jim Palmer	20.00
TP	Tony Perez	25.00
GP	Gaylord Perry	15.00
GP1	Gaylord Perry	15.00
JR	Jim Rice	20.00
BR	Brooks Robinson	30.00
FR	Frank Robinson/25	40.00
AR	Al Rosen	15.00

JS	Johan Santana	40.00
RS	Ron Santo	25.00
BS	Ben Sheets	15.00
SU	Don Sutton	15.00
MT	Mark Teixeira	25.00
LT	Luis Tiant	15.00
LT1	Luis Tiant	15.00
BU	B.J. Upton	15.00
RW	Rickie Weeks	20.00
BW	Billy Williams	20.00
MW	Maury Wills	15.00
RY	Robin Yount/25	70.00

Signature Hits

Production 1-125

BM	Stan Musial, Lou Brock/35	125.00
MY	Robin Yount, Paul Molitor/125	75.00
WG	Dave Winfield, Tony Gwynn/35	90.00
YB	Wade Boggs, Carl Yastrzemski/35	100.00

Signature HRs

NM/M
Production 1-250

BS	Mike Schmidt, Ernie Banks/25	180.00
GM	Ken Griffey Jr., Willie McCovey/250	100.00
KM	Willie McCovey, Harmon Killebrew/35	75.00
RG	Frank Robinson, Ken Griffey Jr./250	85.00

Signature MVPs

NM/M
Production 1-250

BM	Don Mattingly, Yogi Berra/175	100.00
BS	Ernie Banks, Ryne Sandberg/25	200.00
CM	Stan Musial, Orlando Cepeda/100	75.00
DS	Ryne Sandberg, Andre Dawson/175	80.00
EF	Dennis Eckersley, Rollie Fingers/250	30.00
FC	George Foster, Rod Carew/125	40.00
GM	Joe Morgan, Ken Griffey Jr./250	75.00
HY	Robin Yount, Keith Hernandez/200	50.00
JR	Ivan Rodriguez, Chipper Jones/35	125.00
KC	Harmon Killebrew, Rod Carew/100	80.00
KM	Harmon Killebrew, Willie McCovey/35	80.00
LM	Fred Lynn, Joe Morgan/200	30.00
LW	Maury Wills, Barry Larkin/250	35.00
MB	Joe Morgan, Johnny Bench/100	60.00
MG	Denny McLain, Bob Gibson/175	40.00
MY	Robin Yount, Dale Murphy/175	60.00
PR	Dave Parker, Jim Rice/250	40.00
SF	Mike Schmidt, Rollie Fingers/175	60.00
SS	Mike Schmidt, Ryne Sandberg/75	140.00
TB	Frank Thomas, Jeff Bagwell/50	90.00
YC	Orlando Cepeda, Carl Yastrzemski/100	65.00
YS	Carl Yastrzemski, Jim Rice/250	75.00

Signature No-Hitters

NM/M
Production 1-250

BG	Bob Gibson, Jim Bunning/125	60.00
CL	Don Larsen, David Cone/250	40.00
FR	Nolan Ryan, Bob Feller/25	150.00
GP	Bob Gibson, Jim Palmer/125	50.00

Signature Numbers

NM/M
Production 1-49

Platinum: No Pricing
Production One Set

WB	Wade Boggs/26	40.00
GB	George Brett/5	
LB	Lou Brock/20	
MC	Miguel Cabrera/24	50.00
JC	Jose Canseco/33	50.00
CA	Rod Carew/29	35.00
SC	Steve Carlton/32	25.00
OC	Orlando Cepeda/30	25.00
WC	Will Clark/22	60.00
CL	Roger Clemens/22	200.00
RF	Rollie Fingers/34	20.00
CF	Carlton Fisk/22	40.00
EG	Eric Gagne/38	40.00
BG	Bob Gibson/45	25.00
GL	Tom Glavine/47	40.00
KG	Ken Griffey Jr./30	125.00
VG	Vladimir Guerrero/27	50.00
RG	Ron Guidry/49	60.00
TG	Tony Gwynn/19	80.00
MI	Monte Irvin/20	30.00
FJ	Fergie Jenkins/31	20.00
RJ	Randy Johnson/41	75.00
MA	Juan Marichal/27	40.00
DM	Don Mattingly/23	125.00
WM	Willie McCovey/44	40.00
EM	Eddie Murray/33	120.00
DO	David Ortiz/34	50.00
RO	Roy Oswalt/44	25.00
JP	Jim Palmer/22	30.00
PI	Mike Piazza/31	100.00
MP	Mark Prior/22	60.00
KP	Kirby Puckett/34	85.00
FR	Frank Robinson/20	50.00
SR	Scott Rolen/27	40.00
NR	Nolan Ryan/34	120.00
TS	Tom Seaver/41	75.00
JS	John Smoltz/29	60.00
FT	Frank Thomas/35	80.00
BW	Billy Williams/26	30.00
DW	Dave Winfield/31	35.00
KW	Kerry Wood/34	40.00
RY	Robin Yount/19	75.00

Signature ROYs

NM/M
Production 1-250

CM	Willie McCovey, Orlando Cepeda/75	65.00
CS	Rod Carew, Tom Seaver/25	100.00
DM	Andre Dawson, Eddie Murray/25	70.00
FB	Carlton Fisk, Johnny Bench/35	80.00
FL	Fred Lynn/125, Carlton Fisk/125	60.00
GR	Nomar Garciaparra, Scott Rolen/200	85.00
GS	Dwight Gooden, Tom Seaver/100	60.00
JG	Derek Jeter, Nomar Garciaparra/75	185.00
RA	Frank Robinson, Luis Aparicio/125	50.00
RJ	Derek Jeter, Cal Ripken Jr./75	300.00
SG	Dwight Gooden, Darryl Strawberry/250	40.00
WD	Andre Dawson, Billy Williams/250	30.00

Signature Supremacy

NM/M
Production 15-99

LA	Luis Aparicio/50	40.00
JB	Jeff Bagwell/50	75.00
CB	Carlos Beltran/50	30.00
BE	Johnny Bench/25	60.00
YB	Yogi Berra/25	60.00
HB	Hank Blalock/50	25.00
WB	Wade Boggs/25	60.00
LB	Lou Brock/25	40.00
BU	Jim Bunning/99	25.00
MC	Miguel Cabrera/99	40.00
JC	Jose Canseco/25	40.00
CA	Rod Carew/25	35.00
SC	Steve Carlton/99	20.00
OC	Orlando Cepeda/99	20.00
EC	Eric Chavez/99	15.00
WC	Will Clark/50	40.00
AD	Andre Dawson/99	20.00
BD	Bobby Doerr/99	20.00
BF	Bob Feller/99	25.00
RF	Rollie Fingers/99	15.00
CF	Carlton Fisk/50	40.00
EG	Eric Gagne/50	25.00
KG	Ken Griffey Jr./99	80.00
RG	Ron Guidry/50	25.00
TH	Tim Hudson/50	25.00
MI	Monte Irvin/99	20.00
DJ	Derek Jeter/50	200.00
AK	Al Kaline/50	60.00

GK	George Kell/99	25.00
HK	Harmon Killebrew/50	40.00
RK	Ralph Kiner/25	40.00
JU	Juan Marichal/25	50.00
MA	Don Mattingly/25	80.00
BM	Bill Mazeroski/50	40.00
PM	Paul Molitor/50	40.00
JM	Joe Morgan/25	30.00
MM	Mark Mulder/99	15.00
DM	Dale Murphy/99	25.00
MU	Stan Musial/25	125.00
DN	Don Newcombe/99	20.00
DO	David Ortiz/99	40.00
RO	Roy Oswalt/99	15.00
JP	Jim Palmer/99	25.00
TP	Tony Perez/99	25.00
MP	Mark Prior/99	60.00
JR	Jim Rice/99	15.00
RR	Robin Roberts/99	30.00
BR	Brooks Robinson/99	30.00
FR	Frank Robinson/25	40.00
SR	Scott Rolen/25	50.00
AR	Al Rosen/99	25.00
SA	Ryne Sandberg/25	85.00
JS	Johan Santana/99	40.00
RS	Ron Santo/25	25.00
MS	Mike Schmidt/25	100.00
TS	Tom Seaver/25	50.00
BS	Ben Sheets/99	20.00
OS	Ozzie Smith/25	50.00
SM	John Smoltz/50	50.00
AS	Alfonso Soriano/25	40.00
MT	Mark Teixeira/99	25.00
FT	Frank Thomas/25	80.00
BW	Billy Williams/99	25.00
DW	Dave Winfield/25	40.00
CY	Carl Yastrzemski/25	100.00
RY	Robin Yount/25	75.00

Signs of October

NM/M

Production 1-250

BW	Mookie Wilson, Bill Buckner/250	40.00
CS	John Smoltz, Joe Carter/250	50.00
EG	Kirk Gibson, Dennis Eckersley/200	40.00
FM	Carlton Fisk, Joe Morgan/100	50.00
GB	Bob Gibson, Lou Brock/100	70.00
GG	Ron Guidry, Steve Garvey/250	30.00
GL	Mickey Lolich, Bob Gibson/100	40.00
JG	Derek Jeter, Tony Gwynn/250	185.00
LB	Yogi Berra, Don Larsen/250	85.00
MP	Jack Morris, Kirby Puckett/100	85.00
PS	Ozzie Smith, Kirby Puckett/35	125.00
RR	Frank Robinson, Brooks Robinson/250	65.00
SB	George Brett, Ozzie Smith	150.00
SY	Ozzie Smith, Robin Yount/100	85.00
TG	Kirk Gibson, Alan Trammell/250	40.00

2006 Upper Deck

NM/M

Complete Series 1 (500): 150.00
Complete Series 2 (500): 100.00
Complete Update (250):
Common Player: .15
Common Update SP: 4.00
Inserted 1:2 Update
Series 1 Pack (8): 3.50

Series 1 Box (24):		70.00
Series 2 Pack (6):		3.50
Series 2 Box (24):		75.00
Update Pack (8):		3.00
Update Box (24):		60.00
1	Adam Kennedy	.15
2	Bartolo Colon	.25
3	Bengie Molina	.15
4	Casey Kotchman	.15
5	Chone Figgins	.15
6	Dallas McPherson	.15
7	Darin Erstad	.15
8	Ervin Santana	.25
9	Francisco Rodriguez	.15
10	Garret Anderson	.25
11	Jarrod Washburn	.15
12	John Lackey	.15
13	Juan Rivera	.15
14	Orlando Cabrera	.15
15	Paul Byrd	.15
16	Steve Finley	.15
17	Vladimir Guerrero	.75
18	Alex Cintron	.15
19	Brandon Lyon	.15
20	Brandon Webb	.15
21	Chad Tracy	.15
22	Chris Snyder	.15
23	Claudio Vargas	.15
24	Conor Jackson (RC)	.15
25	Craig Counsell	.15
26	Javier Vazquez	.15
27	Jose Valverde	.15
28	Luis Gonzalez	.15
29	Royce Clayton	.15
30	Russ Ortiz	.15
31	Shawn Green	.15
32	Dustin Nippert (RC)	.15
33	Tony Clark	.15
34	Troy Glaus	.25
35	Adam LaRoche	.15
36	Andruw Jones	.50
37	Craig Hansen RC	3.00
38	Chipper Jones	.75
39	Horacio Ramirez	.15
40	Jeff Francoeur	.25
41	John Smoltz	.25
42	Joey Devine RC	.50
43	Johnny Estrada	.15
44	Anthony Lerew (RC)	.15
45	Julio Franco	.15
46	Kyle Farnsworth	.15
47	Marcus Giles	.15
48	Mike Hampton	.15
49	Rafael Furcal	.25
50	Chuck James (RC)	.25
51	Tim Hudson	.40
52	B.J. Ryan	.15
53	Bernie Castro	.15
54	Brian Roberts	.15
55	Walter Young	.15
56	Daniel Cabrera	.15
57	Eric Byrnes	.15
58	Alejandro Freire RC	.50
59	Erik Bedard	.15
60	Javy Lopez	.25
61	Jay Gibbons	.15
62	Jorge Julio	.15
63	Luis Matos	.15
64	Melvin Mora	.40
65	Miguel Tejada	.25
66	Rafael Palmeiro	.25
67	Rodrigo Lopez	.15
68	Sammy Sosa	.75
69	Alejandro Machado	.15
70	Bill Mueller	.15
71	Bronson Arroyo	.15
72	Curt Schilling	.75
73	David Ortiz	.75
74	David Wells	.15
75	Edgar Renteria	.25
76	Ryan Jorgensen RC	.25
77	Jason Varitek	.50
78	Johnny Damon	.75
79	Keith Foulke	.15
80	Kevin Youkilis	.15
81	Manny Ramirez	.75
82	Matt Clement	.15
83	Hanley Ramirez (RC)	.50
84	Tim Wakefield	.15
85	Trot Nixon	.15
86	Wade Miller	.15
87	Aramis Ramirez	.40
88	Carlos Zambrano	.25
89	Corey Patterson	.15
90	Derrek Lee	.50
91	Geovany Soto (RC)	.15
92	Greg Maddux	1.00
93	Jeromy Burnitz	.15
94	Jerry Hairston	.15
95	Kerry Wood	.25
96	Mark Prior	.50
97	Matt Murton	.15
98	Michael Barrett	.15
99	Neifi Perez	.15
100	Nomar Garciaparra	.50
101	Rich Hill	.15
102	Ryan Dempster	.15
103	Todd Walker	.15
104	A.J. Pierzynski	.15
105	Aaron Rowand	.15
106	Bobby Jenks	.15
107	Carl Everett	.15
108	Dustin Hermanson	.15
109	Frank Thomas	.40
110	Freddy Garcia	.15
111	Jermaine Dye	.15
112	Joe Crede	.15
113	Jon Garland	.15
114	Jose Contreras	.25
115	Juan Uribe	.15
116	Mark Buehrle	.25
117	Orlando Hernandez	.15
118	Paul Konerko	.40
119	Scott Podsednik	.15
120	Tadahito Iguchi	.25
121	Aaron Harang	.15
122	Adam Dunn	.50
123	Austin Kearns	.25
124	Brandon Claussen	.15
125	Chris Denorfia (RC)	.15
126	Edwin Encarnacion	.15
127	Miguel Perez (RC)	.15
128	Felipe Lopez	.15
129	Jason LaRue	.15
130	Ken Griffey Jr.	1.50
131	Chris Booker	.15
132	Luke Hudson	.15
133	Jason Bergmann RC	.50
134	Ryan Freel	.15
135	Sean Casey	.15
136	Wily Mo Pena	.15
137	Aaron Boone	.15
138	Ben Broussard	.15
139	Ryan Garko (RC)	.15
140	C.C. Sabathia	.15
141	Casey Blake	.15
142	Cliff Lee	.15
143	Coco Crisp	.15
144	David Riske	.15
145	Grady Sizemore	.40
146	Jake Westbrook	.15
147	Jhonny Peralta	.25
148	Josh Bard	.15
149	Kevin Millwood	.25
150	Ronnie Belliard	.15
151	Scott Elarton	.15
152	Travis Hafner	.40
153	Victor Martinez	.25
154	Aaron Cook	.15
155	Aaron Miles	.15
156	Brad Hawpe	.15
157	Mike Esposito	.15
158	Chin-Hui Tsao	.15
159	Clint Barmes	.15
160	Cory Sullivan	.15
161	Garrett Atkins	.15
162	J.D. Closser	.15
163	Jason Jennings	.15
164	Jeff Baker	.15
165	Jeff Francis	.15
166	Luis Gonzalez	.15
167	Matt Holliday	.50
168	Todd Helton	.50
169	Brandon Inge	.15
170	Carlos Guillen	.15
171	Carlos Pena	.15
172	Chris Shelton	.15
173	Craig Monroe	.15
174	Curtis Granderson	.15
175	Dmitri Young	.15
176	Ivan Rodriguez	.40
177	Jason Johnson	.15
178	Jeremy Bonderman	.15
179	Magglio Ordonez	.15
180	Mark Woodyard (RC)	.15
181	Nook Logan	.15
182	Omar Infante	.15
183	Placido Polanco	.15
184	Chris Heintz RC	.50
185	A.J. Burnett	.15
186	Alex Gonzalez	.15
187	Josh Johnson (RC)	.15
188	Carlos Delgado	.40
189	Dontrelle Willis	.25
190	Josh Wilson (RC)	.15
191	Jason Vargas	.15
192	Jeff Conine	.15
193	Jeremy Hermida (RC)	.15
194	Josh Beckett	.25
195	Juan Encarnacion	.15
196	Juan Pierre	.15
197	Luis Castillo	.15
198	Miguel Cabrera	.75
199	Mike Lowell	.15
200	Paul LoDuca	.15
201	Todd Jones	.15
202	Adam Everett	.15
203	Andy Pettitte	.40
204	Brad Ausmus	.15
205	Brad Lidge	.15
206	Brandon Backe	.15
207	Charlton Jimerson	.15
208	Chris Burke	.15
209	Craig Biggio	.25
210	Daniel Wheeler	.15
211	Jason Lane	.15
212	Jeff Bagwell	.50
213	Lance Berkman	.40
214	Luke Scott	.15
215	Morgan Ensberg	.25
216	Roger Clemens	2.00
217	Roy Oswalt	.25
218	Willy Taveras	.15
219	Andres Blanco	.15
220	Angel Berroa	.15
221	Ruben Gotay	.15
222	David DeJesus	.15
223	Emil Brown	.15
224	J.P. Howell	.15
225	Jeremy Affeldt	.15
226	Jimmy Gobble	.15
227	John Buck	.15
228	Jose Lima	.15
229	Mark Teahen	.15
230	Matt Stairs	.15
231	Mike MacDougal	.15
232	Mike Sweeney	.15
233	Runelvys Hernandez	.15
234	Terrence Long	.15
235	Zack Greinke	.15
236	Ron Flores RC	.50
237	Brad Penny	.15
238	Cesar Izturis	.15
239	D.J. Houlton	.15
240	Derek Lowe	.15
241	Eric Gagne	.25
242	Hee Seop Choi	.15
243	J.D. Drew	.15
244	Jason Phillips	.15
245	Jason Repko	.15
246	Jayson Werth	.15
247	Jeff Kent	.25
248	Jeff Weaver	.15
249	Milton Bradley	.15
250	Odalis Perez	.15
251	Hong-Chih Kuo	.15
252	Oscar Robles	.15
253	Ben Sheets	.25
254	Bill Hall	.15
255	Brady Clark	.15
256	Carlos Lee	.25
257	Chris Capuano	.15
258	Nelson Cruz (RC)	.15
259	Derrick Turnbow	.15
260	Doug Davis	.15
261	Geoff Jenkins	.15
262	J.J. Hardy	.15
263	Lyle Overbay	.15
264	Prince Fielder (RC)	.75
265	Rickie Weeks	.25
266	Russell Branyan	.15
267	Tomokazu Ohka	.15
268	Jonah Bayliss RC	.75
269	Brad Radke	.15
270	Carlos Silva	.15
271	Francisco Liriano (RC)	.50
272	Jacque Jones	.15
273	Joe Mauer	.25
274	Travis Bower	.15
275	Joe Nathan	.15
276	Johan Santana	.50
277	Justin Morneau	.15
278	Kyle Lohse	.15
279	Lew Ford	.15
280	Matthew LeCroy	.15
281	Michael Cuddyer	.15
282	Nick Punto	.15
283	Scott Baker	.15
284	Shannon Stewart	.15
285	Torii Hunter	.25
286	Braden Looper	.15
287	Carlos Beltran	.50
288	Cliff Floyd	.15
289	David Wright	.75
290	Doug Mientkiewicz	.15
291	Anderson Hernandez (RC)	.15
292	Jose Reyes	.50
293	Kazuo Matsui	.15
294	Kris Benson	.15
295	Miguel Cairo	.15
296	Mike Cameron	.15
297	Robert Andino RC	.50
298	Mike Piazza	.75
299	Pedro Martinez	.75
300	Tom Glavine	.25
301	Victor Diaz	.15
302	Tim Hamulack	.15
303	Alex Rodriguez	2.00
304	Bernie Williams	.25
305	Carl Pavano	.15
306	Chien-Ming Wang	.40

No.	Player	Price
307	Derek Jeter	2.00
308	Gary Sheffield	.40
309	Hideki Matsui	1.00
310	Jason Giambi	.40
311	Jorge Posada	.25
312	Kevin Brown	.15
313	Mariano Rivera	.25
314	Matt Lawton	.15
315	Mike Mussina	.25
316	Randy Johnson	.75
317	Robinson Cano	.25
318	Michael Vento	.15
319	Tino Martinez	.25
320	Tony Womack	.15
321	Barry Zito	.25
322	Bobby Crosby	.15
323	Bobby Kielty	.15
324	Dan Johnson	.15
325	Danny Haren	.15
326	Eric Chavez	.25
327	Erubiel Durazo	.15
328	Huston Street	.25
329	Jason Kendall	.15
330	Jay Payton	.15
331	Joe Blanton	.15
332	Joe Kennedy	.15
333	Kirk Saarloos	.15
334	Mark Kotsay	.15
335	Nick Swisher	.15
336	Rich Harden	.25
337	Scott Hatteberg	.15
338	Billy Wagner	.25
339	Bobby Abreu	.50
340	Brett Myers	.15
341	Chase Utley	.40
342	Danny Sandoval RC	.50
343	David Bell	.15
344	Gavin Floyd	.15
345	Jim Thome	.50
346	Jimmy Rollins	.40
347	Jon Lieber	.15
348	Kenny Lofton	.15
349	Mike Lieberthal	.15
350	Pat Burrell	.25
351	Randy Wolf	.15
352	Ryan Howard	.75
353	Vicente Padilla	.15
354	Bryan Bullington	.15
355	J.J. Furmaniak (RC)	.15
356	Craig Wilson	.15
357	Matt Capps (RC)	.15
358	Tom Gorzelanny (RC)	.15
359	Jack Wilson	.15
360	Jason Bay	.25
361	Jose Mesa	.15
362	Josh Fogg	.15
363	Kip Wells	.15
364	Steve Stemle RC	.50
365	Oliver Perez	.15
366	Robert Mackowiak	.15
367	Ronny Paulino (RC)	.15
368	Tike Redman	.15
369	Zachary Duke	.15
370	Adam Eaton	.15
371	Scott Feldman RC	.50
372	Brian Giles	.25
373	Brian Lawrence	.15
374	Damian Jackson	.15
375	Dave Roberts	.15
376	Jake Peavy	.25
377	Joe Randa	.15
378	Khalil Greene	.15
379	Mark Loretta	.25
380	Ramon Hernandez	.15
381	Robert Fick	.15
382	Ryan Klesko	.15
383	Trevor Hoffman	.15
384	Woody Williams	.15
385	Xavier Nady	.15
386	Armando Benitez	.15
387	Brad Hennessey	.15
388	Brian Myrow RC	.50
389	Edgardo Alfonzo	.15
390	J.T. Snow	.15
391	Jeremy Accardo RC	.15
392	Jason Schmidt	.25
393	Lance Niekro	.15
394	Matt Cain (RC)	.25
395	Daniel Ortmeier (RC)	.15
396	Moises Alou	.25
397	Doug Clark	.15
398	Omar Vizquel	.15
399	Pedro Feliz	.15
400	Randy Winn	.15
401	Ray Durham	.15
402	Adrian Beltre	.15
403	Eddie Guardado	.15
404	Felix Hernandez	.50
405	Gil Meche	.15
406	Ichiro Suzuki	1.50
407	Jamie Moyer	.15
408	Jeff Nelson	.15
409	Jeremy Reed	.15
410	Joel Pineiro	.15
411	Jaime Bubela (RC)	.15
412	Raul Ibanez	.15
413	Richie Sexson	.40
414	Ryan Franklin	.15
415	Willie Bloomquist	.15
416	Yorvit Torrealba	.15
417	Yuniesky Betancourt	.15
418	Jeff Harris RC	.25
419	Albert Pujols	2.00
420	Chris Carpenter	.25
421	David Eckstein	.15
422	Jason Isringhausen	.15
423	Jason Marquis	.15
424	Adam Wainwright (RC)	.15
425	Jim Edmonds	.25
426	Ryan Theriot (RC)	1.00
427	Chris Duncan	.15
428	Mark Grudzielanek	.15
429	Mark Mulder	.25
430	Matt Morris	.25
431	Reggie Sanders	.15
432	Scott Rolen	.50
433	Tyler Johnson (RC)	.15
434	Yadier Molina	.15
435	Alex Gonzalez	.15
436	Aubrey Huff	.15
437	Tim Corcoran RC	.40
438	Carl Crawford	.25
439	Casey Fossum	.15
440	Danys Baez	.15
441	Edwin Jackson	.15
442	Joey Gathright	.15
443	Jonny Gomes	.25
444	Jorge Cantu	.15
445	Julio Lugo	.15
446	Nick Green	.15
447	Rocco Baldelli	.15
448	Scott Kazmir	.15
449	Seth McClung	.15
450	Toby Hall	.15
451	Travis Lee	.15
452	Craig Breslow RC	.25
453	Alfonso Soriano	.50
454	Chris Young	.15
455	David Dellucci	.15
456	Francisco Cordero	.15
457	Gary Matthews	.15
458	Hank Blalock	.25
459	Juan Dominguez	.15
460	Josh Rupe	.15
461	Kenny Rogers	.15
462	Kevin Mench	.15
463	Laynce Nix	.15
464	Mark Teixeira	.50
465	Michael Young	.25
466	Richard Hidalgo	.15
467	Jason Botts (RC)	.15
468	Aaron Hill	.15
469	Alex Rios	.15
470	Corey Koskie	.15
471	Chris Demaria RC	.50
472	Eric Hinske	.15
473	Frank Catalanotto	.15
474	John-Ford Griffin (RC)	.15
475	Gustavo Chacin	.15
476	Josh Towers	.15
477	Miguel Batista	.15
478	Orlando Hudson	.15
479	Reed Johnson	.15
480	Roy Halladay	.40
481	Shaun Marcum (RC)	.15
482	Shea Hillenbrand	.15
483	Ted Lilly	.15
484	Vernon Wells	.25
485	Brad Wilkerson	.15
486	Darrell Rasner (RC)	.15
487	Chad Cordero	.15
488	Cristian Guzman	.15
489	Esteban Loaiza	.15
490	John Patterson	.15
491	Jose Guillen	.15
492	Jose Vidro	.15
493	Livan Hernandez	.15
494	Marlon Byrd	.15
495	Nick Johnson	.15
496	Preston Wilson	.15
497	Ryan Church	.15
498	Ryan Zimmerman (RC)	.50
499	Tony Armas	.15
500	Vinny Castilla	.15
501	Andy Green	.15
502	Damion Easley	.15
503	Eric Byrnes	.15
504	Jason Grimsley	.15
505	Jeff DaVanon	.15
506	Johnny Estrada	.15
507	Luis Vizcaino	.15
508	Miguel Batista	.15
509	Orlando Hernandez	.15
510	Orlando Hudson	.15
511	Terry Mulholland	.15
512	Chris Reitsma	.15
513	Edgar Renteria	.25
514	John Thomson	.15
515	Jorge Sosa	.15
516	Oscar Villarreal	.15
517	Peter Orr	.15
518	Ryan Langerhans	.15
519	Todd Pratt	.15
520	Wilson Betemit	.15
521	Brian Jordan	.15
522	Lance Cormier	.15
523	Matt Diaz	.15
524	Mike Remlinger	.15
525	Bruce Chen	.15
526	Chris Gomez	.15
527	Chris Ray	.15
528	Corey Patterson	.15
529	David Newhan	.15
530	Ed Rogers (RC)	.25
531	John Halama	.15
532	Kris Benson	.15
533	LaTroy Hawkins	.15
534	Raul Chavez	.15
535	Alex Cora	.15
536	Alex Gonzalez	.15
537	Coco Crisp	.15
538	David Riske	.15
539	Doug Mirabelli	.15
540	Josh Beckett	.25
541	J.T. Snow	.15
542	Mike Timlin	.15
543	Julian Tavarez	.15
544	Rudy Seanez	.15
545	Wily Mo Pena	.15
546	Bob Howry	.15
547	Glendon Rusch	.15
548	Henry Blanco	.15
549	Jacque Jones	.15
550	Jerome Williams	.15
551	John Mabry	.15
552	Juan Pierre	.25
553	Scott Eyre	.15
554	Scott Williamson	.15
555	Wade Miller	.15
556	Will Ohman	.15
557	Alex Cintron	.15
558	Robert Mackowiak	.15
559	Brandon McCarthy	.15
560	Chris Widger	.15
561	Cliff Politte	.15
562	Javier Vazquez	.15
563	Jim Thome	.75
564	Matt Thornton	.15
565	Neal Cotts	.15
566	Pablo Ozuna	.15
567	Ross Gload	.15
568	Brandon Phillips	.15
569	Bronson Arroyo	.15
570	Dave Williams	.15
571	David Ross	.15
572	David Weathers	.15
573	Eric Milton	.15
574	Javier Valentin	.15
575	Kent Mercker	.15
576	Matt Belisle	.15
577	Paul Wilson	.15
578	Rich Aurilia	.15
579	Rick White	.15
580	Scott Hatteberg	.15
581	Todd Coffey	.15
582	Bob Wickman	.15
583	Danny Graves	.15
584	Eduardo Perez	.15
585	Guillermo Mota	.15
586	Jason Davis	.15
587	Jason Johnson	.15
588	Jason Michaels	.15
589	Rafael Betancourt	.15
590	Ramon Vazquez	.15
591	Scott Sauerbeck	.15
592	Todd Hollandsworth	.15
593	Brian Fuentes	.15
594	Danny Ardoin	.15
595	David Cortes	.15
596	Eli Marrero	.15
597	Jamey Carroll	.15
598	Jason Smith	.15
599	Josh Fogg	.15
600	Miguel Ojeda	.15
601	Mike DeJean	.15
602	Ray King	.15
603	Omar Quintanilla (RC)	.25
604	Zach Day	.15
605	Fernando Rodney	.15
606	Kenny Rogers	.15
607	Mike Maroth	.15
608	Nate Robertson	.15
609	Todd Jones	.15
610	Vance Wilson	.15
611	Bobby Seay	.15
612	Chris Spurling	.15
613	Raul Colon	.15
614	Jason Grilli	.15
615	Marcus Thames	.15
616	Ramon Santiago	.15
617	Alfredo Amezaga	.15
618	Brian Moehler	.15
619	Chris Aguila	.15
620	Franklyn German	.15
621	Joe Borowski	.15
622	Logan Kensing (RC)	.25
623	Matt Treanor	.15
624	Miguel Olivo	.15
625	Sergio Mitre	.15
626	Todd Wellemeyer	.15
627	Wes Helms	.15
628	Chad Qualls	.15
629	Eric Bruntlett	.15
630	Mike Gallo	.15
631	Mike Lamb	.15
632	Orlando Palmeiro	.15
633	Russ Springer	.15
634	Dan Wheeler	.15
635	Eric Munson	.15
637	Trever Miller	.15
638	Ambiorix Burgos	.15
639	Andrew Sisco	.15
640	Denny Bautista	.15
641	Doug Mientkiewicz	.15
642	Elmer Dessens	.15
643	Esteban German	.15
644	Joe Nelson (RC)	.25
645	Mark Grudzielanek	.15
646	Mark Redman	.15
647	Mike Wood	.15
648	Paul Bako	.15
649	Reggie Sanders	.15
650	Scott Elarton	.15
651	Shane Costa	.15
652	Tony Graffanino	.15
653	Jason Bulger (RC)	.25
654	Chris Bootcheck (RC)	.25
655	Esteban Yan	.15
656	Hector Carrasco	.15
657	J.C. Romero	.15
658	Jeff Weaver	.15
659	Jose Molina	.15
660	Kelvim Escobar	.15
661	Maicer Izturis	.15
662	Robb Quinlan	.15
663	Scot Shields	.15
664	Tim Salmon	.15
665	Bill Mueller	.15
666	Brett Tomko	.15
667	Dioner Navarro	.15
668	Jae Weong Seo	.15
669	Jose Cruz	.15
670	Kenny Lofton	.15
671	Lance Carter	.15
672	Nomar Garciaparra	.75
673	Olmedo Saenz	.15
674	Rafael Furcal	.15
675	Ramon Martinez	.15
676	Ricky Ledee	.15
677	Sandy Alomar	.15
678	Yhency Brazoban	.15
679	Corey Koskie	.15
680	Dan Kolb	.15
681	Gabe Gross	.15
682	Jeff Cirillo	.15
683	Matt Wise	.15
684	Rick Helling	.15
685	Chad Moeller	.15
686	David Bush	.15
687	Jorge De La Rosa	.15
688	Justin Lehr	.15
689	Jason Bartlett	.15
690	Jesse Crain	.15
691	Juan Rincon	.15
692	Luis Castillo	.15
693	Mike Redmond	.15
694	Rondell White	.15
695	Tony Batista	.15
696	Juan Castro	.15
697	Luis Rodriguez	.15
698	Matt Guerrier	.15
699	Willie Eyre (RC)	.25
700	Aaron Heilman	.15
701	Billy Wagner	.25
702	Carlos Delgado	.50
703	Chad Bradford	.15
704	Chris Woodward	.15
705	Darren Oliver	.15
706	Duaner Sanchez	.15
707	Endy Chavez	.15
708	Jorge Julio	.15
709	Jose Valentin	.15
710	Julio Franco	.15
711	Paul LoDuca	.15
712	Ramon Castro	.15
713	Steve Trachsel	.15
714	Victor Zambrano	.15
715	Xavier Nady	.15
716	Andy Phillips	.15
717	Bubba Crosby	.15
718	Jaret Wright	.15
719	Kelly Stinnett	.15
720	Kyle Farnsworth	.15
721	Mike Meyers	.15
722	Octavio Dotel	.15
723	Ron Villone	.15

#	Player	Value
724	Scott Proctor	.15
725	Shawn Chacon	.15
726	Tanyon Sturtze	.15
727	Adam Melhuse	.15
728	Brad Halsey	.15
729	Esteban Loaiza	.15
730	Frank Thomas	.50
731	Jay Witasick	.15
732	Justin Duchscherer	.15
733	Kiko Calero	.15
734	Marco Scutaro	.15
735	Mark Ellis	.15
736	Milton Bradley	.15
737	Aaron Fultz	.15
738	Aaron Rowand	.15
739	Geoff Geary	.15
740	Arthur Rhodes	.15
741	Chris Coste RC	.40
742	Rheal Cormier	.15
743	Ryan Franklin	.15
744	Ryan Madson	.15
745	Sal Fasano	.15
746	Tom Gordon	.15
747	Abraham Nunez	.15
748	David Dellucci	.15
749	Julio Santana	.15
750	Shane Victorino	.15
751	Damaso Marte	.15
752	Freddy Sanchez	.15
753	Humberto Cota	.15
754	Jeromy Burnitz	.15
755	Joe Randa	.15
756	Jose Castillo	.15
757	Mike Gonzalez	.15
758	Ryan Doumit	.15
759	Sean Burnett	.15
760	Sean Casey	.15
761	Ian Snell	.15
762	John Grabow	.15
763	Jose Hernandez	.15
764	Roberto Hernandez	.15
765	Ryan Vogelsong	.15
766	Victor Sanchez	.15
767	Adrian Gonzalez	.15
768	Alan Embree	.15
769	Brian Sweeney (RC)	.25
770	Chan Ho Park	.15
771	Clay Hensley	.15
772	Dewon Brazelton	.15
773	Doug Brocail	.15
774	Eric Young	.15
775	Geoff Blum	.15
776	Josh Bard	.15
777	Mark Bellhorn	.15
778	Mike Cameron	.15
779	Mike Piazza	.75
780	Rob Bowen	.15
781	Scott Cassidy	.15
782	Scott Linebrink	.15
783	Shawn Estes	.15
784	Terrmel Sledge	.15
785	Vinny Castilla	.15
786	Jeff Fassero	.15
787	Jose Vizcaino	.15
788	Mark Sweeney	.15
789	Matt Morris	.15
790	Steve Finley	.15
791	Tim Worrell	.15
792	Jamey Wright	.15
793	Jason Ellison	.15
794	Noah Lowry	.15
795	Steve Kline	.15
796	Todd Greene	.15
797	Carl Everett	.15
798	George Sherrill	.15
799	J.J. Putz	.15
800	Jake Woods	.15
801	Jose Lopez	.15
802	Julio Mateo	.15
803	Mike Morse	.15
804	Rafael Soriano	.15
805	Roberto Petagine	.15
806	Aaron Miles	.15
807	Braden Looper	.15
808	Gary Bennett	.15
809	Hector Luna	.15
810	Jeff Suppan	.15
811	John Rodriguez	.15
812	Josh Hancock	.15
813	Juan Encarnacion	.15
814	Larry Bigbie	.15
815	Scott Spiezio	.15
816	Sidney Ponson	.15
817	So Taguchi	.15
818	Brian Meadows	.15
819	Damon Hollins	.15
820	Dan Miceli	.15
821	Doug Waechter	.15
822	Jason Childers	.25
823	Josh Paul	.15
824	Julio Lugo	.15
825	Mark Hendrickson	.15
826	Sean Burroughs	.15
827	Shawn Camp	.15
828	Travis Harper	.15
829	Ty Wigginton	.15
830	Adam Eaton	.15
831	Adrian Brown	.15
832	Akinori Otsuka	.15
833	Antonio Alfonseca	.15
834	Brad Wilkerson	.15
835	D'Angelo Jimenez	.15
836	Gerald Laird	.15
837	Joaquin Benoit	.15
838	Kameron Loe	.15
839	Kevin Millwood	.15
840	Mark DeRosa	.15
841	Phil Nevin	.15
842	Rod Barajas	.15
843	Vicente Padilla	.15
844	A.J. Burnett	.15
845	Bengie Molina	.15
846	Gregg Zaun	.15
847	John McDonald	.15
848	Lyle Overbay	.15
849	Russ Adams	.15
850	Troy Glaus	.15
851	Vinnie Chulk	.15
852	B.J. Ryan	.15
853	Justin Speier	.15
854	Pete Walker	.15
855	Scott Downs	.15
856	Scott Schoeneweis	.15
857	Alfonso Soriano	.75
858	Brian Schneider	.15
859	Daryle Ward	.15
860	Felix Rodriguez	.15
861	Gary Majewski	.15
862	Joey Eischen	.15
863	Jon Rauch	.15
864	Marlon Anderson	.15
865	Matthew LeCroy	.15
866	Mike Stanton	.15
867	Ramon Ortiz	.15
868	Robert Fick	.15
869	Royce Clayton	.15
870	Ryan Drese	.15
871	Vladimir Guerrero	.40
872	Craig Biggio	.15
873	Barry Zito	.15
874	Vernon Wells	.15
875	Chipper Jones	.40
876	Prince Fielder	.75
877	Albert Pujols	1.00
878	Greg Maddux	.75
879	Carl Crawford	.15
880	Brandon Webb	.15
881	J.D. Drew	.15
882	Jason Schmidt	.15
883	Victor Martinez	.15
884	Ichiro Suzuki	.75
885	Miguel Cabrera	.40
886	David Wright	.75
887	Alfonso Soriano	.40
888	Miguel Tejada	.40
889	Khalil Greene	.15
890	Ryan Howard	1.00
891	Jason Bay	.25
892	Mark Teixeira	.25
893	Manny Ramirez	.40
894	Ken Griffey Jr.	.75
895	Todd Helton	.25
896	Angel Berroa	.15
897	Ivan Rodriguez	.25
898	Johan Santana	.25
899	Paul Konerko	.15
900	Derek Jeter	1.00
901	Macay McBride (RC)	.25
902	Tony Pena (RC)	.25
903	Peter Moylan RC	.50
904	Aaron Rakers (RC)	.25
905	Chris Britton RC	.50
906	Nicholas Markakis (RC)	.50
907	Sendy Rleal RC	.50
908	Val Majewski (RC)	.25
909	Jermaine Van Buren (RC)	.25
910	Jonathan Papelbon (RC)	4.00
911	Angel Pagan (RC)	.50
912	David Aardsma (RC)	.25
913	Sean Marshall (RC)	.25
914	Brian Anderson (RC)	.25
915	Freddie Bynum (RC)	.25
916	Fausto Carmona (RC)	.25
917	Kelly Stoppach (RC)	.25
918	Choo Freeman (RC)	.25
919	Ryan Shealy (RC)	.25
920	Joel Zumaya (RC)	6.00
921	Jordan Tata RC	1.00
922	Justin Verlander (RC)	1.00
923	Carlos Martinez RC	.50
924	Chris Resop (RC)	.25
925	Dan Uggla (RC)	.50
926	Eric Reed (RC)	.25
927	Hanley Ramirez (RC)	.75
928	Yusmeiro Petit (RC)	.25
929	Josh Willingham (RC)	.25
930	Mike Jacobs (RC)	.25
931	Reggie Abercrombie (RC)	.25
932	Ricky Nolasco (RC)	.25
933	Scott Olsen (RC)	.25
934	Fernando Nieve (RC)	.25
935	Taylor Buchholz (RC)	.25
936	Cody Ross (RC)	.25
937	James Loney (RC)	.25
938	Takashi Saito RC	2.00
939	Tim Hamulack (RC)	.25
940	Chris Demaria RC	.50
941	Jose Capellan (RC)	.25
942	David Gassner (RC)	.25
943	Jason Kubel (RC)	.25
944	Brian Bannister (RC)	.25
945	Mike Thompson RC	.50
946	Cole Hamels (RC)	5.00
947	Paul Maholm (RC)	.25
948	John Van Benschoten (RC)	.25
949	Nate McLouth (RC)	.25
950	Ben Johnson (RC)	.25
951	Josh Barfield (RC)	.25
952	Travis Ishikawa (RC)	.25
953	Jack Taschner (RC)	.25
954	Kenji Johjima RC	5.00
955	Skip Schumaker (RC)	.25
956	Ruddy Lugo (RC)	.25
957	Jason Hammel (RC)	.25
958	Chris Roberson (RC)	.25
959	Fabio Castro RC	.50
960	Ian Kinsler (RC)	.50
961	John Koronka (RC)	.25
962	Brandon Watson (RC)	.25
963	Jon Lester (RC)	5.00
964	Ben Hendrickson (RC)	.25
965	Martin Prado (RC)	.25
966	Erick Aybar (RC)	.25
967	Bobby Livingston (RC)	.25
968	Ryan Spilborghs (RC)	.25
969	Tommy Murphy (RC)	.25
970	Howie Kendrick (RC)	5.00
971	Casey Janssen RC	1.00
972	Michael O'Connor RC	.50
973	Conor Jackson (RC)	.25
974	Jeremy Hermida (RC)	.25
975	Renyel Pinto (RC)	.25
976	Prince Fielder (RC)	1.50
977	Kevin Frandsen (RC)	.25
978	Ty Taubenheim RC	.50
979	Rich Hill (RC)	.25
980	Jonathan Broxton (RC)	.25
981	Jamie Shields RC	.50
982	Carlos Villanueva RC	.50
983	Boone Logan RC	1.00
984	Brian Wilson RC	.50
985	Andre Ethier (RC)	3.00
986	Michael Napoli RC	1.50
987	Agustin Montero (RC)	.25
988	Jack Hannahan RC	.50
989	Boof Bonser (RC)	.25
990	Carlos Ruiz (RC)	.25
991	Jason Botts (RC)	.25
992	Kendry Morales (RC)	.50
993	Alay Soler (RC)	3.00
994	Santiago Ramirez (RC)	.25
995	Saul Rivera (RC)	.25
996	Anthony Reyes (RC)	.25
997	Matthew Kemp (RC)	.50
998	Jae-Kuk Ryu RC	.50
999	Lastings Milledge (RC)	1.00
1000	Jered Weaver (RC)	4.00
1001	Stephen Drew (RC)	1.00
1002	Carlos Quentin (RC)	.50
1003	Livan Hernandez	.15
1004	Chris Young (RC)	.50
1005	Alberto Callaspo/SP (RC)	6.00
1006	Enrique Gonzalez (RC)	.25
1007	Tony Pena (RC)	.25
1008	Bob Melvin	.15
1009	Fernando Tatis	.15
1010	Willy Aybar (RC)	.25
1011	Ken Ray (RC)	.25
1012	Scott Thorman RC	.50
1013	Eric Hinske/SP	4.00
1014	Kevin Barry (RC)	.50
1015	Bobby Cox	.15
1016	Phil Stockman (RC)	.25
1017	Brayan Pena (RC)	.25
1018	Adam Loewen (RC)	.25
1019	Brandon Fahey RC	.50
1020	Jim Hoey RC	.50
1021	Kurt Birkins/SP RC	8.00
1022	Jim Johnson RC	.75
1023	Sam Perlozzo	.15
1024	Cory Morris (RC)	.50
1025	Hayden Penn (RC)	.25
1026	Javy Lopez	.15
1027	Dustin Pedroia (RC)	.50
1028	Kason Gabbard (RC)	.25
1029	David Pauley (RC)	.25
1030	Kyle Snyder	.15
1031	Terry Francona	.15
1032	Craig Breslow (RC)	.50
1033	Bryan Corey (RC)	.25
1034	Manny Delcarmen (RC)	1.00
1035	Carlos Marmol RC	.50
1036	Buck Coats (RC)	.25
1037	Ryan O'Malley/SP RC	10.00
1038	Angel Guzman (RC)	.25
1039	Ronny Cedeno	.15
1040	Juan Mateo RC	.50
1041	Cesar Izturis	.15
1042	Les Walrond (RC)	.25
1043	Geovany Soto (RC)	.50
1044	Sean Tracey (RC)	.25
1045	Ozzie Guillen/SP	6.00
1046	Royce Clayton	.15
1047	Norris Hopper RC	.50
1048	Bill Bray (RC)	.25
1049	Jerry Narron	.15
1050	Brendan Harris (RC)	.25
1051	Brian Shackelford	.15
1052	Jeremy Sowers (RC)	.25
1053	Joe Inglett RC	1.50
1054	Brian Slocum (RC)	.25
1055	Andrew Brown (RC)	.25
1056	Rafael Perez RC	.50
1057	Edward Mujica (RC)	.50
1058	Andy Marte (RC)	.25
1059	Shin-Soo Choo (RC)	.50
1060	Jeremy Guthrie (RC)	.25
1061	Franklin Gutierrez/SP (RC)	6.00
1062	Kazuo Matsui	.15
1063	Chris Iannetta RC	.50
1064	Manny Corpas RC	.50
1065	Clint Hurdle	.15
1066	Ramon Ramirez (RC)	.25
1067	Sean Casey	.15
1068	Zach Miner (RC)	.25
1069	Brent Clevlen/SP (RC)	8.00
1070	Bob Wickman	.15
1071	Jim Leyland	.15
1072	Alexis Gomez (RC)	.25
1073	Anibal Sanchez (RC)	.50
1074	Taylor Tankersley (RC)	.25
1075	Eric Wedge	.15
1076	Jonah Bayliss RC	.50
1077	Paul Hoover/SP (RC)	8.00
1078	Eddie Guardado	.15
1079	Cody Ross (RC)	.25
1080	Aubrey Huff	.15
1081	Jason Hirsh (RC)	.25
1082	Brandon League	.15
1083	Matt Albers (RC)	.25
1084	Chris Sampson RC	1.50
1085	Phil Garner	.15
1086	J.R. House (RC)	.25
1087	Ryan Shealy (RC)	.25
1088	Stephen Andrade (RC)	.25
1089	Bob Keppel (RC)	.25
1090	Buddy Bell	.15
1091	Justin Huber (RC)	.25
1092	Paul Phillips (RC)	.25
1093	Greg Jones/SP	8.00
1094	Jeff Mathis (RC)	.50
1095	Dustin Moseley (RC)	.50
1096	Joe Saunders (RC)	.25
1097	Reggie Willits (RC)	1.50
1098	Mike Scioscia	.15
1099	Greg Maddux	1.50
1100	Wilson Betemit	.15
1101	Chad Billingsley/SP (RC)	8.00
1102	Russell Martin (RC)	.25
1103	Grady Little	.15
1104	David Bell	.15
1105	Kevin Mench	.15
1106	Laynce Nix	.15
1107	Chris Barnwell RC	.50
1108	Tony Gwynn Jr. (RC)	.50
1109	Corey Hart (RC)	.25
1110	Zach Jackson (RC)	.25
1111	Francisco Cordero	.15
1112	Joe Winklesas (RC)	.25
1113	Ned Yost	.15
1114	Matt Garza (RC)	.50
1115	Chris Heintz	.15
1116	Pat Neshek RC	.50
1117	Josh Rabe/SP RC	15.00
1118	Mike Rivera	.15
1119	Ron Gardenhire	.15
1120	Shawn Green	.15
1121	Oliver Perez	.15
1122	Heath Bell	.15
1123	Bartolome Fortunato (RC)	.25
1124	Anderson Garcia RC	.75
1125	John Maine/SP (RC)	10.00
1126	Henry Owens RC	.50
1127	Mike Pelfrey RC	3.00
1128	Royce Ring (RC)	.25
1129	Willie Randolph	.15
1130	Bobby Abreu	.50
1131	Craig Wilson	.15
1132	T.J. Beam (RC)	.25
1133	Colter Bean/SP (RC)	8.00
1134	Melky Cabrera (RC)	.50

1135 Mitch Jones (RC)	.50
1136 Jeffrey Karstens RC	1.00
1137 Wilbert Nieves (RC)	.25
1138 Kevin Reese (RC)	.50
1139 Kevin Thompson (RC)	.50
1140 Jose Veras RC	.15
1141 Joe Torre	.50
1142 Jeremy Brown (RC)	.25
1143 Santiago Casilla (RC)	.25
1144 Shane Komine RC	1.00
1145 Mike Rouse (RC)	.25
1146 Jason Windsor (RC)	.75
1147 Ken Macha	.15
1148 Jamie Moyer	.15
1149 Phil Nevin/SP	8.00
1150 Eude Brito (RC)	.50
1151 Fabio Castro	.15
1152 Jeff Conine	.15
1153 Scott Mathieson (RC)	.25
1154 Brian Sanches (RC)	.25
1155 Matt Smith (RC)	.50
1156 Joe Thurston (RC)	.25
1157 Marlon Anderson/SP	8.00
1158 Xavier Nady	.15
1159 Shawn Chacon	.15
1160 Rajai Davis (RC)	.25
1161 Yurendell de Caster (RC)	.50
1162 Marty McLeary (RC)	.25
1163 Chris Duffy	.15
1164 Joshua Sharpless RC	1.00
1165 Jim Tracy	.15
1166 David Wells	.15
1167 Russell Branyan	.15
1168 Todd Walker	.15
1169 Paul McAnulty (RC)	.25
1170 Bruce Bochy	.15
1171 Shea Hillenbrand	.15
1172 Eliezer Alfonzo RC	.50
1173 Justin Knoedler/SP (RC)	8.00
1174 Jonathan Sanchez (RC)	.25
1175 Travis Smith (RC)	.25
1176 Cha Seung Baek	.15
1177 T.J. Bohn (RC)	.25
1178 Emiliano Fruto RC	.50
1179 Sean Green RC	.50
1180 Jon Huber RC	.50
1181 Adam Jones SP (RC)	8.00
1182 Mark Lowe (RC)	.25
1183 Eric O'Flaherty RC	.50
1184 Preston Wilson	.15
1185 Mike Hargrove	.15
1186 Jeff Weaver	.15
1187 Ronnie Belliard	.15
1188 John Gall (RC)	.25
1189 Josh Kinney/SP RC	10.00
1190 Tony LaRussa	.15
1191 Scott Dunn (RC)	.25
1192 B.J. Upton	.15
1193 Jon Switzer (RC)	.25
1194 Benjamin Zobrist (RC)	.15
1195 Joe Maddon	.15
1196 Carlos Lee	.15
1197 Matt Stairs	.15
1198 Nick Massett (RC)	.25
1199 Nelson Cruz (RC)	.50
1200 Francisco Rosario (RC)	.25
1201 Wes Littleton (RC)	.25
1202 Drew Meyer (RC)	.25
1203 John Rheinecker (RC)	.25
1204 Robinson Tejeda	.15
1205 Jeremy Accardo/SP	8.00
1206 Luis Figueroa RC	.50
1207 John Hattig Jr. (RC)	.25
1208 Dustin McGowan (RC)	.25
1209 Ryan Roberts RC	.50
1210 Davis Romero (RC)	.25
1211 Ty Taubenheim	.15
1212 John Gibbons	.15
1213 Shawn Hill/SP (RC)	8.00
1214 Brandon Harper RC	.25
1215 Travis Hughes (RC)	.25
1216 Chris Schroder RC	.50
1217 Austin Kearns	.15
1218 Felipe Lopez	.15
1219 Roy Corcoran RC	.50
1220 Melvin Dorta RC	.50
1221 Brandon Webb/SP	4.00
1222 Andruw Jones/SP	6.00
1223 Miguel Tejada/SP	6.00
1224 David Ortiz/SP	8.00
1225 Derrek Lee/SP	6.00
1226 Jim Thome/SP	6.00
1227 Ken Griffey Jr./SP	8.00
1228 Travis Hafner/SP	6.00
1229 Todd Helton/SP	6.00
1230 Magglio Ordonez/SP	4.00
1231 Miguel Cabrera/SP	8.00
1232 Lance Berkman/SP	6.00
1233 Mike Sweeney/SP	4.00
1234 Vladimir Guerrero/SP	8.00
1235 Nomar Garciaparra/SP	8.00
1236 Prince Fielder/SP	8.00
1237 Johan Santana/SP	8.00

1238 Pedro Martinez/SP	6.00
1239 Derek Jeter/SP	10.00
1240 Barry Zito/SP	6.00
1241 Ryan Howard/SP	10.00
1242 Jason Bay/SP	6.00
1243 Trevor Hoffman/SP	4.00
1244 Jason Schmidt/SP	6.00
1245 Ichiro Suzuki/SP	8.00
1246 Albert Pujols/SP	10.00
1247 Carl Crawford/SP	4.00
1248 Mark Teixeira/SP	6.00
1249 Vernon Wells/SP	6.00
1250 Alfonso Soriano/SP	8.00

Blue

Blue: 2-4X
Production 299 Sets

Gold

Gold: 2-4X
Production 299 Sets

Silver Spectrum

No Pricing
Production 25 Sets

Rookie Foil Gold

Gold: 4-8X
Production 99 Sets
Platinum: No Pricing
Production 15 Sets

Rookie Foil Silver

Silver: 2-4X
Production 399 Sets

Printing Plates

No Pricing
Production one set per color.

All-Time Legends

		NM/M
	Common Player:	1.00
AT-1	Ty Cobb	3.00
AT-2	Lou Gehrig	4.00
AT-3	Babe Ruth	5.00
AT-4	Jimmie Foxx	3.00
AT-5	Honus Wagner	3.00
AT-6	Lou Brock	2.00
AT-8	Christy Mathewson	2.00
AT-9	Walter Johnson	2.00
AT-10	Mike Schmidt	3.00
AT-11	Al Kaline	2.00
AT-12	Robin Yount	2.00
AT-13	Johnny Bench	2.00
AT-14	Yogi Berra	2.00
AT-15	Rod Carew	1.00
AT-16	Bob Feller	1.00
AT-17	Carlton Fisk	1.00
AT-18	Bob Gibson	2.00
AT-19	Cy Young	2.00
AT-21	Jackie Robinson	3.00
AT-22	Harmon Killebrew	1.00
AT-23	Mickey Cochrane	1.00
AT-24	Eddie Mathews	1.00
AT-25	Bill Mazeroski	1.00
AT-26	Willie McCovey	2.00
AT-27	Eddie Murray	2.00
AT-28	Lefty Grove	1.00
AT-29	Jim Palmer	1.00
AT-30	Pee Wee Reese	1.00
AT-31	Phil Rizzuto	2.00
AT-32	Brooks Robinson	2.00
AT-33	Nolan Ryan	4.00
AT-34	Tom Seaver	2.00
AT-35	Ozzie Smith	2.00
AT-36	Roy Campanella	2.00
AT-37	Thurman Munson	3.00
AT-38	Mel Ott	2.00
AT-39	Satchel Paige	2.00
AT-40	Rogers Hornsby	2.00

All-Upper Deck Team

No Pricing

Amazing Greats

		NM/M
	Complete Set:	25.00
	Common Player:	.50
BA	Bobby Abreu	.75
JB	Jeff Bagwell	.75
CB	Carlos Beltran	1.00
AB	Adrian Beltre	.50
MC	Miguel Cabrera	1.00
RC	Roger Clemens	3.00
CC	Carl Crawford	.50
JD	Johnny Damon	1.00
JE	Jim Edmonds	.50
RF	Rafael Furcal	.50
EG	Eric Gagne	.50
JG	Jason Giambi	.75
TG	Tom Glavine	.50
KG	Ken Griffey Jr.	2.00
HE	Todd Helton	.75
TH	Tim Hudson	.50
DJ	Derek Jeter	3.00
RJ	Randy Johnson	1.00
AJ	Andruw Jones	1.00
CJ	Chipper Jones	1.00
JJ	Jacque Jones	.50
PK	Paul Konerko	.75
CL	Carlos Lee	.50
JL	Javy Lopez	.50
GM	Greg Maddux	2.00
PM	Pedro Martinez	1.00
DO	David Ortiz	1.00
RO	Roy Oswalt	.50
RP	Rafael Palmeiro	.75
CP	Corey Patterson	.50
MP	Mike Piazza	1.00
PR	Mark Prior	.75
AP	Albert Pujols	3.00
MR	Manny Ramirez	1.00
JR	Jose Reyes	.75
IR	Ivan Rodriguez	.75
SR	Scott Rolen	1.00
JS	Johan Santana	1.00
CS	Curt Schilling	1.00
GS	Gary Sheffield	.75
SM	John Smoltz	.50
AS	Alfonso Soriano	.75
SS	Sammy Sosa	1.00
MT	Mark Teixeira	.75
TE	Miguel Tejada	.75
FT	Frank Thomas	.75
JT	Jim Thome	.75
DW	Dontrelle Willis	.50
KW	Kerry Wood	.50
WR	David Wright	1.50

Amazing Greats Materials

Jim Edmonds • Cardinals

		NM/M
	Complete Set:	
	Common Player:	
BA	Bobby Abreu	6.00
JB	Jeff Bagwell	6.00
CB	Carlos Beltran	6.00
AB	Adrian Beltre	4.00
MC	Miguel Cabrera	8.00
RC	Roger Clemens	15.00
CC	Carl Crawford	6.00
JD	Johnny Damon	10.00
JE	Jim Edmonds	6.00
RF	Rafael Furcal	4.00
EG	Eric Gagne	4.00
JG	Jason Giambi	6.00
TG	Tom Glavine	6.00
KG	Ken Griffey Jr.	20.00
HE	Todd Helton	6.00
TH	Tim Hudson	4.00
DJ	Derek Jeter	20.00
RJ	Randy Johnson	8.00
AJ	Andruw Jones	8.00
CJ	Chipper Jones	8.00
JJ	Jacque Jones	4.00
PK	Paul Konerko	6.00
CL	Carlos Lee	4.00
JL	Javy Lopez	4.00
GM	Greg Maddux	12.00
PM	Pedro Martinez	8.00
DO	David Ortiz	8.00
RO	Roy Oswalt	6.00
RP	Rafael Palmeiro	6.00
CP	Corey Patterson	4.00
MP	Mike Piazza	10.00
PR	Mark Prior	6.00
AP	Albert Pujols	20.00
MR	Manny Ramirez	8.00
JR	Jose Reyes	8.00
IR	Ivan Rodriguez	6.00
SR	Scott Rolen	8.00
JS	Johan Santana	8.00
CS	Curt Schilling	8.00
GS	Gary Sheffield	8.00
SM	John Smoltz	6.00
AS	Alfonso Soriano	6.00
SS	Sammy Sosa	10.00
MT	Mark Teixeira	8.00
TE	Miguel Tejada	10.00
FT	Frank Thomas	6.00
JT	Jim Thome	8.00
DW	Dontrelle Willis	6.00
KW	Kerry Wood	4.00
WR	David Wright	15.00

Diamond Collection

		NM/M
Gold:		1-2X
	Production 699 Sets	
AL	Moises Alou	.50
JB	Jeff Bagwell	.75
RB	Rocco Baldelli	.50
OC	Orlando Cabrera	.50

MC	Mike Cameron	.50
EC	Eric Chavez	.50
CO	Jose Contreras	.50
JC	Jesse Crain	.50
BC	Bobby Crosby	.50
JD	Johnny Damon	1.00
AE	Adam Eaton	.50
JE	Jim Edmonds	.50
SF	Steve Finley	.50
FG	Freddy Garcia	.50
GO	Juan Gonzalez	.50
KG	Ken Griffey Jr.	2.00
JG	Jose Guillen	.50
MH	Mike Hampton	.50
AH	Aubrey Huff	.50
EJ	Edwin Jackson	.50
DJ	Derek Jeter	3.00
NJ	Nick Johnson	.50
RJ	Randy Johnson	1.00
JJ	Jacque Jones	.50
SK	Scott Kazmir	.50
KE	Austin Kearns	.50
JK	Jason Kendall	.50
AK	Adam Kennedy	.50
CK	Casey Kotchman	.50
LA	Matt Lawton	.50
ML	Mike Lieberthal	.50
PL	Paul LoDuca	.50
KL	Kenny Lofton	.50
LO	Mike Lowell	.50
GM	Greg Maddux	2.00
MA	Kazuo Matsui	.50
KM	Kevin Millwood	.50
DO	David Ortiz	1.00
AO	Akinori Otsuka	.50
CP	Carl Pavano	.50
JP	Jorge Posada	.50
BR	Brad Radke	.50
IR	Ivan Rodriguez	.75
CC	C.C. Sabathia	.50
CS	Chris Shelton	.50
JS	John Smoltz	.75
SS	Shannon Stewart	.50
JT	Jim Thome	.75
JW	Jayson Werth	.50
PW	Preston Wilson	.50

Diamond Collection Materials

		NM/M
	Common Player:	4.00
AL	Moises Alou	6.00
JB	Jeff Bagwell	6.00
RB	Rocco Baldelli	4.00
OC	Orlando Cabrera	4.00
MC	Mike Cameron	4.00
EC	Eric Chavez	6.00
CO	Jose Contreras	4.00
JC	Jesse Crain	4.00
BC	Bobby Crosby	4.00
JD	Johnny Damon	10.00
AE	Adam Eaton	4.00
JE	Jim Edmonds	6.00
SF	Steve Finley	4.00
FG	Freddy Garcia	4.00
GO	Juan Gonzalez	4.00
KG	Ken Griffey Jr.	20.00
JG	Jose Guillen	4.00
MH	Mike Hampton	4.00
AH	Aubrey Huff	4.00
EJ	Edwin Jackson	4.00
DJ	Derek Jeter	20.00
NJ	Nick Johnson	4.00
RJ	Randy Johnson	8.00
JJ	Jacque Jones	4.00
SK	Scott Kazmir	4.00
KE	Austin Kearns	4.00
JK	Jason Kendall	4.00
AK	Adam Kennedy	4.00
CK	Casey Kotchman	4.00
LA	Matt Lawton	4.00
ML	Mike Lieberthal	4.00
PL	Paul LoDuca	4.00
KL	Kenny Lofton	4.00
LO	Mike Lowell	4.00
GM	Greg Maddux	12.00
MA	Kazuo Matsui	4.00
KM	Kevin Millwood	4.00
DO	David Ortiz	8.00
AO	Akinori Otsuka	4.00
CP	Carl Pavano	4.00
JP	Jorge Posada	6.00

BR	Brad Radke	4.00
IR	Ivan Rodriguez	6.00
CC	C.C. Sabathia	4.00
CS	Chris Shelton	10.00
JS	John Smoltz	8.00
SS	Shannon Stewart	4.00
JT	Jim Thome	8.00
JW	Jayson Werth	4.00
PW	Preston Wilson	4.00

Diamond Debut

		NM/M
	Common Player:	1.00

#'s 1-40 found in Series 1 packs
#'s 41-82 found in Series 2 packs
Inserted 1:4 Walmart packs.

	Series 2 Common Player:	.50
1	Tadahito Iguchi	1.00
2	Huston Street	.50
3	Norihiro Nakamura	.50
4	Chien-Ming Wang	1.00
5	Pedro Lopez	.50
6	Robinson Cano	2.00
7	Tim Stauffer	.50
8	Ervin Santana	.50
9	Brandon McCarthy	.50
10	Hayden Penn	.50
11	Mike Morse	.50
12	Chad Orvella	.50
13	Prince Fielder	3.00
14	Edwin Encarnacion	.50
15	Scott Olsen	.50
16	Chris Resop	.50
17	Justin Verlander	2.00
18	Melky Cabrera	.50
19	Jeff Francoeur	.50
20	Yuniesky Betancourt	.50
21	Conor Jackson	.50
22	Felix Hernandez	1.00
23	Anthony Reyes	.50
24	John-Ford Griffin	.50
25	Adam Wainwright	.50
26	Ryan Garko	.50
27	Chuck James	.50
28	Tom Seaver	2.00
29	Johnny Bench	2.00
30	Reggie Jackson	2.00
31	Rod Carew	2.00
32	Nolan Ryan	4.00
33	Richie Ashburn	.50
34	Yogi Berra	2.00
35	Lou Brock	1.50
36	Carlton Fisk	1.50
37	Joe Morgan	.75
38	Bob Gibson	2.00
39	Willie McCovey	2.00
40	Harmon Killebrew	2.00
41	Takashi Saito	2.00
42	Kenji Johjima	5.00
43	Joel Zumaya	1.50
44	Dan Uggla	1.00
45	Taylor Buchholz	1.00
46	Josh Barfield	1.00
47	Brian Bannister	1.00
48	Nicholas Markakis	1.00
49	Carlos Martinez	1.00
50	Macay McBride	1.00
51	Brian Anderson	1.00
52	Freddie Bynum	1.00
53	Kelly Stoppach	1.00
54	Choo Freeman	1.00
55	Ryan Shealy	1.00
56	Chris Resop	1.00
57	Hanley Ramirez	1.50
58	Mike Jacobs	1.00
59	Cody Ross	1.00
60	Jose Capellan	1.00
61	David Gassner	1.00
62	Jason Kubel	1.00
63	Jered Weaver	4.00
64	Paul Maholm	1.00
65	Nate McLouth	1.00
66	Ben Johnson	1.00
67	Jack Taschner	1.00
68	Skip Schumaker	1.00
69	Brandon Watson	1.00
70	David Wright	3.00
71	David Ortiz	2.50
72	Alex Rodriguez	4.00
73	Johan Santana	2.00
74	Greg Maddux	3.00
75	Ichiro Suzuki	3.00
76	Albert Pujols	4.00
77	Hideki Matsui	3.00
78	Vladimir Guerrero	2.00
79	Pedro Martinez	2.00
80	Mike Schmidt	2.00
81	Al Kaline	2.00
82	Robin Yount	2.00

First Class Cuts

No Pricing
Production One Set

First Class Legends

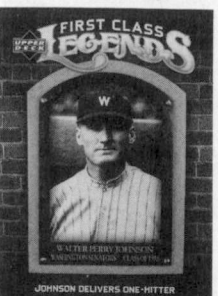

		NM/M
Gold:		1-2X
Production 699 Sets		
Platinum:		2-3X
Production 99 Sets		
Spectrum:		No Pricing
Production One Set		
1	All Babe Ruth's	3.00
21	All Ty Cobb's	2.00
41	All Honus Wagner's	2.00
61	All Christy Mathewson's	1.00
81	All Walter Johnson's	1.00

Game Jersey

		NM/M
	Common Player:	4.00
JB	Jeff Bagwell	6.00
MC	Miguel Cabrera	8.00
EC	Eric Chavez	4.00
RC	Roger Clemens	15.00
JD	Johnny Damon	10.00
JE	Jim Edmonds	6.00
RF	Rafael Furcal	4.00
EG	Eric Gagne	4.00
JG	Jason Giambi	6.00
KG	Ken Griffey Jr.	20.00
VG	Vladimir Guerrero	8.00
RH	Roy Halladay	4.00
DJ	Derek Jeter	20.00
RJ	Randy Johnson	8.00
AJ	Andruw Jones	8.00
CJ	Chipper Jones	8.00
JJ	Jacque Jones	4.00
DL	Derrek Lee	8.00
GM	Greg Maddux	12.00
PM	Pedro Martinez	8.00
DO	David Ortiz	8.00
RP	Rafael Palmeiro	6.00
CP	Corey Patterson	4.00
JP	Jake Peavy	6.00
MP	Mike Piazza	6.00
PO	Jorge Posada	6.00
PR	Mark Prior	6.00
AP	Albert Pujols	20.00
MR	Manny Ramirez	8.00
BR	Brian Roberts	8.00
IR	Ivan Rodriguez	8.00
SR	Scott Rolen	8.00
JS	Johan Santana	8.00
CS	Curt Schilling	8.00
SM	John Smoltz	8.00
AS	Alfonso Soriano	8.00
MT	Mark Teixeira	8.00
TE	Miguel Tejada	8.00
FT	Frank Thomas	8.00
JT	Jim Thome	8.00
DW	Dontrelle Willis	8.00
WR	David Wright	15.00
Series 2		
BA	Bobby Abreu	6.00
GA	Garrett Atkins	4.00
JB	Josh Beckett	8.00
CB	Carlos Beltran	8.00
AB	Adrian Beltre	4.00
BI	Craig Biggio	6.00
HB	Hank Blalock	4.00
SC	Sean Casey	4.00
JD	Johnny Damon	10.00

CD	Carlos Delgado	6.00
AD	Adam Dunn	6.00
PF	Prince Fielder	15.00
TG	Tom Glavine	6.00
GR	Khalil Greene	4.00
KG	Ken Griffey Jr.	20.00
HA	Travis Hafner	6.00
TH	Todd Helton	6.00
RH	Ryan Howard	20.00
TI	Tadahito Iguchi	8.00
DJ	Derek Jeter	20.00
PK	Paul Konerko	6.00
CL	Carlos Lee	6.00
JL	Javy Lopez	4.00
VM	Victor Martinez	6.00
JM	Joe Mauer	8.00
MM	Mike Mussina	6.00
MO	Magglio Ordonez	4.00
RO	Roy Oswalt	6.00
AP	Andy Pettitte	6.00
MP	Mike Piazza	8.00
JR	Jose Reyes	8.00
GS	Gary Sheffield	6.00
SI	Grady Sizemore	10.00
JV	Jason Varitek	8.00
CW	Chien-Ming Wang	15.00
RW	Rickie Weeks	6.00
KW	Kerry Wood	4.00
MY	Michael Young	4.00
RZ	Ryan Zimmerman	15.00
BZ	Barry Zito	6.00

Game Patch

		NM/M
	Inserted 1:288	
JB	Jeff Bagwell	20.00
MC	Miguel Cabrera	25.00
RC	Roger Clemens	30.00
JD	Johnny Damon	25.00
JE	Jim Edmonds	20.00
RF	Rafael Furcal	15.00
KG	Ken Griffey Jr.	40.00
VG	Vladimir Guerrero	25.00
RH	Roy Halladay	15.00
DJ	Derek Jeter	50.00
RJ	Randy Johnson	25.00
AJ	Andruw Jones	20.00
DL	Derrek Lee	20.00
GM	Greg Maddux	25.00
PM	Pedro Martinez	25.00
RP	Rafael Palmeiro	15.00
JP	Jake Peavy	20.00
MP	Mike Piazza	20.00
PR	Mark Prior	20.00
AP	Albert Pujols	50.00
MR	Manny Ramirez	25.00
BR	Brian Roberts	15.00
SR	Scott Rolen	20.00
JS	Johan Santana	20.00
SM	John Smoltz	25.00
TE	Miguel Tejada	20.00
FT	Frank Thomas	20.00
JT	Jim Thome	20.00
DW	Dontrelle Willis	20.00
WR	David Wright	40.00
Series 2:		No Pricing

Inaugural Images

		NM/M
	Common Player:	.50
II-1	Sung-Heon Hong	.50
II-2	Yulieski Gourriel	.50
II-3	Tsuyoshi Nishioka	1.00
II-4	Miguel Cabrera	1.50
II-5	Yung-Chi Chen	.50
II-6	Omari Romero	.50
II-7	Ken Griffey Jr.	2.00
II-8	Bernie Williams	.75
II-9	Daniel Cabrera	.50
II-10	David Ortiz	1.50
II-11	Alex Rodriguez	3.00
II-12	Frederich Cepeda	.50

II-13	Derek Jeter	3.00
II-14	Jorge Cantu	.50
II-15	Alexi Ramirez	.50
II-16	Yoandy Garlobo	.50
II-17	Koji Uehara	.50
II-18	Nobuhiko Matsunaka	.50
II-19	Tomoya Satozaki	.50
II-20	Seung-Yeop Lee	.50
II-21	Yulieski Gourriel	.50
II-22	Adrian Beltre	.50
II-23	Ken Griffey Jr.	2.00
II-24	Jong Beom Lee	.50
II-25	Ichiro Suzuki	2.00
II-26	Yoandy Garlobo	.50
II-27	Daisuke Matsuzaka	15.00
II-28	Yadel Marti	.50
II-29	Chan Ho Park	.50
II-30	Daisuke Matsuzaka	15.00

INKredible

		NM/M
Inserted 1:288		
JB	Joe Blanton	10.00
CA	Miguel Cabrera	40.00
CO	Chad Cordero	20.00
JC	Jesse Crain	10.00
CC	Carl Crawford	20.00
NG	Nomar Garciaparra	60.00
KG	Ken Griffey Jr.	120.00
TH	Travis Hafner	30.00
JH	J.J. Hardy	20.00
TI	Tadahito Iguchi/ SP 91	50.00
DJ	Derek Jeter	200.00
SK	Scott Kazmir	20.00
CK	Casey Kotchman	10.00
VM	Victor Martinez	20.00
JM	Joe Mauer/SP 91	40.00
MO	Justin Morneau	25.00
BM	Brett Myers/SP 72	15.00
LO	Lyle Overbay/SP 91	25.00
JR	Jeremy Reed	15.00
RE	Jose Reyes/SP 91	40.00
AR	Alexis Rios	20.00
BR	Brian Roberts	20.00
MT	Mark Teixeira	25.00
JV	Justin Verlander/ SP 91	40.00
WI	Dontrelle Willis	20.00
DW	David Wright/SP 91	60.00
KY	Kevin Youkilis	25.00
RZ	Ryan Zimmerman/ SP 91	50.00

Player Highlights

		NM/M
Common Player:		.50
PH-1	Andruw Jones	1.00
PH-2	Manny Ramirez	1.00
PH-3	Travis Hafner	1.00
PH-4	Johnny Damon	1.00
PH-5	Miguel Cabrera	1.00
PH-6	Chris Carpenter	.75
PH-7	Derrek Lee	1.00
PH-8	Jason Bay	.75
PH-9	Jason Varitek	1.00
PH-10	Ryan Howard	2.00
PH-11	Mark Teixeira	.75
PH-12	Carlos Delgado	.75
PH-13	Bartolo Colon	.50
PH-14	David Wright	2.00
PH-15	Miguel Tejada	.75
PH-16	Mike Piazza	1.00
PH-17	Paul Konerko	.75
PH-18	Jermaine Dye	.75
PH-19	Ichiro Suzuki	2.00
PH-20	Brad Wilkerson	.50
PH-21	Hideki Matsui	2.00
PH-22	Albert Pujols	3.00
PH-23	Chris Burke	.50
PH-24	Derek Jeter	3.00
PH-25	Brian Roberts	.75

PH-26	David Ortiz	1.50
PH-27	Alex Rodriguez	3.00
PH-28	Ken Griffey Jr.	2.00
PH-29	Prince Fielder	2.00
PH-30	Bobby Abreu	.75
PH-31	Vladimir Guerrero	1.00
PH-32	Tadahito Iguchi	1.00
PH-33	Jose Reyes	1.00
PH-34	Scott Podsednik	.75
PH-35	Gary Sheffield	.75

Run Producers

		NM/M
Common Player:		
RP-1	Ty Cobb	2.00
RP-2	Derrek Lee	1.00
RP-3	Andruw Jones	1.00
RP-4	David Ortiz	1.50
RP-5	Lou Gehrig	3.00
RP-6	Ken Griffey Jr.	2.00
RP-7	Albert Pujols	3.00
RP-8	Derek Jeter	3.00
RP-9	Manny Ramirez	1.00
RP-10	Alex Rodriguez	3.00
RP-11	Gary Sheffield	.75
RP-12	Miguel Cabrera	1.00
RP-13	Hideki Matsui	2.00
RP-14	Vladimir Guerrero	1.00
RP-15	David Wright	2.00
RP-16	Mike Schmidt	2.00
RP-17	Mark Teixeira	.75
RP-18	Babe Ruth	4.00
RP-19	Jimmie Foxx	2.00
RP-20	Honus Wagner	2.00

Signature Sensations

		NM/M
Inserted 1:288 Hobby		
BA	Bronson Arroyo	20.00
GA	Garrett Atkins	10.00
SB	Scott Baker	15.00
KC	Kiko Calero	5.00
JE	Johnny Estrada	8.00
KG	Ken Griffey Jr.	100.00
TR	Travis Hafner	25.00
BH	Bobby Hill	5.00
JJ	Josh Johnson	10.00
AL	Al Leiter	15.00
AM	Aaron Miles	15.00
YM	Yadier Molina	20.00
NP	Nick Punto	8.00
AR	Aaron Rowand	15.00
CS	Cory Sullivan	10.00
JS	Jeff Suppan	15.00
JV	Joe Valentine	10.00
DY	Delmon Young	25.00

Speed to Burn

		NM/M
Common Player:		.50
SB-1	Lou Brock	1.00
SB-3	Alfonso Soriano	1.50
SB-4	Carl Crawford	.75
SB-5	Chone Figgins	.50
SB-6	Ichiro Suzuki	2.00
SB-7	Jose Reyes	1.00
SB-8	Juan Pierre	.50
SB-9	Scott Podsednik	.75
SB-11	Alex Rodriguez	3.00
SB-12	David Wright	2.00

SB-14	Bobby Abreu	.75
SB-15	Brian Roberts	.75

Star Attractions

		NM/M
Gold:		1-2X
Production 699 Sets		
BA	Bobby Abreu	.75
GA	Garret Anderson	.50
JB	Josh Beckett	.50
CB	Carlos Beltran	.75
AB	Adrian Beltre	.50
LB	Lance Berkman	.50
JC	Jose Contreras	.50
JD	Johnny Damon	1.00
CD	Carlos Delgado	.75
JE	Jim Edmonds	.75
EG	Eric Gagne	.50
JG	Jason Giambi	.75
SG	Shawn Green	.50
GR	Khalil Greene	.50
KG	Ken Griffey Jr.	2.00
GU	Jose Guillen	.50
RH	Rich Harden	.50
AH	Aubrey Huff	.50
TH	Torii Hunter	.50
TI	Tadahito Iguchi	.50
DJ	Derek Jeter	3.00
AJ	Andruw Jones	1.00
CJ	Chipper Jones	1.00
JJ	Jacque Jones	.50
CL	Carlos Lee	.50
DL	Derrek Lee	.75
JL	Javy Lopez	.50
GM	Greg Maddux	2.00
PM	Pedro Martinez	1.00
JM	Joe Mauer	.50
MM	Mark Mulder	.50
MO	Magglio Ordonez	.50
DO	David Ortiz	1.00
AP	Andy Pettitte	.75
JP	Jorge Posada	.75
MP	Mark Prior	.75
PU	Albert Pujols	3.00
MR	Manny Ramirez	1.00
JR	Jose Reyes	1.00
CS	Curt Schilling	1.00
JS	Jason Schmidt	.50
GS	Gary Sheffield	.75
SM	John Smoltz	.75
AS	Alfonso Soriano	.75
MT	Mark Teixeira	.75
FT	Frank Thomas	.75
DW	Dontrelle Willis	.50
KW	Kerry Wood	.50
WR	David Wright	1.50
BZ	Barry Zito	.50

Star Attractions Swatches

		NM/M
Common Player:		4.00
BA	Bobby Abreu	6.00
GA	Garret Anderson	4.00
JB	Josh Beckett	4.00
CB	Carlos Beltran	6.00
AB	Adrian Beltre	4.00
LB	Lance Berkman	4.00
JC	Jose Contreras	4.00
JD	Johnny Damon	10.00
CD	Carlos Delgado	6.00
JE	Jim Edmonds	6.00
EG	Eric Gagne	4.00
JG	Jason Giambi	6.00
SG	Shawn Green	4.00
GR	Khalil Greene	4.00
KG	Ken Griffey Jr.	20.00
GU	Jose Guillen	4.00
RH	Rich Harden	6.00
AH	Aubrey Huff	4.00
TH	Torii Hunter	4.00
TI	Tadahito Iguchi	10.00
DJ	Derek Jeter	20.00
AJ	Andruw Jones	8.00
CJ	Chipper Jones	8.00
JJ	Jacque Jones	4.00
CL	Carlos Lee	4.00
DL	Derrek Lee	8.00
JL	Javy Lopez	4.00
GM	Greg Maddux	12.00
PM	Pedro Martinez	8.00
JM	Joe Mauer	4.00

MM	Mark Mulder	4.00
MO	Magglio Ordonez	4.00
DO	David Ortiz	8.00
AP	Andy Pettitte	6.00
JP	Jorge Posada	6.00
MP	Mark Prior	6.00
PU	Albert Pujols	20.00
MR	Manny Ramirez	8.00
JR	Jose Reyes	8.00
CS	Curt Schilling	8.00
JS	Jason Schmidt	4.00
GS	Gary Sheffield	6.00
SM	John Smoltz	8.00
AS	Alfonso Soriano	6.00
MT	Mark Teixeira	8.00
FT	Frank Thomas	6.00
DW	Dontrelle Willis	6.00
KW	Kerry Wood	4.00
WR	David Wright	15.00
BZ	Barry Zito	4.00

Team Pride

		NM/M
Gold:		1-2X
Production 699 Sets		
BA	Bobby Abreu	.75
GA	Garret Anderson	.50
JB	Jeff Bagwell	.75
RB	Rocco Baldelli	.50
SC	Sean Casey	.50
LC	Luis Castillo	.50
EC	Eric Chavez	.50
JD	Johnny Damon	1.00
CD	Carlos Delgado	.75
JE	Jim Edmonds	.75
ME	Morgan Ensberg	.50
KF	Keith Foulke	.50
EG	Eric Gagne	.50
LG	Luis Gonzalez	.50
GR	Khalil Greene	.50
KG	Ken Griffey Jr.	2.00
RH	Rich Harden	.50
TH	Trevor Hoffman	.50
AH	Aubrey Huff	.50
DJ	Derek Jeter	3.00
NJ	Nick Johnson	.50
AJ	Andruw Jones	1.00
CJ	Chipper Jones	1.00
RK	Ryan Klesko	.50
CK	Casey Kotchman	.50
ML	Mike Lieberthal	.50
LO	Mike Lowell	.50
GM	Greg Maddux	2.00
MA	Joe Mauer	.50
JM	Jamie Moyer	.50
DO	David Ortiz	1.00
PE	Andy Pettitte	.75
JP	Jorge Posada	.50
MP	Mark Prior	.75
AP	Albert Pujols	3.00
JR	Jose Reyes	.50
IR	Ivan Rodriguez	.75
CC	C.C. Sabathia	.50
CS	Curt Schilling	1.00
JS	John Smoltz	.75
MS	Mike Sweeney	.50
FT	Frank Thomas	.75
JT	Jim Thome	.75
VA	Jason Varitek	.75
JV	Jose Vidro	.50
BW	Bernie Williams	.50
DW	Dontrelle Willis	.50
KW	Kerry Wood	.50
MY	Michael Young	.50

Team Pride Materials

		NM/M
Common Player:		4.00
BA	Bobby Abreu	6.00
GA	Garret Anderson	4.00
JB	Jeff Bagwell	6.00
RB	Rocco Baldelli	4.00
SC	Sean Casey	4.00
LC	Luis Castillo	4.00
EC	Eric Chavez	4.00
JD	Johnny Damon	10.00
CD	Carlos Delgado	6.00
JE	Jim Edmonds	6.00
ME	Morgan Ensberg	4.00
KF	Keith Foulke	4.00
EG	Eric Gagne	4.00
LG	Luis Gonzalez	4.00

GR	Khalil Greene	4.00
KG	Ken Griffey Jr.	20.00
RH	Rich Harden	4.00
TH	Trevor Hoffman	4.00
AH	Aubrey Huff	4.00
DJ	Derek Jeter	20.00
NJ	Nick Johnson	4.00
AJ	Andruw Jones	8.00
CJ	Chipper Jones	8.00
RK	Ryan Klesko	4.00
CK	Casey Kotchman	4.00
ML	Mike Lieberthal	4.00
LO	Mike Lowell	4.00
GM	Greg Maddux	12.00
MA	Joe Mauer	4.00
JM	Jamie Moyer	4.00
DO	David Ortiz	8.00
PE	Andy Pettitte	6.00
JP	Jorge Posada	6.00
MP	Mark Prior	6.00
AP	Albert Pujols	20.00
JR	Jose Reyes	8.00
IR	Ivan Rodriguez	6.00
CC	C.C. Sabathia	4.00
CS	Curt Schilling	8.00
JS	John Smoltz	8.00
MS	Mike Sweeney	4.00
FT	Frank Thomas	6.00
JT	Jim Thome	8.00
VA	Jason Varitek	6.00
JV	Jose Vidro	4.00
BW	Bernie Williams	6.00
DW	Dontrelle Willis	6.00
KW	Kerry Wood	4.00
MY	Michael Young	4.00
BZ	Barry Zito	4.00

Update Gold

Gold (1001-1250):	4-8X
Gold SP's:	.5-1X
Production 99 Sets	

Update Inkredible

NM/M

Inserted 1:24 Retail

EA	Erick Aybar	10.00
BA	Brandon Backe	10.00
CB	Colter Bean	10.00
YB	Yuniesky Betancourt	10.00
EB	Eude Brito	15.00
BB	Ben Broussard	15.00
AB	Ambiorix Burgos	15.00
GC	Gustavo Chacin	8.00
BC	Brandon Claussen	10.00
CO	Chad Cordero/SP	15.00
CA	Carl Crawford	15.00
CC	Coco Crisp	15.00
CD	Chris Duffy	10.00
JD	Jermaine Dye	15.00
GF	Gavin Floyd	5.00
RF	Ryan Freel	15.00
RG	Ryan Garko	15.00
KG	Ken Griffey Jr./SP	125.00
AH	Aaron Harang	10.00
JH	John Hattig Jr.	10.00
MH	Matt Holliday	15.00
TI	Tadahito Iguchi/SP	30.00
CI	Cesar Izturis	5.00
DJ	Derek Jeter/SP	200.00
AJ	Adam Jones	25.00
JO	Jacque Jones	15.00
JJ	Jorge Julio/SP	10.00
CK	Casey Kotchman	10.00
CL	Cliff Lee	10.00
NL	Noah Lowry	15.00
BM	Brandon McCarthy/SP	15.00
ZM	Zach Miner	10.00
YM	Yadier Molina	15.00
MM	Matt Murton	20.00
LN	Leo Nunez	8.00
AP	Angel Pagan	10.00
PA	John Patterson	5.00
RP	Ronny Paulino	15.00
JP	Jhonny Peralta	15.00
PE	Joel Peralta	8.00
PI	Joel Pineiro	8.00
DR	Darrell Rasner	10.00
KR	Ken Ray	8.00
AR	Alex Rios/SP	30.00
JR	Juan Rivera/SP	20.00
BR	Brian Roberts	15.00
MR	Mike Rouse	10.00
RS	Ryan Shealy	15.00
NS	Nick Swisher	15.00
MT	Mark Teahen	15.00
MV	Michael Vento	8.00
BW	Brian Wilson	8.00
CW	C.J. Wilson	5.00
KY	Kevin Youkilis	15.00

Update Star Attractions

NM/M

Inserted 1:2 Retail

Silver:	2-3X
Production 99 Sets	

BR	Brian Anderson	.50
EA	Erick Aybar	.50
WA	Willy Aybar	.50
JO	Josh Barfield	.50
BI	Chad Billingsley	.75
MC	Matt Cain	.75
RC	Ronny Cedeno	.50
SD	Stephen Drew	1.50
AE	Andre Ethier	1.00
PF	Prince Fielder	1.50
TG	Tony Gwynn Jr.	1.00
CH	Cole Hamels	1.00
HI	Jason Hirsh	.50
HU	Justin Huber	.50
CO	Conor Jackson	.50
JA	Chuck James	.50
KJ	Kenji Johjima	1.50
JJ	Josh Johnson	.50
AJ	Adam Jones	.50
MK	Matthew Kemp	.50
HK	Howie Kendrick	1.00
JK	Jason Kubel	.50
LE	Jon Lester	1.50
FL	Francisco Liriano	1.00
AL	Adam Loewen	.50
NM	Nicholas Markakis	.75
AM	Andy Marte	.50
RM	Russell Martin	.50
MA	Jeff Mathis	.50
DM	Dustin McGowan	.50
LM	Lastings Milledge	1.00
KM	Kendry Morales	.50
SO	Scott Olsen	.50
PA	Jonathan Papelbon	1.00
DP	Dustin Pedroia	.50
PE	Mike Pelfrey	1.50
HP	Hayden Penn	.50
CQ	Carlos Quentin	.50
HR	Hanley Ramirez	1.00
AR	Anthony Reyes	.50
AN	Anibal Sanchez	.50
SW	Jeremy Sowers	.50
DU	Dan Uggla	.50
JV	Justin Verlander	2.00
CY	Chris Young	.50
AW	Adam Wainwright	.50
JW	Jered Weaver	1.00
RZ	Ryan Zimmerman	1.50
JZ	Joel Zumaya	1.00

World Baseball Classic Jersey

DAISUKE MATSUZAKA

NM/M

Inserted 1:24	
Patch:	No Pricing
Production 8 Sets	

JB	Jason Bay	10.00
EB	Erik Bedard	4.00
CB	Carlos Beltran	15.00
MC	Miguel Cabrera	15.00
VC	Vinny Castilla	4.00
FC	Frederich Cepeda	15.00
TC	Tai-San Chang	200.00
RC	Roger Clemens	30.00
JD	Johnny Damon	15.00
CD	Carlos Delgado	10.00
ME	Michel Enriquez	20.00
MF	Maikel Folch	20.00
JF	Jeff Francis	4.00
FR	Jeff Francoeur	15.00
FG	Freddy Garcia	4.00
YG	Yulieski Gourriel	25.00
KG	Ken Griffey Jr.	25.00
JG	Jason Grilli	4.00
HS	Chia-Hsien Hseih	125.00
CH	Chin-Lung Hu	75.00
JH	Justin Huber	4.00
AI	Akinori Iwamura	50.00
AJ	Andruw Jones	15.00
MK	Munenori Kawasaki	50.00
PL	Pedro Lazo	20.00
CL	Carlos Lee	4.00
DL	Derrek Lee	10.00
JL	Jong Beom Lee	8.00
WL	Wei-Chu Lin	180.00
GL	Guangbiao Liu	10.00
VM	Victor Martinez	10.00
NM	Nobuhiko Matsunaka	60.00
DM	Daisuke Matsuzaka	350.00
YM	Yunieski Maya	15.00
JM	Justin Morneau	10.00
TN	Tsuyoshi Nishioka	60.00
MO	Michihiro Ogasawara	60.00
DO	David Ortiz	20.00
WP	Wei-Lun Pan	80.00
EP	Eduardo Paret	20.00
JP	Jin Man Park	15.00
OP	Oliver Perez	4.00
PE	Ariel Pestano	20.00
MP	Mike Piazza	25.00
AP	Albert Pujols	30.00
AR	Alex Rodriguez	25.00
IR	Ivan Rodriguez	10.00
JS	Johan Santana	15.00
MS	Min Han Son	10.00
AS	Alfonso Soriano	15.00
I	Ichiro Suzuki	220.00
HT	Hitoshi Tamura	50.00
MT	Mark Teixeira	10.00
TE	Miguel Tejada	15.00
KU	Koji Uehara	100.00
JV	Jason Varitek	20.00
TW	Tsuyoshi Wada	60.00
WW	Wei Wang	20.00
SW	Shunsuke Watanabe	50.00
GY	Guogang Yang	10.00

2006 Upper Deck World Baseball Classic

NM/M

Complete Set (50):		20.00
Common Player:		.25
1	Derek Jeter	1.50
2	Ken Griffey Jr.	1.00
3	Derrek Lee	.25
4	Dontrelle Willis	.25
5	Alex Rodriguez	1.50
6	Jeff Francoeur	.25
7	Roger Clemens	1.50
8	Johnny Damon	.50
9	Chipper Jones	.50
10	Mark Teixeira	.50
11	Chase Utley	.50
12	Jake Peavy	.50
13	Michael Collins	.25
14	Justin Huber	.25
15	Jason Bay	.50
16	Jeff Francis	.25
17	Justin Morneau	.25
18	Guogang Yang	.25
19	Wei Wang	.25
20	Chia-Hsien Hseih	.25
21	Chin-Lung Hu	.25
22	Wei-Lun Pan	.25
23	Yung-Chi Chen	.25
24	Mike Piazza	.50
25	Albert Pujols	1.50
26	David Ortiz	.50
27	Jose Reyes	.50
28	Miguel Tejada	.50
29	Ichiro Suzuki	1.00
30	Nobuhiko Matsunaka	.25
31	Toshiaki Imae	.25
32	Kazuhiro Wada	.25
33	Shunsuke Watanabe	.25
34	Jung Bong	.25
35	Jong Beom Lee	.25
36	Seung-Yeop Lee	.25
37	Vinny Castilla	.25
38	Oliver Perez	.50
39	Jorge Cantu	.25
40	Andruw Jones	.50
41	Carlos Lee	.50
42	Carlos Beltran	.50
43	Carlos Delgado	.50
44	Ivan Rodriguez	.50
45	Bernie Williams	.50
46	Bobby Abreu	.50
47	Miguel Cabrera	.50
48	Johan Santana	.50
49	Victor Martinez	.50
50	Omar Vizquel	.25

2006 Upper Deck Artifacts

NM/M

Complete Set (100):		35.00
Common Player:		.25
Pack (4):		10.00
Box (10):		90.00
1	Luis Gonzalez	.25
2	Conor Jackson (RC)	.25
3	Joey Devine RC	1.00
4	Andruw Jones	.75
5	Chipper Jones	1.00
6	John Smoltz	.50
7	Jeff Francoeur	.50
8	Brian Roberts	.25
9	Miguel Tejada	.50
10	Nicholas Markakis (RC)	.25
11	Curt Schilling	1.00
12	David Ortiz	1.00
13	Johnny Damon	1.00
14	Manny Ramirez	1.00
15	Jonathan Papelbon (RC)	6.00
16	Aramis Ramirez	.50
17	Carlos Zambrano	.50
18	Derrek Lee	.75
19	Greg Maddux	2.00
20	Mark Prior	.75
21	Mark Buehrle	.50
22	Paul Konerko	.50
23	Adam Dunn	.75
24	Ken Griffey Jr.	2.00
25	Travis Hafner	.50
26	Victor Martinez	.50
27	Todd Helton	.75
28	Ivan Rodriguez	.75
29	Jeremy Bonderman	.25
30	Jeremy Hermida (RC)	.25
31	Carlos Delgado	.50
32	Dontrelle Willis	.50
33	Josh Beckett	.50
34	Miguel Cabrera	1.00
35	Craig Biggio	.50
36	Lance Berkman	.50
37	Roger Clemens	3.00
38	Roy Oswalt	.50
39	Josh Willingham (RC)	.25
40	Hanley Ramirez (RC)	.50
41	Prince Fielder (RC)	2.00
42	Zack Greinke	.25
43	Francisco Rodriguez	.25
44	Vladimir Guerrero	1.00
45	Tim Hamulack (RC)	.25
46	Jeff Kent	.50
47	Ben Sheets	.50
48	Rickie Weeks	.50
49	Francisco Liriano (RC)	4.00
50	Joe Mauer	.75
51	Johan Santana	.75
52	Justin Morneau	.50
53	Torii Hunter	.50
54	Carlos Beltran	.75
55	David Wright	2.00
56	Jose Reyes	.75
57	Mike Piazza	1.00
58	Pedro Martinez	1.00
59	Alex Rodriguez	3.00
60	Derek Jeter	3.00
61	Hideki Matsui	2.00
62	Randy Johnson	1.00
63	Justin Verlander (RC)	1.00
64	Bobby Crosby	.25
65	Eric Chavez	.50
66	Brian Anderson (RC)	.25
67	Bobby Abreu	.50
68	Pat Burrell	.50
69	Jason Bay	.50
70	Oliver Perez	.25
71	Chuck James (RC)	.25
72	Brian Giles	.25
73	Jake Peavy	.50
74	Khalil Greene	.25

75	Jason Schmidt	.50
76	Kenji Johjima RC	4.00
77	Jeremy Accardo RC	.50
78	Adrian Beltre	.25
79	Ichiro Suzuki	2.00
80	Jeff Harris RC	.50
81	Felix Hernandez	.75
82	Albert Pujols	3.00
83	Chris Carpenter	.75
84	Jim Edmonds	.50
85	Scott Rolen	.75
86	Mike Jacobs (RC)	.25
87	Carl Crawford	.50
88	Anderson Hernandez (RC)	.25
89	Scott Kazmir	.50
90	Josh Rupe (RC)	.25
91	Scott Feldman RC	.50
92	Alfonso Soriano	.75
93	Hank Blalock	.50
94	Mark Teixeira	.75
95	Michael Young	.50
96	Roy Halladay	.50
97	Vernon Wells	.50
98	Jason Bergmann RC	.25
99	Ryan Zimmerman (RC)	4.00
100	Jose Vidro	.25

AL/NL Artifacts

NM/M

Common Player:		4.00
Production 325 Sets		
Red:		.75-1.5X
Production 100-250		
Green:		.75-1.5X
Production 150 Sets		
GA	Garrett Atkins	4.00
JB	Jeff Bagwell	8.00
SB	Scott Baker	4.00
RB	Rocco Baldelli	4.00
CL	Clint Barmes	4.00
JA	Jason Bay	8.00
HB	Hank Blalock	4.00
BL	Joe Blanton	4.00
JB	Jeremy Bonderman	6.00
BB	Ben Broussard	4.00
MB	Mark Buehrle	6.00
CB	Chris Burke	4.00
MC	Miguel Cabrera	8.00
MA	Matt Cain	6.00
JC	Jorge Cantu	4.00
CA	Chris Capuano	4.00
CC	Chris Carpenter	10.00
GC	Gustavo Chacin	4.00
EC	Eric Chavez	4.00
RC	Ryan Church	4.00
CH	Chad Cordero	4.00
CC	Carl Crawford	6.00
CR	Joe Crede	4.00
CO	Coco Crisp	6.00
ZD	Zachary Duke	4.00
AD	Adam Dunn/250	8.00
JE	Jim Edmonds	6.00
ME	Morgan Ensberg	4.00
PF	Prince Fielder	15.00
JF	Jeff Francoeur	6.00
EG	Eric Gagne	4.00
GA	Jon Garland	4.00
MG	Marcus Giles	4.00
JG	Jonny Gomes	6.00
KG	Ken Griffey Jr.	15.00
VG	Vladimir Guerrero	8.00
TH	Travis Hafner	8.00
BH	Bill Hall/235	4.00
AH	Aaron Harang	4.00
DH	Danny Haren	4.00
TH	Todd Helton	6.00
FH	Felix Hernandez	6.00
RH	Ramon Hernandez	4.00
TR	Trevor Hoffman	4.00
MH	Matt Holliday	6.00
RY	Ryan Howard	15.00

TI	Tadahito Iguchi	8.00
CO	Conor Jackson	4.00
DJ	Derek Jeter	25.00
DA	Dan Johnson	4.00
NJ	Nick Johnson	4.00
RJ	Randy Johnson/235	8.00
CJ	Chipper Jones	8.00
SK	Scott Kazmir	6.00
LE	Carlos Lee	6.00
CL	Cliff Lee	4.00
DL	Derek Lee	8.00
BL	Brad Lidge	4.00
FL	Felipe Lopez	4.00
ML	Mark Loretta	4.00
NL	Noah Lowry	4.00
PM	Pedro Martinez	8.00
VM	Victor Martinez	6.00
JM	Joe Mauer	10.00
BM	Brian McCann	4.00
BM	Brandon McCarthy	4.00
YM	Yadier Molina	4.00
JU	Justin Morneau	6.00
JN	Joe Nathan	4.00
DO	David Ortiz	10.00
RO	Roy Oswalt	6.00
JP	Jake Peavy	6.00
PE	Jhonny Peralta	4.00
JP	Joel Pineiro	4.00
SP	Scott Podsednik	6.00
MP	Mark Prior	6.00
AP	Albert Pujols/250	20.00
MR	Manny Ramirez	8.00
JR	Jose Reyes	8.00
IR	Ivan Rodriguez	6.00
ES	Ervin Santana	4.00
CS	Chris Shelton	4.00
GS	Grady Sizemore	10.00
JS	John Smoltz/250	250.00
AS	Alfonso Soriano	8.00
HS	Huston Street	4.00
NS	Nick Swisher	4.00
MT	Miguel Tejada	6.00
CU	Chase Utley	10.00
JV	Jason Varitek	8.00
RW	Rickie Weeks	6.00
JW	Jake Westbrook	4.00
DW	Dontrelle Willis	8.00
JW	Jack Wilson/200	4.00
WR	David Wright	20.00
DY	Dmitri Young	4.00
MY	Michael Young	4.00
RZ	Ryan Zimmerman	15.00

Apparel

NM/M

Common Player:		4.00
Production 325 Sets		
Gold:		.75-1.5X
Production 150 Sets		
Silver:		1X
Production 250 Sets		
Rare Apparel:		No Pricing
Production One Set		
AT	Garrett Atkins	4.00
HB	Harold Baines	4.00
SB	Scott Baker	6.00
RB	Rocco Baldelli	4.00
BA	Clint Barmes	4.00
BY	Jason Bay	8.00
YB	Yuniesky Betancourt	4.00
JO	Joe Blanton	4.00
JE	Jeremy Bonderman	4.00
BB	Ben Broussard	4.00
CB	Chris Burke	4.00
MC	Miguel Cabrera	8.00
MA	Matt Cain	6.00
JU	Jorge Cantu	4.00
CS	Chris Capuano	4.00
CH	Chris Carpenter	10.00
GC	Gustavo Chacin	4.00
RC	Ryan Church	4.00
WC	Will Clark	8.00
CD	Chad Cordero	4.00
CA	Carl Crawford	6.00
CO	Coco Crisp	6.00
PF	Prince Fielder	15.00
CF	Carlton Fisk	8.00
GF	Gavin Floyd	4.00
GA	Jon Garland	4.00
SG	Steve Garvey	8.00
MG	Marcus Giles	4.00
JG	Jonny Gomes	4.00
GO	Adrian Gonzalez	4.00

GG	Rich "Goose" Gossage	4.00
KG	Ken Griffey Jr.	15.00
AH	Aaron Harang	4.00
DH	Danny Haren	4.00
JH	Jeremy Hermida	4.00
FH	Felix Hernandez	8.00
RH	Ramon Hernandez	4.00
MH	Matt Holliday	8.00
HO	Ryan Howard	15.00
TI	Tadahito Iguchi	8.00
BO	Bo Jackson	10.00
CJ	Conor Jackson	4.00
DJ	Derek Jeter	25.00
DA	Dan Johnson	4.00
SK	Scott Kazmir	8.00
KE	Jason Kendall	4.00
CK	Casey Kotchman	4.00
JK	John Kruk	8.00
JL	Jason Lane	4.00
DO	Don Larsen	15.00
LE	Carlos Lee	6.00
CL	Cliff Lee	4.00
DL	Derek Lee	8.00
BL	Brad Lidge	4.00
FL	Felipe Lopez	4.00
NL	Noah Lowry	4.00
BI	Bill Madlock	4.00
JM	Joe Mauer	10.00
BC	Brian McCann	8.00
BM	Brandon McCarthy	4.00
FM	Fred McGriff	8.00
YM	Yadier Molina	4.00
MO	Justin Morneau	8.00
JN	Joe Nathan	4.00
GN	Graig Nettles	4.00
OR	Magglio Ordonez	4.00
RO	Roy Oswalt	6.00
PE	Jake Peavy	6.00
JP	Jhonny Peralta	4.00
GP	Gaylord Perry	6.00
PI	Joel Pineiro	4.00
SP	Scott Podsednik	6.00
BP	Boog Powell	4.00
JY	Jeremy Reed	4.00
JR	Jose Reyes	8.00
CR	Cal Ripken Jr.	20.00
BR	Brian Roberts	4.00
AR	Aaron Rowand	4.00
ES	Ervin Santana	4.00
RS	Ron Santo	15.00
MS	Mike Schmidt	10.00
SH	Chris Shelton	4.00
GS	Grady Sizemore	10.00
HS	Huston Street	4.00
NS	Nick Swisher	8.00
ST	So Taguchi	6.00
CU	Chase Utley	10.00
AV	Andy Van Slyke	4.00
RW	Rickie Weeks	6.00
JW	Jake Westbrook	4.00
DW	Dontrelle Willis	6.00
WR	David Wright	20.00
CY	Carl Yastrzemski	15.00
DY	Dmitri Young	4.00
MY	Michael Young	4.00
RZ	Ryan Zimmerman	15.00

Apparel Autographs

NM/M

Production 30 Sets		
Patch Auto.:		No Pricing
Production 10 Sets		
AT	Garrett Atkins	20.00
HB	Harold Baines	20.00
SB	Scott Baker	15.00
BA	Clint Barmes	15.00
BY	Jason Bay	30.00
YB	Yuniesky Betancourt	25.00
JO	Joe Blanton	20.00
JE	Jeremy Bonderman	30.00
BB	Ben Broussard	15.00
CB	Chris Burke	15.00
MC	Miguel Cabrera	40.00
MA	Matt Cain	40.00
CS	Chris Capuano	20.00
CH	Chris Carpenter	50.00
GC	Gustavo Chacin	15.00
RC	Ryan Church	20.00
WC	Will Clark	40.00
CD	Chad Cordero	20.00
CA	Carl Crawford	25.00
CO	Coco Crisp	40.00
JD	Jermaine Dye	20.00
PF	Prince Fielder	75.00
CF	Carlton Fisk	40.00
SG	Steve Garvey	25.00
MG	Marcus Giles	25.00
JG	Jonny Gomes	25.00
GO	Adrian Gonzalez	20.00
GG	Rich "Goose" Gossage	35.00
KG	Ken Griffey Jr.	100.00

AH	Aaron Harang	15.00
DH	Danny Haren	20.00
JH	Jeremy Hermida	25.00
FH	Felix Hernandez	50.00
RH	Ramon Hernandez	15.00
HO	Ryan Howard/23	85.00
TI	Tadahito Iguchi	50.00
BO	Bo Jackson	100.00
CJ	Conor Jackson	40.00
DJ	Derek Jeter	200.00
DA	Dan Johnson	20.00
SK	Scott Kazmir	40.00
CK	Casey Kotchman	25.00
JK	John Kruk	30.00
DO	Don Larsen	25.00
LE	Carlos Lee	25.00
CL	Cliff Lee	15.00
DL	Derek Lee	40.00
BL	Brad Lidge	20.00
FL	Felipe Lopez	25.00
NL	Noah Lowry	40.00
BI	Bill Madlock	15.00
JM	Joe Mauer	50.00
BM	Brandon McCarthy	15.00
YM	Yadier Molina	40.00
MO	Justin Morneau	30.00
JN	Joe Nathan	25.00
GN	Graig Nettles	30.00
OR	Magglio Ordonez	35.00
RO	Roy Oswalt	25.00
PE	Jake Peavy	40.00
JP	Jhonny Peralta	15.00
GP	Gaylord Perry	25.00
PI	Joel Pineiro	25.00
SP	Scott Podsednik	30.00
BP	Boog Powell	25.00
JR	Jose Reyes	40.00
CR	Cal Ripken Jr.	180.00
AR	Aaron Rowand	20.00
RS	Ron Santo	75.00
MS	Mike Schmidt	60.00
SH	Chris Shelton	15.00
HS	Huston Street	20.00
NS	Nick Swisher	25.00
CU	Chase Utley	75.00
AV	Andy Van Slyke	25.00
RW	Rickie Weeks	25.00
JW	Jake Westbrook	20.00
DW	Dontrelle Willis	35.00
WR	David Wright	85.00
CY	Carl Yastrzemski	65.00
DY	Dmitri Young	15.00
MY	Michael Young	25.00
RZ	Ryan Zimmerman	75.00

Autofacts

NM/M

Production 5-800		
JA	Jeremy Accardo/800	15.00
LA	Luis Aparicio/250	15.00
GA	Garrett Atkins/800	15.00
CB	Clint Barmes/800	10.00
JB	Jason Bay/200	20.00
GB	George Bell/715	20.00
BE	Jason Bergmann/800	10.00
BY	Clete Boyer/485	15.00
MC	Miguel Cabrera/250	30.00
MA	Matt Cain/700	20.00
CP	Jose Capellan/800	10.00
CA	Chris Capuano/800	15.00
CH	Chris Carpenter/51	40.00
JC	Joe Carter/400	15.00
GC	Gustavo Chacin/800	10.00
CC	Chris Chambliss/400	15.00
RC	Ryan Church/800	10.00
CK	Jack Clark/800	10.00
CO	Coco Crisp/600	25.00
ED	Eric Davis/487	15.00
AD	Andre Dawson/300	20.00
CD	Chris Demaria/800	10.00
DA	Chris Denorfia/659	10.00
DE	Joey Devine/150	10.00
JD	Jermaine Dye/652	15.00
LD	Lenny Dykstra/412	15.00
SF	Scott Feldman/800	10.00
PF	Prince Fielder/200	50.00
GF	George Foster/300	10.00
SG	Steve Garvey/300	15.00
MG	Marcus Giles/350	15.00
GO	Jonny Gomes/700	10.00
GG	Rich "Goose" Gossage/300	20.00
KG	Ken Griffey Jr./800	60.00

TH	Travis Hafner/400	20.00
TM	Tim Hamulack/742	10.00
AH	Aaron Harang/800	10.00
DH	Danny Haren/800	15.00
JE	Jeff Harris/800	10.00
FH	Felix Hernandez/300	30.00
KH	Kent Hrbek/239	15.00
TI	Tadahito Iguchi/700	30.00
BO	Bo Jackson/250	50.00
CJ	Conor Jackson/800	15.00
RJ	Reggie Jackson/200	50.00
DJ	Derek Jeter/100	150.00
AJ	Andruw Jones/150	50.00
IK	Ian Kinsler/800	20.00
JK	Jason Kubel/400	10.00
JL	Jason Lane/800	10.00
BL	Barry Larkin/300	35.00
CL	Cliff Lee/600	10.00
DL	Derrek Lee/300	30.00
BI	Bill Madlock/300	15.00
PM	Pedro Martinez/100	60.00
JM	Joe Mauer/400	35.00
AM	Aaron Miles/494	15.00
YM	Yadier Molina/800	20.00
JN	Joe Nathan/800	15.00
GN	Graig Nettles/300	20.00
TO	Tony Oliva/300	15.00
MO	Magglio Ordonez/437	25.00
JP	Jhonny Peralta/700	15.00
TP	Tony Perez/251	25.00
HR	Hanley Ramirez/500	20.00
RE	Chris Resop/800	10.00
JR	Jim Rice/200	20.00
CR	Cal Ripken Jr./100	100.00
BR	Brian Roberts/200	15.00
AR	Aaron Rowand/520	15.00
JS	Johan Santana/150	50.00
CS	Chris Shelton/350	15.00
HS	Huston Street/500	15.00
NS	Nick Swisher/700	20.00
WT	Willy Taveras/500	10.00
CU	Chase Utley/200	50.00
AV	Andy Van Slyke/800	25.00
JV	Justin Verlander/700	40.00
RW	Rickie Weeks/91	25.00
JW	Jake Westbrook/650	10.00
WI	Dontrelle Willis/500	20.00
MW	Maury Willis/150	15.00
DW	David Wright/300	65.00
CY	Chris Young/700	15.00
DY	Dmitri Young/300	10.00
MY	Michael Young/600	20.00
CZ	Carlos Zambrano/200	25.00
RZ	Ryan Zimmerman/800	40.00

Awesome Artifacts

NM/M

Common Player: 10.00
Production 45 unless noted.

BA	Jeff Bagwell	12.00
HB	Harold Baines	10.00
SB	Scott Baker	10.00
RB	Rocco Baldelli	10.00
CB	Clint Barmes	10.00
JB	Jason Bay	12.00
HA	Hank Blalock	10.00
BL	Joe Blanton	10.00
MB	Mark Buehrle	10.00
BU	Chris Burke	10.00
MC	Miguel Cabrera	15.00
CA	Matt Cain	10.00
CH	Chris Carpenter	15.00
GC	Gustavo Chacin	10.00
EC	Eric Chavez	10.00
WC	Will Clark	12.00
CC	Carl Crawford	12.00
DD	Don Drysdale/25	25.00
ZD	Zachary Duke	10.00
AD	Adam Dunn	15.00
JE	Jim Edmonds	12.00
ME	Morgan Ensberg	10.00
PF	Prince Fielder	20.00
CF	Carlton Fisk	15.00
FG	Gavin Floyd	10.00
JF	Jeff Francoeur	12.00
EG	Eric Gagne	10.00
FG	Freddy Garcia/21	15.00
GA	Jon Garland	10.00
SG	Steve Garvey	15.00
JG	Jonny Gomes	10.00
KG	Ken Griffey Jr.	30.00
VG	Vladimir Guerrero	15.00
BH	Bill Hall	10.00
AH	Aaron Harang	10.00
DH	Danny Haren	10.00
TH	Todd Helton	10.00
FH	Felix Hernandez	15.00
TR	Trevor Hoffman	10.00
RH	Rogers Hornsby/25	100.00
RY	Ryan Howard	25.00
BO	Bo Jackson	15.00

CO	Conor Jackson	10.00
DJ	Derek Jeter	40.00
DA	Dan Johnson	10.00
NJ	Nick Johnson	10.00
RA	Randy Johnson	15.00
CJ	Chipper Jones	15.00
JL	Jason Lane	10.00
DL	Don Larsen/30	25.00
CL	Cliff Lee	10.00
DE	Derrek Lee	15.00
NL	Noah Lowry	15.00
PM	Pedro Martinez	15.00
EM	Eddie Mathews	15.00
BR	Brian McCann	15.00
BM	Brandon McCarthy	10.00
JM	Johnny Mize/25	20.00
YM	Yadier Molina	10.00
JU	Justin Morneau	12.00
DO	David Ortiz	25.00
RO	Roy Oswalt	10.00
SP	Satchel Paige	100.00
DP	Dave Parker	10.00
JP	Jake Peavy	10.00
PE	Jhonny Peralta	10.00
GP	Gaylord Perry	10.00
JO	Joel Pineiro	10.00
MP	Mark Prior	10.00
AP	Albert Pujols	40.00
MR	Manny Ramirez	15.00
CR	Cal Ripken Jr.	40.00
IR	Ivan Rodriguez	10.00
AR	Aaron Rowand	10.00
ES	Ervin Santana	10.00
RS	Ron Santo	10.00
JA	Jason Schmidt	10.00
CS	Chris Shelton	10.00
GS	Grady Sizemore	15.00
JS	John Smoltz	15.00
AS	Alfonso Soriano	15.00
HS	Huston Street	10.00
NS	Nick Swisher	10.00
MI	Miguel Tejada	10.00
FT	Frank Thomas	15.00
CU	Chase Utley	20.00
AV	Andy Van Slyke	10.00
JV	Jason Varitek	20.00
RW	Rickie Weeks	10.00
DW	David Wells	10.00
WE	Jake Westbrook	10.00
WI	Dontrelle Willis	12.00
JW	Jack Wilson	10.00
WR	David Wright	30.00
CY	Carl Yastrzemski/25	40.00
RZ	Ryan Zimmerman	25.00

2006 Upper Deck Epic

NM/M

Complete Set (300):
Common Player: 2.00
Production 450 Sets
Pack (3): 35.00
Box (5): 150.00

1	Conor Jackson (RC)	2.00
2	Brandon Webb	3.00
3	Craig Counsell	2.00
4	Luis Gonzalez	2.00
5	Miguel Batista	2.00
6	Orlando Hudson	2.00
7	Russ Ortiz	2.00
8	Shawn Green	2.00
9	Andruw Jones	4.00
10	Chipper Jones	5.00
11	Edgar Renteria	3.00
12	Jeff Francoeur	2.00
13	John Smoltz	3.00
14	Marcus Giles	2.00
15	Mike Hampton	2.00
16	Tim Hudson	3.00
17	Erik Bedard	2.00
18	Brian Roberts	2.00
19	Javy Lopez	2.00
20	Jay Gibbons	2.00
21	Jeff Conine	2.00
22	Melvin Mora	2.00
23	Miguel Tejada	4.00
24	Daniel Cabrera	2.00
25	Rodrigo Lopez	2.00
26	Ramon Hernandez	2.00
27	Bronson Arroyo	2.00
28	Curt Schilling	5.00
29	David Ortiz	5.00
30	David Wells	2.00
31	Jason Varitek	4.00
32	Josh Beckett	3.00
33	Kevin Youkilis	3.00
34	Manny Ramirez	5.00
35	Matt Clement	2.00
36	Mike Lowell	2.00
37	Tim Wakefield	2.00
38	Trot Nixon	2.00
39	Aramis Ramirez	3.00
40	Carlos Zambrano	3.00
41	Derrek Lee	4.00
42	Greg Maddux	10.00

43	Juan Pierre	2.00
44	Kerry Wood	2.00
45	Mark Prior	4.00
46	Michael Barrett	2.00
47	Ryan Dempster	2.00
48	Todd Walker	2.00
49	Wade Miller	2.00
50	A.J. Pierzynski	2.00
51	Brian Anderson (RC)	2.00
52	Frank Thomas	4.00
53	Javier Vazquez	2.00
54	Jim Thome	4.00
55	Joe Crede	2.00
56	Jon Garland	2.00
57	Juan Uribe	2.00
58	Mark Buehrle	3.00
59	Paul Konerko	3.00
60	Scott Podsednik	2.00
61	Tadahito Iguchi	3.00
62	Aaron Harang	2.00
63	Adam Dunn	4.00
64	Austin Kearns	3.00
65	Edwin Encarnacion	2.00
66	Eric Milton	2.00
67	Felipe Lopez	2.00
68	Jason LaRue	2.00
69	Ken Griffey Jr.	10.00
70	Wily Mo Pena	2.00
71	Aaron Boone	2.00
72	Ben Broussard	2.00
73	C.C. Sabathia	2.00
74	Casey Blake	2.00
75	Cliff Lee	2.00
76	Grady Sizemore	3.00
77	Jake Westbrook	2.00
78	Josh Bard	2.00
79	Travis Hafner	4.00
80	Victor Martinez	2.00
81	Chin-Hui Tsao	2.00
82	Clint Barmes	2.00
83	Garrett Atkins	2.00
84	Josh Wilson (RC)	2.00
85	Luis Gonzalez	2.00
86	Matt Holliday	2.00
87	Todd Helton	4.00
88	Brandon Inge	2.00
89	Carlos Guillen	2.00
90	Chris Shelton	2.00
91	Craig Monroe	2.00
92	Dmitri Young	2.00
93	Ivan Rodriguez	4.00
94	Jeremy Bonderman	3.00
95	Magglio Ordonez	2.00
96	Alberto Callaspo	2.00
97	Brian Moehler	2.00
98	Dontrelle Willis	3.00
99	Jeremy Hermida (RC)	3.00
100	Jason Vargas	2.00
101	Miguel Cabrera	5.00
102	Adam Everett	2.00
103	Andy Pettitte	3.00
104	Brad Ausmus	2.00
105	Brad Lidge	2.00
106	Craig Biggio	3.00
107	Dan Wheeler	2.00
108	Jeff Bagwell	4.00
109	Lance Berkman	3.00
110	Morgan Ensberg	2.00
111	Preston Wilson	2.00
112	Roger Clemens	10.00
113	Roy Oswalt	3.00
114	David Gassner (RC)	2.00
115	Angel Berroa	2.00
116	Doug Mientkiewicz	2.00
117	Joe Mays	2.00
118	Mark Grudzielanek	2.00
119	Mike Sweeney	2.00
120	Reggie Sanders	2.00
121	Runelvys Hernandez	2.00
122	Scott Elarton	2.00
123	Brandon Watson (RC)	2.00
124	Zack Greinke	2.00
125	Brad Penny	2.00
126	Derek Lowe	2.00
127	Eric Gagne	2.00
128	J.D. Drew	3.00
129	Jayson Werth	2.00
130	Jeff Kent	3.00
131	Nomar Garciaparra	4.00
132	Olmedo Saenz	2.00
133	Rafael Furcal	3.00
134	Ben Sheets	3.00
135	Bill Hall	2.00
136	Carlos Lee	3.00
137	Geoff Jenkins	2.00
138	Prince Fielder (RC)	10.00
139	Rickie Weeks	3.00
140	Jose Capellan (RC)	2.00
141	Brad Radke	2.00
142	Joe Mauer	6.00
143	Joe Nathan	2.00
144	Johan Santana	5.00
145	Justin Morneau	3.00
146	Kyle Lohse	2.00

147	Lew Ford	2.00
148	Luis Castillo	2.00
149	Matthew LeCroy	2.00
150	Michael Cuddyer	2.00
151	Shannon Stewart	2.00
152	Torii Hunter	3.00
153	Billy Wagner	2.00
154	Carlos Beltran	5.00
155	Carlos Delgado	4.00
156	Cliff Floyd	2.00
157	David Wright	10.00
158	Jose Reyes	8.00
159	Kazuo Matsui	2.00
160	Mike Piazza	6.00
161	Paul LoDuca	2.00
162	Pedro Martinez	5.00
163	Tom Glavine	3.00
164	Victor Diaz	2.00
165	Alex Rodriguez	15.00
166	Bernie Williams	3.00
167	Carl Pavano	2.00
168	Chien-Ming Wang	5.00
169	Derek Jeter	15.00
170	Gary Sheffield	4.00
171	Hideki Matsui	8.00
172	Jason Giambi	4.00
173	Johnny Damon	5.00
174	Jorge Posada	4.00
175	Robinson Cano	5.00
176	Mariano Rivera	4.00
177	Mike Mussina	4.00
178	Randy Johnson	5.00
179	Miguel Cairo	2.00
180	Barry Zito	3.00
181	Bobby Crosby	2.00
182	Bobby Kielty	2.00
183	Eric Chavez	3.00
184	Josh Barfield (RC)	2.00
185	Esteban Loaiza	2.00
186	Huston Street	3.00
187	Jason Kendall	2.00
188	Nick Swisher	3.00
189	Aaron Rowand	2.00
190	Bobby Abreu	3.00
191	Chase Utley	5.00
192	Gavin Floyd	2.00
193	Jimmy Rollins	4.00
194	Mike Lieberthal	2.00
195	Pat Burrell	3.00
196	Ryan Howard	8.00
197	Craig Wilson	2.00
198	Jack Wilson	2.00
199	Jason Bay	4.00
200	Joe Randa	2.00
201	Josh Fogg	2.00
202	Kip Wells	2.00
203	Sean Casey	2.00
204	Zachary Duke	2.00
205	Brian Giles	3.00
206	Dave Roberts	2.00
207	Jake Peavy	4.00
208	Khalil Greene	2.00
209	Mike Cameron	2.00
210	Ryan Klesko	2.00
211	Trevor Hoffman	2.00
212	Vinny Castilla	2.00
213	Armando Benitez	2.00
214	Jason Schmidt	3.00
215	Matt Morris	2.00
216	Moises Alou	3.00
217	Omar Vizquel	2.00
218	Ray Durham	2.00
219	Adrian Beltre	2.00
220	Carl Everett	2.00
221	Kenji Johjima RC	15.00
222	Felix Hernandez	4.00
223	Ichiro Suzuki	10.00
224	Jamie Moyer	2.00
225	Jeremy Reed	2.00
226	Joel Pineiro	2.00
227	Raul Ibanez	2.00
228	Rickie Sexson	3.00
229	Albert Pujols	15.00
230	Chris Carpenter	5.00
231	David Eckstein	2.00
232	Jason Marquis	2.00
233	Jeff Suppan	2.00
234	Jim Edmonds	4.00
235	Yadier Molina	2.00
236	Mark Mulder	3.00
237	Scott Rolen	5.00
238	Alex Gonzalez	2.00
239	Aubrey Huff	2.00
240	Carl Crawford	3.00
241	Casey Fossum	2.00
242	Joey Gathright	2.00
243	Scott Kazmir	2.00
244	Toby Hall	2.00
245	Travis Lee	2.00
246	Adam Eaton	2.00
247	Francisco Cordero	2.00
248	Hank Blalock	3.00
249	Kevin Mench	2.00
250	Kevin Millwood	2.00

No.	Player	Price
251	Laynce Nix	2.00
252	Mark Teixeira	4.00
253	Michael Young	2.00
254	A.J. Burnett	2.00
255	Alex Rios	3.00
256	B.J. Ryan	2.00
257	Corey Koskie	2.00
258	Josh Towers	2.00
259	Lyle Overbay	2.00
260	Reed Johnson	2.00
261	Roy Halladay	3.00
262	Russ Adams	2.00
263	Troy Glaus	3.00
264	Vernon Wells	3.00
265	Alfonso Soriano	4.00
266	John Patterson	2.00
267	Damian Jackson	2.00
268	Jose Guillen	2.00
269	Jose Vidro	2.00
270	Livan Hernandez	2.00
271	Adam Kennedy	2.00
272	Bartolo Colon	2.00
273	Bengie Molina	2.00
274	Casey Kotchman	2.00
275	Chone Figgins	2.00
276	Matt Cain (RC)	5.00
277	Darin Erstad	2.00
278	Edgardo Alfonzo	2.00
279	Francisco Rodriguez	2.00
280	Garret Anderson	2.00
281	Vladimir Guerrero	5.00
282	Chris Denorfia (RC)	2.00
283	Joey Devine RC	4.00
284	Justin Verlander (RC)	10.00
285	Scott Feldman RC	5.00
286	Jason Bergmann RC	4.00
287	Jeremy Accardo RC	4.00
288	Adam Wainwright (RC)	8.00
289	Hanley Ramirez (RC)	5.00
290	Josh Johnson (RC)	3.00
291	Ryan Zimmerman (RC)	20.00
292	Anderson Hernandez (RC)	4.00
293	Francisco Liriano (RC)	20.00
294	Josh Willingham (RC)	3.00
295	Hong-Chih Kuo (RC)	8.00
296	Steve Stemle RC	4.00
297	Jeff Harris RC	4.00
298	John Van Benschoten (RC)	4.00
299	Jonathan Papelbon (RC)	25.00
300	Jason Kubel (RC)	10.00

Awesome 8 Materials
Production 1-10

Epic Endorsements
NM/M
Production 10-45

ID	Player	Price
JB	Jason Bay/45	30.00
BE	Johnny Bench/10	
CB	Craig Biggio/30	60.00
WB	Wade Boggs/30	75.00
LB	Lou Brock/30	75.00
JI	Jim Bunning/30	30.00
MC1	Miguel Cabrera/30	50.00
MC2	Miguel Cabrera/30	50.00
RC	Rod Carew/30	50.00
SC1	Steve Carlton/27	35.00
SC2	Steve Carlton/27	35.00
EC	Eric Chavez/30	50.00
WC	Will Clark/23	50.00
AD	Adam Dunn/45	40.00
BF1	Bob Feller/45	40.00
BF2	Bob Feller/45	40.00
PF	Prince Fielder/45	75.00
CF	Carlton Fisk/30	50.00
SG	Steve Garvey/45	30.00
BG	Bob Gibson/30	60.00
KG1	Ken Griffey Jr./30	150.00
KG2	Ken Griffey Jr./30	150.00
KG3	Ken Griffey Jr./30	150.00
TG	Tony Gwynn/30	75.00
JH1	Jeremy Hermida/45	30.00
JH2	Jeremy Hermida/45	30.00
FH1	Felix Hernandez/30	50.00
FH2	Felix Hernandez/30	50.00
RH	Ryan Howard/45	100.00
BO	Bo Jackson/30	85.00
DJ1	Derek Jeter/30	200.00
DJ2	Derek Jeter/30	200.00
DJ3	Derek Jeter/30	200.00
AJ	Andruw Jones/30	40.00
LA	Don Larsen/30	40.00
FL	Fred Lynn/45	25.00
BM	Bill Mazeroski/30	60.00
PM1	Paul Molitor/30	40.00
PM2	Paul Molitor/30	40.00
TO	Tony Oliva/45	30.00
DO	David Ortiz/30	85.00
RO1	Roy Oswalt/45	40.00
RO2	Roy Oswalt/45	40.00
JP1	Jim Palmer/30	40.00
JP2	Jim Palmer/30	40.00
JA	Jake Peavy/45	25.00
TP	Tony Perez/45	40.00
AP	Albert Pujols/15	400.00
CR	Cal Ripken Jr./15	280.00
BN	Brian Roberts/45	30.00
BR1	Brooks Robinson/30	75.00
BR2	Brooks Robinson/30	75.00
FR	Frank Robinson/30	40.00
RS1	Ryne Sandberg/45	100.00
CS	Curt Schilling/15	75.00
TS	Tom Seaver/30	60.00
OS	Ozzie Smith/30	75.00
SM	John Smoltz/30	150.00
AS	Alfonso Soriano/30	40.00
DS	Don Sutton/30	30.00
CU	Chase Utley/45	50.00
BW	Billy Williams/45	25.00
DW1	Dontrelle Willis/30	40.00
DW2	Dontrelle Willis/30	40.00
MW	Maury Wills/45	25.00
WR	David Wright/25	100.00
CY	Carl Yastrzemski/15	
RZ1	Ryan Zimmerman/30	100.00
RZ2	Ryan Zimmerman/30	100.00

Epic Events
NM/M
Common Player: 2.00
Production 675 Sets

ID	Player	Price
EE1	Ryan Howard	4.00
EE2	Tadahito Iguchi	2.00
EE3	Paul Konerko	2.00
EE4	Craig Biggio	2.00
EE5	Alex Rodriguez	6.00
EE6	Ichiro Suzuki	5.00
EE7	David Ortiz	4.00
EE8	Miguel Cabrera	3.00
EE9	Dontrelle Willis	2.00
EE10	Mark Teixeira	3.00
EE11	Hideki Matsui	5.00
EE12	Albert Pujols	8.00
EE13	Albert Pujols	8.00
EE14	Greg Maddux	5.00
EE15	Greg Maddux	5.00
EE16	Manny Ramirez	3.00
EE17	Mark Teixeira	3.00
EE18	Alex Rodriguez	6.00
EE19	Manny Ramirez	3.00
EE20	Randy Johnson	3.00
EE21	Jason Varitek	3.00
EE22	Vladimir Guerrero	3.00
EE23	Roger Clemens	8.00
EE24	Manny Ramirez	3.00
EE25	Curt Schilling	3.00
EE26	Johnny Damon	3.00
EE27	David Ortiz	4.00
EE28	David Wright	6.00
EE29	Ichiro Suzuki	5.00
EE30	Ichiro Suzuki	5.00
EE31	Adam Dunn	3.00
EE32	Adrian Beltre	2.00
EE33	Javy Lopez	2.00
EE34	Greg Maddux	5.00
EE35	Randy Johnson	3.00
EE36	Jim Thome	3.00
EE37	Adam Dunn	3.00
EE38	Bobby Abreu	2.00
EE39	Felix Hernandez	3.00
EE40	Greg Maddux	5.00
EE41	Ken Griffey Jr.	6.00
EE42	Randy Johnson	3.00
EE43	Johan Santana	3.00
EE44	Magglio Ordonez	2.00
EE45	Josh Beckett	2.00
EE46	Ivan Rodriguez	3.00
EE47	Alfonso Soriano	3.00
EE48	Eric Gagne	2.00
EE49	Hank Blalock	2.00
EE50	Roger Clemens	8.00
EE51	Derek Jeter	8.00
EE52	Derek Jeter	8.00
EE53	Barry Zito	2.00
EE54	Alex Rodriguez	6.00
EE55	Nomar Garciaparra	3.00
EE56	Torii Hunter	2.00
EE57	Ichiro Suzuki	5.00
EE58	Randy Johnson	3.00
EE59	Ichiro Suzuki	5.00
EE60	Albert Pujols	8.00
EE61	Albert Pujols	8.00
EE62	Ichiro Suzuki	5.00
EE63	Derek Jeter	8.00
EE64	Pedro Martinez	3.00
EE65	Chris Shelton	2.00
EE66	Ivan Rodriguez	3.00
EE67	Chipper Jones	3.00
EE68	Pedro Martinez	3.00
EE69	Ken Griffey Jr.	6.00
EE70	Jeff Bagwell	3.00
EE71	Nomar Garciaparra	3.00
EE72	Mark Prior	3.00
EE73	Kerry Wood	2.00
EE74	Andruw Jones	3.00
EE75	Derek Jeter	8.00
EE76	Cal Ripken Jr.	10.00
EE77	Ken Griffey Jr.	6.00
EE78	Ken Griffey Jr.	6.00
EE79	Mike Piazza	6.00
EE80	Nolan Ryan	6.00
EE81	Greg Maddux	5.00
EE82	Greg Maddux	5.00
EE83	Roger Clemens	8.00
EE84	Ozzie Smith	4.00
EE85	Tom Seaver	4.00
EE86	Thurman Munson	4.00
EE87	Reggie Jackson	3.00
EE88	Johnny Bench	4.00
EE89	Mike Schmidt	4.00
EE90	Carlton Fisk	2.00
EE91	Eddie Mathews	3.00
EE92	Roy Campanella	4.00
EE93	Jackie Robinson	6.00
EE94	Joe DiMaggio	6.00
EE95	Jimmie Foxx	3.00
EE96	Lou Gehrig	10.00
EE97	Babe Ruth	10.00
EE98	Ty Cobb	6.00
EE99	Honus Wagner	5.00
EE100	Cy Young	5.00

Four Barrel
No Pricing
Production One Set

Foursome Fabrics
NM/M
Production 5-50

ID	Players	Price
CMBF	Carlton Fisk, Thurman Munson, Johnny Bench, Gary Carter/25	70.00
GRSM	Tom Seaver, Nolan Ryan, Juan Marichal, Bob Gibson/30	60.00
MBSP	Albert Pujols, Lou Brock, Stan Musial, Ozzie Smith/30	100.00
PJGG	Ken Griffey Jr., Derek Jeter, Vladimir Guerrero, Albert Pujols/50	100.00
RCJP	Mark Prior, Nolan Ryan, Roger Clemens, Randy Johnson/50	50.00
WRRJ	Pee Wee Reese, Honus Wagner, Cal Ripken Jr., Derek Jeter/20	300.00
WYBS	Ted Williams, Wade Boggs, Curt Schilling, Carl Yastrzemski/50	85.00

Materials
NM/M
Production 10-185
No pricing production 15 or less.

Orange:	.75-1.5X
Production 5-185	
Red:	.75-1.5X
Production 10-185	
Light Purple:	.75-1.5X
Production 4-185	
Dark Purple:	.75-1.5X
Production 3-185	
Blue:	.75-1.5X
Production 3-99	
Teal:	.75-1.5X
Production 5-99	
Green:	1-1.5X
Production 3-75	
Dark Green:	1-2X
Production 3-50	
Grey:	1-2X
Production 3-40	
Gold:	1-1.25X
Production 1-25	

ID	Player	Price
EB	Ernie Banks/155	15.00
JB1	Johnny Bench/155	10.00
JB2	Johnny Bench/155	10.00
WB1	Wade Boggs/185	10.00
WB2	Wade Boggs/185	10.00
LB1	Lou Brock/48	15.00
LB2	Lou Brock/48	15.00
RC1	Roger Clemens/155	20.00
RC2	Roger Clemens/155	20.00
RC3	Roger Clemens/155	20.00
CL1	Roberto Clemente/50	75.00
TC	Ty Cobb/10	
JD1	Joe DiMaggio/185	65.00
JD2	Joe DiMaggio/173	65.00
JD3	Joe DiMaggio/99	75.00
CF	Carlton Fisk/169	10.00
CF2	Carlton Fisk/185	10.00
WF	Whitey Ford/155	15.00
LG1	Lou Gehrig/15	165.00
LG2	Lou Gehrig/15	165.00
LG3	Lou Gehrig/15	165.00
BG	Bob Gibson/155	10.00
BG2	Bob Gibson/155	15.00
HG	Hank Greenberg/50	40.00
KG1	Ken Griffey Jr./175	15.00
KG2	Ken Griffey Jr./175	15.00
KG3	Ken Griffey Jr./175	15.00
VG	Vladimir Guerrero/145	8.00
VG2	Vladimir Guerrero/145	8.00
GH	Gil Hodges/39	15.00
RH	Rogers Hornsby/50	75.00
RE1	Reggie Jackson/52	12.00
RE2	Reggie Jackson/52	12.00
RE3	Reggie Jackson/52	12.00
DJ1	Derek Jeter/185	25.00
DJ2	Derek Jeter/185	25.00
DJ3	Derek Jeter/185	25.00
RJ1	Randy Johnson/145	10.00
RJ2	Randy Johnson/145	10.00
HK	Harmon Killebrew/155	15.00
JM	Juan Marichal/155	8.00
ED	Eddie Mathews/185	15.00
DM1	Don Mattingly/185	15.00
DM2	Don Mattingly/185	15.00
WM	Willie McCovey/155	15.00
WM2	Willie McCovey/155	15.00
WM3	Willie McCovey/155	15.00
PM1	Paul Molitor/155	10.00
PM2	Paul Molitor/155	10.00
JO	Joe Morgan/145	8.00
JO2	Joe Morgan/145	8.00
TH1	Thurman Munson/35	30.00
TH2	Thurman Munson/35	30.00
EM1	Eddie Murray/185	8.00
EM2	Eddie Murray/165	8.00
EM3	Eddie Murray/185	8.00
SM1	Stan Musial/55	25.00
SM2	Stan Musial/75	25.00
MP1	Mike Piazza/145	12.00
MP2	Mike Piazza/145	12.00
MA	Mark Prior/185	8.00
MA2	Mark Prior/185	8.00
KP1	Kirby Puckett/155	15.00
KP2	Kirby Puckett/155	15.00
AP1	Albert Pujols/185	20.00
AP2	Albert Pujols/185	20.00
AP3	Albert Pujols/185	20.00
PR1	Pee Wee Reese/145	15.00
PR2	Pee Wee Reese/145	15.00
CR1	Cal Ripken Jr./155	25.00
CR2	Cal Ripken Jr./177	25.00
CR3	Cal Ripken Jr./155	25.00
RO	Brooks Robinson/49	15.00
RO2	Brooks Robinson/99	15.00
FR1	Frank Robinson/130	10.00
FR2	Frank Robinson/130	10.00
JR	Jackie Robinson/10	
BR1	Babe Ruth/15	250.00
BR2	Babe Ruth/15	250.00
NR1	Nolan Ryan/155	20.00
NR2	Nolan Ryan/155	20.00
NR3	Nolan Ryan/155	20.00
RS1	Ryne Sandberg/155	15.00
RS2	Ryne Sandberg/155	15.00
RS3	Ryne Sandberg/155	15.00
MS1	Mike Schmidt/185	15.00
MS2	Mike Schmidt/185	15.00
MS3	Mike Schmidt/185	15.00
TS	Tom Seaver/155	15.00
TS2	Tom Seaver/155	15.00
OS1	Ozzie Smith/185	15.00
OS2	Ozzie Smith/185	15.00
HW	Honus Wagner/16	200.00
TW1	Ted Williams/125	50.00
TW2	Ted Williams/125	50.00
CY1	Carl Yastrzemski/185	15.00
CY2	Carl Yastrzemski/185	15.00
CY3	Carl Yastrzemski/185	15.00
RY1	Robin Yount/155	10.00
RY2	Robin Yount/155	10.00

Materials Signatures
No Pricing
Production 5 Sets

Pairings
NM/M
Production 5-99

ID	Players	Price
BB	Wade Boggs, Brooks Robinson/99	25.00
BM	Johnny Bench, Joe Morgan/99	20.00

BR	Bob Gibson, Nolan Ryan/99	30.00
BS	Lou Brock, Ozzie Smith/99	30.00
BS2	Wade Boggs, Ryne Sandberg/99	25.00
CJ	Roger Clemens, Randy Johnson/99	25.00
CR	Roger Clemens, Nolan Ryan/99	40.00
DG	Joe DiMaggio, Lou Gehrig/25	220.00
FB	Carlton Fisk, Johnny Bench/99	20.00
FP	Carlton Fisk, Mike Piazza/99	20.00
GB	Bob Gibson, Lou Brock/99	25.00
GC	Hank Greenberg, Ty Cobb/25	150.00
GG	Ken Griffey Jr., Vladimir Guerrero/99	40.00
GP	Ken Griffey Jr., Kirby Puckett/99	35.00
GR	Lou Gehrig, Cal Ripken Jr./45	180.00
JD	Derek Jeter, Joe DiMaggio/99	125.00
JG	Derek Jeter, Ken Griffey Jr./99	75.00
JJ	Reggie Jackson, Derek Jeter/99	40.00
JK	Reggie Jackson, Harmon Killebrew/99	30.00
JM	Derek Jeter, Don Mattingly/99	80.00
JS	Reggie Jackson, Mike Schmidt/99	30.00
KP	Harmon Killebrew, Kirby Puckett/99	30.00
MB	Thurman Munson, Johnny Bench/30	40.00
MM	Juan Marichal, Willie McCovey/99	25.00
MM2	Don Mattingly, Thurman Munson/30	75.00
MR	Eddie Mathews, Brooks Robinson/50	50.00
MS	Eddie Mathews, Mike Schmidt/50	40.00
MY	Paul Molitor, Robin Yount/99	25.00
PH	Albert Pujols, Rogers Hornsby/99	75.00
PM	Albert Pujols, Stan Musial/99	60.00
RJ	Pee Wee Reese, Derek Jeter/99	35.00
RM	Cal Ripken Jr., Eddie Murray/99	40.00
RR2	Brooks Robinson, Frank Robinson/99	25.00
RY	Frank Robinson, Carl Yastrzemski/99	40.00
SB	Ryne Sandberg, Ernie Banks/99	40.00
SM	Ryne Sandberg, Joe Morgan/99	30.00
SR	Tom Seaver, Nolan Ryan/99	40.00
SS	Ryne Sandberg, Ozzie Smith/99	35.00
WC	Honus Wagner, Roberto Clemente/25	225.00
WD	Ted Williams, Joe DiMaggio/45	200.00
WM	Ted Williams, Stan Musial/45	75.00
YW	Carl Yastrzemski, Ted Williams/50	100.00

Swatch

NM/M

Common Player:		10.00
Production 50 Sets		
JB	Jason Bay	15.00
EC	Eric Chavez	10.00
RC	Roger Clemens	30.00
CF	Carlton Fisk	15.00
KG1	Ken Griffey Jr.	30.00
KG2	Ken Griffey Jr.	30.00
VG	Vladimir Guerrero	15.00
TG	Tony Gwynn	25.00
DJ1	Derek Jeter	50.00
DJ2	Derek Jeter	50.00
RJ	Randy Johnson	20.00
PM	Pedro J. Martinez	15.00
JM	Joe Morgan	10.00
DO	David Ortiz	25.00
RO	Roy Oswalt	10.00
JP	Jake Peavy	10.00
MP	Mark Prior	10.00
AP	Albert Pujols	40.00
MR	Manny Ramirez	15.00
JR	Jose Reyes	15.00
CR	Cal Ripken Jr.	40.00
IR	Ivan Rodriguez	12.00
SR	Scott Rolen	20.00
JS	Johan Santana	10.00
CS	Curt Schilling	15.00
MT	Mark Teixeira	12.00
MI	Miguel Tejada	10.00
DW	Dontrelle Willis	10.00
CY	Carl Yastrzemski	20.00
RZ	Ryan Zimmerman	30.00

Triple Materials

NM/M

Production 3-99

BER	Eddie Murray, Brooks Robinson, Johnny Bench/60	35.00
BMR	Brooks Robinson, Wade Boggs, Paul Molitor/99	30.00
BSP	Ryne Sandberg, Ernie Banks, Mark Prior/99	40.00
CDG	Ken Griffey Jr., Ty Cobb, Joe DiMaggio/15	300.00
FJJ	Whitey Ford, Reggie Jackson, Derek Jeter/99	60.00
FMJ	Don Mattingly, Reggie Jackson, Whitey Ford/51	40.00
GJC	Randy Johnson, Roger Clemens, Bob Gibson/99	40.00
GMG	Eddie Murray, Hank Greenberg, Lou Gehrig/25	150.00
GPS	Tom Seaver, Bob Gibson, Mark Prior/99	30.00
GRM	Ken Griffey Jr., Willie McCovey, Frank Robinson/99	40.00
JGK	Vladimir Guerrero, Reggie Jackson, Harmon Killebrew/99	40.00
JKR	Harmon Killebrew, Frank Robinson, Reggie Jackson/99	40.00
JMM	Derek Jeter, Don Mattingly, Thurman Munson/25	125.00
JPG	Albert Pujols, Ken Griffey Jr., Derek Jeter/99	100.00
MBF	Carlton Fisk, Thurman Munson, Johnny Bench/99	40.00
MBG	Johnny Bench, Joe Morgan, Ken Griffey Jr./99	50.00
MBP	Albert Pujols, Lou Brock, Stan Musial/24	90.00
MFM	Carlton Fisk, Eddie Murray, Thurman Munson/99	30.00
MMG	Steve Garvey, Eddie Murray, Don Mattingly/49	40.00
MPS	Tom Seaver, Mike Piazza, Eddie Murray/99	30.00
MSY	Ozzie Smith, Paul Molitor, Robin Yount/49	40.00
RBS	Cal Ripken Jr., Wade Boggs, Mike Schmidt/99	50.00
RCJ	Nolan Ryan, Roger Clemens, Randy Johnson/75	50.00
RJD	Reggie Jackson, Joe DiMaggio, Babe Ruth/99	300.00
RRM	Jackie Robinson, Frank Robinson, Willie McCovey/50	50.00
SMH	Ryne Sandberg, Rogers Hornsby, Joe Morgan/25	80.00
WSR	Honus Wagner, Pee Wee Reese, Ozzie Smith/99	100.00
YRJ	Cal Ripken Jr., Derek Jeter, Robin Yount/99	60.00
YWB	Ted Williams, Wade Boggs, Carl Yastrzemski/25	140.00

2006 Upper Deck First Pitch

NM/M

Complete Set (220):	35.00
Common Player:	.10
Pack (5):	1.50
Box (36):	40.00

1	Chad Tracy	.10
2	Conor Jackson (RC)	.10
3	Craig Counsell	.10
4	Javier Vazquez	.10
5	Luis Gonzalez	.10
6	Shawn Green	.25
7	Troy Glaus	.25
8	Joey Devine RC	1.00
9	Andruw Jones	.40
10	Chipper Jones	.50
11	John Smoltz	.25
12	Marcus Giles	.10
13	Jeff Francoeur	.25
14	Tim Hudson	.25
15	Brian Roberts	.10
16	Erik Bedard	.10
17	Javy Lopez	.10
18	Melvin Mora	.10
19	Miguel Tejada	.40
20	Alejandro Freire RC	1.00
21	Sammy Sosa	.75
22	Craig Hansen RC	3.00
23	Curt Schilling	.50
24	David Ortiz	.50
25	Edgar Renteria	.25
26	Johnny Damon	.50
27	Manny Ramirez	.50
28	Matt Clement	.10
29	Trot Nixon	.10
30	Aramis Ramirez	.25
31	Carlos Zambrano	.25
32	Derek Lee	.50
33	Greg Maddux	1.00
34	Jeromy Burnitz	.10
35	Kerry Wood	.25
36	Mark Prior	.40
37	Nomar Garciaparra	.50
38	Aaron Rowand	.10
39	Chris Demaria RC	.25
40	Jon Garland	.10
41	Mark Buehrle	.25
42	Paul Konerko	.25
43	Scott Podsednik	.25
44	Tadahito Iguchi	.25
45	Adam Dunn	.40
46	Austin Kearns	.10
47	Felipe Lopez	.10
48	Ken Griffey Jr.	1.00
49	Ryan Freel	.10
50	Sean Casey	.10
51	Wily Mo Pena	.10
52	C.C. Sabathia	.10
53	Cliff Lee	.10
54	Coco Crisp	.10
55	Grady Sizemore	.25
56	Jake Westbrook	.10
57	Travis Hafner	.25
58	Victor Martinez	.25
59	Aaron Miles	.10
60	Clint Barmes	.10
61	Garrett Atkins	.10
62	Jeff Baker	.10
63	Jeff Francis	.10
64	Matt Holliday	.25
65	Todd Helton	.40
66	Carlos Guillen	.10
67	Chris Shelton	.10
68	Dmitri Young	.10
69	Ivan Rodriguez	.40
70	Jeremy Bonderman	.10
71	Magglio Ordonez	.25
72	Placido Polanco	.10
73	A.J. Burnett	.10
74	Carlos Delgado	.40
75	Dontrelle Willis	.25
76	Josh Beckett	.25
77	Juan Pierre	.10
78	Ryan Jorgensen RC	.50
79	Miguel Cabrera	.50
80	Robert Andino RC	.50
81	Andy Pettitte	.25
82	Brad Lidge	.10
83	Craig Biggio	.25
84	Jeff Bagwell	.40
85	Lance Berkman	.25
86	Morgan Ensberg	.25
87	Roger Clemens	1.50
88	Roy Oswalt	.25
89	Angel Berroa	.10
90	David DeJesus	.10
91	Steve Stemle RC	1.00
92	Jonah Bayliss RC	2.00
93	Mike Sweeney	.10
94	Ryan Theriot (RC)	1.00
95	Zack Greinke	.25
96	Brad Penny	.10
97	Cesar Izturis	.10
98	Brian Myrow RC	1.00
99	Eric Gagne	.25
100	J.D. Drew	.10
101	Jeff Kent	.25
102	Milton Bradley	.10
103	Odalis Perez	.10
104	Ben Sheets	.25
105	Brady Clark	.10
106	Carlos Lee	.25
107	Geoff Jenkins	.10
108	Lyle Overbay	.10
109	Prince Fielder (RC)	.50
110	Rickie Weeks	.25
111	Jacque Jones	.10
112	Joe Mauer	.25
113	Joe Nathan	.10
114	Johan Santana	.50
115	Justin Morneau	.20
116	Chris Heintz RC	1.00
117	Torii Hunter	.25
118	Carlos Beltran	.40
119	Cliff Floyd	.10
120	David Wright	.75
121	Jose Reyes	.40
122	Mike Cameron	.10
123	Mike Piazza	.50
124	Pedro Martinez	.50
125	Tom Glavine	.25
126	Alex Rodriguez	1.50
127	Derek Jeter	1.50
128	Gary Sheffield	.40
129	Hideki Matsui	.75
130	Jason Giambi	.25
131	Jorge Posada	.25
132	Mariano Rivera	.25
133	Mike Mussina	.25
134	Randy Johnson	.50
135	Barry Zito	.25
136	Bobby Crosby	.10
137	Danny Haren	.10
138	Eric Chavez	.25
139	Huston Street	.10
140	Ron Flores RC	.50
141	Nick Swisher	.10
142	Rich Harden	.25
143	Bobby Abreu	.25
144	Danny Sandoval RC	.50
145	Chase Utley	.25
146	Jim Thome	.40
147	Jimmy Rollins	.25
148	Pat Burrell	.25
149	Ryan Howard	.50
150	Craig Wilson	.10
151	Jack Wilson	.10
152	Jason Bay	.25
153	Matt Lawton	.10
154	Oliver Perez	.10
155	Robert Mackowiak	.10
156	Zachary Duke	.10
157	Brian Giles	.25
158	Jake Peavy	.25
159	Craig Breslow RC	1.00
160	Khalil Greene	.10
161	Mark Loretta	.10
162	Ryan Klesko	.10
163	Trevor Hoffman	.10
164	J.T. Snow	.10
165	Jason Schmidt	.25
166	Marquis Grissom	.10
167	Moises Alou	.25
168	Omar Vizquel	.10
169	Pedro Feliz	.10
170	Jeremy Accardo RC	.50
171	Adrian Beltre	.25
172	Ichiro Suzuki	1.00
173	Felix Hernandez	.50
174	Jeff Harris RC	.25
175	Randy Winn	.10
176	Raul Ibanez	.10
177	Richie Sexson	.25
178	Albert Pujols	1.50
179	Chris Carpenter	.25
180	David Eckstein	.10
181	Jim Edmonds	.25
182	Larry Walker	.25
183	Matt Morris	.10
184	Reggie Sanders	.25
185	Scott Rolen	.40
186	Aubrey Huff	.10
187	Jonny Gomes	.10
188	Carl Crawford	.25
189	Tim Corcoran RC	1.00
190	Julio Lugo	.10
191	Rocco Baldelli	.10
192	Scott Kazmir	.10
193	Alfonso Soriano	.40
194	Hank Blalock	.25
195	Kenny Rogers	.10
196	Scott Feldman RC	1.00
197	Laynce Nix	.10
198	Mark Teixeira	.50
199	Michael Young	.10
200	Aaron Hill	.10
201	Alex Rios	.10
202	Eric Hinske	.10
203	Gustavo Chacin	.10
204	Roy Halladay	.25
205	Shea Hillenbrand	.10
206	Vernon Wells	.25

207	Brad Wilkerson	.10
208	Chad Cordero	.10
209	Jose Guillen	.10
210	Jose Vidro	.10
211	Livan Hernandez	.10
212	Preston Wilson	.10
213	Jason Bergmann RC	1.00
214	Bartolo Colon	.25
215	Chone Figgins	.10
216	Darin Erstad	.25
217	Francisco Rodriguez	.25
218	Garret Anderson	.25
219	Steve Finley	.25
220	Vladimir Guerrero	.50

Diamond Stars

		NM/M
Complete Set (35):		30.00
Common Player:		.50
Inserted 1:3		
1	Luis Gonzalez	.50
2	Andruw Jones	1.00
3	John Smoltz	.75
4	Miguel Tejada	1.00
5	Johnny Damon	1.50
6	Manny Ramirez	1.50
7	Derrek Lee	.75
8	Mark Prior	1.00
9	Mark Buehrle	.50
10	Ken Griffey Jr.	3.00
11	Travis Hafner	.75
12	Todd Helton	1.00
13	Ivan Rodriguez	.75
14	Miguel Cabrera	1.50
15	Roger Clemens	4.00
16	Mike Sweeney	.50
17	Jeff Kent	.75
18	Carlos Lee	.50
19	Johan Santana	1.50
20	Torii Hunter	.50
21	Pedro Martinez	1.50
22	Alex Rodriguez	4.00
23	Derek Jeter	4.00
24	Eric Chavez	.75
25	Bobby Abreu	.75
26	Jason Bay	.75
27	Jake Peavy	.75
28	Moises Alou	.50
29	Ichiro Suzuki	3.00
30	Albert Pujols	4.00
31	Carl Crawford	.75
32	Mark Teixeira	1.50
33	Roy Halladay	.50
34	Jose Guillen	.50
35	Vladimir Guerrero	1.50

Goin' Deep

		NM/M
Complete Set (35):		20.00
Common Player:		.50
Inserted 1:3		
1	Adam Dunn	1.00
2	Albert Pujols	4.00
3	Alex Rodriguez	4.00
4	Alfonso Soriano	1.00
5	Andruw Jones	1.00
6	Aramis Ramirez	.75
7	Bobby Abreu	.75
8	Brian Giles	.50
9	Carlos Delgado	.75
10	Carlos Lee	.50
11	Chipper Jones	1.50
12	David Ortiz	1.50
13	David Wright	2.00
14	Derrek Lee	1.00
15	Eric Chavez	.50
16	Gary Sheffield	.75
17	Hideki Matsui	2.50
18	Jeff Kent	.75
19	Jim Edmonds	.75
20	Ken Griffey Jr.	3.00
21	Luis Gonzalez	.50
22	Manny Ramirez	1.50
23	Mark Teixeira	1.00
24	Miguel Cabrera	1.50
25	Miguel Tejada	1.00
26	Moises Alou	.50
27	Pat Burrell	.75
28	Paul Konerko	.75
29	Rafael Palmeiro	.75
30	Richie Sexson	.75
31	Todd Helton	1.00
32	Torii Hunter	.50
33	Travis Hafner	.50
34	Vernon Wells	.50
35	Vladimir Guerrero	1.50

Hot Stove Headlines

		NM/M
Complete Set (20):		15.00
Common Player:		.50
Inserted 1:3		
1	Alex Rodriguez	3.00

2	Carlos Beltran	.75
3	Carlos Delgado	.50
4	Curt Schilling	1.00
5	Derrek Lee	.75
6	Greg Maddux	2.00
7	Hideki Matsui	2.00
8	Ichiro Suzuki	2.00
9	Ivan Rodriguez	.50
10	Jim Thome	.50
11	Johnny Damon	1.00
12	Ken Griffey Jr.	2.00
13	Manny Ramirez	1.00
14	Miguel Tejada	.75
15	Nomar Garciaparra	1.00
16	Pedro Martinez	1.00
17	Randy Johnson	1.00
18	Roger Clemens	3.00
19	Scott Rolen	.75
20	Vladimir Guerrero	.75

Signature Stars

		NM/M
Common Player:		
DR	J.D. Drew	25.00
JE	Johnny Estrada	10.00
RH	Rich Harden	15.00
PL	Paul LoDuca	15.00
VM	Victor Martinez	15.00
YM	Yadier Molina	10.00
GQ	Guillermo Quiroz	10.00
RI	Juan Rivera	15.00
IS	Ian Snell	10.00
RW	Ryan Wagner	10.00

2006 Upper Deck Future Stars

		NM/M
Complete Set (159):		
Common Player (1-75):		.25
Common Autograph		
(76-159):		5.00
Some SP Auto.'s not priced yet.		
Pack (4):		4.00
Box (24):		80.00
1	Miguel Tejada	.75
2	Brian Roberts	.25
3	Brandon Webb	.25
4	Luis Gonzalez	.25
5	Andruw Jones	.75
6	Chipper Jones	1.00
7	John Smoltz	.75
8	Curt Schilling	1.00
9	Josh Beckett	.25
10	David Ortiz	1.00
11	Manny Ramirez	1.00
12	Jim Thome	1.00
13	Paul Konerko	.75
14	Jermaine Dye	.25
15	Derrek Lee	.75
16	Greg Maddux	2.00
17	Ken Griffey Jr.	2.00
18	Adam Dunn	.75
19	Felipe Lopez	.25
20	Travis Hafner	.75
21	Victor Martinez	.25
22	Grady Sizemore	.75
23	Todd Helton	.75
24	Matt Holliday	.50
25	Jeremy Bonderman	.25
26	Ivan Rodriguez	.75
27	Miguel Cabrera	1.00
28	Dontrelle Willis	.25
29	Roger Clemens	2.00
30	Roy Oswalt	.25
31	Lance Berkman	.75
32	Reggie Sanders	.25
33	Vladimir Guerrero	1.00
34	Chone Figgins	.25
35	Jeff Kent	.25
36	Eric Gagne	.25
37	Carlos Lee	.25
38	Rickie Weeks	.25

39	Johan Santana	1.00
40	Torii Hunter	.25
41	Alex Rodriguez	2.00
42	Derek Jeter	2.50
43	Randy Johnson	1.00
44	Hideki Matsui	1.50
45	Johnny Damon	1.00
46	Pedro Martinez	1.00
47	David Wright	2.00
48	Carlos Beltran	.75
49	Rich Harden	.25
50	Eric Chavez	.25
51	Huston Street	.25
52	Ryan Howard	2.00
53	Bobby Abreu	.75
54	Chase Utley	.75
55	Jason Bay	.75
56	Jake Peavy	.75
57	Brian Giles	.25
58	Trevor Hoffman	.25
59	Jason Schmidt	.25
60	Randy Winn	.25
61	Kenji Johjima	.75
62	Ichiro Suzuki	1.50
63	Felix Hernandez	.75
64	Albert Pujols	2.50
65	Chris Carpenter	.75
66	Jim Edmonds	.25
67	Carl Crawford	.25
68	Scott Kazmir	.25
69	Jonny Gomes	.25
70	Mark Teixeira	.75
71	Michael Young	.25
72	Vernon Wells	.75
73	Roy Halladay	.25
74	Nick Johnson	.25
75	Alfonso Soriano	.75
76	Adam Wainwright (RC)	20.00
77	Anderson Hernandez (RC)	5.00
78	Andre Ethier/SP (RC)	40.00
79	Colter Bean/SP (RC)	10.00
80	Ben Johnson (RC)	5.00
81	Boof Bonser/SP (RC)	20.00
82	Boone Logan RC	8.00
83	Brian Anderson (RC)	5.00
84	Brian Bannister (RC)	8.00
85	Chris Denorfia/SP (RC)	8.00
86	Chad Billingsley/SP (RC)	25.00
87	Cody Ross (RC)	5.00
88	Cole Hamels/SP (RC)	50.00
89	Conor Jackson (RC)	15.00
90	Dan Uggla/SP (RC)	8.00
91	Dave Gassner/SP (RC)	8.00
92	Jordan Tata RC	10.00
93	Eric Reed (RC)	8.00
94	Fausto Carmona (RC)	15.00
95	Luis Figueroa/SP RC	
96	Francisco Liriano/SP (RC)	35.00
97	Freddie Bynum (RC)	5.00
98	Hanley Ramirez/SP (RC)	30.00
99	Hong-Chih Kuo/SP (RC)	50.00
100	Ian Kinsler (RC)	20.00
101	Nelson Cruz SP (RC)	15.00
102	Ruddy Lugo (RC)	5.00
103	Jason Kubel (RC)	15.00
104	Jeff Harris (RC)	5.00
105	Santiago Ramirez (RC)	5.00
106	Jered Weaver/SP (RC)	
107	Jeremy Accardo/SP RC	15.00
108	Jeremy Hermida/SP (RC)	20.00
109	Joel Zumaya SP (RC)	40.00
110	Joey Devine (RC)	8.00
111	John Koronka (RC)	5.00
112	Jonathan Papelbon (RC)	40.00
113	Jose Capellan (RC)	5.00
114	Josh Johnson (RC)	10.00
115	Josh Rupe/SP (RC)	10.00
116	Josh Willingham/SP (RC)	15.00
117	Josh Wilson (RC)	8.00
118	Justin Verlander/SP (RC)	
119	Kelly Shoppach (RC)	8.00
120	Kendry Morales (RC)	15.00
121	Sean Tracey (RC)	8.00
122	Macay McBride (RC)	8.00
123	Martin Prado/SP (RC)	
124	Matt Cain (RC)	20.00
125	Russell Martin (RC)	20.00
126	Tim Hamulack/SP (RC)	8.00
127	Mike Jacobs (RC)	8.00
128	Ben Hendrickson (RC)	5.00

129	Jack Taschner (RC)	5.00
130	Nate McLouth (RC)	10.00
131	Jeremy Sowers/SP (RC)	15.00
132	Paul Maholm (RC)	5.00
133	Stephen Drew/SP (RC)	
134	Jason Bergmann (RC)	10.00
135	Rich Hill/SP (RC)	25.00
136	Melky Cabrera/SP (RC)	
137	Scott Dunn (RC)	5.00
138	Ryan Zimmerman (RC)	40.00
139	Anibal Sanchez (RC)	15.00
140	Sean Marshall (RC)	10.00
141	Takashi Saito/SP RC	40.00
142	Taylor Buchholz (RC)	10.00
143	Carlos Quentin/SP (RC)	15.00
144	Matt Garza (RC)	20.00
145	Wilbert Nieves (RC)	8.00
146	Jamie Shields RC	10.00
147	Jon Lester SP (RC)	
148	Craig Hansen SP RC	
149	Aaron Rakers (RC)	5.00
150	Bobby Livingston (RC)	8.00
151	Brendan Harris (RC)	5.00
152	Alay Soler/SP RC	
153	Chris Britton (RC)	10.00
154	Howie Kendrick/SP (RC)	40.00
155	Jermaine Van Buren (RC)	8.00
156	Choo Freeman/SP (RC)	
157	Matt Capps (RC)	10.00
158	Peter Moylan RC	5.00
159	Ty Taubenheim RC	15.00

Black

Black (1-75):	8-15X
Production 50 Sets	

Blue

Blue (1-75):	4-8X
Production 99 Sets	

Gold

Gold (1-75):	15-25X
Production 25 Sets	

Green

Green (1-75):	2-4X
Production 499 Sets	

Purple

Purple (1-75):	1-2X
Production 1,799 Sets	

Red

Red (1-75):	3-5X
Production 299 Sets	

Patch to History Triple Signature

		NM/M
BSJ	Andruw Jones, Alfonso Soriano, Jason Bay	40.00
CUK	Carl Crawford, Scott Kazmir, B.J. Upton	50.00
DRR	Jose Reyes, Stephen Drew, Hanley Ramirez	75.00
GEH	Andre Ethier, Jeremy Hermida, Tony Gwynn Jr.	40.00
MML	Justin Morneau, Joe Mauer, Francisco Liriano	75.00
MOH	Travis Hafner, Justin Morneau, Lyle Overbay	60.00
NHP	Trevor Hoffman, Joe Nathan, Jonathan Papelbon	60.00
PSO	Ben Sheets, Roy Oswalt, Jake Peavy	50.00
PVW	Justin Verlander, Jonathan Papelbon, Jered Weaver	100.00
SBH	Chad Billingsley, Alay Soler, Cole Hamels	40.00
SHL	Francisco Liriano, Jeremy Sowers, Cole Hamels	60.00
TZU	Ryan Zimmerman, B.J. Upton, Troy Tulowitzki	60.00
VBZ	Jeremy Bonderman, Justin Verlander, Joel Zumaya	100.00

Future Stars

	NM/M
Common Player:	1.00
Black:	8-15X
Production 50 Sets	
Blue:	4-8X
Production 99 Sets	
Gold:	15-25X
Production 25 Sets	
Green:	2-4X
Production 499 Sets	
Purple:	1-2X
Production 1,799 Sets	
Red:	3-5X
Production 299 Sets	
1 Adam Loewen	1.00
2 Nan Wang	2.00
3 Yi Feng	1.50
4 Chien-Ming Chang	2.00
5 Yung-Chi Chen	2.00
6 Chin-Lung Hu	1.50
7 Yadel Marti	1.00
8 Frederich Cepeda	1.00
9 Pedro Luis Lazo	1.00
10 Osmany Urrutia	1.00
11 Yoandy Garlobo	1.00
12 Nobuhiko Matsunaka	2.00
13 Daisuke Matsuzaka	5.00
14 Tsuyoshi Nishioka	2.00
15 Tomoya Satozaki	1.00
16 Koji Uehara	1.00
17 Shunsuke Watanabe	2.00
18 Jong Beom Lee	1.00
19 Sidney de Jong	1.00
20 Shairon Martis	1.00
21 Len Pecota	1.00
22 Dicky Gonzalez	1.00
23 Nicholas Dempsey	1.00
24 Jason Kubel	1.00
25 Chase Utley	2.00

Rookie Signatures Red Ink

Red Ink (76-159):	1.5-2X
Production 35 Sets	

2006 Upper Deck Ovation

	NM/M
Complete Set (126):	
Common (1-84):	.25
Common SP (85-126):	5.00
Production 999	
Pack (5):	5.00
Box (18):	75.00
1 Vladimir Guerrero	.75
2 Bartolo Colon	.25
3 Chone Figgins	.25
4 Lance Berkman	.40
5 Roy Oswalt	.40
6 Craig Biggio	.40
7 Rich Harden	.25
8 Eric Chavez	.40
9 Huston Street	.25
10 Vernon Wells	.40
11 Roy Halladay	.50
12 Troy Glaus	.40
13 Andruw Jones	.50
14 Chipper Jones	.75
15 John Smoltz	.40
16 Carlos Lee	.40
17 Rickie Weeks	.40
18 J.J. Hardy	.25
19 Albert Pujols	2.00
20 Chris Carpenter	.50
21 Scott Rolen	.75
22 Derrek Lee	.50
23 Mark Prior	.50
24 Aramis Ramirez	.40
25 Carl Crawford	.40

26 Scott Kazmir	.40
27 Luis Gonzalez	.25
28 Brandon Webb	.25
29 Chad Tracy	.25
30 Jeff Kent	.40
31 J.D. Drew	.40
32 Jason Schmidt	.40
33 Randy Winn	.25
34 Travis Hafner	.50
35 Victor Martinez	.40
36 Grady Sizemore	.40
37 Ichiro Suzuki	1.50
38 Felix Hernandez	.40
39 Adrian Beltre	.25
40 Miguel Cabrera	.75
41 Dontrelle Willis	.40
42 David Wright	1.50
43 Jose Reyes	.50
44 Pedro Martinez	.75
45 Carlos Beltran	.50
46 Alfonso Soriano	.75
47 Livan Hernandez	.25
48 Jose Guillen	.25
49 Miguel Tejada	.50
50 Brian Roberts	.25
51 Melvin Mora	.25
52 Jake Peavy	.40
53 Brian Giles	.25
54 Khalil Greene	.25
55 Bobby Abreu	.40
56 Ryan Howard	1.00
57 Chase Utley	.50
58 Jason Bay	.40
59 Sean Casey	.25
60 Mark Teixeira	.50
61 Michael Young	.40
62 Hank Blalock	.40
63 Manny Ramirez	.75
64 David Ortiz	.75
65 Josh Beckett	.40
66 Jason Varitek	.50
67 Ken Griffey Jr.	1.50
68 Adam Dunn	.50
69 Todd Helton	.50
70 Garrett Atkins	.25
71 Reggie Sanders	.25
72 Mike Sweeney	.25
73 Chris Shelton	.25
74 Ivan Rodriguez	.50
75 Johan Santana	.75
76 Torii Hunter	.40
77 Justin Morneau	.50
78 Jim Thome	.50
79 Paul Konerko	.40
80 Scott Podsednik	.40
81 Derek Jeter	2.00
82 Hideki Matsui	1.50
83 Johnny Damon	.75
84 Alex Rodriguez	2.00
85 Conor Jackson (RC)	8.00
86 Joey Devine RC	5.00
87 Jonathan Papelbon (RC)	20.00
88 Freddie Bynum (RC)	5.00
89 Chris Denorfia (RC)	8.00
90 Ryan Shealy (RC)	5.00
91 Josh Wilson (RC)	5.00
92 Brian Anderson (RC)	5.00
93 Justin Verlander (RC)	15.00
94 Jeremy Hermida (RC)	5.00
95 Josh Johnson (RC)	5.00
96 Hanley Ramirez (RC)	8.00
97 Josh Willingham (RC)	8.00
98 Cole Hamels (RC)	10.00
99 Hong-Chih Kuo (RC)	15.00
100 Cody Ross (RC)	8.00
101 Jose Capellan (RC)	5.00
102 Prince Fielder (RC)	15.00
103 Dave Gassner (RC)	5.00
104 Jason Kubel (RC)	5.00
105 Francisco Liriano (RC)	10.00
106 Anderson Hernandez (RC)	5.00
107 Bonser (RC)	8.00
108 Boof Bonser (RC)	8.00
109 Jered Weaver (RC)	15.00
110 Ben Johnson (RC)	5.00
111 Jeff Harris RC	
112 Stephen Drew (RC)	10.00
113 Matt Cain (RC)	5.00
114 Skip Schumaker (RC)	5.00
115 Adam Wainwright (RC)	8.00
116 Jeremy Sowers (RC)	5.00
117 Jason Bergmann RC	5.00
118 Chad Billingsley (RC)	10.00
119 Ryan Zimmerman (RC)	15.00
120 Macay McBride (RC)	5.00
121 Aaron Rakers (RC)	5.00
122 Alay Soler RC	5.00
123 Melky Cabrera (RC)	15.00
124 Tim Hamulack (RC)	5.00
125 Andre Ethier (RC)	15.00
126 Kenji Johjima RC	15.00

Gold

Gold (1-84):	4-8X
Production 499 Sets	

Gold Autographs

	NM/M
Production 99 Sets	
85 Conor Jackson	25.00
86 Joey Devine	15.00
87 Jonathan Papelbon	75.00
88 Freddie Bynum	10.00
89 Chris Denorfia	10.00
90 Ryan Shealy	20.00
92 Brian Anderson	10.00
93 Justin Verlander	50.00
94 Jeremy Hermida	20.00
95 Mike Jacobs	10.00
96 Josh Johnson	20.00
97 Hanley Ramirez	25.00
98 Josh Willingham	25.00
99 Cole Hamels	60.00
101 Cody Ross	20.00
102 Jose Capellan	15.00
105 Jason Kubel	15.00
106 Francisco Liriano	50.00
107 Anderson Hernandez	10.00
108 Boof Bonser	15.00
109 Jered Weaver	40.00
110 Ben Johnson	15.00
111 Jeff Harris	15.00
113 Matt Cain	25.00
114 Skip Schumaker	15.00
115 Adam Wainwright	25.00
116 Jeremy Sowers	15.00
117 Jason Bergmann	10.00
118 Chad Billingsley	25.00
119 Ryan Zimmerman	90.00
120 Macay McBride	15.00
121 Aaron Rakers	10.00
122 Alay Soler	10.00
123 Melky Cabrera	50.00
124 Tim Hamulack	20.00
125 Andre Ethier	70.00

Apparel

	NM/M
Common Player:	4.00
BA Jason Bay	8.00
LB Lance Berkman	8.00
JB Jeremy Bonderman	8.00
AB A.J. Burnett	6.00
EC Eric Chavez	6.00
CC Carl Crawford	6.00
JE Jim Edmonds	8.00
PF Prince Fielder	10.00
CF Chone Figgins	6.00
JF Jeff Francoeur	10.00
JG Jonny Gomes	6.00
KG Khalil Greene	8.00
GR Ken Griffey Jr.	20.00
VG Vladimir Guerrero	8.00
HA Travis Hafner	8.00
JH J.J. Hardy	4.00
HE Todd Helton	8.00
FH Felix Hernandez	8.00
TH Trevor Hoffman	8.00
RH Ryan Howard	20.00
HU Torii Hunter	6.00
DJ Derek Jeter	25.00
JK Jeff Kent	6.00
RK Ryan Klesko	4.00
CL Carlos Lee	6.00
VM Victor Martinez	8.00
JM Joe Mauer	8.00
TN Trot Nixon	6.00
DO David Ortiz	15.00
RO Roy Oswalt	8.00
AO Akinori Otsuka	6.00
MP Mark Prior	6.00
AP Albert Pujols	25.00
MR Manny Ramirez	10.00
SR Scott Rolen	8.00
CS Chris Shelton	4.00
GS Grady Sizemore	8.00
HS Huston Street	6.00
MT Mark Teixeira	8.00
VW Vernon Wells	8.00
DW David Wright	15.00
RZ Ryan Zimmerman/SP	25.00

Center Stage

	NM/M
Common Player:	1.00
JB Josh Beckett	1.00
DC Daniel Cabrera	1.00
CA Miguel Cabrera	3.00
JC Jose Contreras	1.00
AC Aaron Cook	1.00
BC Bobby Crosby	1.00
MC Michael Cuddyer	1.00
DD David DeJesus	1.00
SD Stephen Drew	2.00
JF Jason Frasor	1.00

KG Ken Griffey Jr.	5.00
VG Vladimir Guerrero	3.00
FH Felix Hernandez	2.00
RH Runelvys Hernandez	1.00
DJ Derek Jeter	8.00
DL Derrek Lee	2.00
YM Yadier Molina	1.00
MP Mark Prior	2.00
AP Albert Pujols	8.00
FS Freddy Sanchez	1.00
CS Chris Shelton	1.00
IS Ian Snell	1.00
MT Mark Teixeira	2.00
CW Chien-Ming Wang	10.00
DW David Wright	4.00

Center Stage Signatures

No Pricing	
Production 25 Sets	

Curtain Calls

	NM/M
Common Player:	1.00
DC Daniel Cabrera	1.00
EC Eric Chavez	1.00
JC Jose Contreras	1.00
BC Bobby Crosby	1.00
DD David DeJesus	1.00
KG1 Ken Griffey Jr.	4.00
KG2 Ken Griffey Jr.	4.00
RH Rich Harden	1.00
HE Runelvys Hernandez	1.00
YM Yadier Molina	1.00
TO Tomokazu Ohka	1.00
MP Mark Prior	2.00
HR Horacio Ramirez	1.00
FS Freddy Sanchez	1.00
CS Chris Shelton	1.00
MT Miguel Tejada	2.00
CW Chien-Ming Wang	10.00
JE Jered Weaver	2.00
JW Josh Willingham	1.00
MY Michael Young	1.00

Curtain Calls Signatures

No Pricing	
Production 25 Sets	

Ovation Nation

	NM/M
Common Player:	2.00
JB Jason Bay	3.00
DC Daniel Cabrera	2.00
MC Miguel Cabrera	4.00
FC Frederich Cepeda	2.00
YG Yoandy Garlobo	2.00
KG Ken Griffey Jr.	8.00
DJ Derek Jeter	8.00
AJ Andruw Jones	4.00
SL Seung-Yeop Lee	4.00
DM Daisuke Matsuzaka	5.00
NM Nobuhiko Matsunaka	4.00
AP Albert Pujols	8.00
JS Johan Santana	3.00
JA Jae Weong Seo	2.00
MT Miguel Tejada	3.00

Ovation Nation Signatures

No Pricing	
Production 25 Sets	

Spotlight Signatures

	NM/M
Common Autograph:	10.00
JB Josh Beckett/SP	40.00
DC Daniel Cabrera	15.00
CA Miguel Cabrera	25.00
SC Shawn Camp	10.00
EC Eric Chavez/SP	15.00
JC Jose Contreras	30.00
AC Aaron Cook	6.00
LC Lance Cormier	10.00
BC Bobby Crosby	10.00
MC Michael Cuddyer/SP	10.00
DD David DeJesus	15.00
JD Jorge De La Rosa	10.00
JF Jason Frasor	15.00
FG Franklyn German	10.00
MG Mike Gonzalez	10.00
AG Andy Green	6.00
KG1 Ken Griffey Jr.	85.00
KG2 Ken Griffey Jr.	85.00
HA Rich Harden/SP	15.00
RH Runelvys Hernandez	10.00
EJ Edwin Jackson	10.00
YM Yadier Molina	25.00
FN Fernando Nieve	10.00
TO Tomokazu Ohka	30.00
MP Mark Prior	25.00

HR	Horacio Ramirez/SP	10.00
DR	David Ross	20.00
KS	Kirk Saarloos	10.00
FS	Freddy Sanchez	25.00
CS1	Chris Shelton	10.00
CS2	Chris Shelton	10.00
TE	Miguel Tejada/SP	25.00
MT	Matt Thornton	10.00
TR	Matt Treanor	20.00
RW	Ryan Wagner	10.00
CW	Chien-Ming Wang	200.00
JW	Josh Willingham/SP	15.00
MW	Mike Wuertz	15.00
MY	Michael Young	15.00

Superstar Theatre

		NM/M
Common Player:		1.00
BA	Jason Bay	2.00
JB	Josh Beckett	1.00
DC	Daniel Cabrera	1.00
MC	Miguel Cabrera	3.00
CC	Chris Carpenter	2.00
JC	Jose Contreras	1.00
BC	Bobby Crosby	1.00
DD	David DeJesus	1.00
KG1	Ken Griffey Jr.	6.00
KG2	Ken Griffey Jr.	6.00
TH	Travis Hafner	2.00
RH	Rich Harden	1.00
DJ	Derek Jeter	8.00
AJ	Andruw Jones	2.00
DL	Derrek Lee	3.00
PM	Pedro Martinez	3.00
HM	Hideki Matsui	4.00
YM	Yadier Molina	1.00
TO	Tomokazu Ohka	1.00
DO	David Ortiz	3.00
MP	Mark Prior	2.00
AP	Albert Pujols	8.00
MR	Manny Ramirez	3.00
AR	Alex Rodriguez	6.00
CS	Chris Shelton	1.00
IS	Ichiro Suzuki	6.00
TE	Mark Teixeira	2.00
MT	Miguel Tejada	2.00
CW	Chien-Ming Wang	10.00
MY	Michael Young	2.00

Superstar Theatre Signatures

No Pricing
Production 25 Sets

2006 Upper Deck Special FX

		NM/M
Complete Set (1025):		
Common Player:		.25
Common RC (901-1025):		.50
Pack (4):		5.00
Box (16):		75.00
1	Adam Kennedy	.25
2	Bartolo Colon	.25
3	Bengie Molina	.25
4	Casey Kotchman	.25
5	Chone Figgins	.25
6	Dallas McPherson	.25
7	Darin Erstad	.25
8	Ervin Santana	.50
9	Francisco Rodriguez	.25
10	Garret Anderson	.25
11	Jarrod Washburn	.25
12	John Lackey	.25
13	Juan Rivera	.25
14	Orlando Cabrera	.25
15	Paul Byrd	.25
16	Steve Finley	.25
17	Vladimir Guerrero	1.00
18	Alex Cintron	.25
19	Brandon Lyon	.25
20	Brandon Webb	.50
21	Chad Tracy	.25
22	Chris Snyder	.25
23	Claudio Vargas	.25
24	Conor Jackson	.50
25	Craig Counsell	.25
26	Javier Vazquez	.25
27	Jose Valverde	.25
28	Luis Gonzalez	.25
29	Royce Clayton	.25
30	Russ Ortiz	.25
31	Shawn Green	.25
32	Dustin Nippert	.25
33	Tony Clark	.25
34	Troy Glaus	.50
35	Adam LaRoche	.25
36	Andruw Jones	1.00
37	Craig Hansen	.50
38	Chipper Jones	1.00
39	Horacio Ramirez	.25
40	Jeff Francoeur	.50
41	John Smoltz	.50
42	Joey Devine	.25
43	Johnny Estrada	.25
44	Anthony Lerew	.25
45	Julio Franco	.25
46	Kyle Farnsworth	.25
47	Marcus Giles	.25
48	Mike Hampton	.25
49	Rafael Furcal	.50
50	Chuck James	.25
51	Tim Hudson	.50
52	B.J. Ryan	.25
53	Bernie Castro	.25
54	Brian Roberts	.25
55	Walter Young	.25
56	Daniel Cabrera	.25
57	Eric Byrnes	.25
58	Alejandro Freire	.25
59	Erik Bedard	.50
60	Javy Lopez	.25
61	Jay Gibbons	.25
62	Jorge Julio	.25
63	Luis Matos	.25
64	Melvin Mora	.25
65	Miguel Tejada	.75
66	Rafael Palmeiro	.75
67	Rodrigo Lopez	.25
68	Sammy Sosa	1.00
69	Alejandro Machado	.25
70	Bill Mueller	.25
71	Bronson Arroyo	.25
72	Curt Schilling	.75
73	David Ortiz	1.00
74	David Wells	.25
75	Edgar Renteria	.25
76	Ryan Jorgensen	.25
77	Jason Varitek	.75
78	Johnny Damon	1.00
79	Keith Foulke	.25
80	Kevin Youkilis	.50
81	Manny Ramirez	1.00
82	Matt Clement	.25
83	Hanley Ramirez	.50
84	Tim Wakefield	.25
85	Trot Nixon	.25
86	Wade Miller	.25
87	Aramis Ramirez	.50
88	Carlos Zambrano	.50
89	Corey Patterson	.25
90	Derek Lee	.75
91	Geovany Soto	.25
92	Greg Maddux	2.00
93	Jeromy Burnitz	.25
94	Jerry Hairston Jr.	.25
95	Kerry Wood	.50
96	Mark Prior	.75
97	Matt Murton	.25
98	Michael Barrett	.25
99	Neifi Perez	.25
100	Nomar Garciaparra	1.00
101	Rich Hill	.25
102	Ryan Dempster	.25
103	Todd Walker	.25
104	A.J. Pierzynski	.25
105	Aaron Rowand	.25
106	Bobby Jenks	.25
107	Carl Everett	.25
108	Dustin Hermanson	.25
109	Frank Thomas	1.00
110	Freddy Garcia	.25
111	Jermaine Dye	.25
112	Joe Crede	.50
113	Jon Garland	.25
114	Jose Contreras	.25
115	Juan Uribe	.25
116	Mark Buehrle	.25
117	Orlando Hernandez	.25
118	Paul Konerko	.75
119	Scott Podsednik	.25
120	Tadahito Iguchi	.25
121	Aaron Harang	.25
122	Adam Dunn	.75
123	Austin Kearns	.25
124	Brandon Claussen	.25
125	Chris Denorfia	.25
126	Edwin Encarnacion	.25
127	Miguel Perez	.25
128	Felipe Lopez	.25
129	Jason LaRue	.25
130	Ken Griffey Jr.	2.00
131	Chris Booker	.25
132	Luke Hudson	.25
133	Jason Bergmann	.25
134	Ryan Freel	.25
135	Sean Casey	.25
136	Wily Mo Pena	.25
137	Aaron Boone	.25
138	Ben Broussard	.25
139	Ryan Garko	.25
140	C.C. Sabathia	.25
141	Casey Blake	.25
142	Cliff Lee	.25
143	Coco Crisp	.25
144	David Riske	.25
145	Grady Sizemore	.50
146	Jake Westbrook	.25
147	Jhonny Peralta	.25
148	Josh Bard	.25
149	Kevin Millwood	.25
150	Ronnie Belliard	.25
151	Scott Elarton	.25
152	Travis Hafner	.50
153	Victor Martinez	.25
154	Aaron Cook	.25
155	Aaron Miles	.25
156	Brad Hawpe	.25
157	Mike Esposito	.25
158	Chin-Hui Tsao	.25
159	Clint Barmes	.25
160	Cory Sullivan	.25
161	Garrett Atkins	.25
162	J.D. Closser	.25
163	Jason Jennings	.25
164	Jeff Baker	.25
165	Jeff Francis	.25
166	Luis Gonzalez	.25
167	Matt Holliday	.50
168	Todd Helton	.75
169	Brandon Inge	.25
170	Carlos Guillen	.25
171	Carlos Pena	.25
172	Chris Shelton	.25
173	Craig Monroe	.25
174	Curtis Granderson	.25
175	Dmitri Young	.25
176	Ivan Rodriguez	.75
177	Jason Johnson	.25
178	Jeremy Bonderman	.50
179	Magglio Ordonez	.25
180	Mark Woodyard	.25
181	Nook Logan	.25
182	Omar Infante	.25
183	Placido Polanco	.25
184	Chris Heintz	.25
185	A.J. Burnett	.25
186	Alex Gonzalez	.25
187	Josh Johnson	.25
188	Carlos Delgado	.75
189	Dontrelle Willis	.50
190	Josh Wilson	.25
191	Jason Vargas	.25
192	Jeff Conine	.25
193	Jeremy Hermida	.50
194	Josh Beckett	.25
195	Juan Encarnacion	.25
196	Juan Pierre	.25
197	Luis Castillo	.25
198	Miguel Cabrera	1.00
199	Mike Lowell	.25
200	Paul LoDuca	.25
201	Todd Jones	.25
202	Adam Everett	.25
203	Andy Pettitte	.50
204	Brad Ausmus	.25
205	Brad Lidge	.25
206	Brandon Backe	.25
207	Charlton Jimerson	.25
208	Chris Burke	.25
209	Craig Biggio	.50
210	Dan Wheeler	.25
211	Jason Lane	.25
212	Jeff Bagwell	.50
213	Lance Berkman	.50
214	Luke Scott	.25
215	Morgan Ensberg	.25
216	Roger Clemens	2.50
217	Roy Oswalt	.50
218	Willy Taveras	.25
219	Andres Blanco	.25
220	Angel Berroa	.25
221	Ruben Gotay	.25
222	David DeJesus	.25
223	Emil Brown	.25
224	J.P. Howell	.25
225	Jeremy Affeldt	.25
226	Jimmy Gobble	.25
227	John Buck	.25
228	Jose Lima	.25
229	Mark Teahen	.25
230	Matt Stairs	.25
231	Mike MacDougal	.25
232	Mike Sweeney	.25
233	Runelvys Hernandez	.25
234	Terrence Long	.25
235	Zack Greinke	.25
236	Ron Flores	.25
237	Brad Penny	.25
238	Cesar Izturis	.25
239	D.J. Houlton	.25
240	Derek Lowe	.25
241	Eric Gagne	.25
242	Hee Seop Choi	.25
243	J.D. Drew	.50
244	Jason Phillips	.25
245	Jason Repko	.25
246	Jayson Werth	.25
247	Jeff Kent	.50
248	Jeff Weaver	.25
249	Milton Bradley	.25
250	Odalis Perez	.25
251	Hong-Chih Kuo	.25
252	Oscar Robles	.25
253	Ben Sheets	.50
254	Bill Hall	.25
255	Brady Clark	.25
256	Carlos Lee	.50
257	Chris Capuano	.25
258	Nelson Cruz	.25
259	Derrick Turnbow	.25
260	Doug Davis	.25
261	Geoff Jenkins	.25
262	J.J. Hardy	.25
263	Lyle Overbay	.25
264	Prince Fielder	.75
265	Rickie Weeks	.50
266	Russell Branyan	.25
267	Tomokazu Ohka	.25
268	Jonah Bayliss	.25
269	Brad Radke	.25
270	Carlos Silva	.25
271	Francisco Liriano	.50
272	Jacque Jones	.25
273	Joe Mauer	.50
274	Travis Bowyer	.25
275	Joe Nathan	.25
276	Johan Santana	1.00
277	Justin Morneau	.75
278	Kyle Lohse	.25
279	Lew Ford	.25
280	Matthew LeCroy	.25
281	Michael Cuddyer	.25
282	Nick Punto	.25
283	Scott Baker	.25
284	Shannon Stewart	.25
285	Torii Hunter	.50
286	Braden Looper	.25
287	Carlos Beltran	.75
288	Cliff Floyd	.25
289	David Wright	1.50
290	Doug Mientkiewicz	.25
291	Anderson Hernandez	.25
292	Jose Reyes	1.00
293	Kazuo Matsui	.25
294	Kris Benson	.25
295	Miguel Cairo	.25
296	Mike Cameron	.25
297	Robert Andino	.25
298	Mike Piazza	1.00
299	Pedro Martinez	1.00
300	Tom Glavine	.50
301	Victor Diaz	.25
302	Tim Hamulack	.25
303	Alex Rodriguez	2.50
304	Bernie Williams	.50
305	Carl Pavano	.25
306	Chien-Ming Wang	1.00
307	Derek Jeter	2.50
308	Gary Sheffield	.50
309	Hideki Matsui	1.50
310	Jason Giambi	.75
311	Jorge Posada	.50
312	Kevin Brown	.25
313	Mariano Rivera	.50
314	Matt Lawton	.25
315	Mike Mussina	.50
316	Randy Johnson	1.00
317	Robinson Cano	.50
318	Michael Vento	.25
319	Tino Martinez	.25
320	Tony Womack	.25
321	Barry Zito	.50
322	Bobby Crosby	.25
323	Bobby Kielty	.25
324	Dan Johnson	.25
325	Danny Haren	.25
326	Eric Chavez	.50
327	Erubiel Durazo	.25
328	Huston Street	.25
329	Jason Kendall	.25
330	Jay Payton	.25
331	Joe Blanton	.25
332	Joe Kennedy	.25
333	Kirk Saarloos	.25
334	Mark Kotsay	.25
335	Nick Swisher	.50
336	Rich Harden	.25
337	Scott Hatteberg	.25
338	Billy Wagner	.25
339	Bobby Abreu	.50
340	Brett Myers	.25
341	Chase Utley	1.00
342	Danny Sandoval	.25
343	David Bell	.25
344	Gavin Floyd	.25
345	Jim Thome	.75
346	Jimmy Rollins	.50
347	Jon Lieber	.25
348	Kenny Lofton	.25
349	Mike Lieberthal	.25
350	Pat Burrell	.25
351	Randy Wolf	.25
352	Ryan Howard	1.50

#	Name		#	Name		#	Name		#	Name	
353	Vicente Padilla	.25	457	Gary Matthews	.25	561	Cliff Politte	.25	665	Bill Mueller	.25
354	Bryan Bullington	.25	458	Hank Blalock	.50	562	Javier Vazquez	.25	666	Brett Tomko	.25
355	J.J. Furmaniak	.25	459	Juan Dominguez	.25	563	Jim Thome	.75	667	Dioner Navarro	.25
356	Craig Wilson	.25	460	Josh Rupe	.25	564	Matt Thornton	.25	668	Jae Weong Seo	.25
357	Matt Capps	.25	461	Kenny Rogers	.25	565	Neal Cotts	.25	669	Jose Cruz	.25
358	Tom Gorzelanny	.25	462	Kevin Mench	.25	566	Pablo Ozuna	.25	670	Kenny Lofton	.25
359	Jack Wilson	.25	463	Laynce Nix	.25	567	Ross Gload	.25	671	Lance Carter	.25
360	Jason Bay	.50	464	Mark Teixeira	.75	568	Brandon Phillips	.25	672	Nomar Garciaparra	1.00
361	Jose Mesa	.25	465	Michael Young	.25	569	Bronson Arroyo	.25	673	Olmedo Saenz	.25
362	Josh Fogg	.25	466	Richard Hidalgo	.25	570	Dave Williams	.25	674	Rafael Furcal	.25
363	Kip Wells	.25	467	Jason Botts	.25	571	David Ross	.25	675	Ramon Martinez	.25
364	Steve Stemle	.25	468	Aaron Hill	.25	572	David Weathers	.25	676	Ricky Ledee	.25
365	Oliver Perez	.25	469	Alex Rios	.25	573	Eric Milton	.25	677	Sandy Alomar	.25
366	Robert Mackowiak	.25	470	Corey Koskie	.25	574	Javier Valentin	.25	678	Yhency Brazoban	.25
367	Ronny Paulino	.25	471	Chris Demaria	.25	575	Kent Mercker	.25	679	Corey Koskie	.25
368	Tike Redman	.25	472	Eric Hinske	.25	576	Matt Belisle	.25	680	Danny Kolb	.25
369	Zachary Duke	.25	473	Frank Catalanotto	.25	577	Paul Wilson	.25	681	Gabe Gross	.25
370	Adam Eaton	.25	474	John-Ford Griffin	.25	578	Rich Aurilia	.25	682	Jeff Cirillo	.25
371	Scott Feldman	.25	475	Gustavo Chacin	.25	579	Rick White	.25	683	Matt Wise	.25
372	Brian Giles	.25	476	Josh Towers	.25	580	Scott Hatteberg	.25	684	Rick Helling	.25
373	Brian Lawrence	.25	477	Miguel Batista	.25	581	Todd Coffey	.25	685	Chad Moeller	.25
374	Damian Jackson	.25	478	Orlando Hudson	.25	582	Bob Wickman	.25	686	David Bush	.25
375	Dave Roberts	.25	479	Reed Johnson	.25	583	Danny Graves	.25	687	Jorge De La Rosa	.25
376	Jake Peavy	.50	480	Roy Halladay	.50	584	Eduardo Perez	.25	688	Justin Lehr	.25
377	Joe Randa	.25	481	Shaun Marcum	.25	585	Guillermo Mota	.25	689	Jason Bartlett	.25
378	Khalil Greene	.25	482	Shea Hillenbrand	.25	586	Jason Davis	.25	690	Jesse Crain	.25
379	Mark Loretta	.25	483	Ted Lilly	.25	587	Jason Johnson	.25	691	Juan Rincon	.25
380	Ramon Hernandez	.25	484	Vernon Wells	.50	588	Jason Michaels	.25	692	Luis Castillo	.25
381	Robert Fick	.25	485	Brad Wilkerson	.25	589	Rafael Betancourt	.25	693	Mike Redmond	.25
382	Ryan Klesko	.25	486	Darrell Rasner	.25	590	Ramon Vazquez	.25	694	Rondell White	.25
383	Trevor Hoffman	.25	487	Chad Cordero	.25	591	Scott Sauerbeck	.25	695	Tony Batista	.25
384	Woody Williams	.25	488	Cristian Guzman	.25	592	Todd Hollandsworth	.25	696	Juan Castro	.25
385	Xavier Nady	.25	489	Esteban Loaiza	.25	593	Brian Fuentes	.25	697	Luis Rodriguez	.25
386	Armando Benitez	.25	490	John Patterson	.25	594	Danny Ardoin	.25	698	Matt Guerrier	.25
387	Brad Hennessey	.25	491	Jose Guillen	.25	595	David Cortes	.25	699	Willie Eyre	.25
388	Brian Myrow	.25	492	Jose Vidro	.25	596	Eli Marrero	.25	700	Aaron Heilman	.25
389	Edgardo Alfonzo	.25	493	Livan Hernandez	.25	597	Jamey Carroll	.25	701	Billy Wagner	.25
390	J.T. Snow	.25	494	Marlon Byrd	.25	598	Jason Smith	.25	702	Carlos Delgado	.75
391	Jeremy Accardo	.25	495	Nick Johnson	.25	599	Josh Fogg	.25	703	Chad Bradford	.25
392	Jason Schmidt	.50	496	Preston Wilson	.25	600	Miguel Ojeda	.25	704	Chris Woodward	.25
393	Lance Niekro	.25	497	Ryan Church	.25	601	Mike DeJean	.25	705	Darren Oliver	.25
394	Matt Cain	.25	498	Ryan Zimmerman	.50	602	Ray King	.25	706	Duaner Sanchez	.25
395	Daniel Ortmeier	.25	499	Tony Armas	.25	603	Omar Quintanilla	.25	707	Endy Chavez	.25
396	Moises Alou	.50	500	Vinny Castilla	.25	604	Zach Day	.25	708	Jorge Julio	.25
397	Doug Clark	.25	501	Andy Green	.25	605	Fernando Rodney	.25	709	Jose Valentin	.25
398	Omar Vizquel	.25	502	Damion Easley	.25	606	Kenny Rogers	.25	710	Julio Franco	.25
399	Pedro Feliz	.25	503	Eric Byrnes	.25	607	Mike Maroth	.25	711	Paul LoDuca	.25
400	Randy Winn	.25	504	Jason Grimsley	.25	608	Nate Robertson	.25	712	Ramon Castro	.25
401	Ray Durham	.25	505	Jeff DaVanon	.25	609	Todd Jones	.25	713	Steve Trachsel	.25
402	Adrian Beltre	.50	506	Johnny Estrada	.25	610	Vance Wilson	.25	714	Victor Zambrano	.25
403	Eddie Guardado	.25	507	Luis Vizcaino	.25	611	Bobby Seay	.25	715	Xavier Nady	.25
404	Felix Hernandez	.50	508	Miguel Batista	.25	612	Chris Spurling	.25	716	Andy Phillips	.25
405	Gil Meche	.25	509	Orlando Hernandez	.25	613	Ramon Colon	.25	717	Bubba Crosby	.25
406	Ichiro Suzuki	1.50	510	Orlando Hudson	.25	614	Jason Grilli	.25	718	Jaret Wright	.25
407	Jamie Moyer	.25	511	Terry Mulholland	.25	615	Marcus Thames	.25	719	Kelly Stinnett	.25
408	Jeff Nelson	.25	512	Chris Reitsma	.25	616	Ramon Santiago	.25	720	Kyle Farnsworth	.25
409	Jeremy Reed	.25	513	Edgar Renteria	.25	617	Alfredo Amezaga	.25	721	Mike Meyers	.25
410	Joel Pineiro	.25	514	John Thomson	.25	618	Brian Moehler	.25	722	Octavio Dotel	.25
411	Jaime Bubela	.25	515	Jorge Sosa	.25	619	Chris Aguila	.25	723	Ron Villone	.25
412	Raul Ibanez	.25	516	Oscar Villarreal	.25	620	Franklyn German	.25	724	Scott Proctor	.25
413	Richie Sexson	.50	517	Peter Orr	.25	621	Joe Borowski	.25	725	Shawn Chacon	.25
414	Ryan Franklin	.25	518	Ryan Langerhans	.25	622	Logan Kensing	.25	726	Tanyon Sturtze	.25
415	Willie Bloomquist	.25	519	Todd Pratt	.25	623	Matt Treanor	.25	727	Adam Melhuse	.25
416	Yorvit Torrealba	.25	520	Wilson Betemit	.25	624	Miguel Olivo	.25	728	Brad Halsey	.25
417	Yuniesky Betancourt	.25	521	Brian Jordan	.25	625	Sergio Mitre	.25	729	Esteban Loaiza	.25
418	Jeff Harris	.25	522	Lance Cormier	.25	626	Todd Wellemeyer	.25	730	Frank Thomas	1.00
419	Albert Pujols	2.50	523	Matt Diaz	.25	627	Wes Helms	.25	731	Jay Witasick	.25
420	Chris Carpenter	.75	524	Mike Remlinger	.25	628	Chad Qualls	.25	732	Justin Duchscherer	.25
421	David Eckstein	.50	525	Bruce Chen	.25	629	Eric Bruntlett	.25	733	Kiko Calero	.25
422	Jason Isringhausen	.25	526	Chris Gomez	.25	630	Mike Gallo	.25	734	Marco Scutaro	.25
423	Jason Marquis	.25	527	Chris Ray	.25	631	Mike Lamb	.25	735	Mark Ellis	.25
424	Adam Wainwright	.25	528	Corey Patterson	.25	632	Orlando Palmeiro	.25	736	Milton Bradley	.25
425	Jim Edmonds	.50	529	David Newhan	.25	633	Russ Springer	.25	737	Aaron Fultz	.25
426	Ryan Theriot	.25	530	Ed Rogers	.25	634	Dan Wheeler	.25	738	Aaron Rowand	.25
427	Tim Duncan	.25	531	John Halama	.25	635	Eric Munson	.25	739	Geoff Geary	.25
428	Mark Grudzielanek	.25	532	Kris Benson	.25	636	Preston Wilson	.25	740	Arthur Rhodes	.25
429	Mark Mulder	.50	533	LaTroy Hawkins	.25	637	Trever Miller	.25	741	Chris Coste	.25
430	Matt Morris	.25	534	Raul Chavez	.25	638	Ambiorix Burgos	.25	742	Rheal Cormier	.25
431	Reggie Sanders	.25	535	Alex Cora	.25	639	Andrew Sisco	.25	743	Ryan Franklin	.25
432	Scott Rolen	1.00	536	Alex Gonzalez	.25	640	Denny Bautista	.25	744	Ryan Madson	.25
433	Tyler Johnson	.25	537	Coco Crisp	.25	641	Doug Mientkiewicz	.25	745	Sal Fasano	.25
434	Yadier Molina	.25	538	David Riske	.25	642	Elmer Dessens	.25	746	Tom Gordon	.25
435	Alex Gonzalez	.25	539	Doug Mirabelli	.25	643	Esteban German	.25	747	Abraham Nunez	.25
436	Aubrey Huff	.25	540	Josh Beckett	.50	644	Joe Nelson	.25	748	David Dellucci	.25
437	Tim Corcoran	.25	541	J.T. Snow	.25	645	Mark Grudzielanek	.25	749	Julio Santana	.25
438	Carl Crawford	.50	542	Mike Timlin	.25	646	Mark Redman	.25	750	Shane Victorino	.25
439	Casey Fossum	.25	543	Julian Tavarez	.25	647	Mike Wood	.25	751	Damaso Marte	.25
440	Danys Baez	.25	544	Rudy Seanez	.25	648	Paul Bako	.25	752	Freddy Sanchez	.25
441	Edwin Jackson	.25	545	Wily Mo Pena	.25	649	Reggie Sanders	.25	753	Humberto Cota	.25
442	Joey Gathright	.25	546	Bob Howry	.25	650	Scott Elarton	.25	754	Jeromy Burnitz	.25
443	Jonny Gomes	.25	547	Glendon Rusch	.25	651	Shane Costa	.25	755	Joe Randa	.25
444	Jorge Cantu	.25	548	Henry Blanco	.25	652	Tony Graffanino	.25	756	Jose Castillo	.25
445	Julio Lugo	.25	549	Jacque Jones	.25	653	Jason Bulger	.25	757	Mike Gonzalez	.25
446	Nick Green	.25	550	Jerome Williams	.25	654	Chris Bootcheck	.25	758	Ryan Doumit	.25
447	Rocco Baldelli	.25	551	John Mabry	.25	655	Esteban Yan	.25	759	Sean Burnett	.25
448	Scott Kazmir	.50	552	Juan Pierre	.25	656	Hector Carrasco	.25	760	Sean Casey	.25
449	Seth McClung	.25	553	Scott Eyre	.25	657	J.C. Romero	.25	761	Ian Snell	.25
450	Toby Hall	.25	554	Scott Williamson	.25	658	Jeff Weaver	.25	762	John Grabow	.25
451	Travis Lee	.25	555	Wade Miller	.25	659	Jose Molina	.25	763	Jose Hernandez	.25
452	Craig Breslow	.25	556	Will Ohman	.25	660	Kelvim Escobar	.25	764	Roberto Hernandez	.25
453	Alfonso Soriano	1.00	557	Alex Cintron	.25	661	Maicer Izturis	.25	765	Ryan Vogelsong	.25
454	Chris Young	.25	558	Robert Mackowiak	.25	662	Robb Quinlan	.25	766	Victor Sanchez	.25
455	David Dellucci	.25	559	Brandon McCarthy	.25	663	Scot Shields	.25	767	Adrian Gonzalez	.25
456	Francisco Cordero	.25	560	Chris Widger	.25	664	Tim Salmon	.25	768	Alan Embree	.25

769	Brian Sweeney	.25
770	Chan Ho Park	.25
771	Clay Hensley	.25
772	Dewon Brazelton	.25
773	Doug Brocail	.25
774	Eric Young	.25
775	Geoff Blum	.25
776	Josh Bard	.25
777	Mark Bellhorn	.25
778	Mike Cameron	.25
779	Mike Piazza	1.00
780	Rob Bowen	.25
781	Scott Cassidy	.25
782	Scott Linebrink	.25
783	Shawn Estes	.25
784	Terrmel Sledge	.25
785	Vinny Castilla	.25
786	Jeff Fassero	.25
787	Jose Vizcaino	.25
788	Mark Sweeney	.25
789	Matt Morris	.25
790	Steve Finley	.25
791	Tim Worrell	.25
792	Jamey Wright	.25
793	Jason Ellison	.25
794	Noah Lowry	.25
795	Steve Kline	.25
796	Todd Greene	.25
797	Carl Everett	.25
798	George Sherrill	.25
799	J.J. Putz	.25
800	Jake Woods	.25
801	Jose Lopez	.25
802	Julio Mateo	.25
803	Mike Morse	.25
804	Rafael Soriano	.25
805	Roberto Petagine	.25
806	Aaron Miles	.25
807	Braden Looper	.25
808	Gary Bennett	.25
809	Hector Luna	.25
810	Jeff Suppan	.25
811	John Rodriguez	.25
812	Josh Hancock	.25
813	Juan Encarnacion	.25
814	Larry Bigbie	.25
815	Scott Spiezio	.25
816	Sidney Ponson	.25
817	So Taguchi	.25
818	Brian Meadows	.25
819	Damon Hollins	.25
820	Dan Miceli	.25
821	Doug Waechter	.25
822	Jason Childers	.25
823	Josh Paul	.25
824	Julio Lugo	.25
825	Mark Hendrickson	.25
826	Sean Burroughs	.25
827	Shawn Camp	.25
828	Travis Harper	.25
829	Ty Wigginton	.25
830	Adam Eaton	.25
831	Adrian Brown	.25
832	Akinori Otsuka	.25
833	Antonio Alfonseca	.25
834	Brad Wilkerson	.25
835	D'Angelo Jimenez	.25
836	Gerald Laird	.25
837	Joaquin Benoit	.25
838	Kameron Loe	.25
839	Kevin Millwood	.25
840	Mark DeRosa	.25
841	Phil Nevin	.25
842	Rod Barajas	.25
843	Vicente Padilla	.25
844	A.J. Burnett	.25
845	Bengie Molina	.25
846	Gregg Zaun	.25
847	John McDonald	.25
848	Lyle Overbay	.25
849	Russ Adams	.25
850	Troy Glaus	.50
851	Vinnie Chulk	.25
852	B.J. Ryan	.25
853	Justin Speier	.25
854	Pete Walker	.25
855	Scott Downs	.25
856	Scott Schoeneweis	.25
857	Alfonso Soriano	1.00
858	Brian Schneider	.25
859	Daryle Ward	.25
860	Felix Rodriguez	.25
861	Gary Majewski	.25
862	Joey Eischen	.25
863	Jon Rauch	.25
864	Marlon Anderson	.25
865	Matthew LeCroy	.25
866	Mike Stanton	.25
867	Ramon Ortiz	.25
868	Robert Fick	.25
869	Royce Clayton	.25
870	Ryan Drese	.25
871	Vladimir Guerrero	.50
872	Craig Biggio	.25
873	Barry Zito	.25
874	Vernon Wells	.25
875	Chipper Jones	.50
876	Prince Fielder	.50
877	Albert Pujols	1.50
878	Greg Maddux	1.00
879	Carl Crawford	.25
880	Brandon Webb	.25
881	J.D. Drew	.25
882	Jason Schmidt	.25
883	Victor Martinez	.25
884	Ichiro Suzuki	.75
885	Miguel Cabrera	.50
886	David Wright	.75
887	Alfonso Soriano	.50
888	Miguel Tejada	.25
889	Khalil Greene	.25
890	Ryan Howard	1.00
891	Jason Bay	.25
892	Mark Teixeira	.50
893	Manny Ramirez	.75
894	Ken Griffey Jr.	1.00
895	Todd Helton	.50
896	Angel Berroa	.25
897	Ivan Rodriguez	.50
898	Johan Santana	.50
899	Paul Konerko	.50
900	Derek Jeter	1.50
901	Macay McBride (RC)	.50
902	Tony Pena (RC)	.50
903	Peter Moylan RC	.75
904	Aaron Rakers (RC)	.50
905	Chris Britton RC	.75
906	Nicholas Markakis (RC)	1.00
907	Sendy Rleal RC	.50
908	Val Majewski (RC)	.50
909	Jermaine Van Buren (RC)	.50
910	Jonathan Papelbon (RC)	3.00
911	Angel Pagan (RC)	.50
912	David Aardsma (RC)	.50
913	Sean Marshall (RC)	.50
914	Brian Anderson (RC)	.50
915	Freddie Bynum (RC)	.50
916	Fausto Carmona (RC)	.50
917	Kelly Shoppach (RC)	.50
918	Choo Freeman (RC)	.50
919	Ryan Shealy (RC)	.50
920	Joel Zumaya (RC)	2.00
921	Jordan Tata RC	1.00
922	Justin Verlander (RC)	2.00
923	Carlos Martinez RC	.50
924	Chris Resop (RC)	.50
925	Dan Uggla (RC)	.50
926	Eric Reed (RC)	.50
927	Hanley Ramirez (RC)	1.00
928	Yusmeiro Petit (RC)	.50
929	Josh Willingham (RC)	.50
930	Mike Jacobs (RC)	.50
931	Reggie Abercrombie (RC)	.50
932	Ricky Nolasco (RC)	.50
933	Scott Olsen (RC)	.50
934	Fernando Nieve (RC)	.50
935	Taylor Buchholz (RC)	.50
936	Cody Ross (RC)	.50
937	James Loney (RC)	.50
938	Takashi Saito RC	1.00
939	Tim Hamulack RC	.50
940	Chris Demaria RC	.50
941	Jose Capellan (RC)	.50
942	Dave Gassner (RC)	.50
943	Jason Kubel (RC)	.50
944	Brian Bannister (RC)	.50
945	Mike Thompson RC	.50
946	Cole Hamels (RC)	2.00
947	Paul Maholm (RC)	.50
948	John Van Benschoten (RC)	.50
949	Nate McLouth (RC)	.50
950	Ben Johnson (RC)	.50
951	Josh Barfield (RC)	.50
952	Travis Ishikawa (RC)	.50
953	Jack Taschner (RC)	.50
954	Kenji Johjima RC	3.00
955	Skip Schumaker (RC)	.50
956	Ruddy Lugo (RC)	.50
957	Jason Hammel (RC)	.50
958	Chris Roberson (RC)	.50
959	Fabio Castro RC	.50
960	Ian Kinsler (RC)	.50
961	John Koronka (RC)	.50
962	Brandon Watson (RC)	.50
963	Jon Lester RC	3.00
964	Ben Hendrickson (RC)	.50
965	Martin Prado (RC)	.50
966	Felix Aybar (RC)	.50
967	Bobby Livingston (RC)	.50
968	Ryan Spilborghs (RC)	.50
969	Tommy Murphy (RC)	.50
970	Howie Kendrick (RC)	1.50
971	Casey Janssen RC	.50
972	Michael O'Connor RC	.50
973	Conor Jackson (RC)	1.00
974	Jeremy Hermida (RC)	.50
975	Renyel Pinto (RC)	.50
976	Prince Fielder (RC)	2.00
977	Kevin Frandsen (RC)	.50
978	Ty Taubenheim RC	.50
979	Rich Hill (RC)	.50
980	Jonathan Broxton (RC)	.50
981	Jamie Shields RC	.50
982	Carlos Villanueva RC	1.00
983	Boone Logan RC	.50
984	Brian Wilson RC	.50
985	Andre Ethier (RC)	2.00
986	Michael Napoli (RC)	1.00
987	Agustin Montero (RC)	.50
988	Jack Hannahan (RC)	.50
989	Boof Bonser (RC)	.50
990	Carlos Ruiz (RC)	.50
991	Jason Botts (RC)	.50
992	Kendry Morales (RC)	.50
993	Alay Soler RC	.50
994	Santiago Ramirez (RC)	.50
995	Saul Rivera (RC)	.50
996	Anthony Reyes (RC)	1.00
997	Matthew Kemp (RC)	1.00
998	Jae-Kuk Ryu RC	1.50
999	Lastings Milledge (RC)	1.00
1000	Jered Weaver (RC)	2.00
1001	Jeremy Sowers (RC)	1.00
1002	Chad Billingsley (RC)	1.00
1003	Stephen Drew (RC)	2.00
1004	Tony Gwynn (RC)	.50
1005	Melky Cabrera (RC)	1.00
1006	Eliezer Alfonzo RC	.50
1007	Dana Eveland (RC)	.50
1008	Luis Figueroa RC	.50
1009	Emiliano Fruto RC	.50
1010	Clay Hensley (RC)	.50
1011	Zach Jackson (RC)	.50
1012	Bobby Keppel (RC)	.50
1013	Carlos Marmol (RC)	1.00
1014	Russell Martin (RC)	1.00
1015	Leo Nunez (RC)	.50
1016	Ken Ray (RC)	.50
1017	Mike Rouse (RC)	.50
1018	Kevin Thompson (RC)	.50
1019	C.J. Wilson (RC)	.50
1020	Steve Andrade (RC)	.50
1021	Ed Rogers (RC)	.50
1022	Joe Nelson (RC)	.50
1023	Omar Quintanilla (RC)	.50
1024	Chris Bootcheck (RC)	.50
1025	Jason Childers RC	.50

Blue

Blue (1-900):	1-1.5X
Blue RC:	1X
Inserted 1:4	

Green

Green (1-900):	2-3X
Green RC:	1-2X
Production 99 Sets	

Purple

Purple (1-900):	2-3X
Purple RC:	1-2X
Production 150 Sets	

Red

Red (1-900):	3-4X
Red RC:	2-3X
Production 50 Sets	

Materials

		NM/M
	Common Player:	5.00
JB	Jason Bay	8.00
LB	Lance Berkman	5.00
MC	Miguel Cabrera	10.00
MA	Matt Cain	10.00
CA	Chris Carpenter	5.00
CC	Carl Crawford	5.00
CR	Coco Crisp	5.00
AD	Adam Dunn	8.00
PF	Prince Fielder	15.00
RF	Rafael Furcal	5.00
JG	Jason Giambi	8.00
TG	Troy Glaus	5.00
KG	Ken Griffey Jr.	15.00
VG	Vladimir Guerrero	8.00
TH	Travis Hafner	8.00
HA	Roy Halladay	5.00
CH	Cole Hamels	15.00
JH	Jeremy Hermida	5.00
FH	Felix Hernandez	10.00
RH	Ryan Howard	20.00
DJ	Derek Jeter	20.00
KJ	Kenji Johjima	15.00
AJ	Andruw Jones	8.00
SK	Scott Kazmir	5.00
IK	Ian Kinsler	5.00
DL	Derek Lee	10.00
FL	Francisco Liriano	10.00
PM	Pedro Martinez	8.00
VM	Victor Martinez	5.00
JM	Joe Mauer	10.00
LM	Lastings Milledge	10.00
KM	Kendry Morales	5.00
DO	David Ortiz	15.00
JP	Jonathan Papelbon	15.00
AP	Albert Pujols	20.00
HR	Hanley Ramirez	5.00
JR	Jose Reyes	15.00
JS	Johan Santana	10.00
GS	Grady Sizemore	10.00
AS	Alfonso Soriano	8.00
MT	Mark Teixeira	8.00
TE	Miguel Tejada	8.00
JT	Jim Thome	10.00
CU	Chase Utley	15.00
JV	Justin Verlander	15.00
WE	Jered Weaver	10.00
RW	Rickie Weeks	10.00
JW	Josh Willingham	5.00
RZ	Ryan Zimmerman	15.00

Player Highlights

		NM/M
	Common Player:	.50
1	Andruw Jones	1.00
2	Manny Ramirez	1.00
3	Travis Hafner	.75
4	Johnny Damon	1.00
5	Miguel Cabrera	1.00
6	Chris Carpenter	1.00
7	Derek Lee	1.00
8	Jason Bay	.75
9	Jason Varitek	1.00
10	Ryan Howard	3.00
11	Mark Teixeira	1.00
12	Carlos Delgado	.75
13	Bartolo Colon	.50
14	David Wright	2.00
15	Miguel Tejada	.75
16	Mike Piazza	1.50
17	Paul Konerko	.75
18	Jermaine Dye	.50
19	Ichiro Suzuki	2.00
20	Brad Wilkerson	.50
21	Hideki Matsui	2.00
22	Albert Pujols	3.00
23	Chris Burke	.50
24	Derek Jeter	3.00
25	Brian Roberts	.50
26	David Ortiz	1.00
27	Alex Rodriguez	2.00
28	Ken Griffey Jr.	2.00
29	Prince Fielder	.75
30	Bobby Abreu	.75
31	Vladimir Guerrero	1.00
32	Tadahito Iguchi	.50
33	Jose Reyes	.75
34	Scott Podsednik	.50
35	Gary Sheffield	.75

Run Producers

		NM/M
	Common Player:	1.00
1	Ty Cobb	3.00
2	Derek Lee	1.50
3	Andruw Jones	1.50
4	David Ortiz	1.50
5	Lou Gehrig	4.00
6	Ken Griffey Jr.	4.00
7	Albert Pujols	5.00
8	Derek Jeter	5.00
9	Manny Ramirez	1.50
10	Alex Rodriguez	5.00
11	Gary Sheffield	1.00
12	Miguel Cabrera	1.50
13	Hideki Matsui	3.00
14	Vladimir Guerrero	1.50
15	David Wright	3.00
16	Mike Schmidt	1.50
17	Mark Teixeira	1.50
18	Babe Ruth	5.00
19	Jimmie Foxx	3.00
20	Honus Wagner	3.00

Special Endorsements

		NM/M
	Common Player:	5.00
	Inserted 1:16	
RA	Reggie Abercrombie	5.00
AC	Jeremy Accardo	5.00
BA	Brian Anderson	5.00
AN	Robert Andino	5.00
BR	Brian Bannister	8.00
JB	Jason Bay	20.00
BW	Craig Breslow	8.00
CB	Chris Britton	5.00
TB	Taylor Buchholz	10.00
FB	Freddie Bynum	8.00
MI	Miguel Cabrera	20.00
MC	Matt Cain	20.00
JC	Jose Capellan/SP	8.00

CM	Matt Capps	5.00
FC	Fausto Carmona	8.00
TC	Tim Corcoran	5.00
DE	Chris Denorfia	8.00
JD	Joey Devine	8.00
AE	Andre Ethier	20.00
EV	Dana Eveland	10.00
RF	Ron Flores	5.00
KF	Kevin Frandsen	8.00
DG	Dave Gassner	8.00
KG	Ken Griffey Jr.	60.00
TH	Travis Hafner	15.00
CH	Cole Hamels	40.00
HC	Craig Hansen/SP	
BH	Brendan Harris	5.00
HA	Jeff Harris	5.00
HG	Keith Hattig	8.00
HE	Jeremy Hermida	15.00
AH	Anderson Hernandez/SP	5.00
JU	Justin Huber	8.00
JA	Conor Jackson	15.00
MJ	Mike Jacobs	8.00
DJ	Derek Jeter	200.00
BJ	Ben Johnson	8.00
JJ	Josh Johnson	10.00
KE	Howie Kendrick	20.00
IK	Ian Kinsler	15.00
KO	John Koronka	8.00
JK	Jason Kubel	8.00
HK	Hong-Chih Kuo	40.00
FL	Francisco Liriano	20.00
BL	Boone Logan	5.00
RL	Ruddy Lugo	5.00
PM	Paul Maholm	8.00
SM	Sean Marshall	10.00
NI	Nick Massett	8.00
MM	Macay McBride	8.00
NM	Nate McLouth	8.00
KM	Kendry Morales	10.00
PE	Peter Moylan	8.00
FN	Fernando Nieve	5.00
WN	Wilbert Nieves	8.00
JP	Jonathan Papelbon	30.00
AA	Aaron Rakers	5.00
HR	Hanley Ramirez	20.00
RE	Chris Resop	5.00
RB	Chris Roberson	8.00
CR	Cody Ross	8.00
RC	Carlos Ruiz	10.00
RU	Josh Rupe	8.00
TS	Takashi Saito	25.00
RS	Ryan Shealy	10.00
JS	James Shields	20.00
KS	Kelly Shoppach	8.00
MS	Matt Smith	8.00
GS	Geovany Soto	8.00
DU	Dan Uggla	15.00
CU	Chase Utley	30.00
JV	John Van Benschoten	5.00
VE	Justin Verlander/SP	30.00
AW	Adam Wainwright	20.00
JW	Jered Weaver	20.00
RW	Rickie Weeks	15.00
WI	Josh Willingham	15.00
DW	Dontrelle Willis	15.00
JO	Josh Wilson	8.00
RZ	Ryan Zimmerman/SP	40.00
JZ	Joel Zumaya	15.00

Star Attractions

NM/M

Common Player: .50
Inserted 1:8

BA	Bobby Abreu	.75
JB	Josh Beckett	.50
CB	Carlos Beltran	1.00
LB	Lance Berkman	.75
JC	Jose Contreras	.50
JD	Johnny Damon	1.50
CD	Carlos Delgado	.75
JE	Jim Edmonds	.75
JG	Jason Giambi	1.00
KG	Ken Griffey Jr.	3.00
RH	Rich Harden	.50
DJ	Derek Jeter	4.00
AJ	Andruw Jones	1.00
CJ	Chipper Jones	1.50
DL	Derrek Lee	1.50
GM	Greg Maddux	3.00
PM	Pedro Martinez	1.50
JM	Joe Mauer	1.00
MO	Magglio Ordonez	.50
DO	David Ortiz	1.50
PU	Albert Pujols	4.00
MR	Manny Ramirez	1.50
JR	Jose Reyes	1.50
CS	Curt Schilling	1.50
JS	Jason Schmidt	.50
SM	John Smoltz	.75
AS	Alfonso Soriano	1.50
MT	Mark Teixeira	1.00
DW	Dontrelle Willis	.50
WR	David Wright	2.50

WBC Counterparts

NM/M

Common Duo: 1.00
Inserted 1:6

1	Yulieski Gourriel, Daisuke Matsuzaka	5.00
2	Ken Griffey Jr., Yoandy Garlobo	3.00
3	Ken Griffey Jr., Ichiro Suzuki	3.00
4	Derek Jeter, Chin-Lung Hu	4.00
5	Frederich Cepeda, Jong Beom Lee	1.00
6	Nobuhiko Matsunaka, Seung-Yeop Lee	2.00
7	Tsuyoshi Nishioka, Guangbiao Liu	1.00
8	Ichiro Suzuki, Osmany Urrutia	2.50
9	Daisuke Matsuzaka, Roger Clemens	8.00
10	Yadel Marti, Chan Ho Park	1.00
11	Koji Uehara, Jae Weong Seo	1.00
12	Shunsuke Watanabe, Bartolo Colon	2.00
13	Daisuke Matsuzaka, Johan Santana	5.00
14	Pedro Luis Lazo, Freddy Garcia	1.00
15	Koji Uehara, Roger Clemens	3.00

2006 Upper Deck Sweet Spot

NM/M

Complete Set (184):		
Common Player:		.25
Common Auto. (101-184):		15.00
Production 45-275		
Pack (5):		10.00
Box (12):		110.00
1	Bartolo Colon	.25
2	Garret Anderson	.25
3	Francisco Rodriguez	.25
4	Dallas McPherson	.25
5	Andy Pettitte	.40
6	Lance Berkman	.50
7	Willy Taveras	.25
8	Bobby Crosby	.25
9	Danny Haren	.25
10	Nick Swisher	.40
11	Vernon Wells	.50
12	Orlando Hudson	.25
13	Roy Halladay	.50
14	Andruw Jones	.75
15	Chipper Jones	.75
16	Jeff Francoeur	.40
17	John Smoltz	.50
18	Carlos Lee	.40
19	Rickie Weeks	.40
20	Bill Hall	.25
21	Jim Edmonds	.40
22	David Eckstein	.25
23	Mark Mulder	.40
24	Aramis Ramirez	.25
25	Greg Maddux	1.50
26	Nomar Garciaparra	.75
27	Carlos Zambrano	.40
28	Scott Kazmir	.40
29	Jorge Cantu	.25
30	Carl Crawford	.40
31	Luis Gonzalez	.25
32	Troy Glaus	.40
33	Shawn Green	.25
34	Jeff Kent	.40
35	Milton Bradley	.25
36	Cesar Izturis	.25
37	Omar Vizquel	.25
38	Moises Alou	.40
39	Randy Winn	.25
40	Jason Schmidt	.40
41	Coco Crisp	.25
42	C.C. Sabathia	.40
43	Cliff Lee	.25
44	Ichiro Suzuki	1.50
45	Richie Sexson	.25
46	Jeremy Reed	.25
47	Carlos Delgado	.50
48	Miguel Cabrera	.75
49	Luis Castillo	.25
50	Carlos Beltran	.50
51	Tom Glavine	.50
52	David Wright	1.50
53	Cliff Floyd	.25
54	Chad Cordero	.25
55	Jose Vidro	.25
56	Jose Guillen	.25
57	Nick Johnson	.25
58	Miguel Tejada	.50
59	Melvin Mora	.25
60	Javy Lopez	.25
61	Khalil Greene	.25
62	Brian Giles	.25
63	Trevor Hoffman	.25
64	Bobby Abreu	.40
65	Jimmy Rollins	.50
66	Pat Burrell	.40
67	Billy Wagner	.25
68	Jack Wilson	.25
69	Zachary Duke	.25
70	Craig Wilson	.25
71	Mark Teixeira	.50
72	Hank Blalock	.40
73	David Dellucci	.25
74	Manny Ramirez	.75
75	Johnny Damon	.75
76	Jason Varitek	.50
77	Trot Nixon	.25
78	Adam Dunn	.50
79	Felipe Lopez	.25
80	Brandon Claussen	.25
81	Sean Casey	.25
82	Todd Helton	.50
83	Clint Barmes	.25
84	Matt Holliday	.50
85	Mike Sweeney	.25
86	Zack Greinke	.25
87	David DeJesus	.25
88	Ivan Rodriguez	.50
89	Jeremy Bonderman	.25
90	Magglio Ordonez	.25
91	Torii Hunter	.40
92	Joe Nathan	.25
93	Michael Cuddyer	.25
94	Paul Konerko	.50
95	Jermaine Dye	.25
96	Jon Garland	.25
97	Alex Rodriguez	2.00
98	Hideki Matsui	1.50
99	Jason Giambi	.50
100	Mariano Rivera	.40
101	Adrian Beltre/99	25.00
102	Matt Cain/99 (RC)	30.00
103	Craig Biggio/99	35.00
104	Eric Chavez/99	25.00
105	J.D. Drew/99	25.00
106	Eric Gagne/99	50.00
107	Tim Hudson/99	40.00
108	Tom Glavine/275	40.00
109	David Ortiz/99	85.00
110	Scott Rolen/275	40.00
111	Johan Santana/99	50.00
112	Curt Schilling/96	75.00
113	John Smoltz/99	75.00
114	Alfonso Soriano/99	40.00
115	Kerry Wood/99	25.00
116	Edwin Jackson/99	20.00
117	Felix Hernandez/125	50.00
118	Prince Fielder/99 (RC)	100.00
119	Vladimir Guerrero/86	50.00
120	Roger Clemens/99	140.00
121	Albert Pujols/45	250.00
122	Chris Carpenter/99	50.00
123	Derrek Lee/99	40.00
124	Dontrelle Willis/99	30.00
125	Roy Oswalt/99	35.00
126	Ryan Garko/275 (RC)	25.00
127	Tadahito Iguchi/275	60.00
128	Mark Loretta/275	25.00
129	Joe Mauer/275	40.00
130	Victor Martinez/275	30.00
131	Wily Mo Pena/275	30.00
132	Oliver Perez/274	15.00
133	Corey Patterson/275	25.00
134	Ben Sheets/275	20.00
135	Michael Young/275	25.00
136	Jonny Gomes/275	25.00
137	Derek Jeter/275	175.00
138	Ken Griffey Jr./275	100.00
139	Ryan Zimmerman/275 (RC)	60.00
140	Scott Baker/275 (RC)	20.00
141	Huston Street/275	30.00
142	Jason Bay/275	25.00
143	Ryan Howard/275	75.00
144	Travis Hafner/275	35.00
145	Brian Myrow/275 (RC)	20.00
146	Scott Podsednik/275	35.00
147	Brian Roberts/275	25.00
148	Miguel Cabrera	.75

146	Brian Myrow/275 (RC)	20.00
147	Scott Podsednik/275	35.00
148	Brian Roberts/275	25.00
149	Grady Sizemore/135	45.00
150	Chris Demaria/275 RC	15.00
151	Jonah Bayliss/275 RC	20.00
152	Geovany Soto/275 (RC)	20.00
153	Lyle Overbay/275	20.00
154	Joey Devine/275 RC	20.00
155	Alejandro Freire/275 RC	15.00
156	Conor Jackson/275 (RC)	35.00
157	Danny Sandoval/275 RC	15.00
158	Chase Utley/275	50.00
159	Jeff Harris/275 RC	20.00
160	Ron Flores/275 RC	20.00
161	Scott Feldman/275 RC	20.00
162	Yadier Molina/275	30.00
163	Tim Corcoran/275 RC	20.00
164	Craig Hansen/275 RC	40.00
165	Jason Bergmann/275 RC	25.00
166	Craig Breslow/275 RC	25.00
167	Jhonny Peralta/275	30.00
168	Jeremy Hermida/275 (RC)	30.00
169	Scott Kazmir/275	25.00
170	Bobby Crosby/99	25.00
171	Rich Harden/275	25.00
172	Casey Kotchman/275	15.00
173	Tim Hamulack/275 (RC)	15.00
174	Justin Morneau/275	30.00
175	Jake Peavy/275	30.00
176	Yuniesky Betancourt/275	30.00
177	Jeremy Accardo/275 RC	20.00
178	Jorge Cantu/200	25.00
179	Marlon Byrd/275	20.00
180	Ryan Jorgensen/275 RC	20.00
181	Chris Denorfia/275 (RC)	20.00
182	Steve Stemle/275	15.00
183	Robert Andino/275 RC	20.00
184	Chris Heintz/275 RC	15.00

Signature Bat Barrel Black Ink

NM/M

Production 13-25

107	Tim Hudson/25	50.00
110	Scott Rolen/25	50.00
111	Johan Santana/25	60.00
115	Kerry Wood/25	30.00
117	Felix Hernandez/25	60.00
118	Prince Fielder/25	100.00
119	Vladimir Guerrero/25	75.00
121	Albert Pujols/25	275.00
125	Roy Oswalt/25	40.00
127	Tadahito Iguchi/25	90.00
131	Wily Mo Pena/25	40.00
139	Ryan Zimmerman/25	100.00
143	Ryan Howard/25	90.00
151	Jonah Bayliss/25	30.00
153	Lyle Overbay/25	30.00
154	Joey Devine/25	30.00
160	Ron Flores/25	30.00
167	Jhonny Peralta/25	30.00
174	Justin Morneau/25	50.00
178	Jorge Cantu/25	40.00
182	Steve Stemle/25	25.00

Signature Bat Barrel Blue Ink

No Pricing
Production 3-5 Sets

Signature Black Stitch Black Ink

No Pricing
Production One Set
Blue Ink: No Pricing
Production One Set

Signature Glove Leather Black Ink

No Pricing
Production 5-15
Blue Ink: No Pricing
Production 5-15

Signature Red Stitch Blue Ink

NM/M

Production 15-150

101	Adrian Beltre/25	35.00
102	Matt Cain/150	40.00
103	Craig Biggio/25	50.00
106	Eric Gagne/25	60.00
107	Tim Hudson/25	40.00
109	David Ortiz/25	120.00
110	Scott Rolen/150	40.00
111	Johan Santana/25	60.00
112	Curt Schilling/25	100.00
113	John Smoltz/25	90.00
116	Edwin Jackson/150	20.00
118	Prince Fielder/25	100.00
119	Vladimir Guerrero/25	80.00
122	Chris Carpenter/25	60.00
123	Derrek Lee/25	50.00
124	Dontrelle Willis/25	40.00
125	Roy Oswalt/25	40.00
126	Ryan Garko/150	25.00
127	Tadahito Iguchi/150	75.00
128	Mark Loretta/114	35.00
129	Joe Mauer/99	40.00
130	Victor Martinez/150	35.00
131	Wily Mo Pena/150	30.00
132	Oliver Perez/135	15.00
133	Corey Patterson/150	30.00
134	Ben Sheets/150	25.00
135	Michael Young/150	30.00
136	Jonny Gomes/150	40.00
137	Derek Jeter/50	200.00
138	Ken Griffey Jr./150	100.00
139	Ryan Zimmerman/150	60.00
140	Scott Baker/150	20.00
141	Huston Street/150	40.00
142	Jason Bay/150	35.00
143	Ryan Howard/150	75.00
144	Mike Piazza/100	100.00
145	Travis Hafner/99	40.00
146	Brian Myrow/150	20.00
147	Scott Podsednik/150	40.00
148	Brian Roberts/150	25.00
149	Grady Sizemore/75	50.00
150	Chris Demaria/150	20.00
151	Jonah Bayliss/150	20.00
152	Geovany Soto/150	20.00
153	Lyle Overbay/150	20.00
154	Joey Devine/150	20.00
155	Alejandro Freire/150	40.00
156	Conor Jackson/150	40.00
157	Danny Sandoval/150	20.00
158	Chase Utley/150	50.00
159	Jeff Harris/150	20.00
160	Ron Flores/150	20.00
161	Scott Feldman/150	20.00
162	Yadier Molina/135	30.00
163	Tim Corcoran/150	20.00
164	Craig Hansen/150	40.00
165	Jason Bergmann/150	20.00
166	Craig Breslow/150	25.00
167	Jhonny Peralta/120	30.00
168	Jeremy Hermida/150	35.00
169	Scott Kazmir/150	35.00
170	Bobby Crosby/150	35.00
171	Rich Harden/150	25.00
172	Casey Kotchman/150	20.00
173	Tim Hamulack/150	20.00
174	Justin Morneau/150	35.00
175	Jake Peavy/150	30.00
176	Yuniesky Betancourt/150	30.00
177	Jeremy Accardo/150	25.00
178	Jorge Cantu/25	40.00
179	Marlon Byrd/40	30.00
180	Ryan Jorgensen/150	20.00
181	Chris Denorfia/150	25.00
182	Steve Stemle/150	15.00
183	Robert Andino/150	25.00
184	Chris Heintz/150	20.00

Signature Red-Blue Stitch Black Ink

NM/M

Production 25-99

101	Adrian Beltre/50	30.00
102	Matt Cain/99	40.00
103	Craig Biggio/50	50.00
105	J.D. Drew/50	30.00
106	Eric Gagne/50	50.00
107	Tim Hudson/50	40.00
108	Tom Glavine/99	50.00
109	David Ortiz/50	85.00
110	Scott Rolen/99	40.00
111	Johan Santana/50	50.00
112	Curt Schilling/45	80.00
113	John Smoltz/50	80.00
114	Alfonso Soriano/50	80.00
115	Kerry Wood/49	30.00
116	Edwin Jackson/50	20.00

117	Felix Hernandez/60	65.00
118	Prince Fielder/50	100.00
119	Vladimir Guerrero/50	50.00
120	Roger Clemens/50	150.00
121	Albert Pujols/25	250.00
122	Chris Carpenter/50	50.00
123	Derrek Lee/50	40.00
124	Dontrelle Willis/50	30.00
125	Roy Oswalt/50	40.00
126	Ryan Garko/99	30.00
127	Tadahito Iguchi/99	75.00
128	Mark Loretta/99	35.00
129	Joe Mauer/99	40.00
130	Victor Martinez/99	35.00
131	Wily Mo Pena/99	30.00
132	Oliver Perez/99	15.00
133	Corey Patterson/99	30.00
134	Ben Sheets/99	25.00
135	Michael Young/99	30.00
136	Jonny Gomes/99	40.00
137	Derek Jeter/50	175.00
138	Ken Griffey Jr./99	100.00
139	Ryan Zimmerman/99	75.00
140	Scott Baker/99	20.00
141	Huston Street/99	40.00
142	Jason Bay/99	35.00
143	Ryan Howard/99	75.00
145	Travis Hafner/99	40.00
146	Brian Myrow/99	20.00
147	Scott Podsednik/99	40.00
148	Brian Roberts/99	25.00
149	Grady Sizemore/99	50.00
150	Chris Demaria/99	20.00
151	Jonah Bayliss/99	20.00
152	Geovany Soto/99	20.00
153	Lyle Overbay/99	20.00
154	Joey Devine/99	20.00
155	Alejandro Freire/99	20.00
156	Conor Jackson/99	40.00
157	Danny Sandoval/99	20.00
158	Chase Utley/99	50.00
159	Jeff Harris/99	20.00
160	Ron Flores/99	20.00
161	Scott Feldman/99	20.00
162	Yadier Molina/99	30.00
163	Tim Corcoran/99	20.00
164	Craig Hansen/99	40.00
165	Jason Bergmann/99	20.00
166	Craig Breslow/99	25.00
167	Jhonny Peralta/90	30.00
168	Jeremy Hermida/99	35.00
169	Scott Kazmir/99	35.00
170	Bobby Crosby/99	25.00
171	Rich Harden/99	25.00
172	Casey Kotchman/99	20.00
173	Tim Hamulack/99	20.00
174	Justin Morneau/99	35.00
175	Jake Peavy/99	30.00
176	Yuniesky Betancourt/99	30.00
177	Jeremy Accardo/99	25.00
178	Jorge Cantu/99	30.00
179	Marlon Byrd/99	25.00
180	Ryan Jorgensen/99	20.00
181	Chris Denorfia/99	25.00
182	Steve Stemle/99	15.00
183	Robert Andino/91	25.00
184	Chris Heintz/99	20.00

Signature Red-Blue Stitch Blue Ink

NM/M

Production 10-50

102	Matt Cain/40	40.00
110	Scott Rolen/50	40.00
116	Edwin Jackson/50	20.00
127	Tadahito Iguchi/50	75.00
128	Mark Loretta/50	40.00
129	Joe Mauer/50	40.00
130	Victor Martinez/50	35.00
131	Wily Mo Pena/50	35.00
132	Oliver Perez/30	20.00
133	Corey Patterson/50	30.00
134	Ben Sheets/50	25.00
136	Jonny Gomes/50	30.00
138	Ken Griffey Jr./50	125.00
139	Ryan Zimmerman/50	75.00
140	Scott Baker/50	20.00
141	Huston Street/50	40.00
142	Jason Bay/50	40.00
143	Ryan Howard/50	75.00
144	Mike Piazza/50	140.00
145	Travis Hafner/50	50.00
146	Brian Myrow/50	20.00
147	Scott Podsednik/50	40.00
148	Brian Roberts/50	30.00
149	Grady Sizemore/25	60.00
150	Chris Demaria/50	20.00
151	Jonah Bayliss/50	20.00
152	Geovany Soto/50	20.00
153	Lyle Overbay/50	20.00
154	Joey Devine/50	20.00
155	Alejandro Freire/50	20.00

156	Conor Jackson/50	40.00
157	Danny Sandoval/50	20.00
158	Chase Utley/50	60.00
159	Jeff Harris/50	20.00
160	Ron Flores/50	20.00
161	Scott Feldman/50	20.00
162	Yadier Molina/30	40.00
163	Tim Corcoran/50	20.00
164	Craig Hansen/50	50.00
165	Jason Bergmann/50	20.00
166	Craig Breslow/50	25.00
167	Jhonny Peralta/50	35.00
168	Jeremy Hermida/50	40.00
170	Bobby Crosby/50	25.00
171	Rich Harden/50	25.00
172	Casey Kotchman/50	20.00
173	Tim Hamulack/50	20.00
174	Justin Morneau/50	35.00
175	Jake Peavy/49	30.00
177	Jeremy Accardo/50	25.00
178	Jorge Cantu/10	
180	Ryan Jorgensen/50	20.00
181	Chris Denorfia/50	25.00
182	Steve Stemle/50	15.00
183	Robert Andino/50	25.00
184	Chris Heintz/50	20.00

Super Sweet Swatch

NM/M

Production 299 Sets

Gold: 1-2X

Production 75 Sets

Platinum: 1.5-3X

Production 45 Sets

BA	Bobby Abreu	8.00
GA	Garret Anderson	5.00
AT	Garrett Atkins	5.00
JL	Jeff Bagwell	10.00
RB	Rocco Baldelli	8.00
JB	Jason Bay	10.00
BE	Josh Beckett	5.00
LB	Lance Berkman	10.00
CB	Craig Biggio	6.00
HB	Hank Blalock	6.00
MI	Miguel Cabrera	12.00
MA	Matt Cain	10.00
EC	Eric Chavez	5.00
BC	Brandon Claussen	5.00
MC	Matt Clement	5.00
CR	Bobby Crosby/136	5.00
CD	Carlos Delgado	8.00
ZD	Zachary Duke	5.00
AD	Adam Dunn	8.00
DY	Jermaine Dye	5.00
AE	Adam Eaton	5.00
ED	Jim Edmonds	8.00
JE	Johnny Estrada	5.00
PF	Prince Fielder	20.00
FR	Jeff Francoeur	10.00
EG	Eric Gagne	5.00
FG	Freddy Garcia	5.00
JG	Jason Giambi	10.00
BG	Brian Giles	5.00
MG	Marcus Giles	5.00
TG	Troy Glaus/160	8.00
GL	Tom Glavine	8.00
KG	Ken Griffey Jr.	30.00
VG	Vladimir Guerrero	12.00
HA	Travis Hafner	10.00
HY	Roy Halladay	8.00
TO	Todd Helton/232	10.00
FH	Felix Hernandez	10.00
HE	Ramon Hernandez	5.00
HO	Trevor Hoffman	5.00
RH	Ryan Howard	20.00
TH	Tim Hudson	8.00
HU	Torii Hunter	6.00
DJ	Derek Jeter	30.00
NJ	Nick Johnson	5.00
AJ	Andruw Jones	10.00
CJ	Chipper Jones	10.00
JJ	Jacque Jones	5.00
SK	Scott Kazmir	8.00
RK	Ryan Klesko	5.00
KO	Paul Konerko	10.00
DL	Derrek Lee	10.00
ML	Mark Loretta	6.00
NL	Noah Lowry	5.00
PM	Pedro Martinez	15.00
VM	Victor Martinez	8.00
JM	Joe Mauer	12.00
JU	Justin Morneau	8.00
MM	Mark Mulder	5.00
TN	Trot Nixon	5.00
DO	David Ortiz	12.00
RO	Roy Oswalt	8.00
JA	Jay Payton	5.00
PE	Jake Peavy	8.00
AN	Andy Pettitte	8.00
PI	Mike Piazza	15.00
JP	Jorge Posada	12.00
MP	Mark Prior	10.00
AP	Albert Pujols	30.00
MR	Manny Ramirez	12.00

JR	Jose Reyes	8.00
IR	Ivan Rodriguez/193	10.00
SR	Scott Rolen	10.00
SA	Johan Santana	10.00
CS	Curt Schilling	10.00
JS	Jason Schmidt	8.00
RS	Richie Sexson	10.00
BS	Ben Sheets	5.00
GS	Gary Sheffield	10.00
GR	Grady Sizemore	20.00
JO	John Smoltz	10.00
ST	Huston Street	8.00
MS	Mike Sweeney	5.00
NS	Nick Swisher	10.00
TX	Mark Teixeira	10.00
MT	Miguel Tejada	10.00
FT	Frank Thomas	10.00
JV	Jason Varitek	15.00
RW	Rickie Weeks	10.00
WE	David Wells	5.00
VW	Vernon Wells	10.00
BW	Bernie Williams	8.00
DW	Dontrelle Willis	8.00
JW	Jack Wilson	5.00
KW	Kerry Wood	5.00
RZ	Ryan Zimmerman	15.00
BZ	Barry Zito	6.00

2006 UD Sweet Spot Update

NM/M

Complete Set (182):	
Common Player (1-100):	.25
Common Auto. (101-184):	10.00
Production 98-499	
Pack (5):	10.00
Box (12):	110.00

1	Luis Gonzalez	.25
2	Chad Tracy	.25
3	Brandon Webb	.25
4	Andruw Jones	1.00
5	Chipper Jones	1.00
6	John Smoltz	.50
7	Tim Hudson	.50
8	Miguel Tejada	.50
9	Brian Roberts	.25
10	Ramon Hernandez	.25
11	Curt Schilling	.75
12	David Ortiz	1.00
13	Manny Ramirez	1.00
14	Jason Varitek	1.00
15	Josh Beckett	.50
16	Greg Maddux	2.00
17	Derrek Lee	.75
18	Mark Prior	.75
19	Aramis Ramirez	.50
20	Jim Thome	.75
21	Paul Konerko	.75
22	Scott Podsednik	.50
23	Jose Contreras	.25
24	Ken Griffey Jr.	2.00
25	Adam Dunn	.75
26	Felipe Lopez	.25
27	Travis Hafner	.50
28	Victor Martinez	.50
29	Grady Sizemore	.75
30	Jhonny Peralta	.25
31	Todd Helton	.75
32	Garrett Atkins	.25
33	Clint Barmes	.25
34	Ivan Rodriguez	.75
35	Chris Shelton	.25
36	Jeremy Bonderman	.50
37	Miguel Cabrera	1.00
38	Dontrelle Willis	.50
39	Lance Berkman	.50
40	Morgan Ensberg	.25
41	Roy Oswalt	.50
42	Reggie Sanders	.25
43	Mike Sweeney	.25
44	Vladimir Guerrero	1.00
45	Bartolo Colon	.50

#	Player	Value
46	Chone Figgins	.25
47	Nomar Garciaparra	1.00
48	Jeff Kent	.50
49	J.D. Drew	.50
50	Carlos Lee	.50
51	Ben Sheets	.50
52	Rickie Weeks	.50
53	Johan Santana	1.00
54	Torii Hunter	.50
55	Joe Mauer	.75
56	Pedro Martinez	1.00
57	David Wright	2.00
58	Carlos Beltran	.75
59	Carlos Delgado	.75
60	Jose Reyes	.75
61	Derek Jeter	3.00
62	Alex Rodriguez	2.50
63	Randy Johnson	1.00
64	Hideki Matsui	2.00
65	Gary Sheffield	.75
66	Rich Harden	.50
67	Eric Chavez	.50
68	Huston Street	.25
69	Bobby Crosby	.25
70	Bobby Abreu	.50
71	Ryan Howard	2.00
72	Chase Utley	1.00
73	Pat Burrell	.50
74	Jason Bay	.50
75	Sean Casey	.25
76	Mike Piazza	1.50
77	Jake Peavy	.50
78	Brian Giles	.25
79	Milton Bradley	.25
80	Omar Vizquel	.25
81	Jason Schmidt	.50
82	Ichiro Suzuki	2.00
83	Felix Hernandez	.50
84	Kenji Johjima	.50
85	Albert Pujols	3.00
86	Chris Carpenter	.75
87	Scott Rolen	1.00
88	Jim Edmonds	.50
89	Carl Crawford	.50
90	Jonny Gomes	.25
91	Scott Kazmir	.50
92	Mark Teixeira	.75
93	Michael Young	.50
94	Phil Nevin	.25
95	Vernon Wells	.50
96	Roy Halladay	.50
97	Troy Glaus	.50
98	Alfonso Soriano	1.00
99	Nick Johnson	.25
100	Jose Vidro	.25
101	Adam Wainwright/100 (RC)	40.00
102	Anderson Hernandez/100 (RC)	15.00
103	Andre Ethier/150 (RC)	35.00
104	Jason Botts/100 (RC)	15.00
105	Ben Johnson/400 (RC)	10.00
106	Boof Bonser/100 (RC)	20.00
107	Boone Logan/200 RC	10.00
108	Brian Anderson/200 (RC)	10.00
109	Brian Bannister/100 (RC)	15.00
110	Chris Denorfia/100 (RC)	10.00
111	Agustin Montero/100 (RC)	15.00
112	Cody Ross/100 (RC)	10.00
113	Cole Hamels/399 (RC)	35.00
114	Conor Jackson/400 (RC)	10.00
115	Dan Uggla/125 (RC)	25.00
116	Dave Gassner/100 (RC)	10.00
117	C.J. Wilson/150 (RC)	10.00
118	Eric Reed/100 (RC)	10.00
119	Fausto Carmona/99 (RC)	10.00
120	Fernando Nieve/100 (RC)	10.00
121	Francisco Liriano/499 (RC)	25.00
122	Freddie Bynum/100 (RC)	10.00
123	Hanley Ramirez/100 (RC)	30.00
124	Hong-Chih Kuo/100 (RC)	125.00
125	Ian Kinsler/100 (RC)	40.00
126	Carlos Marmol/100 RC	15.00
127	Bobby Keppel/200 (RC)	10.00
128	Jason Kubel/100 (RC)	15.00
129	Jeff Harris/100 RC	10.00
130	Alay Soler/100 RC	15.00
131	Jered Weaver/100 (RC)	30.00
132	Carlos Quentin/100 (RC)	30.00
133	Jeremy Hermida/100 (RC)	20.00
134	Joel Zumaya/100 (RC)	50.00
135	Joey Devine/100 RC	15.00
136	John Koronka/98 (RC)	10.00
137	Jonathan Papelbon/399 (RC)	40.00
138	Jose Capellan/240 (RC)	15.00
139	Josh Johnson/100 (RC)	20.00
140	Josh Rupe/100 (RC)	10.00
141	Josh Willingham/100 (RC)	20.00
143	Justin Verlander/100 (RC)	40.00
144	Kelly Shoppach/100 (RC)	10.00
145	Kendry Morales/100 (RC)	20.00
146	Kevin Thompson/100 (RC)	10.00
147	Macay McBride/100 (RC)	15.00
148	Martin Prado/100 (RC)	10.00
149	Matt Cain/150 (RC)	25.00
150	Clay Hensley/100 (RC)	10.00
151	Ty Taubenheim/100 RC	30.00
152	Mike Jacobs/200 (RC)	15.00
153	Saul Rivera/100 (RC)	15.00
154	Mike Thompson/100 RC	15.00
155	Nate McLouth/100 (RC)	15.00
156	Michael Vento/100 (RC)	15.00
157	Paul Maholm/200 (RC)	10.00
159	Reggie Abercrombie/100 (RC)	15.00
160	Mike Rouse/100 (RC)	10.00
161	Ken Ray/100 (RC)	15.00
162	Ron Flores/100 RC	15.00
163	Ryan Zimmerman/100 (RC)	50.00
164	Erick Aybar/100 (RC)	20.00
165	Sean Marshall/150 (RC)	20.00
166	Takashi Saito/100 RC	40.00
167	Taylor Buchholz/100 (RC)	15.00
168	Matt Murton/100 (RC)	30.00
169	Luis Figueroa/100 RC	15.00
170	Wilbert Nieves/100 (RC)	15.00
171	James Shields/100 RC	20.00
172	Jon Lester/399 (RC)	30.00
173	Craig Hansen/100 RC	30.00
174	Aaron Rakers/100 (RC)	10.00
175	Bobby Livingston/100 (RC)	15.00
176	Brendan Harris/100 (RC)	10.00
177	Zach Jackson/100 (RC)	15.00
178	Chris Britton/100 RC	15.00
179	Howie Kendrick/399 (RC)	25.00
180	Zach Miner/100 (RC)	15.00
181	Kevin Frandsen/100 (RC)	10.00
182	Matt Capps/100 (RC)	10.00
183	Peter Moylan/100 RC	15.00
184	Melky Cabrera/100 (RC)	50.00

Dual Signatures

NM/M

Production 1-55

Code	Players	Value
BN	Taylor Buchholz, Fernando Nieve/55	30.00
CK	Scott Kazmir, Carl Crawford/55	40.00
CU	Carl Crawford, B.J. Upton/45	40.00
CW	Chris Carpenter, Dontrelle Willis/35	50.00
CZ	Miguel Cabrera, Ryan Zimmerman/35	75.00
EG	Andre Ethier, Tony Gwynn Jr./35	40.00
GG	Vladimir Guerrero, Ken Griffey Jr./35	150.00
GT	Ken Griffey Jr., Jim Thome/35	150.00
HD	Dan Uggla, Howie Kendrick/55	40.00
HK	Jeremy Hermida, Jason Kubel/55	30.00
HW	Jeremy Hermida, Josh Willingham/55	30.00
KR	Brian Roberts, Howie Kendrick/35	40.00
KU	B.J. Upton, Scott Kazmir/55	35.00
KW	Scott Kazmir, Dontrelle Willis/35	35.00
LN	Francisco Liriano, Joe Nathan/35	50.00
MM	Joe Mauer, Justin Morneau/35	60.00
MO	Justin Morneau, Lyle Overbay/35	40.00
PL	Jonathan Papelbon, Jon Lester/5	
PO	Jake Peavy, Roy Oswalt/35	40.00
PZ	Jonathan Papelbon, Joel Zumaya/35	90.00
RO	Alex Rios, Lyle Overbay/35	30.00
RR	Jose Reyes, Hanley Ramirez/35	60.00
SN	Huston Street, Joe Nathan/35	30.00
TI	Jim Thome, Tadahito Iguchi/35	100.00
TJ	Jeremy Sowers, Travis Hafner/35	40.00
UD	Stephen Drew, B.J. Upton/35	75.00
UH	Cole Hamels, Chase Utley/35	90.00
UU	Chase Utley, Dan Uggla/35	50.00
UW	Dan Uggla, Josh Willingham/55	30.00
ZU	Ryan Zimmerman, B.J. Upton/35	60.00

Signature Red/Blue Stitch Red Ink

NM/M

Production 40-225

#	Player	Value
101	Adam Wainwright/50	40.00
103	Andre Ethier/50	40.00
105	Ben Johnson/100	10.00
106	Boof Bonser/50	20.00
107	Boone Logan/50	15.00
108	Brian Anderson/100	10.00
109	Brian Bannister/100	15.00
111	Chris Denorfia/50	10.00
112	Cody Ross/50	10.00
113	Cole Hamels/225	40.00
114	Conor Jackson/100	10.00
115	Dan Uggla/30	30.00
117	C.J. Wilson/50	10.00
118	Eric Reed/100	10.00
119	Fausto Carmona/50	10.00
120	Fernando Nieve/50	10.00
121	Francisco Liriano/175	30.00
122	Freddie Bynum/100	10.00
123	Hanley Ramirez/50	40.00
124	Hong-Chih Kuo/50	200.00
125	Ian Kinsler/45	50.00
126	Carlos Marmol/20	10.00
127	Bobby Keppel/100	10.00
128	Jason Kubel/50	20.00
130	Alay Soler/50	20.00
131	Jered Weaver/50	40.00
132	Carlos Quentin/50	20.00
133	Jeremy Hermida/50	20.00
134	Joel Zumaya/50	50.00
135	Joey Devine/50	20.00
136	John Koronka/50	10.00
137	Jonathan Papelbon/175	50.00
138	Jose Capellan/50	10.00
139	Josh Johnson/100	20.00
140	Josh Rupe/50	10.00
141	Josh Willingham/50	20.00
143	Justin Verlander/50	50.00
144	Kelly Shoppach/50	15.00
146	Kevin Thompson/50	10.00
147	Macay McBride/50	15.00
150	Clay Hensley/49	10.00
151	Ty Taubenheim/50	35.00
152	Mike Jacobs/50	15.00
153	Saul Rivera/50	15.00
154	Mike Thompson/50	15.00
155	Nate McLouth/50	15.00
156	Michael Vento/50	15.00
159	Reggie Abercrombie/50	15.00
160	Mike Rouse/50	10.00
161	Ken Ray/50	15.00
162	Ron Flores/50	10.00
163	Ryan Zimmerman/50	60.00
164	Erick Aybar/50	20.00
165	Sean Marshall/50	30.00
167	Taylor Buchholz/50	15.00
168	Matt Murton/50	40.00
169	Luis Figueroa/50	20.00
170	Wilbert Nieves/50	20.00
171	James Shields/50	20.00
172	Jon Lester/175	40.00
174	Aaron Rakers/50	10.00
175	Bobby Livingston/50	20.00
176	Brendan Harris/50	10.00
177	Zach Jackson/50	20.00
178	Chris Britton/50	10.00
179	Howie Kendrick/175	30.00
181	Kevin Frandsen/50	10.00
182	Matt Capps/50	10.00
183	Peter Moylan/50	15.00

Signatures Black Stitch/Ink

No Pricing
Production One Set

Signatures Barrels Black Ink

NM/M

Production 34-70
Blue Ink: No Pricing
Production 9-20
Silver Ink: No Pricing
Production One Set

#	Player	Value
101	Adam Wainwright/35	50.00
103	Andre Ethier/35	50.00
105	Ben Johnson/35	20.00
106	Boof Bonser/35	25.00
107	Boone Logan/35	20.00
108	Brian Anderson/35	20.00
109	Brian Bannister/35	25.00
110	Chris Denorfia/35	20.00
112	Cody Ross/35	20.00
113	Cole Hamels/70	50.00
114	Conor Jackson/35	25.00
115	Dan Uggla/35	35.00
116	Dave Gassner/35	20.00
117	C.J. Wilson/35	15.00
118	Eric Reed/35	20.00
119	Fausto Carmona/35	20.00
120	Fernando Nieve/35	15.00
121	Francisco Liriano/70	40.00
122	Freddie Bynum/35	15.00
123	Hanley Ramirez/35	50.00
124	Hong-Chih Kuo/35	200.00
125	Ian Kinsler/35	60.00
126	Carlos Marmol/35	25.00
127	Bobby Keppel/35	15.00
128	Jason Kubel/35	20.00
130	Alay Soler/35	25.00
132	Carlos Quentin/35	30.00
133	Jeremy Hermida/35	25.00
134	Joel Zumaya/35	65.00
135	Joey Devine/35	20.00
136	John Koronka/35	15.00
137	Jonathan Papelbon/70	60.00
138	Jose Capellan/35	20.00
139	Josh Johnson/35	20.00
141	Josh Willingham/35	50.00
143	Justin Verlander/35	50.00
144	Kelly Shoppach/35	20.00
146	Kevin Thompson/35	25.00
147	Macay McBride/35	15.00
149	Matt Cain/35	40.00
150	Clay Hensley/35	20.00
151	Ty Taubenheim/35	35.00
152	Mike Jacobs/35	20.00
153	Saul Rivera/35	15.00
154	Mike Thompson/35	20.00
155	Nate McLouth/35	25.00
156	Michael Vento/35	20.00
157	Paul Maholm/35	25.00
159	Reggie Abercrombie/35	20.00
160	Mike Rouse/35	15.00
161	Ken Ray/35	15.00
162	Ron Flores/35	15.00
163	Ryan Zimmerman/35	65.00
164	Erick Aybar/35	25.00
165	Sean Marshall/35	25.00
167	Taylor Buchholz/35	15.00
168	Matt Murton/35	50.00
169	Luis Figueroa/34	20.00
170	Wilbert Nieves/30	25.00
171	Jamie Shields/35	35.00
172	Jon Lester/70	50.00
174	Aaron Rakers/35	15.00
175	Bobby Livingston/35	20.00
176	Brendan Harris/35	15.00

177	Zach Jackson/35	20.00
178	Chris Britton/35	20.00
179	Howie Kendrick/70	40.00
181	Kevin Frandsen/35	15.00
182	Matt Capps/35	15.00
183	Peter Moylan/35	20.00

Signatures Leather
Black Ink

NM/M
Production 20-40
Blue Ink: No Pricing
Production 5-10
Silver Ink: No Pricing
Production One Set

113	Cole Hamels/40	60.00
121	Francisco Liriano/40	60.00
137	Jonathan Papelbon/40	75.00
172	Jon Lester/40	60.00
179	Howie Kendrick/40	50.00

Spokesmen Signatures
No Pricing
Production 5 Sets

Sweet Beginnings Swatches

NM/M

	Common Player:	5.00
AB	Adrian Beltre	5.00
AE	Andre Ethier/SP	
AI	Akinori Iwamura	30.00
AJ	Andruw Jones	10.00
AP	Ariel Pestano	5.00
AR	Alex Rios	8.00
AS	Alfonso Soriano	10.00
BA	Bobby Abreu	5.00
BB	Brian Bannister	5.00
BI	Chad Billingsley	10.00
BW	Bernie Williams	10.00
CA	Miguel Cabrera	10.00
CB	Carlos Beltran	10.00
CD	Carlos Delgado	8.00
CH	Chin-Lung Hu	50.00
CJ	Conor Jackson	8.00
CL	Carlos Lee	5.00
CM	Matt Cain	10.00
CU	Chris Duncan	10.00
CZ	Carlos Zambrano	8.00
DL	Derrek Lee	8.00
DO	David Ortiz	15.00
EB	Erik Bedard	10.00
EP	Eduardo Paret	8.00
FA	Fausto Carmona	5.00
FC	Frederich Cepeda	8.00
FL	Francisco Liriano/SP	35.00
GY	Guogang Yang	5.00
HA	Cole Hamels	15.00
HC	Hee Seop Choi	5.00
HT	Hitoshi Tamura	30.00
IK	Ian Kinsler	10.00
IR	Ivan Rodriguez	10.00
IS	Ichiro Suzuki	150.00
JB	Jason Bay	10.00
JD	Johnny Damon	10.00
JF	Jeff Francis	5.00
JH	Jeremy Hermida	8.00
JL	Jong Beom Lee	8.00
JM	Justin Morneau	15.00
JP	Jin Man Park	8.00
JS	Johan Santana	15.00
JV	Jason Varitek	20.00
JZ	Joel Zumaya	15.00
KE	Matthew Kemp	10.00
KG	Ken Griffey Jr.	20.00
KJ	Kenji Johjima/SP	35.00
KU	Koji Uehara	30.00
LO	Javy Lopez	8.00
MA	Moises Alou	8.00
MC	Michael Collins	8.00
ME	Michel Enriquez	8.00
MF	Maikel Folch	5.00
MJ	Mike Jacobs	8.00
MK	Munenori Kawasaki	40.00
MN	Michael Napoli	8.00
MO	Michihiro Ogasawara	30.00
MP	Mike Piazza	15.00
MS	Min Han Son	10.00
MT	Miguel Tejada	8.00
NM	Nobuhiko Matsunaka	30.00
NS	Naoyuki Shimizu	25.00
OU	Osmany Urrutia	10.00
PF	Prince Fielder/SP	25.00
PL	Pedro Luis Lazo	5.00
PU	Albert Pujols	25.00
RO	Alex Rodriguez	20.00
SH	Jamie Shields	10.00
SW	Shunsuke Watanabe	30.00
TN	Tsuyoshi Nishioka	30.00
TW	Tsuyoshi Wada	30.00
VE	Justin Verlander	20.00
VM	Victor Martinez	8.00
VO	Vicyohandry Odelin	5.00
WI	Josh Willingham	8.00
WL	Wei-Chu Lin	50.00
YG	Yulieski Gourriel	10.00
YM	Yuneiski Maya	10.00
RM	Russell Martin/SP	

Sweet Beginnings Patch

NM/M

	Common Player:	
AB	Adrian Beltre	30.00
AE	Andre Ethier	50.00
AJ	Andruw Jones	40.00
AP	Ariel Pestano	30.00
AS	Alfonso Soriano	75.00
BA	Bobby Abreu	60.00
BB	Brian Bannister	40.00
BI	Chad Billingsley	40.00
BW	Bernie Williams	80.00
CA	Miguel Cabrera	60.00
CB	Carlos Beltran	60.00
CD	Carlos Delgado	50.00
CJ	Conor Jackson	60.00
CL	Carlos Lee	40.00
CM	Matt Cain	75.00
CU	Chris Duncan	50.00
CZ	Carlos Zambrano	50.00
DL	Derrek Lee	60.00
DO	David Ortiz	75.00
DU	Dan Uggla	35.00
EB	Erik Bedard	40.00
EP	Eduardo Paret	30.00
FA	Fausto Carmona	40.00
FC	Frederich Cepeda	50.00
FL	Francisco Liriano	50.00
HA	Cole Hamels	50.00
HK	Hong-Chih Kuo	200.00
JB	Jason Bay	50.00
JD	Johnny Damon	50.00
JF	Jeff Francis	40.00
JH	Jeremy Hermida	40.00
JJ	Josh Johnson	40.00
JO	Josh Barfield	40.00
JS	Johan Santana	80.00
JV	Jason Varitek	50.00
JZ	Joel Zumaya	50.00
KE	Matthew Kemp	50.00
KJ	Kenji Johjima	150.00
KU	Koji Uehara	200.00
LE	Jon Lester	50.00
LO	Javy Lopez	50.00
MC	Michael Collins	50.00
ME	Michel Enriquez	50.00
MF	Maikel Folch	40.00
MJ	Mike Jacobs	40.00
MK	Munenori Kawasaki	250.00
MN	Michael Napoli	40.00
MO	Michihiro Ogasawara	200.00
MP	Mike Piazza	85.00
MS	Min Han Son/SP	140.00
NI	Nicholas Markakis	60.00
NM	Nobuhiko Matsunaka	75.00
NS	Naoyuki Shimizu	120.00
OU	Osmany Urrutia	50.00
PA	Jonathan Papelbon	85.00
PE	Mike Pelfrey	75.00
PL	Pedro Luis Lazo	40.00
PU	Albert Pujols	150.00
RN	Ricky Nolasco	40.00
RZ	Ryan Zimmerman	60.00
TW	Tsuyoshi Wada	250.00
VE	Justin Verlander	60.00
VM	Victor Martinez	50.00
VO	Vicyohandry Odelin	30.00
WE	Jered Weaver	40.00
WI	Josh Willingham	40.00
YG	Yulieski Gourriel	75.00
YM	Yuneiski Maya	60.00
RM	Russell Martin	60.00

Veteran Red Stitch
Blue Ink

NM/M
Production 30-525

AG	Tony Gwyn Jr./425	20.00
AH	Aaron Harang/425	20.00
AP	Albert Pujols/30	250.00
AZ	Aramis Ramirez/225	25.00
BJ	B.J. Upton/193	15.00
BR	Brian Roberts/300	15.00
CC	Carl Crawford/425	15.00
CU	Chase Utley/425	40.00
DJ	Derek Jeter/75	200.00
DW	Dontrelle Willis/125	25.00
HS	Huston Street/200	15.00
JB	Jason Bay/425	20.00
JM	Joe Mauer/57	40.00
JN	Joe Nathan/200	20.00
JS	Jeremy Sowers/425	20.00
JT	Jim Thome/75	50.00
KG	Ken Griffey Jr./359	80.00
KG2	Ken Griffey Jr./358	80.00
KY	Kevin Youkilis/425	25.00
LO	Lyle Overbay/525	15.00
MC	Miguel Cabrera/525	25.00
MO	Justin Morneau/425	25.00
RC	Roger Clemens/30	150.00
SD	Stephen Drew/525	25.00
SK	Scott Kazmir/522	20.00
SM	John Smoltz/507	35.00
SP	Scott Podsednik/247	15.00
SS	Mark Mulder/300	15.00
TH	Travis Hafner/525	25.00
TI	Tadahito Iguchi/425	30.00
VM	Victor Martinez/71	20.00

Veterans Barrels
Black Ink

NM/M
Production 10-35
Blue Ink: No Pricing
Production 1-20
Silver Ink: No Pricing
Production One Set

AG	Tony Gwyn Jr./35	30.00
AH	Aaron Harang/35	35.00
AZ	Aramis Ramirez/35	30.00
BJ	B.J. Upton/35	35.00
BR	Brian Roberts/35	25.00
CC	Carl Crawford/35	30.00
CU	Chase Utley/35	70.00
HS	Huston Street/35	35.00
JB	Jason Bay/35	30.00
JN	Joe Nathan/35	30.00
JS	Jeremy Sowers/35	35.00
KG	Ken Griffey Jr./28	100.00
KG2	Ken Griffey Jr./27	100.00
KY	Kevin Youkilis/35	40.00
LO	Lyle Overbay/35	25.00
MC	Miguel Cabrera/35	50.00
MO	Justin Morneau/35	35.00
SD	Stephen Drew/35	60.00
SK	Scott Kazmir/33	30.00
SM	John Smoltz/35	50.00
SO	Scott Podsednik/35	25.00
SS	Mark Mulder/35	25.00
TH	Travis Hafner/35	40.00
TI	Tadahito Iguchi/35	60.00
VM	Victor Martinez/35	30.00

Veteran Lether
Black Ink

Production 5-20
Blue Ink: No Pricing
Production 1-5
Silver Ink: No Pricing
Production One Set

2006 UD Exquisite Collection

NM/M
Common Auto. RC (1-90): 20.00
1-90 Production 55
Autos. 91-100: No Pricing
Production 10
Issued as exchange cards in 06 products.

1	Melky Cabrera, Jeremy Hermida	25.00
2	Fausto Carmona, Craig Hansen	25.00
3	Andre Ethier, Jason Kubel	25.00
4	Boof Bonser, Chad Billingsley	30.00
5	Jeremy Sowers, Fausto Carmona	50.00
6	Josh Willingham, Ronny Paulino	25.00
7	Andre Ethier, Takashi Saito	50.00
8	Cole Hamels, James Shields	100.00
9	Carlos Quentin, Chris Denorfia	30.00
10	Jason Hammel, James Shields	30.00
11	Ian Kinsler, Dan Uggla	40.00
12	Matt Cain, Jeremy Accardo	40.00
13	Jeremy Sowers, Paul Maholm	20.00
14	Jeremy Sowers, Cole Hamels	50.00
15	Boof Bonser, Francisco Liriano	40.00
16	Justin Verlander, Joel Zumaya	80.00
17	Stephen Drew, Hanley Ramirez	50.00
18	Alay Soler, Brian Bannister	20.00
19	Boof Bonser, Dave Gassner	20.00
20	Ryan Theriot, Angel Pagan	65.00
21	Jeremy Hermida, Dan Uggla	30.00
23	Fausto Carmona, Cole Hamels	60.00
24	Hong-Chih Kuo, Takashi Saito	90.00
25	Paul Maholm, Sean Marshall	20.00
26	Dan Uggla, Howie Kendrick	50.00
27	Josh Johnson, Yusmeiro Petit	20.00
29	Andre Ethier, Russell Martin	80.00
30	Francisco Liriano, Jered Weaver	50.00
31	Cole Hamels, Zach Jackson	50.00
32	Jonathan Papelbon, Craig Hansen	50.00
34	Chris Denorfia, Jeremy Hermida	25.00
35	Cody Ross, Josh Willingham	25.00
36	Stephen Drew, Jered Weaver	60.00
38	Scott Dunn, James Shields	40.00
39	Kendry Morales, Howie Kendrick	50.00
40	Paul Maholm, Matt Capps	25.00
41	Ian Kinsler, Howie Kendrick	40.00
42	Matt Cain, Alay Soler	40.00
44	Justin Verlander, Jeremy Sowers	50.00
46	Josh Willingham, Hanley Ramirez	50.00
47	Hanley Ramirez, Jeremy Hermida	40.00
48	Josh Willingham, Dan Uggla	30.00
49	Alay Soler, Cole Hamels	50.00
50	Boof Bonser, Jason Kubel	25.00
51	Mike Jacobs, Kendry Morales	25.00
52	Jonathan Papelbon, Takashi Saito	50.00
53	Justin Verlander, Jonathan Papelbon	75.00
54	Andre Ethier, Chad Billingsley	35.00
55	Jeremy Hermida, Tony Gwynn Jr.	40.00
56	Ryan Zimmerman, Stephen Drew	80.00
57	Josh Barfield, Tony Gwynn Jr.	30.00
58	Clay Hensley, Mike Thompson	25.00
59	Josh Johnson, Justin Verlander	50.00
62	Andre Ethier, Tony Gwynn Jr.	40.00
63	Carlos Quentin, Stephen Drew	50.00
64	Conor Jackson, Carlos Quentin	40.00
65	Ryan Zimmerman, Brendan Harris	50.00
66	Russell Martin, Takashi Saito	80.00
67	Josh Willingham, Mike Jacobs	25.00
68	Mike Jacobs, Hanley Ramirez	30.00
71	Craig Hansen, Cole Hamels	50.00
72	Freddie Bynum, Hanley Ramirez	30.00
74	Taylor Buchholz, Fernando Nieve	25.00
75	Josh Johnson, Adam Wainwright	40.00
76	Josh Willingham, Russell Martin	40.00
77	Wilbert Nieves, Russell Martin	30.00
78	Ben Johnson, Mike Thompson	20.00

79	Ben Hendrickson, Zach Jackson	20.00
80	Jonathan Papelbon, Joel Zumaya	50.00
81	Ben Hendrickson, Jose Capellan	20.00
82	Joey Devine, Ken Ray	20.00
84	Russell Martin, Kelly Stoppach	30.00
85	Josh Johnson, Alay Soler	20.00
86	Alay Soler, Craig Hansen	25.00
87	Chad Billingsley, Craig Hansen	30.00
88	Chad Billingsley, Matt Cain	40.00
89	Francisco Liriano, Craig Hansen	40.00
90	Conor Jackson, Mike Jacobs	25.00

Gold

Gold (1-90):	.75-1.5X
Production 30 Sets	
Gold (91-100):	No Pricing
Production 5 Sets	

Platinum

Production One Set

Cuts

	NM/M
Common Auto.:	
Production 25-65	
AC	Al Campanis/65	100.00
BD	Bill Dickey/65	100.00
BG	Burleigh Grimes/65	120.00
BH	Billy Herman/65	100.00
CG	Charlie Gehringer/65	100.00
CH	Carl Hubbell/65	140.00
DC	Dolph Camilli/65	100.00
DD	Dizzy Dean/30	
EA	Earl Averill/65	120.00
EM	Eddie Mathews/65	150.00
ER	Edd Roush/65	120.00
GE	George Selkirk/65	150.00
GS	George Sisler/65	200.00
HG	Hank Greenberg/65	200.00
JC	Joe Cronin/65	100.00
JM	Johnny Mize/65	120.00
LA	Luke Appling/65	100.00
LB	Lou Boudreau/65	100.00
LG	Lefty Gomez/65	120.00
MC	Max Carey/65	120.00
PW	Pee Wee Reese/65	150.00
RR	Red Ruffing/52	150.00
RS	Ray Schalk/30	250.00
SC	Stan Coveleski/65	80.00
VW	Vic Wertz/65	100.00
WG	Warren Giles/65	100.00
WH	Waite Hoyt/65	100.00
WS	Warren Spahn/65	120.00

Dual Cuts

No Pricing
Production 5 Sets

Endorsed Emblems

	NM/M
Production 25 Sets	
AB	A.J. Burnett	
AD	Adam Dunn	50.00
AJ	Andruw Jones	75.00
AR	Alex Rios	50.00
BJ	B.J. Upton	50.00
BR	Brian Roberts	60.00
BS	Ben Sheets	50.00
CB	Craig Biggio	125.00
CU	Chase Utley	60.00
CZ	Carlos Zambrano	75.00
DL	Derrek Lee	100.00
DO	David Ortiz	200.00
FL	Francisco Liriano	80.00
HS	Huston Street	50.00
JM	Joe Mauer	100.00
JO	Jonathan Papelbon	125.00
JP	Jake Peavy	80.00
JR	Jose Reyes	250.00
JS	Jeremy Sowers	50.00
JT	Jim Thome	125.00
JU	Justin Morneau	100.00
JU2	Justin Morneau	100.00
JV	Justin Verlander	100.00
JW	Jered Weaver	60.00
KG	Ken Griffey Jr.	200.00
KG2	Ken Griffey Jr.	200.00
KG3	Ken Griffey Jr.	200.00
KH	Khalil Greene	60.00
MC	Miguel Cabrera	150.00
MG	Marcus Giles	40.00
MH	Matt Holliday	50.00

MT	Mark Teixeira	50.00
MY	Michael Young	50.00
NS	Nick Swisher	60.00
RW	Rickie Weeks	60.00
SD	Stephen Drew	100.00
SM	John Smoltz	140.00
TH	Travis Hafner	100.00
TR	Trevor Hoffman	80.00

Endorsements

	NM/M
Production 40 Sets	
AP	Albert Pujols	
AS	Alay Soler	25.00
BF	Bob Feller	50.00
BJ	B.J. Upton	40.00
BR	Brooks Robinson	40.00
CC	Chris Carpenter	60.00
CF	Carlton Fisk	60.00
CH	Cole Hamels	75.00
CJ	Chipper Jones	80.00
CR	Cal Ripken Jr.	150.00
DJ	Derek Jeter	
DO	David Ortiz	80.00
DW	Dontrelle Willis	40.00
FH	Felix Hernandez	100.00
FL	Francisco Liriano	40.00
FR	Frank Robinson	50.00
GP	Gaylord Perry	40.00
HK	Howie Kendrick	50.00
JB	Johnny Bench	60.00
JM	Joe Mauer	75.00
JO	Jonathan Papelbon	60.00
JP	Jake Peavy	60.00
JR	Jose Reyes	100.00
JS	Jeremy Sowers	20.00
JV	Justin Verlander	60.00
JW	Jered Weaver	40.00
KG	Ken Griffey Jr.	100.00
KG2	Ken Griffey Jr.	100.00
MC	Miguel Cabrera	60.00
MT	Mark Teixeira	40.00
NR	Nolan Ryan	140.00
PM	Paul Molitor	40.00
RC	Roger Clemens	180.00
RJ	Reggie Jackson	75.00
RO	Roy Oswalt	60.00
RS	Ryne Sandberg	75.00
RZ	Ryan Zimmerman	50.00
SD	Stephen Drew	50.00
SK	Scott Kazmir	80.00
SM	Stan Musial	80.00
TH	Travis Hafner	60.00
TI	Tadahito Iguchi	60.00
VG	Vladimir Guerrero	75.00
VM	Victor Martinez	40.00
WC	Will Clark	40.00

Endorsements Dual

No Pricing
Production 20 Sets

Endorsements Triple

No Pricing
Production 15 Sets

Endorsements Quad

No Pricing
Production 10 Sets

Ensemble Dual Patch

No Pricing
Production 25 Sets

Ensemble Triple Patch

No Pricing
Production 15 Sets

Ensemble Quad Patch

No Pricing
Production 10 Sets

Legends Memorabilia

	NM/M
Production 15 Sets	
Platinum:	No Pricing
Production One Set	
AK	Al Kaline	40.00
BD	Bill Dickey	60.00
BD2	Bill Dickey	60.00
BM	Bill Mazeroski	50.00
BM2	Bill Mazeroski	50.00
BR	Babe Ruth	900.00
BR2	Babe Ruth	900.00
CF	Carlton Fisk	40.00
CR	Cal Ripken Jr.	100.00
CR2	Cal Ripken Jr.	100.00
CR3	Cal Ripken Jr.	100.00
DM	Don Mattingly	80.00
FR	Frank Robinson	40.00
JB	Johnny Bench	50.00
JB2	Johnny Bench	50.00
JC	Joe Cronin	40.00
JD	Joe DiMaggio	180.00

JD2	Joe DiMaggio	180.00
JF	Jimmie Foxx	250.00
JM	Joe Morgan	30.00
LG	Lou Gehrig	400.00
LG2	Lou Gehrig	400.00
MO	Mel Ott	150.00
MS	Mike Schmidt	40.00
NR	Nolan Ryan	100.00
NR2	Nolan Ryan	100.00
OC	Orlando Cepeda	30.00
RC	Roberto Clemente	225.00
RC2	Roberto Clemente	225.00
RH	Rogers Hornsby	120.00
RH2	Rogers Hornsby	120.00
RJ	Reggie Jackson	40.00
RJ2	Reggie Jackson	40.00
RO	Brooks Robinson	40.00
RS	Ryne Sandberg	60.00
SM	Stan Musial	60.00
TG	Tony Gwynn	50.00
TG2	Tony Gwynn	50.00
TM	Thurman Munson	100.00
TM2	Thurman Munson	100.00
TW	Ted Williams	200.00
WB	Wade Boggs	50.00

Material Cuts

Production 2 Sets

Maximum Patch

	NM/M
Production 25 Sets	
AD	Adam Dunn	75.00
AP	Albert Pujols	250.00
AS	Alfonso Soriano	80.00
CA	Carl Crawford	80.00
CB	Carlos Beltran	100.00
CC	Chris Carpenter	100.00
CD	Carlos Delgado	80.00
CJ	Chipper Jones	120.00
CR	Craig Biggio	80.00
CS	Curt Schilling	75.00
DJ	Derek Jeter	350.00
DO	David Ortiz	125.00
FH	Felix Hernandez	120.00
FL	Francisco Liriano	75.00
FT	Frank Thomas	120.00
JF	Jeff Francoeur	100.00
JG	Jason Giambi	120.00
JM	Justin Morneau	120.00
JO	Jonathan Papelbon	75.00
JP	Jake Peavy	75.00
JR	Jose Reyes	120.00
JS	Johan Santana	80.00
JT	Jim Thome	75.00
JV	Justin Verlander	75.00
JW	Jered Weaver	75.00
KG	Ken Griffey Jr.	140.00
MC	Miguel Cabrera	75.00
MI	Miguel Tejada	75.00
MT	Mark Teixeira	75.00
MY	Michael Young	60.00
PF	Prince Fielder	100.00
PM	Pedro Martinez	100.00
TG	Troy Glaus	60.00
TH	Todd Helton	75.00
TO	Tom Glavine	100.00
TR	Travis Hafner	75.00
VG	Vladimir Guerrero	75.00
VM	Victor Martinez	60.00

Memorabilia

	NM/M
Production 45 Sets	
Gold:	.75-1.5X
Production 25 Sets	
Platinum:	No Pricing
Production 15 Sets	
Mem. 1:	No Pricing
Production One Set	
AD	Adam Dunn	15.00
AD2	Adam Dunn	15.00
AJ	Andruw Jones	15.00
AJ2	Andruw Jones	15.00
AP	Albert Pujols	50.00
AP2	Albert Pujols	50.00
AR	Alex Rodriguez	50.00
AS	Alfonso Soriano	20.00
AS2	Alfonso Soriano	20.00
BR	Babe Ruth	450.00
BR2	Babe Ruth	450.00
BZ	Barry Zito	15.00
BZ2	Barry Zito	15.00
CB	Carlos Beltran	20.00
CB2	Carlos Beltran	20.00
CF	Carlton Fisk	15.00
CF2	Carlton Fisk	15.00
CJ	Chipper Jones	25.00
CJ2	Chipper Jones	25.00
CR	Cal Ripken Jr.	50.00
CR2	Cal Ripken Jr.	50.00
CR3	Cal Ripken Jr.	50.00
CS	Curt Schilling	15.00
CU	Chase Utley	35.00

CU2	Chase Utley	35.00
CY	Carl Yastrzemski	25.00
CY2	Carl Yastrzemski	25.00
DA	Daisuke Matsuzaka	250.00
DJ	Derek Jeter	60.00
DJ2	Derek Jeter	60.00
DL	Derrek Lee	60.00
DM	Don Mattingly	40.00
DO	David Ortiz	30.00
DO2	David Ortiz	30.00
FL	Francisco Liriano	20.00
FL2	Francisco Liriano	20.00
GM	Greg Maddux	25.00
GM2	Greg Maddux	25.00
HO	Ryan Howard	25.00
HO2	Ryan Howard	25.00
IS	Ichiro Suzuki	200.00
JA	Jason Bay	15.00
JA2	Jason Bay	15.00
JB	Jeff Bagwell	20.00
JB2	Jeff Bagwell	20.00
JD	Joe DiMaggio	200.00
JM	Joe Mauer	25.00
JP	Jake Peavy	20.00
JP2	Jake Peavy	20.00
JS	Johan Santana	20.00
JS2	Johan Santana	20.00
JT	Jim Thome	20.00
JT2	Jim Thome	20.00
JV	Justin Verlander	35.00
JV2	Justin Verlander	35.00
JW	Jered Weaver	15.00
JW2	Jered Weaver	15.00
KG	Ken Griffey Jr.	30.00
KG2	Ken Griffey Jr.	30.00
KG3	Ken Griffey Jr.	30.00
KJ	Kenji Johjima	30.00
KJ2	Kenji Johjima	30.00
MA	Manny Ramirez	20.00
MA2	Manny Ramirez	20.00
MA3	Manny Ramirez	20.00
MC	Miguel Cabrera	20.00
MC2	Miguel Cabrera	20.00
MI	Miguel Tejada	15.00
MI2	Miguel Tejada	15.00
MR	Mariano Rivera	35.00
MR2	Mariano Rivera	35.00
MS	Mike Schmidt	25.00
MS2	Mike Schmidt	25.00
MT	Mark Teixeira	15.00
NR	Nolan Ryan	50.00
NR2	Nolan Ryan	50.00
PE	Pedro Martinez	30.00
PF	Prince Fielder	30.00
PF2	Prince Fielder	30.00
PM	Paul Molitor	20.00
PM2	Paul Molitor	20.00
RC	Roger Clemens	35.00
RC2	Roger Clemens	35.00
RC3	Roger Clemens	35.00
RE	Reggie Jackson	30.00
RE2	Reggie Jackson	30.00
RH	Roy Halladay	15.00
RH2	Roy Halladay	15.00
RJ	Randy Johnson	20.00
RO	Roy Oswalt	15.00
RO2	Roy Oswalt	15.00
RY	Robin Yount	25.00
RY2	Robin Yount	25.00
SM	Stan Musial	40.00
SM2	Stan Musial	40.00
TG	Tony Gwynn	35.00
TH	Travis Hafner	20.00
VG	Vladimir Guerrero	25.00
VG2	Vladimir Guerrero	25.00
WB	Wade Boggs	20.00

Patch

	NM/M
Production 25 Sets	
Patch 10:	No Pricing
Production 10 Sets	
Patch 1:	No Pricing
Production One Set	
AD	Adam Dunn	40.00
AD2	Adam Dunn	40.00
AJ	Andruw Jones	50.00
AJ2	Andruw Jones	50.00
AP	Albert Pujols	150.00
AP2	Albert Pujols	150.00
AS	Alfonso Soriano	60.00
AS2	Alfonso Soriano	60.00
BZ	Barry Zito	40.00
BZ2	Barry Zito	40.00
CB	Carlos Beltran	50.00
CB2	Carlos Beltran	50.00
CF	Carlton Fisk	50.00
CF2	Carlton Fisk	50.00
CJ	Chipper Jones	80.00
CJ2	Chipper Jones	80.00
CR	Cal Ripken Jr.	120.00
CR2	Cal Ripken Jr.	120.00
CR3	Cal Ripken Jr.	120.00
CS	Curt Schilling	60.00

CU	Chase Utley	60.00
CU2	Chase Utley	60.00
DJ	Derek Jeter	150.00
DJ2	Derek Jeter	150.00
DL	Derrek Lee	50.00
DM	Don Mattingly	100.00
DO	David Ortiz	75.00
DO2	David Ortiz	75.00
FL	Francisco Liriano	40.00
FL2	Francisco Liriano	40.00
GM	Greg Maddux	75.00
GM2	Greg Maddux	75.00
HO	Ryan Howard	100.00
HO2	Ryan Howard	100.00
JA	Jason Bay	40.00
JA2	Jason Bay	40.00
JM	Joe Mauer	60.00
JP	Jake Peavy	50.00
JP2	Jake Peavy	50.00
JS	Johan Santana	60.00
JS2	Johan Santana	60.00
JT	Jim Thome	50.00
JT2	Jim Thome	50.00
JV	Justin Verlander	60.00
JV2	Justin Verlander	60.00
JW	Jered Weaver	50.00
JW2	Jered Weaver	50.00
KG	Ken Griffey Jr.	120.00
KG2	Ken Griffey Jr.	120.00
KG3	Ken Griffey Jr.	120.00
KJ	Kenji Johjima	50.00
KJ2	Kenji Johjima	50.00
MA	Manny Ramirez	50.00
MA2	Manny Ramirez	50.00
MA3	Manny Ramirez	50.00
MC	Miguel Cabrera	50.00
MC2	Miguel Cabrera	50.00
MI	Miguel Tejada	40.00
MI2	Miguel Tejada	40.00
MR	Mariano Rivera	60.00
MR2	Mariano Rivera	60.00
MS	Mike Schmidt	40.00
MS2	Mike Schmidt	40.00
MT	Mark Teixeira	40.00
NR	Nolan Ryan	120.00
NR2	Nolan Ryan	120.00
PE	Pedro Martinez	50.00
PF	Prince Fielder	60.00
PF2	Prince Fielder	60.00
PM	Paul Molitor	30.00
PM2	Paul Molitor	30.00
RC	Roger Clemens	75.00
RC2	Roger Clemens	75.00
RC3	Roger Clemens	75.00
RE	Reggie Jackson	50.00
RE2	Reggie Jackson	50.00
RH	Roy Halladay	50.00
RH2	Roy Halladay	50.00
RJ	Randy Johnson	40.00
RO	Roy Oswalt	40.00
RO2	Roy Oswalt	40.00
RY	Robin Yount	75.00
RY2	Robin Yount	75.00
SM	Stan Musial	40.00
SM2	Stan Musial	40.00
TG	Tony Gwynn	80.00
TH	Travis Hafner	50.00
VG	Vladimir Guerrero	50.00
VG2	Vladimir Guerrero	50.00
WB	Wade Boggs	40.00

Signature Patch

NM/M

Production 30 Sets		
Triple:	No Pricing	
Production One Set		
Dual:	No Pricing	
Production One Set		
AB	A.J. Burnett	
AD	Adam Dunn	60.00
AJ	Andruw Jones	75.00
AR	Alex Rios	60.00
BJ	B.J. Upton	50.00
BR	Brian Roberts	50.00
BS	Ben Sheets	40.00
CB	Craig Biggio	90.00
CC	Chris Carpenter	75.00
CL	Carlos Lee	50.00
CU	Chase Utley	100.00
CZ	Carlos Zambrano	50.00
DJ	Derek Jeter	300.00
DL	Derrek Lee	100.00
DO	David Ortiz	180.00
FH	Felix Hernandez	150.00
JP	Jake Peavy	60.00
JR	Jose Reyes	200.00
JS	Jeremy Sowers	40.00
JT	Jim Thome	80.00
JU	Justin Morneau	75.00
JU2	Justin Morneau	75.00
JV	Justin Verlander	150.00
JW	Jered Weaver	60.00
KH	Khalil Greene	75.00
MC	Miguel Cabrera	120.00

MG	Marcus Giles	40.00
MH	Matt Holliday	75.00
MT	Mark Teixeira	50.00
MY	Michael Young	50.00
NS	Nick Swisher	50.00
RO	Roy Oswalt	60.00
RW	Rickie Weeks	60.00
SD	Stephen Drew	80.00
SK	Scott Kazmir	80.00
TH	Travis Hafner	100.00
TI	Tadahito Iguchi	50.00
VM	Victor Martinez	60.00

2006 UD Ultimate Collection

NM/M

Complete Set (290):		
Common Player (1-100):		1.50
Common RC Auto.		
(101-175):		10.00
Production 180 unless noted.		
Common (191-290):		2.00
Production 799		
Pack (4):		80.00
Box (4):		300.00
1	Babe Ruth	8.00
2	Chad Tracy	1.50
3	Brandon Webb	1.50
4	Andruw Jones	3.00
5	Chipper Jones	4.00
6	John Smoltz	2.00
7	Eddie Mathews	4.00
8	Miguel Tejada	3.00
9	Brian Roberts	1.50
10	Mickey Cochrane	2.00
11	Curt Schilling	3.00
12	David Ortiz	4.00
13	Manny Ramirez	4.00
14	Johnny Bench	4.00
15	Cy Young	2.00
16	Greg Maddux	5.00
17	Derrek Lee	3.00
18	Yogi Berra	4.00
19	Walter Johnson	2.00
20	Jim Thome	3.00
21	Paul Konerko	2.00
22	Lou Gehrig	6.00
23	Jose Contreras	1.50
24	Ken Griffey Jr.	5.00
25	Adam Dunn	3.00
26	Reggie Jackson	3.00
27	Travis Hafner	2.00
28	Victor Martinez	1.50
29	Grady Sizemore	3.00
30	Casey Stengel	3.00
31	Todd Helton	3.00
32	Nolan Ryan	8.00
33	Clint Barmes	1.50
34	Ivan Rodriguez	3.00
35	Chris Shelton	1.50
36	Ty Cobb	5.00
37	Miguel Cabrera	4.00
38	Dontrelle Willis	2.00
39	Lance Berkman	2.00
40	Tom Seaver	4.00
41	Roy Oswalt	2.00
42	Christy Mathewson	3.00
43	Luis Aparicio	1.50
44	Vladimir Guerrero	4.00
45	Bartolo Colon	1.50
46	Roy Campanella	2.00
47	George Sisler	1.50
48	Jeff Kent	1.50
49	J.D. Drew	1.50
50	Carlos Lee	1.50
51	Willie Stargell	3.00
52	Rickie Weeks	1.50
53	Johan Santana	4.00
54	Torii Hunter	1.50
55	Joe Mauer	2.00
56	Pedro Martinez	4.00
57	David Wright	5.00
58	Carlos Beltran	3.00
59	Jimmie Foxx	4.00
60	Jose Reyes	3.00
61	Derek Jeter	8.00
62	Alex Rodriguez	6.00
63	Randy Johnson	4.00
64	Hideki Matsui	5.00
65	Thurman Munson	4.00
66	Rich Harden	1.50
67	Eric Chavez	2.00
68	Don Drysdale	3.00
69	Bobby Crosby	1.50
70	Pee Wee Reese	1.50
71	Ryan Howard	6.00
72	Chase Utley	4.00
73	Jackie Robinson	5.00
74	Jason Bay	3.00
75	Honus Wagner	4.00
76	Lefty Grove	3.00
77	Jake Peavy	3.00
78	Brian Giles	1.50

79	Eddie Murray	3.00
80	Omar Vizquel	1.50
81	Jason Schmidt	2.00
82	Ichiro Suzuki	5.00
83	Felix Hernandez	3.00
84	Kenji Johjima	8.00
85	Albert Pujols	8.00
86	Chris Carpenter	3.00
87	Brooks Robinson	3.00
88	Dizzy Dean	3.00
89	Carl Crawford	2.00
90	Rogers Hornsby	3.00
91	Scott Kazmir	2.00
92	Mark Teixeira	3.00
93	Michael Young	2.00
94	Johnny Mize	1.50
95	Vernon Wells	3.00
96	Roy Halladay	2.00
97	Mel Ott	1.50
98	Alfonso Soriano	4.00
99	Joe Morgan	3.00
100	Satchel Paige	4.00
101	Adam Wainwright (RC)	30.00
102	Anderson Hernandez (RC)	10.00
103	Andre Ethier (RC)	35.00
104	Ben Johnson (RC)	15.00
105	Boof Bonser (RC)	20.00
106	Boone Logan RC	10.00
107	Brian Anderson (RC)	10.00
108	Brian Bannister (RC)	15.00
109	Chris Demaria RC	10.00
110	Chris Denorfia (RC)	10.00
111	Cody Ross (RC)	10.00
112	Cole Hamels (RC)	50.00
113	Conor Jackson (RC)	20.00
114	Dan Uggla (RC)	25.00
115	Dave Gassner (RC)	10.00
116	Eric Reed (RC)	10.00
117	Fausto Carmona (RC)	10.00
118	Fernando Nieve (RC)	10.00
119	Francisco Liriano (RC)	50.00
120	Freddie Bynum (RC)	10.00
121	Hanley Ramirez (RC)	25.00
122	Hong-Chih Kuo (RC)	85.00
123	Ian Kinsler (RC)	50.00
124	Jason Hammel (RC)	10.00
125	Jason Kubel (RC)	10.00
126	Jeff Harris RC	10.00
127	Jered Weaver/150 (RC)	60.00
128	Jeremy Accardo (RC)	10.00
129	Jeremy Hermida (RC)	20.00
130	Joel Zumaya (RC)	30.00
131	Joey Devine (RC)	10.00
132	John Koronka (RC)	15.00
133	John Van Benschoten (RC)	10.00
134	Jonathan Papelbon (RC)	50.00
135	Jose Capellan (RC)	10.00
136	Josh Johnson (RC)	15.00
137	Josh Rupe (RC)	10.00
138	Josh Willingham (RC)	15.00
139	Josh Wilson (RC)	10.00
140	Justin Verlander (RC)	60.00
141	Kelly Shoppach (RC)	10.00
142	Kendry Morales (RC)	15.00
143	Macay McBride (RC)	10.00
144	Martin Prado (RC)	10.00
145	Matt Cain (RC)	30.00
146	Mike Jacobs (RC)	10.00
147	Mike Thompson RC	10.00
148	Nate McLouth (RC)	10.00
149	Paul Maholm (RC)	10.00
150	Prince Fielder (RC)	50.00
151	Reggie Abercrombie (RC)	10.00
152	Rich Hill (RC)	40.00
153	Ron Flores RC	15.00
154	Ruddy Lugo (RC)	10.00
155	Ryan Zimmerman (RC)	60.00
156	Sean Marshall (RC)	20.00
157	Takashi Saito RC	30.00
158	Taylor Buchholz (RC)	15.00
159	Tony Pena (RC)	10.00
160	Wilbert Nieves (RC)	10.00
161	Jamie Shields RC	20.00
162	Jon Lester (RC)	10.00
163	Craig Hansen RC	40.00
164	Aaron Rakers (RC)	10.00
165	Yusmeiro Petit (RC)	10.00
166	Bobby Livingston (RC)	10.00
167	Brendan Harris (RC)	10.00
169	Carlos Ruiz (RC)	15.00
170	Chris Britton RC	10.00
171	Howie Kendrick (RC)	40.00
172	Jermaine Van Buren	10.00
173	Kevin Frandsen (RC)	20.00
174	Matt Capps (RC)	10.00

175	Peter Moylan RC	10.00
191	Richie Ashburn/799	3.00
192	Lou Brock	4.00
193	Lou Boudreau	2.00
194	Orlando Cepeda	2.00
195	Bobby Doerr	2.00
196	Dennis Eckersley	2.00
197	Bob Feller	3.00
198	Rollie Fingers	2.00
199	Carlton Fisk	4.00
200	Bob Gibson	3.00
201	Jim "Catfish" Hunter	3.00
202	Fergie Jenkins	3.00
203	Al Kaline	5.00
204	Harmon Killebrew	5.00
205	Ralph Kiner	3.00
206	Buck Leonard	3.00
207	Juan Marichal	4.00
208	Bill Mazeroski	4.00
209	Willie McCovey	4.00
210	Jim Palmer	2.00
211	Tony Perez	2.00
212	Gaylord Perry	2.00
213	Phil Rizzuto	2.00
214	Robin Roberts	2.00
215	Mike Schmidt	6.00
216	Enos Slaughter	2.00
217	Ozzie Smith	5.00
218	Billy Williams	2.00
219	Robin Yount	5.00
220	Carlos Quentin (RC)	4.00
221	Jeff Francoeur	2.00
222	Brian McCann	2.00
223	Nicholas Markakis (RC)	6.00
224	Josh Beckett	2.00
225	Jason Varitek	2.00
226	Mark Prior	4.00
227	Aramis Ramirez	3.00
228	Jermaine Dye	2.00
229	Tadahito Iguchi	2.00
230	Bobby Jenks	2.00
231	C.C. Sabathia	2.00
232	Jeff Francis	2.00
233	Matt Holliday	2.00
234	Magglio Ordonez	2.00
235	Kenny Rogers	2.00
236	Roger Clemens	8.00
237	Andy Pettitte	3.00
238	Craig Biggio	3.00
239	Chone Figgins	2.00
240	John Lackey	2.00
241	Nomar Garciaparra	4.00
242	Prince Fielder (RC)	6.00
243	Ben Sheets	3.00
244	Bill Hall	2.00
245	Justin Morneau	2.00
246	Joe Nathan	2.00
247	Carlos Delgado	2.00
248	Shawn Green	2.00
249	Billy Wagner	2.00
250	Jason Giambi	4.00
251	Mike Mussina	4.00
252	Mariano Rivera	4.00
253	Robinson Cano	4.00
254	Bobby Abreu	3.00
255	Huston Street	2.00
256	Frank Thomas	4.00
257	Danny Haren	2.00
258	Jason Kendall	2.00
259	Nick Swisher	3.00
260	Pat Burrell	2.00
261	Tom Gordon	2.00
262	Freddy Sanchez	2.00
263	Trevor Hoffman	2.00
264	Khalil Greene	2.00
265	Adrian Gonzalez	2.00
266	Moises Alou	2.00
267	Matt Morris	2.00
268	Pedro Feliz	2.00
269	Richie Sexson	2.00
270	Hoyt Wilhelm	2.00
271	Adrian Beltre	2.00
272	Jim Edmonds	3.00
273	Scott Rolen	2.00
274	Jason Isringhausen	2.00
275	Jorge Cantu	2.00
276	Hank Blalock	2.00
277	Kevin Millwood	2.00
278	Alex Rios	2.00
279	Troy Glaus	3.00
280	B.J. Ryan	2.00
281	Nick Johnson	2.00
282	Chad Cordero	2.00
283	Austin Kearns	2.00
284	Ricky Nolasco (RC)	2.00
285	Travis Ishikawa (RC)	2.00
286	Lastings Milledge (RC)	4.00
287	James Loney (RC)	4.00
288	Red Schoendienst	3.00
289	Warren Spahn	4.00
290	Early Wynn (RC)	2.00

Printing Plates

No Pricing
Production one set per color.

Ensemble Materials 3

Production 25 Sets
Patch: No Pricing
Production 20 Sets

Ensemble Materials 4

Production 20 Sets
Patch: No Pricing
Production 15 Sets

Ensemble Signature 3

NM/M

Production 50 Sets
Triple 15: No Pricing
Production 15 Sets
Triple 1 of 1: No Pricing

AHW	Josh Willingham, Reggie Abercrombie, Jeremy Hermida	40.00
BBB	Jeff Bagwell, Craig Biggio, Lance Berkman	100.00
BBW	Taylor Buchholz, Adam Wainwright, Brian Bannister	50.00
BDD	George Bell, Eric Davis, Andre Dawson	50.00
BHR	Roy Halladay, A.J. Burnett, Alex Rios	40.00
BKM	Ralph Kiner, Bill Mazeroski, Jason Bay	85.00
BNO	Taylor Buchholz, Roy Oswalt, Fernando Nieve	30.00
BSH	A.J. Burnett, Rich Harden, Ben Sheets	40.00
BUK	Craig Biggio, Chase Utley, Ian Kinsler	75.00
BWC	Matt Cain, Brian Bannister, Adam Wainwright	40.00
BWV	Justin Verlander, Boof Bonser, Jered Weaver	85.00
CBP	Oliver Perez, Jason Bay, Sean Casey	30.00
CBS	Ron Cey, Dusty Baker, Don Sutton	50.00
CBZ	Boof Bonser, Joel Zumaya, Matt Cain	50.00
CDV	Jack Clark, Eric Davis, Andy Van Slyke	50.00
CHK	Jason Kubel, Melky Cabrera, Jeremy Hermida	50.00
CHO	Chris Carpenter, Roy Oswalt, Rich Harden	60.00
CKH	Rich Harden, Bobby Crosby, Jason Kendall	40.00
CKS	Carl Crawford, Scott Kazmir, Jamie Shields	50.00
CLH	Cole Hamels, Fausto Carmona, Francisco Liriano	80.00
CMH	Victor Martinez, Travis Hafner, Fausto Carmona	60.00
CNS	Graig Nettles, Ron Cey, Ron Santo	50.00
CPC	Carl Crawford, Coco Crisp, Scott Podsednik	40.00
CSS	John Smoltz, Roger Clemens, Curt Schilling	200.00
CWW	Josh Willingham, Dontrelle Willis, Miguel Cabrera	50.00
CZC	Miguel Cabrera, Eric Chavez, Ryan Zimmerman	80.00
DJH	Hanley Ramirez, Derek Jeter, Jose Reyes	200.00
DPA	Scott Podsednik, Jermaine Dye, Brian Anderson	40.00
DPI	Jermaine Dye, Scott Podsednik, Tadahito Iguchi	60.00
FGC	David Cone, Dwight Gooden, Sid Fernandez	75.00

FJM	Prince Fielder, Conor Jackson, Kendry Morales	50.00
FWL	Rickie Weeks, Prince Fielder, Carlos Lee	60.00
GCN	Graig Nettles, Rich "Goose" Gossage, Chris Chambliss	50.00
GCS	Bret Saberhagen, Dwight Gooden, David Cone	30.00
GJB	Derek Jeter, Ken Griffey Jr., Jason Bay	250.00
GJP	Derek Jeter, Albert Pujols, Ken Griffey Jr.	500.00
GLK	Dave Gassner, Jason Kubel, Francisco Liriano	50.00
GPN	Joe Nathan, Eric Gagne, Jonathan Papelbon	50.00
GRS	Alex Rios, Alfonso Soriano, Vladimir Guerrero	90.00
HBS	Rich Harden, Nick Swisher, Joe Blanton	50.00
HKP	Boog Powell, John Kruk, Kent Hrbek	40.00
HMK	Mark Mulder, Scott Kazmir, Cole Hamels	60.00
HNP	Jonathan Papelbon, Trevor Hoffman, Joe Nathan	75.00
HOT	David Ortiz, Travis Hafner, Mark Teixeira	100.00
HWU	Josh Willingham, Jeremy Hermida, Dan Uggla	30.00
IKU	Dan Uggla, Ian Kinsler, Tadahito Iguchi	85.00
JCN	Melky Cabrera, Wilbert Nieves, Derek Jeter	150.00
JGS	Ken Griffey Jr., Andruw Jones, Alfonso Soriano	120.00
JRR	Derek Jeter, Jose Reyes, Hanley Ramirez	200.00
JWV	Jered Weaver, Justin Verlander, Josh Johnson	75.00
KGJ	John Kruk, Mark Grace, Wally Joyner	80.00
KLB	Francisco Liriano, Boof Bonser, Jason Kubel	50.00
KUU	Ian Kinsler, Dan Uggla, Chase Utley	65.00
KWM	Josh Willingham, Victor Martinez, Jason Kendall	30.00
LGB	Francisco Liriano, Boof Bonser, Dave Gassner	40.00
LHC	Felix Hernandez, Fausto Carmona, Francisco Liriano	50.00
LPO	Derrek Lee, David Ortiz, Albert Pujols	250.00
MCN	Ron Cey, Graig Nettles, Bill Madlock	50.00
MMK	Jason Kendall, Joe Mauer, Victor Martinez	40.00
MNL	Joe Mauer, Francisco Liriano, Joe Nathan	50.00
MWC	Chris Carpenter, Mark Mulder, Adam Wainwright	75.00
MWP	Josh Willingham, Russell Martin, Ronny Paulino	30.00
NLP	Jonathan Papelbon, Brad Lidge, Joe Nathan	50.00
OBL	Brad Lidge, Roy Oswalt, Taylor Buchholz	40.00
PCL	Oliver Perez, Francisco Liriano, Fausto Carmona	
PHL	Cole Hamels, Francisco Liriano, Oliver Perez	65.00
PSO	Roy Oswalt, Jake Peavy, Ben Sheets	40.00
PVW	Justin Verlander, Jered Weaver, Jonathan Papelbon	90.00
RHW	Jeremy Hermida, Josh Willingham, Cody Ross	30.00

RMM	Victor Martinez, Joe Mauer, Ivan Rodriguez	65.00
RRB	Jose Reyes, Yuniesky Betancourt, Hanley Ramirez	60.00
SGM	Greg Maddux, John Smoltz, Tom Glavine	180.00
SJF	Prince Fielder, Mike Jacobs, Chris Shelton	40.00
SKM	Russell Martin, Takashi Saito, Hong-Chih Kuo	200.00
SWB	Taylor Buchholz, Jamie Shields, Jered Weaver	60.00
TGB	Frank Thomas, Ken Griffey Jr., Jeff Bagwell	150.00
TKY	Michael Young, Mark Teixeira, Ian Kinsler	75.00
UHC	Jeremy Hermida, Dan Uggla, Miguel Cabrera	75.00
URC	Miguel Cabrera, Dan Uggla, Hanley Ramirez	40.00
URW	Hanley Ramirez, Dan Uggla, Josh Willingham	35.00
VBZ	Justin Verlander, Jeremy Bonderman, Joel Zumaya	120.00
VWL	Jered Weaver, Francisco Liriano, Justin Verlander	120.00
WJC	Josh Johnson, Jered Weaver, Matt Cain	70.00
WJO	Scott Olsen, Josh Johnson, Dontrelle Willis	40.00
WSV	Justin Verlander, Jered Weaver, Jamie Shields	65.00
ZBC	Joel Zumaya, Matt Cain, Boof Bonser	60.00
ZHZ	Carlos Zambrano, Felix Hernandez, Joel Zumaya	60.00

Ensemble Signatures 4

No Pricing
Production 25 Sets

Ensemble Signatures 5

No Pricing
Production 15 Sets

Ensemble Signatures 6

No Pricing
Production 10 Sets

Ensemble Signatures 8

Production One Set

Game Materials

		NM/M
Common Player:		8.00

Production 50 Sets

AB	A.J. Burnett	8.00
AD	Adam Dunn	10.00
AJ	Andruw Jones	12.00
AP	Albert Pujols	30.00
AR	Alex Rios	8.00
AS	Alfonso Soriano	10.00
BA	Brian Bannister	8.00
BG	Brian Giles	8.00
BM	Bill Mazeroski	15.00
BO	Jeremy Bonderman	10.00
BR	Brian Roberts	8.00
CA	Melky Cabrera	15.00
CC	Carl Crawford	10.00
CH	Chris Carpenter	15.00
CJ	Conor Jackson	10.00
CL	Carlos Lee	10.00
CR	Coco Crisp	10.00
CS	Chris Shelton	8.00
CU	Chase Utley	20.00
CZ	Carlos Zambrano	10.00
DJ	Derek Jeter	30.00
DJ2	Derek Jeter	30.00
DL	Derrek Lee	30.00
DU	Dan Uggla	10.00

DW	Dontrelle Willis	10.00
FH	Felix Hernandez	12.00
FL	Francisco Liriano	15.00
GA	Garrett Atkins	8.00
GP	Gaylord Perry	10.00
HA	Cole Hamels	15.00
HB	Hank Blalock	10.00
HC	Craig Hansen	15.00
HO	Trevor Hoffman	10.00
HR	Hanley Ramirez	15.00
HT	Tim Hudson	10.00
HU	Torii Hunter	10.00
HY	Roy Halladay	10.00
IK	Ian Kinsler	10.00
IR	Ivan Rodriguez	10.00
JB	Jason Bay	12.00
JD	Jermaine Dye	10.00
JH	Jeremy Hermida	8.00
JJ	Josh Johnson	8.00
JK	Jason Kendall	8.00
JM	Joe Mauer	10.00
JN	Joe Nathan	10.00
JP	Jake Peavy	10.00
JR	Jose Reyes	15.00
JS	Johan Santana	12.00
JV	Justin Verlander	15.00
JW	Jered Weaver	15.00
JZ	Joel Zumaya	15.00
KG	Ken Griffey Jr.	25.00
KG2	Ken Griffey Jr.	25.00
KH	Khalil Greene	8.00
KJ	Kenji Johjima	20.00
KM	Kendry Morales	8.00
KU	Jason Kubel	8.00
KY	Kevin Youkilis	10.00
LA	Luis Aparicio	10.00
LM	Lastings Milledge	10.00
LY	Fred Lynn	8.00
MA	Matt Cain	15.00
MC	Miguel Cabrera	15.00
MG	Marcus Giles	8.00
MH	Matt Holliday	15.00
ML	Mark Loretta	8.00
MM	Melvin Mora	8.00
MO	Justin Morneau	12.00
MS	Mike Schmidt	20.00
MT	Mark Teixeira	12.00
MU	Mark Mulder	10.00
MY	Michael Young	10.00
NS	Nick Swisher	10.00
PA	Jonathan Papelbon	20.00
PF	Prince Fielder	15.00
PM	Paul Molitor	15.00
RC	Cal Ripken Jr.	40.00
RH	Rich Harden	10.00
RI	Jim Rice	15.00
RO	Roy Oswalt	10.00
RW	Rickie Weeks	10.00
RZ	Ryan Zimmerman	20.00
SK	Scott Kazmir	10.00
SP	Scott Podsednik	10.00
TE	Miguel Tejada	12.00
TG	Tony Gwynn	15.00
TH	Travis Hafner	10.00
TI	Tadahito Iguchi	10.00
TP	Tony Perez	10.00
VM	Victor Martinez	10.00
WC	Will Clark	15.00
WI	Josh Willingham	8.00
YB	Yuniesky Betancourt	8.00

Game Materials Signatures

NM/M

Production 35 Sets

AB	A.J. Burnett	25.00
AD	Adam Dunn	25.00
AJ	Andruw Jones	50.00
AP	Albert Pujols	250.00
AR	Alex Rios	25.00
AS	Alfonso Soriano	60.00
BA	Brian Bannister	25.00
BG	Brian Giles	25.00
BM	Bill Mazeroski	40.00
BO	Jeremy Bonderman	50.00
BR	Brian Roberts	25.00
CA	Melky Cabrera	40.00
CC	Carl Crawford	25.00
CH	Chris Carpenter	30.00
CJ	Conor Jackson	35.00
CL	Carlos Lee	25.00
CR	Coco Crisp	30.00
CS	Chris Shelton	25.00
CU	Chase Utley	60.00
CZ	Carlos Zambrano	40.00
DJ	Derek Jeter	250.00
DJ2	Derek Jeter	250.00
DL	Derrek Lee	35.00
DU	Dan Uggla	40.00
DW	Dontrelle Willis	30.00
FH	Felix Hernandez	40.00
FL	Francisco Liriano	50.00
GA	Garrett Atkins	25.00

GP	Gaylord Perry	25.00
HA	Cole Hamels	60.00
HB	Hank Blalock	25.00
HC	Craig Hansen	40.00
HO	Trevor Hoffman	30.00
HR	Hanley Ramirez	60.00
HT	Tim Hudson	30.00
HU	Torii Hunter	25.00
HY	Roy Halladay	25.00
IK	Ian Kinsler	30.00
IR	Ivan Rodriguez	35.00
JB	Jason Bay	30.00
JD	Jermaine Dye	25.00
JH	Jeremy Hermida	25.00
JJ	Josh Johnson	35.00
JK	Jason Kendall	25.00
JM	Joe Mauer	40.00
JN	Joe Nathan	25.00
JP	Jake Peavy	30.00
JR	Jose Reyes	40.00
JS	Johan Santana	50.00
JV	Justin Verlander	60.00
JW	Jered Weaver	40.00
JZ	Joel Zumaya	60.00
KG	Ken Griffey Jr.	120.00
KG2	Ken Griffey Jr.	120.00
KH	Khalil Greene	35.00
KM	Kendry Morales	30.00
KU	Jason Kubel	25.00
KY	Kevin Youkilis	25.00
LA	Luis Aparicio	25.00
LY	Fred Lynn	25.00
MA	Matt Cain	40.00
MC	Miguel Cabrera	50.00
MG	Marcus Giles	25.00
MH	Matt Holliday	30.00
ML	Mark Loretta	25.00
MM	Melvin Mora	25.00
MO	Justin Morneau	40.00
MS	Mike Schmidt	50.00
MU	Mark Mulder	25.00
MY	Michael Young	25.00
NS	Nick Swisher	25.00
PA	Jonathan Papelbon	60.00
PM	Paul Molitor	35.00
RC	Cal Ripken Jr.	150.00
RH	Rich Harden	30.00
RI	Jim Rice	30.00
RO	Roy Oswalt	30.00
RW	Rickie Weeks	25.00
RZ	Ryan Zimmerman	65.00
SK	Scott Kazmir	30.00
SP	Scott Podsednik	25.00
TE	Miguel Tejada	30.00
TG	Tony Gwynn	60.00
TH	Travis Hafner	30.00
TI	Tadahito Iguchi	40.00
TP	Tony Perez	30.00
VM	Victor Martinez	30.00
WC	Will Clark	35.00
WI	Josh Willingham	25.00
YB	Yuniesky Betancourt	25.00

Legendary Materials
NM/M
Production 5-55

AR	Al Rosen/55	15.00
BD	Bill Dickey/55	30.00
BD2	Bill Dickey/55	30.00
BG	Bob Gibson/25	20.00
BM	Bill Mazeroski/25	20.00
BO	Bo Jackson/55	20.00
BO2	Bo Jackson/55	20.00
CF	Carlton Fisk/55	10.00
CF2	Carlton Fisk/55	10.00
CW	Rod Carew/55	10.00
CW2	Rod Carew/55	10.00
CY	Carl Yastrzemski/25	20.00
CY2	Carl Yastrzemski/25	20.00
GP	Gaylord Perry/55	10.00
GP2	Gaylord Perry/55	10.00
JB	Johnny Bench/55	20.00
JO	Joe Morgan/55	10.00
JO2	Joe Morgan/55	10.00
JU	Juan Marichal/55	10.00
KI	Kirk Gibson/55	10.00
KP	Kirby Puckett/55	20.00
KP2	Kirby Puckett/55	20.00
MA	Don Mattingly/55	25.00
MA2	Don Mattingly/55	25.00
MW	Maury Wills/41	10.00
NR	Nolan Ryan/55	35.00
NR2	Nolan Ryan/25	40.00
NR3	Nolan Ryan/25	40.00
OS	Ozzie Smith/55	20.00
OS2	Ozzie Smith/55	20.00
PM	Paul Molitor/55	10.00
PM2	Paul Molitor/55	10.00
PN	Phil Niekro/55	10.00
PN2	Phil Niekro/55	10.00
RJ	Reggie Jackson/25	20.00
RJ2	Reggie Jackson/25	15.00
RK	Ralph Kiner/25	20.00
RO	Brooks Robinson/35	15.00

RO2	Brooks Robinson/35	15.00
RS	Ryne Sandberg/35	25.00
RY	Robin Yount/25	15.00
RY2	Robin Yount/25	15.00
SC	Steve Carlton/55	10.00
SC2	Steve Carlton/55	10.00
SU	Don Sutton/55	10.00
SU2	Don Sutton/55	10.00
TG	Tony Gwynn/55	20.00
TG2	Tony Gwynn/55	20.00
TP	Tony Perez/55	15.00
TP2	Tony Perez/55	15.00
WB	Wade Boggs/55	15.00
WB2	Wade Boggs/55	15.00
WC	Will Clark/45	15.00
WC2	Will Clark/45	15.00

Legendary Ensemble Signatures
No Pricing
Production 25 Sets

Maximum Materials
Production 25 Sets
Patch: No Pricing
Production 15 Sets

Numbers Materials
NM/M
Production 35 Sets

AB	A.J. Burnett	10.00
AD	Adam Dunn	12.00
AJ	Andruw Jones	15.00
AP	Albert Pujols	40.00
AR	Alex Rios	10.00
AS	Alfonso Soriano	15.00
BA	Brian Bannister	10.00
BG	Brian Giles	10.00
BM	Bill Mazeroski	15.00
BO	Jeremy Bonderman	15.00
BR	Brian Roberts	10.00
CA	Melky Cabrera	15.00
CC	Carl Crawford	10.00
CH	Chris Carpenter	15.00
CJ	Conor Jackson	15.00
CL	Carlos Lee	10.00
CR	Coco Crisp	10.00
CS	Chris Shelton	10.00
CU	Chase Utley	20.00
CZ	Carlos Zambrano	15.00
DJ	Derek Jeter	40.00
DJ2	Derek Jeter	40.00
DL	Derrek Lee	15.00
DU	Dan Uggla	15.00
DW	Dontrelle Willis	15.00
FH	Felix Hernandez	15.00
FL	Francisco Liriano	20.00
GA	Garrett Atkins	10.00
GP	Gaylord Perry	15.00
HA	Cole Hamels	25.00
HB	Hank Blalock	10.00
HC	Craig Hansen	20.00
HO	Trevor Hoffman	10.00
HR	Hanley Ramirez	20.00
HT	Tim Hudson	10.00
HU	Torii Hunter	10.00
HY	Roy Halladay	10.00
IK	Ian Kinsler	10.00
IR	Ivan Rodriguez	15.00
JB	Jason Bay	15.00
JD	Jermaine Dye	10.00
JH	Jeremy Hermida	10.00
JJ	Josh Johnson	12.00
JK	Jason Kendall	10.00
JM	Joe Mauer	15.00
JN	Joe Nathan	10.00
JP	Jake Peavy	10.00
JR	Jose Reyes	20.00
JS	Johan Santana	20.00
JV	Justin Verlander	20.00
JW	Jered Weaver	20.00
JZ	Joel Zumaya	20.00
KG	Ken Griffey Jr.	35.00
KG2	Ken Griffey Jr.	35.00
KH	Khalil Greene	10.00
KJ	Kenji Johjima	30.00
KM	Kendry Morales	10.00
KU	Jason Kubel	10.00
KY	Kevin Youkilis	15.00
LA	Luis Aparicio	10.00
LM	Lastings Milledge	15.00
LY	Fred Lynn	10.00
MA	Matt Cain	15.00
MC	Miguel Cabrera	15.00
MG	Marcus Giles	10.00
MH	Matt Holliday	10.00
ML	Mark Loretta	10.00
MM	Melvin Mora	10.00
MO	Justin Morneau	15.00
MS	Mike Schmidt	25.00
MT	Mark Teixeira	15.00
MU	Mark Mulder	10.00
MY	Michael Young	10.00

NS	Nick Swisher	10.00
PA	Jonathan Papelbon	25.00
PF	Prince Fielder	20.00
PM	Paul Molitor	15.00
RC	Cal Ripken Jr.	75.00
RH	Rich Harden	10.00
RI	Jim Rice	15.00
RO	Roy Oswalt	15.00
RW	Rickie Weeks	10.00
RZ	Ryan Zimmerman	25.00
SK	Scott Kazmir	10.00
SP	Scott Podsednik	10.00
TE	Miguel Tejada	15.00
TG	Tony Gwynn	20.00
TH	Travis Hafner	15.00
TI	Tadahito Iguchi	15.00
TP	Tony Perez	15.00
VM	Victor Martinez	10.00
WC	Will Clark	15.00
WI	Josh Willingham	10.00
YB	Yuniesky Betancourt	10.00

Numbers Patch
NM/M
Production 35 unless noted.

AB	A.J. Burnett	20.00
AD	Adam Dunn	25.00
AJ	Andruw Jones	25.00
AP	Albert Pujols	80.00
AR	Alex Rios	20.00
AS	Alfonso Soriano	25.00
BA	Brian Bannister	15.00
BG	Brian Giles	20.00
BO	Jeremy Bonderman	25.00
BR	Brian Roberts	20.00
CA	Melky Cabrera	20.00
CC	Carl Crawford	20.00
CH	Chris Carpenter	25.00
CJ	Conor Jackson	20.00
CL	Carlos Lee	20.00
CR	Coco Crisp	20.00
CS	Chris Shelton	15.00
CU	Chase Utley	40.00
CZ	Carlos Zambrano	25.00
DJ	Derek Jeter	65.00
DJ2	Derek Jeter	65.00
DL	Derrek Lee	25.00
DU	Dan Uggla	25.00
DW	Dontrelle Willis	25.00
FH	Felix Hernandez	25.00
FL	Francisco Liriano	30.00
GA	Garrett Atkins	20.00
HA	Cole Hamels	40.00
HB	Hank Blalock	20.00
HO	Trevor Hoffman	20.00
HR	Hanley Ramirez	30.00
HT	Tim Hudson	20.00
HU	Torii Hunter	20.00
HY	Roy Halladay	20.00
IK	Ian Kinsler	20.00
IR	Ivan Rodriguez	25.00
JB	Jason Bay	25.00
JD	Jermaine Dye	20.00
JH	Jeremy Hermida	20.00
JJ	Josh Johnson	20.00
JK	Jason Kendall	20.00
JM	Joe Mauer	40.00
JN	Joe Nathan	20.00
JP	Jake Peavy	20.00
JR	Jose Reyes	40.00
JS	Johan Santana	30.00
JV	Justin Verlander	40.00
JW	Jered Weaver	30.00
JZ	Joel Zumaya	35.00
KG	Ken Griffey Jr.	50.00
KG2	Ken Griffey Jr.	50.00
KH	Khalil Greene	20.00
KJ	Kenji Johjima	50.00
KM	Kendry Morales	20.00
KU	Jason Kubel	20.00
KY	Kevin Youkilis	20.00
LA	Luis Aparicio	20.00
LM	Lastings Milledge	20.00
LY	Fred Lynn	20.00
MA	Matt Cain	30.00
MC	Miguel Cabrera	25.00
MG	Marcus Giles	20.00
MH	Matt Holliday	20.00
ML	Mark Loretta	20.00
MM	Melvin Mora	20.00
MO	Justin Morneau	25.00
MS	Mike Schmidt	50.00
MT	Mark Teixeira	25.00
MU	Mark Mulder	20.00
MY	Michael Young	20.00
NS	Nick Swisher	20.00
PF	Prince Fielder	30.00
PM	Paul Molitor	30.00
RC	Cal Ripken Jr.	100.00
RH	Rich Harden	20.00
RI	Jim Rice	25.00
RO	Roy Oswalt	20.00
RW	Rickie Weeks	20.00
RZ	Ryan Zimmerman	35.00
SK	Scott Kazmir	20.00

SP	Scott Podsednik	20.00
TE	Miguel Tejada	25.00
TG	Tony Gwynn	30.00
TH	Travis Hafner	25.00
TI	Tadahito Iguchi	25.00
VM	Victor Martinez	20.00
WC	Will Clark	25.00
WI	Josh Willingham	20.00
YB	Yuniesky Betancourt	15.00

Signature Patch
No Pricing
Production 10 Sets

Ultimate Patch
NM/M
Production 50 unless noted.
Patch Signature: No Pricing
Production 10 Sets

AB	A.J. Burnett	15.00
AD	Adam Dunn	20.00
AJ	Andruw Jones	20.00
AP	Albert Pujols	60.00
AR	Alex Rios	15.00
AS	Alfonso Soriano	25.00
BA	Brian Bannister	15.00
BG	Brian Giles	15.00
BO	Jeremy Bonderman	25.00
BR	Brian Roberts	15.00
CA	Melky Cabrera	15.00
CC	Carl Crawford	15.00
CH	Chris Carpenter	20.00
CJ	Conor Jackson	15.00
CL	Carlos Lee	15.00
CR	Coco Crisp	15.00
CS	Chris Shelton	15.00
CU	Chase Utley	35.00
CZ	Carlos Zambrano	20.00
DJ	Derek Jeter	50.00
DJ2	Derek Jeter	50.00
DL	Derrek Lee	20.00
DU	Dan Uggla	20.00
DW	Dontrelle Willis	15.00
FH	Felix Hernandez	20.00
FL	Francisco Liriano	25.00
GA	Garrett Atkins	15.00
GP	Gaylord Perry/27	20.00
HA	Cole Hamels	25.00
HB	Hank Blalock	15.00
HO	Trevor Hoffman	15.00
HR	Hanley Ramirez	25.00
HT	Tim Hudson	15.00
HU	Torii Hunter	15.00
HY	Roy Halladay	15.00
IR	Ivan Rodriguez	20.00
JB	Jason Bay	20.00
JD	Jermaine Dye	15.00
JH	Jeremy Hermida	20.00
JJ	Josh Johnson	20.00
JK	Jason Kendall	20.00
JM	Joe Mauer	25.00
JN	Joe Nathan	15.00
JP	Jake Peavy	15.00
JR	Jose Reyes	30.00
JS	Johan Santana	25.00
JV	Justin Verlander	40.00
JW	Jered Weaver	25.00
JZ	Joel Zumaya/47	20.00
KG	Ken Griffey Jr.	50.00
KG2	Ken Griffey Jr.	50.00
KH	Khalil Greene	15.00
KJ	Kenji Johjima	35.00
KM	Kendry Morales	20.00
KU	Jason Kubel	15.00
KY	Kevin Youkilis/10	
LA	Luis Aparicio	20.00
LM	Lastings Milledge	30.00
LY	Fred Lynn	15.00
MA	Matt Cain	25.00
MC	Miguel Cabrera	25.00
MG	Marcus Giles	15.00
MH	Matt Holliday	30.00
ML	Mark Loretta/40	15.00
MM	Melvin Mora	15.00
MO	Justin Morneau	20.00
MS	Mike Schmidt	30.00
MT	Mark Teixeira	20.00
MU	Mark Mulder	15.00
MY	Michael Young	20.00
NS	Nick Swisher	20.00
PF	Prince Fielder	25.00
PM	Paul Molitor	20.00
RC	Cal Ripken Jr.	75.00
RH	Rich Harden	20.00
RI	Jim Rice/31	20.00
RO	Roy Oswalt	25.00
RW	Rickie Weeks	20.00
RZ	Ryan Zimmerman	50.00
SK	Scott Kazmir	20.00
SP	Scott Podsednik	15.00
TE	Miguel Tejada	30.00
TG	Tony Gwynn	30.00
TH	Travis Hafner	20.00
TI	Tadahito Iguchi	30.00

VM	Victor Martinez	15.00
WC	Will Clark	20.00
WI	Josh Willingham	15.00
YB	Yuniesky Betancourt	15.00

Tandem Materials

NM/M

Production 25 Sets		
Signature:	No Pricing	
Production 15 Sets		
Signature Patch:	No Pricing	
Production 5 Sets		
Signature Logo:	No Pricing	
Production One Set		
AA	Alfonso Soriano, Alex Rios	20.00
AH	Garrett Atkins, Matt Holliday	10.00
BH	Felix Hernandez, Yuniesky Betancourt	20.00
BM	Brian Bannister, Lastings Milledge	20.00
BR	Yuniesky Betancourt, Hanley Ramirez	25.00
BV	Justin Verlander, Jeremy Bonderman	40.00
CL	Coco Crisp, Mark Loretta	20.00
CP	Carl Crawford, Scott Podsednik	15.00
CS	Cole Hamels, Scott Kazmir	25.00
CW	Dontrelle Willis, Chris Carpenter	15.00
CZ	Miguel Cabrera, Ryan Zimmerman	25.00
FP	Tony Perez, Prince Fielder	20.00
FW	Prince Fielder, Rickie Weeks	20.00
GP	Ken Griffey Jr., Albert Pujols	50.00
HB	Matt Holliday, Jason Bay	15.00
HF	Prince Fielder, Travis Hafner	20.00
HG	Trevor Hoffman, Brian Giles	10.00
HJ	Andruw Jones, Torii Hunter	15.00
HK	Jeremy Hermida, Jason Kubel	10.00
HM	Travis Hafner, Victor Martinez	10.00
HN	Trevor Hoffman, Joe Nathan	10.00
HO	Roy Oswalt, Rich Harden	15.00
HP	Trevor Hoffman, Jonathan Papelbon	25.00
HR	Hanley Ramirez, Jeremy Hermida	15.00
HW	Jeremy Hermida, Josh Willingham	10.00
ID	Jermaine Dye, Tadahito Iguchi	15.00
JB	Bill Mazeroski, Jason Bay	20.00
JG	Derek Jeter, Ken Griffey Jr.	40.00
JR	Derek Jeter, Cal Ripken Jr.	60.00
KB	Brian Giles, Khalil Greene	10.00
KM	Joe Mauer, Jason Kendall	15.00
KU	Ian Kinsler, Dan Uggla	10.00
KY	Ian Kinsler, Michael Young	10.00
LF	Prince Fielder, Carlos Lee	20.00
MH	Livan Hernandez, Kendry Morales	10.00
MM	Joe Mauer, Victor Martinez	20.00
MP	Tony Perez, Kendry Morales	15.00
MR	Melvin Mora, Brian Roberts	10.00
MW	Rickie Weeks, Paul Molitor	20.00
NJ	Joe Mauer, Joe Nathan	20.00
NM	Joe Mauer, Joe Nathan	15.00
PO	Roy Oswalt, Jake Peavy	15.00
PP	Jake Peavy, Gaylord Perry	15.00
SH	Rich Harden, Nick Swisher	15.00
TY	Michael Young, Mark Teixeira	15.00

VM	Justin Verlander, Jack Morris	20.00
WM	Josh Willingham, Joe Mauer	20.00
YL	Kevin Youkilis, Mark Loretta	15.00
ZJ	Josh Johnson, Joel Zumaya	20.00
ZZ	Joel Zumaya, Carlos Zambrano	20.00

Tandem Patch

NM/M

Production 35 Sets		
AA	Alfonso Soriano, Alex Rios	15.00
AH	Garrett Atkins, Matt Holliday	15.00
AJ	Luis Aparicio, Derek Jeter	40.00
BH	Felix Hernandez, Yuniesky Betancourt	20.00
BM	Brian Bannister, Lastings Milledge	15.00
BR	Yuniesky Betancourt, Hanley Ramirez	20.00
BV	Justin Verlander, Jeremy Bonderman	40.00
CH	Melky Cabrera, Jeremy Hermida	20.00
CL	Coco Crisp, Mark Loretta	15.00
CM	Lastings Milledge, Melky Cabrera	25.00
CO	Roy Oswalt, Roger Clemens	50.00
CP	Carl Crawford, Scott Podsednik	15.00
CR	Miguel Cabrera, Hanley Ramirez	20.00
CS	Cole Hamels, Scott Kazmir	50.00
CV	Justin Verlander, Matt Cain	40.00
CW	Dontrelle Willis, Chris Carpenter	30.00
CZ	Miguel Cabrera, Ryan Zimmerman	30.00
DH	Hanley Ramirez, Derek Jeter	60.00
FW	Prince Fielder, Rickie Weeks	30.00
GD	Adam Dunn, Ken Griffey Jr.	40.00
GG	Tony Gwynn, Brian Giles	30.00
GP	Ken Griffey Jr., Albert Pujols	80.00
GR	Ken Griffey Jr., Alex Rios	40.00
GT	Ken Griffey Jr., Frank Thomas	50.00
HB	Matt Holliday, Jason Bay	20.00
HF	Prince Fielder, Travis Hafner	30.00
HG	Trevor Hoffman, Brian Giles	15.00
HJ	Andruw Jones, Torii Hunter	25.00
HK	Jeremy Hermida, Jason Kubel	15.00
HM	Travis Hafner, Victor Martinez	15.00
HN	Trevor Hoffman, Joe Nathan	15.00
HO	Roy Oswalt, Rich Harden	20.00
HP	Trevor Hoffman, Jonathan Papelbon	30.00
HR	Hanley Ramirez, Jeremy Hermida	25.00
HW	Jeremy Hermida, Josh Willingham	15.00
ID	Jermaine Dye, Tadahito Iguchi	25.00
JC	Derek Jeter, Melky Cabrera	65.00
JG	Derek Jeter, Ken Griffey Jr.	80.00
JJ	Derek Jeter, Reggie Jackson	60.00
JK	Kendry Morales, Jered Weaver	30.00
JM	Kenji Johjima, Victor Martinez	30.00
JR	Derek Jeter, Cal Ripken Jr.	100.00
KB	Brian Giles, Khalil Greene	20.00
KC	Scott Kazmir, Carl Crawford	15.00
KM	Joe Mauer, Jason Kendall	25.00

KU	Ian Kinsler, Dan Uggla	20.00
KY	Ian Kinsler, Michael Young	15.00
LC	Fred Lynn, Coco Crisp	20.00
LF	Prince Fielder, Carlos Lee	20.00
LH	Francisco Liriano, Cole Hamels	40.00
MF	Kendry Morales, Prince Fielder	25.00
MH	Livan Hernandez, Kendry Morales	15.00
ML	Francisco Liriano, Joe Mauer	35.00
MM	Joe Mauer, Victor Martinez	25.00
MR	Melvin Mora, Brian Roberts	15.00
MW	Rickie Weeks, Paul Molitor	20.00
NJ	Joe Mauer, Joe Nathan	20.00
NL	Joe Nathan, Francisco Liriano	30.00
NM	Joe Mauer, Joe Nathan	30.00
NP	Joe Nathan, Jonathan Papelbon	30.00
PC	Matt Cain, Gaylord Perry	30.00
PH	Jonathan Papelbon, Craig Hansen	50.00
PO	Roy Oswalt, Jake Peavy	20.00
PP	Jake Peavy, Gaylord Perry	15.00
RC	Coco Crisp, Alex Rios	15.00
RM	Lastings Milledge, Jose Reyes	30.00
RR	Jose Reyes, Hanley Ramirez	40.00
RS	Mike Schmidt, Cal Ripken Jr.	75.00
RU	Hanley Ramirez, Dan Uggla	25.00
RV	Ivan Rodriguez, Justin Verlander	35.00
SH	Rich Harden, Nick Swisher	15.00
SJ	Conor Jackson, Chris Shelton	25.00
SZ	Ryan Zimmerman, Mike Schmidt	40.00
TY	Michael Young, Mark Teixeira	20.00
UK	Chase Utley, Ian Kinsler	40.00
UM	Chase Utley, Joe Morgan	40.00
UR	Brian Roberts, Dan Uggla	15.00
VM	Justin Verlander, Jack Morris	40.00
VZ	Justin Verlander, Joel Zumaya	40.00
WM	Josh Willingham, Joe Mauer	25.00
WR	Hanley Ramirez, Josh Willingham	25.00
WV	Justin Verlander, Jered Weaver	40.00
YL	Kevin Youkilis, Mark Loretta	20.00
ZA	Garrett Atkins, Ryan Zimmerman	40.00
ZC	Ryan Zimmerman, Miguel Cabrera	40.00
ZJ	Josh Johnson, Joel Zumaya	20.00
ZZ	Joel Zumaya, Carlos Zambrano	30.00

Tri-Marks Signatures

No Pricing
Production 15 Sets

2007 Upper Deck

NM/M

Complete Set (1020):		
Common Player:		.15
Rookie Redemption:		75.00
Hobby Pack (15):		5.00
Hobby Box (16):		70.00
1	Doug Slaten RC	.50
2	Miguel Montero (RC)	.25
3	Brian Burres (RC)	.25
4	Devern Hansack RC	2.00
5	David Murphy (RC)	.25
6	Jose Reyes RC	.25
7	Scott Moore (RC)	.25
8	Josh Fields (RC)	.50
9	Chris Stewart RC	.50
10	Jerry Owens (RC)	.25
11	Ryan Sweeney (RC)	.25
12	Kevin Kouzmanoff (RC)	.50
13	Jeff Baker (RC)	.25
14	Justin Hampson (RC)	.25
15	Jeff Salazar (RC)	.25
16	Alvin Colina RC	.25
17	Troy Tulowitzki (RC)	.50
18	Andrew Miller RC	4.00
19	Mike Rabelo RC	1.00
20	Jose Diaz (RC)	.50
21	Angel Sanchez RC	.50
22	Ryan Braun (RC)	1.00
23	Delwyn Young (RC)	.25
24	Drew Anderson (RC)	.25
25	Dennis Sarfate (RC)	.25
26	Vinny Rottino (RC)	.25
27	Glen Perkins (RC)	.25
28	Alexi Casilla RC	1.00
29	Philip Humber (RC)	.50
30	Andy Cannizaro RC	.50
31	Jeremy Brown	.25
32	Sean Henn (RC)	.25
33	Brian Rogers	.15
34	Carlos Maldonado (RC)	.25
35	Juan Morillo (RC)	.25
36	Fred Lewis (RC)	.25
37	Patrick Misch (RC)	.25
38	Billy Sadler (RC)	.25
39	Ryan Feierabend (RC)	.25
40	Cesar Jimenez RC	.75
41	Oswaldo Navarro RC	.50
42	Travis Chick (RC)	.25
43	Delmon Young (RC)	1.00
44	Shawn Riggans (RC)	.25
45	Brian Stokes (RC)	.25
46	Juan Salas (RC)	.25
47	Joaquin Arias (RC)	.25
48	Adam Lind (RC)	.50
49	Beltran Perez (RC)	.25
50	Brett Campbell RC	.50
51	Brian Roberts	.25
52	Miguel Tejada	.50
53	Brandon Fahey	.15
54	Jay Gibbons	.15
55	Corey Patterson	.25
56	Nicholas Markakis	.25
57	Ramon Hernandez	.15
58	Kris Benson	.15
59	Adam Loewen	.15
60	Erik Bedard	.25
61	Chris Ray	.15
62	Chris Britton	.15
63	Daniel Cabrera	.15
64	Sendy Rleal	.15
65	Manny Ramirez	.75
66	David Ortiz	.75
67	Gabe Kapler	.15
68	Alex Cora	.15
69	Dustin Pedroia	.15
70	Trot Nixon	.15
71	Doug Mirabelli	.15
72	Mark Loretta	.15
73	Curt Schilling	.75
74	Jonathan Papelbon	.50
75	Tim Wakefield	.50
76	Jon Lester	.25
77	Craig Hansen	.15
78	Keith Foulke	.15
79	Jermaine Dye	.15
80	Jim Thome	.50
81	Tadahito Iguchi	.15
82	Robert Mackowiak	.15
83	Brian Anderson	.15
84	Juan Uribe	.15
85	A.J. Pierzynski	.15
86	Alex Cintron	.15
87	Jon Garland	.15
88	Jose Contreras	.15
89	Neal Cotts	.15
90	Bobby Jenks	.15
91	Mike MacDougal	.15

No	Player	Price	No	Player	Price	No	Player	Price	No	Player	Price
92	Javier Vazquez	.15	196	Ichiro Suzuki	1.00	300	Todd Coffey	.15	404	Joe Randa	.15
93	Travis Hafner	.40	197	Raul Ibanez	.15	301	David Weathers	.15	405	Jason Bay	.40
94	Jhonny Peralta	.25	198	Chris Snelling SP	.15	302	Eric Milton	.15	406	Chris Duffy	.15
95	Ryan Garko	.15	199	Felix Hernandez	.50	303	Todd Helton	.50	407	Jose Bautista	.15
96	Victor Martinez	.25	200	Cha Sueng Baek	.15	304	Clint Barmes	.15	408	Ronny Paulino	.15
97	Hector Luna	.15	201	Joel Pineiro	.15	305	Kazuo Matsui	.15	409	Ian Snell	.25
98	Casey Blake	.15	202	Julio Mateo	.15	306	Jamey Carroll	.15	410	Zachary Duke	.15
99	Jason Michaels	.15	203	J.J. Putz	.15	307	Yorvit Torrealba	.15	411	Tom Gorzelanny	.15
100	Shin-Soo Choo	.15	204	Rafael Soriano	.15	308	Matt Holliday	.50	412	Shane Youman	.15
101	C.C. Sabathia	.25	205	Jorge Cantu	.15	309	Choo Freeman	.15	413	Mike Gonzalez	.15
102	Paul Byrd	.15	206	B.J. Upton	.25	310	Brad Hawpe	.25	414	Matt Capps	.15
103	Jeremy Sowers	.15	207	Ty Wigginton	.15	311	Jason Jennings	.15	415	Adrian Gonzalez	.25
104	Cliff Lee	.15	208	Greg Norton	.15	312	Jeff Francis	.25	416	Josh Barfield	.25
105	Rafael Betancourt	.15	209	Dioner Navarro	.15	313	Josh Fogg	.15	417	Todd Walker	.15
106	Francisco Cruceta	.15	210	Carl Crawford	.40	314	Aaron Cook	.15	418	Khalil Greene	.15
107	Sean Casey	.15	211	Jonny Gomes	.15	315	Ubaldo Jimenez	.15	419	Mike Piazza	.75
108	Brandon Inge	.15	212	Damon Hollins	.15	316	Manny Corpas	.15	420	Dave Roberts	.15
109	Placido Polanco	.15	213	Scott Kazmir	.25	317	Miguel Cabrera	.75	421	Mike Cameron	.15
110	Omar Infante	.15	214	Casey Fossum	.15	318	Dan Uggla	.15	422	Geoff Blum	.15
111	Ivan Rodriguez	.50	215	Ruddy Lugo	.15	319	Hanley Ramirez	.50	423	Jake Peavy	.40
112	Magglio Ordonez	.25	216	James Shields	.15	320	Wes Helms	.15	424	Chris Young	.25
113	Craig Monroe	.15	217	Tyler Walker	.15	321	Miguel Olivo	.15	425	Woody Williams	.15
114	Marcus Thames	.15	218	Shawn Camp	.15	322	Jeremy Hermida	.15	426	Clay Hensley	.15
115	Justin Verlander	.50	219	Mark Teixeira	.50	323	Cody Ross	.15	427	Cla Meredith	.15
116	Todd Jones	.15	220	Hank Blalock	.25	324	Josh Willingham	.15	428	Trevor Hoffman	.15
117	Kenny Rogers	.15	221	Ian Kinsler	.25	325	Dontrelle Willis	.25	429	Shea Hillenbrand	.15
118	Joel Zumaya	.25	222	Jerry Hairston Jr.	.15	326	Anibal Sanchez	.15	430	Pedro Feliz	.15
119	Jeremy Bonderman	.50	223	Gerald Laird	.15	327	Josh Johnson	.15	431	Ray Durham	.15
120	Nate Robertson	.15	224	Carlos Lee	.40	328	Jose Garcia	.15	432	Mark Sweeney	.15
121	Mark Teahen	.15	225	Gary Matthews	.15	329	Joe Borowski	.15	433	Eliezer Alfonzo	.15
122	Ryan Shealy	.25	226	Mark DeRosa	.15	330	Taylor Tankersley	.15	434	Moises Alou	.25
123	Mitch Maier (RC)	.25	227	Kip Wells	.15	331	Lance Berkman	.50	435	Steve Finley	.15
124	Doug Mientkiewicz	.15	228	Akinori Otsuka	.15	332	Craig Biggio	.40	436	Todd Linden	.15
125	Mark Grudzielanek	.15	229	Vicente Padilla	.15	333	Aubrey Huff	.15	437	Jason Schmidt	.25
126	Shane Costa	.15	230	John Koronka	.15	334	Adam Everett	.15	438	Matt Cain	.25
127	John Buck	.15	231	Kevin Millwood	.25	335	Brad Ausmus	.15	439	Noah Lowry	.15
128	Reggie Sanders	.15	232	Wes Littleton	.15	336	Willy Taveras	.25	440	Brad Hennessey	.15
129	Mike Sweeney	.15	233	Troy Glaus	.40	337	Luke Scott	.15	441	Armando Benitez	.15
130	Mark Redman	.15	234	Lyle Overbay	.25	338	Chris Burke	.15	442	Jonathan Sanchez	.15
131	Todd Wellemeyer	.15	235	Aaron Hill	.15	339	Roger Clemens	1.50	443	Albert Pujols	2.00
132	Scott Elarton	.15	236	John McDonald	.15	340	Andy Pettitte	.40	444	Ronnie Belliard	.15
133	Ambiorix Burgos	.15	237	Bengie Molina	.15	341	Brandon Backe	.15	445	David Eckstein	.15
134	Joe Nelson	.15	238	Vernon Wells	.25	342	Hector Gimenez	.15	446	Aaron Miles	.15
135	Howie Kendrick	.40	239	Reed Johnson	.15	343	Brad Lidge	.15	447	Yadier Molina	.15
136	Chone Figgins	.15	240	Frank Catalanotto	.15	344	Dan Wheeler	.15	448	Jim Edmonds	.25
137	Orlando Cabrera	.25	241	Roy Halladay	.40	345	Nomar Garciaparra	.75	449	Chris Duncan	.15
138	Maicer Izturis	.15	242	B.J. Ryan	.15	346	Rafael Furcal	.25	450	Juan Encarnacion	.15
139	Jose Molina	.15	243	Gustavo Chacin	.15	347	Wilson Betemit	.15	451	Chris Carpenter	.50
140	Vladimir Guerrero	.75	244	Scott Downs	.15	348	Julio Lugo	.15	452	Jeff Suppan	.15
141	Darin Erstad	.15	245	Casey Janssen	.15	349	Russell Martin	.25	453	Jason Marquis	.15
142	Juan Rivera	.15	246	Justin Speier	.15	350	Andre Ethier	.25	454	Jeff Weaver	.15
143	Jered Weaver	.40	247	Stephen Drew	.40	351	Matthew Kemp	.25	455	Jason Isringhausen	.15
144	John Lackey	.25	248	Conor Jackson	.25	352	Kenny Lofton	.15	456	Braden Looper	.15
145	Joe Saunders	.15	249	Orlando Hudson	.15	353	Brad Penny	.15	457	Ryan Zimmerman	.40
146	Bartolo Colon	.15	250	Chad Tracy	.15	354	Derek Lowe	.25	458	Nick Johnson	.15
147	Scot Shields	.15	251	Johnny Estrada	.15	355	Chad Billingsley	.25	459	Felipe Lopez	.25
148	Francisco Rodriguez	.25	252	Luis Gonzalez	.15	356	Greg Maddux	1.00	460	Brian Schneider	.15
149	Justin Morneau	.50	253	Eric Byrnes	.15	357	Takashi Saito	.15	461	Alfonso Soriano	.75
150	Jason Bartlett	.15	254	Carlos Quentin	.15	358	Jonathan Broxton	.15	462	Austin Kearns	.15
151	Luis Castillo	.15	255	Brandon Webb	.25	359	Prince Fielder	1.00	463	Ryan Church	.15
152	Nick Punto	.15	256	Claudio Vargas	.15	360	Rickie Weeks	.40	464	Alex Escobar	.15
153	Shannon Stewart	.15	257	Juan Cruz	.15	361	Bill Hall	.25	465	Ramon Ortiz	.15
154	Michael Cuddyer	.15	258	Jorge Julio	.15	362	J.J. Hardy	.15	466	Tony Armas	.15
155	Jason Kubel	.15	259	Luis Vizcaino	.15	363	Jeff Cirillo	.15	467	Michael O'Connor	.15
156	Joe Mauer	.50	260	Livan Hernandez	.15	364	Tony Gwynn Jr.	.15	468	Chad Cordero	.15
157	Francisco Liriano	.25	261	Chipper Jones	.75	365	Corey Hart	.15	469	Jon Rauch	.15
158	Joe Nathan	.25	262	Edgar Renteria	.25	366	Laynce Nix	.15	470	Pedro Astacio	.15
159	Dennys Reyes	.15	263	Adam LaRoche	.25	367	Doug Davis	.15	471	Miguel Tejada	.25
160	Brad Radke	.15	264	Willy Aybar	.15	368	Ben Sheets	.40	472	David Ortiz	.50
161	Boof Bonser	.15	265	Brian McCann	.40	369	Chris Capuano	.15	473	Jermaine Dye	.25
162	Juan Rincon	.15	266	Ryan Langerhans	.15	370	David Bush	.15	474	Travis Hafner	.25
163	Derek Jeter	2.00	267	Jeff Francoeur	.40	371	Derrick Turnbow	.15	475	Magglio Ordonez	.25
164	Jason Giambi	.50	268	Matt Diaz	.15	372	Francisco Cordero	.15	476	Mark Teahen	.15
165	Robinson Cano	.50	269	Tim Hudson	.25	373	Jose Reyes	1.00	477	Vladimir Guerrero	.50
166	Andy Phillips	.15	270	John Smoltz	.40	374	Carlos Delgado	.50	478	Justin Morneau	.50
167	Bobby Abreu	.40	271	Oscar Villarreal	.15	375	Julio Franco	.15	479	Derek Jeter	1.00
168	Gary Sheffield	.50	272	Horacio Ramirez	.15	376	Jose Valentin	.15	480	Nick Swisher	.25
169	Bernie Williams	.40	273	Bob Wickman	.15	377	Paul LoDuca	.15	481	Ichiro Suzuki	.50
170	Melky Cabrera	.25	274	Chad Paronto	.15	378	Carlos Beltran	.50	482	Scott Kazmir	.25
171	Mike Mussina	.50	275	Derrek Lee	.50	379	Shawn Green	.15	483	Mark Teixeira	.25
172	Chien-Ming Wang	.50	276	Ryan Theriot	.15	380	Lastings Milledge	.25	484	Vernon Wells	.25
173	Mariano Rivera	.50	277	Cesar Izturis	.15	381	Endy Chavez	.15	485	Brandon Webb	.25
174	Scott Proctor	.15	278	Ronny Cedeno	.15	382	Pedro Martinez	.75	486	Andruw Jones	.40
175	Jaret Wright	.15	279	Michael Barrett	.25	383	John Maine	.15	487	Carlos Zambrano	.25
176	Kyle Farnsworth	.15	280	Juan Pierre	.15	384	Orlando Hernandez	.15	488	Adam Dunn	.25
177	Eric Chavez	.25	281	Jacque Jones	.15	385	Steve Trachsel	.15	489	Matt Holliday	.50
178	Bobby Crosby	.15	282	Matt Murton	.25	386	Billy Wagner	.15	490	Miguel Cabrera	.50
179	Frank Thomas	.50	283	Carlos Zambrano	.25	387	Ryan Howard	1.50	491	Lance Berkman	.25
180	Dan Johnson	.15	284	Mark Prior	.25	388	Chase Utley	.75	492	Nomar Garciaparra	.50
181	Marco Scutaro	.15	285	Rich Hill	.40	389	Jimmy Rollins	.50	493	Prince Fielder	1.00
182	Nick Swisher	.40	286	Sean Marshall	.15	390	Chris Coste	.15	494	Carlos Beltran	.40
183	Milton Bradley	.25	287	Ryan Dempster	.15	391	Jeff Conine	.15	495	Ryan Howard	1.00
184	Jay Payton	.15	288	Ryan O'Malley	.15	392	Aaron Rowand	.15	496	Jason Bay	.25
185	Joe Blanton	.15	289	Scott Hatteberg	.15	393	Shane Victorino	.15	497	Adrian Gonzalez	.25
186	Barry Zito	.40	290	Brandon Phillips	.15	394	David Dellucci	.15	498	Matt Cain	.15
187	Rich Harden	.25	291	Edwin Encarnacion	.15	395	Cole Hamels	.40	499	Albert Pujols	1.00
188	Esteban Loaiza	.15	292	Rich Aurilia	.15	396	Jamie Moyer	.15	500	Ryan Zimmerman	.25
189	Huston Street	.25	293	David Ross	.15	397	Ryan Madson	.15	501	Daisuke	
190	Chad Gaudin	.15	294	Ken Griffey Jr.	1.00	398	Brett Myers	.25		Matsuzaka RC	30.00
191	Richie Sexson	.40	295	Ryan Freel	.15	399	Tom Gordon	.15	501a	Daisuke Matsuzaka/	
192	Yuniesky Betancourt	.15	296	Chris Denorfia	.15	400	Geoff Geary	.15		Ball/150	
193	Willie Bloomquist	.15	297	Bronson Arroyo	.15	401	Freddy Sanchez	.15	502	Kei Igawa RC	5.00
194	Ben Broussard	.15	298	Aaron Harang	.15	402	Xavier Nady	.15	503	Akinori Iwamura RC	6.00
195	Kenji Johjima	.25	299	Brandon Claussen	.15	403	Jose Castillo	.15	521	Randy Johnson	.75

No.	Player	Value
522	Brandon Lyon	.15
523	Robby Hammock	.15
524	Micah Owings (RC)	.15
525	Doug Davis	.15
526	Brian Barden RC	.50
527	Alberto Callaspo	.15
528	Stephen Drew	.25
529	Chris Young	.25
530	Edgar Gonzalez	.15
531	Brandon Medders	.15
532	Tony Pena	.15
533	Jose Valverde	.15
534	Chris Snyder	.15
535	Tony Clark	.15
536	Scott Hairston	.15
537	Jeff DaVanon	.15
538	Randy Johnson	.40
539	Mark Redman	.15
540	Andruw Jones	.50
541	Rafael Soriano	.15
542	Scott Thorman	.15
543	Chipper Jones	.75
544	Mike Gonzalez	.15
545	Lance Cormier	.15
546	Kyle Davies	.15
547	Mike Hampton	.15
548	Chuck James	.15
549	Macay McBride	.15
550	Tanyon Sturtze	.15
551	Tyler Yates	.15
552	Peter Orr	.15
553	Craig Wilson	.15
554	Chris Woodward	.15
556	Chipper Jones	.40
557	Chad Bradford	.15
558	John Parrish	.15
559	Jeremy Guthrie	.15
560	Steve Trachsel	.15
561	Scott Williamson	.15
562	Jaret Wright	.15
563	Paul Bako	.15
564	Chris Gomez	.15
565	Melvin Mora	.15
566	Freddie Bynum	.15
567	Aubrey Huff	.15
568	Jay Payton	.15
569	Miguel Tejada	.50
570	Kurt Birkins	.15
571	Danys Baez	.15
572	Brian Roberts	.25
573	Josh Beckett	.50
574	Matt Clement	.15
575	Hideki Okajima RC	5.00
576	Javier Lopez	.15
577	Joel Pineiro	.15
578	J.C. Romero	.15
579	Kyle Snyder	.15
580	Julian Tavarez	.15
581	Mike Timlin	.15
582	Jason Varitek	.50
583	Mike Lowell	.25
584	Kevin Youkilis	.25
585	Coco Crisp	.15
586	J.D. Drew	.25
587	Eric Hinske	.15
588	Wily Mo Pena	.15
589	Julio Lugo	.15
590	David Ortiz	.75
591	Manny Ramirez	.75
592	Daisuke Matsuzaka	5.00
593	Scott Eyre	.15
594	Angel Guzman	.15
595	Bob Howry	.15
596	Ted Lilly	.15
597	Juan Mateo	.15
598	Wade Miller	.15
599	Carlos Zambrano	.25
600	Will Ohman	.15
601	Mike Wuertz	.15
602	Henry Blanco	.15
603	Aramis Ramirez	.40
604	Cliff Floyd	.15
605	Kerry Wood	.25
606	Alfonso Soriano	.75
607	Daryle Ward	.15
608	Jason Marquis	.15
609	Mark DeRosa	.15
610	Neal Cotts	.15
611	Derrek Lee	.50
612	Aramis Ramirez	.25
613	David Aardsma	.15
614	Mark Buehrle	.25
615	Nick Massett	.15
616	Andrew Sisco	.15
617	Matt Thornton	.15
618	Toby Hall	.15
619	Joe Crede	.15
620	Paul Konerko	.25
621	Darin Erstad	.15
622	Pablo Ozuna	.15
623	Scott Podsednik	.15
624	Jim Thome	.50
625	Jermaine Dye	.15
626	Jim Thome	.25
627	Adam Dunn	.50
628	Bill Bray	.15
629	Alex Gonzalez	.15
630	Josh Hamilton (RC)	1.00
631	Matt Belisle	.15
632	Rheal Cormier	.15
633	Kyle Lohse	.15
634	Eric Milton	.15
635	Kirk Saarloos	.15
636	Mike Stanton	.15
637	Javier Valentin	.15
638	Juan Castro	.15
639	Jeff Conine	.15
640	Jon Coutlangus (RC)	.50
641	Ken Griffey Jr.	1.50
642	Ken Griffey Jr.	.75
643	Fernando Cabrera	.15
644	Fausto Carmona	.15
645	Jason Davis	.15
646	Aaron Fultz	.15
647	Roberto Hernandez	.15
648	Jake Westbrook	.15
649	Kelly Stoppach	.15
650	Josh Barfield	.25
651	Andy Marte	.15
652	Joe Inglett	.15
653	David Dellucci	.15
654	Joe Borowski	.15
655	Franklin Gutierrez	.15
656	Trot Nixon	.15
657	Grady Sizemore	.50
658	Mike Rouse	.15
659	Travis Hafner	.40
660	Victor Martinez	.40
661	C.C. Sabathia	.40
662	Grady Sizemore	.25
663	Jeremy Affeldt	.15
664	Taylor Buchholz	.15
665	Brian Fuentes	.15
666	LaTroy Hawkins	.15
667	Byung-Hyun Kim	.15
668	Brian Lawrence	.15
669	Rodrigo Lopez	.15
670	Jeff Francis	.15
671	Chris Iannetta	.15
672	Garrett Atkins	.25
673	Todd Helton	.50
674	Steve Finley	.15
675	John Mabry	.15
676	Willy Taveras	.15
677	Jason Hirsh	.15
678	Ramon Ramirez	.15
679	Matt Holliday	.75
680	Todd Helton	.25
681	Roman Colon	.15
682	Chad Durbin	.15
683	Jason Grilli	.15
684	Wilfredo Ledezma	.15
685	Mike Maroth	.15
686	Jose Mesa	.15
687	Justin Verlander	.50
688	Fernando Rodney	.15
689	Vance Wilson	.15
690	Carlos Guillen	.15
691	Neifi Perez	.15
692	Curtis Granderson	.15
693	Gary Sheffield	.50
694	Justin Verlander	.25
695	Kevin Gregg	.15
696	Logan Kensing	.15
697	Randy Messenger	.15
698	Sergio Mitre	.15
699	Ricky Nolasco	.15
700	Scott Olsen	.25
701	Renyel Pinto	.15
702	Matt Treanor	.15
703	Alfredo Amezaga	.15
704	Aaron Boone	.15
705	Mike Jacobs	.15
706	Miguel Cabrera	.75
707	Joe Borchard	.15
708	Jorge Julio	.15
709	Rick Vanden Hurk RC	2.00
710	Lee Gardner (RC)	.50
711	Matt Lindstrom (RC)	.50
712	Henry Owens	.15
713	Hanley Ramirez	.50
714	Alejandro De Aza RC	.50
715	Hanley Ramirez	.25
716	Dave Borkowski	.15
717	Jason Jennings	.15
718	Trever Miller	.15
719	Roy Oswalt	.40
720	Wandy Rodriguez	.15
721	Humberto Quintero	.15
722	Morgan Ensberg	.15
723	Mike Lamb	.15
724	Mark Loretta	.15
725	Jason Lane	.15
726	Carlos Lee	.40
727	Orlando Palmeiro	.15
728	Woody Williams	.15
729	Chad Qualls	.15
730	Lance Berkman	.40
731	Rick White	.15
732	Chris Sampson	.15
733	Carlos Lee	.15
734	Jorge De La Rosa	.15
735	Octavio Dotel	.15
736	Jimmy Gobble	.15
737	Zack Greinke	.15
738	Luke Hudson	.15
739	Gil Meche	.15
740	Joel Peralta	.15
741	Odalis Perez	.15
742	David Riske	.15
743	Jason LaRue	.15
744	Tony Pena	.15
745	Esteban German	.15
746	Ross Gload	.15
747	Emil Brown	.15
748	David DeJesus	.15
749	Brandon Duckworth	.15
750	Alex Gordon RC	3.00
751	Jered Weaver	.50
752	Vladimir Guerrero	.75
753	Hector Carrasco	.15
754	Kelvim Escobar	.15
755	Darren Oliver	.15
756	Dustin Moseley	.15
757	Ervin Santana	.15
758	Mike Napoli	.15
759	Shea Hillenbrand	.15
760	Casey Kotchman	.15
761	Reggie Willits	.15
762	Robb Quinlan	.15
763	Garret Anderson	.15
764	Gary Mathews	.15
765	Justin Speier	.15
766	Jered Weaver	.25
767	Joe Beimel	.15
768	Yhency Brazoban	.15
769	Elmer Dessens	.15
770	Mark Hendrickson	.15
771	Hong-Chih Kuo	.25
772	Jason Schmidt	.25
773	Brett Tomko	.15
774	Randy Wolf	.15
775	Mike Lieberthal	.15
776	Marlon Anderson	.15
777	Jeff Kent	.25
778	Ramon Martinez	.15
779	Olmedo Saenz	.15
780	Luis Gonzalez	.25
781	Juan Pierre	.25
782	Jason Repko	.15
783	Nomar Garciaparra	.75
784	Wilson Valdez	.15
785	Jason Schmidt	.15
786	Greg Aquino	.15
787	Brian Shouse	.15
788	Jeff Suppan	.15
789	Carlos Villanueva	.15
790	Matt Wise	.15
791	Johnny Estrada	.15
792	Craig Counsell	.15
793	Tony Graffanino	.15
794	Corey Koskie	.15
795	Claudio Vargas	.15
796	Brady Clark	.15
797	Gabe Gross	.15
798	Geoff Jenkins	.15
799	Kevin Mench	.15
800	Bill Hall	.25
801	Sidney Ponson	.15
802	Jesse Crain	.15
803	Matt Guerrier	.15
804	Pat Neshek	.15
805	Ramon Ortiz	.15
806	Johan Santana	.75
807	Carlos Silva	.15
808	Mike Redmond	.15
809	Jeff Cirillo	.15
810	Luis Rodriguez	.15
811	Lew Ford	.15
812	Torii Hunter	.40
813	Jason Tyner	.15
814	Rondell White	.15
815	Justin Morneau	.50
816	Joe Mauer	.40
817	Johan Santana	.40
818	David Newhan	.15
819	Aaron Sele	.15
820	Ambiorix Burgos	.15
821	Pedro Feliciano	.15
822	Tom Glavine	.50
823	Aaron Heilman	.15
824	Guillermo Mota	.15
825	Jose Reyes	1.00
826	Oliver Perez	.15
827	Duaner Sanchez	.15
828	Scott Schoeneweis	.15
829	Ramon Castro	.15
830	Damion Easley	.15
831	David Wright	1.50
832	Moises Alou	.25
833	Carlos Beltran	.50
834	Dave Williams	.15
835	David Wright	.75
836	Brian Bruney	.15
837	Mike Myers	.15
838	Carl Pavano	.15
839	Andy Pettitte	.40
840	Luis Vizcaino	.15
841	Jorge Posada	.40
842	Miguel Cairo	.15
843	Doug Mientkiewicz	.15
844	Derek Jeter	2.00
845	Alex Rodriguez	2.00
846	Johnny Damon	.75
847	Hideki Matsui	1.00
848	Josh Phelps	.15
849	Phil Hughes (RC)	4.00
850	Roger Clemens	2.00
851	Jason Giambi	.25
852	Kiko Calero	.15
853	Justin Duchscherer	.15
854	Alan Embree	.15
855	Todd Walker	.15
856	Rich Harden	.15
857	Danny Haren	.40
858	Joe Kennedy	.15
859	Jason Kendall	.15
860	Adam Melhuse	.15
861	Mark Ellis	.15
863	Mark Kotsay	.15
864	Shannon Stewart	.15
865	Mike Piazza	.75
866	Mike Piazza	.40
867	Antonio Alfonseca	.15
868	Carlos Ruiz	.15
869	Adam Eaton	.15
870	Freddy Garcia	.15
871	Jon Lieber	.15
872	Matt Smith	.15
873	Rod Barajas	.15
874	Wes Helms	.15
875	Abraham Nunez	.15
876	Pat Burrell	.25
877	Jayson Werth	.15
878	Greg Dobbs	.15
879	Joseph Bisenius RC	.50
880	Michael Bourn (RC)	.50
881	Chase Utley	.75
882	Ryan Howard	1.50
883	Chase Utley	.40
884	Tony Armas	.15
885	Shawn Chacon	.15
886	John Grabow	.15
887	Paul Maholm	.15
888	Damaso Marte	.15
889	Salomon Torres	.15
890	Humberto Cota	.15
891	Ryan Doumit	.15
892	Adam LaRoche	.25
893	Jack Wilson	.15
894	Nate McLouth	.15
895	Brad Eldred	.15
896	Jonah Bayliss	.15
897	Juan Perez RC	.50
898	Jason Bay	.40
899	Adam LaRoche	.15
900	Doug Brocail	.15
901	Scott Cassidy	.15
902	Scott Linebrink	.15
903	Greg Maddux	1.50
904	Jake Peavy	.40
905	Mike Thompson	.15
906	David Wells	.15
907	Josh Bard	.15
908	Rob Bowen	.15
909	Marcus Giles	.15
910	Russell Branyan	.15
911	Jose Cruz	.15
912	Terrmel Sledge	.15
913	Trevor Hoffman	.25
914	Brian Giles	.15
915	Trevor Hoffman	.25
916	Vinnie Chulk	.15
917	Kevin Correia	.15
918	Tim Lincecum RC	25.00
919	Matt Morris	.15
920	Russ Ortiz	.15
921	Barry Zito	.25
922	Bengie Molina	.15
923	Rich Aurilia	.15
924	Omar Vizquel	.25
925	Jason Ellison	.15
926	Ryan Klesko	.15
927	Dave Roberts	.15
928	Randy Winn	.15
929	Barry Zito	.25
930	Miguel Batista	.15
931	Horacio Ramirez	.15
932	Chris Reitsma	.15
933	George Sherrill	.15
934	Jarrod Washburn	.15
935	Jeff Weaver	.15
936	Jake Woods	.15
937	Adrian Beltre	.25
938	Jose Lopez	.15
939	Ichiro Suzuki	1.50

940	Jose Vidro	.15
941	Jose Guillen	.15
942	Sean White RC	.50
943	Brandon Morrow RC	4.00
944	Felix Hernandez	.50
945	Felix Hernandez	.25
946	Randy Flores	.15
947	Ryan Franklin	.15
948	Kelvin Jimenez RC	.50
949	Tyler Johnson	.15
950	Mark Mulder	.15
951	Anthony Reyes	.15
952	Russ Springer	.15
953	Brad Thompson	.15
954	Adam Wainwright	.15
955	Kip Wells	.15
956	Gary Bennett	.15
957	Adam Kennedy	.15
958	Scott Rolen	.75
959	Scott Spiezio	.15
960	So Taguchi	.15
961	Preston Wilson	.15
962	Skip Schumaker	.15
963	Albert Pujols	2.00
964	Chris Carpenter	.50
965	Chris Carpenter	.25
966	Edwin Jackson	.15
967	Jae-Kuk Ryu	.15
968	Jae Weong Seo	.15
969	Jon Switzer	.15
970	Josh Paul	.15
971	Benjamin Zobrist	.15
972	Rocco Baldelli	.15
973	Scott Kazmir	.25
974	Carl Crawford	.25
975	Delmon Young	.50
976	Bruce Chen	.15
977	Joaquin Benoit	.15
978	Scott Feldman	.15
979	Eric Gagne	.15
980	Kameron Loe	.15
981	Brandon McCarthy	.15
982	Robinson Tejeda	.15
983	C.J. Wilson	.15
984	Mark Teixeira	.50
985	Michael Young	.25
986	Kenny Lofton	.25
987	Brad Wilkerson	.15
988	Nelson Cruz	.15
989	Sammy Sosa	.75
990	Michael Young	.25
991	Vernon Wells	.40
992	Matt Stairs	.15
993	Jeremy Accardo	.15
994	A.J. Burnett	.15
995	Jason Frasor	.15
996	Roy Halladay	.40
997	Shaun Marcum	.15
998	Tomokazu Ohka	.15
999	Josh Towers	.15
1000	Gregg Zaun	.15
1001	Royce Clayton	.15
1002	Jason Smith	.15
1003	Alex Rios	.25
1004	Frank Thomas	.75
1005	Roy Halladay	.25
1006	Jesus Flores RC	.50
1007	Dmitri Young	.15
1008	Ray King	.15
1009	Micah Bowie	.15
1010	Shawn Hill	.15
1011	John Patterson	.15
1012	Levale Speigner RC	.50
1013	Ryan Wagner	.15
1014	Jerome Williams	.15
1015	Ryan Zimmerman	.50
1016	Cristian Guzman	.15
1017	Nook Logan	.15
1018	Chris Snelling	.15
1019	Ronnie Belliard	.15
1020	Nick Johnson	.15

Gold

Gold: 8-15X
Production 75 Sets

Printing Plates

No Pricing
Production one set per color.

Ripken Jr. and Tony Gwynn Road to the Hall

2007 Upper Deck Cal Ripken Box Set

	NM/M
Complete Set (45):	35.00
Common Ripken:	1.000

Cal Ripken Jr. Chronicles

	NM/M
Common Ripken:	8.00

Cal Ripken Jr./ Lou Gehrig Iron Man

	NM/M
Common Ripken/Gehrig:	20.00
Autograph:	No Pricing
Production One	

Cooperstown Calling

		NM/M
Common Player:		1.00
AJ	Andruw Jones	1.50
AP	Albert Pujols	5.00
AR	Alex Rodriguez	5.00
AS	Alfonso Soriano	2.00
BI	Craig Biggio	1.00
BW	Billy Wagner	1.00
CA	Chris Carpenter	1.50
CB	Carlos Beltran	2.00
CC	Carl Crawford	1.00
CD	Carlos Delgado	1.50
CJ	Chipper Jones	2.00
CR	Cal Ripken Jr.	5.00
CS	Curt Schilling	2.00
DJ	Derek Jeter	5.00
DO	David Ortiz	2.00
FT	Frank Thomas	1.50
GM	Greg Maddux	3.00
GS	Gary Sheffield	1.50
HA	Travis Hafner	1.00
HE	Todd Helton	1.50
HO	Ryan Howard	4.00
IR	Ivan Rodriguez	1.50
IS	Ichiro Suzuki	3.00
JD	Johnny Damon	2.00
JG	Jason Giambi	1.50
JK	Jeff Kent	1.00
JM	Justin Morneau	2.00
JS	Johan Santana	2.00
JT	Jim Thome	1.50
KG	Ken Griffey Jr.	4.00
MC	Miguel Cabrera	2.00
MM	Mike Mussina	1.50
MP	Mike Piazza	3.00
MR	Manny Ramirez	2.00
MT	Mark Teixeira	1.50
OV	Omar Vizquel	1.00
PE	Andy Pettitte	1.00
PM	Pedro Martinez	2.00
RH	Roy Halladay	1.00
RI	Mariano Rivera	1.50
RJ	Randy Johnson	2.00
RO	Roy Oswalt	1.00
SI	Grady Sizemore	2.00
SM	John Smoltz	1.50
SR	Scott Rolen	1.50
SS	Sammy Sosa	2.00
TE	Miguel Tejada	1.50
TG	Tom Glavine	1.00
TH	Trevor Hoffman	1.00
VG	Vladimir Guerrero	2.00

Cooperstown Calling Autograph

No Pricing

Game Materials

		NM/M
Common Player:		4.00
Patch:		2-4X
AJ	Andruw Jones	8.00
AP	Albert Pujols	20.00
BE	Josh Beckett	6.00
BR	Brian Roberts	6.00
BS	Ben Sheets	6.00
CA	Chris Carpenter	6.00
CB	Carlos Beltran	10.00
CC	Carl Crawford	6.00
CD	Carlos Delgado	8.00
CL	Carlos Lee	6.00
CP	Corey Patterson	4.00
CS	C.C. Sabathia	6.00
DJ	Derek Jeter	20.00
DO	David Ortiz	10.00
DW	Dontrelle Willis	6.00
EC	Eric Chavez	4.00
FH	Felix Hernandez	8.00
HU	Torii Hunter	6.00
IR	Ivan Rodriguez	8.00
JB	Jason Bay	6.00
JG	Jason Giambi	8.00
JM	Joe Mauer	8.00
JR	Jose Reyes	10.00
JS	Johan Santana	8.00
JU	Juan Uribe	4.00
JV	Justin Verlander	15.00
KG	Ken Griffey Jr.	15.00

MC	Miguel Cabrera	8.00
MH	Matt Holliday	8.00
MM	Melvin Mora	4.00
MO	Justin Morneau	10.00
MR	Manny Ramirez	8.00
MS	Mike Sweeney	4.00
MT	Miguel Tejada	6.00
MU	Mike Mussina	8.00
OR	Magglio Ordonez	8.00
PF	Prince Fielder	15.00
RH	Roy Halladay	6.00
RZ	Ryan Zimmerman	8.00
SR	Scott Rolen	8.00
TH	Tim Hudson	4.00
VM	Victor Martinez	6.00
Series 2:		5.00
AB	A.J. Burnett	4.00
AP	Albert Pujols	20.00
AR	Alex Rios	4.00
BA	Bobby Abreu	5.00
BC	Bartolo Colon	4.00
BJ	Bobby Jenks	4.00
CC	Carl Crawford	5.00
CJ	Chipper Jones	10.00
CS	Curt Schilling	8.00
CU	Chase Utley	10.00
DJ	Derek Jeter	20.00
EB	Erik Bedard	12.00
EN	Juan Encarnacion	4.00
FR	Jeff Francoeur/SP	5.00
GS	Gary Sheffield	8.00
HB	Hank Blalock	4.00
HO	Trevor Hoffman	4.00
JD	Johnny Damon	8.00
JE	Jim Edmonds	5.00
JF	Jeff Francis	4.00
JS	John Smoltz	10.00
JT	Jim Thome	8.00
JV	Jose Vidro	4.00
KG	Ken Griffey Jr.	15.00
LB	Lance Berkman	4.00
LG	Luis Gonzalez	4.00
MR	Manny Ramirez	8.00
MT	Mark Teixeira	8.00
RB	Rocco Baldelli	4.00
RJ	Randy Johnson	8.00
RN	Ricky Nolasco	4.00
RO	Roy Oswalt	8.00
RW	Rickie Weeks	4.00
SD	Stephen Drew	8.00
SK	Scott Kazmir	4.00
SR	Scott Rolen	8.00
TG	Tom Glavine	8.00
TH	Todd Helton	8.00
TN	Trot Nixon	4.00
VG	Vladimir Guerrero	8.00
ZD	Zachary Duke	4.00

Ken Griffey Jr. Chronicles

	NM/M
Common Griffey:	5.00

Playoff Predictors

		NM/M
Common Predictor:		3.00
1	Arizona Diamondbacks	5.00
2	Atlanta Braves	5.00
3	Baltimore Orioles	3.00
4	Boston Red Sox	25.00
5	Chicago Cubs	5.00
6	Chicago White Sox	5.00
7	Cincinnati Reds	3.00
8	Cleveland Indians	5.00
9	Colorado Rockies	5.00
10	Detroit Tigers	5.00
11	Florida Marlins	3.00
12	Houston Astros	5.00
13	Kansas City Royals	3.00
14	Los Angeles Angels	5.00
15	Los Angeles Dodgers	5.00
16	Milwaukee Brewers	5.00
17	Minnesota Twins	5.00
18	New York Mets	5.00
19	New York Yankees	15.00
20	Oakland Athletics	5.00
21	Philadelphia Phillies	5.00
22	Pittsburgh Pirates	3.00
23	San Diego Padres	5.00
24	San Francisco Giants	5.00
25	Seattle Mariners	5.00
26	St. Louis Cardinals	5.00
27	Tampa Bay Devil Rays	3.00
28	Texas Rangers	5.00
29	Toronto Blue Jays	5.00
30	Washington Nationals	3.00

Rookie of the Year Predictor

Lee Gardner

		NM/M
Common Player:		3.00
1	Doug Slaten	3.00
2	Miguel Montero	3.00
4	Kory Casto	3.00
5	Jesus Flores	3.00
6	John Danks	3.00
7	Daisuke Matsuzaka	60.00
9	Chris Stewart	3.00
10	Kevin Cameron	3.00
13	Kevin Kouzmanoff	5.00
14	Jeff Baker	3.00
15	Donald Kelly	3.00
16	Troy Tulowitzki	8.00
18	Cesar Jimenez	3.00
20	Jose Garcia	3.00
21	Micah Owings	3.00
22	Josh Hamilton	6.00
24	Jamie Burke	3.00
25	Mike Rabelo	3.00
26	Elijah Dukes	3.00
27	Travis Buck	3.00
28	Kei Igawa	5.00
29	Sean Henn	3.00
32	Michael Bourn	5.00
33	Alex Gordon	20.00
35	Matt Chico	3.00
38	Gustavo Molina	3.00
39	Jared Burton	3.00
40	Jay Marshall	3.00
42	Akinori Iwamura	20.00
43	Delmon Young	8.00
44	Juan Salas	3.00
45	Zack Segovia	3.00
46	Brian Stokes	3.00
47	Joaquin Arias	3.00
48	Hector Gimenez	3.00
49	Ryan Braun	3.00
50	Juan Perez	3.00

Star Power

		NM/M
Inserted 2:1 Fat Packs		
AJ	Andruw Jones	1.50
AP	Albert Pujols	5.00
AR	Alex Rodriguez	5.00
BR	Brian Roberts	1.00
BZ	Barry Zito	.75
CA	Chris Carpenter	1.50
CB	Carlos Beltran	1.50
CC	Carl Crawford	1.00
CJ	Chipper Jones	2.00
CS	Curt Schilling	1.50
CU	Chase Utley	1.50
CZ	Carlos Zambrano	1.00
DA	Johnny Damon	1.50
DJ	Derek Jeter	5.00
DO	David Ortiz	2.00
DW	Dontrelle Willis	.75
FS	Freddy Sanchez	.75
FT	Frank Thomas	1.50
HA	Roy Halladay	1.00
HO	Trevor Hoffman	.75
IS	Ichiro Suzuki	3.00
JB	Jason Bay	1.00
JD	Jermaine Dye	.75
JM	Joe Mauer	1.50
JP	Jake Peavy	1.00
JR	Jose Reyes	2.00
JS	Johan Santana	1.50
JT	Jim Thome	1.50
JU	Justin Morneau	1.50
JV	Justin Verlander	1.50
KG	Ken Griffey Jr.	4.00
KR	Kenny Rogers	.75
LB	Lance Berkman	1.00
MA	Matt Cain	1.00
MC	Miguel Cabrera	2.00
MH	Matt Holliday	1.00

MO	Magglio Ordonez	.75
MR	Manny Ramirez	1.50
MT	Mark Teixeira	1.00
MY	Michael Young	1.00
NG	Nomar Garciaparra	1.50
NS	Nick Swisher	1.00
PF	Prince Fielder	1.50
RH	Ryan Howard	3.00
RO	Roy Oswalt	1.00
RZ	Ryan Zimmerman	1.00
SM	John Smoltz	1.00
TH	Travis Hafner	1.00
VG	Vladimir Guerrero	1.50
WR	David Wright	2.00

Star Signings

		NM/M
Common Auto.:		5.00
AB	Ambiorix Burgos	8.00
AC	Aaron Cook	5.00
AH	Aubrey Huff/SP	15.00
AR	Alex Rios	20.00
BA	Bobby Abreu	35.00
BL	Joe Blanton	8.00
BO	Jeremy Bonderman	30.00
BR	Brandon Backe	8.00
CJ	Conor Jackson	15.00
CO	Chad Cordero	10.00
CP	Corey Patterson	10.00
CS	Chris Shelton	8.00
CY	Chris Young/SP	20.00
DH	Danny Haren	10.00
DJ	Derek Jeter	150.00
DU	Chris Duffy	10.00
GA	Garrett Atkins	10.00
GC	Gustavo Chacin	8.00
HS	Huston Street	15.00
HU	Torii Hunter	15.00
IS	Ian Snell/SP	20.00
JA	Jeremy Accardo	8.00
JB	Jason Bergmann/SP	8.00
JD	Joey Devine	8.00
JG	Jonny Gomes	8.00
JJ	Jorge Julio	8.00
JK	Jason Kubel	8.00
JM	Justin Morneau	25.00
JN	Joe Nathan	15.00
JS	Jason Bay	15.00
KW	Jake Westbrook	10.00
KF	Keith Foulke	10.00
KG	Ken Griffey Jr.	75.00
KM	Kevin Mench	10.00
KS	Kirk Saarloos	8.00
KY	Kevin Youkilis	20.00
LN	Laynce Nix/SP	8.00
LO	Lyle Overbay	10.00
MA	Matt Cain/SP	
MH	Matt Holliday	25.00
MK	Mark Kotsay	10.00
MM	Melvin Mora	8.00
NM	Nate McLouth/SP	15.00
RC	Ryan Church	8.00
RG	Ryan Garko	15.00
RI	Juan Rivera/SP	8.00
RJ	Reed Johnson	15.00
RU	Carlos Ruiz	10.00
SC	Sean Casey/SP	10.00
SD	Stephen Drew	25.00
SP	Scott Podsednik/SP	20.00
TI	Tadahito Iguchi	25.00
VE	Justin Verlander	30.00
WM	Wily Mo Pena	15.00
XN	Xavier Nady	15.00
YB	Yuniesky Betancourt	20.00
Common Player:		10.00
AC	Alberto Callaspo	10.00
AG	Alex Gordon	40.00
AI	Akinori Iwamura/SP	30.00
AS	Angel Sanchez	10.00
BA	Jeff Baker	10.00
BB	Brian Burres	10.00
BE	Josh Beckett/SP	40.00
BO	Ben Broussard	10.00
BU	B.J. Upton/SP	40.00
CB	Craig Biggio/SP	40.00
CC	Carl Crawford/SP	20.00
CR	Cal Ripken Jr./SP	125.00
DJ	Derek Jeter	140.00
DY	Delmon Young/SP	20.00
ED	Elijah Dukes	15.00
FH	Felix Hernandez	30.00
IK	Ian Kinsler/SP	15.00
IS	Ian Snell	15.00
JD	J.D. Drew/SP	15.00
KG	Ken Griffey Jr./SP	75.00
KI	Kei Igawa/SP	50.00
NC	Nelson Cruz	10.00
OP	Oliver Perez/SP	20.00
SA	Juan Salas	10.00
SH	Sean Henn	10.00
YO	Chris Young	20.00
ZS	Zack Segovia	15.00

Ticket to Stardom

		NM/M
Common Player:		2.00
AG	Alex Gordon	8.00
AI	Akinori Iwamura	4.00
AS	Angel Sanchez	2.00
BN	Jared Burton	2.00
BU	Jamie Burke	2.00
CH	Matt Chico	2.00
CJ	Cesar Jimenez	2.00
CS	Chris Stewart	2.00
DA	John Danks	2.00
DK	Donald Kelly	2.00
DM	Daisuke Matsuzaka	2.00
DS	Doug Slaten	2.00
DY	Delmon Young	4.00
ED	Elijah Dukes	2.00
GM	Gustavo Molina	2.00
HG	Hector Gimenez	2.00
JA	Joaquin Arias	2.00
JB	Jeff Baker	2.00
JF	Jesus Flores	2.00
JG	Jose Garcia	2.00
JH	Josh Hamilton	4.00
JM	Jay Marshall	2.00
JP	Juan Perez	2.00
KC	Kevin Cameron	2.00
KI	Kei Igawa	4.00
KK	Kevin Kouzmanoff	3.00
KO	Kory Casto	2.00
MB	Michael Bourn	2.00
MM	Miguel Montero	2.00
MO	Micah Owings	2.00
MR	Mike Rabelo	2.00
RB	Ryan Braun	2.00
SA	Juan Salas	2.00
SH	Sean Henn	2.00
SO	Joakim Soria	2.00
ST	Brian Stokes	2.00
TB	Travis Buck	2.00
TT	Troy Tulowitzki	4.00
ZS	Zack Segovia	2.00

Ticket to Stardom Autograph

No Pricing

1989 Reprints

Jackie Robinson

		NM/M
Common Player:		1.00
AK	Al Kaline	2.00
BF	Bob Feller	1.00
BR	Babe Ruth	5.00
CA	Rod Carew	1.00
CF	Carlton Fisk	1.00
CM	Christy Mathewson	1.00
CS	Casey Stengel	1.00
CY	Cy Young	1.00
DR	Don Drysdale	1.00
FR	Frank Robinson	1.00
GE	Lou Gehrig	3.00
HW	Honus Wagner	2.00
JB	Johnny Bench	1.50
JF	Jimmie Foxx	2.00
JR	Jackie Robinson	2.00
LG	Lefty Grove	1.00
LJ	LeBron James	3.00
MJ	Michael Jordan	5.00
MO	Mel Ott	1.00
RB	Reggie Bush	3.00
RC	Roy Campanella	1.00
RH	Rogers Hornsby	1.00
RJ	Reggie Jackson	1.50
RO	Brooks Robinson	1.50
SC	Sidney Crosby	4.00
SM	Stan Musial	1.50
SP	Satchel Paige	2.00
TC	Ty Cobb	3.00
TM	Thurman Munson	3.00
WJ	Walter Johnson	1.00

1989 Rookie Reprints

Joakim Soria

		NM/M
Common Player:		1.00
AG	Alex Gordon	3.00
AI	Akinori Iwamura	3.00
AS	Angel Sanchez	1.00
BN	Jared Burton	1.00
BU	Jamie Burke	1.00
CJ	Cesar Jimenez	1.00
CS	Chris Stewart	1.00
DK	Donald Kelly	1.00
DM	Daisuke Matsuzaka	20.00
DY	Delmon Young	2.00
ED	Elijah Dukes	1.00
GM	Gustavo Molina	1.00
HG	Hector Gimenez	1.00
JA	Joaquin Arias	1.00
JB	Jeff Baker	1.00
JD	John Danks	1.00
JF	Jesus Flores	1.00
JG	Jose Garcia	1.00
JH	Josh Hamilton	2.00
JM	Jay Marshall	1.00
JP	Juan Perez	1.00
KC	Kevin Cameron	1.00
KI	Kei Igawa	2.00
KK	Kevin Kouzmanoff	2.00
KO	Kory Casto	1.00
MB	Michael Bourn	1.00
MC	Matt Chico	1.00
MM	Miguel Montero	1.00
MO	Micah Owings	1.00
MR	Mike Rabelo	1.00
SA	Juan Salas	1.00
SH	Sean Henn	1.00
SL	Doug Slaten	1.00
SO	Joakim Soria	1.00
ST	Brian Stokes	1.00
TB	Travis Buck	1.00
TT	Troy Tulowitzki	2.00
ZS	Zack Segovia	1.00

1989 Rookie Reprint Signatures

No Pricing
Production 5 Sets

2007 Upper Deck Artifacts

justin verlander

		NM/M
Complete Set (100):		35.00
Common Player:		.25
Pack (4):		10.00
Box (10):		90.00
1	Miguel Tejada	.50
2	David Ortiz	1.00
3	Manny Ramirez	1.00
4	Curt Schilling	.75

5	Jim Thome	.75
6	Paul Konerko	.50
7	Jermaine Dye	.50
8	Travis Hafner	.50
9	Victor Martinez	.50
10	Grady Sizemore	.50
11	Ivan Rodriguez	.75
12	Magglio Ordonez	.50
13	Justin Verlander	.75
14	Mark Teahen	.25
15	Vladimir Guerrero	1.00
16	Jered Weaver	.50
17	Justin Morneau	.75
18	Joe Mauer	.50
19	Torii Hunter	.50
20	Johan Santana	1.00
21	Derek Jeter	3.00
22	Alex Rodriguez	3.00
23	Johnny Damon	.75
24	Huston Street	.25
25	Nick Swisher	.50
26	Ichiro Suzuki	2.00
27	Richie Sexson	.50
28	Carl Crawford	.50
29	Scott Kazmir	.50
30	Michael Young	.50
31	Mark Teixeira	.75
32	Vernon Wells	.50
33	Roy Halladay	.50
34	Brandon Webb	.50
35	Stephen Drew	.50
36	Chipper Jones	1.00
37	Andruw Jones	.75
38	Derrek Lee	.75
39	Aramis Ramirez	.75
40	Ken Griffey Jr.	2.00
41	Adam Dunn	.50
42	Todd Helton	.75
43	Matt Holliday	.50
44	Miguel Cabrera	1.00
45	Hanley Ramirez	1.00
46	Dontrelle Willis	.50
47	Lance Berkman	.50
48	Roy Oswalt	.50
49	Craig Biggio	.50
50	Nomar Garciaparra	1.00
51	Derek Lowe	.25
52	Prince Fielder	1.00
53	Rickie Weeks	.25
54	Jose Reyes	2.00
55	David Wright	2.00
56	Carlos Beltran	.75
57	Ryan Howard	2.00
58	Chase Utley	1.00
59	Jimmy Rollins	.75
60	Jason Bay	.50
61	Freddy Sanchez	.25
62	Trevor Hoffman	.50
63	Adrian Gonzalez	.50
64	Omar Vizquel	.25
65	Matt Cain	.50
66	Albert Pujols	3.00
67	Jim Edmonds	.50
68	Chris Carpenter	.75
69	David Eckstein	.25
70	Ryan Zimmerman	.50
71	Alexi Casilla RC	.50
72	Andrew Miller RC	5.00
73	Andy Cannizaro RC	1.00
74	Brian Stokes (RC)	.50
75	Carlos Maldonado (RC)	.50
76	Cesar Jimenez RC	1.00
77	Daisuke Matsuzaka RC	8.00
78	Delmon Young (RC)	1.00
79	Delwyn Young (RC)	.50
80	Fred Lewis (RC)	1.00
81	Glen Perkins (RC)	.50
82	Jeff Baker (RC)	.50
83	Jeff Fiorentino (RC)	.50
84	Jeff Salazar (RC)	.50
85	Jerry Owens (RC)	.50
86	Josh Fields (RC)	.50
87	Juan Perez RC	.50
88	Juan Salas (RC)	.50
89	Justin Hampson (RC)	.50
90	Kevin Kouzmanoff (RC)	.50
91	Michael Bourn (RC)	.50
92	Miguel Montero (RC)	.50
93	Mike Rabelo RC	.50
94	Oswaldo Navarro RC	.50
95	Philip Humber (RC)	.50
96	Ryan Braun RC	2.00
97	Ryan Sweeney (RC)	.50
98	Sean Henn (RC)	.50
99	Jose Reyes RC	1.00
100	Troy Tulowitzki (RC)	1.00

Antiquity Artifacts

		NM/M
Production 199 Sets		
Patch:		1.5-3X
Production 50 Sets		
AB	Adrian Beltre	6.00

Antiquity

AJ	Andruw Jones	6.00
AL	Adam LaRoche	4.00
AP	Albert Pujols	20.00
AR	Aramis Ramirez	6.00
AT	Garrett Atkins	4.00
BA	Bobby Abreu	6.00
BC	Bartolo Colon	8.00
BE	Carlos Beltran	8.00
BG	Brian Giles	4.00
BO	Jeremy Bonderman	6.00
BR	Brian Roberts	4.00
BU	B.J. Upton	6.00
BW	Billy Wagner	4.00
BZ	Barry Zito	4.00
CA	Miguel Cabrera	8.00
CB	Craig Biggio	6.00
CC	Carl Crawford	6.00
CF	Chone Figgins	4.00
CH	Chris Carpenter	8.00
CJ	Chipper Jones	8.00
CL	Carlos Lee	6.00
CR	Cal Ripken Jr.	25.00
CS	Curt Schilling	8.00
CU	Chase Utley	10.00
DJ	Derek Jeter	20.00
DO	David Ortiz	10.00
DR	J.D. Drew	4.00
DU	Dan Uggla	4.00
DW	Dontrelle Willis	4.00
EC	Eric Chavez	4.00
ED	Jim Edmonds	6.00
FG	Freddy Garcia	6.00
FH	Felix Hernandez	6.00
FL	Francisco Liriano	8.00
FT	Frank Thomas	8.00
GA	Garret Anderson	4.00
GJ	Geoff Jenkins	4.00
GM	Greg Maddux	10.00
GR	Ken Griffey Jr.	20.00
GS	Grady Sizemore	8.00
HA	Rich Harden	4.00
HB	Hank Blalock	4.00
HO	Trevor Hoffman	4.00
HR	Hanley Ramirez	8.00
HS	Huston Street	6.00
HU	Torii Hunter	6.00
IR	Ivan Rodriguez	6.00
JA	Jason Bay	6.00
JC	Jorge Cantu	4.00
JD	Jermaine Dye	4.00
JE	Johnny Estrada	4.00
JF	Jeff Francoeur	8.00
JG	Jason Giambi	4.00
JJ	Josh Johnson	4.00
JK	Jeff Kent	4.00
JM	Joe Mauer	8.00
JP	Jake Peavy	8.00
JR	Jimmy Rollins	8.00
JS	Jason Schmidt	4.00
JT	Jim Thome	8.00
JV	Justin Verlander	8.00
JZ	Joel Zumaya	6.00
KG	Khalil Greene	4.00
LB	Lance Berkman	6.00
LG	Luis Gonzalez	4.00
MO	Justin Morneau	8.00
MR	Manny Ramirez	8.00
MT	Mark Teixeira	8.00
MY	Michael Young	6.00
NS	Nick Swisher	6.00
OR	Magglio Ordonez	4.00
PA	Jonathan Papelbon	10.00
PB	Pat Burrell	4.00
PE	Jhonny Peralta	4.00
PF	Prince Fielder	10.00
PK	Paul Konerko	6.00
PM	Pedro Martinez	8.00
PO	Jorge Posada	8.00
RC	Roger Clemens	10.00
RE	Jose Reyes	10.00
RH	Roy Halladay	6.00
RJ	Randy Johnson	8.00
RO	Roy Oswalt	6.00
RW	Rickie Weeks	4.00
RZ	Ryan Zimmerman	6.00
SA	Johan Santana	8.00
SK	Scott Kazmir	4.00
SM	John Smoltz	6.00
SR	Scott Rolen	6.00
TE	Miguel Tejada	6.00
TG	Tom Glavine	6.00
TH	Todd Helton	8.00
TI	Tim Hudson	4.00
VA	Jason Varitek	6.00
VG	Vladimir Guerrero	8.00
VM	Victor Martinez	6.00
VW	Vernon Wells	4.00

Apparel

NM/M
Production 199 unless noted.
Rare Apparel: No Pricing
Production One Set
Gold: 1X
Production 130 Sets

AB	Adrian Beltre	6.00
AD	Adam Dunn	8.00
AJ	Andruw Jones/25	10.00
AL	Adam LaRoche	6.00
AP	Albert Pujols	20.00
AR	Aramis Ramirez	10.00
AT	Garrett Atkins	6.00
BA	Bobby Abreu	6.00
BC	Bartolo Colon	4.00
BG	Brian Giles	4.00
BI	Craig Biggio	6.00
BO	Jeremy Bonderman	10.00
BR	Brian Roberts	6.00
BU	B.J. Upton	8.00
BW	Billy Wagner	6.00
BZ	Barry Zito	6.00
CB	Carlos Beltran	6.00
CC	Carl Crawford	6.00
CH	Cole Hamels	10.00
CJ	Chipper Jones	8.00
CL	Carlos Lee	8.00
CR	Cal Ripken Jr.	25.00
CS	Curt Schilling	8.00
CU	Chase Utley	10.00
DJ	Derek Jeter	25.00
DO	David Ortiz	15.00
DU	Dan Uggla	6.00
DW	Dontrelle Willis	6.00
DY	Jermaine Dye	4.00
EC	Eric Chavez	6.00
ES	Johnny Estrada	8.00
FG	Freddy Garcia	4.00
FH	Felix Hernandez	6.00
FL	Francisco Liriano	8.00
FT	Frank Thomas	8.00
GA	Garret Anderson	4.00
GJ	Geoff Jenkins	4.00
GM	Greg Maddux	10.00
GR	Khalil Greene	8.00
GS	Grady Sizemore	10.00
HA	Roy Halladay	6.00
HB	Hank Blalock	4.00
HE	Todd Helton	6.00
HO	Trevor Hoffman	6.00
HR	Hanley Ramirez	8.00
HU	Torii Hunter	6.00
IR	Ivan Rodriguez	6.00
JB	Jason Bay	6.00
JC	Jorge Cantu	4.00
JD	J.D. Drew	6.00
JE	Jim Edmonds	6.00
JF	Jeff Francoeur	10.00
JG	Jason Giambi	8.00
JJ	Josh Johnson	4.00
JK	Jeff Kent	6.00
JM	Joe Mauer	8.00
JN	Joe Nathan	4.00
JO	Johnny Damon	8.00
JP	Jake Peavy	6.00
JR	Jimmy Rollins	10.00
JS	Jason Schmidt	4.00
JT	Jim Thome	8.00
JV	Justin Verlander	10.00
JZ	Joel Zumaya	8.00
KG	Ken Griffey Jr.	20.00
LB	Lance Berkman	6.00
LG	Luis Gonzalez	4.00
MC	Miguel Cabrera/67	10.00
MO	Justin Morneau	8.00
MR	Manny Ramirez	8.00
MT	Mark Teixeira	8.00
MY	Michael Young	8.00
OR	Magglio Ordonez	8.00
PA	Jonathan Papelbon	15.00
PB	Pat Burrell	6.00
PE	Jhonny Peralta	6.00
PF	Prince Fielder	15.00
PM	Pedro Martinez	10.00
PO	Jorge Posada	8.00
RC	Roger Clemens	15.00
RE	Jose Reyes	15.00
RH	Rich Harden	4.00
RI	Mariano Rivera	10.00
RJ	Randy Johnson	8.00
RO	Roy Oswalt	6.00
RW	Rickie Weeks	8.00
RZ	Ryan Zimmerman	10.00
SA	Johan Santana	8.00
SK	Scott Kazmir/31	6.00
SM	John Smoltz	8.00
SR	Scott Rolen	8.00
TG	Tom Glavine	8.00
TH	Tim Hudson	8.00
TR	Travis Hafner	6.00
VA	Jason Varitek	10.00
VG	Vladimir Guerrero/99	8.00
VM	Victor Martinez	8.00
VW	Vernon Wells	8.00

Apparel Autograph

NM/M
Production 25 unless noted.

AT	Garrett Atkins/55	15.00
BI	Craig Biggio	40.00
BO	Jeremy Bonderman	50.00
BR	Brian Roberts	40.00
BU	B.J. Upton	25.00
CC	Carl Crawford/55	20.00
CH	Cole Hamels	40.00
CL	Carlos Lee	25.00
CR	Cal Ripken Jr.	180.00
CS	Curt Schilling	50.00
DO	David Ortiz	60.00
DW	Dontrelle Willis	20.00
EC	Eric Chavez	20.00
ES	Johnny Estrada	20.00
FH	Felix Hernandez/23	10.00
FT	Frank Thomas	75.00
GA	Garret Anderson/55	20.00
GR	Khalil Greene/55	25.00
HA	Roy Halladay	35.00
HR	Hanley Ramirez	25.00
JB	Jason Bay/55	20.00
JJ	Josh Johnson	15.00
JP	Jake Peavy	30.00
JT	Jim Thome	50.00
JZ	Joel Zumaya	25.00
MC	Miguel Cabrera	35.00
MO	Justin Morneau	40.00
PA	Jonathan Papelbon	30.00
PE	Jhonny Peralta	20.00
PM	Pedro Martinez	80.00
RC	Roger Clemens	120.00
RH	Rich Harden	20.00
0W	Rickie Weeks	20.00
SK	Scott Kazmir	25.00
VG	Vladimir Guerrero	50.00
VW	Victor Martinez	30.00

Autofacts

NM/M

Common Auto.:		10.00
AD	Adam Dunn	20.00
AK	Austin Kearns	10.00
AL	Adam LaRoche	10.00
AM	Andrew Miller	40.00
AS	Angel Sanchez	10.00
BC	Bobby Crosby	10.00
BE	Josh Beckett	25.00
BO	Jeremy Bonderman/SP	35.00
BT	Jason Bartlett	10.00
BU	Ambiorix Burgos/SP	10.00
CJ	Cesar Jimenez	10.00
CL	Carlos Lee/SP	15.00
CR	Cal Ripken Jr.	125.00
CY	Chris Young	20.00
CZ	Carlos Zambrano	30.00
DJ	Derek Jeter	140.00
DO	David Ortiz/SP	50.00
DW	Dontrelle Willis	15.00
DY	Delmon Young/SP	15.00
EC	Eric Chavez	15.00
GA	Garrett Atkins	10.00
HA	Rich Harden	15.00
HG	Hector Gimenez	10.00
HK	Hong-Chih Kuo	30.00
HR	Hanley Ramirez	20.00
IK	Ian Kinsler	15.00
JA	Joaquin Arias	10.00
JB	Jason Bay	15.00
JC	Jesse Crain	15.00
JE	Johnny Estrada	15.00
JG	Jonny Gomes	10.00
JJ	Josh Johnson	15.00
JW	Jered Weaver	15.00
JZ	Joel Zumaya/SP	20.00
KE	Howie Kendrick	15.00
KG	Ken Griffey Jr.	75.00
KM	Kendry Morales	10.00
KN	Jon Knott	10.00
KW	Kerry Wood	15.00
MJ	Mike Jacobs	10.00
MM	Miguel Montero	10.00
PA	Jonathan Papelbon	25.00
PE	Jhonny Peralta	15.00
PH	Philip Humber	10.00
RA	Chris Ray	10.00
RC	Roger Clemens	100.00
RH	Rich Hill	15.00
RW	Rickie Weeks	15.00
SB	Scott Baker	10.00
SD	Stephen Drew	15.00
SK	Scott Kazmir	15.00
SR	Scott Rolen/SP	20.00
TI	Tadahito Iguchi	20.00
TT	Troy Tulowitzki	20.00
UP	B.J. Upton	15.00
VE	Justin Verlander	20.00
VG	Vladimir Guerrero/SP	40.00
VM	Victor Martinez	15.00
WI	Josh Willingham	10.00
YB	Yuniesky Betancourt	15.00
ZG	Zack Greinke	10.00
ZS	Zack Segovia	15.00

Awesome Artifacts

NM/M
Production 50 Sets

AD	Adam Dunn	15.00
AG	Adrian Gonzalez	15.00
AP	Albert Pujols	40.00
AR	Aramis Ramirez	15.00
AS	Alfonso Soriano	20.00
BA	Bobby Abreu	15.00
BC	Bartolo Colon	10.00
BG	Brian Giles	10.00
BI	Craig Biggio	15.00
BR	Brian Roberts	15.00
BW	Billy Wagner	15.00
BZ	Barry Zito	15.00
CA	Carl Crawford	15.00
CB	Carlos Beltran	20.00
CC	Carl Crawford	15.00
CD	Carlos Delgado	15.00
CF	Chone Figgins	15.00
CJ	Chipper Jones	20.00
CL	Carlos Lee	15.00
CR	Cal Ripken Jr.	40.00
CS	Curt Schilling	15.00
CU	Chase Utley	20.00
DJ	Derek Jeter	40.00
DO	David Ortiz	20.00
DU	Dan Uggla	15.00
DW	Dontrelle Willis	15.00
EC	Eric Chavez	15.00
FG	Freddy Garcia	10.00
FH	Felix Hernandez	15.00
FL	Francisco Liriano	15.00
FT	Frank Thomas	15.00
GA	Garret Anderson	15.00
GM	Greg Maddux	25.00
GR	Khalil Greene	15.00
GS	Grady Sizemore	20.00
HA	Roy Halladay	15.00
HB	Hank Blalock	15.00
HE	Todd Helton	15.00
HR	Hanley Ramirez	20.00
HS	Huston Street	15.00
HU	Torii Hunter	15.00
IK	Ian Kinsler	15.00
IR	Ivan Rodriguez	15.00
JA	Jason Bay	15.00
JB	Jeremy Bonderman	20.00
JC	Jorge Cantu	10.00
JD	Jermaine Dye	10.00
JE	Jim Edmonds	15.00
JF	Jeff Francoeur	20.00
JG	Jason Giambi	15.00
JH	Johnny Damon	20.00
JJ	Josh Johnson	10.00
JK	Jeff Kent	15.00
JM	Joe Mauer	15.00
JO	Josh Barfield	15.00
JP	Jake Peavy	15.00
JR	Jimmy Rollins	15.00
JS	Jason Schmidt	15.00
JT	Jim Thome	15.00
JV	Justin Verlander	20.00

JW	Jered Weaver	15.00
JZ	Joel Zumaya	15.00
KG	Ken Griffey Jr.	30.00
KM	Kendry Morales	15.00
MC	Miguel Cabrera	20.00
MO	Justin Morneau	15.00
MR	Manny Ramirez	20.00
MT	Mark Teixeira	15.00
MY	Michael Young	15.00
OR	Magglio Ordonez	15.00
OS	Roy Oswalt	15.00
PA	Jonathan Papelbon	20.00
PB	Pat Burrell	15.00
PE	Jhonny Peralta	15.00
PF	Prince Fielder	20.00
PO	Jorge Posada	20.00
RC	Robinson Cano	20.00
RE	Jose Reyes	30.00
RF	Rafael Furcal	15.00
RH	Rich Harden	15.00
RJ	Randy Johnson	20.00
RO	Roger Clemens	25.00
RW	Rickie Weeks	15.00
RZ	Ryan Zimmerman	20.00
SK	Scott Kazmir	15.00
SM	John Smoltz	15.00
SR	Scott Rolen	20.00
TG	Tom Glavine	20.00
TH	Trevor Hoffman	15.00
TI	Tim Hudson	15.00
TR	Travis Hafner	15.00
VA	Jason Varitek	20.00
VG	Vladimir Guerrero	15.00
VM	Victor Martinez	15.00
VW	Vernon Wells	15.00

Bat Knobs

Production One Set

Divisional Artifacts

		NM/M
Common Player:		
Production 199 Sets		
Gold:		1X
Production 130 Sets		
AA	Aaron Rowand	6.00
AD	Adam Dunn	6.00
AJ	Andruw Jones	8.00
AL	Adam LaRoche	6.00
AR	Aramis Ramirez	10.00
BA	Bobby Abreu	6.00
BC	Bartolo Colon	4.00
BE	Carlos Beltran	8.00
BG	Brian Giles	6.00
BO	Jeremy Bonderman	10.00
BR	Brian Roberts	6.00
BW	Billy Wagner	6.00
BZ	Barry Zito	6.00
CA	Robinson Cano	10.00
CB	Craig Biggio	6.00
CC	Carl Crawford	6.00
CD	Carlos Delgado/178	8.00
CH	Chris Carpenter	6.00
CJ	Chipper Jones	8.00
CL	Carlos Lee	6.00
CR	Cal Ripken Jr.	25.00
CS	Curt Schilling	8.00
CU	Chase Utley	10.00
DJ	Derek Jeter	25.00
DO	David Ortiz	15.00
DU	Dan Uggla	6.00
DW	Dontrelle Willis	6.00
EC	Eric Chavez	6.00
FG	Freddy Garcia	4.00
FH	Felix Hernandez	6.00
FL	Francisco Liriano	6.00
FT	Frank Thomas	8.00
GA	Garret Anderson	4.00
GM	Greg Maddux	10.00
GR	Ken Griffey Jr.	20.00
GS	Grady Sizemore	10.00
HA	Rich Harden	4.00
HB	Hank Blalock	4.00
HO	Trevor Hoffman	4.00
HR	Hanley Ramirez	8.00
HU	Torii Hunter	6.00
IK	Ian Kinsler	6.00
IR	Ivan Rodriguez	8.00
JA	Jason Bay	6.00
JC	Jorge Cantu	4.00
JD	Jermaine Dye	6.00
JE	Jim Edmonds	6.00

JF	Jeff Francoeur	10.00
JG	Jason Giambi	8.00
JJ	Josh Johnson	4.00
JK	Jeff Kent	6.00
JM	Joe Mauer	8.00
JN	Joe Nathan	4.00
JO	Josh Barfield	4.00
JP	Jake Peavy	6.00
JR	Jimmy Rollins	10.00
JS	Jason Schmidt	4.00
JT	Jim Thome	8.00
JV	Justin Verlander	10.00
JW	Jered Weaver	8.00
JZ	Joel Zumaya	8.00
KG	Khalil Greene	8.00
KM	Kendry Morales	4.00
LB	Lance Berkman	6.00
MC	Miguel Cabrera	8.00
ME	Melky Cabrera	8.00
MO	Justin Morneau	8.00
MR	Manny Ramirez	8.00
MT	Mark Teixeira	8.00
MY	Michael Young	8.00
NS	Nick Swisher	6.00
OR	Magglio Ordonez	6.00
PA	Jonathan Papelbon	15.00
PB	Pat Burrell	6.00
PE	Jhonny Peralta	6.00
PF	Prince Fielder	15.00
PK	Paul Konerko	8.00
PO	Jorge Posada	8.00
RC	Roger Clemens	15.00
RE	Jose Reyes	15.00
RH	Roy Halladay	6.00
RJ	Randy Johnson	8.00
RO	Roy Oswalt	6.00
RW	Rickie Weeks	8.00
RZ	Ryan Zimmerman	10.00
SK	Scott Kazmir	6.00
SM	John Smoltz	8.00
SR	Scott Rolen	8.00
TG	Tom Glavine	8.00
TH	Todd Helton	8.00
TI	Tim Hudson	6.00
TR	Travis Hafner/117	6.00
VA	Jason Varitek	10.00
VG	Vladimir Guerrero	8.00
VM	Victor Martinez	8.00
VW	Vernon Wells	8.00

Divisional Artifacts Autographs

		NM/M
Production 25 unless noted.		
BO	Jeremy Bonderman	50.00
BR	Brian Roberts	40.00
CB	Craig Biggio	40.00
CC	Carl Crawford/55	20.00
CL	Carlos Lee	25.00
CR	Cal Ripken Jr.	180.00
CS	Curt Schilling	50.00
DO	David Ortiz	60.00
DW	Dontrelle Willis/55	40.00
EC	Eric Chavez	20.00
FH	Felix Hernandez/55	50.00
FT	Frank Thomas	75.00
GA	Garret Anderson/55	20.00
HA	Rich Harden	20.00
HR	Hanley Ramirez/55	25.00
IK	Ian Kinsler	20.00
JA	Jason Bay	20.00
JD	Jermaine Dye	20.00
JJ	Josh Johnson/55	15.00
JM	Joe Mauer	40.00
JP	Jake Peavy	30.00
JT	Jim Thome	50.00
JZ	Joel Zumaya	25.00
KG	Khalil Greene	25.00
KM	Kendry Morales/55	15.00
MC	Miguel Cabrera	35.00
MO	Justin Morneau	40.00
MY	Michael Young	20.00
PA	Jonathan Papelbon	30.00
PE	Jhonny Peralta	20.00
PM	Pedro Martinez	80.00
RC	Roger Clemens	120.00
RH	Roy Halladay	35.00
RW	Rickie Weeks	25.00
SK	Scott Kazmir	25.00
TI	Tim Hudson	30.00
VG	Vladimir Guerrero	50.00
VM	Victor Martinez	30.00

2007 Upper Deck Elements

	NM/M
Complete Set (252):	.50
Common player (1-126):	.25
Common RC (127-252):	5.00
Production 550	
Pack (3):	10.00
Box (15):	125.00

Justin Morneau
Twins / 1B

1	Stephen Drew	.50
2	Andruw Jones	1.00
3	Chipper Jones	1.00
4	Miguel Tejada	.75
5	David Ortiz	1.00
6	Manny Ramirez	1.00
7	Derrek Lee	.75
8	Alfonso Soriano	1.00
9	Jermaine Dye	.50
10	Jim Thome	.75
11	Ken Griffey Jr.	2.00
12	Adam Dunn	.75
13	Travis Hafner	.50
14	Grady Sizemore	1.00
15	Todd Helton	.75
16	Gary Sheffield	.75
17	Miguel Cabrera	1.00
18	Lance Berkman	.50
19	Mark Teahen	.25
20	Vladimir Guerrero	1.00
21	Jered Weaver	.50
22	Rafael Furcal	.50
23	Prince Fielder	1.00
24	Justin Morneau	.50
25	Johan Santana	1.00
26	David Wright	2.00
27	Jose Reyes	2.00
28	Derek Jeter	3.00
29	Alex Rodriguez	3.00
30	Nick Swisher	.50
31	Ryan Howard	2.00
32	Jason Bay	.50
33	Adrian Gonzalez	.50
34	Ray Durham	.25
35	Ichiro Suzuki	2.00
36	Albert Pujols	3.00
37	Scott Rolen	.75
38	Carl Crawford	.50
39	Mark Teixeira	.50
40	Michael Young	.50
41	Vernon Wells	.50
42	Ryan Zimmerman	.50
43	Stephen Drew	.50
44	Andruw Jones	1.00
45	Chipper Jones	1.00
46	Miguel Tejada	.75
47	David Ortiz	1.00
48	Manny Ramirez	1.00
49	Derrek Lee	.75
50	Alfonso Soriano	1.00
51	Jermaine Dye	.50
52	Jim Thome	.75
53	Ken Griffey Jr.	2.00
54	Adam Dunn	.75
55	Travis Hafner	.50
56	Grady Sizemore	1.00
57	Todd Helton	.75
58	Gary Sheffield	.75
59	Miguel Cabrera	1.00
60	Lance Berkman	.50
61	Mark Teahen	.25
62	Vladimir Guerrero	1.00
63	Jered Weaver	.50
64	Rafael Furcal	.50
65	Prince Fielder	1.00
66	Justin Morneau	.75
67	Johan Santana	1.00
68	David Wright	2.00
69	Jose Reyes	2.00
70	Derek Jeter	3.00
71	Alex Rodriguez	3.00
72	Nick Swisher	.50
73	Ryan Howard	2.00
74	Jason Bay	.50
75	Adrian Gonzalez	.50
76	Ray Durham	.25
77	Ichiro Suzuki	2.00
78	Albert Pujols	3.00
79	Scott Rolen	.50
80	Carl Crawford	.50
81	Mark Teixeira	.50
82	Michael Young	.50
83	Vernon Wells	.50

84	Ryan Zimmerman	.50
85	Stephen Drew	.50
86	Andruw Jones	1.00
87	Chipper Jones	1.00
88	Miguel Tejada	.75
89	David Ortiz	1.00
90	Manny Ramirez	1.00
91	Derrek Lee	.75
92	Alfonso Soriano	1.00
93	Jermaine Dye	.50
94	Jim Thome	.75
95	Ken Griffey Jr.	2.00
96	Adam Dunn	.75
97	Travis Hafner	.50
98	Grady Sizemore	1.00
99	Todd Helton	.75
100	Gary Sheffield	.75
101	Miguel Cabrera	1.00
102	Lance Berkman	.50
103	Mark Teahen	.25
104	Vladimir Guerrero	1.00
105	Jered Weaver	.50
106	Rafael Furcal	.50
107	Prince Fielder	1.00
108	Justin Morneau	1.00
109	Johan Santana	1.00
110	David Wright	2.00
111	Jose Reyes	2.00
112	Derek Jeter	3.00
113	Alex Rodriguez	3.00
114	Nick Swisher	.50
115	Ryan Howard	2.00
116	Jason Bay	.50
117	Adrian Gonzalez	.50
118	Ray Durham	.25
119	Ichiro Suzuki	2.00
120	Albert Pujols	3.00
121	Scott Rolen	.75
122	Carl Crawford	.50
123	Mark Teixeira	.75
124	Michael Young	.50
125	Vernon Wells	.50
126	Ryan Zimmerman	.50
127	Miguel Montero (RC)	5.00
128	Doug Slaten RC	5.00
129	Hunter Pence (RC)	30.00
130	Brian Burres (RC)	5.00
131	Daisuke Matsuzaka RC	25.00
132	Hideki Okajima RC	10.00
133	Devern Hansack RC	5.00
134	Felix Pie (RC)	8.00
135	Ryan Sweeney (RC)	5.00
136	Chris Stewart RC	5.00
137	Jarrod Saltalamacchia (RC)	8.00
138	John Danks (RC)	8.00
139	Travis Buck (RC)	5.00
140	Troy Tulowitzki (RC)	8.00
141	Chase Wright RC	8.00
142	Matt DeSalvo (RC)	5.00
143	Micah Owings (RC)	5.00
144	Jeff Baker (RC)	5.00
145	Andy LaRoche (RC)	10.00
146	Billy Butler (RC)	10.00
147	Jose Garcia RC	5.00
148	Angel Sanchez (RC)	5.00
149	Alex Gordon RC	25.00
150	Glen Perkins (RC)	5.00
151	Alexi Casilla R	8.00
152	Joe Smith (RC)	5.00
153	Kei Igawa RC	15.00
154	Sean Henn (RC)	5.00
155	Phil Hughes (RC)	20.00
156	Michael Bourn (RC)	5.00
157	Josh Hamilton (RC)	10.00
158	Kevin Kouzmanoff (RC)	5.00
159	Tim Lincecum RC	50.00
160	Brandon Morrow RC	10.00
161	Brandon Wood (RC)	8.00
162	Akinori Iwamura RC	10.00
163	Delmon Young (RC)	8.00
164	Juan Salas (RC)	5.00
165	Elijah Dukes RC	8.00
166	Joaquin Arias (RC)	5.00
167	Adam Lind (RC)	5.00
168	Matt Chico (RC)	5.00
169	Miguel Montero (RC)	5.00
170	Doug Slaten RC	5.00
171	Hunter Pence (RC)	30.00
172	Brian Burres (RC)	5.00
173	Daisuke Matsuzaka RC	25.00
174	Hideki Okajima RC	10.00
175	Devern Hansack RC	5.00
176	Felix Pie (RC)	8.00
177	Ryan Sweeney (RC)	5.00
178	Chris Stewart RC	5.00
179	Jarrod Saltalamacchia (RC)	8.00
180	John Danks (RC)	8.00
181	Travis Buck (RC)	5.00
182	Troy Tulowitzki (RC)	8.00

183	Chase Wright RC	8.00
184	Matt DeSalvo (RC)	5.00
185	Micah Owings (RC)	5.00
186	Jeff Baker (RC)	5.00
187	Andy LaRoche (RC)	10.00
188	Billy Butler (RC)	10.00
189	Jose Garcia RC	5.00
190	Angel Sanchez RC	5.00
191	Alex Gordon RC	25.00
192	Glen Perkins (RC)	5.00
193	Alexi Casilla RC	8.00
194	Joe Smith RC	5.00
195	Kei Igawa RC	15.00
196	Sean Henn (RC)	5.00
197	Phil Hughes (RC)	20.00
198	Michael Bourn (RC)	5.00
199	Josh Hamilton (RC)	10.00
200	Kevin Kouzmanoff (RC)	5.00
201	Tim Lincecum RC	50.00
202	Brandon Morrow RC	10.00
203	Brandon Wood (RC)	8.00
204	Akinori Iwamura (RC)	10.00
205	Delmon Young (RC)	8.00
206	Juan Salas (RC)	5.00
207	Elijah Dukes RC	8.00
208	Joaquin Arias (RC)	5.00
209	Adam Lind (RC)	5.00
210	Matt Chico (RC)	5.00
211	Miguel Montero (RC)	5.00
212	Doug Slaten RC	5.00
213	Hunter Pence (RC)	30.00
214	Brian Burres (RC)	5.00
215	Daisuke Matsuzaka RC	25.00
216	Hideki Okajima RC	10.00
217	Devern Hansack RC	5.00
218	Felix Pie (RC)	8.00
219	Ryan Sweeney (RC)	5.00
220	Chris Stewart RC	5.00
221	Jarrod Saltalamacchia (RC)	8.00
222	John Danks (RC)	8.00
223	Travis Buck (RC)	5.00
224	Troy Tulowitzki (RC)	8.00
225	Chase Wright RC	8.00
226	Matt DeSalvo (RC)	5.00
227	Micah Owings (RC)	5.00
228	Jeff Baker (RC)	5.00
229	Andy LaRoche (RC)	10.00
230	Billy Butler (RC)	10.00
231	Jose Garcia RC	5.00
232	Angel Sanchez RC	5.00
233	Alex Gordon RC	25.00
234	Glen Perkins RC	5.00
235	Alexi Casilla RC	8.00
236	Joe Smith RC	5.00
237	Kei Igawa RC	15.00
238	Sean Henn RC	5.00
239	Phil Hughes (RC)	20.00
240	Michael Bourn (RC)	5.00
241	Josh Hamilton (RC)	10.00
242	Kevin Kouzmanoff (RC)	5.00
243	Tim Lincecum RC	50.00
244	Brandon Morrow RC	10.00
245	Brandon Wood (RC)	8.00
246	Akinori Iwamura (RC)	10.00
247	Delmon Young (RC)	8.00
248	Juan Salas (RC)	5.00
249	Elijah Dukes (RC)	8.00
250	Joaquin Arias (RC)	5.00
251	Adam Lind (RC)	5.00
252	Matt Chico (RC)	5.00

Printing Plates

Production one set per color.

Clear-Cut Elements

NM/M

Production 350 unless noted.

Gold:		1X
Production 49-199 Sets		
Silver:		1.5X
Production 13-99 Sets		
AH	Aaron Harang	20.00
AK	Austin Kearns/234	15.00
AS	Alfonso Soriano	40.00
BB	Brian Bannister	15.00
BR	Brian Roberts	20.00
CA	Matt Cain	20.00
CC	Chris Carpenter	20.00
CP	Corey Patterson	15.00
CR	Cal Ripken Jr.	100.00
CR	Carl Crawford	20.00
DJ	Derek Jeter	200.00
DW	Dontrelle Willis	15.00
FL	Francisco Liriano	25.00
GR	Ken Griffey Jr.	75.00
HR	Hanley Ramirez	25.00
JB	Jason Bay	20.00
JG	Jonny Gomes	10.00
JH	Jeremy Hermida	15.00
JP	Jake Peavy	20.00
JT	Jim Thome	30.00

JV	Justin Verlander	30.00
JZ	Joel Zumaya	20.00
KG	Khalil Greene	15.00
KW	Kerry Wood	15.00
MC	Miguel Cabrera	30.00
MG	Marcus Giles	10.00
MH	Matt Holliday	20.00
ML	Mark Loretta	10.00
MM	Melvin Mora	10.00
MT	Miguel Tejada	25.00
RH	Rich Harden	10.00
RJ	Reed Johnson	10.00
RZ	Ryan Zimmerman	25.00
SA	Johan Santana	30.00
SK	Scott Kazmir	20.00
SR	Scott Rolen	25.00
TH	Travis Hafner	20.00
VM	Victor Martinez	20.00

Dual Elements

NM/M

Production 50 unless noted.

BB	Craig Biggio	15.00
BB	Lance Berkman	15.00
BM	Josh Beckett	60.00
BM	Daisuke Matsuzaka	60.00
BS	Freddy Sanchez	15.00
BS	Jason Bay	15.00
CA	Carlos Beltran	20.00
CA	Alfonso Soriano	20.00
CB	Carl Crawford	10.00
CB	Rocco Baldelli	10.00
CM	Mark Mulder	15.00
CM	Chris Carpenter	15.00
DB	Carlos Delgado	20.00
DB	Carlos Beltran	20.00
DG	Ken Griffey Jr. /29	25.00
DG	Adam Dunn	25.00
DJ	Derek Jeter	40.00
DJ	Johnny Damon	40.00
GG	Brian Giles	10.00
GG	Marcus Giles	10.00
GJ	Ken Griffey Jr.	50.00
GJ	Derek Jeter	50.00
GM	Tom Glavine	25.00
GM	Pedro Martinez	25.00
GS	Vladimir Guerrero	20.00
GS	Alfonso Soriano	20.00
GT	Ken Griffey Jr.	30.00
GT	Frank Thomas	30.00
HB	Roy Halladay	15.00
HB	A.J. Burnett	15.00
HU	Chase Utley	25.00
HU	Cole Hamels	25.00
JJ	Andruw Jones	25.00
JJ	Chipper Jones	25.00
JR	Derek Jeter	50.00
JR	Jose Reyes	50.00
JT	Derek Jeter	30.00
JT	Miguel Tejada	30.00
LP	Jon Lester	30.00
LP	Jonathan Papelbon	30.00
MM	Victor Martinez	15.00
MM	Joe Mauer	15.00
MS	Greg Maddux	30.00
MS	John Smoltz	30.00
MT	Justin Morneau	20.00
MT	Joe Mauer	20.00
OR	Manny Ramirez	30.00
OR	David Ortiz	30.00
PG	Ken Griffey Jr.	50.00
PG	Albert Pujols	50.00
PZ	Jonathan Papelbon	25.00
PZ	Joel Zumaya	25.00
RH	Mariano Rivera	15.00
RH	Trevor Hoffman	15.00
RR	Jose Reyes	30.00
RR	Hanley Ramirez	30.00
RW	Vernon Wells	15.00
RW	Alex Rios	15.00
SB	Curt Schilling	30.00
SB	Josh Beckett	30.00
SH	Travis Hafner	25.00
SH	Grady Sizemore	25.00
SZ	Barry Zito	20.00
SZ	Johan Santana	20.00
TH	Jim Thome	20.00
TH	Travis Hafner	20.00
TK	Jim Thome	20.00
TK	Paul Konerko	20.00
TM	Mark Teixeira	20.00
TM	Justin Morneau	20.00
TR	Miguel Tejada	20.00
TR	Brian Roberts	20.00
TY	Michael Young	20.00
TY	Mark Teixeira	20.00
UU	Chase Utley	20.00
UU	Dan Uggla	20.00
VB	Jeremy Bonderman	20.00
VB	Justin Verlander	20.00
WH	Vernon Wells	15.00
WH	Torii Hunter	15.00
WJ	Randy Johnson	20.00
WJ	Brandon Webb	20.00

WS	Johan Santana	25.00
WS	Brandon Webb	25.00
ZR	Scott Rolen	25.00
ZR	Ryan Zimmerman	25.00

Elemental Autographs

NM/M

Common Autograph:		10.00
AI	Akinori Iwamura	30.00
AL	Adam LaRoche	15.00
BA	Bronson Arroyo	20.00
BH	Bill Hall	15.00
BL	Joe Blanton	10.00
BN	Brendan Harris	10.00
BO	Jeremy Bonderman	20.00
BR	Jared Burton	20.00
BT	Jason Bartlett	10.00
BU	Brian Burres	10.00
BW	Brandon Wood	15.00
CB	Cha Sueng Baek	20.00
CO	Jon Coutlangus	20.00
CR	Cal Ripken Jr.	100.00
CU	Chase Utley	20.00
CW	Chase Wright	25.00
DB	Denny Bautista	15.00
DC	Daniel Cabrera	15.00
DJ	Derek Jeter	200.00
DU	Dan Uggla	15.00
DW	Dontrelle Willis	15.00
FP	Felix Pie	15.00
GA	Garrett Atkins	10.00
GC	Gustavo Chacin	15.00
GO	Alex Gordon	40.00
GP	Glen Perkins	10.00
HA	Rich Harden	10.00
HE	Sean Henn	10.00
HR	Hanley Ramirez	25.00
IK	Ian Kinsler	15.00
JA	Joaquin Arias	10.00
JB	Jason Bay	20.00
JC	Jesse Crain	10.00
JG	Jonny Gomes	10.00
JH	Josh Hamilton	20.00
JK	Jon Knott	10.00
JO	Josh Willingham	10.00
JP	Jake Peavy	20.00
JV	Justin Verlander	25.00
JW	Jayson Werth	15.00
KE	Howie Kendrick	15.00
KI	Kei Igawa	30.00
KM	Kendry Morales	10.00
KY	Kevin Youkilis	20.00
LA	Andy LaRoche	15.00
LI	Bobby Livingston	15.00
LS	Luke Scott	15.00
PA	Jonathan Papelbon	25.00
PE	Jhonny Peralta	15.00
RC	Roger Clemens	80.00
RH	Rich Hill	15.00
RL	Ruddy Lugo	10.00
RO	Scott Rolen	20.00
RT	Ryan Theriot	35.00
SD	Stephen Drew	20.00
SH	James Shields	15.00
SK	Scott Kazmir	15.00
SO	Jeremy Sowers	10.00
SS	Skip Schumaker	15.00
ST	Scott Thorman	10.00
TB	Travis Buck	15.00
TH	Travis Hafner	15.00
TI	Tadahito Iguchi	20.00
VM	Victor Martinez	20.00
WO	Jason Wood	10.00

Elemental Autographs Dual

Production 15 Sets

Elemental Autographs Triple

Production 5 Sets

Elemental Autographs Quad

Production One Set

Essential Elements

NM/M

Common Player:	5.00
Patches:	2-4x

AB	Adrian Beltre	5.00
AD	Adam Dunn	8.00
AJ	Andruw Jones	8.00
AP	Andy Pettitte	8.00
AR	Aramis Ramirez	8.00
AS	Alfonso Soriano	8.00
BA	Bobby Abreu	5.00
BC	Bobby Crosby	5.00
BE	Carlos Beltran	8.00
BG	Brian Giles	5.00
BO	Jeremy Bonderman	15.00
BR	Brian Roberts	8.00
BU	B.J. Upton	5.00
BW	Billy Wagner	5.00
BZ	Barry Zito	5.00
CA	Miguel Cabrera	10.00
CB	Craig Biggio	8.00
CC	Carl Crawford	8.00
CH	Cole Hamels	20.00
CJ	Chipper Jones	10.00
CS	Curt Schilling	5.00
CU	Chase Utley	20.00
DA	Johnny Damon	10.00
DM	Daisuke Matsuzaka	60.00
DO	David Ortiz	15.00
DR	J.D. Drew	5.00
DU	Dan Uggla	8.00
DW	Dontrelle Willis	5.00
EC	Eric Chavez	5.00
ED	Jim Edmonds	5.00
FG	Freddy Garcia	5.00
FH	Felix Hernandez	8.00
FL	Francisco Liriano	8.00
FT	Frank Thomas	15.00
GA	Garret Anderson	5.00
GJ	Geoff Jenkins	5.00
GM	Greg Maddux	20.00
GS	Grady Sizemore	20.00
HA	Rich Harden	5.00
HB	Hank Blalock	5.00
HO	Trevor Hoffman	8.00
HS	Huston Street	8.00
HU	Torii Hunter	8.00
IR	Ivan Rodriguez	8.00
JA	Jason Bay	8.00
JB	Josh Beckett	8.00
JC	Jorge Cantu	5.00
JD	Jermaine Dye	5.00
JE	Johnny Estrada	5.00
JF	Jeff Francoeur	15.00
JG	Jason Giambi	8.00
JJ	Josh Johnson	5.00
JK	Jeff Kent	5.00
JM	Joe Mauer	8.00
JP	Jake Peavy	5.00
JR	Jimmy Rollins	8.00
JS	Johan Santana	10.00
JT	Jim Thome	8.00
JV	Justin Verlander	10.00
KG	Khalil Greene	8.00
LB	Lance Berkman	5.00
LG	Luis Gonzalez	5.00
MM	Mike Mussina	10.00
MO	Justin Morneau	10.00
MP	Mike Piazza	20.00
MR	Manny Ramirez	10.00
MT	Mark Teixeira	10.00
MY	Michael Young	8.00
OR	Magglio Ordonez	10.00
PA	Jonathan Papelbon	15.00
PB	Pat Burrell	8.00
PE	Jhonny Peralta	8.00
PF	Prince Fielder	
PO	Jorge Posada	10.00
PU	Albert Pujols	25.00
RE	Jose Reyes	15.00
RH	Roy Halladay	10.00
RI	Mariano Rivera	10.00
RJ	Randy Johnson	15.00
RO	Roy Oswalt	8.00
RW	Rickie Weeks	8.00
RZ	Ryan Zimmerman	15.00
SK	Scott Kazmir	8.00
SM	John Smoltz	10.00
SR	Scott Rolen	10.00
TE	Miguel Tejada	8.00
TH	Todd Helton	10.00
TI	Tim Hudson	10.00
TR	Travis Hafner	8.00
VG	Vladimir Guerrero	10.00
VM	Victor Martinez	8.00

Quad Elements

No Pricing
Production 10 Sets

Triple Elements

Production 25 Sets

2007 Upper Deck First Edition

	NM/M
Complete Set (300):	35.00
Common Player:	.10
Pack (10):	1.00
Box (36):	30.00

1	Doug Slaten **RC**	.25
2	Miguel Montero **(RC)**	.25
3	Brian Burres **(RC)**	.25
4	Devern Hansack **RC**	1.00
5	David Murphy **(RC)**	.25
6	Jose Reyes **RC**	.25
7	Scott Moore **(RC)**	.25
8	Josh Fields **(RC)**	.25
9	Chris Stewart **RC**	.25
10	Jerry Owens **(RC)**	.25
11	Ryan Sweeney **(RC)**	.25
12	Kevin Kouzmanoff **(RC)**	.40
13	Jeff Baker **(RC)**	.25
14	Justin Hampson **(RC)**	.25
15	Jeff Salazar **(RC)**	.25
16	Alvin Colina **RC**	.25
17	Troy Tulowitzki **(RC)**	.50
18	Andrew Miller **RC**	3.00
19	Mike Rabelo **RC**	.25
20	Jose Diaz **(RC)**	.25
21	Angel Sanchez **RC**	.25
22	Ryan Braun **(RC)**	.25
23	Delwyn Young **(RC)**	.25
24	Drew Anderson **(RC)**	.25
25	Dennis Sarfate **(RC)**	.25
26	Vinny Rottino **(RC)**	.25
27	Glen Perkins **(RC)**	.25
28	Alexi Casilla **RC**	.25
29	Philip Humber **(RC)**	.25
30	Andy Cannizaro **RC**	.25
31	Jeremy Brown	.10
32	Sean Henn **(RC)**	.25
33	Brian Rogers **(RC)**	.25
34	Carlos Maldonado **(RC)**	.25
35	Juan Morillo **(RC)**	.25
36	Fred Lewis **(RC)**	.25
37	Patrick Misch **(RC)**	.25
38	Billy Sadler **(RC)**	.25
39	Ryan Feierabend **(RC)**	.25
40	Cesar Jimenez **RC**	.25
41	Oswaldo Navarro **RC**	.25
42	Travis Chick **(RC)**	.25
43	Delmon Young **(RC)**	.50
44	Shawn Riggans **(RC)**	.25
45	Brian Stokes **(RC)**	.25
46	Juan Salas **(RC)**	.25
47	Joaquin Arias **(RC)**	.25
48	Adam Lind **(RC)**	.50
49	Beltran Perez **(RC)**	.25
50	Brett Campbell **RC**	.25
51	Miguel Tejada	.40
52	Brandon Fahey	.10
53	Jay Gibbons	.10
54	Nicholas Markakis	.25
55	Kris Benson	.10
56	Erik Bedard	.25
57	Chris Ray	.10
58	Chris Britton	.10
59	Manny Ramirez	.50
60	David Ortiz	.50
61	Alex Cora	.10
62	Trot Nixon	.10
63	Doug Mirabelli	.10
64	Curt Schilling	.50
65	Jonathan Papelbon	.50
66	Craig Hansen	.10
67	Jermaine Dye	.25
68	Jim Thome	.40
69	Robert Mackowiak	.10
70	Brian Anderson	.10
71	A.J. Pierzynski	.10
72	Alex Cintron	.10
73	Jose Contreras	.10
74	Bobby Jenks	.10
75	Mike MacDougal	.10
76	Travis Hafner	.40
77	Ryan Garko	.10
78	Victor Martinez	.25
79	Casey Blake	.10
80	Shin-Soo Choo	.10
81	Paul Byrd	.10
82	Jeremy Sowers	.10
83	Cliff Lee	.10
84	Sean Casey	.10
85	Brandon Inge	.10
86	Omar Infante	.10
87	Magglio Ordonez	.10
88	Marcus Thames	.10
89	Justin Verlander	.50
90	Todd Jones	.10
91	Joel Zumaya	.25
92	Nate Robertson	.10
93	Mark Teahen	.25
94	Ryan Shealy	.10
95	Mark Grudzielanek	.10
96	Shane Costa	.10
97	Reggie Sanders	.10
98	Mark Redman	.10
99	Todd Wellemeyer	.10
100	Ambiorix Burgos	.10
101	Joe Nelson	.10
102	Orlando Cabrera	.25
103	Maicer Izturis	.10
104	Vladimir Guerrero	.50
105	Juan Rivera	.10
106	Jered Weaver	.40
107	Joe Saunders	.10
108	Bartolo Colon	.10
109	Francisco Rodriguez	.25
110	Justin Morneau	.50
111	Luis Castillo	.10
112	Michael Cuddyer	.10
113	Joe Mauer	.40
114	Francisco Liriano	.25
115	Joe Nathan	.25
116	Brad Radke	.10
117	Juan Rincon	.10
118	Derek Jeter	1.50
119	Jason Giambi	.40
120	Bobby Abreu	.40
121	Gary Sheffield	.40
122	Melky Cabrera	.25
123	Chien-Ming Wang	.50
124	Mariano Rivera	.40
125	Jaret Wright	.10
126	Kyle Farnsworth	.10
127	Frank Thomas	.50
128	Dan Johnson	.10
129	Marco Scutaro	.10
130	Jay Payton	.10
131	Joe Blanton	.10
132	Rich Harden	.25
133	Esteban Loaiza	.10
134	Chad Gaudin	.10
135	Yuniesky Betancourt	.10
136	Willie Bloomquist	.10
137	Ichiro Suzuki	1.00
138	Raul Ibanez	.10
139	Chris Snelling	.10
140	Cha Sueng Baek	.10
141	Julio Mateo	.10
142	Rafael Soriano	.10
143	Jorge Cantu	.10
144	B.J. Upton	.25
145	Dioner Navarro	.10
146	Carl Crawford	.40
147	Damon Hollins	.10
148	Casey Fossum	.10
149	Ruddy Lugo	.10
150	Tyler Walker	.10
151	Shawn Camp	.10
152	Ian Kinsler	.25
153	Jerry Hairston Jr.	.10
154	Gerald Laird	.10
155	Mark DeRosa	.10
156	Kip Wells	.10
157	Vicente Padilla	.10
158	John Koronka	.10
159	Wes Littleton	.10
160	Lyle Overbay	.10
161	Aaron Hill	.10
162	John McDonald	.10
163	Vernon Wells	.10
164	Frank Catalanotto	.10
165	Roy Halladay	.25
166	B.J. Ryan	.10
167	Casey Janssen	.10
168	Stephen Drew	.50
169	Conor Jackson	.10
170	Chad Tracy	.10
171	Johnny Estrada	.10
172	Eric Byrnes	.10
173	Carlos Quentin	.10
174	Brandon Webb	.25
175	Jorge Julio	.10
176	Luis Vizcaino	.10
177	Chipper Jones	.50
178	Adam LaRoche	.25
179	Brian McCann	.25
180	Ryan Langerhans	.10
181	Matt Diaz	.10
182	John Smoltz	.25
183	Oscar Villarreal	.10
184	Chad Paronto	.10
185	Derrek Lee	.40
186	Ryan Theriot	.10
187	Ronny Cedeno	.10
188	Juan Pierre	.10
189	Matt Murton	.10
190	Carlos Zambrano	.25
191	Mark Prior	.25
192	Ryan Dempster	.10
193	Ryan O'Malley	.10
194	Brandon Phillips	.10
195	Rich Aurilia	.10
196	Ken Griffey Jr.	1.00
197	Ryan Freel	.10
198	Aaron Harang	.10
199	Brandon Claussen	.10
200	David Weathers	.10
201	Eric Milton	.10
202	Kazuo Matsui	.10
203	Jamey Carroll	.10
204	Matt Holliday	.25
205	Brad Hawpe	.10
206	Jason Jennings	.10
207	Josh Fogg	.10
208	Aaron Cook	.10
209	Miguel Cabrera	.50
210	Dan Uggla	.10
211	Hanley Ramirez	.40
212	Jeremy Hermida	.10
213	Cody Ross	.10
214	Josh Willingham	.10
215	Anibal Sanchez	.10
216	Jose Garcia	.10
217	Taylor Tankersley	.10
218	Lance Berkman	.40
219	Craig Biggio	.25
220	Brad Ausmus	.10
221	Willy Taveras	.10
222	Chris Burke	.10
223	Roger Clemens	1.00
224	Brandon Backe	.10
225	Brad Lidge	.10
226	Dan Wheeler	.10
227	Wilson Betemit	.10
228	Julio Lugo	.10
229	Russell Martin	.25
230	Kenny Lofton	.10
231	Brad Penny	.10
232	Chad Billingsley	.10
233	Greg Maddux	1.00
234	Jonathan Broxton	.10
235	Rickie Weeks	.25
236	Bill Hall	.25
237	Tony Gwynn Jr.	.10
238	Corey Hart	.10
239	Laynce Nix	.10
240	Ben Sheets	.25
241	David Bush	.10
242	Francisco Cordero	.10
243	Jose Reyes	.50
244	Carlos Delgado	.40
245	Paul LoDuca	.10
246	Carlos Beltran	.40
247	Lastings Milledge	.25
248	Pedro Martinez	.50
249	John Maine	.10
250	Steve Trachsel	.10
251	Ryan Howard	1.00
252	Jimmy Rollins	.25
253	Chris Coste	.10
254	Jeff Conine	.10
255	David Dellucci	.10
256	Cole Hamels	.25
257	Ryan Madson	.10
258	Brett Myers	.25
259	Freddy Sanchez	.10
260	Xavier Nady	.10
261	Jose Castillo	.10
262	Jason Bay	.25
263	Jose Bautista	.10
264	Ronny Paulino	.10
265	Zachary Duke	.10
266	Shane Youman	.10
267	Matt Capps	.10
268	Adrian Gonzalez	.25
269	Josh Barfield	.10
270	Mike Piazza	.75
271	Dave Roberts	.10
272	Geoff Blum	.10
273	Chris Young	.10
274	Woody Williams	.10
275	Cla Meredith	.10
276	Trevor Hoffman	.25
277	Ray Durham	.10
278	Mark Sweeney	.10
279	Eliezer Alfonzo	.10
280	Todd Linden	.10
281	Jason Schmidt	.25
282	Noah Lowry	.10
283	Brad Hennessey	.10
284	Jonathan Sanchez	.10
285	Albert Pujols	1.50
286	David Eckstein	.10
287	Jim Edmonds	.25
288	Chris Duncan	.10
289	Juan Encarnacion	.10
290	Jeff Suppan	.10
291	Jeff Weaver	.10
292	Braden Looper	.10
293	Ryan Zimmerman	.25
294	Nick Johnson	.10
295	Alfonso Soriano	.50
296	Austin Kearns	.10
297	Alex Escobar	.10
298	Tony Armas	.10
299	Chad Cordero	.10
300	Jon Rauch	.10

Printing Plates

No Pricing
Production one set per color.

Aces

		NM/M
Common Player:		.50
Inserted 1:6		
BW	Brandon Webb	.50
CC	Chris Carpenter	.75
CS	Curt Schilling	.75
CZ	Carlos Zambrano	.50
DW	Dontrelle Willis	.50
FH	Felix Hernandez	.50
JS	Johan Santana	.75
JV	Justin Verlander	.75
PM	Pedro Martinez	.75
RC	Roger Clemens	2.00
RH	Roy Halladay	.50
SA	C.C. Sabathia	.50
SM	John Smoltz	.50
RJ	Randy Johnson	.75
SK	Scott Kazmir	.50

Foundations

		NM/M
Common Player:		.50
Inserted 1:6		
AL	Adam Lind	1.00
AM	Andrew Miller	3.00
DM	David Murphy	.50
DY	Delmon Young	1.00
FL	Fred Lewis	.50
GP	Glen Perkins	.50

JA Joaquin Arias .50
JF Josh Fields .50
JO Jerry Owens .50
JS Jeff Salazar .50
MM Mitch Maier .50
MO Miguel Montero .50
PH Philip Humber .50
RB Ryan Braun .50
RS Ryan Sweeney .50
SM Scott Moore .50
SR Shawn Riggans .50
TC Travis Chick .50
TT Troy Tulowitzki 1.00
UJ Ubaldo Jimenez .50

Leading Off

NM/M
Common Player: .50
Inserted 1:6
AS Alfonso Soriano 1.00
BR Brian Roberts .50
CF Chone Figgins .50
DR Dave Roberts .50
FR Ryan Freel .50
GS Grady Sizemore 1.00
HR Hanley Ramirez 1.00
IS Ichiro Suzuki 2.00
JD Johnny Damon 1.00
JP Juan Pierre .50
JR Jose Reyes 2.00
RF Rafael Furcal .50
RO Jimmy Rollins .75
SP Scott Podsednik .50
WT Willy Taveras .50

Momentum Swing

NM/M
Common Player: .50
Inserted 1:6
AD Adam Dunn .75
AJ Andruw Jones 1.00
AP Albert Pujols 2.50
AR Alex Rodriguez 2.50
AS Alfonso Soriano 1.00
CB Carlos Beltran 1.00
CD Carlos Delgado .75
DL Derrek Lee .75
DO David Ortiz 1.00
JB Jason Bay .75
JD Jermaine Dye .50
JG Jason Giambi .75
JM Justin Morneau 1.00
JT Jim Thome .75
LB Lance Berkman .75
MC Miguel Cabrera 1.00
MT Mark Teixeira .75
RH Ryan Howard 2.00
TH Travis Hafner .75
VG Vladimir Guerrero .75

Pennant Chasers

NM/M
Common Player: .25
Inserted 1:4
AR Aramis Ramirez .75
CC Carl Crawford .75
CG Carlos Guillen .25
CJ Chipper Jones 1.00
CU Chase Utley 1.00
DA Johnny Damon 1.00
DU Dan Uggla .25
DW David Wright 1.50
FS Freddy Sanchez .25
JM Joe Mauer .75
JR Juan Rivera .25
KG Ken Griffey Jr. 2.00
MH Matt Holliday .50
MR Manny Ramirez 1.00
MT Miguel Tejada .50
MY Michael Young .50
NG Nomar Garciaparra .75
NS Nick Swisher .50
OH Orlando Hudson .25
PF Prince Fielder .75
PK Paul Konerko .50
RD Ray Durham .25
RI Raul Ibanez .25
RO Roy Oswalt .50
RZ Ryan Zimmerman .75
SR Scott Rolen .25
TE Mark Teahen .25
TH Trevor Hoffman .50
VM Victor Martinez .50
VW Vernon Wells .50

2007 Upper Deck Future Stars

NM/M
Common Player (1-100): .25
Common RC Auto.
(101-189): 8.00
Pack (4): 4.00
Box (24): 90.00

1 Brandon Webb .40
2 Conor Jackson .25
3 Stephen Drew .40
4 Chipper Jones .75
5 Andruw Jones .40
6 Jeff Francoeur .75
7 John Smoltz .40
8 Miguel Tejada .50
9 Nicholas Markakis .50
10 Brian Roberts .25
11 David Ortiz .75
12 Manny Ramirez .75
13 Josh Beckett .50
14 Curt Schilling .50
15 Derrek Lee .50
16 Aramis Ramirez .50
17 Carlos Zambrano .50
18 Alfonso Soriano .75
19 Jim Thome .50
20 Paul Konerko .50
21 Jon Garland .25
22 Ken Griffey Jr. 1.50
23 Adam Dunn .25
24 Aaron Harang .25
25 Travis Hafner .50
26 Victor Martinez .50
27 Grady Sizemore .75
28 C.C. Sabathia .50
29 Todd Helton .50
30 Matt Holliday .50
31 Garrett Atkins .50
32 Ivan Rodriguez .50
33 Magglio Ordonez .40
34 Gary Sheffield .50
35 Justin Verlander .50
36 Miguel Cabrera .75
37 Hanley Ramirez .75
38 Dontrelle Willis .25
39 Lance Berkman .50
40 Roy Oswalt .50
41 Carlos Lee .50
42 Gil Meche .25
43 Emil Brown .25
44 Mark Teahen .25
45 Vladimir Guerrero .75
46 Jered Weaver .40
47 Howie Kendrick .25
48 Juan Pierre .40
49 Nomar Garciaparra .50
50 Rafael Furcal .40
51 Jeff Kent .40
52 Prince Fielder 1.00
53 Ben Sheets .40
54 Rickie Weeks .25
55 Justin Morneau .50
56 Joe Mauer .50
57 Torii Hunter .40
58 Johan Santana .75
59 Jose Reyes .75
60 David Wright .75
61 Carlos Delgado .50
62 Carlos Beltran .50
63 Derek Jeter 2.00
64 Alex Rodriguez 2.00
65 Johnny Damon .50
66 Jason Giambi .50
67 Bobby Abreu .50
68 Mike Piazza .75
69 Nick Swisher .40
70 Eric Chavez .25
71 Ryan Howard 1.00
72 Chase Utley .75
73 Jimmy Rollins .50
74 Jason Bay .40
75 Freddy Sanchez .25
76 Zachary Duke .25
77 Greg Maddux 1.00
78 Adrian Gonzalez .25
79 Jake Peavy .40
80 Ray Durham .25
81 Barry Zito .25
82 Matt Cain .25
83 Ichiro Suzuki 1.50
84 Felix Hernandez .50
85 Richie Sexson .40
86 Albert Pujols 2.00
87 Scott Rolen .75
88 Chris Carpenter .40
89 Chris Duncan .25
90 Carl Crawford .40
91 Rocco Baldelli .25
92 Scott Kazmir .50
93 Michael Young .50
94 Mark Teixeira .50
95 Ian Kinsler .50
96 Troy Glaus .40
97 Vernon Wells .50
98 Roy Halladay .40
99 Ryan Zimmerman .50
100 Nick Johnson .25
101 Zack Segovia (RC) 8.00
102 Joaquin Arias (RC) 8.00
104 Travis Buck (RC) 10.00
105 Mike Schultz RC 8.00

107 Sean Henn (RC) 8.00
108 Ryan Braun RC 10.00
109 Rick Vanden Hurk RC 10.00
110 Carlos Gomez/SP RC 35.00
111 Mike Rabelo RC 10.00
112 Felix Pie (RC) 15.00
113 Miguel Montero (RC) 8.00
114 Michael Bourn (RC) 15.00
115 Micah Owings/
SP (RC) 15.00
116 Matt Lindstrom (RC) 8.00
117 Matt Chico (RC) 8.00
118 Levale Speigner RC 8.00
119 Lee Gardner (RC) 8.00
120 Kory Casto (RC) 8.00
121 Kevin
Kouzmanoff(RC) 15.00
122 Kevin Cameron RC 8.00
124 Tyler Clippard (RC) 15.00
125 Juan Perez RC 10.00
126 Josh Hamilton/
SP (RC) 20.00
127 Joseph Bisenius RC 10.00
128 Jose Garcia RC 8.00
129 Jon Knott RC 8.00
130 Jon Coutlangus (RC) 10.00
131 John Danks (RC) 8.00
132 Joe Smith RC 10.00
133 Matt Brown RC 10.00
134 Joakim Soria RC 20.00
135 Jesus Flores RC 10.00
136 Jeff Baker RC 8.00
137 Jay Marshall RC 10.00
138 Jared Burton RC 8.00
139 Jamie Vermilyea RC 8.00
140 Jamie Burke (RC) 8.00
141 Ryan Rowland-
Smith RC 10.00
142 Connor Robertson RC 8.00
143 Hector Gimenez (RC) 8.00
144 Gustavo Molina RC 8.00
145 Glen Perkins (RC) 8.00
146 Joba Chamberlain/
SP RC 250.00
147 Doug Slaten RC 8.00
148 Ryan Braun (RC) 60.00
149 Delmon Young/
SP (RC) 40.00
150 Garrett Jones (RC) 8.00
152 Cesar Jimenez RC 8.00
153 Brian Stokes (RC) 8.00
154 Brian Burres (RC) 15.00
155 Brian Barden/SP RC 15.00
156 Kyle Kendrick RC 25.00
157 Andrew Miller RC 20.00
158 Alexi Casilla RC 10.00
159 Alex Gordon/SP RC 60.00
159 A.J. Murray RC 8.00
162 Adam Lind (RC) 8.00
163 Chase Wright RC 15.00
164 Dallas Braden RC 8.00
165 Rocky Cherry RC 15.00
166 Andy Gonzalez RC 8.00
167 Neal Musser RC 10.00
168 Mark Reynolds RC 20.00
169 Dennis Dove (RC) 10.00
170 Justin Hampson (RC) 8.00
171 Phil Hughes/SP (RC) 60.00
172 Kelvin Jimenez RC 8.00
173 Hunter Pence/
SP (RC) 50.00
174 Brad Salmon RC 10.00
175 Ryan Sweeney (RC) 10.00
176 Brandon Wood (RC) 15.00
177 Billy Butler/SP (RC) 40.00
178 Ben Francisco (RC) 8.00
180 Yoel Hernandez (RC) 8.00
181 Tim Lincecum SP 60.00
182 Danny Putnam (RC) 8.00
183 Jarrod Saltalamacchia/
SP (RC) 15.00
184 Andy LaRoche/
SP (RC) 20.00
185 Matt DeSalvo (RC) 10.00
186 Fred Lewis (RC) 8.00
187 Anthony Lerew (RC) 8.00
188 Jesse Litsch (RC) 8.00
189 Daisuke Matsuzaka/
SP RC 250.00

Gold

Gold (1-100, 189): 3-6X
Production 99 Sets

Red

Red (1-100, 189): 2-4X
Production 199 Sets

All-Star Futures

NM/M
Common Player: 2.00
Production 500 Sets
AD Alejandro De Aza 2.00
AG Alex Gordon 8.00

AI Akinori Iwamura 3.00
AL Adam Lind 2.00
AM Andrew Miller 4.00
BA Jeff Baker 2.00
BI Billy Butler 5.00
BM Brandon Morrow 3.00
BU B.J. Upton 3.00
BW Brandon Wood 3.00
CA Alexi Casilla 2.00
CG Carlos Gomez 3.00
CW Chase Wright 2.00
CY Chris Young 2.00
DM Daisuke Matsuzaka 15.00
DP Danny Putnam 2.00
DY Delmon Young 4.00
FL Fred Lewis 2.00
FP Felix Pie 3.00
GP Glen Perkins 2.00
HA Josh Hamilton 4.00
HK Howie Kendrick 3.00
HP Hunter Pence 8.00
IK Ian Kinsler 3.00
JA Joaquin Arias 2.00
JD John Danks 2.00
JS Jarrod Saltalamacchia 2.00
JV Justin Verlander 3.00
KC Kory Casto 2.00
KI Kei Igawa 2.00
KK Kevin Kouzmanoff 2.00
LA Andy LaRoche 3.00
MA Matt Chico 3.00
MB Michael Bourn 2.00
MC Matt Cain 2.00
MI Miguel Montero 2.00
ML Matt Lindstrom 2.00
MO Micah Owings 2.00
PF Prince Fielder 4.00
PH Phil Hughes 6.00
RB Ryan Braun 10.00
RS Ryan Sweeney 2.00
RZ Ryan Zimmerman 4.00
SD Stephen Drew 3.00
SM Joe Smith 2.00
SO Joakim Soria 2.00
TB Travis Buck 2.00
TL Tim Lincecum 8.00
TP Tony Pena 2.00
TT Troy Tulowitzki 4.00

All-Star Futures Autographs

NM/M
Common Auto.: 8.00
AG Alex Gordon/SP 60.00
AI Akinori Iwamura/SP 8.00
AL Adam Lind 8.00
AM Andrew Miller 20.00
BA Jeff Baker 8.00
BI Billy Butler 40.00
BU B.J. Upton 8.00
BW Brandon Wood 15.00
CA Alexi Casilla 8.00
CG Carlos Gomez 35.00
CW Chase Wright 15.00
CY Chris Young 15.00
DM Daisuke
Matsuzaka/SP 250.00
DP Danny Putnam 8.00
DY Delmon Young/SP 8.00
FL Fred Lewis 10.00
FP Felix Pie 15.00
GP Glen Perkins 8.00
HA Josh Hamilton 20.00
HK Howie Kendrick 25.00
HP Hunter Pence 50.00
IK Ian Kinsler 15.00
JA Joaquin Arias 8.00
JD John Danks 8.00
JS Jarrod
Saltalamacchia 15.00
JV Justin Verlander/SP 8.00
KC Kory Casto 8.00
KI Kei Igawa/SP 8.00
KK Kevin Kouzmanoff 10.00
LA Andy LaRoche 15.00
MA Matt Chico 8.00
MC Matt Cain 15.00
MI Miguel Montero 8.00
ML Matt Lindstrom 8.00
MO Micah Owings 15.00
PF Prince Fielder/SP 60.00
PH Phil Hughes/SP 60.00
RB Ryan Braun 60.00
RS Ryan Sweeney 10.00
RZ Ryan Zimmerman/SP 8.00
SD Stephen Drew/SP 8.00
SM Joe Smith 10.00
SO Joakim Soria 15.00
TB Travis Buck 10.00
TL Tim Lincecum 60.00
TP Tony Pena 8.00
TT Troy Tulowitzki 30.00

Clear Path to History Triple Autographs

NM/M

Some not priced due to scarcity.

CCH	Eric Chavez, Bobby Crosby, Rich Harden	20.00
CWR	Miguel Cabrera, Dontrelle Willis, Hanley Ramirez	60.00
DMY	Chris Young, Stephen Drew, Miguel Montero	30.00
FEG	Luis Gonzalez, Andre Ethier, Rafael Furcal	40.00
GKW	Vladimir Guerrero, Howie Kendrick, Jered Weaver/SP	100.00
GPC	Vladimir Guerrero, Albert Pujols, Miguel Cabrera/SP	200.00
HAT	Garrett Atkins, Matt Holliday, Troy Tulowitzki	100.00
HMS	Travis Hafner, Victor Martinez, Jeremy Sowers	50.00
KUC	Carl Crawford, Scott Kazmir, B.J. Upton	60.00
KUK	Ian Kinsler, Dan Uggla, Howie Kendrick	25.00
MPM	Melvin Mora, Corey Patterson, Nick Markakis	25.00
VZR	Justin Verlander, Ryan Zimmerman, Hanley Ramirez	50.00

Cy Young Futures

NM/M

Common Player: 2.00
Production 500 Sets

AL	Anthony Lerew	2.00
AM	Andrew Miller	4.00
BM	Brandon Morrow	3.00
CH	Cole Hamels	4.00
CW	Chase Wright	2.00
DM	Daisuke Matsuzaka	15.00
GP	Glen Perkins	2.00
JD	John Danks	2.00
JG	Jose Garcia	2.00
JL	Jon Lester	4.00
JS	Jeremy Sowers	2.00
JV	Justin Verlander	3.00
JZ	Joel Zumaya	2.00
KI	Kei Igawa	3.00
MA	Matt Chico	2.00
MC	Matt Cain	2.00
MO	Micah Owings	2.00
PH	Phil Hughes	6.00
RV	Rick Vanden Hurk	2.00
SK	Scott Kazmir	3.00
SM	Joe Smith	2.00
TC	Tyler Clippard	2.00
TL	Tim Lincecum	8.00
ZS	Zack Segovia	2.00

Cy Young Futures Auto.

NM/M

Common Auto.: 8.00

AL	Anthony Lerew	8.00
AM	Andrew Miller	20.00
CW	Chase Wright	15.00
DM	Daisuke Matsuzaka/SP	250.00
GP	Glen Perkins	8.00
JD	John Danks	8.00
JG	Jose Garcia	8.00
JZ	Joel Zumaya	15.00
MA	Matt Chico	8.00
MC	Matt Cain	15.00
MO	Micah Owings	15.00
PH	Phil Hughes/SP	60.00
RV	Rick Vanden Hurk	10.00
SH	Sean Henn	8.00
SM	Joe Smith	10.00
TC	Tyler Clippard	15.00
TL	Tim Lincecum	60.00
ZS	Zack Segovia	8.00

MVP Futures

NM/M

Common Player: 2.00
Production 500 Sets

AD	Alejandro De Aza	2.00
AG	Alex Gordon	8.00
AI	Akinori Iwamura	3.00
AL	Adam Lind	2.00
DM	Daisuke Matsuzaka	15.00
DY	Delmon Young	4.00
FP	Felix Pie	3.00
HP	Hunter Pence	8.00
IK	Ian Kinsler	3.00
JA	Joaquin Arias	2.00
JB	Jeff Baker	2.00
JH	Josh Hamilton	2.00
JS	Jarrod Saltalamacchia	2.00
JV	Justin Verlander	3.00
KI	Kei Igawa	2.00
KK	Kevin Kouzmanoff	2.00
LA	Andy LaRoche	3.00
MB	Michael Bourn	2.00
MM	Miguel Montero	2.00
PF	Prince Fielder	4.00
RB	Ryan Braun	10.00
RS	Ryan Sweeney	2.00
RZ	Ryan Zimmerman	4.00
TB	Travis Buck	2.00
TT	Troy Tulowitzki	4.00

MVP Futures Autographs

NM/M

Common Auto.: 8.00

AG	Alex Gordon/SP	60.00
AL	Adam Lind	8.00
DM	Daisuke Matsuzaka/SP	250.00
FP	Felix Pie	15.00
HP	Hunter Pence	50.00
IK	Ian Kinsler	15.00
JA	Joaquin Arias	8.00
JB	Jeff Baker	8.00
JH	Josh Hamilton	20.00
JS	Jarrod Saltalamacchia	15.00
KK	Kevin Kouzmanoff	10.00
LA	Andy LaRoche	20.00
MB	Michael Bourn	15.00
MM	Miguel Montero	8.00
PF	Prince Fielder	60.00
RB	Ryan Braun	60.00
RS	Ryan Sweeney	10.00
TB	Travis Buck	10.00

Rookie Dated Debuts

NM/M

Common Player: 2.00
Production 999 Sets
Autographs: No Pricing
Production 10 Sets

AC	Alexi Casilla	2.00
AD	Alejandro De Aza	2.00
AG	Alex Gordon	5.00
AI	Akinori Iwamura	2.00
AL	Adam Lind	2.00
BA	Jeff Baker	2.00
BB	Brian Barden	2.00
BI	Joseph Bisenius	2.00
BM	Brandon Morrow	2.00
BW	Brandon Wood	2.00
CA	Kory Casto	2.00
CG	Carlos Gomez	3.00
CR	Cal Ripken Jr.	10.00
CW	Chase Wright	2.00
DA	John Danks	2.00
DJ	Derek Jeter	10.00
DM	Daisuke Matsuzaka	10.00
DY	Delmon Young	3.00
ED	Elijah Dukes	2.00
FL	Fred Lewis	2.00
FP	Felix Pie	2.00
GM	Gustavo Molina	2.00
GP	Glen Perkins	2.00
HO	Hideki Okajima	3.00
HP	Hunter Pence	6.00
JA	Joaquin Arias	2.00
JC	Jon Coutlangus	2.00
JF	Jesus Flores	2.00
JH	Josh Hamilton	2.00
JM	Jay Marshall	2.00
JP	Juan Perez	2.00
JS	Joakim Soria	2.00
KC	Kevin Cameron	2.00
KG	Ken Griffey Jr.	8.00
KI	Kei Igawa	2.00
KK	Kevin Kouzmanoff	2.00
LA	Andy LaRoche	3.00
LG	Lee Gardner	2.00
MB	Michael Bourn	2.00
MC	Matt Chico	2.00
MM	Miguel Montero	2.00
MO	Micah Owings	2.00
MR	Mike Rabelo	2.00
PH	Phil Hughes	5.00
RS	Ryan Sweeney	2.00
SA	Jarrod Saltalamacchia	2.00
SM	Joe Smith	2.00
TB	Travis Buck	2.00
TL	Tim Lincecum	5.00
TT	Troy Tulowitzki	4.00

Two for the Bigs

NM/M

Common Duo: 2.00
Production 999 Sets
Autographs: No pricing
Production 10 Sets

AS	Joaquin Arias, Chris Stewart	2.00
BB	Michael Bourn, Joseph Bisenius	2.00
BD	Travis Buck, Elijah Dukes	2.00
BG	Ryan Braun, Alex Gordon	8.00
BS	Ryan Braun, Joakim Soria	2.00
BT	Jeff Baker, Troy Tulowitzki	4.00
CF	Kory Casto, Jesus Flores	2.00
CL	Matt Chico, Tim Lincecum	4.00
CP	Alexi Casilla, Glen Perkins	2.00
CS	Matt Chico, Levale Speigner	2.00
DG	Alejandro De Aza, Lee Gardner	2.00
DK	Daisuke Matsuzaka, Kei Igawa	6.00
DM	John Danks, Gustavo Molina	2.00
DT	Stephen Drew, Troy Tulowitzki	4.00
DV	Alejandro De Aza, Rick Vanden Hurk	2.00
DW	Chase Wright, Matt DeSalvo	2.00
DY	Chris Young, Stephen Drew	3.00
GB	Alex Gordon, Billy Butler	5.00
GF	Hector Gimenez, Jesus Flores	2.00
GI	Alex Gordon, Akinori Iwamura	5.00
GL	Alex Gordon, Andy LaRoche	5.00
GM	Alex Gordon, Daisuke Matsuzaka	8.00
GP	Hector Gimenez, Hunter Pence	4.00
HB	Josh Hamilton, Jared Burton	2.00
HD	Josh Hamilton, Alejandro De Aza	2.00
HL	Phil Hughes, Tim Lincecum	8.00
HP	Josh Hamilton, Hunter Pence	4.00
II	Akinori Iwamura, Kei Igawa	3.00
KC	Kevin Kouzmanoff, Kevin Cameron	2.00
LG	Matt Lindstrom, Lee Gardner	2.00
LV	Adam Lind	2.00
MG	Hector Gimenez, Miguel Montero	2.00
MI	Daisuke Matsuzaka, Akinori Iwamura	5.00
MO	Daisuke Matsuzaka, Hideki Okajima	5.00
MR	Gustavo Molina, Mike Rabelo	2.00
MW	Brandon Morrow, Sean White	2.00
OL	Micah Owings, Tim Lincecum	2.00
OM	Micah Owings, Miguel Montero	2.00
PB	Danny Putnam, Travis Buck	2.00
PD	Hunter Pence, Alejandro De Aza	4.00
PH	Josh Hamilton, Felix Pie	2.00
PP	Felix Pie, Hunter Pence	4.00
RS	Mike Rabelo, Chris Stewart	2.00
SM	Jarrod Saltalamacchia, Miguel Montero	2.00
ST	Jarrod Saltalamacchia, Troy Tulowitzki	4.00
SW	Joe Smith, Chase Wright	2.00
TB	Travis Buck, Billy Butler	3.00
WH	Chase Wright, Phil Hughes	4.00
YD	Delmon Young, Elijah Dukes	2.00
YM	Delmon Young, Daisuke Matsuzaka	5.00

2007 Upper Deck Goudey

NM/M

Complete Set (288):	
Common Player (1-200):	.15
Common SP (201-240):	1.50
Inserted 1:6	
Common Heads Up (241-288):	2.00
Inserted 1:10	
Hobby Pack (8):	5.00
Hobby Box (24):	100.00
1	A.J. Burnett	.25

1	A.J. Burnett	.25
2	Aaron Boone	.15
3	Aaron Rowand	.25
4	Adam Dunn	.50
5	Adrian Beltre	.25
6	Albert Pujols	2.00
7	Ivan Rodriguez	.50
8	Alfonso Soriano	.75
9	Andruw Jones	.50
10	Andy Pettitte	.50
11	Aramis Ramirez	.40
12	B.J. Upton	.25
13	Barry Zito	.25
14	Bartolo Colon	.15
15	Ben Sheets	.25
16	Bobby Abreu	.25
17	Bobby Crosby	.15
18	Brian Giles	.15
19	Brian Roberts	.25
20	C.C. Sabathia	.40
21	Carlos Beltran	.75
22	Carlos Delgado	.50
23	Carlos Lee	.25
24	Carlos Zambrano	.25
25	Chad Cordero	.15
26	Chad Tracy	.15
27	Chipper Jones	.75
28	Craig Biggio	.25
29	Curt Schilling	.50
30	Danny Haren	.25
31	Darin Erstad	.15
32	David Ortiz	.75
33	Billy Wagner	.15
34	Derek Jeter	2.00
35	Derek Lee	.50
36	Dontrelle Willis	.25
37	Edgar Renteria	.25
38	Eric Chavez	.25
39	Felix Hernandez	.25
40	Garret Anderson	.25
41	Garrett Atkins	.25
42	Gary Sheffield	.50
43	Grady Sizemore	.75
44	Greg Maddux	1.50
45	Hank Blalock	.25
46	Hanley Ramirez	.75
47	J.D. Drew	.25
48	Jacque Jones	.15
49	Jake Peavy	.40
50	Jake Westbrook	.15
51	Jason Bay	.25
52	Jason Giambi	.25
53	Jason Schmidt	.25
54	Jason Varitek	.40
55	Troy Tulowitzki	.40
56	Jeff Francoeur	.40
57	Jeff Kent	.25
58	Jeremy Bonderman	.25
59	Jim Edmonds	.25
60	Jim Thome	.50
61	Jimmy Rollins	.50
62	Joe Mauer	.25
63	Johan Santana	.75
64	John Smoltz	.40
65	Johnny Damon	.25
66	Jose Reyes	.75
67	Josh Beckett	.40
68	Justin Morneau	.50
69	Ken Griffey Jr.	1.50
70	Kerry Wood	.15
71	Khalil Greene	.25
72	Lance Berkman	.25
73	Livan Hernandez	.15
74	Manny Ramirez	.75
75	Mark Mulder	.25
76	Chase Utley	.75
77	Mark Teixeira	.50
78	Miguel Tejada	.40
79	Miguel Cabrera	.75
80	Mike Piazza	.75
81	Pat Burrell	.25
82	Paul LoDuca	.15
83	Pedro Martinez	.75
84	Prince Fielder	1.00
85	Rafael Furcal	.25
86	Randy Johnson	.75
87	Richie Sexson	.25
88	Robinson Cano	.75
89	Roy Halladay	.40
90	Roy Oswalt	.40
91	Scott Rolen	.50

#	Player	Price
92	Tim Hudson	.25
93	Todd Helton	.50
94	Tom Glavine	.50
95	Torii Hunter	.40
96	Travis Hafner	.40
97	Trevor Hoffman	.25
98	Vernon Wells	.40
99	Vladimir Guerrero	.75
100	Zachary Duke	.15
101	Alex Rodriguez	2.00
102	Ryan Howard	1.00
103	Michael Barrett	.15
104	Ichiro Suzuki	1.50
105	Hideki Matsui	1.50
106	Jered Weaver	.40
107	Dan Uggla	.25
108	Ryan Freel	.15
109	Bill Hall	.25
110	Ray Durham	.15
111	Morgan Ensberg	.15
112	Shawn Green	.25
113	Brandon Webb	.40
114	Frank Thomas	.75
115	Corey Patterson	.15
116	Edwin Encarnacion	.15
117	Mike Cameron	.15
118	Matt Holliday	.40
119	Jhonny Peralta	.25
120	Nick Swisher	.25
121	Brad Penny	.15
122	Kenji Johjima	.25
123	Francisco Rodriguez	.15
124	Mark Teahen	.15
125	Jonathan Papelbon	.50
126	Carlos Guillen	.15
127	Freddy Sanchez	.15
128	Chien-Ming Wang	.75
129	Andre Ethier	.15
130	Matt Cain	.25
131	Austin Kearns	.15
132	Ramon Hernandez	.15
133	Chris Carpenter	.40
134	Michael Cuddyer	.15
135	Stephen Drew	.25
136	David Wright	.75
137	David DeJesus	.15
138	Gary Matthews	.15
139	Brandon Phillips	.15
140	Josh Barfield	.15
141	Alex Gordon	1.00
142	Scott Kazmir	.15
143	Luis Gonzalez	.15
144	Mike Sweeney	.15
145	Luis Castillo	.15
146	Huston Street	.15
147	Phil Hughes	1.00
148	Adrian Gonzalez	.25
149	Raul Ibanez	.15
150	Joe Crede	.15
151	Mark Loretta	.15
152	Adam LaRoche	.25
153	Troy Glaus	.40
154	Conor Jackson	.15
155	Michael Young	.25
156	Scott Podsednik	.15
157	David Eckstein	.15
158	Mike Jacobs	.15
159	Nomar Garciaparra	.75
160	Mariano Rivera	.50
161	Pedro Feliz	.15
162	Josh Hamilton	.15
163	Ryan Langerhans	.15
164	Willy Taveras	.15
165	Carl Crawford	.25
166	Melvin Mora	.15
167	Francisco Liriano	.25
168	Orlando Cabrera	.25
169	Chris Duncan	.15
170	Johnny Estrada	.15
171	Ryan Zimmerman	.50
172	Rickie Weeks	.15
173	Paul Konerko	.40
174	Jack Wilson	.15
175	Jorge Posada	.40
176	Magglio Ordonez	.15
177	Nick Johnson	.15
178	Geoff Jenkins	.15
179	Reggie Sanders	.15
180	Moises Alou	.25
181	Glen Perkins	.15
182	Brad Lidge	.15
183	Kevin Kouzmanoff	.15
184	Jorge Cantu	.15
185	Carlos Quentin	.15
186	Rich Harden	.15
187	Jose Vidro	.15
188	Aaron Harang	.15
189	Noah Lowry	.15
190	Jermaine Dye	.25
191	Victor Martinez	.25
192	Chone Figgins	.25
193	Aubrey Huff	.15
194	Jason Isringhausen	.15
195	Brian McCann	.40
196	Juan Pierre	.15
197	Delmon Young	.50
198	Felipe Lopez	.15
199	Brad Hawpe	.15
200	Justin Verlander	.40
201	Mike Schmidt	3.00
202	Nolan Ryan	4.00
203	Cal Ripken Jr.	4.00
204	Harmon Killebrew	3.00
205	Reggie Jackson	2.00
206	Johnny Bench	2.00
207	Carlton Fisk	2.00
208	Yogi Berra	3.00
209	Al Kaline	3.00
210	Alan Trammell	1.50
211	Bill Mazeroski	2.00
212	Bob Gibson	2.00
213	Brooks Robinson	3.00
214	Carl Yastrzemski	3.00
215	Don Mattingly	3.00
216	Fergie Jenkins	1.50
217	Jim Rice	1.50
218	Lou Brock	2.00
219	Rod Carew	2.00
220	Stan Musial	3.00
221	Tom Seaver	3.00
222	Tony Gwynn	3.00
223	Wade Boggs	2.00
224	Alex Rodriguez	4.00
225	David Wright	3.00
226	Ryan Howard	3.00
227	Ichiro Suzuki	3.00
228	Ken Griffey Jr.	3.00
229	Daisuke Matsuzaka	4.00
230	Kei Igawa	1.50
231	Akinori Iwamura	2.00
232	Derek Jeter	4.00
233	Albert Pujols	4.00
234	Greg Maddux	3.00
235	David Ortiz	3.00
236	Manny Ramirez	2.00
237	Johan Santana	2.00
238	Pedro Martinez	2.00
239	Roger Clemens	4.00
240	Vladimir Guerrero	2.00
241	Ken Griffey Jr.	4.00
242	Derek Jeter	5.00
243	Ichiro Suzuki	4.00
244	Cal Ripken Jr.	5.00
245	Daisuke Matsuzaka	5.00
246	Kei Igawa	2.00
247	Joe Mauer	2.00
248	Babe Ruth	5.00
249	Johnny Bench	3.00
250	Reggie Jackson	3.00
251	Carlton Fisk	3.00
252	Albert Pujols	5.00
253	Nolan Ryan	5.00
254	Ryan Howard	4.00
255	Mike Schmidt	4.00
256	Brooks Robinson	4.00
257	Harmon Killebrew	4.00
258	Alex Rodriguez	5.00
259	David Ortiz	4.00
260	David Wright	4.00
261	Al Kaline	4.00
262	Justin Verlander	3.00
263	Chase Utley	4.00
264	Justin Morneau	3.00
265	Ken Griffey Jr.	4.00
266	Derek Jeter	5.00
267	Ichiro Suzuki	4.00
268	Cal Ripken Jr.	5.00
269	Daisuke Matsuzaka	5.00
270	Kei Igawa	2.00
271	Joe Mauer	2.00
272	Babe Ruth	5.00
273	Johnny Bench	3.00
274	Reggie Jackson	3.00
275	Carlton Fisk	3.00
276	Albert Pujols	5.00
277	Nolan Ryan	5.00
278	Ryan Howard	4.00
279	Mike Schmidt	4.00
280	Brooks Robinson	4.00
281	Harmon Killebrew	4.00
282	Alex Rodriguez	5.00
283	David Ortiz	4.00
284	David Wright	4.00
285	Al Kaline	4.00
286	Justin Verlander	3.00
287	Chase Utley	4.00
288	Justin Morneau	3.00

Graphs

		NM/M
	Common Autograph:	5.00
AC	Alberto Callaspo	10.00
AH	Aaron Harang	20.00
AK	Al Kaline/SP	150.00
AM	Andy Marte	8.00
AR	Aaron Rowand	20.00
BA	Brian Anderson	5.00
BB	Brian Bannister	15.00
BE	Johnny Bench/SP	150.00
BO	Boof Bonser	10.00
BU	B.J. Upton	20.00
CC	Carl Crawford	10.00
CF	Carlton Fisk/SP	50.00
CL	Cliff Lee	8.00
CO	Coco Crisp	20.00
CR	Cal Ripken Jr./SP	160.00
CY	Chris Young	15.00
DJ	Derek Jeter	150.00
FH	Felix Hernandez	30.00
GA	Garrett Atkins	10.00
GP	Glen Perkins	5.00
HA	Bill Hall	10.00
HI	Rich Hill	15.00
HR	Hanley Ramirez	25.00
IS	Ian Snell	15.00
JB	Jason Bay	10.00
JW	Jered Weaver	15.00
JZ	Joel Zumaya	15.00
KG	Ken Griffey Jr./SP	100.00
KJ	Kelly Johnson	15.00
KK	Kevin Kouzmanoff	15.00
LS	Luke Scott	8.00
MO	Justin Morneau	25.00
MS	Mike Schmidt/SP	80.00
RA	Reggie Abercrombie	8.00
RT	Ryan Theriot	25.00
RZ	Ryan Zimmerman	30.00
SA	Anibal Sanchez	5.00
SK	Scott Kazmir	15.00
TB	Taylor Buchholz	8.00
VM	Victor Martinez	15.00
YB	Yogi Berra/SP	75.00

Immortals
Memorabilia

Inserted 1:288

Memorabilia

#	Player	NM/M
	Common Player:	4.00
1	A.J. Burnett	4.00
3	Aaron Rowand	4.00
4	Adam Dunn	8.00
5	Adrian Beltre	6.00
6	Albert Pujols	20.00
7	Ivan Rodriguez	8.00
8	Alfonso Soriano	15.00
9	Andruw Jones	6.00
10	Andy Pettitte	8.00
11	Aramis Ramirez	6.00
12	B.J. Upton	6.00
13	Barry Zito	6.00
14	Bartolo Colon/SP	6.00
15	Ben Sheets	6.00
16	Bobby Abreu/SP	6.00
17	Bobby Crosby	4.00
18	Brian Giles	4.00
19	Brian Roberts	6.00
20	C.C. Sabathia	8.00
21	Carlos Beltran	6.00
22	Carlos Delgado	6.00
23	Carlos Lee	6.00
24	Carlos Zambrano	6.00
26	Chad Tracy	4.00
27	Chipper Jones	8.00
28	Craig Biggio	6.00
29	Curt Schilling	8.00
31	Darin Erstad	4.00
32	David Ortiz	10.00
33	Billy Wagner	6.00
34	Derek Jeter	20.00
35	Derrek Lee	8.00
36	Dontrelle Willis	6.00
37	Edgar Renteria	4.00
38	Eric Chavez	4.00
39	Felix Hernandez	8.00
40	Garret Anderson	4.00
41	Garrett Atkins	4.00
42	Gary Sheffield	8.00
43	Grady Sizemore	8.00
44	Greg Maddux	15.00
45	Hank Blalock	4.00
46	Hanley Ramirez	10.00
47	J.D. Drew	4.00
49	Jake Peavy	6.00
50	Jake Westbrook	4.00
51	Jason Bay	8.00
52	Jason Giambi	6.00
54	Jason Varitek	10.00
56	Jeff Francoeur	10.00
57	Jeff Kent	6.00
58	Jeremy Bonderman	6.00
59	Jim Edmonds	6.00
60	Jim Thome	6.00
61	Jimmy Rollins	8.00
62	Joe Mauer	6.00
63	Johan Santana	8.00
64	John Smoltz	8.00
65	Jose Reyes	20.00
66	Josh Beckett	8.00
67	Josh Beckett	8.00
68	Justin Morneau	8.00
69	Ken Griffey Jr.	15.00
70	Kerry Wood	6.00
71	Khalil Greene	6.00
72	Lance Berkman	6.00
73	Livan Hernandez	4.00
74	Manny Ramirez	8.00
75	Mark Mulder	4.00
76	Chase Utley	15.00
77	Mark Teixeira	8.00
78	Miguel Tejada	6.00
79	Miguel Cabrera	8.00
80	Mike Piazza	10.00
81	Pat Burrell	6.00
82	Paul LoDuca	4.00
83	Pedro Martinez	8.00
84	Prince Fielder	15.00
85	Rafael Furcal	6.00
86	Randy Johnson	8.00
87	Richie Sexson	6.00
88	Robinson Cano	8.00
89	Roy Halladay	8.00
90	Roy Oswalt	8.00
91	Scott Rolen	8.00
92	Tim Hudson	6.00
93	Todd Helton	8.00
94	Tom Glavine	8.00
95	Torii Hunter	6.00
96	Travis Hafner	6.00
97	Trevor Hoffman	6.00
98	Vernon Wells	6.00
99	Vladimir Guerrero	8.00
100	Zachary Duke	4.00

Sports Royalty

		NM/M
	Common Card:	2.00
AI	Akinori Iwamura	2.00
AP	Albert Pujols	8.00
AS	Alfonso Soriano	3.50
CC	Chris Carpenter	2.00
CR	Cal Ripken Jr.	15.00
DJ	Derek Jeter	8.00
DM	Daisuke Matsuzaka	8.00
DO	David Ortiz	4.00
DS	Dean Smith	3.00
ES	Emmitt Smith	8.00
GH	Gordie Howe	10.00
GM	Greg Maddux	5.00
HI	Martina Hingis	4.00
HR	Hanley Ramirez	3.00
JM	Justin Morneau	5.00
JN	Joe Namath	5.00
JV	Justin Verlander	2.00
JW	John Wooden	5.00
KB	Kobe Bryant	4.00
KD	Kevin Durant	8.00
KG	Ken Griffey Jr.	8.00
KH	Katie Hoff	4.00
KI	Kei Igawa	2.00
LE	Jeanette Lee	2.00
LJ	LeBron James	10.00
LT	LaDainian Tomlinson	8.00
MH	Mia Hamm	5.00
MJ	Michael Jordan	15.00
NR	Nolan Ryan	15.00
PI	Mike Piazza	4.00
PM	Peyton Manning	8.00
RH	Roy Halladay	2.00
RJ	Randy Johnson	3.00
RL	Ryan Lochte	2.00
SA	Johan Santana	3.00
SC	Sidney Crosby	15.00
TH	Trevor Hoffman	2.00
TW	Tiger Woods	20.00
VG	Vladimir Guerrero	3.00

Sports Royalty
Autographs

		NM/M
	Common Autograph:	25.00
AI	Akinori Iwamura	25.00
CR	Cal Ripken Jr.	180.00
DJ	Derek Jeter	140.00
DM	Daisuke Matsuzaka	250.00
DO	David Ortiz	75.00
GH	Gordie Howe	100.00
GM	Greg Maddux	160.00
HI	Martina Hingis	100.00
HR	Hanley Ramirez	25.00
JM	Justin Morneau	25.00
JV	Justin Verlander	60.00
JW	John Wooden	125.00
KG	Ken Griffey Jr.	100.00
KH	Katie Hoff	75.00
KI	Kei Igawa	30.00
LE	Jeanette Lee	150.00
LJ	LeBron James	300.00
LT	LaDainian Tomlinson	150.00
MH	Mia Hamm	125.00
RH	Roy Halladay	30.00
RL	Ryan Lochte	65.00
SC	Sidney Crosby	200.00

933 Goudey Originals

Inserted 2:Case
See 1933 Goudey Pricing

1934-36 Diamond Stars

No Pricing
Production 15 Sets
Autographs: No Pricing
Production One Set

1941 Double Play

No Pricing
Production 15 Sets
Autographs: No Pricing
Production One Set

2007 Upper Deck Premier

		NM/M
Common Player (1-200):		4.00
Production 99 Sets		
Common RC (201-244):		4.00
Production 199 Sets		
Box (1):		300.00
1	Roy Campanella	10.00
2	Ty Cobb	12.00
3	Mickey Cochrane	4.00
4	Dizzy Dean	8.00
5	Don Drysdale	8.00
6	Jimmie Foxx	10.00
7	Lou Gehrig	15.00
8	Lefty Grove	4.00
9	Rogers Hornsby	10.00
10	Walter Johnson	10.00
11	Eddie Mathews	10.00
12	Christy Mathewson	10.00
13	Johnny Mize	8.00
14	Thurman Munson	10.00
15	Mel Ott	8.00
16	Satchel Paige	10.00
17	Jackie Robinson	10.00
18	Babe Ruth	20.00
19	George Sisler	4.00
20	Honus Wagner	10.00
21	Cy Young	10.00
22	Luis Aparicio	4.00
23	Johnny Bench	10.00
24	Yogi Berra	10.00
25	Rod Carew	4.00
26	Orlando Cepeda	6.00
27	Bob Feller	8.00
28	Carlton Fisk	8.00
29	Bob Gibson	8.00
30	Jim "Catfish" Hunter	4.00
31	Reggie Jackson	8.00
32	Al Kaline	8.00
33	Harmon Killebrew	8.00
34	Buck Leonard	4.00
35	Juan Marichal	4.00
36	Bill Mazeroski	6.00
37	Willie McCovey	6.00
38	Joe Morgan	6.00
39	Eddie Murray	6.00
40	Jim Palmer	6.00
41	Tony Perez	6.00
42	Pee Wee Reese	4.00
43	Brooks Robinson	8.00
44	Nolan Ryan	20.00
45	Mike Schmidt	10.00
46	Tom Seaver	8.00
47	Enos Slaughter	4.00
48	Willie Stargell	8.00
49	Early Wynn	4.00
50	Robin Yount	8.00
51	Tony Gwynn	8.00
52	Cal Ripken Jr.	20.00
53	Ernie Banks	10.00
54	Wade Boggs	8.00
55	Steve Carlton	6.00
56	Will Clark	8.00
57	Fergie Jenkins	4.00
58	Bo Jackson	10.00
59	Don Mattingly	15.00
60	Stan Musial	10.00
61	Frank Robinson	8.00
62	Ryne Sandberg	10.00
63	Ozzie Smith	10.00
64	Carl Yastrzemski	10.00
65	Dave Winfield	8.00
66	Paul Molitor	8.00
67	Jason Bay	6.00
68	Freddy Sanchez	4.00
69	Josh Beckett	6.00
70	Carlos Beltran	8.00
71	Craig Biggio	6.00
72	Matt Holliday	6.00
73	A.J. Burnett	4.00
74	Miguel Cabrera	8.00
75	Dontrelle Willis	6.00
76	Chris Carpenter	8.00
77	Roger Clemens	15.00
78	Johnny Damon	8.00
79	Jermaine Dye	4.00
80	Jim Thome	8.00
81	Vladimir Guerrero	8.00
82	Travis Hafner	6.00
83	Victor Martinez	6.00
84	Trevor Hoffman	4.00
85	Derek Jeter	20.00
86	Ken Griffey Jr.	15.00
87	Randy Johnson	8.00
88	Andruw Jones	8.00
89	Derrek Lee	8.00
90	Greg Maddux	10.00
91	Magglio Ordonez	4.00
92	David Ortiz	10.00
93	Jake Peavy	6.00
94	Roy Oswalt	4.00
95	Mike Piazza	10.00
96	Jose Reyes	15.00
97	Ivan Rodriguez	8.00
98	Johan Santana	8.00
99	Scott Rolen	8.00
100	Curt Schilling	6.00
101	John Smoltz	6.00
102	Alfonso Soriano	8.00
103	Miguel Tejada	6.00
104	Frank Thomas	8.00
105	Chase Utley	10.00
106	Joe Mauer	8.00
107	Alex Rodriguez	20.00
108	Alex Rios	6.00
109	Justin Verlander	8.00
110	Ryan Howard	15.00
111	Jered Weaver	6.00
112	Francisco Liriano	6.00
113	David Wright	10.00
114	Felix Hernandez	8.00
115	Jeremy Sowers	4.00
116	Cole Hamels	8.00
117	B.J. Upton	6.00
118	Chien-Ming Wang	35.00
119	Justin Morneau	8.00
120	Jonny Gomes	4.00
121	Adrian Gonzalez	6.00
122	Bill Hall	6.00
123	Rich Harden	4.00
124	Rich Hill	4.00
125	Tadahito Iguchi	4.00
126	Scott Kazmir	6.00
127	Howie Kendrick	6.00
128	Dan Uggla	4.00
129	Hanley Ramirez	8.00
130	Josh Willingham	4.00
131	Nicholas Markakis	6.00
132	Grady Sizemore	8.00
133	Ian Snell	6.00
134	Jonathan Papelbon	8.00
135	Ryan Zimmerman	8.00
136	Stephen Drew	6.00
137	Adam Wainwright	4.00
138	Joel Zumaya	6.00
139	Prince Fielder	10.00
140	Carl Crawford	6.00
141	Huston Street	4.00
142	Matt Cain	8.00
143	Andre Ethier	6.00
144	Brian McCann	4.00
145	Josh Barfield	4.00
146	Anibal Sanchez	4.00
147	Brian Roberts	6.00
148	Brandon Webb	8.00
149	Chipper Jones	10.00
150	Tim Hudson	4.00
151	Adam LaRoche	4.00
152	Jeff Francoeur	8.00
153	Marcus Giles	4.00
154	Jason Varitek	8.00
155	Coco Crisp	4.00
156	Manny Ramirez	8.00
157	Trot Nixon	4.00
158	Carlos Zambrano	6.00
159	Mark Prior	6.00
160	Aramis Ramirez	6.00
161	Mark Buehrle	4.00
162	Paul Konerko	6.00
163	Adam Dunn	8.00
164	C.C. Sabathia	6.00
165	Todd Helton	8.00
166	Garrett Atkins	4.00
167	Jeremy Bonderman	6.00
168	Curtis Granderson	4.00
169	Sean Casey	4.00
170	Lance Berkman	6.00
171	Brad Lidge	4.00
172	Reggie Sanders	4.00
173	Brad Penny	4.00
174	Nomar Garciaparra	8.00
175	Jeff Kent	4.00
176	Chone Figgins	4.00
177	Ben Sheets	6.00
178	Rickie Weeks	4.00
179	Joe Nathan	4.00
180	Torii Hunter	6.00
181	Carlos Delgado	8.00
182	Tom Glavine	6.00
183	Paul LoDuca	4.00
184	Mariano Rivera	8.00
185	Robinson Cano	8.00
186	Bobby Abreu	6.00
187	Hideki Matsui	10.00
188	Barry Zito	6.00
189	Eric Chavez	4.00
190	Jimmy Rollins	6.00
191	Khalil Greene	4.00
192	Brian Giles	4.00
193	Jason Schmidt	4.00
194	Ichiro Suzuki	30.00
195	David Eckstein	4.00
196	Jim Edmonds	6.00
197	Mark Teixeira	8.00
198	Michael Young	6.00
199	Vernon Wells	4.00
200	Roy Halladay	6.00
201	Delmon Young (RC)	8.00
202	Andrew Miller (RC)	20.00
203	Troy Tulowitzki (RC)	6.00
204	Jeff Fiorentino (RC)	4.00
205	David Murphy (RC)	4.00
206	Jeff Baker (RC)	4.00
207	Kevin Hooper (RC)	4.00
208	Kevin Kouzmanoff (RC)	4.00
209	Adam Lind (RC)	6.00
210	Mike Rabelo RC	6.00
211	Craig Hansen (RC)	4.00
212	Mitch Maier RC	4.00
213	Ryan Braun (RC)	4.00
214	Vinny Rottino (RC)	4.00
215	Drew Anderson (RC)	4.00
216	Alexi Casilla RC	6.00
217	Glen Perkins (RC)	4.00
218	Cesar Jimenez RC	4.00
219	Tim Gradoville RC	4.00
220	Shane Youman RC	4.00
221	Billy Sadler (RC)	4.00
222	Patrick Misch (RC)	4.00
223	Juan Salas (RC)	4.00
224	Beltran Perez (RC)	4.00
225	Hector Gimenez (RC)	4.00
226	Philip Humber (RC)	4.00
227	Eric Stults RC	8.00
228	Dennis Sarfate (RC)	4.00
229	Andy Cannizaro RC	4.00
230	Juan Morillo (RC)	6.00
231	Fred Lewis (RC)	4.00
232	Ryan Sweeney (RC)	4.00
233	Chris Narveson (RC)	4.00
234	Michael Bourn (RC)	4.00
235	Joaquin Arias (RC)	4.00
236	Carlos Maldonado (RC)	4.00
237	Alvin Colina RC	4.00
238	Jon Knott (RC)	4.00
239	Justin Hampson (RC)	4.00
240	Jeff Salazar (RC)	4.00
241	Josh Fields (RC)	4.00
242	Delwyn Young (RC)	4.00
243	Daisuke Matsuzaka RC	75.00
244	Kei Igawa RC	15.00

Bronze

Bronze (201-244):	1X
Production 75 Sets	

Printing Plates

Production one set per color.

Gold

Gold (201-244):	1-1.5X
Production 49 Sets	

Platinum

Production One Set

Silver

Silver (201-244):	1X
Production 99 Sets	

Autograph Parallel

No Pricing
Production 25 Sets

Emerging Stars Dual Autographs

		NM/M
Production 50 Sets		
Bronze:		1-1.5X
Production 25 Sets		
Gold:		No Pricing
Production 10 Sets		
Platinum:		No Pricing
Production One Set		
BU	Josh Barfield, Dan Uggla	25.00
BV	Jeremy Bonderman, Justin Verlander	50.00
CA	Carlos Rios, Carl Crawford	30.00
FJ	Felix Hernandez, Jered Weaver	50.00
GB	Josh Barfield, Adrian Gonzalez	25.00
GC	Carl Crawford, Jonny Gomes	25.00
HP	Philip Humber, Mike Pelfrey	35.00
HS	Huston Street, Rich Harden	30.00
HV	Rich Harden, Justin Verlander	40.00
IK	Tadahito Iguchi, Ian Kinsler	25.00
KL	Francisco Liriano, Scott Kazmir	35.00
KS	Scott Kazmir, Jeremy Sowers	25.00
LH	Jon Lester, Craig Hansen	40.00
MB	Jeremy Brown, Joe Mauer	35.00
MG	Justin Morneau, Adrian Gonzalez	40.00
MH	Andrew Miller, Cole Hamels	65.00
MZ	Andrew Miller, Joel Zumaya	50.00
PH	Jonathan Papelbon, Craig Hansen	50.00
PW	Jonathan Papelbon, Adam Wainwright	50.00
QD	Carlos Quentin, Stephen Drew	30.00
RB	Rickie Weeks, Bill Hall	40.00
RD	Jose Reyes, Stephen Drew	60.00
RR	Hanley Ramirez, Jose Reyes	75.00
RY	Alex Rios, Delmon Young	40.00
SH	Jeremy Sowers, Cole Hamels	25.00
SJ	Anibal Sanchez, Josh Johnson	20.00
SW	Adam Wainwright, Huston Street	30.00
TD	Stephen Drew, Troy Tulowitzki	30.00
TR	Troy Tulowitzki, Hanley Ramirez	30.00
UG	Jonny Gomes, B.J. Upton	25.00
UR	Dan Uggla, Hanley Ramirez	30.00
UU	Chase Utley, Dan Uggla	50.00
VH	Felix Hernandez, Justin Verlander	75.00
VM	Justin Verlander, Andrew Miller	75.00
WE	Josh Willingham, Andre Ethier	25.00
WK	Jered Weaver, Howie Kendrick	40.00
WL	Jered Weaver, Francisco Liriano	50.00
YT	Delmon Young, Troy Tulowitzki	40.00
ZW	Joel Zumaya, Adam Wainwright	30.00

Emerging Stars Triple Autographs

	NM/M
Production 50 Sets	
Bronze:	1-1.5X
Production 25 Sets	
Gold:	No Pricing
Production 10 Sets	
Platinum:	No Pricing

Production One Set

ELS	James Loney, Andre Ethier, Takashi Saito	50.00
HHL	Cole Hamels, Rich Hill, Francisco Liriano	75.00
HQE	Carlos Quentin, Matt Holliday, Andre Ethier	40.00
KUK	Howie Kendrick, Dan Uggla, Ian Kinsler	40.00
LBG	Matt Garza, Francisco Liriano, Boof Bonser	50.00
MHL	Francisco Liriano, Cole Hamels, Andrew Miller	80.00
MKL	Jason Kubel, Francisco Liriano, Justin Morneau	40.00
MSK	Scott Kazmir, Jeremy Sowers, Andrew Miller	40.00
MVB	Andrew Miller, Justin Verlander, Jeremy Bonderman	100.00
MYE	Andre Ethier, Nicholas Markakis, Delmon Young	70.00
PSW	Adam Wainwright, Huston Street, Jonathan Papelbon	50.00
QEY	Carlos Quentin, Delmon Young, Andre Ethier	40.00
RRD	Hanley Ramirez, Stephen Drew, Jose Reyes	75.00
SHK	Scott Kazmir, Jeremy Sowers, Cole Hamels	50.00
TDR	Troy Tulowitzki, Stephen Drew, Hanley Ramirez	50.00
THA	Matt Holliday, Garrett Atkins, Troy Tulowitzki	50.00
UKW	Howie Kendrick, Chase Utley, Rickie Weeks	60.00
UUW	Rickie Weeks, Chase Utley, Dan Uggla	50.00
UYK	B.J. Upton, Scott Kazmir, Delmon Young	50.00
VMZ	Justin Verlander, Joel Zumaya, Andrew Miller	80.00
WHV	Jered Weaver, Justin Verlander, Felix Hernandez	85.00
WZS	Adam Wainwright, Joel Zumaya, Takashi Saito	40.00
YER	Alex Rios, Delmon Young, Andre Ethier	40.00

Hallmarks Autographs

NM/M
Production 5-57
Gold: No Pricing
Production 25 Sets
Platinum: No Pricing
Production One Set

LA	Luis Aparicio/57	25.00
MS	Mike Schmidt/48	40.00
OS	Ozzie Smith/57	50.00
PM	Paul Molitor/39	25.00
RJ	Reggie Jackson/47	50.00
RS	Ryne Sandberg/40	60.00
RY	Robin Yount/46	40.00
SC	Steve Carlton/37	35.00
WF	Whitey Ford/25	50.00
WM	Willie McCovey/45	30.00

Insignias Autographs

NM/M
Production 50 Sets
Gold: 1-1.5X
Production 25 Sets
Platinum: No Pricing
Production One Set

AK	Al Kaline	35.00
AM	Andrew Miller	60.00
BU	B.J. Upton	25.00
CR	Cal Ripken Jr.	100.00
DJ	Derek Jeter	150.00
DL	Derrek Lee	30.00
DM	Don Mattingly	60.00
DY	Delmon Young	30.00
EB	Ernie Banks	50.00
FH	Felix Hernandez	50.00
JM	Joe Mauer	40.00
JP	Jake Peavy	30.00

JR	Jose Reyes	80.00
JT	Jim Thome	50.00
JW	Jered Weaver	30.00
KG	Ken Griffey Jr.	90.00
MO	Justin Morneau	30.00
OS	Ozzie Smith	50.00
PA	Jim Palmer	20.00
TG	Tony Gwynn	40.00
TT	Troy Tulowitzki	25.00
WC	Will Clark	25.00

Noteworthy Autographs

NM/M
Production 1-86 15.00
Gold: No Pricing
Production 25 Sets
Platinum: No Pricing
Production One Set

AD	Andre Dawson/50	50.00
AK	Al Kaline/50	50.00
AS	Alfonso Soriano/35	35.00
BA	Jeff Bagwell/75	75.00
BE	Josh Beckett/50	40.00
BJ	Bo Jackson/35	75.00
BR	Brooks Robinson/35	40.00
CB	Craig Biggio/65	40.00
CC	Chris Carpenter/50	40.00
DB	Dusty Baker/25	30.00
DE	Dennis Eckersley/75	15.00
DS	Don Sutton/35	15.00
FJ	Fergie Jenkins/74	15.00
FR	Frank Robinson/31	40.00
GS	Gary Sheffield/86	30.00
JB	Jim Bunning/54	30.00
JC	Jack Clark/75	15.00
JM	Juan Marichal/65	25.00
JP	Jim Palmer/65	20.00
JS	Johan Santana	50.00
KW	Kerry Wood/35	20.00
LA	Luis Aparicio/35	15.00
MM	Mark Mulder/35	15.00
MO	Justin Morneau/30	30.00
MT	Miguel Tejada/50	25.00
PE	Jake Peavy/55	30.00
PM	Paul Molitor/40	25.00
RS	Ryne Sandberg/45	50.00
TG	Tom Glavine/47	60.00
TH	Torii Hunter/26	30.00
WB	Wade Boggs/45	25.00
AP	Albert Pujols/49	200.00
BF	Bob Feller/62	30.00
CF	Carlton Fisk/37	40.00
CR	Cal Ripken Jr./34	125.00
DJ	Derek Jeter/44	150.00
DM	Don Mattingly/35	75.00
HR	Hanley Ramirez/51	30.00
JB	Johnny Bench/45	50.00
JM	Joe Mauer/36	40.00
JT	Jim Thome/52	40.00
JZ	Joel Zumaya/62	15.00
KG	Ken Griffey Jr./56	75.00
RY	Robin Yount/29	50.00
TG	Tony Gwynn/56	40.00

Foursomes

No Pricing
Production 15 Sets

Octographs

No Pricing
Production 5 Sets

Pairings

NM/M
Production 25 Sets

AK	Andruw Jones, Ken Griffey Jr.	125.00
BD	Dave Winfield, Bo Jackson	75.00
BF	Johnny Bench, Carlton Fisk	75.00
BJ	Yogi Berra, Derek Jeter	250.00
BM	Don Mattingly, Wade Boggs	120.00
BU	Chase Utley, Craig Biggio	75.00
CG	Chris Carpenter, Bob Gibson	50.00
CO	Chris Carpenter, Roy Oswalt	60.00
CR	Craig Biggio, Ryne Sandberg	100.00
ER	Ernie Banks, Ryne Sandberg	150.00
FO	Bob Feller, Roy Oswalt	125.00
GF	Bob Feller, Bob Gibson	50.00
GR	Cal Ripken Jr., Ken Griffey Jr.	250.00

JG	Ken Griffey Jr., Derek Jeter	250.00
JW	Dave Winfield, Reggie Jackson	75.00
MC	Don Mattingly, Will Clark	80.00
MG	Tony Gwynn, Stan Musial	125.00
MM	Joe Mauer, Victor Martinez	50.00
MR	Frank Robinson, Eddie Murray	75.00
OY	Carl Yastrzemski, David Ortiz	125.00
PG	Albert Pujols, Ken Griffey Jr.	250.00
RG	Tony Gwynn, Cal Ripken Jr.	200.00
RJ	Cal Ripken Jr., Derek Jeter	250.00
RN	Roger Clemens, Nolan Ryan	275.00
RP	Ivan Rodriguez, Mike Piazza	75.00
RR	Cal Ripken Jr., Brooks Robinson	180.00
SA	Luis Aparicio, Ozzie Smith	75.00
SB	Brooks Robinson, Scott Rolen	60.00
SG	Alfonso Soriano, Vladimir Guerrero	80.00
SM	Ryne Sandberg, Joe Morgan	75.00
TM	Willie McCovey, Jim Thome	60.00
WC	Dontrelle Willis, Miguel Cabrera	50.00
YM	Paul Molitor, Robin Yount	80.00

Patches Dual

NM/M
Production 75 unless noted.
Platinum: No Pricing
Production 5-10
Masterpiece: No Pricing
Production One Set
Gold: .75-1X
Production 6-58
No pricing prod. 25 or less.

AD	Adam Dunn	20.00
AP	Albert Pujols	60.00
AS	Alfonso Soriano	20.00
BU	B.J. Upton	20.00
CH	Cole Hamels	25.00
CR	Cal Ripken Jr.	50.00
CU	Chase Utley	25.00
DJ	Derek Jeter	40.00
DJ2	Derek Jeter	40.00
DM	Don Mattingly	35.00
ED	Jim Edmonds	15.00
FL	Francisco Liriano	15.00
GM	Greg Maddux	30.00
IR	Ivan Rodriguez	20.00
JB	Johnny Bench	25.00
JG	Jason Giambi	15.00
JM	Joe Mauer	20.00
JO	Randy Johnson	20.00
JP	Jake Peavy	15.00
JR	Jose Reyes	40.00
JT	Jim Thome	20.00
JT2	Jim Thome	20.00
JV	Justin Verlander/42	25.00
JW	Jered Weaver	20.00
KG	Ken Griffey Jr.	40.00
KG2	Ken Griffey Jr.	40.00
KM	Kendry Morales	15.00
LB	Lance Berkman	15.00
MC	Miguel Cabrera	20.00
MR	Manny Ramirez	25.00
MS	Mike Schmidt	20.00
MT	Mark Teixeira	20.00
NR	Nolan Ryan	50.00
PF	Prince Fielder	40.00
PM	Pedro Martinez	30.00
RJ	Reggie Jackson	25.00
RS	Ryne Sandberg	30.00
RZ	Ryan Zimmerman	35.00
SA	Johan Santana	25.00
TE	Miguel Tejada	20.00
TG	Tony Gwynn	25.00
TO	Tom Glavine	30.00
VG	Vladimir Guerrero	25.00
VG2	Vladimir Guerrero	25.00

Patches Dual Autographs

NM/M
Production 25 Sets

AD	Adam Dunn	40.00
BR	Brooks Robinson	50.00
BU	B.J. Upton	40.00
CH	Cole Hamels	50.00

CR	Cal Ripken Jr.	180.00
DJ	Derek Jeter	200.00
DM	Don Mattingly	140.00
FL	Francisco Liriano	40.00
IR	Ivan Rodriguez	50.00
JB	Johnny Bench	60.00
KM	Kendry Morales	30.00
NR	Nolan Ryan	150.00
RJ	Reggie Jackson	75.00
RS	Ryne Sandberg	75.00

Patches Triple

NM/M
Production 1-99
Gold: .75-1X
Production 1-57
No pricing prod. 25 or less.
Platinum: No Pricing
Production 5 Sets
Masterpiece: No Pricing
Production One Set

AJ	Andruw Jones/97	30.00
CC	Chris Carpenter/97	30.00
CD	Carlos Delgado/94	25.00
CJ	Chipper Jones/95	40.00
CL	Carlos Lee/99	20.00
CR	Cal Ripken Jr./82	40.00
CS	Curt Schilling/90	30.00
EM	Eddie Murray/77	30.00
FR	Frank Robinson/56	25.00
FT	Frank Thomas/80	40.00
GM	Greg Maddux/87	40.00
JT	Jim Thome/91	20.00
KG	Ken Griffey Jr./89	50.00
MR	Manny Ramirez/94	30.00
OS	Ozzie Smith/78	50.00
RJ	Randy Johnson/89	30.00
RO	Roy Halladay/99	25.00
TE	Miguel Tejada/98	20.00
TG	Tony Gwynn/82	40.00
TS	Tom Seaver/67	35.00
VG	Vladimir Guerrero/97	30.00
WB	Wade Boggs/82	30.00
JT2	Jim Thome/91	20.00
KG2	Ken Griffey Jr./89	50.00

Patches Triple Autographs

No Pricing
Production 15 Sets

Penmanship Autographs

NM/M
Production 1-98
Masterpiece: No Pricing
Production One Set

AK	Al Kaline/53	30.00
BF	Bob Feller/36	25.00
BJ	Bo Jackson/86	40.00
BR	Brooks Robinson/57	30.00
CB	Craig Biggio/88	50.00
CC	Chris Carpenter/97	40.00
CF	Carlton Fisk/72	25.00
CR	Cal Ripken Jr./82	100.00
CR2	Cal Ripken Jr./82	100.00
CY	Carl Yastrzemski/61	60.00
DJ	Derek Jeter/96	150.00
DJ2	Derek Jeter/96	150.00
DL	Derrek Lee/97	25.00
DM	Don Mattingly/83	50.00
DM2	Don Mattingly/83	50.00
EB	Ernie Banks/54	60.00
GM	Greg Maddux/87	80.00
IR	Ivan Rodriguez/91	40.00
JB	Johnny Bench/68	50.00
JI	Jim Palmer/65	25.00
JS	John Smoltz/88	75.00
JT	Jim Thome/91	40.00
KG	Ken Griffey Jr./89	75.00
KG2	Ken Griffey Jr./89	75.00
LA	Luis Aparicio/56	50.00
MS	Mike Schmidt/73	50.00
NR	Nolan Ryan/68	100.00
OZ	Ozzie Smith/78	50.00
PM	Paul Molitor/78	35.00
PM2	Paul Molitor/78	35.00
RA	Randy Johnson/89	50.00
RC	Roger Clemens/84	50.00
RJ	Reggie Jackson/68	65.00
RS	Ryne Sandberg/82	50.00
RY	Robin Yount/74	40.00
SC	Steve Carlton/67	25.00
SM	Stan Musial/42	60.00
SR	Scott Rolen/35	35.00
TE	Miguel Tejada/98	25.00
TG	Tony Gwynn/82	40.00
TG2	Tony Gwynn	40.00
TP	Tony Perez/85	30.00
VG	Vladimir Guerrero/97	60.00
WB	Wade Boggs/82	35.00
WC	Will Clark/86	25.00

WF	Whitey Ford/50	50.00
WM	Willie McCovey/59	40.00
YB	Yogi Berra/47	50.00

Penmanship Autograph Jersey Number

		NM/M
Production 1-58		
AM	Andrew Miller/50	60.00
CF	Carlton Fisk/27	40.00
CH	Cole Hamels/35	50.00
CZ	Carlos Zambrano/38	25.00
DL	Derrek Lee/25	35.00
DW	Dontrelle Willis/35	25.00
DY	Delmon Young/35	30.00
FH	Felix Hernandez/34	50.00
FL	Francisco Liriano/47	30.00
GM	Greg Maddux/36	100.00
JG	Jonny Gomes/31	20.00
JP	Jake Peavy/44	40.00
JS	John Smoltz/29	65.00
JV	Justin Verlander/35	50.00
JW	Jered Weaver/56	25.00
JZ	Joel Zumaya/54	30.00
MO	Justin Morneau/33	30.00
NR	Nolan Ryan/34	100.00
NS	Nick Swisher/33	30.00
PA	Jonathan Papelbon/58	50.00
PH	Philip Humber/49	20.00
RA	Randy Johnson/41	60.00
RO	Roy Oswalt/45	25.00
SA	Johan Santana/57	40.00
SC	Steve Carlton/32	25.00
SR	Scott Rolen/27	40.00
VG	Vladimir Guerrero/27	50.00
VM	Victor Martinez/41	25.00
WB	Wade Boggs/26	40.00
WM	Willie McCovey/44	40.00

Preeminence

		NM/M
Production 50 Sets		
Gold:		1-1.5X
Production 25 Sets		
Platinum:		No Pricing
Production One Set		
AP	Albert Pujols	200.00
BJ	Bo Jackson	60.00
BR	Brooks Robinson	25.00
CC	Chris Carpenter	25.00
CR	Cal Ripken Jr.	120.00
CY	Carl Yastrzemski	50.00
DJ	Derek Jeter	150.00
GM	Greg Maddux	100.00
JB	Johnny Bench	50.00
JM	Joe Mauer	40.00
JT	Jim Thome	40.00
JV	Justin Verlander	50.00
KG	Ken Griffey Jr.	75.00
MS	Mike Schmidt	50.00
NR	Nolan Ryan	90.00
RC	Roger Clemens	100.00
RJ	Reggie Jackson	50.00
RS	Ryne Sandberg	50.00
SM	Stan Musial	60.00
TG	Tony Gwynn	40.00
VG	Vladimir Guerrero	50.00

Rare Patches Dual

		NM/M
Production 50 Sets		
Gold:		1-1.5X
Production 25 Sets		
Platinum:		No Pricing
Production 10 Sets		
Masterpiece:		No Pricing
Production One Set		
BM	Joe Mauer, Johnny Bench	40.00
BR	Brian Roberts, Robinson Cano	25.00
BS	Anibal Sanchez, A.J. Burnett	20.00
CP	Jake Peavy, Chris Carpenter	30.00
CW	Miguel Cabrera, Dontrelle Willis	30.00
DB	Carlos Beltran, Carlos Delgado	30.00
DT	Miguel Tejada, Stephen Drew	25.00
ER	Scott Rolen, Jim Edmonds	40.00
FM	Justin Morneau, Prince Fielder	35.00
FW	Prince Fielder, Rickie Weeks	40.00
GP	Albert Pujols, Ken Griffey Jr.	75.00
HR	Trevor Hoffman, Mariano Rivera	40.00

HS	Jeremy Sowers, Cole Hamels	30.00
JG	Ken Griffey Jr., Derek Jeter	75.00
JJ	Andruw Jones, Chipper Jones	40.00
MG	Tom Glavine, Greg Maddux	70.00
MH	Travis Hafner, Victor Martinez	25.00
MJ	Derek Jeter, Don Mattingly	80.00
OT	Jim Thome, David Ortiz	35.00
PO	Roy Oswalt, Jake Peavy	25.00
PS	Curt Schilling, Jonathan Papelbon	50.00
RC	Roger Clemens, Nolan Ryan	80.00
RD	Derek Jeter, Reggie Jackson	50.00
RG	Cal Ripken Jr., Tony Gwynn	75.00
RJ	Roy Halladay, Johan Santana	40.00
RU	Jimmy Rollins, Chase Utley	50.00
SG	Alfonso Soriano, Vladimir Guerrero	40.00
SH	Johan Santana, Felix Hernandez	40.00
SM	Joe Morgan, Ryne Sandberg	50.00
TR	Miguel Tejada, Jose Reyes	40.00
TT	Jim Thome, Frank Thomas	40.00
UC	Carl Crawford, B.J. Upton	40.00
WJ	Josh Johnson, Dontrelle Willis	20.00
WL	Francisco Liriano, Jered Weaver	30.00
YM	Robin Yount, Paul Molitor	40.00
ZU	Ryan Zimmerman, B.J. Upton	40.00

Rare Patches Triple

		NM/M
Production 25 Sets		
Gold:		No Pricing
Production 10 Sets		
Platinum:		No Pricing
Production 5 Sets		
Masterpiece:		No Pricing
Production One Set		
CRM	Nolan Ryan, Greg Maddux, Roger Clemens	125.00
MRM	Victor Martinez, Joe Mauer	40.00
POG	Albert Pujols, David Ortiz, Vladimir Guerrero	80.00
RGM	Cal Ripken Jr., Tony Gwynn, Paul Molitor	100.00
SHK	Scott Kazmir, Jeremy Sowers, Cole Hamels	30.00
UWR	Chase Utley, Rickie Weeks, Brian Roberts	40.00
WLV	Francisco Liriano, Justin Verlander, Jered Weaver	50.00

Rare Remnants Quad

No Pricing		
Production 25 Sets		
Gold:		No Pricing
Production 10 Sets		
Platinum:		No Pricing
Production 5 Sets		
Masterpiece:		No Pricing
Production One Set		
BMP	Tony Perez, Joe Morgan, Johnny Bench	30.00
BZV	Jeremy Bonderman, Justin Verlander, Joel Zumaya	40.00

Rare Remnants Triple

		NM/M
Production 50 Sets		
Gold:		1-1.5X
Production 25 Sets		
Platinum:		No Pricing
Production 10 Sets		
Masterpiece:		No Pricing
Production One Set		

CBF	Brooks Robinson, Frank Robinson, Cal Ripken Jr.	50.00
CFY	Jimmie Foxx, Joe Cronin, Carl Yastrzemski	60.00
CMK	Ralph Kiner, Bill Mazeroski, Roberto Clemente	100.00
CPR	Chris Carpenter, Albert Pujols, Scott Rolen	40.00
DMP	Jorge Posada, Thurman Munson, Bill Dickey	50.00
DMR	Pedro Martinez, Carlos Delgado, Jose Reyes	40.00
DRB	Jose Reyes, Carlos Delgado, Carlos Beltran	40.00
FBM	Carlton Fisk, Thurman Munson, Johnny Bench	35.00
FGG	Hank Greenberg, Lou Gehrig, Jimmie Foxx	180.00
FMT	Justin Morneau, Mark Teixeira, Prince Fielder	30.00
GGJ	Andruw Jones, Ken Griffey Jr., Vladimir Guerrero	40.00
JCM	Greg Maddux, Randy Johnson, Roger Clemens	40.00
JJR	Derek Jeter, Randy Johnson, Mariano Rivera	50.00
JMM	Thurman Munson, Don Mattingly, Reggie Jackson	75.00
KUC	B.J. Upton, Carl Crawford, Scott Kazmir	25.00
KVJ	Joe Mauer, Victor Martinez, Kenji Johjima	25.00
LMS	Joe Mauer, Francisco Liriano, Johan Santana	25.00
LSH	Francisco Liriano, Jeremy Sowers, Cole Hamels	25.00
OPS	Jake Peavy, Roy Oswalt, Ben Sheets	20.00
OTB	Lance Berkman, David Ortiz, Jim Thome	25.00
PJG	Derek Jeter, Ken Griffey Jr., Albert Pujols	50.00
PMH	Albert Pujols, Stan Musial, Rogers Hornsby	80.00
RCD	Nolan Ryan, Don Drysdale, Roger Clemens	50.00
RDG	Lou Gehrig, Joe DiMaggio, Babe Ruth	475.00
RFS	Bruce Sutter, Rollie Fingers, Mariano Rivera	25.00
RRR	Nolan Ryan	60.00
RWH	Nolan Ryan, Felix Hernandez, Jered Weaver	30.00
RYS	Robin Yount, Cal Ripken Jr., Ozzie Smith	40.00
SGA	Vladimir Guerrero, Bobby Abreu, Alfonso Soriano	25.00
SHM	Joe Morgan, Rogers Hornsby, Ryne Sandberg	50.00
SJZ	Randy Johnson, Barry Zito, Johan Santana	25.00
SRB	Brooks Robinson, Wade Boggs, Mike Schmidt	40.00
TJY	Miguel Tejada, Derek Jeter, Michael Young	30.00
TTH	Mark Teixeira, Jim Thome, Todd Helton	20.00
VWJ	Josh Johnson, Justin Verlander, Jered Weaver	25.00
YBM	Paul Molitor, Wade Boggs, Robin Yount	25.00

Remnants Triple Autograph

No Pricing	
Production 25 Sets	

Remnants Triple

	NM/M
Production 75 Sets	

Gold:		.75-1.5X
Production 6-60		
No pricing prod. 25 or less.		
Platinum:		No Pricing
Production 10 Sets		
Masterpiece:		No Pricing
Production One Set		
AP	Albert Pujols	30.00
AP2	Albert Pujols	30.00
AS	Alfonso Soriano	15.00
BM	Bill Mazeroski	20.00
BR	Babe Ruth	400.00
CA	Roy Campanella	35.00
CF	Carlton Fisk	15.00
CJ	Chipper Jones	25.00
CL	Roger Clemens	25.00
CR	Cal Ripken Jr.	30.00
CS	Curt Schilling	15.00
CU	Chase Utley	25.00
CY	Carl Yastrzemski	25.00
DJ	Derek Jeter	30.00
DJ2	Derek Jeter	30.00
DM	Don Mattingly	40.00
DO	David Ortiz	25.00
EM	Eddie Mathews	30.00
FR	Frank Robinson	20.00
HO	Rogers Hornsby	80.00
JB	Johnny Bench	20.00
JD	Joe DiMaggio	125.00
JO	Jose Reyes	30.00
JR	Jackie Robinson	75.00
JT	Jim Thome	15.00
KG	Ken Griffey Jr.	25.00
KG2	Ken Griffey Jr.	25.00
MO	Mel Ott	50.00
MR	Manny Ramirez	15.00
MS	Mike Schmidt	25.00
NR	Nolan Ryan	40.00
PM	Paul Molitor	15.00
PR	Pee Wee Reese	25.00
RC	Roberto Clemente	75.00
RJ	Reggie Jackson	30.00
RO	Brooks Robinson	15.00
RS	Ryne Sandberg	25.00
RY	Robin Yount	25.00
SM	Stan Musial	30.00
TG	Tony Gwynn	20.00
TM	Thurman Munson	35.00
VG	Vladimir Guerrero	15.00

Remnants Quad

		NM/M
Production 1-96		
Gold:		.75-1.5X
Production 2-57		
No pricing prod. 25 or less.		
Platinum:		No Pricing
Production 5 Sets		
Masterpiece:		No Pricing
Production One Set		
AK	Al Kaline/53	35.00
BM	Bill Mazeroski/56	30.00
CL	Roberto Clemente/55	120.00
CR	Cal Ripken Jr./82	50.00
CY	Carl Yastrzemski/61	30.00
DJ	Derek Jeter/96	50.00
DM	Don Mattingly/83	35.00
EM	Eddie Mathews/52	40.00
HK	Harmon Killebrew/55	40.00
JB	Johnny Bench/68	25.00
JD	Joe DiMaggio/36	125.00
JF	Jimmie Foxx/27	100.00
JR	Jackie Robinson/47	100.00
JT	Jim Thome/91	15.00
KG	Ken Griffey Jr./89	30.00
LG	Lou Gehrig/25	400.00
MI	Johnny Mize/36	40.00
MS	Mike Schmidt/73	30.00
NR	Nolan Ryan/68	50.00
RC	Roger Clemens/84	30.00
RJ	Reggie Jackson/68	25.00
RN	Brooks Robinson/57	25.00
RO	Roy Campanella/48	25.00
SM	Stan Musial/42	50.00
TM	Thurman Munson/70	40.00

Remnants Quad Autograph

Production 15 Sets	

Six

Production 10 Sets	

Stitchings

		NM/M
Production 50 Sets		
Stitchings 35:		1X
Production 35 Sets		
1	Babe Ruth	40.00
2	Babe Ruth	40.00
3	Babe Ruth	40.00
4	Ty Cobb	25.00

5	Ty Cobb	25.00
6	Lou Gehrig	30.00
7	Lou Gehrig	30.00
8	Joe DiMaggio	30.00
9	Joe DiMaggio	30.00
12	Roberto Clemente	30.00
13	Roberto Clemente	30.00
14	Jackie Robinson	30.00
15	Jackie Robinson	30.00
16	Cy Young	15.00
17	Cy Young	15.00
18	Nolan Ryan	30.00
19	Nolan Ryan	30.00
20	Reggie Jackson	15.00
21	Reggie Jackson	15.00
22	Ken Griffey Jr.	25.00
23	Ken Griffey Jr.	25.00
24	Derek Jeter	30.00
25	Derek Jeter	30.00
26	Jimmie Foxx	20.00
27	Jimmie Foxx	20.00
28	Rogers Hornsby	25.00
30	Walter Johnson	25.00
31	Walter Johnson	25.00
32	Ernie Banks	25.00
33	Ernie Banks	25.00
34	Christy Mathewson	15.00
35	Johnny Mize	15.00
36	Thurman Munson	25.00
37	Thurman Munson	25.00
38	Mel Ott	15.00
39	Satchel Paige	20.00
40	George Sisler	15.00
41	Casey Stengel	15.00
42	Honus Wagner	25.00
43	Honus Wagner	25.00
44	Roy Campanella	20.00
45	Mickey Cochrane	15.00
46	Dizzy Dean	15.00
47	Don Drysdale	15.00
48	Lefty Grove	15.00
49	Roger Clemens	25.00
50	Roger Clemens	25.00
51	Cal Ripken Jr.	40.00
52	Cal Ripken Jr.	40.00
53	Tony Gwynn	20.00
54	Tony Gwynn	20.00
55	Johnny Bench	20.00
56	Yogi Berra	20.00
57	Carlton Fisk	15.00
58	Joe Morgan	15.00
59	Brooks Robinson	15.00
60	Mike Schmidt	25.00
61	Willie Stargell	20.00
62	Tom Seaver	20.00
63	Ozzie Smith	25.00
64	Albert Pujols	30.00
65	Albert Pujols	30.00
66	Ryan Howard	20.00
67	David Ortiz	20.00
68	Randy Johnson	25.00
69	Greg Maddux	20.00
70	Greg Maddux	20.00
71	Johan Santana	15.00
72	Al Kaline	15.00
73	Ryne Sandberg	20.00
74	Robin Yount	20.00
75	Frank Robinson	15.00
76	Frank Robinson	15.00
78	Stan Musial	20.00
79	Carl Yastrzemski	20.00
80	Don Mattingly	30.00
81	Ichiro Suzuki	30.00
82	Yogi Berra	15.00
83	Carlton Fisk, Johnny Bench	20.00
84	Johnny Bench, Thurman Munson	25.00
85	Babe Ruth, Lou Gehrig	30.00
86	Yogi Berra, Whitey Ford	20.00
87	Yogi Berra, Don Larsen	20.00
88	Dennis Eckersley, Kirk Gibson	15.00
90	Pee Wee Reese, Jackie Robinson	20.00
91	Jackie Robinson, Satchel Paige	25.00
92	Lou Gehrig, Cal Ripken Jr.	30.00
93	George Sisler, Ichiro Suzuki	30.00
94	Steve Carlton, Roger Clemens, Randy Johnson, Nolan Ryan	40.00
95	Dave Concepcion, Tony Perez, Johnny Bench, Joe Morgan	25.00
96	Babe Ruth, Jimmie Foxx, Mel Ott, Eddie Mathews	40.00
97	Roger Clemens, Greg Maddux, Tom Seaver, Nolan Ryan	40.00
98	Roberto Clemente, Tony Gwynn, Stan Musial, Cal Ripken Jr.	40.00
DM	Daisuke Matsuzaka	60.00
KI	Kei Igawa	25.00
MI	Daisuke Matsuzaka, Kei Igawa	50.00

Stitchings Autograph

No Pricing
Production 25 Sets

Stitchings Cuts

Production One Set

Trios Autographs

No Pricing
Production 20 Sets

World Series Ticket

Production One

2007 Upper Deck Spectrum

		NM/M
Complete Set (149):		
Common Player (1-100):		.25
Common Auto. (101-149):		10.00
Pack (5):		6.00
Box (20):		110.00
1	Miguel Tejada	.50
2	Brian Roberts	.40
3	Melvin Mora	.25
4	David Ortiz	1.00
5	Manny Ramirez	.75
6	Jason Varitek	.50
7	Curt Schilling	.75
8	Jim Thome	.50
9	Paul Konerko	.40
10	Jermaine Dye	.40
11	Travis Hafner	.50
12	Victor Martinez	.40
13	Grady Sizemore	.50
14	C.C. Sabathia	.40
15	Ivan Rodriguez	.50
16	Magglio Ordonez	.25
17	Carlos Guillen	.25
18	Justin Verlander	.50
19	Shane Costa	.25
20	Emil Brown	.25
21	Mark Teahen	.25
22	Vladimir Guerrero	.75
23	Jered Weaver	.50
24	Juan Rivera	.25
25	Justin Morneau	.75
26	Joe Mauer	.50
27	Torii Hunter	.40
28	Johan Santana	.75
29	Derek Jeter	2.00
30	Alex Rodriguez	2.00
31	Johnny Damon	.75
32	Jason Giambi	.50
33	Frank Thomas	.50
34	Nick Swisher	.40
35	Eric Chavez	.40
36	Ichiro Suzuki	1.50
37	Raul Ibanez	.25
38	Richie Sexson	.40
39	Carl Crawford	.40
40	Rocco Baldelli	.40
41	Scott Kazmir	.40
42	Michael Young	.40
43	Mark Teixeira	.50
44	Carlos Lee	.50
45	Gary Matthews	.25
46	Vernon Wells	.40
47	Roy Halladay	.50
48	Lyle Overbay	.25

49	Brandon Webb	.50
50	Conor Jackson	.25
51	Stephen Drew	.50
52	Chipper Jones	.75
53	Andruw Jones	.50
54	Adam LaRoche	.25
55	John Smoltz	.50
56	Derek Lee	.50
57	Aramis Ramirez	.50
58	Carlos Zambrano	.50
59	Ken Griffey Jr.	1.50
60	Adam Dunn	.50
61	Aaron Harang	.40
62	Todd Helton	.50
63	Matt Holliday	.50
64	Garrett Atkins	.40
65	Miguel Cabrera	.75
66	Hanley Ramirez	.50
67	Dontrelle Willis	.50
68	Lance Berkman	.50
69	Roy Oswalt	.50
70	Roger Clemens	1.50
71	J.D. Drew	.40
72	Nomar Garciaparra	.75
73	Rafael Furcal	.40
74	Jeff Kent	.40
75	Prince Fielder	1.00
76	Bill Hall	.40
77	Rickie Weeks	.40
78	Jose Reyes	.75
79	David Wright	1.00
80	Carlos Delgado	.50
81	Carlos Beltran	.50
82	Ryan Howard	1.50
83	Chase Utley	.75
84	Jimmy Rollins	.50
85	Jason Bay	.40
86	Freddy Sanchez	.25
87	Zachary Duke	.25
88	Trevor Hoffman	.25
89	Adrian Gonzalez	.25
90	Mike Piazza	.75
91	Ray Durham	.25
92	Omar Vizquel	.25
93	Jason Schmidt	.40
94	Albert Pujols	2.00
95	Scott Rolen	.75
96	Jim Edmonds	.40
97	Chris Carpenter	.50
98	Alfonso Soriano	.75
99	Ryan Zimmerman	.50
100	Nick Johnson	.25
101	Adam Lind **(RC)**	15.00
102	Alexi Casilla/SP **RC**	40.00
103	Andrew Miller **RC**	50.00
104	Andy Cannizaro **RC**	15.00
105	Angel Sanchez/ SP **RC**	20.00
106	Brian Stokes **(RC)**	10.00
107	Carlos Maldonado **(RC)**	15.00
108	Cesar Jimenez **RC**	10.00
109	Chris Stewart **RC**	10.00
111	David Murphy **(RC)**	10.00
112	Delmon Young/ SP **(RC)**	30.00
113	Delwyn Young **(RC)**	15.00
114	Dennis Sarfate/ SP **(RC)**	10.00
116	Drew Anderson **(RC)**	10.00
117	Fred Lewis **(RC)**	10.00
118	Glen Perkins **(RC)**	15.00
119	Hector Gimenez/ SP **(RC)**	10.00
120	Jeff Baker **(RC)**	10.00
121	Jeff Fiorentino **(RC)**	10.00
122	Jeff Salazar **(RC)**	10.00
124	Joaquin Arias/ SP **(RC)**	10.00
125	Jon Knott/SP **(RC)**	15.00
128	Juan Morillo **RC**	10.00
129	Juan Perez SP **RC**	15.00
130	Juan Salas **(RC)**	10.00
131	Justin Hampson **(RC)**	10.00
132	Kevin Hooper/ SP **(RC)**	25.00
133	Kevin Kouzmanoff **(RC)**	15.00
134	Michael Bourn **(RC)**	15.00
135	Miguel Montero/ SP **(RC)**	15.00
136	Mike Rabelo/SP **RC**	25.00
137	Mitch Maier **(RC)**	15.00
138	Oswaldo Navarro/ SP **RC**	15.00
139	Patrick Misch **(RC)**	10.00
140	Philip Humber **(RC)**	20.00
141	Ryan Braun **(RC)**	15.00
142	Ryan Sweeney **(RC)**	10.00
143	Scott Moore **(RC)**	10.00
145	Sean Henn/SP **(RC)**	20.00
146	Shawn Riggans/ SP **(RC)**	20.00
148	Troy Tulowitzki **(RC)**	25.00
149	Ubaldo Jimenez **(RC)**	10.00

Gold

Stars (1-100):		5-10X
Production 99 Sets		

Red

Stars (1-100):		5-10X
Production 99 Sets		

Aligning the Stars

		NM/M
Production 99 Sets		
BPO	David Ortiz, Lance Berkman, Albert Pujols	30.00
CJM	Roger Clemens, Greg Maddux, Randy Johnson	30.00
CRR	Scott Rolen, Aramis Ramirez, Miguel Cabrera	25.00
DBF	Lance Berkman, Prince Fielder, Carlos Delgado	20.00
GRS	Manny Ramirez, Gary Sheffield, Ken Griffey Jr.	35.00
HRW	Trevor Hoffman, Mariano Rivera, Billy Wagner	20.00
HTT	Travis Hafner, Frank Thomas, Jim Thome	20.00
JDB	Andruw Jones, Carlos Beltran, Adam Dunn	25.00
JGC	Jason Giambi, Derek Jeter, Robinson Cano	60.00
JTY	Derek Jeter, Miguel Tejada, Michael Young	30.00
LHP	Albert Pujols, Derrek Lee, Todd Helton	30.00
LVP	Francisco Liriano, Justin Verlander, Jonathan Papelbon	30.00
MKT	Mark Teixeira, Justin Morneau, Paul Konerko	20.00
MOW	Pedro Martinez, Roy Oswalt, Dontrelle Willis	20.00
RFR	Jose Reyes, Jimmy Rollins, Rafael Furcal	20.00
RMM	Ivan Rodriguez, Victor Martinez, Joe Mauer	20.00
RSV	Jason Varitek, Curt Schilling, Manny Ramirez	30.00
SBA	Carlos Beltran, Alfonso Soriano, Bobby Abreu	25.00
SCF	Carl Crawford, Grady Sizemore, Chone Figgins	20.00
SHS	Johan Santana, Roy Halladay, C.C. Sabathia	20.00
WGD	Vladimir Guerrero, Vernon Wells, Johnny Damon	20.00

Grand Slamarama

		NM/M
Common Player:		10.00
AD	Adam Dunn	15.00
AP	Albert Pujols	50.00
AR	Alex Rodriguez	40.00
BA	Bobby Abreu	15.00
BG	Brian Giles	10.00
CD	Carlos Delgado	20.00
CJ	Chipper Jones	30.00
DA	Johnny Damon	25.00
DO	David Ortiz	30.00
DW	David Wright	40.00
HA	Travis Hafner	15.00
JD	Jermaine Dye	15.00
JM	Justin Morneau	20.00
JT	Jim Thome	25.00

...en Griffey Jr.	40.00
Manny Ramirez	25.00
NG Nomar Garciaparra	15.00
RH Ryan Howard	40.00
RS Richie Sexson	20.00
VG Vladimir Guerrero	20.00

Jersey Number

Jersey # (25-57): 5-10X
No pricing production 1-24.
Cards are #'d to jersey number.

Ripken Road to the Hall

	NM/M
Common Ripken:	8.00

Production 99 Sets
Autographs: No Pricing
Production 5 Sets

Rookie Retrospectrum

P • Jon Lester

	NM/M
Common Player:	.50
Red:	2-4X

Production 99 Sets

AE	Andre Ethier	.50
AW	Adam Wainwright	1.00
BA	Josh Barfield	.50
BB	Boof Bonser	.50
BO	Jason Botts	.50
CA	Matt Capps	.50
CB	Chad Billingsley	.50
CD	Chris Demaria	.50
CF	Choo Freeman	.50
CH	Clay Hensley	.50
CQ	Carlos Quentin	.50
DE	Chris Denorfia	.50
DU	Dan Uggla	.50
FC	Fausto Carmona	.50
FL	Francisco Liriano	1.00
HA	Cole Hamels	1.00
HK	Howie Kendrick	1.00
HR	Hanley Ramirez	1.00
JA	Jeremy Accardo	.50
JB	Jason Bergmann	.50
JC	Jose Capellan	.50
JD	Joey Devine	.50
JH	Jeremy Hermida	.50
JK	Jason Kubel	.50
JL	Jon Lester	1.00
JP	Jonathan Papelbon	1.00
JV	Justin Verlander	1.00
JW	Jered Weaver	1.00
JZ	Joel Zumaya	1.00
KM	Kendry Morales	.50
LM	Lastings Milledge	1.00
MA	Nicholas Markakis	1.00
MC	Matt Cain	1.00
ME	Melky Cabrera	.50
MG	Matt Garza	1.00

MJ	Mike Jacobs	.50
MM	Matt Murton	.50
NM	Nate McLouth	.50
PF	Prince Fielder	1.00
RA	Reggie Abercrombie	.50
RG	Ryan Garko	.50
RM	Russell Martin	.50
RP	Ronny Paulino	.50
RS	Ryan Shealy	.50
RZ	Ryan Zimmerman	1.00
SD	Stephen Drew	1.00
TB	Taylor Buchholz	.50
TG	Tony Gwynn Jr.	.50
TS	Takashi Saito	.50
WI	Josh Willingham	.50

Retrospectrum Signatures

	NM/M

Production 199 unless noted.

BB	Boof Bonser	15.00
BO	Jason Botts	10.00
CA	Matt Capps/134	10.00
CD	Chris Demaria	8.00
CF	Choo Freeman	8.00
CH	Clay Hensley	10.00
CQ	Carlos Quentin	25.00
DU	Dan Uggla	15.00
FC	Fausto Carmona/158	10.00
FL	Francisco Liriano	25.00
HA	Cole Hamels/90	35.00
HK	Howie Kendrick	20.00
HR	Hanley Ramirez	25.00
JA	Jeremy Accardo/32	20.00
JC	Jose Capellan	6.00
JD	Joey Devine	8.00
JH	Jeremy Hermida	10.00
JK	Jason Kubel	10.00
JL	Jon Lester	20.00
JP	Jonathan Papelbon	40.00
JW	Jered Weaver/99	40.00
JZ	Joel Zumaya	20.00
KM	Kendry Morales	15.00
MG	Matt Garza	20.00
MJ	Mike Jacobs	20.00
MM	Matt Murton	20.00
RA	Reggie Abercrombie	8.00
RG	Ryan Garko	15.00
RM	Russell Martin	25.00
RS	Ryan Shealy	15.00
RZ	Ryan Zimmerman	40.00
SD	Stephen Drew	25.00
TB	Taylor Buchholz	10.00
TS	Takashi Saito	30.00
WI	Josh Willingham	15.00

Season Retrospectrum

	NM/M
Common Player:	.50
Red:	2-4X

Production 99 Sets

AH	Aaron Harang	.50
AP	Albert Pujols	4.00
AR	Aramis Ramirez	1.00
AS	Alfonso Soriano	1.50
BA	Bobby Abreu	.50
BH	Bill Hall	.50
BL	Joe Blanton	.50
CA	Miguel Cabrera	1.50
CB	Carlos Beltran	1.00
CC	Chris Carpenter	1.00
CD	Carlos Delgado	1.00
CO	Jose Contreras	1.00
CU	Chase Utley	1.50
CW	Chien-Ming Wang	1.50
CY	Chris Young	1.00
CZ	Carlos Zambrano	1.00
DJ	Derek Jeter	4.00
DO	David Ortiz	1.50
FS	Freddy Sanchez	.50
FT	Frank Thomas	1.00
GM	Greg Maddux	2.50
GS	Grady Sizemore	1.50
HO	Trevor Hoffman	.50
HR	Hanley Ramirez	1.00
JB	Jason Bay	1.00
JC	Joe Crede	1.50
JD	Johnny Damon	1.50
JM	Joe Mauer	1.00
JR	Jose Reyes	1.50
JS	Jeff Suppan	1.50
JT	Jim Thome	1.00
KG	Ken Griffey Jr.	3.00
MC	Michael Cuddyer	.50
MH	Matt Holliday	.50
ML	Mark Loretta	.50
MO	Justin Morneau	1.50
MY	Michael Young	1.00
NG	Nomar Garciaparra	1.50
OR	Magglio Ordonez	1.00
OV	Omar Vizquel	.50

RC	Roger Clemens	3.00
RF	Rafael Furcal	.50
RH	Ryan Howard	3.00
SA	Johan Santana	1.50
SK	Scott Kazmir	.50
TH	Travis Hafner	1.00
TI	Tadahito Iguchi	.50
VG	Vladimir Guerrero	1.50
VW	Vernon Wells	.50
WT	Willy Taveras	.50

Retrospectrum Signatures

	NM/M

Production 25 unless noted.

AH	Aaron Harang	
AR	Aramis Ramirez/3	
AS	Alfonso Soriano	75.00
BA	Bobby Abreu	40.00
BH	Bill Hall	20.00
BL	Joe Blanton	15.00
CA	Miguel Cabrera	50.00
CU	Chase Utley	65.00
CZ	Carlos Zambrano	35.00
DJ	Derek Jeter	180.00
DO	David Ortiz	80.00
FT	Frank Thomas	75.00
GM	Greg Maddux	150.00
HO	Trevor Hoffman	30.00
HR	Hanley Ramirez	25.00
JB	Jason Bay	30.00
JM	Joe Mauer	30.00
KG	Ken Griffey Jr.	120.00
MH	Matt Holliday	35.00
ML	Mark Loretta	15.00
MO	Justin Morneau	30.00
RC	Roger Clemens	120.00
RF	Rafael Furcal	30.00
SA	Johan Santana	50.00
SK	Scott Kazmir	25.00
TH	Travis Hafner	40.00
TI	Tadahito Iguchi	40.00
VG	Vladimir Guerrero	60.00

Rookie Signatures Gold Die-Cut

	NM/M

Production 50 Sets

101	Adam Lind	40.00
103	Andrew Miller	100.00
104	Andy Cannizaro	25.00
105	Angel Sanchez	30.00
106	Brian Stokes	15.00
109	Chris Stewart	15.00
111	David Murphy	20.00
112	Delmon Young	40.00
113	Delwyn Young	25.00
114	Dennis Sarfate	20.00
116	Drew Anderson	15.00
117	Fred Lewis	20.00
118	Glen Perkins	20.00
120	Jeff Baker	20.00
121	Jeff Fiorentino	15.00
122	Jeff Salazar	15.00
125	Jon Knott	25.00
128	Juan Morillo	15.00
131	Justin Hampson	15.00
132	Kevin Hooper	40.00
133	Kevin Kouzmanoff	25.00
134	Michael Bourn	25.00
137	Mitch Maier	25.00
139	Patrick Misch	15.00
140	Philip Humber	30.00
141	Ryan Braun	20.00
143	Ryan Sweeney	20.00
144	Scott Moore	15.00
145	Sean Henn	30.00
146	Shawn Riggans	30.00
148	Troy Tulowitzki	35.00
149	Ubaldo Jimenez	15.00

Shining Star Signatures

	NM/M

Production 15-99

AD	Adam Dunn/99	25.00
AG	Adrian Gonzalez/99	20.00
AR	Alex Rios/99	20.00
BH	Bill Hall/99	20.00
CZ	Carlos Zambrano/99	30.00
DJ	Derek Jeter/54	200.00
DL	Derrek Lee/99	30.00
DO	David Ortiz/99	60.00
GA	Garrett Atkins/99	15.00
HR	Hanley Ramirez/99	25.00
JB	Jason Bay/99	25.00
JM	Joe Mauer/99	25.00
JR	Jose Reyes/99	30.00
JS	Johan Santana/99	50.00
KG	Ken Griffey Jr./99	70.00
KY	Kevin Youkilis/99	25.00
MH	Matt Holliday/99	25.00

MO	Justin Morneau/99	30.00
RI	Juan Rivera/99	15.00
TH	Travis Hafner/72	30.00

Signature Patch

	NM/M

Production 6-25

AG	Adrian Gonzalez/25	40.00
AS	Alfonso Soriano/25	65.00
BA	Bobby Abreu/25	50.00
BJ	B.J. Upton/25	30.00
BS	Ben Sheets/25	35.00
CR	Bobby Crosby/25	25.00
CZ	Carlos Zambrano/25	40.00
DJ	Derek Jeter/25	200.00
DL	Derrek Lee/25	40.00
DO	David Ortiz/25	100.00
DU	Dan Uggla/25	35.00
DW	Dontrelle Willis/25	40.00
GA	Garrett Atkins/25	30.00

Spectrum Swatches

	NM/M

Production 199 Sets
Gold: 1X
Production 75 Sets
Patch: 2-3X
Production 50 Sets

AB	Adrian Beltre	4.00
AG	Adrian Gonzalez	6.00
AH	Aaron Hill	4.00
AK	Austin Kearns	4.00
AP	Albert Pujols	25.00
AR	Aaron Rowand	4.00
AS	Alfonso Soriano	10.00
BA	Bobby Abreu	6.00
BC	Bartolo Colon	4.00
BG	Brian Giles	4.00
BI	Brandon Inge	4.00
BJ	B.J. Upton	6.00
BL	Joe Blanton	4.00
BR	B.J. Ryan	4.00
BS	Ben Sheets	6.00
BW	Billy Wagner	6.00
CA	Jorge Cantu	4.00
CB	Clint Barmes	4.00
CC	Chad Cordero	4.00
CD	Chris Duffy	4.00
CG	Carlos Guillen	4.00
CK	Casey Kotchman	4.00
CO	Coco Crisp	4.00
CR	Bobby Crosby	4.00
CS	C.C. Sabathia	4.00
CU	Chase Utley	15.00
CY	Chris Young	6.00
CZ	Carlos Zambrano	8.00
DA	Johnny Damon	10.00
DC	Daniel Cabrera	6.00
DH	Danny Haren	6.00
DJ	Derek Jeter	25.00
DL	Derrek Lee	8.00
DM	Dallas McPherson	4.00
DO	David Ortiz	15.00
DU	Dan Uggla	6.00
DW	Dontrelle Willis	6.00
ES	Johnny Estrada	6.00
FG	Freddy Garcia	4.00
FL	Francisco Liriano	10.00
FS	Freddy Sanchez	4.00
GA	Garrett Atkins	8.00
GC	Gustavo Chacin	4.00
GR	Curtis Granderson	8.00
GS	Grady Sizemore	10.00
HR	Hanley Ramirez	8.00
HS	Huston Street	6.00
HU	Aubrey Huff	4.00
IS	Ian Snell	8.00
JB	Jeremy Bonderman	10.00
JC	Joe Crede	6.00
JD	J.D. Drew	8.00
JE	Jermaine Dye	6.00
JF	Jeff Francoeur	8.00
JH	J.J. Hardy	6.00
JM	Joe Mauer	10.00
JN	Joe Nathan	6.00
JP	Jake Peavy	8.00
JR	Jose Reyes	15.00
JT	Jim Thome	8.00
JU	Justin Duchscherer	4.00
JW	Jake Westbrook	4.00
KG	Ken Griffey Jr.	25.00
KH	Khalil Greene	6.00
LN	Laynce Nix	4.00
MA	Matt Cain	8.00
MB	Mark Buehrle	4.00
MC	Mike Cameron	4.00
ME	Morgan Ensberg	4.00
MH	Matt Holliday	8.00
MI	Michael Cuddyer	6.00
MM	Melvin Mora	4.00
MO	Justin Morneau	10.00
MT	Miguel Tejada	8.00
NL	Noah Lowry	4.00
NS	Nick Swisher	6.00

OR	Magglio Ordonez	6.00
PA	Jonathan Papelbon	15.00
PE	Jhonny Peralta	6.00
PF	Prince Fielder	10.00
PL	Paul LoDuca	6.00
RA	Aramis Ramirez	8.00
RF	Rafael Furcal	8.00
RH	Rich Harden	8.00
RJ	Reed Johnson	4.00
RO	Brian Roberts	8.00
RQ	Robb Quinlan	4.00
RW	Rickie Weeks	8.00
RZ	Ryan Zimmerman	8.00
SC	Sean Casey	4.00
SK	Scott Kazmir	6.00
TH	Torii Hunter	8.00
TI	Tadahito Iguchi	6.00
TN	Trot Nixon	6.00
VM	Victor Martinez	6.00
WT	Willy Taveras	6.00
YM	Yadier Molina	8.00
ZD	Zachary Duke	8.00
ZG	Zack Greinke	6.00

Super Swatches

NM/M

Production 50 Sets

AD	Adam Dunn	10.00
AJ	Andruw Jones	15.00
AP	Albert Pujols	35.00
AR	Aramis Ramirez	10.00
BA	Bobby Abreu	10.00
BC	Bobby Crosby	10.00
BE	Josh Beckett	10.00
BU	B.J. Upton	15.00
BZ	Barry Zito	10.00
CB	Carlos Beltran	20.00
CC	Carl Crawford	10.00
CD	Carlos Delgado	15.00
CJ	Chipper Jones	15.00
CL	Roger Clemens	25.00
CS	Curt Schilling	15.00
CU	Chase Utley	20.00
DA	Johnny Damon	15.00
DJ	Derek Jeter	35.00
DL	Derek Lee	15.00
DO	David Ortiz	25.00
FT	Frank Thomas	15.00
GS	Gary Sheffield	15.00
HA	Travis Hafner	10.00
HR	Hanley Ramirez	10.00
JB	Jeremy Bonderman	15.00
JD	J.D. Drew	10.00
JR	Jose Reyes	25.00
JS	Johan Santana	15.00
JT	Jim Thome	15.00
JV	Jason Varitek	15.00
JW	Jered Weaver	15.00
KG	Ken Griffey Jr.	30.00
KJ	Kenji Johjima	15.00
LB	Lance Berkman	10.00
MT	Miguel Tejada	10.00
PE	Andy Pettitte	10.00
PF	Prince Fielder	15.00
PK	Paul Konerko	10.00
RB	Rocco Baldelli	10.00
RC	Robinson Cano	20.00
RH	Roy Halladay	10.00
RJ	Randy Johnson	15.00
RS	Richie Sexson	10.00
SR	Scott Rolen	15.00
TH	Todd Helton	10.00
VE	Justin Verlander	15.00
VG	Vladimir Guerrero	15.00
VW	Vernon Wells	10.00

2007 UD Masterpieces

NM/M

Complete Set (90):	50.00
Common player (1-90):	.50
Pack (4):	8.00
Box (18):	120.00

1	Babe Ruth	4.00
2	Babe Ruth	4.00
3	Bobby Thomson	.50
4	Bill Mazeroski	1.00
5	Carlton Fisk	1.00
6	Kirk Gibson	1.00
7	Don Larsen	2.00
8	Lou Gehrig	3.00
9	Roger Maris	3.00
10	Cal Ripken Jr.	4.00
11	Bucky Dent	.50
12	Ryan Howard	3.00
13	Brooks Robinson	2.00
14	David Ortiz	2.00
15	Hideki Matsui	3.00
16	Roger Clemens	4.00
17	Sandy Koufax	5.00
18	Reggie Jackson	2.00
19	Ozzie Smith	3.00
20	Ty Cobb	3.00
21	Walter Johnson	2.00
22	Babe Ruth	4.00
23	Roy Campanella	2.00
24	Jackie Robinson	3.00
25	Carl Yastrzemski	3.00
26	Sandy Koufax	5.00
27	Daisuke Matsuzaka **RC**	8.00
28	Kei Igawa **RC**	1.00
29	Ken Griffey Jr.	3.00
30	Derek Jeter	4.00
31	David Ortiz	2.00
32	Vladimir Guerrero	2.00
33	Chase Utley	2.00
34	Troy Tulowitzki **(RC)**	2.00
35	Joe Mauer	1.00
36	Travis Hafner	1.00
37	Miguel Cabrera	2.00
38	Albert Pujols	4.00
39	Frank Thomas	2.00
40	Mike Piazza	2.00
41	Josh Hamilton	.50
42	Cal Ripken Jr., Tony Gwynn	3.00
43	Ichiro Suzuki	3.00
44	Hideki Matsui	3.00
45	Ken Griffey Jr.	3.00
46	Michael Jordan	4.00
47	John F. Kennedy	2.00
48	Randy Johnson	2.00
49	Albert Pujols	4.00
50	Carlos Beltran	1.50
51	Delmon Young **(RC)**	1.00
52	Johan Santana	2.00
53	Cal Ripken Jr.	4.00
54	Yogi Berra, Jackie Robinson	3.00
55	Cal Ripken Jr.	3.00
56	Hanley Ramirez	2.00
57	Victor Martinez	1.00
58	Cole Hamels	2.00
59	Bobby Doerr	1.00
60	Bruce Sutter	.50
61	Jason Bay	1.00
62	Luis Aparicio	.50
63	Stephen Drew	1.00
64	Jered Weaver	1.00
65	Alex Gordon **RC**	5.00
66	Howie Kendrick	.50
67	Ryan Zimmerman	1.00
68	Akinori Iwamura **RC**	1.00
69	Chien-Ming Wang	2.00
70	David Wright	2.00
71	Ryan Howard	3.00
72	Alex Rodriguez	4.00
73	Justin Morneau	1.50
74	Andrew Miller **RC**	3.00
75	Richard Nixon	1.00
76	Bill Clinton	1.00
77	Phil Hughes **(RC)**	3.00
78	Tom Glavine	1.00
79	Chipper Jones	2.00
80	Craig Biggio	1.00
81	Chris Chambliss	.50
82	Tim Lincecum **RC**	5.00
83	Billy Butler **(RC)**	1.00
84	Andy LaRoche **(RC)**	1.00
85	1969 New York Mets	2.00
86	2004 Boston Red Sox	2.00
87	Roberto Clemente	3.00
88	Chase Utley	2.00
89	Reggie Jackson	2.00
90	Curt Schilling	2.00

Printing Plates

No Pricing
Production one set per color.

Artist's Proof

Production One Set

Black Linen

Black Linen (1-90): 4-6X
Production 99 Sets

Blue Steel

Blue Steel (1-90): 4-8X
Production 50 Sets

Bronze

Production One Set

Celestial Blue

Production One Set

Deep Blue

Black Linen (1-90): 4-6X
Production 75 Sets

Green Linen

Green (1-90): 2-3X

Hades

Hades (1-90): 4-8X
Production 50 Sets

Ionised

Production One Set

Persian Blue Linen

Production One Set

Pinot Red

Pinot Red (1-90): 4-6X
Production 75 Sets

Red Linen

Production One Set

Rusted

Rusted (1-90): 4-8X
Production 50 Sets

Black

Black (1-90): 4-6X
Production 99 Sets

Urban Gray

Production One Set

Captured on Canvas

NM/M

Common Player:	4.00
Bronze:	No Pricing
Forest Green:	No Pricing

Production One Set

AB	Adrian Beltre	4.00
AD	Adam Dunn	8.00
AI	Akinori Iwamura	15.00
AJ	Andruw Jones	6.00
AP	Albert Pujols	25.00
BA	Bobby Abreu	6.00
BC	Bobby Crosby	4.00
BE	Carlos Beltran	8.00
BG	Brian Giles	4.00
BL	Brad Lidge	4.00
BO	Jeremy Bonderman	6.00
BR	Brian Roberts	6.00
BS	Ben Sheets	6.00
CA	Chris Carpenter	8.00
CB	Craig Biggio	6.00
CC	Carl Crawford	6.00
CF	Carlton Fisk	8.00
CJ	Chipper Jones	10.00
CL	Carlos Lee	6.00
CR	Coco Crisp	4.00
CS	C.C. Sabathia	6.00
CU	Chase Utley	15.00
CY	Carl Yastrzemski	10.00
DJ	Derek Jeter	25.00
DL	Derek Lee	8.00
DM	Don Mattingly	20.00
DO	David Ortiz	10.00
DR	J.D. Drew	4.00
DW	Dontrelle Willis	4.00
EB	Erik Bedard	6.00
EC	Eric Chavez	6.00
EG	Eric Gagne	4.00
FH	Felix Hernandez	8.00
FL	Francisco Liriano	6.00
GA	Garrett Atkins	6.00
GL	Tom Glavine	8.00
GR	Khalil Greene	6.00
GS	Grady Sizemore	10.00
HA	Roy Halladay	8.00
HB	Hank Blalock	6.00
HE	Todd Helton	8.00
HR	Hanley Ramirez	10.00
HS	Huston Street	4.00
IR	Ivan Rodriguez	8.00
JA	Jason Bay	6.00
JB	Josh Beckett	8.00
JH	J.J. Hardy	6.00
JK	Jason Kendall	4.00
JM	Joe Mauer	6.00
JN	Joe Nathan	6.00
JP	Jake Peavy	8.00
JR	Jose Reyes	15.00

JS	John Smoltz	8.00
JV	Jason Varitek	8.00
JW	Jered Weaver	6.00
KG	Ken Griffey Jr.	20.00
LB	Lance Berkman	6.00
MA	Daisuke Matsuzaka	50.00
MC	Miguel Cabrera	8.00
MG	Marcus Giles	4.00
MH	Matt Holliday	8.00
MO	Magglio Ordonez	6.00
MR	Mariano Rivera	8.00
MT	Miguel Tejada	6.00
MY	Michael Young	6.00
PA	Jonathan Papelbon	15.00
RA	Manny Ramirez	8.00
RB	Rocco Baldelli	6.00
RC	Roger Clemens	15.00
RH	Rich Harden	4.00
RI	Cal Ripken Jr.	20.00
RJ	Randy Johnson	8.00
RO	Roy Oswalt	8.00
RW	Rickie Weeks	6.00
RZ	Ryan Zimmerman	10.00
SA	Johan Santana	10.00
SC	Curt Schilling	10.00
SH	Gary Sheffield	8.00
SK	Scott Kazmir	6.00
SR	Scott Rolen	8.00
TE	Mark Teixeira	8.00
TG	Tony Gwynn	15.00
TH	Tim Hudson	6.00
TR	Travis Hafner	6.00
VG	Vladimir Guerrero	8.00
VM	Victor Martinez	8.00
WC	Will Clark	8.00

Stroke of Genius

Signatures

NM/M

Common Autograph:	10.00
Parallel:	No Pricing

Production One Set

AG	Adrian Gonzalez	15.00
AL	Andy LaRoche	15.00
BA	Bronson Arroyo	25.00
BB	Billy Butler	30.00
BO	Boof Bonser	10.00
BR	Brooks Robinson	40.00
BS	Ben Sheets	15.00
BU	B.J. Upton	15.00
CD	Chris Duffy	10.00
CF	Chone Figgins	15.00
CH	Cole Hamels	40.00
CQ	Carlos Quentin	15.00
CR	Cal Ripken Jr.	125.00
DH	Danny Haren	15.00
DJ	Derek Jeter	150.00
DO	David Ortiz	50.00
DU	Dan Uggla	15.00
DW	Dontrelle Willis	15.00
EC	Eric Chavez	10.00
GO	Alex Gordon	40.00
GP	Glen Perkins	10.00
HA	Justin Hampson	10.00
HI	Rich Hill	15.00
HK	Howard Kendrick	15.00
HP	Hunter Pence	50.00
HR	Hanley Ramirez	25.00
HS	Huston Street	10.00
HU	Torii Hunter	20.00
IK	Ian Kinsler	15.00
JA	Jason Bay	15.00
JB	Jeff Baker	10.00
JH	Josh Hamilton	20.00
JP	Jonathan Papelbon	35.00
JT	Jim Thome	35.00
JU	Justin Morneau	25.00
JV	Justin Verlander	30.00
JW	Jered Weaver	20.00
JZ	Joel Zumaya	15.00
KE	Austin Kearns	10.00
KG	Ken Griffey Jr.	80.00
KK	Kevin Kouzmanoff	15.00
LE	Cliff Lee	10.00
LI	Adam Lind	10.00
MB	Michael Bourn	15.00
MC	Matt Cain	15.00
MO	Micah Owings	20.00
MS	Mike Schmidt	50.00
PS	Phil Hughes	75.00
RA	Aramis Ramirez	20.00
RC	Roger Clemens	100.00
RH	Rich Harden	10.00
RO	Roy Oswalt	20.00
RZ	Ryan Zimmerman	30.00
SD	Stephen Drew	15.00
SH	Sean Henn	10.00
SO	Jeremy Sowers	10.00
TL	Tim Lincecum	50.00
TR	Travis Hafner	15.00
TT	Troy Tulowitzki	40.00
VM	Victor Martinez	20.00
XN	Xavier Nady	15.00

5x7 Box Topper

		NM/M
Common Payer:		5.00
Inserted 1:Box		
1	Cal Ripken Jr.	15.00
2	Ken Griffey Jr.	10.00
3	Derek Jeter	15.00
4	Sandy Koufax	15.00
5	Babe Ruth	15.00
6	Lou Gehrig	15.00
7	Travis Hafner	5.00
8	Victor Martinez	5.00
9	Jered Weaver	5.00
10	Phil Hughes	8.00
11	Bobby Doerr	5.00
12	Billy Butler	5.00
13	Andy LaRoche	5.00
14	Josh Hamilton	5.00
15	Reggie Jackson	8.00
16	Hanley Ramirez	8.00
17	Don Larsen	8.00
18	Ken Griffey Jr.	10.00
19	Jason Bay	5.00
20	Daisuke Matsuzaka	15.00

5x7 Box Topper Autograph

		NM/M
Inserted 1:Case		
2	Ken Griffey Jr.	85.00
3	Derek Jeter	150.00
7	Travis Hafner	35.00
8	Victor Martinez	25.00
9	Jered Weaver	30.00
10	Phil Hughes	60.00
11	Bobby Doerr	50.00
12	Billy Butler	50.00
13	Andy LaRoche	20.00
14	Josh Hamilton	25.00
15	Reggie Jackson	50.00
16	Hanley Ramirez	35.00
17	Don Larsen	65.00
18	Ken Griffey Jr.	85.00
19	Jason Bay	20.00
20	Daisuke Matsuzaka	275.00

2007 UD Sweet Spot Classic

		NM/M
Common Player:		2.00
Production 575 Sets		
Tin (5):		100.00
1	Phil Niekro	2.00
2	Fred McGriff	3.00
3	Bob Horner	2.00
4	Earl Weaver	2.00
5	Boog Powell	2.00
6	Eddie Murray	4.00
7	Fred Lynn	2.00
8	Dwight Evans	2.00
9	Jim Rice	3.00
10	Carlton Fisk	4.00
11	Luis Tiant	2.00
12	Robin Yount	4.00
13	Bobby Doerr	3.00
14	Ryne Sandberg	5.00
15	Billy Williams	3.00
16	Andre Dawson	3.00
17	Mark Grace	3.00
18	Ron Santo	3.00
19	Shawon Dunston	2.00
20	Harold Baines	2.00
21	Carlton Fisk	4.00
22	Sparky Anderson	2.00
23	George Foster	2.00
24	Dave Parker	2.00
25	Ken Griffey Jr.	2.00
26	Dave Concepcion	2.00
27	Rafael Palmeiro	3.00
28	Al Rosen	2.00
29	Kirk Gibson	2.00
30	Alan Trammell	3.00
31	Jack Morris	2.00
32	Willie Horton	2.00
33	J.R. Richard	2.00
34	Jose Cruz	2.00
36	Willie Wilson	2.00
37	Bo Jackson	4.00
38	Nolan Ryan	8.00
39	Don Baylor	2.00
40	Maury Wills	2.00
41	Tommy John	2.00
42	Ron Cey	2.00
43	Davey Lopes	2.00
44	Tommy Lasorda	2.00
45	Burt Hooton	2.00
46	Reggie Smith	2.00
47	Rollie Fingers	2.00
48	Cecil Cooper	2.00
49	Paul Molitor	4.00
50	Vern Stephens	2.00
51	Tony Oliva	2.00
52	Andres Galarraga	2.00
53	Tim Raines	2.00
54	Dennis Martinez	2.00
55	Lee Mazzilli	2.00
56	Rusty Staub	2.00
57	David Cone	2.00
58	Reggie Jackson	4.00
59	Ron Guidry	2.00
60	Tino Martinez	3.00
61	Don Mattingly	6.00
62	Chris Chambliss	2.00
63	Sparky Lyle	2.00
64	Rich "Goose" Gossage	2.00
65	Dave Righetti	2.00
66	Phil Garner	2.00
67	Bill Madlock	2.00
68	Kent Hrbek	2.00
69	Al Oliver	2.00
70	John Kruk	2.00
71	Greg Luzinski	2.00
72	Dick Allen	2.00
73	Richie Ashburn	3.00
74	Gary Matthews	2.00
76	Mike Schmidt	5.00
77	Waite Hoyt	2.00
78	Bruce Sutter	2.00
79	Roger Maris	6.00
80	Joe Torre	3.00
81	Kevin Mitchell	2.00
82	John Montefusco	2.00
83	Rick Reuschel	2.00
84	Will Clark	3.00
85	Jack Clark	2.00
86	Matt Williams	2.00
87	Steve Garvey	2.00
88	Dave Winfield	3.00
89	Jay Buhner	2.00
90	Edgar Martinez	2.00
91	Carney Lansford	2.00
92	Sal Bando	2.00
93	Dave Stewart	2.00
94	Dennis Eckersley	3.00
95	Jose Canseco	3.00
96	Dennis Eckersley	3.00
97	Roberto Alomar	3.00
98	George Bell	2.00
99	Joe Carter	2.00
100	Frank Howard	2.00
101	Brooks Robinson	4.00
102	Frank Robinson	4.00
103	Jim Palmer	3.00
104	Cal Ripken Jr.	8.00
105	Warren Spahn	4.00
106	Cy Young	4.00
107	Waite Hoyt	2.00
108	Carl Yastrzemski	4.00
109	Johnny Pesky	3.00
110	Wade Boggs	3.00
111	Jackie Robinson	4.00
112	Roy Campanella	4.00
113	Pee Wee Reese	2.00
114	Don Newcombe	2.00
115	Rod Carew	4.00
116	Ernie Banks	4.00
117	Fergie Jenkins	2.00
118	Al Lopez	2.00
119	Luis Aparicio	2.00
120	Toby Harrah	2.00
121	Joe Morgan	3.00
122	Johnny Bench	4.00
123	Tony Perez	3.00
124	Ted Kluszewski	2.00
125	Bob Feller	3.00
126	Bob Lemon	2.00
127	Larry Doby	3.00
128	Lou Boudreau	2.00
129	George Kell	3.00
130	Hal Newhouser	2.00
131	Al Kaline	4.00
132	Ty Cobb	5.00
133	Denny McLain	2.00
134	Buck Leonard	3.00
135	Dean Chance	2.00
136	Don Drysdale	3.00
137	Don Sutton	3.00
138	Eddie Mathews	4.00
139	Paul Molitor	4.00
140	Kirby Puckett	5.00
141	Rod Carew	3.00
142	Harmon Killebrew	4.00
143	Monte Irvin	3.00
144	Mel Ott	3.00
145	Christy Mathewson	4.00
146	Hoyt Wilhelm	2.00
147	Tom Seaver	4.00
148	Joe McCarthy	2.00
149	Joe DiMaggio	5.00
150	Lou Gehrig	6.00
151	Babe Ruth	8.00
152	Casey Stengel	3.00
153	Phil Rizzuto	4.00
154	Thurman Munson	5.00
155	Johnny Mize	2.00
156	Yogi Berra	4.00
157	Roger Maris	5.00
158	Don Larsen	3.00
159	Bill "Moose" Skowron	2.00
160	Lou Piniella	3.00
161	Joe Pepitone	2.00
162	Ray Dandridge	2.00
163	Rollie Fingers	2.00
165	Reggie Jackson	4.00
166	Mickey Cochrane	3.00
167	Jimmie Foxx	4.00
168	Lefty Grove	3.00
169	Gus Zernial	2.00
170	Jim Bunning	2.00
171	Steve Carlton	3.00
172	Robin Roberts	3.00
173	Ralph Kiner	3.00
174	Willie Stargell	4.00
175	Roberto Clemente	6.00
176	Bill Mazeroski	2.00
177	Honus Wagner	5.00
178	Pie Traynor	3.00
179	Elroy Face	2.00
180	Dick Groat	2.00
181	Tony Gwynn	4.00
182	Willie McCovey	3.00
183	Gaylord Perry	2.00
184	Juan Marichal	3.00
185	Orlando Cepeda	3.00
186	Satchel Paige	4.00
187	George Sisler	3.00
188	Rogers Hornsby	4.00
189	Stan Musial	4.00
190	Dizzy Dean	3.00
191	Bob Gibson	4.00
192	Red Schoendienst	2.00
193	Lou Brock	3.00
194	Enos Slaughter	2.00
195	Nolan Ryan	8.00
196	Mickey Vernon	2.00
197	Walter Johnson	4.00
198	Rick Ferrell	2.00
199	Roy Sievers	2.00
200	Judy Johnson	2.00

Classic Memorabilia

		NM/M
Common Player:		5.00
Patch:		2-4X
Production 55 Sets		
AD	Andre Dawson	8.00
AK	Al Kaline	10.00
AO	Al Oliver	8.00
BE	Johnny Bench	15.00
BJ	Bo Jackson	15.00
BM	Bill Madlock	5.00
BO	Wade Boggs	8.00
BR	Babe Ruth/SP	200.00
BS	Bruce Sutter	5.00
CL	Roberto Clemente	40.00
CM	Christy Mathewson/SP	125.00
CR	Cal Ripken Jr.	20.00
CS	Casey Stengel	10.00
CY	Carl Yastrzemski	10.00
DD	Dizzy Dean	30.00
DE	Dennis Eckersley	5.00
DM	Don Mattingly	15.00
DP	Dave Parker	5.00
DR	Don Drysdale	10.00
DS	Don Sutton	5.00
DW	Dave Winfield	10.00
ED	Eddie Murray	8.00
EM	Eddie Mathews	15.00
EV	Dwight Evans	5.00
EW	Early Wynn	8.00
FG	Fred McGriff	5.00
FR	Frank Robinson	10.00
GF	George Foster	5.00
GG	Rich "Goose" Gossage	8.00
GI	Kirk Gibson	5.00
GP	Gaylord Perry	5.00
GW	Tony Gwynn	10.00
HB	Harold Baines/SP	
HK	Harmon Killebrew/SP	10.00
JB	Jim Bunning	8.00
JD	Joe DiMaggio	60.00
JI	Jim Rice	8.00
JM	Jack Morris	5.00
JP	Jim Palmer	8.00
JU	Juan Marichal	5.00
KG	Ken Griffey Jr.	5.00
KH	Kent Hrbek	5.00
KP	Kirby Puckett	15.00
LA	Luis Aparicio	5.00
LB	Lou Brock	8.00
LG	Lou Gehrig	150.00
MA	Don Mattingly	15.00
ME	Eddie Murray	8.00
MG	Mark Grace	8.00
MO	Mel Ott	20.00
MP	Paul Molitor	10.00
MR	Edgar Martinez	5.00
MS	Mike Schmidt	15.00
MW	Maury Wills	5.00
NR	Nolan Ryan	20.00
PA	Dave Parker	5.00
PE	Tony Perez	5.00
PM	Paul Molitor	10.00
PN	Phil Niekro	5.00
PR	Pee Wee Reese/SP	25.00
RF	Rollie Fingers	5.00
RG	Ron Guidry	10.00
RH	Rogers Hornsby	25.00
RK	Ralph Kiner	10.00
RM	Roger Maris	30.00
RO	Roy Campanella	15.00
RS	Ron Santo	10.00
RY	Nolan Ryan	20.00
SC	Red Schoendienst	8.00
SG	Steve Garvey	5.00
ST	Steve Carlton	8.00
SU	Bruce Sutter	5.00
TG	Tony Gwynn	10.00
TM	Thurman Munson	20.00
TO	Tony Oliva	8.00
TP	Tony Perez	5.00
TR	Tim Raines	5.00
WB	Wade Boggs	8.00
WC	Will Clark	5.00
WM	Willie McCovey	8.00
WS	Willie Stargell	8.00
YO	Robin Yount	10.00
CF1	Carlton Fisk	8.00
CF2	Carlton Fisk	8.00
FR1	Frank Robinson	10.00
MI1	Johnny Mize	10.00
MI2	Johnny Mize	10.00
RC1	Rod Carew	8.00
RC2	Rod Carew	8.00
RJ1	Reggie Jackson	10.00
RJ2	Reggie Jackson	10.00
RJ3	Reggie Jackson	10.00

Dual Sig Red Stitch-Blue Ink

		NM/M
Production 50 Sets		
Black Stitch Red Ink:		No Pricing
Production One Set		
Gold Stitch Black Ink:		No Pricing
Production 15 Sets		
AG	Luis Aparicio, Ozzie Guillen	30.00
BF	Carlton Fisk, Johnny Bench	75.00
BG	Harold Baines, Ozzie Guillen	50.00
BR	Robin Roberts, Jim Bunning	60.00
CG	Tony Gwynn, Rod Carew	90.00
CO	Tony Oliva, Rod Carew	40.00
FE	Dennis Eckersley, Rollie Fingers	50.00
FG	Elroy Face, Dick Groat	50.00
FM	Mike Schmidt, Frank Robinson	80.00
FR	Carlton Fisk, Jim Rice	50.00
GR	Bob Gibson, J.R. Richard	50.00
GS	Steve Garvey, Reggie Smith	30.00
GW	Tony Gwynn, Dave Winfield	80.00
HK	Al Kaline, Willie Horton	80.00
JS	Reggie Smith, Reggie Jackson	50.00
KM	Ralph Kiner, Bill Mazeroski	75.00
LT	Tim Raines, Lou Brock	40.00
MC	Jack Clark, Willie McCovey	75.00
MG	Juan Marichal, Bob Gibson	60.00
MK	Stan Musial, Al Kaline	125.00
MM	Don Mattingly, Tino Martinez	80.00
MR	Edgar Martinez, Harold Reynolds	50.00
OH	Tony Oliva, Kent Hrbek	40.00
RR	Nolan Ryan, J.R. Richard	150.00
RS	Cal Ripken Jr., Mike Schmidt	180.00
SB	Ron Santo, Ernie Banks	125.00
SC	Mike Schmidt, Steve Carlton	80.00

SD Ryne Sandberg, Shawon Dunston 80.00
SF Rollie Fingers, Bruce Sutter 60.00
SS Ron Santo, Ryne Sandberg 125.00
SV Mickey Vernon, Roy Sievers 30.00
YP Carl Yastrzemski, Johnny Pesky 100.00

Immortal Signatures
Common Player

Legendary Lettermen
NM/M
Represents total cards produced.
LL1 Babe Ruth/100 150.00
LL2 Ty Cobb/100 75.00
LL3 Christy Mathewson/90 50.00
LL4 Jackie Robinson/80 60.00
LL5 Roy Campanella/100 50.00
LL6 Lou Gehrig/90 150.00
LL7 Mel Ott/75 25.00
LL8 Jimmie Foxx/100 50.00
LL9 Satchel Paige/125 40.00
LL10 Don Drysdale/200 30.00
LL11 Rogers Hornsby/175 60.00
LL12 Honus Wagner/150 50.00
LL13 Babe Ruth/105 150.00
LL14 Dizzy Dean/100 50.00
LL15 Ty Cobb/60 75.00
LL16 Walter Johnson/105 50.00
LL17 Walter Johnson/80 50.00
LL18 Cal Ripken Jr./200 100.00
LL19 Sandy Koufax/150 250.00
LL20 Thurman Munson/150 40.00
LL21 Thurman Munson/70 40.00
LL22 Cal Ripken Jr./175 100.00
LL23 Tony Gwynn/125 50.00
LL24 Nolan Ryan/80 50.00
LL25 Nolan Ryan/165 50.00
LL26 Jackie Robinson/70 60.00
LL27 Carlton Fisk/80 40.00
LL28 Carl Yastrzemski/165 60.00
LL29 Johnny Bench/125 50.00
LL30 Ryne Sandberg/200 100.00
LL31 Don Mattingly/135 75.00
LL32 Ernie Banks/165 40.00
LL33 Bill Mazeroski/135 50.00
LL34 Ernie Banks/125 40.00
LL35 Bob Gibson/150 50.00
LL36 Mike Schmidt/175 60.00
LL37 Al Kaline/150 40.00
LL38 Reggie Jackson/175 50.00
LL39 Stan Musial/150 50.00
LL40 Bo Jackson/175 50.00
LL41 Bo Jackson/105 50.00
LL42 Stan Musial/150 50.00

Ripken Immortal Membership
Production One Set

Signatures Black Ink
NM/M
Common Signature: 15.00
Production 175 unless noted.
AG Andres Galarraga 20.00
AK Al Kaline 30.00
AO Al Oliver 15.00
BJ Bo Jackson 50.00
BM Bill Mazeroski 40.00
BO Wade Boggs/75 40.00
BS Bruce Sutter/75 20.00
CF Carlton Fisk/75 35.00
DA Dick Allen 20.00
DL Don Larsen 30.00
DM Don Mattingly/75 60.00
EC Dennis Eckersley 20.00
EM Edgar Martinez 30.00
FM Fred McGriff 25.00
GP Gaylord Perry 20.00
HB Harold Baines 15.00
JB Johnny Bench/75 60.00
JK John Kruk 20.00
MO Jack Morris 20.00
MS Mike Schmidt/75 50.00
NR Nolan Ryan/75 80.00
OG Ozzie Guillen 20.00
RA Roberto Alomar 25.00
RI Jim Rice 20.00
RJ Reggie Jackson/75 60.00
RS Ryne Sandberg/75 60.00
SA Ron Santo 30.00
SM Reggie Smith 20.00

TG Tony Gwynn/75 50.00
TM Tino Martinez 35.00
TP Tony Perez 25.00
TR Tim Raines 20.00
WB Wade Boggs/75 40.00
WD Willie Davis/75 20.00
WM Willie McCovey/75 50.00
YB Yogi Berra/75 80.00
BR Brooks Robinson 30.00
BW Billy Williams 30.00
CL Carney Lansford 20.00
CO Dave Concepcion 25.00
CY Carl Yastrzemski 50.00
DG Dick Groat 30.00
DS Don Sutton 20.00
DW Dave Winfield 25.00
EB Ernie Banks 60.00
EF Elroy Face 20.00
EV Dwight Evans 20.00
FL Fred Lynn 15.00
FR Frank Robinson/35 50.00
GI Bob Gibson 40.00
JI Jim Bunning 20.00
JP Johnny Pesky 30.00
JR Jim Rice 20.00
KG Ken Griffey Sr. 15.00
KO Sandy Koufax 350.00
LA Luis Aparicio 25.00
LB Lou Brock/75 40.00
MA Juan Marichal 25.00
MG Mark Grace 30.00
MU Stan Musial/75 80.00
MV Mickey Vernon 20.00
OS Ozzie Smith/75 60.00
PN Phil Niekro 20.00
RC Rod Carew 30.00
RF Rollie Fingers 20.00
RK Ralph Kiner/75 40.00
RR Robin Roberts 40.00
RY Robin Yount 40.00
SC Steve Carlton 30.00
SD Shawon Dunston 25.00
SG Steve Garvey 25.00
SK Bill "Moose" Skowron 15.00
TH Toby Harrah 15.00
TO Tony Oliva 20.00
WH Willie Horton 20.00

Signatures Blue Ink
NM/M
Common Signature: 20.00
Production 125 unless noted.
AG Andres Galarraga 20.00
AK Al Kaline 30.00
AO Al Oliver 20.00
BJ Bo Jackson 50.00
BM Bill Mazeroski 40.00
BO Wade Boggs/35 50.00
BS Bruce Sutter/35 25.00
CF Carlton Fisk/35 40.00
DA Dick Allen 20.00
DL Don Larsen 30.00
DM Don Mattingly/35 60.00
EC Dennis Eckersley 20.00
EM Edgar Martinez 20.00
FM Fred McGriff 30.00
GP Gaylord Perry 20.00
HB Harold Baines 20.00
JB Johnny Bench/35 60.00
JK John Kruk 20.00
MO Jack Morris 20.00
MS Mike Schmidt/35 75.00
NR Nolan Ryan/35 120.00
OG Ozzie Guillen 20.00
RA Roberto Alomar 25.00
RI Jim Rice 20.00
RJ Reggie Jackson/35 60.00
RS Ryne Sandberg/35 60.00
SA Ron Santo 20.00
SM Reggie Smith 20.00
TG Tony Gwynn/35 50.00
TM Tino Martinez 40.00
TP Tony Perez 25.00
TR Tim Raines 20.00
WB Wade Boggs/35 50.00
WD Willie Davis/35 20.00
WM Willie McCovey/35 50.00
YB Yogi Berra/35 80.00
BR Brooks Robinson 30.00
BW Billy Williams 30.00
CL Carney Lansford 15.00
CO Dave Concepcion 20.00
CY Carl Yastrzemski 60.00
DG Dick Groat 25.00
DS Don Sutton 20.00
DW Dave Winfield 30.00
EB Ernie Banks 60.00
EF Elroy Face 20.00
EV Dwight Evans 20.00
FL Fred Lynn 15.00
FR Frank Robinson/35 40.00
GI Bob Gibson 20.00
JI Jim Bunning 20.00
JP Johnny Pesky 25.00

JR Jim Rice 20.00
KG Ken Griffey Sr. 20.00
KO Sandy Koufax 300.00
LA Luis Aparicio 20.00
LB Lou Brock/35 40.00
MA Juan Marichal 30.00
MG Mark Grace 25.00
MU Stan Musial/35 80.00
MV Mickey Vernon 20.00
OS Ozzie Smith/35 60.00
PN Phil Niekro 15.00
RC Rod Carew 30.00
RF Rollie Fingers 20.00
RK Ralph Kiner/35 40.00
RR Robin Roberts 40.00
RY Robin Yount 40.00
SC Steve Carlton 25.00
SD Shawon Dunston 25.00
SG Steve Garvey 20.00
SK Bill "Moose" Skowron 20.00
TH Toby Harrah 15.00
TO Tony Oliva 20.00
WH Willie Horton 20.00

Signatures Sepia Black Ink
NM/M
Production 16-199
Red Ink: No Pricing
Production 15 Sets
CF Carlton Fisk/124 30.00
CY Carl Yastrzemski/124 50.00
DM Don Mattingly/124 50.00
DS Duke Snider/30 75.00
JM Juan Marichal/124 30.00
JR Jim Rice/85 30.00
MU Dale Murphy/183 25.00
NR Nolan Ryan/123 80.00
OS Ozzie Smith/183 50.00
RS Ryne Sandberg/199 50.00
TG Tony Gwynn/199 50.00
TS Tom Seaver/16

Signatures Barrel Black Ink
NM/M
Production 50 or 15
Barrel Blue Ink: 1X
Production 25 or 75
No pricing for production 15 or 25.
AG Andres Galarraga/50 25.00
AK Al Kaline/50 50.00
AO Al Oliver/50 30.00
BJ Bo Jackson/50 50.00
BM Bill Mazeroski/50 50.00
DL Don Larsen/50 30.00
EC Dennis Eckersley/50 30.00
EM Edgar Martinez/50 40.00
FM Fred McGriff/50 50.00
GP Gaylord Perry/50 30.00
HB Harold Baines/50 25.00
JK John Kruk/50 30.00
MO Jack Morris/50 30.00
OG Ozzie Guillen/50 25.00
RA Roberto Alomar/50 40.00
RI Jim Rice/50 30.00
SM Reggie Smith/50 25.00
TM Tino Martinez/50 30.00
TP Tony Perez/50 30.00
TR Tim Raines/50 30.00
EV Dwight Evans/50 30.00
JI Jim Bunning/50 25.00
KG Ken Griffey Sr./50 20.00
LA Luis Aparicio/50 20.00
MA Juan Marichal/50 20.00
WH Willie Horton/50 30.00

Signatures Sepia Blue Ink
NM/M
Production 15-199
AK Al Kaline/199 30.00
BW Billy Williams/199 30.00
CF Carlton Fisk/78 30.00
CY Carl Yastrzemski/90 60.00
DM Don Mattingly/9 60.00
DS Duke Snider/199 40.00
EM Edgar Martinez/74 40.00
JM Juan Marichal/84 25.00
JR Jim Rice/75 25.00
LM Lee Mazzilli/199 15.00
MU Dale Murphy/9 20.00
NR Nolan Ryan/80 80.00
OS Ozzie Smith/75 60.00
RC Rocky Colavito/199 50.00
TG Tony Gwynn/199 50.00
WC Will Clark/199 25.00
WF Whitey Ford/15

Signatures Black Barrel Silver Ink
NM/M
Production 3-47
Gold Ink: No Pricing
Production One Set
EC Dennis Eckersley/43 30.00
FM Fred McGriff/27 40.00
GP Gaylord Perry/35 25.00
JK John Kruk/29 30.00
MO Jack Morris/47 25.00
TM Tino Martinez/24 50.00
TP Tony Perez/24 40.00
TR Tim Raines/30 40.00
EV Dwight Evans/24 35.00
KG Ken Griffey Sr./30 35.00
WH Willie Horton/23 35.00

Signatures Black Leather Silver Ink
NM/M
Production 3-47
Green Ink: No Pricing
Production One Set
BS Bruce Sutter/42 30.00
CF Carlton Fisk/27 40.00
EC Dennis Eckersley/43 30.00
FM Fred McGriff/27 40.00
GP Gaylord Perry/36 25.00
JK John Kruk/29 30.00
MO Jack Morris/47 25.00
NR Nolan Ryan/30 140.00
RJ Reggie Jackson/44 60.00
TM Tino Martinez/24 50.00
TP Tony Perez/24 40.00
TR Tim Raines/30 40.00
WM Willie McCovey/44 60.00
BW Billy Williams/26 25.00
DG Dick Groat/24 50.00
DW Dave Winfield/31 30.00
EF Elroy Face/26 30.00
EV Dwight Evans/24 35.00
GI Bob Gibson/45 50.00
KG Ken Griffey Sr./24 50.00
KO Sandy Koufax/32 350.00
MA Juan Marichal/35 35.00
PN Phil Niekro/35 35.00
RC Rod Carew/29 30.00
RF Rollie Fingers/34 20.00
RR Robin Roberts/36 40.00
SC Steve Carlton/32 30.00
SD Shawon Dunston/12
SG Steve Garvey/6
SK "Moose" Skowron/14
TH Toby Harrah/11
TO Tony Oliva/6
WH Willie Horton/23 35.00

Signatures Gold Stitch Black Ink
NM/M
Production 25 or 99
Blue Ink: 1-1.5X
Production 15 or 50
AG Andres Galarraga/99 20.00
AK Al Kaline/99 40.00
AO Al Oliver/99 15.00
BJ Bo Jackson/99 60.00
BM Bill Mazeroski/99 40.00
BO Wade Boggs/25 40.00
CF Carlton Fisk/25 40.00
DA Dick Allen/99 20.00
DL Don Larsen/99 30.00
DM Don Mattingly/25 75.00
EC Dennis Eckersley/99 30.00
EM Edgar Martinez/99 40.00
FM Fred McGriff/99 20.00
GP Gaylord Perry/99 20.00
HB Harold Baines/99 20.00
JK John Kruk/99 25.00
MO Jack Morris/25 15.00
MS Mike Schmidt/25 80.00
OG Ozzie Guillen/99 20.00
RA Roberto Alomar/99 30.00
RI Jim Rice/99 20.00
RS Ryne Sandberg/99 80.00
SA Ron Santo/99 40.00
SM Reggie Smith/99 20.00
TG Tony Gwynn/99 75.00
TM Tino Martinez/99 30.00
TP Tony Perez/99 20.00
TR Tim Raines/99 15.00
WB Wade Boggs/25 40.00
WD Willie Davis/25 30.00
WM Willie McCovey/25 60.00
YB Yogi Berra/25 80.00
BR Brooks Robinson/99 35.00
BW Billy Williams/99 25.00
CL Carney Lansford/99 20.00
CO Dave Concepcion/99 25.00
CY Carl Yastrzemski/99 65.00

DG	Dick Groat/99	30.00
DS	Don Sutton/99	20.00
DW	Dave Winfield/99	30.00
EB	Ernie Banks/99	65.00
EF	Elroy Face/99	25.00
EV	Dwight Evans/99	20.00
FL	Fred Lynn/99	20.00
FR	Frank Robinson/25	40.00
GI	Bob Gibson/99	40.00
JI	Jim Bunning/99	25.00
JP	Johnny Pesky/99	30.00
JR	Jim Rice/99	25.00
KG	Ken Griffey Sr./99	20.00
KO	Sandy Koufax/99	300.00
LA	Luis Aparicio/99	20.00
LB	Lou Brock/25	40.00
MA	Juan Marichal/99	30.00
MG	Mark Grace/99	30.00
MU	Stan Musial/99	100.00
MV	Mickey Vernon/99	25.00
OS	Ozzie Smith/25	75.00
PN	Phil Niekro/99	20.00
RC	Rod Carew/99	35.00
RF	Rollie Fingers/99	20.00
RK	Ralph Kiner/25	60.00
RR	Robin Roberts/99	30.00
RY	Robin Yount/99	40.00
SC	Steve Carlton/99	30.00
SD	Shawon Dunston/99	20.00
SG	Steve Garvey/99	20.00
SK	"Moose" Skowron/99	20.00
TH	Toby Harrah/99	15.00
TO	Tony Oliva/99	20.00
WH	Willie Horton/99	20.00

Signatures Leather Blue Ink

NM/M

Production 75 unless noted.

Gold Ink: 1-1.5X

Production 15 or 50

AG	Andres Galarraga	25.00
AK	Al Kaline	50.00
AO	Al Oliver	25.00
BJ	Bo Jackson	75.00
BM	Bill Mazeroski	50.00
BO	Wade Boggs/25	40.00
CF	Carlton Fisk/25	40.00
DA	Dick Allen	20.00
DL	Don Larsen	40.00
DM	Don Mattingly/25	75.00
EC	Dennis Eckersley	30.00
EM	Edgar Martinez	50.00
FM	Fred McGriff	40.00
GP	Gaylord Perry	20.00
HB	Harold Baines	20.00
JK	John Kruk	20.00
MO	Jack Morris	20.00
MS	Mike Schmidt/25	80.00
OG	Ozzie Guillen	20.00
RA	Roberto Alomar	50.00
RI	Jim Rice	25.00
RS	Ryne Sandberg/25	80.00
SA	Ron Santo	50.00
SM	Reggie Smith	20.00
TG	Tony Gwynn/25	75.00
TM	Tino Martinez	30.00
TP	Tony Perez	30.00
TR	Tim Raines	20.00
WB	Wade Boggs/25	40.00
WD	Willie Davis/25	30.00
WM	Willie McCovey/25	60.00
YB	Yogi Berra/25	80.00
BR	Brooks Robinson/25	60.00
CL	Carney Lansford/25	20.00
CO	Dave Concepcion/25	20.00
CY	Carl Yastrzemski/25	80.00
DG	Dick Groat/25	25.00
DS	Don Sutton/25	20.00
DW	Dave Winfield/25	40.00
EB	Ernie Banks/25	80.00
EF	Elroy Face/25	25.00
EV	Dwight Evans	25.00
FL	Fred Lynn/25	20.00
FR	Frank Robinson/25	50.00
JI	Jim Bunning	25.00
JP	Johnny Pesky/25	35.00
JR	Jim Rice/25	25.00
KG	Ken Griffey Sr.	15.00
KO	Sandy Koufax/25	350.00
LA	Luis Aparicio	30.00
LB	Lou Brock/25	30.00
MA	Juan Marichal	35.00
MG	Mark Grace/25	30.00
MU	Stan Musial/25	100.00
MV	Mickey Vernon/25	30.00
OS	Ozzie Smith/25	80.00
PN	Phil Niekro	25.00
RC	Rod Carew/25	50.00
RF	Rollie Fingers/25	30.00
RK	Ralph Kiner/25	50.00
RR	Robin Roberts/25	40.00
RY	Robin Yount/25	60.00
SC	Steve Carlton/25	25.00
SD	Shawon Dunston/25	25.00
SG	Steve Garvey/25	30.00
SK	"Moose" Skowron/25	30.00
TH	Toby Harrah/25	20.00
TO	Tony Oliva/25	30.00
WH	Willie Horton/25	30.00

Signatures Silver Stitch Blue Ink

NM/M

Production 3-47

Black Ink: No Pricing

Production 15 or 25

BS	Bruce Sutter/42	25.00
CF	Carlton Fisk/27	40.00
EC	Dennis Eckersley/43	30.00
FM	Fred McGriff/27	40.00
GP	Gaylord Perry/36	25.00
JK	John Kruk/29	30.00
MO	Jack Morris/47	25.00
NR	Nolan Ryan/30	140.00
RJ	Reggie Jackson/44	60.00
TM	Tino Martinez/24	50.00
TP	Tony Perez/24	40.00
TR	Tim Raines/30	40.00
WB	Wade Boggs/46	50.00
WM	Willie McCovey/44	60.00
BW	Billy Williams/26	25.00
DG	Dick Groat/24	50.00
DW	Dave Winfield/31	40.00
EF	Elroy Face/26	30.00
EV	Dwight Evans/24	35.00
GI	Bob Gibson/45	50.00
KG	Ken Griffey Sr./30	25.00
KO	Sandy Koufax/32	350.00
MA	Juan Marichal/27	40.00
PN	Phil Niekro/35	35.00
RC	Rod Carew/29	40.00
RF	Rollie Fingers/34	20.00
RR	Robin Roberts/36	40.00
SC	Steve Carlton/32	30.00

2007 UD SP Rookie Edition

NM/M

Complete Set (284):	
Common Player (1-100):	.25
Common RC (101-142):	.50
Common SP (143-234):	1.00
Inserted 1:2	
Common (235-284):	.25
Pack (8):	5.00
Box (14):	65.00

1	Chipper Jones	.75
2	Andruw Jones	.50
3	Jeff Francoeur	.75
4	Stephen Drew	.25
5	Randy Johnson	.75
6	Brandon Webb	.50
7	Alfonso Soriano	.75
8	Derrek Lee	.50
9	Aramis Ramirez	.50
10	Carlos Zambrano	.40
11	Ken Griffey Jr.	1.50
12	Adam Dunn	.50
13	Bronson Arroyo	.25
14	Todd Helton	.50
15	Jeff Francis	.25
16	Matt Holliday	.50
17	Hanley Ramirez	.75
18	Dontrelle Willis	.25
19	Miguel Cabrera	.75
20	Lance Berkman	.40
21	Roy Oswalt	.50
22	Carlos Lee	.50
23	Nomar Garciaparra	.75
24	Jason Schmidt	.25
25	Juan Pierre	.40
26	Rafael Furcal	.40
27	Rickie Weeks	.25
28	Prince Fielder	.75
29	Ben Sheets	.40
30	David Wright	1.00
31	Jose Reyes	.75
32	Pedro Martinez	.75
33	Carlos Beltran	.50
34	Cole Hamels	.50
35	Jimmy Rollins	.50
36	Ryan Howard	1.00
37	Jason Bay	.40
38	Freddy Sanchez	.25
39	Zachary Duke	.25
40	Jake Peavy	.40
41	Greg Maddux	1.50
42	Trevor Hoffman	.25
43	Matt Cain	.25
44	Barry Zito	.25
45	Omar Vizquel	.25
46	Albert Pujols	2.00
47	Chris Carpenter	.50
48	Jim Edmonds	.40
49	Scott Rolen	.50
50	Ryan Zimmerman	.50
51	Felipe Lopez	.25
52	Austin Kearns	.25
53	Miguel Tejada	.50
54	Erik Bedard	.40
55	Chris Ray	.25
56	David Ortiz	.75
57	Curt Schilling	.50
58	Manny Ramirez	.50
59	Jonathan Papelbon	.50
60	Jim Thome	.50
61	Paul Konerko	.40
62	Bobby Jenks	.25
63	Grady Sizemore	.75
64	Victor Martinez	.40
65	C.C. Sabathia	.40
66	Ivan Rodriguez	.50
67	Justin Verlander	.50
68	Joel Zumaya	.25
69	Jeremy Bonderman	.40
70	Gil Meche	.25
71	Mike Sweeney	.25
72	Mark Teahen	.25
73	Vladimir Guerrero	.75
74	Howie Kendrick	.25
75	Francisco Rodriguez	.25
76	Johan Santana	.75
77	Justin Morneau	.50
78	Joe Mauer	.50
79	Joe Nathan	.25
80	Alex Rodriguez	2.00
81	Derek Jeter	2.00
82	Johnny Damon	.75
83	Mariano Rivera	.50
84	Rich Harden	.25
85	Mike Piazza	.75
86	Nick Swisher	.40
87	Ichiro Suzuki	1.50
88	Felix Hernandez	.50
89	Kenji Johjima	.40
90	Richie Sexson	.40
91	Carl Crawford	.40
92	Scott Kazmir	.40
93	B.J. Upton	.40
94	Michael Young	.40
95	Mark Teixeira	.50
96	Eric Gagne	.25
97	Hank Blalock	.25
98	Vernon Wells	.40
99	Roy Halladay	.40
100	Frank Thomas	.75
101	Joaquin Arias (RC)	.50
102	Jeff Baker (RC)	.50
103	Brian Barden RC	.50
104	Michael Bourn (RC)	.50
105	Kevin Slowey (RC)	1.50
106	Chase Wright RC	1.00
107	Kory Casto (RC)	.50
108	Matt Chico (RC)	.50
109	Matt DeSalvo (RC)	1.00
110	Homer Bailey (RC)	1.00
111	Ryan Braun (RC)	3.00
112	Felix Pie (RC)	1.00
113	Jesus Flores RC	.50
114	Ryan Sweeney (RC)	.50
115	Ryan Braun RC	.50
116	Alex Gordon RC	1.50
117	Josh Hamilton (RC)	1.50
118	Sean Henn (RC)	.50
119	Kei Igawa RC	1.00
120	Akinori Iwamura RC	1.50
121	Andy LaRoche (RC)	1.50
122	Kevin Kouzmanoff (RC)	1.50
123	Matt Lindstrom (RC)	.50
124	Tim Lincecum (RC)	4.00
125	Daisuke Matsuzaka RC	4.00
126	Gustavo Molina RC	.50
127	Miguel Montero (RC)	.50
128	Brandon Morrow RC	1.50
129	Hideki Okajima RC	1.50
130	Adam Lind (RC)	.50
131	Mike Rabelo RC	.50
132	Micah Owings (RC)	.50
133	Brandon Wood (RC)	.50
134	Alexi Casilla RC	1.00
135	Joe Smith RC	.50
136	Hunter Pence (RC)	3.00
137	Glen Perkins (RC)	.50
138	Chris Stewart RC	.50
139	Troy Tulowitzki (RC)	2.00
140	Billy Butler (RC)	1.00
141	Delmon Young (RC)	1.00
142	Phil Hughes (RC)	2.00
143	Joaquin Arias	1.00
144	Jeff Baker	1.00
145	Brian Barden	1.00
146	Michael Bourn	1.00
147	Kevin Slowey	2.00
148	Chase Wright	2.00
149	Kory Casto	1.00
150	Matt Chico	1.00
151	Shawn Riggans	1.00
152	Juan Salas	1.00
153	Ryan Braun	5.00
154	Felix Pie	1.00
155	Jesus Flores	1.00
156	Ryan Sweeney	1.00
157	Ryan Braun	1.00
158	Alex Gordon	4.00
159	Josh Hamilton	2.00
160	Sean Henn	1.00
161	Kei Igawa	2.00
162	Akinori Iwamura	2.00
163	Andy LaRoche	1.00
164	Kevin Kouzmanoff	2.00
165	Matt Lindstrom	1.00
166	Tim Lincecum	6.00
167	Daisuke Matsuzaka	6.00
168	Gustavo Molina	1.00
169	Miguel Montero	1.00
170	Brandon Morrow	2.00
171	Hideki Okajima	3.00
172	Adam Lind	1.00
173	Mike Rabelo	1.00
174	Micah Owings	1.00
175	Brandon Wood	1.00
176	Alexi Casilla	2.00
177	Joe Smith	1.00
178	Hunter Pence	5.00
179	Glen Perkins	1.00
180	Chris Stewart	1.00
181	Troy Tulowitzki	3.00
182	Billy Butler	2.00
183	Delmon Young	2.00
184	Phil Hughes	3.00
185	Joaquin Arias	1.00
186	Jeff Baker	1.00
187	Mark Reynolds	1.50
188	Joseph Bisenius	1.00
189	Michael Bourn	1.00
190	Zack Segovia	1.00
191	Kevin Slowey	2.00
192	Chase Wright	1.00
193	Rocky Cherry	1.00
194	Danny Putnam	1.50
195	Kory Casto	1.00
196	Matt Chico	1.00
197	John Danks	1.00
198	Homer Bailey	1.50
199	Ryan Braun	5.00
200	Felix Pie	1.00
201	Jesus Flores	1.00
202	Andy Gonzalez	1.00
203	Ryan Sweeney	1.00
204	Jarrod Saltalamacchia	1.50
205	Alex Gordon	4.00
206	Josh Hamilton	2.00
207	Sean Henn	1.00
208	Kei Igawa	2.00
209	Akinori Iwamura	2.00
210	Andy LaRoche	1.00
211	Rick Vanden Hurk	1.00
212	Kevin Kouzmanoff	2.00
213	Matt Lindstrom	1.00
214	Tim Lincecum	6.00
215	Daisuke Matsuzaka	6.00
216	Gustavo Molina	1.00
217	Miguel Montero	1.00
218	Brandon Morrow	2.00
219	Hideki Okajima	2.00
220	Adam Lind	1.00
221	Mike Rabelo	1.00
222	Brian Burres	1.00
223	Micah Owings	1.00
224	Brandon Wood	1.00
225	Alexi Casilla	2.00
226	Joe Smith	1.00
227	Hunter Pence	5.00
228	Glen Perkins	1.00
229	Chris Stewart	1.00
230	Ben Francisco	1.00
231	Troy Tulowitzki	3.00
232	Billy Butler	1.00
233	Delmon Young	2.00
234	Phil Hughes	3.00
235	Joaquin Arias	.50
236	Jeff Baker	.50
237	Mark Reynolds	.50
238	Joseph Bisenius	.50
239	Michael Bourn	.50
240	Zack Segovia	.50
241	Travis Buck	.50
242	Chase Wright	.50
243	Rocky Cherry	1.00
244	Danny Putnam	.50
245	Kory Casto	.50
246	Matt Chico	.50
247	John Danks	.50
248	Juan Salas	.50
249	Ryan Braun	3.00
250	Felix Pie	1.00
251	Jesus Flores	.50
252	Andy Gonzalez	.50
253	Ryan Sweeney	.50
254	Jarrod Saltalamacchia	1.00
255	Alex Gordon	1.50

256	Josh Hamilton	1.50
257	Sean Henn	.50
258	Kei Igawa	1.00
259	Akinori Iwamura	1.50
260	Andy LaRoche	1.50
261	Rick Vanden Hurk	.50
262	Kevin Kouzmanoff	1.50
263	Matt Lindstrom	.50
264	Tim Lincecum	4.00
265	Daisuke Matsuzaka	4.00
266	Gustavo Molina	.50
267	Miguel Montero	.50
268	Brandon Morrow	1.50
269	Hideki Okajima	1.50
270	Adam Lind	.50
271	Mike Rabelo	.50
272	Brian Burres	.50
273	Micah Owings	.50
274	Brandon Wood	.50
275	Alexi Casilla	1.00
276	Joe Smith	.50
277	Hunter Pence	3.00
278	Glen Perkins	.50
279	Chris Stewart	.50
280	Ben Francisco	.50
281	Troy Tulowitzki	2.00
282	Billy Butler	1.00
283	Delmon Young	1.00
284	Phil Hughes	2.00

Autographs

		NM/M
	Common Autograph:	8.00
101	Joaquin Arias	8.00
102	Jeff Baker	8.00
103	Brian Barden	8.00
104	Michael Bourn	10.00
105	Kevin Slowey	15.00
106	Chase Wright	15.00
107	Kory Casto	8.00
108	Matt Chico	8.00
109	Matt DeSalvo	15.00
110	Homer Bailey	20.00
111	Ryan Braun	75.00
112	Felix Pie	15.00
113	Jesus Flores	15.00
114	Ryan Sweeney	8.00
115	Ryan Braun	10.00
116	Alex Gordon/SP	60.00
117	Josh Hamilton	20.00
118	Sean Henn	8.00
121	Andy LaRoche	15.00
122	Kevin Kouzmanoff	15.00
123	Matt Lindstrom	8.00
124	Tim Lincecum/SP	100.00
125	Daisuke Matsuzaka/SP	275.00
126	Gustavo Molina	15.00
127	Miguel Montero	8.00
128	Brandon Morrow	15.00
130	Adam Lind	10.00
131	Mike Rabelo	10.00
132	Micah Owings	15.00
133	Brandon Wood	15.00
134	Alexi Casilla	10.00
135	Joe Smith	10.00
136	Hunter Pence/SP	50.00
137	Glen Perkins	8.00
138	Chris Stewart	8.00
139	Troy Tulowitzki/SP	30.00
140	Billy Butler	25.00
142	Phil Hughes/SP	80.00
143	Joaquin Arias	8.00
144	Jeff Baker	8.00
145	Brian Barden	8.00
146	Michael Bourn	10.00
147	Kevin Slowey	15.00
148	Chase Wright	15.00
149	Kory Casto	8.00
150	Matt Chico	8.00
151	Shawn Riggans	8.00
152	Juan Salas	8.00
153	Ryan Braun	75.00
154	Felix Pie	15.00
155	Jesus Flores	15.00
156	Ryan Sweeney	8.00
157	Ryan Braun	10.00
158	Alex Gordon/SP	60.00
159	Josh Hamilton	20.00
160	Sean Henn	8.00
163	Andy LaRoche	15.00
164	Kevin Kouzmanoff	15.00
165	Matt Lindstrom	8.00
166	Tim Lincecum/SP	100.00
167	Daisuke Matsuzaka/SP	275.00
168	Gustavo Molina	15.00
169	Miguel Montero	8.00
170	Brandon Morrow	15.00
172	Adam Lind	10.00
173	Mike Rabelo	8.00
174	Micah Owings	15.00
175	Brandon Wood	15.00
176	Alexi Casilla	10.00
177	Joe Smith	10.00
178	Hunter Pence	50.00
179	Glen Perkins	8.00
180	Chris Stewart	8.00
181	Troy Tulowitzki	30.00
182	Billy Butler	25.00
184	Phil Hughes/SP	80.00
185	Joaquin Arias	8.00
186	Jeff Baker	8.00
188	Joseph Bisenius	8.00
189	Michael Bourn	8.00
190	Zack Segovia	8.00
191	Kevin Slowey	15.00
192	Chase Wright	15.00
193	Rocky Cherry	20.00
194	Danny Putnam	20.00
195	Kory Casto	8.00
196	Matt Chico	8.00
197	John Danks	8.00
198	Homer Bailey	20.00
199	Ryan Braun	75.00
200	Felix Pie	15.00
201	Jesus Flores	15.00
202	Andy Gonzalez	8.00
203	Ryan Sweeney/SP	10.00
204	Jarrod Saltalamacchia	15.00
205	Alex Gordon/SP	60.00
206	Josh Hamilton/SP	20.00
207	Sean Henn	8.00
210	Andy LaRoche	15.00
211	Rick Vanden Hurk	8.00
212	Kevin Kouzmanoff	15.00
213	Matt Lindstrom	8.00
214	Tim Lincecum/SP	100.00
215	Daisuke Matsuzaka/SP	275.00
216	Gustavo Molina	15.00
217	Miguel Montero	8.00
218	Brandon Morrow	15.00
220	Adam Lind	10.00
221	Mike Rabelo	10.00
222	Brian Burres	8.00
223	Micah Owings	15.00
224	Brandon Wood/SP	15.00
225	Alexi Casilla	10.00
226	Joe Smith	10.00
227	Hunter Pence/SP	50.00
228	Glen Perkins	8.00
229	Chris Stewart	8.00
230	Ben Francisco	8.00
231	Troy Tulowitzki/SP	30.00
232	Billy Butler/SP	25.00
234	Phil Hughes/SP	80.00
235	Joaquin Arias	8.00
236	Jeff Baker	8.00
238	Joseph Bisenius	8.00
239	Michael Bourn	10.00
240	Zack Segovia	10.00
242	Chase Wright	15.00
243	Rocky Cherry	20.00
244	Danny Putnam	20.00
245	Kory Casto	8.00
246	Matt Chico	8.00
247	John Danks	8.00
248	Juan Salas	8.00
249	Ryan Braun/SP	75.00
250	Felix Pie	15.00
251	Jesus Flores	15.00
252	Andy Gonzalez	8.00
253	Ryan Sweeney	8.00
254	Jarrod Saltalamacchia/SP	15.00
255	Alex Gordon/SP	60.00
256	Josh Hamilton	20.00
257	Sean Henn	8.00
260	Andy LaRoche	15.00
261	Rick Vanden Hurk	8.00
262	Kevin Kouzmanoff	15.00
263	Matt Lindstrom	8.00
264	Tim Lincecum/SP	100.00
265	Daisuke Matsuzaka/SP	275.00
266	Gustavo Molina	15.00
267	Miguel Montero	8.00
268	Brandon Morrow	15.00
270	Adam Lind	10.00
271	Mike Rabelo	10.00
272	Brian Burres	8.00
273	Micah Owings	15.00
274	Brandon Wood	15.00
275	Alexi Casilla	10.00
276	Joe Smith	10.00
277	Hunter Pence/SP	50.00
278	Glen Perkins	8.00
279	Chris Stewart	8.00
280	Ben Francisco	8.00
281	Troy Tulowitzki/SP	30.00
282	Billy Butler SP	25.00
284	Phil Hughes/SP	80.00

Z

1995 Zenith

		NM/M
	Complete Set (150):	15.00
	Common Player:	.10
	Pack (6):	1.50
	Wax Box (24):	17.50
1	Albert Belle	.10
2	Alex Fernandez	.10
3	Andy Benes	.10
4	Barry Larkin	.10
5	Barry Bonds	2.50
6	Ben McDonald	.10
7	Bernard Gilkey	.10
8	Billy Ashley	.10
9	Bobby Bonilla	.10
10	Bret Saberhagen	.10
11	Brian Jordan	.10
12	Cal Ripken Jr.	2.50
13	Carlos Baerga	.10
14	Carlos Delgado	.35
15	Cecil Fielder	.10
16	Chili Davis	.10
17	Chuck Knoblauch	.10
18	Craig Biggio	.10
19	Danny Tartabull	.10
20	Dante Bichette	.10
21	Darren Daulton	.10
22	Dave Justice	.10
23	Dave Winfield	.75
24	David Cone	.10
25	Dean Palmer	.10
26	Deion Sanders	.20
27	Dennis Eckersley	.65
28	Derek Bell	.10
29	Don Mattingly	1.50
30	Edgar Martinez	.10
31	Eric Karros	.10
32	Erik Hanson	.10
33	Frank Thomas	.75
34	Fred McGriff	.10
35	Gary Sheffield	.45
36	Gary Gaetti	.10
37	Greg Maddux	1.25
38	Gregg Jefferies	.10
39	Ivan Rodriguez	.65
40	Kenny Rogers	.10
41	J.T. Snow	.10
42	Hal Morris	.10
43	Eddie Murray (3,000 Hit)	.50
44	Javier Lopez	.10
45	Jay Bell	.10
46	Jeff Conine	.10
47	Jeff Bagwell	.75
48	Hideo Nomo RC	2.00
49	Jeff Kent	.10
50	Jeff King	.10
51	Jim Thome	.65
52	Jimmy Key	.10
53	Joe Carter	.10
54	John Valentin	.10
55	John Olerud	.10
56	Jose Canseco	.45
57	Jose Rijo	.10
58	Jose Offerman	.10
59	Juan Gonzalez	.45
60	Ken Caminiti	.10
61	Ken Griffey Jr.	1.75
62	Kenny Lofton	.10
63	Kevin Appier	.10
64	Kevin Seitzer	.10
65	Kirby Puckett	1.25
66	Kirk Gibson	.10
67	Larry Walker	.10
68	Lenny Dykstra	.10
69	Manny Ramirez	.75
70	Mark Grace	.10
71	Mark McGwire	2.00
72	Marquis Grissom	.10
73	Jim Edmonds	.10
74	Matt Williams	.10
75	Mike Mussina	.45
76	Mike Piazza	1.75
77	Mo Vaughn	.10
78	Moises Alou	.10
79	Ozzie Smith	1.25
80	Paul O'Neill	.10
81	Paul Molitor	.75
82	Rafael Palmeiro	.65
83	Randy Johnson	.75
84	Raul Mondesi	.10
85	Ray Lankford	.10
86	Reggie Sanders	.10
87	Rickey Henderson	.75
88	Rico Brogna	.10
89	Roberto Alomar	.25
90	Robin Ventura	.10
91	Roger Clemens	1.50
92	Ron Gant	.10
93	Rondell White	.10
94	Royce Clayton	.10
95	Ruben Sierra	.10
96	Rusty Greer	.10
97	Ryan Klesko	.10
98	Sammy Sosa	1.25
99	Shawon Dunston	.10
100	Steve Ontiveros	.10
101	Tim Naehring	.10
102	Tim Salmon	.10
103	Tino Martinez	.10
104	Tony Gwynn	1.25
105	Travis Fryman	.10
106	Vinny Castilla	.10
107	Wade Boggs	1.25
108	Wally Joyner	.10
109	Wil Cordero	.10
110	Will Clark	.10
111	Chipper Jones	1.25
112	C.J. Nitkowski	.10
113	Curtis Goodwin	.10
114	Tim Unroe	.10
115	Vaughn Eshelman	.10
116	Marty Cordova	.10
117	Dustin Hermanson	.10
118	Rich Becker	.10
119	Ray Durham	.10
120	Shane Andrews	.10
121	Scott Ruffcorn	.10
122	Mark Grudzielanek RC	.25
123	James Baldwin	.10
124	Carlos Perez RC	.10
125	Julian Tavarez	.10
126	Joe Vitiello	.10
127	Jason Bates	.10
128	Edgardo Alfonzo	.10
129	Juan Acevedo	.10
130	Bill Pulsipher	.10
131	Bob Higginson RC	.25
132	Russ Davis	.10
133	Charles Johnson	.10
134	Derek Jeter	2.50
135	Phil Nevin	.10
136	LaTroy Hawkins	.10
137	Brian Hunter	.10
138	Roberto Petagine	.10
139	Jim Pittsley	.10
140	Garret Anderon	.10
141	Ugueth Urbina	.10
142	Antonio Osuna	.10
143	Michael Tucker	.10
144	Benji Gil	.10
145	Jon Nunnally	.10
146	Alex Rodriguez	2.00
147	Todd Hollandworth	.10
148	Alex Gonzalez	.10
149	Hideo Nomo RC	2.00
150	Shawn Green	.30
---	Numeric Checklist	.10
---	Chase Program Checklist	.10

All-Star Salute

		NM/M
	Complete Set (19):	16.00
	Common Player:	.50
1	Cal Ripken Jr.	3.00
2	Frank Thomas	1.00
3	Mike Piazza	2.00
4	Kirby Puckett	1.50
5	Manny Ramirez	1.00
6	Tony Gwynn	1.50
7	Hideo Nomo	.75
8	Matt Williams	.50
9	Randy Johnson	1.00
10	Raul Mondesi	.50
11	Albert Belle	.50
12	Ivan Rodriguez	1.00
13	Barry Bonds	3.00
14	Carlos Baerga	.50
15	Ken Griffey Jr.	2.00

		NM/M
16	Jeff Conine	.50
17	Frank Thomas	1.00
18	Cal Ripken Jr., Barry Bonds	2.00

Rookie Roll Call

		NM/M
Complete Set (18):		17.50
Common Player:		.60
1	Alex Rodriguez	6.00
2	Derek Jeter	7.50
3	Chipper Jones	5.00
4	Shawn Green	1.50
5	Todd Hollandsworth	.60
6	Bill Pulsipher	.60
7	Hideo Nomo	1.50
8	Ray Durham	.60
9	Curtis Goodwin	.60
10	Brian Hunter	.60
11	Julian Tavarez	.60
12	Marty Cordova	.60
13	Michael Tucker	.60
14	Edgardo Alfonzo	.60
15	LaTroy Hawkins	.60
16	Carlos Perez	.60
17	Charles Johnson	.60
18	Benji Gil	.60

Z-Team

		NM/M
Complete Set (18):		85.00
Common Player:		2.00
1	Cal Ripken Jr.	15.00
2	Ken Griffey Jr.	10.00
3	Frank Thomas	6.00
4	Matt Williams	2.00
5	Mike Piazza	10.00
6	Barry Bonds	15.00
7	Raul Mondesi	2.00

8	Greg Maddux	7.50
9	Jeff Bagwell	6.00
10	Manny Ramirez	6.00
11	Larry Walker	2.00
12	Tony Gwynn	7.50
13	Will Clark	2.00
14	Albert Belle	2.00
15	Kenny Lofton	2.00
16	Rafael Palmeiro	4.50
17	Don Mattingly	9.00
18	Carlos Baerga	2.00

1996 Zenith

		NM/M
Complete Set (150):		15.00
Common Player:		.10
Common Artist's Proofs:		2.00
Star Artist's Proofs:		12X
Pack (6):		1.50
Wax Box (24):		25.00
1	Ken Griffey Jr.	2.00
2	Ozzie Smith	1.50
3	Greg Maddux	1.50
4	Rondell White	.10
5	Mark McGwire	2.50
6	Jim Thome	.75
7	Ivan Rodriguez	.75
8	Marc Newfield	.10
9	Travis Fryman	.10
10	Fred McGriff	.10
11	Shawn Green	.25
12	Mike Piazza	2.00
13	Dante Bichette	.10
14	Tino Martinez	.10
15	Sterling Hitchcock	.10
16	Ryne Sandberg	1.50
17	Rico Brogna	.10
18	Roberto Alomar	.25
19	Barry Larkin	.10
20	Bernie Williams	.10
21	Gary Sheffield	.50
22	Frank Thomas	1.00
23	Gregg Jefferies	.10
24	Jeff Bagwell	1.00
25	Marty Cordova	.10
26	Jim Edmonds	.10
27	Jay Bell	.10
28	Ben McDonald	.10
29	Barry Bonds	3.00
30	Mo Vaughn	.10
31	Johnny Damon	.35
32	Dean Palmer	.10
33	Ismael Valdes	.10
34	Manny Ramirez	1.00
35	Edgar Martinez	.10
36	Cecil Fielder	.10
37	Ryan Klesko	.10
38	Ray Lankford	.10
39	Tim Salmon	.10
40	Joe Carter	.10
41	Jason Isringhausen	.10
42	Rickey Henderson	1.00
43	Lenny Dykstra	.10
44	Andre Dawson	.25
45	Paul O'Neill	.10
46	Ray Durham	.10
47	Raul Mondesi	.10
48	Jay Buhner	.10
49	Eddie Murray	1.00
50	Henry Rodriguez	.10
51	Hal Morris	.10
52	Mike Mussina	.50
53	Wally Joyner	.10
54	Will Clark	.10
55	Chipper Jones	1.50
56	Brian Jordan	.10
57	Larry Walker	.10
58	Wade Boggs	1.50
59	Melvin Nieves	.10
60	Charles Johnson	.10
61	Juan Gonzalez	.50
62	Carlos Delgado	.35
63	Reggie Sanders	.10
64	Brian Hunter	.10
65	Edgardo Alfonzo	.10
66	Kenny Lofton	.10
67	Paul Molitor	1.00
68	Mike Bordick	.10
69	Garret Anderson	.10
70	Orlando Merced	.10
71	Craig Biggio	.10
72	Chuck Knoblauch	.10
73	Mark Grace	.10

74	Jack McDowell	.10
75	Randy Johnson	1.00
76	Cal Ripken Jr.	3.00
77	Matt Williams	.10
78	Benji Gil	.10
79	Moises Alou	.10
80	Robin Ventura	.10
81	Greg Vaughn	.10
82	Carlos Baerga	.10
83	Roger Clemens	1.75
84	Hideo Nomo	.50
85	Pedro Martinez	1.00
86	John Valentin	.10
87	Andres Galarraga	.10
88	Andy Pettitte	.30
89	Derek Bell	.10
90	Kirby Puckett	1.50
91	Tony Gwynn	1.50
92	Brady Anderson	.10
93	Derek Jeter	3.00
94	Michael Tucker	.10
95	Albert Belle	.10
96	David Cone	.10
97	J.T. Snow	.10
98	Tom Glavine	.35
99	Alex Rodriguez	2.50
100	Sammy Sosa	1.50
101	Karim Garcia	.15
102	Alan Benes	.10
103	Chad Mottola	.10
104	Robin Jennings RC	.10
105	Bob Abreu	.10
106	Tony Clark	.10
107	George Arias	.10
108	Jermaine Dye	.10
109	Jeff Suppan	.10
110	Ralph Milliard RC	.10
111	Ruben Rivera	.10
112	Billy Wagner	.10
113	Jason Kendall	.10
114	Mike Grace RC	.10
115	Edgar Renteria	.10
116	Jason Schmidt	.10
117	Paul Wilson	.10
118	Rey Ordonez	.10
119	Rocky Coppinger RC	.10
120	Wilton Guerrero RC	.10
121	Brooks Kieschnick	.10
122	Raul Casanova	.10
123	Alex Ochoa	.10
124	Chan Ho Park	.10
125	John Wasdin	.10
126	Eric Owens	.10
127	Justin Thompson	.10
128	Chris Snopek	.10
129	Terrell Wade	.10
130	Darin Erstad RC	1.50
131	Albert Belle	.10
132	Cal Ripken Jr.	1.50
133	Frank Thomas	.60
134	Greg Maddux	.75
135	Ken Griffey Jr.	1.00
136	Mo Vaughn	.10
137	Chipper Jones	.75
138	Mike Piazza	1.00
139	Ryan Klesko	.10
140	Hideo Nomo	.20
141	Roberto Alomar	.10
142	Manny Ramirez	.60
143	Gary Sheffield	.10
144	Barry Bonds	1.50
145	Matt Williams	.10
146	Jim Edmonds	.10
147	Derek Jeter	1.50
148	Sammy Sosa	.75
149	Kirby Puckett	.75
150	Tony Gwynn	.75

Artist's Proofs

	NM/M
Common Player:	2.00
Stars:	12X

(See 1996 Zenith for checklist and base card values.)

Diamond Club

		NM/M
Complete Set (20):		17.50
Common Player:		.45
Diamond Versions:		12X
1	Albert Belle	.45
2	Mo Vaughn	.45
3	Ken Griffey Jr.	1.50
4	Mike Piazza	1.50
5	Cal Ripken Jr.	2.50
6	Jermaine Dye	.45
7	Jeff Bagwell	1.00
8	Frank Thomas	1.00
9	Alex Rodriguez	2.00
10	Ryan Klesko	.45
11	Roberto Alomar	.60
12	Sammy Sosa	1.25
13	Matt Williams	.45
14	Gary Sheffield	.75
15	Ruben Rivera	.45
16	Darin Erstad	.60
17	Randy Johnson	1.00
18	Greg Maddux	1.25
19	Karim Garcia	.60
20	Chipper Jones	1.25

Mozaics

		NM/M
Complete Set (25):		30.00
Common Card:		.45
1	Greg Maddux, Chipper Jones, Ryan Klesko	3.00
2	Juan Gonzalez, Will Clark, Ivan Rodriguez	1.00
3	Frank Thomas, Robin Ventura, Ray Durham	1.00
4	Matt Williams, Barry Bonds, Osvaldo Fernandez	5.00
5	Ken Griffey Jr., Randy Johnson, Alex Rodriguez	4.00
6	Sammy Sosa, Ryne Sandberg, Mark Grace	4.00
7	Jim Edmonds, Tim Salmon, Garret Anderson	.45
8	Cal Ripken Jr., Roberto Alomar, Mike Mussina	5.00
9	Mo Vaughn, Roger Clemens, John Valentin	3.50
10	Barry Larkin, Reggie Sanders, Hal Morris	.45
11	Ray Lankford, Brian Jordan, Ozzie Smith	1.50

12	Dante Bichette, Larry Walker, Andres Galarraga	.45
13	Mike Piazza, Hideo Nomo, Raul Mondesi	4.00
14	Ben McDonald, Greg Vaughn, Kevin Seitzer	.45
15	Joe Carter, Carlos Delgado, Alex Gonzalez	.60
16	Gary Sheffield, Charles Johnson, Jeff Conine	.45
17	Rondell White, Moises Alou, Henry Rodriguez	.45
18	Albert Belle, Manny Ramirez, Carlos Baerga	1.00
19	Kirby Puckett, Paul Molitor, Chuck Knoblauch	1.50
20	Tony Gwynn, Rickey Henderson, Wally Joyner	2.00
21	Mark McGwire, Mike Bordick, Scott Brosius	4.00
22	Paul O'Neill, Bernie Williams, Wade Boggs	1.50
23	Jay Bell, Orlando Merced, Jason Kendall	.45
24	Rico Brogna, Paul Wilson, Jason Isringhausen	.45
25	Jeff Bagwell, Craig Biggio, Derek Bell	1.00

Z-Team

		NM/M
Complete Set (18):		100.00
Common Player:		3.00
1	Ken Griffey Jr.	12.50
2	Albert Belle	3.00
3	Cal Ripken Jr.	20.00
4	Frank Thomas	7.50
5	Greg Maddux	10.00
6	Mo Vaughn	3.00
7	Chipper Jones	10.00
8	Mike Piazza	12.50
9	Ryan Klesko	3.00
10	Hideo Nomo	4.50
11	Roberto Alomar	3.00
12	Manny Ramirez	6.00
13	Gary Sheffield	3.50
14	Barry Bonds	20.00
15	Matt Williams	3.00
16	Jim Edmonds	3.00
17	Kirby Puckett	10.00
18	Sammy Sosa	10.00

1997 Zenith

		NM/M
Complete Set (50):		15.00
Common Player:		.10
Pack (5 cards, 2 8x10):		2.00
Wax Box (12):		25.00
1	Frank Thomas	.75
2	Tony Gwynn	1.00
3	Jeff Bagwell	.75
4	Paul Molitor	.75
5	Roberto Alomar	.20
6	Mike Piazza	1.25
7	Albert Belle	.10
8	Greg Maddux	1.00
9	Barry Larkin	.10
10	Tony Clark	.10
11	Larry Walker	.10
12	Chipper Jones	1.00
13	Juan Gonzalez	.40
14	Barry Bonds	2.00
15	Ivan Rodriguez	.65

16	Sammy Sosa	1.00
17	Derek Jeter	2.00
18	Hideo Nomo	.40
19	Roger Clemens	1.00
20	Ken Griffey Jr.	1.25
21	Andy Pettitte	.25
22	Alex Rodriguez	1.50
23	Tino Martinez	.10
24	Bernie Williams	.10
25	Ken Caminiti	.10
26	John Smoltz	.10
27	Javier Lopez	.10
28	Mark McGwire	1.50
29	Gary Sheffield	.50
30	David Justice	.10
31	Randy Johnson	.75
32	Chuck Knoblauch	.10
33	Mike Mussina	.40
34	Deion Sanders	.20
35	Cal Ripken Jr.	2.00
36	Darin Erstad	.30
37	Kenny Lofton	.10
38	Jay Buhner	.10
39	Brady Anderson	.10
40	Edgar Martinez	.10
41	Mo Vaughn	.10
42	Ryne Sandberg	1.00
43	Andruw Jones	.75
44	Nomar Garciaparra	1.00
45	Hideki Irabu RC	.25
46	Wilton Guerrero	.10
47	Jose Cruz Jr. RC	.45
48	Vladimir Guerrero	.75
49	Scott Rolen	.65
50	Jose Guillen	.10

V-2

		NM/M
Complete Set (8):		45.00
Common Player:		5.00
1	Ken Griffey Jr.	7.50
2	Andruw Jones	5.00
3	Frank Thomas	5.00
4	Mike Piazza	7.50
5	Alex Rodriguez	10.00
6	Cal Ripken Jr.	12.00
7	Derek Jeter	12.00
8	Vladimir Guerrero	5.00

Z-Team

		NM/M
Complete Set (9):		60.00

Common Player:		3.00
1	Ken Griffey Jr.	9.00
2	Larry Walker	3.00
3	Frank Thomas	6.00
4	Alex Rodriguez	10.00
5	Mike Piazza	9.00
6	Cal Ripken Jr.	12.50
7	Derek Jeter	12.50
8	Andruw Jones	6.00
9	Roger Clemens	7.50

8x10 and 8x10 Dufex

		NM/M
Complete Set (24):		20.00
Common Player:		.50
Dufex Versions:		1X
Samples:		1X
1	Frank Thomas	1.00
2	Tony Gwynn	1.50
3	Jeff Bagwell	1.00
4	Ken Griffey Jr.	2.00
5	Mike Piazza	2.00
6	Greg Maddux	1.50
7	Ken Caminiti	.50
8	Albert Belle	.50
9	Ivan Rodriguez	.75
10	Sammy Sosa	1.50
11	Mark McGwire	2.50
12	Roger Clemens	1.75
13	Alex Rodriguez	2.50
14	Chipper Jones	1.50
15	Juan Gonzalez	.60
16	Barry Bonds	3.00
17	Derek Jeter	3.00
18	Hideo Nomo	.60
19	Cal Ripken Jr.	3.00
20	Hideki Irabu	.50
21	Andruw Jones	1.00
22	Nomar Garciaparra	1.50
23	Vladimir Guerrero	1.00
24	Scott Rolen	.75

1998 Zenith

		NM/M
Complete Set (100):		25.00
Common Player:		.10
Silvers:		2X
Inserted 1:7		
Pack (3):		2.50
Wax Box (18):		35.00
1	Larry Walker	.10
2	Ken Griffey Jr.	1.75
3	Cal Ripken Jr.	2.50
4	Sammy Sosa	1.50
5	Andruw Jones	1.00
6	Frank Thomas	1.00
7	Tony Gwynn	1.50
8	Rafael Palmeiro	.75
9	Tim Salmon	.10
10	Randy Johnson	1.00
11	Juan Gonzalez	.50
12	Greg Maddux	1.50
13	Vladimir Guerrero	1.00

14	Mike Piazza	1.75
15	Andres Galarraga	.10
16	Alex Rodriguez	2.00
17	Derek Jeter	2.50
18	Nomar Garciaparra	1.50
19	Ivan Rodriguez	.75
20	Chipper Jones	1.50
21	Barry Larkin	.10
22	Mo Vaughn	.10
23	Albert Belle	.10
24	Scott Rolen	.65
25	Sandy Alomar Jr.	.10
26	Roberto Alomar	.30
27	Andy Pettitte	.30
28	Chuck Knoblauch	.10
29	Jeff Bagwell	1.00
30	Mike Mussina	.30
31	Fred McGriff	.10
32	Roger Clemens	1.50
33	Rusty Greer	.10
34	Edgar Martinez	.10
35	Paul Molitor	1.00
36	Mark Grace	.10
37	Darin Erstad	.30
38	Kenny Lofton	.10
39	Tom Glavine	.35
40	Javier Lopez	.10
41	Will Clark	.10
42	Tino Martinez	.10
43	Raul Mondesi	.10
44	Brady Anderson	.10
45	Chan Ho Park	.10
46	Jason Giambi	.75
47	Manny Ramirez	1.00
48	Jay Buhner	.10
49	Dante Bichette	.10
50	Jose Cruz Jr.	.10
51	Charles Johnson	.10
52	Bernard Gilkey	.10
53	Johnny Damon	.35
54	David Justice	.10
55	Justin Thompson	.10
56	Bobby Higginson	.10
57	Todd Hundley	.10
58	Gary Sheffield	.50
59	Barry Bonds	2.50
60	Mark McGwire	2.00
61	John Smoltz	.10
62	Tony Clark	.10
63	Brian Jordan	.10
64	Jason Kendall	.10
65	Mariano Rivera	.20
66	Pedro Martinez	1.00
67	Jim Thome	.75
68	Neifi Perez	.10
69	Kevin Brown	.10
70	Hideo Nomo	.50
71	Craig Biggio	.10
72	Bernie Williams	.10
73	Jose Guillen	.10
74	Ken Caminiti	.10
75	Livan Hernandez	.10
76	Ray Lankford	.10
77	Jim Edmonds	.10
78	Matt Williams	.10
79	Mark Kotsay	.10
80	Moises Alou	.10
81	Antone Williamson	.10
82	Jaret Wright	.10
83	Jacob Cruz	.10
84	Abraham Nunez	.10
85	Raul Ibanez	.10
86	Miguel Tejada	.10
87	Derek Lee	.50
88	Juan Encarnacion	.10
89	Todd Helton	.75
90	Travis Lee	.10
91	Ben Grieve	.10
92	Ryan McGuire	.10
93	Richard Hidalgo	.10
94	Paul Konerko	.15
95	Shannon Stewart	.10
96	Homer Bush	.10
97	Lou Collier	.10
98	Jeff Abbott	.10
99	Brett Tomko	.10
100	Fernando Tatis	.10

Value quoted in this guide reflect the retail price of a card, the price a collector can expect to pay when buying a card from a dealer.

Z-Silver

		NM/M
Common Player:		1.00
Stars/RC's:		2X
Inserted 1:7		

(See 1998 Zenith for checklist and base card values.)

Z-Gold

		NM/M
Common Player:		3.00
Stars/Rookies:		12X
Production 100 Sets		

(See 1998 Zenith for checklist and base card values.)

Epix

		NM/M
Complete Set (24):		95.00
Common (Orange) Card:		1.50
Purples:		1X
Emeralds:		2X
1	Ken Griffey Jr./S	7.50
2	Juan Gonzalez/S	2.50
3	Jeff Bagwell/S	4.50
4	Ivan Rodriguez/S	4.00
5	Nomar Garciaparra/S	6.00
6	Ryne Sandberg/S	6.00
7	Frank Thomas/M	4.50
8	Derek Jeter/M	12.00
9	Tony Gwynn/M	6.00
10	Albert Belle/M	1.50
11	Scott Rolen/M	3.50
12	Barry Larkin/M	1.50
13	Alex Rodriguez/P	9.00
14	Cal Ripken Jr./P	12.00
15	Chipper Jones/P	6.00
16	Roger Clemens/P	6.50
17	Mo Vaughn/P	1.50
18	Mark McGwire/P	9.00
19	Mike Piazza/G	7.50
20	Andruw Jones/G	4.50
21	Greg Maddux/G	6.00
22	Barry Bonds/G	12.00
23	Paul Molitor/G	4.50
24	Eddie Murray/G	4.50

Raising the Bar

		NM/M
Complete Set (15):		25.00

Z-Silver (insert checklist)

Common Player:		1.25
Inserted 1:25		
1	Ken Griffey Jr.	3.00
2	Frank Thomas	1.50
3	Alex Rodriguez	3.50
4	Tony Gwynn	2.50
5	Mike Piazza	3.00
6	Ivan Rodriguez	1.25
7	Cal Ripken Jr.	4.50
8	Greg Maddux	2.50
9	Hideo Nomo	1.25
10	Mark McGwire	3.50
11	Juan Gonzalez	1.25
12	Andruw Jones	1.50
13	Jeff Bagwell	1.50
14	Chipper Jones	2.50
15	Nomar Garciaparra	2.50

Rookie Thrills

		NM/M
Complete Set (15):		20.00
Common Player:		1.50
Inserted 1:25		
1	Travis Lee	1.50
2	Juan Encarnacion	1.50
3	Derrek Lee	1.50
4	Raul Ibanez	1.50
5	Ryan McGuire	1.50
6	Todd Helton	3.00
7	Jacob Cruz	1.50
8	Abraham Nunez	1.50
9	Paul Konerko	2.00
10	Ben Grieve	1.50
11	Jeff Abbott	1.50
12	Richard Hidalgo	1.50
13	Jaret Wright	1.50
14	Lou Collier	1.50
15	Miguel Tejada	2.00

Z-Team

		NM/M
Complete Set (18):		35.00
Common Player:		1.25
Golds:		2X
Inserted 1:175		
1	Frank Thomas	2.50
2	Ken Griffey Jr.	3.50
3	Mike Piazza	3.50
4	Cal Ripken Jr.	6.00
5	Alex Rodriguez	5.00
6	Greg Maddux	3.00
7	Derek Jeter	6.00
8	Chipper Jones	3.00
9	Roger Clemens	3.25
10	Ben Grieve	1.25
11	Derrek Lee	1.75
12	Jose Cruz Jr.	1.25
13	Nomar Garciaparra	3.00
14	Travis Lee	1.50
15	Todd Helton	2.00
16	Paul Konerko	1.75
17	Miguel Tejada	1.25
18	Scott Rolen	2.00

5x7

		NM/M
Complete Set (80):		30.00
Common Player:		.25
Impulse Silvers:		1.5X
Inserted 1:7		
1	Nomar Garciaparra	2.00
2	Andres Galarraga	.25
3	Greg Maddux	2.00
4	Frank Thomas	1.00
5	Mark McGwire	3.00
6	Rafael Palmeiro	.75
7	John Smoltz	.25
8	Jeff Bagwell	1.00
9	Andruw Jones	1.00
10	Rusty Greer	.25
11	Paul Molitor	1.00
12	Bernie Williams	.25
13	Kenny Lofton	.25
14	Alex Rodriguez	3.00
15	Derek Jeter	4.00
15s	Derek Jeter ("SAMPLE" overprint on back.)	4.00
16	Scott Rolen	.65
17	Albert Belle	.25
18	Mo Vaughn	.25
19	Chipper Jones	2.00
20	Chuck Knoblauch	.25
21	Mike Piazza	3.00
22	Tony Gwynn	2.00
22s	Tony Gwynn ("SAMPLE" overprint on back.)	2.00
23	Juan Gonzalez	.50
24	Andy Pettitte	.35
25	Tim Salmon	.25
26	Brady Anderson	.25
27	Mike Mussina	.40
28	Edgar Martinez	.25
29	Jose Guillen	.25
30	Hideo Nomo	.50
31	Jim Thome	.65
32	Mark Grace	.25
33	Darin Erstad	.50
34	Bobby Higginson	.25
35	Ivan Rodriguez	.75
36	Todd Hundley	.25
37	Sandy Alomar Jr.	.25
38	Gary Sheffield	.40
39	David Justice	.25
40	Ken Griffey Jr.	2.50
40s	Ken Griffey Jr. ("SAMPLE" overprint on back.)	2.50
41	Vladimir Guerrero	1.00
42	Larry Walker	.25
43	Barry Bonds	4.00
44	Randy Johnson	1.00
45	Roger Clemens	2.25
46	Raul Mondesi	.25
47	Tino Martinez	.25
48	Jason Giambi	.50
49	Matt Williams	.25
8	Chipper Jones	3.00
9	Roger Clemens	3.25
10	Ben Grieve	1.25
11	Derrek Lee	1.75
12	Jose Cruz Jr.	1.25
13	Nomar Garciaparra	3.00
14	Travis Lee	1.50
15	Todd Helton	2.00
16	Paul Konerko	1.75
17	Miguel Tejada	1.25
18	Scott Rolen	2.00
50	Cal Ripken Jr.	4.00
51	Barry Larkin	.25
52	Jim Edmonds	.25
53	Ken Caminiti	.25
54	Sammy Sosa	2.00
55	Tony Clark	.25
56	Manny Ramirez	1.00
57	Bernard Gilkey	.25
58	Jose Cruz Jr.	.25
59	Brian Jordan	.25
60	Kevin Brown	.25
61	Craig Biggio	.25
62	Javier Lopez	.25
63	Jay Buhner	.25
64	Roberto Alomar	.40
65	Justin Thompson	.25
66	Todd Helton	.75
67	Travis Lee	.25
68	Paul Konerko	.35
69	Jaret Wright	.25
70	Ben Grieve	.25
71	Juan Encarnacion	.25
72	Ryan McGuire	.25
73	Derrek Lee	.60
74	Abraham Nunez	.25
75	Richard Hidalgo	.25
76	Miguel Tejada	.25
77	Jacob Cruz	.25
78	Homer Bush	.25
79	Jeff Abbott	.25
80	Lou Collier	.25
	Checklist	.10

5x7 Impulse Silver

		NM/M
Common Player:		2.00
Stars/RC's:		1.5X
Inserted 1:7		

(See 1998 Zenith 5x7 for checklist and base card values.)

5x7 Impulse Gold

		NM/M
Common Player:		5.00
Stars/RC's:		20X
Inserted 1:7		

(See 1998 Zenith 5x7 for checklist and base card values.)